THE AUTHORITY SINCE 1868

THE WORLD ALMANAC

ALMANAC

AND BOOK OF FACTS

1990

WORLD ALMANAC
AN IMPRINT OF PHAROS BOOKS • A SCRIPPS HOWARD COMPANY
NEW YORK

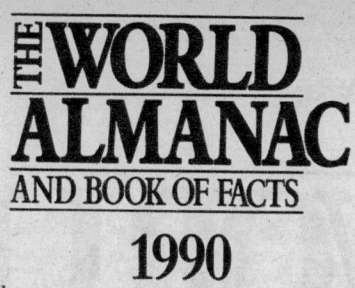

THE WORLD ALMANAC AND BOOK OF FACTS 1990

Editor: Mark S. Hoffman
Associate Editor: June Foley   **Senior Assistant Editor:** Thomas McGuire
Chronology & Special Features: Donald Young   **Index:** Deborah G. Felder
Administrative Assistant: Aris Georgiadis

Pharos Books
Senior Vice President & Publisher: David Hendin
Vice President & Associate Publisher: Phyllis Henrici
Editor-in-Chief: Hana Umlauf Lane   **Sales Manager:** Kevin McDonough
Publicity Manager: Martha Clarke   **Production Manager:** Randy Lang
Editorial Assistant: Jo-Anne Mercado Volkers

The editors acknowledge with thanks the many letters of helpful comment and criticism from readers of THE WORLD ALMANAC, and invite further suggestions and observations. Because of the volume of mail directed to the editorial offices, it is not possible to reply to each letter writer. However, every communication is read by the editors and all comments and suggestions receive careful attention. Inquiries regarding contents should be sent to: Editor, The World Almanac, 200 Park Avenue, New York, NY 10166.

THE WORLD ALMANAC is published annually in November.

THE WORLD ALMANAC does not decide wagers.

The first edition of THE WORLD ALMANAC, a 120-page volume with 12 pages of advertising, was published by the New York World in 1868, 122 years ago. Annual publication was suspended in 1876. Joseph Pulitzer, publisher of the New York World, revived THE WORLD ALMANAC in 1886 with the goal of making it a "compendium of universal knowledge." It has been published annually since then. In 1931, it was acquired by the Scripps Howard Newspapers; until 1951, it bore the imprint of the New York World-Telegram and thereafter, until 1967, that of the New York World-Telegram and Sun. It is now published in paper and clothbound editions by Pharos Books, a Scripps Howard company.

THE WORLD ALMANAC & BOOK OF FACTS 1990
Copyright© Newspaper Enterprise Association, Inc. 1989
Library of Congress Catalog Card Number 4-3781
International Standard Serial Number (ISSN) 0084-1382
Pharos Books (softcover) ISBN 0-88687-559-5
Pharos Books (hardcover) ISBN 0-88687-560-9
Microform Edition since 1868: University Microfilms Intl.
Printed in the United States of America
The softcover and hardcover editions distributed to the trade in the United States
by St. Martin's Press.

WORLD ALMANAC
An Imprint of Pharos Books
A Scripps Howard Company
200 Park Avenue, New York, NY 10166

1990 HIGHLIGHTS

GENERAL INDEX

— F —

Addenda, Late News, Changes

AIDS (p. 161)

Federal health officials, Sept. 1989, permitted the experimental drug, DDI, to be widely distributed while it is still being tested.

Area codes (pp. 589-590)

In Texas, the area codes for the following places should be 409: Bridge City, Port Neches, Silsbee, and Vidor.

Airline Safety (p. 151)

By mid-October, there were 10 fatal accidents involving large U.S. commercial jets, the worst since 1968 when there were 12. The accidents caused 275 deaths, the highest toll since 1979 when 348 died.

Awards
Broadcasting and Theater (p. 354)

Emmy Awards, by Academy of Television Arts and Sciences, for nighttime programs, 1988-89: Dramatic series: *L.A. Law*, NBC; actress, Dana Delany, *China Beach*, ABC; actor: Carroll O'Connor, *In the Heat of the Night*, NBC; supporting actress: Melanie Mayron, *thirtysomething*, ABC; supporting actor: Larry Drake, *L.A. Law*, NBC. Comedy series: *Cheers*, NBC; actress: Candice Bergen, *Murphy Brown*, CBS; actor: Richard Mulligan, *Empty Nest*, NBC; supporting actress: Rhea Perlman, *Cheers*, NBC; supporting actor: Woody Harrelson, *Cheers*, NBC. Miniseries: *War and*

Remembrance, ABC; actress: Holly Hunter, *Roe vs. Wade*, NBC; actor: James Woods, *Hallmark Hall of Fame: My Name Is Bill W.*, ABC; supporting actress: Colleen Dewhurst, *Those She Left Behind*, NBC; supporting actor: Derek Jacobi, *Hallmark Hall of Fame: The Tenth Man*, CBS. Drama-Comedy Special: (tie) *Day One*, CBS; *Roe vs. Wade*, NBC. Variety, Music or Comedy Program: *The Tracey Ullman Show*, Fox. Performance in a Variety or Musical Program: Linda Ronstadt, *Great Performances: Canciones de mi Padre*, PBS. Children's Program: *Free to Be...a Family*, ABC. Classical Program in Performing Arts: *Great Performances: Bernstein at 70!*, PBS; Governor's Award: Lucille Ball.

Miscellaneous (p. 355)

Country Music Awards, by Country Music Assn.: Entertainer: George Strait; single: "I'm No Stranger to the Rain," Keith Whitley; album: "Will the Circle Be Unbroken, Vol. II," Nitty Gritty Dirt Band; song: "Chiseled in Stone," Max D. Barnes, Vern Gosdin; vocal duo: The Judds; female vocalist: Kathy Mattea; male vocalist: Ricky Van Shelton; vocal group: Highway 101; vocal event: Hank Williams Jr., Hank Williams Sr., "There's a Tear in My Beer;" Horizon Award: Clint Black; Hall of Fame: Jack Staton, Cliffie Stone, Hank Thompson.

Nobel Prizes (p. 343-345)

(Each 1989 Nobel Prize carried a cash award of from $455,000 to $470,000.)

Physiology or Medicine: J. Michael Bishop and Harold E. Varmus, American cancer researchers at the Univ. of Calif. Medical School in San Francisco, shared the award.

Chemistry: Sidney Altman of Yale Univ. and Thomas R. Cech of the Univ. of Colorado shared the award. Independently, each discovered that the crucial genetic substance RNA was not merely a passive carrier of genetic information, but could actively aid chemical reactions in the cells. Cech is an American; Altman, born in Montreal, is a citizen of both Canada and the U.S.

Physics: Norman F. Ramsey of Harvard Univ. won the award, which was also shared by Hans G. Dehmelt of the Univ. of Washington and Wolfgang Paul of the Univ. of Bonn. Ramsey's work led to the development of the atomic clock, which measures the vibrations of atoms to create a time standard used around the world. Dehmelt and Paul developed methods to isolate atoms and subatomic particles for study.

Peace: The Dailai Lama, Tibet's exiled religious and political leader, was awarded the prize in recognition of his nonviolent campaign over nearly 40 years to end China's domination of his homeland.

Memorial Prize in Economics: Trygve Haavelmo, a Norwegian, won the award for his pioneering work in methods for testing economic theories, which helped prepare the way for modern economic forecasting.

Literature: Camilo José Cela, who broke literary taboos after the Spanish Civil War, won the award.

Miss America (p. 355)

Miss Missouri, Debbye Turner, was crowned Miss American 1990 on Sept. 16, 1989 in Atlantic City, N.J.

Chronology—July 1989 (p. 59)

Man Convicted of Killing Swedish Premier; Released in October—Carl Gustav Christer Pettersson was found guilty in a Stockholm court, July 27, of the 1986 shooting death of Swedish Prime Minister Olof Palme, and was later sentenced to life in prison. On Oct. 12, an appeals court overturned the conviction saying the evidence was inadequate, and Pettersson was released.

Congress (pp. 304; 299; 302)

Rep. Mickey Leland (D, Tex.) was killed in the crash of a small plane operated by the Ethiopian Relief and Rehabilitation Commission.

Pete Geren won a special election to fill the House seat from Texas of former Speaker Jim Wright, who resigned on June 30, 1989.

Gary Condit was elected to the House seat of Tony Coelho, who resigned in June. Gene Taylor (D., Miss.) won a special election on Oct. 17, 1989, to succeed Rep. Larkin Smith.

Corporate Mergers and Acquisitions (p. 87)

Sony Corp. agreed to buy Columbia Pictures from Coca-Cola for $3.4 billion.

Counties (p. 593)

The correct area for Yuma County, Arizona is 5,564 sq. mi.

HDTV (p. 163)

At the end of Sept. 1989, the Commerce Dept. announced it had abandoned its plans for a focused initiative on HDTV.

Meteorological Data (p. 228)

The 1988 temperatures, worldwide, were the highest in the 130 years that reliable records had been kept. The average temperature was put at 57.61°F.

Nations (pp. 686; 692; 723; 733; 738)

Algeria: Kasdi Merbah was dismissed as prime minister.
Bolivia: Jaime Paz Zamora was elected president.
Italy: Giulio Andreotti was named prime minister.
Malta: Dr. Censu Tabone was named president.
New Zealand: Geoffrey Palmer was chosen prime minister.

Original Names of Entertainers (p. 412)

The original name of Sting is Gordon Somner.

Stock Market (p. 66)

The stock market regained stability during the week of Oct. 16-20.

Trade and Transportation (p. 140)

France introduced, Sept. 20, 1989, the T.G.V. Atlantique, at 186-m.p.h., the world's fastest train to be put into commercial service. Run by France's state-owned railway, it connects Paris with cities on France's Atlantic coast.

Late Additions

Please see p. 959 for late news: Northern California earthquake and change of leadership in East Germany.

Heroes of Young America: The Tenth Annual Poll

Michael Jordan, the basketball star of the Chicago Bulls, was named the "Top Hero" of Young America in *The World Almanac*'s tenth annual poll of high school students. The students in grades 8 through 12 were asked to select those individuals in public life they admired most. The schools chosen to participate represented a geographic cross-section of the United States. In addition to choosing a top hero, the teenagers were asked to make selections in 8 other categories.

The Top Hero

Born in Brooklyn, N.Y. in 1963 and raised in North Carolina, Michael Jordan has become not only one of the leading stars in the National Basketball Assn., but one of the most popular personalities in America. Jordan, who was also named the top sports hero (for the third consecutive year), has gained fame beyond the basketball arena through his many endorsements (fast foods, breakfast cereal, sneakers and clothing, soft drink, etc.) as well as his involvement in charities and other community services.

In a tie for second place were businessman Donald Trump and former president Ronald Reagan. The third place finisher was Tom Cruise, the top hero in 1987, followed by two-time top hero winner Eddie Murphy and former top hero Bill Cosby. In sixth place was Soviet leader Mikhail Gorbachev, which marks the first time that a leader of a nation other than the U.S. has appeared on the list. Jesse Jackson finished in seventh place and was followed by basketball star Magic Johnson, and Patrick Swayze.

While no woman finished in the top ten, the write-in for "Mom" received more votes than any female individual. "Parents" and "Dad" also received many write-in votes in the top hero category.

Books, Songs, and TV Shows

When asked to name their **all-time favorite book**, the students chose S.E. Hinton's *The Outsiders*. Other books receiving substantial mention included Stephen King's *Pet Sematary*, *The Bible*, and J.D. Salinger's *The Catcher in the Rye*.

The overwhelming selection for **favorite song** of 1989 was "Patience" by Guns N' Roses. The **least favorite song** of 1989 was Madonna's "Like a Prayer," which was followed closely by Bobby McFerrin's "Don't Worry, Be Happy" and "Wild Thing" by Tone-Loc.

The **favorite television show** for 1989 was "Roseanne," followed by "The Cosby Show" and "The Wonder Years." The **least favorite show** among the students was "Alf." Among the other least favorite TV shows named were "Roseanne" and "Married With Children."

Listed below are the top male and female vote getters in each category. The winner is listed first.

Top Hero

Michael Jordan, basketball player, Chicago Bulls
Mom, a write-in

Movie Performers/Non-Comedy

Dustin Hoffman, *Rain Man*
Whoopie Goldberg, *The Color Purple*

Television Performers/Non-Comedy

Johnny Depp, "21 Jump Street"
Oprah Winfrey, "The Oprah Winfrey Show"

Comedy

Roseanne Barr, "Roseanne"
Eddie Murphy, *Coming to America*

Music and Dance

Debbie Gibson, pop singer
Eddie Van Halen, rock guitarist, singer

Sports

Michael Jordan, Chicago Bulls
Florence Griffith-Joyner, Olympic champion

News and Sports Media

Barbara Walters, "20/20"
Tom Brokaw, NBC News

Artists and Writers

Stephen King, *Pet Sematary*
Judy Blume, *Tiger Eyes*

Politicians and Newsmakers

Neil Armstrong, former astronaut
Sandra Day O'Connor, Supreme Court Justice

The Heroes of Young America: 1980-1989

1980	Burt Reynolds	1984	Michael Jackson	1987	Tom Cruise
1981	Burt Reynolds	1985	Eddie Murphy	1988	Eddie Murphy
1982	Alan Alda	1986	Bill Cosby	1989	Michael Jordan
1983	Sylvester Stallone				

"The true function of the hero lies in the realm of imagination. Heroes give a child access to what the novelist Cynthia Ozick calls *the grand as if*. When a young girl dreams of heroes, she dreams as if she were free: Limitations of height or weight or sex or race become irrelevant. A hero represents not so much a specific achievement as a whole range of human possibilities, an awe-inspiring glimpse of perfection."

This summary of the function of a hero is from an article by writer Susan Jacoby entitled "The First Girl at Second Base," in which Jacoby discusses her dreams of becoming a major league baseball player. Her definition seems appropriate when trying to capsulize the results of the past ten years of *The World Almanac*'s polling of high school students. Given this definition, it is not surprising that the list of Top Heroes of Young America comes exclusively from the fields of entertainment and sports. If a hero is someone who symbolizes the ideal of a group, someone admired and emulated for his/her achievements and qualities, then it is to be expected that actors who portray larger-than-life characters or athletes whose accomplishments seem "superhuman" are the heroes of America's youth. It also is important to remember that it is often the fictional characters that are played by actors or the persona an entertainer presents that is admired rather than, or in addition to, the real-life personality.

An examination of the list of top heroes reveals that these men represent a combination of the traditional, male-dominated notion of heroism (strength, courage, "machismo") with many character traits associated with adolescence (anti-authoritarian, individualistic, wise-cracking). In Burt Reynolds, the image on the screen is one of physical and mental toughness, while his off-the-screen persona, as demonstrated in his late night talk show appearances, is one of glibness and good humor. Alan Alda's portrayal of Hawkeye Pierce on one of television's all-time successes, "MASH," also presents a wise-cracking, anti-authoritarian individual. Perhaps the most typical male notion of heroism has been captured by Sylvester Stallone's "winners" in the "Rocky" and "Rambo" movie series. It is Stallone's characters that have the strong appeal to his fans, and it is Rocky's overachievement and Rambo's John Wayne-like assaults on the "enemy" that have captivated millions of viewers. The popularity of Tom Cruise's *Top Gun* and his appeal to young women as a romantic lead were directly responsible for his selection as a top hero.

One of the most interesting factors to arise from the ten years of polling is the clear evidence that when selecting a hero, American teenagers are not restricted

(continued)

by racial barriers. Five of the ten top heroes are black and represent a wide range of qualities. In 1984, there was no bigger star than Michael Jackson. While Jackson certainly does not fit into the mold of some of the other heroes, his dynamic performances and his enormous popularity as a recording artist and song writer made him an idol for young people of all races and backgrounds. Jackson's image (before so much was known about his private life) as a drug-free, family oriented pop star had great appeal not only to teenagers, but to music lovers of all ages.

Two-time winner Eddie Murphy, like Jackson, Cruise, and Michael Jordan, has the special appeal to young people of being a big star at a very young age. It is worthwhile noting that most of the recent top heroes have been young men. Bill Cosby's selection in 1986 came as his number one rated TV show was at the peak of its popularity. In Dr. Heathcliff Huxtable, America's youth sees a highly successful professional, a loving but strict father, and a man who is proud of his race. As is the case with his weekly situation comedy, Cosby's popularity crosses all so-called "color lines."

This year's choice for top hero, Michael Jordan, exemplifies "an awe-inspiring glimpse of perfection" on the basketball court, and his image off the court of a clean-cut, hard-working, charitable young man solidifies his position as someone to be admired and emulated by America's youth.

A glance at the list of top heroes reveals that while race does not seem to be a factor, the sex of those admired is relevant. There have been no women named the top hero, and only Oprah Winfrey, in 1988, was named among the top ten finishers. However, in 1989, "Mom" (as in "my Mom") received more votes than any individual female personality. While no women have been able to break this apparent sex barrier, it is probably unfair to assume that teenagers are any more

sexist than the general population. Not only has the poll revealed the continuing notion of heroism as a male domain, but the segments of society from which we choose our heroes continue to be dominated by males. The top box office stars, television personalities, athletes, and business leaders (as demonstrated by annual surveys of the most influential Americans) are, for the most part, male. It can be assumed from the polling that in a period when more than 50 percent of mothers are in the workforce, many teenagers look up to their mothers as role models and as women whose everyday behavior is admired.

In order to gain a better understanding of what concerns the youth of America, this year's poll included a question pertaining to the **most important event in the past ten years.** The idea that teenagers are only interested in celebrities and "superhumans" is dispelled by the results of this survey. The most important event in the 1980s according to the high school students was the explosion and loss of life of the space shuttle *Challenger* in 1986. For many of the students, this tragedy was the equivalent of the Pres. Kennedy or Martin Luther King Jr. assassinations. In addition to watching the event on television, the catastrophe had added impact for this audience because of the death of school teacher Christa McAuliffe. In years to come, it is conceivable that this generation will be asking "Where were you when the *Challenger* exploded?" The other events that dominated the 80s included the signing of the INF Treaty, the AIDS crisis, and the holding of 52 American hostages in Iran in 1980-1981.

In *The Power of Myth*, Joseph Campbell states that "One of the many distinctions between the celebrity and the hero is that one lives only for self while the other acts to redeem society." If we accept this idea, then it is also important to remember that part of the maturing process is sorting out the difference between heroes and celebrities.

M.S.H., Editor

Attitudes Toward Aging

For the first time, *The World Almanac* and Maturity News Service(distributed by United Feature Syndicate) contracted ICR Survey Research Group to conduct a study concerning various issues about the elderly. A total of 1,006 respondents (half male and half female) were contacted by phone to complete the study. Respondents were aged 18 years and older. The data were weighted to provide nationally representative and projectable estimates of the adult population. The range of error for the total sample is ± 3.09 percent.

A summary of the results of the poll follows.

1. **At what age do you consider a person to be old?**—On average, 65 years was considered old. As the respondents' age increased so did their perceptions of a person as being old. Those between age 18 and 34 felt a person 63 years was old, while those 65 and older felt that 72 was old.

2. **At what age should people retire?**—Overall, age 62 was the point at which the population thought people should retire. (It is interesting that this age is a few years younger than the age at which this group considers a person to be old.) More than one-third of all respondents (36%) said that it depended on the person and did not give a specific age.

3. **Will the Social Security System be secure in 20 years?**—The majority (51%) did not believe the Social Security System would be secure in 20 years. Those under the age of 45 were significantly more likely to have doubts (67%) than those aged 45 years and older (30%). Those living in the Northeast had the most faith in the system (50%) as compared to those in the West who had the least faith (32%).

4. **Do you attend regular religious services?**—Differences in age and sex clearly separated the respondents on this question. While 54.2% of those over 65 said they did attend religious services, only 42.6% of those between 18-34 answered yes. Over fifty percent (52.5%) of females said they regularly attended religious services compared to 41.9% males. Geographically, those in the West attended the least with 39.1% responding yes.

5. **Do you believe in God?**—Almost all respondents (97%) said that they do believe in God. The belief in God was proportional across the various age groups and sex.

6. **For what purpose would you accept a tax increase?**—For education, 80%; to create a comprehensive health program, 77%; helping the poor, 75%; more funds for law enforcement and prisons, 59%; more military spending, 22%; and none of the above, 5%.

7. **Old Americans are mostly . . .?**—(Respondents were read a series of paired statements.) Overall, the result of this question showed that most Americans thought older Americans were the same as everybody else. Those statements receiving the most mentions were: poor and struggling (40%); compassionate and giving (41%); and live in the past (37%). Only 6.7% of the respondents felt that older Americans were "too self-centered," and 13.6% felt that older citizens were "open to new ideas." Over 10% of those between 18-34 felt that older Americans were "well-fixed financially" compared to 1.9% of those over 65.

The World Almanac

and Book of Facts for 1990

The Top 10 News Stories

Just when it seemed that massive economic reforms were moving China to a more capitalistic system, student demonstrations calling for a government based on democracy and less political corruption were crushed by military force resulting in many deaths and arrests.

Alaska's Prince William Sound was the site of one of the largest oil spills after the Exxon Valdez struck a reef; the resulting environmental damage and cleanup was still being debated 6 months later.

Mismanagement by Poland's Communist Party and the severe economic problems of the nation led to the rise to power of Solidarity and the forming of a new government under the premiership of a long-time adviser to Lech Walesa.

Elected by 54 percent of the voters, former V.P. George Bush became the 41st president of the United States.

Sharply divided (5-4), the Supreme Court ruled in favor of putting new restraints on a woman's right to have an abortion, although it did not overturn Roe v. Wade.

Demands for independence and autonomy in the Baltic republics and continued economic difficulties were the most pressing domestic issues faced by Soviet leader Mikhail Gorbachev, as he continued to call for sweeping political reform and international disarmament.

Involvement of U.S. military forces in the attempted overthrow of Panama's Manuel Noriega and assistance to the Colombian government in its attempt to control the powerful drug cartels marked the Bush administration's efforts to curb the growing international illegal drug trade, as the President presented his plan to fight drug abuse to the nation.

Xenophiles' attention was focused on Hungary as it cut down its barbed-wire fence along its border with Austria and became a passageway for E. Germans fleeing to W. Germany; a new Hungarian constitution will go into effect in 1990 moving the nation away from Communist domination.

Over 40,000 Americans have full-fledged AIDS and another 100,000 to 200,000 are infected with the AIDS virus and have mild symptoms according to government health officials.

Natural disasters took a heavy toll as an earthquake hit the San Francisco Bay area causing at least 59 deaths and massive property damage; Hurricane Hugo swept through the Caribbean and into S. Carolina causing more than 50 deaths and immense property damage.

The Decade in Review: Heroes, Victims, and Villains of the 1980s

Ten years ago, The World Almanac's "Review of the 1970s" identified the "heroes, victims, and villains" who "embodied the trends and issues of the decade." The personalities profiled were: Richard Nixon and Henry Kissinger; Deng Xiaoping; Leonid Brezhnev; Andrei Sakharov and Aleksandr Solzhenitsyn; Anwar Sadat; Yasir Arafat; the Shah of Iran; Idi Amin Dada; Patty Hearst; Robert Woodward and Carl Bernstein; Gloria Steinem and Phyllis Shlafly; and Betty Ford.

Which personalities might best symbolize the 1980s?

Ronald Reagan's 1980 campaign promised "morning again in America" to a nation demoralized by double-digit inflation, a gasoline crunch, and the Carter administration's failure to rescue American hostages in Iran. As Reagan took the oath of office on Jan. 20, 1981, the 52 American hostages held for 444 days were released. "Reaganomics" was one byword of the 80s: budget cuts and tax reductions did result in economic growth. Reagan increased defense spending while cutting back on social spending, which opponents called unjust to less advantaged Americans. But in the 1984 election campaign, when the president asked Americans if they were "better off . . . than four years ago," the answer was a landslide re-election. Reagan's second term was marked by massive tax reform (Tax Reform Act of 1986) and arms agreements (INF Treaty), with the USSR. However, it was clouded by the Iran-contra scandal, including the Tower Commission's criticism of the president's detached management style; the 1987 stockmarket crash; questions about the ethics of many in the Reagan administration; the savings and loan institution crisis; the trade deficit; and the budget deficit that reached $3.2 trillion in 1988. Still, Reagan left office as one of the most popular presidents in history. And his personal appeal, along with his legacy of peace and prosperity, were among the major factors that made George Bush the first vice president elected to the Oval Office since 1836.

Elected general secretary of the Central Committee of the Communist Party of the USSR on March 11, 1985, Mikhail Gorbachev promoted radical political and economic reform within the Soviet Union and a restructuring of its relations with the outside world. Frequent foreign trips enhanced his reputation abroad, although at home he encountered resistance to change, nationalist movements, and continued economic problems that brought, in 1989, the worst series of strikes since 1917. The USSR agreed, on Feb. 8, 1988, to withdraw its troops from Afghanistan. At a third summit with Pres. Reagan on Dec. 8, 1987, Gorbachev and the U.S. president signed the INF treaty, eliminating all U.S. and Soviet intermediate range nuclear missiles. Gorbachev's maneuvering had produced, by late 1988, a Politburo and a Central Committee Secretariat likely to back up "glasnost" and "perestroika." He assumed the presidency of the USSR on Oct. 1, 1988. In a U.N. speech in Dec., 1988, he announced a unilateral reduction of 500,000 Soviet troops over the next 2 years, and a withdrawal of 10,000 tanks from Eastern Europe. The Soviet legislature, as of fall 1989, was weighing the legalization of alternative political parties having equal rights with the Communist Party. (See "Communism" in Index for details.)

Lech Walesa, almost a decade after signing the Gdansk agreement that founded the free trade union Solidarity, remained a symbol of Poland's struggle for freedom and democracy. After Solidarity was outlawed and martial law imposed, on Dec. 13, 1981, Walesa spent 11 months in confinement. He was awarded the Nobel Peace Prize in 1983. After a series of strikes, the Jaruzelski regime chose to link its hopes for economic reform to a "historic compromise." The Polish government and its non-communist opposition, led by Walesa, agreed on Apr. 5, 1989 to a new government structure, including a bicameral national legislature. The agreement also restored Solidarity's legal status.

The June 1989 voting routed the Communists. Solidarity's total of 260 legislators represented the first formal political opposition in a Soviet-bloc government since the post-WW II period. Walesa persuaded Peasant and Democratic party leaders to support Solidarity's candidate for prime minister, Tadeuz Mazowieki, who was duly elected on Aug. 24, 1989.

Ayatollah Ruhollah Khomeini headed the 1979 revolution that overthrew 2,500 years of monarchy and transformed the relatively Westernized Iran into an extremist Islamic nation. Khomeini termed the U.S. and the USSR "the Great Satans." As supreme religious and political leader for life, he persecuted religious minorities, refused recognition to Islamic sects other than his own Shiite sect, and curtailed women's rights. He led his country in an 8-year war against neighboring Iraq, and expressed bitterness over accepting a U.N.-sponsored cease-fire in July 1988. Khomeini supported militants' seizing the U.S. embassy in Teheran on Nov. 4, 1979, and holding its staff hostage for 444 days. In 1989, he called on Moslems around the world to kill British citizen Salman Rushdie, whose novel, *Satanic Verses,* was said to blaspheme Islam. Khomeini died on June 3, 1989 at 86 or 89; in the area around his burial site, mourners numbered 3 to 10 million.

The 80s were marked by a surge of **terrorism.** In Jan. 1989 the Pentagon issued a report describing 52 terrorist groups. Among the most dramatic terrorist acts of the decade were the TNT-laden terrorist's blowing up of U.S. Marine headquarters in Beirut, killing 241 Americans, while a truck bomb blew up a French paratroop barracks, killing 58, in 1984; and the 1985 hijacking of the Italian luxury liner *Achille Lauro,* the killing of an elderly American passenger, and the subsequent interception by U.S. aircraft of the Egyptian plane flying the terrorists to safety. Almost 700 acts of terrorism worldwide, including attacks in London, Paris, Rome, and Vienna took place in 1985. On Apr. 14-15, U.S. bombers raided the Libyan cities of Tripoli and Benghazi, in retaliation against alleged Libyan involvement in terrorism in Europe. Casualties, military and civilian, numbered 130, including the adopted daughter of Libyan leader Col. Muammar al-Qaddafy. In 1987, terrorist incidents rose to 832, and in 1988 to more than 1,000, although the U.S. State Dept. noted a decrease in the number of "spectacular" attacks.

In Feb. 1988 grand juries in the U.S. indicted **Gen. Manuel Noriega,** head of Panama's National Defense Forces and de facto head of state, on charges of providing protection for international drug traffickers and permitting drug profits to be laundered through Panamanian banks. The U.S. froze millions of dollars in assets belonging to the government of Panama, and the State Dept. began talks with Noriega, seeking his removal. On Jan. 16, 1989, Noriega opened his own bank in Panama City. After a 2-year investigation, a Senate subcommittee concluded on Apr. 3, 1989 that "one of the most serious foreign policy failures" of the Reagan administration was "turning a blind eye" to corruption and drug dealing by Noriega. At Panamanian presidential elections on May 7, 1989, Noriega's candidate claimed victory, but foreign observers alleged fraud, and on May 10 the Panamanian government annulled the vote, charging foreign interference. Pres. Bush, on May 13, 1989, called on Panamanian citizens and the Panama Defense Forces to overthrow Noriega.

Latin America was the world's leading producer of cocaine and an important producer of marijuana and heroin in the 1980s. Colombian and other Latin American **drug-trafficking** groups were exporting, by the late 80s, an estimated 100-200 tons of cocaine annually. Huge profits in the illegal trade were accompanied by widespread government corruption and violence against enforcers and rival drug lords, not just in the main drug-producing countries but throughout the continent.

Illicit retail drug sales in the U.S. in 1980 totalled more than $79 billion. In March 1981, Pres. Reagan advocated a national drug abuse program, to focus on young people; and in 1982 he proposed 12 regional antidrug task forces that would focus on organized crime. The use of cocaine, in the cheap, potent form of "crack," began to be a special problem in late 1985. In Aug. 1986, Pres. Reagan declared a "war" on illegal drugs; Nancy Reagan promoted a "Just Say No" antidrug campaign aimed at young people. Pres. Reagan signed an antidrug bill on Nov. 18, 1988, establishing a cabinet-level office to direct policy and develop strategies to combat drug use.

Anti-apartheid sentiment gathered force in the 80s. In Nov. 1983, South African white voters approved a constitution that for the first time gave "Coloureds" and Asians a limited voice, while still excluding blacks—70% of the population. **Bishop Desmond Tutu,** a black Anglican clergyman who headed the South African Council of Churches, was awarded the Nobel Peace Prize in 1984 as a "unifying force in the campaign to resolve the problem of apartheid." Tutu criticized Pres. Reagan's policy of "constructive engagement" with the white minority government in South Africa as an "unmitigated disaster." Face to face with Reagan, on Dec. 7, 1984, he asked the U.S. president to speak out against abuses in South Africa. Congress passed economic sanctions against South Africa over Reagan's veto in 1986. That year, the South African government called a "state of emergency," which curtailed open resistance, and which would continue throughout 1987 and 1988. The Bush administration, reviewing its South Africa policy in May and June 1989, conferred with Tutu, now an Archbishop, who expressed cautious optimism. In Sept. 1989, P.W. Botha, South Africa's president during the 80s, was succeeded by F.W. de Klerk, on a platform of "evolutionary" change through negotiation with the black population. DeKlerk soon allowed 35,000 protestors to March through Cape Town. On Sept. 28, 1989, Johannesburg eliminated the last remnants of "petty apartheid," by opening recreation centers and swimming pools to all races, with buses to be desegregated within weeks.

In July 1987, during 6 days of nationally televised Iran-contra hearings, **Lt. Col. Oliver North** of the U.S. Marines telegenically defended the covert activities of the National Security Council, including the arms deal with Iran and the use of Iranian funds for the Nicaraguan rebels; he admitted ordering the shredding of documents, and lying to investigators. Expressing no regrets, he said he was a patriotic American, following orders in a just cause. North was convicted on May 4, 1989, on one count each of aiding and abetting the obstruction of Congress, destroying government documents, and receiving a home security system as an illegal gratuity. He was acquitted on 9 other counts. Fined $150,000, he received a 3-year suspended sentence, because of "the many highly commendable aspects" of his life. North was not a leader in the arms scandal, the judge also said, but "a low-ranking subordinate working to carry out initiatives of a few cynical superiors."

Rev. Jesse Jackson was the first black man to make a serious attempt at the U.S. presidency. A Baptist minister, onetime associate of Rev. Martin Luther

King Jr., and founder of Operation PUSH, a black self-help group, Jackson had never held elective office when he made his first bid for the presidency in 1984. His candidacy brought increased voter registration among black Americans. Jackson won about 3.2 million votes during those Democratic primaries, calling for a "Rainbow Coalition" of voters of every race to defeat Reagan. In 1988, Jackson was the only real rival of Mass. Gov. Michael S. Dukakis at the campaign's end. The final convention count on July 21, 1988 was 2,876.25 for Dukakis, 1,218.5 for Jackson. Two days earlier, Jackson had roused the convention crowd with an eloquent and impassioned speech, ending with the exhortation to "Keep hope alive!"

The U.S. observed the first federal holiday in honor of Rev. Martin Luther King Jr. on Jan. 20, 1986. In 1989, Rep. William H. Gray III (Dem., Pa.) became the first black elected majority whip; Ronald H. Brown, the first black to head a major U.S. political party; Gen. Colin L. Powell the first black chairman of the Joint Chiefs of Staff; and Bill White the first black to head a major baseball league. The 80s also saw **black Americans** make enormous contributions to popular culture, through such entertainers as Bill Cosby, Oprah Winfrey, Michael Jackson, and Eddie Murphy; such athletes as Michael Jordan; and such writers as Alice Walker and Toni Morrison. However, in 1987 U.S. whites had a life expectancy of 75.6 years, blacks a life expectancy of 69.4 years; the infant mortality rate for whites was 8.6%, the rate for blacks 17.9%;, and an astounding 45.8% of black children were living in poverty. In 1986, black unemployment levels were double the white rate, with the rate for black teenagers 41%. The average white income was almost double that of blacks in July 1986. The gap was widening between the proportion of white and black high school graduates who completed college. The decade was also marked by an increase in racial violence, and by a surge of racist incidents on college campuses.

Donald Trump might best represent what Pres. Reagan, in his farewell address, called a "booming" entrepreneurship. Son of an apartment building developer and manager in Queens, New York, Trump made his first big solo real estate deal in the 80s. The Trump Tower, a luxury high-rise apartment building, was erected next to Tiffany's on Manhattan's Fifth Avenue in 1983. By the end of the decade, Trump's empire included Manhattan's luxurious Trump Parc and the Plaza; Trump's Castle and Trump's Plaza, his hotels and casinos in Atlantic City; and the Eastern Airlines Shuttle, renamed the Trump Shuttle. Trump's 1987 book, *Trump: The Art of the Deal*, became a bestseller; at the end of 1989 he was negotiating a TV game show to be called "Trump Card."

The 1985 death of actor Rock Hudson brought to America's attention the plight of some other representatives of the 80s—the **AIDS victims.** A study, released on June 26, 1989 by the General Accounting Office, concluded that earlier government estimates of the number of AIDS cases in the U.S. had seriously underestimated the extent of the disease. The GAO predicted that 300,000 to 480,000 cases of AIDS would be diagnosed by the end of 1991, a figure one-third higher than that of the federal Centers for Disease Control. Further, although as of Nov. 1988 changes in sexual practices seemed to be slowing the epidemic somewhat in developed countries, the World Health Organization described the situation in African and other third world nations, where the transmission was primarily

heterosexual, as potentially devastating. One hopeful note: federal health officials announced, on Aug. 17, 1989, that the drug AZT was shown to delay the onset of AIDS in people infected with the disease who had shown no symptoms, "a turning point in the battle to change AIDS from a fatal disease to a treatable one."

Amid a boom in real estate in the 80s, many Americans lacked a roof over their heads. It was uncertain what percentages of the **homeless** were mentally ill, drug or alcohol abusers, or victims of the shortage of low-income housing. However, on Nov. 21, 1988, the head of the General Accounting Office told Pres.-elect Bush that the federal government must address a number of serious problems neglected by the Reagan administration, including the homeless. The GAO recommended $20 billion to repair public housing, and noted that perhaps 3 million Americans were now homeless, with the supply of low-income rental housing shrinking, and "very deep federal subsidies" possibly needed to encourage private investment.

Prominent among other **social problems** of the 80s was child abuse, including sexual child abuse. The decade also saw increased white collar crime in the stock and commodities markets, notably insider trading; and computer crime made an impact. Ethical questions were posed by a rise in corporate mergers and takeovers, with the increased use of junk bonds and leveraged buyout. Sports scandals of the 80s included steroid use; college sports controversies included favoritism to athletes regarding scholastic requirements. Ethical questions accompanied the results of many scientific and technological achievements, such as the actual and potential environmental damage of the "greenhouse effect," acid rain, toxic waste, and unsafe nuclear power plants. Artificial insemination of a surrogate mother resulted in the controversial "Baby M" legal battle. The "right to die" became an issue as medical science advanced. At the end of the decade, the U.S. was the only Western country to use the death penalty.

With the defeat of the Equal Rights Amendment as the 80s began, the **women's movement** lacked a strong focus for much of the decade. Some 300,000 advocates of women's right to choose whether to have an abortion marched on Washington, D.C. in April 1989; but on July 3, the Supreme Court upheld, 5-4, the restrictive Missouri abortion law that opened up the possibility of dismantling Roe v. Wade, the 1973 decision recognizing a constitutional right to abortion.

Sandra Day O'Connor became the first female Supreme Court justice in 1981, Sally Ride the first female astronaut in 1983, and Geraldine Ferraro the first female vice presidential candidate of a major party in 1984. More women than ever were in the work force in the 1980s. As of 1987, 50.8% of mothers were back in the job market within a year of giving birth, compared with 31% in 1976. Wives who worked outside the home year-round and full-time earned 57% of husband's earnings as of 1987. Whether married or unmarried, women employed year-round and full-time in 1987 earned 65 cents for every dollar earned by men. Most working wives continued to hold major responsibility for children and household in the 80s. Concern about the "Mommy track" for women in business and the professions came to the fore in 1989. The poverty rate for female-headed households with no spouse present was 34.7% in 1987.

June Foley, history editor

The Changing Face of Communism

China

The Chinese people have historically believed that their leaders are invested with a certain moral authority, a "mandate from heaven." But Mao Zedong, founder of the Communist state, had said, "Political power grows out of the barrel of a gun." Through their control of the army, the Chinese leaders still held the guns in 1989, but their moral authority was brought into doubt.

Deng, China's paramount leader, had replaced the drab egalitarian poverty of the Mao era with some free-market economic incentives, and had introduced his people to such Western attractions as color television and jewelry. Capitalism took root in "special economic zones."

The new economic freedoms in China had created new opportunities for official corruption and favoritism. Young people, impatient with the pace of reform, emboldened by an apparent growing tolerance of dissent, and believing that democracy was the answer to corruption, were primed to speak out against the regime by early 1989. Though exposed to Western ideas in the classroom, many had an innocent view of what they wanted. "I don't know exactly what democracy is, but we need more of it," a physics student said.

The immediate cause of the massive public protests was the death in April of Hu Yaobang, former general secretary and chairman of the Chinese Community Party. He had been forced from a leadership role in 1987 by conservatives who disapproved of his reformist sympathies. Student marches supporting Hu began immediately after his death, and soon swelled to 100,000 in size. Gathering in Tiananmen Square in Beijing, they called for freedom of speech and assembly, and for increased expenditures for education. The unrest spread to other cities. University students in Beijing began boycotting classes, Apr. 24. Student leaders met with several officials, but some students said later that their principal complaints had not been addressed. Premier Li Peng said in April that China had no plans to implement the type of political changes, e.g., multicandidate elections, that were taking place in the Soviet Union.

A major diplomatic development, the visit of Soviet leader Mikhail Gorbachev to China, was overshadowed by the demonstrations. The world's 2 largest Communist countries, China and the Soviet Union, had become bitter antagonists in the 1960s. Although tensions had eased in recent years, no Soviet leader had visited China since 1959. That hiatus ended May 15 when Gorbachev arrived in Beijing, where 150,000 persons were camped in Tiananmen Square near the Great Hall of the People, headquarters for China's leadership. The Soviet visitors' itinerary was changed to avoid the demonstrators.

Gorbachev met with Deng Li and Zhao Ziang, head of the Chinese Communist Party. It was reported later that no agreement had been reached on Cambodia, where the Communist superpowers were backing different factions. Zhao reportedly told Gorbachev that economic reforms were possible without political restructuring. Referring to the demonstrators, Gorbachev reportedly told Zhao that he had little sympathy for "hotheads" who advocated overnight change.

On May 17, more than 1 million persons, including many workers, packed the square, and crowds formed in at least 20 other cities. Li and Zhao visited hunger strikers in a Beijing hospital. After Gorbachev left China, they visited the square. Zhao said that the demonstrators had "good intentions" but that they must be patient.

Li announced the imposition of martial law 2 days later, and military units took up positions on the outskirts of the capital. Western observers saw this as an indication that Li and Deng, who were considered hard-liners, had won an internal power struggle. In response, a million persons again filled the streets of Beijing. They blocked military convoys and urged soldiers to turn back. Some 500,000 persons marched in Hong Kong in support of the demonstrators, and other protests were staged around the world.

In late May, the number of protestors declined, and Zhao's influence in the leadership was reported to have waned. Chinese art students erected a 33-foot Goddess of Liberty statute in the square suggestive of the Statue of Liberty.

The leadership abandoned restraint in early June and ordered the troops to put an end to the demonstrations. The "People's Army" opened fire on citizens, some armed with stones, and swept through Beijing at night shooting and literally rolling over protestors with their tanks. Estimates of the death toll, mostly in Beijing, ranged from 500 to 7,000. The leadership denied that many had died, and said that most of the victims had been soldiers. As many as 10,000 persons may have been injured.

China's rulers then began to round up dissident leaders. Some of the student organizers fled abroad. By late summer, perhaps 10,000 persons had been arrested, though apparently fewer than half of them were students and intellectuals. Of these, at least 31 were tried and executed for alleged acts of resistance against the authorities. None of the initial group executed in Beijing and Shanghai were students. They were peasants, workers, or men with criminal records.

The ouster of Zhao as Communist Party Chief was announced at the end of a Central Committee meeting in June. He had shown conciliation toward the students. Hu Qili, the party's propaganda chief, was also replaced, as were a number of other party and government officials. And yet, many lower-ranking officials who had been sympathetic—some of them had even joined the marches—were not replaced. Zhao was accused of fostering "counterrevolutionary rebellion."

In July, the Politburo adopted reforms aimed at combating official corruption. Children and spouses of top officials could not engage in "commercial activities." The importation of limousines for leaders was prohibited, as was the use of public funds for entertaining.

After 3 months out of the public eye, Deng reappeared in September. While reaffirming that the regime would adhere to the tenets of communism, he said China would keep its door open to the West and preserve the economic policies of the past decade. It was reported that he had chosen Jiang Zemin, the new party secretary and a comparative moderate, as his successor.

The Soviet Union

Few world leaders, and certainly no previous Soviet leader, had attained the level of international popularity that Mikhail Gorbachev experienced in 1989. A visit to New York and a speech to the United Nations in December 1988 had gone well. The general secretary had announced sharp cuts in Soviet military forces and endorsed the broadening of human rights in the USSR.

In February, the Soviet military withdrawal from Afghanistan was completed, clearing away a major impediment to better relations between the Soviet Union and the rest of the world. The Afghan retreat, leaving the Soviet puppet regime to cope largely by itself with anti-Communist rebels, was a clear signal that Soviet military intervention in other countries was a forsaken policy. Three months later, the summit in Beijing foreshadowed an opportunity to cut back costly defenses along the border between the 2 Communist powers.

Visiting France in July, Gorbachev reiterated his hopes for a "common European home," and he said interference by any nation in the domestic affairs of other nations was "inadmissible." Gorbachev's objectives in this "peace offensive" included increased trade with the West and access to its more advanced technology.

In domestic politics, on the surface at least, Gorbachev appeared to be consolidating his power. At his behest, the Supreme Soviet in December 1988 had approved changes in the constitution that provided for a new legislature. The 2,250-member upper house, the Congress of People's Deputies, would be chosen in elections in which candidates could run against each other, a dramatic departure from the era of handpicked party stalwarts who ran unopposed. The much smaller lower house, also to be called the Supreme Soviet, would be chosen by the Congress and would serve as a standing legislature. The president, to be chosen by the legislature for a maximum of two 5-year terms, would have broad authority.

The elections to the Congress in the spring saw the defeat of a number of veteran Communist Party stalwarts, amid evidence that many voters wished to see Gorbachev implement reforms more quickly. Boris Yeltsin, who had been scolding Gorbachev for years for his timidity, was elected to the Congress from Moscow with 89 percent of the vote.

The Congress convened in Moscow, and Gorbachev was elected president. Although 85 percent of the members were party loyalists, some 400 seats were occupied by radical reformers and by nationalists whose primary loyalties appeared to rest with their respective ethnic groups.

The Supreme Soviet, with 542 members, convened in June and soon established another Soviet precedent by rejecting 6 of 71 nominees for ministerial posts offered by Premier Nikolai Ryzhkov.

As general secretaryof the Communist Party, Gorbachev continued to clean house, forcing the retirement of many officials, mostly proteges of his predecessors. In April, the retirement of 98 members or candidate members of the party's Central Committee was announced. In Spetember, 3 full members and 2 nonvoting members of the ruling Politburo were removed. In a streamlined Politburo of only 11 members, Gorbachev appeared to have a working majority for the first time, although the chief skeptic of his reforms, Yegor Ligachev, remained.

Gorbachev's goal of "perestroika," or restructuring of the Soviet system, had proved realistic insofar as the creation of a new national government was concerned, but efforts to revive the economy proved unavailing. Virtually all the economic statistics were grim. U.S. intelligence estimates showed that the Soviet economy had grown only 1.5 percent in 1988, the same as in 1987. *Izvestia* reported in January that the budget deficit would reach US$160 billion at the official exchange rate by 1990. Premier Ryzhkov, reporting in June that the deficit was running at 6.2 percent of the gross national product, called for large annual cuts in the defense budget through 1995. Inflationary pressures were

revealed in official figures showing that wage increases were outstripping increases in productivity 2-1.

In March, the party's Central Committee endorsed sweeping changes aimed at revitalizing agriculture. Nearly one-half of all Soviet farms lost money or were only marginally profitable. Because of a failed distribution system, one-third of all produce rotted before it reached consumers. The changes, again backed by Gorbachev, didn't call for the breakup of the collective-farm system, but now farmers would be able to lease land and equipment from collectives and grow what they chose. They wouldn't be required to sell all their produce on the state market.

The industrial sector was also in turmoil in 1989. Coal miners, angered by low pay and poor—even hazardous—working conditions, struck at mines across the country in July. At one time, some 500,000 miners had walked out. The costly settlement finally approved by the government would cost between 3 and 5.5 billion rubles—a significant addition to the budget to be financed largely by the printing of more money.

During the miners' strike, Gorbachev had called for "fresh blood" in the party. In this, as in other crises facing the country, he found himself caught in the middle between radicals hoping to exploit the unrest to push for greater reform, and hard-liners who hoped to see the iron hand of discipline imposed on protestors.

The rapid rise of vocal ethnic nationalism threatened the very existence of the polyglot Soviet Union in its present form. Russians constituted barely half of the USSR's population, and many people of other national origins translated their various displeasures with the economy or the political system into demands for more autonomy within the Soviet Union, or even total independence from it. Of significance (as in China), younger people, from a generation supposedly fully indoctrinated in the virtues of a larger Socialist brotherhood, were often in the vanguard of protest.

Gorbachev often warned of the dangers inherent in the ethnic unrest—an "irresponsible game," as he described it in September. He said that the roots of the restlessness could be found in the past mistreatment of ethnic groups, such as the mass deportations of some peoples under Stalin. The Politburo, in August, issued a statement saying that each of the 15 republics should have limited regional autonomy, and each could decide on its own system of economic management within the central government. Furthermore, each republic could challenge national laws that affected it.

The independent states of Estonia, Latvia, and Lithuania had been annexed by the Soviet Union in 1940, ostensibly to protect them from Nazi Germany. In fact, the fate of the 3 Baltic countries had been settled as part of a secret agreement between Germany and the Soviet Union in August 1939. In August 1989, on the 50th anniversary of the agreement, 1 million citizens formed a human chain to show their solidarity. By that time, popular fronts had been formed in all 3 republics, and the Lithuanian legislature had already declared Lithuania's annexation by the USSR invalid. The legislature also asked that Lithuanian recruits into the Soviet army receive their training in Lithuania. Soviet Defense Minister Dmitri Yazov denounced this, suggesting the aim was armed resistance to Moscow.

In May, the Estonian and Lithuanian parliaments passed resolutions declaring their republics' right to create their own monetary system.

The Baltic republics contain major port facilities and missile installations. The Supreme Soviet approved a resolution in July supporting development of an autonomous free-market economic system in Lithuania and Estonia. The 2 republics would have to negotiate with the central government on the management of railroads, natural resources, energy plants, and industries supplying goods to the government.

In August, however, the party's Central Committee said, "Things have gone too far. The fate of the Baltic peoples is in serious danger. ... The consequences could be disastrous. ..." And Gorbachev said in September that there was no basis for questioning the "choice" of the Baltic peoples to enter the Soviet Union.

Heavy loss of life occurred in other republics that experienced ethnic unrest. Armenians and Azerbaijanis clashed repeatedly over the status of an area occupied by Armenians within the republic of Azerbaijan. In Uzbekistan, in June, Uzbeki youths appeared primarily responsible for the perpetration of violence against the Meskhetians, a Turkish group, and at least 90 were reported dead. Nineteen persons died and some 200 were injured in April in Tbilisi, the capital of Georgia, as Georgians demonstrated in behalf of secession from the USSR. A revelation that poison gas had been used by the army prompted an official investigation.

Some Ukranians also called for secession, posing potentially the most serious threat yet to the survival of the country. The Ukraine, with a population of 52 million, provided 25 percent of the nation's food output and accounted for one-third of its industry.

Eastern Europe

Poland's independent trade union, Solidarity, began 1989 without any legal status, and 8 months later its leaders were running the government. The Central Committee of the United Workers' (Communist) Party called in January for its gradual legalization, and a 3-judge panel in April restored the union's legal status.

Although Poland had abundant zinc, copper, and coal and although its agricultural sector was believed able to meet the country's food needs (if farmers were paid fairly), 40 years of Communist mismanagement, combined with the sullen hostility of most of the population, had left the nation's economy in a shambles and its shelves largely bare. The annual inflation rate was 100 percent or more. In this context, dramatic political events unfolded during the year.

Facing up to the need to loosen their firm grip on the country, the regime agreed to the creation of a new parliament having a lower house in which 35 percent of the members would be elected from among opposition and independent candidates. The head of state, the president, heretofore largely a figurehead, would have real power. A judiciary more independent from party control would be established, and opposition media outlets would be allowed. Also in April, the old parliament granted official recognition to the Roman Catholic Church.

In elections to the new parliament, Solidarity captured 99 of 100 seats in the upper house, or Senate, and all 161 seats for which it was allowed to compete in the lower house, the Sejm. The Communists and their allies in 2 small parties held the other 299 seats. Pres. George Bush, visiting Poland in July, allied himself with the movement toward reform, but his promise of only modest financial aid disappointed the Poles.

In July, Gen. Wojciech Jaruzelski was elected president by parliament and then resigned as head of the United Workers' Party, the position from which he had dominated Polish politics for nearly a decade. Solidarity rejected an overture from the Communists to join a coalition government. But then, the Communist premier tapped by Jaruzelski proved unable to form a government, and the 2 minor parties long affiliated with the Communists indicated they would support a government led by Solidarity.

Lech Walesa, whose organizing and negotiating skills had first propelled Solidarity into the forefront of Polish politics, declined to be considered for the premiership, but he had pressed Jaruzelski for a Solidarity-led government, and the latter finally chose one of his recommendations. That was Tadeusz Mazowiecki, a prominent writer and intellectual, and a longtime adviser to Walesa. He succeeded in forming a government in September, but with the interior (police) and defense ministries retained by the Communists. Altogether, his cabinet had 11 members of Solidarity, 4 Communists, and 7 members of the minor parties. Symbolizing the rush toward change, the new finance minister called for private enterprise and free markets.

In **Hungary**, it appeared that the biggest news headlines would be written in 1990, when a new constitution would go into effect. The Hungarians were also clearly moving away from Communist domination, even though (unlike Poland) food was ample and the shops were full of other consumer goods.

In March, the Hungarian government submitted to parliament a draft constitution that omitted mention of a leading role for the Socialist Workers' (Communist) Party. There would be no fixed block of seats set aside in parliament for the Communists. The document contained a bill of rights and a U.S.-style tripartite separation of powers. Gorbachev assured party leader Karoly Grosz, in March, that the Soviet Union would not interfere in the reform movement.

In July, a court declared that former Premier Imre Nagy and 8 of his associates who had also been convicted of treason were in fact innocent.

Hungary's relations with its Socialist neighbors were strained. Czechoslovakia was angered when Hungary, responding to complaints from environmentalists, halted its work on a joint dam project on the Danube River. Hungarian and Romanian leaders clashed over the alleged mistreatment of ethnic Hungarians in Romania, and Hungarian Foreign Minister Gyula Horn said Romania had made military threats.

Hungary's decision in May to cut down its barbed-wire fence along its border with neutral Austria sent shock waves through the Communist world. Hungary soon became a passageway for East German refugees fleeing to West Germany. In the first 9 months of 1989, 20,000 refugees traveled to the West through Hungary. Many of them had come to Hungary as "tourists" and then camped for weeks in Budapest before getting permission to cross into Austria. Hungary, eager to develop better relations with the West, dropped its original reluctance to help the refugees and actually facilitated their departure.

All in all, **East Germany** had a serious refugee problem. In the first 8 months of 1989, 60,000 refugees had left for West Germany with the permission of the regime, and thousands more had crowded into West German diplomatic facilities in Prague and East Berlin in addition to the embassy in Budapest. With East German assent, some 7,000 departed Prague in one day in October. Most of the refugees were young and brought skills that West Germany welcomed.

Although East Germany had the strongest economy in Eastern Europe, growth was stagnating, and consumer goods were growing scarce. Pres. Erich Honecker, 77, was ill, and an opposition group was pressing for the right to run candidates in parliamentary elections scheduled for 1990. The shift of Poland toward neutrality raised questions concerning the supply of 380,000 Soviet troops stationed in East Germany.

(see October Chronology and p. 959 for additional details.)

Don Young, Chronology editor

CHRONOLOGY OF THE YEAR'S EVENTS

Reported Month by Month in 3 Categories: National, International, and General
Nov. 1, 1988 to Oct. 15, 1989

NOVEMBER

National

Index of Economic Indicators Slips — The Commerce Dept. said, Nov. 1, that the index of leading economic indicators had declined by 0.1 percent in September. Several other declines within the past year had not been followed by a slump in the nation's generally robust economy. The Labor Dept. said, Nov. 4, that the unemployment rate had edged downward to 5.2 percent in October, and said, Nov. 10, that the prices charged by producers for finished goods had held steady in October. The Commerce Dept. said, Nov. 16, that the U.S. deficit in merchandise trade had declined to $10.46 billion in September. The Labor Dept. reported, Nov. 22, that consumer prices had jumped 0.4 percent in October. The prime lending rate charged by major U.S. banks rose from 10 percent to 10.5 percent on Nov. 28, and stood at its highest level since May 1985. The Commerce Dept. said, Nov. 29, that the nation's economy, as measured by the gross national product, had grown at an annual rate of 2.6 percent in the third quarter, a figure somewhat higher than the earlier 2.2 percent estimate.

George Bush Elected President — George Herbert Walker Bush, whose long record of public service had included 8 years as vice president under Pres. Ronald Reagan, was elected the 41st president of the U.S. on Nov. 8. The election was the first since 1928 in which a presidential candidate was elected to succeed a president of his own party. Bush became the first vice president since Martin Van Buren in 1836 to be elected directly to the presidency. His running mate, Sen. Dan Quayle of Indiana, was elected vice president. They defeated the Democratic presidential and vice-presidential nominees, Gov. Michael Dukakis of Mass. and Sen. Lloyd Bentsen of Texas. Bush and Quayle carried 40 states with 426 electoral votes, and Dukakis and Bentsen won 10 states and the District of Columbia collecting 112 electoral votes. One of the Dukakis electors actually cast his presidential vote for Bentsen. The nationwide popular vote was closer, about 54 to 46 percent in Bush's favor. In other voting on Nov. 8, the Democrats gained one seat in the U.S. Senate for a margin of 55 to 45, and they added 2 seats in the U.S. House of Representatives for a margin of 260 to 175. The Democrats gained a governorship for a nationwide advantage of 28 to 22, and they also gained a little ground in state legislatures.

Baker Chosen to Head State Department — President-elect George Bush's transition team was headed by two of his campaign strategists, Robert Teeter and Craig Fuller. On Nov. 9, a day after he was elected president, Bush named James Baker 3d as his secretary of state. This and other appointments to his Cabinet would be subject to confirmation by the Senate. Baker, like Bush a Texan, had been White House chief of staff during the first term of Pres. Ronald Reagan, and had then served as secretary of the treasury. He had resigned from the latter position in mid-1988 to become chairman of the Bush presidential campaign. On Nov. 15, Bush announced that he had asked Nicholas Brady to continue as Treasury secretary in his administration. He chose Gov. John Sununu of New Hampshire, Nov. 17, to be his White House chief of staff. Sununu, a conservative, had managed Bush's crucial victory in the New Hampshire primary in February. Bush chose campaign strategist, Lee Atwater, Nov. 17, to serve as chairman of the Republican Party. On Nov. 21, Bush asked 2 more of Reagan's Cabinet members, Attorney General Richard Thornburgh and Education Secretary Lauro Cavazos, to continue in those positions. He also named Richard Darman, former deputy treasury secretary, to head the Office of Management and Budget. On Nov. 23, he picked Brent Scowcroft as his national security adviser. Scowcroft, a retired Air Force general, had held the same post under Pres. Gerald Ford. In an effort to heal any wounds left over from the campaign, Bush met with 2 unsuccessful presidential aspirants, Sen. Robert Dole, the republican minority leader (Nov. 28), and the Rev. Jesse Jackson (Nov. 30).

Need for Higher Taxes Foreseen — In a report issued Nov. 19, the General Accounting Office concluded that higher taxes were probably unavoidable if there was to be any realistic chance of reducing the deficit. Comptroller Gen. Charles Bowsher, head of the GAO, told President-elect George Bush, Nov. 21, that many serious problems neglected by the Reagan administration would have to be confronted, and that the cost of doing so would be "staggering." Bowsher cited these probable outlays: $100-$130 billion to modernize nuclear weapons plants, $20 billion to repair public housing, and $50 billion to rescue floundering savings and loan institutions. "Smaller" expenditures would include $5 billion to build prisons. Former presidents Gerald Ford and Jimmy Carter, Nov. 21, urged Bush to "face reality" and raise taxes, drop some popular domestic programs, and cut Social Security increases.

Reagan Vetoes Ethics Bill — Pres. Ronald Reagan announced, Nov. 23, that he would pocket-veto a bill that would have tightened restrictions on lobbying by former government officials. For the first time, the bill would also have imposed similar restrictions on members of Congress, and one provision would have permanently barred contact by most ex-White House staffers and high U.S. officials with any government executives. Reagan called the bill excessive and discriminatory, and said it would discourage qualified people from entering government service.

Mitchell to Lead Senate Democrats — Democrats who would serve in the Senate in the upcoming 101st Congress caucused, Nov. 29, and elected Sen. George Mitchell (Me.) as their leader. He succeeded Sen. Robert Byrd (W.Va.) who did not seek reelection to the post. With the Democrats holding a 55-45 majority, Mitchell was certain to be elected Senate majority leader. Mitchell, who fell one vote short of a majority on the first ballot, won after his 2 challengers, Sen. Daniel Inouye (Ha.) and J. Bennett Johnston (La.), withdrew before the 2d ballot. Mitchell, an articulate speaker with a moderate image, had gained national recognition with his penetrating questions during the Iran-contra hearings in 1987. On Nov. 30, Republicans reelected Sen. Robert Dole (Kan.) to be their leader.

International

Israeli Election Stalemated — Israeli voters, sharply divided about how to deal with the Palestinian uprising in the occupied territoriries, went to the polls, Nov. 1, to elect members of the Knesset (parliament). The Likud Party, headed by Prime Minister Yitzhak Shamir, had taken a hard line against the Palestinians,

41

and had rejected the Labor Party platform's call for an international peace conference at which the idea of trading "land for peace" would be considered. Labor, led by Foreign Minister Shimon Peres, also wanted to explore the "Jordanian option," which envisioned negotiations between Israel and a Jordanian-Palestinian delegation. Labor and Likud had governed Israel in a shaky "national unity" coalition since the inconclusive 1984 election. The 1988 voting was equally indecisive. Labor and its allied parties won 49 seats. Likud and its allies won 47 seats. The religious parties won 18 seats, and the Arab bloc won 6 seats. With 61 seats needed to form a government, negotiations got under way. Shamir, **Nov. 11,** promised the leaders of the religious parties that he would support their "Who is a Jew" amendment to Israel's Law of Return. The religious leaders wanted to stipulate that people converted to Judaism by Reform or Conservative (rather than Orthodox) rabbis would not be considered Jews. Therefore, they would not automatically become eligible for citizenship. Even while trying to reach an agreement with the religious parties, Shamir also began negotiations with Labor on continuing the unity government.

Thatcher Rebukes Polish Hosts — British Prime Minister Margaret Thatcher visited Poland and stunned her hosts by publicly criticizing their policies. On **Oct. 31,** the government had announced that it would close the Lenin Shipyard in Gdansk, stronghold of the outlawed Solidarity trade union. The government said this was an economic move, but the workers were outraged. On **Nov. 2,** the day Thatcher arrived in Poland, the Polish leader, Gen. Wojciech Jaruzelski, warned that she must not meddle in Polish affairs. In meetings with Polish leaders, **Nov. 3,** Thatcher reportedly rejected a plea for British economic assistance. At a state dinner, **Nov. 3,** she called for more freedom in Poland and throughout Eastern Europe. Huge throngs greeted Thatcher, **Nov. 4,** on her visit to Gdansk, where she met with Solidarity founder Lech Walesa. Thatcher flew to Washington, D.C., **Nov. 16,** for a farewell visit with Pres. Ronald Reagan, whom she had strongly supported. She met with President-elect George Bush, **Nov. 17.** In an interview, **Nov. 17,** Thatcher praised the policies of Soviet leader Mikhail Gorbachev and said, "We're not in a Cold War now."

Ex-President Apologizes to Koreans — Former Pres. Chun Doo Hwan apologized to South Koreans for "wrongdoings and mistakes" during his 8 years in office. Reports of corruption under Chun had circulated for some time. On **Nov. 3,** 20,000 students demonstrated against Chun, calling for his arrest. During a demonstration, **Nov. 5,** in Seoul by 10,000 students, rocks and fire-bombs were thrown at police. The National Assembly conducted televised hearings, **Nov. 7-9,** into allegations against the Chun administration. Charges were made that Chun had pressured wealthy businessmen into donating large sums of money to a research institute that funneled substantial sums to Chun and his associates. Chun, in a televised broadcast, **Nov. 23,** admitted responsibility for corruption during his presidency. He said he would return his accumulated wealth, $3 million in personal property and $20 million in political donations. He said he would enter exile at an undisclosed location in South Korea.

Estonians Challenge Soviet Domination — In response to Soviet leader Mikhail Gorbachev's plan to reorganize the Supreme Soviet into a bicameral legislature headed by himself as president, an Estonian delegation that included both Communist Party officials and nationalists **Nov. 9,** in Moscow, proclaimed its opposition to constitutional changes that would give the new legislature ultimate control over economic, social, and political programs in the republics. Soviet leaders,

Nov. 10, said they would take new initiatives to broaden autonomy at the regional level. On **Nov. 16,** Estonia's Supreme Soviet asserted the right to veto national laws affecting Estonia. By amending the republic's constitution, the Estonian legislature invited a response from the Presidium of the national Supreme Soviet, which said, **Nov. 17,** that the action was "inconsistent" with the national constitution. The Presidium, **Nov. 26,** declared the action unconstitutional. In a speech to the Presidium, **Nov. 27,** Gorbachev deplored the "disastrous" rise of nationalism, citing Estonia, and the republics of Armenia and Azerbaijan.

Agreement Reached on Angola, Namibia — Meeting in Geneva, U.S., Cuban, South African, and Angolan negotiators agreed, **Nov. 15,** on a timetable for withdrawing Cuban troops from Angola and on independence for Namibia. The latter was now controlled by South Africa. It was reported that under the plan Cuba would withdraw its 50,000 troops over a period of 27 months. However, no cease-fire was agreed to between the Angolan government and rebels led by Jonas Savimbi and backed by South Africa and the U.S.. The Angolan and Cuban governments approved the agreement, **Nov. 18,** and South Africa followed suit, **Nov. 22,** although Foreign Minister Roelof Botha said that a lasting peace in Angola would depend on settling the civil war. Angola, Cuba, and South Africa signed the agreement, **Dec. 13,** in Brazzaville, Congo. The final, formal signing of the accords took place, **Dec. 22,** at the United Nations in New York.

Palestinian State Proclaimed — The Palestine National Council, meeting in Algiers, **Nov. 15,** proclaimed the establishment of the independent Palestinian state. The PNC, the legislative body of the Palestine Liberation Organization, also voted to accept U.N. Security Council resolutions 242 and 338 as the basis for a peace conference to resolve the Palestinian question. The PNC also "rejected terrorism in all its forms." The PNC plan ultimately envisioned a confederation between the states of Jordan and Palestine. In announcing the proclamation of a new state, PLO Chairman Yasir Arafat cited U.N. General Assembly resolution 181 (1947), which had called for separate Jewish and Arab states in Palestine. Resolution 242 (1967) called on Israel to withdraw from the territories and recognized the right of all states in the region "to live in peace within secure and recognized boundaries." Resolution 338 called for negotiations to implement 242. The PLO had previously resisted accepting 242 because it would mean the implicit recognition of Israel. The U.S. State Department, **Nov. 16,** said that "implied or indirect reference to Israel's right to exist is not sufficient." But within a few days more than two dozen nations had extended recognition to the newly proclaimed state. Israeli leaders rejected the proclamation. Notwithstanding Arafat's conciliatory gestures, Secretary of State George Shultz, **Nov. 26,** denied him permission to travel to New York to address the U.N. General Assembly because of his "association with terrorism." U.N. Secretary General Javier Perez de Cuellar said, **Nov. 27,** that Shultz's action would harm diplomatic efforts in the Middle East.

Bhutto's Party Wins in Pakistan — Benazir Bhutto, daughter of executed former Pres. Zulkifar Ali Bhutto, emerged as the big winner in the Pakistan National Assembly elections, **Nov. 16.** Her father had been overthrown in 1977 in a military coup led by Mohammad Zia ul-Haq. Bhutto was hanged in 1979 on a murder conviction. His daughter returned from exile in 1986 to lead the political opposition to Zia, who died in a mysterious plane crash in August 1988. In the November voting, Benazir Bhutto's Pakistani People's Party won 92 of the 205 contested seats, and no other faction won more than 55 seats. Bhutto, **Nov. 17,** called on acting Pres. Ghulam Ishaq Khan to allow her to form a new government.

Mulroney Keeps Power in Canada — Canadian Prime Minister Brian Mulroney won a second term in parliamentary elections, **Nov. 21.** The dominant issue in the campaign was free trade, specifically whether the U.S.-Canada trade accord should be approved. Mulroney's government had negotiated the agreement. Opposition leaders, former Liberal Prime Minister John Turner and Edward Broadbent of the New Democratic Party, warned that the concept of free trade embodied in the agreement would prove disadvantageous to Canada's economic and cultural interests. Final approval of the free-trade bill turned on the outcome of the voting. Mulroney's Progressive Conservative Party, which had trailed in the polls for much of the campaign, won a decisive victory, taking 170 of 295 seats in the House of Commons. The Liberals won 82 seats and the NDP 43. The nationwide popular vote was closer: PC 43 percent, Liberals 32 percent, NDP 20 percent. Turner said, **Nov. 22,** that his party would no longer seek to prevent approval of the free-trade agreement.

General

$25 Billion Bid Buys RJR Nabisco — One of the wildest takeover fights in American corporate history reached a resolution, **Nov. 30,** when RJR Nabisco, the food and tobacco giant, was acquired for $25.07 billion. This figure was about twice the size of any other merger. The management group of Kohlberg Kravis Roberts & Co. made the offer that was accepted by the outside directors of RJR Nabisco. A slightly higher offer by a management group led by RJR Pres. F. Ross Johnson was rejected. In October, the company's shares had been priced at $55, but the final offer was equivalent to $109 a share.

Disasters — An earthquake in southwest China, near the Burmese border, **Nov. 6,** claimed 730 lives. ... Five days of heavy rainfall, **Nov. 19-23,** in southern Thailand, sent floodwaters, mud slides, and heavy logs sweeping through low-lying villages; officials estimated, **Nov. 26,** that nearly 1,000 persons had died. ... A cyclone, **Nov. 29,** in Bangladesh killed at least 800 and left hundreds of thousands homeless.

DECEMBER

National

Changes in Economic Data Are Minor — The Commerce Dept. reported, **Dec. 1,** that the leading economic indicators had risen in October by 0.1 percent— a figure later raised to 0.4 percent. The Labor Dept. said, **Dec. 2,** that unemployment in November had edged upward by 0.1 percent to 5.4 percent. The Commerce Dept. reported, **Dec. 14,** that the U.S. merchandise trade deficit had shrunk slightly to $10.35 billion in October. The Labor Dept. said, **Dec. 16,** that prices charged by producers for finished goods rose in November by 0.3 percent, and on **Dec. 20,** it said consumer prices had risen in November by 0.3 percent. The leading indicators edged downward 0.2 percent in November, the Commerce Dept. said, **Dec. 30.** On **Dec. 30,** the last trading day of 1988, the Dow Jones industrial average closed at 2168.57, 11.8 percent above its 1987 close. The year's gain of 229.74 points still left it far below the 1987 pre-collapse high of 2722.42.

Reagan, Bush Subpoenaed in North Trial — Pres. Ronald Reagan and Pres.-elect George Bush received subpoenas to testify for the defense in the trial of former National Security Council staff member Oliver North. Responding, **Dec. 1,** to a request by North's lawyers for 3,500 secret documents, Reagan said his administration had a duty to withhold the classified papers. Ruling, **Dec. 12,** that North's request was an attempt "to frustrate the prosecution," Judge Gerhard Gesell limited the defense's access to 300 documents.

Bush Builds His Administration — On **Dec. 2** Pres.-elect George Bush met with the defeated members of the Democratic national ticket, Massachusetts Gov. Michael Dukakis and Texas Sen. Lloyd Bentsen. On **Dec. 6,** Bush named Houston businessman Robert Mosbacher, Sr., as commerce secretary, career diplomat Thomas Pickering as U.S. ambassador to the United Nations, Stanford University economist Michael Boskin as chairman of his Council of Economic Advisers, and Washington, D.C., lawyer Carla Hills as U.S. trade representative. William Webster was renamed director of the Central Intelligence Agency. Clayton Yeutter, the Reagan administration's trade representative, was named secretary of agriculture, **Dec. 14.** Speculation on the position of defense secretary ended, **Dec. 16,** when Bush chose former Texas Sen. John Tower, widely acknowledged as a leading specialist in the field. Bush said he was "totally satisfied" with the results of an FBI background check on Tower concerning rumors about his personal life. Bush, **Dec. 19,** named former Rep. Jack Kemp (N.Y.) as secretary for housing and urban development. On **Dec. 22,** Bush named Samuel Skinner secretary of transportation, Manuel Lujan as secretary of the interior, Edward Derwinski as the first secretary of veterans affairs, William Reilly as administrator of the Environmental Protection Agency, and Louis Sullivan as secretary of health and human services. Dr. Sullivan, who would be the highest-ranking black in the administration, had met some criticism among conservatives because of what were perceived as less-than-firm views against abortion. On **Dec. 24,** Bush named Elizabeth Dole, secretary of transportation in the Reagan administration, as secretary of labor.

Shuttle Completes Secret Mission — The U.S. space shuttle *Atlantis* and a 5-man crew lifted off from Cape Canaveral, Fla., **Dec. 2,** on a secret mission. It was believed that a new radar reconnaissance satellite, able to "see" through clouds and at night, was put into orbit, **Dec. 3.** The shuttle landed, **Dec. 6,** at Edwards Air Force Base in California.

Raises Proposed for U.S. Leaders — The president's Commission on Executive, Legislative, and Judicial Salaries proposed, **Dec. 13,** that salaries of U.S. government leaders be increased by at least 50 percent. Members of Congress, for example, would go from $89,500 to $135,000 and the president from $200,000 to $350,000. Judges and cabinet officers would be among others getting similar increases. By law, the increases would take effect within a month after the president approved the recommendation, unless rejected by both houses of Congress. Pres. Ronald Reagan gave his approval to the commission's recommendations, **Jan. 5.**

LaRouche Convicted of Conspiracy — Former presidential candidate Lyndon LaRouche was convicted by a federal jury in Virginia, **Dec. 16,** of conspiracy and mail fraud. He and 6 associates were found guilty on charges relating to $30 million in loans solicited by their organization. LaRouche was sentenced, **Jan. 27,** to 15 years in prison.

Securities Firm Accepts Huge Penalty — The securities company Drexel Burnham Lambert agreed, **Dec. 21,** to plead guilty to 6 violations of federal law and to penalties totaling $650 million. The settlement, by far the largest in a securities fraud case, included $300 million in fines and the creation of a $350 million account to satisfy claims by parties who could prove that they had been defrauded by Drexel. The charges related mostly to dealings between Drexel and financier Ivan Boesky, who had been convicted previously. They included insider trading, stock manipulation, and falsified records. The agreement between the government and Drexel also required that Drexel settle civil charges previously brought against it. Michael Milken, the "junk-bond king" who had helped to bring Drexel to prominence on Wall Street, was not a party to the settlement, and faced the possibility of a criminal indictment.

Closing of Bases Recommended — The Defense Secretary's Commission on Base Realignment and Closure issued its recommendation, **Dec. 29.** To save an estimated total of $5.6 billion over 20 years, it proposed the closing of 54 bases, the partial shutdown of 5, and the "realignment" of 54 others. The defense secretary and Congress would have to accept the recommendation on an "all-or-nothing" basis.

International

Soviet Political Reform Approved — The Supreme Soviet, the Soviet Union's nominal parliament, approved sweeping changes, **Dec. 1,** in the country's political structure. The changes had been endorsed by Gen. Secretary Mikhail Gorbachev in June. Under the plan, the Supreme Soviet would become more representative and have real power. The upper house, the Congress of People's Deputies, would have 2,250 members, who in turn would name the 400 or more members of the lower house, the Supreme Soviet. The plan created a new office of president, limited to 2 five-year terms. Before the existing Supreme Soviet voted to approve the plan, a Latvian delegate asked that all republics be allowed to veto new national laws. In the vote to approve the changes, 5 Latvians dissented and 27 Lithuanians and Estonians abstained. The constitutional debate unfolded against a backdrop of regional turmoil. Pravda reported, **Dec. 1,** that 28 persons had died in renewed religious and ethnic strife in Armenia and Azerbaijan. The violence in the region had driven 100,000 people from their homes.

Bhutto Becomes Pakistani Prime Minister — The acting prsident of Pakistan, **Dec. 1,** named Benazir Bhutto as the new prime minister of the country. Bhutto's party had won a decisive victory in the November election. Fundamentalist Islamic leaders had opposed her succession, arguing that the Koran forbade a woman from heading a government. On being sworn in, **Dec. 2,** Bhutto promised to free political prisoners, obey the rule of law, and work for an end to restrictions on unions, the press, and the rights of women.

Soviets Meet with Afghan Rebels — Soviet diplomats and representatives of the Afghan rebel movement met in Taif, Saudi Arabia, **Dec. 3-5,** to discuss the Soviet withdrawal from Afghanistan, scheduled for completion by mid-February. The talks were believed to be the first such contact between the Soviet Union and the anti-Communist rebels since the Soviet invasion in 1979. The participants reportedly discussed the transitional government, safe passage for departing Soviet soldiers, prisoner exchanges, and war reparations.

Gorbachev Meets With Reagan, Bush, and Addresses the U.N. — Soviet leader Mikhail Gorbachev conferred with Pres. Ronald Reagan and Pres.-elect George Bush in New York, and told the U.N. General Assembly that the Soviet Union, acting unilaterally, would reduce its conventional forces. He then pledged to reduce Soviet military forces by 500,000, or about 10 percent, by 1991. Some 10,000 tanks, 8,500 artillery pieces, and 800 aircraft would be removed from East-

ern Europe. Overall, the Soviet Union would assume a defensive posture. None of these actions were to be tied to any concessions by the United States or the North Atlantic Treaty Organization. He also said that most Soviet troops stationed in Mongolia would be withdrawn. Gorbachev promised greater human rights in the Soviet Union, fewer restrictions on emigration, and a moratorium of up to 100 years on debt-service payments from developing countries on Soviet loans. Gorbachev's visit to New York was ended abruptly, **Dec. 8,** after the great magnitude of the earthquake in Soviet Armenia became apparent. He returned home immediately, postponing planned visits to Cuba and Great Britain. Although Reagan had joined other world leaders in praising the Soviet Union's planned military cutbacks, Adm. William Crowe, chairman of the U.S. joint chiefs of staff, said, **Dec. 8,** that the reduction would "fall far short of redressing the conventional balance in Europe."

U.S. Opens Dialogue With PLO — Palestine Liberation Organization Chairman Yasir Arafat, meeting in Sweden, **Dec. 7,** with a delegation of 5 American Jews, said that the PLO accepted Israel and condemned terrorism. A seaborne Israeli force raided a PLO guerrilla base near Beirut, **Dec. 8-9,** and in the fight an Israeli officer and 20 Palestinian fighters were reportedly killed. Arafat addressed the U.N. General Assembly in Geneva, **Dec. 13;** the United States had refused to grant him a visa to speak in New York. He supported an international conference in which "the state of Palestine, Israel, and other neighbors" would work out a comprehensive settlement. He also condemned terrorism "in all its forms." Israeli Prime Minister Yitzhak Shamir, in reaction to Arafat's statements, rejected any thought of talking with the PLO. After U.S. officials said Arafat had not gone far enough, he affirmed, **Dec. 14,** "the right of all parties," including Israel, "to exist in peace and security." Pres. Ronald Reagan then announced that the PLO had met all U.S. conditions and authorized the State Department to enter a dialogue with the PLO. Shamir called the decision a "grave mistake." But worldwide response to the U.S. decision was strongly favorable. A U.S. diplomat, Robert Pelletreau, Jr., met in Tunisia with PLO representatives, **Dec. 16,** the first such contact since the U.S. banned them in 1975 in an agreement with Israel.

Coalition Rule Continues in Israel — Israel's 2 leading political parties worked out an agreement, **Dec. 19,** on a coalition government similar to one that had been in effect for 4 years. This time, however, Yitzhak Shamir would serve as prime minister for all 4 years rather than rotate in the office with Shimon Peres, the Labor Party leader. Peres would shift from foreign minister to finance minister. The agreement shut out the small religious parties, who had appeared to hold the balance of power after the inconclusive November election. Many Jews, especially those in America, had been angered by the demands of the religious parties. The governing groups of both major parties approved the coalition government, **Dec. 21.**

270 Killed When Bomb Destroys Pan Am Plane Over Scotland — On **Dec. 21,** an explosion 31,000 feet in the sky sent pieces of a Pan Am jetliner showering onto the town of Lockerbie, Scotland and the surrounding countryside. The disaster, which was caused by a bomb that had been placed aboard the airplane, resulted in the death of all 259 persons aboard and of 11 others on the ground.

Flight 103 had originated in Frankfurt, West Germany, and had continued from London's Heathrow Airport on a Boeing 747. Its destination was New York's Kennedy International Airport. The plane, which was jammed with holiday travelers, also carried 35 exchange students from Syracuse University.

A wing from the plane tore a crater 50 yards long in Lockerbie, flaming fuel spilled onto houses, and bodies and other pieces of the plane were scattered across fields and woods for many miles.

The Federal Aviation Administration said, **Dec. 22**, that a caller in Helsinki, Finland had warned the U.S. Embassy there, **Dec. 5**, that a Pan Am plane flying from Frankfurt to the United States would be the target of a bombing attempt within 2 weeks. The U.S. State Department then alerted its personnel, some of whom changed their travel plans. The U.S. public, however, was not warned of the threat, one of many received by the government. Finnish police interrogated the tipster and concluded that he had nothing to do with the bombing.

A pro-Iranian Islamic group claimed responsibility for the bombing in a phone call to a wire service, **Dec. 22**.

British investigators said, **Dec. 28**, that a powerful plastic explosive had destroyed the plane. "Conclusive evidence" of an explosive device had been found in a metal luggage holder in the wreckage. On **Feb. 16**, they said that the bomb had been concealed in a radio-cassette player stored in a forward luggage compartment, and that the baggage containing it had probably come from Frankfurt.

General

Devastating Earthquake Hits Armenia — A severe earthquake struck the Soviet republic of Armenia, **Dec. 7**. A government estimate put the death toll at 25,000, and some 500,000 persons were homeless. The city of Leninakan, population 290,000, was nearly leveled; at least 32 mountain villages were destroyed. Soviet leader Mikhail Gorbachev and his wife, having cut short a foreign tour, visited the ruined areas, **Dec. 10** and **11**. At least 60 countries provided relief supplies, and several sent search-and-rescue experts and medical teams. Much of the damage was blamed on the flimsiness of buildings. Pravda reported that buildings constructed within the past 15 years had suffered the most damage.

Bess Myerson Acquitted — Bess Myerson, a former Miss America, was acquitted, **Dec. 22**, by a New York City jury of bribery, fraud, and conspiracy charges. The prosecution had claimed that she had improperly influenced the judge presiding over the divorce case of Carl Capasso, who was Myerson's boy friend. Capasso and the retired judge, Hortense Gabel, were also acquitted.

Disasters — At least 60 students were killed in Yaounde, Cameroon, **Dec. 5**, when they were trampled or jumped to their deaths after hearing a false alarm that the school was about to collapse. ... At least 62 persons were killed and at least 80 were injured, **Dec. 11**, when illegal fireworks exploded and sent a fire racing through a crowded market in Mexico City. ... Some 250 persons were missing and feared drowned when a river ferry capsized and sank en route to Dhaka, in Bangladesh, **Dec. 27**. ... At least 51 persons died, **Dec. 31**, when a boat transporting New Year's Eve celebrants sank at the entrance of the bay in Rio de Janiero, Brazil.

JANUARY

National

Bush Inaugurated as President — On **Jan. 20**, George Bush and Dan Quayle were inaugurated as president and vice president of the U.S. As vice president, Bush presided, **Jan. 4**, over a joint session of Congress—the first day of business for the 101st Congress. The principal task was the announcement of the votes cast for president and vice president by the members of the Electoral College. Bush announced his own victory—426 votes for himself as the Republican presidential candidate and 111 for Gov. Michael Dukakis of Massachusetts, the Democratic candidate. One Democratic elector voted for Sen. Lloyd Bentsen (Tex.) for president, who had been Dukakis's running mate. In a farewell address to the nation, **Jan. 11**, Pres. Ronald Reagan said he saw his administrations as a time of "rediscovery of our values and our common sense." He defined the country as "More prosperous, more secure and happier than it was eight years ago." Bush, **Jan. 12**, named Adm. James Watkins (ret.) as secretary of energy and William Bennett, former education secretary, as the nation's first "drug czar." Chief Justice William Rehnquist swore in Bush as the 41st president at noon, **Jan. 20**, at an outdoor ceremony at the U.S. Capitol. In his address, Bush urged Americans to rise above materialism and "to make kinder the face of the nation and gentler the face of the world." He noted that problems, including crime and poverty, faced the nation but that the federal government acting alone could not achieve solutions. Speaking of the drug problem, he said, "This scourge will stop." Nine inaugural balls were held that evening in the capital. The cost of the week's events, mostly covered by private donations, was $30 million, by far the greatest for any inauguration. Signalling a more open style, Bush personally welcomed tourists at the White House, **Jan. 21**. On **Jan. 23**, Bush telephoned Soviet leader Mikhail Gorbachev and other world leaders. He spoke by phone to an antiabortion rally in Washington. On **Jan. 25**, Bush appointed an 8-member commission to propose a code of ethics for government officials.

Reagan Submits Last Budget — On **Jan. 4**, the Congressional Budget Office estimated that the federal deficit for the 1990 fiscal year would be $141 billion, much higher than the $125 billion estimate by the White House. CBO calculations were based on higher interest rates and slower economic growth, compared with White House estimates. Pres. Ronald Reagan submitted his final budget—for fiscal 1990—on **Jan. 9**. He proposed to spend $1.15 trillion, with a deficit of $92.5 billion. Defense spending would grow 2 percent faster than inflation. More money was targeted for AIDS, rescuing insolvent savings and loan institutions, and cleaning up contaminated nuclear weapons facilities. Reagan also proposed elimination of 82 federal programs. Democrats in Congress tended to dismiss the budget as irrelevant in light of the forthcoming inauguration of George Bush as president.

Two Iran-Contra Charges Dropped — Two of the principal charges against former Lt. Col. Oliver North in the Iran-Contra case were dropped. Lawrence Walsh, the independent counsel, moved, **Jan. 5**, to dismiss the 2 counts in his case against the onetime National Security Council staff member in the Reagan White House. North had contended that he needed thousands of pages of documents to defend himself against the charges, that he had conspired to defraud the U.S. and had stolen government property. Judge Gerhard Gesell had supported North's right to gain access to at least some of the documents, but the administration had refused to provide some of the secret documents, citing national security. Gesell, responding to Walsh's motion, **Jan. 13**, dismissed the counts, saying the court was "totally powerless" to pursue them. The defense had subpoenaed Presidents Ronald Reagan and George Bush, but Gesell held, **Jan. 30**, that there was no evidence that Bush had "any specific information relevant and material" to the defense. Gesell kept open the possibility that Reagan might be called. North's trial on the 12 charges remaining against him opened, **Jan. 31.**

Six Indicted in Pentagon Case — Teledyne Industries of Newbury Park, Calif., and 6 individuals were indicted, **Jan. 6,** by a grand jury in Alexandria, Va., in connection with the Pentagon procurement scandal. These were the first indictments in the investigation, which had come to light in June 1988. The men indicted included a Navy procurement specialist, 2 private consultants, and 3 employees of Teledyne. Charges filed against one or more of them included bribery conspiracy, racketeering, theft of government property, making false statements, and conspiracy to defraud the government. Teledyne was indicted for allegedly paying $160,000 for confidential government information. Hazeltine Corp. of Greenlawn, N.Y., and 3 men—2 former executives and a Teledyne lobbyist—pleaded guilty, **Jan. 6,** to various conspiracy charges related to the case and agreed to cooperate with the investigation. Two former executives of Unisys Corp., a major defense contractor, pleaded guilty, **Jan. 27,** to making illegal campaign donations to members of Congress. A civilian employee of the Marine Corps pleaded guilty, **Jan. 27,** to accepting $43,500 in bribes from a defense consultant to whom he provided confidential information.

Unemployment at a Low at Year's End — The Labor Dept. reported, **Jan. 6,** that unemployment stood at 5.3 percent, a 14-year low, at the end of 1988. The department said, **Jan. 13,** that prices paid by producers for finished goods rose 4 percent in all of 1988. The merchandise trade deficit widened to $12.51 billion in November, the Commerce Dept. said, **Jan. 18.** The Labor Dept. said, **Jan. 19,** that consumer prices rose 4.4 percent in 1988, matching the 1987 increase and much higher than the 1.1 increase in 1986. The slow but steady advance in stock prices continued on Wall Street, and on **Jan. 27,** the Dow Jones industrial average closed above 2300 — at 2322.86 — for the first time since the October 1987 market crash. The Commerce Dept. reported, **Jan. 27,** that the gross national product grew at an annual rate of 2 percent in the 4th quarter of 1988, reflecting the impact of the summer 1988 drought on farm output. For the year as a whole, however, the economy grew at 3.8 percent, its strongest showing in 4 years.

Justice Department Rebukes Meese — Former Attorney Gen. Edwin Meese was criticized, **Jan. 17,** in an internal report issued by the Justice Dept. that he once headed. The report, prepared by the Office of Professional Responsibility, found that ethical breaches by Meese would have called for disciplinary action by the president were Meese still in office. The report asserted that Meese had violated departmental standards of conduct and an executive order on ethics. It cited assistance to a friend and sometime creditor, E. Robert Wallach; a delay in paying income taxes; and his ownership of telecommunications stock while dealing with matters in the department related to telephone companies. Meese's lawyers said there was "no basis" for criticizing his conduct.

International

Two Libyan Jets Downed by U.S. Navy — Two U.S. Navy F-14 fighters and 2 Libyan MiG-23 fighters tangled in international waters off the Libyan coast, **Jan. 4,** and both Libyan planes were downed. Defense Secretary Frank Carlucci said that the U.S. pilots took evasive action, but that the Libyans closed in with apparent "hostile intent." One MiG was then shot down with an air-to-air missile, the other with a heat-seeking missile. Meanwhile, the U.S. continued to press a charge that the Libyans were building a chemical weapons factory 40 miles southwest of Tripoli. Libya said it was a pharmaceutical factory. The U.S. also asserted that 5 West German companies had helped Libya build the facility. West German Chancellor Helmut Kohl at first rejected that claim, saying, **Jan. 10,** that to make accusations without proof was "not the way to behave among friends." But the German government retreated in the face of growing evidence of ties to the plant, and Kohl faced a serious scandal after new allegations were made about German corporate involvement with lethal aid to both Libya and Iraq.

Japan's Emperor Hirohito Dies — After a reign of 62 years, Emperor Hirohito of Japan died in Tokyo, **Jan. 7,** of cancer. During his lifetime, Japan had evolved through war and devastation into a modern industrial power. Crown Prince Akihito succeeded his father to become Japan's 125th emperor. Expressions of sympathy to Hirohito's family and to the Japanese people came in from around the world. His death, however, revived discussion as to his role in World War II, which had never been completely clear. Pres. Ronald Reagan paid tribute to Hirohito's efforts after the war to reconcile the Japanese and American people.

149 Nations Condemn Chemical Weapons — At a conference in Paris, **Jan. 11,** representatives of 149 nations adopted a statement saying that they "solemnly affirm their commitments not to use chemical weapons and condemn such use." Pres. Francois Mitterrand of France had called the conference. The statement reaffirmed the 1925 Geneva Protocol renouncing the use of chemical weapons in war. Soviet Foreign Minister Eduard Shevardnadze told the conference, **Jan. 8,** that the USSR would begin to destroy its stockpile of chemical weapons soon. To preserve unanimity at the conference, Iraq was not challenged on its recent use of chemical weapons against Iran and against its own Kurdish citizens.

Communists Favor Legalizing Solidarity — The long struggle by the Solidarity trade union in Poland to gain recognition seemed near a resolution on **Jan. 18,** when the Central Committee of the United Workers' (Communist) Party called for its eventual legalization. Gen. Wojciech Jaruzelski, the party's leader, allied himself with party moderates during the debate at the committee, saying, "times have changed" and "We are aiming for new solutions." His resolution was passed 228-32. Under its provisions, Solidarity would undergo a 2-year trial period, during which it must not strike and would cooperate with Polish authorities.

Final Soviet Afghan Pullout Begins — The Soviet Union, **Jan. 20,** began airlifting food and fuel to Kabul, the capital of Afghanistan, to keep the city supplied while the Soviet army withdrew from the country. The Soviet foreign ministry announced, **Jan. 25,** that the final "withdrawal process" was under way. On **Jan. 21,** as warfare between rebels and the Soviet-supported Afghan regime drew closer, West Germany announced that it was removing its last 3 envoys from the capital. In the face of growing danger, other Western nations followed suit. On **Jan. 26,** U.S. Secretary of State James Baker ordered the closing of the U.S. Embassy. On **Jan. 30,** the U.S. government criticized stepped-up Soviet bombing of Afghanistan as a "scorched-earth policy." The Soviet commander said the attacks were necessary because rebels had not allowed safe passage for the withdrawing Soviet troops.

New Peace Plan Signed for Lebanon — In Damascas, **Jan. 30,** the foreign ministers of Syria and Iran signed a peace pact aimed at ending violent fighting between rival Shiite Moslem militias in Lebanon. Syria had supported Amal, a moderate group, and Iran supported Hizballah (Party of God), a radical militia. More than 500 persons had been killed since warfare between the militias broke out in April 1988. Under the new truce, Amal would control security in southern Lebanon, and Hizballah could also remain in the area.

General

Death Toll From Smoking Rises — Dr. C. Everett Koop, the U.S. Surgeon General, said, **Jan. 11,** that cigarette smoking had claimed 390,000 lives in 1985, a figure higher than previous annual estimated totals. The results of that study, from the American Cancer Society, were part of a report released by Koop on the 25th anniversary of the 1964 pioneer government study on smoking and health. He called the original report "the most significant health statement ever made by the government." The new report also showed that lung cancer, not breast cancer, was the leading cause of cancer death among women. It also reported that smoking was more common among blue-collar workers and less-educated persons.

Gunman Kills 5 Children — A former student at the Cleveland Elementary School in Stockton, Calif., returned to the school, **Jan. 17,** armed with a semiautomatic rifle and 2 pistols. He opened fire on the school grounds, killing 5 students and wounding 29 others and a teacher. The gunman, Patrick Edward Purdy, who was in his 20s, then shot himself to death with a pistol. The 5 children who were slain were all refugees from Cambodia and Vietnam. Purdy had purchased his Chinese-made AK-47 rifle at a gun shop in Oregon.

Serial Killer Executed in Florida — Theodore Bundy, a former law student, was executed, **Jan. 24,** in the electric chair at the Florida State Prison in Starke. He had been convicted of killing a 12-year-old girl from Lake City, Fla. and 2 women students from Florida State University. Investigators believed he may have killed several dozen women altogether. Under a death sentence for 10 years, he had defended himself tenaciously, insisting on his innocence. Bundy had been the subject of 5 books and a television movie. In the last days of his life, he confessed to at least 16 other murders, but Gov. Bob Martinez of Florida refused to stay his execution to learn any further details. Bundy's execution provoked a celebration outside the prison by revenge-minded people carrying signs and slogans such as "Thank God It's Fryday" and "Roast in Peace."

Trial Focuses Attention on Child Abuse — A former criminal lawyer, Joel Steinberg, was found guilty of 1st-degree manslaughter in New York City, **Jan. 30,** in the death by beating of his 6-year-old illegally adopted daughter, Lisa. Damaging testimony against the defendant had been given by Hedda Nussbaum, Steinberg's lover. Steinberg was found not guilty of 2d-degree murder, which would have required a conclusion that he had acted with a depraved indifference to human life. The shocking details of Steinberg's behavior as described in the trial drew nationwide attention to the problem of child abuse. Steinberg, **Mar. 24,** received the maximum sentence of 8⅓ to 25 years in prison.

Disasters — After running out of fuel, a ferry sank off the Caribbean coast of Guatemala, **Jan. 1,** resulting in the death of 79 of some 120 aboard. ... A mail train and an express train carrying religious pilgrims crashed head-on in Bangladesh, **Jan. 15,** killing 170 people and injuring 1,000. ... At least 51 persons, including 35 schoolgirls, were killed, **Jan. 17,** when a train struck a bus in southern Sri Lanka. ... 274 persons died, **Jan. 23,** when an earthquake hit the Soviet republic of Tadzhikistan.

FEBRUARY

National

Committee Rejects Tower Nomination — The nomination of former Texas Sen. John Tower to be Secretary of Defense was rejected by the Senate Armed Services Committee. In damaging testimony before the committee, **Jan. 31,** Paul M. Weyrich, a leading conservative, said that on several occasions he had observed Tower in a drunken condition and socializing with women who were not his wife. Testifying **Feb. 1,** Tower denied he had a drinking problem. The Federal Bureau of Investigation reopened its investigation of Tower, and the committee, **Feb. 2,** postponed a vote on Tower. Following more published reports unfavorable to Tower, the committee, **Feb. 8,** again postponed a vote. The FBI delivered its report to the White House and the committee, **Feb. 20.** It reportedly found that Tower had a drinking problem in the 1970s but that there was no proof he still had a problem. Defending Tower, **Feb. 21,** Pres. George Bush noted that anti-Tower rumors were not supported by known facts. Before voting on the nomination, **Feb. 23,** members of the Armed Services Committee debated Tower's fitness. Chairman Sam Nunn (D, Ga.) said Tower's "record of alcohol abuse ... cannot be ignored." He said that a military officer with Tower's background would not receive a command. But the ranking Republican, John Warner (R, Va.) contended that not a single senator could recall an instance in which Tower's personal habits interfered with his public duties. Voting strictly along party lines, the committee turned down the nomination, 11-9. Determined to carry the fight to the full Senate, Tower said, **Feb. 26,** that he had never been an alcoholic and that he would stop drinking altogether if confirmed.

Consumer and Producer Prices Jump — The Commerce Dept. reported, **Feb. 1,** that the leading economic indicators had risen 0.6 percent in December. Leading banks raised their prime lending rate, **Feb. 10,** to 11 percent from 10.5 percent, putting the prime at its highest level since 1984. Reporting the largest increase since October 1985, the Labor Dept. said, **Feb. 10,** that prices paid to producers for finished goods jumped 1.0 percent in January. The Commerce Dept. said, **Feb. 17,** that, for the first time in 8 years, the U.S. merchandise trade deficit had declined in 1988, to $137.34 billion from $170.32 billion in 1987. The Labor Dept. said, **Feb. 22,** that consumer prices had risen 0.6 percent in January, the largest monthly increase since January 1987. The Federal Reserve Board increased its discount rate—the rate on loans paid by financial institutions—by 0.5 percent to 7.0 percent, **Feb. 24.** The rate stood at its highest level in almost 3 years.

Federal Pay Raises Rejected — Congress rejected a proposal to increase salaries for themselves, federal judges and top officials in the executive branch. A presidential advisory commission and former Pres. Ronald Reagan had approved the increases, running to 50 percent or more, and only explicit rejection by Congress could prevent their taking effect. The proposed increases, coming at a time of belt-tightening at the federal level, outraged many Americans, and polls showed lopsided public opposition. Members of Congress were swamped with critical mail. The Senate, **Feb. 2,** turned down the pay-increase package 95-5.

House Speaker Jim Wright (D, Tex.) proposed a compromise under which only a 30 percent increase would be approved. But vocal House members demanded and got a **Feb. 7** vote to reject the increases altogether. They prevailed, 380-48. The Senate reaffirmed its opposition, 94-6, and Pres. George Bush, who had previously supported the increases, signed the disapproval resolution.

Bush Acts in Savings & Loan Crisis — Pres. George Bush, **Feb. 6**, proposed to close or sell 350 savings and loan institutions that were in financial trouble. The projected $50 billion cost would be covered by the issuance of government bonds. The thrift industry would pay the principal on the bonds, and the industry and the taxpayers would provide the interest on the bonds.

Bush Aides in Ethics Disputes — It was reported that C. Boyden Gray, the chief ethics adviser to Pres. George Bush, had received outside income and had controlled his investments directly while serving as counsel to Vice-Pres. Bush from 1981 to 1988. Gray said, **Feb. 6**, that he would resign as chairman of Summit Communications, which had paid him $225,000 in fees while he worked for Bush. He also said he would put his assets in a blind trust. Gray, in turn, was reportedly the source of published reports that Secretary of State James Baker owned stock in Chemical New York Corporation. Chemical had made large loans to developing countries, and Baker faced the appearance of a conflict of interest because of his role in the administration as architect of policies dealing with 3d-world debt. Baker said, **Feb. 14**, that he would divest himself of all stock in publicly traded companies. Baker's aides reportedly believed that Gray had leaked information on Baker to take the spotlight away from himself.

Bush Rejects Ban on Semiautomatic Guns — The killing in January of 5 schoolchildren in California by a gunman using a semiautomatic rifle revived the national debate on gun control. A ban on the sale or possession of semiautomatic weapons was approved unanimously, **Feb. 7**, by the Los Angeles city council, and Mayor Tom Bradley signed the bill into law. Pres. George Bush said, **Feb. 16**, he would not support adoption of a law banning the import or sale of such weapons, which he said had a legitimate hunting purpose.

Bush Submits First Budget — Addressing Congress assembled in joint session, **Feb. 9**, Pres. George Bush presented his first budget, for fiscal year 1990. His priorities did not differ greatly from those of his predecessor, Ronald Reagan. Bush would reduce the top tax rate on capital gains from 33 percent to 15 percent, and he also endorsed tax breaks for independent oil and gas drillers. On the spending side, military outlays would be increased only by the rate of inflation. The president proposed few new domestic initiatives. He did call for a new Clean Air Act that would include curbs on acid rain. Bush favored a $5 billion cut in Medicare spending, but did not embrace Reagan's proposed $1.5 billion cut in Medicaid. All of this added up to expenditures of $1.16 trillion and a projected deficit of $91.1 billion. Richard Darman, the White House budget director, said, **Feb. 12**, that tax increases, heretofore apparently ruled out by the White House, would be considered "on the merits" if proposed by the Democrats.

Democrats Elect a Black as Chairman — Ronald Brown, a lawyer in Washington, D.C., was elected chairman of the Democratic National Committee, **Feb. 10**, becoming the first black to lead a major American political party. After 4 other aspirants dropped out, Brown was elected by acclamation. He succeeded Paul Kirk, Jr.

Iran-Contra Trial Under Way — After long delays caused by a search for a jury and disputes over classified documents, the first of the Iran-contra trials got going in federal district court in Washington, D.C., **Feb. 21**. The accused was former National Security Council staff member Oliver North. The trial prosecutor, John Keker, portrayed North as a liar who had misled investigators of the Iran-contra affair and who had thought himself "above the law." Brendan Sullivan, North's attorney, described his client as a patriotic Marine who had followed orders of the "highest-ranking officials" in the government. The first prosecution witness, Rep. Lee Hamilton (D, Ind.) testified, **Feb. 22-23**, that Reagan administration officials, including North, had told him in 1985 and 1986 that the Boland Amendment barring U.S. intelligence agencies from helping the contras had not been violated in any way. Adolfo Calero, a leader of the contras, testified, **Feb. 23**, that North had given him $32 million in 1984 and 1985 while U.S. aid to the contras was forbidden by law. In testimony from **Feb. 24** to **Mar. 1**, Robert Owen, North's courier to the contras, said that North had provided detailed military advice and intelligence data to the contras from 1984 to 1986.

Chicago Voters Back Daley — Richard M. Daley, the Cook County State's Attorney, won the Democratic Party primary for mayor of Chicago, **Feb. 28**. He defeated the acting mayor, Eugene Sawyer, Chicago's second black mayor, who had been named to his office in 1987 following the death of Mayor Harold Washington. The voting divided largely along racial lines. In the general election, **Apr. 4**, Daley was elected mayor with 55.5 percent of the vote. Timothy Evans, an independent candidate, won 41 percent.

International

Stroessner Ousted in Paraguay — Pres. Alfredo Stroessner, who had run Paraguay since seizing power in a military coup in 1954, was overthrown, **Feb. 2-3**, in a coup led by a longtime associate. Gen. Andrés Rodríguez, an ally of Stroessner since the latter came to power, spearheaded the revolt. Western diplomats estimated that up to 300 persons died in the fighting. Rodríguez, the new president, and a 9-member cabinet were sworn in, **Feb. 3**. Stroessner, 76, flew into exile in Brazil, **Feb. 5**. Rodríguez announced, **Feb. 6**, that presidential and congressional elections would be held May 1, and he denied any involvement in drug trafficking. Rodríguez was overwhelmingly elected president, **May 1**.

Japanese Premier Meets With Bush — Prime Minister Noboru Takeshita met with Pres. George Bush in Washington, **Feb. 2**. It was the first meeting between the new president and a foreign leader since his inauguration. The 2 men reportedly participated in a general discussion of important political, military, and economic matters. Japan's trade surplus with the U.S. remained the principal source of stress between the two countries.

Quayle Visits Latin Countries — Vice Pres. Dan Quayle undertook his first diplomatic mission in Venezuela, where he met with the outgoing and incoming presidents and then attended the inauguration, **Feb. 2**, of Pres. Carlos Andrés Pérez. Quayle criticized former Pres. Jimmy Carter, who was also in Caracas, for meeting with Pres. Daniel Ortega of Nicaragua. In El Salvador, **Feb. 3**, Quayle warned that U.S. aid might be lost if the nation's human-rights record did not improve.

Soviets Complete Afghan Withdrawal — The Soviet Union's 9-year military intervention in Afghanistan ended as the last Soviet troops left Kabul, the capital, **Feb. 5.** Tass, the Soviet news agency, reported that Pres. Najibullah had effectively put the city under martial law. Fulfilling their commitment to do so, the last Soviet soldiers left Afghanistan, **Feb. 15,** crossing a bridge from Heiratan into Termez, in the Soviet Union. Lt. Gen. Boris Gromov, the Soviet commander, was the last soldier to cross the bridge. Soviet figures indicated that some 15,000 of their soldiers had been killed in fighting against anticommunist Moslem rebels, and that 37,000 had been wounded. It was estimated that some 250 Soviet diplomats, intelligence agents, and military advisers remained in the country. The Soviet-supported Afghan army numbered about 140,000 soldiers. The government held the cities of Kabul and Jalalabad, outside of which, respectively, 30,000 and 15,000 rebels were massed. The Afghan premier resigned, **Feb. 20,** and a military council assumed most government functions. Representatives of 7 rebel groups based in Pakistan, **Feb. 23,** elected an interim government-in-exile. Iran's leader, Ayatollah Ruhollah Khomeini, told Soviet Foreign Minister Eduard Shevardnadze, **Feb. 26,** in Teheran, that the Soviet withdrawal cleared the way for closer Soviet-Iranian ties.

U.S. Rebukes Israel on Human Rights — The U.S. State Department's annual review of human-rights problems around the world, issued **Feb. 7,** criticized the conduct of the Israeli army in the occupied territories, noting that 366 Palestinians had been killed and more than 20,000 injured in 1988. The Palestinian intifada, or uprising, against Israeli rule had begun in late 1987. The report found that the Israelis often used excessive force, "causing many avoidable deaths and injuries." The report also criticized mass detentions without trial, arbitrary arrests, and deportations. Israeli officials rejected the conclusions in the report.

Mulroney, Bush Meet in Ottawa — In his first foreign trip as president, George Bush met with Canadian Prime Minister Brian Mulroney in Ottawa, **Feb. 10.** They discussed trade, defense, the environment, Central America, and East-West relations. Bush said he told Mulroney that the U.S. would move against acid rain, long a source of complaint north of the border. Bush said he would introduce legislation aimed at reducing acid rain and that a bilateral accord would follow.

Ayatollah Calls for Author's Execution — Anger over a new novel, *The Satanic Verses,* spread throughout the Islamic world as the leader of Iran, Ayatollah Ruhollah Khomeini, called on Moslems around the world to kill author Salman Rushdie and those involved in publishing the book. Rushdie, was born into a Moslem family in India and was now a citizen of Great Britain. A character in the novel experiences a dream in which a character resembling Mohammed, the founder of Islam, is depicted in an irreverent manner. Mass demonstrations against the book took place in a number of countries. Police killed 6 protesters in Pakistan, **Feb. 12** and 3 in India, **Feb. 13.** On **Feb. 15,** one of Khomeini's aides offered $1 million for the killing of Rushdie. Rushdie went into hiding. Many bookstores in the U.S. and elsewhere took the book off the shelves because of concern for the safety of their employees, but some stores restocked the book after many people rushed to buy it. Rushdie issued a statement, **Feb. 18,** that said, "I profoundly regret the distress that publication has occasioned to sincere followers of Islam." Khomeini rejected the apology, **Feb. 19.** Many western nations withdrew their ambassadors from Iran in protest, and Pres. George Bush said, **Feb.**

21, that "inciting murder and offering rewards for its perpetration are deeply offensive to the norms of civilized behavior." West Germany halted plans to assist the economic rebuilding of Iran. Authors organized demonstrations in behalf of Rushdie. During an anti-Rushdie riot in Bombay, **Feb. 24,** Indian police shot and killed 12 people and wounded 40.

Accord Signed on Disarming Contras — Five Central American presidents signed an agreement in El Salvador, **Feb. 14,** that would disarm and repatriate contra rebels opposing the Nicaraguan regime who were based in Honduras. The contras could be relocated in other countries, along with their families. Nicaragua, for its part, agreed to hold an election by February 1990 and to allow outside observers to monitor it. Nicaragua also agreed to free contra prisoners as well as former members of the National Guard under Pres. Anastasio Somoza. Pres. George Bush, whose administration had been taken by surprise when the accord was announced, said that the U.S. should be wary of promises made by Pres. Daniel Ortega of Nicaragua.

Black Leaders Denounce Mrs. Mandela — Black leaders in South Africa broke publicly with Winnie Mandela, the wife of the imprisoned black-nationalist leader Nelson Mandela. Although once thought of among blacks as the mother of the nation, Mrs. Mandela had been suffering from declining reputation for some time. Many had objected in 1987, for example, when she built a palatial home in Soweto with donated money. The immediate controversy focused on the United Mandela Football Club, who guarded her. In December 1988, they abducted 4 black youths from a home operated by a white Methodist minister in Soweto. Three youths later signed affidavits saying that Mrs. Mandela and her bodyguards beat them at her home. The 4th boy disappeared, but police announced, **Feb. 15,** that a decomposing body found in a field had been identified as that of the 14-year-old boy. The 4 youths apparently were suspected by Mandela's guards of being police informers. A doctor who examined the boy later found dead, while he was still at Mandela's home, was himself murdered by unknown assailants shortly thereafter. Major antiapartheid organizations in South Africa, **Feb. 16,** formally disowned Mrs. Mandela and said she had abused the trust of the black community.

Venezuelans Riot Over Price Increases — Venezuelans rioted in protest against government-imposed increases in transportation fares and gasoline prices. The new president, Carlos Andrés Pérez, had acted, **Feb. 16,** to satisfy the International Monetary Fund, with which Venezuela had been negotiating on a loan. The nation's currency, the bolivar, was devalued. After the price increases were announced, **Feb. 27,** riots spread around the country. Pérez declared martial law, **Feb. 28.** Although wage increases were announced **Mar. 1,** new riots erupted. Pérez said, **Mar. 3,** that 300 had died in the violence.

Emperor Hirohito Is Buried — Emperor Hirohito of Japan, who had died in January, was buried, **Feb. 24,** in Tokyo in a daylong Shinto ceremony. Pres. George Bush was among 55 heads of state in attendance. Altogether, some 160 countries were represented. Bush, a former envoy to China, flew on to Beijing, **Feb. 25,** and on **Feb. 26,** he met with China's supreme leader, Deng Xiaoping. In South Korea, **Feb. 27,** Bush met with opposition leaders and addressed the National Assembly.

$470 Million Settlement in Bhopal Disaster — Four years of litigation led, **Feb. 14,** to a costly settlement in the disastrous chemical-plant leak in Bhopal, India in 1984. The Indian Supreme Court ordered Union Carbide Corporation to pay $470 million to victims of the gas leak. According to the Indian government, exposure to the gas, methyl isocyanate, had killed 3,329 people, and 20,000 continued to suffer from its effects. The court issued the order after the company and the government agreed to a proposal by the chief justice. Union Carbide was to pay the $470 million in a lump sum by March 31, 1989. All other civil and criminal charges relating to the incident would be dropped. The court did not consider the question of liability for the tragedy.

Disasters — All 144 persons aboard a chartered jet airliner died, **Feb. 8,** when it crashed into a fog-shrouded mountain in the Azores Islands. The plane was carrying Italian tourists to the Caribbean.

MARCH

National

Senate Defeats Tower Nomination — In a rare rebuff to a president, the U.S. Senate rejected George Bush's nomination of John Tower to be secretary of defense. Tower fought to the end, even acknowledging some shortcomings publicly. He told the National Press Club Mar. 1, "I have broken wedding vows. I think I am probably not alone in that connection." The Senate began debate on the nomination, **Mar. 2.** Carl Levin (D, Mich.) said that the nation was entitled to have a secretary in whom it had confidence, and that Tower had fallen short "in the area of sensitivity to appearances" because he had moved so swiftly from senator to arms negotiator to consultant for defense companies. Sen. Phil Gramm (R, Tex.) said the 70 senators who had served with Tower would acknowledge that he had "the ability to provide effective leadership." When the Senate decided the issue, **Mar. 9,** all but 3 Democrats voted against the nomination. They were joined by one Republican, Nancy Kassebaum (Kan.), and Tower was turned down, 53-47. For only the 9th time—and the first time in 30 years—the Senate had rejected a Cabinet nominee. Tower, observing that no one within his memory "had his human foibles bared to such intensive and demeaning public scrutiny," said he would return to private life in Texas. Bush said he regretted the "cruel ordeal" Tower had experienced. On **Mar. 10,** Bush nominated Dick Cheney, who had been chief of staff for Pres. Gerald Ford and who was now a Republican representative from Wyoming, to be secretary of defense. Cheney, a conservative who was popular on Capitol Hill, was confirmed unanimously by the Senate Armed Services Committee, **Mar. 16,** and by the full Senate, **Mar. 17.**

Witness Ties Reagan to Iran-Contra — The prosecution's case against former National Security Council staff member Oliver North continued with Maj. Gen. John Singlaub (ret.) testifying, **Mar. 1,** that Oliver North knew his efforts in behalf of the contras violated the Boland Amendment. In another court, **Mar. 3,** Robert McFarlane, a former National Security adviser to Pres. Ronald Reagan, was sentenced to 2 years' probation and fined $20,000 for his role in the arms scandal. The first former presidential aide to be sentenced in the affair, McFarlane had already pleaded guilty to 4 misdemeanor counts. In the North trial, former contra fund-raiser Carl Channell testified, **Mar. 8,** that he had heard North say that he was prepared to deceive Congress and go to jail, if he had to. McFarlane testified, **Mar. 10,** that Reagan had approved 3d-country support for the contras and warned aides not to tell Congress about it. Under cross-examination, **Mar. 15,** McFarlane said Reagan had approved an April 1985 plan to give Honduras $110 million in aid in return for Honduran support for the contras. Glenn Robinette, a

former Central Intelligence Agency official, testified, **Mar. 21,** that he and North had falsified documents to conceal the fact that Air Force Maj. Gen. Richard Secord (ret.) had paid for a $13,800 security fence at North's home. Fawn Hall, North's former secretary, testified, **Mar. 22-23,** about her role in helping North alter or destroy relevant documents. Testifying **Mar. 28-29,** former Attorney Gen. Edwin Meese said that as the scandal unfolded the administration had feared the possibility that Reagan would be impeached.

Jobless Rate at 15-Year Low — The Commerce Dept. reported, **Mar. 3,** that the leading economic indicators had risen 0.6 percent in January. The Labor Dept. said, **Mar. 10,** that the unemployment rate had dipped 0.3 percentage points in February to 5.1 percent, a level not reached since May 1974. The U.S. deficit on merchandise trade fell to $9.49 billion in January, the Commerce Dept. said, **Mar. 15.** In February, for the second consecutive month producer prices climbed 1 percent, according to the Labor Dept., **Mar. 17.** Wall Street had anticipated a much lower figure, and the Dow Jones industrial average fell almost 50 points. The Labor Dept. said, **Mar. 21,** that consumer prices had risen 0.4 percent in February. The Commerce Dept. reported, **Mar. 29,** that the leading economic indicators had declined 0.3 percent in February.

Eastern Airlines Files for Bankruptcy — A long labor controversy culminated, **Mar. 4,** in a strike of Eastern Airlines by its machinists. Pilots and flight attendants supported the strike. The carrier was losing money, and the machinists had offered to forgo any raises for 15 months. Frank Lorenzo, chairman of the parent Texas Air Corp., was unpopular with his own employees, though he denied their contention that he had shown hostility toward unions. Pres. George Bush explained, **Mar. 7,** that he had chosen not to use his authority to postpone the strike because he said it should be resolved through the free collective bargaining process. Although the airline was virtually shut down, it kept its popular Northeast shuttle operation going and slashed fares to attract customers. On **Mar. 9,** the company filed for bankruptcy.

Bush Bars Import of Assault Rifles — In the wake of the killing of 5 California schoolchildren in January, opposition to assault rifles continued to grow. The California Senate, **Mar. 9,** and the Assembly, **Mar. 13,** passed differing versions of a bill barring the sale, possession, or manufacture of semiautomatic assault weapons. In a reversal of policy, the Bush administration **Mar. 14,** banned imports of semiautomatic assault rifles indefinitely. Law enforcement officials said that such weapons were preferred by drug dealers. The Soviet AK-47 and the Israeli Uzi were 2 well-known makes affected by the ban. U.S.-manufactured weapons of that type were not affected by the ban.

Grapes, Apples Cause Concern — Responding to an anonymous tipster, the U.S. Food and Drug Administration inspected crates of grapes from Chile in Philadelphia, **Mar. 11** and **12,** and found traces of cyanide in 2 grapes. The FDA, **Mar. 13,** quarantined all fruit from Chile, a major supplier. Chilean exporters halted all shipments of fruit, **Mar. 14.** The Chilean government, **Mar. 14,** blamed the outlawed Communist Party for the tainted grapes. Pres. Augusto Pinochet said, **Mar. 16,** that the impact of the quarantine had been "catastrophic" on Chile's economy, and that the United States had overreacted. Growing concern about another fruit, the apple, prompted 3 federal agencies, **Mar. 16,** to assert that eating apples was safe for both adults and children. The public had been worried by reports that some apples were treated with daminozide, sold under the name Alar, which was suspected as a cause of cancer. The chemical was used to improve apples' appearance, freshness, and texture. The 3 agencies said that a report by the Natural Resources Defense Council had greatly exaggerated the threat posed by daminozide. The FDA, **Mar. 17**, lifted its quarantine on Chilean grapes and berries. The Uniroyal Chemical Company announced, **June 2**, that it was halting domestic sales of Alar.

Shuttle Crew Films Damage to Earth — The space shuttle *Discovery*, with a 5-person crew, was launched, **Mar. 13**, from Cape Canaveral, Fla., and about 6 hours later the crew deployed a tracking and data relay satellite. The crew filmed the Earth in an effort to document damage to the planet from various natural and human causes.

House Republicans Elect Gingrich — Republican members of the U.S. House, **Mar 22**, elected Newt Gingrich (Ga.) to the position of party whip. The office had been vacated by Rep. Dick Cheney (Wyo.), who had been appointed secretary of defense. In winning the No. 2 position in the Republican leadership, Gingrich edged out Rep. Edward Madigan (Ill.) by 87-85. The Georgian, an outspoken conservative, had gained attention with his vigorous criticism of the ethics of House Speaker Jim Wright (D, Tex.).

Huge Oil Spill Fouls Alaskan Waters — The largest oil spill in U.S. history occurred after a tanker struck a reef in Alaska's Prince William Sound, **Mar. 24**. The Exxon *Valdez* struck Bligh Reef, about 25 miles from the town of Valdez, the southern terminus of the pipeline that carried oil from northern Alaska. The tanker, which was off course, was being piloted by the third mate instead of by the captain, Joseph Hazelwood. Exxon Corporation announced, **Mar. 25**, that it accepted full financial responsibility for the spill, which was initially estimated at 240,000 barrels. The 987-foot tanker had been carrying 1,260,000 barrels of crude oil, some of which was being siphoned into another ship. Alyeska Pipeline Service Company, the oil-company consortium that operated the pipeline, had said that there would be a spill containment team at Valdez, but that turned out to consist only of a barge that happened to be in drydock with a hole in its side. A skimming technique removed only a small portion of the oil. Exxon announced, **Mar. 26**, it was ready to deploy a dispersant, but winds up to 73 miles an hour, **Mar. 27**, thwarted that effort. The economic and environmental dimensions of the disaster grew daily. The fishing industry was temporarily wiped out, and the pictures on television of dying birds and otters, soaked with oil, stunned the nation. Exxon said, **Mar. 28**, that it was impossible to contain the spill. Valdez Mayor John Devens said, **Mar. 28**, that his community felt betrayed by Exxon. By **Mar. 29**, the spill extended 45 miles. On hearing a report from federal officials after their return from Alaska, Pres. George Bush called the spill "a major tragedy," but the administration decided not to take over the cleanup. Having tested Capt. Hazelwood, the Coast Guard announced, **Mar. 30**, that he had an unacceptably high level of alcohol in his blood. The FBI opened an investigation into the spill, **Mar. 31**.

5 Plead Guilty in Pentagon Case — Five more men entered guilty pleas in Alexandria, Va. in federal court in connection with the Pentagon procurement scandal. They included Charles Gardner, a former vice president of Unisys Corporation, who pleaded guilty, **Mar. 9**, to tax evasion, bribing a public official, and making false statements. Stuart Berlin, a Navy contract specialist, pleaded guilty, **Mar. 23**, to wire fraud and receiving bribes as part of a plan to help Teledyne Electronics win an Air Force electronics contract. Teledyne pleaded guilty to conspiracy. William Parkin, a defense consultant, pleaded guilty, **Mar. 27**, to bribing a public official (Berlin), wire fraud, and fraud conspiracy.

International

Iran Breaks Ties With Britain — The controversy over Salman Rushdie's novel *The Satanic Verses* led Iran, **Mar. 7**, to break diplomatic relations with Great Britain. Iran had demanded that Britain denounce Rushdie, a British citizen, and his book. The leader of Belgium's Moslem community and a colleague were shot to death in Brussels, **Mar. 29**. A pro-Iranian terrorist group in Lebanon claimed, **Mar. 31**, that it had killed the leader because he had criticized Iran's demand that Rushdie be killed.

Tibetans Demand Independence — Led by 13 Buddhist monks and nuns, up to 2,000 Tibetans marched in a demonstration for independence in Lhasa, the capital of Tibet, **Mar. 5**. Police checked the demonstration with gunfire, and Chinese authorities reported that a policeman and 10 protesters and onlookers were killed. After 3 days of violence, the Chinese government imposed martial law, **Mar. 7**. Officially, 16 people were killed in the clashes, but Tibetans told Westerners that the toll could be as high as 100. The government ordered all tourists out of the city, **Mar. 9**.

Right-Wing Nominee Wins in El Salvador — Alfredo Christiani was elected president of El Salvador, **Mar. 19**, with 54 percent of the vote. The candidate of the Nationalist Republican Alliance (ARENA), Christiani defeated the nominee of the ruling Christian Democratic Party. Leftist rebels had sought without success to disrupt the election. ARENA's founder, Roberto D'Aubuisson, had been accused of human-rights abuses, which he denied. Christiani, **Mar. 21**, called for a cease-fire in the civil war and negotiations with the rebels.

23 Dead in Yugoslav Riots — Clashes between police and ethnic Albanians left at least 23 dead in Kosovo province, in Yugoslavia. Kosovo, which had an Albanian majority, was an autonomous region of the republic of Serbia. On **Mar. 23**, Kosovo's legislature voted to give Serbia direct control over the province's courts and police. Demonstrations, which began immediately, quickly turned violent and spread to several cities.

Bush, Congress Agree on Contra Aid — Pres. George Bush and leaders of Congress in both parties signed an agreement, **Mar. 24**, on continued aid to the contras opposing the Sandinista regime in Nicaragua. Under the accord, which would have to be approved by both houses, the contras would receive $4.5 million a month for food, clothing, shelter, and medical supplies through February 1990, by which time the Nicaraguan government had promised to hold elections. The aid would end if the contras initiated military action prior to the scheduled elections. Leading Democrats who had criticized Reagan administration policy toward Nicaragua praised the agreement with the Bush administration. Congress approved the agreement, **Apr. 13**.

Soviet Elections Stun Leadership — An historic election in the Soviet Union, **Mar. 26**, provided a strong signal that the citizenry wanted to see a faster pace in economic, social, and political reform. At stake were 1,500 seats in the new Congress of People's Deputies. Later, 750 more seats would be filled by the Communist Party and by labor, social, and youth organizations. For the first time since 1917, voters could participate in a nationwide multicandidate parliamentary election. The most prominent antiestablishment candidate was Boris Yeltsin, who had lost his leadership of the Moscow Communist Party because of outspoken criticism of conservative elements in the national leadership. Yeltsin's comeback in the March voting was dramatic, as he polled 89 percent against the party favorite in winning Moscow's at-large seat in the parliament. Elsewhere, radical reformers and ethnic nationalists won over party regulars in many districts. Even a number of party stalwarts who ran unopposed—in Moscow, Leningrad, the Ukraine, and elsewhere—failed to win election because they received less than 50 percent of the vote. Voters simply crossed out their names.

General

EC Ministers Act to Protect Ozone Layer — Environmental ministers representing 12 members of the European Community agreed in Brussels, **Mar. 2,** to ban production of chlorofluorocarbons (CFCs) by the year 2000. CFCs, blamed for contributing to the depletion of the Earth's ozone layer, were used in solvents, refrigerators, foam insulation, and spray cans. The ozone layer prevents harmful ultraviolet radiation—linked to skin cancer and crop damage—from reaching the Earth. Representatives of 123 nations, meeting in London, **Mar. 7,** called for speeding up the timetable provided in an existing international agreement for phasing out use of CFCs. That agreement, approved in 1987, provided for a 50 percent reduction in CFCs by 2000.

Time, Inc., Warner Approve Merger — Time, Inc. and Warner Communications, Inc. agreed, **Mar. 4,** to merge. With annual revenue of more than $10 billion, the merged company would be the world's largest in media and entertainment. The companies decided to merge to compete more effectively with international media companies.

"Junk-Bond King" Is Indicted — Michael Milken, head of the so-called junk-bond department at Drexel Burnham Lambert, was indicted, **Mar. 29,** along with his brother and a 3d Drexel employee, on 98 counts of racketeering, mail fraud, securities fraud, and other criminal charges. The indictment charged that Milken had led a conspiracy to defraud Drexel clients, shareholders, and the investing public. Milken's use of high-risk securities to finance corporate takeovers and leveraged buyouts had added a chapter to Wall Street history and had made Milken very rich: in 1987 alone he had received $550 million in compensation from Drexel. Milken said he would plead not guilty to the charges.

Disasters — Up to 130 Vietnamese refugees drowned, **Mar. 8,** when their fishing boat collided in the South China Sea off Malaysia with a Japanese supertanker.

APRIL

National

Damage From Alaskan Oil Spill Spreads — Oil dumped into Alaskan waters by the *Exxon Valdez* continued to spread in April, and the cleanup proceeded slowly. Alaskan officials canceled the herring season in Prince William Sound, **Apr. 3,** because spawning areas were contaminated. The tanker was refloated, **Apr. 5.** Its captain, Joseph Hazelwood, facing charges that he was drunk when the tanker struck a reef, was jailed in Suffolk County, N.Y., **Apr. 5,** after a judge set bail at $1 million. Hazelwood was freed, **Apr. 6,** after another judge reduced bail to $25,000. Amid reports that the cleanup was proceeding slowly, Pres. George Bush said, **Apr. 7,** that he would send troops, military equipment, and other federal assistance. Adm. Paul A. Yost, Jr., commandant of the Coast Guard, was put in charge of the cleanup. After he and Gov. Steve Cowper of Alaska toured the fouled beaches, **Apr. 14,** Cowper said the state and the Coast Guard were not satisfied with Exxon's efforts to clean up the oil. Ordered by Yost to come up with a cleanup plan, Exxon, **Apr. 15,** proposed to hire 4,000 people to scrub 305 miles of shoreline by Sept. 15. Yost approved the plan, **Apr. 17,** but doubted it was realistic. In fact, at that point, only about 10 percent of the 24,000 barrels of oil had been recovered. The oil continued to spread far from Prince William Sound, touching the shores of Katmai and Kenai Fjords national parks in Alaska.

North Testifies at Iran/Contra Trial — Oliver North, the former National Security Council staff member on trial in Washington, D.C., testified in his own defense in April. The defense, **Apr. 6,** released a document revealing that Pres. Ronald Reagan and Vice Pres. George Bush had done more than previously acknowledged to get help for the Nicaraguan contras. It showed that Reagan had approved a plan in February 1985 to increase assistance to Honduras in return for Honduran support of the contras. A letter explaining the plan was to be delivered to Honduras by a "discreet emissary," not identified. Four weeks later Bush met in Honduras with Pres. Roberto Suazo and told him aid from the U.S. would be resumed or expedited. North testified, **Apr. 6,** that 3 superiors had ordered him to aid the contras. Bush said, **Apr. 7,** that he would not discuss the Reagan administration's efforts to help the contras while the trial was in progress. North admitted, **Apr. 7,** that he had lied to Congress but that he had been ordered by superiors not to discuss details of the effort to help the contras. North testified, **Apr. 12,** that he had been "led to believe" that everything he did was at the direction of the president. After closing arguments, **Apr. 18** and **19,** Judge Gerhard Gesell sent the case to the jury, **Apr. 20.** He told the jury that no one, including the president, had the legal right to tell anyone else to violate the law.

Decline in Unemployment Continues — The decline in the nation's unemployment rate continued in March, the Labor Dept. reported, **Apr. 7.** The rate of 4.9 percent, lowest since 1973, was considered by some economists as virtually equivalent to full employment. The Commerce Dept. reported, **Apr. 14,** that the U.S. merchandise trade deficit had risen sharply to $10.5 billion in February. The Labor Dept. said, **Apr. 14,** that the producer price index, after rising a full percentage point in each of the previous 2 months, had risen by only 0.4 percent in March. The department said, **Apr. 18,** that consumer prices, led by energy prices, had risen 0.5 percent in March. On Wall Street, the Dow Jones industrial average closed above 2400, **Apr. 21,** for the first time since the sharp decline in stock prices began in the summer of 1987. The Commerce Dept. reported, **Apr. 26,** that the economy had shown strength in the first quarter of 1989, with the gross national product expanding at an annual rate of 5.5 percent. The department reported, **Apr. 28,** that leading economic indicators had declined 0.7 percent in March.

Huge Rally Supports Abortion — There was a massive turnout of people, officially estimated at 300,000, in Washington, D.C., **Apr. 9,** advocating a woman's right to choose to have an abortion. The rally, sponsored by the National Organization for Women, was aimed at focusing attention on the issue in advance of the impending Supreme Court decision in a case that could curtail legal abortions.

Bush, Congress Leaders Agree on Budget — Pres. Bush announced, **Apr. 14,** that he and leaders of Congress had reached an agreement on the framework for the federal budget for the 1990 fiscal year. Their budget projected a deficit of $99.4 billion, just under the mandated limit of $100 billion. The budget, not greatly different from the one proposed by Bush in February, foresaw $8.5 billion in increased revenues and $4.7 billion in defense cuts. Domestic spending and interest would be reduced by $9.1 billion. Many specifics were not worked out, most notably the question of where the $5.3 billion in new tax revenue would be found.

Speaker Accused of Breaking House Rules — The House Ethics Committee, consisting of 6 Democrats and 6 Republicans, released a report, **Apr. 17,** that held, unanimously, that there was reason to believe that Speaker Jim Wright (D, Tex.) had violated House rules. The 69 separate instances cited by the committee related to the acceptance of gifts and outside income, and were the legislative equivalent to an indictment. Rep. Julian Dixon (D., Cal.) was chairman of the committee. One group of charges related to bulk sales of Wright's book, *Reflections of a Public Man,* which the committee asserted were part of a "scheme" to evade House rules on outside earned income. Other allegations related to $145,000 in "apparent gifts" from George Mallick, a Texas businessman and longtime friend of Wright. The gifts were in the form of housing, an automobile, and a salary paid to Mrs. Betty Wright. They were not reported on Wright's financial disclosure forms. The committee said it had reason to believe Mallick had a direct interest in legislation, which would have limited Wright to accepting no more than $100 a year from him. Wright said, **Apr. 17,** "I know in my heart I have not violated any rules," and on **Apr. 18,** he vigorously defended his wife's employment by Mallick's company. The committee's next task was to determine if there was "clear and convincing proof" that Wright was guilty of the alleged violations.

Explosion on Ship Kills 47 Sailors — An explosion inside a gun turret on the *U.S.S. Iowa,* **Apr. 19,** killed 47 sailors. The 6-story turret housed three 16-inch battery guns (the world's largest naval guns), stocks of ammunition, and powder charges. The 47-year-old battleship, which had seen action in World War II, was participating in a naval exercise about 300 miles north of Puerto Rico. The crew was loading the guns when the explosion occurred. The Navy began an investigation of the cause of the disaster.

International

Gorbachev in Ireland, Cuba, Britain — Soviet leader Mikhail Gorbachev visited Ireland, **Apr. 2,** where he conferred with Prime Minister Charles Haughey. Gorbachev then flew to Cuba, where he met, **Apr. 3,** with Pres. Fidel Castro. Castro had publicly opposed the type of social and economic reforms Gorbachev was promoting in the Soviet Union. However, Castro, who relied heavily on economic aid from the Soviet Union, had scaled back his criticisms. In an apparent warning to his hosts, Gorbachev, in addressing the National Assembly, **Apr. 4,** said the Soviet Union "categorically opposed . . . the export of revolution or counterrevolution and all forms of foreign interference in the affairs of sovereign states." He said the Soviet Union would stop aiding Nicaragua if the U.S. halted military aid to its Central American allies. In London, **Apr. 6,** Gorbachev and British Prime Minister Margaret Thatcher held day-long talks. He reportedly opposed Thatcher's insistance that U.S. short-range nuclear missiles in West Germany must be modernized. At a state dinner, Gorbachev called himself a "confirmed opponent" of nuclear weapons. Speaking at London's Guildhall, **Apr. 7,** Gorbachev said the Soviet Union was seeking to build an "open, democratic and free society." He

lunched with Queen Elizabeth II at Windsor Castle, **Apr. 7.**

Bush Meets With Mubarak, Shamir — Pres. George Bush conferred with Egyptian Pres. Hosni Mubarak in Washington, **Apr. 3,** and Bush declared that the 2 countries "share the goals of security for Israel, the end of the occupation, and achievement of Palestinian political rights." Israeli Prime Minister Yitzhak Shamir, meeting with Bush in Washington, **Apr. 6,** said Israel would be willing to hold elections in the occupied territories that could lead to a "self-governing administration."

Vietnamese Troops to Leave Cambodia — Vietnam officials said, **Apr. 5,** that it would pull out all of its troops from Cambodia by Sept. 30. Vietnamese forces had entered the country a decade ago to overthrow the regime headed by Pol Pot. Cambodian guerillas, backed by China, were still resisting the Vietnamese and the regime that they had installed. Prince Norodom Sihanouk, leader of the resistance, urged, **Apr. 6,** that the United Nations monitor the withdrawal.

Polish Regime Reaches Accord With Opposition — The long confrontation between the Polish government and its non-Communist opposition appeared to be ending in April. The government and its adversaries, led by Lech Walesa, agreed, **Apr. 5,** to a new structure for government that would include a new bicameral national legislature. A new Senate would have 100 seats, and the existing parliament would become the lower house. It would have 460 seats, 65 percent of which would be reserved for the Communist Party and its allies. Opposition figures and independents would fill the remaining seats. The legislature would elect a president having a 6-year term and strong executive powers. The signed agreement permitted official opposition media outlets, and the outlawed trade union Solidarity was to be restored to legal status. Agreement was also announced, **Apr. 5,** on a law to grant official recognition to the Roman Catholic Church. A major goal of the Polish factions was increased help from the U.S., and on **Apr. 17,** Pres. George Bush announced a package of economic aid, including elimination of U.S. tariffs on some Polish goods, loans to Poland (subject to Congressional approval), and an effort to expand the role of U. S. companies in Poland.

Accident on Soviet Nuclear Sub Fatal to 42 — A Soviet nuclear-powered submarine caught fire and sank off Norway, **Apr. 7.** When fire broke out, the sub surfaced and the crew fought it for 3 hours before abandoning the vessel. Soviet fishing boats rescued 27 crewmen in rafts. Most of the deaths were attributed to drowning or exposure. Tass, the Soviet news agency, said, **Apr. 9,** that the submarine carried 2 torpedoes with nuclear warheads. A Soviet admiral indicated, **Apr. 11,** that the USSR would attempt to recover the vessel.

Soviet Troops Use Poison Gas — Soviet Troops sprayed demonstrators with poison gas in Tbilisi, the capital of Georgia, **Apr. 9.** Georgian nationalists had been demonstrating since February, and on **Apr. 9,** 10,000 gathered in Lenin Square in the capital. Troops beat them, and others were trampled in the panic that followed. The official death count was 20, with 200—including 75 troops—injured. *Izvestia,* the government newspaper, reported, **Apr. 20,** that some demonstrators had died from "chemical agents." The Soviet foreign ministry said, **Apr. 20,** that nothing stronger than tear gas had been used. But a Georgian paper reported, **Apr. 27,** that a toxicologist had confirmed that a poison gas had been used. An investigation ordered by the Politburo was underway.

Drug Cultists Slay 15 in Mexico — Fifteen mutilated bodies were found buried near Matamoros, Mexico, **April 11-16**, near the U.S. border. Five suspects were arrested who said that the victims had been sacrificed to ensure that their killers, who were drug traffickers, would be protected from police. Police closed in on 7 more suspected cultists in an apartment building in Mexico City, **May 6**. Five were taken alive, but the alleged leader of the cult and his bodyguard were found shot to death. A surviving cultist said the leader had asked him to kill him.

Scandal Topples Japanese Premier — Japanese Prime Minister Noboru Takeshita announced that he would resign as a result of his involvement in a major scandal. A number of government officials and businessmen had resigned or had been arrested as a result of involvement in alleged wrongdoing with the Recruit Co. The government was nearly paralyzed by the revelations, and Takeshita's personal popularity had declined sharply. On **Apr. 11**, appearing before the Diet (parliament), Takeshita answered questions on the matter. He said he had received the equivalent of about $700,000 from the company. Although he said that the political donations were legal, some had not been reported, and some legislators suggested that they exceeded campaign funding limits and may have been made in exchange for political favors. A newspaper reported, **Apr. 22**, that Takeshita had received a $380,000 loan from Recruit, later repaid. Saying he wanted to take responsibility for the distrust in his government, Takeshita announced, **Apr. 25**, that he would resign after the 1989 budget was approved by parliament. The prime minister's secretary, Ihei Aoki, who had been called a middleman in financial dealings between Takeshita and Recruit, committed suicide, **Apr. 26**.

NATO Countries Argue Over Missiles — A dispute continued in the NATO alliance over short-range missiles based in West Germany. NATO's foreign ministers agreed, **Apr. 20**, that no immediate decision need be made on upgrading the U.S. short-range missiles. This was the concession to West German Chancellor Helmut Kohl, who was under public pressure in Germany to oppose the modernization of the arsenal. The U.S. and Great Britain had been arguing for the replacement of the weapons. But differences became apparent, **Apr. 30**, when Kohl met in West Germany with Prime Minister Margaret Thatcher of Britain. Kohl urged talks with the Soviet Union aimed at producing cuts in the number of short-range missiles. But Thatcher, along with the Bush administration, had been opposing such talks, and Thatcher reiterated her opposition after the meeting with Kohl.

Soviet Party Old-Timers Purged — Soviet leader Mikhail Gorbachev strengthened his hand, **Apr. 25**, by orchestrating the mass resignations of 110 officials, including 74 full members of the Central Committee of the Communist Party. Most of those who retired, supposedly voluntarily, were holdovers from the time when Leonid Brezhnev ran the party and the country. Vadim Medvedev, the party ideologist, called the resignations an important milestone in perestroika, or restructuring. Former Pres. Andrei Gromyko was among those who resigned.

General

Nurses Killed 49 Patients — Police announced in Vienna, **Apr. 10**, that 4 nurses had admitted killing 49 elderly patients since 1983. The nurses reportedly said that these were mercy killings, but a police investigator said they had also killed patients whom they regarded as a nuisance. The nurses reportedly had given the vic-

tims overdoses of medication or had forced water into their lungs. Press reports said the number of victims could be much higher.

Drexel Settles SEC Civil Charges — The Wall Street securities firm Drexel Burnham Lambert Inc. settled civil charges brought against it by the U.S. Securities and Exchange Commission. Under the **Apr. 13** settlement, Drexel would be under probation for 3 years. It would pay a $15 million fine, put $350 million in a fund for those injured by its violations, dismiss its indicted junk-bond "king" Michael Milken, and appoint or elect leaders acceptable to the SEC. Drexel had previously pleaded guilty to criminal charges. Milken resigned from Drexel, **June 15**, and announced he would form his own financial consulting firm.

95 Soccer Fans Die in Crush — Ninety-five persons attending a soccer game in Sheffield, South Yorkshire, England were killed, **Apr. 15**, when fans pushing into the stadium crushed the victims crowded in front of them. Some 200 others were injured. Just before the game started, some 4,000 fans were massed at an entrance eager to enter the stadium. When it appeared they could not enter easily through the turnstiles, an exit was opened and they flooded in. Those in front of them were pushed forward, and many of those who died were crushed against metal fences.

Disasters — Some 1,000 persons were killed and about 12,000 were injured, **Apr. 26**, when a tornado, which also destroyed 20 villages, stuck central Bangladesh.

MAY

National

Exxon Valdez Oil Spill — Federal officials heard testimony on what occurred aboard ship before the *Exxon Valdez* struck a reef in March and spilled an immense amount of oil. Exxon, **May 1**, released a cleanup plan covering 364 miles of beaches, but about half of that total was to be cleaned up by natural processes. Although Exxon announced an expanded plan, **May 10**, with increased manpower, Adm. Paul Yost, commandant of the Coast Guard, told a Senate hearing, **May 10**, that it would be almost impossible to clean up the beaches on the schedule Exxon projected. Gregory Cousins, the 3d mate, who was in charge of the ship at the time of the accident, testified before hearings conducted in Anchorage, Alaska by the National Transportation Safety Board. He said, **May 16**, that the Captain, Joseph Hazelwood, had set the ship on automatic pilot and left the bridge. Cousins, who was not licensed to pilot the vessel in Prince William Sound, said that before the collision with the reef he took the *Valdez* off automatic pilot, but that it was moving too fast to be piloted effectively in the dangerous area. Testimony by Cousins and by a Coast Guard official, **May 18**, suggested Hazelwood may have been intoxicated. Hazelwood declined to testify. Federal officials reported to Pres. George Bush, **May 18**, that the response by the industry and the government to the spill had been "wholly insufficient."

Shuttle Deploys Craft to Venus — The shuttle *Atlantis*, with 5 crew members aboard, lifted off from Cape Canaveral, Fla, **May 4**. Later that day the crew deployed the *Magellan* spacecraft on a 15-month, 800-million-mile trip to Venus. The *Magellan's* mission was to utilize radar to map 90 percent of the surface of Venus. The shuttle landed at Edwards Air Force Base, Calif., **May 8**.

North Convicted in Iran-Contra Trial — Former National Security Council staff member Oliver North, a retired Lt. Col. in the Marine Corps, became the first person, **May 4**, to be convicted in a jury trial in connection with the Iran-Contra scandal. A jury had deliberated in federal district court in Washington, D.C. for 12 days before reaching a verdict. They acquitted North on 9 charges but found him guilty of 3 others: (1) aiding and abetting the obstruction of Congress by preparing a false chronology of the Reagan administration's arms sales to Iran; (2) altering, destroying, removing, or concealing NSC documents relating to North's efforts to assist the Nicaraguan contras when it was forbidden by law;and (3) receiving as an illegal gratuity a $13,800 security system for his home. North's lawyers said an appeal would be filed. Pres. George Bush, **May 4**, denied that he had offered increased aid to Honduras in 1985 (while he was vice president) in exhange for that country's support for the contras. A document made public during the North trial had revealed that Pres. Ronald Reagan had agreed to such an exchange and that Bush had visited Honduras less than a month later.

Economy Slowing Down a Bit — Data released in May indicated that the U.S. economy was not growing as fast as previously thought. The Labor Dept. said, **May 5**, that unemployment, after hitting a 15-year low, had edged upward 0.3 percent to 5.2 percent in April. The Department said, **May 12**, that the prices asked by producers for finished goods had risen 0.4 percent in April, for the second straight month. The Commerce Dept. reported, **May 17**, that the merchandise trade deficit shrank slightly to $8.86 billion in March. According to the Labor Dept., **May 18**, energy prices were primarily responsible for the 0.7 percent jump in consumer prices recorded in April. Gasoline alone soared 11.4 percent, a record, in April. The advance in stock prices continued, with the Dow Jones industrial average closing above 2500 on **May 19**, a runup of nearly 425 points, or 20 percent, in 6 months. The Commerce Dept., **May 25**, revised downward its calculation of the growth of the gross national product during the first quarter. The new figure, 4.3 percent, compared with the previous 5.5 percent, was welcomed by the Bush administration and many economists, who believed that tightening of credit by the Federal Reserve would control inflation and slow the economy without causing a recession. The Department said, **May 31**, that the leading economic indicators had risen 0.8 percent in April.

Congress OKs Compromise Budget — Congress approved the compromise budget plan worked out in April between Pres. George Bush and Senate and House leaders. Differences between Senate and House versions were reconciled, **May 11**, and the House, **May 17**, and the Senate, **May 18**, then gave final approval. However, even some of its supporters acknowledged that some of the deficit-cutting tactics were illusory.

HUD Fees to Consultants Investigated — Congressional committees began an investigation into millions of dollars in consulting fees paid by the Dept. of Housing and Urban Development to former federal officials and other prominent Republicans. An internal audit released by HUD, **April 26**, had shown that the Moderate Rehabilitation Program, which involved payments to developers to restore housing for families with low or moderate incomes, was the focus of questionable financial arrangements. Ironically, the Reagan administration had tried to kill the program. HUD's inspector general, Paul Adams, found that many contracts had gone to developers represented by ex-HUD employees or political figures. In testimony before a House subcommittee, **May 11**, former Housing Commissioner Thomas Demery, who had helped some developers obtain federal funding, said his involvement had been directed by former HUD Secretary Samuel

Pierce and Pierce's executive assistant, Deborah Gore Dean. Two consultants who testified before the Senate Banking Committee, **May 17**, acknowledged that they had little understanding of housing issues, but that they had earned substantial fees after making contacts. Testifying before the House subcommittee, **May 25**, Pierce acknowledged that he had been lobbied by former officials, and he said he had asked his staff to give "careful consideration" to certain projects, but he denied that any projects had received special treatment.

House Speaker Jim Wright to Resign — Speaker of the House Jim Wright, who faced serious ethical charges, announced that he would resign as speaker and from the House. On **May 26**, a few days before Wright's announcement, the Democratic majority in the House suffered another shock when Rep. Tony Coelho (Cal.) announced that he would resign as majority whip and from the House. Coelho, who ranked third in the Democratic leadership ranks, had hoped to move up a notch in the event that Wright resigned. But then he, too, had become a potential subject of ethical inquiries concerning the possible use of $100,000 in campaign funds to buy junk bonds underwritten by Drexel Burnham Lambert, Inc. In announcing his impending resignations, Coelho denied using campaign funds for that purpose, but he said he had not reported a $50,000 loan used to cover half of the bond purchase on his financial disclosure forms. Wright's announcement of resignation came in a long, impassioned speech to the House, **May 31**. He defended himself against 69 charges brought in April by the House Ethics Committee, and he urged an end to the "period of mindless cannibalism" that prevailed in the House. In recent months, partisan animosities had run high, and many unflattering rumors about members, mostly unsubstantiated, had been circulating.

International

Panama Presidentail Election Voided — The citizens of Panama voted for a president, but the regime dominated by Gen. Manuel Noriega then voided the results. Noriega had allowed the election in the apparent belief that his supporters could engineer the election of his hand-picked candidate, Carlos Duque. Pres. George Bush said, **May 2**, that the United States would not recognize the results of a fraudulent election designed to keep Noriega in power. International observers, including former U.S. Pres. Jimmy Carter, were on hand, **May 7**, when the nation voted for president and for legislators. Independent tallies showed that the opposition candidate, Guillermo Endara, had won in a landslide. Bush declared, **May 9**, that the opposition had won a "clear-cut, overwhelming victory." However, the Electoral Tribunal said, **May 10**, that Duque was ahead by 2 to 1. The government annulled the election, **May 10**, complaining of foreign interference. Published reports that the Bush administration had given the opposition $10 million in covert aid fortified that view. Also on **May 10**, members of paramilitary squads attacked Endara and 2 of his running mates and beat them up in the street. Bush, **May 11**, ordered 2,000 additional combat troops to Panama to protect U.S. citizens and property. Bush, **May 13**, called on the people of Panama to overthrow Noriega, and the Organization of American States denounced him, **May 17**.

Hungary Removing Fence at Border — Hungary began, on **May 2**, to dismantle a 150-mile long fence along the border between Austria and Hungary. The barbed-wire fence had been put up in 1969, replacing a mine field. Hungary thus became the first country in Eastern Europe to open a border with the West, as it made several moves toward political and economic reform. The Central Committee of the Communist Party agreed, **May 8**, to convene a party conference to deal with political reform. On **May 10**, Premier Miklos Nemeth replaced 6 Cabinet ministers with appointees he said were "fighters for political and economic reforms."

Bush, Gorbachev Propose Arms Cuts — Secretary of State James Baker and Soviet Foreign Minister Eduard Shevardnadze agreed, **May 10**, to the reopening of the Strategic Arms Reduction Talks in Geneva. At a meeting with Baker, **May 11**, Soviet leader Mikhail Gorbachev said that the USSR would cut back substantially on its nuclear arsenal in Eastern Europe. He also offered a proposal that both the Warsaw Pact and the NATO alliance cut back one million troops and reduce their conventional armaments. Many Western analysts said Gorbachev had seized the initiative in the international dialogue on arms reduction. Pres. George Bush declared, **May 12**, that it was "time to move beyond containment" and to "seek the integration of the Soviet Union into the community of nations." In Brussels, **May 29**, at the 40th anniversary observance of NATO, Bush proposed that both NATO and the Warsaw Pact cut back on their conventional forces in Europe. He proposed specific ceilings for each class of weaponry and also recommended that the U.S. cut its combat forces in Europe to 275,000 or about 20 percent. Other NATO leaders supported the plan, and Shevardnadze said, **May 30**, that he welcomed it. At the conventional forces talks in Vienna, **May 30**, the Warsaw Pact put forth its proposals for ceilings on personnel and weapons for both sides. At the NATO summit, a compromise was reached, **May 30**, on the dispute on short-range U.S. missiles based in West Germany. Under the agreement, the 2 alliances would first reach an accord on reducing conventional forces. Then, the U.S., in consultations with its allies, would enter negotiations with the Soviet Union to achieve a partial reduction in land-based short-range missiles. The president flew on to Bonn, **May 30**, and, **May 31**, met with West German Chancellor Helmut Kohl. The main objective of the visit was to ease tensions between the 2 allies exacerbated by the dispute over the missiles. Bush met with Prime Minister Margaret Thatcher in London, **June 1**.

Peronist Wins Argentine Presidency — The candidate of the Peronist party was elected president of Argentina, **May 14**. Carlos Saul Menem won 47 percent of the vote to 37 percent for this nearest rival, the candidate of the ruling party. Under the constitution, Menem would not succeed Pres. Raul Alfonsin until December. Runaway inflation was the principal issue in the campaign. Prices were rising 2 percent a day, or 6,000 percent a year. Austerity efforts by the government had failed, and business was crippled as checks and credit cards were rejected for purchases. The Peronist tradition was one of populist or leftist authoritarian government. As the economic situation deteriorated, food riots broke out, and on **May 29**, Alfonsin declared a 30-day state of siege.

Bombardments in Beirut Kill Hundreds — Fighting in Beirut, Lebanon, between Christian and Moslem forces increased in intensity in the spring of 1989. Each side attacked the other with artillery bombardments, and by May, the death toll was put at 350, with some 1,200 wounded. Most of the victims were civilians. Property destruction was heavy, and hundreds of thousands of people fled the city. The Spanish ambassador was killed, **April 16**, when a projectile struck his residence. The religious leader of Lebanon's Sunni Moslems and 21 other people were killed, **May 16**, by a car bomb.

TWA Hijacker Convicted of Murder — Mohammed Ali Hamadei, a Lebanese, was convicted by a West German court, **May 17**, of hijacking a TWA jetliner in 1985 and of killing an American passenger. Hamadei, a pro-Iranian Shiite Moslem, said he had not participated in the murder of the American, Navy diver Robert Stethem. Hamadei was sentenced to life in prison.

Gorbachev Elected Soviet President — Mikhail Gorbachev was elected president of the Soviet Union by the new Soviet parliament, the Congress of People's Deputies. Some 2,250 deputies, most of them chosen in elections by the citizenry, attended the first session in the Kremlin, **May 25**. Most were supporters of the Communist Party, but some 400 were radical reformers and ethnic nationalists. Before the vote on president, many deputies, while endorsing Gorbachev, complained about economic conditions and the lack of progress under perestroika (restructuring). In a secret ballot, Gorbachev received 95.6 percent of the vote. On **May 27**, the deputies chose from their ranks 542 members of the Supreme Soviet, which would be in session most of the year and deal directly with legislation. After reformers were virtually shut out in this voting, some 10,000 supporters of Boris Yeltsin, a radical reformer from Moscow, gathered to protest. On **May 29**, Gorbachev engineered the seating of Yeltsin on the Supreme Soviet, with one of the chosen members agreeing to step aside. Accepting the presidency, **May 30**, Gorbachev promised that defense spending would be cut by 14 percent in 1990-91. In other speeches, deputies denounced the slayings of demonstrators in Soviet Georgia, the brutality of the KGB (state security service), and the restraints on nationalist autonomy.

U.S. Calls 3 Trading Partners Unfair — Pres. George Bush named Japan, Brazil, and India, **May 25**, as unfair trading partners. He acted under a provision of the 1988 Trade Act. Japan was cited for restricting purchases of satellites, superconductors, and forest products. Reportedly, the others were named to avoid Japan being singled out. Under the law, if the 3 countries failed to eliminate the unfair practices within 18 months, they would be subject to U.S. trade retaliation.

General

80 Nations Act on Ozone Threat — Representatives of 80 nations meeting in Helsinki, **May 2**, agreed by consensus to support a ban on production of chemicals that endanger the ozone layer in the atmosphere. The declaration called for chlorofluorocarbons to be phased out by the year 2000 at the latest. A treaty approved in 1987 in Montreal had called for production of CFCs to be cut in half by 1998.

Scientists Defend Fusion Experiment — In the face of growing doubts, 2 scientists who had announced a breakthrough in "cold fusion"—fusion at room temperatures—defended their experiment at a meeting, **May 9**, of the Electrochemical Society in Los Angeles. They stepped up their claim, asserting that the experiment was producing 10 to 50 times more energy than had been put in. By now, dozens of labs had sought to repeat the experiment, but only a few reported achieving confirming evidence. At a conference in Sante Fe, **May 23-25**, sponsored by the U.S. Energy Department, Norman Hackman of Rice University reported, "We have reached no consensus" on whether the experiment was valid.

Surgeon General Speaks Out on Alcohol — Dr. C. Everett Koop, who was about to step down as U.S. surgeon general, called, **May 31**, for a major effort against alcohol abuse and drunk driving. He urged the alcoholic beverage industry to stop sponsoring entertainment events and using celebrities in advertising, and he asked restaurants and bars to end "happy hours" and other similar promotions. He proposed an increase in excise taxes on alcoholic beverages, and tougher enforcement of laws suspending licenses of drivers who had been drinking.

JUNE

National

Key Interest Rate Cut — U.S. banks cut their prime lending rate, reversing a recent trend. The Labor Dept. reported, **June 2**, that the unemployment rate had dropped one-tenth of a percentage point to 5.1 percent in May. Leading banks cut their prime rate by one-half a percentage point, **June 5**, to 11 percent. The rate had been climbing for a year. The drop of other interest rates in recent weeks was seen as a sign of an economic downturn. The Labor Dept. reported, **June 9**, that producer prices for finished goods had risen 0.9 percent in May. The Commerce Dept. said, **June 15**, that the merchandise trade deficit had narrowed in April to $8.26 billion. The Labor Dept. said, **June 16**, that consumer prices had risen 0.6 percent in May. On Wall Street, the Dow Jones industrial average closed, **June 23**, at 2531.87, fewer than 200 points below its all-time high in August 1987, before the big slide in stock prices began.

Largest Unmanned U.S. Rocket Lifts Off — A Titan 4, launched from Cape Canaveral, Fla., **June 4**, became the largest unmanned U.S. rocket ever to rise into space. Including the payload, the rocket was 204 feet in length. This was the first of a fleet of Titan 4's, which were designed to lift military payloads. The rocket's payload was not announced, but some experts said it was a satellite designed to warn of nuclear attack.

Foley Elected Speaker of House — Rep. Tom Foley (D, Wash.) was elected Speaker of the U.S. House of Representatives, **June 6**. He succeeded Jim Wright (D, Tex.), who had resigned. In a straight-line party vote, Foley won over Rep. Robert Michel (R, Ill.), the minority leader. Foley had held the position of majority leader. In an address, Foley called for an end to partisan controversy over ethical conduct. Responding, Michel said that part of the problem was that Democrats had abused the majority status they had held for 35 years. As Foley was elected, the Republican National Committee was circulating a memorandum headlined "Tom Foley: Out of the Liberal Closet." His voting record was compared with that of Rep. Barney Frank (D, Mass.), an acknowledged homosexual. Both Democrats and Republicans deplored the memorandum, and Mark Goodin, communications director of the RNC, took responsibility for it, **June 7**, and resigned. Pres. George Bush said, **June 8**, that Lee Atwater, the Republican national chairman, had assured him that he had not known of the memo. On **June 14**, House Democrats elected Richard Gephardt (Mo.) as their new majority leader and William Gray 3d (Pa.) as majority whip. Gephardt had sought the Democratic presidential nomination in 1988. Gray was the first black to hold a top leadership position in Congress.

Housing Department Scandal Broadens — Evidence of mismanagement and corruption in the U.S. Dept. of Housing and Urban Development grew in June. Testifying before a House subcommittee, **June 9**, former Interior Secretary James Watt said that he had earned more than $400,000 as a private consultant for developers of housing projects, although he had no background in housing issues. He made a few phone calls and personally lobbied Housing Secretary Samuel Pierce Jr. Citing her 5th Amendment right against self-incrimination, Deborah Gore Dean, who had been Pierce's executive assistant, refused to answer the committee's questions, **June 13**. HUD's inspector general, Paul Adams, testified, **June 16**, that escrow agents, retained by HUD to collect proceeds on sales of foreclosed houses, had in many cases kept all the money for themselves and HUD had not sought to collect it. Marilyn Louise Harrell, an agent, admitted to the committee, **June 16**, that she had stolen about $5.5 million in HUD money, but said that she had given much of it to the poor; she won the media nickname of "Robin HUD." Another escrow agent had already pleaded guilty. Paul Manafort, a political consultant to Presidents Reagan and Bush, testified, **June 20**, that he had used his influence to win a HUD contract for a housing project in which he had a financial interest.

Bush Presents Clean Air Program — Pres. George Bush offered a series of proposals, **June 12**, for cleaning up the nation's air. The plan, presented to Congress, would represent a broad revision of the Clean Air Act. To blunt the adverse effects of acid rain, the plan would reduce sulfur emissions from coal-fired power plants by 50 percent. Plants would be required to use cleaner fuel or install scrubbers. Alternative fuels for automobiles, including methanol, ethanol, or natural gas, were to be encouraged, with the industry required to produce one million alternative-fueled cars by 1997. Substantial reductions in tailpipe emissions and gasoline vapor levels were also proposed. If enacted, the plan was expected to cost the automobile industry from $14 to $19 billion a year.

Quayle Revisits Central America — Vice Pres. Dan Quayle made his second trip of 1989 to Central America. He met, **June 12**, with Pres. Vinicio Cerezo of Guatemala, and before leaving the country Quayle charged that Nicaragua was still exporting terrorism. He described Nicaragua, Panama, and Cuba as an antidemocratic axis. He met with Pres. José Azcona of Honduras, **June 12**, and on **June 13**, met with 4 commanders of the Nicaraguan contras. His discussions with political leaders in El Salvador, **June 13**, included a meeting with Roberto D'Aubuisson, the controversial founder of the right-wing ARENA party. Quayle stressed the importance of human rights to D'Aubuisson, who had been linked with death squads. The vice president then visited Costa Rica, where Pres. Oscar Arias, **June 14**, supported Quayle's view that open elections were not possible at the present time in Nicaragua.

Bush Vetoes Minimum Wage Bill — Pres. George Bush cast his first veto, **June 13**, rejecting a bill that would have increased the minimum wage from $3.35 an hour to $4.55 an hour. He said the increase was too great and would cause young people to lose jobs. Bush also objected to a provision limiting to 60 days the period in which an employer could pay a subminimum wage. Bush favored a 6-month period. The president supported an increase in the minimum wage to $4.25. The House, **June 14**, failed to override the veto; the 247-178 vote being well short of the required two-thirds majority.

Court Ruling Stirs Flag Controversy — A Supreme Court ruling that permitted the burning of the American flag as a form of political protest led to an effort to pass a constitutional amendment to prohibit desecration of the flag. The Court's 5-4 decision was announced, **June 21**. Writing for the majority, Justice William Brennan Jr. said, "The government may not prohibit expression simply because it disagrees with its message." Dissenting, Chief Justice William Rehnquist

called the flag "the visible symbol embodying our nation." Pres. George Bush and congressional leaders denounced the decision, and the Senate, **June 22**, 97-3,
expressed its "profound disappointment." Bush announced, **June 27**, his support for a Constitutional
amendment barring desecration of the flag. Civil liberties groups objected, however, saying such an amendment would infringe on First Amendment protection
of free speech. The House, **June 27**, 411-5, expressed
its concern over the ruling.

Court Overturns Nofziger's Conviction — Lyn Nofziger, a former Reagan administration official, who
had been found guilty of illegal lobbying in 1988, won
a reversal of his conviction, **June 27**. A federal appeals
court ruled, 2-1, that prosecutors had failed to prove
the Nofziger knew his lobbying was against the law.

International

Uno Elected Premier of Japan — Foreign Minister
Sousuke Uno was elected president of Japan's ruling
Liberal Democratic Party, **June 2**, and then, on the
same day, was elected prime minister. He succeeded
Noboru Takeshita, who had resigned because of his
involvement in the Recruit company scandal. Uno said
he would seek reforms to clean up Japanese politics.

Iran's Leader, Ayatollah Khomeini, Dies — Ayatollah Ruhollah Khomeini, the political and religious
leader of Iran, died, **June 3**, Khomeini, a Shiite Moslem who was 86 or 89, had ruled Iran since returning
from exile in 1979. On **June 4**, Shiite leaders chose
Pres. Ali Khamenei to succeed him. Pres. George Bush
said, **June 4**, that he hoped Iran would cease being a
"terrorist state" and assume "a responsible role in the
international community." Khomeini was buried, **June
6**, after a chaotic scene in which up to 10 million
mourners demonstrated their grief.

90 Die in Clashes in Uzbekistan — Another Soviet
republic erupted in ethnic violence when bloody
clashes occurred in Uzbekistan between Uzbeks and
Meskhetians. Both were Moslem Turkish ethnic
groups, but the Uzbeks were mostly of the Sunni sect
and the Meskhetians were mainly Shiites. Meskhetians
had been calling for a return to their homeland near
the Turkish border, from which they had been removed during World War II because of supposed sympathy with Turkey. The Uzbeks appeared to have initiated most of the fighting between **June 3 and 10**, in
which at least 90 persons, mostly Meskhetians, were
killed. More than 1,000 persons were reported injured.

Polish Voters Rebuff Communist Regime — For the
first time in more than 40 years, Poles participated in
an open election, and the result was a humiliating setback for the Communist regime. The first round of
voting was held, **June 4**, with runoffs conducted on
June 18. In the Senate, or upper house of Parliament,
candidates supported by the trade union Solidarity
won 99 of the 100 seats. In the 460-member Sejm, or
lower house, Solidarity captured all 161 seats alloted
to opposition (non-communist) candidates. The United
Workers' (Communist) Party and its allies were alloted
the remaining 299 seats. Nonetheless, voters rejected
most of the senior officials of the Workers' party, first
by striking out their names in the first round and then
by supporting candidates with reformist sympathies
where they ran in the runoff.

. **Argentine President Resigns** — Pres. Raúl Alfonsín
announced, **June 12**, that he would resign, effective
June 30. Carlos Saul Menem, who had been elected
president in May, was not scheduled to be sworn in
until December. However, the economic situation was
worsening rapidly. The government reported, **June 7**,
that retail prices had risen 78.5 percent in May alone,

and figures issued, **June 12**, showed that inflation of
309,907 percent had been recorded since Alfonsín became president in 1983. Civic and government leaders
urged Alfonsín to step down to end the political vacuum.

Gorbachev Visits West Germany — Soviet Pres.
Mikhail Gorbachev received an enthusiastic public reception during a visit to West Germany. After arriving
in Bonn, **June 12**, he met with Chancellor Helmut
Kohl and Pres. Richard von Weizsaecker. At a ban-
quet, he welcomed NATO's proposal for a reduction
in conventional arms in Europe, but reiterated Soviet
support for a complete elimination of nuclear weapons
in Europe. Gorbachev and Kohl, **June 13**, signed a
declaration affirming that every state has a right to
freely choose its own political and social system. Polls
showed a high level of popularity for the Soviet president, who attracted cheering crowds in his public appearances.

Hungary Honors Executed Premier — Hungary
honored Imre Nagy, who had been executed in 1958
for his part in the revolt against Soviet domination in
1956. In a move reflecting the reformist movement
within the ruling Socialist Workers' (Communist)
Party, the party's Central Committee announced, **May
30**, that Nagy's trial had been "judicially unlawful."
On **June 13**, the regime and leading political opponents began talks on transition to a multiparty system.
On **June 16**, with the approval of the regime, a memorial service for Nagy and 4 of his aides, all of whom
had been executed or died in captivity, was held in Budapest. Some 100,000 or more persons attended the
ceremony, in which 6 flag-draped coffins were displayed. The 6th, which was empty, represented all of
the hundreds of other Hungarians executed after the
uprising. Nagy and his aides, who had been buried in
an unmarked mass grave, were then reburied in
marked graves. The Central Committee, **June 24**, established a collective presidency of 4 officials in which
reformers appeared to be in control.

European Parliament Shifts to Left — Voting on
June 15 and 18 gave leftist and environmental parties a
small majority among the 518 members of the European Parliament. The Socialists remained the largest
single grouping, but the environmentalists, also called
greens, increased their membership from 20 to 39. In
Great Britain the Labour party won more seats than
did the country's ruling Conservatives. Elected for 5
years, the members would be serving in the Strasbourg
assembly at the time when the European Community's
internal open market became operative in 1992.

Angolan Foes Agree to Truce — An end to the 14-
year civil war in Angola appeared to be in sight in
June. During a summit of African leaders in Zaire,
June 22, Angolan Pres. José Eduardo dos Santos and
the rebel leader, Jonas Savimbi, came to a unantici-
pated agreement. Few details of the agreement were
announced beyond the date of the cease-fire, **June 24**.
Zaire, Congo, and Gabon would be represented on a
national reconciliation commission for Angola.
Savimbi's forces, supported by South Africa and the
United States, had been fighting the regime, which had
been supported by Soviet arms and Cuban troops. U.S.
officials praised the accord.

General

11,000 Attend AIDS Conference — More than
11,000 researchers and public health officials met in
Montreal, **June 4-9**, for the 5th International Conference on acquired immune deficiency syndrome. A
group based in New York, the AIDS Coalition to Un-
leash Power (ACT UP), disrupted parts of the pro-

ram with demands that better drugs to fight the condition be found and that laws be passed to prevent
discrimination against those who were infected.
Stephen Joseph, public health commissioner for New
York City, recommended, **June 5**, that public health
officials be notified of the names of victims and that
notification should also be given to those at risk of
contracting AIDS from victims. CD4, an experimental
drug, was described, **June 6**, as having no convincing
effect on raising of T-cell white blood cells in AIDS
patients or in reducing levels of the virus in their
blood. But another report, **June 8**, said that CD4 had
reduced the level of the virus in 8 of 9 patients. Dr. Jonas Salk and others reported, **June 8**, that the injection
of an experimental vaccine had eliminated the virus
from 2 chimpanzees.

Paramount Seeks to Buy Time Inc. — The planned
friendly merger of Time Inc. and Warner Communications was thrown off course, **June 6**, when Paramount
Communications Corp. made a $10.7 billion cash
tender offer for Time. The move by Paramount, which
had just changed its name from Gulf + Western Industries, outraged Time executives. Time Chairman J.
Richard Munro said that it raised "serious questions"
about the "integrity and motives" of Paramount
Chariman Martin Davis. Speculation on Wall Street
that Time was "in play" and would attract other bid-
ders drove up the price of its stock. Time, **June 16**, rejected Paramount's offer, sued Paramount in an attempt to block the takeover offer, completed a stock
swap with Warner to discourage prospective suitors,
and agreed to acquire Warner for $14 billion as a
means of further discouraging buyers. Paramount,
June 23, raised its offer to $12.2 billion ($200 a share),
but Time rejected it, **June 26**.

Disasters — Some 400 persons died after a gas pipeline explosion engulfed 2 passing trains, **June 3**, near
the town of Ufa in the Ural Mountains of the Soviet
Union. Pres. Mikhail Gorbachev said that a pipeline
leak had allowed gas to accumulate and a spark from a
train had set off the explosion. ... Sri Lankan officials
said, **June 4**, that floods and landslides caused by
heavy rains had killed 171 persons in central Sri
Lanka. ... A jetliner crashed near Paramaribo, the
capital of Suriname, **June 7**, killing 169 of the 182 persons aboard.

JULY

National

Court's Abortion Ruling Stirs Action in States—
The U.S. Supreme Court, in a sharply divided 5-4 decision, announced **July 3**, put new restraints on a
woman's right to have an abortion. The ruling set the
stage for conflicts across the nation in legislative arenas between supporters and opponents of abortion. In
1973, in Roe v. Wade, the Court had recognized a constitutional right to have an abortion. But in its new decision, in Webster v. Reproductive Health Services, the
Court majority upheld a Missouri law prohibiting public employees from performing abortions unless the
mother's life was endangered, barring abortions in
public buildings, and requiring medical tests on any
fetus more than 20 weeks old to determine if it could
live outside the womb. Chief Justice William Rehnquist, in upholding the Missouri law, said support for
Roe v. Wade could not be found in the Constitution,
and he wrote that any restriction on abortion should
be judged by whether it "permissibly furthers the
state's interest in protecting potential human life." Justice Harry Blackmun, the author of the 1973 decision,
wrote in dissent, "I fear for the future. ... The signs

are evident and very ominous, and a chill wind blows."
Predictions were made that the Court would eventually
overturn Roe altogether. In the meantime, opponents
of abortion in many states prepared to push legislation
imposing restrictions on the procedure, including those
upheld in the Missouri case. They received support
from Pres. George Bush, who reiterated his support,
July 3, for a Constitutional amendment barring abortions in most cases. Florida's Gov. Bob Martinez (R)
said, **July 5**, he would call a special session of the state
legislature to consider controls on abortion. The Louisiana state Senate voted, **July 7**, to ask the state to enforce strict antiabortion laws in effect before the
Court's 1973 decision.

North Sentenced in Iran-Contra Case—Former National Security Council aide Oliver North, who had
been convicted in May in the Iran-Contra arms scandal, received his sentence in U.S. District Court in
Washington, D.C., **July 6**. Before sentencing, North
acknowledged to Judge Gerhard Gesell that he grieved
over what had happened and that he had made "many
mistakes." Gesell gave North a 3-year suspended prison sentence, put him on probation for 2 years, ordered him to perform 1,200 hours of community service, and fined him $150,000. The judge said, "I do not
think in this area you were a leader at all, but really a
low-ranking subordinate working to carry out initiatives of a few cynical superiors."

Inflation Fears Ease—Figures released by the government in July eased concerns about inflation. The
Labor Dept. reported, **July 7**, that the unemployment
rate had risen 0.1 percentage point in June to 5.2 percent. The department reported, **July 14**, that producer
prices for finished goods had declined 0.1 percent in
June and that the annual rate of advance (5.1 percent)
in the second quarter had been only half of the advance reported for the first quarter. The Commerce
Dept. said, **July 18**, that the merchandise trade deficit
had widened to $10.24 billion in May. An increase in
consumer prices of 0.2 percent in June, reported by the
Labor Dept., **July 19**, was the smallest in 16 months.
The Commerce Dept. reported, **July 27**, that the gross
national product grew at an annual rate of 1.7 percent
in the second quarter, its slowest rate of expansion in 3
years.

HUD Scandal Continues to Unfold—Jack Kemp,
secretary of Housing and Urban Development, acknowledged, **July 11**, that scandals in the department
were "a discredit to the previous administration," and
he estimated that $2 billion had been lost because of
fraud and mismanagement during the tenure of his predecessor, Samuel Pierce. Kemp said he thought the department had been run in a "slipshod manner." R.
Hunter Cushing, formerly a deputy assistant secretary
at HUD, declined to testify before a House subcommittee, **July 17**, citing his 5th amendment right against
possible self-incrimination. Carla Hills, another former
HUD secretary and currently the U.S. trade representative, testified, **July 17**, and said she had done nothing wrong while acting as a lawyer in behalf of a company currently being investigated for issuing bad loans
under HUD's co-insurance program.

Bush Sets New Goals For Space Program—In an
address in Washington, D.C., **July 20**, commemorat-
ing the 20th anniversary of the landing of 2 U.S. astronauts on the moon, Pres. George Bush called for a new
national commitment in space. Saying he wanted to
establish the United States as "the pre-eminent space-
faring nation," Bush advocated an orbiting space station, a manned base on the moon, and a manned mission to Mars. It was estimated that these ventures
would cost several hundred billion dollars.

International

Japan's New Premier Resigns—Premier Sousuke Uno, after holding office for only 7 weeks, announced that he would resign because his party had suffered setbacks at the polls. His Liberal Democratic Party continued to suffer from the Recruit scandal, and the Japanese media also reported that Uno had had extramarital affairs with several geishas, who are paid female escorts. A sales tax on consumer goods and the opening of agricultural markets to foreign exporters also worked to the disadvantage of the LDP, which had led Japan since 1955. In elections, **July 2**, for the Tokyo metropolitan assembly, the LDP won only 43 seats, a drop of 20. The party suffered a major setback, **July 23**, trailing the Socialist Party in voting for half of the seats to the upper house of the Diet (parliament). As a result, Uno's party held only 109 seats in the upper house to 143 for all the opposition parties. Although the LDP still controlled the more powerful lower house of the parliament, Uno announced, **July 24**, that he took responsibility for the defeat of the previous day and that he would step down when a replacement was chosen.

Gorbachev Visits France—Soviet Pres. Mikhail Gorbachev met with French Pres. Francois Mitterrand, **July 4 and 5**. The two nations signed 21 accords and the leaders also issued a declaration calling for an immediate cease-fire in Lebanon and an end to the arming of the various factions there. Gorbachev told reporters, **July 5**, that he was prepared to develop normal relations with Solidarity leaders in Poland, but he also called Pres. George Bush's appeal for a Soviet troop withdrawal from Poland "propaganda." In Strasbourg, **July 6**, Gorbachev addressed the Council of Europe, a parliament representing Western European nations. In an apparent assurance that the Soviet Union would not intervene in the liberalization movements underway in Poland and Hungary, he said, "Any interference in domestic affairs and any attempt to restrict the sovereignty of states ... are inadmissible." He renewed a call for negotiations on reducing or eliminating short-range nuclear missiles in Europe, but Bush replied, **July 6**, that a reduction in conventional arms must come first.

Jaruzelski Elected Polish President—Poland's new bicameral parliament convened, **July 4**, with the independent trade union Solidarity holding almost half of the seats. Premier Mieczyslaw Rakowski and his cabinet tendered their resignations, but agreed to stay on until parliament elected a president who would appoint a new premier. On **July 14**, Lech Walesa, Solidarity's founder, said he would support Gen. Wojciech Jaruzelski or any other Communist party leader put forth by the parliamentary majority, which included the Communists and 2 smaller parties. Jaruzelski was elected president, **July 19**, the members approving him narrowly, 270-233, with 34 abstaining. He then resigned as Communist Party leader, **July 29**, and was replaced by Rakowski.

Mandela Meets S. African President—The black nationalist leader Nelson Mandela, who had been in prison in South Africa since 1962, met secretly, **July 5**, with South African Pres. Pieter Botha in the latter's office. After the meeting became publicly known, the government gave no indication it planned to free Mandela. Although Mandela was "banned,"—not permitted to be quoted in the press—the government made an exception, **July 12**, and Mandela said that the government could achieve peace in South Africa only by negotiating "with the mass democratic movemement and, in particular, the African National Congress. ..."

Shamir Modifies Peace Plan—Israeli Prime Minister Yitzhak Shamir came under intense pressure from the right wing of his own Likud Party. He was supporting a peace plan that called for elections in the occupied territories to choose Palestinians who could discuss autonomy measures and a peace settlement with Israel. But on **July 5**, Shamir agreed to demands by Likud hard-liners, as follows: elections would not take place until the Palestinian uprising ended; Arabs in East Jerusalem could not run for office or vote; Jewish settlement of the territories would continue; and no Palestinian state would ever be established. Shimon Peres, leader of the Labor Party and a partner of Shamir in the coalition government, said the latter's concessions had jeopardized the peace process. The Palestine Liberation Organization denounced Shamir's shift. A Palestinian extremist grabbed the wheel of a bus west of Jerusalem, **July 6**, and caused it to crash and kill 16 passengers. In the face of a Labor threat to leave the government, Shamir appeared to shift again, and on **July 23**, with Shamir in the majority, the Cabinet endorsed his original plan. But Shamir did not renounce the hard-liners' conditions, which were still seen as significant factors in future negotiations with the Palestinians.

Bush Visits Poland, Hungary—Pres. George Bush arrived in Warsaw, **July 9**, to begin his first visit to Eastern Europe as president. He met with the leader of Poland's Communist regime, Gen. Wojciech Jaruzelski, **July 10**, and then addressed the Polish parliament. Taking note of the tide of democratic reform in Poland, Bush said, "A profound cycle of turmoil and great change is sweeping the world. ..." He announced a plan for U.S. economic aid for Poland that included $100 million for investment in Polish business (subject to approval by Congress), support for the rescheduling of Poland's foreign debt, support for World Bank loans to assist industry and agriculture, and $15 million to clean up industrial pollution, also subject to Congressional approval. On **July 11**, Pres. and Mrs. Bush lunched at the home of Lech Walesa, founder of the Solidarity movement, and Bush then addressed workers at the Lenin Shipyard in Gdansk. Bush flew to Budapest, Hungary, **July 11**, and was soon shaking hands with members of a crowd at an enthusiastic though rain-soaked rally. In an interview published, **July 11**, Premier Miklos Nemeth announced that Hungary's economic reforms, most liberal in the Soviet bloc, would continue. Bush met with Hungary's leaders, **July 12**, and spoke at Karl Marx University. Nemeth presented Bush with strips of barbed wire removed from the fence along the Austrian border that Hungary was removing. Bush announced a $25 million investment package, subject to Congressional approval.

Coal Miners Strike in Soviet Union—Coal miners walked out in a series of wildcat strikes in the Soviet Union in July. Their complaints included low wages, dangerous working conditions, poor housing and medical care, environmental hazards, and a shortage of food and other basic items. Some 500,000 miners were involved in the protest strikes. Miners in Mezhdurechensk, in Siberia, left their jobs, **July 10**, and by **July 17**, the walkout had embraced the surrounding Kuznetsky Basin, a major coal region. Miners at 8 mines in the Donetsk Basin, in the Ukraine, walked out, **July 17**. The strikes became a factor in the debate over perestroika, or restructuring, the program for reforming the Soviet Union supported by Pres. Mikhail Gorbachev. The president, **July 18**, called for "a flow of fresh blood" within the Communist Party. Addressing the party's Central Committee, he warned that he was ready to purge more leaders of the party. The Siberian strikes were settled, **July 19,** after workers won promises from the government for better pay, better living and working conditions, and "full economic and legal independence." As strikes erupted elsewhere in the country, Ukrainian strikers called for the ouster of some party officials. Gorbachev acknowledged, **July 23,** in a television interview that they had legitimate grievances. The strikes were fading by late July after the government offered terms similar to those in Siberia.

Summit Meeting Held in Paris—The heads of government of the 7 major noncommunist industrial nations met in Paris for their annual summit. The summit was scheduled in conjunction with the observance of the bicentennial of the French Revolution. On **July 14,** the 200th anniversary of the storming of the Bastille, 33 heads of government and some one million persons watched a parade on the Champs-Elysees. On **July 15,** the 7 leaders endorsed increased Western economic aid for Poland and Hungary, where far-ranging reforms were taking place. In a statement issued **July 16,** the leaders focused far more on the environment than in the past. They called for more effort to limit the emission of gases that threatened to alter the world's climate. They endorsed debt restructuring as a means of encouraging developing countries to protect their natural resources. After the summit, Pres. Bush visited the Netherlands, **July 17.**

Mexico Agrees to Reduce Debt—Pres. Carlos Salinas announced, **July 23,** that negotiations between Mexico and a committee representing some 500 creditor banks had resulted in an agreement that would reduce the nation's $54 billion commercial bank debt. The agreement marked the first success for the Bush administration's strategy to head off the debt crisis in developing countries, and the first time commercial-bank creditors had agreed to significant reduction of debt during the crisis. Under the plan, creditors could choose one of 3 broad options—reducing the principal, reducing interest, or extending more credit.

Captors Claim They Killed U.S. Hostage—Terrorists in Lebanon claimed that they had executed a U.S. Marine hostage whom they had abducted in 1988. The incident that may have precipitated the execution occurred **July 28,** when Israeli commandos abducted Sheik Abdul Karim Obeid, a spiritual chief in southern Lebanon of the Party of God, a Shiite Moslem group. An Israeli army statement said Sheik Obeid had been "arrested" for planning attacks against Israel. On **July 30,** the Organization of the Oppressed of the World, a mysterious Shiite group that had kidnapped Lt. Col. William Higgins in Lebanon in February 1988, said they would execute Higgins unless Israel freed Obeid. Higgins had headed the U.N. Truce Supervision Organization in Lebanon. The "Oppressed" group announced, **July 31,** that it had hanged Higgins and it distributed a videotape of a hanged man who resembled Higgins. Another terrorist group, the Revolutionary Justice Organization, announced that it would kill another U.S. hostage, Joseph Cicippio, an American University official seized in 1986, unless the Israelis freed Obeid. Pres. George Bush cut short a cross-country trip, denounced Higgins's "brutal murder," and returned to Washington to meet with government and congressional leaders.

General

Pilot Survives Bizarre Flight, Crash—A lone pilot who said he was unconscious most of the way, survived a 1,000-mile flight and crash. Thomas Root, a Washington lawyer, took off alone from Washington National Airport at 6:33 A.M., **July 13,** in a single-engine Cessna. His destination was a business meeting in North Carolina. He radioed at 8:30 that he was having difficulty breathing. He put the plane on automatic pilot and then apparently became unconscious. The Cessna dived into the ocean near Eleuthera Island, where Root emerged from the plane and swam to rescuers as it sank. Police disclosed, **July 14,** that Root had been shot once in the abdomen after the Cessna had taken off. Root told investigators he had no idea how he had been shot, but that he carried a loaded revolver in the glove compartment because his business carried him to remote locations. Federal officials confirmed a report that they had been watching Root as a possible drug trafficker because of "suspicious" trips to the Caribbean.

Time Buys Warner, Averts Takeover—The struggle to control the future of Time, Inc. ended in July. A Delaware Chancery Court, **July 14,** rejected an attempt by Paramount Communications and some Time stockholders to prevent Time's purchase of Warner Communications. Time sought to buy Warner to prevent its own hostile takeover by Paramount. The latter had entered the picture in June after Time and Warner had announced merger plans. A Delaware Supreme Court panel, **July 24,** upheld the lower court. Paramount withdrew its offer and Time immediately acquired Warner for $70 a share, or $14 billion. The new Time Warner Inc. would have annual revenues of more than $10 billion, making it one of the world's largest media and entertainment companies.

Plane Crash Kills 111; 185 Survive—A tense drama in the Midwestern sky ended, **July 19,** in the crash of a United Airlines DC-10 jetliner en route from Denver to Chicago. Although 111 persons died in the tragedy, 185 others survived. While the plane was at 37,000 feet, an engine in the tail exploded and heavily damaged the plane's hydraulic system. For the next 41 minutes the pilot, Al Haynes, struggled to control the craft as he brought it in for a pre-arranged emergency landing at Sioux City municipal airport. Just before touchdown, the right wingtip touched the ground and the plane flipped over and crashed in a fireball. Because the plane broke up—the forward coach section landed in a cornfield—many passengers had easy means of fleeing the wreckage. A 700-person rescue team was prepared for the landing. The cause of the engine explosion was not immediately determined.

Disaster—A Korean Air DC-10 jetliner, en route from Seoul to Tripoli, Libya, crashed in fog while trying to land at Tripoli, **July 27.** At least 82 died in the crash, but more than 100 on the plane survived.

AUGUST

National

Justice Department Nominee Rejected — William Lucas, nominated by Pres. George Bush to serve as assistant attorney general for civil rights, failed to win approval from the Senate Judiciary Committee, **Aug. 1.** The committee, voting nearly along party lines, defeated his nomination on a 7-7 tie vote, and then, by the same vote, declined to send his nomination to the full Senate. Critics found his knowledge of civil rights issues and his experience in litigation insufficient.

Commodities Traders Indicted — The indictment of 46 futures traders at the Chicago Mercantile Exchange and the Chicago Board of Trade was announced, **Aug. 2,** by the U.S. Justice Dept. Of these, 21 charged with racketeering under the Racketeer Influenced and Corrupt Organization Act faced the loss of their assets. The 46 were charged on a variety of other counts that included mail fraud, wire fraud, tax fraud, and filing false tax returns. The Federal Bureau of Investigation had been conducting an investigation in Chicago for more than 2 years.

Consultants' Role in HUD Scandal Described — Paul Adams, inspector general of the Dept. of Housing and Urban Development, told a Senate subcommittee, **Aug. 2,** that 20 consultants had received $5.7 million in fees for lobbying the department. He said that a disproportionate share of HUD money had gone to states that had relatively little need for it, but where highly paid consultants, often with influence in the Reagan administration, had landed contracts for developers. Documents from the files of former Housing and Urban Development Sec. Samuel Pierce were released, **Aug. 3.** They appeared to contradict Pierce's testimony in May that he had had only a small role in selecting projects to receive money from HUD.

Inflation Worries Ease — Figures released in August indicated that inflation remained well under control. The Labor Dept. reported, **Aug. 4,** that unemployment had held steady at 5.2 percent in July. The department said, **Aug. 11,** that producer prices for finished goods declined 0.4 percent in July, the largest decline in 3 years. The Commerce Dept. said, **Aug. 17,** that the U.S. merchandise trade deficit had declined to $8.17 billion in June, the smallest deficit since 1984. The Labor Dept. reported, **Aug. 18,** that consumer prices had risen 0.2 percent in July for the second consecutive month. On Wall Street, the Dow Jones industrial average closed at an all-time high of 2734.64 on **Aug. 24,** completely erasing the plunge in stock values that had begun precisely 2 years earlier. The Commerce Dept. said, **Aug. 29,** that the economy grew at a 2.7 percent annual rate in the 2d quarter, much higher than the previous 1.7 percent estimate.

Congressman Die in Plane Crashes — Rep. Mickey Leland (D, Tex.) and all 15 other persons aboard were killed, **Aug. 7,** when their plane crashed into a mountain while en route from Addis Ababa, Ethiopia, to a refugee camp. Leland, a former chairman of the Congressional Black Caucus, was in the midst of his 6th trip to the Ethiopia-Sudan region in his capacity as head of the House Select Committee on Hunger. Failure of the plane to arrive at its destination triggered an energetic search of the vast remote countryside, but the plane was not found until **Aug. 13.** Rep. Larkin Smith (R, Miss.) died in the crash of a small plane near New Augusta, Miss., **Aug. 13.**

More Wedtech Convictions Obtained — The 6th corruption trial involving the Wedtech Corporation resulted, **Aug. 8,** in the conviction of 3 more men. One of those convicted by a jury in a federal district court in New York City was E. Robert Wallach, a longtime friend of former Attorney Gen. Edwin Meese. Wallach, a San Francisco lawyer, was convicted of racketeering for accepting $425,000 in payoffs from Wedtech executives in exchange for using his influence with Meese and others in government to win defense contracts for Wedtech. W. Franklyn Chinn and Rusty Kent London were convicted of defrauding the company's stockholders.

Bush Signs Rescue of 'Thrifts' — Legislation passed by Congress to rescue the savings and loans industry was signed into law, **Aug. 9,** by Pres. George Bush. The bill provided $166 billion over 10 years to close or merge insolvent S & Ls, also called thrifts. The total cost of rescuing and restructuring the industry was put at $300 billion over 30 years, most of which would be paid by taxpayers. Many of the institutions had made bad loans and offered excessive interest rates. Many had folded, leaving their insured depositors looking to the government for help. The bill created the Resolution Trust Corporation, whose responsibility would include liquidating failing thrifts and helping stronger institutions affiliate with or become commercial banks.

Powell Named to Head Joint Chiefs — Army Gen. Colin Powell was nominated, **Aug. 10,** by Pres. George Bush to serve as chairman of the Joint Chiefs of Staff. The incumbent chairman, Adm. William Crowe, had announced that he would retire, Sept. 30. Powell had served as national security adviser to Pres. Ronald Reagan in 1987 and 1988. On confirmation by the Senate, Powell would become the first black to head the joint chiefs and, at 52, he would also be the youngest to hold the position.

International

Solidarity Leader Heads Polish Government — A leader of the Solidarity trade-union movement was chosen to serve as premier of Poland. It appeared to be the first time that power had passed from a ruling Communist party by democratic means. The Communist party choice for premier was Gen. Czeslaw Kiszczak. On **Aug. 1,** a leader of the Peasant Party, a party allied with the Communists in parliament, said that Kiszczak was an unacceptable choice because he had been the chief enforcer of the 1981 martial-law decree. Nonetheless, he was confirmed, **Aug. 2,** with the votes of 237 of 420 deputies present in the Sejm, or lower house of parliament. The new premier proposed that the United Workers' (Communist) Party and Solidarity form a "grand coalition" government, which the latter declined. Solidarity leader Lech Walesa, **Aug. 7,** proposed that Solidarity form a government in combination with the Peasant Party and the Democratic Party. Both minor parties had been Communist allies for 40 years. On **Aug. 14,** Kiszczak announced that he was unable to form a government. He resigned, **Aug. 17,** and Pres. Wojciech Jaruzelski accepted Walesa's proposal. Declining the honor himself, Walesa proposed 3 possible alternatives for the premiership, and Jaruzelski chose Tadeusz Mazowiecki, **Aug. 19.** On **Aug. 24,** Mazowiecki, who was a journalist and a prominent Roman Catholic intellectual, and a longtime adviser to Walesa was approved by the Sejm, 378-4, with 41 abstentions. He had vowed to move Poland "from a communist system of ownership to capitalism." The Soviet Union's Council of Ministers, **Aug. 24,** congratulated the new premier and said that friendship and cooperation between the 2 countries would continue.

Rafsanjani Becomes Iran's President — Having been elected president, July 28, in a landslide vote, Hojatolislam Hashemi Rafsanjani, the speaker of the Iranian parliament, was sworn in to his new office on **Aug. 3.** He succeeded Ali Khamenei, who was elevated to the country's supreme religious leader after the death of Ayatollah Ruhollah Khomeini in June. On **Aug. 29,** parliament approved all 22 of his cabinet nominees, which was seen as a strong endorsement of a shift toward less radical policies.

Contra Bases to Be Dismantled — Five Central American presidents reached an agreement on the dismantling of contra bases in Honduras. On **Aug. 4,** the government of Nicaragua reached agreement with opposition political parties on a plan to demobilize the rebels. The terms included free elections and no curbs on campaigning. The 5 presidents, meeting in Honduras, **Aug. 7,** agreed to repatriate the 10,000 to 12,000 contras and their families by Dec. 5. A U.N. commission would oversee the return of the contras to Nicaragua or their relocation to other countries, and would collect their arms.

E. German Refugees Create Tensions — West Germany said 44,263 East Germans had emigrated to

West Germany from January to June 1989—most, but not all, with East Germany's permission. East German-Hungarian relations had cooled after Hungary removed its barbed-wire fence with Austria in the spring. Thereafter, small but gradually increasing numbers of East Germans fled to the West through Hungary, and Hungarian guards became less diligent in discouraging them. By early August, several hundred East Germans had taken refuge in West German diplomatic facilities in East Berlin, Budapest, and Prague. On **Aug. 7,** after West Germany had refused to expel the refugees, East Germany warned of "serious consequences."

Japan Elects Kaifu Premier — Japan got its third premier of 1989 when former Education Minister Toshiki Kaifu, one of the few leaders of the ruling Liberal Democratic Party who was untouched by the Recruit scandal, was chosen as party leader, **Aug. 8.** On **Aug. 9,** he was formally elected premier by the Diet (parliament).

Baltic Republics Denounce 1939 Pact — The popular fronts in the Soviet republics of Estonia, Latvia, and Lithuania led protests against the 1939 Hitler-Stalin pact that had resulted in their absorbtion into the Soviet Union. Estonia's parliament, **Aug. 8,** approved legislation establishing residency requirements for voting and running for office. Clearly aimed at non-Estonians, the law provoked a strike by ethnic Russians in Estonia and by mid-August, 50,000 had walked off their jobs. Aleksandr Yakovlev, the Soviet Communist Party official in charge of foreign policy, said **Aug. 18,** that the 1939 pact had contained secret protocols, and he condemned the agreement as a "deviation from Leninist principles." The pact had cleared the way for the Soviet Union to seize the then-independent Baltic states on the pretext that they sought protection from the Nazis. On **Aug. 23,** the 50th anniversary of the pact, one million persons joined hands in the Baltic states to form a line 400 miles long, as a means of showing unity against their current status in the Soviet Union. The Lithuanian popular front called for complete independence. All 3 popular fronts issued a joint statement saying that the Soviet Union had "infringed on the historical right of the Baltic nations to self-determination," and they denounced Soviet terror and violence.

President of South Africa Resigns — Pres. Pieter Botha of South Africa resigned after a bitter confrontation with members of his cabinet. Earlier in 1989, Botha had suffered a stroke and resigned as leader of the National Party. The president thereafter became openly critical of Frederik de Klerk, who had succeeded him as party leader. On **Aug. 10,** Pres. Kenneth Kaunda of Zambia said he would soon meet with de Klerk. Botha, **Aug. 11,** publicly disputed an assertion by his foreign minister that he had been consulted on the meeting between de Klerk and Kaunda. De Klerk, who was also education minister, then met, **Aug. 12,** with most of the cabinet members but without Botha. At an emergency meeting of the cabinet, called by Botha, **Aug. 14,** the president clashed with rebellious ministers. That evening, in a nationwide address, Botha resigned. He again criticized de Klerk and said, "I am being ignored by ministers serving in my cabinet." The cabinet, **Aug. 15,** confirmed de Klerk as acting president. He would serve until national elections, scheduled in September. De Klerk's first crisis was growing protests by blacks across the nation, aimed at ending apartheid, and upgrading the quality of health care for blacks.

Direct Combat Erupts in Lebanon — Direct fighting broke out on the ground in Lebanon between the major forces. Artillery bombardments, which had begun in March, had killed more than 700 people in Beirut. Many of the 1.5 million residents of Beirut had fled the capital. On **Aug. 13,** Syrian troops, supported by Druse and Palestinian fighters attacked the Christian stronghold in East Beirut with tanks and infantry. The foreign ministers of Syria and Iran met with their Lebanese allies in Damascus, **Aug. 15,** for a council of war seeking to form a united front aimed at toppling the Christian "clique." Pope John Paul II, **Aug. 15,** denounced the "genocide" in Lebanon and singled out Syria as a culprit.

Colombian Presidential Candidate Slain — The assassination of a Colombian presidential candidate prompted a new crackdown on illegal drug traffickers. The candidate, Luis Carlos Galán, was shot fatally at a rally in a suburb of Bogotá, **Aug. 18.** Galán, a senator, was a vocal opponent of the drug dealers and exporters. A judge and a police chief were also slain within a 3-day period. Some 4,500 judges went on strike and threatened to resign unless the government provided more protection. Pres. Virgilio Barco, **Aug. 19,** reinstated a decree that permitted drug figures to be extradited to the U.S. for trial. Colombian police and army units confiscated more than $125 million in property, including hundreds of planes and houses as well as helicopters and yachts, from the traffickers. Pres. George Bush said, **Aug. 22,** that Barco had told him that additional financial aid was needed, but that sending in U.S. troops would not be necessary. On **Aug. 24,** the drug barons issued a communiqué vowing "total and absolute war" on the government, and in fact began a new wave of bombings and arson. The Extraditables, a paramilitary group, said, **Aug. 24,** that 10 judges would be killed for every Colombian extradited to the United States. Bush, **Aug. 25,** announced a $65 million military-aid package for Colombia. The U.S. State Department, **Aug. 30,** advised U.S. citizens to consider leaving Colombia. Some 11,000 persons had been arrested after the Galán assassination, and 3,000 remained in custody as of the end of the month.

General

Pete Rose Banned From Baseball — Pete Rose, a baseball legend, was banned from the game for life on **Aug. 24,** by the commissioner of major league baseball, A. Bartlett Giamatti. In making the announcement, Giamatti said he had concluded that Rose had gambled on baseball games, including games involving the Cincinnati Reds, the team Rose managed. Rose, a hero in Cincinnati where he had spent most of his career, had more base hits than any other player in the history of the game. An investigation of Rose had continued for several months, and the gambling charges were supported in a 225-page report prepared for the commissioner by John Dowd, a Washington, D.C. lawyer. Major League Rule 21 provides for the lifetime suspension of anyone who bets on a game in which his team is involved. Rose vehemently denied that he had bet on baseball games. In announcing his suspension, Giamatti said that a signed agreement with Rose affirmed that nothing in it could be deemed as either an admission or denial by Rose that he had bet on baseball games. Giamatti said his decision was based on the Dowd report. Rose had declined to participate in a hearing. He would be eligible to apply for reinstatement after one year. On **Sept. 1,** 8 days after banning Rose, Giamatti, 51, died of a heart attack.

Disasters — Up to 150 persons were killed, **Aug. 9,** when a passenger train derailed and plunged into the San Rafael de Bamoa River in northwestern Mexico. ... Hundreds of people may have been killed, **Aug. 17,** in an explosion at a secret missile installation

60 miles south of Baghdad. ... Fifty-one persons died, **Aug. 20,** when a gravel barge struck a chartered party boat crowded mostly with young people in the River Thames in London; 86 persons on the boat were rescued.

SEPTEMBER

National

U.S. Economic Data Encouraging — Government statistics released in September appeared to bode well for the U.S. economy. The Labor Dept. reported, **Sept. 1,** that in August the unemployment rate edged downward one-tenth of a percentage point to 5.1 percent. The index of leading economic indicators turned upward by 0.2 percent in July after 2 down months, the Commerce Dept. said, **Sept. 1.** The department said, **Sept. 15,** that the U.S. merchandise trade deficit fell to $7.58 billion in July, a level not attained since 1984. Following revised declines in both June and July, the index of producer prices for finished goods fell again in August by 0.4 percent, the Labor Department said, **Sept. 15.** The department said, **Sept. 19,** that the consumer price index had held steady in August, the first time since April 1986 that it had not shown an increase.

Bush Outlines Fight Against Drugs — Pres. George Bush, speaking to the nation on television from the White House for the first time, **Sept. 5,** announced a broad plan to combat drug use and trafficking. The plan called for outlays of $7.9 billion in the 1990 fiscal year, but only $716 million of this represented new spending. The money would be spent on law enforcement, treatment of addicts, education and prevention, and assistance to other countries trying to stop internal drug production. Many Democrats criticized the plan as neither bold enough nor sufficiently well financed. A Colombian linked to the Medellin drug cartel, Eduardo Martinez, was extradited to the U.S., **Sept. 6.** He was the first person sent to the U.S. since Colombia resumed extraditing suspected drug operatives for trial. In what was described as the biggest drug haul in history, federal agents seized at least 20 tons of cocaine and $10 million in Los Angeles, **Sept. 29.**

Iowa **Disaster Linked to Dead Sailor** — A U.S. Navy report issued, **Sept. 7,** concluded that the explosion on the battleship *Iowa* in April was "probably" the result of an act of suicide by a sailor. The sailor, Gunner's Mate 2d Class Clayton Hartwig, was one of 47 sailors killed in the blast. The report said Hartwig had an interest in explosives and was a "loner." It offered no motive, but conjectured that Hartwig had placed a detonating device in with gunpowder and that the powder exploded as it was being rammed into the gun tube during a firing exercise. Investigators found evidence of foreign chemical elements in the gun tube. Hartwig's family denounced the report and demanded a Congressional investigation.

New York Mayor Defeated in Primary — Mayor Edward Koch of New York, seeking a 4th term in the Democratic primary, **Sept. 12,** was defeated by Manhattan Borough Pres. David Dinkins. Dinkins, the first black to be nominated by a major party for mayor of New York, would oppose Rudolph Giuliani, a former U.S. attorney, who won the Republican nomination, in the November election.

Ex-HUD Secretary Declines to Testify — Samuel R. Pierce, Jr., secretary of Housing and Urban Development under Pres. Ronald Reagan, declined to answer questions put to him by members of a House subcommittee. Pierce said, **Sept. 14,** that he would not appear before the subcommittee the next day because he had just hired lawyers and had not had time to prepare his testimony. The subcommittee was investigating payments of large fees to well-connected Republicans and other matters related to the awarding of HUD grants. The subcommittee then subpoenaed Pierce. Appearing before the subcommittee, **Sept. 26,** Pierce answered no questions, citing his Fifth Amendment right against possible self-incrimination. On **Sept. 27,** Lance Wilson, a former executive assistant to Pierce at HUD, asserted the same right.

Exxon Halts Oil Spill Cleanup — As winter approached in Alaska, Exxon Corp., **Sept. 15,** halted its cleanup of the 11-million-gallon oil spill from the tanker *Exxon Valdez.* The spill, largest in U.S. history, had occurred in Prince William Sound in March. Exxon said the cost of the cleanup was approaching $2 billion. Although the company said 1,100 miles of the shoreline had been made "environmentally stable," Alaskan Gov. Steve Cowper said "plenty more" had to be done, and that Alaska would bill Exxon for the cleanup being continued by the state.

Curb on Financing of Arts Rejected — A Senate and House conference committee, **Sept. 29,** rejected an attempt to forbid federal financing of art that violated certain moral standards. A furor over public funding of the arts began earlier in the year. In June, the Corcoran Gallery of Art in Washington, D.C. canceled an exhibition of photographs by Robert Mapplethorpe that included images depicting homoerotic and sadomasochistic activities. The exhibition was to be financed in part by the National Endowment for the Arts, whose appropriation bill was being considered by Congress. The Senate approved a proposal by Sen. Jesse Helms (R, N.C.) to cut off grants for any art found to be "obscene or indecent" or that "denigrates the objects or beliefs of the adherents of a particular religion or nonreligion." Cancellation of the exhibition created much criticism in the art world, and many in Congress argued that support for the arts must be extended to that which was controversial or unpopular. In rejecting the Helms proposal, the Senate and House conferees substituted a restriction that would prevent any support for art defined as obscene by a 1973 Supreme Court decision. Few serious works of art were likely to be rejected on that basis.

International

Convent at Death Camp Stirs Debate — The presence of a Roman Catholic convent on the grounds at Auschwitz, the German Nazi death camp in Poland, provoked a heated debate. Jewish leaders had objected to the presence of the convent at the site where 2 million Jews were killed during World War II. Poland's Catholic primate, Cardinal Jozef Glemp, said, **Sept. 2,** that he objected to a 1987 agreement to move the convent to a nearby ecumenical center. Three of the 4 cardinals who had approved the agreement in 1987 reaffirmed their support for it, **Sept. 3.** On **Sept. 19,** the Vatican offered financial aid for the construction of the ecumenical center. In a letter made public, **Sept. 21,** Glemp reversed his position and supported the removal of the convent to the center.

U.S. Closes Embassy in Lebanon — The U.S. closed its embassy in Beirut as 1,000 persons blockaded the embassy compound and demanded that the United States recognize the government of Gen. Michel Aoun, head of the Christian regime in Lebanon, **Sept. 5.** The U.S. then evacuated its entire staff, **Sept. 6,** the first time since the Lebanese civil war began in 1975 that there was no U.S. diplomatic representation in the country.

Ruling Party Slips in South Africa — The National Party lost ground, Sept. 6, in voting for white parliamentary seats in the South African elections. The NP emerged with 93 seats (a loss of 30) to 39 for the far-right Conservative Party and 33 for the more liberal Democratic Party. Nonetheless, acting Pres. Frederik de Klerk called the results a mandate for his plan for a gradual reform of the nation's apartheid system of racial segregation. Hundreds of thousands of blacks joined a general strike to protest their exclusion from the election. Unofficially, 25 deaths were linked to election violence. De Klerk said, Sept. 7, that South Africa would evolve toward a society dominated by neither blacks nor whites. Parliament, Sept. 14, elected De Klerk to a 5-year term as president.

Gorbachev Shakes Up Politburo — Soviet Pres. Mikhail Grobachev changed the lineup in the ruling Politburo as ethnic and nationalist unrest continued to rise across the Soviet Union. A Ukrainian popular movement, holding its founding congress, Sept. 8-10, approved a resolution calling for transforming the nation into a confederation of autonomous republics. On national television, Sept. 9, Gorbachev took note of "threats of approaching chaos and talk of a threatened coup, and even civil war." He said strikes and violence were not an answer to the country's problems. Gorbachev met in Moscow with government and party leaders of the Baltic republics, Sept. 13. He reportedly opposed separatist movements in the Baltic region, but was also reported to have been conciliatory. By the end of the 2d day, Sept. 20, of a meeting of the Communist Party Central Committee, Gorbachev had succeeded in removing 3 members of the ruling Politburo and 2 candidate members. As a result, it appeared that—with new appointments—the Politburo contained a clear majority in support for Gorbachev's reforms for the first time. Gorbachev, Sept. 25, warned leaders of the republics of Armenia and Azerbaijan that they had 2 days to negotiate an end to the rail blockade, apparently supported by Azerbaijani authorities, that had prevented Armenia from getting badly needed supplies. His threat appeared to bring an easing of tensions between the 2 republics. With Gorbachev present in the Ukraine, Sept. 28, the Ukrainian Communist Party replaced the party boss who had been trying to cope with the rising nationalist sentiment there.

Departures From East Germany Increase — The number of refugees fleeing from E. Germany continued to rise in September. On Sept. 10, Foreign Minister Gyula Horn of Hungary announced suspension of an agreement with E. Germany that Hungary would not permit East Germans to go to the West through Hungary. In the next 4 days, Sept. 11-14, more than 13,000 refugees left Hungary for West Germany via Austria. The E. German government filed a diplomatic protest, Sept. 12, but the Soviet foreign ministry declined to criticize Hungary. Later in the month, as several thousand East Germans crowded into the W. German embassy in Prague, W. German Foreign Minister Hans-Dietrich Genscher flew to the Czechoslovak capital, Sept. 30. His negotiations with E. German authorities opened the way for the refugees to leave by bus, Sept. 30, on the first leg of a trip to W. Germany.

Polish Parliament Approves Cabinet — The lower house of the Polish parliament, the Sejm, Sept. 12, approved the 23-member coalition cabinet put together by Prime Minister Tadeusz Mazowiecki. The cabinet included 11 members of Solidarity, 4 from the United Workers' (Communist) Party, 7 from minor parties, and 1 independent. Solidarity held most of the economic portfolios, but the Communists would continue to control the army and the police. The prime minister, in a speech to the Sejm, reaffirmed a commitment to

keep Poland in the Warsaw Pact and he announced new economic austerity measures. The Bush administration said, Sept. 14, that it would double its pledge of food aid to Poland in the next year, to $100 million.

First Bush-Gorbachev Summit Set — Sec. of State James Baker and Soviet Foreign Minister Eduard Shevardnadze, meeting in Jackson, Wyoming, Sept. 22, announced that Pres. George Bush and Soviet Pres. Mikhail Gorbachev would hold their first summit conference in the spring or summer of 1990. They also signed agreements on the monitoring of chemical weapons, the environment, and on principles for verifying limits on strategic forces and nuclear tests. Addressing the United Nations General Assembly, Sept. 25, Bush said the U.S. would destroy 80 percent of its chemical weapons if the Soviet Union cut its stockpile to the American level. Speaking to the Assembly, Sept. 26, Shevardnadze went further, proposing to ban production of the most advanced types of chemical weapons altogether.

Vietnamese Forces Leave Cambodia — Vietnam completed its withdrawal of its military forces from Cambodia, Sept. 26. The Vietnamese had entered Cambodia in 1978 and had succeeded in overthrowing the brutal regime of Pol Pot, the Khmer Rouge. But fighting had continued, and 25,300 Vietnamese soldiers were killed and 55,000 wounded. In Phnom Penh, Heng Samrin, general secretary of the Cambodian Communist Party, called on his countrymen, Sept. 26, to unite to fight the Khmer Rouge, who still threatened the government.

General

Gunman Kills 7 in Louisville — Returning to a printing plant in Louisville, Ky. where he once worked, a gunman killed 7 people and wounded 13, Sept. 14, before killing himself. The man, Joseph Wesbecker, had been put on permanent disability leave in 1988. He was armed with an AK-47 assault rifle, 3 semiautomatic pistols, a handgun, and a bayonet.

Hurricane Causes Wide Devastation — Hurricane Hugo swept through the Caribbean and struck the mainland in South Carolina, taking a heavy human toll and causing immense property damage. Moving northwest, the hurricane struck Guadeloupe, Sept. 16, Montserrat, Sept. 17, and the U.S. Virgin Islands and Puerto Rico, Sept. 18. On Montserrat, the most devastated island, 80 percent of property was destroyed and 99 percent of its 12,000 inhabitants were homeless. On St. Thomas and St. Croix in the Virgins, it was estimated that 80 percent of the buildings were damaged. Several small towns on the east coast of Puerto Rico were virtually destroyed. Following 2 days of looting, Pres. George Bush, Sept. 20, sent 1,000 military police to the Virgin Islands. With winds of 135 miles an hour, the center of the storm hit Charleston, S.C. on the night of Sept. 21-22. High tides and torrential rains soaked the barrier islands and the coast, damaging private and commercial property as well as many of the city's historical buildings. The death toll was put at 51, including 24 in the U.S. Congress, Sept. 28, approved $1.1 billion in emergency aid, but many complained that the government was slow to respond effectively to the destruction.

Mass Murderer Convicted in L.A. — Richard Ramirez, a 29-year-old Texan, was convicted by a jury in Los Angeles, Sept. 20, of 13 murders and 30 other crimes. The so-called "night stalker" had struck repeatedly in southern California in 1985, breaking into houses in residential neighborhoods.

Woman Gets Custody of Frozen Embryos — A Tennessee state court, Sept. 21, gave temporary custody of

7 frozen embryos to a woman who was separated from her husband. The woman, Mary Sue Davis, hoped to become pregnant, but her husband, Junior Davis, who had sued for divorce, said he no longer wanted to become a father. Judge W. Dale Young held that "human life begins at the moment of conception," and he treated the case as a normal custody battle.

20 Die in School Bus Crash — A collision between a truck and a school bus in Alton, Tex., **Sept. 21**, took the lives of 20 students. More than 60 were injured. The truck struck the bus as it passed through an intersection, and the bus then plunged 40 feet into a waterfilled gravel pit.

Disasters — About 150 persons died, **Sept. 3**, when a Cuban airliner carrying Italian tourists crashed on takeoff from Havana airport. ... A chartered plane carrying Norwegian shipping company employees crashed into the ocean off Denmark, **Sept. 8**, killing all 55 aboard. ... At least 161 people drowned, **Sept. 10**, when a Romanian pleasure boat and a Bulgarian barge collided on the Danube River ... An explosion on a French jetliner flying to Paris from the Congo, **Sept. 19**, caused the death of all 171 aboard. An examination of the wreckage, scattered in Niger, indicated that the cause was a bomb.

OCTOBER

National

Congress Debates Changes in Medicare — A program providing expanded health benefits to 33 million Medicare beneficiaries was intensely debated in the House and Senate in October. The law, which had been signed into law in July 1988, put a cap on fees Medicare patients pay for hospitals and doctors, expanded nursing home coverage, and provided some coverage for prescription drugs. This Medicare Catastrophic Coverage Act soon provoked outcries from more affluent older Americans, who objected to paying the surtax that funded the program. Many had retirement benefits that duplicated what was provided under the law. In response, the House, **Oct. 4**, voted 360-66 to repeal the program and the taxes and premiums that paid for it. Dr. Louis Sullivan, secretary of Health and Human Services, criticized the vote, **Oct. 5**, and said he supported a compromise plan in the Senate. The Senate, **Oct. 6**, voted 99-0 to scale back the program and eliminate the surtax. The Senate kept the limit elderly people must pay in hospital expenses, but repealed the ceiling on payments to doctors, coverage for drugs, and nursing home benefits.

Producer Prices Jump — Producer prices rose after declining for 3 months. The Labor Dept. reported, **Oct. 6**, that the nation's unemployment rate had inched up 0.1 percentage point in September to 5.2 percent. The 0.9 percent surge in September in the Producer Price Index for finished goods, reported by the department, **Oct. 13**, sparked worries that the rate of inflation might soon increase.

Foes of Abortion Suffer Setbacks — Legislative action proved to be disappointing to opponents of abortion. A U.S. Supreme Court decision in July had opened the way to tougher state laws against abortion, and Gov. Bob Martinez (R) of Florida had called the State Legislature into special session to deal with the issue. But legislative committees, **Oct. 10** and **11**, rejected all 5 bills supported by the governor. The outcome was attributed to the greater activism on the part of those who supported the right of a woman to choose to have an abortion. Reversing an earlier stand, the U.S. House of Representatives, **Oct. 11**, voted

216-206 to allow the Federal Government to pay for abortions for poor women if their pregnancies occurred as a result of rape or incest.

Stock Prices Drop Sharply — Stock prices, which had been advancing fairly steadily since their big plunge in October 1987, suddenly fell again in October 1989. After slipping for several days, values tumbled sharply on Friday, **Oct. 13**, when the Dow Jones industrial average declined 190.58 points to a close of 2,569.26. This was the 2d highest one-day decline in points ever, but the percentage decline of 6.9 percent was only the 12th worst ever. The immediate cause of the selloff was attributed primarily to the failure of a group of investors to arrange financing of a takeover of United Airlines. Their setback was seen as an indicator that the era of the "junk bond" financing of corporate takeovers might be nearing an end. Investors were also concerned about the rise in producer prices and by the apparent failure of Congress to approve a reduction in the capital-gains tax.

International

East Germany Has Tense Anniversary — The German Democratic Republic (East Germany) celebrated its 40th anniversary in October, but street protests and an outward flow of refugees marred the occasion. On **Oct. 1**, more than 6,000 East Germans who had taken refuge in West German embassies in Prague and Warsaw arrived by train in West Germany. The East German regime had agreed to their departure. An additional 2,500 East Germans crowded into the West German embassy in Prague, **Oct. 2**. By **Oct. 3**, with more than 8,000 persons either inside the embassy or milling around outside, East Germany agreed to let them depart for West Germany. But East Germany then said it was suspending passport- and visa-free travel to Czechoslovakia. As trains carrying the refugees to the West passed through East Germany, **Oct. 4** and **5**, thousands more crowded into train stations and sought to scramble aboard. In Dresden, **Oct. 5**, police held off some 10,000 persons seeking to board the trains. Pres. Mikhail Gorbachev of the Soviet Union arrived in East Berlin for the anniversary, and, in apparent response to speculation that he wanted to see the East German government move more quickly toward reform, said that matters relating to the government would be decided "not in Moscow, but in Berlin." On **Oct. 7**, he and the East German leader, Erich Honecker, reviewed a military parade. Honecker, 77, who had recently been ill, was regarded as an obstacle to reform. Protestors, calling for more freedom and chanting "Gorby, Gorby," filled the streets of cities throughout East Germany, **Oct. 8**, and clashed with police. As tens of thousands of people continued to demonstrate in Leipzig and Dresden, **Oct. 9**, there were reports that local authorities were willing to consider their demands. The East German Politburo said, **Oct. 11**, that it was time to examine societal problems and why nearly 50,000 persons had fled to the West. Honecker spoke, **Oct. 13**, of the need to change economic and social policies.

Soviet Workers Get Right to Strike — Soviet Pres. Mikhail Gorbachev warned, **Oct. 2**, that the economy was at the brink of collapse, and he called for a 15-month ban on strikes. However, the Soviet legislature, **Oct. 9**, approved a law granting workers the legal right to strike, but it banned strikes in defense, power, and communications industries as well as in civil aviation and surface public transportation. Strikes intended to "over-throw the Soviet state and social system" were also banned. A tense internal situation appeared to ease, **Oct. 10**, when Azerbaijani nationalists agreed to end a rail embargo that had prevented fuel and other essential supplies from reaching Armenia.

Attempt to Oust Noriega Fails — Rebel officers in the Panama Defense Forces led an unsuccessful attempt, **Oct. 3,** to overthrow the nation's strongman, Gen. Manuel Noriega. Many details of the coup, and of the U.S. role in it, remained unclear or in dispute well after it was suppressed. The Bush administration knew in advance that an attempt would be made to topple Noriega, who was under indictment in the U.S. for drug trafficking. The rebels, led by Maj. Moisés Giroldi, attacked the Panamanian military headquarters and, for a time, Noriega was under the control of the rebels. The rebels and U.S. officials were in contact, but subsequent accounts differed on what terms, if any, Noriega would be turned over to U.S. forces. U.S. troops blocked 2 roads leading to the scene of the fighting, but a 3d road was left open, and Noriega loyalist soldiers traveled along it and came to the general's rescue. By early afternoon, the coup had collapsed, and it was reported that Noriega shot Giroldi, heretofore a loyalist who had helped Noriega put down a previous coup. It was believed that about 240 rebels had launched the attack. The death toll was relatively low, and some of those killed may have been executed after surrendering. U.S. administration officials said, **Oct. 4,** that there had not been a full-fledged military effort in behalf of the coup because of the possibility that it might be a trap devised by Noriega to embarrass the United States. In ensuing days, Pres. George Bush and his advisers came under broad criticism for failing to have a plan in place to deal with the coup and for failing to act quickly enough in response to it.

Hungarian Communists Reorganize — Speaking at a congress of the Socialist Workers Party (its formal name) on **Oct. 6,** Rezso Nyers, the party president, said it should be succeeded by a new party that would be a synthesis of both communist and social democratic traditions, and that would seek improved ties with both the Soviet Communist Party and the Western socialist parties. The delegates, **Oct. 7,** voted, 1,005 to 159, to transform the party into a socialist party. Those in the majority believed that the change would permit the party to compete more effectively in free democratic national elections planned for the spring of

1990. Nyers was elected president of the party, **Oct. 9.** Some delegates who were in the minority said they would continue the Socialist Workers Party as a separate organization. On **Oct. 12,** Roland Antoniewicz, leader of a group loyal to Marxist-Leninist principles, denounced the action taken at the congress as "treason."

South Africa Frees Black Leaders — South Africa's government, **Oct. 15,** freed 8 prominent black nationalist leaders. Seven were affiliated with the banned African National Congress, and all had been imprisoned for many years. The best known, Walter Sisulu, 77, had been in prison since 1963, serving a life term for treason. After his release, Sisulu called for the release of Nelson Mandela, leader of the black nationalist movement in South Africa.

General

TV Evangelist Jim Bakker Convicted — Jim Bakker, the television evangelist, was convicted of fraud and conspiracy in a Federal court in Charlotte, N.C. The prosecution, pressing 24 charges of fraud and conspiracy, contended that Bakker solicited donations for vacations he could not provide at his Christian theme park in South Carolina and that he spent $3.7 million of the donations on his lavish life style. Testifying, **Oct. 2,** Bakker blamed fellow evangelist Jerry Falwell, who took over the PTL ministry for a time in 1987, for its financial collapse. Bakker was convicted on all counts, **Oct. 5.** His lawyers said he would appeal.

Dalai Lama Wins Peace Prize — The Norwegian Nobel Committee announced, **Oct. 6,** that it had awarded its Peace Prize to the Dalai Lama, 54, the exiled religious and political leader of Tibet. For nearly 40 years he had symbolized the resistance of the people of Tibet to rule by the Chinese, who had dominated the mountain nation since the 1950s.

Tass Says Aliens Landed in Russia — Tass, the Soviet press agency, reported that alien creatures landed in a space vehicle in a park in the Russian city of Voronezh, 300 miles southeast of Moscow. Tass said scientists had confirmed it, and that a crowd had observed the extraterrestrials. One was described as 9 feet tall and as having 3 eyes. Tass insisted, **Oct. 10,** that the reports were not a joke or a hoax.

See p. 959 for late-breaking October 1989 stories.

Major Decisions of the U.S. Supreme Court, 1988-89

(For further information, see *Supreme Court, Chronology,* and *Addenda.*)

The Supreme Court began its 1988-89 term on Oct. 3, 1988. Summaries of notable actions follow. The Court:

Ruled, 6-3, to strike down a racially discriminatory zoning ordinance that confined private construction of multifamily housing projects to areas where most of a town's minorities lived. (Nov. 7)

Declined to review, thus let stand, a federal appellate court decision ruling out the use of racial quotas to maintain integration at a huge subsidized housing project in Brooklyn, New York. (Nov. 7)

Declined to review, thus let stand, an Indiana Supreme Court ruling that a husband had no right to veto his wife's decision on abortion. (Nov. 14)

Ruled, 6-3, that a conviction was constitutional even though police negligence had eliminated evidence that might have brought exoneration. The majority maintained that "Unless a criminal defendant can show bad faith on the part of the police, failure to preserve potentially useful evidence does not constitute a denial of the due process of law."(Nov. 29)

Ruled, 8-1, that indigent defendants had the right to legal representation on appeal of conviction. (Nov. 29)

Ruled, 5-4, that the Labor Dept. had wrongly denied disability benefits to some 100,000 miners with black-lung disease. The Court also ruled, unanimously, to disallow reopening most of the cases, confining the effect of its ruling to the 7,000 or so cases still pending. (Dec. 6)

Ruled, 5-4, that the Natl. Collegiate Athletic Assn. did not violate the constitutional rights of basketball coach Jerry Tarkanian when it attempted to discipline him for violations, including recruiting, at the Univ. of Nevada. (Dec. 12)

Ruled, unanimously, to uphold an Illinois tax on interstate telephone calls that were billed to addresses in that state. (Jan. 10)

Ruled, 8-1, that states could prevent utilities from billing consumers for the costs of planning and constructing nuclear plants and other facilities that were canceled before they were used. (Jan. 11)

Ruled, 6-3, to uphold a 1982 congressional redistricting in California that had been seen as gerrymandering favoring the Democrats. (Jan. 17)

Ruled, 8-1, that a recent major revision of federal sentencing rules was constitutional. The system was designed to reduce disparities in sentencing for similar crimes and to increase the likelihood of imprisonment for crimes involving drugs and for such white-collar offenses as tax evasion, price-fixing, and insider trading. (Jan. 18)

Ruled, unanimously, that an antiracketeering law could not be used to close an adult bookstore without a prior court finding that the materials for sale were obscene. (Feb. 21)

Ruled, 6-3, that a Texas law exempting the Bible and other religious publications from sales tax was unconstitutional. (Feb. 21)

Ruled, 6-3, that the Constitution did not hold local officials liable for failure to protect a child from physical harm from a parent. (Feb. 22)

Declined to review, thus let stand, the conviction of Bernhard Goetz for illegal possession of a handgun in the New York City subway shooting of four youths he claimed were about to rob him. (Feb. 27)

Ruled, 6-3, that striking railroad and airline workers could not claim their jobs back after the strike if the jobs had been filled by nonstriking workers, despite any seniority claim. (Feb. 28)

Ruled, unanimously, that a city could be held liable for violating an individual's constitutional rights if it failed to adequately train police and other officials, provided that the city acted with "deliberate indifference." (Feb. 28)

Declined to review, thus let stand, an appeals court ruling to strike down a Michigan law requiring that 7% of state contracts be awarded to minority-owned businesses and 5% to businesses owned by women. (Feb. 28)

Ruled, unanimously, that the right to a jury trial was not constitutionally guaranteed to drunk-driving defendants. (Mar. 6)

Ruled, 9-0, that the Federal Savings and Loan Insurance Corp. did not have exclusive jurisdiction to adjudicate a creditor's claim against insolvent savings and loan associations that were government-insured. (Mar. 21)

Ruled, 7-2, to uphold federal drug-testing programs for workers in jobs involving public health and safety. Also ruled, 5-4, that the Customs Service policy of testing applicants for drug-enforcement jobs was not unconstitutional. (Mar. 21)

Ruled, 9-0, that the Freedom of Information Act did not mandate the Federal Bureau of Investigation's disclosure of its criminal identification files. (Mar. 22)

Ruled, 9-0, that New York City's Board of Estimate, its main governing body, was unconstitutional in its violation of the principle of one person, one vote. New York's five borough presidents had equal votes on the Board, although the boroughs varied in population from Brooklyn's 2.2 million to Staten Island's 350,000. (Mar. 22)

Ruled, unanimously, that civil rights plaintiffs were entitled to reimbursement if they won on a "significant" issue in a suit, but not necessarily on the "central" issue. (Mar. 28)

Ruled, unanimously, that the Constitution's protection of religious liberty extended to personal beliefs as well as those of organized religion. The Court overturned an appellate ruling that denied unemployment benefits to a man who had refused to work on Sunday because "as a Christian" he considered it "wrong." (Mar. 29)

Ruled, unanimously, to uphold a New Jersey corporate tax law that prohibited companies from deducting from income their federal windfall profits tax payments. (Apr. 3)

Ruled, 7-2, that it was not unconstitutional for drug agents to detain airline passengers for brief searches if they exhibited behavior that fit the pattern of a drug courier. (Apr. 3)

Ruled, 6-3, that Indian tribes had jurisdiction over child custody cases involving babies born off the reservation to people who lived on the reservation. (Apr. 3)

Ruled, 7-0, to uphold state laws allowing those who experienced indirect financial losses as a result of violations of state antitrust law to sue the violators. "Congress intended the federal antitrust laws to supplement, not displace state antitrust remedies," the Court maintained. (Apr. 18)

Ruled, 9-0, to uphold a system of user fees to pay for a safety program for oil, natural gas, and hazardous liquid pipelines. The system had been established and fees collected by the Transportation Secretary under the authority of Congress as part of the 1986 Budget Reconciliation Act. (Apr. 25)

Ruled, 6-3, to place the burden of proof on employers to justify their decisions on hiring and promoting, once a woman presented direct evidence of sex discrimination. The majority maintained that the employer must prove by a "preponderance of the evidence" that the same decision would have been made, even if gender had not been a factor. (May 1)

Ruled, 5-4, that arbitration agreements to resolve disputes over the purchase of securities were binding. (May 15)

Ruled, unanimously, that a challenge to police use of force against a suspect should be determined on the basis of "objective reasonableness" rather than the intent of the police. The U.S. Court of Appeals in Richmond, Va., had ruled that such litigants must prove that police acted "maliciously and sadistically" in order to recover damages. (May 15)

Ruled, unanimously, that a civil penalty could not be imposed on a person also convicted of a crime for the same act, since this would violate the Fifth Amendment guarantee against double jeopardy. (May 15)

Ruled, 7-2, that a veteran's disability benefits were not subject to property division in a divorce proceeding. (May 30)

Declined to review, thus let stand, a federal appeals court ruling that it was unconstitutional for public high schools to begin football games with a Christian prayer, because it violated the First Amendment stricture against official establishment of religion. (May 30)

Ruled, 9-0, that the ownership of a copyright for commissioned works of art could be shared by the artist and the patron. (June 5)

Ruled, 5-4, to place the burden of proof on minority workers who alleged racial discrimination in employment. The majority held that an employer could justify policies that had a discriminatory effect by providing a reasonable business explanation. (June 5)

Ruled, 5-4, that white workers who claimed unfair treatment due to affirmative action programs could seek redress under civil rights legislation, with no time limit for filing such claims. The case involved white firefighters in Birmingham, Ala., who had challenged an 8-year-old, court-approved settlement aiming to increase the number of blacks hired and promoted. The whites contended that the plan deprived them of promotions because of their race. (June 12)

Ruled, 5-3, that challenges to the seniority system as discriminatory must be made at the time the system is adopted. (June 12)

Ruled, 5-4, to override a ban agaist the use of "victim impact statements" by prosecutors to persuade juries to impose the death penalty in murder cases. (June 12)

Ruled, 9-0, to uphold a landmark 1976 civil rights decision implementing a post-Civil War era rights law. However, the Court ruled, 5-4, to narrow the application of the older law to exclude claims of racial harassment in the workplace. (June 15)

Ruled, 7-2, that railroads and airlines could give periodic drug tests to employees without negotiating the issue with their unions. (June 19)

Ruled, 5-4, that railroads had the right to sell assets and restructure their operations without negotiating with their unions. (June 21)

Ruled, 5-4, that states could be sued by private parties to recover the costs of cleanup of hazardous waste sites under the federal Superfund law. (June 21)

Ruled, 5-4, to strike down the use of the Civil Rights Act of 1866 to bring damage suits against state or local governments for racial discrimination. The majority held that local officials were not liable unless it was proven that the discrimination resulted from an official policy or government-sanctioned custom. (June 22)

Ruled, 5-4, to uphold the federal seizure before trial of a criminal defendant's assets that could be used to pay for the defendant's defense. (June 22)

Ruled, 7-2, that federal law prohibiting age discrimination in employment did not bar employers from making age variations in benefit plans. The majority said that older workers alleging unfairness must prove that the employer adopted the plan with the intent to discriminate. (June 23)

Ruled, 5-4, that indigent inmates on death row did not have a constitutional right to a lawyer to assist them in a second round of state court appeals. (June 23)

Ruled, 5-4, to uphold the death sentence of a man who committed murder in 1979. The man was mentally retarded with an I.Q. of 54 and the mental age of a child six and a half years old. However, the Court also ruled, 5-4, that mental retardation must be considered as a mitigating factor in imposing sentences in such cases, and returned the above case for resentencing. (June 26)

Ruled, unanimously, not to restrict criminal prosecutions and civil lawsuits under the federal Racketeer Influenced and Corrupt Organization (RICO) law. RICO was not limited to organized crime activities or to multiple illegal schemes, the Court said, but could be involved in evidence of a single, continuing fraud scheme or "pattern" of misconduct. (June 26)

Ruled, 5-4, that a Nativity scene displayed in the Allegheny County, Pa. courthouse was unconstitutional, but a display of a Hanukkah menorah on the steps of a Pittsburgh City Hall was constitutional. The majority held that the Nativity scene, standing alone without other more secular Christmas symbols, conveyed an impression of the county government's endorsement of Christianity. However, the menorah, displayed next to a Christmas tree and under a banner with the mayor's name declaring a "salute to liberty," was seen as conveying "the city's secular recognition of different traditions for celebrating the winter-holiday season." (July 3)

Ruled, 5-4, to uphold a restrictive Missouri abortion law. The law prohibited public employees from performing abortions unless the mother's life was in danger, banned the use of public buildings for performing abortions, and required doctors performing abortions after 20 weeks of pregnancy to perform tests to determine whether the fetus could live outside the womb. In reference to *Roe v. Wade*, the 1973 decision that recognized a constitutional right to abortion, the majority held that "to the extent indicated in our opinion, we would modify and narrow *Roe* and succeeding cases." (July 3)

Cases accepted for the 1989-90 term included 3 abortion cases, one church-state case, and the Supreme Court's first "right-to-die" case. Some 80 cases were carried over from the 1988-89 term.

Major Actions of the 101st Congress, 1989

(For further information, see *Congress, Chronology,* and *Addenda.*)

Vice President George Bush presided over the opening of the 101st Congress on Jan. 4, 1989, and certified his own election as president.

Legislation Passed by Congress and Signed or Vetoed by Pres. Bush

Whistleblower Protection. Legislation aiming to protect federal employees from retaliation if they reported fraud and abuse in their agencies was signed by Pres. Bush, April 10. A previous version had been vetoed in Oct. 1988 by then-Pres. Ronald Reagan. The main revisions: (1) Whistleblowers would have to prove only that their whistleblowing activity was a "contributing factor" in steps taken against them, rather than having to prove that it was a "substantial" or "predominant" factor; (2) The agencies would have to give "clear and convincing evidence" that they would have taken the same personnel action against the employee despite the whistleblowing activity. In addition, whistleblowers could seek court appeal of their own cases, and would be guaranteed confidentiality. The final version was adopted unanimously by both Houses of Congress, the Senate on Mar. 16 and the House on Mar. 21.

Minimum Wage. Pres. George Bush cast his first veto, June 13, rejecting a bill that would have increased the minimum wage from $3.35 an hour to $4.55 an hour. He favored an increase to $4.25, contending that the greater increase would result in the loss of jobs for young people. He also objected to a provision limiting to 60 days the period in which an employer could pay a wage below the minimum. He favored a 6-month period. The House failed to override the veto, June 14, in a 247-178 vote.

Supplemental Spending. A bill to provide $3.2 billion in supplemental funds for fiscal 1989 was signed by Pres. Bush, June 30. The major items: $1.2 billion for the Veterans Affairs Dept., $892 million for guaranteed student loans, $342 million to restore funds used for fighting forest fires the previous summer, $125 million for contributions to United Nations peacekeeping forces, $100 million to contend with increased Soviet immigration, and $6.6 million in subsides for continued airplane service to rural areas. There was also a provision that allotted $7.3 million to help pay for the cleanup of the Alaska oil spill. Controversy over antidrug funding was resolved in a compromise whereby $75 million was allotted, rather than the original $822

(continued)

million. It was approved by a Senate voice vote, June 22, and by a 318-6 House vote, June 23.

Savings and Loan Rescue. Thrift industry bailout legislastion was signed by Pres. Bush, Aug. 9, with the final bill closely resembling the original proposal he submitted in Feb. It would provide some $166 billion over 10 years to close or merge insolvent thrift institutions, with some three-fourths of the total amount supplied by U.S. taxpayers. Over 30 years, the savings and loan industry bailout was expected to cost more than $300 billion, with $225 million paid by taxpayers. Under the legislation: tangible capital would have to equal 1.5% of thrift assets within four months, and 3% of assets by the end of 1994; commercial bank deposit insurance premiums would increase to $1.50 from $0.80 for each $1,000 of deposits, while savings and loan premiums would rise to $2.30 from $2.08 per $1,000; thrifts would be barred from investing directly in high-yield junk bonds, and would have to increase their mortgage-related investments to 70% of their portfolios from 60%. The Resolution Funding Corps, a government-sponsored enterprise created to finance the thrift rescue, would sell over $300 billion in real estate owned by insolvent thrifts. The Senate cleared the bill by a 17-7 standing vote, the remaining members already on their summer recess. The House approved, 201-175, in a roll call vote.

Other Legislation

Child Care. Legislation that greatly increased the federal government's role in providing child care assistance was approaching completion in Congress, Oct. 9. Pres. Bush had originally proposed legislation that would cost an estimated $2.5 billion a year by 1993 through an income tax credit for lower-income families. His proposal did not include direct spending for day care centers, but did include a $250 million increase in spending for the Head Start Program of preschool education. Two Democratic bills, calling for expanding tax credits and also for grants to the states to provide money for direct assistance for child care, were estimated to cost from $10.3 billion to more than $14 billion over 4 years. A House plan to expand tax credits alone, which was supported by Pres. Bush, failed the first week of Oct., 285-140, in the House. Another plan supported by the Bush administration had been previously rejected by the Senate. A House and Senate conference committee were working toward reconciling differences in 2 Democratic versions of the bill passed by the House in early Oct. with a measure adopted by the Senate in June. The measures approved in both the House and Senate created a system of tax credits combined with increased grants to the states for child care. However, the Bush administration expressed opposition to several provisions, including one that would require states to meet federal quality standards of care that Republicans maintained would duplicate state regulations and create unnecessary bureaucracy. A Presidential veto was a possibility.

Lawmakers' Access to C.I.A. Files. The House voted, Oct. 12, 369-31, to grant lawmakers broad access to the Central Intelligence Agency's most private analysis of its own problems. The Senate was preparing to vote on a similar bill. The legislation was part of a bill authorizing the fiscal 1990 budget for intelligence agencies. The provision would require the C.I.A. to submit, at the request of the intelligence committee of either house of Congress, any audits or investigative or other reports undertaken by the agency's inspector general. Both intelligence committees already reviewed the inspector general's reports about C.I.A. violations of law, but Congress reportedly had experienced little success in obtaining reports concerning mismanagement and waste.

Flag Desecration Ban. The House of Representatives approved, Oct. 12, 371-43, legislation outlawing flag desecration, as amended by the Senate. The legislation declared that burning or otherwise defacing a flag was punishable by a fine and imprisonment of up to one year. The measure was one of the responses to the Supreme Court decision in June that flag-burning was a form of speech protected by the Constitution. Pres. Bush soon announced his support for a constitutional amendment to overturn that ruling. Democratic leaders who objected to the proposed amendment offered the above legislation instead, aiming to protect the flag while satisfying the Supreme Court's First Amendment concerns. The White House did not say Pres. Bush would veto the measure. It was suggested that he might permit the bill to become law without his signature. On Oct. 19, the Senate rejected a proposed constitutional amendment to outlaw desecration of the flag.

Medicare Physicians' Fees. Heading for the Senate, as of Oct. 12, was a measure approved the first week of Oct. by the House and the Senate Finance Committee, which would replace the current Medicare practice of paying doctors on the basis of "customary, prevailing and reasonable fees" with a standard based on the total costs of the services provided, including the costs of a doctor's training and equipment and the relative value of the technical skills needed. The measure would apply only to what the government paid doctors to treat 33 million elderly people under Medicare.

Aid for Abortions. The House voted, 216-206, on Oct. 11, to allow the federal government to pay for abortions for poor women whose pregnancies resulted from incest or rape. This was an important policy reversal campaigned for by abortion rights advocates following the Supreme Court's decision in July to give states new latitude to restrict abortion. The new measure would permit the government to pay for poor women's abortions only "when such rape or incest has been reported promptly to a law enforcement agency or public health service." The measure went to the Senate, where it was expected to win final passage. Pres. Bush said, Oct. 13, that he saw room for some "flexibility" over the interpretation of the measure. However, on Oct. 21, he vetoed it.

Smoking Ban. House and Senate negotiators agreed, Oct. 16, to prohibit smoking on all commercial airline flights within the contiental U.S. and on most flights to Hawaii and Alaska. This would expand current rules banning smoking on flights of two hours or less, about 80 percent of all flights. The Senate voted to ban all smoking a few weeks earlier. The measure was said to be virtually certain to be passed by the House and sent to Pres. Bush.

Deficit Reduction. The Senate approved, 87-7, on Oct. 13, a $14 billion plan to reduce the federal budget deficit. Democratic and Republican leaders compromised by agreeing to limit the crucial budget legislation for fiscal 1990 to raising revenue and reducing spending, eliminating program expansions that members of both parties had desired. Provisions that were jettisoned included Medicare reform, child care assistance, improvements in benefits for low-income women and children, an increase in the earnings limit for Social Security recipients and tax credits for low-income housing. The package went to the House, which, the previous week, had approved its own $11 billion measure to cut the deficit. It was believed that House negotiators would not accept a bill with provisions solely devised by the Senate. The temporary cut in the capital gains tax rate was one of the measures included in the House version but not in the Senate version of the deficit reduction plan.

How a Bill Becomes a Law

1. A Senator or Representative introduces a bill by sending it to the clerk of the House, who assigns it a number and title. This procedure is termed the *first reading*. The clerk then refers the bill to the appropriate Senate or House committee.

2. If the committee opposes the bill, they immediately *table*, or kill it. Otherwise, the committee holds hearings to listen to opinions and facts offered by members and other interested people. The committee then debates the bill and possibly offers amendments. A vote is taken, and if favorable, the bill is sent back to the clerk of the House.

3. The clerk reads the bill to the House. This is termed the *second reading*. Members may then debate the bill and suggest amendments.

4. *The third reading* is simply by title, and the bill is put to a voice or roll call vote.

5. The bill then goes to the other house, where it may be defeated, or passed with or without amendments. If defeated, the bill dies. If passed with amendments, a

joint Congressional committee works out the differences and arrives at a compromise.

6. After its final passage by both houses, the bill is sent to the President. If he signs it, the bill becomes a law. However, he may *veto* the bill by refusing to sign it and sending it back to the house where it originated, with his reasons for the veto.

7. The President's objections are then read and debated, and a roll-call vote taken. If the bill receives less than a two-thirds vote, it is defeated. If it receives at least two-thirds, it is sent to the other house. If that house also passes it by at least two-thirds, the President's veto is *overridden*, and the bill becomes a law.

8. If the President wishes neither to sign nor to veto the bill, he may retain it for 10 days—not including Sunday—after which it automatically becomes a law even without his signature. However, if Congress has adjourned within those 10 days, the bill is automatically killed; this indirect rejection is termed a *pocket veto*.

Historical Anniversaries

1965—25 Years Ago

Lyndon B. Johnson was inaugurated as the 36th U.S. president. In his State of the Union address, he outlined anti-poverty programs that would create a "Great Society."

The Vietnam War was "Americanized," with a policy of bombing North Vietnam, and the first full-scale combat offensive by U.S. troops. The USSR admitted supplying arms to Hanoi. North Vietnam Leader Ho Chi Minh rejected peace talks with the U.S. Pres. Johnson announced a doubling of draft calls, and the 23,000 U.S. forces in Vietnam at the end of 1964 rose to 180,000 by the end of 1965.

Charles De Gaulle was elected president of France.

Ian Smith, head of the white-minority government of Rhodesia, unilaterally declared his county's independence from Britain. The British governor at Salisbury declared Smith and his government deposed; London ordered economic sanctions against Rhodesia.

Rev. Martin Luther King, Jr. launched a voter registration drive in Selma, Ala. Following demonstrations, arrests, and "Bloody Sunday," when peaceful marchers were attacked by police with tear gas, whips, and nightsticks, the campaign concluded with a "freedom march" of 25,000 people from Selma to Montgomery, the capital. Outside Montgomery, a civil rights activist was shot and killed by Ku Klux Klansmen. Pres. Johnson appealed to Congress for a voting rights law, which was soon enacted; federal examiners began registering voters in Alabama, Louisiana, and Mississippi.

Malcolm X, head of the Organization of Afro-American Unity, was shot and killed. It was not discovered whether his killers were members of the Black Muslim sect from which he had broken a year earlier.

In Watts, a section of Los Angeles, more than 10,000 blacks burned and looted some 500 square

blocks; 15,000 police and Natl. Guardsmen were called in, 34 people killed, nearly 4,000 arrested, and more than 200 businesses destroyed.

Federal legislation liberalized unemployment compensation, expanded employment opportunities for the young, and extended the food stamp program.

Medicaid and Medicare were created, as amendments to the Social Security Act. Medicaid used federal, state, and local money to underwrite medical care for the poor; Medicare, part of the Social Security system, was the first U.S. government-operated health insurance system for the elderly.

Congress founded a Natl. Clearinghouse for Smoking and Health, and ordered that cigarette packages be labeled "Caution: Cigarette smoking may be hazardous to your health."

The U.S. Dept. of Transportation, and the U.S. Department of Housing and Urban Affairs (HUD) were established.

The U.S. production of soft-top convertibles peaked at 507,000 for the 1965 model year.

Unsafe at Any Speed, by consumer advocate Ralph Nader, detailed defects in American cars, and criticized manufacturers for attending to speed and style over safety.

The greatest power failure in history blacked out most of seven states and Ontario, affecting 30 million people.

The miniskirt—6 inches above the knee—designed by Mary Quant, of London, made its first appearance.

Diet Pepsi was introduced.

Books: *The Psychedelic Reader*, by Timothy Leary; *The Autobiography of Malcolm X*, by Malcolm X and

(continued)

Alex Haley; *Everything That Rises Must Converge*, by Flannery O'Connor (posthumously); *The Painted Bird*, by Jerzy Kosinski; *God Bless You, Mr. Rosewater*, by Kurt Vonnegut, Jr.; *The Magus*, by John Fowles; *Thunderball*, by Ian Fleming; *77 Dream Songs* (poetry), by John Berryman.

Art: "Campbell's Tomato Soup Can" by Andy Warhol; "Self-Portrait," by Picasso; "Op Art."

Theater: "Loot," by Joe Orton; "The Odd Couple," by Neil Simon, with Walter Matthau and Art Carney; "On a Clear Day You Can See Forever"; "Man of La Mancha."

Pop music: "(I Can't Get No) Satisfaction," by the Rolling Stones; "Yesterday," and "Michelle," by the Beatles; "Sounds of Silence," by Paul Simon and Art Garfunkel; "I Got You Babe," by Sonny and Cher; "Like a Rolling Stone," by Bob Dylan.

Movies: David Lean's "Doctor Zhivago," with Omar Shariff, Julie Christie; Sidney Lumet's "The Pawnbroker," with Rod Steiger; "Cat Ballou," with Jane Fonda, Lee Marvin; John Schlesinger's "Darling," with Julie Christie; Federico Fellini's "Juliet of the Spirits," with Giuletta Massini; Michelangelo Antonioni's "Red Desert."

1940—50 Years Ago

France, Belgium, the Netherlands, Luxembourg, Denmark, Norway, and Romania fell to the Germans.

Neville Chamberlain resigned, and Winston Churchill was elected British prime minister. "I have nothing to offer but blood, toil, tears, and sweat," Churchill said. He set the nation's objective: "Victory: victory at all costs, victory in spite of all terror, victory however long and hard the road may be: for without victory there is no survival."

Hitler's Luftwaffe intensified the Blitzkrieg (lightning war) in London; the RAF began the night-bombing of Germany.

The Axis was created at Berlin, joining Germany, Italy, and Japan in a 10-year military and economic alliance; later in the year, Hungary and Romania joined.

Soviet Russia took 16,173 square miles of Finland, and the Baltic nations of Estonia, Latvia, and Lithuania, with German concurrence

The Russian revolutionary Leo Trotsky was killed in Mexico on Stalin's orders.

The Popular Democratic Party came to power in Puerto Rico with the election of party founder Luis Muñoz Marín as president of the Senate.

Franklin D. Roosevelt was re-elected to an unprecedented third term as U.S. president, defeating Republican Wendell L. Willkie.

The first peacetime military draft in U.S. history began.

The Alien Registration Act (Smith Act) mandated the fingerprinting of aliens and made it illegal to advocate the overthrow of the U.S. government or to belong to any group advocating this.

A giant cyclotron was built at the Univ. of California, for producing mesotrons from atomic nuclei.

The first transuranium element was discovered at the Univ. of California, Berkeley.

The world's first electron microscope was demonstrated at RCA Laboratories, Camden, N.J.

The Lascaux caves, whose wall drawings of humans dated from 16,000 years earlier, were found by schoolboys near Periguex, France.

The RH blood factor was discovered by Karl Landsteiner, with Alexander S. Wiener, at the Rockefeller Institute, N.Y.

A continuous coal-digging machine was developed by the Consolidation Coal Co.

The Pennsylvania Turnpike, the first tunneled U.S. superhighway, was completed; as was the Arroyo Seco Parkway, the first Los Angeles freeway.

The first FM radio station was begun in Chicago.

A freeze-drying process for food preservation was discovered.

The first Social Security checks were processed.

Meat wrapped in cellophane was sold for the first time, at the A&P.

McDonald hamburger stands began in a drive-in opened near Pasadena, Calif.

M&M candy began, as a candy-coated chocolate produced for the U.S. military.

Tiffany & Co. moved from 37th Street to the first fully air-conditioned store of any kind, on Fifth Avenue at 57th Street.

Gourmet magazine was founded.

The first nylon stockings were sold in the U.S

"Brenda Starr," a cartoon strip by Dale Messick, began publication.

Books: *For Whom the Bell Tolls*, by Ernest Hemingway; *You Can't Go Home Again*, by Thomas Wolfe (posthumously); *The Power and the Glory*, by Graham Greene; *Native Son*, by Richard Wright; *My Name Is Aram* (stories), by William Saroyan; *Cantos* (poetry) by Ezra Pound.

Painting: "The Romanian Blouse," by Matisse; "Sky Blue," by Kandinsky; "Circus Caravan," by Max Beckmann; "Stump in Red Hills," by Georgia O'Keeffe; "The Hailstorm," by Thomas Hart Benton; "Death and Fire," by Paul Klee.

Theater: "The Male Animal," by James Thurber and Elliott Nugent; "There Shall Be No Night," by Robert Sherwood; "The Fifth Column," by Ernest Hemingway and Benjamin Glazer; "George Washington Slept Here," by George S. Kaufman and Moss Hart; "My Sister Eileen," by Joseph A. Fields and Jerome Chodorov. Musicals: "Cabin in the Sky," with Ethel Waters, Todd Duncan, Dooley Wilson, Reg Ingram; "Panama Hattie," with Ethel Merman; "Pal Joey," with Gene Kelly.

Music: "Les Illuminations" song cycle, by Benjamin Britten; "Concerto for Violin and Orchestra," by Paul Hindemith; "Divertimento for String Orchestra," by Bela Bartok; "Concerto for Violin and Orchestra" and "Kammerosimphonie No. 2," by Arnold Schoenberg.

Pop music: "The Last Time I Saw Paris," "Tuxedo Junction," "Beat Me, Daddy, Eight to the Bar," "Blueberry Hill," "Back in the Saddle Again," "You Are My Sunshine."

Radio: "Truth or Consequences," a giveaway quiz show, was created and emceed by Ralph Edwards. The Metropolitan Opera of the Air, and the Bell Telephone Hour began.

Movies: John Ford's "The Grapes of Wrath," with Henry Fonda, Jane Darwell; George Cukor's "The Philadelphia Story," with Katharine Hepburn, Cary Grant, James Stewart; Raoul Walsh's "They Drive by Night," with George Raft, Humphrey Bogart, Ann Sheridan, Ida Lupino; Preston Sturges's "The Great McGinty," with Brian Donlevy; "Kitty Foyle," with Ginger Rogers, Dennis Morgan; "Pride and Prejudice," with Laurence Olivier, Greer Garson, Edna May Oliver; "The Thief of Bagdad," with Sabu; "The Bank Dick," with W.C. Fields, Mae West; Walt Disney's "Fantasia," and "Pinocchio."

1890—100 Years Ago

Idaho became the 43rd state, Wyoming the 44th.

Congress passed the Sherman Anti-Trust Act, to combat business monopolies and unfair restraints on competition.

The United Mine Workers was founded, and soon affiliated with the American Federation of Labor.

Cattlemen and sheepmen engaged in open conflict in the western states.

The Battle of Wounded Knee, in which some 350 men, women, and children were killed by the 7th Cavalry, ended the last major Indian resistance to white settlement in America.

Mississippi's 1890 constitution specified that a prospective voter could be required to read and interpret any of its provisions. Used to disenfranchise the black population, the constitution became the model for other southern states.

Yosemite National Park and Sequoia National Park were created by Acts of Congress.

The Daughters of the American Revolution, and the Colonial Dames of America were founded.

The "Gibson Girl," by illustrator Charles Dana Gibson, made her first appearance, in *Life* magazine.

The first tetanus antitoxin and the first diphtheria antitoxin were produced by a Berlin bacteriologist, Emil von Behring.

Rubber gloves were first used in surgery, at Johns Hopkins Hospital, in Baltimore.

The first commercial dry cell battery was introduced, under the name of Ever Ready, by the National Carbon Company.

Milk was pasteurized by law in many U.S. communities.

Peanut butter was invented by a St. Louis physician as a health food.

The first aluminum saucepan was produced, by Henry W. Avery, in Cleveland.

Prince Otto von Bismark was forced to resign as Germany's prime minister.

The Grand Duchy of Luxembourg split from the Netherlands.

Books: *The Kreutzer Sonata,* by Leo Tolstoy; *The Picture of Dorian Gray,* by Oscar Wilde; *Hunger,* by Knut Hamsun; *Poems by Emily Dickinson* (posthumously); *The Lake Isle of Inisfree* (poetry), by W.B. Yeats; *The Golden Bough* (vol. 1), by anthropologist James G. Frazer; *The Principles of Psychology,* by William James; *How the Other Half Lives,* by Jacob Riis.

Theater; "Hedda Gabler," by Henrik Ibsen. Ballet: "The Sleeping Beauty," music by Tchaikovsky. Opera: "Cavalleria Rusticana," by Mascagni; "Prince Igor," by Borodin, Rimski-Korsakov, and Glazunov; "The Trojans," by Berlioz.

Art: "Poplars," by Monet; "The Cardplayers," by Cezanne; "A Field Under a Starry Sky," and "Crows Over the Wheat Fields," by van Gogh.

Sports: Pitcher Cy Young signed with the Cleveland Indians of the National League. The first Army-Navy football game was played, Annapolis beating West Point, 24-0.

1790—200 Years Ago

King Louis XVI of France accepted the constitution drafted by French revolutionists.

Philadelphia was named the U.S. capital, but later in the year a new capital site was selected on the banks of the Potomac River. Pres. Washington appointed Pierre L'Enfant, a French-American engineer, to design the federal city and the Capitol building.

The U.S. Supreme Court held its first session.

The first U.S. patent office was established.

The Indian Nonintercourse Act prohibited taking land from Indian tribes without congressional approval.

Lavoisier published his *Table of Thirty-One Chemical Elements.*

Mozart wrote the opera "Cosi fan tutte."

Robert Burns wrote the poem "Tam O'Shanter."

1690—300 Years Ago

Calcutta was founded by an East India Company administrator, Job Charnock.

Dutch mariners smuggled coffee plants from the Arab port of Mocha, planted some in the Java colony and sent others to Amsterdam's botanical gardens.

Nantucket colonists began an offshore whaling industry.

John Locke published "An Essay Concerning Human Understanding."

1590—400 Years Ago

The compound microscope was invented by Zacharias Janssen, a Dutch optician.

The first three books of Edmund Spenser's poem

"The Faerie Queen" were published.

El Greco painted "St. Jerome."

1490—500 Years Ago

Portuguese explorers followed the Congo for some 200 miles, converted the king of the Congo Empire to Christianity, and established a post at São Salvador.

The first orphanages were founded in Italy and Holland.

Botticelli completed his painting "The Annunciation."

1290—700 Years Ago

The Ottoman Empire was founded.

Lisbon University was established.

Eyeglasses to correct faulty vision were invented in Italy.

Dante wrote *La Vita Nuova,* an autobiographical account in 31 poems, of his love, from first sight, for Beatrice.

890—1,100 Years Ago

King Alfred the Great extended the power of his courts, established a regular English navy and militia,

and instituted fairs and markets.

ECONOMICS

U.S. Budget Receipts and Outlays—1985-1988

Source: U.S. Treasury Department, Financial Management Service
(Fiscal years end Sept. 30)
(millions of dollars)

Classification	Fiscal 1985[1]	Fiscal 1986	Fiscal 1987	Fiscal 1988
Net Receipts				
Individual income taxes	$334,560	$348,959	$392,557	$401,181
Corporation income taxes	61,331	63,143	83,926	94,195
Social insurance taxes and contributions:				
Federal old-age and survivors insurance	169,882	182,518	194,541	220,337
Federal disability insurance	16,348	17,711	18,861	18,889
Federal hospital insurance	44,871	51,335	55,992	59,859
Railroad retirement fund	2,213	2,103	3,634	3,743
Total employment taxes and contributions	**234,646**	**255,062**	**273,028**	**305,093**
Other insurance and retirement:				
Unemployment	25,758	24,098	25,575	24,584
Federal employees retirement	4,672	4,645	4,613	4,537
Civil service retirement and disability	87	96	102	122
Total social insurance taxes and contributions	**265,163**	**283,901**	**303,318**	**334,335**
Excise taxes	35,992	32,919	32,457	35,540
Estate and gift taxes	6,422	6,958	7,493	7,594
Customs duties	12,079	13,323	15,085	16,198
Deposits of earnings-Federal Reserve Banks	17,059	18,374	16,817	17,163
All other miscellaneous receipts	1,451	1,514	2,490	2,746
Net Budget Receipts	**$734,057**	**$769,091**	**$854,143**	**$908,953**
Net Outlays				
Legislative Branch	$1,610	$1,665	$1,812	$1,852
The Judiciary	966	1,069	1,178	1,137
Executive Office of the President:				
The White House Office	24	23	25	26
Office of Management and Budget	41	37	37	41
Total Executive Office	**111**	**107**	**109**	**121**
Funds appropriated to the President:				
International security assistance	9,295	10,371	6,820	4,273
Multinational assistance	1,763	1,838	1,306	1,498
Agency for International Development	1,208	1,220	1,294	1,404
International Development Assistance	3,008	3,121	2,673	2,980
Total funds appropriated to the President	**12,050**	**11,379**	**10,406**	**7,252**
Agriculture Department:				
Food stamp program	11,701	12,443	12,405	13,144
Farmer's Home Admin.	11,093	8,001	3,748	7,277
Total Agriculture Department	**55,523**	**58,666**	**49,593**	**44,003**
Commerce Department	2,140	2,083	2,156	2,279
Bureau of the Census	—	—	217	216
Defense Department:				
Military personnel	67,842	71,511	72,020	76,337
Operation and maintenance	72,348	75,259	76,178	84,480
Procurement	70,381	76,517	80,744	77,166
Research, development, test, evaluation	27,103	32,283	33,596	34,792
Military construction	4,260	5,067	5,853	5,874
Total Defense Department (military)	**245,371**	**265,636**	**273,938**	**281,940**
Defense Department (civil)	18,842	20,243	20,659	22,074
Education Department	16,682	17,673	16,800	18,246
Energy Department	10,586	11,025	10,688	11,161
Health and Human Services Department:				
Food and Drug Administration	418	417	422	463
National Institutes of Health	4,670	5,115	5,222	6,334
Public Health Service	8,866	9,504	9,886	11,408
Health Care Financing Adm.	113,359	119,307	130,472	144,654
Human Development Services	6,056	5,412	5,448	5,886
Total Health and Human Services Dept.	**132,103**	**143,252**	**148,893**	**158,991**
Social Security	183,434	190,684	202,422	214,178
Housing and Urban Development Department	28,720	14,139	15,464	18,956
Interior Department	4,826	4,791	5,045	5,152
Justice Department:				
Federal Bureau of Investigation	1,072	1,183	1,216	1,384
Total Justice Department	**3,586**	**3,768**	**4,333**	**5,426**
Labor Department:				
Unemployment Trust Fund	23,826	21,819	20,527	18,598
Total Labor Department	**23,893**	**24,141**	**23,453**	**21,870**
State Department	2,645	2,865	2,788	3,421
Transportation Department	25,022	27,365	25,431	26,404
Treasury Department:				
Internal Revenue Service	6,746	7,188	7,513	9,363
Interest on the public debt	178,945	190,151	195,390	214,145
Total Treasury Department	**164,987**	**179,189**	**180,345**	**202,472**
Environmental Protection Agency	4,511	4,869	4,903	4,872
General Services Administration	−214	286	74	−285
National Aeronautics and Space Administration	7,251	7,403	7,591	9,092
Office of Personnel Management	23,727	23,955	26,966	29,191
Small Business Administration	680	490	−72	−54

(continued)

Classification	Fiscal 1985[1]	Fiscal 1986	Fiscal 1987	Fiscal 1988
Net Receipts				
Small Business Administration.............	680	490	−72	−54
Veterans Administration	26,333	26,536	26,952	29,244
Independent agencies:				
Action	129	154	159	153
Board for International Broadcasting.......	97	127	156	194
Corporation for Public Broadcasting.......	151	160	200	214
District of Columbia	548	530	560	550
Equal Employment Opportunity Commission ..	158	159	158	176
Export-Import Bank of the United States	−384	−1,167	−2,300	−894
Federal Communications Commission......	94	92	79	52
Federal Deposit Insurance Corporation	−1,942	705	−1,438	2,146
Federal Emergency Management Agency ...	469	656	531	352
Federal Home Loan Bank Board.........	414	1,071	4,755	8,088
Federal Trade Commission	65	62	66	69
Intragovernmental Agencies	278	218	203	200
Legal Services Corporation............	300	305	309	306
National Archives & Record Adm.	100	96	96	102
National Foundation on the Arts and Humanities	317	320	310	322
National Labor Relations Board	134	132	127	132
National Science Foundation	1,313	1,550	1,562	1,665
Nuclear Regulatory Commission.........	468	421	393	232
Railroad Retirement Board	4,129	3,980	4,196	4,147
Securities and Exchange Commission......	103	104	108	126
Smithsonian Institution...............	226	224	242	260
Tennessee Valley Authority............	1,010	906	1,091	1,089
U.S. Information Agency	694	780	830	843
Total independent agencies	9,580	11,865	14,266	23,361
Undistributed offsetting receipts	−58,973	−64,914	−72,400	−78,473
Net Budget Outlays.................	945,987	990,231	1,003,804	1,064,055
Less net receipts..................	734,057	769,091	854,143	908,953
Deficit........................	−211,931	−221,140	−149,661	−155,102

(1) In accordance with the Balanced Budget and Emergency Deficit Control Act of 1985, all former off-budget entities are now presented on-budget. The Federal Financing Bank activities are now shown as separate accounts under the agencies that use the FFB to finance their programs. In addition, 2 Social Security trust funds (Federal old-age survivors insurance and Federal disability insurance trust funds) have been moved off-budget.

U.S. Net Receipts and Outlays

Source: U.S. Treasury Department; annual statements for year ending June 30[1] (thousands of dollars)

Yearly average	Receipts	Outlays	Yearly average	Receipts	Outlays	Yearly average	Receipts	Outlays
1789-1800[1]	5,717	5,776	1871-1875	336,830	287,460	1911-1915	710,227	720,252
1801-1810[2]	13,056	9,086	1876-1880	288,124	255,598	1916-1920[6]	3,483,652	8,065,333
1811-1820[2]	21,032	23,943	1881-1885	366,961	257,691	1921-1925	4,306,673	3,578,989
1821-1830[2]	21,928	16,162	1886-1890	375,448	279,134	1926-1930	4,069,138	3,182,807
1831-1840[2]	30,461	24,495	1891-1895	352,891	363,599	1931-1935[4]	2,770,973	5,214,874
1841-1850[2]	28,545	34,097	1896-1900	434,877	457,451	1936-1940[4]	4,960,614	10,192,367
1851-1860	60,237	60,163	1901-1905	559,481	535,559	1941-1945[4]	25,951,137	66,037,928
1861-1865	160,907	683,785	1906-1910	628,507	639,178	1946-1950[5][7]	39,047,243	42,334,534
1866-1870	447,301	377,642						

Fiscal Year	Receipts	Outlays	Fiscal year	Receipts	Outlays	Fiscal year	Receipts	Outlays
1955	60,389,744	64,569,973	1974	264,847,484	268,342,952	1981	602,612,295	660,544,033
1960	77,763,460	76,539,413	1975	281,037,466	324,641,586	1982	617,766,000	728,424,000
1964	89,458,664	97,684,375	1976	300,005,077	365,610,129	1983	600,562,000	795,916,000
1965	93,071,797	96,506,904	1976 Trans[3]	81,772,766	94,472,996	1984	666,457,000	841,800,000
1968[9]	153,675,705	172,803,186	1977[3]	356,861,331	401,896,376	1985[10]	734,057,000	945,987,000
1970	193,843,791	194,968,258	1978	401,997,000	450,758,000	1986	769,091,000	990,231,000
1971	188,332,129	210,652,667	1979	465,954,656	493,607,095	1987	854,143,000	1,003,804,000
1972[8]	215,262,639	238,285,907	1980	520,056,012	579,602,970	1988	908,953,000	1,064,055,000
1973	232,191,842	246,603,359						

(1) Average for period March 4, 1789, to Dec. 31, 1800. (2) Years ended Dec. 31, 1801 to 1842; average for 1841-1850 is for the period Jan. 1, 1841, to June 30, 1850. (3) Effective fiscal year 1977, fiscal year is reckoned Oct. 1-Sept. 30; transition quarter covers July 1, 1976-Sept. 30, 1976. (4) Expenditures for years 1932 through 1946 have been revised to include Government corps. (wholly owned) etc. (net). (5) Effective January 3, 1949, amounts refunded by the Government, principally for the overpayment of taxes, are being reported as deductions from total receipts rather than as expenditures. Also, effective July 1, 1948, payments to the Treasury, principally by wholly owned Government corporations for retirement of capital stock and for disposition of earnings, are excluded in reporting both budget receipts and expenditures. Neither of these changes affects the size of the budget surplus or deficit. Beginning 1931 figures in each case have been adjusted accordingly for comparative purposes. (6) Figures for 1918 through 1946 are revised to exclude statutory debt retirement (sinking fund, etc.). (7) Excludes $3 billion transferred to Foreign Economics Corporation Trust Fund, and includes $3 billion representing expenditures made from the FEC Trust Fund. (8) Effective fiscal year 1972 loan repayments and loan disbursements will be netted against expenditures and known as outlays. (9) From 1968, figures include trust funds (e.g. Social Security). (10) Since 1985, off-budget items are incl.; some social security trust funds moved off-budget.

Third World Debt

Outstanding external debt of Third World nations totaled over $1.3 trillion at the end of 1988, according to a survey by the World Bank. The following were the leading debtor nations in 1988.

Country	Dollars	Country	Dollars	Country	Dollars
Brazil	120 billion	Philippines	30 billion	Peru.............	19 billion
Mexico	107 billion	Yugoslavia	22 billion	Colombia.........	17 billion
Argentina	60 billion	Morocco	22 billion	Cote D'Ivoire	14 billion
Venezuela	35 billion	Chile	21 billion	Ecuador	11 billion
Nigeria	31 billion				

Public Debt of the U.S.

Source: U.S. Treasury Department, Financial Management Service, Bureau of the Census

Fiscal year	Debt (billions)	Per. cap. (dollars)	Interest paid (billions)	Pct. of federal outlays	Fiscal year	Debt (billions)	Per. cap. (dollars)	Interest paid (billions)	Pct. of federal outlays
1870	$2.4	$61.06	—	—	1973	457.3	2,164	24.2	9.8
1880	2.0	41.60	—	—	1974	474.2	2,223	29.3	10.9
1890	1.1	17.80	—	—	1975	533.2	2,475	32.7	9.8
1900	1.2	16.60	—	—	1976	620.4	2,852	37.1	10.0
1910	1.1	12.41	—	—	1977	698.8	3,170	41.9	10.2
1920	24.2	228	—	—	1978	771.5	3,463	48.7	10.6
1930	16.1	131	—	—	1979	826.5	3,669	59.8	11.9
1940	43.0	325	1.0	10.5	1980	907.7	3,985	74.9	12.7
1945	258.7	1,849	3.8	4.1	1981	997.9	4,338	95.6	14.1
1950	256.1	1,688	5.7	13.4	1982	1,142.0	4,913	117.4	15.7
1955	272.8	1,651	6.4	9.4	1983	1,377.2	5,870	128.8	15.9
1960	284.1	1,572	9.2	10.0	1984	1,572.3	6,640	153.8	18.1
1965	313.8	1,613	11.3	9.6	1985	1,823.1	7,598	178.9	18.9
1970	370.1	1,814	19.3	9.9	1986	2,125.3	8,774	190.2	19.2
1971	397.3	1,921	21.0	10.0	1987	2,350.3	9,615	195.4	19.5
1972	426.4	2,037	21.8	9.4	1988	2,602.3	10,534	214.1	20.1

Note: Through 1976 the fiscal year ended June 30. From 1977 on, fiscal year ends Sept. 30.

Foreign Direct Investment in the U.S.

Source: Bureau of Economic Analysis; U.S. Commerce Department

(billions of dollars)

	1970	1975	1980	1985	1986	1987	1988
All Countries	13.2	27.6	83.0	184.6	220.4	271.7	328.8
Canada	3.1	5.3	12.1	17.1	20.3	24.0	27.3
Europe	9.5	18.5	54.4	121.4	144.1	186.0	216.4
Netherlands	2.1	5.3	19.1	37.0	40.7	49.1	48.9
Switzerland	1.5	2.1	5.0	10.5	12.0	14.6	15.8
United Kingdom	4.1	6.3	14.1	43.5	55.9	79.6	101.9
W. Germany	0.680	1.4	7.5	14.8	17.2	20.3	23.8
Japan	0.229	0.591	4.7	19.3	26.8	35.1	53.3
Middle East	—	—	—	—	—	4.9	5.8

Foreign Investment in U.S. Companies

Source: U.S. Commerce Dept.

Foreign investors spent $65 billion to buy or establish 1,012 businesses in 1988 according to the U.S. Commerce Department. This was an increase of 61 percent from 1987, and included 12 multibillion-dollar purchases. The leading foreign buyers in 1988 were Great Britain, $21.5 billion; Japan, $14.2 billion; and Canada, $10.4 billion.

The following is the dollar value of U.S. affiliates of foreign manufacturing companies as a percent of all U.S. businesses in manufacturing in 1977 and 1986, the most recent year available.

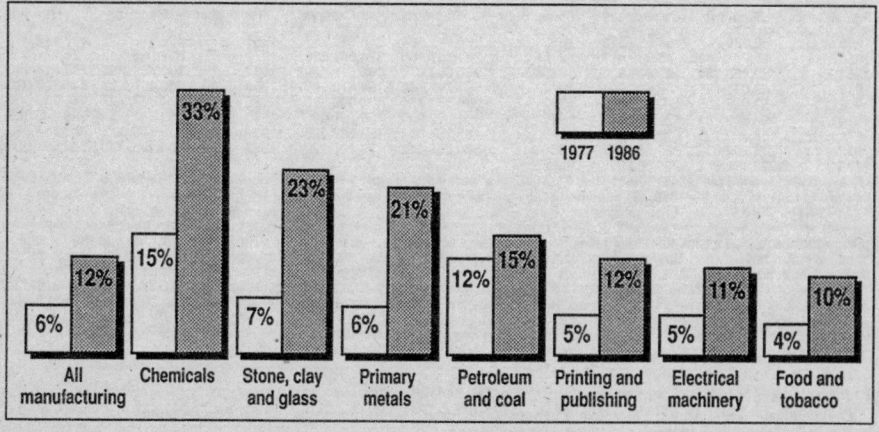

Foreign buying of American companies has skyrocketed in the 1980s. Direct investment in U.S. companies rose to $304.2 billion in 1988, from $90 billion in 1980.

The nations with the largest direct investment in the U.S. at the end of 1988 were Great Britain, 29 percent; The Netherlands, 17 percent; Japan, 16 percent; Canada, 8 percent; and West Germany, 7 percent.

U.S. International Transactions

Source: Bureau of Economic Analysis, U.S. Commerce Department

(millions of dollars)

	1960	1965	1970	1975	1980	1985	1987	1988
Exports of goods and services[1] . . .	**28,861**	**41,087**	**65,674**	**155,729**	**342,485**	**371,212**	**446,138**	**529,806**
Merchandise, adjusted, excluding military[2]	19,650	26,461	42,469	107,088	224,269	215,935	250,266	319,251
Transfers under U.S. military agency sales contracts	335	830	1,501	4,049	8,274	8,626	11,238	10,050
Travel	919	1,380	2,331	4,697	10,588	17,937	23,505	29,202
Passenger fares	175	271	544	1,039	2,591	4,388	5,546	8,860
Other transportation	1,607	2,175	3,125	5,840	11,618	14,674	16,999	18,930
Royalties and license fees[3]	837	1,534	2,331	4,300	7,085	5,995	9,070	10,735
Other private services from unaffiliated foreigners	570	714	1,294	2,920	5,158	13,948	22,959	24,331
U.S. Government miscellaneous services	153	285	332	446	398	878	526	672
Receipts of income on U.S. assets abroad:								
Direct investment	3,621	5,506	8,169	16,595	37,146	33,202	54,754	48,264
Other private receipts	646	1,421	2,671	7,644	32,798	50,131	44,638	52,840
U.S. Government receipts	349	510	907	1,112	2,562	5,499	5,331	6,672
Transfers of goods and services under U.S. military grant programs, net	**1,695**	**1,636**	**2,713**	**2,207**	**756**	**46**	**58**	**92**
Imports of goods and services . . .	**-23,670**	**-32,708**	**-59,901**	**-132,745**	**-333,020**	**-468,468**	**-575,626**	**-641,698**
Merchandise, adjusted, excluding military[2]	-14,758	-21,510	-39,866	-98,185	-249,749	-338,083	-409,766	-446,466
Direct defense expenditures	-3,087	-2,952	-4,855	-4,795	-10,511	-12,183	-14,095	-14,656
Travel	-1,750	-2,438	-3,980	-6,417	-10,397	-24,517	-26,000	-32,112
Passenger fares	-513	-717	-1,215	-2,263	-3,607	-6,671	-7,423	-7,872
Other transportation	-1,402	-1,951	-2,843	-5,708	-11,790	-15,643	-18,062	-19,641
Royalties and license fees[3]	-74	-135	-244	-472	-724	-891	-1,365	-2,048
Other private services	-593	-461	-827	-1,551	-2,909	-5,847	-11,390	-11,400
U.S. Government miscellaneous services	-254	-457	-576	-789	-1,214	-1,732	-1,891	-1,955
Payments of income on foreign assets in the U.S.								
Direct investment	-394	-657	-875	-2,234	-8,635	-6,079	-9,500	-16,748
Other private payments	-511	-942	-3,617	-5,788	-20,893	-35,516	-48,868	-59,746
U.S. Government payments	-332	-489	-1,024	-4,542	-12,592	-21,306	-24,052	-29,054
U.S. military grants of goods and services, net	**-1,695**	**-1,636**	**-2,713**	**-2,207**	**-756**	**-46**	**-53**	**-92**
Unilateral transfers (excl. military grants of goods and services), net	**-2,367**	**-2,948**	**-3,443**	**-4,868**	**-7,593**	**-15,426**	**-14,212**	**-14,656**
U.S. Government grants (excluding military grants of goods and services)	-1,672	-1,808	-1,736	-2,894	-4,731	-11,222	-10,149	-10,377
U.S. Government pensions and other transfers	-273	-463	-611	-1,068	-1,818	-2,138	-2,212	-2,491
Private remittances and other transfers	-423	-677	-1,096	-906	-1,044	-2,067	-1,851	-1,788
U.S. assets abroad, net (increase/ capital outflow (-))	**-4,099**	**-5,716**	**-9,337**	**-39,703**	**-86,118**	**-32,628**	**-76,218**	**-82,110**
U.S. official reserve assets, net . . .	2,145	1,225	2,481	-849	-8,155	-3,858	9,149	3,566
U.S. Government assets, other than official reserve assets, net	-1,100	-1,605	-1,589	-3,474	-5,162	-2,821	997	2,999
U.S. private assets, net	-5,144	-5,336	-10,229	-35,380	-72,802	-25,950	-86,363	-81,543
Foreign assets in U.S., net (increase/ capital inflow (+))	2,294	742	6,359	15,670	58,112	130,012	218,039	219,299
Statistical discrepancy (sum of above items with sign reversed)	-1,019	-157	-219	5,917	24,982	15,298	1,878	-10,641
Memoranda:								
Balance on merchandise trade	**5,191**	**8,378**	**5,773**	**22,984**	**9,466**	**-97,256**	**-129,488**	**-111,892**
Balance on goods and services .								
Balance on goods, services, and remittances	4,496	7,238	4,067	21,011	6,604	-100,460	-133,551	-116,171
Balance on current account	2,824	5,431	2,331	18,116	1,873	-112,692	-143,700	-126,548

(1) Excludes transfers of goods and services under U.S. military grant programs. (2) Excludes exports of goods under U.S. military agency sales contracts identified in Census export documents, excludes imports of goods under direct defense expenditures identified in Census import documents, and reflects various other adjustments. (3) Redefined in 1982.

U.S. Direct Investment Abroad in Selected Countries

Source: Bureau of Economic Analysis, U.S. Commerce Department

(millions of dollars)

	1986	1987	1988		1986	1987	1988
All countries	259,562	307,983	326,900	Portugal	278	412	425
Africa	4,313	4,488	4,603	Spain	2,612	3,789	4,368
Egypt	1,814	1,680	1,705	United Kingdom	35,692	42,031	47,991
Libya	196	310	312	Other Europe	23,693	26,177	25,730
Nigeria	575	1,159	1,342	Austria	386	714	1,167
Asia and Pacific	16,577	16,695	18,860	Finland	292	389	413
Hong Kong	3,980	4,390	5,028	Norway	3,626	3,844	3,834
India	446	439	457	Sweden	1,002	1,111	1,089
Indonesia	4,395	3,050	3,006	Switzerland	17,842	19,518	18,672
Malaysia	1,109	1,019	1,363	Turkey	242	207	193
Philippines	1,135	1,220	1,305	Other	302	394	362
Singapore	2,238	2,462	3,005	Japan	11,332	14,671	16,868
South Korea	800	1,003	1,302	South America	18,644	20,690	21,687
Taiwan	870	1,280	1,546	Argentina	2,919	2,673	2,390
Thailand	1,079	1,274	1,126	Brazil	9,187	10,288	11,810
Other	525	556	721	Chile	224	343	731
Australia	9,120	11,143	13,058	Colombia	2,033	3,241	2,429
Canada	49,994	58,377	61,244	Ecuador	468	466	448
Europe	122,165	146,243	152,232	Peru	1,131	1,084	1,064
European Communities	98,472	120,066	126,502	Venezuela	2,139	2,036	2,273
Belgium	5,229	6,757	7,224	Other	543	560	543
Denmark	1,113	1,091	1,191	Central America	9,571	11,657	12,441
France	8,857	11,771	12,495	Mexico	4,750	4,898	5,516
Germany, West	20,849	24,792	21,673	Panama	4,293	6,131	6,140
Greece	172	132	194	Middle East	4,590	4,589	4,090
Ireland	4,395	5,135	5,743	Israel	600	653	722
Italy	6,935	9,008	9,075	Saudi Arabia	1,972	2,140	2,047
Luxembourg	726	787	756	United Arab Emirates	857	703	680
Netherlands	11,618	14,361	15,367				

National Income by Industry

Source: Bureau of Economic Analysis, U.S. Commerce Department

(billions of dollars)

	1960	1965	1970	1975	1980	1987	1988
National income without capital consumption adjustment	428.6	583.6	835.1	1,315.0	2,263.9	3,638.3	3,952.8
Domestic industries	425.1	577.8	827.8	1,297.4	2,216.3	3,607.8	3,919.5
Private industries	371.6	500.8	695.4	1,088.3	1,894.5	3,078.5	3,352.6
Agriculture, forestry, fisheries	17.8	21.0	25.9	46.5	61.4	90.8	90.4
Mining	5.6	6.1	8.4	21.2	43.8	30.5	34.4
Construction	22.5	32.3	47.4	69.9	126.6	197.2	211.2
Manufacturing	125.3	171.6	215.6	317.5	532.1	718.7	788.6
Durable goods	73.4	105.6	127.7	185.0	313.7	422.9	455.0
Nondurable goods	52.0	66.1	87.9	132.5	218.4	295.8	333.6
Transportation, public utilities	35.8	47.0	64.4	101.1	177.3	278.7	300.2
Transportation	18.5	23.7	31.5	48.0	85.8	120.0	131.1
Communication	8.2	11.5	17.6	26.8	48.1	80.6	83.6
Electric, gas, and sanitary services	9.1	11.7	15.2	26.2	43.4	78.1	85.5
Wholesale trade	25.0	32.5	47.5	83.0	143.3	214.9	234.5
Retail trade	41.3	55.1	79.9	123.1	189.4	313.3	335.6
Finance, insurance, and real estate	51.3	67.4	96.4	143.9	279.5	520.0	568.8
Services	46.9	67.9	109.8	182.1	341.0	714.4	789.0
Government, government enterprises	53.5	76.9	132.4	209.1	321.8	529.3	566.9
Rest of the world	3.5	5.8	7.3	17.5	47.6	30.5	33.3

National Income by Type of Income

Source: Bureau of Economic Analysis, U.S. Commerce Department

(billions of dollars)

	1960	1965	1970	1975	1980	1987	1988
National income	424.9	585.2	832.6	1,289.1	2,203.5	3,665.4	3,972.6
Compensation of employees	296.7	399.8	618.3	948.7	1,638.2	2,690.0	2,907.6
Wages and salaries	272.8	363.7	551.5	814.7	1,372.0	2,249.4	2,429.0
Government	49.2	69.9	117.1	176.1	260.1	419.2	446.5
Other	223.7	293.8	434.3	638.6	1,111.8	1,830.1	1,982.5
Supplements to wages, salary	23.8	36.1	66.8	134.0	266.3	440.7	478.6
Employer contrib. for social ins.	12.6	18.3	34.3	68.0	127.9	227.8	249.7
Other labor income	11.2	17.8	32.5	65.9	138.4	212.8	228.9
Proprietors' income	52.1	65.1	80.2	125.4	180.7	311.6	327.8
Farm	11.6	13.0	14.7	25.4	20.5	41.6	39.8
Nonfarm	40.5	52.1	65.4	100.0	160.1	49.6	47.3
Rental income of persons	15.3	18.1	18.2	13.5	6.6	-8.0	-7.5
Corp. prof., with inv. adjust.	49.8	76.2	69.5	123.9	194.0	270.0	288.0
Corp. profits before tax	49.9	77.4	76.0	134.8	237.1	238.9	259.2
Corp. profits tax liability	22.7	30.9	34.4	50.9	84.8	-1.0	-1.5
Corp. profits after tax	27.2	46.5	41.7	83.9	152.3	32.2	30.3
Dividends	12.9	19.1	22.5	29.6	54.7	13.4	15.7
Undistributed profits	14.3	27.4	19.2	54.3	97.6	61.2	65.4
Inventory valuation adjustment	-.2	-1.2	-6.6	-11.0	-43.1	-47.9	-49.8
Net interest	11.3	20.9	41.2	83.8	200.9	298.7	328.6

Gross National Product, Net National Product, National Income, and Personal Income

Source: Bureau of Economic Analysis. U.S. Commerce Department
(billions of dollars)

	1960	1970	1975	1980	1987	1988
Gross national product	515.3	1,015.5	1,598.4	2,732.0	4,524.3	4,880.6
Less: Capital consumption allowances.	46.4	88.8	161.8	303.8	486.7	513.6
Equals: Net national product	468.9	926.6	1,436.6	2,428.1	4,037.6	4,367.1
Less: Indirect business tax and nontax liability .	45.3	94.0	140.0	213.3	367.8	393.5
Business transfer payments	2.0	4.1	7.4	12.1	26.7	29.0
Statistical discrepancy	−2.8	−1.1	2.5	4.9	−4.7	−9.6
Plus: Subsidies less current surplus of government enterprises	.4	2.9	2.4	5.7	17.6	18.5
Equals: National income	424.9	832.6	1,289.1	2,203.5	3,665.4	3,972.6
Less: Corporate profits with inventory valuation and capital consumption adjustment	49.5	74.7	117.6	177.2	298.7	328.6
Net interest	11.3	41.2	83.8	200.9	351.7	392.9
Contributions for social insurance	21.9	62.2	118.5	216.5	400.8	444.6
Wage accruals less disbursement	.0	.0	.1	.0	0	0
Plus: Government transfer payment to persons.	27.5	81.8	185.7	312.6	521.5	555.7
Personal interest income	24.9	69.3	122.5	271.9	·523.2	571.1
Personal dividend income	12.9	22.2	28.7	52.9	92.0	102.2
Business transfer payments	2.0	4.1	7.4	12.1	26.7	29.0
Equals: Personal income	409.4	831.8	1,313.4	2,258.5	3,777.6	4,064.5

Stock Exchanges
N.Y. Stock Exchange Transactions

Year	Yearly volumes Stock shares	Bonds par values	Year	Yearly volumes Stock shares	Bonds par values
1900	138,981,000	$579,293,000	1970	2,937,359,448	$4,494,864,600
1905	260,569,000	1,026,254,000	1975	4,693,427,000	5,178,300,000
1910	163,705,000	634,863,000	1980	11,352,294,000	5,190,304,000
1915	172,497,000	961,700,000	1981	11,853,740,659	5,733,071,000
1920	227,636,000	3,868,422,000	1982	16,458,036,768	7,155,443,000
1925	459,717,623	3,427,042,210	1983	21,589,576,997	7,572,315,000
1929	1,124,800,410	2,996,398,000	1984	23,071,031,447	6,982,291,000
1930	810,632,546	2,720,301,800	1985	27,510,706,353	9,046,453,000
1935	381,635,752	3,339,458,000	1986	35,680,016,341	10,475,399,000
1940	207,599,749	1,669,438,000	1987	47,801,308,660	9,726,244,000
1950	524,799,621	1,112,425,170	1988	40,438,346,358	7,594,644,000
1960	766,693,818	1,346,419,750			

American Stock Exchange Transactions

Year	Yearly volume Stock shares	Bonds[1] princ. amts.	Year	Yearly volume Stock shares	Bonds[1] princ. amts.	Year	Yearly volume Stock shares	Bonds[1] princ. amts.
1929	476,140,375	$513,551,000	1970	843,116,260	$641,270,000	1984	1,545,010,000	$371,990,000
1930	222,270,065	863,541,000	1980	1,626,072,625	355,723,000	1985	2,100,860,000	645,182,000
1940	42,928,337	303,902,000	1981	1,343,400,220	301,226,000	1986	2,978,540,000	810,264,000
1945	143,309,392	167,333,000	1982	1,485,831,536	325,240,000	1987	3,505,950,000	684,965,000
1950	107,792,340	47,549,000	1983	2,081,270,000	395,190,000	1988	2,515,210,000	604,950,000
1960	286,039,982	32,670,000						

(1) Corporate

Components of Dow Jones Industrial Average

Allied-Signal
Aluminum Co. of Amer.
American Express
AT&T
Bethlehem Steel
Boeing
Chevron
Coca-Cola
DuPont
Eastman Kodak
Exxon

General Electric
General Motors
Goodyear
IBM
International Paper
McDonald's
Merck
Minn. Mining & Manuf.
Navistar
Philip Morris

Primerica
Procter & Gamble
Sears Roebuck
Texaco
Union Carbide
United Technologies
USX Corp.
Westinghouse
Woolworth

Components of Dow Jones Transportation Average

AMR Corp.
Airborne Freight
Alaska Air
American President
Burlington Northern
CSX
Carolina Freight

Consolidated Freightways
Consolidated Rail
Delta Air Lines
Federal Express
Norfolk Southern
Pan Am
Ryder System

Santa Fe Southern Pacific
Southwest Air Lines
UAL
Union Pacific
USAir Group
XTRA Corp

Components of Dow Jones Utility Average

American Electric Power
Centerior Energy
Columbia Gas System
Commonwealth Edison
Consolidated Edison

Consolidated Natural Gas
Detroit Edison
Houston Industries
Niagara Mohawk Power
Pacific Gas & Electric

Panhandle Eastern
Peoples Energy
Philadelphia Electric
Public Service Enterprises
SCE

Dow Jones Industrial Average Since 1954

High		Year	Low		High		Year	Low	
Dec. 31	404.39	1954	Jan. 11	279.87	Jan. 11	1051.70	1973	Dec. 5	788.31
Dec. 30	488.40	1955	Jan. 17	388.20	Mar. 13	891.66	1974	Dec. 6	577.60
Apr. 6	521.05	1956	Jan. 23	462.35	July 15	881.81	1975	Jan. 2	632.04
July 12	520.77	1957	Oct. 22	419.79	Sept. 21	1014.79	1976	Jan. 2	858.71
Dec. 31	583.65	1958	Feb. 25	436.89	Jan. 3	999.75	1977	Nov. 2	800.85
Dec. 31	679.36	1959	Feb. 9	574.46	Sept. 8	907.74	1978	Feb. 28	742.12
Jan. 5	685.47	1960	Oct. 25	566.05	Oct. 5	897.61	1979	Nov. 7	796.67
Dec. 13	734.91	1961	Jan. 3	610.25	Nov. 20	1000.17	1980	Apr. 21	759.13
Jan. 3	726.01	1962	June 26	535.76	Apr. 27	1024.05	1981	Sept. 25	824.01
Dec. 18	767.21	1963	Jan. 2	646.79	Dec. 27	1070.55	1982	Aug. 12	776.92
Nov. 18	891.71	1964	Jan. 2	766.08	Nov. 29	1287.20	1983	Jan. 3	1027.04
Dec. 31	969.26	1965	June 28	840.59	Jan. 6	1286.64	1984	July 24	1086.57
Feb. 9	995.15	1966	Oct. 7	744.32	Dec. 16	1553.10	1985	Jan. 4	1184.96
Sept. 25	943.08	1967	Jan. 3	786.41	Dec. 2	1955.57	1986	Jan. 22	1502.29
Dec. 3	985.21	1968	Mar. 21	825.13	Aug. 25	2722.42	1987	Oct. 19	1738.74
May 14	968.85	1969	Dec. 17	769.93	Oct. 21	2183.50	1988	Jan. 20	1879.14
Dec. 29	842.00	1970	May 6	631.16	Sept. 1	2752.09	1989*	Oct. 9	2791.41
Apr. 28	950.82	1971	Nov. 23	797.97				*As of	10/9/89
Dec. 11	1036.27	1972	Jan. 26	889.15					

Most Active Common Stocks in 1988

New York Exchange		American Exchange		NASDAQ	
Stock	Volume (millions of shares)	Stock	Volume (millions of shares)	Stock	Volume (millions of shares)
AT&T	421.6	Wang Labs B	96.8	MCI	473.5
IBM	366.0	Texas Air	94.6	Intel	456.5
General Electric	354.4	Amdahl	82.4	Apple Computer	369.1
Exxon	349.2	Magma Copper	79.0	Seagate	235.6
Occidental Petroleum	335.6	Lorimar-Telepictures	77.1	Sun Microsystems	195.6
Southern Co.	323.3	Echo Bay Mines	58.4	Lotus	194.0
Texaco	313.4	Diasonics	50.1	Micro Tech	185.1
Pacific Gas and Electric	301.2	New York Times A	42.4	Tele-communications A	178.8
RJR Nabisco	287.6	First Australia Prime	39.5	Liz Claiborne	167.3
Ford Motor	284.5	BAT Industries	37.0	Miniscribe	131.2
Philadelphia Electric	266.7	Western Digital	35.1	Ashton Tate	122.2
Union Carbide	264.0	Fruit of the Loom	32.5	Microsoft	121.4
General Motors	263.6	Home Shopping	31.8	Intergraph	113.9
Eastman Kodak	255.4	Energy Service Co.	28.9	Apollo Computer	112.0
Houston Industries	247.9	Telesphere International	26.9	Oracle Systems	108.2
Navistar	246.6				

Stock Ownership—Characteristics of Shareowners

Source: N.Y. Stock Exchange
(in thousands)

	1970	1980	1983	1985
Total[1]	30,850	30,200	42,360	47,040
Male	15,689	15,666	20,864	23,689
Female	15,161	14,534	21,496	23,341
Age:				
Under 21 years	2,221	2,308	2,749	2,260
21-34 years	4,500	6,407	10,552	11,093
35-44 years	5,801	5,925	8,346	10,982
45-54 years	7,556	5,456	6,586	7,899
55-64 years	6,084	5,144	6,850	8,217
65 years and over . . .	4,330	4,589	7,277	6,589
Education:				
High school:				
3 years or less	3,566	1,746	2,356	2,513
4 years	8,697	5,737	8,788	7,869
College:				
1-3 years	5,867	9,353	13,529	13,937

	1970	1980	1983	1985
4 years or more . . .	9,999	10,613	14,375	19,854
Minors[2]	2,221	2,308	2,749	2,260
Income[3]:				
Under $5,000	2,389			
$5,000-$9,999	5,779	1,742	1,460	2,151
$10,000-$14,999 . . .	8,346	3,180	2,596	1,193
$15,000-$24,999 . . .	7,670	6,930	8,579	7,116
$25,000-$49,999		11,623	17,168	21,369
$50,000 and over . . .	4,114	3,982	7,918	11,321
Residence by MSA size:				
Under 100,000	175	204	262	307
100,000-249,999 . . .	2,245	1,883	3,060	3,448
250,000-499,999	2,686	2,921	3,962	4,293
500,000-999,999	3,712	4,345	6,555	6,950
1,000,000 and over . . .	14,881	15,447	21,730	24,751
Nonmetropolitan areas . . .	6,913	5,400	6,791	7,291

(1) Represents all publicly owned issues of common and preferred stock, incl. stock mutual funds. Data based on national probability samples; (2) Those whose stock holdings are registered in accordance with the Gifts to Minors Statutes; (3) Adults only.

Foreign Stock Markets

The following shows how the world's stock market indexes performed in the first half of 1989, and how the dollar rose or fell against the local currencies. The net result—net index change—is about what a U.S. investor in each market would have realized in paper gains or losses.

Market/index	1st-half stock index	Change in dollar vs. currency	Net index change	Market/index	1st-half stock index	Change in dollar vs. currency	Net index change
Singapore (Str. Times)	+25.9%	+1.0%	+24.7%	Frankfurt (FAZ)	+11.5	+9.1	+2.3
Dow Industrials	+12.5	—	+12.5	Paris (CAC 40)	+10.1	+8.7	+1.3
Toronto (300 comp.)	+10.7	nil	+10.7	Tokyo (Nikkei)	+9.3	+14.9	−5.0
Amsterdam (CBS)	+17.8	+9.1	+8.0	Sydney (All Ordin.)	+2.3	+12.9	−9.0
Zurich (Swissindex)	+16.6	+11.7	+4.4	Hong Kong (Hang Seng)	−15.4	−0.2	−15.0
London (FTSE 100)	+20.0	+16.5	+3.1				

Top Mutual Funds

Source: Lipper Analytical Services Inc.

Ten Years 12/31/78 To 12/31/88	Percent	Five Years 12/31/83 To 12/31/88	Percent	1988 12/31/87 To 12/31/88	Percent
Fidelity Magellan	1279.62	New England Zenith Cap		Kaufmann Fund	58.57
Loomis-Sayles Capital	682.34	Growth	354.29	Integrated Eq: Agg Growth	48.45
Phoenix Stock	660.42	Merrill Pacific A	279.23	Columbia Special	42.55
Quasar Associates	655.18	Japan Fund	266.54	Parnassus Fund	42.44
Phoenix: Growth Fund	652.44	Trustees Commingled		Calvert Fund: Ariel Growth	39.97
Lindner Fund	634.06	International	208.84	Gabelli Growth	39.10
Merrill Pacific A	628.33	Vanguard World: International		Fidelity Sel Retail	38.71
Aim Equity: Weingarten Eq	616.27	Growth	205.48	Fidelity Sel Trans	38.45
Vanguard High Yield	599.11	BB&K International	202.18	Harbor International	37.71
New England: Growth	598.53	Alliance International	183.59	Fidelity Capital Appreciation	37.62
United Vanguard	596.41	T Rowe Price Intl	180.93	Equity Strategies	37.18
Mutual Shares	580.99	Pru-Bache Utility	174.36	Shearson Lehman Small Cap	37.03
Twentieth Century: Select	578.88	Putnam International Equities	170.66	Convertible Sec & Income	36.24
American Capital Pace	575.65	Scudder International	166.65	Security Omni	36.10
Steinroe Special	569.86	Transatlantic Growth	166.31	Gintel Capital Appreciation	35.60
Windsor Fund	565.70	Kemper International	155.07	Fam Value	35.50
Franklin Gold	565.00	Evergreen Limited Market	150.33	Southeastern Asset Mgt Val	35.27
Fidelity Destiny I	562.35	Templeton Foreign	145.65	Pasadena Inv: Growth Fund	35.25
Lindner Dividend	557.02	Keystone International	144.60	Carnegie Cappiello Growth	34.93
New York Venture	555.76	American		Baron Asset	34.59
Sogen International	549.68	Telecommun-Income	140.25	Plymouth Fund: Growth Opp	33.28
International Investors	545.43	Windsor Fund	139.67	Merrill Phoenix A	33.18
IDS New Dimensions	544.75	Vanguard Hi Yield Stock	139.31	Alliance International	32.71
Fidelity Equity-Income	542.06	Mutual Qualified	139.17	Babson Enterprise	32.47
Twentieth Century: Growth	536.35	Mutual Shares	135.86	Oppenheimer Target	32.39
		GT Pacific Growth	134.72		
		United Intl Growth	126.94		
		Fidelity Special Situation:			
		Initial	126.68		
		Merrill Phoenix A	125.13		

Employee Stock Ownership Plans

Source: National Center for Employee Ownership

One of the fastest growing forms of employee compensation is the employee stock ownership plan (ESOP). The following table shows how ESOPs have grown during the 1980s.

Year	Number of plans	Employees in ESOPs (millions)	Year	Number of plans	Employees in ESOPs (millions)	Year	Number of plans	Employees in ESOPs (millions)
1980	5,009	4.048	1984	6,904	6.576	1987	8,777	8.860
1981	5,680	4.537	1985	7,402	7.353	1988	9,000	9.000
1982	6,082	4.745	1986	8,046	7.860	1989	10,000[1]	10,000[2]
1983	6,456	5.397						

(1) Estimated. (2) As of May 25, 1989.

NASDAQ in 1988

NASDAQ, The National Association of Securities Dealers Automated Quotations, reported turnover volume of 27.1 billion shares in 1988. This was a decrease of 23.6% over 1987. The number of companies with shares traded in this market was more than 5,500 in 1989, making NASDAQ the third-largest market in the world, after the New York and Tokyo exchanges.

Bankruptcy Petitions, 1905-87

(In thousands)

Source: Administrative Office of the U.S. Courts, Annual Report of the Director

Year	Filed	Pending	Year	Filed	Pending	Year	Filed	Pending	Year	Filed	Pending
1905	17	28	1935	69	65	1965	180	162	1983	375	537
1910	18	28	1940	53	55	1970	194	191	1984	344	578
1915	28	44	1945	13	21	1975	254	202	1985	365	609
1920	14	30	1950	33	38	1980	278	346	1986	478	729
1925	46	60	1955	59	56	1981	360	362	1987	561	809
1930	63	61	1960	110	95	1982	368	461			

For fiscal years ending in year shown. Covers all U.S. bankruptcy courts. Bankruptcy petitions "Filed" means the commencement of a proceeding through the presentation of a petition to the clerk of the bankruptcy court; "Pending" is a proceeding in which the administration has not been completed.

Capital Gains Tax

Source: U.S. Chamber of Commerce

The following shows how the top effective tax rate on capital gains has changed since 1960.

Year	Effective rate (percent)	Year	Effective rate (percent)	Year	Effective rate (percent)	Year	Effective rate (percent)
1960	25.0	1970	32.2	1976	49.1	1987	28.0
1968	26.9	1971	34.4	1979	28.0	1988	33.0
1969	27.5	1972	45.5	1981	20.0		

Financial Data on Selected Companies

(For additional information on the companies see pages 814-820)

Company	Ticket Symbol	1987 Gross Revenues	Earnings per share 1986	1987	1988	Price[1]	PE[1] Ratio	Dividend[1] Yield %
Abbott Laboratories	ABT	$4.9 bln.	$2.32	$2.78	$3.33	$62¼	17	2.2
Albertson's Inc.	ABS	6.7 bln.	1.50	1.88	2.44	53¼	20	1.5
American Home Products	AHP	5.5 bln.	5.18	5.73	6.38	100	15	3.9
Anheuser-Busch	BUD	8.9 bln.	1.69	2.04	2.45	41⅛	16	2.1
Armstrong World Industries	ACK	2.6 bln.	2.54	3.18	3.51	46⅜	13	2.3
Bausch & Lomb	BOL	978 mln.	2.47	2.81	3.27	58¾	17	2.0
Borden	BN	7.2 bln.	3.00	3.62	4.22	71½	16	3.9
Bristol-Myers	BMY	5.9 bln.	2.07	2.47	2.88	51⅛	17	2.7
Burlington Coat Factory	BCF	584 mln.	1.48	1.73	1.85	22⅞	11	—
Clayton Homes	CMH	212 mln.	0.52	0.63	0.87	9⅞	10	—
Clorox	CLX	1.2 bln.	1.80	1.96	2.46	42¾	16	2.9
Compaq Computer	CPQ	2.0 bln.	1.52	3.59	6.30	90	12	—
Coors (Adolph)	ACCOB	1.5 bln.	1.65	1.32	1.28	21	21	2.4
Consolidated Freightways	CNF	2.6 bln.	2.31	1.93	3.00	33¾	13	3.1
Cross (A.T.)	ATXA	227 mln.	1.29	1.74	2.13	37¾	17	3.3
Digital Equipment	DEC	11.4 bln.	4.81	8.53	9.90	100	12	—
Echlin	ECH	1.2 bln.	1.11	0.88	1.12	17⅛	16	4.1
Emerson Electric	EMR	6.6 bln.	1.87	2.00	2.31	36¾	14	3.0
Exxon	XON	88 bln.	3.71	3.43	3.95	43⅞	14	5.5
Genuine Parts	GPC	2.9 bln.	1.52	1.88	2.35	42⅛	17	2.8
Giant Food	GFSA	2.9 bln.	0.78	1.26	1.63	31⅛	18	1.6
Hartmarx	HMX	1.1 bln.	1.20	2.01	2.03	27¼	15	4.4
Hasbro	HAS	1.3 bln.	1.71	0.82	1.24	22⅜	17	0.7
Hewlett-Packard	HWP	9.8 bln.	2.02	2.50	3.36	51⅜	15	0.8
Home Depoot	HD	1.9 bln.	0.40	0.75	1.00	34½	29	0.3
Jamesway	JMY	782 mln.	0.85	0.82	0.69	10⅝	20	0.8
Kellogg	K	4.3 bln.	2.58	3.20	3.90	77⅛	19	2.2
Kimberly-Clark	KMB	5.3 bln.	2.94	3.73	4.71	68⅛	14	3.8
L.A. Gear	LA	223 mln.	0.28	0.54	2.58	62⅛	15	—
Limited, The	LTD	4.0 bln.	1.21	1.25	1.36	37½	23	0.9
Longs Drug Stores	LDG	1.9 bln.	1.78	2.33	2.75	43¼	15	2.2
Marriott	MHS	7.3 bln.	1.40	1.67	1.95	39¼	19	0.6
MCA	MCA	3.0 bln.	2.02	1.82	2.26	62½	23	1.1
Melville	MES	6.7 bln.	2.20	2.63	3.26	52⅛	16	2.5
Merck	MRK	5.9 bln.	1.62	2.23	3.05	72¼	21	2.5
Motorola	MOT	8.2 bln.	1.53	2.39	3.43	55⅜	15	1.4
National Service Ind.	NS	1.4 bln.	1.45	1.54	1.75	27⅝	15	3.0
NCR	NCR	5.9 bln.	3.42	4.51	5.33	65¼	12	2.0
Noxell	NOXLB	521 nln.	0.93	1.08	1.26	21½	17	2.3
NYNEX	NYN	12.6 bln.	6.01	6.26	6.63	79¾	13	5.5
Olsten	OLS	516 mln.	0.75	1.06	1.40	21¾	18	1.1
Parker Hannifen	PH	2.2 bln.	1.98	1.88	2.20	30¼	14	2.8
Pall	PLL	429 mln.	1.12	1.31	1.55	34	24	1.4
Petrie Stores	PST	1.2 bln.	1.58	1.02	0.75	23⅞	31	0.8
Pfizer	PFE	5.3 bln.	3.90	4.08	4.70	68½	16	3.2
PPG Ind.	PPG	5.6 bln.	2.66	3.19	4.26	44½	10	3.4
Raytheon	RTN	8.1 bln.	5.10	6.12	7.35	79½	10	2.8
Reebok	RBK	1.7 bln.	1.27	1.49	1.20	16¼	14	1.8
Rohr Ind.	RHR	906 mln.	2.70	1.53	1.85	31⅝	16	—
Royal Dutch Petroleum	RD	59 bln.	4.32	5.71	6.27	66⅝	6	5.0
Rubbermaid	RBD	1.1 bln.	0.96	1.15	1.35	32⅜	22	1.4
Sara Lee	SLE	10.4 bln.	2.02	2.35	2.83	57¾	17	2.5
Schering-Plough	SGP	2.9 bln.	2.17	2.73	3.48	76⅛	20	2.4
Seagram	VO	5.0 bln.	4.45	5.46	6.12	80¾	13	1.7
Sears, Roebuck	S	50.2 bln.	3.62	4.35	2.72	45	14	4.4
Snap-on Tools	SNA	854 mln.	1.59	2.13	2.72	35⅞	13	3.0
Stride Rite	SRR	378 mln.	1.13	1.60	3.53	24¾	17	1.6
Tambrands	TMB	563 mln.	3.12	3.45	3.83	73¼	19	2.8
Tandy	TAN	3.7 bln.	2.22	2.70	3.54	46¾	13	1.3
Tootsie Roll	TR	126.6 mln.	1.37	1.55	1.77	34¼	18	0.7
Toys "R" Us	TOY	4.0 bln.	0.78	1.04	1.36	35⅜	25	—
Toro	TTC	609 mln.	1.34	1.52	1.84	23¾	12	2.0
TRW	TRW	6.9 bln.	3.56	4.01	4.29	47½	11	3.6
Union Camp	UCC	2.6 bln.	1.77	2.83	4.25	39⅞	9	3.7
Upjohn	UPJ	2.7 bln.	1.35	1.63	1.90	40⅜	20	2.2
USAir Group	U	5.7 bln.	3.34	5.28	3.81	50	11	0.2
UST	UST	618 mln.	0.92	1.13	1.41	27⅝	18	3.3
VF Corp	VFC	2.5 bln.	2.05	2.58	2.55	35½	14	2.5
Wal-Mart	WMT	20.6 bln.	0.80	1.11	1.48	41⅛	25	0.5
Walgreen	WAL	4.8 bln.	1.67	1.68	2.10	46⅝	19	1.5
Weyerhaeuser	WY	10.0 bln.	1.27	2.12	2.68	30½	11	3.9
Winn-Dixie	WIN	9.0 bln.	2.84	2.72	2.87	53⅝	17	3.6
Winnebago	WGO	425 mln.	0.77	0.78	0.11	7¼	35	5.5
Woolworth	Z	8.0 bln.	3.25	3.81	4.47	67⅛	15	2.8
Wrigley	WWY	891 mln.	1.28	1.69	2.18	44⅞	19	1.8
Zurn Ind.	ZRN	484 mln.	1.43	1.56	1.98	39⅜	19	1.7

(1) As of Sept. 7, 1989. d = deficit.

Federal Reserve System

(as of Aug. 1989)

The Federal Reserve System is the central bank for the United States. The system was established on December 23, 1913, originally to give the country an elastic currency, to provide facilities for discounting commercial paper, and to improve the supervision of banking. Since then, the System's responsibilities have been broadened. Over the years, stability and growth of the economy, a high level of employment, stability in the purchasing power of the dollar, and reasonable balance in transactions with foreign countries have come to be recognized as primary objectives of governmental economic policy.

The Federal Reserve System consists of the Board of Governors, the 12 District Reserve Banks and their branch offices, and the Federal Open Market Committee. Several advisory councils help the Board meet its varied responsibilities.

The hub of the System is the seven member Board of Governors in Washington. The members of the Board are appointed by the President and confirmed by the Senate, to serve 14-year terms. The President also appoints the Chairman and Vice-Chairman of the Board from among the board members for 4-year terms that may be renewed. Currently, the board members are: Alan Greenspan, Chairman; Manuel H. Johnson, Vice Chairman; Edward W. Kelley, Jr.; Martha R. Seger; Wayne D. Angell; John P. La Ware.

The Board is the policy-making body. In addition to its policy making responsibilities, it supervises the budget and operations of the Reserve Banks, approves the appointments of their presidents and appoints 3 of each District Bank's directors, including the chairman and vice chairman of each Reserve Bank's board.

The 12 Reserve Banks and their branch offices serve as the decentralized portion of the System, carrying out day-to-day operations such as circulating currency and coin, providing fiscal agency functions and payments mechanism services. The District Banks are located in Boston, New York, Philadelphia, Cleveland, Richmond, Atlanta, Chicago, St. Louis, Minneapolis, Kansas City, Dallas and San Francisco.

The System's principal function is monetary policy, which it controls using three tools: reserve requirements, the discount rate and open market operations. Uniform reserve requirements, set by the Board, are applied to the transaction accounts and nonpersonal time deposits of all depository institutions. Responsibility for setting the discount rate (the interest rate at which depository institutions can borrow money from the Reserve Banks) is shared by the Board of Governors and the Reserve Banks. Changes in the discount rate are recommended by the individual Boards of Directors of the Reserve Banks and are subject to approval by the Board of Governors. The most important tool of monetary policy is open market operations (the purchase and sale of government securities). Responsibility for influencing the cost and availability of money and credit through the purchase and sale of government securities lies with the Federal Open Market Committee (FOMC). This committee is composed of the 7 members of the Board of Governors, the president of the Federal Reserve Bank of New York, and 4 other Federal Reserve Bank presidents, who serve one-year terms on a rotating basis. The committee bases its decisions on current economic and financial developments and outlook, setting yearly growth objectives for key measures of money supply and credit. The decisions of the committee are carried out by the Domestic Trading Desk of the Federal Reserve Bank of New York.

The Federal Reserve Act prescribes a Federal Advisory Council, consisting of one member from each Federal Reserve District, elected annually by the Board of Directors of each of the 12 Federal Reserve Banks. They meet with the Federal Reserve Board four times a year to discuss business and financial conditions and to make advisory recommendations.

The Consumer Advisory Council is a statutory body, including both consumer and creditor representatives, which advises the Board of Governors on its implementation of consumer regulations and other consumer-related matters.

Following the passage of the Monetary Control Act of 1980, the Board of Governors established the Thrift Institutions Advisory Council to provide information and views on the special needs and problems of thrift institutions. The group is comprised of representatives of mutual savings banks, savings and loan associations, and credit unions.

Federal Reserve Board Discount Rate

The discount rate is the rate of interest set by the Federal Reserve that member banks are charged when borrowing money through the Federal Reserve System.

Effective Date	Rate	Effective Date	Rate	Effective Date	Rate	Effective Date	Rate
1980: Feb. 15	13	1981: May 5	14	Nov. 22	9	1986: March 7	7
May 30	12	Nov. 2	13	Dec. 15	8½	April 21	6½
June 13	11	Dec. 4	12	1984: April 9	9	July 11	6
July 28	10	1982: July 20	11½	Nov. 21	8½	Aug. 21	5½
Sept. 26	11	Aug. 2	11	Dec. 24	8	1987: Sept. 4	6
Nov. 17	12	Aug. 16	10½	1985: May 20	7½	1988: Aug. 9	6½
Dec. 5	13	Aug. 27	10			1989: Feb. 24	7
		Oct. 12	9½			In effect Sept. 1, 1989	6½

The Savings & Loan Crisis by State

Source: Federal Home Loan Bank Board

(as of Feb. 1989)

	Savings & loans total	Insolvent		Savings & Loans total	insolvent		Savings & Loans total	insolvent
Alabama	37	5	Louisiana	94	30	Ohio	223	17
Alaska	3	2	Maine	16	0	Oklahoma	39	6
Arizona	11	2	Maryland	99	5	Oregon	12	3
Arkansas	37	13	Massachusetts	32	0	Pennsylvania	169	5
California	197	25	Michigan	49	5	Rhode Island	4	0
Colorado	37	11	Minnesota	32	3	South Carolina	49	2
Connecticut	27	1	Mississippi	42	9	South Dakota	12	2
Delaware	5	0	Missouri	80	10	Tennessee	60	5
D.C.	5	0	Montana	11	1	Texas	244	114
Florida	147	21	North Carolina	134	6	Utah	13	3
Georgia	71	7	North Dakota	6	2	Vermont	4	0
Hawaii	6	0	Nebraska	24	9	Virginia	63	6
Idaho	6	0	Nevada	6	0	Washington	35	3
Illinois	252	45	New Hampshire	12	0	West Virginia	16	0
Indiana	107	6	New Jersey	134	11	Wisconsin	73	2
Iowa	47	5	New Mexico	25	5	Wyoming	11	3
Kansas	55	16	New York	96	6			
Kentucky	64	1						

Largest U.S. Commercial Banks

Source: American Banker; based on deposits Dec. 31, 1988.

(thousands)

Rank	Deposits	Rank	Deposits
Citibank NA, New York	$104,996,000	First Fidelity Bank NA, Newark, N.J.	7,967,395
Bank of America NT&SA, San Francisco	69,640,000	Michigan National Bank, Farmington Hills	7,694,746
Chase Manhattan Bank NA, New York	58,241,477	Connecticut Bank & Trust Co. NA, Hartford.	7,509,700
Morgan Guaranty Trust Co., New York	45,471,746	NCNB National Bank of Florida, Tampa	7,387,750
Manufacturers Hanover Trust Co., New York.	42,876,000	Crestar Bank, Richmond	7,291,054
Security Pacific National Bank, Los Angeles	36,095,333	Comerica Bank-Detroit	7,217,355
Wells Fargo Bank NA, San Francisco	35,109,059	Philadelphia National Bank	7,131,118
Chemical Bank, New York	33,298,000	First Union National Bank of Florida, Jackson-	
Bankers Trust Co., New York.	33,261,373	ville	7,122,471
First National Bank, Chicago	27,372,439	Fidelity Bank NA, Malvern, Pa.	6,837,703
NCNB Texas National Bank, Dallas	20,474,765	Maryland National Bank, Baltimore	6,793,502
Continental Bank NA, Chicago	17,763,339	AmeriTrust Co. NA, Cleveland	6,542,938
First National Bank, Boston	17,687,897	Manufacturers National Bank, Detroit	6,521,981
Bank of New York	16,665,898	Harris Trust & Savings Bank, Chicago.	6,508,050
Marine Midland Bank NA, Buffalo, N.Y.	16,659,085	Texas Commerce Bank NA, Houston	6,453,537
First Interstate Bank of California, Los Angeles	16,613,623	Provident National Bank, Philadelphia	6,432,758
Mellon Bank NA, Pittsburgh.	15,603,197	United States National Bank, Portland, Ore.	6,095,867
Boston Safe Deposit & Trust Co.	15,464,313	First Interstate Bank of Texas NA, Houston	6,073,573
Irving Trust Co., New York	14,154,588	Florida National Bank, Jacksonville	6,066,205
Republic National Bank, New York.	13,897,318	Huntington National Bank, Columbus, Oh.	6,055,783
National Bank of Detroit	11,989,495	First National Bank, Atlanta	6,017,771
Union Bank, San Francisco	11,911,043	Meridian Bank, Reading, Pa.	6,010,077
National Westminster Bank USA, New York	11,389,004	First Interstate Bank of Arizona NA, Phoenix	5,818,569
NCNB National Bank of North Carolina, Char-		AmSouth Bank NA, Birmingham, Ala.	5,692,601
lotte.	11,054,684	Security Pacific Bank Washington, Seattle	5,686,248
Bank of New England NA, Boston	10,904,043	Bank of Hawaii, Honolulu	5,602,067
First Bank NA, Minneapolis	10,674,583	Norwest Bank Minneapolis NA	5,540,745
Wachovia Bank & Trust Co. NA, Winston-Sa-		Fleet National Bank, Providence, R.I.	5,539,747
lem, N.C.	10,517,863	National City Bank, Cleveland	5,512,392
Southeast Bank NA, Miami	10,287,300	Bank of Tokyo Trust Co., New York	5,497,629
Pittsburgh National Bank	10,045,593	State Street Bank & Trust Co., Boston	5,390,469
Sovran Bank NA, Richmond	9,779,420	Riggs National Bank, Washington, D.C.	5,253,756
Seattle-First National Bank	8,870,643	Northern Trust Co., Chicago	5,165,804
First Union National Bank, Charlotte, N.C.	8,784,792	Sanwa Bank California, San Francisco	5,137,163
Valley National Bank, Phoenix	8,639,762	Shawmut Bank NA, Boston	5,059,673
Citizens & Southern National Bank, Atlanta	8,454,641	Signet Bank/Virginia, Richmond	5,040,448
Connecticut National Bank, Hartford.	8,045,283		

Largest Foreign Banks

Source: American Banker; based on deposits Dec. 31, 1988, or nearest fiscal year-end.

(thousands of U.S. dollars)

Bank, country	Deposits	Bank, country	Deposits
Dai-Ichi Kangyo Bank Ltd., Tokyo, Japan	$312,465,781	Daiwa Bank, Ltd., Osaka, Japan	134,466,778
Sumitomo Bank Ltd., Osaka, Japan	296,000,827	Bank of Tokyo, Ltd., Japan	132,147,474
Fugi Bank, Ltd., Tokyo, Japan	283,585,351	Yasuda Trust & Banking Co. Ltd., Tokyo, Japan	131,788,381
Mitsubishi Bank Ltd., Tokyo, Japan.	269,427,020	Societe Generale, Paris, France	123,187,087
Sanwa Bank Ltd., Osaka, Japan	269,032,279	Dresdner Bank, Frankfurt, W. Germany	120,317,120
Industrial Bank of Japan, Ltd., Tokyo, Japan	215,397,605	Toyo Trust & Banking Co. Ltd., Tokyo, Japan.	105,384,007
Norinchukin Bank, Tokyo, Japan	210,759,455	Hongkong and Shanghai Banking Corp., Hong	
Mitsubishi Trust & Banking Corp., Tokyo, Japan	185,955,516	Kong	101,841,280
Sumitomo Trust & Banking Co., Ltd., Osaka, Ja-		Nippon Credit Bank, Ltd., Tokyo, Japan	96,733,830
pan	177,932,182	Commerzbank, Frankfurt, W. Germany	94,904,206
Tokai Bank Ltd., Nagoya, Japan	175,600,895	Union Bank of Switzerland, Zurich, Switzerland.	93,750,145
Mitsui Trust & Banking Co., Ltd., Tokyo, Japan	161,228,496	Swiss Bank Corp., Basle, Switzerland	89,572,067
Mitsui Bank, Ltd., Tokyo, Japan.	159,039,606	Midland Bank Plc, London, UK	86,753,264
Banque Nationale de Paris, France	158,549,122	Westdeutsche Landesbank Girozentrale, Dussel-	
Barclays Bank Plc, London, UK.	157,357,472	dorf, W. Germany	86,730,534
Deutsche Bank, Frankfurt, W. Germany	154,974,576	Bayerische Vereinsbank, Munich, W. Germany.	85,089,724
National Westminster Bank Plc, London, U.K.	153,645,648	Lloyds Bank Plc, London, U.K.	82,911,264
Credit Lyonnais, Paris, France	148,842,971	Shoko Chukin Bank, Tokyo, Japan.	81,968,920
Long-Term Credit Bank of Japan Ltd., Tokyo, Ja-		Kyowa Bank, Ltd, Tokyo, Japan	81,096,761
pan	147,426,607	Zenshinren Bank, Tokyo, Japan	77,741,067
Credit Agricole Mutuel, Paris, France	141,973,000	Banca Nazionale del Lavoro, Rome, Italy	76,309,515
Taiyo Kobe Bank, Ltd., Kobe, Japan.	138,986,023		

Bank Failures

Source: Federal Deposit Insurance Corp

Year	Closed	Year	Closed	Year	Closed	Year	Closed
1934	61	1960	2	1971	6	1981	10
1935	32	1961	9	1972	3	1982	42
1936	72	1963	2	1973	6	1983	48
1937	84	1964	8	1975	14	1984	79
1938	81	1965	9	1976	17	1985	120
1939	72	1966	8	1978	7	1986	138
1940	48	1967	4	1979	10	1987	184
1955	5	1969	9	1980	10	1988	200
1959	3	1970	8				

All Banks in U.S.—Number, Deposits

Source: Federal Reserve System

Comprises all national banks in the United States and all state commercial banks, trust companies, mutual stock savings banks, private and industrial banks, and special types of institutions that are treated as banks by the federal bank supervisory agencies. Data as of June 30 prior to 1975.

Year	Total all banks	Number of banks — F.R.S. members Total	Number of banks — F.R.S. members Nat'l	Number of banks — F.R.S. members State	Nonmembers Mutual savings	Nonmembers Other	Total all banks	Total deposits (millions of dollars) — F.R.S. members Total	Total deposits — F.R.S. members Nat'l	Total deposits — F.R.S. members State	Nonmembers Mutual savings	Nonmembers Other
1925..	26,479	9,538	8,066	1,472	621	18,320	51,641	32,457	19,912	12,546	7,089	12,095
1930..	23,855	8,315	7,247	1,068	604	14,936	59,828	38,069	23,235	14,834	9,117	12,642
1935..	16,047	6,410	5,425	985	569	9,068	51,149	34,938	22,477	12,461	9,830	6,381
1940..	14,955	6,398	5,164	1,234	551	8,008	70,770	51,729	33,014	18,715	10,631	8,410
1945..	14,542	6,840	5,015	1,825	539	7,163	151,033	118,378	76,534	41,844	14,413	18,242
1950..	14,674	6,885	4,971	1,914	527	7,262	163,770	122,707	82,430	40,277	19,927	21,137
1955..	14,309	6,611	4,744	1,867	525	7,173	208,850	154,670	98,636	56,034	27,310	26,870
1960..	14,006	6,217	4,542	1,675	513	7,276	249,163	179,519	116,178	63,341	35,316	34,328
1965..	14,295	6,235	4,803	1,432	504	7,556	362,611	259,743	171,528	88,215	50,980	51,889
1970..	14,167	5,805	4,638	1,167	496	7,866	502,542	346,289	254,322	91,967	69,285	86,968
1975..	15,108	5,787	4,741	1,046	475	8,846	896,879	590,999	447,590	143,409	110,569	195,311
1980..	15,145	5,422	4,425	997	460	9,263	1,333,399	843,030	651,848	191,182	150,000	340,369
1984..	14,739	5,973	4,905	1,068	267	8,498	1,759,000	1,170,013	945,033	224,980	121,559	467,433
1985..	14,713	6,044	4,964	1,080	344	8,325	1,973,816	1,285,562	1,033,631	251,931	137,535	500,179
1986..	14,513	5,979	4,871	1,108	360	8,174	2,104,713	1,406,949	1,126,092	280,857	148,465	549,299
1987..	14,068	5,736	4,630	1,106	371	7,961	2,150,569	1,415,436	1,139,441	275,995	168,320	566,813
1988..	13,488	5,430	4,357	1,073	375	7,683	2,286,248	1,510,535	1,223,011	287,524	182,795	592,918

Federal Deposit Insurance Corporation (FDIC)

The primary purpose of the Federal Deposit Insurance Corporation (FDIC) is to insure deposits in all banks approved for insurance coverage benefits under the Federal Deposit Insurance Act. The major functions of the FDIC are to pay off depositors of insured banks closed without adequate provision having been made to pay depositors' claims, to act as receiver for all national banks placed in receivership and for state banks placed in receivership when appointed receiver by state authorities, and to prevent the continuance or development of unsafe and unsound banking practices. The FDIC's entire income consists of assessments on insured banks and income from investments; it receives no appropriations from Congress. It may borrow from the U.S. Treasury not to exceed $3 billion outstanding, but has made no such borrowings since it was organized in 1933. The FDIC surplus (Deposit Insurance Fund) as of Jan. 1, 1989 was $14.1 billion.

Year-End Assets and Liabilities of Individuals in the U.S.[1]

Source: Federal Reserve System

(billions of dollars)

	1960	1965	1970	1975	1980	1985	1987	1988
Total financial assets..................	1005.8	1502.7	1968.3	2622.2	4632.0	7995.1	9344.9	10197.0
Checkable deposits & currency........	91.5	107.3	137.2	187.3	291.6	457.1	569.5	589.6
Time & savings deposits.............	164.0	288.4	426.3	765.0	1271.9	2005.5	2193.5	2342.2
Money market fund shares...........	—	—	—	3.7	64.9	214.5	277.6	298.3
Securities........................	511.2	764.2	923.3	912.6	1598.8	2775.4	3189.9	3451.6
U.S. savings bonds...............	45.6	49.7	52.1	67.4	72.5	79.8	101.1	109.6
Other U.S. Treasury securities......	24.1	24.9	31.1	51.6	133.0	396.4	424.8	467.8
U.S. Govt. agency securities.......	2.3	.7	19.6	11.7	41.4	81.5	141.9	221.7
Tax-exempt obligations...........	30.8	36.4	46.0	68.1	88.4	223.2	249.7	267.9
Corporate & foreign bonds.........	10.9	9.0	35.6	67.1	58.8	47.6	84.8	72.1
Open-market paper...............	2.0	5.7	11.8	9.3	40.9	58.7	66.6	79.2
Mutual fund shares..............	17.0	34.4	44.5	38.7	52.1	203.0	409.1	417.5
Other corporate equities.........	378.4	600.5	682.7	598.6	1111.8	1685.3	1711.9	1816.0
Private life insurance res...........	78.8	98.9	123.3	158.5	207.4	246.5	289.5	302.0
Private insured pension res..........	18.9	27.3	41.0	72.3	172.0	400.0	538.9	631.7
Private noninsured pen. res..........	38.1	74.4	112.0	225.0	469.6	848.1	1000.8	1140.0
Govt. insurance & pen. res..........	40.2	60.8	95.2	154.7	283.6	563.7	716.3	824.3
Miscellaneous financial assets.......	63.1	81.5	109.9	143.1	272.3	484.2	568.9	617.2
Total liabilities...................	280.5	444.9	650.4	1090.8	2044.9	3656.4	4411.2	4786.3
Mtg. debt on nonfarm homes........	137.3	214.3	290.0	469.7	943.3	1485.4	1937.8	2156.0
Other mortgage debt[2].............	35.7	65.3	119.4	247.8	422.4	748.1	895.6	957.4
Consumer credit.................	65.0	103.1	143.1	219.6	374.4	601.8	692.7	743.7
Security credit..................	5.4	9.1	10.4	12.1	27.2	56.8	50.4	53.0
Policy loans....................	5.7	8.3	17.0	25.5	42.6	55.3	55.3	55.3
Other debt[2]...................	31.4	44.8	70.3	116.1	708.8	708.8	779.4	820.9

(1) Combined statement for households, farm business, and nonfarm noncorporate business. (2) Includes corporate farms.

Federal Home Loan Bank Board

The Federal Home Loan Bank Board was established by the Federal Home Loan Bank Act, approved July 22, 1932, and made an independent agency in the executive branch in the Housing Amendments of 1955.

All of the Bank Board's activities are self-supporting and do not require the appropriation of U.S. Treasury funds.

Leading Businesses in 1988

Source: FORTUNE Magazine; World Almanac Research

(millions of sales, unless otherwise noted)

Aerospace

United Technologies	$18,088
Boeing	16,962
McDonnell Douglas	15,072
Rockwell International	11,946
Allied-Signal	11,909
Lockheed	10,667
General Dynamics	9,551
Textron	7,111
Northrop	5,797
Martin Marietta	5,727

Apparel

VF	$2,516
Claiborne (Liz)	1,184
Hartmarx	1,174
Fruit of the Loom	1,005
Kellwood	698
Leslie Fay	683
Warnaco	657
Oxford Industries	591
Phillips-Van Heusen	567

Beverages

Pepsico	$13,007
Anheuser-Busch	8,924
Coca-Cola	8,338
Coca-Cola	3,874
Seagram (Jos. E.)	2,199
Coors (Adolph)	1,522
Brown-Forman	1,067
Dr Pepper/Seven-Up	510

Building Materials

American Standard	$3,716
Owens-Illinois	3,572
Owens-Corning Fiber.	2,831
USG	2,811
Hillsborough	2,507
Manville	2,209
Corning Glass Works	2,122
Nortek	1,425
Norton	1,410
Lafarge	1,309

Chemicals

Du Pont (E.I.) De Nemours	$32,514
Dow Chemical	16,682
Union Carbide	8,324
Monsanto	8,293
Hanson Ind. NA	6,494
Grace (W.R.)	6,199
Hoechst Celanese	5,679
PPG Industries	5,617
BASF	5,000
Bayer USA	4,719

Computers (incl. office equip.)

IBM	$59,681
Digital Equipment	11,475
Unisys	9,902
Hewlett-Packard	9,831
NCR	5,990
Apple Computer	4,071
Control Data	3,628
Wang Laboratories	3,068
Zenith Electronics	2,686
Pitney Bowes	2,665

Electronics

General Electric	$49,414
Westinghouse Electric	12,500
Motorola	8,250
Raytheon	8,192
Honeywell	7,148
TRW	6,982
Emerson Electric	6,652
Texas Instruments	6,295
North American Philips	5,424
Whirlpool	4,421

Food

RJR Nabisco	$16,956
Sara Lee	10,424
Conagra	9,475
Beatrice	7,505
Borden	7,244
Archer Daniels	6,798
Pillsbury	6,191
Ralston Purina	6,176

General Mills	5,778
Quaker Oats	5,330

Forest Products

Weyerhauser	$10,004
International Paper	9,533
Georgia-Pacific	9,509
Kimberly-Clark	5,394
Champion International	5,129
James River	5,098
Scott Paper	4,726
Mead	4,464
Boise Cascade	4,095
Stone Container	3,742

Furniture

Interco	$3,341
Masco	2,439
Leggett & Platt	810
Mohasco	791
Miller (Herman)	714
Ohio Mattress	662
Hon Industries	575
Kimball International	530

Industrial and Farm Equip.

Tenneco	$15,707
Caterpillar	10,435
Deere	5,365
Dresser Industries	3,942
Cummins Engine	3,310
Ingersoll-Rand	3,021
Baker Hughes	2,316
Black & Decker	2,281
Parker Hannifin	2,252
Dover	1,954

Life Insurance[1]

Prudential	$116,481.0
Metropolitan Life	94,232.0
Equitable Life	50,415.5
Aetna Life	48,884.9
Teachers Insurance & Annuity	38,631.4
New York Life	35,153.8
Connecticut General	31,095.5
Travelers	30,672.2
John Hancock	28,315.2
Northwestern Mutual	25,349.0

Metal Products

Triangle Industries	$4,104
Gillette	3,581
Combustion Engineering	3,484
Emhart	2,763
Illinois Tool Works	1,930
Stanley Works	1,909
Crown Cork & Seal	1,834
Harsco	1,279
Ball	1,073
Tyler	996

Metals

Aluminum Co. of America	$9,795
LTV	7,526
Reynolds Metals	5,567
Bethlehem Steel	5,489
Inland Steel Ind.	4,068
AMAX	3,944
Armco	3,227
National Steel	2,599
Phelps Dodge	2,320
Asarco	1,988

Motor Vehicles & Parts

General Motors	$121,085
Ford Motor	92,446
Chrysler	35,473
Dana	5,172
Eaton	4,237
Navistar	4,080
Borg-Warner	3,218
Paccar	3,112
Freuhauf	2,143
Mack Trucks	2,102

Petroleum Refining

Exxon	$79,557
Mobil	48,198
Texaco	35,544

Chevron	25,196
Amoco	21,150
Shell Oil	21,070
Atlantic Richfield	17,626
USX	15,792
Phillips Petroleum	11,304
Unocal	8,853

Pharmaceuticals

Johnson & Johnson	$9,000
Bristol-Myers	5,973
Merck	5,940
American Home Products	5,501
Pfizer	5,385
Abbott Laboratories	4,937
Smithkline Beckman	4,749
Lilly (Eli)	4,070
Warner-Lambert	3,908
Schering-Plough	2,969

Publishing & Printing

Time Inc.	$4,507
Gannett	3,314
Times Mirror	3,259
Donnelly (R.R.)	2,878
Tribune	2,335
Knight-Ridder	2,194
Berkshire Hathaway	1,992
McGraw-Hill	1,818
New York Times	1,755
Dow Jones	1,603

Retail[2]

Sears Roebuck	50,251.0
K Mart	27,301.0
Wal-Mart	20,649.0
Kroger	19,053.0
American Stores	18,478.4
J.C. Penney	14,833.0
Safeway	13,612.4
Dayton Hudson	12,204.0
May Department Stores	11,921.0
Great Atlantic & Pacific Tea	9,531.8

Scientific and Photographic Equi

Eastman Kodak	$17,034
Xerox	16,441
Minnesota Mining	10,581
Baxter International	6,861
Litton Industries	4,864
Henley Group	2,903
Polaroid	1,863
Becton Dickinson	1,847
Perkin-Elmer	1,429
Tektronix	1,412

Soaps, Cosmetics

Procter & Gamble	$19,336
Unilever U.S.	6,956
Colgate-Palmolive	5,484
Avon Products	3,365
Revlon Group	2,477
Clorox	1,260
International Flavors	840
Alberto Culver	605
Faberge	593
Noxell	522

Textiles

Armstrong World Ind.	$2,680
Burlington Holdings	2,452
West Point-Pepperell	2,151
Springs Industries	1,825
Fieldcrest Cannon	1,338
DWG	1,168
Shaw Industries	958
United Merchants	723
Dixie Yarns	606
Guilford Mills	578

Tobacco

Philip Morris	$25,860
American Brands	7,477
Universal	2,414
Lorillard	1,410
Standard Commercial	750
UST	607
Dibrell Brothers	555

(continued)

Transportation[3]					
United Parcel Service	$11,032.1	USAIR Group	5,707.0	Bell Atlantic	24,729.2
UAL	9,014.6	NWA	5,650.4	US West	22,415.9
AMR	8,824.3	Santa Fe Southern Pacific	4,934.9	Pacific Telesis Group	21,191.0
CSX	8,668.0	**Utilities[1]**		Pacific Gas & Electric	21,067.7
Texas Air	8,572.9	GTE	$31,103.9	Southwestern Bell	20,985.1
Delta Air Lines	6,915.4	Bellsouth	28,472.4	Southern	19,729.0
Union Pacific	6,794.0	NYNEX	25,362.0	American Information Tech.	19,163.0

(1) Millions of assets as of Dec. 31, 1988; (2) Includes revenues from nonretailing activities; (3) Includes revenues from nontransportation activities.

U.S. Industrial Corporations with Largest Sales in 1988

Source: *FORTUNE Magazine*

Company (1987 rank)	Sales[1] (billions)	Income[1] (or loss) (millions)	Company (1987 rank)	Sales[1] (billions)	Income[1] (or loss) (millions)
General Motors (1)	$121.1	$4,856	Westinghouse Electric (33)	$12.5	$822
Ford Motor (3)	92.4	5,300	Rockwell International (27)	11.9	811
Exxon (2)	79.6	5,260	Allied-Signal (28)	11.9	463
IBM (4)	59.7	5,806	Digital Equipment (38)	11.5	1,305
General Electric (6)	49.4	3,386	Phillips Petroleum (32)	11.3	650
Mobil (5)	48.2	2,087	Goodyear (35)	10.8	350
Chrysler (10)	35.5	1,050	Lockheed (30)	10.7	624
Texaco (7)	33.5	1,304	Minnesota Mining & Manufacturing (37)	10.6	1,154
Du Pont (9)	32.5	2,190	Caterpillar (48)	10.4	616
Philip Morris (12)	25.9	2,337	Sara Lee (40)	10.0	325
Chevron (11)	25.2	1,768	Weyerhaeuser (58)	10.0	564
Amoco (14)	21.2	2,063	Unisys (36)	9.9	680
Shell Oil (13)	21.1	1,239	Hewlett-Packard (49)	9.8	816
Occidental Petroleum (16)	19.4	302	ALCOA (51)	9.8	861
Procter & Gamble (17)	19.3	1,020	General Dynamics (39)	9.6	379
United Technologies (15)	18.1	659	International Paper (52)	9.5	754
Atlantic Richfield (18)	17.6	1,583	Georgia Pacific (44)	9.5	467
Eastman Kodak (25)	17.0	1,397	ConAgra (41)	9.5	154
Boeing (20)	17.0	614	Johnson & Johnson (50)	9.0	974
RJR Nabisco (19)	17.0	1,393	Anheuser-Busch (47)	8.9	715
Dow Chemical (24)	16.7	2,398	Unocal (46)	8.9	480
Xerox (34)	16.4	388	Sun (43)	8.6	7
USX (23)	15.8	756	Coca-Cola (54)	8.3	1,044
Tenneco (21)	15.7	822	Union Carbide (59)	8.3	662
McDonnell Douglas (26)	15.1	350			
Pepsico (29)	13.0	762			

(1) Fiscal year.

Largest Corporate Mergers or Acquisitions in U.S.

(as of mid-1989)

Company	Acquirer	Dollars	Year	Company	Acquirer	Dollars	Year
RJR Nabisco	Kohlberg Kravis Roberts	24.9 bln.	1988	Texasgulf	Elf Aquitaine	4.2 bln.	1981
Warner Communications	Time	13.9 bln.	1989	Cities Service	Occidental Petroleum	4.0 bln.	1982
Gulf Oil	Chevron	13.3 bln.	1984	Dome Petroleum	Amoco	3.8 bln.	1987
Kraft	Philip Morris	11.5 bln.	1988	R.H. Macy	various investors	3.7 bln.	1986
Squibb	Bristol-Myers	11.5 bln.	1989	American Hospital	Baxter Travenol	3.7 bln.	1986
Getty Oil	Texaco	10.1 bln.	1984	Owens-Illinois	Kohlberg Kravis Roberts	3.6 bln.	1987
Conoco	DuPont	8.0 bln.	1981	Belridge Oil	Shell Oil	3.6 bln.	1979
Standard Oil	British Petroleum	7.9 bln.*	1987	NWA	Checchi Group	3.6 bln.	1988
Federated Dept. Stores	Campeau	7.4 bln.	1988	Allied Stores	Campeau	3.5 bln.	1986
Marathon Oil	U.S. Steel	6.5 bln.	1981	Fort Howard Paper	Morgan Stanley Group	3.5 bln.	1988
Beatrice	Kohlberg Kravis Roberts	6.2 bln.	1986	ABC Broadcasting	Capital Cities Comm.	3.5 bln.	1985
RCA	General Electric	6.2 bln.	1986	Viacom	National Amusements	3.4 bln.	1987
Superior Oil	Mobil Oil	5.7 bln.	1984	Panhandle Eastern	Texas Eastern	3.2 bln.	1989
Pillsbury	Grand Metropolitan	5.7 bln.	1988	Chesebrough-Ponds	Unilever N.V.	3.1 bln.	1987
General Foods	Philip Morris	5.6 bln.	1986	MidCon	Occidental Petroleum	3.0 bln.	1986
Safeway Stores	Kohlberg Kravis Roberts	5.3 bln.	1986	Texas Oil and Gas	USX Corp.	3.0 bln.	1986
				Emhart	Black & Decker	2.8 bln.	1989
Farmers Group	B.A.T. Industries	5.2 bln.	1988	Carnation	Nestle	2.8 bln.	1984
Southern Pacific	Santa Fe Railroad	5.2 bln.	1983	Celanese	American Hoechst	2.7 bln.	1987
Southland	J.T. Acquisition	5.1 bln.	1987	G.D. Searle	Monsanto	2.7 bln.	1985
Hughes Aircraft	General Motors	5.0 bln.	1985	Esmark	Beatrice Foods	2.7 bln.	1984
Nabisco	R.J. Reynolds	4.9 bln.	1985	G.D. Searle	Monsanto	2.7 bln.	1986
Signal Cos.	Allied Corp.	4.9 bln.	1986	Continental Group	Kiewit-Murdock	2.7 bln.	1984
Sperry	Burroughs	4.8 bln.	1986	St. Joe Minerals	Fluor	2.6 bln.	1981
Connecticut General	INA	4.3 bln.	1981	Electronic Data Systems	General Motors	2.6 bln.	1984
Borg-Warner	AV Holdings	4.2 bln.	1987	Firestone Tire	Bridgestone	2.6 bln.	1988
				Macmillan	Maxwell Comm.	2.6 bln.	1988
				Associated Dry Goods	May Dept. Stores	2.5 bln.	1986

*For the 45% of Standard Oil that British Petroleum did not already own.

In 1988, there were 3,637 mergers and acquisitions completed, a sharp rise from the 3,565 mergers of 1987. The value of the deals was a record $311.4 billion, compared with $219 billion in 1987.

Consumer Price Index

The Consumer Price Index (CPI) is a measure of the average change in prices over time of basic consumer goods and services. From Jan. 1978, the Bureau of Labor Statistics began publishing CPI's for two population groups: (1) a CPI for All Urban Consumers (CPI-U) which covers about 80% of the total population; and (2) a CPI for Urban Wage Earners and Clerical Workers (CPI-W) which covers about 32% of the total population. The CPI-U includes, in addition to wage earners and clerical workers, groups such as professional, managerial, and technical workers, the self-employed, short-term workers, the unemployed, retirees and others not in the labor force.

The CPI is based on prices of food, clothing, shelter, and fuels, transportation fares, charges for doctors' and dentists'

services, drugs, and the other goods and services bought for day-to-day living. The index had been measuring price changes from a designated reference date—1967—which equaled 100.0.

Beginning with the release of data for January 1988, the standard reference base period for the Consumer Price Index is 1982-84. The rebasing is in keeping with the government's policy that index bases should be updated periodically. The 1982-84 period was chosen to coincide with the time period of the updated CPI's expenditure weights, which are based upon the Consumer Expenditure Surveys for 1982, 1983, and 1984. All of the CPI figures in the following tables have been changed to reflect the new reference base.

Consumer Price Indexes, 1989

Source: Bureau of Labor Statistics, U.S. Labor Department

(seasonally adjusted indexes)

(1982-84=100)	Apr. CPI-U	Apr. CPI-W	May CPI-U	May CPI-W	June CPI-U	June CPI-W
Food, beverages.......	123.9	123.7	124.7	124.4	125.0	124.8
Housing............	121.8	120.0	122.3	120.4	122.6	120.7
Apparel, upkeep.......	119.4	118.2	120.4	118.5	119.1	117.7
Transportation........	115.0	114.8	116.1	116.0	115.9	115.9
Medical care.........	146.6	147.0	147.6	147.9	148.7	148.8
Entertainment........	125.4	124.8	125.5	124.9	126.2	125.5
Other goods, services....	145.6	145.1	146.6	146.1	147.7	147.3
Services............	130.6	129.6	131.2	130.1	131.6	130.5
Special Indexes						
All items less food......	123.0	121.2	123.7	121.8	123.8	122.0
Commodities less food ...	112.4	111.9	113.3	112.7	113.1	112.7
Nondurables[1].........	118.4	118.1	119.3	119.1	119.0	118.8
Energy............	96.1	96.0	97.6	97.7	96.6	96.7
All items less energy.....	127.2	125.8	127.8	126.3	128.1	126.7

(1) Not seasonally adjusted.

Consumer Price Indexes for Selected Items and Groups

Source: Bureau of Labor Statistics, U.S. Labor Dept.

(all urban consumers = CPI-U)

(1982-84 = 100. Annual averages of monthly figures)

	1970	1975	1980	1984	1985	1986	1987	1988
All Items	38.8	53.8	82.4	103.9	107.6	109.6	113.6	118.3
Food and beverages.............	40.1	60.2	86.7	103.2	105.6	109.1	113.5	118.2
Food...................	39.2	59.8	86.8	103.2	105.6	109.0	113.5	118.2
Food at home	39.9	61.8	88.4	102.8	104.3	107.3	111.9	116.6
Cereals, bakery prods..	37.1	62.9	83.9	103.9	107.9	110.9	114.8	122.1
Meats, poultry, fish, eggs..	44.6	67.0	92.0	101.3	100.1	104.5	110.5	114.3
Dairy prods..........	44.7	62.6	90.9	101.3	103.2	103.3	105.9	108.4
Fruits, vegetables......	37.8	56.9	82.1	105.7	108.4	109.4	119.1	128.1
Sugar, sweets........	30.5	65.3	90.5	103.2	105.8	109.0	111.0	114.0
Fats, oils...........	39.2	73.5	89.3	106.6	106.9	106.5	108.1	113.1
Nonalcoholic beverages ...	27.1	41.3	91.4	102.3	104.3	110.4	107.5	107.5
Other prepared foods	39.6	58.9	83.6	103.0	106.4	109.2	113.8	118.0
Food away from home	37.5	54.5	83.4	104.2	108.3	112.5	117.0	121.8
Alcoholic beverages	52.1	65.9	86.4	103.0	106.4	111.1	114.1	118.6
Housing..................	36.4	50.7	81.1	103.6	107.7	110.9	114.2	118.5
Shelter	35.5	48.8	81.0	104.0	109.8	115.8	121.3	127.1
Rent	47.6	59.4	80.9	105.3	111.8	118.3	123.1	127.8
Maintenance, repairs....	35.8	54.1	82.4	103.7	106.5	107.9	111.8	114.7
Fuel, other utilities......	29.1	45.4	75.4	104.8	106.5	104.1	103.0	104.4
Electricity	31.8	50.0	75.8	105.3	108.9	110.4	110.0	111.5
Household furnishings & operation.	46.8	63.4	86.3	101.9	103.8	105.2	107.1	109.4
House furnishings......	55.5	69.8	88.5	101.2	101.7	102.2	103.6	105.1
Apparel & upkeep.............	59.2	72.5	90.9	102.1	105.0	105.9	110.6	115.4
Apparel commodities	66.3	79.6	95.6	103.1	106.0	106.3	111.7	113.7
Men's & boys'........	62.2	75.5	89.4	102.1	105.0	106.2	109.1	113.4
Women's & girls'......	71.8	85.5	96.0	101.3	104.9	104.0	110.4	114.9
Footwear............	56.8	69.6	91.8	101.1	102.3	101.9	105.1	109.9
Transportation...............	37.5	50.1	83.1	103.7	106.4	102.3	105.4	108.7
Private...............	37.5	50.6	84.2	103.6	106.2	101.2	104.2	107.6
Automobiles, new.......	53.0	62.9	88.4	102.8	106.1	110.6	114.6	116.9
Automobiles, used.......	31.2	43.8	62.3	98.7	112.5	113.7	108.8	118.0
Gasoline............	27.9	45.1	97.5	99.4	97.8	98.6	77.0	80.8
Auto insurance........	42.0	48.4	82.0	108.2	119.2	135.0	146.2	156.6
Public................	35.2	43.5	69.0	105.7	110.5	117.0	121.1	123.3
Airline fares	28.3	38.0	68.0	105.8	112.5	117.1	122.8	124.2
Medical care..............	34.0	47.5	74.9	106.8	113.5	122.0	130.1	138.6

(continued)

	1970	1975	1980	1984	1985	1986	1987	1988
Prescription drugs	47.4	51.2	72.5	109.7	120.1	130.4	140.8	152.0
Physicians' services	34.5	48.1	76.5	107.0	113.3	121.5	130.4	139.8
Dental services	39.2	53.2	78.9	107.5	114.2	120.6	128.8	137.5
Hospital room	23.6	38.3	68.0	109.0	115.4	122.3	131.1	143.3
Entertainment	47.5	62.0	83.6	103.8	107.9	111.6	115.3	120.3
Other goods & services	40.9	53.9	75.2	107.9	114.5	121.4	128.5	137.0
Tobacco products	43.1	54.7	72.0	110.1	116.7	124.7	133.6	145.8
Personal care	43.5	57.9	81.9	104.3	108.3	111.9	115.1	119.4
Toilet goods	42.7	58.0	79.6	104.2	107.6	111.3	113.9	118.1
Personal care services	44.2	57.7	83.7	104.4	108.9	112.5	116.2	120.7
Personal, educational expenses	35.5	48.7	70.9	109.7	119.1	128.6	138.5	147.9

Consumer Price Indexes Annual Percent Change

Source: Bureau of Labor Statistics, U.S. Labor Department

The Consumer Price Index (CPI-U) measures the average change in prices of goods and services purchased by urban wage earners and clerical workers.

	1977[1]	1978	1979	1980	1981	1982	1983	1984	1985	1986	1987	1988
All items	6.5	7.7	11.3	13.5	10.4	6.1	3.2	4.3	3.6	1.9	3.6	4.1
Food	6.3	10.0	10.9	8.6	7.9	4.0	2.1	3.8	2.3	3.2	4.1	4.1
Shelter	6.8	10.1	13.9	17.5	11.7	7.1	2.3	4.9	5.6	5.5	4.7	4.8
Rent, residential	6.1	6.8	7.3	8.9	8.7	7.6	5.8	5.2	6.1	5.8	4.1	3.8
Fuel & other utilities	10.7	6.9	10.8	16.4	14.6	9.8	5.6	4.6	1.6	−2.3	−1.1	1.4
Apparel and upkeep	4.5	3.5	4.4	7.1	4.8	2.6	2.5	1.9	2.9	0.9	4.4	4.3
Private transportation	7.3	4.8	14.8	17.4	11.4	3.6	2.2	4.3	2.5	−4.7	3.0	3.3
Automobiles, new	5.3	7.6	7.9	8.0	6.1	3.9	2.5	2.9	3.2	4.2	3.6	1.8
Gasoline	5.8	4.3	35.3	39.0	11.3	−5.3	−3.3	−1.6	.8	−21.9	4.0	0.9
Public transportation	4.7	3.0	6.7	25.6	24.0	10.9	4.8	6.2	4.6	5.9	3.5	1.8
Medical care	9.6	8.4	9.3	10.9	10.8	11.6	8.7	6.2	6.2	7.5	6.6	6.5
Entertainment	4.9	5.3	6.7	8.9	7.8	6.5	4.3	3.7	3.9	3.4	3.3	4.3
Commodities	5.8	7.1	11.4	12.2	8.4	4.0	2.9	3.4	2.1	−0.9	3.2	3.5

(1) Change from 1976.

Consumer Price Index by Region and Selected Cities

Source: Bureau of Labor Statistics, U.S. Labor Department

Area (1982-84 = 100)	CPI-U Indexes			Percent change to May 1989 from— May 1988	CPI-W Indexes			Percent change to May 1989 from— May 1988
	Mar. 1989	Apr. 1989	May 1989		Mar. 1989	Apr. 1989	May 1989	
U.S. city average	122.3	123.1	123.8	5.4	120.8	121.8	122.5	5.4
Northeast urban	126.7	127.4	128.3	6.3	125.4	126.2	127.1	6.4
More than 1,200,000	127.4	128.0	128.7	5.8	125.2	125.9	126.7	6.0
500,000 to 1,200,000	125.1	126.1	127.2	7.0	123.9	124.9	126.0	7.1
50,000 to 500,000	125.5	126.2	127.6	7.5	127.8	128.6	130.0	7.3
North Central urban	119.8	120.8	121.3	5.0	117.9	118.9	119.4	5.1
More than 1,200,000	121.1	121.9	122.2	5.3	118.4	119.2	119.5	5.3
360,000 to 1,200,000	119.2	120.6	120.8	4.4	116.8	118.2	118.5	4.5
50,000 to 360,000	119.9	121.2	122.2	5.3	118.7	120.1	121.1	5.4
Less than 50,000	115.5	116.3	116.8	4.1	115.1	116.1	116.8	4.4
South urban	119.8	120.8	121.3	4.9	119.1	120.3	120.9	5.2
More than 1,200,000	120.5	121.4	122.0	4.5	119.6	120.6	121.3	4.8
450,000 to 1,200,000	121.0	122.2	122.4	5.3	118.8	120.1	120.5	5.7
50,000 to 450,000	118.5	119.4	120.0	4.7	119.0	120.0	120.6	4.9
Less than 50,000	118.0	119.4	120.4	5.9	118.7	120.2	121.3	6.0
West urban	123.1	123.8	124.5	5.1	121.7	122.6	123.3	5.2
More than 1,250,000	124.7	125.3	126.2	5.1	121.9	122.7	123.5	5.2
50,000 to 330,000	120.7	122.1	122.5	5.2	120.1	121.5	121.9	5.2
Selected areas								
Chicago, Ill.–Gary-Lake County, Ill., Ind., Wis.	123.0	123.6	123.9	5.9	119.1	119.8	120.1	6.0
L.A.–Long Beach, Anaheim, Riverside, Cal.	126.2	127.2	128.3	5.2	122.9	124.0	125.0	5.1
New York, N.Y.–Northern N.J., Long Island, N.Y.	128.9	129.5	130.2	6.1	126.8	127.5	128.2	6.2
Philadelphia, Wilmington, Trenton, Pa., Del., N.J.	126.0	126.7	127.9	5.8	125.8	126.7	127.9	5.9
San Francisco–Oakland, San Jose, Cal.	125.9	125.4	126.3	5.5	124.6	124.8	125.7	5.9
Baltimore, Md.	122.8	—	124.1	5.3	122.3	—	123.7	5.4
Boston, Lawrence, Salem, Mass., N.H.	129.7	—	130.5	6.0	129.7	—	130.6	6.1
Cleveland, Akron, Lorain Oh.	121.5	—	122.8	5.3	116.2	—	117.7	5.4
Miami, Ft. Lauderdale, Fla.	119.8	—	120.9	4.0	118.7	—	120.0	4.3
St. Louis, E. St. Louis, Mo.–Ill.	119.4	—	121.5	6.5	119.1	—	121.2	6.6
Washington, D.C.–Md.–Va.	126.1	—	127.1	5.8	125.6	—	126.6	6.1
Dallas–Fort Worth, Tex.	—	118.7	—	—	—	118.6	—	—
Detroit, Ann Arbor, Mich.	—	121.7	—	—	—	119.0	—	—
Houston, Galveston, Brazoria, Tex.	—	113.2	—	—	—	113.5	—	—
Pittsburgh, Beaver Valley, Pa.	—	119.2	—	—	—	114.7	—	—

Producer Price Indexes

Source: Bureau of Labor Statistics, U.S. Labor Department

Producer Price Indexes measure average changes in prices received in primary markets of the U.S. by producers of commodities in all stages of processing.

Commodity group (1982 = 100)	Annual Avg.		1988		1989	
	1987	1988	Jan.	June	Jan.	June
All commodities.	102.8	106.9	105.8	107.4	110.5	112.8
Farm products processed foods and feeds.	103.7	110.0	106.5	111.3	115.0	115.2
Farm products.	95.5	104.8	99.0	106.4	112.0	111.4
Processed foods and feeds	107.9	112.8	110.3	113.9	116.6	117.3
Industrial commodities	102.6	106.3	105.6	106.5	109.6	112.3
Textile products and apparel.	105.1	109.2	108.7	109.3	111.0	112.1
Hides, skins, leathers, and related products	120.4	131.5	134.4	131.4	131.2	134.9
Fuels and related products and power	70.2	66.8	67.5	68.7	68.1	75.7
Chemicals and allied products.	106.4	116.4	113.8	115.2	123.7	124.2
Rubber and plastic products	103.0	109.4	107.8	109.3	111.9	112.8
Lumber and wood products	112.8	118.9	119.2	119.4	120.1	127.3
Pulp, paper, and allied products	121.8	130.4	128.7	130.1	135.1	138.0
Metals and metal products.	107.1	118.7	116.8	118.0	125.3	123.7
Machinery and equipment	110.4	113.2	112.6	113.2	115.6	117.3
Furniture and household durables.	109.9	113.1	112.4	112.4	115.0	116.7
Nonmetallic mineral products	110.0	111.2	111.1	111.4	111.8	112.8
Transportation equipment	112.2	114.2	113.4	114.2	116.8	117.5
Miscellaneous products.	114.9	120.2	119.3	119.7	124.0	126.4

Index of Leading Economic Indicators

Source: Bureau of Economic Analysis, U.S. Dept. of Commerce

The index of leading economic indicators, which is issued to project the economy's performance six months or a year ahead, gained 0.21 percent in July 1989. Analysts said that the increase suggests that the economy is not on the verge of a recession.

The index is made up of twelve measurements of economic activity that tend to change direction long before the overall economy does. The volatility of the index, caused in part by the fact that many of the statistics covered do not reach the Commerce Department until weeks after the initial report, usually results in at least one revision after the initial reporting.

Two companion indexes—those of coincident and lagging indicators—rose in July by 0.5 percent and fell 0.4 percent, respectively. The coincident index reflects current economic conditions. Its components are: employees on nonagricultural payrolls; personal income less transfer payments; industrial production; and manufacturing and trade sales. The lagging index consists of items that tend to lag behind the business cycle.

Leading Indicators: Component Analysis

Components	Contribution to change June to July 1989	Components	Contribution to change June to July 1989
Average workweek of production workers in manufacturing	0.00	adjusted for inflation	+0.05
Average weekly claims for state unemployment insurance[1]	−0.08	New building permits issued	−0.06
New orders for consumer goods and materials, adjusted for inflation	−0.20	Change in manufactureres unfilled orders, durable goods	+0.01
Vendor performance (companies receiving slower deliveries from suppliers)	−0.03	Change in sensitive materials prices	−0.29
Contracts and orders for plant and equipment,		Index of stock prices	+0.14
		Money supply: M-2, adjusted for inflation	+0.27
		Index of consumer expectations	+0.26
		Leading indicators index, percent change	**0.21**

(1) Series is inverted in computing index; that is, a decrease in the series is considered upward movement.

Distribution of Total Personal Income

Source: Bureau of Economic Analysis; U.S. Commerce Department

(in billions)

Year	Personal income	Personal taxes	Disposable Personal income	Personal outlays	Personal Savings Amount	As a pct. of disposable income
1960	$ 402.3	$ 50.4	$ 352.0	$ 332.3	$ 19.7	5.6%
1965	540.7	64.9	475.8	442.1	33.7	7.1
1970	811.1	115.8	695.3	639.5	55.8	8.0
1973	1,065.2	150.7	914.5	835.5	79.0	8.6
1974	1,168.6	170.2	998.3	913.2	85.1	8.5
1975	1,265.0	168.9	1,096.1	1,001.8	94.3	8.6
1976	1,391.2	196.8	1,194.4	1,111.9	82.5	6.9
1977	1,540.4	226.4	1,314.0	1,236.0	78.0	5.9
1978	1,732.7	258.7	1,474.0	1,384.6	89.4	6.1
1979	1,951.2	301.0	1,650.2	1,553.5	96.7	5.9
1980	2,165.3	336.5	1,828.9	1,718.7	110.2	6.0
1981	2,429.5	387.7	2,041.7	1,904.3	137.4	6.7
1982	2,584.6	404.1	2,180.5	2,044.5	136.0	6.2
1983	2,838.6	410.5	2,428.1	2,297.4	130.6	5.4
1984	3,108.7	440.2	2,668.6	2,504.5	164.1	6.1
1985	3,325.3	486.6	2,838.7	2,713.3	125.4	4.4
1986	3,526.2	512.9	3,013.3	2,888.5	124.9	4.1
1987	3,776.6	571.7	3,205.9	3,104.1	101.8	3.2
1988	4,064.5	586.6	3,477.8	3,333.1	144.7	4.2

Personal Consumption Expenditures in the U.S.

Source: Bureau of Economic Analysis, U.S. Commerce Department

(billions of dollars)

	1983	1984	1985	1986	1987	1988
Personal consumption expenditures	2,234.5	2,430.5	2,629.0	2,797.4	3,010.8	3,235.1
Food & Tobacco	450.1	479.0	503.8	533.7	564.8	596.6
Food purchased for off-premise consumption	290.4	305.8	322.7	339.1	353.7	372.6
Purchased meals and beverages	123.5	134.1	139.9	151.6	165.5	176.6
Tobacco products	28.2	30.5	32.2	33.6	35.6	36.9
Clothing, accessories, jewelry	167.2	181.8	193.3	207.5	220.5	234.2
Shoes	20.2	21.6	22.9	24.3	25.7	26.8
Clothing and accessories less shoes	114.7	125.0	133.4	142.4	151.4	160.0
Jewelry and watches	18.0	19.9	20.5	22.8	24.2	25.1
Personal care	34.1	36.4	38.8	41.4	44.4	48.5
Toilet articles, preparations	20.3	21.9	23.1	24.6	26.2	27.9
Barbershops, beauty parlors, baths, health clubs	13.8	14.5	15.7	16.8	18.2	20.7
Housing	344.1	371.3	403.0	434.2	467.7	501.3
Owner-occupied nonfarm dwellings space rent	233.9	252.3	272.7	293.7	317.1	339.3
Tenant-occupied nonfarm dwellings rent	84.7	92.2	103.8	114.3	123.5	132.7
Rental value of farm dwellings	12.1	12.2	10.9	9.7	9.1	9.5
Household operation	294.1	316.9	334.1	347.5	363.0	386.4
Furniture, incl. bedding	23.8	26.5	28.0	30.4	31.7	33.5
Kitchen, other household applicances	19.6	21.6	23.7	25.5	26.7	28.4
China, glassware, tableware, utensils	11.2	12.2	13.0	14.3	15.0	15.7
Other durable house furnishings	24.4	27.1	28.2	30.6	33.2	35.6
Semidurable house furnishings	12.3	13.3	14.0	15.2	15.8	16.6
Cleaning, household supplies, paper products	23.6	25.1	26.4	27.8	29.1	30.8
Household utilities	110.8	117.5	124.2	122.4	126.3	135.1
Telephone, telegraph	37.9	39.8	40.4	42.7	44.1	47.1
Medical care	268.7	298.4	327.5	357.6	399.3	443.0
Drug preparations, sundries	24.4	26.3	28.1	30.2	32.3	34.5
Physicians	61.1	67.1	73.5	80.6	93.8	105.0
Dentists	18.5	19.8	21.5	22.8	25.0	27.0
Privately controlled hospitals and sanitariums	119.6	130.6	140.2	154.2	166.3	182.3
Health insurance	16.0	19.0	21.6	22.4	25.9	29.8
Personal business	136.7	145.8	169.9	192.5	223.2	234.4
Brokerage charges, investment counseling	11.8	11.6	14.8	19.7	20.5	17.6
Bank service charges, trust services, safe deposit box rental	9.0	10.2	11.7	13.0	14.6	15.6
Legal services	21.7	24.6	28.0	30.9	34.9	39.4
Funeral, burial expenses	5.2	5.6	6.3	6.6	7.0	7.6
Transportation	295.4	329.5	359.5	366.3	377.1	406.4
User-operated transportation	270.5	301.6	330.1	335.9	343.4	369.7
New autos	66.2	77.6	87.4	101.3	93.5	101.2
Used autos	21.6	30.2	35.1	33.6	38.2	43.0
Accessories & other parts	21.9	23.3	25.2	26.5	28.7	31.3
Repair, greasing, washing, parking, storage, rental	38.4	42.8	49.1	52.0	55.5	62.5
Gasoline and oil	90.2	90.0	90.6	73.5	75.2	76.8
Tolls	1.2	1.3	1.4	1.7	1.9	2.0
Insurance premiums less claims paid	10.3	10.0	9.9	12.6	15.4	16.8
Purchased local transportation	6.5	6.9	7.2	7.8	8.2	8.4
Transit systems	3.1	3.4	3.6	3.8	4.0	4.1
Taxicab	2.9	3.0	3.1	3.3	3.5	3.8
Railway (commutation)	.4	.5	.5	.6	.7	.5
Purchased intercity transportation	18.4	21.0	22.2	22.6	25.5	28.2
Railway (excl. commutation)	.5	.6	.6	.7	.7	.8
Bus	1.2	1.2	1.2	1.1	1.4	1.6
Airline	15.3	17.5	18.5	18.8	21.2	23.3
Recreation	152.1	168.3	185.7	201.2	224.5	246.8
Books, maps	7.2	7.8	8.1	8.6	9.4	9.8
Magazines, newspapers, sheet music	12.0	12.7	13.2	13.9	15.2	16.0
Nondurable toys and sport supplies	18.0	19.7	21.1	23.1	26.2	28.1
Wheel goods, durable toys, sports equipment, boats, pleasure aircraft	20.4	24.8	26.7	29.7	33.7	36.5
Radio and TV receivers, records, musical instruments	28.2	31.5	37.0	38.8	42.5	48.8
Flowers, seeds, potted plants	4.8	5.2	5.5	5.8	6.6	6.8
Admissions to specified spectator amusements	8.6	9.5	9.5	10.2	11.3	11.9
Motion picture theaters	3.6	3.9	3.6	3.9	4.2	4.2
Legitimate theater, opera	2.4	2.7	3.0	3.3	4.0	4.4
Spectator sports	2.6	2.9	2.9	2.9	3.0	3.2
Clubs, fraternal organizations	4.2	4.5	4.8	5.0	5.5	5.9
Commerical amusements	13.6	14.1	15.1	16.0	17.1	18.9
Private education, research	35.8	39.1	43.3	46.6	51.1	58.0
Higher education	13.2	14.4	15.7	16.9	17.9	19.3
Elementary and secondary schools	11.8	12.6	13.8	14.5	15.6	16.9
Religious and welfare activities	47.8	52.6	57.1	62.9	68.2	76.1
Foreign travel and other, net	8.5	11.3	13.1	7.0	7.0	3.2

Top Paid Business Executives in 1988

Source: *Business Week*

Compensation for business executives in 1988 rose 17 percent over the previous year in a survey of 708 executives from 354 companies conducted by Business Week magazine. Compensation includes stock options and other performance bonuses.

Executive, Company	1988 Compensation	Executive, Company	1988 Compensation
Mike Eisner, Disney chairman	$40.1 mlns.	John Sculley, Apple chairman	$9.5 mlns.
Ed Horrigan, RJR Nabisco v. chairman	21.7 mlns.	Phil Rooney, Waste Management president	
Ross Johnson, RJR Nabisco CEO	21.1 mlns.	dent	7.5 mlns.
Martin Davis, Gulf+Western chairman	16.3 mlns.	Roy Vagelos, Merck chairman	6.9 mlns.
Hugh Liedtke, Pennzoil chairman	11.5 mlns.	Roger Smith, GM chairman	3.8 mlns.
Paul Fireman, Reebok chairman	11.4 mlns.	Lee Iacocca, Chrysler chairman	3.7 mlns.
Ken Olsen, DEC chairman	10.0 mlns.	Jack Welch, GE chairman	2.4 mlns.
Don Petersen, Ford chairman	9.9 mlns.	Lawrence Rawl, Exxon chairman	1.4 mlns.

State Finances

Revenues, Expenditures, Debts, Taxes, and U.S. Aid

(fiscal year 1987)

Source: Census Bureau, U.S. Commerce Dept.

	Revenue (thousands)	Expenditures (thousands)	Debt (thousands)	Per cap. debt	Per cap. taxes	Per cap. U.S. aid
Alabama.	$7,076,621	$6,332,995	$3,728,623	$913	$789	$382
Alaska	4,888,975	4,416,197	6,188,794	11,788	2,024	1,188
Arizona	6,673,432	5,904,421	1,936,738	572	1,025	351
Arkansas	3,887,600	3,473,218	1,440,955	603	791	422
California	70,335,509	62,480,553	22,405,137	810	1,294	398
Colorado	6,723,277	5,456,448	2,319,634	704	777	350
Connecticut . . .	7,595,226	6,665,581	8,013,818	2,496	1,358	1,489
Delaware	1,980,252	1,553,454	2,786,999	4,328	1,463	468
Florida	17,394,294	15,426,277	7,805,781	649	819	262
Georgia	10,240,549	9,060,704	2,600,784	418	856	404
Hawaii	3,164,485	2,614,194	2,867,947	2,648	1,567	424
Idaho	1,867,960	1,605,160	613,692	615	831	392
Illinois	20,632,044	18,820,800	12,665,135	1,094	900	386
Indiana.	9,037,469	8,341,879	2,731,350	494	863	358
Iowa	5,480,709	5,074,819	1,775,728	627	939	385
Kansas.	4,111,666	3,628,853	369,936	149	842	342
Kentucky	6,926,425	6,333,832	4,668,955	1,253	945	457
Louisiana	9,257,378	8,459,791	11,075,130	2,483	773	430
Maine	2,651,426	2,287,295	1,621,025	1,366	1,085	580
Maryland	9,699,876	8,714,466	5,336,095	1,177	1,148	441
Massachusetts .	14,001,086	14,015,247	12,800,267	2,186	1,446	2,986
Michigan.	21,493,252	18,790,798	7,700,322	837	1,071	456
Minnesota	10,642,746	9,204,956	3,586,866	845	1,306	480
Mississippi. . . .	4,413,493	3,956,009	1,322,458	504	740	485
Missouri	7,761,163	7,094,780	4,306,689	844	773	377
Montana.	1,815,739	1,697,461	1,146,145	1,417	731	667
Nebraska	2,474,930	2,282,431	1,478,397	927	755	381
Nevada	2,474,505	2,009,586	1,226,184	1,218	1,123	391
New Hampshire.	1,684,177	1,483,600	2,362,126	2,235	532	368
New Jersey. . . .	19,542,176	17,174,895	17,488,666	2,280	1,237	434
New Mexico. . .	3,842,192	3,306,466	1,780,016	1,187	1,050	519
New York	55,571,707	47,504,647	40,630,801	2,279	1,384	669
North Carolina .	11,874,419	10,133,313	2,725,698	425	972	339
North Dakota . .	1,545,404	1,585,321	791,706	1,178	853	623
Ohio	25,066,860	20,752,558	9,439,644	875	901	406
Oklahoma. . . .	5,781,282	5,509,891	4,105,135	1,255	816	403
Oregon	6,146,378	5,139,882	7,143,426	2,622	821	456
Pennsylvania . .	23,803,151	20,571,383	8,819,566	739	953	442
Rhode Island . .	2,575,306	2,258,828	2,785,175	2,825	1,065	550
South Carolina .	6,766,034	5,958,522	3,722,490	1,087	922	374
South Dakota . .	1,241,301	1,281,619	1,544,118	2,178	587	621
Tennessee	7,382,628	6,584,051	2,260,765	466	742	416
Texas	24,038,018	21,717,262	5,328,886	317	669	289
Utah	3,400,495	3,262,466	1,417,516	844	856	467
Vermont	1,294,204	1,153,449	955,067	1,743	982	314
Virginia.	11,173,692	9,692,887	4,198,991	711	936	323
Washington . . .	11,575,124	9,981,590	3,841,031	846	1,243	436
West Virginia . .	3,965,237	3,884,292	2,240,820	1,181	965	542
Wisconsin	12,167,435	9,427,415	4,795,159	998	1,180	448
Wyoming	1,802,112	1,629,661	780,377	1,593	1,289	916
United States .	**$516,941,419**	**$455,696,203**	**$265,676,763**	**$1,094**	**$1,017**	**$437**

Federal Aid to State and Local Governments

Source: U.S. Office of Management and Budget
(million of dollars)

Type of aid, function, and major program	1970	1975	1980	1985	1987	1988[1]
Grant-in-aid shared revenue	24,065	49,791	91,451	105,897	108,392	116,666
National defense.	37	74	93	157	193	210
Natural resources & environment	411	2,437	5,363	4,069	4,073	3,864
Energy	25	43	499	529	455	414
Agriculture	604	404	569	2,420	2,092	1,751
Transportation[2].	4,599	5,864	13,087	17,055	16,919	17,854
Airports	83	292	590	789	917	979
Highways	4,395	4,702	9,209	12,841	12,649	13,270
Railroads.	—	(z)	54	35	22	26
Urban mass transit	105	689	3,129	2,797	3,253	3,483
Commerce & housing credit	4	2	3	2	1	2
Community & regional development . . .	1,780	2,842	6,486	5,221	4,235	4,498
Education, employment, training, social services[2]	6,393	12,133	21,862	17,817	18,657	21,336
Health[2]	3,849	8,810	15,758	24,451	29,466	32,846
Alcohol, drug abuse, & mental health[2] .	146	590	679	501	622	714
Medicaid[3]	2,727	6,840	13,957	22,655	27,435	30,664
Income security[2]	5,819	9,352	18,495	27,153	29,972	31,494
Assistance payment program	4,142	5,121	6,888	8,592	10,540	10,784
Food stamps, administration.	559	136	413	886	1,108	1,154
Child nutrition & special milk programs[3]	379	1,565	3,388	3,480	3,922	4,278
Housing assistance[3]	436	1,326	3,435	6,407	7,375	8,279
Veterans benefits & services.	18	33	90	91	95	106
Administration of justice.	42	725	529	95	234	336
General government[4]	49	101	138	182	2,000	1,956

(1) Estimate. (2) Includes items not shown separately. (3) Incl. grants for payments to individuals. (4) Incl. general purpose fiscal assistance. z = not applicable.

Philanthropy in the U.S.

Source: Giving USA, 1988; a publication of the American Association of Fund-Raising Counsel Trust for Philanthropy

(Billions of Dollars)

Sources of Contributors

Corporations[1]		Foundations		Bequests[2]		Individuals		Total Amount	
1970.	.797	1970.	1.90	1970.	2.13	1970.	16.19	1970.	21.02
1975.	1.202	1975.	1.65	1975.	2.23	1975.	23.53	1975.	28.61
1977.	1.791	1977.	2.00	1977.	2.99	1977.	29.55	1977.	36.34
1978.	2.084	1978.	2.17	1978.	2.60	1978.	32.10	1978.	38.95
1979.	2.288	1979.	2.42	1979.	2.23	1979.	36.59	1979.	43.69
1980.	2.359	1980.	2.81	1980.	2.86	1980.	40.71	1980.	48.74
1981.	2.514	1981.	3.07	1981.	3.58	1981.	46.42	1981.	55.58
1982.	2.906	1982.	3.16	1982.	5.21	1982.	48.52	1982.	59.80
1983.	3.627	1983.	3.60	1983.	3.88	1983.	53.54	1983.	64.65
1984.	4.057	1984.	3.95	1984.	4.04	1984.	58.50	1984.	70.55
1985.	4.472	1985.	4.90	1985.	4.77	1985.	66.17	1985.	80.31
1986.	4.600	1986.	5.43	1986.	5.70	1986.	76.19	1986.	91.92
1987.	4.600	1987.	5.88	1987.	6.58	1987.	80.76	1987.	97.92
1988.	4.750	1988.	6.13	1988.	6.79	1988.	86.70	1988.	104.37

Uses of Contributions

	Religion	Education	Health	Human service	Arts, culture & humanities	Public/society benefit	Other
1970	9.34	2.60	3.44	2.92	.663	.455	2.64
1975	12.81	2.83	3.61	2.94	1.56	.790	4.40
1977	16.98	3.62	4.09	3.57	2.32	1.22	3.66
1978	18.35	4.11	4.52	3.87	2.40	1.08	4.62
1979	20.17	4.54	4.94	4.48	2.73	1.23	5.27
1980	22.23	4.96	5.34	4.91	3.15	1.46	6.68
1981	25.05	5.77	5.79	5.62	3.66	1.79	7.90
1982	28.06	6.00	6.15	6.33	4.96	1.68	6.62
1983	31.86	6.65	6.68	7.16	4.21	1.89	6.22
1984	35.43	7.29	6.84	7.88	4.50	1.94	6.67
1985	37.46	8.17	7.72	8.50	5.08	2.22	11.16
1986	41.68	9.39	8.44	9.13	5.83	2.38	15.07
1987	44.54	9.84	9.22	9.84	6.31	2.70	15.37
1988	48.21	9.78	9.52	10.49	6.82	3.02	16.53

(1) IRS-based data through 1984. IRS figures include giving by corporations to nonprofit organizations and to their own foundations. They do not include giving by corporate foundations to other nonprofits.

Key Economic Indicators: 1989 Performance and 1990 Forecast

Source: Gary S. Meyers, The Meyers Report; Bloomberg Financial Services (historical data)

Consumer Loans	Jan. 1989	Oct. 1989	1990 Range	Comments
30 yr-fixed mortgage	10.77%	10.17%	9.25-10.25%	Plenty of funds available, hot housing market, rates to fall though 1st quarter, then rise by end of 3rd quarter 1990.
15 yr-fixed mortgage	10.53%	9.88%	8.85-10.01%	
48-mo new auto	11.49%	12.06%	11.23-12.25%	Auto incentives to keep lending competitive and rates low.
Unsec. pers. loan	16.00%	16.44%	15.95-16.40%	Not much movement here, slight down, then a slight up.
Credit card	17.83%	17.83%	17.50-18.50%	Rates generally not expected to change.
Savings Instruments (at banks and thrifts)				
Money market acct.	6.12%	6.51%	6.00-6.40%	Ranges indicate the forecast 1990 high and low. Rate movements should decline through Feb., then level. Look for rate hikes by the end of the 3rd quarter or 4th, as the economy noticeably gains steam. Plenty of funds available will limit rate hikes here.
1yr CD	8.12%	8.30%	7.75-8.45%	
30 mo CD	8.24%	8.19%	7.50-8.50%	
42 mo CD	8.31%	8.18%	7.55-8.60%	
5 yr	8.45%	8.20%	7.75-8.65%	
Key Institutional Interest Rates				
Prime	10.50%	10.50%	9.75-10.50%	Rates to fall, but banks will stall for profits.
Fed Funds	9.04%	9.18%	8.25-9.25%	Rates should fall. Fed must cut—but they still fear inflation.
Discount	6.50%	7.00%	6.25-7.00%	
Treasury Yields				
90 day T-bill	8.04%	8.00%	7.20-8.25%	Tough call, volatility to rule 1990—confuses investors on short term securities. Rates to fall then rise by Sept.
60 mo T-bill	8.74%	8.25%	7.25-8.35%	
1 yr T-bill	9.10%	8.35%	7.33-8.50%	Plenty of funds available for this popular term security.
30 yr T-bill	9.08%	8.16%	7.33-8.15%	T-bond will follow rate trend: down then up at yearend.
Currencies (per $U.S.)				
Japanese Yen	120	133	115-130	Dollar needs to fail; how far could be a shocker. This is key economic scenario: Japan has low unemployment and high inflation. Bundesbank will help lower dollar with rate hikes; Swiss follow W. Germany. British have their own problems.
W. Ger. D-Mark	1.71	1.79	1.75-1.98	
Swiss Franc	1.44	1.79	1.75-1.98	
British Pound	0.53	0.59	0.50-0.58	
Economic Indicators (P.A.)				
Retail sales	19.2%	8.4%	2.75-3.75%	Consumer buying up; store profits fall—too many stores.
CPI	6%	2.4%	2.5-3.65%	Inflation moderate, price volatility confuses analysts and press.
Food prices	14.4%	2.4%	1.75-3.25%	Drought over, yields up, price volatile throughout year.
Producer Price index	10.8%	-4.8%	1.50-3.40%	Over supply of commodities holds prices; rises at yearend.
Housing starts (millions)	1.7	1.4	1.61-17.5	Lower mortgage rates help.
Unemployment	5.4%	5.2%	5.5-6.0%	Economy slows; 1st quarter talk-recession, 4th quarter talk-inflation. Dollar falls and economy and exports grow.
GNP	3.7 (1st Q)	2.7 (2nd Q)	2.1-3.25%	

Note: All forecasts were made on 10/6/89, and cannot reflect major economic, political, and natural events that occurred later.

Gold Reserves of Central Banks and Governments

Source: IMF, *International Financial Statistics*
(Million fine troy ounces)

Year end	All countries[1]	United States	Canada	Japan	Belgium	France	West Germany	Italy	Nether- lands	Switzer- land	United Kingdom
1972	1,019.68	275.97	21.95	21.10	43.08	100.69	117.36	82.37	54.17	83.11	21.08
1973	1,022.24	275.97	21.95	21.11	42.17	100.91	117.61	82.48	54.33	83.20	21.01
1974	1,020.24	275.97	21.95	21.11	42.17	100.93	117.61	82.48	54.33	83.20	21.01
1975	1,018.71	274.71	21.95	21.11	42.17	100.93	117.61	82.48	54.33	83.20	21.03
1976	1,014.23	274.68	21.62	21.11	42.17	101.02	117.61	82.48	54.33	83.20	21.03
1977	1,029.19	277.55	22.01	21.62	42.45	101.67	118.30	82.91	54.63	83.28	21.03
1978	1,036.82	276.41	22.13	23.97	42.59	101.99	118.64	83.12	54.78	83.28	22.23
1979	944.44	264.60	22.18	24.23	34.21	81.92	95.25	66.71	43.97	83.28	22.83
1980	952.99	264.32	20.98	24.23	34.18	81.85	95.18	66.67	43.94	83.28	18.25
1981	953.72	264.11	20.46	24.23	34.18	81.85	95.18	66.67	43.94	83.28	18.84
1982	949.16	264.03	20.26	24.23	34.18	81.85	95.18	66.67	43.94	83.28	19.03
1983	947.84	263.39	20.17	24.23	34.18	81.85	95.18	66.67	43.94	83.28	19.01
1984	946.79	262.79	20.14	24.23	34.18	81.85	95.18	66.67	43.94	83.28	19.01
1985	949.39	262.65	20.11	24.33	34.18	81.85	95.18	66.67	43.94	83.28	19.03
1986	949.11	262.04	19.72	24.23	34.18	81.85	95.18	66.67	43.94	83.28	19.03
1987	944.49	262.38	18.52	24.23	33.63	81.85	95.18	66.67	43.94	83.28	19.01
1988	944.76	261.87	17.38	24.23	33.67	81.85	95.18	66.67	43.94	83.28	19.00

(1) Covers IMF members with reported gold holdings. For countries not listed above, see *International Financial Statistics*, a monthly publication of the International Monetary Fund.

United States Mint

Source: United States Mint, U.S. Treasury Department

The United States Mint was created by Act of April 2, 1792, which established the U.S. national coinage system. Initially, operations were conducted at Philadelphia, then the nation's capital. Supervision of the Mint was a function of the secretary of state, but in 1799, it became an independent agency reporting directly to the president. The Mint was made a statutory bureau of the Treasury Department in 1873, with a director appointed by the president to oversee its operations from headquarters offices in the Treasury Department in Washington, D.C.

The Mint manufactures all U.S. coins and distributes them through the Federal Reserve banks and branches. The Mint also maintains physical custody of the treasury's monetary stocks of gold and silver, moving, storing and releasing from custody as authorized. There are 6 field facilities. Mints are located in Philadelphia and Denver; the San Francisco Mint and San Francisco Old Mint perform coinage operations and numismatic functions; two depositories, one at Fort Knox, Ky., for the storage of gold, and the other at West Point, N.Y., where gold and silver are stored and coinage is produced by congressional authorization. A museum is maintained at the San Francisco Old Mint.

The traditional 90% silver coinage was phased out and cupronickel clad coinage introduced when the Coinage Act of 1965 removed all silver from the dime and quarter and reduced the silver content of the half dollar to 40%. In 1970, legislative action removed the remaining silver from the half dollar and in providing for the resumption of dollar coinage, directed that both denominations produced for circulation also be cupronickel clad metal. Changes in the design, weight and size of the standard silver dollar were approved by Congress in 1978, and beginning in 1979, a smaller cupronickel dollar coin bearing the likeness of Susan B. Anthony and the Apollo II moon landing was released.

A change in the composition of the cent was effected in 1982, when the current copper-plated zinc cent was introduced to replace the traditional 95% copper cent.

The Mint manufactures and sells bronze medals of a national character, produces numismatic coins and coin sets, and as scheduling permits, manufactures coinage for foreign governments. Special government-sponsored numismatic coinage includes congressionally authorized 90% silver half dollars produced in 1982 to mark the 250th anniversary of George Washington's birth, and 90% gold $10 coins dated 1984 and two 90% silver dollars dated 1983 and 1984, respectively, commemorating the 1984 Olympic games, and a 90% gold $5 coin, a 90% silver dollar coin and a cupronickel half dollar for the Statue of Liberty Centennial in 1986. The Mint issued a 1987 dated 90% gold $5 coin and a 1987 dated 90% silver dollar coin honoring the 200th Anniversary of the U.S. Constitution. Congress has also directed the U.S. Mint to commence the production and sale of legal tender gold and silver bullion coins designated as "American Eagle Bullion Coins" by the mint. The coins in the series contain .9167 fine gold, and have a face value of $50 (1 oz.), $25 (1/2 oz.), $10 (1/4 oz.), and $5 (1/10 oz.). The American Eagle silver bullion coin has a face value of $1 and contains 1 troy ounce of .999 fine silver. Information concerning these and other Mint coin programs and coin availability, may be secured from the United States Mint, 10001 Aerospace Road, Lanham, MD 20706.

Domestic Coin Production

	Cents	Nickels	Dimes	Quarters	Halves	Total[1]
1979	10,157,872,254	789,055,672	706,361,184	1,005,497,780	84,127,422	13,500,728,056
1980	12,554,803,660	1,095,327,448	1,454,524,321	1,154,159,487	77,590,449	16,426,066,073
1981	12,864,985,677	1,022,305,843	1,388,934,143	1,177,438,833	57,383,533	16,520,790,029
1982	16,725,504,368	666,081,544	1,062,188,584	980,973,788	23,959,102	19,458,707,386
1983	14,219,554,428	1,098,341,276	1,377,154,224	1,291,341,446	52,291,158	17,821,554,250
1984	13,720,317,906	1,264,444,146	1,561,472,976	1,223,028,064	38,520,996	14,670,235,999
1985	10,935,889,813	1,106,862,408	1,293,180,932	1,295,781,850	28,473,778	12,072,913,262
1986	8,934,262,191	898,702,633	1,155,976,667	1,055,497,993	28,473,778	12,072,913,262
1987	9,561,856,445	782,090,085	1,415,912,883	1,238,094,177	99,481	12,998,053,071
1988	11,346,550,443	1,435,131,652	1,992,935,488	1,158,862,687	25,626,096	15,959,106,366
1989*	8,573,470,000	899,492,000	1,436,610,000	948,508,000	35,774,172	11,893,854,172

* As of Aug. 31 (1) Incl. dollars, 1979-81.

Portraits on U.S. Treasury Bills, Bonds, Notes and Savings Bonds

Denomination	Savings bonds	Treas. bills	Treas. bonds	Treas. notes
25	Washington			
50	F.D. Roosevelt		Jefferson	
75	Truman			
100	Eisenhower		Jackson	
200	Kennedy			
500	Wilson		Washington	
1,000	T. Roosevelt	H. McCulloch	Lincoln	Lincoln
5,000	McKinley	J.G. Carlisle	Monroe	Monroe
10,000	Cleveland	J. Sherman	Cleveland	Cleveland
50,000		C. Glass		
100,000		A Gallatin	Grant	Grant
1,000,000		O. Wolcott	T. Roosevelt	T. Roosevelt
100,000,000				Madison
500,000,000				McKinley

Large Denominations of U.S. Currency Discontinued

The largest denomination of United States currency now being issued is the $100 bill. Issuance of currency in denominations larger than $100 was discontinued in 1969.

As large denomination bills reach the Federal Reserve Bank they are removed from circulation.

Because some of the discontinued currency is expected to be in the hands of holders for many years, the description of the various denominations below is continued:

Amt.	Portrait	Embellishment on back	Amt.	Portrait	Embellishment on back
$ 1	Washington	Great Seal of U.S.	$ 100	Franklin	Independence Hall
2	Jefferson	Signers of Declaration	500	McKinley	Ornate denominational marking
5	Lincoln	Lincoln Memorial	1,000	Cleveland	Ornate denominational marking
10	Hamilton	U.S. Treasury	5,000	Madison	Ornate denominational marking
20	Jackson	White House	10,000	Chase	Ornate denominational marking
50	Grant	U.S. Capitol	100,000*	Wilson	Ornate denominational marking

*For use only in transactions between Federal Reserve System and Treasury Department.

U.S. Currency and Coin

Source: U.S. Treasury Department; Financial Management Service (June 30, 1989)

Amounts Outstanding and in Circulation

Currency	Amounts outstanding	Less amounts held by: United States Treasury	Less amounts held by: Federal Reserve Banks[1]	Amounts in circulation
Federal Reserve notes[1]	$272,981,202,586	$5,111,363	$42,133,317,033	$230,842,774,190
United States notes	322,539,016	31,954,339	213	290,584,464
Currency no longer issued.	267,371,114	251,794	20,524	267,098,796
Total	$273,571,112,716	$37,317,496	$42,133,337,770	$231,400,457,450
Coin[2]				
Dollars[3]	$2,024,703,898	$331,217,520	$108,549,861	$1,584,936,517
Fractional coin	16,638,341,000	103,754,628	337,301,998	16,197,284,374
Total	18,663,044,898	434,972,148	445,851,859	17,782,220,891
Total currency and coin.	$292,234,157,614	$472,289,644	$42,579,189,629	$249,182,678,341

Currency in Circulation by Denominations

Denomination	Total currency in circulation	Federal Reserve Notes[1]	U.S. Notes	Currency no longer issued
1 Dollar	$4,592,665,922	$4,440,975,371	$143,481	$151,547,070
2 Dollars	788,212,466	655,359,544	132,839,958	12,964
5 Dollars	5,750,982,850	5,602,325,465	111,906,705	36,750,680
10 Dollars	11,823,664,200	11,799,300,650	5,950	24,357,600
20 Dollars	63,316,206,660	63,296,045,060	3,380	20,158,220
50 Dollars	30,197,011,250	30,185,439,700	—	11,571,550
100 Dollars	114,602,020,000	114,534,177,400	45,684,900	22,157,700
500 Dollars	150,324,500	150,135,000	—	189,500
1,000 Dollars	174,129,000	173,921,000	—	208,000
5,000 Dollars	1,790,000	1,745,000	—	45,000
10,000 Dollars	3,450,000	3,350,000	—	100,000
Fractional parts	487	—	—	487
Partial notes[4]	115	—	90	25
Total currency	$231,400,457,450	$230,842,774,190	$290,584,464	$267,098,796

Comparative Totals of Money in Circulation — Selected Dates

Date	Dollars (in millions)	Per capita[5]	Date	Dollars (in millions)	Per capita[5]	Date	Dollars (in millions)	Per capita[5]
June 30, 1989	249,182.7	1,002.54	June 30, 1975	81,196.4	380.08	June 30, 1940	7,847.5	59.40
June 30, 1988	235,415.9	956.57	June 30, 1970	54,351.0	265.39	June 30, 1935	5,567.1	43.75
June 30, 1987	215,158.6	883.45	June 30, 1965	39,719.8	204.14	June 30, 1930	4,522.0	36.74
June 30, 1986	199,309.2	883.45	June 30, 1960	32,064.6	177.47	June 30, 1925	4,815.2	41.56
June 30, 1985	185,890.7	778.58	June 30, 1955	30,229.3	182.90	June 30, 1920	5,467.6	51.36
June 30, 1984	175,059.6	739.64	June 30, 1950	27,156.3	179.03	June 30, 1915	3,319.6	33.01
June 30, 1980	127,097.2	558.28	June 30, 1945	26,746.4	191.14	June 30, 1910	3,148.7	34.07

(1) Issued on and after July 1, 1929. (2) Excludes coin sold to collectors at premium prices. (3) Includes $481,781,898 in standard silver dollars. (4) Represents value of certain partial denominations not presented for redemption. (5) Based on Bureau of the Census estimates of population.

The requirement for a gold reserve against U.S. notes was repealed by Public Law 90-269 approved Mar. 18, 1968. Silver certificates issued on and after July 1, 1929 became redeemable from the general fund on June 24, 1968. The amount of security after those dates has been reduced accordingly.

Seigniorage on Coin and Silver Bullion

Source: U.S. Treasury Department, Financial Management Service

Seigniorage is the profit from coining money; it is the difference between the monetary value of coins and their cost, including the manufacturing expense.

Fiscal year	Dollars	Fiscal year	Dollars
Jan. 1, 1935–June 30, 1965, cumulative	2,525,927,763.84	1983	477,479,387.58
1968	383,141,339.00[1]	1984	498,371,724.09
1970	274,217,884.01	1985	515,906,969.31
1972	580,586,683.00	1986	392,445,674.57
1974	320,706,638.49	1987	458,070,694.43
1975	660,898,070.69	1988	470,409,480.20
1980	662,814,791.48	Cumulative Jan. 1, 1935-Sept. 30, 1988	13,727,374,271.32

(1) Revised to include seigniorage on clad coins.

EMPLOYMENT

U.S. Labor Force, Employment and Unemployment

Source: Bureau of Labor Statistics, U.S. Labor Department

The unemployment rate fell in 1988 for the fifth year in a row, to a yearly average of 5.5%. The decline in the unemployment rate occurred even though many more people, particularly women, have sought work, and even though American industry has been streamlining its operations to meet increasing foreign competition.

(numbers in thousands)

Employment status	Annual averages 1986	1987	1988	1989 Jan.	March	May	July
Civilian labor force	117,834	119,865	121,869	123,428	123,264	123,610	123,955
Employed	109,597	112,440	114,988	116,711	117,136	117,215	117,459
Unemployed	8,237	7,425	6,701	6,716	6,128	6,395	6,497
Unemployment rate	7.0	6.2	5.5	5.4	5.0	5.2	5.2

Selected Unemployment Indicators

(quarterly averages, seasonally adjusted)

Category Characteristic	1986 II	III	IV	1987 I	II	III	IV	1988 I	II	III	IV	1989 I	II
Total (all civilian workers) . . .	7.2	7.0	8.8	6.8	6.3	6.0	6.9	6.7	6.5	6.5	6.3	6.2	6.3
Men, 20 years and over . . .	6.2	6.2	6.1	5.8	5.8	5.2	5.0	4.9	4.7	4.7	4.7	4.5	4.4
Women, 20 years and over .	5.4	6.1	6.0	6.4	5.4	5.3	5.2	5.0	4.9	4.9	4.7	4.8	4.8
Both sexes, 16 to 19 years .	19.0	18.2	17.8	17.8	17.1	18.0	18.7	18.0	18.2	18.3	14.8	15.0	15.1
White	6.2	6.0	5.9	5.7	5.4	5.1	5.0	4.8	4.7	4.8	4.8	4.4	4.5
Black and other	13.4	13.1	12.7	12.4	11.7	11.3	11.0	11.1	10.6	9.9	9.9	10.3	9.8
Black	14.7	14.7	14.3	13.9	13.1	12.8	12.3	12.4	11.9	11.2	11.3	11.6	11.2
Hispanic origin	10.6	10.9	10.1	9.8	8.7	8.2	8.5	8.0	8.8	8.0	7.8	7.2	8.1
Married men, spouse present	4.4	4.4	4.4	4.1	4.1	3.8	3.5	3.4	3.2	3.2	3.2	3.0	3.0
Married women, spouse present	5.4	6.1	4.9	4.6	4.3	4.2	4.2	4.0	3.9	3.9	3.7	3.6	3.9
Women who maintain families	9.8	9.8	9.6	9.7	9.4	9.1	9.6	8.2	8.2	8.0	7.9	8.0	7.9
Full-time workers	6.8	6.8	6.5	6.2	5.9	5.8	5.5	5.3	5.1	5.1	5.0	4.9	4.9
Part-time workers	9.3	9.2	9.0	9.0	8.2	8.2	8.2	8.0	7.6	7.6	7.2	7.1	7.3
Unemployed 15 weeks and over[1]	1.9	1.9	1.9	1.8	1.7	1.6	1.5	1.4	1.3	1.3	1.2	1.1	1.1
Labor force time lost[2]	8.1	7.9	7.7	7.4	7.2	8.8	8.7	8.6	8.3	8.4	8.2	8.0	8.0
Industry													
Nonagricultural private wage and salary workers	7.2	7.0	6.9	6.6	6.3	6.0	5.8	5.7	5.5	5.6	5.4	5.3	5.3
Mining	13.6	15.9	14.7	12.3	10.8	8.2	7.8	7.9	8.1	7.0	8.6	7.0	4.6
Construction	12.6	12.9	14.1	12.1	12.0	11.5	10.9	11.1	10.5	10.2	10.3	9.9	9.7
Manufacturing	7.2	7.0	7.2	6.7	6.1	6.7	5.4	5.4	5.2	5.4	5.2	6.0	6.0
Durable goods	7.1	8.7	7.0	5.6	5.0	5.6	5.1	5.4	4.6	5.0	5.0	4.7	4.6
Nondurable goods	7.4	7.4	7.5	6.9	6.3	5.8	6.0	5.5	5.8	5.9	5.5	5.4	5.6
Transportation and public utilities	5.3	5.1	4.7	4.5	4.6	4.3	4.4	3.9	4.0	3.7	3.8	3.9	4.1
Wholesale and retail trade. . .	7.9	7.6	7.3	7.3	7.1	6.7	6.5	6.4	6.0	6.2	6.2	6.8	6.8
Finance and service industries.	5.7	5.6	6.2	6.2	4.9	4.8	4.7	4.8	4.5	4.4	4.4	4.4	4.8
Agricultural wage and salary workers	14.4	12.3	11.2	11.1	9.2	9.9	11.2	11.0	11.1	10.9	4.4	9.1	10.6

(1) Unemployment as a percent of the civilian labor force. (2) Aggregate hours lost by the unemployed and persons on part time for economic reasons as a percent of potentially available labor force hours.

Employed Persons by Occupation, Sex, and Age

Source: Bureau of Labor Statistics

(in thousands)

Occupation	Total 16 years and over 1987	1988	Men 16 years and over 1987	1988	Women 16 years and over 1987	1988
Total.	112,440	114,968	62,107	63,273	50,334	51,696
Managerial and professional specialty	27,742	29,190	15,457	16,139	12,286	13,050
Executive, administration and managerial.	13,316	14,215	8,263	8,526	5,063	5,690
Professional specialty	14,426	14,974	7,194	7,513	7,232	7,460
Technical, sales and administrative support	35,082	35,532	12,378	12,494	22,704	23,038
Technicians and related support	3,336	3,521	1,721	1,833	1,824	1,688
Sales occupations	13,480	13,747	7,015	7,025	6,486	6,722
Administrative support, including clerical.	18,256	18,264	3,642	3,636	14,814	14,628
Service occupations	15,054	15,332	5,924	6,056	9,130	9,275
Private household	934	909	34	34	900	875
Protective service	1,907	1,944	1,637	1,884	271	279
Service, except private household and protective	12,213	12,479	4,253	4,358	7,960	8,121
Precision production, craft, and repair.	13,568	13,664	12,418	12,474	1,153	1,190
Mechanics and repairers	4,445	4,454	4,295	4,307	150	147
Construction trades	5,011	5,098	4,915	4,991	95	107
Other precision production, craft, and repair	4,112	4,112	3,205	3,176	907	938
Operators, fabricators, and laborers	17,488	17,814	12,978	13,234	4,508	4,580
Machine operators, assemblers, and inspectors	7,994	8,117	4,899	4,806	3,295	3,311
Transportation and material moving occupations	4,712	4,831	4,317	4,397	395	434
Handlers, equipment cleaners, helpers, and laborers	4,779	4,866	3,962	4,031	817	835

97

Employment and Unemployment in the U.S.

Source: Bureau of Labor Statistics

Civilian labor force, persons 16 years of age and over (in thousands)

Year*	Employed	Unemployed	Unemployment Rate	Year*	Employed	Unemployed	Unemployment Rate
1940[1]	47,520	8,120	14.6%	1981	100,397	8,273	7.6
1950	58,918	3,288	5.0	1982	99,526	10,678	9.7
1960	65,778	3,852	5.5	1983	100,834	10,717	9.6
1965	71,088	3,366	4.5	1984	105,005	8,539	7.5
1970	78,678	4,093	4.9	1985	107,150	8,312	7.2
1975	85,846	7,929	8.5	1986[2]	109,597	8,237	7.0
1978	96,048	6,202	6.1	1987[2]	112,440	7,425	6.2
1980	99,303	7,637	7.1	1988[2]	114,988	6,701	5.5

(1) Persons 14 years of age and over; (2) Not strictly comparable with prior years.
*Early unemployment rates: 1915, 9.7; 1916, 4.8; 1917, 4.8; 1918, 1.4; 1919, 2.3; 1920, 4.0; 1921, 11.9; 1922, 7.6; 1923, 3.2; 1924, 5.5; 1925, 4.0; 1926, 1.9; 1927, 4.1; 1928, 4.4; 1929, 3.2; 1930, 8.7; 1931, 15.9; 1932, 23.6; 1933, 24.9; 1934, 21.7; 1935, 20.1; 1936, 16.9; 1937, 14.3; 1938, 19.0; 1939, 17.2.

Average Annual Pay, by State

Source: Bureau of Labor Statistics

State	Average annual pay[1] 1987	1988[2]	% Change 1987-88[3]	State	Average annual pay[1] 1987	1988[2]	% Change 1987-88[3]
U.S.	$20,857	$21,871	4.9	Missouri	$19,601	$20,295	3.5
Alabama	18,318	19,003	3.7	Montana	16,438	16,957	3.2
Alaska	28,008	28,033	.1	Nebraska	16,526	17,190	4.0
Arizona	19,610	20,383	3.9	Nevada	19,521	20,556	5.3
Arkansas	16,529	17,023	3.0	New Hampshire	19,414	20,749	6.9
California	23,100	24,124	4.4	New Jersey	23,842	25,748	8.0
Colorado[4]	20,830	21,472	3.1	New Mexico	17,767	18,259	2.8
Connecticut	24,322	26,244	7.9	New York	24,634	26,347	7.0
Delaware	20,764	21,977	5.8	North Carolina	17,861	18,637	4.3
District of Columbia	28,477	30,254	6.2	North Dakota	16,157	16,508	2.2
Florida	18,674	19,520	4.5	Ohio	20,568	21,500	4.5
Georgia	19,651	20,501	4.3	Oklahoma	18,615	19,098	2.6
Hawaii	19,091	20,444	7.1	Oregon	18,888	19,637	4.0
Idaho	17,062	17,648	3.4	Pennsylvania	20,408	21,485	5.3
Illinois	22,250	23,606	6.1	Rhode Island	18,858	20,206	7.1
Indiana	19,692	20,437	3.8	South Carolina	17,280	18,009	4.2
Iowa	17,292	17,928	3.7	South Dakota	14,963	15,424	3.1
Kansas	18,424	19,030	3.3	Tennessee	18,501	19,209	3.8
Kentucky	18,008	18,545	3.0	Texas	20,463	21,130	3.3
Louisiana	18,707	19,330	3.3	Utah	18,303	18,910	3.3
Maine	17,447	18,347	5.2	Vermont	17,703	18,640	5.3
Maryland	21,324	22,500	5.5	Virginia	19,963	21,052	5.5
Massachusetts	22,486	24,143	7.4	Washington	20,110	20,806	3.5
Michigan	23,081	24,193	4.8	West Virginia	18,820	19,341	2.8
Minnesota	20,450	21,481	5.0	Wisconsin	18,390	19,743	4.5
Mississippi	15,938	16,522	3.7	Wyoming	18,817	19,097	1.5

(1) Includes workers covered by Unemployment Insurance (UI) and Unemployment Compensation for Federal Employees (UCFE) programs. (2) Data are preliminary. (3) Percent changes were computed from unrounded average annual pay data and may differ from those computed using data rounded to the nearest dollar.

Average Weekly Earnings of Production Workers[1] by Major Industry, 1965-1988

Source: Bureau of Labor Statistics

(annual averages)

Year	Mining	Construction	Manufacturing	Transportation and public utilities	Wholesale trade
1965	$123.52	$138.38	$107.53	$125.14	$106.49
1966	130.24	146.26	112.19	128.13	111.11
1967	135.89	154.95	114.49	130.82	116.06
1968	142.71	164.49	122.51	138.85	122.31
1969	154.80	181.54	129.51	147.74	129.85
1970	164.40	195.45	133.33	155.93	137.26
1971	172.14	211.67	142.44	168.82	144.18
1972	189.14	221.19	154.71	187.86	151.69
1973	201.40	235.89	166.46	203.31	160.34
1974	219.14	249.25	176.80	217.48	170.33
1975	249.31	266.08	190.79	233.44	183.05
1976	273.90	283.73	209.32	256.71	194.66
1977	301.20	295.65	228.90	278.90	209.13
1978	332.88	318.69	249.27	302.80	228.14
1979	365.07	342.99	269.34	325.58	247.93
1980	397.06	367.78	288.62	351.25	267.96
1981	438.75	399.26	318.00	382.18	291.06
1982	459.88	426.82	330.26	402.48	309.85
1983	479.40	442.97	354.08	420.81	329.18
1984	503.58	458.51	374.03	438.13	342.27
1985	519.93	464.46	386.37	450.30	351.74
1986	525.69	466.75	396.01	458.64	358.11
1987	530.85	479.68	406.31	471.58	365.38
1988	539.33	493.08	418.40	484.18	378.71

(1) Production or nonsupervisory workers or private nonagriculture payrolls

Employed Wage and Salary Workers by Occupation, Industry, and Union Affiliation

Source: Bureau of Labor Statistics
(in thousands)

Occupation	Total employed	1988 Members of unions[1] Total	Percent of employed	Represented by unions[2] Total	Percent of employed
Managerial and professional specialty	24,369	3,644	15.0	4,470	18.3
Executive, administrative, and managerial	11,337	734	6.5	977	8.6
Professional specialty	13,032	2,910	22.3	3,493	26.8
Technical, sales, and administrative support	32,271	3,312	10.3	3,976	12.3
Technicians and related support	3,462	391	11.3	469	13.5
Sales occupations	11,019	587	5.3	689	6.2
Administrative support, including clerical	17,790	2,333	13.1	2,818	15.8
Service occupations	14,178	1,989	14.0	2,225	15.7
Protective service	1,969	765	38.9	839	42.6
Service, except protective service	12,209	1,224	10.0	1,387	11.4
Precision production, craft and repair	11,766	3,164	26.9	3,374	28.7
Operators, fabricators, and laborers	17,010	4,815	28.3	5,105	30.0
Machine operators, assemblers, and inspectors	7,879	2,327	29.5	2,453	31.1
Transportation and material moving occupations	4,418	1,330	30.1	1,407	31.8
Handlers, equipment cleaners, helpers, and laborers	4,713	1,158	24.6	1,245	26.4
Farming, forestry, and fishing	1,813	77	4.2	91	5.0
Industry					
Agricultural wage and salary workers	1,492	30	2.0	35	2.4
Private nonagricultural wage and salary workers	82,741	10,674	12.9	11,723	14.2
Mining	711	133	18.7	146	20.5
Construction	5,193	1,096	21.1	1,151	22.2
Manufacturing	20,430	4,516	22.1	4,854	23.8
Durable goods	12,170	2,875	23.6	3,095	25.4
Nondurable goods	8,260	1,041	19.9	1,759	21.3
Transportation and public utilities	6,053	2,001	33.1	2,144	35.4
Transportation	3,412	1,104	32.3	1,153	33.8
Communications and public utilities	2,640	897	34.0	992	37.6
Wholesale and retail trade	20,597	1,386	6.7	1,559	7.6
Wholesale trade	3,873	290	7.5	336	8.7
Retail trade	16,724	1,095	6.6	1,223	7.3
Finances, insurance, and real estate	6,812	178	2.6	238	3.5
Services	22,944	1,365	5.9	1,631	7.1
Government workers	17,175	6,298	36.7	7,483	43.6

(1) Data refer to members of a labor union or an employee association similar to a union; (2) Data refer to members of a labor union or an employee association similar to a union as well as workers who report no union affiliation but whose jobs are covered by a union or an employee association contract.
note: Data refer to the sole or principal job of full- and part-time workers. Excluded are self-employed workers whose businesses are incorporated although they technically qualify as wage and salary workers.

Characteristics of New Mothers in the Work Force, 1976-1988

Source: U.S. Bureau of the Census

(Women age 18-44 who gave birth in the preceding 12 months; numbers in thousands.)

	July 1987-June 1988 Number of women who gave birth	% in labor force	July 1975-June 1976 Number of women who gave birth	% in labor force
Total	3,667	50.9	2,797	31.0
Years of school completed:				
Less than high school	656	33.7	783	26.0
High school, 4 years	1,583	49.1	1,273	31.6
College, 1 to 3 years	778	61.6	413	32.1
College, 4 or more years	649	59.8	328	39.0
Age:				
18 to 24 years	1,146	46.3	1,291	30.9
25 to 29 years	1,238	52.3	929	33.1
30 to 44 years	1,283	53.6	577	27.6
Birth order and age of woman at birth:				
First birth	1,282	57.7	1,082	39.0
18 to 24 years	628	50.3	694	35.7
25 to 29 years	382	62.2	306	45.0
30 to 44 years	273	68.4	82	44.4
Second or higher order birth	2,385	47.2	1,715	25.9
18 to 24 years	518	41.3	597	25.3
25 to 29 years	857	47.8	623	27.2
30 to 44 years	1,010	49.7	495	24.9
Race and Hispanic origin[1]:				
White	2,894	49.4	2,328	28.6
Black	595	58.6	407	43.2
Hispanic	406	36.6	(NA)	(NA)
Not Hispanic	3,261	52.6	(NA)	(NA)
Marital status:				
Married, husband present	2,700	51.6	2,331	30.4
Widowed, divorced or separated[2]	361	50.3	225	32.3
Never married	606	47.9	241	34.8

(NA) = Not available. (1) Persons of Hispanic origin may be of any race. (2) Includes married, husband absent.

New Mothers in the Work Force, 1976-1988

Source: U.S. Bureau of the Census

(Women 18-44 years old who gave birth in the preceding 12 months; numbers in thousands.)

	Number of women	In the labor force Number	%		Number of women	In the labor force Number	%
1988	3,667	1,866	50.9	1982	3,433	1,508	43.9
1987	3,701	1,881	50.8	1981	3,381	1,411	41.7
1986	3,625	1,805	49.8	1980	3,247	1,233	38.0
1985	3,497	1,691	48.4	1978	3,168	1,120	35.3
1984	3,311	1,547	46.7	1976	2,797	865	31.0
1983	3,625	1,563	43.1				

Earnings by Occupation and Sex

Source: U.S. Bureau of Labor Statistics

(Median usual weekly earnings of full-time wage and salary workers by occupation and sex, annual averages)

Occupation and Sex Men	Number of Workers (in thousands) 1987	1988	Median weekly earnings 1987	1988
Managerial and professional specialty	11,555	11,968	636	666
Executive, administrative, and managerial	6,117	6,238	647	682
Professional specialty	5,438	5,730	625	651
Technical, sales, and administrative support	9,241	9,267	453	472
Technicians and support	1,533	1,647	500	510
Sales occupations	4,580	4,519	479	488
Administrative support, including clerical	3,128	3,101	402	418
Service occupations	4,143	4,317	296	299
Private household	16	8	(¹)	(¹)
Protective service	1,481	1,543	427	424
Service, except private household and protective	2,646	2,766	251	257
Precision production, craft, and repair	10,125	10,249	431	446
Mechanics and repairers	3,681	3,713	423	441
Construction trades	3,548	3,622	416	423
Other precision production, craft, and repair	2,896	2,914	463	477
Operators, fabricators, and laborers	10,926	11,026	344	352
Machine operators, assemblers, and inspectors	4,423	4,454	353	366
Transportation and material moving occupations	3,612	3,636	386	394
Handlers, equipment cleaners, helpers, and laborers	2,890	2,936	289	287
Farming, forestry, and fishing	1,171	1,221	219	234

(1) Data not shown where base is less than 50,000.

Occupation and Sex Women	Number of Workers (in thousands) 1987	1988	Median weekly earnings 1987	1988
Managerial and professional specialty	9,339	9,802	441	465
Executive, administrative, and managerial	4,099	4,487	416	430
Professional specialty	5,240	5,315	458	485
Technical, sales, and administrative support	15,439	15,664	293	305
Technicians and support	1,264	1,313	368	384
Sales occupations	3,077	3,222	246	264
Administrative support, including clerical	11,098	11,129	294	305
Service occupations	4,171	4,352	199	208
Private household	305	320	130	139
Protective service	186	204	314	347
Service, except private household and protective	3,680	3,828	201	210
Precision production, craft, and repair	867	926	302	302
Mechanics and repairers	131	137	456	392
Construction trades	38	69	(¹)	335
Other precision production, craft, and reair	699	721	286	284
Oprators, fabricators, and laborers	3,716	3,737	231	238
Machine operators, assemblers, and inspectors	2,962	2,952	227	236
Transportation and material moving occupations	186	216	299	286
Handlers, equipment cleaners, helpers, and laborers	568	569	233	237
Farming, forestry, and fishing	142	161	191	201

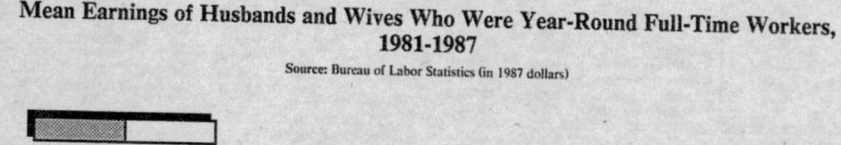

Mean Earnings of Husbands and Wives Who Were Year-Round Full-Time Workers, 1981-1987

Source: Bureau of Labor Statistics (in 1987 dollars)

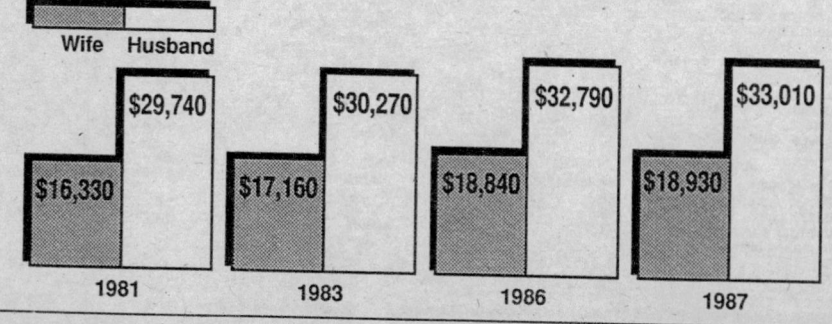

Wife   Husband

1981	1983	1986	1987
$16,330 / $29,740	$17,160 / $30,270	$18,840 / $32,790	$18,930 / $33,010

Earnings of Husbands and Wives, 1981-1987

Source: U.S. Bureau of the Census

Work experience of husbands and wives	Mean earnings In current dollars				Percent change, real income		
	1987	1986	1983	1981	1986-1987	1983-1987	1981-1987
Husbands							
Total	$29,154	$27,882	$22,980	$20,866	0.9	*11.2	*11.8
Worked at full-time jobs	30,606	29,279	24,138	21,870	0.8	*11.2	*12.0
50 to 52 weeks	33,005	31,638	26,532	23,800	0.6	*9.0	*11.0
40 to 49 weeks	22,498	22,468	19,395	17,051	−3.4	1.7	*5.6
27 to 39 weeks	16,609	16,705	13,778	13,519	−4.1	5.7	−1.7
26 weeks or less	9,414	9,658	7,484	6,626	−6.0	10.3	13.7
Worked at part-time jobs	8,790	8,512	7,875	6,835	−0.4	−2.1	2.9
50 to 52 weeks	12,196	12,464	12,032	9,341	−5.6	−11.1	4.5
49 weeks or less	6,013	5,729	4,915	5,145	1.3	7.2	−6.5
Wives							
Total	13,245	12,496	10,164	8,598	*2.3	*14.2	*23.3
Worked at full-time jobs	16,603	15,726	12,900	10,957	*1.9	*12.8	*21.3
50 to 52 weeks	18,929	18,180	15,041	13,067	0.5	*10.3	*15.9
40 to 49 weeks	14,089	13,784	11,951	9,917	−1.4	3.3	*13.7
27 to 39 weeks	11,212	9,981	8,302	7,025	*8.4	*18.4	*27.7
26 weeks or less	4,856	4,225	3,578	3,398	*10.9	*19.0	*14.4
Worked at part-time jobs	5,959	5,466	4,603	3,831	*5.2	*13.5	*24.5
50 to 52 weeks	8,387	8,000	6,849	5,878	1.1	*7.3	*14.2
49 weeks or less	3,770	3,439	2,848	2,566	*5.8	*16.0	*17.6

*Statistically significant at 90% confidence level

Highest-Paying Occupations

Source: U.S. Dept. of Labor

Men	1988 Median weekly salary	% Increase 1983-88	Women	1988 Median weekly salary	% Increase 1983-88
Lawyer	$930	42	Lawyer	$774	33
Airplane pilot	823	33	Engineer	639	28
Aerospace engineer	820	29	Mathematical and computer specialist	575	29
Physician	815	58	Personnel and labor-relations manager	563	NA
Financial manager	788	37	College professor	555	39
Chemical engineer	785	24	Physician	553	33
Personnel and labor-relations manager	785	30	Natural scientist	540	30
Securities and financial-services salesman	768	25	Urban planner	531	39
Education administrator	757	30	Guidance counselor	522	37
College professor	752	46	Registered nurse	515	30
Electrical engineer	749	21	Education administrator	499	28
Civil engineer	734	27	Computer programer	497	21
Mathematical and computer specialist	733	23	High-school teacher	491	35
Pharmacist	720	37	Librarian	465	25
Economist	719	3			

NA = Not available. Note: Figures exclude people who are self-employed or in private practice. Percentage change for airline pilot represents increase since 1984.

Injuries and Illnesses in Industry

Source: Bureau of Labor Statistics

(in thousands)

Industry division	Total cases[1]		Lost workday cases		Nonfatal cases without lost workdays		Lost workdays	
	1986	1987	1986	1987	1986	1987	1986	1987
Injuries and illnesses[2]	5,629.0	6,035.9	2,590.3	2,801.6	3,034.6	3,230.6	46,725.7	50,941.4
Agriculture, forestry, and fishing[3]	90.3	99.6	44.9	50.8	45.3	48.8	736.4	837.7
Mining[3]	67.4	61.5	32.2	35.1	25.0	26.2	979.5	1,039.5
Construction	647.1	638.3	293.1	295.0	353.3	342.3	5,707.5	5,895.3
Manufacturing	1,948.8	2,212.6	861.3	976.5	1,086.6	1,235.2	15,609.1	17,689.9
Durable goods	1,213.8	1,385.6	526.6	597.0	686.5	788.1	9,572.7	10,699.2
Nondurable goods	735.0	827.0	334.7	379.5	400.1	447.1	6,036.4	6,990.7
Transportation and public utilities	406.0	429.2	238.2	250.6	167.0	178.1	5,025.4	5,497.2
Wholesale and retail trade	1,431.6	1,470.5	621.5	654.8	809.4	815.1	10,093.4	10,725.2
Wholesale trade	391.6	408.7	197.4	205.4	193.8	202.9	3,381.8	3,523.7
Retail trade	1,040.1	1,061.8	424.1	449.4	615.6	612.3	6,711.6	7,199.4
Finance, insurance, and real estate	115.4	115.3	50.6	51.2	64.6	63.9	966.5	832.9
Services	932.4	1,009.0	448.6	487.5	483.4	521.0	7,587.8	8,423.6
Injuries	5,492.0	5,845.5	2,533.2	2,721.3	2,955.1	3,120.8	45,383.8	49,069.6
Illnesses	136.9	190.4	57.1	80.3	79.4	109.8	1,341.9	1,871.7

(1) Includes fatalities; (2) Excludes farms with fewer than 11 employees; (3) Excludes independent mining contractors. **Note:** Because of rounding, components may not add to totals.

Employment and Training Services and Unemployment Insurance

Source: Employment and Training Administration, U.S. Department of Labor

Employment Service

The Federal-State Employment Service consists of the United States Employment Service and affiliated state employment services which make up the nation's public employment service system. During program year 1987, the public employment service listed 7.2 million job openings and placed more than 3.8 million people in jobs.

The employment service refers employable applicants to job openings that use their highest skills and helps the unemployed obtain services or training to make them employable. It also provides special attention to handicapped workers, migrants and seasonal farmworkers, workers who lose their jobs because of foreign trade competition, and other worker groups. Veterans receive priority services including referral to jobs and training. During program year 1987, 455,813 veterans were placed in jobs.

Job Training

The Job Training Partnership Act (JTPA), which became fully operational on October 1, 1983, provides job training and employment services for economically disadvantaged youth and adults, dislocated workers, and others who face significant employment barriers. The goal of the Act is to move as many jobless workers as possible into permanent, unsubsidized, self-sustaining employment.

Since its inception, JTPA has provided approximately four and a half million Americans with training and employment services. Its placement rate is 68 percent, making it one of the most successful job and training efforts ever undertaken.

Title I of the Act's five titles basically establishes an administrative structure for the delivery of job and training services. Generally, state governors receive bloc grants from the Labor Department, and the funds are then distributed to Service Delivery Areas — areas of 200,000 population or more where local elected officials work with Private Industry Councils to plan and conduct local training projects.

Title II is in two parts, with Title II-A spelling out the Act's provision of employment and training projects for the economically disadvantaged. In program year 1987 (July 1, 1987 to June 30, 1988), these projects served more than 1.3 million people.

Title II-A outlines a summer youth program offering basic and remedial education, institutional and on-the-job training, work experience, and supportive services. This program had nearly 640,000 participants in program year 1987.

Title III, Economic Dislocation and Worker Adjustment Assistance, provides for job and training help for dislocated workers — workers who lose jobs and are unlikely to return to their previous industries or occupations. This includes workers who lose their jobs because of plant closings or mass layoffs; long-term unemployed persons with limited local opportunities for jobs in their fields; farmers, ranchers, and other self-employed persons who become jobless due to general economic conditions or natural disasters; and, under certain circumstances, displaced homemakers. Such assistance benefitted nearly 183,000 workers in program year 1987.

Title IV authorizes programs to address the employment and training needs of specific groups facing significant barriers to productive employment, including Native Americans, migrant and seasonal farmworkers, and the disabled. In program year 1987, these programs served 33,000 Native Americans; 46,800 migrant and seasonal farmworkers; and 8,550 disabled persons.

In addition, Title IV includes the Job Corps, which each year enrolls approximately 100,000 young people between the ages of 16 and 21 in 107 residential job training centers throughout the United States; the National Commission for Employment Policy; and nationally administered programs for technical assistance, labor market information, research and evaluation, and pilots and demonstrations.

Title V contains miscellaneous provisions, including amendments to the Wagner-Peyser Act of 1933 — the legislation authorizing the federal-state Employment Service.

Trade Ajustment Assistance for Workers

The Trade Adjustment Assistance (TAA) is available to workers who lose their jobs or whose hours of work and wages are reduced as a result of increased imports. TAA includes a variety of benefits and reemployment services to help unemployed workers prepare for and obtain suitable employment. Workers may be eligible for training, job search, relocation and other reemployment services. Additionally, weekly trade readjustment allowances (TRA) may be payable to eligible workers following their exhaustion of unemployment insurance benefits. In fiscal year 1988, about 46,700 workers received $186 million in TRA payments; about 9,700 workers entered training; about 1,200 workers were involved in job search visits; and about 1,300 workers relocated in order to obtain long term jobs.

The TAA program is administered by the Employment and Training Administration's Office of Trade Adjustment Assistance. State employment security agencies serve as agents of the U.S., under an agreement with the Secretary of Labor, for administering the TAA benefit provisions in the Trade Act of 1974.

Unemployment Insurance

Unlike old-age and survivors insurance, entirely a federal program, the unemployment insurance program is a Federal-State system that provides insured wage earners with partial replacement of wages lost during involuntary unemployment. The program protects most workers. During calendar year 1988, an estimated 100.6 million workers in commerce, industry, agriculture, and government, including the armed forces, were covered under the Federal-State system. In addition, an estimated 312,000 railroad workers were insured against unemployment by the Railroad Retirement Board.

Each state, as well as the District of Columbia, Puerto Rico, and the Virgin Islands, has its own law and operates its own program. The amount and duration of the weekly benefits are determined by state laws, based on prior wages and length of employment. States are required to extend the duration of benefits when unemployment rises to and remains above specified state levels; costs of extended benefits are shared by the state and federal governments.

Under the Federal Unemployment Tax Act, as amended in 1985, the tax rate is 6.2% on the first $7,000 paid to each employee of employers with one or more employees in 20 weeks of the year or a quarterly payroll of $1,500. A credit of up to 5.4% is allowed for taxes paid under state unemployment insurance laws that meet certain criteria, leaving the federal share at 0.8% of taxable wages.

Social Security Requirement

The Social Security Act requires, as a condition of such grants, prompt payment of due benefits. The Federal Unemployment Tax Act provides safeguards for workers' right to benefits if they refuse jobs that fail to meet certain labor standards. Through the Unemployment Insurance Service of the Employment and Training Administration, the Secretary of Labor determines whether states qualify for grants and for tax offset credit from employers.

Benefits are financed solely by employer contributions, except in Alaska, Alabama, Pennsylvania, New Jersey, and West Virginia, where employees also contribute. Benefits are paid through the states' public employment offices, at which unemployed workers must register for work and to which they must report regularly for referral to a possible job during the time when they are drawing weekly benefit payments. During the fiscal year 1988, $13.46 billion in benefits was paid under state unemployment insurance programs to 7 million beneficiaries. They received an average weekly payment of $140.37 for total unemployment for an average of 13.8 weeks.

Selected Unemployment Insurance Data by State

Calendar year 1988, state programs only.

	Insured claimants[1]	Beneficiaries[2]	Exhaustions[3]	Initial claims[4]	Benefits paid[5]	Avg. weekly benefit for total unemployment	Employers subject to state law
AL. . . .	165,138	146,918	28,791	348,271	$140,631,009	$101.09	77,886
AK	38,805	38,090	18,670	70,682	86,313,243	156.57	14,893
AZ	54,952	67,064	21,394	172,895	121,816,220	113.91	76,127
AR	115,653	83,544	20,796	208,608	122,964,861	125.61	48,208
CA	1,252,894	968,239	304,607	2,507,833	1,689,234,179	122.29	753,514
CO	107,964	84,338	29,181	155,717	173,384,672	158.32	94,882
CT	116,618	97,417	15,333	177,415	183,444,231	179.23	90,981
DE	23,502	20,168	2,393	36,890	41,295,300	169.68	16,021
DC	26,254	19,796	9,195	35,357	67,302,919	187.98	20,121
FL.	221,878	186,897	57,556	345,780	287,549,720	139.50	290,842
GA	261,607	194,724	38,827	395,081	221,765,831	128.63	134,998
HI	28,803	21,891	4,789	52,540	48,233,877	168.41	24,738
ID	43,002	37,628	11,408	98,882	57,613,970	136.48	23,260
IL	378,155	285,470	102,849	643,033	731,809,323	152.17	235,083
IN	115,048	107,930	26,189	297,361	121,702,565	104.15	100,727
IA	80,068	67,023	16,125	126,727	118,739,602	149.50	59,873
KS	81,561	70,404	21,510	141,811	148,872,693	162.43	59,206
KY	143,014	103,523	21,271	228,588	147,759,881	115.13	68,366
LA	141,806	117,638	54,814	290,951	223,905,292	125.86	82,471
ME	43,886	35,033	7,358	96,875	49,486,579	139.64	31,178
MD	122,983	90,318	20,864	199,171	182,253,679	158.33	103,961
MA	104,043	185,470	52,662	349,266	526,057,671	197.93	141,324
MI	250,641	332,913	107,936	867,537	958,455,883	183.82	169,104
MN	137,014	113,485	36,819	223,090	301,435,050	181.31	94,579
MS	96,882	72,794	20,805	205,694	86,236,700	101.28	45,863
MO	186,252	145,766	43,081	407,238	222,813,416	119.59	122,309
MT	21,509	22,737	7,996	52,417	37,743,806	130.50	23,716
NE	37,852	30,671	8,267	60,009	42,375,393	117.30	38,775
NV	48,339	35,175	7,893	73,946	62,593,664	146.37	24,283
NH	25,415	19,051	338	35,214	12,397,308	125.06	33,372
NJ	287,084	238,880	77,912	447,763	612,561,275	179.84	192,437
NM	36,181	30,694	10,803	64,902	59,605,997	122.49	31,812
NY	509,023	460,903	152,155	959,440	1,092,033,147	143.48	429,989
NC	272,040	207,950	25,802	680,109	190,173,656	133.45	128,095
ND	19,185	16,919	7,239	35,102	29,093,337	132.28	17,637
OH	253,127	291,651	71,111	593,163	576,894,107	151.33	199,869
OK	65,857	59,246	20,084	133,042	107,923,411	142.68	66,776
OR	116,691	102,608	23,903	266,109	187,139,747	146.75	69,878
PA	454,490	378,573	83,259	951,915	842,176,722	164.47	221,764
PR	103,763	74,617	37,178	201,470	89,284,617	77.38	49,053
RI	49,752	41,235	9,560	85,236	80,965,226	166.91	28,462
SC	136,383	84,536	15,808	277,216	85,123,801	110.94	65,503
SD	10,405	8,553	1,207	21,804	12,521,766	121.08	17,919
TN	197,062	154,505	39,142	400,790	182,564,950	105.34	89,782
TX	471,975	356,608	146,129	741,179	789,842,337	158.55	314,092
UT	44,293	35,164	11,029	62,695	67,313,514	157.04	31,258
VT	20,369	15,054	2,103	27,363	23,727,430	132.61	17,676
VA	165,879	125,626	21,164	332,162	135,969,896	134.71	118,999
VI	2,290	1,586	319	3,211	2,534,471	121.44	3,095
WA	201,919	175,028	48,339	464,715	364,159,884	151.51	106,198
WV	59,096	51,808	13,119	88,877	101,681,358	141.42	33,907
WI	177,327	164,752	38,383	349,740	285,505,577	148.59	99,072
WY	16,121	11,544	3,820	32,922	26,700,011	158.79	15,032
Total. . .	8,141,850	6,864,153	1,979,285	16,123,804	13,161,684,774	144.91	5,448,964

(1) Claimants whose base-period earnings or whose employment, covered by the unemployment insurance program, was sufficient to make them eligible for unemployment insurance benefits as provided by state law. (2) First payments. (3) Final payments. Claimants who exhaust their benefit rights in one benefit year may be entitled to further benefits in the following benefit year. (4) Excludes intrastate transitional claims. (5) Adjusted for voided benefit checks and transfers under interstate combined wage plan.

Spells of Job Search and Layoff, by Major Age-Sex Groups, Race, and Hispanic Origin

Source: U.S. Bureau of the Census

(Covers spells that began in 1984 and were completed in 1984, 1985, or early 1986. In percent)

| Age, sex, race, and Hispanic origin | \- Total months in spells lasting— | | | | |
	1 month	2 months	3 months	4 months	5 months or more
Total	9.6	10.9	10.4	19.5	49.6
Both sexes:					
16 to 24 years	10.2	11.1	10.8	18.9	49.0
55 years and over	10.7	9.4	10.5	28.8	40.6
Men, 25-54 years	8.0	10.9	10.1	14.7	56.3
Women, 25-54 years	9.7	10.9	9.9	22.3	47.2
White	10.2	11.7	11.1	19.0	48.1
Black	7.6	8.4	8.4	20.3	55.4
Hispanic[1]	9.0	10.1	11.8	27.8	41.4

(1) Persons of Hispanic origin may be of any race. Note: Components may not add to totals because of rounding. Users of spell estimates should be aware that the associated standard errors may be underestimated.

Employed Wage and Salary Workers Paid at or Below Minimum Hourly Wage Rate, 1987

Source: Bureau of Labor Statistics

Characteristic	Number of Workers[1](1,000)			Percent Distribution			Percent of all Workers Paid Hourly Rates	
	Total paid hourly rates	At $3.35	Below $3.35	Total paid Hourly rates	At $3.35	Below $3.35	At $3.35	Below $3.35
Total, 16 years and over[2]	59,552	3,229	1,468	100.0	100.0	100.0	5.4	2.5
16 to 24 years	15,725	1,958	730	26.4	60.6	49.7	12.5	4.6
16 to 19 years	5,954	1,272	434	10.0	39.4	29.6	21.4	7.3
25 years and over	43,827	1,271	738	73.6	39.4	50.3	2.9	1.7
Male, 16 years and over	30,474	1,283	364	51.2	39.7	24.8	4.2	1.2
16 to 24 years	8,140	910	205	13.7	28.2	14.0	11.2	2.5
16 to 19 years	2,982	611	127	5.0	18.9	8.7	20.5	4.3
25 years and over	22,335	373	158	37.5	11.6	10.8	1.7	.7
Women, 16 years and over	29,078	1,946	1,105	48.8	60.3	75.3	6.7	3.8
16 to 24 years	7,586	1,049	525	12.7	32.5	35.8	13.8	6.9
16 to 19 years	2,972	660	308	5.0	20.4	21.0	22.2	10.4
25 years and over	21,492	898	580	36.1	27.8	39.5	4.2	2.7
White	50,180	2,598	1,311	84.3	80.5	89.3	5.2	2.6
Black	7,667	547	123	12.9	16.9	8.4	7.1	1.6
Hispanic origin[3]	5,155	342	74	8.7	10.6	5.0	6.6	1.4
Full-time workers	44,462	1,089	505	74.7	33.7	34.4	2.4	1.1
Part-time workers[4]	15,090	2,140	963	25.3	66.3	65.6	14.2	6.4
Private sector	51,965	2,919	1,395	87.3	90.4	95.0	5.6	2.7
Goods-producing industries[5]	19,126	447	99	32.1	13.8	6.7	2.3	.5
Service-producing industries[6]	32,840	2,473	1,297	55.1	76.6	88.4	7.5	3.9
Retail trade	12,588	1,576	839	21.1	48.8	57.2	12.5	6.7
Services	12,960	768	426	21.8	23.8	29.0	5.9	3.3
Public sector	7,587	310	73	12.7	9.6	5.0	4.1	1.0

(1) Excludes the incorporated self-employed. (2) Includes races not shown separately. (3) Persons of Hispanic origin may be of any race. (4) Working fewer than 35 hours per week. (5) Includes agriculture, mining, construction, and manufacturing. (6) Includes transportation and public utilities; wholesale trade; finance, insurance, and real estate; private households; and other service industries, not shown separately.

Federal Minimum Hourly Wage Rates Since 1950

Source: U.S. Department of Labor.

(Employee estimates as of September 1984, except as indicated. The Fair Labor Standards Act of 1938 and subsequent amendments provide for minimum wage coverage applicable to specified nonsupervisory employment categories. Exempt from coverage are executives and administrators or professionals.)

Effective date	Minimum Rates for Nonfarm Workers			Minimum rates for farm workers[4]	Effective date	Minimum Rates for Nonfarm Workers			Minimum rates for farm workers[4]
	Laws prior to 1966[1]	Percent, avg earnings[2]	1966 and later[3]			Laws prior to 1966[1]	Percent, avg earnings[2]	1966 and later[3]	
Jan. 25, 1950	$.75	54	(X)	(X)	Jan. 1, 1975	2.10	45	2.00	1.80
Mar. 1, 1956	1.00	52	(X)	(X)	Jan. 1, 1976	2.30	46	2.20	2.00
Sept. 3, 1961	1.15	50	(X)	(X)	Jan. 1, 1977	(5)	(5)	2.30	2.20
Sept. 3, 1963	1.25	51	(X)	(X)	Jan. 1, 1978	2.65	44	2.65	2.65
Feb. 1, 1967	1.40	50	$1.00	$1.00	Jan. 1, 1979	2.90	45	2.90	2.90
Feb. 1, 1968	1.60	54	1.15	1.15	Jan. 1, 1980	3.10	45	3.10	3.10
Feb. 1, 1969	(5)	(5)	1.30	1.30	Jan. 1, 1981	3.35	43	3.35	3.35
Feb. 1, 1970	(5)	(5)	1.45	(5)	Sept. 1, 1985	(5)	(5)	(5)	(5)
Feb. 1, 1971	(5)	(5)	1.60	(5)					
May 1, 1974	2.00	46	1.90	1.60					

(X) Not applicable. (1) Applies to workers covered prior to 1961 Amendments and, after Sept. 1965, to workers covered by 1961 Amendments. Rates set by 1961 Amendments were: Sept. 1961, $1.00; Sept. 1964, $1.15; and Sept. 1965, $1.25. (2) Percent of gross average hourly earnings of production workers in manufacturing. (3) Applies to workers newly covered by Amendments of 1966, 1974, and 1977, and Title IX of Education Amendments of 1972. (4) Included in coverage as of 1966, 1974, and 1977 Amendments. (5) No change in rate.

On June 13, 1989 Pres. George Bush vetoed a bill to raise the minimum wage to $4.55 an hour in 3 years. A House vote, June 14, failed to override the veto.

Work Stoppages (Strikes) in the U.S.

Source: Bureau of Labor Statistics

(involving 1,000 workers or more)

Year	Number stoppages[1]	Workers involved[1] (thousands)	Work days idle[1] (thousands)		Year	Number stoppages[1]	Workers involved[1] (thousands)	Work days idle[1] (thousands)
1955	363	2,055	21,100		1969	412	1,576	29,397
1960	222	896	13,260		1970	381	2,468	52,761
1965	268	999	15,140		1971	298	2,516	35,538
1966	321	1,300	16,000		1972	250	975	16,764
1967	381	2,192	31,320		1973	317	1,400	16,260
1968	392	1,855	35,567					(continued)

Year	Number stoppages[1]	Workers involved[1] (thousands)	Work days idle[1] (thousands)		Number stoppages[1]	Workers involved[1] (thousands)	Work days idle[1] (thousands)
1974	424	1,796	31,809	1982	96	656	9,061
1975	235	965	17,563	1983	81	909	17,461
1976	231	1,519	23,962	1984	62	376	8,499
1977	298	1,212	21,258	1985	54	324	7,079
1978	219	1,006	23,774	1986	69	533	11,861
1979	235	1,021	20,409	1987	46	174	4,481
1980	187	795	20,844	1988	40	118	4,364
1981	145	729	16,908				

(1) The number of stoppages and workers relate to stoppages that began in the year. Days of idleness include all stoppages in effect. Workers are counted more than once if they were involved in more than one stoppage during the year.

Drug Testing and Employee Assistance Programs: 1988

Source: Bureau of Labor Statistics
(Private nonagricultural establishments and employees, summer 1988.)

These findings are from a survey of 7,500 business establishments, undertaken in accordance with the Drug Abuse Act of 1986. It is the first survey on this subject to provide comprehensive coverage of the private nonfarm business sector, encompassing all industries and establishment sizes.

Many testing programs are limited to employees suspected of drug use, and others are conducted on a random basis. Overall, about 950,000 employees were tested in the 12 months preceding the survey; of these, about 9 percent tested positive for drug use. Among the 3.9 million job applicants tested, 12 percent had positive test results.

Establishments in the mining, communications and public utilities, and transportation industries were most likely to have drug testing programs.

Presence of program	Total	Size of establishment							
		1 to 9 employees	10 to 49 employees	50 to 249 employees	100 to 249 employees	250 to 499 employees	500 to 999 employees	1,000 to 4,999 employees	5,000 employees or more
Establishments									
Total (thousands)	4,542.8	3,140.9	1,083.7	195.6	84.4	23.1	9.5	5.2	0.4
Percent:									
With a drug-testing program	3.2	.8	6.4	12.4	17.2	29.7	30.6	41.8	59.8
With an employee assistance program	6.5	3.7	9.7	15.7	29.4	45.3	53.9	70.4	83.0
With both a drug-testing and an employee assistance program	1.4	.4	2.7	3.8	9.4	20.9	22.7	35.2	56.2
With neither a drug-testing nor an employee assistance program	91.7	95.9	86.6	75.7	62.7	45.9	38.3	23.0	13.4
Considering implementation of:									
A drug-testing program	3.9	2.3	5.6	14.8	12.6	12.7	14.9	14.1	11.2
An employee assistance program	3.2	1.9	4.7	10.0	13.8	10.7	12.7	10.7	7.5
With a formal policy on drug use.	13.1	6.4	24.0	35.9	50.4	53.5	59.9	71.2	82.9
Employees									
Total (thousands)	84,965.7	10,700.1	20,584.2	12,254.5	13,309.4	8,220.1	6,469.2	9,569.2	3,831.8
Percent in establishments:									
With a drug-testing program	19.6	1.1	7.3	12.3	17.8	29.2	30.4	43.6	67.6
With an employee assistance program	31.0	4.2	11.2	16.6	30.7	45.2	54.2	71.9	86.8
With both a drug-testing and an employee assistance program	13.8	.7	3.5	3.9	9.7	20.7	22.8	36.4	64.4
With neither a drug-testing nor an employee assistance program	63.2	95.5	84.9	75.0	61.3	46.3	38.2	20.9	10.0
Considering implementation of:									
A drug-testing program	10.1	2.4	6.2	15.1	12.8	13.1	14.3	12.5	8.1
An employee assistance program	8.6	2.0	5.3	9.8	14.1	10.7	13.0	10.0	6.7
With a formal policy on drug use.	42.5	8.2	27.5	35.6	51.7	52.5	58.8	71.7	86.6

Note: The individual categories will sum to more than 100 percent because many establishments had more than 1 program or policy.

Favorite Business Locations

A survey, commissioned by Cushman & Wakefield, a real estate firm, of the chief executive officers of some 400 companies showed that Atlanta was the most popular city for locating a business. The CEOs were asked to rank 31 major cities according to 12 business climate criteria such as cost of labor, taxes, regulatory climate, and employees' quality of life.

Rank 1988	Rank 1987	*City	Rank 1988	Rank 1987	*City		Percent planning to locate new office space in next 12 months 1988	1987
1	1	Atlanta, Ga.	17	12	Cincinnati, Oh.	**New York, N.Y.	18	23
2	2	San Diego, Cal.	18	—	San Antonio, Tex.	Los Angeles, Cal.	15	14
3	5	Boston, Mass.	19	24	St. Louis, Mo.	Chicago, Ill.	15	12
4	6	Chicago, Ill.	20	25	Kansas City, Mo.	Atlanta Ga.	14	10
5	11	Dallas/Fort Worth, Tex.	21	17	Philadelphia Pa.	San Francisco, Cal.	10	12
6	4	Los Angeles, Cal.	22	14	Pittsburgh, Pa.	Boston, Mass.	10	9
7	10	Washington, D.C.	23	20	Portland, Ore.	Houston, Tex.	9	4
8	15	Phoenix, Ariz.	24	22	Houston, Tex.	Washington, D.C.	8	10
9	9	Columbus, Oh.	25	28	Miami, Fla.	Dallas, Tex.	8	9
10	13	Minneapolis/St. Paul, Minn.	26	19	Baltimore, Md.	Detroit/Ann Arbor, Mich.	6	3
11	23	Norfolk, Va.	27	21	Denver, Col.	Seattle, Wash.	5	5
12	16	Seattle, Wash.	28	30	Detroit, Mich.	Philadelphia, Pa.	5	5
13	18	Sacramento, Cal.	29	27	Milwaukee, Wis.	Phoenix, Ariz.	5	4
14	7	New York, N.Y.	30	29	Cleveland, Oh.	Tampa, Fla.	5	4
15	3	Tampa, Fla.	31	26	New Orleans, La.			
16	8	San Francisco, Cal.						

*Cities incl. surrounding suburbs. ** Inc. N.Y. City, Nassau, Suffolk, Westchester counties, No. New Jersey, and So. Connecticut.

Civilian Employment of the Federal Government

Source: Workforce Analysis and Statistics Division, U.S. Office of Personnel Management as of May 1989
(Payroll in thousands of dollars)

	All Areas Employment	Payroll	United States Employment	Payroll	Wash., D.C. MSA Employment	Payroll	Overseas Employment	Payroll
Total, all agencies[1]	3,151,329	7,446,535	3,004,586	7,141,936	357,170	1,026,836	146,743	304,599
Legislative branch	38,068	102,540	38,010	102,326	35,750	95,816	58	214
Congress	19,861	51,287	19,861	51,287	19,861	51,287	—	—
U.S. Senate	7,554	19,535	7,554	19,535	7,554	19,535	—	—
House of Rep Summary	12,293	31,712	12,293	31,712	7,554	19,535	—	—
Comm. on Scty & Coop in Eur	14	40	14	40	12,293	31,712	—	—
Architect of the Capitol	2,183	4,721	14	40	14	40	—	—
Botanic Garden	52	123	2,183	4,721	2,183	4,721	—	—
Comm Int Mig&Coop Econ Dev	15	36	52	123	52	123	—	—
Congressional Budget Ofc	218	976	15	36	15	36	—	—
Copyright Royalty Tribunal	7	31	218	976	218	976	—	—
General Accounting Ofc	5,272	17,259	7	31	7	31	—	—
Government Printing Ofc	5,057	14,184	5,221	17,083	3,426	11,563	51	176
Library of Congress	4,829	12,276	5,057	14,184	4,597	13,213	—	—
Monit Retri Storage Comm	9	31	4,822	12,238	4,822	13,213	—	—
Nat Comm Prev Infant Mort	8	22	9	31	4,822	12,238	7	38
Ofc Technology Assessment	194	432	8	22	9	31	—	—
Physician Payment Rev Comm	1	432	194	432	8	22	—	—
Prosptv Paymt Assessmt Com	16	4	1	—	194	432	—	—
U.S. Tax Court	346	1,158	16	—	1	—	—	—
			346	4	16	4	—	—
Judicial Branch	21,562	56,240	346	1,158	16	—	—	—
			21,312	1,158	341	1,139	—	—
Supreme Court	320	829	320	55,575	1,843	5,283	250	665
U.S. Courts	21,242	55,411	320	829	320	829	—	—
			20,992	54,746	1,523	4,454	250	665
Executive Branch	3,091,699	7,287,755	2,945,264	6,984,035	319,577	925,737	146,435	303,720
Exec Ofc of the President	1,602	5,148	1,592	5,103	1,592	5,103	10	45
White House Office	370	1,069	370	1,069	370	1,069	—	—
Ofc of Vice President	24	78	24	78	24	78	—	—
Ofc of Mgt & Budget	559	2,001	559	2,001	559	2,001	—	—
Office of Administration	209	505	209	505	209	505	—	—
Council Economic Advisors	32	104	32	104	32	104	—	—
Council on Environ Qual	10	38	10	38	10	38	—	—
Ofc of Policy Development	36	105	36	105	36	105	—	—
Exec Residence at WH	90	285	90	285	90	285	—	—
National Security Council	59	218	59	218	59	218	—	—
National Space Council	3	7	3	7	3	7	—	—
Ofc of Natl Drug Control	35	113	35	113	35	113	—	—
Ofc of Sci and Tech Policy	9	34	9	34	9	34	—	—
Ofc of U.S. Trade Rep	166	591	156	546	156	546	10	45
Executive Departments	2,078,796	4,925,773	1,952,998	4,672,583	240,074	693,184	125,798	253,190
State	25,453	75,522	9,097	31,509	8,082	28,061	16,356	44,013
Treasury	165,776	357,095	164,690	353,695	20,861	61,090	1,086	3,400
Defense, total	1,075,009	2,507,407	974,646	2,321,625	89,719	239,645	100,363	185,782
Dept of the Army	381,425	713,748	335,900	641,308	28,123	48,157	45,525	72,440
Army, Mil Func Total	349,836	637,231	304,444	565,072	26,864	44,608	45,392	72,159
Army, Civil Func Total	31,589	76,517	31,456	76,236	1,259	3,549	133	281
Corps of Engineers	31,455	76,170	31,322	75,889	1,125	3,202	133	281
Cemeterial Expenses	134	347	134	347	134	347	—	—
Dept of the Navy	346,176	882,517	320,765	860,689	38,696	117,005	25,417	21,828
Dept of the Air Force	252,180	673,758	236,660	619,091	6,556	17,443	15,520	54,667
Defense Log Agcy	52,991	112,293	52,653	110,848	3,328	10,216	358	1,445
Other Defense Activities	42,237	125,091	28,688	89,689	13,016	46,824	13,549	35,402
Justice	79,277	219,801	77,854	215,310	19,560	57,292	1,423	4,491
Interior	76,801	172,337	76,420	171,312	9,217	25,838	381	1,025
Agriculture	118,382	245,107	116,910	242,621	12,408	34,399	1,472	2,486
Commerce	52,668	98,621	51,942	96,380	19,055	53,773	726	2,241
Labor	18,343	53,550	18,299	53,396	6,210	19,286	44	154
Health and Human Services	122,322	295,348	121,596	293,557	26,968	78,008	726	1,791
Housing & Urban Dev	13,454	35,087	13,324	34,744	3,384	10,647	130	343
Transportation	64,946	227,593	64,437	225,671	9,163	33,160	509	1,922
Energy	17,121	53,266	17,113	53,221	6,019	20,644	8	45
Education	4,694	13,520	4,691	13,511	3,255	9,704	3	9
Veterans Affairs	244,550	571,519	241,979	566,031	6,173	21,637	2,571	5,488
Independent agencies[1]	1,011,301	2,356,834	990,674	2,306,349	77,911	227,450	20,627	50,485
Environmtl Protect Agcy	15,615	42,795	15,597	42,737	5,282	16,204	18	58
Equal Employ Opp Comm	2,843	7,480	2,843	7,480	685	2,079	—	—
Federal Deposit Ins Corp	8,295	22,899	8,281	22,848	1,168	3,881	14	51
Fed Emergency Mgmt Agcy	2,628	7,555	2,621	7,542	1,310	3,994	7	13
General Svcs Admin	19,865	49,896	19,786	49,683	6,660	19,507	79	213
Natl Archives & Recds, Admin	3,101	4,745	3,101	4,745	1,131	2,511	—	—
Natl Aero Space Admin	23,835	88,600	23,826	88,558	5,162	20,199	9	42
Nuclear Regulatory Comm	3,319	14,281	3,319	14,281	2,181	9,592	—	—
Office of Personnel Mgmt	6,822	12,964	6,794	12,929	2,677	6,645	28	35
Panama Canal Commission	8,810	15,934	18	62	7	40	8,792	15,872
Small Business Admin	4,592	18,061	4,508	17,764	908	4,153	84	297
Smithsonian, Summary	5,130	11,287	5,002	10,924	4,743	10,210	128	363
Tennessee Valley Auth	25,616	82,985	25,616	82,985	20	58	—	—
U.S. Information Agency	8,759	29,332	4,355	15,631	4,086	14,281	4,404	13,701
U.S. Intnatl Dev Coop Agcy	4,907	16,229	2,463	8,054	2,460	8,038	2,444	8,175
U.S. Postal Service	842,197	1,858,961	838,493	1,849,235	23,167	57,114	3,704	9,726

(1) Included in total are other independent agencies with fewer than 2,500 employees.

Labor Union Directory
Source: Bureau of Labor Statistics; World Almanac questionnaire
(*) Independent union; all others affiliated with AFL-CIO.

American Federation of Labor & Congress of Industrial Organizations (AFL-CIO), 815 16th St. NW, Washington, DC 20006; 14.1 mln. members.

Actors and Artistes of America, Associated (AAAA), 165 W. 46th St., New York, NY 10036; founded 1919; Theodore Bikel, Pres.; no individual members, 9 National Performing Arts Unions are affiliates; approx. 220,000 combined membership.

Actors' Equity Association, 165 W. 46th St., New York, NY 10036; founded 1913; Colleen Dewhurst, Pres.; 39,000 active members.

Air Line Pilots Association, 1625 Massachusetts Ave. NW, Washington, DC 20036. Henry A. Duffy, Pres.; 41,000 members.

Aluminum Brick & Glass Workers International Union (ABG-WIU), 3362 Hollenberg Drive, Bridgeton, MO 63044; founded 1953; Ernie Labaff, Pres. (since 1985); 55,000 members, 415 locals.

Automobile, Aerospace & Agricultural Implement Workers of America, International Union, United (UAW), 8000 E. Jefferson Ave., Detroit, MI 48214; founded 1935; Owen Bieber, Pres. (since 1983); 1,000,000 members, 1,194 locals.

Bakery, Confectionery & Tobacco Workers International Union (BC&T), 10401 Connecticut Ave., Kensington, MD 20895; founded 1886; John DeConcini, Pres. (since 1978); 127,373 members, 135 locals.

Boilermakers, Iron Shipbuilders, Blacksmiths, Forgers and Helpers, International Brotherhood of (IBBISB/BF&H), 570 New Brotherhood Bldg., 8th and State Ave., Kansas City, KS 66101; founded 1880; Charles W. Jones, Pres. (since 1983) 102,000 members, 500 locals.

Bricklayers and Allied Craftsmen, International Union of, 815 15th St. NW, Washington, DC 20005; John T. Joyce, Pres.; 106,000 members, 543 locals.

Carpenters and Joiners of America, United Brotherhood of, 101 Constitution Ave. NW, Washington, DC 20001; founded 1881; Sigurd Lucassen, Gen. Pres.; 595,000 members, 1,500 locals.

Chemical Workers Union, International (ICWU), 1655 West Market St., Akron, OH 44313; founded 1944; Frank D. Martino, Pres. (since 1975); 50,000 members, 350 locals.

Clothing and Textile Workers Union, Amalgamated (ACTWU), 15 Union Square, New York, NY 10003; founded 1976; union founded 1914; Jack Sheinkman, Pres. (since 1987); 272,669 members, 1,490 locals.

Communications Workers of America, (AFL-CIO, CLC) 1925 K St. NW, Washington, DC 20006; Morton Bahr, Pres.; 700,000 members, 1,200 locals.

Distillery, Wine & Allied Workers International Union (DWU), 66 Grand Ave., Englewood, NJ 07631; founded 1940; George J. Orlando, Pres. (since 1984); 15,500 members, 57 locals.

***Education Association, National**, 1201 16th St. NW, Washington, DC 20036; Keith Geiger, Pres. (since 1989); 2,000,000 members, 12,000 affiliates.

Electrical Workers, International Brotherhood of (IBEW), 1125 15th St., NW, Washington, DC 20005; founded 1891; J.J. Barry, Int'l Pres. (since 1986); 1,000,000 members, 1,400 locals.

Electronic, Electrical, Salaried, Machine and Furniture Workers, International Union of (IUE), 1126 16th St. NW, Washington, DC 20036; founded 1949; William H. Bywater, Pres. (since 1982); 190,000 members, 530 locals.

Farm Workers of America, United (UFW), P.O. Box 62, Keene, CA 93531; founded 1962; Cesar E. Chavez, Pres. (since 1962); 100,000 members.

***Federal Employees, National Federation of (NFFE)**, 1016 16th St. NW, Washington, DC 20036; founded 1917; James M. Peirce Jr., Pres. (since 1976); 60,000+ members, 487 locals.

Fire Fighters, International Association of, 1750 New York Ave. NW, Washington, DC 20006; John A. Gannon, Pres.; 172,401 members, 1,943 locals.

Firemen and Oilers, International Brotherhood of, 1100 Circle 75 Parkway, Suite 350, Atlanta, GA 30339; Jimmy L. Walker, Pres.; 30,000 members.

Food and Commercial Workers International Union, United, (UFCW) 1775 K St., NW, Washington, DC 20006; founded 1979 following merger; William H. Wynn, Int'l Pres. (since 1977); 1.3 million members, 600 locals.

Garment Workers of America, United (UGWA), 4207 Lebanon Rd., Hermitage, TN 37076; founded 1891; Earl W. Carroll, Gen. Pres. (since 1987); 25,000 members, 125 locals.

Glass, Molders, Pottery, Plastics & Allied Workers Intl. Union (GMP), 608 E. Baltimore Pike, P.O. Box 607, Media, PA 19063; founded 1842; James E. Hatfield, Int'l Pres. (since 1977); 90,000 members, 435 locals.

Government Employees, American Federation of (AFGE) AFL-CIO, 80 F St., NW, Washington, DC 20001; founded 1932; John N. Sturdivant, Natl. Pres. (since 1976); 210,000 members, 1,300 locals.

Grain Millers, American Federation of (AFGM), 4949 Olson Memorial Hwy., Minneapolis, MN 55422; founded 1948; Robert W. Willis, Gen. Pres.; 35,000 members, 210 locals.

Graphic Communications International Union (GCIU), 1900 L St., NW, Washington, DC 20036; founded 1983; James J. Norton, Pres. (since 1985); 191,291 members, 602 locals.

Hotel Employees and Restaurant Employees International Union, 1219-28th St., NW, Washington, DC 20007; Edward T. Henley, Gen. Pres.; 330,000 members, 190 locals.

Industrial Workers of America, International Union, Allied (AIW), 3520 W. Oklahoma Ave., Milwaukee, WI 53215; founded 1935; Dominick D'Ambrosio, Intl. Pres. (since 1975); 65,000 members, 350 locals.

Iron Workers, International Association of Bridge Structural and Ornamental, 1750 New York Ave. NW, Washington, DC 20006; Jake West, Gen. Pres.; 150,000 members, 300 locals.

Laborers' International Union of North America (LIUNA), 905 16th St. NW, Washington, DC 20006; founded 1903; Angelo Fosco, Gen. Pres. (since 1976); 450,000 members, 713 locals.

Ladies Garment Workers Union, International (ILGWU), 1710 Broadway, New York, NY 10019; founded 1900; Jay Mazur, Pres. (since 1986); 200,000 members, 340 locals.

Leather Goods, Plastic and Novelty Workers' Union, International, 265 W. 14th St., New York, NY 10011; Domenic DiPaolo, Gen. Pres.; 20,000 members, 85 locals.

Letter Carriers, National Association of (NALC), 100 Indiana Ave. NW, Washington, DC 20001; founded 1889; Vincent R. Sombrotto, Pres. (since 1978); 315,281 members, 3,622 locals.

***Locomotive Engineers, Brotherhood of (BLE)**, 1370 Ontario St., Cleveland, OH 44113; founded 1863; R.E. Delaney, Pres. (since 1986); 55,456 members, 636 divisions.

Longshoremen's Association, International, 17 Battery Pl., New York, NY 10004; Thomas W. Gleason, Pres.; 76,579 members, 367 locals.

***Longshoremen's & Warehousemen's Union, International (ILWU)**, 1188 Franklin St., San Francisco, CA 94109; founded 1937; James R. Herman, Pres. (since 1977); 55,000 members, 58 locals.

Machinists and Aerospace Workers, International Association of (IAM), 1300 Connecticut Ave. NW, Washington, DC 20036; founded 1888; George J. Kourpias , Int'l Pres.; 826,875 members, 1,700 locals.

Maintenance of Way Employes, Brotherhood of (BMWE), 12050 Woodward Ave., Detroit, MI 48203; founded 1887; Geoffrey N. Zeh, Pres. (since 1986); 75,000 members, 910 locals.

Marine & Shipbuilding Workers of America, Industrial Union of (IUMSWA), 5101 River Rd., #110, Bethesda, MD 20816; founded 1934; (merged with Machinists and Aerospace Workers, effective Jan. 1, 1989).

Marine Engineer Beneficial Assn./National Maritime Union (MEBA/NMU), 444 N. Capitol St. NW, Suite 800, Washington, D.C. 20001; C.E. DeFries, Pres.; 50,000 members.

***Mine Workers of America, United (UMWA)**, 900 15th St. NW, Washington, DC 20005; founded 1890; Richard Trumka, Int'l Pres. (since 1982); 186,000 members, 800 locals.

Musicians of the United States and Canada, American Federation of (AF of M), 1501 Broadway, Suite 600, New York, NY 10036; founded 1896; J. Martin Emerson, Pres. (since 1987); 206,000 members, 480 locals.

Newspaper Guild, The (TNG), 8611 Second Ave., Silver Spring, MD 20910; founded 1933; Charles Dale, Pres. (since 1987); 33,000 members, 80 locals.

Novelty & Production Workers, Intl. Union of Allied, 1815 Franklin Ave., Valley Stream, NY 11581; Julius Isaacson, Pres. 30,000 members, 18 locals.

*Nurses Association, American, 2420 Pershing Rd., Kansas City, MO 64108; Lucille A. Joel, Ed.D, R.N., F.A.A.N., Pres.; 53 constituent state assns.

Office and Professional Employees International Union (OPEIU), 265 W. 14th St., New York, NY 10011; founded 1945 (AFL Charter); John Kelly, Int'l Pres. (since 1979); 135,00 members, 300 locals.

Oil, Chemical and Atomic Workers International Union (OCAW), PO Box 2812, Denver, CO 80201; Joseph M. Misbrener, Pres. (since 1983); 100,000 members, 500 locals.

Operating Engineers, International Union of (IUOE), 1125 17th St. NW, Washington, DC 20036; founded 1896; Larry Dugan, Jr., Gen. Pres. (since 1985); 375,000 members, 200 locals.

Painters and Allied Trades, International Brotherhood of (IBPAT), 1750 New York Ave. NW, Washington, DC 20006; founded 1887; William A. Duval, Gen. Pres. (since 1984); 161,516 members, 667 locals.

Paperworkers International Union, United (UPIU), 3340 Perimeter Hill Dr., Nashville, TN 37202; founded 1884; Wayne E. Glenn, Pres. (since 1978); 230,000 members, 1,100 locals.

*Plant Guard Workers of America, International Union, United (UPGWA), 25510 Kelly Rd., Roseville, MI 48066; founded 1948; Henry E. Applen, Pres.; 28,000 members, 176 locals.

Plasterers' and Cement Mason's International Association of the United States & Canada; Operative, 1125 17th St. NW, Washington, DC 20036; Robert J. Holton, Pres.; Vincent J. Panepinto, Secy.-Treas.; 65,000 members, 365 locals.

Plumbing and Pipe Fitting Industry of the United States and Canada, United Association of Journeymen and Apprentices of the, 901 Massachusetts Ave. NW, Washington, DC 20001; Marvin J. Boede, Pres.; 325,000 members.

*Police, Fraternal Order of, 2100 Gardiner Lane, Louisville, KY 40205; Dewey R. Stokes, Natl. Pres. and Charles M. Orms, Natl. Secy.; 203,342 members, 1,843 affiliates.

*Postal Supervisors, National Association of, 490 L'Enfant Plaza SW, Suite 3200, Washington, DC 20024-2120; Rubin Handelman, Pres.; 44,000 members, 443 locals.

Postal Workers Union, American (APWU), 1300 L St. NW, Washington, DC 20005; founded 1971; Moe Biller, Pres. (since 1980); 330,000 members, 2,500 locals.

Railway Carmen Division of Transportation Communications Int'l. Union (BRC Division/TCU), 4929 Main St., Kansas City, MO 64112; founded 1888; W.G. Fairchild, Gen. Pres. (since 1989); 50,000 members, 358 locals.

Retail, Wholesale and Department Store Union, 30 E. 29th St., New York, NY 10016; Lenore Miller, Pres.; 200,000 members, 250 locals.

Roofers, Waterproofers & Allied Workers, United Union of, 1125 17th St. NW, Washington, DC 20036; Earl J. Kruse, Pres.; 27,000 members, 138 locals.

Rubber, Cork, Linoleum and Plastic Workers of America, United (URW), 87 South High St., Akron, OH 44308; founded 1935; Milan Stone; Int'l Pres. (since 1981); 109,000 members, 411 locals.

*Rural Letter Carriers' Association, National, Suite 100, 1448 Duke St., Alexandria, VA 22314; founded 1903; Dallas N. Fields, Pres. (since 1987); 72,000 members; state organizations, 47.

Seafarers International Union of North America (SIUNA), 5201 Auth Way, Camp Springs, MD 20746; founded 1938; Michael Sacco, Pres.; 90,000 members.

Service Employees International Union (SEIU), 1313 L St. NW, Washington, DC 20005; founded 1921; John J. Sweeney, Pres. (since 1980); 850,000 members, 300 locals.

Sheet Metal Workers' International Association (SMWIA), 1750 New York Ave. NW, Washington, DC 20006; founded 1888; Edward J. Carlough, Gen. Pres. (since 1970); 150,000 members, 245 locals.

State, County and Municipal Employees, American Federation of, 1625 L St. NW, Washington, DC 20036; Gerald McEntee, Pres.; 1,200,000 members, 2,991 locals.

Steelworkers of America, United (USWA), 5 Gateway Center, Pittsburgh, PA 15222; founded 1936; Lynn Williams, Int'l Pres. (since 1984); 750,000 members, 3,500 locals.

Teachers, American Federation of (AFT), 555 New Jersey Ave. NW, Washington, DC 20001; founded 1916; Albert Shanker, Pres. (since 1974); 700,000 members, 2,200 locals.

*Teamsters, Chauffeurs, Warehousemen and Helpers of America, International Brotherhood of (IBT), 25 Louisiana Ave. NW, Washington, DC 20001; founded 1903; William J. McCarthy, Gen. Pres.; 1,600,000 members, 700 locals.

Television and Radio Artists, American Federation of, 260 Madison Ave., New York, NY 10016; founded 1937; Frank Maxwell, Pres.; 67,000 members, 38 locals.

Textile Workers of America, United (UTWA), 2 Echelon Plaza, Laurel Rd., P.O. Box 749, Voorhees, NJ 08043-0749; founded 1901; Vernon Mustard, Intl. Pres. (since 1986); 26,000 members, 180 locals.

Theatrical Stage Employes and Moving Picture Machine Operators of the United States and Canada, International Alliance of, 1515 Broadway, New York, NY 10036; Alfred W. Di Tolla, Pres.; 61,471 members, 750 locals.

Transit Union, Amalgamated (ATU), 5025 Wisconsin Ave. NW, Washington, DC 20016; founded 1892; James La Sala, Intl. Pres. (since 1981); 165,000 members, 275 locals.

Transport Workers Union of America, 80 West End Ave., New York, NY 10023; founded 1934; George Leitz, Int'l Pres. (since 1985); 100,000 members, 94 locals.

Transportation Communications International Union (TCU), 3 Research Place, Rockville, MD 20850; Richard I. Kilroy, Int'l Pres. (since 1981); 160,000 members, 750 locals.

*Transportation Union, United (UTU), 14600 Detroit Ave., Cleveland, OH 44107; founded 1969; Fred A. Hardin, Pres. (since 1979); 120,000 members, 862 locals.

*Treasury Employees Union, National (NTEU), 1730 K St. NW, Suite 1101, Washington, DC 20006; founded 1938; Robert M. Tobias, Natl. Pres. (since 1983); 120,000 represented, 250 chapters.

*University Professors, American Association of (AAUP), 1012-14th St., Washington, DC 20005; founded 1915; Carol Simpson Stern, Pres.; 40,000 members, 600 chapters.

Upholsterers' International Union of North America (UIU), 25 N. 4th St., Philadelphia, PA 19106; founded 1882; John Serembus, Pres.; 31,827 members, 133 locals.

Utility Workers Union of America (UWUA), 815 16th St. NW, Washington, DC 20006; founded 1945; James Joy Jr., Natl. Pres. (since 1986); 60,000 members, 220 locals.

International Woodworkers of America —U.S. (IWA—U.S.), 25 Cornell, Gladstone, OR 97027; founded 1987; Wilson (Bill) Hubbell, Natl. Pres.; 28,000 members, 100 locals.

U.S. Union Membership, 1930-88

Source: Bureau of Labor Statistics

Year	Labor[1] Force (thousands)	Union[2] Members (thousands)	Percent	Year	Labor[1] Force (thousands)	Union[2] Members (thousands)	Percent
1930	29,424	3,401	11.6	1975	76,945	19,611	25.5
1935	27,053	3,584	13.2	1980	90,564	19,843	21.9
1940	32,376	8,717	26.9	1983	88,290	17,717	20.1
1945	40,394	14,322	35.5	1984	92,194	17,340	18.8
1950	45,222	14,267	31.5	1985	94,521	16,996	18.0
1955	50,675	16,802	33.2	1986	96,903	16,975	17.5
1960	54,234	17,049	31.4	1987	99,303	16,913	17.0
1965	60,815	17,299	28.4	1988	101,407	17,002	16.8
1970	70,920	19,381	27.3				

(1) Does not include agricultural employment; from 1983 data do not include self-employed or unemployed persons. (2) From 1930 to 1980 data are the number of dues paying members of traditional trade unions with members counted regardless of employment status; from 1983 members include employee associations that engage in collective bargaining with employers.

TAXES

Federal Income Tax

Source: George W. Smith III. CPA. *Cut Your Own Taxes and Save*. Pharos Books.

With the passage of the Tax Reform Act of 1986, Congress enacted the most dramatic changes in our tax law in over fifty years. Its purpose was to create a more equitable income tax system for all taxpayers. Many of the provisions resulting from this massive piece of legislation and the Medicare Catastrophic Coverage Act and the Technical and Miscellaneous Revenue Act of 1988 will affect all taxpayers filing their 1989 income tax returns.

Tax Law Changes
and
Recent Developments

• Parents may elect to include on their income tax return the unearned income of a dependent child under age 14 whose income is more than $500 but less than $5,000. The income must consist solely of interest, dividends or Alaska Permanent Fund dividends. Form 8814, Parents's Election to Report Child's Interest and Dividends, is required to report this income.

• Interest earned on Series EE bonds issued after 1989 that is used to pay for higher education may be excluded from taxable income. This exclusion is subject to an income phaseout, eligibility requirements and certain education expense limitations.

• For individuals age 55 or over, the 3 out of 5 year home use rule for the sale of a principal residence has been expanded. Certain incapacitated individuals who reside in state licensed facilities may exclude from gross income up to $125,000 of gain resulting from the sale if the house was used as their principal residence for at least *one* year out of the last 5 years.

• To be eligible for the child and dependent care credit, a dependent must now be under 13 years of age (previously 15). The taxpayer must also report the name, address, and taxpayer's identification number of the child care provider on their income tax return or the taxpayer will not be entitled to the credit.

• An individual may not claim for 1989 an exemption for a dependent child who is a full time student and has attained the age of 24 *unless* the child's gross income is less than $2,000.

• For 1989, a taxpayer must list the social security number of any dependent claimed on their income tax return who is at least 2 years old by the end of the tax year. There is a penalty for noncompliance.

• Beginning in 1989, senior citizens may owe a Supplemental Medicare premium. This premium is subject to some limitations and only assessed to individuals who are eligible for Medicare Part A (hospital insurance) benefits for more than 6 full months of 1989 and who have an income tax liability of $150 or more. The 1989 premium is based on a rate of $22.50 for each $150 of income tax owed. The premium cannot exceed $800 for a single person. If married and filing a joint return, and both husband and wife are Medicare elegible for more than 6 full months, the premium cannot be more than $1,600. If only one individual is eligible, then the premium cannot be more than $800. If husband and wife file separate returns and lived together during the year, the maximum premium is $1,600 on *each* return if both individuals are Medicare eligible for more than 6 full months. If you file separate returns but did not live together during the year, your premium is figured as if you were single.

• Starting in 1989, the base rate on the first telephone line into a personal residence is not allowed as a business deduction. This does not affect the deductibility of long distance calls or optional services such as call waiting, call forwarding, three-way calling or extra directory listings as long as they are business related.

• Personal exemptions may not be deducted in figuring alternative minimum taxable income. This change retroactively applies to alternative minimum tax computations starting with 1987 income tax returns.

• IRA investments are allowed for certain gold and silver coins issued by the U.S. Government. Investments also may include certain coins issued by a state government. However, only state coins issued after November 10, 1988 qualify.

• Jury duty pay surrendered by an employee to an employer in return for his normal salary is deductible as an adjustment to income—not as an itemized deduction.

Tax Rates

Once again there will be only two rates for 1989 — 15% and 28%. The dollar bracket amounts have been adjusted for inflation.

Married Filing Joint Return or Qualifying Widow(er)

Tax Rates	Bracket
15%	$0 to $30,950
28%	Over $30,950

Married Filing Separately

Tax Rate	Bracket
15%	$0 to $15,475
28%	Over $15,475

Head of Household

Tax Rate	Bracket
15%	$0 to $24,850
28%	Over $24,850

Single

Tax Rate	Bracket
15%	$0 to $18,550
28%	Over $18,550

Certain higher incomes will be subject to an additional 5% tax. This 5% rate adjustment phases out the benefit of the 15% tax rate. For married taxpayers filing jointly the five percent phaseout begins with taxable income of $74,850 and is fully phased out at $155,320.

Heads of household with taxable income between $64,200 and $128,810 will be subject to the five percent adjustment, as will single individuals with taxable income between $44,900 and $93,130. The phaseout for married taxpayers filing separately will apply when taxable income between $37,425 and $117,895.

Standard Deduction

The standard deduction is a flat amount that is subtracted from adjusted gross income for taxpayers who do not itemize their deductions. The amount of the basic standard deduction depends upon the taxpayer's filing status.

Taxpayers with itemized deductions such as medical expenses, charitable contributions, interest, taxes, etc., totaling more than the standard deduction amount should not use the standard deduction. Instead, they should itemize their deductions.

Basic Standard Deduction for 1989

Married filing joint return or qualifying Widow(er)	$5,200
Head of households	$4,550
Single	$3,100
Married filing separately	$2,600

Individuals claimed as a dependent on another person's income tax return may claim on their returns the larger of *(continued)*

$500, or the amount of their earned income up to the amount of the standard deduction, which the taxpayer would normally be allowed. Earned income includes wages, salaries, commissions, tips, net profit from self-employment—any money received as compensation for personal services rendered. It also includes any part of a scholarship or fellowship grant that must be included in gross income.

Example: A dependent parent, age 60, had unearned income (interest and dividends) of $1,700 during 1988. He had no earned income. His basic standard deduction would be $500. He would have taxable income of $1,200

Example: A dependent son had $10,000 of unearned income and $100 of earned income. He is entitled to a $500 standard deduction. He is limited to this amount because he is a dependent and his earned income is less than $500. The taxpayer would, therefore, have $9,600 in taxable income.

Example: A dependent daughter with $4,000 of earned income and $600 of unearned income would claim a maximum $3,100 standard deduction because her earned income of $4,000 is greater than the standard deduction. She would have taxable income of $1,500.

Additional Standard Deduction for Age and Blindness

Elderly or blind taxpayers may also claim an additional standard deduction. Taxpayers who are age 65 or over or blind at the end of 1989, qualify for the additional standard deduction for age and blindness. Taxpayers who claim the additional standard deduction for blindness must attach a doctor's statement to their income tax return. Taxpayers who itemize their deductions will lose the additional standard deduction.

Additional Standard Deduction for 1989
Married filing jointly, age 65 or over or blind (per person) $600
Married filing jointly, age 65 or over and blind (per person) $1,200
Single, age 65 or over or blind $750
Single, age 65 or over and blind $1,500

Examples: In 1989, a sixty-five year old woman would claim $3,850 for her standard deduction computed as follows:

Basic standard deduction for a single person	$3,100
Additional standard deduction for age	750
Total	$3,850

For a married couple filing jointly, a seventy year old husband and a fifty-eight year old blind wife would be entitled to a standard deduction of 1989 totalling $6,400 computed as follows:

Basic standard deduction for Married filing jointly	$5,200
Additional standard deduction for (husband's) age	600
Additional standard deduction for (wife's) blindness	600
Total	$6,400

Exemptions

The personal exemption amount for 1989 is $2,000. Starting in 1990, the personal exemption amount will be adjusted each year for inflation.

Adjustments to Income

Individual Retirement Arrangements (IRAs)

All taxpayers with earned income may still make contributions to their IRAs; however, there may be limits on the amount they can deduct on their income tax return if they are covered by a qualified retirement plan by their employer. Income earned from IRAs will remain tax-free until the taxpayer withdraws it.

For 1989, married taxpayers filing jointly with adjusted gross income of less than $40,000 may take an IRA deduction whether or not they are active participants in a qualified retirement plan. Single taxpayers in qualified retirement plans may also deduct IRAs if their adjusted gross income is below $25,000. The IRA deduction phases out over the next $10,000 of adjusted gross income if taxpayers are active participants in a qualified retirement plan. Consequently, married couples filing jointly with adjusted gross income over $50,000 or single filers with adjusted gross income over $35,000 may not deduct any contributions to their IRAs.

Taxpayers who don't have a qualified retirement plan where they work may take an IRA deduction up to the lesser of $2,000 or the amount of their earned income *regardless of their total income.*

Taxpayers who are eligible to participate in their employers' qualified plans are considered to belong to the plan even if they choose not to participate.

For computing an IRA deduction, adjusted gross income does not include deductible IRAs, but does include taxable Social Security benefits and passive loss limitations.

A qualified retirement plan generally includes: (1) a qualified pension, profit-sharing or stock bonus plan; (2) a qualified annuity plan; (3) a simplified employee pension plan; or (4) a plan established for its employees by the federal, state or other political subdivision or by an agency of these entities.

Itemized Deductions

- Medical expenses are deductible if they exceed 7.5 percent of adjusted gross income. The Medicare Catastrophic premium is not a medical deduction.
- Nonbusiness interest expense will be phased out over the next three years as indicated in the following table:

Tax Year	Amount of Personal Interest Deductible
1989	20%
1990	10%
1991	0

- Investment interest for 1989 is deductible to the extent of net investment income plus up to 20% of the next $10,000 of investment interest expense ($5,000 for a married person filing separately).
- Mortgage interest on a taxpayer's first and second homes remains fully deductible. However, there are limitations.
- Home equity loans are deductible up to the first $100,000 in equity debt.

- Charitable contributions to qualified charities are deductible if the taxpayer itemizes deductions.
- State and local income taxes, real estate taxes, and personal property taxes remain fully deductible.
- Casualty and theft losses are deductible subject to the 10% and $100 limitations.

Moving Expenses

Taxpayers who changed jobs during the year can usually deduct some of their moving expenses. These expenses include the cost of moving household goods, travel to the new home, househunting trips, temporary living quarters, and other related expenses. To qualify, the move must be job-related and it must meet several other requirements including a distance and time test. The expenses for moving household goods and traveling to a new home have some limitations. All other deductible moving expenses, such as househunting trips or temporary living quarters, are subject to a $3,000

(continued)

ceiling. Only 80% of meal expenses are deductible. Moving expenses are deductible only if the taxpayer itemizes deductions on Schedule A of Form 1040.

Employee Business Expense

All employee business expenses including travel and entertainment (except reimbursed expenses) are allowed only as itemized miscellaneous deductions. Only 80 percent of the cost of meals and entertaining customers is deductible. These expenses are then subject to the 2%-of-adjusted-gross-income limit on miscellaneous deductions.

Reimbursed employee buisness expense are reported on Form 2106 and can only be deducted on Form 1040 as an adjustment to income.

Earned Income Credit

Low income workers who have dependent children and maintain a household are eligible for a refundable credit. The credit for 1989 is calculated on earned income with a maximum earned income credit of $910. For income of more than $10,240 the credit begins to phase out until it is completely phased out at $19,340.

If an individual qualifies, the credit is refundable even if the taxpayer is not required to file an income tax return. However, a return must be filed in order to receive the credit. To assist individuals, the IRS publishes a table showing the earned income credit at various levels of income.

Taxing Income of Children

Children who may be claimed as a dependent by another taxpayer may not claim their own exemption on their return. Further, children under age 14 with at least one living parent may use up to $500 of their standard deduction against unearned income. Unearned income includes dividends and interest income. If the child's unearned income is more than $1,000, that income will be taxed at the child's tax rate or the parent's rate, whichever is higher.

The effect of this is to charge a higher tax rate on children's unearned income by taxing it at the parent's rate when that rate is higher. However, because only the amount of unearned income over $1,000 is subject to this treatment, the child does get the benefit of a lower rate on the first $1,000.

For example, assuming the child $3,000 of interest income, the child's taxable income would be $2,500, allowing for the $500 standard deduction. Assuming that the parent's rate is 28%, the child's tax rate would be $635 (15% × $500 + 28% × $2,000). At the parent's rate, the total income of $3,000 would be taxed at a straight 28%, or $840. The tax is lower on the child's return. The difference saved is $205.

Who Must File

Whether U.S. citizens or resident aliens must file an income tax return depends on their gross income, filing status and age.

Generally, U.S. citizens or resident aliens will have to file a tax return if their gross income for the year is at least as much as the amount shown for their situation in the table below.

Filing Status	1989 Gross Income
• Single	
Under 65	$5,100
65 or older	5,850
• Married Filing Joint Return	
Both spouses under 65	9,200
One spouse 65 or older	9,800
Both spouses 65 or older	$10,400
• Married Filing Separate Return	2,000
• Head of Household	
Under 65	6,550
65 or older	7,300
• Qualifying Widow(er)	
Under 65	7,200
65 or older	7,800

Example: John and Mary Smith intend to file a joint return for 1989. John's income is all from wages. Mary receives no income subject to tax. Neither John nor Mary is blind. John is 67 years old but Mary will not be 65 until 1990. In 1989, their combined gross income subject to tax will be $10,000. They will have to file a return for 1989 because their gross income will be at least $9,800.

If Mary was 65 by the end of 1989, they would not have to file a 1989 tax return because their gross income would be less than $10,400 as shown in the table above.

When To File

For 1989, your income tax return is required to be filed with the Internal Revenue Service no later than Monday, April 16, 1990.

If you file later, you may have to pay penalties and interest on any unpaid tax liability.

If you know that you cannot file by the due date, you should request an extension for additional time by filing Form 4868, Application for Automatic Extension of Time To File U.S. Individual Income Tax Return.

Which Form To File

You may be able to use the short Form 1040EZ if:
• You are single and do not claim any dependents.
• You are not 65 or older or blind.
• You have only wages, salaries, tips, taxable scholarships or fellowships, and not more than $400 of interest income.
• Your taxable income is less than $50,000.
• You do not itemize deductions or claim any adjustments to income or tax credits.

You may be able to use Form 1040A if:
• You have income only from wages, salaries, tips, taxable scholarships or fellowships, unemployment compensation, interest, or dividends.
• Your taxable income is less than $50,000.
• You do not itemize deductions.

You can claim a deduction for qualified contributions to an Individual Retirement Arrangement (IRA).

• You can claim a credit for child and dependent care expenses.

Your should use either Form 1040EZ or Form 1040A unless filing Form 1040 allows you to pay a lesser tax. Forms 1040EZ and 1040A are easier to complete than the longer Form 1040. However, even if you meet the above tests, you will have to file Form 1040 if any of the following situations apply to you.

You must use Form 1040 if:
• Your taxable income is $50,000 or more.
• You itemize deductions.
• You receive as a nominee, interest or dividends that belong to another person.
• You receive any nontaxable dividends or capital gain distributions.
• You have foreign accounts and/or foreign trusts.
• You have business, farm or rental income.
• You have taxable social security or railroad retirement benefits.
• You have miscellaneous income not allowed on Form 1040EZ or 1040A such as alimony or pension income.

(continued)

- You have adjustments to income (such as alimony paid) except for an IRA which can also be deducted on Form 1040A.
- You can claim a foreign tax credit or certain other credits to which you are entitled.
- You have paid estimated income tax.
- You have other taxes such as self-employment tax or the alternative minimum tax.

- You file any of these forms:

    Form 1040-ES, Estimated Tax for Individuals, for 1989 (or if you want to apply any part of your 1989 overpayment to estimated tax for 1990).

    Form 2210, Underpayment of Estimated Tax by Individuals.

    Form 2555, Foreign Earned Income.

Frequently Used Tax Forms

706
United States Estate (and Generation Skipping Transfer) Tax Return.
Used for the estate of a deceased United States resident or citizen.

709—A
United States Short Form Gift Tax Return.
Used by married couples to report nontaxable gifts or more than $10,000 but less than $20,000.

1040
U.S. Individual Income Tax Return.
Used by citizens and residents of the United States to report income tax. Also see Form 1040A and Form 1040EZ.

1040-ES
Estimated Tax for Individuals.
Used to make estimated tax payments as a means for paying currently any income tax (including self-employment tax and the alternative minimum tax) due in excess of the tax withheld from wages, salaries, and other payments for personal services. It is not required unless the total tax exceeds withholding (if any) and applicable tax credits by $500 or more.

1040NR
U.S. Nonresident Alien Income Tax Return.
Used by all nonresident alien individuals who file a U.S. tax return, whether or not engaged in a trade or business within the United States. Also used as required for filing nonresident alien fiduciary (estate and trust) returns.

1040X
Amended U.S. Individual Income Tax Return.
Used to claim refund of income taxes, pay additional income taxes, or designate dollar(s) to the Presidential Election Campaign Fund.

1041
U.S. Fiduciary Income Tax Return.
Used by a fiduciary for domestic estate or domestic trust.

1065
U.S. Partnership Return of Income.
Used by partnerships as an information return.

1116
Computation of Foreign Tax Credit—Individual, Fiduciary, or Nonresident Alien Individual.
Used to figure and support the foreign tax credit claimed for the amount of any income, war profits, and excess profits taxes paid or accrued during the tax year to any foreign country or U.S. possession.

1120
U.S. Corporation Income Tax Return.
Used by a corporation to report income tax.

1120S
U.S. Income Tax Return for an S Corporation.
Used by S corporations to report taxes

under Sub-chapter S of the IRC and as an information return.

1139
Corporation Application for Tentative Refund.
Used by corporations that have certain carrybacks and desire a quick refund of taxes.

1310
Statement of Person Claiming Refund Due a Deceased Taxpayer.
Used by a claimant to secure payment of refund on behalf of a deceased taxpayer.

2106
Employee Business Expenses.
For use by employees to support deductions from income tax for travel, transportation, outside salesperson, and reimbursed expenses (except moving expenses).

2119
Sale or Exchange of Principal Residence.
For use by individuals who sold their principal residence. Also used by those individuals 55 or older who elect to exclude gain on the sale of their principal residence.

2120
Multiple Support Declaration.
Used as a statement to disclaim as an income tax exemption an individual to whose support the taxpayer and others have contributed.

2441
Credit for Child and Dependent Care Expenses.
Used to figure the credit for child and dependent care expenses.

2688
Application for Additional Extension of Time To File U.S. Individual Income Tax Return.
Used to apply for an additional extension of time to file Form 1040.

2848
Power of Attorney and Declaration of Representative.
Used as an authorization for one person to act for another in any tax matter (except alcohol and tobacco taxes and firearms activities).

3903
Moving Expenses.
For optional use to support deductions from income for expenses of travel, transportation (including meals and lodging), and certain expenses of selling an old residence and buying a new residence for employees or self-employment individuals moving to a new job location in the U.S. or its possessions.

4562
Depreciation and Amortization.
For use by individuals, estates and trusts, partnerships, and corporations claiming depreciation, amortization, and section

179 expense deduction. Also used to provide required information for automobiles and all other "listed property."

4684
Casualties and Thefts.
For use by all taxpayers for reporting gains and losses from casualties and thefts.

4868
Application for Automatic Extension of Time To File U.S. Individual Income Tax Return.
Used to apply for an automatic 4-month extension of time to file Form 1040.

5498
Individual Retirement Arrangement Information
Used to report contributions to IRAs and the value of the account at the end of the year.

5500EZ
Annual Return of One-Participant (Owners and Their Spouses) Pension Benefit Plan.
Used to report on a pension, profit-sharing, etc., plan covering an individual, partner or an individual and spouse or partners and spouses who wholly own a business.

6251
Alternative Minimum Tax—Individuals.
Used by individuals to report tax preference items and to figure their alternative minimum tax liability.

7004
Application for Automatic Extension of Time To File Corporation Income Tax Return.
Used by corporations and certain exempt organizations to request an automatic extension of 6 months to file their income tax returns.

8283
Noncash Charitable Contributions.
Used by taxpayers to report contributions of property in which the total claimed fair market value of all property contributed exceeds $500.

8582
Passive Activity Loss Limitations.
Used to determine limitations on passive activity losses.

8606
Nondeductible IRA Contributions, IRA Basis, and Nontaxable IRA Distributions.
Used to determine the nondeductible amount of IRA, contributions and distributions. It is also used to determine IRA basis.

8615
Computation of Tax for Children Under Age 14 Who Have Investment Income of More Than $1,000.
Used to figure the tax on unearned income of more than $1,000 belonging to a child under age 14.

Internal Revenue Service Audit

    There are two important considerations you should know regarding the IRS audit program. First, fewer than two out of every hundred individual tax returns will be audited in 1990. Second, the IRS is good at selecting returns for audit

that will yield additional income taxes.

    Returns to be audited are chosen by one of the following six methods and also be random selection:

(continued)

- The Discriminate Function System (DIF)
- Taxpayer Compliance Measurement Program (TCMP)
- Matching Information Documents
- Targeted Group Projects
- Discrepancies in Your Return
- Tips from Informants.

If your return is audited and you feel you are not being treated fairly, or that proper attention is not being paid to your statements, you have a right to ask for a hearing at the IRS appellate level. If you are still dissatisfied, you can take your case to the United States Tax Court. If the total amount in question is less than $10,000, your case can be handled under the Small Tax Case procedures. If you are still dissatisfied, your next move would be the United States Circuit Court of Appeals.

Your Rights As a Taxpayer

Congress responded to complaints that taxpayers were not being treated fairly by the IRS and passed a comprehensive law to force the IRS to explain, in easy to understand language, the actions it proposes to take against a taxpayer and to relax some of its audit and collection procedures. This law is called "The Taxpayer Bill of Rights."

Some of the highlights of this bill of rights are:

- Plain English statements
- Audit recordings of conferences
- Taxpayers are not required to attend the examination

- New audit location rules
- Guidelines for installment payment of taxes
- Acting on wrong IRS advice
- Hardship relief
- Specific basis of IRS decision
- Levies on property
- Suing IRS for damages

You can obtain this IRS Publication free by calling 1-800-424-FORM. Ask for Publication 1, "Your Rights As a Taxpayer."

Federal Estate and Gift Tax

Source: Tax Foundation, Inc. from Commerce Clearing House data. compiled July 15, 1989.

Estate Tax

As a result of the Economic Recovery Tax Act of 1981, the lifetime unified credit against combined estate and gift taxes increased in steps from $47,000 in 1981 to $192,800 in 1987 and thereafter. Thus, cumulative transfers exempt from estate and gift taxes increased from $175,625 in 1981 to $600,000 in 1987 and thereafter. The maximum estate and gift tax rate, which was 70 percent in 1981, has been reduced gradually to 55% from 1987 to 1992, and 50% in 1993 and later years. The current schedule is shown below.

Estate taxes are computed by applying the unified rate schedule, shown below, to the total estate minus allowable deductions, such as funeral expenses, administrative expenses, debts and charitable contributions, plus taxable gifts made after 1976. Gift taxes paid are subtracted from tax due, and credit also may be taken for state death taxes. The amount of the state tax credit is determined by the schedule shown in the table below or the actual state taxes paid, whichever is less. No state tax credit is available to an adjusted taxable estate (i.e., taxable estate minus $60,000) smaller than $40,000. Transfers to a surviving spouse are generally tax exempt.

The law provides for real property passed on to family members for use in a closely held business, such as farming, to be valued on basis of such use, rather than fair market value on basis of highest and best use. In no case may this special valuation reduce the gross estate by more than $750,000.

The generation-skipping transfer tax effective since April 30, 1976 was expanded by the Tax Reform Act of 1986. Under prior law, terminations or distributions from trusts were subject to taxes substantially equivalent to those that would have been imposed had the property been transferred outright to each successive generation. The tax now also applies to "direct skips" which are generation-skipping transfers, such as gifts or transfers of property to a trust, occuring after October 22, 1986 with some exceptions. The tax rate is 55% from 1987 through 1992 and 50% thereafter. Each grantor is allowed a lifetime exemption of $1 million, as well as, prior to 1990, up to $2 million for "direct skips" to each grandchild.

A return must be filed for the estate of every U.S. citizen or resident whose gross estate exceeds $600,000 in 1987 and thereafter ($60,000 for the estate of a nonresident not a citizen). The return is due nine months after death unless an extension is granted.

Gift Tax

Any citizen or resident alien whose gifts to any one person exceed $10,000 within a calender year will be liable for payment of a gift tax, at rates determined under the unified estate and gift tax schedule. Gift tax returns are filed on an annual basis and ordinarily are due by April 15 of the following year.

Gifts made by a husband and wife to a third party may be considered as having been made one-half by each, provided both spouses consent to such division.

Unified Rate Schedule for Estate and Gift Tax[1]

If the amount with respect to which the tentative tax to be computed is:			The tentative tax is:		
Not over $10,000			18 percent of such amount.		
Over	$10,000	but not over	$20,000.	$1,800, plus 20%	of the excess over	$10,000.
Over	$20,000	but not over	$40,000.	$3,800, plus 22%	of the excess over	$20,000.
Over	$40,000	but not over	$60,000.	$8,200, plus 24%	of the excess over	$40,000.
Over	$60,000	but not over	$80,000.	$13,000, plus 26%	of the excess over	$60,000.
Over	$80,000	but not over	$100,000.	$18,200, plus 28%	of the excess over	$80,000.
Over	$100,000	but not over	$150,000.	$23,800, plus 30%	of the excess over	$100,000.
Over	$150,000	but not over	$250,000.	$38,800, plus 32%	of the excess over	$150,000.
Over	$250,000	but not over	$500,000.	$70,800, plus 34%	of the excess over	$250,000.
Over	$500,000	but not over	$750,000.	$155,800, plus 37%	of the excess over	$500,000.
Over	$750,000	but not over	$1,000,000.	$248,300, plus 39%	of the excess over	$750,000.
Over	$1,000,000	but not over	$1,250,000.	$345,800, plus 41%	of the excess over	$1,000,000.
Over	$1,250,000	but not over	$1,500,000.	$448,300, plus 43%	of the excess over	$1,250,000.
Over	$1,500,000	but not over	$2,000,000.	$555,800, plus 45%	of the excess over	$1,500,000.
Over	$2,000,000	but not over	$2,500,000.	$780,800, plus 49%	of the excess over	$2,000,000.
Over	$2,500,000	but not over	$3,000,000.	$1,025,800, plus 53%	of the excess over	$2,500,000.
Over	$3,000,000			$1,290,800 plus 55%	of the excess over	$3,000,000.

Add an additional 5% for amounts between $10,000,000 and $21,040,000.

(1) The unified tax credit against estates and gifts for estates of decedents dying during 1987 and thereafter is $192,800.

(continued)

State Death Tax Credit for Estate Tax

Adjusted taxable estate from	to	Credit = +	%	Of excess over	Adjusted taxable estate from	to	Credit = +	%	Of excess over
$ 0	$ 40,000	0	0	$ 0	2,040,000	2,540,000	106,800	8	2,040,000
40,000	90,000	0	.8	40,000	2,540,000	3,040,000	146,800	8.8	2,540,000
90,000	140,000	400	1.6	90,000	3,040,000	3,540,000	190,800	9.6	3,040,000
140,000	240,000	1,200	2.4	140,000	3,540,000	4,040,000	238,800	10.4	3,540,000
240,000	440,000	3,600	3.2	240,000	4,040,000	5,040,000	290,800	11.2	4,040,000
440,000	640,000	10,000	4	440,000	5,040,000	6,040,000	402,800	12	5,040,000
640,000	840,000	18,000	4.8	640,000	6,040,000	7,040,000	522,800	12.8	6,040,000
840,000	1,040,000	27,600	5.6	840,000	7,040,000	8,040,000	650,800	13.6	7,040,000
1,040,000	1,540,000	38,800	6.4	1,040,000	8,040,000	9,040,000	786,800	14.4	8,040,000
1,540,000	2,040,000	70,800	7.2	1,540,000	9,040,000	10,040,000	930,800	15.2	9,040,000
					10,040,000		1,082,800	16	10,040,000

State Individual Income Taxes: Rates, Exemptions

Source: Tax Foundation, Inc. from Commerce Clearing House data as of July 15, 1989
Footnotes at end of table.

State	Taxable[10] income	Percentage[10] rates	Taxable income	Percentage rates	Personal exemp.[1] Single	Married family head	Each dependent
Alabama[2,4]	First $1,000 1,001-6,000	2 4	Over $6,000	5	$1,500	$3,000	$300
Arizona[2,3,4,5] . . .	First 1,229 1,229-2,458 2,458-3,687	2 3 Less $12 4 Less $37	3,687-4,916 4,916-6,145 6,145-7,374 Over 7,374	5 Less $74 6 Less $123 7 Less $184 8 Less $258	2,125	4,250	1,275
Arkansas	First 2,999 3,000-5,999 6,000-8,999	1 2.5 3.5	9,000-14,999 15,000-24,999 25,000 and over	4.5 6 7	20* *Tax credit	40*	20*
California[2,3,5,7] . .	First 7,636 7,636-18,096 18,096-28,556	1 2 4	28,556-39,644 39,644-50,104 Over 50,104	6 8 9.3 *Tax credit	52*	104*	52*
Colorado[7]	5% of modified federal taxable income.						
Connecticut . . .	7% tax on adjusted capital gains; tax on dividends and interest earned if modified federal adjusted gross income is greater than or equal to $54,000; tax ranges from 1% on $54,000 through 14% on $100,000 and over.				100* *exemptions applied to capital gains.	200*	
Delaware	First 2,000 2,001-5,000 5,001-10,000 10,001-20,000	0 3.2 5.0 6.0	20,001-25,000 25,001-30,000 30,001-40,000 Over 40,000	6.6 7.0 7.6 7.7	1,250	2,500	1,250
Dist. of Col.[9] . . .	First 10,000 10,001-20,000	6 8	Over 20,000	9.5	1,160 *If spouse has no gross income.	2,320*	1,160
Georgia[2]	First 1,000 1,001-3,000 3,001-5,000	1 2 3	5,001-7,000 7,001-10,000 Over 10,000	4 5 6	1,500	3,000	1,500
Hawaii[2]	First $3,000 3,000-5,000 5,000-7,000 7,000-11,000	2.0 4.0 6.0 7.25	$11,000-21,000 21,000-31,000 31,000-41,000 Over 41,000	8 8.75 9.5 10.00	$1,040	$2,080	$1,040
Idaho[2,5]	First 999 1,000-1,999 2,000-2,999 3,000-3,999	2 4 4.5 5.5	4,000-4,999 5,000-7,499 7,500-19,999 Over 20,000	6.5 7.5 7.8 8.2	2,000	4,000	2,000
Illinois	Taxable net income 3*		*Rate to July 1, 1989 is 2.5%		1,000	2,000	1,000
Indiana	Adjusted gross income	3.4			1,000	2,000	1,000
Iowa[3,4,7]	First 1,000 1,001-2,000 2,001-4,000 4,001-9,000 9,001-15,000	0.4 0.8 2.7 5 6.8	15,001-20,000 20,000-30,000 30,001-45,000 Over 45,000	7.2 7.55 8.8 9.98	20* *Tax credit No income tax is imposed on net incomes of $5,000 or less.	40*	15*

(continued)

State	Taxable[10] income	Percentage[10] rates	Taxable income	Percentage rates	Personal exemp.[1] Single	Married family head	Each dependent
Kansas[2,6]	First 35,000	3.65	Over 35,000	5.15	2,000	4,000	2,000
Kentucky[4]	First 3,000	2	4,001-5,000	4	20*	40*	20*
	3,001-4,000	3	5,001-8,000	5	*Tax credit	If spouse has no gross income	
			Over 8,000	6			
Louisiana[4,5]	First 10,000	2	Over 50,000	6	4,500*	9,000*	1,000*
	10,001-50,000	4			*Combined exemption and standard deduction.		
Maine[2]	First 7,999	2	16,000-31,999	7	2,000	4,000	2,000
	8,000-15,999	4.5	Over 32,000	8.5			
Maryland[9]	First 1,000	2	2,001-3,000	4	1,100	2,200	1,100
	1,001-2,000	3	Over 3,000	5			
Massachusetts	Earned and business income:	5*	*No tax on adjusted gross income below $12,000 for husband and wife or $8,000 for single individual. Rates shown apply above these amounts. Exemptions apply to earned income only.		2,200	4,400	1,000
	Interest, divs., net income capital gains	10*					
Michigan[9]	All taxable income	4.6			2,000	4,000	2,000
Minnesota[2,7]	First 19,000	6	75,501-165,000	8.5	Federal exemptions.		
	19,001-75,000	8	Over 165,000	8 plus $447.50			
Mississippi	First 5,000	3	Next 5,000	4	6,000	9,500	1,500
			Over 10,000	5			
Missouri[4]	First 1,000	1.5	5,001-6,000	4	1,200	2,400	400
	1,001-2,000	2	6,001-7,000	4.5			
	2,001-3,000	2.5	7,001-8,000	5			
	3,001-4,000	3	8,001-9,000	5.5			
	4,001-5,000	3.5	Over 9,000	6			
Montana[3,4]	First 1,400	2	11,400-14,300	7	1,140	2,280	1,140
	1,400-2,900	3	14,300-20,000	8			
	2,900-5,700	4	20,000-28,600	9			
	5,700-8,600	5	28,600-50,000	10			
	8,600-11,400	6	Over 50,000	11			
Nebraska[2,7]	First 3,000	2.0	28,001-45,000	4.8	1,180	2,360	1,180
	3,001-28,000	3.1	Over 45,000	5.9			
	No tax if no federal tax liability and Nebraska additions to income of less than $5,000.						
New Hampshire	Interest and dividends (with some exceptions).	5	$1,200 each income is exempt.				
New Jersey	First $20,000	2			$1,000	$2,000	$1,000
	20,000-50,000	2.5					
	Over 50,000	3.5					
	A taxpayer or married couple filing jointly with gross income of $3,000 ($1,500 if filing separately) or less is not taxable.						
New Mexico[2,5]	First 8,000	2.4	36,001-48,000	6.9	Federal exemptions.		
	8,001-16,000	3.8	48,001-64,000	7.7			
	16,001-24,000	4.8	Over 64,000	8.5			
	24,001-36,000	5.9					
New York[2,7,9]	First 11,000	4	22,001-26,000	7	1,000	2,000	1,000
	11,001-16,000	5	Over 26,000	7.875			
	16,001-22,000	6					
North Carolina	First 2,000	3	6,001-10,000	6	1,100	2,200*	800
	2,001-4,000	4	Over 10,000	7	*An additional exemption of $1,100 is allowed the spouse having the lower income; joint returns are not permitted.		
	4,001-6,000	5					
North Dakota[4*]	First 3,000	3.24	25,001-35,000	11.33	Federal exemptions.		
	3,001-5,000	4.86	35,001-50,000	12.96			
	5,001-8,000	6.47	Over 50,000	14.57			
	8,000-15,000	8.1					
	15,001-25,000	9.71	*Optional tax is 17% of federal income tax liability.				
Ohio	First 5,000	0.743	20,001-40,000	4.457	650	1,300	650
	5,001-10,000	1.486	40,001-80,000	5.201			
	10,001-15,000	2.972	80,001-100,000	5.943			
	15,001-20,000	3.715	Over 100,000	6.9			

State	Taxable[10] income	Percentage[10] rates	Taxable income	Percentage rates	Personal exemp.[1] Single	Married family head	Each dependent
Oklahoma[2, 6]	First 2,000 2,001-5,000 5,001-7,500 7,501-10,000	0.5 1 2 3	10,001-12,500 12,501-15,000 Over 15,000	4 5 6	1,000	2,000	1,000
Oregon[2, 3, 4, 5]	First 2,000 2,001-5,000	5 7	Over 5,000	9	89* *Tax credit	178*	89*
Pennsylvania	2.1% of specified classes of taxable income, including earned income.						
Rhode Island	22.96% of modified federal income tax liability.						
South Carolina[3, 8]	First 2,000 2,000-4,000 4,001-6,000 6,001-8,000	2.5 or 2.75 3 4 5	8,001-10,000 Over 10,000	6 7	Federal exemptions. Credit for married persons filing jointly is .7% of the lesser of $30,000 or the qualified earned income of the spouse with the lower income.		
Tennessee	Interest and dividends	6			No tax on the first $1,250 for each individual return; or $2,500 of combined income for persons filing jointly; or from persons 65 or older with certain income levels.		
Utah[2, 4]	First 1,500 1,501-3,000 3,001-4,500	2.6 3.55 4.5	4,501-6,000 6,001-7,500 Over 7,500	5.45 6.4 7.35	25% of federal exemptions.		
Vermont	25% of modified federal income tax liability.						
Virginia[9]	First $3,000 3,001-5,000	2 3	$5,001-16,000 Over 16,000	5 5.75	$800	$1,600	$800
West Virginia[7]	First 10,000 10,001-25,000 25,001-40,000	3 4 4.5	40,001-60,000 Over 60,000	6 6.5	2,000	4,000	2,000
Wisconsin[2, 7]	First 10,000 10,001-20,000	4.9 6.55	Over 20,000	6.93	50* *Tax credit	100*	50*

(1) Does not include exemptions or credits for age or blindness, to offset sales or property taxes paid, or for any special purpose. (2) Rates shown are for married persons filing jointly in Alabama, California, Georgia, Hawaii, Kansas, Maine, Minnesota, Nebraska, New Mexico, New York, Oklahoma, Utah, and Wisconsin; separate rate schedules apply for single taxpayers and in some cases to heads of households or married persons filing separately. Rates shown for Arizona, Idaho, and Oregon are for single taxpayers; in the case of joint returns, the tax is twice the tax that would be due if taxable income of husband and wife were cut in half. (3) Income brackets and/or exemptions are subject to annual adjustment for inflation. Data here are for 1988 tax year. (4) All or part of federal income tax liability is deductible in computing state income tax. (5) Community property state in which, in general, half of community income is taxed to each spouse. (6) Different rate schedules and higher rates apply for taxpayers who choose to deduct Federal income tax in Kansas and Oklahoma. (7) Alternative minimum tax imposed. (8) In South Carolina the first $2,000 will be taxed at 2.5% if the general fund offset account is fully funded; and at 2.75% otherwise. (9) In D.C., Maryland, Michigan, New York, and Virginia rate tables and/or exemptions change in the 1990 tax year. See also footnote 3. (10) For taxpayers with income below a specified amount, many states and D.C. provide special tax rate tables.

State General Sales and Use Taxes

Source: Tax Foundation from data reported by Commerce Clearing house through July 15, 1989

State	Percentage rate	State	Percentage rate	State	Percentage rate
Alabama	4(a)	Louisiana	4(a)	Ohio	5(a)
Arizona	5(a)	Maine	5	Oklahoma	4(a)
Arkansas	4(a)	Maryland	5	Pennsylvania	6
California	4.75(a)	Massachusetts	5	Rhode Island	6
Colorado	3(a)	Michigan	4	South Carolina	5
Connecticut	8	Minnesota	6(a)	South Dakota	4(a)
District of Columbia	6	Mississippi	6	Tennessee	5.5(a)
Florida	6(a)	Missouri	4.225(a)	Texas	6(a)
Georgia	4(a)	Nebraska	4(a)	Utah	5.094(a)
Hawaii	4	Nevada	5.75(a)	Vermont	4
Idaho.en	5	New Jersey	6	Virginia	3.5(a)
Illinois	5(a)	New Mexico	4.75(a)	Washington	6.5(a)
Indiana	5	New York	4(a)	West Virginia	6
Iowa	4(a)	North Carolina	3(a)	Wisconsin	5(a)
Kansas	4.25(a)	North Dakota	6	Wyoming	3(a)
Kentucky	5(a)				

(a) Local sales taxes are additional.
NOTE: Alaska, Delaware, Montana, New Hampshire and Oregon have no statewide sales and use taxes.

State Inheritance Tax Rates and Exemptions

Source: Tax Foundation from Commerce Clearing House data.
Law as of July 15, 1989

State (a)	Spouse, child, or parent	Rates (b) (percent) Brother or sister	Other than relative	Max. rate applies above ($1,000)	Exemptions (c) ($1,000) Spouse	Child or parent	Brother or sister	Other than relative
Connecticut (d)	3-8	4-10	8-14	1,000	All	50	6	1
Delaware	1-6	5-10	10-16	200	70	25	5	1
Indiana	1-10	7-15	10-20	1,500	All	10(5)(e)	0.5	0.1
Iowa (g)	1-8	5-10	10-15	150	All	50(15)(e)	None	None
Kansas	1-5(j)	3-12.5(j)	10-15(j)	500	All	30	5	None
Kentucky	2-10	4-16	6-16	500	All	5(r)	1	0.5
Louisiana	2-3	5-7	5-10	20	25(f)	25	1	0.5
Maryland (g)	1	10	10	(h)	(i)	.15(i)	0.15(i)	0.15(i)
Michigan	2-10 (j)	2-10 (j)	12-17 (j)	750	65(k)	10	10	None
Montana	2-8	4-16	8-32	100	All	All(7)(e)	1	None
Nebraska	1	1	6-18	60	All	10	10	0.5
New Hampshire	(l)	15	15	(h)	(l)	(l)	None	None
New Jersey	(l)	11-16	15-16	(s)	(l)	(l)	0.5(m)	0.5(m)
North Carolina	1-12	4-16	8-17	3,000	All	(n)	None	None
Pennsylvania	6	15	15	(h)	None(o)	None(o)	None	None
South Dakota	3-15 (t)	4-20 (t)	6-30	100	All	30(3)(e)	0.5	0.1
Tennessee	5.5-9.5	5.5-9.5	5.5-9.5	440	600(p)	600	600	600 (q)
Wisconsin	2.5-10(u)	5-20(u)	10-20(u)	100	All	50	1	0.5

(a) In addition to an inheritance tax, all states listed also levy an estate tax, generally to assure full absorption of the federal credit. Iowa, Kansas, Maryland, North Carolina, and Tennessee also impose a generation-skipping transfer tax to absorb the federal tax credit.

(b) Rates generally apply to excess above graduated absolute amounts.

(c) Generally, transfers to governments or to solely charitable, educational, scientific, religious, literary, public, and other similar organizations in the U.S. are wholly exempt. Some states grant additional exemptions, e.g., for insurance, homestead, joint deposits, and for previously or later taxed transfers. In many states, exemptions are deducted from the first bracket only. Adopted and mutually acknowledged children generally receive the same consideration as natural children.

(d) An additional inheritance tax equal to 30% of the basic tax is imposed. A second additional tax equal to 10% of the basic tax and the first additional tax is imposed, except on the farmland passing to a descendant.

(e) Exemption for child (in thousands): $50 in Iowa ($15 per parent) and $30 in S.D. ($3 per parent). Exemption for minor child is (in thousands): $10 in Indiana ($5 per parent and child over 21). In Montana, all property transferred to a child is exempt.

(f) Transfers to surviving spouse are fully exempt after 1991.

(g) Where property of a decedent after deducting debts is $10,000 or less in Iowa, $20,000 in Maryland, no inheritance taxes are due.

(h) Rate applies to entire share.

(i) All real property and the first $100,000 of non-real property transferred to a spouse is exempt. For other beneficiaries, no exemption if share exceeds amount stated.

(j) There is no tax on the share of any beneficiary if the value of the share is less than $100 in Mich.; $200 in Kansas after deductions.

(k) All exempt if transfer qualifies for federal marital deduction. If not, spouse is entitled to another $10,000 deduction. A widow receives $5,000 for every minor child to whom no property is transferred in addition to the normal exemptions for a spouse.

(l) Spouses, children, parents, and children in the decedent's line of succession are entirely exempt.

(m) No exemption if share exceeds amount stated.

(n) Tax credit of $26,150.

(o) However, the $2,000 family exemption is specifically allowed as a deduction.

(p) There is a marital deduction equal to 50% of the value of the taxable transfer.

(q) $350,000 in 1989.

(r) $20,000 for an infant child or child declared mentally disabled.

(s) Maximum rate is $1,700,000 for brother and sister; $700,000 for others.

(t) Top rate 7.5% for children. Rate of 3-15% for brothers or sisters engaged in farming or business with decedent for 10 years if the property inherited is real or personal property used in the enterprise.

(u) Tax reduced by 40% for transfers in 1989; 60% in 1990; phased out by January 1, 1992 and replaced with estate tax in amount of federal credit.

Residential Property Tax Rates in Selected Large Cities: 1987

Source: Government of the District of Columbia, Department of Finance and Revenue.

City	Effective tax rate per $100 Rank	Rate	Assessment level (percent)	Nominal rate per $100	City	Effective tax rate per $100 Rank	Rate	Assessment level (percent)	Nominal rate per $100
Newark, NJ	1	4.20	31.7	13.26	Memphis, TN	16	1.77	25.0	7.09
Detroit, MI	2	4.09	49.9	8.20	Burlington, VT	17	1.72	81.0	2.12
Milwaukee, WI	3	3.48	96.7	3.60	Portland, ME	18	1.71	55.0	3.11
Des Moines, IA	4	2.96	77.4	3.82	Manchester, VT	19	1.71	20.0	8.56
Bridgeport, CT	5	2.95	46.6	6.33	Houston, TX	20	1.71	100.0	1.71
Portland, OR	6	2.75	100.0	2.75	Boise City, ID	21	1.70	99.6	1.71
Baltimore, MD	7	2.68	43.2	6.21	Chicago, IL	22	1.66	16.0	10.35
Providence, RI	8	2.58	35.6	7.25	Indianapolis, IN	23	1.56	15.0	10.37
Philadelphia, PA	9	2.54	34.0	7.48	Fargo, ND	24	1.56	4.5	34.70
Sioux Falls, SD	10	2.32	35.3	6.59	Wilmington, DE	25	1.48	100.0	1.48
Omaha, NE	11	2.18	85.6	2.55	Louisville, KY	26	1.39	100.0	1.39
Minneapolis, MN	12	2.14	18.5	11.58	Jackson, MS	27	1.30	10.0	12.98
Cleveland, OH	13	2.08	35.0	5.95	Billings, MT	28	1.30	3.9	33.35
Atlanta, GA	14	2.00	40.0	5.00	New Orleans, LA	29	1.26	10.0	12.62
Jacksonville, FL	15	1.96	98.1	2.00					(continued)

City	Effective tax rate per $100 Rank	Rate	Assessment level (percent)	Nominal rate per $100	City	Effective tax rate per $100 Rank	Rate	Assessment level (percent)	Nominal rate per $100
Seattle, WA	30	1.22	95.0	1.29	Charleston, WV	41	1.07	62.0	1.73
Boston, MA	31	1.20	100.0	1.20	St. Louis, MO	42	1.02	19.0	5.37
Charlotte, NC	32	1.19	97.4	1.22	Oklahoma City, OK	43	.95	10.7	8.92
New York City, NY	33	1.18	12.7	9.33	Las Vegas, NV	44	.91	34.4	2.64
Wichita, KS	34	1.13	8.0	14.11	Little Rock, AR	45	.89	19.2	4.66
Columbia, SC	35	1.13	4.0	28.18	Denver, CO	46	.89	18.0	4.97
Washington, DC	36	1.11	91.1	1.22	Birmingham, AL	47	.70	10.0	6.95
Anchorage, AK	37	1.10	87.9	1.26	Casper, WY	48	.70	9.1	7.74
Albuquerque, NM	38	1.10	33.3	3.29	Phoenix, AZ	49	.64	5.4	11.83
Norfolk, VA	39	1.10	88.0	1.25	Los Angeles, CA	50	.64	61.2	1.05
Salt Lake City, UT	40	1.08	60.0	1.80	Honolulu, HI	51	.59	89.0	.66

Estimated State and Local Taxes Paid by a Family of Four in Selected Large Cities, by Income Level: 1987

Source: Government of the District of Columbia, Department of Finance and Revenue

(Preliminary. Data based on average family of four, two wage earners and two school age children, owning their own home and living in a city where taxes apply. Comprises state and local sales, income, auto, and real estate taxes.

City	Total Taxes Paid by Gross Family Income Level (dol.) $20,000	$35,000	$50,000	$75,000	$100,000	Percent of Income by Income Level $20,000	$35,000	$50,000	$75,000	$100,000
Albuquerque, NM	1,504	2,594	4,056	6,448	8,996	7.5	7.4	8.1	8.6	9.0
Atlanta, GA	1,897	3,388	5,263	7,946	10,365	9.5	9.7	10.5	10.6	10.4
Baltimore, MD	2,148	3,767	5,669	8,525	11,236	10.7	10.8	11.3	11.4	11.2
Bridgeport, CT	2,742	4,374	6,514	9,566	12,019	13.7	12.5	13.0	12.8	12.0
Burlington, VT	1,570	2,709	4,225	7,035	9,895	7.8	7.7	8.4	9.4	9.9
Charleston, WV	1,560	2,695	4,393	7,043	9,565	7.8	7.7	8.8	9.4	9.6
Charlotte, NC	1,663	2,887	4,562	6,920	9,198	8.3	8.2	9.1	9.2	9.2
Chicago, IL	1,707	2,821	4,150	6,008	7,748	8.5	8.1	8.3	8.0	7.7
Cleveland, OH	1,832	3,260	4,940	7,682	10,567	9.2	9.3	9.9	10.2	10.6
Columbia, SC	1,568	2,918	4,739	7,262	9,620	7.8	8.3	9.5	9.7	9.6
Des Moines, IA	2,027	3,586	5,569	8,410	11,041	10.1	10.2	11.1	11.2	11.0
Detroit, MI	2,400	4,102	6,139	9,280	12,262	12.0	11.7	12.3	12.4	12.3
Honolulu, HI	1,905	3,380	5,240	8,012	10,700	9.5	9.7	10.5	10.7	10.7
Indianapolis, IN	1,648	2,672	3,936	5,831	7,441	8.2	7.6	7.9	7.8	7.4
Jackson, MS	1,508	2,685	4,300	6,546	8,529	7.5	7.7	8.6	8.7	8.5
Louisville, KY	1,800	3,104	4,610	6,733	8,652	9.0	8.9	9.2	9.0	8.7
Memphis, TN	1,601	2,366	3,222	4,536	5,788	8.0	6.8	6.4	6.0	5.8
Milwaukee, WI	2,542	4,671	7,009	10,620	13,946	12.7	13.3	14.0	14.2	13.9
Newark, NJ	2,706	4,711	6,906	10,474	13,707	13.5	13.5	13.8	14.0	13.7
New York City, NY	1,913	3,932	6,462	10,199	13,950	9.6	11.2	12.9	13.6	13.9
Norfolk, VA	1,619	2,757	4,283	7,051	8,542	8.1	7.9	8.6	9.4	8.5
Omaha, NE	1,642	2,714	4,237	6,648	8,977	8.2	7.8	8.5	8.9	9.0
Philadelphia, PA	2,527	4,173	5,799	8,446	10,924	12.6	11.9	11.6	11.3	10.9
Portland, ME	1,570	3,055	5,140	8,625	12,903	7.9	8.7	10.3	11.5	12.9
Portland, OR	2,281	4,008	6,163	9,558	12,643	11.4	11.5	12.3	12.7	12.6
Providence, RI	2,297	3,865	6,168	9,840	13,224	11.5	11.0	12.3	13.1	13.2
St. Louis, MO	1,557	2,607	3,998	5,816	7,213	7.8	7.4	8.0	7.8	7.2
Salt Lake City, UT	1,866	3,304	5,168	7,766	10,279	9.3	9.4	10.3	10.4	10.3
Sioux Falls, SD	1,912	2,903	3,991	5,558	6,950	9.6	8.3	8.0	7.4	6.9
Washington, DC	2,086	3,797	5,623	8,726	11,935	10.4	10.8	11.2	11.6	11.9

Tax Revenues—Selected Countries: 1975 to 1986

Source: Organization for Economic Cooperation and Development

(Covers national and local taxes and Social Security contributions.)

Country	Tax Revenues, 1986 Total (bil. dol.)	Per capita (dol.)	Tax Revenues as Percent of Gross Domestic Product 1975	1980	1985	1986	Percent Change in Total Tax Revenue as Expressed in National Currency 1975–1980	1980–1985	1985–1986
United States	$1,194.5	$4,944	29.0	29.5	29.2	28.9	76.7	46.5	5.3
Australia	54.6	3,419	27.9	29.2	30.3	31.4	88.9	80.4	12.5
Austria	40.0	5,281	38.6	41.2	42.5	42.6	61.5	41.8	5.1
Belgium	52.3	5,302	41.1	43.6	46.9	45.4	61.5	47.2	3.5
Canada	123.8	4,820	32.4	31.6	33.1	33.2	75.5	59.1	7.0
Denmark	41.7	8,151	41.4	45.5	49.2	50.6	90.1	77.6	11.7
Finland	27.0	5,499	35.3	33.3	37.3	38.4	73.7	95.1	10.6
France	321.3	5,802	37.4	42.5	45.6	44.2	116.2	78.2	6.6
Greece	14.6	1,461	24.6	28.6	35.1	36.7	195.7	231.9	25.5
Italy	217.3	3,798	25.1	30.0	34.7	36.2	195.7	139.2	15.8
Japan	570.3	4,698	20.9	25.5	28.0	28.8	222.0	43.5	7.3
Netherlands	79.9	5,483	43.7	45.8	45.0	45.5	95.7	21.7	4.2
New Zealand	9.1	2,775	31.3	33.0	34.3	32.9	60.6	99.7	14.8
Norway	34.8	8,346	44.8	47.1	47.8	49.8	120.1	77.3	8.1
Portugal	9.4	968	24.7	28.7	31.1	32.4	101.1	208.1	26.7
Spain	69.3	1,798	19.6	24.1	28.8	30.4	286.4	119.8	20.6
Sweden	70.2	8,385	43.9	49.4	50.5	53.5	210.3	68.0	14.8
Switzerland	44.0	6,707	29.6	30.8	32.1	32.6	96.4	39.2	8.5
United Kingdom	213.6	3,762	35.4	35.3	38.1	39.0	26.3	64.5	8.9
West Germany	334.8	5,484	35.7	38.0	37.8	37.5	116.6	23.6	4.6

AGRICULTURE

U.S. Farms, 1989

Source: U.S. Department of Agriculture

The Department of Agriculture estimated the number of U.S. farms in June, 1989 at 2.17 million, a drop of 1.1 percent from June, 1988, when there were 2.19 million farms. The decline continued a slide that began in 1982, when there were 2.4 million farms. The size of the average U.S. farm increased in 1989 to 456 acres, from 453 acres in 1988. Overall, about 991 million U.S. acres were devoted to agriculture, as of June 1989.

State	Number of Farms	% Change
Alabama	47,000	−2.1
Alaska	600	−3.2
Arizona	8,100	0.0
Arkansas	49,000	0.0
California	84,000	0.0
Colorado	27,300	0.0
Connecticut	4,000	0.0
Delaware	3,000	0.0
Florida	41,000	0.0
Georgia	48,000	−2.0
Hawaii	4,650	0.0
Idaho	22,300	−0.9
Illinois	86,000	−2.3
Indiana	71,000	−4.1
Iowa	105,000	−1.9
Kansas	69,000	0.0
Kentucky	96,000	
Louisiana	35,000	6.1
Maine	7,300	0.0
Maryland	15,600	−2.5
Mass.	6,900	0.0
Michigan	55,000	−1.8
Minnesota	90,000	−2.2
Mississippi	41,000	−2.4
Missouri	108,000	−1.8
Montana	24,700	0.4
Nebraska	57,000	−1.7
Nevada	2,500	−3.8
New Hampshire	3,200	0.0
New Jersey	8,300	0.0
New Mexico	14,000	0.0
New York	39,000	−4.9
N. Carolina	65,000	−4.4
N. Dakota	33,500	0.0
Ohio	87,000	2.4
Oklahoma	69,000	−1.4
Oregon	37,000	1.4
Pennsylvania	54,000	−1.8
Rhode Island	770	0.0
S. Carolina	25,500	−1.9
S. Dakota	35,000	0.0
Tennessee	91,000	0.0
Texas	186,000	−0.5
Utah	13,000	−2.3
Vermont	7,100	0.0
Virginia	47,000	−2.1
Washington	38,000	0.0
West Virginia	21,000	0.0
Wisconsin	81,000	−1.2
Wyoming	8,900	0.0
Total	2,173,220	−1.1

Farm Income—Marketings and Goverment Payments

Source: Economic Research Service, U.S. Department of Agriculture

(1,000 dollars)

State	1987 Farm marketings Total	1987 Crops	1987 Livestock and products	1988 Farm marketings Total	1988 Crops	1988 Livestock and products	Government payment
AL	2,154.4	633.1	1,521.4	2,400.4	705.8	1,694.6	114.5
AK	29.5	18.8	10.7	30.2	20.4	9.8	1.8
AZ	1,759.9	987.3	772.6	1,959.5	1,166.9	792.5	77.8
AR	3,195.0	1,111.6	2,083.3	3,974.1	1,695.7	2,278.4	343.9
CA	15,808.3	11,382.3	4,426.0	16,598.3	11,894.5	4,703.8	335.1
CO	3,207.2	884.7	2,322.6	3,692.0	1,037.1	2,654.9	280.5
CT	385.1	194.0	191.1	382.1	202.2	179.9	10.5
DE	486.7	116.4	370.3	592.3	148.8	443.5	32.0
FL	5,454.1	4,368.2	1,085.9	5,810.8	4,696.9	1,114.0	174.0
GA	3,123.8	1,298.9	1,824.9	3,544.4	1,533.4	2,010.9	0.4
HI	560.3	472.6	87.7	567.6	479.0	88.6	
ID	2,088.9	1,164.5	924.4	2,291.3	1,257.9	1,033.4	166.8
IL	6,098.7	3,849.8	2,248.9	6,461.0	4,217.5	2,243.5	1,374.0
IN	3,705.7	1,831.9	1,873.8	4,116.8	2,367.4	1,749.3	616.3
IA	8,764.7	3,563.0	5,201.7	9,074.0	4,028.9	5,045.1	1,665.0
KS	5,881.9	1,962.6	3,919.4	6,594.3	2,328.8	4,265.5	848.0
KY	2,447.9	940.5	1,507.5	2,530.2	992.1	1,538.1	160.9
LA	1,475.9	964.6	511.3	1,885.4	1,298.7	586.7	190.1
ME	411.5	183.9	227.6	404.1	188.0	216.1	7.3
MD	1,139.7	405.3	734.4	1,226.2	458.6	767.6	42.7
MA	379.2	258.6	120.6	402.4	297.4	105.0	2.8
MI	2,593.8	1,311.3	1,282.5	2,669.7	1,464.0	1,205.6	303.0
MN	5,831.1	2,270.1	3,561.0	6,106.7	2,742.5	3,364.2	1,035.9
MS	1,986.6	944.6	1,042.0	2,340.7	1,164.4	1,176.3	242.5
MO	3,687.3	1,585.7	2,101.6	3,825.6	1,814.3	2,011.4	456.9
MT	1,355.4	608.1	747.3	1,386.1	569.9	816.2	386.7
NE	6,823.6	1,966.8	4,856.8	7,978.7	2,642.5	5,336.2	1,091.5
NV	232.3	68.6	163.7	229.3	78.8	150.5	6.3
NH	139.0	71.7	67.3	137.0	76.6	60.4	1.9
NJ	632.7	437.7	195.0	642.2	450.4	191.9	10.8
NM	1,167.9	350.9	817.0	1,272.5	362.2	910.3	71.4
NY	2,609.5	800.2	1,809.4	2,605.1	824.0	1,781.2	146.0
NC	3,768.3	1,657.7	2,110.7	4,172.7	1,993.8	2,178.9	715.1
ND	2,362.8	1,600.7	762.1	2,422.9	1,573.6	849.3	381.9
OH	3,477.8	1,862.0	1,65.8	3,629.0	2,024.7	1,604.2	288.4
OK	2,876.7	810.7	2,066.0	3,410.4	1,126.6	2,283.8	97.8
OR	1,890.5	1,235.8	654.7	2,096.1	1,428.8	669.3	64.9
PA	3,213.0	903.5	2,309.5	3,283.7	935.4	2,348.3	0.1
RI	76.9	64.2	12.8	78.5	65.5	13.0	
SC	929.3	479.3	449.9	1,078.4	590.3	488.1	76.9
SD	2,726.4	819.7	1,906.7	2,910.7	945.5	1,965.2	496.0
TN	1,983.5	873.7	1,109.8	2,045.7	965.3	1,080.4	140.4
TX	8,998.4	2,906.7	6,091.7	10,281.1	3,782.9	6,498.2	1,155.3
UT	599.6	133.9	465.6	687.4	150.5	537.0	38.4
VT	422.2	45.3	376.9	404.5	52.5	352.0	5.9
VA	1,758.5	484.0	1,274.5	1,885.9	592.0	1,293.9	64.3
WA	2,861.7	1,880.2	981.5	3,286.7	2,145.9	1,140.8	207.9
WV	234.4	59.9	174.5	248.4	69.8	178.6	12.2
WI	5,015.4	799.2	4,216.2	5,047.9	767.1	4,280.8	409.4
WY	655.1	126.7	528.4	730.2	155.5	574.7	37.7
U.S.	139,468.4	63,751.4	75,717.0	151,430.8	72,569.0	78,861.7	14,479.8

Farms—Number and Acreage by State, 1980 and 1989

Source: Natl. Agricultural Statistics Service: U.S. Agricultural Department

State	Farms (1,000) 1980	1989	Acreage (mil.) 1980	1989	Acreage per Farm 1980	1989
U.S.	2,433	2,173	1,039	991	427	456
Alabama	59	47	12	11	207	226
Alaska	(z)	1	2	1	3,378	1,683
Arizona	8	8	38	36	5,080	4,444
Arkansas	59	49	17	16	280	320
California	81	84	34	31	417	373
Colorado	27	27	36	34	1,358	1,241
Connecticut	4	4	(z)	(z)	117	110
Delaware	4	3	1	1	186	197
Florida	39	41	13	11	344	273
Georgia	59	48	15	13	254	263
Hawaii	4	5	2	2	458	370
Idaho	24	22	15	14	623	614
Illinois	107	86	29	29	269	331
Indiana	87	71	17	16	193	231
Iowa	119	105	34	34	284	319
Kansas	75	69	48	48	644	694
Kentucky	102	96	15	14	143	148
Louisiana	37	35	10	9	273	266
Maine	8	7	2	1	195	199
Maryland	18	16	3	2	157	147
Massachusetts	6	7	1	1	116	99
Michigan	65	55	11	11	175	196
Minnesota	104	90	30	30	291	333
Mississippi	55	41	15	13	265	324
Missouri	120	108	31	30	261	281
Montana	24	25	62	61	2,601	2,453
Nebraska	65	57	48	47	734	826
Nevada	3	3	9	9	3,100	3,560
New Hampshire	3	3	1	1	160	159
New Jersey	9	8	1	1	109	106
New Mexico	14	14	47	45	3,467	3,179
New York	47	39	9	8	200	215
North Carolina	93	65	12	10	126	154
North Dakota	40	34	42	41	1,043	1,209
Ohio	95	87	16	16	171	182
Oklahoma	72	69	35	33	481	478
Oregon	35	37	18	18	517	481
Pennsylvania	62	54	9	8	145	152
Rhode Island	1	1	(z)	(z)	87	95
South Carolina	34	26	6	3	188	208
South Dakota	39	35	45	44	1,169	1,266
Tennessee	96	91	14	13	142	138
Texas	189	186	138	132	731	710
Utah	14	13	12	11	919	869
Vermont	8	7	2	2	226	214
Virginia	58	47	10	9	169	191
Washington	38	38	16	16	429	421
West Virginia	22	21	4	4	191	176
Wisconsin	93	81	19	18	200	217
Wyoming	9	9	35	35	3,846	3,910

(z) Less than 500 farms or 500,000 acres

Livestock on Farms in the U.S.

Source: Natl. Agricultural Statistics, Service: U.S. Agriculture Department (thousands)

Year (On Jan. 1)	All cattle	Milk cows	All sheep	Hogs[3]
1890	60,014	15,000	44,518	48,130
1900	59,739	16,544	48,105	51,055
1910	58,993	19,450	50,239	48,072
1920	70,400	21,455	40,743	60,159
1925	63,373	22,575	38,543	55,770
1930	61,003	23,032	51,565	55,705
1935	68,846	26,082	51,808	39,066
1940	68,309	24,940	52,107	61,165
1945	85,573	27,770	46,520	59,373
1950	77,963	23,853	29,826	58,937
1955	96,592	23,462	31,582	50,474
1960	96,236	19,527	33,170	59,026
1965	109,000	16,981[2]	25,127	56,106
1970	112,369	13,303	20,423	57,046
1975	132,028	11,220	14,515	54,693
1980	111,242	10,758	12,699	67,318
1985	109,749	10,805	10,443	54,073
1986	105,468	11,177	9,983	52,313
1988[1]	99,524	10,298	10,784	54,620
1989	99,484	10,217	10,802	55,299

(1) Total estimated value on farms as of Jan. 1, 1989, was (avg. value per head in parentheses): cattle & calves $60,394,509,000 ($607); sheep & lambs $889,765,000 ($82.40); hogs & pigs $3,665,069,000 ($66.30). (2) New series, milk cows & heifers that have calved, from 1965. (3) As of Dec. 1 of preceding year.

U.S. Meat and Lard Production and Consumption

Source: Economic Research Service, U.S. Agriculture Department (million lbs.)

Year	Beef Production	Beef Consumption	Veal Production	Veal Consumption	Lamb and mutton Production	Consumption	Pork (exclud. lard) Production	Consumption	All meats Production	Consumption	Lard Production	Consumption[1]
1940	7,175	7,257	981	981	876	873	10,044	9,701	19,076	18,812	2,288	1,901
1950	9,534	9,529	1,230	1,206	597	596	10,714	10,390	22,075	21,721	2,631	1,891
1960	14,728	15,465	1,109	1,118	769	857	13,905	14,057	30,511	31,497	2,562	1,358
1970	21,685	23,391	588	610	551	663	14,699	14,871	37,523	39,535	1,913	939
1980	21,643	23,513	400	418	318	349	16,617	16,690	38,978	40,953	1,207	588
1985	23,728	25,472	515	533	359	386	14,807	15,733	39,409	42,125	927	425
1988	23,589	25,188	395	410	335	386	15,684	16,434	40,004	42,418	932	429

(1) Direct use. Excludes lard used in indirect food use such as table spreads and shortenings.

Selected Indexes of Farm Inputs: 1960 to 1987

Source: Economic Research Service, U.S. Agriculture Department

(1977 = 100. Inputs based on physical quantities of resources used in production.)

Input	1960	1965	1970	1975	1980	1981	1982	1983	1985	1986	1987[1]
Total	99	97	96	97	103	102	99	97	92	87	86
Farm labor	177	144	112	106	96	96	93	97	85	80	78
Farm real estate[2]	103	103	105	97	103	104	102	101	95	93	90
Mechanical power and machinery	83	80	85	96	101	98	92	88	80	75	76
Agricultural chemicals[3]	32	49	75	83	123	129	118	105	123	110	111
Feed, seed, and livestock purchases[4]	77	86	96	93	114	108	108	110	106	103	108
Taxes and interest	95	101	102	100	100	99	92	97	91	93	98

(1) Preliminary. (2) Includes service buildings, improvements. (3) Includes fertilizer, lime, and pesticides. (4) Nonfarm portion.

Consumption of Major Food Commodities per Person

Source: Economic Research Service: U.S. Agriculture Department

Commodity[1]	1986	1987	1988	Commodity[1]	1986	1987	1988
Red Meats[2,3]	118.3	113.3	115.1	Fresh[6]	95.9	101.4	96.9
Beef[2]	74.1	69.2	68.2	Citrus[6]	26.7	26.4	26.5
Veal[2]	1.6	1.3	1.1	Noncitrus[6]	69.2	75.1	70.4
Lamb and mutton[2]	1.0	1.0	1.0	Processed:			
Pork[2]	41.6	41.9	44.7	Canned fruit	8.7	8.8	8.8
Poultry[2,3]	51.1	55.3	57.3	Frozen fruit	3.6	3.9	3.8
Chicken[2]	40.6	43.3	44.6	Dried fruit	3.0	2.7	2.9
Turkey[2]	10.5	11.9	12.7	Vegetables:			
Fish[2]	14.7	15.4	15.0	Fresh[6,7]	95.3	98.5	100.3
Eggs	31.7	31.6	31.0	For canning[6]	87.6	87.0	82.8
Dairy products:				For freezing[6]	15.8	16.8	17.5
Cheese (natural equivalent)	23.0	24.0	23.6	Potatoes[6]	124.5	122.4	124.8
Condensed and evaporated milk	7.9	8.0	7.7	Grains:			
Fluid milk and cream	239.6	237.5	236.2	Wheat flour	123.5	127.1	127.5
Whole milk	116.0	111.4	106.1	Rice	11.6	13.4	14.3
Lowfat milk	98.2	100.1	101.6	Pasta	14	17.1	NA
Skim milk	13.4	14.0	16.2	Caloric and noncaloric sweeteners[8]	152.0	151.8	153.4
Cream[4]	4.7	4.6	4.7	Caloric sweeteners	133.5	132.8	133.9
Yogurt	4.4	4.5	4.6	Refined cane and beet sugar	60.8	62.4	62.4
Specialty products[5]	2.9	3.0	3.0	Corn sweeteners	67.5	69.0	70.1
Ice cream	18.3	18.3	17.2	High fructose	47.5	47.4	48.3
Fats and Oils—Total fat content	64.1	62.7	NA	Low-calorie sweeteners[9]	18.5	19.0	19.5
Butter	4.6	4.6	4.5	Other:			
Margarine	11.4	10.5	10.3	Coffee (beans)	10.2	10.2	10.2
Lard	1.7	1.8	1.7	Tea	0.7	0.7	0.7
Edible tallow	1.8	1.0	0.8	Cocoa (beans)	4.8	4.9	5.0
Shortening	22.0	21.3	21.4	Peanuts (shelled)	6.4	6.3	6.8
Salad and cooking oils	24.1	24.7	25.0	Tree nuts	2.2	2.2	2.5
Other edible fats and oils	1.7	1.3	1.3	Dry edible beans	6.7	7.9	NA
Fruits:							

(1) Quantity in pounds, retail weight unless otherwise shown. Data on calendar year basis except for dried fruits, fresh citrus fruits, peanuts, and rice which are on a crop-year basis, and eggs which are on a marketing year basis. Data are as of August 1989. (2) Boneless, trimmed weight. (3) Total may not add due to rounding. (4) Includes heavy cream, light cream, and half and half. (5) Includes buttermilk and sour cream and dip. (6) Farm weight. (7) Commercial production for sale as fresh produce. (8) Dry weight. (9) Sugar-sweetness equivalent. NA = not available.

U.S. Egg Production

Source: Economic Research Service, U.S. Agriculture Department (millions of eggs)

State	1985	1986	1987	1988	State	1985	1986	1987	1988	State	1985	1986	1987	1988
Ala.	2,794	2,723	2,605	2,596	La.	348	336	323	311	Oh.	3,592	3,873	4,351	4,477
Alas.	11.7	12.8	6.6	1.7	Me.	1,237	1,239	1,827	1,300	Okla.	868	809	805	803
Ariz.	99	121	98	86	Md.	813	890	926	932	Ore.	649	659	638	617
Ark.	3,655	3,731	3,874	3,784	Mass.	257	315	273	262	Pa.	4,774	4,692	4,853	5,302
Cal.	8,052	7,850	8,023	7,718	Mich.	1,693	1,644	1,656	1,553	R.I.	80	58	55	52
Col.	568	575	641	784	Minn.	2,267	2,312	2,263	2,250	S.C.	1,573	1,615	1,604	1,432
Conn.	1,173	1,281	1,200	1,121	Miss.	1,251	1,274	1,259	1,251	S.D.	391	395	358	348
Del.	126	135	144	146	Mo.	1,357	1,351	1,397	1,526	Tenn.	756	663	670	532
Fla.	2,692	2,683	2,568	2,758	Mont.	202	201	205	194	Tex.	3,131	3,355	3,424	3,363
Ga.	4,282	4,318	4,476	4,294	Neb.	844	829	869	902	Ut.	418	457	496	493
Ha.	220.5	227	223	224	Nev.	2.2	2.2	2.2	2	Vt.	67	57	60	54
Ida.	239	230	238	217	N.H.	121	95	76	51	Va.	850	914	937	911
Ill.	732	663	709	780	N.J.	474	501	475	486	Wash.	1,355	1,295	1,303	1,327
Ind.	5,538	5,561	5,750	5,644	N.M.	273	280	302	287	W. Va.	121	109	128	126
Ia.	1,600	1,441	1,534	1,979	N.Y.	1,710	1,523	1,115	1,013	Wis.	836	830	877	873
Kan.	472	463	486	396	N.C.	3,294	3,400	3,251	3,396	Wyo.	6.8	4.5	4.3	3
Ky.	431	420	466	457	N.D.	120	118	61	59	Total[*]	68,407	68,398	69,351	69,476

Note: The egg and chicken production year runs from Dec. 1 of the previous year through Nov. 30. (1) Included are eggs destroyed because of possible PCB contamination. [*] States may not add to total.

Farm-Real Estate Debt Outstanding by Lender Groups[1]

Source: Economic Research Service, U.S. Agriculture Department

Dec. 31	Total farm-real estate debt[2] $1,000	Federal land banks[2] $1,000	Amounts held by principal lender groups — Farmers Home Administration[3] $1,000	Life insurance companies[4] $1,000	All commercial banks $1,000	Other[5] $1,000
1955	9,048,676	1,480,000	413,000	2,272,000	1,275,000	3,572,000
1960	12,867,524	2,539,000	723,000	2,975,000	1,592,000	4,991,000
1965	21,220,912	4,240,000	1,497,000	4,802,000	2,607,000	8,041,000
1970	30,492,357	7,145,363	2,440,043	5,610,300	3,772,377	11,378,000
1975	49,852,888	16,029,468	3,368,747	6,726,000	6,296,286	17,262,000
1980	97,486,996	36,196,103	8,163,270	12,927,800	8,563,457	30,180,000
1981	107,230,493	43,825,202	8,876,989	13,073,900	8,342,245	31,770,000
1982	111,312,036	47,821,589	9,169,874	12,801,546	8,391,800	32,000,000
1985	105,739,201	44,583,842	10,426,971	11,830,400	11,384,920	27,200,000
1986	95,879,799	37,757,626	10,348,597	10,940,200	12,710,650	24,000,000
1987	87,717,601	32,637,687	10,083,239	9,895,800	14,455,162	20,600,000
1988	82,952,518	30,326,707	9,606,796	9,581,700	15,416,700	18,000,000

(1) Includes opertator households. (2) Includes data for joint stock land banks and Federal Farm Mortgage Corporations. (3) Includes loans made directly by FmHA for farm ownership, soil and water loans to individuals, Indian tribe land acquisition, grazing associations, and irrigation drainage and soil conservation associations. Also includes loans for rural housing on farm tracts and labor housing. (4) American Council of Life Insurance. (5) Estimated by ERS, USDA.

Average Prices Received by U.S. Farmers

Source: Natl. Agricultural Statistics Service, U.S. Agriculture Department

The figures represent dollars per 100 lbs. for hogs, beef cattle, veal calves, sheep, lamb, and milk (wholesale); dollars per head for milk cows; cents per lb. for milk fat (in cream), chickens, broilers, turkeys, and wool; cents for eggs per dozen.

Weighted calendar year prices for livestock and livestock products other than wool. 1943 through 1963, wool prices are weighted on marketing year basis. The marketing year has been changed (1964) from a calendar year to a Dec.-Nov. basis for hogs, chickens, broilers and eggs.

Year	Hogs	Cattle (beef)	Calves (veal)	Sheep	Lambs	Cows (milk)	All milk	Chickens (excl. broilers)	Broilers	Turkeys	Eggs	Wool
1930	8.84	7.71	9.68	4.74	7.76	74	2.21	...	...	20.2	23.7	19.5
1940	5.39	7.56	8.83	3.95	8.10	61	1.82	13.0	17.3	15.2	18.0	28.4
1950	18.00	23.30	26.30	11.60	25.10	198	3.89	22.2	27.4	32.8	36.3	62.1
1960	15.30	20.40	22.90	5.61	17.90	223	4.21	12.2	16.9	25.4	36.1	42.0
1970	22.70	27.10	34.50	7.51	26.40	332	5.71	9.1	13.6	22.6	39.1	35.4
1975	46.10	32.20	27.20	11.30	42.10	412	8.75	9.9	26.3	34.8	54.5	44.8
1979	41.80	66.10	88.80	26.30	66.70	1,040	12.00	14.4	25.9	41.3	58.3	86.3
1980	38.00	62.40	76.80	21.30	63.60	1,190	13.05	11.0	27.7	41.3	56.3	88.1
1983	46.80	55.50	61.70	15.70	53.90	1,030	13.58	12.7	28.6	38.0	61.1	61.3
1984	47.10	57.30	59.90	16.40	60.10	895	13.46	15.9	33.7	48.9	72.3	79.5
1985	44.00	53.70	62.10	23.90	67.70	860	12.75	14.8	30.1	49.1	57.1	63.3
1986	49.30	52.60	61.10	25.60	69.00	820	12.50	12.5	34.5	47.1	61.6	66.8
1987	51.20	61.10	78.50	29.50	77.60	920	12.53	11.0	28.7	34.8	54.9	91.7
1988	42.30	66.60	89.20	25.60	69.10	990	12.22	9.2	33.1	38.6	52.8	1.38

The figures represent cents per lb. for cotton, apples, and peanuts; dollars per bushel for oats, wheat, corn, barley, and soybeans; dollars per 100 lbs. for rice, sorghum, and potatoes; dollars per ton for cottonseed and baled hay.

Weighted crop year prices. Crop years are as follows: apples, June-May; wheat, oats, barley, hay and potatoes, July-June; cotton, rice, peanuts and cottonseed, August-July; soybeans, September-August; and corn and sorghum grain, October-September.

	Corn	Wheat	Upland cotton[1]	Oats	Barley	Rice	Soybeans	Sorghum	Peanuts	Cottonseed	Hay	Potatoes	Apples
1930	.598	.663	9.46	0.311	.420	1.74	1.34	1.02	5.01	22.00	11.00	1.47	...
1940	.618	.674	9.83	0.298	.393	1.80	.892	.873	3.72	21.70	9.78	.850	...
1950	1.52	2.00	39.90	0.788	1.19	5.09	2.47	1.88	10.9	86.60	21.10	1.50	...
1960	13.00	1.74	30.08	0.599	.840	4.55	2.13	1.49	10.0	42.50	21.70	2.00	2.72
1970	1.33	1.33	21.86	0.623	.973	5.17	2.85	2.04	12.8	56.40	26.10	2.21	6.52
1975	2.54	3.55	51.10	1.45	2.42	8.35	4.92	4.21	19.6	97.00	52.10	4.48	8.80
1979	2.52	3.78	62.3	1.36	2.29	10.50	6.28	4.18	20.6	121.00	59.50	3.43	15.40
1980	3.11	3.91	74.4	1.79	2.86	12.80	7.57	5.25	25.1	129.00	71.00	6.55	12.1
1983	3.21	3.51	65.3	1.62	2.47	8.57	7.83	4.89	24.6	166.00	75.80	5.82	14.9
1984	2.63	3.39	58.7	1.67	2.29	8.04	5.84	4.15	27.9	99.50	72.70	5.69	15.5
1985	2.23	3.08	56.8	1.23	1.98	6.53	5.05	3.45	24.4	66.00	67.60	3.92	17.3
1986	1.50	2.42	51.5	1.21	1.61	3.75	4.78	2.45	29.2	80.00	59.70	5.03	19.1
1987	1.94	2.57	63.7	1.56	1.81	7.27	5.88	3.04	27.7	82.50	65.10	4.35	12.7
1988	2.55	3.72	54.8	2.61	2.79	6.70	7.55	4.07	26.9	119.00	87.10	5.49	10.8

(1) Beginning 1964, 480 lb. net weight bales.

Grain Storage Capacity at Principal Grain Centers in U.S.

Source: Chicago Board of Trade Market Information Department, Aug. 1989

(bushels)

Cities	Capacity	Cities	Capacity
Atlantic Coast	31,700,000	Southwest	
Great Lakes		Fort Worth	70,700,000
		Texas High Plains	96,300,000
Toledo	53,600,000	Enid	79,700,000
Buffalo	15,200,000	**Gulf Points**	
Chicago	52,400,000	South Mississippi	44,700,000
Milwaukee	9,600,000	North Texas Gulf	30,000,000
Duluth	64,300,000	South Texas Gulf	14,800,000
River Points		**Plains**	
		Wichita	37,400,000
Minneapolis	111,700,000	Topeka	56,200,000
Peoria	3,300,000	Salina	51,200,000
St. Louis	17,700,000	Hutchinson	42,000,000
Sioux City	7,800,000	Hastings-Grand Island	26,600,000
Omaha-Council Bluffs	30,700,000	Lincoln	33,700,000
Atchison	16,500,000	**Pacific N.W.**	
St. Joseph	20,100,000	Puget Sound (incl. Portland)	39,800,000
Kansas City, Mo.	80,000,000	California ports	NA

Atlantic Coast — Albany, N.Y., Philadelphia, Pa., Baltimore, Md., Norfolk, Va. **Gulf Points** — New Orleans, Baton Rouge, Ama. Belle Chase, La., Mobile, Ala. **North Texas Gulf** — Houston, Galveston, Beaumont, Port Arthur, Texas. **South Texas Gulf** — Corpus Christi, Brownsville, Texas. **Pacific N.W.** — Seattle, Tacoma, Wash., Portland, Oreg., Columbia River. **Texas High Plains** — Amarillo, Lubbock, Hereford, Plainview, Texas. NA = Not available.

Production of Chief U.S. Crops

Source: National Agricultural Statistics Service: U.S. Agriculture Department

Year	Corn for grain 1,000 bushels	Oats 1,000 bushels	Barley 1,000 bushels	Sorghum for grain 1,000 bushels	All Wheat 1,000 bushels	Rye 1,000 bushels	Flax- seed 1,000 bushels	Cotton lint 1,000 bales	Cotton seed 1,000 tons
1970 ..	4,152,243	915,236	416,091	683,179	1,351,558	36,840	29,416	10,192	4,068
1975 ..	5,828,961	638,960	379,162	754,354	2,126,927	15,924	15,553	8,302	3,218
1980 ..	6,639,396	458,792	361,135	579,343	2,380,934	15,958	7,728	11,122	4,470
1982 ..	8,235,101	592,630	515,935	835,083	2,764,967	19,533	10,278	11,963	4,744
1984 ..	7,674,020	473,661	599,204	866,241	2,594,777	32,463	7,022	12,982	5,149
1985 ..	8,876,706	520,800	591,383	1,120,271	2,425,105	20,537	8,293	13,432	5,279
1986 ..	8,249,864	386,356	610,522	938,124	2,091,635	19,522	11,538	9,731	3,801
1987 ..	7,072,073	374,000	529,530	739,249	2,107,480	19,818	7,444	14,760	5,769
1988 ..	4,921,191	218,773	290,505	577,551	1,811,261	15,047	1,615	15,446	6,054

Year	Tobacco 1,000 lbs.	All Hay 1,000 tons	Beans dry edible 1,000 cwt.	Peas dry edible 1,000 cwt.	Peanuts 1,000 lbs.	Soy- beans 1,000 bushels	Pota- toes 1,000 cwt.	Sweet pota- toes 1,000 cwt.
1970	1,906,453	126,969	17,399	3,315	2,983,121	1,127,100	325,716	13,164
1975	2,182,304	132,397	17,442	2,731	3,846,722	1,548,344	321,978	12,891
1980	1,786,225	130,740	26,729	3,285	2,302,762	1,797,543	303,905	10,953
1982	1,994,494	149,241	25,563	NA	3,440,255	2,190,297	355,131	14,833
1984	1,727,962	150,648	21,070	NA	4,405,745	1,860,863	362,612	12,986
1985	1,511,638	148,601	22,175	NA	4,122,787	2,098,531	407,109	14,853
1986	1,163,940	155,529	22,886	3,196	3,700,745	1,940,101	361,511	12,674
1987	1,190,674	149,302	25,909	3,385	3,619,440	1,922,762	385,774	12,064
1988	1,348,124	126,817	19,230	3,868	4,011,070	1,538,666	349,973	11,832

Year	Rice 1,000 cwt.	Sugar- cane 1,000 tons	Sugar beets 1,000 tons	Pecans 1,000 tons	Al- monds 1,000 tons	Wal- nuts 1,000 tons	Fil- berts 1,000 tons	Oranges* 1,000 boxes	Grape- fruit* 1,000 boxes
1970	NA	23,996	26,378	NA	NA	111.8	9.3	185,770	53,910
1975	NA	28,344	29,704	NA	NA	199.3	12.1	237,810	61,610
1980	146,150	26,963	23,502	91.8	264.4	197.0	15.4	273,630	73,200
1982	153,637	29,770	20,894	135.0	200.7	234.0	18.8	176,690	70,550
1984	138,810	27,340	22,134	116.2	467.1	213.0	13.4	169,510	53,610
1985	134,913	28,213	22,529	122.2	373.8	219.0	24.6	158,750	55,860
1986	133,356	30,311	25,167	136.4	201.3	180.0	15.1	175,710	57,470
1987	129,603	29,218	28,077	131.1	519.0	247.0	21.8	181,175	63,225
1988	159,547	30,347	24,794	154.0	451.9	206.0	16.5	200,040	68,050

NA = Not available. *Crop year ending in year cited.

Harvested Acreage of Principal U.S. Crops

Source: National Agricultural Statistics Service: U.S. Department of Agriculture (thousands of acres)

State	1988p	1987	1986	State	1988p	1987	1986
Alabama	2,364	2,269	2,520	Nebraska	16,765	15,927	17,533
Arizona	789	729	683	Nevada	568	577	584
Arkansas	7,538	7,132	7,359	New Hampshire	105	108	112
California	5,075	4,990	5,070	New Jersey	373	389	437
Colorado	5,609	5,654	6,167	New Mexico	912	974	1,179
Connecticut.	128	140	140	New York.	3,448	3,570	3,855
Delaware	504	531	536	North Carolina	4,179	4,185	4,581
Florida	1,096	1,113	1,224	North Dakota	16,235	19,510	20,571
Georgia	3,754	3,602	3,811	Ohio	9,731	9,698	10,207
Hawaii.	86	87	90	Oklahoma	8,447	8,357	8,568
Idaho	4,018	4,141	4,730	Oregon	2,198	2,345	2,711
Illinois	21,581	20,235	21,900	Pennsylvania	4,262	4,291	4,411
Indiana	11,086	10,586	11,660	Rhode Island	11	13	15
Iowa	23,042	20,856	23,796	South Carolina	2,024	1,916	2,129
Kansas	18,996	19,874	20,674	South Dakota	13,538	14,761	15,966
Kentucky	5,014	4,937	5,131	Tennessee	4,635	4,462	4,586
Louisiana	4,208	3,905	4,300	Texas	16,525	16,267	17,749
Maine	364	369	385	Utah	1,016	1,060	1,132
Maryland	1,474	1,496	1,580	Vermont.	491	497	530
Massachusetts	162	164	166	Virginia	2,737	2,830	2,790
Michigan	6,413	6,245	6,990	Washington.	3,892	3,937	4,713
Minnesota	18,767	17,497	19,096	West Virginia	714	732	683
Mississippi	5,149	4,944	4,878	Wisconsin.	8,400	8,219	9,013
Missouri	12,799	12,409	13,202	Wyoming	1,738	1,856	1,963
Montana	7,118	9,242	9,415	*Total U.S..	290,077	289,628	311,519

P = Preliminary. * States may not add due to rounding.

Agricultural Products — U.S. and World Production and Exports

Source: Foreign Agricultural Service, U.S. Agriculture Department

1987/88 Commodity	Unit	Production U.S.	World	% U.S.	Exports[1] U.S.	World	% U.S.
Wheat	MMT	57.4	501.8	11.4	43.3	115.8	37.4
Oats	MMT	5.4	43.3	12.5	0.0	1.4	1.5
Corn	MMT	179.6	447.4	40.2	44.0	64.8	67.8
Barley	MMT	11.5	180.7	6.4	2.7	20.9	13.2
Rice (milled basis)	MMT	4.1	313.2	1.3	2.3	12.2	18.7
Sorghum	MMT	18.8	56.0	33.5	5.9	8.4	70.1
Soybeans	MMT	52.3	103.3	50.6	21.8	30.4	71.9
Tobacco, unmfd.	MMT	0.5	5.6	8.8	0.2	1.4	14.3
Edible, Veg. Oils	MMT	7.0	51.7	13.5	1.4	17.5	8.0
Cotton (lint)	MB	14.8	80.8	18.3	6.6	23.2	28.3

(1) Standard trade years Wheat: July-June (87/88); Oats: Oct.-Sept. (87/88); Corn: Oct.-Sept. (87/88); Barley: Oct.-Sept. (87/88); Rice: Aug.-July (87/88); Sorghum: Oct.-Sept. (87/88); Soybeans: Sept.-Aug. (87/88); Tobacco: Jan.-Dec. (87); Edible Vegetable Oils: Veg. Oils years a combination of varying years; Cotton: Aug.-July (87/88). (2) Production reported farm weight basis; exports are dried weight basis. (3) Million Bales (480 lb. net).

Grain, Hay, Potato, Cotton, Soybean, Tobacco Production

Source: Economic Research Service, U.S. Agriculture Department

1988 State	Barley 1,000 bushels	Corn, grain 1,000 bushels	Cotton lint 1,000 bales[1]	All Hay 1,000 tons	Oats 1,000 bushels	Potatos 1,000 cwt.	Soybeans 1,000 bushels	Tobacco 1,000 pounds	All Wheat 1,000 bushels
Alabama	—	7,480	380	1,500	1,100	—	14,250	—	8,600
Alaska	—	—	—	—	—	1,139	—	—	—
Arizona	1,352	2,210	1,120	1,325	—	1,246	—	—	7,730
Arkansas	—	6,000	1,050	1,671	3,150	—	80,000	—	56,710
California	17,080	27,115	2,853	8,652	2,450	16,765	—	—	43,785
Colorado	11,725	128,000	—	3,957	3,000	20,156	—	—	79,540
Connecticut	—	—	—	185	—	113	—	2,971	—
Delaware	2,160	9,800	—	68	—	1,806	6,075	—	3,276
Florida	—	3,770	30	729	—	8,173	3,335	17,152	2,035
Georgia	—	31,000	370	1,254	2,835	—	22,500	85,880	21,500
Hawaii	—	—	—	—	—	—	—	—	—
Idaho	51,000	6,500	—	3,881	3,060	99,320	—	—	75,520
Illinois	—	700,800	—	3,310	9,180	736	234,900	—	67,500
Indiana	—	415,000	—	1,868	3,000	756	115,500	10,945	35,000
Iowa	—	898,800	—	6,760	26,400	289	248,000	—	1,050
Kansas	2,975	143,750	1	5,175	5,850	—	46,000	—	323,000
Kentucky	1,078	80,300	—	3,821	400	—	24,115	355,024	20,520
Louisiana	—	11,875	950	891	—	20	50,875	—	11,070
Maine	—	—	—	414	2,925	22,000	—	—	—
Maryland	4,761	27,300	—	619	884	460	14,105	11,970	9,010
Massachusetts	—	—	—	292	—	572	—	767	—
Michigan	1,216	112,000	—	4,220	6,000	8,610	33,880	—	26,040
Minnesota	27,200	347,800	—	6,960	24,750	13,557	124,800	—	51,730
Mississippi	—	9,000	1,830	1,300	—	—	49,500	—	20,700
Missouri	—	153,520	310	5,160	1,440	—	109,980	4,410	77,500
Montana	30,000	2,200	—	2,790	2,790	2,156	—	—	59,970
Nebraska	1,920	818,400	—	6,510	12,160	2,818	70,800	—	72,000
Nevada	2,480	—	—	1,336	—	2,480	—	—	—
New Hampshire	—	—	—	185	—	—	—	—	—
New Jersey	603	5,880	—	256	200	1,170	2,780	—	1,395
New Mexico	455	8,525	128	1,177	—	3,060	—	—	6,960
New York	—	41,225	—	4,940	7,540	6,420	—	—	4,950
North Carolina	2,730	78,120	132	797	3,575	2,904	38,070	553,627	24,000
North Dakota	42,000	22,040	—	2,010	7,200	14,375	12,420	—	103,390
Ohio	—	255,000	—	3,543	9,000	1,697	99,900	14,497	46,000
Oklahoma	960	6,840	290	3,931	2,925	—	4,860	—	172,800
Oregon	14,800	3,002	—	2,775	6,500	20,735	—	—	51,800
Pennsylvania	3,630	59,150	—	4,716	13,000	3,690	7,200	18,175	9,010
Rhode Island	—	—	—	20	—	300	—	—	—
South Carolina	840	19,430	148	504	2,928	—	18,170	100,125	14,030
South Dakota	8,100	132,000	—	3,910	20,000	1,600	41,520	—	38,006
Tennessee	—	38,690	590	2,310	—	91	34,320	93,142	21,500
Texas	540	129,600	5,260	5,350	9,000	3,397	6,300	—	89,600
Utah	9,625	2,728	—	2,138	1,008	1,617	—	—	6,768
Vermont	—	—	—	771	—	—	—	—	—
Virginia	5,325	23,305	4	2,220	636	2,048	15,540	92,177	10,400
Washington	34,720	13,600	—	2,833	2,479	63,250	—	—	124,620
West Virginia	—	2,320	—	876	288	—	—	2,720	414
Wisconsin	2,550	130,650	—	4,925	19,720	20,000	8,970	7,080	5,152
Wyoming	8,680	6,466	—	1,982	1,400	447	—	—	5,340
Total U.S.	290,505	4,921,191	15,446	126,817	218,773	349,973	1,538,666	1,369,662	1,811,261

(1) Equiv. to 480 lbs.

U.S. Farms, 1850-1970

Source: U.S. Bureau of the Census

	Farm population		Number of farms (1,000)	Farm land Total (1,000 acres)	Property value Total (mil. dol.)	Avg. value per farm of land & buildings (dol.)	Avg. value per acre of land & buildings (dol.)	Index of Avg. value of farm real estate per acre (1967=100)
	Total (1,000)	% of total popula-						
1970....	9,712	4.8	2,954	1,102,769	265,744	70,485	193.23	117
1969....	10,307	5.1	2,730	1,063,346	...	75,725	194.43	113
1968....	10,454	5.3	3,071	1,115,231	243,222	63,075	177.54	107
1968....	10,875	5.5	3,162	1,123,456	230,291	57,703	167.05	100
1967....	11,595	5.9	3,257	1,131,844	217,170	52,973	157.28	94
1966....	12,363	6.4	3,356	1,139,597	200,913	47,956	146.18	87
1965....	12,954	6.8	3,158	1,110,185	...	50,646	143,81	82
1963....	13,367	7.1	3,572	1,151,572	183,802	40,267	129.75	77
1962....	14,313	7.7	3,685	1,161,383	176,672	37,437	124.12	78
1965....	14,803	8.1	3,821	1,169,899	169,177	34,481	118.23	74
1960....	15,635*	8.7*	3,962	1,176,946	167,564	32,854	116.49	72
1959....	16,592	9.4	3,711*	1,123,508*	...	34,763*	115.08*	71
1958....	17,128	9.9	4,233	1,184,944	149,936	27,388	102.80	65
1957....	17,656	10.4	4,372	1,191,340	141,658	25,257	97.25	61
1956....	18,712	11.2	4,514	1,197,070	132,901	22,803	90.06	57
1955....	19,078	11.6	4,654	1,201,900	127,977	21,094	85.32	57
1954....	19,019	11.8	4,782	1,158,192	...	20,405	84.25	53
1953....	19,874	12.5	4,984	1,205,740	128,711	19,369	83.34	55
1952....	21,748	13.9	5,198	1,204,930	131,279	18,291	82.08	55
1951....	21,890	14.2	5,428	1,203,500	117,817	15,952	74.74	49
1950....	23,048	15.3	5,388[2]	1,161,420[2]	99,324	14,005[2]	64.97[2]	43
1949....	24,194	16.3	5,722	1,155,174	101,117	13,391	66.33	44
1948....	24,383	16.7	5,803	1,151,784	94,287	12,694	63.96	43
1947....	25,829	18.0	5,871	1,148,394	85,717	11,661	59.62	39
1946....	25,403	18.0	5,926	1,145,003	76,151	10,301	53.31	35
1945....	24,420	17.5	5,859	1,141,615	69,369	7,918	40.63	31
1944....	24,815	18.0	6,003	1,125,461	63,323	8,029	42.83	28
1943....	26,186	19.2	6,089	1,109,308	56,195	6,833	37.50	25
1942....	28,914	21.5	6,202	1,093,155	48,608	6,054	34.35	23
1941....	30,118	22.6	6,293	1,077,002	42,979	5,466	31.94	21
1940....	30,547	23.2	6,102[2]	1,065,114[2]	41,829	5,532[2]	31.69[2]	21
1939....	30,840	23.6	6,441	1,059,582	42,213	5,290	32.17	23
1938....	30,980	23.9	6,527	1,058,315	43,202	5,388	33.23	23
1937....	31,266	24.3	6,636	1,057,047	42,926	5,306	33.31	23
1936....	31,737	24.8	6,739	1,055,780	41,803	5,084	32.45	22
1935....	32,161	25.3	6,812	1,054,515	38,959	4,823	31.16	21
1934....	32,305	25.6	6,776	1,040,963	37,538	4,752	30.93	20
1933....	32,393	25.8	6,741	1,027,415	36,249	4,569	29.98	19
1932....	31,388	25.2	6,687	1,013,865	43,651	5,560	36.67	24
1931....	30,845	24.9	6,608	1,000,317	51,806	6,618	43.72	28
1930....	30,529	24.9	6,295[2]	990,112[2]	57,689	7,624[2]	48.47[2]	31
1929....	30,580	25.2	6,512	974,277	57,738	7,369	49.25	32
1928....	30,548	25.4	6,470	961,787	56,727	7,347	49.42	22
1927....	30,530	25.7	6,458	949,297	56,393	7,383	50.23	33
1926....	30,979	26.5	6,462	936,806	57,412	7,583	52.31	34
1925....	31,190	27.0	6,372	924,319	57,439	7,764	53.52	35
1924....	31,177	27.5	6,480	930,628	58,519	7,791	54.25	36
1923....	31,490	28.2	6,492	936,941	60,902	8,107	56.17	37
1922....	32,109	29.3	6,500	943,253	61,982	8,315	57.30	39
1921....	32,123	29.7	6,511	949,566	71,401	9,449	64.79	44
1920....	31,974	30.1	6,564[2]	958,677[2]	78,386	10,295[2]	69.31[2]	48
1915....	32,440	32.4	6,458	917,335	47,715	6,130	43.16	28
1910....	32,077	34.9	6,366[2]	881,431[2]	40,959	5,480[2]	39.58[2]	...
1900....	29,875	41.9	5,740[2]	841,202[2]	20,365	2,895[2]	19.82[2]	...
1890....	24,771	42.3	4,565	623,219	16,439	2,909	21.31	...
1880....	21,973	43.8	4,009	536,082	12,404	2,544	19.02	...
1870....	...	...	2,660	407,735	9,412	2,799	18.26	...
1860....	...	...	2,044	407,213	7,980	3,251	16.32	...
1850....	...	...	1,449	293,561	3,967	2,258	11.14	...

*Except as indicated by footnote 2, denotes 1st year for which figures include Alaska and Hawaii; (1) Excludes District of Columbia; (2) Includes Alaska and Hawaii; (3) Cropland harvested only.

Foreign Ownership of U.S. Agricultural Land: 1987

Source: U.S. Dept. of Agriculture

	Acreage Owned[1] Total (1,000)	Percent	Acreage Acquired[2] Total (1,000)	Percent		Acreage Owned[1] Total (1,000)	Percent	Acreage Acquired[2] Total (1,000)	Percent
Canada	1,452	11.6	75	23.1	Switzerland	247	2.0	19	5.8
Japan	115	0.9	2	0.6	United Kingdom .	284	2.3	7	2.2
Netherlands. ...	141	1.1	1	0.3	West Germany ..	717	5.7	23	7.1
Netherlands					Total[3]	12,535	—	325	—
Antilles	486	3.9							

(1) Landholdings by foreign interests as of 12/31. (2) Acquisitions by foreign interests from 1/1-12/31/87. (3) Includes other countries not shown separately.

Government Payments by Programs and State[1]

Source: Economic Research Service. U.S. Agriculture Department (thousands)

1988 State	Feed Grain	Wheat	Rice	Cotton	Wool Act	Conservation[2]	Miscellaneous[3]	Total
Alabama	$16,581	$8,688	0	$35,491	$10	$26,834	$26,902	$114,506
Alaska	124	2	0	0	2	1,603	29	1,760
Arizona	3,983	5,401	0	62,806	1,850	1,782	2,012	77,834
Arkansas	28,358	39,214	$189,827	51,252	78	13,341	21,804	343,874
California	28,464	40,237	87,435	118,600	6,949	12,879	40,514	335,078
Colorado	94,992	67,569	0	0	6,023	94,927	17,019	280,530
Connecticut	1,567	0	0	0	28	344	919	2,858
Delaware	8,540	446	0	0	4	343	1,171	10,504
Florida	7,951	1,787	174	2,379	14	7,779	11,950	32,034
Georgia	53,817	26,013	0	26,522	28	28,512	39,070	173,962
Hawaii	0	0	0	0	0	396	0	396
Idaho	23,763	72,047	0	0	2,967	35,548	32,499	166,824
Illinois	1,070,663	33,581	0	0	658	36,747	232,323	1,373,972
Indiana	520,121	18,218	0	0	337	19,001	58,659	616,336
Iowa	1,305,766	802	0	0	1,940	129,063	227,420	1,664,991
Kansas	360,124	300,668	0	0	1,129	147,515	38,558	847,994
Kentucky	99,724	9,689	0	0	135	27,757	23,573	160,878
Louisiana	14,091	6,635	72,696	68,419	30	7,051	21,203	190,125
Maine	1,208	4	0	0	67	4,664	1,376	7,319
Maryland	31,380	1,637	0	0	94	1,666	7,903	42,680
Massachusetts	650	0	0	0	48	484	1,616	2,798
Michigan	216,887	19,066	0	0	730	11,969	54,373	303,025
Minnesota	580,676	84,674	0	0	1,201	94,621	274,767	1,035,939
Mississippi	14,426	14,627	37,690	128,867	16	33,250	13,608	242,484
Missouri	227,145	46,755	13,226	16,544	572	96,492	56,158	456,892
Montana	34,221	126,095	0	0	5,843	90,993	129,582	386,734
Nebraska	833,725	69,176	0	0	997	74,647	112,976	1,091,251
Nevada	514	980	0	0	788	1,065	3,002	6,349
New Hampshire	437	0	0	0	36	539	937	1,949
New Jersey	6,556	573	0	0	24	491	3,189	10,833
New Mexico	19,405	9,539	3	6,948	5,482	22,380	7,665	71,422
New York	58,583	4,365	0	0	287	7,919	15,633	86,767
North Carolina	94,479	11,404	0	8,608	50	10,178	21,304	146,023
North Dakota	101,638	235,851	0	0	1,307	76,569	299,703	715,068
Ohio	309,942	26,454	0	0	1,064	14,252	30,139	381,851
Oklahoma	23,746	161,559	127	25,917	1,262	54,827	20,968	288,406
Oregon	7,465	45,382	0	0	2,685	31,340	10,933	97,805
Pennsylvania	40,873	1,325	0	0	504	7,238	14,980	64,920
Rhode Island	4	0	0	0	13	57	58	132
South Carolina	31,578	11,153	0	13,247	3	12,678	8,283	76,942
South Dakota	232,658	74,958	0	0	4,621	46,596	137,213	496,046
Tennessee	43,922	13,098	40	28,646	45	24,989	29,648	140,388
Texas	315,901	127,785	63,330	329,511	51,431	175,523	91,851	1,155,332
Utah	5,060	5,507	0	0	5,287	12,953	9,571	38,378
Vermont	1,299	0	0	0	77	1,251	3,251	5,881
Virginia	35,895	5,667	0	106	680	6,476	15,453	64,277
Washington	25,904	105,161	0	0	474	53,210	23,174	207,923
West Virginia	4,034	109	0	0	342	2,243	5,439	12,167
Wisconsin	274,579	2,597	0	0	447	30,543	101,205	409,371
Wyoming	6,041	5,382	0	0	8,118	13,854	4,315	37,710
Total U.S.	$7,219,460	$1,841,883	$464,548	$923,863	$116,777	$1,607,379	$2,305,898	$14,479,808

(1) Includes both cash payments and payment-in-kind (PIK); (2) Includes amount paid under agriculture and conservation programs (Conservation Bonus, Conservation Reserve, Agriculture Conservation, Emergency Conservation, and Great Plains Program); (3) Programs included: Rural Clean Water, Clean Lakes, Animal Waste Management, Forest Incentive, Water Bank, Dairy Indemnity, Dairy Termination, Emergency Feed, Extended Warehouse Storage, Extended Farm Storage, Milk Diversion, Disaster Program Crops, Disaster Program Non-Crops, Colorado River Salinity, Warehouse Storage Deduction, Livestock Emergency Assistance, Interest Penalty Payments and Disaster.

Federal Food Assistance Programs

Source: Food and Nutrition Service. U.S. Agriculture Department (millions of dollars)

	1980[1]	1981	1982	1983	1984	1985	1986	1987	1988	1989
Food Stamp Pgm.[2,6]	8,362	10,328	10,159	11,863	11,595	11,715	11,696	11,643	12,338	12,691
P.R. Nutrition Asstnce. Grant[3]	854	908	898	825	825	824	824	853	879	908
Natl. School Lunch Pgm.[3]	3,184	3,276	2,951	3,175	3,328	3,390	3,551	3,685	3,690	3,864
School Breakfast Pgm.	288	332	317	344	364	385	412	447	473	510
Special Supp. Food Pgm. for Women, Infants, Children	725	874	948	1,123	1,386	1,494	1,581	1,680	1,802	1,929
Summer Food Service Pgm.	118	110	93	98	106	113	123	129	137	150
Child Care Food Pgm.[3]	239	335	310	353	407	453	503	548	768	838
Special Milk Pgm.	145	101	18	17	17	16	16	15	22	21
Nutrition Pgm. for the Elderly[3]	75	94	101	119	127	127	137	139	147	151
Needy Family Pgm.[3]	28	39	39	46	53	60	61	63	66	68
Commodity Supp. Food Pgm.[3,8]	21	24	31	41	46	47	44	56	60	79
Food Distribution to Charities Inst.[4,5]	71	78	111	151	190	171	234	158	157	157
Other Costs[6]	56	56	233	1,079	1,126	1,080	952	904	NA	NA
Total[5]	14,174	16,562	16,212	19,237	19,574	19,886	20,132	20,370	NA	NA

(1) 1988 and prior years' data are updated per current reports; data for 1989 represents the program level under current law in the 1990 budget; (2) Excludes Puerto Rico; (3) Includes the value of COC and Section 32 bonus commodities, as do figures for other programs utilizing commodities; (4) Includes summer camps; (5) Excludes food program administration (all years) and food service equipment assistance (FY 1980), Northern Marianas Block, and Disaster Relief; (6) Includes SAE and other costs and program transfers, and excludes a block grant for the Northern Marianas ($.09 million in FY 1982; $3.7 million per year in FY 1982 forward; (7) Includes Child Nutrition State Admin. Expenses, Nutrition Studies & Education (CN), Temporary Emergency Food Assist. Pgm. (minus admin. expenses), & TEFAP Admin. Expenses. (8) Includes Elderly Feeding Projects.

World Wheat, Rice and Corn Production, 1987

Source: U.N. Food and Agriculture Organization

(thousands of metric tons)

Country	Wheat	Rice	Corn	Country	Wheat	Rice	Corn
World, total	516,780	454,320	457,365	Japan	864[2]	13,300[2]	1[1]
Afghanistan	2,850[1]	475[1]	800[1]	Kampuchea	n/a	1,700[1]	105[1]
Argentina	10,100[2]	445	9,250	Korea	800[1]	6,200[1]	2,900[1]
Australia.	12,190	548	158	Korean Republic	5[2]	7,596[2]	110[1]
Austria.	1,451	n/a	1,534	Laos	n/a	1,183	36[1]
Bangladesh	1,091	22,250	1[1]	Madagascar	n/a	2,230[2]	153[1]
Belgium[3]	1,078	n/a	49	Malaysia.	n/a	1,875[2]	27[2]
Brazil	5,709	10,460	26,824	Mexico.	4,409	584	10,988
Bulgaria	3,500[2]	62[1]	1,800[2]	Nepal	701	2,372	805
Burma	192	13,722	350[1]	Netherlands.	785	n/a	5[1]
Canada.	26,342	n/a	7,008	New Zealand	310	n/a	200[1]
Chile	1,874	147	617	Pakistan	12,016	4,768	1,000[2]
China	87,724[2]	176,530	76,495	Panama	n/a	166[2]	90[2]
Colombia	69	1,879	888	Peru	124	1,187	919
Cuba.	n/a	466	95	Philippines.	n/a	8,683	4,276
Czechoslovakia.	6,154	n/a	1,160	Poland.	7,942	n/a	146
Denmark	2,311	n/a	n/a	Portugal	538	144	673
Ecuador	20	417	330[2]	Romania.	6,880[2]	160[1]	22,000[1]
Egypt	2,722	2,400[2]	4,100[2]	South Africa.	2,766	3[1]	7,372
Ethiopia	800[1]	n/a	1,450	Soviet Union	85,000[1]	2,700	14,800
Finland.	281	n/a	n/a	Spain	5,768	490	3,555
France	27,434	55	12,052	Sri Lanka	n/a	2,128	41[1]
German Dem. Rep.	4,140[2]	n/a	1[1]	Sweden	1,558	n/a	n/a
Germany, Fed. Rep.	9,774	n/a	1,208	Switzerland	460[2]	n/a	168[2]
Greece	2,147	114	2,370	Syria	1,656	n/a	61
Hungary	5,714	46	7,187	Thailand	n/a	17,650	2,736
India	45,576	77,960[1]	6,500[1]	Turkey	18,932	280	2,400
Indonesia	n/a	38,676	4,800[2]	United Kingdom.	11,800	n/a	1[1]
Iran	7,960	1,920[2]	60[2]	United States	57,295	5,793	179,437
Iraq.	722	150[2]	35[2]	Uruguay	350[2]	354	104
Ireland	355[2]	n/a	n/a	Venezuela.	1[2]	300	1,200[2]
Israel.	298[2]	n/a	25[2]	Vietnam	n/a	15,300[1]	550[1]
Italy.	9,359	1,060	5,720	Yugoslavia	5,272	49	8,863

(1) FAO estimate; (2) Unofficial figure; (3) Includes Luxembourg; NA = Not available.

Wheat, Rice and Corn—Exports and Imports of 10 Leading Countries

Source: Economic Research Service. U.S. Agriculture Department

(thousands of metric tons.)

Leading Exporters	Exports[1] 1980	1987	1988[p]	Leading Importers	Imports[1] 1980	1987	1988[p]
Wheat				**Wheat**			
United States	41,204	43,327	38,782	China.	13,789	15,000	15,500
France	13,423	16,441	18,500	USSR	16,000	21,500	15,500
Canada	16,262	23,500	12,400	Egypt	5,423	7,073	6,600
Australia	9,577	9,850	11,100	Italy.	3,028	4,271	5,500
Argentina	3,845	3,705	3,700	Japan	5,840	5,653	5,200
Italy.	1,620	2,591	3,600	Algeria	2,294	3,800	4,200
Germany, Fed Rep.	1,502	3,440	3,300	Iraq.	1,366	2,700	3,200
United Kingdom.	1,100	2,520	2,200	Iran	1,896	4,000	3,000
Saudi Arabia	0	1,225	2,000	South Korea.	2,095	4,459	2,800
Hungary	700	1,050	1,900	Pakistan	320	505	2,200
Rice				**Rice**			
Thailand	3,049	4,791	5,800	China.	110	400	1,200
United States	3,028	2,290	2,762	Iran	583	400	900
Pakistan	1,163	1,033	900	Iraq.	350	650	600
Vietnam	5	75	850	USSR	1,283	498	550
Australia	468	430	500	Saudi Arabia	356	431	525
India	900	200	450	India	70	650	500
Italy.	475	541	425	Hong Kong	362	400	380
Burma	674	350	400	Senegal	340	315	355
China.	580	697	300	Malaysia	167	280	350
Uruguay	184	240	240	Bangladesh	84	691	300
Corn				**Corn**			
United States	61,163	43,982	53,342	USSR	11,800	7,300	19,000
France	2,380	6,395	6,700	Japan	13,989	16,697	16,000
South Africa	4,955	745	5,000	South Korea.	2,355	5,100	6,200
China.	125	4,054	4,000	Taiwan	2,703	4,459	4,100
Thailand	2,142	802	1,600	Mexico	3,833	3,150	3,000
Argentina	9,098	4,340	1,200	Spain	4,251	1,855	2,150
Belgium/Luxembourg	1,742	467	480	Netherlands	2,638	1,933	1,933
Spain.	1	600	450	Malaysia	717	1,414	1,500
Zimbabwe	305	500	400	Belgium/Luxembourg	2,927	1,326	1,490
Austria	1	229	215	United Kingdom.	2,349	1,385	1,350

(1) Marketing years; (p) Preliminary.

MANUFACTURES AND MINERALS

General Statistics for Major Industry Groups

Source: Bureau of the Census

The data in the following table are based upon information from the 1987 Annual Survey of Manufacturers.

Industry	All employees		Production workers			Value added by mfr. (millions)
	Number (1,000)	Payroll (millions)	Number (1,000)	Hours (millions)	Wages (millions)	
Food and kindred products	1,449.6	$30,247.5	1,029.9	2,036.5	$18,900.7	$124,186.6
Tobacco products	44.8	1,488.5	32.7	61.4	995.0	14,738.4
Textile mill products	689.6	11,544.2	590.3	1,211.0	8,831.0	26,592.3
Apparel, other textile prods..	1,076.6	13,915.5	904.2	1,603.3	9,846.3	33,126.5
Lumber and wood products.	695.8	12,636.6	578.6	1,145.5	9,472.3	28,391.7
Furniture and fixtures	511.3	9,104.8	409.9	806.9	6,261.7	20,265.4
Paper and allied products	617.3	16,984.2	470.4	991.8	11,880.8	49,724.9
Printing and publishing.	1,500.2	33,594.6	799.8	1,546.5	15,664.8	90,204.3
Chemicals, allied products	817.7	24,978.0	467.3	965.9	12,369.2	120,866.5
Petroleum and coal products	119.8	4,129.3	79.0	165.2	2,536.8	19,095.3
Rubber, misc. plastics prod..	857.7	18,060.4	662.5	1,324.4	11,965.5	45,562.0
Leather, leather products	128.0	1,804.0	107.8	205.8	1,286.5	4,246.2
Stone, clay, glass products	520.2	12,253.5	400.6	822.8	8,704.3	32,553.0
Primary metal industries.	701.9	19,888.2	541.8	1,115.6	14,230.2	47,136.6
Fabricated metal products	1,473.6	35,435.4	1,085.8	2,251.5	22,989.9	76,054.7
Machinery, except electric	1,870.6	51,156.8	1,155.8	2,343.1	26,184.7	117,538.0
Electric, electronic equip..	1,599.8	39,295.3	1,021.1	2,001.0	19,915.8	98,332.2
Transportation equipment.	1,834.5	59,557.5	1,213.6	2,456.6	35,083.8	139,090.8
Instruments, related prods..	964.9	28,165.9	491.8	993.4	11,223.7	70,939.8
Misc. manufacturing indus.	377.6	6,938.6	273.7	522.7	4,075.4	17,826.5
All industries	17,851.5	431,178.3	12,316.6	24,570.9	252,418.4	1,176,471.7

Manufacturing Production Worker Statistics

Source: Bureau of Labor Statistics, U.S. Labor Department (p — preliminary)

Year	All employees	Production workers	Constant Dollars[1]	Avg. weekly earnings	Avg. hourly earnings	Avg. hrs. per wk.
1955	16,882,000	13,288,000	—	$75.30	$1.85	40.7
1960	16,796,000	12,586,000	183.5	89.72	2.26	39.7
1965	18,062,000	13,434,000	206.4	107.53	2.61	41.2
1970	19,367,000	14,044,000	208.0	133.33	3.35	39.8
1975	18,323,000	13,043,000	214.9	190.79	4.83	39.5
1980	20,285,000	14,214,000	212.0	288.62	7.27	39.7
1985	19,260,000	13,092,000	220.15	386.37	9.54	40.5
1986	18,965,000	12,877,000	222.23	396.01	9.73	40.7
1987	19,024,000	12,970,000	220.10	406.31	9.91	41.0
1988	19,403,000	13,254,000	217.80	418.40	10.18	41.1
1989p Jan.	19,516,000	13,312,000	216.26	425.17	10.37	41.0
Feb.	19,518,000	13,318,000	214.54	423.50	10.38	40.9

(1) Earnings in current dollars divided by the Consumer Price Index on a 1977 basis.

International Manufacturing Productivity and Labor Costs

Source: Bureau of Labor Statistics, U.S. Labor Department (1977 = 100)

Output per hour

Country	1960	1965	1970	1975	1980	1985	1986	1987	1988
United States	62.2	76.6	80.8	92.9	101.4	123.6	127.7	132.0	136.2
Canada	50.7	65.0	75.6	88.6	98.2	117.3	117.7	120.5	124.3
Japan	23.2	35.0	64.8	87.7	122.7	161.1	163.7	176.5	190.0
France	36.4	49.2	69.6	88.5	112.0	132.7	135.2	136.8	144.1
West Germany	40.3	54.0	71.2	90.1	108.6	128.4	128.3	129.9	135.9
Italy	36.5	52.9	72.7	91.1	116.9	156.8	158.3	162.3	167.1
Norway	54.6	64.4	81.7	96.8	106.7	126.8	125.9	134.2	NA
Sweden	42.3	58.5	80.7	100.2	112.7	136.1	136.0	141.8	145.0
United Kingdom	55.5	65.7	79.7	95.2	101.7	134.1	138.6	147.6	154.9

Unit Labor Costs in U.S. dollars

Country	1960	1965	1970	1975	1980	1985	1986	1987	1988
United States	58.7	55.8	71.0	91.7	130.6	142.7	143.3	141.7	142.1
Canada	59.4	50.4	64.5	93.1	121.5	128.9	132.1	142.3	157.8
Japan	28.5	35.4	39.1	86.7	116.8	105.6	154.4	170.5	188.4
France	41.7	48.4	46.8	99.5	154.1	109.5	146.3	174.2	172.9
West Germany	25.9	32.6	42.9	88.7	147.9	101.2	143.0	177.0	180.3
Italy	32.5	41.2	50.6	104.3	141.4	103.8	137.4	164.0	168.8
Norway	21.7	26.9	34.5	81.4	129.3	99.8	124.7	153.7	NA
Sweden	30.1	35.4	41.1	83.2	125.3	81.1	105.4	121.5	131.1
United Kingdom	44.2	51.0	54.2	103.7	220.5	143.5	168.6	188.3	210.5

NOTE: The data relate to all employed persons (wage & salary, the self-employed, and unpaid family workers) in the U.S. and Canada, and all employees (wage & salary earners) in the other countries.

Sales and Profits of Manufacturing Corporations by Industry Group

Source: Bureau of the Census—Economic Surveys Division

(millions of dollars)

	Sales			Income after taxes		
	1Q	4Q	1Q	1Q	4Q	1Q
Industry group	1988	1988	1989	1988	1988	1989
All manufacturing corporations	614,176	681,846	664,518	37,060	37,632	37,885
Nondurable manufacturing corporations	313,377	341,140	335,756	21,574	21,299	21,309
Food and kindred products	86,520	100,391	94,549	4,469	4,751	3,668
Textile mill products	11,978	12,584	12,495	394	377	387
Paper and allied products	25,561	26,990	27,281	1,745	1,911	1,979
Printing and publishing	29,495	34,330	32,190	1,979	1,550	1,660
Chemicals and allied products	62,732	66,259	69,268	6,484	5,659	6,882
Industrial chemicals and synthetics	27,533	29,547	30,593	2,478	2,103	3,026
Drugs	11,710	11,802	12,464	2,313	2,208	2,106
Petroleum and coal products	62,630	64,364	63,218	5,050	6,147	5,240
Rubber and miscellaneous plastics products.	17,197	19,079	18,902	921	363	796
Other nondurable manufacturing corporations. . . .	17,263	17,144	17,853	532	542	696
Durable manufacturing corporations	300,800	340,706	328,762	15,485	16,333	16,576
Stone, clay, and glass products	12,238	13,642	12,221	96	556	(8)
Primary metal industries	25,844	28,630	29,242	1,233	1,631	1,710
Iron and steel	12,985	13,644	14,350	369	515	476
Nonferrous metals	12,859	14,986	14,892	864	1,116	1,234
Fabricated metal products	32,998	37,541	36,661	1,567	642	2,116
Machinery, except electrical	54,530	61,493	59,509	3,122	3,632	2,666
Electrical and electronic equipment	48,548	57,024	52,559	2,399	2,762	2,396
Transportation equipment	82,567	91,375	88,048	4,521	4,294	5,205
Motor vehicles and equipment	53,043	57,594	58,974	3,294	3,272	3,867
Aircraft, guided missiles, and parts	26,631	30,871	26,410	1,216	937	1,304
Instruments and related products	21,059	24,160	24,046	1,754	2,079	1,582
Other durable manufacturing corporations	23,015	26,842	26,476	793	737	908
All mining corporations*	8,497	10,714	10,240	286	16	610
All retail trade corporations*	121,058	155,796	NA	1,841	4,937	NA
All wholesale trade corporations*	142,656	164,691	164,486	1,708	2,034	1,801

*With assets over $50 million.

Annual Percent Change in Productivity and Related Data, 1977-1988

Source: Bureau of Labor Statistics, U.S. Labor Department

Item	1977	1978	1979	1980	1981	1982	1983	1984	1985	1986	1987	1988
Business sector:												
Output per hour of all persons	1.8	0.9	1.1	−0.3	1.5	−0.7	2.4	2.6	2.0	2.3	1.2	1.8
Real compensation per hour .	1.4	0.9	−1.4	−2.6	−0.9	1.2	0.6	−0.2	0.8	3.3	0.2	0.8
Unit labor cost	6.0	7.7	11.1	10.9	7.7	8.3	1.4	1.5	2.3	2.8	2.6	3.1
Unit nonlabor payments. . . .	7.1	6.7	5.3	5.4	13.5	1.4	7.3	7.0	2.8	0.7	2.6	2.7
Implicit price deflator	6.4	7.3	9.0	9.0	9.6	5.9	3.3	3.3	2.5	2.1	2.6	2.9
Nonfarm business sector:												
Output per hour of all persons	1.7	1.9	−1.5	−0.4	1.1	−0.9	3.0	2.1	1.3	2.0	1.1	2.1
Real compensation per hour .	1.3	1.0	−1.6	−2.6	−0.7	1.1	0.7	−0.4	0.5	3.2	−0.1	0.7
Unit labor cost	6.1	7.7	11.2	11.0	8.3	8.4	1.0	1.8	2.8	3.0	2.6	2.7
Unit nonlabor payments. . . .	7.5	5.6	4.5	7.1	12.7	2.2	8.7	5.5	3.6	0.9	2.7	2.6
Implicit price deflator	6.6	7.0	8.9	9.7	9.7	6.3	3.5	3.0	3.0	2.3	2.6	2.7
Manufacturing:												
Output per hour of all persons	3.1	1.6	0.0	0.0	2.3	2.5	5.2	5.4	4.5	3.8	3.7	3.6
Real compensation per hour .	2.1	0.6	−1.4	−1.6	−0.5	2.6	−0.7	−0.9	1.2	2.6	−1.0	0.4
Unit labor cost	5.4	6.6	9.7	11.7	7.3	6.2	−2.5	−1.9	0.3	0.7	−1.0	0.9
Unit nonlabor payments. . . .	6.9	1.8	−2.9	−1.2	14.4	1.8	12.9	7.9	−5.9	3.8	1.8	N.A
Implicit price deflator	5.9	5.2	.6.2	8.4	8.9	5.1	1.1	0.7	−1.5	1.6	0.2	N.A

N.A.—Not available.

U.S. Reliance on Foreign Supplies of Minerals

Source: Bureau of Mines, U.S. Interior Department

Mineral	Percent imported in 1988	Major sources (1984-87)	Major uses
Columbium	100%	Brazil, Canada, Thailand	Steelmaking and aerospace alloys
Graphite*	100	Mexico, China, Brazil, Madagascar	Metallurgical processes
Manganese	100	Australia, Brazil, Gabon	Steelmaking
Mica (sheet)	100	India, Belgium, France, Japan	Electronic and electrical equipment
Strontium (Celestite)	100	Mexico, Spain, China	Television picture tubes, pyrotechnics
Bauxite and alumina	97	Australia, Guinea, Jamaica, Suriname	Aluminum production
Fluorspar	91	Mexico, South Africa	Raw material for metallurgical and chemical industries
Diamonds (industrial)	90	South Africa, Britain, Ireland, Zaire	Machinery for grinding and cutting
Tantalum	89	Thailand, Brazil, Australia, Canada	Electronic components
Platinum group*	88	South Africa, Britain, USSR	Catalytic converters for autos, electrical and electronic equipment
Cobalt	84	Zaire, Zambia, Canada, Norway	Aerospace alloys
Tungston	75	China, Canada Bolivia	Lamp filaments
Chromium	75	South Africa, Zimbabwe, Turkey, Yugoslavia	Stainless steel
Nickel	75	Canada, Australia, Norway	Stainless steel and other alloys
Tin	73	Thailand, Brazil, Indonesia, Malaysia	Cans, electrical construction
Barite	71	China, Morocco, India	Oil drilling fluids
Potash	70	Canada, Israel, East Germany, USSR	Fertilizer
Zinc	69	Canada, Mexico, Peru, Australia	Construction and transportation materials
Silver	57	Canada, Mexico, Britain, Peru	Photography, electrical and electronic components
Cadmium	47	Canada, Australia, Mexico, West Germany	Plating and coating of metals

*Percent of imports in 1987.

Minerals

Source: Bureau of Mines, U.S. Interior Department, as of mid-1989

Aluminum: the most abundant metal element in the Earth's crust. Bauxite is the main source of aluminum; convert to aluminum equivalent by multiplying by 0.211. Guinea and Australia have 46 percent of the world's reserves. Aluminum is used in the U.S. in packaging 28%, transportation 19% and building 19%.

Chromium: some 99 percent of the world's chromite is found in South Africa and Zimbabwe. The chemical and metallurgical industries use about 90% of the chromite consumed in the U.S.

Cobalt: used in superalloys for jet engines; chemicals (paint driers, catalysts, magnetic coatings); permanent magnets; and cemented carbides for cutting tools. Principal cobalt producing countries include Zaire, Zambia, and the USSR. The U.S. uses about one-third of total world consumption. Although its resources are relatively large, the U.S. has produced no cobalt since 1971; cobalt resources are low grade and production from these deposits is not economically feasible.

Columbium: used mostly as an alloying element in steels and superalloys. Brazil and Canada are the world's leading producers. There is no U.S. columbium mining industry.

Copper: main uses of copper in the U.S. are in nonelectrical building construction 18%, electrical and electronic products 66%, industrial machinery and equipment 7%, transportation 4%. The leading producer is Chile, followed by the U.S., USSR, Canada, Zambia, and Zaire. Principal mining states are Arizona, New Mexico, and Utah.

Gold: used in the U.S. in jewelry and arts 55%, industrial (mainly electronic) 37%, dental 8%. South Africa has about half of the world's resources; significant quantities are also present in the U.S., Canada, USSR, and Brazil. Gold mining in the U.S. takes place in nearly all of the western states and Alaska.

Iron ore: the source of primary iron for the world's iron and steel industries. Major iron ore producers include the USSR, Brazil, Australia, and China.

Lead: the U.S. is the world's largest producer and consumer of lead metal. Transportation accounted for the major end use in the U.S. with 71% used in batteries, gasoline additives, and other applications. Other uses include emergency power supply batteries, construction sheeting, sporting am-

munition and TV tubes. Other major mine producers include the USSR, Australia, and Canada.

Manganese: essential to iron and steel production. The U.S., Japan, and Western Europe are all nearly deficient in economically minable manganese. South Africa and the USSR have over 70% of the world's reserves.

Nickel: vital to the iron and steel industry and played a key role in the development of the chemical and aerospace industries. Leading producers include the USSR, Canada, Japan and Australia.

Platinum-Group Metals: the platinum group comprises 6 closely related metals: platinum, palladium, rhodium, ruthenium, iridium, and osmium. They commonly occur together in nature and are among the scarcest of the metallic elements. They are consumed in the U.S. by the following industries: automotive 43%, electrical and electronic 21%, and dental and medical 18%. The USSR and South Africa have over 90% of the world's reserves.

Silver: used in the following U.S. industries: photography 48%; electrical and electronic products 25%; sterlingware, electroplated ware, and jewelry 10%. Silver is mined in more than 54 countries. Idaho produces over 30% of the U.S. silver.

Tantalum: a refractory metal with unique electrical, chemical, and physical properties which is mostly used in the U.S in electrical machinery and transportation industries. Thailand, Australia, and Brazil are the leading producers. There is no U.S. tantalum mining industry.

Titanium: a metal which is mostly used in jet engines, airframes, and space and missile applications. It is produced in the USSR, Japan, and the western and central U.S.

Vanadium: used as an alloying element in steel, as an alloying agent in aerospace titanium alloys, and as a catalyst in the production of sulfuric acid and maleic anhyorice. The USSR and South Africa are the world's largest producers.

Zinc: used as protective coating on steel, as diecastings, as an alloying metal with copper to make brass, and as chemical compounds in rubber and paints. It is mined in over 50 countries with Canada the leading producer, followed by the USSR, Australia, Peru and Spain. In the U.S., mine production comes mostly from Tennessee, Missouri, and New York.

World Mineral Reserve Base

Source: Bureau of Mines, U.S. Interior Department

Mineral	Reserve Base[1]	Mineral	Reserve Base[1]
Aluminum	23,200 mln. metric tons[2]	Nickel	120,600 thousand short tons
Chromium	6,800 mln. metric tons	Platinum—	
Cobalt	9,200 thou. short tons	Group Metals	2,140 mln. troy oz.
Columbium	9,100 mln. lbs.	Silver	14,000 mln. troy oz.
Copper	560 mln. metric tons	Tantalum	76 mln. lbs.
Gold	1,550 mln. troy oz.	Titanium	NA
Iron	213,000 mln. long tons[3]	Vanadium	18,300 thousand short tons
Lead	125 mln. metric tons	Zinc	295 mln. metric tons
Manganese	3,900,000 thousand short tons		

(1) Includes demonstrated resources that are currently economic (reserves), marginally economic (marginal reserves), and some of those that are currently subeconomic. (2) Bauxite. (3) Crude ore.

U.S. Nonfuel Mineral Production—Leading States in 1987

Source: Bureau of Mines, U.S. Interior Department

State	Value (thousands)	Principal minerals
California	$2,551,284	Cement, boron minerals, sand and gravel (construction), stone (crushed).
Arizona	1,791,553	Copper, gold, sand and gravel.
Nevada	1,446,814	Gold, sand & gravel (construction), cement, silver.
Texas	1,430,730	Cement, stone (crushed), sand and gravel (construction).
Michigan	1,365,610	Cement, sand & gravel, stone.
Florida	1,346,237	Stone (crushed), cement, phosphate rock.
Georgia	1,212,370	Clays, stone (crushed), cement.
Minnesota	1,142,749	Iron ore, sand and gravel (construction), stone (crushed).
Pennsylvania	1,016,496	Cement, stone (crushed), lime, sand and gravel (construction).
Missouri	863,041	Cement, lead, stone, lime.
Ohio	768,781	Stone (crushed), sand and gravel (construction), salt, lime.
New Mexico	737,675	Sand & gravel, potassium salts, copper.

U.S. Nonfuel Mineral Production

Source: Bureau of Mines, U.S. Interior Department

Production as measured by mine shipments, sales, or marketable production (including consumption by producers)

Metals	1986 Quantity	1986 Value (thousands)	1987 Quantity	1987 Value (thousands)
Antimony (ore and concentrate) . . . . short tons	W	W	W	W
Bauxite . . . . thousand metric tons, dried equivalent	510	$10,361	576	$10,871
Copper (recoverable content of ores, etc.) . . . . metric tons	1,147,277	1,670,660	1,255,914	2,284,156
Gold (recoverable content of ores, etc.) . . . . troy ounces	3,739,105	1,376,855	4,966,382	2,224,691
Iron ore, usable (excluding byproduct iron sinter) thousand long tons, gross weight	W	W	W	W
Iron oxide pigments, crude . . . . short tons	40,987	2,908	42,773	3,598
Lead (recoverable content of ores, etc.) . . . . metric tons	339,987	2,908	311,298	246,654
Magnesium metal . . . . short tons	138,493	423,788	137,123	381,914
Manganiferous ore (5% to 35% Mn) . . . . short tons, gross weight	14,320	W	19,087	W
Mercury . . . . 76-pound flasks	W	W	W	W
Molybdenum (content of ore and concentrate) . . . thousand pounds	95,006	240,484	69,868	179,286
Nickel (content of ore and concentrate) . . . . short tons	1,175	W	—	—
Silver (recoverable content of ores, etc.) . . . . thousand troy ounces	34,524	187,846	39,790	278,930
Titanium concentrate:				
Ilmenite . . . . short tons, gross weight	W	W	W	W
Tungsten ore and concentrate . . . . metric tons	817	5,774	W	W
Vanadium (ore and concentrate) . . . . short tons	W	W	W	W
Zinc (recoverable content of ores, etc.) . . . . metric tons	202,983	170,050	216,981	200,529
Combined value of beryllium concentrates, magnesium chloride for magnesium metal, rare-earth metal concentrates, tin, titanium concentrates (rutile), zircon concentrate, and values indicated by symbol W	XX	1,562,566	XX	1,636,688
Total metals	**XX**	**5,817,000**	**XX**	**7,447,000**

Industrial Minerals (except fuels)				
Abrasive stones[2] . . . . short tons	W	W	12,773	957
Asbestos . . . . metric tons	51,437	17,367	50,600	17,198
Barite . . . . thousand short tons	297	12,326	448	15,810
Boron minerals . . . . do	1,251	426,086	1,385	475,092
Bromine . . . . thousand pounds	310,000	93,000	335,000	107,000
Calcium chloride . . . . short tons	W	W	W	W
Cement:				
Masonry . . . . thousand short tons	3,525	231,551	3,680	259,926
Portland . . . . do	75,181	3,759,942	74,868	3,646,561
Clays . . . . do	44,620	1,095,179	47,657	1,202,284
Diatomite . . . . do	628	128,362	658	134,239
Emory[1] . . . . short tons . . .	2,878	W	1,945	W
Feldspar . . . . short tons	735,000	26,100	720,000	26,100
Fluorspar . . . . do	78,000	W	68,839	11,725
Garnet (abrasive) . . . . do	32,296	2,603	42,277	4,350
Gem stones	NA	9,247	NA	21,389
Gypsum . . . . thousand short tons	15,403	199,570	15,612	106,977
Helium (crude) . . . . million cubic feet	432	9,504	730	16,068
Helium (Grade A) . . . . million cubic feet	1,941	72,788	2,230	82,540
Lime . . . . thousand short tons	14,474	757,867	15,733	786,125
Mica (scrap) . . . . thousand short tons	148	7,108	161	8,201
Peat . . . . do	1,038	23,988	958	26,170
Perlite . . . . do	507	15,646	533	16,494
Phosphate rock . . . . thousand metric tons	40,320	897,131	40,954	793,280
Potassium salts . . . . thousand metric tons, K[2]O equivalent	1,147	152,000	1,485	195,700
Pumice . . . . thousand short tons	554	5,756	392	4,493
Salt . . . . thousand short tons	ᵖ36,663	665,400	36,493	684,170
Sand and gravel (construction) . . . . do	883,000	2,747,200	896,200	3,002,500
Sand and gravel (industrial) . . . . do	27,420	359,300	28,010	364,100
Sodium sulfate (natural) . . . . do	396	34,102	382	33,086
Stone[3] (crushed) . . . . do	1,023,200	4,255,000	1,200,100	5,248,600
Stone[3] (dimension) . . . . do	1,163	173,269	1,184	190,153
Sulfur, Frasch process . . . . thousand metric tons	4,180	508,512	3,610	386,834
Talc and pyrophillite . . . . thousand short tons	1,302	31,227	1,349	28,785
Tripoli . . . . short tons	117,174	918	114,926	975
Vermiculite . . . . thousand short tons	317	34,400	303	33,105
Combined value of aplite, asphalt (native), graphite, iodine, kyanite, lithium minerals, magnesite, marl (greensand), olivine, sodium carbonate (natural), staurolite, wollastonite, and values indicated by symbol W	XX	994,446	XX	374,118
Total nonmetals	**XX**	**17,647,000**	**XX**	**18,899,000**
Grand total	**XX**	**23,464,000**	**XX**	**26,346,000**

(W) Withheld to avoid disclosing company proprietary data; included in "Combined value" figures. (XX) Not applicable. (NA) Not available.
(1) Not reported in 1985.
(2) Grindstones, pulpstones, sharpening stones, excludes mill liners & grinding pebbles.
(3) Excludes abrasive stone, bituminous limestone and sandstone; all included elsewhere in table.

U.S. Pig Iron and Steel Output

Source: American Iron and Steel Institute (net tons)

Year	Total pig iron	Raw steel	Year	Total pig iron	Raw steel
1940	46,071,666	66,982,686	1975	101,208,000	116,642,000
1945	53,223,169	79,701,648	1980	68,721,000	111,835,000
1950	64,586,907	96,836,075	1984	51,904,000	92,528,000
1955	76,857,417	117,036,085	1985	50,446,000	88,259,000
1960	66,480,648	99,281,601	1986	43,952,000	81,606,000
1965	88,184,901	131,461,601	1987	48,410,000	89,151,000
1970	91,435,000	131,514,000	1988	55,745,000	99,924,000

Steel figures include only that portion of the capacity and production of steel for castings used by foundries which were operated by companies producing steel ingots.

U.S. Copper, Lead, and Zinc Production

Source: Bureau of Mines. U.S. Interior Department

Year	Copper Quantity (metric tons)	Copper Value ($1,000)	Lead Quantity (metric tons)	Lead Value ($1,000)	Zinc Quantity (metric tons)	Zinc Value ($1,000)	Year	Copper Quantity (metric tons)	Copper Value ($1,000)	Lead Quantity (metric tons)	Lead Value ($1,000)	Zinc Quantity (metric tons)	Zinc Value ($1,000)
1950	827	379,122	390,839	113,078	565,516	167,000	1982	1,147	1,840,856	512,516	288,579	303,160	257,116
1960	1,037	733,706	223,774	57,722	395,013	112,365	1983	1,038	1,751,476	449,295	214,745	275,294	251,204
1965	1,226	957,028	273,196	93,959	554,429	178,284	1984	1,103	1,625,116	322,677	181,745	252,768	270,833
1970	1,560	1,984,484	518,698	178,609	484,560	163,650	1985	1,106	1,632,483	413,955	174,008	226,545	201,607
1975	1,282	1,814,763	563,783	267,230	425,792	366,097	1986	1,154	1,670,660	339,793	165,150	202,983	170,050
1980	1,181	2,666,931	550,366	515,189	317,103	261,671	1987	1,256	2,284,156	311,298	246,654	216,281	200,529

World Gold Production

(Troy Ounces)

Year	World prod.	South Africa	Ghana	Zaire	United States	Canada	Mexico	Colombia	Australia	China	Philippines	USSR
1972	44,843,374	29,245,273	724,051	140,724	1,449,943	2,078,567	146,061	188,137	754,866	—	606,730	—
1975	38,476,371	22,937,820	523,889	103,217	1,052,252	1,653,611	144,710	308,864	526,821	—	502,577	—
1976	39,024,485	22,936,018	532,473	91,093	1,048,037	1,691,806	162,811	300,307	502,741	—	501,210	—
1977	38,906,145	22,501,886	480,884	80,418	1,100,347	1,733,609	212,709	257,070	624,270	—	558,554	—
1978	38,983,019	22,648,558	402,034	76,077	998,832	1,735,077	202,003	246,446	647,579	—	586,531	—
1979	38,768,978	22,617,179	362,000	69,992	964,390	1,644,265	190,364	269,369	596,910	—	535,166	—
1980	39,197,315	21,669,468	353,000	39,963	969,782	1,627,477	195,991	510,439	547,591	—	753,452	8,425,000
1982	43,082,814	21,355,111	331,000	62,233	1,465,686	2,081,230	214,349	472,674	866,815	1,800,000	834,439	8,550,000
1983	45,163,364	21,847,310	276,000	192,930	2,002,526	2,363,411	198,177	426,517	983,522	1,850,000	816,536	8,600,000
1984	46,929,444	21,860,933	287,000	117,115	2,084,615	2,682,786	270,998	730,670	1,295,963	1,900,000	827,149	8,650,000
1985	49,283,691	21,565,230	299,363	63,022	2,427,232	2,815,118	265,693	1,142,385	1,881,491	1,950,000	1,062,997	8,700,000
1986	51,534,056	20,513,665	287,127	167,827	3,739,015	3,364,700	250,615	1,285,878	2,413,842	2,100,000	1,296,400	8,850,000
1987p	53,033,614	19,176,500	327,598	140,561	4,947,040	3,724,000	256,822	853,600	3,558,954	2,300,000	1,048,081	8,850,000
1988e	58,453,814	19,881,126	372,979	140,000	6,459,539	4,110,000	296,689	933,000	4,887,000	2,500,000	1,134,920	9,000,000

(e) estimated (p) preliminary

U.S. and World Silver Production

Source: Bureau of Mines. U.S. Interior Department

(troy ounces)
Largest production of silver in the United States in 1915—74,961,075 troy ounces.

Year	United States	World	Year	United States	World	Year	United States	World
1930 ..	50,748,127	248,708,426	1960 ..	36,000,000	241,300,000	1983 ..	43,431,000	387,711,000
1935 ..	45,924,454	220,704,231	1965 ..	39,806,033	257,415,000	1984 ..	44,592,000	420,065,000
1940 ..	69,585,734	275,387,000	1970 ..	45,006,000	310,891,000	1985 ..	39,433,000	424,416,000
1945 ..	29,063,255	162,000,000	1975 ..	34,938,000	303,112,000	1986 ..	34,524,000	419,433,000
1950 ..	43,308,739	203,300,000	1980 ..	32,329,000	339,382,000	1987p ..	39,790,000	443,050,000
1955 ..	36,469,610	224,000,000	1982 ..	40,248,000	371,159,000	1988e ..	53,416,000	443,073,000

(p) preliminary. (e) estimate.

Aluminum Summary, 1970 to 1987

Source: Bureau of Mines. U.S. Interior Department

Item	Unit	1970	1975	1980	1984	1985	1986	1987
U.S. production	Mil. sh. ton	4.8	4.9	6.5	6.4	5.8	5.3	5.9
Primary aluminum	Mil. sh. ton	4.0	3.9	5.1	4.5	3.9	3.3	3.7
Plant capacity	Mil. sh. ton	4.3	5.0	5.5	5.4	5.2	4.5	4.3
Secondary aluminum[1]	Mil. sh. ton	.8	1.0	1.4	1.9	1.9	2.0	2.2
Price (cents per lb[2])	Cents/lb	28.7	39.8	71.6	81.0	81.0	81.0	72.3
Imports for consumption[3] . . .	1,000 sh. ton	468	550	713	1,628	1,565	2,168	2,039
Exports[3]	1,000 sh. ton	612	440	1,483	809	1,001	830	1,010
World production, est.	Mil. sh. ton	10.6	13.4	17.0	17.3	16.9	16.9	17.7
World plant capacity	Mil. sh. ton	12.0	16.4	18.7	20.1	19.9	19.7	19.7

(1) Recoverable aluminum content from scrap, old and new; (2) Average prices for primary aluminum, quoted by *Metals Week*, after 1975; (3) Crude and semicrude (including metal and alloys, plates, bars, etc., and scrap).

TRADE AND TRANSPORTATION

U.S. Foreign Trade with Leading Countries

Source: Office of Industry and Trade Information, U.S. Commerce Department

(millions of dollars)

Exports from the U.S. to the following areas and countries and imports into the U.S. from those areas and countries:	Exports 1980	Exports 1987	Exports 1988	Imports 1980	Imports 1987	Imports 1988
Total	220,705	252,866	320,385	240,834	424,082	459,925
Western Hemisphere	74,114	94,795	113,155	78,489	120,605	135,135
Canada	35,395	59,814	69,233	41,455	71,510	81,434
20 Latin American Republics	36,030	31,574	40,077	29,851	46,427	51,194
Central American Common Market	1,951	1,873	2,254	1,849	2,158	2,154
Dominican Republic	795	1,142	1,362	786	1,217	1,479
Panama	699	743	633	330	402	297
Bahamas	396	782	741	1,382	450	426
Jamaica	305	601	758	383	422	472
Netherlands Antilles	448	507	432	2,564	557	440
Trinidad and Tobago	680	361	328	2,378	859	773
Western Europe	71,372	69,718	87,995	47,849	99,934	105,035
OECD countries (excludes depend. and Yugo.)	66,654	69,091	87,236	45,952	98,996	103,996
European Economic Community	53,679	60,575	75,926	35,958	84,876	88,748
Belgium and Luxembourg	6,661	6,189	7,405	1,914	4,359	4,719
Denmark	863	893	970	725	1,882	1,756
France	7,485	7,943	10,086	5,247	11,177	12,689
Germany, Federal Republic of	10,960	11,748	14,331	11,681	28,028	27,421
Ireland	836	1,810	2,182	411	1,155	1,425
Italy	5,511	5,530	6,782	4,313	11,698	12,277
Netherlands	8,669	8,217	10,095	1,910	4,236	4,874
United Kingdom	12,694	14,114	18,404	9,755	17,988	18,740
Austria	448	549	748	388	979	1,137
Finland	505	515	763	439	1,085	1,297
Iceland	79	84	98	200	300	200
Norway	843	842	932	2,632	1,514	1,561
Portugal	911	581	752	256	713	738
Sweden	1,767	1,894	2,705	1,617	4,981	5,217
Switzerland	3,781	3,151	4,207	2,787	4,363	4,745
Greece	922	402	649	292	529	589
Spain	3,179	3,148	4,217	1,209	3,101	3,470
Turkey	540	1,483	1,843	175	897	1,071
Yugoslavia	756	461	534	446	871	925
Eastern Europe	3,860	2,200	3,650	1,433	2,118	2,385
USSR	1,513	1,480	2,768	453	470	649
Asia	60,168	73,268	99,705	78,848	184,195	200,360
Near East	11,900	9,502	10,857	17,280	11,602	12,483
Iran	23	54	73	339	1,752	9
Iraq	724	683	1,156	352	526	1,605
Israel	2,045	3,130	3,248	943	2,724	3,068
Jordan	407	365	373	3	12	13
Kuwait	886	505	690	472	587	507
Lebanon	303	97	123	33	34	42
Saudi Arabia	5,769	3,373	3,799	12,509	4,887	6,237
Syria	239	93	89	26	66	42
Japan	20,790	28,249	37,732	30,701	83,074	93,168
East and South Asia	27,478	31,995	46,061	30,867	77,608	85,438
Bangladesh	292	193	258	85	419	413
China, People's Republic of	3,755	3,497	5,039	1,054	6,911	9,270
China (Taiwan)	4,337	7,413	12,131	6,850	26,407	26,256
Hong Kong	2,686	3,983	5,691	4,736	10,490	10,810
India	1,689	1,463	2,498	1,098	2,725	3,167
Indonesia	1,545	763	1,056	5,183	3,719	3,494
Korea, Republic of	4,685	8,099	11,290	4,147	17,991	21,209
Malaysia	1,337	1,897	2,139	2,577	3,053	3,853
Pakistan	642	128	1,093	733	438	498
Philippines	1,999	1,599	1,880	1,730	2,481	2,906
Singapore	3,033	4,053	5,770	1,920	6,395	8,226
Thailand	1,263	1,544	1,964	816	2,387	3,424
Oceania	4,876	6,526	8,242	3,392	4,550	5,299
Australia	4,093	5,495	6,981	2,509	3,287	3,856
New Zealand and Samoa	599	821	946	703	1,183	1,306
Africa	9,060	6,283	7,431	32,251	12,680	11,710
Algeria	542	426	733	6,577	2,144	1,972
Botswana		29	41	...	7	9
Egypt	1,874	2,210	2,340	458	498	243
Gabon	48	53	56	278	379	199
Ghana	127	115	117	206	260	210
Ivory Coast	185	82	75	288	405	313
Kenya	141	95	92	54	85	69
Liberia	113	70	68	128	101	116
Libya	509	.1	(z)	7,124	(z)	.1
Morocco	344	383	428	35	54	102
Nigeria	1,150	295	356	10,905	3,767	3,536
South Africa, Rep. of	2,464	1,281	1,690	3,321	1,399	1,589
Sudan	143	152	109	17	23	24
Tunisia	174	119	185	60	73	46
Zaire	155	104	125	361	321	384

133

U.S. Exports and Imports of Leading Commodities

Source: Office of Industry and Trade Information, U.S. Commerce Department (millions of dollars)

Commodity	Exports 1980	Exports 1987	Exports 1988	Imports 1980	Imports 1987	Imports 1988
Food and live animals	27,744	19,179	26,415	15,763	20,547	20,107
Cattle, except for breeding	...	...	...	228	417	595
Meat and preparations	1,293	1,768	2,430	2,346	2,786	2,738
Dairy products and eggs	255	385	496	318	442	402
Fish	915	1,588	2,177	2,612	4,788	5,327
Grains and preparations	18,079	8,058	12,281	...	...	...
Wheat, including flour	6,586	3,248	5,080	...	...	...
Rice	1,285	576	802	...	...	...
Grains and Animal feed	2,878	3,907	6,064	331	815	1,011
Vegetables and Fruit	...	2,956	3,488	1,188	4,476	4,662
Sugar	...	...	...	1,988	438	436
Coffee, crude	...	...	...	3,872	2,706	2,289
Cocoa or cacao beans	...	...	...	395	504	405
Tea	...	...	...	131	106	130
Beverages and tobacco	2,663	3,667	4,548	2,772	4,105	4,139
Alcoholic beverages	...	...	...	2,220	3,268	3,414
Tobacco, unmanufactured	2,390	1,091	1,252	422	588	448
Crude materials, inedible, except fuels	23,791	20,416	25,135	10,496	11,528	13,398
Hides and skins	694	1,450	1,639	88	82	102
Oilseeds, oil nuts, oil kernels	5,883	4,343	4,816	...	58	94
Synthetic rubber and rubber latex	695	761	858	...	...	...
Lumber and rough wood	2,675	3,007	4,086	2,134	3,341	3,179
Wood pulp and pulpwood	2,454	3,084	4,002	1,725	2,110	2,663
Textile fibers and wastes	2,864	1,631	1,975	242	438	524
Ores and metal scrap	4,518	3,018	4,279	3,696	2,446	3,264
Mineral fuels and related materials	7,982	7,713	8,186	9,058	44,220	41,088
Coal	4,523	6,740	8,054	...	...	...
Petroleum and products	2,833	3,922	3,679	73,771	41,529	38,175
Natural gas	...	...	...	5,155	2,504	2,577
Animal and vegetable oils and fats	1,946	981	945	533	568	849
Chemicals	20,740	26,381	32,300	8,583	16,213	19,876
Medicines and pharmaceuticals	1,932	3,782	3,941	508	1,456	1,859
Fertilizers, manufactured	2,265	2,259	2,497	1,104	795	1,021
Plastic materials and resins	3,884	5,493	7,277	...	...	...
Machinery and transport equip.	84,629	108,596	135,135	60,546	177,809	197,053
Machinery	55,790	69,637	88,432	31,904	99,433	117,281
Aircraft engines and parts	1,915	4,390	5,502	...	4,475	5,168
Auto engines and parts	1,688	2,406	3,812	...	...	...
Agricultural machinery	3,104	1,493	1,956	682	1,836	2,123
Tractors and parts	1,809	625	885	...	391	1,189
Office machines and computers	8,709	18,692	23,128	2,929	18,462	22,601
Transport equipment	28,839	38,959	46,703	28,642	57,024	79,772
Road motor vehicles and parts	14,590	20,879	8,312	24,134	61,598	71,346
Aircraft and parts except engines	12,816	16,903	20,004	1,885	4,475	5,168
Other manufactured goods	42,714	19,409	22,885	55,900	118,539	132,101
Tires and tubes	511	514	772	1,143	2,271	2,448
Wood and manufactures, exc. furniture	2,675	...	...	632	...	...
Paper and manufactures	2,831	3,180	313	3,587	7,310	8,336
Glassware and pottery	...	...	...	1,224	2,871	2,975
Diamonds, excl. industrial	...	...	...	2,252	3,423	4,306
Nonmetallic mineral manuf.	2,209	2,289	2,861	...	...	...
Metal manufactures	4,205	3,534	...	8,053	...	11,415
Pig iron and ferroalloys	3,123	...	2,173	...	...	...
Iron and steel-mill products	2,998	1,229	2,017	6,686	8,490	10,274
Nonferrous base metals	2,964	1,853	...	7,623	7,991	10,302
Textiles, other than clothing	3,632	677	709	2,493	6,511	6,373
Clothing	1,203	1,156	1,574	6,427	20,491	21,518
Footwear	...	...	...	2,808	7,237	8,041
Furniture	521	624	837	...	...	...
Professional, scientific, controlling instruments.	6,763	7,388	8,890	...	4,509	5,173
Printed matter	1,097	1,562	1,918	613	1,494	1,581
Clocks and watches	133	93	125	1,097	1,702	1,909
Toys, games, sporting goods	1,012	885	1,272	1,914	5,987	6,719
Artworks and antiques	...	...	...	2,672	1,925	2,044
Other transactions	8,496	20,381	27,483	7,183	12,672	12,672
Total	220,705	252,866	308,014	240,834	405,901	441,282

Value of U.S. Exports, Imports, and Merchandise Balance

Source: Office of Trade and Investment Analysis, U.S. Dept. of Commerce

(millions of dollars)

	Principal Census trade totals					Other Census totals		
Year	U.S. exports and reexports excluding military grant-aid	U.S. general imports f.a.s. transaction values[1]	U.S. merchandise balance f.a.s.[1]	U.S. general imports c.i.f.	U.S. balance exports f.a.s. imports c.i.f.	Military grant-aid shipments	Exports of domestic merchandise	Re-exports
1950	9,997	8,954	1,043	—	—	282	10,146	133
1955	14,298	11,566	2,732	—	—	1,256	15,426	128
1960	19,659	15,073	4,586	—	—	949	20,408	201
1965	26,742	21,520	5,222	—	—	779	27,178	343
1970	42,681	40,356	2,325	42,833	−152	565	42,612	634
1975	107,652	98,503	9,149	105,935	1,716	461	106,622	1,490
1980	220,626	244,871	−24,245	256,984	−36,358	156	216,668	4,115
1985	213,133	345,276[2]	−132,143	361,626	−148,493	13	206,925	6,221
1987	252,853[3]	405,910[2]	−153,035	424,082	−171,223	13	243,859	9,007
1988	320,378	441,282[2]	−120,913	459,925	−139,547	8	308,014	12,372

Note: Export values include both commercially-financed shipments and shipments under government-financed programs such as AID and PL-480. (1) Prior to 1974, imports are customs values, i.e. generally at prices in principal foreign markets. (2) In 1981 import value changes back to customs value. (3) Includes undocumented exports to Canada.

Total Exports and Exports Financed by Foreign Aid

(millions of dollars)

	1965	1970	1975	1980	1985	1986	1987	1988
Exports, total	27,530	43,224	107,592	220,783	213,146	217,304	252,866	320,385
Agricultural commodities	6,306	7,349	22,097	41,757	29,619	26,619	29,135	37,593
Nonagricultural commodities	20,445	35,310	85,094	178,948	183,527	190,686	223,731	282,793
Manufactured goods (domestic)	17,439	29,343	70,950	143,971	145,384	148,690	171,522	214,793
Military grant—aid	779	565	461	156	13	12	13	8
Export financed under P.L.-480	1,323	1,021	1,181	1,094	1,083	804	829	NA
Sales for foreign currency	899	276	—	—	—	—	—	NA
Donations, including disaster relief	253	255	257	329	270	108	106	NA
Long-term dollar credit sales	152	490	924	765	813	530	614	NA
AID expend. for U.S. goods for export	—	—	665	673	838	378	402	491

NA = Not available

Value of Principal Agricultural Exports

(millions of dollars)

Commodity	Avg. 1961-65	Avg. 1966-70	1965	1970	1975	1980	1985	1987	1988
Wheat and wheat products	1,268	1,197	1,214	1,144	5,292	6,660	3,898	3,279	5,124
Feed grains	841	1,082	1,162	1,099	5,492	9,759	6,023	3,850	5,912
Rice	178	311	244	314	858	1,288	665	576	805
Fodders and feeds	179	386	278	496	987	1,126	1,013	1,458	1,815
Oilseeds and products	774	1,182	1,029	1,642	NA	9,393	5,794	6,378	5,101
Cotton, raw	639	408	495	377	991	2,864	1,633	1,631	1,975

Retail Trade, 1970-1987

Source: U.S. Bureau of the Census

(in billions of dollars)

	1970	1975	1980	1985	1986	1987
Retail trade, total	375.2	588.1	957.3	1,367.3	1,437.5	1,510.6
Durable goods stores, total[1]	114.8	185.9	300.2	497.0	538.6	559.1
Automotive dealers	65.2	107.3	164.7	299.5	320.3	326.9
Motor vehicle, misc. automotive dealers	59.2	97.3	146.2	273.6	294.4	299.8
Motor vehicle dealers	57.2	89.5	137.7	258.7	277.7	280.3
Motor vehicle dealers, franchised	54.3	84.9	130.5	248.7	266.0	267.1
Auto and home supply stores	6.0	10.1	18.5	25.9	25.9	27.0
Building materials, hardware, garden supply, mobile home dealers[2]	18.1	27.3	50.8	70.4	75.8	78.0
Building materials, supply stores	11.3	17.9	35.0	49.1	54.1	57.9
Hardware stores	3.0	5.2	8.3	11.6	12.3	14.1
Furniture, home furnishings, equipment[1]	17.0	27.0	44.2	71.3	80.3	84.1
Furniture, home furnishings stores	10.4	16.5	26.3	37.6	41.9	44.2
Household appliance, radio, TV	5.6	8.2	14.0	29.2	33.3	34.5
Nondurable goods stores, total[1]	260.3	402.2	657.1	870.3	898.9	951.5
Apparel and accessory stores[1]	22.1	32.4	50.4	69.6	74.8	79.1
Men's, boys' clothing, furnishings	4.5	6.6	7.7	8.7	9.0	9.0
Women's clothing, specialty stores, furriers	8.2	12.4	18.7	26.9	29.7	31.2
Women's ready-to-wear stores	7.1	11.4	17.0	24.3	26.7	28.2
Family clothing stores	4.4	6.7	10.8	16.8	17.8	19.5
Shoe stores	4.5	5.8	10.5	12.7	13.4	14.6
Drug and proprietary stores	14.6	20.0	31.0	47.9	51.6	56.0
Eating and drinking places	30.5	51.1	90.1	125.1	135.3	147.6
Eating places	25.5	44.4	80.4	114.2	123.6	135.1
Food stores	90.0	138.7	220.2	288.6	301.8	314.3
Grocery stores	82.6	129.1	205.6	271.9	284.1	296.1
Gasoline service stations	28.9	47.6	94.1	109.6	97.3	103.2
General merchandise group stores	49.1	73.7	106.6	155.9	165.1	175.9
Department stores[2]	37.4	57.5	86.2	129.4	137.2	146.5
Variety stores	6.1	7.9	7.8	9.1	8.3	8.4
Misc. gen. merchandise group stores[3]	5.7	8.3	12.6	17.3	19.6	20.9
Liquor stores	8.4	11.9	16.9	19.3	19.6	19.5
Non-store retailers	9.1	13.4	22.8	25.0	25.7	26.5
Mail-order houses (department store merchandise)	1.8	2.8	4.3	4.2	3.7	3.6

(1) Includes kinds of business, not shown separately. (2) Excludes leased departments. (3) Includes catalog showroom stores.

U.S. Shopping Centers, by State

Source: *Shopping Center World*, Feb. 1988

	Number	Gross leasable area (mil. sq. ft.)	Retail sales (mil. dol.)	% Change, 1986-1987 Number	% Change, 1986-1987 Gross leasable area	% Change, 1986-1987 Retail sales
U.S. . .	30,641	3,723.0	602,294	7.5	5.7	8.2
North East. . .	1,814	196.5	31,595	6.1	4.8	6.6
ME . .	149	13.8	2,286	5.7	.9	3.6
NH . .	130	13.1	2,153	10.2	4.0	6.8
VT . .	82	5.6	934	3.8	1.9	3.8
MA . .	750	84.4	13,535	5.3	3.1	5.0
RI . . .	160	14.0	2,250	8.1	5.3	7.4
CT . .	543	65.6	10,436	6.1	8.2	9.5
Mid-Atlantic. .	3,008	431.4	68,186	6.5	5.1	7.2
NY . .	1,228	171.6	27,314	4.6	2.6	5.2
NJ . .	677	101.5	16,198	6.8	8.9	11.0
PA . .	1,103	158.3	24,674	8.5	5.5	7.0
East North Central.	4,309	568.3	89,793	8.2	4.7	6.8
OH . .	1,158	167.9	26,215	6.6	3.5	5.3
IN . . .	689	85.0	13,565	4.7	4.2	6.5
IL . . .	1,271	159.9	25,382	12.5	6.4	8.6
MI. . .	730	100.3	15,788	6.6	4.4	6.1
WI. . .	461	55.1	8,842	9.2	4.9	8.2
West North Central.	1,960	249.7	39,829	7.0	4.2	6.9
MN . .	366	51.8	8,303	6.7	3.0	6.3
IA . . .	229	30.6	4,835	7.0	3.4	6.4
MO . .	698	87.3	13,889	7.2	5.1	7.6
ND . .	62	8.2	1,297	6.9	3.1	6.2
SD . .	36	5.0	799	12.5	5.7	9.7
NE . .	176	22.5	3,582	8.6	4.4	7.4
KS . .	393	44.3	7,125	5.7	4.2	6.5
South Atlantic	6,689	805.4	131,814	10.6	8.7	11.5
DE . .	89	15.2	2,415	4.7	3.1	7.2
MD . .	624	90.8	14,453	7.8	7.7	9.7
DC . .	51	6.6	1,066	4.1	—	2.9
VA . .	835	110.7	17,762	9.3	8.5	10.5
WV . .	125	16.2	2,548	6.8	9.5	10.9
NC . .	976	103.5	16,935	15.6	11.8	14.5
SC . .	555	56.3	9,258	8.2	7.1	10.1
GA . .	1,065	107.7	17,903	10.3	8.7	11.6
FL . .	2,369	298.4	49,474	11.2	8.9	12.2
East South Central.	2,154	232.4	37,498	6.7	6.3	8.3
KY . .	501	54.3	8,712	6.6	5.2	7.3
TN . .	787	85.5	13,795	9.2	9.5	11.2
AL . .	524	60.4	9,671	5.4	5.0	6.8
MS . .	342	32.2	5,320	3.6	2.7	5.4
West South Central.	4,014	452.3	74,466	4.3	3.3	6.1
AR . .	311	29.1	4,730	2.6	1.7	3.8
LA . .	590	71.3	11,530	2.6	2.4	4.8
OK . .	503	51.1	8,355	3.1	1.8	4.6
TX . .	2,610	300.8	49,851	5.2	3.9	6.9
Mountain . . .	2,158	248.1	40,984	7.7	4.9	8.3
MT . .	74	.75	1,231	4.2	.2	3.3
ID . . .	101	12.7	2,046	5.2	1.7	5.1
WY . .	43	5.4	858	4.9	—	3.0
CO . .	616	77.8	12,660	5.3	4.3	7.0
NM . .	228	22.4	3,709	4.6	3.7	6.4
AZ . .	741	77.3	13,102	9.3	5.6	9.8
UT . .	153	23.9	3,851	10.1	4.3	8.2
NV . .	202	21.1	3,528	15.4	12.2	15.7
Pacific . . .	4,535	538.9	88,130	7.1	6.0	8.7
WA . .	500	63.8	10,172	8.9	8.0	10.2
OR . .	306	34.6	5,548	5.5	5.8	7.4
CA . .	3,561	421.8	69,283	7.1	5.8	8.6
AK . .	45	5.9	1,003	7.1	9.0	13.0
HI . . .	123	12.7	2,124	5.1	3.1	6.5

— Represents zero.

Top 50 U.S. Industrial Exporters

Source: *FORTUNE Magazine*, July 17, 1989

Rank 1988	1987	Company	Export sales $ Millions	Export sales % change 1987-88	Exports as % of Sales
1	1	General Motors	9,392.0	7.6	7.8
2	2	Ford Motor	8,822.0	15.9	9.5
3	3	Boeing	7,849.0	24.9	46.3
4	4	General Electric	5,744.0	19.0	11.6
5	5	IBM	4,951.0	24.0	8.3
6	8	Chrysler	4,343.9	42.3	12.2
7	6	E.I. du Pont de Nemours	4,196.0	19.0	12.9
8	7	McDonnell Douglas	3,471.0	7.0	23.0
9	10	Caterpillar	2,930.0	33.8	28.1
10	11	United Technologies	2,848.1	37.5	15.8
11	9	Eastman Kodak	2,301.0	26.0	13.5
12	12	Digital Equipment	2,083.0	6.2	18.2
13	14	Hewlett-Packard	2,064.0	29.3	21.0
14	18	Unisys	2,012.9	68.0	20.3
15	13	Philip Morris	1,863.0	9.6	7.2
16	17	Motorola	1,742.0	33.7	21.1
17	16	Occident Petroleum	1,684.0	28.0	8.7
18	20	General Dynamics	1,597.1	0.7	16.7
19	15	Allied-Signal	1,464.0	3.4	12.3
20	19	Weyerhaeuser	1,398.0	20.6	14.0
21	23	Union Carbide	1,388.0	30.4	16.7
22	24	Raytheon	1,307.0	24.8	16.0
23	27	Textron	1,127.0	26.5	15.8
24	22	Westinghouse Electric	1,115.0	1.7	8.9
25	26	Dow Chemical	1,109.0	13.4	6.6
26	25	Archer Daniels Midland	1,087.7	10.8	16.0
27	28	Monsanto	1,083.0	22.1	13.1
28	29	International Paper	1,000.0	28.7	10.5
29	32	Hoechst Celanese	967.0	43.9	17.0
30	21	Exxon	937.0	(17.0)	1.2
31	35	Intel	925.6	72.2	32.2
32	31	Minnesota Mining & Mfg.	836.0	24.2	7.9
33	—	Bayer USA	700.0	16.7	14.8
34	41	Lockheed	686.0	21.6	6.4
35	44	Phillips Petroleum	675.0	21.6	6.0
36	—	Warner Communications	673.5	15.6	16.0
37	33	FMC	647.3	5.6	19.7
38	47	Deere	622.0	61.6	11.6
39	38	Rockwell Int'l	620.0	23.3	5.2
40	37	Merck	619.4	25.9	10.4
41	—	Compaq Computer	611.7	101.9	29.6
42	34	Honeywell	610.0	5.0	8.5
43	—	Aluminum Co. of America	590.6	75.1	6.0
44	—	North American Philips	588.1	26.4	10.8
45	39	Dresser Industries	584.6	23.0	14.8
46	38	Amoco	578.0	17.5	2.7
47	48	Combustion Engineering	560.0	46.0	16.1
48	—	Abbott Laboratories	547.0	36.1	11.1
49	49	Ethyl	542.7	47.6	20.0
50	—	Baxter International	521.0	44.3	7.6
		Total	$96,615.3		

Major Merchant Fleets of the World

Source: Maritime Administration, U.S. Commerce Department

Fleets of oceangoing steam and motor ships totalling 1 million gross tons and over as of Jan. 1, 1989. Excludes ships operating exclusively on the Great Lakes and inland waterways and special types such as channel ships, icebreakers, cable ships, etc., and merchant ships owned by any military force. Gross tonnage is a volume measurement; each cargo gross ton represents 100 cubic ft. of enclosed space. Deadweight tonnage is the carrying capacity of a ship in long tons (2,240 lbs.). Tonnage figures may not add, due to rounding.

(tonnage in thousands)

	Total			Type of Vessel Freighters			Bulk Carriers			Tankers		
	Number	Gross Tons	Dwt. Tons	Number	Gross Tons	Dwt. Tons	Number	Cross Tons	Dwt. Tons	Number	Gross Tons	Dwt. Tons
All Countries	23,468	371,357	601,919	12,518	95,932	118,077	5,332	130,225	227,515	5,250	140,833	254,796
United States²	675	16,807	25,576	381	6,764	7,247	26	740	1,270	247	9,005	16,708
Privately owned³	424	13,641	21,601	178	4,474	4,599	26	740	1,270	215	8,322	15,686
Government Owned	251	3,166	3,975	203	2,290	2,827	—	—	—	32	682	1,022
Reserve fleet	185	2,254	2,910	148	1,491	1,890	—	—	—	27	634	941
Other⁴	66	911	1,064	55	800	937	—	—	—	5	49	81
Argentina	144	1,814	2,849	75	642	896	19	532	920	50	641	1,033
Australia	73	2,382	3,675	18	204	233	33	1,201	2,028	22	978	1,414
Belgium	61	1,865	3,108	21	293	340	22	1,141	2,103	17	418	650
Brazil	331	6,446	10,590	134	990	1,280	99	3,112	5,311	95	2,339	3,995
British Colonies	545	14,029	24,180	246	1,730	2,263	183	5,911	10,235	110	6,362	11,674
*Bulgaria	116	1,295	1,896	52	326	386	46	667	1,038	15	291	461
*China (Mainland)	1,235	12,192	18,437	833	5,906	8,241	224	4,423	7,429	166	1,736	2,700
Cyprus	1,140	17,998	31,832	587	3,576	5,364	423	9,033	15,938	125	5,354	10,516
Denmark (Dis)	151	3,759	5,753	97	1,453	1,458	6	225	405	48	2,082	3,890
France	158	3,728	6,032	76	983	1,137	17	474	768	59	2,222	4,107
Germany (Fed Rep)	390	3,404	4,299	321	2,604	3,123	13	318	479	50	417	663
German Dem. Rep.	149	1,310	1,681	127	917	1,092	17	324	512	4	50	75
Greece	974	20,553	37,130	266	2,119	3,130	470	10,320	18,539	205	7,871	15,358
India	312	6,124	10,053	122	1,214	1,770	114	2,916	4,927	70	1,959	3,329
Indonesia	336	1,487	2,228	223	707	1,023	12	138	194	92	606	995
Iran	121	3,997	7,238	37	399	534	51	1,071	1,767	33	2,527	4,938
Isle of Man	94	1,999	3,568	22	195	252	14	464	833	58	1,341	2,483
Italy	500	6,730	10,765	194	1,118	1,369	69	2,407	4,242	223	2,903	5,036
Japan	1,118	26,070	39,699	473	5,226	4,278	316	10,985	19,703	314	9,713	15,664
Korea (Rep. of)	434	7,064	11,382	221	1,595	1,818	148	4,438	7,858	65	1,031	1,707
Kuwait	44	1,095	1,572	27	504	677	—	—	—	17	591	895
Liberia	1,405	48,435	89,200	285	3,485	4,157	505	14,896	27,900	602	29,711	57,065
Malaysia	164	1,554	2,229	103	527	737	20	402	672	41	625	820
Malta	240	2,774	4,675	123	609	938	63	1,097	1,836	52	1,049	1,895
Mexico	79	1,197	1,828	19	124	163	14	277	411	46	797	1,254
Nassau Bahamas	430	9,875	16,547	167	1,115	1,476	104	2,697	4,550	133	5,570	10,415
Netherlands	367	2,851	3,862	283	1,673	2,168	17	370	602	61	694	1,073
Norway	108	1,139	1,883	59	131	220	10	113	182	31	862	1,472
Norway (NIS)	366	10,922	19,335	85	680	846	96	3,254	6,157	176	6,774	12,289
Panama	3,304	46,371	72,977	1,742	14,561	17,583	895	18,761	32,191	628	12,321	22,974
Philippines	562	8,875	14,770	239	1,420	1,811	272	7,026	12,230	38	366	696
Poland	261	3,187	4,375	156	1,371	1,514	95	1,649	2,609	7	146	242
*Romania	299	3,448	5,263	219	1,212	1,561	68	1,668	2,706	12	569	997
Saudi Arabia	96	2,131	3,641	42	475	657	4	202	358	47	1,442	2,617
Singapore	417	7,341	11,752	218	2,345	2,941	72	2,090	3,650	127	2,907	5,161
Spain	346	3,462	6,380	200	530	812	57	1,080	1,952	87	1,832	3,614
Sweden	156	1,557	1,744	80	989	940	14	183	281	59	355	510
Taiwan	221	4,919	7,238	150	2,327	2,701	55	2,051	3,585	15	539	952
Turkey	342	2,810	4,774	228	786	1,231	57	1,240	2,152	52	760	1,383
United Kingdom	242	4,505	5,766	107	1,668	1,644	33	809	1,390	88	1,728	2,654
*U.S.S.R.	2,434	19,122	25,481	1,716	9,974	11,747	240	4,046	6,386	444	4,807	7,270
Yugoslavia	264	3,409	5,374	167	1,403	1,987	82	1,678	2,859	12	314	525

(1) Includes Combination Passenger & Cargo Ships; (2) Excludes 226 non-merchant type and/or Navy-owned vessels that are currently in the Nat. Reserve Fleet; (3) Comprised of vessels under general agency agreement, bareboat charter, and in the custody of the Dept. of Defense, State & Interior. *Source material limited.

Commerce at Principal U.S. Ports

Source: Corps of Engineers, Department of the Army (by tonnage, 1987)

	Total	Foreign		Total	Foreign
New Orleans, La.	167,917,822	65,764,746	St. Louis, Metro., Mo.	27,571,883	0
New York, N.Y.	154,536,680	52,041,272	Portland, Ore.	26,812,547	15,584,174
Houston, Tex.	112,546,187	57,503,865	Richmond, Cal.	21,431,418	4,805,610
Valdez-Harbor, Ak.	106,867,415	10,030	Chicago, Il.	20,705,271	2,595,585
Baton Rouge, La.	73,401,202	22,809,806	Port Arthur, Tex.	20,615,945	12,716,555
Corpus Christi, Tex.	53,539,806	31,373,836	Boston, Ma., Port of	19,829,871	10,922,416
Long Beach, Calif.	45,898,541	22,520,138	Newport News, Va.	19,264,649	16,738,640
Tampa Harbor, Fla.	44,303,389	19,163,412	Huntington, WVa.	18,722,337	0
Los Angeles, Calif.	40,460,556	19,163,211	Seattle, Wa.	18,552,750	11,090,772
Norfolk Harbor, Va.	39,993,313	29,990,116	Paulsboro, NJ.	17,936,169	11,134,367
Baltimore Hrbr., Md.	37,488,624	24,799,814	Tacoma Hrbr., Wa.	17,129,788	11,622,123
Philadelphia, Pa.	37,336,977	23,259,377	Toledo Harbor, Oh.	16,211,727	7,833,809
Texas City, Tex.	37,233,420	18,797,162	Lorain Harbor, Oh.	14,372,412	54,085
Duluth-Supr., Minn.	36,462,867	4,804,286	Detroit, Mi.	14,129,844	2,030,397
Mobile, Ala.	32,384,042	15,186,783	Port Everglades, Fla.	14,045,487	4,350,001
Lake Charles, La.	31,730,771	19,061,638	Freeport, Tex.	13,980,280	5,498,156
Beaumont, Tex.	29,758,759	9,952,545	Cleveland, Oh.	13,914,047	2,658,445
Pittsburgh, Pa.	28,840,424	0	Anacortes, Wa.	13,687,075	2,743,665
Marcus Hook, Pa.	28,154,337	16,575,797	Jacksonville, Fla.	13,483,675	6,052,491
Pascagoula, Miss.	27,824,815	17,469,569	San Juan, P.R.	13,452,284	5,262,131

Commerce on U.S. Inland Waterways

Source: Corps of Engineers, Department of the Army, 1987

Mississippi River System and Gulf Intracoastal Waterway

Waterway	Tons
Mississippi River, Minneapolis to the Gulf	425,004,518
Mississippi River, Minneapolis to St. Louis	81,617,560
Mississippi River, St. Louis to Cairo	104,491,828
Mississippi River, Cairo to Baton Rouge	167,759,000
Mississippi River, Baton Rouge to New Orleans. .	289,380,806
Mississippi River, New Orleans to Gulf	255,972,635
Gulf Intracoastal Waterway	107,032,420
Mississippi River System.	583,398,214

Ton-Mileage of Freight Carried on Inland Waterways

System	Ton-miles
Atlantic Coast Waterways	25,875,650
Gulf Coast Waterways	37,900,545
Pacific Coast Waterways	22,840,744
Mississippi River System, including Ohio River and Tributaries.	251,577,202
Great Lakes System, U.S. Commerce only	72,542,831
Total:	**410,736,972**

Important Waterways and Canals

The **St. Lawrence & Great Lakes Waterway**, the largest inland navigation system on the continent, extends from the Atlantic Ocean to Duluth at the western end of Lake Superior, a distance of 2,342 miles. With the deepening of channels and locks to 27 ft., ocean carriers are able to penetrate to ports in the Canadian interior and the American midwest.

The major canals are those of the St. Lawrence Great Lakes waterway — the 3 new canals of the St. Lawrence Seaway, with their 7 locks, providing navigation for vessels of 26-foot draught from Montreal to Lake Ontario; the Welland Ship Canal by-passing the Niagara River between Lake Ontario and Lake Erie with its 8 locks, and the Sault Ste. Marie Canal and lock between Lake Huron and Lake Superior. These 16 locks overcome a drop of 580 ft. from the head of the lakes to Montreal. From Montreal to Lake Ontario the former bottleneck of narrow, shallow canals and of slow passage through 22 locks has been overcome, giving faster and safer movement for larger vessels. The new locks and linking channels now accommodate all but the largest ocean-going vessels and the upper St. Lawrence and Great Lakes are open to 80% of the world's saltwater fleet.

Subsidiary Canadian canals or branches include the St. Peters Canal between Bras d'Or Lakes and the Atlantic Ocean in Nova Scotia; the St. Ours and Chambly Canals on the Richelieu River, Quebec; the Ste. Anne and Carillon Canals on the Ottawa River; the Rideau Canal between the Ottawa River and Lake Ontario, the Trent and Murrary Canals between Lake Ontario and Georgian Bay in Ontario and the St. Andrew's Canal on the Red River. The commercial value of these canals is not great but they are maintained to control water levels and permit the passage of small vessels and pleasure craft. The Canso Canal, completed 1957, permits shipping to pass through the causeway connecting Cape Breton Island with the Nova Scotia mainland.

The **Welland Canal** overcomes the 326-ft. drop of Niagara Falls and the rapids of the Niagara River. It has 8 locks, each 859 ft. long, 80 ft. wide and 30 ft. deep. Regulations permit ships of 730-ft. length and 75-ft. beam to transit.

Shortest Navigable Distances Between Ports

Source: Distances Between Ports. (Pub. 151 5th Edition 1985) Defense Mapping Agency Hydrographic/Topographic Center

Distances shown are in nautical miles (1,852 meters or about 6,076.115 feet). To get statute miles, multiply by 1.15.

TO	FROM New York	Montreal	Colon[1]
Algiers, Algeria	3,600	3,592	4,737
Amsterdam, Netherlands	3,411	3,318	4,829
Baltimore, Md.	410	1,820	1,901
Barcelona, Spain	3,721	3,695	4,840
Boston, Mass.	378	1,308	2,157
Buenos Aires, Argentina	5,845	6,440	5,344
Cape Town, S. Africa[2]	6,789	7,115	6,425
Cherbourg, France	3,127	3,034	4,545
Cobh, Ireland	2,878	2,780	4,320
Copenhagen, Denmark	3,934	3,841	5,352
Dakar, Senegal	3,336	3,562	3,689
Galveston, Tex.	1,862	3,224	1,485
Gibraltar[3]	3,210	3,184	4,329
Glasgow, Scotland	3,324	3,231	4,742
Halifax, N.S.	600	958	2,295
Hamburg, W. Germany	3,636	3,543	5,054
Hamilton, Bermuda	697	1,621	1,659
Havana, Cuba	1,199	2,473	990
Helsinki, Finland	4,484	4,391	5,902
Istanbul, Turkey	5,006	4,980	6,125
Kingston, Jamaica	1,472	2,690	555
Lagos, Nigeria	4,870	5,130	5,033
Lisbon, Portugal	2,980	2,941	4,155
Marseille, France	3,896	3,870	5,015
Montreal, Quebec	1,516		3,190
Naples, Italy	4,185	4,159	5,304
Nassau, Bahamas	961	2,274	1,165
New Orleans, La.	1,707	3,069	1,403
New York, N.Y.		1,516	1,974
Norfolk, Va.	287	1,700	1,779
Oslo, Norway	3,888	3,795	5,306
Piraeus, Greece	4,687	4,661	5,806
Port Said, Egypt	5,119	5,093	6,238
Rio de Janeiro, Brazil	4,743	5,342	4,246
St. John's, Nfld.	1,097	1,038	2,697
San Juan, Puerto Rico	1,399	2,445	992
Southampton, England	3,156	3,063	4,514

TO	FROM San. Fran.	Vancouver	Panama[1]
Acapulco, Mexico	1,833	2,612	1,426
Anchorage, Alas.	1,872	1,347	5,127
Bombay, India	9,791	9,513	9,248
Calcutta, India	9,006	8,728	10,929
Colon, Panama[1]	3,290	4,065	44
Jakarta, Indonesia	7,642	7,413	10,570
Haiphong, Vietnam	6,657	6,358	9,806
Hong Kong	6,044	5,756	9,195
Honolulu, Hawaii	2,091	2,423	4,685
Los Angeles, Cal.	369	1,162	2,913
Manila, Philippines	6,221	5,946	9,347
Melbourne, Australia	6,970	7,342	7,928
Pusan, S. Korea	4,914	4,623	8,074
Ho Chi Min City, Vietnam	6,878	6,606	10,017
San Francisco, Cal.		812	3,245
Seattle, Wash.	796	126	4,020
Shanghai, China	5,398	5,110	8,566
Singapore	7,353	7,078	10,495
Suva, Fiji	4,749	5,183	6,325
Valparaiso, Chile	5,140	5,915	2,616
Vancouver, B.C.	812		4,032
Vladivostok, USSR	4,563	4,262	7,739
Yokohama, Japan	4,536	4,262	7,682

TO	FROM Port Said	Cape Town[2]	Singapore
Bombay, India	3,046	4,599	2,441
Calcutta, India	4,691	5,489	1,649
Dar es Salaam, Tanzania	3,238	2,369	4,042
Jakarta, Indonesia	5,293	5,184	526
Hong Kong	6,474	7,071	1,454
Kuwait	3,306	5,169	3,845
Manila, Philippines	6,355	6,952	1,330
Melbourne, Australia	7,837	6,104	3,842
Ho Chi Min City, Vietnam	5,660	6,263	649
Singapore	5,014	5,611	
Yokohama, Japan	7,906	8,503	2,889

(1) Colon on the Atlantic is 44 nautical miles from Panama (port) on the Pacific. (2) Cape Town is 35 nautical miles northwest of the Cape of Good Hope. (3) Gibraltar (port) is 24 nautical miles east of the Strait of Gibraltar.

Notable Ocean Passages by Ships

Compiled by N.R.P. Bonsor

Sailing Vessels

Date	Ship	From	To	Nautical miles	Time D. H. M	Speed (knots)
1846	Yorkshire	Liverpool	New York	3150	16. 0. 0	8.46†
1853	Northern Light	San Francisco	Boston	—	76. 6. 0	—
1854	James Baines	Boston Light	Light Rock	—	12. 6. 0	—
1854	Flying Cloud	New York	San Francisco	15091	89. 0. 0	7.07†
1868-9	Thermopylae	Liverpool	Melbourne	—	63.18.15	—
—	Red Jacket	New York	Liverpool	3150	13. 1.25	10.05†
—	Starr King	50 S. Lat	Golden Gate	—	36. 0. 0	—
—	Golden Fleece	Equator	San Francisco	—	12.12. 0	—
1905	Atlantic	Sandy Hook	England	3013	12. 4. 0	10.32

Atlantic Crossing by Passenger Steamships

Date	Ship		From	To	Nautical miles	Time D. H. M	Speed (knots)
1819 (5/22 - 6/20)	Savannah (a)	US	Savannah	Liverpool	—	29. 4. 0	—
1838 (5/7 - 5/22)	Great Western (b)	Br	New York	Avonmouth	3218	14.15.59	9.14
1840 (8/4 - 8/14)	Britannia (b)	Br	Halifax	Liverpool	2610	9.21.44	10.98†
1854 (6/28 - 7/7)	Baltic	US	Liverpool	New York	3037	9.16.52	13.04
1856 (8/6 - 8/15)	Persia	Br	Sandy Hook	Liverpool	3046	8.23.19	14.15†
1876 (12/16-12/24)	Britannic	Br	Sandy Hook	Queenstown	2882	7.12.41	15.94
1895 (5/18 - 5/24)	Lucania	Br	Sandy Hook	Queenstown	2897	5.11.40	22.00
1898 (3/30 - 4/5)	Kaiser Wilhelm der Grosse	Ger	Needles	Sandy Hook	3120	5.20. 0	22.29
1901 (7/10 - 7/17)	Deutschland	Ger	Sandy Hook	Eddystone	3082	5.11. 5	23.51
1907 (10/6 - 10/10)	Lusitania	Br	Queenstown	Sandy Hook	2780	4.19.52	23.99
1924 (8/20 - 8/25)	Mauretania	Br	Ambrose	Cherbourg	3198	5. 1.49	26.25
1929 (7/17 - 7/22)	Bremen*	Ger	Cherbourg	Ambrose	3164	4.17.42	27.83
1933 (6/27 - 7/2)	Europa	Ger	Cherbourg	Ambrose	3149	4.16.48	27.92
1933 (8/11 - 8/16)	Rex	It	Gibraltar	Ambrose	3181	4.13.58	28.92
1935 (5/30 - 6/3)	Normandie*	Fr	Bishop Rock	Ambrose	2971	4. 3. 2	29.98
1938 (8/10 - 8/14)	Queen Mary	Br	Ambrose	Bishop Rock	2938	3.20.42	31.69
1952 (7/11 - 7/15)	United States	US	Bishop Rock	Ambrose	2906	3.12.12	34.51
1952 (7/3 - 7/7)	United States* (e)	US	Ambrose	Bishop Rock	2942	3.10.40	35.59

Other Ocean Passages

Date	Ship	From	To	Nautical miles	Time D. H. M	Speed (knots)
1928 (June)	USS Lexington	San Pedro	Honolulu	2226	3. 0.36	30.66
1944 (Jul-Sep)	St. Roch (c) (Can)	Halifax	Vancouver	7295	86. 0. 0	—
1945 (7/16-7/19)	USS Indianapolis (d)	San Francisco	Oahu, Hawaii	2091	3. 2.20	28.07
1945 (11/26)	USS Lake Champlain	Gibraltar	Newport News	3360	4. 8.51	32.04
1950 (Jul-Aug)	USS Boxer	Japan	San Francisco	5000	7.18.36	26.80†
1951 (6/1-6/9)	USS Philippine Sea	Yokohama	Alameda	5000	7.13. 0	27.62†
1958 (2/25-3/4)	USS Skate (f)	Nantucket	Portland, Eng	3161	8.11. 0	15.57
1958 (3/23-3/29)	USS Skate (f)	Lizard, Eng	Nantucket	—	7. 5. 0	—
1958 (7/23-8/7)	USS Nautilus (g)	Pearl Harbor	Iceland (via N. Pole)	—	15. 0. 0	—
1960 (2/16-5/10)	USS Triton (h)	New London	Rehoboth, Del	41500	84. 0. 0	20.59†
1960 (8/15-8/20)	USS Seadragon (i)	Baffin Bay	NW Passage, Pac	850	6. 0. 0	—
1962 (10/30-11/11)	African Comet* (U.S.)	New York	Cape Town	6786	12.16.22	22.03
1973 (8/20)	Sea-Land Exchange (k) (U.S.)	Bishop Rock	Ambrose	2912	3.11.24	34.92
1973 (8/24)	Sea-Land Trade (U.S.)	Kobe	Race Rock, BC	4126	5. 6. 0	32.75

† The time taken and/or distance covered is approximate and so, therefore, is the average speed.

* Maiden voyage. (a) The Savannah, a fully rigged sailing vessel with steam auxiliary (over 300 tons, 98.5 ft. long, beam 25.8 ft., depth 12.9 ft.) was launched in the East River in 1818. It was the first ship to use steam in crossing any ocean. It was supplied with engines and detachable iron paddle wheels. On its famous voyage it used steam 105 hours. (b) First Cunard liner. (c) First ship to complete NW Passage in one season. (d) Carried Hiroshima atomic bomb in World War II. (e) Set world speed record; average speed eastbound on maiden voyage 35.59 knots (about 41 m.p.h.). (f) First atomic submarine to cross Atlantic both ways submerged. (g) World's first atomic submarine also first to make undersea voyage under polar ice cap, 1,830 mi. from Point Barrow, Alaska, to Atlantic Ocean, Aug. 1-4, 1958, reaching North Pole Aug. 3. Second undersea transit of the North Pole made by submarine USS Skate Aug. 11, 1958, during trip from New London, Conn., and return. (h) World's largest submarine. Nuclear-powered Triton was submerged during nearly all its voyage around the globe. It duplicated the route of Ferdinand Magellan's circuit (1519-1522) 30,708 mi., starting from St. Paul Rocks off the NE coast of Brazil, Feb. 24-Apr. 25, 1960, then sailed to Cadiz, Spain, before returning home. (i) First underwater transit of Northwest Passage. (k) Fastest freighter crossing of Atlantic.

Recreational Vehicles, 1970-1987

Source: Recreation Vehicle Industry Assn., Reston, Va.

(numbers in thousands)

	Total	Motorized homes	Travel trailers	Folding camping trailers	Truck campers
1970	380.3	30.3	138.0	116.1	95.9
1973	528.8	129.0	212.3	97.7	89.8
1974	295.8	68.9	126.3	55.2	45.4
1975	339.6	96.6	150.6	48.1	44.3
1976	541.1	256.1	189.7	53.3	42.0
1977	533.9	280.2	167.9	53.9	31.9
1978	526.3	293.6	159.8	48.2	24.7
1979	307.7	172.6	90.2	31.1	13.8
1980	181.4	99.9	52.0	24.5	5.0
1981	239.1	135.2	63.8	35.0	5.1
1982	258.0	152.5	65.5	34.3	5.7
1983	358.0	223.7	90.0	37.5	6.8
1984	398.2	257.3	92.4	40.9	7.6
1985	359.2	233.5	82.9	35.9	6.9
1986	379.5	249.6	86.0	36.5	7.4
1987	400.2	255.7	92.8	41.6	10.1

Passenger Transit Industry, 1970-1987

Source: American Public Transit Assn., Washington, D.C.

		1970	1975	1980	1981	1982	1983	1984	1985	1986[P]	1987[P]
Operating systems	Number	1,079	947	1,044	1,035	1,036	1,036	4,973	4,973	5,019	5,048
Motorbus systems[1]	Number	1,075	941	1,040	1,030	1,031	1,031	2,604	2,632	2,654	2,672
Publicly owned systems[1]	Number	144	333	576	578	581	599	(NA)	(NA)	(NA)	(NA)
Passenger vehicles owned[2]	Number	61,428	62,261	71,018	72,098	73,838	73,813	95,603	88,691	91,219	91,115
Motorbuses[2]	Number	49,700	50,811	59,411	60,393	62,114	62,093	63,497	57,285	58,000	57,687
Heavy rail[2]	Number	9,286	9,556	9,641	9,749	9,815	9,891	9,083	9,326	10,386	10,168
Other electric[2,3]	Number	2,442	1,894	1,966	1,956	1,909	1,829	1,527	1,623	1,519	1,581
Suburban rail	Number	(NA)	(NA)	(NA)	(NA)	(NA)	(NA)	4,075	4,035	4,440	4,656
All other	Number	(NA)	(NA)	(NA)	(NA)	(NA)	(NA)	17,421	16,422	16,873	17,023
Total revenue	Mil. dol	(NA)	3,451	6,510	7,366	8,044	8,526	11,623	12,195	13,147	13,968
Passenger revenue	Mil. dol	1,639	1,861	2,557	2,701	3,077	3,172	4,448	4,575	5,011	5,156
Other operating revenue[4]	Mil. dol	68	183	248	344	380	333	780	702	743	771
Operating assistance	Mil. dol	(NA)	1,408	3,705	4,321	4,587	5,023	6,395	6,918	7,393	8.041
Federal	Mil. dol	(NA)	302	1,094	1,095	1,005	827	996	940	912	894
State and local	Mil. dol	(NA)	1,106	2,611	3,226	3,582	4,195	5,399	5,978	6,481	7,147
Total expense	Mil. dol	1,996	3,752	6,711	7,623	8,314	8,736	12,957	14,077	15,080	15,997
Operating expense	Mil. dol	(NA)	3,537	6,246	7,024	7,553	7,956	11,574	12,381	13,353	13,967
Transportation	Mil. dol	(NA)	1,877	3,248	3,596	3,882	3,931	5,142	5,655	6,106	6,019
Maintenance	Mil. dol	(NA)	814	1,774	1,946	2,168	2,392	3,062	3,672	3,965	4,310
Administration	Mil. dol	(NA)	846	1,224	1,482	1,503	1,634	3,370	3,054	3,282	3,638
Reconciling expense	Mil. dol	(NA)	215	464	597	761	780	1,383	1,696	1,727	2,030
Capital expenditure, Federal	Mil. dol	(NA)	1,287	2,787	2,946	2,544	3,162	2,876	2,510	3,137	2,476
Vehicle-miles operated	Million	1,884	1,989	2,094	2,134	2,129	2,117	2,749	2,791	2,890	2,962
Motorbus	Million	1,409	1,526	1,677	1,685	1,669	1,678	1,845	1,863	1,896	1,927
Heavy rail	Million	407	423	385	420	429	408	436	451	476	490
Other electric[3]	Million	68	40	32	29	31	31	32	33	33	34
Suburban rail	Million	(NA)	(NA)	(NA)	(NA)	(NA)	(NA)	168	183	186	189
All other	Million	(NA)	(NA)	(NA)	(NA)	(NA)	(NA)	268	261	299	322
Passengers carried[5]	Million	7,361	6,988	8,249	7,978	7,766	7,903	8,851	8,659	8,801	8,340
Motorbus[5]	Million	5,034	5,084	5,837	5,594	5,324	5,422	5,908	5,675	5,748	5,207
Heavy rail[3,5]	Million	1,881	1,673	2,108	2,094	2,115	2,167	2,231	2,290	2,333	2,402
Other electric[3]	Million	446	231	304	290	316	314	329	303	304	300
Suburban rail	Million	(NA)	(NA)	(NA)	(NA)	(NA)	(NA)	267	275	303	311
All other	Million	(NA)	(NA)	(NA)	(NA)	(NA)	(NA)	116	116	113	113
Avg. revenue per passenger	Cents	22.4	26.7	31.0	33.9	39.7	40.2	50.3	52.8	56.9	61.8
Employees, number (avg.)	1,000	138	160	187	192	194	195	263	270	276	275
Payroll, employee	Mil. dol	1,274	2,236	3,281	3,494	3,731	3,921	5,488	5,843	6,228	6,540

NA = Not available; P = preliminary. (1) Includes systems with combined services including motorbuses, heavy rail, light rail cars, trolley coaches, cable cars, inclined plane cars. Beginning 1984, combined services also include suburban rail cars, urban ferry boats, vanpools, aerila tramways, automated guideways, and demand response vehicles. (2) Beginning 1984, includes active vehicles only. (3) Includes light rail, trolley coach, cable car, inclined plane, aerial tramway, and automated guideways. (4) Includes other operating revenue, non-operating revenue, and auxiliary income. (5) Data for 1970 and 1975 are not comparable with later years.

Fastest Scheduled Passenger Train Runs in U.S. and Canada

Source: Donald M. Steffee, figures are based on 1989 timetables

Railroad	Train	From	To	Dis. miles	Time min.	Speed mph.
Amtrak	Metroliners 112-116	Baltimore	Wilmington	68.4	40	102.6
Amtrak	27 Metroliners	Wilmington[1]	Baltimore	68.4	41	100.1
Amtrak	Five trains	Metro Park	Trenton	33.5	21	95.7
Amtrak	Metroliner 101	Metro Park	Princeton Jct.	23.9	15	95.6
Amtrak	Nine trains	Wilmington	Baltimore	68.4	43	95.4
Amtrak	Two trains	Newark (Del)[1]	Baltimore	56.8	36	94.7
Amtrak	Seven trains	Wilmington[1]	Baltimore	68.4	44	93.3
Amtrak	Four trains	Wilmington	Aberdeen	38.7	25	92.9
Amtrak	Three trains	Newark[1]	Trenton	47.9	31	92.7
Amtrak	Metroliner 103	Metro Park	Philadelphia	66.3	43	92.5
Amtrak	Three trains	Metro Park	Trenton	33.5	22	91.4
Amtrak	Five trains	Baltimore	Wilmington	68.4	45	91.2
Amtrak	Four trains	Newark	Trenton	47.9	32	89.8
Amtrak	Fast Mail	Philadelphia	Baltimore	94.2	63	89.7
Amtrak	Metroliner 101	Philadelphia	Newark	80.7	54	89.7
Amtrak	Benjamin Franklin	Metro Park	Princeton Junction	23.9	16	89.6
Amtrak	Nite Owl	Wilmington	Aberdeen	38.7	26	89.5
Amtrak	Five trains	Philadelphia	Metro Park	66.3	45	88.4
Amtrak	Six trains	Newark[1]	Philadelphia	80.7	55	88.0
Amtrak	Valley Forge	Newark	No. Philadelphia	76.2	52	87.9
Amtrak	Senator	Trenton	Metro Park	33.5	23	87.4
Amtrak	Bankers	Baltimore	Wilmington	68.4	47	87.3
Amtrak	Two trains	Newark	Trenton	47.9	33	87.1

Fastest Scheduled Passenger Train Runs in Foreign Countries

France	TGV trains (2 runs)	Paris	Macon	225.7	100	135.4
Japan	Yamabiko trains (6 runs)	Morica	Sendi	106.3	50	127.6
Great Britain	High Speed Trains (3 runs)	Swindon	Reading	41.5	23	108.3
West Germany	Intercity trains (7 runs)	Celle	Uelzen	32.5	19	102.6
Italy	IC501	Milan	Bologna	135.8	86	94.7
Soviet Union	High Speed Train[2]	Leningrad[1]	Moscow[3]	403.6	270	89.7
Sweden	Seven trains	Skvode	Hallsberg	70.8	48	88.5
Spain	Talgos 120 and 121	Alcazar[1]	Albacete	80.7	57	84.9
Australia	Riverina XPT	Culcairn	Wagga Wagga	47.0	35	80.6

(1) Runs listed in both directions. (2) Once weekly: Thursday from Leningrad, Fri. from Moscow. (3) Probable operating stop at Bologuye; times unavailable

Motorcycles, 1970-1986

Source: Federal Highway Administration

Year	Number of registered vehicles (1,000)	Travel (mil. veh. miles)	Average travel per vehicle (miles)	Fuel Consumption Total (mil. gal.)	Fuel Consumption Average per vehicle (gal.)	Average miles per gallon consumed
1970	2,824	2,979	1,055	59.6	21	50
1975	4,964	5,629	1,134	112.6	23	50
1976	4,933	6,003	1,217	120.1	24	50
1978	4,868	7,158	1,470	143.2	29	50
1979	5,422	8,637	1,593	172.7	32	50
1980	5,694	10,214	1,794	204.3	36	50
1981	5,831	10,690	1,833	213.8	37	50
1982	5,754	9,910	1,722	198.2	34	50
1983	5,585	8,760	1,568	175.2	31	50
1984	5,480	8,784	1,603	175.7	32	50
1985	5,444	9,086	1,669	181.7	33	50
1986	5,262	9,414	1,789	188.3	36	50

Best-Selling Cars of 1987

Source: Ward's Automotive Reports

Model	Number Sold	Suggested '88 Retail Price	Model	Number Sold	Suggested '88 Retail Price
Ford Escort	392,360	$6,895	Pontiac Grand Am	211,192	$10,269
Ford Taurus	354,971	11,806	Toyota Camry	186,633	11,248
Honda Accord	334,876	10,925	Chevrolet Caprice	177,344	12,510
Chevrolet Cavalier	307,028	7,395	Honda Civic	173,110	6,195
Chevrolet Celebrity	306,480	11,010	Ford Mustang	172,602	9,209
Hyundai	263,610	5,395	Oldsmobile 88	168,853	14,978
Oldsmobile Ciera	244,607	11,420	Toyota Corolla	164,300	8,998
Nissan Sentra	235,945	6,449	Buick Century	147,797	12,068
Ford Tempo	219,296	9,056	Cadillac de Ville	146,174	23,574
Chevrolet Corsica/Beretta	214,074	9,955	Buick LeSabre	141,126	14,885

Passenger Car Production, U.S. Plants

Source: Motor Vehicle Manufacturers Association

	1986	1987	1988		1986	1987	1988
Renault Alliance	46,095	16,004	—	Cavalier	395,151	315,328	357,807
Renault Encore	3,408	—	—	Camaro	172,584	121,550	99,820
Total Eagle	49,503	16,004	—	Beretta—Corsica	17,200	348,806	434,313
Horizon	171,882	45,663	78,794	Celebrity	257,983	285,111	189,912
Reliant	151,695	136,109	100,462	Monte Carlo	110,048	72,745	—
Sundance	36,856	89,678	104,310	Chevrolet	223,842	200,583	203,494
Acclaim	—	—	7,241	Corvette	28,410	28,514	22,878
Caravelle	44,368	42,955	9,834	**Total Chevrolet**	1,499,230	1,515,571	1,381,967
Gran Fury	17,818	7,180	13,059	Acadian	19,490	—	—
Total Plymouth	422,619	321,585	313,700	1000	16,814	—	—
Laser	25,327	—	—	Sunbird	130,167	89,470	113,736
LeBaron	83,163	64,089	7,912	Fiero	69,735	33,935	13,296
LeBaron GTS	68,699	37,508	9,539	Firebird	105,110	77,731	66,456
Le Baron J	3,996	113,858	90,449	Grand Am	231,318	247,701	242,121
Fifth Avenue	122,442	65,675	33,280	6000	132,385	67,943	94,663
New Yorker (C)	—	18,916	106,832	Bonneville H	42,543	125,014	121,914
New Yorker (E)	64,964	57,102	—	**Total Pontiac**	794,737	657,281	806,356
Total Chrysler-Plymouth	791,210	678,733	561,712	Firenza	38,212	17,978	5,230
Omni	163,416	40,039	77,332	Calais	120,629	115,085	119,690
Shadow	35,107	96,073	103,190	Ciera	236,613	108,766	38,053
Daytona	33,063	64,054	79,657	Cutlass Supreme	107,036	76,751	140,513
Aries	126,311	127,948	91,998	Delta 88	291,346	193,737	167,785
Spirit	—	—	8,090	Oldsmobile 98	114,558	73,004	76,341
Dodge 600	64,063	39,773	8,549	Toronado	18,779	16,453	15,308
Lancer	47,817	23,123	9,365	**Total Oldsmobile**	927,173	601,774	562,920
Dynasty	—	8,486	114,156	Skyhawk	82,429	34,517	28,037
Diplomat	35,593	15,188	18,796	Somerset and Skylark	112,773	63,612	55,343
Total Dodge	506,370	414,684	511,133	Century	230,137	152,892	142,454
Total Chrysler Corp.	1,297,580	1,109,421	1,072,845	Regal	60,897	40,425	—
Thunderbird	131,289	157,507	111,533	LeSabre	172,061	152,836	144,924
Taurus	335,689	405,640	395,512	Electra	91,559	94,485	92,099
Tempo	198,824	145,812	183,124	Riviera	26,110	13,468	13,631
Escort	378,341	394,699	414,596	**Total Buick**	775,966	552,567	484,851
Mustang	177,728	214,128	200,054	Cimarron	23,241	10,404	3,693
Total Ford	1,221,871	1,317,786	1,304,819	Cadillac	248,076	218,741	200,118
Cougar	101,788	138,464	87,765	Eldorado	25,246	20,538	35,385
Sable	127,343	121,641	135,436	Seville	22,474	21,395	23,514
Topaz	57,560	46,975	70,565	Allante	—	4,803	2,320
Lynx	60,297	21,352	—	**Total Cadillac**	319,037	275,881	265,030
Capri	12,344	—	—	**Total General Motors**	4,316,143	3,603,074	3,501,124
Town Car	137,280	142,017	123,110	Honda	238,159	324,065	366,354
Mark	26,126	28,546	28,734	Mazda	—	4,200	163,289
Continental	19,626	13,595	55,312	Nissan	65,117	117,334	109,897
Total Lincoln—Mercury	542,364	512,590	500,922	Toyota	13,649	43,744	55,480
Total Ford Motor Co.	1,764,235	1,830,376	1,805,741	Volkswagen of America	84,397	66,696	35,998
Geo, Prizm, Nova	191,475	142,934	73,743	**Total Passenger Cars**	7,828,783	7,098,910	7,110,728
Chevette	102,537	—	—				

Selected Motor Vehicle Statistics

Source: Federal Highway Adm.; National Transportation Safety Board; Insurance Institute for Highway Safety

State	Driver's age Jan. 1, 1989 (1) Regular	(2) Juvenile	1988 Licensed drivers[3] (mlns.)	1988 Registered autos, buses & trucks[3] (mlns.)	State gas tax gal. cents (Jan. 1, 1989)	1987 Vehicle-Miles of Travel (mlns.)	1988 Motorfuel consumption[3] Highway (min) gallons	Non-Highway (min) gallons	Safety belt use law[4] (July 1, 1989)
Alabama	16	—	2.7	3.6	13	37,426	2,412	63	No
Alaska	16	—	.3	.4	8	3,900	241	40	No
Arizona	16	—	2.3	2.5	17	31,728	1,908	52	No
Arkansas	16	—	1.7	1.5	13.5	18,395	1,537	68	No
California	16/18	14	19.1	21.3	9	226,301	14,242	386	S
Colorado	18	16	2.3	3.1	18	26,968	1,714	43	S
Connecticut	16/18	—	2.4	2.7	20	26,775	1,627	32	P
Delaware	16/18	—	.5	.5	16	6,086	394	10	No
Dist. of Col.	18	16	.4	.3	15.5	3,368	200	5	S
Florida	16	—	8.8	11.1	9.7	93,639	6,871	298	S
Georgia	16	—	4.3	5.2	7.5	60,293	4,246	113	S
Hawaii	15	—	.6	.7	11	7,218	368	20	P
Idaho	16	14	.7	1.0	18	8,119	560	36	S
Illinois	16/18	—	7.3	7.9	13	75,756	5,547	119	S
Indiana	16/18	—	3.6	3.7	15	44,122	3,206	86	S
Iowa	16/18	—	1.8	2.8	18	20,808	1,633	90	P
Kansas	16	14	1.7	2.2	11	20,561	1,613	67	S
Kentucky	16	—	2.4	2.8	15	30,320	2,258	71	No
Louisiana	15/17	15	2.6	2.9	16	30,599	2,257	100	S
Maine	15/17	15	.9	.9	16	10,766	773	31	No
Maryland	16/18	16	3.1	3.4	18.5	36,493	2,313	64	S
Massachusetts	17/18	16½	4.0	3.9	11	42,305	2,774	72	No
Michigan	16/18	14	6.4	7.0	15	75,706	4,703	146	S
Minnesota	16/18	15	2.5	3.2	20	35,167	2,351	147	S
Mississippi	15	—	1.8	1.8	17	20,173	1,602	61	No
Missouri	16	—	3.5	3.8	11	43,379	3,237	81	S
Montana	15/16	13	6.1	.6	20	8,074	535	34	S
Nebraska	16	14	1.1	1.3	18.3	13,091	965	71	No
Nevada	16	14	.7	.9	18	8,396	710	18	S
New Hampshire	16/18	16	.8	.9	14	9,167	574	10	No
New Jersey	17	16	6.1	5.6	10.5	57,071	4,031	90	S
New Mexico	15/16	—	1.1	1.3	14	15,116	1,018	27	P
New York	17/18	16	10.2	10.0	8	98,002	6,567	159	P
North Carolina	16/18	—	4.4	5.0	15.7	54,600	4,072	124	P
North Dakota	16	14	.4	.7	17	5,681	450	55	P*
Ohio	16/18	14	7.4	8.8	14.8	79,157	5,750	167	S
Oklahoma	16	—	2.2	2.9	16	31,606	1,948	73	S
Oregon	16	14	2.1	2.3	14	23,332	1,509	48	No
Pennsylvania	17/18	16	7.8	7.9	12	78,626	5,545	106	S
Rhode Island	16/18	—	.7	.7	15	6,003	436	14	No
South Carolina	16	15	2.2	2.4	15	30,224	2,059	78	S
South Dakota	16	14	.5	.7	18	6,209	459	39	No
Tennessee	16	14	3.2	4.1	17	42,126	3,211	68	S
Texas	16/18	15	11.3	12.2	15	151,186	10,081	420	P
Utah	16/18	—	1.0	1.1	19	12,679	881	22	S
Vermont	18	16	.4	.5	13	5,039	328	10	No
Virginia	16/19	—	4.2	4.7	17.5	54,834	3,541	80	S
Washington	16/18	—	3.2	3.9	18	38,520	2,484	73	S
West Virginia	16/18	16	1.3	1.2	10.5	13,742	986	30	No
Wisconsin	16/18	14	3.3	3.1	20.9	40,196	2,436	95	S
Wyoming	16	14	.3	.5	8	5,367	497	27	S
Total[5]			164.2	183.5		1,924,327	131,660	4,239	

(1) Unrestricted operation of private passenger car. When 2 ages are shown, license is issued at lower age upon completion of approved driver education course. (2) Juvenile license issued with consent of parent or guardian. (3) Estimated, 1988. (4) P = an officer may stop a vehicle for a violation (primary); S = an officer may only issue a seat belt citation when the vehicle is stopped for another moving violation (secondary); (5) Figures may not add, due to rounding. *Law went into effect 7/12/89.

Automobile Factory Sales

Source: Motor Vehicle Manufacturers Association

Year	Passenger cars Number	Motor trucks, buses Number	Total Number	Year	Passenger cars Number	Motor trucks, buses Number	Total Number
1900	4,192	—	4,190	1981	6,255,340	1,700,908	7,956,248
1910	181,000	6,000	187,000	1982	5,049,184	1,906,455	6,955,639
1920	1,905,560	321,789	2,227,349	1983	6,739,223	2,413,897	9,153,120
1930	2,787,456	575,364	3,362,820	1985	8,002,259	3,356,905	11,359,164
1940	3,717,385	754,901	4,472,286	1986	7,516,189	3,392,885	10,909,074
1950	6,665,863	1,337,193	8,003,056	1987	7,085,147	3,821,410	10,906,557
1960	6,665,863	1,194,475	7,869,271	1988	7,104,617	4,120,574	11,225,191
1970	6,546,817	1,692,440	8,239,257				

After July 1, 1964 all tactical vehicles are excluded. Federal excise taxes are excluded in all years.

Road Mileage Between Selected U.S. Cities

	Atlanta	Boston	Chicago	Cincinnati	Cleveland	Dallas	Denver	Des Moines	Detroit	Houston
Atlanta, Ga. . . .	. . .	1,037	674	440	672	795	1,398	870	699	789
Boston, Mass. . . .	1,037	. . .	963	840	628	1,748	1,949	1,280	695	1,804
Chicago, Ill.	674	963	. . .	287	335	917	996	327	266	1,067
Cincinnati, Oh. . .	440	840	287	. . .	244	920	1,164	571	259	1,029
Cleveland, Oh. . .	672	628	335	244	. . .	1,159	1,321	652	170	1,273
Dallas Tex.	795	1,748	917	920	1,159	. . .	781	684	1,143	243
Denver, Col.	1,398	1,949	996	1,164	1,321	781	. . .	669	1,253	1,019
Detroit, Mich. . . .	699	695	266	259	170	1,143	1,253	584	. . .	1,265
Houston, Tex. . . .	789	1,804	1,067	1,029	1,273	243	1,019	905	1,265	. . .
Indianapolis, Ind. .	493	906	181	106	294	865	1,058	465	278	987
Kansas City, Mo. .	798	1,391	499	591	779	489	600	195	743	710
Los Angeles, Cal.	2,182	2,979	2,054	2,179	2,367	1,387	1,059	1,727	2,311	1,538
Memphis, Tenn. .	371	1,296	530	468	712	452	1,040	599	713	561
Milwaukee, Wis. .	761	1,050	87	374	422	991	1,029	361	353	1,142
Minneapolis, Minn.	1,068	1,368	405	692	740	936	841	252	671	1,157
New Orleans, La. .	479	1,507	912	786	1,030	496	1,273	978	1,045	356
New York, N.Y. . .	841	206	802	647	473	1,552	1,771	1,119	637	1,608
Omaha, Neb. . . .	986	1,412	459	693	784	644	537	132	716	865
Philadelphia, Pa. .	741	296	738	567	413	1,452	1,691	1,051	573	1,508
Pittsburgh, Pa. . .	687	561	452	287	129	1,204	1,411	763	287	1,313
Portland Ore. . . .	2,601	3,046	2,083	2,333	2,418	2,009	1,238	1,786	2,349	2,205
St. Louis, Mo. . . .	541	1,141	289	340	529	630	857	333	513	779
San Francisco . . .	2,496	3,095	2,142	2,362	2,467	1,753	1,235	1,815	2,399	1,912
Seattle, Wash. . .	2,618	2,976	2,013	2,300	2,348	2,078	1,307	1,749	2,279	2,274
Tulsa, Okla.	772	1,537	683	736	925	257	681	443	909	478
Washington, D.C. .	608	429	671	481	346	1,319	1,616	984	506	1,375

	Indianapolis	Kansas City	Los Angeles	Louisville	Memphis	Milwaukee	Minneapolis	New Orleans	New York	Omaha
Atlanta, Ga.	493	798	2,182	382	371	761	1,068	479	841	986
Boston, Mass. . . .	906	1,391	2,979	941	1,296	1,050	1,368	1,507	206	1,412
Chicago, Ill.	181	499	2,054	292	530	87	405	912	802	459
Cincinnati, Oh. . .	106	591	2,179	101	468	374	692	786	647	693
Cleveland Oh. . .	294	779	2,367	345	712	422	740	1,030	473	784
Dallas, Tex.	865	489	1,387	819	452	991	936	496	1,552	644
Denver, Col.	1,058	600	1,059	1,120	1,040	1,029	841	1,273	1,771	537
Detroit, Mich. . . .	278	743	2,311	360	713	353	671	1,045	637	716
Houston, Tex. . . .	987	710	1,538	928	561	1,142	1,157	356	1,608	865
Indianapolis, Ind. .	. . .	485	2,073	111	435	268	586	796	713	587
Kansas City, Mo. .	485	. . .	1,589	520	451	537	447	806	1,198	201
Los Angeles, Cal.	2,073	1,589	. . .	2,108	1,817	2,087	1,889	1,883	2,786	1,595
Memphis, Tenn. .	435	451	1,817	367	. . .	612	826	390	1,100	652
Milwaukee, Wis. .	268	537	2,087	379	612	. . .	332	994	889	493
Minneapolis, Minn.	586	447	1,889	697	826	332	. . .	1,214	1,207	357
New Orleans, La. .	796	806	1,883	685	390	994	1,214	. . .	1,311	1,007
New York, N.Y. . .	713	1,198	2,786	748	1,100	889	1,207	1,311	. . .	1,251
Omaha, Neb. . . .	587	201	1,595	687	652	493	357	1,007	1,251	. . .
Philadelphia, Pa. .	633	1,118	2,706	668	1,000	825	1,143	1,211	100	1,183
Pittsburgh, Pa. . .	353	838	2,426	388	752	539	857	1,070	368	895
Portland, Ore. . . .	1,227	1,809	959	2,320	2,259	2,010	1,678	2,505	2,885	1,654
St. Louis, Mo. . . .	235	257	1,845	263	285	363	552	673	948	449
San Francisco . . .	2,256	1,835	379	2,349	2,125	2,175	1,940	1,940	2,934	1,683
Seattle, Wash. . .	2,194	1,839	1,131	2,305	2,290	1,940	1,608	2,574	2,815	1,638
Tulsa, Okla.	631	248	1,452	659	401	757	695	647	1,344	387
Washington, D.C. .	558	1,043	2,631	582	867	758	1,076	1,078	233	1,116

	Philadelphia	Pittsburgh	Portland	St. Louis	Salt Lake City	San Francisco	Seattle	Toledo	Tulsa	Washington
Atlanta, Ga.	741	687	2,601	541	1,878	2,496	2,618	640	772	608
Boston, Mass. . . .	296	561	3,046	1,141	2,343	3,095	2,976	739	1,537	429
Chicago, Ill.	738	452	2,083	289	1,390	2,142	2,013	232	683	671
Cincinnati, Oh. . .	567	287	2,333	340	1,610	2,362	2,300	200	736	481
Cleveland Oh. . .	413	129	2,418	529	1,715	2,467	2,078	111	925	346
Dallas, Tex.	1,452	1,204	2,009	630	1,242	1,753	2,078	1,084	257	1,319
Denver, Col.	1,691	1,411	1,238	857	504	1,235	1,307	1,218	681	1,616
Detroit, Mich. . . .	576	287	2,349	513	1,647	2,399	2,279	59	909	506
Houston, Tex. . . .	1,508	1,313	2,205	779	1,438	1,912	2,274	1,206	478	1,375
Indianapolis, Ind. .	633	353	2,227	235	1,504	2,256	2,194	219	631	558
Kansas City, Mo. .	1,118	838	1,809	257	1,086	1,839	687	248	1,043	
Los Angeles, Cal.	2,706	2,426	959	1,845	715	379	1,131	2,276	1,452	2,631
Memphis, Tenn. .	1,000	752	2,259	285	1,535	2,125	2,290	654	401	867
Milwaukee, Wis. .	825	539	2,010	363	1,423	2,175	1,940	319	757	758
Minneapolis, Minn.	1,143	857	1,678	552	1,186	1,940	1,608	637	695	1,076
New Orleans, La. .	1,211	1,070	2,505	673	1,738	2,249	2,574	986	647	1,078
New York, N.Y. . .	100	368	2,885	948	2,182	2,934	2,815	578	1,344	233
Omaha, Neb. . . .	1,183	895	1,654	449	931	1,683	1,638	681	387	1,116
Philadelphia, Pa. .	. . .	288	2,821	868	2,114	2,866	2,751	514	1,264	133
Pittsburgh, Pa. . .	288	. . .	2,535	588	1,826	2,578	2,465	228	984	221
Portland, Ore. . . .	2,821	2,535	. . .	2,060	767	636	172	2,315	1,913	2,754
St. Louis, Mo. . . .	868	588	2,060	. . .	1,337	2,089	2,081	454	396	793
San Francisco . . .	2,866	2,578	636	2,089	752	. . .	808	2,364	1,760	2,799
Seattle, Wash. . .	2,751	2,465	172	2,081	836	808	. . .	2,245	1,982	2,684
Tulsa, Okla.	1,264	984	1,913	396	1,172	1,760	1,982	850	. . .	1,189
Washington, D.C. .	133	221	2,754	793	2,047	2,799	2,684	447	1,189	. . .

Air Distances Between Selected World Cities in Statute Miles

Point-to-point measurements are usually from City Hall

	Bangkok	Berlin	Cairo	Cape Town	Caracas	Chicago	Hong Kong	Honolulu	Lima	London
Bangkok	...	5,352	4,523	6,300	10,555	8,570	1,077	6,609	12,244	5,944
Berlin	5,352	...	1,797	5,961	5,238	4,414	5,443	7,320	6,896	583
Cairo	4,523	1,797	...	4,480	6,342	6,141	5,066	8,848	7,726	2,185
Cape Town	6,300	5,961	4,480	...	6,366	8,491	7,376	11,535	6,072	5,989
Caracas	10,555	5,238	6,342	6,366	...	2,495	10,165	6,021	1,707	4,655
Chicago	8,570	4,414	6,141	8,491	2,495	...	7,797	4,256	3,775	3,958
Hong Kong	1,077	5,443	5,066	7,376	10,165	7,797	...	5,556	11,418	5,990
Honolulu	6,609	7,320	8,848	11,535	6,021	4,256	5,556	...	5,947	7,240
London	5,944	583	2,185	5,989	4,655	3,958	5,990	7,240	6,316	...
Los Angeles	7,637	5,782	7,520	9,969	3,632	1,745	7,240	2,557	4,171	5,439
Madrid	6,337	1,165	2,087	5,308	4,346	4,189	6,558	7,872	5,907	785
Melbourne	4,568	9,918	8,675	6,425	9,717	9,673	4,595	5,505	8,059	10,500
Mexico City	9,793	6,056	7,700	8,519	2,234	1,690	8,788	3,789	2,639	5,558
Montreal	8,338	3,740	5,427	7,922	2,438	745	7,736	4,918	3,970	3,254
Moscow	4,389	1,006	1,803	6,279	6,177	4,987	4,437	7,047	7,862	1,564
New York	8,669	3,979	5,619	7,803	2,120	714	8,060	4,969	3,639	3,469
Paris	5,877	548	1,998	5,786	4,732	4,143	5,990	7,449	6,370	214
Peking	2,046	4,584	4,698	8,044	8,950	6,604	1,217	5,077	10,349	5,074
Rio de Janeiro	9,994	6,209	6,143	3,781	2,804	5,282	11,009	8,288	2,342	5,750
Rome	5,494	737	1,326	5,231	5,195	4,824	5,774	8,040	6,750	895
San Francisco	7,931	5,672	7,466	10,248	3,902	1,859	6,905	2,398	4,518	5,367
Singapore	883	6,164	5,137	6,008	11,402	9,372	1,605	6,726	11,689	6,747
Stockholm	5,089	528	2,096	6,423	5,471	4,331	5,063	6,875	7,166	942
Tokyo	2,865	5,557	5,958	9,154	5,471	6,314	1,791	3,859	9,631	5,959
Warsaw	5,033	322	1,619	5,935	5,559	4,679	5,147	7,366	7,215	905
Washington, D.C.	8,807	4,181	5,822	7,895	2,047	596	8,155	4,838	3,509	3,674

	Los Angeles	Madrid	Melbourne	Mexico City	Montreal	Moscow	New Delhi	New York	Paris	Peking
Bangkok	7,637	6,337	4,568	9,793	8,338	4,389	1,813	8,669	5,877	2,046
Berlin	5,782	1,165	9,918	6,056	3,740	1,006	3,598	3,979	548	4,584
Cairo	7,520	2,087	8,675	7,700	5,427	1,803	2,758	5,619	1,998	4,698
Cape Town	9,969	5,308	6,425	8,519	7,922	6,279	5,769	7,803	5,786	8,044
Caracas	3,632	4,346	9,717	2,234	2,438	6,177	8,833	2,120	4,732	8,950
Chicago	1,745	4,189	9,673	1,690	745	4,987	7,486	714	4,143	6,604
Hong Kong	7,240	6,558	4,595	8,788	7,736	4,437	2,339	8,060	5,990	1,217
Honolulu	2,557	7,872	5,505	3,789	4,918	7,047	7,412	4,969	7,449	5,077
London	5,439	785	10,500	5,558	3,254	1,564	4,181	3,469	214	5,074
Los Angeles	...	5,848	7,931	1,542	2,427	6,068	7,011	2,451	5,601	6,250
Madrid	5,848	...	10,758	5,643	3,448	2,147	4,530	3,593	655	5,745
Melbourne	7,931	10,758	...	8,426	10,395	8,950	6,329	10,359	10,430	5,643
Mexico City	1,542	5,643	8,426	...	2,317	6,676	9,120	2,090	5,725	7,753
Montreal	2,427	3,448	10,395	2,317	...	4,401	7,012	331	3,432	6,519
Moscow	6,068	2,147	8,950	6,676	4,401	...	2,698	4,683	1,554	3,607
New York	2,451	3,593	10,359	2,090	331	4,683	7,318	...	3,636	6,844
Paris	5,601	655	10,430	5,725	3,432	1,554	4,102	3,636	...	5,120
Peking	6,250	5,745	5,643	7,753	6,519	3,607	2,353	6,844	5,120	...
Rio de Janeiro	6,330	5,045	8,226	4,764	5,078	7,170	8,753	4,801	5,684	10,768
Rome	6,326	851	9,929	6,377	4,104	1,483	3,684	4,293	690	5,063
San Francisco	347	5,803	7,856	1,887	2,543	5,885	7,691	2,572	5,577	5,918
Singapore	8,767	7,080	3,759	10,327	9,203	5,228	2,571	9,534	6,673	2,771
Stockholm	5,454	1,653	9,630	6,012	3,714	716	3,414	3,986	1,003	4,133
Tokyo	5,470	6,706	5,062	7,035	6,471	4,660	3,638	6,757	6,053	1,307
Warsaw	5,922	1,427	9,598	6,337	4,022	721	3,277	4,270	852	4,325
Washington, D.C.	2,300	3,792	10,180	1,885	489	4,876	7,500	205	3,840	6,942

	Rio de Janeiro	Rome	San Francisco	Singapore	Stockholm	Teheran	Tokyo	Vienna	Warsaw	Wash., D.C.
Bangkok	9,994	5,494	7,931	883	5,089	3,391	2,865	5,252	5,033	8,807
Berlin	6,209	737	5,672	6,164	528	2,185	5,557	326	322	4,181
Cairo	6,143	1,326	7,466	5,137	2,096	1,234	5,958	1,481	1,619	5,822
Cape Town	3,781	5,231	10,248	6,008	6,423	5,241	9,154	5,656	5,935	7,895
Caracas	2,804	5,195	3,902	11,402	5,471	7,320	8,808	5,372	5,559	2,047
Chicago	5,282	4,824	1,859	9,372	4,331	6,502	6,314	4,698	4,679	596
Hong Kong	11,009	5,774	6,905	1,605	5,063	3,843	1,791	5,431	5,147	8,155
Honolulu	8,288	8,040	2,398	6,726	6,875	8,070	3,859	7,632	7,366	4,838
London	5,750	895	5,367	6,747	942	2,743	5,959	771	905	3,674
Los Angeles	6,330	6,326	347	8,767	5,454	7,682	5,470	6,108	5,922	2,300
Madrid	5,045	851	5,803	7,080	1,653	2,978	6,706	1,128	1,427	3,792
Melbourne	8,226	9,929	7,856	3,759	9,630	7,826	5,062	9,790	9,598	10,180
Mexico City	4,764	6,377	1,887	10,327	6,012	8,184	7,035	6,320	6,337	1,885
Montreal	5,078	4,104	2,543	9,203	3,714	5,880	6,471	4,009	4,022	489
Moscow	7,170	1,483	5,885	5,228	716	1,532	4,660	1,043	721	4,876
New York	4,801	4,293	2,572	9,534	3,986	6,141	6,757	4,234	4,270	205
Paris	5,684	690	5,577	6,673	1,003	2,625	6,053	645	852	3,840
Peking	10,768	5,063	5,918	2,771	4,133	3,490	1,307	4,648	4,325	6,942
Rio de Janeiro	...	5,707	6,613	9,785	6,683	7,374	11,532	6,127	6,455	4,779
Rome	5,707	...	6,259	6,229	1,245	2,127	6,142	477	820	4,497
San Francisco	6,613	6,259	...	8,448	5,399	7,362	5,150	5,994	5,854	2,441
Singapore	9,785	6,229	8,448	...	5,936	4,103	3,300	6,035	5,843	9,662
Stockholm	6,683	1,245	5,399	5,936	...	2,173	5,053	780	494	4,183
Tokyo	11,532	6,142	5,150	3,300	5,053	4,775	...	5,689	5,347	6,791
Warsaw	6,455	820	5,854	5,843	494	1,879	5,689	347	...	4,472
Washington, D.C.	4,779	4,497	2,441	9,662	4,183	6,341	6,791	4,438	4,472	...

AEROSPACE
Memorable Manned Space Flights
Sources: National Aeronautics and Space Administration and The World Almanac.

Crew, date	Mission name	Orbits[1]	Duration	Remarks
Yuri A. Gagarin (4/12/61)	Vostok 1	1	1h 48m.	First manned orbital flight.
Alan B. Shepard Jr. (5/5/61)	Mercury-Redstone 3	(2)	15m 22s . .	First American in space. Spacecraft sank. Grissom rescued.
Virgil I. Grissom (7/21/61)	Mercury-Redstone 4	(2)	15m 37s . .	
Gherman S. Titov (8/6-7/61)	Vostok 2	16	25h 18m.	First space flight of more than 24 hrs.
John H. Glenn Jr. (2/20/62)	Mercury-Atlas 6	3	4h 55m 23s . .	First American in orbit. Manual retrofire error caused 250 mi. landing overshoot.
M. Scott Carpenter (5/24/62)	Mercury-Atlas 7	3	4h 56m 05s . .	Vostok 3 and 4 made first group flight.
Andrian G. Nikolayev (8/11-15/62)	Vostok 3	64	94h 22m.	On first orbit it came within 3 miles of Vostok 3.
Pavel R. Popovich (8/12-15/62)	Vostok 4	48	70h 57m.	Closest splashdown to target to date (4.5 mi.).
Walter M. Schirra Jr. (10/3/62)	Mercury-Atlas 8	6	9h 13m 11s . .	First U.S. evaluation of effects on man of one day in space.
L. Gordon Cooper (5/15-16/63)	Mercury-Atlas 9	22	34h 19m 49s . .	Vostok 5 and 6 made 2d group flight.
Valery F. Bykovsky (6/14-6/19/63)	Vostok 5	81	119h 06m.	
Valentina V. Tereshkova (6/16-19/63)	Vostok 6	48	70h 50m.	First woman in space.
Vladimir M. Komarov, Konstantin P. Feoktistov, Boris B. Yegorov (10/12/64)	Voskhod 1	16	24h 17m.	First 3-man orbital flight: first without space suits.
Pavel I. Belyayev, Aleksei A. Leonov (3/18/65)	Voskhod 2	17	26h 02m.	Leonov made first "space walk" (10 min.)
Virgil I. Grissom, John W. Young (3/23/65). . . .	Gemini-Titan 3	3	4h 53m 00s . .	First manned spacecraft to change its orbital path.
James A. McDivitt, Edward H. White 2d, (6/3-7/65).	Gemini-Titan 4	62	97h 56m 11s . .	White was first American to "walk in space" (20 min.).
L. Gordon Cooper Jr., Charles Conrad Jr. (8/21-29/65)	Gemini-Titan 5	120	190h 55m 14s . .	First use of fuel cells for electric power; evaluated guidance and navigation system.
Frank Borman, James A. Lovell Jr. (12/4-18/65) . .	Gemini-Titan 7	206	330h 35m 31s . .	Longest duration Gemini flight
Walter M. Schirra Jr., Thomas P. Stafford (12/15-16/65)	Gemini-Titan 6-A	16	25h 51m 24s . .	Completed world's first space rendezvous with Gemini 7.
Neil A. Armstrong, David R. Scott (3/16-17/66)	Gemini-Titan 8	6.5	10h 41m 26s . .	First docking of one space vehicle with another; mission aborted, control malfunction.
John W. Young, Michael Collins (7/18-21/66)	Gemini-Titan 10	43	70h 46m 39s . .	First use of Agena target vehicle's propulsion systems. Docked, made 2 revolutions of earth tethered; set Gemini altitude record (739.2 mi.).
Charles Conrad Jr., Richard F. Gordon Jr. (9/12-15/66)	Gemini-Titan 11	44	71h 17m 08s . .	Final Gemini mission; record 5½ hrs. of extravehicular activity.
James A. Lovell Jr., Edwin E. Aldrin Jr. (11/11-15/66)	Gemini-Titan 12	59	94h 34m 31s . .	
Vladimir M. Komarov (4/23/67)	Soyuz 1	17	26h 40m.	Crashed after re-entry killing Komarov.
Walter M. Schirra Jr., Donn F. Eisele, R. Walter Cunningham (10/11-22/68)	Apollo-Saturn 7	163	260h 09m 03s . .	First manned flight of Apollo spacecraft command-service module only. Made rendezvous with unmanned Soyuz 2.
Georgi T. Beregovoi (10/26-30/68)	Soyuz 3	64	94h 51m.	
Frank Borman, James A. Lovell Jr., William A. Anders (12/21-27/68) .	Apollo-Saturn 8	10[3]	147h 00m 42s	First flight to moon (command-service module only); views of lunar surface televised to earth.
Vladimir A. Shatalov (1/14-17/69)	Soyuz 4	45	71h 14m.	Docked with Soyuz 5.
Boris V. Volyanov, Aleksei S. Yeliseyev, Yevgeny V. Khrunov (1/15-18/69)	Soyuz 5	46	72h 46m.	Docked with Soyuz 4; Yeliseyev and Khrunov transferred to Soyuz 4.
James A. McDivitt, David R. Scott, Russell L. Schweickart (3/3-13/69) .	Apollo-Saturn 9	151	241h 00m 54s . .	First manned flight of lunar module.

(continued)

Crew, date	Mission name	Orbits[1]	Duration	Remarks
Thomas P. Stafford, Eugene A. Cernan, John W. Young (5/18-26/69)	Apollo-Saturn 10	31[4]	192h 03m 23s . .	First lunar module orbit of moon.
Neil A. Armstrong, Edwin E. Aldrin Jr., Michael Collins (7/16-24/69)	Apollo-Saturn 11	30[3]	195h 18m 35s . .	First lunar landing made by Armstrong and Aldrin; collected 48.5 lbs. of soil, rock samples; lunar stay time 21 h, 36m, 21 s.
Georgi S. Shonin, Valery N. Kubasov (10/11-16/69)	Soyuz 6	79	118h 42m.	First welding of metals in space.
Anatoly V. Filipchenko, Vladislav N. Volkov, Viktor V. Gorbatko (10/12-17/69)	Soyuz 7	79	118h 41m.	Space lab construction tests made; Soyuz 6, 7 and 8 — first time 3 spacecraft 7 crew orbited earth at once.
Charles Conrad Jr., Richard F. Gordon, Alan L. Bean (11/14-24/69)	Apollo-Saturn 12	45[3]	244h 36m 25s . .	Conrad and Bean made 2d moon landing; collected 74.7 lbs. of samples, lunar stay time 31 h, 31 m.
James A. Lovell Jr., Fred W. Haise Jr., John L. Swigart Jr. (4/11-17/70)	Apollo-Saturn 13	. . .	142h 54m 41s . .	Aborted after service module oxygen tank ruptured; crew returned safely using lunar module oxygen and power.
Alan B. Shepard Jr., Stuart A. Roosa, Edgar D. Mitchell (1/31-2/9/71).	Apollo-Saturn 14	34[3]	216h 01m 57s . .	Shepard and Mitchell made 3d moon landing, collected 96 lbs. of lunar samples; lunar stay 33 h, 31 m.
Georgi T. Dobrovolsky, Vladislav N. Volkov, Viktor I. Patsayev (6/6-30/71)	Soyuz 11	360	569h 40m.	Docked with Salyut space station; and orbited in Salyut for 23 days; crew died during re-entry from loss of pressurization.
David R. Scott, Alfred M. Worden, James B. Irwin (7/26-8/7/71).	Apollo-Saturn 15	74[3]	295h 11m 53s . .	Scott and Irwin made 4th moon landing; first lunar rover use; first deep space walk; 170 lbs. of samples; 66 h, 55 m, stay.
Charles M. Duke Jr., Thomas K. Mattingly, John W. Young (4/16-27/72)	Apollo-Saturn 16	64[3]	265h 51m 05s . .	Young and Duke made 5th moon landing; collected 213 lbs. of lunar samples; lunar stay line 71 h, 2 m.
Eugene A. Cernan, Ronald E. Evans, Harrison H. Schmitt (12/7-19/72)	Apollo-Saturn 17	75[3]	301h 51m 59s . .	Cernan and Schmitt made 6th manned lunar landing; collected 243 lbs. of samples; record lunar stay of 75 h.
Charles Conrad Jr., Joseph P. Kerwin, Paul J. Weitz (5/25-6/22/73)	Skylab 2	. . .	672h 49m 49s . .	First American manned orbiting space station; made long-flights tests, crew repaired damage caused during boost.
Alan L. Bean, Jack R. Lousma, Owen K. Garriott (7/28-9/25/73)	Skylab 3	. . .	1,427h 09m 04s . .	Crew systems and operational tests, exceeded pre-mission plans for scientific activities; space walk total 13h, 44 m.
Gerald P. Carr, Edward G. Gibson, William Pogue (11/16/73-2/8/74) . . .	Skylab 4	. . .	2,017h 16m 30s . .	Final Skylab mission; record space walk of 7 h, 1 m., record space walks total for a mission 22 h, 21 m.
Alexi Leonov, Valeri Kubason (7/15-7/21/75) .	Soyuz 19	96	143h 31m	
Vance Brand, Thomas P. Stafford, Donald K. Slayton (7/15-7/24/75) .	Apollo 18	136	217h 30m.	U.S.-USSR joint flight. Crews linked-up in space, conducted experiments, shared meals, and held a joint news conference.
Leonid Kizim, Vladmir Solovyov, Oleg Atkov (2/8-10/2/84).	Salyut 7	. . .	237 days.	Set space endurance record. (since broken)

(1) The U.S. measures orbital flights in revolutions while the Soviets use "orbits." (2) Suborbital. (3) Moon orbits in command module. (4) Moon orbits.

Fire aboard spacecraft Apollo I on the ground at Cape Kennedy, Fla. killed Virgil I. Grissom, Edward H. White and Roger B. Chaffee on Jan. 27, 1967. They were the only U.S. astronauts killed in space tests.

U.S. Space Shuttles

Name, date	Crew	Name, date	Crew
Columbia (4/12-14/81) . . .	Robert L. Crippen, John W. Young.	Challenger (4/4-9/83)	Paul Weitz, Karol Bobko, Story Musgrave, Donald Peterson.
Columbia (11/12-14/81) .	Joe Engle, Richard Truly.		
Columbia (3/22-30/82) . . .	Jack Lousma, C. Gordon Fullerton.	Challenger (6/18-24/83) `. .	Robert L. Crippen, Norman Thagard, John Fabian, Frederick Hauck, Sally K. Ride (1st U.S. woman in space).
Columbia (6-27/7-4/82) . . .	Thomas Mattingly 2d, Henry Hartsfield Jr.		
Columbia (11/11-16/82) . .	Vance Brand, Robert Overmyer, William Lenoir, Joseph Allen.		

(continued)

U.S. Space Shuttles

Name, date	Crew
Challenger (8/30-9/5/83) . .	Richard Truly, Daniel Brandenstein, William Thornton, Guion Bluford (1st U.S. black in space), Dale Gardner.
Columbia (11/28-12/8/83) . .	John Young, Brewster Shaw Jr., Robert Parker, Owen Garriott, Byron Lichtenberg, Ulf Merbold.
Challenger (2/3-11/84) . . .	Vance Brand, Robert Gibson, Ronald McNair, Bruce McCandless, Robert Stewart.
Challenger (4/6-13/84) . . .	Robert L. Crippen, Francis R. Scobee, George D. Nelson, Terry J. Hart, James D. Van Hoften.
Discovery (8/30-9/5/84) . .	Henry W. Hartsfield Jr., Michael L. Coats, Steven A. Hawley, Judith A. Resnik, Richard M. Mullane, Charles D. Walker.
Challenger (10/5-13/84) . .	Robert L. Crippen, Jon A. McBride, Kathryn D. Sullivan, Sally K. Ride, Marc Garneau (first Canadian), David C. Leestma, Paul D. Scully-Power.
Discovery (11/8-16/84) . . .	Frederick H. Hauck, David M. Walker, Dr. Anna L. Fisher, Joseph P. Allen, Dale A. Gardner.
Discovery (1/24-27/85) . . .	Thomas K. Mattingly, Loren J. Shriver, James F. Buchli, Ellison S. Onizuka, Gary E. Payton.
Discovery (4/12-19/85) . . .	Karol J. Bobko, Donald E. Williams, Sen. Jake Garn, Charles D. Walker, Jeffrey A. Hoffman, S. David Griggs, M. Rhea Seddon.
Challenger (4/29-5/6/85) . .	Robert F. Overmyer, Frederick D. Gregory, Don L. Lind, Taylor G. Wang, Lodewijk van den Berg, Norman Thagard, William Thornton.
Discovery (6/17-6/24/85) . .	John O. Creighton, Shannon W. Lucid, Steven R. Nagel, Daniel C. Brandenstein, John W. Fabian, Prince Sultan Salman al-Saud (first Arab), Patrick Baudry.
Challenger (7/29-8/6/85) . .	Roy D. Bridges Jr., Anthony W. England, Karl G. Henize, F. Story Musgrave, C. Gordon Fullerton, Loren W. Acton, John-David F. Bartoe.
Discovery (8/27-9/3/85) . .	John M. Lounge, James D. van Hoften, William F. Fisher, Joe H. Engle, Richard O. Covey.
Atlantis (10/4-10/7/85) . . .	Karol J. Bobko, Ronald J. Grabe, David C. Hilmers, William A. Pailes, Robert C. Stewart.
Challenger (10/30-11/6/85) .	Henry W. Hartsfield Jr., Steven R. Nagel, Bonnie J. Dunbar, James F. Buchli, Guion S. Bluford Jr., Ernst Messerschmid, Reinhard Furrer, Wubbo J. Ockels.
Atlantis (11/26-12/3/85) . .	Brewster H. Shaw Jr., Bryan D. O'Connor, Charles Walker, Rodolfo Neri (first Mexican), Jerry L. Ross, Sherwood C. Spring, Mary L. Cleave.
Columbia (1/12-1/18/86) . .	Robert L. Gibson, Charles F. Bolden Jr., George D. Nelson, Bill Nelson (first congressman), Franklin R. Chang-Diaz, Steven A. Hawley, Robert J. Cenker.
Challenger (1/28/86-exploded after takeoff) . .	Francis R. Scobee, Michael J. Smith, Ronald E. McNair, Ellison S. Onizuka, Judith A. Resnik, Gregory B. Jarvis, Sharon Christa McAuliffe.
Discovery (9/29-10/3/88) . .	Frederick H. Hauck, Richard O. Covey, David C. Hilmers, George D. Nelson, John M. Lounge.
Atlantis (12/3-12/6/88) . . .	Robert L. Gibson, Guy S. Gardner, Richard M. Mullane, Jerry L. Ross, William M. Shepherd.
Discovery (3/13-3/18/89) . .	Michael L. Coats, John E. Blaha, James F. Buchli, Robert C. Springer, James P. Bagian.
Atlantis (5/4-5/8/89)	David M. Walker, Ronald J. Grabe, Mary L. Cleave, Norman E. Thagard, Mark C. Lee.
Columbia (8/8-8/13/89) . . .	Brewster H. Shaw Jr., Richard N. Richards, David C. Leestma, James C. Adamson, Mark N. Brown.

Notable U.S. Unmanned and Planetary Missions

Spacecraft	Launch date (GMT)	Mission	Remarks
Mariner 2	Aug. 27, 1962	Venus	Passed within 22,000 miles from Venus 12/14/62; contact lost 1/3/63 at 54 million miles
Ranger 7	July 28, 1964	Moon	Yielded over 4,000 photos
Mariner 4	Nov. 28, 1964	Mars	Passed behind Mars 7/14/65; took 22 photos from 6,000 miles
Ranger 8	Feb. 17, 1965	Moon	Yielded over 7,000 photos
Surveyor 3	Apr. 17, 1967	Moon	Scooped and tested lunar soil
Mariner 5	June 14, 1967	Venus	In solar orbit; closest Venus fly-by 10/19/67
Mariner 6	Feb. 25, 1969	Mars	Came within 2,000 miles of Mars 7/31/69; sent back data, photos
Mariner 7	Mar. 27, 1969	Mars	Came within 2,000 miles of Mars 8/5/69
Mariner 9	May 30, 1971	Mars	First craft to orbit Mars 11/13/71; sent back over 7,000 photos
Pioneer 10	Mar. 3, 1972	Jupiter	Passed Jupiter 12/3/73; exited the solar system 6/14/83

(continued)

Mariner 10	Nov. 3, 1973	Venus, Mercury	Passed Venus 2/5/74; arrived Mercury 3/29/74. First time gravity of one planet (Venus) used to whip space-craft toward another (Mercury)
Viking 1	Aug. 20, 1975	Mars	Landed on Mars 7/20/76; did scientific research, sent photos; functioned 6 1/2 years
Viking 2	Sept. 9, 1975	Mars	Landed on Mars 9/3/76; functioned 3 1/2 years
Voyager 1	Sept. 5, 1977	Jupiter, Saturn	Encountered Jupiter 3/5/79; Saturn 11/13/80
Voyager 2	Aug. 20, 1977	Jupiter, Saturn, Uranus, Neptune	Encountered Jupiter 7/9/79; Saturn 8/26/81; Uranus 1/8 and 1/27/86; Neptune 8/24/89
Pioneer 12	May 20, 1978	Venus	Entered Venus orbit 12/4/78
Pioneer 13	Aug. 8, 1978	Venus	Encountered Venus 12/9/78
Titan 4	June 14, 1989	Orbit Earth	First of 41 such rockets whose primary purpose is defense

Successful Space Launches: 1957 to 1987

(Criterion of success is attainment of Earth orbit or Earth escape)

Year Total	Total[1]	USSR	United States	Japan	European Space Agency	India	China
1957-1959	2,976	2,016	875	34	16	3	19
1957-1959	21	6	15	—	—	—	—
1960-1964	268	76	192	—	—	—	—
1965-1969	586	302	279	—	—	—	—
1970-1974	555	405	139	—	—	—	—
1975-1979	607	461	126	5	—	—	2
1980	105	89	13	10	1	—	6
1981	123	98	18	2	—	1	—
1982	121	101	18	3	2	1	1
1983	127	98	22	1	—	—	1
1984	129	97	22	3	2	1	1
1985	121	98	17	3	4	—	3
1986	103	91	6	2	3	—	1
1987	110	95	8	3	2	—	2

(1) Incl. launches in countries not shown.

NASA Outlays for Research and Development

Source: U.S. Office of Management and Budget
(millions of dollars)

Year	Total outlays	Percent change	Performance Total	Performance Space flight	Performance Space science applications	Performance Air transport and other	Facilities Total	Facilities Space flight	Facilities Space science applications	Facilities Air transport and other
1968	$4,726	−12.9[1]	$4,599	$3,028	$1,061	$510	$127	$69	$29	$29
1970	3,753	−11.7	3,699	2,195	963	541	54	14	21	19
1975	3,266	.3	3,181	1,500	1,076	606	85	35	9	42
1980	4,850	15.8	4,710	2,556	1,341	813	140	38	5	97
1985	7,251	2.9	7,004	3,852	1,834	1,318	247	70	23	154
1987	7,591	2.5	7,277	4,018	1,583	1,676	314	119	25	170

(1) Change from 1967.

National Aviation Hall of Fame

The National Aviation Hall of Fame at Dayton, Oh., is dedicated to honoring the outstanding pioneers of air and space.

Allen, William M.
Andrews, Frank M.
Armstrong, Neil A.
Arnold, Henry H. "Hap"
Atwood, John Leland
Baichen, Bernt
Baldwin, Thomas S.
Beachey, Lincoln
Beech, Olive A.
Beech, Walter H.
Bell, Alexander Graham
Bell, Lawrence D.
Boeing, William E.
Bong, Richard I.
Borman, Frank
Boyd, Albert
Brown, George "Scratchley"
Byrd, Richard E.
Cessna, Clyde V.
Chamberlin, Clarence D.
Chanute, Octave
Chennault, Claire L.
Cochran (Odlum), Jacqueline
Collins, Michael
Conrad Jr., Charles
Crossfield, A. Scott
Cunningham, Alfred A.
Curtiss, Glenn H.
deSeversky, Alexander P.
Doolittle, James H.
Douglas, Donald W.

Draper, Charles S.
Eaker, Ira C.
Earhart, (Putnam), Amelia
Eielson, C. Benjamin
Ellyson, Theodore G.
Ely, Eugene B.
Fairchild, Sherman M.
Fleet, Reuben H.
Fokker, Anthony H.G.
Ford, Henry
Foss, Joseph
Foulois, Benjamin D.
Gabreski, Francis S.
Glenn Jr., John H.
Goddard, George W.
Goddard, Robert H.
Godfrey, Arthur
Goldwater, Barry M.
Grissom, Virgil I.
Gross, Robert E.
Grumman, Leroy R.
Guggenheim, Harry F.
Haughton, Daniel J.
Hegenberger, Albert F.
Heinemann, Edward H.
Hoover, Robert A.
Hughes, Howard R.
Ingalls, David S.
Johnson, Clarence L.
Kenney, George C.
Kettering, Charles F.

Kindelberger, James H.
Knabenshue, A. Roy
Knight, William J.
Lahm, Frank P.
Langley, Samuel P.
Lear, William P. Sr.
LeMay, Curtis E.
LeVier, Anthony W.
Lindbergh, Anne M.
Lindbergh, Charles A.
Link, Edwin A.
Lockheed, Allan H.
Loening, Grover
Luke Jr., Frank
Macready, John A.
Martin, Glenn L.
McDonnell, James S.
Meyer, John C.
Mitchell, William "Billy"
Montgomery, John J.
Moorer, Thomas H.
Moss, Sanford A.
Neumann, Gerhard
Northrop, John K.
Patterson, William T.
Piper Sr., William T.
Post, Wiley H.
Read, Albert C.
Reeve, Robert C.
Rentschler, Frederick B.
Richardson, Holden C.

Rickenbacker, Edward V.
Rodgers, Calbraith P.
Rogers, Will
Ryan, T. Claude
Schirra, Walter M.
Schriever, Bernard A.
Selfridge, Thomas E.
Shepard Jr., Alan B.
Sikorsky, Igor I.
Six, Robert F.
Smith, C.R.
Spaatz, Carl A.
Sperry Sr., Elmer A.
Sperry Sr., Lawrence B.
Stapp, John P.
Taylor, Charles E.
Towers, John H.
Trippe, Juan T.
Turner, Roscoe
Twining, Nathan F.
von Braun, Wernher
von Karman, Theodore
Wade, Leigh
Walden, Henry W.
Wilson, Thornton A.
Wright, Orville
Wright, Wilbur
Yeager, Charles E.
Young, John W.

Notable Around the World and Intercontinental Trips

	From/To	Miles	Time	Date
Nellie Bly	New York/New York		72d 06h 11m	1889
George Francis Train	New York/New York		67d 12h 03m	1890
Charles Fitzmorris	Chicago/Chicago		60d 13h 29m	1901
J. W. Willis Sayre	Seattle/Seattle		54d 09h 42m	1903
J. Alcock-A.W. Brown (1)	Newfoundland/Ireland	1,960	16h 12m	June 14-15, 1919
Two U.S. Army airplanes	Seattle/Seattle	26,103	35d 01h 11m	1924
Richard E. Byrd (2)	Spitsbergen/N. Pole	1,545	15h 30m	May 9, 1926
Amundsen-Ellsworth-Nobile Expedition	Spitsbergen/Teller, Alaska		80h	May 11-14,1926
E.S. Evans and L. Wells (N. Y.World) (3)	New York/New York	18,400	28d 14h 36m 05s	June 16-July 14, 1926
Charles Lindbergh (4)	New York/Paris	3,610	33h 29m 30s	May 20-21, 1927
Amelia Earhart, W. Stultz, L. Gordon	Newfoundland/Wales		20h 40m	June 17-18, 1928
Graf Zepppelin	Friedrichshafen, Ger./Lakehurst, N.J.	6,630	4d 15h 46m	Oct. 11-15, 1928
Graf Zeppelin	Friedrichshafen, Ger./Lakehurst, N.J.	21,700	20d 04h	Aug. 14-Sept. 4, 1929
Wiley Post and Harold Gatty (Monoplane Winnie Mae)	New York/New York	15,474	8d 15h 51m	July 1, 1931
C. Pangborn-H. Herndon Jr. (5)	Misawa, Japan/Wenatchee, Wash.	4,458	41h 34m	Oct. 3-5, 1931
Amelia Earhart (6)	Newfoundland/Ireland	2,026	14h 56m	May 20-21, 1932
Wiley Post (Monoplane Winnie Mae) (7)	New York/New York	15,596	115h 36m 30s	July 15-22, 1933
Hindenburg Zeppelin	Lakehurst, N.J./Frankfort, Ger.		42h 53m	Aug. 9-11, 1936
H. R. Ekins (Scripps-Howard Newspapers in race) (Zeppelin Hindenburg to Germany air planes from Frankfurt)	Lakehurst, N.J./Lakehurst, N.J.	25,654	18d 11h 14m 33s	Sept. 30-Oct. 19, 1936
Howard Hughes and 4 assistants	New York/New York	14,824	3d 19h 08m 10s	July 10-13, 1938
Douglas Corrigan	New York/Dublin		28h 13m	July 17-18, 1938
Mrs. Clara Adams (Pan American Clipper)	Port Washington, N.Y./Newark, N.J.		16d 19h 04m	June 28-July 15, 1939
Globester, U.S. Air Transport Command	Wash., D.C./Wash., D.C.	23,279	149h 44m	Oct. 4, 1945
Capt. William P. Odom (A-26 Reynolds Bombshell)	New York/New York	20,000	78h 55m 12s	Apr. 12-16, 1947
America, Pan American 4-engine Lockheed Constellation (8)	New York/New York	22,219	101h 32m	June 17-30, 1947
Col. Edward Eagan	New York/New York	20,559	147h 15m	Dec. 13, 1948
USAF B-50 Lucky Lady II (Capt. James Gallagher) (9)	Ft. Worth, Tex./Ft. Worth, Tex.	23,452	94h 01m	Feb. 26-Mar. 2, 1949
Col. D. Schilling, USAF (10)	England/Limestone, Me.	3,300	10h 01m	Sept. 22, 1950
C.F. Blair Jr.	Norway/Alaska	3,300	10h 29m	May 29, 1951
Two U.S. S-55.	Massachusetts/Scotland	3,410	42h 30m	July 15-31, 1952
Canberra Bomber (11)	N. Ireland/Newfoundland	2,073	04h 34m	Aug. 26, 1952
	Newfoundland/N. Ireland	2,073	03h 25m	Aug. 26, 1952
Three USAF B-52 Stratofortresses (12).	Merced, Cal./Cal.	24,325	45h 19m	Jan. 15-18, 1957
Max Conrad	Chicago/Rome	5,000	34h 03m	Mar. 5-6, 1959
USSR TU-114 (13)	Moscow/New York	5,092	11h 06m	June 28, 1959
Boeing 707-320	New York/Moscow	c.5090	08h 54m	July 23, 1959
Peter Gluckmann (solo)	San Francisco/San Francisco	22,800	29d	Aug. 22-Sept. 20, 1959
Sue Snyder	Chicago/Chicago	21,219	62h 59m	June 22-24, 1960
Max Conrad (solo)	Miami/Miami	25,946	8d 18h 35m 57s	Feb. 28-Mar. 8, 1961
Sam Miller & Louis Fodor	New York/New York		46h 28m	Aug. 3-4, 1963
Robert & Joan Wallick	Manila/Manila	23,129	05d 06h 17m 10s	June 2-7, 1966
Arthur Godfrey, Richard Merrill, Fred Austin, Karl Keller	New York/New York	23,333	86h 9m 01s	June 4-7, 1966
Trevor K. Brougham	Darwin, Australia/Darwin	24,800	5d 05h 57m	Aug. 5-10, 1972
Walter H. Mullikin, Albert Frink, Lyman Watt, Frank Cassaniti, Edward Shields	New York/New York	23,137	1d 22h 50s	May 1-3,1976
David Kunst (15)	Waseca, Minn./Waseca, Minn.	14,500	4yrs 3mos 16d	June 10, 1970-Oct. 5, 1974
Arnold Palmer	Denver/Denver	22,985	57h 25m 42s	May 17-19, 1976
Boeing 747 (14)	San Francisco/San Francisco	26,382	54h 7m 12s	Oct. 28-31, 1977
Concorde	London/Wash., D.C.	1,023 mph	03h 34m 48s	May 29, 1976
Concorde	Paris/New York	1,037.50 mph	03h 30m 11s	Aug. 22, 1978
Richard Rutan & Jeana Yeager (16)	Edwards AFB, Cal.	25,012	09d 03m 44s	Dec. 14-23, 1986

(1) Non-stop transtlantic flight. (2) Polar flight. (3) Mileage by train and auto, 4,110; by plane, 6,300; by steamship, 8,000. (4) Solo transatlantic flight in the Ryan monoplane the "Spirit of St. Louis". (5) Non-stop Pacific flight. (6) Woman's transoceanic solo flight. (7) First to fly solo around northern circumference of the world, also first to fly twice around the world. (8) Inception of regular commercial global air service. (9) First non-stop round-the-world flight, refueled 4 times in flight. (10) Non-stop jet transatlantic flight. (11) Transatlantic round trip on same day. (12) First non-stop global flight by jet planes; refueled in flight by KC-97 aerial tankers; average speed approx. 525 mph. (13) Non-stop between Moscow and New York. (14) Speed record around the world over both the earth's poles. (15) First to circle the earth on foot. (16) Circled the earth nonstop without refueling.

International Aeronautical Records

Source: The National Aeronautic Association, 1763 R St. NW, Washington, DC 20009, representative in the United States of the Federation Aeronautique Internationale, certifying agency for world aviation and space records. The International Aeronautical Federation was formed in 1905 by representatives from Belgium, France, Germany, Great Britain, Spain, Italy, Switzerland, and the United States, with headquarters in Paris. Regulations for the control of official records were signed Oct. 14, 1905. World records are defined as maximum performance, regardless of class or type of aircraft used. Records to mid-1989.

World Absolute Records—Maximum Performance in Any Class

Speed over a straight course — 3,529.56 kph. (2,193.16 mph) — Capt. Elden W. Joersz, USAF, Lockheed SR-71; Beale AFB, Cal., July 28, 1976.

Speed over a closed circuit — 3,367.221 kph. (2,092.294 mph) — Maj. Adolphus H. Bledsoe Jr., USAF, Lockheed SR-71; Beale AFB, Cal., July 27, 1976.

Speed around the world, non-stop, nonrefueled — 186.11 kmh (115.65 mph) — Richard Rutan & Jeana Yeager, U.S., Voyager, Edwards AFB, Cal., Dec. 14-23, 1986.

Altitude — 37,650 meters (123,523.58 feet) — Alexander Fedotov, USSR, E-266M; Podmoskovnoye, USSR, Aug. 31, 1977.

Altitude in horizontal flight — 25,929.031 meters (85,068.997 ft.) — Capt. Robert C. Helt, USAF, Lockheed SR-71; Beale AFB, Cal., July 28, 1976.

Class K Spacecraft

Duration — 326 days — Col. Yuri V. Romanenko, USSR, space station *MIR;* Dec. 29, 1987.

Altitude — 377,668.9 kms (234,672.5 mi.) — Frank Borman, James A. Lovell Jr., William Anders, Apollo 8; Dec. 21-27, 1968.

Greatest mass lifted — 127,980 kgs. (282,197 lbs.) — Frank Borman, James A. Lovell Jr., William Anders, Apollo 8; Dec. 21-27, 1968.

Distance — 140,800,200 kms. (87,436,800 mi.) — Anatoly Beresovoy & Valentin Lebedev, USSR, Salyut 7, Soyuz T5, Soyuz T7; May 13-Dec. 10, 1982.

World "Class" Records

All other records, international in scope, are termed World "Class" records and are divided into classes: airships, free balloons, airplanes, seaplanes, amphibians, gliders, and rotorplanes. Airplanes (Class C) are sub-divided into four groups: Group I — piston engine aircraft, Group II — turboprop aircraft, Group III — jet aircraft, Group IV — rocket powered aircraft. A partial listing of world records follows:

Airplanes (Class C-I, Group I—piston engine)

Distance, closed circuit — 40,212,139 kms (24,986.727 mi.) — Richard Rutan & Jeana Yeager, U.S., Voyager; Edwards AFB, Cal., Dec. 14-23, 1986.

Speed for 100 kilometers (62.137 miles) without payload — 755.668 kph. (469.549 mph.) — Jacqueline Cochran, U.S.; North American P-51; Coachella Valley, Cal., Dec. 10, 1947.

Speed for 1,000 kilometers (621.369 miles) without payload — 693.78 kph. (431.09 mph.) — Jacqueline Cochran, U.S.; North American P-51; Santa Rosasummit, Cal. — Flagstaff, Ariz. course, May 24, 1948.

Speed for 5,000 kilometers (3,106.849 miles) without payload — 544.59 kph. (338.39 mph.) — Capt. James Bauer, USAF, Boeing B-29; Dayton, Oh., June 28, 1946.

Speed Around the World — 490.51 kph. (304.80 mph.) — Joe Harnish, U.S., Gulfstream Commander 695A, Elkhart, Ind., Mar. 21-24, 1983. **Speed around the world** — 327.73 kph (203.64 mph) — D.N. Dalton, Australia; Beechcraft Duke; Brisbane, Aust., July 20-25, 1975. Time: 5 days, 2 hours, 19 min., 57 sec.

Light Airplanes—(Class C-1.d)

Great Circle distance without landing — 12,760.00 km (7,929.71 mi.) — Peter Wilkins, Australia, Piper Malibu, Sydney, Aust. to Phoenix, Ariz., Mar. 30-Apr. 1, 1987.

Speed for 100 kilometers — (62,137 miles) in a closed circuit — 519.480 kph. (322.780 mph.) — Ms. R. M. Sharpe, Great Britain; Vickers Supermarine Spitfire 5-B; Wolverhampton, June 17, 1950.

Helicopters (Class E-1)

Great Circle distance without landing — 3,561.55 kms. (2,213.04 miles) — Robert G. Ferry, U.S.; Hughes YOH-6A helicopter; Culver City, Cal., to Ormond Beach, Fla., Apr. 6-7, 1966.

Speed around the world —56.97 kph. (35.40 mph.) — H. Ross Perot Jr.; Bell 206 L-11 Long Ranger N39112; Dallas, Tex.–Dallas, Tex.; Sept. 1-30, 1982; 29 days, 3 hrs., 8 min., 13 sec.

Gliders (Class D-I—single seater)

Distance, straight line — 1,460.8 kms. (907.7 miles) — Hans Werner Grosse, West Germany; ASK 12 sailplane; Luebeck to Biarritz, Apr. 25, 1972.

Distance to a goal & return — 1,646.68 kms. (1,023.25 miles) — Thomas Knauff, U.S. Nimbus III; Williamsport, Pa., Apr. 25, 1983.

Airplanes (Class C-I, Group II—Turboprop)

Great Circle distance without landing — 14,052.95 kms. (8,732.09 miles) — Lt. Col. Edgar L. Allison Jr., USAF, Lockheed HC-130 Hercules aircraft; Taiwan to Scott AFB, Ill.; Feb. 20, 1972.

Altitude — 15,549 meters (51,014 ft.) — Donald R. Wilson, U.S.; LTV L450F aircraft; Greenville, Tex., Mar. 27, 1972.

Speed for 1,000 kilometers (621.369 miles) without payload — 871.38 kph. (541.449 mph.) — Ivan Soukhomline, USSR; TU-114 aircraft; Sternberg, USSR; Mar. 24, 1960.

Speed for 5,000 kilometers (3,106.849 miles) without payload — 877.212 kph. (545.072 mph.) — Ivan Soukhomline, USSR; TU-114 aircraft; Sternberg, USSR; Apr. 9, 1960.

Speed around the world —490.51 kph (304.80 mph) — Joe Harnish, U.S., Gulfstream Commander 695A, Elkhart, Ind., Mar. 21-24, 1983.

Airplanes (Class C-1, Group III—Jet-Engine)

Great Circle distance without landing — 20,168.78 kms. (12,532.28 mi.) — Maj. Clyde P. Evely, USAF, Boeing B-52-H, Kadena, Okinawa to Madrid, Spain, Jan. 10-11, 1962.

Distance in a closed circuit — 20,150.92 kms. (12,521.78 miles) — Vladimir Tersky, USSR, AN-124, Podmoskovnoye, USSR, May 6-7, 1987.

Altitude — 36,650 meters (123,523.58 ft.) — Alexander Fedotov, USSR; E-226M airplane; Podmoskovnoye, USSR, Aug. 31, 1977.

Speed for 100 kilometers in a closed circuit — 2,605 kph. (1,618.7 mph.) — Alexander Fedotov, USSR; E-266 airplane, Apr. 8, 1973.

Speed for 500 kilometers in a closed circuit — 2,981.5 kph. (1,852.61 mph.) — Mikhail Komarov, USSR; E-266 airplane, Oct. 5, 1967.

Speed for 1,000 kilometers in a closed circuit — 3,367.221 kph (2,092.294 mph) — Maj. Adolphus H. Bledsoe Jr., USAF; Lockheed SR-71; Beale AFB, Cal., July 27, 1976.

Speed for 2,000 kilometers without payload — 2,012,257 kph. (1,250.42 mph.) — S. Agapov, USSR; Podmoscovnde, USSR; July 20, 1983.

Speed around the world — 1,026.26 kmh. (637.71 mph) — Allen E. Paulson, U.S., Gulfstream IV, Houston, Tex., Feb. 26-28, 1988.

Balloons-Class A

Altitude — 34,668 meters (113,739.9 feet) — Cmdr. Malcolm D. Ross, USNR; Lee Lewis Memorial Winzen Research Balloon; Gulf of Mexico, May 4, 1961.

Distance —8,382.4 kms. (5,208.67 mi.) — Ben Abruzzo; Raven Experimental; Nagashima, Japan to Covello, Cal., Nov. 9-12, 1981.

Duration —137 hr., 5 min., 50 sec. — Ben Abruzzo and Maxie Anderson; Double Eagle II; Presque Isle, Maine to Miserey, France (3,107.61 mi.); Aug. 12-17, 1978.

FAI Course Records

Los Angeles to New York — 1,954.79 kph (1,214.65 mph) — Capt. Robert G. Sowers, USAF; Convair B-58 Hustler; elapsed time: 2 hrs. 58.71 sec., Mar. 5, 1962.

New York to Los Angeles — 1,741 kph (1,081.80 mph) — Capt. Robert G. Sowers, USAF; Convair B-58 Hustler; elapsed time: 2 hrs. 15 min. 50.08 sec., Mar. 5, 1962.

New York to Paris — 1,753.068 kph (1,089.36 mph) — Maj. W. R. Payne, U.S.; Convair B-58 Hustler; elapsed time: 3 hrs 19 min. 44 sec., May 26, 1961.

London to New York — 945.423 kph (587.457 mph) — Maj. Burl Davenport, USAF; Boeing KC-135; elapsed time: 5 hrs. 53 min. 12.77 sec.; June 27, 1958.

Baltimore to Moscow, USSR — 906.64 kph (563.36 mph) — Col. James B. Swindal, USAF; Boeing VC-137 (707); elapsed time: 8 hrs. 33 min. 45.4 sec., May 19, 1963.

New York to London — 2,908.026 kph (1,806.964 mph) — Maj. James V. Sullivan, USAF; Lockheed SR-71; elapsed time 1 hr. 54 min. 56.4 sec., Sept. 1, 1974.

London to Los Angeles — 2,310.353 kph (1,435.587 mph) — Capt. Harold B. Adams, USAF; Lockheed SR-71; elapsed time: 3 hrs. 47 min. 39 sec., Sept. 13, 1974.

The Busiest U.S. Airports in 1988

Source: Air Transport Association of America (Passengers arriving & departing)

Chicago O'Hare	56,678,991	Newark	22,495,568
Atlanta	45,900,098	St. Louis	20,170,060
Los Angeles	44,398,611	Honolulu	20,155,834
Dallas/Ft. Worth	44,271,038	Detroit	19,780,029
New York (JFK)	31,165,676	Pittsburgh	17,987,040
San Francisco	30,506,794	Minneapolis/St. Paul	17,733,837
Denver	30,011,802	Orlando	16,354,215
Miami	24,525,302	Phoenix	15,924,698
New York (LGA)	24,158,780	Washington (DCA)	15,750,993
Boston	23,732,959	Philadelphia	15,639,558

U.S. Scheduled Airline Traffic

Source: Air Transport Association of America (thousands)

	1986	1987	1988
Passenger traffic			
Revenue passengers enplaned	418,946	447,678	454,614
Revenue passenger miles	366,545,855	404,471,484	423,301,559
Available seat miles	607,435,847	648,720,938	676,802,327
Revenue passenger load factor(%)	60.3	62.3	62.5
Cargo traffic (ton miles)	9,025,467	10,016,111	11,469,193
Freight and express	7,344,054	8,260,278	9,632,219
U.S. Mail	1,648,143	1,721,263	1,809,959
Foreign Mail	33,270	34,570	27,015
Overall traffic and service			
Total revenue ton miles—charter service	3,202,486	4,448,871	4,539,030
Total revenue ton miles—all services	48,883,854	54,917,632	58,338,680
Total available ton miles—all services	90,243,958	99,152,795	105,270,796

U.S. Airline Safety

Source: National Transportation Safety Board

	Departures (millions)	Fatal accidents	Fatalities	Fatal accidents per 100,000 departures		Departures (millions)	Fatal accidents	Fatalities	Fatal accidents per 100,000 departures
1976	4.8	2	38	0.041	1983	5.0	4	15	0.079
1977	4.9	3	78	0.061	1984	5.4	1	4	0.018
1978	5.0	5	160	0.100	1985	5.8	4	197	0.069
1979	5.4	4	351	0.074	1986	6.4	2	1	0.031
1980	5.4	0	0	0.000	1987	6.6	4[1]	231	0.046[1]
1981	5.2	4	4	0.077	1988	6.7	3[1]	285	0.030[1]
1982	5.0	4	233	0.060					

(1) Sabotage-caused accidents are incl. in the Accidents but not in the Accident rates.

Busiest Foreign Airports in 1988*

Source: Airport Operators Council International (passengers arriving & departing)

London, UK, Heathrow	37,525,300	Amsterdam, Netherlands, Schiphol	14,510,042
Tokyo, Japan, Haneda	32,177,040	Stockholm, Sweden, Arlanda	13,145,940
Frankfurt, W. Germany	24,442,966	Sydney, Australia, Kingsford Smith	12,492,689
Paris, France, Orly	22,205,823	Singapore, Changi	11,380,950
London, UK, Gatwick	20,761,200	Copenhagen, Denmark	11,133,147
Osaka, Japan	20,060,795	Zurich, Switzerland	10,791,427
Toronto, Canada, Lester B. Pearson	19,053,271	Fukuoka, Japan	10,720,711
Paris, France, Charles De Gaulle	17,887,294	Bangkok, Thailand	10,554,757
Hong Kong	15,276,789	Dusseldorf, W. Germany	9,981,930

*Does not include airports that did not respond to the AOCI survey.

Leading Passenger Airlines in 1988

(In thousands)

Airline	Passengers	Airline	Passengers	Airline	Passengers
American	64,296	Piedmont	27,117	Braniff	4,322
Delta	59,969	Trans World	25,124	Midway	4,258
United	56,326	Southwest	16,842	Aloha	3,426
Continental	37,636	Pan American	16,755	Air Wisconsin	2,420
Northwest	35,784	America West	12,651	PSA	2,365
Eastern	35,621	Hawaiian	5,497	Horizon Air	1,397
USAir	32,466	Alaska	4,772		

Notable Proposed U.S. Space Missions

Source: National Aeronautics and Space Administration

Year, Month		Mission	Purpose
1989	Dec.	Hubble Space Telescope (b)	Study stars and galaxies
1990	Feb.	Roentgen Satellite (a)	Study X-ray emissions from stars and galaxies
	Mar.	Astronomy/Broad Band X-ray Telescope (c)	Obtain ultraviolet and X-ray data on stars
	April	Gamma Ray Observatory (b)	Investigate black holes, neutron stars and other gamma-ray emitters
	June	Space Life Sciences Lab (c)	First of a series of missions to study effects of weightlessness
		Combined Release and Radiation Satellite	Study effects of radiation on spacecraft components
	Oct.	Ulysses (b)	Study Sun's environment
1991	Jan.	Tethered Satellite System (c)	Study gas clouds and electrical fields in space
	Feb.	International Microgravity Lab (c)	Establish system for life-science studies
	May	Atmospheric Lab for Applications & Science (c)	Study variations in solar spectrum and Earth's atmosphere
	July	Spacelab (c)	Low-gravity experiments
	Aug.	Extreme Ultraviolet Explorer (a)	Catalog ultraviolet spectrum of stars and galaxies
	Oct.	Upper Atmosphere Research Satellite (c)	Study physical processes of upper atmosphere
	Nov.	Doppler Imaging Interferometer (c)	Study upper-atmospheric winds
		Small Explorer-1 (a)	First of a series to study space physics and atmospheric science
1992	May	Space Radar Lab (c)	Acquire radar images of Earth's surface
	June	TOPEX/Poseidon (a)	Study relationship of ocean systems to climate
	Sept.	Mars Observer (a)	Study climate and surface of Mars
		Shuttle High-energy Astrophysics Lab (c)	Study X-ray sources and spectrum in space
1993	June	Gravity Probe (b)	Prototype of mission to test Einstein's theory of relativity
		Polar (a)	Study physical properties of the aurora borealis
	Nov.	Waves in Space Plasmas (c)	Study gaslike particles in space with radio-signal experiments
1994		X-ray Timing Explorer (a)	Study compact X-ray sources such as neutron stars and black holes
1995		Advanced X-ray Astronomy Facility (b)	Observatory with high-resolution telescope; to be in orbit 15 years
1996		Comet Rendezvous Asteroid Flyby (a)	Study origin and evolution of solar system
1997		Earth Observing System (a)	Orbit and study Earth
1998		Cassini (a)	Study Saturn
1999		Space Infrared Telescope Facility (b)	Measure infrared emissions from Milky Way to get clearer picture of galaxy
2000		Mars Rover Sample Return (d)	Collect Martian-soil samples and return to Earth for observation

(a) Launched by expendable rocket. (b) Launched by shuttle. (c) Carried aboard shuttle. (d) To be determined.

International Space Projects

Source: Omni Space Almanac, Pharos Books

Date	Event
1988-1989	Olympus, Europe's new generation comsat, launched.
1990	Gamma Ray Observatory launched, a joint effort of Britain, the Netherlands, the United States, and West Germany.
1990	Russian space shuttle operational.
1990	Tethered Satellite System (built by Italy) launched by the space shuttle.
1991	Eureca, Europe's first free-flying, retrievable space platform, launched.

Date	Event
1992	Japan's H-2 launch rocket operational.
1995	Europe's Columbus module and Japan's space station module launched.
1995	Europe's Ariane 5 heavy-lift launch vehicle becomes operational.
1997	Europe's spaceplane, Hermes, built by France, is operational.
2004	Britain's HOTOL spaceship, a one-stage-to orbit, air-breathing scramjet, offers secheduled service to orbit.

ENERGY
World Nuclear Power

Source: International Atomic Energy Agency, April, 1989

Country	Reactors in Operation # of Units	Reactors in Operation Total MW(e)[1]	Reactors under Construction # of Units	Reactors under Construction Total MW(e)[1]	Nuclear Electricity Supplied, 1988 TW(e).h[1]	Nuclear Electricity Supplied, 1988 % of Total	Total Operating Experience to December 31, 1988 Years	Total Operating Experience to December 31, 1988 Months
Argentina	2	935	1	692	5.1	11.2	20	7
Belgium	7	5,480	—	—	40.6	65.5	86	7
Brazil	1	626	1	1,245	0.6	0.3	6	9
Bulgaria	5	2,585	2	1,906	16.0	35.6	43	8
Canada	18	12,185	4	3,524	78.2	16.0	206	0
China	—	—	3	2,148	—	—	—	—
Cuba	—	—	2	816	—	—	—	1
Czechoslovakia	8	3,264	8	5,120	21.7	26.7	44	1
Finland	4	2,310	—	—	18.4	36.0	39	4
France	55	52,588	9	2,245	260.2	69.9	488	1
East Germany	5	1,694	6	3,432	10.9*	9.9	72	5
West Germany	23	21,491	2	1,520	137.8	34.0	279	3
Hungary	4	1,645	—	—	12.6	48.9	14	2
India	6	1,154	8	1,760	5.4	3.0	72	8
Iran	—	—	2	2,392	—	—	77	10
Italy	2	1,120	—	—			394	0
Japan	38	8,253	12	10,931	167.8*	23.4	36	4
South Korea	8	6,270	1	900	38.0	46.9	36	
Mexico	—	—	2	1,308	—	—	—	9
Netherlands	2	508	—	—	3.5	5.3	35	3
Pakistan	1	125	—	—	0.2	0.6	17	
Poland	—	—	2	880	—	—	—	—
Romania	—	—	5	3,300	—	—	—	—
South Africa	2	1,842	—	—	10.5	7.3	8	3
Spain	10	7,519	—	—	48.3	36.1	82	7
Sweden	12	9,693	—	—	66.3	46.9	135	2
Switzerland	5	2,952	—	—	21.5	7.4	68	10
Taiwan	6	4,924	—	—	29.3*	1.0*	44	1
United Kingdom	40	11,921	2	1,833	55.5	19.3	810	10
United States	108	95,273	7	7,689	526.9	19.5	1,261	10
Soviet Union	56	33,823	26	21,230	215.7	12.6	687	2
Yugoslavia	1	632	—	—	3.9	5.2	7	3
Total	**429**	**310,812**	**105**	**84,871**	**1,794.9**	—	**5,040**	**9**

[1]IAEA estimate; 1 terawatt-hour (TW(e).h) = 10^6 megawatt-hour (MW(e).h). For an average power plant, 1 TW(e).h = 0.39 megatonnes of coal equivalent (input) and 0.23 megatonnes of oil equivalent (input).

U.S. Nuclear Power Plant Operations

Source: Energy Information Administration, Monthly Energy Review, March 1989

	Operable Reactors Number	Nuclear-Based Electricity Generation Million Net Kilowatthours	Nuclear Portion of Domestic Electricity Generation Percent		Operable Reactors Number	Nuclear-Based Electricity Generation Million Net Kilowatthours	Nuclear Portion of Domestic Electricity Generation Percent
1976	61	191,104	9.4	1984	86	327,634	13.6
1977	65	250,883	11.8	1985	95	383,691	15.5
1978	70	276,403	12.5	1986	100	414,038	16.6
1979	68	255,155	11.4	1987	107	455,270	17.7
1980	70	251,116	11.0	1988	108	526,901	19.5
1981	74	272,674	11.9	1989 January	108	46,328	20.0
1982	77	282,773	12.6	1989 February	108	36,725	17.7
1983	80	293,677	12.7	1989 March	108	39,636	17.5

Status of U.S. Nuclear Reactor Units

Source: Energy Information Administration, Monthly Energy Review, March 1989

	Licensed for Operation Operable	Licensed for Operation In Startup	Construction Permits Granted	Construction Permits Pending	On Order	Announced	Total	Total Design Capacity Million Net Kilowatts
				Number of Reactor Units				
1976	61	0	72	66	16	19	234	236
1977	65	1	80	52	13	9	220	220
1978	70	0	90	32	9	4	205	204
1979	68	0	91	21	3	0	183	179
1980	70	2	82	12	3	0	163	163
1981	74	2	75	11	3	0	163	157
1982	77	2	60	3	2	0	144	135
1983	80	3	53	0	2	0	138	129
1984	86	6	38	0	2	0	132	123
1985	95	3	30	0	2	0	130	121
1986	100	7	19	0	2	0	128	119
1987	107	4	14	0	2	0	127	119
1988	108	3	13	0	0	0	124	116
1989 January	108	3	13	0	0	0	124	116
1989 February	108	3	13	0	0	0	124	116
1989 March	108	3	13	0	0	0	124	116

U.S. Total Energy Production by Source, 1954-1988

Source: Energy Information Administration. Annual Energy Review. 1988 (quadrillion Btu, except as noted)

Year	Coal	Natural Gas[1]	Crude Oil[2]	Natural Gas Plant Liquids	Hydroelectric Power[3]	Nuclear Electric Power[4]	Geothermal[4]	Total	Percent Change[5]
1954	10.54	8.68	13.43	1.11	1.36	0	0	35.13	4.5
1955	12.37	9.34	14.41	1.24	1.36	0	0	38.73	10.2
1956	13.31	10.00	15.18	1.28	1.43	0	0	41.21	6.4
1957	13.06	10.61	15.18	1.29	1.52	0	0	41.65	1.1
1958	10.78	10.94	14.20	1.29	1.59	(6)	0	38.81	−6.8
1959	10.78	11.95	14.93	1.38	1.55	(6)	0	40.60	4.6
1960	10.82	12.66	14.93	1.46	1.61	0.01	0	41.49	2.2
1961	10.45	13.10	15.21	1.55	1.66	0.02	(6)	41.99	1.2
1962	10.90	13.72	15.52	1.59	1.82	0.03	(6)	43.58	3.8
1963	11.85	14.51	15.97	1.71	1.77	0.04	(6)	45.85	5.2
1964	12.52	15.30	16.16	1.80	1.89	0.04	(6)	47.72	4.1
1965	13.06	15.78	16.52	1.88	2.06	0.04	(6)	49.34	3.4
1966	13.47	17.01	17.56	2.00	2.06	0.06	(6)	52.17	5.7
1967	13.83	17.94	18.65	2.18	2.35	0.09	0.01	55.04	5.5
1968	13.61	19.07	19.31	2.32	2.35	0.14	0.01	56.81	3.2
1969	13.86	20.45	19.56	2.42	2.65	0.15	0.01	59.10	4.0
1970	14.61	21.67	20.40	2.51	2.63	0.24	0.01	62.07	5.0
1971	13.19	22.28	20.03	2.54	2.82	0.41	0.01	61.29	−1.3
1972	14.09	22.21	20.04	2.60	2.86	0.58	0.03	62.42	1.8
1973	13.99	22.19	19.49	2.57	2.86	0.91	0.04	62.06	−0.6
1974	14.07	21.21	18.57	2.47	3.18	1.27	0.05	60.84	−2.0
1975	14.99	19.64	17.73	2.37	3.15	1.90	0.07	59.86	−1.6
1976	15.65	19.48	17.26	2.33	2.98	2.11	0.08	59.89	0.1
1977	15.76	19.57	17.45	2.33	2.33	2.70	0.08	60.22	0.5
1978	14.91	19.49	18.43	2.25	2.94	3.02	0.06	61.10	1.5
1979	17.54	20.08	18.10	2.29	2.93	2.78	0.08	63.80	4.4
1980	18.60	19.91	18.25	2.25	2.90	2.74	0.11	64.76	1.5
1981	18.38	19.70	18.15	2.31	2.76	3.01	0.12	64.42	−0.5
1982	18.64	18.25	18.31	2.19	3.26	3.13	0.10	63.89	−0.8
1983	17.25	16.53	18.39	2.18	3.50	3.20	0.13	61.19	−4.2
1984	19.72	17.93	18.85	2.27	3.31	3.55	0.16	65.81	7.6
1985	19.33	16.92	18.99	2.24	2.94	4.15	0.20	64.78	−1.6
1986	19.51	16.47	18.38	2.15	3.03	4.47	0.22	64.25	−0.8
1987	20.14	17.05	17.67	2.22	2.59	4.91	0.23	64.82	0.9
1988[p]	20.94	17.19	17.26	2.26	2.32	5.68	0.22	65.88	1.6

(1) Dry natural gas; (2) Includes lease condensate; (3) Electric utility and industrial generation of hydroelectric power; (4) Generated by electric utilities; (5) Percent change from previous year calculated from data prior to rounding; (6) Less than 0.005 quadrillion Btu; (p) = preliminary.

U.S. Total Energy Consumption by Source, 1954-1988

Source: Energy Information Administration. Annual Energy Review. 1988 (quadrillion Btu, except as noted)

Year	Coal	Natural Gas	Petroleum[1]	Hydroelectric Power[2]	Nuclear Electric Power[3]	Geothermal[3]	Total	Percent Change[4]
1954	9.71	8.33	15.84	1.39	0	0	35.27	2.8
1955	11.17	9.00	17.25	1.41	0	0	38.82	10.1
1956	11.35	9.61	17.94	1.49	0	0	40.38	4.0
1957	10.82	10.19	17.93	1.56	0	0	40.48	0.3
1958	9.53	10.66	18.53	1.63	(5)	0	40.35	−0.3
1959	9.52	11.72	19.32	1.59	(5)	0	42.14	4.4
1960	9.84	12.39	19.92	1.66	0.01	(5)	43.80	3.9
1961	9.62	12.93	20.22	1.68	0.02	(5)	44.46	1.5
1962	9.91	13.73	21.05	1.82	0.03	(5)	46.53	4.7
1963	10.41	14.40	21.70	1.77	0.04	(5)	48.32	3.9
1964	10.96	15.29	22.30	1.91	0.04	(5)	50.50	4.5
1965	11.58	15.77	23.25	2.06	0.04	(5)	52.68	4.3
1966	12.14	17.00	24.40	2.07	0.06	(5)	55.66	5.6
1967	11.91	17.94	25.28	2.34	0.09	0.01	57.57	3.4
1968	12.33	19.21	26.98	2.34	0.14	0.01	61.00	6.0
1969	12.38	20.68	28.34	2.66	0.15	0.01	64.19	5.2
1970	12.26	21.79	29.52	2.65	0.24	0.01	66.43	3.5
1971	11.60	22.47	30.56	2.86	0.41	0.01	67.89	2.2
1972	12.08	22.70	32.95	2.86	0.58	0.03	71.26	5.0
1973	12.97	22.51	34.84	2.94	0.91	0.04	74.28	4.2
1974	12.66	21.73	33.45	3.01	1.27	0.05	72.54	−2.3
1975	12.66	19.95	32.73	3.31	1.90	0.07	70.55	−2.8
1976	13.58	20.35	35.17	3.22	2.11	0.08	74.36	5.4
1977	13.92	19.93	37.12	3.07	2.70	0.08	76.29	2.6
1978	13.77	20.00	37.97	2.51	3.02	0.06	78.09	2.4
1979	15.04	20.67	37.12	3.14	2.78	0.08	78.90	1.0
1980	15.42	20.39	34.20	3.14	2.74	0.11	75.96	−3.7
1981	15.91	19.93	31.93	3.12	3.01	0.12	73.99	−2.6
1982	15.32	18.51	30.23	3.11	3.13	0.10	70.84	−4.3
1983	15.90	17.36	30.05	3.56	3.20	0.13	70.50	−0.5
1984	17.07	18.51	31.05	3.87	3.55	0.16	74.06	5.1
1985	17.48	17.85	30.92	3.72	4.15	0.20	73.96	−0.1
1986	17.26	16.71	32.20	3.36	4.47	0.22	74.26	0.4
1987	18.01	17.67	32.87	3.40	4.91	0.23	76.77	3.4
1988[p]	18.81	18.60	33.96	3.07	5.68	0.22	79.94	4.1

(1) Petroleum products supplied including natural gas plant liquids and crude oil burned as fuel; (2) Electric utility and industrial generation of hydroelectric power and net electricity imports; (3) Generated by electric utilities; (4) Percent change from previous year calculated from data prior to rounding; (5) Less than 0.005 quadrillion Btu; (p) = preliminary.

World Production of Crude Oil[1], 1960-1988

Source: Energy Information Administration, Annual Energy Review, 1988 (millions of barrels per day)

Year	Total[2] OPEC	Canada	China	Mexico	United Kingdom	United States	U.S.S.R.	Other Non-OPEC	Total World
1960	8.70	0.52	0.10	0.27	[3]	7.04	2.91	1.42	20.96
1961	9.36	0.61	0.11	0.29	[3]	7.18	3.28	1.60	22.43
1962	10.51	0.67	0.12	0.31	[3]	7.33	3.67	1.71	24.32
1963	11.51	0.71	0.13	0.32	[3]	7.54	4.07	1.85	26.13
1964	12.98	0.75	0.18	0.32	[3]	7.61	4.60	1.92	28.36
1965	14.34	0.81	0.23	0.32	[3]	7.80	4.79	2.01	30.30
1966	15.77	0.88	0.29	0.33	[3]	8.30	5.23	2.13	32.93
1967	16.85	0.96	0.28	0.37	[3]	8.81	5.68	2.42	35.37
1968	18.79	1.19	0.30	0.39	[3]	9.10	6.08	2.79	38.64
1969	20.91	1.13	0.48	0.46	[3]	9.24	6.48	2.99	41.69
1970	23.41	1.26	0.60	0.49	[3]	9.64	6.97	3.50	45.87
1971	25.33	1.35	0.78	0.49	[3]	9.46	7.44	3.64	48.48
1972	27.09	1.53	0.90	0.51	[3]	9.44	7.88	3.77	51.13
1973	30.99	1.80	1.09	0.47	[3]	9.21	8.33	3.80	55.68
1974	30.73	1.55	1.32	0.57	[3]	8.77	8.86	3.86	55.66
1975	27.15	1.43	1.49	0.71	0.01	8.38	9.47	4.14	52.78
1976	30.74	1.31	1.67	0.83	0.25	8.13	9.99	4.36	57.27
1977	31.30	1.32	1.87	0.98	0.77	8.25	10.49	4.62	59.59
1978	29.88	1.32	2.08	1.21	1.08	8.71	10.95	4.78	60.00
1979	31.00	1.50	2.12	1.46	1.57	8.55	11.19	5.09	62.48
1980	26.99	1.44	2.11	1.94	1.62	8.60	11.46	5.20	59.35
1981	22.84	1.29	2.01	2.31	1.81	8.57	11.55	5.39	55.78
1982	19.15	1.27	2.05	2.75	2.07	8.65	11.62	5.65	53.18
1983	17.89	1.36	2.12	2.69	2.29	8.69	11.68	6.25	52.97
1984	17.86	1.44	2.30	2.78	2.48	8.88	11.58	6.90	54.20
1985	16.63	1.47	2.51	2.75	2.53	8.97	11.25	7.54	53.65
1986	18.75	1.47	2.62	2.44	2.55	8.68	11.54	7.85	55.89
1987	18.58	1.53	2.69	2.48	2.48	8.35	11.69	8.23	56.10
1988p	20.52	1.60	2.69	2.51	2.27	8.13	11.68	8.69	58.09

(1) Includes lease condensate, excludes natural gas plant liquids; (2) Current membership of the Organization of the Petroleum Exporting Countries includes Algeria, Ecuador, Gabon, Indonesia, Iran, Iraq, Kuwait, Libya, Nigeria, Qatar, Saudi Arabia, United Arab Emirates, and Venezuela; (3) Less than 5,000 barrels per-day; (p) = preliminary.

U.S. Coal Production and Consumption, 1950-1988

Source: Energy Information Administration, Annual Energy Review, 1988 (million short tons)

Year	Production Bituminous Coal	Production Sub-bituminous Coal	Production Lignite	Production Anthracite	Production Total	Consumption Electric Utilities	Consumption Coke Plants	Consumption Transportation	Consumption Residential & Commercial	Consumption Total
1950	516.3	(1)	(1)	44.1	560.4	91.9	104.0	63.0	114.6	494.1
1951	533.7	(1)	(1)	42.7	576.3	105.8	113.7	56.2	101.5	505.9
1952	466.8	(1)	(1)	40.6	507.4	107.1	97.8	39.8	92.3	454.1
1953	457.3	(1)	(1)	30.9	488.2	115.9	113.1	29.6	79.2	454.8
1954	391.7	(1)	(1)	29.1	420.8	118.4	85.6	18.6	69.1	389.9
1955	464.6	(1)	(1)	26.2	490.8	143.8	107.7	17.0	68.4	447.0
1956	500.9	(1)	(1)	28.9	529.8	158.3	106.3	13.8	64.2	456.9
1957	492.7	(1)	(1)	25.3	518.0	160.8	108.4	9.8	49.0	434.5
1958	410.4	(1)	(1)	21.2	431.6	155.7	76.8	4.7	47.9	385.7
1959	412.0	(1)	(1)	20.6	432.7	168.4	79.6	3.6	40.8	385.1
1960	415.5	(1)	(1)	18.8	434.3	176.7	81.4	3.0	40.9	398.1
1961	403.0	(1)	(1)	17.4	420.4	182.2	74.2	0.8	37.3	390.4
1962	422.1	(1)	(1)	16.9	439.0	193.3	74.7	0.7	36.5	402.3
1963	458.9	(1)	(1)	18.3	477.2	211.3	78.1	0.7	31.5	423.5
1964	487.0	(1)	(1)	17.2	504.2	225.4	89.2	0.7	27.2	445.7
1965	512.1	(1)	(1)	14.9	527.0	244.8	95.3	0.7	25.7	472.0
1966	533.9	(1)	(1)	12.9	546.8	266.5	96.4	0.6	25.6	497.7
1967	552.6	(1)	(1)	12.3	564.9	274.2	92.8	0.5	22.1	491.4
1968	545.2	(1)	(1)	11.5	556.7	297.8	91.3	0.4	20.0	509.8
1969	547.2	8.3	5.0	10.5	571.0	310.6	93.4	0.3	18.9	516.4
1970	578.5	16.4	8.0	9.7	612.7	320.2	96.5	0.3	16.1	523.2
1971	521.3	22.2	8.7	8.7	560.9	327.3	83.2	0.2	15.2	501.6
1972	556.8	27.5	11.0	7.1	602.5	351.8	87.7	0.2	11.7	524.3
1973	543.5	33.9	14.3	6.8	598.6	389.2	94.1	0.1	11.1	562.6
1974	545.7	42.2	15.5	6.6	610.0	391.8	90.2	0.1	11.4	558.4
1975	577.5	51.1	19.8	6.2	654.6	406.0	83.6	(2)	9.4	562.6
1976	588.4	64.8	25.5	6.2	684.9	448.4	84.7	(2)	8.9	603.8
1977	581.0	82.1	28.2	5.9	697.2	477.1	77.7	(2)	9.0	625.3
1978	534.0	96.8	34.4	5.0	670.2	481.2	71.4	(2)	9.5	625.2
1979	612.3	121.5	42.5	4.8	781.1	527.1	77.4	(2)	8.4	680.5
1980	628.8	147.7	47.2	6.1	829.7	569.3	66.7	(2)	6.5	702.7
1981	608.0	159.7	50.7	5.4	823.8	596.8	61.0	(2)	7.4	732.6
1982	620.2	160.9	52.4	4.6	838.1	593.7	40.9	(2)	8.2	706.9
1983	568.6	151.0	58.3	4.1	782.1	625.2	37.0	(2)	8.4	736.7
1984	649.5	179.2	63.1	4.2	895.9	664.4	44.0	(2)	9.1	791.3
1985	613.9	192.7	72.4	4.7	883.6	693.8	41.1	(2)	7.8	818.0
1986	620.1	189.6	76.4	4.3	890.3	685.1	36.0	(2)	7.7	804.3
1987	636.6	200.2	78.4	3.6	918.8	717.9	37.0	(2)	7.7	836.9
1988p	647.9	221.4	86.1	3.5	958.9	756.8	41.0	(2)	6.9	881.4

(1) Included in bituminous; (2) Less than 0.05 million short tons; (p) = preliminary.

U.S. Household Energy Consumption by Census Region, 1978-82, 1984, and 1987

Source: Energy Information Administration. Annual Energy Review, 1988 (quadrillion Btu, except as noted)

Census Region	1978	1979	1980	1981	1982	1984[2]	1987[p]
Northeast							
Natural Gas	1.14	1.05	0.92	1.06	0.99	0.93	1.05
Electricity[3]	0.39	0.39	0.39	0.42	0.38	0.41	0.45
Distillate Fuel Oil and Kerosene	1.32	1.03	1.09	0.96	0.79	0.93	0.85
Liquefied Petroleum Gases	0.03	0.03	0.03	0.03	0.02	0.03	0.02
Total[1]	2.89	2.50	2.43	2.47	2.18	2.29	2.36
Consumption per household (million Btu)	166	145	138	138	122	125	124
North Central							
Natural Gas	2.53	2.48	2.02	2.24	1.76	1.99	1.84
Electricity[3]	0.60	0.59	0.60	0.57	0.57	0.55	0.61
Distillate Fuel Oil and Kerosene	0.46	0.31	0.16	0.17	0.15	0.13	0.14
Liquefied Petroleum Gases	0.12	0.10	0.15	0.13	0.11	0.13	0.13
Total	3.70	3.48	2.92	3.12	2.60	2.80	2.73
Consumption per household (million Btu)	180	168	139	147	122	129	123
South							
Natural Gas	0.96	0.91	1.11	1.16	1.13	1.15	1.09
Electricity[3]	1.00	0.97	1.06	1.03	1.05	1.06	1.21
Distillate Fuel Oil and Kerosene	0.32	0.28	0.27	0.16	0.17	0.16	0.16
Liquefied Petroleum Gases	0.15	0.14	0.15	0.12	0.12	0.12	0.11
Total	2.43	2.30	2.59	2.46	2.46	2.50	2.58
Consumption per household (million Btu)	99	92	96	89	88	85	83
West							
Natural Gas	0.95	0.88	0.89	0.93	0.89	0.91	0.87
Electricity[3]	0.48	0.47	0.41	0.46	0.42	0.47	0.48
Distillate Fuel Oil and Kerosene	0.09	0.09	0.04	0.03	0.03	0.04	0.02
Liquefield Petroleum Gases	0.03	0.04	0.04	0.04	0.04	0.03	0.05
Total	1.54	1.47	1.38	1.47	1.38	1.45	1.41
Consumption per household (million Btu)	110	100	86	90	84	85	77
United States							
Natural Gas	5.58	5.31	4.94	5.39	4.77	4.98	4.84
Electricity[3]	2.47	2.42	2.46	2.48	2.42	2.48	2.75
Distillate Fuel Oil and Kerosene	2.19	1.71	1.55	1.33	1.14	1.26	1.17
Liquefied Petroleum Gases	0.33	0.31	0.36	0.31	0.29	0.31	0.32
Total	10.56	9.74	9.32	9.51	8.62	9.04	9.08
Consumption per household (million Btu)	138	126	114	114	103	105	100

(1) Major energy items only, as shown; (2) Data for April of year shown through March of following year; (3) Includes electricity generated for distribution from wood, waste, geothermal, wind, photovoltaic, and solar thermal energy.

Net Electricity Generation at Electric Utilities by Energy Source

Source: Energy Information Administration. Annual Energy Review, 1988 (billion kilowatthours)

	Coal	Petroleum	Natural Gas	Nuclear Electric Power	Hydro-electric Power	Other[1]	Total
1974	828	301	320	114	301	3	1,867
1975	853	289	300	173	300	3	1,918
1976	944	320	295	191	284	4	2,038
1977	985	358	306	251	220	4	2,124
1978	976	365	305	276	280	3	2,206
1979	1,075	304	329	255	280	4	2,247
1980	1,162	246	346	251	276	6	2,286
1981	1,203	206	346	273	261	6	2,295
1982	1,192	147	305	283	309	5	2,241
1983	1,259	144	274	294	332	6	2,310
1984	1,342	120	297	328	321	9	2,416
1985	1,402	100	292	384	281	11	2,470
1986	1,386	137	249	414	281	12	2,487
1987	1,464	118	273	455	291	12	2,572
1988[p]	1,537	149	253	527	223	12	2,701

(1) Electricity produced from geothermal, wood, waste, wind, photovoltaic, and solar thermal energy sources connected to electric utility distribution systems; p = preliminary.

U.S. Passenger Car Efficiency, 1966-1987

Source: Energy Information Administration. Annual Energy Review, 1988

Year	Mileage Thousand Miles per Car	Mileage Index 1973 = 100.0	Fuel Consumption Gallons per Car	Fuel Consumption Index 1973 = 100.0	Fuel Rate Miles per Gallon	Fuel Rate Index 1973 = 100.0
1966	9.92	96.7	703	91.2	14.1	106.0
1968	10.14	98.8	731	94.8	13.9	104.5
1970	10.27	100.0	760	98.6	13.5	101.5
1973	10.26	100.0	771	100.0	13.3	100.0
1975	9.69	94.4	716	93.9	13.5	101.5
1977	9.88	96.3	716	93.9	13.8	103.8
1980	9.14	89.1	591	76.7	15.5	116.5
1981	9.19	89.6	576	74.7	15.9	119.6
1982	9.43	91.9	566	73.4	16.7	125.6
1983	9.48	92.4	553	71.7	17.1	128.6
1984	9.56	93.2	536	69.5	17.8	133.8
1985	9.56	93.2	525	68.1	18.2	136.8
1986	9.61	93.7	526	68.2	18.3	137.6
1987[p]	9.88	96.3	515	66.8	19.2	144.4

(p) = preliminary

U.S. Net Imports of Energy by Source, 1953-88

Source: Energy Information Administration, Annual Energy Review, 1988 (quadrillion Btu)

Year	Coal	Petroleum[2]	Natural Gas (Dry)	Other[3]	Total	Year	Coal	Petroleum[2]	Natural Gas (Dry)	Other[3]	Total
1953	-0.97	1.44	-0.02	0.02	0.47	1971	-1.54	8.07	0.88	(4)	7.41
1954	-0.91	1.58	-0.02	0.02	0.67	1972	-1.53	9.83	0.97	0.05	9.32
1955	-1.46	1.98	-0.02	0.04	0.54	1973	-1.42	12.98	0.98	0.14	12.68
1956	-1.98	2.26	-0.03	0.04	0.30	1974	-1.57	12.66	0.91	0.19	12.19
1957	-2.16	2.26	(4)	0.02	0.12	1975	-1.74	12.51	0.90	0.08	11.75
1958	-1.41	3.14	0.10	0.03	1.86	1976	-1.57	15.20	0.92	0.09	14.65
1959	-1.04	3.46	0.12	0.03	2.57	1977	-1.40	18.24	0.98	0.20	18.02
1960	-1.02	3.57	0.15	0.04	2.74	1978	-1.00	17.06	0.94	0.33	17.32
1961	-0.98	3.82	0.22	0.02	3.08	1979	-1.70	16.93	1.24	0.27	16.75
1962	-1.08	4.20	0.40		3.53	1980	-2.39	13.50	0.96	0.18	12.25
1963	-1.35	4.21	0.40	-0.01	3.25	1981	-2.92	11.38	0.86	0.33	9.65
1964	-1.33	4.53	0.44	0.01	3.65	1982	-2.77	9.05	0.90	0.28	7.46
1965	-1.37	5.01	0.44	-0.02	4.06	1983	-2.01	9.08	0.89	0.35	8.31
1966	-1.35	5.21	0.47	-0.01	4.32	1984	-2.12	9.89	0.79	0.39	8.95
1967	-1.35	4.91	0.50	-0.02	4.04	1985	-2.39	8.95	0.89	0.41	7.87
1968	-1.37	5.73	0.58	-0.02	4.90	1986	-2.19	11.53	0.69	0.35	10.38
1969	-1.53	6.42	0.70	-0.02	5.56	1987	-2.05	12.53	0.94	0.48	11.90
1970	-1.93	6.92	0.77	-0.04	5.72	1988ᵖ	-2.45	13.44	1.22	0.34	12.55

(1) Net imports = imports minus exports; (2) Includes imports to Strategic Petroleum Reserve, from 1977; (3) Coal Coke and small amounts of electricity transmitted across U.S. borders with Canada and Mexico; (4) Less than 0.005 quadrillion Btu; (p) = preliminary.

Net Imports of Crude Oil and Petroleum Products by Country of Origin, 1961-1987

Source: Energy Information Administration, Annual Energy Review, 1988 (thousand barrels per day, except as shown)

Year	Organization of Petroleum Exporting Countries (OPEC) Total OPEC[1]	Arab Members of OPEC[2]	Canada	Mexico	United Kingdom	Virgin Is. and Puerto Rico	Total Net Imports	Total Net Imports Percent of Consumption[3]	U.S. Dependence on OPEC Percent of Net Imports[4]	Percent of Consumption[5]
1961	1,283	284	167	27	-10	42	1,743	17.5	73.6	12.9
1962	1,210	241	229	35	-6	40	1,913	18.4	63.3	11.6
1963	1,282	258	243	29	-7	43	1,915	17.8	67.0	11.9
1964	1,359	293	272	23	-9	45	2,057	18.7	66.1	12.3
1965	1,475	324	297	21	-11	45	2,281	19.8	64.7	12.8
1966	1,470	291	352	6	-6	58	2,375	19.7	61.9	12.2
1967	1,258	177	400	13	-51	89	2,230	17.8	56.4	10.0
1968	1,302	272	468	15	13	143	2,609	19.5	49.9	9.7
1969	1,336	276	564	10	7	186	2,933	20.8	45.5	9.4
1970	1,343	196	736	9	-1	270	3,161	21.5	42.5	9.1
1971	1,671	327	831	-14	1	365	3,701	24.3	45.2	11.0
1972	2,061	529	1,082	-20	-1	428	4,519	27.6	45.6	12.6
1973	2,991	914	1,294	-28	(6)	426	6,025	34.8	49.6	17.3
1974	3,277	752	1,038	-27	1	475	5,892	35.4	55.6	19.7
1975	3,599	1,382	824	29	7	484	5,846	35.8	61.6	22.0
1976	5,063	2,423	571	53	24	488	7,090	40.6	71.4	29.0
1977	6,190	3,184	446	155	117	560	8,565	46.5	72.3	33.6
1978	5,747	2,962	359	291	173	436	8,002	42.5	71.8	30.5
1979	5,633	3,054	438	418	196	353	7,985	43.1	70.5	30.4
1980	4,293	2,549	347	506	169	256	6,365	37.3	67.4	25.2
1981	3,315	1,844	358	497	370	169	5,401	33.6	61.4	20.6
1982	2,136	852	397	632	442	154	4,298	28.1	49.7	14.0
1983	1,843	630	471	802	374	178	4,312	28.3	42.7	12.1
1984	2,037	817	547	714	388	184	4,715	30.0	43.2	13.0
1985	1,821	470	696	755	295	114	4,286	27.3	42.5	11.6
1986	2,828	1,160	721	642	342	152	5,439	33.4	52.0	17.4
1987	3,055	1,273	765	585	346	118	5,914	35.5	51.7	18.3
1988ᵖ	3,421	1,826	892	670	301	112	6,353	37.0	53.8	19.9

(1) Includes Nigeria, Saudi Arabia, Venezuela, Ecuador, Gabon, Indonesia, Iran, Iraq, Kuwait, Libya, Qatar, and United Arab Emirates; (2) Includes Algeria, Iraq, Kuwait, Libya, Qatar, Saudi Arabia, and United Arab Emirates; (3) Calculated by dividing total net petroleum imports by total U.S. petroleum products supplied; (4) Calculated by dividing net petroleum imports from OPEC countries by total net petroleum imports; (5) Calculated by dividing net petroleum imports from OPEC countries by total U.S. petroleum product supplied; (6) Less than 500 barrels per day; (p) = preliminary.

World's Largest Capacity Hydro Plants

Source: U.S. Committee on Large Dams, of the Intl. Commission on Large Dams, Sept. 1989

Rank order	Name	Country	Rated capacity now (MW)	Rated capacity planned (MW)	Rank order	Name	Country	Rated capacity now (MW)	Rated capacity planned (MW)
1	Turukhansk (Lower Tungu-ska)*	USSR		20,000	4	Guri (Raúl Leoni)	Venezuela	10,300	10,300
2	Itaipu	Brazil/Paraguay	7,400	13,320	5	Tucuruí	Brazil	2,640	7,260
3	Grand Coulee	USA	7,460	10,830	6	Sayano Shu-shensk*	USSR	6,400	6,400

(continued)

Rank order	Name	Country	Rated capacity now (MW)	Rated capacity planned (MW)	Rank order	Name	Country	Rated capacity now (MW)	Rated capacity planned (MW)
7=	Corpus Posadas	Argentina/Paraguay	4,700	6,000	17=	Rogun*	USSR		3,600
7=	Krasnoyarsk	USSR	6,000	6,000	17=	Oak Creek	USA	3,600	3,600
9	La Grande 2	Canada	5,328	5,328	19	Paulo Afonso I	Brazil		3,409
10	Churchill Falls	Canada	5,225	5,225	20	Pati*	Argentina	1,524	3,300
11	Xingo	Brazil	3,012	5,020	21=	Ilha Solteira	Brazil	3,200	3,200
12	Tarbela	Pakistan	1,750	4,678	21=	Brumley Gap	USA	3,200	3,200
13=	Bratsk	USSR	4,500	4,500	23	Chapetón*	Argentina		3,000
13=	Ust-Ilim	USSR	3,675	4,500	24	Gezhouba	China	2,715	2,715
15	Cabora Bassa	Mozambique	2,425	4,150	25	John Day	USA	2,160	2,700
16	Boguchany	USSR		4,000	25	Nurek	USSR	900	2,700
					25=	Yacyreta*	Argentina/Paraguay		2,700

*Planned or under construction.

Major Dams of the World

Source: U.S. Committee on Large Dams, of the Intl. Commission of Large Dams; September, 1989

World's Highest Dams

Rank order	Name	Country	Height above lowest formation (m)	Rank order	Name	Country	Height above lowest formation (m)
1	Rogun*	USSR	335	14	El Cajón	Honduras	234
2	Nurek	USSR	300	15	Chirkei	USSR	233
3	Grand Dixence	Switzerland	285	16	Oroville	USA	230
4	Inguri	USSR	272	17	Bhakra	India	226
5	Chicoasén	Mexico	261	18	Hoover	USA	221
6	Tehri*	India	261	19	Contra	Switzerland	220
7	Kishau*	India	253	20	Mratinje	Yugoslavia	220
8=	Ertan	China	245	21	Dworshak	USA	219
9=	Sayano-Shushensk*	USSR	245	22	Glen Canyon	USA	216
10	Guavio*	Colombia	243	23=	Toktogue	USSR	215
11	Mica	Canada	242	24	Daniel Johnson	Canada	214
12	Mauvoisin	Switzerland	237	25	San Roque	Philippines	210
13	Chivor	Colombia	237				

*Under construction.

World's Largest Volume Embankment Dams

Rank order	Name	Country	Volume cubic meters × 1000	Rank Order	Name	Country	Volume cubic meters × 1000
1	Tarbella	Pakistan	148,500	14	Oroville	USA	59,635
2	Fort Peck	USA	96,050	15	San Luis	USA	59,559
3	Tucurui	Brazil	85,200	16	Nurek	USSR	58,000
4	Ataturk*	Turkey	85,000	17	Tanda	Pakistan	57,250
5	Yacireta*	Argentina	81,000	18	Garrison	USA	50,843
6	Rogun*	USSR	75,500	19	Chochiti	USA	50,228
7	Oahe	USA	70,339	20	Oosterschelde	Netherlands	50,000
8	Guri	Venezuela	70,000	21	Zhanghe	China	46,232
9	Parambikulam	India	69,165	22	Tabqua	Syria	46,000
10	High Island West	Hong Kong	67,000	23	Aswan High	Egypt	44,300
11	Gardiner	Canada	65,000	24	W A C Bennett	Canada	43,733
12	Afsluitdijk	Netherlands	63,400	25	San Roque	Philippines	43,150
13	Mangla	Pakistan	63,379				

*Under construction.

World's Largest Capacity Manmade Reservoirs

Rank order	Name	Country	Capacity cubic meters × 1000	Rank Order	Name	Country	Capacity cubic meters × 1000
1	Owen Falls	Uganda	204,800	14	Ust-Ilim	USSR	59,300
2	Bratsk	USSR	169,000	15	Boguchany*	USSR	58,200
3	Aswan (High)	Egypt	162,000	16	Kuibyshev	USSR	58,000
4	Kariba	Zimbabwe/Zambia	160,368	17	Serra de Mesa	Brazil	54,400
5	Akosombo	Ghana	147,960	18	Caniapiscau Barrage KA 3	Canada	53,790
6	Daniel Johnson	Canada	141,851				
7	Guri	Venezuela	135,000	19	Bukhtarma	USSR	49,800
8	Krasnoyarsk	USSR	73,300	20	Ataturk	Turkey	48,700
9	W A C Bennett (Portage Mt.)	Canada	70,309	21	Irkutsk	USSR	46,000
10	Zeya	USSR	68,400	22	Tucurui	Brazil	45,500
11	Cabora Bassa	Mozambique	63,000	23	Vilyui	USSR	35,900
12	La Grande 2	Canada	61,715	24	Sanmenxia	China	35,400
13	La Grande 3	Canada	60,020	25	Hoover	USA	34,852

*Under construction

Major U.S. Dams and Reservoirs

Source: Committee on Register of Dams, Corps of Engineers, U.S. Army; September, 1989

Highest Dams

Order	Dam Name	River	State	Type	Height Feet	Height Meters	Year Complete
1	Oroville	Feather	Cal.	E	754	230	1968
2	Hoover	Colorado	Nev.	A	725	221	1936
3	Dworshak	N Fork Clearwater	Id.	G	718	219	1973
4	Glen Canyon	Colorado	Ariz.	A	708	216	1966
5	New Bullards Bar	North Yuba	Cal.	A	636	194	1970
6	New Melones	Stanislaus	Cal.	R	626	191	1979
7	Swift	Lewis	Wash.	E	610	186	1958
8	Mossyrock	Cowlitz	Wash.	A	607	185	1968
9	Shasta	Sacramento	Cal.	G	600	183	1945
10	Hungry Horse	S Fork Flathead	Mon.	A	564	172	1953
11	Grand Coulee	Columbia	Wash.	G	551	168	1942
12	Ross	Skagit	Wash.	A	541	165	1949

E = Embankment, Earthfill; R = Embankment, Rockfill; G = Gravity; A = Arch.

Largest Embankment Dams

Order	Dam Name	River	State	Type	Volume Cubic yards X 1000	Volume Cubic Meters X 1000	Year Complete
1	Fort Peck	Missouri	Mon.	E	125,624	96,050	1937
2	Oahe	Missouri	S.D.	E	91,996	70,339	1958
3	Oroville	Feather	Cal.	E	77,997	59,635	1968
4	San Luis	San Luis Creek	Cal.	E	77,897	59,559	1967
5	Garrison	Missouri	N.D.	E	66,498	50,843	1953
6	Cochiti	Rio Grande	N.M.	E	65,693	50,228	1975
7	Earthquake Lake	Madison	Mon.	E-G	49,998	38,228	1959
8	Fort Randall	Missouri	S.D.	E	49,962	38,200	1952
9	Castaic	Castaic Creek	Cal.	E	43,998	33,640	1973
10	Ludington P/S	Lake Michigan	Mich.	E	37,699	28,824	1973
11	Kingsley	N. Platte	Neb.	E	31,999	24,466	1941
12	Warm Springs	Dry Creek	Cal.	E	29,977	22,920	1982

E = Embankment, Earthfill; R = Embankment, Rockfill; E-R = Embankment, Earth & Rockfill; G = Gravity; A = Arch.

Largest Man-Made Reservoirs

Order	Dam Name	Reservoir	Location	Reservoir Capacity Acre-Feet	Reservoir Capacity Cubic Meters x 1000	Year Completed
1	Hoover	Lake Meade	Nev.	28,253,000	34,850,000	1936
2	Glen Canyon	Lake Powell	Ariz.	26,997,000	33,300,000	1966
3	Garrison	Lake Sakakawea	N.D.	22,635,000	27,920,000	1953
4	Oahe	Lake Oahe	S.D.	22,238,000	27,430,000	1958
5	Fort Peck	Fort Peck Lake	Mon.	17,933,000	22,120,000	1937
6	Grand Coulee	F D Roosevelt Lake	Wash.	9,558,000	11,790,000	1942
7	Libby	Lake Koocanusa	Mon.	5,813,000	7,170,000	1973
8	Fort Randall	Lake Francis Case	S.D.	4,621,000	5,700,000	1952
9	Shasta	Lake Shasta	Cal.	4,548,000	5,610,000	1945
10	Toledo Bend	Toledo Bend Lake	La.	4,475,000	5,520,000	1968
11	Wolf Creek	Cumberland Lake	Ky.	3,997,000	4,930,000	1951
12	Flaming Gorge	Flaming Gorge Reservoir	Ut.	3,786,000	4,670,000	1964

1 acre foot = 1 acre of water, 1 foot deep

Largest Hydropower Projects

Order	Dam Name	River	Location	Rated Capacity mw
1	Grand Coulee	Columbia	Wash.	6,180
2	Chief Joseph	Columbia	Wash.	2,457
3	John Day	Columbia	Ore.	2,160
4	Bath County P/S	Little Back Ck	Va.	2,100
5	Robert Moses-Niagara	Niagara	N.Y.	1,950
6	The Dalles	Columbia	Ore.	1,805
7	Luddington	Lake Michigan	Mich.	1,657
8	Raccoon Mtn	Tennessee River	Tenn.	1,530
9	Hoover	Colorado	Nev.	1,434
10	Pyramid	California Aqueduct	Cal.	1,250
11	Rocky Reach	Columbia	Wash.	1,213
12	Bonneville	Columbia	Ore.	1,092

SCIENCE AND TECHNOLOGY

Scientific Achievements and Discoveries: 1989

Origins of Life on Earth

Archeologists in Israel found a 60,000 year-old Neanderthal skeleton that indicates for the first time that the primitive **hominids** were anatomically **able to talk.** Along with other recent findings, this discovery raises the possibility that Neanderthals and the more advanced, anatomically modern humans could talk to each other. The latest Neanderthal discovery, made at Kebara Cave in Israel, is that of a skeleton containing a hyoid bone, which lies between the chin and the larynx and anchors the muscles that move the tongue, lower jaw, and larynx. According to Baruch Arensburg of Tel Aviv Univ., the shape, size, and position of Neanderthal hyoid bone is identical to that of modern humans and indicates that "the anatomy of speech was the same" in both, and that they "could speak in the same way." Whether they did speak is unknown because of doubt about the capabilities of the Neanderthal brain.

Analysis of grooves on ancient teeth has led to a consensus that these are the marks of heavy **toothpick use by human ancestors.** The earliest known example of the grooved-teeth phenomena was found in 1.8 million-year-old fossils of Homo habilis, an ancestral species, excavated at Omo in Ethiopia. This evidence has led to the conclusion that toothpicks may have been one of the first human-made tools. Christy G. Turner 2d of Arizona State Univ. concluded, "As far as can be empirically documented, the oldest human habit is picking one's teeth."

An analysis of charcoal and some snails found along with broken stone tools and bison bones in Oklahoma, dated as far back as 26,000 to 40,000 years, may be evidence of the **earliest known presence of humans in North America.** Don Wycoff, leader of the Oklahoma Archeological Survey team, emphasized the preliminary nature of the findings. If confirmed, the findings would dramatically alter the current belief that dates human occupation in North America to 11,000 to 11,500 years ago.

A strong consensus is developing among archeologists who believe that **complex human cultures,** with permanent communities and economic and social systems, were established **before the development of agriculture.** The emergence of farming about 10,000 years ago has generally been accepted as the event that led to the rise of cities, writing, and recorded history. Among the findings that have led archeologists to rethink past theories are: beads and pendants, produced in Western Europe around 32,000 years ago by standardized methods and worn to denote social identity; settlements of mammoth-bone houses in central Russia (dating to around 20,000 years ago); and elaborate villages occupied by Middle Eastern foragers nearly 13,000 years ago. According to T. Douglas Price of the Univ. of Wisconsin, "Agriculture by itself was not the revolutionizing force we thought it was." The developing theory also dispels the belief that humans progressed broadly and uniformly through the ages, moving from one clear stage of advancement to another in a preordained series of cultural and technological revolutions. The new theory postulates that development took place with a series of disjointed cultural fluctuations.

Neptune and other Astronomical Findings

After a journey of 12 years and 4.4 billion miles, *Voyager 2* passed within 3,000 miles of Neptune's frigid methane clouds sending back pictures and data about the distant planet and its environment. Among the discoveries concerning Neptune, which is 2.8 billion miles from Earth, *Voyager 2* found the planet to be a pale blue object glowing with auroras and crackling and hissing from radio noise of charged particles trapped by magnetic fields. It also discovered that Neptune has 8 moons. The largest, Triton, was found to be the coldest known object in the solar system, and was believed to contain icy volcanoes. The length of Neptune's day was found to be 16 hours, 3 minutes. Time-lapse photography revealed tremendous velocities of Neptunian winds and a "great dark spot," reminding scientists of the Great Red Spot on Jupiter, which is a giant storm system. Three distinct rings were found around Neptune. One of them consists of at least 3 dense clumps of orbiting debris that stand out from the more diffuse ring particles. The radio messages sent by *Voyager 2* took 4 hours and 6 minutes to reach the Jet Propulsion Laboratory in Pasadena, Calif.

Researchers at Cornell Univ. and the Arecibo radiotelescope in Puerto Rico discovered what they believe is a **galaxy being born,** which would be the first proto-galaxy to be found in the state of gestation. The finding appears to demonstrate that contrary to current belief, galaxies are still being formed, and were not all produced shortly after the cataclysmic explosion, "Big Bang," that is believed to have created the universe. A proto-galaxy is a mass of hydrogen with few or no stars and is big enough to form a galaxy when its hydrogen collapses under the strain of gravitational pull and great masses of material clump together. The vast hydrogen cloud is about 65 million light-years from Earth.

The Big Bang theory of the creation of the universe is being challenged by scientists who believe that hot electrically charged gases known as plasma have played a critical role in shaping the universe. This new theory contends that electric and magnetic forces of plasmas provided the framework and much of the power, along with gravity, to organize matter into galaxies and other large structures. The universe of **plasma cosmology** has existed forever, without a beginning and with no end in sight. The Big Bang theory assumes gravity is the dominant shaping force and rests on Einstein's interpretation of gravity and his general study of relativity. Hannes Alfven, a Swedish physicist who won the Nobel Prize in 1970, is plasma cosmology's most ardent advocate.

Medicine

The discovery of the **gene that causes cystic fibrosis** has led scientists to believe that they will be able to learn how the disease attacks the body and to develop treatments that might save the lives of many patients. Cystic fibrosis is a disorder of the breathing system, pancreas, and sweat glands. It is the most common lethal genetic disease in North America. About 30,000 people in the U.S. have the disease, and approximately 1,000 new cases are diagnosed each year. About 5 percent of all Americans carry the gene for cystic fibrosis, but a child must inherit it from both parents to be affected. The principal researchers are Francis Collins of the Univ. of Michigan and La-Chee Tsui of the Hospital for Sick Children in Toronto.

A new drug, deprenyl, **prevents the death of brain cells** and slows the progress of **Parkinson's disease.** The development of the drug marks the first time that any drug has been shown to delay the symptoms of any neurological disease. The researchers, James W. Tetrud and J. William Langston of the California Parkinson's Foundation in San Jose, cautioned that their study was small and that without an autopsy it was impossible to prove that the drug prevented the death of brain cells in a Parkinson's patient. About 400,000 Americans have Parkinson's disease.

According to a study led by Charles H. Hennekens of Harvard Medical School and Brigham and Women's Hospital in Boston, healthy men over 50 years old who take one **aspirin** every other day **cut the risk of having a heart attack** nearly in half. Aspirin's benefits appeared to be the greatest in men with low cholesterol levels. Doctors from Mount Sinai Medical Center in New York City cautioned that "Aspirin is not a magic pill with regard to heart attacks," but agreed with the potential value of acetylsalicylic acid (aspirin) for high risk patients.

A National Institutes of Health study found that a **blood test** commonly used to measure kidney function is a **highly accurate predictor of heart attacks and stroke** in patients with high blood pressure. The findings showed that people whose blood had high levels of creatinine, a natural byproduct of the breakdown of muscle tissue, were 5 times more likely to die of heart attack or stroke than those with low levels. The study was based on data compiled during an 8-year project that followed 10,500 patients.

While more Americans are **donating organs for transplants**, according to the United Network for Organ Sharing, there is still a critical short supply primarily due to medical advances which are making more people candidates for transplants. A record 16,792 people were awaiting transplants in the U.S. (as of March 1989); the vast majority of them were in need of kidneys. A 15-month study ending in December 1988 showed increases in liver, heart, pancreas, and kidney donations.

AIDS

Researchers have found that **AZT** (azidothymidine), the only medication licensed for the treatment of AIDS in the U.S., can significantly **delay the onset of the disease** in people who are infected but show only mild or even no symptoms of immune system damage. Previously, the drug was thought to benefit only those patients who already had full-fledged AIDS or certain other symptoms including severely debilitated immune systems. As many as 100,000 to 200,000 Americans infected with the AIDS virus have mild symptoms according to Anthony S. Fauci, director of the National Institute of Allergy and Infectious Diseases. Government health officials estimate that 40,000 Americans have full-fledged AIDS and would qualify for AZT under the current standards, and that about 25,000 are taking it. AZT does not cure AIDS, but it does slow the multiplication of the virus. Dr. Fauci said that people who are at risk for being infected with AIDS, even if they have "absolutely no symptoms, it behooves them to get themselves tested."

The Food and Drug Admin. approved a drug, **aerosol pentamidine**, that **helps prevent a type of pneumonia** that is the leading cause of death among AIDS patients. The drug treatment might help 100,000 people infected with the virus who are at risk of developing the pneumonia. Approximately 65 percent of AIDS patients develop the usually fatal strain of pneumonia.

An experimental drug, for the treatment of AIDS, dideoxyinosine or **DDI**, was found to produce **improvements** in patients **without causing toxic side effects** sometimes associated with AZT. In a study of 26 patients, the 13 patients who received the highest doses of the drug showed increases in their immune system cells and decreases in AIDS viral proteins in their blood, as well as weight gain. Researchers cautioned that their findings were preliminary and that their data did not prove that DDI can slow the progress of AIDS infections.

Genetics

According to Judith Hall of the Univ. of British Columbia, different characteristics given to sets of genes by mothers and fathers may be responsible for many kinds of cancer and inherited diseases. New findings suggest that contrary to a fundamental law of genetics, **genes from the mother and those from the father may differ** in ways that help explain some inherited diseases. For example, cancer research has found that in some cases losing a chromosome from a mother is more likely to cause cancer than losing a chromosome from a father. People have 23 pairs of chromosomes, and normally receive one set from each parent. Scientists have believed it made no difference to a child whether it inherited a genetic trait from its mother or its father.

The Federal Bureau of Investigation has begun using **DNA profiling** to obtain positive identification of suspects in criminal investigations. By using the F.B.I. laboratory, any police department in the U.S. can obtain positive identification of a suspect, or exclude him or her based on the unique genetic material in each specimen of blood, semen, other bodily fluids, or tissue. The new method is most useful in sex crimes. Ultimately, the F.B.I. expects to be able to reconstruct a physical profile of a criminal including hair and eye color. The technology is considered even more valuable than fingerprinting because biological evidence like hair or skin is found at crime scenes much more often than fingerprints.

In May 1989, the first federally approved **transfer of cells containing foreign genes** into a human was accomplished at the Clinical Center of the National Institutes of Health. Cancer-fighting cells that had been altered by insertion of a foreign gene were infused into the bloodstream of a cancer patient who had volunteered for the experiment. The main purpose of the procedure was to make the cells easily identifiable so that doctors could track them in the patient's body. The cells, tumor infiltrating lymphocytes, had been taken from the patient's cancerous tissue and treated in the laboratory to increase their numbers and therefore their ability to attack the cancer tissues.

The Brain

Data gathered by Joseph LeDoux, a psychologist at the Center for Neural Science at New York Univ., and other researchers indicate that the brain is arranged so key aspects of **emotional life**, like primitive fears, **can operate largely independent of thought.** This arrangement may explain why certain emotional reactions, like phobias or reactions to experiences early in life are so strong despite their obvious irrationality. Dr. LeDoux said: "Emotional reactions and emotional memories can be formed without any conscious, cognitive participation at all, because anatomically the emotional system can act independently."

Behavior

A research project, conducted by David M. Buss of the Univ. of Michigan, has defined the **points of conflict that arise between men and women** in a wide

(continued)

range of relationships. The findings are similar for couples who are dating, are newlyweds, or are unhappily married. Among the differences between the sexes that the study revealed are: women's feelings of being neglected and men's irritations about women's self-absorption; men's condescension and women's moodiness; and men's complaint that women too often turned down their sexual overtures and women's complaint that men were too aggressive sexually. "The evolutionary model that I use holds that conflicts occur when one sex does something that interferes with the other's strategy for reproduction," Dr. Buss said. His theory is based on the belief that women are more discriminating than men about sexual partners because biologically women have to invest more time and energy in reproduction than do men.

Redford B. Williams, a psychiatrist at Duke Univ., reported that **angry, cynical people** are 5 times as **likely to die before age 50** as people who are calm and trusting. People with so-called type A behavior (fast-talking workaholics) are not more prone to premature death from heart disease, but people who are hostile are more likely to suffer premature death from all causes. "Such toxic personalities can be traced to biological differences that are likely present from birth," said Dr. Williams.

Technology

The largest scientific instrument ever built, the **Large Electron-Positron Collider** (LEP), went into operation in August 1989. LEP is a circular tunnel 16.6 miles in circumference that passes under villages, farms, and the Jura mountains along the border between France and Switzerland. It was built by a consortium of 14 European nations, taking 7 years to complete and costing nearly $1 billion. It is designed to help scientists explore the **nature of matter.** LEP will collide electrons and their antimatter equivalents, positrons. In the collisions, the electrons and positrons annihilate each other, their combined energies merge, and this energy is transformed into heavy, very short-lived particles.

Cold Fusion

B. Stanley Pons of the Univ. of Utah and Martin Fleischmann of the Univ. of Southhampton, England announced in March 1989 that they had achieved **nucler fusion** at room temperature in a jar of water. Nuclear fusion is the force that powers the sun, the stars, and hydrogen bombs, fusing atoms together rather than breaking them apart as is done in nuclear reactors. Harnessing the process could result in an unlimited source of inexpensive electric power. Previously, fusion had been achieved only at high pressures and temperatures, using powerful laser beams or magnets. The announcement was followed by much controversy and skepticism. In May 1989, hundreds of scientists gathered to evaluate "cold fusion," and the concensus was that the findings had no practical use and that Pons and Fleischmann had misinterpreted their results. J. Robert Schrieffer, director of the Institute for Theoretical Physics at the Univ. of California at Santa Barbara, a co-chairman of the conference of scientists, said, "I personally do not believe that the Pons-Fleischmann heat is due to anything but chemical energies." The negative views reflected the failure of many major laboratories around the world to produce the same amount of heat that Pons and Fleishmann claimed to have achieved.

Patents

In 1988, the U.S. Patent and Trademark Office issued 77,924 patents. Of these patents, residents of countries other than the U.S. received 48 percent, with the Japanese receiving 16,158 (21 percent of the total), more than double the number issued to Japanese in 1975, when 35 percent of the patents were issued to residents of foreign nations.

The 10 corporations that received the most U.S. patents in 1988 were: Hitachi, Toshiba, Canon, General Electric, Fuji Photo Film, Philips, Siemens, I.B.M., Mitsubishi Denki, and Bayer.

Computer Software

Software programmers and companies are becoming concerned over the recent push to patent basic programs previously regarded as being in the public domain. Software producers have traditionally depended on copyrights to protect their intellectual property, just as authors or composers do. The Patent Office does not count software patents as a separate category, but patent lawyers reported that there has been a proliferation of such patents issued in 1989 that were applied for a number of years ago. Companies fear that broad patents on basic software could block the creation of new programs, which is often a highly derivative process that refines old ideas.

Equations

A growing number of patents have been applied for and issued for mathematical equations (algorithms). In the past, the courts have ruled that mathematical equations could not be patented because they were similar to the laws of nature. However, in recent years, new technologies have brought into question the distinction between what is natural and what is man-made. One of the best known algorithms recently granted a patent belongs to AT&T's Bell Laboratories, which developed an equation used by large organizations to decide methods of allocating resources.

Inventors of the Year

Four scientists at Genentech, Inc., South San Francisco, Calif. were named "inventors of the year" by Intellectual Property Owners Foundation. The 1989 winners were chosen for their invention of the drug t-PA, used in dissolving blood clots in heart attack victims. The winners were David V. Goeddel, William J. Korh, Diane Pennica, and Gordon A. Behar.

Inventions of 1989

Some of the more "interesting" inventions issued patents during 1989 were: a **drink dispensing machine** for use in **outer space** by the Coca-Cola Co.; a shampoo called "Skunked" that can wash skunk spray out of fur, hair, and clothing; a **synthetic bagpipe** bag that will last longer than traditional bags made from sheepskin, elk hide, or cowhide; a recording system that creates the illusion of **3-dimensional sound** (cycle-acoustic cueing); a tool to cut microscopic grooves in the cornea of the eye to correct the most severe cases of nearsightedness (myopia); an **exercise machine that simulates crawling** for use by sedentary people or those who suffer from lower back pain; a new form of pectin, the additive that makes jellies and jams gel; a chemical solution that preserves human organs to be used in transplants; a "baby cry muffler" designed to quiet a baby's screaming without causing any danger of suffocation; fins that are wide enough to keep an adult afloat for the time it takes to make one running step; and a **better mousetrap** in which the mouse trips a sensor that causes a chamber to lift up and dump the rodent into a plastic bag, causing suffocation.

Computer Virus

Beginning Nov. 2, 1988, a so-called virus spread through many of the university, military, and corporate computers operating in the United States. The virus is a form of computer sabotage. An individual creates a set of instructions designed to copy themselves and spread from computer to computer through networks or shared disks. In this case, the intent appeared to be malicious. Computers linked to the 60,000-member Internet network were affected as the virus filled up the memory capacity of the computers it attacked. As computers ran out of memory, they became inoperable. However, no information was destroyed. Robert Morris Jr., a Cornell graduate student, had designed the virus to test the security of computer systems.

High-Definition Television

High-definition television (HDTV), which produces images as sharp and as detailed as those for movies, is expected to be a $50 billion industry by the year 2000. HDTV is also expected to have wide applications in other areas including personal computers, semiconductors, and telecommunications. While some believe that HDTV will not have great commercial success due to the very high cost of the necessary video screens, the Bush administration is being pressured by U.S. electronics corporations to finance the needed research to enable those companies to better compete with Japan in the HDTV market. The U.S. Defense Department's Defense Advanced Research Projects Agency will provide $30 million in grants in 1989 for research in high-definition television, but the electronics industry is asking for $1.35 billion more. The industry's immediate goal is a 27-inch HDTV set that would sell for $1,500 after production begins in 1993-1994. In June 1989, Japan began the world's first daily broadcasts of HDTV programs. The programs in Japan will be seen only by a select group; receivers cost about $60,000 and are not yet commercially available.

Inventions and Discoveries

Invention	Date	Inventor	Nation.
Adding machine	1642	Pascal	French
Adding machine	1885	Burroughs	U.S.
Addressograph	1892	Rotheim	Norwegian
Aerosol spray	1926	Goodhue	U.S.
Air brake	1868	Westinghouse	U.S.
Air conditioning	1911	Carrier	U.S.
Air pump	1654	Guericke	German
Airplane, automatic pilot	1912	Sperry	U.S.
Airplane, experimental	1896	Langley	U.S.
Airplane jet engine	1939	Ohain	German
Airplane with motor	1903	Wright bros.	U.S.
Airplane, hydro.	1911	Curtiss	U.S.
Airship	1852	Giffard	French
Airship, rigid dirigible	1900	Zeppelin	German
Arc welder	1919	Thomson	U.S.
Autogyro	1920	de la Cierva	Spanish
Automobile, differential gear	1885	Benz	German
Automobile, electric	1892	Morrison	U.S.
Automobile, exp'mtl	1864	Marcus	Austrian
Automobile, gasoline	1889	Daimler	German
Automobile, gasoline	1892	Duryea	U.S.
Automobile magneto	1897	Bosch	German
Automobile muffler	...	Maxim, H.P.	U.S.
Automobile self-starter	1911	Kettering	U.S.
Babbitt metal	1839	Babbitt	U.S.
Bakelite	1907	Baekeland Belg.	U.S.
Balloon	1783	Montgolfier	French
Barometer	1643	Torricelli	Italian
Bicycle, modern	1885	Starley	English
Bifocal lens	1780	Franklin	U.S.
Block signals, railway	1867	Hall	U.S.
Bomb, depth	1916	Tait	U.S.
Bottle machine	1895	Owens	U.S.
Braille printing	1829	Braille	French
Burner, gas	1855	Bunsen	German
Calculating machine	1833	Babbage	English
Camera—see also Photography			
Camera, Kodak	1888	Eastman, Walker	U.S.
Camera, Polaroid Land	1948	Land	U.S.
Car coupler	1873	Janney	U.S.
Carburetor, gasoline	1893	Maybach	German
Card time recorder	1894	Cooper	U.S.
Carding machine	1797	Whittemore	U.S.
Carpet sweeper	1876	Bissell	U.S.
Cash register	1879	Ritty	U.S.
Cathode ray tube	1878	Crookes	English
Cellophane	1908	Brandenberger	Swiss
Celluloid	1870	Hyatt	U.S.
Cement, Portland	1824	Aspdin	English
Chronometer	1761	Harrison	English
Circuit breaker	1925	Hilliard	U.S.
Clock, pendulum	1657	Huygens	Dutch
Coaxial cable system	1929	Affel, Espensched	U.S.
Coke oven	1893	Hoffman	Austrian
Compressed air rock drill	1871	Ingersoll	U.S.
Comptometer	1887	Felt	U.S.
Computer, automatic sequence	1944	Aiken et al.	U.S.
Condenser microphone (telephone)	1916	Wente	U.S.
Corn, hybrid	1917	Jones	U.S.
Cotton gin	1793	Whitney	U.S.
Cream separator	1878	DeLaval	Swedish
Cultivator, disc	1878	Mallon	U.S.
Cystoscope	1878	Nitze	German
Diesel engine	1895	Diesel	German
Dynamite	1866	Nobel	Swedish
Dynamo, continuous current	1871	Gramme	Belgian
Dynamo, hydrogen cooled	1915	Schuler	U.S.
Electric battery	1800	Volta	Italian
Electric fan	1882	Wheeler	U.S.
Electrocardiograph	1903	Einthoven	Dutch
Electroencephalograph	1929	Berger	German
Electromagnet	1824	Sturgeon	English
Electron spectrometer	1944	Deutsch, Elliott, Evans	U.S.
Electron tube multigrid	1913	Langmuir	U.S.
Electroplating	1805	Brugnatelli	Italian
Electrostatic generator	1929	Van de Graaff	U.S.
Elevator brake	1852	Otis	U.S.
Elevator, push button	1922	Larson	U.S.
Engine, coal-gas 4-cycle	1876	Otto	German
Engine, compression ignition	1883	Daimler	German
Engine, electric ignition	1883	Benz	German
Engine, gas, compound	1926	Eickemeyer	U.S.
Engine, gasoline	1872	Brayton, Geo.	U.S.
Engine, gasoline	1889	Daimler	German
Engine, steam, piston	1705	Newcomen	English
Engine, steam, piston	1769	Watt	Scottish
Engraving, half-tone	1852	Talbot	U.S.
Filament, tungsten	1913	Coolidge	U.S.
Flanged rail	1831	Stevens	U.S.
Flatiron, electric	1882	Seely	U.S.
Furnace (for steel)	1858	Siemens	German
Galvanometer	1820	Sweigger	German
Gas discharge tube	1922	Hull	U.S.
Gas lighting	1792	Murdoch	Scottish
Gas mantle	1885	Welsbach	Austrian
Gasoline (lead ethyl)	1922	Midgley	U.S.
Gasoline, cracked	1913	Burton	U.S.
Gasoline, high octane	1930	Ipatieff	Russian
Geiger counter	1913	Geiger	German

Invention	Date	Inventor	Nation.
Glass, laminated safety	1909	Benedictus	French
Glider	1853	Cayley	English
Gun, breechloader	1811	Thornton	U.S.
Gun, Browning	1897	Browning	U.S.
Gun, magazine	1875	Hotchkiss	U.S.
Gun, silencer	1908	Maxim, H.P.	U.S.
Guncotton	1847	Schoenbein	German
Gyrocompass	1911	Sperry	U.S.
Gyroscope	1852	Foucault	French
Harvester-thresher	1818	Lane	U.S.
Helicopter	1939	Sikorsky	U.S.
Hydrometer	1768	Baume	French
Ice-making machine	1851	Gorrie	U.S.
Iron lung	1928	Drinker, Slaw.	U.S.
Kaleidoscope	1817	Brewster	Scottish
Kinetoscope	1889	Edison	U.S.
Lacquer, nitrocellulose	1921	Flaherty	U.S.
Lamp, arc	1847	Staite	English
Lamp, incandescent	1879	Edison	U.S.
Lamp, incand., frosted	1924	Pipkin	U.S.
Lamp, incand., gas	1913	Langmuir	U.S.
Lamp, Klieg	1911	Kliegl, A.&J.	U.S.
Lamp, mercury vapor	1912	Hewitt	U.S.
Lamp, miner's safety	1816	Davy	English
Lamp, neon	1909	Claude	French
Lathe, turret	1845	Fitch	U.S.
Launderette	1934	Cantrell	U.S.
Lens, achromatic	1758	Dollond	English
Lens, fused bifocal	1908	Borsch	U.S.
Leydenjar (condenser)	1745	von Kleist	German
Lightning rod	1752	Franklin	U.S.
Linoleum	1860	Walton	English
Linotype	1884	Mergenthaler	U.S.
Lock, cylinder	1851	Yale	U.S.
Locomotive, electric	1851	Vail	U.S.
Locomotive, exp'mtl	1802	Trevithick	English
Locomotive, exp'mtl	1812	Fenton et al.	English
Locomotive, exp'mtl	1813	Hedley	English
Locomotive, exp'mtl	1814	Stephenson	English
Locomotive practical	1829	Stephenson	English
Locomotive, 1st U.S.	1830	Cooper, P.	U.S.
Loom, power	1785	Cartwright	English
Loudspeaker, dynamic	1924	Rice, Kellogg	U.S.
Machine gun	1861	Gatling	U.S.
Machine gun, improved	1872	Hotchkiss	U.S.
Machine gun (Maxim)	1883	Maxim, H.S.	U.S., Eng.
Magnet, electro	1828	Henry	U.S.
Mantle, gas	1885	Welsbach	Austrian
Mason jar	1858	Mason, J.	U.S.
Match, friction	1827	John Walker	English
Mercerized textiles	1843	Mercer, J.	English
Meter, induction	1888	Shallenberg	U.S.
Metronome	1816	Malezel	German
Micrometer	1636	Gascoigne	English
Microphone	1877	Berliner	U.S.
Microscope, compound	1590	Janssen	Dutch
Microscope, electronic	1931	Knoll, Ruska	German
Microscope, field ion.	1951	Mueller	Germany
Monitor, warship	1861	Ericsson	U.S.
Monotype	1887	Lanston	U.S.
Motor, AC	1892	Tesla	U.S.
Motor, DC	1837	Davenport	U.S.
Motor, induction	1887	Tesla	U.S.
Motorcycle	1885	Daimler	German
Movie machine	1894	Jenkins	U.S.
Movie, panoramic	1952	Waller	U.S.
Movie, talking	1927	Warner Bros.	U.S.
Mower, lawn	1831	Budding, Ferrabee	English
Mowing machine	1822	Bailey	U.S.
Neoprene	1930	Carothers	U.S.
Nylon synthetic	1930	Carothers	U.S.
Nylon	1937	Du Pont lab.	U.S.
Oil cracking furnace	1891	Gavrilov	Russian
Oil filled power cable	1921	Emanueli	Italian
Oleomargarine	1869	Mege-Mouries	French
Ophthalmoscope	1851	Helmholtz	German
Paper machine	1809	Dickinson	U.S.
Parachute	1785	Blanchard	French
Pen, ballpoint	1888	Loud	U.S.
Pen, fountain	1884	Waterman	U.S.

Invention	Date	Inventor	Nation.
Pen, steel	1780	Harrison	English
Pendulum	1583	Galileo	Italian
Percussion cap	1807	Forsythe	Scottish
Phonograph	1877	Edison	U.S.
Photo, color	1892	Ives	U.S.
Photo film, celluloid	1893	Reichenbach	U.S.
Photo film, transparent	1884	Eastman, Goodwin	U.S.
Photoelectric cell	1895	Elster	German
Photographic paper	1835	Talbot	English
Photography	1835	Talbot	English
Photography	1835	Daguerre	French
Photography	1816	Niepce	French
Photophone	1880	Bell	U.S.-Scot.
Phototelegraphy	1925	Bell Labs	U.S.
Piano	1709	Cristofori	Italian
Piano, player	1863	Fourneaux	French
Pin, safety	1849	Hunt	U.S.
Pistol (revolver)	1836	Colt	U.S.
Plow, cast iron	1785	Ransome	English
Plow, disc	1896	Hardy	U.S.
Pneumatic hammer	1890	King	U.S.
Powder, smokeless	1884	Vieille	French
Printing press, rotary	1845	Hoe	U.S.
Printing press, web	1865	Bullock	U.S.
Propeller, screw	1804	Stevens	U.S.
Propeller, screw	1837	Ericsson	Swedish
Punch card accounting	1889	Hollerith	U.S.
Radar	1940	Watson-Watt	Scottish
Radio amplifier	1906	De Forest	U.S.
Radio beacon	1928	Donovan	U.S.
Radio crystal oscillator	1918	Nicolson	U.S.
Radio receiver, cascade tuning	1913	Alexanderson	U.S.
Radio receiver, heterodyne	1913	Fessenden	U.S.
Radio transmitter triode modulation	1914	Alexanderson	U.S.
Radio tube-diode	1905	Fleming	English
Radio tube oscillator	1915	De Forest	U.S.
Radio tube triode	1906	De Forest	U.S.
Radio, signals	1895	Marconi	Italian
Radio, magnetic detector	1902	Marconi	Italian
Radio FM 2-path	1933	Armstrong	U.S.
Rayon	1883	Swan	English
Razor, electric	1928	Schick	U.S.
Razor, safety	1895	Gillette	U.S.
Reaper	1834	McCormick	U.S.
Record, cylinder	1887	Bell, Tainter	U.S.
Record, disc	1887	Berliner	U.S.
Record, long playing	1947	Goldmark	U.S.
Record, wax cylinder	1888	Edison	U.S.
Refrigerants, low-boiling fluorine compound	1930	Midgely and co-workers	U.S.
Refrigerator car	1868	David	U.S.
Resin, synthetic	1931	Hill	English
Rifle, repeating	1860	Spencer	U.S.
Rocket engine	1926	Goddard	U.S.
Rubber, vulcanized	1839	Goodyear	U.S.
Saw, band	1808	Newberry	English
Saw, circular	1777	Miller	English
Searchlight, arc	1915	Sperry	U.S.
Sewing machine	1846	Howe	U.S.
Shoe-sewing machine	1860	McKay	U.S.
Shrapnel shell	1784	Shrapnel	English
Shuttle, flying	1733	Kay	English
Sleeping-car	1865	Pullman	U.S.
Slide rule	1620	Oughtred	English
Soap, hardwater	1928	Bertsch	German
Spectroscope	1859	Kirchoff, Bunsen	German
Spectroscope (mass)	1918	Dempster	U.S.
Spinning jenny	1767	Hargreaves	English
Spinning mule	1779	Crompton	English
Steamboat, exp'mtl	1778	Jouffroy	French
Steamboat, exp'mtl	1785	Fitch	U.S.
Steamboat, exp'mtl	1787	Rumsey	U.S.
Steamboat, exp'mtl	1788	Miller	Scottish
Steamboat, exp'mtl	1803	Fulton	U.S.
Steamboat, exp'mtl	1804	Stevens	U.S.
Steamboat, practical	1802	Symington	Scottish
Steamboat, practical	1807	Fulton	U.S.
Steam car	1770	Cugnot	French
Steam turbine	1884	Parsons	English
Steel (converter)	1856	Bessemer	English

Invention	Date	Inventor	Nation.
Steel alloy	1891	Harvey	U.S.
Steel alloy, high-speed	1901	Taylor, White	U.S.
Steel, electric	1900	Heroult	French
Steel, manganese	1884	Hadfield	English
Steel, stainless	1916	Brearley	English
Stereoscope	1838	Wheatstone	English
Stethoscope	1819	Laennec	French
Stethoscope, binaural	1840	Cammann	U.S.
Stock ticker	1870	Edison	U.S.
Storage battery, rechargeable	1859	Plante	French
Stove, electric	1896	Hadaway	U.S.
Submarine	1891	Holland	U.S.
Submarine, even keel	1894	Lake	U.S.
Submarine, torpedo	1776	Bushnell	U.S.
Tank, military	1914	Swinton	English
Tape recorder, magnetic	1899	Poulsen	Danish
Telegraph, magnetic	1837	Morse	U.S.
Telegraph, quadruplex	1864	Edison	U.S.
Telegraph, railroad	1887	Woods	U.S.
Telegraph, wireless high frequency	1895	Marconi	Italian
Telephone	1876	Bell	U.S.-Scot.
Telephone amplifier	1912	De Forest	U.S.
Telephone, automatic	1891	Stowger	U.S.
Telephone, radio	1900	Poulsen, Fessenden	Danish
Telephone, radio	1906	De Forest	U.S.
Telephone, radio, l. d	1915	AT&T	U.S.
Telephone, recording	1898	Poulsen	Danish
Telephone, wireless	1899	Collins	Neth.
Telescope	1608	Lippershey	Neth.
Telescope	1609	Galileo	Italian
Telescope, astronomical	1611	Kepler	German
Teletype	1928	Morkrum, Kleinschmidt	U.S.
Television, iconoscope	1923	Zworykin	U.S.
Television, electronic	1927	Farnsworth	U.S.
Television, (mech. scanner)	1923	Baird	Scottish
Thermometer	1593	Galileo	Italian
Thermometer	1730	Reaumur	French
Thermometer, mercury	1714	Fahrenheit	German
Time recorder	1890	Bundy	U.S.
Time, self-regulator	1918	Bryce	U.S.
Tire, double-tube	1845	Thomson	Scottish
Tire, pneumatic	1888	Dunlop	Scottish
Toaster, automatic	1918	Strite	U.S.
Tool, pneumatic	1865	Law	English
Torpedo, marine	1804	Fulton	U.S.
Tractor, crawler	1904	Holt	U.S.
Transformer A.C.	1885	Stanley	U.S.
Transistor	1947	Shockley, Brattain, Bardeen	U.S.
Trolley car, electric	1884	Van DePoele,	U.S.
	-87	Sprague	U.S.
Tungsten, ductile	1912	Coolidge	U.S.
Turbine, gas	1849	Bourdin	French
Turbine, hydraulic	1849	Francis	U.S.
Turbine, steam	1884	Parsons	English
Type, movable	1447	Gutenberg	German
Typewriter	1867	Sholes, Soule, Glidden	U.S.
Vacuum cleaner, electric	1907	Spangler	U.S.
Washer, electric	1901	Fisher	U.S.
Welding, atomic hydrogen	1924	Langmuir, Palmer	U.S.
Welding, electric	1877	Thomson	U.S.
Wind tunnel	1912	Eiffel	French
Wire, barbed	1874	Glidden	U.S.
Wire, barbed	1875	Haisn	U.S.
Wrench, double-acting	1913	Owen	U.S.
X-ray tube	1913	Coolidge	U.S.
Zipper	1891	Judson	U.S.

Discoveries and Innovations: Chemistry, Physics, Biology, Medicine

	Date	Discoverer	Nation.
Acetylene gas	1892	Wilson	U.S.
ACTH	1949	Armour & Co.	U.S.
Adrenalin	1901	Takamine	Japanese
Aluminum, electrolytic process	1886	Hall	U.S.
Aluminum, isolated	1825	Oersted	Danish
Analine dye	1856	Perkin	English
Anesthesia, ether	1842	Long	U.S.
Anesthesia, local	1885	Koller	Austrian
Anesthesia, spinal	1898	Bier	German
Anti-rabies	1885	Pasteur	French
Antiseptic surgery	1867	Lister	English
Antitoxin, diphtheria	1891	Von Behring	German
Argyrol	1901	Barnes	U.S.
Arsphenamine	1910	Ehrlich	German
Aspirin	1889	Dresser	German
Atabrine	...	Mietzsch, et al.	German
Atomic numbers	1913	Moseley	English
Atomic theory	1803	Dalton	English
Atomic time clock	1947	Libby	U.S.
Atom-smashing theory	1919	Rutherford	English
Aureomycin	1948	Duggar	U.S.
Bacitracin	1945	Johnson, et al.	U.S.
Bacteria (described)	1676	Leeuwenhoek	Dutch
Barbital	1903	Fischer	German
Bleaching powder	1798	Tennant	English
Blood, circulation	1628	Harvey	English
Bordeaux mixture	1885	Millardet	French
Bromine from sea	1924	Edgar Kramer	U.S.
Calcium carbide	1888	Wilson	U.S.
Calculus	1670	Newton	English
Camphor synthetic	1896	Haller	French
Canning (food)	1804	Appert	French
Carbomycin	1952	Tanner	U.S.
Carbon oxides	1925	Fisher	German
Chlorine	1774	Scheele	Swedish
Chloroform	1831	Guthrie, S.	U.S.
Chloromycetin	1947	Burkholder	U.S.
Classification of plants and animals	1735	Linnaeus	Swedish
Cocaine	1860	Niermann	German
Combustion explained	1777	Lavoisier	French
Conditioned reflex	1914	Pavlov	Russian
Conteben	1950	Belmisch, Mietzsch, Domagk	German
Cortisone	1936	Kendall	U.S.
Cortisone, synthesis	1946	Sarett	U.S.
Cosmic rays	1910	Gockel	Swiss
Cyanimide	1905	Frank, Caro.	German
Cyclotron	1930	Lawrence	U.S.
DDT	1874	Zeidler	German
(not applied as insecticide until 1939)			
Deuterium	1932	Urey, Brickwedde, Murphy	U.S.
DNA (structure)	1951	Crick	English
		Watson	U.S.
		Wilkins	English.
Electric resistance (law)	1827	Ohm	German
Electric waves	1888	Hertz	German
Electrolysis	1852	Faraday	English
Electromagnetism	1819	Oersted	Danish
Electron	1897	Thomson, J.	English
Electron diffraction	1936	Thomson, G.	English
		Davisson	U.S.
Electroshock treatment	1938	Cerletti, Bini	Italian
Erythromycin	1952	McGuire.	U.S.
Evolution, natural selection	1858	Darwin	English
Falling bodies, law	1590	Galileo	Italian
Gases, law of combining volumes	1808	Gay-Lussac	French
Geometry, analytic	1619	Descartes	French
Gold (cyanide process for extraction)	1887	MacArthur, Forest	British
Gravitation, law	1687	Newton	English
Holograph	1948	Gabor	British
Human heart transplant	1967	Barnard	S. African

	Date	Discoverer	Nation.
Indigo, synthesis of	1880	Baeyer	German
Induction, electric	1830	Henry	U.S.
Insulin	1922	Banting, Best,	Canadian,
		Macleod	Scottish
Intelligence testing	1905	Binet, Simon	French
Isinazid	1952	Hoffman-	
		La-Roche	U.S.
		Domagk	German
Isotopes, theory	1912	Soddy	English
Laser (light amplification by stimulated emission			
of radiation)	1958	Townes, Schaw-	
		low	U.S.
Light, velocity	1675	Roemer	Danish
Light, wave theory	1690	Huygens	Dutch
Lithography	1796	Senefelder	Bohemian
Lobotomy	1935	Egas Moniz	Portuguese
LSD-25	1943	Hoffman	Swiss
Mendelian laws	1866	Mendel	Austrian
Mercator projection			
(map)	1568	Mercator (Kremer)	Flemish
Methanol	1925	Patard	French
Milk condensation	1853	Borden	U.S.
Molecular hypothesis	1811	Avogadro	Italian
Motion, laws of	1687	Newton	English
Neomycin	1949	Waksman,	
		Lechevalier	U.S.
Neutron	1932	Chadwick	English
Nitric acid	1648	Glauber	German
Nitric oxide	1772	Priestley	English
Nitroglycerin	1846	Sobrero	Italian
Oil cracking process	1891	Dewar	U.S.
Oxygen	1774	Priestley	English
Ozone	1840	Schonbein	German
Paper, sulfite process	1867	Tilghman	U.S.
Paper, wood pulp,			
sulfate process	1884	Dahl	German
Penicillin	1929	Fleming	Scottish
practical use	1941	Florey, Chain	English
Periodic law and			
table of elements	1869	Mendeleyev	Russian
Planetary motion, laws	1609	Kepler	German
Plutonium fission	1940	Kennedy, Wahl,	
		Seaborg, Segre	U.S.
Polymixin	1947	Ainsworth	English
Positron	1932	Anderson	U.S.
Proton	1919	Rutherford	N. Zealand

	Date	Discoverer	Nation.
Psychoanalysis	1900	Freud	Austrian
Quantum theory	1900	Planck	German
Quasars	1963	Matthews,	
		Sandage	U.S.
Quinine synthetic	1918	Rabe	German
Radioactivity	1896	Becquerel	French
Radium	1898	Curie, Pierre	French
		Curie, Marie	Pol.-Fr.
Relativity theory	1905	Einstein	German
Reserpine	1949	Jal Vaikl	Indian
Salvarsan (606)	1910	Ehrlich	German
Schick test	1913	Schick	U.S.
Silicon	1823	Berzelius	Swedish
Streptomycin	1945	Waksman	U.S.
Sulfadiazine	1940	Roblin	U.S.
Sulfanilamide	1934	Domagk	German
Sulfanilamide theory	1908	Gelmo	German
Sulfapyridine	1938	Ewins, Phelps	English
Sulfathiazole	...	Fosbinder, Walter	U.S.
Sulfuric acid	1831	Phillips	English
Sulfuric acid, lead	1746	Roebuck	English
Terramycin	1950	Finlay, et al.	U.S.
Tuberculin	1890	Koch	German
Uranium fission		Hahn, Meitner,	
(theory)	1939	Strassmann	German
		Bohr	Danish
		Fermi	Italian
		Einstein, Pegram,	
		Wheeler	U.S.
Uranium fission,		Fermi,	
atomic reactor	1942	Szilard	U.S.
Vaccine, measles	1954	Enders, Peebles	U.S.
Vaccine, polio	1953	Salk	U.S.
Vaccine, polio, oral	1955	Sabin	U.S.
Vaccine, rabies	1885	Pasteur	French
Vaccine, smallpox	1796	Jenner	English
Vaccine, typhus	1909	Nicolle	French
Van Allen belts,			
radiation	1958	Van Allen	U.S.
Vitamin A	1913	McCollum, Davis	U.S.
Vitamin B	1916	McCollum	U.S.
Vitamin C	1912	Holst, Froelich	Norwegian
Vitamin D	1922	McCollum	U.S.
Wassermann test	1906	Wassermann	German
Xerography	1938	Carlson	U.S.
X-ray	1895	Roentgen	German

Chemical Elements, Discoverers, Atomic Weights

Atomic weights, based on the exact number 12 as the assigned atomic mass of the principal isotope of carbon, carbon 12, are provided through the courtesy of the International Union of Pure and Applied Chemistry and Butterworth Scientific Publications.
For the radioactive elements, with the exception of uranium and thorium, the mass number of either the isotope of longest half-life (*) or the better known isotope (**) is given.

Chemical element	Symbol	Atomic number	Atomic weight	Year discov.	Discoverer
Actinium	Ac	89	227*	1899	Debierne
Aluminum	Al	13	26.9815	1825	Oersted
Americium	Am	95	243*	1944	Seaborg, et al.
Antimony	Sb	51	121.75	1450	Valentine
Argon	Ar	18	39.948	1894	Rayleigh, Ramsay
Arsenic	As	33	74.9216	13th c.	Albertus Magnus
Astatine	At	85	210*	1940	Corson, et al.
Barium	Ba	56	137.34	1808	Davy
Berkelium	Bk	97	249**	1949	Thompson, Ghiorso, Seaborg
Beryllium	Be	4	9.0122	1798	Vauquelin
Bismuth	Bi	83	208.980	15th c.	Valentine
Boron	B	5	10.811a	1808	Gay-Lussac, Thenard
Bromine	Br	35	79.904b	1826	Balard
Cadmium	Cd	48	112.40	1817	Stromeyer
Calcium	Ca	20	40.08	1808	Davy
Californium	Cf	98	251*	1950	Thompson, et al.
Carbon	C	6	12.01115a	B.C.	
Cerium	Ce	58	140.12	1803	Klaproth
Cesium	Cs	55	132.905	1860	Bunsen, Kirchhoff
Chlorine	Cl	17	35.453b	1774	Scheele
Chromium	Cr	24	51.996b	1797	Vauquelin
Cobalt	Co	27	58.9332	1735	Brandt
Copper	Cu	29	63.546b	B.C.	

Chemical element	Symbol	Atomic number	Atomic weight	Year discov.	Discoverer
Curium	Cm	96	247*	1944	Seaborg, James, Ghiorso
Dysprosium	Dy	66	162.50	1886	Boisbaudran
Einsteinium	Es	99	254*	1952	Ghiorso, et al.
Erbium	Er	68	167.26	1843	Mosander
Europium	Eu	63	151.96	1901	Demarcay
Fermium	Fm	100	257*	1953	Ghiorso, et al.
Fluorine	F	9	18.9984	1771	Scheele
Francium	Fr	87	223*	1939	Perey
Gadolinium	Gd	64	157.25	1886	Marignac
Gallium	Ga	31	69.72	1875	Boisbaudran
Germanium	Ge	32	72.59	1886	Winkler
Gold	Au	79	196.967	B.C.	
Hafnium	Hf	72	178.49	1923	Coster, Hevesy
Hahnium	Ha	105	262*	1970	Ghiorso, et al.
Helium	He	2	4.0026	1868	Janssen, Lockyer
Holmium	Ho	67	164.930	1878	Soret, Delafontaine
Hydrogen	H	1	1.00797a	1766	Cavendish
Indium	In	49	114.82	1863	Reich, Richter
Iodine	I	53	126.9044	1811	Courtois
Iridium	Ir	77	192.2	1804	Tennant
Iron	Fe	26	55.847b	B.C.	
Krypton	Kr	36	83.80	1898	Ramsay, Travers
Lanthanum	La	57	138.91	1839	Mosander
Lawrencium	Lr	103	262*	1961	Ghiorso, T. Sikkeland, A.E. Larsh, and R.M. Latimer
Lead	Pb	82	207.19	B.C.	
Lithium	Li	3	6.939	1817	Arfvedson
Lutetium	Lu	71	174.97	1907	Welsbach, Urbain
Magnesium	Mg	12	24.312	1829	Bussy
Manganese	Mn	25	54.9380	1774	Gahn
Mendelevium	Md	101	258*	1955	Ghiorso, et al.
Mercury	Hg	80	200.59	B.C.	
Molybdenum	Mo	42	95.94	1782	Hjelm
Neodymium	Nd	60	144.24	1885	Welsbach
Neon	Ne	10	20.183	1898	Ramsay, Travers
Neptunium	Np	93	237*	1940	McMillan, Abelson
Nickel	Ni	28	58.71	1751	Cronstedt
Niobium†	Nb	41	92.906	1801	Hatchett
Nitrogen	N	7	14.0067	1772	Rutherford
Nobelium	No	102	259*	1958	Ghiorso, et al.
Osmium	Os	76	190.2	1804	Tennant
Oxygen	O	8	15.9994a	1774	Priestley, Scheele
Palladium	Pd	46	106.4	1803	Wollaston
Phosphorus	P	15	30.9738	1669	Brand
Platinum	Pt	78	195.09	1735	Ulloa
Plutonium	Pu	94	242**	1940	Seaborg, et al.
Polonium	Po	84	210**	1898	P. and M. Curie
Potassium	K	19	39.102	1807	Davy
Praseodymium	Pr	59	140.907	1885	Welsbach
Promethium	Pm	61	147**	1945	Glendenin, Marinsky, Coryell
Protactinium	Pa	91	231*	1917	Hahn, Meitner
Radium	Ra	88	226*	1898	P. & M. Curie, Bemont
Radon	Rn	86	222*	1900	Dorn
Rhenium	Re	75	186.2	1925	Noddack, Tacke, Berg
Rhodium	Rh	45	102.905	1803	Wollaston
Rubidium	Rb	37	85.47	1861	Bunsen, Kirchhoff
Ruthenium	Ru	44	101.07	1845	Klaus
Rutherfordium	Rf	104	261*	1969	Ghiorso, et al.
Samarium	Sm	62	150.35	1879	Boisbaudran
Scandium	Sc	21	44.956	1879	Nilson
Selenium	Se	34	78.96	1817	Berzelius
Silicon	Si	14	28.086a	1823	Berzelius
Silver	Ag	47	107.868b	B.C.	
Sodium	Na	11	22.9898	1807	Davy
Strontium	Sr	38	87.62	1790	Crawford
Sulfur	S	16	32.064a	B.C.	
Tantalum	Ta	73	180.948	1802	Ekeberg
Technetium	Tc	43	99**	1937	Perrier and Segre
Tellurium	Te	52	127.60	1782	Von Reichenstein
Terbium	Tb	65	158.924	1843	Mosander
Thallium	Tl	81	204.37	1861	Crookes
Thorium	Th	90	232.038	1828	Berzelius
Thulium	Tm	69	168.934	1879	Cleve
Tin	Sn	50	118.69	B.C.	
Titanium	Ti	22	47.90	1791	Gregor
Tungsten (Wolfram)	W	74	183.85	1783	d'Elhujar
Uranium	U	92	238.03	1789	Klaproth
Vanadium	V	23	50.942	1830	Sefstrom
Xenon	Xe	54	131.30	1898	Ramsay, Travers
Ytterbium	Yb	70	173.04	1878	Marignac
Yttrium	Y	39	88.905	1794	Gadolin
Zinc	Zn	30	65.37	B.C.	
Zirconium	Zr	40	91.22	1789	Klaproth

(1) Formerly Columbium. (a) Atomic weights so designated are known to be variable because of natural variations in isotopic composition. The observed ranges are: hydrogen±0.0001; boron±0.003; carbon±0.005; oxygen±0.0001; silicon±0.001; sulfur±0.003. (b) Atomic weights so designated are believed to have the following experimental uncertainties: chlorine±0.001; chromium±0.001; iron±0.003; bromine±0.001; silver±0.001; copper±0.001.

HEALTH
Ethics on Care of the Terminally Ill

The Supreme Court, on July 3, 1989, agreed to decide, during its next term, whether a state can require an unconscious person to be maintained indefinitely by medical technology against the wishes of family members who believe the patient would prefer to die.

As of January, 1988, hospitals are required by the Joint Commission Accreditation to have formal policies specifying when doctors and nurses can refrain from trying to resuscitate terminally ill patients. The policy must be developed in consultation with the medical staff and the nursing staff, adopted by the medical staff and then approved by the hospital's governing body. The policy must define the roles of physicians, nursing personnel, and members of the patient's family in any decision to withhold resuscitation. It must also include "provisions designed to assure that a patient's rights are respected."

In March 1986, the American Medical Association announced that it would be ethical for doctors to withhold "all means of life prolonging medical treatment," including food and water, from patients in irreversible comas even if death was not imminent. The withholding of such therapy should occur only when a patient's coma "is beyond doubt irreversible and there are adequate safeguards to confirm the accuracy of the diagnosis," the association's judicial council said. The opinion could affect at least 10,000 Americans who are in irreversible comas.

While the opinion of the 271,000-member association does not constitute a hard and fast rule for doctors, it opens the way for them to withdraw life prolonging treatment with less fear of being taken to court, and to use the opinion as a defense if they are challenged. The A.M.A. said that stopping therapy is a decision that each physician and each patient's family and legal guardians would address on a case by case basis.

The A.M.A. opinion also said: "Life prolonging medical treatment includes medication and artificially or technologically supplied respiration, nutrition or hydration. In treating a terminally ill or irreversibly comatose patient, the physician should determine whether the benefits of treatment outweigh its burdens. At all times, the dignity of the patient should be maintained."

Many states have tried to clear the issue of treating the comatose who are terminally ill by acting to define brain death. In at least 37 states, legislatures or courts have worked out a definition modeled along the lines of a recommendation previously released by the A.M.A. that said a person is brain dead when he has suffered "irreversible cessation of the functions of the entire brain, including the brain stem."

A number of states have "living will" statutes that set out a procedure for a mentally competent person to declare that he or she does not wish to be subjected to a "death-prolonging" procedure.

Immunization Schedule for Children

Source: American Academy of Pediatrics

Age	Type of Vaccination	Disease Immunized Against	Age	Type of Vaccination	Disease Immunized Against
2 months	DTP	Diphtheria, Tetanus (Lockjaw), Pertussis (Whooping Cough)	18 months	DTP Booster	
	Oral Polio Vaccine	Poliomyelitis	(2)	Oral Polio Booster	
4 months	DTP		School Entry	DTP Booster Oral Polio Booster	Measles, Mumps, Rubella
	Oral Polio Vaccine		Kinder-garten³	MMR Booster	Measles, Mumps, Rubella
6 months	DTP		Junior High⁴	MMR Booster	Measles, Mumps, Rubella
15 months	Measles, Mumps Rubella Vaccine¹ (MMR)	Measles, Mumps, Rubella (German Measles)			

(1) MMR may be given as early as 12 months. (2) The American Academy of Pediatrics and national Center for Disease Control advises immunization of children 18 months and older against Haemophilus influenza type B, which causes the most common and serious form of meningitis in children under age 5 years and can also cause pneumonia, bronchitis, and ear infections. (3) The Advisory Committee on Immunization Practices plans to target school entry for the MMR booster. (4) The American Academy of Pediatrics has targeted junior high school entry for the MMR booster in an effort to more quickly prevent measles outbreaks in schools.
Note: The American College of Physicians recommends that adolescents and adults consult with their physicians about further vaccinations. Those without natural infection or proper immunization against childhood diseases like measles, mumps, rubella, and poliomyelitis may be at increased risk for such disease and their complications as adults; in addition, tetanus and diphtheria should be boosted periodically; and various ages, occupations, lifestyles, environmental risks, and outbreaks of disease may call for adult immunization.

Heart and Blood Vessel Disease
Warning Signs

Source: American Heart Association, Dallas

Of Heart Attack
- Uncomfortable pressure, fullness, squeezing or pain in the center of the chest lasting more than two minutes or longer
- Pain may radiate to the shoulder, arm, neck or jaw
- Sweating may accompany pain or discomfort
- Nausea and vomiting may also occur
- Shortness of breath, dizziness, or fainting may accompany other signs

The American Heart Association advises immediate action at the onset of these symptoms. The Association points out that more than half of heart attack victims die before they reach the hospital and that the average victim waits 2 hours before seeking help.

Of Stroke
- Sudden temporary weakness or numbness of face or limbs on one side of the body
- Temporary loss of speech, or trouble speaking or understanding speech
- Temporary dimness or loss of vision, particularly in one eye
- Unexplained dizziness, unsteadiness, or sudden falls

Major Risk Factors

Blood pressure—High blood pressure increases the risk of stroke, heart attack, kidney failure and congestive heart failure.

Cholesterol—A cholesteral concentration over 240 mg/dl approximately doubles the risk of coronary heart disease; about 25% of the U.S. adult population falls into this category. Blood cholesterol values between 200 and 240 mg/dl are in a zone of moderate and increasing risk.

Cigarettes—Cigarette smokers have more than twice the risk of heart attack and 2 to 4 times the risk of sudden cardiac death than non-smokers. Young smokers have a higher risk for early death due to stroke.

Cardiovascular Diseases Statistical Summary

1987
Prevalence — 66,890,000 Americans have one or more forms of heart and blood vessel disease.
- hypertension — 60,990,000.
- coronary heart disease — 5,000,000.
- rheumatic heart disease — 2,180,000.
- stroke — 2,060,000.

Mortality — 976,700 in 1987 (45.9% of all deaths).
- nearly one-fifth of all persons killed by CVD are under age 65.
Congenital or inborn heart defects —
- post-natal mortality from heart defects was estimated at more than 5,600 in 1987.

Heart attack — caused 513,700 deaths in 1987.
- 5,000,000 alive today have history of heart attack and/or angina pectoris.
- As many as 1,500,000 Americans will have a heart attack this year and over 500,000 of them will die.

Stroke — killed 149,200 in 1987; afflicts 2,060,000.

Hypertension (high blood pressure) — 60,990,000 Americans age 6 and above—nearly one in 3 adults.
Rheumatic heart disease — afflicts 2,180,000.
- killed about 6,100 in 1987.
Note: 1987 mortality data are estimates based on 1987 provisional data as published by the National Center for Health Statistics.

Estimated Cost of Cardiovascular Disease, 1990

According to the American Heart Association, the estimated cost of cardiovascular diseases in 1990 will be $94.5 billion: hospital and nursing home services, $60.7 billion; lost output due to disability, $15.4 billion; physician and nursing services, $13.6 billion; and medications, $4.7 billion. These estimates are an extrapolation from "Health Care Expenditures for Major Diseases in 1980," *Health Care Financing Review.*

Cancer Prevention

Source: American Cancer Society, 1989

PRIMARY PREVENTION: steps that might be taken to avoid those factors that might lead to the development of cancer.

Smoking — Cigarette smoking is responsible for 85% of lung cancer cases among men, 75% among women— about 83% overall. Smoking accounts for about 30% of all cancer deaths. Those who smoke two or more packs of cigarettes a day have lung cancer mortality rates 15-25 times greater than non-smokers.

Nutrition — Risk for colon, breast and uterine cancers increases for obese people. High-fat diet may be a factor in the development of certain cancers such as breast, colon and prostate. High-fiber foods may help reduce risk of colon cancer. Foods rich in vitamins A and C may help lower risk for cancers of larynx, esophagus, stomach, and lung. Eating cruciferous vegetables such as cabbage, broccoli, brussels sprouts, kohlrabi and cauliflower, may help protect against certain cancers. Salt-cured, smoked and nitrite-cured foods have been linked to esophageal and stomach cancer. The heavy use of alcohol, especially when accompanied by cigarette smoking or chewing tobacco, increases risk of cancers of the mouth, larynx, throat, esophagus, and liver.

Sunlight — Almost all of the more than 500,000 cases of non-melanoma skin cancer developed each year in the U.S. are considered to be sun-related. Such exposure is a major factor in the development of melanoma, and the incidence increases for those living near the equator.

Alcohol — Oral cancer and cancers of the larynx, throat, esophagus, and liver occur more frequently among heavy drinkers of alcohol.

Smokeless Tobacco — Increased risk factor for cancers of the mouth, larynx, throat, and esophagus.

Estrogen — For mature women, certain risks associated with estrogen treatment to control menopausal symptoms, including an increased risk of endometrial cancer. Use of estrogen needs careful discussion by the menopausal woman and her physician.

Radiation — Excessive exposure to radiation can increase cancer risk. Most medical X rays are adjusted to deliver the lowest dose possible without sacrificing image quality. The ACS believes there is a potential problem of radon in the home. If levels are found to be too high, remedial actions should be taken.

Occupational hazards — Exposure to a number of industrial agents (nickel, chromate, asbestos, vinyl chloride, etc.) increases risk. Risk factor greatly increased when combined with smoking.

SECONDARY PREVENTION: steps to be taken to diagnose a cancer or precursor as early as possible after it has developed.

Colorectal tests — The ACS recommends 3 tests for the early detection of colon and rectum cancer in people without symptoms: The digital rectal examination performed by a physician during an office visit, every year after the age of 40; the stool blood test every year after 50; and the proctosigmoidoscopy examination every 3 to 5 years after the age of 50 following 2 annual exams with negative results.

Pap test — For cervical cancer, women who are or have been sexually active, or have reached 18 years, should have an annual Pap test and pelvic examination. After a woman has had 3 or more consecutive satisfactory normal exams, the Pap test may be performed less frequently at the discretion of her physician.

Breast cancer detection — The ACS recommends the monthly practice of breast self-examination by women 20 years and older. Physical examination of the breast should be done every 3 years from ages 20-40 and then every year. The ACS recommends a mammogram every year for asymptomatic women age 50 and over, and a baseline mammogram between ages 35-39. Women 40-49 should have mammography every 1-2 years, depending on physical and mammographic findings.

Estimated New Cancer Cases and Deaths By Sex for Selected Sites, 1989*

Source: American Cancer Society

	Estimated New Cases			Estimated Deaths		
	Total	Male	Female	Total	Male	Female
All Sites	1,010,000	505,000[1]	505,000[1]	502,000	266,000	236,000
Oral	30,600	20,600	10,000	8,650	5,775	2,875
Colon-Rectum	107,000	50,000	57,000	53,500	26,000	27,500
Lung	155,000	101,000	54,000	142,000	93,000	49,000
Skin	27,000[2]	14,500[2]	12,500[2]	8,200+[3]	5,200	3,000
Breast	142,900[4]	900[4]	142,000[4]	43,300	300	43,000
Uterus	13,000[4]	—	13,000[4]	6,000	—	6,000

*Note: The estimates of new cancer cases are offered as a rough guide and should not be regarded as definitive. (1) Carcinoma in situ and non-melanoma skin cancers are not included in totals. Carcinoma in situ of the uterine cervix accounts for more than 50,000 new cases annually, and carcinoma in situ of the female breast accounts for about 10,000 new cases annually. Non-melanoma skin cancer accounts for more than 500,000 new cases annually. (2) Melanoma only. (3) Melanoma 6,000; other skin 2,200. (4) Invasive cancer of the cervix and uteri, only.

Cancer's 7 Warning Signals*

Source: American Cancer Society

1. A change in bowel or bladder habits.
2. A sore that does not heal.
3. Unusual bleeding or discharge.
4. Thickening or lump in breast or elsewhere.

5. Indigestion or difficulty in swallowing.
6. Obvious change in wart or mole.
7. Nagging cough or hoarseness.
*If you have a warning signal, see your doctor.

AIDS Cases by Age Group, Exposure Category, and Sex, July 1988-June 1989 and Cumulative Totals

Source: U.S. Dept. of Health and Human Services, Centers for Disease Control, HIV/AIDS Surveillance Report, July 1989

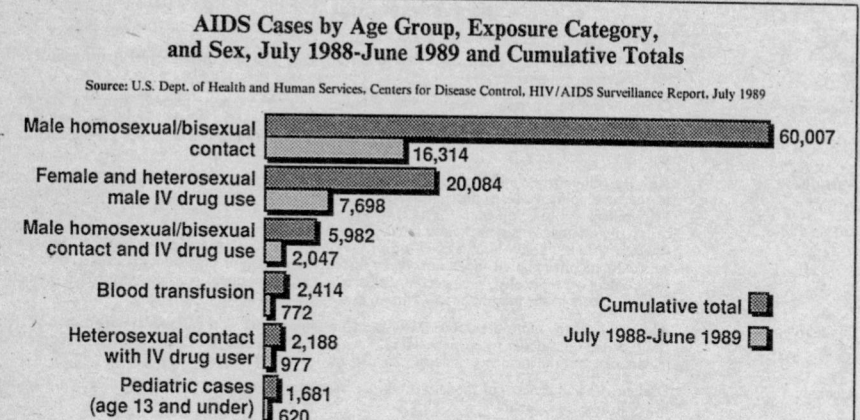

Male homosexual/bisexual contact — 60,007 / 16,314
Female and heterosexual male IV drug use — 20,084 / 7,698
Male homosexual/bisexual contact and IV drug use — 5,982 / 2,047
Blood transfusion — 2,414 / 772
Heterosexual contact with IV drug user — 2,188 / 977
Pediatric cases (age 13 and under) — 1,681 / 620

Cumulative total
July 1988-June 1989

AIDS Cases and Incidence Rates Per 100,000 Population, By Metropolitan Area

Source: Centers for Disease Control, HIV/AIDS Surveillance Report, July 1989

Metropolitan area	July 1987-June 1988 Incidence No.	Rate	July 1988-June 1989 Incidence No.	Rate	Cumlative Total
Anaheim, Calif.	239	10.7	271	11.9	822
Atlanta, Ga.	460	17.0	774	28.0	1,856
Baltimore, Md.	289	12.6	383	16.7	951
Bergen-Passaic, N.J.	320	24.5	240	18.4	901
Boston, Mass.	441	11.8	606	16.2	1,702
Chicago, Ill.	714	11.4	897	14.3	2,456
Dallas, Tex.	554	21.9	548	21.0	1,708
Denver, Colo.	221	12.9	288	16.5	828
Detroit, Mich.	215	5.0	359	8.5	829
Fort Lauderdale, Fla.	341	28.7	469	38.8	1,296
Houston, Tex.	911	26.7	844	24.1	2,985
Jersey City, N.J.	403	72.4	409	73.5	1,249
Los Angeles, Calif.	1,860	22.0	1,790	20.8	6,912
Miami, Fla.	483	26.8	863	47.5	2,502
Nassau-Suffolk, N.Y.	289	10.8	336	12.5	1,088
New Orleans, La.	277	20.5	257	18.9	859
New York, N.Y.	4,929	57.6	5,546	64.5	20,177

Metropolitan area	July 1987-June 1988 Incidence No.	Rate	July 1988-June 1989 Incidence No.	Rate	Cumulative Total
Newark, N.J.	1,019	54.2	1,008	53.6	2,920
Oakland, Calif.	342	17.1	319	15.7	1,172
Philadelphia, Pa.	654	13.5	761	15.7	2,128
Phoenix, Ariz.	230	11.1	182	8.5	579
Riverside-San Bernardino, Calif.	206	9.7	221	10.0	620
San Diego, Calif.	407	17.7	449	19.1	1,344
San Francisco, Calif.	1,525	92.6	1,804	108.3	6,506
San Juan, P.R.	414	37.0	883	78.6	1,564
Seattle, Wash.	326	18.1	350	19.1	1,027
Tampa, Fla.	293	14.6	448	21.8	959
Washington, D.C.	865	23.8	852	23.1	2,851
West Palm Beach, Fla.	243	30.2	325	39.0	879
Metropolitan area subtotal*	23,862	16.8	27,960	19.4	85,779
Non-metropolitan areas	4,233	4.0	5,672	5.3	14,157
Total	28,095	11.3	33,632	13.4	99,936

*Includes data from all metropolitan areas with 50,000 or more population.

Drug Usage: America's High School Students

Source: National Institute on Drug Abuse/Univ. of Michigan Inst. for Social Research

Drug use among American high school and college students continued to decline in 1988. The downturn in cocaine use, which began in 1987, continued in 1988, as did the use of "crack" by high school seniors.

Among the findings reported from the 1988 survey are the following: current **daily marijuana use** has fallen from 10.7 percent in 1978 to 2.7 percent in 1988 (in 1978, 35 percent thought there was a "great risk" associated with regular marijuana use, whereas in 1988 the percentage was 77); between 1987 and 1988 the proportion of seniors who said they believe that **experimentation with crack** involves great risk rose from 57 percent to 62 percent, while the percent saying it was readily available rose slightly. "We really can't say with much certainty whether a similar decline in crack use is occurring among the high school dropout segment of the population, which constitutes about 15 percent of the age group," stated Univ. of Michigan research scientist Dr. Lloyd Johnston.

Results are based on large, representative sample surveys of 135 graduating classes enrolled in public and private high schools across the United States.

	Class of 1975	Class of 1978	Class of 1980	Class of 1981	Class of 1983	Class of 1984	Class of 1985	Class of 1986	Class of 1987	Class of 1988	'87-'88 change
				Percent ever used							
Marijuana/Hashish	47.3	59.2	60.3	59.5	57.0	54.9	54.2	50.9	50.2	47.2	−3.0ss
Inhalants	NA	12.0	11.9	12.3	13.6	14.4	15.4	15.9	17.0	16.7	−0.3
Inhalants Adjusted[1]	NA	NA	17.6	17.4	18.8	19.0	18.1	20.1	18.6	17.5	−1.1
Amyl & Butyl Nitrites	NA	NA	11.1	10.1	8.4	8.1	7.9	8.6	4.7	3.2	−1.5s
Hallucinogens	16.3	14.3	13.3	13.3	11.9	10.7	10.3	9.7	10.3	8.9	−1.4s
Hallucinogens Adjusted[2]	NA	NA	15.7	15.7	14.7	13.3	12.1	11.9	10.6	9.2	−1.4s
LSD	11.3	9.7	9.3	9.8	8.9	8.0	7.5	7.2	8.4	7.7	−0.7
PCP	NA	NA	9.6	7.8	5.6	5.0	4.9	4.8	3.0	2.9	−0.1
Cocaine	9.0	12.9	15.7	16.5	16.2	16.1	17.3	16.9[5]	15.2	12.1	−3.1sss
"Crack"	NA	NA	NA	NA	NA	1.3	1.2	1.1	1.2	1.1	−0.1
Heroin	2.2	1.6	1.1	1.1	1.2	1.2	1.2	1.1	1.2	1.1	−0.1
Other opiates[3]	9.0	9.9	9.8	10.1	9.4	9.7	10.2	9.0	9.2	8.6	−0.6
Stimulants[3]	22.3	22.9	26.4	32.2	35.4	NA	NA	NA	NA	NA	NA
Stimulants Adjusted[3,4]	NA	NA	NA	NA	26.9	27.9	26.2	23.4	21.6	19.8	−1.8s
Sedatives[3]	18.2	16.0	14.9	16.0	14.4	13.3	11.8	10.4	8.7	7.8	−0.9
Barbiturates[3]	16.9	13.7	11.0	11.3	9.9	9.9	9.2	8.4	7.4	6.7	−0.7
Methaqualone[3]	8.1	7.9	9.5	10.6	10.1	8.3	6.7	5.2	4.0	3.3	−0.7
Tranquilizers[3]	17.0	17.0	15.2	14.7	13.3	12.4	11.9	10.9	10.9	9.4	−1.5s
Alcohol	90.4	93.1	93.2	92.6	92.6	92.6	92.2	91.3	92.2	92.0	−0.2
Cigarettes	73.6	75.3	71.0	71.0	70.6	69.7	68.8	67.6	67.2	66.4	−0.8

NA=Not available. Level of significance between the two most recent classes: s=.05, ss=.01, sss=.001.
(1) Adjusted for underreporting of amyl and butyl nitrites. (2) Adjusted for underreporting of PCP. (3) Only drug use which was not under a doctor's orders. (4) Adjusted for overreporting of the non-prescription stimulants. (5) In 1986, 12.6 percent of those who used cocaine used it in powder form, while 4.1 percent used the "crack" form.

Drug Usage: America's College Students

Source: National Institute on Drug Abuse/University of Michigan Institute for Social Research

Percent who used in last twelve months

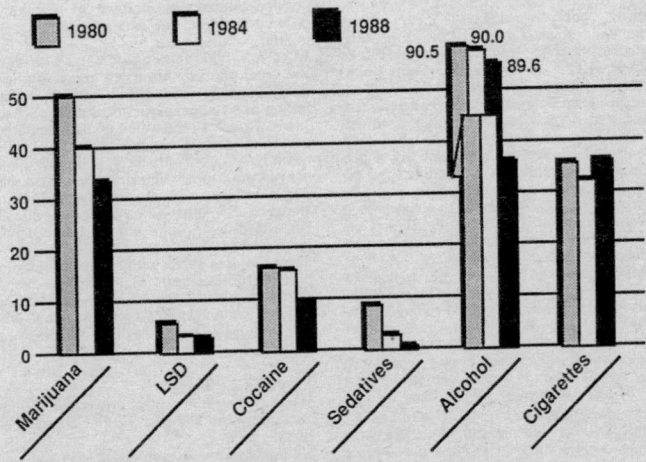

Effects of Commonly Abused Drugs

Source: National Institute on Drug Abuse

Tobacco
Effects and dangers: Nicotine, the active ingredient in tobacco, acts as a stimulant on the heart and nervous system.

When tobacco smoke is inhaled the immediate effects on the body are a faster heart beat and elevated blood pressure.

These effects, however, are quickly dissipated. Tar (in the smoke) contains many carcinogens. These compounds, many of which are in polluted air but are found in vastly greater quantities in cigarette smoke, have been identified as major causes of cancer and respiratory difficulties. Even relatively young smokers can have shortness of breath, nagging cough, or develop cardiovascular and respiratory difficulties. A third principal component of cigarette smoke, carbon monoxide, is also a cause of some of the more serious health effects of smoking. Carbon monoxide can reduce the blood's ability to carry oxygen to body tissues and can promote the development of arteriosclerosis (hardening of the arteries). Long-term effects of smoking cigarettes are emphysema, chronic bronchitis, heart disease, lung cancer, and cancer in other parts of the body.

Risks during pregnancy: Women who smoke during pregnancy are more likely to have babies that weigh less, and more frequently lose their babies through stillbirth or death soon after birth.

Alcohol

Effects: Like sedatives, it is a central nervous system depressant. In small doses, it has a tranquilizing effect on most people, although it appears to stimulate others. Alcohol first acts on those parts of the brain which affect self-control and other learned behaviors; lowered self-control often leads to the aggressive behavior associated with some people who drink.

Dangers: In large doses, alcohol can dull sensation and impair muscular coordination, memory, and judgment. Taken in larger quantities over a long period time, alcohol can damage the liver and heart and can cause permanent brain damage. A large dose of alcohol, which can be as little as a pint or less of whiskey consumed at once, can interfere with the part of the brain that controls breathing. The respiratory failure which results can bring death. Delirium tremens, the most extreme manifestation of alcohol withdrawal, can also cause death. On the average, heavy drinkers shorten their life span by about 10 years.

Risks during pregnancy: Women who drink heavily during pregnancy (more than 3 ounces of alcohol per day or about 2 mixed drinks) run a higher risk than other women of delivering babies with physical, mental and behavioral abnormalities.

Dependence: Repeated drinking produces tolerance to the drug's effects and dependence. The drinker's body then needs alcohol to function. Once dependent, drinkers experience withdrawal symptoms when they stop drinking.

Marijuana ("grass", "pot", "weed")

What is it?: A common plant (*Cannabis sativa*), its chief psychoactive ingredient is delta-9-tetrahydrocannabinol, or THC. The amount of THC in the marijuana cigarette (joint) primarily determines its psychoactive potential.

Effects: Most users experience an increase in heart rate, reddening of the eyes, and dryness in the mouth and throat. Studies indicate the drug temporarily impairs short-term memory, alters sense of time, and reduces the ability to perform tasks requiring concentration, swift reactions, and coordination. Many feel that their hearing, vision, and skin sensitivity are enhanced by the drug, but these reports have not been objectively confirmed by research. Feelings of euphoria, relaxation, altered sense of body image, and bouts of exaggerated laughter are also commonly reported.

Dangers: Scientists believe marijuana can be particularly harmful to lungs because users typically inhale the unfiltered smoke deeply and hold it in their lungs for prolonged periods of time. Marijuana smoke has been found to have more cancer-causing agents than are found in cigarette smoke (see above). Because marijuana use increases heart rate as much as 50% and brings on chest pain in people who have a poor blood supply to the heart (and more rapidly than tobacco smoke does), doctors believe people with heart conditions or who are at high risk for heart ailments, should not use marijuana. Findings also suggest that regular use may reduce fertility in women and that men with marginal fertility or endocrine functioning should avoid marijuana use and that it is especially harmful during adolescence, a period of rapid physical and sexual development.

Risks during pregnancy: Research is limited, but scientists believe marijuana which crosses the placental barrier, may have a toxic effect on embryos and fetuses.

Dependence: Tolerance to marijuana, the need to take more and more of the drug over time to get the original effect, has been proven in humans and animals. Physical dependence has been demonstrated in research subjects who ingested an amount equal to smoking 10 to 20 joints a day. When the drug was discontinued, subjects experienced withdrawal symptoms—irritability, sleep disturbances, loss of appetite and weight, sweating, and stomach upset.

Bad reactions: Most commonly reported immediate adverse reaction to marijuana use is the "acute panic anxiety reaction," usually described as an exaggeration of normal marijuana effects in which intense fears of losing control accompany severe anxiety. The symptoms often disappear in a few hours when the acute drug effects have worn off.

Hallucinogens ("psychodelics")

What are they?: Drugs which affect perception, sensation, thinking, self-awareness, and emotion.

(1) LSD (lysergic acid diethylamide), a synthetic, is converted from lysergic acid which comes from fungus (ergot).

Effects: Vary greatly according to dosage, personality of the user, and conditions under which the drug is used. Basically, it causes changes in sensation. Vision alters; users describe changes in depth perception and in the meaning of the perceived object. Illusions and hallucinations often occur. Physical reactions range from minor changes such as dilated pupils, a rise in temperature and heartbeat, or a slight increase in blood pressure, to tremors. High doses can greatly alter the state of consciousness. Heavy use of the drug may produce flashbacks, recurrences of some features of a previous LSD experience days or months after the last dose.

Dangers: After taking LSD, a person loses control over normal thought processes. Although many perceptions are pleasant, others may cause panic or may make a person believe that he or she cannot be harmed. Longer-term harmful reactions include anxiety and depression, or "breaks from reality" which may last from a few days to months. Heavy users sometimes develop signs of organic brain damage, such as impaired memory and attention span, mental confusion, and difficulty with abstract thinking. It is not known yet whether such mental changes are permanent.

(2) Mescaline: Comes from peyote cactus and its effects are similar to those of LSD.

Phencyclidine (PCP or "angel dust")

What is it?: A drug that was developed as a surgical anesthetic for humans in the late 1950s. Because of its unpleasant and unusual side effects, PCP was soon restricted to its only current legal use as a veterinary anesthetic and tranquilizer.

Effects: Vary according to dosage. Low doses may provide the usual releasing effects of many psychoactive drugs. A floaty euphoria is described, sometimes associated with a feeling of numbness (part of the drug's anesthetic effects). Increased doses produce an excited, confused intoxication, which may include muscle rigidity, loss of concentration and memory, visual disturbances, delirium, feelings of isolation, convulsions, speech impairment, violent behavior, fear of death, and changes in the user's perceptions of their bodies.

Dangers: PCP intoxication can produce violent and bizarre behavior even in people not otherwise prone to such behavior. Violent actions may be directed at themselves or others and often account for serious injuries and death. More people die from accidents caused by the erratic behavior produced by the drug than from the drug's direct effect on the body. A temporary, schizophrenic-like psychosis, which can last for days or weeks, has also occurred in users of moderate or higher doses.

Stimulants ("Uppers")

What are they?: A class of drugs which stimulate the central nervous system and produce an increase in alertness and activity.

(1) Amphetamines promote a feeling of alertness and increase in speech and general physical activity. Under medical supervision, the drugs are taken to control appetite.

Effects and dangers: Even small, infrequent doses can produce toxic effects in some people. Restlessness, anxiety, mood swings, panic, circulatory and cardiac disturbances, paranoid thoughts, hallucinations, convulsions, and coma have all been reported. Heavy, frequent doses can produce brain damage which results in speed disturbances and difficulty in turning thoughts into words. Death can result from injected amphetamine overdose. Long-term users often have acne resembling a measles rash; trouble with teeth, gums and nails, and dry lifeless hair. As heavy users who inject amphetamines accumulate larger amounts of the drug in their bodies, the resulting toxicity can produce amphetamine psychosis. People in this extremely suspicious, paranoid state, frequently exhibit bizarre, sometimes violent behavior.

Dependence: People with a history of sustained low-dose use quite often become dependent and feel they need the drug to get by.

(2) **Cocaine** is a stimulant extracted from the leaves of the coca plant. It is available in many forms, the most available of which is cocaine hydrochloride. Cocaine hydrochloride is often used medically as a local anesthetic, but is also sold illegally on the street in large pieces called rocks. Street cocaine is a white, crystal-like powder that is most commonly inhaled or snorted, though some users ingest, inject, or smoke a form of the drug called freebase or crack.

Freebase and crack are formed by chemically converting street cocaine to a purified substance that is more suitable for smoking. Smoking freebase or crack produces a shorter, but more intense high than other ways of using the drug. It is the most direct and rapid means of getting the drug to the brain, and because larger amounts are reaching the brain more quickly, the effects of the drug are more intense and the dangers associated with its use are greater.

Effects: The drug's usual effects are dilated pupils and increased blood pressure, heart rate, breathing rate, and body temperature. Even small doses may elicit feelings of euphoria; illusions of increased mental and physical strength and sensory awareness; and a decrease in hunger, pain, and the perceived need for sleep. Large doses significantly magnify these effects, sometimes causing irrational behavior and confusion.

Dangers: Paranoia is not an uncommon response to heavy doses. Psychosis may be triggered in users prone to mental instability. Repeated inhalation often results in nostril and nasal membrane irritation. Some regular users have reported feelings of restlessness, irritability, and anxiety. Others have experienced hallucinations of touch, sight, taste, or smell. When people stop using cocaine after taking it for a long time, they frequently become depressed. They tend to fight off this depression by taking more cocaine, just as in the up/down amphetamine cycle.

Cocaine is toxic. Although few people realize it, overdose deaths, though rare, have occurred as a result of injecting, ingesting and even snorting cocaine. The deaths are a result of seizures followed by respiratory arrest and coma, or sometimes by cardiac arrest. Other dangers associated with cocaine include the risk of infection, such as hepatitis, resulting from the use of unsterile needles and the risk of fire or explosion resulting from the use of volatile substances necessary for freebase preparation.

Dependence: Cocaine is not a narcotic; no evidence suggests that it produces a physical dependence. However, cocaine is psychologically a very dangerous, dependence-producing drug. Smoking freebase or crack increases this risk of dependence.

(3) **Caffeine** may be the world's most popular drug. It is primarily consumed in coffee and tea, but is also found in cocoa, cola and other soft drinks, as well as in many over-the-counter medicines.

Effects: Two to four cups of coffee increase heart rate, body temperature, urine production, and gastric juice secretion. Caffeine can also raise sugar levels and cause tremors, loss of coordination, decreased appetite, and postponement of fatigue. It can interfere with the depth of sleep and the amount of dream sleep by causing more rapid eye movement (REM) sleep at first, but less than average over an entire night. Extremely high doses may cause diarrhea, sleeplessness, trembling, severe headache, and nervousness.

Dependence: A form of physical dependence may result with regular consumption. In such cases, withdrawal symptoms may occur if caffeine use is stopped or interrupted. These symptoms include headache, irritability, and fatigue. Tolerance may develop with the use of six to eight cups or more a day. A regular user of caffeine who has developed a tolerance may also develop a craving for the drug's effects.

Dangers: Poisonous doses of caffeine have occurred occasionally and have resulted in convulsions, breathing failure, and even death. However, it is almost impossible to die from drinking too much coffee or tea. The deaths that have been reported have resulted from the misuse of tablets containing caffeine.

Sedatives (Tranquilizers, sleeping pills)

What are they?: Drugs which depress the central nervous system, more appropriately called sedative-hypnotics because they include drugs which calm the nerves (the sedation effect) and produce sleep (the hypnotic effect). Of drugs in this class, barbiturates ("barbs", "downers", "reds") have the highest rate of abuse and misuse. The most commonly abused barbiturates include pentobarbital (Nembutal), secobarbital (Seconal), and amobarbital (Amytal). These all have legitimate use as sedatives or sleeping aids. Among the most commonly abused nonbarbiturate drugs are glutethimide (Doriden), meprobamate (Miltown), methyprylon (Noludar), ethchlorvynol (Placidyl), and methaqualone (Sopor, Quaalude). These are prescribed to help people sleep. Benzodiazepines, especially diazepam (Valium), prescribed to relieve anxiety, are commonly abused, and their rate of abuse and misuse is increasing.

Dangers: These can kill. Barbiturate overdose is implicated in nearly one-third of all reported drug-induced deaths. Accidental deaths may occur when a user takes an unintended larger or repeated dose of sedatives because of confusion or impairment in judgment caused by initial intake of the drug. With lesser, but still large doses, users can go into coma. Moderately large doses often produce an intoxicated stupor. Users' speech is often slurred, memory vague, and judgment impaired. Taken along with alcohol, the combination can be fatal. Tranquilizers act somewhat differently from other sedatives and are considered less hazardous. But even by themselves, or in combination with other drugs (especially alcohol and other sedatives) they can be quite dangerous.

Dependence: Potential for dependence is greatest with barbiturates, but all sedatives, tranquilizers, can be addictive. Barbiturate withdrawal is often more severe than heroin withdrawal.

Narcotics

What they are?: Drugs that relieve pain and often induce sleep. The opiates, which are narcotics, include opium and drugs derived from opium, such as morphine, codeine, and heroin. Narcotics also include certain synthetic chemicals that have a morphine-like action, such as methadone.

Which are abused?: Heroin ("junk," "smack") accounts for 90% of narcotic abuse in the U.S. Sometimes medicinal narcotics are also abused, including paregoric containing codeine, and methadone, meperidine, and morphine.

Dependence: Anyone can become heroin dependent if he or she takes the drug regularly. Although environmental stress and problems of coping have often been considered as factors that lead to heroin addiction, physicians or psychologists do not agree that some people just have an "addictive personality" and are prone to dependence. All we know for certain is that continued use of heroin causes dependence.

Dangers: Physical dangers depend on the specific drug, its source, and the way it is used. Most medical problems are caused by the uncertain dosage level, use of unsterile needles and other paraphernalia, contamination of the drug, or combination of a narcotic with other drugs, rather than by the effects of the heroin (or another narcotic) itself. The life expectancy of a heroin addict who injects the drug intravenously is significantly lower than that of one who does not. An overdose can result in death. If, for example, an addict obtains pure heroin and is not tolerant of the dose, he or she may die minutes after injecting it. Infections from unsterile needles, solutions, syringes, cause many diseases. Serum hepatitis is common. Skin abscesses, inflammation of the veins and congestion of the lungs also occur.

Withdrawal: When a heroin-dependent person stops taking the drug, withdrawal begins within 4-6 hours after the last injection. Full-blown withdrawal symptoms—which include shaking, sweating, vomiting, a running nose and eyes, muscle aches, chills, abdominal pains, and diarrhea—begin some 12-16 hours after the last injection. The intensity of symptoms depends on the degree of dependence.

Basic First Aid

First aid experts stress that knowing what to do for an injured person until a doctor or trained person gets to an accident scene can save a life, especially in cases of stoppage of breath, severe bleeding, and shock.

People with special medical problems, such as diabetes, cardiovascular disease, epilepsy, or allergy, are also urged to wear some sort of emblem identifying it, as a safeguard against use of medication that might be injurious or fatal in an emergency. Emblems may be obtained from Medic Alert Foundation, Turlock, CA 95380.

Most accidents occur in homes. National Safety Council figures show that home accidents exceed those in other locations, such as in autos, at work, or in public places.

In all cases, get medical assistance as soon as possible.

Animal bite — Wound should be washed with soap under running water and animal should be caught alive for rabies test.

Asphyxiation — Start mouth-to-mouth resuscitation immediately after getting patient to fresh air.

Bleeding — Elevate the wound above the heart if possible. Press hard on wound with sterile compress until bleeding stops. Send for doctor if it is severe.

Burn — If mild, with skin unbroken and no blisters, plunge into ice water until pain subsides. Apply a dry dressing if necessary. Send for physician if burn is severe. Apply sterile compresses and keep patient quiet and comfortably warm until doctor's arrival. Do not try to clean burn, or to break blisters.

Chemical in eye — With patient lying down, pour cupsful of water immediately into corner of eye, letting it run to other side to remove chemicals thoroughly. Cover with sterile compress. Get medical attention immediately .

Choking — Do not use back slaps to dislodge obstruction. (See Abdominal Thrust)

Convulsions — Place person on back on bed or rug. Loosen clothing. Turn head to side. Do not place a blunt object between the victim's teeth. If convulsions do not stop, get medical attention immediately.

Cut (minor) — Apply mild antiseptic and sterile compress after washing with soap under warm running water.

Drowning — (See Mouth-to-Mouth Resuscitation) Artificial breathing must be started at once, before victim is out of the water, if possible. If the victim's stomach is bloated with water, put victim on stomach, place hands under stomach, and lift. If no pulse is felt, begin cardio-pulmonary resuscitation. This should only be done by those professionally trained. If necessary, treat for shock. (See Shock)

Electric shock — If possible, turn off power. Don't touch victim until contact is broken; pull him from contact with electrical source using rope, wooden pole, or loop of dry cloth. Start mouth-to-mouth resuscitation if breathing has stopped.

Foreign body in eye — Touch object with moistened corner of handkerchief if it can be seen. If it cannot be seen or does not come out after a few attempts, take patient to doctor. Do not rub eye.

Fainting — If victim feels faint, lower head to knees. Lay him down with head turned to side if he becomes unconscious. Loosen clothing and open windows. Keep patient lying quietly for at least 15 minutes after he regains consciousness. Call doctor if faint lasts for more than a few minutes.

Fall — Send for physician if patient has continued pain. Cover wound with sterile dressing and stop any severe bleeding. Do not move patient unless absolutely necessary — as in case of fire — if broken bone is suspected. Keep patient warm and comfortable.

Loss of Limb — If a limb is severed, it is important to properly protect the limb so that it can possibly be reattached to the victim. After the victim is cared for, the limb should be placed in a clean plastic bag, garbage can or other suitable container. Pack ice around the limb on the OUTSIDE of the bag to keep the limb cold. Call ahead to the hospital to alert them of the situation.

Poisoning — Call doctor. Use antidote listed on label if container is found. Call local Poison Control Center if possible. Except for lye, other caustics, and petroleum products, induce vomiting unless victim is unconscious. Give milk if poison or antidote is unknown.

Shock (injury-related) — Keep the victim lying down; if uncertain as to his injuries, keep him flat on his back. Maintain the victim's normal body temperature; if the weather is cold or damp, place blankets or extra clothing over and under the victim; if weather is hot, provide shade.

Snakebite — Immediately get victim to a hospital. If there is mild swelling or pain, apply a constricting band 2 to 4 inches above the bite.

Sting from insect — If possible, remove stinger and apply solution of ammonia and water, or paste of baking soda. Call physician immediately if body swells or patient collapses.

Unconsciousness — Send for doctor and place person on his back. Start resuscitation if he stops breathing. Never give food or liquids to an unconscious person.

Abdominal Thrust

The American Red Cross and the American Heart Association both agree that the recommended first aid for choking victims is the abdominal thrust, also known as the Heimlich maneuver, after its creator, Dr. Henry Heimlich. Slaps on the back are no longer advised and may even prove detrimental in an attempt to assist a choking victim.

- Get behind the victim and wrap your arms around him above his waist.
- Make a fist with one hand and place it, with the thumb knuckle pressing inward, just below the point of the "v" of the rib cage.
- Grasp the wrist with the other hand and give one or more upward thrusts or hugs.
- Start mouth-to-mouth resuscitation if breathing stops.

Mouth-to-Mouth Resuscitation

Stressing that your breath can save a life, the American Red Cross gives the following directions for mouth-to-mouth resuscitation if the victim is not breathing:

- Determine consciousness by tapping the victim on the shoulder and asking loudly, "Are you okay?"
- Tilt the victim's head back so that his chin is pointing upward. Do not press on the soft tissue under the chin, as this might obstruct the airway. If you suspect that an accident victim might have neck or back injuries, open the airway by placing the tips of your index and middle fingers on the corners of the victim's jaw to lift it forward without tilting the head.
- Place your cheek and ear close to the victim's mouth and nose. Look at the victim's chest to see if it rises and falls. Listen and feel for air to be exhaled for about 5 seconds.
- If there is no breathing, pinch the victim's nostrils shut with the thumb and index finger of your hand that is pressing on the victim's forehead. Another way to prevent leakage of air when the lungs are inflated is to press your cheek against the victim's nose.
- Blow air into victim's mouth by taking a deep breath and then sealing your mouth tightly around the victim's mouth. Initially, give two, quick (approx. 1.5 seconds each), full breaths without allowing the lungs to deflate completely between each breath.
- Watch the victim's chest to see if it rises.
- Stop blowing when the victim's chest is expanded. Raise your mouth; turn your head to the side and listen for exhalation.
- Watch the chest to see if it falls.
- Repeat the blowing cycle until the victim starts breathing.

Note: Infants (up to one year) and children (1 to 8 years) should be administered mouth-to-mouth resuscitation as described above, except for the following:

- Do not tilt the head as far back as an adult's head.
- Both the mouth and nose of the infant should be sealed by the mouth.
- Give breaths to a child once every four seconds.
- Blow into the infant's mouth and nose once every three seconds with less pressure and volume than for a child.

Stress: How Much Can Affect Your Health?

Source: Reprinted with permission from the *Journal of Psychosomatic Research*, Vol. 11, pp. 213-218, T.H. Holmes, M.D., R.H. Rahe, M.D.; The Social Readjustment Rating Scale © 1967, Pergamon Press, Ltd.

Change, both good and bad, can create stress and stress, if sufficiently severe, can lead to illness. Drs. Thomas Holmes and Richard Rahe, psychiatrists at the University of Washington in Seattle, have developed the Social Readjustment Rating Scale. In their study, they gave a point value to stressful events. The psychiatrists discovered that in 79 percent of the persons studied, major illness followed the accumulation of stress-related changes totaling over 300 points in one year.

The Social Readjustment Rating Scale

Life Event	Value	Life Event	Value
Death of Spouse	100	In-law troubles	29
Divorce	73	Outstanding personal achievement	28
Marital separation from mate	65	Wife beginning or ceasing work outside the home	26
Detention in jail or other institution	63	Beginning or ceasing formal schooling	26
Death of a close family member	63	Major change in living conditions (e.g., building a new home, remodeling, deterioration of home or neighborhood)	25
Major personal injury or illness	53		
Marriage	50		
Being fired at work	47	Revision of personal habits (dress, manners, association, etc.)	24
Marital reconciliation with mate	45	Troubles with the boss	23
Retirement from work	45	Major change in working hours or conditions	20
Major change in the health or behavior of a family member	44	Change in residence	20
		Changing to a new school	20
Pregnancy	40	Major change in usual type and/or amount of recreation	19
Sexual difficulties	39		
Gaining a new family member (e.g., through birth, adoption, moving in, etc.)	39	Major change in church activities (e.g., a lot more or a lot less than usual)	19
Major business readjustment (e.g., merger, reorganization, bankruptcy, etc.)	39	Major change in social activities (e.g., clubs, dancing, movies, visiting, etc.)	18
Major change in financial state (e.g., a lot worse off or a lot better off than usual)	38	Taking out a mortgage or loan for a lesser purchase (e.g., for a car, TV, freezer, etc.)	17
Death of a close friend	37	Major change in sleeping habits (a lot more or a lot less sleep, or change in part of day when asleep)	16
Changing to a different line of work	36		
Major change in the number of arguments with spouse (e.g., either a lot more or a lot less than usual regarding child-rearing, personal habits, etc.)	35	Major change in number of family get-togethers (e.g., a lot more or a lot less than usual)	15
Taking out a mortgage or loan for a major purchase (e.g. for a home, business, etc.)	31	Major change in eating habits (a lot more or a lot less food intake, or very different meal hours or surroundings)	15
Foreclosure on a mortgage or loan	30	Vacation	13
Major change in responsibilities at work (e.g., promotion, demotion, lateral transfer)	29	Christmas	12
Son or daughter leaving home (e.g., marriage, attending college, etc.)	29	Minor violations of the law (e.g., traffic tickets, jaywalking, disturbing the peace, etc.)	11

A Patient's Bill of Rights

Source: American Hospital Association. © copyright 1972.

Often, as a hospital patient, you feel you have little control over your circumstances. You do, however, have some important rights. They have been enumerated by the American Hospital Association.

1. The patient has the right to considerate and respectful care.
2. The patient has the right to obtain from his physician complete current information concerning his diagnosis, treatment, and prognosis in terms the patient can be expected to understand. When it is not medically advisable to give such information to the patient, the information should be made available to an appropriate person in his behalf. He has the right to know, by name, the physician responsible for coordinating his care.
3. The patient has the right to receive from his physician information necessary to give informed consent prior to the start of any procedure and/or treatment. Except in emergencies, such information for informed consent should include but not necessarily be limited to the specific procedure and/or treatment, the medically significant risks involved, and the probable duration of incapacitation. Where medically significant alternatives for care or treatment exist, or when the patient requests information concerning medical alternatives, the patient has the right to such information. The patient also has the right to know the name of the person responsible for the procedures and/or treatment.
4. The patient has the right to refuse treatment to the extent permitted by law and to be informed of the medical consequences of his action.
5. The patient has the right to every consideration of his privacy concerning his own medical care program. Case discussion, consultation, examination, and treatment are confidential and should be conducted discreetly. Those not directly involved in his care must have the permission of the patient to be present.
6. The patient has the right to expect that all communications and records pertaining to his care should be treated as confidential.
7. The patient has the right to expect that within its capacity a hospital must make reasonable response to the request of a patient for services. The hospital must provide evaluation, service, and/or referral as indicated by the urgency of the case. When medically permissable, a patient may be transferred to another facility only after he has received complete information and explanation concerning the need for and alternatives to such a transfer. The receiving institution must first have accepted the patient for transfer.
8. The patient has the right to obtain information as to any relationship of his hospital to other health care and education institutions insofar as this care is concerned. The patient has the right to obtain information as to the existence of any professional relationships among individuals, by name, who are treating him.
9. The patient has the right to be advised if the hospital proposes to engage in or perform human experimentation affecting his care or treatment. The patient has the right to refuse to participate in such research projects.
10. The patient has the right to expect reasonable continuity of care. He has the right to know in advance what appointment times and physicians are available and where. The patient has the right to expect that the hospital will provide a mechanism whereby he is informed by his physician of the patient's continuing health care requirements following discharge.
11. The patient has the right to examine and receive an explanation of his bill, regardless of the source of payment.
12. The patient has the right to know what hospital rules and regulations apply to his conduct as a patient.

Nutritive Value of Food (Calories, Proteins, etc.)

Source: Home and Garden Bulletin No. 72; available from Supt. of Documents, U. S. Government Printing Office, Washington, DC 20402

Food	Measure	Grams	Food Energy (calories)	Protein (grams)	Fat (grams)	Saturated fats (grams)	Carbohydrate (grams)	Calcium (milligrams)	Iron (milligrams)	Vitamin A (I.U.)	Thiamin (milligrams)	Riboflavin (milligrams)
Dairy products												
Cheese, cheddar	1 oz.	28	115	7	9	6.1	T	204	.2	300	.01	.11
Cheese, cottage, small curd	1 cup	210	220	26	9	6.0	6	126	.3	340	.04	.34
Cheese, cream	1 oz.	28	100	2	10	6.2	1	23	.3	400	T	.06
Cheese, Swiss	1 oz.	28	105	8	8	5.0	1	272	T	240	.01	.10
Cheese, pasteurized process spread, American	1 oz.	28	82	5	6	3.8	2	159	.1	220	.01	.12
Half-and-Half	1 tbsp.	15	20	T	2	1.1	1	16	T	20	.01	.02
Cream, sour	1 tbsp.	15	25	T	3	1.6	1	14	T	90	T	.02
Milk, whole	1 cup	244	150	8	8	5.1	11	291	.1	310	.09	.40
Milk, nonfat (skim)	1 cup	244	85	8	T	.3	12	302	.1	500	.09	.37
Buttermilk	1 cup	245	100	8	2	1.3	12	285	.1	80	.08	.38
Milkshake, chocolate	10.6 oz.	300	355	9	8	5.0	63	396	.9	260	.14	.67
Ice Cream, hardened	1 cup	133	270	5	14	8.9	32	176	.1	540	.05	.33
Sherbet	1 cup	193	270	2	4	2.4	59	103	.3	190	.03	.09
Yogurt, fruit-flavored	8 oz.	227	230	10	3	1.8	42	343	.2	120	.08	.40
Eggs												
Fried in butter	1	46	85	5	6	2.4	1	26	.9	290	.03	.13
Hard-cooked	1	50	80	6	6	1.7	1	28	1.0	260	.04	.14
Scrambled in butter (milk added)	1	64	95	6	7	2.8	1	47	.9	310	.04	.16
Fats & oils												
Butter	1 tbsp.	14	100	T	12	7.2	T	3	T	430	T	T
Margarine	1 tbsp.	14	100	T	12	2.1	T	3	T	470	T	T
Salad dressing, blue cheese	1 tbsp.	15	75	1	8	1.6	1	12	T	30	T	.02
Salad dressing, French	1 tbsp.	16	65	T	6	1.1	3	2	.1	-	-	-
Salad dressing, Italian	1 tbsp.	15	85	T	9	1.6	1	2	T	T	T	T
Mayonnaise	1 tbsp.	14	100	T	11	2.0	T	3	.1	40	T	.01
Meat, poultry, fish												
Bluefish, baked with butter or margarine	3 oz.	85	135	22	4	-	0	25	0.6	40	.09	.08
Clams, raw, meat only	3 oz.	85	65	11	1	-	2	59	5.2	90	.08	.15
Crabmeat, white or king, canned	1 cup	135	135	24	3	.6	1	61	1.1	-	.11	.11
Fish sticks, breaded, cooked, frozen	1 oz.	28	50	5	3	-	2	3	.1	0	.01	.02
Salmon, pink, canned	3 oz.	85	120	17	5	.9	0	167	.7	60	.03	.16
Sardines, Atlantic, canned in oil	3 oz.	85	175	20	9	3.0	0	372	2.5	190	.02	.17
Shrimp, French fried	3 oz.	85	190	17	9	2.3	9	61	1.7	-	.03	.07
Tuna, in oil	3 oz.	85	170	24	7	1.7	0	7	1.6	70	.04	.10
Bacon, broiled or fried crisp	2 slices	15	85	4	8	2.5	T	2	.5	0	.08	.05
Ground beef, broiled, 10% fat	3 oz.	85	185	23	10	4.0	0	10	3.0	20	.08	.20
Roast beef, relatively lean	3 oz.	85	165	25	7	2.8	0	11	3.2	10	.06	.19
Beef steak, lean and fat	3 oz.	85	330	20	27	11.3	0	9	2.5	50	.05	.15
Beef & vegetable stew	1 cup	245	220	16	11	4.9	15	29	2.9	2,400	.15	.17
Lamb, chop, lean and fat	3.1 oz.	89	360	18	32	14.8	0	8	1.0	-	.11	.19
Liver, beef	3 oz.	85	195	22	9	2.5	5	9	7.5	45,390	.22	3.56
Ham, light cure, lean and fat	3 oz.	85	245	18	19	6.8	0	8	2.2	0	.40	.15
Pork, chop, lean and fat	2.7 oz	78	305	19	25	8.9	0	9	2.7	0	.75	.22
Bologna	1 slice	28	85	3	8	3.0	T	2	.5	-	.05	.06
Frankfurter, cooked	1	56	170	7	15	5.6	1	3	.8	-	.08	.11
Sausage, pork link, cooked	1 link	13	60	2	6	2.1	T	1	.3	0	.10	.04
Veal, cutlet, fried, bones removed	3 oz.	85	185	23	9	4.0	0	9	2.7	-	.06	.21
Chicken, drumstick, fried, bones removed	1.3 oz	38	90	12	4	1.1	T	6	.9	50	.03	.15
Chicken, half broiler, broiled, bones removed	6.2 oz.	176	240	42	7	2.2	0	16	3.0	160	.09	.34
Chicken a la king	1 cup	245	470	27	34	12.7	12	127	2.5	1,130	.10	.42
Chicken potpie, baked, 1/3 of 9 in. diam. pie	1 piece	232	545	23	31	11.3	42	70	3.0	3,090	.34	.31
Fruits & products												
Apple, raw, 2-3/4 in. diam.	1	138	80	T	1	-	20	10	.4	120	.04	.03
Applejuice	1 cup	248	120	T	T	-	30	15	1.5	-	.02	.05
Applesauce, canned, sweetened	1 cup	255	230	1	T	-	61	10	1.3	100	.05	.03
Apricots, raw	3	107	55	1	T	-	14	18	.5	2,890	.03	.04
Banana, raw	1	119	100	1	T	-	26	10	.8	230	.06	.07
Cherries, sweet, raw	10	68	45	1	T	-	12	15	.3	70	.03	.04
Fruit cocktail, canned, in heavy syrup	1 cup	255	195	1	T	-	50	23	1.0	360	.05	.03
Grapefruit, raw, medium, white	1/2	241	45	1	T	-	12	19	.5	10	.05	.02
Grapes, Thompson seedless	10	50	35	T	T	-	9	6	.2	50	.03	.02
Lemonade, frozen, diluted	1 cup	248	105	T	T	-	28	2	.1	10	.01	.02
Cantaloupe, 5-in. diam.	1/2	477	80	2	T	-	20	38	1.1	9,240	.11	.08
Orange, 2-5/8 in. diam.	1	131	65	1	T	-	16	54	.5	260	.13	.05
Orange juice, frozen, diluted	1 cup	249	120	2	T	-	29	25	.2	540	.23	.03
Peach, raw, 2-1/2 in. diam.	1	100	40	1	T	-	10	9	.5	1,330	.02	.05
Peaches, canned in syrup	1 cup	256	200	1	T	-	51	10	.8	1,100	.03	.05
Pear, raw, Bartlett, 2-1/2 in. diam.	1	164	100	1	1	-	25	13	.5	30	.03	.07
Pineapple, heavy syrup pack, crushed, chunks	1 cup	255	190	1	T	-	49	28	.8	130	.20	.05
Raisins, seedless	1 cup	145	420	4	T	-	112	90	5.1	30	.16	.12
Strawberries, whole	1 cup	149	55	1	1	-	13	31	1.5	90	.04	.10
Watermelon, 4 by 8 in. wedge	1 wedge	926	110	2	1	-	27	30	2.1	2,510	.13	.13
Grain products												
Bagel, egg	1	55	165	6	2	.5	28	9	1.2	30	.14	.10
Biscuit, 2 in. diam., from home recipe	1	28	105	2	5	1.2	13	34	.4	T	.08	.08
Bread, raisin	1 slice	25	65	2	1	.2	13	18	.6	T	.09	.06
Bread, white, enriched, soft-crumb	1 slice	25	70	2	1	.2	13	21	.6	T	.10	.06
Bread, whole wheat, soft-crumb	1 slice	28	65	3	1	.1	14	24	.8	T	.09	.03
Oatmeal or rolled oats	1 cup	240	130	5	2	.4	23	22	1.4	0	.19	.05
Bran flakes (40% bran), added sugar, salt, iron, vitamins	1 cup	35	105	4	1	-	28	19	12.4	1,650	.41	.49
Corn flakes, added sugar, salt, iron, vitamins	1 cup	25	95	2	T	-	21	*	0.6	1,180	.29	.35
Rice, puffed, added iron, thiamin, niacin	1 cup	15	60	1	T	-	13	3	.3	0	.07	.01

Food	Measure	Grams	Food Energy (calories)	Protein (grams)	Fat (grams)	Saturated fats (grams)	Carbohydrate (grams)	Calcium (milligrams)	Iron (milligrams)	Vitamin A (I.U.)	Thiamin (milligrams)	Riboflavin (milligrams)
Wheat, shredded, plain, 1 biscuit or 1/2 cup	1 serving	25	90	2	1	-	20	11	.9	0	.06	.03
Cake, angel food, 1/12 of cake	1	53	135	3	T	-	32	50	.2	0	.03	.08
Coffeecake, 1/6 cake	1	72	230	5	7	2.0	38	44	1.2	120	.14	.15
Cupcake, 2-1/2 in. diam., with chocolate icing	1	36	130	2	5	2.0	21	47	.4	60	.05	.06
Boston cream pie with custard filling, 1/12 of cake	1	69	210	3	6	1.9	34	46	.7	140	.09	.11
Fruitcake, dark, 1/30 of loaf	1	15	55	1	2	.5	9	11	.4	20	.02	.02
Cake, pound, 1/17 of loaf	1	33	160	2	10	2.5	16	6	.5	80	.05	.06
Brownies, with nuts, from commercial recipe	1	20	85	1	4	.9	13	9	.4	20	.03	.02
Cookies, chocolate chip, from home recipe	4	40	205	2	12	3.5	24	14	.8	40	.06	.06
Vanilla wafers	10	40	185	2	6	-	30	16	.6	50	.10	.09
Crackers, graham	2	14	55	1	1	.3	10	6	.5	0	.02	.08
Crackers, saltines	4	11	50	1	1	.3	8	2	.5	0	.05	.05
Danish pastry, round piece	1	65	275	5	15	4.7	30	33	1.2	200	.18	.19
Doughnut, cake type	1	25	100	1	5	1.2	13	10	.4	20	.05	.05
Macaroni and cheese, from home recipe	1 cup	200	430	17	22	8.9	40	362	1.8	860	.20	.40
Muffin, corn	1	40	125	3	4	1.2	19	42	.7	120	.10	.10
Noodles, enriched, cooked	1 cup	160	200	7	2	-	37	16	1.4	110	.22	.13
Pancake, plain, from home recipe	1	27	60	2	2	.5	9	27	.4	30	.06	.07
Pie, apple, 1/7 of pie	1	135	345	3	15	3.9	51	11	.9	40	.15	.11
Pie, banana cream, 1/7 of pie	1	130	285	6	12	3.8	40	86	1.0	330	.11	.22
Pie, cherry, 1/7 of pie	1	135	350	4	15	4.0	52	19	.9	590	.16	.12
Pie, lemon meringue, 1/7 of pie	1	120	305	4	12	3.7	45	17	1.0	200	.09	.12
Pie, pecan, 1/7 of pie	1	118	495	6	27	4.0	61	55	3.7	190	.26	.14
Pie, pumpkin, 1/7 of pie	1	130	275	5	15	5.4	32	66	1.0	3,210	.11	.18
Pizza, cheese, 1/8 of 12 in. diam. pie	1	60	145	6	4	1.7	22	86	1.1	230	.16	.18
Popcorn, popped, plain	1 cup	6	25	1	T	T	5	5	.2	-	-	.01
Pretzels, stick	10	3	10	T	T	-	2	1	T	0	.01	.01
Rice, white, enriched, instant, cooked	1 cup	165	180	4	T	-	40	5	1.3	0	.21	**
Rolls, enriched, brown & serve	1	26	85	2	2	.4	14	20	.5	T	.10	.06
Rolls, frankfurter & hamburger	1	40	120	3	2	.5	21	30	.8	T	.16	.10
Spaghetti with meat balls & tomato sauce, from home recipe	1 cup	248	330	*9	12	3.3	39	124	3.7	1,590	.25	.30
Legumes, nuts, seeds												
Beans, Great Northern, cooked	1 cup	180	210	14	1	-	38	90	4.9	0	.25	.13
Peanuts, roasted in oil, salted	1 cup	144	840	37	72	13.7	27	107	3.0	-	.46	.19
Peanut butter	1 tbsp.	16	95	4	8	1.5	3	9	.3	-	.02	.02
Sunflower seeds	1 cup	145	810	35	69	8.2	29	174	10.3	70	2.84	.33
Sugars & sweets												
Candy, caramels	1 oz.	28	115	1	3	1.6	22	42	.4	T	.01	.05
Candy, milk chocolate	1 oz.	28	145	2	9	5.5	16	65	.3	80	.02	.10
Fudge, chocolate	1 oz.	28	115	1	3	1.3	21	22	.3	T	.01	.03
Candy, hard	1 oz.	28	110	0	T	-	28	6	.5	0	0	0
Honey	1 tbsp.	21	65	T	0	0	17	1	.1	0	T	.01
Jams & Preserves	1 tbsp.	20	55	T	T	-	14	4	.2	T	T	.01
Sugar, white, granulated	1 tbsp.	12	45	0	0	0	12	0	T	0	0	0
Vegetables												
Asparagus, canned, spears	4 spears	80	15	2	T	-	3	15	1.5	640	.05	.08
Beans, lima, thick-seeded	1 cup	170	170	10	T	-	32	34	2.9	390	.12	.09
Beans, green, from frozen, cuts	1 cup	135	35	2	T	-	8	54	.9	780	.09	.12
Beets, canned, diced or sliced	1 cup	170	65	2	T	-	15	32	1.2	30	.02	.05
Broccoli, cooked	1 stalk	180	45	6	1	-	8	158	1.4	4,500	.16	.36
Cabbage, raw, coarsely shredded or sliced	1 cup	70	15	1	T	-	4	34	.3	90	.04	.04
Carrots, raw, 7-1/2 by 1-1/8 in.	1	72	30	1	T	-	7	27	.5	7,930	.04	.04
Cauliflower, raw	1 cup	115	31	3	T	-	6	29	1.3	70	.13	.12
Celery, raw	1 stalk	40	5	T	T	-	2	16	.1	110	.01	.01
Collards, cooked	1 cup	190	65	7	1	-	10	357	1.5	14,820	.21	.38
Corn, sweet, cooked	1 ear	140	70	2	1	-	16	2	.5	310	.09	.08
Corn, cream style	1 cup	256	210	5	2	-	51	8	1.5	840	.08	.13
Cucumber, with peel	6-8 slices	28	5	T	T	-	1	7	.3	70	.01	.01
Lettuce, Iceberg, chopped	1 cup	55	5	T	T	-	2	11	.3	180	.03	.03
Mushrooms, raw	1 cup	70	20	1	T	-	3	4	.6	T	.07	.32
Onions, raw, chopped	1 cup	170	65	3	T	-	15	46	.9	T	.05	.07
Peas, frozen, cooked	1 cup	160	110	8	T	-	19	30	3.0	960	.43	.14
Potatoes, baked, peeled	1	156	145	4	T	-	33	14	1.1	T	.15	.07
Potatoes, frozen, French fried	10	50	110	2	4	1.1	17	5	.9	T	.07	.01
Potatoes, mashed, milk added	1 cup	210	135	4	2	.7	27	50	.8	40	.17	.11
Potato chips	10	20	115	1	8	2.1	10	8	.4	T	.04	.01
Potato salad	1 cup	250	250	7	7	2.0	41	80	1.5	350	.20	.18
Sauerkraut, canned	1 cup	235	40	2	T	-	9	85	1.2	120	.07	.09
Spinach, chopped, from frozen	1 cup	205	45	6	1	-	8	232	4.3	16,200	.14	.31
Squash, summer, cooked	1 cup	210	30	2	T	-	7	53	.8	820	.11	.17
Sweet potatoes, baked in skin, peeled	1	114	160	2	1	-	37	46	1.0	9,230	.10	.08
Tomatoes, raw	1	135	25	1	T	-	6	16	.6	1,110	.07	.05
Tomato catsup	1 tbsp.	15	15	T	T	-	4	3	.1	210	.01	.01
Tomato juice	1 cup	243	45	2	T	-	10	17	2.2	1,940	.12	.07
Miscellaneous												
Beer	12 fl. oz.	360	150	1	0	0	14	18	T	-	.01	.11
Gin, rum, vodka, whisky, 86 proof	1-1/2 fl. oz.	42	105	-	0	0	T	-	-	-	-	-
Wine, table	3-1/2 fl. oz.	102	85	T	0	0	4	9	.4	-	T	.01
Cola-type beverage	12 fl. oz.	369	145	0	0	0	37	-	-	0	0	0
Ginger ale	12 fl. oz	366	115	0	0	0	29	-	-	0	0	0
Gelatin dessert	1 cup	240	140	4	0	0	34	-	-	-	-	-
Mustard, prepared	1 tsp.	5	5	T	T	-	T	4	.1	-	-	-
Olives, pickled, green	4 medium	16	15	T	2	.2	T	8	.2	40	-	-
Pickles, dill, whole	1	65	5	T	T	-	1	17	.7	70	T	.01
Popsicle, 3 fl. oz.	1	95	70	0	0	0	18	0	T	0	0	0
Soup, cream of chicken, prepared with milk	1 cup	245	180	7	10	4.2	15	172	.5	610	.05	.27
Soup, cream of mushroom, prepared with milk	1 cup	245	215	7	14	5.4	16	191	.5	250	.05	.34
Soup, tomato, prepared with water	1 cup	245	90	2	3	.5	16	15	.7	1,000	.05	.05

T — Indicates trace * — Varies by brand

Food and Nutrition

Food contains proteins, carbohydrates, fats, water, vitamins and minerals. Nutrition is the way your body takes in and uses these ingredients to maintain proper functioning.

In March 1989, the Natl. Research Council reported on the role of diet in cardiovascular diseases, cancer, chronic liver and kidney diseases, diabetes, osteoporosis, obesity, and dental cavities. Major recommendations included: reducing fat intake to 30 percent or less of total calories, reducing saturated fat to less than 10 percent of calories, and reducing cholesterol to less than 300 milligrams daily; eating five or more half-cup servings per day of vegetables and fruits, especially green and yellow vegetables and citrus fruits; eating six or more servings daily of bread, cereals, and legumes, for a total of more than 55 percent of calories; eating no more than twice the recommended daily allowance of protein, and no more than 1.6 grams per day per kilogram of body weight; eating less than six grams a day of salt, limiting its use in cooking, avoiding it at the table, and consuming salty foods sparingly; and maintaining an adequate intake of calcium.

Protein

Proteins are composed of amino acids and are indispensable in the diet. They build, maintain, and repair the body. Best sources: eggs, milk, fish, meat, poultry, soybeans, nuts. High quality proteins such as eggs, meat, or fish supply all 8 amino acids needed in the diet. Low quality proteins such as nuts and grain do not.

Fats

Fats provide energy by furnishing calories to the body, and by carrying vitamins A, D, E, and K. They are the most concentrated source of energy in the diet. Best sources: butter, margarine, salad oils, nuts, cream, egg yolks, most cheeses, lard, meat.

Carbohydrates

Carbohydrates provide energy for body function and activity by supplying immediate calories. The carbohydrate group includes sugars, starches, fiber, and starchy vegetables. Best sources: grains, legumes, nuts, potatoes, fruits.

Water

Water dissolves and transports other nutrients throughout the body, aiding the processes of digestion, absorption, circulation, and excretion. It also helps regulate body temperature. We get water from all foods.

Vitamins

Vitamin A—promotes good eyesight and helps keep the skin and mucous membranes resistant to infection. Best sources: liver, carrots, sweet potatoes, kale, collard greens, turnips, fortified milk.

Vitamin B$_1$ (thiamine)—prevents beriberi. Essential to carbohydrate metabolism and health of nervous system.

Vitamin B$_2$ (riboflavin)—protects skin, mouth, eye, eyelids, and mucous membranes. Essential to protein and energy metabolism. Best sources: liver, milk, meat, poultry, broccoli, mushrooms.

Vitamin B$_6$ (pyridoxine)—important in the regulation of the central nervous system and in protein metabolism. Best sources: whole grains, meats, nuts, brewers' yeast.

Vitamin B$_{12}$ (cobalamin)—needed to form red blood cells. Best sources: liver, meat, fish, eggs, soybeans.

Niacin—maintains the health of skin, tongue, and digestive system. Best sources: poultry, peanuts, fish, organ meats, enriched flour and bread.

Other B vitamins—biotin, choline, folic acid (folacin), inositol, PABA (para-aminobenzoic acid), and pantothenic acid.

Vitamin C (ascorbic acid)—maintains collagen, a protein necessary for the formation of skin, ligaments, and bones. It helps heal wounds and mend fractures, and aids in resisting some types of virus and bacterial infections. Best sources: citrus fruits and juices, turnips, broccoli, Brussels sprouts, potatoes and sweet potatoes, tomatoes, cabbage.

Vitamin D—important for bone development. Best sources: sunlight, fortified milk and milk products, fish-liver oils, egg yolks, organ meats.

Vitamin E (tocopherol)—helps protect red blood cells. Best sources: vegetable oils, wheat germ, whole grains, eggs, peanuts, organ meats, margarine, green leafy vegetables.

Vitamin K—necessary for formation of prothrombin, which helps blood to clot. Also made by intestinal bacteria. Best dietary sources: green leafy vegetables, tomatoes.

Minerals

Calcium—the most abundant mineral in the body, works with phosphorus in building and maintaining bones and teeth. Best sources: milk and milk products, cheese, and blackstrap molasses.

Phosphorus—the 2d most abundant mineral, performs more functions than any other mineral, and plays a part in nearly every chemical reaction in the body. Best source: whole grains, cheese, milk.

Iron—Necessary for the formation of myoglobin, which transports oxygen to muscle tissue, and hemoglobin, which transports oxygen in the blood. Best sources: organ meats, beans, green leafy vegetables, and shellfish.

Other minerals—chromium, cobalt, copper, fluorine, iodine, magnesium, manganese, molybdenum, potassium, selenium, sodium, sulfur, and zinc.

Recommended Daily Dietary Allowances

Source: Food and Nutrition Board, National Academy of Sciences—National Research Council; 1980

	Age (years)	Weight (lbs.)	Protein (grams)	Vitamin A [1]	Vitamin D [2]	Vitamin E [3]	Vitamin C (mg.)	Thiamin (mg.)	Riboflavin (mg.)	Niacin (mg.) [4]	Vitamin B$_6$ (mg.)	Folacin (micrograms)	Vitamin B$_{12}$ (micrograms)	Calcium (mg.)	Phosphorus (mg.)	Magnesium (mg.)	Iron (mg.)	Zinc (mg.)	Iodine (micrograms)
Infants . . . to 6 mos.		13	kg × 2.2	420	10	3	35	0.3	0.4	6	0.3	30	0.5	360	240	50	10	3	40
to 1 yr.		20	kg × 2.0	400	10	4	35	0.5	0.6	8	0.6	45	1.5	540	360	70	15	5	50
Children .	1-3	29	23	400	10	5	45	0.7	0.8	9	0.9	100	2.0	800	800	150	15	10	70
	4-6	44	30	500	10	6	45	0.9	1.0	11	1.3	200	2.5	800	800	200	10	10	90
	7-10	62	34	700	10	7	45	1.2	1.4	16	1.6	300	3.0	800	800	250	10	10	120
Males . . .	11-14	99	45	1000	10	8	50	1.4	1.6	18	1.8	400	3.0	1200	1200	350	18	15	150
	15-18	145	56	1000	10	10	60	1.4	1.7	18	2.0	400	3.0	1200	1200	400	18	15	150
	19-22	154	56	1000	7.5	10	60	1.5	1.7	19	2.2	400	3.0	800	800	350	10	15	150
	23-50	154	56	1000	5	10	60	1.4	1.6	18	2.2	400	3.0	800	800	350	10	15	150
	51+	154	56	1000	5	10	60	1.2	1.4	16	2.2	400	3.0	800	800	350	10	15	150
Females .	11-14	101	46	800	10	8	50	1.1	1.3	15	1.8	400	3.0	1200	1200	300	18	15	150
	15-18	120	46	800	10	8	60	1.1	1.3	14	2.0	400	3.0	1200	1200	300	18	15	150
	19-22	120	44	800	7.5	8	60	1.1	1.3	14	2.0	400	3.0	800	800	300	18	15	150
	23-50	120	44	800	5	8	60	1.0	1.2	13	2.0	400	3.0	800	800	300	18	15	150
	51+	120	44	800	5	8	60	1.0	1.2	13	2.0	400	3.0	800	800	300	10	15	150
Pregnant			+30	+200	+5	+2	+20	+0.4	+0.3	+2	+0.6	+400	+1.0	+400	+400	+150	[5]	+5	+25
Lactating			+20	+400	+5	+3	+40	+0.5	+0.5	+5	+0.5	+100	+1.0	+400	+400	+150	[5]	+10	+50

(1) Retinol equivalents. (2) Micrograms of cholecalciferol. (3) Milligrams alpha-tocopherol equivalents. (4) Niacin equivalents. (5) The use of 30-60 milligrams of supplemental iron is recommended.

EDUCATION

Educational Attainment by Age, Race, and Sex

Source: U.S. Bureau of the Census unpublished data as of March, 1988 (Number of persons in thousands)

Race, age, and sex	All persons	Less than high school, 4 years	High school, 4 years	College, 1 to 3 years	College, 4 years or more	Less than high school, 4 years	High school, 4 years	College, 1 to 3 years	College, 4 years or more
		Years of school completed				Percent			
March 1988									
All races									
18 to 24 years	26,060	5,627	11,254	7,148	2,029	21.6	43.2	27.4	7.8
25 years and over	151,616	36,114	58,940	25,783	30,779	38.9	38.9	17.0	20.3
25 to 34 years	42,970	5,836	17,889	9,069	10,174	13.6	41.6	21.1	23.7
35 to 44 years	34,682	4,841	13,200	7,309	9,332	14.0	38.1	21.1	26.9
45 to 54 years	23,795	5,230	9,860	3,698	5,008	22.0	41.4	15.5	21.0
55 to 64 years	21,642	7,024	8,580	2,793	3,246	32.5	39.6	12.9	15.0
65 years and over.	28,527	13,183	9,412	2,915	3,018	46.2	33.0	10.2	10.6
Male, 25 years and over . . .	71,941	16,944	25,674	12,052	17,269	23.6	35.7	16.8	24.0
Female, 25 years and over . .	79,676	19,171	33,266	13,730	13,510	24.1	41.8	17.2	17.0
White									
18 to 24 years	21,552	4,400	9,295	6,041	1,819	20.4	43.1	28.0	8.4
25 years and over	131,092	29,282	51,795	22,599	27,416	22.3	39.5	17.2	20.9
25 to 34 years	36,148	4,613	15,052	7,621	8,861	12.8	41.6	21.1	24.5
35 to 44 years	29,783	3,804	11,339	6,351	8,290	12.8	38.1	21.3	27.8
45 to 54 years	20,448	4,099	8,645	3,281	4,424	20.0	42.3	16.0	21.6
55 to 64 years	19,074	5,672	7,854	2,562	2,985	29.7	41.2	13.4	15.6
65 years and over.	25,639	11,095	8,905	2,784	2,857	43.3	34.7	10.9	11.1
Male, 25 years and over . . .	62,679	13,959	22,541	10,572	15,608	22.3	36.0	16.9	24.9
Female, 25 years and over . .	68,414	15,323	29,255	12,027	11,808	22.4	42.8	17.6	17.3
Black									
18 to 24 years	3,619	1,065	1,627	791	134	29.4	45.0	21.9	3.7
25 years and over	15,929	5,838	5,914	2,382	1,796	36.7	37.1	15.0	11.3
25 to 34 years	5,272	1,029	2,446	1,104	693	19.5	46.4	20.9	13.1
35 to 44 years	3,700	841	1,563	724	571	22.7	42.2	19.6	15.4
45 to 54 years	2,501	969	969	290	274	38.7	38.7	11.6	11.0
55 to 64 years	2,074	1,175	580	172	146	56.7	28.0	8.3	7.0
65 years and over.	2,383	1,824	357	91	111	76.5	15.0	3.8	4.7
Male, 25 years and over . . .	7,067	2,571	2,612	1,091	792	36.4	37.0	15.4	11.2
Female, 25 years and over . .	8,863	3,267	3,302	1,291	1,003	36.9	37.3	14.6	11.3
Hispanic Origin[1]									
18 to 24 years	2,665	1,106	1,040	438	80	41.5	39.0	16.4	3.0
25 years and over	9,940	4,874	2,815	1,257	995	49.0	28.3	12.6	10.0
25 to 34 years	3,785	1,449	1,239	647	450	38.3	32.7	17.1	11.9
35 to 44 years	2,624	1,157	823	363	282	44.1	31.4	13.8	10.7
45 to 54 years	1,488	820	386	126	155	55.1	25.9	8.5	10.4
55 to 64 years	1,142	749	240	82	71	65.6	21.0	7.2	6.2
65 years and over.	903	701	126	39	37	77.6	14.0	4.3	4.1
Male, 25 years and over . . .	4,889	2,346	1,332	625	585	48.0	27.2	12.8	12.0
Female, 25 years and over . .	5,051	2,528	1,482	632	410	50.0	29.3	12.5	8.1

(1) Persons of Hispanic origin may be of any race.

Historical Summary of Public Elementary and Secondary Schools
Source: National Center for Education Statistics, U.S. Dept. of Education

	1899-1900	1909-10	1919-20	1929-30	1939-40	1949-50	1959-60	1969-70	1979-80	1986-87
Pupils and teachers (thousands) .										
Total U.S. population	75,995	90,492	104,512	121,770	130,880	148,665	179,323	203,212	224,567	241,096
Population 5-17 years of age	21,573	24,009	27,556	31,417	30,150	30,168	43,881	52,490	48,040	45,148
Percent aged 5-17 years.	28.4	26.5	26.4	25.8	23.0	20.3	24.5	25.8	21.4	18.7
Enrollment (thousands)										
Elementary and secondary	15,503	17,814	21,578	25,678	25,434	25,111	36,087	45,619	41,645	39,837
Percent pop. 5-17 enrolled	71.9	74.2	78.3	81.7	84.4	83.2	82.2	86.9	86.7	88.2
Percent in high schools	3.3	5.1	10.2	17.1	26.0	22.7	23.5	28.5	32.9	31.2
High school graduates.	62	111	231	592	1,143	1,063	1,627	2,589	2,748	2,433
Average school term (in days). . . .	144.3	157.5	161.9	172.7	175.0	177.9	178.0	178.9	178.5	. . .
Total instructional staff	. . .	. . .	678	880	912	962	1,464	2,253	2,441	. . .
Teachers, librarians: Men	127	110	93	140	195	195	402	691	782[4]	. . .
Women	296	413	565	703	681	719	985	1,440	1,518[4]	. . .
Percent men	29.9	21.1	14.1	16.6	22.2	21.3	29.0	33.4	34.0[4]	. . .
Revenue & expenditures (millions)										
Total revenue	$219	$433	$970	$2,088	$2,260	$5,437	$14,746	$40,267	$96,881	$158,827
Total expenditures	214	426	1,036	2,316	2,344	5,837	15,613	40,683	95,962	160,900[4]
Current elem. and secondary. . .	179	356	861	1,843	1,941	4,687	12,329	34,218	86,984[1]	. . .
Capital outlay.	35	69	153	370	257	1,014	2,661	4,659	6,506	. . .
Interest on school debt	. . .	. . .	18	92	130	100	489	1,171	1,874	. . .
Other	. . .	. . .	3	9	13	35	132	636	598	. . .
Salaries and pupil cost	(Data in unadjusted dollars)									
Average annual teacher salary[2]. . .	$325	$485	$871	$1,420	$1,441	$3,010	$5,174	$8,840	$16,715	$27,746
Expenditure per capita total pop. . .	2.83	4.71	9.91	19.03	17.91	39	87	200	424	667[4]
Current expenditure per pupil ADA[3].	16.67	27.85	53.32	86.70	88.09	209	375	816	2,272	3,977

(1) Because of a modification of the scope, "current expenditures for elementary and secondary schools" data for 1959-60 and later years are not entirely comparable with data for prior years. (2) Includes supervisors, principals, teachers and other non-supervisory instructional staff. (3) "ADA" means average daily attendance in elementary and secondary day schools. (4) Estimated.

Fall Enrollment and Teachers in Full-time Day Schools
Elementary and Secondary Day Schools, Fall 1987
Source: National Center for Education Statistics, U.S. Dept. of Education; National Education Assn.

	Local school districts Total	Total enrollment	Pupils per teacher	Classroom teachers	Teacher's average pay (1987-1988)	Instructional aides	Expenditure per pupil
United States	15,577	40,024,244	17.6	2,278,813	$28,044	337,061	$3,977
Alabama	129	729,234	19.3	37,716	23,320	3,677	2,573
Alaska	55	105,678	17.3	6,113	40,424	277	8,010
Arizona	240	572,421	18.6	30,707	27,388	6,564	3,544
Arkansas	331	437,036	17.1	25,572	20,340	2,587	2,733
California	1,084	4,489,322	22.9	195,864	33,159	49,985	3,728
Colorado	177	560,236	18.0	31,168	28,651	4,052	4,147
Connecticut	166	465,465	13.3	35,050	33,487	—	5,435
Delaware	19	95,659	16.1	5,951	29,575	718	4,825
District of Columbia . . .	1	86,435	13.9	6,232	34,705	636	5,742
Florida	67	1,664.774	17.4	95,857	25,198	17,564	3,794
Georgia	186	1,110,947	17.8	62,280	26,177	11,898	3,374
Hawaii.	1	166,160	21.6	7,684	28,785	1,339	3,787
Idaho	115	212,444	20.7	10,258	22,242	923	2,585
Illinois	986	1,811,446	17.2	105,217	29,663	11,555	4,106
Indiana	303	964,129	17.9	53,749	27,386	9,637	3,556
Iowa	436	480,826	15.6	30,873	24,867	3,050	3,808
Kansas	304	421,112	15.4	27,317	24,647	2,523	3,933
Kentucky	178	642,696	18.2	35,239	24,274	5,182	2,733
Louisiana	66	793,093	18.5	42,920	21,209	7,477	3,069
Maine	200	211,817	14.9	14,204	23,425	2,683	3,850
Maryland	24	683,797	17.1	40,093	30,933	5,316	4,777
Massachusetts	396	825,320	13.9	59,517	30,019	8,024	5,145
Michigan	563	1,606,344	20.1	80,081	32,926	12,457	4,353
Minnesota	436	721,481	17.1	42,132	29,900	6,389	4,180
Mississippi	152	505,550	—	—	20,669		2,350
Missouri.	544	802,060	16.2	49,632	24,703	3,540	3,472
Montana	550	152,207	15.8	9,659	23,798	1,011	4,194
Nebraska	891	268,100	15.1	17,713	23,246	2,472	3,756
Nevada	17	168,353	20.2	8,348	27,600	—	3,573
New Hampshire	173	166,045	16.0	10,363	24,091	1,501	3,933
New Jersey	604	1,092,982	14.0	78,335	30,720	8,193	5,953
New Mexico	88	287,229	18.9	15,175	24,351	3,070	3,558
New York	722	2,594,070	15.2	170,236	34,500	23,825	6,497
North Carolina	140	1,085,976	18.2	59,771	24,900	17,002	3,129
North Dakota	303	119,004	15.6	7,632	21,660	899	3,437
Ohio.	703	1,793,411	18.0	99,641	27,606	7,721	3,671
Oklahoma	611	584,212	16.9	34,515	22,006	3,750	3,099
Oregon	304	455,895	18.3	24,911	28,060	3,995	4,337
Pennsylvania	501	1,668,542	16.2	103,307	29,174	10,187	4,616
Rhode Island	40	134,061	15.0	8,934	32,858	901	4,985
South Carolina	91	614,921	17.2	35,701	24,241	5,652	3,237
South Dakota	194	126,817	15.5	8,172	19,750	1,178	3,097
Tennessee	141	823,783	19.6	42,082	23,785	7,401	2,827
Texas	1,063	3,236,787	17.3	187,159	25,655	27,945	3,409
Utah.	40	423,386	24.7	17,124	22,621	2,561	2,415
Vermont	275	92,755	13.4	6,938	23,397	1,279	4,399
Virginia	136	979,417	16.3	59,928	27,436	8,405	3,780
Washington.	296	775,755	20.2	38,344	28,116	5,120	3,964
West Virginia	55	344,236	15.2	22,702	21,736	2,888	3,784
Wisconsin.	431	772,363	16.2	47,721	28,998	5,812	4,523
Wyoming	49	98,455	14.5	6,798	27,260	1,266	5,201

Programs for the Handicapped
Source: Office of Special Educ. and Rehabilitative Services, U.S. Dept. of Education

Number of children 3 to 21 years old served annually in educational programs for the handicapped and percent of total public school enrollment.

Type of Handicapped	1980-81	1981-82	1982-83	1983-84	1984-85	1985-86	1986-87	1987-88
	Number Served, in Thousands							
All conditions.	4,142	4,198	4,255	4,298	4,315	4,317	4,374	4,446
Learning disabled	1,462	1,622	1,741	1,806	1,832	1,862	1,914	1,928
Speech impaired	1,168	1,135	1,131	1,128	1,126	1,125	1,136	953
Mentally retarded	829	786	757	727	694	660	643	582
Seriously emotionally disturbed . .	346	339	352	361	372	375	383	373
Hard of hearing and deaf	79	75	73	72	69	66	65	56
Orthopedically handicapped	58	58	57	56	56	57	57	47
Visually handicapped	31	29	28	29	28	27	26	22
Deaf-blind.	3	2	2	2	2	2	2	1
	As Percent of Total Enrollment							
All conditions.	10.11	10.47	10.73	10.92	10.98	10.93	10.97	11.10
Learning disabled	3.57	4.05	4.39	4.59	4.66	4.71	4.80	4.82
Speech impaired.	2.85	2.83	2.85	2.87	2.87	2.85	2.85	2.38
Mentally retarded	2.02	1.96	1.91	1.85	1.77	1.67	1.61	1.45
Seriously emotionally disturbed . .	.85	.85	.89	.92	.95	.95	.96	.93
Hard of hearing and deaf	.19	.19	.18	.18	.17	.17	.16	.14
Orthopedically handicapped	.14	.14	.14	.14	.14	.14	.14	.12
Visually handicapped	.08	.07	.07	.07	.07	.07	.07	.06
Deaf-blind.	.01	.01	.01	.01	.01	.01	.01	.01

Note: Counts are based on reports from the 50 States, District of Columbia and Puerto Rico (i.e., figures from U.S. territories are not included). Percentages of total enrollment are based on the total annual enrollment of U.S. public schools, preprimary through 12th grade. Details may not add to totals because of rounding.

Federal Funds for Education, 1980-1989

Source: U.S. Office of Management and Budget

Federal funds obligated for programs administered by the Department of Education: Fiscal years 1980 to 1989
(In thousands of dollars)

	1980	1982	1984	1986	1988	1989[1]
Total.............	$14,102,165	$15,069,598	$17,072,698	$18,940,681	$20,697,311	$24,058,528
Elementary and secondary education.............	4,239,022	3,802,234	4,294,269	4,447,153	5,682,997	6,112,813
Grants for the disadvantaged..	3,204,664	3,063,651	3,501,383	3,557,026	4,357,970	4,591,299
Special programs.........	788,918	524,730	549,117	658,676	1,067,213	1,252,548
Bilingual education.........	169,540	136,292	173,051	167,534	191,470	197,394
Indian education.........	75,900	77,561	70,718	63,917	66,344	71,572
School assistance in federally affected areas..........	812,873	457,227	608,791	677,055	731,241	770,028
Maintenance and operations ..	690,000	438,498	555,300	636,405	685,498	708,396
Construction	110,873	15,951	28,491	21,267	35,640	39,302
Disaster assistance	12,000	2,778	25,000	19,383	10,103	22,330
Other	—	—	—	—	—	—
Education for the handicapped.	1,555,253	2,023,536	2,416,799	2,573,399	3,075,456	4,165,970
State grant programs.......	815,805	933,657	1,082,180	1,087,249	1,115,333	1,905,951
Early childhood education[2] ...	38,745	40,673	53,164	15,991	210,752	439,718
Special centers, projects, and research	55,075	35,057	54,871	54,629	78,600	80,526
Captioned films and media services.............	17,778	11,438	14,000	36,105	13,026	13,403
Personnel training	55,375	48,911	55,540	68,339	66,153	67,095
Handicapped rehabilitation Service and research	572,475	953,800	1,157,044	1,311,086	1,591,592	1,659,277
Vocational education and adult programs.............	1,153,743	751,118	954,320	1,016,302	1,000,055	1,125,433
Basic programs[3]	744,653	530,669	689,324	862,979	823,299	903,309
Consumer and homemaking ..	63,169	29,363	36,792	30,311	32,752	33,157
Program improvement and supportive services	162,512	91,650	117,249	—	—	—
State planning and advisory councils..............	13,423	8,800	11,200	6,761	7,681	8,271
Adult education, grants to States	153,724	90,636	99,755	109,791	129,183	164,389
Other	16,262	—	—	6,460	7,140	16,307
Postsecondary student financial assistance	5,108,534	6,584,012	7,478,401	8,932,803	8,807,929	10,451,431
Educational opportunity grants[4].	2,534378	2,546,167	3,565,209	4,460,266	4,620,133	5,091,899
Work-study	596,065	523,910	561,322	576,145	604,445	612,142
Direct student loans	322,749	193,686	191,962	212,696	216,963	217,262
Guaranteed student loans....	1,597,877	3,297,776	3,130,939	3,658,502	3,297,305	4,455,902
Other student assistance programs.............	57,465	22,473	28,969	25,194	69,083	74,226
Direct aid to postsecondary institutions..........	277,068	284,467	311,221	294,681	341,063	415,216
Aid to minority and developing institutions	114,680	119,829	132,081	125,895	135,222	195,959
Special programs for the disadvantaged	147,389	150,238	164,740	168,786	205,841	219,257
Cooperative education......	14,999	14,400	14,400	—	—	—
Higher education facilities.....	268,493	449,191	216,893	206,017	162,528	90,204
Construction loans and insurance	35,362	38,690	54,105	26,800	89,820	39,546
Interest subsidy grants......	24,626	23,759	23,925	23,981	24,466	30,735
College housing loans	208,505	386,742	138,863	155,236	48,242	19,923
Other higher education programs.............	34,927	38,226	82,410	64,032	79,305	75,142
International education and foreign languages	19,977	23,923	30,800	—	—	—
Fund for Improvement of Postsecondary Education. ..	12,000	11,503	11,710	62,835	65,813	72,189
Other	2,950	2,800	39,900	1,197	13,492	2,953
Public Library services......	101,218	80,074	107,895	117,998	135,731	150,871
Public Library services......	66,451	60,000	65,000	71,774	78,922	81,009
Interlibrary cooperation		11,520	15,000	17,226	18,395	19,102
Public Library construction ...	—	—	21,015	17,514	23,577	35,995
Research Libraries.........	5,992	5,760	6,000	5,742	5,744	5,675
Other	28,775	2,794	880	5,742	9,093	9,090
Payments to special institutions	273,860	251,570	249,610	255,297	271,658	284,063
American Printing House for the Blind...............	4,349	5,000	5,000	5,263	5,266	5,335
National Technical Institute for the Deaf..............	19,799	26,300	28,000	30,624	31,594	33,326
Gallaudet College	49,409	64,815	56,288	59,334	62,195	65,998
Howard University	200,303	155,455	160,322	160,076	172,603	179,404
Departmental accounts	277,174	347,943	352,089	355,944	409,348	417,357

(continued)

	1980	1982	1984	1986	1988	1989[1]
Educational research and improvement	51,415	61,550	57,165	57,514	68,147	78,201
Departmental management account	223,857	283,906	293,351	298,397	341,171	338,984
Other	1,875	2,290	1,401	—	—	—
Trust funds	27	197	172	33	30	172

(1) Estimated. (2) Includes preschool incentive grants. (3) Includes programs of national significance and special programs for the disadvantaged. (4) Includes Pell Grants, Supplemental Education Opportunity Grants and State Student Incentive Grants, and Income Contingent Loans. (—) Data are not available or not applicable.
NOTE: Because of rounding, details may not add to totals.

Public Libraries

Source: World Almanac questionnaire (1988)

City	No. bound Volumes	Circulation	Annual Acquisitions Expend.	City	No. bound Volumes	Circulation	Annual Acquisitions Expend.
Akron, Oh.*,a (18)	1,200,677	1,953,376	NA	Miami, Fla. (28)	2,386,204	4,200,000	$2,200,000
Albuquerque, N.M. (11)	610,502	2,283,512	$1,168,447	Milwaukee, Wis. (12)	2,051,114	3,382,982	1,360,814
Anaheim, Cal. (4)	383,000	1,361,538	611,212	Minneapolis, Minn. (14)	1,806,925	2,728,157	1,500,000
Anchorage, Alas. (8)	477,679	1,149,982	759,220	Mobile, Ala. (5)	363,511	949,993	460,513
Arlington, Tex.* (4)	343,891	1,455,702	226,555	Nashville, Tenn.* (16)	608,346	1,945,454	871,515
Atlanta, Ga.* (25)	1,300,000	2,100,000	2,600,000	New Orleans, La. (14)	966,301	1,063,395	859,931
Baltimore, Md. (31)	2,037,132	1,519,716	1,560,764	New York, N.Y. (research)	9,189,489	—	—
Baton Rouge, La.*,a (10)	493,506	1,640,686	NA	Branches (81)	3,180,866	9,669,316	14,931,000
Birmingham, Ala. (19)	1,092,285	2,072,444	916,174	Brooklyn (58)	4,637,167	8,610,459	5,133,434
Boston, Mass.a (25)	4,916,277	1,454,414	NA	Queens (61)	5,500,000	11,320,000	5,500,000
Buffalo, N.Y.* (53)	3,602,478	6,237,516	2,023,551	Norfolk, Va. (11)	835,860	868,600	588,400
Charlotte, N.C. (19)	930,000	3,187,097	1,042,186	Oklahoma City, Okla. (10)	855,305	3,350,113	1,387,725
Cincinnati, Oh. (39)	3,700,000	7,179,389	4,205,140	Oakland, Cal. (16)	907,082	1,627,320	806,836
Cleveland, Oh. (30)	2,626,475	4,044,885	3,413,704	Omaha, Neb. (10)	588,013	1,860,728	892,109
Colorado Springs, Col.* (7)	535,463	1,342,986	1,002,347	Philadelphia, Pa. (53)	3,164,632	5,084,446	4,393,914
Columbus, Oh. (20)	1,424,799	5,354,746	2,412,107	Phoenix, Az.a (9)	1,332,400	4,137,000	NA
Corpus Christi, Tex. (4)	293,452	750,138	284,750	Pittsburgh, Pa.a (21)	1,907,373	2,837,534	NA
Dallas, Tex.a (18)	1,777,073	3,874,425	NA	Portland, Ore.* (15)	4,000,000	2,000,000	1,400,000
Dayton, Oh.*,a (19)	1,344,584	5,012,236	NA	Richmond, Va. (10)	730,581	852,911	406,366
Denver, Col.a (21)	1,177,785	2,570,396	NA	Rochester, N.Y.a (11)	959,207	1,457,210	NA
Des Moines, Ia.a (5)	548,244	1,218,816	NA	Sacramento, Cal. (26)	1,375,121	4,000,000	1,701,736
Detroit, Mich. (25)	2,684,116	1,843,049	2,000,000	St. Louis, Mo.a (19)	1,457,314	1,101,640	NA
District of Columbia (25)	1,507,556	1,843,098	1,530,000	St. Paul, Minn. (13)	935,151	2,294,534	5,998,596
El Paso, Tex. (9)	600,000	1,200,000	842,000	San Diego, Cal. (31)	1,561,232	4,568,116	1,862,547
Ft. Worth, Tex. (8)	1,140,859	2,361,816	1,068,249	San Francisco, Cal.a (26)	1,749,129	2,470,091	NA
Fresno, Cal.* (35)	941,715	1,960,000	485,000	Shreveport, La. (19)	376,069	956,907	394,686
Honolulu, Ha.a (47)	442,482	517,066	NA	Syracuse, N.Y.*,a (8)	509,386	1,189,319	NA
Indianapolis, Ind.* (21)	1,602,000	4,926,758	1,841,747	Tampa, Fla.* (15)	880,000	2,500,000	1,800,000
Jersey City, N.J. (11)	744,383	395,266	447,465	Toledo, Oh.* (18)	1,500,000	4,400,000	NA
Kansas City, Mo.a (14)	1,346,364	875,040	NA	Tucson, Ariz.*,a (15)	760,000	3,900,000	NA
Los Angeles, Cal. (62)	5,663,240	10,382,321	4,469,364	Tulsa, Okla.* (20)	780,000	2,829,245	900,000
Louisville, Ky. (14)	903,084	3,084,620	979,836	Wichita, Kan. (12)	894,942	1,396,667	400,000
Memphis, Tenn.* (24)	3,455,774	2,410,470	1,201,663	Yonkers, N.Y.a (3)	230,347	849,529	NA
Mesa, Ariz. (2)	450,342	2,013,478	1,197,531				

(*) County library system. (a) Has not provided up-to-date information. Figure in parentheses denotes number of branches. (NA) Not available.

Preprimary School Enrollment of Children 3 to 5 Years Old: 1970 to 1988

Source: U.S. Bureau of the Census

Civilian noninstitutional population. Includes public and non-public nursery school and kindergarten programs. Excludes 5 year olds enrolled in elementary school.

	Number of children (1,000)							Enrollment rate			
	1970	1975	1980	1985	1987	1988	1970	1985	1987	1988
Population, 3–5 years old	10,877	10,183	9,284	10,252	10,733	10,872	10,994				
Total Enrolled[1]	4,075	4,954	4,878	5,385	5,865	5,932	5,977	37.5	54.6	54.6	54.4
Nursery	1,093	1,745	1,982	2,347	2,477	2,555	2,621	10.0	23.1	23.5	23.8
Kindergarten	2,982	3,209	2,896	3,038	3,388	3,377	3,356	27.4	31.6	31.1	30.5
White	3,414	4,105	3,994	4,430	4,757	4,748	4,891	37.8	54.7	54.1	55.4
Black	585	731	725	758	919	893	814	34.9	55.8	54.2	48.2
Hispanic origin[3]	NA	NA	370	406	496	587	544	NA	43.3	45.5	44.2
3 years old	454	683	857	1,005	1,035	1,022	1,028	13.0	28.8	28.6	27.6
4 years old	1,003	1,418	1,423	1,619	1,765	1,717	1,768	27.9	49.1	47.7	49.1
5 years old	2,617	2,852	2,598	2,762	3,065	3,192	3,183	69.2	86.5	86.1	86.6
Labor Force Status of Mother											
All races:[2] With mother in labor force[4]	1,345	2,168	2,480	2,853	3,306	3,422	3,478	38.8	58.1	58.2	57.4
3 and 4 years old	526	973	1,252	1,453	1,656	1,568	1,619	23.5	43.6	41.6	41.1
5 years old	818	1,195	1,229	1,399	1,649	1,854	1,859	66.6	87.2	87.9	87.5
Employed	1,246	1,948	2,256	2,578	2,999	3,180	3,258	39.3	59.1	58.9	57.8
Full-time	770	1,236	1,445	1,655	1,969	2,085	2,140	38.6	57.4	57.9	57.6
Mother not in labor force	2,694	2,704	2,266	2,378	2,372	2,250	2,197	37.0	50.4	50.1	50.6

(NA) Not available. (1) Includes children with mothers whose labor force status is unknown and children with no mother present in household, not shown separately. (2) Includes other races not shown separately. (3) Person of Hispanic origin may be of any race. (4) Includes children with mothers who are unemployed, not shown separately.

High School Graduation and Dropout Rates, 1987

Source: National Center for Education Statistics, U.S. Dept. of Education

	Graduation rate, rank	Dropout rate, rank		Graduation rate, rank	Dropout rate rank
U.S.	73.1%	26.9%	Mo.	76.1% (26)	23.9% (26)
Ala.	69.5 (39)	30.5 (13)	Mont.	84.5 (6)	15.5 (46)
Alaska	73.6 (32)	26.4 (20)	Neb.	86.7 (4)	13.3 (48)
Ariz.	70.0 (38)	30.0 (14)	Nev.	81.3 (12)	18.7 (40)
Ark.	78.6 (19)	21.4 (33)	N.H.	74.6 (31)	25.4 (21)
Calif.	68.5 (41)	31.5 (11)	N.J.	79.7 (14)	20.3 (38)
Colo.	76.0 (27)*	24.0 (24)*	N.M.	73.2 (33)	26.8 (19)
Conn.	78.2 (20)	21.8 (32)	N.Y.	66.7 (45)	33.3 (7)
Del.	71.0 (36)	29.0 (16)	N.C.	69.1 (40)	30.9 (12)
D.C.	59.5 (51)	40.5 (1)	N.D.	88.4 (2)	11.6 (50)
Fla.	63.5 (49)	36.5 (3)	Ohio	79.2 (17)	20.8 (35)
Ga.	65.0 (48)	35.0 (4)	Okla.	75.8 (30)	24.2 (22)
Hawaii.	84.5 (7)	15.5 (45)	Ore.	70.8 (37)	29.2 (15)
Idaho	79.6 (15)*	20.4 (36)*	Penn.	81.1 (13)	18.9 (39)
Ill.	77.8 (22)	22.2 (30)	R.I.	72.0 (34)	28.0 (18)
Ind.	75.9 (29)	24.1 (23)	S.C.	67.8 (43)	32.2 (9)
Iowa	86.6 (5)	13.4 (47)	S.D.	86.9 (3)	13.1 (49)
Kan.	84.1 (8)	15.9 (44)	Tenn.	67.2 (44)	32.8 (8)
Ky.	67.9 (42)	32.1 (10)	Tex.	65.9 (46)	34.1 (6)
La.	61.6 (50)	38.4 (2)	Utah.	82.5 (11)	17.5 (41)
Me.	78.8 (18)	21.2 (34)	Vt.	82.7 (10)	17.3 (42)
Md.	76.5 (25)	23.5 (27)	Va.	76.6 (24)	23.4 (28)
Mass.	76.0 (27)*	24.0 (24)*	Wash.	78.1 (21)	21.9 (31)
Mich.	71.4 (35)	28.6 (17)	W.V.	77.1 (23)	22.9 (29)
Minn.	88.7 (1)	11.3 (51)	Wis.	83.7 (9)	16.3 (43)
Miss.	65.6 (47)	34.4 (5)	Wyo.	79.6 (15)*	20.4 (36)*

*Tie.

Characteristics of Private Elementary and Secondary Schools and Teachers, by Level and Affiliation of School: 1986

Source: National Center for Education Statistics, U.S. Dept. of Education.

Item	Total	Level of School				Religious Affiliation		
		Elementary	Secondary	Combined	Other	Catholic	Other	None
Number of schools	25,616	15,303	2,438	4,949	2,926	9,911	10,771	4,934
Percent Distribution								
Years in operation:								
10 years or less	25.5	20.2	9.9	41.4	39.2	1.7	45.2	30.2
25 years or more	50.3	63.3	62.6	21.9	20.0	84.1	29.3	28.2
Minority enrollment:								
Less than 5 percent	38.9	45.1	27.8	37.1	18.7	45.8	40.5	21.6
5 to 14 percent	22.4	19.8	36.1	23.4	22.9	20.4	20.9	29.4
15 to 24 percent	10.6	7.7	14.4	11.6	21.1	8.9	12.7	9.8
25 to 49 percent	10.0	7.8	11.8	5.1	28.6	7.2	8.4	19.3
50 to 89 percent	9.9	9.2	4.4	18.2	4.6	6.3	12.1	12.7
90 percent or more	8.1	10.4	5.4	4.6	4.1	11.5	5.4	7.1
Annual tuition:								
Less than $500	13.0	18.8	4.8	5.4	1.1	25.6	6.3	1.1
$500 to $1,000	27.9	35.1	4.4	29.6	5.0	37.1	30.8	1.0
$1,001 to $1,500	26.4	29.1	34.4	22.7	9.3	25.7	30.7	17.6
$1,501 to $2,500	14.6	8.3	28.7	18.0	31.8	7.7	20.4	16.0
More than $2,500	18.2	8.8	27.8	24.4	52.9	3.9	11.9	64.3
Mean enrollment	234	218	541	211	94	363	142	174
Number of teachers[1] (1,000)	404	190	83	96	35	185	127	92
Percent Distribution								
Age: Under 30	24.0	25.2	18.0	22.3	36.3	21.9	27.2	23.7
30 to 39 years old	37.6	36.2	39.2	38.1	40.4	36.7	37.8	39.2
40 to 49 years old	23.2	23.2	25.0	25.5	13.0	23.6	21.8	24.6
50 to 59 years old	10.5	10.3	12.3	10.5	7.9	11.8	9.6	9.5
60 years old and over	4.6	5.1	5.6	3.6	2.4	6.0	3.6	3.1
Sex: Male	24.1	10.3	48.6	29.9	25.4	(NA)	(NA)	(NA)
Female	75.9	89.7	51.5	70.1	74.6	(NA)	(NA)	(NA)
Race:								
White, non-Hispanic	92.2	91.1	95.0	92.6	91.1	93.5	91.9	90.2
Black, non-Hispanic	3.8	4.8	1.4	3.3	5.0	2.5	4.0	5.9
Hispanic	2.9	2.9	2.9	3.3	2.4	3.4	2.9	2.2
Education: Bachelor's	64.0	74.1	48.5	58.0	62.5	66.7	63.6	59.3
Master's	29.4	19.8	48.6	32.0	29.9	29.5	26.4	33.6
Experience:								
Less than 5 years	24.8	25.2	18.6	23.7	40.6	20.8	27.5	29.4
5 to 9 years	27.0	27.7	22.6	29.2	27.5	24.5	30.7	26.8
10 years or more	48.2	47.1	58.8	47.1	31.9	54.8	41.8	43.8
Average salary[2]:								
Base salary	$14,400	$12,900	$17,100	$14,900	$14,900	$13,900	$13,600	$16,500
Earned income	$15,600	$13,700	$19,000	$16,500	$16,600	$15,100	$14,800	$18,000

(NA) Not available. (1) Full- and part-time. (2) Full-time teachers with salaries.

Scholastic Aptitude Test (SAT) Mean Scores and Characteristics of College Bound Seniors: 1967 to 1988

Source: College Entrance Examination Board

(For school year ending in year shown)

Type of Test and Characteristic Test Scores[1]	Unit	1967	1970	1975	1980	1981	1982	1984	1985	1986	1987	1988
Verbal, total[1]	Point	466	460	434	424	424	426	426	431	431	430	428
Male	Point	463	459	437	428	430	431	433	437	437	435	435
Female	Point	468	461	431	420	418	421	420	425	426	425	422
Math, total[2]	Point	492	488	472	466	466	467	471	475	475	476	476
Male	Point	514	509	495	491	492	493	495	499	501	500	498
Female	Point	467	465	449	443	443	443	449	452	451	453	455
Participants												
Total	1,000	NA	NA	996	992	994	989	965	977	1,001	1,080	1,134
Male	Percent	NA	NA	49.9	48.2	48.0	48.1	48.2	48.3	48.1	48.0	48.0
White	Percent	NA	NA	86.0	82.1	81.9	81.7	80.3	80.0	NA	78.0	77.0
Black	Percent	NA	NA	7.9	9.1	9.0	8.9	9.1	8.9	NA	9.0	9.0
Obtaining scores of—600 or above:												
Verbal	Percent	NA	NA	7.9	7.2	7.0	7.1	7.0	7.0	8.0	8.0	7.0
Math	Percent	NA	NA	15.6	15.1	14.4	15.3	17.0	17.0	17.0	18.0	17.0
Below 400:												
Verbal	Percent	NA	NA	37.8	41.8	41.6	40.2	40.0	40.0	38.0	40.0	42.0
Math	Percent	NA	NA	28.5	30.2	29.5	29.5	29.0	28.0	28.0	29.0	27.0

(NA) Not available. (1) Minimum score, 200; maximum score, 800. (2) 1967 and 1970 are estimates based on total number of persons taking SAT.

American College Testing (ACT) Program Mean Scores and Characteristics of College-Bound Students: 1970 to 1988

Source: The American College Testing Program

Data for academic year ending in year shown.

Type of Test and Mean Test Scores[1]	Unit	1970	1975	1980	1981	1982	1984	1985	1986	1987	1988
Composite	Point	19.9	18.6	18.5	18.5	18.4	18.5	18.6	18.8	18.7	18.8
Male	Point	20.3	19.5	19.3	19.3	19.2	19.3	19.4	19.6	19.5	19.6
Female	Point	19.4	17.8	17.9	17.8	17.8	17.9	17.9	18.1	18.1	18.1
English	Point	18.5	17.7	17.9	17.8	17.9	18.1	18.1	18.5	18.4	18.5
Male	Point	17.6	17.1	17.3	17.3	17.3	17.5	17.6	17.9	17.9	18.0
Female	Point	19.4	18.3	18.3	18.2	18.4	18.6	18.6	18.9	18.9	19.0
Math	Point	20.0	17.6	17.4	17.3	17.2	17.3	17.2	17.3	17.2	17.2
Male	Point	21.1	19.3	18.9	18.9	18.6	18.6	18.8	18.8	18.6	18.4
Female	Point	18.8	16.2	16.2	16.0	16.0	16.1	16.0	16.0	16.1	16.1
Social Studies	Point	19.7	17.4	17.2	17.2	17.3	17.3	17.4	17.6	17.5	17.4
Male	Point	20.3	18.7	18.2	18.3	18.1	18.1	18.3	18.6	18.4	18.4
Female	Point	19.0	16.4	16.4	16.4	16.4	16.5	16.6	16.9	16.7	16.6
Natural Science	Point	20.8	21.1	21.1	21.0	20.8	21.0	21.2	21.4	21.4	21.4
Male	Point	21.6	22.4	22.4	22.3	22.2	22.4	22.6	22.7	22.9	22.8
Female	Point	20.0	20.0	20.0	20.0	19.7	19.9	20.0	20.2	20.1	20.2
Participants											
Total	1,000	788	714	822	836	805	849	739	730	777	842
Male	Percent	52	46	45	45	45	46	46	46	46	46
White	Percent	(NA)	77	83	83	83	82	82	82	81	81
Black	Percent	4	7	8	8	8	9	8	8	8	9
Obtaining composite scores of—											
26 or above	Percent	14	14	13	13	13	13	14	14	14	14
15 or below	Percent	21	33	33	33	34	33	32	31	31	31

(NA) Not available. (1) Minimum score, 1; maximum score, 36. (2) Test scores and characteristics of college-bound students based on a 10% sample through 1984. Begining in 1985, these data are now based on the performance of all ACT-tested students who graduated in the spring of a given school year and who took the ACT Assessment during junior or senior year of high school.

College Freshmen Attitudes

The 23rd annual survey of incoming freshmen, taken by the American Council on Education and the Higher Education Research Inst. at the Univ. of California at Los Angeles, revealed that students are increasingly interested in college as a path leading to a high-paying job, and that they are receiving less financial assistance from the federal government.

While the majority of students took liberal positions when asked about specific issues as pollution, disarmament, abortion, and consumer protection, 22 percent (the highest ever in the history of the survey) identified their political views as conservative or far right. The students were particularly conservative on matters related to crime and the death penalty. Two-thirds of the freshmen agreed that the best way to control AIDS was through widespread, mandatory testing. In addition, 71 percent felt that employers should be allowed to test employees or job applicants for drug abuse. "Making more money" was a very important factor in the decision to attend college for 73 percent of those polled, and a record 59 percent of the freshmen said they were interested in pursuing advanced degrees.

The lowest level since the survey began, 16 percent, took part in the government's major aid program, Pell grants, for students from low- and middle-income families. In 1980, the survey showed that 32 percent of those polled had participated in the program. The Education Dept. reported that 11 percent of the Pell grants went to vocational students in 1980 compared with 27 percent in 1988.

The findings are based on questionnaires filled out by 308,007 freshmen entering 585 two- and four-year colleges and universities.

College Faculty Salaries and Benefits: 1970-1988

Source: *Annual Report on the Economic Status of the Profession,* American Assn. of University Professors

(thousands of dollars)

[For academic year ending in year shown. Figures are for 9 months teaching for full-time faculty members in four-year colleges and universities.]

Type of control and academic rank	1970	1975	1978	1980	1981	1982	1983	1984	1985	1986	1987	1988
Average Salaries												
Public: All ranks	13.1	16.6	19.3	22.1	23.9	26.2	28.6	29.4	31.2	33.4	35.8	37.2
Professor	17.3	21.7	25.4	28.8	31.0	33.7	36.0	37.1	39.6	42.3	45.3	47.2
Associate professor	13.2	16.7	19.5	21.9	23.4	25.7	27.5	28.4	30.2	32.2	34.2	35.6
Assistant professor	10.9	13.7	16.0	18.0	19.2	21.2	22.6	23.5	25.0	26.7	28.5	29.6
Instructor	9.1	11.2	13.1	14.8	15.1	16.7	17.7	19.1	19.5	20.9	21.8	22.2
Private:[1] All ranks	13.1	16.6	19.4	22.1	24.4	26.8	29.2	31.1	33.0	35.4	37.8	39.7
Professor	17.8	22.4	26.2	30.1	32.7	35.8	38.8	41.5	44.1	47.0	50.3	52.2
Associate professor	12.6	16.0	18.7	21.0	23.1	25.4	27.5	29.4	30.9	32.9	34.9	36.6
Assistant professor	10.3	13.0	15.1	17.0	18.4	20.4	22.1	23.7	25.0	26.8	28.3	30.1
Instructor	8.6	10.9	12.1	13.3	14.4	15.9	17.6	18.4	19.0	19.8	20.4	22.7
Average fringe benefits												
All ranks combined:												
Public	1.9	2.5	3.0	3.9	4.7	5.1	5.4	6.0	7.0	7.3	7.8	8.2
Private[1]	2.2	2.8	3.3	4.1	4.9	5.4	5.7	6.4	7.2	8.0	8.6	9.2

(1) Excludes church-related colleges and universities.

College Enrollment and Labor Force Status of Recent High School Graduates and Dropouts

Source: Bureau of Labor Statistics

School enrollment status	Total — Civilian noninstitutional population (1,000)	Total — Labor force participation rate	Total — Unemployment rate	Men — Civilian noninstitutional population (1,000)	Men — Labor force participation rate	Men — Unemployment rate	Women — Civilian noninstitutional population (1,000)	Women — Labor force participation rate	Women — Unemployment rate
1978									
High school graduates	3,178	64.5	13.8	1,500	67.9	11.2	1,679	61.5	16.3
Enrolled in college	1,593	42.9	13.0	767	45.0	11.3	827	41.0	14.7
Not enrolled in college	1,585	86.3	14.0	733	91.8	11.2	852	81.3	17.0
High school dropouts	839	68.8	27.6	479	80.2	24.0	360	53.4	34.4
1983									
High school graduates	2,964	63.6	22.3	1,390	67.5	22.6	1,574	60.2	22.0
Enrolled in college	1,562	44.9	17.0	721	47.7	17.4	841	42.6	16.5
Not enrolled in college	1,402	84.5	25.5	669	88.8	25.6	733	80.5	25.4
High school dropouts	597	63.1	31.6	329	75.4	32.7	268	48.1	29.5
1988									
High school graduates	2,673	62.7	13.5	1,334	65.1	13.4	1,339	60.3	13.7
Enrolled in college	1,575	47.4	11.6	761	47.6	9.5	814	47.3	13.6
Not enrolled in college	1,098	84.7	15.1	572	88.5	16.2	526	80.6	13.7
High school dropouts	552	59.2	26.7	307	74.4	28.5	245	40.1	22.4

A record 59 percent of high school graduates in 1988 were enrolled in college by October 1988.

The percentage of high school graduates going on to college has risen nearly 10 percent over the past decade. The college enrollment rate of black high school graduates (45 percent) has remained below that of whites (61 percent) and hispanics (57 percent).

About 100,000 graduates not in college were enrolled in at least one vocational education course. These courses include secretarial, trade, or technical classes.

Institutions of Higher Education—Charges: 1970 to 1988

Source: National Center for Education Statistics, U.S. Dept. of Education.

Data are for the entire academic year ending in year shown. Figures for 1970 are average charges for full-time resident degree-credit students; figures for later years are average charges per full-time equivalent student. Room and board are based on full-time students.

Academic Control and year	Tuition and Required Fees — All institutions	Tuition and Required Fees — 2-yr. colleges	Tuition and Required Fees — 4-yr. universities	Board Rates — All institutions	Board Rates — 2-yr. colleges	Board Rates — 4-yr. universities	Dormitory Charges — All institutions	Dormitory Charges — 2-yr. colleges	Dormitory Charges — 4-yr. universities
Public:									
1970	$323	$178	$427	$511	$465	$540	$369	$308	$395
1975	432	277	599	625	638	634	506	424	527
1980	583	355	840	867	894	898	715	572	749
1985	971	584	1,386	1,241	1,302	1,276	1,196	921	1,237
1988, est.	1,160	690	1,750	1,520	1,490	1,600	1,350	1,050	1,410
Private:									
1970	1,533	1,034	1,809	561	546	608	436	413	503
1975	2,117	1,367	2,614	700	660	771	586	564	691
1980	3,130	2,062	3,811	955	924	1,078	827	769	999
1985	5,314	3,485	6,843	1,462	1,294	1,647	1,426	1,424	1,753
1988, est.	6,820	3,910	8,770	1,900	1,600	2,310	1,760	1,360	2,250

American Colleges and Universities

General Information for the 1988–89 Academic Year
Source: Peterson's Guides

These listings include all accredited undergraduate degree-granting institutions in the United States and U.S. territories that have a total institutional enrollment of 600 or more. Four-year colleges (those that award a bachelor's as their highest undergraduate degree) are listed first, followed by two-year colleges (those that award an associate as their highest or primary undergraduate degree).

All institutions are coeducational except those where the zip code is followed by: (1)–men only, (2)–primarily men, (3)–women only, (4)–primarily women.

Year is that of founding.

Governing official is the chief executive officer.

Institutional control: 1–independent (nonprofit), 2–independent-religious, 3–proprietary (profit making), 4–federal, 5–state, 7–commonwealth (Puerto Rico), 8–territory (U.S. territories), 9–county, 10–district, 11–city, 12–state and local, 13–state related.

Highest degree offered: B–bachelor's, M–master's, D–doctorate.

Enrollment is the total number of matriculated undergraduate and (if applicable) graduate students.

Faculty is the total number of faculty members teaching undergraduate and graduate courses.

Any data not reported are indicated as NR.

Four-Year Colleges

Name, address	Year	Governing official, control, and highest degree offered		Enrollment	Faculty
Abilene Christian U, Abilene, TX 79699	1906	Dr. William J. Teague	2-D	4,223	230
Acad of Art Coll, San Francisco, CA 94108	1929	Dr. Donald Haight	3-M	2,140	140
Adams State Coll, Alamosa, CO 81102	1921	Dr. William M. Fulkerson, Jr.	5-M	2,476	115
Adelphi U, Garden City, NY 11530	1896	Dr. Peter Diamandopoulos	1-D	9,062	770
Adrian Coll, Adrian, MI 49221	1859	Dr. Daniel W. Behring	2-B	1,229	125
Alabama Agricultural and Mechanical U, Normal, AL 35762	1875	Dr. Carl Marbury	5-D	4,244	314
Alabama State U, Montgomery, AL 36195	1874	Dr. Leon Howard	5-M	4,045	270
Alaska Pacific U, Anchorage, AK 99508	1959	Dr. F. Thomas Trotter	2-D	851	58
Albany Coll of Pharmacy of Union U, Albany, NY 12208	1881	Dr. Kenneth W. Miller	1-B	652	129
Albany State Coll, Albany, GA 31705	1903	Dr. Billy C. Black	5-M	2,105	151
Albion Coll, Albion, MI 49224	1835	Dr. Melvin L. Vulgamore	2-B	1,705	120
Albright Coll, Reading, PA 19612	1856	Dr. David G. Ruffer	2-B	1,326	128
Alcorn State U, Lorman, MS 39096	1871	Dr. Walter Washington	5-M	2,757	183
Alderson-Broaddus Coll, Philippi, WV 26416	1871	Dr. W. Christian Sizemore	2-B	759	74
Alfred U, Alfred, NY 14802	1836	Dr. Edward G. Coll, Jr.	1-D	2,593	175
Allegheny Coll, Meadville, PA 16335	1815	Dr. Daniel F. Sullivan	2-M	1,981	186
Allentown Coll of St Francis de Sales, Center Valley, PA 18034	1962	Very Rev. Daniel Gambet	2-M	1,700	90
Alma Coll, Alma, MI 48801	1886	Dr. Alan J. Stone	2-B	1,198	99
Alvernia Coll, Reading, PA 19607	1958	Sr. M. Dolorey	2-B	1,076	93
Alverno Coll, Milwaukee, WI 53215 (3)	1887	Joel Read	1-B	2,191	161
Amber U, Garland, TX 75041	1971	Dr. Douglas W. Warner	1-M	926	50
American Coll for the Applied Arts, Atlanta, GA 30326	1977	Rafael A. Lago	3-B	735	55
American International Coll, Springfield, MA 01109	1885	Dr. Harry J. Courniotes	1-D	1,681	85
American U, Washington, DC 20016	1893	Dr. Richard Berendzen	2-D	10,153	1,060
American U of Puerto Rico, Bayamón, PR 00619	1963	Juan B. Nazario Negron	1-B	4,255	250
Amherst Coll, Amherst, MA 01002	1821	Peter R. Pouncey	1-B	1,585	152
Anderson U, Anderson, IN 46012	1917	Dr. Robert A. Nicholson	2-M	2,050	167
Andrews U, Berrien Springs, MI 49104	1874	Dr. W. Richard Lesher	2-D	2,469	282
Angelo State U, San Angelo, TX 76909	1928	Dr. Lloyd Drexell Vincent	5-M	6,334	213
Anna Maria Coll for Men and Women, Paxton, MA 01612	1946	Sr. Bernadette Madore	2-M	1,060	138
Antillian Coll, Mayagüez, PR 00709	1957	Dr. James Unger	2-B	790	55
Appalachian State U, Boone, NC 28608	1899	Dr. John E. Thomas	5-M	11,130	537
Aquinas Coll, Grand Rapids, MI 49506	1886	Dr. Peter D. O'Connor	2-M	2,535	169
Arizona State U, Tempe, AZ 85287	1885	Dr. J. Russell Nelson	5-D	43,426	2,713
Arkansas Coll, Batesville, AR 72503	1872	E. Graham Holloway	2-B	825	61
Arkansas State U, State University, AR 72467	1909	Dr. Eugene W. Smith	5-M	9,026	360
Arkansas Tech U, Russellville, AR 72801	1909	Dr. Kenneth G. Kersh	5-M	3,588	196
Armstrong State Coll, Savannah, GA 31419	1935	Dr. Robert A. Burnett	5-M	3,232	166
Art Ctr Coll of Design, Pasadena, CA 91103	1930	Mr. David R. Brown	1-M	1,285	208
Art Inst of Fort Lauderdale, Fort Lauderdale, FL 33316	1968	Ms. Miryam Drucker	3-B	2,000	100
Asbury Coll, Wilmore, KY 40390	1890	Dr. Dennis F. Kinlaw	2-B	993	96
Ashland Coll, Ashland, OH 44805	1878	Dr. Joseph Shultz	2-M	4,072	139
Assumption Coll, Worcester, MA 01615	1904	Joseph H. Hagan	2-M	2,000	140
Athens State Coll, Athens, AL 35611	1822	Dr. James R. Chasteen	5-B	2,100	110
Atlantic Christian Coll, Wilson, NC 27893	1902	Dr. James B. Hemby	2-B	1,354	99
Atlantic Union Coll, South Lancaster, MA 01561	1882	Dr. Lawrence T. Geraty	2-B	752	76
Auburn U, Auburn University, AL 36849	1856	Dr. James E. Martin	5-D	20,553	1,144
Augsburg Coll, Minneapolis, MN 55454	1869	Dr. Charles S. Anderson	2-M	2,532	123
Augusta Coll, Augusta, GA 30910	1925	Dr. Richard S. Wallace	5-M	4,461	190
Augustana Coll, Rock Island, IL 61201	1860	Dr. Thomas Tredway	2-B	2,241	158
Augustana Coll, Sioux Falls, SD 57197	1860	Dr. Lloyd Svendsbye	2-M	2,048	176
Aurora U, Aurora, IL 60506	1893	Thomas H. Zarle	1-M	2,079	193
Austin Coll, Sherman, TX 75091	1849	Dr. Harry E. Smith	2-M	1,269	89
Austin Peay State U, Clarksville, TN 37044	1927	Dr. Oscar Page	5-M	5,013	251
Averett Coll, Danville, VA 24541	1859	Dr. Frank R. Campbell	2-M	982	65
Avila Coll, Kansas City, MO 64145	1916	Dr. Larry Kramer	2-M	1,640	152
Azusa Pacific U, Azusa, CA 91702	1899	Dr. Paul E. Sago	2-M	2,833	180
Babson Coll, Babson Park, MA 02157	1919	Dr. William R. Dill	1-M	2,973	152
Baker Coll, Flint, MI 48507	1911	Mr. Edward J. Kurtz	1-B	2,675	98
Baker Coll of Owosso, Owosso, MI 48867	1984	NR	1-B	900	37
Baker U, Baldwin City, KS 66006	1858	Dr. Daniel M. Lambert	2-M	879	68
Baldwin-Wallace Coll, Berea, OH 44017	1845	Dr. Neal Malicky	2-M	4,564	263
Ball State U, Muncie, IN 47306	1918	Dr. John E. Worthen	5-D	18,156	973
Baltimore Hebrew U, Baltimore, MD 21215	1919	Dr. Leivy Smolar	1-D	606	33

Name, address	Year	Governing official, control, and highest degree offered	Enroll-ment	Faculty
Baptist Bible Coll, Springfield, MO 65803	1950	NR 2-M	823	37
Baptist Bible Coll of Pennsylvania, Clarks Summit, PA 18411	1932	Milo Thompson, Jr. 2-M	620	36
Baptist Coll at Charleston, Charleston, SC 29411	1964	Dr. Jairy C. Hunter, Jr. 2-M	1,926	85
Barat Coll, Lake Forest, IL 60045	1858	Lucy S. Morros 2-B	674	92
Bard Coll, Annandale-on-Hudson, NY 12504	1860	Dr. Leon Botstein 1-M	996	109
Barnard Coll, New York, NY 10027 (3)	1889	Ms. Ellen V. Futter 1-B	2,200	260
Barry U, Miami Shores, FL 33161	1940	Sr. Jeanne O'Laughlin 2-D	5,238	364
Baruch Coll of the City U of New York, New York, NY 10010	1968	Dr. Joel Segall 12-M	18,100	850
Bates Coll, Lewiston, ME 04240	1855	Dr. Thomas H. Reynolds 1-B	1,500	150
Bayamón Central U, Bayamón, PR 00621	1970	Rev. Vincent A. M. Van Rooij, OP 2-M	2,796	132
Baylor U, Waco, TX 76798	1845	Dr. Herbert H. Reynolds . . . 2-D	11,772	563
Beaver Coll, Glenside, PA 19038	1853	Dr. Bette E. Landman 2-M	2,199	128
Belhaven Coll, Jackson, MS 39202	1883	Dr. Newton Wilson 2-B	700	76
Bellarmine Coll, Louisville, KY 40205	1950	Dr. Eugene V. Petrik 2-M	2,584	196
Bellevue Coll, Bellevue, NE 68005	1965	Dr. John B. Muller 1-B	1,862	58
Belmont Abbey Coll, Belmont, NC 28012	1876	Dr. John R. Dempsey 2-B	1,055	84
Belmont Coll, Nashville, TN 37212	1951	Dr. William E. Troutt 2-M	2,688	237
Beloit Coll, Beloit, WI 53511	1846	Dr. Roger H. Hull 1-M	1,125	115
Bemidji State U, Bemidji, MN 56601	1919	Dr. Lowell R. Gillett 5-M	5,021	250
Benedict Coll, Columbia, SC 29204	1870	Dr. Marshall C. Grigsby . . . 2-B	1,448	116
Benedictine Coll, Atchison, KS 66002	1859	Thomas O. James 2-B	803	88
Bennett Coll, Greensboro, NC 27401 (3)	1873	Dr. Gloria Scott 2-B	602	51
Bennington Coll, Bennington, VT 05201	1932	Dr. Elizabeth Coleman 1-M	613	78
Bentley Coll, Waltham, MA 02154	1917	Dr. Gregory H. Adamian . . . 1-M	7,150	363
Berea Coll, Berea, KY 40404	1855	Dr. John B. Stephenson . . . 1-B	1,527	130
Berklee Coll of Music, Boston, MA 02215	1945	Mr. Lee Eliot Berk 1-B	2,829	NR
Bethany Coll, Lindsborg, KS 67456	1881	Dr. Peter J. Ristuben 2-B	722	84
Bethany Coll, Bethany, WV 26032	1840	Dr. D. Duane Cummins 2-B	844	71
Bethel Coll, North Newton, KS 67117	1887	Dr. Harold J. Schultz 2-B	621	77
Bethel Coll, St Paul, MN 55112	1871	Dr. George K. Brushaber . . . 2-B	1,800	149
Bethune-Cookman Coll, Daytona Beach, FL 32015	1904	Dr. Oswald P. Bronson, Sr. . . 2-B	1,860	173
Biola U, La Mirada, CA 90639	1908	Dr. Clyde Cook 2-D	2,552	224
Birmingham-Southern Coll, Birmingham, AL 35254	1856	Dr. Neal R. Berte 2-M	1,836	146
Black Hills State Coll, Spearfish, SD 57783	1883	Dr. Clifford Trump 5-M	2,282	106
Bloomfield Coll, Bloomfield, NJ 07003	1868	Dr. John F. Noonan 2-B	1,484	124
Bloomsburg U of Pennsylvania, Bloomsburg, PA 17815	1839	Dr. Harry Ausprich 5-M	6,804	389
Bluefield State Coll, Bluefield, WV 24701	1895	Dr. Gregory D. Adkins 5-B	2,558	125
Bluffton Coll, Bluffton, OH 45817	1899	Dr. Elmer Neufeld 2-B	608	55
Bob Jones U, Greenville, SC 29614	1927	Dr. Bob Jones, III 2-D	4,390	NR
Boise State U, Boise, ID 83725	1932	Dr. John H. Keiser 5-M	11,429	449
Boston Coll, Chestnut Hill, MA 02167	1863	Rev. J. Donald Monan, SJ . . 2-D	14,561	914
Boston U, Boston, MA 02215	1839	Dr. John Silber 1-D	28,557	2,707
Bowdoin Coll, Brunswick, ME 04011	1794	Dr. A. LeRoy Greason 1-B	1,350	130
Bowie State U, Bowie, MD 20715	1865	Dr. James E. Lyons, Sr. . . . 5-M	3,327	167
Bowling Green State U, Bowling Green, OH 43403	1910	Dr. Paul J. Olscamp 5-D	17,882	845
Bradley U, Peoria, IL 61625	1897	Dr. Martin G. Abegg 1-M	5,174	369
Brandeis U, Waltham, MA 02254	1948	Dr. Evelyn E. Handler 1-D	3,689	496
Brenau Professional Coll, Gainesville, GA 30501	1878	Dr. John S. Burd 1-M	1,222	150
Brescia Coll, Owensboro, KY 42301	1950	Dr. Ruth Gehres 2-B	946	61
Brewton-Parker Coll, Mt Vernon, GA 30445	1904	Dr. Y. Lynn Holmes 2-B	1,472	72
Briar Cliff Coll, Sioux City, IA 51104	1930	Dr. Margaret Wick 2-B	1,103	82
Bridgewater Coll, Bridgewater, VA 22812	1880	Dr. Wayne F. Geisert 2-B	976	73
Bridgewater State Coll, Bridgewater, MA 02324	1840	Dr. Robert J. Dillman 5-M	5,339	324
Brigham Young U, Provo, UT 84602	1875	Dr. Jeffrey R. Holland 2-D	28,001	1,586
Brigham Young U-Hawaii Cmps, Laie, Oahu, HI 96762	1955	Dr. Alton L. Wade 2-B	2,142	138
Bristol U, Bristol, TN 37620	1895	Mr. Ronald Cosby 3-M	1,014	19
Brooklyn Coll of the City U of New York, Brooklyn, NY 11210	1930	Dr. Robert Hess 12-M	16,615	993
Brooks Inst of Photography, Santa Barbara, CA 93108	1945	Mr. Ernest H. Brooks, II . . . 3-M	645	37
Brown U, Providence, RI 02912	1764	Vartan Gregorian 1-D	7,612	548
Bryant Coll, Smithfield, RI 02917	1863	Dr. William T. O'Hara 1-M	5,827	180
Bryn Mawr Coll, Bryn Mawr, PA 19010 (4)	1885	Mary Patterson McPherson . . 1-D	1,847	196
Bucknell U, Lewisburg, PA 17837	1846	Dr. Gary A. Sojka 1-M	3,519	246
Buena Vista Coll, Storm Lake, IA 50588	1891	Dr. Keith G. Briscoe 2-B	1,086	87
Butler U, Indianapolis, IN 46208	1855	Mr. John G. Johnson 1-M	3,912	392
Cabrini Coll, Radnor, PA 19087	1957	Sr. Eileen Currie, MSC . . . 2-M	1,264	97
Caldwell Coll, Caldwell, NJ 07006	1939	Sr. Vivien Jennings 2-B	950	79
California Baptist Coll, Riverside, CA 92504	1950	Dr. Russell R. Tuck 2-B	666	64
California Coll of Arts and Crafts, Oakland, CA 94618	1907	Mr. Neil J. Hoffman 1-M	1,119	167
California Inst of Tech, Pasadena, CA 91125	1891	Dr. Thomas E. Everhart . . . 1-D	1,841	270
California Inst of the Arts, Valencia, CA 91355	1961	Dr. Steven D. Lavine 1-M	850	175
California Lutheran U, Thousand Oaks, CA 91360	1959	Dr. Jerry H. Miller 2-M	2,757	180
California Polytechnic State U, San Luis Obispo, San Luis Obispo, CA 93407	1901	Dr. Warren J. Baker 5-M	16,553	1,167
California State Polytechnic U, Pomona, Pomona, CA 91768	1938	Dr. Hugh O. La Bounty 5-M	18,930	1,082
California State U, Bakersfield, Bakersfield, CA 93311	1970	Dr. Tomas A. Arciniega . . . 5-M	4,930	257
California State U, Chico, Chico, CA 95929	1887	Dr. Robin Wilson 5-M	16,031	1,051
California State U, Fresno, Fresno, CA 93740	1911	Dr. Harold H. Haak 5-M	19,124	1,143
California State U, Fullerton, Fullerton, CA 92634	1957	Dr. Jewel Plummer Cobb . . . 5-M	24,700	1,398
California State U, Hayward, Hayward, CA 94542	1957	Dr. Ellis E. McCune 5-M	12,637	622
California State U, Long Beach, Long Beach, CA 90840	1949	Dr. Curtis L. McCray 5-M	35,363	2,096
California State U, Northridge, Northridge, CA 91330	1958	Dr. James Cleary 5-M	31,531	1,808
California State U, Sacramento, Sacramento, CA 95819	1947	Dr. Donald R. Gerth 5-M	25,153	1,378
California State U, Stanislaus, Turlock, CA 95380	1957	Dr. John W. Moore 5-M	5,282	300
California U of Pennsylvania, California, PA 15419	1852	Dr. John Pierce Watkins . . . 5-M	6,313	354
Calumet Coll of Saint Joseph, Whiting, IN 46394	1951	Dr. Dennis C. Rittenmeyer . . 2-B	1,059	83
Calvin Coll, Grand Rapids, MI 49506	1876	Dr. Anthony J. Diekema . . . 2-M	4,505	291
Cameron U, Lawton, OK 73505	1908	Dr. Don Davis 5-M	5,574	234
Campbellsville Coll, Campbellsville, KY 42718	1906	Dr. Kenneth W. Winters . . . 2-B	734	56
Campbell U, Buies Creek, NC 27506	1887	Dr. Norman A. Wiggins . . . 2-D	4,195	154
Canisius Coll, Buffalo, NY 14208	1870	Rev. James M. Demske, SJ . . 1-M	4,515	309
Capital U, Columbus, OH 43209	1830	Dr. Brian Freeman 2-D	3,016	163
Capitol Coll, Laurel, MD 20708	1964	Dr. G. William Troxler 1-B	777	59

Name, address	Year	Governing official, control, and highest degree offered	Enroll-ment	Faculty
Cardinal Stritch Coll, Milwaukee, WI 53217	1937	Sr. M. Camille Kliebhan	2-M	3,050	167
Carleton Coll, Northfield, MN 55057	1866	Dr. Stephen R. Lewis, Jr.	1-B	1,885	151
Carlow Coll, Pittsburgh, PA 15213 (4)	1929	Grace Ann Geibel, RSM	2-M	962	122
Carnegie Mellon U, Pittsburgh, PA 15213	1900	Dr. Richard M. Cyert	1-D	6,993	737
Carroll Coll, Waukesha, WI 53186	1846	Dr. Dan C. West	2-B	1,393	133
Carroll Coll of Montana, Helena, MT 59625	1909	Dr. Matthew Quinn	2-B	1,414	109
Carson-Newman Coll, Jefferson City, TN 37760	1851	Dr. J. Cordell Maddox	2-M	2,003	122
Carthage Coll, Kenosha, WI 53141	1847	Dr. F. Gregory Campbell	2-M	1,842	113
Case Western Reserve U, Cleveland, OH 44106	1826	Dr. Agnar Pytte	1-D	8,333	1,674
Castleton State Coll, Castleton, VT 05735	1787	Dr. Lyle A. Gray	5-M	1,803	135
Catawba Coll, Salisbury, NC 28144	1851	Dr. Stephen H. Wurster	2-M	1,030	74
Catholic U of America, Washington, DC 20064	1887	Rev. William J. Byron, SJ	2-D	6,687	570
Catholic U of Puerto Rico, Ponce, PR 00732	1948	Rev. F. Tosello Giangiacomo	2-M	11,495	471
Cedar Crest Coll, Allentown, PA 18104 (4)	1867	Dr. Gene S. Cesari	2-B	1,039	123
Cedarville Coll, Cedarville, OH 45314	1887	Dr. Paul H. Dixon	2-B	1,879	143
Centenary Coll, Hackettstown, NJ 07840 (4)	1867	Dr. Stephanie M. Bennett	2-B	820	88
Centenary Coll of Louisiana, Shreveport, LA 71134	1825	Dr. Donald A. Webb	2-M	1,041	102
Ctr for Creative Studies—Coll of Art and Design, Detroit, MI 48202	1926	Jerome Grove	1-B	954	208
Central Bible Coll, Springfield, MO 65803	1922	H. Maurice Lednicky	2-B	886	51
Central Connecticut State U, New Britain, CT 06050	1849	Dr. John W. Shumaker	5-M	14,198	732
Central Methodist Coll, Fayette, MO 65248	1854	Dr. Joe A. Howell	2-B	714	70
Central Michigan U, Mount Pleasant, MI 48859	1892	Dr. Edward B. Jakubauskas	5-D	17,032	789
Central Missouri State U, Warrensburg, MO 64093	1871	Dr. Ed Elliott	5-M	10,104	461
Central State U, Wilberforce, OH 45384	1887	Dr. Arthur E. Thomas	5-B	2,515	138
Central State U, Edmond, OK 73060	1890	Dr. Bill J. Lillard	5-M	13,866	NR
Central U of Iowa, Pella, IA 50219	1853	Dr. Kenneth J. Weller	2-B	1,680	110
Central Washington U, Ellensburg, WA 98926	1891	Dr. Donald L. Garrity	5-M	7,109	312
Centre Coll, Danville, KY 40422	1819	Mr. William H. Breeze	2-B	860	81
Chadron State Coll, Chadron, NE 69337	1911	Dr. Samuel H. Rankin	5-M	2,450	96
Chaminade U of Honolulu, Honolulu, HI 96816	1955	Fr. Raymond A. Roesch, SM	2-M	2,556	195
Chapman Coll, Orange, CA 92666	1861	Dr. James Doti	2-M	2,185	138
Charter Oak Coll, Farmington, CT 06032	1973	Dr. William T. Slater	5-B	810	NR
Chatham Coll, Pittsburgh, PA 15232 (3)	1869	Rebecca Stafford	1-B	684	61
Chestnut Hill Coll, Philadelphia, PA 19118 (4)	1924	Sr. Matthew Anita MacDonald	2-M	1,031	100
Chicago State U, Chicago, IL 60628	1867	Dr. George E. Ayers	5-M	6,134	406
Christian Brothers Coll, Memphis, TN 38104	1871	Br. Theodore Drahmann	2-M	1,740	120
Christopher Newport Coll, Newport News, VA 23606	1961	Dr. Anthony Santoro	5-B	4,650	171
The Citadel, The Military Coll of South Carolina, Charleston, SC 29409 (1)	1842	Maj. Gen. James A. Grimsley	5-M	3,488	152
City Coll of the City U of New York, New York, NY 10031	1847	Bernard W. Harleston	12-D	12,780	1,352
City U, Bellevue, WA 98008	1973	Dr. Michael A. Pastore	1-M	3,920	260
Claflin Coll, Orangeburg, SC 29115	1869	Oscar A. Rogers	2-B	742	59
Clarion U of Pennsylvania, Clarion, PA 16214	1867	Mr. Jack L. Stark	1-B	856	104
Clark Coll, Atlanta, GA 30314	1869	Dr. Thomas A. Bond	5-M	6,601	383
Clarke Coll, Dubuque, IA 52001	1843	Dr. Thomas Cole, Jr.	2-M	2,127	145
Clarkson U, Potsdam, NY 13676	1896	Dr. Catherine Dunn, BVM	2-M	830	55
Clark U, Worcester, MA 01610	1887	Dr. Richard H. Gallagher	1-D	3,665	231
Clayton State Coll, Morrow, GA 30260	1969	Dr. Richard P. Traina	1-D	2,899	269
Cleary Coll, Ypsilanti, MI 48197	1883	NR	5-B	3,667	156
Clemson U, Clemson, SC 29634	1889	Dr. Harry Howard	1-B	1,200	67
Cleveland State U, Cleveland, OH 44115	1964	Dr. Max Lennon	5-D	14,794	1,050
Clinch Valley Coll of the U of Virginia, Wise, VA 24293	1954	Dr. John A. Flower	5-D	17,821	780
Coe Coll, Cedar Rapids, IA 52402	1851	Dr. Jimmy A. Knight	5-B	1,688	113
Colby Coll, Waterville, ME 04901	1813	Dr. John E. Brown	2-B	1,242	121
Coleman Coll, La Mesa, CA 92041	1963	William R. Cotter	1-B	1,736	164
Colgate U, Hamilton, NY 13346	1819	Dr. Coleman Furr	1-B	841	86
Coll for Human Services, New York, NY 10014	1964	Dr. Neil R. Grabois	1-M	2,766	246
Coll Misericordia, Dallas, PA 18612	1924	Audrey C. Cohen	1-M	763	53
Coll of Aeronautics, Flushing, NY 11371 (2)	1932	Dr. Bruce L. Wilson	2-M	1,114	120
Coll of Boca Raton, Boca Raton, FL 33431	1963	Dr. George W. Brush	1-B	1,300	70
Coll of Charleston, Charleston, SC 29424	1770	Dr. Donald E. Ross	1-M	1,150	75
Coll of Great Falls, Great Falls, MT 59405	1932	Dr. Harry M. Lightsey, Jr.	5-M	6,205	348
Coll of Idaho, Caldwell, ID 83605	1891	Dr. William A. Shields	2-M	1,200	80
Coll of Insurance, New York, NY 10007	1962	Mr. Robert L. Hendren, Jr.	2-M	989	101
Coll of Mount Saint Joseph, Cincinnati, OH 45051	1920	Ellen Thrower	1-M	1,064	82
Coll of Mount Saint Vincent, Riverdale, NY 10471 (4)	1847	Francis Marie Thrailkill, OSU	2-M	2,566	197
Coll of New Rochelle, New Rochelle, NY 10805 (4)	1904	Sr. Doris Smith	1-M	1,120	83
Coll of Notre Dame, Belmont, CA 94002	1851	Sr. Dorothy A. Kelly	2-M	2,240	173
Coll of Notre Dame of Maryland, Baltimore, MD 21210 (4)	1873	Sr. Veronica Skillin	2-M	1,052	94
Coll of Saint Benedict, Saint Joseph, MN 56374 (3)	1887	Sr. Kathleen Feeley	2-B	2,461	75
Coll of St Catherine, St Paul, MN 55105 (3)	1905	Sr. Colman O'Connell, OSB	2-B	2,196	130
Coll of Saint Elizabeth, Convent Station, NJ 07961 (4)	1899	Dr. Anita Pampusch	2-B	2,729	153
Coll of St Francis, Joliet, IL 60435	1920	Sr. Jacqueline Burns	2-B	1,040	103
Coll of Saint Mary, Omaha, NE 68124 (4)	1923	Dr. John C. Orr	2-M	1,856	85
Coll of Saint Rose, Albany, NY 12203	1920	Dr. Kenneth Nielsen	2-B	1,133	139
Coll of St Scholastica, Duluth, MN 55811	1906	Dr. Louis C. Vaccaro	1-M	2,853	216
Coll of St Thomas, St Paul, MN 55105	1885	Dr. Daniel H. Pilon	2-M	1,835	142
Coll of Santa Fe, Santa Fe, NM 87501	1947	Msgr. Terrence J. Murphy	2-D	8,790	495
Coll of Staten Island of the City U of New York, Staten Island, NY 10301	1955	Dr. James A. Fries	2-M	1,602	63
Coll of the Holy Cross, Worcester, MA 01610	1843	Dr. Edmond L. Volpe	12-M	10,673	634
Coll of William and Mary, Williamsburg, VA 23185	1693	Rev. John E. Brooks, SJ	2-B	2,558	231
Coll of Wooster, Wooster, OH 44691	1866	Dr. Paul R. Verkuil	5-D	7,372	716
Colorado Coll, Colorado Springs, CO 80903	1874	Dr. Henry J. Copeland	2-B	1,904	159
Colorado Sch of Mines, Golden, CO 80401	1874	Dr. Gresham Riley	1-M	1,967	228
Colorado State U, Fort Collins, CO 80523	1870	Dr. George S. Ansell	5-D	2,343	224
Colorado Tech Coll, Colorado Springs, CO 80907	1965	Dr. Philip E. Austin	5-D	19,885	NR
Columbia Bible Coll and Sem, Columbia, SC 29230	1923	Dr. David D. O'Donnell	3-B	1,147	50
Columbia Coll, Chicago, IL 60605	1890	Mr. J. Robertson McQuilkin	2-D	929	32
Columbia Coll, Columbia, MO 65216	1851	Mr. Mirron Alexandroff	1-M	6,045	575
Columbia Coll, New York, NY 10027	1754	Dr. Donald B. Ruthenberg	2-B	714	56
Columbia Coll, Columbia, SC 29203 (3)	1854	Robert E. Pollack	1-B	3,229	420
Columbia Union Coll, Takoma Park, MD 20912	1904	Dr. Peter T. Mitchell	2-M	1,218	83
		Dr. William A. Loveless	2-B	1,204	164
Columbia U, Sch of Engineering & Applied Sci, New York, NY 10027	1864	Dr. Robert Gross	1-D	1,934	156

Name, address	Year	Governing official, control, and highest degree offered	Enrollment	Faculty
Columbia U, Sch of General Studies, New York, NY 10027	1947	Ward H. Dennis 1-M	1,320	450
Columbia U, Sch of Nursing, New York, NY 10032 (4)	1935	NR 1-M	90	41
Columbus Coll, Columbus, GA 31993	1958	Dr. Frank D. Brown . . . 5-M	3,803	NR
Columbus Coll of Art and Design, Columbus, OH 43215	1879	Mr. Joseph V. Canzani . . 1-B	1,293	92
Concord Coll, Athens, WV 24712	1872	Dr. Jerry L. Beasley . . . 5-B	2,450	135
Concordia Coll, River Forest, IL 60305	1864	Dr. Eugene L. Krentz . . . 2-M	1,187	144
Concordia Coll, Moorhead, MN 56560	1891	Dr. Paul J. Dovre 2-B	2,880	234
Concordia Coll, St Paul, MN 55104	1893	Dr. Herman Wentzel . . . 2-B	1,133	85
Concordia Coll Wisconsin, Mequon, WI 53092	1881	Dr. R. John Buuck 2-M	1,276	75
Concordia Teachers Coll, Seward, NE 68434	1894	Ralph L. Reinke 2-M	780	75
Connecticut Coll, New London, CT 06320	1911	Claire Gaudiani 1-M	2,024	230
Converse Coll, Spartanburg, SC 29301 (3)	1889	Dr. Robert T. Coleman, Jr. . 1-M	1,254	90
Cooper Union for the Advancement of Science & Art, New York, NY 10003	1859	Mr. John Jay Iselin 1-M	1,001	167
Coppin State Coll, Baltimore, MD 21216	1900	Dr. Calvin W. Burnett . . . 5-M	2,240	158
Cornell Coll, Mount Vernon, IA 52314	1853	Dr. David G. Marker 2-B	1,129	84
Cornell U, Ithaca, NY 14853	1865	Dr. Frank H. T. Rhodes . . 1-D	18,088	1,597
Corpus Christi State U, Corpus Christi, TX 78412	1971	Dr. B. Alan Sugg 5-M	4,141	188
Creighton U, Omaha, NE 68178	1878	Rev. Michael G. Morrison, SJ	5,958	1,161
Culver-Stockton Coll, Canton, MO 63435	1853	Dr. Robert Brown 2-B	1,032	60
Cumberland Coll, Williamsburg, KY 40769	1889	Dr. James Taylor 2-M	1,904	118
Cumberland U, Lebanon, TN 37087	1842	M. Walker Buckalew . . . 1-M	707	60
Curry Coll, Milton, MA 02186	1879	Dr. William L. Boyle, Jr. . 1-M	1,032	156
Daemen Coll, Amherst, NY 14226	1947	Dr. Robert S. Marshall . . 1-B	1,532	106
Dakota State Coll, Madison, SD 57042	1881	Dr. Jerald Tunheim 5-B	1,111	54
Dakota Wesleyan U, Mitchell, SD 57301	1885	Dr. James B. Beddow . . . 2-B	668	56
Dallas Baptist U, Dallas, TX 75211	1898	Dr. W. Marvin Watson . . . 2-M	2,018	115
Dartmouth Coll, Hanover, NH 03755	1769	Dr. James O. Freeman . . 1-D	5,400	304
Davenport Coll of Business, Grand Rapids, MI 49503	1866	Donald W. Maine 1-B	5,900	113
David Lipscomb U, Nashville, TN 37204	1891	Dr. Harold Hazelip 2-M	2,311	156
Davidson Coll, Davidson, NC 28036	1837	Dr. John W. Kuykendall . . 2-B	1,376	NR
Davis & Elkins Coll, Elkins, WV 26241	1904	Dr. Dorothy I. MacConkey . 2-B	811	77
Defiance Coll, Defiance, OH 43512	1850	Dr. Marvin J. Ludwig . . . 2-B	1,033	77
Delaware State Coll, Dover, DE 19901	1891	Dr. William B. DeLauder . 5-M	2,510	185
Delaware Valley Coll, Doylestown, PA 18901	1896	Mr. William H. Rorer, III . . 1-B	1,165	80
Delta State U, Cleveland, MS 38733	1925	Dr. F. Kent Wyatt 5-D	3,600	226
Denison U, Granville, OH 43023	1831	Samuel J. Thios 1-B	2,108	176
Denver Tech Coll, Denver, CO 80222	1945	NR 3-B	795	76
DePaul U, Chicago, IL 60604	1898	Rev. John T. Richardson, CM 2-D	14,699	734
DePauw U, Greencastle, IN 46135	1837	Dr. Robert Bottoms 2-M	2,480	218
Detroit Coll of Business, Dearborn, MI 48126	1962	Dr. James Mendola 1-B	2,331	82
Detroit Coll of Business-Flint, Flint, MI 48504	1974	Ralph E. Stingel, Jr. 1-B	728	45
DeVry Inst of Tech, Phoenix, AZ 85021	1967	James A. Dugan 3-B	2,735	60
DeVry Inst of Tech, City of Industry, CA 91746	1983	Paul R. McGuirk 3-B	2,251	55
DeVry Inst of Tech, Kansas City, MO 64131	1931	Mr. Charles R. Levalley . . 3-B	1,607	46
Dickinson Coll, Carlisle, PA 17013	1773	Dr. A. Lee Fritschler . . . 1-B	1,991	146
Dickinson State U, Dickinson, ND 58601	1918	Dr. Albert A. Watrel 5-B	1,417	98
Doane Coll, Crete, NE 68333	1872	Dr. Fred D. Brown 2-B	625	66
Dominican Coll of Blauvelt, Orangeburg, NY 10962	1952	Sr. Kathleen Sullivan . . . 1-B	1,442	162
Dominican Coll of San Rafael, San Rafael, CA 94901	1890	Dr. Joseph H. Fink 2-M	714	95
Dordt Coll, Sioux Center, IA 51250	1955	Dr. John B. Hulst 2-B	987	70
Dowling Coll, Oakdale, NY 11769	1959	Dr. Victor P. Meskill . . . 1-M	4,036	274
Drake U, Des Moines, IA 50311	1881	Dr. Michael Ferrari 1-D	6,618	256
Drew U, Madison, NJ 07940	1866	Dr. W. Scott McDonald . . 2-D	2,364	124
Drexel U, Philadelphia, PA 19104	1891	Dr. Harold M. Myers . . . 1-D	12,265	858
Drury Coll, Springfield, MO 65802	1873	Dr. John E. Moore, Jr. . . 2-M	1,315	110
Duke U, Durham, NC 27706	1838	Dr. H. Keith H. Brodie . . 2-D	10,712	3,200
Duquesne U, Pittsburgh, PA 15282	1878	John E. Murray 2-D	6,370	479
D'Youville Coll, Buffalo, NY 14201	1908	Dr. Denise A. Roche, GNSH . 1-M	1,100	97
Earlham Coll, Richmond, IN 47374	1847	Dr. Richard J. Wood . . . 2-M	1,232	122
East Carolina U, Greenville, NC 27858	1907	Dr. Richard Eakin 5-D	15,579	1,041
East Central U, Ada, OK 74820	1909	Dr. Joe Parsons 2-M	4,251	200
Eastern Coll, Saint Davids, PA 19087	1932	Dr. Roberta Hestenes . . . 2-M	1,178	100
Eastern Connecticut State U, Willimantic, CT 06226	1889	David G. Carter 5-M	4,447	191
Eastern Illinois U, Charleston, IL 61920	1895	Dr. Stanley Rives 5-M	10,510	570
Eastern Kentucky U, Richmond, KY 40475	1906	Dr. Hanly Funderburk . . . 5-M	13,664	785
Eastern Mennonite Coll, Harrisonburg, VA 22801	1917	Dr. Joseph L. Lapp 2-B	967	80
Eastern Michigan U, Ypsilanti, MI 48197	1849	Dr. John W. Porter 5-M	23,641	1,049
Eastern Nazarene Coll, Quincy, MA 02170	1927	Dr. Bruce H. Carpenter . . 2-M	3,994	156
Eastern Montana Coll, Billings, MT 59101	1918	Dr. Stephen W. Nease . . 5-M	979	72
Eastern New Mexico U, Portales, NM 88130	1934	Dr. Robert Matheny 5-M	3,418	200
Eastern Oregon State Coll, La Grande, OR 97850	1929	David E. Gilbert 5-M	1,802	NR
Eastern Washington U, Cheney, WA 99004	1882	Dr. Alexander Schilt . . . 5-M	8,198	469
East Stroudsburg U of Pennsylvania, East Stroudsburg, PA 18301	1893	James Gilbert 5-M	4,909	289
East Tennessee State U, Johnson City, TN 37614	1911	Dr. Ronald E. Beller . . . 5-D	11,000	723
East Texas Baptist U, Marshall, TX 75670	1912	Dr. Robert E. Craig 2-B	716	64
East Texas State U, Commerce, TX 75428	1889	Dr. Jerry D. Morris 5-D	7,315	201
Eckerd Coll, St Petersburg, FL 33733	1958	Dr. Peter H. Armacost . . 2-B	1,325	109
Edgewood Coll, Madison, WI 53711	1927	Dr. James A. Ebben . . . 2-M	1,110	90
Edinboro U of Pennsylvania, Edinboro, PA 16444	1857	Foster F. Diebold 5-M	7,001	343
Electronic Data Processing Coll of Puerto Rico, Hato Rey, PR 00918	1968	NR 3-B	1,176	40
Elizabeth City State U, Elizabeth City, NC 27909	1891	Dr. Jimmy R. Jenkins . . . 5-B	1,643	110
Elizabethtown Coll, Elizabethtown, PA 17022	1899	Dr. Gerhard E. Spiegler . . 2-B	1,773	144
Elmhurst Coll, Elmhurst, IL 60126	1871	Dr. Ivan E. Frick 2-B	3,135	142
Elmira Coll, Elmira, NY 14901	1855	Dr. Thomas K. Meier . . . 1-M	1,998	91
Elms Coll, Chicopee, MA 01013 (3)	1928	Sr. Mary A. Dooley 2-M	650	79
Elon Coll, Elon College, NC 27244	1889	Dr. J. Fred Young 2-M	3,314	175
Embry-Riddle Aeronautical U, Daytona Beach, FL 32014	1926	Kenneth Tallman 1-M	5,317	213
Embry-Riddle Aeronautical U, Coll of Continuing Ed, Daytona Beach, FL 32014	1926	Charles S. Williams 1-M	3,808	NR
Embry-Riddle Aeronautical U, Prescott Cmps, Prescott, AZ 86301	1978	Paul Daly 1-B	1,609	NR
Emerson Coll, Boston, MA 02116	1880	Dr. Allen E. Koenig 1-M	2,460	251
Emmanuel Coll, Boston, MA 02115 (4)	1919	Sr. Janet Eisner 2-M	973	87

Name, address	Year	Governing official, control, and highest degree offered	Enrollment	Faculty
Emory & Henry Coll, Emory, VA 24327	1836	Dr. Charles W. Sydnor, Jr. ... 2-B	788	61
Emory U, Atlanta, GA 30322	1836	Dr. James T. Laney ... 2-D	9,285	337
Emporia State U, Emporia, KS 66801	1863	Dr. Robert E. Glennen ... 5-M	5,763	294
Eugene Lang Coll, New Sch for Social Research, New York, NY 10011	1985	Donald Scott	257	51
Evangel Coll, Springfield, MO 65802	1955	Dr. Robert H. Spence ... 2-B	1,564	122
Evergreen State Coll, Olympia, WA 98505	1967	Dr. Joseph D. Olander ... 5-M	3,250	330
Fairfield U, Fairfield, CT 06430	1942	Rev. Aloysius P. Kelley ... 2-M	4,878	330
Fairleigh Dickinson U, Florham-Madison Cmps, Madison, NJ 07940	1958	Dr. Robert H. Donaldson ... 1-M	3,818	191
Fairleigh Dickinson U, Rutherford Cmps, Rutherford, NJ 07070	1942	Dr. Robert Donaldson ... 1-M	2,455	148
Fairleigh Dickinson U, Teaneck-Hackensack Cmps, Teaneck, NJ 07666	1954	Dr. Robert H. Donaldson ... 1-D	4,886	540
Fairmont State Coll, Fairmont, WV 26554	1865	Dr. Wendell G. Hardway ... 5-B	5,747	316
Fashion Inst of Tech, New York, NY 10001	1944	Dr. Marvin J. Feldman ... 12-M	11,944	789
Faulkner U, Montgomery, AL 36193	1942	Dr. Billy D. Hilyer ... 2-D	1,984	49
Fayetteville State U, Fayetteville, NC 28301	1867	Dr. Charles A. Lyons, Jr. ... 5-M	2,726	177
Felician Coll, Lodi, NJ 07644	1942	Sr. Theresa Martin ... 2-B	647	78
Ferris State U, Big Rapids, MI 49307	1884	Dr. J. William Wenrich ... 5-D	11,762	638
Ferrum Coll, Ferrum, VA 24088	1913	Dr. Jerry M. Boone ... 2-B	1,206	103
Fisk U, Nashville, TN 37208	1866	Dr. Henry Ponder ... 2-M	774	81
Fitchburg State Coll, Fitchburg, MA 01420	1894	Dr. Vincent J. Mara ... 5-M	6,224	274
Flagler Coll, St Augustine, FL 32085	1968	Dr. William L. Proctor ... 1-B	1,166	92
Florida Agricultural and Mechanical U, Tallahassee, FL 32307	1887	Dr. Frederick Humphries ... 5-D	6,408	370
Florida Atlantic U, Boca Raton, FL 33431	1961	Dr. Helen Popovich ... 5-D	8,387	456
Florida Inst of Tech, Melbourne, FL 32901	1958	Dr. Lynn E. Weaver ... 1-D	4,117	683
Florida International U, Miami, FL 33199	1965	Dr. Modesto A. Maidique ... 5-D	17,482	862
Florida Southern Coll, Lakeland, FL 33801	1885	Dr. Robert A. Davis ... 2-M	1,955	154
Florida State U, Tallahassee, FL 32306	1857	Dr. Bernard F. Sliger ... 5-D	23,883	1,434
Fontbonne Coll, St Louis, MO 63105	1917	Dr. Meneve Dunham ... 2-M	1,036	99
Fordham U, New York, NY 10458	1841	Rev. Joseph A. O'Hare, SJ ... 2-D	13,036	933
Fort Hays State U, Hays, KS 67601	1902	Dr. Edward H. Hammond ... 5-M	5,005	NR
Fort Lewis Coll, Durango, CO 81301	1911	Joel M. Jones ... 5-B	3,842	180
Fort Valley State Coll, Fort Valley, GA 31030	1895	Dr. Luther Burse ... 5-M	1,915	148
Franciscan U of Steubenville, Steubenville, OH 43952	1946	Rev. Michael Scanlan ... 2-M	1,369	81
Francis Marion Coll, Florence, SC 29501	1970	Dr. Thomas C. Stanton ... 5-M	3,929	188
Franklin and Marshall Coll, Lancaster, PA 17604	1787	Dr. A. Richard Kneedler ... 1-B	1,850	160
Franklin Coll of Indiana, Franklin, IN 46131	1834	Mr. William Bryan Martin ... 2-B	780	73
Franklin Pierce Coll, Rindge, NH 03461	1962	Dr. Walter Peterson ... 1-B	1,183	94
Franklin U, Columbus, OH 43215	1902	Dr. Paul J. Otte ... 1-B	4,160	206
Freed-Hardeman Coll, Henderson, TN 38340	1869	Dr. E. Claude Gardner ... 2-M	1,169	82
Fresno Pacific Coll, Fresno, CA 93702	1944	Dr. Richard Kriegbaum ... 2-M	1,223	43
Friends U, Wichita, KS 67213	1898	Dr. Richard Felix ... 2-M	1,185	93
Frostburg State U, Frostburg, MD 21532	1898	Dr. Herb F. Reinhard, Jr. ... 5-M	4,525	287
Furman U, Greenville, SC 29613	1826	Dr. John E. Johns ... 2-M	2,794	206
Gallaudet U, Washington, DC 20002	1856	Dr. Robert L. Williams ... 1-D	2,391	330
Gannon U, Erie, PA 16541	1944	Dr. M. Daniel Henry ... 2-M	3,592	156
Gardner-Webb Coll, Boiling Springs, NC 28017	1905	Dr. M. Christopher White ... 2-M	2,189	151
Geneva Coll, Beaver Falls, PA 15010	1848	Dr. Joseph McFarland ... 2-M	1,445	105
George Fox Coll, Newberg, OR 97132	1891	Dr. Edward F. Stevens ... 2-B	820	74
George Mason U, Fairfax, VA 22030	1957	Dr. George W. Johnson ... 5-D	18,965	879
Georgetown Coll, Georgetown, KY 40324	1829	Dr. W. Morgan Patterson ... 2-M	1,471	93
Georgetown U, Washington, DC 20057	1789	Rev. Timothy S. Healy, SJ ... 2-D	11,516	650
George Washington U, Washington, DC 20052	1821	Mr. Stephen J. Trachtenberg ... 1-D	16,973	1,133
Georgia Coll, Milledgeville, GA 31061	1889	Dr. Edwin G. Speir ... 5-M	4,522	168
Georgia Inst of Tech, Atlanta, GA 30332	1885	Dr. John P. Crecine ... 5-D	11,887	547
Georgian Court Coll, Lakewood, NJ 08701 (4)	1908	Sr. Barbara Williams ... 2-M	2,054	131
Georgia Southern Coll, Statesboro, GA 30460	1906	Dr. Nicholas Henry ... 5-M	9,841	492
Georgia Southwestern Coll, Americus, GA 31709	1906	Dr. William H. Capitan ... 5-M	2,250	155
Georgia State U, Atlanta, GA 30303	1913	Dr. William M. Suttles ... 5-D	22,245	NR
Gettysburg Coll, Gettysburg, PA 17325	1832	Dr. Charles E. Glassick ... 2-B	1,900	150
Glassboro State Coll, Glassboro, NJ 08028	1923	Dr. Herman D. James ... 5-M	9,500	445
Glenville State Coll, Glenville, WV 26351	1872	Dr. James L. Peterson ... 5-B	2,204	88
GMI Engineering & Management Inst, Flint, MI 48504	1919	Dr. William B. Cottingham ... 1-M	3,068	NR
Golden Gate U, San Francisco, CA 94105	1901	Dr. Otto W. Butz ... 1-D	9,338	760
Goldey-Beacom Coll, Wilmington, DE 19808	1886	Mr. William R. Baldt ... 1-B	2,500	66
Gonzaga U, Spokane, WA 99258	1887	Rev. Bernard J. Coughlin, SJ ... 2-D	3,896	288
Gordon Coll, Wenham, MA 01984	1889	Dr. Richard F. Gross ... 2-B	1,183	89
Goshen Coll, Goshen, IN 46526	1894	Dr. Victor Stoltzfus ... 2-B	1,085	112
Goucher Coll, Towson, MD 21204	1885	Dr. Rhoda M. Dorsey ... 1-M	982	134
Governors State U, University Park, IL 60466	1969	Dr. Leo Goodman-Malamuth, II ... 5-M	5,092	276
Grace Coll, Winona Lake, IN 46590	1948	Dr. John Davis ... 2-B	769	49
Graceland Coll, Lamoni, IA 50140	1895	Dr. Barbara J. Higdon ... 2-B	909	68
Grand Canyon Coll, Phoenix, AZ 85061	1949	Dr. Bill Williams ... 2-M	1,813	159
Grand Rapids Baptist Coll and Sem, Grand Rapids, MI 49505	1941	Dr. Charles Wagner ... 2-M	929	53
Grand Valley State U, Allendale, MI 49401	1960	Mr. Arend D. Lubbers ... 5-M	8,948	305
Grand View Coll, Des Moines, IA 50316	1896	Dr. Arthur E. Puotinen ... 2-B	1,359	110
Grantham Coll of Engineering, Los Alamitos, CA 90720	1951	Mr. Donald J. Grantham ... 3-B	710	4
Greensboro Coll, Greensboro, NC 27401	1838	Dr. William H. Likins ... 2-B	967	73
Greenville Coll, Greenville, IL 62246	1892	Dr. W. Richard Stephens ... 2-B	702	64
Griffin Coll, Seattle, WA 98121	1909	Wayne P. Wilson ... 3-B	1,800	36
Grinnell Coll, Grinnell, IA 50112	1846	Dr. George A. Drake ... 1-B	1,276	122
Grove City Coll, Grove City, PA 16127	1876	Dr. Charles S. MacKenzie ... 2-B	2,148	124
Guilford Coll, Greensboro, NC 27410	1837	Dr. William R. Rogers ... 2-B	1,250	114
Gustavus Adolphus Coll, St Peter, MN 56082	1862	Dr. John S. Kendall ... 2-B	2,387	188
Gwynedd-Mercy Coll, Gwynedd Valley, PA 19437 (4)	1948	Sr. Isabelle Keiss, RSM ... 2-M	1,812	155
Hahnemann U, Philadelphia, PA 19102	1848	Mr. Iqbal F. Paroo ... 1-D	2,042	430
Hamilton Coll, Clinton, NY 13323	1812	Dr. Harry C. Payne ... 1-B	1,654	159
Hamline U, St Paul, MN 55104	1854	Dr. Larry G. Osnes ... 2-D	2,235	128
Hampden-Sydney Coll, Hampden-Sydney, VA 23943 (1)	1776	Dr. James R. Leutze ... 2-B	937	88
Hampshire Coll, Amherst, MA 01002	1965	Dr. Adele S. Simmons ... 1-B	1,232	112

Name, address	Year	Governing official, control, and highest degree offered		Enroll-ment	Faculty
Hampton U, Hampton, VA 23668	1868	Dr. William R. Harvey	1-M	5,147	368
Hannibal-LaGrange Coll, Hannibal, MO 63401	1858	Dr. Paul Brown	2-B	853	73
Hanover Coll, Hanover, IN 47243	1827	Dr. Russell L. Nichols	2-B	1,070	92
Harding U, Searcy, AR 72143	1924	Dr. David B. Burks, Jr.	2-M	3,204	185
Hardin-Simmons U, Abilene, TX 79698	1891	Dr. Jesse C. Fletcher	2-M	1,747	138
Hartwick Coll, Oneonta, NY 13820	1797	Dr. Philip S. Wilder, Jr.	1-B	1,515	145
Harvard U, Cambridge, MA 02138	1636	Mr. Derek Bok	1-D	17,484	800
Hastings Coll, Hastings, NE 68902	1882	Dr. Thomas J. Reeves	2-M	954	84
Haverford Coll, Haverford, PA 19041	1833	Tom G. Kessinger	1-B	1,105	117
Hawaii Pacific Coll, Honolulu, HI 96813	1965	Mr. Chatt Wright	1-M	4,560	201
Heidelberg Coll, Tiffin, OH 44883	1850	Dr. William C. Cassell	2-M	1,206	NR
Henderson State U, Arkadelphia, AR 71923	1890	Dr. Charles D. Dunn	5-M	3,209	163
Hendrix Coll, Conway, AR 72032	1876	Dr. Joe B. Hatcher	2-B	1,029	73
High Point Coll, High Point, NC 27261	1924	Dr. Jacob C. Martinson, Jr.	2-B	1,917	87
Hillsdale Coll, Hillsdale, MI 49242	1844	Dr. George C. Roche, III	1-B	1,071	100
Hiram Coll, Hiram, OH 44234	1850	Dr. James A. Norton	2-B	1,248	86
Hobart Coll, Geneva, NY 14456 (1)	1822	Mr. Carroll Brewster	2-B	1,127	166
Hofstra U, Hempstead, NY 11550	1935	Dr. James M. Shuart	1-D	12,210	822
Hollins Coll, Roanoke, VA 24020 (3)	1842	Dr. Paula P. Brownlee	1-M	1,030	90
Holy Family Coll, Philadelphia, PA 19114	1954	Sr. M. Francesca	2-B	1,685	162
Holy Names Coll, Oakland, CA 94619	1868	Sr. Lois MacGillivray	2-M	720	79
Hood Coll, Frederick, MD 21701 (4)	1893	Dr. Martha E. Church	2-M	1,874	115
Hope Coll, Holland, MI 49423	1862	Dr. John Jacobson, Jr.	2-B	2,781	228
Houghton Coll, Houghton, NY 14744	1883	Dr. Daniel R. Chamberlain	2-B	1,126	89
Houston Baptist U, Houston, TX 77074	1960	Dr. E. Douglas Hodo	2-M	2,429	160
Howard Payne U, Brownwood, TX 76801	1889	Dr. Don Newbury	2-B	1,247	92
Howard U, Washington, DC 20059	1867	Dr. James E. Cheek	1-D	11,742	1,877
Hunter Coll of the City U of New York, New York, NY 10021	1870	Tilden J. Le Melle	12-M	15,560	NR
Huntingdon Coll, Montgomery, AL 36194	1854	Dr. Allen K. Jackson	2-B	866	71
Husson Coll, Bangor, ME 04401	1898	Dr. William H. Beardsley	1-M	1,792	49
Idaho State U, Pocatello, ID 83209	1901	Dr. Richard Bowen	5-D	7,616	459
Illinois Benedictine Coll, Lisle, IL 60532	1887	Dr. Richard C. Becker	2-M	2,514	195
Illinois Coll, Jacksonville, IL 62650	1829	Dr. Donald C. Mundinger	2-B	842	78
Illinois Inst of Tech, Chicago, IL 60616	1892	Dr. Meyer Feldberg	1-D	6,208	492
Illinois State U, Normal, IL 61761	1857	Thomas P. Wallace	5-D	21,394	1,048
Illinois Wesleyan U, Bloomington, IL 61702	1850	Dr. Wendell W. Hess	2-B	1,750	157
Immaculata Coll, Immaculata, PA 19345 (4)	1920	Sr. Marian William	2-M	2,100	152
Incarnate Word Coll, San Antonio, TX 78209	1881	Dr. Louis J. Agnese, Jr.	2-M	2,240	142
Indiana Inst of Tech, Fort Wayne, IN 46803	1930	Donald J. Andorfer	1-B	623	42
Indiana U, Terre Haute, IN 47809	1865	Dr. Richard G. Landini	5-D	11,677	NR
Indiana U at South Bend, South Bend, IN 46634	1922	H. Daniel Cohen	5-M	6,451	300
Indiana U Bloomington, Bloomington, IN 47405	1820	Kenneth R. R. Gros Louis	5-D	33,776	1,595
Indiana U Northwest, Gary, IN 46408	1959	Dr. Peggy G. Elliott	5-M	4,910	NR
Indiana U of Pennsylvania, Indiana, PA 15705	1875	Dr. John D. Welty	5-D	13,650	818
Indiana U–Purdue U at Fort Wayne, Fort Wayne, IN 46805	1917	Dr. Thomas P. Wallace	5-M	11,073	667
Indiana U–Purdue U at Indianapolis, Indianapolis, IN 46202	1969	Gerald L. Bepko, Jr.	5-D	24,808	1,922
Indiana U Southeast, New Albany, IN 47150	1941	Dr. Leon Rand	5-M	5,267	289
Indiana Wesleyan U, Marion, IN 46953	1920	Dr. James Barnes	2-M	1,002	100
Inter American U of PR, Aguadilla Regional Coll, Aguadilla, PR 00605	1957	NR	1-B	3,266	175
Inter Amer U of PR, Barranquitas Regional Coll, Barranquitas, PR 00618	1957	Mr. Vidal Rivera-Garcia	1-B	1,226	96
Inter American U of PR, Fajardo Regional Coll, Fajardo, PR 00648	1965	Mrs. Yolanda Robles Garcia	1-B	1,813	108
Inter American U of PR, Ponce Regional Coll, Ponce, PR 00715	1962	Mr. Jose I. Correa Colon	1-B	3,155	199
Inter American U of PR, San Germán Cmps, San Germán, PR 00753	1912	Dr. Federico Matheu	1-M	5,700	287
International Acad of Merchandising & Design, Ltd, Chicago, IL 60654	1977	Clem Stein, Jr.	3-B	753	75
Iona Coll, New Rochelle, NY 10801	1940	Br. John G. Driscoll	2-M	6,882	502
Iowa State U of Science and Tech, Ames, IA 50011	1858	Dr. Gordon P. Eaton	5-D	25,448	2,076
Iowa Wesleyan Coll, Mount Pleasant, IA 52641	1842	Robert J. Prins	2-B	679	52
ITT Tech Inst, West Covina, CA 91790	1982	NR	3-B	675	NR
ITT Tech Inst, Fort Wayne, IN 46825	1967	Jack B. Cozad	3-B	1,036	30
ITT Tech Inst, Indianapolis, IN 46268	1966	Alan J. Crews	3-B	1,297	46
ITT Tech Inst, Portland, OR 97218	1971	E. Lynn Thacker	3-B	660	24
Jackson State U, Jackson, MS 39217	1877	Dr. James A. Hefner	5-D	6,777	395
Jacksonville State U, Jacksonville, AL 36265	1883	Dr. Harold J. McGee	5-M	7,511	367
Jacksonville U, Jacksonville, FL 32211	1934	Dr. Frances B. Kinne	1-M	2,257	NR
James Madison U, Harrisonburg, VA 22807	1908	Dr. Ronald E. Carrier	5-M	10,525	668
Jamestown Coll, Jamestown, ND 58401	1883	Dr. James Walker	2-B	796	58
Jersey City State Coll, Jersey City, NJ 07305	1927	Dr. William J. Maxwell	5-M	6,717	420
John Brown U, Siloam Springs, AR 72761	1919	Dr. John E. Brown, III	2-B	874	70
John Carroll U, University Heights, OH 44118	1886	Rev. Michael J. Lavelle, SJ	2-M	4,082	268
John F Kennedy U, Orinda, CA 94563	1964	Dr. Donald J. MacIntyre	1-M	2,000	NR
John Jay Coll of Crim Justice of City U of NY, New York, NY 10019	1964	Dr. Gerald Lynch	12-D	7,312	507
Johns Hopkins U, Baltimore, MD 21218	1876	Dr. Steven Muller	1-D	5,196	704
Johnson & Wales U, Providence, RI 02903	1914	Dr. Morris J. Gaebe	1-M	7,210	240
Johnson C Smith U, Charlotte, NC 28216	1867	Dr. Robert L. Albright	1-B	1,197	91
Johnson State Coll, Johnson, VT 05656	1828	Mr. Eric R. Gilbertson	5-M	1,327	95
Jones Coll, Jacksonville, FL 32211	1918	James M. Patch	1-B	1,500	57
Jordan Coll, Cedar Springs, MI 49319	1967	Lexie K. Coxon	2-B	2,271	176
Juilliard Sch, New York, NY 10023	1905	Dr. Joseph W. Polisi	1-D	850	220
Juniata Coll, Huntingdon, PA 16652	1876	Dr. Robert W. Neff	1-B	1,103	90
Kalamazoo Coll, Kalamazoo, MI 49007	1833	Dr. David Breneman	1-B	1,255	99
Kansas Newman Coll, Wichita, KS 67213	1933	Dr. Robert J. Giroux	2-B	591	61
Kansas State U, Manhattan, KS 66506	1863	Dr. Jon Wefald	5-M	19,301	1,250
Kean Coll of New Jersey, Union, NJ 07083	1855	Dr. Nathan Weiss	5-M	12,372	771
Kearney State Coll, Kearney, NE 68849	1903	Dr. William R. Nester	5-M	9,381	379
Keene State Coll, Keene, NH 03431	1909	Dr. Judith A. Sturnick	5-M	2,893	250
Kendall Coll of Art and Design, Grand Rapids, MI 49503	1928	Dr. Phyllis I. Danielson	1-B	746	62
Kennesaw State Coll, Marietta, GA 30061	1966	Dr. Betty L. Siegel	5-M	8,614	417

Name, address	Year	Governing official, control, and highest degree offered		Enrollment	Faculty
Kent State U, Kent, OH 44242	1910	Dr. Michael Schwartz	5-D	22,753	1,118
Kentucky State U, Frankfort, KY 40601	1886	Dr. Raymond M. Burse	13-M	2,222	128
Kentucky Wesleyan Coll, Owensboro, KY 42302	1858	Dr. Luther W. White	2-B	765	80
Kenyon Coll, Gambier, OH 43022	1824	Dr. Philip H. Jordan, Jr.	1-B	1,573	140
Keuka Coll, Keuka Park, NY 14478	1890	Dr. Arthur F. Kirk, Jr.	1-B	604	67
King's Coll, Wilkes-Barre, PA 18711	1946	Rev. James Lackenmier, CSC	2-B	2,304	162
Knox Coll, Galesburg, IL 61401	1837	Dr. John P. McCall	1-B	1,024	80
Knoxville Coll, Knoxville, TN 37921	1875	Dr. Joe L. Boyer, Jr.	2-B	1,306	51
Kutztown U of Pennsylvania, Kutztown, PA 19530	1866	Dr. Robert Wittman	5-M	7,168	355
Lafayette Coll, Easton, PA 18042	1826	Dr. David W. Ellis	2-B	2,039	195
LaGrange Coll, LaGrange, GA 30240	1831	Dr. Walter Y. Murphy	2-M	956	74
Lake Erie Coll, Painesville, OH 44077	1856	Dr. Clodus R. Smith	1-M	690	60
Lake Forest Coll, Lake Forest, IL 60045	1857	Dr. Eugene Hotchkiss, III	1-M	1,132	105
Lakeland Coll, Sheboygan, WI 53082	1862	Dr. Richard E. Hill	2-B	1,537	39
Lake Superior State U, Sault Sainte Marie, MI 49783	1946	Dr. H. Erik Shaar	5-M	3,155	155
Lamar U, Beaumont, TX 77710	1923	Dr. Bill J. Franklin	5-D	11,848	725
Lambuth Coll, Jackson, TN 38301	1843	Dr. Thomas F. Boyd	2-B	767	52
Lander Coll, Greenwood, SC 29649	1872	Dr. Larry A. Jackson	5-M	2,479	156
Langston U, Langston, OK 73050	1897	Dr. Ernest L. Holloway	5-M	2,514	128
Laredo State U, Laredo, TX 78040	1969	Dr. Leo Sayavedra	5-M	1,077	54
La Roche Coll, Pittsburgh, PA 15237	1963	Sr. Margaret Huber	2-M	1,852	121
La Salle U, Philadelphia, PA 19141	1863	Dr. Patrick Ellis	2-M	6,464	269
Lawrence Tech U, Southfield, MI 48075	1932	Dr. Richard E. Marburger	1-M	5,490	304
Lawrence U, Appleton, WI 54912	1847	Dr. Richard Warch	1-B	1,224	115
Lebanon Valley Coll, Annville, PA 17003	1866	Mr. John A. Synodinos	2-B	1,303	121
Lee Coll, Cleveland, TN 37311	1918	Dr. Paul Conn	2-B	1,535	118
Lees-McRae Coll, Banner Elk, NC 28604	1900	Dr. Bradford L. Crain	2-B	787	58
Lehigh U, Bethlehem, PA 18015	1865	Dr. Peter Likins	1-D	6,569	487
Lehman Coll of the City U of New York, Bronx, NY 10468	1931	Dr. Leonard Lief	12-M	9,598	603
Le Moyne Coll, Syracuse, NY 13214	1946	Rev. Kevin G. O'Connell, SJ	2-B	2,274	186
LeMoyne-Owen Coll, Memphis, TN 38126	1870	Dr. Irving P. McPhail	2-B	1,130	63
Lenoir-Rhyne Coll, Hickory, NC 28603	1891	Dr. John E. Trainer, Jr.	2-M	1,616	135
Lesley Coll, Cambridge, MA 02138 (3)	1909	Margaret A. McKenna	1-D	4,463	46
LeTourneau Coll, Longview, TX 75607	1946	Dr. Alvin O. Austin	2-B	753	55
Lewis and Clark Coll, Portland, OR 97219	1867	Mr. James A. Gardner	1-D	2,552	166
Lewis-Clark State Coll, Lewiston, ID 83501	1894	Dr. Lee A. Vickers	5-B	2,164	107
Lewis U, Romeoville, IL 60441	1932	Br. James Gaffney, FSC	2-M	3,501	151
Liberty U, Lynchburg, VA 24506	1971	Dr. A. Pierre Guillermin	2-M	10,902	255
Limestone Coll, Gaffney, SC 29340	1845	Mr. G. Frederick Payne	1-B	952	63
Lincoln Memorial U, Harrogate, TN 37752	1897	Dr. Gary J. Burchett	1-M	1,582	101
Lincoln U, Jefferson City, MO 65101	1866	Dr. Wendell G. Rayburn	5-M	2,743	127
Lincoln U, Lincoln University, PA 19352	1854	Dr. Niara Sudarkasa	13-M	1,250	131
Lindenwood Coll, St Charles, MO 63301	1827	Dr. James I. Spainhower	1-M	1,766	108
Lindsey Wilson Coll, Columbia, KY 42728	1903	Dr. John B. Begley	2-B	1,060	53
Linfield Coll, McMinnville, OR 97128	1849	Dr. Charles U. Walker	2-B	1,283	150
Livingston U, Livingston, AL 35470	1835	Dr. Asa N. Green	5-M	1,633	92
Lock Haven U of Pennsylvania, Lock Haven, PA 17745	1870	Dr. Craig Dean Willis	5-M	3,012	188
Logan Coll of Chiropractic, Chesterfield, MO 63006	1935	Dr. Beatrice B. Hagen	1-D	694	75
Long Island U, Brooklyn Cmps, Brooklyn, NY 11201	1926	Dr. David J. Steinberg	1-D	5,168	400
Long Island U, C W Post Cmps, Brookville, NY 11548	1954	Dr. David J. Steinberg	1-M	8,771	685
Long Island U, Southampton Cmps, Southampton, NY 11968	1963	Dr. David J. Steinberg	1-M	1,224	131
Longwood Coll, Farmville, VA 23901	1839	Dr. William F. Dorrill	5-M	2,955	184
Loras Coll, Dubuque, IA 52001	1839	Rev. Msgr. James Barta	2-M	2,004	156
Los Angeles Coll of Chiropractic, Whittier, CA 90609	1911	Dr. E. Maylon Drake	1-D	998	84
Louisiana Coll, Pineville, LA 71359	1906	Dr. Robert L. Lynn	2-B	1,017	81
Louisiana State U and A&M Coll, Baton Rouge, LA 70803	1860	Dr. James H. Wharton	5-D	26,564	1,242
Louisiana State U in Shreveport, Shreveport, LA 71115	1965	Dr. E. Grady Bogue	5-M	4,499	218
Louisiana Tech U, Ruston, LA 71272	1894	Dr. Daniel D. Reneau	5-D	10,110	451
Lourdes Coll, Sylvania, OH 43560	1958	Sr. Ann Francis Klimkowski, OSF	2-B	773	108
Loyola Coll, Baltimore, MD 21210	1852	Rev. Joseph A. Sellinger	2-M	5,650	376
Loyola Marymount U, Los Angeles, CA 90045	1911	Rev. James N. Loughran, SJ	2-D	4,869	386
Loyola U, New Orleans, New Orleans, LA 70118	1912	Rev. James C. Carter, SJ	2-D	4,952	340
Loyola U of Chicago, Chicago, IL 60611	1870	Rev. Raymond C. Baumhart, SJ	2-D	14,046	1,290
Lubbock Christian U, Lubbock, TX 79407	1957	Dr. Steven S. Lemley	2-B	1,079	110
Luther Coll, Decorah, IA 52101	1861	Dr. H. George Anderson	2-B	2,214	183
Lycoming Coll, Williamsport, PA 17701	1812	Dr. Frederick E. Blumer	2-B	1,065	98
Lynchburg Coll, Lynchburg, VA 24501	1903	Dr. George N. Rainsford	2-M	2,447	173
Lyndon State Coll, Lyndonville, VT 05851	1911	Dr. Clive C. Veri	5-M	996	85
Macalester Coll, St Paul, MN 55105	1874	Dr. Robert M. Gavin, Jr.	2-B	1,847	214
MacMurray Coll, Jacksonville, IL 62650	1846	Dr. Edward J. Mitchell	2-B	650	74
Maharishi International U, Fairfield, IA 52556	1971	Dr. Bevan Morris	1-D	768	96
Malone Coll, Canton, OH 44709	1892	Dr. Gordon R. Werkema	2-B	1,325	91
Manchester Coll, North Manchester, IN 46962	1889	Dr. William P. Robinson	2-M	1,021	90
Manhattan Coll, Riverdale, NY 10471	1853	Br. Thomas J. Scanlan	1-M	4,341	410
Manhattan Sch of Music, New York, NY 10027	1917	Gideon W. Waldrop	1-D	787	180
Manhattanville Coll, Purchase, NY 10577	1841	Dr. Marcia Savage	1-M	1,500	130
Mankato State U, Mankato, MN 56001	1867	Dr. Margaret R. Preska	5-M	14,206	680
Mansfield U of Pennsylvania, Mansfield, PA 16933	1857	Mr. Rod C. Kelchner	5-M	2,980	185
Marian Coll, Indianapolis, IN 46222	1851	Dr. Louis C. Gatto	2-B	1,215	123
Marian Coll of Fond du Lac, Fond du Lac, WI 54935	1936	Dr. Edward L. Henry	2-M	859	81
Marietta Coll, Marietta, OH 45750	1835	Dr. Sherrill Cleland	1-M	1,339	115
Marist Coll, Poughkeepsie, NY 12601	1929	Dr. Dennis J. Murray	1-M	4,002	279
Marquette U, Milwaukee, WI 53233	1881	Rev. John P. Raynor, SJ	2-D	12,184	1,001
Marshall U, Huntington, WV 25755	1837	Dr. Dale F. Nitzschke	5-D	12,349	537
Mars Hill Coll, Mars Hill, NC 28754	1856	Dr. Fred B. Bentley	2-B	1,344	89
Mary Baldwin Coll, Staunton, VA 24401 (3)	1842	Dr. Cynthia Tyson	2-B	692	84
Marygrove Coll, Detroit, MI 48221	1910	Dr. John E. Shay, Jr.	2-M	1,235	67
Maryland Inst, Coll of Art, Baltimore, MD 21217	1826	Mr. Fred Lazarus	1-M	1,285	112
Marylhurst Coll, Marylhurst, OR 97036	1893	Nancy A. Wilgenbusch	1-M	1,005	274
Marymount Coll, Tarrytown, NY 10591 (4)	1907	Sr. Brigid Driscoll	1-B	1,247	145
Marymount Manhattan Coll, New York, NY 10021 (4)	1936	Sr. Colette Mahoney	1-B	1,300	155
Marymount U, Arlington, VA 22207	1950	Sr. M. Majelia Berg, RSHM	2-M	2,977	215

Name, address	Year	Governing official, control, and highest degree offered		Enrollment	Faculty
Maryville Coll, Maryville, TN 37801	1819	Dr. Richard I. Ferrin	2-B	787	58
Maryville Coll–Saint Louis, St Louis, MO 63141	1872	Dr. Claudius Pritchard	1-M	2,934	214
Mary Washington Coll, Fredericksburg, VA 22401	1908	Dr. William M. Anderson, Jr.	5-M	3,427	196
Marywood Coll, Scranton, PA 18509	1915	Sr. Mary Reap, IHM	2-M	2,395	219
Massachusetts Coll of Art, Boston, MA 02115	1873	Dr. William F. O'Neil	5-M	1,269	105
Mass Coll of Pharm & Allied Health Sciences, Boston, MA 02115	1823	Dr. Louis P. Jeffrey	1-D	1,064	122
Massachusetts Inst of Tech, Cambridge, MA 02139	1861	Dr. Paul E. Gray	1-D	9,425	929
Massachusetts Maritime Acad, Buzzards Bay, MA 02532	1891	Rear Adm. John F. Aylmer	5-B	600	58
Master's Coll, Newhall, CA 91322	1927	Dr. John F. MacArthur, Jr.	2-M	975	70
Mayville State U, Mayville, ND 58257	1889	Dr. James A. Schobel	5-B	755	50
McKendree Coll, Lebanon, IL 62254	1828	Dr. Gerrit J. TenBrink	2-B	976	72
McMurry Coll, Abilene, TX 79697	1923	Dr. Thomas K. Kim	2-B	1,689	118
McNeese State U, Lake Charles, LA 70609	1939	Dr. Robert D. Hebert	5-M	7,423	322
Medaille Coll, Buffalo, NY 14214	1875	Kevin I. Sullivan	1-B	1,053	70
Medgar Evers Coll of the City U of NY, Brooklyn, NY 11225	1969	Dr. Leo A. Corbie	12-B	2,480	323
Medical Coll of Georgia, Augusta, GA 30912	1828	Dr. Francis J. Tedesco	5-D	1,843	NR
Medical U of South Carolina, Charleston, SC 29425	1824	Dr. James B. Edwards	5-D	2,118	1,795
Memphis State U, Memphis, TN 38152	1912	Dr. Thomas G. Carpenter	5-D	20,399	1,120
Mercer U, Macon, GA 31207	1833	Dr. R. Kirby Godsey	2-D	3,725	163
Mercer U Atlanta, Atlanta, GA 30341	1968	Dr. R. Kirby Godsey	2-D	1,911	126
Mercy Coll, Dobbs Ferry, NY 10522	1951	Dr. Wilbert J. LeMelle	1-M	5,548	640
Mercy Coll of Detroit, Detroit, MI 48219	1941	Maureen A. Fay, OP	2-M	2,325	216
Mercyhurst Coll, Erie, PA 16546	1926	Dr. William P. Garvey	2-M	2,037	117
Meredith Coll, Raleigh, NC 27607 (3)	1891	Dr. John E. Weems	2-M	2,124	156
Merrimack Coll, North Andover, MA 01845	1947	Rev. John E. Deegan, OSA	2-B	2,357	274
Mesa State Coll, Grand Junction, CO 81502	1925	Dr. John U. Tomlinson	5-B	3,958	166
Messiah Coll, Grantham, PA 17027	1909	Dr. D. Ray Hostetter	2-B	2,179	141
Methodist Coll, Fayetteville, NC 28311	1956	Dr. M. Elton Hendricks	2-B	1,391	95
Metropolitan State Coll, Denver, CO 80204	1965	Dr. Thomas Brewer, Jr.	5-B	16,500	650
Metropolitan State U, St Paul, MN 55101	1971	Dr. Reatha Clark King	5-M	5,799	584
Miami U, Oxford, OH 45056	1809	Dr. Paul G. Pearson	5-D	16,044	840
Michigan State U, East Lansing, MI 48824	1855	Dr. John DiBiaggio	5-D	42,695	3,990
Michigan Tech U, Houghton, MI 49931	1885	Dr. Dale F. Stein	5-D	6,250	362
MidAmerica Nazarene Coll, Olathe, KS 66061	1966	Dr. Don Owens	2-B	1,121	73
Middlebury Coll, Middlebury, VT 05753	1800	Dr. Olin C. Robison	1-D	1,950	189
Middle Tennessee State U, Murfreesboro, TN 37132	1911	Dr. Sam H. Ingram	5-D	13,165	653
Midland Lutheran Coll, Fremont, NE 68025	1883	Dr. Carl L. Hansen	2-B	910	65
Midwestern State U, Wichita Falls, TX 76308	1922	Dr. Louis J. Rodriguez	5-M	5,394	212
Millersville U of Pennsylvania, Millersville, PA 17551	1854	Dr. Joseph A. Caputo	5-M	7,389	405
Milligan Coll, Milligan College, TN 37682	1866	Dr. Marshall J. Leggett	2-B	658	57
Millikin U, Decatur, IL 62522	1901	Dr. J. Roger Miller	2-B	1,736	162
Millsaps Coll, Jackson, MS 39210	1890	Dr. George M. Harmon	2-M	1,445	115
Mills Coll, Oakland, CA 94613 (3)	1852	Dr. Mary S. Metz	1-M	1,050	167
Milwaukee Sch of Engineering, Milwaukee, WI 53201	1903	Dr. Robert R. Spitzer	1-M	2,807	208
Minneapolis Coll of Art and Design, Minneapolis, MN 55404	1886	G. Richard Slade	1-B	713	92
Minot State U, Minot, ND 58701	1913	Dr. Gordon B. Olson	5-M	3,304	171
Mississippi Coll, Clinton, MS 39058	1826	Dr. Lewis Nobles	2-M	3,485	176
Mississippi State U, Mississippi State, MS 39762	1878	Dr. Donald W. Zacharias	5-D	12,406	802
Mississippi U for Women, Columbus, MS 39701 (4)	1884	Dr. Harvey M. Craft	5-M	2,085	126
Missouri Baptist Coll, St Louis, MO 63141	1968	Dr. Patrick O. Copley	2-B	951	56
Missouri Southern State Coll, Joplin, MO 64801	1937	Dr. Julio Leon	5-B	5,404	237
Missouri Valley Coll, Marshall, MO 65340	1889	Dr. Earl J. Reeves	2-B	1,050	60
Missouri Western State Coll, St Joseph, MO 64507	1915	Dr. Janet Gorman Murphy	5-B	4,153	61
Mobile Coll, Mobile, AL 36613	1961	Dr. Michael A. Magnoli	2-M	1,059	83
Molloy Coll, Rockville Centre, NY 11570	1955	Dr. Janet A. Fitzgerald, OP	1-B	1,384	175
Monmouth Coll, Monmouth, IL 61462	1853	Dr. Bruce Haywood	2-B	687	73
Monmouth Coll, West Long Branch, NJ 07764	1933	Dr. Samuel H. Magill	1-M	4,430	191
Montana Coll of Mineral Science and Tech, Butte, MT 59701	1895	Dr. Lindsay D. Norman, Jr.	5-M	1,818	122
Montana State U, Bozeman, MT 59717	1893	Dr. William J. Tietz	5-D	10,024	550
Montclair State Coll, Upper Montclair, NJ 07043	1908	Dr. Richard A. Lynde	5-M	12,720	701
Moody Bible Inst, Chicago, IL 60610	1886	Dr. Joseph M. Stowell, III	2-M	1,484	102
Moore Coll of Art and Design, Philadelphia, PA 19103 (3)	1844	Dr. Edward C. McGuire	1-B	663	93
Moorhead State U, Moorhead, MN 56560	1887	Dr. Roland Dille	5-M	8,435	NR
Moravian Coll, Bethlehem, PA 18018	1742	Dr. Roger Harry Martin	2-M	1,659	143
Morehead State U, Morehead, KY 40351	1922	Dr. C. Nelson Grote	5-M	7,379	358
Morehouse Coll, Atlanta, GA 30314 (1)	1867	Dr. Leroy Keith, Jr.	1-B	2,685	150
Morgan State U, Baltimore, MD 21239	1867	Dr. Earl Richardson	5-D	3,941	NR
Morningside Coll, Sioux City, IA 51106	1894	Dr. Miles Tommeraasen	2-M	1,216	113
Morris Brown Coll, Atlanta, GA 30314	1881	Dr. Calvert H. Smith	2-B	1,300	NR
Morris Coll, Sumter, SC 29150	1908	Dr. Luns C. Richardson	2-B	774	52
Mount Holyoke Coll, South Hadley, MA 01075 (3)	1837	Mrs. Elizabeth Topham Kennan	1-B	1,947	203
Mount Marty Coll, Yankton, SD 57078	1936	Sr. Jacquelyn Ernster	2-M	871	80
Mount Mary Coll, Milwaukee, WI 53222 (3)	1913	Sr. Ruth Hollenbach	2-M	1,366	137
Mount Mercy Coll, Cedar Rapids, IA 52402	1928	Dr. Thomas R. Feld	2-B	1,568	107
Mount Olive Coll, Mount Olive, NC 28365	1951	Dr. W. Burkette Raper	2-B	997	55
Mount Saint Mary Coll, Newburgh, NY 12550	1930	Dr. Ann Sakac	1-M	1,241	153
Mount Saint Mary's Coll, Los Angeles, CA 90049 (4)	1925	Sr. Magdalen Coughlin	2-M	1,203	141
Mount Saint Mary's Coll, Emmitsburg, MD 21727	1808	Dr. Robert J. Wickenheiser	2-M	1,717	116
Mount Senario Coll, Ladysmith, WI 54848	1962	Mr. Patrick Reidy	1-B	1,056	40
Mount Union Coll, Alliance, OH 44601	1846	Dr. Harold M. Kolenbrander	2-B	1,272	108
Mount Vernon Nazarene Coll, Mount Vernon, OH 43050	1968	Dr. William J. Prince	2-B	1,087	77
Muhlenberg Coll, Allentown, PA 18104	1848	Dr. Jonathan C. Messerli	2-B	1,597	150
Multnomah Sch of the Bible, Portland, OR 97220	1936	Dr. Joseph C. Aldrich	2-M	710	42
Mundelein Coll, Chicago, IL 60660 (4)	1929	Sr. Mary Breslin, BVM	2-M	1,010	97
Murray State U, Murray, KY 42071	1922	Dr. Kala M. Stroup	5-M	7,628	371
Muskegon Coll, Muskegon, MI 49442	1888	Mr. Robert D. Jewell	1-B	1,700	60
Muskingum Coll, New Concord, OH 43762	1837	Dr. Samuel W. Speck, Jr.	2-B	1,101	115
National Coll, Rapid City, SD 57709	1941	Mr. John W. Hauer	3-B	678	47
National Coll of Chiropractic, Lombard, IL 60148	1906	Dr. J. F. Winterstein	1-D	777	92
National Coll of Education, Evanston, IL 60201	1886	NR	1-D	6,208	215
National Ed Ctr–Tampa Tech Inst Cmps, Tampa, FL 33610	1948	Lyle R. Groth	3-B	1,566	63
National U, San Diego, CA 92108	1971	Dr. Frank Hennessy	1-D	12,580	1,817
Nazareth Coll in Kalamazoo, Kalamazoo, MI 49001	1924	Dr. Patrick B. Smith	2-M	730	97

Name, address	Year	Governing official, control, and highest degree offered	Enroll-ment	Faculty
Nazareth Coll of Rochester, Rochester, NY 14610	1924	Dr. Rose Marie Beston 1-M	2,935	153
Nebraska Wesleyan U, Lincoln, NE 68504	1887	Dr. John W. White, Jr. 2-B	1,576	123
Newberry Coll, Newberry, SC 29108	1856	Dr. Hubert H. Setzler, Jr. . . 2-B	686	62
New England Coll, Henniker, NH 03242	1946	William R. O'Connell, Jr. . . 1-M	1,260	116
New England Conservatory of Music, Boston, MA 02115	1867	Andrew Falender 1-M	781	191
New England Inst of Tech, Warwick, RI 02886 (2)	1940	Dr. Richard I. Gouse 1-B	1,585	120
New Hampshire Coll, Manchester, NH 03104	1932	Richard A. Gustafson 1-M	3,373	77
New Jersey Inst of Tech, Newark, NJ 07102	1881	Dr. Saul K. Fenster 13-D	7,668	532
New Mexico Highlands U, Las Vegas, NM 87701	1893	Dr. Gilbert Sanchez 5-M	2,027	98
New Mexico Inst of Mining and Tech, Socorro, NM 87801	1889	Dr. Laurence H. Lattman . . 5-D	1,228	98
New Mexico State U, Las Cruces, NM 88003	1888	Dr. James E. Halligan 5-D	14,284	715
New Sch B A , New Sch for Social Research, New York, NY 10011	1919	Gerald A. Heeger 1-B	207	635
New York Inst of Tech, Old Westbury, NY 11568	1955	Dr. Alexander Schure 1-M	12,575	1,340
New York Sch of Interior Design, New York, NY 10022	1916	Mr. Arthur Satz 1-B	726	70
New York U, New York, NY 10011	1831	Dr. John Brademas 1-D	31,690	5,428
Niagara U, Niagara University, NY 14109	1856	Rev. Donald J. Harrington, CM 1-M	3,050	229
Nicholls State U, Thibodaux, LA 70310	1948	Dr. Donald J. Ayo 5-M	7,165	275
Nichols Coll, Dudley, MA 01570	1815	Dr. Lowell C. Smith 1-M	1,209	49
Norfolk State U, Norfolk, VA 23504	1935	Dr. Harrison B. Wilson . . . 5-M	7,721	511
North Adams State Coll, North Adams, MA 01247	1894	Dr. Catherine Tisinger 5-M	2,584	127
North Carolina A&T State U, Greensboro, NC 27411	1891	Dr. Edward B. Fort 5-M	6,161	410
North Carolina Central U, Durham, NC 27707	1910	Dr. Tyronza R. Richmond . . 5-M	5,182	326
North Carolina Sch of the Arts, Winston-Salem, NC 27117	1963	Dr. Jane E. Milley 5-M	750	122
North Carolina State U, Raleigh, NC 27695	1887	Dr. Bruce R. Poulton 5-D	25,537	1,442
North Carolina Wesleyan Coll, Rocky Mount, NC 27804	1956	Dr. Leslie H. Garner, Jr. . . 2-B	1,516	52
North Central Bible Coll, Minneapolis, MN 55404	1930	Dr. Don H. Argue 2-B	1,167	54
North Central Coll, Naperville, IL 60566	1861	Mr. Gael D. Swing 2-M	2,343	140
North Dakota State U, Fargo, ND 58105	1890	James Ozbun 5-D	9,534	429
Northeastern Illinois U, Chicago, IL 60625	1961	Dr. Gordon Lamb 5-M	9,846	525
Northeastern State U, Tahlequah, OK 74464	1846	Dr. W. Roger Webb 5-D	8,707	329
Northeastern U, Boston, MA 02115	1898	Kenneth G. Ryder 1-D	32,389	2,996
Northeast Louisiana U, Monroe, LA 71209	1931	Dr. Dwight D. Vines 5-D	10,340	428
Northeast Missouri State U, Kirksville, MO 63501	1867	Dr. Charles J. McClain . . . 5-M	6,085	341
Northern Arizona U, Flagstaff, AZ 86011	1899	Dr. Eugene M. Hughes . . . 5-D	15,059	899
Northern Illinois U, De Kalb, IL 60115	1895	Dr. John E. LaTourette . . . 5-D	24,255	1,264
Northern Kentucky U, Highland Heights, KY 41076	1968	Dr. Leon E. Boothe 5-M	9,497	539
Northern Michigan U, Marquette, MI 49855	1899	Dr. James B. Appleberry . . 5-M	7,952	376
Northern Montana Coll, Havre, MT 59501	1929	William C. Merwin 5-M	1,583	103
North Georgia Coll, Dahlonega, GA 30597	1873	Dr. John H. Owen 5-M	2,181	111
Northland Coll, Ashland, WI 54806	1892	Dr. Robert Rue Parsonage . . 2-B	647	62
North Park Coll, Chicago, IL 60625	1891	Dr. David G. Horner 2-B	1,083	85
Northrop U, Los Angeles, CA 90045	1942	Dr. B. J. Shell 1-D	1,813	145
Northwest Coll of the Assemblies of God, Kirkland, WA 98083	1934	Dr. D. V. Hurst 2-B	687	44
Northwestern Coll, Orange City, IA 51041	1882	Dr. James E. Bultman 2-M	965	88
Northwestern Coll, St Paul, MN 55113	1902	Donald Ericksen 2-B	973	78
Northwestern Oklahoma State U, Alva, OK 73717	1897	Dr. Joe J. Struckle 5-M	1,751	93
Northwestern State U of Louisiana, Natchitoches, LA 71497	1884	Dr. Roberts A. Alost 5-M	6,455	246
Northwestern U, Evanston, IL 60208	1851	Dr. Arnold R. Weber 1-D	11,337	729
Northwest Missouri State U, Maryville, MO 64468	1905	Dr. Dean L. Hubbard 5-M	5,337	288
Northwest Nazarene Coll, Nampa, ID 83651	1913	Dr. A. Gordon Wetmore . . . 2-M	1,095	97
Northwood Inst, Midland, MI 48640	1959	Dr. David E. Fry 1-B	1,785	62
Norwich U, Northfield, VT 05663	1819	Lt. Gen. W. Russel Todd . . 1-M	2,246	242
Notre Dame Coll, Manchester, NH 03104	1950	Dr. Carol J. Descoteaux, CSC 2-M	772	80
Notre Dame Coll of Ohio, Cleveland, OH 44121 (3)	1922	Sr. Marla Loehr, SND 2-B	751	79
Nova U, Fort Lauderdale, FL 33314	1964	Dr. Abraham S. Fischler . . 1-D	7,800	65
Nyack Coll, Nyack, NY 10960	1882	Mr. Rexford A. Boda 2-M	814	77
Oakland City Coll, Oakland City, IN 47660	1885	Dr. James W. Murray 2-M	646	NR
Oakland U, Rochester, MI 48063	1957	Dr. Joseph E. Champagne . . 5-D	12,254	617
Oakwood Coll, Huntsville, AL 35896	1896	Dr. Benjamin F. Reaves . . 2-B	1,200	105
Oberlin Coll, Oberlin, OH 44074	1833	S. Frederick Starr 1-M	2,857	230
Occidental Coll, Los Angeles, CA 90041	1887	Dr. John B. Slaughter 1-M	1,694	171
Oglethorpe U, Atlanta, GA 30319	1835	Dr. Donald S. Stanton 1-M	1,047	74
Ohio Dominican Coll, Columbus, OH 43219	1911	Sr. Mary Andrew Matesich . . 2-B	1,331	86
Ohio Northern U, Ada, OH 45810	1871	Dr. DeBow Freed 2-D	2,540	181
Ohio State U, Columbus, OH 43210	1870	Dr. Edward Jennings 5-D	53,669	3,848
Ohio State U–Lima Cmps, Lima, OH 45804	1960	Dr. James S. Biddle 5-B	1,276	41
Ohio State U–Mansfield Cmps, Mansfield, OH 44906	1958	Dr. John O. Riedl, Jr. 5-B	1,277	52
Ohio State U–Marion Cmps, Marion, OH 43302	1957	Francis E. Hazard 5-B	1,137	33
Ohio State U–Newark Cmps, Newark, OH 43055	1957	Dr. Julius S. Greenstein . . 5-B	1,503	41
Ohio U, Athens, OH 45701	1804	Dr. Charles J. Ping 5-D	15,500	950
Ohio U–Chillicothe, Chillicothe, OH 45601	1946	Dr. Delbert Meyer 5-B	1,468	63
Ohio U–Ironton, Ironton, OH 45638	1956	Mr. Bill Dingus 5-B	1,303	89
Ohio U–Lancaster, Lancaster, OH 43130	1968	Dr. Raymond Wilkes 5-M	625	100
Ohio U–Zanesville, Zanesville, OH 43701	1946	Dr. Craig D. Laubenthal . . 5-M	1,230	49
Ohio Wesleyan U, Delaware, OH 43015	1842	Dr. David L. Warren 2-B	1,839	154
Oklahoma Baptist U, Shawnee, OK 74801	1910	Dr. Bob R. Agee 2-B	1,967	128
Oklahoma Christian Coll, Oklahoma City, OK 73136	1950	Dr. Terry Johnson 2-M	1,627	111
Oklahoma City U, Oklahoma City, OK 73106	1904	Dr. Jerald C. Walker 2-M	3,535	212
Oklahoma Panhandle State U, Goodwell, OK 73939	1909	Mr. William Larry Boyd . . . 5-B	1,182	71
Oklahoma State U, Stillwater, OK 74078	1890	Dr. John Campbell 5-D	20,764	664
Old Dominion U, Norfolk, VA 23529	1930	Dr. Joseph M. Marchello . . 5-D	15,656	703
Olivet Coll, Olivet, MI 49076	1844	Dr. Donald A. Morris 2-B	784	63
Olivet Nazarene U, Kankakee, IL 60901	1907	Dr. Leslie Parrott 2-M	1,774	115
Oral Roberts U, Tulsa, OK 74171	1963	Mr. G. Oral Roberts 2-D	4,218	390
Oregon Health Sciences U, Portland, OR 97201	1974	Dr. Peter O. Kohler 5-D	1,246	50
Oregon Inst of Tech, Klamath Falls, OR 97601	1947	Dr. Larry J. Blake 5-B	3,026	144
Oregon State U, Corvallis, OR 97331	1868	Dr. John V. Byrne 5-D	15,637	2,366
Orlando Coll, Orlando, FL 32810	1918	Mrs. Ouida B. Kirby 1-M	846	40
Otis Art Inst of Parsons Sch of Des, New Sch for Soc Res, Los Angeles, CA 90057	1917	Roger Workman 1-M	854	208
Otterbein Coll, Westerville, OH 43081	1847	Dr. C. Brent DeVore 2-B	2,209	164
Ouachita Baptist U, Arkadelphia, AR 71923	1886	Dr. Daniel R. Grant 2-M	1,403	101

Name, address	Year	Governing official, control, and highest degree offered	Enrollment	Faculty
Our Lady of Holy Cross Coll, New Orleans, LA 70131	1916	Rev. Thomas E. Chambers, CSC ... 2-M	848	62
Our Lady of the Lake U of San Antonio, San Antonio, TX 78207	1911	Sr. Elizabeth Anne Sueltenfuss ... 2-M	2,245	130
Pace U, New York, NY 10038	1906	Dr. Edward J. Mortola ... 1-D	9,657	542
Pace U, Pleasantville/Briarcliff Cmps, Pleasantville, NY 10570	1963	Dr. Richard Podgorski ... 1-M	4,104	644
Pace U, White Plains Cmps, White Plains, NY 10603	1923	Dr. Margaret R. Gotti ... 1-D	4,324	644
Pacific Lutheran U, Tacoma, WA 98447	1890	Dr. William O. Rieke ... 2-M	3,975	292
Pacific Union Coll, Angwin, CA 94508	1882	Dr. D. Malcolm Maxwell ... 2-M	1,640	127
Pacific U, Forest Grove, OR 97116	1849	Dr. Robert F. Duvall ... 1-D	1,360	193
Paine Coll, Augusta, GA 30910	1882	Dr. Julius S. Scott, Jr. ... 2-B	606	68
Palm Beach Atlantic Coll, West Palm Beach, FL 33402	1968	Dr. Claude Rhea ... 2-B	1,135	81
Pan American U, Edinburg, TX 78539	1927	Dr. Miguel A. Nevarez ... 5-M	11,218	385
Park Coll, Parkville, MO 64152	1875	Dr. Donald J. Breckon ... 2-M	653	76
Parks Coll of Saint Louis U, Cahokia, IL 62206	1927	Dr. Paul A. Whelan ... 2-B	1,117	60
Parsons Sch of Design, New Sch for Social Research, New York, NY 10011	1896	David Levy ... 1-M	1,820	356
Pembroke State U, Pembroke, NC 28372	1887	Dr. Paul R. Givens ... 5-M	2,835	165
Pennsylvania Coll of Optometry, Philadelphia, PA 19141	1919	Dr. Melvin D. Wolfberg ... 1-D	634	67
Penna State U at Erie, The Behrend Coll, Erie, PA 16563	1926	Dr. John M. Lilley ... 13-M	2,830	151
Penna State U at Harrisburg—The Capital Coll, Middletown, PA 17057	1966	Dr. Ruth Leventhal ... 13-D	3,144	180
Penna State U Univ Park Cmps, University Park, PA 16802	1855	Dr. Bryce Jordan ... 13-D	37,269	1,986
Pepperdine U, Culver City, CA 90230	1937	Dr. David Davenport ... 2-D	3,739	118
Pepperdine U, Malibu, CA 90265	1937	Dr. David Davenport ... 2-D	3,396	279
Peru State Coll, Peru, NE 68421	1867	Dr. Jerry L. Gallentine ... 5-M	1,552	82
Pfeiffer Coll, Misenheimer, NC 28109	1885	Dr. Zane E. Eargle ... 2-M	883	65
Philadelphia Coll of Pharmacy and Science, Philadelphia, PA 19104	1821	Dr. Allen Misher ... 1-D	1,619	161
Philadelphia Coll of Textiles and Science, Philadelphia, PA 19144	1884	Dr. James P. Gallagher ... 1-M	3,417	NR
Phillips U, Enid, OK 73702	1906	Dr. Robert Peck ... 2-D	942	70
Pikeville Coll, Pikeville, KY 41501	1889	Mr. Jerry Waddell ... 2-B	915	64
Pine Manor Coll, Chestnut Hill, MA 02167 (3)	1911	Rosemary Ashby ... 1-B	620	66
Pittsburg State U, Pittsburg, KS 66762	1903	Dr. Donald W. Wilson ... 5-M	5,609	283
Pitzer Coll, Claremont, CA 91711	1963	Dr. Frank L. Ellsworth ... 1-B	770	85
Plymouth State Coll of the U System of NH, Plymouth, NH 03264	1871	Dr. William J. Farrell ... 5-M	3,400	200
Point Loma Nazarene Coll, San Diego, CA 92106	1902	Dr. Jim L. Bond ... 2-M	2,165	NR
Point Park Coll, Pittsburgh, PA 15222	1960	Dr. J. Matthew Simon ... 1-M	2,812	171
Polytechnic U, Brooklyn Cmps, Brooklyn, NY 11201	1854	Dr. George Bugliarello ... 1-D	2,652	393
Polytechnic U, Farmingdale Cmps, Farmingdale, NY 11735	1854	Dr. James J. Conti ... 1-D	1,095	393
Pomona Coll, Claremont, CA 91711	1887	Dr. David Alexander ... 1-B	1,402	189
Portland State U, Portland, OR 97207	1946	Dr. Natale A. Sicuro ... 5-D	16,021	726
Post Coll, Waterbury, CT 06708	1890	Dr. N. Patricia Yarborough ... 1-B	1,654	276
Prairie View A&M U, Prairie View, TX 77446	1878	Dr. Percy A. Pierre ... 5-M	5,307	286
Pratt Inst, Brooklyn, NY 11205	1887	Mr. Richardson Pratt, Jr. ... 1-M	3,536	504
Presbyterian Coll, Clinton, SC 29325	1880	Dr. Kenneth B. Orr ... 2-B	1,112	97
Princeton U, Princeton, NJ 08544	1746	Harold T. Shapiro ... 1-D	6,140	800
Principia Coll, Elsah, IL 62028	1910	Dr. John E. G. Boyman ... 2-B	639	79
Providence Coll, Providence, RI 02918	1917	Rev. John F. Cunningham, OP ... 2-D	4,329	279
Purdue U, West Lafayette, IN 47907	1869	Dr. Steven C. Beering ... 5-D	34,969	NR
Purdue U Calumet, Hammond, IN 46323	1951	Prof. Richard J. Combs ... 5-M	7,386	404
Queens Coll, Charlotte, NC 28274	1857	Dr. Billy O. Wireman ... 2-M	1,384	94
Queens Coll of the City U of New York, Flushing, NY 11367	1937	Dr. Shirley Strum Kenny ... 12-M	16,948	1,183
Quincy Coll, Quincy, IL 62301	1860	Rev. James Toal OFM ... 2-M	1,527	87
Quinnipiac Coll, Hamden, CT 06518	1929	Dr. John L. Lahey ... 1-M	2,925	NR
Radford U, Radford, VA 24142	1910	Dr. Donald N. Dedmon ... 5-M	8,764	418
Ramapo Coll of New Jersey, Mahwah, NJ 07430	1969	Dr. Robert A. Scott ... 5-B	4,058	218
Randolph-Macon Coll, Ashland, VA 23005	1830	Dr. Ladell Payne ... 2-B	1,121	126
Randolph-Macon Woman's Coll, Lynchburg, VA 24503 (3)	1891	Ms. Linda Koch Lorimer ... 2-B	765	87
Reed Coll, Portland, OR 97202	1909	Mr. James L. Powell ... 1-M	1,286	117
Regis Coll, Denver, CO 80221	1877	Rev. David M. Clarke, SJ ... 2-M	5,100	95
Regis Coll, Weston, MA 02193 (3)	1927	Sr. Therese Higgins ... 2-B	1,025	106
Rensselaer Polytechnic Inst, Troy, NY 12180	1824	Roland W. Schmitt ... 1-D	6,371	400
Rhode Island Coll, Providence, RI 02908	1854	Dr. Carol J. Guardo ... 5-M	8,044	422
Rhode Island Sch of Design, Providence, RI 02903	1877	Dr. Thomas F. Schutte ... 1-M	1,918	275
Rhodes Coll, Memphis, TN 38112	1848	Dr. James H. Daughdrill, Jr. ... 2-B	1,346	149
Rice U, Houston, TX 77251	1891	Dr. George Rupp ... 1-D	3,850	454
Rider Coll, Lawrenceville, NJ 08648	1865	Dr. Frank N. Elliott ... 1-M	4,139	275
Rio Grande Coll/Comm Coll, Rio Grande, OH 45674	1876	Dr. Paul C. Hayes ... 1-B	1,884	108
Ripon Coll, Ripon, WI 54971	1851	Mr. William R. Stott, Jr. ... 1-B	857	164
Rivier Coll, Nashua, NH 03060 (3)	1933	Sr. Jeanne Perreault ... 2-M	2,500	53
Roanoke Coll, Salem, VA 24153	1842	Dr. Norman D. Fintel ... 2-B	1,594	116
Roberts Wesleyan Coll, Rochester, NY 14624	1866	Dr. William C. Crothers ... 2-B	820	79
Rochester Inst of Tech, Rochester, NY 14623	1829	Dr. M. Richard Rose ... 1-M	13,181	1,127
Rockford Coll, Rockford, IL 61108	1847	Dr. Gretchen Kreuter ... 1-M	1,480	75
Rockhurst Coll, Kansas City, MO 64110	1910	Rev. Thomas J. Savage, SJ ... 2-M	2,034	173
Rocky Mountain Coll, Billings, MT 59102	1878	Dr. Arthur H. DeRosier, Jr. ... 2-B	705	51
Roger Williams Coll, Bristol, RI 02809	1948	Mr. William H. Rizzini ... 1-B	2,000	208
Rollins Coll, Winter Park, FL 32789	1885	Dr. Thaddeus Seymour ... 1-M	2,051	131
Roosevelt U, Chicago, IL 60605	1945	Dr. Theodore L. Gross ... 1-M	6,142	508
Rosary Coll, River Forest, IL 60305	1848	Sr. Jean Murray ... 2-M	1,625	83
Rose-Hulman Inst of Tech, Terre Haute, IN 47803 (1)	1874	Dr. Samuel F. Hulbert ... 1-M	1,360	97
Rosemont Coll, Rosemont, PA 19010 (3)	1921	Dr. Dorothy McKenna Brown ... 2-B	613	99
Rush U, Chicago, IL 60612	1969	Dr. Leo M. Henikoff ... 1-D	1,126	170
Russell Sage Coll, Troy, NY 12180 (3)	1916	Dr. Sara Chapman ... 1-M	2,227	174
Rust Coll, Holly Springs, MS 38635	1866	Dr. William A. McMillan ... 2-B	925	61
Rutgers, State U of NJ, Camden Coll of Arts and Scis, Camden, NJ 08102	1950	NR ... 5-B	3,063	NR

Name, address	Year	Governing official, control, and highest degree offered		Enrollment	Faculty
Rutgers, State U of NJ, Coll of Engineering, Piscataway, NJ 08855	1864	Dr. Ellis H. Dill	5-B	2,567	NR
Rutgers, State U of NJ, Coll of Nursing, Newark, NJ 07102 (4)	1956	NR	5-B	412	NR
Rutgers, State U of NJ, Coll of Pharmacy, New Brunswick, NJ 08903	1927	Dr. John L. Coldizzi	5-B	774	NR
Rutgers, State U of NJ, Cook Coll, New Brunswick, NJ 08903	1921	NR	5-B	3,009	NR
Rutgers, State U of NJ, Douglass Coll, New Brunswick, NJ 08903 (3)	1918	Dr. Mary S. Hartman	5-B	3,341	NR
Rutgers, State U of NJ, Livingston Coll, New Brunswick, NJ 08903	1969	NR	5-B	3,576	NR
Rutgers, State U of NJ, Mason Gross Sch of Arts, New Brunswick, NJ 08903	1976	NR	5-M	639	NR
Rutgers, State U of NJ, Newark Coll of Arts and Scis, Newark, NJ 07102	1946	Norman Samuels	5-B	3,621	NR
Rutgers, State U of NJ, Rutgers Coll, New Brunswick, NJ 08903	1766	NR	5-B	8,563	NR
Rutgers, State U of NJ, U Coll–Camden, Camden, NJ 08102	1950	NR	5-B	973	NR
Rutgers, State U of NJ, U Coll–Newark, Newark, NJ 07102	1934	Norman Samuels	5-B	1,978	NR
Rutgers, State U of NJ, U Coll–New Brunswick, New Brunswick, NJ 08903	1934	Amy Cohen	5-B	3,101	NR
Sacred Heart U, Fairfield, CT 06432	1963	Dr. Anthony J. Cernera	2-M	4,341	304
Saginaw Valley State U, University Center, MI 48710	1963	Dr. Jack M. Ryder	5-M	5,870	313
St Ambrose U, Davenport, IA 52803	1882	Dr. Edward J. Rogalski	2-M	2,200	157
St Andrews Presbyterian Coll, Laurinburg, NC 28352	1958	Dr. Thomas L. Reuschling	2-B	801	66
Saint Anselm Coll, Manchester, NH 03102	1889	Br. Joachim W. Froehlich, OSB	2-B	1,833	145
Saint Augustine's Coll, Raleigh, NC 27610	1867	Dr. Prezell R. Robinson	2-B	1,828	112
St Bonaventure U, St Bonaventure, NY 14778	1854	Very Rev. Mathia Doyle, OFM	2-M	2,852	199
St Cloud State U, St Cloud, MN 56301	1869	Dr. Brendan McDonald	5-M	16,252	716
Saint Francis Coll, Fort Wayne, IN 46808	1890	Sr. M. JoEllen Scheetz	2-M	1,031	80
St Francis Coll, Brooklyn Heights, NY 11201	1858	Br. Donald Sullivan, OSF	1-B	1,929	128
Saint Francis Coll, Loretto, PA 15940	1847	Rev. Christian R. Oravec	2-M	1,274	81
St John Fisher Coll, Rochester, NY 14618	1948	Dr. William L. Pickett	1-M	1,987	131
Saint John's U, Collegeville, MN 56321 (1)	1857	Fr. Hilary Thimmesh, OSB	2-M	1,998	156
Saint John's U, Jamaica, NY 11439	1870	Very Rev. Joseph T. Cahill, CM	2-D	19,143	916
Saint Joseph Coll, West Hartford, CT 06117 (3)	1932	Dr. M. Paton Ryan, RSM	2-M	1,310	118
Saint Joseph's Coll, Rensselaer, IN 47978	1889	Fr. Charles Banet	2-M	1,001	85
Saint Joseph's Coll, Windham, ME 04062	1912	Loring E. Hart	2-B	622	73
St Joseph's Coll, Brooklyn, NY 11205	1916	Sr. George A. O'Connor	1-B	794	98
St Joseph's Coll, Suffolk Cmps, Patchogue, NY 11772	1916	Sr. George Aquin O'Connor	1-B	1,766	145
Saint Joseph's U, Philadelphia, PA 19131	1851	Rev. Nicholas S. Rashford, SJ	2-M	5,715	160
St Lawrence U, Canton, NY 13617	1856	Patti McGill Peterson	1-M	2,224	194
Saint Leo Coll, Saint Leo, FL 33574	1889	Rev. Msgr. Frank Mouch	2-B	1,120	77
St Louis Coll of Pharmacy, St Louis, MO 63110	1864	Dr. Sumner M. Robinson	1-D	750	54
Saint Louis U, St Louis, MO 63103	1818	Rev. Lawrence Biondi	2-D	11,148	904
Saint Martin's Coll, Lacey, WA 98503	1895	Dr. David Spangler	2-M	635	50
Saint Mary Coll, Leavenworth, KS 66048	1923	Sr. M. Janet McGilley	2-B	1,071	107
Saint Mary of the Plains Coll, Dodge City, KS 67801	1952	Dr. Michael J. McCarthy	2-B	908	87
Saint Mary-of-the-Woods Coll, Saint Mary-of-the-Woods, IN 47876 (3)	1840	Barbara Doherty, SP	2-M	910	55
Saint Mary's Coll, Notre Dame, IN 46556 (3)	1844	Dr. William A. Hickey	2-B	1,821	180
Saint Mary's Coll of California, Moraga, CA 94575	1863	Br. Mel Anderson	2-M	3,310	180
St Mary's Coll of Maryland, St Mary's City, MD 20686	1839	Dr. Edward T. Lewis	5-B	1,345	107
Saint Mary's Coll of Minnesota, Winona, MN 55987	1912	Br. Louis DeThomasis, FSC	2-M	1,686	114
St Mary's U of San Antonio, San Antonio, TX 78284	1852	Rev. John Moder, SM	2-D	3,654	216
Saint Michael's Coll, Winooski, VT 05404	1904	Dr. Paul J. Reiss	2-M	2,287	151
St Norbert Coll, De Pere, WI 54115	1898	Dr. Thomas A. Manion	2-M	1,851	143
St Olaf Coll, Northfield, MN 55057	1874	Dr. Melvin George	2-B	3,121	382
Saint Paul's Coll, Lawrenceville, VA 23868	1888	Dr. Marvin B. Scott	2-B	736	38
Saint Peter's Coll, Jersey City, NJ 07306	1872	Rev. Edward Glynn, SJ	2-M	3,346	452
St Thomas Aquinas Coll, Sparkill, NY 10976	1958	Dr. Donald T. McNelis	1-M	2,063	115
St Thomas U, Miami, FL 33054	1961	Dr. Pasquale DiPasquale, Jr.	2-M	2,500	202
Saint Vincent Coll, Latrobe, PA 15650	1846	Rev. John F. Murtha, OSB	2-B	1,193	85
Saint Xavier Coll, Chicago, IL 60655	1847	Dr. Ronald Champagne	2-M	2,641	195
Salem Coll, Winston-Salem, NC 27108 (3)	1772	Dr. Thomas V. Litzenburg, Jr.	2-B	667	79
Salem Coll, Salem, WV 26426	1888	Dr. Ronald E. Ohl	1-M	750	57
Salem State Coll, Salem, MA 01970	1854	Rolando Bonachea	5-M	8,654	323
Salisbury State U, Salisbury, MD 21801	1925	Dr. Thomas A. Bellavance	5-M	5,260	220
Salve Regina Coll, Newport, RI 02840	1934	Dr. M. Lucille McKillop, RSM	2-M	2,252	203
Samford U, Birmingham, AL 35229	1841	Dr. Thomas E. Corts	2-D	4,089	271
Sam Houston State U, Huntsville, TX 77341	1879	Dr. Elliott T. Bowers	5-D	11,550	387
San Diego State U, San Diego, CA 92182	1897	Dr. Thomas B. Day	5-D	35,821	2,821
San Francisco Art Inst, San Francisco, CA 94133	1871	Dr. William O. Barrett	1-M	723	NR
San Francisco State U, San Francisco, CA 94132	1899	NR	5-D	26,835	1,778
Sangamon State U, Springfield, IL 62794	1969	Dr. Durward Long	5-M	3,942	185
San Jose State U, San Jose, CA 95192	1857	Dr. Gail Fullerton	5-M	28,415	2,033
Santa Clara U, Santa Clara, CA 95053	1851	Rev. Paul L. Locateili, SJ	2-D	7,802	545
Sarah Lawrence Coll, Bronxville, NY 10708	1926	Dr. Alice Stone Ilchman	1-M	1,150	154
Savannah Coll of Art and Design, Savannah, GA 31401	1976	Richard G. Rowan	1-M	1,397	70
Savannah State Coll, Savannah, GA 31404	1890	Dr. Wiley S. Bolden	5-M	1,932	149
Sch for Lifelong Learning of the U System of NH, Durham, NH 03824	1972	Eric Brown	12-B	627	200
Sch of the Art Inst of Chicago, Chicago, IL 60603	1866	Mr. Anthony Jones	1-M	2,149	347
Sch of the Museum of Fine Arts, Boston, MA 02115	1876	Bruce K. MacDonald	1-M	664	61
Sch of the Ozarks, Point Lookout, MO 65726	1906	Dr. Jerry Davis	1-B	1,310	98
Sch of Visual Arts, New York, NY 10010	1947	David Rhodes	3-M	2,188	690
Schreiner Coll, Kerrville, TX 78028	1923	Dr. Sam M. Junkin	2-B	602	57
Scripps Coll, Claremont, CA 91711 (3)	1926	Dr. John H. Chandler	1-B	607	84
Seattle Pacific U, Seattle, WA 98119	1891	Rev. Msgr. John J. Strynkowski	2-M	3,356	240
Seattle U, Seattle, WA 98122	1891	Rev. William J. Sullivan, SJ	2-D	4,379	230

Name, address	Year	Governing official, control, and highest degree offered		Enrollment	Faculty
Seton Hall U, South Orange, NJ 07079	1856	Msgr. John J. Petillo	2-D	8,695	470
Seton Hill Coll, Greensburg, PA 15601 (4)	1883	JoAnne W. Boyle	2-B	870	84
Shawnee State U, Portsmouth, OH 45662	1986	Dr. Robert L. Ewigleben	5-B	2,967	233
Shenandoah Coll and Conservatory, Winchester, VA 22601	1875	Dr. James A. Davis	2-M	1,007	130
Shepherd Coll, Shepherdstown, WV 25443	1871	Dr. James A. Butcher	5-B	4,020	172
Shippensburg U of Pennsylvania, Shippensburg, PA 17257	1871	Dr. Anthony F. Ceddia	5-M	6,352	356
Shorter Coll, Rome, GA 30161	1873	Dr. James D. Jordan	2-B	832	76
Siena Coll, Loudonville, NY 12211	1937	Fr. Hugh F. Hines	2-B	3,604	223
Siena Heights Coll, Adrian, MI 49221	1919	Sr. Cathleen Real, CMH	2-M	1,599	110
Silver Lake Coll, Manitowoc, WI 54220	1869	Sr. Barbara Belinske	2-M	795	108
Simmons Coll, Boston, MA 02115 (3)	1899	William J. Holmes	1-D	2,889	304
Simpson Coll, Indianola, IA 50125	1860	Dr. Stephen G. Jennings	2-B	1,710	134
Sioux Falls Coll, Sioux Falls, SD 57105	1883	Dr. Thomas F. Johnson	2-M	900	66
Skidmore Coll, Saratoga Springs, NY 12866	1911	Dr. David H. Porter	1-B	2,165	220
Slippery Rock U of Pennsylvania, Slippery Rock, PA 16057	1889	Dr. Robert Aebersold	5-M	7,360	381
Smith Coll, Northampton, MA 01063 (3)	1871	Mrs. Mary Maples Dunn	1-D	2,834	296
Sonoma State U, Rohnert Park, CA 94928	1961	Dr. David W. Benson	5-M	6,697	318
South Carolina State Coll, Orangeburg, SC 29117	1896	Dr. Albert E. Smith	5-M	4,399	269
South Dakota Sch of Mines and Tech, Rapid City, SD 57701	1885	Dr. Richard J. Gowen	5-D	2,062	126
South Dakota State U, Brookings, SD 57007	1881	Dr. Robert T. Wagner	5-D	6,871	490
Southeastern Coll of the Assemblies of God, Lakeland, FL 33801	1935	Dr. James Hennesy	2-B	1,155	71
Southeastern Louisiana U, Hammond, LA 70402	1925	Dr. G. Warren Smith	5-M	8,655	377
Southeastern Massachusetts U, North Dartmouth, MA 02747	1895	Dr. John R. Brazil	5-M	6,162	440
Southeastern Oklahoma State U, Durant, OK 74701	1909	Dr. Larry Williams	5-M	3,632	174
Southeastern U, Washington, DC 20024	1879	Dr. W. Robert Higgins	1-M	1,038	163
Southeast Missouri State U, Cape Girardeau, MO 63701	1873	Dr. Bill W. Stacy	5-M	8,778	500
Southern Arkansas U, Magnolia, AR 71753	1909	Dr. Harold T. Brinson	5-M	2,159	116
Southern California Coll, Costa Mesa, CA 92626	1920	Mr. Wayne E. Kraiss	2-M	949	81
Southern Coll of Seventh-Day Adventists, Collegedale, TN 37315	1892	Dr. Donald R. Sahly	2-B	1,443	120
Southern Coll of Tech, Marietta, GA 30060	1948	Dr. Stephen R. Cheshier	5-M	3,778	190
Southern Connecticut State U, New Haven, CT 06515	1893	Mr. Michael J. Adanti	5-M	12,800	677
Southern Illinois U at Carbondale, Carbondale, IL 62901	1869	John C. Guyon	5-D	24,227	NR
Southern Illinois U at Edwardsville, Edwardsville, IL 62026	1957	Earl E. Lazerson	5-D	11,352	743
Southern Methodist U, Dallas, TX 75275	1911	Mr. A. Kenneth Pye	1-D	8,944	NR
Southern Nazarene U, Bethany, OK 73008	1899	Dr. Ponder W. Gilliland	2-M	1,358	104
Southern Oregon State Coll, Ashland, OR 97520	1926	Dr. Joseph Cox	5-M	4,853	288
Southern Utah State Coll, Cedar City, UT 84720	1897	Gerald R. Sherratt	5-M	3,036	145
Southern Vermont Coll, Bennington, VT 05201	1926	Dr. William A. Glasser	1-B	635	56
Southwest Baptist U, Bolivar, MO 65613	1878	Dr. James L. Sells	2-M	2,909	195
Southwestern Adventist Coll, Keene, TX 76059	1894	Dr. Marvin E. Anderson	2-M	778	56
Southwestern Coll, Winfield, KS 67156	1885	Dr. Bruce Blake	2-M	663	72
Southwestern Oklahoma State U, Weatherford, OK 73096	1903	Dr. Leonard G. Campbell	5-M	5,478	237
Southwestern U, Georgetown, TX 78626	1840	Dr. Roy B. Shilling, Jr.	2-B	1,171	111
Southwest Missouri State U, Springfield, MO 65804	1905	Dr. Marshall Gordon	5-M	17,561	803
Southwest State U, Marshall, MN 56258	1963	Dr. Doug Treadway	5-B	2,475	108
Spalding U, Louisville, KY 40203	1814	Dr. Eileen M. Egan	2-D	1,141	91
Spelman Coll, Atlanta, GA 30314 (3)	1881	Dr. Johnetta Cole	1-B	1,742	167
Spring Arbor Coll, Spring Arbor, MI 49283	1873	Dr. Dorsey W. Brause	2-B	782	79
Springfield Coll, Springfield, MA 01109	1885	Dr. Frank S. Falcone	1-D	2,502	259
Spring Garden Coll, Philadelphia, PA 19119	1851	Dr. Daniel N. DeLucca	1-B	1,224	100
Spring Hill Coll, Mobile, AL 36608	1830	Very Rev. Paul S. Tipton, SJ	2-M	1,036	87
Stanford U, Stanford, CA 94305	1891	Dr. Donald Kennedy	1-D	13,224	1,315
State U of NY at Albany, Albany, NY 12222	1844	Vincent I. O'Leary	5-D	16,219	946
State U of NY at Binghamton, Binghamton, NY 13901	1946	Clifford D. Clark	5-D	12,588	756
State U of NY at Buffalo, Buffalo, NY 14260	1846	Dr. Steven B. Sample	5-D	24,942	2,005
State U of NY at Stony Brook, Stony Brook, NY 11794	1957	Dr. John H. Marburger, III	5-D	14,799	1,465
State U of NY Coll at Brockport, Brockport, NY 14420	1867	Dr. John E. Van de Wetering	5-M	7,371	555
State U of NY Coll at Buffalo, Buffalo, NY 14222	1871	Dr. Richard A. Wiesen	5-M	12,718	596
State U of NY Coll at Cortland, Cortland, NY 13045	1868	Dr. James M. Clark	5-M	6,430	380
State U of NY Coll at Fredonia, Fredonia, NY 14063	1867	Dr. Donald A. MacPhee	5-M	4,094	310
State U of NY Coll at Geneseo, Geneseo, NY 14454	1867	Dr. Robert W. MacVittie	5-M	4,557	282
State U of NY Coll at New Paltz, New Paltz, NY 12561	1828	Alice Chandler	5-M	8,128	455
State U of NY Coll at Old Westbury, Old Westbury, NY 11568	1965	Dr. L. Eudora Pettigrew	5-B	3,946	148
State U of NY Coll at Oneonta, Oneonta, NY 13820	1889	Dr. Alan B. Donovan	5-M	6,000	320
State U of NY Coll at Oswego, Oswego, NY 13126	1861	Dr. Stephen Weber	5-M	8,375	427
State U of NY Coll at Plattsburgh, Plattsburgh, NY 12901	1889	Dr. Charles Warren	5-M	5,959	404
State U of NY Coll at Potsdam, Potsdam, NY 13676	1816	Dr. John Marshall	5-M	4,273	263
State U of NY Coll at Purchase, Purchase, NY 10577	1967	Dr. Sheldon Grebstein	5-M	2,410	284
State U of NY Coll of Envmntl Sci & Forestry, Syracuse, NY 13210	1911	Dr. Ross S. Whaley	5-D	1,222	122
State U of NY Coll of Tech at Utica/Rome, Utica, NY 13504	1966	Dr. Peter J. Cayan	5-M	2,620	172
State U of NY Empire State Coll, Saratoga Springs, NY 12866	1971	Dr. James W. Hall	5-M	5,913	333
State U of NY Health Science Ctr at Brooklyn, Brooklyn, NY 11203	1858	Dr. Donald J. Scherl	5-D	1,700	144
State U of NY Health Science Ctr at Syracuse, Syracuse, NY 13210	1950	Dr. John Bernard Henry	5-D	980	NR
State U of NY Maritime Coll, Throgs Neck, NY 10465	1874	Rear Adm. Floyd Miller	5-M	837	109
Stephen F Austin State U, Nacogdoches, TX 75962	1923	Dr. William R. Johnson	5-D	12,564	450
Stephens Coll, Columbia, MO 65215 (4)	1833	Dr. Patsy H. Sampson	1-B	1,256	76
Stetson U, DeLand, FL 32720	1883	Dr. H. Douglas Lee	2-D	2,975	164
Stevens Inst of Tech, Hoboken, NJ 07030	1870	Dr. Harold J. Raveche	1-D	3,200	250
Stockton State Coll, Pomona, NJ 08240	1971	Dr. Vera King Farris	5-B	5,297	243
Stonehill Coll, North Easton, MA 02357	1948	Rev. Bartley MacPhaidin	2-B	1,964	171
Strayer Coll, Washington, DC 20005	1892	Charles E. Palmer, Jr.	3-M	1,587	74
Suffolk U, Boston, MA 02114	1906	Dr. Daniel H. Perlman	1-D	5,444	348
Sul Ross State U, Alpine, TX 79832	1917	Dr. Jack W. Humphries	5-M	2,313	118
Susquehanna U, Selinsgrove, PA 17870	1858	Dr. Joel L. Cunningham	2-B	1,476	143
Swarthmore Coll, Swarthmore, PA 19081	1864	Dr. David W. Fraser	1-B	1,333	179
Syracuse U, Syracuse, NY 13244	1870	Dr. Melvin A. Eggers	1-D	16,821	1,050
Tampa Coll, Tampa, FL 33614	1890	Mr. Donald C. Jones	1-M	1,577	94

Name, address	Year	Governing official, control, and highest degree offered		Enrollment	Faculty
Tarkio Coll, Tarkio, MO 64491	1883	Dr. Roy McIntosh	2-B	784	54
Tarleton State U, Stephenville, TX 76402	1899	Dr. Barry B. Thompson	5-M	5,667	223
Taylor U, Upland, IN 46989	1846	Dr. Jay L. Kesler	1-B	1,661	120
Temple U, Philadelphia, PA 19122	1884	Mr. Peter J. Liacouras	13-D	28,056	2,062
Tennessee State U, Nashville, TN 37209	1912	Dr. Otis Floyd	5-D	8,270	444
Tennessee Tech U, Cookeville, TN 38505	1915	Dr. Angelo A. Volpe	5-D	8,006	674
Tennessee Temple U, Chattanooga, TN 37404	1946	NR	2-D	1,400	114
Tennessee Wesleyan Coll, Athens, TN 37303	1857	Dr. James E. Cheek	2-B	601	56
Texas A&I U, Kingsville, TX 78363	1925	Dr. Steven Altman	5-M	5,612	234
Texas A&M U, College Station, TX 77843	1876	Dr. William H. Moblem	5-D	39,163	2,151
Texas A&M U at Galveston, Galveston, TX 77553	1971	Dr. William J. Merrell	5-B	743	60
Texas Christian U, Fort Worth, TX 76129	1873	Dr. William Tucker	2-D	6,993	385
Texas Lutheran Coll, Seguin, TX 78155	1891	Dr. Charles H. Oestreich	2-B	1,006	79
Texas Southern U, Houston, TX 77004	1947	Dr. William H. Harris	5-D	8,672	448
Texas Tech U, Lubbock, TX 79409	1923	Lauro F. Cavazos	5-D	24,605	1,611
Texas Wesleyan U, Fort Worth, TX 76105	1891	Dr. Jerry G. Bawcom	2-M	1,550	111
Texas Woman's U, Denton, TX 76204 (4)	1901	Dr. Shirley Sears Chater	5-D	8,898	476
Thiel Coll, Greenville, PA 16125	1866	Dr. Louis T. Almen	2-B	941	92
Thomas A Edison State Coll, Trenton, NJ 08625	1972	Dr. George A. Pruitt	5-B	6,844	NR
Thomas Coll, Waterville, ME 04901	1894	Cyril M. Joly, Jr.	1-M	1,068	58
Thomas Jefferson U, Philadelphia, PA 19107	1824	Lewis W. Bluemle, Jr., MD	1-D	1,128	83
Thomas More Coll, Crestview Hills, KY 41017	1921	Dr. Charles J. Bensman	2-B	1,120	120
Tiffin U, Tiffin, OH 44883	1888	Dr. George Kidd, Jr.	1-B	777	47
Toccoa Falls Coll, Toccoa Falls, GA 30598	1907	Dr. Paul L. Alford	2-B	769	50
Tougaloo Coll, Tougaloo, MS 39174	1869	Dr. Adib A. Shakir	2-B	848	62
Touro Coll, New York, NY 10036	1971	Dr. Bernard Lander	1-M	3,609	340
Towson State U, Towson, MD 21204	1866	Dr. Hoke L. Smith	5-M	15,169	957
Transylvania U, Lexington, KY 40508	1780	Dr. Charles L. Shearer	2-B	963	95
Trenton State Coll, Trenton, NJ 08650	1855	Dr. Harold Eickhoff	5-M	7,348	509
Trinity Coll, Hartford, CT 06106	1823	James F. English, Jr.	1-M	2,045	194
Trinity Coll, Washington, DC 20017 (3)	1897	James J. McGrath	2-M	1,125	124
Trinity Coll, Deerfield, IL 60015	1897	Dr. Kenneth M. Meyer	2-B	825	51
Trinity Coll, Burlington, VT 05401 (4)	1925	Sr. Janice Ryan	2-B	999	115
Trinity U, San Antonio, TX 78284	1869	Dr. Ronald K. Calgaard	2-M	2,512	261
Tri-State U, Angola, IN 46703	1884	Dr. Beaumont Davison	1-B	1,054	75
Troy State U, Troy, AL 36082	1887	Dr. Ralph W. Adams	5-M	3,988	206
Troy State U at Dothan, Dothan, AL 36303	1962	Mr. Thomas Harrison	5-M	1,735	82
Troy State U in Montgomery, Montgomery, AL 36195	1957	Dr. Millard E. Elrod	5-M	2,520	132
Tufts U, Medford, MA 02155	1852	Dr. Jean Mayer	1-D	7,868	589
Tulane U, New Orleans, LA 70118	1834	Dr. Eamon M. Kelly	1-D	11,241	709
Tusculum Coll, Greeneville, TN 37743	1794	Donald B. Clardy	2-M	716	133
Tuskegee U, Tuskegee, AL 36088	1881	Dr. Benjamin F. Payton	1-D	3,400	307
Union Coll, Barbourville, KY 40906	1879	Dr. Jack C. Phillips	2-M	1,147	61
Union Coll, Lincoln, NE 68506	1891	John Wagner	2-B	619	69
Union Coll, Schenectady, NY 12308	1795	Dr. John S. Morris	1-D	2,395	197
Union for Experimenting Colleges and Universities, Cincinnati, OH 45202	1964	Robert T. Conley	1-D	1,100	NR
Union U, Jackson, TN 38305	1823	Dr. Hyran E. Barefoot	2-B	2,017	112
United States Air Force Acad, Colorado Springs, CO 80840	1954	Lt. Gen. Charles Hamm	4-B	4,530	568
United States Coast Guard Acad, New London, CT 06320	1876	R. Adm. Richard P. Cueroni	4-B	899	110
United States International U, San Diego, CA 92131	1952	Dr. William C. Rust	1-D	3,307	245
United States Merchant Marine Acad, Kings Point, NY 11024	1943	Rear Adm. P. L. Krinsky	4-B	844	74
United States Military Acad, West Point, NY 10996	1802	Lt. Gen. Dave R. Palmer	4-B	4,420	534
United States Naval Acad, Annapolis, MD 21402	1845	R. Adm. Ronald F. Marryott	4-B	4,500	600
Universidad Politécnica de Puerto Rico, Hato Rey, PR 00919	1974	Ernesto Vazquez-Torres	1-B	2,721	115
U of Akron, Akron, OH 44325	1870	William V. Muse	5-D	27,818	1,647
U of Alabama, Tuscaloosa, AL 35487	1831	Dr. E. Roger Sayers	5-D	18,150	764
U of Alabama in Huntsville, Huntsville, AL 35899	1950	Dr. Louis Padulo	5-D	7,474	466
U of Alaska Anchorage, Anchorage, AK 99508	1954	Dr. M. O. Looney	5-M	13,200	851
U of Alaska Fairbanks, Fairbanks, AK 99775	1917	Dr. Patrick J. O'Rourke	5-D	4,278	524
U of Alaska Southeast, Juneau, AK 99801	1972	Dr. Marshall Lind	5-M	3,484	93
U of Arizona, Tucson, AZ 85721	1885	Dr. Henry Koffler	5-D	34,725	1,865
U of Arkansas at Little Rock, Little Rock, AR 72204	1927	Dr. James H. Young	5-M	10,152	680
U of Arkansas at Monticello, Monticello, AR 71655	1909	Dr. Fred J. Taylor	5-B	1,934	117
U of Arkansas at Pine Bluff, Pine Bluff, AR 71601	1873	Dr. Charles A. Walker	5-D	3,333	163
U of Arkansas for Medical Sciences, Little Rock, AR 72205	1879	Dr. Harry P. Ward	5-D	1,328	NR
U of Baltimore, Baltimore, MD 21201	1925	Dr. H. Mebane Turner	5-D	5,228	257
U of Bridgeport, Bridgeport, CT 06601	1927	Dr. Janet D. Greenwood	1-D	5,376	375
U of California at Berkeley, Berkeley, CA 94720	1868	Ira Michael Heyman	5-D	31,612	NR
U of California, Davis, Davis, CA 95616	1906	Dr. Theodore L. Hullar	5-D	21,838	1,520
U of California, Irvine, Irvine, CA 92717	1965	Jack W. Peltason	5-D	15,874	578
U of California, Los Angeles, Los Angeles, CA 90024	1919	Charles E. Young	5-D	35,730	3,150
U of California, Riverside, Riverside, CA 92521	1954	Dr. Rosemary S. J. Schraer	5-D	7,487	585
U of California, San Diego, La Jolla, CA 92093	1964	Dr. Richard C. Atkinson	5-D	17,227	883
U of California, Santa Barbara, Santa Barbara, CA 93106	1891	Dr. Barbara S. Uehling	5-D	18,000	700
U of California, Santa Cruz, Santa Cruz, CA 95064	1965	Dr. Robert B. Stevens	5-D	8,589	449
U of Central Arkansas, Conway, AR 72032	1907	Winfred L. Thompson	5-M	6,698	263
U of Central Florida, Orlando, FL 32816	1963	Dr. Trevor Colbourn	5-D	18,094	754
U of Charleston, Charleston, WV 25304	1888	Mr. Lewis McManus	1-M	1,407	118
U of Chicago, Chicago, IL 60637	1891	Hanna Holborn Gray	1-D	8,600	603
U of Cincinnati, Cincinnati, OH 45221	1819	Dr. Joseph A. Steger	5-D	26,475	1,457
U of Colorado at Boulder, Boulder, CO 80309	1876	James N. Corbridge, Jr.	5-D	24,072	NR
U of Colorado at Colorado Springs, Colorado Springs, CO 80933	1965	Dr. Dwayne C. Nuzum	5-D	4,402	351
U of Colorado at Denver, Denver, CO 80204	1912	John Buechner	5-D	10,096	624
U of Colorado Health Sciences Ctr, Denver, CO 80262	1883	Dr. Bernard W. Nelson	5-D	1,596	NR
U of Connecticut, Storrs, CT 06268	1881	Dr. John T. Casteen, III	5-D	23,820	1,250
U of Connecticut at Hartford, West Hartford, CT 06117	1946	Dr. Russell F. Farnen	5-B	1,407	91
U of Connecticut at Stamford, Stamford, CT 06903	1951	Ms. Yakira H. Frank	5-M	1,175	93
U of Connecticut at Waterbury, Waterbury, CT 06710	1946	Mr. Alphonse Avitabile	5-B	608	58
U of Dallas, Irving, TX 75062	1956	Dr. Robert F. Sasseen	2-D	2,649	102
U of Dayton, Dayton, OH 45469	1850	Dr. Raymond L. Fitz, SM	2-D	11,090	693
U of Delaware, Newark, DE 19716	1743	Dr. Russel C. Jones	13-D	17,197	930
U of Denver, Denver, CO 80208	1864	Dr. Dwight Smith	1-D	7,020	548
U of Detroit, Detroit, MI 48221	1877	Rev. Robert A. Mitchell, SJ	2-D	6,021	159

Name, address	Year	Governing official, control, and highest degree offered	Enroll-ment	Faculty
U of Dubuque, Dubuque, IA 52001	1852	Dr. Walter F. Peterson 2-D	1,248	66
U of Evansville, Evansville, IN 47722	1854	Dr. James S. Vinson 2-M	3,512	161
U of Findlay, Findlay, OH 45840	1882	Dr. Kenneth E. Zirkle 2-M	1,768	133
U of Florida, Gainesville, FL 32611	1853	Mr. Marshall M. Criser 5-D	34,021	4,233
U of Georgia, Athens, GA 30602	1785	Dr. Charles B. Knapp 5-D	27,176	2,637
U of Guam, Mangilao, GU 96923	1952	Dr. Wilfred P. Leon Guerrezo 8-M	2,096	215
U of Hartford, West Hartford, CT 06117	1877	Hartzel Lebed 1-D	7,710	608
U of Hawaii at Hilo, Hilo, HI 96720	1970	Dr. Edward J. Kormondy . . . 5-B	2,812	200
U of Hawaii at Manoa, Honolulu, HI 96822	1907	Albert J. Simone 5-D	18,477	NR
U of Health Sciences/Chicago Medical Sch, North Chicago, IL 60064	1912	Dr. Herman M. Finch 1-D	892	17
U of Houston, Houston, TX 77004	1927	Richard L. Van Horn 5-D	30,372	2,025
U of Houston–Clear Lake, Houston, TX 77058	1971	Dr. Thomas M. Stauffer . . . 5-M	7,196	321
U of Houston–Downtown, Houston, TX 77002	1974	Manuel T. Pacheco 5-B	7,414	347
U of Idaho, Moscow, ID 83843	1889	Dr. Richard D. Gibb 5-D	9,444	546
U of Illinois at Chicago, Chicago, IL 60680	1965	Dr. Donald N. Langenberg . . 5-D	24,087	2,665
U of Illinois at Urbana-Champaign, Urbana, IL 61801	1867	Dr. Morton W. Weir 5-D	36,036	2,967
U of Indianapolis, Indianapolis, IN 46227	1902	Dr. G. Benjamin Lautz, Jr. . . 2-M	3,131	239
U of Iowa, Iowa City, IA 52242	1847	Dr. Hunter R. Rawling, III . . 5-D	29,230	1,600
U of Kansas, Lawrence, KS 66045	1866	Gene A. Budig 5-D	26,020	1,279
U of Kansas Medical Ctr, Kansas City, KS 66103	1905	D. Kay Clawson, MD 5-D	2,524	130
U of Kentucky, Lexington, KY 40506	1865	Dr. David P. Roselle 5-D	22,336	1,879
U of La Verne, La Verne, CA 91750	1891	Dr. Stephen Morgan 1-D	5,933	506
U of Louisville, Louisville, KY 40292	1798	Dr. Donald C. Swain 5-D	21,096	1,576
U of Lowell, Lowell, MA 01854	1894	Dr. William T. Hogan 5-D	11,456	636
U of Maine, Orono, ME 04469	1865	Dr. Dale W. Lick 5-D	10,967	900
U of Maine at Augusta, Augusta, ME 04330	1965	Dr. George P. Connick 5-B	3,824	218
U of Maine at Farmington, Farmington, ME 04938	1864	Dr. J. Michael Orenduff . . . 5-B	2,427	159
U of Maine at Fort Kent, Fort Kent, ME 04743	1878	Dr. Barbara Leondar 5-B	714	30
U of Maine at Machias, Machias, ME 04654	1909	Mr. Frederic A. Reynolds . . 5-B	851	54
U of Maine at Presque Isle, Presque Isle, ME 04769	1903	Dr. James R. Roach 5-M	1,404	109
U of Mary, Bismarck, ND 58504	1959	Sr. Thomas Welder 2-M	1,352	87
U of Mary Hardin-Baylor, Belton, TX 76513	1845	Dr. Bobby E. Parker 2-M	1,511	75
U of Maryland at Baltimore, Baltimore, MD 21201	1807	Dr. Edward N. Brandt, Jr. . . 5-D	4,563	187
U of Maryland Baltimore County, Baltimore, MD 21228	1966	Dr. Michael K. Hooker 5-D	9,868	575
U of Maryland Coll Park, College Park, MD 20742	1856	Dr. William E. Kirwan 5-D	36,681	1,769
U of Maryland Eastern Shore, Princess Anne, MD 21853	1886	Dr. William P. Hytche 5-D	1,559	130
U of Maryland U Coll, College Park, MD 20742	1947	Dr. T. Benjamin Massey . . . 5-M	36,258	NR
U of Massachusetts at Amherst, Amherst, MA 01003	1863	Joseph Duffey 5-D	25,216	1,412
U of Massachusetts at Boston, Boston, MA 02125	1964	Dr. Sherry H. Penney 6-D	10,961	794
U of Miami, Coral Gables, FL 33124	1925	Dr. Edward T. Foote, II 1-D	11,397	1,934
U of Michigan, Ann Arbor, MI 48109	1817	James J. Duderstadt 5-D	35,220	3,619
U of Michigan–Dearborn, Dearborn, MI 48128	1956	Dr. Blenda Wilson 5-M	6,573	370
U of Michigan–Flint, Flint, MI 48502	1956	Dr. Clinton B. Jones 5-M	6,305	211
U of Minnesota, Morris, Morris, MN 56267	1959	Dr. John Q. Imholte 5-B	1,959	142
U of Minnesota, Twin Cities Cmps, Minneapolis, MN 55455	1851	Richard J. Sauer 5-D	38,172	2,836
U of Mississippi, University, MS 38677	1844	Dr. R. Gerald Turner 5-D	9,639	512
U of Missouri–Columbia, Columbia, MO 65211	1839	Dr. Haskell Monroe 5-D	23,434	1,549
U of Missouri–Kansas City, Kansas City, MO 64110	1933	Dr. George A. Russell 5-D	11,756	952
U of Missouri–Rolla, Rolla, MO 65401	1870	Dr. Martin Jischke 5-D	5,724	381
U of Missouri–St Louis, St Louis, MO 63121	1963	Dr. Marguerite Ross Barnett . 5-D	12,202	635
U of Montana, Missoula, MT 59812	1893	Dr. James V. Koch 5-D	8,879	483
U of Nebraska at Omaha, Omaha, NE 68182	1908	Dr. Del D. Weber 5-M	14,194	534
U of Nebraska-Lincoln, Lincoln, NE 68588	1869	Dr. Martin A. Massengale . . 5-D	25,653	1,467
U of Nebraska Medical Ctr, Omaha, NE 68105	1869	Dr. Charles E. Andrews . . . 5-D	2,279	155
U of Nevada, Las Vegas, Las Vegas, NV 89154	1957	Dr. Robert Maxson 5-D	15,000	521
U of Nevada–Reno, Reno, NV 89557	1874	Dr. Joseph N. Crowley 5-D	9,772	445
U of New England, Biddeford, ME 04005	1939	Dr. Charles W. Ford 1-D	1,071	92
U of New Hampshire, Durham, NH 03824	1866	Dr. Gordon A. Haaland 5-D	11,131	778
U of New Haven, West Haven, CT 06516	1920	Dr. Phillip S. Kaplan 1-D	6,044	428
U of New Mexico, Albuquerque, NM 87131	1889	Gerald May 5-D	24,158	2,047
U of New Orleans, New Orleans, LA 70148	1958	Dr. Gregory M. O'Brien . . . 5-D	16,076	711
U of North Alabama, Florence, AL 35632	1872	Dr. Robert M. Guillot 5-M	5,291	206
U of North Carolina at Asheville, Asheville, NC 28804	1927	Dr. David G. Brown 5-B	3,200	216
U of North Carolina at Chapel Hill, Chapel Hill, NC 27599	1795	Paul Hardin, III 5-D	23,.79	NR
U of North Carolina at Charlotte, Charlotte, NC 28223	1946	Dr. Elbert K. Fretwell, Jr. . . 5-M	12,031	875
U of North Carolina at Greensboro, Greensboro, NC 27412	1891	Dr. William E. Moran 5-D	11,174	678
U of North Carolina at Wilmington, Wilmington, NC 28403	1947	Dr. William H. Wagoner . . . 5-M	6,553	377
U of North Dakota, Grand Forks, ND 58202	1883	Dr. Thomas J. Clifford 5-D	11,658	603
U of Northern Colorado, Greeley, CO 80639	1890	Mr. Robert C. Dickeson . . . 5-D	9,408	500
U of Northern Iowa, Cedar Falls, IA 50614	1876	Dr. Constantine W. Curris . . 5-D	11,472	795
U of North Florida, Jacksonville, FL 32216	1965	Dr. Roy E. McTarnaghan . . . 5-M	7,266	189
U of North Texas, Denton, TX 76203	1890	Dr. Alfred F. Hurley 5-D	24,498	888
U of Notre Dame, Notre Dame, IN 46556	1842	Rev. Edward A. Malloy, CSC 1-D	9,700	800
U of Oklahoma, Norman, OK 73069	1890	David Swank 5-D	20,632	870
U of Oklahoma Health Sciences Ctr, Oklahoma City, OK 73190	1890	Dr. Clayton Rich 5-D	3,158	NR
U of Oregon, Eugene, OR 97403	1872	Paul Olum 5-D	18,530	1,133
U of Osteopathic Medicine and Health Sciences, Des Moines, IA 50312	1898	Dr. J. Leonard Azneer 1-D	1,002	108
U of Pennsylvania, Philadelphia, PA 19104	1740	Dr. F. Sheldon Hackney . . . 1-D	19,600	3,828
U of Phoenix, Phoenix, AZ 85040	1976	William Gibbs 3-M	5,000	850
U of Pittsburgh, Pittsburgh, PA 15260	1787	Dr. Wesley W. Posvar 13-D	28,524	2,960
U of Pittsburgh at Bradford, Bradford, PA 16701	1963	Dr. Richard E. McDowell . . . 13-B	993	89
U of Pittsburgh at Greensburg, Greensburg, PA 15601	1963	Dr. George F. Chambers . . . 13-B	1,520	91
U of Pittsburgh at Johnstown, Johnstown, PA 15904	1927	Dr. Frank H. Blackington, III . 13-B	3,224	172
U of Portland, Portland, OR 97203	1901	Rev. Thomas C. Oddo 2-M	2,367	187
U of Puerto Rico at Arecibo, Arecibo, PR 00613	1967	Ana d. Babilonia 7-B	3,742	182
U of Puerto Rico at Bayamon, Bayamón, PR 00619	1971	Prof. Aida Canals de Bird . . 7-B	4,302	199
U of Puerto Rico at Ponce, Ponce, PR 00732	1970	Mr. Pedro E. Laboy 7-B	2,348	138
U of Puerto Rico, Cayey U Coll, Cayey, PR 00633	1967	Dr. Margarita Benitez 7-B	3,358	191
U of Puerto Rico, Humacao U Coll, Humacao, PR 00661	1962	Elsa I. Berrios de Santos . . 7-B	3,825	234
U of Puerto Rico, Mayagüez Cmps, Mayagüez, PR 00709	1911	Dr. Jose L. M. Pico 7-D	9,432	676
U of Puerto Rico Medical Sciences Cmps, San Juan, PR 00936	1950	Dr. Jose M. Saldana 7-D	3,220	856
U of Puerto Rico, Rio Piedras, Rio Piedras, PR 00931	1903	Dr. Juan R. Fernandez 7-D	22,524	1,461
U of Puget Sound, Tacoma, WA 98416	1888	Dr. Philip M. Phibbs 2-M	3,344	216
U of Redlands, Redlands, CA 92373	1907	Dr. James R. Appleton 1-M	2,900	120

Name, address	Year	Governing official, control, and highest degree offered		Enroll- ment	Faculty
U of Rhode Island, Kingston, RI 02881	1892	Dr. Edward D. Eddy	5-D	11,874	804
U of Richmond, Richmond, VA 23173	1830	Dr. Richard L. Morrill	2-M	4,956	297
U of Rochester, Rochester, NY 14627	1850	G. Dennis O'Brien	1-D	8,114	655
U of St Thomas, Houston, TX 77006	1947	Frank H. Bredeweg, CSB	2-D	1,661	197
U of San Diego, San Diego, CA 92110	1949	Dr. Author E. Hughes	2-D	5,858	405
U of San Francisco, San Francisco, CA 94117	1855	Rev. John J. Lo Schiavo, SJ	2-D	4,826	424
U of Science and Arts of Oklahoma, Chickasha, OK 73018	1908	Dr. Roy Troutt	5-B	1,373	75
U of Scranton, Scranton, PA 18510	1888	Rev. J. A. Panuska, SJ	2-M	4,837	357
U of South Alabama, Mobile, AL 36688	1964	Dr. Frederick P. Whiddon	5-D	10,443	715
U of South Carolina, Columbia, SC 29208	1801	Dr. James B. Holderman	5-D	26,435	1,360
U of South Carolina at Aiken, Aiken, SC 29801	1961	Dr. Robert E. Alexander	5-B	2,528	217
U of South Carolina at Spartanburg, Spartanburg, SC 29303	1967	Dr. Olin B. Sansbury, Jr.	5-B	3,247	219
U of South Carolina–Coastal Carolina Coll, Conway, SC 29526	1954	Dr. Ronald G. Eaglin	5-B	3,989	212
U of South Dakota, Vermillion, SD 57069	1862	NR	5-D	5,836	364
U of Southern California, Los Angeles, CA 90089	1880	Dr. James H. Zumberge	1-D	29,590	3,289
U of Southern Colorado, Pueblo, CO 81001	1933	Dr. Robert Shirley	5-M	3,953	240
U of Southern Indiana, Evansville, IN 47712	1965	Dr. David L. Rice	5-M	5,265	247
U of Southern Maine, Portland, ME 04103	1878	Dr. Patricia Plante	5-D	10,160	458
U of South Mississippi, Hattiesburg, MS 39406	1910	Dr. Aubrey K. Lucus	5-D	11,051	668
U of South Florida, Tampa, FL 33620	1956	Dr. Francis T. Borkowski	5-D	30,003	1,422
U of Southwestern Louisiana, Lafayette, LA 70504	1898	Dr. Ray P. Authement	5-D	15,037	677
U of Tampa, Tampa, FL 33606	1931	Mr. Bruce A. Samson	1-M	2,396	179
U of Tennessee at Chattanooga, Chattanooga, TN 37403	1886	Dr. Frederick W. Obear	5-M	7,526	314
U of Tennessee at Martin, Martin, TN 38238	1927	Dr. Margaret N. Perry	5-M	4,800	NR
U of Tennessee, Knoxville, Knoxville, TN 37996	1794	Dr. Jack E. Reese	5-D	24,361	1,173
U of Tennessee, Memphis, Memphis, TN 38163	1911	Dr. James C. Hunt	5-D	1,773	779
U of Texas at Arlington, Arlington, TX 76019	1895	Dr. Wendell H. Nedderman	5-D	23,383	870
U of Texas at Austin, Austin, TX 78712	1883	Dr. William Cunningham	5-D	50,107	2,301
U of Texas at Dallas, Richardson, TX 75083	1969	Dr. Robert H. Rutford	5-D	7,667	385
U of Texas at El Paso, El Paso, TX 79968	1913	Dr. Diana Natalicio	5-D	14,971	619
U of Texas at San Antonio, San Antonio, TX 78285	1969	Dr. James W. Wagener	5-M	13,134	654
U of Texas at Tyler, Tyler, TX 75701	1972	Dr. George F. Hamm	5-M	3,850	348
U of Texas Health Science Ctr at Houston, Houston, TX 77225	1943	Dr. John C. Ribble	5-D	2,837	106
U of Texas Health Science Ctr at San Antonio, San Antonio, TX 78284	1976	Dr. John P. Howe, III	5-D	2,219	118
U of Texas Medical Branch at Galveston, Galveston, TX 77550	1891	Dr. Thomas N. James	5-D	1,705	609
U of Texas of the Permian Basin, Odessa, TX 79762	1969	Dr. Duane M. Leach	5-M	2,132	105
U of Texas Southwestern Med Ctr at Dallas, Dallas, TX 75235	1972	Dr. C. Kern Wildenthal	5-D	1,458	270
U of the Arts, Philadelphia, PA 19102	1876	NR	1-M	1,371	355
U of the District of Columbia, Washington, DC 20008	1976	Dr. Raphael L. Cordata	10-M	11,263	805
U of the Ozarks, Clarksville, AR 72830	1834	Dr. Fritz H. Ehren	2-B	711	51
U of the Pacific, Stockton, CA 95211	1851	Dr. Bill L. Atchley	1-D	5,800	335
U of the Sacred Heart, Santurce, PR 00914	1939	Jose Alberto Morales, Esq.	2-M	7,480	383
U of the South, Sewanee, TN 37375	1857	Dr. Samuel R. Williamson, Jr.	2-D	1,171	111
U of the State of New York, Regents Coll Degrees, Albany, NY 12230	1971	C. Wayne Williams	13-B	14,400	NR
U of the Virgin Islands, Charlotte Amalie, St Thomas, VI 00602	1962	Dr. Arthur A. Richards	8-M	2,471	175
U of Toledo, Toledo, OH 43606	1872	John Stoepler	5-D	22,806	1,233
U of Tulsa, Tulsa, OK 74104	1894	Dr. J. Paschal Twyman	2-D	4,431	400
U of Utah, Salt Lake City, UT 84112	1850	Dr. Chase N. Peterson	5-D	23,626	924
U of Vermont, Burlington, VT 05405	1791	Dr. Lattie F. Coor	5-D	9,506	922
U of Virginia, Charlottesville, VA 22906	1819	Robert M. O'Neil	13-D	17,198	1,804
U of Washington, Seattle, WA 98195	1861	William P. Gerberding	5-D	33,460	3,118
U of West Florida, Pensacola, FL 32514	1963	Dr. Morris L. Marx	5-M	7,170	383
U of West Los Angeles, Los Angeles, CA 90066	1966	Bernard Jefferson	1-D	670	22
U of Wisconsin–Eau Claire, Eau Claire, WI 54701	1916	Dr. Larry Schnack	5-M	11,038	585
U of Wisconsin–Green Bay, Green Bay, WI 54311	1968	Dr. David L. Outcalt	5-M	5,221	208
U of Wisconsin–La Crosse, La Crosse, WI 54601	1909	Dr. Noel J. Richards	5-M	9,262	523
U of Wisconsin–Madison, Madison, WI 53706	1848	Dr. Donna E. Shalala	5-D	40,949	2,290
U of Wisconsin–Milwaukee, Milwaukee, WI 53201	1956	Dr. Clifford V. Smith, Jr.	5-D	25,212	1,263
U of Wisconsin–Oshkosh, Oshkosh, WI 54901	1871	Dr. Edward M. Penson	5-M	11,228	532
U of Wisconsin–Parkside, Kenosha, WI 53141	1968	Dr. Sheila Kaplan	5-M	5,170	290
U of Wisconsin–Platteville, Platteville, WI 53818	1866	Dr. William W. Chmurny	5-M	5,353	280
U of Wisconsin–River Falls, River Falls, WI 54022	1874	Dr. Gary A. Thibodeau	5-M	5,544	295
U of Wisconsin–Stevens Point, Stevens Point, WI 54481	1894	Dr. Philip R. Marshall	5-M	9,350	410
U of Wisconsin–Stout, Menomonie, WI 54751	1891	Dr. Charles Sorenson	5-M	7,599	411
U of Wisconsin–Superior, Superior, WI 54880	1893	Dr. Terrence MacTaggart	5-M	2,437	162
U of Wisconsin–Whitewater, Whitewater, WI 53190	1868	Dr. James R. Connor	5-M	10,458	496
U of Wyoming, Laramie, WY 82071	1886	Dr. Terry P. Roark	5-D	10,773	812
Upsala Coll, East Orange, NJ 07019	1893	Robert E. Karsten	2-M	1,130	62
Urbana U, Urbana, OH 43078	1850	Dr. Paul G. Bunnell	2-B	768	96
Ursinus Coll, Collegeville, PA 19426	1869	Dr. Richard P. Richter	2-B	1,225	129
Ursuline Coll, Pepper Pike, OH 44124 (4)	1871	Sr. Anne Marie Diederich	2-M	1,297	110
Utah State U, Logan, UT 84322	1888	Dr. Stanford Cazier	5-D	12,132	524
Utica Coll of Syracuse U, Utica, NY 13502	1946	Dr. Michael K. Simpson	1-B	1,600	140
Valdosta State Coll, Valdosta, GA 31698	1906	Dr. Hugh C. Bailey	5-M	6,950	296
Valley City State U, Valley City, ND 58072	1890	Dr. Charles B. House, Jr.	5-B	1,154	66
Valparaiso U, Valparaiso, IN 46383	1859	Dr. Alan F. Harre	2-D	3,952	368
Vanderbilt U, Nashville, TN 37240	1873	Mr. Joe B. Wyatt	1-D	9,021	1,154
Vassar Coll, Poughkeepsie, NY 12601	1861	Frances D. Fergusson	1-M	2,395	217
Villa Julie Coll, Stevenson, MD 21153	1952	Ms. Carolyn Manuszak	1-B	1,279	156
Villa Maria Coll, Erie, PA 16505 (4)	1925	Sr. Leonie Shanley, SSJ	2-M	686	71
Villanova U, Villanova, PA 19085	1842	Rev. John M. Driscoll, OSA	2-D	11,728	920
Virginia Commonwealth U, Richmond, VA 23298	1838	Dr. Edmund F. Ackell	5-D	20,645	2,186
Virginia Military Inst, Lexington, VA 24450 (1)	1839	Gen. Sam S. Walker	5-B	1,310	92
Virginia Polytechnic Inst and State U, Blacksburg, VA 24061	1872	James D. McComas	5-D	22,361	1,607
Virginia State U, Petersburg, VA 23803	1882	Dr. Wesley C. McClure	5-M	3,855	236
Virginia Union U, Richmond, VA 23220	1865	Dr. S. Dallas Simmons	2-M	1,200	NR
Virginia Wesleyan Coll, Norfolk, VA 23502	1961	Dr. Lambuth M. Clarke	2-B	1,261	94
Viterbo Coll, La Crosse, WI 54601	1890	Dr. Robert E. Gibbons	2-M	1,067	89

Name, address	Year	Governing official, control, and highest degree offered	Enrollment	Faculty
Wabash Coll, Crawfordsville, IN 47933 (1)	1832	Dr. Victor M. Powell 1-B	872	78
Wagner Coll, Staten Island, NY 10301	1883	Dr. Norman R. Smith 1-M	1,767	147
Wake Forest U, Winston-Salem, NC 27109	1834	Dr. Thomas K. Hearn, Jr. . . . 2-D	5,337	306
Walla Walla Coll, College Place, WA 99324	1892	Dr. H. J. Bergman 2-M	1,515	168
Walsh Coll, Canton, OH 44720	1958	Dr. Francis Blouin 2-M	1,381	104
Walsh Coll of Accountancy & Business Admin, Troy, MI 48007	1922	Dr. Jeffery W. Barry 1-M	2,697	100
Wartburg Coll, Waverly, IA 50677	1852	Dr. Robert Vogel 2-B	1,358	111
Washburn U of Topeka, Topeka, KS 66621	1865	Dr. John L. Green, Jr. . . . 11-M	6,587	324
Washington and Jefferson Coll, Washington, PA 15301	1781	Dr. Howard J. Burnett 1-B	1,192	96
Washington and Lee U, Lexington, VA 24450	1749	Dr. John D. Wilson 1-D	1,990	161
Washington Coll, Chestertown, MD 21620	1782	Mr. Douglass Cater 1-M	988	81
Washington State U, Pullman, WA 99164	1892	Dr. Samuel H. Smith 5-D	16,352	881
Washington U, St Louis, MO 63130	1853	Dr. William H. Danforth . . . 1-D	9,341	2,811
Wayland Baptist U, Plainview, TX 79072	1908	Dr. Glenn Barnett 2-M	1,935	158
Waynesburg Coll, Waynesburg, PA 15370	1849	Dr. J. Thomas Mills, Jr. . . . 2-M	1,031	60
Wayne State Coll, Wayne, NE 68787	1910	Dr. Donald J. Mash 5-M	2,873	151
Wayne State U, Detroit, MI 48202	1868	Dr. David Adamany 5-D	30,751	1,980
Weber State Coll, Ogden, UT 84408	1889	Dr. Stephen D. Nadauld . . . 5-M	12,146	417
Webster U, St Louis, MO 63119	1915	Dr. Leigh Gerdine 1-D	9,049	353
Wellesley Coll, Wellesley, MA 02181 (3)	1870	Dr. Nannerl Keohane 1-B	2,239	330
Wentworth Inst of Tech, Boston, MA 02115	1904	Dr. Edward T. Kirkpatrick . . . 1-B	3,290	154
Wesleyan U, Middletown, CT 06457	1831	Mr. Colin Campbell 1-D	2,938	346
Wesley Coll, Dover, DE 19901	1873	Dr. Reed M. Stewart 2-B	1,200	98
West Chester U of Pennsylvania, West Chester, PA 19383	1871	Dr. Kenneth L. Perrin 5-M	11,475	549
West Coast U, Los Angeles, CA 90020	1909	Dr. Robert M. L. Baker, Jr. . . 1-M	1,600	250
Western Carolina U, Cullowhee, NC 28723	1889	Dr. Myron L. Coulter 5-M	6,055	379
Western Connecticut State U, Danbury, CT 06810	1903	Dr. Stephen Feldman 5-M	6,380	248
Western Illinois U, Macomb, IL 61455	1899	Dr. Ralph H. Wagoner 5-M	12,500	626
Western International U, Phoenix, AZ 85021	1978	Ronald C. Bauer 1-M	1,146	66
Western Kentucky U, Bowling Green, KY 42101	1906	Dr. Samuel K. Alexander, Jr. . 5-M	14,121	823
Western Maryland Coll, Westminster, MD 21157	1868	Dr. Robert H. Chambers . . . 1-M	2,002	127
Western Michigan U, Kalamazoo, MI 49008	1903	Dr. Diether H. Haenicke . . . 5-D	24,861	1,223
Western Montana Coll of the U of Montana, Dillon, MT 59725	1893	Dr. W. Michael Easton 5-B	792	42
Western New England Coll, Springfield, MA 01119	1919	Dr. Beverly W. Miller 1-D	4,487	303
Western New Mexico U, Silver City, NM 88061	1893	Dr. Kenneth Ladner 5-M	1,680	90
Western Oregon State Coll, Monmouth, OR 97361	1856	Dr. Richard S. Meyers 5-M	3,980	221
Western State Coll of Colorado, Gunnison, CO 81230	1911	Dr. William T. Hamilton 5-B	1,986	100
Western State U Coll of Law of Orange County, Fullerton, CA 92631	1966	NR 3-D	1,158	50
Western Washington U, Bellingham, WA 98225	1893	Dr. Kenneth P. Mortimer . . . 5-M	9,838	456
Westfield State Coll, Westfield, MA 01086	1838	Dr. Irving H. Buchen 5-M	5,311	204
West Georgia Coll, Carrollton, GA 30118	1933	Dr. Maurice K. Townsend . . . 5-M	6,710	300
West Liberty State Coll, West Liberty, WV 26074	1837	Dr. Clyde D. Campbell 5-B	2,435	143
Westminster Coll, Fulton, MO 65251	1851	Dr. J. Harvey Saunders 2-B	707	87
Westminster Coll, New Wilmington, PA 16172	1852	Dr. Oscar E. Remick 2-M	1,475	127
Westminster Coll of Salt Lake City, Salt Lake City, UT 84105	1875	Dr. Charles H. Dick 1-M	1,856	61
Westmont Coll, Santa Barbara, CA 93108	1940	Dr. David K. Winter 2-B	1,283	117
West Texas State U, Canyon, TX 79016	1909	Dr. Ed Roach 5-M	5,756	313
West Virginia Inst of Tech, Montgomery, WV 25136	1895	Dr. Robert C. Gillespie 5-M	2,956	198
West Virginia State Coll, Institute, WV 25112	1891	Hazo W. Carter 5-B	4,514	225
West Virginia U, Morgantown, WV 26506	1867	Dr. Neil S. Bucklew 5-D	18,746	1,313
West Virginia Wesleyan Coll, Buckhannon, WV 26201	1890	Dr. Thomas B. Courtice 2-M	1,484	99
Wheaton Coll, Wheaton, IL 60187	1860	Dr. J. Richard Chase 2-M	2,445	236
Wheaton Coll, Norton, MA 02766	1834	Alice F. Emerson 1-B	1,172	113
Wheeling Jesuit Coll, Wheeling, WV 26003	1954	Fr. Thomas S. Acker, SJ . . . 2-M	1,030	75
Wheelock Coll, Boston, MA 02215 (4)	1888	Dr. Daniel S. Cheever, Jr. . . 1-M	985	117
Whitman Coll, Walla Walla, WA 99362	1859	Mr. Edward F. Forster 1-B	1,230	121
Whittier Coll, Whittier, CA 90608	1887	Dr. Eugene S. Mills 1-D	1,579	90
Whitworth Coll, Spokane, WA 99251	1890	Dr. Arthur J. De Jong 2-M	1,840	91
Wichita State U, Wichita, KS 67208	1895	Dr. Warren B. Armstrong . . . 5-D	17,267	852
Widener U, Chester, PA 19013	1821	Robert J. Bruce 1-D	8,516	296
Wilkes Coll, Wilkes-Barre, PA 18766	1933	Dr. Christopher N. Breiseth . . 1-M	2,962	NR
Willamette U, Salem, OR 97301	1842	Dr. Jerry E. Hudson 2-D	2,098	138
William Jewell Coll, Liberty, MO 64068	1849	Dr. J. Gordon Kingsley 2-B	1,426	125
William Paterson Coll of New Jersey, Wayne, NJ 07470	1855	Dr. Arnold Speert 5-M	9,232	333
William Penn Coll, Oskaloosa, IA 52577	1873	Mr. John D. Wagoner 2-B	675	57
Williams Coll, Williamstown, MA 01267	1793	Dr. Francis C. Oakley 1-M	2,168	266
William Smith Coll, Geneva, NY 14456 (3)	1908	Mr. Carroll W. Brewster . . . 1-B	800	170
William Woods Coll, Fulton, MO 65251 (3)	1870	Dr. John M. Bartholomy . . . 2-B	730	70
Wilmington Coll, New Castle, DE 19720	1967	Dr. Audrey K. Doberstein . . . 1-M	1,482	103
Wilmington Coll, Wilmington, OH 45177	1870	Neil Thorburn 2-B	825	62
Wilson Coll, Chambersburg, PA 17201 (4)	1869	Dr. Mary-Linda Merriam . . . 2-B	665	66
Wingate Coll, Wingate, NC 28174	1895	Dr. Paul R. Corts 2-M	1,729	98
Winona State U, Winona, MN 55987	1858	Dr. Thomas Stark 5-M	7,200	300
Winston-Salem State U, Winston-Salem, NC 27110	1892	Dr. Cleon F. Thompson, Jr. . . 5-B	2,532	186
Winthrop Coll, Rock Hill, SC 29733	1886	Dr. Michael Smith 5-M	5,351	386
Wittenberg U, Springfield, OH 45501	1845	Dr. William A. Kinnison 2-B	2,250	179
Wofford Coll, Spartanburg, SC 29301	1854	Dr. Joab M. Lesesne 2-B	1,135	82
Woodbury U, Burbank, CA 91510	1884	Dr. Wayne L. Miller 1-M	858	83
Worcester Polytechnic Inst, Worcester, MA 01609	1865	Dr. Jon C. Strauss 1-D	3,812	NR
Worcester State Coll, Worcester, MA 01602	1874	Dr. Philip D. Vairo 5-M	4,800	202
Wright State U, Dayton, OH 45435	1964	Dr. Paige E. Mulhollan 5-D	17,104	950
Xavier U, Cincinnati, OH 45207	1831	Albert J. DiUlio, SJ 2-M	6,412	430
Xavier U of Louisiana, New Orleans, LA 70125	1925	Dr. Norman C. Francis 2-M	2,528	179
Yale U, New Haven, CT 06520	1701	Benno C. Schmidt, Jr. 1-D	10,998	718
Yeshiva U, New York, NY 10033	1886	Dr. Norman Lamm 1-D	4,543	164
York Coll of Pennsylvania, York, PA 17403	1787	Dr. Robert V. Iosue 1-M	4,789	273
York Coll of the City U of New York, Jamaica, NY 11451	1967	Mr. Milton G. Bassin 12-B	4,826	200
Youngstown State U, Youngstown, OH 44555	1908	Dr. Neil D. Humphrey 5-M	14,710	887

Two-Year Colleges

The highest undergraduate degree offered for all two-year colleges is the associate degree.

Institution	Year	President	Code	Enrollment	
Abraham Baldwin Agricultural Coll, Tifton, GA 31793	1933	Dr. James A. Burran	5	1,895	89
Adirondack Comm Coll, Glens Falls, NY 12801	1960	Dr. Roger Andersen	12	3,102	140
Aiken Tech Coll, Aiken, SC 29802	1972	Dr. Paul L. Blowers	12	1,350	175
Aims Comm Coll, Greeley, CO 80632	1967	Dr. George R. Conger	10	7,319	362
Alamance Comm Coll, Haw River, NC 27258	1959	Dr. W. Ronald McCarter	5	3,298	145
Alexandria Tech Inst, Alexandria, MN 56308	1961	Frank Starke	5	622	113
Allan Hancock Coll, Santa Maria, CA 93454	1920	Dr. Gary R. Edelbrock	12	8,331	368
Allegany Comm Coll, Cumberland, MD 21502	1961	Dr. Donald L. Alexander	12	2,220	147
Allen County Comm Coll, Iola, KS 66749	1923	Dr. William A. Griffin, Jr.	12	1,141	125
Alpena Comm Coll, Alpena, MI 49707	1952	Dr. Donald L. Newport	12	2,276	122
Alvin Comm Coll, Alvin, TX 77511	1949	Dr. A. R. Allbright	12	4,152	209
Amarillo Coll, Amarillo, TX 79178	1929	Dr. George T. Miller	12	5,394	NR
American Inst of Business, Des Moines, IA 50321	1921	Keith Fenton	1	1,120	60
Anderson Coll, Anderson, SC 29621	1911	Dr. Mark L. Hopkins	2	1,045	58
Angelina Coll, Lufkin, TX 75902	1968	Dr. Jack W. Hudgins	12	2,960	136
Anne Arundel Comm Coll, Arnold, MD 21012	1961	Dr. Thomas E. Florestano	12	11,664	568
Anoka-Ramsey Comm Coll, Coon Rapids, MN 55433	1965	Dr. Richard Carpenter	5	4,624	179
Anson Comm Coll, Ansonville, NC 28007	1962	Dr. Edwin R. Chapman	5	849	36
Antelope Valley Coll, Lancaster, CA 93536	1929	Dr. Allan W. Kurki	12	8,263	346
Arapahoe Comm Coll, Littleton, CO 80160	1965	Dr. James F. Weber	5	6,800	285
Arizona Western Coll, Yuma, AZ 85366	1962	Dr. James R. Carruthers	12	5,200	384
Arkansas State U–Beebe Branch, Beebe, AR 72012	1927	Mr. William H. Owen, Jr.	5	1,202	62
Art Inst of Atlanta, Atlanta, GA 30326	1949	John Knepper	3	1,400	95
Art Inst of Dallas, Dallas, TX 75231	1978	Ms. Deborah G. Wright	3	830	45
Art Inst of Houston, Houston, TX 77006	1978	NR	3	900	NR
Art Inst of Philadelphia, Philadelphia, PA 19103	1966	John R. Knepper	3	1,100	90
Art Inst of Pittsburgh, Pittsburgh, PA 15222	1921	John T. Barclay	3	1,878	87
Art Inst of Seattle, Seattle, WA 98121	1979	George L. Pry	3	1,269	81
Asheville-Buncombe Tech Comm Coll, Asheville, NC 28801	1959	Mr. Harvey L. Haynes	5	3,051	250
Asnuntuck Comm Coll, Enfield, CT 06082	1972	Dr. Harvey S. Irlen	5	2,007	79
Atlanta Metropolitan Coll, Atlanta, GA 30310	1974	Dr. Edwin A. Thompson	5	1,367	NR
Atlantic Comm Coll, Mays Landing, NJ 08330	1966	Dr. William Orth	9	4,165	215
Austin Comm Coll, Austin, MN 55912	1940	Dr. James Flannery	5	1,202	73
Austin Comm Coll, Austin, TX 78768	1972	Dr. Dan Angel	10	21,378	945
Bainbridge Coll, Bainbridge, GA 31717	1972	Dr. Edward D. Mobley	5	808	NR
Bakersfield Coll, Bakersfield, CA 93305	1913	Dr. Richard Wright	12	11,544	448
Barstow Coll, Barstow, CA 92311	1959	Dr. John C. Menzie	12	2,371	92
Barton County Comm Coll, Great Bend, KS 67530	1969	Dr. Jimmie L. Downing	12	3,060	78
Bauder Fashion Coll, Atlanta, GA 30326 (4)	1963	John E. Kettle	3	600	34
Bay de Noc Comm Coll, Escanaba, MI 49829	1963	Dr. Dwight E. Link	9	2,197	125
Bay State Jr Coll, Boston, MA 02116	1946	Dr. Thomas E. Langford	1	703	39
Beaufort County Comm Coll, Washington, NC 27889	1968	Mr. James P. Blanton	5	1,266	95
Becker Jr Coll–East Cmps, Worcester, MA 01609	1887	Arnold C. Weller, Jr.	1	604	46
Beckley Coll, Beckley, WV 25802	1933	Dr. George D. Balsama	1	1,614	71
Bee County Coll, Beeville, TX 78102	1965	Dr. Norman Wallace	12	2,550	139
Belleville Area Coll, Belleville, IL 62221	1946	Dr. Joseph Cipfl	10	12,158	611
Bellevue Comm Coll, Bellevue, WA 98009	1966	Dr. Richard White	5	8,055	452
Belmont Tech Coll, St Clairsville, OH 43950	1971	Dr. Steve Maradian	5	1,901	138
Bergen Comm Coll, Paramus, NJ 07652	1965	Dr. Jose Lopez-Isa	9	6,481	422
Berkeley Sch, West Paterson, NJ 07424	1931	Jack R. Jones	3	689	25
Berkeley Sch, New York, NY 10017	1945	Mr. Louis Cress	3	665	NR
Berkshire Comm Coll, Pittsfield, MA 01201	1960	Dr. Cathryn L. Addy	5	2,150	126
Bessemer State Tech Coll, Bessemer, AL 35021	1966	Dr. W. Michael Bailey	5	1,826	102
Big Bend Comm Coll, Moses Lake, WA 98837	1962	Mr. Greg Fitch	5	1,968	114
Bishop State Comm Coll, Mobile, AL 36690	1965	Dr. Yvonne Kennedy	5	1,824	72
Bismarck State Coll, Bismarck, ND 58501	1939	Dr. Kermit Lidstrom	5	2,492	117
Black Hawk Coll–East Cmps, Kewanee, IL 61443	1967	Dr. Charles Warthen	12	725	63
Black Hawk Coll–Quad-Cities Cmps, Moline, IL 61265	1946	Dr. Herbert C. Lyon	12	5,263	284
Blackhawk Tech Coll, Janesville, WI 53547	1968	Dr. James C. Catania	10	2,000	128
Blair Jr Coll, Colorado Springs, CO 80915	1897	Thomas Twardowski	3	750	40
Blinn Coll, Brenham, TX 77833	1883	Walter C. Schwartz	12	5,915	205
Blue Mountain Comm Coll, Pendleton, OR 97801	1962	Mr. Ronald L. Daniels	9	2,719	175
Blue Ridge Comm Coll, Weyers Cave, VA 24486	1965	Dr. James C. Sears	5	2,483	138
Blue Ridge Tech Coll, Flat Rock, NC 28731	1969	Dr. David W. Sink, Jr.	12	1,244	NR
Borough of Manhattan Comm Coll of City U of NY, New York, NY 10007	1963	Dr. Augusta Souza Kappner	12	12,642	1,108
Bossier Parish Comm Coll, Bossier City, LA 71111	1967	James M. Conerly	12	2,242	94
Bowling Green State U–Firelands Coll, Huron, OH 44839	1968	Dr. Robert DeBard	5	1,275	77
Brainerd Comm Coll, Brainerd, MN 56401	1938	Sally Jane Ihne	5	1,526	77
Brazosport Coll, Lake Jackson, TX 77566	1948	Dr. John R. Grable	12	3,550	135
Brevard Coll, Brevard, NC 28712	1853	Dr. William T. Greer, Jr.	2	680	59
Brevard Comm Coll, Cocoa, FL 32922	1960	Dr. Maxwell C. King	5	12,377	858
Brewer State Jr Coll, Fayette, AL 35555	1969	Dr. Tommy M. Boothe	5	694	38
Briarcliffe Sch, Hicksville, NY 11801 (4)	1966	Richard Turan	3	600	57
Bristol Comm Coll, Fall River, MA 02720	1965	Ms. Eileen Farley	5	2,786	177
Bronx Comm Coll of City U of NY, Bronx, NY 10453	1959	NR	12	5,730	390
Brookhaven Coll, Farmers Branch, TX 75244	1978	Dr. Patsy J. Fulton	9	7,827	343
Brooks Coll, Long Beach, CA 90804	1971	Mr. Steve Sotraidis	3	775	57
Broome Comm Coll, Binghamton, NY 13902	1946	Dr. Donald A. Dellow	12	5,961	453
Broward Comm Coll, Fort Lauderdale, FL 33301	1960	Dr. Willis N. Holcombe	5	21,370	744
Brunswick Coll, Brunswick, GA 31523	1965	Dr. John W. Teel	5	1,338	64
Brunswick Comm Coll, Supply, NC 28462	1979	NR	5	674	56
Bryant and Stratton Business Inst, Buffalo, NY 14202	1854	Mr. James J. Pautler	3	1,568	131
Bryant and Stratton Business Inst, Rochester, NY 14604 (4)	1973	Richard Jarrett	3	1,321	85
Bryant and Stratton Business Inst, Syracuse, NY 13202	1926	Arpad Kozlovary, Jr.	3	1,207	48
Bryant and Stratton Business Inst, E Hills Cmps, Williamsville, NY 14221	1978	Francis J. Gustina	3	1,596	77
Bucks County Comm Coll, Newtown, PA 18940	1964	Dr. William E. Vincent	9	10,006	375
Bunker Hill Comm Coll, Boston, MA 02129	1973	NR	5	3,481	185
Burlington County Coll, Pemberton, NJ 08068	1966	Dr. Robert Messina	9	6,007	150
Butler County Comm Coll, El Dorado, KS 67042	1927	Dr. Rodney Cox	12	4,070	294
Butler County Comm Coll, Butler, PA 16001	1965	Dr. Frederick W. Woodward	9	2,540	120
Butte Coll, Oroville, CA 95965	1966	Dr. Wendell L. Reeder	10	9,993	575

Name, address	Year	Governing official, control	Enrollment	Faculty
Cabrillo Coll, Aptos, CA 95003	1959	Dr. Robert F. Agrella 10	12,087	505
Caldwell Comm Coll and Tech Inst, Hudson, NC 28638	1964	Dr. Eric B. McKeithan 5	2,627	183
California Coll for Health Sciences, National City, CA 92050	1977	NR 3	3,000	4
Camden County Coll, Blackwood, NJ 08012	1967	Dr. Robert W. Ramsay 12	9,200	385
Cañada Coll, Redwood City, CA 94061	1968	D. Robert Stiff 10	7,600	239
Cannon's International Bus Coll of Honolulu, Honolulu, HI 96814	1917	Mrs. Evelyn A. Schemmel 3	750	25
Cape Cod Comm Coll, West Barnstable, MA 02668	1961	Philip R. Day, Jr. 5	2,303	160
Cape Fear Comm Coll, Wilmington, NC 28401	1959	Dr. E. Thomas Satterfield, Jr. . . 5	2,539	77
Carl Albert Jr Coll, Poteau, OK 74953	1934	NR 5	1,716	160
Carl Sandburg Coll, Galesburg, IL 61401	1967	Jack W. Fuller 12	2,800	117
Carteret Comm Coll, Morehead City, NC 28557	1963	Dr. Donald W. Bryant 5	1,460	86
Casper Coll, Casper, WY 82601	1945	Dr. Lester Vierra 10	2,025	171
Catawba Valley Comm Coll, Hickory, NC 28601	1960	Dr. Cuyler A. Dunbar 12	3,000	175
Cayuga County Comm Coll, Auburn, NY 13021	1953	Dr. Lawrence H. Poole 12	2,792	144
Cazenovia Coll, Cazenovia, NY 13035	1824	Dr. Stephen M. Schneeweiss . . 1	920	134
Cecil Comm Coll, North East, MD 21901	1968	Dr. Robert L. Gell 9	1,411	107
Cedar Valley Coll, Lancaster, TX 75134	1977	Dr. Floyd S. Elkins 12	2,849	130
Central Alabama Comm Coll–Alexander City Cmps, Alexander City, AL 35010	1965	Dr. James H. Cornell 5	1,036	81
Central Carolina Comm Coll, Sanford, NC 27330	1962	Dr. Marvin S. Joyner 12	2,527	177
Central City Business Inst, Syracuse, NY 13202	1904	Mr. Donald J. Nelli 3	972	37
Central Comm Coll–Grand Island Cmps, Grand Island, NE 68802	1976	Donald Nelson 12	1,397	76
Central Comm Coll–Hastings Cmps, Hastings, NE 68901	1966	Dr. Carl H. Rolf 12	2,274	116
Central Comm Coll–Platte Cmps, Columbus, NE 68602	1968	Dr. Peter Rush 12	2,346	98
Central Florida Comm Coll, Ocala, FL 32678	1957	Dr. William J. Campion 12	4,000	168
Centralia Coll, Centralia, WA 98531	1925	Dr. Henry P. Kirk 5	1,227	112
Central Ohio Tech Coll, Newark, OH 43055	1971	Dr. Julius S. Greenstein 5	1,445	106
Central Oregon Comm Coll, Bend, OR 97701	1949	Dr. Frederick H. Boyle 10	2,604	195
Central Pennsylvania Business Sch, Summerdale, PA 17093	1922	Mr. Bart A. Milano 3	696	68
Central Piedmont Comm Coll, Charlotte, NC 28235	1963	Dr. Ruth Shaw 12	16,007	1,214
Central Texas Coll, Killeen, TX 76542	1967	Dr. Luis M. Morton 12	6,498	NR
Central Virginia Comm Coll, Lynchburg, VA 24502	1966	Dr. J. E. Merritt 5	3,744	114
Central Wyoming Coll, Riverton, WY 82501	1966	Dr. Edward L. Donovan 12	1,406	58
Cerritos Coll, Norwalk, CA 90650	1956	Dr. Ernest Martinez 12	19,221	613
Chabot Coll, Hayward, CA 94545	1961	Dr. Richard D. Yeo 5	20,467	1,075
Chaffey Coll, Rancho Cucamonga, CA 91701	1883	Dr. Jerry W. Young 10	11,800	500
Champlain Coll, Burlington, VT 05402	1878	Dr. Robert A. Skiff 1	1,590	89
Charles County Comm Coll, La Plata, MD 20646	1958	Dr. John Sine 12	4,773	247
Charles Stewart Mott Comm Coll, Flint, MI 48502	1923	Mr. David G. Moore 9	10,517	436
Chattahoochee Valley State Comm Coll, Phenix City, AL 36867	1974	Dr. James E. Owen 5	1,572	71
Chattanooga State Tech Comm Coll, Chattanooga, TN 37406	1965	Dr. Harry D. Wagner 5	4,480	NR
Chemeketa Comm Coll, Salem, OR 97309	1955	William Segura 12	8,776	NR
Chesapeake Coll, Wye Mills, MD 21679	1965	Dr. Robert C. Schleiger 12	2,247	216
Chesterfield-Marlboro Tech Coll, Cheraw, SC 29520	1967	Dr. Ronald W. Hampton 12	728	47
Chipola Jr Coll, Marianna, FL 32446	1947	Dr. Jerry W. Kandzer 5	1,844	110
Chippewa Valley Tech Coll, Eau Claire, WI 54701	1912	Dr. Norbert K. Wurtzel 10	3,800	400
Chowan Coll, Murfreesboro, NC 27855	1848	Dr. Bruce E. Whitaker 2	966	NR
Cincinnati Tech Coll, Cincinnati, OH 45223	1966	Mr. Frederick B. Schlimm 5	4,479	341
Cisco Jr Coll, Cisco, TX 76437	1940	Dr. Roger Schustereit 12	1,692	98
Citrus Coll, Glendora, CA 91740	1915	Dr. Louis F. Zellers 12	9,205	484
City Coll of San Francisco, San Francisco, CA 94112	1935	Dr. Carlos Brazil Ramirez 12	25,900	970
City Colls of Chicago, Chicago City-Wide Coll, Chicago, IL 60606	1975	Dr. Mark Warden 12	2,684	306
City Colls of Chicago, Harold Washington Coll, Chicago, IL 60601	1962	Dr. Bernice Miller 12	7,184	197
City Colls of Chicago, Harry S Truman Coll, Chicago, IL 60640	1956	Dr. Wallace B. Appelson 12	4,162	170
City Colls of Chicago, Kennedy-King Coll, Chicago, IL 60621	1935	Dr. Harold Pates 12	3,137	163
City Colls of Chicago, Malcolm X Coll, Chicago, IL 60612	1911	Dr. Deila Burt 12	2,310	149
City Colls of Chicago, Olive-Harvey Coll, Chicago, IL 60628	1970	Mr. Homer D. Franklin 12	3,311	135
City Colls of Chicago, Richard J Daley Coll, Chicago, IL 60652	1960	Dr. William P. Conway 12	4,662	152
City Colls of Chicago, Wilbur Wright Coll, Chicago, IL 60634	1934	Mr. Raymond F. LeFevour . . . 12	4,916	161
Clackamas Comm Coll, Oregon City, OR 97045	1966	Dr. John S. Keyser 9	5,501	500
Clarendon Coll, Clarendon, TX 79226	1898	Mr. Kenneth D. Vaughan 12	905	57
Clark Coll, Vancouver, WA 98663	1933	Dr. Earl P. Johnson 5	9,300	320
Clark County Comm Coll, North Las Vegas, NV 89030	1971	Dr. Paul E. Meacham 5	10,519	100
Clark State Comm Coll, Springfield, OH 45501	1962	Mr. Albert Salerno 5	2,200	121
Clatsop Comm Coll, Astoria, OR 97103	1958	Mr. Philip L. Bainer 9	2,752	169
Cleveland Comm Coll, Shelby, NC 28150	1965	Dr. James B. Petty 5	1,511	95
Cleveland Inst of Electronics, Cleveland, OH 44114 (2)	1934	John R. Drinko 3	3,100	6
Cleveland State Comm Coll, Cleveland, TN 37320	1967	Dr. James W. Ford 5	2,977	135
Clinton Comm Coll, Clinton, IA 52732	1946	Dr. Adelbert Purga 12	1,082	64
Clinton Comm Coll, Plattsburgh, NY 12901	1969	Dr. Jay Fennell 12	1,807	130
Cloud County Comm Coll, Concordia, KS 66901	1965	Dr. James P. Ihrig 12	2,507	232
Coastal Carolina Comm Coll, Jacksonville, NC 28540	1964	Dr. Ronald K. Lingle, Jr. 12	3,401	148
Coastline Comm Coll, Fountain Valley, CA 92708	1976	Mr. William M. Vega 12	15,229	490
Cochise Coll, Douglas, AZ 85607	1962	Dr. Dan W. Rehurek 12	4,746	301
Coffeyville Comm Coll, Coffeyville, KS 67337	1923	Dr. Dan Kinney 12	1,747	66
Colby Comm Coll, Colby, KS 67701	1964	Dr. Mikel Ary 12	710	75
Coll of Alameda, Alameda, CA 94501	1970	Donald R. Hongisto 12	5,406	NR
Coll of Eastern Utah, Price, UT 84501	1937	Dr. Michael A. Petersen 5	2,200	80
Coll of Lake County, Grayslake, IL 60030	1967	Dr. Daniel J. La Vista 12	12,581	710
Coll of San Mateo, San Mateo, CA 94402	1922	Dr. Lois A. Callahan 12	14,502	481
Coll of Southern Idaho, Twin Falls, ID 83303	1964	Mr. Gerald R. Meyerhoeffer . . . 12	2,776	108
Coll of The Albemarle, Elizabeth City, NC 27906	1960	Dr. Parker Chesson, Jr. 5	1,603	110
Coll of the Canyons, Valencia, CA 91355	1969	Dr. Dianne G. Van Hook 12	5,119	173
Coll of the Desert, Palm Desert, CA 92260	1959	Dr. David A. George 12	8,475	295
Coll of the Mainland, Texas City, TX 77591	1967	Mr. Larry L. Stanley 12	3,527	180
Coll of the Sequoias, Visalia, CA 93277	1925	Dr. Lincoln H. Hall 12	8,449	380

Name, address	Year	Governing official, control	Enrollment	Faculty
Coll of the Siskiyous, Weed, CA 96094	1957	Dr. Eugene Schumacher 12	2,482	158
Collin County Comm Coll, McKinney, TX 75070	1985	NR 12	3,000	375
Colorado Inst of Art, Denver, CO 80203	1952	Cheryl Murphy 3	1,200	63
Colorado Mountain Coll, Timberline Cmps, Leadville, CO 80461	1965	NR 10	610	47
Columbia Basin Coll, Pasco, WA 99301	1955	Dr. Marv Weiss 5	5,748	350
Columbia-Greene Comm Coll, Hudson, NY 12534	1969	Dr. Murray H. Block 12	1,616	110
Columbia State Comm Coll, Columbia, TN 38401	1966	Dr. Paul Sands 5	2,706	95
Columbus State Comm Coll, Columbus, OH 43216	1963	Dr. Harold M. Nestor 5	9,520	522
Commonwealth Coll, Virginia Beach, Virginia Beach, VA 23452	1880	Joseph A. Kennedy 3	850	30
Comm Coll of Allegheny County Allegheny Cmps, Pittsburgh, PA 15212	1966	Dr. Julius R. Brown 9	6,928	1,379
Comm Coll of Allegheny County Boyce Cmps, Monroeville, PA 15146	1966	Dr. Carl A. Di Sibio 9	3,962	779
Comm Coll of Allegheny County Coll Ctr–North, Pittsburgh, PA 15237	1972	Dr. Fred F. Bartok 9	2,879	1,395
Comm Coll of Allegheny County South Cmps, West Mifflin, PA 15122	1967	Dr. Thomas A. Juravich 9	4,520	760
Comm Coll of Aurora, Aurora, CO 80011	1983	Larry Carter 5	3,700	210
Comm Coll of Baltimore, Baltimore, MD 21215	1947	Dr. Joseph T. Durham 12	6,200	493
Comm Coll of Beaver County, Monaca, PA 15061	1966	Dr. William K. Bauer 5	2,604	150
Comm Coll of Denver, Denver, CO 80204	1970	Dr. Byron McClenney 5	4,185	186
Comm Coll of Philadelphia, Philadelphia, PA 19130	1964	Dr. Judith S. Eaton 12	14,214	976
Comm Coll of Rhode Island, Warwick, RI 02886	1964	Edward Liston 5	8,665	543
Comm Coll of the Air Force, Maxwell Air Force Base, AL 36112	1972	Col. R. A. Gregory, Jr. 4	389,000	10,000
Comm Coll of the Finger Lakes, Canandaigua, NY 14424	1965	Dr. Charles J. Meder 12	3,355	209
Comm Coll of Vermont, Waterbury, VT 05676	1970	Mr. Kenneth G. Kalb 5	1,175	410
Compton Comm Coll, Compton, CA 90221	1927	Dr. Edison O. Jackson 12	5,248	347
Connors State Coll, Warner, OK 74469	1908	Dr. Carl O. Westbrook 5	1,772	62
Contra Costa Coll, San Pablo, CA 94806	1948	Dr. D. Candy Rose 12	8,214	281
Cooke County Coll, Gainesville, TX 76240	1924	Dr. Luther Bud Joyner 9	2,996	143
Copiah-Lincoln Comm Coll, Wesson, MS 39191	1928	Dr. Billy B. Thames 12	1,891	116
Corning Comm Coll, Corning, NY 14830	1956	Dr. Donald H. Hangen 12	2,716	142
Cosumnes River Coll, Sacramento, CA 95823	1970	Dr. Marc E. Hall 10	8,554	264
County Coll of Morris, Randolph, NJ 07869	1966	Dr. Edward J. Yaw 9	9,347	730
Cowley Cty Comm Coll & Voc-Tech Sch, Arkansas City, KS 67005	1922	Dr. Gwendel Nelson 12	2,189	38
Crafton Hills Coll, Yucaipa, CA 92399	1972	Dr. Donald L. Singer 12	4,337	189
Craven Comm Coll, New Bern, NC 28560	1965	Dr. Thurman E. Brock 5	2,154	186
Cuesta Coll, San Luis Obispo, CA 93403	1964	Dr. Frank R. Martinez 10	8,000	273
Culinary Inst of America, Hyde Park, NY 12538	1946	Mr. Ferdinand E. Metz 1	1,833	100
Cumberland County Coll, Vineland, NJ 08360	1963	Dr. Philip S. Phelon 12	2,226	87
Cuyahoga Comm Coll, Eastern Cmps, Warrensville Township, OH 44122	1971	Dr. Grace Carolyn Brown . . . 12	5,475	253
Cuyahoga Comm Coll, Metropolitan Cmps, Cleveland, OH 44115	1963	Dr. Ronald R. Zambetti 12	5,331	NR
Cuyahoga Comm Coll, Western Cmps, Parma, OH 44130	1966	Mr. Ronald M. Sobel 12	11,882	491
Cuyamaca Coll, El Cajon, CA 92019	1978	Dr. Samuel M. Ciccati 5	3,727	143
Cypress Coll, Cypress, CA 90630	1966	Dr. Jack Scott 12	13,400	398
Dalton Coll, Dalton, GA 30720	1963	Dr. Derrell C. Roberts 5	1,866	61
Danville Area Comm Coll, Danville, IL 61832	1946	Dr. Ronald K. Lingle 12	3,368	143
Danville Comm Coll, Danville, VA 24541	1967	Dr. Arnold R. Oliver 5	3,015	132
Darton Coll, Albany, GA 31707	1965	Mrs. Marilyn Malphurs 5	1,893	84
Davenport Coll of Business, Kalamazoo Cmps, Kalamazoo, MI 49007 (4)	1866	C. Dexter Rohm 1	1,059	68
Davenport Coll of Business, Lansing Cmps, Lansing, MI 48933	1979	Don Colizzi 1	963	52
Davidson County Comm Coll, Lexington, NC 27293	1958	Dr. J. Bryan Brooks 5	2,579	153
Daytona Beach Comm Coll, Daytona Beach, FL 32015	1958	Dr. Charles H. Polk 5	8,703	NR
Dean Jr Coll, Franklin, MA 02038	1865	Mr. Richard E. Crockford 1	1,200	102
De Anza Coll, Cupertino, CA 95014	1967	Dr. A. Robert Dehart 12	25,546	897
DeKalb Coll, Decatur, GA 30034	1964	Dr. Marvin M. Cole 5	10,566	NR
Delaware County Comm Coll, Media, PA 19063	1967	Dr. Richard D. De Cosmo . . . 12	8,273	416
Delaware Tech & Comm Coll, Southern Cmps, Georgetown, DE 19947	1967	Mr. Jack F. Owens 5	2,479	166
Delaware Tech & Comm Coll, Stanton/Wilmington Cmps, Newark, DE 19702	1968	Dr. John R. Kotula 5	5,078	323
Delaware Tech & Comm Coll, Terry Cmps, Dover, DE 19901	1972	Dr. Linda Jolly 5	1,605	98
Delgado Comm Coll, New Orleans, LA 70119	1921	Dr. James Caillier 5	7,315	489
Del Mar Coll, Corpus Christi, TX 78404	1935	Mr. B. R. Venters 12	9,972	446
Delta Coll, University Center, MI 48710	1961	Mr. Donald J. Carlyon 10	10,694	413
Denmark Tech Coll, Denmark, SC 29042	1948	Dr. Curtis E. Bryan 5	699	45
Denver Automotive and Diesel Coll, Denver, CO 80223	1963	NR 3	675	43
Denver Inst of Tech, Denver, CO 80221	1953	Kirk T. Riedinger 3	780	48
Des Moines Area Comm Coll, Ankeny, IA 50021	1966	Dr. Joseph Borgen 12	9,861	208
Diablo Valley Coll, Pleasant Hill, CA 94523	1949	Dr. Phyllis L. Peterson 12	21,000	660
Dixie Coll, St George, UT 84770	1911	Dr. Douglas Alder 5	2,300	66
Dodge City Comm Coll, Dodge City, KS 67801	1935	Mr. Gay Dahn 12	1,500	210
Draughons Jr Coll, Knoxville, TN 37919	1903	NR 3	600	38
Draughons Jr Coll, Memphis, TN 38116	1890	NR 3	700	NR
Dundalk Comm Coll, Baltimore, MD 21222	1970	Dr. Martha A. Smith 9	3,206	201
Durham Tech Comm Coll, Durham, NC 27703	1961	Dr. Phail Wynn, Jr. 5	4,484	242
Dutchess Comm Coll, Poughkeepsie, NY 12601	1957	Dr. Jerry Lee 12	6,417	389
Dyersburg State Comm Coll, Dyersburg, TN 38025	1969	Dr. Karen A. Bowyer 5	1,742	114
East Arkansas Comm Coll, Forrest City, AR 72335	1974	Dr. Bob C. Burns 5	1,490	89
East Central Coll, Union, MO 63084	1968	Dr. Charles R. Novak 10	2,684	120
East Central Jr Coll, Decatur, MS 39327	1928	Dr. Eddie M. Smith 12	1,189	53
Eastern Arizona Coll, Thatcher, AZ 85552	1888	Mr. Gherald L. Hoopes, Jr. . . 12	2,065	233
Eastern New Mexico U–Roswell, Roswell, NM 88202	1958	Dr. Loyd R. Hughes 12	1,632	85
Eastern Oklahoma State Coll, Wilburton, OK 74578	1907	NR 5	2,446	89
Eastern Wyoming Coll, Torrington, WY 82240	1948	Mr. Guido Smith 12	1,807	49
Eastfield Coll, Mesquite, TX 75150	1970	Dr. Justus D. Sundermann . . 12	9,125	399
East Georgia Coll, Swainsboro, GA 30401	1973	Dr. Willie D. Gunn 5	617	20

Name, address	Year	Governing official, control	Enrollment	Faculty
East Los Angeles Coll, Monterey Park, CA 91754	1945	Mr. Arthur Avila ... 12	13,000	450
East Mississippi Jr Coll, Scooba, MS 39358	1927	Mr. Clois Cheatham ... 12	939	175
Edgecombe Comm Coll, Tarboro, NC 27886	1968	Mr. Charles B. McIntyre ... 12	1,341	104
Edison Comm Coll, Fort Myers, FL 33906	1962	Dr. David G. Robinson ... 12	7,732	NR
Edison State Comm Coll, Piqua, OH 45356	1973	Kenneth A. Yowell ... 5	2,652	143
Edmonds Comm Coll, Lynnwood, WA 98036	1967	Mr. Thomas C. Nielsen ... 12	5,460	307
El Camino Coll, Torrance, CA 90506	1947	Dr. Sam Schauerman ... 10	26,784	483
El Centro Coll, Dallas, TX 75202	1966	Dr. Wright L. Lassiter, Jr. ... 9	5,534	313
Elgin Comm Coll, Elgin, IL 60123	1949	Dr. Paul Heath ... 12	6,805	332
Ellsworth Comm Coll, Iowa Falls, IA 50126	1890	Duane R. Lloyd ... 12	940	55
El Paso Comm Coll, El Paso, TX 79998	1969	Dr. Robert E. Shepack ... 9	15,290	1,734
El Reno Jr Coll, El Reno, OK 73036	1938	Dr. Bill S. Cole ... 12	1,522	82
Endicott Coll, Beverly, MA 01915 (3)	1939	Dr. Richard E. Wylie ... 1	775	71
Enterprise State Jr Coll, Enterprise, AL 36331	1965	Dr. Joseph D. Talmadge ... 5	2,028	118
Erie Comm Coll, City Cmps, Buffalo, NY 14203	1971	Dr. Louis M. Ricci ... 12	3,112	189
Erie Comm Coll, North Cmps, Williamsville, NY 14221	1946	Dr. Louis M. Ricci ... 12	7,548	286
Erie Comm Coll, South Cmps, Orchard Park, NY 14127	1974	Dr. Louis M. Ricci ... 12	3,405	196
Essex Comm Coll, Baltimore, MD 21237	1957	Dr. John E. Ravekes ... 12	10,218	470
Essex County Coll, Newark, NJ 07102	1966	Dr. Zachary Yamba ... 9	5,694	146
Eugenio Maria de Hostos Comm Coll of City U of NY, Bronx, NY 10451	1968	Dr. I. Santiago ... 12	4,024	NR
Everett Comm Coll, Everett, WA 98201	1941	Mr. Robert Drewel ... 5	3,736	252
Evergreen Valley Coll, San Jose, CA 95135	1975	Dr. Gerald H. Strelitz ... 12	8,758	257
Fairleigh Dickinson U, Edward Williams Coll, Hackensack, NJ 07601	1964	Kenneth T. Vehrkens ... 1	1,597	61
Fashion Inst-Design/Merchandising, LA Cmps, Los Angeles, CA 90017	1969	Ms. Tonian Hohberg ... 3	3,300	160
Fashion Inst-Design/Merchandising, SF Cmps, San Francisco, CA 94108	1969	Jane Bell ... 3	800	55
Fayetteville Tech Comm Coll, Fayetteville, NC 28303	1961	Dr. Craig Allen ... 5	6,040	690
Feather River Coll, Quincy, CA 95971	1968	Dr. Joseph Brennan ... 12	1,102	74
Fergus Falls Comm Coll, Fergus Falls, MN 56537	1960	Mr. Dan F. True ... 5	1,300	89
Fiorello H LaGuardia Comm Coll of City U of NY, Long Island City, NY 11101	1971	Martin G. Moed ... 12	8,963	588
Flathead Valley Comm Coll, Kalispell, MT 59901	1967	Dr. Howard L. Fryett ... 12	1,958	119
Florence-Darlington Tech Coll, Florence, SC 29501	1963	Dr. Michael B. McCall ... 5	1,874	210
Florida Comm Coll at Jacksonville, Jacksonville, FL 32202	1966	Dr. Charles C. Spence ... 5	15,385	1,411
Florida Keys Comm Coll, Key West, FL 33040	1965	Dr. William A. Seeker ... 5	643	92
Floyd Coll, Rome, GA 30163	1970	Dr. David B. McCorkle ... 5	1,259	NR
Foothill Coll, Los Altos Hills, CA 94022	1958	Dr. Thomas H. Clements ... 12	15,728	500
Forsyth Tech Comm Coll, Winston-Salem, NC 27103	1964	Dr. Bob H. Greene ... 5	4,513	193
Fort Scott Comm Coll, Fort Scott, KS 66701	1919	Mr. Richard D. Hedges ... 12	1,700	131
Fox Valley Tech Coll, Appleton, WI 54913	1967	Dr. Stanley J. Spanbauer ... 12	4,749	1,241
Frank Phillips Coll, Borger, TX 79008	1948	Dr. Andy Hicks ... 12	953	93
Frederick Comm Coll, Frederick, MD 21701	1957	Dr. Lee J. Betts ... 12	3,483	205
Fresno City Coll, Fresno, CA 93741	1910	Dr. Ernest R. Leach ... 10	15,728	534
Front Range Comm Coll, Westminster, CO 80030	1968	Dr. Cary Israel ... 5	5,967	450
Fullerton Coll, Fullerton, CA 92634	1913	Dr. Philip W. Borst ... 12	18,383	675
Fulton-Montgomery Comm Coll, Johnstown, NY 12095	1964	Mr. John G. Boshart ... 12	1,745	122
Gadsden State Comm Coll, Gadsden, AL 35999	1965	NR ... 5	4,062	NR
Gainesville Coll, Gainesville, GA 30503	1964	Dr. J. Foster Watkins ... 5	2,160	80
Galveston Coll, Galveston, TX 77550	1967	John E. Pickelman ... 12	2,182	122
Garden City Comm Coll, Garden City, KS 67846	1919	Dr. James H. Tangeman ... 10	1,820	95
Garland County Comm Coll, Hot Springs, AR 71913	1973	NR ... 12	1,729	106
Garrett Comm Coll, McHenry, MD 21541	1966	Dr. Stephen Herman ... 12	612	32
Gaston Coll, Dallas, NC 28034	1963	Dr. W. Wayne Scott ... 12	3,434	220
Gateway Comm Coll, Phoenix, AZ 85034	1968	Ms. Myrna Harrison ... 5	5,432	213
Gateway Tech Coll, Racine, WI 53403	1911	Dr. John R. Birkholz ... 12	7,533	501
Gavilan Coll, Gilroy, CA 95020	1919	Dr. John J. Holleman ... 12	4,029	174
Genesee Comm Coll, Batavia, NY 14020	1966	Dr. Stuart Steiner ... 12	3,015	181
George Corley Wallace State Comm Coll, Selma, AL 36702	1966	Dr. Charles L. Byrd ... 5	1,514	72
George C Wallace State Comm Coll, Dothan, AL 36303	1949	Dr. Nathan L. Hodges ... 5	3,781	163
Georgia Military Coll, Milledgeville, GA 31061	1879	Maj. Gen. William Acker ... 12	1,614	113
Germanna Comm Coll, Locust Grove, VA 22508	1970	Dr. Francis S. Turnage ... 5	1,102	111
Glendale Comm Coll, Glendale, AZ 85302	1965	Dr. John R. Waltrip ... 12	17,948	609
Glendale Comm Coll, Glendale, CA 91208	1927	Dr. John A. Davitt ... 12	12,911	267
Glen Oaks Comm Coll, Centreville, MI 49032	1965	Dr. Philip G. Ward ... 12	1,384	96
Gloucester County Coll, Sewell, NJ 08080	1967	Dr. Richard N. Jones ... 9	3,560	151
Gogebic Comm Coll, Ironwood, MI 49938	1932	Dr. James R. Grote ... 12	1,210	79
Golden West Coll, Huntington Beach, CA 92647	1966	NR ... 5	14,200	430
Gordon Coll, Barnesville, GA 30204	1852	Dr. Jerry M. Williamson ... 5	1,403	83
Grand Rapids Jr Coll, Grand Rapids, MI 49503	1914	Mr. Richard Calkins ... 11	10,993	331
Grays Harbor Coll, Aberdeen, WA 98520	1930	Dr. Joseph A. Malik ... 5	1,212	115
Grayson County Coll, Denison, TX 75020	1964	Dr. Jim M. Williams ... 12	3,185	176
Greater Hartford Comm Coll, Hartford, CT 06105	1967	Walter J. Markiewicz ... 5	2,927	NR
Greater New Haven State Tech Coll, North Haven, CT 06473	1977	George D. Harris ... 5	900	85
Great Lakes Jr Coll of Business, Saginaw, MI 48607	1907	Angelo Guerriero ... 1	1,763	133
Greenfield Comm Coll, Greenfield, MA 01301	1962	Katherine H. Sloan ... 5	1,612	79
Green River Comm Coll, Auburn, WA 98002	1965	Mr. Richard A. Rutkowski ... 5	5,550	267
Greenville Tech Coll, Greenville, SC 29606	1962	Dr. Thomas E. Barton, Jr. ... 5	6,473	493
Grossmont Coll, El Cajon, CA 92020	1961	Dr. Ivan L. Jones ... 12	15,595	570
Guam Comm Coll, Guam Main Facility, GU 96921	1977	John T. Cruz ... 8	1,723	227
Guilford Tech Comm Coll, Jamestown, NC 27282	1958	Dr. Ray Needham ... 12	5,471	539
Gulf Coast Comm Coll, Panama City, FL 32401	1957	Dr. Robert L. McSpadden ... 5	4,975	240
Hagerstown Jr Coll, Hagerstown, MD 21740	1946	Dr. Norman P. Shea ... 9	2,641	152
Halifax Comm Coll, Weldon, NC 27890	1967	Dr. Phillip W. Taylor ... 12	1,051	68
Hamilton Tech Coll, Davenport, IA 52807	1969	Charles Hamilton, Jr. ... 3	943	33
Harcum Jr Coll, Bryn Mawr, PA 19010 (4)	1915	Dr. Norma F. Furst ... 1	707	84
Hardbarger Jr Coll of Business, Raleigh, NC 27602	1924	NR ... 4	650	32
Harford Comm Coll, Bel Air, MD 21014	1957	Dr. Alfred C. O'Connell ... 12	4,425	265
Harrisburg Area Comm Coll, Harrisburg, PA 17110	1964	Dr. Kenneth B. Woodbury, Jr. ... 12	6,686	279
Harry M Ayers State Tech Coll, Anniston, AL 36202	1966	NR ... 5	697	225
Hartford State Tech Coll, Hartford, CT 06106	1946	Mr. Kenneth E. DeRego ... 5	955	82

Name, address	Year	Governing official, control	Enrollment	Faculty
Hartnell Coll, Salinas, CA 93901	1920	Dr. James R. Hardt	10	7,014	272
Hawkeye Inst of Tech, Waterloo, IA 50704	1967	Dr. John E. Hawse	12	1,926	165
Haywood Comm Coll, Clyde, NC 28721	1964	Mr. Joseph H. Nanney	12	1,093	86
Heald Business Coll, San Francisco, CA 94103	1863	Alec Winters	1	850	31
Henry Ford Comm Coll, Dearborn, MI 48128	1938	Dr. Stuart M. Bundy	10	15,938	1,005
Herkimer County Comm Coll, Herkimer, NY 13350	1966	Mr. Ronald F. Williams	12	2,019	86
Hesser Coll, Manchester, NH 03101	1900	Linwood W. Galeucia	3	2,200	60
Hibbing Comm Coll, Hibbing, MN 55746	1916	Dr. Anthony Kuznik	5	1,345	65
Highland Comm Coll, Freeport, IL 61032	1962	Dr. Joseph C. Piland	10	2,878	142
Highland Comm Coll, Highland, KS 66035	1858	Dr. Larry F. Devane	12	1,686	162
Highland Park Comm Coll, Highland Park, MI 48203	1918	Dr. Comer Heath, III	12	2,333	42
Highline Comm Coll, Des Moines, WA 98198	1961	Dr. Shirley B. Gordon	5	8,100	432
Hilbert Coll, Hamburg, NY 14075	1957	Sr. Edmunette Paczesny	1	729	48
Hill Coll of the Hill Jr Coll District, Hillsboro, TX 76645	1923	Dr. W. R. Auvenshine	10	1,500	98
Hillsborough Comm Coll, Tampa, FL 33631	1968	Dr. Andreas A. Paloumpis	5	15,684	527
Hinds Comm Coll, Raymond, MS 39154	1917	NR	12	8,228	506
Hocking Tech Coll, Nelsonville, OH 45764	1968	Dr. John J. Light	5	3,800	252
Holmes Comm Coll, Goodman, MS 39079	1928	NR	12	1,800	130
Holyoke Comm Coll, Holyoke, MA 01040	1946	Dr. David M. Bartley	5	3,389	200
Horry-Georgetown Tech Coll, Conway, SC 29526	1965	Dr. D. Kent Sharples	12	1,658	113
Housatonic Comm Coll, Bridgeport, CT 06608	1966	Dr. Vincent S. Darnowski	5	2,335	92
Houston Comm Coll System, Houston, TX 77270	1971	Mr. J. B. Whiteley	12	30,236	2,085
Howard Coll, Big Spring, TX 79720	1945	Dr. Bob E. Riley	12	1,526	127
Howard Comm Coll, Columbia, MD 21044	1966	Dr. Dwight A. Burrill	12	3,926	245
Hudson County Comm Coll, Jersey City, NJ 07306	1974	NR	12	2,726	NR
Hudson Valley Comm Coll, Troy, NY 12180	1953	Dr. Joseph J. Bulmer	12	8,816	420
Hutchinson Comm Coll, Hutchinson, KS 67501	1928	Dr. James H. Stringer	12	4,064	286
ICM Sch of Business, Pittsburgh, PA 15222	1963	Wayne R. Zanardelli	3	655	55
ICS Ctr for Degree Studies, Scranton, PA 18515	1975	Mr. Gary Keisling	3	12,529	5
Illinois Central Coll, East Peoria, IL 61635	1967	Dr. Leon H. Perley	12	12,360	526
Illinois East Comm Colls, Frontier Comm Coll, Fairfield, IL 62837	1976	Richard Mason	12	2,448	161
Illinois East Comm Colls, Lincoln Trail Coll, Robinson, IL 62454	1969	Dr. Donald E. Donnay	12	940	60
Illinois East Comm Colls, Olney Central Coll, Olney, IL 62450	1960	Dr. Stephen J. Kridelbaugh	12	1,500	83
Illinois East Comm Colls, Wabash Valley Coll, Mount Carmel, IL 62863	1960	Dr. Harry K. Benson	12	1,683	63
Illinois Valley Comm Coll, Oglesby, IL 61348	1924	Dr. Alfred E. Wisgoski	10	4,200	NR
Imperial Valley Coll, Imperial, CA 92251	1922	Dr. John A. DePaoli	12	4,039	143
Independence Comm Coll, Independence, KS 67301	1925	Dr. Jo Ann C. McDowell	10	1,471	127
Indiana Business Coll, Indianapolis, IN 46204	1902	Kenneth J. Konesco	3	1,500	NR
Indiana Vocational Tech Coll–Central Indiana, Indianapolis, IN 46206	1963	Dr. Meredith L. Carter	5	4,956	285
Indiana Vocational Tech Coll–Columbus, Columbus, IN 47203	1963	NR	5	2,378	121
Indiana Vocational Tech Coll–Eastcentral, Muncie, IN 47302	1968	Mr. Richard L. Davidson	5	1,672	92
Indiana Vocational Tech Coll–Kokomo, Kokomo, IN 46901	1968	Mr. Bill Morris	5	2,299	128
Indiana Vocational Tech Coll–Lafayette, Lafayette, IN 47903	1968	Dr. Thomas E. Reckerd	5	1,804	113
Indiana Vocational Tech Coll–Northcentral, South Bend, IN 46619	1968	Dr. Carl F. Lutz	5	2,639	176
Indiana Vocational Tech Coll–Northeast, Fort Wayne, IN 46805	1969	Mr. Jon L. Rupright	5	3,106	164
Indiana Vocational Tech Coll–Northwest, Gary, IN 46409	1963	Mr. Mearle R. Donica	5	3,083	208
Indiana Vocational Tech Coll–Southcentral, Sellersburg, IN 47172	1968	Jonathan W. Thomas	5	1,539	94
Indiana Vocational Tech Coll–Southeast, Madison, IN 47250	1963	Homer B. Smith	5	786	59
Indiana Vocational Tech Coll–Southwest, Evansville, IN 47710	1963	Dr. H. Victor Baldi	5	2,064	116
Indiana Vocational Tech Coll–Wabash Valley, Terre Haute, IN 47802	1966	Mr. Sam E. Borden	5	2,002	123
Indiana Vocational Tech Coll–Whitewater, Richmond, IN 47374	1963	Dr. Judith A. Redwine	5	1,068	78
Indian Hills Comm Coll, Ottumwa, IA 52501	1966	Dr. Lyle A. Hellyer	12	2,598	121
Indian River Comm Coll, Fort Pierce, FL 34954	1960	Dr. Edwin R. Massey	5	10,184	568
Inter American U of PR, Guayama Regional Coll, Guayama, PR 00654	1958	Mr. Pablo I. Rivera Diaz	1	1,304	89
Interboro Inst, New York, NY 10019	1888	Mr. Mischa Lazoff	3	700	36
International Tech Inst, Tampa, FL 33610	1968	NR	1	600	NR
Inver Hills Comm Coll, Inver Grove Heights, MN 55075	1969	Dr. Patrick A. Roche	5	4,800	192
Iowa Central Comm Coll, Fort Dodge, IA 50501	1966	Dr. Harvey D. Martin	12	2,740	155
Iowa Western Comm Coll, Council Bluffs, IA 51502	1966	Dr. Carl L. Heinrich	12	2,604	166
Irvine Valley Coll, Irvine, CA 92720	1979	Ronald A. Kong	12	5,315	227
Isothermal Comm Coll, Spindale, NC 28160	1965	Dr. Willard L. Lewis	5	1,546	85
Itasca Comm Coll, Grand Rapids, MN 55744	1922	Dr. Lawrence N. Dukes	5	1,245	83
Itawamba Comm Coll, Fulton, MS 38843	1947	Dr. W. O. Benjamin	12	2,878	99
ITT Tech Inst, St Louis, MO 63108 (2)	1936	L. Davis Cunningham	3	617	25
ITT Tech Inst, Dayton, OH 45414 (2)	1935	Dennis W. Alspaugh	3	647	25
Jackson Comm Coll, Jackson, MI 49201	1928	Dr. Clyde LeTarte	9	7,000	440
Jackson State Comm Coll, Jackson, TN 38301	1967	Dr. Walter L. Nelms	5	2,774	141
James H Faulkner State Jr Coll, Bay Minette, AL 36507	1965	Dr. Gary L. Branch	5	2,348	117
James Sprunt Comm Coll, Kenansville, NC 28349	1964	Dr. Carl D. Price	5	853	59
Jamestown Comm Coll, Jamestown, NY 14701	1950	Mr. Paul A. Benke	12	3,698	236
Jefferson Coll, Hillsboro, MO 63050	1963	Dr. B. Ray Henry	12	3,294	163
Jefferson Comm Coll, Watertown, NY 13601	1961	Mr. John T. Henderson	12	1,903	180
Jefferson Davis State Jr Coll, Brewton, AL 36427	1965	Sandra K. McLeod	5	900	53
Jefferson State Jr Coll, Birmingham, AL 35215	1965	Dr. Judy M. Merritt	5	6,685	302
Jefferson Tech Coll, Steubenville, OH 43952	1966	Dr. Edward L. Florak	5	1,415	98
J F Drake State Tech Coll, Huntsville, AL 35811	1961	Johnny L. Harris	5	778	NR
John A Logan Coll, Carterville, IL 62918	1967	Dr. Harold R. O'Neil	5	3,838	105
John C Calhoun State Comm Coll, Decatur, AL 35609	1965	Dr. James R. Chasteen	5	6,551	305
John M Patterson State Tech Coll, Montgomery, AL 36116	1962	Mr. J. L. Taunton	5	611	45
Johnson County Comm Coll, Overland Park, KS 66210	1967	Dr. Charles J. Carlsen	12	11,164	447
Johnston Comm Coll, Smithfield, NC 27577	1969	Dr. John L. Tart	5	2,080	145
John Tyler Comm Coll, Chester, VA 23831	1967	Dr. Freddie W. Nicholas, Sr.	12	4,516	186
John Wood Comm Coll, Quincy, IL 62301	1974	Dr. Robert C. Keys	10	3,901	112

Name, address	Year	Governing official, control	Enrollment	Faculty
Jones County Jr Coll, Ellisville, MS 39437	1928	Dr. T. Terrell Tisdale 12	3,368	145
J Sargeant Reynolds Comm Coll, Richmond, VA 23261	1972	Dr. S. A. Burnette 5	4,688	586
Jr Coll of Albany, Albany, NY 12208	1957	Dr. Sara Chapman 1	1,056	85
Kalamazoo Valley Comm Coll, Kalamazoo, MI 49009	1966	Dr. Marilyn J. Schlack 12	9,158	309
Kankakee Comm Coll, Kankakee, IL 60901	1966	Dr. Larry D. Huffman 12	3,300	213
Kansas City Kansas Comm Coll, Kansas City, KS 66112	1923	Dr. Bill Spencer 9	4,230	289
Kansas Coll of Tech, Salina, KS 67401	1965	Dr. Anthony L. Tilmans 5	737	61
Kaskaskia Coll, Centralia, IL 62801	1966	Mr. Raymond D. Woods 12	2,804	192
Katharine Gibbs Sch, Melville, NY 11747 (4)	1971	NR 3	600	17
Katharine Gibbs Sch, New York, NY 10166 (4)	1918	Miss Diana Mazzarella 3	793	50
Kellogg Comm Coll, Battle Creek, MI 49017	1956	Dr. Paul R. Ohm 12	5,276	250
Kent State U, Ashtabula Cmps, Ashtabula, OH 44004	1958	Dr. John K. Mahan 5	866	60
Kent State U, Salem Cmps, Salem, OH 44460	1966	Dr. James F. Cooney 5	798	63
Kent State U, Stark Cmps, Canton, OH 44720	1967	Dr. William G. Bittle 5	1,870	75
Kent State U, Trumbull Cmps, Warren, OH 44483	1954	John N. Cable 5	1,695	90
Kent State U, Tuscarawas Cmps, New Philadelphia, OH 44663	1962	Harold D. Shade 5	952	71
Keystone Jr Coll, La Plume, PA 18440	1868	Robert E. Mooney, Jr. 1	768	88
Kilgore Coll, Kilgore, TX 75662	1935	NR 12	4,289	191
Kingsborough Comm Coll of City U of NY, Brooklyn, NY 11235	1963	Dr. Leon M. Goldstein 12	7,959	669
Kings River Comm Coll, Reedley, CA 93654	1926	Dr. Abel B. Sykes, Jr. 12	3,146	176
Kirkwood Comm Coll, Cedar Rapids, IA 52406	1966	Dr. Norm Nielsen 12	7,053	430
Kirtland Comm Coll, Roscommon, MI 48653	1966	Mr. Raymond D. Homer 10	1,146	75
Kishwaukee Coll, Malta, IL 60150	1967	Dr. Norman L. Jenkins 12	3,583	NR
Labette Comm Coll, Parsons, KS 67357	1923	Dr. Gery C. Hochanadel 12	2,669	261
Lackawanna Jr Coll, Scranton, PA 18505	1894	Mr. Allan P. Mensky 1	660	90
Lake City Comm Coll, Lake City, FL 32055	1962	Dr. Muriel Kay Heimer 5	2,756	300
Lake Land Coll, Mattoon, IL 61938	1966	Dr. David V. Schultz 12	3,952	360
Lakeland Comm Coll, Mentor, OH 44060	1967	Dr. Ralph R. Doty 12	7,840	416
Lake Michigan Coll, Benton Harbor, MI 49022	1946	Dr. Anne E. Mulder 10	3,066	240
Lakeshore Tech Coll, Cleveland, WI 53015	1967	Dr. Dennis Ladwig 12	2,352	702
Lake-Sumter Comm Coll, Leesburg, FL 32788	1961	Dr. Carl C. Andersen 12	2,103	NR
Lake Tahoe Comm Coll, South Lake Tahoe, CA 95702	1975	Dr. James W. Duke 12	1,467	92
Lakewood Comm Coll, White Bear Lake, MN 55110	1967	Dr. Jerry Owens 5	5,321	165
Lamar U—Port Arthur, Port Arthur, TX 77641	1909	Dr. Sam Monroe 5	1,707	85
Lane Comm Coll, Eugene, OR 97405	1964	Dr. Richard M. Turner, III 12	7,623	369
Laney Coll, Oakland, CA 94607	1953	Mr. Odell Johnson 5	9,924	NR
Lansing Comm Coll, Lansing, MI 48901	1957	Dr. Philip J. Gannon 12	23,390	1,000
Laramie County Comm Coll, Cheyenne, WY 82007	1968	Dr. Timothy Davies 9	3,676	213
Laredo Jr Coll, Laredo, TX 78040	1946	Dr. Roger L. Worsley 12	4,981	NR
Lassen Coll, Susanville, CA 96130	1925	Dr. Virginia L. Holten 12	2,808	350
Latter-Day Saints Business Coll, Salt Lake City, UT 84111	1886	Dr. Kenneth H. Beesley 2	801	61
Lawson State Comm Coll, Birmingham, AL 35221	1965	Dr. Perry W. Ward 5	1,105	54
Lee Coll, Baytown, TX 77520	1934	Dr. Vivian Bowling Blevins 10	5,068	251
Lehigh County Comm Coll, Schnecksville, PA 18078	1967	Dr. Robert L. Barthlow 12	3,487	126
Lenoir Comm Coll, Kinston, NC 28502	1960	Dr. Lonnie H. Blizzard 5	2,263	147
Lewis and Clark Comm Coll, Godfrey, IL 62035	1970	NR 10	5,012	304
Lima Tech Coll, Lima, OH 45804	1971	Dr. James S. Biddle 5	1,795	167
Lincoln Land Comm Coll, Springfield, IL 62708	1967	Dr. Robert L. Poorman 10	7,848	402
Lincoln Tech Inst, Allentown, PA 18104	1949	Robert G. Milot 3	870	31
Linn-Benton Comm Coll, Albany, OR 97321	1966	Dr. Thomas Gonzales 12	11,000	640
Long Beach City Coll, Long Beach, CA 90808	1927	Dr. Beverly O'Neil 5	26,044	850
Longview Comm Coll, Lee's Summit, MO 64081	1969	Mr. Aldo W. Leker 10	7,764	314
Lorain County Comm Coll, Elyria, OH 44035	1963	Dr. Roy Church 12	6,089	312
Lord Fairfax Comm Coll, Middletown, VA 22645	1969	Dr. Marilyn C. Beck 12	2,473	110
Los Angeles City Coll, Los Angeles, CA 90029	1929	Dr. Stelle Feuers 12	14,463	700
Los Angeles Harbor Coll, Wilmington, CA 90744	1949	Mr. James L. Heinselman 12	8,990	310
Los Angeles Mission Coll, San Fernando, CA 91340	1974	Mr. Lowell J. Erickson 12	4,870	115
Los Angeles Pierce Coll, Woodland Hills, CA 91371	1947	Dr. David Wolf 12	18,415	399
Los Angeles Southwest Coll, Los Angeles, CA 90047	1967	Dr. Thomas G. Lakin 12	5,063	228
Los Angeles Trade-Tech Coll, Los Angeles, CA 90015	1925	Mr. Thomas L. Stevens, Jr. 12	13,301	250
Los Angeles Valley Coll, Van Nuys, CA 91401	1949	Dr. Mary E. Lee 12	18,503	260
Los Medanos Coll, Pittsburg, CA 94565	1975	Dr. Chester H. Case 10	6,793	200
Louisburg Coll, Louisburg, NC 27549	1787	Dr. J. Allen Norris, Jr. 2	870	56
Louisiana State U at Alexandria, Alexandria, LA 71302	1960	Dr. James W. Firnberg 5	2,203	102
Louisiana State U at Eunice, Eunice, LA 70535	1967	Dr. Anthony Mumphrey 5	1,746	84
Lower Columbia Coll, Longview, WA 98632	1934	Dr. Vernon R. Pickett 5	3,900	143
Lurleen B Wallace State Jr Coll, Andalusia, AL 36420	1969	Dr. William H. McWhorter 5	1,003	39
Luzerne County Comm Coll, Nanticoke, PA 18634	1966	Thomas J. Moran 9	5,850	249
MacCormac Jr Coll, Chicago, IL 60604	1904	Mr. Gordon C. Borchardt 1	700	41
Macon Coll, Macon, GA 31297	1968	Dr. S. Aaron Hyatt 5	3,511	126
Madison Area Tech Coll, Madison, WI 53704	1911	Dr. Jerry C. Kaiser 10	10,611	1,619
Manatee Comm Coll, Bradenton, FL 34207	1957	Dr. Stephen J. Korcheck 5	7,163	234
Manchester Comm Coll, Manchester, CT 06040	1963	Dr. Jonathan M. Daube 5	7,000	200
Maple Woods Comm Coll, Kansas City, MO 64156-	1969	Dr. Stephen R. Brainard 12	3,486	160
Maria Coll, Albany, NY 12208	1958	Sr. Laureen Fitzgerald 1	927	75
Marin Comm Coll, Kentfield, CA 94904	1926	Ms. Myrna R. Miller 12	10,000	NR
Marion Tech Coll, Marion, OH 43302	1971	Dr. John Richard Bryson 13	1,348	105
Marshalltown Comm Coll, Marshalltown, IA 50158	1927	Dr. James W. Blake 10	1,300	98
Martin Comm Coll, Williamston, NC 27892	1968	Dr. W. Travis Martin 5	689	51
Marymount Coll, Palos Verdes, California, Rancho Palos Verdes, CA 90274	1932	Dr. Thomas D. Wood 2	753	70
Massachusetts Bay Comm Coll, Wellesley Hills, MA 02181	1961	Mr. Roger A. Van Winkle 5	4,125	NR
Massasoit Comm Coll, Brockton, MA 02402	1968	Dr. Gerard F. Burke 5	6,591	342
Mattatuck Comm Coll, Waterbury, CT 06708	1967	Dr. Richard L. Sanders 5	3,812	54
Mayland Comm Coll, Spruce Pine, NC 28777	1971	Dr. Virginia Foxx 12	775	35
McDowell Tech Comm Coll, Marion, NC 28752	1964	Dr. Robert M. Boggs 5	612	45
McHenry County Coll, Crystal Lake, IL 60012	1967	Mr. Robert C. Bartlett 12	3,488	140
McLennan Comm Coll, Waco, TX 76708	1965	Dr. Dennis F. Michaelis 9	5,459	246
Mendocino Coll, Ukiah, CA 95482	1973	Dr. Leroy R. Lowery 12	4,195	166
Merced Coll, Merced, CA 95348	1962	Dr. Tom K. Harris, Jr. 12	6,970	368
Mercer County Comm Coll, Trenton, NJ 08690	1966	Mr. John P. Hanley 12	8,651	331
Meridian Comm Coll, Meridian, MS 39305	1937	Dr. William F. Scaggs 12	2,814	230
Merritt Coll, Oakland, CA 94619	1953	NR 12	5,942	NR

Name, address	Year	Governing official, control	Enroll- ment	Faculty
Mesabi Comm Coll, Virginia, MN 55792	1918	Richard Kohlase ... 5	1,011	50
Mesa Comm Coll, Mesa, AZ 85202	1965	Mr. William A. Holt ... 12	19,577	525
Metropolitan Tech Comm Coll, Omaha, NE 68103	1974	Dr. J. Richard Gilliland ... 12	6,630	368
Miami-Dade Comm Coll, Miami, FL 33132	1960	Dr. Robert H. McCabe ... 12	46,035	1,950
Miami U–Hamilton Cmps, Hamilton, OH 45011	1968	Dr. Harriet Taylor ... 5	2,168	160
Miami U–Middletown Cmps, Middletown, OH 45042	1966	Dr. C. Eugene Bennett ... 5	1,915	165
Middle Georgia Coll, Cochran, GA 31014	1884	Dr. Fretwell G. Crider, Jr. ... 5	1,472	80
Middlesex Comm Coll, Middletown, CT 06457	1966	Mr. Robert A. Chapman ... 5	3,080	130
Middlesex Comm Coll, Bedford, MA 01730	1970	Dr. Evan S. Dobelle, Jr. ... 5	3,602	195
Middlesex County Coll, Edison, NJ 08818	1964	Dr. Flora M. Edwards ... 9	11,218	329
Midland Coll, Midland, TX 79705	1969	Dr. Jess H. Parrish ... 12	3,789	192
Midlands Tech Coll, Columbia, SC 29202	1974	Dr. James L. Hudgins ... 12	6,082	NR
Mid Michigan Comm Coll, Harrison, MI 48625	1965	Dr. Eugene F. Schorzmann ... 12	2,013	200
Mid-Plains Comm Coll, North Platte, NE 69101	1965	Mr. Kenneth L. Aten ... 10	1,984	87
Mid-State Tech Coll, Wisconsin Rapids, WI 54494	1917	Dr. M. H. Schneeberg ... 12	2,219	86
Miles Comm Coll, Miles City, MT 59301	1939	Dr. Judson H. Flower ... 12	654	52
Milwaukee Area Tech Coll, Milwaukee, WI 53203	1912	Dr. Rus F. Slicker ... 10	17,031	NR
Mineral Area Coll, Flat River, MO 63601	1922	Dr. Dixie Kohn ... 10	2,205	75
Minneapolis Comm Coll, Minneapolis, MN 55403	1965	Earl W. Bowman ... 5	3,266	175
MiraCosta Coll, Oceanside, CA 92056	1934	Dr. H. Deon Holt ... 5	9,723	295
Mission Coll, Santa Clara, CA 95054	1977	Dr. Betty M. Dean ... 12	11,171	311
Mississippi County Comm Coll, Blytheville, AR 72316	1975	Dr. John P. Sullins ... 5	1,548	106
Mississippi Delta Jr Coll, Moorhead, MS 38761	1926	Dr. J. T. Hall ... 10	1,712	128
Miss Gulf Coast Comm Coll, Jackson County Cmps, Gautier, MS 39553	1965	Mr. Curtis L. Davis ... 10	2,713	131
Miss Gulf Coast Comm Coll, Jefferson Davis Cmps, Gulfport, MS 39507	1965	Mr. Glen W. Cadle ... 12	3,450	156
Miss Gulf Coast Comm Coll, Perkinston Cmps, Perkinston, MS 39573	1925	Dr. Clyde E. Strickland ... 12	869	66
Mitchell Comm Coll, Statesville, NC 28677	1852	Dr. Charles C. Poindexter ... 5	1,452	111
Moberly Area Jr Coll, Moberly, MO 65270	1927	Dr. Andrew Komar, Jr. ... 12	1,326	78
Modesto Jr Coll, Modesto, CA 95350	1921	Dr. Stanley L. Hodges ... 12	7,313	454
Mohave Comm Coll, Kingman, AZ 86401	1971	Dr. Charles W. Hall ... 5	3,890	294
Mohawk Valley Comm Coll, Utica, NY 13501	1946	Dr. Michael I. Schafer ... 12	6,500	343
Mohegan Comm Coll, Norwich, CT 06360	1969	Mr. John D. Hurd ... 5	2,819	128
Monroe Business Inst, Bronx, NY 10468	1933	Stephen J. Jerome ... 3	1,746	100
Monroe Comm Coll, Rochester, NY 14623	1961	Dr. Peter A. Spina ... 12	12,768	699
Monroe County Comm Coll, Monroe, MI 48161	1964	Mr. Gerald D. Welch ... 9	3,118	156
Montcalm Comm Coll, Sidney, MI 48885	1965	Dr. Donald C. Burns ... 12	1,914	NR
Monterey Peninsula Coll, Monterey, CA 93940	1947	Dr. David W. Hopkins, Jr. ... 5	8,500	235
Montgomery Coll–Germantown Cmps, Germantown, MD 20874	1975	Dr. Robert E. Parilla ... 12	3,116	136
Montgomery Coll–Rockville Cmps, Rockville, MD 20850	1965	Dr. Robert E. Parilla ... 12	12,830	649
Montgomery Coll–Takoma Park Cmps, Takoma Park, MD 20912	1946	Dr. Robert E. Parilla ... 12	4,130	208
Montgomery County Comm Coll, Blue Bell, PA 19422	1964	Dr. Edward M. Sweitzer ... 9	7,170	395
Moorpark Coll, Moorpark, CA 93021	1967	Dr. Stanley L. Bowers ... 12	11,312	335
Moraine Park Tech Coll, Fond du Lac, WI 54936	1967	Dr. John J. Shanahan ... 12	4,921	284
Moraine Valley Comm Coll, Palos Hills, IL 60465	1967	Dr. Fred Gaskin ... 12	12,914	545
Morgan Comm Coll, Fort Morgan, CO 80701	1967	Dr. Harold Deselms ... 5	903	138
Morton Coll, Cicero, IL 60650	1924	Mr. Charles P. Ferro ... 12	2,663	272
Motlow State Comm Coll, Tullahoma, TN 37388	1969	Dr. A. Frank Glass ... 5	2,392	217
Mountain Empire Comm Coll, Big Stone Gap, VA 24219	1972	Ruth Mercedes Smith ... 5	2,841	138
Mountain View Coll, Dallas, TX 75211	1970	Dr. William H. Jordan ... 9	5,772	245
Mt Hood Comm Coll, Gresham, OR 97030	1966	Dr. Paul Kreider ... 12	7,530	501
Mount Ida Coll, Newton Centre, MA 02159	1899	Dr. Bryan E. Carlson ... 1	1,650	125
Mt San Antonio Coll, Walnut, CA 91789	1946	Dr. John D. Randall ... 10	21,528	716
Mt San Jacinto Coll, San Jacinto, CA 92383	1963	Dr. Richard H. Lowe ... 12	4,231	166
Mount Wachusett Comm Coll, Gardner, MA 01440	1963	Daniel M. Asquino ... 5	1,891	112
Murray State Coll, Tishomingo, OK 73460	1908	Dr. Clyde R. Kindell ... 5	1,394	NR
Muscatine Comm Coll, Muscatine, IA 52761	1929	Dr. Victor G. McAvoy ... 5	1,060	54
Muskegon Comm Coll, Muskegon, MI 49442	1926	Dr. James L. Stevenson ... 12	5,273	218
Muskingum Area Tech Coll, Zanesville, OH 43701	1969	Dr. Lynn H. Willett ... 12	1,944	180
Napa Valley Coll, Napa, CA 94558	1942	Dr. William H. Feddersen ... 12	5,798	303
Nash Comm Coll, Rocky Mount, NC 27804	1967	Dr. J. Reid Parrott, Jr. ... 5	1,593	88
Nashville State Tech Inst, Nashville, TN 37209	1970	Dr. Sherry Hoppe ... 5	5,392	287
Nassau Comm Coll, Garden City, NY 11530	1959	Dr. Sean A. Fanelli ... 12	16,117	1,308
National Ed Ctr–Allentown Business Sch Cmps, Allentown, PA 18103	1869	Bettie H. Thomas ... 3	900	35
National Ed Ctr–Arkansas Coll of Tech Cmps, Little Rock, AR 72207	1969	Byron D. Thompson ... 3	650	70
National Ed Ctr–Bauder Coll Cmps, Fort Lauderdale, FL 33334	1964	Mr. Dale Oakley ... 3	1,117	41
National Ed Ctr–Brown Inst Cmps, Minneapolis, MN 55407	1946	Bill Johnson ... 3	1,816	NR
National Ed Ctr–Kentucky Coll of Tech Cmps, Louisville, KY 40213	1946	NR ... 3	625	25
National Ed Ctr–National Inst of Tech Cmps, West Des Moines, IA 50265	1964	NR ... 3	650	18
National Ed Ctr–Spartan Sch of Aeronautics Cmps, Tulsa, OK 74158 (2)	1928	Frank D. Iacobocci ... 3	2,249	150
National Sch of Health Tech, Philadelphia, PA 19107	1963	NR ... 3	600	25
Navajo Comm Coll, Tsaile, AZ 86556	1968	Mr. Dean C. Jackson ... 4	1,405	136
Navarro Coll, Corsicana, TX 75110	1946	Dr. Lary L. Reed ... 12	2,310	141
Neosho County Comm Coll, Chanute, KS 66720	1936	George H. VanAllen ... 12	1,200	117
Newbury Coll, Brookline, MA 02146	1962	Mr. Edward J. Tassinari ... 3	947	78
New England Banking Inst, Boston, MA 02111	1909	NR ... 1	2,138	230
New Hampshire Tech Inst, Concord, NH 03302	1964	Dr. David E. Larrabee, Sr. ... 5	1,084	NR
New Hampshire Vocational-Tech Coll, Manchester, NH 03102	1945	Dr. Richard E. Mandeville ... 5	604	50
New Mexico Jr Coll, Hobbs, NM 88240	1965	Dr. Charles D. Hays ... 12	2,613	93
New Mexico State U–Alamogordo, Alamogordo, NM 88310	1958	Dr. Charles R. Reidlinger ... 5	1,680	95
New Mexico State U–Carlsbad, Carlsbad, NM 88220	1950	Dr. Shelton W. Marlow ... 5	1,010	67
New Orleans Baptist Theological Sem, New Orleans, LA 70126	1917	Dr. Landrum P. Leavell, II ... 2	1,708	8
New River Comm Coll, Dublin, VA 24084	1969	Dr. H. Randall Edwards ... 5	1,916	186
New York City Tech Coll of City U of NY, Brooklyn, NY 11201	1946	Dr. Ursula C. Schwerin ... 12	10,323	1,074

Name, address	Year	Governing official, control	Enrollment	Faculty
Niagara County Comm Coll, Sanborn, NY 14132	1962	Dr. Donald J. Donato ... 12	4,693	354
Nicolet Area Tech Coll, Rhinelander, WI 54501	1968	Dr. Patricia A. Travis ... 12	1,311	64
Normandale Comm Coll, Bloomington, MN 55431	1968	Mr. Dale A. Lorenz ... 5	8,560	250
Northampton County Area Comm Coll, Bethlehem, PA 18017	1967	Dr. Robert J. Kopecek ... 12	4,712	225
North Arkansas Comm Coll, Harrison, AR 72601	1974	Dr. Bill Baker ... 12	1,077	75
North Central Michigan Coll, Petoskey, MI 49770	1958	Mr. Alfred D. Shankland ... 9	1,650	93
North Central Missouri Coll, Trenton, MO 64683	1925	Dr. Donald A. Gatzke ... 10	746	92
North Central Tech Coll, Mansfield, OH 44906	1961	Dr. Byron E. Kee ... 5	1,835	136
Northcentral Tech Coll, Wausau, WI 54401	1912	Dr. Donald Hagen ... 10	2,070	184
North Country Comm Coll, Saranac Lake, NY 12983	1967	David W. Petty ... 12	1,575	150
North Dakota State Coll of Science, Wahpeton, ND 58076	1903	Dr. Jerry Olson ... 5	2,385	151
Northeast Alabama State Jr Coll, Rainsville, AL 35986	1963	Dr. Charles M. Pendley ... 5	1,162	60
Northeast Comm Coll, Norfolk, NE 68702	1973	Dr. Robert P. Cox ... 5	2,687	122
Northeastern Jr Coll, Sterling, CO 80751	1941	NR ... 12	2,040	72
Northeastern Oklahoma A&M Coll, Miami, OK 74354	1919	Dr. Bobby R. Wright ... 12	2,472	125
Northeast Iowa Tech Inst–Peosta Cmps, Peosta, IA 52068	1970	Dr. James L. Arneson ... 12	714	50
Northeast Mississippi Comm Coll, Booneville, MS 38829	1948	Joe M. Childers ... 10	2,625	NN
Northeast Texas Comm Coll, Mount Pleasant, TX 75455	1985	NR ... 12	1,673	98
Northeast Wisconsin Tech Coll, Green Bay, WI 54307	1913	Dr. Gerald D. Prindiville ... 5	5,558	191
Northern Essex Comm Coll, Haverhill, MA 01830	1960	Dr. John R. Dimitry ... 5	6,374	238
Northern Nevada Comm Coll, Elko, NV 89801	1967	Dr. William J. Berg ... 5	2,005	124
Northern New Mexico Comm Coll, Española, NM 87532	1909	Dr. Sigredo Maestas ... 5	1,436	117
Northern Oklahoma Coll, Tonkawa, OK 74653	1901	Dr. Edwin E. Vineyard ... 5	1,764	55
Northern Virginia Comm Coll, Annandale, VA 22003	1965	Dr. Richard J. Ernst ... 5	33,466	1,353
North Florida Jr Coll, Madison, FL 32340	1958	Dr. William H. McCoy ... 5	966	48
North Harris County Coll District, Houston, TX 77060	1972	Dr. Joe A. Airola ... 12	13,301	613
North Hennepin Comm Coll, Minneapolis, MN 55445	1966	Dr. John Helling ... 5	5,600	300
North Idaho Coll, Coeur d'Alene, ID 83814	1933	Dr. Carl R. Bennett ... 12	2,565	136
North Iowa Area Comm Coll, Mason City, IA 50401	1918	Dr. David Buettner ... 12	2,532	85
North Lake Coll, Irving, TX 75038	1977	Dr. James F. Horton, Jr. ... 9	6,064	270
Northland Comm Coll, Thief River Falls, MN 56701	1965	Dr. T. A. Easton ... 5	973	42
Northland Pioneer Coll, Holbrook, AZ 86025	1974	Dr. Marvin L. Vasher ... 12	6,524	395
North Seattle Comm Coll, Seattle, WA 98103	1970	Dr. Barbara Daum ... 5	7,898	232
North Shore Comm Coll, Beverly, MA 01915	1965	Dr. George Traicoff ... 5	3,126	200
Northwest Alabama State Jr Coll, Phil Campbell, AL 35581	1961	Dr. Charles W. Britnell ... 5	1,600	83
Northwest Comm Coll, Powell, WY 82435	1946	Mr. John DeWitt, Jr. ... 12	1,739	149
Northwestern Business Coll–Tech Ctr, Lima, OH 45805	1920	Mr. Loren R. Jarvis ... 3	1,221	52
Northwestern Connecticut Comm Coll, Winsted, CT 06098	1965	Dr. Booker T. DeVaughn ... 5	2,346	68
Northwestern Michigan Coll, Traverse City, MI 49684	1951	Dr. Phillip E. Runkel ... 12	4,307	233
Northwest Tech Coll, Archbold, OH 43502	1968	Dr. James O. Miller ... 5	1,869	78
Norwalk Comm Coll, Norwalk, CT 06854	1961	Dr. William H. Schwab ... 5	3,338	151
Norwalk State Tech Coll, Norwalk, CT 06854	1961	Dr. John Karl Fisher ... 5	1,101	56
Oakland Comm Coll, Bloomfield Hills, MI 48013	1964	Dr. R. Stephen Nicholson ... 12	27,827	583
Oakton Comm Coll, Des Plaines, IL 60016	1969	Dr. Thomas TenHoeve ... 10	10,547	350
Ocean County Coll, Toms River, NJ 08753	1964	Dr. Milton Shaw ... 9	6,214	261
Ohio State U Agricultural Tech Inst, Wooster, OH 44691	1972	Dr. Dan D. Garrison ... 5	685	49
Ohlone Coll, Fremont, CA 94539	1967	Dr. Peter Blomerley ... 12	8,514	418
Okaloosa-Walton Comm Coll, Niceville, FL 32578	1963	Dr. James R. Richburg ... 12	4,973	273
Oklahoma City Comm Coll, Oklahoma City, OK 73159	1969	Dr. Donald L. Newport ... 5	8,338	277
Oklahoma Jr Coll of Business and Tech, Tulsa, OK 74133	1919	NR ... 3	1,322	52
Oklahoma State U Tech Branch, Oklahoma City, Oklahoma City, OK 73107	1961	Dr. James Hooper ... 5	3,527	206
Oklahoma State U, Tech Branch, Okmulgee, Okmulgee, OK 74447	1946	Dr. Robert Klabenes ... 5	2,147	137
Olympic Coll, Bremerton, WA 98310	1946	Dr. Wallace A. Simpson ... 5	6,315	294
Onondaga Comm Coll, Syracuse, NY 13215	1962	Dr. Bruce H. Leslie ... 12	7,203	400
Orangeburg-Calhoun Tech Coll, Orangeburg, SC 29115	1968	Mr. M. Rudolph Groomes ... 12	1,145	55
Orange Coast Coll, Costa Mesa, CA 92628	1947	Dr. Donald R. Bronsard ... 12	22,600	807
Orange County Comm Coll, Middletown, NY 10940	1950	Dr. William F. Messner ... 12	4,839	277
Otero Jr Coll, La Junta, CO 81050	1941	Dr. W. L. McDivitt ... 5	827	51
Owens Tech Coll, Findlay, OH 45840	1983	NR ... 5	639	15
Owens Tech Coll, Toledo, OH 43699	1966	NR ... 5	6,653	370
Oxnard Coll, Oxnard, CA 93033	1975	Mr. Roger Boedecker ... 9	4,929	155
Palm Beach Comm Coll, Lake Worth, FL 33461	1933	Dr. Edward M. Eissey ... 5	13,364	650
Palo Alto Coll, San Antonio, TX 78224	1987	NR ... 12	3,711	155
Palomar Coll, San Marcos, CA 92069	1946	Dr. George R. Boggs ... 12	17,557	802
Palo Verde Coll, Blythe, CA 92225	1947	Dr. Wilford J. Beumel ... 12	760	42
Panola Jr Coll, Carthage, TX 75633	1947	Dr. Gary McDaniel ... 12	1,457	61
Paris Jr Coll, Paris, TX 75460	1924	Mr. Bobby R. Walters ... 12	2,288	110
Parkland Coll, Champaign, IL 61821	1967	Dr. Paul J. Magelli ... 10	7,884	457
Parks Jr Coll, Denver, CO 80229	1895	Dr. Morgan Landry ... 3	750	NR
Pasadena City Coll, Pasadena, CA 91106	1924	Dr. Jack A. Scott ... 10	20,207	900
Passaic County Comm Coll, Paterson, NJ 07509	1968	Kenneth E. Wright ... 9	2,839	171
Patrick Henry Comm Coll, Martinsville, VA 24115	1962	NR ... 5	1,165	80
Patrick Henry State Jr Coll, Monroeville, AL 36460	1965	Mr. James R. Allen ... 5	765	41
Paul D Camp Comm Coll, Franklin, VA 23851	1971	Dr. Walter Delany ... 5	1,132	65
Paul Smith's Coll, Paul Smiths, NY 12970	1937	H. David Chamberlain ... 1	784	62
Pearl River Comm Coll, Poplarville, MS 39470	1909	Dr. Ted J. Alexander ... 12	2,337	134
Peirce Jr Coll, Philadelphia, PA 19102	1865	Dr. Raymond C. Lewin ... 1	1,197	74
Pellissippi State Tech Comm Coll, Knoxville, TN 37933	1974	Mr. J. L. Goins ... 5	3,261	137
Peninsula Coll, Port Angeles, WA 98362	1961	Dr. Paul G. Cornaby ... 5	1,103	126
Pennco Tech, Bristol, PA 19007	1961	John Hobyak ... 3	745	25
Penna State U Allentown Cmps, Fogelsville, PA 18051	1912	Mr. John V. Cooney ... 13	781	35
Penna State U Altoona Cmps, Altoona, PA 16603	1929	Dr. James A. Duplass ... 13	2,604	100
Penna State U Beaver Cmps, Monaca, PA 15061	1964	David B. Otto ... 13	1,104	60
Penna State U Berks Cmps, Reading, PA 19610	1924	Dr. Frederick H. Gaige ... 13	1,440	55
Penna State U Delaware County Cmps, Media, PA 19063	1966	Edward S. J. Tomezsko ... 13	1,861	78
Penna State U DuBois Cmps, DuBois, PA 15801	1935	Dr. Jacqueline L. Schoch ... 13	957	47
Penna State U Fayette Cmps, Uniontown, PA 15401	1934	Dr. John D. Sink ... 13	894	44
Penna State U Hazelton Cmps, Hazelton, PA 18201	1934	Dr. James J. Staudenmeier ... 13	1,276	58
Penna State U McKeesport Cmps, McKeesport, PA 15132	1947	Dr. Cash J. Kowalski ... 13	1,463	60
Penna State U Mont Alto Cmps, Mont Alto, PA 17237	1929	Corrinne A. Caldwell ... 13	970	47
Penna State U New Kensington Cmps, New Kensington, PA 15068	1958	Dr. Robert D. Arbuckle ... 13	1,428	76
Penna State U Ogontz Cmps, Abington, PA 19001	1950	Dr. Robert A. Bernoff ... 13	3,502	121

Name, address	Year	Governing official, control	Enrollment	Faculty
Penna State U Schuylkill Cmps, Schuylkill Haven, PA 17972	1934	Dr. Wayne Lammie ... 13	1,122	46
Penna State U Shenango Valley Cmps, Sharon, PA 16146	1965	Dr. Vincent De Sanctis ... 13	1,078	42
Penna State U Wilkes-Barre Cmps, Lehman, PA 18627	1916	Dr. James H. Ryan ... 13	980	55
Penna State U Worthington Scranton Cmps, Dunmore, PA 18512	1923	Dr. James D. Gallagher ...13	1,321	67
Penna State U York Cmps, York, PA 17403	1926	Dr. John J. Romano ...13	1,662	67
Penn Valley Comm Coll, Kansas City, MO 64111	1969	Dr. Zelma Harris ...10	5,320	NR
Pensacola Jr Coll, Pensacola, FL 32504	1948	Dr. Horace E. Hartsell ...5	8,500	938
Phillips Coll, Columbus, GA 31901	1971	NR ...3	644	NR
Phillips County Comm Coll, Helena, AR 72342	1965	Dr. Steven Jones ...12	1,486	72
Phillips Jr Coll, New Orleans, LA 70121	1970	NR ...3	1,100	NR
Phillips Jr Coll of Business, Melbourne, FL 32935	1958	NR ...3	600	35
Phillips Jr Coll of the Mississippi Gulf Coast, Gulfport, MS 39507	1927	Dennis Dollar ...3	750	34
Phoenix Coll, Phoenix, AZ 85013	1920	Dr. William E. Berry ...12	13,146	770
Piedmont Comm Coll, Roxboro, NC 27573	1970	Dr. H. James Owen ...12	991	51
Piedmont Tech Coll, Greenwood, SC 29648	1966	Dr. Lex D. Walters ...5	1,745	NR
Piedmont Virginia Comm Coll, Charlottesville, VA 22901	1972	NR ...5	4,230	262
Pierce Coll, Tacoma, WA 98498	1967	Dr. Brent Knight ...5	6,400	402
Pima Comm Coll, Tucson, AZ 85702	1966	Diego A. Navarrete, Jr. ...5	26,810	1,205
Pitt Comm Coll, Greenville, NC 27835	1961	Dr. Charles E. Russell ...12	3,337	207
Pittsburgh Inst of Aeronautics, Pittsburgh, PA 15236 (2)	1929	Ivan D. Livi ...1	889	112
Plaza Business Inst, Jackson Heights, NY 11372	1916	NR ...3	623	24
Polk Comm Coll, Winter Haven, FL 33881	1964	Dr. Maryli VanLeer Peck ...5	5,600	NR
Porterville Coll, Porterville, CA 93257	1927	Dr. Paul D. Alcantra ...5	2,238	65
Portland Comm Coll, Portland, OR 97219	1961	Dr. Daniel F. Moriarty ...12	34,400	1,136
Potomac State Coll of West Virginia U, Keyser, WV 26726	1901	Joseph M. Gratto ...5	1,105	83
Prairie State Coll, Chicago Heights, IL 60411	1958	Dr. W. Harold Garner ...12	4,477	253
Prince George's Comm Coll, Largo, MD 20772	1958	Dr. Robert I. Bickford ...9	13,500	591
Queensborough Comm Coll of City U of NY, Bayside, NY 11364	1958	Dr. Kurt R. Schmeller ...12	11,941	738
Quincy Jr Coll, Quincy, MA 02169	1958	Dr. O. Clayton Johnson ...11	1,421	69
Quinebaug Valley Comm Coll, Danielson, CT 06239	1971	Dr. Robert E. Miller ...5	1,320	59
Quinsigamond Comm Coll, Worcester, MA 01606	1963	Dr. Clifford S. Peterson ...5	4,411	185
Rainy River Comm Coll, International Falls, MN 56649	1967	Dr. Karen E. Nagle ...5	613	45
Rancho Santiago Coll, Santa Ana, CA 92706	1915	Dr. Robert D. Jensen ...10	21,178	1,648
Randolph Comm Coll, Asheboro, NC 27204	1962	Dr. Larry K. Linker ...5	1,267	80
Rappahannock Comm Coll, Glenns, VA 23149	1970	Dr. John H. Upton ...12	1,910	175
Raritan Valley Comm Coll, Somerville, NJ 08876	1965	Dr. S. Charles Irace ...9	4,582	NR
Reading Area Comm Coll, Reading, PA 19603	1971	Dr. Gust Zogas ...5	1,640	102
Red Rocks Comm Coll, Lakewood, CO 80401	1967	Dr. Thomas K. Thomas ...5	5,148	206
Reinhardt Coll, Waleska, GA 30183	1883	Dr. Floyd A. Falany ...2	600	29
Rend Lake Coll, Ina, IL 62846	1967	Dr. Harry J. Braun ...5	2,880	197
RETS Electronic Inst, Birmingham, AL 35234	1974	Victor L. Riley ...3	650	14
RETS Electronic Inst, Louisville, KY 40219	1935	Frank S. Jordan ...3	778	19
RETS Tech Ctr, Centerville, OH 45459	1953	Michael A. LeMaster ...3	602	20
Richard Bland Coll, Petersburg, VA 23805	1961	Dr. Clarence Maze, Jr. ...5	1,015	44
Richland Coll, Dallas, TX 75243	1972	Dr. Stephen Mittelstet ...12	12,996	646
Richland Comm Coll, Decatur, IL 62521	1971	Mr. Howard Brown ...10	4,250	167
Richmond Comm Coll, Hamlet, NC 28345	1964	Joseph W. Grimsley ...5	940	100
Ricks Coll, Rexburg, ID 83440	1888	Dr. Joe J. Christensen ...2	7,694	288
Rio Hondo Coll, Whittier, CA 90608	1960	Herbert M. Sussman ...12	12,921	710
Rio Salado Comm Coll, Phoenix, AZ 85003	1978	Dr. Charles A. Green ...12	14,000	609
Riverside Comm Coll, Riverside, CA 92506	1916	Dr. Charles A. Kane ...12	16,220	480
Roane State Comm Coll, Harriman, TN 37748	1971	Dr. Cuyler A. Dunbar ...5	3,853	202
Robert Morris Coll, Chicago Cmps, Chicago, IL 60601	1965	Richard D. Pickett ...1	1,529	103
Robeson Comm Coll, Lumberton, NC 28359	1965	Fred W. Williams, Jr. ...5	600	NR
Rochester Comm Coll, Rochester, MN 55904	1915	Dr. Geraldine A. Evans ...5	3,839	160
Rockingham Comm Coll, Wentworth, NC 27375	1964	Dr. N. J. Owens, Jr. ...5	1,690	111
Rockland Comm Coll, Suffern, NY 10901	1959	Dr. F. Thomas Clark ...12	8,580	515
Rock Valley Coll, Rockford, IL 61101	1964	Dr. Karl J. Jacobs ...10	8,218	205
Rogers State Coll, Claremore, OK 74017	1909	Dr. Richard H. Mosier ...5	3,350	191
Rogue Comm Coll, Grants Pass, OR 97527	1971	Dr. Harvey Bennett ...12	3,214	315
Rose State Coll, Midwest City, OK 73110	1971	Dr. Larry Nutter ...5	9,971	341
Rowan-Cabarrus Comm Coll, Salisbury, NC 28144	1963	Dr. Richard L. Brownell ...5	2,700	130
Sacramento City Coll, Sacramento, CA 95822	1916	Dr. Robert M. Harris ...12	15,095	420
Saddleback Coll, Mission Viejo, CA 92692	1967	NR ...12	18,559	660
Saint Augustine Coll, Chicago, IL 60640	1980	Fr. Carlos A. Plazas ...1	884	176
St Bernard Parish Comm Coll, Chalmette, LA 70043	1967	Dr. Daniel Daste ...12	829	47
Saint Charles County Comm Coll, St Charles, MO 63301	1986	NR ...5	2,249	112
St Clair County Comm Coll, Port Huron, MI 48061	1923	Dr. Richard L. Norris ...9	4,075	214
St Johns River Comm Coll, Palatka, FL 32077	1958	Dr. R. L. McLendon, Jr. ...5	2,453	140
St Louis Comm Coll at Florissant Valley, St Louis, MO 63135	1963	Dr. Michael T. Murphy ...10	10,689	379
St Louis Comm Coll at Forest Park, St Louis, MO 63110	1962	Dr. Vernon O. Crawley ...10	6,685	81
St Louis Comm Coll at Meramec, Kirkwood, MO 63122	1963	Dr. Gwendolyn W. Stephenson ...10	13,728	458
St Mary's Cmps of the Coll of St Catherine, Minneapolis, MN 55454	1964	Dr. Anita M. Pampusch ...2	685	79
St Paul Tech Inst, St Paul, MN 55102	1922	Dr. Harlan H. Sheely ...12	2,100	675
St Philip's Coll, San Antonio, TX 78203	1898	Dr. Stephen R. Mitchell ...10	6,027	387
Salem Comm Coll, Carneys Point, NJ 08069	1971	Dr. William Wenzel ...9	1,202	NR
Salish Kootenai Coll, Pablo, MT 59855	1977	NR ...1	767	60
Salt Lake Comm Coll, Salt Lake City, UT 84130	1948	Dr. Orville D. Carnahan ...5	9,577	NR
Sampson Comm Coll, Clinton, NC 28328	1965	Dr. Clifton W. Paderick ...12	909	102
San Antonio Coll, San Antonio, TX 78284	1925	Dr. Max Castillo ...12	23,344	877
San Bernardino Valley Coll, San Bernardino, CA 92410	1926	Dr. Manuel G. Rivera ...12	10,031	NR
Sandhills Comm Coll, Pinehurst, NC 28374	1963	Dr. Raymond A. Stone ...12	2,038	123
San Diego City Coll, San Diego, CA 92101	1914	Jeanne L. Atherton ...12	15,728	NR
San Diego Mesa Coll, San Diego, CA 92111	1962	Dr. Allen Brooks ...10	27,000	887
San Diego Miramar Coll, San Diego, CA 92126	1969	Dr. George F. Yee ...12	6,982	222
San Jacinto Coll-North Cmps, Houston, TX 77049	1974	Dr. Edwin E. Lehr ...12	3,522	174
San Jacinto Coll-South Cmps, Houston, TX 77089	1979	Dr. Parker Williams ...12	4,685	214
San Joaquin Delta Coll, Stockton, CA 95207	1935	Dr. L. H. Horton, Jr. ...10	16,552	610

Name, address	Year	Governing official, control	Enrollment	Faculty
San Jose City Coll, San Jose, CA 95128	1921	Dr. Byron R. Skinner 10	10,384	354
San Juan Coll, Farmington, NM 87401	1958	Dr. James C. Henderson 9	2,855	167
Santa Barbara City Coll, Santa Barbara, CA 93109	1908	Dr. Peter R. MacDougall 10	11,298	463
Santa Fe Comm Coll, Gainesville, FL 32602	1966	Mr. Alan J. Robertson 12	9,918	417
Santa Fe Comm Coll, Santa Fe, NM 87502	1983	William C. Witter 12	2,351	153
Santa Monica Coll, Santa Monica, CA 90405	1929	Dr. Richard L. Moore 12	21,923	634
Santa Rosa Jr Coll, Santa Rosa, CA 95401	1918	Dr. Roy Mikalson 12	24,841	754
Sauk Valley Comm Coll, Dixon, IL 61021	1965	Dr. Richard L. Behrendt 10	4,226	185
Schenectady County Comm Coll, Schenectady, NY 12305	1968	Dr. Peter F. Burnham 12	3,115	155
Schoolcraft Coll, Livonia, MI 48152	1961	Dr. Richard W. McDowell ...10	8,388	360
Scott Comm Coll, Bettendorf, IA 52722	1966	Lenny E. Stone 12	3,012	150
Scottsdale Comm Coll, Scottsdale, AZ 85256	1969	NR 12	8,000	376
Seattle Central Comm Coll, Seattle, WA 98122	1966	Dr. Charles H. Mitchell 5	8,256	380
Seminole Comm Coll, Sanford, FL 32773	1966	Dr. Earl S. Weldon 12	6,181	487
Seminole Jr Coll, Seminole, OK 74868	1931	Gregory G. Fitch 5	1,437	80
Seward County Comm Coll, Liberal, KS 67901	1969	Dr. Theodore W. Wischropp .12	1,589	NR
Shasta Coll, Redding, CA 96099	1948	Kenneth B. Cerreta 12	11,587	385
Shawnee Comm Coll, Ullin, IL 62992	1967	Dr. Barry Gowin 12	2,500	111
Shelby State Comm Coll, Memphis, TN 38174	1972	Dr. Raymond C. Bowen 5	3,822	144
Sheridan Coll, Sheridan, WY 82801	1948	Dr. Stephen Maier 12	2,130	73
Shoreline Comm Coll, Seattle, WA 98133	1964	Dr. Ronald E. Bell 5	7,407	250
Sinclair Comm Coll, Dayton, OH 45402	1887	Dr. David H. Ponitz 12	16,632	884
Skagit Valley Coll, Mount Vernon, WA 98273	1926	Dr. James M. Ford 5	2,494	314
Skyline Coll, San Bruno, CA 94066	1969	Ms. Linda Graef Salter 9	7,833	268
Snead State Jr Coll, Boaz, AL 35957	1935	Dr. William H. Osborn 5	1,399	NR
Snow Coll, Ephraim, UT 84627	1888	Dr. Steven D. Bennion 5	1,534	65
Solano Comm Coll, Suisun City, CA 94585	1945	Dr. Marjorie K. Blaha 5	10,300	432
South Central Comm Coll, New Haven, CT 06511	1968	Dr. Antonio Perez 5	3,158	210
Southeast Comm Coll, Lincoln Cmps, Lincoln, NE 68520	1973	NR 10	4,409	524
Southeast Comm Coll, Milford Cmps, Milford, NE 68405	1941	Dr. Thomas Stone 10	883	85
Southeastern Baptist Theological Sem, Wake Forest, NC 27587	1950	Dr. Lewis A. Drummond 2	828	53
Southeastern Comm Coll, Whiteville, NC 28472	1964	Dr. H. Edwin Beam 5	1,201	110
Southeastern Comm Coll, North Cmps, West Burlington, IA 52655	1968	Dr. R. Gene Gardner 12	1,736	86
Southeastern Illinois Coll, Harrisburg, IL 62946	1960	Dr. Harry W. Abell 5	3,361	163
Southern Arkansas U–El Dorado Branch, El Dorado, AR 71730	1975	Dr. Ben Whitfield 5	736	36
Southern Arkansas U Tech, Camden, AR 71701	1968	Dr. George J. Brown 5	830	61
Southern Coll, Orlando, FL 32807	1969	NR 3	654	34
Southern Jr Coll of Business, Birmingham, AL 35203	1969	Kenneth C. Horne 3	780	40
Southern Maine Vocational-Tech Inst, South Portland, ME 04106	1946	Dr. Wayne H. Ross 5	1,610	148
Southern Ohio Coll, Cincinnati Cmps, Cincinnati, OH 45237	1927	Mr. Duane W. Hawkins 3	766	64
Southern Ohio Coll, Fairfield Cmps, Fairfield, OH 45014	1927	Burton Lipson 3	725	55
Southern State Comm Coll, Hillsboro, OH 45133	1975	Dr. Lewis C. Miller 5	1,289	85
Southern Union State Jr Coll, Wadley, AL 36276	1922	Dr. Richard J. Federinko 5	2,457	119
Southern U, Shreveport–Bossier City Cmps, Shreveport, LA 71107	1964	Dr. Robert H. Smith 5	1,229	73
Southern West Virginia Comm Coll, Logan, WV 25601	1971	Dr. Gregory D. Adkins 5	2,618	127
South Florida Comm Coll, Avon Park, FL 33825	1966	Dr. Catherine P. Cornelius ...5	1,500	112
South Georgia Coll, Douglas, GA 31533	1906	Dr. Edward D. Jackson, Jr. ...5	1,010	51
South Mountain Comm Coll, Phoenix, AZ 85040	1979	Raul Cardenas 12	2,874	124
South Plains Coll, Levelland, TX 79336	1958	Dr. Marvin L. Baker 12	4,393	273
South Puget Sound Comm Coll, Olympia, WA 98502	1970	Dr. Kenneth Minnaert 5	4,470	178
South Seattle Comm Coll, Seattle, WA 98106	1970	Mr. Jerry M. Brockey 5	6,625	234
Southside Virginia Comm Coll, Alberta, VA 23821	1970	Dr. John J. Cavan 5	1,366	175
South Suburban Coll, South Holland, IL 60473	1927	Dr. Richard Fonte 5	9,442	429
Southwestern Coll, Chula Vista, CA 92010	1961	Joseph M. Conte 12	14,066	616
Southwestern Comm Coll, Creston, IA 50801	1966	Richard L. Byerly 5	907	49
Southwestern Comm Coll, Sylva, NC 28779	1964	Dr. Norman K. Myers 5	1,249	186
Southwestern Michigan Coll, Dowagiac, MI 49047	1964	Mr. David C. Briegel 12	3,400	167
Southwest Mississippi Comm Coll, Summit, MS 39666	1918	NR 10	1,353	75
Southwest State Tech Coll, Mobile, AL 36605	1954	Dr. Thomas A. McLeod 5	928	45
Southwest Texas Jr Coll, Uvalde, TX 78801	1946	Dr. Jimmy Goodson 12	2,298	177
Southwest Virginia Comm Coll, Richlands, VA 24641	1968	Dr. Charles R. King 5	6,994	273
Southwest Wisconsin Tech Coll, Fennimore, WI 53809	1967	Mr. Ronald H. Anderson 12	1,102	117
Spartanburg Methodist Coll, Spartanburg, SC 29301	1911	Dr. George D. Fields 2	996	76
Spartanburg Tech Coll, Spartanburg, SC 29305	1961	Dr. Jack A. Powers 5	1,740	NR
Spokane Comm Coll, Spokane, WA 99207	1963	Dr. Donald Bressler 5	4,888	299
Spokane Falls Comm Coll, Spokane, WA 99204	1967	Dr. Vern Loland 5	5,140	867
Spoon River Coll, Canton, IL 61520	1959	Felix T. Haynes 5	2,100	133
Springfield Tech Comm Coll, Springfield, MA 01105	1967	Andrew M. Scibelli 5	3,276	209
Stanly Comm Coll, Albemarle, NC 28001	1971	Dr. Charles H. Byrd 5	1,365	106
Stark Tech Coll, Canton, OH 44720	1970	Dr. John J. McGrath 12	3,275	196
State Comm Coll of East St Louis, East St Louis, IL 62201	1969	Dr. Richard M. Bonner 5	1,200	83
State Fair Comm Coll, Sedalia, MO 65301	1966	Dr. Marvin Fielding 10	1,750	126
State Tech Inst at Memphis, Memphis, TN 38134	1967	Dr. Charles Temple 5	7,398	407
State U of NY Coll of A&T at Cobleskill, Cobleskill, NY 12043	1916	Dr. Neal V. Robbins 5	2,738	160
State U of NY Coll of A&T at Morrisville, Morrisville, NY 13408	1908	Dr. Frederick W. Woodward ...3	3,362	192
State U of NY Coll of Tech at Alfred, Alfred, NY 14802	1908	Dr. John O. Hunter 5	3,775	211
State U of NY Coll of Tech at Canton, Canton, NY 13617	1906	Dr. Earl W. MacArthur 5	2,328	121
State U of NY Coll of Tech at Delhi, Delhi, NY 13753	1913	Mr. Seldon M. Kruger 5	2,453	135
State U of NY Coll of Tech at Farmingdale, Farmingdale, NY 11735	1912	Dr. Frank A. Cipriani 5	10,802	549
Stratton Coll, Milwaukee, WI 53202	1863	Ms. Maritza Samoorian 3	601	30
Suffolk County Comm Coll–Ammerman Cmps, Selden, NY 11784	1962	Mr. Robert T. Kreiling 12	11,729	471
Suffolk County Comm Coll–Eastern Cmps, Riverhead, NY 11901	1977	Steven T. Kenny 12	2,198	120
Suffolk County Comm Coll–Western Cmps, Brentwood, NY 11717	1974	Salvatore J. LaLima 12	4,759	275
Sullivan County Comm Coll, Loch Sheldrake, NY 12759	1962	Dr. John F. Walter 12	1,779	NR
Sullivan Jr Coll of Business, Louisville, KY 40232	1864	Mr. A. R. Sullivan 3	1,968	102
Sumter Area Tech Coll, Sumter, SC 29150	1963	Dr. Herbert C. Robbins 5	1,742	112
Surry Comm Coll, Dobson, NC 27017	1965	Dr. Swanson Richards 5	2,545	94

Name, address	Year	Governing official, control	Enroll-ment	Faculty
Tacoma Comm Coll, Tacoma, WA 98465	1965	Dr. Carleton Opgaard 5	4,653	289
Taft Coll, Taft, CA 93268	1922	Dr. David Cothrun 12	749	65
Tallahassee Comm Coll, Tallahassee, FL 32304	1966	Dr. James H. Hinson, Jr. 12	7,302	313
Tarrant County Jr Coll, Fort Worth, TX 76102	1967	Dr. Joe B. Rushing 9	25,857	850
Tech Career Institutes, New York, NY 10001	1974	J. Raynald Louis 3	2,200	86
Tech Coll of the Lowcountry, Beaufort, SC 29902	1972	Dr. Anne S. McNutt 5	949	NR
Tech Coll of the Municipality of San Juan, Hato Rey, PR 00918	1971	NR 11	946	91
Temple Jr Coll, Temple, TX 76504	1926	Dr. Marvin R. Felder 10	2,462	113
Terra Tech Coll, Fremont, OH 43420	1968	Dr. Richard M. Simon 5	2,614	148
Texas Southmost Coll, Brownsville, TX 78520	1926	Dr. Juliet V. Garcia 10	5,522	200
Texas State Tech Inst–Amarillo Cmps, Amarillo, TX 79111	1970	Mr. Ronald DeSpain 5	861	84
Texas State Tech Inst–Harlingen Cmps, Harlingen, TX 78551	1967	Mr. J. Gilbert Leal 5	2,193	180
Texas State Tech Inst–Sweetwater Cmps, Sweetwater, TX 79556	1970	Dr. Clay G. Johnson 5	748	47
Texas State Tech Inst–Waco Cmps, Waco, TX 76705	1965	Dr. Robert D. Krienke 5	4,022	362
Thames Valley State Tech Coll, Norwich, CT 06360	1963	Dr. R. Eileen Baccus 5	600	47
Thomas Nelson Comm Coll, Hampton, VA 23670	1968	Dr. Robert G. Templin, Jr. ... 5	6,640	258
Three Rivers Comm Coll, Poplar Bluff, MO 63901	1966	Dr. Jack L. Bottenfield 5	1,776	67
Tidewater Comm Coll, Chesapeake Cmps, Chesapeake, VA 23320	1968	Dr. George B. Pass 5	2,335	84
Tidewater Comm Coll, Portsmouth Cmps, Portsmouth, VA 23703	1968	Dr. George B. Pass 5	4,319	205
Tidewater Comm Coll, Virginia Beach Cmps, Virginia Beach, VA 23456	1968	Dr. George B. Pass 5	9,903	388
Tompkins Cortland Comm Coll, Dryden, NY 13053	1968	Eduardo J. Marti 12	2,654	225
Treasure Valley Comm Coll, Ontario, OR 97914	1962	Glenn Mayle 12	2,177	121
Trenholm State Tech Coll, Montgomery, AL 36108	1965	Dr. Thad McClammy 5	703	48
Tri-Cities State Tech Inst, Blountville, TN 37617	1966	Dr. R. Wade Powers 5	1,820	70
Tri-County Comm Coll, Murphy, NC 28906	1964	Mr. Vincent W. Crisp 5	900	47
Tri-County Tech Coll, Pendleton, SC 29670	1962	Dr. Don C. Garrison 5	2,327	NR
Trident Tech Coll, Charleston, SC 29411	1964	Dr. Charles W. Branch 12	5,402	NR
Trinidad State Jr Coll, Trinidad, CO 81082	1925	Dr. Thomas E. Sullivan 5	1,399	90
Trinity Valley Comm Coll, Athens, TX 75751	1946	Mr. Ron Baugh 12	3,893	NR
Triton Coll, River Grove, IL 60171	1964	Dr. James Catanzaro 5	13,338	1,454
Trocaire Coll, Buffalo, NY 14220	1958	Sr. Barbara Ciarico 1	849	94
Tulsa Jr Coll, Tulsa, OK 74135	1968	Dr. Alfred M. Philips 5	18,100	700
Tunxis Comm Coll, Farmington, CT 06032	1969	Ms. Marilyn Menack 5	1,846	152
Tyler Jr Coll, Tyler, TX 75711	1926	Dr. Raymond M. Hawkins ... 12	7,984	364
Ulster County Comm Coll, Stone Ridge, NY 12484	1962	Mr. Robert T. Brown 12	3,150	169
Umpqua Comm Coll, Roseburg, OR 97470	1964	Dr. James Kraby 12	1,718	120
Union County Coll, Cranford, NJ 07016	1933	Dr. Derek Nunney 12	8,741	373
U of Akron–Wayne Coll, Orrville, OH 44667	1972	Dr. William V. Muse 5	1,220	109
U of Alaska Anchorage, Kenai Peninsula Coll, Soldotna, AK 99669	1964	Ginger Steffy 5	1,429	65
U of Alaska Anchorage, Kodiak Coll, Kodiak, AK 99615	1968	Ms. Carol Hagel 5	890	69
U of Alaska Anchorage, Matanuska-Susitna Coll, Palmer, AK 99645	1958	Mr. Glenn F. Massay 5	1,301	96
U of Alaska, Prince William Sound Comm Coll, Valdez, AK 99686	1978	Dr. John S. Devens, Sr. 5	650	60
U of Alaska Southeast, Islands Coll, Sitka, AK 99835	1962	Mr. Richard M. Griffin 5	892	31
U of Alaska Southeast, Ketchikan Cmps, Ketchikan, AK 99901	1954	Dr. Ed Bohart 12	638	62
U of Cincinnati Clermont Coll, Batavia, OH 45103	1972	Dr. Roger J. Barry 5	1,228	95
U of Cincinnati Raymond Walters Coll, Cincinnati, OH 45236	1967	Dr. Ernest G. Muntz 5	2,333	210
U of Hawaii–Kapiolani Comm Coll, Honolulu, HI 96816	1946	Mr. John F. Morton 5	5,465	272
U of Hawaii–Kauai Comm Coll, Lihue, HI 96766	1965	Mr. David Iha 5	1,231	104
U of Hawaii–Windward Comm Coll, Kaneohe, HI 96744	1972	Dr. Peter T. Dyer 5	1,555	NR
U of Kentucky, Ashland Comm Coll, Ashland, KY 41101	1937	Dr. Anthony Newberry 5	2,614	104
U of Kentucky, Elizabethtown Comm Coll, Elizabethtown, KY 42701	1964	Dr. Charles E. Stebbins 5	2,779	99
U of Kentucky, Hazard Comm Coll, Hazard, KY 41701	1968	Dr. G. Edward Hughes 5	1,042	42
U of Kentucky, Henderson Comm Coll, Henderson, KY 42420	1963	Dr. Patrick R. Lake 5	1,251	70
U of Kentucky, Hopkinsville Comm Coll, Hopkinsville, KY 42240	1965	Dr. Thomas L. Riley 5	1,743	62
U of Kentucky, Jefferson Comm Coll, Louisville, KY 40202	1968	Dr. Ronald J. Horvath 5	8,100	282
U of Kentucky, Lexington Comm Coll, Lexington, KY 40506	1965	Dr. Allen G. Edwards 5	3,399	183
U of Kentucky, Madisonville Comm Coll, Madisonville, KY 42431	1968	Dr. Arthur D. Stumpf 5	1,836	117
U of Kentucky, Maysville Comm Coll, Maysville, KY 41056	1967	Dr. James C. Shires 5	872	45
U of Kentucky, Owensboro Comm Coll, Owensboro, KY 42303	1986	NR 5	1,706	63
U of Kentucky, Paducah Comm Coll, Paducah, KY 42002	1932	Dr. Donald J. Clemens 5	2,418	106
U of Kentucky, Prestonsburg Comm Coll, Prestonsburg, KY 41653	1964	Dr. Henry A. Campbell, Jr. ... 5	2,082	89
U of Kentucky, Somerset Comm Coll, Somerset, KY 42501	1965	Dr. Richard G. Carpenter ... 5	1,567	60
U of Kentucky, Southeast Comm Coll, Cumberland, KY 40823	1960	Dr. W. Bruce Ayers 5	1,603	97
U of Minnesota Tech Coll, Crookston, Crookston, MN 56716	1966	Donald G. Sargeant 5	1,221	75
U of Minnesota Tech Coll, Waseca, Waseca, MN 56093	1971	Dr. Edward C. Frederick 5	743	61
U of New Mexico–Gallup Branch, Gallup, NM 87301	1968	Dr. John M. Phillips 5	1,607	110
U of New Mexico–Valencia Cmps, Los Lunas, NM 87031	1981	Dr. Omero Suarez 5	1,060	93
U of North Dakota–Lake Region, Devils Lake, ND 58301	1941	Ms. Sharon L. Etemad 5	661	38
U of South Carolina at Beaufort, Beaufort, SC 29902	1959	Dr. Ron Tuttle 5	850	54
U of South Carolina at Lancaster, Lancaster, SC 29720	1959	Mr. John R. Arnold 5	1,004	60
U of South Carolina at Salkehatchie, Allendale, SC 29810	1965	Dr. Carl A. Clayton 5	646	40
U of South Carolina at Sumter, Sumter, SC 29150	1966	Mr. J. C. Anderson, Jr. 5	1,258	77
U of Wisconsin Ctr–Fond du Lac, Fond du Lac, WI 54935	1968	Bradley M. Gottfried 5	753	36
U of Wisconsin Ctr–Fox Valley, Menasha, WI 54952	1933	Dr. Robert E. Young 5	1,440	55
U of Wisconsin Ctr–Marathon County, Wausau, WI 54401	1933	George Newtown 5	1,193	65
U of Wisconsin Ctr–Rock County, Janesville, WI 53545	1966	Dr. Thomas W. Walterman ... 5	980	40
U of Wisconsin Ctr–Sheboygan County, Sheboygan, WI 53081	1933	Dr. Barbara P. Losty 5	640	30

Name, address	Year	Governing official, control	Enrollment	Faculty
Valencia Comm Coll, Orlando, FL 32802	1967	Dr. Paul C. Gianini, Jr. 5	14,852	606
Vance-Granville Comm Coll, Henderson, NC 27536	1969	Dr. Ben F. Currin 5	1,900	107
Ventura Coll, Ventura, CA 93003	1925	Dr. Robert W. Long 12	11,400	541
Vermont Tech Coll, Randolph Center, VT 05061	1910	Dr. Robert G. Clarke 5	740	75
Vernon Regional Jr Coll, Vernon, TX 76384	1972	Dr. Joe Mills 12	1,729	112
Victoria Coll, Victoria, TX 77901	1925	Dr. Roland E. Bing 9	3,229	120
Victor Valley Coll, Victorville, CA 92392	1960	Dr. Ruth N. Johnson 5	5,500	347
Vincennes U, Vincennes, IN 47591	1801	Dr. Phillip M. Summers 5	5,581	400
Vincennes U–Jasper Ctr, Jasper, IN 47546	1970	NR 5	905	55
Virginia Highlands Comm Coll, Abingdon, VA 24210	1967	Dr. N. DeWitt Moore, Jr. 5	1,975	102
Virginia Western Comm Coll, Roanoke, VA 24038	1966	Dr. Charles L. Downs 5	8,200	202
Vista Coll, Berkeley, CA 94704	1974	Santiago Wood 12	4,613	NR
Volunteer State Comm Coll, Gallatin, TN 37066	1970	Dr. Hal R. Ramer 5	3,474	224
Wake Tech Comm Coll, Raleigh, NC 27603	1958	Dr. Bruce I. Howell 12	5,468	350
Walker Coll, Jasper, AL 35501	1938	Dr. David Rowland 1	827	39
Wallace State Comm Coll, Hanceville, AL 35077	1966	Dr. James C. Bailey 5	3,382	211
Walla Walla Comm Coll, Walla Walla, WA 99362	1967	Dr. Steven L. VanAusdle 5	5,355	120
Walters State Comm Coll, Morristown, TN 37813	1970	Dr. Jack E. Campbell 5	3,513	205
Washington Tech Coll, Marietta, OH 45750	1971	Dr. Carson K. Miller 5	1,723	79
Washtenaw Comm Coll, Ann Arbor, MI 48106	1965	Dr. Gunder A. Myran 12	9,121	460
Waterbury State Tech Coll, Waterbury, CT 06708	1964	Mr. Charles A. Ekstrom 5	1,575	52
Watterson Coll, Louisville, KY 40218	1962	Robert Flynn 3	631	38
Waubonsee Comm Coll, Sugar Grove, IL 60554	1966	Dr. John J. Swalec 10	5,828	370
Waukesha County Tech Coll, Pewaukee, WI 53072	1923	Dr. Richard T. Anderson 12	4,424	520
Wayne Comm Coll, Goldsboro, NC 27533	1957	Dr. G. Herman Porter 12	2,229	156
Wayne County Comm Coll, Detroit, MI 48226	1967	Dr. Ronald J. Temple 12	11,123	417
Weatherford Coll, Weatherford, TX 76086	1869	Dr. E. W. Mince 5	2,354	89
Wenatchee Valley Coll, Wenatchee, WA 98801	1939	Dr. Arnie Heuchert 12	3,100	168
Westark Comm Coll, Fort Smith, AR 72913	1928	Mr. Joel R. Stubblefield 12	4,306	180
Westchester Business Inst, White Plains, NY 10602	1915	Ernest H. Sutkowski 3	870	26
Westchester Comm Coll, Valhalla, NY 10595	1946	Dr. Joseph N. Hankin 12	8,352	536
Western Nebraska Comm Coll, Sidney, NE 69162	1965	Joseph McCann	766	32
Western Nebraska Comm Coll–Scottsbluff Cmps, Scottsbluff, NE 69361	1926	Dr. John N. Harms 12	2,108	51
Western Nevada Comm Coll, Carson City, NV 89703	1971	Dr. Anthony D. Calabro 5	4,736	279
Western Oklahoma State Coll, Altus, OK 73521	1926	Dr. W. C. Burris 5	2,019	94
Western Piedmont Comm Coll, Morganton, NC 28655	1964	Dr. Jim A. Richardson 5	2,297	132
Western Texas Coll, Snyder, TX 79549	1969	Dr. Harry L. Krenek 12	1,026	55
Western Wisconsin Tech Coll, La Crosse, WI 54602	1911	Dr. Beverly S. Simone 10	3,452	172
Western Wyoming Comm Coll, Rock Springs, WY 82901	1959	Dr. Tex L. Boggs 12	2,147	103
West Hills Coll, Coalinga, CA 93210	1932	Stan R. Arterberry 9	2,870	132
Westmoreland County Comm Coll, Youngwood, PA 15697	1970	Dr. Daniel C. Krezenski 5	4,570	303
West Shore Comm Coll, Scottville, MI 49454	1967	Dr. William M. Anderson 10	1,186	68
West Valley Coll, Saratoga, CA 95070	1963	Dr. Dale A. Johnston 5	13,354	882
West Virginia Northern Comm Coll, Wheeling, WV 26003	1972	Dr. Barbara Guthrie-Morse 5	2,633	151
West Virginia U at Parkersburg, Parkersburg, WV 26101	1971	Dr. Eldon L. Miller 5	3,219	158
Wharton County Jr Coll, Wharton, TX 77488	1946	Dr. Elbert C. Hutchins 12	2,551	140
Whatcom Comm Coll, Bellingham, WA 98226	1970	Dr. Harold G. Heiner 5	1,085	104
Wilkes Comm Coll, Wilkesboro, NC 28697	1965	Dr. David E. Daniel 5	1,765	110
William Rainey Harper Coll, Palatine, IL 60067	1965	Dr. Paul N. Thompson 12	18,100	929
Williamsport Area Comm Coll, Williamsport, PA 17701	1965	Dr. Robert Breuder 12	3,706	256
Willmar Comm Coll, Willmar, MN 56201	1961	Harold G. Conradi 5	1,325	66
Willmar Tech Inst, Willmar, MN 56201	1961	NR 12	1,350	107
Wilson Tech Comm Coll, Wilson, NC 27893	1958	Dr. Frank L. Eagles 5	1,367	88
Wisconsin Indianhead Tech Coll, New Richmond Cmps, New Richmond, WI 54017	1972	Marilyn McCarty 10	746	NR
Wisconsin Indianhead Tech Coll, Rice Lake Cmps, Rice Lake, WI 54868	1941	Mary Ellen Filkins 10	715	80
Wisconsin Indianhead Tech Coll, Superior Cmps, Superior, WI 54880	1912	Mr. Richard Parish 10	714	65
Worthington Comm Coll, Worthington, MN 56187	1936	Mr. Conrad W. Burchill 5	744	42
Wor-Wic Tech Comm Coll, Salisbury, MD 21801	1976	NR 12	1,032	69
Wright State U, Lake Cmps, Celina, OH 45822	1969	Donald A. Carlson 5	860	53
Wyoming Tech Inst, Laramie, WY 82070 (2)	1966	NR 3	600	NR
Wytheville Comm Coll, Wytheville, VA 24382	1967	Dr. William F. Snyder 5	1,764	123
Yakima Valley Comm Coll, Yakima, WA 98907	1928	Dr. V. Philip Tullar 5	4,902	401
Yavapai Coll, Prescott, AZ 86301	1966	Dr. Paul Walker 12	6,872	339
York Tech Coll, Rock Hill, SC 29730	1961	Dr. Baxter Hood 5	2,631	215
Yuba Coll, Marysville, CA 95901	1927	Dr. Patricia L. Wirth 12	11,116	267

Tuition and College Costs 1989-90

Based on the Peterson's Guides Annual Survey of Undergraduate Institutions, the average cost of tuition, mandatory fees, and college room and board at four-year private colleges is $11,051. The average cost at four-year public colleges is $4,581 for state residents and $7,334 for nonresidents. Two-year public colleges are the least expensive group of institutions; tuition and fees average $1,150 for state residents and $2,586 for nonresidents. Tuition and fees at two-year private colleges average $4,640.

The most expensive four-year institutions, including tuition, mandatory fees, and college room and board, are Sarah Lawrence College, ($19,980), Bennington College, ($19,975), Brandeis University ($19,970), Barnard College ($19,952), Dartmouth College ($19,700), Boston University ($19,635), Brown University and Johns Hopkins University ($19,510), Bard College ($19,495), and Tufts University ($19,475). Bennington College has the highest tuition of all four-year undergraduate institutions ($16,495). The least expensive are the U.S. service academies, which are all free.

ENVIRONMENT

Environmental Quality Index

Source: Feb.-Mar. 1989 issue of *National Wildlife* magazine

In 1989, *National Wildlife* magazine published the twenty-first in its series of annual reports on the environment. The eighties in general, with 1988 in particular, could be considered as the decade when the planet struck back, according to the report. The frequency with which environmental disasters occurred seemed, for some, to indicate that the earth was saying it could no longer be treated in a negative and destructive manner.

Wildlife: The plight of America's wildlife worsened dramatically during the drought of 1988. Hardest hit were the duck and waterfowl populations. This was attributed to a loss of habitat; the summer drought, compounded with the continuing drainage of wetlands for agriculture, caused the decline of suitable environments for the birds. Salmon, as well as trout and bass, were also in danger of habitat destruction. Major rivers became dangerously low and warm during the year, inhibiting their oxygen-carrying capacity, which in turn threatened the fish populations. The dry conditions affected the food supply of forest dwellers such as squirrels and deer, portending hardship for their predators. This danger to animal habitat did spur the government to take some action. Before leaving office, President Reagan signed into law the reauthorized Endangered Species Act, providing funds to monitor the status of many declining species not yet officially considered threatened or endangered. In the spirit of protecting wetlands, the Environmental Protection Agency rejected a plan to build a recreation area at Lake Alma, in Georgia, and in Illinois the agency fined three developers thousands of dollars for illegally filling marshlands in the state.

Air: The long, hot summer of 1988 saw the worst air pollution in decades. Smog—ozone pollution created by the action of sunlight on such emissions as automobile exhaust—appeared in record proportions far from its usual city haunts. Rural Maine and northern New York state reported excessive ozone levels. According to a study by World Resources Institute in Washington, D.C., such ground-based ozone was causing $5 million in annual U.S. crop losses. Acid rain continued to be a major concern. The EPA indicated that half the streams in the mid-Atlantic and southeastern states—areas not previously considered in the acid rain zone—were either acidic or on the verge of becoming so. Evidence was found of added affects of acid rain, including excessive algae growth, which clogged waterways and absorbed oxygen necessary to sustain marine life. In June this year, Pres. Bush asked that the Clean Air Law of 1970 be amended to halve the allowable emission of sulfur dioxide, a leading component of acid rain.

Water: The closing of beaches last summer that made headline news alerted many to the varied problems of water pollution. A disgusting array of pollutants was washed onto shore by an ocean seemingly unable to absorb any more garbage, from untreated human waste to used medical syringes. Thirty-four East Coast cities chose to ignore the 1972 Clean Water Act, merely screening out large floating objects, rather than removing 85 percent of bacteria and pollutants before discharging municipal sewage. The drought dramatized the water-suppy problem in many regions, causing an increase in water-use restrictions. Water quantity was also a serious issue. Traces of some 400 chemicals were found in the Great Lakes—some from as far away as Latin America—posing a threat to people, due to the poisoning of marine life. The EPA reported the presence of pesticides in well water in many states, with harmful levels found in at least one of every nine wells tested.

Energy: Although there was no change in the country's energy situation in 1988, there were significant changes in perception. Two agencies trusted for their estimates of future trends in the oil industry made significant and startling changes in their figures. The International Energy Agency announced it had underestimated the world's oil consumption by more than a million barrels a day, causing those in the industry to question their ability to meet future oil demand. The U.S. Geological Survey also revealed dramatic misconceptions in its figures. Its estimate of undiscovered oil and gas in the nation was little more than half of that initially projected. These reduced estimates spurred debates over possible oil exploration in Alaska's Arctic National Wildlife Reserve. The **greenhouse effect** was on the minds of many last summer, as the searing heat added to the already existing evidence of the trend in global warming. Elevated levels of carbon dioxide—produced by the burning of fossil fuels—were thought to be responsible for half the greenhouse effect.

Soil: Reminiscent of the Dust Bowl days of the Dirty Thirties, the Midwest was again stricken with duststorms and severe soil erosion that accrued much loss and crop devastation. In North Dakota's fertile Red River Valley, losses of at least 15 tons of topsoil per acre were common, and some areas measured losses of 30 tons per acre. The loss of crops and the low yields from the drought-stricken fields posed a variety of problems. The lack of crop residue on dusty fields meant more severe wind erosion would be likely in the future. There was also a fear of soil loss by water erosion from winter rains and spring runoff, which would mean higher levels of sedimentation in rivers, streams and lakes. A related concern was agricultural chemicals, not decomposed by growth or activated by water, as a threat to downstream water supplies, and affecting the soil chemistry for next year's crop.

Forests: Natural disasters marked the state of the nation's forests in 1988. Wildfires ravaged western woodlands, causing the destruction of 4 million acres in 7 western states and Alaska, including a half million acres in Yellowstone Park. Debates raged as to the soundness of the policy of letting naturally caused wildfires burn in national parks and designated wilderness areas. Yet, the principal threat to America's forests continued to be the seemingly unlimited demand for wood products as the rate of logging again exceeded the rate of timber growth. The Forest Service's plan for the next half century of forest management called for high levels of logging and extensive road building to open up remote areas to logging. In 5 of the 19 national forests, the plans proposed cutting more timber than would be replaced by new growth.

Air Pollutants in Monitored Cities*

Sources: United Nations Environment Program and World Health Organization

Particulate Matter
Annual average number of days in which suspended particulate matter levels exceeded 230 micrograms per cubic meter.

City	Days
New Delhi	294
Xian, China	273
Beijing	272
Calcutta, India	268
Shenyang, China	219
Teheran, Iran	174
Jakarta, Indonesia	173
Shanghai	133
Guangzhou, China	123
Bombay, India	100

Sulfur Dioxide
Annual average number of days in which sulfur dioxide levels exceeded 150 micrograms per cubic meter.

City	Days
Shenyang, China	146
Teheran, Iran	104
Seoul, South Korea	87
Xian, China	71
Beijing	68
Gourdon, France	46
Madrid	35
Guangzhou, China	30
Zagreb, Yugoslavia	30
Milan, Italy	29

Carbon Monoxide
Cities that exceeded W.H.O. guidelines for 8-hour concentrations over a 5-year period (1980-1984). Listed in order from highest level to lowest.

City	Rank
Paris	1
Brisbane, Australia	2
Sao Paulo, Brazil	3
Los Angeles	4
Melbourne, Australia	5
New York	6
Chicago	7
Toronto	8

*50 cities around the world are monitored by the Global Environment Monitoring System, a United Nations program. Because some countries do not participate, the findings are not comprehensive.

U.S. Municipal Solid Waste, 1960-1986

Source: U.S. Environmental Protection Agency

(millions of tons, unless otherwise indicated)

Item, material[1]	1960	1965	1970	1975	1980	1981	1982	1983	1984	1985	1986
Gross waste generated	82.3	98.3	118.3	122.7	139.1	140.9	137.8	144.1	148.1	152.5	157.7
Per person per day (lb.)	2.50	2.77	3.16	3.11	3.35	3.36	3.25	3.37	3.43	3.49	3.58
Materials recovered	5.9	6.2	8.0	9.1	13.4	13.2	12.9	13.9	15.1	15.3	16.9
Per person per day (lb.)	.18	.17	.21	.23	.32	.31	.30	.32	.35	.35	.39
Processed for energy recovery	(NA)	.2	.4	.7	2.7	2.3	3.5	5.0	6.5	7.6	9.6
Per person per day (lb.)	(NA)	.01	.01	.02	.06	.05	.08	.12	.15	.17	.22
Net waste disposed of	76.4	91.9	109.9	112.8	123.0	125.4	121.4	125.2	126.5	129.7	131.2
Per person per day (lb.)	2.32	2.59	2.94	2.86	2.96	2.99	2.86	2.92	2.93	2.97	2.98
Percent distribution of net discards[2]											
Paper and paperboard	32.1	35.0	33.1	30.4	33.6	34.5	33.2	35.3	37.1	35.5	35.6
Glass	8.4	9.2	11.3	11.6	11.3	11.3	11.0	10.4	.97	8.9	8.4
Metals	13.7	11.6	12.2	11.8	10.3	10.0	10.1	9.9	9.6	9.0	8.9
Plastics	.5	1.5	2.7	3.9	6.0	6.1	6.7	7.0	7.2	7.1	7.3
Rubber and leather	2.2	2.4	2.7	3.3	3.3	3.2	3.0	2.6	2.5	2.5	2.8
Textiles	2.6	2.4	2.0	2.2	2.3	2.4	2.4	2.3	2.1	2.0	2.0
Wood	3.9	3.8	3.6	3.8	3.9	3.5	4.0	4.0	3.8	3.9	4.1
Food wastes	14.6	13.1	11.5	11.8	9.2	8.9	8.8	8.5	8.1	9.0	8.9
Yard wastes	20.3	19.2	19.0	19.5	18.2	18.2	18.7	18.1	17.9	20.4	20.1
Other wastes	1.7	1.7	1.7	1.9	1.9	1.9	2.0	1.9	1.9	1.8	1.8

NA = Not Available. (1) Includes post-consumer residential and commercial solid wastes, the major portion of typical municipal collections; excludes mining, agriculture and industrial processing, demolition and construction wastes, sewage sludge, junked cars, and obsolete equipment wastes. (2) Net discards after materials recovery and before energy recovery.

Hazardous Waste Sites

Source: Environmental Protection Agency, Natl. Priorities List Fact Book, March 1989

State	Final Sites	Proposed Sites	Total Sites	State	Final Sites	Proposed Sites	Total Sites
				Nebraska	3	2	5
Alabama	10	2	12	Nevada	0	0	0
Alaska	1	0	1	New Hampshire	15	0	15
Arizona	5	4	10	New Jersey	100	7	107
Arkansas	10	0	10	New Mexico	6	4	10
California	52	36	88	New York	73	3	76
Colorado	13	3	16	North Carolina	15	6	21
Connecticut	8	6	14	North Dakota	2	0	2
Delaware	12	8	20	Ohio	29	3	32
Florida	32	15	47	Oklahoma	8	3	11
Georgia	7	6	13	Oregon	6	1	7
Hawaii	0	6	6	Pennsylvania	71	24	95
Idaho	4	0	4	Rhode Island	8	1	9
Illinois	23	16	39	South Carolina	14	7	21
Indiana	30	7	37	South Dakota	1	0	1
Iowa	9	14	23	Tennessee	10	3	13
Kansas	9	2	11	Texas	24	4	28
Kentucky	12	5	17	Utah	5	5	10
Louisiana	9	2	11	Vermont	4	4	8
Maine	6	2	8	Virginia	12	9	21
Maryland	7	3	10	Washington	25	17	42
Massachusetts	21	1	22	West Virginia	5	1	6
Michigan	65	15	80	Wisconsin	35	4	39
Minnesota	40	0	40	Wyoming	1	1	2
Mississippi	2	1	3	Guam	1	0	1
Missouri	14	7	21	Puerto Rico	8	1	9
Montana	8	2	10	**Total**	**890**	**273**	**1,163**

Endangered and Threatened Species and Recovery Plans

Source: U.S. Fish and Wildlife Service, U.S. Interior Department; June 6, 1989.

Group	Endangered U.S. only	Endangered U.S. & foreign	Endangered Foreign only	Threatened U.S. only	Threatened U.S. & foreign	Threatened Foreign only	Listed species total	Species with plans
Mammals	32	19	241	6	2	23	323	24
Birds	61	15	145	7	3	0	231	57
Reptiles	8	7	59	14	4	14	106	22
Amphibians	5	0	8	3	1	0	17	5
Fishes	45	2	11	24	6	0	88	47
Snails	3	0	1	6	0	0	10	7
Clams	32	0	2	0	0	0	34	22
Crustaceans	8	0	0	1	0	0	9	4
Insects	10	0	0	7	0	0	17	12
Arachnids	3	0	0	0	0	0	3	0
Plants	153	6	1	40	6	2	208	85
Total	**360**	**49**	**468**	**108**	**22**	**39**	**1,046**	**285**

Total U.S. Endangered	409	Approved recovery plans	245
Total U.S. Threatened	130	Species/populations in above plans.	301
Total U.S. listed	**539**	Percentage of listed species covered by 1 or more plans.	52.9%

Note: Separate populations of a species, listed both as Endangered and Threatened, are tallied twice. Those 9 species are: grizzly bear (US = T & Mex = E), leopard, gray wolf, bald eagle, piping plover, roseate tern, Nile crocodile, green sea turtle, and olive Ridley sea turtle. Further, there are 9 species of lemurs; 9 gibbons; 2 each of musk deer, sifakas, and uakaris; and 29–41 species of Oahu tree snails; these are each counted as one species above.

Some Endangered Species in North America

Source: U.S. Fish and Wildlife Service, U.S. Interior Department; as of July, 1989

Common name	Scientific name	Range
Mammals		
Ozark big-eared bat	Plecotus townsendii ingens	U.S. (Mo., Okla., Ariz.)
Brown or grizzly bear	Ursus arctos horribilis	U.S. (48 conterminous states)
Eastern cougar	Felis concolor cougar	Eastern N.A.
Columbian white-tailed deer	Odocoileus virginianus leucurus	U.S. (Wash., Ore.)
San Joaquin kit fox	Vulpes macrotis mutica	U.S. (Cal.)
Fresno kangaroo	Dipodomys nitratoides exiles	U.S. (Cal.)
Southeastern beach mouse	Peromyscus polionotus phasma	U.S. (Fla.)
Ocelot	Felis pardalis	U.S. (Tex., Ariz.)
Southern sea otter	Enhydra lutris hereis	U.S. (Wash., Ore., Cal.)
Florida panther	Felis concolor coryi	U.S. (La., Ark. east to S.C., Fla.)
Utah prairie dog	Cynomys parvidens	U.S. (Ut.)
Morro Bay kangaroo rat	Dipodomys heermanni morroensis	U.S. (Cal.)
Carolina northern flying squirrel	Glaucomys sabrinus coloratus	U.S. (N.C., Tenn.)
Hualapai Mexican vole	Microtus mexicanus hualpaiensis	U.S. (Ariz.)
Red wolf	Canis rufus	U.S. (Southeast to central Tex.)
Birds		
Masked bobwhite (quail)	Colinus virginianus ridgwayi	U.S. (Ariz.)
California condor	Gymnogyps californianus	U.S. (Ore., Cal.)
Whooping crane	Grus americana	U.S. (Rky. Mntns. east to Carolinas), Canada
Eskimo curlew	Numenius borealis	Alaska and N. Canada
Bald eagle	Haliaeetus leucocephalus	U.S. (most states), Canada
American peregrine falcon	Falco peregrinus anatum	Canada to Mexico
Hawaiian hawk	Buteo solitarius	U.S. (Hi.)
Attwater's greater prairie-chicken	Tympanuchus cupido attwateri	U.S. (Tex.)
Bachman's warbler (wood)	Vermivora bachmanii	U.S. (Southeast), Cuba
Kirtland's warbler (wood)	Dendroica kirtlandii	U.S., Canada, Bahama Is.
Ivory-billed woodpecker	Campephilus principalis	U.S. (Southcentral and Southeast), Cuba
Reptiles		
American crocodile	Crocodylus acutus	U.S. (Fla.)
Atlantic salt marsh snake	Nerodia fasciatia taeniata	U.S. (Fla.)
Plymouth red-bellied turtle	Pseudemys rubiventris bangsi	U.S. (Mass.)
Fishes		
Yaqui catfish	Ictalupus pricei	U.S. (Ariz.)
Bonytail chub	Gila elegans	U.S. (Ariz., Cal., Col., Nev., Ut., Wyo.)
Gila trout	Salmo gilae	U.S. (Ariz., N.M.)

Some Endangered Species in the World

Source: U.S. Fish and Wildlife Service, U.S. Interior Department; as of July, 1989

Common name	Scientific name	Historic range
Mammals		
Asian wild ass	Equus hemianus	Southwestern & Central Asia
Bobcat	Felis rufus escuinapae	Central Mexico
Cheetah	Acinonyx jubatus	Africa to India
Chinese river dolphin	Lipotes vexillifer	China
Asian elephant	Elephas maximas	S. Central & E. Africa
Bactrian camel	Camelus bactrianus	Mongolia, China
Gorilla	Gorilla gorilla	Central & W. Africa
Leopard	Panthera pardus	Africa, Asia
Asiatic lion	Panthera leo persica	Turkey to India
Howler monkey	Alouatta pigra	Mexico to S. America
Giant panda	Ailuropoda melanoleuca	China
Black rhinoceros	Diceros bicornis	Sub-Saharan Africa
Tiger	Panthera tigris	Asia
Gray whale	Eschrichtius robustus	N. Pacific Ocean
Wild yak	Bos grunniens	China (Tibet), India
Mountain zebra	Equus zebra zebra	South Africa
Birds		
Hooded crane	Grus monacha	Japan, USSR
Indigo macaw	Anodorhynchus leari	Brazil
West African ostrich	Struthio camelus spatzi	Spanish Sahara
Golden parakeet	Aratinga guarouba	Brazil
Australian parrot	Geopsittacus occidentalis	Australia

Speeds of Animals

Source: Natural History magazine, March 1974.
Copyright © The American Museum of Natural History, 1974.

Animal	Mph	Animal	Mph	Animal	Mph
Cheetah	70	Mongolian wild ass	40	Human	27.89
Pronghorn antelope	61	Greyhound	39.35	Elephant	25
Wildebeest	50	Whippet	35.50	Black mamba snake	20
Lion	50	Rabbit (domestic)	35	Six-lined race runner	18
Thomson's gazelle	50	Mule deer	35	Wild turkey	15
Quarterhorse	47.5	Jackal	35	Squirrel	12
Elk	45	Reindeer	32	Pig (domestic)	11
Cape hunting dog	45	Giraffe	32	Chicken	9
Coyote	43	White-tailed deer	30	Spider (Tegenaria atrica)	1.17
Gray fox	42	Wart hog	30	Giant tortoise	0.17
Hyena	40	Grizzly bear	30	Three-toed sloth	0.15
Zebra	40	Cat (domestic)	30	Garden snail	0.03

Most of these measurements are for maximum speeds over approximate quarter-mile distances. Exceptions are the lion and elephant, whose speeds were clocked in the act of charging; the whippet, which was timed over a 200-yard course; the cheetah over a 100-yard distance; man for a 15-yard segment of a 100-yard run (of 13.6 seconds); and the black mamba, six-lined race runner, spider, giant tortoise, three-toed sloth, and garden snail, which were measured over various small distances.

Gestation, Longevity, and Incubation of Animals

Longevity figures were supplied by Ronald T. Reuther. They refer to animals in captivity; the potential life span of animals is rarely attained in nature. Maximum longevity figures are from the Biology Data Book, 1972. Figures on gestation and incubation are averages based on estimates by leading authorities.

Animal	Gestation (day)	Average longevity (years)	Maximum longevity (yrs., mos.)	Animal	Gestation (day)	Average longevity (years)	Maximum longevity (yrs., mos.)
Ass	365	12	35-10	Leopard	98	12	19-4
Baboon	187	20	35-7	Lion	100	15	25-1
Bear: Black	219	18	36-10	Monkey (rhesus)	164	15	—
Grizzly	225	25	—	Moose	240	12	—
Polar	240	20	34-8	Mouse (meadow)	21	3	—
Beaver	122	5	20-6	Mouse (dom. white)	19	3	3-6
Buffalo (American)	278	15	—	Opossum (American)	14-17	1	—
Bactrian camel	406	12	29-5	Pig (domestic)	112	10	27
Cat (domestic)	63	12	28	Puma	90	12	19
Chimpanzee	231	20	44-6	Rabbit (domestic)	31	5	13
Chipmunk	31	6	8	Rhinoceros (black)	450	15	—
Cow	284	15	30	Rhinoceros (white)	—	20	—
Deer (white-tailed)	201	8	17-6	Sea lion (California)	350	12	28
Dog (domestic)	61	12	20	Sheep (domestic)	154	12	20
Elephant (African)	—	35	60	Squirrel (gray)	44	10	—
Elephant (Asian)	645	40	70	Tiger	105	16	26-3
Elk	250	15	26-6	Wolf (maned)	63	5	—
Fox (red)	52	7	14	Zebra (Grant's)	365	15	—
Giraffe	425	10	33-7				
Goat (domestic)	151	8	18	**Incubation time (days)**			
Gorilla	257	20	39-4	Chicken			21
Guinea pig	68	4	7-6	Duck			30
Hippopotamus	238	25	—	Goose			30
Horse	330	20	46	Pigeon			18
Kangaroo	42	7	—	Turkey			26

Major Venomous Animals

Snakes

Coral snake - 2 to 4 ft. long, in Americas south of Canada; bite is nearly painless; very slow onset of paralysis, difficulty breathing; mortality high without antivenin.

Rattlesnake - 2 to 8 ft. long, throughout W. Hemisphere. Rapid onset of symptoms of severe pain, swelling; mortality low, but amputation of affected limb is sometimes necessary; antivenin. Probably higher mortality rate for Mojave rattler.

Cottonmouth water moccasin - up to 5 ft. long, wetlands of southern U.S. from Virginia to Texas. Rapid onset of symptoms of severe pain, swelling; mortality low, but tissue destruction can be extensive; antivenin.

Copperhead - less than 4 ft. long, from New England to Texas; pain and swelling; very seldom fatal; antivenin seldom available.

Bushmaster - up to 12 ft. long, wet tropical forests of C. and S. America; few bites occur, but mortality rate is high.

Barba Amarilla or Fer-de-lance - up to 7 ft. long, from tropical Mexico to Brazil; severe tissue damage common; moderate mortality; antivenin.

Asian pit vipers - from 2 to 5 ft. long throughout Asia; reactions and mortality vary but most bites cause tissue damage and mortality is generally low.

Sharp-nosed pit viper or One Hundred Pace Snake - up to 5 ft. long, in southern Vietnam and Taiwan, China; the most toxic of Asian pit vipers; very rapid onset of swelling and tissue damage, internal bleeding; moderate mortality; antivenin.

Boomslang - under 6 ft. long, in African savannahs; rapid onset of nausea and dizziness, often followed by slight recovery and then sudden death from internal hemorrhaging; bites rare, mortality high; antivenin.

European vipers - from 1 to 3 ft. long; bleeding and tissue damage; mortality low; antivenins.

Puff adder - up to 5 ft. long, fat; south of the Sahara and throughout the Middle East; rapid large swelling, great pain, dizziness; moderate mortality often from internal bleeding; antivenin.

Gaboon viper - over 6 ft. long, fat; 2-inch fangs; south of the Sahara; massive tissue damage, internal bleeding; few recorded bites.

Saw-scaled or carpet viper - up to 2 ft. long, in dry areas from India to Africa; severe bleeding, fever; high mortality, causes more human fatalities than any other snake; antivenin.

Desert horned viper - in dry areas of Africa and western Asia; swelling and tissue damage; low mortality; antivenin.

Russell's viper or tic-palonga - over 5 ft. long, throughout Asia; internal bleeding; moderate mortality rate; bite reports common; antivenin.

Black mamba - up to 14 ft. long, fast-moving; S. and C. Africa; rapid onset of dizziness, difficulty breathing, erratic heart-beat; mortality high, nears 100% without antivenin.

Kraits - in S. Asia; rapid onset of sleepiness; numbness; up to 50% mortality even with antivenin treatment.

Common or Asian cobra - 4 to 8 ft. long, throughout S. Asia; considerable tissue damage, sometimes paralysis; mortality probably not more than 10%; antivenin.

King cobra - up to 16 ft. long, throughout S. Asia; rapid swelling, dizziness, loss of consciousness, difficulty breathing, erratic heart-beat; mortality varies sharply with amount of venom involved, most bites involve non-fatal amounts; antivenin.

Yellow or Cape cobra - 7 ft. long, in southern Africa; most toxic venom of any cobra; rapid onset of swelling, breathing and cardiac difficulties; mortality high without treatment; antivenin.

Ringhals, or spitting, cobra - 5 ft. and 7 ft. long; southern Africa; squirt venom through holes in front of fangs as a defense; venom is severely irritating and can cause blindness.

Australian brown snakes - very slow onset of symptoms of cardiac or respiratory distress; moderate mortality; antivenin.

Tiger snake - 2 to 6 ft. long, S. Australia; pain, numbness, mental disturbances with rapid onset of paralysis; may be the most deadly of all land snakes though antivenin is quite effective.

Death adder - less than 3 ft. long, Australia; rapid onset of faintness, cardiac and respiratory distress; at least 50% mortality without antivenin.

Taipan - up to 11 ft. long, in Australia and New Guinea; rapid paralysis with severe breathing difficulty; mortality nears 100% without antivenin.

Sea snakes - throughout Pacific, Indian oceans except NE Pacific; almost painless bite, variety of muscle pain, paralysis; mortality rate low, many bites are not envenomed; some antivenins.

Notes: Not all snake bites by venomous snakes are actually envenomed. Any animal bite, however, carries the danger of tetanus and anyone suffering a venomous snake bite should seek medical attention. Antivenins are not certain cures; they are only an aid in the treatment of bites. Mortality rates above are for envenomed bites; low mortality, up to 2% result in death; moderate, 2–5%; high, 5–15%. Even when the victim recovers fully, prolonged hospitalization and extensive medical procedures are usually required.

Lizards

Gila monster - up to 24 inches long with heavy body and tail, in high desert in southwest U.S. and N. Mexico; immediate severe pain followed by vomiting, then, difficulty swallowing, weakness approaching paralysis; no recent mortality.

Mexican beaded lizard - similar to Gila monster, Mexican westcoast; reaction and mortality rate similar to Gila monster.

Insects

Ants, bees, wasps, hornets, etc. Global distribution. Usual reaction is piercing pain in area of sting. Not directly fatal, except in cases of massive multiple stings. Many people suffer allergic reactions - swelling, rashes, partial paralysis –and a few may die within minutes from severe sensitivity to the venom (anaphylactic shock).

Spiders, scorpions

Black widow - small, round-bodied with hour-glass marking; the widow and its relatives are found around the world in tropical and temperate zones; sharp pain, weakness, clammy skin, muscular rigidity, breathing difficulty and, in small children, convulsions; low mortality; antivenin.

Recluse or fiddleback and brown spiders - small, oblong body; throughout U.S.; pain with later ulceration at place of bite; in severe cases fever, nausea, and stomach cramps; ulceration may last months; very low mortality.

Atrax **spiders** - several varieties, often large, in Australia; slow onset of breathing, circulation difficulties; low mortality.

Tarantulas - large, hairy spiders found around the world; American tarantulas, and probably all others, are **harmless,** though their bite may cause some pain and swelling.

Scorpions - crab-like body with stinger in tail, various sizes, many varieties throughout tropical and subtropical areas; various symptoms may include severe pain spreading from the wound, numbness, severe emotional agitation, cramps; severe reactions include vomiting, diarrhea, respiratory failure; low mortality, usually in children; antivenins.

Sea Life

Sea wasps - jellyfish, with tentacles up to 30 ft. long, in the S. Pacific; very rapid onset of circulatory problems; high mortality largely because of speed of toxic reaction; antivenin.

Portuguese man-of-war - jellyfish-like, with tentacles up to 70 ft. long, in most warm water areas; immediate severe pain; not fatal, though shock may cause death in a rare case.

Octopi - global distribution, usually in warm waters; all varieties produce venom but only a few can cause death; rapid onset of paralysis with breathing difficulty.

Stingrays - several varieties of differing sizes, found in tropical and temperate seas and some fresh water; severe pain, rapid onset of nausea, vomiting, breathing difficulties; wound area may ulcerate, gangrene may appear; seldom fatal.

Stonefish - brownish fish which lies motionless as a rock on bottom in shallow water; throughout S. Pacific and Indian oceans; extraordinary pain, rapid paralysis; low mortality.

Cone-shells - molluscs in small, beautiful shells in the S. Pacific and Indian oceans; shoot barbs into victims; paralysis; low mortality.

How Much Water Is Used . . . ?

Source: American Water Works Assn.

1. In the average residence during a year? **107,000 gallons**
2. By an average person daily? **168 gallons**
3. To flush a toilet? **5-7 gallons**
4. To take a shower? **25-50 gallons**
5. To brush your teeth (water running)? **2 gallons**
6. To shave (water running)? **10-15 gallons**
7. To wash dishes by hand? **20 gallons**
8. To run a dishwasher? **2 gallons**

Major U.S. Public Zoological Parks

Source: World Almanac questionnaire, 1989; budget and attendance in millions. (*) park has not provided up-to-date data.

Zoo	Budget	Attend-ance	Acres	Species	Major attractions
Arizona-Sonora Desert Museum (Tucson)	$3.4	0.5	15	200	Mountain Habitat, Sonora Desert Exhibit
Audubon (New Orleans)	9.0	1.0	58	372	Asian Domain, Louisiana Swamp, Australia Exhibit
Bronx (N.Y.C.)	27.4	2.3	265	644	Himalayan Highlands, African Plains, Jungle World, Wild Asia, Mouse House
Buffalo	2.5	0.5	23	270	Habicat, Gorilla Habitat, Children's Zoo
Chicago (Brookfield)	25.0	2.0	204	425	7 Seas Panorama, Tropic World, Australian Walkabout
Cincinnati	10.0	1.5	67	735	Gorilla World, Insect World, white bengal tigers
Cleveland	5.1	0.8	160	440	African Plains, rhino/cheetah, Animals of China
Dallas	5.9	0.5	45	332	Okapi, bongo antelope, hands-on reptile exhibit
Denver*	4.8	0.9	76	339	Bear Mountain, hooved animals, Feline House
Detroit	10.0	0.7	125	300	Reptiles, Bird House, Penguinarium, chimpanzees
Houston*	2.6	2.0	55	649	Children's Zoo, Aquarium
Lincoln Park (Chicago)	10.5	4.0	35	382	Farm in the Zoo, Birds of Prey, Children's Zoo
Los Angeles	1.5	1.7	111	500	Koalas, elephant & camel rides, Aviary
Louisville*	2.5	0.4	73	245	African Panorama, polar bear, Siberian tiger
Memphis*	2.4	0.5	36	380	Tropical Bird House, Aquarium, waterfowl, twin hippo babies
Miami Metrozoo*	6.8	0.8	290	345	koalas, Aviary, cageless exhibits
Milwaukee*	11.0	1.8	185	605	Dolphin Show, Zoomobile, penguins
Minnesota	6.8	0.9	488	398	Tropics Trail, Minnesota Trail, koalas, dolphins
National (Wash. D.C.)	13.0	3.0	163	484	Giant pandas, Komodo dragon lizards, gorillas
Oklahoma City·	6.0	0.5	100	532	Aquaticus dolphin & sea lion shows
Philadelphia	11.0	1.4	42	560	World of Primates, Treehouse, Rare Animal House
Phoenix	6.5	1.0	125	300	African Veldt, Children's Zoo, Arizona exhibit
Rio Grande (Albuquerque)	4.0	0.5	60	263	Ape Country, Cat Walk, Jungle Habitat
Riverbanks (Columbia, S.C.)	2.5	0.7	50	230	Aquarium Reptile Complex, Riverbanks Farm
St. Louis	10.0	2.3	83	619	Big Cat Country, Herpetarium, Primate House
San Antonio	6.0	1.0	50	674	Children's Zoo, elephant shows, Barrier Reef
San Diego	40.0	3.5	100	800	Tiger River, Southeast Asian exhibit, koalas
San Diego (Wild Animal Park)*	16.0	1.3	1,800	225	Mixed-species enclosures; exotic species, monorail
San Francisco*	8.0	1.2	125	270	Primate Discovery Center, Koala Crossing, Gorilla World, Penguin Island
Toledo	5.8	1.3	33	400	Hippoquarium, African Savanna, Children's Zoo
Washington Pk (Portland)	10.5	1.0	64	135	Cascade Stream & Pond, Alaska Tundra, Penguinarium, 3-acre Africa exhibit
Woodland Pk (Seattle)	5.3	1.0	90	250	African Savanna, gorillas, Asian Elephant Forest

Top 50 American Kennel Club Registrations

Breed	Rank 1988	1988	Rank 1987	1987	Breed	Rank 1988	1988	Rank 1987	1987
Cocker Spaniels	1	108,720	1	105,236	Brittanys	26	14,439	24	14,242
Labrador Retrievers	2	86,446	2	81,987	Dalmations	27	14,109	27	11,291
Poodles	3	82,600	3	85,400	Pugs	28	11,659	29	10,400
Golden Retrievers	4	62,950	4	60,936	West Highland White Terriers	29	11,565	28	10,532
German Shepherd Dogs	5	57,139	5	57,612	Bichons Frises	30	9,684	33	8,633
Chow Chows	6	50,781	6	49,096	Bulldogs	31	9,566	31	8,879
Rottweilers	7	42,748	12	36,162	German Shorthaired Pointers	32	9,111	34	8,285
Beagles	8	41,983	7	41,972	Great Danes	33	8,996	30	8,641
Dachshunds	9	41,921	9	40,031	Samoyeds	34	8,986	32	7,011
Miniature Schnauzers	10	41,558	8	41,462	Scottish Terriers	35	8,106	36	7,045
Shih Tzu	11	38,829	11	36,519	Keeshonden	36	7,431	35	6,718
Shetland Sheepdogs	12	38,730	10	37,616	Cairn Terriers	37	7,187	37	6,046
Yorkshire Terriers	13	36,040	13	36,033	Akitas	38	6,518	39	6,123
Pomeranians	14	30,516	16	27,911	Alaskan Malamutes	39	5,811	38	4,678
Lhasa Apsos	15	30,194	14	31,685	Miniature Pinschers	40	5,579	41	5,255
Doberman Pinschers	16	23,928	15	28,783	Airedale Terriers	41	4,687	40	4,252
Chihuahuas	17	23,487	17	21,398	Chesapeake Bay Retrievers	42	4,315	43	4,382
Siberian Huskies	18	21,430	19	20,708	Old English Sheepdogs	43	3,973	42	3,967
Basset Hounds	19	21,423	18	21,082	St. Bernards	44	3,827	44	3,551
Boxers	20	20,604	22	19,553	Pembroke Welsh Corgis	45	3,796	47	3,680
English Springer Spaniels	21	20,238	20	19,969	Weimaraners	46	3,653	45	3,680
Pekingese	22	20,134	21	19,803	Norwegian Elkhounds	47	3,416	45	2,982
Collies	23	18,931	23	18,705	Wire Fox Terriers	48	3,095	50	2,803
Boston Terriers	24	14,988	25	14,015	Silky Terriers	49	2,862	51	3,137
Maltese	25	14,453	26	13,259	Irish Setters	50	2,849	48	

Cat Breeds

There are 27 cat breeds recognized: abyssinian, american shorthair, balinese, birman, bombay, burmese, colorpoint shorthair, egyptian mau, exotic shorthair, havana brown, himalayan, japanese bobtail, korat, leopard cat, lilac foreign shorthair, maine coon cat, manx, ocicat, oriental shorthair, persian, rex, russian blue, scottish fold, siamese, sphynx, turkish angora, wirehair shorthair.

Mammals: Orders and Major Families

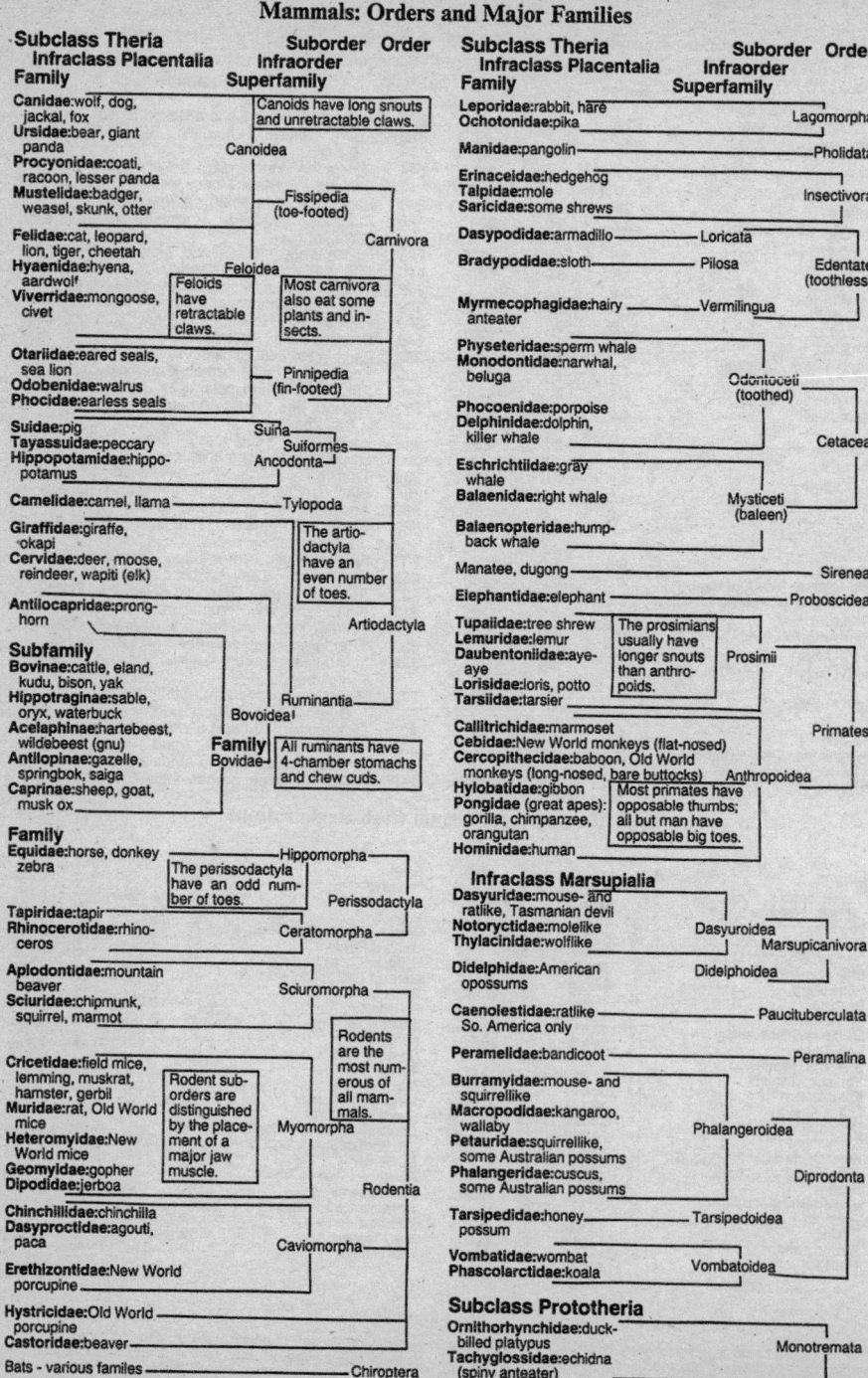

Subclass Theria
Infraclass Placentalia

Family	Suborder Infraorder Superfamily	Order

Canidae:wolf, dog, jackal, fox
Ursidae:bear, giant panda
Procyonidae:coati, racoon, lesser panda
Mustelidae:badger, weasel, skunk, otter
— Canoids have long snouts and unretractable claws.
Canoidea — Fissipedia (toe-footed)

Felidae:cat, leopard, lion, tiger, cheetah
Hyaenidae:hyena, aardwolf
Viverridae:mongoose, civet
Feloidea — Feloids have retractable claws.
Most carnivora also eat some plants and insects.
Carnivora

Otariidae:eared seals, sea lion
Odobenidae:walrus
Phocidae:earless seals
— Pinnipedia (fin-footed)

Suidae:pig
Tayassuidae:peccary
Hippopotamidae:hippopotamus
Suina — Suiformes — Ancodonta

Camelidae:camel, llama — Tylopoda

Giraffidae:giraffe, okapi
Cervidae:deer, moose, reindeer, wapiti (elk)
The artiodactyla have an even number of toes.

Antilocapridae:pronghorn
Artiodactyla

Subfamily
Bovinae:cattle, eland, kudu, bison, yak
Hippotraginae:sable, oryx, waterbuck
Acelaphinae:hartebeest, wildebeest (gnu)
Antilopinae:gazelle, springbok, saiga
Caprinae:sheep, goat, musk ox
Ruminantia
Bovoidea
Family Bovidae
All ruminants have 4-chamber stomachs and chew cuds.

Family
Equidae:horse, donkey, zebra
Hippomorpha
The perissodactyla have an odd number of toes.
Tapiridae:tapir
Rhinocerotidae:rhinoceros
Ceratomorpha
Perissodactyla

Aplodontidae:mountain beaver
Sciuridae:chipmunk, squirrel, marmot
Sciuromorpha

Cricetidae:field mice, lemming, muskrat, hamster, gerbil
Muridae:rat, Old World mice
Heteromyidae: New World mice
Geomyidae:gopher
Dipodidae:jerboa
Rodent suborders are distinguished by the placement of a major jaw muscle.
Rodents are the most numerous of all mammals.
Myomorpha

Chinchillidae:chinchilla
Dasyproctidae:agouti, paca
Erethizontidae: New World porcupine
Hystricidae: Old World porcupine
Castoridae:beaver
Caviomorpha
Rodentia

Bats - various familes — Chiroptera

Subclass Theria
Infraclass Placentalia

Family	Suborder Infraorder Superfamily	Order

Leporidae:rabbit, hare
Ochotonidae:pika
— Lagomorpha

Manidae:pangolin — Pholidata

Erinaceidae:hedgehog
Talpidae:mole
Saricidae:some shrews
Insectivora

Dasypodidae:armadillo — Loricata
Bradypodidae:sloth — Pilosa
Myrmecophagidae:hairy anteater — Vermilingua
Edentate (toothless)

Physeteridae:sperm whale
Monodontidae:narwhal, beluga
Phocoenidae:porpoise
Delphinidae:dolphin, killer whale
Odontoceti (toothed)

Eschrichtiidae:gray whale
Balaenidae:right whale
Balaenopteridae:humpback whale
Mysticeti (baleen)
Cetacea

Manatee, dugong — Sirenea

Elephantidae:elephant — Proboscidea

Tupaiidae:tree shrew
Lemuridae:lemur
Daubentoniidae:aye-aye
Lorisidae:loris, potto
Tarsiidae:tarsier
The prosimians usually have longer snouts than anthropoids.
Prosimii

Callitrichidae:marmoset
Cebidae: New World monkeys (flat-nosed)
Cercopithecidae:baboon, Old World monkeys (long-nosed, bare buttocks)
Hylobatidae:gibbon
Pongidae (great apes): gorilla, chimpanzee, orangutan
Hominidae:human
Most primates have opposable thumbs; all but man have opposable big toes.
Anthropoidea
Primates

Infraclass Marsupialia
Dasyuridae:mouse- and ratlike, Tasmanian devil
Notoryctidae:molelike
Thylacinidae:wolflike
Dasyuroidea
Marsupicanivora

Didelphidae: American opossums — Didelphoidea

Caenolestidae:ratlike So. America only — Paucituberculata

Peramelidae:bandicoot — Peramalina

Burramyidae:mouse- and squirrellike
Macropodidae:kangaroo, wallaby
Petauridae:squirrellike, some Australian possums
Phalangeridae:cuscus, some Australian possums
Phalangeroidea
Diprodonta

Tarsipedidae:honey possum — Tarsipedoidea

Vombatidae:wombat
Phascolarctidae:koala
Vombatoidea

Subclass Prototheria
Ornithorhynchidae:duck-billed platypus
Tachyglossidae:echidna (spiny anteater)
Monotremata

Giant Trees of the U.S.

Source: The American Forestry Association, Washington, D.C.

There are approximately 748 different species of trees native to the continental U.S., including a few imports that have become naturalized to the extent of reproducing themselves in the wild state.

The oldest living trees in the world are reputed to be the bristlecone pines, the majority of which are found growing on the arid crags of California's White Mts. Some of them are estimated to be more than 4,600 years old. The largest known bristlecone pine is the "Patriarch," believed to be 1,500 years old. The oldest known redwoods are about 3,500 years old.

Recognition as the National Champion of each species is determined by total mass of each tree, based on this formula: the circumference in inches as measured at a point 4 1/2 feet above the ground plus the total height of the tree in feet plus 1/4 of the average crown spread in feet. Trees are compared on the basis of this formula. Trees within five points of each other are declared co-champions. The Giant Sequoia champion has the largest circumference, 83 ft. 2 in., Smallflower Paw Paw the smallest, 4 in. Anyone can nominate the candidates for the National Register of Big Trees. For information, write to National Register of Big Trees, American Forestry Assn., P.O. Box 2000, Washington, DC 20013. Or call toll-free at (800) 368-5748. Following is a small selection of the trees registered.

(Figure in parentheses is year of most recent measurement)

Species	Height (ft.)	Location
Acacia, Catclaw (1971)	49	Red Rock, N.M.
Ailanthus (1972)	64	Head of Harbor, L.I.
Alaska Cedar (1972)	120	Olympic Natl. Park, Wash.
Alder, Green (1984)	28	Marquette, Mich.
Alder, White (1984)	37	West Salem, Ore.
Allthorn (1986)	11	Willacy Co., Tex.
Apple, Common (1986)	70	East End, Va.
Ash, Carolina (1987)	48	Chesapeake, Va.
Ash, Texas (1984)	42	Travis Co., Tex.
Aspen, Quaking (1982)	109	Ontonagon Co., Mich.
Avocado (1987)	40	Hallandale, Fla.
Basswood, White (1986)	75	Henderson Co., N.C.
Bayberry, Southern (1984)	31	Dr. George Is., Fla.
Beech, American (1984)	130	Ashtabula Co., Oh.
Birch, Paper (1979)	93	Hartford, Me.
Birch, River (1988)	90	Appleton Comm., Tenn.
Birch, Water (1973)	53	Wallowa Co., Ore.
Blackbead, Ebony (1986)	40	Hidalgo Co., Tex.
Bladdernut, Sierra (1986)	28	Fresno, Co., Cal.
Boxwood, Florida (1986)	27	Monroe Co., Fla.
Buckeye, Red (1983)	64	Kalamazoo Co., Mich.
Buckthorn, Hollyleaf (1976)	22	Greenfield, Cal.
Buffaloberry, Silver (1975)	22	Maleur Co., Ore.
Bumelia, Tough (1987)	41	Amelia Is., Fla.
Butternut (1987)	80	Eugene, Ore.
California Laurel (1978)	88	Siskiyou Natl. For., Ore.
Camphor Tree (1977)	72	Hardee Co., Fla.
Catalpa, Southern (1981)	80	Henderson Co., Ill.
Catclaw, Right (1986)	36	Uvalde Co., Tex.
Cedar, Atlantic white (1985)	88	Escambia Co., Ala.
Cherry, Bitter (1985)	104	Vashon Is., Wash.
Coconut, Palm (1979)	92	Hilo, Hi.
Cypress, McNab (1981)	55	Amador Co., Cal.
Dahoon, Myrtle (1972)	46	Lawtey, Fla.
Desert Willow (1976)	56	Gila Co., Ariz.
Dogwood, Blackfruit (1986)	18	Shasta Co., Cal.
Douglas Fir, Rocky Mtn. (1984)	158	Ochoco Natl. For., Ore.
Elder, American (1987)	16	Jefferson Natl. For., Va.
Elm, American (1985)	125	Southampton Co., Va.
Eucalyptus, Longbeak (1983)	171	Kern Co., Cal.
Fiddlewood, Florida (1987)	39	Dade Co., Fla.
Fig, Shortleaf (1986)	41	Monroe Co., Fla.
Fir, Grand (1987)	251	Olympic Natl. Park, Wash.
Franklinia (1986)	36	Wyndmoor, Pa.
Gallberry, Large (1986)	21	Virginia Beach, Va.
Geiger Tree (1987)	25	Lee Co., Fla.
Guiana Plum (1976)	31	Coral Gables, Fla.
Hackberry, Common (1987)	97	Middletown, Oh.
Hawthorn, Barberry (1982)	12	Angelina Natl. Forest, Tex.
Hawthorne, Fleshy (1988)	8	Kirkwood, Mo.
Hawthorne, Scarlet (1980)	37	Clinton, N.Y.
Hazel, California (1984)	47	Seattle, Wash.
Hemlock, Carolina (1972)	88	Burke Co., N.C.
Hickory, Mockernut (1985)	125	Monroe Co., Ala.
Hickory, Shellbark (1986)	105	Rixeyville, Va.
Holly, Carolina (1986)	25	Jacksonville, Fla.
Honeylocust (1985)	115	Wayne Co., Mich.
Huisache (1987)	48	Big Bend Natl. Park, Tex.
India Almond (1986)	61	Monroe Co., Fla.
Jujube, Common (1977)	40	Bee County, Tex.
Juniper, Western (1983)	86	Stanislaus Natl. Forest, Cal.
Larch, European (1982)	86	Northfield, Vt.
Laurel, English (1987)	32	Seattle, Wash.
Loblolly Bay (1983)	94	Ocala Natl. Forest, Fla.
Locust, Black (1974)	96	Dansville, N.Y.
Madrone, Pacific (1984)	96	Humboldt Co., Cal.
Magnolia, Umbrella (1969)	45	Bucks Co., Pa.
Mahogany, W. Indies (1988)	70	Lee Co., Fla.
Manzanita, Common	29	River Pines, Cal.
Maple, Black	118	Allegan Co., Mich.
Maple, Douglas (1985)	65	Ahsahka, Ida.
Mesquite, Honey (1984)	52	Real County, Tex.
Mountain Ash, Sitka (1981)	50	Gardiner, Ore.
Mulberry, Black (1983)	68	Westminster, Md.
Oak, Bluejack (1985)	68	Cherokee Co., Tex.
Oak, Chestnut (1982)	75	Northport, N.Y.
Oak, Harvard (1986)	30	Yoakum Co., Tex.
Oak, Scarlet (1978)	150	Colbert Co., Ala.
Oysterwood (1986)	24	Monroe Co., Fla.
Palmetto, Dwarf (1979)	27	Brazoria, Tex.
Paloverde, Blue (1976)	53	Riverside Co., Cal.
Paper Mulberry (1987)	40	Norfolk, Va.
Pawpaw, Common (1986)	60	Newton Co., Miss.
Peach (1986)	18	Morrisville, Va.
Pear, Common (1985)	55	Wayne Co., Mich.
Pecan (1980)	143	Cocke Co., Tenn.
Persimmon, Texas (1965)	26	Uvalde Co., Tex.
Pinckneya (1982)	32	Orange Springs, Fla.
Pine, Bishop (1986)	112	Mendocino Co., Cal.
Pine, Intermountain (1978)	47	Inyo Natl. Forest, Cal.
Pine, Limber (1987)	39	Twin Peaks Wilderness Area, Ut.
Pine, Monterey (1968)	125	Downing's Forest, Cal.
Pine, Virginia (1981)	114	Jefferson Co., Ala.
Pistache, Texas (1976)	39	Val Verde Co., Cal.
Plum, Chicasaw (1987)	32	Henderson Co., N.C.
Plum, Mexican (1981)	26	Irving, Tex.
Poison Sumac (1972)	16	Robins Is., N.Y.
Poplar, Balsam (1986)	138	Marquette, Mich.
Portiatree (1968)	42	Kekaha, Ha.
Prickly-Ash, Lime (1987)	25	Lee Co., Fla.
Privet, Japanese (1984)	42	Columbia, S.C.
Redbud, Eastern (1987)	41	Nashville, Tenn.
Rhododendron, Rosebay (1981)	40	Oconee Co., S.C.
Ribbonbush (1977)	23	No. Warner Springs, Cal.
Russian Olive (1982)	58	Cortez, Col.
Saffron Plum (1987)	31	Santa Ana, Tex.
Sassafras (1982)	76	Owensboro, Ky.
Sequoia, Giant (1975)	275	Sequoia Natl. Park, Cal.
Serviceberry, Downy (1986)	60	Burkes Garden, Va.
Silktree, Mimosa (1986)	54	Webster Parish, La.
Silverbell, Carolina (1987)	86	Great Smoky Natl. Park, Tenn.
Sophora, Mescalbean (1983)	27	Comal Co., Tex.
Spruce, Blue (1981)	126	Gunnison Natl. Forest, Col.
Spruce, Norway (1987)	92	Durham, N.H.
Stewartia, Virginia (1987)	18	NW River Park, Va.
Sumac, Shining (1986)	49	Marion Co., Tex.
Sweetgum, American (1986)	136	Craven Co., N.C.
Sycamore, Arizona (1981)	114	Sierra Co., N.M.
Tamarisk (1981)	34	Columbus, N.M.
Thatchpalm, Florida (1986)	23	Monroe Co., Fla.
Tupelo, Swamp (1987)	102	Suffolk Co., Va.
Walnut, Arizona (1987)	85	Mimbres Valley, N.M.
Willow, Sitka (1988)	34	Coupeville, Wash.
Willow, Weeping (1987)	114	Asheville, N.C.
Yew, Florida (1986)	20	Torreya State Park, Fla.
Yucca, Mojave (1987)	24	Needles Resource Area, Cal.
Yucca, Torrey (1987)	23	Lincoln Natl. Forest, N.M.

METEOROLOGY

National Weather Service Watches and Warnings

Source: National Weather Service, NOAA, U.S. Commerce Department; *Glossary of Meteorology*. American Meteorological Society

National Weather Service forecasters issue a Tornado Watch for a specific area where tornadoes are most likely to occur during the valid time of the watch. A Watch alerts people to check for threatening weather, make plans for action, and listen for a Tornado Warning. A Tornado Warning means that a tornado has been sighted or indicated by radar, and that safety precautions should be taken at once. A Hurricane Watch means that an existing hurricane poses a threat to coastal and inland communities in the area specified by the Watch. A Hurricane Warning means hurricane force winds and/or dangerously high water and exceptionally high waves are expected in a specified coastal area within 24 hours.

Tornado—A violent rotating column of air in contact with the ground and pendant from a thundercloud, usually recognized as a funnel-shaped vortex accompanied by a loud roar. With rotating winds est. up to 300 mph., on a local scale, it is the most destructive storm. Tornado paths have varied in length from a few feet to nearly 300 miles (avg. 5 mi.); diameter from a few feet to over a mile (average 220 yards); average forward speed, 30 mph.

Cyclone—An atmospheric circulation of winds rotating counterclockwise in the northern hemisphere and clockwise in the southern hemisphere. Tornadoes, hurricanes, and the lows shown on weather maps are all examples of cyclones having various sizes and intensities. Cyclones are usually accompanied by precipitation or stormy weather.

Hurricane—A severe cyclone originating over tropical ocean waters and having winds 74 miles an hour or higher. (In the western Pacific, such storms are known as typhoons.) The area of strong winds takes the form of a circle or an oval, sometimes as much as 500 miles in diameter. In the lower latitudes hurricanes usually move toward the west or northwest at 10 to 15 mph. When the center approaches 25° to 30° North Latitude, direction of motion often changes to northeast, with increased forward speed.

Blizzard—A severe weather condition characterized by strong winds bearing a great amount of snow. The National Weather Service specifies a wind of 35 miles an hour or higher, and sufficient falling and/or blowing snow to reduce visibility to less than ¼ of a mile for a duration of three hours or longer.

Severe Thunderstorm—A thunderstorm with winds of 58 mph. or greater and/or hail three-fourths of an inch or larger in diameter.

Flood—The condition that occurs when water overflows the natural or artificial confines of a stream or other body of water, or accumulates by drainage over low-lying areas.

National Weather Service Marine Warnings and Advisories

Small Craft Advisory: A Small Craft Advisory alerts mariners to sustained (exceeding two hours) weather and/or sea conditions either present or forecast, potentially hazardous to small boats. Hazardous conditions may include winds of 18 to 33 knots and/or dangerous wave or inlet conditions. It is the responsibility of the mariner, based on his experience and size or type of boat, to determine if the conditions are hazardous. When a mariner becomes aware of a Small Craft Advisory, he should immediately obtain the latest marine forecast to determine the reason for the Advisory.

Gale Warning indicates that winds within the range 34 to 47 knots are forecast for the area.

Tropical Storm Warning indicates that winds of 34 to 63 knots are forecast in a specified coastal area in 24 hours or less. Only issued for winds produced by tropical weather systems.

Storm Warning indicates that winds 48 knots and above, no matter how high the speed, are forecast for the area.

Hurricane Warning indicates that winds 64 knots and above are forecast for the area. Only issued for winds produced by tropical weather systems.

Special Marine Warning: A warning for potentially hazardous weather conditions, usually of short duration (2 hours or less) and producing wind speeds of 34 knots or more, not adequately covered by existing marine warnings.

Primary sources of dissemination are commercial radio, TV, U.S. Coast Guard Radio stations, and NOAA VHF-FM broadcasts. These broadcasts on 162.40 to 162.55 MHz can usually be received 20-40 miles from the transmitting antenna site, depending on terrain and quality of the receiver used. Where transmitting antennas are on high ground, the range is somewhat greater, reaching 60 miles or more.

Speed of Winds in the U.S.

Source: Natl. Climatic Data Center, NESDIS, NOAA, U.S. Department of Commerce
Miles per hour — average through 1988. High through 1988. Wind velocities in true values.

Station	Avg.	High	Station	Avg.	High	Station	Avg.	High
Albuquerque, N.M.	9.0	90	Helena, Mont.	7.8	73	Mt. Washington, N.H.	35.2	231
Anchorage, Alas.	6.9	64	Honolulu, Ha.	11.5	(b)67	New Orleans, La.	8.2	(b)98
Atlanta, Ga.	9.1	60	Houston, Tex.	7.8	51	New York, N.Y.(c)	9.4	70
Baltimore, Md.	9.2	80	Indianapolis, Ind.	9.6	46	Omaha, Neb.	10.6	109
Bismarck, N.D.	10.3	(b)72	Jacksonville, Fla.	8.0	(b)82	Philadelphia, Pa.	9.5	73
Boston, Mass.	12.5	61	Kansas City, Mo.	10.8	70	Phoenix, Ariz.	6.3	86
Buffalo, N.Y.	12.0	91	Lexington, Ky.	9.3	46	Pittsburgh, Pa.	9.1	58
Cape Hatteras, N.C.	11.2	(b)110	Little Rock, Ark.	7.9	65	Portland, Ore.	7.9	88
Casper, Wyo.	12.9	81	Los Angeles, Cal.	6.2	49	St. Louis, Mo.	9.7	(b)60
Chicago, Ill.	10.3	58	Louisville, Ky.	8.3	61	Salt Lake City, Ut.	8.8	71
Cleveland, Oh.	10.3	(b)74	Memphis, Tenn.	8.9	46	San Diego, Cal.	6.9	56
Dallas, Tex.	10.9	73	Miami, Fla.	9.3	(a)74	San Francisco, Cal.	8.7	47
Denver, Col.	8.7	(b)56	Milwaukee, Wis.	11.6	54	Seattle, Wash.	9.0	66
Detroit, Mich.	10.3	48	Minneapolis, Minn.	10.6	(b)92	Spokane, Wash.	8.8	59
Galveston, Tex.	11.0	(d)100	Mobile, Ala.	9.0	63	Washington, D.C.	9.3	78

(a) Highest velocity ever recorded in Miami area was 132 mph. at former station in Miami Beach in September, 1926.
(b) Previous location. (c) Data for Central Park, Battery Place data through 1960. avg. 14.5, high 113. (d) Recorded before anemometer blew away. Estimated high 120.

The Meaning of "One Inch of Rain"

An acre of ground contains 43,560 square feet. Consequently, a rainfall of 1 inch over 1 acre of ground would mean a total of 6,272,640 cubic inches of water. This is equivalent of 3,630 cubic feet.

As a cubic foot of pure water weights about 62.4 pounds, the exact amount varying with the density, it follows that the weight of a uniform coating of 1 inch of rain over 1 acre of surface would be 226,512 pounds, or about 113 short tons. The weight of 1 U.S. gallon of pure water is about 8.345 pounds. Consequently a rainfall of 1 inch over 1 acre of ground would mean 27,143 gallons of water.

Tides and Their Causes

Source: NOAA, National Ocean Service, U.S. Department of Commerce

The tides are a natural phenomenon involving the alternating rise and fall in the large fluid bodies of the earth caused by the combined gravitational attraction of the sun and moon. The combination of these two variable force influences produces the complex recurrent cycle of the tides. Tides may occur in both oceans and seas, to a limited extent in large lakes, the atmosphere, and, to a very minute degree, in the earth itself. The period between succeeding tides varies as the result of many factors and force influences.

The tide-generating force represents the difference between (1) the centrifugal force produced by the revolution of the earth around the common center-of-gravity of the earth-moon system and (2) the gravitational attraction of the moon acting upon the earth's overlying waters. Since, on the average, the moon is only 238,852 miles from the earth compared with the sun's much greater distance of 92,956,000 miles, this closer distance outranks the much smaller mass of the moon compared with that of the sun, and the moon's tide-raising force is, accordingly, $2\frac{1}{5}$ times that of the sun.

The effect of the tide-generating forces of the moon and sun acting tangentially to the earth's surface (the so-called "tractive force") tends to cause a maximum accumulation of the waters of the oceans at two diametrically opposite positions on the surface of the earth and to withdraw compensating amounts of water from all points 90° removed from the positions of these tidal bulges. As the earth rotates beneath the maxima and minima of these tide-generating forces, a sequence of two high tides, separated by two low tides, ideally is produced each day.

Twice in each lunar month, when the sun, moon, and earth are directly aligned, with the moon between the earth and the sun (at new moon) or on the opposite side of the earth from the sun (at full moon), the sun and the moon exert their gravitational force in a mutual or additive fashion. Higher high tides and lower low tides are produced. These are called *spring* tides. At two positions 90° in between, the gravitational forces of the moon and sun — imposed at right angles—tend to counteract each other to the greatest extent, and the range between high and low tides is reduced. These are called *neap* tides. This semi-monthly variation between the spring and neap tides is called the *phase inequality*.

The inclination of the moon's orbit to the equator also produces a difference in the height of succeeding high tides and in the extent of depression of succeeding low tides which is known as the *diurnal inequality*. In extreme cases, this phenomenon can result in only one high tide and one low tide each day.

The actual range of tide in the waters of the open ocean may amount to only one or two feet. However, as this tide approaches shoal waters and its effects are augmented the tidal range may be greatly increased. In Nova Scotia along the narrow channel of the Bay of Fundy, the range of tides or difference between high and low waters, may reach 43 1/2 feet or more (under spring tide conditions) due to resonant amplification.

At New Orleans, the periodic rise and fall of the tide varies with the state of the Mississippi, being about 10 inches at low stage and zero at high. The Canadian Tide Tables for 1972 gave a maximum range of nearly 50 feet at Leaf Basin, Ungava Bay, Quebec.

In every case, actual high or low tide can vary considerably from the average, due to weather conditions such as strong winds, abrupt barometric pressure changes, or prolonged periods of extreme high or low pressure.

The Average Rise and Fall of Tides

Places	Ft.	In.	Places	Ft.	In.	Places	Ft.	In.
Baltimore, Md.	1	1	Mobile, Ala.	1	6[1]	San Diego, Cal.	5	9[1]
Boston, Mass.	9	6	New London, Conn.	2	7	Sandy Hook, N.J.	4	8
Charleston, S.C.	5	3	Newport, R.I.	3	6	San Francisco, Cal.	5	10[1]
Cristobal, Panama	1	1[1]	New York, N.Y.	4	7	Savannah, Ga.	7	5
Eastport, Me.	18	4	Old Pt. Comfort, Va.	2	6	Seattle, Wash.	11	4[1]
Galveston, Tex.	1	5[1]	Philadelphia, Pa.	6	2	Tampa, Fla.	2	10[1]
Halifax, N.S.	4	5	Portland, Me.	9	1	Vancouver, B.C.	10	6[1]
Key West, Fla.	1	10[1]	St. John's, Nfld.	2	7	Washington, D.C.	2	9

(1) Diurnal range.

Hurricane Names in 1990

U.S. government agencies responsible for weather and related communications have used girls' names to identify major tropical storms since 1953. A U.S. proposal that both male and female names be adopted for hurricanes, starting in 1979, was accepted by a committee of the World Meteorological Organization.

Names assigned to Atlantic hurricanes, 1990 — Arthur, Bertha, Cesar, Diana, Edouard, Fran, Gustav, Hortense, Isidore, Josephine, Klaus, Lili, Marco, Nana, Omar, Paloma, Rene, Sally, Teddy, Vicky, Wilfred.

Names assigned to Eastern Pacific hurricanes, 1990 — Alma, Boris, Cristina, Douglas, Elida, Fausto, Genevieve, Hernan, Iselle, Julio, Kenna, Lowell, Marie, Norbert, Odile, Polo, Rachel, Simon, Trudy, Vance, Wallis.

Hurricane Hotlines

When tropical storms or hurricanes threaten, you will be able to get updates on the telephone from the National Oceanic and Atmospheric Administration. Recorded messages will identify areas under a hurricane watch or warning, the location of the storm, its forecast movement and wind speeds and tidal effects.

Two Hurricane Hotlines will be set up, one to be activated when hurricanes or tropical storms threaten the Eastern and Gulf Coast states, another for Hawaii. The number for the East Coast hot line is (900) 410-6622 (or NOAA). For Hawaii, the number is (900) 410-2263 (or CANE).

Callers will be billed 50 cents for the first minute and 45 cents for each additional minute. The average call is expected to cost about 85 cents.

Explanation of Normal Temperatures

Normal temperatures listed in the tables on pages 224 and 225 are based on records of the National Weather Service for the 30-year period from 1951-1980 inclusive. To obtain the average maximum or minimum temperature for any month, the daily temperatures are added; the total is then divided by the number of days in that month.

The normal maximum temperature for January, for example, is obtained by adding the average maximums for Jan., 1951, Jan., 1952, etc., through Jan., 1980. The total is then divided by 30. The normal minimum temperature is obtained in a similar manner by adding the average minimums for each January in the 30-year period and dividing by 30. The normal temperature for January is one half of the sum for the normal maximum and minimum temperatures for that month. The mean temperature for any one day is one-half the total of the maximum and minimum temperatures for that day.

Monthly Normal Temperature and Precipitation

Source: Natl. Climatic Data Center, NESDIS, NOAA, U.S. Department of Commerce

These normals are based on records for the 30-year period 1951 to 1980 inclusive. (See explanation on page 223.) For stations that did not have continuous records from the same instrument site for the entire 30 years, the means have been adjusted to the record at the present site.

Airport station; *city office stations. T, temperature in Fahrenheit; P, precipitation in inches; L, less than .05 inch.

Station	Jan. T.	Jan. P.	Feb. T.	Feb. P.	Mar. T.	Mar. P.	Apr. T.	Apr. P.	May T.	May P.	June T.	June P.	July T.	July P.	Aug. T.	Aug. P.	Sept. T.	Sept. P.	Oct. T.	Oct. P.	Nov. T.	Nov. P.	Dec. T.	Dec. P.
Albany, N.Y.	21	2.4	23	2.3	34	3.0	47	2.9	58	3.3	67	3.3	71	3.0	69	3.3	61	3.2	51	2.9	39	3.0	26	3.0
Albuquerque, N.M.	35	0.4	39	0.4	46	0.5	55	0.4	64	0.5	75	0.5	79	1.3	76	1.5	69	0.9	57	0.9	44	0.4	36	0.5
Anchorage, Alas.	13	0.8	18	0.9	24	0.7	35	0.7	46	0.6	54	1.1	58	2.0	56	2.1	48	2.5	35	1.7	22	1.1	14	1.1
Asheville, N.C.	37	3.5	39	3.6	46	5.1	56	3.8	63	4.2	70	4.2	73	4.4	73	4.8	70	4.0	56	3.3	46	3.3	39	3.5
Atlanta, Ga.	42	4.9	45	4.4	53	5.9	62	4.4	69	4.0	76	3.4	79	4.7	78	3.4	73	3.2	62	2.5	52	3.4	45	4.2
Atlantic City, N.J.	34	3.3	35	3.2	42	3.7	51	3.1	60	2.9	68	2.9	74	3.9	74	4.5	68	2.7	58	2.8	48	3.5	38	3.5
Baltimore, Md.	33	3.0	35	3.0	43	3.7	54	3.4	63	3.4	72	3.8	77	3.9	76	4.6	69	3.5	57	3.1	46	3.1	37	3.4
Barrow, Alas.	-14	0.2	-20	0.2	-16	0.2	-2	0.2	19	0.2	33	0.4	39	0.9	38	1.0	31	0.6	14	0.6	-1	0.3	-13	0.2
Birmingham, Ala.	42	5.2	46	4.7	54	6.6	63	5.0	70	4.5	77	3.7	80	5.4	80	3.9	74	4.3	62	2.7	52	3.6	45	5.0
Bismarck, N.D.	7	0.5	15	0.5	26	0.7	43	1.5	55	2.2	64	3.0	70	2.0	69	1.7	57	1.4	46	0.8	29	0.5	15	0.5
Boise, Ida.	30	1.6	36	1.1	41	1.0	49	1.2	57	1.2	66	1.0	75	0.3	72	0.4	63	0.6	52	0.8	40	1.3	32	1.3
Boston, Mass.	30	4.0	31	3.7	38	4.1	49	3.7	59	3.5	68	2.9	74	2.7	72	3.7	65	3.4	55	3.4	45	4.2	34	4.9
Buffalo, N.Y.	24	3.0	25	2.4	33	3.0	45	3.0	56	2.9	66	2.7	71	3.0	69	4.2	62	3.4	52	2.9	40	3.6	29	3.4
Burlington, Vt.	17	1.9	18	1.7	29	2.2	43	2.8	55	3.0	65	3.6	70	3.4	67	3.9	59	3.2	48	2.8	37	2.8	23	2.4
Caribou, Me.	11	2.4	13	2.1	24	2.4	37	2.6	50	2.9	60	3.2	65	4.0	63	4.0	54	3.5	43	3.1	31	3.2	16	3.1
Charleston, S.C.	49	3.3	51	3.4	57	4.4	66	2.6	73	4.4	79	6.5	82	7.3	81	6.5	77	4.9	68	2.9	59	2.2	52	3.1
Chicago, Ill.	21	1.6	26	1.3	36	2.6	49	3.7	59	3.2	69	4.1	73	3.6	72	3.5	65	3.4	54	2.3	40	2.1	28	2.1
Cleveland, Oh.	26	2.5	27	2.2	37	3.0	48	3.3	58	3.3	68	3.5	72	3.4	70	3.4	64	2.9	53	2.5	42	2.8	31	2.8
Columbus, Oh.	27	2.8	30	2.2	40	3.2	51	3.4	61	3.8	70	4.0	74	4.0	72	3.7	66	2.8	54	1.9	42	2.6	32	2.6
Dallas-Ft. Worth, Tex.	44	1.7	49	1.9	56	2.4	66	3.6	74	4.3	82	2.6	86	2.0	86	1.8	79	3.3	68	2.5	56	1.8	48	1.7
Denver, Col.	30	0.5	34	0.7	38	1.2	47	1.8	57	2.5	67	1.6	73	1.9	71	1.5	63	1.2	52	1.0	39	0.8	33	0.6
Des Moines, Ia.	19	1.0	25	1.1	35	2.2	51	3.2	62	4.0	72	4.2	76	3.2	74	4.1	65	3.1	54	2.2	39	1.5	26	1.5
Detroit, Mich.	23	1.9	26	1.7	35	2.5	47	3.2	58	2.8	68	3.4	72	3.1	71	3.2	63	2.3	52	2.1	40	2.3	29	2.5
Dodge City, Kan.	30	0.5	35	0.5	42	1.5	54	1.8	64	3.3	75	3.0	80	3.1	78	2.5	69	1.9	58	1.3	43	0.8	34	0.5
Duluth, Minn.	6	1.2	12	0.9	23	1.8	38	2.2	50	3.2	59	4.0	65	4.0	63	4.1	54	3.3	44	2.2	28	1.7	14	1.3
Eureka, Cal.*	47	7.0	49	5.2	48	5.1	49	2.9	52	1.6	55	0.6	56	0.1	57	0.4	57	0.9	54	2.7	51	5.9	48	6.2
Fairbanks, Alas.	-13	0.5	-4	0.5	9	0.4	30	0.3	48	0.6	59	1.3	62	1.8	57	1.9	45	1.1	25	0.7	4	0.7	-10	0.7
Fresno, Cal.	46	2.0	51	1.9	54	1.6	60	1.2	68	0.3	75	0.1	81	L	79	L	74	0.2	65	0.4	53	1.2	45	1.6
Galveston, Tex.*	54	3.0	56	2.3	62	2.1	69	2.6	76	3.3	81	3.5	83	3.8	83	4.4	80	5.8	73	2.6	63	3.2	57	3.6
Grand Junction, Col.	26	0.6	34	0.5	42	0.8	52	0.7	62	0.8	72	0.4	79	0.5	76	0.9	67	0.7	55	0.9	40	0.6	28	0.6
Gr. Rapids, Mich.	22	1.9	24	1.5	33	2.5	46	3.6	58	3.0	67	3.9	71	3.0	70	3.5	62	3.1	51	2.9	39	2.9	27	2.6
Hartford, Conn.	25	3.5	28	3.2	37	4.2	49	4.0	59	3.4	69	3.4	73	3.1	71	4.0	63	3.9	52	3.5	42	4.1	29	4.2
Helena, Mon.	18	0.7	26	0.4	32	0.7	42	1.0	52	1.7	60	2.0	68	1.0	66	1.2	56	0.8	45	0.7	31	0.5	23	0.6
Honolulu, Ha.	73	3.8	73	2.7	74	3.5	76	1.5	78	1.2	79	0.5	80	0.5	81	0.6	81	0.6	80	1.9	77	3.2	74	3.4
Houston, Tex.	51	3.2	55	3.3	61	2.7	69	4.2	75	4.7	81	4.0	83	3.3	83	3.7	78	4.9	70	3.7	60	3.4	54	3.7
Huron, S.D.	11	0.4	18	0.8	29	1.2	46	2.0	57	2.7	68	3.3	74	2.3	72	2.0	61	1.4	49	1.4	32	0.7	19	0.5
Indianapolis, Ind.	26	2.7	30	2.5	40	3.6	52	3.7	63	3.7	72	4.0	75	4.3	73	3.5	67	2.7	55	2.5	42	3.0	32	3.0
Jackson, Miss.	46	5.0	49	4.9	56	5.9	65	5.9	73	4.8	79	2.9	82	4.4	81	3.7	76	3.6	65	2.6	55	4.2	49	5.4
Jacksonville, Fla.	53	3.1	55	3.5	61	3.7	68	3.3	74	4.9	79	5.4	81	6.5	81	7.2	78	7.3	70	3.4	61	1.9	55	2.6
Juneau, Alas.	22	3.7	28	3.7	31	3.3	39	2.9	46	3.4	53	3.0	56	4.1	55	5.0	49	6.4	42	7.7	33	5.2	27	4.7
Kansas City, Mo.	26	1.0	32	1.0	42	2.1	55	2.7	65	3.4	76	4.1	79	3.5	77	3.2	68	3.3	58	2.5	43	1.2	32	1.1
Knoxville, Tenn.	38	4.7	42	4.2	50	5.5	60	3.9	67	3.7	74	4.0	78	4.3	77	3.0	72	3.0	60	2.7	49	3.8	41	4.6
Lander, Wyo.	20	0.5	26	0.6	32	1.1	42	2.2	53	2.7	62	1.5	71	0.7	69	0.5	58	0.9	47	1.2	31	0.8	23	0.5
Lexington, Ky.	32	3.6	35	3.3	44	4.8	55	4.0	64	4.2	72	4.3	76	5.0	75	4.0	69	3.3	57	2.3	45	3.3	36	3.8
Little Rock, Ark.	40	3.9	44	3.8	52	4.7	62	5.4	71	5.3	79	3.7	82	3.6	81	3.1	74	4.3	63	2.8	51	4.4	43	4.2
Los Angeles, Cal.*	57	3.7	59	3.0	60	2.4	62	1.2	65	0.2	69	L	74	L	75	0.1	73	0.3	69	0.2	63	1.9	58	2.0
Louisville, Ky.	33	3.4	36	3.2	45	4.7	57	4.1	65	4.2	74	3.6	78	4.1	76	3.3	70	3.6	58	2.6	46	3.5	37	3.5
Marquette, Mich.*	12	2.0	14	1.9	23	2.8	37	3.6	50	4.0	60	3.9	65	3.2	63	3.3	54	3.9	44	3.3	30	2.9	18	2.4
Memphis, Tenn.	40	4.6	44	4.3	52	5.4	63	5.8	71	5.1	79	3.6	82	4.0	81	3.7	74	3.6	63	2.4	51	4.2	43	4.9
Miami, Fla.	67	2.1	68	2.1	72	1.9	75	3.1	79	6.5	81	9.2	83	6.0	83	7.0	82	8.1	78	7.1	73	2.7	69	1.9
Milwaukee, Wis.	19	1.6	23	1.3	32	2.6	45	3.4	55	2.6	65	3.6	71	3.5	69	3.1	62	2.9	51	2.3	37	2.0	25	2.0
Minneapolis, Minn.	11	0.8	18	0.9	29	1.7	46	2.1	59	3.2	68	4.1	73	3.5	71	3.6	61	2.5	50	1.9	33	1.3	19	0.9
Mobile, Ala.	51	4.6	54	4.9	60	6.5	68	5.4	75	5.5	81	5.1	82	7.7	82	6.8	78	6.6	69	2.6	59	3.7	53	5.4
Moline, Ill.	20	1.6	25	1.3	36	2.8	50	4.0	61	4.2	71	4.3	75	4.9	73	3.8	65	3.7	54	2.7	39	2.0	26	1.9
Nashville, Tenn.	37	4.5	40	4.0	49	5.6	60	4.8	68	4.6	76	3.7	79	3.8	78	3.4	72	3.7	60	2.6	49	3.5	41	4.6
Newark, N.J.	31	3.1	33	3.1	41	4.2	52	3.6	62	3.6	72	2.9	77	3.9	76	4.3	68	3.7	57	3.1	47	3.6	36	3.4
New Orleans, La.	52	5.0	55	5.2	61	4.7	69	4.5	75	5.1	80	4.6	82	6.7	82	6.0	79	5.9	69	2.7	60	4.1	55	5.3
New York, N.Y.*	32	3.2	33	3.1	41	4.2	53	3.8	62	3.8	71	3.2	77	3.8	75	4.0	68	3.7	58	3.4	47	4.1	36	3.8
Nome, Alas.	9	0.8	3	0.5	7	0.6	18	0.6	36	0.5	45	1.2	51	2.2	50	3.1	42	2.3	28	1.3	16	0.9	4	0.7
Norfolk, Va.	40	3.7	41	3.3	49	3.9	58	2.9	67	3.8	76	3.5	78	5.2	78	5.3	72	4.4	61	3.4	52	2.9	44	3.2
Okla. City, Okla.	36	1.0	41	1.3	49	2.1	60	2.9	68	5.5	77	3.9	82	3.0	81	2.4	73	3.4	62	2.7	49	1.5	40	1.2
Omaha, Neb.	19	0.8	25	0.9	35	1.9	50	2.9	62	4.3	71	4.1	76	3.6	74	4.1	64	2.5	54	2.1	38	1.3	26	0.8
Pago Pago, Amer. Samoa	81	13	81	13	81	11	81	11	80	11	80	8.6	79	6.5	79	7.1	79	6.7	80	11	80	11	81	14
Philadelphia, Pa.	31	3.2	33	2.8	42	3.9	53	3.5	63	3.2	72	3.9	77	3.9	75	4.1	68	3.4	57	2.8	46	3.3	36	3.5
Phoenix, Ariz.	52	0.7	56	0.6	61	0.8	68	0.3	77	0.1	87	0.2	92	0.7	90	1.0	85	0.6	73	0.6	61	0.5	53	0.8
Pittsburgh, Pa.	27	2.9	29	2.4	39	3.6	50	3.3	60	3.5	68	3.3	72	3.8	71	3.3	64	2.8	53	2.5	42	2.3	31	2.6
Portland, Me.	22	3.8	23	3.6	32	4.0	43	3.9	53	3.3	62	3.1	68	2.8	67	2.8	59	3.3	49	3.8	38	4.7	26	4.5
Portland, Ore.	39	6.2	43	3.9	46	3.6	50	2.3	57	2.1	63	1.5	68	0.5	67	1.1	63	1.6	54	3.1	46	5.2	41	6.4
Providence, R.I.	28	4.1	29	3.7	37	4.3	48	4.0	58	3.5	67	2.8	73	3.0	71	4.0	64	3.5	53	3.8	43	4.2	32	4.5
Raleigh, N.C.	40	3.6	42	3.4	49	3.7	59	2.9	67	3.7	74	3.7	78	4.4	77	4.4	71	3.3	60	2.7	50	2.9	42	3.1
Rapid City, S.D.	21	0.4	26	0.6	33	1.0	45	2.0	56	2.6	65	3.3	73	2.1	71	1.4	61	1.0	50	0.8	35	0.5	26	0.5
Reno, Nev.	32	1.2	37	1.0	41	0.7	46	0.5	55	0.7	62	0.3	70	0.3	67	0.3	60	0.3	50	0.3	40	0.6	33	1.2
Richmond, Va.	37	3.2	39	3.1	47	3.6	58	2.9	66	3.6	74	3.6	78	5.1	77	5.0	70	3.5	59	3.7	49	3.3	40	3.4
St. Louis, Mo.	29	1.7	34	2.1	43	3.3	56	3.6	66	3.5	75	3.7	79	3.6	77	2.6	70	2.7	58	2.3	45	2.5	34	2.2
Salt Lake City, Ut.	29	1.4	34	1.3	41	1.7	49	2.2	59	1.5	68	1.0	78	0.7	75	0.9	65	0.9	53	1.1	40	1.2	30	1.4
San Antonio, Tex.	50	1.6	54	1.9	62	1.3	70	2.7	76	3.7	82	3.0	85	1.9	84	2.7	79	3.8	70	2.9	60	2.3	53	1.4
San Diego, Cal.	57	2.1	58	1.4	59	1.6	61	0.8	63	0.2	66	0.1	70	L	72	0.1	71	0.2	68	0.3	62	1.1	57	1.4
San Francisco, Cal.	49	4.7	52	3.2	53	2.6	55	1.5	58	0.3	61	0.1	62	L	63	0.1	64	0.2	61	1.1	55	2.4	49	3.6
San Juan, P.R.	77	3.0	77	2.0	78	2.3	80	3.6	79	5.6	80	4.7	82	4.9	82	5.9	82	6.0	81	5.9	80	5.6	78	4.7
Sault Ste. Marie, Mich.*	13	2.2	14	1.7	24	2.0	38	2.4	50	2.9	58	3.3	64	3.0	63	3.5	55	3.9	45	2.9	33	3.2	20	2.6
Savannah, Ga.	49	3.1	52	3.2	58	3.8	66	3.2	73	4.6	79	5.7	81	7.4	81	6.7	77	5.2	67	2.3	58	1.9	51	2.8
Seattle, Wash.	39	6.0	43	4.2	44	3.6	49	2.4	55	1.6	60	1.4	65	0.7	64	1.3	60	2.0	52	3.4	45	5.6	41	6.3
Spokane, Wash.	26	2.5	32	1.6	38	1.4	46	1.1	54	1.4	62	1.2	70	0.5	68	0.7	60	0.7	48	1.1	35	2.1	29	2.5
Springfield, Mo.	32	1.6	36	2.1	45	3.4	56	4.0	65	4.3	73	4.7	78	3.6	77	2.8	70	4.2	58	3.2	45	2.9	36	2.6
Syracuse, N.Y.	23	2.6	24	2.7	33	3.1	46	3.3	57	3.2	66	3.6	71	3.8	69	3.8	62	3.3	51	3.1	41	3.5	28	3.2
Tampa, Fla.	60	2.2	61	3.0	66	3.5	72	1.8	77	3.4	81	5.3	82	7.4	82	7.6	81	6.2	74	2.3	67	1.9	61	2.1
Washington, D.C.	31	2.8	34	2.6	42	3.4	53	3.1	62	3.6	71	4.2	76	3.8	74	4.2	67	3.3	55	3.0	45	3.0	35	3.3
Wilmington, Del.	31	3.1	33	3.0	42	3.9	52	3.4	62	3.2	71	3.5	76	3.9	75	4.0	68	3.6	56	2.9	46	3.3	36	3.5

Normal Temperatures, Highs, Lows, Precipitation

Source: Natl. Climatic Data Center, NESDIS, NOAA, U.S. Department of Commerce

These normals are based on records for the thirty-year period 1951-1980. (See explanation on page 223.) The extreme temperatures (through 1988) are listed for the stations shown and may not agree with the states records shown on page 227-228.

Airport stations; * designates city office stations. The minus (−) sign indicates temperatures below zero. Fahrenheit thermometer registration.

State	Station	Normal temperature January Max.	Min.	July Max.	Min.	Extreme temperature Highest	Lowest	annual precipitation (inches)
Alabama	Mobile	61	41	91	73	104	3	64.64
Alabama	Montgomery	57	36	92	72	105	0	49.16
Alaska	Juneau	27	16	64	47	90	−22	53.15
Arizona	Phoenix	65	39	105	80	118	17	7.11
Arkansas	Little Rock	50	30	93	71	112	−5	49.20
California	Los Angeles*	67	48	84	64	110	28	14.85
California	San Francisco	55	42	71	53	106	20	19.71
Colorado	Denver	43	16	88	59	104	−30	15.31
Connecticut	Hartford	34	17	85	62	102	−26	44.39
Delaware	Wilmington	39	23	86	66	102	−14	41.38
Dist. of Col.	Washington	43	28	88	70	104	−5	39.00
Florida	Jacksonville	65	42	91	72	105	7	52.76
Florida	Key West	72	66	89	80	95	41	39.42
Florida	Miami	75	59	89	76	98	30	57.55
Georgia	Atlanta	51	33	88	69	105	−8	48.61
Hawaii	Honolulu	80	65	87	73	94	53	23.47
Idaho	Boise	37	23	91	59	111	−23	11.71
Illinois	Chicago	29	14	83	63	104	−27	33.34
Indiana	Indianapolis	34	18	85	65	104	−22	39.12
Iowa	Des Moines	27	10	86	66	108	−24	30.83
Iowa	Dubuque	24	7	82	62	101	−28	38.59
Kansas	Wichita	40	19	93	70	113	−21	28.61
Kentucky	Louisville	41	24	88	68	105	−20	43.56
Louisiana	New Orleans	62	43	91	74	102	14	59.74
Maine	Portland	31	12	79	57	103	−39	43.52
Maryland	Baltimore	41	24	87	67	105	−7	41.84
Massachusetts	Boston	36	23	82	65	102	−12	43.84
Michigan	Detroit	31	16	83	61	104	−21	30.97
Michigan	Sault Ste. Marie*	21	5	75	52	98	−36	33.48
Minnesota	Minn.-St. Paul	20	2	83	63	105	−34	26.36
Mississippi	Jackson	57	35	93	68	106	2	52.82
Missouri	St. Louis	38	20	89	69	107	−18	33.91
Montana	Helena	28	8	84	52	105	−42	11.37
Nebraska	Omaha	30	10	89	67	114	−23	30.34
Nevada	Las Vegas	45	33	105	76	116	8	4.19
New Hampshire	Concord	31	9	83	56	102	−37	36.53
New Jersey	Atlantic City	41	23	84	65	106	−11	41.93
New Mexico	Albuquerque	47	22	93	65	105	−17	8.12
New Mexico	Roswell	55	27	94	69	109	−9	9.70
New York	Albany	30	12	83	60	100	−28	35.74
New York	New York-La Guardia	37	26	84	69	107	−3	42.82
No. Carolina	Charlotte	50	31	88	69	104	−5	43.16
No. Carolina	Raleigh	50	29	88	67	105	−9	41.76
No. Dakota	Bismarck	18	−4	84	56	109	−44	15.36
Ohio	Cincinnati-Greater	37	20	86	65	102	−25	40.14
Ohio	Cleveland	33	19	82	61	104	−19	35.40
Oklahoma	Oklahoma City	47	25	94	71	110	−4	30.89
Oregon	Portland	44	34	80	56	107	−3	37.39
Pennsylvania	Harrisburg	37	22	86	65	107	−9	39.09
Pennsylvania	Philadelphia	39	24	86	67	104	−7	41.42
Rhode Island	Block Island	37	25	76	64	92	−4	41.91
So. Carolina	Charleston	59	37	89	72	104	6	51.59
So. Dakota	Huron	22	0	87	61	112	−39	18.66
So. Dakota	Rapid City	32	9	87	59	110	−27	16.27
Tennessee	Nashville	46	28	90	69	107	−17	48.49
Texas	Amarillo	49	22	91	66	108	−14	19.10
Texas	Galveston*	59	48	87	79	101	8	40.24
Texas	Houston	62	41	94	73	107	11	44.76
Utah	Salt Lake City	37	20	93	62	107	−30	15.31
Vermont	Burlington	25	8	81	59	101	−30	33.69
Virginia	Norfolk	48	32	90	70	104	−3	45.22
Washington	Seattle-Tacoma	44	34	75	54	99	0	38.60
Washington	Spokane	31	20	84	55	108	−25	16.71
West Virginia	Huntington	41	25	86	65	102	−16	40.74
Wisconsin	Madison	25	7	83	58	104	−37	30.84
Wisconsin	Milwaukee	26	11	80	62	103	−26	30.94
Wyoming	Cheyenne	37	15	83	55	100	−34	13.31
Puerto Rico	San Juan	83	70	88	76	98	60	53.99

Mean Annual Snowfall (inches) based on record through 1980: Boston, Mass. 42; Sault Ste. Marie, Mich., 113; Albany, N.Y. 65.2; Rochester, N.Y. 89.2; Burlington, Vt., 78.6; Cheyenne, Wyo., 53.3; Juneau, Alas. 105.8.

Wettest Spot: Mount Waialeale, Ha., on the island of Kauai, is the rainiest place in the world, according to the National Geographic Society, with an average annual rainfall of 460 inches.

Highest Temperature: A temperature of 136° F. observed at Azizia, Tripolitania in Northern Africa on Sept. 13, 1922, is generally accepted as the world's highest temperature recorded under standard conditions.

The record high in the United States was 134° in Death Valley, Cal., July 10, 1913.

Lowest Temperature: A record low temperature of −128.6° F. was recorded at the Soviet Antarctica station Vostok on July 21, 1983.

The record low in the United States was −80° at Prospect Creek, Alas., Jan. 23, 1971.

The lowest official temperature on the North American continent was recorded at 81 degrees below zero in February, 1947, at a lonely airport in the Yukon called Snag.

These are the meteorological champions—the official temperature extremes—but there are plenty of other claimants to thermometer fame. However, sun readings are unofficial records, since meteorological data to qualify officially must be taken on instruments in a sheltered and ventilated location.

Annual Climatological Data

Source: Natl. Climatic Data Center, NESDIS, NOAA, U.S. Department of Commerce

1987

Station	Elev. ft.	Highest	Date	Lowest	Date	Total (in.)	Greatest in 24 hrs.	Date	Total (in.)	Greatest in 24 hours	Date	MPH	Date	Clear*	Cloudy*	Prec. .01 in. or more	Snow, sleet 1 in. or more
Albany, N.Y.	275	99	7/8	-13	1/15	29.55	2.44	8/28	60.4	13.7	2/12	36	8/5	58	172	127	12
Albuquerque, N.M.	5311	98	7/23	8	12/30	13.11	1.39	8/9	15.3	10.9	4/1	48	11/15	169	99	67	3
Anchorage, Alas.	114	73	7/19	-9	1/28	14.32	0.90	8/29	70.3	4.7	11/21	35	2/3	37	265	110	25
Asheville, N.C.	2140	96	7/8	2	1/11	26.50	1.77	10/1	15.4	14.0	1/7	35	4/7	127	122	109	2
Atlanta, Ga.	1010	99	7/8	16	2/7	45.85	3.52	10/1	4.2	4.2	1/7	35	5/10	140	123	104	1
Baltimore, Md.	148	104	7/16	3	1/11	72.30	1.83	11/27	14.8	8.4	1/7	48	12/28	116	129	99	4
Barrow, Alas.	31	61	8/5	-43	1/26	3.59	0.52	8/17	17.8	2.0	9/20	44	1/1	66	184	60	4
Birmingham, Ala.	678	98	6/26	15	2/7	41.04	2.45	11/19	0.3	0.3	1/7	—	—	—	—	109	0
Bismarck, N.D.	1647	107	6/27	-35	2/11	10.17	1.81	7/1	49.3	10.0	12/26	41	5/28	109	147	84	12
Boise, Ida.	2838	104	6/22	-4	12/28	11.30	0.95	5/28	21.6	3.9	12/21	36	4/14	125	147	78	8
Boston, Mass.	15	99	7/11	-4	1/14	34.78	2.43	7/23	39.8	9.4	1/8	45	6/22	95	165	119	7
Buffalo, N.Y.	705	97	7/6	-9	12/12	38.61	2.22	7/23	57.6	10.4	2/6	46	8/15	48	219	158	17
Burlington, Vt.	332	97	8/3	-16	1/14	26.68	2.32	6/25	58.2	11.0	2/12	37	2/22	49	196	140	16
Charleston, S.C.	40	100	6/24	21	1/28	42.57	2.90	9/8	0.4	0.4	1/15	35	8/28	115	150	104	0
Charleston, W. Va.	939	104	7/16	1	1/6	31.40	1.90	11/19	27.6	3.5	12/17	31	3/26	94	170	127	12
Chicago, Ill.	658	104	6/20	-14	1/6	33.36	3.61	10/17	28.7	5.0	2/10	43	4/6	109	136	107	9
Cincinnati, Oh.	869	103	7/9	-3	1/6	39.97	4.28	7/19	14.9	3.4	2/11	39	2/22	125	140	114	6
Cleveland, Oh.	777	104	6/25	-5	2/6	29.69	1.46	11/5	73.5	7.8	2/3	39	11/16	62	198	158	26
Columbus, Oh.	812	101	6/25	-1	2/6	36.57	3.33	7/20	25.4	4.9	1/25	35	11/20	92	158	130	7
Concord, N.H.	342	96	6/15	-23	1/11	33.30	2.19	8/14	53.2	13.7	2/12	37	2/12	85	164	124	13
Dallas, Tex.	551	107	8/8	16	1/10	25.04	2.75	6/1	3.5	1.4	2/11	43	12/19	142	121	70	2
Denver, Co.	5283	99	6/24	-12	1/4	14.96	2.45	5/18	44.7	7.1	3/30	37	5/6	113	127	73	17
Des Moines, Ia.	938	104	8/17	-16	2/12	22.11	2.35	6/7	11.7	5.1	2/9	43	11/16	145	133	85	2
Detroit, Mich.	633	104	6/25	-3	1/7	26.86	1.72	9/22	36.4	7.6	2/11	39	5/15	85	173	152	10
Dodge City, Kan.	2582	106	8/14	-12	1/9	14.96	1.38	5/27	16.3	8.9	3/23	46	3/27	152	105	61	4
Duluth, Minn.	1428	97	7/7	-33	2/2	32.17	2.68	9/19	78.1	10.9	1/11	37	3/12	98	164	123	20
Fairbanks, Alas.	436	85	7/14	-35	12/2	10.47	1.03	6/15	50.7	3.6	11/29	26	5/29	51	219	120	21
Fresno, Cal.	328	109	8/30	27	12/30	9.39	1.02	4/19	0	0	—	24	4/30	217	90	38	0
Galveston, Tex.	7	95	8/24	31	1/10	39.88	6.84	9/2	T	T	2/7	38	5/21	—	—	74	0
Grand Rapids, Mich.	784	100	7/6	-15	1/7	36.37	3.16	9/22	63.8	4.0	11/6	37	11/16	66	193	147	25
Hartford, Conn.	169	99	7/10	-14	1/11	39.80	2.92	7/23	51.4	10.7	2/12	40	8/29	95	165	109	12
Helena, Mont.	3828	100	6/25	-16	1/5	10.03	1.19	9/17	38.9	5.9	9/17	56	2/21,	—	—	85	16
Honolulu, Ha.	7	94	9/6	57	12/16	16.47	4.17	12/5	0	0	—	29	12/5	96	57	88	0
Houston, Tex.	96	102	8/9	24	2/12	22.93	1.94	8/11	T	T	2/7	41	10/1	112	150	86	0
Huron, S.D.	1281	109	6/24	-37	1/6	19.20	2.67	5/20	45.1	9.9	3/11	50	12/14	129	122	77	14
Indianapolis, Ind.	792	103	7/15	-4	2/13	31.32	1.90	4/6	17.4	5.3	12/28	46	4/6	117	149	116	5
Jackson, Miss.	291	105	6/29	12	2/7	43.99	3.00	10/1	T	T	12/12	35	7/15	124	146	103	0
Jacksonville, Fla.	26	99	6/24	24	12/19	60.68	3.47	9/6	T	T	2/6	31	11/15	106	143	107	0
Kansas City, Mo.	1014	105	8/8	-11	2/11	24.22	5.13	9/15	12.6	5.0	2/3	40	9/28	168	96	67	3
Lander, Wyo.	5557	99	7/30	-12	1/2	7.63	0.70	5/1	63.8	10.1	3/15	54	9/10	126	133	57	14
Little Rock, Ark.	257	105	6/29	7	1/11	48.21	7.81	11/18	16.1	12.1	1/6	—	—	—	—	98	4
Los Angeles, Cal.	97	106	9/4	38	12/28	7.96	1.40	1/17	0	0	—	—	—	166	83	28	0
Louisville, Ky.	477	103	7/9	3	2/6	37.53	3.00	1/19	8.8	5.0	2/11	40	7/17	136	128	96	2
Marquette, Mich.	1415	99	7/28	-19	2/8	41.80	2.97	11/5	202.4	23.3	1/20	—	—	—	—	171	52
Memphis, Tenn.	258	101	6/29	6	2/12	50.24	5.65	11/19	11.2	7.7	1/6	37	12/27	148	132	98	3
Miami, Fla.	7	94	8/9	43	12/14	44.59	3.20	6/12	0	0	—	31	8/14	81	123	118	0
Milford, Ut.	5028	100	6/24	-21	1/20	8.43	0.66	5/29	50.7	10.1	1/17	49	8/11	—	—	67	17
Milwaukee, Wis.	672	103	8/1	-12	1/5	30.43	2.40	9/22	43.6	10.8	2/10	38	11/16	111	142	106	12
Minneapolis, Minn.	834	105	7/31	-18	1/6	19.08	1.99	8/3	53.3	8.7	1/19	39	8/2	129	141	92	16
Mobile, Ala.	211	100	6/27	19	2/7	62.25	4.74	8/8	1.7	1.7	2/5	33	1/19	135	147	117	1
Moline, Ill.	582	104	6/25	-14	2/12	25.75	1.77	8/22	23.1	8.4	2/10	41	1/12	128	129	90	5
Nashville, Tenn.	590	105	7/8	5	2/6	31.41	3.15	11/19	11.6	8.1	1/6	35	11/16	148	126	99	3
Newark, N.J.	7	101	7/16	6	12/12	43.51	3.63	7/19	19.1	6.8	1/8	52	7/17	89	148	102	5
New Orleans, La.	4	96	6/28	25	2/7	74.40	8.08	4/1	T	T	2/5	39	9/10	104	141	117	0
New York, N.Y.	132	99	8/14	5	12/12	44.67	3.37	11/20	15.7	5.8	1/3	29	12/28	—	—	104	4
Norfolk, Va.	24	99	6/23	18	12/17	38.68	1.92	8/19	4.4	4.4	1/7	38	4/13	104	142	119	2
Oklahoma City, Okla.	1285	104	8/8	-4	1/8	31.94	3.10	6/28	15.8	8.9	1/5	46	11/15	153	107	87	2
Omaha, Neb.	997	104	6/21	-15	2/11	19.32	1.36	5/21	12.0	2.6	11/15	52	7/15	126	137*	85	2
Philadelphia, Pa.	5	102	7/17	3	1/11	38.41	3.47	7/21	12.5	3.8	1/8	48	12/28	108	1*	109	5
Phoenix, Ariz.	1110	116	6/22	31	12/30	7.21	2.32	10/14	0	0	—	35	8/27	234	-3	34	0
Pittsburgh, Pa.	1137	103	7/16	-3	2/7	27.09	1.82	2/1	28.4	2.6	3/3	44	5/23	53	196	147	8
Portland, Me.	43	97	6/15	-13	2/6	43.62	4.56	11/1	51.3	12.8	2/12	31	11/2	101	170	131	11
Portland, Ore.	21	105	9/2	22	2/2	31.72	1.62	1/13	0.6	0.4	1/18	39	1/11	68	224	146	0
Providence, R.I.	51	97	7/11	-5	1/15	38.37	2.92	3/26	24.1	7.0	1/8	35	12/28	97	160	103	7
Raleigh, N.C.	434	105	8/18	9	1/12	37.66	2.47	9/4	7.4	7.3	1/7	32	5/24	111	150	110	1
Rapid City, S.D.	3162	106	8/15	-20	1/9	10.92	1.86	5/1	34.2	7.2	12/25	53	3/11	132	110	75	9
Reno, Nev.	4404	103	7/21	-4	12/27	5.30	1.65	11/22	24.0	6.9	12/23	—	—	164	108	36	6
Richmond, Va.	164	101	6/23	4	1/12	37.26	3.84	7/22	9.9	7.5	1/7	38	7/9	109	135	101	3
Rochester, N.Y.	547	98	7/9	-8	12/12	24.60	1.72	7/17	56.5	6.2	2/3	41	11/10	61	198	155	19
St. Louis, Mo.	535	103	8/17	-3	2/12	33.93	2.27	2/1	19.7	4.8	12/27	46	10/17	135	130	88	6
Salt Lake City, Ut.	4221	102	6/24	0	12/27	9.29	0.96	5/17	44.7	5.5	1/5	47	1/11	118	154	75	13
San Antonio, Tex.	788	102	8/10	22	2/12	19.01	4.02	7/20	0.1	0.1	2/7	31	3/13	108	119	59	0
San Diego, Cal.	13	107	9/4	38	12/27	10.26	1.98	4/20	0	0	—	40	1/17	152	89	39	0
San Francisco, Cal.	8	105	7/17	33	12/29	13.67	1.45	1/16	T	T	12/27	46	12/15	156	110	59	0
Sault Ste Marie, Mich.	721	97	7/8	-17	11/14	36.94	2.42	11/4	150.3	15.3	1/5	44	7/15	64	193	180	40
Savannah, Ga.	46	101	6/24	22	1/28	48.17	3.30	9/8	T	T	12/12	29	9/4	129	131	103	0
Seattle, Wash.	400	98	9/2	22	2/1	32.98	1.72	1/13	T	T	12/30	38	2/13	58	228	138	0
Shreveport, La.	254	102	8/6	17	2/12	36.38	2.89	2/17	2.0	1.2	1/6	35	12/27	148	128	95	1
Sioux City, Ia.	1095	108	6/21	-22	2/11	23.25	3.19	8/22	29.4	5.5	1/19	45	10/27	116	133	75	10
Spokane, Wash.	2356	98	9/3	-5	12/26	16.52	1.02	1/14	39.1	4.6	12/29	39	12/12	185	197	104	16
Springfield, Mo.	1268	99	6/26	-7	1/8	48.46	4.18	6/29	26.9	6.3	12/27	35	3/28	138	128	113	6
Syracuse, N.Y.	410	97	7/16	-14	1/14	34.44	1.57	7/21	120.2	9.8	2/12	31	12/15	54	201	176	37
Tampa, Fla.	19	96	7/12	33	1/28	52.33	4.48	11/22	0	0	—	37	7/19	131	98	101	0
Washington, D.C.	10	104	7/16	10	1/11	31.74	1.79	11/27	14.7	8.0	1/7	38	12/28	93	153	107	5
Wilmington, Del.	74	100	7/17	3	1/11	37.80	3.80	7/21	12.5	6.4	1/7	46	12/28	117	137	94	2

*To get partly cloudy days deduct the total of clear and cloudy days from 365 (1 yr.). T—trace. (1) Date shown is the starting date of the storm (in some cases it lasted more than one day).

Record Temperatures by States Through 1988

Source: Natl. Climatic Data Center, NESDIS, NOAA, U.S. Commerce Department

State	Lowest °F	Highest	Latest date	Station	Approximate elevation in feet
Alabama	−27		Jan. 30, 1966	New Market	725
		112	Sept. 5, 1925	Centerville	345
Alaska	−80		Jan. 23, 1971	Prospect Creek Camp	1,100
		100	June 27, 1915	Fort Yukon	419
Arizona	−40		Jan. 7, 1971	Hawley Lake	8,180
		127	July 7, 1905¹	Parker	345
Arkansas	−29		Feb. 13, 1905	Pond	1,250
		120	Aug. 10, 1936	Ozark	396
California	−45		Jan. 20, 1937	Boca	5,532
		134	July 10, 1913	Greenland Ranch	−178
Colorado	−61		Feb. 1, 1985	Maybell	5,920
		118	July 11, 1888	Bennett	5,484
Connecticut	−32		Feb. 16, 1943	Falls Village	585
		105	July 22, 1926	Waterbury	409
Delaware	−17		Jan. 17, 1893	Millsboro	20
		110	July 21, 1930	Millsboro	20
Dist. of Col.	−15		Feb. 11, 1899	Washington	112
		106	July 20, 1930	Washington	112
Florida	−2		Feb. 13, 1899	Tallahassee	193
		109	June 29, 1931	Monticello	207
Georgia	−17		Jan. 27, 1940	CCC Camp F-16	1,000
		112	Jul. 24, 1952	Louisville	132
Hawaii	12		May 17, 1979	Mauna Kea	13,770
		100	Apr. 27, 1931	Pahala	850
Idaho	−60		Jan. 16, 1943	Island Park Dam	6,285
		118	July 28, 1934	Orofino	1,027
Illinois	−35		Jan. 22, 1930	Mount Carroll	817
		117	July 14, 1954	E. St. Louis	410
Indiana	−35		Feb. 2, 1951	Greensburg	954
		116	July 14, 1936	Collegeville	672
Iowa	−47		Jan. 12, 1912	Washta	1,157
		118	July 20, 1934	Keokuk	614
Kansas	−40		Feb. 13, 1905	Lebanon	1,812
		121	July 24, 1936¹	Alton (near)	1,651
Kentucky	−34		Jan. 28, 1963	Cynthiana	719
		114	July 28, 1930	Greensburg	581
Louisiana	−16		Feb. 13, 1899	Minden	194
		114	Aug. 10, 1936	Plain Dealing	268
Maine	−48		Jan. 19, 1925	Van Buren	510
		105	July 10, 1911¹	North Bridgton	450
Maryland	−40		Jan. 13, 1912	Oakland	2,461
		109	July 10, 1936¹	Cumberland and Frederick	623-325
Massachusetts	−35		Jan. 12, 1981	Chester	640
		107	Aug. 2, 1975	Chester and New Bedford	120-640
Michigan	−51		Feb. 9, 1934	Vanderbilt	785
		112	July 13, 1936	Mio	963
Minnesota	−59		Feb. 16, 1903¹	Pokegama Dam	1,280
		114	July 6, 1936¹	Moorhead	904
Mississippi	−19		Jan. 30, 1966	Corinth	420
		115	July 29, 1930	Holly Springs	600
Missouri	−40		Feb. 13, 1905	Warsaw	700
		118	July 14, 1954¹	Warsaw and Union	687-560
Montana	−70		Jan. 20, 1954	Rogers Pass	5,470
		117	July 5, 1937	Medicine Lake	1,950
Nebraska	−47		Feb. 12, 1899	Camp Clarke	3,700
		118	July 24, 1936¹	Minden	2,169
Nevada	−50		Jan. 8, 1937	San Jacinto	5,200
		122	June 23, 1954¹	Overton	1,240
New Hampshire	−46		Jan. 28 1925	Pittsburgh	1,575
		106	July 4, 1911	Nashua	125
New Jersey	−34		Jan. 5, 1904	River Vale	70
		110	July 10, 1936	Runyon	18
New Mexico	−50		Feb. 1, 1951	Gavilan	7,350
		116	July 14, 1934¹	Orogrande	4,171
New York	−52		Feb. 18, 1979	Old Forge	1,720
		108	July 22, 1926	Troy	35
North Carolina	−34		Jan. 21, 1985	Mt. Mitchell	6,525
		110	Aug. 21, 1983	Fayetteville	213
North Dakota	−60		Feb. 15, 1936	Parshall	1,929
		121	July 6, 1936	Steele	1,857
Ohio	−39		Feb. 10, 1899	Milligan	800
		113	July 21, 1934¹	Gallipolis (near)	673
Oklahoma	−27		Jan. 18, 1930	Watts	958
		120	July 26, 1943¹	Tishmoningo	670
Oregon	−54		Feb. 10, 1933¹	Seneca	4,700
		119	Aug. 10, 1938	Pendleton	1,074
Pennsylvania	−42		Jan. 5, 1904	Smethport	1,469
		111	July 10, 1936¹	Phoenixville	100
Rhode Island	−23		Jan. 11, 1942	Kingston	100
		104	Aug. 2, 1975	Providence	51
South Carolina	−19		Jan. 21, 1985	Caesar's Head	3,100
		111	June 28, 1954¹	Camden	170
South Dakota	−58		Feb. 17, 1936	McIntosh	2,277
		120	July 5, 1936	Gannvalley	1,750

State	Lowest °F	Highest	Latest date	Station	Approximate elevation in feet
Tennessee	−32		Dec. 30, 1917	Mountain City	2,471
		113	Aug. 9, 1930 ¹	Perryville	377
Texas	−23		Feb. 8, 1933	Seminole	3,275
		120	Aug. 12, 1936	Seymour	1,291
Utah	−69		Feb. 1, 1985	Peter's Sink	8,092
		117	Jul. 5, 1985	Saint George	2,880
Vermont	−50		Dec. 30, 1933	Bloomfield	915
		105	July 4, 1911	Vernon	310
Virginia	−30		Jan. 22, 1985	Mtn. Lake Bio. Stn.	3,870
		110	July 15, 1954	Balcony Falls	725
Washington	−48		Dec. 30, 1968	Mazama	2,120
	−48		Dec. 30, 1968	Winthrop	1,755
		118	Aug. 5, 1961 ¹	Ice Harbor Dam	475
West Virginia	−37		Dec. 30, 1917	Lewisburg	2,200
		112	July 10, 1936 ¹	Martinsburg	435
Wisconsin	−54		Jan. 24, 1922	Danbury	908
		114	July 13, 1936	Wisconsin Dells	900
Wyoming	−63		Feb. 9, 1933	Moran	6,770
		114	July 12, 1900	Basin	3,500

(1) Also on earlier dates at the same or other places.

International Temperature and Precipitation

Source: Environmental Data Service, U.S. Commerce Department

A standard period of 30 years has been used to obtain the average daily maximum and minimum temperatures and precipitation. The length of record of extreme maximum and minimum temperatures includes all available years of data for a given location and is usually for a longer period.

		Temperature F°						Average
		Average Daily				Extreme		annual
	Elev.	January		July				precipitation
Station	Ft.	Max.	Min.	Max.	Min.	Max.	Min.	(inches)
Addis Ababa, Ethiopia	8,038	75	43	69	50	94	32	48.7
Algiers, Algeria	194	59	49	83	70	107	32	30.0
Amsterdam, Netherlands	5	40	34	69	59	95	3	25.6
Athens, Greece	351	54	42	90	72	109	20	15.8
Auckland, New Zealand	23	73	60	56	46	90	33	49.1
Bangkok, Thailand	53	89	67	90	76	104	50	57.8
Beirut, Lebanon	111	62	51	87	73	107	30	35.1
Belgrade, Yugoslavia	453	37	27	84	61	107	−14	24.6
Berlin, Germany	187	35	26	74	55	96	−15	23.1
Bogota, Colombia	8,355	67	48	64	50	75	30	41.8
Bombay, India	27	88	62	88	75	110	46	71.2
Bucharest, Romania	269	33	20	86	61	105	−18	22.8
Budapest, Hungary	394	35	26	82	61	103	−10	24.2
Buenos Aires, Argentina	89	85	63	57	42	104	22	37.4
Cairo, Egypt	381	65	47	96	70	117	34	1.1
Capetown, South Africa	56	78	60	63	45	103	28	20.0
Caracas, Venezuela	3,418	75	56	78	61	91	45	32.9
Casablanca, Morocco	164	63	45	79	65	110	31	15.9
Copenhagen, Denmark	43	36	29	72	55	91	−3	23.3
Damascus, Syria	2,362	53	36	96	64	113	21	8.6
Dublin, Ireland	155	47	35	67	51	86	8	29.7
Geneva, Switzerland	1,329	39	29	77	58	101	−1	33.9
Havana, Cuba	80	79	65	89	75	104	43	48.2
Hong Kong	109	64	56	87	78	97	32	85.1
Istanbul, Turkey	59	45	36	81	65	100	17	31.5
Jerusalem, Israel	2,654	55	41	87	63	107	26	19.7
Lagos, Nigeria	10	88	74	83	74	104	60	72.3
La Paz, Bolivia	12,001	63	43	62	33	80	26	22.6
Lima, Peru	394	82	66	67	57	93	49	1.6
London, England	149	44	35	73	55	99	9	22.9
Madrid, Spain	2,188	47	33	87	62	102	14	16.5
Manila, Philippines	49	86	69	88	75	101	58	82.0
Mexico City, Mexico	7,340	66	42	74	54	92	24	23.0
Moscow, U.S.S.R.	505	21	9	76	55	96	−27	24.8
Nairobi, Kenya	5,971	77	54	69	51	87	41	37.7
Oslo, Norway	308	30	20	73	56	93	−21	26.9
Paris, France	164	42	32	76	55	105	1	22.3
Prague, Czechoslovakia	662	34	25	74	58	98	−16	19.3
Reykjavik, Iceland	92	36	28	58	48	74	4	33.9
Rome, Italy	377	54	39	88	64	104	20	29.5
San Salvador, El Salvador	2,238	90	60	89	65	105	45	70.0
Santiago, Chile	1,706	85	53	59	37	99	24	14.2
Sao Paolo, Brazil	2,628	77	63	66	53	100	32	57.3
Shanghai, China	16	47	32	91	75	104	10	45.0
Singapore	33	86	73	88	75	97	66	95.0
Stockholm, Sweden	146	31	23	70	55	97	−26	22.4
Sydney, Australia	62	78	65	60	46	114	35	46.5
Teheran, Iran	3,937	45	27	99	72	109	−5	9.7
Tokyo, Japan	19	47	29	83	70	101	17	61.6
Tripoli, Libya	72	61	47	85	71	114	33	15.1
Vienna, Austria	664	34	26	75	59	98	−14	25.6
Warsaw, Poland	294	30	21	75	56	98	−22	22.0

Record Maximum 24-Hour Precipitation by State

(through 1988)

Source: Natl. Climatic Data Center, NESDIS, NOAA, U.S. Department of Commerce

State	Precip. (inches)	Date	Station	Elevation (feet)	State	Precip. (inches)	Date	Station	Elevation (feet)
Ala. . .	20.33	4/13/55	Axis	36	Mont. .	11.50	6/20/21	Circle	2,440
Alas...	15.20	10/12/82	Angoon	15	Neb. . .	13.15	7/8-9/50	York	1,610
Ariz. . .	11.40	9/4-5/70	Workman Creek	6,970	Nev. . .	7.40	3/19/07	Lewer's Ranch	5,200
Ark. . .	14.06	12/3/82	Big Fork	1,100	N.H. . .	10.38	2/10-11/70	Mount Washington	6,260
Cal. . .	26.12	1/22-23/43	Hoegees Camp	2,760	N.J. . .	14.81	8/19/39	Tuckerton	20
Colo. . .	11.08	6/17/65	Holly	3,390	N.M. . .	11.28	5/18-19/55	Lake Maloya	7,400
Conn. .	12.77	8/19/55	Burlington	460	N.Y. . .	11.17	10/9/03	NYC Central Park	130
Del. . .	8.50	7/13/75	Dover	30	N.C. . .	22.22	7/15-16/16	Altapass	2,600
Fla. . .	38.70	9/5/50	Yankeetown	5	N.D. . .	8.10	6/29/75	Litchville	1,470
Ga... .	18.00	8/28/11	St. George	77	Ohio . .	10.51	7/12/66	Sandusky	610
Ha... .	38.00	1/24-25/56	Kilauea Plantation	180	Okla. . .	15.50	9/3-4/40	Sapulpa	740
Id. . . .	7.17	11/23/09	Rattlesnake Creek	4,000	Ore. . .	10.17	12/21/15	Glenora	575
Ill. . . .	16.54	6/14-15/57	East St. Louis	410	Pa. . . .	34.50*	7/17/42	Smethport	1,510
Ind. . . .	10.50	8/6/05	Princeton	480	R.I. . . .	12.13	9/16-17/32	Westerly	40
Ia. . . .	16.70	8/5-6/59	Decatur Co.	1,110	S.C. . .	13.25	7/14-15/16	Effingham	110
Kan. . .	12.59	5/31-6/1/41	Burlington	1,010	S.D. . .	8.00	9/10/00	Elk Point	1,127
Ky. . . .	10.40	6/28/60	Dunmor	610	Tenn. . .	11.00	3/28/02	McMinnville	900
La... .	22.00	8/28-29/62	Hackberry	10	Texas . .	43.00*	7/25-26/79	Alvin	50
Me... .	8.05	9/11/54	Brunswick	70	Utah . .	6.00*	9/5/70	Bug Point	6,600
Md... .	14.75	7/26-27/97	Jewell	152	Vt. . . .	8.77	11/3-4/27	Somerset	2,080
Mass. .	18.15	8/18-19/55	Westfield	220	Va. . . .	27.00*	8/20/69	Nelson Co.	est. 500
Mich...	9.78	8/31-9/1/14	Bloomingdale	750	Wash. . .	12.00	1/21/35	Quinault R.S.	220
Minn...	10.84	7/21-22/72	Fort Ripley	1,140	W.Va. . .	19.00*	7/18/89	Rockport	700
Miss. .	15.68	7/9/68	Columbus	190	Wis. . .	11.72	6/24/46	Mellen	1,150
Mo... .	18.18	7/20/65	Edgarton	850	Wyo...	6.06	8/1/85	Cheyenne	6,126

*Estimated

Wind Chill Table

Source: National Weather Service, NOAA, U.S. Commerce Department

Both temperature and wind cause heat loss from body surfaces. A combination of cold and wind makes a body feel colder than the actual temperature. The table shows, for example, that a temperature of 20 degrees Fahrenheit, plus a wind of 20 miles per hour, causes a body heat loss equal to that in minus 10 degrees with no wind. In other words, the wind makes 20 degrees feel like minus 10.

Top line of figures shows actual temperatures in degrees Fahrenheit. Column at left shows wind speeds.

	35	30	25	20	15	10	5	0	−5	−10	−15	−20	−25	−30	−35	−40	−45
MPH																	
5	33	27	21	16	12	7	0	−5	−10	−15	−21	−26	−31	−36	−42	−47	−52
10	22	16	10	3	−3	−9	−15	−22	−27	−34	−40	−46	−52	−58	−64	−71	−77
15	16	9	2	−5	−11	−18	−25	−31	−38	−45	−51	−58	−65	−72	−78	−85	−92
20	12	4	−3	−10	−17	−24	−31	−39	−46	−53	−60	−67	−74	−81	−88	−95	−103
25	8	1	−7	−15	−22	−29	−36	−44	−51	−59	−66	−74	−81	−88	−96	−103	−110
30	6	−2	−10	−18	−25	−33	−41	−49	−56	−64	−71	−79	−86	−93	−101	−109	−116
35	4	−4	−12	−20	−27	−35	−43	−52	−58	−67	−74	−82	−89	−97	−105	−113	−120
40	3	−5	−13	−21	−29	−37	−45	−53	−60	−69	−76	−84	−92	−100	−107	−115	−123
45	2	−6	−14	−22	−30	−38	−46	−54	−62	−70	−78	−85	−93	−102	−109	−117	−125

(Wind speeds greater than 45 mph have little additional chilling effect.)

Heat Index

The index is a measure of the contribution that high humidity makes with abnormally high temperatures in reducing the body's ability to cool itself. For example, the index shows that for an actual air temperature of 100 degrees Fahrenheit and a relative humidity of 50 percent, the effect on the human body would be same as 120 degrees. Sunstroke and heat exhaustion are likely when the heat index reaches 105. This index is a measure of what hot weather "feels like" to the average person for various temperatures and relative humidities.

Relative Humidity	Air Temperature* 70	75	80	85	90	95	100	105	110	115	120
	Apparent Temperature*										
0%	64	69	73	78	83	87	91	95	99	103	107
10%	65	70	75	80	85	90	95	100	105	111	116
20%	66	72	77	82	87	93	99	105	112	120	130
30%	67	73	78	84	90	96	104	113	123	135	148
40%	68	74	79	86	93	101	110	123	137	151	
50%	69	75	81	88	96	107	120	135	150		
60%	70	76	82	90	100	114	132	149			
70%	70	77	85	93	106	124	144				
80%	71	78	86	97	113	136					
90%	71	79	88	102	122						
100%	72	80	91	108							

*Degrees Fahrenheit.

Average Relative Humidity (%)

Source: Natl. Climatic Data Center, NESDIS, NOAA, U.S. Department of Commerce

(M-morning; A-afternoon; through 1988)

	Jan. M	Jan. A	Feb. M	Feb. A	Mar. M	Mar. A	Apr. M	Apr. A	May M	May A	June M	June A	July M	July A	Aug. M	Aug. A	Sept. M	Sept. A	Oct. M	Oct. A	Nov. M	Nov. A	Dec. M	Dec. A
Mobile, Ala.	80	60	81	55	84	55	87	52	87	54	87	54	89	60	90	61	88	59	86	53	85	57	83	61
Juneau, Alas.	79	75	82	74	83	68	81	63	79	63	80	65	84	70	88	74	91	76	88	78	84	79	83	81
Phoenix, Ariz.	67	32	61	27	58	24	43	16	35	13	32	12	45	20	51	23	51	23	52	23	59	28	68	34
Little Rock, Ark.	80	61	80	59	79	56	82	61	86	58	86	55	87	56	88	57	89	58	86	53	83	59	80	62
Los Angeles, Calif.	63	50	71	52	74	52	78	54	81	55	85	56	84	53	84	55	78	54	76	56	61	49	62	50
San Francisco, Calif.	81	63	83	63	81	61	82	61	89	68	89	72	92	74	93	73	87	66	81	60	82	63	80	63
Denver, Colo.	63	49	66	43	67	40	67	35	70	38	69	35	68	34	68	35	68	34	65	36	68	49	65	51
Hartford, Conn.	71	56	72	54	71	51	68	44	73	47	77	51	77	51	83	53	85	54	83	51	79	56	76	60
Wilmington, Del.	75	60	75	57	73	52	72	50	76	53	78	54	79	54	83	56	85	55	84	54	80	56	77	60
Dist. of Colo.	77	59	78	55	77	52	76	48	83	56	85	57	87	55	89	56	90	56	88	56	83	57	79	58
Jacksonville, Fla.	87	57	86	53	86	50	86	48	85	50	87	57	88	58	91	60	91	63	91	58	89	56	88	58
Miami, Fla.	84	59	83	57	82	56	79	54	81	60	85	66	85	63	86	65	88	67	86	64	85	62	83	60
Atlanta, Ga.	78	59	76	54	77	51	78	50	83	54	84	56	89	61	90	61	89	60	85	54	82	56	79	59
Columbus, Ga.	84	60	83	54	85	52	85	48	85	51	86	53	90	58	91	57	90	57	90	52	88	54	85	58
Honolulu, Ha.	82	62	78	59	73	58	70	56	67	54	67	53	68	52	69	53	68	52	69	55	75	59	79	61
Boise, Ida.	80	70	79	61	74	45	70	36	69	34	67	30	54	22	52	23	60	30	67	40	77	60	81	71
Chicago, Ill.	76	67	77	66	79	61	77	55	77	54	78	56	82	57	85	57	85	58	82	56	81	64	80	70
Indianapolis, Ind.	80	70	80	67	80	63	78	56	82	56	82	57	87	60	90	61	90	59	86	58	85	67	83	73
Des Moines, Ia.	75	67	78	66	78	61	78	56	77	55	79	56	81	57	84	58	84	59	79	56	79	64	79	70
Dubuque, Ia.	74	67	76	65	78	62	76	56	79	57	83	61	84	60	86	61	86	61	82	59	81	65	80	72
Wichita, Kan.	78	63	79	60	77	54	78	52	83	55	82	53	77	48	79	49	82	55	80	54	80	58	80	62
Louisville, Ky.	76	64	76	62	75	57	75	52	82	55	83	57	85	58	88	58	89	58	86	59	79	61	77	65
New Orleans, La.	84	66	83	63	84	60	87	60	89	60	89	62	91	66	91	66	89	65	87	59	86	61	86	66
Portland, Me.	76	61	76	59	75	58	73	55	75	58	79	61	80	59	83	59	86	60	84	59	83	63	79	62
Baltimore, Md.	71	57	71	55	71	50	71	48	76	52	79	52	80	53	83	55	84	55	82	54	77	55	74	57
Boston, Mass.	66	57	67	56	68	57	67	54	71	59	74	59	73	56	76	59	79	60	77	58	74	60	71	60
Detroit, Mich.	79	69	79	65	79	61	78	53	80	54	82	53	86	56	87	57	84	57	84	57	82	66	81	71
Minneapolis-St. Paul, Minn.	73	66	75	66	76	62	75	53	76	52	79	55	80	54	83	56	85	60	82	59	80	66	77	70
Jackson, Miss.	86	65	87	59	87	57	91	55	92	56	91	56	93	59	94	59	94	59	93	54	91	59	88	63
Kansas City, Mo.	74	63	76	64	78	61	78	57	84	59	85	59	83	56	86	59	85	60	81	58	79	63	78	66
St. Louis, Mo.	83	66	83	64	82	60	79	55	83	56	84	57	85	56	89	57	90	59	86	57	85	64	84	69
Helena, Mont.	70	62	71	55	71	46	69	38	70	37	71	37	66	29	66	30	72	37	73	42	74	58	72	65
Omaha, Neb.	77	66	79	64	78	58	77	53	79	54	82	55	83	56	86	59	86	60	82	57	81	63	80	68
Las Vegas, Nev.	55	31	50	26	44	22	35	15	31	13	24	10	29	15	35	17	34	17	38	19	46	27	56	33
Reno, Nev.	79	51	74	40	70	34	67	28	66	25	66	22	65	19	67	20	70	23	73	28	75	42	77	52
Concord, N.H.	74	58	76	56	76	53	74	45	77	48	83	53	84	51	88	53	90	55	87	53	84	60	80	63
Atlantic City, N.J.	77	58	79	56	77	54	76	51	78	55	81	57	83	56	86	57	87	58	87	56	84	58	78	59
Albuquerque, N.M.	71	40	65	32	56	24	49	18	48	18	46	17	60	27	66	30	62	31	62	30	66	36	71	43
Buffalo, N.Y.	79	73	80	71	80	66	76	58	75	56	77	57	78	55	83	58	84	60	82	61	81	70	81	74
New York-LaGuardia, N.Y.	65	57	65	55	66	53	66	50	70	53	72	53	75	55	75	55	79	57	75	58	71	58	68	60
Charlotte, N.C.	78	55	76	52	79	50	78	47	83	53	85	56	87	58	89	59	90	57	87	54	84	54	79	57
Bismarck, N.D.	73	67	77	68	80	63	79	52	78	48	84	53	83	47	83	46	82	50	79	52	80	64	78	70
Cleveland, Ohio	77	70	78	68	77	63	75	56	77	57	79	58	81	57	85	60	84	60	80	60	80	66	77	70
Oklahoma City, Okla.	77	59	78	57	75	52	77	52	83	57	83	56	79	50	81	50	84	56	80	54	80	60	78	58
Eugene, Ore.	92	80	92	73	91	64	90	57	91	54	90	49	88	40	89	43	94	53	93	76	92	82	84	...
Portland, Ore.	86	76	86	68	86	60	86	55	85	53	84	49	82	45	83	46	87	49	90	63	88	74	87	79
Philadelphia, Pa.	72	59	71	56	71	53	70	48	74	52	77	54	79	54	81	54	83	56	80	54	78	56	74	59
Pittsburgh, Pa.	75	65	74	62	74	57	72	50	75	52	78	52	82	53	85	56	85	56	81	54	78	62	76	67
Providence, R.I.	70	56	70	54	70	52	68	47	72	52	75	56	77	55	79	56	81	56	78	53	77	57	74	58
Charleston, S.C.	83	55	81	52	83	50	83	49	85	54	86	59	88	62	90	63	90	62	89	56	86	53	84	55
Huron, S.D.	73	67	78	69	83	66	83	56	84	54	87	57	86	52	89	53	87	54	82	56	82	64	78	69
Memphis, Tenn.	78	63	78	59	78	56	78	54	82	55	83	56	84	57	86	57	86	56	84	52	80	56	79	61
Nashville, Tenn.	81	61	80	59	79	59	78	53	83	51	86	56	87	55	90	57	91	59	90	57	85	58	82	60
Dallas-Ft. Worth, Tex.	79	60	79	59	79	57	82	58	87	60	85	55	80	48	80	50	83	56	82	55	81	57	79	59
Houston, Tex.	85	64	86	60	87	59	89	59	92	62	92	59	92	58	93	59	93	62	91	58	89	60	86	61
Salt Lake City, Ut.	78	69	77	58	71	47	67	39	65	33	60	26	52	21	55	23	62	29	69	41	74	58	78	71
Burlington, Vt.	70	63	73	63	74	59	73	53	75	51	78	56	79	53	83	57	86	62	81	61	78	67	75	69
Norfolk, Va.	74	59	74	57	73	53	73	50	77	55	79	56	82	59	84	61	83	61	83	60	79	56	75	58
Seattle-Tacoma, Wash.	80	74	80	67	82	61	83	57	82	54	81	53	81	49	83	51	86	55	86	67	83	74	82	77
Huntington, W.Va.	80	60	78	62	75	55	75	49	84	53	88	57	90	60	92	60	92	60	87	55	80	61	78	66
Milwaukee, Wis.	75	68	76	67	79	65	78	61	78	60	80	61	82	61	87	63	87	64	82	63	80	67	80	72
Cheyenne, Wyo.	57	50	60	47	64	46	67	41	70	43	70	41	69	38	68	37	66	38	60	41	60	49	58	52
San Juan, P.R.	81	64	79	62	77	60	75	62	78	65	78	66	78	66	79	66	79	67	80	66	81	67	81	66

Average Annual Snowfall

Source: Natl. Climatic Data Center, NESDIS, NOAA, U.S. Department of Commerce

(inches; through 1988)

The following are among the "snowiest" places in the U.S.:

Place	Inches	Place	Inches	Place	Inches
Anchorage, Alas.	68.5	South Bend, Ind.	72.0	Mt. Washington, N.H.	253.5
Bettles, Alas.	78.5	Caribou, Me.	111.7	Albany, N.Y.	65.3
Cold Bay, Alas.	61.6	Portland, Me.	71.2	Binghamton, N.Y.	82.9
Fairbanks, Alas.	65.0	Blue Hill, Mass.	59.9	Buffalo, N.Y.	91.5
Homer, Alas.	58.6	Worcester, Mass.	69.2	Rochester, N.Y.	88.3
Juneau, Alas.	98.3	Alpena, Mich.	85.0	Syracuse, N.Y.	109.9
Kodiak, Alas.	76.8	Grand Rapids, Mich.	71.3	Youngstown, Ohio	56.5
McGrath, Alas.	90.3	Houghton Lake, Mich.		Sexton Summit, Ore.	97.8
Nome, Alas.	55.1	Marquette, Mich.	123.7	Erie, Pa.	84.4
St. Paul Is., Alas.	56.5	Muskegon, Mich.	97.2	Salt Lake City, Ut.	58.2
Talkeetna, Alas.	108.1	Sault St. Marie, Mich.	115.5	Burlington, Vt.	77.6
Valdez, Alas.	303.9	Duluth, Minn.	76.7	Stampede Pass, Wash.	431.9
Yakutat, Alas.	204.5	Intl. Falls, Minn.	61.3	Beckley, W.Va.	61.0
Flagstaff, Ariz.	97.1	Billings, Mont.	56.4	Elkins, W.Va.	74.2
Blue Canyon, Calif.	240.8	Great Falls, Mont.	58.3	Caspar, Wyo.	80.9
Mt. Shasta, Calif.	104.9	Kalispell, Mont.	64.6	Lander, Wyo.	104.6
Denver, Colo.	60.0	Concord, N.H.	64.2	Sheridan, Wyo.	70.7

ASTRONOMY AND CALENDAR

Edited by Dr. Kenneth L. Franklin, Astronomer Emeritus
American Museum-Hayden Planetarium

Celestial Events Highlights, 1990

(Greenwich Mean Time, or as indicated)

As usual, the celestial spectacles this year are dramatic and beautiful, but usually happening somewhere out of our sight, or, at least, inconveniently timed. In the evenings, this year, Jupiter gives us a show early on, giving way to Saturn in mid-year, who hands the stage to Mars in late fall, who, in turn, shares the sky with returning Jupiter at year's end. But in late January and early February, Mercury, Venus, and Saturn give us a pas de trois in the dawn twilight, Mercury quickly leaving the scene to the other two. This duo is joined by Mars as February changes to March, but Saturn soon goes its own way. Gradually, Mars leaves the dawn to Venus to finally become very prominent in the nights of autumn and winter. But Venus and Jupiter become spectacularly intimate, 0°.04 apart, on August 12 in the dawn twilight, but at about 6 PM EST, thus visible only a half a world away from viewers in North America.

Antares is the only bright star occulted this year, but never viewable from North America. Each of the planets but Venus is occulted at least once, but only the August 18 occultation of Jupiter is visible from part of North America, and then only well after sunrise. And of the two solar and two lunar eclipses, none is visible from the northern and western hemispheres, although partial phases of the July 22 solar eclipse can be seen from Alaska, and from the northwest near sunset.

Whenever an event is highlighted in the listing below, regard it as an alert to a close gathering of the participants, thus an opportunity to watch the motions of each as they dance across the starry background. Close approaches of a bright planet to Uranus or Neptune are noted to allow possible binocular or telescopic observation of the distant planets, otherwise difficult to see. These occasions and others may afford challenges to dedicated photographers and sky watchers. Use the moon's passing of bodies as a guide for placing the objects in the sky.

January

Mercury begins the year invisible in the evening sky, approaching inferior conjunction with the sun on the 9th, and passing Neptune twice this month, once on the 13th, and within less than a degree from Neptune on the 27th.

Venus is effectively lost to sight this month, passing through inferior conjunction on the 18th.

Mars appears to be a star of magnitude 1.5, moving eastward in Ophiuchus away from Antares, rising a bit before the sun.

Jupiter, having just passed opposition near the feet of the Gemini twins on Dec 27, is the bright planet that rises in the east while the evening twilight fades in the west.

Saturn is in conjunction with the sun on the 6th, so is lost to view virtually all month.

Moon passes Jupiter the evening of the 9th (EST), occults Antares on the 22nd, passes Mars on the 23rd, Uranus, Mercury, and Neptune on the 24th, and Saturn on the 25th, and annuarily eclipses the sun on the 26th.

Jan. 2—Neptune in conjunction with the sun.

Jan. 3—The Quadrantid meteors is only slightly troubled by the first quarter moon.

Jan. 4—Earth at perihelion, 91.4 million miles from the sun, closest this year.

Jan. 6—Saturn in conjunction with the sun.

Jan. 9—Mercury in inferior conjunction with the sun.

Jan. 10—Moon passes 4° north of Jupiter

Jan. 13—Mercury is 3° north of Neptune.

Jan. 19—Sun enters Capricornus.

Jan. 18—Venus is in inferior conjunction with the sun.

Jan. 20—Mercury stationary, resuming its eastward motion.

Jan. 22—Antares is occulted by the waning crescent moon; find the pair very close together about 3 AM EST.

Jan. 23—Moon passes 4° south of Mars.

Jan. 24—Moon passes 5° south of Mercury.

Jan. 25—Moon passes 3° south of Saturn.

Jan. 26—Moon in annular eclipse of sun.

Jan. 27—Mercury is 0°.8 north of Neptune.

February

Mercury is 25° west of the sun at the beginning of the month and stays west in the dawn sky all month, only 0°.2 north of Saturn on the 3rd, passing Venus on the 4th, and the moon on the 24th.

Venus is stationary on the 8th, passing Saturn on the 7th and 14th, and the moon on the 22nd, achieving greatest brilliancy on the same day.

Mars, slowly climbing out of the dawn twilight in Sagittarius, passes 0°.2 south of Uranus on the 9th, 1°.5 south of Neptune on the 17th, the moon on the 21st, and 1°.0 south of Saturn on the 28th.

Jupiter, still near the feet of the twins, passes the moon on the 6th, and is stationary on the 24th, resuming its direct, eastward, motion.

Saturn is fainter than Mercury, the pair only 0°.2 apart on the 3rd, and very much fainter than Venus which passes on the 7th and 14th; the moon takes its turn moving past Saturn on the 22nd.

Moon passes Jupiter on the 6th, is in total eclipse on the 9th, occults Antares on the 18th, passes Uranus, Neptune, and Mars on the 21st, Saturn and Venus on the 22nd, and Mercury on the 24th.

Feb. 1—Mercury is at greatest western elongation from the sun, 25°.

Feb. 3—Mercury is 0°.2 north of Saturn.

Feb. 4—Mercury is 7° south of Venus.

Feb. 6—Jupiter is 4° south of the moon.

Feb. 7—Venus is 7° south of Saturn.

Feb. 8—Venus is stationary, resuming direct motion.

Feb. 9—Mars is 0°.2 south of Uranus; total lunar eclipse.

Feb. 14—Venus is again 7° south of Saturn.

Feb. 16—Sun enters Aquarius.

Feb. 17—Mars is 1°.5 south of Neptune.

Feb. 18—Antares is occulted by the last quarter moon; look for them close together in this morning's dawn sky.

Feb. 21—Mars is 2° north of the moon; note Saturn and Venus below.

Feb. 22—Crescent Moon passes Saturn and Venus; see the moon below them before dawn today; Venus at greatest brilliancy.

Feb. 23—Pluto stationary, beginning retrogarde motion.

Feb. 24—Mercury 2° south of the moon; Jupiter stationary, resuming its direct motion.

Feb. 28—Mars is 1° south of Saturn.

March

Mercury is lost to view all month, being in superior conjunction on the 20th.

Venus remains close to Mars all month, but Saturn quickly pulls away from both, Venus attaining greatest western elongation, 46° from the sun, on the 30th.

Mars, although gradually brightening until late fall, is now only about 1% the brightness of nearby Venus, as they both play in Capricornus this month.

Jupiter is fading almost imperceptibly, remaining near the feet of Gemini, but still dominating the evening sky.

Saturn is the only bright object in western Sagittarius near Capricornus, as it leaves brilliant Venus and faint Mars behind in the morning sky.

Moon passes Jupiter on the 5th, occults Antares on the 18th, passes Uranus and Neptune on the 20th, Saturn on the 21st, occults Mars on the 22nd, and passes Venus on the 23rd.

Mar. 5—Jupiter 4° south of the moon.

Mar. 11—Sun enters Pisces.

Mar. 18—Moon occults Antares; see them close in the morning sky.

Mar. 20—Mercury in superior conjunction; Vernal equinox, 21:19 GMT (16:19 EST), spring begins in the northern hemisphere, fall in the southern as the sun crosses the equator from south to north.

Mar. 21—Saturn 2° north of the moon.

Mar. 22—Mars 0°.4 south of moon; occultation.

Mar. 23—Venus 2° north of the moon.

Mar. 30—Venus at greatest elongation, 46° west of the sun.

April

Mercury is an evening object all month, but too close to the evening twilight for convenient viewing, although at mid-month eager watchers can give it a try; look to the right of the sun after sunset for a fairly bright speck in the glow, not to be confused with Aldebaran higher up the sky; it is stationary on the 23rd, beginning its retrograde motion prior to inferior conjunction.

Venus is still spectacular in the southeast morning sky, being 4° south of the waning crescent moon on the 22nd.

Mars slides from Capricornus into Aquarius this month, very gradually becoming brighter.

Jupiter is obviously moving into Gemini, away from the feet, this month, and is still the only bright starlike object in the evening sky.

Saturn lazes near the boundary of Sagittarius and Capricornus, gradually slowing its eastward march.

Moon passes Jupiter on the 1st, occults Antares on the 14th, passes Uranus on the 16th, Neptune on the 17th, Saturn on the 18th, Mars on the 20th, Venus on the 22nd, and Jupiter again on the 29th.

Apr. 1—Moon passes 3° north of Jupiter.

Apr. 13—Mercury at greatest elongation, 20° east of the sun.

Apr. 14—Occultation of Antares this morning by the gibbous moon; look for them very close as they rise in the southeast.

Apr. 16—Neptune stationary, beginning its retrograde motion.

Apr. 18—Moon passes 1°.8 south of Saturn; sun enters Aries.

Apr. 20—Moon passes 3° north of Mars.

Apr. 22—Moon passes 4° north of Venus; Lyrid meteor shower may be good.

Apr. 23—Mercury stationary, beginning retrograde motion.

Apr. 29—Moon passes 3° north of Jupiter the 2nd time this month.

May

Mercury is in inferior conjunction, between the earth and the sun, on the 4th, is stationary on the 16th, resuming its direct, eastward motion, and reaches greatest elongation 25° west of the sun on the 31st.

Venus is 7° south of the waning crescent moon on the 21st, a little far for spectacle, but still perhaps worth an early morning sighting.

Mars, while faint, is brighter than anything around, making it easy to find as it moves from Aquarius into Pisces.

Jupiter, in Gemini, has the evening sky all to itself, coming to 2° south of the waxing crescent moon on the 27th GMT (watch on the evening of the 26th, EST).

Saturn, beginning its retrogarde motion on the 4th, slowly turns back into Sagittarius, the constellation it occupies all year.

Moon occults Antares on the 11th, passes Uranus and Neptune on the 14th, Saturn on the 15th, Mars on the 19th, Venus on the 21st, Mercury on the 23rd, and Jupiter on the 27th (26th, EST).

May 4—Mercury in inferior conjunction.

May 5—Saturn stationary, beginning retrograde motion.

May 7—Pluto at opposition.

May 11—Occultation of Antares by the waning gibbous moon; watch them get closer in the morning sky.

May 13—Sun enters Taurus.

May 15—Moon passes 1°.5 south of Saturn.

May 16—Mercury stationary, resuming direct, westward motion.

May 19—Moon passes 6° north of Mars.

May 21—Moon passes 7° north of Venus.

May 23—Moon passes 9° north of Mercury .

May 27—Moon passes 2° north of Jupiter.

May 31—Mercury at greatest elongation, 25° west of the sun.

June

Mercury is difficult to find before dawn, but it is there for the first half of the month before it passes beyond the sun; sky students may find it as it passes 4° to the north of Aldebaran.

Venus still dominates the dawn twilight passing south of the waning crescent moon on the 20th.

Mars, in Pisces all this month, gains nearly a half magnitude in brightness.

Jupiter, if its location is noted each evening this month, will lead the careful observer to the very thin crescent moon in the bright evening twilight of the 23rd, when the moon will be 1°.6 north of the planet.

Saturn is the brightest star-like object in western Sagittarius as it approaches opposition next month.

Moon occults Antares on the 7th, passes Uranus and Neptune on the 10th, Saturn on the 11th, Mars on the 17th, Venus on the 20th, and Jupiter on the 23rd.

Jun. 7—Antares is occulted by the moon; compare their positions last night with those tonight.

Jun. 11—Moon passes 1°.5 south of Saturn.

Jun. 17—Moon passes 7° north of Mars.

Jun. 18—Mercury passes 4° north of Aldebaran.

Jun. 20—Moon passes 7° north of Venus; Sun enters Gemini.

Jun. 21—Summer solstice; the Sun stands still over its most northerly latitude at 15:33 GMT (10:33 EST); summer begins in the northern hemisphere, winter in the southern.

Jun. 23—Moon passes 1°.6 north of Jupiter.

Jun. 29—Uranus at opposition.

July

Mercury, is lost to view for the first half of this month, and is too far south for easy sighting later, but note that it passes 0°.04 north of Regulus on the 29th, thus try for them with binoculars in the evening twilight of the 28th and the 29th to find them close in the sky.

Venus is slowly approaching the sun in our dawn sky, but still an outstanding object.

Mars moves firmly into southern Aries as it brightens to zero magnitude.

Jupiter is lost to view all month as it passes beyond the sun.

Saturn rises about sunset and sets about sunrise, as it passes through opposition to the sun this month.

Moon occults Antares on the 5th (watch during the evening of the 4th), passes Uranus and Neptune on the 7th, Saturn on the 8th, Mars on the 16th, Venus on the 20th, and totally eclipses the sun on the 22nd.

Jul. 2—Mercury in superior conjunction beyond the sun.

Jul. 3—Venus passes 4° north of Aldebaran.

Jul. 4—Earth at aphelion, 94.4 million miles from the sun, the greatest distance this year.

Jul. 5—Occultation of Antares by the waxing gibbous moon; watch them pass very close during the evening of the 4th, between fireworks displays; Neptune at opposition.

Jul. 8—Moon passes 1°.5 south of Saturn.

Jul. 14—Saturn at opposition.

Jul. 15—Jupiter in conjunction, half a sky away from Saturn.

Jul. 16—Moon passes 8° north of Mars.

Jul. 20—Moon passes 7° north of Venus; Sun enters Cancer.

Jul. 22—Total solar eclipse.

Jul. 23—Moon passes 3° south of Mercury.

Jul. 29—Mercury passes 0°.04 north of Regulus.

Jul. 31—Pluto is stationary, resuming its direct motion.

August

Mercury stands 27° east of the sun on the 11th, its greatest elongation this month, but it is too far into the southwest for easy sighting.

Venus, although still in the dawn sky, is still rising earlier than the sun and to its left, getting extremely close to Jupiter on the 12th, but watch them the mornings of the 12th and 13th.

Mars moves from faint Aries into the more prominent zodiacal constellation of Taurus during the month, still brightening along the way.

Jupiter begins to rise earlier, crawling away from the dawn twilight all month, passing extremely close to Venus on the 12th; watch the mornings of the 12th and 13th.

Saturn stays in western Sagittarius, still in retrograde motion following its opposition last month.

Moon occults Antares on the 1st, passes Uranus on the 3rd, Neptune and Saturn on the 4th, partially enters the earth's shadow for an eclipse on the 6th, passes Mars on the 13th, occults Jupiter on the 18th, Venus on the 19th, Mercury on the 22nd, and again Antares on the 28th, again passes Uranus on the 30th, and Neptune on the 31st.

Aug. 1—Antares is occulted by the moon, now past first quarter.

Aug. 4—Moon passes 1°.4 south of Saturn.

Aug. 6—Partial eclipse of the moon.

Aug. 10—Sun enters Leo.

Aug. 11—Mercury at greates elongation, 27° east of the sun.

Aug. 12—Venus and Jupiter pass only 0°.04 from each other about 6 PM EST; look for them close together this morning and tomorrow morning; Perseid meteor shower somewhat bothered by the last quarter moon.

Aug. 13—Moon passes 7° north of Mars.

Aug. 18—Moon occults Jupiter about 8 AM EST, a daytime event for central North America for those with telescopes.

Aug. 19—Moon occults Venus.

Aug. 22—Moon occults Mercury.

Aug. 25—Mercury stationary, beginning its retrograde motion.

Aug. 28—Moon occults Antares.

September

Mercury is lost all month in the glare of the sun.

Venus, after passing 0°.8 north of Regulus on the 6th, is then lost in the sun's glare until the end of the year.

Mars is sensibly slowing its eastward dash among the stars as it crosses the line between Aldebaran and the Pleiades, passing 6° north of Aldebaran in direct motion on the 25th.

Jupiter remains in Cancer for the rest of the year.

Saturn begins its trek out of Sagittarius this month, but won't pass the boundary until next year.

Moon passes Saturn on the 1st, Mars on the 10th, occults Jupiter on the 15th, passes Mercury on the 17th, occults Antares on the 25th, passes Uranus and Neptune on the 27th, and Saturn on the 28th.

Sep. 1—Moon passes 1°.7 south of Saturn.

Sep. 6—Venus passes 0°.8 north of Regulus.

Sep. 8—Mercury at inferior conjunction, between the earth and the sun.

Sep. 14—Uranus stationary, resuming its direct, eastward motion.

Sep. 15—Moon occults Jupiter; see them close in this morning's sky.

Sep. 16—Mercury stationary, resuming its direct motion; Sun enters Virgo.

Sep. 17—Moon passes 2° south of Mercury.

Sep. 23—Saturn stationary, resuming its direct motion; Autumnal equinox, 6:55 GMT (1:55 EST), when the sun moves across the equator into the southern hemisphere, fall beginning in the north, spring in the south; Neptune stationary, resuming its direct motion.

Sep. 24—Mercury achieving its greatest elongation, 18° west of the sun.

Sep. 25—Antares occulted by the waxing crescent moon; see how close they can get on the evening of the 24th; Mars 4° north of Aldebaran.

Sep. 28—Moon passes 1°.5 south of Saturn.

October

Mercury is lost in the sun's glare all month.

Venus is beyond the sun, totally lost to view.

Mars begins its retrograde motion this month, becoming stationary on the 20th in Taurus.

Jupiter rises around midnight by month's end, and is occulted by the last quarter moon on the 12th.

Saturn is still the brightest object in Sagittarius, found in the southwest after sunset.

Moon passes Mars on the 8th, occults Jupiter on the 12th, Antares on the 22nd, passes Uranus on the 24th, passes Neptune and occults Saturn on the 25th.

Oct. 8—Moon passes 5° north of Mars.

Oct. 12—Moon occults Jupiter; see them very close as they rise shortly after midnight.

Oct. 20—Mars stationary, beginning retrograde motion.

Oct. 24—Mercury beyond the sun in superior conjunction; fine crescent moon occults Antares; watch this show begin the evening of the 21st.

Oct. 25—Moon occults Saturn; see them close this evening.

Oct. 30—Sun enters Libra.

November

Mercury is 1°.7 north of the very thin crescent moon on the afternoon of the 18th, a difficult sighting, because both are quite low in the southwestern twilight.

Venus is in superior conjunction with the sun on the first, so invisible in our sky.

Mars, having traveled all the way from near Antares at the first of the year to be near the face of the bull, passing Aldebaran in retrograde motion on the 13th, puts on its best show: closest to the earth on the 20th, and opposite the sun on the 27th.

Jupiter begins its retrograde motion on the 30th, still in Cancer.

Saturn, faithfully residing in Sagittarius, may still be seen low in the southwest in the evening twilight, occulted by the fat crescent moon on the 22nd (watch in the evening on the 21st, EST).

Moon passes Mars on the 5th, Jupiter on the 9th, occults Antares and passes Mercury on the 18th, passes Uranus on the 20th, Neptune on the 21st, and occults Saturn on the 22nd.

Nov. 1—Venus in superior conjunction.

Nov. 5—Moon passes 3° north of Mars.

Nov. 9—Moon passes 1°.6 south of Jupiter.

Nov. 10—Pluto in conjunction.

Nov. 18—Moon, only 30 hours past New, occults Antares; moon passes 1°.8 south of Mercury; Leonid meteors free from lunar interference.

Nov. 20—Mars closest to the earth.

Nov. 22—Moon occults Saturn; watch their close approach the evening of the 21st; sun enters Scorpius.

Nov. 27—Mars at opposition.

Nov. 29—Sun enters Ophiuchus.

Nov. 30—Jupiter, stationary, beginning retrograde motion.

December

Mercury is still difficult to see in the southwestern twilight, but is wholly lost in the sun's glare by the 3rd week.

Venus, while technically an evening star, is still deeply imbedded in the evening twilight, practically invisible until next year.

Mars is the only show in the evening sky, until Jupiter rises to surpass Mars in brightness.

Jupiter lets Mars have the evening spotlight, but clearly takes over by midnight.

Saturn is fading in the western wings as twilight catches it in the southwest.

Moon passes Jupiter on the 6th, occults Antares on the 15th, passes Neptune on the 18th, occults Saturn on the 19th, and passes Mars on the 29th.

Dec. 1—Moon passes 3° north of Mars.

Dec. 6—Mercury at greatest elongation, 21° east of the sun; moon passes 2° south of Jupiter.

Dec. 10—Mercury passes 1°.8 south of Uranus in direct motion.

Dec. 14—Mercury stationary, beginning its retrograde motion; try for the Geminid meteors, known for occasional fireballs.

Dec. 15—Antares occulted by a very thin waning crescent Moon; compare their positions this morning and tomorrow morning.

Dec. 16—Sun enters Sagittarius.

Dec. 18—Mercury passes 0°.6 north of Uranus in retrograde motion; Mercury passes 1°.4 north of Venus.

Dec. 19—Venus passes 0°.6 south of Uranus; Moon occults Saturn.

Dec. 22—Winter Solstice, when the sun reaches its most southerly point over the earth, 3:07 GMT (22:07 EST on the 21st); winter begins in the northern hemisphere, summer in the southern.

Dec. 23—Venus passes 1°.8 south of Neptune.

Dec. 24—Mercury in inferior conjunction.

Dec. 29—Moon passes 2° north of Mars.

Dec. 31—Uranus in conjunction with the sun.

Planets and the Sun

The planets of the solar system, in order of their mean distance from the sun, are Mercury, Venus, Earth, Mars, Jupiter, Saturn, Uranus, Neptune and Pluto. Both Uranus and Neptune are visible through good field glasses, but Pluto is so distant and so small that only large telescopes or long exposure photographs can make it visible.

Since Mercury and Venus are nearer to the sun than is the earth, their motions about the sun are seen from the earth as wide swings first to one side of the sun and then to the other, although they are both passing continuously around the sun in orbits that are almost circular. When their passage takes them either between the earth and the sun, or beyond the sun as seen from the earth, they are invisible to us. Because of the laws which govern the motions of planets about the sun, both Mercury and Venus require much less time to pass between the earth and the sun than around the far side of the sun, so their periods of visibility and invisibility are unequal.

The planets that lie farther from the sun than does the earth may be seen for longer periods of time and are invisible only when they are so located in our sky that they rise and set about the same time as the sun when, of course, they are overwhelmed by the sun's great brilliance. None of the planets has any light of its own but each shines only by reflecting sunlight from its surface. Mercury and Venus, because they are between the earth and the sun, show phases very much as the moon does. The planets farther from the sun are always seen as full, although Mars does occasionally present a slightly gibbous phase — like the moon when not quite full.

The planets move rapidly among the stars because they are very much nearer to us. The stars are also in motion, some of them at tremendous speeds, but they are so far away that their motion does not change their apparent positions in the heavens sufficiently for anyone to perceive that change in a single lifetime. The very nearest star is about 7,000 times as far away as the most distant planet.

Planets of the Solar System

Mercury

Mercury, nearest planet to the sun, is the second smallest of the nine planets known to be orbiting the sun. Its diameter is 3,100 miles and its mean distance from the sun is 36,000,000 miles.

Mercury moves with great speed in its journey about the sun, averaging about 30 miles a second to complete its circuit in 88 of our days. Mercury rotates upon its axis over a period of nearly 59 days, thus exposing all of its surface periodically to the sun. It is believed that the surface passing before the sun may have a temperature of about 800° F., while the temperature on the side turned temporarily away from the sun does not fall as low as might be expected. This night temperature has been described by Russian astronomers as "room temperature" — possibly about 70°. This would contradict the former belief that Mercury did not possess an atmosphere, for some sort of atmosphere would be needed to retain the fierce solar radiation that strikes Mercury. A shallow but dense layer of carbon dioxide would produce the "greenhouse" effect, in which heat accumulated during exposure to the sun would not completely escape at night. The actual presence of a carbon dioxide atmosphere is in dispute. Other research, however, has indicated a nighttime temperature approaching $-300°$.

This uncertainty about conditions upon Mercury and its motion arise from its shorter angular distance from the sun as seen from the earth, for Mercury is always too much in line with the sun to be observed against a dark sky, but is always seen during either morning or evening twilight.

Mariner 10 made 3 passes by Mercury in 1974 and 1975. A large fraction of the surface was photographed from varying distances, revealing a degree of cratering similar to that of the moon. An atmosphere of hydrogen and helium may be made up of gases of the solar wind temporarily concentrated by the presence of Mercury. The discovery of a weak but permanent magnetic field was a surprise. It has been held that both a fluid core and rapid rotation were necessary for the generation of a planetary magnetic field. Mercury may demonstrate these conditions to be unnecessary, or the field may reveal something about the history of Mercury.

Venus

Venus, slightly smaller than the earth, moves about the sun at a mean distance of 67,000,000 miles in 225 of our days. Its synodical revolution — its return to the same relationship with the earth and the sun, which is a result of the combination of its own motion and that of the earth — is 584 days. Every 19 months, then, Venus will be nearer to the earth than any other planet of the solar system. The planet is covered with a dense, white, cloudy atmosphere that conceals whatever is below it. This same cloud reflects sunlight efficiently so that when Venus is favorably situated, it is the third brightest object in the sky, exceeded only by the sun and the moon.

Spectral analysis of sunlight reflected from Venus' cloud tops has shown features that can best be explained by identifying the material of the clouds as sulphuric acid (oil of vitriol). Infrared spectroscopy from a balloon-borne telescope nearly 20 miles above the earth's surface gave indications of a small amount of water vapor present in the same region of the atmosphere of Venus. In 1956, radio astronomers at the Naval Research Laboratories in Washington, D. C., found a temperature for Venus of about 600° F., in marked contrast to minus 125° F., previously found at the cloud tops. Subsequent radio work confirmed a high temperature and produced evidence for this temperature to be associated with the solid body of Venus. With this peculiarity in mind, space scientists devised experiments for the U.S. space probe Mariner 2 to perform when it flew by in 1962. Mariner 2 confirmed the high temperature and the fact that it pertained to the ground rather than to some special activity of the atmosphere. In addition, Mariner 2 was unable to detect any radiation belts similar to the earth's so-called Van Allen belts. Nor was it able to detect the existence of a magnetic field even as weak as 1/100,000 of that of the earth.

In 1967, a Russian space probe, Venera 4, and the American Mariner 5 arrived at Venus within a few hours of each other. Venera 4 was designed to allow an instrument package to land gently on the planet's surface via parachute. It ceased transmission of information in about 75 minutes when the temperature it read went above 500° F. After considerable controversy, it was agreed that it still had 20 miles to go to reach the surface. The U.S. probe, Mariner 5, went around the dark side of Venus at a distance of about 6,000 miles. Again, it detected no significant magnetic field but its radio signals passed to earth through Venus' atmosphere twice — once on the night side and once on the day side. The results are startling. Venus' atmosphere is nearly all carbon dioxide and must exert a pressure at the planet's surface of up to 100 times the earth's normal sea-level pressure of one atmosphere. Since the earth and Venus are about the same size, and were presumably formed at the same time by the same general process from the same mixture of chemical elements, one is faced with the question: which is the planet with the unusual history — earth or Venus?

Radar astronomers using powerful transmitters as well as sensitive receivers and computers have succeeded in determining the rotation period of Venus. It turns out to be 243 days clockwise — in other words, contrary to the spin of most of the other planets and to its own motion around the sun. If it were exactly 243.16 days, Venus would always present the same face toward the earth at every inferior conjunction. This rate and sense of rotation allows a "day" on Venus of 117.4 earth days. Any part of Venus will receive sunlight on its clouds for over 58 days and will be in darkness for 58 days. Recent radar observations have shown surface features below the clouds. Large craters, continent-sized highlands, and extensive, dry "ocean" basins have been identified.

Mariner 10 passed Venus before traveling on to Mercury in 1974. The carbon dioxide molecule found in such abundance in the atmosphere is rather opaque to certain ultraviolet wavelengths, enabling sensitive television cameras to take pictures of the Venusian cloud cover. Photos radioed to earth show a spiral pattern in the clouds from equator to the poles.

In December, 1978, two U. S. Pioneer probes arrived at Venus. One went into orbit about Venus, the other split into 5 separate probes targeted for widely-spaced entry points to sample different conditions. The instrumentation ensemble was selected on the basis of previous missions that had shown the range of conditions to be studied. The probes confirmed expected high surface temperatures and high winds aloft. Winds of about 200 miles per hour, there, may account for the transfer of heat into the night side in spite of the low rotation speed of the planet. Surface winds were light at the time, however. Atmosphere and cloud chemistries were examined in detail, providing much data for continued analysis. The probes detected 4 layers of clouds and more light on the surface than expected solely from sunlight. This light allowed Russian scientists to obtain at least two photos showing rocks on the surface. Sulphur seems to play a large role in the chemistry of Venus, and reactions involving sulphur may be responsible for the glow. To learn more about the weather and atmospheric circulation on Venus, the orbiter takes daily photos of the daylight side cloud cover. It confirms the cloud pattern and its circulation shown by Mariner 10. The ionosphere shows large variability. The orbiter's radar operates in 2 modes: one, for ground elevation variability, and the second for ground reflectivity in 2 dimensions, thus "imaging" the surface. Radar maps of the entire planet that show the features mentioned above have been produced.

Mars

Mars is the first planet beyond the earth, away from the sun. Mars' diameter is about 4,200 miles, although a determination of the radius and mass of Mars by the space-probe, Mariner 4, which flew by Mars on July 14, 1965 at a distance of less than 6,000 miles, indicated that these dimensions were slightly larger than had been previously estimated. While Mars' orbit is also nearly circular, it is somewhat more eccentric than the orbits of many of the other planets, and Mars is more than 30 million miles farther from the sun in some parts of its year than it is at others. Mars takes 687 of our days to make one circuit of the sun, traveling at about 15 miles a second. Mars rotates upon its axis in almost the same period of time that the earth does — 24 hours and 37 minutes. Mars' mean distance from the sun is 141 million miles, so that the temperature on Mars would be lower than that on the earth even if Mars' atmosphere were about the same as ours. The atmosphere is not, however, for Mariner 4 reported that atmospheric pressure on Mars is between 1% and 2% of the earth's atmospheric pressure. This thin atmosphere appears to be largely carbon dioxide. No evidence of free water was found.

There appears to be no magnetic field about Mars. This would eliminate the previous conception of a dangerous radiation belt around Mars. The same lack of a magnetic field would expose the surface of Mars to an influx of cosmic radiation about 100 times as intense as that on earth.

Deductions from years of telescopic observation indicate that 5/8ths of the surface of Mars is a desert of reddish rock, sand, and soil. The rest of Mars is covered by irregular patches that appear generally green in hues that change through the Martian year. These were formerly held to be some sort of primitive vegetation, but with the findings of Mariner 4 of a complete lack of water and oxygen, such growth does not appear possible. The nature of the green areas is now unknown. They may be regions covered with volcanic salts whose color changes with changing temperatures and atmospheric conditions, or they may be gray, rather than green. When large gray areas are placed beside large red areas, the gray areas will appear green to the eye.

Mars' axis of rotation is inclined from a vertical to the plane of its orbit about the sun by about 25° and therefore Mars has seasons as does the earth, except that the Martian seasons are longer because Mars' year

is longer. White caps form about the winter pole of Mars, growing through the winter and shrinking in summer. These polar caps are now believed to be both water ice and carbon dioxide ice. It is the carbon dioxide that is seen to come and go with the seasons. The water ice is apparently in many layers with dust between them, indicating climatic cycles.

The canals of Mars have become more of a mystery than they were before the voyage of Mariner 4. Markings forming a network of fine lines crossing much of the surface of Mars have been seen there by men who have devoted much time to the study of the planet, but no canals have shown clearly enough in previous photographs to be universally accepted. A few of the 21 photographs sent back to earth by Mariner 4 covered areas crossed by canals. The pictures show faint, ill-defined, broad, dark markings, but no positive identification of the nature of the markings.

Mariners 6 & 7 in 1969 sent back many more photographs of higher quality than those of the pioneering Mariner 4. These pictures showed cratering similar to the earlier views, but in addition showed 2 other types of terrain. Some regions seemed featureless for many square miles, but others were chaotic, showing high relief without apparent organization into mountain chains or craters.

Mariner 9, the first artificial body to be placed in an orbit about Mars, has transmitted over 10,000 photographs covering 100% of the planet's surface. Preliminary study of these photos and other data shows that Mars resembles no other planet we know. Using terrestrial terms, however, scientists describe features that seem to be clearly of volcanic origin. One of these features is Nix Olympica, (now called Olympus Mons), apparently a shield volcano whose caldera is over 50 miles wide, and whose outer slopes are over 300 miles in diameter, and which stands about 90,000 feet above the surrounding plain. Some features may have been produced by cracking (faulting) of the surface and the sliding of one region over or past another. Many craters seem to have been produced by impacting bodies such as may have come from the nearby asteroid belt. Features near the south pole may have been produced by glaciers that are no longer present. Flowing water, non-existent on Mars at the present time, probably carved canyons, one 10 times longer and 3 times deeper than the Grand Canyon.

Although the Russians landed a probe on the Martian surface, it transmitted for only 20 seconds. In 1976, the U.S. landed 2 Viking spacecraft on the Martian surface. The landers had devices aboard to perform chemical analyses of the soil in search of evidence of life. The results have been inconclusive. The 2 Viking orbiters have returned the best pictures yet of Martian topographic features. Many features can be explained only if Mars once had large quantities of flowing water.

Mars' position in its orbit and its speed around that orbit in relation to the earth's position and speed bring Mars fairly close to the earth on occasions about two years apart and then move Mars and the earth too far apart for accurate observation and photography. Every 15-17 years, the close approaches are especially favorable to close observation.

Mars has 2 satellites, discovered in 1877 by Asaph Hall. The outer satellite, Deimos, revolves around Mars in about 31 hours. The inner satellite, Phobos, whips around Mars in a little more than 7 hours, making 3 trips around the planet each Martian day. Mariner and Viking photos show these bodies to be irregularly shaped and pitted with numerous craters. Phobos also shows a system of linear grooves, each about 1/3-

mile across and roughly parallel. Phobos measures about 8 by 12 miles and Deimos about 5 by 7.5 miles in size.

Jupiter

Jupiter is the largest of the planets. Its equatorial diameter is 88,000 miles, 11 times the diameter of the earth. Its polar diameter is about 6,000 miles shorter. This is an equilibrium condition resulting from the liquidity of the planet and its extremely rapid rate of rotation: a Jupiter day is only 10 earth hours long. For a planet this size, this rotational speed is amazing, and it moves a point on Jupiter's equator at a speed of 22,000 miles an hour, as compared with 1,000 miles an hour for a point on the earth's equator. Jupiter is at an average distance of 480 million miles from the sun and takes almost 12 of our years to make one complete circuit of the sun.

The only directly observable chemical constituents of Jupiter's atmosphere are methane (CH_4) and ammonia (NH_3), but it is reasonable to assume the same mixture of elements available to make Jupiter as to make the sun. This would mean a large fraction of hydrogen and helium must be present also, as well as water (H_2O). The temperature at the tops of the clouds may be about minus 260° F. The clouds are probably ammonia ice crystals, becoming ammonia droplets lower down. There may be a space before water ice crystals show up as clouds: in turn, these become water droplets near the bottom of the entire cloud layer. The total atmosphere may be only a few hundred miles in depth, pulled down by the surface gravity (= 2.64 times earth's) to a relatively thin layer. Of course, the gases become denser with depth until they may turn into a slush or a slurry. Perhaps there is no surface — no real interface between the gaseous atmosphere and the body of Jupiter. Pioneers 10 and 11 provided evidence for considering Jupiter to be almost entirely liquid hydrogen. Long before a rocky core about the size of the earth is reached, hydrogen mixed with helium becomes a liquid metal at very high temperature and pressure. Jupiter's cloudy atmosphere is a fairly good reflector of sunlight and makes it appear far brighter than any of the stars.

Fourteen of Jupiter's 17 or more satellites have been found through earth-based observations. Four of the moons are large and bright, rivaling our own moon and the planet Mercury in diameter, and may be seen through a field glass. They move rapidly around Jupiter and their change of position from night to night is extremely interesting to watch. The other satellites are much smaller and in all but one instance much farther from Jupiter and cannot be seen except through powerful telescopes. The 4 outermost satellites are revolving around Jupiter clockwise as seen from the north, contrary to the motions of the great majority of the satellites in the solar system and to the direction of revolution of the planets around the sun. The reason for this retrograde motion is not known, but one theory is that Jupiter's tremendous gravitational power may have captured 4 of the minor planets or asteroids that move about the sun between Mars and Jupiter, and that these would necessarily revolve backward. At the great distance of these bodies from Jupiter — some 14 million miles — direct motion would result in decay of the orbits, while retrograde orbits would be stable. Jupiter's mass is more than twice the mass of all the other planets put together, and accounts for Jupiter's tremendous gravitational field and so, probably, for its numerous satellites and its dense atmosphere.

In December, 1973, Pioneer 10 passed about 80,000 miles from the equator of Jupiter and was whipped into a path taking it out of our solar system in about 50 years, and beyond the system of planets, on June 13, 1983. In December, 1974, Pioneer 11 passed within 30,000 miles of Jupiter, moving roughly from south to north, over the poles.

Photographs from both encounters were useful at the time but were far surpassed by those of Voyagers I and II. Thousands of high resolution multi-color pictures show rapid variations of features both large and small. The Great Red Spot exhibits internal counterclockwise rotation. Much turbulence is seen in adjacent material passing north or south of it. The satellites Amalthea, Io, Europa, Ganymede, and Callisto were photographed, some in great detail. Each is individual and unique, with no similarities to other known planets or satellites. Io has active volcanoes that probably have ejected material into a doughnut-shaped ring enveloping its orbit about Jupiter. This is not to be confused with the thin flat disk-like ring closer to Jupiter's surface. Now that such a ring has been seen by the Voyagers, older uncertain observations from Earth can be reinterpreted as early sightings of this structure.

Saturn

Saturn, last of the planets visible to the unaided eye, is almost twice as far from the sun as Jupiter, almost 900 million miles. It is second in size to Jupiter but its mass is much smaller. Saturn's specific gravity is less than that of water. Its diameter is about 71,000 miles at the equator; its rotational speed spins it completely around in a little more than 10 hours, and its atmosphere is much like that of Jupiter, except that its temperature at the top of its cloud layer is at least 100° lower. At about 300° F. below zero, the ammonia would be frozen out of Saturn's clouds. The theoretical construction of Saturn resembles that of Jupiter; it is either all gas, or it has a small dense center surrounded by a layer of liquid and a deep atmosphere.

Until Pioneer 11 passed Saturn in September 1979 only 10 satellites of Saturn were known. Since that time, the situation is quite confused. Added to data interpretations from the fly-by are earth-based observations using new techniques while the rings were edge-on and virtually invisible. It was hoped that the Voyager I and II fly-bys would help sort out the system. It is now believed that Saturn has at least 22 satellites, some sharing orbits. The Saturn satellite system is still confused.

Saturn's ring system begins about 7,000 miles above the visible disk of Saturn, lying above its equator and extending about 35,000 miles into space. The diameter of the ring system visible from Earth is about 170,000 miles; the rings are estimated to be no thicker than 10 miles. In 1973, radar observation showed the ring particles to be large chunks of material averaging a meter on a side.

Voyager I and II observations showed the rings to be considerably more complex than had been believed, so much so that interpretation will take much time. To the untrained eye, the Voyager photographs could be mistaken for pictures of a colorful phonograph record.

Uranus

Voyager II, after passing Saturn in August 1981, headed for a rendezvous with Uranus culminating in a fly-by January 24, 1986. This encounter answered many questions, and raised others.

Uranus, discovered by Sir William Herschel on Mar. 13, 1781, lies at a distance of 1.8 billion miles from the sun, taking 84 years to make its circuit around our star. Uranus has a diameter of about 32,000 miles and spins once in some 16.8 hours, according to fly-by data. One of the most fascinating features of Uranus is how far it is tipped over. Its north pole lies 98° from being directly up and down to its orbit plane. Thus, its seasons are extreme. When the sun rises at the north pole, it stays up for 42 years; then it sets and the north pole will be in darkness (and winter) for 42 years.

The satellite system of Uranus, consisting of at least 15 moons, (the 5 largest having been known before the fly-by) have orbits lying in the plane of the planet's equator. In that plane there is also a complex of rings, 9 of which were discovered in 1978. Invisible from Earth, the 9 original rings were found by observers watching Uranus pass before a star. As they waited, they saw their photoelectric equipment register several short eclipses of the star. Then the planet occulted the star as expected. After the star came out from behind Uranus, the star winked out several more times. Subsequent observations and analyses indicated the 9 narrow, nearly opaque rings circling Uranus. Evidence from the Voyager II fly-by has shown the ring particles to be predominantly a yard or so in diameter.

In addition to the 10 new, very small satellites, Voyager II returned detailed photos of the 5 large satellites. As in the case of other satellites newly observed in the Voyager program, these bodies proved to be entirely different from each other and any others. Miranda has grooved markings, reminiscent of Jupiter's Ganymede, but often arranged in a chevron pattern. Ariel shows rifts and channels. Umbriel is extremely dark, prompting some observers to regard its surface as among the oldest in the system. Titania has rifts and fractures, but not the evidence of flow found on Ariel. Oberon's main feature is its surface saturated with craters, unrelieved by other formations.

The structure of Uranus is subject to some debate. Basically, however, it may have a rocky core surrounded by a thick icy mantle on top of which is a crust of hydrogen and helium that gradually becomes an atmosphere. Perhaps continued analysis of the wealth of data returned by Voyager II will shed some light on this problem.

Neptune

Neptune, currently the most distant planet from the sun (until 1999), lies at an average distance of 2.8 billion miles. Having a diameter of about 31,000 miles and a rotation period of 18.2 hours, it is a virtual twin of Uranus. It is significantly more dense than Uranus, however, and this increases the debate over its internal structure. Neptune circles the sun in 164 years in a nearly circular orbit.

Neptune has 3 satellites, the third being found in 1981. The largest, Triton, is in a retrograde orbit suggesting that it was captured rather than being co-eval

with Neptune. Triton is sufficiently large to raise significant tides on Neptune which will one day, say 100 million years from now, cause Triton to come close enough to Neptune for it to be torn apart. Nereid was found in 1949, and is in a long looping orbit suggesting it, too, was captured. The orbit of the third body is under analysis at this writing. Observations made in 1968 but not interpreted until 1982 suggest that Neptune, too, has a ring system.

As with the other giant planets, Neptune is emitting more energy than it receives from the sun. These excesses are thought to be cooling from internal heat sources and from the heat of the formation of the planets.

Little is known of Neptune beyond its distance, but Voyager II, if all continues to operate, will send us pictures and observations in 1989.

Pluto

Although Pluto on the average stays about 3.6 billion miles from the sun, its orbit is so eccentric that it is now approaching its minimum distance of 2.7 billion miles, less than the current distance of Neptune. Thus Pluto, until 1999, is temporarily planet number 8 from the sun. At its mean distance, Pluto takes 247.7 years to circumnavigate the sun. Until recently that was about all that was known of Pluto.

About a century ago, a hypothetical planet was believed to lie beyond Neptune and Uranus. Little more than a guess, a mass of one Earth was assigned to the mysterious body and mathematical searches were begun. Amid some controversy about the validity of the predictive process, Pluto was found nearly where it was predicted to be. It was found by Clyde Tombaugh at the Lowell Observatory in Flagstaff, Ariz., in 1930.

At the U.S. Naval Observatory, also in Flagstaff, on July 2, 1978, James Christy obtained a photograph of Pluto that was distinctly elongated. Repeated observations of this shape and its variation were convincing evidence of the discovery of a satellite of Pluto. Now named Charon, it may be 500 miles across, at a distance of over 10,000 miles, and taking 6.4 days to move around Pluto, the same length of time Pluto takes to rotate once. Gravitational laws allow these interactions to give us the mass of Pluto as 0.0017 of the Earth and a diameter of 1,500 miles. This makes the density about the same as that of water.

It is now clear that Pluto, the body found by Tombaugh, could not have influenced Neptune and Uranus to go astray. Theorists are again at work looking for a new planet X.

Greenwich Sidereal Time for 0ʰ GMT, 1990

(Add 12 hours to obtain Right Ascension of Mean Sun)

Date	h	m	Date	h	m	Date	h	m	Date	h	m
Jan. 1	06	41.5	11	13	15.8	20	19	50.1	28	02	24.3
11	07	21.0	21	13	55.2	30	20	29.5	Nov. 7	03	03.8
21	08	0.4	May 1	14	34.6	Aug. 9	21	08.9	17	03	43.2
31	08	39.8	11	15	14.1	19	21	48.3	27	04	22.6
Feb. 10	09	19.2	21	15	53.5	29	22	27.8	Dec. 7	05	02.0
20	09	58.7	31	16	32.9	Sept. 8	23	07.2	17	05	41.5
Mar. 2	10	38.1	June 10	17	12.3	18	23	46.6	27	06	20.9
12	11	17.5	20	17	51.8	28	00	26.0	1990 Jan. 6	07	00.3
22	11	56.9	30	18	31.2	Oct. 8	01	05.5			
Apr. 1	12	36.4	July 10	19	10.6	18	01	44.9			

Astronomical Signs and Symbols

☉	The Sun	⊕	The Earth	♅	Uranus	□	Quadrature
☾	The Moon	♂	Mars	♆	Neptune	☍	Opposition
☿	Mercury	♃	Jupiter	♇	Pluto	☊	Ascending Node
♀	Venus	♄	Saturn	☌	Conjunction	☋	Descending Node

Two heavenly bodies are in "conjunction" (☌) when they are due north and south of each other, either in Right Ascension (with respect to the north celestial pole) or in Celestial Longitude (with respect to the north ecliptic pole). If the bodies are seen near each other, they will rise and set at nearly the same time. They are in "opposition" (☍) when their Right Ascensions differ by exactly 12 hours, or their Celestial Longitudes differ by 180°. One of the two objects in opposition will rise while the other is setting. "Quadrature" (□) refers to the arrangement when the coordinates of two bodies differ by exactly 90°. These terms may refer to the relative positions of any two bodies as seen from the earth, but one of the bodies is so frequently the sun that mention of the sun is omitted; otherwise both bodies are named. The geocentric angular separation between sun and object is termed "elongation." Elongation is limited only for Mercury and Venus; the "greatest elongation" for each of these bodies is noted in the appropriate tables and is approximately the time for longest observation. When a planet is in its "ascending" (☊) or "descending" (☋) node, it is passing northward or southward, respectively, through the plane of the earth's orbit, across the celestial circle called the ecliptic. The term "perihelion" means nearest to the sun, and "aphelion," farthest from the sun. An "occultation" of a planet or star is an eclipse of it by some other body, usually the moon.

Planetary Configurations, 1990

Greenwich Mean Time (0 designates midnight; 12 designates noon; * = star; ☽ = moon)

Mo.	D. h. m.		
Jan.	2 18	- ☌ ♆ ☉	
	4 17	-	⊕ Perihelion
	6 21	- ☌ ♄ ☉	
	9 02	- ☌ ☿ ☉	Inferior
	10 00	- ☌ ♃ ☽	♃ 4° S
	13 21	- ☌ ☿ ♆	☿ 3° S
	18 23	- ☌ ♀ ☉	Inferior
	20 03	-	☿ Stationary
	22 08	- ☌ ☽ *	Antares 0°.3 N; Occ'n Occultation
	23 15	- ☌ ♂ ☽	♂ 4° N
	24 13	- ☌ ♅ ☽	♅ 3° N
	24 20	- ☌ ☿ ☽	☿ 5° N
	24 23	- ☌ ♆ ☽	♆ 4° N
	25 10	- ☌ ♄ ☽	♄ 3° N
	26 19	- ☌ ☽ ☉	Annular Solar Eclipse
	27 23	- ☌ ☿ ♆	☿ 0°.8 N
Feb.	1 01	-	☿ Gr Elong. 25° W of ☉
	3 15	- ☌ ☿ ♄	☿ 0°.2 N
	4 06	- ☌ ☿ ♀	☿ 7° S
	6 04	- ☌ ♃ ☽	♃ 4° S
	7 05	- ☌ ♀ ♄	♀ 7° N
	8 04	-	♀ Stationary
	9 14	- ☌ ♂ ♅	♂ 0°.2 S
	9 19	- ☍ ☽ ☉	Total Lunar Eclipse
	14 17	- ☌ ♀ ♄	♀ 7° N
	17 06	- ☌ ♂ ♆	♂ 1°.5 S
	18 16	- ☌ ☽ *	Antares 0°.3 N; Occ'n
	21 00	- ☌ ♅ ☽	♅ 3° N
	21 10	- ☌ ♆ ☽	♆ 4° N
	21 16	- ☌ ♂ ☽	♂ 2° N
	22 00	- ☌ ♄ ☽	♄ 3° N
	22 04	- ☌ ♀ ☽	♀ 8° N
	22 13	-	♀ Gr. Brilliancy
	23 01	-	♇ Stationary
	24 01	- ☌ ☿ ☽	☿ 2° S
	24 19	-	♃ Stationary
	28 17	- ☌ ♂ ♄	♂ 1°.0 S
Mar.	5 09	- ☌ ♃ ☽	♃ 4° S
	18 00	- ☌ ☽ *	Antares 0°.2 N; Occ'n
	20 01	- ☌ ☿ ☉	Superior
	20 11	- ☌ ♅ ☽	♅ 3° N
	20 20	- ☌ ♆ ☽	♆ 4° N
	20 21 19		Vernal Equinox; Spring begins Northern Hemisphere
	21 14	- ☌ ♄ ☽	♄ 2° N
	22 18	- ☌ ♂ ☽	♂ 0°.4 S; Occ'n
	23 07	- ☌ ♀ ☽	♀ 2° N
	30 07	-	♀ Gr Elong. 46° W of ☉
Apr.	1 18	- ☌ ♃ ☽	♃ 3° S
	13 15	-	☿ Gr. Elong. 20° E of ☉

Mo.	D. h. m.		
	13 23	-	♅ Stationary
	14 07	- ☌ ☽ *	Antares 0°.1 S; Occ'n
	16 11	-	♆ Stationary
	16 19	- ☌ ♅ ☽	♅ 3° N
	17 04	- ☌ ♆ ☽	♆ 3° N
	18 01	- ☌ ♄ ☽	♄ 1°.8 N
	20 20	- ☌ ♂ ☽	♂ 3° S
	22 01	- ☌ ♀ ☽	♀ 4° S
	23 15	-	☿ Stationary
	29 08	- ☌ ♃ ☽	♃ 3° S
May	4 00	- ☌ ☿ ☉	Inferior
	5 02	-	♄ Stationary
	7 02	- ☍ ♇ ☉	
	11 13	- ☌ ☽ *	Antares 0°.2 S; Occ'n
	14 00	- ☌ ♅ ☽	♅ 2° N
	14 10	- ☌ ♆ ☽	♆ 3° N
	15 08	- ☌ ♄ ☽	♄ 1°.5 N
	16 07	-	☿ Stationary
	19 20	- ☌ ♂ ☽	♂ 6° S
	21 20	- ☌ ♀ ☽	♀ 7° S
	23 03	- ☌ ☿ ☽	☿ 9° S
	27 02	- ☌ ♃ ☽	♃ 2° S
	31 03	-	☿ Gr. Elong. 25° W of ☉
June	7 19	- ☌ ☽ *	Antares 0°.2 S; Occ'n
	10 05	- ☌ ♅ ☽	♅ 2° N
	10 15	- ☌ ♆ ☽	♆ 3° N
	11 12	- ☌ ♄ ☽	♄ 1°.4 N
	17 16	- ☌ ♂ ☽	♂ 7° S
	18 02	- ☌ ☿ *	☿ 4° N of Aldebaran
	20 11	- ☌ ♀ ☽	♀ 7° S
	21 15 33		Summer Solstice; Summer begins; Northern Hemisphere
	23 22	- ☌ ♃ ☽	♃ 1°.6 S
	29 15	- ☍ ♅ ☉	
July	2 17	- ☌ ☿ ☉	Superior
	3 15	- ☌ ♀ *	♀ 4° N of Aldebaran
	4 05	-	⊕ Aphelion
	5 02	- ☌ ☽ *	Antares 0°.2 S; Occ'n
	5 11	- ☍ ♆ ☉	
	7 09	- ☌ ♅ ☽	♅ 2° N
	7 20	- ☌ ♆ ☽	♆ 3° N
	8 14	- ☌ ♄ ☽	♄ 1°.5 N
	14 18	- ☍ ♄ ☉	
	15 06	- ☌ ♃ ☉	
	16 08	- ☌ ♂ ☽	♂ 8° S
	20 03	- ☌ ♀ ☽	♀ 4° S
	22 03	- ☌ ☽ ☉	Total Solar Eclipse
	23 18	- ☌ ☿ ☽	☿ 3° N
	29 06	- ☌ ☿ *	☿ 0°.04 N of Regulus
	31 02	-	♇ Stationary

Mo.	D. h. m.			
Aug.	1 09	-	☌ ☽ *	Antares 0°.1 S; Occ'n
	3 14	-	☌ ♅ ☽	♅ 2° N
	4 02	-	☌ ♆ ☽	♆ 3° N
	4 18	-	☌ ♄ ☽	♄ 1°.6 N
	6 14	-	☍ ☽ ☉	Partial Lunar Eclipse
	9 05	-	☌ ♀ *	♀ 7° S of Polluse
	11 20	-		☿ Gr. Elong. 27° E of ☉
	12 23	-	☌ ♀ ♃	♀ 0°.04 N
	13 19	-	☌ ♂ ☽	♂ 7° S
	18 13	-	☌ ♃ ☽	♃ 0°.4 S; Occ'n
	19 00	-	☌ ♀ ☽	♀ 0°.5 N; Occ'n
	22 12	-	☌ ☿ ☽	☿ 0°.2 N; Occ'n
	25 00	-		☿ Stationary
	28 17	-	☌ ☽ *	Antares 0°.2 S; Occ'n
	30 21	-	☌ ♅ ☽	♅ 2° N
	31 09	-	☌ ♆ ☽	♆ 3° N
Sept.	1 00	-	☌ ♄ ☽	♄ 1°.7 N
	6 21	-	☌ ♀ *	♀ 0°.8 N of Regulus
	8 04	-	☌ ☿ ☉	Inferior
	10 23	-	☌ ♂ ☽	♂ 6° S
	14 15	-	☌ ☿ ♀	☿ 3° S
	14 19	-		♅ Stationary
	15 06	-	☌ ♃ ☽	♃ 0°.3 N; Occ'n
	16 16	-		☿ Stationary
	17 20	-	☌ ☿ ☽	☿ 2° N
	23 03	-		♄ Stationary
	23 06 55			Autumnal Equinox; Autumn begins, Northern Hemisphere
	23 16	-		♆ Stationary
	24 04	-		☿ Gr Elong. 18° W of ☉
	25 01	-	☌ ☽ *	Antares 0°.4 S; Occ'n
	25 07	-	☌ ♂ *	♂ 4° N of Aldebaran
	27 06	-	☌ ♅ ☽	♅ 2° N
	27 18	-	☌ ♆ ☽	♆ 3° N
	28 08	-	☌ ♄ ☽	♄ 1°.5 N
Oct.	8 19	-	☌ ♂ ☽	♂ 5° S
	12 20	-	☌ ♃ ☽	♃ 1°.0 N; Occ'n

Mo.	D. h. m.			
	20 12	-		♂ Stationary
	22 04	-	☌ ☿ ☉	Superior
	22 08	-	☌ ☽ *	Antares 0°.6 S; Occ'n
	24 15	-	☌ ♅ ☽	♅ 1°.9 N
	25 02	-	☌ ♆ ☽	♆ 3° N
	25 17	-	☌ ♄ ☽	♄ 1°.1 N; Occ'n
Nov.	1 15	-	☌ ♀ ☉	Superior
	5 02	-	☌ ♂ ☽	♂ 3° S
	9 07	-	☌ ♃ ☽	♃ 1°.6 N
	10 09	-	☌ ♇ ☉	
	13 10	-	☌ ♂ *	♂ 6° N of Aldebaran
	17 03	-	☌ ☿ *	☿ 3° N of Antares
	18 15	-	☌ ☽ *	Antares 0°.7 S; Occ'n
	18 20	-	☌ ☿ ☽	☿ 1°.7 N
	20 04	-		♂ Closest approach to ⊕
	20 23	-	☌ ♅ ☽	♅ 1°.6 N
	21 10	-	☌ ♆ ☽	♆ 2° N
	22 04	-	☌ ♄ ☽	♄ 0°.6 N; Occ'n
	27 21	-	☍ ♂ ☉	
	30 13	-		♃ Stationary
Dec.	1 23	-	☌ ♂ ☽	♂ 3° S
	6 07	-		☿ Gr. Elong. 21° E of ☉
	6 16	-	☌ ♃ ☽	♃ 2° N
	10 08	-	☌ ☿ ♅	☿ 1°.3 S
	14 18	-		☿ Stationary
	15 21	-	☌ ☽ *	Antares 0°.7 S; Occ'n
	18 05	-	☌ ☿ ♅	☿ 0°.6 N
	18 18	-	☌ ♆ ☽	♆ 2° N
	18 23	-	☌ ☿ ♀	☿ 1°.4 N
	19 10	-	☌ ♀ ♅	♀ 0°.6 S
	19 15	-	☌ ♄ ☽	♄ 0°.2 N; Occ'n
	22 03 07			Winter Solstice; Winter begins, Northern Hemisphere
	23 03	-	☌ ♀ ♆	♀ 1°.8 S
	24 08	-	☌ ☿ ☉	Inferior
	29 01	-	☌ ♂ ☽	☿ 2° S
	31 16	-	☌ ♅ ☉	

Rising and Setting of Planets, 1990

Greenwich Mean Time (0 designates midnight)

Venus, 1990

		20° N. Latitude Rise	20° N. Latitude Set	30° N. Latitude Rise	30° N. Latitude Set	40° N. Latitude Rise	40° N. Latitude Set	50° N. Latitude Rise	50° N. Latitude Set	60° N. Latitude Rise	60° N. Latitude Set
Jan.	10	7:21	18:38	7:35	18:25	7:51	18:08	8:13	17:46	8:49	17:11
	20	6:16	17:35	6:28	17:22	6:43	17:07	7:04	16:47	7:37	16:14
	30	5:15	16:35	5:27	16:22	5:42	16:07	6:03	15:47	6:35	15:14
Feb.	9	4:29	15:49	4:42	15:36	4:58	15:20	5:19	14:59	6:58	13:22
	19	4:00	15:19	4:14	15:05	4:30	14:49	4:52	14:27	6:22	12:49
Mar.	1	3:43	15:01	3:57	14:48	4:13	14:31	4:36	14:08	5:45	12:15
	11	3:34	14:53	3:47	14:40	4:03	14:24	4:25	14:02	5:01	13:26
	21	3:28	14:51	3:41	14:39	3:56	14:24	4:16	14:04	4:48	13:32
	31	3:25	14:54	3:35	14:43	3:48	14:30	4:06	14:13	4:33	13:46
Apr.	10	3:22	14:59	3:30	14:51	3:40	14:41	3:54	14:27	4:14	14:07
	20	3:19	15:05	3:24	15:00	3:31	14:54	3:40	14:45	3:53	14:32
	30	3:16	15:13	3:18	15:11	3:21	15:08	9:14	15:05	3:29	15:01
May	10	3:12	15:21	3:11	15:23	3:10	15:24	3:07	15:27	3:04	15:31
	20	3:09	15:30	3:05	15:35	2:59	15:42	2:51	15:50	2:38	16:03
	30	3:07	15:41	2:59	15:49	2:49	16:00	2:34	16:14	2:12	16:37
June	9	3:07	15:52	2:55	16:04	2:40	16:19	2:20	16:40	1:48	17:13
	19	3:09	16:05	2:53	16:20	2:35	16:39	2:08	17:06	1:25	17:50
	29	3:13	16:18	2:55	16:36	2:33	16:59	2:01	17:31	1:07	18:25
July	9	3:20	16:32	3:00	16:52	2:35	17:18	1:59	17:54	0:56	18:57
	19	3:30	16:46	3:09	17:08	2:43	17:34	2:04	18:13	0:56	19:22
	29	3:43	16:59	3:22	17:20	2:55	17:47	2:17	18:25	1:08	19:34
Aug.	8	3:58	17:10	3:38	17:30	3:13	17:55	2:37	18:31	1:34	19:33
	18	4:13	17:18	3:56	17:36	3:33	17:58	3:02	18:29	2:08	19:22
	28	4:29	17:24	4:14	17:38	3:56	17:57	3:30	18:22	2:47	19:04
Sept.	7	4:44	17:27	4:33	17:38	4:19	17:51	3:59	18:10	3:29	18:40
	17	4:58	17:28	4:51	17:35	4:42	17:43	4:30	17:55	4:10	18:14
	27	5:12	17:27	5:09	17:30	5:05	17:34	5:00	17:39	4:51	17:47
Oct.	7	5:26	17:26	5:27	17:25	5:28	17:23	5:30	17:21	5:32	17:18
	17	5:40	17:25	5:45	17:20	5:52	17:13	6:00	17:04	6:14	16:50
	27	5:54	17:26	6:04	17:16	6:16	17:04	6:31	16:48	6:56	16:23
Nov.	6	6:10	17:29	6:23	17:15	6:40	16:58	7:03	16:35	7:40	15:58
	16	6:27	17:34	6:44	17:17	7:05	16:55	7:34	16:26	8:23	15:37
	26	6:44	17:42	7:04	17:22	7:29	16:58	8:04	16:22	9:04	15:22
Dec.	6	7:02	17:54	7:23	17:33	7:51	17:05	8:29	16:27	9:38	15:18

		20° N. Latitude		30° N. Latitude		40° N. Latitude		50° N. Latitude		60° N. Latitude	
		Rise	Set	Rise	Set	Rise	Set	Rise	Set	Rise	Set
	16	7:18	18:09	7:40	17:47	8:08	17:19	8:48	16:39	10:00	15:28
	26	7:32	18:26	7:54	18:05	8:21	17:38	8:59	17:00	10:06	15:53

Mars, 1990

		Rise	Set	Rise	Set	Rise	Set	Rise	Set	Rise	Set
Jan.	10	4:15	15:09	4:35	14:48	5:01	14:22	5:38	13:45	6:42	12:41
	20	4:07	14:59	4:29	14:38	4:56	14:11	5:34	13:32	6:42	12:25
	30	4:00	14:51	4:21	14:29	4:49	14:01	5:28	13:23	6:37	12:13
Feb.	9	3:52	14:43	4:13	14:21	4:40	13:54	5:19	13:15	6:28	12:07
	19	3:43	14:36	4:04	14:15	4:31	13:49	5:08	13:11	6:14	12:05
Mar.	1	3:34	14:30	3:54	14:10	4:19	13:44	4:55	13:09	5:57	12:07
	11	3:23	14:24	3:42	14:05	4:06	13:41	4:39	13:08	5:35	12:13
	21	3:12	14:18	3:30	14:01	3:51	13:39	4:21	13:09	5:11	12:20
	31	3:00	14:12	3:16	13:57	3:35	13:38	4:01	13:11	4:44	12:29
Apr.	10	2:47	14:06	3:01	13:52	3:17	13:36	3:39	13:14	4:15	12:38
	20	2:33	13:59	2:44	13:48	2:58	13:35	3:17	13:16	3:46	12:47
	30	2:19	13:52	2:27	13:44	2:38	13:33	2:53	13:19	3:15	12:56
May	10	2:03	13:45	2:10	13:39	2:17	13:31	2:28	13:21	2:44	13:05
	20	1:47	13:37	1:51	13:34	1:56	13:29	2:03	13:23	2:12	13:13
	30	1:31	13:29	1:33	13:28	1:34	13:26	1:37	13:24	1:40	13:21
June	9	1:14	13:21	1:14	13:22	1:12	13:23	1:11	13:25	1:08	13:28
	19	0:58	13:12	0:54	13:15	0:50	13:20	0:45	13:25	0:36	13:34
	29	0:41	13:03	0:35	13:09	0:28	13:16	0:19	13:25	0:04	13:40
July	9	0:23	12:53	0:16	13:01	0:06	13:11	23:51	13:24	23:29	13:45
	19	0:06	12:43	23:54	12:53	23:42	13:05	23:25	13:22	22:58	13:49
	29	23:47	12:32	23:35	12:44	23:20	12:58	23:00	13:18	22:27	13:51
Aug.	8	23:29	12:20	23:15	12:33	22:58	12:50	22:35	13:13	21:57	13:51
	18	23:10	12:06	22:55	12:21	22:36	12:40	22:10	13:06	21:26	13:49
	28	22:50	11:51	22:34	12:07	22:13	12:28	21:44	12:56	20:56	13:44
Sept.	7	22:29	11:33	22:11	11:51	21:49	12:13	21:18	12:44	20:26	13:36
	17	22:05	11:13	21:47	11:31	21:23	11:54	20:50	12:27	19:54	13:24
	27	21:38	10:49	21:19	11:08	20:55	11:32	20:20	12:07	19:21	13:06
Oct.	7	21:08	10:20	20:48	10:40	20:23	11:05	19:47	11:41	18:45	12:43
	17	20:32	9:47	20:12	10:07	19:46	10:33	19:09	11:10	18:04	12:15
	27	19:51	9:07	19:30	9:28	19:04	9:54	18:26	10:32	17:19	11:39
Nov.	6	19:03	8:21	18:42	8:42	18:15	9:08	17:37	9:47	16:29	10:55
	16	18:11	7:29	17:49	7:50	17:23	8:17	16:44	8:55	15:35	10:04
	26	17:15	6:33	16:54	6:54	16:28	7:21	15:50	7:59	14:41	9:07
Dec.	6	16:21	5:38	16:00	5:58	15:34	6:25	14:56	7:02	13:50	8:09
	16	15:30	4:46	15:10	5:06	14:44	5:32	14:07	6:09	13:02	7:14
	26	14:45	4:00	14:25	4:20	13:59	4:46	13:23	5:22	12:18	6:27

Jupiter, 1990

		Rise	Set	Rise	Set	Rise	Set	Rise	Set	Rise	Set
Jan.	10	16:19	5:38	15:57	6:00	15:29	6:28	14:50	7:07	13:38	8:19
	20	15:34	4:54	15:13	5:16	14:45	5:43	14:05	6:23	12:52	7:36
	30	14:51	4:11	14:29	4:32	14:01	5:00	13:21	5:40	12:09	6:53
Feb.	9	14:09	3:28	13:47	3:50	13:19	4:18	12:39	4:58	11:26	6:11
	19	13:28	2:48	13:06	3:09	12:38	3:37	11:58	4:17	10:45	5:30
Mar.	1	12:48	2:08	12:26	2:30	11:59	2:58	11:19	3:38	10:05	4:51
	11	12:10	1:30	11:48	1:52	11:21	2:20	10:40	3:00	9:27	4:14
	21	11:34	0:54	11:12	1:16	10:44	1:43	10:04	2:24	8:50	3:37
	31	10:58	0:18	10:36	0:40	10:09	1:08	9:28	1:48	8:15	3:02
Apr.	10	10:24	23:40	10:02	0:06	9:34	0:34	8:54	1:14	7:41	2:27
	20	9:51	23:07	9:29	23:29	9:01	23:57	8:21	0:40	7:08	1:54
	30	9:19	22:35	8:57	22:57	8:29	23:24	7:49	0:07	6:36	1:20
May	10	8:47	22:03	8:25	22:25	7:58	22:52	7:18	23:32	6:06	0:47
	20	8:16	21:32	7:55	21:53	7:27	22:21	6:48	23:00	5:36	0:15
	30	7:46	21:01	7:24	21:22	6:57	21:49	6:18	22:28	5:07	23:39
June	9	7:16	20:30	6:55	20:51	6:28	21:18	5:49	21:57	4:39	23:06
	19	6:46	19:59	6:25	20:20	5:59	20:47	5:20	21:25	4:12	22:33
	29	6:17	19:29	5:56	19:50	5:30	20:16	4:52	20:53	3:46	22:00
July	9	5:47	18:59	5:27	19:19	5:01	19:45	4:25	20:21	3:20	21:26
	19	5:18	18:28	4:58	18:48	4:33	19:14	3:57	19:49	2:54	20:52
	29	4:49	17:58	4:29	18:17	4:05	18:42	3:29	19:17	2:28	20:18
Aug.	8	4:20	17:27	4:00	17:46	3:36	18:10	3:02	18:45	2:03	19:44
	18	3:50	16:56	3:31	17:15	3:08	17:38	2:34	18:12	1:37	19:09
	28	3:20	16:25	3:02	16:43	2:39	17:06	2:06	17:38	1:11	18:34
Sept.	7	2:50	15:53	2:32	16:10	2:09	16:33	1:38	17:05	0:44	17:58
	17	2:19	15:20	2:01	15:38	1:40	16:00	1:09	16:30	0:17	17:22
	27	1:47	14:47	1:30	15:04	1:09	15:26	0:39	15:56	23:46	16:46
Oct.	7	1:15	14:14	0:58	14:30	0:38	14:51	0:08	15:20	23:17	16:09
	17	0:42	13:40	0:26	13:56	0:05	14:16	23:33	14:45	22:46	15:32
	27	0:08	13:04	23:48	13:20	23:28	13:40	23:00	14:08	22:14	14:55
Nov.	6	23:29	12:28	23:13	12:44	22:53	13:04	22:26	13:31	21:40	14:17
	16	22:52	11:51	22:36	12:07	22:17	12:26	21:50	12:54	21:04	13:39
	26	22:14	11:13	21:58	11:28	21:39	11:48	21:12	12:15	20:27	13:00
Dec.	6	21:34	10:34	21:19	10:49	20:59	11:09	20:32	11:36	19:47	12:21
	16	20:53	9:53	20:38	10:09	20:18	10:29	19:50	10:56	19:05	11:42
	26	20:11	9:11	19:55	9:27	19:35	9:47	19:07	10:15	18:21	11:02

		20° N. Latitude		30° N. Latitude		40° N. Latitude		50° N. Latitude		60° N. Latitude	
		Rise	Set	Rise	Set	Rise	Set	Rise	Set	Rise	Set

Saturn, 1990

		Rise	Set	Rise	Set	Rise	Set	Rise	Set	Rise	Set
Jan.	10	6:26	17:21	6:46	17:01	7:10	16:36	7:46	16:01	8:46	15:01
	20	5:51	16:47	6:11	16:27	6:36	16:03	7:10	15:28	8:10	14:28
	30	5:16	16:13	5:36	15:53	6:01	15:29	6:35	14:54	7:34	13:55
Feb.	9	4:42	15:39	5:01	15:19	5:25	14:55	6:00	14:21	6:58	13:22
	19	4:06	15:04	4:26	14:45	4:50	14:21	5:24	13:47	6:22	12:49
Mar.	1	3:31	14:29	3:50	14:10	4:14	13:46	4:48	13:12	5:45	12:15
	11	2:55	13:53	3:14	13:34	3:38	13:11	4:11	12:37	5:08	11:41
	21	2:19	13:17	2:38	12:59	3:01	12:35	3:34	12:02	4:30	11:06
	31	1:42	12:41	2:01	12:22	2:24	11:59	2:57	11:26	3:53	10:30
Apr.	10	1:04	12:04	1:23	11:45	1:46	11:22	2:19	10:49	3:15	9:54
	20	0:26	11:26	0:45	11:07	1:08	10:44	1:41	10:11	2:36	9:16
	30	23:44	10:47	0:06	10:28	0:30	10:05	1:02	9:33	1:57	8:38
May	10	23:04	10:08	23:23	9:49	23:46	9:26	0:23	8:53	1:18	7:58
	20	22:24	9:28	22:43	9:09	23:07	8:46	23:39	8:13	0:38	7:18
	30	21:44	8:47	22:03	8:28	22:26	8:05	22:59	7:32	23:55	6:36
June	9	21:03	8:06	21:22	7:47	21:45	7:23	22:18	6:50	23:14	5:54
	19	20:21	7:24	20:40	7:05	21:04	6:41	21:37	6:08	22:34	5:11
	29	19:39	6:41	19:58	6:22	20:22	5:58	20:56	5:25	21:53	4:28
July	9	18:57	5:59	19:16	5:40	19:41	5:15	20:14	4:42	21:12	3:44
	19	18:15	5:16	18:34	4:57	18:59	4:32	19:33	3:58	20:31	3:00
	29	17:33	4:34	17:52	4:14	18:17	3:50	18:51	3:15	19:50	2:17
Aug.	8	16:51	3:51	17:11	3:32	17:35	3:07	18:10	2:32	19:09	1:33
	18	16:09	3:09	16:29	2:50	16:54	2:25	17:29	1:50	18:28	0:50
	28	15:28	2:26	15:48	2:08	16:13	1:43	16:48	1:08	17:48	0:08
Sept.	7	14:48	1:47	15:07	1:27	15:32	1:02	16:07	0:27	17:08	23:23
	17	14:08	1:07	14:28	0:47	14:53	0:22	15:28	23:43	16:28	22:42
	27	13:28	0:27	13:48	0:07	14:13	23:39	14:48	23:03	15:49	22:03
Oct.	7	12:50	23:45	13:10	23:25	13:35	23:00	14:10	22:25	15:10	21:24
	17	12:12	23:07	12:32	22:47	12:56	22:22	13:32	21:47	14:32	20:47
	27	11:34	22:30	11:54	22:10	12:19	21:45	12:54	21:10	13:54	20:10
Nov.	6	10:57	21:53	11:17	21:34	11:42	21:09	12:17	20:34	13:17	19:34
	16	10:21	21:17	10:41	20:58	11:05	20:33	11:40	19:59	12:39	18:59
	26	9:45	20:42	10:05	20:22	10:29	19:58	11:04	19:24	12:02	18:25
Dec.	6	9:10	20:07	9:29	19:48	9:53	19:23	10:27	18:49	11:26	17:51
	16	8:35	19:32	8:54	19:13	9:18	18:49	9:52	18:16	10:49	17:18
	26	8:00	18:58	8:19	18:39	8:42	18:15	9:16	17:42	10:12	16:45

Moonrise Tonight

The idea of estimating the time of moonrise tonight may have scared you off in the past because you assumed that it involved a difficult and mysterious series of calculations. The actual process is quite easy to do, however, especially with the little pocket calculators that seem ubiquitous today. The first major step involves finding three numbers for your city obtained from the latitude and longitude figures listed on pages 264–265. If your city is not here, find the information from a map, atlas or other source. These answers are permanent and never need to be determined for that city again. You can write these numbers down and use them every year you stay in that city. The second step involves taking the correct four figures from the tables of moonrise and moonset for the date you want. The third major step involves adjusting this answer to standard time.

Let us determine the time for the rise of full moon in Joplin, Missouri, May 9, 1990.

First, in order to determine the 3 constant numbers for Joplin, find the latitude and longitude from the table on page 264–265.

I. Latitude: 37°05'26" north; longitude: 94°30'00" west from p. 264.

IA. Convert the Lat. and Long. to decimal numbers:
Lat.
26" ÷ 60 = 0.'4333.
5' + 0.'4333 = 5.'4333
5.'4333 ÷ 60 = 0.°0906
37° + 0.°0906 = 37.°0906 for the latitude.
Long.
30' ÷ 60 = 0.'5
94° + 0.°5 = 94.°5 for the longitude.

IB. Fraction between 30° and 40° that Joplin lies:
40° − 30° = 10°
37.°0906 − 30° = 7.°0906
7.°0906 ÷ 10° = .709

IC. Fraction of the world that Joplin lies west of Greenwich meridian:
94.°5 ÷ 360° = 0.2625

ID. Correction from local to standard time:
(Standard Time Meridian for Central Time is 90°.)
94.°5 − 90° = 4.°5 west of the standard me-

ridian, or later by 4 minutes for each degree.
4.5 × 4 = 18 minutes later than local time.

IE. These three numbers, IB, IC, and ID, are good for Joplin for all future rise and set calculations, and never have to be calculated again.

II. Find the time of moonrise for Joplin's latitude:

IIA. From the calendar page 256, find the four times of moonrise: for 30° and 40° for each date, May 9 and May 10.

	30°	40°
May 9	18:44	19:10
May 10	19:40	20:11

IIB. We want to find the time of moonrise at Joplin's latitude for both the 9th and the 10th. This time lies 0.709 (Ans. IB) times the difference between the rise times at 30° and 40° on each date:
For the 9th: 19:10 − 18:44 = 26 minutes
26 × 0.709 = 18.4 minutes
18:44 + 18 = 19:02 at Joplin's latitude, but in Greenwich, England.
For the 10th: 20:11 − 19:40 = 31 minutes
31 × 0.709 = 22 minutes
19:40 + 22 = 20:02.

IIC. Now take the proportion of the time that the earth turned between Greenwich and Joplin (Ans. IC):

    20:02 − 19:02 = 60 minutes
    60 × 0.2625 = 15.8 minutes
    19:02 + 16 = 19:18 local time of moonrise.

IID. Next correct for the standard meridian (Ans.

ID):

19:18 + 18 = 19:36 for the Standard time of moonrise, but daylight time makes us add another hour, so the clock should actually read 20:18 Central Daylight time May 9, 1990, for Joplin, Missouri.

Star Tables

These tables include stars of visual magnitude 2.5 and brighter. Co-ordinates are for mid-1990. Where no parallax figures are given, the trigonometric parallax figure is smaller than the margin for error and the distance given is obtained by indirect methods. Stars of variable magnitude designated by v.

To find the time when the star is on meridian, subtract R.A.M.S. of the sun table on page 238 from the star's right ascension, first adding 24h to the latter, if necessary. Mark this result P.M., if less than 12h; but if greater than 12, subtract 12h and mark the remainder A.M.

Star	Magni-tude	Paral-lax "	Light yrs.	Right ascen. h. m.	Decli-nation ° '	Star	Magni-tude	Paral-lax "	Light yrs.	Right ascen. h. m.	Decli-nation ° '
α Andromedae (Alpheratz)	2.06	0.02	90	0 07.9	29 02	β Ursae Majoris (Merak)	2.37	0.04	78	11 01.3	56 26
β Cassiopeiae	2.27v	0.07	45	0 08.7	59 06	α Ursae Majoris (Dubhe)	1.79	0.03	105	11 03.2	61 48
α Phoenicis	2.39	0.04	93	0 25.8	−42 21	β Leonis (Denebola)	2.14	0.08	43	11 48.6	14 38
α Cassiopeiae (Schedir)	2.23	0.01	150	0 40.0	56 29	γ Ursae Majoris (Phecda)	2.44	0.02	90	11 53.4	53 45
β Ceti	2.04	0.06	57	0 43.1	−18 02	α Crucis	1.58		370	12 26.1	−63 03
γ Cassiopeiae	2.47v	0.03	96	0 56.1	60 40	γ Crucis	1.63		220	12 30.6	−57 04
β Andromedae	2.06	0.04	76	1 09.2	35 34	γ Centauri	2.17		160	12 41.0	−48 55
α Eridani (Achernar)	0.46	0.02	118	1 37.4	−57 17	β Crucis	1.25v		490	12 47.2	−59 39
γ Andromedae	2.26		260	2 03.3	42 17	ε Ursae Majoris (Alioth)	1.77v	0.01	68	12 53.6	56 01
α Arietis	2.00	0.04	76	2 06.6	23 25	ζ Ursae Majoris (Mizar)	2.05	0.04	88	13 23.6	54 59
ο Ceti	2.00v	0.01	103	2 18.9	−3 01	α Virginis (Spica)	0.97v	0.02	220	13 24.7	−11 07
α Ursae Min. (Pole Star)	2.02v		680	2 20.9	89 13	ε Centauri	2.30v		570	13 39.3	−53 25
β Persei (Algol)	2.12v	0.03	105	3 07.5	40 55	η Ursae Majoris (Alkaid)	1.86		210	13 47.2	49 22
α Persei	1.80	0.03	570	3 23.6	49 50	β Centauri	0.61v	0.02	490	14 03.2	−60 20
α Tauri (Aldebaran)	0.85v	0.05	68	4 35.4	16 30	θ Centauri	2.06	0.06	55	14 06.1	−36 20
β Orionis (Rigel)	0.12v		900	5 14.1	−8 13	α Bootis (Arcturus)	−0.04	0.09	36	14 15.2	19 14
α Aurigae (Capella)	0.08	0.07	45	5 16.0	45 59	η Centauri	2.31v		390	14 34.9	−42 07
γ Orionis (Bellatrix)	1.64	0.03	470	5 24.6	6 21	α Centauri	−0.01	0.75	4.3	14 38.9	−60 48
β Tauri (El Nath)	1.65	0.02	300	5 25.7	28 36	α Lupi	2.30v		430	14 41.3	−47 21
δ Orionis	2.23v		1500	5 31.5	0 18	ε Bootis	2.40	0.01	103	14 44.6	27 07
ε Orionis	1.70		1600	5 35.7	−1 12	β Ursae Minoris	2.08	0.03	105	14 50.8	74 12
ζ Orionis	2.05	0.02	1600	5 40.3	−1 57	α Coronae Borealis	2.23v	0.04	76	15 34.3	26 45
κ Orionis	2.06	0.01	2100	5 47.3	−9 40	δ Scorpii	2.32		590	15 59.8	−22 36
α Orionis (Betelgeuse)	0.50v		520	5 54.6	7 24	α Scorpii (Antares)	0.96v	0.02	520	16 28.9	−26 25
β Aurigae	1.90	0.04	88	5 58.8	44 57	α Trianguli Australis	1.92	0.02	82	16 47.7	−69 01
β Canis Majoris	1.98	0.01	750	6 22.3	−17 57	ε Scorpii	2.29	0.05	66	16 49.6	−34 17
α Carinae (Canopus)	−0.72	0.02	98	6 23.7	−52 41	η Ophiuchi	2.43	0.05	69	17 09.9	−15 43
γ Geminorum	1.93	0.03	105	6 37.2	16 25	λ Scorpii	1.63v		310	17 33.0	−37 06
α Canis Majoris (Sirius)	−1.46	0.38	8.7	6 44.7	−16 42	α Ophiuchi	2.08	0.06	58	17 34.5	12 34
ε Canis Majoris	1.50		680	6 58.2	−28 57	θ Scorpii	1.87	0.02	650	17 36.7	−42 60
δ Canis Majoris	1.86		2100	7 08.0	−26 23	κ Scorpii	2.41v		470	17 41.9	−39 02
η Canis Majoris	2.44		2700	7 23.7	−29 17	γ Draconis	2.23	0.02	108	17 56.4	51 29
α Geminorum (Castor)	1.99	0.07	45	7 34.0	31 55	ε Sagittarii	1.85	0.02	124	18 23.6	−34 23
α Canis Minoris (Procyon)	0.38	0.29	11.3	7 38.8	5 15	α Lyrae (Vega)	0.03	0.12	26.5	18 36.7	38 46
β Geminorum (Pollux)	1.14	0.09	35	7 44.7	28 03	σ Sagittarii	2.02		300	18 54.7	−26 19
ζ Puppis	2.25		2400	8 03.2	−39 59	α Aquilae (Altair)	0.77	0.20	16.5	19 50.4	8 51
γ Velorum	1.82		520	8 09.2	−47 19	γ Cygni	2.20		750	20 21.9	40 13
ε Carinae	1.86		340	8 22.3	−59 29	α Pavonis	1.94		310	20 25.0	−56 46
δ Velorum	1.96	0.04	76	8 44.4	−54 41	α Cygni (Deneb)	1.25		1600	20 41.1	45 15
λ Velorum	2.21	0.02	750	9 07.6	−43 24	ε Cygni	2.46	0.04	74	20 45.9	33 56
β Carinae	1.68	0.04	86	9 13.0	−69 41	α Cephei	2.44	0.06	52	21 18.4	62 33
ι Carinae	2.25		750	9 16.8	−59 14	ε Pegasi	2.39		780	21 43.7	9 50
κ Velorum	2.50	0.01	470	9 21.8	−54 58	α Gruis	1.74	0.05	64	22 07.7	−47 00
α Hydrae	1.98	0.02	94	9 27.1	−8 37	β Gruis	2.11v		280	22 42.1	−46 56
α Leonis (Regulus)	1.35	0.04	84	10 07.9	12 01	α Piscis Austrinis (Fomalhaut)	1.16	0.14	22.6	22 57.2	−29 40
γ Leonis	1.90	0.02	90	10 19.5	19 56	β Pegasi	2.42v	0.02	210	23 03.3	28 02
						α Pegasi	2.49	0.03	109	23 04.3	15 09

Constellations

Culturally, constellations are imagined patterns among the stars that, in some cases, have been recognized through millenia of tradition. In the early days of astronomy, knowledge of the constellations was necessary in order to function as an astronomer. For today's astronomers, constellations are simply areas on the entire sky in which interesting objects await observation and interpretation.

Because western culture has prevailed in establishing modern science, equally viable and interesting constellations and celestial traditions of other cultures (of Asia or Africa, for example) are not well known outside of their regions of origin. Even the patterns with which we are most familiar today have undergone considerable change over the centuries, because the western heritage embraces teachings of cultures disparate in time as well as place.

Today, students of the sky the world over recognize 88 constellations that cover the entire celestial sphere. Many of these have their origins in ancient days; many are "modern," contrived out of unformed stars by astronomers a few centuries ago. Unformed stars were those usually too faint or inconveniently placed to be included in depicting the more prominent constellations. When astronomers began to travel to South Africa in the 16th and 17th centuries, they found a sky that itself was unformed, and showing numerous brilliant stars. Thus, we find constellations in the southern hemisphere like the "air pump," the "microscope," the "furnace," and other technological marvels of the time, as well as some arguably traditional forms, such as the "fly."

Many of the commonly recognized constellations had their origins in ancient Asia Minor—Syria, Babylon, etc. These were adopted by the Greeks and Romans who translated their names and stories into their own languages, some details being modified in the process. After the declines of these cultures, most such knowledge entered oral tradition, or remained hidden in monastic libraries. Beginning in the 8th century, the Moslem explosion spread through the Mediterranean world. Wherever possible, everything was translated into Arabic to be taught in the universities the Moslems established all over their new-found world.

In the 13th century, Alphonsus XX of Spain, an avid student of astronomy, succeeded in having Claudius Ptolemy's *Almagest*, as its Arabian title was known, translated into Latin. It thus became widely available to European scholars. In the process, the constellation names were translated, but the star names were retained in their Arabic forms. Transliterating Arabic into the Roman alphabet has never been an exact art, so many of the star names we use today only "seem" Arabic to all but scholars.

Names of stars often indicated what parts of the traditional figures they represented: Deneb, the tail of the swan; Betelgeuse, the armpit of the giant. Thus, the names were an indication of the position in the sky of a particular star, provided one recognized the traditional form of the mythic figure.

In English, usage of the Latin names for the constellations couples often inconceivable creatures, represented in unimaginable configurations, with names that often seem unintelligible. Avoiding traditional names, astronomers may designate the brighter stars in a constellation with Greek letters, usually in order of brightness. Thus, the "alpha star" is often the brightest star of that constellation. The "of" implies possession, so the genetive (possessive) form of the constellation name is used, as in Alpha Orionis, the first star of Orion (Betelgeuse). Astronomers usually use a 3-letter form for the constellation name, understanding it to be read as either the nominative or genitive case of the name.

Until the 1920's, astronomers used curved boundaries for the constellation areas. As these were rather arbitrary at best, the International Astronomical Union adopted boundaries that ran due north-south and east-west, filling the sky much as the contiguous states fill up the area of the "lower 48" United States.

Within these boundaries, and occasionally crossing them, popular "asterisms" are recognized: the Big Dipper is a small part of Ursa Major, the big bear; the Sickle is the traditional head and mane of Leo, the lion; one of the horntips of Taurus, the bull, properly belongs to Auriga, the charioteer; the northeast star of the Great Square of Pegasus is Alpha Andromedae.

It is unlikely that further change will occur in the realm of the celestial constellations.

Name	Genitive	Abbreviation	Meaning
Andromeda	Andromedae	And	Chained Maiden
Antlia	Antliae	Ant	Air Pump
Apus	Apodis	Aps	Bird of Paradise
Aquarius	Aquarii	Aqr	Water Bearer
Aquila	Aquilae	Aql	Eagle
Ara	Arae	Ara	Altar
Aries	Arietis	Ari	Ram
Auriga	Aurigae	Aur	Charioteer
Bootes	Bootis	Boo	Herdsmen
Caelum	Caeli	Cae	Chisel
Camelopardalis	Camelopardalis	Cam	Giraffe
Cancer	Cancri	Cnc	Crab
Canes Venatici	Canum Venaticorum	CVn	Hunting Dogs
Canis Major	Canis Majoris	CMa	Great Dog
Canis Minor	Canis Minoris	CMi	Little Dog
Capricornus	Capricorni	Cap	Sea-goat
Carina	Carinae	Car	Keel
Cassiopeia	Cassiopeiae	Cas	Queen
Centaurus	Centauri	Cen	Centaur
Cepheus	Cephei	Cep	King
Cetus	Ceti	Cet	Whale
Chamaeleon	Chamaeleontis	Cha	Chameleon
Circinus	Circini	Cir	Compasses (art)
Columba	Columbae	Col	Dove
Coma Berenices	Comae Berenices	Com	Berenice's Hair
Corona Australis	Coronae Australis	CrA	Southern Crown
Corona Borealis	Coronae Borealis	CrB	Northern Crown
Corvus	Corvi	Crv	Crow
Crater	Crateris	Crt	Cup
Crux	Crucis	Cru	Cross (southern)
Cygnus	Cygni	Cyg	Swan
Delphinus	Delphini	Del	Dolphin
Dorado	Doradus	Dor	Goldfish
Draco	Draconis	Dra	Dragon
Equuleus	Equulei	Equ	Little Horse
Eridanus	Eridani	Eri	River
Fornax	Fornacis	For	Furnace
Gemini	Geminorum	Gem	Twins
Grus	Gruis	Gru	Crane (bird)
Hercules	Herculis	Her	Hercules
Horologium	Horologii	Hor	Clock
Hydra	Hydrae	Hya	Water Snake (female)
Hydrus	Hydri	Hyi	Water Snake (male)
Indus	Indi	Ind	Indian
Lacerta	Lacertae	Lac	Lizard
Leo	Leonis	Leo	Lion
Leo Minor	Leonis Minoris	LMi	Little Lion
Lepus	Leporis	Lep	Hare
Libra	Librae	Lib	Balance
Lupus	Lupi	Lup	Wolf
Lynx	Lyncis	Lyn	Lynx
Lyra	Lyrae	Lyr	Lyre
Mensa	Mensae	Men	Table Mountain
Microscopium	Microscopii	Mic	Microscope
Monoceros	Monocerotis	Mon	Unicorn
Musca	Muscae	Mus	Fly
Norma	Normae	Nor	Square (rule)
Octans	Octantis	Oct	Octant
Ophiuchus	Ophiuchi	Oph	Serpent Bearer
Orion	Orionis	Ori	Hunter
Pavo	Pavonis	Pav	Peacock
Pegasus	Pegasi	Peg	Flying Horse
Perseus	Persei	Per	Hero
Phoenix	Phoenicis	Phe	Phoenix
Pictor	Pictoris	Pic	Painter
Pisces	Piscium	Psc	Fishes
Piscis Austrinus	Piscis Austrini	PsA	Southern Fish
Puppis	Puppis	Pup	Stern (deck)

Name	Genitive	Abbreviation	Meaning	Name	Genitive	Abbreviation	Meaning
Pyxis	Pyxidis	Pyx	Compass (sea)	Triangulum	Trianguli	Tri	Triangle
Reticulum	Reticuli	Ret	Reticle	Triangulum Australe	Trianguli Australis	TrA	Southern Triangle
Sagitta	Sagittae	Sge	Arrow				
Sagittarius	Sagittarii	Sgr	Archer	Tucana	Tucanae	Tuc	Toucan
Scorpius	Scorpii	Sco	Scorpion	Ursa Major	Ursae Majoris	UMa	Great Bear
Sculptor	Sculptoris	Scl	Sculptor	Ursa Minor	Ursae Minoris	UMi	Little Bear
Scutum	Scuti	Sct	Shield	Vela	Velorum	Vel	Sail
Serpens	Serpentis	Ser	Serpent	Virgo	Virginis	Vir	Maiden
Sextans	Sextantis	Sex	Sextant	Volans	Volantis	Vol	Flying Fish
Taurus	Tauri	Tau	Bull	Vulpecula	Vulpeculae	Vul	Fox
Telescopium	Telescopii	Tel	Telescope				

Aurora Borealis and Aurora Australis.

The Aurora Borealis, also called the Northern Lights, is a broad display of rather faint light in the northern skies at night. The Aurora Australis, a similar phenomenon, appears at the same time in southern skies. The aurora appears in a wide variety of forms. Sometimes it is seen as a quiet glow, almost foglike in character; sometimes as vertical streamers in which there may be considerable motion; sometimes as a series of luminous expanding arcs. There are many colors, with white, yellow, and red predominating.

The auroras are most vivid and most frequently seen at about 20 degrees from the magnetic poles, along the northern coast of the North American continent and the eastern part of the northern coast of Europe. They have been seen as far south as Key West and as far north as Australia and New Zealand, but rarely.

While the cause of the auroras is not known beyond question, there does seem to be a definite correlation between auroral displays and sun-spot activity. It is thought that atomic particles expelled from the sun by the forces that cause solar flares speed through space at velocities of 400 to 600 miles per second. These particles are entrapped by the earth's magnetic field, forming what are termed the Van Allen belts. The encounter of these clouds of the solar wind with the earth's magnetic field weakens the field so that previously trapped particles are allowed to impact the upper atmosphere. The collisions between solar and terrestrial atoms result in the glow in the upper atmosphere called the aurora. The glow may be vivid where the lines of magnetic force converge near the magnetic poles.

The auroral displays appear at heights ranging from 50 to about 600 miles and have given us a means of estimating the extent of the earth's atmosphere.

The auroras are often accompanied by magnetic storms whose forces, also guided by the lines of force of the earth's magnetic field, disrupt electrical communication.

Eclipses, 1990

(E.S.T.)

There are four eclipses, two of the sun and two of the moon.

I. The first eclipse is an annular eclipse of the sun, January 26. The Partial phases are visible generally throughout Antarctica except the shore on the Indian Ocean, from Cape Horn, Chile, Argentina, Uruguay, Paraguay, southern Bolivia, and southwestern Brazil. The line of central eclipse (annularity) begins on the Antarctic Continent, approximately 71 degrees south latitude, and 74 degrees east longitude, swerving southward then northward into the South Atlantic, where it ends.

Circumstances of the Eclipse

Eclipse begins	Jan 26 12:13 pm EST
Central eclipse begins	1:55
Greatest eclipse	2:30
Central eclipse ends	3:06
Eclipse ends	4:48

Duration at Greatest eclipse: 2 minutes 0 seconds.

II The second eclipse is a total eclipse of the moon, February 9. The beginning of the umbral phase is generally visible in New Zealand, Australia, all of Asia, western Pacific Ocean, Alaska, Arctic regions, Europe except the Iberian peninsula, Africa except the northwest extension and the southwest coast, Indian Ocean, and Wilkes Land. The end is generally visible in the western half of Australia, Asia, Philippine Sea, Arctic regions, Greenland, Europe, Africa, eastern Atlantic Ocean, Indian Ocean, and portions of Antarctica.

Circumstances of the Eclipse

Moon enters penumbra	Feb 9 11:20 am EST
Moon enters umbra	12:29 pm
Moon enters totality	1:49
Middle of eclipse	2:11
Moon leaves totality	2:33
Moon leaves umbra	3:54
Moon leaves penumbra	5:03

Magnitude of the eclipse: 1.080.

III The third eclipse is a total eclipse of the sun, July 21/22.

The partial phases are generally visible throughout Siberia, northeast Asia, northern Greenland, northern Canada except the Ungava peninsula, and Alaska. The line of central eclipse (totality) begins in southern Finland, moves along the northern coast of Siberia, crossing the central Aleutian Islands, and ends northeast of Hawaii.

Circumstances of the Eclipse

Eclipse begins	July 21 7:40 pm EST
Central eclipse begins	8:53
Central eclipse, local apparent noon	9:37
Central eclipse ends	11:11
Eclipse ends	July 22 12:24 am

Maximum duration: 2 minutes 36.0 seconds.

IV The fourth eclipse is a partial eclipse of the moon, August 6. The beginning of the umbral phase is generally visible in Antarctica, the Pacific Ocean, California, southern Alaska, eastern Siberia and southeastern Asia, eastern Indian Ocean, Australia, and New Zealand. The end is generally visible in Antarctica, western Pacific Ocean, all of Asia except the west, southern half of the Middle East, east coast of Africa, Indian Ocean, Australia, and New Zealand.

Circumstances of the Eclipse

Moon enters penumbra   August   6 6:30 am   EST

Moon enters umbra	7:44
Middle of the eclipse	9:12
Moon leaves umbra	10:40
Moon leaves penumbra	11:55

Magnitude of the eclipse: 0.682.

The Planets and the Solar System

Planet	Mean daily motion "	Orbital velocity miles per sec.	Sidereal revolution days	Synodical revolution days	Dist. from sun in millions of mi. Max.	Dist. from sun in millions of mi. Min.	Dist. from Earth in millions of mi. Max.	Dist. from Earth in millions of mi. Min.	Light at[1] peri-helion	Light at[1] aphe-lion
Mercury . . .	14732	29.75	88.0	115.9	43.4	28.6	136	50	10.58	4.59
Venus . . .	5768	21.76	224.7	583.9	67.7	66.8	161	25	1.94	1.89
Earth	3548	18.51	365.3	—	94.6	91.4	—	—	1.03	0.97
Mars	1886	14.99	687.0	779.9	155.0	128.5	248	35	0.524	0.360
Jupiter . . .	299	8.12	4332.1	398.9	507.0	460.6	600	368	0.0408	0.0336
Saturn . . .	120	5.99	10825.9	378.1	937.5	838.4	1031	745	0.01230	0.00984
Uranus . .	42	4.23	30676.1	369.7	1859.7	1669.3	1953	1606	0.00300	0.00250
Neptune . .	21	3.38	59911.1	367.5	2821.7	2760.4	2915	2667	0.00114	0.00109
Pluto	14	2.95	90824.2	366.7	4551.4	2756.4	4644	2663	0.00114	0.00042

1. Light at perihelion and aphelion is solar illumination in units of mean illumination at Earth.

Planet	Mean longitude of:[*] ascending node ° ' "	Mean longitude of:[*] perihelion ° ' "	Inclination[*] of orbit to ecliptic ° ' "	Mean distance[**]	Eccentricity[*] of orbit	Mean longitude at the epoch[*] ° ' "
Mercury. . . .	48 11 46	77 16 48	7 00 17	0.387099	0.205629	211 23 37
Venus.	76 34 37	131 37 12	3 23 41	0.723327	0.006792	21 47 25
Earth	— — —	102 45 25	— — —	0.999999	0.016732	335 27 03
Mars	49 28 23	335 51 43	1 50 59	1.523652	0.093273	343 25 58
Jupiter . . .	100 22 23	15 30 22	1 18 18	5.20316	0.048191	49 52 10
Saturn . . .	113 33 25	91 42 43	2 29 13	9.52355	0.054690	271 13 10
Uranus . . .	73 58 52	169 15 36	0 46 21	19.1690	0.047313	264 35 32
Neptune . . .	131 40 48	43 57 36	1 46 13	30.0468	0.010382	280 07 11
Pluto	110 07 08	223 57 04	17 08 44	39.3395	0.246171	222 18 01

*Consistent for the standard Epoch: 1988 Aug. 27 Ephemeris Time **Astronomical units

Sun and planets	Semi-diameter at unit distance "	Semi-diameter at mean least dist. "	in miles mean s.d.	Volume ⊕=1.	Mass. ⊕=1.	Den-sity ⊕=1.	Sidereal period of rotation d.	Sidereal period of rotation h.	Sidereal period of rotation m.	Sidereal period of rotation s.	Gravi-ty at sur-face ⊕=1.	Re-flect-ing power Pct.	Prob-able tem-per-ature °F.
Sun	959.62	—	432560	1303730	332830	0.26	24	16	48	27.9	—	—	+ 10,000
Mercury . . .	3.37	5.5	1515	0.0559	0.0553	0.99	58	21	58		0.37	0.06	+ 620
Venus	8.34	30.1	3760	0.8541	0.8150	0.95	243	R			0.88	0.72	+ 900
Earth	—	—	3963	1.000	1.000	1.00		23	56	4.1	1.00	0.39	+ 72
Moon	2.40	932.4	1080	0.020	0.0123	0.62	27	7	43		0.17	0.07	— 10
Mars	4.69	8.95	2108.4	0.1506	0.1074	0.71		24	37	23	0.38	0.16	— 10
Jupiter . . .	98.35	23.4	44362	1403	317.83	0.23		9	3	30	2.64	0.70	— 240
Saturn . . .	82.83	9.7	37280	832	95.16	0.11		10	30		1.15	0.75	— 300
Uranus . . .	35.4	1.9	15800	63	14.50	0.23		15	36	R	1.15	0.90	— 340
Neptune . . .	33.4	1.2	15100	55	17.20	0.31		18	26		1.12	0.82	— 370
Pluto*	1.9	0.05	930	0.01	0.0025	0.25	6	9	17		0.04	0.14	?	?

*Observers at the U.S. Naval Observatory have derived values similar to these after having discovered that Pluto has a satellite. It apparently revolves about Pluto in a period equal to Pluto's rotation period. (R) retrograde of Venus and Uranus.

Telescopes

Most of the world's major astronomical installations are in the northern hemisphere, while many of astronomy's major problems are found in the southern sky. This imbalance has long been recognized and is being remedied.

In the northern hemisphere the largest reflector is the 236-inch mirror at the Special Astrophysical Observatory in the Caucasus in the Soviet Union. The largest reflectors in the U.S. include 3 in California: at Palomar Mtn., 200 inches; at Lick Observatory, Mt. Hamilton, 120 inches; and at Mt. Wilson Observatory, 100 inches. Also in the U.S. are the Multiple Mirror Telescope (MMT) at Mt. Hopkins Observatory in Amado, AZ, which is a 176-inch single mirror reflector, a 158-inch reflector at Kitt Peak, Arizona, dedicated in June 1973, and a 107-inch telescope at the McDonald Observatory on Mt. Locke in Texas. A telescope at the Crimean Astrophysical Observatory in the Soviet Union has a 104-inch mirror.

Placed in service in 1975 were three large reflectors for the southern hemisphere. Associated Universities for Research in Astronomy (AURA), the operating organization of Kitt Peak National Observatory, dedicated the 158-inch reflector (twin of the telescope on Kitt Peak) at Cerro Tololo International Observatory, Chile; the European Southern Observatory has a 141-inch reflector at La Silla, Chile; and the Anglo-Australian telescope, 152 inches in diameter, is at Siding Spring Observatory in Australia.

Optical Telescopes

Optical astronomical telescopes are of two kinds, refracting and reflecting. In the first, light passes through a lens which brings the light rays into focus, where the image may be examined after being magnified by a second lens, the eye-piece, or directly photographed.

The reflector consists of a concave parabolic mirror, generally of Pyrex or now of a relatively heat insensitive material, cervit, coated with silver or aluminum, which reflects the light rays back toward the upper end of the telescope, where they are either magnified and observed by the eye-piece or, as in the case of the refractors, photographed. In most reflecting telescopes, the light is reflected again by a secondary mirror and comes to a focus after passing through a hole in the side of the telescope, where the eye-piece or camera is located, or after passing through a hole in the center of the primary mirror.

The Sun

The sun, the controlling body of our solar system, is a star whose dimensions cause it to be classified among stars as average in size, temperature, and brightness. Its proximity to the earth makes it appear to us as tremendously large and bright. A series of thermo-nuclear reactions involving the atoms of the elements of which it is composed produces the heat and light that make life possible on earth.

The sun has a diameter of 864,000 miles and is distant, on the average, 92,900,000 miles from the earth. It is 1.41 times as dense as water. The light of the sun reaches the earth in 499.012 seconds or slightly more than 8 minutes. The average solar surface temperature has been measured by several indirect methods which agree closely on a value of 6,000° Kelvin or about 10,000° F. The interior temperature of the sun is about 35,000,000 F.°.

When sunlight is analyzed with a spectroscope, it is found to consist of a continuous spectrum composed of all the colors of the rainbow in order, crossed by many dark lines. The "absorption lines" are produced by gaseous materials in the atmosphere of the sun. More than 60 of the natural terrestrial elements have been identified in the sun, all in gaseous form because of the intense heat of the sun.

Spheres and Corona

The radiating surface of the sun is called the **photosphere**, and just above it is the **chromosphere**. The chromosphere is visible to the naked eye only at times of total solar eclipses, appearing then to be a pinkish-violet layer with occasional great prominences projecting above its general level. With proper instruments the chromosphere can be seen or photographed whenever the sun is visible without waiting for a total eclipse. Above the chromosphere is the **corona**, also visible to the naked eye only at times of total eclipse. Instruments also permit the brighter portions of the corona to be studied whenever conditions are favorable. The pearly light of the corona surges millions of miles from the sun. Iron, nickel, and calcium are believed to be principal contributors to the composition of the corona, all in a state of extreme attenuation and high ionization that indicates temperatures on the order of a million degrees Fahrenheit.

Sunspots

There is an intimate connection between sunspots and the corona. At times of low sunspot activity, the fine streamers of the corona will be much longer above the sun's equator than over the polar regions of the sun, while during high sunspot activity, the corona extends fairly evenly outward from all regions of the sun, but to a much greater distance in space. Sunspots are dark, irregularly-shaped regions whose diameters may reach tens of thousands of miles. The average life of a sunspot group is from two to three weeks, but there have been groups that have lasted for more than a year, being carried repeatedly around as the sun rotated upon its axis. The record for the duration of a sunspot is 18 months. Sunspots reach a low point every 11.3 years, with a peak of activity occurring irregularly between two successive minima.

The sun is 400,000 times as bright as the full moon and gives the earth 6 million times as much light as do all the other stars put together. Actually, most of the stars that can be easily seen on any clear night are brighter than the sun.

The Zodiac

The sun's apparent yearly path among the stars is known as the **ecliptic**. The zone 16° wide, 8° on each side of the ecliptic, is known as the **zodiac**. Inside of this zone are the apparent paths of the sun, moon, earth, and major planets. Beginning at the point on the ecliptic which marks the position of the sun at the vernal equinox, and thence proceeding eastward, the zodiac is divided into twelve signs of 30° each, as shown herewith.

These signs are named from the twelve constellations of the zodiac with which the signs coincided in the time of the astronomer Hipparchus, about 2,000 years ago. Owing to the precession of the equinoxes, that is to say, to the retrograde motion of the equinoxes along the ecliptic, each sign in the zodiac has, in the course of 2,000 years, moved backward 30° into the constellation west of it; so that the sign Aries is now in the constellation Pisces, and so on. The vernal equinox will move from Pisces into Aquarius about the middle of the 26th century. The signs of the zodiac with their Latin and English names are as follows:

Spring	1.	♈ Aries.	The Ram.
	2.	♉ Taurus.	The Bull.
	3.	♊ Gemini.	The Twins.
Summer	4.	♋ Cancer.	The Crab.
	5.	♌ Leo.	The Lion.
	6.	♍ Virgo.	The Virgin.
Autumn	7.	♎ Libra.	The Balance.
	8.	♏ Scorpius.	The Scorpion.
	9.	♐ Sagittarius.	The Archer.
Winter	10.	♑ Capricorn.	The Goat.
	11.	♒ Aquarius.	The Water Bearer.
	12.	♓ Pisces.	The Fishes.

Moon's Perigee and Apogee, 1990

Perigee						Apogee					
Date	GMT	EST	Date	GMT	EST	Date	GMT	EST	Date	GMT	EST
Jan....	7	19	14	Apr....	25	17	12	Jan...	19	16	11	May...	10	0	19*
Feb....	2	3	22*	May...	24	3	22*	Feb...	16	13	8	June...	6	4	23*
Feb...	28	8	3	June...	21	11	6	Mar...	16	8	3	July...	3	16	11
Mar...	28	8	3					Apr...	12	20	15				

(continued)

Perigee						**Apogee**				
Date	GMT	EST	Date	GMT	EST	Date	GMT	EST	Date	GMT	EST
July. . . 19	11	6	Nov. . . 3	23	18	July. . . 31	8	3	Oct. . . 22	16	11
Aug. . . 15	10	5	Dec. . . 2	11	6	Aug. . . 28	3	22*	Nov. . . 19	3	22*
Sept. . . 9	11	6	Dec. . . 31	0	19*	Sept. . . 24	22	17	Dec. . . 16	4	23*
Oct. . . 6	18	13									

*Previous day

Astronomical Constants; Speed of Light

The following were adopted in 1968, in accordance with the resolutions and recommendations of the International Astronomical Union (Hamburg 1964): Speed of light, 299,792.5 kilometers per second, or about 186,282.3976 statute miles per second; solar parallax, 8″.794; constant of nutation, 9″.210; and constant of aberration, 20″.496.

The Moon

The moon completes a circuit around the earth in a period whose mean or average duration is 27 days 7 hours 43.2 minutes. This is the moon's sidereal period. Because of the motion of the moon in common with the earth around the sun, the mean duration of the lunar month — the period from one new moon to the next new moon — is 29 days 12 hours 44.05 minutes. This is the moon's synodical period.

The mean distance of the moon from the earth according to the American Ephemeris is 238,857 miles. Because the orbit of the moon about the earth is not circular but elliptical, however, the maximum distance from the earth that the moon may reach is 252,710 miles and the least distance is 221,463 miles. All distances are from the center of one object to the center of the other.

The moon's diameter is 2,160 miles. If we deduct the radius of the moon, 1,080 miles, and the radius of the earth, 3,963 miles from the minimum distance or perigee, given above, we shall have for the nearest approach of the bodies' surfaces 216,420 miles.

The moon rotates on its axis in a period of time exactly equal to its sidereal revolution about the earth — 27.321666 days. The moon's revolution about the earth is irregular because of its elliptical orbit. The moon's rotation, however, is regular and this, together with the irregular revolution, produces what is called "libration in longitude" which permits us to see first farther around the east side and then farther around the west side of the moon. The moon's variation north or south of the ecliptic permits us to see farther over first one pole and then the other of the moon and this is "libration in latitude." These two libration effects permit us to see a total of about 60% of the moon's surface over a period of time. The hidden side of the moon was photographed in 1959 by the Soviet space vehicle Lunik III. Since then many excellent pictures of nearly all of the moon's surface have been transmitted to earth by Lunar Orbiters launched by the U.S.

The tides are caused mainly by the moon, because of its proximity to the earth. The ratio of the tide-raising power of the moon to that of the sun is 11 to 5.

Harvest Moon and Hunter's Moon

The Harvest Moon, the full moon nearest the Autumnal Equinox, ushers in a period of several successive days when the moon rises soon after sunset. This phenomenon gives farmers in temperate latitudes extra hours of light in which to harvest their crops before frost and winter come. The 1990 Harvest Moon falls on Oct. 4 GMT. Harvest moon in the south temperate latitudes falls on Mar. 11.

The next full moon after Harvest Moon is called the Hunter's Moon, accompanied by a similar phenomenon but less marked; — Nov. 2, northern hemisphere; Apr. 10, southern hemisphere.

The Earth: Size, Computation of Time, Seasons

Size and Dimensions

The earth is the fifth largest planet and the third from the sun. Its mass is 6 sextillion, 588 quintillion short tons. Using the parameters of an ellipsoid adopted by the International Astronomical Union in 1964 and recognized by the International Union of Geodesy and Geophysics in 1967, the length of the equator is 24,901.55 miles, the length of a meridian is 24,859.82 miles, the equatorial diameter is 7,926.41 miles, and the area of this reference ellipsoid is approximately 196,938,800 square miles.

The earth is considered a solid, rigid mass with a dense core of magnetic, probably metallic material. The outer part of the core is probably liquid. Around the core is a thick shell or mantle of heavy crystalline rock which in turn is covered by a thin crust forming the solid granite and basalt base of the continents and ocean basins. Over broad areas of the earth's surface the crust has a thin cover of sedimentary rock such as sandstone, shale, and limestone formed by weathering of the earth's surface and deposition of sands, clays, and plant and animal remains.

The temperature in the earth increases about 1°F. with every 100 to 200 feet in depth, in the upper 100 kilometers of the earth, and the temperature near the core is believed to be near the melting point of the core materials under the conditions at that depth. The heat of the earth is believed to be derived from radioactivity in the rocks, pressures developed within the earth, and original heat (if the earth in fact was formed at high temperatures).

Atmosphere of the Earth

The earth's atmosphere is a blanket composed of nitrogen, oxygen, and argon, in amounts of about 78, 21, and 1% by volume. Also present in minute quantities are carbon dioxide, hydrogen, neon, helium, krypton, and xenon.

Water vapor displaces other gases and varies from nearly zero to about 4% by volume. The height of the ozone layer varies from approximately 12 to 21 miles above the earth. Traces exist as low as 6 miles and as high as 35 miles. Traces of methane have been found.

The atmosphere rests on the earth's surface with the weight equivalent to a layer of water 34 ft. deep. For about 300,000 ft. upward the gases remain in the proportions stated. Gravity holds the gases to the earth. The weight of the air compresses it at the bottom, so that the greatest density is at the earth's surface. Pressure, as well as density, decreases as height increases because the weight pressing upon any layer is always less than that pressing upon the layers below.

The temperature of the air drops with increased height until the **tropopause** is reached. This may vary from 25,000 to 60,000 ft. The atmosphere below the tropopause is the **troposphere;** the atmosphere for about twenty miles above the tropopause is the **stratosphere,** where the temperature generally increases with height except at high latitudes in winter. A temperature maximum near the 30-mile level is called the **stratopause.** Above this boundary is the **mesosphere** where the temperature decreases with height to a minimum, the **mesopause,** at a height of 50 miles. Extending above the mesosphere to the outer fringes of the atmosphere is the **thermosphere,** a region where temperature increases with height to a value measured in thousands of degrees Fahrenheit. The lower portion of this region, extending from 50 to about 400 miles in altitude, is characterized by a high ion density, and is thus called the **ionosphere.** The outer region is called **exosphere;** this is the region where gas molecules traveling at high speed may escape into outer space, above 600 miles.

Latitude, Longitude

Position on the globe is measured by means of meridians and parallels. Meridians, which are imaginary lines drawn around the earth through the poles, determine **longitude.** The meridian running through Greenwich, England, is the **prime meridian of longitude,** and all others are either east or west. Parallels, which are imaginary circles parallel with the equator, determine **latitude.** The length of a degree of longitude varies as the cosine of the latitude. At the equator a degree is 69.171 statute miles; this is gradually reduced toward the poles. Value of a longitude degree at the poles is zero.

Latitude is reckoned by the number of degrees north or south of the equator, an imaginary circle on the earth's surface everywhere equidistant between the two poles. According to the IAU Ellipsoid of 1964, the length of a degree of latitude is 68.708 statute miles at the equator and varies slightly north and south because of the oblate form of the globe; at the poles it is 69.403 statute miles.

Computation of Time

The earth rotates on its axis and follows an elliptical orbit around the sun. The rotation makes the sun appear to move across the sky from East to West. It determines day and night and the complete rotation, in relation to the sun, is called the **apparent** or **true solar day.** This varies but an average determines the **mean solar day** of 24 hours.

The mean solar day is in universal use for civil purposes. It may be obtained from apparent solar time by correcting observations of the sun for the equation of time, but when high precision is required, the mean solar time is calculated from its relation to sidereal time. These relations are extremely complicated, but for most practical uses, they may be considered as follows:

Sidereal time is the measure of time defined by the diurnal motion of the vernal equinox, and is determined from observation of the meridian transits of stars. One complete rotation of the earth relative to the equinox is called the **sidereal day.** The **mean sidereal day** is 23 hours, 56 minutes, 4.091 seconds of mean solar time.

The **Calendar Year** begins at 12 o'clock midnight precisely local clock time, on the night of Dec. 31-Jan. 1. The day and the calendar month also begin at midnight by the clock. The interval required for the earth to make one absolute revolution around the sun is a **sidereal year;** it consisted of 365 days, 6 hours, 9 minutes, and 9.5 seconds of mean solar time (approximately 24 hours per day) in 1900, and is increasing at the rate of 0.0001-second annually.

The **Tropical Year,** on which the return of the seasons depends, is the interval between two consecutive returns of the sun to the vernal equinox. The tropical year consists of 365 days, 5 hours, 48 minutes, and 46 seconds in 1900. It is decreasing at the rate of 0.530 seconds per century.

In 1956 the unit of time interval was defined to be identical with the second of **Ephemeris Time,** 1/31,556,925.9747 of the tropical year for 1900 January 0d 12th hour E.T. A physical definition of the second based on a quantum transition of cesium (atomic second) was adopted in 1964. The atomic second is equal to 9,192,631,770 cycles of the emitted radiation. In 1967 this atomic second was adopted as the unit of time interval for the Intern'l System of Units.

The Zones and Seasons

The five zones of the earth's surface are Torrid, lying between the Tropics of Cancer and Capricorn; North Temperate, between Cancer and the Arctic Circle; South Temperate, between Capricorn and the Antarctic Circle; The Frigid Zones, between the polar Circles and the Poles.

The inclination or tilt of the earth's axis with respect to the sun determines the seasons. These are commonly marked in the North Temperate Zone, where spring begins at the vernal equinox, summer at the summer solstice, autumn at the autumnal equinox and winter at the winter solstice.

In the South Temperate Zone, the seasons are reversed. Spring begins at the autumnal equinox, summer at the winter solstice, etc.

If the earth's axis were perpendicular to the plane of the earth's orbit around the sun there would be no change of seasons. Day and night would be of nearly constant length and there would be equable conditions of temperature. But the axis is tilted 23° 27′ away from a perpendicular to the orbit and only in March and September is the axis at right angles to the sun.

The points at which the sun crosses the equator are the equinoxes, when day and night are most nearly equal. The points at which the sun is at a maximum distance from the equator are the solstices. Days and nights are then most unequal.

In June the North Pole is tilted 23° 27′ toward the sun and the days in the northern hemisphere are longer than the nights, while the days in the southern hemisphere are shorter than the nights. In December the North Pole is tilted 23° 27′ away from the sun and the situation is reversed.

The Seasons in 1990

In 1990 the 4 seasons will begin as follows: add one hour to EST for Atlantic Time; subtract one hour for Central, two hours for Mountain, 3 hours for Pacific, 4 hours for Yukon, 5 hours for Alaska-Hawaii and six hours for Bering Time. Also shown in Greenwich Mean Time.

		Date	GMT	EST
Vernal Equinox	Spring	Mar. 20	21:19	16:19
Summer Solstice	Summer	June 21	15:33	10:33
Autumnal Equinox	Autumn	Sept. 23	6:55	1:55
Winter Solstice	Winter	Dec. 22	3:07	22:07*
*Previous Day				

Poles of The Earth

The geographic (rotation) poles, or points where the earth's axis of rotation cuts the surface, are not absolutely fixed in the body of the earth. The pole of rotation describes an irregular curve about its mean position.

Two periods have been detected in this motion: (1) an annual period due to seasonal changes in barometric pressure, load of ice and snow on the surface and to other phenomena of seasonal character; (2) a period of about 14 months due to the shape and constitution of the earth.

In addition there are small but as yet unpredictable irregularities. The whole motion is so small that the actual pole at any time remains within a circle of 30 or 40 feet in radius centered at the mean position of the pole.

The pole of rotation for the time being is of course the pole having a latitude of 90° and an indeterminate longitude.

Magnetic Poles

The **north magnetic pole** of the earth is that region where the magnetic force is vertically downward and the **south magnetic pole** that region where the magnetic force is vertically upward. A compass placed at the magnetic poles experiences no directive force in azimuth.

There are slow changes in the distribution of the earth's magnetic field. These changes were at one time attributed in part to a periodic movement of the magnetic poles around the geographical poles, but later evidence refutes this theory and points, rather, to a slow migration of "disturbance" foci over the earth.

There appear shifts in position of the magnetic poles due to the changes in the earth's magnetic field. The center of the area designated as the north magnetic pole was estimated to be in about latitude 70.5° N and longitude 96° W in 1905; from recent nearby measurements and studies of the secular changes, the position in 1970 is estimated as latitude 76.2° N and longitude 101° W. Improved data rather than actual motion account for at least part of the change.

The position of the south magnetic pole in 1912 was near 71° S and longitude 150° E; the position in 1970 is estimated at latitude 66° S and longitude 139.1° E.

The direction of the horizontal components of the magnetic field at any point is known as magnetic north at that point, and the angle by which it deviates east or west of true north is known as the magnetic declination, or in the mariner's terminology, the **variation of the compass.**

A compass without error points in the direction of magnetic north. (In general this is *not* the direction of the magnetic north pole.) If one follows the direction indicated by the north end of the compass, he will travel along a rather irregular curve which eventually reaches the north magnetic pole (though not usually by a great-circle route). However, the action of the compass should not be thought of as due to any influence of the distant pole, but simply as an indication of the distribution of the earth's magnetism at the place of observation.

Rotation of The Earth

The speed of rotation of the earth about its axis has been found to be slightly variable. The variations may be classified as:

(A) **Secular.** Tidal friction acts as a brake on the rotation and causes a slow secular increase in the length of the day, about 1 millisecond per century.

(B) **Irregular.** The speed of rotation may increase for a number of years, about 5 to 10, and then start decreasing. The maximum difference from the mean in the length of the day during a century is about 5 milliseconds. The accumulated difference in time has amounted to approximately 44 seconds since 1900. The cause is probably motion in the interior of the earth.

(C) **Periodic.** Seasonal variations exist with periods of one year and six months. The cumulative effect is such that each year the earth is late about 30 milliseconds near June 1 and is ahead about 30 milliseconds near Oct. 1. The maximum seasonal variation in the length of the day is about 0.5 millisecond. It is believed that the principal cause of the annual variation is the seasonal change in the wind patterns of the Northern and Southern Hemispheres. The semiannual variation is due chiefly to tidal action of the sun, which distorts the shape of the earth slightly.

The secular and irregular variations were discovered by comparing time based on the rotation of the earth with time based on the orbital motion of the moon about the earth and of the planets about the sun. The periodic variation was determined largely with the aid of quartz-crystal clocks. The introduction of the cesium-beam atomic clock in 1955 made it possible to determine in greater detail than before the nature of the irregular and periodic variations.

Morning and Evening Stars, 1990

(GMT)

	Morning	Evening		Morning	Evening
Jan.	Mercury from Jan. 9	Mercury Jan. 1 to Jan. 9		Uranus	
	Venus from Jan. 18	Venus Jan. 1 to Jan. 18		Neptune	
	Mars Jan. 1	Jupiter Jan. 1		Pluto	
	Uranus Jan. 1	Saturn Jan. 1 to Jan. 6	**Apr.**	Venus	Mercury
	Neptune from Jan. 2	Neptune to Jan. 2		Mars	Jupiter
	Pluto Jan. 1			Saturn	
Feb.	Mercury			Uranus	
	Venus			Neptune	
	Mars			Pluto	
	Saturn	Jupiter	**May**	Mercury from May 3	Mercury to May 3
	Uranus			Venus	Jupiter
	Neptune			Mars	Pluto from May 7
	Pluto			Saturn	
Mar.	Mercury to Mar. 20	Mercury from Mar. 20		Uranus	
	Venus	Jupiter		Neptune	
	Mars			Pluto to May 7	
	Saturn		**June**	Mercury	Jupiter

Morning	Evening		Morning	Evening
Venus	Uranus from June 29		Jupiter	Neptune
Mars	Pluto			Pluto
Saturn		**Oct.**	Mercury to Oct. 21	Mercury from Oct. 21
Uranus to June 29			Venus	Saturn
Neptune			Mars	Uranus
July Mercury to July 2	Mercury from July 2		Jupiter	Neptune
Venus	Jupiter to July 15			Pluto
Mars	Saturn from July 14	**Nov.**	Venus to Nov. 1	Mercury
Jupiter from July 15	Uranus		Mars to Nov. 27	Venus from Nov. 1
Saturn to July 14	Neptune from July 5		Jupiter	Mars from Nov. 27
Neptune to July 5	Pluto		Pluto from Nov. 10	Uranus
Aug. Venus	Mercury			Neptune
Mars	Saturn			Pluto to Nov. 10
Jupiter	Uranus	**Dec.**	Mercury from Dec. 24	Mercury to Dec. 24
	Neptune		Jupiter	Venus
	Pluto		Uranus from Dec. 31	Mars
Sept. Mercury from Sept. 8	Mercury to Sept. 8		Pluto	Saturn
Venus	Saturn			Uranus to Dec. 31
Mars	Uranus			Neptune

Astronomical Twilight—Meridian of Greenwich

Date 1990	20° Begin h m	20° End h m	30° Begin h m	30° End h m	40° Begin h m	40° End h m	50° Begin h m	50° End h m	60° Begin h m	60° End h m
Jan. 1	5 16	6 50	5 30	6 35	5 45	6 21	6 00	6 07	6 18	5 49
11	5 19	6 56	5 33	6 43	5 46	6 30	6 00	6 17	6 15	6 01
21	5 21	7 01	5 32	6 51	5 43	6 40	5 55	6 30	6 06	6 18
Feb. 1	5 21	7 07	5 29	6 58	5 38	6 51	5 45	6 44	5 51	6 38
11	5 18	7 11	5 24	7 05	5 29	7 01	5 32	6 59	5 32	7 01
21	5 13	7 15	5 17	7 12	5 17	7 12	5 16	7 14	5 09	7 23
Mar. 1	5 08	7 18	5 08	7 19	5 06	7 21	4 59	7 29	4 44	7 45
11	5 00	7 21	4 58	7 24	4 50	7 32	4 38	7 46	4 12	8 12
21	4 52	7 24	4 45	7 32	4 33	7 44	4 14	8 04	3 37	8 43
Apr. 1	4 42	7 28	4 31	7 39	4 14	7 57	3 47	8 25	2 53	9 21
11	4 32	7 32	4 18	7 47	3 56	8 09	3 20	8 47	2 03	10 10
21	4 23	7 36	4 04	7 54	3 37	8 23	2 52	9 11	0 37	11 47
May 1	4 14	7 41	3 52	8 04	3 19	8 37	2 22	9 39		
11	4 08	7 46	3 41	8 13	3 03	8 53	1 49	10 09		
21	4 02	7 52	3 32	8 22	2 48	9 07	1 13	10 46		
June 1	3 58	7 58	3 26	8 30	2 36	9 20	0 21	11 52		
11	3 56	8 03	3 22	8 36	2 29	9 30				
21	3 57	8 06	3 22	8 40	2 28	9 35				
July 1	3 59	8 07	3 25	8 41	2 30	9 35				
11	4 03	8 06	3 30	8 39	2 40	9 30				
21	4 08	8 03	3 39	8 33	2 52	9 18	1 12	11 23		
Aug. 1	4 15	7 56	3 48	8 23	3 09	9 01	1 49	10 20		
11	4 20	7 50	3 56	8 13	3 22	8 46	2 21	9 46		
21	4 24	7 41	4 05	8 01	3 34	8 27	2 47	9 15		
Sept. 1	4 29	7 31	4 14	7 46	3 51	8 08	3 13	8 43	1 40	10 02
11	4 32	7 20	4 20	7 33	4 02	7 50	3 33	8 16	2 36	9 12
21	4 35	7 11	4 26	7 19	4 14	7 31	3 52	7 52	3 11	8 31
Oct. 1	4 38	7 02	4 33	7 05	4 25	7 13	4 10	7 28	3 41	7 54
11	4 40	6 53	4 40	6 53	4 35	6 58	4 26	7 05	4 07	7 23
21	4 43	6 47	4 45	6 44	4 45	6 43	4 41	6 46	4 32	6 55
Nov. 1	4 46	6 41	4 52	6 34	4 56	6 30	4 58	6 27	4 56	6 27
11	4 50	6 38	4 59	6 28	5 06	6 21	5 13	6 14	5 17	6 08
21	4 55	6 36	5 06	6 25	5 16	6 15	5 26	6 04	5 37	5 52
Dec. 1	5 00	6 37	5 13	6 24	5 25	6 11	5 38	5 58	5 53	5 42
11	5 06	6 40	5 20	6 26	5 34	6 12	5 48	5 57	6 06	5 38
21	5 11	6 45	5 25	6 30	5 39	6 16	5 55	6 00	6 15	5 40
31	5 15	6 50	5 30	6 35	5 44	6 21	6 00	6 06	6 18	5 48

Chronological Eras, 1990

The year 1990 of the Christian Era comprises the latter part of the 214th and the beginning of the 215th year of the independence of the United States of America.

Era	Year	Begins in 1990	Era	Year	Begins in 1990
			Japanese	2650	Jan. 1
Byzantine	7499	Sept. 14	Grecian	2302	Sept. 14
Jewish	5751	Sept. 19 (sunset)	(Seleucidae)		or Oct. 14
			Diocletian	1707	Sept. 11
Roman (Ab Urbe Condita)	2743	Jan. 14	Indian (Saka)	1912	Mar. 22
Nabonassar (Babylonian)	2739	Apr. 26	Mohammedan (Hegira)	1411	July 23

Chronological Cycles, 1990

Dominical Letter	G	Golden Number (Lunar Cycle)	XV	Roman Indiction	13
Epact	3	Solar Cycle	11	Julian Period (year of)	6703

1st Month

January, 1990

31 days

NOTE: Light numbers indicate Sun. **Dark** numbers indicate **Moon.** *Degrees are North Latitude.*

FM = full moon; LQ = last quarter; NM = new moon; FQ = first quarter.

CAUTION: Must be converted to local time. For instructions see page 242.

Day of month week year	Sun on Meridian Moon phase h m s	Sun's Declination ° '	20° Rise Sun/Moon h m	20° Set Sun/Moon h m	30° Rise Sun/Moon h m	30° Set Sun/Moon h m	40° Rise Sun/Moon h m	40° Set Sun/Moon h m	50° Rise Sun/Moon h m	50° Set Sun/Moon h m	60° Rise Sun/Moon h m	60° Set Sun/Moon h m
1 Mo	12 3 32	− 23 3	6 35	17 32	6 56	17 11	7 22	16 45	7 59	16 09	9 02	15 05
1			9 45	21 43	9 54	21 37	10 04	21 30	10 18	21 20	10 40	21 04
2 Tu	12 3 60	− 22 58	6 35	17 33	6 56	17 12	7 22	16 46	7 59	16 10	9 02	15 06
2			10 22	22 39	10 25	22 39	10 29	22 39	10 34	22 39	10 41	22 38
3 We	12 4 28	− 22 52	6 36	17 33	6 56	17 13	7 22	16 47	7 58	16 11	9 01	15 08
3			10 59	23 36	10 56	23 42	10 53	23 49	10 49	23 59	10 42	− −
4 Th	12 4 55	− 22 46	6 36	17 34	6 57	17 13	7 22	16 48	7 58	16 12	9 01	15 09
4	10 40 FQ		11 37	− −	11 29	− −	11 18	− −	11 04	− −	10 43	0 14
5 Fr	12 5 22	− 22 40	6 36	17 35	6 57	17 14	7 22	16 49	7 58	16 13	9 00	15 11
5			12 18	0 35	12 04	0 47	11 47	1 02	11 23	1 22	10 46	1 54
6 Sa	12 5 49	− 22 33	6 37	17 35	6 57	17 15	7 22	16 50	7 58	16 14	8 59	15 13
6			13 4	1 37	12 44	1 55	12 20	2 16	11 47	2 47	10 51	3 39
7 Su	12 6 15	− 22 26	6 37	17 36	6 57	17 16	7 22	16 51	7 57	16 15	8 58	15 15
7			13 55	2 42	13 32	3 04	13 01	3 33	12 19	4 14	11 01	5 28
8 Mo	12 6 40	− 22 18	6 37	17 36	6 57	17 17	7 22	16 52	7 57	16 17	8 57	15 17
8			14 53	3 48	14 27	4 14	13 53	4 48	13 03	5 36	11 24	7 14
9 Tu	12 7 05	− 22 10	6 37	17 37	6 57	17 17	7 22	16 53	7 57	16 18	8 56	15 19
9			15 57	4 54	15 29	5 21	14 55	5 56	14 03	6 48	12 18	8 34
10 We	12 7 30	− 22 2	6 37	17 38	6 57	17 18	7 22	16 54	7 56	16 19	8 55	15 21
10			17 02	5 55	16 37	6 21	16 05	6 54	15 18	7 42	13 47	9 15
11 Th	12 7 54	− 21 53	6 37	17 38	6 57	17 19	7 21	16 55	7 56	16 21	8 54	15 23
11	4 57 FM		18 06	6 50	17 45	7 13	17 18	7 41	16 40	8 22	15 32	9 32
12 Fr	12 8 17	− 21 43	6 38	17 39	6 57	17 20	7 21	16 56	7 55	16 22	8 52	15 25
12			19 07	7 38	18 50	7 56	18 30	8 18	18 02	8 49	17 15	9 40
13 Sa	12 8 40	− 21 34	6 38	17 40	6 57	17 21	7 21	16 57	7 54	16 23	8 51	15 27
13			20 04	8 20	19 53	8 33	19 39	8 49	19 21	9 10	18 52	9 44
14 Su	12 9 2	− 21 23	6 38	17 40	6 57	17 21	7 21	16 58	7 54	16 25	8 50	15 29
14			20 57	8 57	20 52	9 04	20 45	9 14	20 36	9 27	20 22	9 46
15 Mo	12 9 23	− 21 13	6 38	17 41	6 57	17 22	7 20	16 59	7 53	16 26	8 48	15 31
15			21 48	9 31	21 48	9 33	21 48	9 37	21 48	9 41	21 48	9 47
16 Tu	12 9 44	− 21 2	6 38	17 42	6 57	17 23	7 20	17 00	7 52	16 28	8 47	15 33
16			22 37	10 03	22 42	10 01	22 49	9 58	22 58	9 54	23 11	9 47
17 We	12 10 4	− 20 50	6 38	17 42	6 56	17 24	7 19	17 01	7 51	16 29	8 45	15 36
17			23 26	10 35	23 37	10 28	23 49	10 19	− −	10 07	− −	9 48
18 Th	12 10 23	− 20 38	6 38	17 43	6 56	17 25	7 19	17 02	7 50	16 31	8 43	15 38
18	21 17 LQ		− −	11 09	− −	10 56	− −	10 41	0 07	10 21	0 34	9 49
19 Fr	12 10 42	− 20 26	6 38	17 44	6 56	17 26	7 18	17 03	7 50	16 32	8 41	15 41
19			0 16	11 44	0 31	11 27	0 50	11 06	1 16	10 38	1 59	9 51
20 Sa	12 11 0	− 20 14	6 38	17 44	6 56	17 27	7 18	17 05	7 49	16 34	8 40	15 43
20			1 08	12 22	1 27	12 01	1 51	11 35	2 26	10 58	3 27	9 55
21 Su	12 11 17	− 20 1	6 38	17 45	6 55	17 27	7 17	17 06	7 48	16 35	8 38	15 45
21			2 01	13 05	2 24	12 40	2 53	12 10	3 36	11 25	4 56	10 03
22 Mo	12 11 34	− 19 47	6 38	17 46	6 55	17 28	7 17	17 07	7 47	16 37	8 36	15 48
22			2 55	13 52	3 21	13 26	3 54	12 52	4 43	12 02	6 22	10 22
23 Tu	12 11 50	− 19 33	6 38	17 46	6 55	17 29	7 16	17 08	7 45	16 39	8 34	15 50
23			3 49	14 45	4 17	14 17	4 52	13 42	5 43	12 51	7 33	11 01
24 We	12 12 5	− 19 19	6 37	17 47	6 54	17 30	7 15	17 09	7 44	16 40	8 32	15 53
24			4 43	15 41	5 09	15 15	5 44	14 42	6 34	13 52	8 15	12 12
25 Th	12 12 19	− 19 5	6 37	17 48	6 54	17 31	7 15	17 11	7 43	16 42	8 30	15 55
25			5 33	16 40	5 58	16 17	6 29	15 47	7 13	15 05	8 35	13 45
26 Fr	12 12 32	− 18 50	6 37	17 48	6 54	17 32	7 14	17 12	7 42	16 44	8 28	15 58
26	19 20 NM		6 21	17 39	6 41	17 21	7 07	16 57	7 43	16 23	8 44	15 25
27 Sa	12 12 45	− 18 35	6 37	17 49	6 53	17 33	7 13	17 13	7 41	16 45	8 26	16 00
27			7 04	18 38	7 20	18 25	7 39	18 08	8 06	17 44	8 49	17 05
28 Su	12 12 57	− 18 19	6 37	17 49	6 53	17 34	7 12	17 14	7 39	16 47	8 24	16 03
28			7 44	19 36	7 55	19 28	8 07	19 19	8 25	19 05	8 51	18 44
29 Mo	12 13 8	− 18 3	6 36	17 50	6 52	17 34	7 12	17 15	7 38	16 49	8 21	16 06
29			8 22	20 34	8 27	20 32	8 33	20 29	8 41	20 26	8 53	20 21
30 Tu	12 13 18	− 17 47	6 36	17 51	6 52	17 35	7 11	17 16	7 37	16 50	8 19	16 08
30			9 00	21 31	8 59	21 35	8 58	21 40	8 56	21 47	8 54	21 58
31 We	12 13 27	− 17 31	6 36	17 51	6 51	17 36	7 10	17 18	7 35	16 52	8 17	16 11
31			9 38	22 30	9 31	22 40	9 23	22 53	9 12	23 10	8 55	23 37

2nd Month · **February, 1990** **28 days**

Greenwich Mean Time

NOTE: Light numbers indicate Sun. **Dark** numbers indicate **Moon.** *Degrees are North Latitude.*

FM = full moon; LQ = last quarter; NM = new moon; FQ = first quarter.

CAUTION: Must be converted to local time. For instructions see page 242.

Day of month week year	Sun on Meridian Moon phase h m s	Sun's Declination °	20° Rise Sun Moon h m	20° Set Sun Moon h m	30° Rise Sun Moon h m	30° Set Sun Moon h m	40° Rise Sun Moon h m	40° Set Sun Moon h m	50° Rise Sun Moon h m	50° Set Sun Moon h m	60° Rise Sun Moon h m	60° Set Sun Moon h m
1 Th 32	12 13 36	−17 14	6 36 10 18	17 52 23 31	6 51 10 05	17 37 23 47	7 09 9 50	17 19 − −	7 34 9 29	16 54 − −	8 15 8 57	16 13 − −
2 Fr 33	12 13 43 18 32 FQ	−16 57	6 35 11 02	17 52 − −	6 50 10 44	17 38 − −	7 08 10 21	17 20 0 07	7 33 9 51	16 55 0 34	8 12 9 01	16 16 1 20
3 Sa 34	12 13 50	−16 40	6 35 11 50	17 53 0 34	6 49 11 28	17 39 0 55	7 07 10 59	17 21 1 22	7 31 10 19	16 57 2 00	8 10 9 09	16 19 3 07
4 Su 35	12 13 56	−16 22	6 35 12 45	17 53 1 39	6 49 12 19	17 40 2 04	7 06 11 46	17 22 2 36	7 30 10 58	16 59 3 22	8 07 9 25	16 21 4 53
5 Mo 36	12 14 1	−16 4	6 34 13 45	17 54 2 43	6 48 13 17	17 40 3 10	7 05 12 42	17 24 3 45	7 28 11 51	17 01 4 36	8 05 10 04	16 24 6 22
6 Tu 37	12 14 6	−15 46	6 34 14 47	17 55 3 44	6 47 14 21	17 41 4 11	7 04 13 48	17 25 4 45	7 26 12 58	17 02 5 35	8 02 11 19	16 27 7 16
7 We 38	12 14 9	−15 27	6 33 15 51	17 55 4 40	6 47 15 28	17 42 5 04	7 03 14 58	17 26 5 35	7 25 14 16	17 04 6 19	8 00 12 58	16 29 7 39
8 Th 39	12 14 12	−15 9	6 33 16 52	17 56 5 30	6 46 16 33	17 43 5 50	7 02 16 10	17 27 6 15	7 23 15 37	17 06 6 50	7 57 14 42	16 32 7 50
9 Fr 40	12 14 14 19 16 FM	−14 50	6 33 17 50	17 56 6 13	6 45 17 37	17 44 6 29	7 01 17 20	17 28 6 48	7 22 16 57	17 08 7 13	7 55 16 20	16 35 7 55
10 Sa 41	12 14 15	−14 30	6 32 18 45	17 57 6 52	6 44 18 37	17 44 7 02	6 59 18 27	17 30 7 15	7 20 18 14	17 09 7 31	7 52 17 53	16 37 7 57
11 Su 42	12 14 15	−14 11	6 32 19 37	17 57 7 27	6 44 19 35	17 45 7 32	6 58 19 32	17 31 7 38	7 18 19 28	17 11 7 46	7 50 19 21	16 40 7 58
12 Mo 43	12 14 15	−13 51	6 31 20 27	17 58 8 01	6 43 20 30	17 46 8 01	6 57 20 34	17 32 8 00	7 17 20 39	17 13 8 00	7 47 20 47	16 43 7 59
13 Tu 44	12 14 14	−13 31	6 31 21 17	17 58 8 33	6 42 21 25	17 47 8 28	6 56 21 35	17 33 8 22	7 15 21 49	17 14 8 13	7 44 22 11	16 45 8 00
14 We 45	12 14 12	−13 11	6 30 22 07	17 59 9 06	6 41 22 20	17 48 8 56	6 55 22 36	17 34 8 44	7 13 22 59	17 16 8 27	7 42 23 35	16 48 8 00
15 Th 46	12 14 9	−12 50	6 29 22 58	17 59 9 41	6 40 23 16	17 48 9 26	6 53 23 38	17 35 9 07	7 11 − −	17 18 8 42	7 39 − −	16 50 8 02
16 Fr 47	12 14 6	−12 30	6 29 23 50	18 00 10 18	6 39 − −	17 49 9 59	6 52 − −	17 37 9 35	7 09 0 09	17 20 9 01	7 36 1 02	16 53 8 05
17 Sa 48	12 14 2 18 48 LQ	−12 9	6 28 − −	18 00 10 58	6 38 0 12	17 50 10 35	6 51 0 40	17 38 10 06	7 08 1 19	17 21 9 25	7 33 2 31	16 56 8 11
18 Su 49	12 13 57	−11 48	6 28 0 44	18 01 11 43	6 37 1 09	17 51 11 18	6 49 1 41	17 39 10 45	7 06 2 27	17 23 9 57	7 31 3 59	16 58 8 24
19 Mo 50	12 13 52	−11 27	6 27 1 38	18 01 12 33	6 37 2 05	17 52 12 06	6 48 2 39	17 40 11 31	7 04 3 30	17 25 10 40	7 28 5 17	17 01 8 52
20 Tu 51	12 13 46	−11 5	6 26 2 31	18 01 13 27	6 36 2 58	17 52 13 00	6 47 3 33	17 41 12 26	7 02 4 24	17 26 11 35	7 25 6 11	17 03 9 49
21 We 52	12 13 39	−10 44	6 26 3 22	18 02 14 24	6 35 3 48	17 53 14 00	6 45 4 21	17 42 13 28	7 00 5 08	17 28 12 42	7 22 6 39	17 06 11 12
22 Th 53	12 13 32	−10 22	6 25 4 11	18 02 15 23	6 34 4 33	17 54 15 03	6 44 5 02	17 44 14 36	6 58 5 42	17 30 13 58	7 20 6 53	17 09 12 50
23 Fr 54	12 13 24	−10 0	6 24 4 56	18 03 16 23	6 33 5 14	17 55 16 07	6 43 5 37	17 45 15 47	6 56 6 08	17 32 15 18	7 17 7 11	17 11 14 31
24 Sa 55	12 13 15	− 9 38	6 24 5 38	18 03 17 22	6 32 5 51	17 55 17 12	6 41 6 01	17 46 16 59	6 54 6 28	17 33 16 41	7 14 7 02	17 14 16 11
25 Su 56	12 13 6 8 54 NM	− 9 16	6 23 6 18	18 03 18 21	6 31 6 25	17 56 18 17	6 40 6 34	17 47 18 11	6 52 6 46	17 35 18 03	7 11 7 04	17 16 17 51
26 Mo 57	12 12 56	− 8 54	6 22 6 57	18 04 19 20	6 30 6 58	17 57 19 22	6 38 7 00	17 48 19 24	6 50 7 02	17 37 19 27	7 08 7 06	17 19 19 31
27 Tu 58	12 12 46	− 8 31	6 22 7 35	18 04 20 20	6 29 7 31	17 57 20 28	6 37 7 25	17 49 20 38	6 48 7 18	17 38 20 51	7 05 7 07	17 21 21 12
28 We 59	12 12 35	− 8 9	6 21 8 16	18 05 21 22	6 27 8 05	17 58 21 36	6 35 7 53	17 50 21 54	6 46 7 35	17 40 22 18	7 02 7 09	17 24 22 57

3rd Month   March, 1990   31 days

Greenwich Mean Time

NOTE: Light numbers indicate Sun. **Dark** numbers indicate **Moon.** *Degrees are North Latitude.*

FM = full moon; LQ = last quarter; NM = new moon; FQ = first quarter.

CAUTION: Must be converted to local time. For instructions see page 242.

Day of month / week / year	Sun on Meridian / Moon phase (h m s)	Sun's Decl (° ')	20° Rise	20° Set	30° Rise	30° Set	40° Rise	40° Set	50° Rise	50° Set	60° Rise	60° Set
1 Th 60 (Sun)	12 12 24	− 7 46	6 20	18 05	6 26	17 59	6 34	17 51	6 44	17 42	6 59	17 27
1 Th 60 (Moon)			9 00	22 26	8 43	22 46	8 23	23 10	7 56	23 45	7 12	– –
2 Fr 61 (Sun)	12 12 12	− 7 23	6 19	18 05	6 25	18 00	6 32	17 53	6 42	17 43	6 56	17 29
2 Fr 61 (Moon)			9 48	23 32	9 26	23 56	9 00	– –	8 22	– –	7 19	0 45
3 Sa 62 (Sun)	12 11 60	− .7 0	6 19	18 06	6 24	18 00	6 31	17 54	6 40	17 45	6 54	17 32
3 Sa 62 (Moon)			10 41	– –	10 16	– –	9 44	0 26	8 58	1 10	7 32	2 34
4 Su 63 (Sun)	12 11 47	− 6 37	6 18	18 06	6 23	18 01	6 29	17 55	6 38	17 47	6 51	17 34
4 Su 63 (Moon)	2 5 FQ		11 39	0 37	11 12	1 03	10 37	1 37	9 46	2 28	8 03	4 10
5 Mo 64 (Sun)	12 11 34	− 6 14	6 17	18 06	6 22	18 02	6 28	17 56	6 36	17 48	6 48	17 37
5 Mo 64 (Moon)			12 40	1 39	12 14	2 06	11 39	2 40	10 49	3 31	9 06	5 15
6 Tu 65 (Sun)	12 11 20	− 5 51	6 16	18 07	6 21	18 02	6 26	17 57	6 34	17 50	6 45	17 39
6 Tu 65 (Moon)			13 42	2 35	13 18	3 01	12 48	3 33	12 03	4 19	10 38	5 46
7 We 66 (Sun)	12 11 6	− 5 28	6 15	18 07	6 20	18 03	6 25	17 58	6 32	17 51	6 42	17 42
7 We 66 (Moon)			14 43	3 26	14 23	3 48	13 58	4 15	13 22	4 53	12 19	5 59
8 Th 67 (Sun)	12 10 51	− 5 4	6 15	18 07	6 19	18 04	6 23	17 59	6 29	17 53	6 39	17 44
8 Th 67 (Moon)			15 41	4 10	15 26	4 28	15 07	4 49	14 41	5 18	13 57	6 05
9 Fr 68 (Sun)	12 10 36	− 4 41	6 14	18 08	6 17	18 04	6 22	18 00	6 27	17 55	6 36	17 47
9 Fr 68 (Moon)			16 36	4 50	16 26	5 02	16 14	5 17	15 57	5 37	15 30	6 09
10 Sa 69 (Sun)	12 10 21	− 4 18	6 13	18 08	6 16	18 05	6 20	18 01	6 25	17 56	6 33	17 49
10 Sa 69 (Moon)			17 29	5 26	17 24	5 33	17 18	5 42	17 11	5 53	16 59	6 10
11 Su 70 (Sun)	12 10 5	− 3 54	6 12	18 08	6 15	18 06	6 19	18 02	6 23	17 58	6 30	17 52
11 Su 70 (Moon)	10 58 FM		18 19	6 00	18 20	6 02	18 21	6 04	18 22	6 07	18 24	6 11
12 Mo 71 (Sun)	12 9 49	− 3 31	6 11	18 09	6 14	18 06	6 17	18 03	6 21	18 00	6 27	17 54
12 Mo 71 (Moon)			19 09	6 32	19 15	6 29	19 22	6 25	19 32	6 20	19 48	6 12
13 Tu 72 (Sun)	12 9 33	− 3 7	6 10	18 09	6 13	18 07	6 15	18 04	6 19	18 01	6 24	17 57
13 Tu 72 (Moon)			19 59	7 05	20 10	6 57	20 24	6 47	20 43	6 34	21 13	6 13
14 We 73 (Sun)	12 9 16	− 2 43	6 10	18 09	6 12	18 07	6 14	18 05	6 17	18 03	6 21	17 59
14 We 73 (Moon)			20 50	7 39	21 06	7 26	21 25	7 10	21 53	6 48	22 39	6 14
15 Th 74 (Sun)	12 8 59	− 2 20	6 09	18 10	6 10	18 08	6 12	18 06	6 14	18 04	6 18	18 02
15 Th 74 (Moon)			21 42	8 15	22 02	7 58	22 27	7 36	23 03	7 06	– –	6 17
16 Fr 75 (Sun)	12 8 42	− 1 56	6 08	18 10	6 09	18 09	6 11	18 07	6 12	18 06	6 15	18 04
16 Fr 75 (Moon)			22 34	8 54	22 58	8 33	23 28	8 06	– –	7 28	0 06	6 22
17 Sa 76 (Sun)	12 8 25	− 1 32	6 07	18 10	6 08	18 09	6 09	18 09	6 10	18 08	6 12	18 06
17 Sa 76 (Moon)			23 28	9 37	23 54	9 13	– –	8 42	0 12	7 56	1 35	6 32
18 Su 77 (Sun)	12 8 8	− 1 9	6 06	18 10	6 07	18 10	6 07	18 10	6 08	18 09	6 09	18 09
18 Su 77 (Moon)			– –	10 25	– –	9 58	0 27	9 24	1 17	8 34	2 57	6 53
19 Mo 78 (Sun)	12 7 50	− 0 45	6 05	18 11	6 06	18 11	6 06	18 11	6 06	18 11	6 06	18 11
19 Mo 78 (Moon)	14 30 LQ		0 21	11 16	0 48	10 49	1 23	10 14	2 14	9 23	4 01	7 36
20 Tu 79 (Sun)	12 7 32	− 0 21	6 04	18 11	6 04	18 11	6 04	18 12	6 04	18 12	6 03	18 14
20 Tu 79 (Moon)			1 12	12 11	1 39	11 45	2 12	11 12	3 01	10 24	4 39	8 47
21 We 80 (Sun)	12 7 15	0 3	6 04	18 11	6 03	18 12	6 02	18 13	6 01	18 14	6 00	18 16
21 We 80 (Moon)			2 01	13 08	2 25	12 45	2 55	12 16	3 39	11 35	4 58	10 17
22 Th 81 (Sun)	12 6 57	0 26	6 03	18 11	6 02	18 12	6 01	18 14	5 59	18 16	5 57	18 19
22 Th 81 (Moon)			2 47	14 06	3 07	13 48	3 32	13 24	4 07	12 51	5 07	11 55
23 Fr 82 (Sun)	12 6 39	0 50	6 02	18 12	6 01	18 13	5 59	18 15	5 57	18 17	5 54	18 21
23 Fr 82 (Moon)			3 29	15 05	3 45	14 51	4 04	14 35	4 30	14 12	5 12	13 34
24 Sa 83 (Sun)	12 6 21	1 14	6 01	18 12	6 00	18 14	5 58	18 16	5 55	18 19	5 51	18 24
24 Sa 83 (Moon)			4 10	16 03	4 20	15 56	4 32	15 46	4 49	15 33	5 15	15 13
25 Su 84 (Sun)	12 6 3	1 37	6 00	18 12	5 58	18 14	5 56	18 17	5 53	18 20	5 48	18 26
25 Su 84 (Moon)			4 49	17 02	4 53	17 01	4 59	16 59	5 06	16 57	5 17	16 52
26 Mo 85 (Sun)	12 5 45	2 1	5 59	18 13	5 57	18 15	5 54	18 18	5 51	18 22	5 45	18 28
26 Mo 85 (Moon)	19 48 NM		5 28	18 03	5 26	18 08	5 25	18 14	5 22	18 22	5 18	18 34
27 Tu 86 (Sun)	12 5 26	2 24	5 58	18 13	5 56	18 15	5 53	18 19	5 48	18 23	5 41	18 31
27 Tu 86 (Moon)			6 09	19 06	6 01	19 17	5 52	19 31	5 39	19 50	5 20	20 20
28 We 87 (Sun)	12 5 8	2 48	5 57	18 13	5 55	18 16	5 51	18 20	5 46	18 25	5 38	18 33
28 We 87 (Moon)			6 52	20 11	6 39	20 28	6 22	20 50	5 59	21 20	5 24	22 10
29 Th 88 (Sun)	12 4 50	3 11	5 57	18 13	5 53	18 17	5 50	18 21	5 44	18 27	5 35	18 36
29 Th 88 (Moon)			7 40	21 18	7 21	21 41	6 57	22 09	6 24	22 49	5 29	– –
30 Fr 89 (Sun)	12 4 32	3 35	5 56	18 14	5 52	18 17	5 48	18 22	5 42	18 28	5 32	18 38
30 Fr 89 (Moon)			8 33	22 26	8 10	22 52	7 40	23 25	6 57	– –	5 41	0 03
31 Sa 90 (Sun)	12 4 14	3 58	5 55	18 14	5 51	18 18	5 46	18 23	5 40	18 30	5 29	18 41
31 Sa 90 (Moon)			9 32	23 31	9 05	23 58	8 31	– –	7 42	0 13	6 05	1 49

4th Month   April, 1990   30 days

Greenwich Mean Time

NOTE: Light numbers indicate Sun. **Dark** numbers indicate **Moon**. *Degrees are North Latitude.*

FM = full moon; LQ = last quarter; NM = new moon; FQ = first quarter.

CAUTION: Must be converted to local time. For instructions see page 242.

Day of month week year	Sun on Meridian **Moon phase** h m s	Sun's Declination °	20° Rise Sun **Moon** h m	20° Set Sun **Moon** h m	30° Rise Sun **Moon** h m	30° Set Sun **Moon** h m	40° Rise Sun **Moon** h m	40° Set Sun **Moon** h m	50° Rise Sun **Moon** h m	50° Set Sun **Moon** h m	60° Rise Sun **Moon** h m	60° Set Sun **Moon** h m
1 Su 91	12 3 56	4 21	5 54	18 14	5 50	18 18	5 45	18 24	5 38	18 31	5 26	18 43
			10 34	– –	10 07	– –	9 32	0 33	8 42	1 23	6 58	3 07
2 Mo 92	12 3 38	4 45	5 53	18 14	5 49	18 19	5 43	18 25	5 35	18 33	5 23	18 45
	10 24 FQ		11 37	0 31	11 12	0 57	10 40	1 29	9 54	2 17	8 24	3 48
3 Tu 93	12 3 21	5 8	5 52	18 15	5 47	18 20	5 41	18 26	5 33	18 34	5 20	18 48
			12 38	1 24	12 17	1 46	11 50	2 15	11 12	2 55	10 03	4 06
4 We 94	12 3 3	5 31	5 51	18 15	5 46	18 20	5 40	18 27	5 31	18 36	5 17	18 50
			13 36	2 10	13 20	2 28	12 59	2 51	12 30	3 23	11 42	4 15
5 Th 95	12 2 46	5 53	5 51	18 15	5 45	18 21	5 38	18 28	5 29	18 38	5 14	18 53
			14 32	2 51	14 20	3 04	14 06	3 21	13 46	3 44	13 15	4 19
6 Fr 96	12 2 29	6 16	5 50	18 16	5 44	18 21	5 37	18 29	5 27	18 39	5 11	18 55
			15 24	3 27	15 18	3 36	15 10	3 46	15 00	4 00	14 43	4 22
7 Sa 97	12 2 11	6 39	5 49	18 16	5 43	18 22	5 35	18 30	5 25	18 41	5 08	18 58
			16 15	4 01	16 14	4 05	16 12	4 09	16 11	4 15	16 08	4 23
8 Su 98	12 1 55	7 1	5 48	18 16	5 42	18 23	5 34	18 31	5 23	18 42	5 05	19 00
			17 04	4 34	17 08	4 32	17 13	4 30	17 20	4 28	17 31	4 24
9 Mo 99	12 1 38	7 24	5 47	18 16	5 40	18 23	5 32	18 32	5 20	18 44	5 02	19 03
			17 54	5 06	18 03	5 00	18 14	4 52	18 30	4 41	18 54	4 25
10 Tu 100	12 1 22	7 46	5 46	18 17	5 39	18 24	5 30	18 33	5 18	18 45	4 59	19 05
	03 18 FM		18 44	5 39	18 58	5 28	19 15	5 14	19 39	4 56	20 19	4 26
11 We 101	12 1 5	8 8	5 46	18 17	5 38	18 25	5 29	18 34	5 16	18 47	4 56	19 07
			19 35	6 15	19 54	5 59	20 17	5 39	20 50	5 12	21 46	4 29
12 Th 102	12 0 50	8 30	5 45	18 17	5 37	18 25	5 27	18 35	5 14	18 49	4 53	19 10
			20 28	6 53	20 50	6 33	21 18	6 08	21 59	5 33	23 14	4 34
13 Fr 103	12 0 34	8 52	5 44	18 18	5 36	18 26	5 26	18 36	5 12	18 50	4 50	19 12
			21 21	7 34	21 46	7 11	22 18	6 41	23 05	5 59	– –	4 42
14 Sa 104	12 0 19	9 14	5 43	18 18	5 35	18 26	5 24	18 37	5 10	18 52	4 47	19 15
			22 14	8 20	22 40	7 54	23 14	7 21	– –	6 33	0 38	5 00
15 Su 105	12 0 4	9 36	5 42	18 18	5 34	18 27	5 23	18 38	5 08	18 53	4 44	19 17
			23 05	9 10	23 32	8 43	– –	8 09	0 05	7 18	1 49	5 34
16 Mo 106	11 59 50	9 57	5 42	18 18	5 33	18 28	5 21	18 39	5 06	18 55	4 42	19 20
			23 54	10 03	– –	9 36	0 06	9 03	0 55	8 14	2 36	6 34
17 Tu 107	11 59 36	10 18	5 41	18 19	5 31	18 28	5 20	18 40	5 04	18 56	4 39	19 22
			– –	10 58	0 19	10 34	0 50	10 04	1 36	9 19	3 01	7 56
18 We 108	11 59 22	10 39	5 40	18 19	5 30	18 29	5 18	18 41	5 02	18 58	4 36	19 25
	07 02 LQ		0 40	11 54	1 01	11 34	1 28	11 08	2 07	10 32	3 13	9 28
19 Th 109	11 59 9	11 0	5 39	18 19	5 29	18 29	5 17	18 42	5 00	19 00	4 33	19 27
			1 22	12 50	1 40	12 35	2 01	12 15	2 31	11 48	3 20	11 03
20 Fr 110	11 58 56	11 21	5 38	18 20	5 28	18 30	5 15	18 43	4 58	19 01	4 30	19 30
			2 03	13 47	2 15	13 37	2 30	13 24	2 51	13 07	3 24	12 39
21 Sa 111	11 58 44	11 42	5 38	18 20	5 27	18 31	5 14	18 44	4 56	19 03	4 27	19 32
			2 41	14 44	2 48	14 40	2 57	14 34	3 08	14 27	3 26	14 15
22 Su 112	11 58 32	12 2	5 37	18 20	5 26	18 31	5 13	18 45	4 54	19 04	4 24	19 35
			3 19	15 43	3 21	15 45	3 22	15 47	3 25	15 49	3 28	15 53
23 Mo 113	11 58 20	12 22	5 36	18 21	5 25	18 32	5 11	18 46	4 52	19 06	4 21	19 37
			3 59	16 44	3 54	16 52	3 49	17 02	3 41	17 15	3 31	17 36
24 Tu 114	11 58 9	12 42	5 36	18 21	5 24	18 33	5 10	18 47	4 50	19 07	4 18	19 40
			4 41	17 49	4 30	18 03	4 17	18 20	4 00	18 44	3 34	19 24
25 We 115	11 57 59	13 2	5 35	18 21	5 23	18 33	5 08	18 48	4 48	19 09	4 16	19 42
	04 27 NM		5 27	18 56	5 11	19 16	4 50	19 41	4 23	20 16	3 39	21 18
26 Th 116	11 57 49	13 22	5 34	18 22	5 22	18 34	5 07	18 49	4 46	19 10	4 13	19 45
			6 19	20 06	5 57	20 30	5 30	21 01	4 52	21 46	3 48	23 11
27 Fr 117	11 57 39	13 41	5 34	18 22	5 21	18 35	5 06	18 50	4 44	19 12	4 10	19 47
			7 17	21 15	6 52	21 42	6 20	22 16	5 33	23 06	4 06	– –
28 Sa 118	11 57 30	14 0	5 33	18 22	5 20	18 35	5 04	18 51	4 42	19 14	4 07	19 50
			8 20	22 19	7 53	22 46	7 19	23 19	6 29	– –	4 48	0 46
29 Su 119	11 57 21	14 19	5 32	18 23	5 19	18 36	5 03	18 52	4 41	19 15	4 04	19 52
			9 25	23 17	9 00	23 41	8 27	– –	7 39	0 08	6 05	1 44
30 Mo 120	11 57 13	14 38	5 32	18 23	5 18	18 36	5 02	18 53	4 39	19 17	4 02	19 55
			10 29	– –	10 07	– –	9 39	0 11	8 58	0 53	7 43	2 10

5th Month   May, 1990   31 days

Greenwich Mean Time

NOTE: Light numbers indicate Sun. **Dark** numbers indicate **Moon**. *Degrees are North Latitude.*

FM = full moon; LQ = last quarter; NM = new moon; FQ = first quarter.

CAUTION: Must be converted to local time. For instructions see page 242.

Day of month / week / year	Sun on Meridian / Moon phase h m s	Sun's Declina-tion °	20° Rise	20° Set	30° Rise	30° Set	40° Rise	40° Set	50° Rise	50° Set	60° Rise	60° Set
1 Tu 121	11 57 6	14 56	5 31	18 23	5 18	18 37	5 01	18 54	4 37	19 18	3 59	19 57
	20 18 FQ		11 30	0 07	11 12	0 26	10 50	0 51	10 18	1 25	9 24	2 22
2 We 122	11 56 59	15 14	5 30	18 24	5 16	18 38	4 59	18 55	4 35	19 20	3 56	20 00
			12 27	0 50	12 14	1 05	11 58	1 23	11 36	1 49	11 0	2 28
3 Th 123	11 56 52	15 32	5 30	18 24	5 16	18 38	4 58	18 56	4 34	19 21	3 53	20 02
			13 21	1 28	13 13	1 38	13 04	1 50	12 51	2 07	12 30	2 32
4 Fr 124	11 56 46	15 50	5 29	18 24	5 15	18 39	4 57	18 57	4 32	19 23	3 51	20 04
			14 12	2 03	14 09	2 08	14 06	2 14	14 02	2 22	13 56	2 34
5 Sa 125	11 56 41	16 7	5 29	18 25	5 14	18 40	4 56	18 58	4 30	19 24	3 48	20 07
			15 01	2 36	15 04	2 36	15 07	2 36	15 12	2 35	15 19	2 35
6 Su 126	11 56 36	16 24	5 28	18 25	5 13	18 40	4 55	18 59	4 28	19 26	3 46	20 09
			15 50	3 08	15 58	3 03	16 07	2 57	16 20	2 49	16 41	2 36
7 Mo 127	11 56 32	16 41	5 28	18 26	5 12	18 41	4 53	19 00	4 27	19 27	3 43	20 12
			16 40	3 41	16 52	3 31	17 08	3 19	17 29	3 03	18 04	2 38
8 Tu 128	11 56 28	16 57	5 27	18 26	5 12	18 42	4 52	19 01	4 25	19 29	3 40	20 14
			17 31	4 15	17 48	4 01	18 09	3 43	18 39	3 19	19 30	2 40
9 We 129	11 56 25	17 14	5 27	18 26	5 11	18 42	4 51	19 02	4 24	19 30	3 38	20 17
	19 31 FM		18 23	4 52	18 44	4 34	19 10	4 11	19 48	3 38	20 56	2 45
10 Th 130	11 56 22	17 30	5 26	18 27	5 10	18 43	4 50	19 03	4 22	19 32	3 35	20 19
			19 16	5 33	19 40	5 11	20 11	4 42	20 56	4 03	22 22	2 52
11 Fr 131	11 56 20	17 45	5 26	18 27	5 09	18 44	4 49	19 04	4 20	19 33	3 33	20 22
			20 09	6 17	20 35	5 52	21 08	5 21	21 58	4 34	23 37	3 07
12 Sa 132	11 56 19	18 1	5 25	18 28	5 09	18 44	4 48	19 05	4 19	19 35	3 30	20 24
			21 01	7 06	21 27	6 39	22 01	6 06	22 51	5 16	- -	3 36
13 Su 133	11 56 18	18 16	5 25	18 28	5 08	18 45	4 47	19 06	4 17	19 36	3 28	20 26
			21 50	7 58	22 15	7 31	22 48	6 58	23 34	6 08	0 32	4 28
14 Mo 134	11 56 17	18 31	5 24	18 28	5 07	18 45	4 46	19 07	4 16	19 37	3 25	20 29
			22 36	8 52	22 59	8 27	23 27	7 56	- -	7 11	1 03	5 43
15 Tu 135	11 56 18	18 45	5 24	18 29	5 07	18 46	4 45	19 08	4 15	19 39	3 23	20 31
			23 19	9 47	23 38	9 26	- -	8 59	0 08	8 20	1 19	7 11
16 We 136	11 56 18	18 59	5 24	18 29	5 06	18 47	4 44	19 09	4 13	19 40	3 21	20 33
			23 59	10 42	- -	10 25	0 01	10 04	0 34	9 34	1 28	8 43
17 Th 137	11 56 20	19 13	5 23	18 30	5 06	18 47	4 43	19 10	4 12	19 42	3 18	20 36
	19 45 LQ		- -	11 37	0 13	11 25	0 31	11 10	0 55	10 49	1 32	10 16
18 Fr 138	11 56 22	19 27	5 23	18 30	5 05	18 48	4 42	19 11	4 11	19 43	3 16	20 38
			0 37	12 32	0 46	12 26	0 57	12 18	1 12	12 06	1 35	11 48
19 Sa 139	11 56 24	19 40	5 23	18 31	5 04	18 49	4 42	19 12	4 09	19 44	3 14	20 40
			1 14	13 28	1 18	13 27	1 22	13 26	1 28	13 25	1 38	13 22
20 Su 140	11 56 28	19 53	5 22	18 31	5 04	18 49	4 41	19 13	4 08	19 46	3 12	20 43
			1 51	14 26	1 50	14 31	1 47	14 37	1 44	14 46	1 40	14 59
21 Mo 141	11 56 31	20 5	5 22	18 31	5 03	18 50	4 40	19 14	4 07	19 47	3 10	20 45
			2 31	15 27	2 23	15 38	2 14	15 52	2 01	16 11	1 42	16 41
22 Tu 142	11 56 36	20 17	5 22	18 32	5 03	18 51	4 39	19 14	4 06	19 48	3 08	20 47
			3 14	16 32	3 00	16 49	2 44	17 10	2 21	17 40	1 47	18 30
23 We 143	11 56 40	20 29	5 22	18 32	5 03	18 51	4 39	19 15	4 04	19 50	3 06	20 49
			4 03	17 41	3 43	18 03	3 20	18 31	2 47	19 11	1 54	20 24
24 Th 144	11 56 46	20 41	5 21	18 32	5 02	18 52	4 38	19 16	4 03	19 51	3 04	20 51
	11 47 NM		4 58	18 51	4 34	19 17	4 04	19 50	3 22	20 37	2 07	22 11
25 Fr 145	11 56 52	20 52	5 21	18 33	5 02	18 52	4 37	19 17	4 02	19 52	3 02	20 53
			6 00	20 00	5 33	20 26	5 00	21 00	4 11	21 50	2 36	23 29
26 Sa 146	11 56 58	21 3	5 21	18 33	5 01	18 53	4 37	19 18	4 01	19 55	3 00	20 56
			7 06	21 02	6 39	21 27	6 06	21 59	5 16	22 45	3 38	- -
27 Su 147	11 57 5	21 13	5 21	18 34	5 01	18 53	4 36	19 19	4 00	19 55	2 58	20 58
			8 13	21 57	7 49	22 19	7 19	22 46	6 35	23 23	5 12	0 09
28 Mo 148	11 57 12	21 23	5 20	18 34	5 01	18 54	4 35	19 19	3 59	19 56	2 56	21 00
			9 18	22 45	8 58	23 01	8 33	23 22	7 58	23 50	6 57	0 27
29 Tu 149	11 57 20	21 33	5 20	18 34	5 00	18 55	4 35	19 20	3 59	19 57	2 55	21 01
			10 18	23 26	10 03	23 38	9 45	23 52	9 20	- -	8 38	0 36
30 We 150	11 57 28	21 42	5 20	18 35	5 00	18 55	4 34	19 21	3 58	19 58	2 53	21 03
			11 14	- -	11 05	- -	10 53	- -	10 37	0 11	10 12	0 41
31 Th 151	11 57 36	21 51	5 20	18 35	5 00	18 56	4 34	19 22	3 57	19 59	2 51	21 05
	8 11 FQ		12 07	0 03	12 03	0 09	11 58	0 17	11 51	0 28	11 41	0 44

6th Month   June, 1990   30 days

Greenwich Mean Time

NOTE: Light numbers indicate Sun. **Dark** numbers indicate **Moon**. *Degrees are North Latitude.*

FM = full moon; LQ = last quarter; NM = new moon; FQ = first quarter.

CAUTION: Must be converted to local time. For instruction see page 242.

Day of month / week / year	Sun on Meridian Moon phase h m s	Sun's Declination ° '	20° Rise Sun/Moon h m	20° Set Sun/Moon h m	30° Rise Sun/Moon h m	30° Set Sun/Moon h m	40° Rise Sun/Moon h m	40° Set Sun/Moon h m	50° Rise Sun/Moon h m	50° Set Sun/Moon h m	60° Rise Sun/Moon h m	60° Set Sun/Moon h m
1 Fr 152	11 57 45	21 59	5 20	18 36	4 59	18 56	4 33	19 22	3 56	20 00	2 50	21 07
			12 58	0 37	12 59	0 38	13 00	0 40	13 02	0 42	13 05	0 45
2 Sa 153	11 57 54	22 8	5 20	18 36	4 59	18 57	4 33	19 23	3 55	20 01	2 48	21 09
			13 47	1 09	13 53	1 06	14 01	1 02	14 11	0 56	14 28	0 47
3 Su 154	11 58 4	22 15	5 20	18 36	4 59	18 57	4 33	19 24	3 55	20 02	2 47	21 10
			14 36	1 42	14 47	1 34	15 01	1 23	15 20	1 10	15 51	0 48
4 Mo 155	11 58 14	22 23	5 20	18 37	4 59	18 58	4 32	19 25	3 54	20 03	2 46	21 12
			15 27	2 16	15 42	2 03	16 02	1 47	16 29	1 25	17 15	0 51
5 Tu 156	11 58 24	22 30	5 20	18 37	4 59	18 58	4 32	19 25	3 53	20 04	2 44	21 14
			16 18	2 52	16 38	2 35	17 03	2 13	17 39	1 43	18 41	0 54
6 We 157	11 58 35	22 36	5 20	18 38	4 59	18 59	4 32	19 26	3 53	20 05	2 43	21 15
			17 11	3 32	17 34	3 10	18 04	2 44	18 47	2 06	20 07	1 01
7 Th 158	11 58 46	22 42	5 20	18 38	4 58	18 59	4 31	19 26	3 52	20 06	2 42	21 16
			18 04	4 15	18 30	3 51	19 03	3 20	19 51	2 36	21 27	1 13
8 Fr 159	11 58 57 11 1 FM	22 48	5 20	18 38	4 58	19 00	4 31	19 27	3 52	20 06	2 41	21 18
			18 57	5 02	19 23	4 36	19 57	4 03	20 47	3 14	22 28	1 37
9 Sa 160	11 59 9	22 54	5 20	18 39	4 58	19 00	4 31	19 28	3 52	20 07	2 40	21 19
			19 47	5 54	20 13	5 27	20 46	4 53	21 33	4 04	23 06	2 22
10 Su 161	11 59 21	22 59	5 20	18 39	4 58	19 01	4 31	19 28	3 51	20 08	2 39	21 20
			20 35	6 47	20 58	6 22	21 27	5 50	22 10	5 04	23 26	3 32
11 Mo 162	11 59 33	23 3	5 20	18 39	4 58	19 01	4 31	19 29	3 51	20 08	2 39	21 21
			21 19	7 43	21 38	7 20	22 03	6 52	22 38	6 12	23 36	4 58
12 Tu 163	11 59 45	23 7	5 20	18 40	4 58	19 01	4 31	19 29	3 51	20 09	2 38	21 22
			21 59	8 38	22 14	8 20	22 34	7 57	23 00	7 24	23 42	6 29
13 We 164	11 59 57	23 11	5 20	18 40	4 58	19 02	4 31	19 30	3 50	20 10	2 37	21 23
			22 37	9 33	22 47	9 19	23 00	9 02	23 18	8 39	23 45	8 01
14 Th 165	12 0 10	23 14	5 20	18 40	4 58	19 02	4 31	19 30	3 50	20 10	2 37	21 24
			23 13	10 27	23 19	10 18	23 25	10 08	23 24	9 54	23 48	9 32
15 Fr 166	12 0 22	23 17	5 20	18 40	4 58	19 02	4 31	19 30	3 50	20 11	2 36	21 25
			23 49	11 21	23 49	11 18	23 49	11 15	23 49	11 10	23 50	11 02
16 Sa 167	12 0 35 4 48 LQ	23 20	5 20	18 41	4 59	19 03	4 31	19 31	3 50	20 11	2 36	21 26
			- -	12 16	- -	12 19	- -	12 23	- -	12 27	23 52	12 35
17 Su 168	12 0 48	23 22	5 21	18 41	4 59	19 03	4 31	19 31	3 50	20 12	2 36	21 26
			0 27	13 14	0 21	13 23	0 14	13 33	0 05	13 48	23 55	14 11
18 Mo 169	12 1 1	23 24	5 21	18 41	4 59	19 03	4 31	19 31	3 50	20 12	2 36	21 27
			1 06	14 15	0 55	14 29	0 42	14 47	0 23	15 12	- -	15 53
19 Tu 170	12 1 15	23 25	5 21	18 41	4 59	19 04	4 31	19 32	3 50	20 12	2 35	21 27
			1 51	15 20	1 34	15 40	1 14	16 05	0 45	16 40	0 00	17 42
20 We 171	12 1 28	23 26	5 21	18 42	4 59	19 04	4 31	19 32	3 50	20 13	2 36	21 28
			2 41	16 28	2 20	16 52	1 53	17 23	1 15	18 07	0 10	19 32
21 Th 172	12 1 41	23 26	5 21	18 42	4 59	19 04	4 31	19 32	3 51	20 13	2 36	21 28
			3 39	17 37	3 14	18 03	2 42	18 37	1 56	19 27	0 30	21 06
22 Fr 173	12 1 54 18 55 NM	23 27	5 22	18 43	5 00	19 04	4 31	19 32	3 51	20 13	2 36	21 28
			4 43	18 43	4 16	19 09	3 42	19 42	2 53	20 30	1 13	22 04
23 Sa 174	12 2 7	23 26	5 22	18 43	5 00	19 04	4 32	19 33	3 51	20 13	2 36	21 28
			5 51	19 42	5 25	20 05	4 53	20 35	4 06	21 16	2 33	22 30
24 Su 175	12 2 20	23 25	5 22	18 43	5 00	19 05	4 32	19 33	3 51	20 13	2 37	21 28
			6 58	20 34	6 36	20 53	6 08	21 17	5 29	21 49	4 17	22 43
25 Mo 176	12 2 33	23 24	5 22	18 43	5 00	19 05	4 32	19 33	3 52	20 13	2 37	21 28
			8 02	21 19	7 45	21 33	7 24	21 50	6 54	22 13	6 04	22 49
26 Tu 177	12 2 46	23 23	5 23	18 43	5 01	19 05	4 33	19 33	3 52	20 13	2 38	21 28
			9 02	21 59	8 50	22 07	8 36	22 18	8 16	22 32	7 44	22 53
27 We 178	12 2 59	23 21	5 23	18 43	5 01	19 05	4 33	19 33	3 53	20 13	2 38	21 27
			9 57	22 38	9 51	22 38	9 44	22 42	9 34	22 47	9 18	22 55
28 Th 179	12 3 11	23 18	5 23	18 43	5 01	19 05	4 33	19 33	3 53	20 13	2 39	21 27
			10 50	23 09	10 49	23 07	10 48	23 05	10 47	23 02	10 45	22 57
29 Fr 180	12 3 23 22 7 FQ	23 15	5 23	18 43	5 02	19 05	4 34	19 33	3 54	20 13	2 41	21 26
			11 41	23 42	11 45	23 35	11 51	23 27	11 58	23 16	12 10	22 59
30 Sa 181	12 3 35	23 12	5 24	18 43	5 02	19 05	4 34	19 33	3 54	20 13	2 41	21 26
			12 31	- -	12 40	- -	12 52	23 50	13 08	23 31	13 34	23 01

7th Month — July, 1990 — 31 days

Greenwich Mean Time

NOTE: Light numbers indicate Sun. **Dark** numbers indicate **Moon.** *Degrees are North Latitude.*

FM = full moon; LQ = last quarter; NM = new moon; FQ = first quarter.

CAUTION: Must be converted to local time. For instruction see page 242.

Day of month / week / year	Sun on Meridian / Moon phase (h m s)	Sun's Declination (° ')	20° Rise Sun/Moon	20° Set Sun/Moon	30° Rise Sun/Moon	30° Set Sun/Moon	40° Rise Sun/Moon	40° Set Sun/Moon	50° Rise Sun/Moon	50° Set Sun/Moon	60° Rise Sun/Moon	60° Set Sun/Moon
1 Su 182	12 3 47	23 8	5 24	18 43	5 02	19 05	4 35	19 33	3 55	20 13	2 42	21 25
			13 21	0 16	13 35	0 04	13 53	– –	14 18	23 48	14 59	23 04
2 Mo 183	12 3 58	23 4	5 24	18 43	5 03	19 05	4 35	19 33	3 55	20 12	2 43	21 24
			14 12	0 51	14 31	0 35	14 54	0 15	15 28	– –	16 25	23 09
3 Tu 184	12 4 10	23 0	5 25	18 44	5 03	19 05	4 36	19 32	3 56	20 12	2 44	21 23
			15 05	1 30	15 27	1 09	15 56	0 44	16 36	0 09	17 51	23 19
4 We 185	12 4 20	22 55	5 25	18 44	5 04	19 05	4 36	19 32	3 57	20 11	2 45	21 23
			15 58	2 12	16 23	1 48	16 55	1 18	17 42	0 36	19 14	23 38
5 Th 186	12 4 31	22 50	5 25	18 44	5 04	19 05	4 37	19 32	3 58	20 11	2 47	21 22
			16 51	2 58	17 17	2 32	17 51	1 59	18 41	1 11	20 23	– –
6 Fr 187	12 4 41	22 44	5 26	18 44	5 04	19 05	4 37	19 32	3 58	20 11	2 48	21 20
			17 43	3 48	18 09	3 21	18 42	2 47	19 31	1 57	21 08	0 16
7 Sa 188	12 4 51	22 38	5 26	18 44	5 05	19 05	4 38	19 31	3 59	20 10	2 49	21 19
			18 32	4 41	18 56	4 16	19 27	3 43	20 11	2 55	21 33	1 18
8 Su 189	12 5 0 / 1 23 FM	22 32	5 26	18 43	5 05	19 04	4 39	19 31	4 00	20 09	2 51	21 18
			19 17	5 37	19 38	5 14	20 04	4 44	20 41	4 01	21 45	2 41
9 Mo 190	12 5 9	22 25	5 27	18 43	5 06	19 04	4 39	19 31	4 01	20 09	2 52	21 17
			19 59	6 33	20 16	6 13	20 37	5 49	21 05	5 14	21 52	4 12
10 Tu 191	12 5 18	22 18	5 27	18 43	5 06	19 04	4 40	19 30	4 02	20 08	2 54	21 15
			20 38	7 28	20 50	7 13	21 05	6 55	21 25	6 29	21 56	5 45
11 We 192	12 5 26	22 10	5 27	18 43	5 07	19 04	4 41	19 30	4 03	20 07	2 56	21 14
			21 15	8 23	21 22	8 13	21 30	8 01	21 41	7 44	21 59	7 17
12 Th 193	12 5 34	22 2	5 28	18 43	5 07	19 04	4 41	19 30	4 04	20 07	2 57	21 12
			21 51	9 17	21 52	9 13	21 54	9 07	21 57	9 00	22 01	8 48
13 Fr 194	12 5 41	21 54	5 28	18 43	5 08	19 03	4 42	19 29	4 05	20 06	2 59	21 11
			22 27	10 12	22 23	10 13	22 18	10 14	22 12	10 16	22 03	10 19
14 Sa 195	12 5 48	21 45	5 29	18 43	5 08	19 03	4 43	19 29	4 06	20 05	3 01	21 09
			23 05	11 08	22 56	11 15	22 44	11 23	22 29	11 35	22 05	11 53
15 Su 196	12 5 55	21 36	5 29	18 43	5 09	19 03	4 43	19 28	4 07	20 04	3 03	21 08
			23 46	12 06	23 32	12 19	23 13	12 34	22 49	12 56	22 09	13 31
16 Mo 197	12 6 1 / 11 4 LQ	21 27	5 29	18 43	5 09	19 02	4 44	19 27	4 08	20 03	3 05	21 06
			– –	13 08	– –	13 26	23 48	13 48	23 14	14 20	22 17	15 14
17 Tu 198	12 6 6	21 17	5 30	18 42	5 10	19 02	4 45	19 27	4 09	20 02	3 07	21 04
			0 33	14 12	0 13	14 35	– –	15 04	23 48	15 45	22 30	17 01
18 We 199	12 6 11	21 7	5 30	18 42	5 11	19 02	4 46	19 26	4 11	20 01	3 09	21 02
			1 26	15 19	1 02	15 45	0 32	16 18	– –	17 06	23 00	18 41
19 Th 200	12 6 15	20 56	5 31	18 42	5 11	19 01	4 47	19 25	4 12	20 00	3 11	21 00
			2 25	16 25	1 59	16 51	1 26	17 25	0 37	18 15	– –	19 54
20 Fr 201	12 6 19	20 45	5 31	18 42	5 12	19 01	4 47	19 25	4 13	19 59	3 13	20 58
			3 30	17 26	3 04	17 51	2 30	18 23	1 41	19 08	0 02	20 32
21 Sa 202	12 6 22	20 34	5 31	18 41	5 12	19 00	4 48	19 24	4 14	19 58	3 15	20 56
			4 37	18 21	4 13	18 42	3 43	19 09	2 59	19 46	1 37	20 50
22 Su 203	12 6 25 / 2 54 NM	20 22	5 32	18 41	5 13	19 00	4 49	19 23	4 15	19 57	3 17	20 54
			5 43	19 10	5 23	19 26	4 59	19 46	4 24	20 14	3 24	20 58
23 Mo 204	12 6 27	20 10	5 32	18 41	5 13	18 59	4 50	19 22	4 17	19 55	3 19	20 52
			6 45	19 52	6 31	20 03	6 13	20 17	5 48	20 35	5 08	21 03
24 Tu 205	12 6 29	19 58	5 32	18 40	5 14	18 59	4 51	19 22	4 18	19 54	3 22	20 50
			7 43	20 30	7 35	20 36	7 24	20 43	7 09	20 52	6 46	21 06
25 We 206	12 6 30	19 45	5 33	18 40	5 15	18 58	4 52	19 21	4 19	19 53	3 24	20 48
			8 38	21 06	8 35	21 06	8 32	21 06	8 26	21 07	8 18	21 08
26 Th 207	12 6 30	19 33	5 33	18 40	5 15	18 57	4 53	19 20	4 21	19 52	3 26	20 45
			9 31	21 40	9 33	21 35	9 36	21 29	9 40	21 21	9 46	21 09
27 Fr 208	12 6 30	19 19	5 33	18 39	5 16	18 57	4 53	19 19	4 22	19 50	3 28	20 43
			10 22	22 14	10 30	22 04	10 39	21 52	10 52	21 36	11 12	21 11
28 Sa 209	12 6 29	19 6	5 34	18 39	5 16	18 56	4 54	19 18	4 23	19 49	3 31	20 41
			11 13	22 49	11 26	22 35	11 41	22 17	12 03	21 53	12 37	21 14
29 Su 210	12 6 28 / 14 1 FQ	18 52	5 34	18 38	5 17	18 56	4 55	19 17	4 25	19 47	3 33	20 38
			12 05	23 26	12 22	23 08	12 43	22 45	13 13	22 12	14 04	21 18
30 Mo 211	12 6 26	18 38	5 35	18 38	5 18	18 55	4 56	19 16	4 26	19 46	3 35	20 36
			12 57	– –	13 18	23 45	13 45	23 17	14 23	22 37	15 31	21 26
31 Tu 212	12 6 23	18 23	5 35	18 38	5 18	18 54	4 57	19 15	4 27	19 44	3 38	20 34
			13 50	0 07	14 14	– –	14 45	23 55	15 30	23 09	16 56	21 41

8th Month   August, 1990   31 days

Greenwich Mean Time

NOTE: Light numbers indicate Sun. **Dark** numbers indicate **Moon.** *Degrees are North Latitude.*

FM = full moon; LQ = last quarter; NM = new moon; FQ = first quarter.

CAUTION: Must be converted to local time. For instruction see page 242.

Day of month / week / year	Sun on Meridian / Moon phase (h m s)	Sun's Declina-tion (° ')	20° Rise	20° Set	30° Rise	30° Set	40° Rise	40° Set	50° Rise	50° Set	60° Rise	60° Set
1 We	12 6 20	18 8	5 35	18 37	5 19	18 53	4 58	19 14	4 29	19 43	3 40	20 31
213			14 43	0 52	15 09	0 27	15 43	– –	16 32	23 50	18 12	22 10
2 Th	12 6 16	17 53	5 36	18 37	5 19	18 53	4 59	19 13	4 30	19 41	3 42	20 29
214			15 35	1 40	16 02	1 14	16 36	0 40	17 26	– –	19 07	23 03
3 Fr	12 6 11	17 38	5 36	18 36	5 20	18 52	5 00	19 12	4 32	19 40	3 45	20 26
215			16 25	2 33	16 51	2 06	17 23	1 33	18 09	0 43	19 38	– –
4 Sa	12 6 6	17 22	5 36	18 36	5 21	18 51	5 01	19 11	4 33	19 38	3 47	20 24
216			17 12	3 28	17 35	3 03	18 03	2 32	18 43	1 47	19 54	0 20
5 Su	12 5 60	17 6	5 37	18 35	5 21	18 50	5 02	19 10	4 34	19 37	3 49	20 21
217			17 56	4 24	18 15	4 03	18 38	3 36	19 10	2 58	20 03	1 50
6 Mo	12 5 54	16 50	5 37	18 35	5 22	18 50	5 03	19 09	4 36	19 35	3 52	20 18
218	14 19 FM		18 37	5 20	18 50	5 04	19 07	4 43	19 31	4 13	20 07	3 24
7 Tu	12 5 47	16 33	5 37	18 34	5 22	18 49	5 04	19 07	4 37	19 33	3 54	20 16
219			19 15	6 16	19 23	6 05	19 34	5 50	19 48	5 30	20 10	4 57
8 We	12 5 39	16 17	5 38	18 33	5 23	18 48	5 05	19 06	4 39	19 32	3 57	20 13
220			19 52	7 12	19 55	7 05	19 59	6 58	20 04	6 47	20 13	6 30
9 Th	12 5 31	15 60	5 38	18 33	5 24	18 47	5 05	19 05	4 40	19 30	3 59	20 10
221			20 28	8 07	20 26	8 06	20 23	8 06	20 20	8 05	20 15	8 03
10 Fr	12 5 22	15 42	5 38	18 32	5 24	18 46	5 06	19 04	4 42	19 28	4 01	20 08
222			21 06	9 03	20 58	9 08	20 49	9 15	20 36	9 23	20 17	9 37
11 Sa	12 5 13	15 25	5 39	18 32	5 25	18 45	5 07	19 02	4 43	19 26	4 04	20 05
223			21 46	10 01	21 33	10 12	21 17	10 25	20 55	10 44	20 20	11 13
12 Su	12 5 3	15 7	5 39	18 31	5 25	18 44	5 08	19 01	4 45	19 24	4 06	20 02
224			22 31	11 01	22 12	11 18	21 49	11 38	21 18	12 07	20 26	12 55
13 Mo	12 4 52	14 49	5 39	18 30	5 26	18 43	5 09	19 00	4 46	19 23	4 09	19 59
225	15 54 LQ		23 21	12 04	22 58	12 26	22 29	12 52	21 49	13 31	20 37	14 40
14 Tu	12 4 42	14 31	5 40	18 30	5 27	18 42	5 10	18 58	4 48	19 21	4 11	19 57
226			– –	13 09	23 51	13 34	23 18	14 06	22 31	14 52	21 00	16 21
15 We	12 4 30	14 12	5 40	18 29	5 27	18 41	5 11	18 57	4 49	19 19	4 13	19 54
227			0 16	14 14	– –	14 40	– –	15 14	23 27	16 04	21 47	17 44
16 Th	12 4 18	13 53	5 40	18 28	5 28	18 40	5 12	18 56	4 51	19 17	4 16	19 51
228			1 18	15 15	0 51	15 41	0 17	16 14	– –	17 01	23 09	18 33
17 Fr	12 4 6	13 34	5 40	18 27	5 28	18 39	5 13	18 54	4 52	19 15	4 18	19 48
229			2 22	16 11	1 57	16 34	1 25	17 03	0 39	17 44	– –	18 56
18 Sa	12 3 53	13 15	5 41	18 27	5 29	18 38	5 14	18 53	4 54	19 13	4 21	19 45
230			3 27	17 01	3 05	17 20	2 38	17 43	1 59	18 15	0 50	19 07
19 Su	12 3 39	12 56	5 41	18 26	5 29	18 37	5 15	18 52	4 55	19 11	4 23	19 43
231			4 30	17 45	4 13	17 59	3 52	18 16	3 23	18 38	2 34	19 13
20 Mo	12 3 25	12 36	5 41	18 25	5 30	18 36	5 16	18 50	4 57	19 09	4 25	19 40
232	12 39 NM		5 29	18 25	5 18	18 33	5 04	18 43	4 45	18 57	4 14	19 17
21 Tu	12 3 11	12 16	5 42	18 25	5 31	18 35	5 17	18 49	4 58	19 07	4 28	19 37
233			6 26	19 02	6 20	19 05	6 13	19 08	6 03	19 12	5 48	19 19
22 We	12 2 56	11 56	5 42	18 24	5 31	18 34	5 18	18 47	5 00	19 05	4 30	19 34
234			7 19	19 37	7 19	19 34	7 19	19 31	7 19	19 27	7 19	19 21
23 Th	12 2 41	11 36	5 42	18 23	5 32	18 33	5 19	18 46	5 01	19 03	4 33	19 31
235			8 12	20 17	8 17	20 03	8 23	19 54	8 32	19 42	8 46	19 23
24 Fr	12 2 25	11 16	5 42	18 22	5 32	18 32	5 20	18 44	5 03	19 01	4 35	19 25
236			9 03	20 46	9 14	20 34	9 27	20 18	9 44	19 58	10 12	19 25
25 Sa	12 2 9	10 55	5 43	18 21	5 33	18 31	5 21	18 43	5 04	18 59	4 37	19 22
237			9 55	21 23	10 10	21 06	10 29	20 45	10 56	20 16	11 39	19 29
26 Su	12 1 52	10 35	5 43	18 21	5 33	18 30	5 22	18 41	5 05	18 57	4 40	19 22
238			10 48	22 02	11 07	21 42	11 32	21 15	12 06	20 39	13 07	19 35
27 Mo	12 1 35	10 14	5 43	18 20	5 34	18 29	5 23	18 40	5 07	18 55	4 42	19 19
239			11 41	22 45	12 04	22 21	12 33	21 51	13 15	21 07	14 34	19 47
28 Tu	12 1 18	9 53	5 43	18 19	5 35	18 28	5 24	18 38	5 08	18 53	4 45	19 16
240	7 34 FQ		12 34	23 32	12 59	23 06	13 32	22 33	14 19	21 45	15 54	20 09
29 We	12 0 60	9 32	5 44	18 18	5 35	18 26	5 25	18 37	5 09	18 51	4 47	19 13
241			13 26	– –	13 53	23 56	14 27	23 23	15 16	22 33	16 58	20 51
30 Th	12 0 41	9 10	5 44	18 17	5 36	18 25	5 25	18 35	5 11	18 49	4 49	19 10
242			14 17	0 23	14 43	– –	15 16	– –	16 04	23 31	17 38	21 58
31 Fr	12 0 23	8 49	5 44	18 16	5 36	18 24	5 26	18 34	5 13	18 47	4 52	19 07
243			15 05	1 16	15 29	0 51	15 59	0 19	16 42	– –	18 00	23 23

9th Month   September, 1990   30 days

Greenwich Mean Time

NOTE: Light numbers indicate Sun. **Dark** numbers indicate **Moon**. *Degrees are North Latitude.*

FM = full moon; LQ = last quarter; NM = new moon; FQ = first quarter.

CAUTION: Must be converted to local time. For instruction see page 242.

Day of month / week / year	Sun on Meridian Moon phase (h m s)	Sun's Declination (° ')	20° Rise Sun/Moon (h m)	20° Set Sun/Moon (h m)	30° Rise Sun/Moon (h m)	30° Set Sun/Moon (h m)	40° Rise Sun/Moon (h m)	40° Set Sun/Moon (h m)	50° Rise Sun/Moon (h m)	50° Set Sun/Moon (h m)	60° Rise Sun/Moon (h m)	60° Set Sun/Moon (h m)
1 Sa	12 0 4	8 27	5 44	18 16	5 37	18 23	5 27	18 32	5 14	18 45	4 54	19 04
244			15 50	2 12	16 10	1 49	16 35	1 21	17 11	0 39	18 11	- -
2 Su	11 59 45	8 5	5 45	18 15	5 37	18 22	5 28	18 30	5 16	18 43	4 56	19 01
245			16 32	3 08	16 48	2 50	17 07	2 26	17 34	1 53	18 18	0 55
3 Mo	11 59 25	7 44	5 45	18 14	5 38	18 21	5 29	18 29	5 17	18 40	4 59	18 58
246			17 11	4 05	17 22	3 51	17 35	3 33	17 53	3 09	18 22	2 30
4 Tu	11 59 6	7 22	5 45	18 13	5 38	18 19	5 30	18 27	5 19	18 38	5 01	18 55
247			17 49	5 01	17 54	4 52	18 01	4 42	18 10	4 27	18 24	4 04
5 We	11 58 46	6 59	5 45	18 12	5 39	18 18	5 31	18 26	5 20	18 36	5 04	18 52
248	01 46 FM		18 26	5 57	18 26	5 54	18 26	5 51	18 26	5 46	18 27	5 38
6 Th	11 58 26	6 37	5 45	18 11	5 39	18 17	5 32	18 24	5 22	18 34	5 06	18 49
249			19 05	6 54	18 59	6 57	18 52	7 01	18 43	7 06	18 29	7 13
7 Fr	11 58 5	6 15	5 46	18 10	5 40	18 16	5 33	18 22	5 23	18 32	5 08	18 46
250			19 45	7 53	19 34	8 02	19 20	8 13	19 01	8 28	18 32	8 51
8 Sa	11 57 45	5 52	5 46	18 09	5 41	18 14	5 34	18 21	5 25	18 30	5 11	18 43
251			20 29	8 54	20 12	9 08	19 52	9 26	19 23	9 52	18 38	10 33
9 Su	11 57 24	5 30	5 46	18 08	5 41	18 13	5 35	18 19	5 26	18 27	5 13	18 40
252			21 18	9 57	20 56	10 17	20 29	10 42	19 52	11 17	18 47	12 19
10 Mo	11 57 3	5 7	5 46	18 08	5 42	18 12	5 36	18 18	5 28	18 25	5 15	18 37
253			22 12	11 02	21 47	11 26	21 16	11 56	20 30	12 40	19 06	14 03
11 Tu	11 56 42	4 44	5 46	18 07	5 42	18 11	5 37	18 16	5 29	18 23	5 18	18 34
254	20 53 LQ		23 12	12 07	22 45	12 33	22 11	13 07	21 22	13 56	19 44	15 33
12 We	11 56 21	4 22	5 47	18 06	5 43	18 10	5 38	18 14	5 31	18 21	5 20	18 31
255			- -	13 09	23 49	13 35	23 16	14 09	22 28	14 57	20 54	16 32
13 Th	11 55 60	3 59	5 47	18 05	5 43	18 08	5 39	18 13	5 32	18 19	5 22	18 28
256			0 14	14 06	- -	14 30	- -	15 00	23 45	15 43	22 29	17 01
14 Fr	11 55 38	3 36	5 47	18 04	5 44	18 07	5 40	18 11	5 34	18 17	5 25	18 25
257			1 18	14 57	0 55	15 17	0 26	15 42	- -	16 17	- -	17 16
15 Sa	11 55 17	3 13	5 47	18 03	5 44	18 06	5 41	18 09	5 35	18 14	5 27	18 22
258			2 20	15 42	2 02	15 57	1 38	16 16	1 06	16 42	0 10	17 23
16 Su	11 54 56	2 50	5 47	18 02	5 45	18 05	5 41	18 08	5 37	18 12	5 29	18 19
259			3 19	16 22	3 06	16 32	2 49	16 45	2 26	17 02	1 49	17 28
17 Mo	11 54 34	2 26	5 48	18 01	5 45	18 03	5 42	18 06	5 38	18 10	5 32	18 16
260			4 16	16 59	4 08	17 04	3 58	17 10	3 45	17 18	3 24	17 31
18 Tu	11 54 13	2 3	5 48	18 00	5 46	18 02	5 43	18 04	5 40	18 08	5 34	18 13
261			5 10	17 34	5 07	17 34	5 04	17 34	5 00	17 33	4 54	17 33
19 We	11 53 52	1 40	5 48	17 59	5 46	18 01	5 44	18 03	5 41	18 05	5 36	18 10
262	0 46 NM		6 02	18 09	6 05	18 03	6 09	17 57	6 14	17 48	6 21	17 35
20 Th	11 53 31	1 17	5 48	17 58	5 47	18 00	5 45	18 01	5 43	18 03	5 39	18 07
263			6 54	18 44	7 02	18 33	7 12	18 21	7 26	18 04	7 48	17 37
21 Fr	11 53 9	0 53	5 49	17 57	5 48	17 58	5 46	17 59	5 44	18 01	5 41	18 04
264			7 46	19 20	7 59	19 05	8 15	18 46	8 38	18 21	9 14	17 41
22 Sa	11 52 48	0 30	5 49	17 57	5 48	17 57	5 47	17 58	5 46	17 59	5 43	18 01
265			8 38	19 59	8 56	19 39	9 18	19 15	9 49	18 42	10 42	17 46
23 Su	11 52 27	0 7	5 49	17 56	5 49	17 56	5 48	17 56	5 47	17 57	5 46	17 58
266			9 31	20 40	9 53	20 18	10 20	19 49	10 59	19 08	12 09	17 56
24 Mo	11 52 6	— 0 17	5 49	17 55	5 49	17 55	5 49	17 54	5 49	17 54	5 48	17 55
267			10 24	21 26	10 49	21 00	11 20	20 28	12 05	19 42	13 32	18 14
25 Tu	11 51 46	— 0 40	5 49	17 54	5 50	17 53	5 50	17 53	5 50	17 52	5 50	17 52
268			11 17	22 14	11 43	21 48	12 16	21 15	13 05	20 25	14 44	18 47
26 We	11 51 25	— 1 3	5 50	17 53	5 50	17 52	5 51	17 51	5 52	17 50	5 53	17 49
269			12 08	23 06	12 34	22 40	13 07	22 08	13 56	21 19	15 33	19 43
27 Th	11 51 4	— 1 27	5 50	17 52	5 51	17 51	5 52	17 50	5 53	17 48	5 55	17 46
270	2 6 FQ		12 56	- -	13 21	23 36	13 52	23 06	14 37	22 22	16 02	21 00
28 Fr	11 50 44	— 1 50	5 50	17 51	5 51	17 50	5 53	17 48	5 55	17 46	5 58	17 43
271			13 42	0 00	14 04	- -	14 31	- -	15 10	23 32	16 17	22 27
29 Sa	11 50 24	— 2 13	5 50	17 50	5 52	17 48	5 54	17 46	5 56	17 44	6 00	17 40
272			14 25	0 55	14 42	0 35	15 04	0 09	15 35	- -	16 26	23 59
30 Su	11 50 4	— 2 37	5 51	17 49	5 53	17 47	5 55	17 45	5 58	17 41	6 02	17 37
273			15 05	1 51	15 18	1 35	15 34	1 14	15 56	0 46	16 31	- -

10th Month   October, 1990   31 days

Greenwich Mean Time

NOTE: Light numbers indicate Sun. **Dark** numbers indicate **Moon.** *Degrees are North Latitude.*

FM = full moon; LQ = last quarter; NM = new moon; FQ = first quarter.

CAUTION: Must be converted to local time. For instruction see page 242.

Day of month week year	Sun on Meridian Moon phase h m s	Sun's Declina-tion	20° Rise Sun Moon h m	20° Set Sun Moon h m	30° Rise Sun Moon h m	30° Set Sun Moon h m	40° Rise Sun Moon h m	40° Set Sun Moon h m	50° Rise Sun Moon h m	50° Set Sun Moon h m	60° Rise Sun Moon h m	60° Set Sun Moon h m
1 Mo 274	11 49 45	− 3 0	5 51	17 48	5 53	17 46	5 56	17 43	5 59	17 39	6 05	17 34
			15 43	2 46	15 51	2 35	16 01	2 22	16 14	2 03	16 34	1 32
2 Tu 275	11 49 25	− 3 23	5 51	17 48	5 54	17 45	5 57	17 41	6 01	17 37	6 07	17 31
			16 20	3 42	16 23	3 37	16 26	3 30	16 31	3 20	16 37	3 05
3 We 276	11 49 6	− 3 47	5 51	17 47	5 54	17 43	5 58	17 40	6 03	17 35	6 09	17 28
			16 59	4 39	16 56	4 39	16 52	4 40	16 47	4 40	16 40	4 40
4 Th 277	11 48 48 / 12 2 FM	− 4 10	5 52	17 46	5 55	17 42	5 59	17 38	6 04	17 33	6 12	17 25
			17 39	5 38	17 30	5 44	17 19	5 52	17 05	6 02	16 43	6 18
5 Fr 278	11 48 30	− 4 33	5 52	17 45	5 55	17 41	6 00	17 37	6 06	17 31	6 14	17 22
			18 23	6 39	18 08	6 51	17 50	7 06	17 26	7 27	16 49	8 00
6 Sa 279	11 48 12	− 4 56	5 52	17 44	5 56	17 40	6 01	17 35	6 07	17 28	6 17	17 19
			19 11	7 44	18 52	8 01	18 27	8 24	17 53	8 55	16 57	9 47
7 Su 280	11 47 54	− 5 19	5 52	17 43	5 57	17 39	6 02	17 33	6 09	17 26	6 19	17 16
			20 05	8 50	19 42	9 13	19 12	9 41	18 29	10 22	17 13	11 36
8 Mo 281	11 47 37	− 5 42	5 53	17 42	5 57	17 38	6 03	17 32	6 10	17 24	6 21	17 13
			21 05	9 58	20 39	10 23	20 06	10 55	19 18	11 43	17 44	13 15
9 Tu 282	11 47 20	− 6 5	5 53	17 42	5 58	17 36	6 04	17 30	6 12	17 22	6 24	17 10
			22 08	11 02	21 42	11 28	21 09	12 02	20 21	12 50	18 46	14 26
10 We 283	11 47 4	− 6 28	5 53	17 41	5 58	17 35	6 05	17 29	6 13	17 20	6 26	17 07
			23 12	12 02	22 48	12 26	22 19	12 57	21 35	13 42	20 15	15 04
11 Th 284	11 46 48 / 3 31 LQ	− 6 50	5 53	17 40	5 59	17 34	6 06	17 27	6 15	17 18	6 29	17 04
			− −	12 54	23 55	13 16	23 30	13 42	22 55	14 19	21 55	15 23
12 Fr 285	11 46 33	− 7 13	5 54	17 39	6 00	17 33	6 07	17 26	6 17	17 16	6 31	17 01
			0 14	13 41	− −	13 58	− −	14 18	− −	14 47	23 33	15 32
13 Sa 286	11 46 18	− 7 36	5 54	17 38	6 00	17 32	6 08	17 24	6 18	17 14	6 34	16 58
			1 14	14 22	0 59	14 34	0 41	14 48	0 15	15 08	− −	15 38
14 Su 287	11 46 4	− 7 58	5 54	17 38	6 01	17 31	6 09	17 23	6 20	17 12	6 36	16 55
			2 10	15 00	2 01	15 06	1 49	15 14	1 33	15 25	1 07	15 41
15 Mo 288	11 45 50	− 8 20	5 55	17 37	6 02	17 30	6 10	17 21	6 21	17 10	6 39	16 52
			3 04	15 35	3 00	15 36	2 55	15 38	2 48	15 40	2 37	15 44
16 Tu 289	11 45 37	− 8 42	5 55	17 36	6 02	17 29	6 11	17 20	6 23	17 08	6 41	16 49
			3 56	16 09	3 57	16 05	3 58	16 01	4 00	15 55	4 03	15 46
17 We 290	11 45 25	− 9 5	5 55	17 35	6 03	17 27	6 12	17 18	6 25	17 06	6 43	16 46
			4 47	16 43	4 54	16 35	5 01	16 24	5 12	16 10	5 28	15 49
18 Th 291	11 45 13 / 15 37 NM	− 9 27	5 56	17 34	6 04	17 26	6 13	17 17	6 26	17 04	6 46	16 43
			5 39	17 19	5 50	17 05	6 04	16 49	6 23	16 27	6 54	15 52
19 Fr 292	11 45 2	− 9 48	5 56	17 34	6 04	17 25	6 14	17 15	6 28	17 02	6 48	16 40
			6 31	17 56	6 46	17 39	7 06	17 17	7 34	16 47	8 20	15 57
20 Sa 293	11 44 51	−10 10	5 56	17 33	6 05	17 24	6 15	17 14	6 29	17 00	6 51	16 38
			7 23	18 37	7 43	18 16	8 08	17 49	8 44	17 11	9 47	16 06
21 Su 294	11 44 41	−10 32	5 57	17 32	6 06	17 23	6 16	17 12	6 31	16 58	6 53	16 35
			8 16	19 21	8 40	18 57	9 09	18 26	9 52	17 42	11 12	16 21
22 Mo 295	11 44 32	−10 53	5 57	17 32	6 06	17 22	6 17	17 11	6 33	16 56	6 56	16 32
			9 09	20 08	9 35	19 43	10 07	19 10	10 54	18 22	12 28	16 48
23 Tu 296	11 44 23	−11 14	5 58	17 31	6 07	17 21	6 19	17 10	6 34	16 54	6 59	16 29
			10 01	20 59	10 27	20 33	11 00	20 00	11 48	19 12	13 25	17 35
24 We 297	11 44 15	−11 35	5 58	17 30	6 08	17 20	6 20	17 08	6 36	16 52	7 01	16 26
			10 50	21 51	11 15	21 27	11 47	20 56	12 33	20 11	14 01	18 44
25 Th 298	11 44 8	−11 56	5 58	17 30	6 08	17 19	6 21	17 07	6 38	16 50	7 04	16 24
			11 36	22 45	11 58	22 23	12 27	21 56	13 08	21 17	14 21	20 06
26 Fr 299	11 44 1 / 20 26 FQ	−12 17	5 59	17 29	6 09	17 18	6 22	17 06	6 39	16 48	7 06	16 21
			12 18	23 39	12 38	23 21	13 02	22 59	13 35	22 28	14 32	21 34
27 Sa 300	11 43 55	−12 37	5 59	17 28	6 10	17 18	6 23	17 04	6 41	16 46	7 09	16 18
			12 58	− −	13 13	− −	13 32	− −	13 58	23 41	14 38	23 04
28 Su 301	11 43 50	−12 57	6 00	17 28	6 11	17 17	6 24	17 03	6 42	16 44	7 11	16 15
			13 36	0 33	13 47	0 20	13 59	0 04	14 16	− −	14 43	− −
29 Mo 302	11 43 46	−13 18	6 00	17 27	6 11	17 16	6 25	17 02	6 44	16 43	7 14	16 13
			14 13	1 27	14 18	1 19	14 25	1 09	14 33	0 56	14 46	0 34
30 Tu 303	11 43 42	−13 37	6 00	17 27	6 12	17 15	6 26	17 00	6 46	16 41	7 16	16 10
			14 51	2 22	14 50	2 20	14 50	2 17	14 50	2 12	14 49	2 05
31 We 304	11 43 39	−13 57	6 01	17 26	6 13	17 14	6 28	16 59	6 47	16 39	7 19	16 07
			15 29	3 19	15 23	3 22	15 16	3 26	15 07	3 32	14 53	3 40

11th Month · November, 1990 · 30 days

Greenwich Mean Time

NOTE: Light numbers indicate Sun. **Dark** numbers indicate **Moon.** *Degrees are North Latitude.*

FM = full moon; LQ = last quarter; NM = new moon; FQ = first quarter.

CAUTION: Must be converted to local time. For instruction see page 242.

Day of month/week/year	Sun on Meridian / Moon phase (h m s)	Sun's Declination (° ')	20° Rise Sun/Moon	20° Set Sun/Moon	30° Rise Sun/Moon	30° Set Sun/Moon	40° Rise Sun/Moon	40° Set Sun/Moon	50° Rise Sun/Moon	50° Set Sun/Moon	60° Rise Sun/Moon	60° Set Sun/Moon
1 Th 305	11 43 37	−14 17	6 01	17 26	6 14	17 13	6 29	16 58	6 49	16 37	7 21	16 05
			16 11	4 19	16 00	4 28	15 46	4 39	15 27	4 55	14 57	5 19
2 Fr 306	11 43 36 / 21 48 FM	−14 36	6 02	17 25	6 14	17 12	6 30	16 57	6 51	16 36	7 24	16 02
			16 58	5 22	16 41	5 37	16 20	5 56	15 51	6 22	15 05	7 04
3 Sa 307	11 43 35	−14 55	6 02	17 25	6 15	17 12	6 31	16 56	6 52	16 34	7 27	16 00
			17 51	6 29	17 29	6 50	17 02	7 15	16 23	7 51	15 17	8 54
4 Su 308	11 43 35	−15 13	6 03	17 24	6 16	17 11	6 32	16 55	6 54	16 32	7 29	15 57
			18 50	7 39	18 25	8 03	17 54	8 34	17 08	9 18	15 42	10 42
5 Mo 309	11 43 36	−15 32	6 03	17 24	6 17	17 10	6 33	16 54	6 56	16 31	7 32	15 55
			19 55	8 47	19 29	9 13	18 56	9 46	18.07	10 34	16 33	12 09
6 Tu 310	11 43 38	−15 50	6 04	17 23	6 17	17 09	6 34	16 52	6 57	16 29	7 34	15 52
			21 01	9 51	20 37	10 16	20 06	10 48	19 21	11 34	17 56	13 01
7 We 311	11 43 41	−16 8	6 04	17 23	6 18	17 09	6 36	16 51	6 59	16 28	7 37	15 50
			22 06	10 48	21 46	11 11	21 19	11 38	20 42	12 18	19 36	13 37
8 Th 312	11 43 45	−16 26	6 05	17 23	6 19	17 08	6 37	16 50	7 01	16 26	7 39	15 47
			23 08	11 38	22 52	11 56	22 32	12 18	22 04	12 49	21 17	13 39
9 Fr 313	11 43 49 / 13 2 LQ	−16 43	6 05	17 22	6 20	17 07	6 38	16 49	7 02	16 25	7 42	15 45
			− −	12 22	23 55	12 35	23 42	12 51	23 23	13 13	22 53	13 47
10 Sa 314	11 43 55	−17 0	6 06	17 22	6 21	17 07	6 39	16 48	7 04	16 23	7 45	15 42
			0 06	13 00	− −	13 08	− −	13 18	− −	13 31	− −	13 51
11 Su 315	11 44 1	−17 17	6 06	17 21	6 21	17 06	6 40	16 47	7 06	16 22	7 47	15 40
			1 01	13 36	0 55	13 39	0 48	13 43	0 39	13 47	0 24	13 54
12 Mo 316	11 44 8	−17 34	6 07	17 21	6 22	17 06	6 41	16 47	7 07	16 20	7 50	15 38
			1 53	14 10	1 52	14 08	1 52	14 06	1 51	14 02	1 51	13 57
13 Tu 317	11 44 16	−17 50	6 07	17 21	6 23	17 05	6 42	16 46	7 09	16 19	7 52	15 36
			2 44	14 44	2 49	14 37	2 54	14 29	3 02	14 17	3 15	13 59
14 We 318	11 44 25	−18 6	6 08	17 21	6 24	17 05	6 44	16 45	7 11	16 18	7 55	15 33
			3 34	15 19	3 44	15 07	3 56	14 53	4 13	14 33	4 39	14 03
15 Th 319	11 44 34	−18 22	6 09	17 20	6 25	17 04	6 45	16 44	7 12	16 16	7 57	15 31
			4 26	15 56	4 40	15 40	4 58	15 20	5 23	14 52	6 04	14 08
16 Fr 320	11 44 45	−18 37	6 09	17 20	6 26	17 04	6 46	16 43	7 14	16 15	8 00	15 29
			5 18	16 35	5 36	16 15	6 00	15 50	6 33	15 15	7 30	14 15
17 Sa 321	11 44 56 / 9 5 NM	−18 52	6 10	17 20	6 26	17 03	6 47	16 42	7 15	16 14	8 02	15 27
			6 11	17 18	6 33	16 55	7 01	16 26	7 41	15 44	8 55	14 28
18 Su 322	11 45 9	−19 7	6 10	17 20	6 27	17 03	6 48	16 42	7 17	16 13	8 05	15 25
			7 03	18 04	7 28	17 39	8 00	17 07	8 45	16 21	10 14	14 51
19 Mo 323	11 45 22	−19 21	6 11	17 20	6 28	17 02	6 49	16 41	7 19	16 12	8 07	15 23
			7 55	18 54	8 21	18 28	8 54	17 55	9 42	17 07	11 18	15 32
20 Tu 324	11 45 36	−19 35	6 12	17 19	6 29	17 02	6 50	16 40	7 20	16 10	8 10	15 21
			8 45	19 46	9 11	19 21	9 43	18 50	10 30	18 03	12 00	16 34
21 We 325	11 45 50	−19 48	6 12	17 19	6 30	17 02	6 52	16 40	7 22	16 09	8 12	15 19
			9 32	20 39	9 55	20 17	10 25	19 48	11 07	19 07	12 24	17 52
22 Th 326	11 46 6	−20 2	6 13	17 19	6 31	17 01	6 53	16 39	7 23	16 08	8 14	15 17
			10 15	21 32	10 36	21 13	11 01	20 49	11 37	20 16	12 38	19 17
23 Fr 327	11 46 22	−20 15	6 13	17 19	6 31	17 01	6 54	16 39	7 25	16 07	8 17	15 15
			10 56	22 25	11 12	22 10	11 32	21 52	12 00	21 26	12 46	20 44
24 Sa 328	11 46 39	−20 27	6 14	17 19	6 32	17 01	6 55	16 38	7 26	16 06	8 19	15 14
			11 33	23 17	11 45	23 08	12 00	22 55	12 20	22 38	12 51	22 11
25 Su 329	11 46 57 / 13 11 FQ	−20 39	6 15	17 19	6 33	17 01	6 56	16 38	7 28	16 06	8 21	15 12
			12 09	− −	12 16	− −	12 25	24 00	12 37	23 52	12 55	23 39
26 Mo 330	11 47 15	−20 51	6 15	17 19	6 34	17 00	6 57	16 37	7 29	16 05	8 24	15 10
			12 45	0 10	12 47	0 06	12 49	− −	12 53	− −	12.58	− −
27 Tu 331	11 47 34	−21 2	6 16	17 19	6 35	17 00	6 58	16 37	7 31	16 04	8 26	15 09
			13 22	1 04	13 18	1 05	13 14	1 06	13 09	1 07	13 01	1 08
28 We 332	11 47 54	−21 13	6 17	17 19	6 36	17 00	6 59	16 36	7 32	16 03	8 28	15 07
			14 01	2 01	13 52	2 07	13 41	2 14	13 27	2 25	13 05	2 41
29 Th 333	11 48 15	−21 24	6 17	17 19	6 36	17 00	7 00	16 36	7 34	16 03	8 30	15 06
			14 44	3 00	14 30	3 12	14 12	3 27	13 48	3 48	13 11	4 20
30 Fr 334	11 48 36	−21 34	6 18	17 19	6 37	17 00	7 01	16 36	7 35	16 02	8 32	15 04
			15 33	4 04	15 13	4 22	14 49	4 44	14 16	5 14	13 20	6 06

12th Month   December, 1990   31 days

Greenwich Mean Time

NOTE: Light numbers indicate Sun. **Dark** numbers indicate **Moon.** *Degrees are North Latitude.*

FM = full moon; LQ = last quarter; NM = new moon; FQ = first quarter.

CAUTION: Must be converted to local time. For instruction see page 242.

Day of month/week/year	Sun on Meridian Moon phase h m s	Sun's Declination ° '	20° Rise Sun/Moon h m	20° Set Sun/Moon h m	30° Rise h m	30° Set h m	40° Rise h m	40° Set h m	50° Rise h m	50° Set h m	60° Rise h m	60° Set h m
1 Sa 335	11 48 58	−21 44	6 18	17 19	6 38	17 00	7 02	16 35	7 36	16 01	8 34	15 03
			16 29	5 12	16 06	5 35	15 36	6 03	14 54	6 43	13 38	7 56
2 Su 336	11 49 21 / 7 50 FM	−21 53	6 19	17 19	6 39	17 00	7 03	16 35	7 38	16 01	8 36	15 02
			17 32	6 22	17 06	6 48	16 34	7 20	15 46	8 07	14 15	9 37
3 Mo 337	11 49 44	−22 2	6 20	17 20	6 40	17 00	7 04	16 35	7 39	16 00	8 38	15 01
			18 40	7 30	18 15	7 56	17 42	8 29	16 55	9 17	15 24	10 49
4 Tu 338	11 50 8	−22 10	6 20	17 20	6 40	17 00	7 05	16 35	7 40	16 00	8 40	15 00
			19 49	8 33	19 26	8 57	18 58	9 27	18 17	10 09	17 03	11 26
5 We 339	11 50 32	−22 18	6 21	17 20	6 41	17 00	7 06	16 35	7 41	15 59	8 42	14 59
			20 55	9 28	20 37	9 48	20 14	10 13	19 42	10 47	18 49	11 44
6 Th 340	11 50 57	−22 26	6 22	17 20	6 42	17 00	7 07	16 35	7 43	15 59	8 44	14 58
			21 56	10 16	21 44	10 31	21 28	10 50	21 06	11 15	20 31	11 54
7 Fr 341	11 51 23	−22 33	6 22	17 20	6 43	17 00	7 08	16 35	7 44	15 59	8 46	14 57
			22 54	10 58	22 47	11 08	22 38	11 20	22 25	11 36	22 06	12 00
8 Sa 342	11 51 49	−22 40	6 23	17 21	6 43	17 00	7 09	16 35	7 45	15 58	8 47	14 56
			23 48	11 36	23 46	11 40	23 44	11 46	23 41	11 53	23 36	12 04
9 Su 343	11 52 15 / 2 4 LQ	−22 46	6 23	17 21	6 44	17 00	7 10	16 35	7 46	15 58	8 49	14 55
			– –	12 11	– –	12 11	– –	12 10	– –	12 08	– –	12 07
10 Mo 344	11 52 42	−22 52	6 24	17 21	6 45	17 01	7 11	16 35	7 47	15 58	8 50	14 55
			0 40	12 45	0 43	12 40	0 47	12 33	0 53	12 24	1 02	12 09
11 Tu 345	11 53 9	−22 58	6 25	17 22	6 45	17 01	7 11	16 35	7 48	15 58	8 52	14 54
			1 31	13 20	1 39	13 10	1 50	12 57	2 04	12 39	2 26	12 13
12 We 346	11 53 37	−23 2	6 25	17 22	6 46	17 01	7 12	16 35	7 49	15 58	8 53	14 54
			2 22	13 56	2 35	13 41	2 51	13 23	3 14	12 57	3 51	12 17
13 Th 347	11 54 6	−23 7	6 26	17 22	6 47	17 01	7 13	16 35	7 50	15 58	8 55	14 53
			3 14	14 34	3 31	14 15	3 53	13 52	4 24	13 19	5 16	12 24
14 Fr 348	11 54 34	−23 11	6 26	17 23	6 47	17 02	7 14	16 35	7 51	15 58	8 56	14 53
			4 06	15 16	4 27	14 54	4 54	14 26	5 32	13 46	6 41	12 35
15 Sa 349	11 55 3	−23 15	6 27	17 23	6 48	17 02	7 14	16 36	7 52	15 58	8 57	14 53
			4 59	16 01	5 23	15 37	5 53	15 05	6 38	14 20	8 02	12 54
16 Su 350	11 55 32	−23 18	6 28	17 23	6 49	17 02	7 15	16 36	7 53	15 58	8 58	14 53
			5 51	16 50	6 17	16 24	6 49	15 51	7 37	15 03	9 11	13 29
17 Mo 351	11 56 1 / 4 22 NM	−23 20	6 28	17 24	6 49	17 03	7 16	16 36	7 53	15 59	8 59	14 53
			6 42	17 42	7 07	17 16	7 40	16 44	8 27	15 57	10 00	14 25
18 Tu 352	11 56 31	−23 22	6 29	17 24	6 50	17 03	7 16	16 37	7 54	15 59	9 00	14 53
			7 30	18 34	7 54	18 11	8 24	17 42	9 08	16 59	10 29	15 40
19 We 353	11 57 0	−23 24	6 29	17 25	6 50	17 04	7 17	16 37	7 55	15 59	9 01	14 53
			8 14	19 28	8 35	19 08	9 02	18 43	9 40	18 07	10 45	17 04
20 Th 354	11 57 30	−23 25	6 30	17 25	6 51	17 04	7 18	16 37	7 55	16 00	9 01	14 54
			8 55	20 21	9 13	20 05	9 35	19 45	10 05	19 17	10 55	18 30
21 Fr 355	11 58 0	−23 26	6 30	17 26	6 52	17 04	7 18	16 38	7 56	16 00	9 02	14 54
			9 33	21 13	9 47	21 02	10 03	20 48	10 25	20 28	11 01	19 57
22 Sa 356	11 58 30	−23 26	6 31	17 26	6 52	17 05	7 19	16 38	7 56	16 01	9 02	14 55
			10 09	22 05	10 18	21 58	10 28	21 50	10 43	21 40	11 05	21 23
23 Su 357	11 58 60	−23 26	6 31	17 27	6 53	17 05	7 19	16 39	7 57	16 01	9 03	14 55
			10 44	22 57	10 48	22 56	10 52	22 54	10 58	22 52	11 08	22 49
24 Mo 358	11 59 30	−23 26	6 32	17 27	6 53	17 06	7 20	16 39	7 57	16 02	9 03	14 56
			11 19	23 50	11 18	23 54	11 16	23 59	11 14	– –	11 11	– –
25 Tu 359	11 59 60 / 3 16 FQ	−23 25	6 32	17 28	6 53	17 07	7 20	16 40	7 58	16 03	9 03	14 57
			11 56	– –	11 49	– –	11 41	– –	11 30	0 06	11 14	0 17
26 We 360	12 0 29	−23 23	6 33	17 28	6 54	17 07	7 20	16 41	7 58	16 03	9 04	14 58
			12 35	0 46	12 23	0 56	12 09	1 08	11 49	1 24	11 18	1 50
27 Th 361	12 0 59	−23 21	6 33	17 29	6 54	17 08	7 21	16 41	7 58	16 04	9 04	14 58
			13 20	1 46	13 02	2 01	12 41	2 19	12 12	2 45	11 26	3 28
28 Fr 362	12 1 28	−23 18	6 34	17 29	6 55	17 08	7 21	16 42	7 58	16 05	9 04	15 00
			14 10	2 49	13 49	3 09	13 22	3 35	12 44	4 10	11 38	5 13
29 Sa 363	12 1 58	−23 15	6 34	17 30	6 55	17 09	7 21	16 43	7 58	16 06	9 03	15 01
			15 09	3 57	14 44	4 20	14 12	4 51	13 27	5 35	12 03	6 58
30 Su 364	12 2 27	−23 12	6 34	17 31	6 55	17 10	7 22	16 43	7 59	16 06	9 03	15 02
			16 14	5 05	15 48	5 31	15 15	6 04	14 27	6 52	12 53	8 26
31 Mo 365	12 2 55 / 18 35 FM	−23 8	6 35	17 31	6 56	17 10	7 22	16 44	7 59	16 07	9 03	15 03
			17 22	6 11	16 58	6 36	16 27	7 08	15 43	7 54	14 18	9 20

Latitude, Longitude, and Altitude of North American Cities

Source: National Oceanic and Atmospheric Administration. U.S. Commerce Department for geographic positions.
Source for Canadian cities: Geodetic Survey of Canada, Dept. of Energy, Mines, and Resources.
Altitudes U.S. Geological Survey and various sources. *Approx. altitude at downtown business area U.S.; in Canada at city hall except where (a) is at tower of major airport.

City	Lat. N °	'	"	Long. W °	'	"	Alt.* feet
Abilene, Tex.	32	27	05	99	43	51	1710
Akron, Oh.	41	05	00	81	30	44	874
Albany, N.Y.	42	39	01	73	45	01	20
Albuquerque, N.M.	35	05	01	106	39	05	4,945
Allentown, Pa.	40	36	11	75	28	06	255
Alert, N.W.T.	82	29	50	62	21	65	95
Altoona, Pa.	40	30	55	78	24	03	1,180
Amarillo, Tex.	35	12	27	101	50	04	3,685
Anchorage, Alas.	61	10	00	149	59	00	118
Ann Arbor, Mich.	42	16	59	83	44	52	880
Asheville, N.C.	35	35	42	82	33	26	1,985
Ashland, Ky.	38	28	36	82	38	23	536
Atlanta, Ga.	33	45	10	84	23	37	1,050
Atlantic City, N.J.	39	21	32	74	25	53	10
Augusta, Ga.	33	28	20	81	58	00	143
Augusta, Me.	44	18	53	69	46	29	45
Austin, Tex.	30	16	09	97	44	37	505
Bakersfield, Cal.	35	22	31	119	01	18	400
Baltimore, Md.	39	17	26	76	36	45	20
Bangor, Me.	44	48	13	68	46	18	20
Baton Rouge, La.	30	26	58	91	11	00	57
Battle Creek, Mich.	42	18	58	85	10	48	820
Bay City, Mich.	43	36	04	83	53	15	595
Beaumont, Tex.	30	05	20	94	06	09	20
Belleville, Ont.	44	09	42	77	23	11	257
Bellingham, Wash.	48	45	34	122	28	36	60
Berkeley, Cal.	37	52	10	122	16	17	40
Bethlehem, Pa.	40	37	16	75	22	34	235
Billings, Mon.	45	47	00	108	30	04	3,120
Biloxi, Miss.	30	23	48	88	53	00	20
Binghamton, N.Y.	42	06	03	75	54	47	865
Birmingham, Ala.	33	31	01	86	48	36	600
Bismarck, N.D.	46	48	23	100	47	17	1,674
Bloomington, Ill.	40	28	58	88	59	36	800
Boise, Ida.	43	37	07	116	11	58	2,704
Boston, Mass.	42	21	24	71	03	25	21
Bowling Green, Ky.	36	59	41	86	26	33	510
Brandon, Man.	49	51	00	99	57	00	1,265(a)
Brantford, Ont.	43	08	34	80	15	39	705(a)
Brattleboro, Vt.	42	51	06	72	33	48	300
Bridgeport, Conn.	41	10	49	73	11	22	10
Brockton, Mass.	42	05	02	71	01	25	130
Brownsville, Tex.	25	54	07	97	29	58	35
Buffalo, N.Y.	42	52	52	78	52	21	585
Burlington, Ont.	43	19	33	79	47	57	284
Burlington, Vt.	44	28	34	73	12	46	110
Butte, Mon.	46	01	06	112	32	11	5,765
Calgary, Alta.	51	02	46	114	03	24	3,427
Cambridge, Mass.	42	22	01	71	06	22	20
Camden, N.J.	39	56	41	75	07	14	30
Canton, Oh.	40	47	50	81	22	37	1,030
Carson City, Nev.	39	10	00	119	46	00	4,680
Cedar Rapids, Ia.	41	58	01	91	39	53	730
Central Islip, N.Y.	40	47	24	73	12	00	80
Champaign, Ill.	40	07	05	88	14	48	740
Charleston, S.C.	32	46	35	79	55	53	9
Charleston, W.Va.	38	21	01	81	37	52	601
Charlotte, N.C.	35	13	44	80	50	45	720
Charlottetown, P.E.I.	46	14	07	63	07	49	31
Chattanooga, Tenn.	35	02	41	85	18	32	675
Cheyenne, Wy.	41	08	09	104	49	07	6,100
Chicago, Ill.	41	52	28	87	38	22	595
Churchill, Man.	58	45	15	94	10	00	94(a)
Cincinnati, Oh.	39	06	07	84	30	35	550
Cleveland, Oh.	41	29	51	81	41	50	660
Colorado Springs	38	50	07	104	49	16	5,980
Columbia, Mo.	38	57	03	92	19	46	730
Columbia, S.C.	34	00	02	81	02	00	190
Columbus, Ga.	32	28	07	84	59	24	265
Columbus, Oh.	39	57	47	83	00	17	780
Concord, N.H.	43	12	22	71	32	25	290
Corpus Christi, Tex.	27	47	51	97	23	45	35
Dallas, Tex.	32	47	09	96	47	37	435
Dartmouth, N.S.	44	39	50	63	34	08	24
Davenport, Ia.	41	31	19	90	34	33	590
Dawson, Yukon	64	03	30	139	26	00	1,211(a)
Dayton, Oh.	39	45	32	84	11	43	574
Daytona Beach, Fla.	29	12	44	81	01	10	7
Decatur, Ill.	39	50	42	88	56	47	682
Denver, Col.	39	44	58	104	59	22	5,280
Des Moines, Ia.	41	35	14	93	37	00	803
Detroit, Mich.	42	19	48	83	02	57	585
Dodge City, Kan.	37	45	17	100	01	09	2,480
Dubuque, Ia.	42	29	55	90	40	08	620
Duluth, Minn.	46	46	56	92	06	24	610
Durham, N.C.	36	00	00	78	54	45	405

City	Lat. N °	'	"	Long. W °	'	"	Alt.* feet
Eau Claire, Wis.	44	48	31	91	29	49	790
Edmonton, Alta.	53	32	43	113	29	21	2,186
El Paso, Tex.	31	45	36	106	29	11	3,695
Elizabeth, N.J.	40	39	43	74	12	59	21
Enid, Okla.	36	23	40	97	52	35	1,240
Erie, Pa.	42	07	15	80	04	57	685
Eugene, Ore.	44	03	16	123	05	30	422
Eureka, Cal.	40	48	08	124	09	46	45
Evansville, Ind.	37	58	20	87	34	21	385
Fairbanks, Alas.	64	48	00	147	51	00	448
Fall River, Mass.	41	42	06	71	09	18	40
Fargo, N.D.	46	52	30	96	47	18	900
Flagstaff, Ariz.	35	11	36	111	39	06	6,900
Flint, Mich.	43	00	50	83	41	33	750
Ft. Smith, Ark.	35	23	10	94	25	36	440
Fort Wayne, Ind.	41	04	21	85	08	26	790
Fort Worth, Tex.	32	44	55	97	19	44.	670
Fredericton, N.B.	45	57	47	66	38	38	29
Fresno, Cal.	36	44	12	119	47	11	285
Gadsden, Ala.	34	00	57	86	00	41	555
Gainesville, Fla.	29	38	56	82	19	19	175
Gallup, N.M.	35	31	30	108	44	30	6,540
Galveston, Tex.	29	18	10	94	47	43	5
Gary, Ind.	41	36	12	87	20	19	590
Grand Junction, Col.	39	04	06	108	33	54	4,590
Grand Rapids, Mich.	42	58	03	85	40	13	610
Great Falls, Mon.	47	29	33	111	18	23	3,340
Green Bay, Wis.	44	30	48	88	00	50	590
Greensboro, N.C.	36	04	17	79	47	25	839
Greenville, S.C.	34	50	50	82	24	01	966
Guelph, Ont.	43	32	35	80	14	54	1,065
Gulfport, Miss.	30	22	04	89	05	36	20
Halifax, N.S.	44	38	54	63	34	30	60
Hamilton, Ont.	43	15	20	79	52	30	329
Hamilton, Oh.	39	23	59	84	33	47	600
Harrisburg, Pa.	40	15	43	76	52	59	365
Hartford, Conn.	41	46	12	72	40	49	40
Helena, Mon.	46	35	33	112	02	24	4,155
Hilo, Hawaii	19	43	30	155	05	24	40
Holyoke, Mass.	42	12	29	72	36	36	115
Honolulu, Ha.	21	18	22	157	51	35	21
Houston, Tex.	29	45	26	95	21	37	40
Hull, Que.	45	25	42	75	42	41	185
Huntington, W.Va.	38	25	12	82	26	33	565
Huntsville, Ala.	34	44	18	86	35	19	640
Indianapolis, Ind.	39	46	07	86	09	46	710
Iowa City, Ia.	41	39	37	91	31	53	685
Jackson, Mich.	42	14	43	84	24	22	940
Jackson, Miss.	32	17	56	90	11	06	298
Jacksonville, Fla.	30	19	44	81	39	42	20
Jersey City, N.J.	40	43	50	74	03	56	20
Johnstown, Pa.	40	19	35	78	55	03	1,185
Joplin, Mo.	37	05	26	94	30	00	990
Juneau, Alas.	58	18	12	134	24	30	50
Kalamazoo, Mich.	42	17	29	85	35	14	755
Kansas City, Kan.	39	07	04	94	38	24	750
Kansas City, Mo.	39	04	56	94	35	20	750
Kenosha, Wis.	42	35	43	87	50	11	610
Key West, Fla.	24	33	30	81	48	12	5
Kingston, Ont.	44	13	53	76	28	48	264
Kitchener, Ont.	43	26	58	80	29	12	1,100
Knoxville, Tenn.	35	57	39	83	55	07	890
Lafayette, Ind.	40	25	11	86	53	39	550
Lancaster, Pa.	40	02	25	76	18	29	355
Lansing, Mich.	42	44	01	84	33	15	830
Laredo, Tex.	27	30	22	99	30	30	440
La Salle, Que.	45	25	30	73	39	00	110
Las Vegas, Nev.	36	10	20	115	08	37	2,030
Laval, Que.	45	33	05	73	44	42	142
Lawrence, Mass.	42	42	16	71	10	08	65
Lethbridge, Alta.	49	41	38	112	49	58	2,985
Lexington, Ky.	38	02	50	84	29	46	955
Lihue, Ha.	21	58	48	159	22	30	210
Lima, Oh.	40	44	35	84	06	20	865
Lincoln, Neb.	40	48	59	96	42	15	1,150
Little Rock, Ark.	34	44	42	92	16	37	286
London, Ont.	42	59	17	81	14	03	822
Long Beach, Cal.	33	46	14	118	11	18	35
Lorain, Oh.	41	28	05	82	10	49	610
Los Angeles, Cal.	34	03	15	118	14	28	340
Louisville, Ky.	38	14	47	85	45	49	450
Lowell, Mass.	42	38	25	71	19	14	100
Lubbock, Tex.	33	35	05	101	50	33	3,195

City	Lat. N °′″			Long. W °′″			Alt.* Feet	City	Lat. N °′″			Long. W °′″			Alt.* Feet
Macon, Ga.	32	50	12	83	37	36	335	Salina, Kan.	38	50	36	97	36	46	1,229
Madison, Wis.	43	04	23	89	22	55	860	Salt Lake City, Ut.	40	45	23	111	53	26	4,390
Manchester, N.H.	42	59	28	71	27	41	175	San Angelo, Tex.	31	27	39	100	26	03	1,845
Marshall, Tex.	32	33	00	94	23	00	410	San Antonio, Tex.	29	25	37	98	29	06	650
Memphis, Tenn.	35	08	46	90	03	13	275	San Bernardino, Cal.	34	06	30	117	17	28	1,080
Meriden, Conn.	41	32	06	72	47	30	190	San Diego, Cal.	32	42	53	117	09	21	20
Mexico City, Mexico.	19	25	45	99	07	00	7,347	San Francisco, Cal.	37	46	39	122	24	40	65
Miami, Fla.	25	46	37	80	11	32	10	San Jose, Cal.	37	20	16	121	53	24	90
Milwaukee, Wis.	43	02	19	87	54	15	635	San Juan, P.R.	18	27	00	66	04	15	35
Minneapolis, Minn.	44	58	57	93	15	43	815	Santa Barbara, Cal.	34	25	18	119	41	55	100
Minot, N.D.	48	14	09	101	17	38	1,550	Santa Cruz, Cal.	36	58	18	122	01	18	20
Mississauga, Ont.	43	33	00	79	35	00	260(a)	Santa Fe, N.M.	35	41	11	105	56	10	6,950
Mobile, Ala.	30	41	36	88	02	33	5	Sarasota, Fla.	27	20	05	82	32	30	20
Moline, Ill.	41	30	31	90	30	49	585	Saskatoon, Sask.	52	07	49	106	39	35	1,587
Moncton, N.B.	46	05	18	64	46	41	38	Sault Ste. Marie, Ont.	46	30	24	84	20	04	589
Montgomery, Ala.	32	22	33	86	18	31	160	Savannah, Ga.	32	04	42	81	05	37	20
Montpelier, Vt.	44	15	36	72	34	41	485	Schenectady, N.Y.	42	48	42	73	55	42	245
Montreal, Que.	45	30	33	73	33	14	90	Scranton, Pa.	41	24	32	75	39	46	725
Moose Jaw, Sask.	50	23	34	105	32	04	1,784	Seattle, Wash.	47	36	32	122	20	12	10
Muncie, Ind.	40	11	28	85	23	16	950	Sheboygan, Wis.	43	45	03	87	42	52	630
								Sherbrooke, Que.	45	24	27	71	51	07	535(a)
Nashville, Tenn.	36	09	33	86	46	55	450	Sheridan, Wy.	44	47	55	106	57	10	3,740
Natchez, Miss.	31	33	48	91	23	30	210	Shreveport, La.	32	30	46	93	44	58	204
Newark, N.J.	40	44	14	74	10	19	55	Sioux City, Ia.	42	29	46	96	24	30	1,110
New Bedford, Mass.	41	38	13	70	55	41	15	Sioux Falls, S.D.	43	32	35	96	43	35	1,395
New Britain, Conn.	41	40	08	72	46	59	200	Somerville, Mass.	42	23	15	71	06	07	13
New Haven, Conn.	41	18	25	72	55	30	40	South Bend, Ind.	41	40	33	86	15	01	710
New Orleans, La.	29	56	53	90	04	10	5	Spartanburg, S.C.	34	57	03	81	56	06	875
New York, N.Y.	40	45	06	73	59	39	55	Spokane, Wash.	47	39	32	117	25	33	1,890
Niagara Falls, N.Y.	43	05	34	79	03	26	570	Springfield, Ill.	39	47	58	89	38	51	610
Niagara Falls, Ont.	43	06	22	79	03	51	590	Springfield, Mass.	42	06	21	72	35	32	60
Nome, Alas.	64	30	00	165	25	00	25	Springfield, Mo.	37	13	03	93	17	32	1,300
Norfolk, Va.	36	51	10	76	17	21	10	Springfield, Oh.	39	55	38	83	48	29	980
North Bay, Ont.	46	18	35	79	27	45	670	Stamford, Conn.	41	03	09	73	32	24	35
								Steubenville, Oh.	40	21	42	80	36	53	660
Oakland, Cal.	37	48	03	122	15	54	25	Stockton, Cal.	37	57	30	121	17	16	20
Ogden, Ut.	41	13	31	111	58	21	4,295	Sudbury, Ont.	46	29	24	80	59	24	850(a)
Oklahoma City.	35	28	26	97	31	04	1,195	Superior, Wis.	46	43	14	92	06	07	630
Omaha, Neb.	41	15	42	95	56	14	1,040	Sydney, N.S.	46	08	15	60	11	48	15
Orlando, Fla.	28	32	42	81	22	38	70	Syracuse, N.Y.	43	03	04	76	09	14	400
Oshawa, Ont.	43	53	46	78	51	57	350								
Ottawa, Ont.	45	26	24	75	41	42	185	Tacoma, Wash.	47	14	59	122	26	15	110
								Tallahassee, Fla.	30	26	30	84	16	56	150
Paducah, Ky.	37	05	13	88	35	56	345	Tampa, Fla.	27	56	58	82	27	25	15
Pasadena, Cal.	34	08	44	118	08	41	830	Terre Haute, Ind.	39	28	03	87	24	26	496
Paterson, N.J.	40	55	01	74	10	21	100	Texarkana, Tex.	33	25	48	94	02	30	324
Pensacola, Fla.	30	24	51	87	12	56	15	Thunder Bay, Ont.	48	22	54	89	14	42	616
Peoria, Ill.	40	41	42	89	35	33	470	Toledo, Oh.	41	39	14	83	32	39	585
Peterborough, Ont.	44	18	32	78	19	13	673	Topeka, Kan.	39	03	16	95	40	23	930
Philadelphia, Pa.	39	56	58	75	09	21	100	Toronto, Ont.	43	39	10	79	23	00	300
Phoenix, Ariz.	33	27	12	112	04	28	1,090	Trenton, N.J.	40	13	14	74	46	13	35
Pierre, S.D.	44	22	18	100	20	54	1,480	Trois-Rivieres, Que.	46	20	36	72	32	37	115(a)
Pittsburgh, Pa.	40	26	19	80	00	00	745	Troy, N.Y.	42	43	45	73	40	58	35
Pittsfield, Mass.	42	26	53	73	15	14	1,015	Tucson, Ariz.	32	13	15	110	58	08	2,390
Pocatello, Ida.	42	51	38	112	27	01	4,460	Tulsa, Okla.	36	09	12	95	59	34	804
Port Arthur, Tex.	29	52	30	93	56	15	10								
Portland, Me.	43	39	33	70	15	19	25	Urbana, Ill.	40	06	42	88	12	06	725
Portland, Ore.	45	31	06	122	40	35	77	Utica, N.Y.	43	06	12	75	13	33	415
Portsmouth, N.H.	43	04	30	70	45	24	20								
Portsmouth, Va.	36	50	07	76	18	14	10	Vancouver, B.C.	49	18	56	123	04	44	141
Prince Rupert, B.C.	54	19	00	130	19	00	125(a)	Victoria, B.C.	48	25	43	123	21	49	57
Providence, R.I.	41	49	32	71	24	41	80								
Provo, Ut.	40	14	06	111	39	24	4,550	Waco, Tex.	31	33	12	97	08	00	405
Pueblo, Col.	38	16	17	104	36	33	4,690	Walla Walla, Wash.	46	04	08	118	20	24	936
								Washington, D.C.	38	53	51	77	00	33	25
Quebec City, Que.	46	48	51	71	12	30	163	Waterbury, Conn.	41	33	13	73	02	31	260
								Waterloo, Ia.	42	29	40	92	20	20	850
Racine, Wis.	42	43	49	87	47	12	630	West Palm Beach, Fla.	26	42	36	80	03	07	15
Rapid City, S.D.	44	04	52	103	13	11	3,230	Wheeling, W. Va.	40	04	03	80	43	20	650
Raleigh, N.C.	35	46	38	78	38	21	365	Whitehorse, Yukon	60	43	17	135	03	03	2,305(a)
Reading, Pa.	40	20	09	75	55	40	265	White Plains, N.Y.	41	02	00	73	45	48	220
Regina, Sask.	50	26	55	104	36	50	1,894(a)	Wichita, Kan.	37	41	30	97	20	16	1,290
Reno, Nev.	39	31	27	119	48	40	4,490	Wichita Falls, Tex.	33	54	34	98	29	28	945
Richmond, Va.	37	32	15	77	26	09	160	Wilkes-Barre, Pa.	41	14	32	75	53	17	640
Roanoke, Va.	37	16	13	79	56	44	905	Wilmington, Del.	39	44	46	75	32	51	135
Rochester, Minn.	44	01	21	92	28	03	990	Wilmington, N.C.	34	14	14	77	56	58	35
Rochester, N.Y.	43	09	41	77	36	21	515	Windsor, Ont.	42	18	56	83	02	10	603
Rockford, Ill.	42	16	07	89	05	48	715	Winnipeg, Man.	49	53	56	97	08	23	762
								Winston-Salem, N.C.	36	05	52	80	14	42	860
Sacramento, Cal.	38	34	57	121	29	41	30	Worcester, Mass.	42	15	37	71	48	17	475
Saginaw, Mich.	43	25	52	83	56	05	595								
St. Catharines, Ont.	43	09	33	79	14	50	362(a)	Yakima, Wash.	46	36	09	120	30	39	1,060
St. Cloud, Minn.	45	34	00	94	10	24	1,040	Yellowknife, N.W.T.	62	27	16	114	22	33	674(a)
Saint John, N.B.	45	16	22	66	03	48	27	Yonkers, N.Y.	40	55	55	73	53	54	10
St. John's, Nfld.	47	33	42	52	42	48	200(a)	York, Pa.	39	57	35	76	43	36	370
St. Joseph, Mo.	39	45	57	94	51	02	850	Youngstown, Oh.	41	05	57	80	39	02	840
St. Louis, Mo.	38	37	45	90	12	22	455	Yuma, Ariz.	32	42	54	114	37	24	160
St. Paul, Minn.	44	57	19	93	06	07	780								
St. Petersburg, Fla.	27	46	18	82	38	19	20	Zanesville, Oh.	39	56′	18	82	00	30	720
Salem, Ore.	44	56	24	123	01	59	155								

World Cities

City	Lat. N °′″			Long. W °′″			Alt.* Feet	City	Lat. N °′″			Long. W °′″			Alt.* Feet
London, UK (Greenwich)	51	30	00N	0	0	0	245	Jerusalem, Israel	31	47	00N	35	13	00E	2,500
Paris, France	48	50	14N	2	20	14E	300	Johannesburg, So. Afr.	26	10	00S	28	02	00E	5,740
Berlin, Germany	52	32	00N	13	25	00E	110	New Delhi, India	28	38	00N	77	12	00E	770
Rome, Italy	41	53	00N	12	30	00E	95	Peking, China	39	54	00N	116	28	00E	600
Warsaw, Poland	52	15	00N	21	00	00E	360	Rio de Janeiro, Brazil	22	53	43S	43	13	22W	30
Moscow, USSR	55	45	00N	37	42	00E	394	Tokyo, Japan	35	45	00N	139	45	00E	30
Athens, Greece	37	58	00N	23	44	00E	300	Sydney, Australia	33	52	00S	151	12	00E	25

Perpetual Calendar

The number shown for each year indicates which Gregorian calendar to use. For 1583-1802, or for Julian calendar, see page 268. For years 1803-1820, use numbers for 1983-2000, respectively.

7

January

S	M	T	W	T	F	S
						1
2	3	4	5	6	7	8
9	10	11	12	13	14	15
16	17	18	19	20	21	22
23	24	25	26	27	28	29
30	31					

February

S	M	T	W	T	F	S
		1	2	3	4	5
6	7	8	9	10	11	12
13	14	15	16	17	18	19
20	21	22	23	24	25	26
27	28					

March

S	M	T	W	T	F	S
		1	2	3	4	5
6	7	8	9	10	11	12
13	14	15	16	17	18	19
20	21	22	23	24	25	26
27	28	29	30	31		

April

S	M	T	W	T	F	S
					1	2
3	4	5	6	7	8	9
10	11	12	13	14	15	16
17	18	19	20	21	22	23
24	25	26	27	28	29	30

May

S	M	T	W	T	F	S
1	2	3	4	5	6	7
8	9	10	11	12	13	14
15	16	17	18	19	20	21
22	23	24	25	26	27	28
29	30	31				

June

S	M	T	W	T	F	S
			1	2	3	4
5	6	7	8	9	10	11
12	13	14	15	16	17	18
19	20	21	22	23	24	25
26	27	28	29	30		

July

S	M	T	W	T	F	S
					1	2
3	4	5	6	7	8	9
10	11	12	13	14	15	16
17	18	19	20	21	22	23
24	25	26	27	28	29	30
31						

August

S	M	T	W	T	F	S
	1	2	3	4	5	6
7	8	9	10	11	12	13
14	15	16	17	18	19	20
21	22	23	24	25	26	27
28	29	30	31			

September

S	M	T	W	T	F	S
				1	2	3
4	5	6	7	8	9	10
11	12	13	14	15	16	17
18	19	20	21	22	23	24
25	26	27	28	29	30	

October

S	M	T	W	T	F	S
						1
2	3	4	5	6	7	8
9	10	11	12	13	14	15
16	17	18	19	20	21	22
23	24	25	26	27	28	29
30	31					

November

S	M	T	W	T	F	S
		1	2	3	4	5
6	7	8	9	10	11	12
13	14	15	16	17	18	19
20	21	22	23	24	25	26
27	28	29	30			

December

S	M	T	W	T	F	S
				1	2	3
4	5	6	7	8	9	10
11	12	13	14	15	16	17
18	19	20	21	22	23	24
25	26	27	28	29	30	31

8

January

S	M	T	W	T	F	S
1	2	3	4	5	6	7
8	9	10	11	12	13	14
15	16	17	18	19	20	21
22	23	24	25	26	27	28
29	30	31				

February

S	M	T	W	T	F	S
			1	2	3	4
5	6	7	8	9	10	11
12	13	14	15	16	17	18
19	20	21	22	23	24	25
26	27	28	29			

March

S	M	T	W	T	F	S
				1	2	3
4	5	6	7	8	9	10
11	12	13	14	15	16	17
18	19	20	21	22	23	24
25	26	27	28	29	30	31

April

S	M	T	W	T	F	S
1	2	3	4	5	6	7
8	9	10	11	12	13	14
15	16	17	18	19	20	21
22	23	24	25	26	27	28
29	30					

May

S	M	T	W	T	F	S
		1	2	3	4	5
6	7	8	9	10	11	12
13	14	15	16	17	18	19
20	21	22	23	24	25	26
27	28	29	30	31		

June

S	M	T	W	T	F	S
					1	2
3	4	5	6	7	8	9
10	11	12	13	14	15	16
17	18	19	20	21	22	23
24	25	26	27	28	29	30

July

S	M	T	W	T	F	S
1	2	3	4	5	6	7
8	9	10	11	12	13	14
15	16	17	18	19	20	21
22	23	24	25	26	27	28
29	30	31				

August

S	M	T	W	T	F	S
			1	2	3	4
5	6	7	8	9	10	11
12	13	14	15	16	17	18
19	20	21	22	23	24	25
26	27	28	29	30	31	

September

S	M	T	W	T	F	S
						1
2	3	4	5	6	7	8
9	10	11	12	13	14	15
16	17	18	19	20	21	22
23	24	25	26	27	28	29
30						

October

S	M	T	W	T	F	S
	1	2	3	4	5	6
7	8	9	10	11	12	13
14	15	16	17	18	19	20
21	22	23	24	25	26	27
28	29	30	31			

November

S	M	T	W	T	F	S
				1	2	3
4	5	6	7	8	9	10
11	12	13	14	15	16	17
18	19	20	21	22	23	24
25	26	27	28	29	30	

December

S	M	T	W	T	F	S
						1
2	3	4	5	6	7	8
9	10	11	12	13	14	15
16	17	18	19	20	21	22
23	24	25	26	27	28	29
30	31					

9

January

S	M	T	W	T	F	S
	1	2	3	4	5	6
7	8	9	10	11	12	13
14	15	16	17	18	19	20
21	22	23	24	25	26	27
28	29	30	31			

February

S	M	T	W	T	F	S
				1	2	3
4	5	6	7	8	9	10
11	12	13	14	15	16	17
18	19	20	21	22	23	24
25	26	27	28	29		

March

S	M	T	W	T	F	S
					1	2
3	4	5	6	7	8	9
10	11	12	13	14	15	16
17	18	19	20	21	22	23
24	25	26	27	28	29	30
31						

April

S	M	T	W	T	F	S
	1	2	3	4	5	6
7	8	9	10	11	12	13
14	15	16	17	18	19	20
21	22	23	24	25	26	27
28	29	30				

May

S	M	T	W	T	F	S
			1	2	3	4
5	6	7	8	9	10	11
12	13	14	15	16	17	18
19	20	21	22	23	24	25
26	27	28	29	30	31	

June

S	M	T	W	T	F	S
						1
2	3	4	5	6	7	8
9	10	11	12	13	14	15
16	17	18	19	20	21	22
23	24	25	26	27	28	29
30						

July

S	M	T	W	T	F	S
	1	2	3	4	5	6
7	8	9	10	11	12	13
14	15	16	17	18	19	20
21	22	23	24	25	26	27
28	29	30	31			

August

S	M	T	W	T	F	S
				1	2	3
4	5	6	7	8	9	10
11	12	13	14	15	16	17
18	19	20	21	22	23	24
25	26	27	28	29	30	31

September

S	M	T	W	T	F	S
1	2	3	4	5	6	7
8	9	10	11	12	13	14
15	16	17	18	19	20	21
22	23	24	25	26	27	28
29	30					

October

S	M	T	W	T	F	S
		1	2	3	4	5
6	7	8	9	10	11	12
13	14	15	16	17	18	19
20	21	22	23	24	25	26
27	28	29	30	31		

November

S	M	T	W	T	F	S
					1	2
3	4	5	6	7	8	9
10	11	12	13	14	15	16
17	18	19	20	21	22	23
24	25	26	27	28	29	30

December

S	M	T	W	T	F	S
1	2	3	4	5	6	7
8	9	10	11	12	13	14
15	16	17	18	19	20	21
22	23	24	25	26	27	28
29	30	31				

10

January

S	M	T	W	T	F	S
		1	2	3	4	5
6	7	8	9	10	11	12
13	14	15	16	17	18	19
20	21	22	23	24	25	26
27	28	29	30	31		

February

S	M	T	W	T	F	S
					1	2
3	4	5	6	7	8	9
10	11	12	13	14	15	16
17	18	19	20	21	22	23
24	25	26	27	28	29	

March

S	M	T	W	T	F	S
						1
2	3	4	5	6	7	8
9	10	11	12	13	14	15
16	17	18	19	20	21	22
23	24	25	26	27	28	29
30	31					

April

S	M	T	W	T	F	S
		1	2	3	4	5
6	7	8	9	10	11	12
13	14	15	16	17	18	19
20	21	22	23	24	25	26
27	28	29	30			

May

S	M	T	W	T	F	S
				1	2	3
4	5	6	7	8	9	10
11	12	13	14	15	16	17
18	19	20	21	22	23	24
25	26	27	28	29	30	31

June

S	M	T	W	T	F	S
1	2	3	4	5	6	7
8	9	10	11	12	13	14
15	16	17	18	19	20	21
22	23	24	25	26	27	28
29	30					

July

S	M	T	W	T	F	S
		1	2	3	4	5
6	7	8	9	10	11	12
13	14	15	16	17	18	19
20	21	22	23	24	25	26
27	28	29	30	31		

August

S	M	T	W	T	F	S
					1	2
3	4	5	6	7	8	9
10	11	12	13	14	15	16
17	18	19	20	21	22	23
24	25	26	27	28	29	30
31						

September

S	M	T	W	T	F	S
	1	2	3	4	5	6
7	8	9	10	11	12	13
14	15	16	17	18	19	20
21	22	23	24	25	26	27
28	29	30				

October

S	M	T	W	T	F	S
			1	2	3	4
5	6	7	8	9	10	11
12	13	14	15	16	17	18
19	20	21	22	23	24	25
26	27	28	29	30	31	

November

S	M	T	W	T	F	S
						1
2	3	4	5	6	7	8
9	10	11	12	13	14	15
16	17	18	19	20	21	22
23	24	25	26	27	28	29
30						

December

S	M	T	W	T	F	S
	1	2	3	4	5	6
7	8	9	10	11	12	13
14	15	16	17	18	19	20
21	22	23	24	25	26	27
28	29	30	31			

11

January

S	M	T	W	T	F	S
			1	2	3	4
5	6	7	8	9	10	11
12	13	14	15	16	17	18
19	20	21	22	23	24	25
26	27	28	29	30	31	

February

S	M	T	W	T	F	S
						1
2	3	4	5	6	7	8
9	10	11	12	13	14	15
16	17	18	19	20	21	22
23	24	25	26	27	28	29

March

S	M	T	W	T	F	S
1	2	3	4	5	6	7
8	9	10	11	12	13	14
15	16	17	18	19	20	21
22	23	24	25	26	27	28
29	30	31				

April

S	M	T	W	T	F	S
			1	2	3	4
5	6	7	8	9	10	11
12	13	14	15	16	17	18
19	20	21	22	23	24	25
26	27	28	29	30		

May

S	M	T	W	T	F	S
					1	2
3	4	5	6	7	8	9
10	11	12	13	14	15	16
17	18	19	20	21	22	23
24	25	26	27	28	29	30
31						

June

S	M	T	W	T	F	S
	1	2	3	4	5	6
7	8	9	10	11	12	13
14	15	16	17	18	19	20
21	22	23	24	25	26	27
28	29	30				

July

S	M	T	W	T	F	S
			1	2	3	4
5	6	7	8	9	10	11
12	13	14	15	16	17	18
19	20	21	22	23	24	25
26	27	28	29	30	31	

August

S	M	T	W	T	F	S
						1
2	3	4	5	6	7	8
9	10	11	12	13	14	15
16	17	18	19	20	21	22
23	24	25	26	27	28	29
30	31					

September

S	M	T	W	T	F	S
		1	2	3	4	5
6	7	8	9	10	11	12
13	14	15	16	17	18	19
20	21	22	23	24	25	26
27	28	29	30			

October

S	M	T	W	T	F	S
				1	2	3
4	5	6	7	8	9	10
11	12	13	14	15	16	17
18	19	20	21	22	23	24
25	26	27	28	29	30	31

November

S	M	T	W	T	F	S
1	2	3	4	5	6	7
8	9	10	11	12	13	14
15	16	17	18	19	20	21
22	23	24	25	26	27	28
29	30					

December

S	M	T	W	T	F	S
		1	2	3	4	5
6	7	8	9	10	11	12
13	14	15	16	17	18	19
20	21	22	23	24	25	26
27	28	29	30	31		

12

January

S	M	T	W	T	F	S
				1	2	3
4	5	6	7	8	9	10
11	12	13	14	15	16	17
18	19	20	21	22	23	24
25	26	27	28	29	30	31

February

S	M	T	W	T	F	S
1	2	3	4	5	6	7
8	9	10	11	12	13	14
15	16	17	18	19	20	21
22	23	24	25	26	27	28
29						

March

S	M	T	W	T	F	S
	1	2	3	4	5	6
7	8	9	10	11	12	13
14	15	16	17	18	19	20
21	22	23	24	25	26	27
28	29	30	31			

April

S	M	T	W	T	F	S
				1	2	3
4	5	6	7	8	9	10
11	12	13	14	15	16	17
18	19	20	21	22	23	24
25	26	27	28	29	30	

May

S	M	T	W	T	F	S
						1
2	3	4	5	6	7	8
9	10	11	12	13	14	15
16	17	18	19	20	21	22
23	24	25	26	27	28	29
30	31					

June

S	M	T	W	T	F	S
		1	2	3	4	5
6	7	8	9	10	11	12
13	14	15	16	17	18	19
20	21	22	23	24	25	26
27	28	29	30			

July

S	M	T	W	T	F	S
				1	2	3
4	5	6	7	8	9	10
11	12	13	14	15	16	17
18	19	20	21	22	23	24
25	26	27	28	29	30	31

August

S	M	T	W	T	F	S
1	2	3	4	5	6	7
8	9	10	11	12	13	14
15	16	17	18	19	20	21
22	23	24	25	26	27	28
29	30	31				

September

S	M	T	W	T	F	S
			1	2	3	4
5	6	7	8	9	10	11
12	13	14	15	16	17	18
19	20	21	22	23	24	25
26	27	28	29	30		

October

S	M	T	W	T	F	S
					1	2
3	4	5	6	7	8	9
10	11	12	13	14	15	16
17	18	19	20	21	22	23
24	25	26	27	28	29	30
31						

November

S	M	T	W	T	F	S
	1	2	3	4	5	6
7	8	9	10	11	12	13
14	15	16	17	18	19	20
21	22	23	24	25	26	27
28	29	30				

December

S	M	T	W	T	F	S
			1	2	3	4
5	6	7	8	9	10	11
12	13	14	15	16	17	18
19	20	21	22	23	24	25
26	27	28	29	30	31	

13

January

S	M	T	W	T	F	S
					1	2
3	4	5	6	7	8	9
10	11	12	13	14	15	16
17	18	19	20	21	22	23
24	25	26	27	28	29	30
31						

February

S	M	T	W	T	F	S
	1	2	3	4	5	6
7	8	9	10	11	12	13
14	15	16	17	18	19	20
21	22	23	24	25	26	27
28	29					

March

S	M	T	W	T	F	S
		1	2	3	4	5
6	7	8	9	10	11	12
13	14	15	16	17	18	19
20	21	22	23	24	25	26
27	28	29	30	31		

April

S	M	T	W	T	F	S
					1	2
3	4	5	6	7	8	9
10	11	12	13	14	15	16
17	18	19	20	21	22	23
24	25	26	27	28	29	30

May

S	M	T	W	T	F	S
1	2	3	4	5	6	7
8	9	10	11	12	13	14
15	16	17	18	19	20	21
22	23	24	25	26	27	28
29	30	31				

June

S	M	T	W	T	F	S
			1	2	3	4
5	6	7	8	9	10	11
12	13	14	15	16	17	18
19	20	21	22	23	24	25
26	27	28	29	30		

July

S	M	T	W	T	F	S
					1	2
3	4	5	6	7	8	9
10	11	12	13	14	15	16
17	18	19	20	21	22	23
24	25	26	27	28	29	30
31						

August

S	M	T	W	T	F	S
	1	2	3	4	5	6
7	8	9	10	11	12	13
14	15	16	17	18	19	20
21	22	23	24	25	26	27
28	29	30	31			

September

S	M	T	W	T	F	S
				1	2	3
4	5	6	7	8	9	10
11	12	13	14	15	16	17
18	19	20	21	22	23	24
25	26	27	28	29	30	

October

S	M	T	W	T	F	S
						1
2	3	4	5	6	7	8
9	10	11	12	13	14	15
16	17	18	19	20	21	22
23	24	25	26	27	28	29
30	31					

November

S	M	T	W	T	F	S
		1	2	3	4	5
6	7	8	9	10	11	12
13	14	15	16	17	18	19
20	21	22	23	24	25	26
27	28	29	30			

December

S	M	T	W	T	F	S
				1	2	3
4	5	6	7	8	9	10
11	12	13	14	15	16	17
18	19	20	21	22	23	24
25	26	27	28	29	30	31

14

January

S	M	T	W	T	F	S
						1
2	3	4	5	6	7	8
9	10	11	12	13	14	15
16	17	18	19	20	21	22
23	24	25	26	27	28	29
30	31					

February

S	M	T	W	T	F	S
		1	2	3	4	5
6	7	8	9	10	11	12
13	14	15	16	17	18	19
20	21	22	23	24	25	26
27	28	29				

March

S	M	T	W	T	F	S
			1	2	3	4
5	6	7	8	9	10	11
12	13	14	15	16	17	18
19	20	21	22	23	24	25
26	27	28	29	30	31	

April

S	M	T	W	T	F	S
						1
2	3	4	5	6	7	8
9	10	11	12	13	14	15
16	17	18	19	20	21	22
23	24	25	26	27	28	29
30						

May

S	M	T	W	T	F	S
	1	2	3	4	5	6
7	8	9	10	11	12	13
14	15	16	17	18	19	20
21	22	23	24	25	26	27
28	29	30	31			

June

S	M	T	W	T	F	S
				1	2	3
4	5	6	7	8	9	10
11	12	13	14	15	16	17
18	19	20	21	22	23	24
25	26	27	28	29	30	

July

S	M	T	W	T	F	S
						1
2	3	4	5	6	7	8
9	10	11	12	13	14	15
16	17	18	19	20	21	22
23	24	25	26	27	28	29
30	31					

August

S	M	T	W	T	F	S
		1	2	3	4	5
6	7	8	9	10	11	12
13	14	15	16	17	18	19
20	21	22	23	24	25	26
27	28	29	30	31		

September

S	M	T	W	T	F	S
					1	2
3	4	5	6	7	8	9
10	11	12	13	14	15	16
17	18	19	20	21	22	23
24	25	26	27	28	29	30

October

S	M	T	W	T	F	S
1	2	3	4	5	6	7
8	9	10	11	12	13	14
15	16	17	18	19	20	21
22	23	24	25	26	27	28
29	30	31				

November

S	M	T	W	T	F	S
			1	2	3	4
5	6	7	8	9	10	11
12	13	14	15	16	17	18
19	20	21	22	23	24	25
26	27	28	29	30		

December

S	M	T	W	T	F	S
					1	2
3	4	5	6	7	8	9
10	11	12	13	14	15	16
17	18	19	20	21	22	23
24	25	26	27	28	29	30
31						

Julian and Gregorian Calendars; Leap Year; Century

Calendars based on the movements of sun and moon have been used since ancient times, but none has been perfect. The Julian calendar, under which western nations measured time until 1582 A.D., was authorized by Julius Caesar in 46 B.C., the year 709 of Rome. His expert was a Greek, Sosigenes. The Julian calendar, on the assumption that the true year was 365 1/4 days long, gave every fourth year 366 days. The Venerable Bede, an Anglo-Saxon monk, announced in 730 A.D. that the 365 1/4-day Julian year was 11 min., 14 sec. too long, making a cumulative error of about a day every 128 years, but nothing was done about it for over 800 years.

By 1582 the accumulated error was estimated to have amounted to 10 days. In that year Pope Gregory XIII decreed that the day following Oct. 4, 1582, should be called Oct. 15, thus dropping 10 days.

However, with common years 365 days and a 366-day leap year every fourth year, the error in the length of the year would have recurred at the rate of a little more than 3 days every 400 years. So 3 of every 4 centesimal years (ending in 00) were made common years, not leap years. Thus 1600 was a leap year, 1700, 1800 and 1900 were not, but 2000 will be. **Leap years** are those divisible by 4 except centesimal years, which are common unless divisible by 400.

The Gregorian calendar was adopted at once by France, Italy, Spain, Portugal and Luxembourg. Within 2 years most German Catholic states, Belgium and parts of Switzerland and the Netherlands were brought under the new calendar, and Hungary followed in 1587. The rest of the Netherlands, along with Denmark and the German Protestant states made the change in 1699-1700 (German Protestants retained the old reckoning of Easter until 1776).

The British Government imposed the Gregorian calendar on all its possessions, including the American colonies, in 1752. The British decreed that the day following Sept. 2, 1752, should be called Sept. 14, a loss of 11 days. All dates

preceding were marked O.S., for Old Style. In addition New Year's Day was moved to Jan. 1 from Mar. 25. (e.g., under the old reckoning, Mar. 24, 1700 had been followed by Mar. 25, 1701.) George Washington's birth date, which was Feb. 11, 1731, O.S., became Feb. 22, 1732, N.S. In 1753 Sweden too went Gregorian, retaining the old Easter rules until 1844.

In 1793 the French Revolutionary Government adopted a calendar of 12 months of 30 days each with 5 extra days in September of each common year and a 6th extra day every 4th year. Napoleon reinstated the Gregorian calendar in 1806.

The Gregorian system later spread to non-European regions, first in the European colonies, then in the independent countries, replacing traditional calendars at least for official purposes. Japan in 1873, Egypt in 1875, China in 1912 and Turkey in 1917 made the change, usually in conjunction with political upheavals. In China, the republican government began reckoning years from its 1911 founding — e.g., 1948 was designated the year 37. After 1949, the Communists adopted the Common, or Christian Era year count, even for the traditional lunar calendar.

In 1918 the revolutionary government in Russia decreed that the day after Jan. 31, 1918, Old Style, would become Feb. 14, 1918, New Style. Greece followed in 1923. (In Russia the Orthodox Church has retained the Julian calendar, as have various Middle Eastern Christian sects.) For the first time in history, all major cultures have one calendar.

To change from the Julian to the Gregorian calendar, add 10 days to dates Oct. 5, 1582, through Feb. 28, 1700; after that date add 11 days through Feb. 28, 1800; 12 days through Feb. 28, 1900; and 13 days through Feb. 28, 2100.

A century consists of 100 consecutive calendar years. The 1st century consisted of the years 1 through 100. The 20th century consists of the years 1901 through 2000 and will end Dec. 31, 2000. The 21st century will begin Jan. 1, 2001.

Julian Calendar

To find which of the 14 calendars printed on pages 266-267 applies to any year, starting Jan. 1, under the Julian system, find the century for the desired year in the three left-hand columns below; read across. Then find the year in the four top rows; read down. The number in the intersection is the calendar designation for that year.

	Year (last two figures of desired year)						
	01 02 03 04	05 06 07 08	09 10 11 12	13 14 15 16	17 18 19 20	21 22 23 24	25 26 27 28
	29 30 31 32	33 34 35 36	37 38 39 40	41 42 43 44	45 46 47 48	49 50 51 52	53 54 55 56
	57 58 59 60	61 62 63 64	65 66 67 68	69 70 71 72	73 74 75 76	77 78 79 80	81 82 83 84
Century	00 85 86 87	88 89 90 91	92 93 94 95	96 97 98 99			
0 700 1400	12 7 1 2	10 5 6 7	8 3 4 5	6 1 2 3	11 6 7 1	9 4 5 6	14 2 3 4
100 800 1500	11 6 7 1	9 4 5 6	14 2 3 4	12 7 1 2	10 5 6 7	8 3 4 5	6 1 2 3
200 900 1600	10 5 6 7	8 3 4 5	6 1 2 3	11 6 7 1	9 4 5 6	14 2 3 4	12 7 1 2
300 1000 1700	9 4 5 6	14 2 3 4	12 7 1 2	10 5 6 7	8 3 4 5	6 1 2 3	11 6 7 1
400 1100 1800	8 4 5 13	1 2 3 11	6 7 1 9	4 5 6 14	2 3 4 12	7 1 2 10	5 6 7 8
500 1200 1900	14 2 3 4	12 7 1 2	10 5 6 7	8 3 4 5	6 1 2 3	11 6 7 1	9 4 5 6
600 1300 2000	13 1 2 3	11 6 7 1	9 4 5 6	14 2 3 4	12 7 1 2	10 5 6 7	8 3 4 5

Gregorian Calendar

Pick desired year from table below or on page 266 (for years 1800 to 2059). The number shown with each year shows which calendar to use for that year, as shown on pages 266-267. (The Gregorian calendar was inaugurated Oct. 15, 1582. From that date to Dec. 31, 1582, use calendar 6.)

1583-1802

1583 . . 7	1603 . . 4	1623 . . 1	1643 . . 5	1663 . . 2	1683 . . 6	1703 . . 2	1723 . . 6	1743 . . 3	1763 . . 7	1783 . . 4
1584 . . 2	1604 . . 12	1624 . . 9	1644 . . 13	1664 . . 10	1684 . . 14	1704 . . 10	1724 . . 14	1744 . . 11	1764 . . 8	1784 . . 12
1585 . . 3	1605 . . 7	1625 . . 4	1645 . . 1	1665 . . 5	1685 . . 2	1705 . . 5	1725 . . 2	1745 . . 6	1765 . . 3	1785 . . 7
1586 . . 4	1606 . . 1	1626 . . 5	1646 . . 2	1666 . . 6	1686 . . 3	1706 . . 6	1726 . . 3	1746 . . 7	1766 . . 4	1786 . . 1
1587 . . 5	1607 . . 2	1627 . . 6	1647 . . 3	1667 . . 7	1687 . . 4	1707 . . 7	1727 . . 4	1747 . . 1	1767 . . 5	1787 . . 2
1588 . . 13	1608 . . 10	1628 . . 14	1648 . . 11	1668 . . 8	1688 . . 12	1708 . . 8	1728 . . 12	1748 . . 9	1768 . . 13	1788 . . 10
1589 . . 1	1609 . . 5	1629 . . 2	1649 . . 6	1669 . . 3	1689 . . 7	1709 . . 3	1729 . . 7	1749 . . 4	1769 . . 1	1789 . . 5
1590 . . 2	1610 . . 6	1630 . . 3	1650 . . 7	1670 . . 4	1690 . . 1	1710 . . 4	1730 . . 1	1750 . . 5	1770 . . 2	1790 . . 6
1591 . . 3	1611 . . 7	1631 . . 4	1651 . . 1	1671 . . 5	1691 . . 2	1711 . . 5	1731 . . 2	1751 . . 6	1771 . . 3	1791 . . 7
1592 . . 11	1612 . . 8	1632 . . 12	1652 . . 9	1672 . . 13	1692 . . 10	1712 . . 13	1732 . . 10	1752 . . 14	1772 . . 11	1792 . . 8
1593 . . 6	1613 . . 3	1633 . . 7	1653 . . 4	1673 . . 1	1693 . . 5	1713 . . 1	1733 . . 5	1753 . . 2	1773 . . 6	1793 . . 3
1594 . . 7	1614 . . 4	1634 . . 1	1654 . . 5	1674 . . 2	1694 . . 6	1714 . . 2	1734 . . 6	1754 . . 3	1774 . . 7	1794 . . 4
1595 . . 1	1615 . . 5	1635 . . 2	1655 . . 6	1675 . . 3	1695 . . 7	1715 . . 3	1735 . . 7	1755 . . 4	1775 . . 1	1795 . . 5
1596 . . 9	1616 . . 13	1636 . . 10	1656 . . 14	1676 . . 11	1696 . . 8	1716 . . 11	1736 . . 8	1756 . . 12	1776 . . 9	1796 . . 13
1597 . . 4	1617 . . 1	1637 . . 5	1657 . . 2	1677 . . 6	1697 . . 3	1717 . . 6	1737 . . 3	1757 . . 7	1777 . . 4	1797 . . 1
1598 . . 5	1618 . . 2	1638 . . 6	1658 . . 3	1678 . . 7	1698 . . 4	1718 . . 7	1738 . . 4	1758 . . 1	1778 . . 5	1798 . . 2
1599 . . 6	1619 . . 3	1639 . . 7	1659 . . 4	1679 . . 1	1699 . . 5	1719 . . 1	1739 . . 5	1759 . . 2	1779 . . 6	1799 . . 3
1600 . . 14	1620 . . 11	1640 . . 8	1660 . . 12	1680 . . 9	1700 . . 6	1720 . . 9	1740 . . 13	1760 . . 10	1780 . . 14	1800 . . 4
1601 . . 2	1621 . . 6	1641 . . 3	1661 . . 7	1681 . . 4	1701 . . 7	1721 . . 4	1741 . . 1	1761 . . 5	1781 . . 2	1801 . . 5
1602 . . 3	1622 . . 7	1642 . . 4	1662 . . 1	1682 . . 5	1702 . . 1	1722 . . 5	1742 . . 2	1762 . . 6	1782 . . 3	1802 . . 6

The Julian Period

How many days have you lived? To determine this, you must multiply your age by 365, add the number of days since your last birthday until today, and account for all leap years. Chances are your answer would be wrong. Astronomers, however, find it convenient to express dates and long time intervals in days rather than in years, months and days. This is done by placing events within the Julian period.

The Julian period was devised in 1582 by Joseph Scaliger and named after his father Julius (not after the Julian calendar). Scaliger had Julian Day (JD) #1 begin at noon, Jan. 1, 4713 B. C., the most recent time that three major chronological cycles began on the same day — 1) the 28-year solar cycle, after which dates in the Julian calendar (e.g., Feb. 11)

return to the same days of the week (e.g., Monday); 2) the 19-year lunar cycle, after which the phases of the moon return to the same dates of the year; and 3) the 15-year indiction cycle, used in ancient Rome to regulate taxes. It will take 7980 years to complete the period, the product of 28, 19, and 15.

Noon of Dec. 31, 1989, marks the beginning of JD 2,447,892; that many days will have passed since the start of the Julian period. The JD at noon of any date in 1989 may be found by adding to this figure the day of the year for that date, which is given in the left hand column in the chart below. Simple JD conversion tables are used by astronomers.

Days Between Two Dates

Table covers period of two ordinary years. Example—Days between Feb. 10, 1989 and Dec. 15, 1990: subtract 41 from 714; answer is 673 days. For leap year, such as 1992, one day must be added: final answer is 674.

Date	Jan.	Feb.	Mar.	April	May	June	July	Aug.	Sept.	Oct.	Nov.	Dec.	Date	Jan.	Feb.	Mar.	April	May	June	July	Aug.	Sept.	Oct.	Nov.	Dec.
1	1	32	60	91	121	152	182	213	244	274	305	335	1	366	397	425	456	486	517	547	578	609	639	670	700
2	2	33	61	92	122	153	183	214	245	275	306	336	2	367	398	426	457	487	518	548	579	610	640	671	701
3	3	34	62	93	123	154	184	215	246	276	307	337	3	368	399	427	458	488	519	549	580	611	641	672	702
4	4	35	63	94	124	155	185	216	247	277	308	338	4	369	400	428	459	489	520	550	581	612	642	673	703
5	5	36	64	95	125	156	186	217	248	278	309	339	5	370	401	429	460	490	521	551	582	613	643	674	704
6	6	37	65	96	126	157	187	218	249	279	310	340	6	371	402	430	461	491	522	552	583	614	644	675	705
7	7	38	66	97	127	158	188	219	250	280	311	341	7	372	403	431	462	492	523	553	584	615	645	676	706
8	8	39	67	98	128	159	189	220	251	281	312	342	8	373	404	432	463	493	524	554	585	616	646	677	707
9	9	40	68	99	129	160	190	221	252	282	313	343	9	374	405	433	464	494	525	555	586	617	647	678	708
10	10	41	69	100	130	161	191	222	253	283	314	344	10	375	406	434	465	495	526	556	587	618	648	679	709
11	11	42	70	101	131	162	192	223	254	284	315	345	11	376	407	435	466	496	527	557	588	619	649	680	710
12	12	43	71	102	132	163	193	224	255	285	316	346	12	377	408	436	467	497	528	558	589	620	650	681	711
13	13	44	72	103	133	164	194	225	256	286	317	347	13	378	409	437	468	498	529	559	590	621	651	682	712
14	14	45	73	104	134	165	195	226	257	287	318	348	14	379	410	438	469	499	530	560	591	622	652	683	713
15	15	46	74	105	135	166	196	227	258	288	319	349	15	380	411	439	470	500	531	561	592	623	653	684	714
16	16	47	75	106	136	167	197	228	259	289	320	350	16	381	412	440	471	501	532	562	593	624	654	685	715
17	17	48	76	107	137	168	198	229	260	290	321	351	17	382	413	441	472	502	533	563	594	625	655	686	716
18	18	49	77	108	138	169	199	230	261	291	322	352	18	383	414	442	473	503	534	564	595	626	656	687	717
19	19	50	78	109	139	170	200	231	262	292	323	353	19	384	415	443	474	504	535	565	596	627	657	688	718
20	20	51	79	110	140	171	201	232	263	293	324	354	20	385	416	444	475	505	536	566	597	628	658	689	719
21	21	52	80	111	141	172	202	233	264	294	325	355	21	386	417	445	476	506	537	567	598	629	659	690	720
22	22	53	81	112	142	173	203	234	265	295	326	356	22	387	418	446	477	507	538	568	599	630	660	691	721
23	23	54	82	113	143	174	204	235	266	296	327	357	23	388	419	447	478	508	539	569	600	631	661	692	722
24	24	55	83	114	144	175	205	236	267	297	328	358	24	389	420	448	479	509	540	570	601	632	662	693	723
25	25	56	84	115	145	176	206	237	268	298	329	359	25	390	421	449	480	510	541	571	602	633	663	694	724
26	26	57	85	116	146	177	207	238	269	299	330	360	26	391	422	450	481	511	542	572	603	634	664	695	725
27	27	58	86	117	147	178	208	239	270	300	331	361	27	392	423	451	482	512	543	573	604	635	665	696	726
28	28	59	87	118	148	179	209	240	271	301	332	362	28	393	424	452	483	513	544	574	605	636	666	697	727
29	29	—	88	119	149	180	210	241	272	302	333	363	29	394	—	453	484	514	545	575	606	637	667	698	728
30	30	—	89	120	150	181	211	242	273	303	334	364	30	395	—	454	485	515	546	576	607	638	668	699	729
31	31	—	90	—	151	—	212	243	—	304	—	365	31	396	—	455	—	516	—	577	608	—	669	—	730

Lunar Calendar, Chinese New Year, Vietnamese Tet

The ancient Chinese lunar calendar is divided into 12 months of either 29 or 30 days (compensating for the fact that the mean duration of the lunar month is 29 days, 12 hours, 44.05 minutes). The calendar is synchronized with the solar year by the addition of extra months at fixed intervals.

The Chinese calendar runs on a sexagenary cycle, i.e., 60 years. The cycles 1876-1935 and 1936-1995, with the years grouped under their twelve animal designations, are printed below. The Year 1990 (Lunar Year 4688) is found in the seventh column, under Horse, and is known as a "Year of the Horse." Readers can find the animal name for the year of their birth, marriage, etc., in the same chart. (Note: the first 3-7 weeks of each of the western years belong to the previous Chinese year and animal designation.)

Both the western (Gregorian) and traditional lunar calendars are used publicly in China, and two New Year's celebrations are held. On Taiwan, in overseas Chinese communities, and in Vietnam, the lunar calendar has been used only to set the dates for traditional festivals, with the Gregorian system in general use.

The four-day Chinese New Year, Hsin Nien, and the three-day Vietnamese New Year festival, Tet, begin at the first new moon after the sun enters Aquarius. The day may fall, therefore, between Jan. 21 and Feb. 19 of the Gregorian calendar. Jan. 27, 1990 marks the start of the new Chinese year. The date is fixed according to the date of the new moon in the Far East. Since this is west of the International Date Line the date may be one day later than that of the new moon in the United States.

Rat	Ox	Tiger	Hare (Rabbit)	Dragon	Snake	Horse	Sheep (Goat)	Monkey	Rooster	Dog	Pig
1876	1877	1878	1879	1880	1881	1882	1883	1884	1885	1886	1887
1888	1889	1890	1891	1892	1893	1894	1895	1896	1897	1898	1899
1900	1901	1902	1903	1904	1905	1906	1907	1908	1909	1910	1911
1912	1913	1914	1915	1916	1917	1918	1919	1920	1921	1922	1923
1924	1925	1926	1927	1928	1929	1930	1931	1932	1933	1934	1935
1936	1937	1938	1939	1940	1941	1942	1943	1944	1945	1946	1947
1948	1949	1950	1951	1952	1953	1954	1955	1956	1957	1958	1959
1960	1961	1962	1963	1964	1965	1966	1967	1968	1969	1970	1971
1972	1973	1974	1975	1976	1977	1978	1979	1980	1981	1982	1983
1984	1985	1986	1987	1988	1989	1990	1991	1992	1993	1994	1995

Standard Time, Daylight Saving Time, and Others

Source: Defense Mapping Agency Hydrographic Center; Department of Transportation; National Inst. of Standards & Technology; U.S. Naval Observatory

Standard Time

Standard time is reckoned from Greenwich, England, recognized as the Prime Meridian of Longitude. The world is divided into 24 zones, each 15° of arc, or one hour in time apart. The Greenwich meridian (0°) extends through the center of the initial zone, and the zones to the east are numbered from 1 to 12 with the prefix "minus" indicating the number of hours to be subtracted to obtain Greenwich Time. Each zone extends $7\frac{1}{2}°$ on either side of its central meridian.

Westward zones are similarly numbered, but prefixed "plus" showing the number of hours that must be added to get Greenwich Time. While these zones apply generally to sea areas, it should be noted that the Standard Time maintained in many countries does not coincide with zone time. A graphical representation of the zones is shown on the Standard Time Zone Chart of the World published by the Defense Mapping Agency Hydrographic/Topographic Center, Washington, DC 20315-0030.

The United States and possessions are divided into eight Standard Time zones, as set forth by the Uniform Time Act of 1966, which also provides for the use of Daylight Saving Time therein. Each zone is approximately 15° of longitude in width. All places in each zone use, instead of their own local time, the time counted from the transit of the "mean sun" across the Standard Time meridian which passes near the middle of that zone.

These time zones are designated as Atlantic, Eastern, Central, Mountain, Pacific, Yukon, Alaska-Hawaii, and Bering (Samoa), and the time in these zones is basically reckoned from the 60th, 75th, 90th, 105th, 120th, 135th, 150th and 165th meridians west of Greenwich. The time wanders to conform to local geographical regions. The time in the various zones is earlier than Greenwich Time by 4, 5, 6, 7, 8, 9, 10, and 11 hours respectively.

24-Hour Time

24-hour time is widely used in scientific work throughout the world. In the United States it is used also in operations of the Armed Forces. In Europe it is frequently used by the transportation networks in preference to the 12-hour a.m. and p.m. system. With the 24-hour system the day begins at midnight and is designated 0000 through 2359.

International Date Line

The Date Line is a zig-zag line that approximately coincides with the 180th meridian, and it is where the calendar dates are separated. The date must be advanced one day when crossing in a westerly direction and set back one day when crossing in an easterly direction.

The line is deflected eastward through the Bering Strait and westward of the Aleutians to prevent separating these areas by date. The line is again deflected eastward of the

Tonga and New Zealand Islands in the South Pacific for the same reason.

Daylight Saving Time

Daylight Saving Time is achieved by advancing the clock one hour. Under the Uniform Time Act, which became effective in 1967, all states, the District of Columbia, and U.S. possessions were to observe Daylight Saving Time beginning at 2 a.m. on the last Sunday in April and ending at 2 a.m. on the last Sunday in October. Any state could, by law, exempt itself; a 1972 amendment to the act authorized states split by time zones to take that into consideration in exempting themselves. Arizona, Hawaii, Puerto Rico, the Virgin Islands, American Samoa, and part of Indiana are now exempt. Some local zone boundaries in Kansas, Texas, Florida, Michigan, and Alaska have been modified in the last several years by the Dept. of Transportation, which oversees the act. To conserve energy Congress put most of the nation on year-round Daylight Saving Time for two years effective Jan. 6, 1974 through Oct. 26, 1975; but a further bill, signed in October, 1974, restored Standard Time from the last Sunday in that month to the last Sunday in February, 1975. At the end of 1975, Congress failed to renew this temporary legislation and the nation returned to the older end-of April to end-of October DST system.

On July 8, 1986, Pres. Ronald Reagan signed legislation moving up the start of daylight saving time to the first Sunday in April. Daylight Saving Time, which used to start the last Sunday in April, will still end the last Sunday in October. The Transportation Dept. estimated that the earlier starting date will help save more than $28 million in traffic accident costs and prevent more than 1,500 injuries and 20 deaths. The new law, opposed by some farm state lawmakers, took effect in 1987.

International

Adjusting clock time to be able to use the added daylight on summer evenings is common throughout the world.

Western Europe is on daylight saving time generally from the last Sunday in March to the last Sunday in September; however, the United Kingdom continues until the last Sunday in October.

The Soviet Union lies over 11 time zones, but maintains its standard time 1 hour fast of the zone designation. Additionally, it proclaims daylight saving time as does Europe.

China lies across 5 time zones, but has decreed that the entire country be placed on zone time minus 8 hours with daylight saving time from April 12 to September 12.

Many of the countries in the Southern Hemisphere maintain daylight saving time generally from October to March; however, most countries near the equator do not deviate from standard time.

Standard Time Differences—World Cities

The time indicated in the table is fixed by law and is called the legal time, or, more generally, Standard Time. Use of Daylight Saving Time varies widely. *Indicates morning of the following day. At 12:00 noon, Eastern Standard Time, the standard time (in 24-hour time) in foreign cities is as follows:

City	Time	City	Time	City	Time	City	Time
Addis Ababa	20 00	Cape Town	19 00	Leningrad	20 00	Santiago (Chile)	13 00
Alexandria	19 00	Caracas	13 00	Lima	12 00	Seoul	2 00*
Amsterdam	18 00	Casablanca	17 00	Lisbon	17 00	Shanghai	1 00*
Athens	19 00	Copenhagen	18 00	Liverpool	17 00	Singapore	1 00*
Auckland	5 00*	Dacca	23 00	London	17 00	Stockholm	18 00
Baghdad	20 00	Delhi	22 30	Madrid	18 00	Sydney (Australia)	3 00*
Bangkok	0 00	Dublin	17 00	Manila	1 00*	Tashkent	23 00
Beijing	1 00*	Gdansk	18 00	Mecca	20 00	Teheran	20 30
Belfast	17 00	Geneva	18 00	Melbourne	3 00*	Tel Aviv	19 00
Berlin	18 00	Havana	12 00	Mexico City	11 00	Tokyo	2 00*
Bogota	12 00	Helsinki	19 00	Montevideo	14 00	Valparaiso	13 00
Bombay	22 30	Ho Chi Minh City	1 00*	Moscow	20 00	Vladivostok	3 00*
Bremen	18 00	Hong Kong	1 00*	Nagasaki	2 00*	Vienna	18 00
Brussels	18 00	Istanbul	19 00	Oslo	18 00	Warsaw	18 00
Bucharest	19 00	Jakarta	0 00	Paris	18 00	Wellington (N.Z.)	5 00*
Budapest	18 00	Jerusalem	19 00	Prague	18 00	Yokohama	2 00*
Buenos Aires	14 00	Johannesburg	19 00	Rangoon	23 30	Zurich	18 00
Cairo	19 00	Karachi	22 00	Rio De Janeiro	14 00		
Calcutta	22 30	Le Havre	18 00	Rome	18 00		

Standard Time Differences — North American Cities

At 12 o'clock noon, Eastern Standard Time, the standard time in N.A. cities is as follows:

Akron, Oh.	12.00	Noon	Frankfort, Ky.	12.00	Noon	*Phoenix, Ariz.	10.00	A.M.
Albuquerque, N.M.	10.00	A.M.	Galveston, Tex.	11.00	A.M.	Pierre, S.D.	11.00	A.M.
Atlanta, Ga.	12.00	Noon	Grand Rapids, Mich.	12.00	Noon	Pittsburgh, Pa.	12.00	Noon
Austin, Tex.	11.00	A.M.	Halifax, N.S.	1.00	P.M.	Portland, Me.	12.00	Noon
Baltimore, Md.	12.00	Noon	Hartford, Conn.	12.00	Noon	Portland, Ore.	9.00	A.M.
Birmingham, Ala.	11.00	A.M.	Helena, Mon.	10.00	A.M.	Providence, R.I.	12.00	Noon
Bismarck, N.D.	11.00	A.M.	*Honolulu, Ha.	7.00	A.M.	*Regina, Sask.	11.00	A.M.
Boise, Ida.	10.00	A.M.	Houston, Tex.	11.00	A.M.	Reno, Nev.	9.00	A.M.
Boston, Mass.	12.00	Noon	*Indianapolis, Ind.	12.00	Noon	Richmond, Va.	12.00	Noon
Buffalo, N.Y.	12.00	Noon	Jacksonville, Fla.	12.00	Noon	Rochester, N.Y.	12.00	Noon
Butte, Mon.	10.00	A.M.	Juneau, Alas.	8.00	A.M.	Sacramento, Cal.	9.00	A.M.
Calgary, Alta.	10.00	A.M.	Kansas City, Mo.	11.00	A.M.	St. John's, Nfld.	1.30	P.M.
Charleston, S.C.	12.00	Noon	Knoxville, Tenn.	12.00	Noon	St. Louis, Mo.	11.00	A.M.
Charleston, W.Va.	12.00	Noon	Lexington, Ky.	12.00	Noon	St. Paul, Minn.	11.00	A.M.
Charlotte, N.C.	12.00	Noon	Lincoln, Neb.	11.00	A.M.	Salt Lake City, Ut.	10.00	A.M.
Charlottetown, P.E.I.	1.00	P.M.	Little Rock, Ark.	11.00	A.M.	San Antonio, Tex.	11.00	A.M.
Chattanooga, Tenn.	12.00	Noon	Los Angeles, Cal.	9.00	A.M.	San Diego, Cal.	9.00	A.M.
Cheyenne, Wy.	10.00	A.M.	Louisville, Ky.	12.00	Noon	San Francisco, Cal.	9.00	A.M.
Chicago, Ill.	11.00	A.M.	*Mexico City	11.00	A.M.	Santa Fe, N.M.	10.00	A.M.
Cleveland, Oh.	12.00	Noon	Memphis, Tenn.	11.00	A.M.	Savannah, Ga.	12.00	Noon
Colorado Spr., Col.	10.00	A.M.	Miami, Fla.	12.00	Noon	Seattle, Wash.	9.00	A.M.
Columbus, Oh.	12.00	Noon	Milwaukee, Wis.	11.00	A.M.	Shreveport, La.	11.00	A.M.
Dallas, Tex.	11.00	A.M.	Minneapolis, Minn.	11.00	A.M.	Sioux Falls, S.D.	11.00	A.M.
*Dawson, Yuk.	9.00	A.M.	Mobile, Ala.	11.00	A.M.	Spokane, Wash.	9.00	A.M.
Dayton, Oh.	12.00	Noon	Montreal, Que.	12.00	Noon	Tampa, Fla.	12.00	Noon
Denver, Col.	10.00	A.M.	Nashville, Tenn.	11.00	A.M.	Toledo, Oh.	12.00	Noon
Des Moines, Ia.	11.00	A.M.	New Haven, Conn.	12.00	Noon	Topeka, Kan.	11.00	A.M.
Detroit, Mich.	12.00	Noon	New Orleans, La.	11.00	A.M.	Toronto, Ont.	12.00	Noon
Duluth, Minn.	11.00	A.M.	New York, N.Y.	12.00	Noon	*Tucson, Ariz.	10.00	A.M.
El Paso, Tex.	10.00	A.M.	Nome, Alas.	8.00	A.M.	Tulsa, Okla.	11.00	A.M.
Erie, Pa.	12.00	Noon	Norfolk, Va.	12.00	Noon	Vancouver, B.C.	9.00	A.M.
Evansville, Ind.	11.00	A.M.	Okla. City, Okla.	11.00	A.M.	Washington, D.C.	12.00	Noon
Fairbanks, Alas.	8.00	A.M.	Omaha, Neb.	11.00	A.M.	Wichita, Kan.	11.00	A.M.
Flint, Mich.	12.00	Noon	Peoria, Ill.	11.00	A.M.	Wilmington, Del.	12.00	Noon
*Fort Wayne, Ind.	12.00	Noon	Philadelphia, Pa.	12.00	Noon	Winnipeg, Man.	11.00	A.M.
Fort Worth, Tex.	11.00	A.M.						

*Cities with an asterisk do not observe daylight saving time. During much of the year, it is necessary to add one hour to the cities which do observe daylight savings time to get the proper time relation.

Legal or Public Holidays, 1990

Technically there are no national holidays in the United States; each state has jurisdiction over its holidays, which are designated by legislative enactment or executive proclamation. In practice, however, most states observe the federal legal public holidays, even though the President and Congress can legally designate holidays only for the District of Columbia and for federal employees.

Federal legal public holidays are New Year's Day, Martin Luther King Day, Washington's Birthday, Memorial Day, Independence Day, Labor Day, Columbus Day, Veterans' Day, Thanksgiving, and Christmas.

Chief Legal or Public Holidays

When a holiday falls on a Sunday or a Saturday it is usually observed on the following Monday or preceding Friday. For some holidays, government and business closing practices vary. In most states, the office of the Secretary of State can provide details of holiday closings. In most states, the following will be legal or public holidays in 1990:

Jan. 1 (Monday) — New Year's Day.

Feb. 12 (Monday) — Lincoln's Birthday.

Feb. 19 (3d Mon. in Feb.) — Washington's Birthday, or Presidents' Day, or Washington-Lincoln Day.

May 28 (last Mon. in May) — Memorial Day, or Decoration Day.

July 4 (Wednesday) — Independence Day.

Sept. 3 (1st Mon. in Sept.) — Labor Day.

Oct. 8 (2d Mon. in Oct.) — Columbus Day, or Discoverers' Day, or Pioneers' Day.

Nov. 11 (Monday) — Veterans' Day.

Nov. 22 (4th Thurs. in Nov.) — Thanksgiving Day.

Dec. 25 (Tuesday) — Christmas Day.

In some states, the following will be legal or public holidays in 1990:

Jan. 15 (Monday) — Martin Luther King Day. In some states, combined with Robert E. Lee Day.

Apr. 13 (Friday) — Good Friday. In some states, observed for half or part of day.

Nov. 6 (1st Tues. after the 1st Mon. in Nov.) — Election Day.

Some Other Legal or Public Holidays

Source: Questionnaires to states

Jan. 19 — Confederate Heroes' Day or Robert E. Lee Day. In various southern states.

Feb. 27 — Mardi Gras Day (Tuesday before Ash Wednesday). In Alabama and Louisiana.

Mar. 2 — Texas Independence Day. In that state.

Mar. 28 — Seward's Day. In Alaska.

Apr. 13 — Thomas Jefferson's Birthday. In Alabama.

Apr. 16 — Jose de Diego Day. In Puerto Rico.

Apr. 16 — Patriot's Day (3d Monday in Apr.) In Maine.

Apr. 21 — San Jacinto Day. In Texas.

Apr. 23 — Confederate Memorial Day. In Alabama and Mississippi; Apr. 26 in Georgia.

May 8 — Harry S. Truman's Birthday. In Missouri.

May 29 — Jefferson Davis's Birthday. In Mississippi.

June 4 — Jefferson Davis's Birthday (1st Mon. in June). In Alabama.

June 3 — Confederate Memorial Day. In Kentucky.

June 11 — King Kamehameha I Day. In Hawaii.

June 20 — West Virginia Day. In that state.

July 24 — Pioneer Day. In Utah.

July 25 — Puerto Rico Constitution Day. In that state.

Aug. 14 — Victory Day. In Rhode Island.

Aug. 16 — Bennington Battle Day. In Vermont.

Aug. 17 — Admission Day. In Hawaii.

Sept. 12 — Defender's Day. In Maryland.

Oct. 18 — Alaska Day. In that state.

Oct. 31 — Nevada Day. In that state.

UNITED STATES GOVERNMENT

LEGISLATIVE BRANCH	EXECUTIVE BRANCH	JUDICIAL BRANCH
CONGRESS Senate House Architect of the Capitol U.S. Botanic Garden General Accounting Office Government Printing Office Library of Congress Office of Technology Assessment Congressional Budget Office Copyright Royalty Tribunal	**PRESIDENT** Vice President Cabinet Executive Office of the President White House Office Office of Management and Budget Council of Economic Advisors National Security Council Office of Policy Development Office of the U.S. Trade Representative Council on Environmental Quality Office of Science and Technology Policy Office of Administration Office of National Drug Control Policy	**Supreme Court of the United States** Courts Of Appeals District Courts Claims Court Court of Appeals for the Federal Circuit Court of International Trade Territorial Courts Court of Military Appeals Tax Court Administrative Office of the Courts Federal Judicial Center

The Bush Administration

As of mid-1989

Terms of office of the president and vice president, from Jan. 20, 1989 to Jan. 20, 1993. No person may be elected president of the United States for more than two 4-year terms.

President — George Bush of Texas receives salary of $200,000 a year taxable; in addition an expense allowance of $50,000 to assist in defraying expenses resulting from his official duties. Also there may be expended not exceeding $100,000, nontaxable, a year for travel expenses and $20,000 for official entertainment available for allocation within the Executive Office of the President. Congress has provided lifetime pensions of $69,630 a year, free mailing privileges, free office space, and up to $96,000 a year for office help for former Presidents except for the first 30 month period during which a former President is entitled to staff assistance for which an amount up to $150,000 a year may be paid, and $20,000 annually for their widows.

Vice President — Dan Quayle of Indiana receives salary of $115,000 a year and $10,000 for expenses, all of which is taxable.

For succession to presidency, see Succession in Index.

The Cabinet
(Salary: $99,500 per annum)

Secretary of State — James A. Baker 3d, Tex.
Secretary of Treasury — Nicholas F. Brady, N.J.
Secretary of Defense — Richard B. Cheney, Wyo.
Attorney General — Richard "Dick" Thornburgh, Pa.
Secretary of Interior — Manual Lujan, N.M.
Secretary of Agriculture — Clayton K. Yeutter, Neb.
Secretary of Commerce — Robert A. Mosbacher, Tex.
Secretary of Labor — Elizabeth Hanford Dole, N.C.
Secretary of Health and Human Services — Louis W. Sullivan, Ga.
Secretary of Housing and Urban Development — Jack F. Kemp, N.Y.
Secretary of Transportation — Samuel K. Skinner, Ill.
Secretary of Energy — James D. Watkins, Cal.
Secretary of Education — Lauro F. Cavazos, Tex.
Secretary of Veterans Affairs — Edward J. Derwinski, Ill.

The White House Staff
1600 Pennsylvania Ave. NW 20500

Chief of Staff — John H. Sununu.
Deputy Chief of Staff — Andrew Card Jr.
Assistants to the President
  Counsel to the President — C. Boyden Gray.

Press Relations — Max Marlin Fitzwater.
Legislative Affairs — Frederick D. McClure.
Communications & Planning — David Demarest Jr.
Domestic Affairs — Roger Porter.
Management Admin. — J. Bonnie Newman.
Cabinet Secy. — David Q. Bates.
National Security Affairs — Brent Scowcroft.

Executive Agencies

Council of Economic Advisers — Michael J. Boskin.
Central Intelligence Agency — William H. Webster, dir.
Office of National Drug Control Policy — William J. Bennett.
Office of Management and Budget — Richard G. Darman.
U.S. Trade Representative — Carla Hills.
Office of Science and Technology Policy — Allan Bromley, dir.
Council on Environmental Quality — Michael Deland, chmn.

Department of State
2201 C St. NW 20520

Secretary of State — James A. Baker 3d.
Deputy Secretary — Lawrence S. Engleburger.
Under Sec. for Political Affairs — Robert M. Kimmitt.
Under Sec. for Security Assistance, Science and Technology — Reginald Bartholomew.
Under Sec. for Economic Agricultural Affairs — Richard T. McCormack.
Under Secretary for Management — Ivan Selin.
Legal Advisor — Abraham D. Sofaer.
Assistant Secretaries for:
  Administration & Information Management — Sheldon Krys.
  African Affairs — Herman J. Cohen.
  East Asian & Pacific Affairs — Richard H. Solomon.
  Consular Affairs — Joan M. Clark.
  Diplomatic Security — Robert E. Lamb.
  Economic & Business Affairs — Eugene J. McAllister.
  European & Canadian Affairs — vacant.
  Human Rights & Humanitarian Affairs — Richard Schifter.
  Intelligence & Research — Douglas P. Mulholland.
  Legislative Affairs — Janet Mullins.
  Inter-American Affairs — Bernard Aronson.

International Narcotics Matters — Melvin Levitsky.
International Organizations — John R. Bolton.
Near-Eastern & S. Asian Affairs — John H. Kelly.
Political-Military Affairs — H. Allen Holmes.
Public Affairs & Spokesman — Margaret DeB. Tutwiler.
Oceans, International Environmental & Scientific Affairs — Frederick M. Bernthal.
Dir. General, Foreign Service & Dir. of Personnel — Edward J. Perkins.
Management Policy — C. Edward Dillery, dir.
Inspector General — Sherman M. Funk.
Policy Planning Staff — Dennis Rose
U.S. Information Agency — Bruce Gelb, dir.
U.S. Rep. to the UN — Thomas R. Pickering.

Treasury Department

1500 Pennsylvania Ave. NW 20220
Secretary of the Treasury — Nicholas F. Brady.
Deputy Sec. of the Treasury — John E. Robson.
Under Sec. for Finance — Robert R. Glauber.
Under Sec. for International Affairs — David C. Mulford.
General Counsel — Edith B. Holiday.
Assistant Secretaries: — Roger Bolton (Public Affairs); Charles H. Dallara (Intl. Affairs); David W. Mullins Jr. (Domestic Finance); Salvatore R. Martoche (Enforcement); Gerald Murphy (Fiscal); Kenneth W. Gideon (Tax Policy); Bryce Larry Harlow (Legislative Affairs); vacant (Economic Policy); Hollis S. McLoughlin (Policy Management).
Bureaus:
Alcohol, Tobacco & Firearms — Stephen E. Higgins, dir.
Comptroller of the Currency — Robert Clarke.
Customs — William von Raab, comm.
Engraving & Printing — Richard H. Daly, dir.
Federal Law Enforcement Training Center — Charles F. Rinkevich, dir.
Financial Management Service — William E. Douglas, comm.
Internal Revenue Service — Fred T. Goldberg, comm.
Mint — Donna Pope, dir.
Public Debt — Richard L. Gregg, comm.
Treasurer of the U.S. — vacant.
U.S. Savings Bond Division — Jerrold B. Speers, dir.
U.S. Secret Service — John R. Simpson, dir.

Department of Defense

The Pentagon 20301
Secretary of Defense — Richard B. Cheney.
Deputy Secretary — Donald J. Atwood Jr.
Under Secy. for Acquisition — vacant.
Under Secy. for Policy — Paul Wolfowitz.
Asst. Secretaries:
Atomic Energy — Robert B. Barker.
Command Control Communications & Intelligence — vacant.
Comptroller — Robert W. Helm.
Force Management & Personnel — vacant.
Health Affairs — vacant.
International Security Affairs — Henry S. Rowen.
International Security Policy — Stephen J. Hadley.
Legislative Affairs — David Gribbin 3d.
Products & Logistics — Jack Katzen.
Program Analysis & Evaluation — David S.C. Chu.
Public Affairs — Pete Williams.
Reserve Affairs — Stephen M. Duncan.
Chairman, Joint Chiefs of Staff — Gen. Colin L. Powell.
General Counsel — vacant.
Admin. & Management — David O. Cooke, dir.

Department of the Army

The Pentagon 20310
Secretary of the Army — John O. Marsh Jr.

Under Secretary — Michael P.W. Stone.
Assistant Secretaries for:
Civil Works — Robert W. Page.
Installations & Logistics — John W. Shannon.
Financial Management — Kenneth B. Kramer.
Research, Development and Acquisition — Jay R. Sculley.
Manpower & Reserve Affairs — vacant.
Chief of Public Affairs — Brig. Gen. Pat H. Brady.
Chief of Staff — Gen. Carl E. Vuono.
Inspector General — vacant.
Deputy Chiefs of Staff:
Logistics — Lt. Gen. Jimmy D. Ross.
Operations & Plans — Lt. Gen. Gordon R. Sullivan.
Personnel — Lt. Gen. Allen K. Ono.
Intelligence — Lt. Gen. Sidney Weinstein.
Commanders:
U.S. Army Materiel Command — Gen. Louis C. Wagner.
U.S. Army Forces Command — vacant.
U.S. Army Training and Doctrine Command — Gen. John W. Foss.
First U.S. Army — Lt. Gen. James E. Thompson.
Second U.S. Army — Lt. Gen. Orren R. Whiddon.
Third U.S. Army — Lt. Gen. John J. Yeosock.
Fourth U.S. Army — Lt. Gen. James R. Hall.
Fifth U.S. Army — Lt. Gen. William H. Schneider.
Sixth U.S. Army — Lt. Gen. William H. Harrison.

Department of the Navy

The Pentagon 20350
Secretary of the Navy — H. Lawrence Garrett 3d.
Under Secretary — Everett Pyatt, act.
Assistant Secretaries for:
Financial Management — vacant.
Manpower, Reserve Affairs — Kenneth Bergquist.
Research, Engineering & Systems — Richard Rumpf, act.
Shipbuilding & Logistics — Everett Pyatt.
Judge Advocate General — RADM E. D. Stumbaugh.
Chief of Naval Operations — ADM Carlisle A.H. Trost.
Chief of Information — RADM Brent Baker.
Military Sealift Command — VADM Paul D. Butcher.
Chief of Naval Personnel — VADM Leon A. Edney.

U.S. Marine Corps:
(Arlington Annex 20380)

Commandant — Gen. A.M. Gray.
Asst. Commandant — Gen. Joseph J. Went.
Chief of Staff — Lt. Gen. L.H. Buehl

Department of the Air Force

The Pentagon 20330
Secretary of the Air Force — Donald B. Rice.
Under Secretary — vacant.
Assistant Secretaries for:
Manpower & Reserve Affairs — Karen R. Keesling.
Acquisition — John J. Welch Jr.
Readiness Support — Eric M. Thorson, act.
Public Affairs — Brig. Gen. Michael P. McRaney.
Office of Space Systems — Brig. Gen. Donald R. Walker.
Chief of Staff — Gen. Larry D. Welch.
Inspector General — Lt. Gen. Buford R. Lary.
Deputy Chiefs of Staff:
Logistics & Engineering — Lt. Gen. Charles C. McDonald.
Programs & Resources — Lt. Gen. James P. McCarthy.
Personnel — Lt. Gen. Thomas J. Hickey.
Plans & Operations — Lt. Gen. Jimmie V. Adams.
Major Air Commands:
AF Logistics Command — Gen. Alfred G. Hansen.
AF Systems Command — Gen. Bernard P. Randolph.

Strategic Air Command — Gen. John T. Chain.
Tactical Air Command — Gen. Robert D. Russ.
Alaskan Air Command — Lt. Gen. Thomas G. McInerney.
Pacific Air Forces — Gen. Merrill A. McPeak.
USAF Europe — Gen. Michael J. Dugan.
Electronic Security Command — Maj. Gen. Paul H. Martin.
AF Communications Command — Maj. Gen. James S. Cassity Jr.
Air Training Command — Lt. Gen. Robert C. Oaks.
Military Airlift Command — Gen. Duane H. Cassidy.
AF Space Command — Lt. Gen. Donald J. Kutyna.

Department of Justice

Constitution Ave. & 10th St. NW 20530
Attorney General — Richard "Dick" Thornburgh.
Deputy Attorney General — vacant.
Solicitor General — Kenneth W. Starr.
Associate Attorney General — vacant.
Liaison Services —Barry H. Stern.
Intelligence Policy & Review — Mary Lawton.
Professional Responsibility —Michael E. Shaheen Jr.
Assistants:
Antitrust Division — James F. Rill.
Civil Division — Stewart Schiffer, act.
Civil Rights Division — James Turner, act.
Criminal Division — Edward S.G. Dennis.
Justice Programs —Richard Abell.
Justice Management Division — Harry H. Flickinger.
Land & Natural Resources Division — Donald A. Carr, act.
Legal Policy — Thomas M. Boyd.
Legal Counsel — William B. Bark.
Legislative Affairs — Carol T. Crawford.
Tax Division — Shirley D. Peterson.
Fed. Bureau of Investigation — William S. Sessions, dir.
Exec. Off. for Immigration Review — David L. Milhollan, dir.
Bureau of Prisons — J. Michael Quinlan.
Comm. Relations Service — Grace F. Hughes.
Office of Inspector General — Anthony C. Moscato, act.
Office of Special Counsel for Immigration Related Unfair Employment Practices — Andrew Strotny, act.
Exec. Off. for U.S. Trustees — Thomas J. Stanton, dir.
Exec. Off. for U.S. Attorneys — Laurence S. McWhorter.
Public Affairs — David R. Runkel, dir.
Immigration and Naturalization Service — James L. Buck, act.
Pardon Attorney — David C. Stephenson.
U.S. Parole Commission — Benjamin F. Baer, chmn.
U.S. Marshals Service — Stanley E. Morris, dir.
Foreign Claims Settlement Comm. — Stanley J. Gold.
Interpol, U.S. Natl. Central Bureau — Richard C. Stiener, chief.

Department of the Interior

C St. between 18th & 19th Sts. NW 20240
Secretary of the Interior — Manual Lujan.
Under Secretary — Frank Bracken.
Assistant Secretaries for:
Fish, Wildlife and Parks — Constance Harriman.
Water & Science — vacant.
Land & Minerals Management — vacant.
Policy, Budget, and Administration — Lou Gallegos.
Indian Affairs — Eddie Frank Brown.
Territorial & Intl. Affairs — Stella Guerra.
Bureau of Land Management — Cy Jamison, dir.
Bureau of Mines — T.S. Ary, dir.
Bureau of Reclamation — vacant.
Fish & Wildlife Service — John F. Turner, dir.
Geological Survey — Dallas L. Peck, dir.
National Park Service — James M. Ridenour.

Public Affairs — I. Stephen Goldstein, dir.
Office of Congressional and Legislative Affairs — John E. Schrote.
Solicitor — Martin L. Allday.

Department of Agriculture

The Mall, 12th & 14th Sts. 20250
Secretary of Agriculture — Clayton Yeutter.
Deputy Secretary — Jack C. Parnell.
Administration — John Franke Jr.
Internatl. Affairs & Commodity Programs — Richard T. Crowder.
Food & Consumer Services — Ann Chadwick, act.
Marketing & Inspection Services — Jo Ann Smith.
Small Community & Rural Development — Roland Vautour.
Economics — Leo Mayer, act.
Congressional Affairs — F. Eugene Bailey.
Natural Resources & Environment — John Evans, act.
General Counsel — Alan Raul.
Science & Education — Charles Hess.
Inspector General — Leon Snead, act.

Department of Commerce

14th St. between Constitution & E St. NW 20230
Secretary of Commerce — Robert Mosbacher.
Deputy Secretary — Thomas Murrin.
General Counsel — Wendell Willkie.
Assistant Secretaries:
Administration — Thomas Collamore.
Congressional Affairs — Marc Stanley.
Economic Development Adm. — Orson G. Swindle.
Intl. Economic Policy — Thomas Duesterberg.
Natl. Telecommunications Information Adm. — vacant.
Patent & Trademark Office — vacant.
Trade Development — Michael Skarzynski.
Bureau of the Census — vacant.
Bureau of Economic Analysis — Allan H. Young, dir.
Under Secy. for International Trade — J. Michael Farren.
Under Secy. for Econ. Affairs — Michael Darby.
Under Secy. for Science & Technology — vacant.
Natl. Oceanic & Atmospheric Admin. — vacant.
Natl. Technical Info. Service — Joseph F. Caponio, dir.
Natl. Institute For Standards & Technology — vacant.
Minority Business Development Agency — Kenneth Bolton.
Public Affairs — Marion Blakey, dir.
Consumer Affairs — John Gibbons.

Department of Labor

200 Constitution Ave. NW 20210
Secretary of Labor — Elizabeth Dole.
Deputy Secretary — Roderick A. DeArment.
Assistant Secretaries for:
Administration and Management — Thomas C. Komarek.
Congressional Affairs — Kathleen Harrington.
Employment & Training — Robert Jones.
Employment Standards — William C. Brooks.
Labor-Management Standards — William White.
Mine Safety & Health — David O'Neal, act.
Occupational Safety & Health — Gerard F. Scannell.
Pension & Welfare Benefit Programs — David Ball.
Policy — Jennifer Lynn Dorn.
Public and Intergovernmental Affairs — Dale Triber Tate.
Veterans Employment — Thomas E. Collins 3d.
Solicitor of Labor — Robert Davis.
Dep. Under Secy. for International Affairs — Shellyn Gae McCaffrey.
Dep. Under Secy. for Labor-Management Relations & Cooperative Programs — John R. Stepp.

Office of Information & Public Affairs — Johanna Schneider, dir.
Women's Bureau — Jill Emery, dir.
Inspector General — J. Brian Hyland.
Comm. of Labor Statistics — Janet L. Norwood.

Department of Health and Human Services

200 Independence Ave. SW 20201

Secretary of HHS — Louis W. Sullivan.
Under Secretary — Constance Horner.
Assistant Secretaries for:
  Management and Budget — Kevin Moley.
  Public Affairs — Kay C. James.
  Health — James Mason.
  Planning and Evaluation — Arnold Tompkins, act.
  Human Development Services — Mary Gall.
  Legislation — Gerald Olson.
  Personnel Administration — Thomas McFee.
  Family Support Admin. — Catherine Bertini, act.
General Counsel — Michael Astrue.
Inspector General — Richard P. Kusserow.
Civil Rights — Edward Mercado.
Surgeon General — vacant.
Health Care Financing Admin. — Louis B. Hays, act.
Social Security Adm. — Gwendolyn S. King.
Consumer Affairs — Bonnie Guiton.

Department of Housing and Urban Development

451 7th St. SW 20410

Secretary of Housing & Urban Development — Jack Kemp.
Under Secretary — Alfred A. DelliBovi.
Deputies — Edwin I. Gardner.
Assistant Secretaries for:
  Administration — Claire E. Freeman.
  Community Planning & Development — S. Anna Kondratas.
  Housing & Federal Housing Commissioner — C. Austin Fitts.
  Legislation & Congressional Relations — Timothy L. Coyle.
  Policy Development & Research — John Weicher.
  Public Affairs — Sherrie S. Rollins.
  Public & Indian Housing — vacant.
  Fair Housing & Equal Opportunity — vacant.
President, Govt. Natl. Mortgage Assn. — vacant.
International Affairs — Theodore Britton Jr.
Labor Relations — Justin Logsdon.
General Counsel — Francis A. Keating 2d.
Inspector General — Paul A. Adams.
Indian & Alaska Native Programs — vacant.
Board of Contract Appeals — David T. Anderson.
Chief Administrative Law Judge — Alan W. Heifetz.

Department of Transportation

400 7th St. SW 20590

Secretary of Transportation — Samuel K. Skinner.
Deputy Secretary — Elaine Chao.
Assistant Secretaries — Jeffrey Shane (Policy and International Affairs); Kate Moore (Budget and Programs); John H. Seymour (Administration); David Prosperi (Public Affairs); Galen Reser (Governmental Affairs).
National Highway Traffic Safety Admin. — Jerry Curry.
U. S. Coast Guard Commandant — Adm. Paul A. Yost Jr.
Federal Aviation Admin. — James Busey.

Federal Highway Admin. — Thomas Larson.
Federal Railroad Admin. — Gilbert Carmichael.
Maritime Admin. — vacant.
Urban Mass Transportation Admin. — Brian Clymer.
Research & Special Programs Admin. — Travis Dungan.
Saint Lawrence Seaway Development Corp. — James L. Emery.

Department of Energy

1000 Independence Ave. SW 20585

Secretary of Energy — James D. Watkins.
Deputy Secy. — W. Henson Moore.
Under Secretary — John C. Tuck.
General Counsel — Eric Fygi, act.
Inspector General — John C. Layton.
Assistant Secretaries — Donna Fitzpatrick (Management & Administration); C. Anson Franklin (Congressional, Intergovernmental & Public Affairs); Troy E. Wade 2d (Defense Programs); David B. Waller (International Affairs & Energy Emergencies); Mary Ann Novak (Nuclear Energy); Helmut A. Merklein (Energy Info. Adm.); James A. Wampler (Fossil Energy); John R. Berg (Conservation & Renewable Energy); Peter N. Brush (Environment, Safety & Health).
Economic Regulatory Adm. — C. L. Van Orman, adm.
Federal Energy Regulatory Comm. — Martha O. Hesse, chmn.
Office of Hearings & Appeals — George B. Breznay, dir.
Office of Energy Research — Robert O. Hunter Jr.
Office of Civilian Radioactive Waste Management — Samuel Rousso.
Office of Minority Economic Impact — Raymond G. Massie, dir.
Board of Contract Appeals — E. Barclay van Doren, chmn.

Department of Education

400 Maryland Ave. SW 20202

Secretary of Education — Lauro F. Cavazos.
Under Secretary — John Theodore Sanders.
Chief of Staff — Bill R. Phillips.
Deputy Under Secretaries — Charles E.M. Kolb, Michelle Easton, Gary Rasmussen.
General Counsel — Steven Winnick, act.
Assistant Secretaries:
  Legislation — Nancy Mohr Kennedy.
  Elementary and Secondary Education — Daniel Bonner, act.
  Postsecondary Education — James Williams, act.
  Educational Research and Improvement — Bruno Manno, act.
  Adult & Vocational Education — Dr. D. Kay Wright, act.
  Special Education and Rehabilitative Services — Robert Davila.
  Civil Rights — William Smith, act.
  Bilingual & Minority Languages — Rita Esquivel.

Department of Veterans Affairs

810 Vermont Ave. NW 20420

Secretary of Veterans Affairs — Edward J. Derwinski.
Deputy — Anthony J. Principi.
Insepector General — vacant.
Veterans Benefits Adm. — vacant.
Veterans Health Services & Research Adm. — vacant.
General Counsel — vacant.

Judiciary of the U.S.

Data as of mid-1989

Justices of the United States Supreme Court

The Supreme Court comprises the chief justice of the United States and 8 associate justices, all appointed by the president with advice and consent of the Senate. Salaries: chief justice $115,000 annually, associate justice $110,000.

Name; apptd from *Chief Justices in italics*	Service Term	Yrs.	Born	Died
John Jay, N.Y.	1789-1795	5	1745	1829
John Rutledge, S.C.	1789-1791	1	1739	1800
William Cushing, Mass.	1789-1810	20	1732	1810
James Wilson, Pa.	1789-1798	8	1742	1798
John Blair, Va.	1789-1796	6	1732	1800
James Iredell, N.C.	1790-1799	9	1751	1799
Thomas Johnson, Md.	1791-1793	1	1732	1819
William Paterson, N.J.	1793-1806	13	1745	1806
John Rutledge, S.C.	1795(a)	—	1739	1800
Samuel Chase, Md.	1796-1811	15	1741	1811
Oliver Ellsworth, Conn.	1796-1800	4	1745	1807
Bushrod Washington, Va.	1798-1829	31	1762	1829
Alfred Moore, N.C.	1799-1804	4	1755	1810
John Marshall, Va.	1801-1835	34	1755	1835
William Johnson, S.C.	1804-1834	30	1771	1834
Henry B. Livingston, N.Y.	1806-1823	16	1757	1823
Thomas Todd, Ky.	1807-1826	18	1765	1826
Joseph Story, Mass.	1811-1845	33	1779	1845
Gabriel Duval, Md.	1811-1835	22	1752	1844
Smith Thompson, N.Y.	1823-1843	20	1768	1843
Robert Trimble, Ky.	1826-1828	2	1777	1828
John McLean, Oh.	1829-1861	32	1785	1861
Henry Baldwin, Pa.	1830-1844	14	1780	1844
James M. Wayne, Ga.	1835-1867	32	1790	1867
Roger B. Taney, Md.	1836-1864	28	1777	1864
Philip P. Barbour, Va.	1836-1841	4	1783	1841
John Catron, Tenn.	1837-1865	28	1786	1865
John McKinley, Ala.	1837-1852	15	1780	1852
Peter V. Daniel, Va.	1841-1860	19	1784	1860
Samuel Nelson, N.Y.	1845-1872	27	1792	1873
Levi Woodbury, N.H.	1845-1851	5	1789	1851
Robert C. Grier, Pa.	1846-1870	23	1794	1870
Benjamin R. Curtis, Mass.	1851-1857	6	1809	1874
John A. Campbell, Ala.	1853-1861	8	1811	1889
Nathan Clifford, Me.	1858-1881	23	1803	1881
Noah H. Swayne, Oh.	1862-1881	18	1804	1884
Samuel F. Miller, Ia.	1862-1890	28	1816	1890
David Davis, Ill.	1862-1877	14	1815	1886
Stephen J. Field, Cal.	1863-1897	34	1816	1899
Salmon P. Chase, Oh.	1864-1873	8	1808	1873
William Strong, Pa.	1870-1880	10	1808	1895
Joseph P. Bradley, N.J.	1870-1892	21	1813	1892
Ward Hunt, N.Y.	1872-1882	9	1810	1886
Morrison R. Waite, Oh.	1874-1888	14	1816	1888
John M. Harlan, Ky.	1877-1911	34	1833	1911
William B. Woods, Ga.	1880-1887	6	1824	1887
Stanley Matthews, Oh.	1881-1889	7	1824	1889
Horace Gray, Mass.	1881-1902	20	1828	1902
Samuel Blatchford, N.Y.	1882-1893	11	1820	1893
Lucius Q. C. Lamar, Miss.	1888-1893	5	1825	1893
Melville W. Fuller, Ill.	1888-1910	21	1833	1910
David J. Brewer, Kan.	1889-1910	20	1837	1910
Henry B. Brown, Mich.	1890-1906	15	1836	1913
George Shiras Jr., Pa.	1892-1903	10	1832	1924
Howell E. Jackson, Tenn.	1893-1895	2	1832	1895
Edward D. White, La.	1894-1910	16	1845	1921
Rufus W. Peckham, N.Y.	1895-1909	13	1838	1909
Joseph McKenna, Cal.	1898-1925	26	1843	1926
Oliver W. Holmes, Mass.	1902-1932	29	1841	1935
William R. Day, Oh.	1903-1922	19	1849	1923
William H. Moody, Mass.	1906-1910	3	1853	1917
Horace H. Lurton, Tenn.	1909-1914	4	1844	1914
Charles E. Hughes, N.Y.	1910-1916	5	1862	1948
Willis Van Devanter, Wy.	1910-1937	26	1859	1941
Joseph R. Lamar, Ga.	1910-1916	5	1857	1916
Edward D. White, La.	1910-1921	10	1845	1921
Mahlon Pitney, N.J.	1912-1922	10	1858	1924
James C. McReynolds, Tenn.	1914-1941	26	1862	1946
Louis D. Brandeis, Mass.	1916-1939	22	1856	1941
John H. Clarke, Oh.	1916-1922	5	1857	1945
William H. Taft, Conn.	1921-1930	8	1857	1930
George Sutherland, Ut.	1922-1938	15	1862	1942
Pierce Butler, Minn.	1922-1939	16	1866	1939
Edward T. Sanford, Tenn.	1923-1930	7	1865	1930
Harlan F. Stone, N.Y.	1925-1941	16	1872	1946
Charles E. Hughes, N.Y.	1930-1941	11	1862	1948
Owen J. Roberts, Pa.	1930-1945	15	1875	1955
Benjamin N. Cardozo, N.Y.	1932-1938	6	1870	1938
Hugo L. Black, Ala.	1937-1971	34	1886	1971
Stanley F. Reed, Ky.	1938-1957	19	1884	1980
Felix Frankfurter, Mass.	1939-1962	23	1882	1965
William O. Douglas, Conn.	1939-1975	36	1898	1980
Frank Murphy, Mich.	1940-1949	9	1890	1949
Harlan F. Stone, N.Y.	1941-1946	5	1872	1946
James F. Byrnes, S.C.	1941-1942	1	1879	1972
Robert H. Jackson, N.Y.	1941-1954	12	1892	1954
Wiley B. Rutledge, Ia.	1943-1949	6	1894	1949
Harold H. Burton, Oh.	1945-1958	13	1888	1964
Fred M. Vinson, Ky.	1946-1953	7	1890	1953
Tom C. Clark, Tex.	1949-1967	18	1899	1977
Sherman Minton, Ind.	1949-1956	7	1890	1965
Earl Warren, Cal.	1953-1969	16	1891	1974
John Marshall Harlan, N.Y.	1955-1971	16	1899	1971
William J. Brennan Jr., N.J.	1956 —	—	1906	—
Charles E. Whittaker, Mo.	1957-1962	5	1901	1973
Potter Stewart, Oh.	1958-1981	23	1915	1985
Byron R. White, Col.	1962 —	—	1917	—
Arthur J. Goldberg, Ill.	1962-1965	3	1908	—
Abe Fortas, Tenn.	1965-1969	4	1910	1982
Thurgood Marshall, N.Y.	1967 —	—	1908	—
Warren E. Burger, Va.	1969-1986	17	1907	—
Harry A. Blackmun, Minn.	1970 —	—	1908	—
Lewis F. Powell Jr., Va.	1972-1987	15	1907	—
William H. Rehnquist, Ariz.	1972-1986	14	1924	—
John Paul Stevens, Ill.	1975 —	—	1920	—
Sandra Day O'Connor, Ariz.	1981 —	—	1930	—
William H. Rehnquist, Ariz.	1986 —	—	1924	—
Antonin Scalia, Va.	1986 —	—	1936	—
Anthony M. Kennedy, Cal.	1988 —	—	1936	—

(a) Rejected Dec. 15, 1795.

U.S. Court of International Trade

New York, NY 10007 (Salaries, $89,500)

Chief Judge — Edward D. Re.

Judges — James L. Watson, Gregory W. Carman, Jane A. Restani, Dominick L. DiCarlo, Thomas J. Aquilino Jr., Nicholas Tsoucalas, R. Kenton Musgrave.

U.S. Claims Court

Washington, D.C. 20005 (Salaries, $89,500)

Chief Judge — Loren A. Smith.

Judges — James F. Merow, John P. Wiese, Robert J. Yock, Reginald W. Gibson, Lawrence S. Margolis, Christine C. Nettesheim, Moody R. Tidwell 3d, Marian Blank Horn, Eric G. Bruggink, John L. Napier, Bohdan A. Futey, Wilkes C. Robinson, Roger B. Andewelt, James T. Turner, Randall R. Rader.

U.S. Tax Court

Washington DC 20217 (Salaries, $89,500)

Chief Judge — Arthur L. Nims 3d.

Judges — Herbert L. Chabot, Edna G. Parker, Jules J. Korner 3d, Meade Whitaker, Mary Ann Cohen, John O. Colvin, Perry Shields, Charles E. Clapp 2d, Lapsley W. Hamblen Jr., Stephen J. Swift, Joel Gerber, Julien I. Jacobs, Lawrence A. Wright, Carolyn

Miller Parr, Robert P. Ruwe, Thomas B. Wells, Laurence J. Whalen. B. John Williams Jr.

U.S. Courts of Appeals

(Salaries, $95,000. CJ means Chief Judge)

Federal Circuit — Howard T. Markey, CJ; Daniel M. Friedman, Giles S. Rich, Edward S. Smith, Helen W. Nies; Pauline Newman, Jean G. Bissell, Glenn L. Archer Jr., H. Robert Mayer, Paul R. Michel; Clerk's Office, Washington, DC 20439.

District of Columbia — Patricia M. Wald, CJ; Spottswood W. Robinson 3d, Abner J. Mikva, Harry T. Edwards, Ruth Bader Ginsburg, Kenneth W. Starr, Laurence H. Silberman; James L. Buckley, Stephen F. Williams, Douglas Ginsburg, David B. Sentelle; Clerk's Office, Washington, DC 20001.

First Circuit (Me., Mass., N.H., R.I., Puerto Rico) — Levin H. Campbell, CJ; Hugh H. Bownes, Stephen Breyer, Juan R. Torruella, Bruce M. Selya; Clerk's Office, Boston, MA 02109.

Second Circuit (Conn., N.Y., Vt.) — Wilfred Feinberg, CJ; James L. Oakes, CJ; Wilfred Freiberg, Thomas J. Meskill, Jon O. Newman, Amalya Lyle Kearse, Richard J. Cardamone, Lawrence W. Pierce, Ralph K. Winter Jr., George C. Pratt, Roger J. Miner, Frank X. Altimari, J. Daniel Mahoney; Clerk's Office, New York, NY 10007.

Third Circuit (Del., N.J., Pa., Virgin Is.) — John J. Gibbons, CJ; A. Leon Higginbotham Jr., Dolores K. Sloviter, Edward R. Becker, Carol Los Mansmann, Walter K. Stapleton, Morton I. Ginsberg, Anthony J. Scirica, William D. Hutchinson, Robert E. Cowen, Richard L. Nygaard; Clerk's Office, Philadelphia, PA 19106.

Fourth Circuit (Md., N.C., S.C., Va., W.Va.) — Sam J. Ervin 3d, CJ; Harrison L. Winter, Kenneth K. Hall, Donald Stuart Russell, H. Emory Widener Jr., James D. Phillips Jr., Francis D. Murnaghan Jr., James M. Sprouse, Robert F. Chapman, J. Harvie Wilkinson 3d, William W. Wilkins Jr.; Clerk's Office, Richmond, VA 23219.

Fifth Circuit (La., Miss., Tex.) — Charles Clark, CJ; Thomas G. Gee, Alvin B. Rubin, Thomas M. Reavley, Henry A. Politz, Carolyn D. King, Samuel D. Johnson, Jerre S. Williams, William L. Garwood, E. Grady Jolly, Patrick E. Higginbotham, W. Eugene Davis, Jerry E. Smith, Edith Hollan Jones, John M. Duhe Jr.; Clerk's Office, New Orleans, LA 70130.

Sixth Circuit (Ky., Mich., Ohio, Tenn.) — Albert J. Engel, CJ; Gilbert S. Merritt, Damon J. Keith, Boyce F. Martin Jr., Nathaniel R. Jones, Robert B. Krupansky, Harry W. Wellford, Cornelia G. Kennedy, H. Ted Milburn, Ralph B. Guy Jr., David A. Nelson, James L. Ryan, Danny J. Boggs, Alan E. Norris; Clerk's Office, Cincinnati, OH 45202.

Seventh Circuit (Ill., Ind., Wis.) — William J. Bauer, CJ; Walter J. Cummings, Harlington Wood Jr., Richard D. Cudahy, Richard A. Posner, John L. Coffey, Joel M. Flaum, Frank H. Easterbrook, Kenneth F. Ripple, Daniel A. Manion, Michael S. Kanne; Clerk's Office, Chicago, IL 60604.

Eighth Circuit (Ark., Ia., Minn., Mo., Neb., N.D., S.D.) — Donald P. Lay, CJ; Theodore McMillian, Richard S. Arnold, John R. Gibson, George C. Fagg, Pasco M. Bowman 2d, Roger L. Wollman, Frank J. Magill, C. Arlen Beam; Clerk's Office, St. Louis, MO 63101.

Ninth Circuit (Alaska, Ariz., Cal., Ha., Ida., Mont., Nev., Ore., Wash., Guam, N. Mariana Islands) — Albert T. Goodwin, CJ; James R. Browning, J. Clifford Wallace, Procter Hug Jr., Thomas Tang, Jerome Farris, Betty B. Fletcher, Mary M. Schroeder, Harry Pregerson, Arthur L. Alarcon, Cecil F. Poole, Dorothy W. Nelson, William C. Canby Jr., William A. Norris, Stephen Reinhardt, Robert R. Beezer, Cynthia M. Hall, Charles E. Wiggins, Melvin Brunetti, Alex Kozinski, David R. Thompson, John T. Noonan, Diarmuid F. O'Scannlain, Edward Leavy, Stephen S. Trout; Clerk's Office, San Francisco, CA 94101.

Tenth Circuit (Col., Kan., N.M., Okla., Ut., Wy.) — William J. Holloway Jr., CJ; Monroe G. McKay, James K. Logan, Stephanie K. Seymour, John P. Moore, Stephen H. Anderson, Deanell R. Tacha, Bobby R. Baldock, Wade Brorby, David M. Ebel; Clerk's Office, Denver, CO 80294.

Eleventh Circuit (Ala. Fla., Ga.)— Paul R. Roney, CJ; Gerald B. Tjoflat, James C. Hill, Peter T. Fay, Robert S. Vance, Phyllis A. Kravitch, Frank M. Johnson Jr., Joseph W. Hatchett, R. Lanier Anderson 3d, Thomas A. Clark, J.L. Edmondson, Emmett R. Cox; Clerk's Office, Atlanta GA 30303.

Temporary Emergency Court of Appeals — Reynaldo G. Garza, CJ; Clerk's Office, Washington, DC 20001 .

U.S. District Courts

(Salaries, $89,500. CJ means Chief Judge)

Alabama — **Northern:** Sam C. Pointer Jr., CJ; James Hughes Hancock, Robert B. Propst, E. B. Haltom Jr., U. W. Clemon, William M. Acker Jr.; Clerk's Office, Birmingham 35203. **Middle:** Tru-

man M. Hobbs, CJ; Myron H. Thompson, Joel F. Dubina; Clerk's Office, Montgomery 36101. **Southern:** Alex T. Howard Jr., CJ; Charles R. Butler Jr.; Clerk's Office, Mobile 36652.

Alaska — H. Russel Holland, CJ; Andrew J. Kleinfeld; Clerk's Office, Anchorage 99513.

Arizona — Richard M. Bilby, CJ; Charles L. Hardy, Alfredo C. Marquez, Earl H. Carroll, William D. Browning, Paul G. Rosenblat, Robert C. Bloomfield, Roger G. Strand; Clerk's Office, Phoenix 85025.

Arkansas — **Eastern:** Garnett Thomas Eisele, CJ; Henry Woods, George Howard Jr., Stephen M. Reasoner; Clerk's Office, Little Rock 72203. **Western:** H. Franklin Waters, CJ; George Howard Jr., Morris S. Arnold; Clerk's Office, Fort Smith 72902.

California — **Northern:** William A. Ingram, CJ; William W. Schwarzer, Robert P. Aguilar, Thelton E. Henderson, Marilyn H. Patel, Eugene F. Lynch, John P. Vukasin Jr, Charles A. Legge, D. Lowell Jensen, Fern M. Smith; Clerk's Office, San Francisco 94102. **Eastern:** Lawrence K. Karlton, CJ; Milton L. Schwartz, Edward Dean Price, Raul A. Ramirez, Robert E. Coyle, Edward J. Garcia; Clerk's Office, Sacramento 95814. **Central:** Manuel L. Real, CJ; Wm. Matthew Byrne Jr., Robert M. Takasugi, Mariana R. Pfaelzer, Terry J. Hatter Jr., A. Wallace Tashima, Consuelo Bland Marshall, David V. Kenyon, Richard A. Gadbois, Edward Rafeedie, Pamela A. Rymer, Harry L. Hupp, Alicemarie H. Stotler, James M. Ideman, William J. Rea, William D. Keller, Ferdinand F. Fernandez, Stephen V. Wilson, J. Spencer Letts, Dickran M. Tevrizian Jr., John G. Davies, Ronald S.W. Lew; Clerk's Office, Los Angeles 90012. **Southern:** Gordon Thompson Jr., CJ; William B. Enright, Judith N. Keep, Earl B. Gilliam, J. Lawrence Irving, Rudi M. Brewster, John S. Rhoades Sr.; Clerk's Office, San Diego 92189.

Colorado — Sherman G. Finesilver, CJ; Richard P. Matsch, Jim R. Carrigan, Zita L. Weinshienk, Lewis T. Babcock; Clerk's Office, Denver 80294.

Connecticut — Ellen B. Burns, CJ; T.F. Gilroy Daly, Warren W. Eginton, Jose A. Cabranes, Peter C. Dorsey, Alan H. Nevas; Clerk's Office, New Haven 06510.

Delaware — Murray M. Schwartz, CJ; Joseph J. Longobardi, Joseph J. Farnan Jr., Jane R. Roth; Clerk's Office, Wilmington 19801.

District of Columbia — Aubrey E. Robinson Jr., CJ; Gerhard A. Gesell, John H. Pratt, Charles R. Richey, Louis F. Oberdorfer, Harold H. Greene, John Garrett Penn, Joyce Hens Green, Norma H. Johnson, Thomas P. Jackson, Thomas F. Hogan, Stanley S. Harris, George H. Revercomb, Stanley Sporkin, Royce C. Lamberth; Clerk's Office, Washington DC 20001.

Florida — **Northern:** William H. Stafford Jr. CJ; Maurice M. Paul, C. Roger Vinson; Clerk's Office, Tallahassee 32301. **Middle:** William Terrell Hodges, CJ; Howell W. Melton, George C. Carr, Susan H. Black, William J. Castagna; John H. Moore 2d, Elizabeth A. Kovachevich, George K. Sharp, Patricia C. Fawsett; Clerk's Office, Jacksonville 32201. **Southern:** James Lawrence King, CJ; Norman C. Roettger Jr.; William M. Hoeveler, Jose A. Gonzalez Jr., James C. Paine, James W. Kehoe, Eugene P. Spellman, Edward B. Davis, Alcee L. Hastings, Lenore C. Nesbitt, Stanley Marcus, Thomas E. Scott, William J. Zloch, Kenneth L. Ryskamp; Clerk's Office, Miami 33128.

Georgia — **Northern:** William C. O'Kelley, CJ; Richard C. Freeman, Harold L. Murphy, Marvin H. Shoob, G. Ernest Tidwell, Orinda Dale Evans, Robert L. Vining Jr., Robert H. Hall, Harold T. Ward, J. Owen Forrester, Jack T. Camp; Clerk's Office, Atlanta 30335. **Middle:** Wilbur D. Owens Jr., CJ; J. Robert Elliott, Duross Fitzpatrick; Clerk's Office, Macon 31202. **Southern:** Anthony A. Alaimo, CJ; B. Avant Edenfield, Dudley H. Bowen Jr.; Clerk's Office, Savannah 31412.

Hawaii — Harold M. Fong, CJ; Alan C. Kay, David A. Ezra; Clerk's Office, Honolulu 96850.

Idaho — Harold L. Ryan, CJ; Marion J. Callister; Clerk's Office, Boise, 83724.

Illinois — **Northern:** John F. Grady, CJ; Nicholas J. Bua, Stanley J. Roszkowski, James B. Moran, Marvin E. Aspen, Milton I. Shadur, Charles P. Kocoras, John A. Nordberg, William T. Hart, Paul E. Plunkett, Ilana Diamond Rovner, Charles R. Norgle Sr., James F. Holderman Jr., Ann C. Williams, Brian Barnett Duff, Harry D. Lienenweber, James B. Zagel, James H. Alesia, Suzanne B. Conlon, George M. Marovich; Clerk's Office, Chicago 60604. **Central:** Harold Albert Baker, CJ; Michael M. Mihm, Richard Mills; Clerk's Office, Springfield 62705. **Southern:** James L. Foreman, CJ; William L. Beatty, William D. Stiehl; Clerk's Office, E. St. Louis 62202.

Indiana — Northern: Allen Sharp, CJ; William C. Lee, James T. Moody, Robert L. Miller Jr., Rudy Lozano; Clerk's Office, South Bend 46601. **Southern:** Gene E. Brooks, CJ; S. Hugh Dillin, Sarah E. Barker, Larry J. McKinney, John D. Tinder; Clerk's Office, Indianapolis 46204.

Iowa — Northern: Donald E. O'Brien, CJ; David R. Hansen; Clerk's Office, Cedar Rapids 52401. **Southern:** Harold D. Vietor, CJ; Charles R. Wolle; Clerk's Office, Des Moines 50309.

Kansas — Earl E. O'Connor, CJ; Dale E. Saffels, Patrick F. Kelly, Sam A. Crow; Clerk's Office, Wichita 67202.

Kentucky — Eastern: Eugene E. Siler Jr., CJ; William Bertelsman, Henry R. Wilhoit Jr., Karl S. Forester; Clerk's Office, Lexington 40586. **Western:** Edward H. Johnstone, CJ; Thomas A. Ballantine, Ronald E. Meredith, Charles R. Simpson 3d; Clerk's Office, Louisville 40202.

Louisiana — Eastern: Frederick J. R. Heebe, CJ; Charles Schwartz Jr., Morley L. Sear, Adrian A. Duplantier, Robert F. Collins, George Arceneaux Jr., Veronica D. Wicker, Patrick E. Carr, Peter Beer, A. J. McNamara, Henry A. Mentz Jr., Martin L. C. Feldman, Marcel Livaudais Jr.; Clerk's Office, New Orleans 70130. **Middle:** John V. Parker, CJ; Frank J. Polozola; Clerk's Office, Baton Rouge 70821. **Western:** Tom Stagg, CJ; Earl Ernest Veron, John M. Shaw, F. A. Little Jr., Donald E. Walter; Clerk's Office, Shreveport 71101.

Maine — Conrad K. Cyr, CJ; Gene Carter; Clerk's Office, Portland 04112.

Maryland — Alexander Harvey 2d, CJ; Joseph C. Howard, Norman P. Ramsey, William E. Black Jr., John R. Hargrove, J. Frederick Motz, Frederic N. Smalkin, Paul V. Niemeyer; Clerk's Office, Baltimore 21201.

Massachusetts — Frank H. Freedman, CJ; Joseph L. Tauro, Walter Jay Skinner, A. David Mazzone, Robert E. Keeton, John J. McNaught, Rya W. Zobel, David S. Nelson, William G. Young, Mark L. Wolf, Douglas P. Woodlock, Edward F. Harrington; Clerk's Office, Boston 02109.

Michigan — Eastern: James P. Churchill, CJ; Julian A. Cook Jr., Stewart A. Newblatt, Avern Cohn, Anna Diggs Taylor, Horace W. Gilmore, George E. Woods, Richard F. Suhrheinrich, George La Plata, Barbara K. Hackett, Lawrence P. Zatkoff, Patrick J. Duggan, Bernard A. Friedman, Paul V. Gadola; Clerk's Office, Detroit 48226. **Western:** Douglas W. Hillman, CJ; Benjamin F. Gibson, Richard A. Enslen, Robert H. Bell; Clerk's Office, Grand Rapids 49503.

Minnesota — Donald D. Alsop, CJ; Harry H. MacLaughlin, Robert G. Renner, Diana E. Murphy, Paul A. Magnuson, James M. Rosenbaum, David S. Doty; Clerk's Office, St. Paul 55101.

Mississippi — Northern: L. T. Senter Jr., CJ; Neal Biggers, Glen H. Davidson; Clerk's Office, Oxford 38655. **Southern:** William H. Barbour Jr., CJ; Walter L. Nixon Jr., Harry T. Wingate, Tom S. Lee, Walter J. Gex 3d; Clerk's Office, Jackson 39201.

Missouri — Eastern: John F. Nangle, CJ; Edward D. Filippine, William L. Hungate, Clyde S. Cahill Jr., Stephen N. Limbaugh, George F. Gunn Jr.; Clerk's Office, St. Louis 63101. **Western:** Scott O. Wright, CJ; Russell G. Clark, Howard F. Sachs, Joseph E. Stevens Jr., D. Brook Bartlett, Dean Whipple; Clerk's Office, Kansas City 64106.

Montana — James F. Battin, CJ; Paul G. Hatfield, Charles C. Lovell; Clerk's Office, Billings 59101.

Nebraska — Lyle E. Strom, CJ; Warren K. Urbom, William G. Cambridge; Clerk's Office, Omaha 68101.

Nevada — Edward C. Reed Jr., CJ; Lloyd D. George, Howard D. McKibben, Philip M. Pro; Clerk's Office, Las Vegas 89101.

New Hampshire — Shane Devine, CJ; Martin F. Loughlin; Clerk's Office, Concord 03301.

New Jersey — John F. Gerry, CJ; Stanley S. Brotman, Anne E. Thompson, D. R. Debevoise, H. Lee Sarokin, Harold A. Ackerman, John W. Bissell, Maryanne Trump Barry, Joseph H. Rodriguez, Garrett E. Brown Jr., Alfred J. Lechner Jr., Nicholas H. Politan, Alfred M. Wolin, John C. Lifland; Clerk's Office, Newark 07102.

New Mexico — Santiago E. Campos, CJ; Juan G. Burciaga, John E. Conway, James A. Parker; Clerk's Office, Albuquerque 87103.

New York — Northern: Neal P. McCurn, CJ; Howard G. Munson, Thomas J. McAvoy, Con G. Cholakis; Clerk's Office, Albany 12201. **Eastern:** Thomas C. Platt Jr., CJ; Jack B. Weinstein, Mark A. Costantino, Charles P. Sifton, Eugene H. Nickerson, Joseph M. McLaughlin, Israel Leo Glasser, Raymond J. Dearie, Leonard D. Wexler, Edward R. Korman, Reena Raggi; Clerk's Office, Brooklyn 11201. **Southern:** Charles L. Brieant, CJ; David N. Edelstein, Thomas P. Griesa, Robert J. Ward, Kevin Thomas Duffy, Richard Owen, Leonard B. Sand, Mary Johnson Lowe, Gerard L. Goettel, Charles S. Haight Jr., Vincent L. Broderick, Pierre N. Leval, Robert W. Sweet, John E. Sprizzo, Shirley Wohl Kram, John F. Keenan, Peter K. Leisure, John M. Walker, Louis L. Stanton, Miriam G. Cedarbaum, Michael B. Mukasey, Kenneth Conboy, Kimba Wood, Robert P. Patterson Jr.; Clerk's Office N. Y. City 10007. **Western:** Michael A. Telesca, CJ; John T. Curtin, Richard J. Arcara, David G. Larimer; Clerk's Office, Buffalo 14202.

North Carolina — Eastern: W. Earl Britt, CJ; James C. Fox, Terrence W. Boyle, Malcolm J. Howard; Clerk's Office, Raleigh 27611. **Middle:** Richard C. Erwin, CJ; Frank W. Bullock Jr., N. Carlton Tilley Jr.; Clerk's Office, Greensboro 27402. **Western:** Robert D. Potter, CJ; James B. McMillan, Richard L. Voorhees; Clerk's Office Asheville 28801.

North Dakota — Patrick A. Conmy, CJ; Rodney S. Webb; Clerk's Office, Bismarck 58502.

Ohio — Northern: Frank J. Battisti, CJ; Thomas D. Lambros, John M. Manos, George W. White, Ann Aldrich, Alvin I. Krenzler, John W. Potter, David D. Dowd Jr., Sam H. Bell, Alice M. Batchelder, Richard B. McQuade Jr.; Clerk's Office, Cleveland 44114. **Southern:** Carl B. Rubin, CJ; John D. Holschuh, Walter H. Rice, S. Arthur Spiegel, Herman J. Weber, James L. Graham, George C. Smith; Clerk's Office, Columbus 43215.

Oklahoma — Northern: H. Dale Cook, CJ; James O. Ellison, Thomas R. Brett, David L. Russell; Clerk's Office, Tulsa 74103. **Eastern:** Frank H. Shey, CJ; David L. Russell; Clerk's Office, Muskogee 74401. **Western:** Ralph G. Thompson, CJ; Wayne Alley, Lee R. West, David L. Russell, Layn R. Phillips; Clerk's Office, Oklahoma City 73102.

Oregon — Owen M. Panner, CJ; James M. Burns, James A. Redden, Helen J. Frye, Malcolm F. Marsh; Clerk's Office, Portland 97205.

Pennsylvania — Eastern: John P. Fullam, CJ; Louis Charles Bechtle, Joseph L. McGlynn Jr., Edward N. Cahn, Louis H. Pollak, Norma L. Shapiro, James T. Giles, James McGirr Kelly, Thomas N. O'Neill Jr., Marvin Katz, Edmund V. Ludwig, Robert F. Kelly, Franklin S. Van Antwerpen, Robert S. Gawthrop, Lowell A. Reed Jr., Jan E. Dubois, Herbert J. Hutton, Jay C. Waldman; Clerk's Office, Philadelphia 19106. **Middle:** Richard P. Conaboy, CJ; Sylvia H. Rambo, William W. Caldwell, Edward M. Kosik; Clerk's Office, Scranton 18501. **Western:** Maurice B. Cohill Jr., CJ; Paul A. Simmons, Gustave Diamond, Donald E. Ziegler, Alan N. Bloch, Glenn E. Mencer, William L. Standish, D. Brooks Smith; Clerk's Office, Pittsburgh 15230.

Rhode Island — Francis J. Boyle, CJ; Ronald R. Lagueux, Ernest C. Torres; Clerk's Office, Providence 02903.

South Carolina — Solomon Blatt Jr., CJ; C. Weston Houck, Falcon B. Hawkins, Matthew J. Perry Jr., George R. Anderson Jr., Clyde H. Hamilton, Karen L. Henderson, Joseph F. Anderson Jr.; Clerk's Office, Columbia 29202.

South Dakota — Donald J. Porter, CJ; Richard H. Battey, John Bailey Jones; Clerk's Office, Sioux Falls 57102.

Tennessee — Eastern: Thomas G. Hull, CJ; James H. Jarvis, R. Allan Edgar, Leon Jordan; Clerk's Office, Knoxville 37901. **Middle:** Thomas A. Wiseman Jr., CJ; Thomas A. Higgins, John T. Nixon; Clerk's Office, Nashville 37203. **Western:** Odell Horton, CJ; Julia S. Gibbons, James D. Todd, Jerome Turner; Clerk's Office, Memphis 38103.

Texas — Northern: Robert W. Porter, CJ; Eldon B. Mahon, Mary Lou Robinson, Barefoot Sanders, David O. Belew Jr., Jerry Buchmeyer, A. Joe Fish, Robert B. Maloney, Sidney A. Fitzwater, Samuel R. Cummings; Clerk's Office, Dallas 75242. **Southern:** James De Anda, CJ; Norman W. Black, George P. Kazen, Hugh Gibson, Filemon B. Vela, Hayden W. Head Jr., Ricardo H. Hinojosa, Lynn N. Hughes, David Hittner, Kenneth M. Hoyt, Simeon T. Lake 3d; Clerk's Office, Houston 77208. **Eastern:** William Wayne Justice, CJ; Robert M. Parker, Howell Cobb, Sam B. Hall Jr., Paul N. Brown; Clerk's Office, Tyler 75702. **Western:** Lucius D. Bunton 3d, CJ; Harry Lee Hudspeth, Hipolito F. Garcia, James R. Nowlin, Edward C. Prado, Walter S. Smith Jr., Emilio M. Garza; Clerk's Office, San Antonio 78206.

Utah — Bruce S. Jenkins, CJ; J. Thomas Greene, David Sam, David K. Winder; Clerk's Office, Salt Lake City 84101.

Vermont — Franklin S. Billings Jr., CJ; Clerk's Office, Burlington 05402.

Virginia — **Eastern:** Albert V. Bryan Jr., CJ; J. Calvitt Clarke, Richard L. Williams, James C. Cacheris, Robert G. Doumar, Claude M. Hilton, James R. Spencer, Thomas S. Ellis 3d; Clerk's Office, Alexandria 22320. **Western:** James C. Turk, CJ; Glen M. Williams, James H. Michael Jr., Jackson L. Kiser; Clerk's Office, Roanoke 24006.

Washington — **Eastern:** Robert J. McNichols, CJ; Justin L. Quackenbush, Alan A. McDonald; Clerk's Office, Spokane 99210. **Western:** Barbara J. Rothstein, CJ; Jack E. Tanner, John C. Coughenour, Carolyn R. Dimmick, Robert J. Bryan, William L. Dwyer, Thomas Zilly; Clerk's Office, Seattle 98104.

West Virginia — **Northern:** Robert Earl Maxwell, CJ; William M. Kidd; Clerk's Office. Elkins 26241. **Southern:** Charles H. Haden 2d, CJ; Robert J. Staker, John T. Copenhaver Jr., Elizabeth V. Hallanan; Clerk's Office, Charleston 25329.

Wisconsin — **Eastern:** Robert W. Warren, CJ; Terence T. Evans, Thomas J. Curran, J.P. Stadtmueller; Clerk's Office, Milwaukee 53202. **Western:** Barbara B. Crabb, CJ; John C. Shabaz; Clerk's Office, Madison 53701.

Wyoming — Clarence A. Brimmer, CJ; Alan B. Johnson; Clerk's Office, Cheyenne 82001.

U.S. Territorial District Courts

Guam — Cristobal C. Duenas; Clerk's Office, Agana 96910.
Puerto Rico — Juan M. Perez-Gimenez, CJ; Gilberto Gierbolini, Carman Consuelo Cerezo, Jaime Pieras Jr., Raymond L. Acosta, Hector M. Laffitte, Jose Antonio Fuste; Clerk's Office, San Juan 00904.
Virgin Islands — David V. O'Brien, CJ; Clerk's Office, Charlotte Amalie, St. Thomas 00801.

State Officials, Salaries, Party Membership

As of mid-1989

Alabama

Governor — Guy Hunt, R., $70,222.
Lt. Gov. — Jim Folsom Jr., D., $40 per legislative day, plus annual salary of $1,900 per month plus $1,500 per month for expenses.
Sec. of State — Glen Browder, D., $36,234.
Atty. Gen. — Don Siegelman, D., $77,420.
Treasurer — George Wallace Jr., D., $49,500.
Legislature: meets annually the 3d Tuesday in Apr. (first year of term of office, first Tuesday in Feb. (2d and 3d years), 2d Tuesday in Jan. (4th year) at Montgomery. Members receive $10 a day salary, plus $1,900 per month expenses, plus $40 per day expenses during legislative sessions, and mileage of 10¢ per mile.
Senate — Dem., 27; Rep., 7; 1 vacancy. Total, 35.
House — Dem., 84; Rep., 19; 2 vacancies. Total, 105.

Alaska

Governor — Steve Cowper, D., $81,648.
Lt. Gov. — Stephen McAlpine, D., $76,188.
Atty. General — Douglas Baily, D., $77,304.
Legislature: meets annually in January at Juneau, for 120 days with a 10-day extension possible upon ⅔ vote. First session in odd years. Members receive $22,140 per year plus $80 a day per diem.
Senate — Dem., 8; Rep., 12. Total, 20.
House — Dem., 24; Rep., 16. Total, 40.

Arizona

Governor — Rose Mofford, D., $75,000.
Sec. of State — Jim Shumway, D., $50,000.
Atty. Gen. — Bob Corbin, R., $70,000.
Treasurer — Ray Rottas, R., $50,000.
Legislature: meets annually in January at Phoenix. Each member receives an annual salary of $15,000.
Senate — Dem., 13; Rep., 17. Total, 30.
House — Dem., 26; Rep., 34. Total, 60.

Arkansas

Governor — Bill Clinton, D., $35,000.
Lt. Gov. — Winston Bryant, D., $14,000.
Sec. of State — W. J. "Bill" McCuen, D., $22,500.
Atty. Gen. — Steve Clark, D., $26,500.
Treasurer — Jimmie Lou Fisher, D., $22,500.
General Assembly: meets odd years in January at Little Rock. Members receive $7,500 per year, $74 a day while in regular session, plus 21 cents a mile travel expense.
Senate — Dem., 31; Rep., 4. Total, 35.
House — Dem., 88; Rep. 11; 1 ind. Total, 100.

California

Governor — George Deukmejian, R., $85,000.
Lt. Gov. — Leo T. McCarthy, D., $72,500.
Sec. of State — March Fong Eu, D., $72,500.
Controller — Gray Davis, D., $72,500.
Atty. Gen. — John Van de Kamp, D., $77,500.
Legislature: meets at Sacramento; regular sessions commence on the first Monday in Dec. of every even-numbered year; each session lasts 2 years. Members receive $40,816 per year plus mileage and $65 per diem.
Senate — Dem., 24; Rep., 15, one ind. Total, 40.
Assembly — Dem., 47; Rep., 33. Total, 80.

Colorado

Governor — Roy Romer, D., $70,000.
Lt. Gov. — Mike Callihan, D., $48,500.
Secy. of State — Natalie Meyer, R., $48,500.
Atty. Gen. — Duane Woodard, R., $60,000.
Treasurer — Gail Schoettler, D., $48,500.
General Assembly: meets annually in January at Denver. Members receive $17,500 annually.
Senate — Dem., 11; Rep., 24. Total, 35.
House — Dem., 26; Rep., 39. Total, 65.

Connecticut

Governor — William A. O'Neill, D., $78,000.
Lt. Gov. — Joseph J. Fauliso, D., $55,000.
Sec. of State — Julia H. Tashjian, D., $50,000.
Treasurer — Francisco Borges, D., $50,000.
Comptroller — J. Edward Caldwell, D., $50,000.
Atty. Gen. — Clarine Nardi Riddle, Act., $60,000.
General Assembly: meets annually odd years in January and even years in February at Hartford. Salary $15,200 per year plus $4,500 (senator), $3,500 (representative) per year for expenses, plus travel allowance.
Senate — Dem., 23; Rep., 13. Total, 36.
House — Dem., 86; Rep., 65. Total, 151.

Delaware

Governor — Michael N. Castle, R., $70,000.
Lt. Gov. — S. B. Woo, D., $30,000.
Sec. of State — Michael Harkins, R., $50,000.
Atty. Gen. — Charles Oberly 3d, D., $52,320.
Treasurer — Janet C. Rzewnicki, R., $33,960.
General Assembly: meets annually at Dover from the 2d Tuesday in January to midnight June 30. Members receive $20,000 base salary.
Senate — Dem., 13; Rep., 8. Total, 21.
House — Dem., 19; Rep., 22. Total, 41.

Florida

Governor — Bob Martinez, R., $90,570.
Lt. Gov. — Bobby Brantley, R., $81,967.
Sec. of State — Jim Smith, R., $81,967.
Comptroller — Gerald Lewis, D., $81,967.
Atty. Gen. — Robert Butterworth, D., $81,967.
Treasurer — Tim Gallagher, R., $81,967.
Legislature: meets annually at Tallahassee. Members receive $18,900 per year plus expense allowance while on official business.
Senate — Dem., 23; Rep., 17. Total, 40.
House — Dem., 75; Rep., 45. Total, 120.

Georgia

Governor — Joe Frank Harris, D., $86,706.
Lt. Gov. — Zell Miller, D., $59,293.
Sec. of State — Max Cleland, D., $69,450.
Insurance Comm. — Warren Evans, D., $69,438.
Atty. Gen. — Michael J. Bowers, $71,048.
General Assembly: meets annually at Atlanta. Members receive $10,000 per year. During session $59 per day for expenses.
Senate — Dem., 44; Rep., 11; 1 NP. Total, 56.
House — Dem., 144; Rep., 36. Total, 180.

Hawaii

Governor — John Waihee, D., $80,000.
Lt. Gov. — Benjamin Cayetano, D., $76,000.
Atty. Gen. — Warren Price. $68,400.
Comptroller — Russel Nagata, $68,400.
Dir. of Budget & Finance — Yukio Takemoto, $68,400.
Legislature: meets annually on 3d Wednesday in January at Honolulu. Members receive $27,000 per year plus expenses.
Senate — Dem., 22. Rep., 3. Total, 25.
House — Dem., 45. Rep., 6. Total, 51.

Idaho

Governor — Cecil D. Andrus, D., $55,000.
Lt. Gov. — C. L. "Butch" Otter, R., $15,000.
Sec. of State — Pete T. Cenarrusa, R., $45,000.
Treasurer — Lydia Justice Edwards, R., $45,000.
Atty. Gen. — Jim Jones, R., $48,000.
Legislature: meets annually the Monday on or nearest the 9th of January at Boise. Members receive $30 per day during session, $15 per day when not in session, plus certain travel and living allowances.
Senate — Dem., 19; Rep., 23. Total. 42.
House — Dem., 20; Rep., 64. Total, 84.

Illinois

Governor — James R. Thompson, R., $93,266.
Lt. Gov. — George H. Ryan, R., $65,835.
Sec. of State — Jim Edgar, R., $82,294.
Comptroller — Roland W. Burris, D., $71,321.
Atty. Gen. — Neil F. Hartigan, D., $82,294.
Treasurer — Jerry Cosentino, D., $71,321.
General Assembly: meets annually in January at Springfield. Members receive $35,661 per annum.
Senate — Dem., 31; Rep., 28. Total, 59.
House — Dem., 67; Rep., 51. Total, 118.

Indiana

Governor — Evan Bayh, D., $77,000 plus discretionary expenses.
Lt. Gov. — Frank O'Bannon, D., $64,000 plus discretionary expenses.
Sec. of State — Joseph Hogsett D., $46,000.
Atty. Gen. — Linley E. Pearson, R., $51,000.
Treasurer — Marjorie H. O'Laughlin, R., $46,000.
Auditor — Ann G. Devore, R., $46,000.
General Assembly: meets annually in January. Members receive $11,600 per year plus $75 per day while in session, $15 per day while not in session.
Senate — Dem., 24; Rep., 26. Total, 50.
House — Dem., 50; Rep., 50. Total, 100.

Iowa

Governor — Terry E. Branstad, R., $70,000.
Lt. Gov. — Jo Ann Zimmerman, D., $23,900.
Sec. of State — Elaine Baxter, D., $53,000.
Atty. Gen. — Tom Miller, D., $62,500.
Treasurer — Michael L. Fitzgerald, D., $53,000.
Auditor — Richard D. Johnson, R., $53,000.
Secy. of Agriculture — Dale M. Cochran, D., $53,000.
General Assembly: meets annually in January at Des Moines. Members receive $16,600 annually plus maximum expense allowance of $40 per day for first 110 days of first session, and first 100 days of 2d session; mileage expenses at 21c a mile.
Senate — Dem., 30; Rep., 20. Total, 50.
House — Dem., 61; Rep., 39. Total, 100.

Kansas

Governor — Mike Hayden, R., $66,950.
Lt. Gov. — Jack Walker, R., $18,753.
Sec. of State — Bill Graves, R., $51,500.
Atty. Gen. — Robert T. Stephan, R., $59,232.
Treasurer — Joan Finney, D., $52,530.
Legislature: meets annually in January at Topeka. Members receive $54 a day plus $66 a day expenses while in session, plus $600 per month while not in session.
Senate — Dem., 16; Rep., 24. Total, 40.
House — Dem., 51; Rep., 74. Total, 125.

Kentucky

Governor — Wallace G. Wilkinson, D., $65,483.
Lt. Gov. — Brereton Jones, D., $55,647.
Sec. of State — Bremer Ehrler, D., $55,647.
Atty. Gen. — Fred Cowan, D., $55,647.
Treasurer — Robert Meade, D., $55,647.
Auditor — Bob Babbage, D., $55,647.
General Assembly: meets even years in January at Frankfort. Members receive $100 per day and $100 per day during session and $950 per month for expenses for interim.

Senate — Dem., 29; Rep., 9. Total, 38.
House — Dem., 72; Rep., 28. Total, 100.

Louisiana

Governor — Charles "Buddy" Roemer, D., $73,440.
Lt. Gov. — Paul Hardy, D., $63,367.
Sec. of State — Fox McKeithen, D., $60,169.
Atty. Gen. — William J. Guste Jr., D., $60,169.
Treasurer — Mary Landrieu, D., $60,169.
Legislature: meets annually for 60 legislative days commencing on 3d Monday in April. Members receive $75 per day and mileage plus annual salary of $16,800.
Senate — Dem., 33; Rep., 6. Total, 39.
House — Dem., 87; Rep., 18. Total, 105.

Maine

Governor — John R. McKernan Jr., R., $70,000.
Sec. of State — G. William Diamond D., $37,523.
Atty. Gen. — James Tierney, D., $58,073.
Treasurer — Samuel Shapiro, D., $50,044.
Legislature: meets annually in December at Augusta. Members receive $9,000 for first regular sessions, $6,000 for second regular session plus expenses; presiding officers receive 50% more.
Senate — Dem., 20; Rep., 15. Total, 35.
House — Dem., 97; Rep., 54. Total, 151.

Maryland

Governor — William Donald Schaefer, D., $85,000.
Lt. Gov. — Melvin Steinberg, D., $72,500.
Comptroller — Louis L. Goldstein, D., $72,500.
Atty. Gen. — J. Joseph Curran Jr., D., $72,500.
Sec. of State — Winfield M. Kelly Jr., D., $45,000.
Treasurer — Lucille Maurer, D., $72,500.
General Assembly: meets 90 consecutive days annually beginning on the 2d Wednesday in January at Annapolis. Members receive $25,000 per year plus expenses.
Senate — Dem., 40; Rep., 7. Total, 47.
House — Dem., 125; Rep., 16. Total, 141.

Massachusetts

Governor — Michael S. Dukakis, D., $75,000.
Lt. Gov. — Evelyn Murphy, $60,000.
Sec. of State — Michael Joseph Connolly, D., $60,000.
Atty. Gen. — James M. Shannon, D., $65,000.
Treasurer — Robert Q. Crane, D., $60,000.
Auditor — A. Joseph DeNucci, D., $60,000.
General Court (Legislature): meets each January in Boston. Salaries $30,000 per annum.
Senate — Dem., 32; Rep., 8. Total, 40.
House — Dem., 129; Rep., 31. Total, 160.

Michigan

Governor — James J. Blanchard, D., $100,100.
Lt. Gov. — Martha W. Griffiths, D., $67,400.
Sec. of State — Richard H. Austin, D., $89,000.
Atty. Gen. — Frank J. Kelley, D., $89,000.
Treasurer — Robert A. Bowman, N-P, $80,300.
Legislature: meets annually in January at Lansing. Members receive $42,670 per year, plus $8,100 expense allowance.
Senate — Dem., 18; Rep., 20. Total, 38.
House — Dem., 61; Rep., 49. Total, 110.

Minnesota

Governor — Rudy Perpich, DFL, $98,914.
Lt. Gov. — Marlene Johnson, DFL, $54,405.
Sec. of State — Joan Anderson Growe, DFL., $54,405.
Atty. Gen. — Hubert H. Humphrey 3d, DFL, $77,274.
Treasurer — Michael McGrath, DFL., $51,469.
Auditor — Arnie Carlson, IR, $59,352.
Legislature: meets for a total of 120 days within every 2 years at St. Paul. Members receive $23,941 per year, plus expense allowance during session.
Senate — DFL., 44; IR. 23. Total, 67.
House — DFL., 81; IR. 53. Total, 134.
(DFL means Democratic-Farmer-Labor. IR means Independent Republican.)

Mississippi

Governor — Ray Mabus, D., $63,000.
Lt. Gov. — Brad Dye, D., $40,800.
Sec. of State — Dick Molpus, D., $54,000.
Atty. Gen. — Mike Moore, D., $61,200.
Treasurer — Marshall Bennett, D., $54,000.
Legislature: meets annually in January at Jackson. Members receive $10,100 per regular session plus travel allowance, and $500 per month while not in session.
Senate — Dem., 45; Rep., 7. Total, 52.
House — Dem., 115; Rep., 7. Total, 122.

Missouri

Governor — John D. Ashcroft, R., $81,000.
Lt. Gov. — Mel Carnahan, D., $50,064.
Sec. of State — Roy D. Blunt, R., $66,744.
Atty. Gen. — William L. Webster, R., $72,312.
Treasurer — Wendell Bailey, R., $66,744.
State Auditor — Margaret Kelly, R., $66,744.
General Assembly: meets annually in Jefferson City on the first Wednesday after first Monday in January. Members receive $19,524 annually.
Senate — Dem., 21; Rep., 13. Total, 34.
House — Dem., 105; Rep., 58. Total, 163.

Montana

Governor — Stan Stephens, R., $50,452.
Lt. Gov. — Alan Kolstad, R., $36,141.
Sec. of State — Mike Cooney, D., $33,342.
Atty. Gen. — Marc Racicot, R., $46,016.
Legislative Assembly: meets odd years in January at Helena. Members receive $59.12 per legislative day plus $50 per day for expenses while in session.
Senate — Dem., 27; Rep., 23. Total, 50.
House — Dem., 52; Rep., 48. Total, 100.

Nebraska

Governor — Kay Orr, R., $58,000.
Lt. Gov. — William Nichol, R., $40,000.
Sec. of State — Allen J. Beermann, R., $40,000.
Atty. Gen. — Robert Spire, R., $57,500.
Treasurer — Frank Marsh, R., $35,000.
Legislature: meets annually in January at Lincoln. Members receive salary of $12,000 annually plus travelling expenses.
Unicameral body composed of 49 members who are elected on a nonpartisan ballot and are classed as senators.

Nevada

Governor — Robert Miller, D., $77,500.
Lt. Gov. — vacant $12,500.
Sec. of State — Frankie Sue Del Papa, D., $50,000.
Comptroller — Darrel Daines, R., $49,000.
Atty. Gen. — Brian McKay, R., $62,500.
Treasurer — Ken Santor, R., $49,000.
Legislature: meets odd years in January at Carson City. Members receive $130 per day for 60 days (20 days for special sessions).
Senate — Dem., 9; Rep., 12. Total, 21.
Assembly — Rep., 12; Dem., 30. Total, 42.

New Hampshire

Governor — Judd Gregg, R., $72,146.
Sec. of State — William M. Gardner, D., $50,675.
Atty. Gen. — Stephen E. Merrill, $58,940.
Treasurer — Georgie A. Thomas, R., $50,675.
General Court (Legislature): meets every year in January at Concord. Members receive $200; presiding officers $250.
Senate — Dem., 8; Rep., 16. Total, 24.
House — Rep., 281; Dem., 119. Total, 400.

New Jersey

Governor — Thomas H. Kean, R., $85,000.
Sec. of State — Jane Burgio, R., $95,000.
Atty. Gen. — Richard N. Perrotti, R., $95,000.
Treasurer — Feather O'Connor, $95,000.
Legislature: meets throughout the year at Trenton. Members receive $25,000 per year, except president of Senate and speaker of Assembly who receive 1/3 more.
Senate — Dem., 24; Rep., 16. Total, 40.
Assembly — Dem., 39; Rep. 41. Total, 80.

New Mexico

Governor — Garrey E. Carruthers, R., $63,000.
Lt. Gov. — Jack Stahl, R., $40,425.
Sec. of State — Rebecca Vigil-Giron, D., $40,425.
Atty. Gen. — Hal Stratton, R., $46,200.
Treasurer — James Lewis, D., $40,425.
Legislature: meets on the 3d Tuesday in January at Sante Fe; odd years for 60 days, even years for 30 days. Members receive $75 per day while in session.
Senate — Dem., 26; Rep., 16. Total, 42.
House — Dem., 45; Rep., 25. Total, 70.

New York

Governor — Mario M. Cuomo, D., $130,000.
Lt. Gov. — Stan Lundine, D., $110,000.
Sec. of State — Gail S. Shaffer, D., $87,338.
Comptroller — Edward V. Regan, R., $110,000.
Atty. Gen. — Robert Abrams, D., $110,000.
Legislature: meets annually in January at Albany. Members receive $57,000 per year.

Senate — Dem., 27; Rep., 34. Total, 61.
Assembly — Dem., 92; Rep., 58. Total, 150.

North Carolina

Governor — James G. Martin, R., $109,728 plus $11,500 per year expenses.
Lt. Gov. — James C. Gardner, R., $66,972 per year, plus $11,500 per year expense allowance.
Sec. of State — Rufus L. Edmisten, D., $66,972.
Atty. Gen. — Lacy Thornberg, D., $66,972.
Treasurer — Harlan E. Boyles, D., $66,972.
General Assembly: meets odd years in January at Raleigh. Members receive $11,124 annual salary and $5,500 annual expense allowance, plus $81 per diem subsistence and travel allowance while in session.
Senate — Dem., 37; Rep., 13. Total, 50.
House — Dem., 74; Rep., 46. Total, 120.

North Dakota

Governor — George A. Sinner, D., $65,000.
Lt. Gov. — Lloyd B. Omdahl, D., $50,000.
Sec. of State — Jim Kusler, D., $46,000.
Atty. Gen. — Nicholas Spaeth, D., $52,000.
Treasurer — Robert Hanson, D., $46,000.
Legislative Assembly: meets odd years in January at Bismarck. Members receive $90 per day expenses during session and $180 per month when not in session.
Senate — Dem., 32; Rep., 21. Total, 53.
House — Dem., 45; Rep., 61. Total, 106.

Ohio

Governor — Richard F. Celeste, D., $65,000.
Lt. Gov. — Paul R. Leonard, $44,903.
Sec. of State — Sherrod Brown, D., $63,814.
Atty. Gen. — Anthony J. Celebrezze Jr., D., $63,814.
Treasurer — Mary Ellen Withrow, D., $63,814.
Auditor — Thomas E. Ferguson, D., $63,814.
General Assembly: meets odd years at Columbus on first Monday in January; no limit on session. Members receive $34,905 per annum.
Senate — Dem., 14; Rep., 19. Total, 33.
House — Dem., 59; Rep., 40. Total, 99.

Oklahoma

Governor — Henry L. Bellmon, R., $70,000.
Lt. Gov. — Robert S. Kerr 3d, D., $40,000.
Sec. of State — Hannah Diggs Atkins, D., $37,500.
Atty. Gen. — Robert H. Henry, D., $55,000.
Treasurer — Ellis Edwards, D., $50,000.
Legislature: meets annually in January at Oklahoma City. Members receive $32,000 annually.
Senate — Dem., 33; Rep., 15. Total, 48.
House — Dem., 69; Rep., 32. Total, 101.

Oregon

Governor — Neil Goldschmidt, D., $75,000, plus $500 monthly expenses.
Sec. of State — Barbara Roberts, D., $57,500.
Atty. Gen. — David B. Frohnmayer, R., $62,000.
Treasurer — Tony Meeker, R., $57,500.
Legislative Assembly: meets odd years in January at Salem. Members receive $937 monthly and $62 expenses per day while in session; $837 per month plus expenses while not in session.
Senate — Dem., 19; Rep., 11. Total, 30.
House — Dem., 32; Rep., 28. Total, 60.

Pennsylvania

Governor — Robert Casey, D., $85,000.
Lt. Gov. — Mark S. Singel, D., $67,500.
Sec. of the Commonwealth — James J. Haggerty, D., $58,000.
Atty. Gen. — Ernest R. Preate, R., $84,000.
Treasurer — Catherine Baker Knoll, D., $84,000.
General Assembly — convenes annually in January at Harrisburg. Members receive $35,000 per year plus expenses.
Senate — Dem., 23; Rep., 27. Total, 50.
House — Dem., 103; Rep., 99; 1 vacancy. Total, 203.

Rhode Island

Governor — Edward DiPrete, R., $69,000.
Lt. Gov. — Roger N. Begin, D., $52,000.
Sec. of State — Kathleen S. Connell, D., $52,000.
Atty. Gen. — James E. O'Neil, D., $55,000.
Treasurer — Anthony J. Solomon, D., $52,000.
General Assembly: meets annually in January at Providence. Members receive $5 per day for 60 days, and travel allowance of 8c per mile.
Senate — Dem., 41; Rep., 9. Total, 50.
House — Dem., 83; Rep., 17. Total, 100.

South Carolina

Governor — Carroll A. Campbell Jr., R., $83,232.
Lt. Gov. — Nick Theodore, D., $36,414.
Sec. of State — John T. Campbell, D., $70,447.
Comptroller Gen. — Earle E. Morris Jr., D., $70,447.
Atty. Gen. — T.T. Medlock, D., $70,447.
Treasurer — G.L. Patterson Jr., D., $70,447.
General Assembly: meets annually in January at Columbia. Members receive $10,000 per year and expense allowance of $74 per day, plus travel and postage allowance.
Senate — Dem., 35; Rep., 11. Total, 46.
House — Dem. 86; Rep., 37; 1 vacancy. Total, 124.

South Dakota

Governor — George S. Mickelson, R., $59,045.
Lt. Gov. — Walter B. Miller, R., $8,219 plus $75 per day during legislative session.
Sec. of State — Joyce Hazeltine, R., $40,108.
Treasurer — David Volk, R., $40,108.
Atty. Gen. — Roger Tellinghuisen, R., $50,135.
Auditor — Vernon Larson, R., $40,108.
Legislature: meets annually in January at Pierre. Members receive $4,267 for 40-day session in odd-numbered years, and $3,733 for 35-day session in even-numbered years, plus $75 per legislative day.
Senate — Dem., 15; Rep., 20. Total, 35.
House — Dem., 24. Rep., 46. Total, 70.

Tennessee

Governor — Ned Ray McWherter, D., $85,000.
Lt. Gov. — John S. Wilder, D., $49,500.
Sec. of State — Gentry Crowell, D., $65,500.
Comptroller — William Snodgrass, D., $65,000.
Atty. Gen. — Charles W. Burson, D., $65,650.
General Assembly: meets annually in January at Nashville. Members receive $16,500 yearly plus $78.00 per diem plus office expenses.
Senate — Dem., 22; Rep., 11. Total, 33.
House — Dem., 60; Rep., 39. Total, 99.

Texas

Governor — William P. Clements, R., $93,342.
Lt. Gov. — Bill Hobby, D., $7,200.
Sec. of State — Jack M. Rains, R., $64,890.
Comptroller — Bob Bullock, D., $74,698.
Atty. Gen. — Jim Mattox, D., $74,698.
Treasurer — Ann W. Richards, D., $74,698.
Legislature: meets odd years in January at Austin. Members receive annual salary not exceeding $7,200, per diem while in session, and travel allowance.
Senate — Dem., 23; Rep., 8. Total, 31.
House — Dem., 94; Rep., 56. Total, 150.

Utah

Governor — Norman Bangerter, R., $60,000.
Lt. Gov. — W. Val Oveson, R., $50,000.
Atty. Gen. — R. Paul Van Dam, D., $49,000.
Treasurer — Edward T. Alter, D., $45,500.
Legislature: convenes for 45 days on 2d Monday in January each year; members receive $25 per day, $15 daily expenses, and mileage.
Senate — Dem., 7; Rep., 22. Total, 29.
House — Dem., 28; Rep., 47. Total, 75.

Vermont

Governor — Madeleine M. Kunin, D., $71,200.
Lt. Gov. — Howard Dean, D., $29,700.
Sec. of State — James H. Douglas, R., $44,800.
Atty. Gen. — Jeffrey Amestoy, R., $53,800.
Treasurer — Paul W. Ruse Jr., D., $44,800.
Auditor of Accounts — Alexander V. Acebo, R., $44,800.
General Assembly: meets odd years in January at Montpelier. Members receive $6,750 plus $80 per day for special session, plus specified expenses.

Senate — Dem., 16; Rep., 14. Total, 30.
House — Dem., 76; Rep., 74. Total, 150.

Virginia

Governor — Gerald L. Baliles, D., $85,000.
Lt. Gov. — L. Douglas Wilder, D., $28,000.
Atty. Gen. — Mary Sue Terry, D., $75,000.
Sec. of the Commonwealth — Sandra D. Bowen, D., $53,085.
Treasurer — Alice W. Handy, $65,000.
General Assembly: meets annually in January at Richmond. Members receive $18,000 annually plus expense and mileage allowances.
Senate — Dem., 30; Rep., 10. Total, 40.
House — Dem., 64; Rep., 35; Ind., 1. Total. 100.

Washington

Governor — Booth Gardner, D., $86,800.
Lt. Gov. — John A. Cherberg, D., $53,800.
Sec. of State — Ralph Munro, R., $53,800.
Atty. Gen. — Ken Eikenberry, R., $63,800.
Treasurer — Robert S. O'Brien, D., $55,700.
Legislature: meets annually in January at Olympia. Members receive $16,000 annually plus per diem of $50 per diem and 10¢ per mile while in session, and $50 per diem for attending meetings during interim.
Senate — Dem., 25; Rep., 24. Total, 49.
House — Dem., 61; Rep., 37. Total, 98.

West Virginia

Governor — Gaston Caperton, D., $72,000.
Sec. of State — Ken Hechler, D., $43,200.
Atty. Gen. — Charlie Brown, D., $50,400.
Treasurer — A. James Manchin, D., $50,400.
Comm. of Agric. — Clive Benedict, R., $46,800.
Auditor — Glen B. Gainer Jr., D., $46,800.
Legislature: meets annually in January at Charleston. Members receive $6,500.
Senate — Dem., 29; Rep., 5. Total, 34.
House — Dem., 79; Rep., 21. Total, 100.

Wisconsin

Governor — Tommy G. Thompson, R., $86,149.
Lt. Gov. — Scott McCallum, R., $46,360.
Sec. of State — Douglas La Follette, D., $42,089.
Treasurer — Charles P. Smith, D., $42,089.
Atty. Gen. — Donald Hanaway, R., $73,930.
Superintendent of Public Instruction — Herbert J. Grover, $66,536.
Legislature: meets in January at Madison. Members receive $31,236 annually plus $55 per day expenses.
Senate — Dem., 20; Rep., 13. Total, 33.
Assembly — Dem., 56; Rep., 43. Total, 99.

Wyoming

Governor — Mike Sullivan, D., $70,000.
Sec. of State — Kathy Karpan, D., $52,500.
Atty. Gen. — Joseph Meyer, $52,500.
Treasurer — Stan Smith, R., $52,500.
Auditor — Jack Sidi, R., $52,500.
Legislature: meets odd years in January, even years in February, at Cheyenne. Members receive $75 per day while in session, plus $60 per day for expenses.
Senate — Dem., 11; Rep., 19. Total, 30.
House — Dem., 23; Rep. 41. Total, 64.

Puerto Rico

Governor — Rafael Hernández-Colón.
Secretary of State — Sila Maria Calderón.
Secy. of Justice — Héctor Rivera-Cruz.
These officials belong to the Popular Democratic Party.
Legislature: composed of a Senate of 27 members and a House of Representatives of 53 members. Majority of the members of both chambers belongs to the Popular Democratic Party. They meet annually on the 2d Monday in January at San Juan.

U.S. Government Independent Agencies

Source: National Archives & Records Administration

Address: Washington, DC. Location and ZIP codes of agencies in parentheses; as of mid-1989.

ACTION — Donna M. Alvarado, dir. (1100 Vermont Ave., NW, 20525).

Administrative Conference of the United States — Marshall J. Breger, chmn. (2120 L St. NW, 20037).

African Development Foundation — Leonard H. Robinson Jr., pres. (1625 Massachusetts Ave. NW, 20036).

American Battle Monuments Commission — Gen. Andrew J. Goodpaster, chmn. (200 Massachusetts Ave. NW, 20314).

Appalachian Regional Commission — Winifred A. Pizzano, federal co-chmn.; Gov. Carroll A. Campbell Jr. of South Carolina, states' co-chmn. (1666 Connecticut Ave. NW, 20235).

Board for International Broadcasting — Malcolm S. Forbes Jr., chmn. (1201 Connecticut Ave., 20036).

Central Intelligence Agency — William H. Webster, dir. (Wash., DC 20505).

Commission of Fine Arts — J. Carter Brown, chmn. (708 Jackson Pl. NW, 20006).

Commission on Civil Rights — William B. Allen, chmn. (1121 Vermont Ave. NW, 20425).

Commodity Futures Trading Commission — Wendy L. Gramm, chmn. (2033 K St. NW, 20581).

Consumer Product Safety Commission — Anne Graham, act. chmn. (5401 Westbard Ave., Bethesda, MD 20207).

Environmental Protection Agency — William K. Reilly, adm. (401 M St., SW, 20460).

Equal Employment Opportunity Commission — Clarence Thomas, chmn. (2401 E St., NW, 20507).

Export-Import Bank of the United States — William F. Ryan, act. pres. and chmn. (811 Vermont Ave. NW 20571).

Farm Credit Administration — Marvin R. Duncan, act. chmn., Federal Farm Credit Board (1501 Farm Credit Drive, McLean, VA 22102).

Federal Communications Commission — Dennis R. Patrick, chmn. (1919 M St. NW, 20554).

Federal Deposit Insurance Corporation — L. William Seidman, chmn. (550 17th St. NW, 20429).

Federal Election Commission — Danny E. McDonald, chmn. (999 E. St. NW, 20463).

Federal Emergency Management Agency — Calvin G. Franklin, dir. (500 C St. SW, 20472).

Federal Home Loan Bank Board — M. Danny Wall, chmn. (1700 G St. NW, 20552).

Federal Labor Relations Authority — Jerry L. Calhoun, chmn. (500 C St. SW, 20424).

Federal Maritime Commission — James J. Carey, act. chmn. (1100 L St. NW 20573).

Federal Mediation and Conciliation Service — Kay McMurray, dir. (2100 K St. NW, 20427).

Federal Reserve System — Chairman, board of governors: Alan Greenspan. (20th St. & Constitution Ave. NW, 20551).

Federal Trade Commission — Daniel Oliver, chmn. (Pennsylvania Ave. at 6th St. NW, 20580).

General Accounting Office — Comptroller General of the U.S.; Charles A. Bowsher (441 G St. NW, 20548).

General Services Administration — Richard G. Austin, act. adm. (18th & F Sts. NW, 20405).

Government Printing Office — Public printer: Joseph E. Jenifer, act. (North Capitol and H Sts. NW, 20401).

Inter-American Foundation — Victor Blanco, chmn. (1515 Wilson Blvd., Rosslyn, VA 22209).

Interstate Commerce Commission — Heather J. Gradison, chmn. (12th St. & Constitution Ave. NW, 20423).

Library of Congress — James H. Billington, librarian (101 Independence Ave. SE, 20540).

Merit Systems Protection Board — Daniel R. Levinson, chmn. (1120 Vermont Ave. NW, 20419).

National Aeronautics and Space Administration — Richard H. Truly, adm. (600 Independence Ave., SW 20546).

National Archives & Records Administration — Don W. Wilson archivist (7th & Pennsylvania Ave. NW, 20408).

National Credit Union Administration — Roger W. Jepsen, chmn. (1776 G St. NW, 20456).

National Foundation on the Arts and the Humanities — Hugh Southern, act. chmn. (arts) 1100 Pennsylvania Ave. NW, 20506; Lynne V. Cheney, chmn. (humanities) same address. Institute of Museum Services: Daphne W. Murray, dir., same address.

National Labor Relations Board — James M. Stephens, chmn. (1717 Pennsylvania Ave. NW, 20570).

National Mediation Board — Walter C. Wallace, chmn. (1425 K St. NW, 20572).

National Science Foundation — Mary L. Good, chmn., National Science Board (1800 G St. NW, 20550).

National Transportation Safety Board — James L. Kolstad, act. chmn. (800 Independence Ave. SW, 20594).

Nuclear Regulatory Commission — Lando W. Zech Jr., chmn. (1717 H St. NW, 20555).

Occupational Safety and Health Review Commission — E. Ross Buckley, chmn. (1825 K St. NW, 20006).

Office of Personnel Management — Constance B. Newman, dir., (1900 E St. NW, 20415).

Peace Corps — Paul D. Coverdell, dir. (1990 K St. NW, 20526).

Postal Rate Commission — Janet D. Steiger, chmn. (1333 H. St. NW, 20268-0001).

Railroad Retirement Board — Thomas J. Simon, chmn. (2000 L. St. NW, 20036), Main Office (844 Rush St., Chicago, IL 60611).

Securities and Exchange Commission — David S. Ruder, chmn. (450 5th St. NW, 20549).

Selective Service System — Samuel K. Lessey Jr., dir. (1023 31st St. NW, 20435).

Small Business Administration — Susan S. Engeleiter, adm. (1441 L St. NW, 20416).

Smithsonian Institution — Robert McC. Adams, secy. (1000 Jefferson Dr. SW, 20560).

Tennessee Valley Authority — Chairman, board of directors: Marvin Runyon. (400 W. Summit Hill Dr., Knoxville, TN 37902 and Capitol Hill Office Bldg., Room 300, 412 1st St. SE, Washington, DC 20444).

United States Arms Control & Disarmament Agency — Ronald F. Lehman 2d, dir. (320 21st St. NW 20451).

United States Information Agency — Bruce S. Gelb, dir. (301 4th St. SW, 20547).

United States International Development Cooperation Agency — Alan Woods, act. dir. (320 21st St. NW 20523).

United States International Trade Commission — Anne E. Brunsdale, chmn. (500 E St. NW, 20436).

United States Postal Service — Anthony M. Frank, postmaster general (475 L'Enfant Plaza West SW, 20260).

Governors of States and Possessions

(as of mid-1989)

State	Capital	Governor	Party	Term years	Term expires	Annual salary
Alabama	Montgomery	Guy Hunt	Rep.	4	Jan. 1991	$70,222
Alaska	Juneau	Steve Cowper	Dem.	4	Dec. 1990	81,648
Arizona	Phoenix	Rose Mofford	Rep.	4	Jan. 1991	75,000
Arkansas	Little Rock	Bill Clinton	Dem.	4	Jan. 1991	35,000
California	Sacramento	George Deukmejian	Rep.	4	Jan. 1991	85,000
Colorado	Denver	Roy Romer	Dem.	4	Jan. 1991	70,000
Connecticut	Hartford	William O'Neill	Dem.	4	Jan. 1991	78,000
Delaware	Dover	Michael N. Castle	Rep.	4	Jan. 1993	70,000
Florida	Tallahassee	Bob Martinez	Rep.	4	Jan. 1991	90,570
Georgia	Atlanta	Joe Frank Harris	Dem.	4	Jan. 1991	86,706
Hawaii	Honolulu	John Waihee	Dem.	4	Dec. 1990	80,000
Idaho	Boise	Cecil D. Andrus	Dem.	4	Jan. 1991	55,000
Illinois	Springfield	James R. Thompson	Rep.	4	Jan. 1991	93,266

(continued)

State	Capital	Governor	Party	Term years	Term expires	Annual salary
Indiana	Indianapolis	Evan Bayh	Dem.	4	Jan. 1993	77,000
Iowa	Des Moines	Terry E. Branstad	Rep.	4	Jan. 1991	70,000
Kansas	Topeka	Mike Hayden	Rep.	4	Jan. 1991	66,950
Kentucky	Frankfort	Wallace G. Wilkinson	Dem.	4	Dec. 1991	65,483
Louisiana	Baton Rouge	Charles "Buddy" Roemer	Dem.	4	May 1992	73,440
Maine	Augusta	John McKernan Jr.	Rep.	4	Jan. 1991	70,000
Maryland	Annapolis	William Donald Schaefer	Dem.	4	Jan. 1991	85,000
Massachusetts	Boston	Michael S. Dukakis	Dem.	4	Jan. 1991	75,000
Michigan	Lansing	James J. Blanchard	Dem.	4	Jan. 1991	100,100
Minnesota	St. Paul	Rudy Perpich	Dem.	4	Jan. 1991	98,914
Mississippi	Jackson	Ray Mabus	Dem.	4	Jan. 1992	63,000
Missouri	Jefferson City	John D. Ashcroft	Rep.	4	Jan. 1993	81,000
Montana	Helena	Stan Stephens	Rep.	4	Jan. 1993	50,452
Nebraska	Lincoln	Kay Orr	Rep.	4	Jan. 1991	58,000
Nevada	Carson City	Robert Miller	Dem.	4	Jan. 1991	77,500
New Hampshire	Concord	Judd Gregg	Rep.	2	Jan. 1991	72,146
New Jersey	Trenton	Thomas H. Kean	Rep.	4	Jan. 1990	85,000
New Mexico	Santa Fe	Garrey E. Carruthers	Rep.	4	Jan. 1991	63,000
New York	Albany	Mario M. Cuomo	Dem.	4	Jan. 1991	130,000
North Carolina	Raleigh	James G. Martin	Rep.	4	Jan. 1993	109,728
North Dakota	Bismarck	George A. Sinner	Dem.	4	Jan. 1993	65,000
Ohio	Columbus	Richard F. Celeste	Dem.	4	Jan. 1991	65,000
Oklahoma	Oklahoma City	Henry Bellmon	Rep.	4	Jan. 1991	70,000
Oregon	Salem	Neil Goldschmidt	Dem.	4	Jan. 1991	75,000
Pennsylvania	Harrisburg	Robert Casey	Dem.	4	Jan. 1991	85,000
Rhode Island	Providence	Edward DiPrete	Rep.	2	Jan. 1993	69,000
South Carolina	Columbia	Carroll A. Campbell Jr.	Rep.	4	Jan. 1991	83,232
South Dakota	Pierre	George S. Mickelson	Rep.	4	Jan. 1991	59,045
Tennessee	Nashville	Ned Ray McWherter	Dem.	4	Jan. 1991	85,000
Texas	Austin	Bill Clements	Rep.	4	Jan. 1991	93,342
Utah	Salt Lake City	Norman Bangerter	Rep.	4	Jan. 1993	60,000
Vermont	Montpelier	Madeleine M. Kunin	Dem.	2	Jan. 1991	71,200
Virginia	Richmond	Gerald L. Baliles	Dem.	4	Jan. 1990	85,000
Washington	Olympia	Booth Gardner	Dem.	4	Jan. 1993	86,800
West Virginia	Charleston	Gaston Caperton	Dem.	4	Jan. 1993	72,000
Wisconsin	Madison	Tommy G. Thompson	Rep.	4	Jan. 1991	86,149
Wyoming	Cheyenne	Mike Sullivan	Dem.	4	Jan. 1991	70,000
Amer. Samoa	Pago Pago	Peter T. Coleman	Rep.	4	Jan. 1993	—
Guam	Agana	Joseph Ada	Dem.	4	Jan. 1991	—
Puerto Rico	San Juan	Rafael Hernandez Colón	P.D.	4	Jan. 1993	—
Virgin Islands	Charlotte Amalie	Alexander Farreley	Dem.	4	Jan. 1991	—

Mayors and City Managers of Selected U.S. Cities

As of mid-1989

*Asterisk before name denotes city manager. All others are mayors. For mayors, dates are those of next election; for city managers, they are dates of appointment.

D. Democrat; R. Republican; N-P, Non-Partisan

City	Name	Term
Abilene, Tex.	Dale E. Ferguson, N-P	1990, May.
Abington, Pa.	*Albert Herrmann	1978, May
Akron, Oh.	D.L. Plusquellic, D	1991, Nov.
Alameda, Cal.	Chuck Corica, N-P	1991, Apr.
Albany, Ga.	*Nicholas M. Meiszer	1985, Sept.
Albany, N.Y.	Thomas M. Whalen,3d,D	1989, Nov.
Albuquerque, N.M.	Ken Schultz, N-P	1989, Oct.
Alexandria, La.	Edward Randolph Jr., D	1990, Oct.
Alexandria, Va.	*Vola Lawson	1985, Sept.
Alhambra, Cal.	*Kevin J. Murphy	1983, May
Allentown, Pa.	Joseph S. Daddona, D	1989, Nov.
Altoona, Pa.	Alan Mikula, D	1989, Nov.
Amarillo, Tex.	*John Ward	1983, June
Ames, Ia.	*Steven L. Schainker	1982, Oct.
Anaheim, Cal.	*Bob Simpson	1987, Dec.
Anchorage, Alas.	Tom Fink, N-P	1991, Nov.
Anderson, Ind.	J. Mark Lawler, D	1991, Nov.
Anderson, S.C.	*Richard Burnette	1976, Sept.
Ann Arbor, Mich.	*Del Borgsdorf	1988, Aug.
Appleton, Wis.	Dorothy Johnson, N-P	1992, Apr.
Arcadia, Cal.	*George J. Watts	1981, Feb.
Arlington, Mass.	*Donald R. Marquis	1966, Nov.
Arlington, Tex.	*William Kirchhoff	1985, Oct.
Arlington Hts. Ill.	William Maki, N-P	1993, Apr.
Arvada, Col.	*Neal G. Berlin	1986, Mar.
Asheville, N.C.	*W. Louis Bissette, R	1989, Nov.
Athens, Ga.	Dwain Chambers, D	1989, Nov.
Atlanta, Ga.	Andrew Young, D	1989, Oct.
Atlantic City, N.J.	James L. Usry, R	1990, May
Auburn, N.Y.	*Bruce Clifford	1966, Aug.
Augusta, Ga.	Charles Devaney, D	1990, Nov.
Aurora, Col.	*James Griesemer	1984, Jan.
Aurora, Ill.	David L. Pierce, N-P	1993, Apr.
Austin, Tex.	*Jorge Carrasco	1984, Mar.
Bakersfield, Cal.	*J. Dale Hawley	1988, Apr.
Baldwin Park, Cal.	*Ralph Webb	1981, Apr.
Baltimore, Md.	Kurt Schmoke, D	1991, Nov.
Bangor, Me.	*John W. Flynn	1977, Feb.
Baton Rouge, La.	Tom Ed McHugh, D	1992, Oct.
Battle Creek, Mich.	*Rance L. Leaders	1988, June
Bay City, Mich.	*David D. Barnes	1979, May
Bayonne, N.J.	Dennis Collins, D	1990, May
Baytown, Tex.	*Robby Roundtree	1989, May
Beaumont, Tex.	*Ray A. Riley	1989, Feb.
Belleville, Ill.	Richard Brauer, N-P	1993, Apr.
Bellevue, Wash.	*Phillip Kushlaw	1985, Feb.
Bellflower, Cal.	M.G. Brassard	1990, Nov.
Beloit, Wis.	*David Wilcox	1986, Feb.
Berkeley, Cal.	*Hal Cronkite	1986, Apr.
Bessemer, Ala.	Ed Porter, N-P	1990, July
Bethlehem, Pa.	Paul M. Marcincin, D	1989, Nov.
Beverly Hills, Cal.	*Edward Kreins	1979, Oct.
Billings, Mont.	*Alan Tandy	1985, May
Biloxi, Miss.	Peter Halat, D	1993, May
Binghamton, N.Y.	Juanita M. Crabb, D	1989, Nov.
Birmingham, Ala.	Richard Arrington Jr., D	1991, Oct.
Bismarck, N.D.	Marlan Haakenson, R	1990, Apr.
Bloomfield, Minn.	*John Pidgeon	1967, Dec.

City	Name	Term
Bloomfield, N.J.	John Crecco, R	1989, Nov.
Bloomington, Ill.	Jesse Smart, D	1993, Apr.
Bloomington, Ind.	Tomilea Allison, D	1991, Nov.
Bloomington, Minn.	*John Pidgeon	1967, Dec.
Boca Raton, Fla.	Emil Danciu, N-P	1991, Mar.
Boise, Ida.	Dirk Kempthorne, N-P	1989, Nov.
Boston, Mass.	Raymond L. Flynn, D	1991 Nov.
Boulder, Col.	*David Knapp	1989, June
Bowie, Md.	*G. Charles Moore	1976, Mar.
Bowling Green, Ky.	*Charles W. Coates.	1977, Feb.
Bridgeport, Conn.	Thomas W. Bucci, D	1989, Nov.
Bristol, Conn.	John Leone, D	1989, Nov.
Brockton, Mass.	Carl Pitaro, D	1991, Nov.
Brooklyn Center, Minn.	*Gerald G. Splinter	1977, Oct.
Brownsville, Tex.	*Steve Fitzgibbons	1987, Jan.
Bryan, Tex.	*Ernest R. Clark	1979, Feb.
Buena Park, Cal.	*Kevin O'Rourke	1985, Nov.
Buffalo, N.Y.	James D. Griffin, D	1989, Nov.
Burbank, Cal.	*Bud Ovrom	1985, June
Burlington, Vt.	Peter Clavelle, N-P	1991, Mar.
Calumet City, Ill.	Robert C. Stefaniak, D	1993, Apr.
Cambridge, Mass.	*Robert Healy.	1974, May
Camden, N.J.	Melvin Primas Jr., D.	1993, May
Canton, Oh.	Sam Purses, D.	1991, Nov.
Cape Girardeau, Mo.	*J. Ronald Fischer	1988, Feb.
Carson, Cal.	*John Dangleis	1984, Nov.
Casper, Wyo.	*Thomas Forslund	1988, June
Cedar Rapids, Ia.	Donald J. Canney, N-P	1989, Nov.
Champaign, Ill.	*Steven C. Carter.	1985, Feb.
Charleston, S.C.	Joseph P. Riley Jr., D	1991, Nov.
Charleston, W. Va.	Charles Gardner, R	1991, Apr.
Charlotte, N.C.	Sue Myrick, R	1989, Nov.
Charlottesville, Va.	*Cole Hendrix	1970, Jan.
Chattanooga, Tenn.	Gene Roberts, R	1991, Apr.
Chesapeake, Va.	*James W. Rein.	1987, Mar.
Chester, Pa.	Willie Mae James Leake, R	1991, Nov.
Cheyenne, Wyo.	Gary Schaeffer, R.	1992, Nov.
Chicago, Ill.	Richard M. Daley, D.	1993, Apr.
Chicago Hts., Ill.	Charles Panici, D	1991, Apr.
Chicopee, Mass.	Joseph Chessey, D	1989, Nov.
Chino, Cal.	*Richard Rowe	1985, Feb.
Chula Vista, Cal.	*John Goss	1983, Jan.
Cincinnati, Oh.	*Scott Johnson	1986, Mar.
Clearwater, Fla.	*Ronald H. Rabun.	1988, Apr.
Cleveland, Oh.	George Voinovich, R	1989, Nov.
Cleveland Hgts., Oh.	*Robert Downey.	1985, Jan.
Col. Spgs., Col.	*Roy Pederson	1989, Jan.
Columbia, Mo.	*Raymond A. Beck	1985, Aug.
Columbia, S.C.	*Graydon V. Olive Jr..	1970, Mar.
Columbus, Ga.	James Jernigan, N-P	1990, Nov.
Columbus, Oh.	Dana Rinehart, R	1991, Nov.
Commerce, Cal.	*Robert Hinderliter	1973, Aug.
Compton, Cal.	*Howard Caldwell.	1989, June
Concord, Cal.	*Michael Uberuaga	1986, May
Coon Rapids., Minn.	*Richard Thistle	1979, July
Coral Gables, Fla.	*H.C. Eads Jr.	1988, May
Corpus Christi, Tex.	*Juan Garza	1988, Apr.
Corvallis, Ore.	*Gerald Seals	1988, Feb.
Costa Mesa, Cal.	*Allan L. Roeder.	1985, Oct.
Council Bluffs, Ia.	Tom Hanafan, D	1990, Nov.
Covington, Ky.	*Arnold Simpson	1986, Nov.
Cranston, R.I.	Michael Traficante, R	1990, Nov.
Crystal, Minn.	*John Irving	1963, Jan.
Culver City, Cal.	*Dale Jones	1967, Sept.
Cuyahoga Falls, Oh.	Don L. Robart, R	1989, Nov.
Dallas, Tex.	*Richard Knight	1986, Dec.
Daly City, Cal.	*David R. Rowe	1969, Sept.
Danbury, Conn.	Joseph Sauer, N-P	1989, Nov.
Danville, Va.	*Charles Church	1981, June
Davenport, Ia.	Thomas W. Hart, R	1989, Nov.
Dayton, Oh.	*Richard Helwig	1984, Nov.
Daytona Bch., Fla.	*Howard D. Tipton	1978, Oct.
Dearborn, Mich.	Michael Guido, N-P	1989, Nov.
Dearborn Hts., Mich.	Lyle Van Houton, R	1989, Nov.
Decatur, Ill.	*James Bacon Jr.	1988, Oct.
Denton, Tex.	*Larry Harrell	1986, Feb.
Denver, Col.	Federico Pena, D	1991, May
Des Moines, Ia.	*John Dorrian, D.	1990, Nov.
Des Plaines, Ill.	John Seitz, N-P	1989, Apr.
Detroit, Mich.	Coleman A. Young, N-P	1989, Nov.
Dotham, Aia.	*Don J. Marnon	1987, May
Dover, Del.	*vacant.	
Downers Grove, Ill.	*James R. Griesemer.	1972, Sept.
Downey, Cal.	*Don Davis.	1985, Oct.
Dubuque, Ia.	*W. Kenneth Gearhart	1979, Aug.
Duluth, Minn.	John Fedo, N-P	1989, Nov.

City	Name	Term
Durham, N.C.	*Orville Powell.	1983, Mar.
E. Chicago, Ind.	Robert A. Pastrick, D	1991, Nov.
E. Cleveland, Oh.	Darryl Pittman, D.	1989, Nov.
E. Detroit.	*S. Wesley McAllister Jr.	1988, Oct.
E. Hartford, Conn.	Robert F. McNulty, D.	1989, Nov.
E. Lansing, Mich.	Joan Hunault, N-P.	1989, Nov.
E. Orange, N.J.	John Hatcher Jr., D.	1989, Nov.
Eau Claire, Wis.	*Eric Anderson	1984, Jan.
Edina, Minn.	*Kenneth Rosland.	1977, Nov.
Edison, N.J.	Anthony Yelencsics, D	1989, Nov.
El Cajon, Cal.	John Reber, D	1990, June
El Monte, Cal.	Don McMillen, N-P	1990, Apr.
El Paso, Tex.	Suzie Azar, N-P	1991, May
Elgin, Ill.	*James J. Cook.	1985, Oct.
Elizabeth, N.J.	Thomas G. Dunn, D	1992, Nov.
Elkhart, Ind.	James Perron, D	1992, Nov.
Elmhurst, Ill.	Charles Garrigues, N-P	1991, Apr.
Elmira, N.Y.	*W. Gregg LaMar	1987, July
Elyria, Oh.	Michael Keys, D	1991, Nov.
Enfield, Conn.	*Robert J. Mulready.	1983, Feb.
Enid, Okla.	*Robert Elliott	1986, June
Erie, Pa.	Louis J. Tullio, D.	1989, Nov.
Escondido, Cal.	*Douglas K. Clark.	1989, July
Euclid, Oh.	David Lynch, R	1991, Nov.
Eugene, Ore.	*Michael Gleason	1981, Jan.
Evanston, Ill.	*Joel Asprooth.	1982, May
Evansville, Ind.	Frank McDonald, D	1991, Nov.
Everett, Mass.	John McCarthy, D.	1989, Nov.
Everett, Wash.	William Moore, N-P	1989, Nov.
Fairborn, Oh.	*Michael Hammond.	1985, Dec.
Fairfield, Cal.	*B. Gale Wilson	1956, Mar.
Fair Lawn, N.J.	*Joseph Garger	1979, Oct.
Fall River, Mass.	Carlton Viveiros, N-P	1989, Nov.
Fargo, N.D.	Jon Lindgren, D	1990, Apr.
Farmington Hills, Mich.	*William M. Costick	1981, Jan.
Fayetteville, Ark.	*James Pennington	1987, Sept.
Fayetteville, N.C.	*John P. Smith.	1981, Jan.
Fitchburg, Mass.	Jeffrey Bean, D	1989, Nov.
Flagstaff, Ariz.	*Frank Abeyta.	1981, Jan.
Flint, Mich.	Matthew Collier, N-P	1991, Nov.
Florissant, Mo.	James J. Eagan, N-P	1991, Apr.
Fond du Lac, Wis.	*Jack Howley	1989, Aug.
Ft. Collins, Col.	*Steven Burkett	1986, Apr.
Ft. Lauderdale, Fla.	*Constance Hoffmann	1980, Oct.
Ft. Lee, N.J.	Nicholas Corbiscello, R.	1991, Nov.
Ft. Smith, Ark.	*William Vines, N-P	1990, Nov.
Ft. Wayne, Ind.	Paul Helmke, R	1991, Nov.
Ft. Worth, Tex.	*Douglas Harman	1985, Mar.
Fountain Valley, Cal.	*Judy Kelsey.	1984, May
Fremont, Cal.	*Charles Kent McClain	1981, May
Fresno, Cal.	*James Aldredge	1986, July
Fullerton, Cal.	*William C. Winter.	1979, Oct.
Gadsden, Ala.	David Nolen, D.	1990, July
Gainesville, Fla.	*W.D. Higginbotham Jr..	1984, Sept.
Galesburg, Ill.	*Robert Knabel	1989, Feb.
Galveston, Tex.	*Douglas W. Matthews	1985, Mar.
Gardena, Cal.	*Kenneth Landau	1985, Apr.
Garden Grove, Cal.	*Delbert L. Powers	1980, July
Garfield Hts., Oh.	Thomas Longo, D	1989, Nov.
Garland, Tex.	*James K. Spore	1985, Mar.
Gary, Ind.	Thomas Barnes, D	1991, Nov.
Gastonia, N.C.	*Gary Hicks	1973, Dec.
Glendale, Ariz.	*Martin Vanacour	1985, Mar.
Glendale, Cal.	*David Ramsay	1988, May
Grand Forks, N.D.	Michael Polovitz, D	1992, Apr.
Grand Island, Neb.	Charles Baasch, R	1990, Nov.
Gr. Prairie, Tex.	*Wendel Hulse	1987, Apr.
Gr. Rapids, Mich.	*Kurt Kimball.	1987, Apr.
Great Falls, Mont.	*G. Allen Johnson	1981, Jan.
Greeley, Col.	*Sam Sasaki.	1987, Mar.
Green Bay, Wis.	Samuel Halloin, N-P	1991, Apr.
Greensboro, N.C.	*T.Z. Osborne	1973, Feb.
Greenville, Miss.	William Burnley Jr., D.	1989, Oct.
Greenville, S.C.	*John Dullea.	1971, Oct.
Greenwich, Conn.	John Margenot, D, first selectman	1989, Nov.
Groton, Conn.	Catherine Kolnaski, D.	1991, May
Hackensack, N.J.	*Robert F. Casey.	1987, Apr.
Hagerstown, Md.	Stephen Sager	1993, May
Hamden, Conn.	John L. Carusone, D	1989, Nov.
Hamilton, Oh.	*Hal Shepherd.	1989, Apr.
Hammond, Ind.	Thomas McDermott, D	1991, Nov.
Hampton, Va.	*Robert O'Neill Jr.	1984, Oct.
Harlingen, Tex.	*G.D. Sotelo.	1981, July
Harrisburg, Pa.	Stephen Reed, D	1989, Nov.
Hartford, Conn.	Carrie Saxon Perry, D	1989, Nov.
Hattiesburg, Miss.	Ed Morgan, D	1993, June
Haverhill, Mass.	Theodore Pelosi, R	1989, Nov.

City	Name	Term
Hawthorne, Cal.	*James Armas, act.	1988, Apr.
Hayward, Cal.	*Louis Garcia	1989, Jan.
Hialeah, Fla.	Raul Martinez, D	1989, Nov.
High Point, N.C.	*H. Lewis Price	1983, July
Hollywood, Fla.	*Irving Rosenbaum	1988, Aug.
Holyoke, Mass.	Michael Dunn, D	1989, Nov.
Honolulu, Ha.	Frank Fasi, R	1992, Nov.
Hot Springs, Ark.	*Michael Wright	1986, Aug.
Houston, Tex.	Kathryn Whitmire, N-P	1989, Nov.
Huntington, W. Va.	Robert Nelson, D	1989, Nov.
Huntington Beach, Cal.	*Charles Thompson	1981, Oct.
Hutchinson, Kan.	*Joe Palacioc	1989, Jan.
Idaho Falls, Ida.	Thomas Campbell, N-P	1989, Nov.
Independence, Mo.	*Robert Svehla	1989, June
Indianapolis, Ind.	William Hudnut, R	1991, Nov.
Inglewood, Cal.	*Paul Eckles	1975, Nov.
Inkster, Mich.	*Grady Holmes	1987, Sept.
Iowa City, Ia.	*Stephen Atkins	1986, July
Irving, Tex.	*Jack Huffman	1974, Jan.
Irvington, N.J.	J. Walter Jonkoski, D	1990, May
Jackson, Mich.	*William P. Buchanan	1985, Nov.
Jackson, Miss.	Kane Ditto, D	1993, May
Jackson, Tenn.	Charles Farmer, D	1991, May
Jacksonville, Fla.	Tommy Hazouri, D	1991, May
Jamestown, N.Y.	Steve Carlson, D	1989, Nov.
Janesville, Wis.	*Steven Sheiffer	1987, May
Jersey City, N.J.	Gerald McCann, N-P	1993, May
Johnson City, Tenn.	*John G. Campbell	1984, June
Johnstown, Pa.	Herbert Pfuhl Jr., R	1989, Nov.
Joliet, Ill.	*John M. Mezera	1987, Jan.
Joplin, Mo.	*Leonard A. Martin	1986, Sept.
Kalamazoo, Mich.	*James Holgersson	1989, June
Kansas City, Kan.	*David Isabell	1985, June
Kansas City, Mo.	Richard Berkley, R	1991, Apr.
Kenner, La.	Aaron Broussard, N-P	1990, June
Kenosha, Wis.	Patrick Moran, N-P	1992, Apr.
Kettering, Oh.	*Robert Walker	1982, Oct.
Key West, Fla.	*Richard H. Witker	1988, Jan.
Killeen, Tex.	*Dion Miller	1989, Apr.
Knoxville, Tenn.	Victor Ashe, R	1991, Nov.
Kokomo, Ind.	Robert Sargent, D	1991, Nov.
LaCrosse, Wis.	Patrick Zielke, N-P	1993, Apr.
La Habra, Cal.	*Lee Risner	1970, Nov.
La Mesa, Cal.	*Ronald Creagh	1988, Oct.
La Mirada, Cal.	*Gary K. Sloan	1981, Apr.
Lafayette, Ind.	James Riehle, D	1990, Nov.
Lafayette, La.	Dud Lastrapes, R	1990, June
Lakeland, Fla.	*E.S. Strickland	1986, Feb.
Lakewood, Cal.	*Howard L. Chambers	1976, June
Lakewood, Col.	*Larry Rice	1986, May
Lakewood, Oh.	Anthony Sinagra, R	1991, Nov.
Lancaster, Pa.	Arthur E. Morris, R	1989, Nov.
Lansing, Mich.	Terry John McKane, N-P	1989, Nov.
Laredo, Tex.	*Marvin Townsend	1982, June
Largo, Fla.	George McGough, R	1991, Apr.
Las Cruces, N.M.	*Dana Miller	1983, Feb.
Las Vegas, Nev.	Ron Lurie, D	1991, June
Lawrence, Kan.	*Buford M. Watson Jr.	1970, Jan.
Lawrence, Mass.	Kevin Sullivan, N-P	1989, Nov.
Lawton, Okla.	*Melissa B. Vossmer	1986, Nov.
Lewiston, Me.	*Lucien Gosselin	1980, July
Lexington, Ky.	Scotty Baesler, N-P	1989, Nov.
Lincoln, Neb.	Bill Harris, D	1991, May
Linden, N.J.	Paul Werkmeister, D	1990, Nov.
Little Rock, Ark.	*Thomas Dalton	1986, June
Livermore, Cal.	*Leland Horner	1978, Oct.
Lombard, Ill.	*William Lichter	1985, Jan.
Long Beach, Cal.	*James Hankla	1987, Mar.
Long Beach, N.Y.	*Edwin Eaton	1979, June
Longmont, Col.	*Geoff Dolan	1987, Jan.
Longview, Tex.	*C. Ray Jackson	1980, Apr.
Lorain, Oh.	Alex Olejko, D	1991, Nov.
Los Angeles, Cal.	Thomas Bradley, N-P	1993, June
Louisville, Ky.	Jerry Abramson, D	1985, Nov.
Lowell, Mass.	*James Campbell	1987, Jan.
L. Merion, Pa.	*Thomas B. Fulweiler	1968, Jan.
Lubbock, Tex.	*Larry Cunningham	1976, Sept.
Lynchburg, Va.	*E. Allen Culverhouse	1979, June
Lynn, Mass.	Albert DiVirgilio, D	1989, Nov.
Lynwood, Cal.	*Charles Gomez	1982, Mar.
Macon, Ga.	William L. Robinson, D	1991, Nov.
Madison, Wis.	Paul Soglin, R	1991, Apr.
Malden, Mass.	James S. Conway, D	1989, Nov.
Manchester, Conn.	Peter DiRosa Jr., D	1989, Nov.
Manchester, N.H.	Emile Beaulieu, D	1989, Nov.
Manitowoc, Wis.	Kevin Crawford, N-P	1991, Apr.
Mansfield, Oh.	Edward Meehan, R	1991, Nov.
Marion, Ind.	Robert Mitchell, D	1991, Nov.
Marion, Oh.	Robert S. Brown, R	1991, Nov.
McAllen, Tex.	Othal Brand, R	1993, Apr.
McKeesport, Pa.	Lou Washowich, D	1991, Nov.
Medford, Mass.	Michael McGlynn, N-P	1989, Nov.
Melbourne, Fla.	*Samuel Halter	1978, July
Memphis, Tenn.	Richard C. Hackett, N-P	1991, Oct.
Mentor, Oh.	*vacant	
Meriden, Conn.	*Michael Aldi	1988, Mar.
Meridian, Miss.	Jimmy Kemp, R	1993, June
Mesa, Ariz.	*C.K. Luster	1979, June
Mesquite, Tex.	*James Prugel	1987, Dec.
Miami, Fla.	*Cesar H. Odio	1985, Dec.
Miami Beach, Fla.	*Rob Parkins	1982, Apr.
Middletown, Conn.	Sebastian Garafalo, R	1989, Nov.
Middletown, Oh.	*William Klosterman	1988, July
Midland, Tex.	Carroll M. Thomas, N-P	1990, May
Midwest City, Okla.	*Charles Johnson	1984, Nov.
Milford, Conn.	Alberta Jagoe, D	1989, Nov.
Milwaukee, Wis.	John Norquist, D	1992, Apr.
Minneapolis, Minn.	Donald Fraser, D	1989, Nov.
Minnetonka, Minn.	*James F. Miller	1980, Jan.
Minot, N.D.	*Robert Schempp, R	1977, Nov.
Mobile, Ala.	Arthur Outlaw, R	1989, Aug.
Modesto, Cal.	*Garth Lipsky	1974, Jan.
Monroe, La.	Robert Powell, D	1992, Apr.
Montclair, N.J.	*Bertrand Kendall	1980, Sept.
Montebello, Cal.	*Richard Torres	1989, May
Monterey Park, Cal.	*Mark Lewis	1988, July
Montgomery, Ala.	Emory Folmar, R	1991, Nov.
Mt. Lebanon, Pa.	*James Cain	1982, Apr.
Mt. Prospect, Ill.	*John F. Dixon	1987, Mar.
Mt. Vernon, N.Y.	Roland Blackwood, D	1991, Nov.
Mountain View, Cal.	*Bruce Liedstrand	1976, June
Muncie, Ind.	James Carey, D	1991, Nov.
Muskegon, Mich.	*Robert Hagemann	1983, Sept.
Muskogee, Okla.	*Walter Beckham	1984, Feb.
Napa, Cal.	*Vern Hamilton	1989 Mar.
Naperville, Ill.	*Ralph DeSantis	1988, June
Nashua, N.H.	James Donchess, N-P	1991, Nov.
Nashville, Tenn.	Bill Boner, D	1991, Aug.
National City, Cal.	*Tom McCabe	1979, Mar.
New Bedford, Mass.	John Bullard, D	1989, Nov.
New Britain, Conn.	William J. McNamara, D	1989, Nov.
New Brunswick, N.J.	John Lynch, D	1990, Nov.
New Castle, Pa.	Richard Christofer, D	1991, Nov.
New Haven, Conn.	Biagio DiLieto, D	1989, Nov.
New London, Conn.	*C.F. Driscoll	1969, May
New Orleans, La.	Sidney Barthelemy, D	1990, Mar.
New Rochelle, N.Y.	*C. Samuel Kissinger	1975, Apr.
New York, N.Y.	Edward Koch, D	1989, Nov.
Newark, N.J.	Sharpe James, D	1990, May
Newark, Oh.	William Moore, R	1991, Nov.
Newport, R.I.	*Francis Edwards	1987, Jan.
Newport Beach, Cal.	*Robert L. Wynn	1971, Aug.
Newport News, Va.	*Ed Maroney	1987, Jan.
Newton, Mass.	Theodore Mann, R	1989, Nov.
Niagara Falls, N.Y.	Michael O'Laughlin, D	1991, Nov.
Norfolk, Va.	*James B. Oliver Jr.	1987, Jan.
Norman, Okla.	*Ron Wood, act	1989, May
Norristown, Pa.	Samuel Vallone, R	1989, Nov.
North Charleston, S.C.	John Bourne Jr., R	1990, May
North Las Vegas	*Michael Dyal	1982, May
No. Little Rock, Ark.	Patrick Hayes, D	1992, Nov.
Norwalk, Cal.	*Ray Gibbs	1984, Feb.
Norwalk, Conn.	Frank Esposito, R	1989, Nov.
Norwich, Conn.	*Ernert Zmyslinski	1988, July
Novato, Cal.	*Phillip J. Brown	1975, May
Oak Park, Ill.	*J.N. Nielsen	1986, July
Oak Ridge, Tenn.	*Jeffrey J. Broughton	1986, Sept.
Oakland, Cal.	*Henry L. Gardner	1981, June
Oceanside, Cal.	*Suzanne Foucault	1982, Nov.
Odessa, Tex.	*John Harrison	1982, Aug.
Ogden, Ut.	L. Clifford Goff, N-P	1989, Nov.
Oklahoma City, Okla.	*Terry L. Childers	1986, Sept.
Omaha, Neb.	P.J. Morgan, D	1993, May
Ontario, Cal.	*Roger Hughbanks, N-P	1975, July
Orange, Cal.	*J. William Little	1984, Jan.
Orange, N.J.	Robert L. Brown, D	1992, May
Orlando, Fla.	Bill Frederick, N-P	1992, Sept.
Oshkosh, Wis.	*W. O. Frueh	1976, Aug.
Overland Park, Kan.	*Donald Pipes	1977, June
Owensboro, Ky.	*Max Rhoads	1959, Sept.
Oxnard, Cal.	*David Mora	1985, July
Pacifica, Cal.	*Daniel Pincetich	1985, Dec.
Palm Springs, Cal.	*Norman R. King	1979, Dec.
Palo Alto, Cal.	*William Zaner	1979, Sept.
Park Ridge, Ill.	*George E. Hagman	1984, July

City	Name	Term	City	Name	Term
Parkersburg, W. Va.	William Nicely, R	1989, Nov.	Sandy City, Ut.	Steve Newton, N-P	1989, Nov.
Parma, Oh.	Michael Ries, D	1991, Nov.	Santa Ana, Cal.	*David Ream	1986, July
Pasadena, Cal.	William Thomson Jr., R	1990, May	Santa Barbara, Cal.	*Richard Thomas	1977, Jan.
Pasadena, Tex.	John Ray Harrison	1993, May	Santa Clara, Cal.	*Jennifer Sparacino	1987, Mar.
Paterson, N.J.	Frank X. Graves Jr., D	1990, May	Santa Cruz, Cal.	*Richard Wilson	1981, June
Pawtucket, R.I.	Brian Sarault	1989, Nov.	Santa Fe, N.M.	Sam Pick, D	1990, Mar.
Peabody, Mass.	Peter Torigian, D	1989, Nov.	Santa Maria, Cal.	*Wayne Schwammel	1989, June
Pekin, Ill.	Larry Homerin, D	1991, Apr.	Santa Monica, Cal.	*John Jalili	1984, Dec.
Pensacola, Fla.	*Steve Garman	1986, June	Santa Rosa, Cal.	*Kenneth Blackman	1970, July
Peoria, Ill.	*Thomas Mikulecky	1987, July	Sarasota, Fla.	*David Sollenberger	1987, Mar.
Perth Amboy, N.J.	George J. Otlowski, D	1992, May	Savannah, Ga.	*Arthur A. Mendonsa	1962, July
Petersburg, Va.	*Richard M. Brown	1984, Oct.	Schenectady, N.Y.	Karen Johnson, D	1991, Nov.
Philadelphia, Pa.	W. Wilson Goode, D	1991, Nov.	Scottsdale, Ariz.	*Jorge Carrasco	1988, Oct.
Phoenix, Ariz.	Terry Goddard, N-P	1989, Oct.	Scranton, Pa.	David Wenzel, R	1989, Nov.
Pico Rivera, Cal.	*Dennis Courtemarche	1984, Nov.	Seattle, Wash.	Charles Royer, D	1989, Nov.
Pine Bluff, Ark	Carolyn Robinson, D	1992, Nov.	Shaker Heights, Oh.	Stephen Alfred, N-P	1989, Nov.
Pittsburgh, Pa.	Sophie Masloff, D	1989, Nov.	Sheboygan, Wis.	Richard Schneider, N-P	1993, Apr.
Pittsfield, Mass.	Anne E. Wojtkowski, D	1989, Nov.	Shreveport, La.	John Hussey, D	1990, Nov.
Plainfield, N.J.	Richard Taylor, D	1989, Nov.	Simi Valley, Cal.	*M.L. Koester	1979, Sept.
Plano, Tex.	*Thomas Muehlenbeck	1987, Dec.	Sioux City, Ia.	Loren Callendar, D	1989, Nov.
Pocatello, Ida.	Richard Finlayson, N-P	1989, Nov.	Sioux Falls, S.D.	Jack White, R	1991, June
Pomona, Cal.	*A.J. Wilson	1988, Feb.	Skokie, Ill.	*Albert Rigoni	1987, Jan.
Pompano Beach, Fla.	*Danny Crew, act.	1988, Dec.	Somerville, Mass.	Eugene Brune, D	1989, Nov.
Pontiac, Mich.	Walter Moore, N-P	1989, Nov.	South Bend, Ind.	Joseph Kernan, D	1991, Nov.
Port Arthur, Tex.	*George Dibrell	1962, Oct.	South Gate, Cal.	Herbert Cranton, D	1990, Apr.
Port Huron, Mich.	*Gerald R. Bouchard	1965, June	Southfield, Mich.	*Robert Block	1985, Jan.
Portland, Me.	*Robert Ganley	1986, Sept.	Sparks, Nev.	*Patricia Thompson	1983, Sept.
Portland, Ore.	Bud Clark, N-P	1992, Nov.	Spartanburg, S.C.	*Wayne Bowers	1984, Sept.
Portsmouth, Oh.	*Barry Feldman	1977, Jan.	Spokane, Wash.	*Terry Novak	1978, July
Portsmouth, Va.	*George Hanbury	1982, June	Springfield, Ill.	Ossie Langfelder, D	1991, Apr.
Poughkeepsie, N.Y.	*William J. Theysohn	1982, Mar.	Springfield, Mass	Richard Neal, N-P	1989, Nov.
Prichard, Ala.	Margie M. Wilson D.	1992, Aug.	Springfield, Mo.	*Don G. Busch	1971, Oct.
Providence, R.I.	Joseph Paolino Jr., D	1990, Nov.	Springfield, Oh.	*Matthew Kridler	1988, Oct.
Provo, Ut.	Joseph Jenkins, R	1989, Nov.	Springfield, Ore.	*Michael Kelly	1989, Jan.
Pueblo, Col.	*Lewis A. Quigley	1987, Jan.	Stamford, Conn.	Thom Serrani, D	1989, Nov.
Quincy, Mass.	Francis X. McCauley, R.	1989, Nov.	Sterling Hts., Mich.	*Steve Duchane	1988, Sept.
Racine, Wis.	N. Owen Davies, N-P	1991, Apr.	Stillwater, Okla.	*Carl Weinaug	1983, Apr.
Raleigh, N.C.	*Dempsey Benton	1983, Dec.	Stockton, Cal.	*Alan N. Harvey	1988, Aug.
Rapid City, S.D.	Keith Carlyle, N-P	1991, Apr.	Stratford, Conn.	*Ronald Owens	1984, July
Reading, Pa.	William Haggerty Jr., D	1991, Nov.	Sunnyvale, Cal.	*Thomas Lewcock	1980, Apr.
Redding, Cal.	*Robert Christofferson	1987, Jan.	Syracuse, N.Y.	Thomas G. Young, D	1989, Nov.
Redlands, Cal.	*John E. Holmes	1983, Apr.	Tacoma, Wash.	*Erling O. Mork	1975, June
Redondo Beach, Cal.	*Timothy Casey	1981, May	Tallahassee, Fla.	*Daniel A. Kleman	1974, Aug.
Redwood City, Cal.	*James M. Smith	1982, Feb.	Tampa, Fla.	Sandra Friedman, N-P	1991, Mar.
Reno, Nev.	*Harold Schilling	1986, Mar.	Taunton, Mass.	Richard Johnson, D	1989, Nov.
Revere, Mass.	George V. Colella, D	1989, Nov.	Taylor, Mich.	Cameron Priebe, D	1989, Nov.
Richardson, Tex.	*Bob Hughey	1974, Mar.	Teaneck, N.J.	*Werner H. Schmid	1959, Mar.
Richfield, Minn.	*James Prosser	1986, Sept.	Tempe, Ariz.	Harry E. Mitchell, D	1990, Mar.
Richmond, Cal.	*Larry Moore	1987, Aug.	Temple, Tex.	*Jack Parker	1985, Apr.
Richmond, Ind.	Frank Waltermann, D	1991, Nov.	Terre Haute, Ind.	P. Pete Chalos, D	1991, Nov.
Richmond, Va.	*Robert C. Bobb.	1986, July	Thornton, Col.	*Jack Ethredge	1985, Jan.
Riverside, Cal.	*Douglas Weiford	1980, Mar.	Thousand Oaks, Cal.	*Grant Brimhall	1978, Jan.
Roanoke, Va.	*W.R. Herbert	1985, Nov.	Titusville, Fla.	*Norman Hickey	1974, June
Rochester, Minn.	*Steven Kvenvold	1979, June	Toledo, Oh.	*Philip Hawkey	1986, May
Rochester, N.Y.	Thomas Ryan Jr., D	1989, Nov.	Topeka, Kan.	Butch Felker, N-P	1993, Apr.
Rock Hill, S.C.	*Joe Lanford	1979, July	Torrance, Cal.	*Leroy J. Jackson	1983, Jan.
Rock Island, Ill.	*John Phillips	1986, Nov.	Trenton, N.J.	Arthur Holland, N-P	1990, May
Rockford, Ill.	Charles Box, D	1993, Apr.	Troy, N.Y.	*Steven Dworsky	1986, July
Rockville, Md.	*Bruce Romer	1988, Sept.	Tucson, Ariz.	*Joel Valdez	1974, May
Rome, N.Y.	Carl Eilenberg, R	1991, Nov.	Tulsa, Okla.	Rodger Randle, D	1990, Apr.
Roseville, Mich.	Jeanne Riesterer, N-P	1989, Nov.	Tuscaloosa, Ala.	Alvin DuPont, D	1989, Oct.
Roswell, N.M.	*Ralph Fresquez	1986, Jan.	Tyler, Tex.	*Gary Gwyn	1982, Nov.
Royal Oak, Mich.	*William Baldridge.	1975, Sept.	Union City, N.J.	Robert Menendez, D	1990, May
Sacramento, Cal.	*Walter Slipe	1976, Mar.	Univ. City, Mo.	*Frank Oliendorff	1980, Mar.
Saginaw, Mich.	*Vernon E. Stoner.	1987, Feb.	Upland, Cal.	*Ray Silver	1988, Dec.
St. Clair Shores, Mich.	*Roy Stype.	1982, May	Upper Arlington, Oh.	*Richard King	1984, Aug.
St. Cloud, Minn.	Robert Huston, N-P	1989, Nov.	Utica, N.Y.	Louis La Polla, R	1991, Nov.
St. Joseph, Mo.	Glenda Kelly, D.	1990, Apr.	Vancouver, Wash.	*Paul Grattet	1980, Aug.
St. Louis, Mo.	Vincent Schoemehl, D	1993, Apr.	Ventura, Cal.	*John Baker	1986, Nov.
St. Louis Park, Minn.	*William C. Dixon	1988, Oct.	Victoria, Tex.	*James J. Miller	1980, June
St. Paul, Minn.	George Latimer, D	1989, Nov.	Vineland, N.J.	Harry Curley, N-P	1992, May
St. Petersburg, Fla.	*Robert Obering.	1985, Oct.	Virginia Beach, Va.	*Aubrey Watts Jr.	1987, Dec.
Salem, Mass.	Anthony V. Salvo, D.	1989, Nov.	Waco, Tex.	*John Harrison	1977, Sept.
Salem, Ore.	*Gary Eide	1988, Jan.	Walnut Creek, Cal.	*Donald Blubaugh	1988, Apr.
Salina, Kan.	*Dennis Kissinger	1988, Jan.	Waltham, Mass.	William Stanley, D	1991, Nov.
Salinas, Cal.	*Roy Herte	1988, Sept.	Warren, Mich.	Ronald Bonkowski, N-P	1991, Nov.
Salt Lake City, Ut.	Palmer DePaulis, D	1991, Nov.	Warren, Oh.	Daniel Sferra, D	1991, Nov.
San Angelo, Tex.	*Stephen Brown	1982, May	Warwick, R.I.	Francis X. Flaherty, D	1990, Nov.
San Antonio, Tex.	Lila Cockrell, D	1991, Apr.	Wash., D.C.	Marion Barry, D	1990, Nov.
San Bernardino, Cal.	Bob Holcomb, D	1993, May	Waterbury, Conn.	Joseph Santopietro, R	1989, Nov.
San Bruno, Cal.	*Gerald Minford	1971, Dec.	Waterloo, Ia.	Bernard L. McKinley, N-P	1989, Apr.
San Diego, Cal.	Maureen O'Connor, N-P	1992, Nov.	Waukegan, Ill.	Haig Paravonian, R	1993, Apr.
San Francisco, Cal.	Art Agnos, D	1991, Nov.	Waukesha, Wis.	Paul Vrakas, N-P	1990, Apr.
San Jose, Cal.	*Leslie White	1989, May	Wausau, Wis.	John Robinson, D	1992, Apr.
San Leandro, Cal.	*Richard H. Randall.	1986, July	Wauwatosa, Wis.	James Brundahl, N-P	1992, Apr.
San Mateo, Cal.	*Richard Delong.	1976, Sept.	W. Allis, Wis.	Fred Cashmore, N-P	1992, Apr.
San Rafael, Cal.	*Pamela Nicolai	1985, Dec.	W. Covina, Cal.	*Herman Fast	1976, Aug.
Sandusky, Oh.	*Frank Link	1972, Jan.	W. Haven, Conn.	Azelio Guerra, D	1989, Nov.

City	Name	Term	City	Name	Term
W. New York, N.J.	Anthony DeFino, D	1991, May	Wilmington, Del.	Daniel Frawley, D	1992, Nov.
W. Orange, N.J.	Samuel Spina, D	1990, May	Wilmington, N.C.	*William B. Farris	1983, May
W. Palm Beach, Fla.	*Paul Steinbrenner	1986, Jan.	Winston-Salem, N.C.	*Bryce A. Stuart	1980, Jan.
Westland, Mich.	Charles T. Griffin, D	1989, Nov.	Woonsocket, R.I.	Charles Baldelli, D	1989, Nov.
Westminster, Cal.	*Jerry Kenny	1989, Jan.	Worcester, Mass.	Jordan Levy, D	1989, Nov.
Westminster, Col.	*William Christopher	1978, June	Wyandotte, Mich.	James R. DeSana, D	1991, Apr.
Wheaton, Ill.	*Donald Rose	1980, Nov.	Wyoming, Mich.	*James Sheeran	1976, Nov.
Wheeling, W. Va.	*Michael Nau	1985, Oct.	Yakima, Wash.	*Richard Zais Jr.	1979, Jan.
White Plains, N.Y.	Alfred Del Vecchio, R	1989, Nov.	Yonkers, N.Y.	*Neil De Luca	1988, Jan.
Whittier, Cal.	Victor Lopez, N-P	1990, Apr.	York, Pa.	William Althaus, R	1989, Nov.
Wichita, Kan.	*Chris Cherches	1985, Oct.	Youngstown, Oh.	Patrick Ungaro, D	1989, Nov.
Wichita Falls, Tex.	*James Berzina	1983, June	Yuma, Ariz.	*Doug Lowe, R	1984, Jan.
Wilkes-Barre, Pa.	Lee Namey, D	1991, Nov.	Zanesville, Oh.	Donald Lewis Mason, R	1991, Nov.
Williamsport, Pa.	Jessie Bloom, D	1992, Nov.			

Number of Local Governments, by Type—States: 1987

Source: U.S. Bureau of the Census.

Governments in existence in January. Limited to governments actually in existence. Excludes, therefore, a few counties and numerous townships and "incorporated places" existing as areas for which statistics can be presented as to population and other subjects, but lacking any separate organized county, township, or municipal government.

State	All local governmental units	County governments	Municipal governments	Township governments[1]	School district governments
U.S.	83,186	3,042	19,200	16,691	14,721
Alabama	1,053	67	436	—	129
Alaska	172	9	149	—	—
Arizona	576	15	81	—	227
Arkansas	1,396	75	483	—	333
California	4,331	57	442	—	1,098
Colorado	1,593	62	266	—	180¹
Connecticut	477	—	31	149	16
Delaware	281	3	57	—	19
District of Columbia	2	—	1	—	—
Florida	965	66	390	—	95
Georgia	1,286	158	532	—	186
Hawaii	18	3	1	—	—
Idaho	1,065	44	198	—	118
Illinois	6,627	102	1,279	1,434	1,029
Indiana	2,806	91	567	1,008	304
Iowa	1,877	99	955	—	451
Kansas	3,803	105	627	1,360	324¹
Kentucky	1,303	119	437	—	178
Louisiana	452	61	301	—	66
Maine	800	16	22	471	88
Maryland	401	23	155	—	—
Massachusetts	836	12	39	312	82
Michigan	2,699	83	534	1,242	590
Minnesota	3,555	87	855	1,798	441
Mississippi	853	82	290	—	171
Missouri	3,147	114	930	325	561
Montana	1,243	54	128	—	547
Nebraska	3,152	93	534	454	952
Nevada	197	16	18	—	17
New Hampshire	524	10	13	221	160
New Jersey	1,625	21	320	247	551
New Mexico	331	33	98	—	88
New York	3,302	57	618	929	720
North Carolina	916	100	495	—	—
North Dakota	2,787	53	366	1,355	310
Ohio	3,377	88	940	1,318	621
Oklahoma	1,802	77	591	—	636
Oregon	1,502	36	240	—	350
Pennsylvania	4,956	66	1,022	1,548	515
Rhode Island	125	—	8	31	3
South Carolina	707	46	269	—	92
South Dakota	1,762	64	309	984	193
Tennessee	904	94	334	—	14
Texas	4,415	254	1,156	—	1,113
Utah	530	29	225	—	40
Vermont	673	14	55	237	272
Virginia	430	95	229	—	—
Washington	1,779	39	266	—	297¹
West Virginia	630	55	230	—	55
Wisconsin	2,719	72	580	1,268	433
Wyoming	424	23	95	—	56

— Represents zero. (1) Includes "town" governments in the 6 New England States and in Minnesota, New York, and Wisconsin.

CABINETS OF THE U. S.

Secretaries of State

The Department of Foreign Affairs was created by act of Congress July 27, 1789, and the name changed to Department of State on Sept. 15.

President	Secretary	Home	Apptd.	President	Secretary	Home	Apptd.
Washington	Thomas Jefferson	Va.	1789	Cleveland	F.T. Frelinghuysen	N.J.	1885
"	Edmund Randolph	"	1794	"	Thomas F. Bayard	Del.	1885
"	Timothy Pickering	Pa.	1795	Harrison, B.	"	"	1889
Adams, J.	"	"	1797	"	James G. Blaine	Me.	1889
"	John Marshall	Va.	1800	Harrison, B.	John W. Foster	Ind.	1892
Jefferson	James Madison	"	1801	Cleveland	Walter Q. Gresham.	Ill.	1893
Madison	Robert Smith	Md.	1809	"	Richard Olney	Mass..	1895
"	James Monroe	Va.	1811	McKinley	"	"	1897
Monroe	John Quincy Adams	Mass...	1817	"	John Sherman	Oh.	1897
Adams, J.Q.	Henry Clay	Ky.	1825	"	William R. Day	"	1898
Jackson	Martin Van Buren	N.Y...	1829	"	John Hay	D.C.	1898
"	Edward Livingston	La.	1831	Roosevelt, T.	"	"	1901
"	Louis McLane	Del.	1833	"	Elihu Root	N.Y.	1905
"	John Forsyth	Ga.	1834	"	Robert Bacon	"	1909
Van Buren	"	"	1837	Taft	"	"	1909
Harrison, W.H.	Daniel Webster	Mass.	1841	"	Philander C. Knox	Pa.	1909
Tyler	"	"	1841	Wilson	"	"	1913
"	Abel P. Upshur	Va.	1843	"	William J. Bryan	Neb.	1913
"	John C. Calhoun	S.C.	1844	"	Robert Lansing	N.Y.	1915
"	"	"	1845	"	Bainbridge Colby	"	1920
Polk	James Buchanan	Pa.	1845	Harding	Charles E. Hughes	"	1921
Taylor	"	"	1849	Coolidge	"	"	1923
				"	Frank B. Kellogg	Minn.	1925
	John M. Clayton	Del.	1849	Hoover	"	"	1929
Fillmore	"	"	1850	"	Henry L. Stimson	N.Y.	1929
"	Daniel Webster	Mass.	1850	Roosevelt, F.D.	Cordell Hull	Tenn.	1933
"	Edward Everett	"	1852	"	E.R. Stettinius Jr.	Va.	1944
Pierce	William L. Marcy	N.Y.	1853	Truman	"	"	1945
Buchanan	"	"	1857	"	James F. Byrnes	S.C.	1945
"	Lewis Cass	Mich.	1857	"	George C. Marshall.	Pa.	1947
"	Jeremiah S. Black	Pa.	1860	"	Dean G. Acheson	Conn.	1949
Lincoln	"	"	1861	Eisenhower	John Foster Dulles	N.Y.	1953
"	William H. Seward	N.Y.	1861	"	Christian A. Herter	Mass.	1959
Johnson, A.	"	"	1865	Kennedy	Dean Rusk	N.Y.	1961
Grant	Elihu B. Washburne	Ill.	1869	Johnson, L.B.	"	"	1963
"	Hamilton Fish	N.Y.	1869	Nixon	William P. Rogers	N.Y.	1969
Hayes	"	"	1877	"	Henry A. Kissinger	D.C.	1973
"	William M. Evarts	"	1877	Ford	"	"	1974
Garfield	"	"	1881	Carter	Cyrus R. Vance	N.Y.	1977
"	James G. Blaine	Me.	1881	"	Edmund S. Muskie	Me.	1980
Arthur	"	"	1881	Reagan	Alexander M. Haig Jr.	Conn.	1981
"	F.T. Frelinghuysen	N.J.	1881	"	George P. Shultz	Cal.	1982
				Bush	James A. Baker 3d	Tex..	1989

Secretaries of the Treasury

The Treasury Department was organized by act of Congress Sept. 2, 1789.

President	Secretary	Home	Apptd.	President	Secretary	Home	Apptd.
Washington	Alexander Hamilton	N.Y.	1789	Lincoln	William P. Fessenden	Me.	1864
"	Oliver Wolcott	Conn.	1795	"	Hugh McCulloch	Ind.	1865
Adams, J.	"	"	1797	Johnson, A.	"	"	1865
"	Samuel Dexter	Mass.	1801	Grant	George S. Boutwell	Mass..	1869
Jefferson	"	"	1801	"	William A. Richardson	Mass..	1873
"	Albert Gallatin	Pa.	1801	"	Benjamin H. Bristow	Ky.	1874
Madison	"	"	1809	"	Lot M. Morrill	Me.	1876
"	George W. Campbell	Tenn.	1814	Hayes	John Sherman	Oh.	1877
"	Alexander J. Dallas	Pa.	1814	Garfield	William Windom	Minn.	1881
"	William H. Crawford	Ga.	1816	Arthur	Charles J. Folger	N.Y.	1881
Monroe	"	"	1817	"	Walter Q. Gresham	Ind.	1884
Adams, J.Q.	Richard Rush	Pa.	1825	"	Hugh McCulloch	Ind.	1884
Jackson	Samuel D. Ingham	Pa.	1829	Cleveland	Daniel Manning	N.Y.	1885
"	Louis McLane	Del.	1831	Cleveland	Charles S. Fairchild.		1887
"	William J. Duane	Pa.	1833	Harrison, B.	William Windom	Minn.	1889
"	Roger B. Taney	Md.	1833	"	Charles Foster	Oh.	1891
"	Levi Woodbury	N.H.	1834	Cleveland	John G. Carlisle	Ky.	1893
Van Buren	"	"	1837	McKinley	Lyman J. Gage	Ill.	1897
Harrison, W.H.	Thomas Ewing	Oh.	1841	Roosevelt, T.	"	"	1901
Tyler	"	"	1841	"	Leslie M. Shaw	Ia.	1902
"	Walter Forward	Pa.	1841	"	George B. Cortelyou	N.Y.	1907
"	John C. Spencer	N.Y.	1843	Taft	Franklin MacVeagh	Ill.	1909
Tyler	George M. Bibb	Ky.	1844	Wilson	William G. McAdoo	N.Y.	1913
Polk	Robert J. Walker	Miss.	1845	"	Carter Glass	Va.	1918
Taylor	William M. Meredith	Pa.	1849	"	David F. Houston	Mo.	1920
Fillmore	Thomas Corwin	Oh.	1850	Harding	Andrew W. Mellon	Pa.	1921
Pierce	James Guthrie	Ky.	1853	Coolidge	"	"	1923
Buchanan	Howell Cobb	Ga.	1857	Hoover	"	"	1929
"	Phillip F. Thomas	Md.	1860	"	Ogden L. Mills	N.Y.	1932
"	John A. Dix	N.Y.	1861	Roosevelt, F.D.	William H. Woodin	"	1933
Lincoln	Salmon P. Chase	Oh.	1861	"	Henry Morgenthau, Jr.	"	1934

President	Secretary	Home	Apptd.	President	Secretary	Home	Apptd.
Truman	Fred M. Vinson	Ky.	1945	Nixon	George P. Shultz	Ill.	1972
"	John W. Snyder	Mo.	1946	"	William E. Simon	N.J.	1974
Eisenhower	George M. Humphrey	Oh.	1953	Ford	"	"	1974
"	Robert B. Anderson	Conn.	1957	Carter	W. Michael Blumenthal	Mich.	1977
Kennedy	C. Douglas Dillon	N.J.	1961	"	G. William Miller	R.I.	1979
Johnson, L.B.	"	"	1963	Reagan	Donald T. Regan	N.Y.	1981
"	Henry H. Fowler	Va.	1965	"	James A. Baker 3d	Tex.	1985
"	Joseph W. Barr	Ind.	1968	"	Nicholas F. Brady	N.J.	1988
Nixon	David M. Kennedy	Ill.	1969	Bush	"	"	1989
"	John B. Connally	Tex.	1971				

Secretaries of Defense

The Department of Defense, originally designated the National Military Establishment, was created Sept. 18, 1947. It is headed by the secretary of defense, who is a member of the president's cabinet.

The departments of the army, of the navy, and of the air force function within the Department of Defense, and their respective secretaries are no longer members of the president's cabinet.

President	Secretary	Home	Apptd.	President	Secretary	Home	Apptd.
Truman	James V. Forrestal	N.Y.	1947	Nixon	Melvin R. Laird	Wis.	1969
"	Louis A. Johnson	W.Va.	1949	"	Elliot L. Richardson	Mass.	1973
"	George C. Marshall	Pa.	1950	"	James R. Schlesinger	Va.	1973
"	Robert A. Lovett	N.Y.	1951	Ford	"	"	1974
Eisenhower	Charles E. Wilson	Mich.	1953	"	Donald H. Rumsfeld	Ill.	1975
"	Neil H. McElroy	Oh.	1957	Carter	Harold Brown	Cal.	1977
"	Thomas S. Gates Jr.	Pa.	1959	Reagan	Caspar W. Weinberger	Cal.	1981
Kennedy	Robert S. McNamara	Mich.	1961	"	Frank C. Carlucci	Pa.	1987
Johnson, L.B.	"	"	1963	Bush	Richard B. Cheney	Wyo.	1989
"	Clark M. Clifford	Md.	1968				

Secretaries of War

The War (and Navy) Department was created by act of Congress Aug. 7, 1789, and Gen. Henry Knox was commissioned secretary of war under that act Sept. 12, 1789.

President	Secretary	Home	Apptd.	President	Secretary	Home	Apptd.
Washington	Henry Knox	Mass.	1789	Grant	John A. Rawlins	Ill.	1869
"	Timothy Pickering	Pa.	1795	"	William T. Sherman	Oh.	1869
"	James McHenry	Md.	1796	"	William W. Belknap	Ia.	1869
Adams, J.	"	"	1797	"	Alphonso Taft	Oh.	1876
"	Samuel Dexter	Mass.	1800	"	James D. Cameron	Pa.	1876
Jefferson	Henry Dearborn	"	1801	Hayes	George W. McCrary	Ia.	1877
Madison	William Eustis	Mass.	1809	"	Alexander Ramsey	Minn.	1879
"	John Armstrong	N.Y.	1813	Garfield	Robert T. Lincoln	Ill.	1881
Madison	James Monroe	Va.	1814	Arthur	"	"	1881
"	William H. Crawford	Ga.	1815	Cleveland	William C. Endicott	Mass.	1885
Monroe	John C. Calhoun	S.C.	1817	Harrison, B.	Redfield Proctor	Vt.	1889
Adams, J.Q.	James Barbour	Va.	1825	"	Stephen B. Elkins	W.Va.	1891
"	Peter B. Porter	N.Y.	1828	Cleveland	Daniel S. Lamont	N.Y.	1893
Jackson	John H. Eaton	Tenn.	1829	McKinley	Russel A. Alger	Mich.	1897
"	Lewis Cass	Mich.	1831	"	Elihu Root	N.Y.	1899
"	Benjamin F. Butler	N.Y.	1837	Roosevelt, T.	"	"	1901
Van Buren	Joel R. Poinsett	S.C.	1837	"	William H. Taft	Oh.	1904
Harrison, W.H.	John Bell	Tenn.	1841	"	Luke E. Wright	Tenn.	1908
Tyler	John Bell	Tenn	1841	Taft	Jacob M. Dickinson	Tenn.	1909
Tyler	John C. Spencer	N.Y.	1841	"	Henry L. Stimson	N.Y.	1911
"	James M. Porter	Pa.	1843	Wilson	Lindley M. Garrison	N.J.	1913
"	William Wilkins	"	1844	"	Newton D. Baker	Oh.	1916
Polk	William L. Marcy	N.Y.	1845	Harding	John W. Weeks	Mass.	1921
Taylor	George W. Crawford	Ga.	1849	Coolidge	"	"	1923
Fillmore	Charles M. Conrad	La.	1850	"	Dwight F. Davis	Mo.	1925
Pierce	Jefferson Davis	Miss.	1853	Hoover	James W. Good	Ill.	1929
Buchanan	John B. Floyd	Va.	1857	Hoover	Patrick J. Hurley	Okla.	1929
"	Joseph Holt	Ky.	1861	Roosevelt, F.D.	George H. Dern	Ut.	1933
Lincoln	Simon Cameron	Pa.	1861	"	Harry H. Woodring	Kan.	1937
"	Edwin M. Stanton	Pa.	1862	Roosevelt, F.D.	Henry L. Stimson	N.Y.	1940
Johnson, A.	"	"	1865	Truman	Robert P. Patterson	N.Y.	1945
"	John M. Schofield	Ill.	1868	"	*Kenneth C. Royall	N.C.	1947

Secretaries of the Navy

The Navy Department was created by act of Congress Apr. 30, 1798.

President	Secretary	Home	Apptd.	President	Secretary	Home	Apptd.
Adams, J.	Benjamin Stoddert	Md.	1798	Van Buren	Mahlon Dickerson	N.J.	1837
Jefferson	"	"	1801	"	James K. Paulding	N.Y.	1838
"	Robert Smith	"	1801	Harrison, W.H.	George E. Badger	N.C.	1841
Madison	Paul Hamilton	S.C.	1809	Tyler	"	"	1841
"	William Jones	Pa.	1813	"	Abel P. Upshur	Va.	1841
"	Benjamin Williams Crowninshield	Mass.	1814	"	David Henshaw	Mass.	1843
Monroe	"	"	1817	"	Thomas W. Gilmer	Va.	1844
"	Smith Thompson	N.Y.	1818	"	John Y. Mason	"	1844
"	Samuel L. Southard	N.J.	1823	Polk	George Bancroft	Mass.	1845
Adams, J.Q.	"	"	1825	"	John Y. Mason	Va.	1846
Jackson	John Branch	N.C.	1829	Taylor	William B. Preston	Va.	1849
"	Levi Woodbury	N.H.	1831	Fillmore	William A. Graham	N.C.	1850
"	Mahlon Dickerson	N.J.	1834	"	John P. Kennedy	Md.	1852
				Pierce	James C. Dobbin	N.C.	1853

President	Secretary	Home	Apptd.	President	Secretary	Home	Apptd.
Buchanan	Isaac Toucey	Conn.	1857	Roosevelt, T.	Paul Morton	Ill.	1904
Lincoln	Gideon Welles	Conn.	1861	"	Charles J. Bonaparte	Md.	1905
Johnson, A.	"	"	1865	"	Victor H. Metcalf	Cal.	1906
Grant	Adolph E. Borie	Pa.	1869	"	Truman H. Newberry	Mich.	1908
"	George M. Robeson	N.J.	1869	Taft	George von L. Meyer	Mass.	1909
Hayes	Richard W. Thompson	Ind.	1877	Wilson	Josephus Daniels	N.C.	1913
"	Nathan Goff Jr.	W.Va.	1881	Harding	Edwin Denby	Mich.	1921
Garfield	William H. Hunt	La.	1881	Coolidge	"	"	1923
Arthur	William E. Chandler	N.H.	1882	"	Curtis D. Wilbur	Cal.	1924
Cleveland	William C. Whitney	N.Y.	1885	Hoover	Charles Francis Adams	Mass.	1929
Harrison, B.	Benjamin F. Tracy	N.Y.	1889	Roosevelt, F.D.	Claude A. Swanson	Va.	1933
Cleveland	Hilary A. Herbert	Ala.	1893	"	Charles Edison	N.J.	1940
McKinley	John D. Long	Mass.	1897	"	Frank Knox	Ill.	1940
Roosevelt, T.	"	"	1901	"	*James V. Forrestal	N.Y.	1944
"	William H. Moody	"	1902	Truman	"	"	1945

*Last members of Cabinet. The War Department became the Department of the Army and it and the Navy Department became branches of the Department of Defense, created Sept. 18, 1947.

Attorneys General

The office of attorney general was organized by act of Congress Sept. 24, 1789. The Department of Justice was created June 22, 1870.

President	Attorney General	Home	Apptd.	President	Attorney General	Home	Apptd.
Washington	Edmund Randolph	Va.	1789	Cleveland	Augustus Garland	Ark.	1885
"	William Bradford	Pa.	1794	Harrison, B.	William H. H. Miller	Ind.	1889
"	Charles Lee	Va.	1795	Cleveland	Richard Olney	Mass.	1893
Adams, J.	"	"	1797	"	Judson Harmon	Oh.	1895
Jefferson	Levi Lincoln	Mass.	1801	McKinley	Joseph McKenna	Cal.	1897
"	John Breckenridge	Ky.	1805	"	John W. Griggs	N.J.	1898
"	Caesar A. Rodney	Del.	1807	"	Philander C. Knox	Pa.	1901
Madison	"	"	1809	Roosevelt, T.	"	"	1901
"	William Pinkney	Md.	1811	"	William H. Moody	Mass.	1904
"	Richard Rush	Pa.	1814	"	Charles J. Bonaparte	Md.	1906
Monroe	"	"	1817	Taft	George W. Wickersham	N.Y.	1909
"	William Wirt	Va.	1817	Wilson	J.C. McReynolds	Tenn.	1913
Adams, J.Q.	"	"	1825	"	Thomas W. Gregory	Tex.	1914
Jackson	John M. Berrien	Ga.	1829	"	A. Mitchell Palmer	Pa.	1919
"	Roger B. Taney	Md.	1831	Harding	Harry M. Daugherty	Oh.	1921
"	Benjamin F. Butler	N.Y.	1833	Coolidge	"	"	1923
Van Buren	"	"	1837	"	Harlan F. Stone	N.Y.	1924
"	Felix Grundy	Tenn.	1838	"	John G. Sargent	Vt.	1925
"	Henry D. Gilpin	Pa.	1840	Hoover	William D. Mitchell	Minn.	1929
Harrison, W.H.	John J. Crittenden	Ky.	1841	Roosevelt, F.D.	Homer S. Cummings	Conn.	1933
Tyler	"	"	1841	"	Frank Murphy	Mich.	1939
"	Hugh S. Legare	S.C.	1841	"	Robert H. Jackson	N.Y.	1940
"	John Nelson	Md.	1843	"	Francis Biddle	Pa.	1941
Polk	John Y. Mason	Va.	1845	Truman	Thomas C. Clark	Tex.	1945
"	Nathan Clifford	Me.	1846	"	J. Howard McGrath	R.I.	1949
"	Isaac Toucey	Conn.	1848	"	J.P. McGranery	Pa.	1952
Taylor	Reverdy Johnson	Md.	1849	Eisenhower	Herbert Brownell Jr.	N.Y.	1953
Fillmore	John J. Crittenden	Ky.	1850	"	William P. Rogers	Md.	1957
Pierce	Caleb Cushing	Mass.	1853	Kennedy	Robert F. Kennedy	Mass.	1961
Buchanan	Jeremiah S. Black	Pa.	1857	Johnson, L.B.	"	"	1963
"	Edwin M. Stanton	Pa.	1860	"	N. de B. Katzenbach	Ill.	1964
Lincoln	Edward Bates	Mo.	1861	"	Ramsey Clark	Tex.	1967
"	James Speed	Ky.	1864	Nixon	John N. Mitchell	N.Y.	1969
Johnson, A.	"	"	1865	"	Richard G. Kleindienst	Ariz.	1972
"	Henry Stanbery	Oh.	1866	"	Elliot L. Richardson	Mass.	1973
"	William M. Evarts	N.Y.	1868	"	William B. Saxbe	Oh.	1974
Grant	Ebenezer R. Hoar	Mass.	1869	Ford	"	"	1974
"	Amos T. Akerman	Ga.	1870	"	Edward H. Levi	Ill.	1975
"	George H. Williams	Ore.	1871	Carter	Griffin B. Bell	Ga.	1977
"	Edwards Pierrepont	N.Y.	1875	"	Benjamin R. Civiletti	Md.	1979
"	Alphonso Taft	Oh.	1876	Reagan	William French Smith	Cal.	1981
Hayes	Charles Devens	Mass.	1877	"	Edwin Meese 3d	Cal.	1985
Garfield	Wayne MacVeagh	Pa.	1881	"	Richard Thornburgh	Pa	1988
Arthur	Benjamin H. Brewster	"	1881	Bush	"	"	1989

Secretaries of the Interior

The Department of Interior was created by act of Congress Mar. 3, 1849.

President	Secretary	Home	Apptd.	President	Secretary	Home	Apptd.
Taylor	Thomas Ewing	Oh.	1849	Grant	Jacob D. Cox	Oh.	1869
Fillmore	Thomas M. T. McKennan	Pa.	1850	"	Columbus Delano		1870
Fillmore	Alex H. H. Stuart	Va.	1850	"	Zachariah Chandler	Mich.	1875
Pierce	Robert McClelland	Mich.	1853	Hayes	Carl Schurz	Mo.	1877
Buchanan	Jacob Thompson	Miss.	1857	Garfield	Samuel J. Kirkwood	Ia.	1881
Lincoln	Caleb B. Smith	Ind.	1861	Arthur	Henry M. Teller	Col.	1882
"	John P. Usher	"	1863	Cleveland	Lucius Q.C. Lamar	Miss.	1885
Johnson, A.	"	"	1865	"	William F. Vilas	Wis.	1888
"	James Harlan	Ia.	1865	Harrison, B.	John W. Noble	Mo.	1889
"	Orville H. Browning	Ill.	1866	Cleveland	Hoke Smith	Ga.	1893

President	Secretary	Home	Apptd.	President	Secretary	Home	Apptd.
Cleveland	David R. Francis	Mo.	1896	Truman	Julius A. Krug	Wis.	1946
McKinley	Cornelius N. Bliss	N.Y.	1897	"	Oscar L. Chapman	Col.	1949
"	Ethan A. Hitchcock	Mo.	1898	Eisenhower	Douglas McKay	Ore.	1953
Roosevelt, T.	"	"	1901	"	Fred A Seaton	Neb.	1956
"	James R. Garfield	Oh.	1907	Kennedy	Stewart L. Udall	Ariz.	1961
Taft	Richard A. Ballinger	Wash.	1909	Johnson, L.B.	"	"	1963
"	Walter L. Fisher	Ill.	1911	Nixon	Walter J. Hickel	Alas.	1969
Wilson	Franklin K. Lane	Cal.	1913	"	Rogers C.B. Morton	Md.	1971
"	John B. Payne	Ill.	1920	Ford	"		1974
Harding	Albert B. Fall	N.M.	1921	"	Stanley K. Hathaway	Wyo.	1975
"	Hubert Work	Col.	1923	"	Thomas S. Kleppe	N.D.	1975
Coolidge	"	"	1923	Carter	Cecil D. Andrus	Ida.	1977
"	Roy O. West	Ill.	1929	Reagan	James G. Watt	Col.	1981
Hoover	Ray Lyman Wilbur	Cal.	1929	"	William P. Clark	Cal.	1983
Roosevelt, F.D.	Harold L. Ickes	Ill.	1933	"	Donald P. Hodel	Ore.	1985
Truman	"	"	1945	Bush	Manuel Lujan	N.M.	1989

Secretaries of Agriculture

The Department of Agriculture was created by act of Congress May 15, 1862. On Feb. 8, 1889, its commissioner was re-named secretary of agriculture and became a member of the cabinet.

President	Secretary	Home	Apptd.	President	Secretary	Home	Apptd.
Cleveland	Norman J. Colman	Mo.	1889	"	Claude R. Wickard	Ind.	1940
Harrison, B.	Jeremiah M. Rusk	Wis.	1889	Truman	Clinton P. Anderson	N.M.	1945
Cleveland	J. Sterling Morton	Neb.	1893	"	Charles F. Brannan	Col.	1948
McKinley	James Wilson	Ia.	1897	Eisenhower	Ezra Taft Benson	Ut.	1953
Roosevelt, T.	"	"	1901	Kennedy	Orville L. Freeman	Minn.	1961
Taft	"	"	1909	Johnson, L.B.	"	"	1963
Wilson	David F. Houston	Mo.	1913	Nixon	Clifford M. Hardin	Ind.	1969
"	Edwin T. Meredith	Ia.	1920	"	Earl L. Butz	Ind.	1971
Harding	Henry C. Wallace	Ia.	1921	Ford	"	"	1974
Coolidge	"	"	1923	"	John A. Knebel	Va.	1976
"	Howard M. Gore	W.Va.	1924	Carter	Bob Bergland	Minn.	1977
"	William M. Jardine	Kan.	1925	Reagan	John R. Block	Ill.	1981
Hoover	Arthur M. Hyde	Mo.	1929	"	Richard E. Lyng	Cal.	1986
Roosevelt, F.D.	Henry A. Wallace	Ia.	1933	Bush	Clayton K. Yeutter	Neb.	1989

Secretaries of Commerce and Labor

The Department of Commerce and Labor, created by Congress Feb. 14, 1903, was divided by Congress Mar. 4, 1913, into separate departments of Commerce and Labor. The secretary of each was made a cabinet member.

President	Secretary	Home	Apptd.	President	Secretary	Home	Apptd.
Secretaries of Commerce and Labor				**Secretaries of Commerce**			
Roosevelt, T.	George B. Cortelyou	N.Y.	1903	Wilson	William C. Redfield	N.Y.	1913
"	Victor H. Metcalf	Cal.	1904	"	Joshua W. Alexander	Mo.	1919
"	Oscar S. Straus	N.Y.	1906	Harding	Herbert C. Hoover	Cal.	1921
Taft	Charles Nagel	Mo.	1909	Coolidge	"	"	1923
Secretaries of Labor				"	William F. Whiting	Mass.	1928
Wilson	William B. Wilson	Pa.	1913	Hoover	Robert P. Lamont	Ill.	1929
Harding	James J. Davis	Pa.	1921	"	Roy D. Chapin	Mich.	1932
Coolidge	"	"	1923	Roosevelt, F.D.	Daniel C. Roper	S.C.	1933
Hoover	"	"	1929	"	Harry L. Hopkins	N.Y.	1939
"	William N. Doak	Va.	1930	"	Jesse Jones	Tex.	1940
Roosevelt, F.D.	Frances Perkins	N.Y.	1933	"	Henry A. Wallace	Ia.	1945
Truman	L.B. Schwellenbach	Wash.	1945	Truman	"		1945
"	Maurice J. Tobin	Mass.	1949	"	W. Averell Harriman	N.Y.	1947
Eisenhower	Martin P. Durkin	Ill.	1953	"	Charles Sawyer	Oh.	1948
"	James P. Mitchell	N.J.	1953	Eisenhower	Sinclair Weeks	Mass.	1953
Kennedy	Arthur J. Goldberg	Ill.	1961	"	Lewis L. Strauss	N.Y.	1958
"	W. Willard Wirtz	Ill.	1962	"	Frederick H. Mueller	Mich.	1959
Johnson, L.B.	"	"	1963	Kennedy	Luther H. Hodges	N.C.	1961
Nixon	George P. Shultz	Ill	1969	Johnson, L.B.	"	"	1963
"	James D. Hodgson	Cal.	1970	"	Jonn T. Connor	N.J.	1965
"	Peter J. Brennan	N.Y.	1973	"	Alex B. Trowbridge	N.J.	1967
Ford	"		1974	"	Cyrus R. Smith	N.Y.	1968
"	John T. Dunlop	Cal.	1975	Nixon	Maurice H. Stans	Minn.	1969
"	W.J. Usery Jr.	Ga.	1976	"	Peter G. Peterson	Ill.	1972
Carter	F. Ray Marshall	Tex.	1977	"	Frederick B. Dent	S.C.	1973
Reagan	Raymond J. Donovan	N.J.	1981	Ford	"	"	1974
"	William E. Brock	Tenn.	1985	"	Rogers C.B. Morton	Md.	1975
"	Ann D. McLaughlin	D.C.	1987	"	Elliot L. Richardson	Mass.	1975
Bush	Elizabeth Hanford Dole	N.C.	1989	Carter	Juanita M. Kreps	N.C.	1977
				"	Philip M. Klutznick	D.C.	1979
				Reagan	Malcolm Baldrige	Conn.	1981
				"	C. William Verity Jr.	Oh.	1987
				Bush	Robert A. Mosbacher	Tex.	1989

Secretaries of Housing and Urban Development

The Department of Housing and Urban Development was created by act of Congress Sept. 9, 1965.

President	Secretary	Home	Apptd.	President	Secretary	Home	Apptd.
Johnson, L.B.	Robert C. Weaver	Wash.	1966	Ford	Carla Anderson Hills	Cal.	1975
"	Robert C. Wood	Mass.	1969	Carter	Patricia Roberts Harris	D.C.	1977
Nixon	George W. Romney	Mich.	1969	"	Moon Landrieu	La.	1979
"	James T. Lynn	Oh.	1973	Reagan	Samuel R. Pierce Jr.	N.Y.	1981
Ford	"	"	1974	Bush	Jack F. Kemp	N.Y.	1989

Secretaries of Transportation

The Department of Transportation was created by act of Congress Oct. 15, 1966.

President	Secretary	Home	Apptd.	President	Secretary	Home	Apptd.
Johnson, L.B.	Alan S. Boyd	Fla.	1966	Carter	Neil E. Goldschmidt	Ore.	1979
Nixon	John A. Volpe	Mass.	1969	Reagan	Andrew L. Lewis Jr.	Pa.	1981
"	Claude S. Brinegar	Cal.	1973	"	Elizabeth Hanford Dole	N.C.	1983
Ford	Claude S. Brinegar	Cal.	1974	"	James H. Burnley	N.C.	1987
"	William T. Coleman Jr.	Pa.	1975	Bush	Samuel K. Skinner	Ill.	1989
Carter	Brock Adams	Wash.	1977				

Secretaries of Energy

The Department of Energy was created by federal law Aug. 4, 1977.

President	Secretary	Home	Apptd.	President	Secretary	Home	Apptd.
Carter	James R. Schlesinger	Va.	1977	Reagan	Donald P. Hodel	Ore.	1982
"	Charles Duncan Jr.	Wyo.	1979	"	John S. Herrington	Cal.	1985
Reagan	James B. Edwards	S.C.	1981	Bush	James D. Watkins	Cal.	1989

Secretaries of Health, Education, and Welfare

The Department of Health, Education and Welfare, created by Congress Apr. 11, 1953, was divided by Congress Sept. 27, 1979, into separate departments of Education, and Health and Human Services. The secretary of each is a cabinet member.

President	Secretary	Home	Apptd.	President	Secretary	Home	Apptd.
Eisenhower	Oveta Culp Hobby	Tex.	1953	Nixon	Robert H. Finch	Cal.	1969
"	Marion B. Folsom	N.Y.	1955	"	Elliot L. Richardson	Mass.	1970
"	Arthur S. Flemming	Oh.	1958	"	Caspar W. Weinberger	Cal.	1973
Kennedy	Abraham A. Ribicoff	Conn.	1961	Ford	"	"	1974
"	Anthony J. Celebrezze	Oh.	1962	"	Forrest D. Mathews	Ala.	1975
Johnson, L.B.	"	"	1963	Carter	Joseph A. Califano, Jr.	D.C.	1977
"	John W. Gardner	N.Y.	1965	"	Patricia Roberts Harris	D.C.	1979
Johnson, L.B.	Wilbur J. Cohen	Mich.	1968				

Secretaries of Health and Human Services

President	Secretary	Home	Apptd.	President	Secretary	Home	Apptd.
Carter	Patricia Roberts Harris	D.C.	1979	Reagan	Otis R. Bowen	Ind.	1985
Reagan	Richard S. Schweiker	Pa.	1981	Bush	Louis W. Sullivan	Ga.	1989
"	Margaret M. Heckler	Mass.	1983				

Secretaries of Education

President	Secretary	Home	Apptd.	President	Secretary	Home	Apptd.
Carter	Shirley Hufstedler	Cal.	1979	Reagan	Lauro F. Cavazos	Tex.	1988
Reagan	Terrel Bell	Ut.	1981	Bush	"	"	1989
Reagan	William J. Bennett	N.Y.	1985				

Secretaries of Veterans Affairs

The Department of Veterans Affairs was created Oct. 25, 1988 when Pres. Reagan signed a bill which made the Veterans Administration into a cabinet post as of Mar. 15, 1989.

President	Secretary	Home	Apptd.
Bush	Edward J. Derwinski	Ill.	1989

Librarians of Congress

Librarian	Served	Appointed by President	Librarian	Served	Appointed by President
John J. Beckley	1802-1807	Jefferson	Herbert Putnam	1899-1939	McKinley
Patrick Magruder	1807-1815	Jefferson	Archibald MacLeish	1939-1944	F. Roosevelt
George Watterston	1815-1829	Madison	Luther H. Evans	1945-1953	Truman
John Silva Meehan	1829-1861	Jackson	L. Quincy Mumford	1954-1974	Eisenhower
John G. Stephenson	1861-1864	Lincoln	Daniel J. Boorstin	1975-1987	Ford
Ainsworth Rand Spofford	1864-1897	Lincoln	James H. Billington	1987-	Reagan
John Russell Young	1897-1899	McKinley			

Presidents Pro Tempore of the Senate

Until 1890, presidents "pro tem" were named "for the occasion only." Beginning with that year, they have served "until the Senate otherwise ordered." Sen. John J. Ingalls, chosen under the old rule in 1887, was again elected, under the new rule, in 1890. Party designations are D, Democrat; R, Republican.

Name	Party	State	Elected	Name	Party	State	Elected
John J. Ingalls	R.	Kan.	Apr. 3, 1890	William H. King	D.	Ut.	Nov. 19, 1940
Charles F. Manderson	R.	Neb.	Mar. 2, 1891	Pat Harrison	D.	Miss.	Jan. 6, 1941
Isham G. Harris	D.	Tenn.	Mar. 22, 1893	Carter Glass	D.	Va.	July 10, 1941
Matt W. Ransom	D.	N.C.	Jan. 7, 1895	Kenneth McKellar	D.	Tenn.	Jan. 6, 1945
Isham G. Harris	D.	Tenn.	Jan. 10, 1895	Arthur H. Vandenberg	R.	Mich.	Jan. 4, 1947
William P. Frye	R.	Me.	Feb. 7, 1896	Kenneth McKellar	D.	Tenn.	Jan. 3, 1949
Charles Curtis	R.	Kan.	Dec. 4, 1911	Styles Bridges	R.	N.H.	Jan. 3, 1953
Augustus O. Bacon	D.	Ga.	Jan. 15, 1912	Walter F. George	D.	Ga.	Jan. 5, 1955
Jacob H. Gallinger	R.	N.H.	Feb. 12, 1912	Carl Hayden	D.	Ariz.	Jan. 3, 1957
Henry Cabot Lodge	R.	Mass.	Mar. 25, 1912	Richard B. Russell	D.	Ga.	Jan. 3, 1969
Frank B. Brandegee	R.	Conn.	May 25, 1912	Allen J. Ellender	D.	La.	Jan. 22, 1971
James P. Clarke	D.	Ark.	Mar. 13, 1913	James O. Eastland	D.	Miss.	July 28, 1972
Willard Saulsbury	D.	Del.	Dec. 14, 1916	Warren G. Magnuson	D.	Wash.	Jan. 23, 1979
Albert B. Cummins	R.	Ia.	May 19, 1919	Strom Thurmond	R.	S.C.	Jan. 5, 1981
George H. Moses	R.	N.H.	Mar. 6, 1925	John C. Stennis	D.	Miss.	Jan. 6, 1987
Key Pittman	D.	Nev.	Mar. 9, 1933	Robert C. Byrd	D.	W.Va.	Jan. 4, 1989

Speakers of the House of Representatives

Party designations: A, American; D, Democratic; DR, Democratic Republican; F, Federalist; R, Republican; W, Whig. *Served only one day.

Name	Party	State	Tenure	Name	Party	State	Tenure
Frederick Muhlenberg	F	Pa.	1789-1791	*Theodore M. Pomeroy	R	N.Y.	1869-1869
Jonathan Trumbull	F	Conn.	1791-1793	James G. Blaine	R	Me.	1869-1875
Frederick Muhlenberg	F	Pa.	1793-1795	Michael C. Kerr	D	Ind.	1875-1876
Jonathan Dayton	F	N.J.	1795-1799	Samuel J. Randall	D	Pa.	1876-1881
Theodore Sedgwick	F	Mass.	1799-1801	Joseph W. Keifer	R	Oh.	1881-1883
Nathaniel Macon	DR	N.C.	1801-1807	John G. Carlisle	D	Ky.	1883-1889
Joseph B. Varnum	DR	Mass.	1807-1811	Thomas B. Reed	R	Me.	1889-1891
Henry Clay	DR	Ky.	1811-1814	Charles F. Crisp	D	Ga.	1891-1895
Langdon Cheves	DR	S.C.	1814-1815	Thomas B. Reed	R	Me.	1895-1899
Henry Clay	DR	Ky.	1815-1820	David B. Henderson	R	Ia.	1899-1903
John W. Taylor	DR	N.Y.	1820-1821	Joseph G. Cannon	R	Ill.	1903-1911
Philip P. Barbour	DR	Va.	1821-1823	Champ Clark	D	Mo.	1911-1919
Henry Clay	DR	Ky.	1823-1825	Frederick H. Gillett	R	Mass.	1919-1925
John W. Taylor	D	N.Y.	1825-1827	Nicholas Longworth	R	Oh.	1925-1931
Andrew Stevenson	D	Va.	1827-1834	John N. Garner	D	Tex.	1931-1933
John Bell	D	Tenn.	1834-1835	Henry T. Rainey	D	Ill.	1933-1935
James K. Polk	D	Tenn.	1835-1839	Joseph W. Byrns	D	Tenn.	1935-1936
Robert M. T. Hunter	D	Va.	1839-1841	William B. Bankhead	D	Ala.	1936-1940
John White	W	Ky.	1841-1843	Sam Rayburn	D	Tex.	1940-1947
John W. Jones	D	Va.	1843-1845	Joseph W. Martin Jr.	R	Mass.	1947-1949
John W. Davis	D	Ind.	1845-1847	Sam Rayburn	D	Tex.	1949-1953
Robert C. Winthrop	W	Mass.	1847-1849	Joseph W. Martin Jr.	R	Mass.	1953-1955
Howell Cobb	D	Ga.	1849-1851	Sam Rayburn	D	Tex.	1955-1961
Linn Boyd	D	Ky.	1851-1855	John W. McCormack	D	Mass.	1962-1971
Nathaniel P. Banks	A	Mass.	1856-1857	Carl Albert	D	Okla.	1971-1977
James L. Orr	D	S.C.	1857-1859	Thomas P. O'Neill Jr.	D	Mass.	1977-1987
William Pennington	R	N.J.	1860-1861	James Wright	D	Tex.	1987-1989
Galusha A. Grow	R	Pa.	1861-1863	Thomas S. Foley	D	Wash.	1989-
Schuyler Colfax	R	Ind.	1863-1869				

National Political Conventions: 1960-1988

Democratic		Republican	
Opening date	Site	Opening date	Site
July 11, 1960	Los Angeles	July 25, 1960	Chicago
Aug. 24, 1964	Atlantic City	July 13, 1964	San Francisco
Aug. 26, 1968	Chicago	Aug. 5, 1968	Miami Beach
July 10, 1972	Miami Beach	Aug. 21, 1972	Miami Beach
July 12, 1976	New York City	Aug. 16, 1976	Kansas City, Mo.
Aug. 11, 1980	New York City	July 14, 1980	Detroit
July 16, 1984	San Francisco	Aug. 20, 1984	Dallas
July 18, 1988	Atlanta	Aug. 15, 1988	New Orleans

Burial Places of the Presidents

Washington	Mt. Vernon, Va.	Fillmore	Buffalo, N.Y.	T. Roosevelt	Oyster Bay, N.Y.
J. Adams	Quincy, Mass.	Pierce	Concord, N.H.	Taft	Arlington Nat'l. Cem'y.
Jefferson	Charlottesville, Va.	Buchanan	Lancaster, Pa.	Wilson	Washington Cathedral
Madison	Montpelier Station, Va.	Lincoln	Springfield, Ill.	Harding	Marion, Oh.
Monroe	Richmond, Va.	A. Johnson	Greeneville, Tenn.	Coolidge	Plymouth, Vt.
J.Q. Adams	Quincy, Mass.	Grant	New York City	Hoover	West Branch, Ia.
Jackson	Nashville, Tenn.	Hayes	Fremont, Oh.	F.D. Roosevelt	Hyde Park, N.Y.
Van Buren	Kinderhook, N.Y.	Garfield	Cleveland, Oh.	Truman	Independence, Mo.
W.H. Harrison	North Bend, Oh.	Arthur	Albany, N.Y.	Eisenhower	Abilene, Kan.
Tyler	Richmond, Va.	Cleveland	Princeton, N.J.	Kennedy	Arlington Nat'l. Cem'y.
Polk	Nashville, Tenn.	B. Harrison	Indianapolis, Ind.	L.B. Johnson	Stonewall, Tex.
Taylor	Louisville, Ky.	McKinley	Canton, Oh.		

Federal Bureau of Investigation

The Federal Bureau of Investigation was created July 26. 1908 and was referred to as Office of Chief Examiner. It became the Bureau of Investigation (Mar. 26, 1909), United States Bureau of Investigation (July 1, 1932), Division of Investigation (Aug. 10, 1933), and Federal Bureau of Investigation (July 1, 1935).

Director	Assumed office	Director	Assumed office
Stanley W. Finch	July 26, 1908	L. Patrick Gray, act.	May 3, 1972
A(lexander) Bruce Bielaski	Apr. 30, 1912	William D. Ruckelshaus, act.	Apr. 27, 1973
William E. Allen, act.	Feb. 10, 1919	Clarence M. Kelley	July 9, 1973
William J. Flynn	July 1, 1919	William H. Webster	Feb. 23, 1978
William J. Burns	Aug. 22, 1921	John E. Otto, act.	May 27, 1987
J. Edgar Hoover, act.	May 10, 1924	William S. Sessions	Nov. 2, 1987
J. Edgar Hoover	Dec. 10, 1924		

Central Intelligence Agency

On June 13, 1942 President Roosevelt established the Office of Strategic Services (OSS) and named William J. Donovan as its director. The OSS was disbanded Oct. 1, 1945 and its functions absorbed by the State and War departments. President Truman, Jan. 22, 1946, established the Central Intelligence Agency Group (CIG) to operate under the direction of the National Intelligence Authority (NIA). The National Security Act of 1947 replaced the NIA with the National Security Council and the CIG with the Central Intelligence Agency.

Director	Served	Appointed by President	Director	Served	Appointed by President
Adm. Sidney W. Souers	1946	Truman	Richard Helms	1966-1973	Johnson
Gen. Hoyt S. Vandenberg	1946-1947	Truman	James R. Schlesinger	1973	Nixon
Adm. Roscoe H. Hillenkoetter	1947-1950	Truman	William E. Colby	1973-1976	Nixon
Gen. Walter Bedell Smith	1950-1953	Truman	George Bush	1976-1977	Ford
Allen W. Dulles	1953-1961	Eisenhower	Adm. Stansfield Turner	1977-1981	Carter
John A. McCone	1961-1965	Kennedy	William J. Casey	1981-1987	Reagan
Adm. William F. Raborn Jr.	1965-1966	Johnson	William H. Webster	1987-	Reagan

Wives and Children of the Presidents

Listed in order of presidential administrations.

Name (Born–died, married)	State	Sons/ daughters	Name (Born–died, married)	State	Sons/ daughters
Martha Dandridge Custis Washington (1732-1802, 1759)	Va.	None	Caroline Lavinia Scott Harrison (1832-1892, 1853)	Oh.	1/1
Abigail Smith Adams (1744-1818, 1764).	Mass.	3/2	Mary Scott Lord Dimmick Harrison (1858-1948, 1896)	Pa.	../1
Martha Wayles Skelton Jefferson (1748-1782, 1772)	Va.	1/5	Ida Saxton McKinley (1847-1907, 1871).	Oh.	../2
Dorothea "Dolley" Payne Todd Madison (1768-1849, 1794)	N.C.	None	Alice Hathaway Lee Roosevelt (1861-1884, 1880)	Mass.	../1
Elizabeth Kortright Monroe (1768-1830, 1786)	N.Y.	../2 (A)	Edith Kermit Carow Roosevelt (1861-1948, 1886)	Conn.	4/1
Louise Catherine Johnson Adams (1775-1852, 1797)	Md.(B)	3/1	Helen Herron Taft (1861-1943, 1886)	Oh.	2/1
Rachel Donelson Robards Jackson (1767-1828, 1791)	Va.	None	Ellen Louise Axson Wilson (1860-1914, 1885)	Ga.	../3
Hannah Hoes Van Buren (1783-1819, 1807)	N.Y.	4/...	Edith Bolling Galt Wilson (1872-1961, 1915)	Va.	None
Anna Symmes Harrison (1775-1864, 1795)	N.J.	6/4	Florence Kling De Wolfe Harding (1860-1924, 1891)	Oh.	None
Letitia Christian Tyler (1790-1842, 1813)	Va.	3/5	Grace Ana Goodhue Coolidge (1879-1957, 1905)	Vt.	2/...
Julia Gardiner Tyler (1820-1889, 1844)	N.Y.	5/2	Lou Henry Hoover (1875-1944, 1899)	la.	2/...
Sarah Childress Polk (1803-1891, 1824)	Tenn.	None	Anna Eleanor Roosevelt Roosevelt (1884-1962, 1905)	N.Y.	4/1 (A)
Margaret Smith Taylor (1788-1852, 1810)	Md.	1/5	Bess Wallace Truman (1885-1982, 1919)	Mo.	../1
Abigail Powers Fillmore (1798-1853, 1826)	N.Y.	1/1	Mamie Geneva Doud Eisenhower (1896-1979, 1916)	la.	1/...(A)
Caroline Carmichael McIntosh Fillmore (1813-1881, 1858)	N.J.	None	Jacqueline Lee Bouvier Kennedy (b. 1929, 1953)	N.Y.	1/1 (A)
Jane Means Appleton Pierce (1806-1863, 1834)	N.H.	3/...	Claudia "Lady Bird" Alta Taylor Johnson (b. 1912, 1934)	Tex.	../2
Mary Todd Lincoln (1818-1882, 1842)	Ky.	4/...	Thelma Catherine Patricia Ryan Nixon (b. 1912, 1940)	Nev.	../2
Eliza McCardle Johnson (1810-1876, 1827)	Tenn.	3/2	Elizabeth Bloomer Warren Ford (b. 1918, 1948)	Ill.	3/1
Julia Dent Grant (1826-1902, 1848)	Mo.	3/1	Rosalynn Smith Carter (b. 1927, 1946)	Ga.	3/1
Lucy Ware Webb Hayes (1831-1889, 1852)	Oh.	7/1	Anne Frances "Nancy" Robbins Davis Reagan (b. 1923, 1952)	N.Y.	1/1 (C)
Lucretia Rudolph Garfield (1832-1918, 1858)	Oh.	4/1	Barbara Pierce Bush (b. 1925, 1945).	N.Y.	4/2
Ellen Lewis Herndon Arthur (1837-1880, 1859)	Va.	2/1			
Frances Folsom Cleveland (1864-1947, 1886)	N.Y.	2/3			

James Buchanan, 15th president, was unmarried. (A) plus one infant, deceased. (B) Born London, father a Md. citizen. (C) President Reagan has a son and daughter from a former marriage.

First Lady: Barbara Bush

The first lady was born Barbara Pierce in Rye, N.Y. on June 8, 1925; the daughter of Marvin and Pauline (Robinson) Pierce. She attended Smith College, 1943-44. She married George Bush, Jan. 6, 1945. They have four sons and a daughter (another daughter died in childhood). Mrs. Bush is best known for her efforts to promote literacy and has served on the board of directors of the Reading is Fundamental and Business Council for Effective Literacy organizations.

National Political Parties

As of mid-1989

Republican Party

National Headquarters—310 First St., SE, Washington, DC 20003.
Chairman—Lee Atwater.
Co-Chairman—Jeanie Austin.
Vice Chairmen—Bernard M. Shanley, Shelia Roberge, Jack Londen, Martha Moore, Peter Secchia, Nelda Barton, Ernest Angelo Jr., Kay Riddle, Elsie Vartanian.
Secretary—Kit Mehrtens.
Treasurer—William J. McManus.
General Counsel—Jan Baran.

Democratic Party

National Headquarters—430 South Capitol St., SE, Washington, DC 20003.
Chairman—Ronald H. Brown.
Vice Chairpersons—Lynn Cutler, Jack Otero, Carmen Perez, James Ruvolo, Lottie Shackelford.
Secretary—Dorothy V. Bush.
Treasurer—Robert Farmer.

Other Major Political Organizations

American Party of the United States
(P.O. Box 597, Provo, UT 84603)
National Chairman—Arly Pedersen.
Secretary—Doris Feimer.
Treasurer—Florence Bale.

American Populist Party
(P.O. Box 1988, Ford City, PA 16226)
National Chairman—Tom McIntyre.

Americans For Democratic Action
(1511 K St., NW, Washington, DC 20005)
President—Charles Rangel.
National Director—Marc A. Pearl.
Chair, Exec. Comm.—James Bishop.

Communist Party U.S.A.
(235 W. 23d St., New York, NY 10011)
General Secretary—Gus Hall.

Conservative Party of the State of N.Y.
(45 E. 29th St., New York, NY 10016)
Chairman—Serphin R. Maltese.
Executive Director—Anthony Rudmann.
Secretary—John J. Flynn.

Liberal Party of New York State
(18 W. 56th St., New York, NY 10019)
Chairman—Frank Marin.
Exec. Director—Carl F. Grillo.

Libertarian Party
(1528 Pennsylvania Ave SE, Wash., DC 20003)
Chair—David Walter.
Vice-Chair—David Bergland.
Secretary—Imad A. Ahmad.
National Director—D. Nick Dunbar.

Prohibition National Committee
(P.O. Box 2635, Denver, CO 80201)
National Chairman—Earl F. Dodge.
National Secretary—Margaret L. Storms.

Socialist Party USA
(516 W. 25th St., New York, NY 10001)

Socialist Labor Party
In Minnesota: Industrial Gov't. Party
(914 Industrial Ave., Palo Alto, CA 94303)
National Secretary—Robert Bills.

Socialist Workers Party
(14 Charles Lane, New York, NY 10014)
National Secretary—Jack Barnes.

America's Third Parties

Since 1860, there have been only 4 presidential elections in which all third parties together polled more than 10% of the vote: the Populists (James Baird Weaver) in 1892, the National Progressives (Theodore Roosevelt) in 1912, the La Follette Progressives in 1924, and George Wallace's American Party in 1968. In 1948, the combined third parties (Henry Wallace's Progressives, Strom Thurmond's States' Rights party or Dixiecrats, Prohibition, Socialists, and others) received only 5.75% of the vote. In most elections since 1860, fewer than one vote in 20 has been cast for a third party. The only successful third party in American history was the Republican Party in the election of Abraham Lincoln in 1860.

Notable Third Parties

Party	Presidential nominee	Election	Issues	Strength in
Anti-Masonic	William Wirt	1832	Against secret societies and oaths	Pa., Vt.
Liberty	James G. Birney	1844	Anti-slavery	North
Free Soil	Martin Van Buren	1848	Anti-slavery	New York, Ohio
American (Know Nothing)	Millard Fillmore	1856	Anti-immigrant	Northeast, South
Greenback	Peter Cooper	1876	For "cheap money,"	
Greenback	James B. Weaver	1880	labor rights	National
Prohibition	John P. St. John	1884	Anti-liquor	National
Populist	James B. Weaver	1892	For "cheap money," end of national banks	South, West
Socialist	Eugene V. Debs	1900-20	For public ownership	National
Progressive (Bull Moose)	Theodore Roosevelt	1912	Against high tariffs	Midwest, West
Progressive	Robert M. LaFollette	1924	Farmer & labor rights	Midwest, West
Socialist	Norman Thomas	1928-48	Liberal reforms	National
Union	William Lemke	1936	Anti "New Deal"	National
States' Rights	Strom Thurmond	1948	For states' rights	South
Progressive	Henry Wallace	1948	Anti-cold war	New York, California
American Independent	George Wallace	1968	For states' rights	South
American	John G. Schmitz	1972	For "law and order"	Far West, Oh., La.
None (Independent)	John B. Anderson	1980	A 3d choice	National

CONGRESS

The One Hundred and First Congress
With 1988 Election Results

The Senate

Terms are for 6 years and end Jan. 3 of the year preceding name. Annual salary $89,500; President Pro Tempore, Majority Leader, and Minority Leader $99,500. To be eligible for the U.S. Senate a person must be at least 30 years of age, a citizen of the United States for at least 9 years, and a resident of the state from which he is chosen. The Congress must meet annually on Jan. 3, unless it has, by law, appointed a different day.

Senate officials (101st Congress): President Pro Tempore Robert Byrd; Majority Leader George Mitchell; Majority Whip Alan Cranston; Minority Leader Bob Dole; Minority Whip Alan Simpson.

Dem., 57; Rep., 43; Total, 100. *Incumbent. Bold face denotes winner.

Official Totals (Source: News Election Service)

Term ends	Senator (Party)	1988 Election	Term ends	Senator (Party)	1988 Election
	Alabama			**Indiana**	
1991	Howell Heflin (D)		1993	Dan Quayle (R)	
1993	Richard C. Shelby (D)		1995	**Richard G. Lugar*** (R)	1,430,525
				Jack Wickes (D)	668,778
	Alaska			**Iowa**	
1991	Ted Stevens (R)		1991	Tom Harkin (D)	
1993	Frank Murkowski (R)		1993	Charles E. Grassley (R)	
	Arizona			**Kansas**	
1993	John McCain (R)		1991	Nancy Landon Kassebaum (R)	
1995	**Dennis DeConcini*** (D)	660,403	1993	Robert J. Dole (R)	
	Keith DeGreen (R)	478,060			
	Arkansas			**Kentucky**	
1991	David Pryor (D)		1991	Mitch McConnell (R)	
1993	Dale Bumpers (D)		1993	Wendell H. Ford (D)	
	California			**Louisiana**	
1993	Alan Cranston (D)		1991	J. Bennett Johnston (D)	
1995	**Pete Wilson*** (R)	5,143,409	1993	John B. Breaux (D)	
	Leo McCarthy (D)	4,287,253		**Maine**	
	Colorado		1991	William S. Cohen (R)	
1991	William L. Armstrong (R)		1995	**George J. Mitchell*** (D)	452,590
1993	Timothy E. Wirth (D)			Jasper S. Wyman (R)	104,105
	Connecticut			**Maryland**	
1993	Christopher J. Dodd (D)		1993	Barbara A. Mikulski (D)	
1995	**Joe Lieberman** (D)	688,499	1995	**Paul S. Sarbanes*** (D)	999,166
	Lowell P. Weicker (R)	678,454		Alan L. Keyes (R)	617,537
	Delaware			**Massachusetts**	
1991	Joseph R. Biden Jr. (D)		1991	John Kerry (D)	
1995	**William V. Roth Jr.*** (R)	151,115	1995	**Edward M. Kennedy*** (D)	1,693,344
	S. B. Woo (D)	92,378		Joseph D. Malone (R)	884,267
	Florida			**Michigan**	
1993	Bob Graham (D)		1991	Carl Levin (D)	
1995	**Connie Mack** (R)	2,049,329	1995	**Donald W. Riegle Jr.*** (D)	2,116,865
	Buddy MacKay (D)	2,015,717		Jim Dunn (R)	1,348,219
	Georgia			**Minnesota**	
1991	Sam Nunn (D)		1991	Rudolph E. Boschwitz (R)	
1993	Wyche Fowler (D)		1995	**David Durenberger*** (R)	1,176,210
	Hawaii			Hubert H. "Skip" Humphrey III (D)	856,694
1993	Daniel K. Inouye (D)			**Mississippi**	
1995	**Spark M. Matsunaga*** (D)	247,941	1991	Thad Cochran (R)	
	Maria M. Hustace (R)	66,987	1995	**Trent Lott** (R)	510,380
	Idaho			Wayne Dowdy (D)	436,339
1991	James A. McClure (R)			**Missouri**	
1993	Steven D. Symms (R)		1993	Christopher "Kit" Bond (R)	
	Illinois		1995	**John C. Danforth*** (R)	1,407,416
1991	Paul Simon (D)			Jeremiah W. "Jay" Nixon (D)	660,045
1993	Alan J. Dixon (D)			**Montana**	
			1991	Max Baucus (D)	

Term ends	Senator (Party)	1988 Election
1995	**Conrad Burns** (R)	**189,445**
	John Melcher* (D)	175,809

Nebraska

1991	J. James Exon (D)	
1995	**Bob Kerrey** (D)	**378,717**
	David Karnes* (R)	278,250

Nevada

1993	Harry M. Reid (D)	
1995	**Richard H. Bryan** (D)	**175,548**
	Chic Hecht* (R)	161,336

New Hampshire

1991	Gordon J. Humphrey (R)	
1993	Warren Rudman (R)	

New Jersey

1991	Bill Bradley (D)	
1995	**Frank R. Lautenberg*** (D)	**1,599,905**
	Peter M. Dawkins (R).	1,349,937

New Mexico

1991	Pete V. Domenici (R)	
1995	**Jeff Bingaman*** (D)	**321,983**
	Bill Valentine (R)	186,579

New York

1993	Alfonse M. D'Amato (R)	
1995	**Daniel Patrick Moynihan*** (D)	**4,048,649**
	Robert R. McMillan (R).	1,875,784

North Carolina

1991	Jesse Helms (R)	
1993	Terry Sanford (D)	

North Dakota

1993	Kent Conrad (D)	
1995	**Quentin N. Burdick*** (D)	**171,899**
	Earl Strinden (R)	112,937

Ohio

1993	John Glenn (D)	
1995	**Howard M. Metzenbaum*** (D)	**2,480,038**
	George V. Voinovich (R)	1,872,716

Oklahoma

1991	David Boren (D)	
1993	Don Nickles (R)	

Oregon

1991	Mark O. Hatfield (R)	
1993	Bob Packwood (R)	

Pennsylvania

1993	Arlen Specter (R)	
1995	**John Heinz*** (R)	**2,901,715**
	Joe Vignola (D)	1,416,764

Term ends	Senator (Party)	1988 Election
Rhode Island		
1991	Claiborne deB. Pell (D)	
1995	**John H. Chafee*** (R)	**217,273**
	Richard A. Licht (D).	180,717

South Carolina

1991	Strom Thurmond (R)	
1993	Ernest Fritz Hollings* (D)	

South Dakota

1991	Larry Pressler (R) `	
1993	Thomas A. Daschle (D)	

Tennessee

1991	Albert Gore Jr. (D)	
1995	**James R. Sasser*** (D)	**1,020,061**
	Bill Andersen (R)	541,033

Texas

1991	Phil Gramm (R)	
1995	**Lloyd Bentsen*** (D)	**3,149,806**
	Beau Boulter (R)	2,129,228

Utah

1993	E. J. "Jake" Garn (R)	
1995	**Orrin G. Hatch*** (R)	**430,084**
	Brian H. Moss (D).	203,364

Vermont

1993	Patrick J. Leahy (D)	
1995	**James M. Jeffords** (R)	**163,201**
	Bill Gray (D)	71,469

Virginia

1991	John William Warner (R)	
1995	**Charles S. Robb** (D).	**1,474,086**
	Maurice A. Dawkins (R)	593,652

Washington

1993	Brock Adams (D)	
1995	**Slade Gorton** (R)	**944,359**
	Mike Lowry (D)	904,183

West Virginia

1991	Jay Rockefeller (D)	
1995	**Robert C. Byrd*** (D)	**410,983**
	M. Jay Wolfe (R)	223,564

Wisconsin

1993	Robert W. Kasten Jr. (R)	
1995	**Herbert H. Kohl** (D)	**1,128,625**
	Susan Engeleiter (R)	1,030,440

Wyoming

1991	Alan Kooi Simpson (R)	
1995	**Malcolm Wallop*** (R)	**91,143**
	John Vinich (D)	89,821

Congress: Incumbents Re-elected, 1962-1986

Source: *Congressional Quarterly*

	Presidential-Year Elections						Midterm Elections						
	1964	1968	1972	1976	1980	1984	1962	1966	1970	1974	1978	1982	1986
Representatives:													
Incumbent candidates	397	409	390	384	398	411	402	411	401	391	382	393	394
Re-elected	344	396	365	368	361	392	368	362	379	343	358	354	385
% of candidates	86.6	96.8	93.6	95.8	90.7	95.3	91.5	88.1	94.5	87.7	93.7	90.1	97.7
Defeated: In primaries.	8	4	12	3	6	3	12	8	10	8	5	10¹	3
In general elections	45	9	13	13	31	16	22	41	12	40	19	29	6
Senators:													
Incumbent candidates	33	28	27	25	29	29	35	32	31	27	25	30	28
Re-elected	28	20	20	16	16	26	29	28	24	23	15	28	21
% of candidates	84.8	71.4	74.1	64.0	55.2	89.7	82.9	87.5	77.4	85.2	60.0	93.3	75.0
Defeated: In primaries.	1	4	2	–	4	–	1	3	1	2	3	–	–
In general elections	4	4	5	9	9	3	5	1	6	2	7	2	7

(–) Represents zero. (1) Six incumbents defeated in primaries by other incumbents due to redistricting.

The House of Representatives

Members' terms to Jan. 3, 1991. Annual salary $89,500; Speaker of the House, $115,000; Majority Leader and Minority Leader $99,500. To be eligible for membership, a person must be at least 25, a U.S. citizen for at least 7 years, and a resident of the state from which he or she is chosen.

House Officials (101st Congress): Speaker Thomas S. Foley; Majority Leader Richard A. Gephardt; Majority Whip William H. Gray 3d; Minority Leader Robert H. Michel; Minority Whip Newt Gingrich.

C-Conservative; D-Democrat; B-Libertarian; I-Independent; L-Liberal; PF-Peace & Freedom; PO-Populist; R-Republican; T-Right to Life.

Dem., 262, Rep., 173. Total 435. *Incumbent. Bold face denotes winner.

Official Totals (Source: News Election Service)

Dist.	Representative (Party)	1988 Election	Dist.	Representative (Party)	1988 Election
	Alabama			Carol Harner (R)	47,957
1.	**H.L."Sonny" Callahan*** (R)	**115,173**	16.	**Leon E. Panetta*** (D)	**177,452**
	John M. Tyson Jr. (D)	77,670		Stanley Monteith (R)	48,375
2.	**William L. Dickinson*** (R)	**Unopposed**	17.	**Charles "Chip" Pashayan*** (R)	**129,568**
3.	**Bill Nichols*** (D)	**Unopposed**		Vincent Lavery (D)	51,730
4.	**Tom Bevill*** (D)	**Unopposed**	18.	**Richard H. Lehman*** (R)	**125,715**
5.	**Ronnie G. Flippo*** (D)	**120,142**		David A. Linn (D)	54,034
	Stan McDonald (R)	64,491	19.	**Robert J. "Bob" Lagomarsino*** (R)	**116,026**
6.	**Ben Erdreich*** (D)	**138,920**		Gary K. Hart (D)	112,033
	Charles Caddis (R)	68,788	20.	**William M. Thomas*** (R)	**162,779**
7.	**Claude Harris** (D)	**136,074**		Lita Reid (D)	62,037
	James E. "Jim" Bacon (R)	63,372	21.	**Elton Gallegly** (R)	**181,413**
				Donald E. Stevens (D)	75,739
	Alaska At Large		22.	**Carlos J. Moorhead*** (R)	**164,699**
	Don Young* (R)	**120,595**		John G. Simmons (D)	61,555
	Peter Gruenstein (D)	71,881	23.	**Anthony C. Beilenson*** (D)	**147,858**
				Jim Salomon (R)	77,184
	Arizona		24.	**Henry A. Waxman*** (D)	**112,038**
1.	**John J. Rhodes III** (R)	**184,639**		John N. Cowles (R)	36,835
	John M. Fillmore (D)	71,388	25.	**Edward R. Roybal*** (D)	**85,378**
2.	**Morris K. Udall*** (D)	**99,895**		Paul Reyes (PF)	8,746
	Joseph D. Sweeney (R)	36,309	26.	**Howard L. Berman*** (D)	**126,930**
3.	**Bob Stump*** (R)	**174,453**		G.C. "Brodie" Broderson (R)	53,518
	Dave Moss (D)	72,417	27.	**Mel Levine*** (D)	**148,814**
4.	**John Kyl*** (R)	**Unopposed**		Dennis Galbraith (R)	65,307
5.	**Jim Kolbe*** (R)	**164,462**	28.	**Julian C. Dixon*** (D)	**109,801**
	Judith E. Belcher (D)	78,115		George Zandivar Adams (R)	28,645
			29.	**Augustus F. "Gus" Hawkins*** (D)	**88,169**
	Arkansas			Reuben D. Franco (R)	14,543
1.	**Bill Alexander*** (D)	**Unopposed**	30.	**Matthew G. "Marty" Martinez*** (D)	**72,253**
2.	**Tommy F. Robinson*** (D)	**168,889**		Ralph R. Ramirez (R)	43,833
	Warren D. Carpenter (R)	33,475	31.	**Mervyn M. Dymally*** (D)	**100,919**
3.	**John Paul Hammerschmidt*** (R)	**161,623**		Arnold C. May (R)	36,017
	David Stewart (D)	54,767	32.	**Glenn M. Anderson*** (D)	**114,666**
4.	**Beryl Anthony Jr.*** (D)	**129,508**		Sanford W. Kahn (R)	50,710
	Roger N. Bell (R)	57,658	33.	**David Dreier*** (R)	**151,704**
				Nelson Gentry (D)	57,586
	California		34.	**Esteban E. Torres*** (D)	**92,087**
1.	**Douglas H. Bosco*** (D)	**159,815**		Charles M. House (R)	50,954
	Samuel "Mark" Vanderbilt (R)	72,189	35.	**Jerry Lewis*** (R)	**181,203**
2.	**Wally Herger** (R)	**139,010**		Paul Sweeney (D)	71,186
	Wayne Meyer (D)	91,088	36.	**George E. Brown Jr.*** (D)	**103,493**
3.	**Robert T. Matsui*** (D)	**183,470**		John Paul Stark (R)	81,413
	Lowell Patrick Landowski (R)	74,296	37.	**Al McCandless*** (R)	**174,284**
4.	**Vic Fazio*** (D)	**Unopposed**		Johnny Pearson (D)	89,666
5.	**Nancy Pelosi*** (D)	**133,530**	38.	**Robert K. "Bob" Dornan*** (R)	**87,690**
	Bruce Michael O'Neill (R)	33,692		Jerry Yudelson (D)	52,399
6.	**Barbara Boxer*** (D)	**176,645**	39.	**William E. "Bill" Dannemeyer*** (R)	**169,360**
	William Steinmetz (R)	64,174		Don E. Marquis (D)	52,162
7.	**George Miller*** (D)	**170,006**	40.	**Christopher Cox** (R)	**181,269**
	Jean Last (R)	78,478		Lida Lenney (D)	80,782
8.	**Ronald V. Dellums*** (D)	**163,221**	41.	**Bill Lowery*** (R)	**187,380**
	John J. Cuddihy Jr. (R)	76,531		Dan Kripke (D)	88,192
9.	**Fortney H. "Pete" Stark*** (D)	**152,866**	42.	**Dana Rohrabacher** (D)	**153,280**
	Howard Hertz (R)	56,656		Guy C. Kimbrough (R)	78,778
10.	**Don Edwards*** (D)	**Unopposed**	43.	**Ron Packard*** (R)	**202,478**
11.	**Tom Lantos*** (D)	**145,484**		Howard Greenebaum (D)	72,499
	G.M. "Bill" Quraishi (R)	50,050	44.	**Jim Bates*** (D)	**90,796**
12.	**Tom Campbell** (R)	**136,384**		Rob Butterfield (R)	55,511
	Anna G. Eschoo (D)	121,523	45.	**Duncan Hunter*** (R)	**166,451**
13.	**Norman Y. Mineta*** (D)	**143,980**		Pete Lepiscopo (D)	54,012
	Luke Sommer (R)	63,959			
14.	**Norman D. Shumway*** (R)	**173,876**		**Colorado**	
	Patricia Malberg (D)	103,889	1.	**Patricia Schroeder*** (D)	**133,922**
15.	**Tony Coelho*** (D)	**118,710**			

Dist.	Representative (Party)	1988 Election
	Joy Wood (R)	57,587
2.	David E. Skaggs (D)	147,437
	Dave Bath (R)	87,578
3.	Ben Nighthorse Campbell (D)	169,284
	Jim Zartman (R)	47,625
4.	Hank Brown* (R)	156,202
	Charles S. Vigil (D)	57,552
5.	Joel Hefley (R)	181,612
	John J. Mitchell (D)	60,116
6.	Daniel Schaefer* (R)	136,487
	Martha M. Ezzard (D)	77,158

Connecticut

Dist.	Representative (Party)	1988 Election
1.	Barbara Bailey Kennelly* (D)	176,463
	Mario Robles Jr. (R)	51,985
2.	Samuel Gejdenson* (D)	143,326
	Glenn Carberry (R)	81,965
3.	Bruce A. Morrison* (D)	147,394
	Gerard B. Patton (R)	74,275
4.	Christopher Shays (R)	147,843
	Roger Pearson (D)	55,751
5.	John G. Rowland* (R)	163,729
	Joseph Marinam Jr. (D)	58,612
6.	Nancy L. Johnson* (R)	157,020
	James L. Griffin (D)	78,814

Delaware At Large

Dist.	Representative (Party)	1988 Election
	Thomas R. Carper* (D)	158,338
	James P. Krapf (R)	76,179

Florida

Dist.	Representative (Party)	1988 Election
1.	Earl Hutto* (D)	142,251
	E. D. Armbruster (R)	70,314
2.	Bill Grant (D)	Unopposed
3.	Charles E. Bennett* (D)	Unopposed
4.	Craig T. James* (R)	125,467
	Bill Chappell (D)	124,735
5.	Bill McCollum* (R)	Unopposed
6.	Cliff Stearns (R)	136,342
	Jon Mills (D)	118,706
7.	Sam M. Gibbons* (D)	Unopposed
8.	C. W. Bill Young* (R)	169,119
	C. Bette Wimbish (D)	62,525
9.	Michael Bilirakis* (R)	Unopposed
10.	Andy Ireland* (R)	156,499
	David B. Higginbottom (D)	56,519
11.	Bill Nelson* (D)	168,294
	Bill Tolley (R)	108,260
12.	Tom Lewis* (R)	Unopposed
13.	Porter Goss (R)	231,063
	Jack Conway (D)	93,651
14.	Harry A. Johnston (D)	173,251
	Ken Adams (R)	142,581
15.	E. Clay Shaw Jr.* (R)	132,044
	Mike A. Kuhle (D)	67,718
16.	Larry Smith* (D)	153,000
	Joseph Smith (R)	67,427
17.	William Lehman* (D)	Unopposed
18.	Ileana Ros-Lehtinen (R)	
19.	Dante B. Fascell* (D)	135,284
	Ralph Carlos Rocheteau (R)	51,565

Georgia

Dist.	Representative (Party)	1988 Election
1.	Lindsay Thomas* (D)	94,531
	John Christian "Chris" Meredith (R)	46,552
2.	Charles Hatcher* (D)	85,029
	Ralph T. Hudgens (R)	52,807
3.	Richard Ray* (D)	Unopposed
4.	Ben Jones (D)	148,394
	Patrick Swindall* (R)	97,745
5.	John Lewis (D)	135,194
	J. W. Tibbs Jr. (R)	37,693
6.	Newt Gingrich* (R)	110,169
	Dave Worley (D)	76,824
7.	George Darden* (D)	135,056
	Robert Lamutt (R)	73,425
8.	J. Roy Rowland* (D)	Unopposed
9.	Ed Jenkins* (D)	121,800

Dist.	Representative (Party)	1988 Election
	Joe Hoffman (R)	71,905
10.	Doug Barnard Jr.* (D)	118,156
	Mark Myers (R)	66,521

Hawaii

Dist.	Representative (Party)	1988 Election
1.	Patricia Saiki (R)	96,848
	Mary Bitterman (D)	76,394
2.	Daniel K. Akaka* (D)	Unopposed

Idaho

Dist.	Representative (Party)	1988 Election
1.	Larry E. Craig* (R)	135,221
	Jeanne Givens (D)	70,328
2.	Richard Stallings* (D)	127,956
	Dane Watkins (R)	68,226

Illinois

Dist.	Representative (Party)	1988 Election
1.	Charles A. Hayes* (D)	164,125
	Stephen J. Evans (R)	6,753
2.	Gus Savage* (D)	138,256
	William T. Hespel (R)	28,831
3.	Martin A. Russo* (D)	132,111
	Joseph J. McCarthy (R)	80,181
4.	George E. Sangmeister (D)	91,282
	Jack Davis (R)	90,243
5.	William O. Lipinski* (D)	93,567
	John J. Holowinski (R)	59,128
6.	Henry J. Hyde* (R)	153,425
	William J. Andrle (D)	54,804
7.	Cardiss Collins* (D)	Unopposed
8.	Dan Rostenkowski* (D)	107,728
	V. Stephen Vetter (R)	34,659
9.	Sidney R. Yates* (D)	135,583
	Herbert Sohn (R)	67,604
10.	John E. Porter* (R)	158,519
	Eugene F. Friedman (D)	60,187
11.	Frank Annunzio* (D)	131,753
	George S. Gottlieb (R)	72,489
12.	Philip M. Crane* (R)	165,913
	John A. Leonardi (D)	54,769
13.	Harris W. Fawell* (R)	174,992
	Evelyn E. Craig (D)	74,424
14.	J. Dennis Hastert (R)	161,146
	Stephen Yonhanaie (D)	57,482
15.	Edward R. Madigan* (R)	140,171
	Thomas J. "Tom" Curl (D)	55,260
16.	Lynn Martin* (R)	128,365
	Steven E. Mahan (D)	72,431
17.	Lane Evans* (D)	132,130
	William E. Stewart (R)	71,560
18.	Robert H. Michel* (R)	114,458
	G. Douglas Stephens (D)	94,763
19.	Terry L. Bruce* (D)	132,889
	Robert F. Kerans (R)	73,981
20.	Richard J. Durbin* (D)	153,341
	Paul E. Jurgens (R)	69,303
21.	Jerry F. Costello* (D)	105,836
	Robert H. Gaffner (R)	95,385
22.	Glenn Poshard (D)	139,392
	Patrick J. Kelley (R)	75,462

Indiana

Dist.	Representative (Party)	1988 Election
1.	Peter J. Visclosky* (D)	138,251
	Owen W. Crumpacker (R)	41,076
2.	Philip R. Sharp* (D)	116,915
	Mike Pence (R)	102,846
3.	John Hiler* (R)	116,309
	Thomas W. Ward (R)	97,934
4.	Dan R. Coats* (R)	132,843
	Jill Long (D)	80,915
5.	James Jontz (D)	116,240
	Patricia L. Williams (R)	90,163
6.	Dan Burton* (R)	192,064
	George Thomas Holland (D)	71,447
7.	John T. Myers* (R)	130,578
	Mark Richard Waterfill (D)	80,741
8.	Francis X. McCloskey (D)	141,355
	John L. Myers (R)	87,321
9.	Lee H. Hamilton* (D)	147,193

Dist.	Representative (Party)	1988 Election
	Floyd Eugene Coates (R)	60,946
10.	Andrew Jacobs Jr.* (D)	105,846
	James C. Cummings (R)	68,978

Iowa

1.	Jim Leach* (R)	112,746
	Bill Gluba (D)	71,280
2.	Thomas J. Tauke* (R)	113,543
	Eric Tabor (D)	86,438
3.	David R. Nagle (D)	129,204
	Donald B. Redfern (R)	74,682
4.	Neal Smith* (D)	157,065
	Paul Lunde (R)	62,056
5.	Jim Ross Lightfoot* (R)	117,761
	Gene Freund (D)	66,599
6.	Fred Grandy (R)	125,859
	Dave O'Brien (D)	69,614

Kansas

1.	Pat Roberts* (R)	Unopposed
2.	Jim Slattery* (D)	135,694
	Phil Meinhardt (R)	49,498
3.	Jan Meyers* (R)	150,223
	Lionel Kunst (D)	53,959
4.	Dan Glickman* (D)	122,777
	Lee Thompson (R)	69,165
5.	Bob Whittaker* (R)	127,722
	John A. Barnes (D)	54,327

Kentucky

1.	Carroll Hubbard Jr.* (D)	117,288
	Hatchett (I)	6,106
2.	William H. Natcher* (D)	92,184
	Martin A. Tori (R)	59,907
3.	Romano L. Mazzoli* (D)	131,981
	Philip Dunnagan (R)	57,387
4.	Jim Bunning (R)	145,609
	Richard V. Beliles (D)	50,575
5.	Harold Rogers* (R)	Unopposed
6.	Larry J. Hopkins* (R)	128,898
	Milton Patton (D)	45,339
7.	Carl C. Perkins* (D)	96,946
	William Thompson "Will" Scott (R)	68,165

Louisiana

1.	Bob Livingston* (R)
2.	Lindy (Mrs. Hale) Boggs* (D)
3.	W.J. "Billy" Tauzin* (D)
4.	Jim McCrery* (R)
5.	Jerry Huckaby* (D)
6.	Richard Hugh Baker (R)
7.	James A. "Jimmy" Hayes (D)
8.	Clyde C. Holloway (R)
	Faye Williams (D)

8.	Clyde C. Holloway (R)	116,241
	Faye Williams (D)	88,564

In Louisiana, all candidates of all parties run against each other in an open primary, unless they are unopposed incumbents in which case they are declared elected. All candidates who receive more than 50 percent of the primary vote are also declared elected, and do not appear on the General Election ballot.

Maine

1.	Joseph E. Brennan (D)	190,989
	Edward S. O'Meara Jr. (R)	111,125
2.	Olympia J. Snowe* (R)	167,226
	Kenneth P. Hayes (D)	85,346

Maryland

1.	Roy Dyson* (D)	96,128
	Wayne T. Gilchrest (R)	94,588
2.	Helen Delich Bentley* (R)	157,956
	Joseph Bartenfelder (D)	63,114
3.	Benjamin L. Cardin (D)	133,779
	Ross Z. Pierpont (R)	49,733
4.	Thomas McMillen (D)	128,624
	Bradlyn McClanahan (R)	59,688
5.	Steny H. Hoyer* (D)	128,437
	John Eugene Sellner (R)	34,909
6.	Beverly B. Byron* (D)	166,753

	Kenneth W. Halsey (R)	54,524
7.	Kweisi Mfume (D)	Unopposed
8.	Constance A. Morella (R)	172,619
	Peter Franchot (D)	102,478

Massachusetts

1.	Silvio O. Conte* (R)	186,356
	John R. Arden (D)	38,907
2.	Richard E. Neal (D)	156,262
	Louis R. Godena (I)	38,446
3.	Joseph D. Early* (D)	Unopposed
4.	Barney Frank* (D)	169,729
	Debra R. Tucker (R)	71,661
5.	Chester Atkins* (D)	Unopposed
6.	Nicholas Mavroules* (D)	177,643
	Paul McCarthy (R)	77,186
7.	Edward J. Markey* (D)	Unopposed
8.	Joseph P. Kennedy II (D)	165,745
	Glenn W. Fiscus (R)	40,316
9.	John Joseph Moakley* (D)	Unopposed
10.	Gerry E. Studds* (D)	187,178
	Jon L. Bryan (R)	93,564
11.	Brian J. Donnelly* (D)	169,692
	Michael G. Gilleran (R)	40,277

Michigan

1.	John Conyers Jr.* (D)	127,800
	Bill Ashe (R)	10,979
2.	Carl D. Pursell* (R)	120,070
	Lana Pollack (D)	98,290
3.	Howard Wolpe* (D)	112,605
	Cal Allgaier (R)	83,769
4.	Fred Upton (R)	132,270
	Norman J. Rivers (D)	54,428
5.	Paul B. Henry* (R)	166,569
	James M. Catchick (D)	62,868
6.	Bob Carr* (D)	120,581
	Scott Schultz (R)	81,079
7.	Dale E. Kildee* (D)	150,832
	Jeff Coad (R)	47,071
8.	Bob Traxler* (D)	139,904
	Lloyd F. Buhl (R)	54,195
9.	Guy Vander Jagt* (R)	149,748
	David John Gawron (D)	64,843
10.	Bill Schuette* (R)	152,646
	Matthias G. Forbes (D)	55,398
11.	Robert W. Davis* (R)	129,085
	Mitch Irwin (D)	86,526
12.	David E. Bonior* (D)	108,158
	Douglas Carl (R)	91,780
13.	George W. Crockett Jr.* (D)	99,751
	John Wright Savage II (R)	13,196
14.	Dennis M. Hertel* (D)	111,612
	Kenneth C. McNealy (R)	64,750
15.	William D. Ford* (D)	104,596
	Burl C. Adkins (R)	56,963
16.	John D. Dingell* (D)	Unopposed
17.	Sander Levin* (D)	135,493
	Dennis M. Flessland (R)	55,197
18.	William S. Broomfield* (R)	195,579
	Gary L. Kohut (D)	57,643

Minnesota

1.	Timothy J. "Tim" Penny* (D)	161,118
	Curt Schrimpf (R)	67,709
2.	Vin Weber* (R)	131,639
	Doug Peterson (D)	96,016
3.	Bill Frenzel* (R)	215,322
	Dave Carlson (D)	99,770
4.	Bruce F. Vento* (D)	181,227
	Ian Maitland (R)	67,073
5.	Martin Olav Sabo* (D)	174,416
	Raymond C. Gilbertson (R)	60,646
6.	Gerry Sikorski* (D)	169,486
	Ray Ploetz (R)	89,209
7.	Arlan Stangeland* (R)	121,396
	Marv Hanson (D)	101,011
8.	James L. Oberstar* (D)	165,656

Dist.	Representative (Party)	1988 Election
	Jerry Shuster (R)	56,630

Mississippi

Dist.	Representative (Party)	1988 Election
1.	Jamie L. Whitten* (D)	137,445
	Jim Bush (R)	38,381
2.	Mike Espy (D)	112,401
	Jack Coleman (R)	59,827
3.	G. V. "Sonny" Montgomery* (D) . .	164,651
	Jimmie Ray Bourland (R)	20,729
4.	Mike Parker (D)	110,184
	Thomas Collins (R)	88,433
5.	vacant	
	Gene Taylor (D)	82,034

Missouri

Dist.	Representative (Party)	1988 Election
1.	William "Bill" Clay* (D)	140,751
	Joseph A. Schwan (R)	53,109
2.	Jack Buechner (R)	186,450
	Robert H. "Bob" Feigenbaum (D) . .	91,645
3.	Richard A. Gephardt* (D)	150,205
	Mark F. "Thor" Hearne (R)	86,763
4.	Ike Skelton* (D)	166,480
	David Eyerly (R)	65,393
5.	Alan Wheat* (D)	149,166
	Mary Ellen Lobb (R)	60,453
6.	E. Thomas Coleman* (R)	135,883
	Doug R. Hughes (D)	93,128
7.	Melton B. "Mel" Hancock (R) . . .	127,939
	Max Bacon (D)	111,244
8.	Bill Emerson* (R)	117,601
	Wayne Cryts (D)	84,801
9.	Harold L. Volkmer* (D)	160,872
	Ken Dudley (R)	76,008

Montana

Dist.	Representative (Party)	1988 Election
1.	Pat Williams* (D)	115,278
	Jim Fenlason (R)	74,405
2.	Ron Marlenee* (R)	97,465
	Buck O'Brien (D)	78,069

Nebraska

Dist.	Representative (Party)	1988 Election
1.	Douglas K. Bereuter* (R)	146,231
	Corky Jones (D)	72,167
2.	Peter Hoagland (D)	112,174
	Jerry Schenken (R)	109,193
3.	Virginia Smith* (R)	170,302
	John D. Racek (D)	45,183

Nevada

Dist.	Representative (Party)	1988 Election
1.	James H. Bilbray* (D)	101,764
	Lucille Lusk (R)	53,588
2.	Barbara F. Vucanovich* (R)	105,981
	Jim Spoo (D)	75,163

New Hampshire

Dist.	Representative (Party)	1988 Election
1.	Robert C. Smith* (R)	131,530
	Joseph F. Keefe (D)	86,546
2.	Chuck Douglas (R)	119,543
	James W. Donchess (D)	89,486

New Jersey

Dist.	Representative (Party)	1988 Election
1.	James J. Florio* (D)	141,988
	Frank A. Cristaudo (R)	60,037
2.	William J. Hughes* (D)	134,505
	Kirk W. Conover (R)	67,759
3.	Frank Pallone Jr. (D)	117,024
	Joseph Azzolina (R)	107,479
4.	Christopher H. Smith* (R)	155,283
	Betty Holland (D)	79,006
5.	Marge Roukema* (R)	175,562
	Lee Monaco (D)	54,828
6.	Bernard J. Dwyer* (D)	120,125
	Peter J. Sica (R)	74,824
7.	Matthew J. Rinaldo* (R)	153,350
	James Hely (D)	52,189
8.	Robert A. Roe* (D)	Unopposed
9.	Robert G. Torricelli* (D)	142,012
	Roger J. Lane (R)	68,363
10.	Donald M. Payne (D)	84,681

Dist.	Representative (Party)	1988 Election
	Michael Webb (R)	13,848
11.	Dean A. Gallo* (R)	154,654
	John C. Shaw (D)	64,773
12.	Jim Courter* (R)	165,918
	Norman J. Weinstein (D)	71,596
13.	H. James Saxton* (R)	167,470
	James B. Smith (D)	73,561
14.	Frank J. Guarini* (D) . . . . . . : .	104,001
	Fred J. Theeming Jr. (R)	47,293

New Mexico

Dist.	Representative (Party)	1988 Election
1.	Steven H. Schiff (R)	89,985
	Tom Udall (D)	84,138
2.	Joe Skeen* (R)	Unopposed
3.	Bill Richardson* (D)	124,938
	Cecilia M. Salazar (R)	45,954

New York

Dist.	Representative (Party)	1988 Election
1.	George J. Hochbrueckner (D) . . .	105,624
	Edward P. Romaine (R)	102,327
2.	Thomas J. Downey* (D)	107,646
	Joseph Cardino Jr. (R)	66,972
3.	Robert J. Mrazek* (D)	128,336
	Robert Previdi (R)	91,122
4.	Norman F. Lent* (R)	151,038
	Francis T. Goban (D)	59,479
5.	Raymond J. McGrath* (R)	134,881
	William G. Kelly (D)	68,930
6.	Floyd H. Flake (D)	94,506
	Robert L. Brandofino (C)	15,547
7.	Gary L. Ackerman* (D)	Unopposed
8.	James H. Scheuer* (D)	Unopposed
9.	Thomas J. Manton* (D)	Unopposed
10.	Charles E. Schumer* (D)	107,056
	George S. Popielarski (R)	24,313
11.	Edolphus Towns* (D)	73,755
	Riaz B. Hussain (R)	7,418
12.	Major R. Owens* (D)	74,304
	Owen Augustin (R)	5,582
13.	Stephen J. Solarz* (D)	81,305
	Anthony M. Curci (R)	27,536
14.	Guy V. Molinari* (R)	99,179
	Jerome X. O'Donovan (D)	57,503
15.	Bill Green* (R)	107,599
	Peter G. Doukas (D)	64,425
16.	Charles B. Rangel* (D)	107,620
	Michael Liccione (C)	1,779
17.	Ted Weiss* (D)	157,339
	Myrna C. Albert (R)	29,156
18.	Robert Garcia* (D)	75,459
	Fred Brown (R)	5,764
19.	Eliot L. Engel (D)	77,158
	Mario Biaggi (R)	37,454
20.	Nita M. Lowey (D)	102,235
	Joe Dioguardi* (R)	96,465
21.	Hamilton Fish Jr.* (R)	150,443
	Lawrence W. Grunberger (D)	47,294
22.	Benjamin A. Gilman* (R)	144,227
	Eleanor F. Burlingham (D)	54,312
23.	Michael R. McNulty (D)	145,040
	Peter M. Bakal (R)	89,858
24.	Gerald B. Solomon* (R)	162,962
	Fred Baye (D)	62,177
25.	Sherwood L. Boehlert* (R)	Unopposed
26.	David O'B. Martin* (R)	131,043
	Donald R. Ravenscroft (D)	43,485
27.	James T. Walsh (R)	124,928
	Rosemary S. Pooler (D)	90,854
28.	Matthew F. McHugh* (D)	141,976
	Mary C. Dixon (T)	10,395
29.	Frank R. Horton* (R)	132,608
	James R. Vogel (D)	51,243
30.	Louise M. Slaughter (D)	128,364
	John D. Bouchard (R)	89,126
31.	William Paxon (R)	117,710
	David J. Swarts (D)	102,777
32.	John J. LaFalce* (D)	133,917
	Emil K. Everett (R)	50,229

Dist.	Representative (Party)	1988 Election
33.	Henry J. Nowak* (D)	Unopposed
34.	Amory Houghton Jr. (R)	131,078
	Ian Kelly Woodward (L)	4,797

North Carolina

Dist.	Representative (Party)	1988 Election
1.	Walter B. Jones* (D)	118,027
	Howard D. Moye (R)	63,013
2.	I.T. "Tim" Valentine Jr.* (D)	Unopposed
3.	Martin Lancaster (D)	Unopposed
4.	David E. Price* (D)	131,896
	Tom Fetzer (R)	95,482
5.	Stephen L. Neal* (D)	110,516
	Lyons Gray (R)	99,540
6.	Howard Coble* (R)	116,534
	Tom Gilmore (D)	70,008
7.	Charles G. Rose III* (D)	102,392
	George G. "Jerry" Thompson (R)	49,855
8.	W. G. "Bill" Hefner* (D)	99,214
	Ted Blanton (R)	93,463
9.	J. Alex McMillan* (R)	139,014
	Mark Sholander (D)	71,802
10.	Cass Ballenger (R)	112,554
	Jack L. Rhyne (D)	71,865
11.	James McClure Clarke (D)	108,436
	Charles H. Taylor (R)	106,907

North Dakota At Large

	Byron L. Dorgan* (D)	212,583
	Steve Sydness (R)	84,475

Ohio

Dist.	Representative (Party)	1988 Election
1.	Thomas A. Luken* (D)	117,682
	Steve Chabot (R)	90,738
2.	Willis D. Gradison Jr.* (R)	153,162
	Chuck R. Stidham (D)	58,637
3.	Tony P. Hall* (D)	141,953
	Ron Crutcher (R)	42,664
4.	Michael G. Oxley* (R)	Unopposed
5.	Paul E. Gillmor (R)	123,838
	Tom Murray (D)	80,472
6.	Bob McEwen* (R)	152,235
	Gordon R. Roberts (D)	52,635
7.	Michael DeWine* (R)	142,597
	Jack Schira (D)	50,423
8.	Donald E. Lukens (R)	154,164
	John Griffin (D)	49,084
9.	Marcy Kaptur* (D)	157,557
	Al Hawkins (R)	36,183
10.	Clarence E. Miller* (R)	143,673
	John M. Buchanan (D)	56,893
11.	Dennis E. Eckart* (D)	124,600
	Margaret Mueller (R)	78,028
12.	John R. Kasich* (R)	204,892
	Mark P. Brown (D)	50,782
13.	Donald J. Pease* (D)	137,074
	Dwight Brown (R)	59,287
14.	Thomas C. Sawyer (D)	148,951
	Loretta A. Lang (R)	50,356
15.	Chalmers P. Wylie* (R)	154,694
	Mark S. Froehlich (D)	51,172
16.	Ralph Regula* (R)	158,824
	Melvin J. Gravely (D)	43,356
17.	James A. Traficant Jr.* (D)	232,221
	Frederick W. Lenz (R)	68,822
18.	Douglas Applegate* (D)	151,306
	William C. Abraham (R)	43,628
19.	Edward F. Feighan* (D)	168,065
	Noel F. Roberts (R)	70,359
20.	Mary Rose Oakar* (D)	146,715
	Michael Sajna (R)	30,944
21.	Louis Stokes* (D)	148,388
	Franklin H. Roski (R)	24,804

Oklahoma

Dist.	Representative (Party)	1988 Election
1.	James M. Inhofe (R)	103,458
	Kurt Glassco (D)	93,101
2.	Mike Synar* (D)	136,009
	Ira Phillips (R)	73,659
3.	Wes Watkins* (D)	Unopposed
4.	Dave McCurdy* (D)	Unopposed
5.	Mickey Edwards* (R)	139,182
	Terry J. Montgomery (D)	53,668
6.	Glenn English* (D)	122,887
	Mike Brown (R)	45,239

Watkins and McCurdy, Unopposed, will not appear on the ballot and are considered elected.

Oregon

Dist.	Representative (Party)	1988 Election
1.	Les AuCoin* (D)	179,915
	Earl Molander (R)	78,626
2.	Bob Smith* (R)	125,366
	Larry Tuttle (D)	74,700
3.	Ron Wyden* (D)	Unopposed
4.	Peter A. DeFazio (D)	108,483
	Jim Howard (R)	42,220
5.	Denny Smith* (R)	111,229
	Mike Kopetski (D)	110,564

Pennsylvania

Dist.	Representative (Party)	1988 Election
1.	Thomas M. Foglietta* (D)	128,076
	William J. O'Brien (R)	39,749
2.	William H. Gray* (D)	184,322
	Richard L. Harsch (R)	12,365
3.	Robert A. Borski* (D)	135,590
	Mark Matthews (R)	78,909
4.	Joseph P. Kolter* (D)	124,041
	Gordon R. Johnson (R)	52,402
5.	Richard T. Schulze* (R)	153,453
	Donald A. Hadley (D)	42,758
6.	Gus Yatron* (D)	114,119
	James R. Erwin (R)	65,278
7.	Curt Weldon (R)	155,387
	David Landau (D)	73,745
8.	Peter H. Kostmayer* (D)	128,153
	Ed Howard (R)	93,648
9.	Bud Shuster* (R, D)	Unopposed
10.	Joseph M. McDade* (R)	140,096
	Robert C. Cordaro (D)	51,179
11.	Paul E. Kanjorski* (D)	Unopposed
12.	John P. Murtha* (D)	Unopposed
13.	Lawrence Coughlin* (R)	152,191
	Bernard Tomkin (D)	76,424
14.	William J. Coyne* (D)	135,181
	Richard E. Caligiuri (R)	36,719
15.	Don Ritter* (R)	106,951
	Ed Reibman (D)	79,127
16.	Robert S. Walker* (R)	136,944
	Ernest Eric Guyll (D)	48,169
17.	George W. Gekas* (R, D)	Unopposed
18.	Doug Walgren* (D)	136,924
	John A. Newman (R)	80,975
19.	William F. Goodling* (R)	145,381
	Paul E. Ritchey (D)	42,819
20.	Joseph M. Gaydos* (D)	137,472
	Richard W. Wilson (PO)	2,144
21.	Thomas J. Ridge* (R)	141,832
	George R. H. Elder (D)	38,288
22.	Austin J. Murphy* (D)	123,428
	William Hodgkiss (R)	47,039
23.	William F. Clinger Jr.* (R)	105,575
	Howard Shakespeare (D)	63,476

Rhode Island

Dist.	Representative (Party)	1988 Election
1.	Ronald K. Machtley (R)	105,506
	Fernand J. St Germain* (D)	84,141
2.	Claudine Schneider* (R)	145,218
	Ruth S. Morgenthau (D)	56,129

South Carolina

Dist.	Representative (Party)	1988 Election
1.	Arthur Ravenel Jr. (R)	101,572
	Wheeler Tillman (D)	57,691
2.	Floyd D. Spence* (R)	94,960
	Jim Leventis (D)	83,978
3.	Butler Derrick* (D)	89,071
	Henry Jordan (R)	75,571
4.	Liz J. Patterson (D)	90,234

Dist.	Representative (Party)	1988 Election
	Knox White (R)	82,793
5.	John Spratt Jr.* (D)	107,959
	Robert K. "Bob" Carley (R)	46,622
6.	Robert Tallon* (D)	120,719
	Bob Cunningham (R)	37,958

South Dakota At Large

	Tim Johnson (D)	223,759
	David Volk (R)	88,157

Tennessee

Dist.	Representative (Party)	1988 Election
1.	James H. "Jimmy" Quillen* (R)	119,526
	Sidney S. Smith (D)	29,469
2.	John J. Duncan Jr.* (R)	99,631
	Dudley W. Taylor (D)	77,540
3.	Marilyn Lloyd* (D)	108,264
	Harold L. Coker (R)	80,372
4.	Jim Cooper* (D)	Unopposed
5.	Bob Clement* (D)	Unopposed
6.	Bart Gordon* (D)	123,652
	Wallace Embry (R)	38,033
7.	Don Sundquist* (R)	142,025
	Kenneth "Ken" Bloodworth (D)	35,237
8.	John Tanner (D)	94,571
	Ed Bryant (R)	56,893
9.	Harold E. Ford* (D)	126,280
	Isaac Richmond (I)	28,522

Texas

Dist.	Representative (Party)	1988 Election
1.	Jim Chapman* (D)	122,566
	Horace McQueen (R)	74,357
2.	Charles Wilson* (D)	145,614
	Gary W. Nelson (B)	20,475
3.	Steve Bartlett* (R)	227,882
	Blake Cowden (D)	50,627
4.	Ralph M. Hall* (D)	139,379
	Randy Sutton (R)	67,337
5.	John Bryant* (D)	95,376
	Lon Williams (R)	59,877
6.	Joe Barton* (R)	164,692
	M. P. "Pat" Kendrick (D)	78,786
7.	Bill Archer* (R)	185,203
	Dianne Richards (D)	48,824
8.	Jack Fields* (R)	Unopposed
9.	Jack Brooks* (D)	Unopposed
10.	J. J. "Jake" Pickle* (D)	232,213
	Vincent J. May (B)	16,281
11.	Marvin Leath* (D)	134,207
	Frederick M. King (B)	6,533
12.	Vacant	
13.	Bill Sarpalius (D)	98,345
	Larry S. Milner (R)	89,105
14.	Greg Laughlin (D)	111,395
	Mac Sweeney* (R)	96,042
15.	E. "Kika" de la Garza* (D)	93,672
	Gloria Joyce Hendrix (B)	6,133
16.	Ronald Coleman* (D)	Unopposed
17.	Charles W. Stenholm* (D)	Unopposed
18.	Mickey Leland* (D)	94,408
	J. Alejandro Snead (B)	7,235
19.	Larry Combest* (R)	113,068
	Gerald McCathern (D)	53,932
20.	Henry B. Gonzalez* (D)	94,527
	Lee Trevino (R)	36,801
21.	Lamar Smith* (R)	203,989
	James A. Robinson (B)	14,801
22.	Tom DeLay* (R)	125,733
	Wayne Walker (D)	58,471
23.	Albert G. Bustamente* (D)	116,423
	Jerome L. "Jerry" Gonzales (R)	60,559
24.	Martin Frost* (D)	135,794
	Leo Sandovy (R)	10,841
25.	Mike Andrews* (D)	113,499
	George Loeffler (R)	44,043
26.	Dick Armey* (R)	194,944
	Jo Ann Reyes (D)	86,490
27.	Solomon P. Ortiz* (D)	Unopposed

Utah

Dist.	Representative (Party)	1988 Election
1.	James V. Hansen* (R)	130,893
	Gunn McKay (D)	87,976
2.	Wayne Owens (D)	112,129
	Richard Snelgrove (R)	80,212
3.	Howard C. Nielson* (R)	129,951
	Robert W. Stringham (D)	60,018

Vermont At Large

	Peter Smith (R)	98,937
	Paul N. Poirier (D)	45,330

Virginia

Dist.	Representative (Party)	1988 Election
1.	Herbert H. "Herb" Bateman* (R)	135,937
	James S. Ellenson (D)	49,614
2.	Owen B. Pickett (D)	106,666
	Jerry R. Curry (R)	62,564
3.	Thomas J. "Tom" Bliley Jr.* (R)	Unopposed
4.	Norman Sisisky* (D)	Unopposed
5.	L. F. Payne Jr.* (D)	97,242
	Charles R. Hawkins (R)	78,396
6.	James R. "Jim" Olin* (D)	118,369
	Charles E. Judd (R)	66,935
7.	D. French Slaughter* (R)	Unopposed
8.	Stan Parris* (R)	154,761
	David G. Brickley (D)	93,561
9.	Frederick C. "Rick" Boucher* (D)	113,309
	John C. Brown (R)	65,410
10.	Frank R. Wolf* (R)	187,850
	Robert L. Weinberg (D)	88,284

Washington

Dist.	Representative (Party)	1988 Election
1.	John Miller* (R)	152,265
	Reese Lindquist (D)	122,646
2.	Al Swift* (D)	Unopposed
3.	Jolene Unsoeld (D)	109,390
	Bill Wight (R)	108,763
4.	Sid Morrison* (R)	142,938
	J. Richard Golob (D)	48,850
5.	Thomas S. Foley* (D)	160,654
	Marilyn A. Derby (R)	49,657
6.	Norman D. Dicks* (D)	125,904
	Kevin P. Cook (R)	60,346
7.	Jim McDermott (D)	173,809
	Robert Edwards (R)	53,902
8.	Rod Chandler* (R)	174,942
	Jim Kean (D)	71,920

West Virginia

Dist.	Representative (Party)	1988 Election
1.	Alan B. Mollohan* (D)	119,256
	Howard K. Tuck (R)	40,732
2.	Harley O. Staggers Jr.* (D)	Unopposed
3.	Bob Wise* (D)	120,192
	Paul W. Hart (R)	41,478
4.	Nick J. Rahall II * (D)	78,812
	Marianne R. Brewster (R)	49,753

Wisconsin

Dist.	Representative (Party)	1988 Election
1.	Les Aspin* (D)	158,552
	Bernard Weaver (R)	49,620
2.	Robert W. Kastenmeier* (D)	151,501
	Ann Haney (R)	107,457
3.	Steven C. Gunderson* (R)	157,513
	Karl Krueger (D)	72,935
4.	Gerald D. Kleczka* (D)	Unopposed
5.	Jim Moody* (D)	140,518
	Helen Barnhill (R)	78,307
6.	Thomas E. Petri* (R)	165,923
	Joseph Garrett (D)	57,552
7.	David R. Obey* (D)	142,197
	Kevin J. Hermening (R)	86,077
8.	Toby Roth* (R)	167,275
	Robert A. Baron (D)	72,708
9.	F. James Sensenbrener Jr.* (R)	185,093
	Thomas J. Hickey (D)	62,003

Wyoming At Large

	Richard B. Cheney* (R)	118,350
	Bryan Sharratt (D)	56,527

Resident Commissioner (Non-Voting)
Puerto Rico
Jaime B. Fuster* (D)
Non-Voting Delegates

District of Columbia
Walter E. Fauntroy* (D)
Mary L. H. King (R)

Guam
Ben G. Blaz* (R)
Virgin Islands
Ron de Lugo* (D)

American Samoa
Eni F.H. Faleomavaega* (D)

Political Divisions of the U.S. Senate and House of Representatives
From 1859 (36th Cong.) to 1989-1991 (101st Cong.)

Source: Clerk of the House of Representatives; Secretary of the Senate

Congress	Years	Senate — Number of Senators	Democrats	Republicans	Other parties	Vacant	House of Representatives — Number of Representatives	Democrats	Republicans	Other parties	Vacant
36th	1859-61	66	38	26	2		237	101	113	23	
37th	1861-63	50	11	31	7	1	178	42	106	28	2
38th	1863-65	51	12	39			183	80	103		
39th	1865-67	52	10	42			191	46	145		
40th	1867-69	53	11	42			193	49	143		1
41st	1869-71	74	11	61		2	243	73	170		
42d	1871-73	74	17	57			243	104	139		
43d	1873-75	74	19	54		1	293	88	203		2
44th	1875-77	76	29	46		1	293	181	107	3	2
45th	1877-79	76	36	39	1		293	156	137		
46th	1879-81	76	43	33			293	150	128	14	1
47th	1881-83	76	37	37	2		293	130	152	11	
48th	1883-85	76	36	40			325	200	119	6	
49th	1885-87	76	34	41		1	325	182	140	2	1
50th	1887-89	76	37	39			325	170	151	4	
51st	1889-91	84	37	47			330	156	173	1	
52d	1891-93	88	39	47	2		333	231	88	14	
53d	1893-95	88	44	38	3	3	356	220	126	10	
54th	1895-97	88	39	44	5		357	104	246	7	
55th	1897-99	90	34	46	10		357	134	206	16	1
56th	1899-1901	90	26	53	11		357	163	185	9	
57th	1901-03	90	29	56	3	2	357	153	198	5	1
58th	1903-05	90	32	58			386	178	207		1
59th	1905-07	90	32	58			386	136	250		
60th	1907-09	92	29	61		2	386	164	222		
61st	1909-11	92	32	59		1	391	172	219		
62d	1911-13	92	42	49		1	391	228	162	1	
63d	1913-15	96	51	44	1		435	290	127	18	
64th	1915-17	96	56	39	1		435	231	193	8	3
65th	1917-19	96	53	42	1		435	'210	216	9	
66th	1919-21	96	47	48	1		435	191	237	7	
67th	1921-23	96	37	59			435	132	300	1	2
68th	1923-25	96	43	51	2		435	207	225	3	
69th	1925-27	96	40	54	1	1	435	183	247	5	
70th	1927-29	96	47	48	1		435	195	237	3	
71st	1929-31	96	39	56	1		435	163	267	1	4
72d	1931-33	96	47	48	1		435	²216	218	1	
73d	1933-35	96	59	36	1		435	313	117	5	
74th	1935-37	96	69	25	2		435	322	103	10	
75th	1937-39	96	75	17	4		435	333	89	13	
76th	1939-41	96	69	23	4		435	262	169	4	
77th	1941-43	96	66	28	2		435	267	162	6	
78th	1943-45	96	57	38	1		435	222	209	4	
79th	1945-47	96	57	38	1		435	243	190	2	
80th	1947-49	96	45	51			435	188	246	1	
81st	1949-51	96	54	42			435	263	171	1	
82d	1951-53	96	48	47	1		435	234	199	2	
83d	1953-55	96	46	48	2		435	213	221	1	
84th	1955-57	96	48	47	1		435	232	203		
85th	1957-59	96	49	47			435	234	201		
86th	1959-61	98	64	34			⁴436	283	153		
87th	1961-63	100	64	36			⁴437	262	175		
88th	1963-65	100	67	33			435	258	176		1
89th	1965-67	100	68	32			435	295	140		
90th	1967-69	100	64	36			435	248	187		
91st	1969-71	100	58	42			435	243	192		
92d	1971-73	100	54	44	2		435	255	180		
93d	1973-75	100	56	42	2		435	242	192	1	
94th	1975-77	100	61	37	2		435	291	144		
95th	1977-79	100	61	38	1		435	292	143		
96th	1979-81	100	58	41	1		435	277	158		
97th	1981-83	100	46	53	1		435	242	190		3
98th	1983-85	100	46	54			435	269	166		
99th	1985-87	100	47	53			435	253	182		
100th	1987-89	100	54	46			435	258	177		
101st	1989-91	100	57	43			435	262	173		

(1) Democrats organized House with help of other parties. (2) Democrats organized House due to Republican deaths. (3) Proclamation declaring Alaska a State issued Jan. 3, 1959. (4) Proclamation declaring Hawaii a State issued Aug. 21, 1959.

Congressional Committees

Senate Standing Committees
(As of Mar. 15, 1989)

Agriculture, Nutrition, and Forestry
Chairman: Patrick J. Leahy, Vt.
Ranking Rep.: Richard G. Lugar, Ind.
Appropriations
Chairman: Robert C. Byrd, W.V.
Ranking Rep.: Mark O. Hatfield, Ore.
Armed Services
Chairman: Sam Nunn, Ga.
Ranking Rep.: John W. Warner, Va.
Banking, Housing, and Urban Affairs
Chairman: Donald W. Riegle Jr., Mich.
Ranking Rep.: Jake Garn, Utah
Budget
Chairman: Jim Sasser, Tenn.
Ranking Rep.: Pete V. Domini
ci, N.M.
Commerce, Science, and Transportation
Chairman: Ernest F. Hollings, S.C.
Ranking Rep.: John C. Danforth, Mo.
Energy and Natural Resources
Chairman: J. Bennett Johnston, La.
Ranking Rep.: James A. McClure, Ida.
Environment and Public Works
Chairman: Quentin N. Burdick, N.D.
Ranking Rep.: John H. Chafee, R.I.
Finance
Chairman: Lloyd Bentsen, Tex.
Ranking Rep.: Bob Packwood, Ore.
Foreign Relations
Chairman: Claiborne Pell, R.I.
Ranking Rep.: Jesse Helms, N.C.
Governmental Affairs
Chairman: John Glenn, Ohio
Ranking Rep.: William V. Roth Jr., Del.
Judiciary
Chairman: Joseph R. Biden Jr., Del.
Ranking Rep.: Strom Thurmond, S.C.
Labor and Human Resources
Chairman: Edward M. Kennedy, Mass.
Ranking Rep.: Orrin G. Hatch, Utah
Rules and Administration
Chairman: Wendell H. Ford, Ky.
Ranking Rep.: Ted Stevens, Alas.
Small Business
Chairman: Dale Bumpers, Ark.
Ranking Rep.: Rudy Boschwitz, Minn.
Veterans' Affairs
Chairman: Alan Cranston, Cal.
Ranking Rep.: Frank H. Murkowski, Alas.

Senate Select and Special Committees
(As of Mar. 15, 1989)

Aging
Chairman: David H. Pryor, Ark.
Ranking Rep.: John Heinz, Pa.
Ethics
Chairman: Howell Heflin, Ala.
Ranking Rep.: Warren Rudman, N.H.
Indian Affairs
Chairman: Daniel K. Inouye, Ha.
Ranking Rep.: Frank H. Murkowski, Alas.
Intelligence
Chairman: David L. Boren, Okla.
V. Chairman: William S. Cohen, Me.

Joint Committees of Congress

Economic
Chairman: Rep. Lee H. Hamilton (D), Ind.
V. Chairman: Sen. Paul S. Sarbanes (D), Md.
Library
Chairman: Rep. Frank Annunzio (D), Ill.
V. Chairman: Sen. Claiborne Pell (D), R.I.
Printing
Chairman: Sen. Wendell H. Ford (D), Ky.
V. Chairman: Rep. Frank Annunzio (D), Ill.

Taxation
Chairman: Sen. Lloyd Bentsen (D), Tex.
V. Chairman: Rep. Dan Rostenkowski (D), Ill.

House Standing Committees
(As of Apr. 14, 1989)

Agriculture
Chairman: E de la Garza, Tex.
Ranking Rep.: Edward R. Madigan, Ill.
Appropriations
Chairman: Jamie L. Whitten, Miss.
Ranking Rep.: Silvio O. Conte, Mass.
Armed Services
Chairman: Les Aspin, Wis.
Ranking Rep.: William L. Dickinson, Ala.
Banking, Finance, and Urban Affairs
Chairman: Henry B. Gonzalez, Tex.
Ranking Rep.: Chalmers P. Wylie, Ohio
Budget
Chairman: Leon E. Panetta, Cal.
Ranking Rep.: Bill Frenzel, Mich.
District of Columbia
Chairman: Ronald V. Dellums, Cal.
Ranking Rep.: Stan Parris, Va.
Education and Labor
Chairman: Augustus F. Hawkins, Cal.
Ranking Rep.: William F. Goodling, Pa.
Energy and Commerce
Chairman: John D. Dingell, Mich.
Ranking Rep.: Norman F. Lent, N.Y.
Foreign Affairs
Chairman: Dante B. Fascell, Fla.
Ranking Rep.: William S. Broomfield, Mich.
Government Operations
Chairman: John Conyers Jr., Mich.
Ranking Rep.: Frank Horton, N.Y.
House Administration
Chairman: Frank Annunzio, Ill.
Ranking Rep.: William M. Thomas, Cal.
Interior and Insular Affairs
Chairman: Morris K. Udall, Ariz.
Ranking Rep.: Don Young, Alas.
Judiciary
Chairman: Jack Brooks, Tex.
Ranking Rep.: Hamilton Fish Jr., N.Y.
Merchant Marine and Fisheries
Chairman: Walter B. Jones, N.C.
Ranking Rep.: Robert W. Davis, Mich.
Post Office and Civil Service
Chairman: William D. Ford, Mich.
Ranking Rep.: Benjamin A. Gilman, N.Y.
Public Works and Transportation
Chairman: Glenn M. Anderson, Cal.
Ranking Rep.: John Paul Hammerschmidt, Ark.
Rules
Chairman: John Moakley, Mass.
Ranking Rep.: James H. Quillen, Tenn.
Science, Space, and Technology
Chairman: Robert A. Roe, N.J.
Ranking Rep.: Robert S. Walker, Pa.
Small Business
Chairman: John J. LaFalce, N.Y.
Ranking Rep.: Joseph M. McDade, Pa.
Standards of Official Conduct
Chairman: Julian C. Dixon, Cal.
Ranking Rep.: John T. Myers, Ind.
Veterans' Affairs
Chairman: G.V. Montgomery, Miss.
Ranking Rep.: Bob Stump, Ariz.
Ways and Means
Chairman: Dan Rostenkowski, Ill.
Ranking Rep.: Bill Archer, Tex.

House Select Committees

Aging
Chairman: Edward R. Roybal, Cal.
Ranking Rep.: Matthew J. Rinaldo, N.J.

Children, Youth, and Families
Chairman: George Miller, Cal.
Ranking Rep.: Thomas J. Bliley Jr., Va.
Hunger
Chairman: vacant
Ranking Rep.: Bill Emerson, Mo.

Intelligence
Chairman: Anthony C. Beilenson, Cal.
Ranking Rep.: Henry J. Hyde, Ill.
Narcotics Abuse and Control
Chairman: Charles B. Rangel, N.Y.
Ranking Rep.: Lawrence Coughlin, Pa.

Congress: Selected Characteristics, 1975-1989

Source: *Congressional Quarterly, Congressional Directory*

(As of beginning of first session of each Congress. Figures for Representatives exclude vacancies.)

	Male	Female	Black	Age Under 40	40-49	50-59	60-69	70-79	80 and over	Seniority[1] Less than 2 years	2-9 years	10-19 years	20-29 years	30 years or more
Representatives														
94th Cong., 1975	416	19	15	69	138	137	75	14	2	96	162	125	42	10
95th Cong., 1977	417	18	16	81	121	147	71	15	–	71	207	116	33	8
96th Cong., 1979	417	16	16	86	125	145	63	14	–	80	206	105	32	10
97th Cong., 1981	416	19	17	94	142	132	54	12	1	77	231	96	23	8
98th Cong., 1983	413	21	21	86	145	132	57	13	1	83	224	88	28	11
99th Cong., 1985	412	22	20	71	154	131	59	17	2	49	237	104	34	10
100th Cong., 1987. . . .	412	23	23	63	153	137	56	24	2	51	221	114	37	12
101st Cong., 1989. . . .	410	25	24	(NA)	(NA)	(NA)	(NA)	(NA)	(NA)	(NA)	(NA)	(NA)	(NA)	(NA)
Senators														
94th Cong., 1975[2] . . .	100	–	1	5	21	35	24	15	–	11	41	34	10	4
95th Cong., 1977	100	–	1	6	26	35	21	10	2	18	41	24	12	5
96th Cong., 1979	99	1	–	10	31	33	17	8	1	20	41	23	12	4
97th Cong., 1981	98	2	–	9	35	36	14	6	–	19	51	17	11	2
98th Cong., 1983	98	2	–	7	28	39	20	3	3	5	61	21	10	3
99th Cong., 1985 . . . . :	98	2	–	4	27	38	25	4	2	8	56	27	7	2
100th Cong., 1987. . . .	98	2	–	5	30	36	22	5	2	14	41	36	7	2
101st Cong., 1989. . . .	98	2	–	(NA)	(NA)	(NA)	(NA)	(NA)	(NA)	(NA)	(NA)	(NA)	(NA)	(NA)

(-) Represents zero. NA = Not available. (1) Represents consecutive years of service. (2) Includes Senator Durkin, NH., seated Sept. 1975.

Congress: Measures Introduced and Enacted, and Time in Session, 1971–1987

Source: *Calendars of the U.S. House of Representatives and History of Legislation; Vital Statistics on Congress, 1987-88.*

(excludes simple and concurrent resolutions)

	92nd Cong., 1971-72	93d Cong., 1973-74	94th Cong., 1975-76	95th Cong., 1977-78	96th Cong., 1979-80	97th Cong., 1981-82	98th Cong., 1983-84	99th Cong., 1985-86	100th Cong., 1987
Measures introduced	22,969	23,396	21,096	19,387	12,583	11,490	11,156	9,885	6.514
Bills	21,363	21,950	19,762	18,045	11,722	10,582	10,134	8,697	5,838
Joint resolutions	1,606	1,446	1,334	1,342	861	908	1,022	1,188	676
Measures enacted	768	774	729	803	736	529	677	483	249
Public	607	651	588	633	613	473	623	466	242
Private	161	123	141	170	123	56	54	17	7
House of Representatives									
Number of days.	298	318	311	323	326	303	266	281	(NA)
Number of hours	1,429	1,487	1,788	1,898	1,876	1,420	1,705	1,794	(NA)
Number of hours per day	4.8	4.7	5.7	5.9	5.8	4.7	6.4	6.4	(NA)
Senate									
Number of days.	348	334	320	337	333	312	281	313	(NA)
Number of hours	2,294	2,028	2,210	2,510	2,324	2,158	1,951	2,531	(NA)
Number of hours per day	6.6	6.1	6.9	7.4	7.0	6.9	6.9	8.1	(NA)

NA = Not available.

Congressional Bills Vetoed, 1789-1989

Source: Senate Library

	Regular vetoes	Pocket vetoes	Total vetoes	Vetoes over-ridden		Regular vetoes	Pocket vetoes	Total vetoes	Vetoes over-ridden
Washington	2	—	2	—	Cleveland	304	110	414	2
John Adams	—	—	—	—	Benjamin Harrison	19	25	44	1
Jefferson	—	—	—	—	Cleveland	42	128	170	5
Madison	5	2	7	—	McKinley	6	36	42	—
Monroe	1	—	1	—	Theodore Roosevelt	42	40	82	1
John Q. Adams	—	—	—	—	Taft	30	9	39	1
Jackson	5	7	12	—	Wilson	33	11	44	6
Van Buren	—	1	1	—	Harding	5	1	6	—
William Harrison	—	—	—	—	Coolidge	20	30	50	4
Tyler	6	4	10	1	Hoover	21	16	37	3
Polk	2	1	3	—	Franklin Roosevelt	372	263	635	9
Taylor	—	—	—	—	Truman	180	70	250	12
Fillmore	—	—	—	—	Eisenhower	73	108	181	2
Pierce	9	—	9	5	Kennedy	12	9	21	—
Buchanan	4	3	7	—	Lyndon Johnson	16	14	30	—
Lincoln	2	5	7	—	Nixon	26	17	43	7
Andrew Johnson	21	8	29	15	Ford	48	18	66	12
Grant	45	48	93	4	Carter	13	18	31	2
Hayes	12	1	13	1	Reagan	39	39	78	9
Garfield	—	—	—	—	Bush[1]	1	0	1	0
Arthur	4	8	12	1					
(1) As of mid-1989.					**Total**	1,420	1,051	2,471	103

PRESIDENTIAL ELECTIONS

Popular and Electoral Vote, 1984 and 1988

Source: News Election Service

States	1988 Electoral Vote Dukakis	Bush	Democrat Dukakis	Republican Bush	1984 Electoral Vote Mondale	Reagan	Democrat Mondale	Republican Reagan
Ala.. . . .	0	9	549,506	815,576	0	9	551,899	872,849
Alas.. . . .	0	3	72,584	119,251	0	3	62,007	138,377
Ariz. . . .	0	7	454,029	702,541	0	7	333,854	681,416
Ark.. . . .	0	6	349,237	466,578	0	6	338,646	534,774
Cal.. . .	0	47	4,702,233	5,054,917	0	47	3,815,947	5,305,410
Col.. . . .	0	8	621,453	728,177	0	8	454,975	821,817
Conn. . . .	0	8	676,584	750,241	0	8	569,597	890,877
Del.. . . .	0	3	108,647	139,639	0	3	101,656	152,190
D.C. . . .	3	0	159,407	27,590	3	0	180,408	29,009
Fla.. . . .	0	21	1,655,851	2,616,597	0	21	1,448,344	2,728,775
Ga.. . . .	0	12	714,792	1,081,331	0	12	706,628	1,068,722
Ha.. . . .	4	0	192,364	158,625	0	4	147,098	184,934
Ida.. . . .	0	4	147,272	253,881	0	4	108,510	297,523
Ill.. . . .	0	24	2,215,940	2,310,939	0	24	2,086,499	2,707,103
Ind.. . . .	0	12	860,643	1,297,763	0	12	841,481	1,377,230
Ia..	8	0	670,557	545,355	0	8	605,620	703,088
Kan. . . .	0	7	422,636	554,049	0	7	332,471	674,646
Ky.	0	9	580,368	734,281	0	9	536,756	815,345
La.	0	10	717,460	883,702	0	10	651,586	1,037,299
Me.. . . .	0	4	243,569	307,131	0	4	214,515	336,500
Md.. . . .	0	10	826,304	876,167	0	10	787,935	879,918
Mass. . .	13	0	1,401,415	1,194,635	0	13	1,239,606	1,310,936
Mich.. . .	0	20	1,675,783	1,965,486	0	20	1,529,638	2,251,571
Minn.. . .	10	0	1,109,471	962,337	10	0	1,036,364	1,032,603
Miss.. . .	0	7	363,921	557,890	0	7	352,192	582,377
Mo.. . . .	0	11	1,001,619	1,084,953	0	11	848,583	1,274,188
Mon.. . .	0	4	168,936	190,412	0	4	146,742	232,450
Neb. . . .	0	5	259,235	397,956	0	5	187,475	459,135
Nev. . . .	0	4	132,738	206,040	0	4	91,655	188,770
N.H. . . .	0	4	163,696	281,537	0	4	120,377	267,051
N.J.. . . .	0	16	1,317,541	1,740,604	0	16	1,261,323	1,933,630
N.M.. . . .	0	5	244,497	270,341	0	5	201,769	307,101
N.Y. . . .	36	0	3,347,882	3,081,871	0	36	3,119,609	3,664,763
N.C. . . .	0	13	890,167	1,237,258	0	13	824,287	1,346,481
N.D. . . .	0	3	127,739	166,559	0	3	104,429	200,336
Oh.. . . .	0	23	1,939,629	2,416,549	0	23	1,825,440	2,678,559
Okla.. . .	0	8	483,423	678,367	0	8	385,080	861,530
Ore. . . .	7	0	616,206	560,126	0	7	536,479	685,700
Pa.. . . .	0	25	2,194,944	2,300,087	0	25	2,228,131	2,584,323
R.I.. . . .	4	0	225,123	177,761	0	4	197,106	212,080
S.C. . . .	0	8	370,554	606,443	0	8	344,459	615,539
S.D. . . .	0	3	145,560	165,415	0	3	116,113	200,267
Tenn.. . .	0	11	679,794	947,233	0	11	711,714	990,212
Tex. . . .	0	29	2,352,748	3,036,829	0	29	1,949,276	3,433,428
Ut.	0	5	207,352	428,442	0	5	155,369	469,105
Vt.. . . .	0	3	115,775	124,331	0	3	95,730	135,865
Va.. . . .	0	12	859,799	1,309,162	0	12	796,250	1,337,078
Wash.. . .	10	0	933,516	903,835	0	10	798,352	1,051,670
W.Va.. . .	6	0	341,016	310,065	0	6	328,125	405,483
Wis. . . .	11	0	1,126,794	1,047,499	0	11	995,740	1,198,584
Wyo.. . . .	0	3	67,113	106,867	0	3	53,370	133,241
Total.. .	112	426	41,805,422	48,881,221	13	525	37,457,215	54,281,858

Presidential Election Returns by Counties

All results are official. Results for New England states are for selected cities or towns due to unavailability of county results. Totals are always statewide.

Source: News Election Service

Alabama

County	1988 Dukakis (D)	Bush (R)	1984 Mondale (D)	Reagan (R)
Autauga	3,667	7,828	3,366	8,350
Baldwin	9,271	25,933	7,272	24,964
Barbour	3,836	4,958	4,591	5,459
Bibb	2,244	2,885	2,167	3,487
Blount	4,485	8,754	3,738	8,508
Bullock	3,122	1,421	3,537	1,697
Butler	3,465	3,923	3,641	4,941
Calhoun	12,451	19,806	12,752	23,291
Chambers	5,103	7,694	5,302	8,024
Cherokee	3,176	2,868	3,029	3,225
Chilton	3,820	8,761	3,924	8,243
Choctaw	3,491	3,629	3,373	3,960
Clarke	4,217	5,708	4,452	6,282
Clay	1,602	3,496	1,456	3,432
Cleburne	1,383	3,071	1,238	3,259
Coffee	4,319	8,890	4,370	10,558
Colbert	10,397	7,775	11,008	9,530
Conecuh	3,022	3,256	2,737	3,538
Coosa	1,860	2,405	1,781	2,585
Covington	3,845	8,130	3,812	9,944
Crenshaw	1,836	2,617	1,904	3,261
Cullman	8,517	14,351	7,989	14,782
Dale	3,476	9,266	3,215	10,319
Dallas	9,660	7,630	10,955	9,585
DeKalb	7,333	11,478	7,212	12,098
Elmore	4,501	10,852	4,198	11,694
Escambia	4,020	6,807	3,853	8,694
Etowah	17,762	17,828	19,074	19,243
Fayette	3,186	4,338	2,533	4,654
Franklin	4,961	5,146	4,601	5,304
Geneva	2,685	5,703	2,330	6,308
Greene	3,295	1,048	3,675	1,361
Hale	3,187	2,414	3,289	2,691
Henry	2,206	3,613	2,231	3,952
Houston	7,001	19,989	6,488	20,834
Jackson	7,418	6,090	7,635	6,730
Jefferson	107,766	148,879	107,506	158,362
Lamar	2,274	3,214	1,910	3,943
Lauderdale	12,862	12,942	12,907	15,354
Lawrence	4,646	3,616	4,866	4,466
Lee	9,078	17,180	9,077	16,757
Limestone	5,455	9,086	5,410	8,423
Lowndes	3,328	1,405	3,567	1,629
Macon	6,351	1,304	7,857	1,543
Madison	25,800	53,575	26,889	50,428
Marengo	4,402	4,241	4,811	5,261
Marion	4,505	5,955	3,918	6,771
Marshall	7,357	12,148	7,704	12,330
Mobile	45,524	72,203	47,252	81,923
Monroe	3,509	5,379	3,725	5,917
Montgomery	28,709	41,131	31,206	43,328
Morgan	10,594	18,679	11,324	24,103
Perry	3,574	2,107	3,731	2,600
Pickens	3,107	3,851	3,586	4,685
Pike	3,813	5,897	3,541	6,231
Randolph	2,462	4,625	2,439	4,940
Russell	6,589	6,333	7,610	6,654
St. Clair	4,335	10,604	4,000	10,408
Shelby	7,138	27,052	5,884	21,858
Sumter	4,390	2,212	4,478	2,493
Talladega	8,291	12,973	8,490	14,067
Tallapoosa	4,598	8,502	4,458	9,045
Tuscaloosa	18,166	27,396	16,066	28,075
Walker	11,338	11,011	10,591	12,852
Washington	3,402	3,741	3,081	4,434
Wilcox	3,369	1,739	2,663	2,337
Winston	2,954	6,235	2,624	6,845
Totals	549,506	815,576	551,899	872,849

Alabama Vote Since 1940

1940, Roosevelt, Dem., 250,726; Willkie, Rep., 42,174; Babson, Proh., 698; Browder, Com., 509; Thomas, Soc., 100.

1944, Roosevelt, Dem., 198,918; Dewey, Rep., 44,540; Watson, Proh., 1,095; Thomas, Soc., 190.

1948, Thurmond, States' Rights, 171,443; Dewey, Rep., 40,930; Wallace, Prog., 1,522; Watson, Proh., 1,085.

1952, Eisenhower, Rep., 149,231; Stevenson, Dem., 275,075; Hamblen, Proh., 1,814.

1956, Stevenson, Dem., 290,844; Eisenhower, Rep. 195,694; Independent electors, 20,323.

1960, Kennedy, Dem., 324,050; Nixon, Rep., 237,981; Faubus, States' Rights, 4,367; Decker, Proh., 2,106; King, Afro-Americans, 1,485; scattering, 236.

1964, Dem. 209,848 (electors unpledged); Goldwater, Rep., 479,085; scattering, 105.

1968, Nixon, Rep., 146,923; Humphrey, Dem., 196,579; Wallace, 3d party, 691,425; Munn, Proh., 4,022.

1972, Nixon, Rep., 728,701; McGovern, Dem., 219,108 plus 37,815 Natl. Demo. Party of Alabama; Schmitz, Conservative, 11,918; Munn., Proh., 8,551.

1976, Carter, Dem., 659,170; Ford, Rep., 504,070; Maddox, Am. Ind., 9,198; Bubar, Proh., 6,669; Hall, Com., 1,954; MacBride, Libertarian, 1,481.

1980, Reagan, Rep., 654,192; Carter, Dem., 636,730; Anderson, Independent, 16,481; Rarick, Amer. Ind., 15,010; Clark, Libertarian, 13,318; Bubar, Statesman, 1,743; Hall, Com., 1,629; DeBerry, Soc. Work., 1,303; McReynolds, Socialist, 1,006; Commoner, Citizens, 517.

1984, Reagan, Rep., 872,849; Mondale, Dem., 551,899; Bergland, Libertarian, 9,504.

1988, Bush, Rep., 815,576; Dukakis, Dem., 549,506; Paul, Lib., 8,460; Fulani, Ind., 3,311.

Alaska

Election District	1988 Dukakis (D)	Bush (R)	1984 Mondale (D)	Reagan (R)
No. 1	3,167	4,564	2,937	5,256
No. 2	1,879	2,274	1,857	2,645
No. 3	1,884	2,313	1,561	2,540
No. 4	6,057	5,963	5,293	7,322
No. 5	3,696	6,874	2,896	8,188
No. 6	1,543	2,347	1,261	2,883
No. 7	2,088	3,806	1,539	4,363
No. 8	3,815	7,629	2,752	8,603
No. 9	3,980	6,876	3,186	8,361
No. 10	3,786	6,241	3,094	7,634
No. 11	2,590	3,189	2,021	5,176
No. 12	3,733	3,511	4,063	5,348
No. 13	2,643	4,968	2,816	6,106
No. 14	3,387	6,164	2,843	7,465
No. 15	3,726	8,949	2,749	8,993
No. 16	4,174	8,851	2,935	9,942
No. 17	1,302	3,093	1,014	3,793
No. 18	1,674	5,998	967	4,858
No. 19	2,737	4,485	1,905	3,880
No. 20	3,389	5,225	2,914	6,538
No. 21	2,816	3,127	2,433	3,629
No. 22	1,377	1,861	1,319	2,075
No. 23	1,390	1,898	1,546	2,165
No. 24	1,381	1,818	1,473	2,321
No. 25	1,430	1,611	1,825	2,004
No. 26	1,568	2,959	1,216	3,019
No. 27	1,372	2,657	1,252	3,270
Totals	72,584	119,251	62,007	138,377

Alaska Vote Since 1960

1960, Kennedy, Dem., 29,809; Nixon, Rep. 30,953.

1964, Johnson, Dem., 44,329; Goldwater, Rep., 22,930.

1968, Nixon, Rep., 37,600; Humphrey, Dem., 35,411; Wallace, 3d party, 10,024.

1972, Nixon, Rep., 55,349; McGovern, Dem., 32,967; Schmitz, American, 6,903.

1976, Carter, Dem., 44,058; Ford, Rep., 71,555; MacBride, Libertarian, 6,785.

1980, Reagan, Rep., 86,112; Carter, Dem., 41,842; Clark, Libertarian, 18,479; Anderson, Ind., 11,155; Write-in, 857.

1984, Reagan, Rep., 138,377; Mondale, Dem., 62,007; Bergland, Libertarian, 6,378.

1988, Bush, Rep., 119,251; Dukakis, Dem., 72,584; Paul, Lib., 5,484; Fulani, New. Alliance, 1,024.

Arizona

County	1988 Dukakis (D)	Bush (R)	1984 Mondale (D)	Reagan (R)
Apache	8,944	5,347	7,277	5,638
Cochise	11,812	15,815	9,671	16,405
Coconino	14,660	16,649	11,528	17,581
Gila	7,147	7,861	6,509	8,543
Graham	3,407	5,120	3,080	5,247
Greenlee	1,733	1,526	1,963	1,801

La Paz	1,746	2,562	1,502	2,757
Maricopa	230,952	442,337	154,833	411,902
Mohave	10,197	17,651	7,436	17,364
Navajo	9,023	10,393	8,017	11,379
Pima	113,824	117,899	91,585	123,830
Pinal	13,850	14,966	11,923	16,464
Santa Cruz	3,268	3,320	2,463	3,855
Yavapai	14,514	27,842	9,609	24,802
Yuma	8,952	13,253	6,458	13,848
Totals	454,029	702,541	333,854	681,416

Arizona Vote Since 1940

1940, Roosevelt, Dem., 95,267; Willkie, Rep., 54,030; Babson, Proh., 742.

1944, Roosevelt, Dem., 80,926; Dewey, Rep., 56,287; Watson, Proh., 421.

1948, Truman, Dem., 95,251; Dewey, Rep., 77,597; Wallace, Prog., 3,310; Watson, Proh., 786; Teichert, Soc. Labor, 121.

1952, Eisenhower, Rep., 152,042; Stevenson, Dem., 108,528.

1956, Eisenhower, Rep., 176,990; Stevenson, Dem., 112,880; Andrews, Ind. 303.

1960, Kennedy, Dem., 176,781; Nixon, Rep., 221,241; Hass, Soc. Labor, 469.

1964, Johnson, Dem., 237,753; Goldwater, Rep., 242,535; Hass, Soc. Labor, 482.

1968, Nixon, Rep., 266,721; Humphrey, Dem., 170,514; Wallace, 3d party, 46,573; McCarthy, New Party, 2,751; Halstead, Soc. Worker, 85; Cleaver, Peace and Freedom, 217; Blomen, Soc. Labor, 75.

1972, Nixon, Rep., 402,812; McGovern, Dem., 198,540; Schmitz, Amer., 21,208; Soc. Workers, 30,945. (Due to ballot peculiarities in 3 counties (particularly Pima), thousands of voters cast ballots for the Socialist Workers Party *and* one of the major candidates. Court ordered both votes counted as official.

1976, Carter, Dem., 295,602; Ford, Rep., 418,642; McCarthy, Ind., 19,229; MacBride, Libertarian, 7,647; Camejo, Soc. Workers, 928; Anderson, Amer., 564; Maddox, Am. Ind., 85.

1980, Reagan, Rep., 529,688; Carter, Dem., 246,843; Anderson, Ind., 76,952; Clark, Libertarian, 18,784; De Berry, Soc. Workers, 1,100; Commoner, Citizens, 551; Hall, Com., 25; Griswold, Workers World, 2.

1984, Reagan, Rep., 681,416; Mondale, Dem., 333,854; Bergland, Libertarian, 10,585.

1988, Bush, Rep., 702,541; Dukakis, Dem., 454,029; Paul, Lib., 13,351; Fulani, New Alliance, 1,662.

Arkansas

	1988		1984	
County	Dukakis (D)	Bush (R)	Mondale (D)	Reagan (R)
Arkansas	3,075	4,007	3,153	4,804
Ashley	4,466	4,111	3,373	5,675
Baxter	4,808	8,614	4,528	10,870
Benton	9,399	24,295	7,306	24,296
Boone	3,998	7,567	3,356	7,961
Bradley	2,167	2,089	2,313	2,690
Calhoun	1,024	1,316	1,058	1,474
Carroll	2,632	4,553	2,263	5,041
Chicot	2,426	1,901	3,407	2,502
Clark	4,675	3,389	4,638	4,185
Clay	3,442	2,766	3,279	3,767
Cleburne	3,404	4,932	3,172	5,769
Cleveland	1,404	1,462	1,378	1,773
Columbia	3,706	5,810	3,680	6,526
Conway	4,134	4,066	3,742	5,049
Craighead	9,083	11,887	8,035	14,047
Crawford	3,582	9,092	3,071	9,551
Crittenden	6,702	7,441	6,520	6,663
Cross	2,989	3,186	2,701	3,917
Dallas	1,990	1,947	2,035	2,361
Desha	2,859	2,334	2,918	2,696
Drew	2,578	2,995	2,638	3,407
Faulkner	7,302	10,678	7,169	11,595
Franklin	2,458	3,588	2,399	4,382
Fulton	2,018	1,918	1,864	2,329
Garland	11,406	19,281	11,484	21,213
Grant	2,142	2,717	2,148	3,167
Greene	5,065	5,161	4,730	6,179
Hempstead	3,841	3,938	3,327	4,904
Hot Spring	5,090	4,181	5,836	5,629
Howard	1,818	2,510	1,746	3,079
Independence	4,523	6,637	4,415	7,428
Izard	2,652	2,824	2,346	2,726
Jackson	4,199	3,049	4,038	3,901
Jefferson	16,664	12,520	18,082	14,514
Johnson	2,818	4,046	3,056	4,720

Lafayette	1,915	1,860	1,695	2,290
Lawrence	3,179	3,205	2,594	4,039
Lee	2,878	1,863	2,541	2,101
Lincoln	2,204	1,557	2,406	1,860
Little River	2,740	2,347	2,090	3,155
Logan	1,254	2,203	3,206	5,663
Lonoke	4,786	7,215	4,636	8,425
Madison	2,106	3,067	2,133	3,516
Marion	2,033	2,993	1,945	3,545
Miller	5,437	7,110	4,686	8,302
Mississippi	6,759	7,841	7,548	10,180
Monroe	2,052	1,862	2,413	2,508
Montgomery	1,362	1,752	1,497	2,221
Nevada	1,732	1,714	1,783	2,352
Newton	1,489	2,504	1,414	2,749
Ouachita	5,229	6,297	5,858	6,700
Perry	1,470	1,627	1,404	2,047
Phillips	5,580	3,892	5,946	4,686
Pike	1,681	2,105	1,443	2,665
Poinsett	3,873	3,644	3,906	5,622
Polk	2,390	4,099	2,101	5,181
Pope	4,941	10,084	5,082	10,667
Prairie	1,688	1,947	1,437	2,407
Pulaski	55,857	70,562	54,237	77,651
Randolph	2,781	2,560	2,507	3,188
St. Francis	4,656	4,298	4,866	5,378
Saline	8,436	12,353	5,977	11,709
Scott	1,707	2,507	1,609	3,066
Searcy	1,340	2,743	1,313	2,819
Sebastian	9,684	24,426	8,688	27,595
Sevier	2,037	2,254	1,942	3,302
Sharp	2,955	3,623	2,492	4,392
Stone	1,728	2,186	1,654	2,325
Union	5,931	10,581	6,208	12,333
Van Buren	2,607	3,562	2,529	4,060
Washington	12,557	23,601	11,319	24,993
White	6,957	11,094	6,603	12,566
Woodruff	1,924	1,097	2,055	1,675
Yell	2,763	3,535	2,679	4,051
Totals	349,237	466,578	338,646	534,774

Arkansas Vote Since 1940

1940, Roosevelt, Dem., 158,622; Willkie, Rep., 42,121; Babson, Proh., 793; Thomas, Soc., 305.

1944, Roosevelt, Dem., 148,965; Dewey, Rep., 63,551; Thomas, Soc. 438.

1948, Truman, Dem., 149,659; Dewey, Rep., 50,959; Thurmond, States' Rights, 40,068; Thomas, Soc., 1,037; Wallace, Prog., 751; Watson, Proh., 1.

1952, Eisenhower, Rep., 177,155; Stevenson, Dem., 226,300; Hamblen, Proh., 886; MacArthur, Christian Nationalist, 458; Hass, Soc. Labor, 1.

1956, Stevenson, Dem., 213,277; Eisenhower, Rep., 186,287; Andrews, Ind., 7,008.

1960, Kennedy, Dem., 215,049; Nixon, Rep., 184,508; Nat'l. States' Rights, 28,952.

1964, Johnson, Dem., 314,197; Goldwater, Rep., 243,264; Kasper, Nat'l. States Rights, 2,965.

1968, Nixon, Rep., 189,062; Humphrey, Dem., 184,901; Wallace, 3d party, 235,627.

1972, Nixon, Rep., 445,751; McGovern, Dem., 198,899; Schmitz, Amer., 3,016.

1976, Carter, Dem., 498,604; Ford, Rep., 267,903; McCarthy, Ind., 639; Anderson, Amer., 389.

1980, Reagan, Rep., 403,164; Carter, Dem., 398,041; Anderson, Ind., 22,468; Clark, Libertarian, 8,970; Commoner, Citizens, 2,345; Bubar, Statesman, 1,350; Hall, Comm., 1,244.

1984, Reagan, Rep., 534,774; Mondale, Dem., 338,646; Bergland, Libertarian, 2,220.

1988, Bush, Rep., 466,578; Dukakis, Dem., 349,237; Duke, Chr. Pop., 5,146; Paul, Lib., 3,297.

California

	1988		1984	
County	Dukakis (D)	Bush (R)	Mondale (D)	Reagan (R)
Alameda	310,283	162,815	279,281	190,029
Alpine	230	306	194	264
Amador	5,197	6,893	4,166	6,970
Butte	30,406	40,143	25,126	44,836
Calaveras	5,674	7,640	3,919	7,339
Colusa	2,022	3,077	1,715	3,362
Contra Costa	169,411	158,652	137,941	167,797
Del Norte	3,587	3,714	2,693	3,989
El Dorado	19,801	30,021	13,969	26,900
Fresno	92,635	94,835	83,416	101,156
Glenn	2,894	4,944	2,480	5,994
Humboldt	29,781	21,460	24,870	27,495
Imperial	10,243	12,889	8,231	13,816
Inyo	2,653	5,042	2,348	5,811

	1988 Dukakis (D)	1988 Bush (R)	1984 Mondale (D)	1984 Reagan (R)
Kern	55,083	90,550	44,523	85,872
Kings	9,142	12,118	7,317	13,357
Lake	9,828	9,366	8,292	10,291
Lassen	3,446	5,157	3,253	5,338
Los Angeles	1,372,352	1,239,716	1,114,578	1,370,813
Madera	10,642	13,255	8,701	13,853
Marin	69,394	46,855	56,796	55,845
Mariposa	2,998	3,768	2,121	3,571
Mendocino	17,152	12,979	14,172	16,107
Merced	20,105	21,717	16,875	25,003
Modoc	1,416	2,518	1,219	2,995
Mono	1,284	2,177	944	2,630
Monterey	48,998	50,022	39,676	54,440
Napa	22,283	23,235	18,234	25,715
Nevada	14,980	21,383	10,941	19,440
Orange	269,013	586,230	200,477	615,099
Placer	27,516	42,096	20,527	36,565
Plumas	4,251	4,603	3,709	5,079
Riverside	133,122	199,979	99,853	178,397
Sacramento	188,557	201,832	153,450	197,957
San Benito	4,559	5,578	3,454	5,530
San Bernardino	151,118	235,167	114,710	217,556
San Diego	333,264	523,143	251,134	487,362
San Francisco	201,887	72,503	190,396	88,683
San Joaquin	61,699	75,309	53,441	81,084
San Luis Obispo	35,667	46,613	26,626	48,331
San Mateo	141,859	109,261	120,853	133,912
Santa Barbara	63,586	77,524	49,505	85,458
Santa Clara	277,810	254,442	224,032	280,425
Santa Cruz	63,133	37,728	47,240	39,862
Shasta	21,171	32,402	19,178	32,854
Sierra	791	860	781	1,078
Siskiyou	8,365	9,056	7,130	10,544
Solano	54,344	50,314	41,435	50,867
Sonoma	91,262	67,725	69,383	74,014
Stanislaus	44,685	51,648	36,599	54,085
Sutter	6,557	14,100	5,526	14,425
Tehama	7,213	9,854	6,511	11,536
Trinity	2,518	3,267	2,204	3,525
Tulare	30,711	46,891	27,707	50,262
Tuolumne	8,717	10,646	7,212	10,376
Ventura	89,065	147,604	64,623	146,647
Yolo	30,429	22,358	25,264	23,604
Yuba	5,444	8,937	4,996	9,265
Totals	4,702,233	5,054,917	3,815,947	5,305,410

California Vote Since 1940

1940, Roosevelt, Dem., 1,877,618; Willkie, Rep., 1,351,419; Thomas, Prog., 16,506; Browder, Com., 13,586; Babson, Proh., 9,400.

1944, Roosevelt, Dem., 1,988,564; Dewey, Rep., 1,512,965; Watson, Proh., 14,770; Thomas, Soc., 3,923; Teichert, Soc. Labor, 327.

1948, Truman, Dem., 1,913,134; Dewey, Rep., 1,895,269; Wallace, Prog., 190,381; Watson, Proh., 16,926; Thomas, Soc., 3,459; Thurmond, States' Rights, 1,228; Teichert, Soc. Labor, 195; Dobbs, Soc. Workers, 133.

1952, Eisenhower, Rep., 2,897,310; Stevenson, Dem., 2,197,548; Hallinan, Prog., 24,106; Hamblen, Proh., 15,653; MacArthur, (Tenny Ticket), 3,326; (Kellems Ticket) 178; Hass, Soc. Labor, 273; Hoopes, Soc., 206; scattered, 3,249.

1956, Eisenhower, Rep., 3,027,668; Stevenson, Dem., 2,420,136; Holtwick, Proh., 11,119; Andrews, Constitution, 6,087; Hass, Soc. Labor, 300; Hoopes, Soc., 123; Dobbs, Soc. Workers, 96; Smith, Christian Nat'l., 8.

1960, Kennedy, Dem., 3,224,099; Nixon, Rep., 3,259,722; Decker, Proh., 21,706; Hass, Soc. Labor, 1,051.

1964, Johnson, Dem., 4,171,877; Goldwater, Rep., 2,879,108; Hass, Soc. Labor, 489; DeBerry, Soc. Worker, 378; Munn, Proh., 305; Hensley, Universal, 19.

1968, Nixon, Rep., 3,467,664; Humphrey, Dem., 3,244,318; Wallace, 3d party, 487,270; Peace and Freedom party, 27,707; McCarthy, Alternative, 20,721; Gregory, write-in, 3,230; Mitchell, Com., 260; Munn, Proh., 59; Blomen, Soc. Labor, 341; Soeters, Defense, 17.

1972, Nixon, Rep. 4,602,096; McGovern, Dem., 3,475,847; Schmitz, Amer., 232,554; Spock, Peace and Freedom, 55,167; Hall, Com., 373; Hospers, Libertarian, 980; Munn, Proh., 53; Fisher, Soc. Labor, 197; Jenness, Soc. Workers, 574; Green, Universal, 21.

1976, Carter, Dem., 3,742,284; Ford, Rep., 3,882,244; MacBride, Libertarian, 56,388; Maddox, Am. Ind., 51,098; Wright, People's, 41,731; Camejo, Soc. Workers, 17,259; Hall, Com., 12,766; write-in, McCarthy, 58,412; other write-in, 4,935.

1980, Reagan, Rep. 4,524,858; Carter, Dem., 3,083,661; Anderson, Ind., 739,833; Clark, Libertarian, 148,434; Com-

moner, Ind. 61,063; Smith, Peace & Freedom, 18,116; Rarick, Amer. Ind., 9,856.

1984, Reagan, Rep. 5,305,410; Mondale, Dem., 3,815,947; Bergland, Libertarian, 48,400.

1988, Bush, Rep., 5,054,917; Dukakis, Dem., 4,702,233; Paul, Lib., 70,105; Fulani, Ind., 31,181.

Colorado

	1988		1984	
County	Dukakis (D)	Bush (R)	Mondale (D)	Reagan (R)
Adams	49,464	43,163	35,285	55,092
Alamosa	2,146	2,567	1,720	2,953
Arapahoe	61,113	95,926	39,891	107,556
Archuleta	795	1,440	584	1,557
Baca	851	1,670	580	1,903
Bent	1,068	1,032	859	1,314
Boulder	57,265	48,174	42,195	53,535
Chaffee	2,548	3,080	1,779	3,680
Cheyenne	399	760	307	892
Clear Creek	1,698	1,820	1,089	2,151
Conejos	1,976	1,455	1,553	1,669
Costilla	1,120	454	997	621
Crowley	630	862	517	993
Custer	310	753	241	832
Delta	3,521	5,449	2,835	6,678
Denver	127,173	77,753	110,200	105,096
Dolores	230	488	173	667
Douglas	6,931	17,035	3,011	12,249
Eagle	3,314	4,366	2,032	4,500
Elbert	1,566	2,805	802	2,605
El Paso	39,995	96,965	28,185	88,377
Fremont	5,278	7,623	3,895	8,250
Garfield	4,620	6,358	3,076	7,111
Gilpin	804	728	634	896
Grand	1,451	2,306	1,017	2,865
Gunnison	1,897	2,520	1,424	3,100
Hinsdale	111	295	98	310
Huerfano	1,876	1,079	1,602	1,581
Jackson	294	584	191	722
Jefferson	81,824	110,820	53,700	124,496
Kiowa	398	645	265	850
Kit Carson	1,196	2,262	778	2,762
Lake	1,516	969	1,324	1,364
La Plata	5,443	7,714	4,040	8,719
Larimer	35,703	45,967	23,896	49,883
Las Animas	4,075	2,162	3,670	2,992
Lincoln	874	1,356	587	1,661
Logan	3,382	4,485	2,155	5,883
Mesa	14,372	22,150	9,938	23,736
Mineral	174	217	117	333
Moffat	1,634	2,757	1,228	3,630
Montezuma	2,233	4,208	1,665	4,753
Montrose	3,748	6,012	2,864	7,162
Morgan	3,728	4,795	2,331	6,097
Otero	3,910	4,265	3,005	5,373
Ouray	439	814	366	914
Park	1,343	1,909	782	2,041
Philips	923	1,317	651	1,689
Pitkin	3,420	2,801	2,293	3,117
Prowers	2,207	2,978	1,467	3,501
Pueblo	32,788	20,119	27,126	24,634
Rio Blanco	803	1,821	484	2,131
Rio Grande	1,545	2,626	1,104	3,122
Routt	2,922	3,264	2,051	4,239
Saguache	1,033	945	867	1,201
San Juan	192	210	183	320
San Miguel	961	798	654	833
Sedgwick	611	921	429	1,146
Summit	2,595	2,893	1,588	3,253
Teller	1,656	3,760	1,043	3,460
Washington	958	1,707	568	2,080
Weld	20,548	26,497	13,863	31,293
Yuma	1,835	2,513	1,121	3,394
Total	621,453	728,177	454,975	821,817

Colorado Vote Since 1940

1940, Roosevelt, Dem., 265,554; Willkie, Rep., 279,576; Thomas, Soc., 1,899; Babson, Proh., 1,597; Browder, Com., 378.

1944, Roosevelt, Dem., 234,331; Dewey, Rep., 268,731; Thomas, Soc., 1,977.

1948, Truman, Dem., 267,288; Dewey, Rep., 239,714; Wallace, Prog., 6,115; Thomas, Soc., 1,678; Dobbs, Soc. Workers, 228; Teichert, Soc. Labor, 214.

1952, Eisenhower, Rep., 379,782; Stevenson, Dem., 245,504; MacArthur, Constitution, 2,181; Hallinan, Prog., 1,919; Hoopes, Soc., 365; Hass, Soc. Labor, 352.

1956, Eisenhower, Rep., 394,479; Stevenson, Dem., 263,997; Hass, Soc. Lab., 3,308; Andrews, Ind., 759; Hoopes, Soc., 531.

1960, Kennedy, Dem., 330,629; Nixon, Rep., 402,242; Hass, Soc. Labor, 2,803; Dobbs, Soc. Workers, 572.

1964, Johnson, Dem., 476,024; Goldwater, Rep., 296,767; Hass, Soc. Labor, 302; DeBerry, Soc. Worker, 2,537; Munn, Proh., 1,356.

1968, Nixon, Rep., 409,345; Humphrey, Dem., 335,174; Wallace, 3d party, 60,813; Blomen, Soc. Labor, 3,016; Gregory, New-party, 1,393; Munn, Proh., 275; Halstead, Soc. Worker, 235.

1972, Nixon, Rep., 597,189; McGovern, Dem., 329,980; Fisher, Soc. Labor, 4,361; Hospers, Libertarian, 1,111; Hall, Com., 432; Jenness, Soc. Workers, 555; Munn, Proh., 467; Schmitz, Amer., 17,269; Spock, Peoples, 2,403.

1976, Carter, Dem., 460,353; Ford, Rep., 584,367; McCarthy, Ind., 26,107; MacBride, Libertarian, 5,330; Bubar, Proh., 2,882.

1980, Reagan, Rep., 652,264; Carter, Dem., 367,973; Anderson, Ind., 130,633; Clark, Libertarian, 25,744; Commoner, Citizens, 5,614; Bubar, Statesman, 1,180; Pulley, Socialist, 520; Hall, Com., 487.

1984, Reagan, Rep., 821,817; Mondale, Dem., 454,975; Bergland, Libertarian, 11,257.

1988, Bush, Rep., 728,177; Dukakis, Dem., 621,453; Paul, Lib., 15,482; Dodge, Proh., 4,604.

Connecticut

City	1988 Dukakis (D)	Bush (R)	1984 Mondale (D)	Reagan (R)
Bridgeport	23,831	17,084	24,332	24,256
Hartford	27,295	8,100	29,327	11,621
New Britain	15,843	9,569	14,608	13,723
New Haven	31,951	11,616	32,518	16,483
Norwalk	14,518	18,618	12,509	22,447
Stamford	20,773	24,877	19,432	29,167
Waterbury	18,202	20,018	18,217	24,764
West Hartford	19,311	16,482	16,882	20,517
Totals	676,584	750,241	569,597	890,877

Connecticut Vote Since 1940

1940, Roosevelt, Dem., 417,621; Willkie, Rep., 361,021; Browder, Com., 1,091; Aiken, Soc. Labor, 971; Willkie, Union, 798.

1944, Roosevelt, Dem., 435,146; Dewey, Rep., 390,527; Thomas, Soc., 5,097; Teichert, Soc. Labor, 1,220.

1948, Truman, Dem., 423,297; Dewey, Rep., 437,754; Wallace, Prog., 13,713; Thomas, Soc., 6,964; Teichert, Soc. Labor, 1,184; Dobbs, Soc. Workers, 606.

1952, Eisenhower, Rep., 611,012; Stevenson, Dem., 481,649; Hoopes, Soc., 2,244; Hallinan, Peoples, 1,466; Hass, Soc. Labor, 535; write-in, 5.

1956, Eisenhower, Rep., 711,837; Stevenson, Dem., 405,079; scattered, 205.

1960, Kennedy, Dem., 657,055; Nixon, Rep., 565,813.

1964, Johnson, Dem., 826,269; Goldwater, Rep., 390,996; scattered, 1,313.

1968, Nixon, Rep., 556,721; Humphrey, Dem., 621,561; Wallace, 3d party, 76,650; scattered, 1,300.

1972, Nixon, Rep., 810,763; McGovern, Dem., 555,498; Schmitz, Amer., 17,239; scattered, 777.

1976, Carter, Dem., 647,895; Ford, Rep., 719,261; Maddox, George Wallace Party, 7,101; LaRouche, U.S. Labor, 1,789.

1980, Reagan, Rep., 677,210; Carter, Dem., 541,732; Anderson, Ind., 171,807; Clark, Libertarian, 8,570; Commoner, Citizens, 6,130; scattered, 836.

1984, Reagan, Rep., 890,877; Mondale, Dem., 569,597.

1988, Bush, Rep., 750,241; Dukakis, Dem., 676,584; Paul, Lib., 14,071; Fulani; New Alliance, 2,491.

Delaware

County	1988 Dukakis (D)	Bush (R)	1984 Mondale (D)	Reagan (R)
Kent	12,996	19,923	11,789	21,531
New Castle	79,147	92,587	76,238	102,322
Sussex	16,504	27,129	13,629	28,337
Totals	108,647	139,639	101,656	152,190

Delaware Vote Since 1940

1940, Roosevelt, Dem., 74,559; Willkie, Rep., 61,440; Babson, Proh., 220; Thomas, Soc., 115.

1944, Roosevelt, Dem., 68,166; Dewey, Rep., 56,747; Watson, Proh., 294; Thomas, Soc., 154.

1948, Truman, Dem., 67,813; Dewey, Rep., 69,688; Wallace, Prog., 1,050; Watson, Proh., 343; Thomas, Soc., 250; Teichert, Soc. Labor, 29.

1952, Eisenhower, Rep., 90,059; Stevenson, Dem., 83,315; Hass, Soc. Labor, 242; Hamblen, Proh., 234; Hallinan, Prog., 155; Hoopes, Soc., 20.

1956, Eisenhower, Rep., 98,057; Stevenson, Dem., 79,421; Oltwick, Proh., 400; Hass, Soc. Labor, 110.

1960, Kennedy, Dem., 99,590; Nixon, Rep., 96,373; Faubus, States' Rights, 354; Decker, Proh., 284; Hass, Soc. Labor, 82.

1964, Johnson, Dem., 122,704; Goldwater, Rep., 78,078; Hass, Soc. Labor, 113; Munn, Proh., 425.

1968, Nixon, Rep., 96,714; Humphrey, Dem., 89,194; Wallace, 3d party, 28,459.

1972, Nixon, Rep., 140,357; McGovern, Dem., 92,283; Schmitz, Amer., 2,638; Munn, Proh., 238.

1976, Carter, Dem., 122,596; Ford, Rep., 109,831; McCarthy, non-partisan, 2,437; Anderson, Amer., 645; LaRouche, U.S. Labor, 136; Bubar, Proh., 103; Levin, Soc. Labor, 86.

1980, Reagan, Rep., 111,252; Carter, Dem., 105,754; Anderson, Ind., 16,288; Clark, Libertarian, 1,974; Greaves, American, 400.

1984, Reagan, Rep., 152,190; Mondale, Dem., 101,656; Bergland, Libertarian, 268.

1988, Bush, Rep., 139,639; Dukakis, Dem., 108,647; Paul, Lib., 1,162; Fulani, New Alliance, 443.

District of Columbia

County	1988 Dukakis (D)	Bush (R)	1984 Mondale (D)	Reagan (R)
Totals	159,407	27,590	180,408	29,009

District of Columbia Vote Since 1964

1964, Johnson, Dem., 169,796; Goldwater, Rep., 28,801.

1968, Nixon, Rep., 31,012; Humphrey, Dem., 139,566.

1972, Nixon, Rep., 35,226; McGovern, Dem., 127,627; Reed, Soc. Workers, 316; Hall, Com., 252.

1976, Carter, Dem., 137,818; Ford, Rep., 27,873; Camejo, Soc. Workers, 545; MacBride, Libertarian, 274; Hall, Com., 219; LaRouche, U.S. Labor, 157.

1980, Reagan, Rep., 23,313; Carter, Dem., 130,231; Anderson, Ind., 16,131; Commoner, Citizens, 1,826; Clark, Libertarian, 1,104; Hall, Com., 369; De Berry, Soc. Work., 173; Griswold, Workers World, 52; write-ins, 690.

1984, Mondale, Dem., 180,408; Reagan, Rep., 29,009; Bergland, Libertarian, 279.

1988, Bush, Rep., 27,590; Dukakis, Dem., 159,407; Fulani, New Alliance, 2,901; Paul, Lib., 554.

Florida

County	1988 Dukakis (D)	Bush (R)	1984 Mondale (D)	Reagan (R)
Alachua	29,375	30,124	26,551	30,582
Baker	1,353	3,414	1,381	3,485
Bay	11,582	31,712	9,381	29,322
Bradford	2,386	4,218	2,341	4,128
Brevard	42,967	104,721	36,963	102,339
Broward	218,211	220,196	194,542	254,501
Calhoun	1,329	2,420	1,312	2,493
Charlotte	15,967	28,879	11,303	27,464
Citrus	12,177	21,052	10,463	20,754
Clay	7,766	25,882	5,488	21,545
Collier	12,768	38,910	9,065	33,003
Columbia	4,072	7,759	4,261	8,807
Dade	216,847	270,672	223,793	324,216
De Soto	2,181	4,237	2,302	4,822
Dixie	1,366	2,027	1,224	2,204
Duval	74,832	127,875	77,459	128,653
Escambia	29,934	64,774	26,798	66,638
Flagler	4,241	6,494	2,999	4,907
Franklin	1,283	1,911	1,089	2,218
Gadsden	6,368	5,987	7,309	5,805
Gilchrist	1,137	1,854	1,051	2,056
Glades	1,034	1,546	1,070	1,987
Gulf	1,687	3,040	1,783	3,573
Hamilton	1,314	2,062	1,401	1,921
Hardee	1,688	3,636	1,536	3,957
Hendry	2,036	3,962	2,018	4,524
Hernando	15,432	21,179	12,204	21,273
Highlands	8,087	16,713	7,217	16,465
Hillsborough	98,969	150,065	86,189	157,827
Holmes	1,639	4,221	1,231	4,547

	1988 Dukakis	1988 Bush	1984 Mondale	1984 Reagan
Indian River	10,447	24,619	8,731	23,694
Jackson	5,002	8,392	4,956	9,086
Jefferson	2,055	2,326	2,055	2,244
Lafayette	722	1,450	862	1,513
Lake	16,762	37,314	12,215	35,304
Lee	40,709	87,247	30,011	85,006
Leon	33,446	36,032	29,654	36,301
Levy	3,433	5,250	3,103	5,561
Liberty	709	1,419	649	1,409
Madison	1,950	2,556	2,101	2,816
Manatee	26,618	51,160	20,887	55,775
Marion	20,679	41,488	16,221	37,796
Martin	11,486	31,270	8,976	28,897
Monroe	10,151	15,919	7,771	16,316
Nassau	4,138	8,366	3,483	8,033
Okaloosa	9,726	40,295	7,289	36,963
Okeechobee	3,007	4,733	2,226	4,447
Orange	53,991	117,141	48,737	122,007
Osceola	9,811	21,350	6,627	18,344
Palm Beach	144,143	181,408	116,071	186,755
Pasco	50,369	63,788	40,961	66,609
Pinellas	152,374	210,971	128,547	240,535
Polk	38,236	77,065	35,505	84,174
Putnam	8,569	11,621	7,821	11,424
St. Johns	7,999	19,164	6,652	16,493
St. Lucie	17,427	32,241	13,039	28,189
Santa Rosa	5,251	18,948	4,646	21,237
Sarasota	42,095	84,585	30,512	87,713
Seminole	22,627	60,328	17,789	56,229
Sumter	3,900	5,933	3,460	6,252
Suwannee	3,126	5,859	2,788	6,079
Taylor	1,762	4,054	1,728	4,030
Union	691	1,643	761	1,804
Volusia	55,437	74,116	43,811	68,317
Wakulla	1,805	3,157	1,469	3,087
Walton	3,231	7,481	2,500	7,117
Washington	2,139	4,366	1,916	4,603
Totals	1,655,851	2,616,597	1,448,344	2,728,775

Florida Vote Since 1940

1940, Roosevelt, Dem., 359,334; Willkie, Rep., 126,158.

1944, Roosevelt, Dem., 339,377; Dewey, Rep., 143,215.

1948, Truman, Dem., 281,988; Dewey, Rep., 194,280; Thurmond, States' Rights, 89,755; Wallace, Prog., 11,620.

1952, Eisenhower, Rep., 544,036; Stevenson, Dem., 444,950; scattered, 351.

1956, Eisenhower, Rep., 643,849; Stevenson, Dem., 480,371.

1960, Kennedy, Dem., 748,700; Nixon, Rep., 795,476.

1964, Johnson, Dem., 948,540; Goldwater, Rep., 905,941.

1968, Nixon, Rep., 886,804; Humphrey, Dem., 676,794; Wallace, 3d party, 624,207.

1972, Nixon, Rep., 1,857,759; McGovern, Dem., 718,117; scattered, 7,407.

1976, Carter, Dem., 1,636,000; Ford, Rep., 1,469,531; McCarthy, Ind., 23,643; Anderson, Amer., 21,325.

1980, Reagan, Rep., 2,046,951; Carter, Dem., 1,419,475; Anderson, Ind., 189,692; Clark, Libertarian, 30,524; write-ins, 285.

1984, Reagan, Rep., 2,728,775; Mondale, Dem., 1,448,344.

1988, Bush, Rep., 2,616,597; Dukakis, Dem., 1,655,851; Paul, Lib., 19,796, Fulani, New Alliance, 6,655.

Georgia

County	1988 Dukakis (D)	1988 Bush (R)	1984 Mondale (D)	1984 Reagan (R)
Appling	1,837	3,000	1,958	2,929
Atkinson	887	1,126	901	944
Bacon	780	1,407	1,010	1,778
Baker	707	629	691	675
Baldwin	4,008	5,852	3,853	5,717
Banks	984	1,590	1,063	1,549
Barrow	2,442	4,738	2,367	4,123
Bartow	4,884	8,039	4,780	7,104
Ben Hill	1,867	2,005	1,859	2,313
Berrien	1,381	2,030	1,670	2,395
Bibb	22,084	22,179	26,427	24,170
Bleckley	1,175	1,950	1,465	1,912
Brantley	1,450	1,539	1,517	1,679
Brooks	1,500	2,136	1,661	2,229
Bryan	1,423	2,802	1,398	2,265
Bulloch	3,417	6,354	3,644	6,117
Burke	2,861	2,988	3,127	3,137
Butts	1,730	2,184	1,820	2,141
Calhoun	901	644	1,077	776
Camden	2,090	2,913	2,164	2,841
Candler	877	1,261	1,014	1,497
Carroll	4,706	10,754	5,590	11,436
Catoosa	3,588	9,319	3,089	7,908
Charlton	943	1,327	1,111	1,368
Chatham	25,063	35,623	28,271	38,482
Chattahoochee	362	454	428	459
Chattooga	2,206	3,665	2,576	2,953
Cherokee	4,378	14,593	3,499	11,146
Clarke	11,154	11,150	10,132	11,503
Clay	595	398	750	419
Clayton	14,689	28,225	11,763	31,553
Clinch	594	863	625	862
Cobb	39,297	106,621	28,414	97,429
Coffee	2,777	4,019	2,633	4,200
Colquitt	2,998	5,653	3,208	5,815
Columbia	4,617	16,401	3,727	12,294
Cook	1,226	1,555	1,510	1,860
Coweta	4,212	9,668	3,650	7,981
Crawford	1,340	1,235	1,423	1,298
Crisp	1,690	2,916	2,128	2,895
Dade	1,120	2,539	1,150	2,750
Dawson	761	1,908	643	1,322
Decatur	2,348	3,866	2,656	4,134
DeKalb	92,521	90,179	77,329	104,697
Dodge	2,164	2,677	2,513	2,765
Dooly	1,613	1,386	1,726	1,435
Dougherty	12,579	15,520	12,904	16,920
Douglas	5,086	13,493	4,371	12,428
Early	1,359	1,918	1,494	2,239
Echols	245	422	227	453
Effingham	1,905	3,933	2,055	4,266
Elbert	2,118	2,796	2,670	3,366
Emanuel	2,387	3,530	2,458	3,920
Evans	1,023	1,707	1,193	1,601
Fannin	2,123	4,271	1,965	4,159
Fayette	4,593	16,443	2,861	12,575
Floyd	8,548	14,697	8,873	15,437
Forsyth	2,347	7,947	2,275	6,841
Franklin	1,842	2,615	1,838	2,549
Fulton	120,752	91,785	125,567	95,149
Gilmer	1,363	3,353	1,234	2,972
Glascock	210	580	317	827
Glynn	6,339	11,126	6,574	11,724
Gordon	2,369	6,051	2,607	5,566
Grady	1,883	2,989	2,261	3,886
Greene	1,818	1,432	1,992	1,599
Gwinnett	20,948	66,372	14,139	54,749
Habersham	2,114	4,871	2,125	4,647
Hall	7,782	17,415	7,421	15,076
Hancock	1,947	621	2,109	644
Haralson	2,404	4,529	1,938	3,945
Harris	1,905	3,414	2,096	3,138
Hart	2,476	3,044	2,496	2,842
Heard	874	1,551	810	1,492
Henry	4,348	10,882	4,096	9,142
Houston	8,664	15,748	9,226	14,255
Irwin	918	1,226	905	1,330
Jackson	2,607	4,407	2,717	4,202
Jasper	1,188	1,474	1,122	1,431
Jeff Davis	1,242	2,050	1,380	2,233
Jefferson	2,346	2,788	2,816	2,999
Jenkins	953	1,288	1,108	1,399
Johnson	927	1,567	1,199	1,733
Jones	2,662	3,618	2,781	3,401
Lamar	1,416	2,035	1,605	2,198
Lanier	698	725	741	852
Laurens	4,879	6,929	5,471	7,181
Lee	995	2,875	1,284	2,972
Liberty	2,906	3,100	2,803	3,229
Lincoln	893	1,417	1,115	1,357
Long	681	858	816	1,099
Lowndes	6,427	10,855	6,167	10,437
Lumpkin	1,286	2,688	1,110	1,991
McDuffie	1,704	3,231	2,006	3,284
McIntosh	1,527	1,273	1,796	1,512
Macon	2,268	1,412	2,521	1,515
Madison	1,639	3,724	1,690	3,768
Marion	844	804	951	846
Meriwether	2,934	3,101	2,864	3,195
Miller	515	1,105	526	1,348
Mitchell	2,260	2,590	2,791	2,737
Monroe	1,970	2,570	2,189	2,420
Montgomery	903	1,228	950	1,365
Morgan	1,508	2,108	1,714	2,301
Murray	1,679	3,996	1,649	3,521
Muscogee	18,772	23,058	20,835	23,816
Newton	3,111	5,809	3,389	5,810
Oconee	1,990	4,265	1,467	3,471
Oglethorpe	1,154	1,951	1,238	2,122
Paulding	2,717	7,329	2,621	6,048
Peach	2,972	2,782	3,369	2,652
Pickens	1,430	3,021	1,329	2,801
Pierce	1,558	1,947	1,501	1,978
Pike	1,176	2,074	1,203	1,855
Polk	2,977	5,454	3,322	5,435
Pulaski	1,476	1,400	1,440	1,509
Putnam	1,532	2,111	1,336	1,830
Quitman	436	296	490	361
Rabun	1,301	2,278	1,267	2,191
Randolph	1,369	1,319	1,454	1,578
Richmond	20,489	27,566	21,208	29,869
Rockdale	4,330	12,413	3,291	10,121
Schley	439	635	403	614
Screven	1,461	2,178	1,747	2,583
Seminole	1,171	1,469	1,350	1,636
Spalding	4,318	7,730	4,878	8,571
Stephens	2,185	4,329	2,272	4,057
Stewart	1,136	832	1,308	805

Sumter	3,332	4,289	3,725	4,607
Talbot	1,248	802	1,494	778
Taliaferro	469	306	550	318
Tattnall	1,694	3,172	1,954	3,641
Taylor	1,134	1,145	1,340	1,292
Telfair	1,765	1,805	2,049	1,980
Terrell	1,383	1,517	1,598	1,744
Thomas	3,530	6,572	4,039	6,427
Tift	2,446	4,760	2,736	4,429
Toombs	1,152	4,433	2,385	4,470
Towns	942	1,783	1,007	1,960
Treutlen	726	970	843	1,086
Troup	4,562	9,484	5,272	9,340
Turner	1,122	1,312	1,270	1,329
Twiggs	1,730	1,261	1,755	1,143
Union	1,258	2,396	1,112	1,914
Upson	2,666	4,614	2,943	4,803
Walker	4,753	10,487	5,000	10,734
Walton	3,091	5,974	2,481	4,995
Ware	4,292	4,819	4,435	5,547
Warren	1,091	897	1,258	1,087
Washington	2,615	2,752	3,034	2,887
Wayne	2,417	3,340	2,434	3,698
Webster	427	361	534	402
Wheeler	658	709	774	833
White	1,028	2,648	1,090	2,369
Whitfield	4,618	12,761	5,284	11,957
Wilcox	1,079	1,235	1,212	1,218
Wilkes	1,549	1,810	1,586	1,837
Wilkinson	1,831	1,546	2,102	1,756
Worth	1,311	2,668	1,685	2,910
Totals	**714,792**	**1,081,331**	**706,628**	**1,068,722**

Georgia Vote Since 1940

1940, Roosevelt, Dem., 265,194; Willkie, Rep., 23,934; Ind. Dem., 22,428; total, 46,362; Babson, Proh., 983.

1944, Roosevelt, Dem., 268,187; Dewey, Rep., 56,506; Watson, Proh., 36.

1948, Truman, Dem., 254,646; Dewey, Rep., 76,691; Thurmond, States' Rights, 85,055; Wallace, Prog., 1,636; Watson, Proh., 732.

1952, Eisenhower, Rep., 198,979; Stevenson, Dem., 456,823; Liberty Party, 1.

1956, Stevenson, Dem., 444,388; Eisenhower, Rep., 222,778; Andrews, Ind., write-in, 1,754.

1960, Kennedy, Dem., 458,638; Nixon, Rep., 274,472; write-in, 239.

1964, Johnson, Dem., 522,557; Goldwater, Rep., 616,600.

1968, Nixon, Rep., 380,111; Humphrey, Dem., 334,440; Wallace, 3d party, 535,550; write-in, 162.

1972, Nixon, Rep., 881,496; McGovern, Dem., 289,529; Schmitz, Amer., 2,288; scattered.

1976, Carter, Dem., 979,409; Ford, Rep., 483,743; write-in, 4,306.

1980, Reagan, Rep., 654,168; Carter, Dem., 890,955; Anderson, Ind., 36,055; Clark, Libertarian, 15,627.

1984, Reagan, Rep., 1,068,722; Mondale, Dem., 706,628.

1988, Bush, Rep., 1,081,331; Dukakis, Dem., 714,792; Paul, Lib., 8,435; Fulani, New Alliance, 5,099.

Hawaii

	1988		1984	
County	Dukakis (D)	Bush (R)	Mondale (D)	Reagan (R)
Hawaii	24,091	17,125	17,856	20,707
Honolulu	138,971	120,258	107,404	140,258
Kauai	11,770	8,298	8,862	9,249
Maui	17,532	12,944	12,966	14,720
Totals	192,364	158,625	147,098	184,934

Hawaii Vote Since 1960

1960, Kennedy, Dem., 92,410; Nixon, Rep., 92,295.

1964, Johnson, Dem., 163,249; Goldwater, Rep., 44,022.

1968, Nixon, Rep., 91,425; Humphrey, Dem., 141,324; Wallace, 3d party, 3,469.

1972, Nixon, Rep., 168,865; McGovern, Dem., 101,409.

1976, Carter, Dem., 147,375; Ford, Rep., 140,003; MacBride, Libertarian, 3,923.

1980, Reagan, Rep., 130,112; Carter, Dem., 135,879; Anderson, Ind., 32,021; Clark, Libertarian, 3,269; Commoner, Citizens, 1,548; Hall, Com., 458.

1984, Reagan, Rep., 184,934; Mondale, Dem., 147,098; Bergland, Libertarian, 2,167.

1988, Bush, Rep., 158,625; Dukakis, Dem., 192,364; Paul, Lib., 1,999; Fulani, New Alliance, 1,003.

Idaho

	1988		1984	
County	Dukakis (D)	Bush (R)	Mondale (D)	Reagan (R)
Ada	30,525	54,951	21,760	60,036
Adams	643	1,107	540	1,381
Bannock	13,074	14,986	9,399	18,742
Bear Lake	867	2,084	481	2,760
Benewah	1,518	1,650	1,447	2,039
Bingham	4,346	10,131	3,064	11,900
Blaine	2,498	3,130	1,971	3,603
Boise	620	1,044	436	1,249
Bonner	5,555	5,721	4,628	6,889
Bonneville	7,032	22,613	4,877	24,392
Boundary	1,336	1,800	1,158	2,159
Butte	521	899	429	1,245
Camas	136	288	123	364
Canyon	10,207	21,426	7,527	24,613
Caribou	867	2,239	535	3,032
Cassia	1,833	5,345	1,036	6,503
Clark	133	281	59	353
Clearwater	1,861	1,659	1,608	2,176
Custer	616	1,253	461	1,653
Elmore	2,078	3,756	1,458	4,595
Franklin	806	2,992	439	3,261
Fremont	1,178	3,401	818	4,006
Gem	2,064	2,926	1,607	3,644
Gooding	1,872	2,908	1,247	3,819
Idaho	2,198	3,541	1,996	4,219
Jefferson	1,198	5,295	743	5,770
Jerome	1,985	3,830	1,284	4,913
Kootenai	11,621	15,093	9,004	17,330
Latah	6,544	6,367	5,571	7,709
Lemhi	1,157	2,378	852	2,810
Lewis	807	786	648	1,000
Lincoln	574	918	386	1,211
Madison	1,009	6,197	483	6,798
Minidoka	2,290	4,623	1,398	5,938
Nez Perce	7,754	7,027	5,981	8,153
Oneida	508	1,269	360	1,528
Owyhee	848	1,707	574	2,141
Payette	1,900	3,786	1,410	4,605
Power	1,095	1,838	678	2,298
Shoshone	3,379	2,134	3,033	3,156
Teton	531	982	370	1,242
Twin Falls	7,078	13,243	4,567	16,974
Valley	1,251	1,897	945	2,299
Washington	1,359	2,380	1,119	3,015
Totals	147,272	253,881	108,510	297,523

Idaho Vote Since 1940

1940, Roosevelt, Dem., 127,842; Willkie, Rep., 106,553; Thomas, Soc., 497; Browder, Com., 276.

1944, Roosevelt, Dem., 107,399; Dewey, Rep., 100,137; Watson, Proh., 503; Thomas, Soc., 282.

1948, Truman, Dem., 107,370; Dewey, Rep., 101,514; Wallace, Prog., 4,972; Watson, Proh., 628; Thomas, Soc., 332.

1952, Eisenhower, Rep., 180,707; Stevenson Dem., 95,081; Hallinan, Prog., 443; write-in, 23.

1956, Eisenhower, Rep., 166,979; Stevenson, Dem., 105,868; Andrews, Ind., 126; write-in, 16.

1960, Kennedy, Dem., 138,853; Nixon, Rep., 161,597.

1964, Johnson, Dem., 148,920; Goldwater, Rep., 143,557.

1968, Nixon, Rep., 165,369; Humphrey, Dem., 89,273; Wallace, 3d party, 36,541.

1972, Nixon, Rep., 199,384; McGovern, Dem., 80,826; Schmitz, Amer., 28,869; Spock, Peoples, 903.

1976, Carter, Dem., 126,549; Ford, Rep., 204,151; Maddox, Amer., 5,935; MacBride, Libertarian, 3,558; LaRouche, U.S. Labor, 739.

1980, Reagan, Rep., 290,699; Carter, Dem., 110,192; Anderson, Ind., 27,058; Clark, Libertarian, 8,425; Rarick, Amer., 1,057.

1984, Reagan, Rep., 297,523; Mondale, Dem., 108,510; Bergland, Libertarian, 2,823.

1988, Bush, Rep., 253,881; Dukakis, Dem., 147,272; Paul, Lib., 5,313; Fulani, Ind., 2,502.

Illinois

	1988		1984	
County	Dukakis (D)	Bush (R)	Mondale (D)	Reagan (R)
Adams	13,768	15,831	10,336	20,225
Alexander	2,693	1,954	2,872	2,574
Bond	3,459	3,608	2,870	4,240
Boone	4,234	6,923	3,717	7,536
Brown	1,267	1,373	959	1,478
Bureau	7,354	8,896	6,925	11,741
Calhoun	1,544	1,238	1,443	1,648

County				
Carroll	2,990	4,464	2,398	5,237
Cass	3,316	2,916	2,937	3,435
Champaign	29,733	33,247	27,266	39,224
Christian	8,295	7,040	7,541	8,534
Clark	3,275	4,508	3,032	5,318
Clay	2,761	3,494	2,524	4,562
Clinton	5,935	7,681	4,628	9,233
Coles	8,327	11,043	7,156	14,044
Cook	1,129,973	878,582	1,112,641	1,055,558
Crawford	3,555	4,951	3,130	6,261
Cumberland	1,904	2,667	1,733	3,002
DeKalb	11,811	17,182	10,942	20,294
DeWitt	2,660	3,942	2,352	4,534
Douglas	3,184	4,378	2,886	5,691
DuPage	94,285	217,907	71,430	227,141
Edgar	3,880	5,538	3,241	6,821
Edwards	1,218	2,212	1,057	2,778
Effingham	4,553	8,431	3,841	9,617
Fayette	4,632	5,452	3,844	6,607
Ford	2,026	4,059	1,763	4,871
Franklin	11,023	7,677	10,667	9,656
Fulton	9,046	6,999	9,131	9,147
Gallatin	2,455	1,580	2,164	1,939
Greene	3,020	3,136	2,563	4,057
Grundy	5,525	8,743	4,671	9,595
Hamilton	2,618	2,622	2,251	3,074
Hancock	4,740	4,568	3,713	6,251
Hardin	1,308	1,504	1,205	1,689
Henderson	2,085	1,726	1,969	2,289
Henry	11,594	11,358	10,679	14,504
Iroquois	4,221	9,596	3,300	11,327
Jackson	11,334	9,687	12,105	13,609
Jasper	2,135	3,024	1,750	3,673
Jefferson	7,729	7,624	7,200	9,642
Jersey	4,376	4,343	3,762	5,146
JoDaviess	4,141	4,923	3,348	5,877
Johnson	1,872	2,797	1,647	3,424
Kane	36,366	66,283	31,875	72,655
Kankakee	15,147	20,316	15,246	23,807
Kendall	4,347	10,653	3,789	10,872
Knox	12,752	10,842	12,027	14,974
Lake	64,327	114,115	53,947	118,401
LaSalle	22,271	22,166	20,532	27,388
Lawrence	3,140	3,655	2,924	4,686
Lee	4,608	8,903	3,919	11,178
Livingston	5,009	10,324	4,567	12,291
Logan	4,727	8,490	4,052	9,932
McDonough	5,247	7,173	4,561	9,383
McHenry	18,919	46,135	14,420	47,282
McLean	18,659	30,572	15,880	32,221
Macon	25,364	23,862	25,463	30,457
Macoupin	12,195	9,362	10,602	12,282
Madison	54,175	44,907	48,352	57,021
Marion	8,592	8,695	7,599	11,300
Marshall	2,742	3,588	2,386	4,060
Mason	3,406	3,424	3,354	4,109
Massac	3,227	3,507	3,194	3,827
Menard	2,103	3,560	1,826	3,925
Mercer	4,204	3,683	3,982	4,907
Monroe	4,529	6,275	3,256	6,936
Montgomery	7,293	6,388	6,360	8,191
Morgan	6,032	8,808	5,361	10,683
Moultrie	3,013	3,167	2,458	3,593
Ogle	5,641	11,644	4,803	13,503
Peoria	35,253	37,605	36,830	45,607
Perry	5,167	4,576	4,584	5,852
Piatt	3,099	4,137	2,840	5,000
Pike	4,614	3,965	3,965	5,295
Pope	996	1,202	940	1,545
Pulaski	1,793	1,666	1,724	1,923
Putnam	1,601	1,516	1,487	1,912
Randolph	7,844	7,396	6,355	9,415
Richland	2,863	4,264	2,182	5,665
Rock Island	40,174	27,412	40,208	35,121
St. Clair	55,465	41,439	52,294	51,046
Saline	6,676	5,798	6,038	7,176
Sangamon	37,729	50,175	34,059	54,086
Schuyler	1,866	2,178	1,533	2,515
Scott	1,243	1,535	943	1,976
Shelby	4,650	5,370	4,317	6,372
Stark	1,274	1,841	1,072	2,228
Stephenson	7,460	11,342	6,723	14,237
Tazewell	24,603	28,861	23,095	33,782
Union	4,197	4,244	3,815	4,721
Vermilion	17,918	16,943	16,530	22,932
Wabash	2,241	3,453	1,795	3,639
Warren	3,617	4,584	3,318	5,846
Washington	2,689	4,127	2,363	5,129
Wayne	3,135	5,481	2,621	6,298
White	4,144	4,354	3,457	5,500
Whiteside	11,328	12,978	11,226	16,743
Will	49,816	73,129	45,193	78,684
Williamson	12,712	12,274	11,614	14,930
Winnebago	45,280	55,699	44,629	64,203
Woodford	4,604	9,474	4,425	10,758
Totals	2,215,940	2,310,939	2,086,499	2,707,103

Illinois Vote Since 1940

1940, Roosevelt, Dem., 2,149,934; Willkie, Rep., 2,047,240; Thomas, Soc., 10,914; Babson, Proh., 9,190.

1944, Roosevelt, Dem., 2,079,479; Dewey, Rep., 1,939,314; Teichert, Soc. Labor, 9,677; Watson, Proh., 7,411; Thomas, Soc., 180.

1948, Truman, Dem., 1,994,715; Dewey, Rep., 1,961,103; Watson, Proh., 11,959; Thomas, Soc., 11,522; Teichert, Soc. Labor, 3,118.

1952, Eisenhower, Rep., 2,457,327; Stevenson, Dem., 2,013,920; Hass, Soc. Labor, 9,363; write-in, 448.

1956, Eisenhower, Rep., 2,623,327; Stevenson, Dem., 1,775,682; Hass, Soc. Labor, 8,342; write-in, 56.

1960, Kennedy, Dem., 2,377,846; Nixon, Rep., 2,368,988; Hass, Soc. Labor, 10,560; write-in, 15.

1964, Johnson, Dem., 2,796,833; Goldwater, Rep., 1,905,946; write-in, 62.

1968, Nixon, Rep., 2,174,774; Humphrey, Dem., 2,039,814; Wallace, 3d party, 390,958; Blomen, Soc. Labor, 13,878; write-in, 325.

1972, Nixon, Rep. 2,788,179; McGovern, Dem., 1,913,472; Fisher, Soc. Labor, 12,344; Schmitz. Amer., 2,471; Hall, Com., 4,541; others, 2,229.

1976, Carter, Dem., 2,271,295; Ford, Rep., 2,364,269; McCarthy, Ind., 55,939; Hall, Com., 9,250; MacBride, Libertarian, 8,057; Camejo, Soc. Workers, 3,615; Levin, Soc. Labor, 2,422; LaRouche, U.S. Labor, 2,018; write-in, 1,968.

1980, Reagan, Rep., 2,358,049; Carter, Dem., 1,981,413; Anderson, Ind., 346,754; Clark, Libertarian, 38,939; Commoner, Citizens, 10,692; Hall, Com., 9,711; Griswold, Workers World, 2,257; DeBerry, Socialist Workers, 1,302; write-ins, 604.

1984, Reagan, Rep., 2,707,103; Mondale, Dem., 2,086,499; Bergland, Libertarian, 10,086.

1988, Bush, Rep., 2,310,939; Dukakis, Dem., 2,215,940; Paul, Lib., 14,944; Fulani, Solid., 10,276.

Indiana

County	1988 Dukakis (D)	1988 Bush (R)	1984 Mondale (D)	1984 Reagan (R)
Adams	3,811	8,137	3,923	7,958
Allen	39,238	74,638	38,462	75,505
Bartholomew	8,804	17,364	8,075	18,704
Benton	1,349	2,698	1,357	3,281
Blackford	2,253	3,336	2,395	3,787
Boone	4,168	11,608	3,982	11,790
Brown	2,115	3,348	2,657	3,517
Carroll	2,952	4,981	2,774	5,528
Cass	5,784	10,970	5,521	12,355
Clark	14,528	16,544	14,138	19,419
Clay	3,724	5,852	3,707	6,957
Clinton	4,412	8,570	4,329	8,969
Crawford	2,036	2,532	2,256	2,633
Daviess	3,483	6,768	3,545	7,721
Dearborn	5,066	8,195	4,920	9,149
Decatur	2,979	6,245	2,766	6,551
Dekalb	4,657	9,018	4,617	8,769
Delaware	20,548	27,348	19,791	30,092
Dubois	5,954	9,995	5,423	9,391
Elkhart	14,236	33,793	13,240	34,621
Fayette	4,118	5,949	4,122	7,142
Floyd	11,024	14,291	10,616	15,466
Fountain	3,279	5,113	2,897	5,450
Franklin	2,472	4,777	2,225	5,202
Fulton	2,788	5,234	2,527	6,057
Gibson	7,031	7,610	7,082	8,618
Grant	10,799	18,441	9,986	20,482
Greene	5,979	7,689	5,297	8,438
Hamilton	8,853	36,654	6,364	30,254
Hancock	5,355	13,374	4,550	12,880
Harrison	4,933	6,702	4,634	7,255
Hendricks	7,643	22,090	6,659	21,307
Henry	7,779	11,280	7,064	11,926
Howard	11,518	19,971	10,458	22,386
Huntington	3,873	11,675	4,598	10,805
Jackson	5,550	9,470	5,163	9,879
Jasper	3,237	6,009	2,821	6,537
Jay	3,212	5,363	3,174	5,975
Jefferson	5,221	6,949	4,952	7,482
Jennings	3,667	5,666	3,264	6,356
Johnson	9,001	24,654	7,715	23,482
Knox	7,006	9,813	6,417	10,872
Kosciusko	5,321	17,761	4,877	17,560
LaGrange	2,029	4,495	1,864	4,772
Lake	105,026	79,929	117,984	94,870
LaPorte	17,585	20,537	15,904	23,346
Lawrence	5,787	10,742	5,608	11,440
Madison	24,443	32,596	22,254	36,510
Marion	128,627	184,519	130,185	184,880
Marshall	5,488	10,490	4,931	11,100
Martin	2,132	3,066	1,937	3,363

County			
Miami	4,613	8,533	4,224	9,551
Monroe	15,855	20,756	14,719	21,772
Montgomery	3,623	10,793	3,626	11,119
Morgan	5,375	14,284	4,627	14,884
Newton	1,744	3,274	1,596	3,560
Noble	4,143	7,889	4,237	8,459
Ohio	1,113	1,412	1,068	1,503
Orange	2,739	5,245	D2,571	5,909
Owen	2,484	3,837	2,082	4,204
Parke	2,563	4,458	2,205	5,052
Perry	4,804	4,720	4,760	4,785
Pike	3,037	3,294	3,231	3,689
Porter	19,390	29,790	17,862	32,505
Posey	4,468	5,987	4,452	6,472
Pulaski	2,213	3,677	2,008	4,167
Putnam	3,850	7,119	3,392	7,820
Randolph	3,990	6,856	3,805	7,793
Ripley	3,605	6,414	3,336	7,143
Rush	2,451	5,112	2,307	5,429
St. Joseph	48,056	49,481	47,513	54,404
Scott	3,378	3,455	3,460	4,110
Shelby	5,382	10,176	5,357	11,056
Spencer	4,061	4,964	4,005	5,816
Starke	4,104	4,458	3,674	5,104
Steuben	3,114	6,855	2,441	6,424
Sullivan	4,320	4,246	4,006	4,771
Switzerland	1,479	1,572	1,484	1,857
Tippecanoe	16,256	27,897	15,789	29,706
Tipton	2,485	5,148	2,328	5,687
Union	946	1,814	816	1,970
Vanderburgh	31,270	38,928	31,049	40,994
Vermillion	4,044	3,674	3,666	4,428
Vigo	19,192	21,929	18,429	26,259
Wabash	4,168	9,153	4,077	9,862
Warren	1,542	2,243	1,309	2,525
Warrick	7,999	10,504	6,345	10,202
Washington	3,370	4,998	3,334	5,874
Wayne	10,209	16,388	10,173	18,955
Wells	3,437	7,712	3,274	7,579
White	3,256	6,220	3,157	7,279
Whitley	3,642	7,679	3,690	7,763
Totals	860,643	1,297,763	841,481	1,377,230

Indiana Vote Since 1940

1940, Roosevelt, Dem., 874,063; Willkie, Rep., 899,466; Babson, Proh., 6,437; Thomas, Soc., 2,075; Aiken, Soc. Labor, 706.

1944, Roosevelt, Dem., 781,403; Dewey, Rep., 875,891; Watson, Proh., 12,574; Thomas, Soc., 2,223.

1948, Truman, Dem., 807,833; Dewey, Rep., 821,079; Watson, Proh., 14,711; Wallace, Prog., 9,649; Thomas, Soc., 2,179; Teichert, Soc. Labor, 763.

1952, Eisenhower, Rep., 1,136,259; Stevenson, Dem., 801,530; Hamblen, Proh., 15,335; Hallinan, Prog., 1,222; Hass, Soc. Labor, 979.

1956, Eisenhower, Rep., 1,182,811; Stevenson, Dem., 783,908; Holtwick, Proh., 6,554; Hass, Soc. Labor, 1,334.

1960, Kennedy, Dem., 952,358; Nixon, Rep., 1,175,120; Decker, Proh., 6,746; Hass, Soc. Labor, 1,136.

1964, Johnson, Dem. 1,170,848; Goldwater, Rep., 911,118; Munn, Proh., 8,266; Hass, Soc. Labor, 1,374.

1968, Nixon, Rep., 1,067,885; Humphrey, Dem., 806,659; Wallace, 3d party, 243,108; Munn, Proh., 4,616; Halstead, Soc. Worker, 1,293; Gregory, write-in, 36.

1972, Nixon, Rep., 1,405,154; McGovern, Dem., 708,568; Reed, Soc. Workers, 5,575; Fisher, Soc. Labor, 1,688; Spock, Peace & Freedom, 4,544.

1976, Carter, Dem., 1,014,714; Ford, Rep., 1,185,958; Anderson, Amer., 14,048; Camejo, Soc. Workers, 5,695; LaRouche, U.S. Labor, 1,947.

1980 Reagan, Rep., 1,255,656; Carter, Dem., 844,197; Anderson, Ind., 111,639; Clark, Libertarian, 19,627; Commoner, Citizens, 4,852; Greaves, American, 4,750; Hall, Com., 702; DeBerry, Soc., 610.

1984 Reagan, Rep., 1,377,230; Mondale, Dem., 841,481; Bergland, Libertarian, 6,741.

1988, Bush, Rep., 1,297,763; Dukakis, Dem., 860,643; Fulani, New Alliance, 10,215.

Iowa

County	1988 Dukakis (D)	Bush (R)	1984 Mondale (D)	Reagan (R)
Adair	2,261	1,833	1,979	2,615
Adams	1,283	1,080	1,221	1,706
Allamakee	2,768	3,186	2,282	3,997
Appanoose	3,209	2,779	3,289	3,412
Audubon	1,863	1,478	1,854	2,306
Benton	5,873	4,011	4,993	5,566

County			
Black Hawk	31,657	24,112	31,467	32,262
Boone	7,232	4,381	6,485	5,746
Bremer	4,961	5,079	4,084	6,895
Buchanan	4,778	3,495	4,129	4,965
Buena Vista	4,580	4,170	4,109	5,193
Butler	2,593	3,523	2,323	4,570
Calhoun	2,990	2,474	2,541	3,311
Carroll	5,437	3,701	4,960	5,021
Cass	2,934	3,962	2,417	5,053
Cedar	4,032	3,373	3,086	4,617
Cerro Gordo	12,857	9,358	11,570	11,214
Cherokee	3,574	3,218	3,349	4,046
Chickasaw	3,530	2,549	3,186	3,661
Clarke	2,262	1,631	2,030	2,262
Clay	4,173	3,641	3,774	4,450
Clayton	4,320	3,839	3,446	5,029
Clinton	12,549	10,243	11,240	13,914
Crawford	3,868	3,375	3,396	4,552
Dallas	7,501	4,858	6,564	6,080
Davis	2,246	1,563	2,187	1,956
Decatur	2,192	1,406	2,098	2,104
Delaware	3,947	3,425	3,158	4,769
Des Moines	11,593	7,652	11,173	9,559
Dickinson	3,342	3,678	3,025	4,064
Dubuque	23,797	14,530	21,876	19,239
Emmet	2,778	2,173	2,746	2,946
Fayette	5,304	4,921	4,677	6,505
Floyd	4,377	3,266	4,154	4,341
Franklin	2,594	2,320	2,349	3,129
Fremont	1,547	1,946	1,426	2,666
Greene	3,011	2,091	2,831	2,579
Grundy	2,211	3,433	1,915	4,527
Guthrie	2,910	2,005	2,517	2,783
Hamilton	4,156	3,277	3,330	4,279
Hancock	2,831	2,731	2,539	3,362
Hardin	5,088	3,856	4,477	5,195
Harrison	2,883	3,108	2,495	4,352
Henry	3,754	3,951	3,377	4,516
Howard	2,330	1,970	2,135	2,718
Humboldt	2,713	2,594	2,406	3,396
Ida	1,787	1,951	1,559	2,618
Iowa	3,338	3,247	2,815	4,352
Jackson	4,864	3,237	4,400	4,811
Jasper	8,940	6,703	8,023	8,576
Jefferson	3,594	3,614	2,961	4,727
Johnson	28,759	15,453	26,000	18,677
Jones	4,641	3,496	3,825	4,907
Keokuk	2,899	2,278	2,649	2,913
Kossuth	5,088	3,938	4,838	4,872
Lee	10,911	6,228	8,912	8,756
Linn	42,993	33,129	38,528	41,061
Louisa	2,268	2,060	1,927	2,623
Lucas	2,454	1,776	2,422	2,630
Lyon	1,706	3,517	1,401	4,178
Madison	3,421	2,410	3,067	3,168
Mahaska	4,451	4,798	4,107	6,086
Marion	6,922	5,914	6,313	7,259
Marshall	9,760	7,657	8,809	10,839
Mills	2,092	3,212	1,434	3,994
Mitchell	2,870	2,338	2,531	3,144
Monona	2,408	2,068	2,159	2,746
Monroe	2,338	1,313	2,342	1,927
Montgomery	1,896	3,166	1,661	4,224
Muscatine	7,059	6,904	5,986	9,069
O'Brien	2,768	4,241	2,479	5,008
Osceola	1,277	1,951	1,146	2,285
Page	2,185	4,583	1,914	5,876
Palo Alto	3,377	2,041	3,018	2,715
Plymouth	4,220	5,316	3,464	6,482
Pocahontas	2,722	1,871	2,481	2,627
Polk	84,476	57,854	75,413	71,413
Pottawattamie	14,958	17,193	12,329	21,527
Poweshiek	4,876	3,683	4,103	4,715
Ringgold	1,609	1,110	1,593	1,512
Sac	2,613	2,411	2,363	3,298
Scott	34,415	31,025	32,550	38,034
Shelby	2,806	3,019	2,291	4,200
Sioux	2,923	10,270	2,585	11,665
Story	19,051	13,782	18,277	19,804
Tama	4,584	3,362	4,061	4,882
Taylor	1,671	1,647	1,499	2,496
Union	3,236	2,751	2,875	3,583
Van Buren	1,612	1,692	1,606	2,138
Wapello	10,177	5,350	10,545	7,098
Warren	9,627	6,424	8,171	8,277
Washington	3,776	3,741	3,079	4,613
Wayne	1,988	1,467	1,927	2,061
Webster	10,267	6,926	9,930	9,619
Winnebago	2,804	2,863	2,569	3,616
Winneshiek	4,443	4,194	3,724	5,277
Woodbury	20,153	18,790	18,951	23,002
Worth	2,440	1,488	2,263	1,985
Wright	3,353	2,658	2,980	3,675
Totals	670,557	545,355	605,620	703,088

Iowa Vote Since 1940

1940, Roosevelt, Dem., 578,800; Willkie, Rep., 632,370; Babson, Proh., 2,284; Browder, Com., 1,524; Aiken, Soc. Labor, 452.

1944, Roosevelt, Dem., 499,876; Dewey, Rep., 547,267; Watson, Proh., 3,752; Thomas, Soc., 1,511; Teichert, Soc. Labor, 193.

1948, Truman, Dem., 522,380; Dewey, Rep., 494,018; Wallace, Prog., 12,125; Teichert, Soc. Labor, 4,274; Watson, Proh., 3,382; Thomas, Soc., 1,829; Dobbs, Soc. Workers, 26.

1952, Eisenhower, Rep., 808,906; Stevenson, Dem., 451,513; Hallinan, Prog., 5,085; Hamblen, Proh., 2,882; Hoopes, Soc., 219; Hass, Soc. Labor, 139; scattering 29.

1956, Eisenhower, Rep., 729,187; Stevenson, Dem., 501,858; Andrews (A.C.P. of Iowa), 3,202; Hoopes, Soc., 192; Hass, Soc. Labor, 125.

1960, Kennedy, Dem., 550,565; Nixon, Rep., 722,381; Hass, Soc. Labor, 230; write-in, 634.

1964, Johnson, Dem., 733,030; Goldwater, Rep., 449,148; Hass, Soc. Labor, 182; DeBerry, Soc. Worker, 159; Munn, Proh., 1,902.

1968, Nixon, Rep., 619,106; Humphrey, Dem., 476,699; Wallace, 3d party, 66,422; Munn, Proh., 362; Halstead, Soc. Worker, 3,377; Cleaver, Peace and Freedom, 1,332; Blomen, Soc. Labor, 241.

1972, Nixon, Rep., 706,207; McGovern, Dem., 496,206; Schmitz, Amer., 22,056; Jenness, Soc. Workers, 488; Fisher, Soc. Labor, 195; Hall, Com. 272; Green, Universal, 199; scattered, 321.

1976, Carter, Dem., 619,931; Ford, Rep., 632,863; McCarthy, Ind., 20,051; Anderson, Amer., 3,040; MacBride, Libertarian, 1,452.

1980, Reagan, Rep., 676,026; Carter, Dem., 508,672; Anderson, Ind., 115,633; Clark, Libertarian, 13,123; Commoner, Citizens, 2,273; McReynolds, Socialist, 534; Hall Com., 298; DeBerry, Soc. Work., 244; Greaves, American, 189; Bubar, Statesman, 150; scattering, 519.

1984, Reagan, Rep., 703,088; Mondale, Dem., 605,620; Bergland, Libertarian, 1,844.

1988, Bush, Rep., 545,355; Dukakis, Dem., 670,557; LaRouche, Ind., 3,526; Paul, Lib., 2,494.

Kansas

County	1988 Dukakis (D)	Bush (R)	1984 Mondale (D)	Reagan (R)
Allen	2,392	3,429	1,779	4,266
Anderson	1,466	1,781	1,155	2,462
Atchison	3,177	3,243	2,641	4,536
Barber	1,118	1,539	805	2,111
Barton	5,024	7,741	3,111	10,234
Bourbon	2,623	3,660	2,174	4,856
Brown	1,719	3,059	1,303	3,894
Butler	7,690	10,976	6,352	12,920
Chase	538	884	393	1,162
Chautauqua	661	1,247	497	1,688
Cherokee	4,069	4,281	3,663	5,081
Cheyenne	594	1,105	356	1,442
Clark	409	876	324	1,075
Clay	1,112	2,997	919	3,559
Cloud	2,022	3,043	1,878	3,856
Coffey	1,246	2,581	1,037	3,063
Comanche	375	738	285	993
Cowley	6,186	7,778	5,153	9,930
Crawford	7,783	6,940	6,722	9,518
Decatur	793	1,291	467	1,769
Dickinson	2,870	5,121	2,168	6,487
Doniphan	1,312	2,162	962	2,818
Douglas	15,752	16,149	12,877	18,804
Edwards	792	993	606	1,352
Elk	608	1,075	452	1,301
Ellis	5,289	5,194	3,457	7,509
Ellsworth	1,219	1,711	905	2,353
Finney	3,408	5,381	2,398	6,943
Ford	3,817	5,685	2,914	6,738
Franklin	3,592	4,777	2,524	6,283
Geary	2,721	3,782	2,301	4,475
Gove	663	966	426	1,310
Graham	702	1,139	480	1,423
Grant	907	1,654	615	2,043
Gray	696	1,180	514	1,580
Greeley	317	506	227	699
Greenwood	1,421	2,217	1,173	2,900
Hamilton	517	801	408	1,037
Harper	1,235	1,941	893	2,696
Harvey	5,503	6,893	4,599	8,507
Haskell	427	964	281	1,151
Hodgeman	439	732	306	939
Jackson	2,261	2,759	1,667	3,464
Jefferson	2,810	3,605	1,990	4,524
Jewell	684	1,546	583	1,992
Johnson	55,183	95,591	37,782	101,042

County				
Kearny	524	1,073	321	1,214
Kingman	1,420	2,205	1,047	2,826
Kiowa	485	1,276	361	1,537
Labette	4,433	5,125	3,631	6,542
Lane	450	768	282	1,008
Leavenworth	8,797	9,913	6,583	11,018
Lincoln	796	1,229	551	1,723
Linn	1,497	2,163	1,152	2,794
Logan	503	988	331	1,235
Lyon	5,314	6,820	4,188	9,796
McPherson	4,354	6,563	3,185	8,630
Marion	2,024	3,685	1,633	4,407
Marshall	2,560	3,140	1,813	4,097
Meade	664	1,322	491	1,804
Miami	4,427	4,807	3,076	5,877
Mitchell	1,145	2,257	919	3,036
Montgomery	5,429	9,067	4,933	12,023
Morris	1,165	1,682	820	2,240
Morton	569	1,074	322	1,353
Nemaha	2,261	2,849	1,761	3,653
Neosho	3,402	3,739	2,679	4,968
Ness	887	1,230	539	1,779
Norton	855	1,923	611	2,515
Osage	2,840	3,496	2,072	4,288
Osborne	943	1,541	686	2,171
Ottawa	953	1,836	698	2,343
Pawnee	1,474	1,825	1,092	2,570
Phillips	960	2,316	626	2,810
Pottawatomie	2,544	3,897	1,798	4,596
Pratt	1,651	2,505	1,253	3,240
Rawlins	612	1,318	412	1,625
Reno	11,545	12,753	9,229	16,621
Republic	1,069	2,346	966	2,974
Rice	2,033	2,503	1,559	3,598
Riley	7,283	9,507	5,974	11,306
Rooks	1,012	1,938	699	2,604
Rush	1,020	1,045	718	1,758
Russell	1,448	2,403	1,055	3,673
Saline	7,998	11,371	6,527	15,242
Scott	717	1,590	427	2,017
Sedgwick	65,618	86,124	55,060	95,972
Seward	1,655	4,089	1,198	5,047
Shawnee	33,940	35,489	26,307	43,435
Sheridan	600	901	429	1,274
Sherman	1,082	1,929	714	2,702
Smith	1,004	1,951	684	2,330
Stafford	1,121	1,532	844	2,062
Stanton	310	592	205	783
Stevens	612	1,642	386	1,862
Summer	4,417	5,394	3,713	6,942
Thomas	1,408	2,342	887	3,106
Trego	795	979	598	1,491
Wabaunsee	1,166	1,737	805	2,276
Wallace	257	655	152	838
Washington	1,063	2,269	889	2,979
Wichita	399	721	232	916
Wilson	1,545	2,743	1,343	3,660
Woodson	761	1,062	596	1,408
Wyandotte	38,678	19,097	35,887	27,267
Totals	422,636	554,049	332,471	674,646

Kansas Vote Since 1940

1940, Roosevelt, Dem., 364,725; Willkie, Rep., 489,169; Babson, Proh., 4,056; Thomas, Soc., 2,347.

1944, Roosevelt, Dem., 287,458; Dewey, Rep., 442,096; Watson, Proh., 2,609; Thomas, Soc., 1,613.

1948, Truman, Dem., 351,902; Dewey, Rep., 423,039; Watson, Proh., 6,468; Wallace, Prog., 4,603; Thomas, Soc., 2,807.

1952, Eisenhower, Rep., 616,302; Stevenson, Dem., 273,296; Hamblen, Proh., 6,038; Hoopes, Soc., 530.

1956, Eisenhower, Rep., 566,878; Stevenson, Dem., 296,317; Holtwick, Proh., 3,048.

1960, Kennedy, Dem., 363,213; Nixon, Rep., 561,474; Decker, Proh., 4,138.

1964, Johnson, Dem., 464,028; Goldwater, Rep., 386,579; Munn, Proh., 5,393; Hass, Soc. Labor, 1,901.

1968, Nixon, Rep., 478,674; Humphrey, Dem., 302,996; Wallace, 3d, 88,921; Munn, Proh., 2,192.

1972, Nixon, Rep., 619,812; McGovern, Dem., 270,287; Schmitz, Cons., 21,808; Munn, Proh., 4,188.

1976, Carter, Dem., 430,421; Ford, Rep., 502,752; McCarthy, Ind., 13,185; Anderson, Amer., 4,724; MacBride, Libertarian, 3,242; Maddox, Cons., 2,118; Bubar, Proh., 1,403.

1980, Reagan, Rep., 566,812; Carter, Dem., 326,150; Anderson, Ind., 68,231; Clark, Libertarian, 14,470; Shelton, American, 1,555; Hall, Com., 967; Bubar, Statesman, 821; Rarick, Conservative, 789.

1984, Reagan, Rep., 674,646; Mondale, Dem., 332,471; Bergland, Libertarian, 3,585.

1988, Bush, Rep., 554,049; Dukakis, Dem., 422,636; Paul,
Ind., 12,553; Fulani, Ind., 3,806.

Kentucky

	1988		1984	
County	Dukakis (D)	Bush (R)	Mondale (D)	Reagan (R)
Adair	1,723	4,346	1,812	4,500
Allen	1,573	3,342	1,521	3,427
Anderson	2,176	3,225	1,717	3,425
Ballard	2,162	1,460	2,002	1,663
Barren	4,799	6,653	4,503	7,717
Bath	2,099	1,614	1,781	2,020
Bell	5,182	5,759	5,490	7,249
Boone	5,382	12,667	4,853	12,690
Bourbon	2,793	3,308	2,649	3,836
Boyd	9,552	9,379	9,601	10,925
Boyle	3,575	4,746	3,378	5,675
Bracken	1,176	1,630	1,136	1,812
Breathitt	3,387	2,149	3,435	2,855
Breckinridge	2,765	3,841	2,669	4,432
Bullitt	6,005	8,859	5,005	9,556
Butler	1,245	3,278	1,055	3,121
Caldwell	2,564	2,952	2,427	3,162
Calloway	5,287	6,225	5,028	6,442
Campbell	9,553	19,387	9,068	21,473
Carlisle	1,428	1,104	1,277	1,308
Carroll	1,913	1,702	1,564	1,824
Carter	4,570	4,325	3,985	4,656
Casey	1,216	3,857	1,122	4,356
Christian	5,704	9,250	5,432	10,708
Clark	4,252	5,329	3,595	6,130
Clay	1,709	4,156	1,634	4,772
Clinton	899	3,248	838	3,459
Crittenden	1,443	2,211	1,483	2,167
Cumberland	753	2,231	766	2,729
Daviess	14,815	17,356	13,347	19,495
Edmonson	1,243	2,555	1,200	3,001
Elliott	1,797	550	1,683	601
Estill	1,692	3,077	1,593	3,512
Fayette	32,554	48,065	28,961	51,993
Fleming	2,086	2,409	1,616	2,824
Floyd	12,327	5,296	10,259	5,218
Franklin	9,271	9,805	7,790	11,057
Fulton	1,531	1,474	1,534	1,780
Gallatin	1,060	881	1,042	1,042
Garrard	1,710	2,681	1,566	3,284
Grant	1,896	2,835	1,685	2,840
Graves	7,153	6,274	6,759	7,287
Grayson	2,575	5,186	2,200	5,524
Green	1,595	3,139	1,611	3,210
Greenup	6,956	6,559	6,923	7,451
Hancock	1,478	1,733	1,287	1,967
Hardin	7,262	13,240	6,329	14,293
Harlan	7,341	5,166	7,663	6,959
Harrison	2,748	2,983	2,405	3,467
Hart	2,519	2,927	2,278	3,065
Henderson	7,648	6,911	6,795	7,389
Henry	2,544	2,286	2,279	2,802
Hickman	1,158	1,142	1,049	1,380
Hopkins	7,453	7,979	6,743	9,368
Jackson	678	3,926	542	3,806
Jefferson	127,936	139,711	119,350	161,283
Jessamine	2,955	7,057	2,379	7,081
Johnson	3,538	4,619	3,078	5,225
Kenton	14,838	30,738	14,642	34,304
Knott	5,185	1,691	4,487	1,728
Knox	2,919	4,903	2,932	5,730
Larue	1,822	2,590	1,514	2,873
Laurel	3,620	9,296	3,267	9,621
Lawrence	2,198	2,294	2,223	2,713
Lee	984	1,588	768	1,862
Leslie	1,105	3,280	1,075	3,385
Letcher	4,697	3,601	4,153	3,676
Lewis	1,568	3,108	1,484	3,445
Lincoln	2,677	3,530	2,498	3,996
Livingston	2,052	1,834	2,007	1,866
Logan	3,379	4,295	3,347	4,889
Lyon	1,337	1,077	1,272	969
McCracken	12,208	12,160	12,535	12,903
McCreary	1,644	3,477	1,609	4,028
McLean	2,269	1,829	1,917	1,942
Madison	6,672	9,958	6,509	11,309
Magoffin	2,895	2,158	2,942	2,343
Marion	3,152	2,500	2,835	3,305
Marshall	5,888	5,256	5,725	5,152
Martin	1,581	2,587	1,471	3,248
Mason	2,721	3,158	2,663	2,751
Meade	3,079	3,441	2,503	3,820
Menifee	1,096	670	956	785
Mercer	2,832	3,904	2,516	4,592
Metcalfe	1,705	2,179	1,575	2,349
Monroe	1,025	4,214	1,052	4,670
Montgomery	3,082	3,435	2,490	3,864
Morgan	2,329	1,452	2,481	1,834
Muhlenberg	6,912	5,369	6,157	6,094
Nelson	4,788	5,283	4,199	6,044
Nicholas	1,242	1,271	1,107	1,535
Ohio	3,612	4,910	3,253	5,119
Oldham	4,025	8,716	2,857	8,112
Owen	1,823	1,468	1,575	1,735
Owsley	345	1,266	375	1,466
Pendleton	1,576	2,487	1,529	2,767
Perry	5,557	5,154	5,258	5,218
Pike	16,339	9,976	15,817	11,869
Powell	2,113	2,126	1,575	2,269
Pulaski	4,788	13,482	4,384	14,434
Robertson	515	511	467	567
Rockcastle	1,041	3,880	1,089	4,328
Rowan	2,968	3,093	2,748	3,698
Russell	1,455	4,292	1,448	4,476
Scott	3,380	4,482	2,606	4,461
Shelby	3,834	4,998	3,326	5,390
Simpson	2,138	2,699	2,140	3,073
Spencer	1,121	1,368	910	1,456
Taylor	2,879	5,362	3,286	5,932
Todd	1,632	2,282	1,505	2,364
Trigg	1,991	2,427	1,905	2,512
Trimble	1,342	1,083	1,088	1,389
Union	3,316	2,292	3,090	2,524
Warren	9,684	16,703	7,937	16,167
Washington	1,950	2,445	1,786	2,804
Wayne	2,057	3,672	2,277	4,449
Webster	3,019	2,159	3,042	2,504
Whitley	3,794	7,337	3,575	7,851
Wolfe	1,516	916	1,394	1,257
Woodford	2,653	4,512	2,290	4,746
Totals	580,368	734,281	536,756	815,345

Kentucky Vote Since 1940

1940, Roosevelt, Dem., 557,222; Willkie, Rep., 410,384;
Babson, Proh., 1,443; Thomas, Soc., 1,014.

1944, Roosevelt, Dem., 472,589; Dewey, Rep., 392,448;
Watson, Proh., 2,023; Thomas, Soc., 535; Teichert, Soc.
Labor, 222.

1948, Truman, Dem., 466,756; Dewey, Rep., 341,210; Thur-
mond, States' Rights, 10,411; Wallace, Prog., 1,567;
Thomas, Soc., 1,284; Watson, Proh., 1,245; Teichert, Soc.
Labor, 185.

1952, Eisenhower, Rep., 495,029; Stevenson, Dem., 495,729;
Hamblen, Proh., 1,161; Hass, Soc. Labor, 893; Hallinan,
Proh., 336.

1956, Eisenhower, Rep., 572,192; Stevenson, Dem., 476,453;
Byrd, States' Rights, 2,657; Holtwick, Proh., 2,145;
Hass, Soc. Labor, 358.

1960, Kennedy, Dem., 521,855; Nixon, Rep., 602,607.

1964, Johnson, Dem., 669,659; Goldwater, Rep., 372,977;
John Kasper, Nat'l. States Rights, 3,469.

1968, Nixon, Rep., 462,411; Humphrey, Dem., 397,547;
Wallace, 3d p., 193,098; Halstead, Soc. Worker, 2,843.

1972, Nixon, Rep., 676,446; McGovern, Dem., 371,159;
Schmitz, Amer., 17,627; Jenness, Soc. Workers, 685; Hall,
Com., 464; Spock, Peoples, 1,118.

1976, Carter, Dem., 615,717; Ford, Rep., 531,852; Anderson, Amer., 8,308; McCarthy, Ind., 6,837; Maddox,
Amer. Ind., 2,328; MacBride, Libertarian, 814.

1980, Reagan, Rep., 635,274; Carter, Dem., 616,417; Anderson, Ind., 31,127; Clark, Libertarian, 5,531; McCormack,
Respect For Life, 4,233; Commoner, Citizens, 1,304; Pulley, Socialist, 393; Hall, Com., 348.

1984, Reagan, Rep., 815,345; Mondale, Dem., 536,756.

1988, Bush, Rep., 734,281; Dukakis, Dem., 580,368; Duke,
Pop., 4,494; Paul, Lib., 2,118.

Louisiana

	1988		1984	
Parish	Dukakis (D)	Bush (R)	Mondale (D)	Reagan (R)
Acadia	11,510	11,319	9,262	14,906
Allen	5,204	3,674	4,842	4,474
Ascension	12,147	10,726	11,048	11,945
Assumption	5,610	4,017	4,660	5,433
Avoyelles	7,353	7,659	6,808	9,402
Beauregard	4,704	6,466	4,199	7,353
Bienville	3,705	3,680	3,530	4,587
Bossier	9,035	20,807	7,006	22,638
Caddo	39,204	54,498	35,727	63,429
Calcasieu	33,932	29,649	33,214	35,566
Caldwell	1,423	2,997	1,348	3,341
Cameron	2,257	1,775	1,608	2,265
Catahoula	1,916	2,862	1,649	3,640
Claiborne	3,158	3,756	2,789	4,349
Concordia	3,461	5,037	3,332	6,177
DeSoto	5,366	5,022	4,642	5,989
E. Baton Rouge	59,270	86,791	56,673	95,704
East Carroll	1,809	1,536	2,089	1,974
East Feliciana	3,659	3,527	4,122	4,166
Evangeline	7,693	7,437	6,981	8,680
Franklin	3,043	5,520	2,937	6,708

Grant	2,628	4,402	2,588	5,334
Iberia	12,166	15,438	10,170	17,727
Iberville	8,678	5,855	8,587	6,455
Jackson	2,842	4,251	2,568	5,034
Jefferson	53,035	110,942	41,163	123,997
Jefferson Davis	6,799	5,851	5,962	8,296
Lafayette	24,133	36,648	19,265	44,344
Lafourche	15,013	16,152	10,186	20,930
LaSalle	1,622	4,559	1,318	5,404
Lincoln	5,427	8,853	5,432	9,087
Livingston	9,659	15,779	8,913	17,465
Madison	2,416	2,334	2,906	2,849
Morehouse	4,496	7,335	4,829	8,585
Natchitoches	6,151	7,224	5,806	8,836
Orleans	116,851	64,763	119,478	86,316
Ouachita	15,429	33,858	15,525	37,270
Plaquemines	3,997	6,084	3,261	7,655
Pointe Coupee	6,308	4,333	6,732	5,477
Rapides	17,928	29,977	16,121	32,879
Red River	2,254	2,266	1,958	3,060
Richland	2,833	5,226	2,918	5,980
Sabine	3,532	4,767	2,980	6,295
St. Bernard	11,406	19,609	8,076	24,428
St. Charles	7,973	9,685	6,784	10,185
St. Helena	3,013	2,006	2,956	2,366
St. James	6,707	3,799	5,989	4,627
St. John The Baptist	8,366	7,464	7,646	9,093
St. Landry	19,091	15,790	17,950	19,055
St. Martin	10,148	7,541	8,589	9,698
St. Mary	10,364	11,540	9,411	15,275
St. Tammany	15,638	38,334	11,719	38,664
Tangipahoa	13,527	16,669	12,799	19,580
Tensas	1,556	1,645	1,628	1,956
Terrebonne	12,686	18,745	9,640	23,696
Union	3,210	5,900	2,916	6,585
Vermilion	12,180	9,224	9,033	12,721
Vernon	4,998	7,453	4,076	9,035
Washington	8,369	9,374	7,680	11,185
Webster	7,434	10,204	6,509	12,055
W. Baton Rouge	4,686	3,972	4,631	4,189
West Carroll	1,607	3,077	1,474	3,874
West Feliciana	2,146	1,854	2,296	2,097
Winn	2,699	4,165	2,633	4,934
Totals	717,460	883,702	651,586	1,037,299

Louisiana Vote Since 1940

1940, Roosevelt, Dem., 319,751; Willkie, Rep., 52,446.

1944, Roosevelt, Dem., 281,564; Dewey, Rep., 67,750.

1948, Thurmond, States' Rights, 204,290; Truman, Dem., 136,344; Dewey, Rep., 72,657; Wallace, Prog., 3,035.

1952, Eisenhower, Rep., 306,925, Stevenson, Dem., 345,027.

1956, Eisenhower, Rep., 329,047; Stevenson, Dem., 243,977; Andrews, States' Rights, 44,520.

1960, Kennedy, Dem., 407,339; Nixon, Rep., 230,890; States' Rights (unpledged) 169,572.

1964, Johnson, Dem., 387,068; Goldwater, Rep., 509,225.

1968, Nixon, Rep., 257,535; Humphrey, Dem., 309,615; Wallace, 3d party, 530,300.

1972, Nixon, Rep., 686,852; McGovern, Dem., 298,142; Schmitz, Amer., 52,099; Jenness, Soc. Workers, 14,398.

1976, Carter, Dem., 661,365; Ford, Rep., 587,446; Maddox, Amer., 10,058; Hall, Com., 7,417; McCarthy, Ind., 6,588; MacBride, Libertarian, 3,325.

1980, Reagan, Rep., 792,853; Carter, Dem., 708,453; Anderson, Ind., 26,345; Rarick, Amer. Ind., 10,333; Clark, Libertarian, 8,240; Commoner, Citizens, 1,584; DeBerry, Soc. Work., 783.

1984, Reagan, Rep., 1,037,299; Mondale, Dem., 651,586; Bergland, Libertarian, 1,876.

1988, Bush, Rep., 883,702; Dukakis, Dem., 717,460; Duke, Pop., 18,612; Paul, Lib., 4,115.

Maine

	1988		1984	
	Dukakis	Bush	Mondale	Reagan
City	(D)	(R)	(D)	(R)
Auburn	4,629	5,947	4,430	6,994
Augusta	4,576	5,182	4,451	5,995
Bangor	6,534	7,194	6,155	8,389
Bath	1,838	2,543	1,714	2,899
Biddeford	5,017	4,375	5,489	4,147
Brewer	1,784	2,908	1,461	3,093
Gardiner	1,395	1,609	1,216	1,942
Lewiston	9,225	7,265	9,853	9,480
Old Town	2,220	1,640	2,217	2,087
Portland	18,234	11,676	17,543	13,315
Rockland	1,198	1,850	1,051	2,169
Saco	3,169	3,852	3,094	3,761
Sanford	3,456	4,541	3,517	4,578
South Portland	5,820	5,744	5,377	6,653
Waterville	4,031	3,158	4,075	3,873
Westbrook	3,648	4,086	3,345	4,456
Totals	243,569	307,131	214,515	336,500

Maine Vote Since 1940

1940, Roosevelt, Dem., 156,478; Willkie, Rep., 165,951; Browder, Com., 411.

1944, Roosevelt, Dem., 140,631; Dewey, Rep., 155,434; Teichert, Soc. Labor, 335.

1948, Truman, Dem., 111,916; Dewey, Rep., 150,234; Wallace, Prog., 1,884; Thomas, Soc., 547; Teichert, Soc. Labor, 206.

1952, Eisenhower, Rep., 232,353; Stevenson, Dem., 118,806; Hallinan, Prog., 332; Hass, Soc. Labor, 156; Hoopes, Soc., 138; scattered, 1.

1956, Eisenhower, Rep., 249,238; Stevenson, Dem., 102,468.

1960, Kennedy, Dem., 181,159; Nixon, Rep., 240,608.

1964, Johnson, Dem., 262,264; Goldwater, Rep., 118,701.

1968, Nixon, Rep., 169,254; Humphrey, Dem., 217,312; Wallace, 3d party, 6,370.

1972, Nixon, Rep., 256,458; McGovern, Dem., 160,584; scattered, 229.

1976, Carter, Dem., 232,279; Ford, Rep., 236,320; McCarthy, Ind., 10,874; Bubar, Proh., 3,495.

1980, Reagan, Rep., 238,522; Carter, Dem., 220,974; Anderson, Ind., 53,327; Clark, Libertarian, 5,119; Commoner, Citizens, 4,394; Hall, Com., 591; write-ins, 84.

1984, Reagan, Rep., 336,500; Mondale, Dem., 214,515.

1988, Bush, Rep., 307,131; Dukakis, Dem., 243,569; Paul, Lib., 2,700; Fulani, New Alliance, 1,405.

Maryland

	1988		1984	
	Dukakis	Bush	Mondale	Reagan
County	(D)	(R)	(D)	(R)
Allegany	11,844	17,462	11,143	19,763
Anne Arundel	55,440	98,540	47,565	94,171
Baltimore	121,570	163,881	106,908	171,929
Calvert	6,376	10,956	5,455	8,303
Caroline	2,440	4,661	2,198	4,876
Carroll	12,368	31,224	8,898	27,230
Cecil	7,807	13,224	6,681	13,111
Charles	11,823	20,828	10,264	16,132
Dorchester	3,709	6,343	3,160	6,699
Frederick	17,061	32,575	13,411	29,606
Garrett	2,557	6,665	2,386	7,042
Harford	19,803	38,493	17,133	37,382
Howard	34,007	44,153	25,713	35,641
Kent	2,925	3,761	2,390	3,897
Montgomery	165,187	154,191	146,036	146,924
Prince George's	133,816	86,545	136,063	95,121
Queen Anne's	3,857	7,803	2,938	6,784
St. Mary's	7,434	12,767	6,420	11,201
Somerset	2,911	4,222	2,439	4,508
Talbot	3,948	8,170	3,198	8,028
Washington	14,408	25,912	13,329	27,118
Wicomico	9,413	16,272	8,160	16,124
Worcester	4,787	8,430	3,770	8,208
Totals	826,304	876,167	787,935	879,918

Maryland Vote Since 1940

1940, Roosevelt, Dem., 384,546; Willkie, Rep., 269,534; Thomas, Soc., 4,093; Browder, Com., 1,274; Aiken, Soc. Labor, 657.

1944, Roosevelt, Dem., 315,490; Dewey, Rep., 292,949.

1948, Truman, Dem., 286,521; Dewey, Rep., 294,814; Wallace, Prog., 9,983; Thomas, Soc., 2,941; Thurmond, States' Rights, 2,476; Wright, write-in, 2,294.

1952, Eisenhower, Rep., 499,424; Stevenson, Dem., 395,337; Hallinan, Prog., 7,313.

1956, Eisenhower, Rep., 559,738; Stevenson, Dem., 372,613.

1960, Kennedy, Dem., 565,800; Nixon, Rep., 489,538.

1964, Johnson, Dem., 730,912; Goldwater, Rep., 385,495; write-in, 50.

1968, Nixon, Rep., 517,995; Humphrey, Dem., 538,310; Wallace, 3d party, 178,734.

1972, Nixon, Rep., 829,305; McGovern, Dem., 505,781; Schmitz, Amer., 18,726.

1976, Carter, Dem., 759,612; Ford, Rep., 672,661.

1980, Reagan, Rep., 680,606; Carter, Dem., 726,161; Anderson, Ind., 119,537; Clark, Libertarian, 14,192.

1984, Reagan, Rep., 879,918; Mondale, Dem., 787,935; Bergland, Libertarian, 5,721.

1988, Bush, Rep., 876,167; Dukakis, Dem., 826,304; Paul, Lib., 6,748; Fulani, Alliance, 5,115.

Massachusetts

	1988		1984	
	Dukakis	Bush	Mondale	Reagan
City	(D)	(R)	(D)	(R)
Boston	122,349	62,202	131,745	75,311
Brockton	14,776	16,056	14,130	17,161
Cambridge	32,027	8,770	32,582	10,007
Fall River	20,184	8,394	20,722	11,463
Framingham	15,826	12,745	14,368	15,074
Lawrence	9,255	8,265	10,986	9,877
Lowell	16,391	13,998	15,042	16,834
Lynn	18,540	12,182	17,103	14,445
New Bedford	22,609	9,901	22,070	13,147
Newton	29,039	13,892	27,343	16,184
Quincy	20,911	18,403	18,971	20,123
Somerville	21,612	8,931	21,065	11,318
Springfield	30,113	16,244	29,376	21,431
Worcester	34,369	24,355	32,525	27,348
Totals	1,401,415	1,194,635	1,239,606	1,310,936

Massachusetts Vote Since 1940

1940, Roosevelt, Dem., 1,076,522; Willkie, Rep., 939,700; Thomas, Soc., 4,091; Browder, Com., 3,806; Aiken, Soc. Labor, 1,492; Babson, Proh., 1,370.

1944, Roosevelt, Dem., 1,035,296; Dewey, Rep., 921,350; Teichert, Soc. Labor, 2,780; Watson, Proh., 973.

1948, Truman, Dem., 1,151,788; Dewey, Rep., 909,370; Wallace, Prog., 38,157; Teichert, Soc. Labor, 5,535; Watson, Proh., 1,663.

1952, Eisenhower, Rep., 1,292,325; Stevenson, Dem., 1,083,525; Hallinan, Prog., 4,636; Hass, Soc. Labor, 1,957; Hamblen, Proh., 886; scattered, 69; blanks, 41,150.

1956, Eisenhower, Rep., 1,393,197; Stevenson, Dem., 948,190; Hass, Soc. Labor, 5,573; Holtwick, Proh., 1,205; others, 341.

1960, Kennedy, Dem., 1,487,174; Nixon, Rep., 976,750; Hass, Soc. Labor, 3,892; Decker, Proh., 1,633; others, 31; blank and void, 26,024.

1964, Johnson, Dem., 1,786,422; Goldwater, Rep., 549,727; Hass, Soc. Labor, 4,755; Munn, Proh., 3,735; scattered, 159; blank, 48,104.

1968, Nixon, Rep., 766,844; Humphrey, Dem., 1,469,218; Wallace, 3d party, 87,088; Blomen, Soc. Labor, 6,180; Munn, Proh., 2,369; scattered, 53; blanks, 25,394.

1972, Nixon, Rep., 1,112,078; McGovern, Dem., 1,332,540; Jenness, Soc. Workers, 10,600; Fisher, Soc. Labor, 129; Schmitz, Amer., 2,877; Spock, Peoples, 101; Hall, Com., 46; Hospers, Libertarian, 43; scattered, 342.

1976, Carter, Dem., 1,429,475; Ford, Rep., 1,030,276; McCarthy, Ind., 65,637; Camejo, Soc. Workers, 8,138; Anderson, Amer., 7,555; La Rouche, U.S. Labor, 4,922; MacBride, Libertarian, 135.

1980, Reagan, Rep., 1,057,631; Carter, Dem., 1,053,802; Anderson, Ind., 382,539; Clark, Libertarian, 22,038; DeBerry, Soc. Workers, 3,735; Commoner, Citizens, 2,056; McReynolds, Socialist, 62; Bubar, Statesman, 34; Griswold, Workers World, 19; scattered, 2,382.

1984, Reagan, Rep., 1,310,936; Mondale, Dem., 1,239,606.

1988, Bush, Rep., 1,194,635; Dukakis, Dem., 1,401,415; Paul, Lib., 24,251; Fulani, New Alliance, 9,561.

Michigan

	1988		1984	
	Dukakis	Bush	Mondale	Reagan
County	(D)	(R)	(D)	(R)
Alcona	1,918	2,966	1,616	3,223
Alger	2,210	1,830	2,018	2,175
Allegan	10,785	22,163	8,389	23,762
Alpena	6,341	6,664	5,136	8,212
Antrim	3,159	5,231	2,507	5,726
Arenac	3,211	3,064	2,436	3,483
Baraga	1,753	1,630	1,818	1,965
Barry	7,983	12,546	5,898	14,245
Bay	28,225	20,710	22,597	26,198
Benzie	2,437	3,240	1,866	3,590
Berrien	21,948	37,799	21,228	43,160
Branch	5,231	9,225	3,860	11,004
Calhoun	22,717	26,771	20,313	34,470
Cass	7,444	10,229	6,634	11,647
Charlevoix	3,875	5,802	3,175	6,355
Cheboygan	3,943	5,395	3,358	6,053
Chippewa	5,222	6,786	4,575	8,135
Clare	4,710	5,663	3,764	6,587
Clinton	9,225	15,497	6,226	17,387
Crawford	1,825	3,097	1,558	3,303
Delta	8,891	7,114	7,934	8,952
Dickinson	6,129	6,158	5,614	6,880
Eaton	15,322	24,193	10,290	27,720
Emmet	4,170	7,105	3,254	7,760
Genesee	104,880	70,922	89,491	92,943
Gladwin	4,164	4,746	3,368	5,401
Gogebic	5,151	3,509	5,554	4,006
Grand Traverse	10,098	17,191	7,271	18,036
Gratiot	5,719	8,447	4,000	10,456
Hillsdale	4,763	10,571	3,616	12,063
Houghton	6,510	7,098	6,434	8,652
Huron	5,714	9,419	3,966	11,073
Ingham	55,984	58,363	46,411	68,753
Ionia	8,160	12,028	5,735	14,162
Iosco	4,929	7,234	3,850	7,907
Iron	3,774	2,866	3,559	3,468
Isabella	7,960	10,362	6,435	12,215
Jackson	21,865	33,885	18,340	40,133
Kalamazoo	39,457	50,205	32,460	58,327
Kalkaska	2,092	3,369	1,595	3,623
Kent	73,467	131,910	66,238	137,417
Keweenaw	631	536	628	599
Lake	1,958	1,713	1,845	2,125
Lapeer	10,736	16,670	7,800	19,222
Leelanau	3,331	5,215	2,498	5,356
Lenawee	13,690	19,115	11,012	22,409
Livingston	13,749	31,331	10,720	31,846
Luce	864	1,528	833	1,715
Mackinac	2,093	3,127	1,949	3,627
Macomb	112,856	175,632	97,816	194,300
Manistee	4,765	5,368	3,917	6,328
Marquette	15,418	11,704	14,074	14,196
Mason	4,531	6,800	3,803	8,202
Mecosta	4,736	8,181	4,048	9,023
Menominee	4,918	5,440	4,425	6,618
Midland	13,452	19,994	10,769	21,521
Missaukee	1,621	3,566	1,256	3,970
Monroe	21,847	26,189	19,617	29,419
Montcalm	7,664	10,963	5,491	13,109
Montmorency	1,563	2,514	1,387	2,913
Muskegon	28,977	33,567	25,247	39,355
Newaygo	5,389	9,896	4,496	10,636
Oakland	174,745	283,359	150,286	306,050
Oceana	3,356	5,693	2,865	6,405
Ogemaw	4,012	4,091	3,132	4,901
Ontonagon	2,517	2,023	2,350	2,464
Osceola	2,860	5,218	2,127	5,923
Oscoda	1,170	1,972	951	2,239
Otsego	2,635	4,620	2,117	4,639
Ottawa	18,769	61,515	15,000	60,142
Presque Isle	3,025	3,614	2,481	4,207
Roscommon	4,394	5,866	3,359	6,419
Saginaw	45,616	42,401	38,420	51,495
St. Clair	20,909	32,336	16,998	36,114
St. Joseph	7,017	13,084	5,795	15,405
Sanilac	5,445	10,653	4,126	12,627
Schoolcraft	2,071	1,802	1,920	2,139
Shiawassee	13,056	15,506	9,514	18,756
Tuscola	9,060	12,093	6,212	14,698
Van Buren	10,668	14,522	8,853	16,426
Washtenaw	61,799	55,029	55,084	58,736
Wayne	450,222	291,996	496,632	367,391
Wexford	4,287	6,043	3,396	7,279
Totals	1,675,783	1,965,486	1,529,638	2,251,571

Michigan Vote Since 1940

1940, Roosevelt, Dem., 1,032,991; Willkie, Rep., 1,039,917; Thomas, Soc., 7,593; Browder, Com., 2,834; Babson, Proh., 1,795; Aiken, Soc. Labor, 795.

1944, Roosevelt, Dem., 1,106,899; Dewey, Rep., 1,084,423; Watson, Proh., 6,503; Thomas, Soc., 4,598; Smith, America First, 1,530; Teichert, Soc. Labor, 1,264.

1948, Truman, Dem., 1,003,448; Dewey, Rep., 1,038,595; Wallace, Prog., 46,515; Watson, Proh., 13,052; Thomas, Soc., 6,063; Teichert, Soc. Labor, 1,263; Dobbs, Soc. Workers, 672.

1952, Eisenhower, Rep., 1,551,529; Stevenson, Dem., 1,230,657; Hamblen, Proh., 10,331; Hallinan, Prog., 3,922; Hass, Soc. Labor, 1,495; Dobbs, Soc. Workers, 655; scattered, 3.

1956, Eisenhower, Rep., 1,713,647; Stevenson, Dem., 1,359,898; Holtwick, Proh., 6,923.

1960, Kennedy, Dem., 1,687,269; Nixon, Rep., 1,620,428; Dobbs, Soc. Workers, 4,347; Decker, Proh., 2,029; Daly, Tax Cut, 1,767; Hass, Soc. Labor, 1,718; Ind. American, 539.

1964, Johnson, Dem., 2,136,615; Goldwater, Rep., 1,060,152; DeBerry, Soc. Workers, 3,817; Hass, Soc. Labor, 1,704; Proh. (no candidate listed), 699, scattering, 145.

1968, Nixon, Rep., 1,370,665; Humphrey, Dem., 1,593,082; Wallace, 3d party, 331,968; Halstead, Soc. Worker, 4,099; Blomen, Soc. Labor, 1,762; Cleaver, New Politics, 4,585; Munn, Proh., 60; scattering, 29.

1972, Nixon, Rep., 1,961,721; McGovern, Dem., 1,459,435; Schmitz, Amer., 63,321; Fisher, Soc. Labor, 2,437; Jenness, Soc. Workers, 1,603; Hall, Com., 1,210.

1976, Carter, Dem., 1,696,714; Ford, Rep., 1,893,742; McCarthy, Ind., 47,905; MacBride, Libertarian, 5,406; Wright, People's, 3,504, Camejo, Soc. Workers, 1,804; LaRouche, U.S. Labor, 1,366; Levin, Soc. Labor, 1,148; scattering, 2,160.

1980, Reagan, Rep., 1,915,225; Carter, Dem., 1,661,532; Anderson, Ind., 275,223; Clark, Libertarian, 41,597; Commoner, Citizens, 11,930; Hall, Com., 3,262; Griswold, Workers World, 30; Greaves, American, 21; Bubar, Statesman, 9.

1984, Reagan, Rep., 2,251,571; Mondale, Dem., 1,529,638; Bergland, Libertarian, 10,055.

1988, Bush, Rep., 1,965,486; Dukakis, Dem., 1,675,783; Paul, Lib., 18,336; Fulani, Ind., 2,513.

Minnesota

County	1988 Dukakis (D)	Bush (R)	1984 Mondale (D)	Reagan (R)
Aitkin	3,863	3,011	3,943	3,422
Anoka	57,953	46,853	50,305	46,578
Becker	5,787	6,738	5,456	7,553
Beltrami	7,566	6,652	7,481	7,414
Benton	5,861	6,060	4,922	6,830
Big Stone	2,026	1,469	1,994	1,821
Blue Earth	12,375	11,959	11,877	14,298
Brown	5,109	6,898	4,469	8,399
Carlton	8,790	4,626	9,189	4,877
Carver	8,439	12,560	6,725	11,963
Cass	5,127	5,895	4,773	6,619
Chippewa	3,238	3,190	3,047	3,964
Chisago	7,875	6,163	6,683	6,279
Clay	11,186	10,380	10,294	11,565
Clearwater	1,769	1,763	1,917	2,066
Cook	1,080	1,078	1,129	1,219
Cottonwood	3,095	3,390	3,073	4,275
Crow Wing	9,474	11,017	8,719	11,362
Dakota	61,942	61,606	49,125	55,119
Dodge	2,925	3,848	2,786	4,428
Douglas	5,803	7,898	5,444	9,005
Faribault	3,879	4,846	3,993	5,690
Fillmore	4,114	5,004	4,351	6,342
Freeborn	8,836	7,226	9,338	8,413
Goodhue	9,438	9,455	8,679	11,171
Grant	1,950	1,693	1,867	2,111
Hennepin	292,909	240,209	272,401	253,921
Houston	3,936	4,777	3,512	5,645
Hubbard	3,306	4,365	2,806	4,621
Isanti	6,075	5,246	5,378	5,660
Itasca	10,517	8,358	11,455	9,306
Jackson	3,275	2,629	3,437	3,131
Kanabec	2,970	2,571	2,660	3,027
Kandiyohi	8,962	8,634	8,402	9,539
Kittson	1,650	1,381	1,610	1,716
Koochiching	3,867	2,842	4,238	3,466
LacQuiParle	2,805	2,116	2,685	2,731
Lake	3,887	1,838	4,468	2,003
Lake O'Woods	798	984	824	1,094
Le Sueur	5,410	5,415	5,070	6,033
Lincoln	1,891	1,479	1,827	1,905
Lyon	5,657	5,969	5,389	7,170
McLeod	5,736	7,967	4,864	8,728
Mahnomen	1,277	1,051	1,241	1,328
Marshall	3,001	2,752	2,705	3,433
Martin	4,922	5,724	4,673	7,308
Meeker	4,544	4,999	4,156	5,511
Mille Lacs	4,327	3,862	4,011	4,307
Morrison	6,469	6,598	6,225	7,556
Mower	11,893	6,969	12,498	8,054
Murray	2,840	2,316	2,741	2,780
Nicollet	6,786	6,878	5,789	7,472
Nobles	4,953	4,348	4,619	4,876
Norman	2,149	1,789	2,202	2,152
Olmsted	19,423	27,683	16,335	28,129
Otter Tail	10,373	14,015	9,714	15,664
Pennington	3,105	2,920	2,913	3,536
Pine	5,540	3,857	5,223	4,493
Pipestone	2,382	2,760	2,391	3,043
Polk	7,523	7,032	7,033	8,617
Pope	3,074	2,627	2,757	3,064
Ramsey	143,767	88,736	141,623	95,667
Red Lake	1,229	918	1,294	1,184
Redwood	3,178	5,076	2,957	6,020
Renville	4,454	4,356	3,972	5,571
Rice	11,570	9,460	10,880	10,456
Rock	2,435	2,737	2,188	2,971
Roseau	2,630	3,500	2,319	3,445
St. Louis	70,344	31,799	77,683	34,162
Scott	11,405	13,050	9,452	12,573
Sherburne	7,959	8,360	6,140	7,738
Sibley	3,154	3,655	2,761	4,638
Stearns	23,798	27,529	20,944	30,216
Steele	5,496	7,981	5,060	8,780
Stevens	2,721	2,679	2,451	3,251
Swift	3,579	2,156	3,531	2,893
Todd	5,023	5,633	4,657	6,585
Traverse	1,399	1,061	1,325	1,399
Wabasha	4,442	4,681	3,872	5,299
Wadena	2,484	3,733	2,454	4,306
Waseca	3,721	4,471	3,527	5,509
Washington	34,952	30,850	28,527	29,046
Watonwan	2,544	2,821	2,425	3,526
Wilkin	1,486	1,933	1,410	2,367
Winona	10,310	11,012	9,577	11,981
Wright	14,177	14,987	12,486	15,399
Yellow Med	3,282	2,925	3,018	3,819
Totals	1,109,471	962,337	1,036,364	1,032,603

Minnesota Vote Since 1940

1940, Roosevelt, Dem., 644,196; Willkie, Rep., 596,274; Thomas, Soc., 5,454; Browder, Com., 2,711; Aiken, Ind., 2,553.

1944, Roosevelt, Dem., 589,864; Dewey, Rep., 527,416; Thomas, Soc., 5,073; Teichert, Ind. Gov't., 3,176.

1948, Truman, Dem., 692,966; Dewey, Rep., 483,617; Wallace, Prog., 27,866; Thomas, Soc., 4,646; Teichert, Soc. Labor, 2,525; Dobbs, Soc. Workers, 606.

1952, Eisenhower, Rep., 763,211; Stevenson, Dem., 608,458; Hallinan, Prog., 2,666; Hass, Soc. Labor, 2,383; Hamblen, Proh., 2,147; Dobbs, Soc. Workers, 618.

1956, Eisenhower, Rep., 719,302; Stevenson, Dem., 617,525; Hass, Soc. Labor (Ind. Gov.), 2,080; Dobbs, Soc. Workers, 1,098.

1960, Kennedy, Dem., 779,933; Nixon, Rep., 757,915; Dobbs, Soc. Workers, 3,077; Industrial Gov., 962.

1964, Johnson, Dem., 991,117; Goldwater, Rep., 559,624; DeBerry, Soc. Workers, 1,177; Hass, Industrial Gov., 2,544.

1968, Nixon, Rep., 658,643; Humphrey, Dem., 857,738; Wallace, 3d party, 68,931; scattered, 2,443; Halstead, Soc. Worker, 808; Blomen, Ind. Gov't., 285; Mitchell, Com., 415; Cleaver, Peace, 935; McCarthy, write-in, 585; scattered, 170.

1972, Nixon, Rep., 898,269; McGovern, Dem., 802,346; Schmitz, Amer., 31,407; Spock, Peoples, 2,805; Fisher, Soc. Labor, 4,261; Jenness, Soc. Workers, 940; Hall, Com., 662; scattered, 962.

1976, Carter, Dem., 1,070,440; Ford, Rep., 819,395; McCarthy, Ind., 35,490; Anderson, Amer., 13,592; Camejo, Soc. Workers, 4,149; MacBride, Libertarian, 3,529; Hall, Com., 1,092.

1980, Reagan, Rep., 873, 268; Carter, Dem., 954,173; Anderson, Ind., 174,997; Clark, Libertarian, 31,593; Commoner, Citizens, 8,406; Hall, Com., 1,117; DeBerry, Soc. Workers, 711; Griswold, Workers World, 698; McReynolds, Socialist, 536; write-ins, 281.

1984, Mondale, Dem., 1,036,364; Reagan, Rep., 1,032,603; Bergland, Libertarian, 2,996.

1988, Bush, 962,337; Dukakis, Dem., 1,109,471; McCarthy, Minn. Prog., 5,403; Paul, Lib., 5,109.

Mississippi

County	1988 Dukakis (D)	Bush (R)	1984 Mondale (D)	Reagan (R)
Adams	7,732	8,116	7,849	9,440
Alcorn	5,335	6,641	4,862	7,203
Amite	2,834	3,333	2,569	3,463
Attala	2,997	4,524	3,327	4,870
Benton	1,718	1,565	1,715	1,737
Bolivar	7,606	6,105	8,769	6,939
Calhoun	2,086	3,375	1,749	3,579
Carroll	1,560	2,628	1,462	2,823
Chickasaw	2,713	3,390	2,329	3,605
Choctaw	1,335	2,297	1,166	2,491
Claiborne	3,083	1,233	3,179	1,294
Clarke	2,576	4,522	2,262	4,551
Clay	3,849	3,645	4,046	4,112
Coahoma	6,139	4,939	6,839	5,759
Copiah	4,175	5,100	4,591	5,806
Covington	2,591	4,005	2,219	4,165
DeSoto	5,449	14,681	4,369	12,576
Forrest	6,953	14,249	6,786	15,719
Franklin	1,563	2,376	1,494	2,564
George	2,435	4,545	1,655	4,346
Greene	1,637	2,837	1,297	2,744
Grenada	3,683	5,352	3,325	5,181
Hancock	3,760	7,763	2,630	7,662
Harrison	14,439	32,892	12,495	33,995
Hinds	41,058	52,749	42,373	56,953

Holmes	5,350	2,737	5,641	3,102
Humphreys	2,644	2,018	2,596	2,309
Issaquena	511	424	501	512
Itawamba	3,143	4,535	2,674	4,587
Jackson	10,328	29,830	8,821	29,585
Jasper	3,184	3,368	3,104	3,727
Jefferson	2,693	702	3,049	856
Jefferson Davis	2,948	2,745	2,644	2,884
Jones	7,383	16,764	7,298	17,586
Kemper	2,069	2,128	2,089	2,354
Lafayette	3,967	5,841	3,646	6,006
Lamar	2,535	9,145	1,964	7,929
Lauderdale	7,967	18,302	7,534	18,807
Lawrence	2,517	3,682	2,274	3,970
Leake	2,787	4,168	2,845	4,663
Lee	6,604	13,767	6,208	13,312
Leflore	5,830	6,409	7,443	7,550
Lincoln	4,534	8,710	4,458	8,898
Lowndes	5,993	11,258	6,078	12,049
Madison	8,242	11,399	8,002	9,298
Marion	4,240	7,019	3,757	7,355
Marshall	6,982	4,668	5,845	4,389
Monroe	4,669	6,447	4,437	7,387
Montgomery	1,893	2,504	1,881	3,093
Neshoba	2,942	6,363	2,630	6,715
Newton	2,332	5,658	2,127	5,911
Noxubee	2,722	1,870	2,928	2,123
Oktibbeha	5,100	7,126	5,097	7,574
Panola	5,222	5,382	5,465	5,850
Pearl River	3,939	10,220	3,085	9,978
Perry	1,326	2,983	1,415	3,098
Pike	6,531	7,637	6,137	8,254
Pontotoc	2,772	4,939	2,434	5,182
Prentiss	3,429	4,348	2,897	4,821
Quitman	2,497	1,832	2,343	2,198
Rankin	6,201	22,937	5,874	22,393
Scott	2,939	5,522	3,274	5,763
Sharkey	1,609	1,277	1,723	1,487
Simpson	3,016	6,151	2,894	5,983
Smith	1,660	4,573	1,573	5,116
Stone	1,452	3,007	1,185	2,960
Sunflower	4,898	4,362	4,913	5,178
Tallahatchie	2,881	2,633	2,725	2,901
Tate	2,872	4,553	2,846	4,677
Tippah	2,958	4,593	2,566	4,706
Tishomingo	3,378	3,646	2,879	3,527
Tunica	1,510	896	1,621	1,109
Union	3,044	5,511	2,766	5,837
Walthall	2,354	3,103	2,219	3,305
Warren	7,437	12,507	8,054	12,959
Washington	10,222	10,229	10,617	12,454
Wayne	2,889	4,496	2,818	5,000
Webster	1,550	3,061	1,397	3,390
Wilkinson	2,678	1,528	2,627	1,722
Winston	3,851	5,317	3,543	5,192
Yalobusha	2,402	2,660	2,337	2,934
Yazoo	4,989	5,538	5,037	6,275
Totals	363,921	557,890	352,192	582,377

Mississippi Vote Since 1940

1940, Roosevelt, Dem., 168,252; Willkie, Ind. Rep., 4,550; Rep., 2,814; total, 7,364; Thomas, Soc., 103.

1944, Roosevelt, Dem., 158,515; Dewey, Rep., 3,742; Reg. Dem., 9,964; Ind. Rep., 7,859.

1948, Thurmond, States' Rights, 167,538; Truman, Dem., 19,384; Dewey, Rep., 5,043; Wallace, Prog., 225.

1952, Eisenhower, Ind. vote pledged to Rep. candidate, 112,966; Stevenson, Dem., 172,566.

1956, Stevenson, Dem., 144,498; Eisenhower, Rep., 56,372; Black and Tan Grand Old Party, 4,313; total, 60,685; Byrd, Ind., 42,966.

1960, Democratic unpledged electors, 116,248; Kennedy, Dem., 108,362; Nixon, Rep., 73,561. Mississippi's victorious slate of 8 unpledged Democratic electors cast their votes for Sen. Harry F. Byrd (D-Va.).

1964, Johnson, Dem., 52,618; Goldwater, Rep., 356,528.

1968, Nixon, Rep., 88,516; Humphrey, Dem., 150,644; Wallace, 3d party, 415,349.

1972, Nixon, Rep., 505,125; McGovern, Dem., 126,782; Schmitz, Amer., 11,598; Jenness, Soc. Workers, 2,458.

1976, Carter, Dem., 381,309; Ford, Rep., 366,846; Anderson, Amer., 6,678; McCarthy, Ind., 4,074; Maddox, Ind., 4,049; Camejo, Soc. Workers, 2,805; MacBride, Libertarian, 2,609.

1980, Reagan, Rep., 441,089; Carter, Dem., 429,281; Anderson, Ind., 12,036; Clark, Libertarian, 5,465; Griswold, Workers World, 2,402; Pulley, Soc. Worker, 2,347.

1984, Reagan, Rep., 582,377; Mondale, Dem., 352,192; Bergland, Libertarian, 2,336.

1988, Bush, Rep., 557,890; Dukakis, Dem., 363,921; Duke, Ind., 4,232; Paul, Lib., 3,329.

Missouri

	1988		1984	
County	Dukakis (D)	Bush (R)	Mondale (D)	Reagan (R)
Adair	3,571	5,721	3,119	6,430
Andrew	3,108	3,407	2,457	4,252
Atchison	1,468	1,761	1,219	2,277
Audrain	5,226	5,072	4,662	7,261
Barry	4,210	7,231	3,483	7,683
Barton	1,603	3,339	1,348	3,996
Bates	3,332	3,574	2,889	4,223
Benton	2,654	3,467	2,251	3,805
Bollinger	1,883	2,710	1,923	2,778
Boone	24,370	22,948	19,364	26,600
Buchanan	18,601	15,336	15,369	19,735
Butler	5,751	7,968	4,699	8,712
Caldwell	1,726	2,074	1,382	2,678
Callaway	5,209	6,687	4,327	8,262
Camden	3,930	7,773	3,088	8,057
Cape Girardeau	7,904	16,583	7,346	17,404
Carroll	2,330	2,811	1,980	3,495
Carter	1,087	1,429	916	1,402
Cass	10,092	12,799	7,517	14,456
Cedar	1,774	2,966	1,440	3,539
Chariton	2,347	2,193	2,244	2,744
Christian	4,724	7,670	3,223	7,634
Clark	1,925	1,493	1,627	2,068
Clay	29,620	30,293	22,586	36,529
Clinton	3,653	3,282	2,778	4,226
Cole	8,259	16,023	6,702	20,366
Cooper	2,510	3,737	2,219	4,603
Crawford	3,107	3,856	2,610	4,716
Dade	1,315	2,154	1,100	2,600
Dallas	2,293	2,898	1,902	3,577
Daviess	1,743	1,765	1,526	2,414
DeKalb	1,970	1,863	1,464	2,188
Dent	2,421	2,975	2,544	3,490
Douglas	1,735	3,225	1,536	3,662
Dunklin	5,281	5,026	4,967	6,092
Franklin	11,891	16,611	8,319	18,669
Gasconade	1,621	4,216	1,130	4,678
Gentry	1,872	1,554	1,600	2,047
Greene	35,475	52,211	27,965	57,250
Grundy	2,052	2,668	1,861	3,156
Harrison	1,776	2,271	1,649	2,844
Henry	4,135	4,167	3,741	5,419
Hickory	1,677	2,043	1,212	2,190
Holt	1,258	1,583	1,026	2,087
Howard	2,446	1,865	2,014	2,360
Howell	4,324	7,277	3,767	8,204
Iron	2,283	1,877	2,023	2,316
Jackson	147,964	107,810	135,067	132,271
Jasper	11,159	19,934	9,259	23,066
Jefferson	27,738	29,279	20,026	34,525
Johnson	5,373	7,512	4,238	8,413
Knox	1,255	1,212	1,097	1,513
Laclede	3,442	6,070	2,665	6,406
Lafayette	5,654	6,825	4,848	8,581
Lawrence	4,432	6,911	3,720	8,370
Lewis	2,460	1,803	1,977	2,438
Lincoln	4,605	5,305	3,290	6,137
Linn	3,150	3,061	3,112	3,822
Livingston	3,077	3,462	2,699	4,090
McDonald	2,299	3,812	2,109	4,521
Macon	3,215	3,406	3,037	4,542
Madison	2,167	2,528	1,862	2,808
Maries	1,552	1,919	1,388	2,267
Marion	5,617	5,034	4,666	6,831
Mercer	877	875	875	1,229
Miller	2,555	5,662	2,054	6,706
Missouri	2,814	2,218	2,524	2,502
Moniteau	1,936	3,502	1,614	4,197
Monroe	2,461	1,542	1,992	2,163
Montgomery	2,064	2,714	1,668	3,261
Morgan	2,604	3,958	2,169	4,392
New Madrid	3,812	3,387	3,776	4,323
Newton	5,798	10,617	4,623	11,709
Nodaway	4,240	4,103	3,615	5,471
Oregon	2,042	1,717	2,026	1,979
Osage	1,771	3,885	1,343	4,381
Ozark	1,329	2,404	1,110	2,614
Pemiscot	3,288	3,066	3,293	3,733
Perry	2,136	3,836	1,837	4,493
Pettis	5,486	9,648	5,413	10,991
Phelps	5,867	8,329	5,074	9,012
Pike	3,816	3,271	3,313	3,933
Platte	11,225	11,838	7,668	12,859
Polk	3,419	5,030	2,819	5,467
Pulaski	3,446	4,642	2,865	5,330
Putnam	803	1,365	797	1,540
Ralls	2,489	1,494	2,011	2,067
Randolph	5,291	4,384	4,471	5,735
Ray	4,879	3,763	3,979	4,875
Reynolds	1,864	1,162	2,026	1,330
Ripley	1,961	2,647	1,883	2,927
St. Charles	29,286	50,005	17,617	47,784
St. Clair	1,864	2,312	1,655	2,667
St. Francois	8,158	7,923	7,137	9,792
Ste. Genevieve	3,612	2,532	2,723	3,245

St. Louis	216,534	262,784	173,144	307,684	Powell	1,174	1,574	1,066	1,877
Saline	5,039	4,625	4,281	6,042	Prairie	343	541	289	693
Schuyler	1,013	1,063	1,141	1,250	Ravalli	4,763	7,418	3,825	8,161
Scotland	1,117	1,248	1,075	1,485	Richland	1,824	2,628	1,382	3,847
Scott	5,914	6,013	5,569	8,727	Roosevelt	2,083	1,957	1,962	2,431
Shannon	1,796	1,696	1,580	1,779	Rosebud	1,869	1,822	1,920	2,413
Shelby	1,818	1,586	1,573	2,243	Sanders	1,959	2,152	1,654	2,467
Stoddard	4,701	5,822	4,294	6,701	Sheridan	1,354	1,381	1,087	1,774
Stone	2,889	5,080	2,119	5,706	Silver Bow	11,422	5,043	11,095	6,637
Sullivan	1,562	1,897	1,784	2,306	Stillwater	1,407	1,920	1,100	2,118
Taney	3,888	7,043	2,912	7,082	Sweet Grass	462	1,242	378	1,417
Texas	3,887	4,584	3,662	5,591	Teton	1,303	1,876	1,102	2,257
Vernon	3,402	4,149	2,984	5,181	Toole	1,070	1,505	789	1,949
Warren	2,935	4,452	1,964	5,150	Treasure	231	291	209	353
Washington	3,744	3,240	2,987	3,755	Valley	2,163	2,467	1,849	3,123
Wayne	2,456	2,648	2,363	2,867	Wheatland	443	667	407	753
Webster	3,890	5,123	2,982	5,529	Wibaux	258	358	216	423
Worth	732	677	734	921	Yellowstone	21,987	28,069	19,437	34,124
Wright	2,232	4,151	1,973	4,687	Totals	168,936	190,412	146,742	232,450
Totals	1,001,619	1,084,953	848,583	1,274,188					

Missouri Vote Since 1940

1940, Roosevelt, Dem., 958,476; Willkie, Rep., 871,009; Thomas, Soc., 2,226; Babson, Proh., 1,809; Aiken, Soc. Labor, 209.

1944, Roosevelt, Dem., 807,357; Dewey, Rep., 761,175; Thomas, Soc., 1,750; Watson, Proh., 1,175; Teichert, Soc. Labor, 221.

1948, Truman, Dem., 917,315; Dewey, Rep., 655,039; Wallace, Prog., 3,998; Thomas, Soc., 2,222.

1952, Eisenhower, Rep., 959,429; Stevenson, Dem., 929,830; Hallinan, Prog., 987; Hamblen, Proh., 885; MacArthur, Christian Nationalist, 302; America First, 233; Hoopes, Soc., 227; Hass, Soc. Labor, 169.

1956, Stevenson, Dem., 918,273; Eisenhower, Rep., 914,299.

1960, Kennedy, Dem., 972,201; Nixon, Rep., 962,221.

1964, Johnson, Dem., 1,164,344; Goldwater, Rep., 653,535.

1968, Nixon, Rep., 811,932; Humphrey, Dem., 791,444; Wallace, 3d party, 206,126.

1972, Nixon, Rep., 1,154,058; McGovern, Dem., 698,531.

1976, Carter, Dem., 999,163; Ford, Rep., 928,808; McCarthy, Ind., 24,329.

1980, Reagan, Rep., 1,074,181; Carter, Dem., 931,182; Anderson, Ind., 77,920; Clark, Libertarian, 14,422; DeBerry, Soc. Workers, 1,515; Commoner, Citizens, 573; write-ins, 31.

1984, Reagan, Rep., 1,274,188; Mondale, Dem., 848,583.

1988, Bush, Rep., 1,084,953; Dukakis, Dem., 1,001,619; Fulani, New Alliance, 6,656; Paul, write-in, 434.

Montana Vote Since 1940

1940, Roosevelt, Dem., 145,698; Willkie, Rep., 99,579; Thomas, Soc., 1,443; Babson, Proh., 664; Browder, Com., 489.

1944, Roosevelt, Dem., 112,556; Dewey, Rep., 93,163; Thomas, Soc., 1,296; Watson, Proh., 340.

1948, Truman, Dem., 119,071; Dewey, Rep., 96,770; Wallace, Prog., 7,313; Thomas, Soc., 695; Watson, Proh., 429.

1952, Eisenhower, Rep., 157,394; Stevenson, Dem., 106,213; Hallinan, Prog., 723; Hamblen, Proh., 548; Hoopes, Soc., 159.

1956, Eisenhower, Rep., 154,933; Stevenson, Dem., 116,238.

1960, Kennedy, Dem., 134,891; Nixon, Rep., 141,841; Decker, Proh., 456; Dobbs, Soc. Workers, 391.

1964, Johnson, Dem., 164,246; Goldwater, Rep., 113,032; Kasper, Nat'l States Rights, 519; Munn, Proh., 499; DeBerry, Soc. Worker, 332.

1968, Nixon, Rep., 138,835; Humphrey, Dem., 114,117; Wallace, 3d party, 20,015; Halstead, Soc. Worker, 457; Munn, Proh., 510; Caton, New Reform, 470.

1972, Nixon, Rep., 183,976; McGovern, Dem., 120,197; Schmitz, Amer., 13,430.

1976, Carter, Dem., 149,259; Ford, Rep., 173,703; Anderson, Amer., 5,772.

1980, Reagan, Rep., 206,814; Carter, Dem., 118,032; Anderson, Ind., 29,281; Clark, Libertarian, 9,825.

1984, Reagan, Rep., 232,450; Mondale, Dem., 146,742; Bergland, Libertarian, 5,185.

1988, Bush, Rep., 190,412; Dukakis, Dem., 168,936; Paul, Lib., 5,047; Fulani, New Alliance, 1,279.

Montana

County	1988		1984	
	Dukakis (D)	Bush (R)	Mondale (D)	Reagan (R)
Beaverhead	1,274	2,668	942	3,044
Big Horn	2,233	1,711	2,681	2,390
Blaine	1,460	1,402	1,229	1,736
Broadwater	592	1,054	458	1,345
Carbon	2,039	2,360	1,657	2,877
Carter	242	686	194	823
Cascade	15,718	15,946	14,252	19,846
Chouteau	1,166	1,980	896	2,425
Custer	2,343	3,007	1,982	3,879
Daniels	571	802	473	984
Dawson	2,120	2,658	1,776	3,468
Deer Lodge	3,185	1,168	3,539	1,901
Fallon	612	1,002	569	1,237
Fergus	2,052	3,948	1,804	4,585
Flathead	10,202	14,461	8,310	17,012
Gallatin	9,527	13,214	8,163	15,643
Garfield	196	631	134	770
Glacier	2,151	1,728	2,167	2,228
Golden Valley	203	335	211	384
Granite	511	789	417	880
Hill	4,219	3,467	3,657	4,635
Jefferson	1,746	2,007	1,324	2,226
Judith Basin	590	902	483	1,050
Lake	4,109	4,883	3,473	5,754
Lewis & Clark	11,932	10,946	8,768	13,569
Liberty	418	771	323	895
Lincoln	3,601	3,500	2,959	4,080
Madison	878	2,045	708	2,308
McCone	567	814	459	1,015
Meagher	337	656	283	771
Mineral	789	616	718	943
Missoula	19,178	15,965	16,540	19,777
Musselshell	898	1,280	781	1,541
Park	2,526	3,823	2,387	4,115
Petroleum	91	204	86	258
Phillips	905	1,462	787	1,934
Pondera	1,245	1,795	1,039	2,239
Powder River	395	815	346	1,066

Nebraska

County	1988		1984	
	Dukakis (D)	Bush (R)	Mondale (D)	Reagan (R)
Adams	4,145	8,063	2,940	9,092
Antelope	933	2,626	697	3,222
Arthur	58	210	33	248
Banner	112	361	58	457
Blaine	72	338	48	363
Boone	976	2,160	690	2,508
Box Butte	2,466	3,253	1,471	4,011
Boyd	480	957	308	1,173
Brown	435	1,335	312	1,513
Buffalo	4,700	9,980	3,083	11,343
Burt	1,458	2,050	1,054	2,645
Butler	1,715	2,083	1,192	2,555
Cass	3,674	4,658	2,495	5,451
Cedar	1,759	2,462	1,201	3,298
Chase	597	1,446	367	1,687
Cherry	642	2,240	463	2,720
Cheyenne	1,333	2,862	857	3,159
Clay	1,097	2,352	811	2,919
Colfax	1,542	2,329	981	2,998
Cuming	1,238	3,201	779	3,931
Custer	1,496	4,202	1,060	4,749
Dakota	2,941	2,744	2,510	3,467
Dawes	1,122	2,618	864	3,325
Dawson	2,184	5,529	1,487	6,878
Deuel	302	769	198	961
Dixon	1,166	1,802	985	2,154
Dodge	6,116	8,412	4,259	10,167
Douglas	76,444	99,806	58,867	112,557
Dundy	333	828	225	992
Fillmore	1,433	1,952	1,009	2,474
Franklin	768	1,294	522	1,597
Frontier	384	1,057	258	1,351
Furnas	791	1,830	579	2,363
Gage	4,008	5,114	2,699	6,102
Garden	366	986	180	1,158

Garfield	234	803	196	899
Gosper	331	694	201	802
Grant	89	301	51	404
Greeley	670	763	485	948
Hall	6,822	12,020	4,615	13,082
Hamilton	1,289	3,019	840	3,417
Harlan	725	1,403	493	1,692
Hayes	160	512	100	591
Hitchcock	480	1,132	341	1,391
Holt	1,327	4,081	893	4,611
Hooker	91	378	55	433
Howard	1,186	1,526	887	1,899
Jefferson	1,819	2,470	1,366	3,114
Johnson	1,162	1,182	821	1,536
Kearney	1,056	2,120	726	2,505
Keith	1,067	2,879	631	3,423
Keya Paha	145	446	126	505
Kimball	540	1,321	339	1,732
Knox	1,477	2,644	1,149	3,364
Lancaster	44,260	44,605	32,780	48,627
Lincoln	6,070	8,395	4,483	10,692
Logan	93	373	66	445
Loup	97	295	79	323
McPherson	60	229	57	295
Madison	2,779	9,135	1,755	9,786
Merrick	1,192	2,376	818	2,696
Morrill	753	1,554	463	1,888
Nance	794	1,185	524	1,391
Nemaha	1,457	2,293	1,004	2,752
Nuckolls	1,114	1,750	947	2,132
Otoe	2,616	3,724	1,868	4,679
Pawnee	767	975	552	1,306
Perkins	467	1,117	307	1,418
Phelps	1,047	3,316	739	3,739
Pierce	914	2,474	545	3,016
Platte	3,285	9,029	2,057	10,035
Polk	944	1,768	610	2,149
Red Willow	1,505	3,325	1,022	4,101
Richardson	1,926	2,702	1,422	3,634
Rock	198	756	147	873
Saline	3,119	2,352	2,385	2,941
Sarpy	10,936	20,179	6,831	20,155
Saunders	3,524	4,454	2,467	5,217
Scotts Bluff	4,454	8,594	3,060	10,676
Seward	2,682	3,467	1,905	3,969
Sheridan	612	2,251	377	2,661
Sherman	839	914	701	1,144
Sioux	194	568	121	732
Stanton	637	1,709	410	2,080
Thayer	1,322	1,981	946	2,578
Thomas	81	383	73	298
Thurston	1,225	1,105	1,077	1,410
Valley	873	1,603	739	2,052
Washington	2,552	4,567	1,561	5,163
Wayne	1,111	2,473	833	3,075
Webster	891	1,314	645	1,694
Wheeler	141	309	97	365
York	1,748	4,744	1,114	5,012
Totals	259,235	397,956	187,475	459,135

Nebraska Vote Since 1940

1940, Roosevelt, Dem., 263,677; Willkie, Rep., 352,201.

1944, Roosevelt, Dem., 233,246; Dewey, Rep., 329,880.

1948, Truman, Dem., 224,165; Dewey, Rep., 264,774.

1952, Eisenhower, Rep., 421,603; Stevenson Dem., 188,057.

1956, Eisenhower, Rep., 378,108; Stevenson, Dem., 199,029.

1960, Kennedy, Dem., 232,542; Nixon, Rep., 380,553.

1964, Johnson, Dem., 307,307; Goldwater, Rep., 276,847.

1968, Nixon, Rep., 321,163; Humphrey, Dem., 170,784; Wallace, 3d party, 44,904.

1972, Nixon, Rep., 406,298; McGovern, Dem., 169,991; scattered 817.

1976, Carter, Dem., 233,287; Ford, Rep., 359,219; McCarthy, Ind., 9,383; Maddox, Amer. Ind., 3,378; MacBride, Libertarian, 1,476.

1980, Reagan, Rep., 419,214; Carter, Dem., 166,424; Anderson, Ind., 44,854; Clark, Libertarian, 9,041.

1984, Reagan, Rep., 459,135; Mondale, Dem., 187,475; Bergland, Libertarian, 2,075.

1988, Bush, Rep., 397,956; Dukakis, Dem., 259,235; Paul, Lib., 2,534; Fulani, New Alliance, 1,740.

Nevada

	1988		1984	
County	Dukakis (D)	Bush (R)	Mondale (D)	Reagan (R)
Churchill	1,481	4,578	1,304	4,479
Clark	78,359	108,110	53,386	94,133
Douglas	3,107	7,074	1,877	6,385
Elko	2,310	5,722	1,566	5,110
Esmeralda	143	380	158	453
Eureka	151	413	124	439
Humboldt	1,024	2,378	862	2,498
Lander	439	1,214	301	1,222
Lincoln	466	1,035	397	1,175
Lyon	2,301	4,390	1,673	4,370
Mineral	978	1,480	766	1,645
Nye	1,748	3,619	1,269	3,573
Pershing	458	867	333	956
Storey	432	651	252	570
Washoe	32,902	52,654	22,321	50,418
White Pine	1,351	1,774	1,275	1,917
Totals	132,738	206,040	91,655	188,770

Nevada Vote Since 1940

1940, Roosevelt, Dem., 31,945; Willkie, Rep., 21,229.

1944, Roosevelt, Dem., 29,623; Dewey, Rep., 24,611.

1948, Truman, Dem., 31,291; Dewey, Rep., 29,357; Wallace, Prog., 1,469.

1952, Eisenhower, Rep., 50,502; Stevenson, Dem., 31,688.

1956, Eisenhower, Rep., 56,049; Stevenson, Dem., 40,640.

1960, Kennedy, Dem., 54,880; Nixon, Rep., 52,387.

1964, Johnson, Dem., 79,339; Goldwater, Rep., 56,094.

1968, Nixon, Rep., 73,188; Humphrey, Dem., 60,598; Wallace, 3d party, 20,432.

1972, Nixon, Rep., 115,750; McGovern, Dem. 66,016.

1976, Carter Dem., 92,479; Ford, Rep., 101,273; MacBride, Libertarian, 1,519; Maddox, Amer. Ind., 1,497; scattered 5,108.

1980, Reagan, Rep., 155,017; Carter, Dem., 66,666; Anderson, Ind., 17,651; Clark, Libertarian, 4,358.

1984, Reagan, Rep., 108,770; Mondale, Dem., 91,655; Bergland, Libertarian, 2,292.

1988, Bush, Rep., 206,040; Dukakis, Dem., 132,738; Paul, Lib., 3,520; Fulani, New Alliance, 835.

New Hampshire

	1988		1984	
City	Dukakis (D)	Bush (R)	Mondale (D)	Reagan (R)
Berlin City	2,271	2,529	1,863	3,261
Claremont	2,254	2,513	2,006	2,868
Concord	6,698	7,439	5,172	7,190
Dover	4,803	5,357	3,826	5,397
Keene	4,466	4,535	3,238	4,975
Laconia	2,111	3,835	1,552	4,151
Manchester	12,567	23,893	10,283	24,780
Nashua	12,833	19,369	9,305	16,961
Portsmith.	5,377	4,827	4,418	4,967
Rochester	3,591	5,368	2,622	5,457
Totals	163,696	281,537	120,377	267,051

New Hampshire Vote Since 1940

1940, Roosevelt, Dem., 125,292; Willkie, Rep., 110,127.

1944, Roosevelt, Dem., 119,663; Dewey, Rep., 109,916; Thomas, Soc., 46.

1948, Truman, Dem., 107,995; Dewey, Rep., 121,299; Wallace, Prog., 1,970; Thomas, Soc., 86; Teichert, Soc. Labor, 83; Thurmond, States' Rights, 7.

1952, Eisenhower, Rep., 166,287; Stevenson, Dem., 106,663.

1956, Eisenhower, Rep., 176,519; Stevenson, Dem., 90,364; Andrews, Const., 111.

1960, Kennedy, Dem., 137,772; Nixon, Rep., 157,989.

1964, Johnson, Dem., 182,065; Goldwater, Rep., 104,029.

1968, Nixon, Rep., 154,903; Humphrey, Dem., 130,589; Wallace, 3d party, 11,173; New Party, 421; Halstead, Soc. Worker, 104.

1972, Nixon, Rep., 213,724; McGovern, Dem., 116,435; Schmitz, Amer., 3,386; Jenness, Soc. Workers, 368; scattered, 142.

1976, Carter, Dem., 147,645; Ford, Rep., 185,935; McCarthy, Ind., 4,095; MacBride, Libertarian 936; Reagan, write-in, 388; La Rouche, U.S. Labor, 186; Camejo, Soc. Workers, 161; Levin, Soc. Labor, 66; scattered, 215.

1980, Reagan, Rep., 221,705; Carter, Dem., 108,864; Anderson, Ind., 49,693; Clark, Libertarian, 2,067; Commoner, Citizens, 1,325; Hall, Com., 129; Griswold, Workers World, 76; DeBerry, Soc. Workers, 72; scattered, 68.

1984, Reagan, Rep., 267,051; Mondale, Dem., 120,377; Bergland, Libertarian, 735.

1988, Bush, Rep., 281,537; Dukakis, Dem., 163,696; Paul, Lib., 4,502; Fulani, New Alliance, 790.

New Jersey

County	1988 Dukakis (D)	1988 Bush (R)	1984 Mondale (D)	1984 Reagan (R)
Atlantic	34,047	44,748	33,240	49,158
Bergen	160,655	226,885	155,039	268,507
Burlington	61,140	87,416	57,467	89,815
Camden	90,704	100,072	90,233	109,749
Cape May	15,105	28,738	13,378	28,768
Cumberland	21,869	26,024	21,141	29,398
Essex	156,098	111,491	173,295	136,798
Gloucester	35,479	51,708	32,702	54,041
Hudson	95,696	81,807	94,304	112,834
Hunterdon	13,758	31,907	10,972	29,737
Mercer	68,712	65,384	66,398	71,195
Middlesex	117,149	143,361	104,905	160,221
Monmouth	91,844	147,320	79,382	152,595
Morris	58,721	127,420	53,201	137,719
Ocean	64,474	124,587	51,012	124,391
Passaic	66,254	88,070	69,590	101,951
Salem	9,956	15,240	8,935	17,368
Somerset	37,406	67,658	31,924	66,303
Sussex	13,676	36,086	11,502	35,680
Union	93,158	112,967	92,056	135,446
Warren	11,640	21,715	10,647	21,938
Totals	**1,317,541**	**1,740,604**	**1,261,323**	**1,933,630**

New Jersey Vote Since 1940

1940, Roosevelt, Dem., 1,016,404; Willkie, Rep., 944,876; Browder, Com., 8,814; Thomas, Soc., 2,823; Babson, Proh., 851; Aiken, Soc. Labor, 446.

1944, Roosevelt, Dem., 987,874; Dewey, Rep., 961,335; Teichert, Soc. Labor, 6,939; Watson, Nat'l. Proh., 4,255; Thomas, Soc., 3,385.

1948, Truman, Dem., 895,455; Dewey, Rep., 981,124; Wallace, Prog., 42,683; Watson, Proh., 10,593; Thomas, Soc., 10,521; Dobbs, Soc. Workers, 5,825; Teichert, Soc. Labor, 3,354.

1952, Eisenhower, Rep., 1,373,613; Stevenson, Dem., 1,015,902; Hoopes, Soc., 8,593; Hass, Soc. Labor, 5,815; Hallinan, Prog., 5,589; Krajewski, Poor Man's, 4,203; Dobbs, Soc. Workers, 3,850; Hamblen, Proh., 989.

1956, Eisenhower, Rep., 1,606,942; Stevenson Dem., 850,337; Holtwick, Proh., 9,147; Hass, Soc. Labor, 6,736; Andrews, Conservative, 5,317; Dobbs, Soc. Workers, 4,004; Krajewski, American Third Party, 1,829.

1960, Kennedy, Dem., 1,385,415; Nixon, Rep., 1,363,324; Dobbs, Soc. Workers, 11,402; Lee, Conservative, 8,708; Hass, Soc. Labor, 4,262.

1964, Johnson, Dem., 1,867,671; Goldwater, Rep., 963,843; DeBerry, Soc. Workers, 8,181; Hass, Soc. Labor, 7,075.

1968, Nixon, Rep., 1,325,467; Humphrey, Dem., 1,264,206; Wallace, 3d party, 262,187; Halstead, Soc. Worker, 8,667; Gregory, Peace Freedom, 8,084; Blomen, Soc. Labor, 6,784.

1972, Nixon, Rep., 1,845,502; McGovern, Dem., 1,102,211; Schmitz, Amer., 34,378; Spock, Peoples, 5,355; Fisher, Soc. Labor, 4,544; Jenness, Soc. Workers, 2,233; Mahalchik, Amer. First, 1,743; Hall, Com., 1,263.

1976, Carter, Dem., 1,444,653; Ford, Rep., 1,509,688; McCarthy, Ind., 32,717; MacBride, Libertarian, 9,449; Maddox, Amer., 7,716; Levin, Soc. Labor, 3,686; Hall, Com., 1,662; LaRouche, U.S. Labor, 1,650; Camejo, Soc. Workers, 1,184; Wright, People's, 1,044; Bubar, Proh., 554; Zeidler, Soc., 469.

1980, Reagan, Rep., 1,546,557; Carter, Dem., 1,147,364; Anderson, Ind., 234,632; Clark, Libertarian, 20,652; Commoner, Citizens, 8,203; McCormack, Right to Life, 3,927; Lynen, Middle Class, 3,694; Hall, Com., 2,555; Pulley, Soc. Workers, 2,198; McReynolds, Soc., 1,973; Gahres, Down With Lawyers, 1,718; Griswold, Workers World, 1,288; Wendelken, Ind., 923.

1984, Reagan, Rep., 1,933,630; Mondale, Dem., 1,261,323; Bergland, Libertarian, 6,416.

1988, Bush, Rep., 1,740,604; Dukakis, Dem., 1,317,541; Lewin, Peace & Freedom, 9,953; Paul, Lib., 8,421.

New Mexico

County	1988 Dukakis (D)	1988 Bush (R)	1984 Mondale (D)	1984 Reagan (R)
Bernalillo	78,346	92,830	67,789	104,694
Catron	490	925	418	970
Chaves	6,730	13,367	5,332	15,248
Cibola	3,458	2,640	3,140	3,578
Colfax	2,785	2,256	2,435	2,994
Curry	3,995	8,032	3,108	9,188
De Baca	480	643	386	756
Dona Ana	19,608	21,582	13,878	22,153
Eddy	8,544	9,805	7,364	11,810
Grant	5,443	4,196	5,755	4,979
Guadalupe	1,243	861	946	990
Harding	291	377	224	401
Hidalgo	901	1,100	860	1,282
Lea	5,879	11,309	4,558	14,569
Lincoln	1,690	3,511	1,134	3,992
Los Alamos	3,275	6,622	2,859	6,882
Luna	3,066	3,415	2,557	4,145
McKinley	9,595	5,694	7,915	6,557
Mora	1,601	923	1,235	1,017
Otero	5,284	9,984	4,167	9,751
Quay	1,901	2,454	1,368	2,842
Rio Arriba	7,503	3,024	6,938	4,116
Roosevelt	2,033	3,589	1,696	4,598
Sandoval	9,332	9,411	7,080	9,005
San Juan	11,094	16,202	8,963	18,690
San Miguel	6,131	2,763	5,227	3,485
Santa Fe	23,581	12,891	18,262	15,886
Sierra	1,595	2,507	1,335	2,663
Socorro	2,960	3,114	2,541	3,403
Taos	6,271	2,897	5,144	4,154
Torrance	1,618	2,252	1,274	2,326
Union	638	1,291	488	1,503
Valencia	7,136	7,874	5,393	8,474
Totals	**244,497**	**270,341**	**201,769**	**307,101**

New Mexico Vote Since 1940

1940, Roosevelt, Dem., 103,699; Willkie, Rep., 79,315.

1944, Roosevelt, Dem., 81,389; Dewey, Rep., 70,688; Watson, Proh., 148.

1948, Truman, Dem., 105,464; Dewey, Rep., 80,303; Wallace, Prog., 1,037; Watson, Proh., 127; Thomas, Soc., 83; Teichert, Soc. Labor, 49.

1952, Eisenhower, Rep., 132,170; Stevenson, Dem., 105,661; Hamblen, Proh., 297; Hallinan, Ind. Prog., 225; MacArthur, Christian National, 220; Hass, Soc. Labor, 35.

1956, Eisenhower, Rep., 146,788; Stevenson, Dem., 106,098; Holtwick, Proh., 607; Andrews, Ind., 364; Hass, Soc. Labor, 69.

1960, Kennedy, Dem., 156,027; Nixon, Rep., 153,733; Decker, Proh., 777; Hass, Soc. Labor, 570.

1964, Johnson, Dem., 194,017; Goldwater, Rep., 131,838; Hass, Soc. Labor, 1,217; Munn, Proh., 543.

1968, Nixon, Rep., 169,692; Humphrey, Dem., 130,081; Wallace, 3d party, 25,737; Chavez, 1,519; Halstead, Soc. Worker, 252.

1972, Nixon, Rep., 235,606; McGovern, Dem., 141,084; Schmitz, Amer., 8,767; Jenness, Soc. Workers, 474.

1976, Carter, Dem., 201,148; Ford, Rep. 211,419; Camejo, Soc. Workers, 2,462; MacBride, Libertarian, 1,110; Zeidler, Soc., 240; Bubar, Proh., 211.

1980, Reagan, Rep., 250,779; Carter, Dem., 167,826; Anderson, Ind., 29,459; Clark, Libertarian, 4,365; Commoner, Citizens, 2,202; Bubar, Statesman, 1,281; Pulley, Soc. Worker, 325.

1984, Reagan, Rep., 307,101; Mondale, Dem., 201,769; Bergland, Libertarian, 4,459.

1988, Bush, Rep., 270,341; Dukakis, Dem., 244,497; Paul, Lib., 3,268; Fulani, New Alliance, 2,237.

New York

County	1988 Dukakis (D)	1988 Bush (R)	1984 Mondale (D)	1984 Reagan (R)
Albany	86,564	59,534	75,447	74,542
Allegany	5,614	11,880	4,720	14,527
Bronx	218,245	76,043	223,112	109,308
Broome	48,130	47,610	37,658	58,109
Cattaraugus	12,447	18,691	10,194	24,162
Cayuga	15,044	16,934	12,207	21,451
Chautauqua	25,814	31,642	22,986	39,597
Chemung	15,966	20,951	14,638	24,909
Chenango	8,021	11,727	6,343	14,254
Clinton	12,670	15,702	10,804	19,549
Columbia	11,585	15,111	8,960	18,814
Cortland	7,673	10,934	6,438	13,691
Delaware	7,463	11,391	5,745	14,002
Dutchess	38,968	62,165	32,867	70,324
Erie	238,779	185,796	237,631	222,882
Essex	6,623	10,350	5,119	12,114
Franklin	7,928	9,135	6,400	10,617
Fulton	9,012	11,757	7,644	14,887
Genesee	9,945	14,182	8,549	16,582
Greene	7,265	11,874	5,858	14,150

Hamilton	976	2,320	737	2,637
Herkimer	12,694	15,104	10,346	18,827
Jefferson	14,137	19,304	10,960	23,445
Kings	363,916	178,961	368,518	230,064
Lewis	4,252	5,787	2,757	7,069
Livingston	9,506	14,004	7,399	16,389
Madison	10,665	14,902	8,291	17,568
Monroe	153,650	155,271	132,109	182,696
Montgomery	11,371	11,128	9,044	14,398
Nassau	250,130	337,430	240,697	392,017
New York	385,675	115,927	379,521	144,281
Niagara	43,801	42,537	41,368	51,289
Oneida	47,665	55,039	42,603	65,377
Onondaga	94,751	104,080	81,777	121,857
Ontario	17,341	21,780	12,844	24,507
Orange	38,465	65,446	32,663	69,413
Orleans	5,913	9,028	4,429	10,453
Oswego	18,430	25,362	14,437	31,481
Otsego	11,069	13,021	9,582	16,777
Putnam	12,158	24,086	9,473	25,707
Queens	325,147	217,049	328,379	285,477
Rensselaer	33,066	35,412	26,755	43,892
Richmond	47,812	77,427	44,345	83,187
Rockland	47,634	63,825	44,687	70,020
St. Lawrence	18,921	20,290	15,963	26,062
Saratoga	31,684	43,498	22,166	47,394
Schenectady	36,483	33,364	30,612	42,808
Schoharie	5,389	7,008	3,996	8,692
Schuyler	2,900	4,291	2,422	5,207
Seneca	6,215	7,221	4,825	9,420
Steuben	12,824	25,359	10,471	28,848
Suffolk	199,215	311,242	171,295	335,485
Sullivan	11,635	15,713	10,475	18,037
Tioga	8,102	12,670	5,860	14,856
Tompkins	21,455	14,932	19,357	18,255
Ulster	30,744	41,173	26,445	47,372
Warren	8,580	15,860	5,886	17,616
Washington	8,201	14,103	5,909	16,580
Wayne	12,959	20,613	9,700	24,171
Westchester	169,860	197,956	160,225	229,005
Wyoming	5,228	9,451	4,381	11,199
Yates	3,507	5,488	2,670	6,367
Totals	**3,347,882**	**3,081,871**	**3,119,609**	**3,664,763**

New York Vote Since 1940

1940, Roosevelt, Dem., 2,834,500; American Lab., 417,418; total, 3,251,918; Willkie, Rep., 3,027,478; Thomas, Soc., 18,950; Babson, Proh., 3,250.

1944, Roosevelt, Dem., 2,478,598; American Lab., 496,405; Liberal, 329,325; total, 3,304,238; Dewey, Rep., 2,987,647; Teichert, Ind. Gov't., 14,352; Thomas, Soc., 10,553.

1948, Truman, Dem., 2,557,642; Liberal, 222,562; total, 2,780,204; Dewey, Rep., 2,841,163; Wallace, Amer. Lab., 509,559; Thomas, Soc., 40,879; Teichert, Ind. Gov't., 2,729; Dobbs, Soc. Workers, 2,675.

1952, Eisenhower, Rep., 3,952,815; Stevenson, Dem., 2,687,890, Liberal, 416,711; total, 3,104,601; Hallinan, American Lab., 64,211; Hoopes, Soc., 2,664; Dobbs, Soc. Workers, 2,212; Hass, Ind. Gov't., 1,560; scattering, 178; blank and void, 87,813.

1956, Eisenhower, Rep., 4,340,340; Stevenson, Dem., 2,458,212; Liberal, 292,557; total, 2,750,769; write-in votes for Andrews, 1,027; Werdel, 492; Hass, 150; Hoopes, 82; others, 476.

1960, Kennedy, Dem., 3,423,909; Liberal, 406,176; total, 3,830,085; Nixon, Rep., 3,446,419; Dobbs, Soc. Workers, 14,319; scattering, 256; blank and void, 88,896.

1964, Johnson, Dem., 4,913,156; Goldwater, Rep., 2,243,559; Hass, Soc. Labor, 6,085; DeBerry, Soc. Workers, 3,215; scattering, 188; blank and void, 151,383.

1968, Nixon, Rep., 3,007,932; Humphrey, Dem., 3,378,470; Wallace, 3d party, 358,864; Blomen, Soc. Labor, 8,432; Halstead, Soc. Worker, 11,851; Gregory, Freedom and Peace, 24,517; blank, void, and scattering, 171,624.

1972, Nixon, Rep., 3,824,642; Conservative, 368,136; McGovern, Dem., 2,767,956; Liberal, 183,128; Reed, Soc. Workers, 7,797; Fisher, Soc. Labor, 4,530; Hall, Com., 5,641; blank, void, or scattered, 161,641.

1976, Carter, Dem., 3,389,558; Ford, Rep., 3,100,791; MacBride, Libertarian, 12,197; Hall, Com., 10,270; Camejo, Soc. Workers, 6,996; LaRouche, U.S. Labor, 5,413; blank, void, or scattered, 143,037.

1980, Reagan, Rep., 2,893,831; Carter, Dem., 2,728,372; Anderson, Lib., 467,801; Clark, Libertarian, 52,648; McCormack, Right To Life, 24,159; Commoner, Citizens, 23,186; Hall, Com., 7,414; DeBerry, Soc. Workers, 2,068; Griswold, Workers World, 1,416; scattering, 1,064.

1984, Reagan, Rep., 3,664,763; Mondale, Dem., 3,119,609; Bergland, Libertarian, 11,949.

1988, Bush, Rep., 3,081,871; Dukakis, Dem., 3,347,882; Marra, Right to Life, 20,497; Fulani, New Alliance, 15,845.

North Carolina

	1988		1984	
	Dukakis	Bush	Mondale	Reagan
County	(D)	(R)	(D)	(R)
Alamance	12,642	24,131	11,230	26,063
Alexander	4,148	7,968	3,581	8,502
Alleghany	2,087	2,174	2,013	2,589
Anson	4,831	2,782	5,015	3,719
Ashe	4,034	6,019	4,009	6,611
Avery	1,367	4,277	1,159	4,702
Beaufort	5,352	8,190	5,987	9,284
Bertie	3,762	2,145	3,953	2,879
Bladen	5,031	3,770	5,064	4,701
Brunswick	7,881	10,007	6,774	9,673
Buncombe	26,964	36,828	23,337	37,698
Burke	10,848	15,933	10,353	18,766
Cabarrus	10,686	22,524	8,477	22,528
Caldwell	7,862	15,176	7,311	17,024
Camden	1,081	1,144	1,075	1,282
Carteret	6,859	11,076	5,882	11,637
Caswell	4,189	3,299	4,157	3,992
Catawba	12,922	28,872	11,700	31,476
Chatham	7,600	6,999	7,458	8,595
Cherokee	2,567	4,557	2,776	4,894
Chowan	1,756	1,884	1,736	2,171
Clay	1,289	2,174	1,340	2,259
Cleveland	10,321	14,039	10,288	17,095
Columbus	9,172	6,659	8,728	9,150
Craven	7,313	12,057	7,186	12,893
Cumberland	23,789	27,057	22,614	31,602
Currituck	1,555	2,443	1,668	2,885
Dare	2,806	5,234	1,839	4,738
Davidson	13,215	28,374	11,469	30,471
Davie	3,166	7,988	2,911	8,201
Duplin	5,945	5,774	6,830	7,708
Durham	35,441	29,928	32,244	29,185
Edgecombe	9,044	6,831	10,545	9,635
Forsyth	39,726	57,688	36,814	59,208
Franklin	5,438	5,499	4,766	5,984
Gaston	14,582	34,775	14,142	39,167
Gates	2,024	1,451	2,225	1,694
Graham	1,313	2,091	1,494	2,514
Granville	5,280	4,880	5,217	6,302
Greene	2,729	2,498	2,772	3,195
Guilford	50,351	66,060	46,027	73,096
Halifax	8,726	7,462	9,278	8,832
Harnett	7,259	9,749	7,106	11,198
Haywood	9,010	8,957	7,958	10,146
Henderson	9,338	19,711	7,222	19,369
Hertford	4,943	2,977	4,498	3,176
Hoke	3,281	2,020	3,214	2,449
Hyde	1,316	940	1,004	1,195
Iredell	10,530	21,536	9,999	23,641
Jackson	4,933	5,166	4,367	5,582
Johnston	8,717	15,563	7,833	16,210
Jones	1,946	1,649	2,025	2,062
Lee	4,231	7,104	3,925	8,198
Lenoir	7,649	10,669	8,556	13,321
Lincoln	6,444	11,651	5,996	12,621
McDowell	4,449	6,526	4,076	7,639
Macon	3,773	6,026	3,570	6,661
Madison	3,033	3,453	2,988	3,666
Martin	3,598	3,341	3,870	4,266
Mecklenburg	71,907	106,236	63,190	106,754
Mitchell	1,377	4,620	1,286	4,737
Montgomery	3,995	4,504	3,831	5,109
Moore	7,642	14,543	7,063	14,681
Nash	8,740	15,906	8,588	17,295
New Hanover	15,401	23,807	12,591	23,771
Northampton	4,599	2,415	5,094	3,198
Onslow	7,162	12,253	5,713	13,928
Orange	22,326	14,503	20,564	15,585
Pamlico	2,188	2,297	2,152	2,554
Pasquotank	3,860	4,006	3,854	4,646
Pender	4,377	4,926	4,354	5,079
Perquimans	1,543	1,781	1,441	1,939
Person	3,777	4,832	3,528	5,854
Pitt	14,777	18,245	13,481	18,983
Polk	2,534	3,874	2,169	4,046
Randolph	8,641	23,881	7,511	25,759
Richmond	7,151	5,073	7,494	6,502
Robeson	16,988	9,908	15,257	12,847
Rockingham	11,551	14,591	10,605	17,895
Rowan	12,127	23,192	10,643	25,207
Rutherford	6,926	10,337	6,862	11,369
Sampson	8,009	8,524	9,115	10,665
Scotland	3,865	3,199	4,028	4,077
Stanly	6,627	11,885	6,138	13,116
Stokes	5,319	8,661	4,950	9,515
Surry	7,245	11,393	7,188	13,340
Swain	1,821	1,795	2,000	2,012
Transylvania	4,280	7,009	3,733	6,956

	1988		1984	
Tyrrell	785	637	807	774
Union	8,820	17,015	7,048	16,885
Vance	5,631	5,625	5,880	6,836
Wake	61,352	81,613	50,323	81,251
Warren	4,249	2,163	3,946	2,664
Washington	2,806	2,186	3,114	2,731
Watauga	6,048	8,662	5,163	9,370
Wayne	9,135	15,292	10,011	17,961
Wilkes	7,230	15,231	6,852	18,670
Wilson	8,214	10,997	8,343	12,243
Yadkin	3,195	7,918	3,075	8,976
Yancey	3,803	4,160	3,651	4,296
Totals	890,167	1,237,258	824,287	1,346,481

North Carolina Vote Since 1940

1940, Roosevelt, Dem., 609,015; Willkie, Rep., 213,633.

1944, Roosevelt, Dem., 527,399; Dewey, Rep., 263,155.

1948, Truman, Dem., 459,070; Dewey, Rep., 258,572; Thurmond, States' Rights, 69,652; Wallace, Prog., 3,915.

1952, Eisenhower, Rep., 558,107; Stevenson, Dem., 652,803.

1956, Eisenhower, Rep., 575,062; Stevenson, Dem., 590,530.

1960, Kennedy, Dem., 713,136; Nixon, Rep., 655,420.

1964, Johnson, Dem., 800,139; Goldwater Rep., 624,844.

1968, Nixon, Rep., 627,192; Humphrey, Dem., 464,113; Wallace, 3d party, 496,188.

1972, Nixon, Rep., 1,054,889; McGovern, Dem., 438,705; Schmitz, Amer., 25,018.

1976, Dem., 927,365; Ford, Rep., 741,960; Anderson, Amer., 5,607; MacBride, Libertarian, 2,219; LaRouche, U.S. Labor, 755.

1980, Reagan, Rep., 915,018; Carter, Dem., 875,635; Anderson, Ind., 52,800; Clark, Libertarian, 9,677; Commoner, Citizens, 2,287; DeBerry, Soc. Workers, 416.

1984, Reagan, Rep., 1,346,481; Mondale, Dem., 824,287; Bergland, Libertarian, 3,794.

1988, Bush, Rep., 1,237,258; Dukakis, Dem., 890,167; Fulani, New Alliance, 5,682; Paul, write-in, 1,263.

North Dakota

	1988		1984	
	Wells	1,317	1,901	1,036	2,426
Williams	4,004	5,653	3,177	8,166
Totals	127,739	166,559	104,429	200,336

North Dakota Vote Since 1940

1940, Roosevelt, Dem., 124,036; Willkie, Rep., 154,590; Thomas, Soc., 1,279; Knutson, Com., 545; Babson, Proh., 325.

1944, Roosevelt, Dem., 100,144; Dewey, Rep., 118,535; Thomas, Soc., 943, Watson, Proh., 549.

1948, Truman, Dem., 95,812; Dewey, Rep., 115,139; Wallace, Prog., 8,391; Thomas, Soc., 1,000, Thurmond, States' Rights, 374.

1952, Eisenhower, Rep., 191,712; Stevenson, Dem., 76,694; MacArthur, Christian Nationalist, 1,075; Hallinan, Prog., 344; Hamblen, Proh., 302.

1956, Eisenhower, Rep., 156,766; Stevenson, Dem., 96,742; Andrews, Amer., 483.

1960, Kennedy, Dem., 123,963; Nixon, Rep., 154,310; Dobbs, Soc. Workers, 158.

1964, Johnson, Dem., 149,784; Goldwater, Rep., 108,207; DeBerry, Soc. Worker, 224; Munn, Proh., 174.

1968, Nixon, Rep., 138,669; Humphrey, Dem., 94,769; Wallace, 3d party, 14,244; Halstead, Soc. Worker, 128; Munn, Prohibition, 38; Troxell, Ind., 34.

1972, Nixon, Rep., 174,109; McGovern, Dem., 100,384; Jenness, Soc. Workers, 288; Hall, Com., 87; Schmitz, Amer., 5,646.

1976, Carter, Dem., 136,078; Ford, Rep., 153,470; Anderson, Amer., 3,698; McCarthy, Ind., 2,952; Maddox, Amer. Ind., 269; MacBride, Libertarian, 256; scattering, 371.

1980, Reagan, Rep., 193,695; Carter, Dem., 79,189; Anderson, Ind., 23,640; Clark, Libertarian, 3,743; Commoner, Libertarian, 429; McLain, Nat'l People's League, 296; Greaves, American, 235; Hall, Com., 93; DeBerry, Soc. Workers, 89; McReynolds, Soc., 82; Bubar, Statesman, 54.

1984, Reagan, Rep., 200,336; Mondale, Dem., 104,429; Bergland, Libertarian, 703.

1988, Bush, Rep., 166,559; Dukakis, Dem., 127,739; Paul, Lib., 1,315; LaRouche, Natl. Econ. Recovery, 905.

	1988		1984	
County	Dukakis (D)	Bush (R)	Mondale (D)	Reagan (R)
Adams	708	1,018	530	1,343
Barnes	2,858	3,631	2,507	4,348
Benson	1,691	1,316	1,599	1,729
Billings	211	437	133	505
Bottineau	1,684	2,530	1,279	3,356
Bowman	737	1,111	562	1,559
Burke	693	971	543	1,298
Burleigh	10,760	18,000	8,781	19,913
Cass	22,107	26,699	18,054	29,221
Cavalier	1,333	2,096	1,110	2,661
Dickey	1,249	2,064	1,051	2,460
Divide	875	869	626	1,165
Dunn	892	1,263	716	1,583
Eddy	748	891	796	1,049
Emmons	925	1,634	620	1,885
Foster	837	1,218	765	1,422
Golden Valley	388	781	325	964
Grand Forks	12,494	14,801	10,050	15,898
Grant	654	1,351	507	1,607
Griggs	846	1,020	828	1,254
Hettinger	698	1,395	524	1,646
Kidder	678	1,039	506	1,240
La Moure	1,223	1,642	1,086	1,978
Logan	540	1,111	401	1,222
McHenry	1,665	1,888	1,283	2,485
McIntosh	598	1,726	427	2,047
McKenzie	1,273	1,949	974	2,610
McLean	2,428	2,906	2,062	3,673
Mercer	1,843	3,013	1,729	3,705
Morton	4,708	5,588	3,996	7,146
Mountrail	1,977	1,443	1,565	1,959
Nelson	1,151	1,078	1,026	1,445
Oliver	526	696	419	915
Pembina	1,616	2,471	1,367	2,895
Pierce	1,008	1,422	691	1,883
Ramsey	2,665	3,103	2,304	4,150
Ransom	1,459	1,362	1,222	1,706
Renville	837	893	592	1,163
Richland	3,523	4,670	3,047	5,980
Rolette	2,426	1,126	2,179	1,479
Sargent	1,306	1,119	1,295	1,385
Sheridan	428	885	306	1,075
Sioux	701	325	655	442
Slope	202	315	174	419
Stark	3,678	6,137	2,759	7,641
Steele	895	690	781	941
Stutsman	4,214	5,375	3,495	6,591
Towner	970	946	789	1,242
Traill	1,940	2,562	1,580	3,037
Walsh	2,646	3,250	2,264	4,347
Ward	9,906	13,179	7,336	16,077

Ohio

	1988		1984	
County	Dukakis (D)	Bush (R)	Mondale (D)	Reagan (R)
Adams	3,740	5,916	3,534	6,113
Allen	13,727	31,021	12,176	33,506
Ashland	6,072	12,726	4,786	14,339
Ashtabula	20,536	17,654	19,344	21,669
Athens	10,795	9,314	10,201	11,548
Auglaize	4,756	13,562	4,102	14,766
Belmont	19,515	12,214	19,458	15,170
Brown	5,047	7,539	4,067	8,221
Butler	33,770	75,725	27,700	76,216
Carroll	4,667	6,179	3,771	6,703
Champaign	4,272	8,995	3,544	9,935
Clark	23,247	32,729	21,154	35,831
Clermont	15,352	37,417	11,713	35,316
Clinton	3,746	8,856	3,332	9,603
Columbiana	21,581	21,175	20,155	24,552
Coshocton	6,020	8,282	4,392	9,842
Crawford	6,018	12,472	4,932	14,688
Cuyahoga	353,401	242,439	362,626	284,094
Darke	6,851	14,914	5,904	16,379
Defiance	5,448	9,566	5,004	10,951
Delaware	7,590	20,693	5,773	19,050
Erie	15,097	16,670	13,508	19,174
Fairfield	12,504	29,208	9,817	30,843
Fayette	2,623	6,186	2,126	6,838
Franklin	147,585	226,265	131,530	250,360
Fulton	5,076	10,230	4,217	11,412
Gallia	4,834	7,399	4,251	8,194
Geauga	11,874	22,339	9,954	22,369
Greene	18,025	34,432	17,129	34,267
Guernsey	5,926	8,507	4,967	10,252
Hamilton	140,354	227,004	140,350	246,288
Hancock	7,435	19,896	5,758	22,169
Hardin	4,145	7,291	3,813	8,722
Harrison	3,881	3,298	3,370	4,276
Henry	3,764	8,618	2,779	9,317
Highland	4,278	8,776	3,784	9,000
Hocking	3,706	5,426	3,280	6,071
Holmes	2,179	5,064	1,737	5,146
Huron	7,794	12,633	6,609	14,388
Jackson	4,505	6,671	4,369	7,411
Jefferson	22,095	14,141	22,832	17,105
Knox	6,882	12,180	5,730	14,062

Lake	39,667	52,963	36,711	54,587
Lawrence	11,628	12,937	11,431	14,973
Licking	16,793	34,540	13,995	37,560
Logan	4,484	11,099	3,645	12,230
Lorain	55,600	50,410	52,970	57,379
Lucas	99,755	83,788	97,293	100,285
Madison	3,421	8,303	2,928	8,979
Mahoning	75,524	43,722	76,514	53,424
Marion	9,596	14,864	8,827	17,392
Medina	19,505	29,962	15,897	30,690
Meigs	3,699	5,486	3,549	6,307
Mercer	4,978	11,162	4,422	11,542
Miami	11,138	24,915	9,695	26,300
Monroe	4,269	2,557	3,611	3,302
Montgomery	95,737	131,596	94,016	137,053
Morgan	2,085	3,713	1,868	3,994
Morrow	3,515	7,130	2,839	8,116
Muskingum	11,691	19,736	10,037	21,821
Noble	2,079	3,155	1,777	3,653
Ottawa	8,038	9,352	7,053	10,920
Paulding	3,114	5,381	2,811	5,545
Perry	5,011	6,602	3,961	7,548
Pickaway	4,905	10,796	4,110	11,942
Pike	5,191	5,611	4,895	6,318
Portage	25,607	26,334	21,719	29,536
Preble	4,937	10,297	4,198	11,065
Putnam	4,004	11,183	3,194	11,936
Richland	19,617	30,047	16,141	35,299
Ross	9,271	14,563	8,020	17,015
Sandusky	9,709	14,203	8,564	17,214
Scioto	14,442	16,029	14,120	18,818
Seneca	9,504	13,704	7,905	16,520
Shelby	5,065	12,198	4,315	13,509
Stark	69,639	87,087	65,157	98,434
Summit	112,612	101,155	109,569	115,637
Trumbull	58,674	38,815	56,902	45,623
Tuscarawas	14,185	17,145	13,149	19,366
Union	3,130	8,846	2,579	9,336
Van Wert	3,848	9,410	3,338	9,570
Vinton	2,385	2,652	1,990	3,041
Warren	11,145	31,419	9,031	29,848
Washington	9,967	14,767	7,920	16,529
Wayne	13,571	22,320	11,323	24,475
Williams	4,666	10,782	3,624	10,804
Wood	18,579	26,013	15,907	29,750
Wyandot	2,936	6,178	2,342	7,204
Totals	1,939,629	2,416,549	1,825,440	2,678,559

Ohio Vote Since 1940

1940, Roosevelt, Dem., 1,733,139; Willkie, Rep., 1,586,773.

1944, Roosevelt, Dem., 1,570,763; Dewey, Rep., 1,582,293.

1948, Truman, Dem., 1,452,791; Dewey, Rep., 1,445,684; Wallace, Prog., 37,596.

1952, Eisenhower, Rep., 2,100,391; Stevenson, Dem., 1,600,367.

1956, Eisenhower, Rep., 2,262,610; Stevenson, Dem., 1,439,655.

1960, Kennedy, Dem., 1,944,248; Nixon, Rep., 2,217,611.

1964, Johnson, Dem., 2,498,331; Goldwater, Rep., 1,470,865.

1968, Nixon, Rep., 1,791,014; Humphrey, Dem., 1,700,586; Wallace, 3d party, 467,495; Gregory, 372; Munn, Proh., 19; Blomen, Soc. Labor, 120; Halstead, Soc. Worker, 69; Mitchell, Com., 23.

1972, Nixon, Rep., 2,441,827; McGovern, Dem., 1,558,889; Fisher, Soc. Labor, 7,107; Hall, Com., 6,437; Schmitz, Amer., 80,067; Wallace, Ind., 460.

1976, Carter, Dem., 2,011,621; Ford, Rep., 2,000,505; McCarthy, Ind., 58,258; Maddox, Amer. Ind., 15,529; MacBride, Libertarian, 8,961; Hall, Com., 7,817; Camejo, Soc. Workers, 4,717; LaRouche, U.S. Labor, 4,335; scattered, 130.

1980, Reagan, Rep., 2,206,545; Carter, Dem., 1,752,414; Anderson, Ind., 254,472; Clark, Libertarian, 49,033; Commoner, Citizens, 8,564; Hall, Com., 4,729; Congress, Ind. 4,029; Griswold, Workers World, 3,790; Bubar, Statesman, 27.

1984, Reagan, Rep., 2,678,559; Mondale, Dem., 1,825,440; Bergland, Libertarian, 5,886.

1988, Bush, Rep., 2,416,549; Dukakis, Dem., 1,939,629; Fulani, Ind., 12,017; Paul, Ind., 11,926.

Oklahoma

	1988		1984	
County	Dukakis (D)	Bush (R)	Mondale (D)	Reagan (R)
Adair	2,624	3,558	2,266	4,423
Alfalfa	1,117	1,960	866	2,715
Atoka	2,565	1,971	2,047	2,361
Beaver	777	2,013	536	2,689
Beckham	3,388	3,463	2,601	5,005
Blaine	1,775	2,889	1,484	4,037
Bryan	6,849	4,615	5,475	6,246
Caddo	5,387	4,689	4,463	6,811
Canadian	7,453	17,872	5,245	20,929
Carter	7,988	8,430	6,161	11,578
Cherokee	6,483	5,838	5,307	7,614
Choctaw	3,362	2,217	2,801	3,155
Cimarron	470	1,153	359	1,420
Cleveland	22,067	36,313	16,512	42,806
Coal	1,365	891	1,284	1,259
Comanche	11,441	17,464	8,890	21,382
Cotton	1,482	1,266	1,264	1,796
Craig	2,940	2,463	2,515	3,629
Creek	9,512	11,308	7,465	15,011
Custer	3,697	6,735	2,700	8,191
Delaware	4,889	5,248	3,789	6,690
Dewey	963	1,543	664	2,098
Ellis	786	1,422	562	1,881
Garfield	8,067	15,248	5,730	19,642
Garvin	5,438	5,109	4,215	7,505
Grady	6,689	7,994	4,846	11,042
Grant	1,249	1,690	825	2,470
Greer	1,256	1,225	1,220	1,664
Harmon	890	611	785	1,009
Harper	593	1,281	373	1,748
Haskell	2,963	1,822	2,535	2,417
Hughes	3,259	2,037	2,901	2,663
Jackson	3,542	4,423	2,996	5,773
Jefferson	1,767	1,063	1,496	1,656
Johnston	2,042	1,518	1,820	2,195
Kay	7,751	12,646	6,044	16,731
Kingfisher	1,777	4,011	1,125	5,528
Kiowa	2,296	2,030	2,016	2,951
Latimer	2,365	1,830	1,858	2,210
Le Flore	6,594	6,964	5,990	8,604
Lincoln	4,225	6,409	3,020	8,088
Logan	4,603	6,947	3,551	8,356
Love	1,889	1,361	1,359	1,833
McClain	3,594	4,771	2,549	6,056
McCurtain	4,928	4,920	3,994	6,381
Mcintosh	4,041	2,665	3,479	3,646
Major	982	2,638	619	3,385
Marshall	2,730	1,911	2,039	2,488
Mayes	6,691	6,115	5,154	8,585
Murray	2,697	2,056	2,229	3,073
Muskogee	13,760	11,147	12,343	14,652
Noble	1,661	3,015	1,238	4,018
Nowata	2,203	2,000	1,687	3,030
Okfuskee	2,209	1,851	1,684	2,443
Oklahoma	75,812	135,376	60,235	159,974
Okmulgee	8,262	5,674	7,380	8,704
Osage	7,778	7,162	6,095	10,083
Ottawa	6,658	5,026	5,781	7,666
Pawnee	2,781	3,324	2,165	4,699
Payne	10,568	16,027	7,653	20,811
Pittsburg	8,623	7,594	6,860	9,778
Pontotoc	6,484	6,609	5,526	8,301
Pottawatomie	8,873	12,099	6,966	16,143
Pushmataha	2,430	1,841	2,079	2,499
Roger Mills	866	1,132	680	1,550
Rogers	8,771	12,940	6,013	16,137
Seminole	4,911	4,078	3,957	6,009
Sequoyah	4,951	5,710	4,202	7,042
Stephens	7,833	9,844	6,359	12,871
Texas	1,717	4,971	1,033	5,968
Tillman	2,148	1,754	1,674	2,637
Tulsa	69,044	127,512	58,274	159,549
Wagoner	7,378	10,219	5,271	12,534
Washington	6,971	14,613	5,476	19,043
Washita	2,290	2,402	1,547	3,847
Woods	1,735	2,835	1,231	3,741
Woodward	2,408	4,996	1,647	6,376
Totals	483,423	678,367	385,080	861,530

Oklahoma Vote Since 1940

1940, Roosevelt, Dem., 474,313; Willkie, Rep., 348,872; Babson, Proh., 3,027.

1944, Roosevelt, Dem., 401,549; Dewey, Rep., 319,424; Watson, Proh., 1,663.

1948, Truman, Dem., 452,782; Dewey, Rep., 268,817.

1952, Eisenhower, Rep., 518,045; Stevenson, Dem., 430,939.

1956, Eisenhower, Rep., 473,769; Stevenson, Dem., 385,581.

1960, Kennedy, Dem., 370,111; Nixon, Rep., 533,039.

1964, Johnson, Dem., 519,834; Goldwater, Rep. 412,665.

1968, Nixon, Rep., 449,697; Humphrey, Dem., 301,658; Wallace, 3d party, 191,731.

1972, Nixon, Rep. 759,025; McGovern, Dem., 247,147; Schmitz, Amer., 23,728.

1976, Carter, Dem., 532,442; Ford, Rep., 545,708; McCarthy, Ind., 14,101.

1980, Reagan, Rep., 695,570; Carter, Dem., 402,026; Anderson, Ind., 38,284; Clark, Libertarian, 13,828.

1984, Reagan, Rep., 861,530; Mondale, Dem., 385,080; Bergland, Libertarian, 9,066.

1988, Bush, Rep., 678,367; Dukakis, Dem., 483,423; Paul, Lib., 6,261; Fulani, New Alliance, 2,985.

Oregon

	1988		1984	
	Dukakis	Bush	Mondale	Reagan
County	(D)	(R)	(D)	(R)
Baker.	2,896	3,696	2,591	5,204
Benton	16,930	14,004	16,073	17,836
Clackamas	59,799	61,381	47,254	68,630
Clatsop.	8,074	5,956	7,525	7,522
Columbia.	8,983	6,424	8,219	7,811
Coos	13,996	10,153	13,562	13,637
Crook	2,719	3,049	2,268	3,773
Curry.	4,015	4,761	3,423	5,363
Deschutes	14,264	16,425	11,671	19,323
Douglas	17,255	20,120	14,609	25,243
Gilliam	417	470	369	700
Grant	1,437	2,264	1,344	2,695
Harney	1,379	1,833	1,290	2,197
Hood River	3,275	3,257	3,022	4,531
Jackson	28,028	32,516	22,230	37,895
Jefferson.	2,346	2,509	1,920	3,283
Josephine	10,646	15,876	8,539	19,470
Klamath	8,429	13,484	7,575	17,686
Lake	1,237	2,161	1,184	2,466
Lane	69,883	47,563	63,999	61,493
Lincoln	9,598	7,364	8,637	9,110
Linn.	17,007	18,312	16,161	23,463
Malheur	2,965	6,285	2,611	8,441
Marion	41,193	45,292	36,440	54,535
Morrow.	1,375	1,529	1,254	2,130
Multnomah.	161,361	95,561	144,179	119,932
Polk.	9,626	10,553	8,709	12,678
Sherman.	435	555	398	828
Tillamook	5,529	4,297	4,988	5,267
Umatilla	8,327	10,254	8,246	14,211
Union.	4,682	5,061	4,134	6,645
Wallowa	1,425	1,993	1,204	2,619
Wasco	5,141	4,462	5,526	6,905
Washington	59,837	67,018	44,602	75,877
Wheeler	274	367	253	504
Yamhill	11,423	13,321	9,450	15,797
Totals	616,206	560,126	536,479	685,700

Oregon Vote Since 1940

1940, Roosevelt, Dem., 258,415; Willkie, Rep., 219,555; Aiken, Soc. Labor, 2,487; Thomas, Soc., 398; Browder, Com., 191; Babson, Proh., 154.

1944, Roosevelt, Dem., 248,635; Dewey, Rep., 225,365; Thomas, Soc., 3,785; Watson, Proh., 2,362.

1948, Truman, Dem., 243,147; Dewey, Rep., 260,904; Wallace, Prog., 14,978; Thomas, Soc., 5,051.

1952, Eisenhower, Rep., 420,815; Stevenson, Dem., 270,579; Hallinan, Ind., 3,665.

1956, Eisenhower, Rep., 406,393; Stevenson, Dem., 329,204.

1960, Kennedy, Dem., 367,402; Nixon, Rep., 408,060.

1964, Johnson, Dem., 501,017; Goldwater, Rep., 282,779; write-in, 2,509.

1968, Nixon, Rep., 408,433; Humphrey, Dem., 358,866; Wallace, 3d party, 49,683; write-in, McCarthy, 1,496; N. Rockefeller, 69; others, 1,075.

1972, Nixon, Rep., 486,686; McGovern, Dem., 392,760; Schmitz, Amer., 46,211; write-in, 2,289.

1976, Carter, Dem., 490,407; Ford, Rep., 492,120; McCarthy, Ind., 40,207; write-in, 7,142.

1980, Reagan, Rep., 571,044; Carter, Dem., 456,890; Anderson, Ind., 112,389; Clark, Libertarian, 25,838; Commoner, Citizens, 13,642; scattered, 1,713.

1984, Reagan, Rep., 658,700; Mondale, Dem., 536,479.

1988, Bush, Rep., 560,126; Dukakis, Dem., 616,206; Paul, Lib., 14,811; Fulani, Ind., 6,487.

Pennsylvania

	1988		1984	
	Dukakis	Bush	Mondale	Reagan
County	(D)	(R)	(D)	(R)
Adams	8,299	15,650	7,289	16,786
Allegheny	348,814	231,137	372,576	284,692
Armstrong	13,892	11,509	14,525	13,709
Beaver	50,327	25,764	54,765	32,052
Bedford	5,754	11,123	5,424	13,085
Berks	41,040	70,153	37,849	74,605
Blair	15,588	25,623	15,651	30,104
Bradford	6,635	13,568	5,474	14,808
Bucks	82,472	127,563	74,568	130,119
Butler.	22,341	27,777	24,735	31,676
Cambria	38,517	25,626	39,865	32,173

	1988		1984	
	Dukakis	Bush	Mondale	Reagan
	(D)	(R)	(D)	(R)
Cameron.	901	1,731	990	2,031
Carbon.	9,104	10,232	8,836	10,701
Centre	18,357	23,875	16,194	27,802
Chester	44,853	93,522	38,870	92,221
Clarion	5,616	8,026	5,407	9,836
Clearfield	12,235	14,296	11,963	18,653
Clinton	5,759	5,735	4,525	6,678
Columbia.	7,767	12,114	8,254	14,402
Crawford	13,021	17,249	12,792	20,181
Cumberland	24,613	47,292	21,374	49,282
Dauphin	35,079	48,917	33,576	54,330
Delaware	96,144	147,656	98,207	161,754
Elk	5,879	6,737	5,486	8,470
Erie	53,913	48,306	52,471	55,860
Fayette.	33,098	16,915	35,098	21,314
Forest	895	1,159	839	1,468
Franklin	12,368	27,086	11,480	27,243
Fulton	1,532	3,086	1,309	3,254
Greene	9,126	4,879	9,365	6,376
Huntingdon	4,752	8,800	4,430	10,220
Indiana.	16,514	14,983	15,791	18,845
Jefferson.	6,235	9,743	5,950	11,334
Juniata	2,834	4,881	2,624	5,059
Lackawanna	45,591	42,083	45,851	48,132
Lancaster	38,982	96,979	31,308	99,090
Lawrence	21,884	15,829	23,981	19,277
Lebanon	11,912	24,415	10,520	27,008
Lehigh	42,801	56,363	41,089	61,799
Luzerne	58,553	59,059	58,482	69,169
Lycoming	13,528	24,792	13,147	28,498
McKean	5,300	9,323	4,818	10,963
Mercer	24,278	21,301	24,658	24,211
Mifflin.	4,790	8,170	5,178	9,106
Monroe.	9,859	17,185	8,193	16,109
Montgomery	109,834	170,294	99,741	181,426
Montour	2,031	3,617	2,055	4,174
Northampton . . .	39,264	42,748	37,979	44,648
Northumberland. .	14,255	20,207	13,748	22,109
Perry	3,910	8,545	3,692	9,365
Philadelphia	449,566	219,053	501,369	267,178
Pike.	3,097	6,659	2,503	6,343
Potter.	2,119	4,432	1,789	5,164
Schuylkill.	24,797	32,666	25,758	37,330
Snyder.	2,658	9,054	2,383	8,968
Somerset	13,815	16,809	13,900	19,502
Sullivan.	1,091	1,808	952	1,926
Susquehanna	4,871	9,077	4,471	10,566
Tioga	4,807	9,471	4,060	10,532
Union	3,163	7,912	2,747	7,792
Venango	8,624	11,468	9,114	13,507
Warren	6,790	8,991	6,244	10,838
Washington	47,527	28,651	50,911	34,782
Wayne	3,775	9,926	3,155	10,061
Westmoreland . . .	76,710	61,472	79,906	71,377
Wyoming	2,797	6,607	2,518	7,230
York	37,691	72,408	33,359	75,020
Totals	2,194,944	2,300,087	2,228,131	2,584,323

Pennsylvania Vote Since 1940

1940, Roosevelt, Dem., 2,171,035; Willkie, Rep., 1,889,848; Thomas, Soc., 10,967; Browder, Com., 4,519; Aiken, Ind. Gov., 1,518.

1944, Roosevelt, Dem., 1,940,479; Dewey, Rep., 1,835,054; Thomas, Soc., 11,721; Watson, Proh., 5,750; Teichert, Ind. Gov., 1,789.

1948, Truman, Dem., 1,752,426; Dewey, Rep., 1,902,197; Wallace, Prog., 55,161; Thomas, Soc., 11,325; Watson, Proh., 10,338; Dobbs, Militant Workers, 2,133; Teichert, Ind. Gov., 1,461.

1952, Eisenhower, Rep., 2,415,789; Stevenson, Dem., 2,146,269; Hamblen, Proh., 8,771; Hallinan, Prog., 4,200; Hoopes, Soc., 2,684; Dobbs, Militant Workers, 1,502; Hass, Ind. Gov., 1,347; scattered, 155.

1956, Eisenhower, Rep., 2,585,252; Stevenson, Dem., 1,981,769; Hass, Soc. Labor, 7,447; Dobbs, Militant Workers, 2,035.

1960, Kennedy, Dem., 2,556,282; Nixon, Rep., 2,439,956; Hass, Soc. Labor, 7,185; Dobbs, Soc. Workers, 2,678; scattering, 440.

1964, Johnson, Dem., 3,130,954; Goldwater, Rep., 1,673,657; DeBerry, Soc. Workers, 10,456; Hass, Soc. Labor, 5,092; scattering, 2,531.

1968, Nixon, Rep., 2,090,017; Humphrey, Dem., 2,259,405; Wallace, 3d party, 378,582; Blomen, Soc. Labor, 4,977; Halstead, Soc. Workers, 4,862; Gregory, 7,821; others, 2,264.

1972, Nixon, Rep., 2,714,521; McGovern, Dem., 1,796,951; Schmitz, Amer., 70,593; Jenness, Soc. Workers, 4,639; Hall, Com., 2,686; others, 2,715.

1976, Carter, Dem., 2,328,677; Ford, Rep., 2,205,604; McCarthy, Ind., 50,584; Maddox, Constitution, 25,344;

Camejo, Soc. Workers, 3,009; LaRouche, U.S. Labor, 2,744; Hall, Com., 1,891; others, 2,934.

1980, Reagan, Rep., 2,261,872; Carter, Dem., 1,937,540; Anderson, Ind., 292,921; Clark, Libertarian, 33,263; De-Berry, Soc. Workers, 20,291; Commoner, Consumer, 10,430; Hall, Com., 5,184.

1984, Reagan, Rep., 2,584,323; Mondale, Dem., 2,228,131; Bergland, Libertarian, 6,982.

1988, Bush, Rep., 2,300,087; Dukakis, Dem., 2,194,944; McCarthy, Consumer, 19,158; Paul, Lib., 12,051.

Rhode Island

City	1988 Dukakis (D)	Bush (R)	1984 Mondale (D)	Reagan (R)
Cranston	19,711	17,129	17,742	19,517
East Providence	11,948	8,181	11,064	10,332
Pawtucket	15,985	9,359	14,109	12,460
Providence	34,806	15,310	35,751	19,748
Warwick	21,662	18,052	19,278	22,276
Totals	225,123	177,761	197,106	212,080

Rhode Island Vote Since 1940

1940, Roosevelt, Dem., 182,182; Willkie, Rep., 138,653; Browder, Com., 239; Babson, Proh., 74.

1944, Roosevelt, Dem., 175,356; Dewey, Rep., 123,487; Watson, Proh., 433.

1948, Truman, Dem., 188,736; Dewey, Rep., 135,787; Wallace, Prog., 2,619; Thomas, Soc., 429; Teichert, Soc. Labor, 131.

1952, Eisenhower, Rep., 210,935; Stevenson, Dem., 203,293; Hallinan, Prog., 187; Hass, Soc. Labor, 83.

1956, Eisenhower, Rep., 225,819; Stevenson, Dem., 161,790.

1960, Kennedy, Dem., 258,032; Nixon, Rep., 147,502.

1964, Johnson, Dem., 315,463; Goldwater, Rep., 74,615.

1968, Nixon, Rep., 122,359; Humphrey, Dem., 246,518; Wallace, 3d party, 15,678; Halstead, Soc. Worker, 383.

1972, Nixon, Rep., 220,383; McGovern, Dem., 194,645; Jenness, Soc. Workers, 729.

1976, Carter, Dem., 227,636; Ford, Rep., 181,249; MacBride, Libertarian, 715; Camejo, Soc. Workers, 462; Hall, Com., 334; Levin, Soc. Labor, 188.

1980, Reagan, Rep., 154,793; Carter, Dem., 198,342; Anderson, Ind., 59,819; Clark, Libertarian, 2,458; Hall, Com., 218; McReynolds, Socialist, 170; DeBerry, Soc. Worker, 90; Griswold, Workers World, 77.

1984, Reagan, Rep., 212,080; Mondale, Dem., 197,106; Bergland, Libertarian, 277.

1988, Bush, Rep., 177,761; Dukakis, Dem., 225,123; Paul, Lib., 825; Fulani, New Alliance, 280.

South Carolina

County	1988 Dukakis (D)	Bush (R)	1984 Mondale (D)	Reagan (R)
Abbeville	3,629	3,738	3,051	3,798
Aiken	10,598	27,665	9,872	25,872
Allendale	1,796	1,295	2,170	1,570
Anderson	12,281	25,939	10,324	24,123
Bamberg	2,830	2,403	2,892	2,908
Barnwell	2,564	4,467	2,811	4,346
Beaufort	8,691	16,184	7,347	13,668
Berkeley	9,312	16,779	7,380	16,972
Calhoun	2,175	2,585	2,315	2,742
Charleston	32,977	49,149	29,470	53,779
Cherokee	4,322	7,763	4,101	8,655
Chester	3,737	3,968	3,559	4,441
Chesterfield	4,699	4,999	4,593	5,451
Clarendon	5,030	4,337	5,591	5,102
Colleton	4,508	4,962	4,910	6,200
Darlington	7,625	9,854	7,456	11,100
Dillon	3,251	3,793	3,360	4,646
Dorchester	7,371	14,756	7,037	15,289
Edgefield	3,020	3,814	3,227	3,224
Fairfield	3,827	2,714	4,117	3,147
Florence	12,531	19,490	14,639	22,753
Georgetown	5,402	7,032	6,392	7,370
Greenville	27,188	67,371	24,137	66,766
Greenwood	6,511	9,096	6,339	10,887
Hampton	3,435	2,826	3,736	3,464
Horry	13,316	24,843	8,940	20,396
Jasper	2,894	2,004	3,753	3,102
Kershaw	4,494	8,877	4,323	8,822
Lancaster	6,181	9,152	5,804	10,383
Laurens	5,930	9,731	5,312	9,729
Lee	3,423	2,936	3,912	3,548
Lexington	11,366	41,467	8,828	38,628
McCormick	1,722	1,172	1,526	1,186
Marion	5,008	4,403	5,043	4,698
Marlboro	3,937	2,921	4,294	3,951
Newberry	3,825	6,427	3,790	7,176
Oconee	4,299	10,184	3,333	8,625
Orangeburg	14,655	13,281	15,121	14,286
Pickens	6,103	17,448	4,481	15,155
Richland	36,420	43,841	32,212	46,773
Saluda	1,984	3,225	1,962	3,515
Spartanburg	22,964	40,801	20,130	41,553
Sumter	9,502	13,161	9,566	12,909
Union	4,420	6,019	4,424	6,331
Williamsburg	7,343	5,914	7,586	6,492
York	11,458	21,657	9,273	20,008
Totals	370,554	606,443	344,459	615,539

South Carolina Vote Since 1940

1940, Roosevelt, Dem., 95,470; Willkie, Rep., 1,727.

1944, Roosevelt, Dem., 90,601; Dewey, Rep., 4,547; Southern Democrats, 7,799; Watson, Proh., 365; Rep. Tolbert faction, 63.

1948, Thurmond, States' Rights, 102,607; Truman, Dem., 34,423; Dewey, Rep., 5,386; Wallace, Prog., 154; Thomas, Soc., 1.

1952, Eisenhower ran on two tickets. Under state law vote cast for two Eisenhower slates of electors could not be combined. Eisenhower, Ind., 158,289; Rep., 9,793; total, 168,082; Stevenson, Dem., 173,004; Hamblen, Proh., 1.

1956, Stevenson, Dem., 136,372; Byrd, Ind., 88,509; Eisenhower, Rep., 75,700; Andrews, Ind., 2.

1960, Kennedy, Dem., 198,129; Nixon, Rep., 188,558; write-in, 1.

1964, Johnson, Dem., 215,700; Goldwater, Rep., 309,048; write-ins: Nixon, 1, Wallace, 5; Powell, 1; Thurmond, 1.

1968, Nixon, Rep., 254,062; Humphrey, Dem., 197,486; Wallace, 3d party, 215,430.

1972, Nixon, Rep., 477,044; McGovern, Dem., 184,559, United Citizens, 2,265; Schmitz, Amer., 10,075; write-in, 17.

1976, Carter, Dem., 450,807; Ford, Rep., 346,149; Anderson, Amer., 2,996; Maddox, Amer. Ind., 1,950; write-in, 681.

1980, Reagan, Rep., 439,277; Carter, Dem., 428,220; Anderson, Ind., 13,868; Clark, Libertarian, 4,807; Rarick, Amer. Ind., 2,086.

1984, Reagan, Rep., 615,539; Mondale, Dem., 344,459; Bergland, Libertarian, 4,359.

1988, Bush, Rep., 606,443; Dukakis, Dem., 370,554; Paul, Lib., 4,935; Fulani, United Citizens, 4,077.

South Dakota

County	1988 Dukakis (D)	Bush (R)	1984 Mondale (D)	Reagan (R)
Aurora	987	856	840	1,029
Beadle	4,523	4,611	3,523	5,876
Bennett	579	663	453	856
Bon Homme	1,574	1,826	1,408	2,478
Brookings	4,860	5,394	4,089	6,679
Brown	8,673	8,537	6,852	10,541
Brule	991	971	961	1,578
Buffalo	334	151	236	253
Butte	1,256	2,291	784	2,865
Campbell	334	909	214	1,035
Chas. Mix	2,205	1,966	1,879	2,660
Clark	1,164	1,247	960	1,748
Clay	2,859	2,307	2,711	3,057
Codington	4,570	5,050	3,528	6,108
Corson	722	710	792	955
Custer	1,180	1,806	858	2,183
Davison	3,705	4,024	3,248	4,783
Day	2,137	1,616	1,932	2,150
Deuel	1,246	1,251	941	1,537
Dewey	1,007	765	772	941
Douglas	695	1,438	536	1,713
Edmunds	1,259	1,327	1,007	1,553
Fall River	1,380	2,002	1,115	2,748
Faulk	714	842	579	1,124
Grant	1,988	2,148	1,606	2,738
Gregory	1,138	1,566	780	1,777
Haakon	379	958	237	1,168
Hamlin	1,258	1,380	963	1,782
Hand	1,101	1,461	846	2,030
Hanson	776	786	625	898
Harding	259	633	186	723
Hughes	2,853	4,545	2,072	4,985
Hutchinson	1,594	2,700	1,237	3,372
Hyde	436	546	350	797
Jackson	450	671	365	903
Jerauld	751	777	542	1,012
Jones	261	521	206	689

Kingsbury	1,472	1,592	1,249	2,121
Lake	2,663	2,439	2,367	3,027
Lawrence	3,705	5,570	2,565	5,949
Lincoln	3,190	3,537	2,626	3,988
Lyman	631	843	478	1,120
McCook	1,492	1,501	1,448	1,902
McPherson	571	1,358	418	1,813
Marshall	1,372	1,142	1,111	1,529
Meade	3,212	5,189	2,093	5,908
Mellette	385	460	303	616
Miner	955	795	960	1,004
Minnehaha	29,135	26,765	23,042	29,908
Moody	1,715	1,161	1,586	1,633
Pennington	12,068	19,510	8,224	21,947
Perkins	851	1,326	714	1,686
Potter	701	1,175	482	1,551
Roberts	2,267	2,012	2,063	2,767
Sanborn	770	815	611	1,080
Shannon	1,206	256	1,489	324
Spink	2,071	1,969	1,680	2,627
Stanley	511	698	351	942
Sully	393	571	266	836
Todd	1,117	535	1,022	679
Tripp	1,219	2,113	935	2,483
Turner	1,780	2,436	1,486	3,086
Union	2,612	1,907	2,221	2,431
Walworth	1,094	1,940	779	2,396
Yankton	3,777	4,186	2,932	5,161
Ziebach	427	362	359	429
Totals	**145,560**	**165,415**	**116,113**	**200,267**

South Dakota Vote Since 1940

1940, Roosevelt, Dem., 131,862; Willkie, Rep., 177,065.

1944, Roosevelt, Dem., 96,711; Dewey, Rep., 135,365.

1948, Truman, Dem., 117,653; Dewey, Rep., 129,651; Wallace, Prog., 2,801.

1952, Eisenhower, Rep., 203,857; Stevenson, Dem., 90,426.

1956, Eisenhower, Rep., 171,569; Stevenson, Dem., 122,288.

1960, Kennedy, Dem., 128,070; Nixon, Rep., 178,417.

1964, Johnson, Dem., 163,010; Goldwater, Rep., 130,108.

1968, Nixon, Rep., 149,841; Humphrey, Dem., 118,023; Wallace, 3d party, 13,400.

1972, Nixon, Rep., 166,476; McGovern, Dem., 139,945; Jenness, Soc. Workers, 994.

1976, Carter, Dem., 147,068; Ford, Rep., 151,505; MacBride, Libertarian, 1,619; Hall, Com., 318; Camejo, Soc. Workers, 168.

1980, Reagan, Rep., 198,343; Carter, Dem., 103,855; Anderson, Ind., 21,431; Clark, Libertarian, 3,824; Pulley, Soc. Workers, 250.

1984, Reagan, Rep., 200,267; Mondale, Dem., 116,113.

1988, Bush, Rep., 165,415; Dukakis, Dem., 145,560; Paul, Lib., 1,060; Fulani, New Alliance, 730.

Tennessee

	1988		1984	
County	Dukakis (D)	Bush (R)	Mondale (D)	Reagan (R)
Anderson	9,589	15,056	10,415	16,783
Bedford	4,046	4,856	4,499	4,699
Benton	2,826	2,167	3,398	2,481
Bledsoe	1,274	1,858	1,316	1,950
Blount	9,602	20,027	9,188	20,525
Bradley	6,122	15,829	6,085	16,322
Campbell	4,188	5,197	4,692	5,685
Cannon	1,726	1,604	1,846	1,669
Carroll	4,151	5,635	4,568	6,017
Carter	4,634	12,036	4,642	13,153
Cheatham	3,067	4,132	3,007	4,109
Chester	1,757	2,781	1,854	2,793
Claiborne	2,977	4,071	2,870	4,474
Clay	1,183	1,291	1,281	1,338
Cocke	2,115	5,430	2,068	6,665
Coffee	5,686	7,837	5,691	7,695
Crockett	1,742	2,214	1,937	2,479
Cumberland	3,964	7,557	3,605	7,083
Davidson	89,270	98,599	89,498	98,115
Decatur	1,880	2,286	2,031	2,390
De Kalb	2,452	2,098	2,645	2,337
Dickson	5,129	5,343	5,809	5,846
Dyer	3,690	6,508	3,991	6,610
Fayette	3,292	3,573	3,634	3,733
Fentress	1,856	3,103	1,755	2,922
Franklin	5,442	5,381	5,846	5,705
Gibson	7,542	8,415	8,334	9,484
Giles	3,918	3,518	3,812	3,875
Grainger	1,423	2,734	1,565	3,212
Greene	5,077	11,947	4,763	13,215
Grundy	2,415	1,429	2,596	1,396
Hamblen	5,061	10,418	4,922	11,144
Hamilton	40,990	68,111	41,449	69,626
Hancock	737	1,303	619	1,491
Hardeman	3,526	3,547	3,797	3,712
Hardin	2,808	4,252	3,051	4,632
Hawkins	5,212	9,356	4,802	9,863
Haywood	2,923	2,687	3,308	2,839
Henderson	2,296	5,418	2,426	5,362
Henry	5,138	4,784	5,407	5,376
Hickman	2,643	2,246	2,941	2,370
Houston	1,467	882	1,716	882
Humphreys	3,037	2,132	3,668	2,249
Jackson	1,962	1,168	2,894	1,544
Jefferson	3,168	6,832	3,185	7,721
Johnson	1,329	3,715	999	3,853
Knox	41,829	73,092	43,448	76,965
Lake	935	806	1,191	878
Lauderdale	3,296	3,308	3,506	3,566
Lawrence	4,903	6,273	5,458	6,034
Lewis	1,419	1,324	1,556	1,733
Lincoln	3,672	4,288	4,103	3,982
Loudon	3,480	7,122	3,227	7,113
McMinn	4,568	8,462	5,141	9,604
McNairy	3,510	4,625	3,825	4,776
Macon	1,538	2,962	1,747	3,330
Madison	11,001	16,952	12,006	17,819
Marion	4,175	4,407	3,942	4,337
Marshall	2,795	2,975	2,935	3,416
Maury	6,280	8,397	6,950	9,008
Meigs	1,048	1,507	1,012	1,575
Monroe	4,000	6,355	4,223	6,665
Montgomery	9,145	12,599	9,939	13,228
Moore	731	786	808	863
Morgan	1,941	2,576	2,121	2,903
Obion	4,785	6,037	4,769	6,384
Overton	2,511	1,873	2,749	2,054
Perry	1,208	854	1,316	948
Pickett	634	1,118	706	1,246
Polk	2,073	2,297	2,112	2,785
Putnam	6,606	9,547	7,443	8,999
Rhea	2,595	5,144	2,804	5,692
Roane	6,535	10,881	6,623	11,882
Robertson	5,884	5,714	5,756	5,445
Rutherford	12,245	20,397	11,618	19,503
Scott	1,611	2,562	1,810	3,107
Sequatchie	1,196	1,659	1,238	1,785
Sevier	3,643	11,920	3,384	12,517
Shelby	149,759	157,457	169,717	165,947
Smith	2,522	2,138	3,256	2,393
Stewart	1,979	1,302	2,174	1,285
Sullivan	17,396	32,996	16,925	36,516
Sumner	11,702	19,523	11,535	18,442
Tipton	3,824	6,052	3,895	5,945
Trousdale	1,193	969	1,142	781
Unicoi	1,794	3,664	1,696	4,249
Union	1,431	2,110	1,495	2,447
Van Buren	796	780	810	718
Warren	4,646	4,529	4,813	4,811
Washington	10,087	19,615	9,452	21,762
Wayne	1,516	3,405	1,534	3,332
Weakley	4,239	5,701	4,752	6,480
White	2,562	2,646	3,033	2,895
Williamson	7,864	20,847	6,929	17,975
Wilson	8,360	13,317	8,433	12,858
Totals	**679,794**	**947,233**	**711,714**	**990,212**

Tennessee Vote Since 1940

1940, Roosevelt, Dem., 351,601; Willkie, Rep., 169,153; Babson, Proh., 1,606; Thomas, Soc., 463.

1944, Roosevelt, Dem., 308,707; Dewey, Rep., 200,311; Watson, Proh., 882; Thomas, Soc., 892.

1948, Truman, Dem., 270,402; Dewey, Rep., 202,914; Thurmond, States' Rights, 73,815; Wallace, Prog., 1,864; Thomas, Soc., 1,288.

1952, Eisenhower, Rep., 446,147; Stevenson, Dem., 443,710; Hamblen, Proh., 1,432; Hallinan, Prog., 885; MacArthur, Christian Nationalist, 379.

1956, Eisenhower, Rep., 462,288; Stevenson, Dem., 456,507; Andrews, Ind., 19,820; Holtwick, Proh., 789.

1960, Kennedy, Dem., 481,453; Nixon, Rep., 556,577; Faubus, States' Rights, 11,304; Decker, Proh., 2,458.

1964, Johnson, Dem. 635,047; Goldwater, Rep., 508,965; write-in, 34.

1968, Nixon, Rep., 472,592; Humphrey, Dem., 351,233; Wallace, 3d party, 424,792.

1972, Nixon, Rep., 813,147; McGovern, Dem., 357,293; Schmitz, Amer., 30,373; write-in, 369.

1976, Carter, Dem., 825,879; Ford, Rep., 633,969; Anderson, Amer., 5,769; McCarthy, Ind., 5,004; Maddox, Am. Ind., 2,303; MacBride, Libertarian, 1,375; Hall, Com., 547; LaRouche, U.S. Labor, 512; Bubar, Proh., 442; Miller, Ind., 316; write-in, 230.

1980, Reagan, Rep., 787,761; Carter, Dem., 783,051; Anderson, Ind., 35,991; Clark, Libertarian, 7,116; Commoner, Citizens, 1,112; Bubar, Statesman, 521; McReynolds, So-

cialist, 519; Hall. Com., 503; DeBerry. Soc. Worker, 490; Griswold. Workers World, 400; write-ins. 152.
1984, Rèagan, Rep., 990,212; Mondale, Dem., 711,714; Bergland, Libertarian, 3,072.
1988, Bush. Rep., 947,233; Dukakis, Dem., 679,794; Paul, Ind., 2,041; Duke, Ind., 1,807.

Texas

County	1988 Dukakis (D)	1988 Bush (R)	1984 Mondale (D)	1984 Reagan (R)
Anderson	6,128	7,858	4,747	8,634
Andrews	1,122	3,052	820	3,918
Angelina	10,849	12,738	9,054	14,685
Aransas	2,305	3,858	1,696	4,352
Archer	1,627	2,010	1,089	2,487
Armstrong	314	720	238	791
Atascosa	4,657	4,777	3,547	5,279
Austin	2,593	4,524	1,941	4,872
Bailey	876	1,459	684	1,888
Bandera	1,251	3,435	771	3,152
Bastrop	8,004	5,991	4,744	6,439
Baylor	1,153	914	1,019	1,314
Bee	4,616	4,620	3,659	5,377
Bell	17,751	29,382	13,322	31,117
Bexar	174,036	193,192	136,947	203,319
Blanco	1,012	1,680	700	1,957
Borden	169	283	140	325
Bosque	2,670	3,458	2,046	3,923
Bowie	12,331	15,454	10,077	18,244
Brazoria	23,436	34,028	18,609	39,166
Brazos	14,885	29,369	12,348	34,733
Brewster	1,569	1,708	1,462	2,066
Briscoe	574	464	471	538
Brooks	2,859	608	2,702	896
Brown	4,763	6,810	4,070	8,468
Burleson	3,085	2,242	2,578	3,076
Burnet	4,343	5,120	2,983	5,895
Caldwell	4,649	3,553	3,401	4,315
Calhoun	3,314	3,183	2,586	4,434
Callahan	2,017	2,887	1,305	3,538
Cameron	30,972	24,263	26,394	29,545
Camp	2,121	1,908	1,917	2,238
Carson	1,034	2,100	826	2,412
Cass	5,941	5,305	5,053	6,677
Castro	1,436	1,604	1,009	2,026
Chambers	3,035	3,694	2,632	4,322
Cherokee	5,604	7,520	4,494	8,187
Childress	1,060	1,201	900	1,574
Clay	2,288	2,043	1,844	2,569
Cochran	681	771	557	1,117
Coke	674	863	532	1,060
Coleman	1,978	2,340	1,420	2,790
Collin	22,934	67,776	13,604	61,095
Collingsworth	809	872	742	1,396
Colorado	2,847	3,723	2,428	4,528
Comal	5,716	13,994	4,179	13,452
Comanche	2,622	2,120	2,248	2,678
Concho	643	617	580	821
Cooke	4,217	7,196	3,278	8,260
Coryell	4,026	7,461	3,113	9,056
Cottle	690	379	623	507
Crane	596	1,219	392	1,473
Crockett	881	932	589	1,094
Crosby	1,435	1,121	1,212	1,376
Culberson	557	417	407	509
Dallam	645	1,205	496	1,594
Dallas	243,198	347,094	203,592	405,444
Dawson	2,155	3,154	1,781	3,685
Deaf Smith	1,930	3,744	1,485	4,762
Delta	1,244	849	973	1,024
Denton	26,204	57,444	16,772	52,865
DeWitt	2,579	3,628	1,882	4,401
Dickens	696	435	692	594
Dimmit	2,735	900	2,546	1,338
Donley	661	1,043	529	1,297
Duval	4,177	907	3,748	1,201
Eastland	3,215	3,929	2,522	4,841
Ector	10,825	23,155	8,913	31,228
Edwards	368	556	159	626
Ellis	11,169	16,422	8,029	16,873
El Paso	62,622	55,573	51,917	66,114
Erath	4,113	5,427	3,234	6,122
Falls	2,877	2,344	2,834	3,133
Fannin	5,163	4,024	4,399	4,692
Fayette	3,390	4,551	2,379	5,711
Fisher	1,516	721	1,384	965
Floyd	1,391	1,741	1,023	2,092
Foard	513	306	448	472
Fort Bend	23,351	39,818	18,729	41,370
Franklin	1,453	1,439	1,104	1,836
Freestone	2,916	3,159	2,489	3,624
Frio	3,016	1,505	2,656	2,003
Gaines	1,310	2,265	797	2,714
Galveston	38,633	34,913	36,092	40,262
Garza	989	1,183	521	1,219
Gillespie	1,588	5,662	1,137	5,496
Glasscock	143	384	128	403
Goliad	1,358	1,427	836	1,540
Gonzales	2,897	2,983	2,196	3,962
Gray	2,460	7,259	2,003	8,955
Grayson	14,347	18,825	11,803	22,554
Gregg	12,486	26,465	10,700	29,697
Grimes	2,735	2,820	2,370	3,365
Guadalupe	7,111	13,265	5,060	14,382
Hale	3,502	6,284	3,202	7,670
Hall	1,029	714	984	1,058
Hamilton	1,355	1,718	1,130	2,118
Hansford	443	1,967	259	2,213
Hardeman	1,143	855	927	1,238
Hardin	8,245	6,897	6,782	8,380
Harris	342,919	464,217	334,135	536,029
Harrison	8,974	11,957	7,773	12,618
Hartley	505	1,229	356	1,419
Haskell	1,715	1,193	1,434	1,701
Hays	11,187	11,716	6,663	12,467
Hemphill	527	1,170	413	1,650
Henderson	9,819	11,005	7,302	12,725
Hidalgo	54,330	29,246	44,147	35,059
Hill	4,381	4,796	3,420	5,344
Hockley	2,850	4,368	2,044	5,462
Hood	4,255	7,400	3,063	6,817
Hopkins	4,984	5,133	3,707	5,772
Houston	3,846	3,882	3,275	4,542
Howard	4,445	6,024	4,115	7,519
Hudspeth	406	405	362	557
Hunt	8,820	12,331	6,971	14,303
Hutchinson	2,950	7,526	2,052	9,078
Irion	326	539	199	619
Jack	1,521	1,542	945	1,825
Jackson	2,141	2,954	1,804	3,661
Jasper	6,613	4,985	5,787	5,965
Jeff Davis	325	524	299	511
Jefferson	55,649	35,754	54,846	45,124
Jim Hogg	1,630	510	1,703	608
Jim Wells	8,495	4,335	7,795	5,896
Johnson	12,507	17,509	9,148	18,254
Jones	2,898	3,000	2,343	4,017
Karnes	2,529	2,383	1,802	3,068
Kaufman	7,358	8,466	5,554	9,343
Kendall	1,446	4,875	938	4,568
Kenedy	119	76	110	96
Kent	398	274	253	332
Kerr	3,587	11,207	3,102	11,829
Kimble	551	1,061	442	1,333
King	64	111	53	141
Kinney	669	771	486	774
Kleberg	5,367	4,443	4,924	5,712
Knox	1,013	765	921	1,027
Lamar	7,553	8,021	5,504	9,273
Lamb	2,230	3,064	1,919	3,892
Lampasas	1,954	3,000	1,356	3,285
LaSalle	1,651	693	1,504	1,007
Lavaca	3,531	4,377	2,464	5,058
Lee	2,527	2,513	1,659	2,967
Leon	2,316	2,778	1,821	3,207
Liberty	8,343	8,524	6,292	10,504
Limestone	3,476	3,257	3,228	4,063
Lipscomb	377	1,111	241	1,461
Live Oak	1,573	2,277	1,260	2,481
Llano	2,629	3,550	1,894	4,042
Loving	23	54	16	57
Lubbock	22,202	50,760	18,793	57,151
Lynn	1,086	1,279	1,009	1,617
McCulloch	1,665	1,618	1,433	2,060
McLennan	27,545	38,606	23,206	42,232
McMullen	94	302	61	337
Madison	1,835	1,896	1,384	2,158
Marion	2,255	1,857	2,111	2,336
Martin	632	1,017	512	1,218
Mason	671	975	570	1,168
Matagorda	5,675	6,787	5,201	8,452
Maverick	4,395	1,592	3,063	1,783
Medina	4,227	5,722	3,053	5,737
Menard	614	552	394	725
Midland	8,487	30,618	7,214	33,706
Milam	4,865	3,512	3,734	4,384
Mills	842	1,043	688	1,262
Mitchell	1,773	1,596	1,332	2,007
Montague	3,689	3,475	2,602	4,406
Montgomery	18,394	40,360	13,293	41,230
Moore	1,537	3,710	1,129	4,649
Morris	3,522	2,104	2,925	2,778
Motley	262	429	282	533
Nacogdoches	6,886	11,767	5,694	13,063
Navarro	6,749	6,455	5,672	7,816
Newton	3,640	1,659	3,296	2,123
Nolan	2,853	2,734	2,524	3,608
Nueces	49,209	46,337	46,721	54,333
Ochiltree	579	2,928	419	3,492
Oldham	303	691	226	762
Orange	17,834	11,959	16,816	15,386
Palo Pinto	3,930	4,649	3,349	5,701
Panola	4,123	4,642	3,179	5,676
Parker	8,517	14,090	6,050	13,647
Parmer	764	2,061	567	2,524
Pecos	1,960	2,483	1,596	3,451
Polk	5,943	5,831	3,898	5,987
Potter	9,563	16,400	8,365	20,396

Presidio	1,176	586	992	837
Rains	1,448	1,281	1,027	1,560
Randall	8,492	27,986	6,044	30,249
Reagan	418	935	243	1,079
Real	483	795	360	1,004
Red River	3,165	2,475	2,518	2,979
Reeves	2,812	1,724	2,396	2,461
Refugio	1,831	1,883	1,559	2,421
Roberts	135	441	106	539
Robertson	3,630	2,184	3,339	2,663
Rockwall	2,659	7,214	1,639	6,688
Runnels	1,720	2,417	1,179	2,968
Rusk	5,140	9,117	4,599	11,081
Sabine	2,053	1,925	1,940	2,045
San Augustine	2,118	1,946	1,583	1,937
San Jacinto	2,972	2,691	2,466	3,174
San Patricio	9,920	9,159	8,838	11,074
San Saba	1,165	1,099	1,070	1,566
Schleicher	494	653	326	854
Scurry	2,119	3,749	1,564	5,028
Shackelford	681	865	415	1,181
Shelby	4,261	3,999	3,610	4,863
Sherman	340	1,145	246	1,269
Smith	18,719	34,658	15,227	40,740
Somervell	983	1,304	635	1,422
Starr	6,958	1,218	5,047	1,658
Stephens	1,519	2,342	1,046	2,898
Sterling	188	464	129	577
Stonewall	724	421	643	599
Sutton	571	996	465	1,251
Swisher	1,893	1,271	1,642	1,611
Tarrant	151,310	242,660	120,147	248,050
Taylor	13,073	28,563	9,628	34,444
Terrell	390	296	289	407
Terry	1,941	2,645	1,535	3,181
Throckmorton	534	455	388	586
Titus	4,357	4,247	3,631	5,069
Tom Green	12,263	21,463	8,981	23,847
Travis	127,783	105,915	94,124	124,944
Trinity	2,657	2,448	2,115	2,599
Tyler	4,198	3,070	3,119	3,638
Upshur	5,242	5,991	4,614	7,325
Upton	544	1,189	380	1,603
Uvalde	3,684	4,266	2,482	4,790
Val Verde	5,044	5,109	3,857	5,909
Van Zandt	6,153	7,371	4,506	8,474
Victoria	8,923	15,056	7,037	18,787
Walker	5,826	8,473	4,263	8,809
Waller	3,957	3,607	3,828	4,116
Ward	1,858	2,709	1,188	3,474
Washington	2,960	6,041	2,483	6,506
Webb	16,227	7,528	12,308	8,582
Wharton	5,935	6,978	5,072	8,495
Wheeler	1,067	1,703	805	2,251
Wichita	17,956	23,324	16,009	28,932
Wilbarger	2,248	2,669	2,011	3,644
Willacy	3,165	1,750	3,037	2,340
Williamson	19,589	27,322	9,911	25,774
Wilson	3,953	4,436	2,829	4,588
Winkler	947	1,656	752	2,213
Wise	5,288	6,064	3,856	6,958
Wood	4,553	6,216	3,449	7,144
Yoakum	727	1,762	456	2,204
Young	3,007	4,156	2,203	5,282
Zapata	2,171	958	1,577	1,214
Zavala	3,338	628	2,937	924
Totals	2,352,748	3,036,829	1,949,276	3,433,428

Texas Vote Since 1940

1940, Roosevelt, Dem., 840,151; Willkie, Rep., 199,152; Babson, Proh., 925; Thomas, Soc., 728; Browder, Com., 212.

1944, Roosevelt, Dem., 821,605; Dewey, Rep., 191,425; Texas Regulars, 135,439; Watson, Proh., 1,017; Thomas, Soc., 594; America First, 250.

1948, Truman, Dem., 750,700; Dewey, Rep., 282,240; Thurmond, States' Rights, 106,909; Wallace, Prog., 3,764; Watson, Proh., 2,758; Thomas, Soc., 874.

1952, Eisenhower, Rep., 1,102,878; Stevenson, Dem., 969,228; Hamblen, Proh., 1,983; MacArthur, Christian Nationalist, 833; MacArthur, Constitution, 730; Hallinan, Prog., 294.

1956, Eisenhower, Rep., 1,080,619; Stevenson, Dem., 859,958; Andrews, Ind., 14,591.

1960, Kennedy, Dem., 1,167,932; Nixon, Rep., 1,121,699; Sullivan, Constitution, 18,169; Decker, Proh., 3,870; write-in, 15.

1964, Johnson, Dem., 1,663,185; Goldwater, Rep., 958,566; Lightburn, Constitution, 5,060.

1968, Nixon, Rep., 1,227,844; Humphrey, Dem., 1,266,804; Wallace, 3d party, 584,269; write-in, 489.

1972, Nixon, Rep., 2,298,896; McGovern, Dem., 1,154,289; Schmitz, Amer., 6,039; Jenness, Soc. Workers, 8,664; others, 3,393.

1976, Carter, Dem., 2,082,319; Ford, Rep., 1,953,300; McCarthy, Ind., 20,118; Anderson, Amer., 11,442; Camejo, Soc. Workers, 1,723; write-in, 2,982.

1980, Reagan, Rep., 2,510,705; Carter, Dem., 1,881,147; Anderson, Ind., 111,613; Clark, Libertarian, 37,643; write-in, 528.

1984, Reagan, Rep., 3,433,428; Mondale, Dem., 1,949,276.

1988, Bush, Rep., 3,036,829; Dukakis, Dem., 2,352,748; Paul, Lib., 30,355; Fulani, New Alliance, 7,208.

Utah

	1988		1984	
County	Dukakis (D)	Bush (R)	Mondale (D)	Reagan (R)
Beaver	816	1,286	708	1,516
Box Elder	2,736	12,585	1,983	13,243
Cache	5,871	21,766	4,123	22,127
Carbon	5,521	3,019	4,357	4,393
Daggett	132	272	227	296
Davis	16,868	50,469	11,727	49,863
Duchesne	1,227	3,118	746	4,437
Emery	1,788	2,322	1,326	3,081
Garfield	370	1,470	315	1,609
Grand	1,287	1,895	876	2,463
Iron	1,736	6,038	1,342	6,856
Juab	974	1,505	917	1,902
Kane	398	1,788	294	1,710
Millard	1,124	3,515	1,192	4,345
Morgan	647	1,889	481	1,934
Piute	206	476	151	606
Rich	234	621	131	797
Salt Lake	107,453	163,557	78,488	183,536
San Juan	1,407	2,377	1,145	2,598
Sanpete	1,822	4,579	1,227	5,507
Sevier	1,403	4,747	1,072	5,736
Summit	2,545	3,881	1,539	4,093
Tooele	4,166	5,539	3,584	6,478
Uintah	1,799	5,341	1,186	7,337
Utah	18,533	68,134	14,801	72,284
Wasatch	1,451	2,487	1,015	2,789
Washington	3,054	13,306	1,846	12,049
Wayne	353	784	224	930
Weber	21,431	39,676	18,346	44,590
Totals	207,352	428,442	155,369	469,105

Utah Vote Since 1940

1940, Roosevelt, Dem., 154,277; Willkie, Rep., 93,151; Thomas, Soc., 200; Browder, Com., 191.

1944, Roosevelt, Dem., 150,088; Dewey, Rep., 97,891; Thomas, Soc., 340.

1948, Truman, Dem., 149,151; Dewey, Rep., 124,402; Wallace, Prog., 2,679; Dobbs, Soc. Workers, 73.

1952, Eisenhower, Rep., 194,190; Stevenson, Dem., 135,364.

1956, Eisenhower, Rep., 215,631; Stevenson, Dem., 118,364.

1960, Kennedy, Dem., 169,248; Nixon, Rep., 205,361; Dobbs, Soc. Workers, 100.

1964, Johnson, Dem., 219,628; Goldwater, Rep., 181,785.

1968, Nixon, Rep., 238,728; Humphrey, Dem., 156,665; Wallace, 3d party, 26,906; Halstead, Soc. Worker, 89; Peace and Freedom, 180.

1972, Nixon, Rep., 323,643; McGovern, Dem., 126,284; Schmitz, Amer., 28,549.

1976, Carter, Dem., 182,110; Ford, Rep., 337,908; Anderson, Amer., 13,304; McCarthy, Ind., 3,907; MacBride, Libertarian, 2,438; Maddox, Am. Ind., 1,162; Camejo, Soc. Workers, 268; Hall, Com., 121.

1980, Reagan, Rep., 439,687; Carter, Dem., 124,266; Anderson, Ind., 30,284; Clark, Libertarian, 7,226; Commoner, Citizens, 1,009; Greaves, American, 965; Rarick, Amer. Ind., 522; Hall, Com., 139; DeBerry, Soc. Worker, 124.

1984, Reagan, Rep., 469,105; Mondale, Dem., 155,369; Bergland, Libertarian, 2,447.

1988, Bush, Rep., 428,442; Dukakis, Dem., 207,352; Paul, Lib., 7,473; Dennis, American, 2,158.

Vermont

	1988		1984	
City	Dukakis (D)	Bush (R)	Mondale (D)	Reagan (R)
Barre City	2,132	2,100	1,903	2,195
Bennington	3,180	2,748	2,879	3,237
Brattleboro	3,136	2,044	2,741	2,645
Burlington	9,748	6,382	10,080	7,857
Montpelier	2,351	2,013	2,120	2,257

Rutland City.....	3,590	3,631	3,298	3,970
St. Albans City..	1,441	1,295	1,346	1,748
St. Johnsbury...	1,188	1,974	915	2,152
South Burlington..	3,373	3,136	2,728	3,443
Winooski.......	1,426	1,014	1,361	1,264
Totals........	115,775	124,331	95,730	135,865

Vermont Vote Since 1940

1940, Roosevelt, Dem., 64,269; Willkie, Rep., 78,371; Browder, Com., 411.

1944, Roosevelt, Dem., 53,820; Dewey, Rep., 71,527.

1948, Truman, Dem., 45,557; Dewey, Rep., 75,926; Wallace, Prog., 1,279; Thomas, Soc., 585.

1952, Eisenhower, Rep., 109,717; Stevenson, Dem., 43,355; Hallinan, Prog., 282; Hoopes, Soc., 185.

1956, Eisenhower, Rep., 110,390; Stevenson, Dem., 42,549; scattered, 39.

1960, Kennedy, Dem., 69,186; Nixon, Rep., 98,131.

1964, Johnson, Dem., 107,674; Goldwater, Rep., 54,868.

1968, Nixon, Rep., 85,142; Humphrey, Dem., 70,255; Wallace, 3d party, 5,104; Halstead, Soc. Worker, 295; Gregory, New Party, 579.

1972, Nixon, Rep., 117,149; McGovern, Dem., 68,174; Spock, Liberty Union, 1,010; Jenness, Soc. Workers, 296; scattered, 318.

1976, Carter, Dem., 77,798; Carter, Ind. Vermonter, 991; Ford, Rep., 100,387; McCarthy, Ind., 4,001; Camejo, Soc. Workers, 430; LaRouche, U.S. Labor, 196; scattered, 99.

1980, Reagan, Rep., 94,598; Carter, Dem., 81,891; Anderson, Ind., 31,760; Commoner, Citizens, 2,316; Clark, Libertarian, 1,900; McReynolds, Liberty Union, 136; Hall, Com. 118; DeBerry, Soc. Worker, 75; scattering, 413.

1984, Reagan, Rep., 135,865; Mondale, Dem., 95,730; Bergland, Libertarian, 1,002.

1988, Bush, Rep., 124,331; Dukakis, Dem., 115,775; Paul, Lib., 1,000; LaRouche, Ind., 275.

Virginia

	1988		1984	
County	Dukakis (D)	Bush (R)	Mondale (D)	Reagan (R)
Accomack......	4,443	6,926	4,355	8,047
Albemarle......	10,363	15,117	7,982	14,455
Alleghany......	2,316	2,555	1,932	3,067
Amelia........	1,359	2,187	1,432	2,336
Amherst.......	3,567	6,507	3,409	7,004
Appomattox.....	1,740	3,205	1,498	3,386
Arlington......	40,314	34,191	37,031	34,848
Augusta.......	4,170	13,251	3,899	15,308
Bath.........	881	1,273	727	1,434
Bedford.......	5,406	10,702	4,754	10,371
Bland........	937	1,556	867	1,812
Botetourt......	3,763	5,687	3,243	5,959
Brunswick.....	3,070	2,742	3,040	2,950
Buchanan.....	6,935	3,912	7,828	5,053
Buckingham....	1,941	2,481	1,879	2,627
Campbell......	4,574	12,713	4,380	13,388
Caroline......	3,186	3,065	3,111	2,949
Carroll	3,190	6,377	2,914	7,056
Charles City.....	1,839	826	1,776	776
Charlotte......	1,923	2,699	1,811	2,999
Chesterfield....	18,723	58,828	13,739	54,896
Clarke.......	1,478	2,502	1,215	2,529
Craig........	864	1,112	845	1,173
Culpeper......	2,555	5,896	2,255	5,596
Cumberland....	1,132	1,978	1,237	2,027
Dickenson.....	4,461	3,091	4,848	3,921
Dinwiddie.....	3,405	4,165	3,485	4,547
Essex........	1,294	2,038	1,300	2,120
Fairfax.......	125,711	200,631	107,295	183,181
Fauquier......	4,837	11,733	4,056	10,319
Floyd........	1,727	2,921	1,599	3,431
Fluvanna......	1,562	2,447	1,332	2,247
Franklin.......	5,734	7,391	4,903	7,684
Frederick......	3,707	9,921	2,671	9,542
Giles	3,042	3,490	3,047	4,340
Gloucester.....	3,372	7,646	2,830	7,109
Goochland.....	2,209	3,765	2,178	3,404
Grayson......	2,441	3,968	2,319	4,508
Greene.......	899	2,234	760	2,216
Greensville.....	2,083	1,610	2,352	2,304
Halifax.......	4,282	5,671	4,231	6,726
Hanover......	5,985	20,570	4,831	18,800
Henrico.......	26,980	✶ 62,284	21,336	63,864
Henry........	7,536	10,871	6,976	12,693
Highland......	456	807	398	997
Isle of Wight....	3,747	5,779	3,650	5,664
James City.....	4,642	8,945	3,486	7,104
King George....	1,519	2,587	1,450	2,356
King and Queen...	1,309	1,376	1,201	1,449
King William.....	1,561	2,735	1,448	2,803
Lancaster......	1,551	3,380	1,559	3,416
Lee..........	4,906	4,080	5,085	5,365
Loudoun......	10,101	20,448	8,227	17,765
Louisa........	2,789	3,831	2,703	3,789
Lunenburg......	1,870	2,530	1,754	2,713
Madison.......	1,427	2,501	1,302	2,723
Mathews.......	1,235	2,752	1,106	2,868
Mecklenburg....	3,275	5,887	3,438	6,777
Middlesex......	1,361	2,571	1,206	2,612
Montgomery.....	8,909	12,326	7,202	12,428
Nelson........	2,272	2,502	2,021	2,777
New Kent......	1,427	2,917	1,204	2,679
Northampton...	2,242	2,562	2,226	2,906
Northumberland...	1,506	2,984	1,407	3,166
Nottoway......	2,217	3,161	2,296	3,418
Orange........	2,592	4,319	2,285	4,483
Page.........	2,499	5,013	2,437	5,021
Patrick.......	2,093	3,990	1,908	4,703
Pittsylvania.....	6,612	12,229	7,791	15,743
Powhatan.....	1,467	4,040	1,381	3,921
Prince Edward....	2,434	3,147	2,589	3,454
Prince George....	2,469	4,982	2,136	4,999
Prince William...	19,198	39,654	15,631	34,992
Pulaski.......	4,686	6,844	4,364	8,242
Rappahannock...	1,003	1,657	999	1,696
Richmond	924	1,862	830	1,869
Roanoke......	12,938	22,011	10,569	23,348
Rockbridge.....	2,412	3,541	2,098	4,067
Rockingham.....	4,716	13,241	4,220	13,480
Russell........	6,222	4,374	6,760	5,738
Scott.........	3,616	4,986	3,904	5,804
Shenandoah.....	3,276	8,612	2,771	9,048
Smyth........	3,989	7,446	4,102	8,593
Southampton....	3,000	3,439	3,300	4,669
Spotsylvania.....	5,486	10,978	4,012	8,207
Stafford.......	5,380	12,234	4,429	10,283
Surry........	1,602	1,246	1,875	1,462
Sussex........	1,958	1,822	2,408	2,183
Tazewell......	8,098	7,165	8,014	9,645
Warren.......	2,769	4,700	2,551	5,016
Washington.....	5,819	10,722	5,573	12,132
Westmoreland....	2,311	2,974	2,363	3,219
Wise.........	7,017	6,189	7,303	7,909
Wythe........	3,201	5,827	2,996	6,773
York.........	4,639	11,103	4,063	10,214
City				
Alexandria......	24,358	20,913	23,552	21,166
Bedford.......	960	1,322	997	1,553
Bristol........	2,446	4,407	2,429	5,012
Buena Vista.....	828	1,121	724	1,335
Charlottesville....	7,671	5,817	7,317	6,947
Chesapeake.....	18,828	29,738	16,740	27,542
Clifton Forge.....	961	759	896	965
Colonial Heights...	1,581	6,001	1,218	6,387
Covington......	1,567	1,274	1,391	1,722
Danville.......	7,353	12,221	5,846	12,141
Emporia.......	977	1,289	807	1,252
Fairfax........	3,430	5,576	3,263	6,234
Falls Church.....	2,484	2,470	2,398	2,684
Franklin.......	1,630	1,557	1,537	1,561
Fredericksburg....	2,683	3,401	2,439	3,500
Galax........	907	1,278	814	1,548
Hampton......	19,106	24,034	18,180	25,537
Harrisonburg....	2,799	5,376	2,384	5,221
Hopewell......	2,566	4,672	2,564	5,661
Lexington......	997	994	946	1,197
Lynchburg.....	8,279	15,323	8,542	17,447
Manassas......	2,658	5,980	1,824	4,615
Manassas Park...	434	993	375	975
Martinsville.....	2,794	3,360	2,942	4,234
Newport News...	21,413	32,570	21,834	33,614
Norfolk.......	37,778	30,538	38,913	36,360
Norton	795	608	842	806
Petersburg.....	8,177	4,231	9,248	5,753
Poquoson.....	877	3,840	647	3,667
Portsmouth....	19,698	16,087	21,623	18,940
Radford.......	1,855	2,481	1,781	2,855
Richmond.....	42,155	31,586	49,408	38,754
Roanoke......	17,185	15,389	17,300	19,008
Salem........	3,760	5,694	3,347	6,419
South Boston....	936	1,694	974	1,899
Staunton......	2,457	5,775	2,012	6,137
Suffolk.......	8,080	9,742	8,842	10,128
Virginia Beach....	33,780	76,481	24,703	72,571
Waynesboro....	2,038	4,672	1,579	4,465
Williamsburg....	1,534	1,648	1,469	1,913
Winchester.....	2,300	4,497	2,064	5,055
Total........	859,799	1,309,162	796,250	1,337,078

Virginia Vote Since 1940

1940, Roosevelt, Dem., 235,961; Willkie, Rep., 109,363; Babson, Proh., 882; Thomas, Soc., 282; Browder, Com., 71; Aiken, Soc. Labor, 48.

1944, Roosevelt, Dem., 242,276; Dewey, Rep., 145,243; Watson, Proh., 459; Thomas, Soc., 417; Teichert, Soc. Labor, 90.

1948, Truman, Dem., 200,786; Dewey, Rep., 172,070; Thurmond, States' Rights, 43,393; Wallace, Prog., 2,047; Thomas, Soc., 726; Teichert, Soc. Labor, 234.

1952, Eisenhower, Rep., 349,037; Stevenson, Dem., 268,677; Hass, Soc. Labor, 1,160; Hoopes, Social Dem., 504; Hallinan, Prog., 311.

1956, Eisenhower, Rep., 386,459; Stevenson, Dem., 267,760; Andrews, States' Rights, 42,964; Hoopes, Soc. Dem., 444; Hass, Soc. Labor, 351.

1960, Kennedy, Dem., 362,327; Nixon, Rep., 404,521; Coiner, Conservative, 4,204; Hass, Soc. Labor, 397.

1964, Johnson, Dem., 558,038; Goldwater, Rep., 481,334; Hass, Soc. Labor, 2,895.

1968, Nixon, Rep., 590,319; Humphrey, Dem., 442,387; Wallace, 3d party, *320,272; Blomen, Soc. Labor, 4,671; Munn, Proh., 601; Gregory, Peace and Freedom, 1,680.

*10,561 votes for Wallace were omitted in the count.

1972, Nixon, Rep., 988,493; McGovern, Dem., 438,887; Schmitz, Amer., 19,721; Fisher, Soc. Labor, 9,918.

1976, Carter, Dem., 813,896; Ford, Rep., 836,554; Camejo, Soc. Workers, 17,802; Anderson, Amer., 16,686; LaRouche, U.S. Labor, 7,508; MacBride, Libertarian, 4,648.

1980, Reagan, Rep., 989,609; Carter, Dem., 752,174; Anderson, Ind., 95,418; Commoner, Citizens, 14,024; Clark, Libertarian, 12,821; DeBerry, Soc. Worker, 1,986.

1984, Reagan, Rep., 1,337,078; Mondale, Dem., 796,250.

1988, Bush, Rep., 1,309,162; Dukakis, Dem., 859,799; Fulani, Ind., 14,312; Paul, Lib., 8,336.

Washington

County	1988 Dukakis (D)	Bush (R)	1984 Mondale (D)	Reagan (R)
Adams	1,612	2,612	1,311	3,449
Asotin	3,422	2,874	3,042	3,876
Benton	14,817	28,688	13,784	32,307
Chelan	8,183	11,601	6,978	13,667
Clallam	11,123	11,200	9,701	13,605
Clark	40,021	37,285	35,248	40,681
Columbia	730	1,172	673	1,404
Cowlitz	16,090	12,009	15,361	14,858
Douglas	3,760	5,378	3,127	6,443
Ferry	972	972	935	1,232
Franklin	4,772	6,488	4,328	7,724
Garfield	593	714	493	913
Grant	7,564	10,859	6,298	12,888
Grays Harbor	14,097	8,860	14,050	11,286
Island	8,510	12,552	6,850	13,548
Jefferson	5,270	4,184	4,602	4,543
King	349,663	290,574	289,620	332,987
Kitsap	33,748	34,743	29,681	36,101
Kittitas	5,318	5,048	4,830	6,580
Klickitat	2,991	2,920	2,712	3,910
Lewis	8,629	14,184	7,634	15,846
Lincoln	1,884	2,689	1,671	3,474
Mason	7,826	7,426	7,007	8,410
Okanogan	5,630	5,856	5,330	7,476
Pacific	5,017	3,073	4,679	3,613
Pend Oreille	1,925	1,802	1,655	2,374
Pierce	96,688	94,167	79,498	112,877
San Juan	3,008	2,660	2,514	2,900
Skagit	15,159	16,550	13,947	18,840
Skamania	1,748	1,356	1,552	1,736
Snohomish	80,694	84,158	66,728	90,362
Spokane	68,520	68,787	59,620	88,043
Stevens	5,068	6,576	4,304	8,211
Thurston	33,860	31,980	26,840	34,442
Wahkiakum	961	629	930	776
Walla Walla	7,448	9,683	6,804	12,361
Whatcom	25,571	23,820	22,670	27,228
Whitman	7,403	7,680	6,621	10,021
Yakima	23,221	30,026	24,724	40,678
Totals	933,516	903,835	796,352	1,051,670

Washington Vote Since 1940

1940, Roosevelt, Dem., 462,145; Willkie, Rep., 322,123; Thomas, Soc., 4,586; Browder, Com., 2,626; Babson, Proh., 1,686; Aiken, Soc. Labor, 667.

1944, Roosevelt, Dem., 486,774; Dewey, Rep., 361,689; Thomas, Soc., 3,824; Watson, Proh., 2,396; Teichert, Soc. Labor, 1,645.

1948, Truman, Dem., 476,165; Dewey, Rep., 386,315; Wallace, Prog., 31,692; Watson, Proh., 6,117; Thomas, Soc., 3,534; Teichert, Soc. Labor, 1,133; Dobbs, Soc. Workers, 103.

1952, Eisenhower, Rep., 599,107; Stevenson, Dem., 492,845; MacArthur, Christian Nationalist, 7,290; Hallinan, Prog.,

2,460; Hass, Soc. Labor, 633; Hoopes, Soc., 254; Dobbs, Soc. Workers, 119.

1956, Eisenhower, Rep., 620,430; Stevenson, Dem., 523,002; Hass, Soc. Labor, 7,457.

1960, Kennedy, Dem., 599,298; Nixon, Rep., 629,273; Hass, Soc. Labor, 10,895; Curtis, Constitution, 1,401; Dobbs, Soc. Workers, 705.

1964, Johnson, Dem., 779,699; Goldwater, Rep., 470,366; Hass, Soc. Labor, 7,772; DeBerry, Freedom Soc., 537.

1968, Nixon, Rep., 588,510; Humphrey, Dem., 616,037; Wallace, 3d party, 96,990; Blomen, Soc. Labor, 488; Cleaver, Peace and Freedom, 1,609; Halstead, Soc. Worker, 270; Mitchell, Free Ballot, 377.

1972, Nixon, Rep., 837,135; McGovern, Dem., 568,334; Schmitz, Amer., 58,906; Spock, Ind., 2,644; Fisher, Soc. Labor, 1,102; Jenness, Soc. Worker, 623; Hall, Com., 566; Hospers, Libertarian, 1,537.

1976, Carter, Dem., 717,323; Ford, Rep., 777,732; McCarthy, Ind., 36,986; Maddox, Amer. Ind., 8,585; Anderson, Amer., 5,046; MacBride, Libertarian, 5,042; Wright, People's, 1,124; Camejo, Soc. Workers, 905; LaRouche, U.S. Labor, 903; Hall, Com., 817; Levin, Soc. Labor, 713; Zeidler, Soc., 358.

1980, Reagan, Rep., 865,244; Carter, Dem., 650,193; Anderson, Ind., 185,073; Clark, Libertarian, 29,213; Commoner, Citizens, 9,403; DeBerry, Soc. Worker, 1,137; McReynolds, Socialist, 956; Hall, Com., 834; Griswold, Workers World, 341.

1984, Reagan, Rep., 1,051,670; Mondale, Dem., 798,352; Bergland, Libertarian, 8,844.

1988, Bush, Rep., 903,835; Dukakis, Dem., 933,516; Paul, Lib., 17,240; LaRouche, Ind., 4,412.

West Virginia

County	1988 Dukakis (D)	Bush (R)	1984 Mondale (D)	Reagan (R)
Barbour	3,221	3,023	3,108	3,877
Berkeley	6,313	10,761	6,181	12,887
Boone	6,539	2,786	7,121	4,656
Braxton	3,377	2,024	3,350	2,902
Brooke	6,258	4,006	6,636	4,819
Cabell	15,368	17,197	15,513	21,815
Calhoun	1,644	1,395	1,473	1,765
Clay	2,263	1,536	2,117	1,667
Doddridge	955	1,880	836	2,343
Fayette	11,009	5,143	11,650	7,360
Gilmer	1,661	1,387	1,494	1,953
Grant	893	3,215	828	3,715
Greenbrier	6,091	5,395	5,599	7,337
Hampshire	2,085	3,253	2,102	4,065
Hancock	8,338	5,882	8,708	7,326
Hardy	1,689	2,581	1,641	2,938
Harrison	17,005	13,364	14,969	19,400
Jackson	4,573	5,696	4,147	7,117
Jefferson	4,334	5,349	4,216	5,884
Kanawha	41,144	38,140	37,832	51,499
Lewis	3,272	3,602	2,693	5,297
Lincoln	5,049	3,457	5,467	4,405
Logan	11,317	4,244	10,892	6,425
McDowell	7,204	2,463	8,546	4,284
Marion	14,441	9,229	13,833	13,106
Marshall	7,903	6,793	7,947	8,615
Mason	5,468	5,332	5,701	6,648
Mercer	10,152	10,221	9,164	13,910
Mineral	4,059	6,015	3,832	7,291
Mingo	7,429	2,896	8,434	4,275
Monongalia	14,178	12,091	13,236	14,972
Monroe	2,427	2,719	2,333	3,612
Morgan	1,545	3,002	1,457	3,469
Nicholas	5,173	3,731	4,588	4,656
Ohio	10,121	10,341	10,163	13,447
Pendleton	1,595	1,901	1,464	2,047
Pleasants	1,421	1,761	1,458	2,255
Pocahontas	1,958	1,876	1,903	2,479
Preston	4,357	5,804	4,054	6,955
Putnam	6,640	8,163	5,208	9,238
Raleigh	14,302	10,395	14,442	14,571
Randolph	5,233	4,746	4,839	6,100
Ritchie	1,446	2,874	1,231	3,355
Roane	2,447	2,861	2,468	3,751
Summers	3,072	2,231	2,670	2,975
Taylor	2,852	2,816	2,754	4,007
Tucker	1,869	1,699	1,766	2,240
Tyler	1,501	2,365	1,395	3,170
Upshur	3,065	4,813	2,468	5,951
Wayne	8,621	7,123	8,378	8,811
Webster	2,185	1,016	2,355	1,565
Wetzel	3,928	3,381	3,549	4,626
Wirt	929	1,125	868	1,450
Wood	12,959	19,450	11,357	24,821

Wyoming	6,138	3,516	5,691	5,379
Totals	**341,016**	**310,065**	**328,125**	**405,483**

West Virginia Vote Since 1940

1940, Roosevelt, Dem., 495,662; Willkie, Rep., 372,414.

1944, Roosevelt, Dem., 392,777; Dewey, Rep., 322,819.

1948, Truman, Dem., 429,188; Dewey, Rep., 316,251; Wallace, Prog., 3,311.

1952, Eisenhower, Rep., 419,970; Stevenson, Dem., 453,578.

1956, Eisenhower, Rep., 449,297; Stevenson, Dem., 381,534.

1960, Kennedy, Dem., 441,786; Nixon, Rep., 395,995.

1964, Johnson, Dem., 538,087; Goldwater, Rep., 253,953.

1968, Nixon, Rep., 307,555; Humphrey, Dem., 374,091; Wallace, 3d party, 72,560.

1972, Nixon, Rep., 484,964; McGovern, Dem., 277,435.

1976, Carter, Dem., 435,864; Ford, Rep., 314,726.

1980, Reagan, Rep., 334,206; Carter, Dem., 367,462; Anderson, Ind., 31,691; Clark, Libertarian, 4,356.

1984, Reagan, Rep., 405,483; Mondale, Dem., 328,125.

1988, Bush, Rep., 310,065; Dukakis, Dem., 341,016; Fulani, New Alliance, 2,230.

Wisconsin

	1988		1984	
County	Dukakis (D)	Bush (R)	Mondale (D)	Reagan (R)
Adams	3,598	3,258	2,713	3,644
Ashland	4,526	2,926	4,680	3,517
Barron	8,951	8,527	8,060	9,587
Bayfield	4,323	3,095	4,034	3,474
Brown	41,788	43,625	30,208	51,186
Buffalo	3,481	2,783	2,921	3,325
Burnet	3,537	2,884	3,328	3,528
Calumet	6,481	8,107	4,735	8,969
Chippewa	11,447	9,757	10,200	10,983
Clark	6,642	6,296	5,647	8,098
Columbia	9,132	10,475	8,124	11,658
Crawford	3,608	3,238	3,435	4,411
Dane	105,414	69,143	94,638	74,009
Dodge	12,663	17,003	11,052	20,455
Door	5,425	6,907	3,915	8,264
Douglas	13,907	6,440	14,290	7,066
Dunn	9,205	7,273	7,709	8,472
Eau Claire	21,150	17,664	19,344	20,394
Florence	1,018	1,106	870	1,227
Fond duLac	15,887	21,985	13,982	26,067
Forest	2,142	1,845	2,213	2,296
Grant	9,421	10,049	7,890	13,427
Green	5,153	6,636	4,367	7,826
Green Lake	3,033	5,205	2,441	6,198
Iowa	4,268	4,240	3,842	4,982
Iron	2,090	1,599	1,967	1,667
Jackson	3,924	3,555	3,427	4,383
Jefferson	11,816	14,309	10,788	17,779
Juneau	3,734	4,869	3,151	5,627
Kenosha	30,089	21,661	29,233	26,112
Kewaunee	4,786	4,330	3,444	5,705
La Crosse	22,204	21,548	17,787	25,717
La Fayette	3,521	3,665	2,959	4,582
Langlade	4,254	4,884	3,675	5,828
Lincoln	5,819	5,257	5,352	6,681
Manitowoc	19,680	16,020	17,249	19,635
Marathon	24,658	24,482	20,126	27,077
Marinette	8,030	9,637	6,798	11,439
Marquette	2,463	3,059	2,031	3,404
Menominee	1,028	381	832	392
Milwaukee	268,287	168,363	259,134	196,259
Monroe	6,437	7,073	5,564	8,225
Oconto	6,549	7,084	5,288	8,713
Oneida	7,414	8,130	6,416	9,782
Outagamie	27,771	33,113	19,789	36,765
Ozaukee	12,661	22,899	10,763	23,896
Pepin	1,906	1,311	1,629	1,555
Pierce	8,659	6,045	7,285	7,611
Polk	8,981	6,866	8,033	8,101
Portage	16,317	12,057	14,399	13,603
Price	3,987	3,450	3,479	4,286
Racine	39,631	36,342	36,953	42,085
Richland	3,643	4,026	2,844	4,857
Rock	29,576	28,178	26,430	32,483
Rusk	3,888	3,063	3,843	4,061
St. Croix	11,392	9,960	10,126	11,365
Sauk	8,324	10,225	7,157	11,067
Sawyer	3,231	3,260	2,981	3,911
Shawano	6,587	8,362	5,469	10,635
Sheboygan	23,429	23,471	21,111	26,343
Taylor	3,785	4,254	3,271	4,918
Trempealeau	6,212	4,902	5,405	6,007
Vernon	5,754	5,226	5,051	6,468
Vilas	3,781	5,842	2,940	5,963
Walworth	12,203	18,259	9,876	20,590
Washburn	3,393	3,074	3,188	3,847
Washington	15,907	24,328	12,966	25,278
Waukesha	57,598	90,467	47,308	92,415
Waupaca	7,078	11,559	5,894	13,097
Waushara	3,535	4,953	2,782	5,768
Winnebago	28,508	35,085	22,791	39,014
Wood	16,074	16,549	12,118	20,525
Totals	**1,126,794**	**1,047,499**	**995,740**	**1,198,584**

Wisconsin Vote Since 1940

1940, Roosevelt, Dem., 704,821; Willkie, Rep., 679,260; Thomas, Soc., 15,071; Browder, Com., 2,394; Babson, Proh., 2,148; Aiken, Soc. Labor, 1,882.

1944, Roosevelt, Dem., 650,413; Dewey, Rep., 674,532; Thomas, Soc., 13,205; Teichert, Soc. Labor, 1,002.

1948, Truman, Dem., 647,310; Dewey, Rep., 590,959; Wallace, Prog., 25,282; Thomas, Soc., 12,547; Teichert, Soc. Labor, 399; Dobbs, Soc. Workers, 303.

1952, Eisenhower, Rep., 979,744; Stevenson, Dem., 622,175; Hallinan, Ind., 2,174; Dobbs, Ind., 1,350; Hoopes, Ind., 1,157; Hass, Ind., 770.

1956, Eisenhower, Rep., 954,844; Stevenson, Dem., 586,768; Andrews, Ind., 6,918; Hoopes, Soc., 754; Hass, Soc. Labor, 710; Dobbs, Soc. Workers, 564.

1960, Kennedy, Dem., 830,805; Nixon, Rep., 895,175; Dobbs, Soc. Workers, 1,792; Hass, Soc. Labor, 1,310.

1964, Johnson, Dem., 1,050,424; Goldwater, Rep., 638,495; DeBerry, Soc. Worker, 1,692; Hass, Soc. Labor, 1,204.

1968, Nixon, Rep., 809,997; Humphrey, Dem., 748,804; Wallace, 3d party, 127,835; Blomen, Soc. Labor, 1,338; Halstead, Soc. Worker, 1,222; scattered, 2,342.

1972 Nixon, Rep., 989,430; McGovern, Dem., 810,174; Schmitz, Amer., 47,525; Spock, Ind., 2,701; Fisher, Soc. Labor, 998; Hall, Com., 663; Reed, Ind., 506; scattered, 893.

1976, Carter, Dem., 1,040,232; Ford, Rep., 1,004,987; McCarthy, Ind., 34,943; Maddox, Amer. Ind., 8,552; Zeidler, Soc., 4,298; MacBride, Libertarian, 3,814; Camejo, Soc. Workers, 1,691; Wright, People's, 943; Hall, Com., 749; LaRouche, U.S. Lab., 738; Levin, Soc. Labor, 389; scattered, 2,839.

1980, Reagan, Rep., 1,088,845; Carter, Dem., 981,584; Anderson, Ind., 160,657; Clark, Libertarian, 29,135; Commoner, Citizens, 7,767; Rarick, Constitution, 1,519; McReynolds, Socialist, 808; Hall, Com., 772; Griswold, Workers World, 414; DeBerry, Soc. Workers, 383; scattering, 1,337.

1984, Reagan, Rep., 1,198,584; Mondale, Dem., 995,740; Bergland, Libertarian, 4,883.

1988, Bush, Rep., 1,047,499; Dukakis, Dem., 1,126,794; Paul, Lib., 5,157; Duke, Pop., 3,056.

Wyoming

	1988		1984	
County	Dukakis (D)	Bush (R)	Mondale (D)	Reagan (R)
Albany	5,486	5,653	4,708	7,452
Big Horn	1,469	3,258	1,175	4,019
Campbell	2,288	6,702	1,525	8,387
Carbon	2,555	3,336	2,295	4,557
Converse	1,301	2,885	929	3,542
Crook	553	1,939	450	2,286
Fremont	5,020	7,681	3,969	9,885
Goshen	1,875	3,075	1,364	3,776
Hot Springs	800	1,490	672	1,943
Johnson	707	2,081	558	2,634
Laramie	11,851	15,561	10,110	19,348
Lincoln	1,592	3,237	1,021	3,854
Natrona	9,148	14,005	7,598	18,488
Niobrara	354	825	239	1,098
Park	2,646	6,884	1,965	7,994
Platte	1,482	2,253	1,232	2,813
Sheridan	4,655	5,980	3,648	7,460
Sublette	576	1,636	389	1,976
Sweetwater	6,720	6,780	5,230	8,308
Teton	2,217	3,616	1,565	3,487
Uinta	1,922	3,464	1,276	4,075
Washakie	1,197	2,538	970	3,245
Weston	699	1,988	482	2,614
Totals	**67,113**	**106,867**	**53,370**	**133,241**

Wyoming Vote Since 1940

1940, Roosevelt, Dem., 59,287; Willkie, Rep., 52,633; Babson, Proh., 172; Thomas, Soc., 148.

1944, Roosevelt, Dem., 49,419; Dewey, Rep., 51,921.

1948, Truman, Dem., 52,354; Dewey, Rep., 47,947; Wallace, Prog., 931; Thomas, Soc., 137; Teichert, Soc. Labor, 56.

1952, Eisenhower, Rep., 81,047; Stevenson, Dem., 47,934; Hamblen, Proh., 194; Hoopes, Soc., 40; Haas, Soc. Labor, 36.

1956, Eisenhower, Rep., 74,573; Stevenson, Dem., 49,554.

1960, Kennedy, Dem., 63,331; Nixon, Rep., 77,451.

1964, Johnson, Dem., 80,718; Goldwater, Rep., 61,998.

1968, Nixon, Rep., 70,927; Humphrey, Dem., 45,173; Wallace, 3d party, 11,105.

1972, Nixon, Rep., 100,464; McGovern, Dem., 44,358; Schmitz, Amer., 748.

1976, Carter, Dem., 62,239; Ford, Rep., 92,717; McCarthy, Ind., 624; Reagan, Ind., 307; Anderson, Amer., 290; MacBride, Libertarian, 89; Brown, Ind., 47; Maddox, Amer. Ind., 30.

1980, Reagan, Rep., 110,700; Carter, Dem., 49,427; Anderson, Ind., 12,072; Clark, Libertarian, 4,514.

1984, Reagan, Rep., 133,241; Mondale, Dem., 53,370; Bergland, Libertarian, 2,357.

1988, Bush, Rep., 106,867; Dukakis, Dem., 67,113; Paul, Lib., 2,026; Fulani, New Alliance, 545.

Official 1988 Presidential General Election Results

Source: Federal Election Commission

Candidate	Party[1]	Official Popular Vote Total	Percent of Total Vote
George Bush	Republican	48,886,097	53.37
Michael S. Dukakis	Democratic	41,809,074	45.65
Delmar Dennis	American	3,475	0.00
Earl Dodge	Prohibition	8,002	0.01
David Duke	Populist	47,047	0.05
Lenora B. Fulani	New Alliance	217,219	0.24
James C. Griffin	American Independent	27,818	0.03
Jack Herer	GrassRoots	1,949	0.00
Larry Holmes	Workers World	7,846	0.01
Willa Kenoyer	Socialist	3,882	0.00
Lyndon H. LaRouche	National Economic	25,542	0.03
Herbert Lewin	Peace & Freedom	10,370	0.01
William A. Marra	Right to Life	20,504	0.02
John G. Martin	Third World Assembly	236	0.00
Eugene J. McCarthy	Consumer	30,905	0.03
Ronald E. Paul	Libertarian	432,116	0.47
James Mac Warren	Socialist Workers	15,604	0.02
Edward Winn	Workers League	18,662	0.02
Louie G. Youngkeit	Independent	372	0.00
Write-In		21,039	0.02
None of Above	(Nevada Option)	6,934	0.01
Total Votes		**91,594,693**	

Voting Age Population: 182,628,000
(Census Bureau Estimate)

[1] Party designations may vary from one state to another.

Presidential Primaries—Votes Cast and Percent of Voting-Age Population Casting Votes, by Party: 1988

Source: Committee for the Study of the American Electorate

State	Voting age population (VAP) (1,000)	Votes cast in Democratic Primary Total (1,000)	Percent of VAP	Votes cast in Republican Primary Total (1,000)	Percent of VAP	State	Voting age population (VAP) (1,000)	Votes cast in Democratic Primary Total (1,000)	Percent of VAP	Votes cast in Republican Primary Total (1,000)	Percent of VAP
Ala.	3,010	406	13.5	214	7.1	Nebr.	1,167	164	14.1	203	17.4
Ariz.	1,761	498	28.3	68	3.9	NH.	823	124	15.0	158	19.2
Cal.	20,875	3,139	15.0	2,243	10.8	NJ.	5,943	671	11.3	282	4.8
Conn.	2,492	241	9.7	104	4.2	N Mex.	1,101	189	17.1	89	8.1
DC.	489	86	17.7	7	1.5	NY.	13,480	1,575	11.7	–	–
Fla.	9,614	1,273	13.2	901	9.4	NC.	4,913	680	13.8	274	5.6
Ga.	4,665	623	13.4	401	8.6	Ohio.	7,970	1,376	17.3	787	9.9
Idaho.	701	51	7.3	68	9.7	Okla.	2,404	393	16.3	209	8.7
Ill.	8,550	1,496	17.5	858	10.0	Oreg.	2,051	401	19.6	274	13.4
Ind.	4,068	646	15.9	438	10.8	Pa.	9,060	1,508	16.6	871	9.6
Ky.	2,746	319	11.6	121	4.4	RI.	764	49	6.4	16	2.1
La.	3,175	624	19.7	145	4.6	S Dak.	509	72	14.1	93	18.4
Md.	3,491	531	15.2	201	5.8	Tenn.	3,661	576	15.7	254	6.9
Mass.	4,535	714	15.7	241	5.3	Tex.	12,270	1,767	14.4	1,015	8.3
Miss.	1,867	359	19.3	159	8.5	Va.	4,544	365	8.0	234	5.2
Mo.	3,821	528	13.8	400	10.5	W Va.	1,398	340	24.3	143	10.2
Mont.	586	122	20.8	86	14.7	Wis.	3,536	1,015	28.7	359	10.2

(–) Represents zero.
Presidential primaries were not held in Ark, Ariz, Col, Del, Ha, Iowa, Kans, Maine, Mich, Minn, Nev, N Dak, SC, Utah, Vt, Wash, and Wyo.

Major Parties' Popular and Electoral Vote for President

(F) Federalist; (D) Democrat; (R) Republican; (DR) Democrat Republican; (NR) National Republican;
(W) Whig; (P) People's; (PR) Progressive; (SR) States' Rights; (LR) Liberal Republican; Asterisk (*)—See notes.

Year	President elected	Popular	Elec.	Losing candidate	Popular	Elec.
1789	George Washington (F)	Unknown	69	No opposition	—	—
1792	George Washington (F)	Unknown	132	No opposition	—	—
1796	John Adams (F)	Unknown	71	Thomas Jefferson (DR)	Unknown	68
1800*	Thomas Jefferson (DR)	Unknown	73	Aaron Burr (DR)	Unknown	73
1804	Thomas Jefferson (DR)	Unknown	162	Charles Pinckney (F)	Unknown	14
1808	James Madison (DR)	Unknown	122	Charles Pinckney (F)	Unknown	47
1812	James Madison (DR)	Unknown	128	DeWitt Clinton (F)	Unknown	89
1816	James Monroe (DR)	Unknown	183	Rufus King (F)	Unknown	34
1820	James Monroe (DR)	Unknown	231	John Quincy Adams (DR)	Unknown	1
1824*	John Quincy Adams (DR)	105,321	84	Andrew Jackson (DR)	155,872	99
				Henry Clay (DR)	46,587	37
				William H. Crawford (DR)	44,282	41
1828	Andrew Jackson (D)	647,231	178	John Quincy Adams (NR)	509,097	83
1832	Andrew Jackson (D)	687,502	219	Henry Clay (NR)	530,189	49
1836	Martin Van Buren (D)	762,678	170	William H. Harrison (W)	548,007	73
1840	William H. Harrison (W)	1,275,017	234	Martin Van Buren (D)	1,128,702	60
1844	James K. Polk (D)	1,337,243	170	Henry Clay (W)	1,299,068	105
1848	Zachary Taylor (W)	1,360,101	163	Lewis Cass (D)	1,220,544	127
1852	Franklin Pierce (D)	1,601,474	254	Winfield Scott (W)	1,386,578	42
1856	James C. Buchanan (D)	1,927,995	174	John C. Fremont (R)	1,391,555	114
1860	Abraham Lincoln (R)	1,866,352	180	Stephen A. Douglas (D)	1,375,157	12
				John C. Breckinridge (D)	845,763	72
				John Bell (Const. Union)	589,581	39
1864	Abraham Lincoln (R)	2,216,067	212	George McClellan (D)	1,808,725	21
1868	Ulysses S. Grant (R)	3,015,071	214	Horatio Seymour (D)	2,709,615	80
1872*	Ulysses S. Grant (R)	3,597,070	286	Horace Greeley (D-LR)	2,834,079	—
1876*	Rutherford B. Hayes (R)	4,033,950	185	Samuel J. Tilden (D)	4,284,757	184
1880	James A. Garfield (R)	4,449,053	214	Winfield S. Hancock (D)	4,442,030	155
1884	Grover Cleveland (D)	4,911,017	219	James G. Blaine (R)	4,848,334	182
1888*	Benjamin Harrison (R)	5,444,337	233	Grover Cleveland (D)	5,540,050	168
1892	Grover Cleveland (D)	5,554,414	277	Benjamin Harrison (R)	5,190,802	145
				James Weaver (P)	1,027,329	22
1896	William McKinley (R)	7,035,638	271	William J. Bryan (D-P)	6,467,946	176
1900	William McKinley (R)	7,219,530	292	William J. Bryan (D)	6,358,071	155
1904	Theodore Roosevelt (R)	7,628,834	336	Alton B. Parker (D)	5,084,491	140
1908	William H. Taft (R)	7,679,006	321	William J. Bryan (D)	6,409,106	162
1912	Woodrow Wilson (D)	6,286,214	435	Theodore Roosevelt (PR)	4,216,020	88
				William H. Taft (R)	3,483,922	8
1916	Woodrow Wilson (D)	9,129,606	277	Charles E. Hughes (R)	8,538,221	254
1920	Warren G. Harding (R)	16,152,200	404	James M. Cox (D)	9,147,353	127
1924	Calvin Coolidge (R)	15,725,016	382	John W. Davis (D)	8,385,586	136
				Robert M. LaFollette (PR)	4,822,856	13
1928	Herbert Hoover (R)	21,392,190	444	Alfred E. Smith (D)	15,016,443	87
1932	Franklin D. Roosevelt (D)	22,821,857	472	Herbert Hoover (R)	15,761,841	59
				Norman Thomas (Socialist)	884,781	—
1936	Franklin D. Roosevelt (D)	27,751,597	523	Alfred Landon (R)	16,679,583	8
1940	Franklin D. Roosevelt (D)	27,243,466	449	Wendell Willkie (R)	22,304,755	82
1944	Franklin D. Roosevelt (D)	25,602,505	432	Thomas E. Dewey (R)	22,006,278	99
1948	Harry S Truman (D)	24,105,812	303	Thomas E. Dewey (R)	21,970,065	189
				J. Strom Thurmond (SR)	1,169,021	39
				Henry A. Wallace (PR)	1,157,172	—
1952	Dwight D. Eisenhower (R)	33,936,252	442	Adlai E. Stevenson (D)	27,314,992	89
1956*	Dwight D. Eisenhower (R)	35,585,316	457	Adlai E. Stevenson (D)	26,031,322	73
1960*	John F. Kennedy (D)	34,227,096	303	Richard M. Nixon (R)	34,108,546	219
1964	Lyndon B. Johnson (D)	43,126,506	486	Barry M. Goldwater (R)	27,176,799	52
1968	Richard M. Nixon (R)	31,785,480	301	Hubert H. Humphrey (D)	31,275,166	191
				George C. Wallace (3d party)	9,906,473	46
1972*	Richard M. Nixon (R)	47,165,234	520	George S. McGovern (D)	29,170,774	17
1976*	Jimmy Carter (D)	40,828,929	297	Gerald R. Ford (R)	39,148,940	240
1980	Ronald Reagan (R)	43,899,248	489	Jimmy Carter (D)	35,481,435	49
				John B. Anderson (independent)	5,719,437	—
1984	Ronald Reagan (R)	54,281,858	525	Walter F. Mondale (D)	37,457,215	13
1988*	George Bush (R)	48,881,221	426	Michael S. Dukakis (D)	41,805,422	111

1800—Elected by House of Representatives because of tied electoral vote. **1824**—Elected by House of Representatives. No candidate polled a majority. In 1824, the Democrat Republicans had become a loose coalition of competing political groups. By 1828, the supporters of Jackson were known as Democrats, and the J.Q. Adams and Henry Clay supporters as National Republicans. **1872**—Greeley died Nov. 29, 1872. His electoral votes were split among 4 individuals. **1876**—Fla., La., Ore., and S. C. election returns were disputed. Congress in joint session (Mar. 2, 1877) declared Hayes and Wheeler elected President and Vice-President. **1888**—Cleveland had more votes than Harrison but the 233 electoral votes cast for Harrison against the 168 for Cleveland elected Harrison president. **1956**—Democrats elected 74 electors but one from Alabama refused to vote for Stevenson. **1960**—Sen. Harry F. Byrd (D-Va.) received 15 electoral votes. **1972**—John Hospers of Cal. and Theodora Nathan of Ore. received one vote from an elector of Virginia. **1976**—Ronald Reagan of Cal. received one vote from an elector of Washington. **1988**—Sen. Lloyd Bentsen (D.-Tex.) received 1 electoral vote.

The Electoral College

The president and the vice president of the United States are the only elective federal officials not elected by direct vote of the people. They are elected by the members of the Electoral College, an institution that has survived since the founding of the nation despite repeated attempts in Congress to alter or abolish it. In the elections of 1824, 1876 and 1888 the presidential candidate receiving the largest popular vote failed to win a majority of the electoral votes.

On presidential election day, the first Tuesday after the first Monday in November of every 4th year, each state chooses as many electors as it has senators and representatives in Congress. In 1964, for the first time, as provided by the 23d Amendment to the Constitution, the District of Columbia voted for 3 electors. Thus, with 100 senators and 435 representatives, there are 538 members of the Electoral College, with a majority of 270 electoral votes needed to elect the president and vice president.

Political parties customarily nominate their lists of electors at their respective state conventions. An elector cannot be a member of Congress or any person holding federal office.

Some states print the names of the candidates for president and vice president at the top of the November ballot while others list only the names of the electors. In either case, the electors of the party receiving the highest vote are elected. The electors meet on the first Monday after the 2d Wednesday in December in their respective state capitals or in some other place prescribed by state legislatures. By long-established custom they vote for their party nominees, although the Constitution does not require them to do so. All of the state's electoral votes are then awarded to the winners. The only Constitutional requirement is that at least one of the persons each elector votes for shall not be an inhabitant of that elector's home state.

Certified and sealed lists of the votes of the electors in each state are mailed to the president of the U.S. Senate. He opens them in the presence of the members of the Senate and House of Representatives in a joint session held on Jan. 6 (the next day if that falls on a Sunday), and the electoral votes of all the states are then counted. If no candidate for president has a majority, the House of Representatives chooses a president from among the 3 highest candidates, with all representatives from each state combining to cast one vote for that state. If no candidate for vice president has a majority, the Senate chooses from the top 2, with the senators voting as individuals.

Voting for President

Source: Federal Election Commission; Commission for Study of American Electorate

Candidates		Voter Participation (% of voting-age population)	Candidates		Voter Participation (% of voting-age population)
1932	Roosevelt-Hoover	52.4	1964	Johnson-Goldwater	61.9
1936	Roosevelt-Landon	56.0	1968	Humphrey-Nixon	60.9
1940	Roosevelt-Wilkie	58.9	1972	McGovern-Nixon	55.2(a)
1944	Roosevelt-Dewey	56.0	1976	Carter-Ford	53.5
1948	Truman-Dewey	51.1	1980	Carter-Reagan	54.0
1952	Stevenson-Eisenhower	61.6	1984	Mondale-Reagan	53.1
1956	Stevenson-Eisenhower	59.3	1988	Dukakis-Bush	50.1
1960	Kennedy-Nixon	62.8			

(a) The sharp drop in 1972 reflects the expansion of eligibility with the enfranchisement of 18 to 21 year olds.

In 1988, there were 91,594,693 votes cast for the Presidential candidates, 1 million less than the total in the 1984 election.

There were 2.9% fewer voting-age population voters in the 1988 Presidential election, according to a state-by-state tabulation of votes compiled by the Federal Election Commission.

The report, which is based on official counts provided to the FEC by voting authorities of each of the 50 states and the District of Columbia, shows 91,609,655 votes were cast for the President out of the 1988 estimated voting age population of 182,628,000.

In 1984, there were 92,652,842 votes cast for the Presiden-

tial candidates appearing on various state ballots, plus write-ins.

Because of the variety of state laws governing registration, there is no official record of total registered voters in the United States. Estimated voting age population figures, upon which the FEC bases its statistics, are provided each year by the Bureau of the Census.

Also, because the FEC figures are obtained from official state election sources, the counts are based on individual state definitions of a valid vote cast and counted for a candidate.

Characteristics of the Voting-Age Population: November 1984 and 1988

Source: U.S. Bureau of the Census

Characteristic		1984 Number of persons (thousands)	1984 Percent registered	1984 Percent voted	1988 Number of persons (thousands)	1988 Percent registered	1988 Percent voted
Total, 18 years and over		169,963	68.3	59.9	178,098	66.6	57.4
White		146,761	69.6	61.4	152,848	67.9	59.1
Black		18,432	66.3	55.8	19,692	64.5	51.5
Hispanic[1]		9,471	40.1	32.6	12,893	35.5	28.8
Male		80,327	67.3	59.0	84,531	65.2	56.4
Female		89,636	69.3	60.8	93,568	67.8	58.3
18 to 24 years		27,976	51.3	40.8	25,569	48.2	36.1
25 to 44 years		71,023	66.6	58.4	77,863	63.0	53.9
45 to 64 years		44,307	76.6	69.8	45,862	75.5	67.8
65 years and over		26,658	76.9	67.7	28,804	78.4	68.8
Northeast		36,868	66.6	59.7	37,874	64.8	57.4
Midwest		42,136	74.6	65.7	43,309	72.5	62.9
South		57,587	66.9	56.8	60,725	65.6	54.5
West		33,372	64.7	58.5	36,190	63.0	55.6
Years of school completed:							
Elementary: 0 to 8 years		20,580	53.4	42.9	19,145	47.5	36.7
High school: 1 to 3 years		22,068	54.9	44.4	21,052	52.8	41.3
4 years		67,807	67.3	58.7	70,003	64.6	54.7
College: 1 to 3 years		30,915	75.7	67.5	34,264	73.5	64.5
4 years or more		28,593	83.8	79.1	33,604	83.1	77.6

(1) Hispanics may be of any race.

Electoral Votes for President

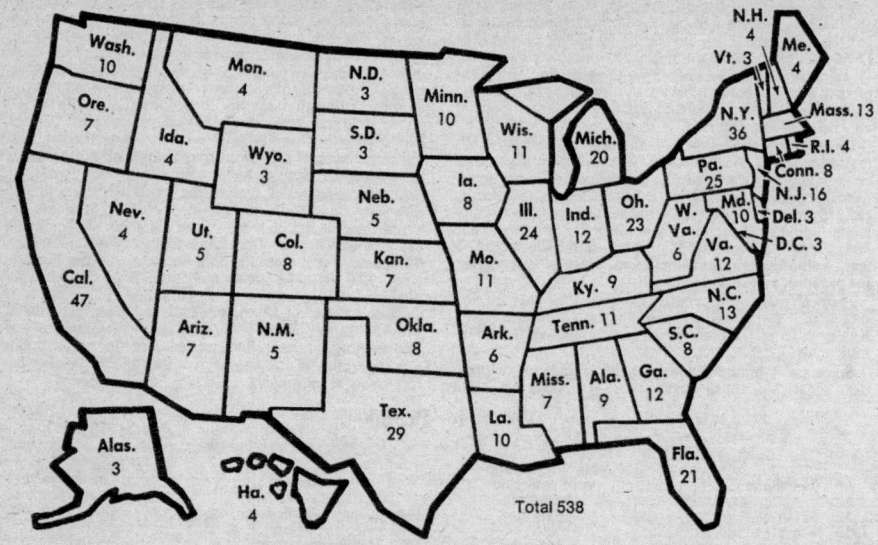

Total 538

Voting Age Population Turnout in Presidential Elections
Source: Committee for the Study of the American Electorate

	1988 % VAP Voted	1984 % VAP Voted	+/− 88-84		1988 % VAP Voted	1984 % VAP Voted	+/− 88-84		1988 % VAP Voted	1984 % VAP Voted	+/− 88-84
Ala.	45.80	49.85	−4.06	Ky.	48.16	50.77	−2.61	N.D.	61.54	62.67	−1.13
Alas.	51.98	59.15	−7.17	La.	51.28	54.55	−3.27	Oh.	55.13	58.20	−3.07
Ariz.	44.99	45.23	−.25	Me.	62.15	64.77	−2.62	Okla.	48.17	52.15	−3.43
Ark.	47.00	51.84	−4.84	Md.	49.11	51.41	−2.30	Ore.	58.59	61.82	−3.23
Cal.	47.36	49.56	−2.19	Mass.	58.06	57.60	.45	Pa.	50.07	53.98	−3.91
Col.	55.14	55.05	.09	Mich.	54.03	57.90	−3.87	R.I.	52.95	55.85	−2.89
Conn.	57.92	61.10	−3.17	Minn.	66.33	68.16	−1.83	S.C.	38.91	40.66	−1.75
Del.	51.00	55.46	−4.46	Miss.	51.02	52.23	−1.21	S.D.	61.49	62.57	−1.08
D.C.	39.44	43.21	−3.77	Mo.	54.80	57.25	−2.45	Tenn.	44.69	49.05	−4.36
Fla.	44.75	48.24	−3.49	Mon.	62.41	65.04	−2.63	Tex.	44.23	47.20	−2.96
Ga.	38.79	41.98	−3.19	Neb.	56.68	55.64	1.04	Ut.	60.02	61.55	−1.53
Ha.	43.02	44.31	−1.29	Nev.	44.88	41.49	3.39	Vt.	59.06	59.84	−.78
Ida.	58.34	59.93	−1.59	N.H.	54.74	52.98	1.76	Va.	48.23	50.69	−2.46
Ill.	53.32	57.11	−3.79	N.J.	52.06	56.68	−4.52	Wash.	54.59	58.09	−3.51
Ind.	53.31	55.92	−2.62	N.M.	47.35	51.33	−3.99	W.Va.	46.73	51.74	−5.01
Ia.	59.72	62.25	−2.99	N.Y.	48.11	51.18	−3.06	Wis.	61.98	63.46	−1.48
Kan.	54.29	56.84	−2.55	N.C.	43.44	47.36	−3.92	Wy.	50.30	53.38	−3.08

Party Nominees for President and Vice President
Asterisk (*) denotes winning ticket

	Democratic		Republican	
Year	President	Vice President	President	Vice President
1920	James M. Cox	Franklin D. Roosevelt	Warren G. Harding	Calvin Coolidge
1920	James M. Cox	Franklin D. Roosevelt	Warren G. Harding*	Calvin Coolidge
1924	John W. Davis	Charles W. Bryan	Calvin Coolidge*	Charles G. Dawes
1928	Alfred E. Smith	Joseph T. Robinson	Herbert Hoover*	Charles Curtis
1932	Franklin D. Roosevelt*	John N. Garner	Herbert Hoover	Charles Curtis
1936	Franklin D. Roosevelt*	John N. Garner	Alfred M. Landon	Frank Knox
1940	Franklin D. Roosevelt*	Henry A. Wallace	Wendell L. Willkie	Charles McNary
1944	Franklin D. Roosevelt*	Harry S. Truman	Thomas E. Dewey	John W. Bricker
1948	Harry S. Truman*	Alben W. Barkley	Thomas E. Dewey	Earl Warren
1952	Adlai E. Stevenson	John J. Sparkman	Dwight D. Eisenhower*	Richard M. Nixon
1956	Adlai E. Stevenson	Estes Kefauver	Dwight D. Eisenhower*	Richard M. Nixon
1960	John F. Kennedy*	Lyndon B. Johnson	Richard M. Nixon	Henry Cabot Lodge
1964	Lyndon B. Johnson*	Hubert H. Humphrey	Barry M. Goldwater	William E. Miller
1968	Hubert H. Humphrey	Edmund S. Muskie	Richard M. Nixon*	Spiro T. Agnew
1972	George S. McGovern	R. Sargent Shriver Jr.	Richard M. Nixon*	Spiro T. Agnew
1976	Jimmy Carter*	Walter F. Mondale	Gerald R. Ford	Robert J. Dole
1980	Jimmy Carter	Walter F. Mondale	Ronald Reagan*	George Bush
1984	Walter F. Mondale	Geraldine Ferraro	Ronald Reagan*	George Bush
1988	Michael S. Dukakis	Lloyd Bentsen	George Bush*	J. Danforth "Dan" Quayle

Presidents of the U.S.

No.	Name	Politics	Born	in	Inaug.	at age	Died	at age
1	George Washington	Fed.	1732, Feb. 22	Va.	1789	57	1799, Dec. 14	67
2	John Adams	Fed.	1735, Oct. 30	Mass.	1797	61	1826, July 4	90
3	Thomas Jefferson	Dem.-Rep.	1743, Apr. 13	Va.	1801	57	1826, July 4	83
4	James Madison	Dem.-Rep.	1751, Mar. 16	Va.	1809	57	1836, June 28	85
5	James Monroe	Dem.-Rep.	1758, Apr. 28	Va.	1817	58	1831, July 4	73
6	John Quincy Adams	Dem.-Rep.	1767, July 11	Mass.	1825	57	1848, Feb. 23	80
7	Andrew Jackson	Dem.	1767, Mar. 15	S.C.	1829	61	1845, June 8	78
8	Martin Van Buren	Dem.	1782, Dec. 5	N.Y.	1837	54	1862, July 24	79
9	William Henry Harrison	Whig	1773, Feb. 9	Va.	1841	68	1841, Apr. 4	68
10	John Tyler	Whig	1790, Mar. 29	Va.	1841	51	1862, Jan. 18	71
11	James Knox Polk	Dem.	1795, Nov. 2	N.C.	1845	49	1849, June 15	53
12	Zachary Taylor	Whig	1784, Nov. 24	Va.	1849	64	1850, July 9	65
13	Millard Fillmore	Whig	1800, Jan. 7	N.Y.	1850	50	1874, Mar. 8	74
14	Franklin Pierce	Dem.	1804, Nov. 23	N.H.	1853	48	1869, Oct. 8	64
15	James Buchanan	Dem.	1791, Apr. 23	Pa.	1857	65	1868, June 1	77
16	Abraham Lincoln	Rep.	1809, Feb. 12	Ky.	1861	52	1865, Apr. 15	56
17	Andrew Johnson	(1)	1808, Dec. 29	N.C.	1865	56	1875, July 31	66
18	Ulysses Simpson Grant	Rep.	1822, Apr. 27	Oh.	1869	46	1885, July 23	63
19	Rutherford Birchard Hayes	Rep.	1822, Oct. 4	Oh.	1877	54	1893, Jan. 17	70
20	James Abram Garfield	Rep.	1831, Nov. 19	Oh.	1881	49	1881, Sept. 19	49
21	Chester Alan Arthur	Rep.	1829, Oct. 5	Vt.	1881	51	1886, Nov. 18	57
22	Grover Cleveland	Dem.	1837, Mar. 18	N.J.	1885	47	1908, June 24	71
23	Benjamin Harrison	Rep.	1833, Aug. 20	Oh.	1889	55	1901, Mar. 13	67
24	Grover Cleveland	Dem.	1837, Mar. 18	N.J.	1893	55	1908, June 24	71
25	William McKinley	Rep.	1843, Jan. 29	Oh.	1897	54	1901, Sept. 14	58
26	Theodore Roosevelt	Rep.	1858, Oct. 27	N.Y.	1901	42	1919, Jan. 6	60
27	William Howard Taft	Rep.	1857, Sept. 15	Oh.	1909	51	1930, Mar. 8	72
28	Woodrow Wilson	Dem.	1856, Dec. 28	Va.	1913	56	1924, Feb. 3	67
29	Warren Gamaliel Harding	Rep.	1865, Nov. 2	Oh.	1921	55	1923, Aug. 2	57
30	Calvin Coolidge	Rep.	1872, July 4	Vt.	1923	51	1933, Jan. 5	60
31	Herbert Clark Hoover	Rep.	1874, Aug. 10	Ia.	1929	54	1964, Oct. 20	90
32	Franklin Delano Roosevelt	Dem.	1882, Jan. 30	N.Y.	1933	51	1945, Apr. 12	63
33	Harry S. Truman	Dem.	1884, May 8	Mo.	1945	60	1972, Dec. 26	88
34	Dwight David Eisenhower	Rep.	1890, Oct. 14	Tex.	1953	62	1969, Mar. 28	78
35	John Fitzgerald Kennedy	Dem.	1917, May 29	Mass.	1961	43	1963, Nov. 22	46
36	Lyndon Baines Johnson	Dem.	1908, Aug. 27	Tex.	1963	55	1973, Jan. 22	64
37	Richard Milhous Nixon (2)	Rep.	1913, Jan. 9	Cal.	1969	56		
38	Gerald Rudolph Ford	Rep.	1913, July 14	Neb.	1974	61		
39	Jimmy (James Earl) Carter	Dem.	1924, Oct. 1	Ga.	1977	52		
40	Ronald Reagan	Rep.	1911, Feb. 6	Ill.	1981	69		
41	George Bush	Rep.	1924, June 12	Mass.	1989	64		

(1) Andrew Johnson — a Democrat, nominated vice president by Republicans and elected with Lincoln on National Union ticket. (2) Resigned Aug. 9, 1974.

Presidents, Vice Presidents, Congresses

	President	Service		Vice President	Congress
1	George Washington	Apr. 30, 1789—Mar. 3, 1797	1	John Adams	1, 2, 3, 4
2	John Adams	Mar. 4, 1797—Mar. 3, 1801	2	Thomas Jefferson	5, 6
3	Thomas Jefferson	Mar. 4, 1801—Mar. 3, 1805	3	Aaron Burr	7, 8
	"	Mar. 4, 1805—Mar. 3, 1809	4	George Clinton	9, 10
4	James Madison	Mar. 4, 1809—Mar. 3, 1813		"(1)	11, 12
	"	Mar. 4, 1813—Mar. 3, 1817	5	Elbridge Gerry (2)	13, 14
5	James Monroe	Mar. 4, 1817—Mar. 3, 1825	6	Daniel D. Tompkins	15, 16, 17, 18
6	John Quincy Adams	Mar. 4, 1825—Mar. 3, 1829	7	John C. Calhoun	19, 20
7	Andrew Jackson	Mar. 4, 1829—Mar. 3, 1833		"(3)	21, 22
	"	Mar. 4, 1833—Mar. 3, 1837	8	Martin Van Buren	23, 24
8	Martin Van Buren	Mar. 4, 1837—Mar. 3, 1841	9	Richard M. Johnson	25, 26
9	William Henry Harrison (4)	Mar. 4, 1841—Apr. 4, 1841	10	John Tyler	27
10	John Tyler	Apr. 6, 1841—Mar. 3, 1845			27, 28
11	James K. Polk	Mar. 4, 1845—Mar. 3, 1849	11	George M. Dallas	29, 30
12	Zachary Taylor (4)	Mar. 5, 1849—July 9, 1850	12	Millard Fillmore	31
13	Millard Fillmore	July 10, 1850—Mar. 3, 1853			31, 32
14	Franklin Pierce	Mar. 4, 1853—Mar. 3, 1857	13	William R. King (5)	33, 34
15	James Buchanan	Mar. 4, 1857—Mar. 3, 1861	14	John C. Breckinridge	35, 36
16	Abraham Lincoln	Mar. 4, 1861—Mar. 3, 1865	15	Hannibal Hamlin	37, 38
	"(4)	Mar. 4, 1865—Apr. 15, 1865	16	Andrew Johnson	39
17	Andrew Johnson	Apr. 15, 1865—Mar. 3, 1869			39, 40
18	Ulysses S. Grant	Mar. 4, 1869—Mar. 3, 1873	17	Schuyler Colfax	41, 42
	"	Mar. 4, 1873—Mar. 3, 1877	18	Henry Wilson (6)	43, 44
19	Rutherford B. Hayes	Mar. 4, 1877—Mar. 3, 1881	19	William A. Wheeler	45, 46
20	James A. Garfield (4)	Mar. 4, 1881—Sept. 19, 1881	20	Chester A. Arthur	47
21	Chester A. Arthur	Sept. 20, 1881—Mar. 3, 1885			47, 48
22	Grover Cleveland (7)	Mar. 4, 1885—Mar. 3, 1889	21	Thomas A. Hendricks (8)	49, 50
23	Benjamin Harrison	Mar. 4, 1889—Mar. 3, 1893	22	Levi P. Morton	51, 52
24	Grover Cleveland (7)	Mar. 4, 1893—Mar. 3, 1897	23	Adlai E. Stevenson	53, 54
25	William McKinley	Mar. 4, 1897—Mar. 3, 1901	24	Garret A. Hobart (9)	55, 56
	"(4)	Mar. 4, 1901—Sept. 14, 1901	25	Theodore Roosevelt	57
26	Theodore Roosevelt	Sept. 14, 1901—Mar. 3, 1905			57, 58
	"	Mar. 4, 1905—Mar. 3, 1909	26	Charles W. Fairbanks	59, 60
27	William H. Taft	Mar. 4, 1909—Mar. 3, 1913	27	James S. Sherman (10)	61, 62
28	Woodrow Wilson	Mar. 4, 1913—Mar. 3, 1921	28	Thomas R. Marshall	63, 64, 65, 66
29	Warren G. Harding (4)	Mar. 4, 1921—Aug. 2, 1923	29	Calvin Coolidge	67

Presidents, Vice Presidents, Congresses

President	Service	Vice President	Congress
30 Calvin Coolidge	Aug. 3, 1923—Mar. 3, 1925		68
"	Mar. 4, 1925—Mar. 3, 1929	30 Charles G. Dawes	69, 70
31 Herbert C. Hoover	Mar. 4, 1929—Mar. 3, 1933	31 Charles Curtis	71, 72
32 Franklin D. Roosevelt (16)	Mar. 4, 1933—Jan. 20, 1941	32 John N. Garner	73, 74, 75, 76
"	Jan. 20, 1941—Jan. 20, 1945	33 Henry A. Wallace	77, 78
"(4)	Jan. 20, 1945—Apr. 12, 1945	34 Harry S. Truman	79
33 Harry S. Truman	Apr. 12, 1945—Jan. 20, 1949		79, 80
"	Jan. 20, 1949—Jan. 20, 1953	35 Alben W. Barkley	81, 82
34 Dwight D. Eisenhower	Jan. 20, 1953—Jan. 20, 1961	36 Richard M. Nixon	83, 84, 85, 86
35 John F. Kennedy (4)	Jan. 20, 1961—Nov. 22, 1963	37 Lyndon B. Johnson	87, 88
36 Lyndon B. Johnson	Nov. 22, 1963—Jan. 20, 1965		88
"	Jan. 20, 1965—Jan. 20, 1969	38 Hubert H. Humphrey	89, 90
37 Richard M. Nixon	Jan. 20, 1969—Jan. 20, 1973	39 Spiro T. Agnew (11)	91, 92, 93
"(12)	Jan. 20, 1973—Aug. 9, 1974	40 Gerald R. Ford (13)	93
38 Gerald R. Ford (14)	Aug. 9, 1974—Jan. 20, 1977	41 Nelson A. Rockefeller (15)	93, 94
39 Jimmy (James Earl) Carter	Jan. 20, 1977—Jan. 20, 1981	42 Walter F. Mondale	95, 96
40 Ronald Reagan	Jan. 20, 1981—Jan. 20, 1989	43 George Bush	97, 98, 99, 100
41 George Bush	Jan. 20, 1989—	44 Dan Quayle	101

(1) Died Apr. 20, 1812. (2) Died Nov. 23, 1814. (3) Resigned Dec. 28, 1832, to become U.S. Senator. (4) Died in office. (5) Died Apr. 18, 1853. (6) Died Nov. 22, 1875. (7) Terms not consecutive. (8) Died Nov. 25, 1885. (9) Died Nov. 21, 1899. (10) Died Oct. 30, 1912. (11) Resigned Oct. 10, 1973. (12) Resigned Aug. 9, 1974. (13) First non-elected vice president, chosen under 25th Amendment procedure. (14) First non-elected president. (15) 2d non-elected vice president. (16) First president to be inaugurated under 20th Amendment, Jan. 20, 1937.

Vice Presidents of the U.S.

The numerals given vice presidents do not coincide with those given presidents, because some presidents had none and some had more than one.

	Name	Birthplace	Year	Home	Inaug.	Politics	Place of death	Year	Age
1	John Adams	Quincy, Mass.	1735	Mass.	1789	Fed.	Quincy, Mass.	1826	90
2	Thomas Jefferson	Shadwell, Va.	1743	Va.	1797	Dem.-Rep.	Monticello, Va.	1826	83
3	Aaron Burr	Newark, N.J.	1756	N.Y.	1801	Dem.-Rep.	Staten Island, N.Y.	1836	80
4	George Clinton	Ulster Co., N.Y.	1739	N.Y.	1805	Dem.-Rep.	Washington, D.C.	1812	73
5	Elbridge Gerry	Marblehead, Mass.	1744	Mass.	1813	Dem.-Rep.	Washington, D.C.	1814	70
6	Daniel D. Tompkins	Scarsdale, N.Y.	1774	N.Y.	1817	Dem.-Rep.	Staten Island, N.Y.	1825	51
7	John C. Calhoun (1)	Abbeville, S.C.	1782	S.C.	1825	Dem.-Rep.	Washington, D.C.	1850	68
8	Martin Van Buren	Kinderhook, N.Y.	1782	N.Y.	1833	Dem.	Kinderhook, N.Y.	1862	79
9	Richard M. Johnson	Louisville, Ky.	1780	Ky.	1837	Dem.	Frankfort, Ky.	1850	70
10	John Tyler	Greenway, Va.	1790	Va.	1841	Whig	Richmond, Va.	1862	71
11	George M. Dallas	Philadelphia, Pa.	1792	Pa.	1845	Dem.	Philadelphia, Pa.	1864	72
12	Millard Fillmore	Summerhill, N.Y.	1800	N.Y.	1849	Whig	Buffalo, N.Y.	1874	74
13	William R. King	Sampson Co., N.C.	1786	Ala.	1853	Dem.	Dallas Co., Ala.	1853	67
14	John C. Breckinridge	Lexington, Ky.	1821	Ky.	1857	Dem.	Lexington, Ky.	1875	54
15	Hannibal Hamlin	Paris, Me.	1809	Me.	1861	Rep.	Bangor, Me.	1891	81
16	Andrew Johnson	Raleigh, N.C.	1808	Tenn.	1865	(2)	Carter Co., Tenn.	1875	66
17	Schuyler Colfax	New York, N.Y.	1823	Ind.	1869	Rep.	Mankato, Minn.	1885	62
18	Henry Wilson	Farmington, N.H.	1812	Mass.	1873	Rep.	Washington, D.C.	1875	63
19	William A. Wheeler	Malone, N.Y.	1819	N.Y.	1877	Rep.	Malone, N.Y.	1887	68
20	Chester A. Arthur	Fairfield, Vt.	1829	N.Y.	1881	Rep.	New York, N.Y.	1886	57
21	Thomas A. Hendricks	Muskingum Co., Oh.	1819	Ind.	1885	Dem.	Indianapolis, Ind.	1885	66
22	Levi P. Morton	Shoreham, Vt.	1824	N.Y.	1889	Rep.	Rhinebeck, N.Y.	1920	96
23	Adlai E. Stevenson (3)	Christian Co., Ky.	1835	Ill.	1893	Dem.	Chicago, Ill.	1914	78
24	Garret A. Hobart	Long Branch, N.J.	1844	N.J.	1897	Rep.	Paterson, N.J.	1899	55
25	Theodore Roosevelt	New York, N.Y.	1858	N.Y.	1901	Rep.	Oyster Bay, N.Y.	1919	60
26	Charles W. Fairbanks	Unionville Centre, Oh.	1852	Ind.	1905	Rep.	Indianapolis, Ind.	1918	66
27	James S. Sherman	Utica, N.Y.	1855	N.Y.	1909	Rep.	Utica, N.Y.	1912	57
28	Thomas R. Marshall	N. Manchester, Ind.	1854	Ind.	1913	Dem.	Washington, D.C.	1925	71
29	Calvin Coolidge	Plymouth, Vt.	1872	Mass.	1921	Rep.	Northampton, Mass.	1933	60
30	Charles G. Dawes	Marietta, Oh.	1865	Ill.	1925	Rep.	Evanston, Ill.	1951	85
31	Charles Curtis	Topeka, Kan.	1860	Kan.	1929	Rep.	Washington, D.C.	1936	76
32	John Nance Garner	Red River Co., Tex.	1868	Tex.	1933	Dem.	Uvalde, Tex.	1967	98
33	Henry Agard Wallace	Adair County, Ia.	1888	Iowa	1941	Dem.	Danbury, Conn.	1965	77
34	Harry S. Truman	Lamar, Mo.	1884	Mo.	1945	Dem.	Kansas City, Mo.	1972	88
35	Alben W. Barkley	Graves County, Ky.	1877	Ky.	1949	Dem.	Lexington, Va.	1956	78
36	Richard M. Nixon	Yorba Linda, Cal.	1913	Cal.	1953	Rep.			
37	Lyndon B. Johnson	Johnson City, Tex.	1908	Tex.	1961	Dem.	San Antonio, Tex.	1973	64
38	Hubert H. Humphrey	Wallace, S.D.	1911	Minn.	1965	Dem.	Waverly, Minn.	1978	66
39	Spiro T. Agnew (4)	Baltimore, Md.	1918	Md.	1969	Rep.			
40	Gerald R. Ford	Omaha, Neb.	1913	Mich.	1973	Rep.			
41	Nelson A. Rockefeller	Bar Harbor, Me.	1908	N.Y.	1974	Rep.	New York, N.Y.	1979	70
42	Walter F. Mondale	Ceylon, Minn.	1928	Minn.	1977	Dem.			
43	George Bush	Milton, Mass.	1924	Tex.	1981	Rep.			
44	Dan Quayle	Indianapolis, Ind.	1947	Ind.	1989	Rep.			

(1) John C. Calhoun resigned Dec. 28, 1832, having been elected to the Senate to fill a vacancy. (2) Andrew Johnson — a Democrat nominated by Republicans and elected with Lincoln on the National Union Ticket. (3) Adlai E. Stevenson, 23d vice president, was grandfather of Democratic candidate for president, 1952 and 1956. (4) Resigned Oct. 10, 1973.

AWARDS — MEDALS — PRIZES

The Alfred B. Nobel Prize Winners

Alfred B. Nobel, inventor of dynamite, bequeathed $9,000,000, the interest to be distributed yearly to those who had most benefited mankind in physics, chemistry, medicine-physiology, literature, and peace. The first Nobel Memorial Prize in Economics was awarded in 1969. No awards given for years omitted. In 1988, each prize was worth approximately $390,000.

Physics

1988 Leon M. Lederman, Melvin Schwartz, Jack Steinberger, all U.S.
1987 K. Alex Muller, Swiss; J. Georg Bednorz, W. German
1986 Ernest Ruska, German, Gerd Binnig, W. German, Heinrich Rohrer, Swiss
1985 Klaus von Klitzing, W. German
1984 Carlo Rubbia, Italian, Simon van der Meere, Dutch
1983 Subrahmanyan Chandrasekhar, William A. Fowler, both U.S.
1982 Kenneth G. Wilson, U.S.
1981 Nicolass Bloembergen, Arthur Schaalow, both U.S.; Kai M. Siegbahn, Swedish
1980 James W. Cronin, Val L. Fitch, U.S.
1979 Steven Weinberg, Sheldon L. Glashow, both U.S.; Abdus Salam, Pakistani
1978 Pyotr Kapitsa, USSR; Arno Penzias, Robert Wilson, both U.S.
1977 John H. Van Vleck, Philip W. Anderson, both U.S.; Nevill F. Mott, British
1976 Burton Richter, U.S. Samuel C.C. Ting, U.S.
1975 James Rainwater, U.S. Ben Mottelson, U.S.-Danish, Aage Bohr, Danish
1974 Martin Ryle, British Antony Hewish, British
1973 Ivar Giaever, U.S. Leo Esaki, Japan Brian D. Josephson, British
1972 John Bardeen, U.S. Leon N. Cooper, U.S. John R. Schrieffer, U.S.
1971 Dennis Gabor, British
1970 Louis Neel, French Hannes Alfven, Swedish
1969 Murray Gell-Mann, U.S.
1968 Luis W. Alvarez, U.S.
1967 Hans A. Bethe, U.S.

1966 Alfred Kastler, French
1965 Richard P. Feynman, U.S. Julian S. Schwinger, U.S. Shinichiro Tomonaga, Japanese
1964 Nikolai G. Basov, USSR Aleksander M. Prochorov, USSR Charles H. Townes, U.S.
1963 Maria Goeppert-Mayer, U.S. J. Hans D. Jensen, German Eugene P. Wigner, U.S.
1962 Lev. D. Landau, USSR
1961 Robert Hofstadter, U.S. Rudolf L. Mossbauer, German
1960 Donald A. Glaser, U.S.
1959 Owen Chamberlain, U.S. Emilio G. Segre, U.S.
1958 Pavel Cherenkov, Ilya Frank, Igor Y. Tamm, all USSR
1957 Tsung-dao Lee, Chen Ning Yang, both U.S.
1956 John Bardeen, U.S. Walter H. Brattain, U.S. William Shockley, U.S.
1955 Polykarp Kusch, U.S. Willis E. Lamb, U.S.
1954 Max Born, British Walter Bothe, German
1953 Frits Zernike, Dutch
1952 Felix Bloch, U.S. Edward M. Purcell, U.S.
1951 Sir John D. Cockroft, British Ernest T. S. Walton, Irish
1950 Cecil F. Powell, British
1949 Hideki Yukawa, Japanese
1948 Patrick M. S. Blackett, British
1947 Sir Edward V. Appleton, British
1946 Percy Williams Bridgman, U.S.
1945 Wolfgang Pauli, U.S.
1944 Isidor Isaac Rabi, U.S.
1943 Otto Stern, U.S.
1939 Ernest O. Lawrence, U.S.
1938 Enrico Fermi, U.S.
1937 Clinton J. Davisson, U.S. Sir George P. Thomson, British
1936 Carl D. Anderson, U.S.

Victor F. Hess, Austrian
1935 Sir James Chadwick, British
1933 Paul A. M. Dirac, British Erwin Schrodinger, Austrian
1932 Werner Heisenberg, German
1930 Sir Chandrasekhara V. Raman, Indian
1929 Prince Louis-Victor de Broglie, French
1928 Owen W. Richardson, British
1927 Arthur H. Compton, U.S. Charles T. R. Wilson, British
1926 Jean B. Perrin, French
1925 James Franck, Gustav Hertz, both German
1924 Karl M. G. Siegbahn, Swedish
1923 Robert A. Millikan, U.S.
1922 Niels Bohr, Danish
1921 Albert Einstein, Ger.-U.S.
1920 Charles E. Guillaume, French
1919 Johannes Stark, German
1918 Max K. E. L. Planck, German
1917 Charles G. Barkla, British
1915 Sir William H. Bragg, British Sir William L. Bragg, British
1914 Max von Laue, German
1913 Heike Kamerlingh-Onnes, Dutch
1912 Nils G. Dalen, Swedish
1911 Wilhelm Wien, German
1910 Johannes D. van der Waals, Dutch
1909 Carl F. Braun, German Guglielmo Marconi, Italian
1908 Gabriel Lippmann, French
1907 Albert A. Michelson, U.S.
1906 Sir Joseph J. Thomson, British
1905 Philipp E. A. von Lenard, Ger.
1904 John W. Strutt, Lord Rayleigh, British
1903 Antoine Henri Becquerel, French Marie Curie, Polish-French Pierre Curie, French
1902 Hendrik A. Lorentz, Pieter Zeeman, both Dutch
1901 Wilhelm C. Roentgen, German

Chemistry

1988 Johann Deisenhofer, Robert Huber, Hartmut Michel, all W. German
1987 Donald J. Cram, Charles J. Pederson, both U.S.; Jean-Marie Lehn, French
1986 Dudley Herschbach, Yuan T. Lee, both U.S.; John C. Polanyi, Canadian
1985 Herbert A. Hauptman, Jerome Karle, both U.S.
1984 Bruce Merrifield, U.S.
1983 Henry Taube, Canadian
1982 Aaron Klug, S. African
1981 Kenichi Fukui, Japan., Roald Hoffmann, U.S.
1980 Paul Berg., U.S.; Walter Gilbert, U.S., Frederick Sanger, U.K.
1979 Herbert C. Brown, U.S. George Wittig, German
1978 Peter Mitchell, British
1977 Ilya Prigogine, Belgian
1976 William N. Lipscomb, U.S.
1975 John Cornforth, Austral.-Brit., Vladimir Prelog, Yugo.-Switz.
1974 Paul J. Flory, U.S.
1973 Ernst Otto Fischer, W. German Geoffrey Wilkinson, British
1972 Christian B. Anfinsen, U.S.

Stanford Moore, U.S. William H. Stein, U.S.
1971 Gerhard Herzberg, Canadian
1970 Luis F. Leloir, Arg.
1969 Derek H. R. Barton, British Odd Hassel, Norwegian
1968 Lars Onsager, U.S.
1967 Manfred Eigen, German Ronald G. W. Norrish, British George Porter, British
1966 Robert S. Mulliken, U.S.
1965 Robert B. Woodward, U.S.
1964 Dorothy C. Hodgkin, British
1963 Giulio Natta, Italian Karl Ziegler, German
1962 John C. Kendrew, British Max F. Perutz, British
1961 Melvin Calvin, U.S.
1960 Willard F. Libby, U.S.
1959 Jaroslav Heyrovsky, Czech
1958 Frederick Sanger, British
1957 Sir Alexander R. Todd, British
1956 Sir Cyril N. Hinshelwood, British Nikolai N. Semenov, USSR
1955 Vincent du Vigneaud, U.S.
1954 Linus C. Pauling, U.S.
1953 Hermann Staudinger, German
1952 Archer J. P. Martin, British Richard L. M. Synge, British

1951 Edwin M. McMillan, U.S. Glenn T. Seaborg, U.S.
1950 Kurt Alder, German Otto P. H. Diels, German
1949 William F. Giauque, U.S.
1948 Arne W. K. Tiselius, Swedish
1947 Sir Robert Robinson, British
1946 James B. Sumner, John H. Northrop, Wendell M. Stanley, U.S.
1945 Artturi I. Virtanen, Finnish
1944 Otto Hahn, German
1943 Georg de Hevesy, Hungarian
1939 Adolf F. J. Butenandt, German Leopold Ruzicka, Swiss
1938 Richard Kuhn, German
1937 Walter N. Haworth, British Paul Karrer, Swiss
1936 Peter J. W. Debye, Dutch
1935 Frederic Joliot-Curie, French Irene Joliot-Curie, French
1934 Harold C. Urey, U.S.
1932 Irving Langmuir, U.S.
1931 Friedrich Bergius, German Karl Bosch, German
1930 Hans Fischer, German
1929 Sir Arthur Harden, British Hans von Euler-Chelpin, Swed.
1928 Adolf O. R. Windaus, German
1927 Heinrich O. Wieland, German

343

1926 Theodor Svedberg, Swedish
1925 Richard A. Zsigmondy, German
1923 Fritz Pregl, Austrian
1922 Francis W. Aston, British
1921 Frederick Soddy, British
1920 Walther H. Nernst, German
1918 Fritz Haber, German
1915 Richard M. Willstatter, German

1914 Theodore W. Richards, U.S.
1913 Alfred Werner, Swiss
1912 Victor Grignard, French
     Paul Sabatier, French
1911 Marie Curie, Polish-French
1910 Otto Wallach, German
1909 Wilhelm Ostwald, German
1908 Ernest Rutherford, British

1907 Eduard Buchner, German
1906 Henri Moissan, French
1905 Adolf von Baeyer, German
1904 Sir William Ramsay, British
1903 Svante A. Arrhenius, Swedish
1902 Emil Fischer, German
1901 Jacobus H. van't Hoff, Dutch

Physiology or Medicine

1988 Gertrude B. Elion, George H. Hitchings, both U.S; Sir James Black, Brit.
1987 Susumu Tonegawa, Japanese
1986 Rita Levi-Montalcini, It.-U.S., Stanley Cohen, both U.S.
1985 Michael S. Brown, Joseph L. Goldstein, both U.S.
1984 Cesar Milstein, Brit.-Argentina; Georges J. F. Koehler, German; Niels K. Jerne, Brit.-Danish
1983 Barbara McClintock, U.S.
1982 Sune Bergstrom, Bengt Samuelsson, both Swedish; John R. Vane, British.
1981 Roger W. Sperry, David H. Hubel, Tosten N. Wiesel, all U.S.
1980 Baruj Benacerraf, George Snell, both U.S.; Jean Dausset, France
1979 Alian M. Cormack, U.S. Geoffrey N. Hounsfield, British
1978 Daniel Nathans, Hamilton O. Smith, both U.S.; Werner Arber, Swiss
1977 Rosalyn S. Yalow, Roger C.L. Guillemin, Andrew V. Schally, U.S.
1976 Baruch S. Blumberg, U.S. Daniel Carleton Gajdusek, U.S.
1975 David Baltimore, Howard Temin, both U.S.; Renato Dulbecco, Ital.-U.S.
1974 Albert Claude, Lux.-U.S.; George Emil Palade, Rom.-U.S.; Christian Rene de Duve, Belg.
1973 Karl von Frisch, Ger.; Konrad Lorenz, Ger.-Austrian; Nikolaas Tinbergen, Brit.
1972 Gerald M. Edelman, U.S. Rodney R. Porter, British
1971 Earl W. Sutherland Jr., U.S.
1970 Julius Axelrod, U.S. Sir Bernard Katz, British Ulf von Euler, Swedish
1969 Max Delbruck, Alfred D. Hershey, Salvador Luria, all U.S.
1968 Robert W. Holley, H. Gobind Khorana,

Marshall W. Nirenberg, all U.S.
1967 Ragnar Granit, Swedish Haldan Keffer Hartline, U.S. George Wald, U.S.
1966 Charles B. Huggins, Francis Peyton Rous, both U.S.
1965 Francois Jacob, Andre Lwoff, Jacques Monod, all French
1964 Konrad E. Bloch, U.S. Feodor Lynen, German
1963 Sir John C. Eccles, Australian Alan L. Hodgkin, British Andrew F. Huxley, British
1962 Francis H. C. Crick, British James D. Watson, U.S. Maurice H. F. Wilkins, British
1961 Georg von Bekesy, U.S.
1960 Sir F. MacFarlane Burnet, Australian Peter B. Medawar, British
1959 Arthur Kornberg, U.S. Severo Ochoa, U.S.
1958 George W. Beadle, U.S. Edward L. Tatum, U.S. Joshua Lederberg, U.S.
1957 Daniel Bovet, Italian
1956 Andre F. Cournand, U.S. Werner Forssmann, German Dickinson W. Richards, Jr., U.S.
1955 Alex H. T. Theorell, Swedish
1954 John F. Enders, Frederick C. Robbins, Thomas H. Weller, all U.S.
1953 Hans A. Krebs, British Fritz A. Lipmann, U.S.
1952 Selman A. Waksman, U.S.
1951 Max Theiler, U.S.
1950 Philip S. Hench, Edward C. Kendall, both U.S. Tadeus Reichstein, Swiss
1949 Walter R. Hess, Swiss Antonio Moniz, Portuguese
1948 Paul H. Müller, Swiss
1947 Carl F. Cori, Gerty T. Cori, both U.S. Bernardo A. Houssay, Arg.
1946 Hermann J. Muller, U.S.
1945 Ernst B. Chain, British

Sir Alexander Fleming, British
Sir Howard W. Florey, British
1944 Joseph Erlanger, U.S. Herbert S. Gasser, U.S.
1943 Henrik C. P. Dam, Danish Edward A. Doisy, U.S.
1939 Gerhard Domagk, German
1938 Corneille J. F. Heymans, Belg.
1937 Albert Szent-Gyorgyi, Hung.-U.S.
1936 Sir Henry H. Dale, British Otto Loewi, U.S.
1935 Hans Spemann, German
1934 George R. Minot, Wm. P. Murphy, G. H. Whipple, all U.S.
1933 Thomas H. Morgan, U.S.
1932 Edgar D. Adrian, British Sir Charles S. Sherrington, Brit.
1931 Otto H. Warburg, German
1930 Karl Landsteiner, U.S.
1929 Christiaan Eijkman, Dutch Sir Frederick G. Hopkins, British
1928 Charles J. H. Nicolle, French
1927 Julius Wagner-Jauregg, Aus.
1926 Johannes A. G. Fibiger, Danish
1924 Willem Einthoven, Dutch
1923 Frederick G. Banting, Canadian John J. R. Macleod, Scottish
1922 Archibald V. Hill, British Otto F. Meyerhof, German
1920 Schack A. S. Krogh, Danish
1919 Jules Bordet, Belgian
1914 Robert Barany, Austrian
1913 Charles R. Richet, French
1912 Alexis Carrel, French
1911 Allvar Gullstrand, Swedish
1910 Albrecht Kossel, German
1909 Emil T. Kocher, Swiss
1908 Paul Ehrlich, German Elie Metchnikoff, French
1907 Charles L. A. Laveran, French
1906 Camillo Golgi, Italian Santiago Ramon y Cajal, Sp.
1905 Robert Koch, German
1904 Ivan P. Pavlov, Russian
1903 Niels R. Finsen, Danish
1902 Sir Ronald Ross, British
1901 Emil A. von Behring, German

Literature

1988 Naguib Mahfouz, Egyptian
1987 Joseph Brodsky, USSR-U.S.
1986 Wole Soyinka, Nigerian
1985 Claude Simon, French
1984 Jaroslav Siefert, Czech.
1983 William Golding, British
1982 Gabriel Garcia Marquez, Colombian-Mex.
1981 Elias Canetti, Bulgarian-British
1980 Czeslaw Milosz, Polish-U.S.
1979 Odysseus Elytis, Greek
1978 Isaac Bashevis Singer, U.S. (Yiddish)
1977 Vicente Aleixandre, Spanish
1976 Saul Bellow, U.S.
1975 Eugenio Montale, Ital.
1974 Eyvind Johnson, Harry Edmund Martinson, both Swedish
1973 Patrick White, Australian
1972 Heinrich Boll, W. German
1971 Pablo Neruda, Chilean
1970 Aleksandr I. Solzhenitsyn, Russ.
1969 Samuel Beckett, Irish
1968 Yasunari Kawabata, Japanese
1967 Miguel Angel Asturias, Guate.
1966 Samuel Joseph Agnon, Israeli Nelly Sachs, Swedish

1962 Mikhail Sholokhov, Russian
1964 Jean Paul Sartre, French (Prize declined)
1963 Giorgos Seferis, Greek
1962 John Steinbeck, U.S.
1961 Ivo Andric, Yugoslavian
1960 Saint-John Perse, French
1959 Salvatore Quasimodo, Italian
1958 Boris L. Pasternak, Russian (Prize declined)
1957 Albert Camus, French
1956 Juan Ramon Jimenez, Puerto Rican-Span.
1955 Halldor K. Laxness, Icelandic
1954 Ernest Hemingway, U.S.
1953 Sir Winston Churchill, British
1952 Francois Mauriac, French
1951 Par F. Lagerkvist, Swedish
1950 Bertrand Russell, British
1949 William Faulkner, U.S.
1948 T.S. Eliot, British
1947 Andre Gide, French
1946 Hermann Hesse, Swiss
1945 Gabriela Mistral, Chilean
1944 Johannes V. Jensen, Danish
1939 Frans E. Sillanpaa, Finnish
1938 Pearl S. Buck, U.S.

1937 Roger Martin du Gard, French
1936 Eugene O'Neill, U.S.
1934 Luigi Pirandello, Italian
1933 Ivan A. Bunin, French
1932 John Galsworthy, British
1931 Erik A. Karlfeldt, Swedish
1930 Sinclair Lewis, U.S.
1929 Thomas Mann, German
1928 Sigrid Undset, Norwegian
1927 Henri Bergson, French
1926 Grazia Deledda, Italian
1925 George Bernard Shaw, British
1924 Wladyslaw S. Reymont, Polish
1923 William Butler Yeats, Irish
1922 Jacinto Benavente, Spanish
1921 Anatole France, French
1920 Knut Hamsun, Norwegian
1919 Carl F. G. Spitteler, Swiss
1917 Karl A. Gjellerup, Danish Henrik Pontoppidan, Danish
1916 Verner von Heidenstam, Swed.
1915 Romain Rolland, French
1913 Rabindranath Tagore, Indian
1912 Gerhart Hauptmann, German
1911 Maurice Maeterlinck, Belgian
1910 Paul J. L. Heyse, German
1909 Selma Lagerlof, Swedish

1908 Rudolf C. Eucken, German	1904 Frederic Mistral, French	1902 Theodor Mommsen, German
1907 Rudyard Kipling, British	Jose Echegaray, Spanish	1901 Rene F. A Sully Prudhomme,
1906 Giosue Carducci, Italian	1903 Bjornsterne Bjornson, Norw.	French
1905 Henryk Sienkiewicz, Polish		

Nobel Memorial Prize in Economics

		Friedrich A. von Hayek, Austrian
1988 Maurice Allais, French	1979 Theodore W. Schultz, U.S.,	
1987 Robert M. Solow, U.S.	Sir Arthur Lewis, British	1973 Wassily Leontief, U.S.
1986 James M. Buchanon, U.S.	1978 Herbert A. Simon, U.S.	1972 Kenneth J. Arrow, U.S.
1985 Franco Modigliani, It.-U.S.	1977 Bertil Ohlin, Swedish	John R. Hicks, British
1984 Richard Stone, British	James E. Meade, British	1971 Simon Kuznets, U.S.
1983 Gerard Debreu, Fr.-U.S.	1976 Milton Friedman, U.S.	1970 Paul A. Samuelson, U.S.
1982 George J. Stigler, U.S.	1975 Tjalling Koopmans, Dutch-U.S.,	1969 Ragnar Frisch, Norwegian
1981 James Tobin, U.S.	Leonid Kantorovich, USSR	Jan Tinbergen, Dutch
1980 Lawrence R. Klein, U.S.	1974 Gunnar Myrdal, Swed.,	

Peace

	League of Red Cross Societies	Ludwig Quidde, German
1988 United Nations Peacekeeping	1962 Linus C. Pauling, U.S.	1926 Aristide Briand, French
Forces	1961 Dag Hammarskjold, Swedish	Gustav Stresemann, German
1987 Oscar Arias Sanchez, Costa Rican	1960 Albert J. Luthuli, South African	1925 Sir J. Austen Chamberlain, Brit.
1986 Elie Wiesel, Romania-U.S.	1959 Philip J. Noel-Baker, British	Charles G. Dawes, U.S.
1985 Intl. Physicians for the Prevention of	1958 Georges Pire, Belgian	1922 Fridtjof Nansen, Norwegian
Nuclear War, U.S.	1957 Lester B. Pearson, Canadian	1921 Karl H. Branting, Swedish
1984 Bishop Desmond Tutu, So. African	1954 Office of the UN High	Christian L. Lange, Norwegian
1983 Lech Walesa, Polish	Commissioner for Refugees	1920 Leon V.A. Bourgeois, French
1982 Alva Myrdal, Swedish; Alfonso	1953 George C. Marshall, U.S.	1919 Woodrow Wilson, U.S.
Garcia Robles, Mexican	1952 Albert Schweitzer, French	1917 International Red Cross
1981 Office of U.N. High Commissioner	1951 Leon Jouhaux, French	1913 Henri La Fontaine, Belgian
for Refugees	1950 Ralph J. Bunche, U.S.	1912 Elihu Root, U.S.
1980 Adolfo Perez Esquivel, Argentine	1949 Lord John Boyd Orr of Brechin	1911 Tobias M.C. Asser, Dutch
1979 Mother Teresa of Calcutta,	Mearns, British	Alfred H. Fried, Austrian
Albanian-Indian	1947 Friends Service Council, Brit.	1910 Permanent Intl. Peace Bureau
1978 Anwar Sadat, Egyptian	Amer. Friends Service Com.	1909 Auguste M. F. Beernaert, Belg.
Menachem Begin, Israeli	1946 Emily G. Balch,	Paul H. B. B. d'Estournelles de
1977 Amnesty International	John R. Mott, both U.S.	Constant, French
1976 Mairead Corrigan, Betty Williams,	1945 Cordell Hull, U.S.	1908 Klas P. Arnoldson, Swedish
N. Irish	1944 International Red Cross	Fredrik Bajer, Danish
1975 Andrei Sakharov, USSR	1938 Nansen International Office	1907 Ernesto T. Moneta, Italian
1974 Eisaku Sato, Japanese, Sean	for Refugees	Louis Renault, French
MacBride, Irish	1937 Viscount Cecil of Chelwood, Brit.	1906 Theodore Roosevelt, U.S.
1973 Henry Kissinger, U.S.	1936 Carlos de Saavedra Lamas, Arg.	1905 Baroness Bertha von Suttner,
Le Duc Tho, N. Vietnamese	1935 Carl von Ossietzky, German	Austrian
(Tho declined)	1934 Arthur Henderson, British	1904 Institute of International Law
1971 Willy Brandt, W. German	1933 Sir Norman Angell, British	1903 Sir William R. Cremer, British
1970 Norman E. Borlaug, U.S.	1931 Jane Addams, U.S.	1902 Elie Ducommun,
1969 Intl. Labor Organization	Nicholas Murray Butler, U.S.	Charles A. Gobat, both Swiss
1968 Rene Cassin, French	1930 Nathan Soderblom, Swedish	1901 Jean H. Dunant, Swiss
1965 U.N. Children's Fund (UNICEF)	1929 Frank B. Kellogg, U.S.	Frederic Passy, French
1964 Martin Luther King Jr., U.S.	1927 Ferdinand E. Buisson, French	
1963 International Red Cross,		

Pulitzer Prizes in Journalism, Letters, and Music

The Pulitzer Prizes were endowed by Joseph Pulitzer (1847-1911), publisher of The World, New York, N.Y., in a bequest to Columbia University, and are awarded annually by the president of the university on recommendation of the Pulitzer Prize Board for work done during the preceding year. The administrator is Robert C. Christopher of Columbia Univ. All prizes are $3,000 (originally $500) in each category, except Meritorious Public Service for which a gold medal is given.

Journalism

Meritorious Public Service

For distinguished and meritorious public service by a United States newspaper.

1918—New York Times. Also special award to Minna Lewinson and Henry Beetle Hough.
1919—Milwaukee Journal.
1921—Boston Post.
1922—New York World.
1923—Memphis (Tenn.) Commercial Appeal.
1924—New York World.
1926—Enquirer-Sun, Columbus, Ga.
1927—Canton (Oh.) Daily News.
1928—Indianapolis Times.
1929—Evening World, New York.
1931—Atlanta (Ga.) Constitution.
1932—Indianapolis (Ind.) News.
1933—New York World-Telegram.
1934—Medford (Ore.) Mail-Tribune.
1935—Sacramento (Cal.) Bee.
1936—Cedar Rapids (Ia.) Gazette.
1937—St.Louis Post-Dispatch.
1938—Bismarck (N.D.) Tribune.

1939—Miami (Fla.) Daily News.
1940—Waterbury (Conn.) Republican and American.
1941—St.Louis Post-Dispatch.
1942—Los Angeles Times.
1943—Omaha World Herald.
1944—New York Times.
1945—Detroit Free Press.
1946—Scranton (Pa.) Times.
1947—Baltimore Sun.
1948—St. Louis Post-Dispatch.
1949—Nebraska State Journal.
1950—Chicago Daily News; St. Louis Post-Dispatch.
1951—Miami (Fla.) Herald and Brooklyn Eagle.
1952—St. Louis Post-Dispatch.
1953—Whiteville (N.C.) News Reporter; Tabor City (N.C.) Tribune.
1954—Newsday (Long Island, N.Y.)
1955—Columbus (Ga.) Ledger and Sunday Ledger-Enquirer.
1956—Watsonville (Cal.) Register-Pajaronian.
1957—Chicago Daily News.
1958—Arkansas Gazette, Little Rock.
1959—Utica (N.Y.) Observer-Dispatch and Utica Daily Press.
1960—Los Angeles Times.
1961—Amarillo (Tex.) Globe-Times.

1962—Panama City (Fla.) News-Herald.
1963—Chicago Daily News.
1964—St.Petersburg (Fla.) Times.
1965—Hutchinson (Kan.) News.
1966—Boston Globe.
1967—The Louisville Courier-Journal; The Milwaukee Journal.
1968—Riverside (Cal.) Press-Enterprise.
1969—Los Angeles Times.
1970—Newsday (Long Island, N.Y.).
1971—Winston Salem (N.C.) Journal & Sentinel.
1972—New York Times.
1973—Washington Post.
1974—Newsday (Long Island, N.Y.).
1975—Boston Globe.
1976—Anchorage Daily News.
1977—Lufkin (Tex.) News.
1978—Philadelphia Inquirer.
1979—Point Reyes (Cal.) Light.
1980—Gannett News Service.
1981—Charlotte (N.C.) Observer.
1982—Detroit News.
1983—Jackson (Miss.) Clarion-Ledger.
1984—Los Angeles Times.
1985—Ft. Worth (Tex.) Star-Telegram.
1986—Denver Post.
1987—Pittsburgh Press.
1988—Charlotte Observer.
1989—Anchorage Daily News.

Reporting

This category originally embraced all fields, local, national, and international. Later separate categories were created for the different fields of reporting.

1917—Herbert Bayard Swope, New York World.
1918—Harold A. Littledale, New York Evening Post.
1920—John J. Leary, Jr., New York World.
1921—Louis Seibold, New York World.
1922—Kirke L. Simpson, Associated Press.
1923—Alva Johnston, New York Times.
1924—Magner White, San Diego Sun.
1925—James W. Mulroy and Alvin H. Goldstein, Chicago Daily News.
1926—William Burke Miller, Louisville Courier-Journal.
1927—John T. Rogers, St. Louis Post-Dispatch.
1929—Paul Y. Anderson, St. Louis Post-Dispatch.
1930—Russell D. Owens, New York Times. Also $500 to W.O. Dapping, Auburn (N.Y.) Citizen.
1931—A.B. MacDonald, Kansas City (Mo.) Star.
1932—W.C. Richards, D.D. Martin, J.S. Pooler, F.D. Webb, J.N.W. Sloan, Detroit Free Press.
1933—Francis A. Jamieson, Associated Press.
1934—Royce Brier, San Francisco Chronicle.
1935—William H.Taylor, New York Herald Tribune.
1936—Lauren D.Lyman, New York Times.
1937—John J. O'Neill, N.Y.Herald Tribune; William L. Laurence, N.Y Times; Howard W. Blakeslee, A.P.; Gobind Behari Lal, Universal Service; and David Dietz, Scripps-Howard Newspapers.
1938—Raymond Sprigle, Pittsburgh Post-Gazette.
1939—Thomas L. Stokes, Scripps-Howard Newspaper Alliance.
1940—S.Burton Heath, New York World-Telegram.
1941—Westbrook Pegler, New York World-Telegram.
1942—Stanton Delaplane, San Francisco Chronicle.
1943—George Weller, Chicago Daily News.
1944—Paul Schoenstein, N.Y.Journal-American.
1945—Jack S. McDowell, San Francisco Call-Bulletin.
1946—William L. Laurence, New York Times.
1947—Frederick Woltman, N.Y.World-Telegram.
1948—George E. Goodwin, Atlanta Journal.
1949—Malcolm Johnson, New York Sun.
1950—Meyer Berger, New York Times.
1951—Edward S. Montgomery, San Francisco Examiner.
1952—Geo. de Carvalho, San Francisco Chronicle.

(1) General or Spot; (2) Special or Investigative

1953—(1) Providence (R.I.) Journal and Evening Bulletin; (2) Edward J. Mowery, N.Y.World-Telegram & Sun.
1954—(1) Vicksburg (Miss.) Sunday Post-Herald; (2) Alvin Scott McCoy, Kansas City (Mo.) Star.
1955—(1) Mrs. Caro Brown, Alice (Tex.) Daily Echo; (2) Roland K. Towery, Cuero (Tex.) Record.
1956—(1) Lee Hills, Detroit Free Press; (2) Arthur Daley, New York Times.
1957—(1) Salt Lake Tribune, Salt Lake City, Ut.; (2) Wallace Turner and William Lambert, Portland Oregonian.
1958—(1) Fargo, (N.D.) Forum; (2) George Beveridge, Evening Star, Washington, D.C.
1959—(1) Mary Lou Werner, Washington Evening Star; (2) John Harold Brislin, Scranton (Pa.) Tribune, and The Scrantonian.

1960—(1) Jack Nelson, Atlanta Constitution; (2) Miriam Ottenberg, Washington Evening Star.
1961—(1) Sanche de Gramont, N.Y.Herald Tribune; (2) Edgar May, Buffalo Evening News.
1962—(1) Robert D.Mullins, Deseret News, Salt Lake City; (2) George Bliss, Chicago Tribune.
1963—(1) Shared by Sylvan Fox, William Longgood, and Anthony Shannon, N.Y.World-Telegram & Sun; (2) Oscar Griffin, Jr., Pecos (Tex.) Independent and Enterprise.
1964—(1) Norman C.Miller, Wall Street Journal; (2) Shared by James V. Magee, Albert V. Gaudiosi, and Frederick A. Meyer, Philadelphia Bulletin.
1965—(1) Melvin H.Ruder, Hungry Horse News (Columbia Falls, Mon.); (2) Gene Goltz, Houston Post.
1966—(1) Los Angeles Times Staff; (2) John A. Frasca, Tampa (Fla.) Tribune.
1967—(1) Robert V.Cox, Chambersburg (Pa.) Public Opinion; (2) Gene Miller, Miami Herald.
1968—Detroit Free Press Staff; (2) J. Anthony Lukas, N.Y. Times.
1969—(1) John Fetterman, Louisville Courier-Journal and Times; (2) Albert L.Delugach, St.Louis Globe Democrat, and Denny Walsh, Life.
1970—(1) Thomas Fitzpatrick, Chicago Sun-Times; (2) Harold Eugene Martin, Montgomery Advertiser & Alabama Journal.
1971—(1) Akron Beacon Journal Staff, (2) William Hugh Jones, Chicago Tribune.
1972—(1) Richard Cooper and John Machacek, Rochester Times-Union; (2) Timothy Leland, Gerard M. O'Neill, Stephen A. Kurkjian and Anne De Santis, Boston Globe.
1973—(1) Chicago Tribune; (2) Sun Newspapers of Omaha.
1974—(1) Hugh F. Hough, Arthur M. Petacque, Chicago Sun-Times; (2) William Sherman, N.Y. Daily News.
1975—(1) Xenia (Oh.) Daily Gazette; (2) Indianapolis Star.
1976—(1) Gene Miller, Miami Herald; (2) Chicago Tribune.
1977—(1) Margo Huston, Milwaukee Journal; (2) Acel Moore, Wendell Rawls Jr., Philadelphia Inquirer.
1978—(1) Richard Whitt, Louisville Courier-Journal; (2) Anthony R. Dolan, Stamford (Conn.) Advocate.
1979—(1) San Diego (Cal.) Evening Tribune; (2) Gilbert M. Gaul, Elliot G.Jaspin, Pottsville (Pa.) Republican.
1980—(1) Philadelphia Inquirer; (2) Stephen A. Kurkjian, Alexander B.Hawes Jr., Nils Bruzelius, Joan Vennochi, Robert M. Porterfield, Boston Globe.
1981—(1) Longview (Wash.) Daily News staff; (2) Clark Hallas and Robert B. Lowe, Arizona Daily Star.
1982—(1) Kansas City Star, Kansas City Times; (2) Paul Henderson, Seattle Times.
1983—(1) Fort Wayne (Ind.) News-Sentinel; (2) Loretta Tofani, Washington Post.
1984—(1) Newsday (N.Y.); (2) Boston Globe.
1985—(1) Thomas Turcol, Virginian-Pilot and Ledger-Star, Norfolk, Va.; (2) William K.Marimow, Philadelphia Inquirer; Lucy Morgan & Jack Reed, St. Petersburg (Fla.) Times.
1986—(1) Edna Buchanan, Miami Herald; (2) Jeffrey A. Marx & Michael M. York, Lexington (Ky.) Herald-Leader.
1987—(1) Akron Beacon Journal; (2) Daniel R. Biddle, H.G. Bissinger, Fredric N. Tulsky, Philadelphia Inquirer; John Woestendiek, Philadelphia Inquirer.
1988—(1) Alabama Journal; Lawrence (Mass.) Eagle-Tribune; (2) Walt Bogdanich, Wall Street Journal.
1989—(1) Louisville Courier-Journal; (2) Bill Dedman, Atlanta Journal and Constitution.

Criticism or Commentary

(1) Criticism; (2) Commentary

1970—(1) Ada Louise Huxtable, N.Y. Times; (2) Marquis W. Childs, St.Louis Post-Dispatch.
1971—(1) Harold C.Schonberg, N.Y. Times; (2) William A. Caldwell, The Record, Hackensack, N.J.
1972—(1) Frank Peters Jr., St. Louis Post-Dispatch; (2) Mike Royko, Chicago Daily News.
1973—(1) Ronald Powers, Chicago Sun-Times; (2) David S. Broder, Washington Post.
1974—(1) Emily Genauer, Newsday, (N.Y.); (2) Edwin A. Roberts, Jr., National Observer.
1975—(1) Roger Ebert, Chicago Sun Times; (2) Mary McGrory, Washington Star.
1976—(1) Alan M.Kriegsman, Washington Post; (2) Walter W. (Red) Smith, N.Y. Times.
1977—(1) William McPherson, Washington Post; (2) George F. Will, Wash. Post Writers Group.
1978—(1) Walter Kerr, New York Times; (2) William Safire, New York Times.
1979—(1) Paul Gapp, Chicago Tribune; (2) Russell Baker, New York Times.
1980—(1) William A. Henry III, Boston Globe; (2) Ellen Goodman, Boston Globe.
1981—(1) Jonathan Yardley, Washington Star; (2) Dave Ander-

son, New York Times.
1982—(1) Martin Bernheimer, Los Angeles Times; (2) Art Buchwald, Los Angeles Times Syndicate.
1983—(1) Manuela Hoelterhoff, Wall St. Journal; (2) Claude Sitton, Raleigh (N.C.) News & Observer.
1984—Paul Goldberger, New York Times; (2) Vermont Royster, Wall St. Journal
1985—(1) Howard Rosenberg, Los Angeles Times; (2) Murray Kempton, Newsday (N.Y.).
1986—(1) Donal J. Henahan, New York Times; (2) Jimmy Breslin, N.Y. Daily News.
1987—(1) Richard Eder, Los Angeles Times; (2) Charles Krauthammer, Washington Post.
1988—(1) Tom Shales, Washington Post; (2) Dave Barry, Miami Herald.
1989—(1) Michael Skube, News and Observer, Raleigh, N.C.; (2) Clarence Page, Chicago Tribune.

National Reporting

1942—Louis Stark, New York Times.
1944—Dewey L. Fleming, Baltimore Sun.
1945—James B. Reston, New York Times.
1946—Edward A. Harris, St. Louis Post-Dispatch.
1947—Edward T. Folliard, Washington Post.
1948—Bert Andrews, New York Herald Tribune; Nat S. Finney, Minneapolis Tribune.
1949—Charles P. Trussell, New York Times.
1950—Edwin O. Guthman, Seattle Times.
1952—Anthony Leviero, New York Times.
1953—Don Whitehead, Associated Press.
1954—Richard Wilson, Des Moines Register.
1955—Anthony Lewis, Washington Daily News.
1956—Charles L. Bartlett, Chattanooga Times.
1957—James Reston, New York Times.
1958—Relman Morin, AP; Clark Mollenhoff, Des Moines Register & Tribune.
1959—Howard Van Smith, Miami (Fla.) News.
1960—Vance Trimble, Scripps-Howard, Washington, D.C.
1961—Edward R. Cony, Wall Street Journal.
1962—Nathan G. Caldwell and Gene S. Graham, Nashville Tennessean.
1963—Anthony Lewis, New York Times.
1964—Merriman Smith, UPI.
1965—Louis M. Kohlmeier, Wall Street Journal.
1966—Haynes Johnson, Washington Evening Star.
1967—Monroe Karmin and Stanley Penn, Wall Street Journal.
1968—Howard James, Christian Science Monitor; Nathan K. Kotz, Des Moines Register.
1969—Robert Cahn, Christian Science Monitor.
1970—William J. Eaton, Chicago Daily News.
1971—Lucinda Franks & Thomas Powers, UPI.
1972—Jack Anderson, United Feature Syndicate.
1973—Robert Boyd and Clark Hoyt, Knight Newspapers.
1974—James R. Polk, Washington Star-News; Jack White, Providence Journal-Bulletin.
1975—Donald L. Barlett and James B. Steele, Philadelphia Inquirer.
1976—James Risser, Des Moines Register.
1977—Walter Mears, Associated Press.
1978—Gaylord D. Shaw, Los Angeles Times.
1979—James Risser, Des Moines Register.
1980—Charles Stafford, Bette Swenson Orsini, St. Petersburg (Fla.) Times.
1981—John M. Crewdson, New York Times.
1982—Rick Atkinson, Kansas City Times.
1983—Boston Globe.
1984—John Noble Wilford, New York Times.
1985—Thomas J. Knudson, Des Moines (Ia.) Register.
1986—Craig Flournoy & George Rodrigue, Dallas Morning News; Arthur Howe, Philadelphia Inquirer.
1987—Miami Herald; and New York Times.
1988—Tim Weiner, Philadelphia Inquirer.
1989—Donald L. Barlett & James B. Steele, Philadelphia Inquirer.

International Reporting

1942—Laurence Edmund Allen, Associated Press.
1943—Ira Wolfert, No. Am. Newspaper Alliance.
1944—Daniel DeLuce, Associated Press.
1945—Mark S. Watson, Baltimore Sun.
1946—Homer W. Bigart, New York Herald Tribune.
1947—Eddy Gilmore, Associated Press.
1948—Paul W. Ward, Baltimore Sun.
1949—Price Day, Baltimore Sun.
1950—Edmund Stevens, Christian Science Monitor.
1951—Keyes Beech and Fred Sparks, Chicago Daily News; Homer Bigart and Marguerite Higgins, New York Herald Tribune;

Relman Morin and Don Whitehead, AP.
1952—John M. Hightower, Associated Press.
1953—Austin C. Wehrwein, Milwaukee Journal.
1954—Jim G. Lucas, Scripps-Howard Newspapers.
1955—Harrison Salisbury, New York Times.
1956—William Randolph Hearst, Jr., Frank Conniff, Hearst Newspapers; Kingsbury Smith, INS.
1957—Russell Jones, United Press.
1958—New York Times.
1959—Joseph Martin and Philip Santora, N.Y. News.
1960—A.M. Rosenthal, New York Times.
1961—Lynn Heinzerling, Associated Press.
1962—Walter Lippmann, N.Y. Herald Tribune Synd.
1963—Hal Hendrix, Miami (Fla.) News.
1964—Malcolm W. Browne, AP; David Halberstam, N.Y. Times.
1965—J.A. Livingston, Philadelphia Bulletin.
1966—Peter Arnett, AP.
1967—R. John Hughes, Christian Science Monitor.
1968—Alfred Friendly, Washington Post.
1969—William Tuohy, L.A. Times.
1970—Seymour M. Hersh, Dispatch News Service.
1971—Jimmie Lee Hoagland, Washington Post.
1972—Peter R. Kann, Wall Street Journal.
1973—Max Frankel, N.Y. Times.
1974—Hedrick Smith, N.Y. Times.
1975—William Mullen and Ovie Carter, Chicago Tribune.
1976—Sydney H. Schanberg, N.Y. Times.
1978—Henry Kamm, N.Y. Times.
1979—Richard Ben Cramer, Philadelphia Inquirer.
1980—Joel Brinkley, Jay Mather, Louisville (Ky.) Courier-Journal.
1981—Shirley Christian, Miami Herald.
1982—John Darnton, New York Times.
1983—Thomas L. Friedman, New York Times; Loren Jenkins, Washington Post.
1984—Karen Elliot House, Wall St. Journal
1985—Josh Friedman, Dennis Bell, Ozler Muhammad, Newsday (N.Y.).
1986—Lewis M. Simons, Pete Carey, Katherine Ellison, San Jose (Calif.) Mercury News.
1987—Michael Parks, Los Angeles Times.
1988—Thomas L. Friedman, N.Y. Times.
1989—Glenn Frankel, Washington Post; Bill Keller, New York Times.

Correspondence

For Washington or foreign correspondence. Category was merged with those in national and international reporting in 1948.
1929—Paul Scott Mowrer, Chicago Daily News.
1930—Leland Stowe, New York Herald Tribune.
1931—H.R. Knickerbocker, Philadelphia Public Ledger and New York Evening Post.
1932—Walter Duranty, New York Times, and Charles G. Ross, St. Louis Post-Dispatch.
1933—Edgar Ansel Mowrer, Chicago Daily News.
1934—Frederick T. Birchall, New York Times.
1935—Arthur Krock, New York Times.
1936—Wilfred C. Barber, Chicago Tribune.
1937—Anne O'Hare McCormick, New York Times.
1938—Arthur Krock, New York Times.
1939—Louis P. Lochner, Associated Press.
1940—Otto D. Tolischus, New York Times.
1941—Bronze plaque to commemorate work of American correspondents on war fronts.
1942—Carlos P. Romulo, Philippines Herald.
1943—Hanson W. Baldwin, New York Times.
1944—Ernest Taylor Pyle, Scripps-Howard Newspaper Alliance.
1945—Harold V. (Hal) Boyle, Associated Press.
1946—Arnaldo Cortesi, New York Times.
1947—Brooks Atkinson, New York Times.

Editorial Writing

1917—New York Tribune.
1918—Louisville (Ky.) Courier-Journal.
1920—Harvey E. Newbranch, Omaha Evening World-Herald.
1922—Frank M. O'Brien, New York Herald.
1923—William Allen White, Emporia Gazette.
1924—Frank Buxton, Boston Herald. Special Prize. Frank I. Cobb, New York World.
1925—Robert Lathan, Charleston (S.C.) News and Courier.
1926—Edward M. Kingsbury, N. Y. Times.
1927—F. Lauriston Bullard, Boston Herald.
1928—Grover C. Hall, Montgomery Advertiser.
1929—Louis Isaac Jaffe, Norfolk Virginian-Pilot.
1931—Chas. Ryckman, Fremont (Neb.) Tribune.
1933—Kansas City (Mo.) Star.
1934—E. P. Chase, Atlantic (Ia.) News Telegraph.

1936—Felix Morley, Washington Post. George B. Parker, Scripps-Howard Newspapers.
1937—John W. Owens, Baltimore Sun.
1938—W.W. Waymack, Des Moines (Ia.) Register and Tribune.
1939—Ronald G. Callvert, Portland Oregonian.
1940—Bart Howard, St. Louis Post-Dispatch.
1941—Reuben Maury, Daily News, N.Y.
1942—Geoffrey Parsons, New York Herald Tribune.
1943—Forrest W. Seymour, Des Moines (Ia.) Register and Tribune.
1944—Henry J. Haskell, Kansas City (Mo.) Star.
1945—George W. Potter, Providence (R.I.) Journal-Bulletin.
1946—Hodding Carter, Greenville (Miss.) Delta Democrat-Times.
1947—William H. Grimes, Wall Street Journal.
1948—Virginius Dabney, Richmond (Va.) Times-Dispatch.
1949—John H. Crider, Boston (Mass.) Herald, Herbert Elliston, Washington Post.
1950—Carl M. Saunders, Jackson (Mich.) Citizen-Patriot.
1951—William H. Fitzpatrick, New Orleans States.
1952—Louis LaCoss, St. Louis Globe Democrat.
1953—Vermont C. Royster, Wall Street Journal.
1954—Don Murray, Boston Herald.
1955—Royce Howes, Detroit Free Press.
1956—Lauren K. Soth, Des Moines (Ia.) Register and Tribune.
1957—Buford Boone, Tuscaloosa (Ala.) News.
1958—Harry S. Ashmore, Arkansas Gazette.
1959—Ralph McGill, Atlanta Constitution.
1960—Lenoir Chambers, Norfolk Virginian-Pilot.
1961—William J. Dorvillier, San Juan (Puerto Rico) Star.
1962—Thomas M. Storke, Santa Barbara (Cal.) News-Press.
1963—Ira B. Harkey, Jr., Pascagoula (Miss.) Chronicle.
1964—Hazel Brannon Smith, Lexington (Miss.) Advertiser.
1965—John R. Harrison, The Gainesville (Fla.) Sun.
1966—Robert Lasch, St. Louis Post-Dispatch.
1967—Eugene C. Patterson, Atlanta Constitution.
1968—John S. Knight, Knight Newspapers.
1969—Paul Greenberg, Pine Bluff (Ark.) Commercial.
1970—Philip L. Geyelin, Washington Post.
1971—Horance G. Davis, Jr., Gainesville (Fla.) Sun.
1972—John Strohmeyer, Bethlehem (Pa.) Globe-Times.
1973—Roger B. Linscott, Berkshire Eagle, Pittsfield, Mass.
1974—F. Gilman Spencer, Trenton (N.J.) Trentonian.
1975—John D. Maurice, Charleston (W. Va.) Daily Mail.
1976—Philip Kerby, Los Angeles Times.
1977—Warren L. Lerude, Foster Church, and Norman F. Cardoza, Reno (Nev.) Evening Gazette and Nevada State Journal.
1978—Meg Greenfield, Washington Post.
1979—Edwin M. Yoder, Washington Star.
1980—Robert L. Bartley, Wall Street Journal.
1982—Jack Rosenthal, New York Times.
1983—Editorial board, Miami Herald.
1984—Albert Scardino, Georgia Gazette.
1985—Richard Aregood, Philadelphia Daily News.
1986—Jack Fuller, Chicago Tribune.
1987—Jonathan Freedman, The Tribune (San Diego).
1988—Jane Healy, Orlando Sentinel.
1989—Lois Wille, Chicago Tribune.

Editorial Cartooning

1922—Rollin Kirby, New York World.
1924—Jay N. Darling, Des Moines Register.
1925—Rollin Kirby, New York World.
1926—D. R. Fitzpatrick, St. Louis Post-Dispatch.
1927—Nelson Harding, Brooklyn Eagle.
1928—Nelson Harding, Brooklyn Eagle.
1929—Rollin Kirby, New York World.
1930—Charles Macauley, Brooklyn Eagle.
1931—Edmund Duffy, Baltimore Sun.
1932—John T. McCutcheon, Chicago Tribune.
1933—H. M. Talburt, Washington Daily News.
1934—Edmund Duffy, Baltimore Sun.
1935—Ross A. Lewis, Milwaukee Journal.
1937—C. D. Batchelor, New York Daily News.
1938—Vaughn Shoemaker, Chicago Daily News.
1939—Charles G. Werner, Daily Oklahoman.
1940—Edmund Duffy, Baltimore Sun.
1941—Jacob Burck, Chicago Times.
1942—Herbert L. Block, Newspaper Enterprise Assn.
1943—Jay N. Darling, Des Moines Register.
1944—Clifford K. Berryman, Washington Star.
1945—Bill Mauldin, United Feature Syndicate.
1946—Bruce Alexander Russell, Los Angeles Times.
1947—Vaughn Shoemaker, Chicago Daily News.
1948—Reuben L. (Rube) Goldberg, N. Y. Sun.
1949—Lute Pease, Newark (N.J.) Evening News.
1950—James T. Berryman, Washington Star.

1951—Reginald W. Manning, Arizona Republic.
1952—Fred L. Packer, New York Mirror.
1953—Edward D. Kuekes, Cleveland Plain Dealer.
1954—Herbert L. Block, Washington Post & Times-Herald.
1955—Daniel R. Fitzpatrick, St. Louis Post-Dispatch.
1956—Robert York, Louisville (Ky.) Times.
1957—Tom Little, Nashville Tennessean.
1958—Bruce M. Shanks, Buffalo Evening News.
1959—Bill Mauldin, St. Louis Post-Dispatch.
1961—Carey Orr, Chicago Tribune.
1962—Edmund S. Valtman, Hartford Times.
1963—Frank Miller, Des Moines Register.
1964—Paul Conrad, Denver Post.
1966—Don Wright, Miami News.
1967—Patrick B. Oliphant, Denver Post.
1968—Eugene Gray Payne, Charlotte Observer.
1969—John Fischetti, Chicago Daily News.
1970—Thomas F. Darcy, Newsday.
1971—Paul Conrad, L. A. Times.
1972—Jeffrey K. MacNelly, Richmond News-Leader.
1974—Paul Szep, Boston Globe.
1975—Garry Trudeau, Universal Press Syndicate.
1976—Tony Auth, Philadelphia Inquirer.
1977—Paul Szep, Boston Globe.
1978—Jeffrey K. MacNelly, Richmond News Leader.
1979—Herbert L. Block, Washington Post.
1980—Don Wright, Miami (Fla.) News.
1981—Mike Peters, Dayton (Oh.) Daily News.
1982—Ben Sargent, Austin American-Statesman.
1983—Richard Lochner, Chicago Tribune.
1984—Paul Conrad, Los Angeles Times.
1985—Jeffrey K. MacNelly, Chicago Tribune.
1986—Jules Feiffer, Village Voice (N.Y. City)
1987—Berke Breathed, Washington Post.
1988—Doug Marlette, Atlanta Constitution, Charlotte Observer.
1989—Jack Higgins, Chicago Sun-Times.

Spot News Photography

1942—Milton Brooks, Detroit News.
1943—Frank Noel, Associated Press.
1944—Frank Filan, AP; Earl L. Bunker, Omaha World-Herald.
1945—Joe Rosenthal, Associated Press, for photograph of planting American flag on Iwo Jima.
1947—Arnold Hardy, amateur, Atlanta, Ga.
1948—Frank Cushing, Boston Traveler.
1949—Nathaniel Fein, New York Herald Tribune.
1950—Bill Crouch, Oakland (Cal.) Tribune.
1951—Max Desfor, Associated Press.
1952—John Robinson and Don Ultang, Des Moines Register and Tribune.
1953—William M. Gallagher, Flint (Mich.) Journal.
1954—Mrs. Walter M. Schau, amateur.
1955—John L. Gaunt, Jr., Los Angeles Times.
1956—New York Daily News.
1957—Harry A. Trask, Boston Traveler.
1958—William C. Beall, Washington Daily News.
1959—William Seaman, Minneapolis Star.
1960—Andrew Lopez, UPI.
1961—Yasushi Nagao, Mainichi Newspapers, Tokyo.
1962—Paul Vathis, Associated Press.
1963—Hector Rondon, La Republica, Caracas, Venezuela.
1964—Robert H. Jackson, Dallas Times-Herald.
1965—Horst Faas, Associated Press.
1966—Kyoichi Sawada, UPI.
1967—Jack R. Thornell, Associated Press.
1968—Rocco Morabito, Jacksonville Journal.
1969—Edward Adams, AP.
1970—Steve Starr, AP.
1971—John Paul Filo, Valley Daily News & Daily Dispatch of Tarentum & New Kensington, Pa.
1972—Horst Faas and Michel Laurent, AP.
1973—Huynh Cong Ut, AP.
1974—Anthony K. Roberts, AP.
1975—Gerald H. Gay, Seattle Times.
1976—Stanley Forman, Boston Herald American.
1977—Neal Ulevich, Associated Press; Stanley Forman, Boston Herald American.
1978—John H. Blair, UPI.
1979—Thomas J. Kelly III, Pottstown (Pa.) Mercury.
1980—UPI.
1981—Larry C. Price, Ft. Worth (Tex.) Star-Telegram.
1982—Ron Edmonds, Associated Press.
1983—Bill Foley, AP.
1984—Stan Grossfeld, Boston Globe.
1985—The Register, Santa Ana, Calif.
1986—Carol Guzy & Michel duCille, Miami Herald.
1987—Kim Komenich, San Francisco Examiner.

1988—Scott Shaw, Odessa (Tex.) American.
1989—Ron Olshwanger, St. Louis Post-Dispatch.

Feature Photography

1968—Toshio Sakai, UPI.
1969—Moneta Sleet Jr., Ebony.
1970—Dallas Kinney, Palm Beach Post.
1971—Jack Dykinga, Chicago Sun-Times.
1972—Dave Kennerly, UPI.
1973—Brian Lanker, Topeka Capitol-Journal.
1974—Slava Veder, AP.
1975—Matthew Lewis, Washington Post.
1976—Louisville Courier-Journal and Louisville Times.
1977—Robin Hood, Chattanooga News-Free Press.
1978—J. Ross Baughman, AP.
1979—Staff Photographers, Boston Herald American.
1980—Erwin H. Hagler, Dallas Times-Herald.
1981—Taro M. Yamasaki, Detroit Free Press.
1982—John H. White, Chicago Sun-Times.
1983—James B. Dickman, Dallas Times-Herald.
1984—Anthony Suad, Denver Post.
1985—Stan Grossfeld, Boston Globe; Larry C. Price, Philadelphia Inquirer.
1986—Tom Gralish, Philadelphia Inquirer.
1987—David Peterson, Des Moines Register.
1988—Michel duCille, Miami Herald.
1989—Manny Crisostomo, Detroit Free Press.

Special Citation

1938—Edmonton (Alberta) Journal, bronze plaque.
1941—New York Times.
1944—Byron Price and Mrs. William Allen White. Also to Richard Rodgers and Oscar Hammerstein 2d, for musical, Oklahoma!
1945—Press cartographers for war maps.
1947—(Pulitzer centennial year.) Columbia Univ. and the Graduate School of Journalism, and St. Louis Post-Dispatch.
1948—Dr. Frank Diehl Fackenthal.
1951—Cyrus L. Sulzberger, New York Times.
1952—Max Kase, New York Journal-American, Kansas City Star.
1953—The New York Times; Lester Markel.
1957—Kenneth Roberts, for his historical novels.
1958—Walter Lippmann, New York Herald Tribune.
1960—Garrett Mattingly, for The Armada.

1961—American Heritage Picture History of the Civil War.
1964—The Gannett Newspapers.
1973—James T. Flexner, for biography of George Washington.
1976—John Hohenberg, for services to American journalism.
1977—Alex Haley, for Roots.
1978—Richard Lee Strout, Christian Science Monitor and New Republic.
   —E.B. White.
1984—Theodore Geisel ("Dr. Seuss").
1985—William Schuman, composer, educational leader.
1987—Joseph Pulitzer Jr.

Feature Writing

1979—Jon D. Franklin, Baltimore Evening Sun.
1980—Madeleine Blais, Miami Herald Tropic Magazine. Janet Cooke, Washington Post.
1981—Teresa Carpenter, Village Voice, New York City.
1982—Saul Pett, Associated Press.
1984—Peter M. Rinearson, Seattle Times.
1985—Alice Steinbach, Baltimore Sun.
1986—John Camp, St. Paul Pioneer Press & Dispatch
1987—Steve Twomey, Philadelphia Inquirer.
1988—Jacqui Banaszynski, St. Paul Pioneer Press Dispatch.
1989—David Zucchino, Philadelphia Inquirer.

Explanatory Journalism

1985—Jon Franklin, Baltimore Evening Sun.
1986—New York Times Staff.
1987—Jeff Lyon & Peter Gorner, Chicago Tribune.
1988—Daniel Hertzberg, James B. Stewart, Wall Street Journal.
1989—David Hanners, William Snyder, Karen Blessen, Dallas Morning News.

Specialized Reporting

1985—Randall Savage, Jackie Crosby, Macon (Ga.) Telegraph and News.
1986—Andrew Schneider & Mary Pat Flaherty, Pittsburgh Press.
1987—Alex S. Jones, New York Times.
1988—Dean Baquet, William Gaines, Ann Marie Lipinski, Chicago Tribune.
1989—Edward Humes, Orange County (Calif.) Register.

Letters

Fiction

For fiction in book form by an American author, preferably dealing with American life.
1918—Ernest Poole, His Family.
1919—Booth Tarkington, The Magnificent Ambersons.
1921—Edith Wharton, The Age of Innocence.
1922—Booth Tarkington, Alice Adams.
1923—Willa Cather, One of Ours.
1924—Margaret Wilson, The Able McLaughlins.
1925—Edna Ferber, So Big.
1926—Sinclair Lewis, Arrowsmith. (Refused prize.)
1927—Louis Bromfield, Early Autumn.
1928—Thornton Wilder, Bridge of San Luis Rey.
1929—Julia M. Peterkin, Scarlet Sister Mary.
1930—Oliver LaFarge, Laughing Boy.
1931—Margaret Ayer Barnes, Years of Grace.
1932—Pearl S. Buck, The Good Earth.
1933—T. S. Stribling, The Store.
1934—Caroline Miller, Lamb in His Bosom.
1935—Josephine W. Johnson, Now in November.
1936—Harold L. Davis, Honey in the Horn.
1937—Margaret Mitchell, Gone with the Wind.
1938—John P. Marquand, The Late George Apley.
1939—Marjorie Kinnan Rawlings, The Yearling.
1940—John Steinbeck, The Grapes of Wrath.
1942—Ellen Glasgow, In This Our Life.
1943—Upton Sinclair, Dragon's Teeth.
1944—Martin Flavin, Journey in the Dark.
1945—John Hersey, A Bell for Adano.
1947—Robert Penn Warren, All the King's Men.
1948—James A Michener, Tales of the South Pacific.
1949—James Gould Cozzens, Guard of Honor.
1950—A. B. Guthrie Jr., The Way West.
1951—Conrad Richter, The Town.
1952—Herman Wouk, The Caine Mutiny.
1953—Ernest Hemingway, The Old Man and the Sea.
1955—William Faulkner, A Fable.
1956—MacKinlay Kantor, Andersonville.

1958—James Agee, A Death in the Family.
1959—Robert Lewis Taylor, The Travels of Jaimie McPheeters.
1960—Allen Drury, Advise and Consent.
1961—Harper Lee, To Kill a Mockingbird.
1962—Edwin O'Connor, The Edge of Sadness.
1963—William Faulkner, The Reivers.
1965—Shirley Ann Grau, The Keepers of the House.
1966—Katherine Anne Porter, Collected Stories of Katherine Anne Porter.
1967—Bernard Malamud, The Fixer.
1968—William Styron, The Confessions of Nat Turner.
1969—N. Scott Momaday, House Made of Dawn.
1970—Jean Stafford, Collected Stories.
1972—Wallace Stegner, Angle of Repose.
1973—Eudora Welty, The Optimist's Daughter.
1975—Michael Shaara, The Killer Angels.
1976—Saul Bellow, Humboldt's Gift.
1978—James Alan McPherson, Elbow Room.
1979—John Cheever, The Stories of John Cheever.
1980—Norman Mailer, The Executioner's Song.
1981—John Kennedy Toole, A Confederacy of Dunces.
1982—John Updike, Rabbit is Rich.
1983—Alice Walker, The Color Purple.
1984—William Kennedy, Ironweed.
1985—Alison Lurie, Foreign Affairs.
1986—Larry McMurtry, Lonesome Dove.
1987—Peter Taylor, A Summons to Memphis.
1988—Toni Morrison, Beloved.
1989—Anne Tyler, Breathing Lessons.

Drama

For an American play, preferably original and dealing with American life.
1918—Jesse Lynch Williams, Why Marry?
1920—Eugene O'Neill, Beyond the Horizon.
1921—Zona Gale, Miss Lulu Bett.
1922—Eugene O'Neill, Anna Christie.

1923—Owen Davis, Icebound.
1924—Hatcher Hughes, Hell-Bent for Heaven.
1925—Sidney Howard, They Knew What They Wanted.
1926—George Kelly, Craig's Wife.
1927—Paul Green, In Abraham's Bosom.
1928—Eugene O'Neill, Strange Interlude.
1929—Elmer Rice, Street Scene.
1930—Marc Connelly, The Green Pastures.
1931—Susan Glaspell, Alison's House.
1932—George S. Kaufman, Morrie Ryskind and Ira Gershwin, Of Thee I Sing.
1933—Maxwell Anderson, Both Your Houses.
1934—Sidney Kingsley, Men in White.
1935—Zoe Akins, The Old Maid.
1936—Robert E. Sherwood, Idiot's Delight.
1937—George S. Kaufman and Moss Hart, You Can't Take It With You.
1938—Thornton Wilder, Our Town.
1939—Robert E. Sherwood, Abe Lincoln in Illinois.
1940—William Saroyan, The Time of Your Life.
1941—Robert E. Sherwood, There Shall Be No Night.
1943—Thornton Wilder, The Skin of Our Teeth.
1945—Mary Chase, Harvey.
1946—Russel Crouse and Howard Lindsay, State of the Union.
1948—Tennessee Williams, A Streetcar Named Desire.
1949—Arthur Miller, Death of a Salesman.
1950—Richard Rodgers, Oscar Hammerstein 2d, and Joshua Logan, South Pacific.
1952—Joseph Kramm, The Shrike.
1953—William Inge, Picnic.
1954—John Patrick, Teahouse of the August Moon.
1955—Tennessee Williams, Cat on a Hot Tin Roof.
1956—Frances Goodrich and Albert Hackett, The Diary of Anne Frank.
1957—Eugene O'Neill, Long Day's Journey Into Night.
1958—Ketti Frings, Look Homeward, Angel.
1959—Archibald MacLeish, J. B.
1960—George Abbott, Jerome Weidman, Sheldon Harnick and Jerry Bock, Fiorello.
1961—Tad Mosel, All the Way Home.
1962—Frank Loesser and Abe Burrows, How To Succeed In Business Without Really Trying.
1965—Frank D. Gilroy, The Subject Was Roses.
1967—Edward Albee, A Delicate Balance.
1969—Howard Sackler, The Great White Hope.
1970—Charles Gordone, No Place to Be Somebody.
1971—Paul Zindel, The Effect of Gamma Rays on Man-in-the-Moon Marigolds.
1973—Jason Miller, That Championship Season.
1975—Edward Albee, Seascape.
1976—Michael Bennett, James Kirkwood, Nicholas Dante, Marvin Hamlisch, Edward Kleban, A Chorus Line.
1977—Michael Cristofer, The Shadow Box.
1978—Donald L. Coburn, The Gin Game.
1979—Sam Shepard, Buried Child.
1980—Lanford Wilson, Talley's Folly.
1981—Beth Henley, Crimes of the Heart.
1982—Charles Fuller, A Soldier's Play.
1983—Marsha Norman, 'night, Mother.
1984—David Mamet, Glengarry Glen Ross.
1985—Stephen Sondheim, James Lapine, Sunday in the Park with George.
1987—August Wilson, Fences.
1988—Alfred Uhry, Driving Miss Daisy.
1989—Wendy Wasserstein, The Heidi Chronicles.

History

For a book on the history of the United States.
1917—J. J. Jusserand, With Americans of Past and Present Days.
1918—James Ford Rhodes, History of the Civil War.
1920—Justin H. Smith, The War with Mexico.
1921—William Sowden Sims, The Victory at Sea.
1922—James Truslow Adams, The Founding of New England.
1923—Charles Warren, The Supreme Court in United States History.
1924—Charles Howard McIlwain, The American Revolution: A Constitutional Interpretation.
1925—Frederick L. Paxton, A History of the American Frontier.
1926—Edward Channing, A History of the U.S.
1927—Samuel Flag Bemis, Pinckney's Treaty.
1928—Vernon Louis Parrington, Main Currents in American Thought.
1929—Fred A. Shannon, The Organization and Administration of the Union Army, 1861-65.
1930—Claude H. Van Tyne, The War of Independence.
1931—Bernadotte E. Schmitt, The Coming of the War, 1914.
1932—Gen. John J. Pershing, My Experiences in the World War.

1933—Frederick J. Turner, The Significance of Sections in American History.
1934—Herbert Agar, The People's Choice.
1935—Charles McLean Andrews, The Colonial Period of American History.
1936—Andrew C. McLaughlin, The Constitutional History of the United States.
1937—Van Wyck Brooks, The Flowering of New England.
1938—Paul Herman Buck, The Road to Reunion, 1865-1900.
1939—Frank Luther Mott, A History of American Magazines.
1940—Carl Sandburg, Abraham Lincoln: The War Years.
1941—Marcus Lee Hansen, The Atlantic Migration, 1607-1860.
1942—Margaret Leech, Reveille in Washington.
1943—Esther Forbes, Paul Revere and the World He Lived In.
1944—Merle Catton, The Growth of American Thought.
1945—Stephen Bonsal, Unfinished Business.
1946—Arthur M. Schlesinger Jr., The Age of Jackson.
1947—James Phinney Baxter 3d, Scientists Against Time.
1948—Bernard De Voto, Across the Wide Missouri.
1949—Roy F. Nichols, The Disruption of American Democracy.
1950—O. W. Larkin, Art and Life in America.
1951—R. Carlyle Buley, The Old Northwest: Pioneer Period 1815-1840.
1952—Oscar Handlin, The Uprooted.
1953—George Dangerfield, The Era of Good Feelings.
1954—Bruce Catton, A Stillness at Appomattox.
1955—Paul Horgan, Great River: The Rio Grande in North American History.
1956—Richard Hofstadter, The Age of Reform.
1957—George F. Kennan, Russia Leaves the War.
1958—Bray Hammond, Banks and Politics in America—From the Revolution to the Civil War.
1959—Leonard D. White and Jean Schneider, The Republican Era; 1869-1901.
1960—Margaret Leech, In the Days of McKinley.
1961—Herbert Feis, Between War and Peace: The Potsdam Conference.
1962—Lawrence H. Gibson, The Triumphant Empire: Thunderclouds Gather in the West.
1963—Constance McLaughlin Green, Washington: Village and Capital, 1800-1878.
1964—Sumner Chilton Powell, Puritan Village: The Formation of A New England Town.
1965—Irwin Unger, The Greenback Era.
1966—Perry Miller, Life of the Mind in America.
1967—William H. Goetzmann, Exploration and Empire: the Explorer and Scientist in the Winning of the American West.
1968—Bernard Bailyn, The Ideological Origins of the American Revolution.
1969—Leonard W. Levy, Origin of the Fifth Amendment.
1970—Dean Acheson, Present at the Creation: My Years in the State Department.
1971—James McGregor Burns, Roosevelt: The Soldier of Freedom.
1972—Carl N. Degler, Neither Black Nor White.
1973—Michael Kammen, People of Paradox: An Inquiry Concerning the Origins of American Civilization.
1974—Daniel J. Boorstin, The Americans: The Democratic Experience.
1975—Dumas Malone, Jefferson and His Time.
1976—Paul Horgan, Lamy of Santa Fe.
1977—David M. Potter, The Impending Crisis.
1978—Alfred D. Chandler, Jr., The Visible Hand: The Managerial Revolution in American Business.
1979—Don E. Fehrenbacher, The Dred Scott Case: Its Significance in American Law and Politics.
1980—Leon F. Litwack, Been in the Storm So Long.
1981—Lawrence A. Cremin, American Education: The National Experience, 1783-1876.
1982—C. Vann Woodward, ed., Mary Chestnut's Civil War.
1983—Rhys L. Issac, The Transformation of Virginia, 1740-1790.
1985—Thomas K. McCraw, Prophets of Regulation.
1986—Walter A. McDougall, . . . The Heavens and the Earth.
1987—Bernard Bailyn, Voyagers to the West.
1988—Robert V. Bruce, The Launching of Modern American Science 1846-1876.
1989—Taylor Branch, Parting the Waters: America in the King Years, 1954-63; and James M. McPherson, Battle Cry of Freedom: The Civil War Era.

Biography or Autobiography

For a distinguished biography or autobiography by an American author.
1917—Laura E. Richards and Maude Howe Elliott, assisted by Florence Howe Hall, Julia Ward Howe.
1918—William Cabell Bruce, Benjamin Franklin, Self-Revealed.
1919—Henry Adams, The Education of Henry Adams.
1920—Albert J. Beveridge, The Life of John Marshall.

1921—Edward Bok, The Americanization of Edward Bok.
1922—Hamlin Garland, A Daughter of the Middle Border.
1923—Burton J. Hendrick, The Life and Letters of Walter H. Page.
1924—Michael Pupin, From Immigrant to Inventor.
1925—M. A. DeWolfe Howe, Barrett Wendell and His Letters.
1926—Harvey Cushing, Life of Sir William Osler.
1927—Emory Holloway, Whitman: An Interpretation in Narrative.

1928—Charles Edward Russell, The American Orchestra and Theodore Thomas.
1929—Burton J. Hendrick, The Training of an American: The Earlier Life and Letters of Walter H. Page.
1930—Marquis James, The Raven (Sam Houston).
1931—Henry James, Charles W. Eliot.
1932—Henry F. Pringle, Theodore Roosevelt.
1933—Allan Nevins, Grover Cleveland.
1934—Tyler Dennett, John Hay.
1935—Douglas Southall Freeman, R. E. Lee.
1936—Ralph Barton Perry, The Thought and Character of William James.
1937—Allan Nevins, Hamilton Fish: The Inner History of the Grant Administration.
1938—Divided between Odell Shepard, Pedlar's Progress; Marquis James, Andrew Jackson.
1939—Carl Van Doren, Benjamin Franklin.
1940—Ray Stannard Baker, Woodrow Wilson, Life and Letters.
1941—Ola Elizabeth Winslow, Jonathan Edwards.
1942—Forrest Wilson, Crusader in Crinoline.
1943—Samuel Eliot Morison, Admiral of the Ocean Sea (Columbus).
1944—Carleton Mabee, The American Leonardo: The Life of Samuel F. B. Morse.
1945—Russell Blaine Nye, George Bancroft; Brahmin Rebel.
1946—Linny Marsh Wolfe, Son of the Wilderness.
1947—William Allen White, The Autobiography of William Allen White.
1948—Margaret Clapp, Forgotten First Citizen: John Bigelow.
1949—Robert E. Sherwood, Roosevelt and Hopkins.
1950—Samuel Flag Bemis, John Quincy Adams and the Foundations of American Foreign Policy.
1951—Margaret Louise Colt, John C. Calhoun: American Portrait.
1952—Merlo J. Pusey, Charles Evans Hughes.
1953—David J. Mays, Edmund Pendleton, 1721-1803.
1954—Charles A. Lindbergh, The Spirit of St. Louis.
1955—William S. White, The Taft Story.
1956—Talbot F. Hamlin, Benjamin Henry Latrobe.
1957—John F. Kennedy, Profiles in Courage.
1958—Douglas Southall Freeman (decd. 1953), George Washington, Vols. I-VI; John Alexander Carroll and Mary Wells Ashworth, Vol. VII.
1959—Arthur Walworth, Woodrow Wilson: American Prophet.
1960—Samuel Eliot Morison, John Paul Jones.
1961—David Donald, Charles Sumner and The Coming of the Civil War.
1963—Leon Edel, Henry James: Vol. II. The Conquest of London, 1870-1881; Vol. III, The Middle Years, 1881-1895.
1964—Walter Jackson Bate, John Keats.
1965—Ernest Samuels, Henry Adams.
1966—Arthur M. Schlesinger Jr., A Thousand Days.
1967—Justin Kaplan, Mr. Clemens and Mark Twain.
1968—George F. Kennan, Memoirs (1925-1950).
1969—B. L. Reid, The Man from New York: John Quinn and his Friends.
1970—T. Harry Williams, Huey Long.
1971—Lawrence Thompson, Robert Frost: The Years of Triumph, 1915-1938.
1972—Joseph P. Lash, Eleanor and Franklin.
1973—W. A. Swanberg, Luce and His Empire.
1974—Louis Sheaffer, O'Neill, Son and Artist.
1975—Robert A. Caro, The Power Broker: Robert Moses and the Fall of New York.
1976—R.W.B. Lewis, Edith Wharton: A Biography.
1977—John E. Mack, A Prince of Our Disorder, The Life of T.E. Lawrence.
1978—Walter Jackson Bate, Samuel Johnson.
1979—Leonard Baker, Days of Sorrow and Pain: Leo Baeck and the Berlin Jews.
1980—Edmund Morris, The Rise of Theodore Roosevelt.
1981—Robert K. Massie, Peter the Great: His Life and World.
1982—William S. McFeely, Grant: A Biography.
1983—Russell Baker, Growing Up.
1984—Louis R. Harlan, Booker T. Washington.
1985—Kenneth Silverman, The Life and Times of Cotton Mather.
1986—Elizabeth Frank, Louise Bogan: A Portrait.
1987—David J. Garrow, Bearing the Cross: Martin Luther King Jr. and the Southern Christian Leadership Conference.

1988—David Herbert Donald, Look Homeward: A Life of Thomas Wolfe.
1989—Richard Ellmann, Oscar Wilde.

American Poetry

Before this prize was established in 1922, awards were made from gifts provided by the Poetry Society: 1918—Love Songs, by Sara Teasdale. 1919—Old Road to Paradise, by Margaret Widemer; Corn Huskers, by Carl Sandburg.
1922—Edwin Arlington Robinson, Collected Poems.
1923—Edna St. Vincent Millay, The Ballad of the Harp-Weaver; A Few Figs from Thistles; Eight Sonnets in American Poetry, 1922; A Miscellany.
1924—Robert Frost, New Hampshire: A Poem with Notes and Grace Notes.
1925—Edwin Arlington Robinson, The Man Who Died Twice.
1926—Amy Lowell, What's O'Clock.
1927—Leonora Speyer, Fiddler's Farewell.
1928—Edwin Arlington Robinson, Tristram.
1929—Stephen Vincent Benet, John Brown's Body.
1930—Conrad Aiken, Selected Poems.
1931—Robert Frost, Collected Poems.
1932—George Dillon, The Flowering Stone.
1933—Archibald MacLeish, Conquistador.
1934—Robert Hillyer, Collected Verse.
1935—Audrey Wurdemann, Bright Ambush.
1936—Robert P. Tristram Coffin, Strange Holiness.
1937—Robert Frost, A Further Range.
1938—Marya Zaturenska, Cold Morning Sky.
1939—John Gould Fletcher, Selected Poems.
1940—Mark Van Doren, Collected Poems.
1941—Leonard Bacon, Sunderland Capture.
1942—William Rose Benet, The Dust Which Is God.
1943—Robert Frost, A Witness Tree.
1944—Stephen Vincent Benet, Western Star.
1945—Karl Shapiro, V-Letter and Other Poems.
1947—Robert Lowell, Lord Weary's Castle.
1948—W. H. Auden, The Age of Anxiety.
1949—Peter Viereck, Terror and Decorum.
1950—Gwendolyn Brooks, Annie Allen.
1951—Carl Sandburg, Complete Poems.
1952—Marianne Moore, Collected Poems.
1953—Archibald MacLeish, Collected Poems.
1954—Theodore Roethke, The Waking.
1955—Wallace Stevens, Collected Poems.
1956—Elizabeth Bishop, Poems, North and South.
1957—Richard Wilbur, Things of This World.
1958—Robert Penn Warren, Promises: Poems 1954-1956.
1959—Stanley Kunitz, Selected Poems 1928-1958.
1960—W. D. Snodgrass, Heart's Needle.
1961—Phyllis McGinley, Times Three: Selected Verse from Three Decades.
1962—Alan Dugan, Poems.
1963—William Carlos Williams, Pictures From Breughel.
1964—Louis Simpson, At the End of the Open Road.
1965—John Berryman, 77 Dream Songs.
1966—Richard Eberhart, Selected Poems.
1967—Anne Sexton, Live or Die.
1968—Anthony Hecht, The Hard Hours.
1969—George Oppen, Of Being Numerous.
1970—Richard Howard, Untitled Subjects.
1971—William S. Merwin, The Carrier of Ladders.
1972—James Wright, Collected Poems.
1973—Maxine Winokur Kumin, Up Country.
1975—Gary Snyder, Turtle Island.
1976—John Ashbery, Self-Portrait in a Convex Mirror.
1977—James Merrill, Divine Comedies.
1978—Howard Nemerov, Collected Poems.
1979—Robert Penn Warren, Now and Then: Poems 1976-1978.
1980—Donald Justice, Selected Poems.
1981—James Schuyler, The Morning of the Poem.
1982—Sylvia Plath, The Collected Poems.
1983—Galway Kinnell, Selected Poems.
1984—Mary Oliver, American Primitive.
1985—Carolyn Kizer, Yin.
1986—Henry Taylor, The Flying Change.
1987—Rita Dove, Thomas and Beulah.
1988—William Meredith, Partial Accounts: New and Selected Poems.
1989—Richard Wilbur, New and Collected Poems.

General Non-Fiction

1962—Theodore H. White, The Making of the President 1960.
1963—Barbara W. Tuchman, The Guns of August.
1964—Richard Hofstadter, Anti-Intellectualism in American Life.
1965—Howard Mumford Jones, O Strange New World.
1966—Edwin Way Teale, Wandering Through Winter.

1967—David Brion Davis, The Problem of Slavery in Western Culture.
1968—Will and Ariel Durant, Rousseau and Revolution.
1969—Norman Mailer, The Armies of the Night; and Rene Jules Dubos, So Human an Animal: How We Are Shaped by Surroundings and Events.
1970—Eric H. Erikson, Gandhi's Truth.
1971—John Toland, The Rising Sun.
1972—Barbara W. Tuchman, Stilwell and the American Experience in China, 1911-1945.
1973—Frances FitzGerald, Fire in the Lake: The Vietnamese and the Americans in Vietnam; Robert Coles, Children of Crisis, Volumes II & III.
1974—Ernest Becker, The Denial of Death.
1975—Annie Dillard, Pilgrim at Tinker Creek.
1976—Robert N. Butler, Why Survive? Being Old in America.
1977—William W. Warner, Beautiful Swimmers.

1978—Carl Sagan, The Dragons of Eden.
1979—Edward O. Wilson, On Human Nature.
1980—Douglas R. Hofstadter, Gödel, Escher, Bach: An Eternal Golden Braid.
1981—Carl E. Schorske, Fin-de-Siecle Vienna: Politics and Culture.
1982—Tracy Kidder, The Soul of a New Machine.
1983—Susan Sheehan, Is There No Place on Earth for Me?
1984—Paul Starr, Social Transformation of American Medicine.
1985—Studs Terkel, The Good War.
1986—Joseph Lelyveld, Move Your Shadow; J. Anthony Lukas, Common Ground.
1987—David K. Shipler, Arab and Jew.
1988—Richard Rhodes, The Making of the Atomic Bomb.
1989—Neil Sheehan, A Bright Shining Lie: John Paul Vann and America in Vietnam.

Music

For composition by an American (before 1977, by a composer resident in the U.S.), in the larger forms of chamber, orchestra or choral music or for an operatic work including ballet. A special posthumous award was granted in 1976 to Scott Joplin.
1943—William Schuman, Secular Cantata No. 2, A Free Song.
1944—Howard Hanson, Symphony No. 4, Op. 34.
1945—Aaron Copland, Appalachian Spring.
1946—Leo Sowerby, The Canticle of the Sun.
1947—Charles E. Ives, Symphony No. 3.
1948—Walter Piston, Symphony No. 3.
1949—Virgil Thomson, Louisiana Story.
1950—Gian-Carlo Menotti, The Consul.
1951—Douglas Moore, Giants in the Earth.
1952—Gail Kubik, Symphony Concertante.
1954—Quincy Porter, Concerto for Two Pianos and Orchestra.
1955—Gian-Carlo Menotti, The Saint of Bleecker Street.
1956—Ernest Toch, Symphony No. 3.
1957—Norman Dello Joio, Meditations on Ecclesiastes.
1958—Samuel Barber, Vanessa.
1959—John La Montaine, Concerto for Piano and Orchestra.
1960—Elliott Carter, Second String Quartet.
1961—Walter Piston, Symphony No. 7.
1962—Robert Ward, The Crucible.
1963—Samuel Barber, Piano Concerto No. 1.
1966—Leslie Bassett, Variations for Orchestra.

1967—Leon Kirchner, Quartet No. 3.
1968—George Crumb, Echoes of Time and The River.
1969—Karel Husa, String Quartet No. 3.
1970—Charles W. Wuorinen, Time's Encomium.
1971—Mario Davidovsky, Synchronisms No. 6.
1972—Jacob Druckman, Windows.
1973—Elliott Carter, String Quartet No. 3.
1974—Donald Martino, Notturno. (Special citation) Roger Sessions.
1975—Dominick Argento, From the Diary of Virginia Woolf.
1976—Ned Rorem, Air Music.
1977—Richard Wernick, Visions of Terror and Wonder.
1978—Michael Colgrass, Deja Vu for Percussion and Orchestra.

1979—Joseph Schwantner, Aftertones of Infinity.
1980—David Del Tredici, In Memory of a Summer Day.
1982—Roger Sessions, Concerto For Orchestra. (Special Citation) Milton Babbitt.
1983—Ellen T. Zwilich, Three Movements for Orchestra.
1984—Bernard Rands, Canti del Sole.
1985—Stephen Albert, Symphony, RiverRun.
1986—George Perle, Wind Quintet IV.
1987—John Harbison, The Flight Into Egypt.
1988—William Bolcom, 12 New Etudes for Piano.
1989—Roger Reynolds, Whispers Out of Time.

Special Awards

Awarded in 1988 or 1989

Books, Allied Arts

Academy of American Poets Awards: fellowship for distinguished achievement, $20,000: Richard Howard; Lamont Poetry Selection, $1,000: Minnie Bruce Pratt, *Crime Against Nature;* Landon Translation Award, $1,000: Martin Greenberg, *Five Plays* by Heinrich von Kleist; Lavan Younger Poet Awards, $1,000 each: Marie Howe, Naomi Shihab Nye, John Yau; Whitman Award, $1,000: Martha Hollander.

American Academy and Institute of Arts and Letters Awards: gold medal: Isaac Bashevis Singer; Distinguished Service to the Arts: Vartan Gregorian; new literary Academy member: Mary McCarthy; new literary Institute members: Don DeLillo, Peter Gay, John Guare, Donald Hall, Alison Lurie.

Bancroft Prizes, by Columbia Univ., for American history book, $4,000 each: Eric Foner, *Reconstruction: America's Unfinished Revolution 1863-1877;* Edmund S. Morgan, *Inventing the People: The Rise of Popular Sovereignty in England and America.*

Bobst Awards in Arts and Letters, by New York Univ.: Edward Albee, Robert Giroux, Toni Morrison, Reynolds Price.

Bollingen Prize in Poetry, by Yale Univ., $10,000: Edgar Bowers.

Caldecott Medal, by Amer. Library Assn., for children's book illustration: Stephen Gammell, *Song and Dance Man* by Karen Ackerman.

Christopher Awards, by Christopher Foundation, for affirmation of human values, bronze medallions: books for adults: *Alicia: My Story,* Alicia Appleman-Jurman; *Balm in Gilead: Journey of a Healer,* Sara Lawrence Lightfoot; *Battle*

Cry of Freedom: The Civil War Era, James M. McPherson; *Beyond the Frozen Sea: Visions of Antarctica,* Edwin Mickleburgh; *Fear No Evil,* Natan Sharansky; *Getting Better: Inside Alcoholics Anonymous,* Nan Robertson; *Grey Is the Color of Hope,* Irina Ratushinskaya; *Morning Glory Babies: Children with Aids and the Celebration of Life,* Tolbert McCarroll; *Murdered in Central America: The Stories of Eleven U.S. Missionaries,* Donna Whitson Brett and Edward T. Brett; *No Place But Here: A Teacher's Vocation in a Rural Community,* Garret Keizer; *Parting the Waters: America in the King Years 1954-63,* Taylor Branch; *Rachel and Her Children: Homeless Families in America,* Jonathan Kozol; *With All Our Heart & Mind: The Spiritual Works of Mercy in a Psychological Age,* Sidney Callahan.

Edgar Awards, by Mystery Writers of America: Grand Master: Hillary Waugh; lifetime achievement: Joan Kahn; novel: Stuart M. Kaminsky, *A Cold Red Sunrise;* first novel: David Stout, *Carolina Skeletons;* original paperback: Timothy Findley, *The Telling of Lies;* fact crime: Harry N. MacLean, *In Broad Daylight;* critical/biographical: Francis M. Nevins Jr., *Cornell Woolrich: First You Dream, Then You Die;* young adult novel: Sonia Levitin, *Incident at Loring Groves;* juvenile: Willo Davis Roberts, *Megan's Island;* short story, Bill Crenshaw, "Flicks"; Fish Award for short story: Linda O. Johnston, "Different Drummers."

Food and Beverage Book Award, by Intl. Assn. of Cooking Professionals & Joseph E. Seagram & Sons: book of the year: *The Cake Bible,* Rose Levy Beranbaum.

Golden Kite Awards, by Society of Children's Book Writers: fiction: George Ella Lyon, *Borrowed Children;* non-fiction: James Giblin, *Let There Be Light;* picture-illustration: Susan Jeffers, *Forest of Dreams.*

Lilly Poetry Prize, by Modern Poetry Assn., Poetry magazine, and American Council for the Arts, $25,000: Mona Van Duyn.

Los Angeles Times Book Prizes: $1,000 each: fiction: Gabriel Garcia Marquez, *Love in the Time of Cholera;* poetry: Richard Wilbur, *New and Collected Poetry;* history: Eric Foner, *Reconstruction;* biography: Brenda Maddox, *Nora: The Real Life of Molly Bloom;* current interest: William Greider, *Secrets of the Temple: How the Federal Reserve Runs the Country;* Kirsch Award, for work on West: Thomas Gunn.

Mitchell Prizes, for books on fine arts: Mitchell Prize, $10,000: Thomas DaCosta Kauffmann, *The School of Prague: Painting at the Court of Rudolf II;* Eric Mitchell Prize, for first book, $3,000: Stanley Meltzoff, *Botticelli, Signorelli and Savonarola: 'Theologica Poetica' and Painting from Boccaccio and Poliziano;* 20th Century Prize, $3,000: Angelica Zander Rudenstine, *Modern Painting, Drawing and Sculpture Collected by Emily and Joseph Pulitzer Jr.*

National Book Awards, by American publishers, $10,000 and Nevelson sculpture each: fiction: Pete Dexter, *Paris Trout;* nonfiction: Neil Sheehan, *A Bright Shining Lie;* distinguished contribution to American letters: Jason Epstein.

National Book Critics Circle Awards: fiction: Bharati Mukherjee, *The Middleman and Other Stories;* nonfiction: Taylor Branch, *Parting the Waters;* biography: Richard Ellmann, *Oscar Wilde;* poetry: Donald Hall, *The One Day;* criticism: Clifford Geertz, *Works and Lives: The Anthropologist as Author.*

New York Times Awards for Best Illustrated Children's Books: *Sir Francis Drake, His Daring Deeds,* Roy Gerrard; *Theodor and Mr. Balbini,* Petra Mathers; *Cats Are Cats,* Nancy Larrick, il. Ed Young; *Fire Came to the Earth People,* Susan L. Roth; *Swan Sky, Tejima; Shaka: King of the Zulus,* Diane Stanley and Peter Vennema, il. Diane Stanley; *Look! Look! Look!,* Tana Hoban; *A River Dream,* Allen Say; *I Want to Be an Astronaut,* Byron Barton; *Stringbean's Trip to the Shining Sea,* Vera B. Williams; il. Vera B. Williams and Jennifer Williams.

PEN/Faulkner Award for Fiction, $7,500: James Salter, *Dusk and Other Stories.*

Rhea Award, for contribution to short story form, $25,000: Tobias Wolff.

Whiting Writers' Awards, $25,000 each: Michael Burkard, *Fictions from the Self;* Lydia Davis, *Break It Down;* Bruce Duffy, *The World as I Found It;* Gerald Early, *Tuxedo Junction;* Jonathan Franzen, *The Twenty-Seventh City;* Mary La Chapelle, *Houses of Heroes and Other Stories;* Li-Young Lee, *Rose;* Sylvia Moss, *Cities in Motion;* Geoffrey O'Brien, *Dream Time: Chapters from the Sixties;* William Vollmann, *You Bright and Risen Angels.*

Wilder Award, by American Library Assn., for body of work: Elizabeth George Spear.

Journalism Awards

Cabot Prizes, by Columbia Univ., for advancement of inter-American understanding, $1,000 and gold medal each: Stephen Kinzer, *New York Times;* Nicholas Clark Asheshov, *Lima Times* and *Andean Report,* Lima, Peru; Roberto Civita, *Veja,* São Paulo, Brazil; Hermenegildo Sabat, *Clarin,* Buenos Aires.

Catholic Press Assn. Awards: general excellence, general interest magazines: *New Catholic World;* general interest newsletters: *U.S. Parish;* general excellence, national newspapers: *National Catholic Register.*

Distinguished Writing Awards, by American Society of Newspaper Editors, $2,500 each: deadline writing: Francis X. Clines, *New York Times* and David J. Remnick, *Washington Post;* state and local government: Mark Davis, *Tampa Tribune;* editorial: Samuel T. Francis, *Washington Times;* non-deadline: James Lileks, *St. Paul Pioneer Press Dispatch;* Michael Skube, *Raleigh* (N.C.) *News and Observer.*

Livingston Awards for Young Journalists, $5,000 each: international reporting: Anne Nelson, "In the Grotto of the Pink Sisters," *Mother Jones* magazine; national reporting: Dave Von Drehler, "The Death Penalty: A Failure of Execution," *Miami Herald;* local reporting: Bonita Brodt, "Chicago Public Schools: 'Worst in America,' " *Chicago Tribune.*

National Journalism Awards, by Scripps Howard Foundation, $39,000: Schulz Award, for college cartoonist: Christopher Kalb, Yale College: Stone Award, for editorial writing: Ann Daly Goodwin, *St. Paul Pioneer Press Dispatch;* Meeman Awards, for environmental journalism: Dennis Anderson, *St. Paul Pioneer Press Dispatch; Charleston* (W.Va.) *Gazette;* E.W. Scripps Award, for First Amendment service: *Eagle-Tribune,* Lawrence, Mass.; C.E. Scripps Award, for newspaper literacy: *Lesher Communications,* Northern Calif.; Howard public service awards: *Philadelphia Inquirer, Anchorage Daily News;* Pyle Award, for human interest writing: John Kifner, *New York Times.*

National Magazine Awards, by American Society of Magazine Editors: general excellence: *Sports Illustrated, Vanity Fair, American Heritage, The Sciences;* personal service: *Good Housekeeping;* special interest: *Condé Nast Traveler;* feature writing: *Esquire;* public interest: *California;* design: *Rolling Stone;* photography: *National Geographic;* essays and

criticism: *Harper's;* single-topic issue: *Hippocrates;* fiction: *New Yorker;* reporting: *New Yorker.*

Pictures of the Year Awards, by Univ. of Missouri-Columbia School of Journalism: newspaper photographer: John Kaplan, *Pittsburgh Press;* magazine photographer: James Nachtwey, Magnum Photography Services; Canon Photo Essayist Award: Eugene Richards, Magnum; Kodak Crystal Eagle Award: Charles Moore, Black Star.

Polk Awards in Journalism, by Long Island Univ.: foreign reporting: John Kifner, *New York Times;* national: Keith Schneider, *New York Times;* local: David Gomez, Patricia Guthrie, *Albuquerque* (N.M.) *Tribune;* Donald L. Barlett, James B. Steele, *Philadelphia Inquirer;* environmental: Mary Bishop, *Roanoke* (Va.) *Times and World News;* financial: *National Thrift News;* cultural: Lawrence Wechsler, *Shapkinsky's Karma, Boggs's Bills;* photojournalism: Mary Ellen Mark; career award: William Shawn, *New Yorker.*

Reuben Awards, by National Cartoonists Society: cartoonist of the year: Bill Watterson, "Calvin and Hobbes," United Press Syndicate; category winners: advertising: Bob Bindig; animation: Bill Melendez; comic books: Will Eisner, "The Spirit"; editorial: Jim Borgman, *Cincinnati Enquirer;* humor strip: Bill Watterson, "Calvin and Hobbes"; illustration: Arnold Roth; magazine gag: Eldon Dedini; special feature: Mort Drucker, *Mad* magazine; sports: Bill Gallo, *New York Daily News;* story strip: Jim Scanarelli, "Gasoline Alley;" syndicated panel: Gary Larson, "The Far Side."

Science-in-Society Journalism Awards, by National Assn. of Science Writers, $1,000 each: newspapers: Gayle Golden, *Dallas Morning News;* magazines: Nolan Hester, *Albuquerque* (N.M.) *Journal.*

Society of Professional Journalists Awards: First Amendment: *Riverdale Press,* Bronx, N.Y.; general reporting: Gary Thatcher, *Christian Science Monitor;* Peggy O'Crowley, *News Tribune,* Woodbridge and Perth Amboy, N.J.; Washington: James O'Shea, *Chicago Tribune;* foreign: Douglas Farah, *Washington Post;* editorial: Fred Brown, Jack Cox, Chuck Green, *Denver Post;* public service: *Anchorage Daily News;* James Steele and Donald Barlett, *Philadelphia Inquirer.*

Movie, Radio, TV, and Theater Awards

Directors Guild of America: Barry Levinson, *Rain Man.*

Drama Desk Awards: musical: "Jerome Robbins's Broadway;" play: "The Heidi Chronicles," Wendy Wasserstein; revival: "Our Town;" actor: Philip Bosco, "Lend Me a Tenor;" actress: Pauline Collins, "Shirley Valentine;" featured actress: Tovah Feldshuh, "Lend Me a Tenor;" fea-

tured actor: Peter Frechette, "Eastern Standard;" actor, musical: Jason Alexander, "Jerome Robbins's Broadway;" actress, musical: Toni DiBuono, "Forbidden Broadway;" director: Jerry Zaks, "Lend Me a Tenor;" costume design: William Ivey Long, "Lend Me a Tenor;" set design: Santo Loquasto, "Cafe Crown" and "Italian American Reconciliation;" lighting design: Jennifer Tipton, "Jerome Robbins's Broadway," "Long Day's Journey Into Night," "Waiting for Godot;" unique theatrical experience: Bill Irwin, "Largely New York."

DuPont-Columbia Univ. Awards, for broadcast journalism: golden baton: "60 Minutes," CBS; silver batons: "CBS Evening News" for Iran-Iraq War coverage; NBC News, for Tom Brokaw interview with Mikhail Gorbachev; ABC News, for "Nightline" broadcasts from Jerusalem; WWOR, Secaucus, N.J.; WCVC, Boston; WUSA, Washington; WSMV, Nashville; WCAX, Burlington, Vt.; WBRZ and John Camp, Baton Rouge, La.; Public Affairs Television and Alvin H. Perlmutter, for "Joseph Campbell and the Power of Myth;" radio: silver baton: Nina Totenberg, National Public Radio, for Supreme Court coverage.

Emmy Awards, by Academy of Television Arts and Sciences, for nighttime programs, 1987-88: Dramatic series: *thirtysomething,* ABC; actress, drama: Tyne Daly, *Cagney & Lacey;* actor, drama: Richard Kiley, *A Year in the Life,* NBC; supporting actress: Patricia Wettig, *thirtysomething,* ABC; supporting actor: Larry Drake, *L.A. Law, NBC.* Comedy series: *The Wonder Years,* ABC; actress: Beatrice Arthur, *The Golden Girls,* NBC; actor: Michael J. Fox, *Family Ties,* NBC; supporting actress: Estelle Getty, *The Golden Girls,* NBC; supporting actor: John Larroquette, *Night Court,* NBC. Drama-Comedy special: *Inherit the Wind,* NBC. Miniseries: *The Murder of Mary Phagan,* NBC; actress, miniseries or special: Jessica Tandy, *Foxfire,* CBS; actor, miniseries or special: Jason Robards, *Inherit the Wind,* NBC; supporting actress: Jane Seymour, *Onassis,* ABC; supporting actor: John Shea, *Baby M.,* ABC. Variety, music, or comedy special: *Irving Berlin's 100th Birthday Celebration,* CBS; individual performance, variety or music program: Robin Williams, *ABC Presents a Royal Gala,* ABC.

Daytime Emmy Awards: dramatic series: *Santa Barbara,* NBC; actress: Marcy Walker, *Santa Barbara;* actor: David Canary, *All My Children,* ABC; writing: *Santa Barbara,* Anne Howard Bailey and Charles Pratt Jr., head writers; directing: *The Young and the Restless,* CBS; Frank Pacelli, Heather Hill, Randy Robbins, Rudy Vejar; supporting actress: Debbi Morgan, *All My Children;* and Nancy Lee Grahn, *Santa Barbara;* supporting actor: Justin Deas, *Santa Barbara;* juvenile female, Robin Scorpio, *General Hospital,* ABC; juvenile male: Justin Gocke, *Santa Barbara;* costume design: *Another World,* NBC, Margarita Delgado and Charles Schoonmaker; talk/service show: *The Oprah Winfrey Show;* talk/service show host: Sally Jessy Raphael; game/audience participation show: *The $25,000 Pyramid,* CBS; game show host: Alex Trebek, *Jeopardy!;* children's series: *Newton's Apple,* PBS; children's special: "Taking a Stand," *ABC Afterschool Special,* ABC; animated program: "The New Adventures of Winnie the Pooh," ABC.

Helen Hayes Awards, for Washington professional theater: resident shows: play: "Six Characters in Search of an Author," Arena Stage; musical: "The Cocoanuts," Arena Stage; new play: "The Night Hank Williams Died," Larry L. King, New Playwrights' Theater; lead actress: Jennifer Mendenhall, "Aunt Dan & Lemon," Woolly Mammoth Theater Company; lead actor: Michael Willis, "The Boys Next Door," Round House Theater; supporting actress: Sarah C. Marshall, "Baby With the Bathwater," Round House Theater; supporting actor: Edward Gero, "MacBeth," Shakespeare Theater at the Folger; actress, musical: Kim Criswell, "Side by Side by Sondheim," Olney Theater; actor, musical: Charles Janasz, "The Cocoanuts;" director: Liviu Ciulei, "Six Characters in Search of an Author;" lighting design: Allen Lee Hughes, "Six Characters in Search of an Author;" costume design: William Pucilowsky, "The Constant Wife," Washington Stage Guild; set design: Russell Metheny, "eleemosynary," Horizons Theater; nonresident shows: production: "The Search for Signs of Intelligent Life

in the Universe," by Jane Wagner, Kennedy Center; actor: Victor Garber, "Wenceslas Square," Kennedy Center; actress: Lily Tomlin, "The Search for Signs of Intelligent Life in the Universe;" director: Jane Wagner, "The Search . . .;" supporting performer: Bruce Norris, "Wenceslas Square."

Hull-Warriner Award, by Dramatists Guild, for controversial play, $11,000: "The Heidi Chronicles," by Wendy Wasserstein.

Kennedy Center Honors, for performing artists: Alvin Ailey, George Burns, Myrna Loy, Alexander Schneider, Roger L. Stevens.

National Journalism Awards, by Scripps Howard Foundation, for broadcast journalism: Charles E. Scripps literacy award: KOCO, Oklahoma City, Okla; Jack R. Howard Awards, for TV: WBRZ, Baton Rouge, La.; WFAA, Dallas; for radio: KTAR-AM, Phoenix.

National Society of Arts and Letters, lifetime achievement award: Geraldine Fitzgerald.

New York Drama Critics Circle Awards: new play, $1,000: "The Heidi Chronicles," Wendy Wasserstein; new foreign play: "Aristocrats," Brian Friel; special citation: Bill Irwin, "Largely New York."

New York Film Critics' Circle Awards: best film: "The Accidental Tourist;" actor: Jeremy Irons, "Dead Ringers;" actress: Meryl Streep, "A Cry in the Dark;" supporting actor: Dean Stockwell, "Married to the Mob," and "Tucker;" supporting actress: Diane Venora, "Bird;" foreign film: "Woman on the Verge of a Nervous Breakdown;" screenplay: "Bull Durham;" director: Chris Menges, "A World Apart;" cinematography: Henri Alekan, "Wings of Desire" and "The Thin Blue Line."

Outer Critics Circle Awards: play: "The Heidi Chronicles," Wendy Wasserstein; musical: "Jerome Robbins's Broadway;" Gassner Award for American playwright: Jerry Sterner, "Other People's Money;" off-Broadway play: "Other People's Money;" actor: Ken Conway, "Other People's Money;" actress: Pauline Collins, "Shirley Valentine;" musical actor: Jason Alexander, "Jerome Robbins's Broadway;" musical actress: Ruth Brown, "Black and Blue;" director: Jerry Zaks, "Lend Me a Tenor;" acting debuts: Peter Frechette, "Eastern Standard;" Toni DiBuono, "Forbidden Broadway;" revival: "Our Town;" design: "Lend Me a Tenor," Tony Walton, William Ivey Long, Paul Gallo; special awards: Jewish Repertory Theater; Mikhail Baryshnikov, "Metamorphosis;" ensemble acting in "Lend Me a Tenor."

Theater Hall of Fame: new members: George Balanchine; Dorothy and Herbert Fields; Max Gordon; Elliot Norton; Danny Kaye, Ruby Dee; Siobhan McKenna; Eli Wallach; special awards: Arthur Birsh, *Playbill;* Gregory Mosher, Bernard Gerstein, Lincoln Center Theater.

Tony (Antoinette Perry) **Awards** play: "The Heidi Chronicles," Wendy Wasserstein; musical: "Jerome Robbins's Broadway;" revival: "Our Town;" actor: Philip Bosco, "Lend Me a Tenor;" actress: Pauline Collins, "Shirley Valentine;" musical actor: Jason Alexander, "Jerome Robbins's Broadway;" musical actress: Ruth Brown, "Black and Blue;" featured actor: Boyd Gaines, "The Heidi Chronicles;" featured actress: Christine Baranski, "Rumors;" featured musical actor: Scott Wise, "Jerome Robbins's Broadway;" featured musical actress: Debbie Shapiro, "Jerome Robbins's Broadway;" direction: Jerry Zaks, "Lend Me a Tenor;" musical direction: Jerome Robbins, "Jerome Robbins's Broadway;" scenic design: Santo Loquasto, "Cafe Crown;" costume design: Claudio Segovia, Hector Orezzoli, "Black and Blue;" lighting design: Jennifer Tipton, "Jerome Robbins's Broadway;" choreography: Cholly Atkins, Henry LeTang, Frankie Manning, Fayard Nicholas, "Black and Blue."

Miscellaneous Awards

American Academy and Institute of Arts and Letters Awards: non-literary awards: gold medal: Louise Bourgeois; Brunner architecture prize: Richard Rogers; new Academy members: Jasper Johns, John Cage; new Institute members: Christo, Jane Freilicher, Agnes Martin, George McNeil, Ralph Shapey.

Bruhn Prize, for young ballet dancers, $15,000: Silja Wendrup-Schandorff, Royal Danish Ballet; Stephen Legate, National Ballet of Canada.

Cliburn International Piano Competition, $15,000, Carnegie Hall recital, and 2 years of concert touring: Aleksei Sultanov, U.S.S.R.; second prize, $10,000, New York City recital: Jose Cocarelli, Brazil; third prize, $7,500, New York City recital: Benedetto Lupo, Italy; fourth: Aleksandr Shtarkman, U.S.S.R.; fifth: Ying Tian, China-U.S.; sixth: Eliso Bolkvadze, U.S.S.R.

Council of Fashion Designers of America: lifetime achievement: Nancy Reagan, Richard Avedon; Perry Ellis Award, for new talent: Isaac Mizrahi; men's wear: Bill Robinson; Eugenia Sheppard Award, for fashion journalism: Nina Hyde, Washington Post; special awards: Judy Peabody; Grace Mirabella; Geoffrey Beene, House of Chanel, Karl Lagerfeld.

Country Music Awards (See *Addenda*)

Fermi Award, U.S. Department of Energy, for achievement in atomic energy development, use, or control, gold medal and $100,000 each: Victor F. Weisskopf, M.I.T.;

Richard B. Setlow, Brookhaven National Laboratory.

Grawemeyer Award for Music, by Univ. of Kentucky, $150,000: Chinary Ung, Arizona State Univ., Tempe, "Inner Voices."

Monk International Jazz Piano Competition, $10,000: Ted Rosenthal, New York City.

National Spelling Bee (See *Language*)

National Teacher of the Year, by Council of Chief State School Officers, *Encyclopaedia Britannica,* and *Good Housekeeping Magazine,* crystal apple: Mary V. Bicouvaris, Bethel High School, Hampton, Va.

Pritzker Architecture Prize, $100,000: Frank O. Gehry.

Songwriter's Hall of Fame: new members: Leslie Bricusse and Anthony Newley; Roy Orbison; Lee Adams; Eddie DeLange.

The Spingarn Medal

The Spingarn Medal has been awarded annually since 1914 by the National Association for the Advancement of Colored People for the highest achievement by a black American.

1946 Dr. Percy L. Julian	1959 Langston Hughes	1974 Henry (Hank) Aaron
1947 Channing H. Tobias	1960 Kenneth B. Clark	1975 Alvin Ailey
1948 Ralph J. Bunche	1961 Robert C. Weaver	1976 Alex Haley
1949 Charles Hamilton Houston	1962 Medgar Wiley Evers	1977 Andrew Young
1950 Mabel Keaton Staupers	1963 Roy Wilkins	1978 Mrs. Rosa L. Parks
1951 Harry T. Moore	1964 Leontyne Price	1979 Dr. Rayford W. Logan
1952 Paul R. Williams	1965 John H. Johnson	1980 Coleman Young
1953 Theodore K. Lawless	1966 Edward W. Brooke	1981 Dr. Benjamin Elijah Mays
1954 Carl Murphy	1967 Sammy Davis Jr.	1982 Lena Horne
1955 Jack Roosevelt Robinson	1968 Clarence M. Mitchell Jr.	1983 Thomas Bradley
1956 Martin Luther King Jr.	1969 Jacob Lawrence	1984 Bill Cosby
1957 Mrs. Daisy Bates and the Little	1970 Leon Howard Sullivan	1985 Dr. Benjamin L. Hooks
Rock Nine	1971 Gordon Parks	1986 Percy E. Sutton
1958 Edward Kennedy (Duke)	1972 Wilson C. Riles	1987 Frederick Douglass Patterson
Ellington	1973 Damon Keith	1988 Jesse Jackson

Miss America Winners

1921 Margaret Gorman, Washington, D.C.	1960 Lynda Lee Mead, Natchez, Mississippi
1922-23 Mary Campbell, Columbus, Ohio	1961 Nancy Fleming, Montague, Michigan
1924 Ruth Malcolmson, Philadelphia, Pennsylvania	1962 Maria Fletcher, Asheville, North Carolina
1925 Fay Lamphier, Oakland, California	1963 Jacquelyn Mayer, Sandusky, Ohio
1926 Norma Smallwood, Tulsa, Oklahoma	1964 Donna Axum, El Dorado, Arkansas
1927 Lois Delaner, Joliet, Illinois	1965 Vonda Kay Van Dyke, Phoenix, Arizona
1933 Marion Bergeron, West Haven, Connecticut	1966 Deborah Irene Bryant, Overland Park, Kansas
1935 Henrietta Leaver, Pittsburgh, Pennsylvania	1967 Jane Anne Jayroe, Laverne, Oklahoma
1936 Rose Coyle, Philadelphia, Pennsylvania	1968 Debra Dene Barnes, Moran, Kansas
1937 Bette Cooper, Bertrand Island, New Jersey	1969 Judith Anne Ford, Belvidere, Illinois
1938 Marilyn Meseke, Marion, Ohio	1970 Pamela Anne Eldred, Birmingham, Michigan
1939 Patricia Donnelly, Detroit, Michigan	1971 Phyllis Ann George, Denton, Texas
1940 Frances Marie Burke, Philadelphia, Pennsylvania	1972 Laurie Lea Schaefer, Columbus, Ohio
1941 Rosemary LaPlanche, Los Angeles, California	1973 Terry Anne Meeuwsen, DePere, Wisconsin
1942 Jo-Caroll Dennison, Tyler, Texas	1974 Rebecca Ann King, Denver, Colorado
1943 Jean Bartel, Los Angeles, California	1975 Shirley Cothran, Fort Worth, Texas
1944 Venus Ramey, Washington, D.C.	1976 Tawney Elaine Godin, Yonkers, N.Y.
1945 Bess Myerson, New York City, N.Y.	1977 Dorothy Kathleen Benham, Edina, Minnesota
1946 Marilyn Buferd, Los Angeles, California	1978 Susan Perkins, Columbus, Ohio
1947 Barbara Walker, Memphis, Tennessee	1979 Kylene Barker, Galax, Virginia
1948 BeBe Shopp, Hopkins, Minnesota	1980 Cheryl Prewitt, Ackerman, Mississippi
1949 Jacque Mercer, Litchfield, Arizona	1981 Susan Powell, Elk City, Oklahoma
1951 Yolande Betbeze, Mobile, Alabama	1982 Elizabeth Ward, Russellville, Arkansas
1952 Coleen Kay Hutchins, Salt Lake City, Utah	1983 Debra Maffett, Anaheim, California
1953 Neva Jane Langley, Macon, Georgia	1984 Vanessa Williams, Milwood, New York*
1954 Evelyn Margaret Ay, Ephrata, Pennsylvania	Suzette Charles, Mays Landing, New Jersey
1955 Lee Meriwether, San Francisco, California	1985 Sharlene Wells, Salt Lake City, Utah
1956 Sharon Ritchie, Denver, Colorado	1986 Susan Akin, Meridian, Mississippi
1957 Marian McKnight, Manning, South Carolina	1987 Kellye Cash, Memphis, Tennessee
1958 Marilyn Van Derbur, Denver, Colorado	1988 Kaye Lani Rae Rafko, Monroe, Michigan
1959 Mary Ann Mobley, Brandon, Mississippi	1989 Gretchen Carlson, Anoka, Minnesota

*Resigned July 23, 1984.

Motion Picture Academy Awards (Oscars)

1927-28
Actor: Emil Jannings, *The Way of All Flesh.*
Actress: Janet Gaynor, *Seventh Heaven.*
Director: Frank Borzage, *Seventh Heaven;* Lewis Milestone, *Two Arabian Knights.*
Picture: *Wings,* Paramount.

1928-29
Actor: Warner Baxter, *In Old Arizona.*
Actress: Mary Pickford, *Coquette.*
Director: Frank Lloyd, *The Divine Lady.*
Picture: *Broadway Melody,* MGM.

1929-30
Actor: George Arliss, *Disraeli.*
Actress: Norma Shearer, *The Divorcee.*
Director: Lewis Milestone, *All Quiet on the Western Front.*
Picture: *All Quiet on the Western Front,* Univ.

1930-31
Actor: Lionel Barrymore, *Free Soul.*
Actress: Marie Dressler, *Min and Bill.*
Director: Norman Taurog, *Skippy.*
Picture: *Cimarron,* RKO.

1931-32
Actor: Fredric March, *Dr. Jekyll and Mr. Hyde;* Wallace
  Beery, *The Champ* (tie).
Actress: Helen Hayes, *Sin of Madelon Claudet.*
Director: Frank Borzage, *Bad Girl.*
Picture: *Grand Hotel,* MGM.
Special: Walt Disney, *Mickey Mouse.*

1932-33
Actor: Charles Laughton, *Private Life of Henry VIII.*
Actress: Katharine Hepburn, *Morning Glory.*
Director: Frank Lloyd, *Cavalcade.*
Picture: *Cavalcade,* Fox.

1934
Actor: Clark Gable, *It Happened One Night.*
Actress: Claudette Colbert, *It Happened One Night.*
Director: Frank Capra, *It Happened One Night.*
Picture: *It Happened One Night,* Columbia.

1935
Actor: Victor McLaglen, *The Informer.*
Actress: Bette Davis, *Dangerous.*
Director: John Ford, *The Informer.*
Picture: *Mutiny on the Bounty,* MGM.

1936
Actor: Paul Muni, *Story of Louis Pasteur.*
Actress: Luise Rainer, *The Great Ziegfeld.*
Sup. Actor: Walter Brennan, *Come and Get It.*
Sup. Actress: Gale Sondergaard, *Anthony Adverse.*
Director: Frank Capra, *Mr. Deeds Goes to Town.*
Picture: *The Great Ziegfeld,* MGM.

1937
Actor: Spencer Tracy, *Captains Courageous.*
Actress: Luise Rainer, *The Good Earth.*
Sup. Actor: Joseph Schildkraut, *Life of Emile Zola.*
Sup. Actress: Alice Brady, *In Old Chicago.*
Director: Leo McCarey, *The Awful Truth.*
Picture: *Life of Emile Zola,* Warner.

1938
Actor: Spencer Tracy, *Boys Town.*
Actress: Bette Davis, *Jezebel.*
Sup. Actor: Walter Brennan, *Kentucky.*
Sup. Actress: Fay Bainter, *Jezebel.*
Director: Frank Capra, *You Can't Take It With You.*
Picture: *You Can't Take It With You,* Columbia.

1939
Actor: Robert Donat, *Goodbye Mr. Chips.*
Actress: Vivien Leigh, *Gone With the Wind.*
Sup. Actor: Thomas Mitchell, *Stage Coach.*
Sup. Actress: Hattie McDaniel, *Gone With the Wind.*
Director: Victor Fleming, *Gone With the Wind.*
Picture: *Gone With the Wind,* Selznick International.

1940
Actor: James Stewart, *The Philadelphia Story.*
Actress: Ginger Rogers, *Kitty Foyle.*
Sup. Actor: Walter Brennan, *The Westerner.*
Sup. Actress: Jane Darwell, *The Grapes of Wrath.*
Director: John Ford, *The Grapes of Wrath.*
Picture: *Rebecca,* Selznick International.

1941
Actor: Gary Cooper, *Sergeant York.*
Actress: Joan Fontaine, *Suspicion.*
Sup. Actor: Donald Crisp, *How Green Was My Valley.*
Sup. Actress: Mary Astor, *The Great Lie.*
Director: John Ford, *How Green Was My Valley.*
Picture: *How Green Was My Valley,* 20th Cent.-Fox.

1942
Actor: James Cagney, *Yankee Doodle Dandy.*
Actress: Greer Garson, *Mrs. Miniver.*
Sup. Actor: Van Heflin, *Johnny Eager.*
Sup. Actress: Teresa Wright, *Mrs. Miniver.*
Director: William Wyler, *Mrs. Miniver.*
Picture: *Mrs. Miniver,* MGM.

1943
Actor: Paul Lukas, *Watch on the Rhine.*
Actress: Jennifer Jones, *The Song of Bernadette.*
Sup. Actor: Charles Coburn, *The More the Merrier.*
Sup. Actress: Katina Paxinou, *For Whom the Bell Tolls.*
Director: Michael Curtiz, *Casablanca.*
Picture: *Casablanca,* Warner.

1944
Actor: Bing Crosby, *Going My Way.*
Actress: Ingrid Bergman, *Gaslight.*
Sup. Actor: Barry Fitzgerald, *Going My Way.*
Sup. Actress: Ethel Barrymore, *None But the Lonely Heart.*
Director: Leo McCarey, *Going My Way.*
Picture: *Going My Way,* Paramount.

1945
Actor: Ray Milland, *The Lost Weekend.*
Actress: Joan Crawford, *Mildred Pierce.*
Sup. Actor: James Dunn, *A Tree Grows in Brooklyn.*

Sup. Actress: Anne Revere, *National Velvet.*
Director: Billy Wilder, *The Lost Weekend.*
Picture: *The Lost Weekend,* Paramount.

1946
Actor: Fredric March, *Best Years of Our Lives.*
Actress: Olivia de Havilland, *To Each His Own.*
Sup. Actor: Harold Russell, *The Best Years of Our Lives.*
Sup. Actress: Anne Baxter, *The Razor's Edge.*
Director: William Wyler, *The Best Years of Our Lives.*
Picture: *The Best Years of Our Lives,* Goldwyn, RKO.

1947
Actor: Ronald Colman, *A Double Life.*
Actress: Loretta Young, *The Farmer's Daughter.*
Sup. Actor: Edmund Gwenn, *Miracle on 34th Street.*
Sup. Actress: Celeste Holm, *Gentleman's Agreement.*
Director: Elia Kazan, *Gentleman's Agreement.*
Picture: *Gentleman's Agreement,* 20th Cent.-Fox.

1948
Actor: Laurence Olivier, *Hamlet.*
Actress: Jane Wyman, *Johnny Belinda.*
Sup. Actor: Walter Huston, *Treasure of Sierra Madre.*
Sup. Actress: Claire Trevor, *Key Largo.*
Director: John Huston, *Treasure of Sierra Madre.*
Picture: *Hamlet,* Two Cities Film, Universal International.

1949
Actor: Broderick Crawford, *All the King's Men.*
Actress: Olivia de Havilland, *The Heiress.*
Sup. Actor: Dean Jagger, *Twelve O'Clock High.*
Sup. Actress: Mercedes McCambridge, *All the King's Men.*
Director: Joseph L. Mankiewicz, *Letter to Three Wives.*
Picture: *All the King's Men,* Columbia.

1950
Actor: Jose Ferrer, *Cyrano de Bergerac.*
Actress: Judy Holliday, *Born Yesterday.*
Sup. Actor: George Sanders, *All About Eve.*
Sup. Actress: Josephine Hull, *Harvey.*
Director: Joseph L. Mankiewicz, *All About Eve.*
Picture: *All About Eve,* 20th Century-Fox.

1951
Actor: Humphrey Bogart, *The African Queen.*
Actress: Vivien Leigh, *A Streetcar Named Desire.*
Sup. Actor: Karl Malden, *A Streetcar Named Desire.*
Sup. Actress: Kim Hunter, *A Streetcar Named Desire.*
Director: George Stevens, *A Place in the Sun.*
Picture: *An American in Paris,* MGM.

1952
Actor: Gary Cooper, *High Noon.*
Actress: Shirley Booth, *Come Back, Little Sheba.*
Sup. Actor: Anthony Quinn, *Viva Zapata!*
Sup. Actress: Gloria Grahame, *The Bad and the Beautiful.*
Director: John Ford, *The Quiet Man.*
Picture: *Greatest Show on Earth,* C.B. DeMille, Para-
  mount.

1953
Actor: William Holden, *Stalag 17.*
Actress: Audrey Hepburn, *Roman Holiday.*
Sup. Actor: Frank Sinatra, *From Here to Eternity.*
Sup. Actress: Donna Reed, *From Here to Eternity.*
Director: Fred Zinnemann, *From Here to Eternity.*
Picture: *From Here to Eternity,* Columbia.

1954
Actor: Marlon Brando, *On the Waterfront.*
Actress: Grace Kelly, *The Country Girl.*
Sup. Actor: Edmond O'Brien, *The Barefoot Contessa.*
Sup. Actress: Eva Marie Saint, *On the Waterfront.*
Director: Elia Kazan, *On the Waterfront.*
Picture: *On the Waterfront,* Horizon-American, Colum.

1955
Actor: Ernest Borgnine, *Marty.*
Actress: Anna Magnani, *The Rose Tattoo.*
Sup. Actor: Jack Lemmon, *Mister Roberts.*
Sup. Actress: Jo Van Fleet, *East of Eden.*
Director: Delbert Mann, *Marty.*
Picture: *Marty,* Hecht and Lancaster's Steven Prods., U.A.

1956
Actor: Yul Brynner, *The King and I.*
Actress: Ingrid Bergman, *Anastasia.*
Sup. Actor: Anthony Quinn, *Lust for Life.*
Sup. Actress: Dorothy Malone, *Written on the Wind.*
Director: George Stevens, *Giant.*
Picture: *Around the World in 80 Days,* Michael Todd, U.A.

1957
Actor: Alec Guinness, *The Bridge on the River Kwai.*
Actress: Joanne Woodward, *The Three Faces of Eve.*
Sup. Actor: Red Buttons, *Sayonara.*
Sup. Actress: Miyoshi Umeki, *Sayonara.*
Director: David Lean, *The Bridge on the River Kwai.*
Picture: *The Bridge on the River Kwai,* Columbia.

1958
Actor: David Niven, *Separate Tables.*
Actress: Susan Hayward, *I Want to Live.*
Sup. Actor: Burl Ives, *The Big Country.*
Sup. Actress: Wendy Hiller, *Separate Tables.*
Director: Vincente Minnelli, *Gigi.*
Picture: *Gigi.* Arthur Freed Production, MGM.

1959
Actor: Charlton Heston, *Ben-Hur.*
Actress: Simone Signoret, *Room at the Top.*
Sup. Actor: Hugh Griffith, *Ben-Hur.*
Sup. Actress: Shelley Winters, *Diary of Anne Frank.*
Director: William Wyler, *Ben-Hur.*
Picture: *Ben-Hur,* MGM.

1960
Actor: Burt Lancaster, *Elmer Gantry.*
Actress: Elizabeth Taylor, *Butterfield 8.*
Sup. Actor: Peter Ustinov, *Spartacus.*
Sup. Actress: Shirley Jones, *Elmer Gantry.*
Director: Billy Wilder, *The Apartment.*
Picture: *The Apartment,* Mirisch Co., U.A.

1961
Actor: Maximilian Schell, *Judgment at Nuremberg.*
Actress: Sophia Loren, *Two Women.*
Sup. Actor: George Chakiris, *West Side Story.*
Sup. Actress: Rita Moreno, *West Side Story.*
Director: Jerome Robbins, Robert Wise, *West Side Story.*
Picture: *West Side Story,* United Artists.

1962
Actor: Gregory Peck, *To Kill a Mockingbird.*
Actress: Anne Bancroft, *The Miracle Worker.*
Sup. Actor: Ed Begley, *Sweet Bird of Youth.*
Sup. Actress: Patty Duke, *The Miracle Worker.*
Director: David Lean, *Lawrence of Arabia.*
Picture: *Lawrence of Arabia,* Columbia.

1963
Actor: Sidney Poitier, *Lilies of the Field.*
Actress: Patricia Neal, *Hud.*
Sup. Actor: Melvyn Douglas, *Hud.*
Sup. Actress: Margaret Rutherford, *The V.I.P.s.*
Director: Tony Richardson, *Tom Jones.*
Picture: *Tom Jones,* Woodfall Prod., UA-Lopert Pictures.

1964
Actor: Rex Harrison, *My Fair Lady.*
Actress: Julie Andrews, *Mary Poppins.*
Sup. Actor: Peter Ustinov, *Topkapi.*
Sup. Actress: Lila Kedrova, *Zorba the Greek.*
Director: George Cukor, *My Fair Lady.*
Picture: *My Fair Lady,* Warner Bros.

1965
Actor: Lee Marvin, *Cat Ballou.*
Actress: Julie Christie, *Darling.*
Sup. Actor: Martin Balsam, *A Thousand Clowns.*
Sup. Actress: Shelley Winters, *A Patch of Blue.*
Director: Robert Wise, *The Sound of Music.*
Picture: *The Sound of Music,* 20th Century-Fox.

1966
Actor: Paul Scofield, *A Man for All Seasons.*
Actress: Elizabeth Taylor, *Who's Afraid of Virginia Woolf?*
Sup. Actor: Walter Matthau, *The Fortune Cookie.*
Sup. Actress: Sandy Dennis, *Who's Afraid of Virginia Woolf?*
Director: Fred Zinnemann, *A Man for All Seasons.*
Picture: *A Man for All Seasons,* Columbia.

1967
Actor: Rod Steiger, *In the Heat of the Night.*
Actress: Katharine Hepburn, *Guess Who's Coming to Dinner.*
Sup. Actor: George Kennedy, *Cool Hand Luke.*
Sup. Actress: Estelle Parsons, *Bonnie and Clyde.*
Director: Mike Nichols, *The Graduate.*
Picture: *In the Heat of the Night.*

1968
Actor: Cliff Robertson, *Charly.*
Actress: Katharine Hepburn, *The Lion in Winter;* Barbra Streisand, *Funny Girl* (tie).
Sup. Actor: Jack Albertson, *The Subject Was Roses.*
Sup. Actress: Ruth Gordon, *Rosemary's Baby.*
Director: Sir Carol Reed, *Oliver!*
Picture: *Oliver!*

1969
Actor: John Wayne, *True Grit.*
Actress: Maggie Smith, *The Prime of Miss Jean Brodie.*
Sup. Actor: Gig Young, *They Shoot Horses, Don't They?*
Sup. Actress: Goldie Hawn, *Cactus Flower.*
Director: John Schlesinger, *Midnight Cowboy.*
Picture: *Midnight Cowboy.*

1970
Actor: George C. Scott, *Patton* (refused).
Actress: Glenda Jackson, *Women in Love.*

Sup. Actor: John Mills, *Ryan's Daughter.*
Sup. Actress: Helen Hayes, *Airport.*
Director: Franklin Schaffner, *Patton.*
Picture: *Patton.*

1971
Actor: Gene Hackman, *The French Connection.*
Actress: Jane Fonda, *Klute.*
Sup. Actor: Ben Johnson, *The Last Picture Show.*
Sup. Actress: Cloris Leachman, *The Last Picture Show.*
Director: William Friedkin, *The French Connection.*
Picture: *The French Connection.*

1972
Actor: Marlon Brando, *The Godfather* (refused).
Actress: Liza Minnelli, *Cabaret.*
Sup. Actor: Joel Grey, *Cabaret.*
Sup. Actress: Eileen Heckart, *Butterflies are Free.*
Director: Bob Fosse, *Cabaret.*
Picture: *The Godfather.*

1973
Actor: Jack Lemmon, *Save the Tiger.*
Actress: Glenda Jackson, *A Touch of Class.*
Sup. Actor: John Houseman, *The Paper Chase.*
Sup. Actress: Tatum O'Neal, *Paper Moon.*
Director: George Roy Hill, *The Sting.*
Picture: *The Sting.*

1974
Actor: Art Carney, *Harry and Tonto.*
Actress: Ellen Burstyn, *Alice Doesn't Live Here Anymore.*
Sup. Actor: Robert DeNiro, *The Godfather, Part II.*
Sup. Actress: Ingrid Bergman, *Murder on the Orient Express.*
Director: Francis Ford Coppola, *The Godfather, Part II.*
Picture: *The Godfather, Part II.*

1975
Actor: Jack Nicholson, *One Flew Over the Cuckoo's Nest.*
Actress: Louise Fletcher, *One Flew Over the Cuckoo's Nest.*
Sup. Actor: George Burns, *The Sunshine Boys.*
Sup. Actress: Lee Grant, *Shampoo.*
Director: Milos Forman, *One Flew Over the Cuckoo's Nest.*
Picture: *One Flew Over the Cuckoo's Nest.*

1976
Actor: Peter Finch, *Network.*
Actress: Faye Dunaway, *Network.*
Sup. Actor: Jason Robards, *All the President's Men.*
Sup. Actress: Beatrice Straight, *Network.*
Director: John G. Avildsen, *Rocky.*
Picture: *Rocky.*

1977
Actor: Richard Dreyfuss, *The Goodbye Girl.*
Actress: Diane Keaton, *Annie Hall.*
Sup. Actor: Jason Robards, *Julia.*
Sup. Actress: Vanessa Redgrave, *Julia.*
Director: Woody Allen, *Annie Hall.*
Picture: *Annie Hall.*

1978
Actor: Jon Voight, *Coming Home.*
Actress: Jane Fonda, *Coming Home.*
Sup. Actor: Christopher Walken, *The Deer Hunter.*
Sup. Actress: Maggie Smith, *California Suite.*
Director: Michael Cimino, *The Deer Hunter.*
Picture: *The Deer Hunter.*

1979
Actor: Dustin Hoffman, *Kramer vs. Kramer.*
Actress: Sally Field, *Norma Rae.*
Sup. Actor: Melvyn Douglas, *Being There.*
Sup. Actress: Meryl Streep, *Kramer vs. Kramer.*
Director: Robert Benton, *Kramer vs. Kramer.*
Picture: *Kramer vs. Kramer.*

1980
Actor: Robert DeNiro, *Raging Bull.*
Actress: Sissy Spacek, *Coal Miner's Daughter.*
Sup. Actor: Timothy Hutton, *Ordinary People.*
Sup. Actress: Mary Steenburgen, *Melvin & Howard.*
Director: Robert Redford, *Ordinary People.*
Picture: *Ordinary People.*

1981
Actor: Henry Fonda, *On Golden Pond.*
Actress: Katharine Hepburn, *On Golden Pond.*
Sup. Actor: John Gielgud, *Arthur.*
Sup. Actress: Maureen Stapleton, *Reds.*
Director: Warren Beatty, *Reds.*
Picture: *Chariots of Fire.*

1982
Actor: Ben Kingsley, *Gandhi.*
Actress: Meryl Streep, *Sophie's Choice.*
Sup. Actor: Louis Gossett, Jr., *An Officer and a Gentleman.*
Sup. Actress: Jessica Lange, *Tootsie.*
Director: Richard Attenborough, *Gandhi.*
Picture: *Gandhi.*

1983
Actor: Robert Duvall, *Tender Mercies.*
Actress: Shirley MacLaine, *Terms of Endearment.*
Supporting Actor: Jack Nicholson, *Terms of Endearment.*
Supporting Actress: Linda Hunt, *The Year of Living Dangerously.*
Director: James L. Brooks, *Terms of Endearment.*
Picture: *Terms of Endearment.*

1984
Actor: F. Murray Abraham, *Amadeus.*
Actress: Sally Field, *Places in the Heart.*
Supporting Actor: Haing S. Ngor, *The Killing Fields.*
Supporting Actress: Peggy Ashcroft, *A Passage to India.*
Director: Milos Forman, *Amadeus.*
Picture: *Amadeus.*

1985
Actor: William Hurt, *Kiss of the Spider Woman.*
Actress: Geraldine Page, *The Trip to Bountiful.*
Supporting Actor: Don Ameche, *Cocoon.*
Supporting Actress: Anjelica Huston, *Prizzi's Honor.*
Director: Sydney Pollack, *Out of Africa.*
Picture: *Out of Africa.*

1986
Actor: Paul Newman, *The Color of Money.*
Actress: Marlee Matlin, *Children of a Lesser God.*
Supporting Actor: Michael Caine, *Hannah and Her Sisters.*
Supporting Actress: Dianne Wiest, *Hannah and Her Sisters.*
Director: Oliver Stone, *Platoon.*
Picture: *Platoon.*

1987
Actor: Michael Douglas, *Wall Street.*
Actress: Cher, *Moonstruck.*
Supporting Actor: Sean Connery, *The Untouchables.*
Supporting Actress: Olympia Dukakis, *Moonstruck.*
Director: Bernardo Bertolucci, *The Last Emperor.*
Picture: *The Last Emperor.*

1988
Picture: *Rain Man.*
Actor: Dustin Hoffman, *Rain Man.*
Actress: Jodie Foster, *The Accused.*
Supporting Actor: Kevin Kline, *A Fish Called Wanda.*
Supporting Actress: Geena Davis, *The Accidental Tourist.*
Director: Barry Levinson, *Rain Man.*
Foreign-language Film: *Pelle the Conqueror.*
Original Screenplay: Ronald Bass, Barry Morrow, *Rain Man.*
Screenplay Adaptation: Christopher Hampton, *Dangerous Liaisons.*
Cinematography: Peter Biziou, *Mississippi Burning.*
Editing: Arthur Schmidt, *Who Framed Roger Rabbit.*
Original Score: Dave Grusin, *The Milagro Beanfield War.*
Original Song: Carly Simon, "Let the River Run," *Working Girl.*
Costume Design: James Acheson, *Dangerous Liaisons.*
Visual Effects: Ken Ralston, Richard Williams, Edward Jones, George Gibbs, *Who Framed Roger Rabbit*
Documentary Feature: *Hotel Terminus: The Life and Times of Klaus Barbie.*
Documentary Short: *You Don't Have to Die.*
Animated Short: *Tin Toy.*
Live Short: *The Appointments of Dennis Jennings.*

Grammy Awards

Source: National Academy of Recording Arts & Sciences

1958
Record: Domenico Modugno, *Nel Blu Dipinto Di Blu (Volare).*
Album: Henry Mancini, *The Music from Peter Gunn.*

1959
Record: Bobby Darin, *Mack the Knife.*
Album: Frank Sinatra, *Come Dance With Me.*

1960
Record: Percy Faith, *Theme From A Summer Place.*
Album: Bob Newhart, *Button Down Mind.*

1961
Record: Henry Mancini, *Moon River.*
Album: Judy Garland, *Judy At Carnegie Hall.*

1962
Record: Tony Bennett, *I Left My Heart in San Francisco.*
Album: Vaughn Meader, *The First Family.*

1963
Record: Henry Mancini, *The Days of Wine and Roses.*
Album: *The Barbra Streisand Album.*

1964
Record: Stan Getz and Astrud Gilberto, *The Girl From Ipanema.*
Album: *Getz/Gilberto.*

1965
Record: Herb Alpert, *A Taste Of Honey.*
Album: Frank Sinatra, *September of My Years.*

1966
Record: Frank Sinatra, *Strangers in the Night.*
Album: Frank Sinatra, *A Man and His Music.*

1967
Record: 5th Dimension, *Up, Up and Away.*
Album: The Beatles, *Sgt. Pepper's Lonely Hearts Club Band.*

1968
Record: Simon & Garfunkel, *Mrs. Robinson.*
Album: Glen Campbell, *By the Time I Get to Phoenix.*

1969
Record: 5th Dimension, *Aquarius/Let the Sunshine In.*
Album: *Blood, Sweat and Tears.*

1970
Record: Simon & Garfunkel, *Bridge Over Troubled Waters.*
Album: *Bridge Over Troubled Waters.*

1971
Record: Carole King, *It's Too Late.*
Album: Carole King, *Tapestry.*

1972
Record: Roberta Flack, *The First Time Ever I Saw Your Face.*
Album: *The Concert For Bangla Desh.*

1973
Record: Roberta Flack, *Killing Me Softly with His Song.*
Album: Stevie Wonder, *Innervisions.*

1974
Record: Olivia Newton-John, *I Honestly Love You.*
Album: Stevie Wonder, *Fulfullingness' First Finale.*

1975
Record: Captain & Tennille, *Love Will Keep Us Together.*
Album: Paul Simon, *Still Crazy After All These Years.*

1976
Record: George Benson, *This Masquerade.*
Album: Stevie Wonder, *Songs in the Key of Life.*

1977
Record: Eagles, *Hotel California.*
Album: Fleetwood Mac, *Rumours.*

1978
Record: Billy Joel, *Just the Way You Are.*
Album: Bee Gees, *Saturday Night Fever.*

1979
Record: The Doobie Brothers, *What a Fool Believes.*
Album: Billy Joel, *52nd Street.*

1980
Record: Christopher Cross, *Sailing.*
Album: Christopher Cross, *Christopher Cross.*

1981
Record: Kim Carnes, *Bette Davis Eyes.*
Album: John Lennon, Yoko Ono, *Double Fantasy.*

1982
Record: Toto, *Rosanna.*
Album: Toto, *Toto IV.*

1983
Record: Michael Jackson, *Beat It.*
Album: Michael Jackson, *Thriller.*

1984
Record: Tina Turner, *What's Love Got to Do With It.*
Album: Lionel Richie, *Can't Slow Down.*

1985
Record: USA for Africa, *We Are the World.*
Album: Phil Collins, *No Jacket Required.*

1986
Record: Steve Winwood, *Higher Love.*
Album: Paul Simon, *Graceland.*

1987
Record: Paul Simon, *Graceland.*
Album: U2, *The Joshua Tree.*

1988
Record: Bobby McFerrin, *Don't Worry, Be Happy.*
Album: George Michael, *Faith.*

ARTS AND MEDIA

Notable New York Theater Openings, 1988-89 Season

Ain't Misbehavin', revival of the revue based on the music of Fats Waller; with Nell Carter, Armelia McQueen, Charlaine Woodard, Andre De Shields, and Ken Page.

Black and Blue, revue conceived by Claudio Segovia and Hector Orezzoli as a tribute to a great black American jazz and blues artists; with Ruth Brown, Carrie Smith, Linda Hopkins.

Born Yesterday, revival of the 1946 Garson Kanin comedy; with Ed Asner, Madeline Kahn, and Daniel Hugh Kelly.

Brilliant Traces, play by Cindy Lou Johnson; with Joan Cusack and Kevin Anderson.

Call Me Ethel, one-woman musical that chronicles the life of Ethel Merman; with Rita McKenzie.

Coriolanus, Shakespeare's drama; with Christopher Walken, Irene Worth, Keith David, Moses Gunn, and Larry Bryggman.

Ghetto, drama by Joshua Sobol; with George Hearn, Helen Schneider, and Donal Donnelly.

Hizzoner, one-man play about famed New York City mayor Fiorello LaGuardia; with Tony Lo Bianco.

Jerome Robbins Broadway, anthology of the best musical numbers staged by the famed choreographer and director; with Charlotte D'Amboise, Jason Alexander, and Faith Prince.

Largely New York, comedy written and directed by Bill Irwin; with Irwin.

Legs Diamond, musical by Peter Allen; with Allen.

Lend Me a Tenor, play by Ken Ludwig; with Philip Bosco, Victor Garber, Tovah Feldshuh, and Ron Holgate.

Metamorphosis, play adapted by Steven Berkoff from a Franz Kafka short story; with Mikhail Baryshnikov and Rene Auberjonois.

Our Town, revival of the Thornton Wilder classic; with Spalding Gray, Eric Stoltz, and Penelope Ann Miller.

Spoils of War, drama by Michael Weller; with Kate Nelligan, Christopher Collet, and Jeffrey De Munn.

Rumors, comedy by Neil Simon; with Ron Leibman, Jessica Walter, Joyce Van Patten, and Ken Howard.

Run For Your Wife, comedy by Ray Cooney; with Cooney, Paxton Whitehead, Hilary Labow, and Kay Walbye.

Shirley Valentine, one-woman play by Willy Russell; with Pauline Collins.

Starmites, musical by Barry Keating; with Liz Larsen and Brian Lane Green.

The Cocktail Hour, comedy by A.R. Gurney; with Nancy Marchand, Keene Curtis, and Bruce Davison.

The Devil's Disciple, revival of the George Bernard Shaw play; with Philip Bosco, Victor Garber, Roxanne Hart, and Remak Ramsey.

The Heidi Chronicles, play by Wendy Wasserstein; with Joan Allen, Peter Friedman, Boyd Gaines, and Ellen Parker.

The Pajama Game, New York City Opera's production of the 1954 musical; with Judy Kaye, Richard Muenz, and Avery Saltzman.

The Winter's Tale, the Shakespeare tragedy; with Mandy Patinkin, Diane Venora, Christopher Reeve, and Alfre Woodard.

Welcome to the Club, musical-comedy by Cy Coleman and A.E. Hotchner; with Avery Schreiber, Sally Mayes, and Marilyn Sokol.

What the Butler Saw, revival of the 1967 Joe Orton farce; with Carole Shelley, Joseph Maher, and Charles Keating.

Record Long Run Broadway Plays[1]

Source: *Variety*

Show	Perf.	Show	Perf.	Show	Perf.
*Oh, Calcutta (revival)	5,892	La Cage aux Folles	1,761	Oh! Calcutta! (original)	1,314
*Chorus Line	5,792	Hair	1,750	Brighton Beach Memoirs	1,299
42d Street	3,486	The Wiz	1,672	Angel Street	1,295
Grease	3,388	Born Yesterday	1,642	Lightnin'	1,291
Fiddler on the Roof	3,242	Ain't Misbehavin'	1,604	Promises, Promises	1,281
Life With Father	3,224	Best Little Whorehouse in Texas	1,584	The King and I	1,246
Tobacco Road	3,182	Mary, Mary	1,572	Cactus Flower	1,234
Hello Dolly	2,844	Evita	1,567	Sleuth	1,222
*Cats	2,813	Voice of the Turtle	1,557	Torch Song Trilogy	1,222
My Fair Lady	2,717	Barefoot in the Park	1,530	"1776"	1,217
Annie	2,377	Dreamgirls	1,521	*Me and My Girl	1,212
Man of La Mancha	2,328	Mame	1,508	Equus	1,209
Abie's Irish Rose	2,327	Same Time, Next Year	1,453	Sugar Babies	1,208
Oklahoma!	2,212	Arsenic and Old Lace	1,444	Guys and Dolls	1,200
Pippin	1,944	The Sound of Music	1,443	Amadeus	1,181
South Pacific	1,925	How To Succeed in Business		Cabaret	1,165
Magic Show	1,920	Without Really Trying	1,417	Mister Roberts	1,157
Deathtrap	1,792	Hellzapoppin	1,404	Annie Get Your Gun	1,147
Gemini	1,788	The Music Man	1,375	Seven Year Itch	1,141
Harvey	1,775	Funny Girl	1,348	Butterflies Are Free	1,128
Dancin'	1,774	Mumenschanz	1,326	Pins and Needles	1,108

(1) Number of performances through July 2, 1989. *Still running July 2, 1989.

Top Road Grossers, 1988-89

(outside New York City)

Source: *Variety*

Show	Totals	Show	Totals	Show	Totals
Les Miserables		South Pacific	9,804,746	Penn & Teller	5,698,769
(2 companies)	$77,735,722	The Search for Signs of Intelligent Life in		Elvis	5,109,560
Cats (2 companies)	30,168,516	the Universe (Lily Tomlin)	8,933,701	Oba-Oba	4,765,324
Me And My Girl	14,379,639	Into the Woods	8,584,304	Anything Goes	3,738,941
Cabaret	11,090,334	Driving Miss Daisy	7,461,314	Broadway Bound	3,637,295
Can-Can	10,014,214				

Notable Movies of the Year (Aug. 1988 to July 1989)

Movie	Stars	Director
A Cry in the Dark	Meryl Streep, Sam Neill	Fred Schepisi
Another Woman	Gena Rowlands, Mia Farrow, Gene Hackman, Ian Holm	Woody Allen
Batman	Michael Keaton, Jack Nicholson, Kim Basinger	Tim Burton
Beaches	Bette Midler, Barbara Hershey	Garry Marshall
Betrayed	Debra Winger, Tom Berenger	Costa-Gavras
Bird	Forest Whitaker, Diana Verora	Clint Eastwood
Buster	Phil Collins, Julie Walters	David Green
Clara's Heart	Whoopi Goldberg, Michael Ontkean, Kathleen Quinlan	Robert Mulligan
Clean and Sober	Michael Keaton, Kathy Baker, Morgan Freeman	Glenn Gordon Caron
Cocoon: The Return	Don Ameche, Wilford Brimley, Hume Cronin, Maureen Stapleton, Jessica Tandy	Daniel Petrie
Cousins	Ted Danson, Isabella Rossellini, Sean Young, Lloyd Bridges	Joel Schumacher
Crossing Delancy	Amy Irving, Peter Riegert	Joan Micklin Silver
Dangerous Liaisons	Glenn Close, Michelle Pfeiffer, John Malkovich	Stephen Frears
Dead Poets Society	Robin Williams, Robert Sean Leonard	Peter Weir
Dead Ringers	Jeremy Irons, Genevieve Bujold	David Cronenberg
Dirty Rotten Scoundrels	Steve Martin, Michael Caine	Frank Oz
Do the Right Thing	Danny Aiello, Ossie Davis, Ruby Dee, Spike Lee	Spike Lee
Eight Men Out	John Cusack, D.B. Sweeney, Clifton James, Charlie Sheen	John Sayles
Everybody's All-American	Dennis Quaid, Jessica Lange, Timothy Hutton	Taylor Hackford
Farewell to the King	Nick Nolte, Nigel Havens	John Milius
Field of Dreams	Kevin Costner, Amy Madigan, James Earl Jones, Burt Lancaster	Phil Alden Robinson
Ghostbusters II	Bill Murray, Dan Aykroyd, Harold Ramis, Sigourney Weaver	Ivan Reitman
Gorillas in the Mist	Sigourney Weaver, Bryan Brown	Michael Apted
Great Balls of Fire	Dennis Quaid, Winona Ryder, Alec Baldwin	Jim McBride
Indiana Jones and the Last Crusade	Harrison Ford, Sean Connery, Alison Doody	Steven Spielberg
Jackknife	Robert De Niro, Ed Harris, Kathy Baker	David Jones
Lean on Me	Morgan Freeman, Robert Guillaume, Beverly Todd	John V. Avildsen
Lethal Weapon II	Mel Gibson, Danny Glover	Richard Donner
Licence To Kill	Timothy Dalton, Carey Lowell, Robert Davi	John Glen
Little Dorrit	Alec Guinness, Derek Jacobi, Sarah Pickering	Christine Edzard
Major League	Tom Berenger, Corbin Bernsen, Charlie Sheen	Davis S. Wood
Married to the Mob	Michelle Pfeiffer, Matthew Modine, Dean Stockwell	Jonathan Demme
Memories of Me	Billy Crystal, Alan King, JoBeth Williams	Henry Winkler
Miles From Home	Richard Gere, Kevin Anderson, John Malkovich	Gary Sinise
Miss Firecracker	Holly Hunter, Mary Steenburgen, Tim Robbins, Alfre Woodard	Thomas Schlamme
Mississippi Burning	Gene Hackman, Willem Dafoe, Frances McDormand	Alan Parker
Moon Over Parador	Richard Dreyfuss, Sonia Braga, Raul Julia	Paul Mazursky
New York Stories	Woody Allen, Mia Farrow, Nick Nolte, Talia Shire	Woody Allen, Francis Coppola, Martin Scorsese
Physical Evidence	Burt Reynolds, Theresa Russell, Ned Beatty	Michael Crichton
Punchline	Tom Hanks, Sally Field	David Seltzer
Rain Man	Dustin Hoffman, Tom Cruise	Barry Levinson
Running On Empty	Judd Hirsch, Christine Lahti, River Phoenix, Martha Plimpton	Sidney Lumet
Say Anything	John Cusack, Ione Skye	Cameron Crowe
Scrooged	Bill Murray, Karen Allen, Robert Mitchem, John Forsythe	Richard Donner
See No Evil, Hear No Evil	Richard Pryor, Gene Wilder	Arthur Hiller
Skin Deep	John Ritter, Vincent Gardenia, Alyson Reed	Blake Edwards
Star Trek V	William Shatner, Leonard Nimoy	William Shatner
Sweet Hearts Dance	Don Johnson, Susan Sarandon, Jeff Daniels	Robert Greenwald
Talk Radio	Eric Bogosian, Alec Baldwin, Ellen Greene, Leslie Hope	Oliver Stone
Tap	Gregory Hines, Sammy Davis Jr., Suzzanne Douglas	Nick Castle
Tequila Sunrise	Mel Gibson, Michelle Pfeiffer, Kurt Russell	Robert Towne
The Accused	Kelly McGillis, Jodie Foster	Jonathan Kaplan
The Accidental Tourist	William Hurt, Kathleen Turner, Geena Davis	Lawrence Kasdan
The Burbs	Tom Hanks, Bruce Dern, Carrie Fisher	Joe Dante
The Dream Team	Michael Keaton, Christopher Lloyd, Peter Boyle	Howard Zieff
The Good Mother	Diane Keaton, Jason Robards, James Naughton	Leonard Nimoy
The Last Temptation of Christ	Willem Dafoe, Harvey Keitel, Barbara Hershey	Martin Scorsese
The Naked Gun	Leslie Nielsen, Priscilla Presley	David Zucker
Things Change	Don Ameche, Joe Mantegna, Robert Prosky	David Mamet
Torch Song Trilogy	Harvey Firestein, Anne Bancroft, Matthew Broderick	Paul Bogart
True Believer	James Woods, Robert Downey Jr.	Joseph Ruben
Tucker: The Man and His Dream	Jeff Bridges, Martin Landau, Dean Stockwell	Francis Coppola
Twins	Arnold Schwarzenegger, Danny DeVito	Ivan Reitman
Vampire's Kiss	Nicolas Cage, Maria Conchita Alonso, Jennifer Beals	Robert Bierman
When Harry Met Sally	Billy Crystal, Meg Ryan, Carrie Fisher	Rob Reiner
Without a Clue	Michael Caine, Ben Kingsley	Thom Eberhardt
Working Girl	Melanie Griffith, Sigourney Weaver, Harrison Ford	Mike Nichols

Top Movie Rentals, 1988

Source: *Variety*, January, 1989

Figures represent U.S. and Canadian rentals accruing to distributors, not total ticket sales receipts taken in at theaters.

Title	Total Rentals	Title	Total Rentals	Title	Total Rentals
1. Who Framed Roger Rabbit	$78,000,000	18. Bull Durham	21,900,000	36. Shoot To Kill	12,478,000
2. Coming to America	65,000,000	19. Colors	21,200,000	37. Dirty Rotten Scoundrels	12,000,000
3. Good Morning, Vietnam	58,103,000	20. Rain Man	21,000,000	38. Ernest Saves Christmas	12,000,000
4. Crocodile Dundee II	57,300,000	21. Young Guns	19,500,000	39. Gorillas In The Mist	12,000,000
5. Big	50,800,000	22. Biloxi Blues	19,466,043	40. Working Girl	12,000,000
6. Three Men And A Baby	36,300,000	23. The Great Outdoors	19,104,434	41. Funny Farm	11,800,000
7. Die Hard	35,000,000	24. The Dead Pool	19,000,000	42. Alien Nation	11,300,000
8. Cocktail	35,000,000	25. Bambi (reissue)	18,865,000	43. Betrayed	11,126,475
9. Moonstruck	34,393,000	26. Midnight Run	18,263,413	44. The Fox And The Hound (reissue)	10,605,000
10. Beetlejuice	33,200,000	27. Big Business	17,768,000	45. Punchline	10,200,000
11. Scrooged	33,000,000	28. The Land Before Time	17,000,000	46. Fatal Attraction	10,000,000
12. Twins	32,000,000	29. Red Heat	16,000,000	47. The Presidio	9,600,000
13. Rambo III	28,000,000	30. The Last Emperor	16,000,000	48. License To Drive	9,330,000
14. Willow	27,835,000	31. Oliver & Company	15,000,000	49. Friday The 13th Part VII—The New Blood	9,100,000
15. A Fish Called Wanda	26,577,000	32. Tequila Sunrise	15,000,000	50. Police Academy 5: Assignment Miami Beach	9,100,000
16. The Naked Gun	26,000,000	33. Broadcast News	14,900,000		
17. A Nightmare On Elm Street 4: The Dream Master	22,000,000	34. The Accused	14,000,000		
		35. Child's Play	14,000,000		

All-Time Top 50 Movies

Source: *Variety*, January, 1989

Rental figures are in absolute dollars, reflecting actual amounts received by the distributors (estimated for movies in current release). Ticket price inflation favors recent films, but older films have the advantage of numerous reissues adding to their totals.

Title	Total Rentals	Title	Total Rentals	Title	Total Rentals
1. E.T. the Extra-Terrestrial; 1982	$228,618,939	1987	80,857,776	1937	61,752,000
2. Star Wars; 1977	193,500,000	19. The Sound of Music; 1965	79,748,000	36. On Golden Pond; 1981	61,174,744
3. Return of the Jedi; 1983	168,002,414	20. Gremlins; 1984	79,500,000	37. Kramer Vs. Kramer; 1979	59,986,335
4. The Empire Strikes Back; 1980	141,600,000	21. Top Gun; 1986	79,400,000	38. One Flew Over the Cuckoo's Nest; 1975	59,939,701
5. Ghostbusters; 1984	130,211,324	22. Rambo: First Blood Part II; 1985	78,919,250	39. 9 to 5; 1980	59,100,000
6. Jaws; 1975	129,549,325	23. The Sting; 1973	78,212,000	40. Smokey And the Bandit; 1977	58,949,938
7. Raiders of the Lost Ark; 1981	115,598,000	24. Who Framed Roger Rabbit; 1988	78,000,000	41. Stir Crazy; 1980	58,364,420
8. Indiana Jones and the Temple of Doom	109,000,000	25. Gone With the Wind; 1939	77,641,106	42. The Karate Kid Part II; 1986	58,362,026
9. Beverly Hills Cop; 1984	108,000,000	26. Rocky IV; 1985	76,023,246	43. Good Morning, Vietnam; 1987	58,103,000
10. Back to the Future; 1985	104,408,738	27. Saturday Night Fever; 1977	74,100,000	44. Crocodile Dundee II; 1988	57,300,000
11. Grease; 1978	96,300,000	28. National Lampoon's Animal House; 1978	70,826,000	45. Star Trek IV: the Voyage Home; 1986	56,820,071
12. tootsie; 1982	96,292,736	29. Crocodile Dundee; 1986	70,227,000	46. Rocky; 1976	56,524,972
13. the Exorcist; 1973	89,000,000	30. Fatal Attraction; 1987	70,000,000	47. Star Trek; 1979	56,000,000
14. the Godfather; 1972	86,275,000	31. Platoon; 1986	69,742,143	48. An Officer and A Gentleman; 1982	55,223,000
15. Superman; 1978	82,800,000	32. Rocky III; 1982	66,262,796	49. American Graffiti; 1973	55,128,175
16. Close Encounters of the Third Kind; 1977/1980	82,750,000	33. Superman II; 1981	65,100,000	50. Porky's; 1982	54,000,000
17. Three Men and a Baby; 1977	81,313,000	34. Coming to America; 1988	65,000,000		
18. Beverly Hills Cop II;		35. Snow White and the Seven Dwarfs;			

U.S. Book Production

Source: *Publishers Weekly*, Mar. 10, 1989

Hardcover and Paperback

Category	1986	1987	1988[p]	Category	1986	1987	1988[p]
Agriculture	564	652	575	Literature	2,145	2,358	1,982
Art	1,697	1,693	1,338	Medicine	3,445	3,995	3,376
Biography	2,152	2,259	1,994	Music	356	352	273
Business	1,604	1,462	1,375	Philosophy, Psychology	1,669	1,845	1,656
Education	1,029	1,081	979	Poetry, Drama	1,278	1,236	1,106
Fiction	5,578	6,298	5,144	Religion	2,788	2,850	2,306
General Works	2,484	2,620	2,083	Science	3,360	3,658	3,118
History	2,471	2,882	2,550	Sociology, Economics	7,912	8,115	7,119
Home Economics	1,103	1,168	929	Sports, Recreation	1,192	1,263	941
Juveniles	4,516	4,642	4,212	Technology	2,698	2,756	2,216
Language	668	699	534	Travel	543	629	554
Law	1,385	1,544	1,129	Total	52,637	56,027	47,489

p = preliminary

Notable Books of 1988

Source: American Library Association

Fiction

Eva Luna, Isabel Allende
Where I'm Calling From, Raymond Carver
Libra, Don DeLillo
Paris Trout, Pete Dexter
Selected Stories, Andre Dubus
Tracks, Louise Erdrich
Love in the Time of Cholera, Gabriel Garcia Marquez
Of Such Small Differences, Joanne Greenberg

The Fifth Child, Doris Lessing
The Middleman and Other Stories, Bharati Mukherjee
Mama Day, Gloria Naylor
Wheat That Springeth Green, J.F. Powers
Points of Light, Linda Gray Sexton
Fair and Tender Ladies, Lee Smith
A Far Cry from Kensington, Muriel Spark
Breathing Lessons, Anne Tyler

Nonfiction

The Arctic Grail, Pierre Berton
We Are Not Afraid, Seth Cagin and Dray Philip
Oscar Wilde, Richard Ellmann
Freud, Peter Gay
Remembering America, Richard N. Goodwin
Stranger in the Forest, Eric Hansen

Lovesong, Julius Lester
Battle Cry of Freedom, James M. McPherson
Nora, Brenda Maddox
Adam, Eve, and the Serpent, Elaine Pagels
Fear No Evil, Natan Sharansky

Bestselling Children's Books of 1988

Source: *Publishers Weekly,* Apr. 28, 1989

(All books are hardcover.)

1. *Dear Mili,* Wilhelm Grimm, translated by Ralph Manheim, illus. by Maurice Sendak
2. *Where's Waldo,* Martin Handford
3. *Downy Duckling,* Demi
4. *Sing a Song of Popcorn,* compiled by Beatrice Schenk de Regniers, et al.
5. *The Story of the Easter Bunny,* Sheila Black, illus. by Robyn Officer
6. *Owl Moon,* Jane Yolen, illustrated by John Schoenherr
7. *Cuddly Chick,* Demi
8. *Baby's First Christmas,* Tomie dePaola
9. *The Way Things Work,* David Macaulay
10. *Spot's Big Book of Words,* Eric Hill
11. *Find Waldo Now,* Martin Handford
12. *I Am Not Going to Get Up Today,* Dr. Seuss, illus. by James Stevenson
13. *Just As Long As We're Together,* Judy Blume
14. *Baby Donald's Busy Play Group,* illus. by Darrell Baker
15. *Nothing to Do,* Liza Alexander, illus. by Tom Cooke
16. *Just Like Ernie,* Emily Thompson, illus. by Tom Cooke
17. *The Glow-in-the-Dark Night Sky Book,* Clint Hatchett, illus. by Stephen Marchesi
18. *The Little Engine That Could,* Watty Piper
19. *Spot's First Easter,* Eric Hill
20. *The Little Engine That Could Pudgy Word Book,* Deborah Shine, illus. by Christine Ong

All-Time Bestselling Paperback Books

Source: *Publisher's Weekly,* May 26, 1989; figures are publishers' estimates.

1. *Baby and Child Care,* Dr. Benjamin Spock, 39,200,000
2. *Merriam Webster Dictionary,* 19,700,000
3. *New American Roget's College Thesaurus,* 17,620,000
4. *How to Win Friends and Influence People,* Dale Carnegie, 17,400,000
5. *The Hobbit,* J.R.R. Tolkien, 14,500,000
6. *The American Heritage Dictionary,* 12,983,480
7. *1984,* George Orwell, 12,800,000
8. *The New American Webster's Handy College Dictionary,* 12,600,000
9. *The Exorcist,* William Peter Blatty, 12,400,000
10. *French/English, English/French Dictionary,* La Rousse, 11,300,000
11. *The Thorn Birds,* Colleen McCullough, 10,880,000
12. *Spanish/English, English/Spanish Dictionary,* ed. Carlos Castillo & Otto F. Bond, 10,800,000
13. *Animal Farm,* George Orwell, 10,470,000
14. *Mythology,* Edith Hamilton, 10,000,000
15. *The Catcher in the Rye,* J.D. Salinger, 9,650,000
16. *Love Story,* Erich Segal, 9,500,000
17. *Peyton Place,* Grace Metalious, 9,468,566
18. *Valley of the Dolls,* Jacqueline Susann, 9,451,000
19. *The Pearl,* John Steinbeck, 9,430,000
20. *The Sensuous Woman,* "J", 9,377,592
21. *The Fellowship of the Ring,* J.R.R. Tolkien, 8,400,000
22. *Jaws,* Peter Benchley, 8,286,000
23. *Everything You Always Wanted to Know About Sex ...,* David R. Reuben, M.D., 8,243,000
24. *God's Little Acre,* Erskine Caldwell, 8,230,000
25. *Hoyle's Rules of Games,* ed. Albert Morehead & G. Mott-Smith, 7,810,000
26. *Exodus,* Leon Uris, 7,520,000
27. *A Separate Peace,* John Knowles, 7,520,000
28. *The Happy Hooker,* Xaviera Hollander, 7,498,276
29. *One Flew Over the Cuckoo's Nest,* Ken Kesey, 7,440,000
30. *Of Mice and Men,* John Steinbeck, 7,422,000
31. *The Other Side of Midnight,* Sidney Sheldon, 7,389,162
32. *Jonathan Livingston Seagull,* Richard Bach, 7,282,000
33. *I Never Promised You a Rose Garden,* Joanne Greenberg, 7,100,000
34. *Simple Solution to Rubik's Cube,* James Nourse, 7,053,000
35. *How to Buy Stocks,* Louis Engel, 7,025,000
36. *Chariots of the Gods,* Erich Von Daniken, 7,025,000
37. *Complete Scarsdale Medical Diet,* Herman Tarnower, M.D. & Samm Sinclair Baker, 6,833,020
38. *The Two Towers,* J.R.R. Tolkien, 6,815,000
39. *Rich Man, Poor Man,* Irwin Shaw, 6,794,370
40. *The Return of the King,* J.R.R. Tolkien, 6,775,000
41. *Helter Skelter,* Vincent Bugliosi and Curt Gentry, 6,625,000
42. *Shogun,* James Clavell, 6,620,571
43. *I the Jury,* Mickey Spillane, 6,610,000
44. *All Quiet on the Western Front,* Erich Marie Remarque, 6,475,000
45. *I'm OK, You're OK,* Thomas Harris, 6,435,000
46. *The Amityville Horror,* Jay Anson, 6,422,000
47. *Dr. Atkins' Diet Revolution,* Dr. Robert Atkins, 6,230,000
48. *Airport,* Arthur Hailey, 6,120,000
49. *Fear of Flying,* Erica Jong, 6,110,000
50. *Webster's New World Dictionary,* ed. David B. Guralnik, 5,957,000

Best-Selling Books of 1988

Source: *New York Times*; numbers in parentheses show rank on *Publishers Weekly* bestseller lists.

Hardcover Fiction

1. *The Cardinal of the Kremlin*, Tom Clancy (6)
2. *The Bonfire of the Vanities*, Tom Wolfe (1)
3. *The Icarus Agenda*, Robert Ludlum (4)*
4. *Alaska*, James Michener (4)*
5. *The Sands of Time*, Sidney Sheldon
6. *Zoya*, Danielle Steel (5)
7. *Love in the Time of Cholera*, Gabriel Garcia Marquez (2)
8. *The Shell Seekers*, Rosamunde Pilcher (3)
9. *The Queen of the Damned*, Anne Rice
10. *'Till We Meet Again*, Judith Krantz (7)
* tie

Hardcover Nonfiction

1. *A Brief History of Time*, Stephen W. Hawking (4)*
2. *Trump*, Donald J. Trump with Tony Schwartz (2)
3. *All I Really Need to Know I Learned in Kindergarten*, Robert Fulghum
4. *Talking Straight*, Lee Iacocca with Sonny Kleinfield (6)
5. *Gracie*, George Burns
6. *The Rise and Fall of the Great Powers*, Paul Kennedy (5)
7. *For the Record*, Donald T. Regan
8. *Thriving on Chaos*, Tom Peters (4)*
9. *Love, Medicine & Miracles*, Bernie S. Siegel
10. *Child Star*, Shirley Temple Black
* tie

Hardcover How-to, Advice, Other

1. *The 8-Week Cholesterol Cure*, Robert E. Kowalski (1)
2. *Swim With the Sharks Without Being Eaten Alive*, Harvey Mackay (3)
3. *Webster's Ninth New Collegiate Dictionary*

4. *The Frugal Gourmet Cooks American*, Jeff Smith
5. *Elizabeth Takes Off*, Elizabeth Taylor

Paperback Fiction

1. *Presumed Innocent*, Scott Turow
2. *Patriot Games*, Tom Clancy
3. *Fine Things*, Danielle Steel
4. *The Prince of Tides*, Pat Conroy
5. *Fallen Hearts*, V.C. Andrews
6. *Kaleidoscope*, Danielle Steel
7. *Misery*, Stephen King
8. *The Tommyknockers*, Stephen King
9. *Weep No More, My Lady*, Mary Higgins Clark
10. *The Bonfire of the Vanities*, Tom Wolfe

Paperback Nonfiction

1. *Love, Medicine & Miracles*, Bernie S. Siegel
2. *The Road Less Traveled*, M. Scott Peck
3. *Communion*, Whitley Strieber
4. *The Power of Myth*, Joseph Campbell with Bill Moyers
5. *The Cat Who Came for Christmas*, Cleveland Amory
6. *Small Sacrifices*, Ann Rule
7. *The Closing of the American Mind*, Allan Bloom
8. *Spycatcher*, Peter Wright with Paul Greengrass
9. *Necessary Losses*, Judith Viorst
10. *Time Flies*, Bill Cosby

Paperback How-to, Advice, Other

1. *Something Under the Bed Is Drooling*, Bill Watterson
2. *Dianetics*, L. Ron Hubbard
3. *Calvin and Hobbes*, Bill Watterson
4. *Rand McNally Road Atlas*
5. *The Essential Calvin and Hobbes*, Bill Watterson

Circulation of Leading U.S. Magazines

Source: Audit Bureau of Circulations, Schaumburg, Ill.

General magazines, exclusive of groups and comics; also exclusive of magazines that failed to file reports to ABC by press time. Based on total average paid circulation during the 6 months prior to Dec. 31, 1988.

Magazine	Circulation	Magazine	Circulation	Magazine	Circulation
Modern Maturity	19,301,820	U.S. News & World Report	2,300,197	The American Rifleman	1,358,967
NRTA/AARP News Bulletin	19,000,184	Southern Living	2,288,695	Bon Appetit	1,344,050
Reader's Digest	16,452,422	Smithsonian	2,262,015	New Woman	1,332,586
TV Guide	16,302,705	Glamour	2,190,027	Golf Digest	1,314,434
National Geographic Magazine	10,574,562	Penthouse	2,109,256	True Story	1,300,829
		Field & Stream	2,032,020	Mademoiselle	1,283,242
Better Homes and Gardens	8,143,083	Popular Science	1,844,323	Rolling Stone	1,273,681
Family Circle	5,922,530	Country Living	1,833,816	The Family Handyman	1,260,373
Woman's Day	5,581,573	Money	1,821,625	Sesame Street Magazine	1,260,274
Good Housekeeping	5,217,147	Motorland	1,812,625	Self	1,229,791
McCall's	5,142,463	Parents Magazine	1,772,633	Vogue	1,202,471
Ladies' Home Journal	5,086,714	Seventeen	1,752,308	Home Mechanix	1,229,727
Time	4,648,454	Life	1,749,936	Soap Opera Digest	1,147,884
National Enquirer	4,285,707	Popular Mechanics	1,668,096	Travel & Leisure	1,125,788
Guideposts	4,258,806	1,001 Home Ideas	1,536,706	National Examiner	1,120,434
Redbook	3,950,489	The Elks Magazine	1,526,010	'Teen	1,093,051
The American Legion Magazine	3,824,260	Globe	1,525,745	Rodale's Organic Gardening	1,086,406
Star	3,682,796	Outdoor Life	1,514,400	Changing Times	1,040,677
Playboy	3,555,663	Adventure Road	1,484,143	Discover	1,030,228
People	3,349,401	Sunset	1,430,860	Health	1,026,164
Sports Illustrated	3,329,415	Woman's World	1,413,575	Scouting	1,009,086
Newsweek	3,227,391	Boys' Life	1,392,535	Yankee	1,003,948
Prevention	3,136,447	US Magazine	1,379,602	Weight Watchers	1,003,347
Cosmopolitan	2,760,010	The Workbasket	1,402,785	(continued)	
		The American Hunter	1,359,307		

Magazine	Circulation	Magazine	Circulation	Magazine	Circulation
Weekly World News	990,177	Scientific American	644,998	Audubon	436,196
American Health	981,626	Inc.	639,549	3-2-1 Contact	435,911
Country Home	972,178	Endless Vacation	638,890	Home Office Computing	434,565
Sport	947,005	Colonial Homes	627,296	Success!	425,341
Golf Magazine	937,232	The Saturday Evening Post	626,339	New York Magazine	423,901
Car and Driver	935,315	The New Yorker	613,275	Town & Country	423,868
Psychology Today	931,859	Working Mother	605,951	Car Craft	416,231
Omni	925,345	Muscle & Fitness	603,071	Savvy	409,416
Home Magazine	923,493	House & Garden	601,112	Crafts	400,596
Working Woman	905,358	Catholic Digest	592,889	Club	400,192
House Beautiful	890,745	Flower & Garden Magazine	592,445	Capper's	393,391
YM	887,571	Cooking Light	584,588	Brides	387,252
Hot Rod	884,669	Guns & Ammo	582,162	Gallery Magazine	378,678
Business Week (NA)	879,334	Decorating Remodeling	567,339	Golf Illustrated	382,086
Nation's Business	855,424	Ms.	548,708	Satellite Orbit	363,848
Essence	850,007	Inside Sports	545,295	Parenting Magazine	360,649
Workbench	845,673	Turtle Magazine	544,336	Petersen's Hunting	352,946
Elle	826,877	Tennis	533,925	Modern Bride	350,531
Gourmet	806,304	McCall's Needlework &		Frequent Flyer Magazine	350,323
National News	801,733	Crafts	523,569	Rural Kentuckian	341,687
Food & Wine	798,366	Sports Afield	523,174	Woman's Sports & Fitness	347,690
Traveller	796,678	The Rotarian	521,827	Carolina Country	347,033
Motor Trend	784,919	Grit	520,019	TV Crosswords	337,903
Four Wheeler	769,947	Woman	518,943	Easyriders	336,649
Esquire	753,730	Natural History	517,354	Connoisseur	334,142
Conde Nast Traveler	753,381	New Choices for the Best		Hippocrates	333,188
Harper's Bazaar	753,262	Years	507,062	Cycle	331,266
Mother Earth News	742,774	Personal Computing	501,440	High Fidelity	327,248
VFW Auxiliary Magazine	732,757	Stereo Review	504,582	Country Journal	325,165
Forbes	741,731	Bassmaster Magazine	505,895	Trailer Life	322,165
Popular Photography	726,572	Sylvia Porter's Personal		Flying	320,779
Homeowner	724,017	Finance	500,532	Baseball Digest	320,711
Practical Homeowner	719,730	Westways	474,264	The Tennessee Magazine	314,059
Games	716,271	The Atlantic	474,027	Bicycling	312,372
Metropolitan Home	704,194	Ski Magazine	465,819	Air & Space-Smithsonian	311,133
Road & Track	703,899	Video Review	462,612	Crafts 'n Things	310,028
Shape Magazine	700,867	Video	453,290	Fishing World	307,835
Modern Photography	689,058	Venture	450,239	Automobile	305,652
Good Food	674,492	Skiing Magazine	451,552	Financial World	303,316
Gentleman's Quarterly	669,923	Runner's World	444,860	Early American Life	300,445
Fortune (NA)	658,616	The Sun	441,150	Texas Monthly	300,105
Architectural Digest	656,783	World Tennis	441,076		
Vanity Fair	652,310	Country Music	439,609		

Selected U.S. Daily Newspaper Circulation

Source: Audit Bureau of Circulations report of average paid circulation for 6 months to Mar. 31, 1989.

Newspaper	Daily	Newspaper	Daily	Newspaper	Daily
Akron Beacon Journal(m)	152,929	Daytona Beach		Journal(m)	*80,498
Albuquerque Journal(m)	†119,400	News-Journal(m)	92,394	Middletown (N.Y.) Times	
Albuquerque Tribune(e)	†40,636	Dubuque Telegraph-Herald(e)	34,177	Herald Record(m)	82,878
Amarillo News(m)	43,265	El Paso Herald-Post(e)	†29,439	Mobile Press(e)	*†43,650
Amarillo Globe-Times(e)	†23,798	Erie (Pa.) News(m)	*29,711	Mobile Register(m)	*156,736
Anchorage Times(e)	31,559	Erie (Pa.) Times(e)	*40,825	Modesto (Cal.) Bee(m)	†79,058
Ann Arbor News(e)	48,103	Evansville (Ind.) Courier(m)	62,888	Montgomery Advertiser(m)	*51,524
Asbury Park (N.J.) Press(e)	144,526	Evansville (Ind.) Press(e)	36,475	Montgomery Journal(e)	*17,183
Athens (Ga.) News(m)	12,357	Everett (Wash.) Herald(e)	56,304	Nashville Banner(e)	63,078
Athens (Ga.) Banner-Herald(e)	13,782	Fargo (N.D.) Forum(m)	55,134	Newport News (Va.) Press(m)	*175,744
Augusta (Ga.) Chronicle(m)	66,540	Ft. Lauderdale News(e)	*31,607	Newport News (Va.) Times	
Augusta (Ga.) Herald(e)	14,081	Ft. Myers (Fla.) News-Press(m)	91,958	Herald(e)	*†31,460
Bakersfield Californian(m)	†82,248	Ft. Wayne Journal-Gazette(m)	†61,777	Pensacola News-Journal(m)	†60,131
Bangor (Me.) News(m)	*79,448	Gary Post-Tribune(m)	73,969	Peoria Journal Star(a)	*93,443
Baton Rouge Advocate(m)	77,259	Greenville (S.C.) News(m)	*86,506	Phoenix Gazette(e)	†112,223
Baton Rouge State-Times(e)	28,004	Greenville (S.C.) Piedmont(e)	*25,658	Portland (Me.) Press Herald(m)	58,924
Bergen Co. (N.J.) Record(e)	*155,433	Honolulu Advertiser(m)	98,025	Reno Gazette Journal(m)	63,448
Billings (Mont.) Gazette(m)	53,870	Honolulu Star-Bulletin(e)	96,074	Roanoke Times & World	
Binghamton (N.Y.) Press & Sun		Huntington (W.Va.)		News(m&e)	124,010
Bulletin(m)	68,248	Herald-Dispatch(m)	†43,587	Rochester Times-Union(e)	*90,472
Birmingham Post-Herald(m)	*63,021	Hyannis: Cape Cod Times(m)	40,548	Rockford (Ill.) Register-Star(m)	74,080
Bismark (N.D.) Tribune(m)	29,972	Jackson (Miss.)		Salem (Ore.)	
Bloomington (Ill.)		Clarion-Ledger(m)	†80,044	Statesman-Journal(m)	56,811
Pantagraph(a)	51,859	Jacksonville Times-Union(m)	173,272	Salt Lake City Tribune(m)	111,356
Bridgeport (Conn.) Post(e)	*†56,117	Kalamazoo Gazette(e)	62,045	San Bernardino Sun(m)	86,316
Bristol (Va.) Herald-Courier		Knoxville News-Sentinel(m)	100,353	Sarasota Herald-Tribune(m)	†133,926
Tennessean(a)	†43,212	Lansing (Mich.) State		Savannah News(m)	53,817
Camden (N.J.) Courier-Post(e)	†103,497	Journal(m)	63,379	Savannah Press(e)	18,523
Casper (Wyo.) Star Tribune(m)	35,330	Las Vegas Review-Journal(a)	†134,491	Scranton Times(e)	*52,787
Charleston (W.Va.) Gazette(m)	55,456	Lubbock (Tex.) Avalanche		Scrantonian Tribune(m)	38,028
Chattanooga News-Free		Journal(m)	†65,854	Sioux City Journal(m)	*50,451
Press(e)	57,233	Lynchburg (Va.) News &		Sioux Falls (S.D.)	
Columbia (S.C.) State(m)	139,963	Advance(a)	†41,751	Argus-Leader(a)	45,820
Columbus (Ga.)		Macon (Ga.) Telegraph &		Spokane Daily Chronicle(e)	*26,274
Ledger-Enquirer(m)	56,044	News(m)	73,134	Springfield (Ill.) State Journal	
Corpus Christi Caller-Times(m)	†67,628	Madison (Wis.) State		Register(a)	68,336

Newspaper	Daily	Newspaper	Daily	Newspaper	Daily
Springfield (Mass.) Union		Terre Haute Tribune Star(m)	34,980	Winston-Salem Journal(m)	94,652
News(a)	112,229	Toledo Blade(e)	154,592	Worcester Gazette(e)	*†71,542
Stockton (Cal.) Record(m)	54,456	Topeka Capital-Journal(m)	†67,680	Worcester Telegram(m)	*†58,388
Syracuse Herald-Journal(e)	95,791	Tucson Daily Star(m)	†90,498	Yakima (Wash.)	
Syracuse Post-Standard(m)	83,201	Tulsa Tribune(e)	†68,990	Herald-Republic(a)	†40,074
Tacoma News Tribune(m)	†117,246	Wilmington Journal(e)	120,132	Youngstown Vindicator(e)	†90,608
Tallahassee Democrat(m)	59,534	Wilmington (N.C.) Star(m)	49,079		

(m) morning; (e) evening; (a) all day; *Mon.-Fri. average; †3 months.

Top 50 U.S. Daily Newspapers

Source: Audit Bureau of Circulations, Schaumburg, Ill.; circulation for 6-month period ending Mar. 31, 1989.

From Oct. 1, 1988 through March 31, 1989, 21 of the 50 top newspapers reported declines in daily circulation; in the 12 months before, 18 of the 50 had reported declines. The biggest circulation gain was at the Ft. Lauderdale Sun Sentinel, up 18.9%. The biggest loss was 11.3%, at the Chicago Sun-Times. Of the top 50 papers, 14 reported declines in Sunday circulation.

	Aug. daily Circ.	12 mos. prev.	Sunday	12 mos. prev.		Aug. daily Circ.	12 mos. prev.	Sunday	12 mos. prev.
1. Wall Street Journal	1,931,410	-4.6%	NA	NA	28. (Portland) Oregonian	327,603	-1.7%	415,926	+1.3%
2. USA Today	1,341,811	NA	NA	NA	29. Houston Post	322,193	+6.6%	362,847	+5.2%
3. (New York) Daily News	1,230,186	-4.1%	1,526,413	-6.0%	30. Buffalo News	320,003	+1.5%	384,157	+1.5%
4. Los Angeles Times	1,119,840	-1.2%	1,423,310	+0.3%	31. Tampa Tribune Sun.: Tribune & Times	287,289³	+5.9%	382,842³	+5.6%
5. New York Times	1,117,376	+3.6%	1,663,530	+1.0%					
6. Washington Post	812,419	+0.3%	1,140,856	+1.5%	32. Atlanta Constitution Sun.: w/ Journal	282,442	+3.6%	665,186	+0.8%
7. Chicago Tribune	740,154	-4.4%	1,137,447	+0.7%					
8. Newsday	697,509	+4.9%	707,787	+0.8%	33. (New Orleans) Times-Picayune	281,851³	-2.2%	338,978³	-2.6%
9. Detroit News	676,025	-1.8%	820,655	-1.9%					
10. Detroit Free Press	629,275	-2.9%	693,943	-3.8%	34. San Jose Mercury-News	277,010	+1.0%	331,998	+3.4%
11. San Francisco Chronicle Sun.: w/ Examiner	556,196	-2.3%	700,989	-3.1%	35. Milwaukee Journal	275,778	-2.9%	506,517	-1.2%
					36. Kansas City (Missouri) Times	275,016	-2.0%	NA	NA
12. Chicago Sun-Times	554,670	-11.3%	595,311	-6.6%	37. Orlando Sentinel	273,544	+7.1%	377,935	+6.7%
13. New York Post	535,407	-3.6%	402,136²	NA	38. San Diego Union	269,190³	+2.3%	437,784³	+3.4%
14. Boston Globe	509,573	+2.3%	787,385	-0.3%	39. Columbus (Ohio) Dispatch	257,366	-0.1%	380,375	-1.2%
15. Philadelphia Inquirer	500,136	-0.8%	1,010,530	+0.9%	40. Sacramento Bee	251,120³	+0.3%	306,574³	+2.0%
16. (Newark) Star-Ledger	458,049³	-0.4%	675,980³	+0.3%	41. Denver Post	241,386	+4.7%	401,843	-1.9%
17. (Cleveland) Plain Dealer	447,822	-0.3%	570,737	+0.6%	42. Los Angeles Herald Examiner	238,392	+0.3%	183,122	-3.2%
18. Miami Herald	442,976	+2.8%	546,801	+1.5%	43. Philadelphia Daily News	237,822	-1.7%	NA	NA
19. Houston Chronicle	427,844	+3.9%	585,845	+5.9%	44. Seattle Times Sun.: w/ Post-Intelligencer	236,563	+0.4%	504,993	-0.1%
20. Minneapolis Star Tribune	403,300	-0.7%	650,317	+0.3%					
21. St. Louis Post-Dispatch	378,225	+0.02%	560,618	+1.1%	45. Charlotte (N.C.) Observer	235,739	+3.4%	292,828	+3.0%
22. St. Petersburg Times	375,870³	+4.0%	471,472³	+4.2%	46. (Louisville) Courier-Journal	235,414⁵	-0.9%	326,767	-0.9%
23. (Phoenix) Arizona Republic	372,209³	+4.4%	566,510³	+0.5%	47. Fort Lauderdale Sun-Sentinel Sun.: w/ News	232,650	+18.9%	340,474	+5.9%
24. (Denver) Rocky Mountain News	365,493	+2.4%	411,023	+3.4%					
25. Boston Herald	360,046	+1.6%	251,851	-0.1%	48. (Baltimore) Sun	231,990	+1.4%	485,269	+1.0%
26. Dallas Morning News	359,976	⁴	534,843	+1.5%	49. Indianapolis Star	230,787³	+1.7%	406,099³	+1.3%
27. Orange County Register	344,965	+6.1%	392,695	+6.2%	50. (Okla. City) Oklahoman	229,008	-3.6%	323,118	+3.1%

NA = Not applicable; (1) Daily circ. Mon.-Thurs.; (2) Starting Mar. 5, 1989; (3) Average for 3 months; (4) Circ. Mon.-Thurs. & Sat.; (5) Changed from all-day to morning.

U.S. Opera Companies with Budgets of $500,000 or More

Source: Central Opera Service, Lincoln Center, New York, N.Y. 10023; August, 1988

Anchorage Opera; vacant, gen. mgr.
Arizona Opera Co. (Tucson); Glynn Ross, gen. dir.
Fullerton Civic Light Opera (Calif.); R. G. Duncan, gen. mgr.
Long Beach Opera (Calif.); Micheal Milenski, gen. dir.
Long Beach Civic Light Opera (Calif.); Harvey Waggoner, exec. dir.
Los Angeles Music Center Opera Assn.; Peter Hemmings, exec. dir.
Opera Pacific (Costa Mesa, Calif.); David DiChiera, gen. dir.

Sacramento Opera Assn. (Calif.); Marianne Oaks, gen. dir.
San Diego Civic Light Opera; Leon Drew, gen mgr.
San Diego Opera Assn.; Ian Campbell, gen. dir.
San Francisco Opera; Lotti Mansouri, gen. dir.
San Francisco Opera Center (inc. Western Opera Theater); Christine Bullin, mgr.
Opera San José (Calif.); Irene Dalis, exec. dir.
San José Civic Light Opera (Calif.); Stewart Slater, dir.
Central City Opera (Denver); Daniel Rule, gen. mgr.
Opera Colorado (Denver); Nathaniel Merrill, art. dir.

(continued)

Connecticut Opera (Hartford); George Osborne, gen. dir.
Goodspeed Opera House (E. Haddam, Conn.); Michael Price, exec. dir.
Washington Opera (D.C.); Martin Feinstein, gen. dir.
Greater Miami Opera Assn.; Robert Heuer, gen. mgr.
Orlando Opera Co. (Fla.); Richard Owens, gen. dir.
Palm Beach Opera; H. P. Benn, gen. dir.
Sarasota Opera Assn. (Fla.); Deane Allyn, exec. dir.
Atlanta Opera (Ga.); Alfred Kennedy, gen. mgr.
Hawaii Opera Theatre; Beebe Freitas, art. dir.
Chicago Opera Theater; Alan Stone, art. dir.
Lyric Opera of Chicago; Ardis Krainik, gen. mgr.
Indianapolis Opera; Robert Driver, art. dir.
Des Moines Metro Opera (Indianola); Robert Larsen, art. dir.
Music Theatre of Wichita; John Holly, prod. dir.
Kentucky Opera Assn. (Louisville); Thomson Smillie, gen. dir.
New Orleans Opera Assn.; Arthur Cosenza, gen. dir.
Baltimore Opera Co.; vacant, gen. mgr.
Opera Company of Boston; Sarah Caldwell, art. dir.
Michigan Opera Theatre (Detroit); David DiChiera, gen. dir.
Minnesota Opera Co. (St. Paul); Kevin Smith, gen. dir.
Lyric Opera of Kansas City (Missouri); Russell Patterson, gen. dir. & art. dir.
Opera Theatre of St. Louis (Missouri); Charles MacKay, gen. dir.
Opera/Omaha (Neb.); Mary Robert, gen. dir.
Nevada Opera (Reno); Ted Puffer, gen. dir.
New Jersey State Opera (Newark); Alfredo Silipigni, art. dir.
Santa Fe Opera (New Mexico); John Crosby, gen. dir.
Tri-Cities Opera (Binghamton, N.Y.); P. Hibbitt & C. Savoca, art. dirs.
Chautauqua Opera (N.Y.); Linda Jackson, gen. mgr.

Glimmerglass Opera (Cooperstown, N.Y.); Paul Kellogg, gen. mgr.
Syracuse Opera; Robert Swedberg, gen. dir.
Metropolitan Opera Assn. (New York City); Bruce Crawford, gen. mgr.
New York City Opera; Beverly Sills, gen. dir.
New York City Opera Natl. Co.; Nancy Kelly, adm. dir.
Opera Orchestra of N.Y. (N.Y.C.); Eve Queler, art dir.
Opera Carolina (Charlotte, N.C.); James Wright, gen. dir.
Cincinnati Opera Assn.; James deBlasis, art. dir.
Cleveland Opera; David Bamberger, gen. dir.
Opera/Columbus (Oh.); Michael Harrison, gen. dir.
Dayton Opera Assn. (Oh.); Dennis Hanthorn, mng. dir.
Tulsa Opera (Oklahoma); Myrna S. Ruffner, gen. mgr.
Portland Opera Assn. (Oregon); Robert Bailey, exec. dir.
American Music Theater Festival (Phila.); Marjorie Samoff, prod. dir.
Opera Company of Philadelphia; Margaret Anne Everitt, gen. dir.
Pennsylvania Opera Theater (Phila.); Barbara Silverstein, art dir. & gen. mgr.
Pittsburgh Civic Light Opera; Charles Gray, exec. dir.
Pittsburgh Opera; Tito Capobianco, gen. dir.
Opera Memphis (Tenn.); Robert Driver, gen. & art. dir.
Dallas Opera; Plato Karayanis, gen. dir.
Lyric Opera of Dallas (Tex.); John Burrows, art. dir.
Fort Worth Opera; J. Mario Ramos, mng. dir.
Houston Grand Opera Assn.; R. David Gockley, gen. dir.
Texas Opera Theater (Houston); Ann Tomfohrde, dir.
Theatre Under the Stars (Houston); Frank Young, exec. dir.
Utah Opera (Salt Lake City); Glade Peterson, gen. dir.
Virginia Opera (Norfolk); Peter Mark, gen. dir.
Seattle Opera Assn.; Speight Jenkins, gen. dir.
Florentine Opera of Milwaukee; John Gage, gen. mgr.
Skylight Comic Opera (Milwaukee); Colin Cabot, mng. dir.

Notable U.S. Dance Companies
Source: Dance/USA, July 1989

Aman Folk Ensemble, Los Angeles, CA
American Ballet Theatre, New York, NY
Armitage Ballet, New York, NY
Ballet Arizona, Pheonix, AZ
Ballet Chicago, Chicago, IL
Ballet Hispanico of New York, New York, NY
Ballet Metropolitan, Columbus, OH
Ballet West, Salt Lake City, UT
Bill T. Jones/Arnie Zane Company, New York, NY
Boston Ballet, Newton, MA
Caribbean Dance Company, St. Croix, VI
Chuck Davis African-American Dance Ensemble, Durham, NC
Cincinnati/New Orleans City Ballet, Cincinnati, OH
Cleveland/San Jose Ballet, Cleveland, OH
Cunningham Dance Foundation, New York, NY
Dan Wagoner and Dancers, New York, NY
Dance Exchange, Washington, DC
Dance Theatre of Harlem, New York, NY
Danceteller, Philadelphia, PA
David Gordon/Pick Up Co., New York, NY
David Parsons Company, New York, NY
Dayton Ballet Association, Dayton, OH
Dayton Contemporary Dance Company, Dayton, OH
Elisa Monte Dance Company, New York, NY
Feld Ballet, New York, NY
Fort Worth Ballet, Fort Worth, TX
Garth Fagan's Bucket Dance Theatre, Rochester, NY
HARRY, New York, NY
Hartford Ballet, Hartford, CT
Houston Ballet, Houston, TX
Hubbard Street Dance Company, Chicago, IL
Jazz Tap Ensemble, Los Angeles, CA
Jennifer Muller and the Works, New York, NY
Jose Limon Dance Company, New York, NY
Joyce Trisler Danscompany, New York, NY
KHADRA International Folk Ballet, San Francisco, CA
Lar Lubovitch Dance Company, New York, NY
Laura Dean Dancers and Musicians, New York, NY

Lewitzky Dance Foundation, Los Angeles, CA
Louisville Ballet, Louisville, KY
Lucinda Childs Dance Company, New York, NY
Margaret Jenkins Dance Company, San Francisco, CA
Miami City Ballet, Miami Beach, FL
Milwaukee Ballet, Milwaukee, WI
Mordine & Company, Chicago, IL
New Dance Ensemble, Minneapolis, MN
New York City Ballet, New York, NY
Nina Wiener and Dancers, New York, NY
North Carolina Dance Theater, Winston Salem, NC
Oakland Ballet, Oakland, CA
ODC/San Francisco, San Francisco, CA
Ohio Ballet, Akron, OH
Pacific Northwest Ballet, Seattle, WA
Paul Taylor Dance Company, New York, NY
Pennsylvania Ballet, Philadelphia, PA
Philadanco, Philadelphia, PA
Pilobolus, Washington, CT
Pittsburgh Ballet Theatre, Pittsburgh, PA
Pittsburgh Dance Alloy, Pittsburgh, PA
Princeton Ballet, New Brunswick, NJ
Rebecca Kelly Dance Company, New York, NY
Repertory Dance Theatre, Salt Lake City, UT
Richmond Ballet, Richmond, VA
Ririe-Woodbury Dance Company, Salt Lake City, UT
Rosalind Newman and Dancers, New York, NY
San Francisco Ballet, San Francisco, CA
Solomons Company/Dance, New York, NY
State Ballet of Missouri, Kansas City, MO
Stuart Pimsler Dance & Theater, Columbus, OH
Tandy Beal and Company, Santa Cruz, CA
Trisha Brown Company, New York, NY
Tulsa Ballet Theatre, Tulsa, OK
Washington Ballet, Washington, DC
Zenon Dance Company, Minneapolis, MN
ZeroMoving Dance Company, Philadelphia, PA
Zivili Kolo-Ensemble, Granville, OH

Symphony Orchestras of the U.S.

Source: American Symphony Orchestra League, 777 14th St. NW, Washington, DC 20005 (as of July 13, 1989)

Classifications are based on annual incomes or budgets of orchestras.

Major Orchestras	Music Director
Atlanta Symphony	Yoel Levi[1]
Baltimore Symphony	David Zinman
Boston Symphony	Seiji Ozawa
Buffalo Philharmonic	Semyon Bychkov
Chicago Symphony	Sir Georg Solti
Cincinnati Symphony	Jesus Lopez-Cobos
Cleveland Orchestra	Christoph von Dohnanyi
Columbus Symphony	Christian Badea[2]
Dallas Symphony	Eduardo Mata
Denver Symphony	Vacant
Detroit Symphony	Gunther Herbig
Houston Symphony	Christoph Eschenbach
Indianapolis Symphony	Raymond Leppard
Los Angeles Philharmonic	Andre Previn
Milwaukee Symphony	Zdenek Macal
Minnesota Orchestra	Edo de Waart
National Symphony (D.C.)	Mstislav Rostropovich
New Jersey Symphony (Newark)	Hugh Wolf
New Orleans Symphony	Maxim Shostakovich
New York Philharmonic	Zubin Mehta
Oregon Symphony	James DePreist[1]
Philadelphia Orchestra	Riccardo Muti[1]
Phoenix Symphony	Theo Alcantara[3]
Pittsburgh Symphony	Lorin Maazel
Rochester Philharmonic	Jerzy Semkow[4]
St. Louis Symphony	Leonard Slatkin[1]
St. Paul Chamber Orchestra	Hugh Wolff,[5] Christopher Hogwood[6]
San Antonio Symphony	Zdenek Macal[2]
San Diego Symphony	Vacant
San Francisco Symphony	Herbert Blomstedt[1]
Seattle Symphony	Gerard Schwarz
Syracuse Symphony	Kazuyoshi Akiyama
Utah Symphony	Joseph Silverstein

Regional Orchestras	Music Director
Alabama Symphony	Paul Polivnick[1]
American Symphony (N.Y.C.)	Vacant
Austin Symphony (Tex.)	Sung Kwak
Brooklyn Philharmonic	Lukas Foss[1]
Charlotte Symphony (N.C.)	Leo B. Driehuys
Colorado Springs Symphony	Vacant

Concerto Soloists Chamber (Phila.)	Marc S. Mostovoy[1]
Dayton Philharmonic (Ohio)	Isaiah Jackson[1]
Philharmonic of Florida	James Judd
Florida Orchestra	Jahja Ling
Florida Symphony (Orlando)	Kenneth Jean
Ft. Worth Symphony (Tex.)	John Giordano
Grand Rapids Symphony (Mich.)	Catherine Comet
Grant Park Symphony (Chicago)	Zdenek Macal[5]
Hartford Symphony	Michael Lankester
Honolulu Symphony	Donald Johanos
Hudson Valley Philharmonic (Poughkeepsie, N.Y.)	Imre Pallo
Jacksonville Symphony (Fla.)	Roger Nierenberg
Kansas City Symphony	William McGlaughlin
Long Beach Symphony (Cal.)	Jo Ann Falletta[7]
Long Island Philharmonic (N.Y.)	Christopher Keene
Los Angeles Chamber	Iona Brown
Louisville Orchestra (Ky.)	Lawrence Leighton Smith
Memphis Symphony (Tenn.)	Alan Balter[1]
New Haven Symphony (Conn.)	Michael Palmer[6]
New Mexico Symphony (Albuquerque)	Neal H. Stulberg[9]
New World Symphony (Miami Beach, Fla.)	Michael Tilsan[10]
North Carolina Symphony (Raleigh)	Gergardt Zimmerman[1]
Omaha Symphony	Bruce Hangen
Orpheus Chamber (N.Y.C.)	Vacant
Pacific Symphony (Santa Ana, Cal.)	Vacant
Puerto Rico Symphony (Santurce)	Vacant
Richmond Symphony (Va.)	George Manahan
Sacramento Symphony (Cal.)	Carter Nice[1]
San Jose Symphony (Cal.)	George Cleve[1]
Spokane Symphony (Wash.)	Bruce Ferdon
Springfield Symphony (Mass.)	Raymond C. Harvey[1]
Toledo Symphony (Ohio)	Yuval Zaliouk
Tucson Symphony (Ariz.)	Robert E. Bernhardt
Tulsa Symphony (Okla.)	Bernard Rubenstein
Virginia Symphony (Norfolk)	Winston Dan Vogel[1]
Wichita Symphony (Kan.)	Michael Palmer[1]

Metropolitan Orchestras

Akron Symphony (Ohio)
Albany Symphony (N.Y.)
Amarillo Symphony (Tex.)
American Composers Orch. (NYC)
Anchorage Symphony (Alas.)
Arkansas Symphony (Little Rock)
Baton Rouge Symphony (La)
BC Pops (Binghamton, N.Y.)
Binghamton Symphony & Choral Society (N.Y.)
Boise Philharmonic (Ida.)
Brevard Symphony (Melbourne, Fla.)
Cabrillo Music Festival (Aptos, Cal.)
Canton Symphony (Ohio)
Cathedral Symphony (Newark, N.J.)
Cedar Rapids Symphony (Ia.)
Charleston Symphony (S.C.)
Chattanooga Symphony & Opera (Tenn.)
Colorado Music Festival (Boulder)
Columbus Symphony (Ga.)
Corpus Christi Symphony (Tex.)
Delaware Symphony (Wilmington)
Denver Chamber Orchestra (Col.)
Des Moines Symphony (Ia.)
Duluth-Superior Symphony (Minn.)
Eastern Philhar. (Greensboro, N.C.)
El Paso Symphony (Tex.)
Elgin Symphony (Ill.)
Erie Philharmonic (Pa.)
Eugene Symphony (Ore.)
Evansville Philharmonic (Ind.)
Fairfax Symphony (Annandale, Va.)
Flint Symphony (Mich.)
Florida Symphonic Pops (Boca Raton)

Florida West Coast Symphony (Sarasota)
Ft. Wayne Philharmonic (Ind.)
Fresno Philharmonic (Cal.)
Glendale Symphony (Cal.)
Greensboro Symphony (N.C.)
Handel and Hayden Society (Boston)
Harrisburg Symphony (Pa.)
Kalamazoo Symphony (Mich.)
Knoxville Symphony (Tenn.)
Lake Forest Symphony (Ill.)
Lansing Symphony (Mich.)
Lexington Philharmonic (Ky.)
Lincoln Symphony (Neb.)
Little Orchestra Soc. of N.Y. (NYC)
Lubbock Symphony (Tex.)
Madison Symphony (Wis.)
Marin Symphony (San Rafael, Cal.)
Midland-Odessa Symphony & Chorale (Tex.)
Mississippi Symphony (Jackson)
Modesto Symphony (Cal.)
Monterey Country Symphony (Carmel, Cal.)
Music of the Baroque (Chicago)
National Repertory Orchestra (Evergreen, Col.)
Orchestra New England (New Haven, Conn.)
New Hampshire Symphony (Manchester)
Northeastern Pa. Philharmonic (Avoca)
Pasadena Symphony (Cal.)

Peoria Symphony (Ill.)
Philharmonia Baroque (San Francisco)
Philharmonia Virtuosi (Dobbs Ferry, N.Y.)
Portland Symphony (Maine)
Quad City Symphony (Davenport, Ia.)
Queens Symphony (Rego Park, N.Y.)
Reading Symphony (Pa.)
Rhode Island Philharmonic (Providence)
Rochester Symphony (Minn.)
Saginaw Symphony (Mich.)
Santa Barbara Symphony (Cal.)
Santa Rosa Symphony (Cal.)
Savannah Symphony (Ga.)
Shreveport Symphony (La.)
Sioux City Symphony (Ia.)
So. Bend Symphony (Ind.)
So. Carolina Philharmonic & Chamber (S.C.)
So. Dakota Symphony (Sioux Falls)
Springfield Symphony (Ill.)
Springfield Symphony (Mo.)
Stamford Symphony (Cal.)
Stockton Symphony (Cal.)
Ventura County Symphony (Cal.)
Vermont Symphony (Burlington)
Virginia Beach Pops (Va.)
W. Virginia Symphony (Charleston)
New Orchestra of Westchester (Hartsdale, N.Y.)
Wheeling Symphony (W.V.)
Winston-Salem Symphony (N.C.)
Youngstown Symphony (Ohio)

(1) Music Director/Conductor; (2) Artistic Director & Principal Conductor; (3) Musical Director/Principal Conductor; (4) Musical Advisor/Principal Conductor; (5) Principal Conductor; (6) Director of Music; (7) Conductor; (8) Music Director—Designate; (9) Conductor/Music Director; (10) Music Advisor.

All-time Top Television Programs

Source: A.C. Nielsen estimates, Jan. 30, 1960 through Apr. 17, 1989, excluding unsponsored or joint network telecasts or programs under 30 minutes long.

Ranked by percent of average audience.

	Program	Date	Network	Households (000)		Program	Date	Network	Households (000)
1	M*A*S*H Special	2/28/83	CBS	50,150		Day After)	11/20/83	ABC	38,550
2	Dallas	11/21/80	CBS	41,470	16	Roots Pt. VI	1/28/77	ABC	32,680
3	Roots Pt. VIII	1/30/77	ABC	36,380	16	The Fugitive	8/29/67	ABC	25,700
4	Super Bowl XVI	1/24/82	CBS	40,020	18	Super Bowl XXI	1/25/87	CBS	40,030
5	Super Bowl XVII	1/30/83	NBC	40,480	19	Roots Pt. V	1/27/77	ABC	32,540
6	Super Bowl XX	1/26/86	NBC	41,490	20	Ed Sullivan	2/9/64	CBS	23,240
7	Gone With The Wind-Pt. 1	11/7/76	NBC	33,960	21	Bob Hope Christmas Special	1/14/71	NBC	27,050
8	Gone With The Wind-Pt. 2	11/8/76	NBC	33,750	22	Roots Pt. III	1/25/77	ABC	31,900
9	Super Bowl XII	1/15/78	CBS	34,410	23	Super Bowl XI	1/9/77	NBC	31,610
10	Super Bowl XIII	1/21/79	NBC	35,090	23	Super Bowl XV	1/25/81	NBC	34,540
11	Bob Hope Christmas Show	1/15/70	NBC	27,260	25	Super Bowl VI	1/16/72	CBS	27,450
12	Super Bowl XVIII	1/22/84	CBS	38,800	26	Roots Pt. II	1/24/77	ABC	31,400
12	Super Bowl XIX	1/20/85	ABC	39,390	27	Beverly Hillbillies	1/8/64	CBS	22,570
14	Super Bowl XIV	1/20/80	CBS	35,330	28	Roots Pt. IV	1/26/77	ABC	31,190
15	ABC Theater (The				28	Ed Sullivan	2/16/64	CBS	22,445
					30	Super Bowl XXIII	1/22/89	NBC	39,320

Network TV Program Ratings

Source: Nielsen Media Research, Feb. 1989

Program or type	TV Households Rating %	TV Households No. (000)	Women (18+)	Men (18+)	Teens 12-17	Children 2-11
Today Show	4.5	4,080	2,980	1,720	95	170
This Morning	2.5	2,220	1,580	1,090	70	150
Good Morning America	4.2	3,750	2,850	1,410	90	160
Daytime Drama	6.5	5,890	5,080	1,530	410	680
Q & A Participation	4.1	3,720	2,800	1,440	140	500
All 10am-4:30pm	5.5	4,930	4,100	1,430	300	600
Evening						
Informational	11.4	10,350	7,930	5,970	500	840
General Drama	12.2	11,020	9,200	5,840	870	1,330
Susp. & Mystery Drama	14.4	13,040	10,580	7,990	1,060	1,700
Situation Comedy	17.6	15,920	12,540	7,700	2,470	4,400
Adventure	9.7	8,770	6,850	5,560	860	1,510
Feature Film	16.1	14,580	11,650	9,260	1,400	1,830
All 7-11pm Reg.	14.3	12,920	10,360	7,340	1,340	2,240

Audience Composition (000) spans Women (18+), Men (18+), Teens 12-17, Children 2-11.

Network TV Ratings Decline in 1988-89

The combined rating for the three TV networks declined in prime time to 41.3 from 42.8 in the 1988-89 season, which ended April 16. This was the sixth straight year of decline. Each rating point represents 904,000 homes, which means the networks lost viewers in about 1,356,000 homes. Further, the total share of the TV audience controlled by network TV fell from 70.7 percent in 1987-88 to 67.2 percent in 1988-89. Network spokesmen conceded that the majority of the audience was lost to cable TV, which gained two of the three share points lost by the networks. Independent TV stations, including those carrying the programs of the FOX network, gained the other point.

U.S. Television Sets and Stations Received

Set Ownership
(Nielsen est. as of Jan. 1, 1989)
Total TV Households 90,400,000
(98% of U.S. households own at least one TV set)

Homes with:

Color TV sets	87,300,000	97%
B&W only	3,070,000	3%
2 or more sets	56,600,000	63%
One set	33,810,000	37%
Cable (May 1989)	50,241,840	56%

Total Persons 2+ 232,800,000
Total Women 18+ . . . 93,410,000
Total Men 18+ 84,470,000
Total Teens 12-17 19,900,000
Total Children 2-11 . . . 35,020,000

Stations Receivable
(Nielsen, September 1988)
% of TV homes receiving:
1-6	9%
7-10	33%
11-14	32%
15-19	20%
20-29	6%

America's Favorite Television Programs: 1988

Source: Nielsen Media Research
(Percent of TV households and persons in TV households)

Regularly Scheduled Network Programs (February 1989)

(Nielsen People Meter Average Audience Estimates)

Program	TV Households	Women	Men	Teens	Children	Program	TV Households	Women	Men	Teens	Children
Bill Cosby Show	27.2	20.9	14.3	22.7	23.7	Amen		14.4			
A Different World	24.7	18.8	12.5	22.7	21.6	ABC Mystery Movie			12.2		
Roseanne	24.0	18.2	12.1	18.7	19.5	NBC Sunday Night Movie			11.9		
60 Minutes	23.8	18.4	17.2			L.A. Law			11.4		
Cheers	23.2	17.6	13.5	16.5	13.0	Growing Pains				15.5	14.0
Murder, She Wrote	23.1	20.1	14.9			Head of the Class				15.1	13.8
Golden Girls	23.0	19.8	11.6	11.9		Hogan Family				14.2	16.8
Who's The Boss?	21.7	16.2		16.8	17.5	Wonder Years				14.1	
Empty Nest	20.2	17.2				Family Ties				12.4	13.8
CBS Sunday Movie	19.5	16.9	12.9			Day By Day				11.3	
Hunter	19.1	15.4	11.9			Full House				11.0	15.5
Unsolved Mysteries	18.9	14.7	12.7			Bugs Bunny/ Tweety Show II					14.4
Alf	18.9			16.2	20.9	Magical World of Disney					14.4
Night Court	18.6		11.8			Garfield and Friends					13.6
Dear John	18.6			11.9		Mr. Belvedere					13.5
Matlock		15.1	11.5								
Knots Landing		14.4									

Favorite Syndicated Programs*

Source: Nielsen Media Research. February. 1989

(Ratings based on Designated Market Area coverage as reported by Nielsen's Cassandra Report)

Program	TV households	Women	Men	Teens	Children	Program	TV households	Women	Men	Teens	Children
Wheel of Fortune	17.0	14.3	10.2	4.9	5.2	Donahue	7.9	6.2	2.9	1.2	0.6
Jeopardy	14.3	11.8	8.0	4.2	3.0	Family Feud	7.9	6.3	3.9	5.7	4.1
Cosby Show	12.1	8.8	6.2	12.6	11.6	Night Court	7.9	5.1	5.2	7.8	5.0
Oprah Winfrey Show	11.8	10.0	3.7	3.8	1.3	Cheers	7.6	5.2	5.2	4.5	2.7
Star Trek Next Generation	10.4	6.3	8.4	6.7	6.4	Inside Edition	6.8	5.1	3.8	1.9	1.1
PM Magazine	9.3	7.0	5.7	2.5	2.5	Family Ties	6.7	4.1	3.1	8.0	6.6
Current Affair	8.5	6.2	5.2	3.5	1.9	M*A*S*H	6.7	4.5	4.6	2.7	1.7
Entertainment Tonight	8.0	6.1	4.6	2.7	1.6	USA Today: TV Show	6.7	4.7	4.0	1.4	1.0

Average Television Viewing Time

Source: Nielsen Media Research, Feb. 1989 (hours: minutes, per week)

		Mon.-Fri. 10am-4:30pm	Mon.-Fri. 4:30pm-7:30pm	Mon.-Sun. 8-11pm	Sat. 7am-1pm	Mon.-Fri. 11:30pm-1am
Total Persons	age 2+	4:53	3:58	8:57	:52	1:13
Total Women	age 18+	6:26	5:08	10:19	:42	1:27
	18-24	5:41	3:50	7:05	:40	1:08
	25-54	5:43	4:20	9:47	:44	1:28
	55+	8:04	7:08	12:19	:38	1:34
Total Men	age 18+	3:40	3:58	9:10	:40	1:24
	18-24	3:11	2:51	6:06	:35	1:21
	25-54	2:58	3:19	8:58	:41	1:24
	55+	5:35	6:09	11:32	:39	1:26
Female Teens	12-17	3:15	4:06	6:31	:47	:35
Male Teens	12-17	2:26	3:49	7:07	:56	:50
Children	2-5	7:19	4:39	6:37	1:44	:23
Children	6-11	3:05	5:05	5:50	1:53	:25

Recordings & Music Videos

The Recording Industry of America, Inc. confers Gold Awards on single records that sell 1 million units, albums and their tape equivalents that sell 500,000 units, and music videos that sell 25,000 units. Platinum Awards go to single records that sell 2 million units, to albums and tapes that sell 1 million, and to music videos that sell 50,000. Multi-Platinum Awards are conferred on single records that sell 3 million units or more, albums and tapes that sell 2 million or more, and music videos that sell 100,000 units or more. Multi-Platinum and Platinum Awards for music released in 1988 and 1989 follow.

Artists, Recording Titles

Albums, Multi-Platinum
(Number in parentheses indicates millions of albums sold.)
Paula Abdul; Forever Your Girl (2).
Baker, Anita; Giving You the Best That I Got (3).
Bon Jovi; New Jersey (5).
Bobby Brown; Don't Be Cruel (4).
Tracy Chapman; Tracy Chapman (3).
Cinderella; Long Cold Winter (2).
DJ Jazzy Jeff & Fresh Prince; He's the DJ, I'm the Rapper (2).
Fine Young Cannibals; The Raw & the Cooked (2).
Debbie Gibson; Electric Youth (2).
Guns 'N' Roses; G 'N R Lies (2).
Journey; Greatest Hits (2).
Kenny G; Silhouette (2).
Madonna; Like a Prayer (2).
Metallica; And Justice for All (2).
New Kids on the Block; Hangin' Tough (3).
Poison; Open Up and Say . . .Ahh (4).
Soundtrack; Cocktail (4).
Tone Loc; Loc'ed after Dark (2).
Traveling Wilburys; Traveling Wilburys (2).
U2; Rattle and Hum (3).
Van Halen; OU812 (3).
Various; Dirty Dancing (3).
Steve Winwood; Roll with It (2).

Albums, Platinum
AC/DC; Blow Up Your Video.
Bangles; Everything.
Rob Base & D.J. E-Z Rock; It Takes Two.
The Boys; Messages from the Boys.
Edie Brickell & the New Bohemians; Shooting Rubberbands at the Stars.
Cheap Trick; Lap of Luxury.
Chicago; 19.
John Cougar Mellancamp; Big Daddy.
Crosby, Stills, Nash & Young; American Dream.
Eazy-E; Eazy-Duz-It.
Europe; Out of This World.
Fleetwood Mac; Greatest Hits.
Lita Ford; Lita.
Great White; Twice Shy.
Guy; Guy.
Hall & Oates; Ooh Yeah!
M.C. Hammer; Let's Get It Started.
Bruce Hornsby and the Range; Scenes from the Southside.
Joan Jett & the Blackhearts; Up Your Alley.
Journey; Greatest Hits.
The Judds; The Judds Greatest Hits.
Kiss; Smashes, Thrashes & Hits.
Huey Lewis & the News; Small World.
Living Colour; Vivid.
Richard Marx; Repeat Offender.
Bobby McFerrin; Simple Pleasures.
Bette Midler; Beaches (Soundtrack).
Midnight Oil; Diesel and Dust.
Milli Vanilli; Girl You Know It's True.
N.W.A.; Straight Outta Compton.
New Edition; Heart Break.
Billy Ocean; Tear Down These Walls.

Roy Orbison; Mystery Girl.
Ozzy Osbourne; No Rest for the Wicked.
Robert Palmer; Heavy Nova.
Tom Petty; Full Moon Fever.
Pink Floyd; Delicate Sound of Thunder.
Robert Plant; Now and Zen.
R.E.M.; Green.
David Lee Roth; Skyscrapper.
Run-D.M.C.; Tougher Than Leather.
Sade; Stronger Than Pride.
Scorpions; Savage Amusement.
Skid Row; Skid Row.
Soundtrack; Good Morning Vietnam.
Rod Stewart; Out of Order.
Barbra Streisand; Till I Loved You.
Al B. Sure!; In Effect Mode.
Dayne Taylor; Tell It to My Heart.
Tiffany; Hold an Old Friend's Hand.
Randy Travis; Old 8 X 10.
Luther Vandross; Any Love.
Karyn White; Karyn White.
Winger; Winger.

Singles, Multi-Platinum
Tone Loc; Wild Thing (2).

Singles, Platinum
Paula Abdul; Straight Up.
The Beach Boys; Kokomo.
Milli Vanilli; Girl You Know It's True.
Tone Loc; Funky Cold Medina.

Music Videos, Multi-Platinum
(number in parentheses indicates thousands of music videos sold)
Bon Jovi; Slippery When Wet (100).
California Raisins; Meet the Raisins (100).
Def Leppard; Historia (200).
Michael Jackson; Moonwalker (800).
Madonna; The Virgin Tour (100).
Metallica; Cliff 'Em All (150).
Motley Crue; Uncensored (100).
Prince & the Revolution; Prince & the Revolution "Live" (100).
Raffi; A Young Children's Concert (100).
Raffi; Raffi in Concert with Rise & Shine Band (100).
Bruce Springsteen; Video Anthology 1978-1988 (350).

Music Videos, Platinum
Neil Diamond; Greatest Hits Live.
Dokken; Unchain the Night.
The Doors; The Doors Live at the Hollywood Bowl.
The Doors; Dance on Fire.
Debbie Gibson; Out of the Blue.
Debbie Gibson; Live in Concert—The Out of the Blue Tour.
Inxs; Kick the Video Flick.
Madonna; Ciao Italia—Live from Italy.
George Michael; Faith.
Prince; Sign O' the Times.
Lionel Richie; The Making of Dancing on the Ceiling.
Rush; A Show of Hands.
George Strait; George Strait Live.
Various; Natural States.
Whitesnake; Trilogy.

100 Leading U.S. Advertisers, 1987

Source: *Advertising Age*, Sept. 28, 1988 © Crain Communications Inc. 1988.

Rank	Advertiser	Ad spending (millions)	Rank	Advertiser	Ad spending (millions)	Rank	Advertiser	Ad spending (millions)
1	Philip Morris	$1,557.8	35	Schering-Plough	$250.2	70	Seagram	$122.3
2	Procter & Gamble	1,386.7	36	Walt Disney	249.8	71	Cosmair	117.2
3	General Motors	1,024.9	37	Honda Motor	245.4	72	CPC International	115.3
4	Sears, Roebuck	886.5	38	H.J. Heinz	245.3	73	Kroger	115.3
5	RJR Nabisco	839.6	39	IBM	240.8	74	Loews	115.2
6	PepsiCo	704.0	40	Grand Metropolitan	231.6	75	Dr Pepper/Seven-Up	114.1
7	Eastman Kodak	658.2	41	Campbell Soup	230.7	76	Subaru of America	113.2
8	McDonald's	649.5	42	Tandy	225.1	77	Wm. Wrigley Jr.	112.5
9	Ford Motor	639.5	43	BCI Holdings	223.2	78	Prudential Insurance	111.3
10	Anheuser-Busch	635.1	44	American Express	212.5	79	Warner Communications	110.4
11	K mart	631.8	45	Time	196.6	80	Delta Air Lines	108.6
12	Unilever	580.7	46	Pfizer	182.1	81	Wendy's Internatl.	107.6
13	General Mills	572.2	47	Nissan Motor	181.4	82	Philips	107.2
14	Chrysler	568.7	48	IC Industries	169.3	83	B.A.T. Industries	105.3
15	Warner-Lambert	558.1	49	Volkswagen	167.3	84	Daimler-Benz	105.0
16	AT&T	531.0	50	Mobil	166.3	85	Gillette	103.8
17	Kellogg	524.9	51	Revlon	165.2	86	Stroh Brewery	102.9
18	J.C. Penney	513.5	52	Hyundai	164.3	87	Clorox	102.1
19	Pillsbury	473.9	53	U.S. Dairy	161.4	88	BMW	99.5
20	Johnson & Johnson	459.3	54	Beecham	153.3	89	S.C. Johnson & Son	96.4
21	Ralston Purina	436.6	55	AMR	152.6	90	Goodyear Tire & Rubber	95.0
22	Kraft	400.7	56	Mazda Motor	151.9	91	Hallmark Cards	93.9
23	American Home Prods.	390.4	57	American Brands	151.4	92	E&J Gallo Winery	93.6
24	Mars	378.6	58	ITT	151.3	93	MCA	91.4
25	Coca-Cola	364.7	59	Du Pont	149.7	94	Marriott	88.5
26	Bristol-Myers	358.9	60	Bayer	145.4	95	Franklin Mint	86.6
27	Quaker Oats	344.4	61	Adolph Coors	144.7	96	Southland	86.1
28	Nestle	340.8	62	Nynex	142.8	97	United Biscuits (Holdings)	84.8
29	U.S. Government	311.3	63	Bell Atlantic	138.6	98	Borden	84.7
30	Colgate-Palmolive	279.8	64	UAL	137.8	99	Monsanto	84.7
31	Sara Lee	278.1	65	Dow Chemical	135.7	100	Ameritech	83.4
32	General Electric	272.6	66	Noxell	134.9			
33	Toyota Motor	257.7	67	Hasbro	134.3			
34	American Cyanamid	250.4	68	Texas Air	124.3			
			69	Hershey Foods	122.8			

Media Spending by 35 Leading Advertisers

Source: *Advertising Age*, Sept. 28, 1988; copyright © Crain Communications Inc., 1988.

(In thousands; totals also include business and farm publications, newspaper supplements, and outdoor ads.)

Rank 1987	Rank 1986	Advertiser	Newspaper	Magazine	Network TV	Spot TV	Network cable TV	Network radio	Spot radio
1	2	Philip Morris	$49,740	$243,331	$330,778	$111,888	$20,522	$8,937	$29,489
2	1	Procter & Gamble	5,576	79,611	377,552	238,049	23,713	23,665	7,906
3	5	General Motors	174,889	153,985	272,953	103,522	7,968	18,906	34,829
4	3	Sears, Roebuck	NA	21,608	89,973	25,765	2,327	52,701	21,211
5	4	RJR Nabisco	20,242	105,674	209,777	31,272	14,688	2,226	8,788
6	8	PepsiCo	8,178	936	140,342	271,069	3,742	5,203	19,766
7	9	Eastman Kodak	2,866	32,884	145,961	15,000	7,989	3,941	960
8	10	McDonald's	NA	7,192	216,067	129,010	1,820	0	4,548
9	6	Ford Motor	100,690	125,491	161,177	50,292	6,118	19,766	14,861
10	7	Anheuser-Busch	11,409	11,893	186,948	83,767	22,943	23,456	43,550
11	11	K mart	NA	23,482	18,238	30,942	2,632	6,824	3,696
12	14	Unilever	1,567	58,259	211,923	58,017	4,865	8,627	3,319
13	13	General Mills	501	19,983	133,724	137,028	18,582	2,873	1,060
14	16	Chrysler	70,166	100,446	151,569	82,836	6,684	4,874	17,345
15	12	Warner-Lambert	1,497	14,227	102,472	41,682	2,123	24,614	2,397
16	15	American Telephone & Telegraph	35,920	76,270	146,418	34,790	6,440	15,004	6,864
17	23	Kellogg	483	3,406	237,985	61,925	4,496	17	0
18	17	J.C. Penney	NA	9,044	48,507	12,951	2,847	2,612	292
19	18	Pillsbury	753	5,246	104,335	118,776	1,300	0	16,366
20	21	Johnson & Johnson	790	32,816	181,999	8,953	2,569	138	1,349
21	19	Ralston Purina	2,467	18,471	102,545	25,152	4,342	4,963	2,570
22	20	Kraft	2,183	29,787	71,245	67,914	1,331	678	5,964
23	22	American Home Prods.	216	13,907	182,057	14,917	7,254	2,534	1,208
24	27	Mars	650	10,991	130,271	38,439	14,877	8,569	1,388
25	24	Coca-Cola	5,467	4,087	111,153	71,061	8,766	2,449	13,051
26	26	Bristol-Myers	553	37,964	134,419	8,239	4,615	0	1,157
27	29	Quaker Oats	2,032	26,147	104,107	32,877	3,156	1,212	6,641
28	28	Nestle	2,476	25,044	86,607	48,924	3,847	3,620	4,198
29	25	U.S. Government	3,996	44,160	55,659	35,342	2,714	10,124	8,844
30	34	Colgate-Palmolive	1,754	7,810	68,572	22,614	342	197	749
31	35	Sara Lee	5,360	27,438	66,917	24,814	1,121	2,701	781
32	32	General Electric	22,816	37,727	38,356	8,580	390	3,091	1,022
33	33	Toyota Motor	28,409	27,105	46,298	66,294	2,229	2,301	4,831
34	37	American Cyanamid	97	7,929	23,501	16,109	2,124	2,330	2,891
35	40	Schering-Plough	235	29,202	66,038	8,186	2,870	10,641	3,696

NOTED PERSONALITIES

Widely Known Americans of the Present

Statesmen, authors of nonfiction, military men, and other prominent persons not listed in other categories; as of mid-1989.

Name (Birthplace)	Birthdate	Name (Birthplace)	Birthdate
Abrams, Elliott (New York, N.Y.)	1/24/48	Friedan, Betty (Peoria, Ill.)	2/4/21
Arledge, Roone (Forest Hills, N.Y.)	7/8/31	Friedman, Milton (Brooklyn, N.Y.)	7/31/12
Anderson, Jack (Long Beach, Cal.)	10/19/22	Galbraith, John Kenneth (Ontario, Can.)	10/15/08
Armstrong, Neil (Wapakoneta, Oh.)	8/5/30	Gephardt, Richard (St. Louis, Mo.)	1/31/41
Armstrong, William L. (Fremont, Neb.)	1937	Giamatti, A. Bartlett (Boston, Mass.)	4/4/38
Ash, Mary Kay (Hot Wells, Tex.)	—	Gingrich, Newt (Harrisburg, Pa.)	6/17/43
Aspin, Les (Milwaukee, Wis.)	7/21/38	Ginsberg, Allen (Paterson, N.J.)	6/3/21
Bailey, F. Lee (Waltham, Mass.)	6/10/33	Giuliani, Rudolph W. (New York, N.Y.)	5/28/44
Baker, Howard (Huntsville, Tenn.)	11/15/25	Glenn, John (Cambridge, Oh.)	7/18/21
Baker, James A. (Houston, Tex.)	4/28/30	Goldwater, Barry M. (Phoenix, Ariz.)	1/1/09
Baker, Russell (Loudoun Co., Va.)	8/14/25	Goodman, Ellen (Newton, Mass.)	4/11/41
Barthelmy, Sidney K. (New Orleans, La.)	3/17/42	Gore, Albert Jr. (Washington, D.C.)	3/31/48
Belli, Melvin (Sonora, Cal.)	7/29/07	Gottlieb, Robert A. (New York)	4/9/31
Bennett, William J. (Salem, Oh.)	5/4/38	Gould, Stephen Jay (New York, N.Y.)	9/10/41
Bentsen, Lloyd (Missian, Tex.)	2/11/21	Graham, Billy (Charlotte, N.C.)	11/7/18
Biden, Joseph R. Jr. (Scranton, Pa.)	11/20/42	Graham, Katharine (New York, N.Y.)	6/16/17
Blackmun, Harry (Nashville, Ill.)	11/12/08	Gramm, Phil (Ft. Bennington, Ga.)	7/8/42
Blass, Bill (Ft. Wayne, Ind.)	6/22/22	Gray, William H. 3d (Baton Rouge, La.)	8/20/41
Bombeck, Erma (Dayton, Oh.)	2/21/27	Greenfield, Meg (Seattle, Wash.)	12/27/30
Boorstin, Daniel (Atlanta, Ga.)	10/1/14	Greenspan, Alan (New York, N.Y.)	3/6/26
Bradlee, Ben (Boston, Mass.)	8/26/21	Gumble, Bryant (New Orleans, La.)	9/29/48
Bradley, Bill (Crystal City, Mo.)	7/28/43	Hammer, Armand (New York, N.Y.)	5/21/98
Bradley, Ed (Philadelphia, Pa.)	6/22/41	Hart, Gary (Ottawa, Kan.)	11/28/37
Bradley, Thomas (Calvert, Tex.)	12/29/17	Harvey, Paul (Tulsa, Okla.)	9/4/18
Brady, Nicholas (New York, N.Y.)	4/11/30	Hatch, Orrin (Homestead, Pa.)	3/22/34
Brennan, William J. (Newark, N.J.)	4/25/06	Hatfield, Mark O. (Dallas, Ore.)	7/12/22
Breslin, Jimmy (Jamaica, N.Y.)	10/17/30	Heflin, Howell (Poulan, Ga.)	6/19/21
Brinkley, David (Wilmington, N.C.)	7/10/20	Hefner, Hugh (Chicago, Ill.)	4/9/26
Brody, Jane (Brooklyn, N.Y.)	5/19/41	Helms, Jesse (Monroe, N.C.)	10/18/21
Brokaw, Tom (Webster, S. Dak.)	2/6/40	Heloise (Waco, Tex.)	4/15/51
Brothers, Joyce (New York, N.Y.)	9/20/28	Hollings, Ernest (Charleston, S.C.)	1/1/22
Brown, Helen Gurley (Green Forest, Ark.)	2/18/22	Iacocca, Lee A. (Allentown, Pa.)	10/15/24
Buchwald, Art (Mt. Vernon, N.Y.)	10/20/25	Icahn, Carl (New York, N.Y.)	1936
Buckley, William F. (New York, N.Y.)	11/24/25	Inouye, Daniel K. (Honolulu, Ha.)	9/7/24
Bumpers, Dale (Charleston, Ark.)	8/12/25	Jackson, Jesse (Greenville, N.C.)	10/8/41
Buscaglia, Leo (Los Angeles, Cal.)	3/31/24	Jennings, Peter (Toronto, Ont.)	8/29/38
Bush, Barbara (Rye, N.Y.)	6/8/25	Johnson, Lady Bird (Karnack, Tex.)	12/22/12
Byrd, Robert (N. Wilkesboro, N.C.)	11/20/17	Jordan, Barbara (Houston, Tex.)	2/21/36
Carlucci, Frank (Scranton, Pa.)	10/18/30	Kael, Pauline (Petaluma, Calif.)	6/19/19
Carter, Jimmy (Plains, Ga.)	10/1/24	Karan, Donna (Forest Hills, N.Y.)	10/2/48
Carter, Rosalynn (Plains, Ga.)	8/18/27	Kassebaum, Nancy (Topeka, Kan.)	7/29/32
Chancellor, John (Chicago, Ill.)	7/14/27	Keillor, Garrison (Anoka, Minn.)	8/7/42
Chavez, Cesar (Yuma, Ariz.)	3/31/27	Kemp, Jack (Los Angeles, Cal.)	7/13/35
Cheney, Richard B. (Lincoln, Neb.)	1/30/41	Kennedy, Anthony (Sacramento, Cal.)	7/23/36
Child, Julia (Pasadena, Cal.)	8/15/12	Kennedy, Edward M. (Brookline, Mass.)	2/22/32
Chisholm, Shirley (Brooklyn, N.Y.)	11/30/24	Kennedy, Rose (Boston, Mass.)	7/22/90
Chung, Connie (Washington, D.C.)	8/20/46	Kerr, Walter (Evanston, Ill.)	7/8/13
Claiborne, Craig (Sunflower, Miss.)	9/4/20	King, Coretta Scott (Marion, Ala.)	4/27/27
Clark, William (Dallas, Tex.)	12/11/30	King, Larry (Brooklyn, N.Y.)	11/19/34
Collins, Martha (Shelby Cty, Ky.)	12/7/36	Kirkland, Lane (Camden, S.C.)	3/12/22
Commager, Henry Steele (Pittsburgh, Pa.)	10/25/02	Kirkpatrick, Jeane (Duncan, Okla.)	11/19/26
Cooney, Joan Ganz (Phoenix, Ariz.)	10/30/29	Kissinger, Henry (Fuerth, Germany)	5/27/23
Cosell, Howard (Winston-Salem, N.C.)	3/25/20	Klein, Calvin (New York, N.Y.)	11/19/42
Cousins, Norman (Union Hill, N.J.)	6/24/12	Koch, Edward I. (New York, N.Y.)	12/12/24
Cranston, Alan (Palo Alto, Cal.)	6/19/14	Koop, C. Everett (Brooklyn, N.Y.)	10/14/16
Crist, Judith (New York, N.Y.)	5/22/22	Koppel, Ted (Lancashire, Eng.)	2/8/40
Cronkite, Walter (St. Joseph, Mo.)	11/4/16	Kuhn, Maggie (Buffalo, N.Y.)	1905
Crowe, Adm. William J. Jr. (La Grange, Ky.)	1/2/25	Landers, Ann (Sioux City, Ia.)	7/4/18
Cuomo, Mario (Queens, N.Y.)	6/15/32	Lauder, Estee (New York, N.Y.)	—
Daley, Richard M. (Chicago, Ill.)	4/24/42	Lauren, Ralph (Bronx, N.Y.)	10/14/39
Dellums, Ronald (Oakland, Cal.)	11/24/35	Leahy, Patrick (Montpelier, Vt.)	3/31/40
Dingell, John D. Jr. (Colorado Spngs., Col.)	7/8/26	Lear, Norman (New Haven, Conn.)	7/27/22
Dodd, Christopher (Willimantic, Conn.)	5/27/44	Lehrer, Jim (Wichita, Kan.)	5/19/34
Dole, Elizabeth (Salisbury, N.C.)	7/29/36	Leland, Mickey (Lubbock, Tex.)	11/27/44
Dole, Robert (Russell, Kan.)	7/22/23	Lindbergh, Anne Morrow (Englewood, N.J.)	1906
Domenici, Pete (Albuquerque, N.M.)	5/7/32	Lorenzo, Frank (New York, N.Y.)	5/19/40
Donaldson, Sam (El Paso, Tex.)	3/11/34	Lott, Trent (Grenada, Miss.)	10/9/41
Dukakis, Michael S. (Boston, Mass.)	11/3/33	Lugar, Richard G. (Indianapolis, Ind.)	4/4/32
Dymally, Mervyn (Trinidad, W.I.)	5/12/26	MacNeil, Robert (Montreal, Que.)	1/19/31
Eisner, Michael (New York, N.Y.)	3/7/42	Madden, John (Austin, Minn.)	1936
Ephron, Nora (New York, N.Y.)	5/19/41	Marshall, Thurgood (Baltimore, Md.)	7/2/08
Falwell, Jerry (Lynchburg, Va.)	8/11/33	McCarver, Tim (Memphis, Tenn.)	10/16/41
Feinstein, Dianne (San Francisco, Cal.)	6/22/33	Metzenbaum, Howard (Cleveland, Oh.)	6/4/17
Feldstein, Martin (New York, N.Y.)	11/25/39	Michel, Robert H. (Peoria, Ill.)	3/2/23
Ferraro, Geraldine (Newburgh, N.Y.)	8/26/35	Mikulski, Barbara (Baltimore, Md.)	7/20/36
Fitzwater, Marlin (Salina, Kan.)	11/24/42	Mitchell, George (Waterville, Me.)	8/20/33
Foley, Thomas S. (Spokane, Wash.)	3/6/29	Mondale, Walter (Ceylon, Minn.)	1/5/28
Forbes, Malcolm (New York, N.Y.)	8/19/19	Mosbacher, Robert (Mt. Vernon, N.Y.)	3/11/27
Ford, Betty (Chicago, Ill.)	4/8/18	Moyers, Bill (Hugo, Okla.)	6/5/34
Ford, Gerald R. (Omaha, Neb.)	7/14/13	Moynihan, Daniel P. (Tulsa, Okla.)	3/16/27

Mudd, Roger (Washington, D.C.)	2/9/28
Murdoch, Rupert (Melbourne, Austr.)	5/11/31
Nader, Ralph (Winsted, Conn.)	2/27/34
Nidetch, Jean (Brooklyn, N.Y.)	10/12/23
Nixon, Pat (Ely, Nev.)	3/16/12
Nixon, Richard (Yorba Linda, Cal.)	1/9/13
North, Oliver (San Antonio, Tex.)	10/7/43
Norton, Eleanor Holmes (Washington, D.C.)	6/13/37
Nunn, Sam (Perry, Ga.)	9/8/38
O'Connor, Cardinal John (Phila., Pa.)	1/15/20
O'Connor, Sandra Day (nr. Duncan, Ariz.)	3/26/30
Onassis, Jacqueline (Southampton, N.Y.)	7/28/29
O'Neill, Thomas P. (Cambridge, Mass.)	12/9/12
Packwood, Bob (Portland, Ore.)	9/11/32
Paley, William S. (Chicago, Ill.)	9/28/01
Pauley, Jane (Indianapolis, Ind.)	10/31/50
Pauling, Linus (Portland, Ore.)	2/28/01
Pepper, Claude (Dudleyville, Ala.)	9/8/00
Phelan, Richard (Chicago, Ill.)	3/29/37
Pickens, T. Boone (Holdenville, Okla.)	5/22/28
Pickering, Thomas (Orange, N.J.)	11/5/31
Porter, Sylvia (Patchogue, N.Y.)	6/18/13
Proxmire, William (Lake Forest, Ill.)	1/11/15
Quayle, Dan (Indianapolis, Ind.)	2/4/47
Quinn, Jane Bryant (Niagara Falls, N.Y.)	2/5/39
Rangel, Charles (New York, N.Y.)	6/11/30
Rather, Dan (Wharton, Tex.)	10/31/31
Reagan, Nancy (New York, N.Y.)	7/6/23
Reagan, Ronald (Tampico, Ill.)	2/6/11
Reasoner, Harry (Dakota City, Ia.)	4/17/23
Rehnquist, William (Milwaukee, Wis.)	10/1/24
Ride, Sally K. (Encino, Calif.)	1952
Roberts, Oral (nr. Ada, Okla.)	1/24/18
Robertson, Pat (Lexington, Va.)	3/22/30
Rockefeller, David (New York, N.Y.)	6/12/15
Rockefeller, John D. 4th "Jay" (New York, N.Y.)	6/18/37
Rockefeller, Laurance S. (New York, N.Y.)	5/26/10
Rooney, Andy (Albany, N.Y.)	1/14/19
Rostenkowski, Dan (Chicago, Ill.)	1/2/28
Rozelle, Pete (S. Gate, Calif.)	3/1/26
Rukeyser, Louis (New York, N.Y.)	1/30/33
Safer, Morley (Toronto, Ontario)	11/8/31
Safire, William (New York, N.Y.)	12/17/29
Sagan, Carl (New York, N.Y.)	11/9/34
Salk, Jonas (New York, N.Y.)	10/28/14
Sawyer, Diane (Glasgow, Ky.)	12/22/45
Scalia, Antonin (Trenton, N.J.)	3/11/36
Schlesinger, Arthur Jr. (Columbus, Oh.)	10/15/17
Schroeder, Patricia (Portland, Ore.)	7/30/40
Schuller, Robert (Alton, Ia.)	9/16/26
Scowcroft, Brent (Ogden, Ut.)	3/19/25
Seaborg, Glenn T. (Ishpeming, Mich.)	4/19/12
Shanker, Albert (New York, N.Y.)	9/14/28
Shriver, Maria (Chicago, Ill.)	11/6/55
Shultz, George P. (New York, N.Y.)	12/13/20
Silverstein, Shel (Chicago, Ill.)	1932
Simmons, Richard (New Orleans, La.)	7/12/48
Simon, Paul (Eugene, Ore.)	11/29/28
Simpson, Alan K. (Cody, Wyo.)	9/2/31
Smith, Liz (Ft. Worth, Tex.)	2/2/23
Solarz, Stephen J. (New York, N.Y.)	9/2/40
Spock, Benjamin (New Haven, Conn.)	5/2/03
Stahl, Lesley (Lynn, Mass.)	12/16/41
Steinbrenner, George (Rocky River, Oh.)	7/4/30
Steinem, Gloria (Toledo, Oh.)	3/25/34
Stern, David J. (New York, N.Y.)	9/22/42
Stevens, John Paul (Chicago, Ill.)	4/20/20
Sullivan, Louis (Atlanta, Ga.)	11/3/33
Sulzberger, Arthur Ochs (New York, N.Y.)	2/5/26
Sununu, John H. (Havana, Cuba)	7/2/39
Terkel, Studs (New York, N.Y.)	5/16/12
Thornburgh, Dick (Pittsburgh, Pa.)	7/16/32
Thurmond, J. Strom (Edgefield, S.C.)	12/5/02
Tinker, Grant (Stamford, Conn.)	1/11/26
Tisch, Laurence (New York, N.Y.)	3/15/23
Toland, John (LaCrosse, Wis.)	6/29/12
Tower, John (Houston, Tex.)	9/29/25
Trillin, Calvin (Kansas City, Mo.)	12/5/35
Truman, Margaret (Independence, Mo.)	2/17/24
Trump, Donald (New York, N.Y.)	1946
Turner, Ted (Cincinnati, Oh.)	1938
Udall, Morris K. (St. Johns, Ariz.)	6/15/22
Ueberroth, Peter (Chicago, Ill.)	9/2/37
Van Buren, Abigail (Sioux City, Ia.)	7/4/18
Volcker, Paul A. (Cape May, N.J.)	9/5/27
Wallace, George (Clio, Ala.)	8/25/19
Wallace, Mike (Brookline, Mass.)	5/9/18
Walters, Barbara (Boston, Mass.)	9/25/31
Walton, Sam (Kingfisher, Okla.)	1920
Webster, William H. (St. Louis, Mo.)	3/6/24
Weinberger, Caspar (San Francisco, Cal.)	8/18/17
Wenner, Jann (New York, N.Y.)	1/7/46
Westheimer, Ruth (Germany)	1928
White, Bill (Lakewood, Fla.)	1/28/34
White, Byron (Ft. Collins, Col.)	6/8/17
Wiesel, Elie (Sighet, Transyl.)	9/30/28
Will, George (Champaign, Ill.)	1941
Wright, James C. Jr. (Ft. Worth, Tex.)	12/22/22
Yard, Molly (Shanghai, China)	
Young, Andrew (New Orleans, La.)	3/12/32
Young, Coleman (Tuscaloosa, Ala.)	5/24/18
Ziegler, John (Grosse Point, Mich.)	2/9/34

Noted Black Americans

Names of black athletes and entertainers are not included here as they are listed elsewhere in The World Almanac.

The Rev. Dr. Ralph David Abernathy, b. 1926, organizer, 1957, and president, 1968, of the Southern Christian Leadership Conference.

Crispus Attucks, c. 1723-1770, agitator who led group that precipitated the "Boston Massacre," Mar. 5, 1770.

James Baldwin, 1924-1987, author, playwright; *The Fire Next Time, Blues for Mister Charlie, Just Above My Head.*

Benjamin Banneker, 1731-1806, inventor, astronomer, mathematician, and gazeteer; served on commission that surveyed and laid out Washington, D. C.

Imamu Amiri Baraka, b. LeRoi Jones, 1934, poet, playwright.

James P. Beckwourth, 1798-c. 1867, western fur-trader, scout, after whom Beckwourth Pass in northern California is named.

Dr. Mary McCleod Bethune, 1875-1955, adviser to presidents Roosevelt, Truman; division administrator, Natl. Youth Administration, 1935; founder, pres. Bethune-Cookman College.

Henry Blair, 19th century, obtained patents (believed the first issued to a black) for a corn-planter, 1834, and for a cotton-planter, 1836.

Julian Bond, b. 1940, civil rights leader first elected to the Georgia state legislature, 1965; helped found Student Nonviolent Coordinating Committee.

Edward Bouchet, 1852-1918, first black to earn a Ph.D., Yale, 1876, at a U. S. university; first black elected to Phi Beta Kappa.

Thomas Bradley, b. 1917, elected mayor of Los Angeles, 1973.

Andrew F. Brimmer, b. 1926, first black member, 1966, Federal Reserve Board.

Edward W. Brooke, b. 1919, attorney general, 1962, of Massachusetts; first black elected to U. S. Senate, 1967, since 19th century Reconstruction.

Gwendolyn Brooks, b. 1917, poet, novelist; first black to win a Pulitzer Prize, 1950, for *Annie Allen.*

Sterling A. Brown, 1901-1989, poet, literature professor; helped establish Afro-American literary criticism.

William Wells Brown, 1815-1884, novelist, dramatist; first American black to publish a novel.

Dr. Ralph Bunche, 1904-1971, first black to win the Nobel Peace Prize, 1950; undersecretary of the UN, 1950.

Sherian Grace Cadoria, b. 1940, brigadier general; highest ranking black woman in U.S. armed forces.

Alexa Canady, b. 1950, first black woman neurosurgeon in U.S.

George E. Carruthers, b. 1940, physicist developed the Apollo 16 lunar surface ultraviolet camera/spectograph.

George Washington Carver, 1861-1943, botanist, chemurgist, and educator; his extensive experiments in soil building and plant diseases revolutionized the economy of the South.

Charles Waddell Chestnutt, 1858-1932, author known primarily for his short stories, including *The Conjure Woman.*

Shirley Chisholm, b. 1924, first black woman elected to House of Representatives, Brooklyn, N. Y., 1968.

Bishop Philip R. Cousin, b. 1933, Pres., Natl. Council of Churches of Christ in the USA, 1985-.

Countee Cullen, 1903-1946, poet; won many literary prizes.

Lt. Gen. Benjamin O. Davis Jr. b. 1912, West Point, 1936, first black Air Force general, 1954.

Brig. Gen. Benjamin O. Davis Sr., 1877-1970, first black general, 1940, in U. S. Army.

William L. Dawson, 1886-1970, Illinois congressman, first black chairman of a major House of Representatives committee.

Isaiah Dorman, 19th century, U. S. Army interpreter, killed with Custer, 1876, at Battle of the Little Big Horn.

Aaron Douglas, 1900-1979, painter; called father of black American art.

Frederick Douglass, 1817-1895, author, editor, orator, diplomat; edited the abolitionist weekly, The North Star, in Rochester, N. Y.; U.S. minister and consul general to Haiti.

Dr. Charles Richard Drew, 1904-1950, pioneer in development of blood banks; director of American Red Cross blood donor project in World War II.

William Edward Burghardt Du Bois, 1868-1963, historian, sociologist; a founder of the National Association for the Advancement of Colored People (NAACP), 1909, and founder of its magazine The Crisis; author, *The Souls of Black Folk.*

Paul Laurence Dunbar, 1872-1906, poet, novelist; won fame with *Lyrics of Lowly Life,* 1896.

Jean Baptiste Point du Sable, c. 1750-1818, pioneer trader and first settler of Chicago, 1779.

Marian Wright Edelman, b. 1939, founder, pres. of Children's Defense Fund.

Ralph Ellison, b. 1914, novelist, essayist, *Invisible Man.*

Estevanico, explorer; led Spanish expedition of 1538 into the American Southwest.

James Farmer, b. 1920, a founder of the Congress of Racial Equality, 1942; asst. secretary, Dept. of HEW, 1969.

Henry O. Flipper, 1856-1940, first black to graduate, 1877, from West Point.

Charles Fuller, b. 1939, Pulitzer Prize-winning playwright; *A Soldier's Play.*

Mary Hatwood Futrell, b. 1940, president, Natl. Education Assn., 1983-.

Marcus Garvey, 1887-1940, founded Universal Negro Improvement Assn., 1911.

Kenneth Gibson, b. 1932, Newark, N.J., mayor, 1970-1986.

Charles Gordone, b. 1925, won 1970 Pulitzer Prize in Drama, with *No Place to Be Somebody.*

Vice Adm. Samuel L. Gravely Jr. b. 1922, first black admiral, 1971, served in World War II, Korea, and Vietnam; commander, Third Fleet.

William H. Gray 3d, b. 1941, U.S. representative from Pa., 1978—; chairman, Budget Committee, 1985-88; chairman, House Democratic Caucus, 1988-89; majority whip, 1989-.

Alex Haley, b. 1921, Pulitzer Prize-winning author; *Roots, The Autobiography of Malcolm X.*

Jupiter Hammon, c. 1720-1800, poet; the first black American to have his works published, 1761.

Lorraine Hansberry, 1930-1965, playwright; won New York Drama Critics Circle Award, 1959, with *Raisin in the Sun.*

Barbara Harris, b. 1931, first woman Episcopal bishop.

Patricia Roberts Harris, 1924-1985, U. S. ambassador to Luxembourg, 1965-67; secretary; Dept. of HUD, 1977-1979, Dept. of HHS, 1979-1981.

William H. Hastie, 1904-1976 first black federal judge, appointed 1937; governor of Virgin Islands, 1946-49; judge, U.S. Circuit Court of Appeals, 1949.

Chester Himes, 1909-1984, novelist, *Cotton Comes to Harlem.*

Matthew A. Henson, 1866-1955, member of Peary's 1909 expedition to the North Pole; placed U.S. flag at the Pole.

Dr. William A. Hinton, 1883-1959, developed the Hinton and Davies-Hinton tests for detection of syphilis; first black professor, 1949, at Harvard Medical School.

Benjamin L. Hooks, b. 1925, first black member, 1972-1979, Federal Communications Comm.; exec. dir., NAACP, 1977—.

Langston Hughes, 1902-1967, poet; story, song lyric author.

Charlayne Hunter-Gault, b. 1942, first black woman admitted to Univ. of Ga., 1961; ran *N.Y. Times* Harlem Bureau, 1968-1977; broadcast journalist, 1978—.

The Rev. Jesse Jackson, b. 1941, national director, Operation Bread Basket; campaigned for Democratic presidential nomination, 1984, 1988.

Maynard Jackson, b. 1938, elected mayor of Atlanta, 1973.

Gen. Daniel James Jr. 1920-1978, first black 4-star general, 1975; Commander, North American Air Defense Command.

Pvt. Henry Johnson, 1897-1929, the first American decorated by France in World War I with the Croix de Guerre.

James Weldon Johnson, 1871-1938, poet, lyricist, novelist; first black admitted to Florida bar; U.S. consul in Venezuela and Nicaragua.

John H. Johnson, b. 1918, publisher, editor of Ebony, Jet, Ebony Jr. magazines, from 1942.

Barbara Jordan, b. 1936, former congresswoman from Texas; member, House Judiciary Committee.

Vernon E. Jordan, b. 1935, exec. dir. Natl. Urban League, 1972.

Ernest E. Just, 1883-1941, marine biologist, studied egg development; author, *Biology of Cell Surfaces,* 1941.

Leontine T.C. Kelly, b. 1920, United Methodist bishop; first black woman bishop of a major American denomination.

The Rev. Dr. Martin Luther King Jr., 1929-1968, led 382-day Montgomery, Ala., boycott that brought 1956 U.S. Supreme Court decision holding segregation on buses unconstitutional; founder, president, Southern Christian Leadership Conference, 1957; won Nobel Peace Prize, 1964.

Lewis H. Latimer, 1848-1928, associate of Edison; supervised installation of first electric street lighting in N.Y.C.

Malcolm X, 1925-1965, leading spokesman for black pride, founded, 1963, Organization of Afro-American Unity.

Thurgood Marshall, b. 1908, first black U.S. solicitor general 1965; first black justice of the U. S. Supreme Court, 1967; as a lawyer led the legal battery that won the historic decision from the Supreme Court declaring racial segregation of public schools unconstitutional, 1954.

Jan Matzeliger, 1852-1889, invented lasting machine, patented 1883, which revolutionized the shoe industry.

Benjamin Mays, 1895-1984, educator, civil rights leader; headed Morehouse College, 1940-1967.

Wade H. McCree Jr., b. 1920, solicitor general of the U.S., 1977-1981.

Donald E. McHenry, b. 1936, U.S. ambassador to the United Nations, 1979-1981.

Ronald McNair, 1950-1986, physicist, first black astronaut; killed in *Challenger* explosion.

Dorie Miller, 1919-1943, Navy hero of Pearl Harbor attack; awarded the Navy Cross.

Ernest N. Morial, b. 1929, elected first black mayor of New Orleans, 1977.

Toni Morrison, novelist; *Song of Solomon, Tar Baby;* won 1988 Pulitzer prize for *Beloved.*

Willard Motley, 1912-1965, novelist; *Knock on Any Door.*

Elijah Muhammad, 1897-1975, founded Black Muslims, 1931.

Pedro Alonzo Nino, navigator of the Nina, one of Columbus' 3 ships on his first voyage of discovery to the New World, 1492.

Rosa Parks, b. 1913, Montgomery Ala. Citizen arrested for refusing to move to the back of the bus, Dec. 1, 1955, bringing a 382-day bus boycott led by Martin Luther King Jr.

Frederick D. Patterson, 1901-1988, founder of United Negro College Fund, 1944; Tuskegee Institute's third pres., 1935-1953.

Adam Clayton Powell, 1908-1972, early civil rights leader, congressman 1945-1969; chairman, House Committee on Education and Labor, 1960-1967.

Joseph H. Rainey, 1832-1887, first black elected to House of Representatives, 1869, from South Carolina.

A. Philip Randolph, 1889-1979, organized the Brotherhood of Sleeping Car Porters, 1925; organizer of 1941 and 1963 March on Washington movements; vice president, AFL-CIO.

Charles Rangel, b. 1930, congressman from N.Y.C. from 1970; member, Ways and Means Committee; chairman, Select Committee on Narcotics Abuse & Control.

Hiram R. Revels, 1822-1901, first black U.S. senator, elected in Mississippi, served 1870-1871.

Lloyd Richards, b. 1922(?), first black to direct a Broadway play, 1959; dean, Yale Univ. School of Drama & artistic director of Yale Repertory Theatre, 1979—.

Wilson C. Riles, b. 1917, elected, 1970, California State Superintendent of Public Instruction.

Norbert Rillieux, 1806-1894; invented a vacuum pan evaporator, 1846, revolutionizing the sugar-refining industry.

Paul Robeson, 1898-1976, actor and concert singer, graduated 1st in class at Rutgers, 1918, Phi Beta Kappa; grad. Columbia Univ. law school, 1923; associated with communist causes.

Carl T. Rowan, b. 1925, prize-winning journalist; director of the U.S. Information Agency, 1964, the first black to sit on the National Security Council; U. S. ambassador to Finland, 1963.

John B. Russwurm, 1799-1851, with **Samuel E. Cornish,** 1793-1858, founded, 1827, the nation's first black newspaper, Freedom's Journal, in N.Y.C.

Bayard Rustin, 1910-1987, organizer of the 1963 March on Washington; executive director, A. Philip Randolph Institute.

Peter Salem, at the Battle of Bunker Hill, June 17, 1775, shot and killed British commander Maj. John Pitcairn.

Ntozake Shange, b. 1948, writer, *For Colored Girls Who Have Considered Suicide/When the Rainbow is Enuf.*

Bishop Stephen Spottswood, 1897-1974, board chairman of NAACP, 1961-1974.

The Rev. Leon H. Sullivan, b. 1922, economic development planner, first black on General Motors Bd. of Directors.

Willard Townsend, 1895-1957, organized the United Transport Service Employees, 1935 (redcaps, etc.); vice pres. AFL-CIO.

Sojourner Truth, 1797-1883, born Isabella Baumfree; preacher, abolitionist; raised funds for Union in Civil War; worked for black educational opportunities.

Harriet Tubman, 1823-1913, Underground Railroad conductor served as nurse and spy for Union Army in the Civil War.

Nat Turner, 1800-1831, led the most significant of over 200 slave revolts in U.S., in Southampton, Va.; hanged.

Alice Walker, b. 1944, novelist, essayist, *The Color Purple.*

Booker T. Washington, 1856-1915, founder, 1881, and first president of Tuskegee Institute; author, *Up From Slavery.*

Dr. Robert C. Weaver, b. 1907, first black member of the U.S. Cabinet, secretary, Dept. of HUD, 1966.

Clifton R. Wharton Jr., b. 1926, first black pres. of major U.S. univ.; chancellor, nation's largest univ. system, 8 yrs.; chairman & CEO, country's largest pension fund, 1987—.

Phillis Wheatley, c. 1753-1784, poet; 2d American woman and first black woman to have her works published, 1770.

Bill White, b. 1934, first black baseball league president; named Natl. League head, 1989.

Walter White, 1893-1955, exec. secretary, NAACP, 1931-1955.

Roy Wilkins, 1901-1981, exec. director, NAACP, 1955-1977.

Dr. Daniel Hale Williams, 1858-1931, performed one of first 2 open-heart operations, 1893; founded Provident, Chicago's first Negro hospital; first black elected a fellow of the American College of Surgeons.

August Wilson, b. 1945, playwright, won 1987 Pulitzer Prize, Tony Award for *Fences*.

Granville T. Woods, 1856-1910, invented the third-rail system now used in subways, a complex railway telegraph device that helped reduce train accidents, and an automatic air brake.

Dr. Carter G. Woodson, 1875-1950, historian; founded Assn. for the Study of Negro Life and History, 1915, and Journal of Negro History, 1916.

Richard Wright, 1908-1960, novelist; *Native Son, Black Boy.*

Frank Yerby, b. 1916, first best-selling American black novelist; *The Foxes of Harrow, Vixen.*

Andrew Young, b. 1932, civil rights leader, congressman from Georgia, U.S. ambassador to the United Nations, 1977-79; mayor of Atlanta, 1982-.

Whitney M. Young Jr., 1921-1971, exec. director, 1961, National Urban League; author, lecturer, newspaper columnist.

About 5,000 blacks served in the Continental Army during the **American Revolution,** mostly in integrated units, some in all-black combat units. Some 200,000 blacks served in the Union Army during the **Civil War;** 38,000 gave their lives; 22 won the Medal of Honor, the nation's highest award. Of 367,000 blacks in the armed forces during **World War I,** 100,000 served in France. More than 1,000,000 blacks served in the armed forces during **World War II;** all-black fighter and bomber AAF units and infantry divisions gave distinguished service. In 1954 the policy of all-black units was finally abolished. Of 274,937 blacks who served in the armed forces during the **Vietnam War** (1965-1974), 5,681 were killed in combat.

As of Jan., 1988, there were 301 black mayors, 2,621 members of municipal governing boards, 406 state legislators, and 23 U.S. representatives. There are now 6,829 blacks holding elected office in the U.S. and Virgin Islands, an increase of 14.8% over the previous year, according to a survey by the Joint Center for Political Studies, Washington, D.C.,

Notable Living American Fiction Writers and Playwrights

Name (Birthplace)	Birthdate
Adams, Alice (Fredericksburg, Va.)	8/14/26
Albee, Edward (Washington, D.C.)	3/12/28
Asimov, Isaac (Petrovichi, Russia)	1/2/20
Auchincloss, Louis (Lawrence, N.Y.)	9/27/17
Barth, John (Cambridge, Md.)	5/27/30
Beattie, Ann (Washington, D.C.)	9/7/47
Bellow, Saul (Quebec, Canada)	7/10/15
Benchley, Peter (New York, N.Y.)	5/8/40
Berger, Thomas (Cincinnati, Oh.)	7/20/24
Blume, Judy (Elizabeth, N.J.)	2/12/38
Bradbury, Ray (Waukegan, Ill.)	8/22/20
Brooks, Gwendolyn (Topeka, Kan.)	6/7/17
Calisher, Hortense (New York, N.Y.)	12/20/11
Clark, Mary Higgins (New York, N.Y.)	12/24/31
Clavell, James (England)	10/10/24
Cleary, Beverly (McMinnville, Ore.)	1916
Connell, Evan S. (Kansas City, Mo.)	8/17/24
Conroy, Pat (Atlanta, Ga.)	10/26/45
Crews, Harry (Alma, Ga.)	6/6/35
Crichton, Michael (Chicago, Ill.)	10/23/42
Dailey, Janet (Storm Lake, Ia.)	5/21/44
De Vries, Peter (Chicago, Ill.)	2/27/10
Didion, Joan (Sacramento, Cal.)	12/5/34
Doctorow, E. L. (New York, N.Y.)	1/6/31
Dunne, John Gregory (Hartford, Conn.)	5/25/32
Elkin, Stanley (New York, N.Y.)	5/11/30
Ellison, Ralph (Oklahoma City, Okla.)	3/1/14
Fast, Howard (New York, N.Y.)	11/11/14
French, Marilyn (New York, N.Y.)	11/21/29
Fuller, Charles (Philadelphia, Pa.)	3/5/39
Gaddis, William (New York, N.Y.)	1922
Geisel, Theodore ("Dr. Seuss," Springfield, Mass.)	3/2/04
Gilroy, Frank (New York, N.Y.)	10/13/25
Godwin, Gail (Birmingham, Ala.)	6/18/37
Gold, Herbert (Cleveland, Oh.)	3/9/24
Goldman, William (Chicago, Ill.)	8/12/31
Gordon, Mary (Long Island, N.Y.)	12/8/49
Grau, Shirley Ann (New Orleans, La.)	7/8/29
Guare, John (New York, N.Y.)	2/5/38
Hailey, Arthur (Luton, England)	4/5/20
Haley, Alex (Ithaca, N.Y.)	8/11/21
Hawkes, John (Stamford, Conn.)	8/17/25
Heinlein, Robert (Butler, Mon.)	7/7/07
Heller, Joseph (Brooklyn, N.Y.)	5/1/23
Helprin, Mark (New York, N.Y.)	6/28/47
Hersey, John (Tientsin, China)	6/17/14
Irving, John (Exeter, N.H.)	3/2/42
Jong, Erica (New York, N.Y.)	3/26/42
Kennedy, William (Albany, N.Y.)	1/16/28
Kerr, Jean (Scranton, Pa.)	7/10/23
King, Stephen (Portland, Me.)	9/21/47
Knowles, John (Fairmont, W. Va.)	9/16/26
Kosinski, Jerzy (Lódz, Poland)	6/14/33

Name (Birthplace)	Birthdate
Krantz, Judith (New York, N.Y.)	1/9/28
LeGuin, Ursula (Berkeley, Cal.)	10/21/29
L'Engle, Madeleine (New York, N.Y.)	11/29/18
Leonard, Elmore (New Orleans, La.)	10/11/25
Levin, Ira (New York, N.Y.)	8/27/29
Ludlum, Robert (New York, N.Y.)	5/25/27
Lurie, Alison (Chicago, Ill.)	9/3/26
Mailer, Norman (Long Branch, N.J.)	1/31/23
Mamet, David (Chicago, Ill.)	11/30/47
McGuane, Thomas (Wyandotte, Mich.)	12/11/39
McMurtry, Larry (Wichita Falls, Tex.)	6/3/36
Michener, James A. (New York, N.Y.)	2/3/07
Miller, Arthur (New York, N.Y.)	10/17/15
Morris, Wright (Central City, Neb.)	1/6/10
Morrison, Toni (Lorain, Oh.)	—
Oates, Joyce Carol (Lockport, N.Y.)	6/16/38
Ozick, Cynthia (New York, N.Y.)	4/17/28
Paley, Grace (New York, N.Y.)	12/11/22
Percy, Walker (Birmingham, Ala.)	5/28/16
Piercy, Marge (Detroit, Mich.)	3/31/36
Potok, Chaim (New York, N.Y.)	2/17/29
Price, Reynolds (Macon, N.C.)	2/1/33
Puzo, Mario (New York, N.Y.)	10/15/20
Pynchon, Thomas (Glen Cove, N.Y.)	5/8/37
Rabe, David (Dubuque, Ia.)	3/10/40
Reed, Ishmael (Chattanooga, Tenn.)	2/22/38
Roth, Henry (Austria-Hungary)	2/8/06
Roth, Philip (Newark, N.J.)	3/19/33
Salinger, J. D. (New York, N.Y.)	1/1/19
Sanders, Lawrence (New York, N.Y.)	1920
Sendak, Maurice (New York, N.Y.)	6/10/28
Shepard, Sam (Ft. Sheridan, Ill.)	11/5/43
Simon, Neil (New York, N.Y.)	7/4/27
Singer, Isaac Bashevis (Radzymin, Poland)	7/14/04
Spillane, Mickey (Brooklyn, N.Y.)	3/9/18
Stegner, Wallace (Lake Mills, Ia.)	2/18/09
Stone, Irving (San Francisco, Cal.)	7/14/03
Stone, Robert (Brooklyn, N.Y.)	8/21/37
Taylor, Peter (Trenton, Tenn.)	1/8/17
Theroux, Paul (Medford, Mass.)	4/10/41
Tyler, Anne (Minneapolis, Minn.)	10/25/41
Updike, John (Shillington, Pa.)	3/18/32
Uris, Leon (Baltimore, Md.)	8/3/24
Vidal, Gore (West Point, N.Y.)	10/3/25
Vonnegut, Kurt Jr. (Indianapolis, Ind.)	11/11/22
Walker, Alice (Eatonton, Ga.)	1944
Wallace, Irving (Chicago, Ill.)	3/18/16
Wambaugh, Joseph (East Pittsburgh, Pa.)	1/22/37
Warren, Robert Penn (Guthrie, Ky.)	4/24/05
Welty, Eudora (Jackson, Miss.)	4/13/09
Wilson, August (Pittsburgh, Pa.)	4/27/45
Wilson, Lanford (Lebanon, Mo.)	4/13/37
Wolfe, Tom (Richmond, Va.)	3/2/31
Wolff, Tobias (Birmingham, Ala.)	6/19/45
Wouk, Herman (New York, N.Y.)	5/27/15

American Architects and Some of Their Achievements

Max Abramovitz, b. 1908, Avery Fisher Hall, Lincoln Center, N.Y.C.

Henry Bacon, 1866-1924, Lincoln Memorial.

Pietro Belluschi, b. 1899, Juilliard School of Music, Lincoln Center, N.Y.C.

Marcel Breuer, 1902-1981, Whitney Museum of American Art, N.Y.C. (with Hamilton Smith).

Charles Bulfinch, 1763-1844, State House, Boston; Capitol, Wash. D.C., (part).

Gordon Bunshaft, b. 1909, Lever House, Park Ave, N.Y.C.; Hirshhorn Museum, Wash., D.C.

Daniel H. Burnham, 1846-1912, Union Station, Wash. D.C.; Flatiron, N.Y.C.

Irwin Chanin, 1892-1988, New York City theaters, skyscrapers.

Ralph Adams Cram, 1863-1942, Cathedral of St. John the Divine, N.Y.C.; U.S. Military Academy (part).

R. Buckminster Fuller, 1895-1983, U.S. Pavilion, Expo 67, Montreal (geodesic domes).

Cass Gilbert, 1859-1934, Custom House, Woolworth Bldg., N.Y.C.; Supreme Court bldg., Wash., D.C.

Bertram G. Goodhue, 1869-1924, Capitol, Lincoln, Neb.; St. Thomas, St. Bartholomew, N.Y.C.

Walter Gropius, 1883-1969, Pan Am Building, N.Y.C. (with Pietro Belluschi).

Peter Harrison, 1716-1775, Touro Synagogue, Redwood Library, Newport, R.I.

Wallace K. Harrison, 1895-1981, Metropolitan Opera House, Lincoln Center, N.Y.C.

Thomas Hastings, 1860-1929, Public Library, Frick Mansion, N.Y.C.

James Hoban, 1762-1831, The White House.

Raymond Hood, 1881-1934, Rockefeller Center, N.Y.C. (part); Daily News, N.Y.C.; Tribune, Chicago.

Richard M. Hunt, 1827-1895, Metropolitan Museum, N.Y.C. (part); Natl. Observatory, Wash., D.C.

William Le Baron Jenney, 1832-1907, Home Insurance, Chicago (demolished 1931).

Philip C. Johnson, b. 1906, N.Y. State Theater, Lincoln Center, N.Y.C.

Albert Kahn, 1869-1942, Athletic Club Bldg., General Motors Bldg., Detroit.

Louis Kahn, 1901-1974, Salk Laboratory, La Jolla, Cal.; Yale Art Gallery.

Christopher Grant LaFarge, 1862-1938, Roman Catholic Chapel, West Point.

Benjamin H. Latrobe, 1764-1820, U.S. Capitol (part).

William Lescaze, 1896-1969, Philadelphia Savings Fund Society; Borg-Warner Bldg., Chicago.

Charles F. McKim, 1847-1909, Public Library, Boston, Columbia Univ., N.Y.C. (part).

Charles M. McKim, b. 1920, KUHT-TV Transmitter Building, Houston; Lutheran Church of the Redeemer, Houston.

Ludwig Mies van der Rohe, 1886-1969, Seagram Building, N.Y.C. (with Philip C. Johnson); National Gallery, Berlin.

Robert Mills, 1781-1855, Washington Monument.

Richard J. Neutra, 1892-1970, Mathematics Park, Princeton; Orange Co. Courthouse, Santa Ana, Cal.

Gyo Obata, b. 1923, Natl. Air & Space Mus., Smithsonian Institution; Dallas-Ft. Worth Airport.

Frederick L. Olmsted, 1822-1903, Central Park, N.Y.C.; Fairmount Park, Philadelphia.

I(eoh) M(ing) Pei, b. 1917, National Center for Atmospheric Research, Boulder, Col.; East Wing, Natl. Gallery of Art, Wash., D.C.; Pyramid, The Louvre, Paris.

William Pereira, 1909-1985, Cape Canaveral; Transamerica Bldg., San Francisco.

John Russell Pope, 1874-1937, National Gallery.

John Portman, b. 1924, Peachtree Center, Atlanta.

James Renwick Jr., 1818-1895, Grace Church, St. Patrick's Cathedral, N.Y.C.; Smithsonian, Corcoran Galleries, Wash., D.C.

Henry H. Richardson, 1838-1886, Trinity Church, Boston.

Kevin Roche, b. 1922, Oakland Cal. Museum; Fine Arts Center, U. of Mass.

James Gamble Rogers, 1867-1947, Columbia-Presbyterian Medical Center, N.Y.C.; Northwestern Univ., Chicago.

John Wellborn Root, 1887-1963, Palmolive Building, Chicago; Hotel Statler, Washington; Hotel Tamanaco, Caracas.

Paul Rudolph, b. 1918, Jewitt Art Center, Wellesley College; Art & Architecture Bldg., Yale.

Charles M. Russell, 1866-1926, Western life.

Eero Saarinen, 1910-1961, Gateway to the West Arch, St. Louis; Trans World Flight Center, N.Y.C.

Louis Skidmore, 1897-1962, AEC town site, Oak Ridge, Tenn.; Terrace Plaza Hotel, Cincinnati.

Clarence S. Stein, 1882-1975, Temple Emanu-El, N.Y.C.

Edward Durell Stone, 1902-1978, U.S. Embassy, New Delhi, India; (H. Hartford) Gallery of Modern Art, N.Y.C.

Louis H. Sullivan, 1856-1924, Auditorium, Chicago.

Richard Upjohn, 1802-1878, Trinity Church, N.Y.C.

Ralph T. Walker, 1889-1973, N.Y. Telephone Hdqrs., N.Y.C.; IBM Research Lab., Poughkeepsie, N.Y.

Roland A. Wank, 1898-1970, Cincinnati Union Terminal; head architect TVA, 1933-44.

Stanford White, 1853-1906, Washington Arch; first Madison Square Garden, N.Y.C.

Frank Lloyd Wright, 1867 (or 1869)-1959, Imperial Hotel, Tokyo; Guggenheim Museum, N.Y.C.; Unity Church, Oak Park, Ill; Robie House, Chicago; Taliesin, Wis.

William Wurster, 1895-1973, Ghirardelli Sq., San Francisco; Cowell College, U. Cal., Berkeley.

Minoru Yamasaki, 1912-1986, World Trade Center, N.Y.C.

Noted American Cartoonists

Charles Addams, 1912-1988, macabre cartoons.

Brad Anderson, b. 1924, Marmaduke.

Peter Arno, 1904-1968, urban characterizations.

Tex Avery, 1908-1980, Friz Freleng, b. 1905?, Chuck Jones, b. 1912, animators of Bugs Bunny, Porky Pig, Daffy Duck.

George Baker, 1915-1975, The Sad Sack.

C. C. Beck, b. 1910, Captain Marvel.

Jim Berry, b. 1932, Berry's World.

Herb Block (Herblock), b. 1909, leading political cartoonist.

George Booth, b. 1926, New Yorker cartoonist.

Berke Breathed, b. 1957, Bloom County.

Clare Briggs, 1875-1930, Mr. & Mrs.

Dik Browne, 1917-1989, Hi & Lois, Hagar the Horrible.

Ernie Bushmiller, 1905-1982, Nancy.

Milton Caniff, 1907-1988, Terry & the Pirates; Steve Canyon.

Al Capp, 1909-1979, Li'l Abner.

Paul Conrad, 1924, political cartoonist.

Roy Crane, 1901-1977, Captain Easy; Buz Sawyer.

Robert Crumb, b. 1943, "Underground" cartoonist.

Jay N. Darling (Ding), 1876-1962, political cartoonist.

Jim Davis, b. 1945, Garfield.

Billy DeBeck, 1890-1942, Barney Google.

Rudolph Dirks, 1877-1968, The Katzenjammer Kids.

Walt Disney, 1901-1966, producer of animated cartoons; created Mickey Mouse & Donald Duck.

Steve Ditko, b. 1927, Spider-Man.

Mort Drucker, b. 1929, Mad magazine.

Jules Feiffer, b. 1929, satirical Village Voice cartoonist.

Bud Fisher, 1884-1954, Mutt & Jeff.

Ham Fisher, 1900-1955, Joe Palooka.

James Montgomery Flagg, 1877-1960, illustrator; created the famous Uncle Sam recruiting poster during WWI.

Max Fleischer, 1883-1972, creator of Betty Boop, Popeye cartoons.

Hal Foster, 1892-1982, Tarzan; Prince Valiant.

Fontaine Fox, 1884-1964, Toonerville Folks.

Rube Goldberg, 1883-1970, Boob McNutt.

Chester Gould, 1900-1985, Dick Tracy.

Harold Gray, 1894-1968, Little Orphan Annie.

Cathy Guisewite, b. 1950, Cathy.

Bill Hanna, b. 1910, & Joe Barbera, b. 1911, animators of Tom & Jerry, Huckleberry Hound, Yogi Bear, Flintstones.

Johnny Hart, b. 1931, BC, Wizard of Id.

Jimmy Hatlo, 1898-1963, Little Iodine.

John Held Jr., 1889-1958, "Jazz Age" cartoonist.

George Herriman, 1881-1944, Krazy Kat.

Harry Hershfield, 1885-1974, Abie the Agent.

Al Hirschfeld, b. 1903, N.Y. Times theater caricaturist.

Burne Hogarth, b. 1911, Tarzan.

Helen Hokinson, 1900-1949, satirized clubwomen.

Bil Keane, b. 1922, The Family Circus.

Walt Kelly, 1913-1973, Pogo.

Hank Ketcham, b. 1920, Dennis the Menace.

Ted Key, b. 1912, Hazel.

Frank King, 1883-1969, Gasoline Alley.

Jack Kirby, b. 1917, Fantastic Four.

Rollin Kirby, 1875-1952, political cartoonist.

B(ernard) Kliban, b. 1935, cat books.

Edward Koren, b. 1935, New Yorker woolly characters.

Walter Lantz, b. 1900, Woody Woodpecker.

Gary Larson, b. 1950, The Far Side.

Mell Lazarus, b. 1929, Momma, Miss Peach.

Noted Personalities — Cartoonists; Political Leaders

Stan Lee, b. 1922, Marvel Comics.
Don Martin, b. 1931, *Mad* magazine.
Bill Mauldin, b. 1921, depicted squalid life of the G.I. in WWII.
Jeff MacNelly, b. 1947, political cartoonist, and strip Shoe.
Winsor McCay, 1872-1934, Little Nemo.
John T. McCutcheon, 1870-1949, midwestern rural life.
George McManus, 1884-1954, Bringing Up Father.
Dale Messick, b. 1906, Brenda Starr.
Norman Mingo, 1896-1980, Alfred E. Neuman.
Bob Montana, 1920-1975, Archie.
Dick Moores, 1909-1986, Gasoline Alley.
Willard Mullin, 1902-1978, sports cartoonist; created Dodgers "Bum" and Mets "Kid".
Russell Myers, b. 1938, Broom Hilda.
Thomas Nast, 1840-1902, political cartoonist; created the Democratic donkey and Republican elephant.
Pat Oliphant, b. 1935, political cartoonist.
Frederick Burr Opper, 1857-1937, Happy Hooligan.
Richard Outcault, 1863-1928, Yellow Kid; Buster Brown.
Mike Peters, b. 1943, editorial cartoons; Mother Goose & Grimm.
George Price, b. 1901, New Yorker lower-class life.

Alex Raymond, 1909-1956, Flash Gordon; Jungle Jim.
Art Sansom, b. 1920, The Born Loser.
Charles Schulz, b. 1922, Peanuts.
Elzie C. Segar, 1894-1938, Popeye.
Jerry Siegel, b. 1914, & Joe Shuster, b. 1914, Superman.
Sydney Smith, 1887-1935, The Gumps.
Otto Soglow, 1900-1975, Little King; Canyon Kiddies.
William Steig, b. 1907, New Yorker cartoonist.
James Swinnerton, 1875-1974, Little Jimmy.
Paul Terry, 1887-1971, animator of Mighty Mouse.
Bob Thaves, b. 1924, Frank and Ernest.
James Thurber, 1894-1961, New Yorker cartoonist.
Garry Trudeau, b. 1948, Doonesbury.
Mort Walker, b. 1923, Beetle Bailey.
Bill Watterson, b. 1958, Calvin and Hobbes.
Russ Westover, 1887-1966, Tillie the Toiler.
Frank Willard, 1893-1958, Moon Mullins.
J. R. Williams, 1888-1957, The Willets Family; Out Our Way.
Gahan Wilson, b. 1930, cartoonist of the macabre.
Tom Wilson, b. 1931, Ziggy.
Art Young, 1866-1943, political radical and satirist.
Chic Young, 1901-1973, Blondie.

Noted Political Leaders of the Past

(U.S. presidents and most vice presidents, Supreme Court justices, signers of Declaration of Independence, listed elsewhere.)

Abu Bakr, 573-634, Mohammedan leader, first caliph, chosen successor to Mohammed.
Dean Acheson, 1893-1971, (U.S.) secretary of state, chief architect of cold war foreign policy.
Samuel Adams, 1722-1803, (U.S.) patriot, Boston Tea Party firebrand.
Konrad Adenauer, 1876-1967, (G.) West German chancellor.
Emilio Aguinaldo, 1869-1964, (Philip.) revolutionary, fought against Spain and the U.S.
Akbar, 1542-1605, greatest Mogul emperor of India.
Salvador Allende Gossens, 1908-1973, (Chil.) president, advocate of democratic socialism.
Herbert H. Asquith, 1852-1928, (Br.) Liberal prime minister, instituted an advanced program of social reform.
Atahualpa, ?-1533, Inca (ruling chief) of Peru.
Kemal Atatürk, 1881-1938, (Turk.) founded modern Turkey.
Clement Attlee, 1883-1967, (Br.) Labour party leader, prime minister, enacted national health, nationalized many industries.
Stephen F. Austin, 1793-1836, (U.S.) led Texas colonization.
Mikhail Bakunin, 1814-1876, (R.) revolutionary, leading exponent of anarchism.
Arthur J. Balfour, 1848-1930, (Br.) as foreign secretary under Lloyd George issued Balfour Declaration expressing official British approval of Zionism.
Bernard M. Baruch, 1870-1965, (U.S.) financier, gvt. adviser.
Fulgencio Batista y Zaldivar, 1901-1973, (Cub.) ruler overthrown by Castro.
Lord Beaverbrook, 1879-1964, (Br.) financier, statesman, newspaper owner.
Eduard Benes, 1884-1948, (Czech.) president during interwar and post-WW II eras.
David Ben-Gurion, 1886-1973, (Isr.) first premier of Israel.
Thomas Hart Benton, 1782-1858, (U.S.) Missouri senator, championed agrarian interests and westward expansion.
Lavrenti Beria, 1899-1953, (USSR) Communist leader prominent in political purges under Stalin.
Aneurin Bevan, 1897-1960, (Br.) Labour party leader.
Ernest Bevin, 1881-1951, (Br.) Labour party leader, foreign minister, helped lay foundation for NATO.
Otto von Bismarck, 1815-1898, (G.) statesman known as the Iron Chancellor, uniter of Germany, 1870.
James G. Blaine, 1830-1893, (U.S.) Republican politician, diplomat, influential in launching Pan-American movement.
Léon Blum, 1872-1950, (F.) socialist leader, writer, headed first Popular Front government.
Simón Bolívar, 1783-1830, (Venez.) South American revolutionary who liberated much of the continent from Spanish rule.
William E. Borah, 1865-1940, (U.S.) isolationist senator, instrumental in blocking U.S. membership in League of Nations and the World Court.
Cesare Borgia, 1476-1507, (It.) soldier, politician, an outstanding figure of the Italian Renaissance.
Leonid Brezhnev, 1906-1982, (USSR) leader of the Soviet Union, 1964-82.
Aristide Briand, 1862-1932, (F.) foreign minister, chief architect of Locarno Pact and anti-war Kellogg-Briand Pact.
William Jennings Bryan, 1860-1925, (U.S.) Democratic, populist leader, orator, 3 times lost race for presidency.
Nikolai Bukharin, 1888-1938, (USSR) communist leader.
William C. Bullitt, 1891-1967, (U.S.) diplomat, first ambassador to USSR, ambassador to France.

Ralph Bunche, 1904-1971, (U.S.) a founder and key diplomat of United Nations for more than 20 years.
John C. Calhoun, 1782-1850, (U.S.) political leader, champion of states' rights and a symbol of the Old South.
Robert Castlereagh, 1769-1822, (Br.) foreign secy, guided Grand Alliance against Napoleon.
Camillo Benso Cavour, 1810-1861, (It.) statesman, largely responsible for uniting Italy under the House of Savoy.
Austen Chamberlain, 1863-1937, (Br.) Conservative party leader, largely responsible for Locarno Pact of 1925.
Neville Chamberlain, 1869-1940, (Br.) Conservative prime minister whose appeasement of Hitler led to Munich Pact.
Salmon P. Chase, 1808-1873, (U.S.) public official, abolitionist, jurist, 6th Supreme Court chief justice.
Chiang Kai-shek, 1887-1975, (Chin.) Nationalist Chinese president whose govt. was driven from mainland to Taiwan.
Chou En-lai, 1898-1976, (Chin.) diplomat, prime minister, a leading figure of the Chinese Communist party.
Winston Churchill, 1874-1965, (Br.) prime minister, soldier, author, guided Britain through WW II.
Galeazzo Ciano, 1903-1944, (It.) fascist foreign minister, helped create Rome-Berlin Axis, executed by Mussolini.
Henry Clay, 1777-1852, (U.S.) "The Great Compromiser," one of most influential pre-Civil War political leaders.
Georges Clemenceau, 1841-1929, (F.) twice premier, Wilson's chief antagonist at Paris Peace Conference after WW I.
DeWitt Clinton, 1769-1828, (U.S.) political leader, responsible for promoting idea of the Erie Canal.
Robert Clive, 1725-1774, (Br.) first administrator of Bengal, laid foundation for British Empire in India.
Jean Baptiste Colbert, 1619-1683, (F.) statesman, influential under Louis XIV, created the French navy.
Oliver Cromwell, 1599-1658, (Br.) Lord Protector of England, led parliamentary forces during Civil War.
Curzon of Kedleston, 1859-1925, (Br.) viceroy of India, foreign secretary, major force in dealing with post-WW I problems in Europe and Far East.
Édouard Daladier, 1884-1970, (F.) radical socialist politician, arrested by Vichy, interned by Germans until liberation in 1945.
Georges Danton, 1759-1794, (F.) a leading figure in the French Revolution.
Jefferson Davis, 1808-1889, (U.S.) president of the Confederate States of America.
Charles G. Dawes, 1865-1951, (U.S.) statesman, banker, advanced Dawes Plan to stabilize post-WW I German finances.
Alcide De Gasperi, 1881-1954, (It.) premier, founder of the Christian Democratic party.
Charles DeGaulle, 1890-1970, (F.) general, statesman, and first president of the Fifth Republic.
Eamon De Valera, 1882-1975, (Ir.-U.S.) statesman, led fight for Irish independence.
Thomas E. Dewey, 1902-1971, (U.S.) New York governor, twice loser in try for presidency.
Ngo Dinh Diem, 1901-1963, (Viet.) South Vietnamese president, assassinated in government take-over.
Everett M. Dirksen, 1896-1969, (U.S.) Senate Republican minority leader, orator.
Benjamin Disraeli, 1804-1881, (Br.) prime minister, considered founder of modern Conservative party.
Engelbert Dollfuss, 1892-1934, (Aus.) chancellor, assassinated by Austrian Nazis.

Andrea Doria, 1466-1560, (It.) Genoese admiral, statesman, called "Father of Peace" and "Liberator of Genoa."

Stephen A. Douglas, 1813-1861, (U.S.) Democratic leader, orator, opposed Lincoln for the presidency.

John Foster Dulles, 1888-1959, (U.S.) secretary of state under Eisenhower, cold war policy maker.

Friedrich Ebert, 1871-1925, (G.) Social Democratic movement leader, instrumental in bringing about Weimar constitution.

Sir Anthony Eden, 1897-1977, (Br.) foreign secretary, prime minister during Suez invasion of 1956.

Ludwig Erhard, 1897-1977, (G.) economist, West German chancellor, led nation's economic rise after WW II.

Hamilton Fish, 1808-1893, (U.S.) secretary of state, successfully mediated disputes with Great Britain, Latin America.

James V. Forrestal, 1892-1949, (U.S.) secretary of navy, first secretary of defense.

Francisco Franco, 1892-1975, (Sp.) leader of rebel forces during Spanish Civil War and dictator of Spain.

Benjamin Franklin, 1706-1790, (U.S.) printer, publisher, author, inventor, scientist, diplomat.

Louis de Frontenac, 1620-1698, (F.) governor of New France (Canada); encouraged explorations, fought Iroquois.

Hugh Gaitskell, 1906-1963, (Br.) Labour party leader, major force in reversing its stand for unilateral disarmament.

Albert Gallatin, 1761-1849, (U.S.) secretary of treasury who was instrumental in negotiating end of War of 1812.

Léon Gambetta, 1838-1882, (F.) statesman, politician, one of the founders of the Third Republic.

Indira Gandhi, 1917-1984, (Ind.) succeeded father, Jawaharlal Nehru, as prime minister, assassinated.

Mohandas K. Gandhi, 1869-1948, (Ind.) political leader, ascetic, led nationalist movement against British rule.

Giuseppe Garibaldi, 1807-1882, (It.) patriot, soldier, a leading figure in the Risorgimento, the Italian unification movement.

Genghis Khan, c. 1167-1227, brilliant Mongol conqueror, ruler of vast Asian empire.

William E. Gladstone, 1809-1898, (Br.) prime minister 4 times, dominant force of Liberal party from 1868 to 1894.

Paul Joseph Goebbels, 1897-1945, (G.) Nazi propagandist, master of mass psychology.

Klement Gottwald, 1896-1953, (Czech.) communist leader ushered communism into his country.

Che (Ernesto) Guevara, 1928-1967, (Arg.) guerilla leader, prominent in Cuban revolution, killed in Bolivia.

Haile Selassie, 1891-1975, (Eth.) emperor, maintained monarchy through invasion, occupation, internal resistance.

Alexander Hamilton, 1755-1804, (U.S.) first treasury secretary, champion of strong central government.

Dag Hammarskjold, 1905-1961, (Swed.) statesman, UN secretary general.

John Hancock, 1737-1793, (U.S.) revolutionary leader, first signer of Declaration of Independence.

John Hay, 1838-1905, (U.S.) secretary of state, primarily associated with Open Door Policy toward China.

Patrick Henry, 1736-1799, (U.S.) major revolutionary figure, remarkable orator.

Édouard Herriot, 1872-1957, (F.) Radical Socialist leader, twice premier, president of National Assembly.

Theodor Herzl, 1860-1904, (Aus.) founder of modern Zionism.

Heinrich Himmler, 1900-1945, (G.) chief of Nazi SS and Gestapo, primarily responsible for the Holocaust.

Paul von Hindenburg, 1847-1934, (G.) field marshal, president.

Hirohito, 1902-1989; emperor of Japan from 1926.

Adolf Hitler, 1889-1945, (G.) dictator, founder of National Socialism.

Ho Chi Minh, 1890-1969, (Viet.) North Vietnamese president, Vietnamese Communist leader, national hero.

Harry L. Hopkins, 1890-1946, (U.S.) New Deal administrator, closest adviser to FDR during WW II.

Edward M. House, 1858-1938, (U.S.) diplomat, confidential adviser to Woodrow Wilson.

Samuel Houston, 1793-1863, (U.S.) leader of struggle to win control of Texas from Mexico.

Cordell Hull, 1871-1955, (U.S.) secretary of state, initiated reciprocal trade to lower tariffs, helped organize UN.

Hubert H. Humphrey, 1911-1978, (U.S.) Minnesota Democrat, senator, vice president, spent 32 years in public service.

Ibn Saud, c. 1888-1953, (S. Arab.) founder of Saudi Arabia and its first king.

Jacob Javits, 1904-1986 (U.S.) U.S. senator from New York for 24 years.

Jinnah, Muhammed Ali, 1876-1948, (Pak.) founder, first governor-general of Pakistan.

Benito Juarez, 1806-1872, (Mex.) rallied countrymen against foreign threats, sought to create democratic, federal republic.

Kamehameha I, c. 1758-1819, (Haw.) founder, first monarch of unified Hawaii.

Frank B. Kellogg, 1856-1937, (U.S.) secretary of state, negotiated Kellogg-Briand Pact to outlaw war.

Robert F. Kennedy, 1925-1968, (U.S.) attorney general, senator, assassinated while seeking presidential nomination.

Aleksandr Kerensky, 1881-1970, (R.) revolutionary, served as premier after Feb. 1917 revolution until Bolshevik overthrow.

Nikita Khrushchev, 1894-1971, (USSR) premier, first secretary of Communist party, initiated de-Stalinization.

Lajos Kossuth, 1802-1894, (Hung.) principal figure in 1848 Hungarian revolution.

Pyotr Kropotkin, 1842-1921, (R.) anarchist, championed the peasants but opposed Bolshevism.

Kublai Khan, c. 1215-1294, Mongol emperor, founder of Yüan dynasty in China.

Béla Kun, 1886-c.1939, (Hung.) communist, member of 3d International, tried to foment worldwide revolution.

Robert M. LaFollette, 1855-1925, (U.S.) Wisconsin public official, leader of progressive movement.

Pierre Laval, 1883-1945, (F.) politician, Vichy foreign minister, executed for treason.

Andrew Bonar Law, 1858-1923, (Br.) Conservative party politician, led opposition to Irish home rule.

Vladimir Ilyich Lenin (Ulyanov), 1870-1924, (USSR) revolutionary, founder of Bolshevism, Soviet leader 1917-1924.

Ferdinand de Lesseps, 1805-1894, (F.) diplomat, engineer, conceived idea of Suez Canal.

Rene Levesque, 1922-1987 (Can.) Premier of Quebec, 1976-85; led unsuccessful fight to separate from Canada.

Liu Shao-ch'i, c.1898-1974, (Chin.) communist leader, fell from grace during "cultural revolution."

Maxim Litvinov, 1876-1951, (USSR) revolutionary, commissar of foreign affairs, favored cooperation with Western powers.

David Lloyd George, 1863-1945, (Br.) Liberal party prime minister, laid foundations for modern welfare state.

Henry Cabot Lodge, 1850-1924, (U.S.) Republican senator, led opposition to participation in League of Nations.

Huey P. Long, 1893-1935, (U.S.) Louisiana political demagogue, governor, assassinated.

Rosa Luxemburg, 1871-1919, (G.) revolutionary, leader of the German Social Democratic party and Spartacus party.

J. Ramsay MacDonald, 1866-1937, (Br.) first Labour party prime minister of Great Britain.

Harold MacMillan, 1895-1987 (Br.) prime minister of Great Britain, 1957-63.

Joseph R. McCarthy, 1908-1957, (U.S.) senator notorious for his witch hunt for communists in the government.

Makarios III, 1913-1977, (Cypr.) Greek Orthodox archbishop, first president of Cyprus.

Malcolm X (Malcolm Little), 1925-1965, (U.S.) black separatist leader, assassinated.

Mao Tse-tung, 1893-1976, (Chin.) chief Chinese Marxist theorist, soldier, led Chinese revolution establishing his nation as an important communist state.

Jean Paul Marat, 1743-1793, (F.) revolutionary, politician, identified with radical Jacobins, assassinated.

José Marti, 1853-1895, (Cub.) patriot, poet, leader of Cuban struggle for independence.

Jan Masaryk, 1886-1948, (Czech.) foreign minister, died by mysterious suicide following communist coup.

Thomas G. Masaryk, 1850-1937, (Czech.) statesman, philosopher, first president of Czechoslovak Republic.

Jules Mazarin, 1602-1661, (F.) cardinal, statesman, prime minister under Louis XIII and queen regent Anne of Austria.

Tom Mboya, 1930-1969, (Kenyan) political leader, instrumental in securing independence for his country.

Cosimo I de' Medici, 1519-1574, (It.) Duke of Florence, grand duke of Tuscany.

Lorenzo de' Medici, the Magnificent, 1449-1492, (It.) merchant prince, a towering figure in Italian Renaissance.

Catherine de Medicis, 1519-1589, (F.) queen consort of Henry II, regent of France, influential in Catholic-Huguenot wars.

Golda Meir, 1898-1979, (Isr.) prime minister, 1969-74.

Klemens W.N.L. Metternich, 1773-1859, (Aus.) statesman, arbiter of post-Napoleonic Europe.

Anastas Mikoyan, 1895-1978, (USSR) prominent Soviet leader from 1917; president 1964-65.

Guy Mollet, 1905-1975, (F.) social politician, resistance leader.

Henry Morgenthau Jr., 1891-1967, (U.S.) secretary of treasury, raised funds to finance New Deal and U.S. WW II activities.

Gouverneur Morris, 1752-1816, (U.S.) statesman, diplomat, financial expert who helped plan decimal coinage system.

Wayne Morse, 1900-1974, (U.S.) senator, long-time critic of Vietnam War.

Muhammad Ali, 1769?-1849, (Egypt) pasha, founder of dynasty that encouraged emergence of modern Egyptian state.

Benito Mussolini, 1883-1945, (It.) dictator and leader of the Italian fascist state.

Imre Nagy, c. 1895-1958, (Hung.) communist premier, assassinated after Soviets crushed 1956 uprising.

Gamal Abdel Nasser, 1918-1970, (Egypt.) leader of Arab unification, second Egyptian president.

Jawaharlal Nehru, 1889-1964, (Ind.) prime minister, guided India through its early years of independence.

Kwame Nkrumah, 1909-1972, (Ghan.) dictatorial prime minister, deposed in 1966.

Frederick North, 1732-1792, (Br.) prime minister, his inept policies led to loss of American colonies.

Daniel O'Connell, 1775-1847, (Ir.) political leader, known as The Liberator.

Omar, c.581-644, Mohammedan leader, 2d caliph, led Islam to become an imperial power.

Ignace Paderewski, 1860-1941, (Pol.) statesman, pianist, composer, briefly prime minister, an ardent patriot.

Viscount Palmerston, 1784-1865, (Br.) Whig-Liberal prime minister, foreign minister, embodied British nationalism.

George Papandreou, 1888-1968, (Gk.) Republican politician, served three times as prime minister.

Franz von Papen, 1879-1969, (G.) politician, played major role in overthrow of Weimar Republic and rise of Hitler.

Charles Stewart Parnell, 1846-1891, (Ir.) nationalist leader, "uncrowned king of Ireland."

Lester Pearson, 1897-1972, (Can.) diplomat, Liberal party leader, prime minister.

Robert Peel, 1788-1850, (Br.) reformist prime minister, founder of Conservative party.

Juan Perón, 1895-1974, (Arg.) president, dictator.

Joseph Pilsudski, 1867-1935, (Pol.) statesman, instrumental in re-establishing Polish state in the 20th century.

Charles Pinckney, 1757-1824, (U.S.) founding father, his Pinckney plan was largely incorporated into constitution.

William Pitt, the Elder, 1708-1778, (Br.) statesman, called the "Great Commoner," transformed Britain into imperial power.

William Pitt, the Younger, 1759-1806, (Br.) prime minister during French Revolutionary wars.

Georgi Plekhanov, 1857-1918, (R.) revolutionary, social philosopher, called "father of Russian Marxism."

Raymond Poincaré, 1860-1934, (F.) 9th president of the Republic, advocated harsh punishment of Germany after WW I.

Georges Pompidou, 1911-1974, (F.) Gaullist political leader, president from 1969 to 1974.

Grigori Potemkin, 1739-1791, (R.) field marshal, favorite of Catherine II.

Edmund Randolph, 1753-1813, (U.S.) attorney, prominent in drafting, ratification of constitution.

John Randolph, 1773-1833, (U.S.) southern planter, strong advocate of states' rights.

Jeannette Rankin, 1880-1973, (U.S.) pacifist, first woman member of U.S. Congress.

Walter Rathenau, 1867-1922, (G.) industrialist, social theorist, statesman.

Sam Rayburn, 1882-1961, (U.S.) Democratic leader, representative for 47 years, House speaker for 17.

Paul Reynaud, 1878-1966, (F.) statesman, premier in 1940 at the time of France's defeat by Germany.

Syngman Rhee, 1875-1965, (Kor.) first president of the Republic of Korea.

Cecil Rhodes, 1853-1902, (Br.) imperialist, industrial magnate, established Rhodes scholarships in his will.

Cardinal de Richelieu, 1585-1642, (F.) statesman, known as "red eminence," chief minister to Louis XIII.

Maximilien Robespierre, 1758-1794, (F.) leading figure of French Revolution, responsible for much of Reign of Terror.

Nelson Rockefeller, 1908-1979, (U.S.) Republican gov. of N.Y., 1959-73; U.S. vice president, 1974-77.

Eleanor Roosevelt, 1884-1962, (U.S.) humanitarian, United Nations diplomat.

Elihu Root, 1845-1937, (U.S.) lawyer, statesman, diplomat, leading Republican supporter of the League of Nations.

John Russell, 1792-1878, (Br.) Liberal prime minister during the Irish potato famine.

Anwar el-Sadat, 1918-1981, (Egypt) president, 1970-1981, promoted peace with Israel.

António de O. Salazar, 1899-1970, (Port.) statesman, long-time dictator.

José de San Martín, 1778-1850, South American revolutionary, protector of Peru.

Eisaku Sato, 1901-1975, (Jap.) prime minister, presided over Japan's post-WW II emergence as major world power.

Philipp Scheidemann, 1865-1939, (G.) Social Democratic leader, first chancellor of the German republic.

Robert Schuman, 1886-1963, (F.) statesman, founded European Coal and Steel Community.

Carl Schurz, 1829-1906, (U.S.) German-American political leader, journalist, orator, dedicated reformer.

Kurt Schuschnigg, 1897-1977, (Aus.) chancellor, unsuccessful in stopping his country's annexation by Germany.

William H. Seward, 1801-1872, (U.S.) anti-slavery activist, as Lincoln's secretary of state purchased Alaska.

Carlo Sforza, 1872-1952, (It.) foreign minister, anti-fascist.

Alfred E. Smith, 1873-1944, (U.S.) New York Democratic governor, first Roman Catholic to run for presidency.

Jan C. Smuts, 1870-1950, (S.Af.) statesman, philosopher, soldier, prime minister.

Paul Henri Spaak, 1899-1972, (Belg.) statesman, socialist leader.

Joseph Stalin, 1879-1953, (USSR) Soviet dictator, 1924-53.

Edwin M. Stanton, 1814-1869, (U.S.) Lincoln's secretary of war during the Civil War.

Edward R. Stettinius Jr., 1900-1949, (U.S.) industrialist, secretary of state who coordinated aid to WW II allies.

Adlai E. Stevenson, 1900-1965, (U.S.) Democratic leader, diplomat, Illinois governor, presidential candidate.

Henry L. Stimson, 1867-1950, (U.S.) statesman, served in 5 administrations, influenced foreign policy in 1930s and 1940s.

Gustav Stresemann, 1878-1929, (G.) chancellor, foreign minister, dedicated to regaining friendship for post-WW I Germany.

Sukarno, 1901-1970, (Indon.) dictatorial first president of the Indonesian republic.

Sun Yat-sen, 1866-1925, (Chin.) revolutionary, leader of Kuomintang, regarded as the father of modern China.

Robert A. Taft, 1889-1953, (U.S.) conservative Senate leader, called "Mr. Republican."

Charles de Talleyrand, 1754-1838, (F.) statesman, diplomat, the major force of the Congress of Vienna of 1814-15.

U Thant, 1909-1974 (Bur.) statesman, UN secretary-general.

Norman M. Thomas, 1884-1968, (U.S.) social reformer, 6 times unsuccessful Socialist party presidential candidate.

Josip Broz Tito, 1892-1980, (Yug.) president of Yugoslavia from 1953, World War II guerrilla chief, postwar rival of Stalin, leader of 3d world movement.

Palmiro Togliatti, 1893-1964, (It.) major leader of Italian Communist party.

Hideki Tojo, 1885-1948, (Jap.) statesman, soldier, prime minister during most of WW II.

François Toussaint L'Ouverture, c. 1744-1803, (Hait.) patriot, martyr, thwarted French colonial aims.

Leon Trotsky, 1879-1940, (USSR) revolutionary, founded Red Army, expelled from party in conflict with Stalin.

Rafael L. Trujillo Molina, 1891-1961, (Dom.) absolute dictator, assassinated.

Moïse K. Tshombe, 1919-1969, (Cong.) politician, president of secessionist Katanga, premier of Republic of Congo (Zaire).

William M. Tweed, 1823-1878, (U.S.) politician, absolute leader of Tammany Hall, NYC's Democratic political machine.

Walter Ulbricht, 1893-1973, (G.) communist leader of German Democratic Republic.

Arthur H. Vandenberg, 1884-1951, (U.S.) senator, proponent of anti-communist bipartisan foreign policy after WW II.

Eleutherios Venizelos, 1864-1936, (Gk.) most prominent Greek statesman in early 20th century; expanded territory.

Hendrik F. Verwoerd, 1901-1966, (S.Af.) prime minister, rigorously applied apartheid policy despite protest.

Robert Walpole, 1676-1745, (Br.) statesman, generally considered Britain's first prime minister.

Daniel Webster, 1782-1852, (U.S.) orator, politician, advocate of business interests during Jacksonian agrarianism.

Chaim Weizmann, 1874-1952, Zionist leader, scientist, first Israeli president.

Wendell L. Willkie, 1892-1944, (U.S.) Republican who tried to unseat FDR when he ran for his 3d term.

Emiliano Zapata, c. 1879-1919, (Mex.) revolutionary, major influence on modern Mexico.

Notable Military and Naval Leaders of the Past

Creighton Abrams, 1914-1974, (U.S.) commanded forces in Vietnam, 1968-72.

Harold Alexander, 1891-1969, (Br.) led Allied invasion of Italy, 1943.

Ethan Allen, 1738-1789, (U.S.) headed Green Mountain Boys; captured Ft. Ticonderoga, 1775.

Edmund Allenby, 1861-1936, (Br.) in Boer War, WW1; led Egyptian expeditionary force, 1917-18.

Benedict Arnold, 1741-1801, (U.S.) victorious at Saratoga; tried to betray West Point to British.

Henry "Hap" Arnold, 1886-1950, (U.S.) commanded Army Air Force in WW2.

Petr Bagration, 1765-1812, (R.) hero of Napoleonic wars.

John Barry, 1745-1803, (U.S.) won numerous sea battles during revolution.

Pierre Beauregard, 1818-1893, (U.S.) Confederate general ordered bombardment of Ft. Sumter that began the Civil War.

Gebhard v. Blücher, 1742-1819, (G.) helped defeat Napoleon at Waterloo.

Napoleon Bonaparte, 1769-1821, (F.) defeated Russia and Austria at Austerlitz, 1805; invaded Russia, 1812; defeated at Waterloo, 1815.

Edward Braddock, 1695-1755, (Br.) commanded forces in French and Indian War.

Omar N. Bradley, 1893-1981, (U.S.) headed U.S. ground troops in Normandy invasion, 1944.

John Burgoyne, 1722-1792, (Br.) defeated at Saratoga.

Claire Chennault, 1890-1958, (U.S.) headed Flying Tigers in WW2.

Mark Clark, 1896-1984, (U.S.) led forces in WW2 and Korean War.

Karl v. Clausewitz, 1780-1831, (G.) wrote books on military theory.

Henry Clinton, 1738-1795, (Br.) commander of forces in America, 1778-81.

Lucius D. Clay, 1897-1978, (U.S.) led Berlin airlift, 1948-49.

Charles Cornwallis, 1738-1805, (Br.) victorious at Brandywine, 1777; surrendered at Yorktown.

Crazy Horse, 1849-1877, (U.S.) Sioux war chief victorious at Little Big Horn.

George A. Custer, 1839-1876, (U.S.) defeated and killed at Little Big Horn.

Moshe Dayan, 1915-1981, (Isr.) directed campaigns in the 1967, 1973 wars.

Stephen Decatur, 1779-1820, (U.S.) naval hero of Barbary wars, War of 1812.

Anton Denikin, 1872-1947, (R.) led White forces in Russian civil war.

George Dewey, 1837-1917, (U.S.) destroyed Spanish fleet at Manila, 1898.

Hugh C. Dowding, 1883-1970, (Br.) headed RAF, 1936-40.

Jubal Early, 1816-1894, (U.S.) Confederate general led raid on Washington, 1864.

Dwight D. Eisenhower, 1890-1969, (U.S.) commanded Allied forces in Europe, WW2.

David Farragut, 1801-1870, (U.S.) Union admiral captured New Orleans, Mobile Bay.

Ferdinand Foch, 1851-1929, (F.) headed victorious Allied armies, 1918.

Nathan Bedford Forrest, 1821-1877, (U.S.) Confederate general led cavalry raids against Union supply lines.

Frederick the Great, 1712-1786, (G.) led Prussia in The Seven Years War.

Nathanael Greene, 1742-1786, (U.S.) defeated British in Southern campaign, 1780-81.

Charles G. Gordon, 1833-1885, (Br.) led forces in China; killed at Khartoum.

Horatio Gates, 1728-1806, (U.S.) commanded army at Saratoga.

Ulysses S. Grant, 1822-1885, (U.S.) headed Union army, 1864-65; forced Lee's surrender, 1865.

Heinz Guderian, 1888-1953, (G.) tank theorist led panzer forces in Poland, France, Russia.

Douglas Haig, 1861-1928, (Br.) led British armies in France, 1915-18.

William F. Halsey, 1882-1959, (U.S.) defeated Japanese fleet at Leyte Gulf, 1944.

Sir Arthur Travers Harris, 1895-1984, (Br.) led Britain's WWII bomber command.

Richard Howe, 1726-1799, (Br.) commanded navy in America, 1776-78; first of June victory against French, 1794.

William Howe, 1729-1814, (Br.) commanded forces in America, 1776-78.

Isaac Hull, 1773-1843, (U.S.) sunk British frigate Guerriere, 1812.

Thomas (Stonewall) Jackson, 1824-1863, (U.S.) Confederate general led forces in the Shenandoah Valley campaign.

Joseph Joffre, 1852-1931, (F.) headed Allied armies, won Battle of the Marne, 1914.

John Paul Jones, 1747-1792, (U.S.) raided British coast; commanded Bonhomme Richard in victory over Serapis, 1779.

Stephen Kearny, 1794-1848, (U.S.) headed Army of the West in Mexican War.

Ernest J. King, 1878-1956, (U.S.) chief naval strategist in WW2.

Horatio H. Kitchener, 1850-1916, (Br.) led forces in Boer War; victorious at Khartoum; organized army in WW1.

Lavrenti Kornilov, 1870-1918, (R.) Commander-in-Chief, 1917; led counter-revolutionary march on Petrograd.

Thaddeus Kosciusko, 1746-1817, (P.) aided American cause in revolution.

Mikhail Kutuzov, 1745-1813, (R.) fought French at Borodino, 1812; abandoned Moscow; forced French retreat.

Marquis de Lafayette, 1757-1834, (F.) aided American cause in the revolution.

Thomas E. Lawrence (of Arabia), 1888-1935, (Br.) organized revolt of Arabs against Turks in WW1.

Henry (Light-Horse Harry) Lee, 1756-1818, (U.S.) cavalry officer in revolution.

Robert E. Lee, 1807-1870, (U.S.) Confederate general defeated at Gettysburg; surrendered to Grant, 1865.

Lyman Lemnitzer, 1899-1988, (U.S.) WWII hero, later general, chairman of Joint Chiefs of Staff.

James Longstreet, 1821-1904, (U.S.) aided Lee at Gettysburg.

Douglas MacArthur, 1880-1964, (U.S.) commanded forces in SW Pacific in WW2; headed occupation forces in Japan, 1945-51; UN commander in Korean War.

Francis Marion, 1733-1795, (U.S.) led guerrilla actions in S.C. during revolution.

Duke of Marlborough, 1650-1722, (Br.) led forces against Louis XIV in War of the Spanish Sucession.

George C. Marshall, 1880-1959, (U.S.) chief of staff in WW2; authored Marshall Plan.

George B. McClellan, 1826-1885, (U.S.) Union general commanded Army of the Potomac, 1861-62.

George Meade, 1815-1872, (U.S.) commanded Union forces at Gettysburg.

Billy Mitchell, 1879-1936, (U.S.) air-power advocate; court-martialed for insubordination, later vindicated.

Helmuth v. Moltke, 1800-1891, (G.) victorious in Austro-Prussian, Franco-Prussian wars.

Louis de Montcalm, 1712-1759, (F.) headed troops in Canada; defeated at Quebec, 1759.

Bernard Law Montgomery, 1887-1976, (Br.) stopped German offensive at Alamein, 1942; helped plan Normandy invasion.

Daniel Morgan, 1736-1802, (U.S.) victorious at Cowpens, 1781.

Louis Mountbatten, 1900-1979, (Br.) Supreme Allied Commander of SE Asia, 1943-46.

Joachim Murat, 1767-1815, (F.) leader of cavalry at Marengo, 1800; Austerlitz, 1805; and Jena, 1806.

Horatio Nelson, 1758-1805, (Br.) naval commander destroyed French fleet at Trafalgar.

Michel Ney, 1769-1815,. (F.) commanded forces in Switzerland, Austria, Russia; defeated at Waterloo.

Chester Nimitz, 1885-1966, (U.S.) commander of naval forces in Pacific in WW2.

George S. Patton, 1885-1945, (U.S.) led assault on Sicily, 1943; headed 3d Army invasion of German-occupied Europe.

Oliver Perry, 1785-1819, (U.S.) won Battle of Lake Erie in War of 1812.

John Pershing, 1860-1948, (U.S.) commanded Mexican border campaign, 1916; American expeditionary forces in WW1.

Henri Philippe Pétain, 1856-1951, (F.) defended Verdun, 1916; headed Vichy government in WW2.

George E. Pickett, 1825-1875, (U.S.) Confederate general famed for "charge" at Gettysburg.

Hyman Rickover, 1900-1986 (U.S.) father of the nuclear navy.

Erwin Rommel, 1891-1944, (G.) headed Afrika Korps.

Karl v. Rundstedt, 1875-1953, (G.) supreme commander in West, 1943-45.

Aleksandr Samsonov, 1859-1914, (R.) led invasion of E. Prussia, defeated at Tannenberg, 1914.

Winfield Scott, 1786-1866, (U.S.) hero of War of 1812; headed forces in Mexican war, took Mexico City.

Philip Sheridan, 1831-1888, (U.S.) Union cavalry officer headed Army of the Shenandoah, 1864-65.

William T. Sherman, 1820-1891, (U.S.) Union general sacked Atlanta during "march to the sea," 1864.

Carl Spaatz, 1891-1974, (U.S.) directed strategic bombing against Germany, later Japan, in WW2.

Raymond Spruance, 1886-1969, (U.S.) victorious at Midway Island, 1942.

Joseph W. Stilwell, 1883-1946, (U.S.) headed forces in the China, Burma, India theater in WW2.

J.E.B. Stuart, 1833-1864, (U.S.) Confederate cavalry commander.

George H. Thomas, 1816-1870, (U.S.) saved Union army at Chattanooga, 1863; victorious at Nashville, 1864.

Semyon Timoshenko, 1895-1970, (USSR) defended Moscow, Stalingrad; led winter offensive, 1942-43.

Alfred v. Tirpitz, 1849-1930, (G.) responsible for submarine blockade in WW1.

Jonathan M. Wainwright, 1883-1953, (U.S.) forced to surrender on Corregidor, 1942.

George Washington, 1732-1799, (U.S.) led Continental army, 1775-83.

Archibald Wavell, 1883-1950, (Br.) commanded forces in N. and E. Africa, and SE Asia in WW2.

Anthony Wayne, 1745-1796, (U.S.) captured Stony Point, 1779; defeated Indians at Fallen Timbers, 1794.
Duke of Wellington, 1769-1852, (Br.) defeated Napoleon at Waterloo.

James Wolfe, 1727-1759, (Br.) captured Quebec from French, 1759.
Georgi Zhukov, 1895-1974, (USSR) defended Moscow, 1941; led assault on Berlin.

Poets Laureate of England

There is no authentic record of the origin of the office of Poet Laureate of England. According to Warton, there was a Versificator Regis, or King's Poet, in the reign of Henry III (1216-1272), and he was paid 100 shillings a year. Geoffrey Chaucer (1340-1400) assumed the title of Poet Laureate, and in 1389 got a royal grant of a yearly allowance of wine. In the reign of Edward IV (1461-1483), John Kay held the post. Under Henry VII (1485-1509), Andrew Bernard was the Poet Laureate, and was succeeded under Henry VIII (1509-1547) by John Skelton. Next came Edmund Spenser, who died in 1599; then Samuel Daniel, appointed 1599, and

then Ben Jonson, 1619. Sir William D'Avenant was appointed in 1637. He was a godson of William Shakespeare.
Others were John Dryden, 1670; Thomas Shadwell, 1688; Nahum Tate, 1692; Nicholas Rowe, 1715; the Rev. Laurence Eusden, 1718; Colley Cibber, 1730; William Whitehead, 1757, on the refusal of Gray; Rev. Thomas Warton, 1785, on the refusal of Mason; Henry J. Pye, 1790; Robert Southey, 1813, on the refusal of Sir Walter Scott; William Wordsworth, 1843; Alfred, Lord Tennyson, 1850; Alfred Austin, 1896; Robert Bridges, 1913; John Masefield, 1930; Cecil Day Lewis, 1967; Sir John Betjeman, 1972; Ted Hughes, 1984.

U.S. Poet Laureate

Robert Penn Warren, the poet, novelist, and essayist, was named the country's first official Poet Laureate on Feb. 26, 1986. The only writer to have won the Pulitzer Prize for fiction and poetry (twice), Warren was chosen by Daniel J.

Boorstin, the Librarian of Congress. The appointment began in September, 1986. On April 17, 1987, Richard Wilbur was named the second Poet Laureate. In May, 1988, Howard Nemerov was named the third Poet Laureate.

Noted Writers of the Past

Henry Adams, 1838-1918, (U.S.) historian, philosopher. *The Education of Henry Adams.*
George Ade, 1866-1944, (U.S.) humorist. *Fables in Slang.*
Conrad Aiken, 1889-1973, (U.S.) poet, critic.
Louisa May Alcott, 1832-1888, (U.S.) novelist. *Little Women.*
Sholom Aleichem, 1859-1916. (R.) Yiddish writer. *Tevye's Daughter, The Great Fair.*
Vicente Aleixandre, 1898-1984, (Sp.) poet. 1977 Nobel Prize winner.
Horatio Alger, 1832-1899, (U.S.) "rags-to-riches" books.
Hans Christian Andersen, 1805-1875, (Den.) author of fairy tales. *The Princess and the Pea, The Ugly Duckling.*
Maxwell Anderson, 1888-1959, (U.S.) playwright. *What Price Glory?, High Tor, Winterset, Key Largo.*
Sherwood Anderson, 1876-1941, (U.S.) author. *Winesburg, Ohio.*
Matthew Arnold, 1822-1888, (Br.) poet, critic. "Thrysis," "Dover Beach."
Jane Austen, 1775-1817, (Br.) novelist. *Pride and Prejudice, Sense and Sensibility, Emma, Mansfield Park, Persuasion.*
Isaac Babel, 1894-1941, (R.) short-story writer, playwright. *Odessa Tales, Red Cavalry.*
James M. Barrie, 1860-1937, (Br.) playwright, novelist. *Peter Pan, Dear Brutus, What Every Woman Knows.*
Honoré de Balzac, 1799-1850, (Fr.) novelist. *Le Père Goriot, Cousine Bette, Eugénie Grandet, The Human Comedy.*
Charles Baudelaire, 1821-1867, (Fr.) symbolist poet. *Les Fleurs du Mal.*
L. Frank Baum, 1856-1919, (U.S.) children's author. *Wizard of Oz series.*
Simone de Beauvoir, 1908-1986, (Fr.) novelist, essayist. *The Second Sex.*
Brendan Behan, 1923-1964, (Ir.) playwright. *The Quare Fellow, The Hostage, Borstal Boy.*
Robert Benchley, 1889-1945, (U.S.) humorist. *From Bed to Worse, My Ten Years in a Quandary.*
Stephen Vincent Benét, 1898-1943, (U.S.) poet, novelist. *John Brown's Body.*
John Berryman, 1914-1972, (U.S.) poet. *Homage to Mistress Bradstreet.*
Ambrose Bierce, 1842-1914, (U.S.) short-story writer, journalist. *In the Midst of Life, The Devil's Dictionary.*
William Blake, 1757-1827, (Br.) poet, mystic, artist. *Songs of Innocence, Songs of Experience.*
Giovanni Boccaccio, 1313-1375, (It.) poet, storyteller. *Decameron, Filostrato.*
Jorge Luis Borges, 1900-1986 (Arg.) short-story writer, poet, essayist. *Labyrinths.*
James Boswell, 1740-1795, (Sc.) author. *The Life of Samuel Johnson.*
Anne Bradstreet, c. 1612-1672, (U.S.) poet. *The Tenth Muse Lately Sprung Up in America.*
Bertolt Brecht, 1898-1956, (G.) dramatist, poet. *The Threepenny Opera, Mother Courage and Her Children.*
Charlotte Brontë, 1816-1855, (Br.) novelist. *Jane Eyre.*
Emily Brontë, 1818-1848, (Br.) novelist. *Wuthering Heights.*

Elizabeth Barrett Browning, 1806-1861, (Br.) poet. *Sonnets from the Portuguese.*
Robert Browning, 1812-1889, (Br.) poet. "My Last Duchess," "Fra Lippo Lippi."
Pearl Buck, 1892-1973, (U.S.) novelist. *The Good Earth.*
Mikhail Bulgakov, 1891-1940, (R.) novelist, playwright. *The Heart of a Dog, The Master and Margarita.*
John Bunyan, 1628-1688, (Br.) writer. *Pilgrim's Progress.*
Robert Burns, 1759-1796, (Sc.) poet. "Flow Gently, Sweet Afton," "My Heart's in the Highlands," "Auld Lang Syne."
Edgar Rice Burroughs, 1875-1950, (U.S.) novelist. *Tarzan of the Apes.*
George Gordon Lord Byron, 1788-1824, (Br.) poet. *Don Juan, Childe Harold.*
Italo Calvino, 1923-1985 (It.) novelist, short story writer. *If on a Winter's Night a Traveler . . .*
Albert Camus, 1913-1960, (F.) novelist. *The Plague, The Stranger, Caligula, The Fall.*
Lewis Carroll, 1832-1898, (Br.) writer, mathematician. *Alice's Adventures in Wonderland, Through the Looking Glass.*
Karel Capek, 1890-1938, (Czech.) playwright, novelist, essayist. *R.U.R. (Rossum's Universal Robots).*
Giacomo Casanova, 1725-1798, (It.) Venetian adventurer, author, world famous for his memoirs.
Willa Cather, 1876-1947, (U.S.) novelist, essayist. *O Pioneers!, My Ántonia.*
Miguel de Cervantes Saavedra, 1547-1616, (Sp.) novelist, dramatist, poet. *Don Quixote de la Mancha.*
Raymond Chandler, 1888-1959, (U.S.) writer of detective fiction. *Philip Marlowe series.*
Geoffrey Chaucer, c. 1340-1400, (Br.) poet. *The Canterbury Tales.*
John Cheever, 1912-1983, (U.S.) short story writer, novelist. *The Wapshot Scandal, "The Country Husband."*
Anton Chekhov, 1860-1904, (R.) short-story writer, dramatist. *Uncle Vanya, The Cherry Orchard, The Three Sisters.*
G.K. Chesterton, 1874-1936, (Br.) author. Fr. Brown series.
Agatha Christie, 1891-1976, (Br.) mystery writer. *And Then There Were None, Murder on the Orient Express.*
Jean Cocteau, 1889-1963, (F.) writer, visual artist, filmmaker. *The Beauty and the Beast, Enfants Terribles.*
Samuel Taylor Coleridge, 1772-1834, (Br.) poet, man of letters. "Kubla Khan," "The Rime of the Ancient Mariner."
(Sidonie) Colette, 1873-1954, (F.) novelist. *Claudine, Gigi.*
Joseph Conrad, 1857-1924, (Br.) novelist. *Lord Jim, Heart of Darkness, The Nigger of the Narcissus.*
James Fenimore Cooper, 1789-1851, (U.S.) novelist. *Leather-Stocking Tales.*
Pierre Corneille, 1606-1684, (F.) Dramatist. *Medeé, Le Cid, Horace, Cinna, Polyeucte.*
Hart Crane, 1899-1932, (U.S.) poet. "The Bridge."
Stephen Crane, 1871-1900, (U.S.) novelist. *The Red Badge of Courage.*
e.e. cummings, 1894-1962, (U.S.) poet. *Tulips and Chimneys.*
Gabriele D'Annunzio, 1863-1938, (It.) poet, novelist, dramatist. *The Child of Pleasure, The Intruder, The Victim.*
Dante Alighieri, 1265-1321, (It.) poet. *The Divine Comedy.*

Daniel Defoe, 1660-1731, (Br.) writer. *Robinson Crusoe, Moll Flanders, Journal of the Plague Year.*

Charles Dickens, 1812-1870, (Br.) novelist. *David Copperfield, Oliver Twist, Great Expectations, The Pickwick Papers.*

Emily Dickinson, 1830-1886, (U.S.) poet.

Isak Dinesen (Karen Blixen), 1885-1962, (Dan.) author. *Out of Africa, Seven Gothic Tales, Winter's Tales.*

John Donne, 1573-1631, (Br.) poet. *Songs and Sonnets, Holy Sonnets*, "Death Be Not Proud."

John Dos Passos, 1896-1970, (U.S.) author. *U.S.A.*

Fyodor Dostoyevsky, 1821-1881, (R.) author. *Crime and Punishment, The Brothers Karamazov, The Possessed.*

Arthur Conan Doyle, 1859-1930, (Br.) author, created Sherlock Holmes.

Theodore Dreiser, 1871-1945, (U.S.) novelist. *An American Tragedy, Sister Carrie.*

John Dryden, 1631-1700, (Br.) poet, dramatist, critic. *Fables, Ancient and Modern.*

Alexandre Dumas, 1802-1870, (F.) novelist, dramatist. *The Three Musketeers, The Count of Monte Cristo.*

Alexandre Dumas (fils), 1824-1895, (F.) dramatist, novelist. *La Dame aux camélias, Le Demi-Monde.*

Ilya G. Ehrenburg, 1891-1967, (R.) novelist, journalist. *The Thaw.*

George Eliot, 1819-1880, (Br.) novelist. *Adam Bede, Silas Marner, The Mill on the Floss, Middlemarch.*

T.S. Eliot, 1888-1965, (Br.) poet, critic. *The Waste Land*, "The Love Song of J. Alfred Prufrock," "Murder in the Cathedral."

Ralph Waldo Emerson, 1803-1882, (U.S.) poet, essayist. "The Concord Hymn," "Brahma," *Nature.*

James T. Farrell, 1904-1979, (U.S.) novelist. Studs Lonigan trilogy.

William Faulkner, 1897-1962, (U.S.) novelist. *Sanctuary, Light in August, The Sound and the Fury, Absalom, Absalom!*

Edna Ferber, 1885-1968, (U.S.) novelist, dramatist. *Show Boat, Saratoga Trunk, Giant, Dinner at Eight.*

Henry Fielding, 1707-1754, (Br.) novelist. *Tom Jones.*

F. Scott Fitzgerald, 1896-1940, (U.S.) short-story writer, novelist. *The Great Gatsby, Tender is the Night.*

Gustave Flaubert, 1821-1880, (F.) novelist. *Madame Bovary.*

C.S. Forester, 1899-1966, (Br.) novelist. Horatio Hornblower series.

E.M. Forster, 1879-1970, (Br.) novelist. *A Passage to India.*

Anatole France, 1844-1924, (F.) writer. *Penguin Island, My Friend's Book, Le Crime de Sylvestre Bonnard.*

Robert Frost, 1874-1963, (U.S.) poet. "Birches," "Fire and Ice," "Stopping by Woods on a Snowy Evening."

John Galsworthy, 1867-1933, (Br.) novelist, dramatist. *The Forsyte Saga, A Modern Comedy.*

Erle Stanley Gardner, 1889-1970, (U.S.) author, lawyer. Perry Mason series.

Jean Genet, 1911-1986, (Fr.) playwright, novelist. "The Blacks."

André Gide, 1869-1951, (F.) writer, *The Immoralist, The Pastoral Symphony, Strait is the Gate.*

Jean Giraudoux, 1882-1944, (F.) novelist, dramatist. *Electra, The Madwoman of Chaillot, Ondine, Tiger at the Gate.*

Johann W. von Goethe, 1749-1832, (G.) poet, dramatist, novelist. *Faust.*

Nikolai Gogol, 1809-1852, (R.) short-story writer, dramatist, novelist. *Dead Souls, The Inspector General.*

Oliver Goldsmith, 1730?-1774, (Br.-Ir.) writer. *The Vicar of Wakefield, She Stoops to Conquer.*

Maxim Gorky, 1868-1936, (R.) writer, founder of Soviet realism. *Mother, The Lower Depths.*

Robert Graves, 1895-1985, (Br.) poet, classical scholar, novelist. *The White Goddess.*

Thomas Gray, 1716-1771, (Br.) poet. "Elegy Written in a Country Churchyard."

Zane Grey, 1875-1939, (U.S.) writer of western stories.

Jakob Grimm, 1785-1863, (G.) philologist, folklorist. *German Methodology, Grimm's Fairy Tales.*

Wilhelm Grimm, 1786-1859, (G.) philologist, folklorist. *Grimm's Fairy Tales.*

Edgar A. Guest, 1881-1959, (U.S.) poet. *A Heap of Livin'*

Dashiell Hammett, 1894-1961, (U.S.) writer of detective fiction, created Sam Spade.

Knute Hamsun, 1859-1952 (Nor.) novelist. *Hunger.*

Thomas Hardy, 1840-1928, (Br.) novelist, poet. *The Return of the Native, Tess of the D'Urbervilles, Jude the Obscure.*

Joel Chandler Harris, 1848-1908, (U.S.) short-story writer. Uncle Remus series.

Moss Hart, 1904-1961, (U.S.) playwright. *Once in a Lifetime, You Can't Take It With You.*

Bret Harte, 1836-1902, (U.S.) short-story writer, poet. *The Luck of Roaring Camp.*

Jaroslav Hasek, 1883-1923, (Czech.) writer. *The Good Soldier Schweik.*

Nathaniel Hawthorne, 1804-1864, (U.S.) novelist, short story writer. *The Scarlet Letter, The House of the Seven Gables.*

Heinrich Heine, 1797-1856, (G.) poet. *Book of Songs.*

Lillian Hellman, 1905-1984, (U.S.) playwright, author of memoirs, "The Little Foxes," *An Unfinished Woman.*

Ernest Hemingway, 1899-1961, (U.S.) novelist, short-story writer. *A Farewell to Arms, For Whom the Bell Tolls.*

O. Henry (W.S. Porter), 1862-1910, (U.S.) short-story writer. "The Gift of the Magi."

Hermann Hesse, 1877-1962, (G.) novelist, poet. *Death and the Lover, Steppenwolf, Siddhartha.*

Oliver Wendell Holmes, 1809-1894, (U.S.) poet, novelist. *The Autocrat of the Breakfast-Table.*

Alfred E. Housman, 1859-1936, (Br.) poet. *A Shropshire Lad.*

William Dean Howells, 1837-1920, (U.S.) novelist, critic, dean of late 19th century American letters.

Langston Hughes, 1902-1967, (U.S.) poet, playwright. *The Weary Blues, One-Way Ticket, Shakespeare in Harlem.*

Victor Hugo, 1802-1885, (F.) poet, dramatist, novelist. *Notre Dame de Paris, Les Misérables.*

Aldous Huxley 1894-1963, (Br.) author. *Point Counter Point, Brave New World.*

Henrik Ibsen, 1828-1906, (Nor.) dramatist, poet. *A Doll's House, Ghosts, The Wild Duck, Hedda Gabler.*

William Inge, 1913-1973, (U.S.) playwright. *Come Back Little Sheba, Bus Stop, The Dark at the Top of the Stairs, Picnic.*

Washington Irving, 1783-1859, (U.S.) essayist, author. "Rip Van Winkle," "The Legend of Sleepy Hollow."

Shirley Jackson, 1919-1965, (U.S.) writer. "The Lottery."

Henry James, 1843-1916, (U.S.) novelist, critic. *Washington Square, Portrait of a Lady, The American.*

Robinson Jeffers, 1887-1962, (U.S.) poet, dramatist. *Tamar and Other Poems, Medea.*

Samuel Johnson, 1709-1784, (Br.) author, scholar, critic. *Dictionary of the English Language.*

Ben Jonson, 1572-1637, (Br.) dramatist, poet. *Volpone.*

James Joyce, 1882-1941, (Ir.) novelist. *Ulysses, A Portrait of the Artist as a Young Man, Finnegans Wake.*

Franz Kafka, 1883-1924, (G.) novelist, short-story writer. *The Trial, America, The Castle, The Metamorphosis.*

George S. Kaufman, 1889-1961, (U.S.) playwright. *The Man Who Came to Dinner, You Can't Take It With You, Stage Door.*

Nikos Kazantzakis, 1883?-1957, (Gk.) novelist. *Zorba the Greek, A Greek Passion.*

John Keats, 1795-1821, (Br.) poet. *On a Grecian Urn, La Belle Dame Sans Merci.*

Joyce Kilmer, 1886-1918, (U.S.) poet, "Trees."

Rudyard Kipling, 1865-1936, (Br.) author, poet. "The White Man's Burden," "Gunga Din," *The Jungle Book.*

Jean de la Fontaine, 1621-1695, (F.) poet. *Fables choisies.*

Pär Lagerkvist, 1891-1974, (Swed.) poet, dramatist, novelist. *Barabbas, The Sybil.*

Selma Lagerlöf, 1858-1940, (Swed.) novelist. *Jerusalem, The Ring of the Lowenskolds.*

Alphonse de Lamartine, 1790-1869, (F.) poet, novelist, statesman. *Méditations poétiques.*

Charles Lamb, 1775-1834, (Br.) essayist. *Specimens of English Dramatic Poets, Essays of Elia.*

Giuseppe di Lampedusa, 1896-1957, (It.) novelist. *The Leopard.*

Ring Lardner, 1885-1933, (U.S.) short story writer, humorist. *You Know Me, Al.*

D. H. Lawrence, 1885-1930, (Br.) novelist. *Sons and Lovers, Women in Love, Lady Chatterley's Lover.*

Mikhail Lermontov, 1814-1841, (R.) novelist, poet. "Demon," *Hero of Our Time.*

Alain-René Lesage, 1668-1747, (F.) novelist. *Gil Blas de Santillane.*

Gotthold Lessing, 1729-1781, (G.) dramatist, philosopher, critic. *Miss Sara Sampson, Minna von Barnhelm.*

Sinclair Lewis, 1885-1951, (U.S.) novelist, playwright. *Babbitt, Arrowsmith, Dodsworth, Main Street.*

Vachel Lindsay, 1879-1931, (U.S.) poet. *General William Booth Enters into Heaven, The Congo.*

Hugh Lofting, 1886-1947, (Br.) Dr. Doolittle series.

Jack London, 1876-1916, (U.S.) novelist, journalist. *Call of the Wild, The Sea-Wolf.*

Henry Wadsworth Longfellow, 1807-1882, (U.S.) poet. *Evangeline, The Song of Hiawatha.*

Amy Lowell, 1874-1925, (U.S.) poet, critic. "Lilacs."

James Russell Lowell, 1819-1891, (U.S.) poet, editor. *Poems, The Bigelow Papers.*

Robert Lowell, 1917-1977, (U.S.) poet. "Lord Weary's Castle," "For the Union Dead."

Emil Ludwig, 1881-1948, (G.) biographer. *Goethe, Beethoven, Napoleon, Bismarck.*

Niccolò Machiavelli, 1469-1527, (It.) author, statesman. *The Prince, Discourses on Livy.*

Bernard Malamud, 1914-1986, (U.S.) short story writer, novelist. "The Magic Barrel," *The Assistant, The Fixer.*
Stéphane Mallarmé, 1842-1898, (F.) poet. *The Afternoon of a Faun.*
Thomas Malory, ?-1471, (Br.) writer. *Morte d'Arthur.*
Andre Malraux, 1901-1976, (F.) novelist. *Man's Fate.*
Osip Mandelstam, 1891-1938, (R.) Acmeist poet.
Thomas Mann, 1875-1955, (G.) novelist, essayist. *Buddenbrooks, Death in Venice, The Magic Mountain.*
Katherine Mansfield, 1888-1923, (Br.) short story writer. "Bliss," "The Garden Party."
Christopher Marlowe, 1564-1593, (Br.) dramatist, poet. *Tamburlaine the Great, Dr. Faustus, The Jew of Malta.*
John Masefield, 1878-1967, (Br.) poet. "Sea Fever," "Cargoes," *Salt Water Ballads.*
Edgar Lee Masters, 1869-1950, (U.S.) poet, biographer. *Spoon River Anthology.*
W. Somerset Maugham, 1874-1965, (Br.) author. *Of Human Bondage, The Razor's Edge, The Moon and Sixpence.*
Guy de Maupassant, 1850-1893, (F.) novelist, short-story writer. "A Life," "Bel-Ami," "The Necklace."
François Mauriac, 1885-1970, (F.) novelist, dramatist. *Viper's Tangle, The Kiss to the Leper.*
Vladimir Mayakovsky, 1893-1930, (R.) poet, dramatist. *The Cloud in Trousers.*
Carson McCullers, 1917-1967, (U.S.) novelist. *The Heart is a Lonely Hunter, Member of the Wedding.*
Herman Melville, 1819-1891, (U.S.) novelist, poet. *Moby Dick, Typee, Billy Budd, Omoo.*
H.L. Mencken, 1880-1956, (U.S.) author, critic, editor. *Prejudices, The American Language.*
George Meredith, 1828-1909, (Br.) novelist, poet. *The Ordeal of Richard Feverel, The Egoist.*
Prosper Mérimée, 1803-1870, (F.) author. *Carmen.*
Edna St. Vincent Millay, 1892-1950, (U.S.) poet. *The Harp Weaver and Other Poems, A Few Figs from Thistles.*
A.A. Milne, 1882-1956, (Br.) author. *Winnie-the-Pooh.*
John Milton, 1608-1674, (Br.) poet. *Paradise Lost.*
Gabriela Mistral, 1889-1957, (Chil.) poet. *Sonnets of Death, Desolación, Tala, Lagar.*
Margaret Mitchell, 1900-1949, (U.S.) novelist. *Gone With the Wind.*
Jean Baptiste Molière, 1622-1673, (F.) dramatist. *Le Tartuffe, Le Misanthrope, Le Bourgeois Gentilhomme.*
Ferenc Molnár, 1878-1952, (Hung.) dramatist, novelist. *Liliom, The Guardsman, The Swan.*
Michel de Montaigne, 1533-1592, (F.) essayist. *Essais.*
Eugenio Montale, 1896-1981, (It.) poet.
Clement C. Moore, 1779-1863, (U.S.) poet, educator. "A Visit from Saint Nicholas."
Marianne Moore, 1887-1972, (U.S.) poet. *O to Be a Dragon.*
Thomas More, 1478-1535, (Br.) author. *Utopia.*
H.H. Munro (Saki), 1870-1916, (Br.) author. *Reginald, The Chronicles of Clovis, Beasts and Super-Beasts.*
Alfred de Musset, 1810-1857, (F.) poet, dramatist. *Confession d'un enfant du siècle.*
Vladimir Nabokov, 1899-1977, (Rus.-U.S.) author. *Lolita.*
Ogden Nash, 1902-1971, (U.S.) poet. *Hard Lines, I'm a Stranger Here Myself, The Private Dining Room.*
Pablo Neruda, 1904-1973, (Chil.) poet. *Twenty Love Poems and One Song of Despair, Toward the Splendid City.*
Sean O'Casey, 1884-1964, (Ir.) dramatist. *Juno and the Paycock, The Plough and the Stars.*
Flannery O'Connor, 1925-1964, (U.S.) novelist, short story writer. *Wise Blood,* "A Good Man Is Hard to Find."
Clifford Odets, 1906-1963, (U.S.) playwright. *Waiting for Lefty, Awake and Sing, Golden Boy, The Country Girl.*
John O'Hara, 1905-1970, (U.S.) novelist. *From the Terrace, Appointment in Samarra.*
Omar Khayyam, c. 1028-1122, (Per.) poet. *Rubaiyat.*
Eugene O'Neill, 1888-1953, (U.S.) playwright. *Emperor Jones, Anna Christie, Long Day's Journey into Night.*
George Orwell, 1903-1950, (Br.) novelist, essayist. *Animal Farm, Nineteen Eighty-Four.*
Thomas (Tom) Paine, 1737-1809, (U.S.) author, political theorist. *Common Sense.*
Dorothy Parker, 1893-1967, (U.S.) poet, short-story writer. *Enough Rope, Laments for the Living.*
Boris Pasternak, 1890-1960, (R.) poet, novelist. *Doctor Zhivago, My Sister, Life.*
Samuel Pepys, 1633-1703, (Br.) public official, author of the English diary in the English language.
S. J. Perelman, 1904-1979, (U.S.) humorist. *The Road to Miltown, Under the Spreading Atrophy.*
Francesco Petrarca, 1304-1374, (It.) poet, humanist. *Africa, Trionfi, Canzoniere, On Solitude.*
Luigi Pirandello, 1867-1936, (It.) novelist, dramatist. *Six Characters in Search of an Author.*

Edgar Allan Poe, 1809-1849, (U.S.) poet, short-story writer, critic. "Annabel Lee," "The Raven," "The Purloined Letter."
Alexander Pope, 1688-1744, (Br.) poet. *The Rape of the Lock, An Essay on Man.*
Katherine Anne Porter, 1890-1980, (U.S.) novelist, short story writer. *Ship of Fools.*
Ezra Pound, 1885-1972, (U.S.) poet. *Cantos.*
Marcel Proust, 1871-1922, (F.) novelist. *A la recherche du temps perdu (Remembrance of Things Past).*
Aleksandr Pushkin, 1799-1837, (R.) poet, prose writer. *Boris Godunov, Eugene Onegin, The Bronze Horseman.*
François Rabelais, 1495-1553, (F.) writer, physician. *Gargantua, Pantagruel.*
Jean Racine, 1639-1699, (F.) dramatist. *Andromaque, Phèdre, Bérénice, Britannicus.*
Ayn Rand, 1905-1982, (Rus.-U.S.) novelist, philosopher. *The Fountainhead, Atlas Shrugged.*
Erich Maria Remarque, 1898-1970, (Ger.-U.S.) novelist. *All Quiet on the Western Front.*
Samuel Richardson, 1689-1761, (Br.) novelist. *Clarissa Harlowe, Pamela; or, Virtue Rewarded.*
James Whitcomb Riley, 1849-1916, (U.S.) poet. "When the Frost is on the Pumpkin," "Little Orphant Annie."
Rainer Maria Rilke, 1875-1926, (G.) poet. *Life and Songs, Divine Elegies, Sonnets to Orpheus.*
Arthur Rimbaud, 1854-1891, (F.) *A Season in Hell.*
Edwin Arlington Robinson, 1869-1935, (U.S.) poet. "Richard Cory," "Miniver Cheevy."
Theodore Roethke, 1908-1963, (U.S.) poet. *Open House, The Waking, The Far Field.*
Romain Rolland, 1866-1944, (F.) novelist, biographer. *Jean-Christophe.*
Pierre de Ronsard, 1524-1585, (F.) poet. *Sonnets pour Hélène.*
Edmond Rostand, 1868-1918, (F.) poet, dramatist. *Cyrano de Bergerac.*
Damon Runyon, 1880-1946, (U.S.) short-story writer, journalist. *Guys and Dolls, Blue Plate Special.*
John Ruskin, 1819-1900, (Br.) critic, social theorist. *Modern Painters, The Seven Lamps of Architecture.*
Antoine de Saint-Exupery, 1900-1944, (F.) writer, aviator. *Wind, Sand and Stars, Le Petit Prince.*
George Sand, 1804-1876, (F.) novelist. *Consuelo, The Haunted Pool, Les Maitres sonneurs.*
Carl Sandburg, 1878-1967, (U.S.) poet. *Chicago Poems, Smoke and Steel, Harvest Poems.*
George Santayana, 1863-1952, (U.S.) poet, essayist, philosopher. *The Sense of Beauty, The Realms of Being.*
William Saroyan, 1908-1981, (U.S.) playwright, novelist. *The Time of Your Life, The Human Comedy.*
Jean-Paul Sartre, 1905-1980, (Fr.) philosopher, novelist, playwright. *Nausea, No Exit.*
Friedrich von Schiller, 1759-1805, (G.) dramatist, poet, historian. *Don Carlos, Maria Stuart, Wilhelm Tell.*
Sir Walter Scott, 1771-1832, (Sc.) novelist, poet. *Ivanhoe, Rob Roy, The Bride of Lammermoor.*
Jaroslav Seifert, 1902-1986, (Cz.) poet.
William Shakespeare, 1564-1616, (Br.) dramatist, poet. *Romeo and Juliet, Hamlet, King Lear, The Merchant of Venice.*
George Bernard Shaw, 1856-1950, (Ir.) playwright, critic. *St. Joan, Pygmalion, Major Barbara, Man and Superman.*
Mary Wollstonecraft Shelley, 1797-1851, (Br.) author. *Frankenstein.*
Percy Bysshe Shelley, 1792-1822, (Br.) poet. *Prometheus Unbound, Adonais,* "Ode to the West Wind," "To a Skylark."
Richard B. Sheridan, 1751-1816, (Br.) dramatist. *The Rivals, School for Scandal.*
Robert Sherwood, 1896-1955, (U.S.) playwright. *The Petrified Forest, Abe Lincoln in Illinois, Reunion in Vienna.*
Mikhail Sholokhov, 1906-1984 (U.S.S.R.) author, 1965 Nobel laureate. *And Quiet Flows the Don.*
Upton Sinclair, 1878-1968, (U.S.) novelist. *The Jungle.*
Edmund Spenser, 1552-1599, (Br.) poet. *The Faerie Queen.*
Christina Stead, 1903-1983 (Austral.) novelist, short-story writer. *The Man Who Loved Children.*
Richard Steele, 1672-1729, (Br.) essayist, playwright, began the Tatler and Spectator. *The Conscious Lovers.*
Lincoln Steffens, 1866-1936, (U.S.) editor, author. *The Shame of the Cities.*
Gertrude Stein, 1874-1946, (U.S.) author. *Three Lives.*
John Steinbeck, 1902-1968, (U.S.) novelist. *Grapes of Wrath, Of Mice and Men, Winter of Our Discontent.*
Stendhal (Marie Henri Beyle), 1783-1842, (F.) poet, novelist. *The Red and the Black, The Charterhouse of Parma.*
Laurence Sterne, 1713-1768, (Br.) novelist. *Tristram Shandy.*
Wallace Stevens, 1879-1955, (U.S.) poet. *Harmonium, The Man With the Blue Guitar, Transport to Summer.*
Robert Louis Stevenson, 1850-1894, (Br.) novelist, poet, essayist. *Treasure Island, A Child's Garden of Verses.*

Rex Stout, 1886-1975, (U.S.) novelist, created Nero Wolfe.

Harriet Beecher Stowe, 1811-1896, (U.S.) novelist. *Uncle Tom's Cabin.*

Lytton Strachey, 1880-1932, (Br.) biographer, critic. *Eminent Victorians, Queen Victoria, Elizabeth and Essex.*

August Strindberg, 1849-1912, (Swed.) dramatist, novelist. *The Father, Miss Julie, The Creditors.*

Jonathan Swift, 1667-1745, (Br.) author. *Gulliver's Travels.*

Algernon C. Swinburne, 1837-1909, (Br.) poet, critic. *Songs Before Sunrise.*

John M. Synge, 1871-1909, (Ir.) poet, dramatist. *Riders to the Sea, The Playboy of the Western World.*

Rabindranath Tagore, 1861-1941, (Ind.), author, poet. *Sadhana, The Realization of Life, Gitanjali.*

Booth Tarkington, 1869-1946, (U.S.) novelist. *Seventeen, Alice Adams, Penrod.*

Sara Teasdale, 1884-1933, (U.S.) poet. *Helen of Troy and Other Poems, Rivers to the Sea, Flame and Shadow.*

Alfred Lord Tennyson, 1809-1892, (Br.) poet. *Idylls of the King, In Memoriam,* "The Charge of the Light Brigade."

William Makepeace Thackeray, 1811-1863, (Br.) novelist. *Vanity Fair.*

Dylan Thomas, 1914-1953, (Welsh) poet. *Under Milk Wood, A Child's Christmas in Wales.*

Henry David Thoreau, 1817-1862, (U.S.) transcendentalist thinker, writer. *Walden.*

James Thurber, 1894-1961, (U.S.) humorist, artist. *The New Yorker, The Owl in the Attic, Thurber Carnival.*

J.R.R. Tolkien, 1892-1973, (Br.) author. *The Hobbit, Lord of the Rings.*

Leo Tolstoy, 1828-1910, (r.) novelist. *War and Peace, Anna Karenina.*

Anthony Trollope, 1815-1882, (Br.) novelist. *The Warden, Barchester Towers, The Palliser novels.*

Ivan Turgenev, 1818-1883, (r.) novelist, short-story writer. *Fathers and Sons, First Love, A Month in the Country.*

Mark Twain (Samuel Clemens), 1835-1910, (U.S.) novelist, humorist. *The Adventures of Huckleberry Finn, Tom Sawyer.*

Sigrid Undset, 1881-1949, (Nor.) novelist, poet. *Kristin Lavransdatter.*

Paul Valéry, 1871-1945, (F.) poet, critic. *La Jeune Parque, The Graveyard by the Sea.*

Jules Verne, 1828-1905, (F.) novelist, originator of modern science fiction. *Twenty Thousand Leagues Under the Sea.*

François Villon, 1431-1463?, (F.) poet. *Le petit et le Grand, Testament.*

Evelyn Waugh, 1903-1966, (Br.) satirist. *The Loved One.*

H.G. Wells, 1866-1946, (Br.) author. *The Time Machine, The Invisible Man, The War of the Worlds.*

Rebecca West, 1893-1983 (Br.) author. *Black Lamb and Grey Falcon.*

Edith Wharton, 1862-1937, (U.S.) novelist. *The Age of Innocence, The House of Mirth.*

E.B. White, 1899-1985 (U.S.), essayist, children's book author. *Here is New York, Charlotte's Web, Stuart Little.*

T.H. White, 1906-1964, (Br.) author. *The Once and Future King.*

Walt Whitman, 1819-1892, (U.S.) poet. *Leaves of Grass.*

John Greenleaf Whittier, 1807-1892, (U.S.) poet, journalist. *Snow-bound.*

Oscar Wilde, 1854-1900, (Ir.) author, wit. *The Picture of Dorian Gray, The Importance of Being Earnest.*

Thornton Wilder, 1897-1975, (U.S.) playwright. *Our Town, The Skin of Our Teeth, The Matchmaker.*

Tennessee Williams, 1912-1983 (U.S.) playwright. *A Streetcar Named Desire, Cat on a Hot Tin Roof, The Glass Menagerie.*

William Carlos Williams, 1883-1963, (U.S.) poet, physician. *Tempers, Al Que Quiere!, Paterson.*

Edmund Wilson, 1895-1972, (U.S.) author, literary and social critic. *Axel's Castle, To the Finland Station.*

P.G. Wodehouse, 1881-1975, (U.S.) poet, dramatist. The "Jeeves" novels, *Anything Goes.*

Thomas Wolfe, 1900-1938, (U.S.) novelist. *Look Homeward, Angel, You Can't Go Home Again, Of Time and the River.*

Virginia Woolf, 1882-1941, (Br.) novelist, essayist. *Mrs. Dalloway, To the Lighthouse, The Waves.*

William Wordsworth, 1770-1850, (Br.) poet. "Tintern Abbey," "Ode: Intimations of Immortality."

William Butler Yeats, 1865-1939, (Ir.) poet, playwright. *The Wild Swans at Coole, The Tower, Last Poems.*

Émile Zola, 1840-1902, (F.) novelist. *Nana, The Dram Shop.*

Noted Artists and Sculptors of the Past

Artists are painters unless otherwise indicated.

Washington Allston, 1779-1843, (U.S.) landscapist. *Belshazzar's Feast.*

Albrecht Altdorfer, 1480-1538, (Ger.) landscapist. *Battle of Alexander.*

Andrea del Sarto, 1486-1530, frescoes. *Madonna of the Harpies.*

Fra Angelico, c. 1400-1455, (It.) Renaissance muralist. *Madonna of the Linen Drapers' Guild.*

Alexsandr Archipenko, 1887-1964, (U.S.) sculptor. *Boxing Match, Medranos.*

John James Audubon, 1785-1851, (U.S.) *Birds of America.*

Hans Baldung Grien, 1484-1545, (Ger.) *Todentanz.*

Ernst Barlach, 1870-1938, (Ger.) Expressionist sculptor. *Man Drawing a Sword.*

Frederic-Auguste Bartholdi, 1834-1904, (Fr.) *Liberty Enlightening the World, Lion of Belfort.*

Fra Bartolommeo, 1472-1517, (It.) *Vision of St. Bernard.*

Aubrey Beardsley, 1872-1898, (Br.) illustrator. *Salome, Lysistrata.*

Max Beckmann, 1884-1950, (Ger.) Expressionist. *The Descent from the Cross.*

Gentile Bellini, 1426-1507, (It.) Renaissance. *Procession in St. Mark's Square.*

Giovanni Bellini, 1428-1516, (It.) *St. Francis in Ecstasy.*

Jacopo Bellini, 1400-1470, (It.) *Crucifixion.*

George Wesley Bellows, 1882-1925, (U.S.) sports artist. *Stag at Sharkey's.*

Thomas Hart Benton, 1889-1975, (U.S.) American regionalist. *Threshing Wheat, Arts of the West.*

Gianlorenzo Bernini, 1598-1680, (It.) Baroque sculpture. *The Assumption.*

Albert Bierstadt, 1830-1902, (U.S.) landscapist. *The Rocky Mountains, Mount Corcoran.*

George Caleb Bingham, 1811-1879, (U.S.) *Fur Traders Descending the Missouri.*

William Blake, 1752-1827, (Br.) engraver. *Book of Job, Songs of Innocence, Songs of Experience.*

Rosa Bonheur, 1822-1899, (Fr.) *The Horse Fair.*

Pierre Bonnard, 1867-1947, (Fr.) Intimist. *The Breakfast Room.*

Gutzon Borglum, 1871-1941, (U.S.) sculptor. *Mt. Rushmore Memorial.*

Hieronymus Bosch, 1450-1516, (Flem.) religious allegories. *The Crowning with Thorns.*

Sandro Botticelli, 1444-1510, (It.) Renaissance. *Birth of Venus.*

Constantin Brancusi, 1876-1957, (Rum.) Nonobjective sculptor. *Flying Turtle, The Kiss.*

Georges Braque, 1882-1963, (Fr.) Cubist. *Violin and Palette.*

Pieter Bruegel the Elder, c. 1525-1569, (Flem.) *The Peasant Dance.*

Pieter Bruegel the Younger, 1564-1638, (Flem.) *Village Fair, The Crucifixion.*

Edward Burne-Jones, 1833-1898, (Br.) Pre-Raphaelite artist-craftsman. *The Mirror of Venus.*

Alexander Calder, 1898-1976, (U.S.) sculptor. *Lobster Trap and Fish Tail.*

Michelangelo Merisi da Caravaggio, 1573-1610, (It.) Baroque. *The Supper at Emmaus.*

Emily Carr, 1871-1945, (Can.) landscapist. *Blunden Harbour, Big Raven.*

Carlo Carra, 1881-1966, (It.) Metaphysical school. *Lot's Daughters.*

Mary Cassatt, 1845-1926, (U.S.) Impressionist. *Woman Bathing.*

George Catlin, 1796-1872, (U.S.) American Indian life. *Gallery of Indians.*

Benvenuto Cellini, 1500-1571, (It.) Mannerist sculptor, goldsmith. *Perseus.*

Paul Cezanne, 1839-1906, (Fr.) *Card Players, Mont-Sainte-Victoire with Large Pine Trees.*

Marc Chagall, 1887-1985, (Rus.) Jewish life and folklore. *I and the Village.*

Jean Simeon Chardin, 1699-1779, (Fr.) still lifes. *The Kiss, The Grace.*

Frederic Church, 1826-1900, (U.S.) Hudson River school. *Niagara, Andes of Ecuador.*

Giovanni Cimabue, 1240-1302, (It.) Byzantine mosaicist. *Madonna Enthroned with St. Francis.*

Claude Lorrain, 1600-1682, (Fr.) ideal-landscapist. *The Enchanted Castle.*

Thomas Cole, 1801-1848, (U.S.) Hudson River school. *The Ox-Bow.*

John Constable, 1776-1837, (Br.) landscapist. *Salisbury Cathedral from the Bishop's Grounds.*

John Singleton Copley, 1738-1815, (U.S.) portraitist. Samuel Adams, Watson and the Shark.

Lovis Corinth, 1858-1925, (Ger.) Expressionist. Apocalypse.

Jean-Baptiste-Camille Corot, 1796-1875, (Fr.) landscapist. Souvenir de Mortefontaine, Pastorale.

Correggio, 1494-1534, (It.) Renaissance muralist. Mystic Marriages of St. Catherine.

Gustave Courbet, 1819-1877, (Fr.) Realist. The Artist's Studio.

Lucas Cranach the Elder, 1472-1553, (Ger.) Protestant Reformation portraitist. Luther.

Nathaniel Currier, 1813-1888, and **James M. Ives,** 1824-1895, (both U.S.) lithographers. A Midnight Race on the Mississippi.

John Steuart Curry, 1897-1946, (U.S.) Americana, murals. Baptism in Kansas.

Salvador Dali, 1904-1989, (Sp.) Surrealist. Persistence of Memory.

Honore Daumier, 1808-1879, (Fr.) caricaturist. The Third-Class Carriage.

Jacques-Louis David, 1748-1825, (Fr.) Neoclassicist. The Oath of the Horatii.

Arthur Davies, 1862-1928, (U.S.) Romantic landscapist. Unicorns.

Edgar Degas, 1834-1917, (Fr.) The Ballet Class.

Eugene Delacroix, Co. 1789-1863, (Fr.) Romantic. Massacre at Chios.

Paul Delaroche, 1797-1856, (Fr.) historical themes. Children of Edward IV.

Luca Della Robbia, 1400-1482, (It.) Renaissance terracotta artist. Cantoria (singing gallery), Florence cathedral.

Donatello, 1386-1466, (It.) Renaissance sculptor. David, Gattamelata.

Jean Dubuffet, 1902-1985, (Fr.) painter, sculptor, printmaker. Group of Four Trees.

Marcel Duchamp, 1887-1968, (Fr.) Nude Descending a Staircase.

Raoul Dufy, 1877-1953, (Fr.) Fauvist. Chateau and Horses.

Asher Brown Durand, 1796-1886, (U.S.) Hudson River school. Kindred Spirits.

Albrecht Durer, 1471-1528, (Ger.) Renaissance engraver, woodcuts. St. Jerome in His Study, Melancholia I, Apocalypse.

Anthony van Dyck, 1599-1641, (Flem.) Baroque portraitist. Portrait of Charles I Hunting.

Thomas Eakins, 1844-1916, (U.S.) Realist. The Gross Clinic.

Jacob Epstein, 1880-1959, (Br.) religious and allegorical sculptor. Genesis, Ecce Homo.

Jan van Eyck, 1380-1441, (Flem.) naturalistic panels. Adoration of the Lamb.

Anselm Feuerbach, 1829-1880, (Ger.) Romantic Classicism. Judgement of Paris, Iphigenia.

John Bernard Flannagan, 1895-1942, (U.S.) animal sculptor. Triumph of the Egg.

Jean-Honore Fragonard, 1732-1806, (Fr.) Rococo. The Swing.

Daniel Chester French, 1850-1931, (U.S.) The Minute Man of Concord; seated Lincoln, Lincoln Memorial, Washington, D.C.

Caspar David Friedrich, 1774-1840, (Ger.) Romantic landscapes. Man and Woman Gazing at the Moon.

Thomas Gainsborough, 1727-1788, (Br.) portraitist. The Blue Boy.

Paul Gauguin, 1848-1903, (Fr.) Post-impressionist. The Tahitians.

Lorenzo Ghiberti, 1378-1455, (It.) Renaissance sculptor. Gates of Paradise baptistry doors, Florence.

Alberto Giacometti, 1901-1966, (It.) attenuated sculptures of solitary figures. Man Pointing.

Giorgione, c. 1477-1510, (It.) Renaissance. The Tempest.

Giotto di Bondone, 1267-1337, (It.) Renaissance. Presentation of Christ in the Temple.

Francois Girardon, 1628-1715, (Fr.) Baroque sculptor of classical themes. Apollo Tended by the Nymphs.

Vincent van Gogh, 1853-1890, (Dutch) The Starry Night, L'Arlesienne.

Arshile Gorky, 1905-1948, (U.S.) Surrealist. The Liver Is the Cock's Comb.

Francisco de Goya y Lucientes, 1746-1828, (Sp.) The Naked Maja, The Disasters of War (etchings).

El Greco, 1541-1614, View of Toledo.

Horatio Greenough, 1805-1852, (U.S.) Neo-classical sculptor. George Washington.

Matthias Grünewald, 1480-1528, (Ger.) mystical religious themes. The Resurrection.

Frans Hals, c. 1580-1666, (Dutch) portraitist. Laughing Cavalier, Gypsy Girl.

Childe Hassam, 1859-1935, (U.S.) Impressionist. Southwest Wind.

Edward Hicks, 1780-1849, (U.S.) folk painter. The Peaceable Kingdom.

Hans Hofmann, 1880-1966, (U.S.) early Abstract Expressionist. Spring. The Gate.

William Hogarth, 1697-1764, (Br.) caricaturist. The Rake's Progress.

Katsushika Hokusai, 1760-1849, (Jap.) printmaker. Crabs.

Hans Holbein the Elder, 1460-1524, (Ger.) late Gothic. Presentation of Christ in the Temple.

Hans Holbein the Younger, 1497-1543, (Ger.) portraitist. Henry VIII.

Winslow Homer, 1836-1910, (U.S.) marine themes. Marine Coast, High Cliff.

Edward Hopper, 1882-1967, (U.S.) realistic urban scenes. Sunlight in a Cafeteria.

Jean-Auguste-Dominique Ingres, 1780-1867, (Fr.) Classicist. Valpincon Bather.

George Inness, 1825-1894, (U.S.) luminous landscapist. Delaware Water Gap.

Vasily Kandinsky, 1866-1944, (Rus.) Abstractionist. Capricious Forms.

Paul Klee, 1879-1940, (Swiss) Abstractionist. Twittering Machine.

Oscar Kokoschka, 1886-1980, (Aus.) Expressionist. View of Prague.

Kathe Kollwitz, 1867-1945, (Ger.) printmaker, social justice themes. The Peasant War.

Gaston Lachaise, 1882-1935, (U.S.) figurative sculptor. Standing Woman.

John La Farge, 1835-1910, (U.S.) muralist. Red and White Peonies.

Fernand Leger, 1881-1955, (Fr.) machine art. The Cyclists.

Leonardo da Vinci, 1452-1519, (It.) Mona Lisa, Last Supper, The Annunciation.

Emanuel Leutze, 1816-1868, (U.S.) historical themes. Washington Crossing the Delaware.

Jacques Lipchitz, 1891-1973, (Fr.) Cubist sculptor. Harpist.

Filippino Lippi, 1457-1504, (It.) Renaissance. The Vision of St. Bernard.

Fra Filippo Lippi, 1406-1469, (It.) Renaissance. Coronation of the Virgin.

Morris Louis, 1912-1962, (U.S.) Abstract Expressionist. Signa, Stripes.

Aristide Maillol, 1861-1944, (Fr.) sculptor. The Mediterranean.

Edouard Manet, 1832-1883, (Fr.) forerunner of Impressionism. Luncheon on the Grass, Olympia.

Andrea Mantegna, 1431-1506, (It.) Renaissance frescoes. Triumph of Caesar.

Franz Marc, 1880-1916, (Ger.) Expressionist. Blue Horses.

John Marin, 1870-1953, (U.S.) expressionist seascapes. Maine Island.

Reginald Marsh, 1898-1954, (U.S.) satirical artist. Tattoo and Haircut.

Masaccio, 1401-1428, (It.) Renaissance. The Tribute Money.

Henri Matisse, 1869-1954, (Fr.) Fauvist. Woman with the Hat.

Michelangelo Buonarroti, 1475-1564, (It.) Pieta, David, Moses, The Last Judgment, Sistine Ceiling.

Jean-Francois Millet, 1814-1875, (Fr.) painter of peasant subjects. The Gleaners, The Man with a Hoe.

Amedeo Modigliani, 1884-1920, (It.) Reclining Nude.

Piet Mondrian, 1872-1944, (Dutch) Abstractionist. Composition.

Claude Monet, 1840-1926, (Fr.) Impressionist. The Bridge at Argenteuil, Haystacks.

Henry Moore, 1898-1986, (Br.) sculptor of large-scale, abstract works. Reclining Figure (several).

Gustave Moreau, 1826-1898, (Fr.) Symbolist. The Apparition, Dance of Salome.

James Wilson Morrice, 1865-1924, (Can.) landscapist. The Ferry, Quebec, Venice, Looking Over the Lagoon.

Grandma Moses, 1860-1961, (U.S.) folk painter. Out for the Christmas Trees.

Edvard Munch, 1863-1944, (Nor.) Expressionist. The Cry.

Bartolome Murillo, 1618-1682, (Sp.) Baroque religious artist. Vision of St. Anthony. The Two Trinities.

Barnett Newman, 1905-1970, (U.S.) Abstract Expressionist. Stations of the Cross.

Isamu Noguchi, 1904-1988, (U.S.) trad. Japanese art, modern techniques.

Georgia O'Keeffe, 1887-1986, (U.S.) Southwest motifs. Cow's Skull.

Jose Clemente Orozco, 1883-1949, (Mex.) frescoes. House of Tears.

Charles Willson Peale, 1741-1827, (U.S.) American Revolutionary portraitist. Washington, Franklin, Jefferson, John Adams.

Rembrandt Peale, 1778-1860, (U.S.) portraitist. Thomas Jefferson.

Pietro Perugino, 1446-1523, (It.) Renaissance. Delivery of the Keys to St. Peter.

Pablo Picasso, 1881-1973, (Sp.) Guernica, Dove, Head of a Woman.

Piero della Francesca, c. 1415-1492, (It.) Renaissance. Duke of Urbino, Flagellation of Christ.

Camille Pissarro, 1830-1903, (Fr.) Impressionist. Morning Sunlight.

Jackson Pollock, 1912-1956, (U.S.) Abstract Expressionist. Autumn Rhythm.

Nicolas Poussin, 1594-1665, (Fr.) Baroque pictorial classicism. St. John on Patmos.

Maurice B. Prendergast, c. 1860-1924, (U.S.) Post-impressionist water colorist. Umbrellas in the Rain.

Pierre-Paul Prud'hon, 1758-1823, (Fr.) Romanticist. Crime pursued by Vengeance and Justice.

Pierre Cecile Puvis de Chavannes, 1824-1898, (Fr.) muralist. The Poor Fisherman.

Raphael Sanzio, 1483-1520, (It.) Renaissance. Disputa, School of Athens, Sistine Madonna.

Man Ray, 1890-1976, (U.S.) Dadaist. Observing Time, The Lovers.

Odilon Redon, 1840-1916, (Fr.) Symbolist lithographer. In the Dream.

Rembrandt van Rijn, 1606-1669, (Dutch) The Bridal Couple, The Night Watch.

Frederic Remington, 1861-1909, (U.S.) painter, sculptor, portrayer of the American West. Bronco Buster.

Pierre-Auguste Renoir, 1841-1919, (Fr.) impressionist. The Luncheon of the Boating Party.

Joshua Reynolds, 1723-1792, (Br.) portraitist. Mrs. Siddons as the Tragic Muse.

Diego Rivera, 1886-1957, (Mex.) frescoes. The Fecund Earth.

Norman Rockwell, 1894-1978, (U.S.) illustrator. Saturday Evening Post covers.

Auguste Rodin, 1840-1917, (Fr.) sculptor. The Thinker, The Burghers of Calais.

Mark Rothko, 1903-1970, (U.S.) Abstract Expressionist. Light, Earth and Blue.

Georges Rouault, 1871-1958, (Fr.) Expressionist. The Old King.

Henri Rousseau, 1844-1910, (Fr.) primitive exotic themes. The Snake Charmer.

Theodore Rousseau, 1812-1867, (Swiss-Fr.) landscapist. Under the Birches, Evening.

Peter Paul Rubens, 1577-1640, (Flem.) Baroque. Mystic Marriage of St. Catherine.

Jacob van Ruisdael, c. 1628-1682, (Dutch) landscapist. Jewish Cemetery.

Salomon van Ruysdael, c. 1600-1670, (Dutch) landscapist. River with Ferry-Boat.

Albert Pinkham Ryder, 1847-1917, (U.S.) seascapes and allegories. Toilers of the Sea.

Augustus Saint-Gaudens, 1848-1907, (U.S.) memorial statues. Farragut, Mrs. Henry Adams (Grief).

Andrea Sansovino, 1460-1529, (It.) Renaissance sculptor. Baptism of Christ.

Jacopo Sansovino, 1486-1570, (It.) Renaissance sculptor. St. John the Baptist.

John Singer Sargent, 1856-1925, (U.S.) Edwardian society portraitist. The Wyndham Sisters, Madam X.

Georges Seurat, 1859-1891, (Fr.) Pointillist. Sunday Afternoon on the Island of Grande Jatte.

Gino Severini, 1883-1966, (It.) Futurist and Cubist. Dynamic Hieroglyph of the Bal Tabarin.

Ben Shahn, 1898-1969, (U.S.) social and political themes. Sacco and Vanzetti series, Seurat's Lunch, Handball.

Charles Sheeler, 1883-1965, (U.S.) Abstractionist. Upper Deck.

David Alfaro Siqueiros, 1896-1974, (Mex.) political muralist. March of Humanity.

John F. Sloan, 1871-1951, (U.S.) depictions of New York City. Wake of the Ferry.

David Smith, 1906-1965, (U.S.) welded metal sculpture. Hudson River Landscape, Zig, Cubi series.

Gilbert Stuart, 1755-1828, (U.S.) portraitist. George Washington.

Thomas Sully, 1783-1872, (U.S.) portraitist. Col. Thomas Handasyd Perkins, The Passage of the Delaware.

Yves Tanguy, 1900-1955, (Fr.) Surrealist. Rose of the Four Winds.

Giovanni Battista Tiepolo, 1696-1770, (It.) Rococo frescoes. The Crucifixion.

Jacopo Tintoretto, 1518-1594, (It.) Mannerist. The Last Supper.

Titian, c. 1485-1576, (It.) Renaissance. Venus and the Lute Player, The Bacchanal.

Henri de Toulouse-Lautrec, 1864-1901, (Fr.) At the Moulin Rouge.

John Trumbull, 1756-1843, (U.S.) historical themes. The Declaration of Independence.

Joseph Mallord William Turner, 1775-1851, (Br.) Romantic landscapist. Snow Storm.

Paolo Uccello, 1397-1475, (It.) Gothic-Renaissance. The Rout of San Romano.

Maurice Utrillo, 1883-1955, (Fr.) Impressionist. Sacre-Coeur de Montmartre.

John Vanderlyn, 1775-1852, (U.S.) Neo-classicist. Ariadne Asleep on the Island of Naxos.

Diego Velazquez, 1599-1660, (Sp.) Baroque. Las Meninas, Portrait of Juan de Pareja.

Jan Vermeer, 1632-1675, (Dutch) interior genre subjects. Young Woman~with a Water Jug.

Paolo Veronese, 1528-1588, (It.) devotional themes, vastly peopled canvases. The Temptation of St. Anthony.

Andrea del Verrocchio, 1435-1488, (It.) Florentine sculptor. Colleoni.

Maurice de Vlaminck, 1876-1958, (Fr.) Fauvist landscapist. The Storm.

Andy Warhol, 1928-1987 (U.S.) Pop Art, Campbell's Soup Cans.

Antoine Watteau, 1684-1721, (Fr.) Rococo painter of "scenes of gallantry". The Embarkation for Cythera.

George Frederic Watts, 1817-1904, (Br.) painter and sculptor of grandiose allegorical themes. Hope, Physical Energy.

Benjamin West, 1738-1820, realistic historical themes. Death of General Wolfe.

James Abbott McNeill Whistler, 1834-1903, (U.S.) Arrangement in Grey and Black, No. 1: The Artist's Mother.

Archibald M. Willard, 1836-1918, (U.S.) The Spirit of '76.

Grant Wood, 1891-1942, (U.S.) Midwestern regionalist. American Gothic, Daughters of Revolution.

Ossip Zadkine, 1890-1967, (Rus.) School of Paris sculptor. The Destroyed City, Musicians, Christ.

Noted Philosophers and Religionists of the Past

Lyman Abbott, 1835-1922, (U.S.) clergyman, reformer; advocate of Christian Socialism.

Pierre Abelard, 1079-1142, (F.) philosopher, theologian, and teacher, used dialectic method to support Christian dogma.

Felix Adler, 1851-1933, (U.S.) German-born founder of the Ethical Culture Society.

St. Augustine, 354-430, Latin bishop considered the founder of formalized Christian theology.

Averroes, 1126-1198, (Sp.) Islamic philosopher.

Roger Bacon, c.1214-1294, (Br.) philosopher and scientist.

Karl Barth, 1886-1968, (Sw.) theologian, a leading force in 20th-century Protestantism.

St. Benedict, c.480-547, (It.) founded the Benedictines.

Jeremy Bentham, 1748-1832, (Br.) philosopher, reformer, founder of Utilitarianism.

Henri Bergson, 1859-1941, (F.) philosopher of evolution.

George Berkeley, 1685-1753, (Ir.) philosopher, churchman.

John Biddle, 1615-1662, (Br.) founder of English Unitarianism.

Jakob Boehme, 1575-1624, (G.) theosophist and mystic.

William Brewster, 1567-1644, (Br.) headed Pilgrims, signed Mayflower Compact.

Emil Brunner, 1889-1966, (Sw.) theologian.

Giordano Bruno, 1548-1600, (It.) philosopher.

Martin Buber, 1878-1965, (G.) Jewish philosopher, theologian, wrote I and Thou.

Buddha (Siddhartha Gautama), c.563-c.483 BC, (Ind.) philosopher, founded Buddhism.

John Calvin, 1509-1564, (F.) theologian, a key figure in the Protestant Reformation.

Rudolph Carnap, 1891-1970, (U.S.) German-born philosopher, a founder of logical positivism.

William Ellery Channing, 1780-1842, (U.S.) clergyman, early spokesman for Unitarianism.

Auguste Comte, 1798-1857, (F.) philosopher, the founder of positivism.

Confucius, 551-479 BC, (Chin.) founder of Confucianism.

John Cotton, 1584-1652, (Br.) Puritan theologian.

Thomas Cranmer, 1489-1556, (Br.) churchman, wrote much of Book of Common Prayer; promoter of English Reformation.

René Descartes, 1596-1650, (F.) philosopher, mathematician.

John Dewey, 1859-1952, (U.S.) philosopher, educator; helped inaugurate the progressive education movement.

Denis Diderot, 1713-1784, (F.) philosopher, creator of first modern encyclopedia.

Mary Baker Eddy, 1821-1910, (U.S.) founder of Christian Science.

Jonathan Edwards, 1703-1758, (U.S.) preacher, theologian.

(Desiderius) Erasmus, c.1466-1536, (Du.) Renaissance humanist.

Johann Fichte, 1762-1814, (G.) philosopher, the first of the Transcendental Idealists.

George Fox, 1624-1691, (Br.) founder of Society of Friends.

St. Francis of Assisi, 1182-1226, (It.) founded Franciscans.

al Ghazali, 1058-1111, Islamic philosopher.

Georg W. Hegel, 1770-1831, (G.) Idealist philosopher.

Martin Heidegger, 1889-1976, (G.) existentialist philosopher, affected fields ranging from physics to literary criticism.

Johann G. Herder, 1744-1803, (G.) philosopher, cultural historian; a founder of German Romanticism.

David Hume, 1711-1776, (Sc.) philosopher, historian.

Jan Hus, 1369-1415, (Czech.) religious reformer.

Edmund Husserl, 1859-1938, (G.) philosopher, founded the Phenomenological movement.

Thomas Huxley, 1825-1895, (Br.) philosopher, educator.

Ignatius of Loyola, 1491-1556, (Sp.) founder of the Jesuits.

William Inge, 1860-1954, (Br.) theologian, explored the mystic aspects of Christianity.

William James, 1842-1910, (U.S.) philosopher, psychologist; advanced theory of the pragmatic nature of truth.

Karl Jaspers, 1883-1969, (G.) existentialist philosopher.

Immanuel Kant, 1724-1804, (G.) metaphysician, preeminent founder of modern critical philosophy.

Soren Kierkegaard, 1813-1855, (Den.) philosopher, considered the father of Existentialism.

John Knox, 1505-1572, (Sc.) leader of the Protestant Reformation in Scotland.

Lao-Tzu, 604-531 BC, (Chin.) philosopher, considered the founder of the Taoist religion.

Gottfried von Leibniz, 1646-1716, (G.) philosopher, mathematician.

Martin Luther, 1483-1546, (G.) leader of the Protestant Reformation, founded Lutheran church.

Maimonides, 1135-1204, (Sp.) Jewish philosopher.

Jacques Maritain, 1882-1973, (F.) Neo-Thomist philosopher.

Cotton Mather, 1663-1728, (U.S.) defender of orthodox Puritanism; founded Yale, 1703.

Philipp Melanchthon, 1497-1560, (G.) theologian, humanist; an important voice in the Reformation.

Thomas Merton, 1915-1968, (U.S.) Trappist monk, spiritual writer.

Mohammed, c.570-632, Arab prophet of the religion of Islam.

Dwight Moody, 1837-1899, (U.S.) evangelist.

George E. Moore, 1873-1958, (Br.) ethical theorist.

Elijah Muhammad, 1897-1975, (U.S.) leader of the Black Muslim sect.

Heinrich Muhlenberg, 1711-1787, (G.) organized the Lutheran Church in America.

John H. Newman, 1801-1890, (Br.) Roman Catholic cardinal, led Oxford Movement.

Reinhold Niebuhr, 1892-1971, (U.S.) Protestant theologian, social and political critic.

Friedrich Nietzsche, 1844-1900, (G.) moral philosopher.

Blaise Pascal, 1623-1662, (F.) philosopher and mathematician.

St. Patrick, c.389-c.461, brought Christianity to Ireland.

St. Paul, ?-c.67, a founder of the Christian religion.

Charles S. Peirce, 1839-1914, (U.S.) philosopher, logician; originated concept of Pragmatism, 1878.

Josiah Royce 1855-1916, (U.S.) Idealist philosopher.

Charles T. Russell, 1852-1916, (U.S.) founder of Jehovah's Witnesses.

Fredrich von Schelling, 1775-1854, (G.) philosopher.

Friedrich Schleiermacher, 1768-1834, (G.) theologian, a founder of modern Protestant theology.

Arthur Schopenhauer, 1788-1860, (G.) philosopher.

Joseph Smith, 1805-1844, (U.S.) founded Latter Day Saints (Mormon) movement, 1830.

Herbert Spencer, 1820-1903, (Br.) philosopher of evolution.

Baruch Spinoza, 1632-1677, (Du.) rationalist philosopher.

Billy Sunday, 1862-1935, (U.S.) evangelist.

Daisetz Teitaro Suzuki, 1870-1966, (Jap.) Buddhist scholar.

Emanuel Swedenborg, 1688-1722, (Swed.) philosopher, mystic.

Thomas à Becket, 1118-1170, (Br.) archbishop of Canterbury, opposed Henry II.

Thomas à Kempis, c.1380-1471, (G.) theologian probably wrote Imitation of Christ.

Thomas Aquinas, 1225-1274, (It.) theologian, philosopher.

Paul Tillich, 1886-1965, (U.S.) German-born philosopher and theologian.

John Wesley, 1703-1791, (Br.) theologian, evangelist; founded Methodism.

Alfred North Whitehead, 1861-1947, (Br.) philosopher, mathematician.

William of Occam, c.1285-c.1349 (Br.) philosopher.

Roger Williams, c.1603-1683, (U.S.) clergyman, championed religious freedom and separation of church and state.

Ludwig Wittgenstein, 1889-1951, (Aus.) philosopher.

John Wycliffe, 1320-1384, (Br.) theologian, reformer.

Brigham Young, 1801-1877, (U.S.) Mormon leader, colonized Utah.

Huldrych Zwingli, 1484-1531, (Sw.) theologian, led Swiss Protestant Reformation.

Noted Social Reformers and Educators of the Past

Jane Addams, 1860-1935, (U.S.) co-founder of Hull House; won Nobel Peace Prize, 1931.

Susan B. Anthony, 1820-1906, (U.S.) a leader in temperance, anti-slavery, and women's suffrage movements.

Henry Barnard, 1811-1900, (U.S.) public school reformer.

Thomas Barnardo, 1845-1905, (Br.) social reformer, pioneered in the care of destitute children.

Clara Barton, 1821-1912, (U.S.) organizer of the American Red Cross.

Henry Ward Beecher, 1813-1887, (U.S.) clergyman, abolitionist.

Sarah G. Blanding, 1899-1985, (U.S.) head of Vassar College, 1946-64.

Amelia Bloomer, 1818-1894, (U.S.) social reformer, women's rights advocate.

William Booth, 1829-1912, (Br.) founded the Salvation Army.

Nicholas Murray Butler, 1862-1947, (U.S.) educator headed Columbia Univ., 1902-45; won Nobel Peace Prize, 1931.

Frances X. (Mother) Cabrini, 1850-1917, (U.S.) Italian-born nun founded charitable institutions; first American canonized.

Carrie Chapman Catt, 1859-1947, (U.S.) suffragette, helped win passage of the 19th amendment.

Dorothy Day, 1897-1980, (U.S.) founder of Catholic Worker Movement.

Eugene V. Debs, 1855-1926, (U.S.) labor leader, led Pullman strike, 1894; 4-time Socialist presidential candidate.

Melvil Dewey, 1851-1931, (U.S.) devised decimal system of library-book classification.

Dorothea Dix, 1802-1887, (U.S.) crusader for humane care of mentally ill.

Frederick Douglass, 1817-1895, (U.S.) abolitionist.

W.E.B. DuBois, 1868-1963, (U.S.) Negro-rights leader, educator, and writer.

William Lloyd Garrison, 1805-1879, (U.S.) abolitionist, reformer.

Giovanni Gentile, 1875-1944, (It.) philosopher, educator; reformed Italian educational system.

Samuel Gompers, 1850-1924, (U.S.) labor leader; a founder and president of AFL.

William Green, 1873-1952, (U.S.) president of AFL, 1924-52.

Sidney Hillman, 1887-1946, (U.S.) labor leader, helped organize CIO.

John Holt, 1924-1985, (U.S.) educator and author, How Children Fail.

Samuel G. Howe, 1801-1876, (U.S.) social reformer, changed public attitudes toward the handicapped.

Helen Keller, 1880-1968, (U.S.) crusader for better treatment for the handicapped.

Martin Luther King Jr., 1929-1968, (U.S.) civil rights leader; won Nobel Peace Prize, 1964.

John L. Lewis, 1880-1969, (U.S.) labor leader, headed United Mine Workers, 1920-60.

Horace Mann, 1796-1859, (U.S.) pioneered modern public school system.

William H. McGuffey, 1800-1873, (U.S.) author of Reader, the mainstay of 19th century U.S. public education.

Alexander Meiklejohn, 1872-1964, (U.S.) British-born educator, championed academic freedom and experimental curricula.

Lucretia Mott, 1793-1880, (U.S.) reformer, pioneer feminist.

Philip Murray, 1886-1952, (U.S.) Scotch-born labor leader.

Florence Nightingale, 1820-1910, (Br.) founder of modern nursing.

Emmeline Pankhurst, 1858-1928, (Br.) woman suffragist.

Elizabeth P. Peabody, 1804-1894, (U.S.) education pioneer, founded 1st kindergarten in U.S., 1860.

Walter Reuther, 1907-1970, (U.S.) labor leader, headed UAW.

Jacob Riis, 1849-1914, (U.S.) crusader for urban reforms.

Margaret Sanger, 1883-1966, (U.S.) social reformer, pioneered the birth control movement.

Elizabeth Seton, 1774-1821, (U.S.) established parochial school education in U.S.

Earl of Shaftesbury (A.A. Cooper), 1801-1885, (Br.) social reformer.

Elizabeth Cady Stanton, 1815-1902, (U.S.) women's suf-
frage pioneer.
Lucy Stone, 1818-1893, (U.S.) feminist, abolitionist.
Harriet Tubman, c.1820-1913, (U.S.) abolitionist, ran Under-
ground Railroad.
Booker T. Washington, 1856-1915, (U.S.) educator, re-
former; championed vocational training for blacks.
Walter F. White, 1893-1955, (U.S.) headed NAACP, 1931-55.

William Wilberforce, 1759-1833, (Br.) social reformer, prominent in struggle to abolish the slave trade.
Emma Hart Willard, 1787-1870, (U.S.) pioneered higher education for women.
Frances E. Willard, 1839-1898, (U.S.) temperance, woman's
rights leader.
Whitney M. Young Jr., 1921-1971, (U.S.) civil rights leader,
headed National Urban League, 1961-71.

Noted Historians, Economists, and Social Scientists of the Past

Brooks Adams, 1848-1927, (U.S.) historian, political theoreti-
cian.
Francis Bacon, 1561-1626, (Br.) philosopher, essayist, and
statesman.
George Bancroft, 1800-1891, (U.S.) historian, wrote 10-vol-
ume History of the United States.
Charles A. Beard, 1874-1948, (U.S.) historian, attacked mo-
tives of the Founding Fathers.
Bede (the Venerable), c.673-735, (Br.) scholar, historian.
Ruth Benedict, 1887-1948, (U.S.) anthropologist, studied
Indian tribes of the Southwest.
Louis Blanc, 1811-1882, (F.) Socialist leader and historian
whose ideas were a link between utopian and Marxist socialism.
Leonard Bloomfield, 1887-1949, (U.S.) linguist. Language.
Franz Boas, 1858-1942, (U.S.) German-born anthropologist,
studied American Indians.
Van Wyck Brooks, 1886-1963, (U.S.) cultural historian, critic.
Edmund Burke, 1729-1797, (Ir.) British parliamentarian and
political philosopher; influenced many Federalists.
Joseph Campbell, 1904-1987, (U.S.) authored books on my-
thology, folklore.
Thomas Carlyle, 1795-1881, (Sc.) philosopher, historian, and
critic.
Edward Channing, 1856-1931, (U.S.) historian, wrote 6-vol-
ume A History of the United States.
John R. Commons, 1862-1945, (U.S.) economist, labor his-
torian.
Benedetto Croce, 1866-1952, (It.) philosopher, statesman,
and historian.
Bernard A. De Voto, 1897-1955, (U.S.) historian, won Pulitzer prize in 1948 for Across the Wide Missouri.
Ariel Durant, 1898-1981, (U.S.) historian, collaborated with
husband on 11-volume The Story of Civilization.
Will Durant, 1885-1981, (U.S.) historian. The Story of Civilization, The Story of Philosophy.
Emile Durkheim, 1858-1917, (F.) a founder of modern sociol-
ogy.
Friedrich Engels, 1820-1895, (G.) political writer, with Marx
wrote the Communist Manifesto.
Irving Fisher, 1867-1947, (U.S.) economist, contributed to the
development of modern monetary theory.
John Fiske, 1842-1901, (U.S.) historian and lecturer, popular-
ized Darwinian theory of evolution.
Charles Fourier, 1772-1837, (F.) utopian socialist.
Henry George, 1839-1897, (U.S.) economist, reformer, led
single-tax movement.
Edward Gibbon, 1737-1794, (Br.) historian, wrote The History
of the Decline and Fall of the Roman Empire.
Francesco Guicciardini, 1483-1540, (It.) historian, wrote
Storia d'Italia, principal historical work of the 16th-century.
Alvin Hansen, 1887-1975, (U.S.) economist.
Thomas Hobbes, 1588-1679, (Br.) social philosopher.
Richard Hofstadter, 1916-1970, (U.S.) historian, wrote The
Age of Reform.
John Maynard Keynes, 1883-1946, (Br.) economist, principal
advocate of deficit spending.
Alfred L. Kroeber, 1876-1960, (U.S.) cultural anthropologist,
studied Indians of North and South America.
James L. Laughlin, 1850-1933, (U.S.) economist, helped es-
tablish Federal Reserve System.
Lucien Lévy-Bruhl, 1857-1939, (F.) philosopher, studied the
psychology of primitive societies.
Kurt Lewin, 1890-1947, (U.S.) German-born psychologist,
studied human motivation and group dynamics.
John Locke, 1632-1704, (Br.) political philosopher.
Konrad Lorenz, 1904-1989, (Aus.) ethologist, pioneer in
study of animal behavior.
Thomas B. Macauley, 1800-1859, (Br.) historian, statesman.
Bronisław Malinowski, 1884-1942, (Pol.) anthropologist, con-
sidered the father of social anthropology.
Thomas R. Malthus, 1766-1834, (Br.) economist, famed for
Essay on the Principle of Population.
Karl Mannheim, 1893-1947, (Hung.) sociologist, historian.
Karl Marx, 1818-1883, (G.) political philosopher, proponent of
modern communism.
Giuseppe Mazzini, 1805-1872, (It.) political philosopher.
George H. Mead, 1863-1931, (U.S.) philosopher and social
psychologist.

Margaret Mead, 1901-1978, (U.S.) cultural anthropologist,
popularized field.
James Mill, 1773-1836, (Sc.) philosopher, historian, and econ-
omist; a proponent of Utilitarianism.
John Stuart Mill, 1806-1873, (Br.) philosopher, political econ-
omist.
Perry G. Miller, 1905-1963, (U.S.) historian, interpreted 17th-
century New England.
Theodor Mommsen, 1817-1903, (G.) historian, wrote The
History of Rome.
Charles-Louis Montesquieu, 1689-1755, (F.) social philoso-
pher.
Samuel Eliot Morison, 1887-1976, (U.S.) historian, chroni-
cled voyages of early explorers.
Gunnar Myrdal, 1898-1987, (Swe.) economist, social scientist.
Allan Nevins, 1890-1971, (U.S.) historian, biographer; twice
won Pulitzer prize.
Jose Ortega y Gasset, 1883-1955, (Sp.) philosopher and
humanist; advocated control by an elite.
Robert Owen, 1771-1858, (Br.) political philosopher, re-
former.
Vilfredo Pareto, 1848-1923, (It.) economist, sociologist.
Francis Parkman, 1823-1893, (U.S.) historian, wrote 8-vol-
ume France and England in North America, 1851-92.
Marco Polo, c.1254-1324, (It.) narrated an account of his
travels to China.
William Prescott, 1796-1859, (U.S.) early American historian.
Pierre Joseph Proudhon, 1809-1865, (F.) social theorist,
regarded as the father of anarchism.
Francois Quesnay, 1694-1774, (F.) economic theorist, dem-
onstrated circular flow of economic activity through society.
David Ricardo, 1772-1823, (Br.) economic theorist, advo-
cated free international trade.
James H. Robinson, 1863-1936, (U.S.) historian, educator.
Carl Rogers, 1902-1987, (U.S.) psychotherapist, author.
Jean-Jacques Rousseau, 1712-1778, (F.) social philosopher,
author.
Edward Sapir, 1884-1939 (Ger.-U.S.) anthropologist, studied
ethnology and linguistics of some U.S. Indian groups.
Ferdinand de Saussure, 1857-1913, (Swiss) a founder of
modern linguistics.
Hjalmar Schacht, 1877-1970, (G.) economist.
Joseph Schumpeter, 1883-1950, (U.S.) Czech.-born econo-
mist, championed big business, capitalism.
Albert Schweitzer, 1875-1965, (Alsatian) social philosopher,
theologian, and humanitarian.
George Simmel, 1858-1918, (G.) sociologist, philosopher.
Adam Smith, 1723-1790, (Br.) economist, advocated laissez-
faire economy and free trade.
Jared Sparks, 1789-1866, (U.S.) historian, among first to do
research from original documents.
Oswald Spengler, 1880-1936, (G.) philosopher and historian,
wrote The Decline of the West.
William G. Sumner, 1840-1910, (U.S.) social scientist, econo-
mist; championed laissez-faire economy, Social Darwinism.
Hippolyte Taine, 1828-1893, (F.) historian.
Frank W. Taussig, 1859-1940, (U.S.) economist, educator.
Nikolaas Tinbergen, 1907-1988, (Dutch-Br.) ethologist, pio-
neer in study of animal behavior.
Alexis de Tocqueville, 1805-1859, (F.) political scientist, his-
torian.
Francis E. Townsend, 1867-1960, (U.S.) author of old-age
pension plan.
Arnold Toynbee, 1889-1975, (Br.) historian, wrote 10-volume
A Study of History.
Heinrich von Treitschke, 1834-1896, (G.) historian, political
writer.
George Trevelyan, 1838-1928, (Br.) historian, statesman.
Barbara Tuchman, 1912-1989, (U.S.) author of Pulitzer Prize-
winning history books, The Guns of August.
Frederick J. Turner, 1861-1932, (U.S.) historian, educator.
Thorstein B. Veblen, 1857-1929, (U.S.) economist, social
philosopher.
Giovanni Vico, 1668-1744, (It.) historian, philosopher.
Voltaire (F.M. Arouet), 1694-1778, (F.) philosopher, historian,
and poet.
Izaak Walton, 1593-1683, (Br.) author, wrote first biographical
works in English literature.

Sidney J., 1859-1947, and wife Beatrice, 1858-1943, Webb (Br.) leading figures in Fabian Society and British Labour Party.
Walter P. Webb, 1888-1963, (U.S.) historian of the West.

Max Weber, 1864-1920, (G.) sociologist. *The Protestant Ethic and the Spirit of Capitalism.*

Noted Scientists of the Past

Howard H. Aiken, 1900-1973, (U.S.) mathematician, credited with designing forerunner of digital computer.

Albertus Magnus, 1193-1280, (G.) theologian, philosopher, scientist, established medieval Christian study of natural science.

Andre-Marie Ampère, 1775-1836, (F.) scientist known for contributions to electrodynamics.

Amedeo Avogadro, 1776-1856, (It.) chemist, physicist, advanced important theories on properties of gases.

A.C. Becquerel, 1788-1878, (F.) physicist, pioneer in electrochemical science.

A.H. Becquerel, 1852-1908, (F.) physicist, discovered radioactivity in uranium.

Alexander Graham Bell, 1847-1922, (U.S.) inventor, first to patent and commercially exploit the telephone, 1876.

Daniel Bernoulli, 1700-1782, (Swiss) mathematician, advanced kinetic theory of gases and fluids.

Jöns Jakob Berzelius, 1779-1848, (Swed.) chemist, developed modern chemical symbols and formulas.

Henry Bessemer, 1813-1898, (Br.) engineer, invented Bessemer steel-making process.

Louis Blériot, 1872-1936, (F.) engineer, pioneer aviator, invented and constructed monoplanes.

Niels Bohr, 1885-1962, (Dan.) physicist, leading figure in the development of quantum theory.

Max Born, 1882-1970, (G.) physicist known for research in quantum mechanics.

Satyendranath Bose, 1894-1974, (In.) physicist, chemist, mathematician known for Bose statistics, forerunner of modern quantum theory.

Walter Brattain, 1902-1987, (U.S.) inventor, worked on invention of transistor.

Louis de Broglie, 1893-1987, (F.) physicist, best known for wave theory.

Robert Bunsen, 1811-1899, (G.) chemist, invented Bunsen burner.

Luther Burbank, 1849-1926, (U.S.) plant breeder whose work developed plant breeding into a modern science.

Vannevar Bush, 1890-1974, (U.S.) electrical engineer, developed differential analyzer, first electronic analogue computer.

Alexis Carrel, 1873-1944, (F.) surgeon, biologist, developed methods of suturing blood vessels and transplanting organs.

George Washington Carver, 1860?-1943, (U.S.) agricultural chemist, experimenter, benefactor of South, a black hero.

Henry Cavendish, 1731-1810, (Br.) chemist, physicist, discovered hydrogen.

James Chadwick, 1891-1974, (Br.) physicist, discovered the neutron.

Jean M. Charcot, 1825-1893, (F.) neurologist known for work on hysteria, hypnotism, sclerosis.

Albert Claude, 1899-1983, (Belg.) a founder of modern cell biology.

John D. Cockcroft, 1897-1967, (Br.) nuclear physicist, constructed first atomic particle accelerator with E.T.S. Walton.

William Crookes, 1832-1919, (Br.) physicist, chemist, discovered thallium, invented a cathode-ray tube, radiometer.

Marie Curie, 1867-1934, (Pol.-F.) physical chemist known for work on radium and its compounds.

Pierre Curie, 1859-1906, (F.) physical chemist known for work with his wife on radioactivity.

Gottlieb Daimler, 1834-1900, (G.) engineer, inventor, pioneer automobile manufacturer.

John Dalton, 1766-1844, (Br.) chemist, physicist, formulated atomic theory, made first table of atomic weights.

Charles Darwin, 1809-1882, (Br.) naturalist, established theory of organic evolution.

Humphry Davy, 1778-1829, (Br.) chemist, research in electrochemistry led to isolation of potassium, sodium, calcium, barium, boron, magnesium, and strontium.

Lee De Forest, 1873-1961, (U.S.) inventor, pioneer in development of wireless telegraphy, sound pictures, television.

Max Delbrück, 1907-1981, (U.S.) pioneer in modern molecular genetics.

Rudolf Diesel, 1858-1913, (G.) mechanical engineer, patented Diesel engine.

Thomas Dooley, 1927-1961, (U.S.) "jungle doctor," noted for efforts to supply medical aid to underdeveloped countries.

Christian Doppler, 1803-1853, (Aus.) physicist, demonstrated Doppler effect (change in energy wavelengths caused by motion).

Thomas A. Edison, 1847-1931, (U.S.) inventor, held over 1,000 patents, including incandescent electric lamp, phonograph.

Paul Ehrlich, 1854-1915, (G.) bacteriologist, pioneer in modern immunology and bacteriology.

Albert Einstein, 1879-1955, (Ger.-U.S.) theoretical physicist, known for formulation of relativity theory.

John F. Enders, 1897-1985, (U.S.) virologist who helped discover vaccines against polio, measles, and mumps.

Leonhard Euler, 1707-1783, (Swiss) mathematician, physicist, authored first calculus book.

Gabriel Fahrenheit, 1686-1736, (G.) physicist, introduced Fahrenheit scale for thermometers.

Michael Faraday, 1791-1867, (Br.) chemist, physicist, known for work in field of electricity.

Pierre de Fermat, 1601-1665, (F.) mathematician, discovered analytic geometry, founded modern theory of numbers and calculus of probabilities.

Enrico Fermi, 1901-1954, (It.) physicist, one of chief architects of the nuclear age.

Galileo Ferraris, 1847-1897, (It.) physicist, electrical engineer, discovered principle of rotary magnetic field.

Richard Feynman, 1918-1988, (U.S.) a leading theoretical physicist of the postwar generation.

Camille Flammarion, 1842-1925, (F.) astronomer, popularized study of astronomy.

Alexander Fleming, 1881-1955, (Br.) bacteriologist, discovered penicillin.

Jean B.J. Fourier, 1768-1830, (F.) mathematician, discovered theorem governing periodic oscillation.

James Franck, 1882-1964, (G.) physicist, proved value of quantum theory.

Sigmund Freud, 1856-1939, (Aus.) psychiatrist, founder of psychoanalysis.

Galileo Galilei, 1564-1642, (It.) astronomer, physicist, a founder of the experimental method.

Luigi Galvani, 1737-1798, (It.) physician, physicist, known as founder of galvanism.

Carl Friedrich Gauss, 1777-1855, (G.) mathematician, astronomer, physicist, made important contributions to almost every field of physical science, founded a number of new fields.

Joseph Gay-Lussac, 1778-1850, (F.) chemist, physicist, investigated behavior of gases, discovered law of combining volumes.

Josiah W. Gibbs, 1839-1903, (U.S.) theoretical physicist, chemist, founded chemical thermodynamics.

Robert H. Goddard, 1882-1945 (U.S.) physicist, father of modern rocketry.

George W. Goethals, 1858-1928, (U.S.) army engineer, built the Panama Canal.

William C. Gorgas, 1854-1920, (U.S.) sanitarian, U.S. army surgeon-general, his work to prevent yellow fever, malaria helped insure construction of Panama Canal.

Ernest Haeckel, 1834-1919, (G.) zoologist, evolutionist, a strong proponent of Darwin.

Otto Hahn, 1879-1968, (G.) chemist, worked on atomic fission.

J.B.S. Haldane, 1892-1964, (Sc.) scientist, known for work as geneticist and application of mathematics to science.

James Hall, 1761-1832, (Br.) geologist, chemist, founded experimental geology, geochemistry.

Edmund Halley, 1656-1742, (Br.) astronomer, calculated the orbits of many planets.

William Harvey, 1578-1657, (Br.) physician, anatomist, discovered circulation of the blood.

Hermann v. Helmholtz, 1821-1894, (G.) physicist, anatomist, physiologist, made fundamental contributions to physiology, optics, electrodynamics, mathematics, meteorology.

William Herschel, 1738-1822, (Br.) astronomer, discovered Uranus.

Heinrich Hertz, 1857-1894, (G.) physicist, his discoveries led to wireless telegraphy.

David Hilbert, 1862-1943, (G.) mathematician, formulated first satisfactory set of axioms for modern Euclidean geometry.

Edwin P. Hubble, 1889-1953, (U.S.) astronomer, produced first observational evidence of expanding universe.

Alexander v. Humboldt, 1769-1859, (G.) explorer, naturalist, propagator of earth sciences, originated ecology, geophysics.

Julian Huxley, 1887-1975, (Br.) biologist, a gifted exponent and philosopher of science.

Edward Jenner, 1749-1823, (Br.) physician, discovered vaccination.

William Jenner, 1815-1898, (Br.) physician, pathological anatomist.

Frederic Joliot-Curie, 1900-1958, (F.) physicist, with his wife continued work of Curies on radioactivity.

Irene Joliot-Curie, 1897-1956, (F.) physicist, continued work of Curies in radioactivity.

James P. Joule, 1818-1889, (Br.) physicist, determined relationship between heat and mechanical energy (conservation of energy).

Carl Jung, 1875-1961, (Sw.) psychiatrist, founder of analytical psychology.

Wm. Thomson Kelvin, 1824-1907, (Br.) mathematician, physicist, known for work on heat and electricity.

Sister Elizabeth Kenny, 1886-1952, (Austral.) nurse, developed method of treatment for polio.

Johannes Kepler, 1571-1630, (G.) astronomer, discovered important laws of planetary motion.

Joseph Lagrange, 1736-1813, (F.) geometer, astronomer, worked in all fields of analysis, and number theory, and analytical and celestial mechanics.

Jean B. Lamarck, 1744-1829, (F.) naturalist, forerunner of Darwin in evolutionary theory.

Irving Langmuir, 1881-1957, (U.S.) physical chemist, his studies of molecular films on solid and liquid surfaces opened new fields in colloid research and biochemistry.

Pierre S. Laplace, 1749-1827, (F.) astronomer, physicist, put forth nebular hypothesis of origin of solar system.

Antoine Lavoisier, 1743-1794, (F.) chemist, founder of modern chemistry.

Ernest O. Lawrence, 1901-1958, (U.S.) physicist, invented the cyclotron.

Louis Leakey, 1903-1972, (Br.) anthropologist, discovered important fossils, remains of early hominids.

Anton van Leeuwenhoek, 1632-1723, (Du.) microscopist, father of microbiology.

Gottfried Wilhelm Leibniz, 1646-1716, (G.) mathematician, developed theories of differential and integral calculus.

Justus von Liebig, 1803-1873, (G.) chemist, established quantitative organic chemical analysis.

Joseph Lister, 1827-1912, (Br.) pioneer of antiseptic surgery.

Percival Lowell, 1855-1916, (U.S.) astronomer, predicted the existence of Pluto.

Guglielmo Marconi, 1874-1937, (It.) physicist, known for his development of wireless telegraphy.

James Clerk Maxwell, 1831-1879, (Sc.) physicist, known especially for his work in electricity and magnetism.

Maria Goeppert Mayer, 1906-1972, (G.-U.S.) physicist, independently developed theory of structure of atomic nuclei.

Lise Meitner, 1878-1968, (Aus.) physicist whose work contributed to the development of the atomic bomb.

Gregor J. Mendel, 1822-1884, (Aus.) botanist, known for his experimental work on heredity.

Franz Mesmer, 1734-1815, (G.) physician, developed theory of animal magnetism.

Albert A. Michelson, 1852-1931, (U.S.) physicist, established speed of light as a fundamental constant.

Robert A. Millikan, 1868-1953, (U.S.) physicist, noted for study of elementary electronic charge and photoelectric effect.

Thomas Hunt Morgan, 1866-1945, (U.S.) geneticist, embryologist, established chromosome theory of heredity.

Isaac Newton, 1642-1727, (Br.) natural philosopher, mathematician, discovered law of gravitation, laws of motion.

J. Robert Oppenheimer, 1904-1967, (U.S.) physicist, director of Los Alamos during development of the atomic bomb.

Wilhelm Ostwald, 1853-1932, (G.) physical chemist, philosopher, chief founder of physical chemistry.

Louis Pasteur, 1822-1895, (F.) chemist, originated process of pasteurization.

Max Planck, 1858-1947, (G.) physicist, originated and developed quantum theory.

Henri Poincaré, 1854-1912, (F.) mathematician, physicist, influenced cosmology, relativity, and topology.

Joseph Priestley, 1733-1804, (Br.) chemist, one of the discoverers of oxygen.

Rabi, Isidor Isaac, 1899-1988 (U.S.) physicist, pioneered atom exploration.

Walter S. Reed, 1851-1902, (U.S.) army pathologist, bacteriologist, proved mosquitos transmit yellow fever.

Bernhard Riemann, 1826-1866, (G.) mathematician, contributed to development of calculus, complex variable theory, and mathematical physics.

Wilhelm Roentgen, 1845-1923, (G.) physicist, discovered X-rays.

Bertrand Russell, 1872-1970, (Br.) logician, philosopher, one of the founders of modern logic, wrote *Principia Mathematica.*

Ernest Rutherford, 1871-1937, (Br.) physicist, discovered the atomic nucleus.

Giovanni Schiaparelli, 1835-1910, (It.) astronomer, hypothesized canals on the surface of Mars.

Angelo Secchi, 1818-1878, (It.) astronomer, pioneer in classifying stars by their spectra.

Harlow Shapley, 1885-1972, (U.S.) astronomer, noted for his studies of the galaxy.

Charles P. Steinmetz, 1865-1923, (G.-U.S.) electrical engineer, developed basic ideas on alternating current systems.

Leo Szilard, 1898-1964, (Hung.-U.S.) physicist, helped create first sustained nuclear reaction.

Nikola Tesla, 1856-1943, (Croatia-U.S.) electrical engineer, contributed to most developments in electronics.

Rudolf Virchow, 1821-1902, (G.) pathologist, a founder of cellular pathology.

Alessandro Volta, 1745-1827, (It.) physicist, pioneer in electricity.

Alfred Russell Wallace, 1823-1913, (Br.) naturalist, proposed concept of evolution similar to Darwin.

August v. Wasserman, 1866-1925, (G.) bacteriologist, discovered reaction used as test for syphilis.

James E. Watt, 1736-1819, (Sc.) mechanical engineer, inventor, invented modern steam condensing engine.

Alfred L. Wegener, 1880-1930, (G.) meteorologist, geophysicist, postulated theory of continental drift.

Norbert Wiener, 1894-1964, (U.S.) mathematician, founder of the science of cybernetics.

Sewall Wright, 1890-1988 (U.S.) a leading evolutionary theorist.

Ferdinand v. Zeppelin, 1838-1917 (G.) soldier, aeronaut, airship designer.

Noted Business Leaders, Industrialists, and Philanthropists of the Past

Elizabeth Arden (F.N. Graham), 1884-1966, (U.S.) Canadian-born businesswoman founded and headed cosmetics empire.

Philip D. Armour, 1832-1901, (U.S.) industrialist, streamlined meat packing.

John Jacob Astor, 1763-1848, (U.S.) German-born fur trader, banker, real estate magnate; at death, richest in U.S.

Francis W. Ayer, 1848-1923, (U.S.) ad industry pioneer.

August Belmont, 1816-1890, (U.S.) German-born financier.

James B. (Diamond Jim) Brady, 1856-1917, (U.S.) financier, philanthropist, legendary bon vivant.

Adolphus Busch, 1839-1913, (U.S.) German-born businessman, established brewery empire.

Asa Candler, 1851-1929, (U.S.) founded Coca-Cola Co.

Andrew Carnegie, 1835-1919, (U.S.) Scots-born industrialist, founded U.S. Steel; financed over 2,800 libraries.

William Colgate, 1783-1857, (U.S.) British-born businessman, philanthropist; founded soap-making empire.

Jay Cooke, 1821-1905, (U.S.) financier, sold $1 billion in Union bonds during Civil War.

Peter Cooper, 1791-1883, (U.S.) industrialist, inventor, philanthropist.

Ezra Cornell, 1807-1874, (U.S.) businessman, philanthropist; headed Western Union, established univ.

Erastus Corning, 1794-1872, (U.S.) financier, headed N.Y. Central.

Charles Crocker, 1822-1888, (U.S.) railroad builder, financier.

Samuel Cunard, 1787-1865, (Can.) pioneered trans-Atlantic steam navigation.

Marcus Daly, 1841-1900, (U.S.) Irish-born copper magnate.

Walt Disney, 1901-1966, (U.S.) pioneer in cinema animation, built entertainment empire.

Herbert H. Dow, 1866-1930, (U.S.) Canadian-born founder of chemical co.

James Duke, 1856-1925, (U.S.) founded American Tobacco, Duke Univ.

Eleuthere I. du Pont, 1771-1834, (U.S.) French-born gunpowder manufacturer; founded one of world's largest business empires.

Thomas C. Durant, 1820-1885, (U.S.) railroad official, financier.

William C. Durant, 1861-1947, (U.S.) industrialist, formed General Motors.

George Eastman, 1854-1932, (U.S.) inventor, manufacturer of photographic equipment.

Marshall Field, 1834-1906, (U.S.) merchant, founded Chicago's largest department store.

Harvey Firestone, 1868-1938, (U.S.) industrialist, founded tire co.

Henry M. Flagler, 1830-1913, (U.S.) financier, helped form Standard Oil; developed Florida as resort state.

Henry Ford, 1863-1947, (U.S.) auto maker, developed first popular low-priced car.

Henry Ford 2d, 1917-1987, (U.S.) headed auto company founded by grandfather.

Henry C. Frick, 1849-1919, (U.S.) industrialist, helped organize U.S. Steel.

Jakob Fugger (Jakob the Rich), 1459-1525, (G.) headed leading banking house, trading concern, in 16th-century Europe.

Alfred C. Fuller, 1885-1973, (U.S.) Canadian-born businessman, founded brush co.

Elbert H. Gary, 1846-1927, (U.S.) U.S. Steel head, 1903-27.

Amadeo P. Giannini, 1870-1949, (U.S.) founded Bank of America.

Stephen Girard, 1750-1831, (U.S.) French-born financier, philanthropist; richest man in U.S. at his death.

Jean Paul Getty, 1892-1976, (U.S.) founded oil empire.

Jay Gould, 1836-1892, (U.S.) railroad magnate, financier, speculator.

Hetty Green, 1834-1916, (U.S.) financier, the "witch of Wall St."; richest woman in U.S in her day.

William Gregg, 1800-1867, (U.S.) launched textile industry in the South.

Meyer Guggenheim, 1828-1905, (U.S.) Swiss-born merchant, philanthropist; built merchandising, mining empires.

Edward H. Harriman, 1848-1909, (U.S.) railroad financier, administrator; headed Union Pacific.

William Randolph Hearst, 1863-1951, (U.S.) a dominant figure in American journalism; built vast publishing empire.

Henry J. Heinz, 1844-1919, (U.S.) founded food empire.

James J. Hill, 1838-1916, (U.S.) Canadian-born railroad magnate, financier; founded Great Northern Railway.

Conrad N. Hilton, 1888-1979, (U.S.) intl. hotel chain founder.

Howard Hughes, 1905-1976, (U.S.) industrialist, financier, movie maker.

H.L. Hunt, 1889-1974, (U.S.) oil magnate.

Collis P. Huntington, 1821-1900, (U.S.) railroad magnate.

Henry E. Huntington, 1850-1927, (U.S.) railroad builder, philanthropist.

Walter L. Jacobs, 1898-1985, (U.S.) founder of the first rental car agency, which later became Hertz.

Howard Johnson, 1896-1972, (U.S.) founded restaurant chain.

Henry J. Kaiser, 1882-1967, (U.S.) industrialist, built empire in steel, aluminum.

Minor C. Keith, 1848-1929, (U.S.) railroad magnate; founded United Fruit Co.

Will K. Kellogg, 1860-1951, (U.S.) businessman, philanthropist, founded breakfast food co.

Richard King, 1825-1885, (U.S.) cattleman, founded half-million acre King Ranch in Texas.

William S. Knudsen, 1879-1948, (U.S.) Danish-born auto industry executive.

Samuel H. Kress, 1863-1955, (U.S.) businessman, art collector, philanthropist; founded "dime store" chain.

Ray A. Kroc, 1902-1984, (U.S.) builder of McDonald's fast food empire; owner, San Diego Padres baseball team.

Alfred Krupp, 1812-1887, (G.) armaments magnate.

Albert Lasker, 1880-1952, (U.S.) businessman, philanthropist.

Thomas Lipton, 1850-1931, (Ir.) merchant, built tea empire.

James McGill, 1744-1813, (Can.) Scots-born fur trader, founded univ.

Andrew W. Mellon, 1855-1937, (U.S.) financier, industrialist; benefactor of National Gallery of Art.

Charles E. Merrill, 1885-1956, (U.S.) financier, developed firm of Merrill Lynch.

John Pierpont Morgan, 1837-1913, (U.S.) most powerful figure in finance and industry at the turn-of-the-century.

Malcolm Muir, 1885-1979, (U.S.) created *Business Week* magazine; headed *Newsweek*, 1937-61.

Samuel Newhouse, 1895-1979, (U.S.) publishing and broadcasting magnate, built communications empire.

Aristotle Onassis, 1900-1975, (Gr.) shipping magnate.

George Peabody, 1795-1869, (U.S.) merchant, financier, philanthropist.

James C. Penney, 1875-1971, (U.S.) businessman, developed department store chain.

William C. Procter, 1862-1934, (U.S.) headed soap co.

John D. Rockefeller, 1839-1937, (U.S.) industrialist, established Standard Oil; became world's wealthiest person.

John D. Rockefeller Jr., 1874-1960, (U.S.) philanthropist, established foundation; provided land for United Nations.

Meyer A. Rothschild, 1743-1812, (G.) founded international banking house.

Thomas Fortune Ryan, 1851-1928, (U.S.) financier, dominated N.Y. City public transportation; helped found American Tobacco.

Russell Sage, 1816-1906, (U.S.) financier.

David Sarnoff, 1891-1971, (U.S.) broadcasting pioneer, established first radio network, NBC.

Richard W. Sears, 1863-1914, (U.S.) founded mail-order co.

(Ernst) Werner von Siemens, 1816-1892, (G.) industrialist, inventor.

Alfred P. Sloan, 1875-1966, (U.S.) industrialist, philanthropist; headed General Motors.

A. Leland Stanford, 1824-1893, (U.S.) railroad official, philanthropist; founded univ.

Nathan Strauss, 1848-1931, (U.S.) German-born merchant, philanthropist; headed Macy's.

Levi Strauss, c.1829-1902, (U.S.) pants manufacturer.

Clement Studebaker, 1831-1901, (U.S.) wagon, carriage manufacturer.

Gustavus Swift, 1839-1903, (U.S.) pioneer meat-packer; promoted refrigerated railroad cars.

Gerard Swope, 1872-1957, (U.S.) industrialist, economist; headed General Electric.

James Walter Thompson, 1847-1928, (U.S.) ad executive.

Theodore N. Vail, 1845-1920, (U.S.) organized Bell Telephone system, headed ATT.

Cornelius Vanderbilt, 1794-1877, (U.S.) financier, established steamship, railroad empires.

Henry Villard, 1835-1900, (U.S.) German-born railroad executive, financier.

Charles R. Walgreen, 1873-1939, (U.S.) founded drugstore chain.

DeWitt Wallace, 1890-1981, (U.S.) and **Lila Wallace,** 1890-1984, (U.S.) co-founders of *Reader's Digest* magazine, philanthropists.

John Wanamaker, 1838-1922, (U.S.) pioneered department-store merchandising.

Aaron Montgomery Ward, 1843-1913, (U.S.) established first mail-order firm.

Thomas J. Watson, 1874-1956, (U.S.) headed IBM, 1924-49.

John Hay Whitney, 1905-1982, (U.S.) publisher, sportsman, philanthropist.

Charles E. Wilson, 1890-1961, (U.S.) auto industry executive; public official.

Frank W. Woolworth, 1852-1919, (U.S.) created 5 & 10 chain.

William Wrigley Jr., 1861-1932, (U.S.) founded chewing gum co.

Composers of the Western World

Carl Philipp Emanuel Bach, 1714-1788, (G.) Prussian and Wurtembergian Sonatas.

Johann Christian Bach, 1735-1782, (G.) Concertos; sonatas.

Johann Sebastian Bach, 1685-1750, (G.) St. Matthew Passion, The Well-Tempered Clavichord.

Samuel Barber, 1910-1981, (U.S.) Adagio for Strings, Vanessa.

Bela Bartok, 1881-1945, (Hung.) Concerto for Orchestra, The Miraculous Mandarin.

Ludwig Van Beethoven, 1770-1827, (G.) Concertos (Emperor); sonatas (Moonlight, Pastorale, Pathetique); symphonies (Eroica).

Vincenzo Bellini, 1801-1835, (It.) La Sonnambula, Norma, I Puritani.

Alban Berg, 1885-1935, (Aus.) Wozzeck, Lulu.

Hector Berlioz, 1803-1869, (F.) Damnation of Faust, Symphonie Fantastique, Requiem.

Leonard Bernstein, b. 1918, (U.S.) Jeremiah, West Side Story.

Georges Bizet, 1838-1875, (F.) Carmen, Pearl Fishers.

Ernest Bloch, 1880-1959, (Swiss) Schelomo, Voice in the Wilderness, Sacred Service.

Luigi Boccherini, 1743-1805, (It.) Cello Concerto in B Flat, Symphony in C.

Alexander Borodin, 1833-1887, (R.) Prince Igor, In the Steppes of Central Asia.

Johannes Brahms, 1833-1897, (G.) Liebeslieder Waltzes, Rhapsody in E Flat Major, Opus 119 for Piano, Academic Festival Overture; symphonies; quartets.

Benjamin Britten, 1913-1976, (Br.) Peter Grimes, Turn of the Screw, Ceremony of Carols, War Requiem.

Anton Bruckner, 1824-1896, (Aus.) Symphonies (Romantic), Intermezzo for String Quintet.

Ferruccio Busoni, 1866-1924, (It.) Doctor Faust, Comedy Overture.

Dietrich Buxtehude, 1637-1707, (D.) Cantatas, trio sonatas.

William Byrd, 1543-1623, (Br.) Masses, sacred songs.

(Alexis-) Emmanuel Chabrier, 1841-1894, (Fr.) Le Roi Malgre Lui, Espana.

Gustave Charpentier, 1860-1956, (Fr.) Louise.

Frederic Chopin, 1810-1849, (P.) Polonaises, mazurkas, waltzes, etudes, nocturnes. Polonaise No. 6 in A Flat Major (Heroic); sonatas.

Aaron Copland, b. 1900, (U.S.) Appalachian Spring.

(Achille-) Claude Debussy, 1862-1918, (F.) Pelleas et Melisande, La Mer, Prelude to the Afternoon of a Faun.

C.P. Leo Delibes, 1836-1891, (F.) Lakme, Coppelia, Sylvia.

Norman Dello Joio, b. 1913, (U.S.) Triumph of St. Joan, Psalm of David.

Gaetano Donizetti, 1797-1848, (It.) Elixir of Love, Lucia Di Lammermoor, Daughter of the Regiment.

Paul Dukas, 1865-1935, (Fr.) Sorcerer's Apprentice.

Antonin Dvorak, 1841-1904, (C.) Symphony in E Minor (From the New World).

Edward Elgar, 1857-1934, (Br.) Pomp and Circumstance.

Manuel de Falla, 1876-1946, (Sp.) La Vide Breve, El Amor Brujo.

Gabriel Faure, 1845-1924, (Fr.) Requiem, Ballade.

Friedrich von Flotow, 1812-1883, (G.) Martha.

Cesar Franck, 1822-1890, (Belg.) D Minor Symphony.

George Gershwin, 1898-1937, (U.S.) Rhapsody in Blue, American in Paris, Porgy and Bess.

Umberto Giordano, 1867-1948, (It.) Andrea Chenier.

Alexander K. Glazunoff, 1865-1936, (R.) Symphonies, Stenka Razin.

Mikhail Glinka, 1804-1857, (R.) Ruslan and Ludmilla.

Christoph W. Gluck, 1714-1787, (G.) Alceste, Iphigenie en Tauride.

Charles Gounod, 1818-1893, (F.) Faust, Romeo and Juliet.

Edvard Grieg, 1843-1907, (Nor.) Peer Gynt Suite, Concerto in A Minor.

George Frederick Handel, 1685-1759, (G., Br.) Messiah, Xerxes, Berenice.

Howard Hanson, 1896-1981, (U.S.) Symphonies No. 1 (Nordic) and 2 (Romantic).

Roy Harris, 1898-1979, (U.S.) Symphonies, Amer. Portraits.

Joseph Haydn, 1732-1809, (Aus.) Symphonies (Clock); oratorios; chamber music.

Paul Hindemith, 1895-1963, (U.S.) Mathis Der Maler.

Gustav Holst, 1874-1934, (Br.) The Planets.

Arthur Honegger, 1892-1955, (Swiss) Judith, Le Roi David, Pacific 231.

Alan Hovhaness, b. 1911, (U.S.) Symphonies, Magnificat.

Engelbert Humperdinck, 1854-1921, (G.) Hansel and Gretel.

Charles Ives, 1874-1954, (U.S.) Third Symphony.

Aram Khachaturian, 1903-1978, (Armen.) Gayane (ballet), symphonies.

Zoltan Kodaly, 1882-1967, (Hung.) Hary Janos, Psalmus Hungaricus.

Fritz Kreisler, 1875-1962, (Aus.) Caprice Viennois, Tambourin Chinois.

Rodolphe Kreutzer, 1766-1831, (F.) 40 etudes for violin.

Edouard V.A. Lalo, 1823-1892, (F.) Symphonie Espagnole.

Ruggiero Leoncavallo, 1857-1919, (It.) Pagliacci.

Franz Liszt, 1811-1886, (Hung.) 20 Hungarian rhapsodies; symphonic poems.

Edward MacDowell, 1861-1908, (U.S.) To a Wild Rose.

Gustav Mahler, 1860-1911, (Aus.) Lied von der Erde.

Pietro Mascagni, 1863-1945, (It.) Cavalleria Rusticana.

Jules Massenet, 1842-1912, (F.) Manon, Le Cid, Thais.

Felix Mendelssohn, 1809-1847, (G.) Midsummer Night's Dream, Songs Without Words.

Gian-Carlo Menotti, b. 1911, (It.-U.S.) The Medium, The Consul, Amahl and the Night Visitors.

Giacomo Meyerbeer, 1791-1864, (G.) Robert le Diable, Les Huguenots.

Claudio Monteverdi, 1567-1643, (It.) Opera; masses; madrigals.

Wolfgang Amadeus Mozart, 1756-1791, (Aus.) Magic Flute, Marriage of Figaro; concertos; symphonies, etc.

Modest Moussorgsky, 1835-1881, (R.) Boris Godunov, Pictures at an Exhibition.

Jacques Offenbach, 1819-1880, (F.) Tales of Hoffmann.

Carl Orff, 1895-1982, (G.) Carmina Burana.

Ignace Paderewski, 1860-1941, (P.) Minuet in G.

Giovanni P. da Palestrina, c. 1525-1594, (It.) Masses; madrigals.

Amilcare Ponchielli, 1834-1886, (It.) La Gioconda.

Francis Poulenc, 1899-1963, (F.) Dialogues des Carmelites.

Serge Prokofiev, 1891-1953, (R.) Love for Three Oranges, Lt. Kije, Peter and the Wolf.

Giacomo Puccini, 1858-1924, (It.) La Boheme, Manon Lescaut, Tosca, Madame Butterfly.

Sergei Rachmaninov, 1873-1943, (R.) 24 preludes, E concerti, 4 symphonies. Prelude in C Sharp Minor.

Maurice Ravel, 1875-1937, (Fr.) Bolero, Daphnis et Chloe, Rapsodie Espagnole.

Nikolai Rimsky-Korsakov, 1844-1908, (R.) Golden Cockerel, Capriccio Espagnol, Scheherazade, Russian Easter Overture.

Gioacchino Rossini, 1792-1868, (It.) Barber of Seville, Semiramide, William Tell.

Chas. Camille Saint-Saens, 1835-1921, (F.) Samson and Delilah, Danse Macabre.

Alessandro Scarlatti, 1660-1725, (It.) Cantatas; concertos.

Domenico Scarlatti, 1685-1757, (It.) Harpsichord sonatas.

Arnold Schoenberg, 1874-1951, (Aus.) Pelleas and Melisande, Transfigured Night, De Profundis.

Franz Schubert, 1797-1828, (A.) Lieder; symphonies (Unfinished); overtures (Rosamunde).

William Schuman, b. 1910, (U.S.) Credendum, New England Triptych.

Robert Schumann, 1810-1856, (G.) Symphonies, songs.

Aleksandr Scriabin, 1872-1915, (R.) Prometheus.

Dimitri Shostakovich, 1906-1975, (R.) Symphonies, Lady Macbeth of Mzensk, The Nose.

Jean Sibelius, 1865-1957, (Finn.) Finlandia, Karelia.

Bedrich Smetana, 1824-1884, (Cz.) The Bartered Bride.

Karlheinz Stockhausen, b. 1928, (G.) Kontrapunkte, Kontakte.

Richard Strauss, 1864-1949, (G.) Salome, Elektra, Der Rosenkavalier, Thus Spake Zarathustra.

Igor F. Stravinsky, 1882-1971, (R.-U.S.) Oedipus Rex, Le Sacre du Printemps, Petrushka.

Peter I. Tchaikovsky, 1840-1893, (R.) Nutcracker Suite, Swan Lake, Eugene Onegin.

Ambroise Thomas, 1811-1896, (F.) Mignon.

Virgil Thomson, b. 1896, (U.S.) Opera, ballet; Four Saints in Three Acts.

Ralph Vaughan Williams, 1872-1958, (Br.) Job, London Symphony, Symphony No. 7 (Antartica).

Giuseppe Verdi, 1813-1901, (It.) Aida, Rigoletto, Don Carlo, Il Trovatore, La Traviata, Falstaff, Macbeth.

Heitor Villa-Lobos, 1887-1959, (Brazil) Choros.

Antonio Vivaldi, 1678-1741, (It.) Concerti, The Four Seasons.

Richard Wagner, 1813-1883, (G.) Rienzi, Tannhauser, Lohengrin, Tristan und Isolde.

Carl Maria von Weber, 1786-1826, (G.) Der Freischutz.

Composers of Operettas, Musicals, and Popular Music

Richard Adler, b. 1921, (U.S.) *Pajama Game; Damn Yankees.*

Milton Ager, 1893-1979, (U.S.) I Wonder What's Become of Sally; Hard Hearted Hannah; Ain't She Sweet?

Leroy Anderson, 1908-1975, (U.S.) Syncopated Clock.

Paul Anka, b. 1941, (Can.) My Way; She's a Lady; Tonight Show theme.

Harold Arlen, 1905-1986, (U.S.) Stormy Weather; Over the Rainbow; Blues in the Night; That Old Black Magic.

Burt Bacharach, b. 1928, (U.S.) Raindrops Keep Fallin' on My Head; Walk on By; What the World Needs Now is Love.

Ernest Ball, 1878-1927, (U.S.) Mother Machree; When Irish Eyes Are Smiling.

Irving Berlin, b. 1888, (U.S.) *This is the Army; Annie Get Your Gun; Call Me Madam;* God Bless America; White Christmas.

Leonard Bernstein, b. 1918, (U.S.) *On the Town; Wonderful Town; Candide; West Side Story.*

Eubie Blake, 1883-1983, (U.S.) *Shuffle Along;* I'm Just Wild about Harry.

Jerry Bock, b. 1928, (U.S.) *Mr. Wonderful; Fiorello; Fiddler on the Roof; The Rothschilds.*

Carrie Jacobs Bond, 1862-1946, (U.S.) I Love You Truly.

Nacio Herb Brown, 1896-1964, (U.S.) Singing in the Rain; You Were Meant for Me; All I Do Is Dream of You.

Hoagy Carmichael, 1899-1981, (U.S.) Stardust; Georgia on My Mind; Old Buttermilk Sky.

George M. Cohan, 1878-1942, (U.S.) Give My Regards to Broadway; You're A Grand Old Flag; Over There.

Cy Coleman, b. 1929, (U.S.) *Sweet Charity;* Witchcraft.

Noel Coward, 1899-1973 (Br.) *Bitter Sweet;* Mad Dogs and Englishmen; Mad About the Boy.

Walter Donaldson, 1893-1947, (U.S.) My Buddy; Carolina in the Morning; You're Driving Me Crazy; Makin' Whoopee.

Neil Diamond, b. 1941, (U.S.) I'm a Believer; Sweet Caroline.

Vernon Duke, 1903-1969, (U.S.) April in Paris.

Bob Dylan, b. 1941, (U.S.) Blowin' in the Wind.

Gus Edwards, 1879-1945, (U.S.) School Days; By the Light of the Silvery Moon; In My Merry Oldsmobile.

Sherman Edwards, 1919-1981, (U.S.) See You in September; Wonderful! Wonderful!

Duke Ellington, 1899-1974, (U.S.) Sophisticated Lady; Satin Doll; It Don't Mean a Thing; Solitude.

Sammy Fain, b. 1902, I'll Be Seeing You; Love Is a Many-Splendored Thing.

Fred Fisher, 1875-1942, (U.S.) Peg O' My Heart; Chicago.

Stephen Collins Foster, 1826-1864, (U.S.) My Old Kentucky Home; Old Folks At Home.

Rudolf Friml, 1879-1972, (naturalized U.S.) *The Firefly; Rose Marie; Vagabond King; Bird of Paradise.*

John Gay, 1685-1732, (Br.) *The Beggar's Opera.*

George Gershwin, 1898-1937, (U.S.) Someone to Watch Over Me; I've Got a Crush on You; Embraceable You.

Ferde Grofe, 1892-1972, (U.S.) Grand Canyon Suite.

W. C. Handy, 1873-1958, (U.S.) St. Louis Blues.

Ray Henderson, 1896-1970, (U.S.) *George White's Scandals;* That Old Gang of Mine; Five Foot Two, Eyes of Blue.

Victor Herbert, 1859-1924, (Ir.-U.S.) *Mlle. Modiste; Babes in Toyland; The Red Mill; Naughty Marietta; Sweethearts.*

Jerry Herman, b. 1932, (U.S.) *Hello Dolly; Mame.*

Brian Holland, b. 1941, **Lamont Dozier,** b. 1941, **Eddie Holland,** b. 1939, (all U.S.) Heat Wave; Stop! In the Name of Love; Baby, I Need Your Loving.

Scott Joplin, 1868-1917, (U.S.) *Treemonisha.*

John Kander, b. 1927, (U.S.) *Cabaret; Chicago; Funny Lady.*

Jerome Kern, 1885-1945, (U.S.) *Sally; Sunny; Show Boat.*

Carole King, b. 1942, (U.S.) Will You Love Me Tomorrow?; Natural Woman; One Fine Day; Up on the Roof.

Burton Lane, b. 1912, (U.S.) *Finian's Rainbow.*

Franz Lehar, 1870-1948, (Hung.) *Merry Widow.*

Jerry Leiber & **Mike Stoller,** both b. 1933, (both U.S.) Hound Dog; Searchin'; Yakety Yak; Love Me Tender.

Mitch Leigh, b. 1928, (U.S.) *Man of La Mancha.*

John Lennon, 1940-1980, & **Paul McCartney,** b. 1942, (both Br.) I Want to Hold Your Hand; She Loves You; Hard Day's Night; Can't Buy Me Love; And I Love Her.

Frank Loesser, 1910-1969, (U.S.) *Guys and Dolls; Where's Charley?; The Most Happy Fella; How to Succeed . . . .*

Frederick Loewe, b. 1901, (Aust.-U.S.) *The Day Before Spring; Brigadoon; Paint Your Wagon; My Fair Lady; Camelot.*

Henry Mancini, b. 1924, (U.S.) Moon River; Days of Wine and Roses; Pink Panther Theme.

Barry Mann, b. 1939, & **Cynthia Weil,** b. 1937, (both U.S.) You've Lost That Loving Feeling, Saturday Night at the Movies.

Jimmy McHugh, 1894-1969 (U.S.) Don't Blame Me; I'm in the Mood for Love; I Feel a Song Coming On.

Joseph Meyer, 1894-1987, (U.S.) If You Knew Susie; California, Here I Come; Crazy Rhythm.

Chauncey Olcott, 1860-1932, (U.S.) Mother Machree.

Cole Porter, 1893-1964, (U.S.) *Anything Goes; Kiss Me Kate; Can Can; Silk Stockings.*

Richard Rodgers, 1902-1979, (U.S.) *Connecticut Yankee; Oklahoma!; Carousel; South Pacific; The King and I; The Sound of Music.*

Smokey Robinson, b. 1940, (U.S.) Shop Around; My Guy; My Girl; Get Ready.

Sigmund Romberg, 1887-1951, (Hung.) *Maytime; The Student Prince; Desert Song; Blossom Time.*

Harold Rome, b. 1908, (U.S.) *Pins and Needles; Call Me Mister; Wish You Were Here; Fanny; Destry Rides Again.*

Vincent Rose, b. 1880-1944, (U.S.) Avalon; Whispering; Blueberry Hill.

Harry Ruby, 1895-1974, (U.S.) Three Little Words; Who's Sorry Now?

Arthur Schwartz, 1900-1984, (U.S.) *The Band Wagon;* Dancing in the Dark; By Myself; That's Entertainment.

Neil Sedaka, b. 1939, (U.S.) Breaking Up Is Hard to Do.

Paul Simon, b. 1942, (U.S.) Sounds of Silence; I Am a Rock; Mrs. Robinson; Bridge Over Troubled Waters.

Stephen Sondheim, b. 1930, (U.S.) *A Little Night Music; Company; Sweeney Todd; Sunday in the Park with George.*

John Philip Sousa. 1854-1932, (U.S.) *El Capitan;* Stars and Stripes Forever.

Oskar Straus, 1870-1954, (Aus.) *Chocolate Soldier.*

Johann Strauss, 1825-1899, (Aus.) *Gypsy Baron; Die Fledermaus;* waltzes: Blue Danube, Artist's Life.

Charles Strouse, b. 1928, (U.S.) *Bye Bye, Birdie; Annie.*

Jule Styne, b. 1905, (b. Br.-U.S.) *Gentlemen Prefer Blondes; Bells Are Ringing; Gypsy; Funny Girl.*

Arthur S. Sullivan, 1842-1900, (Br.) *H.M.S. Pinafore, Pirates of Penzance; The Mikado.*

Deems Taylor, 1885-1966, (U.S.) *Peter Ibbetson.*

Egbert van Alstyne, 1882-1951, (U.S.) In the Shade of the Old Apple Tree; Memories; Pretty Baby.

James Van Heusen, b. 1913, (U.S.) Moonlight Becomes You; Swinging on a Star; All the Way; Love and Marriage.

Albert von Tilzer, 1878-1956, (U.S.) I'll Be With You in Apple Blossom Time; Take Me Out to the Ball Game.

Harry von Tilzer, 1872-1946, (U.S.) Only a Bird in a Gilded Cage; On a Sunday Afternoon.

Fats Waller, 1904-1943, (U.S.) Honeysuckle Rose; Ain't Misbehavin'.

Harry Warren, 1893-1981, (U.S.) You're My Everything; We're in the Money; I Only Have Eyes for You.

Jimmy Webb, b. 1946, (U.S.) Up, Up and Away; By the Time I Get to Phoenix; Didn't We?; Wichita Lineman.

Kurt Weill, 1900-1950, (G.-U.S.) *Threepenny Opera; Lady in the Dark; Knickerbocker Holiday; One Touch of Venus.*

Percy Wenrich, 1887-1952, (U.S.) When You Wore a Tulip; Moonlight Bay; Put On Your Old Gray Bonnet.

Richard A. Whiting, 1891-1938, (U.S.) Till We Meet Again; Sleepytime Gal; Beyond the Blue Horizon; My Ideal.

Meredith Willson, 1902-1984, (U.S.) *The Music Man.*

Stevie Wonder, b. 1950, (U.S.) You Are the Sunshine of My Life; Signed, Sealed, Delivered, I'm Yours.

Vincent Youmans, 1898-1946, (U.S.) *Two Little Girls in Blue; Wildflower; No, No, Nanette; Hit the Deck; Rainbow; Smiles.*

Lyricists

Johnny Burke, 1908-1984, (U.S.) What's New?; Misty; Imagination; Polka Dots and Moonbeams.

Sammy Cahn, b. 1913, (U.S.) High Hopes; Love and Marriage; The Second Time Around; It's Magic.

Betty Comden, b. 1919 (U.S.) and **Adolph Green,** b. 1915 (U.S.) The Party's Over; Just in Time; New York, New York.

Hal David, b. 1921 (U.S.) What the World Needs Now Is Love; Close to You.

Buddy De Sylva, 1895-1950, (U.S.) When Day is Done; Look for the Silver Lining; April Showers.

Howard Dietz, 1896-1983, (U.S.) Dancing in the Dark; You and the Night and the Music; That's Entertainment.

Al Dubin, 1891-1945, (U.S.) Tiptoe Through the Tulips; Anniversary Waltz; Lullaby of Broadway.

Fred Ebb, b. 1936 (U.S.) *Cabaret, Zorba, Woman of the Year.*

Dorothy Fields, 1905-1974, (U.S.) On the Sunny Side of the Street; Don't Blame Me; The Way You Look Tonight.

Ira Gershwin, 1896-1983, (U.S.) The Man I Love; Fascinating Rhythm; S'Wonderful; Embraceable You.

Wm. S. Gilbert, 1836-1911, (Br.) *The Mikado; H.M.S. Pinafore, Pirates of Penzance.*

Mack Gordon, 1905-1959, (Pol.-U.S.) You'll Never Know; The More I See You; Chattanooga Choo-Choo; You Make Me Feel So Young.

Oscar Hammerstein II, 1895-1960, (U.S.) *Ol' Man River; Oklahoma; Carousel.*

E. Y. (Yip) Harburg, 1898-1981, (U.S.) Brother, Can You Spare a Dime; April in Paris; Over the Rainbow.

Lorenz Hart, 1895-1943, (U.S.) Isn't It Romantic; Blue Moon; Lover; Manhattan; My Funny Valentine; Mountain Greenery.

DuBose Heyward, 1885-1940, (U.S.) Summertime; A Woman Is A Sometime Thing.

Gus Kahn, 1886-1941, (U.S.) Memories; Ain't We Got Fun.

Alan J. Lerner, 1918-1986, (U.S.) *Brigadoon; My Fair Lady; Camelot; Gigi; On a Clear Day You Can See Forever.*

Johnny Mercer, 1909-1976, (U.S.) Blues in the Night; Come Rain or Come Shine; Laura; That Old Black Magic.

Bob Merrill, b. 1921, (U.S.) People; Don't Rain on My Parade.

Jack Norworth, 1879-1959, (U.S.) Take Me Out to the Ball Game; Shine On Harvest Moon.

Mitchell Parish, b. 1901, (U.S.) Stairway to the Stars; Stardust.

Andy Razaf, 1895-1973, (U.S.) Honeysuckle Rose, Ain't Misbehavin', S'posin'.

Leo Robin, 1900-1984, (U.S.) Thanks for the Memory; Hooray for Love; Diamonds are a Girl's Best Friend.

Jack Yellen, b. 1892, (U.S.) Down by the O-Hi-O; Ain't She Sweet; Happy Days Are Here Again.

Noted Jazz Artists

Jazz has been called America's only completely unique contribution to Western culture. The following individuals have made major contributions in this field:

Julian "Cannonball" Adderley, 1928-1975: alto sax.

Louis "Satchmo" Armstrong, 1900-1971: trumpet, singer; originated the "scat" vocal.

Mildred Bailey, 1907-1951: blues singer.

Chet Baker, 1929-1988: trumpet.

Count Basie, 1904-1984: orchestra leader, piano.

Sidney Bechet, 1897-1950: early innovator, soprano sax.

Bix Beiderbecke, 1903-1931: cornet, piano, composer.

Bunny Berrigan, 1909-1942: trumpet, singer.

Barney Bigard, 1906-1980: clarinet.

Art Blakey, b. 1919: drums, leader.

Jimmy Blanton, 1921-1942: bass.

Charles "Buddy" Bolden, 1868-1931: cornet; formed the first jazz band in the 1890s.

Big Bill Broonzy, 1893-1958: blues singer, guitar.

Clifford Brown, 1930-1956: trumpet.

Ray Brown, b. 1926: bass.
Dave Brubeck, b. 1920: piano, combo leader.
Don Byas, b. 1912: tenor sax.
Harry Carney, 1910-1974: baritone sax.
Benny Carter, b. 1907: alto sax, trumpet, clarinet.
Ron Carter, b. 1937: bass, cello.
Sidney Catlett, 1910-1951: drums.
Charlie Christian, 1919-1942: guitar.
Kenny Clarke, 1914-1985: pioneer of modern drums.
Buck Clayton, b. 1911: trumpet, arranger.
Al Cohn, 1925-1988: tenor sax, composer.
Cozy Cole, 1909-1981: drums.
Ornette Coleman, b. 1930: saxophone; unorthodox style.
John Coltrane, 1926-1967: tenor sax innovator.
Eddie Condon, 1904-1973: guitar, band leader; promoter of Dixieland.
Chick Corea, b. 1941: pianist, composer.
Tadd Dameron, 1917-1965: piano, composer.
Eddie "Lockjaw" Davis, 1921-1986: tenor sax.
Miles Davis, b. 1926: trumpet; pioneer of cool jazz.
Wild Bill Davison, b. 1906: cornet, leader; prominent in early Chicago jazz.
Buddy De Franco, b. 1933: clarinet.
Paul Desmond, 1924-1977: alto sax.
Vic Dickenson, 1906-1984: trombone, composer.
Warren "Baby" Dodds, 1898-1959: Dixieland drummer.
Johnny Dodds, 1892-1940: clarinet.
Eric Dolphy, 1928-1964: alto sax, composer.
Jimmy Dorsey, 1904-1957: clarinet, alto sax; band leader.
Tommy Dorsey, 1905-1956: trombone; band leader.
Roy Eldridge, 1911-1989: trumpet, drums, singer.
Duke Ellington, 1899-1974: piano, band leader, composer.
Bill Evans, 1929-1980: piano.
Gil Evans, 1912-1988: composer, arranger, piano.
Ella Fitzgerald, b. 1918: singer.
"Red" Garland, 1923-1984: piano.
Erroll Garner, 1921-1977: piano, composer, "Misty."
Stan Getz, b. 1927: tenor sax.
Dizzy Gillespie, b. 1917: trumpet, composer; bop developer.
Benny Goodman, 1909-1986: clarinet, band and combo leader.
Dexter Gordon, b. 1923: tenor sax; bop-derived style.
Stephane Grappelli, b. 1908: violin.
Bobby Hackett, 1915-1976: trumpet, cornet.
Lionel Hampton, b. 1913: vibes, drums, piano, combo leader.
Herbie Hancock, b. 1940: piano, composer.
W. C. Handy, 1873-1958: composer, "St. Louis Blues."
Coleman Hawkins, 1904-1969: tenor sax; 1939 recording of "Body and Soul", a classic.
Roy Haynes, b. 1926: drums.
Fletcher Henderson, 1898-1952: orchestra leader, arranger; pioneered jazz and dance bands of the 30s.
Woody Herman, 1913-87: clarinet, alto sax, band leader.
Jay C. Higginbotham, 1906-1973: trombone.
Earl "Fatha" Hines, 1905-1983: piano, songwriter.
Johnny Hodges, 1906-1971: alto sax.
Billie Holiday, 1915-1959: blues singer, "Strange Fruit."
Sam "Lightnin' " Hopkins, 1912-1982: blues singer, guitar.
Mahalia Jackson, 1911-1972: gospel singer.
Milt Jackson, b. 1923: vibes, piano, guitar.
Illinois Jacquet, b. 1922: tenor sax.
Keith Jarrett, b. 1945: technically phenomenal pianist.
Blind Lemon Jefferson, 1897-1930: blues singer, guitar.
Bunk Johnson, 1879-1949: cornet, trumpet.
James P. Johnson, 1891-1955: piano, composer.
J. J. Johnson, b. 1924: trombone, composer.
Elvin Jones, b. 1927: drums.
Jo Jones, 1911-1985: drums.
Philly Joe Jones, 1923-1985: drums.
Quincy Jones, b. 1933: arranger.
Thad Jones, 1923-1986: trumpet, cornet.
Scott Joplin, 1868-1917: composer; "Maple Leaf Rag."
Stan Kenton, 1912-1979: orchestra leader, composer, piano.
Barney Kessel, b. 1923: guitar.
Lee Konitz, b. 1927: alto sax.
Gene Krupa, 1909-1973: drums, band and combo leader.
Scott LaFaro, 1936-1961: bass.
Huddie Ledbetter (Leadbelly), 1888-1949: blues singer, guitar.
John Lewis, b. 1920: composer, piano, combo leader.

Jimmie Lunceford, 1902-1947: band leader, sax.
Herbie Mann, b. 1930: flute.
Wynton Marsalis, b. 1961: trumpet.
Jimmy McPartland, b. 1907: trumpet.
Marian McPartland, b. 1920: piano.
Glenn Miller, 1904-1944: trombone, dance band leader.
Charles Mingus, 1922-1979: bass, composer, combo leader.
Thelonious Monk, 1920-1982: piano, composer, combo leader; a developer of bop.
Wes Montgomery, 1925-1968: guitar.
"Jelly Roll" Morton, 1885-1941: composer, piano, singer.
Bennie Moten, 1894-1935: piano; an early organizer of large jazz orchestras.
Gerry Mulligan, b. 1927: baritone sax, arranger, leader.
Turk Murphy, 1915-1987: trombone, band leader.
Theodore "Fats" Navarro, 1923-1950: trumpet.
Red Nichols, 1905-1965: cornet, combo leader.
Red Norvo, b. 1908: vibes, band leader.
Anita O'Day, b. 1919: singer.
King Oliver, 1885-1938: cornet, band leader; teacher of Louis Armstrong.
Kid Ory, 1886-1973: trombone, "Muskrat Ramble".
Charlie "Bird" Parker, 1920-1955: alto sax, composer; rated by many as the greatest jazz improviser.
Art Pepper, 1925-1982: alto sax.
Oscar Peterson, b. 1925: piano, composer, combo leader.
Oscar Pettiford, 1922-1960: a leading bassist in the bop era.
Bud Powell, 1924-1966: piano; modern jazz pioneer.
Sun Ra, b. 1915?: big band leader, pianist, composer.
Gertrude "Ma" Rainey, 1886-1939: blues singer.
Don Redman, 1900-1964: composer, arranger; pioneer in the evolution of the large orchestra.
Django Reinhardt, 1910-1953: guitar; Belgian gypsy, first European to influence American jazz.
Buddy Rich, 1917-1987: drums, band leader.
Max Roach, b. 1925: drums.
Sonny Rollins, b. 1929: tenor sax.
Frank Rosolino, 1926-1978: trombone.
Jimmy Rushing, 1903-1972: blues singer.
George Russell, b. 1923: composer, piano.
Pee Wee Russell, 1906-1969: clarinet.
Artie Shaw, b. 1910: clarinet, combo leader.
George Shearing, b. 1919: piano, composer, "Lullaby of Birdland."
Horace Silver, b. 1928: piano, combo leader.
Zoot Sims, 1925-1985: tenor, alto sax; clarinet.
Zutty Singleton, 1898-1975: Dixieland drummer.
Bessie Smith, 1894-1937: blues singer.
Clarence "Pinetop" Smith, 1904-1929: piano, singer; pioneer of boogie woogie.
Willie "The Lion" Smith, 1897-1973: stride style pianist.
Muggsy Spanier, 1906-1967: cornet, band leader.
Billy Strayhorn, 1915-67: composer, piano.
Sonny Stitt, 1924-1982: alto, tenor sax.
Art Tatum, 1910-1956: piano; technical virtuoso.
Billy Taylor, b. 1921: piano, composer.
Cecil Taylor, b. 1933: piano, composer.
Jack Teagarden, 1905-1964: trombone, singer.
Dave Tough, 1908-1948: drums.
Lennie Tristano, 1919-1978: piano, composer.
Joe Turner, 1911-1985: blues singer.
McCoy Tyner, b. 1938: piano, composer.
Sarah Vaughan, b. 1924: singer.
Joe Venuti, 1904-1978: first great jazz violinist.
Thomas "Fats" Waller, 1904-1943: piano, singer, composer. "Ain't Misbehavin' ".
Dinah Washington, 1924-1963: singer.
Chick Webb, 1902-1939: band leader, drums.
Ben Webster, 1909-1973: tenor sax.
Paul Whiteman, 1890-1967: orchestra leader; a major figure in the introduction of jazz to a large audience.
Charles "Cootie" Williams, 1908-1985: trumpet, band leader.
Mary Lou Williams, 1914-1981: piano, composer.
Teddy Wilson, 1912-1986: piano, composer.
Kai Winding, 1922-1983: trombone, composer.
Jimmy Yancey, 1894-1951: piano.
Lester "Pres" Young, 1909-1959: tenor sax, composer; a bop pioneer.

Rock & Roll Notables

For more than a quarter of a century, rock & roll has been an important force in American popular culture. The following individuals or groups have made a significant impact. Next to each is an associated single record or record album.

Alabama: "Tennessee River"
The Allman Brothers Band: "Ramblin' Man"
The Animals: "House of the Rising Sun"

Paul Anka: "Lonely Boy"
The Association: "Cherish"
Frankie Avalon: "Venus"

The Band: "The Weight"
The Beach Boys: "Surfin' U.S.A."
The Beastie Boys: "(You've Got to) Fight for Your Right to Party"
The Beatles: "Hey Jude"
The Bee Gees: "Stayin' Alive"
Pat Benatar: "Hit Me With Your Best Shot"
Chuck Berry: "Johnny B. Goode"
The Big Bopper: "Chantilly Lace"
Black Sabbath: "Paranoid"
Blind Faith: "Can't Find My Way Home"
Blondie: "Heart of Glass"
Blood, Sweat and Tears: "Spinning Wheel"
Bon Jovi: Slippery When Wet
Gary "U.S." Bonds: "Quarter to Three"
Booker T. and the MGs: "Green Onions"
Earl Bostic: "Flamingo"
David Bowie: "Let's Dance"
James Brown: "Papa's Got a Brand New Bag"
Jackson Browne: "Doctor My Eyes"
Buffalo Springfield: "For What It's Worth"
The Byrds: "Turn! Turn! Turn!"
Canned Heat: "Going Up the Country"
The Cars: "Shake It Up"
Ray Charles: "Georgia on My Mind"
Chubby Checker: "The Twist"
Chicago: "Hard Habit to Break"
Eric Clapton: "Layla"
The Coasters: "Yakety Yak"
Eddie Cochran: "Summertime Blues"
Phil Collins: "Against All Odds"
Sam Cooke: "You Send Me"
Alice Cooper: "School's Out"
Elvis Costello: "Allison"
Cream: "Sunshine of Your Love"
Credence Clearwater Revival: "Proud Mary"
Crosby, Stills, Nash and Young: "Suite: Judy Blue Eyes"
The Crystals: "Da Doo Ron Ron"
Danny and the Juniors: "At the Hop"
Bobby Darin: "Splish Splash"
Spencer Davis Group: "Gimme Some Lovin' "
Bo Diddley: "Who Do You Love?"
Dion and the Belmonts: "A Teenager in Love"
Dire Straits: Brothers in Arms
Fats Domino: "Blueberry Hill"
The Doobie Brothers: "What a Fool Believes"
The Doors: "Light My Fire"
The Drifters: "Save the Last Dance for Me"
Duran Duran: "Hungry Like the Wolf"
Bob Dylan: "Like a Rolling Stone"
The Eagles: "Hotel California"
Earth, Wind and Fire: "Shining Star"
Emerson, Lake and Palmer: "From the Beginning"
The Eurythmics: "Sweet Dreams (Are Made of This)"
Everly Brothers: "Wake Up Little Susie"
Jose Feliciano: "Light My Fire"
The Five Satins: "In the Still of the Night"
Fleetwood Mac: Rumours
Dan Fogelberg: "Missing You"
The Four Seasons: "Sherry"
The Four Tops: "I Can't Help Myself"
Aretha Franklin: "Respect"
Marvin Gaye: "I Heard It through the Grapevine"
Genesis: "Land of Confusion"
The J. Geils Band: Freeze-Frame
Grand Funk Railroad: "We're an American Band"
The Grateful Dead: "Truckin' "
Bill Haley and the Comets: "Rock Around the Clock"
Hall and Oates: "Rich Girl"
Jimi Hendrix: Are You Experienced?
Buddy Holly and the Crickets: "That'll Be the Day"
Whitney Houston: "The Greatest Love"
Janis Ian: "At Seventeen"
The Isley Brothers: "It's Your Thing"
The Jackson 5/The Jacksons: "ABC"
Janet Jackson: "Control"
Michael Jackson: "Beat It"
Jay and the Americans: "This Magic Moment"
The Jefferson Airplane/Jefferson Starship: "White Rabbit"
Jethro Tull: Aqualung
Joan Jett: "I Love Rock 'n' Roll"
Billy Joel: "Uptown Girl"
Elton John: "Sad Songs"
Janis Joplin: "Me and Bobby McGee"
Chaka Khan: "I Feel for You"
B.B. King: "The Thrill Is Gone"
Carole King: Tapestry
The Kinks: "You Really Got Me"
Kiss: "Rock' n' Roll All Night"

Gladys Knight and the Pips: "Midnight Train to Georgia"
Cyndi Lauper: "Girls Just Want to Have Fun"
Led Zeppelin: "Stairway to Heaven"
Brenda Lee: "I'm Sorry"
Huey Lewis and the News: Sports
Jerry Lee Lewis: "Whole Lotta Shakin' Going On"
Little Anthony and the Imperials: "Tears on My Pillow"
Little Richard: "Tutti Frutti"
Lovin Spoonful: "Do You Believe in Magic?"
Frankie Lymon: "Why Do Fools Fall in Love?"
Lynyrd Skynyrd: "Freebird"
Madonna: "Material Girl"
The Mamas and the Papas: "Monday, Monday"
Bob Marley: "Jamming"
Martha and the Vandellas: "Dancin' in the Streets"
The Marvelettes: "Please Mr. Postman"
Clyde McPhatter: "Money Honey"
John Cougar Mellencamp: "Hurt So Good"
George Michael: "I Want Your Sex"
Steve Miller Band: "Abracadabra"
Joni Mitchell: "Big Yellow Taxi"
The Monkees: "I'm a Believer"
Moody Blues: "Nights in White Satin"
Rick Nelson: "Hello Mary Lou"
Roy Orbison: "Oh Pretty Woman"
Ozzy Osbourne: "You Can't Kill Rock 'n' Roll"
Carl Perkins: "Blue Suede Shoes"
Tom Petty and the Heartbreakers: "Refugee"
Pink Floyd: Dark Side of the Moon
Poco: Deliverin'
The Police: "Every Breath You Take"
Iggy Pop: "Lust for Life"
Elvis Presley: "Love Me Tender"
The Pretenders: Learning to Crawl
Lloyd Price: "Stagger Lee"
Prince: "Purple Rain"
Procul Harum: "A Whiter Shade of Pale"
Gary Puckett and the Union Gap: "Young Girl"
Queen: "Bohemian Rhapsody"
The Rascals: "Good Lovin' "
Otis Redding: "The Dock of the Bay"
Lou Reed: "Walk on the Wild Side"
REO Speedwagon: "Keep on Lovin' You"
Righteous Brothers: "You've Lost that Lovin' Feeling"
Johnny Rivers: "Poor Side of Town"
Smokey Robinson and the Miracles: "Ooh Baby Baby"
The Rolling Stones: "Satisfaction"
The Ronettes: "Be My Baby"
Linda Ronstadt: "You're No Good"
Run D.M.C.: "Raisin' Hell"
Sam and Dave: "Soul Man"
Santana: "Black Magic Woman"
Neil Sedaka: "Breaking Up is Hard to Do"
Bob Seger: "Old Time Rock and Roll"
Del Shannon: "Runaway"
The Shirelles: "Soldier Boy"
Simon and Garfunkel: "Bridge Over Troubled Water"
Carly Simon: "You're So Vain"
Sly and the Family Stone: "Everyday People"
Patti Smith: "Because the Night"
Southside Johnny and the Asbury Jukes: This Time
Dusty Springfield: "You Don't Have to Say You Love Me"
Bruce Springsteen: "Born in the U.S.A."
Steely Dan: "Rikki Don't Lose That Number"
Steppenwolf: "Born to Be Wild"
Cat Stevens: "Wild World"
Rod Stewart: "Maggie Mae"
Sting: "If You Love Somebody, Set Them Free"
Donna Summer: "Bad Girls"
The Supremes: "Stop! In the Name of Love"
Talking Heads: "Wild Wild Life"
James Taylor: "You've Got a Friend"
The Temptations: "My Girl"
Three Dog Night: "Joy to the World"
Traffic: "Feelin' Alright"
Big Joe Turner: "Shake, Rattle & Roll"
Tina Turner: "What's Love Got to Do with It?"
U2: "With or Without You"
Van Halen: "Jump"
Dionne Warwick: "I'll Never Fall in Love Again"
Muddy Waters: "Rollin' Stone' "
Mary Wells: "My Guy"
The Who: "My Generation"
Jackie Wilson: "That's Why"
Stevie Wonder: "You Are the Sunshine of My Life"
The Yardbirds: "For Your Love"
Yes: "Owner of a Lonely Heart"
Frank Zappa/Mothers of Invention: Sheik Yerbouti

Entertainment Personalities — Where and When Born

Actors, Actresses, Dancers, Musicians, Producers, Radio-TV Performers, Singers
(As of July 15, 1989)

Name	Birthplace	Born	Name	Birthplace	Born
Abbado, Claudio	Milan, Italy	6/26/33	Auberjonois, Rene	New York, N.Y.	6/1/40
Abbott, George	Forestville, N.Y.	6/25/87	Aumont, Jean-Pierre	Paris, France	1/5/09
Abraham, F. Murray	Pittsburgh, Pa.	10/24/39	Austin, Patti	New York, N.Y.	1948
Acuff, Roy	Maynardville, Tenn.	9/15/03	Autry, Gene	Tioga, Tex.	9/29/07
Adams, Don	New York, N.Y.	4/19/26	Avalon, Frankie	Philadelphia, Pa.	9/18/40
Adams, Edie	Kingston, Pa.	4/16/29	Ax, Emmanuel	Lvov, USSR	6/8/49
Adams, Joey	New York, N.Y.	1/6/11	Aykroyd, Dan	Ottawa, Ont.	7/1/52
Adams, Mason	New York, N.Y.	2/26/19	Ayres, Lew	Minneapolis, Minn.	12/28/08
Adams, Maud	Lulea, Sweden	2/12/45	Aznavour, Charles	Paris, France	5/22/24
Adler, Larry	Baltimore, Md.	2/10/14			
Agutter, Jenny	London, England	12/20/52	Bacall, Lauren	New York, N.Y.	9/16/24
Aiello, Danny	New York, N.Y.	6/20/33	Bacon, Kevin	Philadelphia, Pa.	7/8/58
Ailey, Alvin	Rogers, Tex.	1/5/31	Baez, Joan	Staten Island, N.Y.	1/9/41
Aimee, Anouk	Paris, France	4/27/32	Bailey, Pearl	Newport News, Va.	3/29/18
Akins, Claude	Nelson, Ga.	5/25/18	Bain, Conrad	Lethbridge, Alta.	2/4/23
Albanese, Licia	Bari, Italy	7/22/13	Baio, Scott	Brooklyn, N.Y.	9/22/61
Alberghetti, Anna Maria	Pesaro, Italy	5/15/36	Baker, Anita	Toledo, Oh.	1/26/58
Albert, Eddie	Rock Island, Ill.	4/22/08	Baker, Carroll	Johnstown, Pa.	5/28/31
Albert, Edward	Los Angeles, Cal.	2/20/51	Baker, Joe Don	Groesbeck, Tex.	2/12/36
Albright, Lola	Akron, Oh.	7/20/24	Baldwin, Alec	Massapequa, N.Y.	4/3/58
Alda, Alan	New York, N.Y.	1/28/36	Ballard, Kaye	Cleveland, Oh.	11/20/26
Alexander, Jane	Boston, Mass.	10/28/39	Balsam, Martin	New York, N.Y.	11/4/19
Allen, Debbie	Houston, Tex.	1/16/53	Bancroft, Anne	New York, N.Y.	9/17/31
Allen, Karen	Carrollton, Ill.	10/5/51	Banks, Jonathan	Washington, D.C.	1/31/46
Allen, Mel	Birmingham, Ala.	2/14/13	Barber, Red	Columbus, Miss.	2/17/08
Allen, Nancy	New York, N.Y.	6/24/50	Bardot, Brigitte	Paris, France	9/28/34
Allen, Peter	Tenderfield, Australia	2/10/44	Bari, Lynn	Roanoke, Va.	12/18/15
Allen, Steve	New York, N.Y.	12/26/21	Barker, Bob	Darrington, Wash.	12/12/23
Allen, Woody	Brooklyn, N.Y.	12/1/35	Barkin, Ellen	New York, N.Y.	4/16/55
Alley, Kirstie	Wichita, Kan.	1/12/55	Barnes, Priscilla	Ft. Dix, N.J.	12/7/56
Allman, Gregg	Nashville, Tenn.	12/7/47	Barr, Roseanne	Salt Lake City, Ut.	11/3/52
Allyson, June	New York, N.Y.	10/7/17	Barrault, Jean-Louis	Vesinet, France	9/8/10
Alonso, Maria Conchita	Cuba	1957	Barrie, Barbara	Chicago, Ill.	5/23/31
Alpert, Herb	Los Angeles, Cal.	3/31/35	Barrie, Mona	London, England	12/18/09
Altman, Robert	Kansas City, Mo.	2/20/25	Barry, Gene	New York, N.Y.	6/14/19
Ameche, Don	Kenosha, Wis.	5/31/08	Bartholomew, Freddie	London, England	3/28/24
Ames, Ed	Boston, Mass.	7/9/27	Bartok, Eva	Budapest, Hungary	6/18/26
Ames, Leon	Portland, Ind.	1/20/03	Barty, Billy	Millsboro, Pa.	10/25/24
Amos, John	Newark, N.J.	12/27/41	Baryshnikov, Mikhail	Riga, Latvia	1/28/48
Amsterdam, Morey	Chicago, Ill.	12/14/14	Basinger, Kim	Athens, Ga.	12/8/53
Anderson, Harry	Newport, R.I.	10/14/52	Bassey, Shirley	Cardiff, Wales	1/8/37
Anderson, Ian	Dunfermline, Scotland	8/10/47	Bateman, Jason	Rye, N.Y.	1/14/69
Anderson, Judith	Adelaide, Australia	2/10/98	Bateman, Justine	Rye, N.Y.	2/19/66
Anderson, Loni	St. Paul, Minn.	8/5/46	Bates, Alan	Allestree, England	2/17/34
Anderson, Lynn	Grand Forks, N.D.	9/26/47	Baxter-Birney, Meredith	Los Angeles, Cal.	6/21/47
Anderson, Marian	Philadelphia, Pa.	2/17/02	Beal, John	Joplin, Mo.	8/13/09
Anderson, Melissa Sue	Berkeley, Cal.	9/26/62	Bean, Orson	Burlington, Vt.	7/22/28
Anderson, Richard	Long Branch, N.J.	8/8/26	Beasley, Allyce	New York, N.Y.	7/6/54
Anderson, Richard Dean	Minneapolis, Minn.	1/23/53	Beatty, Ned	Louisville, Ky.	7/6/37
Andersson, Bibi	Stockholm, Sweden	11/11/35	Beatty, Robert	Hamilton, Ont.	10/19/09
Andress, Ursula	Bern, Switzerland	3/19/36	Beatty, Warren	Richmond, Va.	3/30/37
Andrews, Anthony	London, England	1948	Beck, John	Chicago, Ill.	1/28/43
Andrews, Dana	Collins, Miss.	1/1/09	Bedelia, Bonnie	New York, N.Y.	3/25/48
Andrews, Julie	Walton, England	10/1/35	Bee Gees		
Andrews, Maxene	Minneapolis, Minn.	1/3/18	Gibb, Barry	Isle of Man, England	9/1/46
Andrews, Patty	Minneapolis, Minn.	2/16/20	Gibb, Robin	" "	12/22/49
Anka, Paul	Ottawa, Ont.	7/30/41	Gibb, Maurice	" "	12/22/49
Ann-Margret	Stockholm, Sweden	4/28/41	Beery, Noah Jr.	New York, N.Y.	8/10/13
Anspach, Susan	New York, N.Y.	11/23/39	Begley, Ed Jr.	Los Angeles, Cal.	9/16/49
Ant, Adam	London, England	11/3/54	Belafonte, Harry	New York, N.Y.	3/1/27
Archer, Anne	Los Angeles, Cal.	8/25/50	Belafonte-Harper, Shari	New York, N.Y.	9/22/54
Arden, Eve	Mill Valley, Cal.	4/30/12	Bel Geddes, Barbara	New York, N.Y.	10/31/22
Arkin, Alan	New York, N.Y.	3/26/34	Bellamy, Ralph	Chicago, Ill.	6/17/04
Arnaz, Desi Jr.	Los Angeles, Cal.	1/19/53	Belmondo, Jean-Paul	Neuilly-sur-Seine, France	4/9/33
Arnaz, Lucie	Hollywood, Cal.	7/17/51	Belushi, Jim	Chicago, Ill.	6/15/54
Arness, James	Minneapolis, Minn.	5/26/23	Benatar, Pat	Brooklyn, N.Y.	1/10/53
Arnold, Eddy	Henderson, Tenn.	5/15/18	Benedict, Dirk	Helena, Mont.	3/1/45
Arquette, Rosanna	New York, N.Y.	8/10/59	Benjamin, Richard	New York, N.Y.	5/22/38
Arrau, Claudio	Chillau, Chile	2/6/03	Bennett, Joan	Palisades, N.J.	2/27/10
Arroyo, Martina	New York, N.Y.	2/2/37	Bennett, Tony	New York, N.Y.	8/3/26
Arthur, Beatrice	New York, N.Y.	5/13/26	Benson, George	Pittsburgh, Pa.	3/22/43
Arthur, Jean	New York, N.Y.	10/17/05	Benson, Robby	Dallas, Tex.	1/21/55
Ashcroft, Peggy	Croyden, England	12/22/07	Beradino, John	Los Angeles, Cal.	5/1/17
Ashley, Elizabeth	Ocala, Fla.	8/30/41	Berenger, Tom	Chicago, Ill.	5/31/50
Asner, Ed	Kansas City, Mo.	11/15/29	Bergen, Candice	Beverly Hills, Cal.	5/9/46
Assante, Armand	New York, N.Y.	10/4/49	Bergen, Polly	Knoxville, Tenn.	7/14/30
Astin, John	Baltimore, Md.	3/30/30	Bergerac, Jacques	Biarritz, France	5/26/27
Atherton, William	New Haven, Conn.	7/30/47	Bergman, Ingmar	Uppsala, Sweden	7/14/18
Atkins, Chet	Luttrell, Tenn.	6/20/24	Berle, Milton	New York, N.Y.	7/12/08
Attenborough, Richard	Cambridge, England	8/29/23	Berlinger, Warren	Brooklyn, N.Y.	8/31/37
			Berman, Lazar	Leningrad, USSR	2/26/30

Name	Birthplace	Born
Berman, Shelley	Chicago, Ill.	2/3/26
Bernsen, Corbin	No. Hollywood, Cal.	9/7/54
Bernstein, Leonard	Lawrence, Mass.	8/25/18
Berry, Chuck	St. Louis, Mo.	10/18/26
Berry, Ken	Moline, Ill.	11/3/33
Bertinelli, Valerie	Wilmington, Del.	4/23/60
Bikel, Theodore	Vienna, Austria	5/2/24
Birney, David	Washington, D.C.	4/23/39
Bishop, Joey	Bronx, N.Y.	2/3/18
Bisoglio, Val	New York, N.Y.	5/7/26
Bisset, Jacqueline	Weybridge, England	9/13/44
Bixby, Bill	San Francisco, Cal.	1/22/34
Black, Karen	Park Ridge, Ill.	7/1/42
Blackstone Jr., Harry	Three Rivers, Mich.	6/30/34
Blades, Ruben	Panama	1948
Blaine, Vivian	Newark, N.J.	11/21/21
Blair, Linda	St. Louis, Mo.	1/22/59
Blake, Amanda	Buffalo, N.Y.	2/20/29
Blake, Robert	Nutley, N.J.	9/18/33
Bledsoe, Tempestt	Chicago, Ill.	8/1/73
Bloom, Claire	London, England	2/15/31
Blyth, Ann	Mt. Kisco, N.Y.	8/16/28
Bochco, Steven	New York, N.Y.	12/16/43
Bogarde, Dirk	London, England	3/28/20
Bogdanovich, Peter	Kingston, N.Y.	7/30/39
Bonet, Lisa	San Francisco, Cal.	11/16/67
Bonham-Carter, Helena	England	1967
Bon Jovi, Jon	Sayreville, N.J.	3/2/61
Bono, Sonny	Detroit, Mich.	2/16/35
Booke, Sorrell	Buffalo, N.Y.	1/4/30
Boone, Debby	Hackensack, N.J.	9/22/56
Boone, Pat	Jacksonville, Fla.	6/1/34
Booth, Shirley	New York, N.Y.	8/30/07
Borge, Victor	Copenhagen, Denmark	1/3/09
Borgnine, Ernest	Hamden, Conn.	1/24/17
Bosco, Philip	Jersey City, N.J.	9/26/30
Bosley, Tom	Chicago, Ill.	10/1/27
Bosson, Barbara	Charleroi, Pa.	11/1/39
Bostwick, Barry	San Mateo, Cal.	2/24/46
Bottoms, Joseph	Santa Barbara, Cal.	4/22/54
Bottoms, Timothy	Santa Barbara, Cal.	8/30/51
Bowie, David	London, England	1/8/47
Boxleitner, Bruce	Elgin, Ill.	5/12/50
Boy George	London, England	6/14/61
Boyle, Peter	Philadelphia, Pa.	10/18/33
Bracco, Lorraine	New York, N.Y.	1955
Bracken, Eddie	New York, N.Y.	2/7/20
Brand, Neville	Kewanee, Ill.	8/13/21
Brando, Marlon	Omaha, Neb.	4/3/24
Brazzi, Rossano	Bologna, Italy	9/18/16
Brendel, Alfred	Wiesenberg, Austria	1/5/31
Brennan, Eileen	Los Angeles, Cal.	9/3/35
Brenner, David	Philadelphia, Pa.	2/4/45
Brewer, Teresa	Toledo, Oh.	5/7/31
Brian, David	New York, N.Y.	8/5/14
Bridges, Beau	Hollywood, Cal.	12/9/41
Bridges, Jeff	Los Angeles, Cal.	12/4/49
Bridges, Lloyd	San Leandro, Cal.	1/15/13
Bridges, Todd	San Francisco, Cal.	5/27/65
Brimley, Wilford	Salt Lake City, Ut.	9/27/34
Broderick, Matthew	New York, N.Y.	3/21/62
Brolin, James	Los Angeles, Cal.	7/18/40
Bronson, Charles	Ehrenfeld, Pa.	11/3/22
Brooks, Albert	Beverly Hills, Cal.	7/22/47
Brooks, Avery	Evansville, Ind.	10/2/-
Brooks, Mel	New York, N.Y.	6/28/26
Brooks, Stephen	Columbus, Oh.	1942
Brosnan, Pierce	Co. Meath, Ireland	5/16/53
Brown, Blair	Washington, D.C.	1948
Brown, Bryan	Australia	1947
Brown, James	Pulaski, Tenn.	6/17/28
Brown, Jim	St. Simons Island, Ga.	2/17/36
Brown, Les	Reinerton, Pa.	3/14/12
Brown, Ray	Pittsburgh, Pa.	10/13/26
Browne, Roscoe Lee	Woodbury, N.J.	5/2/25
Bryant, Anita	Barnsdall, Okla.	3/25/40
Buckley, Betty	Ft. Worth, Tex.	7/3/47
Bujold, Genevieve	Montreal, Que.	7/1/42
Bullock, Jm J.	Casper, Wyo.	2/9/-
Bumbry, Grace	St. Louis, Mo.	1/4/37
Burghoff, Gary	Bristol, Conn.	5/24/40
Burke, Delta	Orlando, Fla.	7/30/56
Burke, Paul	New Orleans, La.	7/21/26
Burnett, Carol	San Antonio, Tex.	4/26/33
Burns, George	New York, N.Y.	1/20/96
Burr, Raymond	New Westminster, B.C.	5/21/17
Burstyn, Ellen	Detroit, Mich.	12/7/32
Burton, LeVar	Landsthul, W. Germany	2/16/57
Busey, Gary	Goose Creek, Tex.	6/29/44
Butkus, Dick	Chicago, Ill.	12/9/42
Button, Dick	Englewood, N.J.	7/18/29
Buttons, Red	New York, N.Y.	2/5/19
Buzzi, Ruth	Westerly, R.I.	7/24/36
Byrne, David	Dumbarton, Scotland	5/14/52
Caan, James	New York, N.Y.	3/26/39
Caballe, Montserrat	Barcelona, Spain	4/12/33
Caesar, Sid	Yonkers, N.Y.	9/8/22
Cage, Nicolas	Long Beach, Cal.	1965
Caine, Michael	London, England	3/14/33
Caldwell, Sarah	Maryville, Mo.	3/6/24
Caldwell, Zoe	Melbourne, Australia	9/14/33
Calhoun, Rory	Los Angeles, Cal.	8/8/23
Callas, Charlie	Brooklyn, N.Y.	12/20/-
Calloway, Cab	Rochester, N.Y.	12/25/07
Cameron, Kirk	Panorama City, Cal.	10/12/70
Camp, Hamilton	London, England	10/30/34
Campanella, Joseph	New York, N.Y.	11/21/27
Campbell, Glen	Billstown, Ark.	4/22/36
Candy, John	Toronto, Ont.	10/31/50
Cannon, Dyan	Tacoma, Wash.	1/4/37
Cantrell, Lana	Sydney, Australia.	8/7/43
Capra, Frank	Palermo, Italy	5/18/97
Cara, Irene	New York, N.Y.	3/18/59
Carey, Macdonald	Sioux City, Ia.	3/15/13
Carey, Phil	Hackensack, N.J.	7/15/25
Carey, Ron	Newark, N.J.	12/11/35
Cariou, Len	Winnipeg, Canada	9/30/39
Carle, Frankie	Providence, R.I.	3/25/03
Carlin, George	New York, N.Y.	5/12/38
Carlisle, Kitty	New Orleans, La	9/3/15
Carmen, Eric	Cleveland, Oh.	8/11/49
Carmichael, Ian	Hull, England	6/18/20
Carnes, Kim	California	1948
Carney, Art.	Mt. Vernon, N.Y.	11/4/18
Carnovsky, Morris	St. Louis, Mo.	9/5/97
Caron, Leslie	Boulogne, France.	7/1/31
Carpenter, John	Carthage, N.Y.	1/16/48
Carr, Vikki	El Paso, Tex.	7/19/41
Carradine, David	Hollywood, Cal.	10/8/36
Carradine, Keith	San Mateo, Cal.	8/8/50
Carreras, Jose.	Barcelona, Spain	12/5/47
Carroll, Diahann	Bronx, N.Y.	7/17/35
Carroll, Pat	Shreveport, La.	5/5/27
Carson, Johnny	Corning, Ia.	10/23/25
Carter, Dixie	McLemoresville, Tenn.	5/25/39
Carter, Jack	New York, N.Y.	6/24/23
Carter, June	Maces Spring, Va.	6/23/29
Carter, Lynda	Phoenix, Ariz.	7/24/51
Carter, Nell	Birmingham, Ala.	9/13/48
Carvey, Dana	Missoula, Mont.	4/2/55
Casadesus, Gaby	Marseilles, France	1902
Cash, Johnny	Kingsland, Ark.	2/26/32
Cash, Rosanne	Memphis, Tenn.	5/24/55
Cass, Peggy	Boston, Mass.	5/21/24
Cassidy, David	New York, N.Y.	4/12/50
Cassidy, Shaun	Los Angeles, Cal.	9/27/58
Cates, Phoebe	New York, N.Y.	1964
Caulfield, Joan	West Orange, N.J.	6/1/22
Cavallaro, Carmen	New York, N.Y.	5/6/13
Cavett, Dick	Gibbon, Neb.	11/19/36
Chamberlain, Richard	Beverly Hills, Cal.	3/31/35
Champion, Marge	Los Angeles, Cal.	9/2/23
Channing, Carol	Seattle, Wash.	1/31/23
Channing, Stockard	New York, N.Y.	2/13/44
Chaplin, Geraldine	Santa Monica, Cal.	7/31/44
Chaplin, Sydney	Beverly Hills, Cal.	3/31/26
Chapman, Tracy	Cleveland, OH.	1964
Charisse, Cyd	Amarillo, Tex.	3/8/21
Charles, Ray	Albany, Ga.	9/23/30
Charo	Murcia, Spain	1/15/51
Chase, Chevy	New York, N.Y.	10/8/43
Checker, Chubby	Philadelphia, Pa.	10/3/41
Cher	El Centro, Cal.	5/20/46
Chong, Rae Dawn.	California	1961
Chong, Thomas	Edmonton, Alta.	5/24/38
Christie, Julie.	Assam, India	4/14/40
Christopher, William	Evanston, Ill.	10/20/32
Christy, June	Springfield, Ill.	11/20/25
Clapton, Eric	Surrey, England.	3/30/45
Clark, Dane	New York, N.Y.	2/18/13
Clark, Dick	Mt. Vernon, N.Y.	11/30/29
Clark, Petula	Ewell, Surrey, England.	11/15/32
Clark, Roy	Meherrin, Va.	4/15/33
Clark, Susan	Sarnia, Ont.	3/8/44
Clary, Robert	Paris, France	3/1/26
Clayburgh, Jill	New York, N.Y.	4/30/44

Name	Birthplace	Born	Name	Birthplace	Born
Cleese, John	England	10/27/39	Daly, Tyne	Madison, Wis.	2/21/47
Cleveland, James	Chicago, Ill.	12/5/31	Damone, Vic	Brooklyn, N.Y.	6/12/28
Cliburn, Van	Shreveport, La.	7/12/34	D'Angelo, Beverly	Columbus, Oh.	1954
Clooney, Rosemary	Maysville, Ky.	5/23/28	Dangerfield, Rodney	Babylon, N.Y.	11/22/22
Close, Glenn	Greenwich, Conn.	3/19/47	Daniels, Charlie	Wilmington, N.C.	10/28/36
Coburn, James	Laurel, Neb.	8/31/28	Daniels, William	Brooklyn, N.Y.	3/31/27
Coca, Imogene	Philadelphia, Pa.	11/18/08	Danner, Blythe	Philadelphia, Pa.	2/3/44
Cohn, Mindy	Los Angeles, Cal.	5/20/66	Danson, Ted	San Diego, Cal.	12/29/47
Colbert, Claudette	Paris, France	9/18/05	Danza, Tony	New York, N.Y.	4/21/50
Cole, Gary	Park Ridge, Ill.	9/20/57	Darby, Kim	Hollywood, Cal.	7/8/48
Cole, Natalie	Los Angeles, Cal.	2/6/50	Darren, James	Philadelphia, Pa.	6/8/36
Cole, Olivia	Memphis, Tenn.	11/26/42	Davidson, John	Pittsburgh, Pa.	12/13/41
Coleman, Dabney	Austin, Tex.	1/3/32	Davis, Ann B.	Schenectady, N.Y.	5/5/26
Coleman, Gary	Zion, Ill.	2/8/68	Davis, Bette	Lowell, Mass.	4/5/08
Collins, Dorothy	Windsor, Ont.	11/18/26	Davis, Clifton	Chicago, Ill.	10/4/45
Collins, Joan	London, England	5/23/33	Davis, Geena	Ware, Mass.	1/21/57
Collins, Judy	Seattle, Wash.	5/1/39	Davis, Judy	Perth, Australia	1956
Collins, Phil	London, England	1/30/51	Davis, Mac	Lubbock, Tex.	1/21/42
Comden, Betty	Brooklyn, N.Y.	5/3/19	Davis, Ossie	Cogdell, Ga.	12/18/17
Como, Perry	Canonsburg, Pa.	5/18/12	Davis, Sammy Jr.	New York, N.Y.	12/8/25
Conner, Nadine	Compton, Cal.	2/20/13	Davis, Skeeter	Dry Ridge, Ky.	12/30/31
Connery, Sean	Edinburgh, Scotland	8/25/30	Dawber, Pam	Farmington Hills, Mich.	10/18/51
Conniff, Ray	Attleboro, Mass.	11/6/16	Dawn, Hazel	Ogden, Ut.	3/23/98
Connors, Chuck	Brooklyn, N.Y.	4/10/21	Dawson, Richard	Hampshire, England	11/20/32
Connors, Mike	Fresno, Cal.	8/15/25	Day, Doris	Cincinnati, Oh.	4/3/24
Conrad, Robert	Chicago, Ill.	3/1/35	Day, Laraine	Roosevelt, Ut.	10/13/20
Conrad, William	Louisville, Ky.	9/27/20	Dean, Jimmy	Plainview, Tex.	8/10/28
Constantine, Michael	Reading, Pa.	5/22/27	De Camp, Rosemary	Prescott, Ariz.	11/14/10
Conti, Tom	Paisley, Scotland	11/22/41	DeCarlo, Yvonne	Vancouver, B.C.	9/1/22
Convy, Bert	St. Louis, Mo.	6/23/39	Dee, Frances	Los Angeles, Cal.	11/26/07
Conway, Tim	Willoughby, Oh.	12/15/33	Dee, Ruby	Cleveland, Oh.	10/27/23
Cook, Barbara	Atlanta, Ga.	10/25/27	Dee, Sandra	Bayonne, N.J.	4/23/42
Cook, Peter	Torquay, England.	11/17/37	Defore, Don	Cedar Rapids, Ia.	8/25/17
Cooke, Alistair	Manchester, England.	11/20/08	DeHaven, Gloria	Los Angeles, Cal.	7/23/25
Coolidge, Rita	Nashville, Tenn.	5/1/45	De Havilland, Olivia	Tokyo, Japan	7/1/16
Cooper, Alice	Detroit, Mich.	2/4/48	Delany, Dana	New York, N.Y.	3/13/56
Cooper, Jackie	Los Angeles, Cal.	9/15/22	Della Chiesa, Vivienne	Chicago, Ill.	10/9/20
Coppola, Francis	Detroit, Mich.	4/7/39	Delon, Alain	Sceaux, France	11/8/35
Corby, Ellen	Racine, Wis.	6/3/13	DeLuise, Dom	Brooklyn, N.Y.	8/1/33
Cord, Alex	New York, N.Y.	8/3/31	De Mille, Agnes	New York, N.Y.	1905
Corea, Chick	Chelsea, Mass.	6/12/41	De Mornay, Rebecca	Santa Rosa, Cal.	1962
Corelli, Franco	Ancona, Italy	4/8/23	Deneuve, Catherine	Paris, France	10/22/43
Corey, Jeff	New York, N.Y.	8/10/14	De Niro, Robert	New York, N.Y.	8/17/43
Cosby, Bill	Philadelphia, Pa.	7/12/37	Dennehy, Brian	Bridgeport, Conn.	7/9/40
Costas, Bob	New York, N.Y.	3/22/52	Denning, Richard	Poughkeepsie, N.Y.	3/27/14
Costello, Elvis	London, England	8/25/54	Dennis, Sandy	Hastings, Neb.	4/27/37
Costner, Kevin	Los Angeles, Cal.	1/18/55	Denver, Bob	New Rochelle, N.Y.	1/9/35
Cotten, Joseph	Petersburg, Va.	5/15/05	Denver, John	Roswell, N.M.	12/31/43
Cougar, John	Seymour, Ind.	10/7/51	DePalma, Brian	Newark, N.J.	9/11/40
Courtenay, Tom	Hull, England	2/25/37	Depp, Johnny	Owensboro, KY.	6/9/63
Cox, Ronny	Cloudcroft, N.M.	8/23/38	Derek, Bo	Long Beach, Cal.	11/20/56
Craddock, Crash	Greensboro, N.C.	6/16/40	Derek, John	Hollywood, Cal.	8/12/26
Crain, Jeanne	Barstow, Cal.	5/25/25	Dern, Bruce	Chicago, Ill.	6/4/36
Crawford, Michael	Salisbury, England	1/19/42	Devane, William	Albany, N.Y.	9/5/37
Crenna, Richard	Los Angeles, Cal.	11/30/27	DeVito, Danny	Neptune, N.J.	11/17/44
Crespin, Regine	Marseilles, France	2/23/26	Dewhurst, Colleen	Montreal, Que.	6/3/26
Cronyn, Hume	London, Ont.	7/18/11	DeWitt, Joyce	Wheeling, W.Va.	4/23/49
Crosby, Bob	Spokane, Wash.	8/23/13	Dey, Susan	Pekin, Ill.	12/10/52
Crosby, Cathy Lee	Los Angeles, Cal.	12/2/48	Diamond, Neil	Brooklyn, N.Y.	1/24/41
Crosby, David	Los Angeles, Cal.	8/14/41	Dickinson, Angie	Kulm, N.D.	9/30/31
Crosby, Norm	Boston, Mass.	9/15/27	Dietrich, Marlene	Berlin, Germany	12/27/01
Cross, Christopher	San Antonio, Tex.	5/3/51	Diller, Phyllis	Lima, Oh.	7/17/17
Crouse, Lindsay	New York, N.Y.	5/12/48	Dillman, Bradford	San Francisco, Cal.	4/14/30
Cruise, Tom	Syracuse, N.Y.	1962	Dillon, Matt	New Rochelle, N.Y.	2/18/64
Crystal, Billy	Long Beach, N.Y.	3/14/47	Dixon, Ivan	New York, N.Y.	4/6/31
Cugat, Xavier	Barcelona, Spain	1/1/00	Dobson, Kevin	New York, N.Y.	3/18/44
Cullen, Bill	Pittsburgh, Pa.	2/18/20	Domingo, Placido	Madrid, Spain	1/21/41
Cullum, John	Knoxville, Tenn.	3/2/30	Domino, Fats	New Orleans, La.	2/26/28
Culp, Robert	Oakland, Cal.	8/16/30	Donahue, Phil	Cleveland, Oh.	12/21/35
Cummings, Constance	Seattle, Wash.	5/15/10	Donahue, Troy	New York, N.Y.	1/27/36
Cummings, Robert	Joplin, Mo.	6/9/10	Donovan	Glasgow, Scotland	5/10/43
Curtin, Jane	Cambridge, Mass.	9/6/47	Dotrice, Roy	Guernsey, England	5/26/23
Curtin, Phyllis	Clarksburg, W.Va.	12/3/30	Douglas, Kirk	Amsterdam, N.Y.	12/9/18
Curtis, Jamie Lee	Los Angeles, Cal.	11/22/58	Douglas, Michael	New Brunswick, N.J.	9/25/44
Curtis, Keene	Salt Lake City, Ut.	2/15/23	Douglas, Mike	Chicago, Ill.	8/11/25
Curtis, Ken	Lamar, Col.	7/2/16	Down, Leslie-Ann	London, England	3/17/54
Curtis, Tony	New York, N.Y.	6/3/25	Downey, Robert Jr.	California	4/4/65
Cusack, Cyril	Durban, S. Africa	11/26/10	Downs, Hugh	Akron, Oh.	2/14/21
Cusack, Joan	Evanston, Ill.	10/11/62	Doyle, David	Lincoln, Neb.	12/1/29
Cusack, John	Chicago, Ill.	1967	Dragon, Daryl	Los Angeles, Cal.	8/27/42
Cushing, Peter	Surrey, England.	5/26/13	Drake, Alfred	Bronx, N.Y.	10/7/14
Dafoe, Willem	Appleton, Wis.	7/22/55	Drake, Larry	Tulsa, Okla.	2/21/-
Dahl, Arlene	Minneapolis, Minn.	8/11/28	Drew, Ellen	Kansas City, Mo.	11/23/15
Dale, Jim	Rothwell, England	8/15/35	Dryer, Fred	Hawthorne, Cal.	7/6/46
Dalton, Abby	Las Vegas, Nev.	8/15/32	Dreyfuss, Richard	Brooklyn, N.Y.	10/29/47
Dalton, Timothy	Wales	3/21/44	Dru, Joanne	Logan, W.Va.	1/31/23
Daltrey, Roger	London, England	3/1/44	Duchin, Peter	New York, N.Y.	7/28/37
Daly, John	Johannesburg, S. Africa	2/20/14	Duff, Howard	Bremerton, Wash.	11/24/17

Name	Birthplace	Born	Name	Birthplace	Born
Duffy, Julia	Minneapolis, Minn.	6/27/51	kia.		2/11/12
Duffy, Patrick	Townsend, Mont.	3/17/49	Firth, Peter	Yorkshire, England	10/27/53
Dufour, Val	New Orleans, La.	2/5/27	Fischer-Dieskau, Dietrich	Berlin, Germany	5/28/25
Dukakis, Olympia	Massachusetts	1932	Fisher, Carrie	Beverly Hills, Cal.	10/21/56
Duke, Patty.	New York, N.Y.	12/14/46	Fisher, Eddie	Philadelphia, Pa.	8/10/28
Dullea, Keir.	Cleveland, Oh.	5/30/36	Fitzgerald, Ella.	Newport News, Va.	4/25/18
Dunaway, Faye	Bascom, Fla.	1/14/41	Fitzgerald, Geraldine	Dublin, Ireland.	11/24/13
Duncan, Sandy	Henderson, Tex.	2/20/46	Flack, Roberta	Black Mountain, N.C.	2/10/39
Dunham, Katherine	Joliet, Ill.	6/22/10	Flanagan, Fionnula	Dublin, Ireland.	12/10/41
Dunn, Nora.	Chicago, Ill.	4/29/52	Flanders, Ed	Minneapolis, Minn.	12/29/34
Dunne, Griffin	California	6/8/55	Fleming, Rhonda	Hollywood, Cal.	8/10/23
Dunne, Irene	Louisville, Ky.	12/20/98	Fletcher, Louise	Birmingham, Ala.	1936
Dunnock, Mildred	Baltimore, Md.	1/25/04	Foch, Nina	Leyden, Netherlands	4/20/24
Durbin, Deanna	Winnipeg, Man.	12/4/21	Fogelberg, Dan	Peoria, Ill.	8/13/51
Durning, Charles.	Highland Falls, N.Y.	2/28/23	Fonda, Jane	New York, N.Y.	12/21/37
Dussault, Nancy	Pensacola, Fla.	6/30/36	Fonda, Peter.	New York, N.Y.	2/23/40
Duvall, Robert	San Diego, Cal.	1/5/31	Fontaine, Joan.	Tokyo, Japan	10/22/17
Duvall, Shelley	Houston, Tex.	1949	Fonteyn, Margot.	Reigate, England	5/18/19
Dylan, Bob	Duluth, Minn.	5/24/41	Ford (Tenn.), Ernie	Bristol, Tenn.	2/13/19
Dysart, Richard	Augusta, Me.	3/30/-	Ford, Glenn	Quebec, Canada	5/1/16
			Ford, Harrison	Chicago, Ill.	7/13/42
Easton, Sheena	Bellshill, Scotland.	4/27/59	Forrest, Steve	Huntsville, Tex.	9/29/24
Eastwood, Clint	San Francisco, Cal.	5/31/30	Forsythe, Henderson	Macon, Mo.	9/11/17
Ebert, Roger	Urbana, Ill.	6/18/42	Forsythe, John.	Penns Grove, N.J.	1/29/18
Ebsen, Buddy	Belleville, Ill.	4/2/08	Foster, Jodie.	New York, N.Y.	11/19/62
Eckstine, Billy	Pittsburgh, Pa.	7/8/14	Fox, James.	London, England	5/19/39
Edelman, Herb.	Brooklyn, N.Y.	11/5/33	Fox, Michael J..	Edmonton, Alta.	6/9/61
Eden, Barbara.	Tucson, Ariz.	8/23/34	Foxworth, Robert	Houston, Tex.	11/1/41
Edwards, Anthony	Santa Barbara, Cal.	1/19/62	Foxx, Redd.	St. Louis, Mo.	12/9/22
Edwards, Blake	Tulsa, Okla.	7/26/22	Frampton, Peter.	Kent, England	4/22/50
Edwards, Ralph	Merino, Col.	6/13/13	Francescatti, Zino	Marseilles, France	8/9/05
Edwards, Vincent	Brooklyn, N.Y..	7/7/28	Franciosa, Anthony	New York, N.Y.	10/25/28
Eggar, Samantha	London, England	3/5/39	Francis, Anne	Ossining, N.Y.	9/16/30
Eichhorn, Lisa	Reading, Pa.	2/4/52	Francis, Arlene	Boston, Mass.	10/20/08
Eikenberry, Jill	New Haven, Conn.	1/21/47	Francis, Connie	Newark, N.J.	12/12/38
Ekberg, Anita	Malmo, Sweden	9/29/31	Francis, Genie	Los Angeles, Cal.	5/26/62
Ekland, Britt	Stockholm, Sweden	10/6/42	Frankenheimer, John	Malba, N.Y.	2/19/30
Elam, Jack	Miami, Ariz.	11/13/16	Franklin, Aretha	Memphis, Tenn.	3/25/42
Elizondo, Hector	New York, N.Y.	12/22/36	Franklin, Bonnie	Santa Monica, Cal.	1/6/44
Elliott, Bob	Boston, Mass.	3/26/23	Franklin, Joe	New York, N.Y.	1929
Elliott, Denholm	London, England	5/31/22	Frann, Mary	St. Louis, Mo.	2/27/43
Elliott, Sam.	Sacramento, Cal.	8/9/44	Franz, Dennis	Chicago, Ill.	10/28/44
Elvira (Cassandra Peter-			Freed, Bert.	New York, N.Y.	11/3/19
son)	Manhattan, Kan.	9/17/51	Freeman Jr., Al	San Antonio, Tex.	3/21/34
Estevez, Emilio	New York, N.Y.	1962	Frick, Mr. (W. Groebli)	Basel, Switzerland	4/21/15
Estrada, Erik	New York, N.Y.	3/16/49	Friedkin, William	Chicago, Ill.	8/29/39
Evans, Dale	Uvalde, Tex..	10/31/12	Frost, David	Tenterden, England	4/7/39
Evans, Gene	Holbrook, Ariz.	7/11/24	Funicello, Annette	Utica, N.Y.	10/22/42
Evans, Linda	Hartford, Conn.	11/18/42	Funt, Allen	New York, N.Y.	9/16/14
Evans, Robert	New York, N.Y.	6/29/30			
Everett, Chad	South Bend, Ind.	6/11/36	Gabor, Eva.	Hungary	1921
Everly, Don.	Brownie, Ky.	2/1/37	Gabor, Zsa Zsa	Hungary	
Everly, Phil	Brownie, Ky.	1/19/38	Gabriel, John.	Niagara Falls, N.Y.	5/25/31
Evigan, Greg	S. Amboy, N.J.	10/14/53	Gabriel, Peter	London, England	5/13/50
Ewell, Tom	Owensboro, Ky.	4/29/09	Gail, Max	Detroit, Mich.	4/5/43
			Gallagher, Megan	Reading, Pa.	2/6/-
Fabares, Shelley	Santa Monica, Cal.	1/19/42	Galloway, Don	Brooksville, Ky.	7/27/37
Fabian (Forte)	Philadelphia, Pa.	2/6/43	Galway, James	Belfast, Ireland	12/8/39
Fabray, Nanette	San Diego, Cal.	10/27/20	Garagiola, Joe	St. Louis, Mo.	2/12/26
Fairbanks, Douglas Jr.	New York, N.Y.	12/9/09	Garbo, Greta.	Stockholm, Sweden	9/18/05
Fairchild, Morgan	Dallas, Tex.	2/3/50	Gardenia, Vincent	Naples, Italy.	1/7/22
Falana, Lola	Philadelphia, Pa.	9/11/46	Gardner, Ava	Smithfield, N.C.	12/24/22
Falk, Peter	New York, N.Y.	9/16/27	Garfunkel, Art	New York, N.Y.	10/13/41
Farentino, James	Brooklyn, N.Y..	2/24/38	Garland, Beverly	Santa Cruz, Cal.	10/17/26
Fargo, Donna	Mt. Airy, N.C.	11/10/45	Garner, James.	Norman, Okla.	4/7/28
Farr, Jamie	Toledo, Oh.	7/1/34	Garr, Teri	Lakewood, Oh.	12/11/49
Farrell, Charles	Onset Bay, Mass.	8/9/01	Garrett, Betty	St. Joseph, Mo.	5/23/19
Farrell, Eileen	Willimantic, Conn.	2/13/20	Garson, Greer	Co. Down, N. Ireland	9/29/08
Farrell, Mike	St. Paul, Minn.	2/6/39	Gatlin, Larry	Seminole, Tex.	5/2/48
Farrow, Mia	Los Angeles, Cal.	2/9/45	Gavin, John	Los Angeles, Cal.	4/8/32
Fawcett, Farrah	Corpus Christi, Tex.	2/2/47	Gayle, Crystal	Paintsville, Ky.	1/9/51
Faye, Alice	New York, N.Y.	5/5/12	Gaynor, Mitzi	Chicago, Ill.	9/4/30
Feld, Fritz.	Berlin, Germany	10/15/00	Gazzara, Ben	New York, N.Y.	8/28/30
Feldon, Barbara	Pittsburgh, Pa.	3/12/41	Geary, Anthony	Coalsville, Ut.	5/29/47
Feldshuh, Tovah.	New York, N.Y.	12/27/52	Gedda, Nicolai	Stockholm, Sweden	7/11/25
Feliciano, Jose.	Lares, Puerto Rico	9/10/45	Geldof, Bob	Co. Dublin, Ire.	10/5/51
Fell, Norman	Philadelphia, Pa.	3/24/24	Gennaro, Peter	Metairie, La.	1924
Fellini, Federico	Rimini, Italy	1/20/20	Gentry, Bobbie.	Chickasaw Co., Miss.	7/27/44
Fellows, Edith	Boston, Mass.	5/20/23	Gere, Richard	Philadelphia, Pa.	8/31/49
Fender, Freddy	San Benito, Tex.	6/4/37	Getty, Estelle	New York, N.Y.	7/25/24
Ferrell, Conchata	Charleston, W. Va.	3/28/43	Ghostley, Alice.	Eve, Mo.	8/14/26
Ferrer, Jose	Santuce, P.R.	1/8/12	Giannini, Giancarlo	Spezia, Italy.	8/1/42
Ferrer, Mel	Elberon, N.J.	8/25/17	Gibb, Cynthia	Bennington, Vt.	12/14/63
Ferrigno, Lou.	Brooklyn, N.Y.	11/9/52	Gibbs, Marla	Chicago, Ill.	6/14/31
Fiedler, John	Platville, Wis.	2/3/25	Gibson, Debbie	Merrick, N.Y.	8/31/70
Field, Sally	Pasadena, Cal.	11/6/46	Gibson, Henry	Germantown, Pa.	9/21/35
Fields, Kim	Los Angeles, Cal.	5/12/69	Gibson, Mel	Peerskill, N.Y.	1/3/51
Finney, Albert	Salford, England	5/9/36	Gielgud, John	London, England	4/14/04
Firkusny, Rudolf	Napajedla, Czechoslova-		Gifford, Frank	Santa Monica, Cal.	8/16/30

Name	Birthplace	Born
Gilbert, Melissa	Los Angeles, Cal.	5/8/64
Gilberto, Astrud	Salvador, Brazil	3/30/40
Gilford, Jack	New York, N.Y.	7/25/07
Gillette, Anita	Baltimore, Md.	8/16/38
Gilley, Mickey	Natchez, Miss.	3/9/36
Ginty, Robert	New York, N.Y.	11/14/48
Gish, Lillian	Springfield, Oh.	10/14/96
Givens, Robin	New York, N.Y.	11/27/64
Glaser, Paul Michael	Cambridge, Mass.	3/25/43
Glass, Ron	Evansville, Ind.	7/10/45
Glenn, Scott	Pittsburgh, Pa.	1/26/42
Gless, Sharon	Los Angeles, Cal.	5/31/43
Glover, Danny	San Francisco, Cal.	1948
Glynn, Carlin	Cleveland, Oh.	2/19/40
Gobel, George	Chicago, Ill.	5/20/19
Godard, Jean Luc	Paris, France	12/3/30
Goddard, Paulette	Great Neck, N.Y.	6/3/11
Godunov, Alexander	Sakhalin Is., USSR	11/28/49
Goldberg, Whoopi	New York, N.Y.	1949
Goldblum, Jeff	Pittsburgh, Pa.	10/22/53
Goldsboro, Bobby	Marianna, Fla.	1/18/42
Goldthwait, Bob	Syracuse, N.Y.	1962
Goodman, John	St. Louis, Mo.	6/20/53
Gordon, Gale	New York, N.Y.	2/2/06
Gorman, Cliff	New York, N.Y.	10/13/36
Gorme, Eydie	Bronx, N.Y.	8/16/32
Gorshin, Frank	Pittsburgh, Pa.	4/5/34
Gossett Jr., Louis	Brooklyn, N.Y.	5/27/36
Gould, Elliott	Brooklyn, N.Y.	8/29/38
Gould, Harold	Schenectady, N.Y.	12/10/23
Gould, Morton	Richmond Hill, N.Y.	12/10/13
Goulding, Ray	Lowell, Mass.	3/20/22
Goulet, Robert	Lawrence, Mass.	11/26/33
Gowdy, Curt	Green River, Wyo.	7/31/19
Graham, Martha	Pittsburgh, Pa.	5/11/94
Graham, Virginia	Chicago, Ill.	7/4/12
Grammer, Kelsey	Virgin Islands	2/20/-
Granger, Farley	San Jose, Cal.	7/1/25
Granger, Stewart	London, England	5/6/13
Grant, Amy	Augusta, Ga.	1961
Grant, Lee	New York, N.Y.	10/31/29
Graves, Peter	Minneapolis, Minn.	3/18/26
Gray, Coleen	Staplehurst, Neb.	10/23/22
Gray, Erin	Honolulu, Ha.	1/7/52
Gray, Linda	Santa Monica, Cal.	9/12/40
Grayson, Kathryn	Winston-Salem, N.C.	2/9/22
Greco, Buddy	Philadelphia, Pa.	8/14/26
Greco, Jose	Abruzzi, Italy	12/23/18
Green, Adolph	New York, N.Y.	12/2/15
Green, Al	Forest City, Ark.	4/13/46
Greene, Ellen	New York, N.Y.	1950
Greene, Michele	Las Vegas, Nev.	2/3/-
Greene, Shecky	Chicago, Ill.	4/8/26
Gregory, Cynthia	Los Angeles, Cal.	7/8/46
Gregory, Dick	St. Louis, Mo.	10/12/32
Gregory, James	Bronx, N.Y.	12/23/11
Grey, Joel	Cleveland, Oh.	4/11/32
Griffin, Merv	San Mateo, Cal.	7/6/25
Griffith, Andy	Mount Airy, N.C.	6/1/26
Griffith, Melanie	New York, N.Y.	8/9/57
Grimes, Tammy	Lynn, Mass.	1/30/34
Grizzard, George	Roanoke Rapids, N.C.	4/1/28
Grodin, Charles	Pittsburgh, Pa.	4/21/35
Groh, David	New York, N.Y.	5/21/41
Grosbard, Ulu	Antwerp, Belgium	1/19/29
Gross, Michael	Chicago, Ill.	6/21/47
Guardino, Harry	New York, N.Y.	12/23/25
Guillaume, Robert	St. Louis, Mo.	11/30/37
Guinness, Alec	London, England	4/2/14
Gunn, Moses	St. Louis, Mo.	10/2/29
Guthrie, Arlo	New York, N.Y.	7/10/47
Guttenberg, Steve	New York, N.Y.	8/24/58
Guy, Jasmine	Boston, Mass.	3/10/-
Gwynne, Fred	New York, N.Y.	7/10/26
Hackett, Buddy	Brooklyn, N.Y.	8/31/24
Hackman, Gene	San Bernardino, Cal.	1/30/30
Hagen, Uta	Gottingen, Germany	6/12/19
Haggard, Merle	Bakersfield, Cal.	4/6/37
Haggerty, Dan	Hollywood, Cal.	11/19/41
Hagman, Larry	Weatherford, Tex.	9/21/31
Hague, Albert	Berlin, Germany	10/13/20
Haid, Charles	San Francisco, Cal.	6/2/43
Hale, Barbara	DeKalb, Ill.	4/18/22
Hall, Arsenio	Cleveland, Oh.	2/12/58
Hall, Daryl	Pottstown, Pa.	10/11/49
Hall, Deidre	Milwaukee, Wis.	10/31/48
Hall, Huntz	New York, N.Y.	8/15/19
Hall, Monty	Winnipeg, Man.	8/25/25

Name	Birthplace	Born
Hall, Tom T.	Olive Hill, Ky.	5/25/36
Hamel, Veronica	Philadelphia, Pa.	11/20/43
Hamill, Mark	Oakland, Cal.	9/25/51
Hamilton, George	Memphis, Tenn.	8/12/39
Hamilton, Linda	Salisbury, Md.	9/26/-
Hamlin, Harry	Pasadena, Cal.	10/30/51
Hampshire, Susan	London, England	5/12/42
Hampton, Lionel	Birmingham, Ala.	4/12/13
Hancock, Herbie	Chicago, Ill.	4/12/40
Hanks, Tom	Oakland, Cal.	7/9/56
Hannah, Daryl	Chicago, Ill.	1961
Harmon, Mark	Burbank, Cal.	9/2/51
Harper, Jessica	Chicago, Ill.	1949
Harper, Tess	Mommoth Springs, Ark.	1952
Harper, Valerie	Suffern, N.Y.	8/22/40
Harrelson, Woody	Midland, Tex.	7/23/-
Harrington, Pat Jr.	New York, N.Y.	8/13/29
Harris, Barbara	Evanston, Ill.	7/25/35
Harris, Ed	Englewood, N.J.	11/28/50
Harris, Emmylou	Birmingham, Ala.	4/2/47
Harris, Julie	Grosse Pte. Park, Mich.	12/2/25
Harris, Phil	Linton, Ind.	6/24/04
Harris, Richard	Co. Limerick, Ireland	10/1/33
Harris, Rosemary	Ashby, England	9/19/30
Harrison, George	Liverpool, England	2/25/43
Harrison, Gregory	Avalon, Cal.	5/31/50
Harrison, Rex	Huyton, England	3/5/08
Harry, Deborah	Miami, Fla.	7/1/45
Harry, Jackee	Winston-Salem, N.C.	8/14/-
Hart, Mary	Sioux Falls, S.D.	1951
Hartley, Mariette	New York, N.Y.	6/21/40
Hartman, David	Pawtucket, R.I.	5/19/35
Hartman, Lisa	Houston, Tex.	6/1/56
Hartman, Phil	Ontario, Canada	9/24/48
Hasselhoff, David	Baltimore, Md.	7/17/52
Hasso, Signe	Stockholm, Sweden	8/15/10
Hauer, Rutger	Netherlands	1/23/44
Haver, June	Rock Island, Ill.	6/10/26
Havoc, June	Seattle, Wash.	11/8/16
Hawn, Goldie	Washington, D.C.	11/21/45
Hayden, Melissa	Toronto, Ont.	4/25/23
Hayes, Helen	Washington, D.C.	10/10/00
Hayes, Isaac	Covington, Tenn.	8/20/42
Hayes, Peter Lind	San Francisco, Cal.	6/25/15
Hays, Robert	Bethesda, Md.	7/24/47
Healy, Mary	New Orleans, La.	4/14/18
Hearn, George	Memphis, Tenn.	1935
Heatherton, Joey	Rockville Centre, N.Y.	9/14/44
Heckart, Eileen	Columbus, Oh.	3/29/19
Helmond, Katherine	Galveston, Tex.	7/5/34
Hemingway, Margaux	Portland, Ore.	2/19/55
Hemingway, Mariel	Mill Valley, Cal.	11/21/61
Hemmings, David	Guildford, England	11/18/41
Hemsley, Sherman	Philadelphia, Pa.	2/1/38
Henderson, Florence	Dale, Ind.	2/14/34
Henderson, Skitch	Halstad, Minn.	1/27/18
Henner, Marilu	Chicago, Ill.	4/6/52
Henning, Doug	Ft. Garry, Man.	5/3/47
Henreid, Paul	Trieste, Austria	1/10/08
Hensley, Pamela	Los Angeles, Cal.	10/3/50
Henson, Jim	Greenville, Miss.	9/24/36
Hepburn, Audrey	Brussels, Belgium	5/4/29
Hepburn, Katharine	Hartford, Conn.	11/8/09
Herman, Pee-wee	Peekskill, N.Y.	1952
Herrmann, Edward	Washington, D.C.	7/21/43
Hershey, Barbara	Los Angeles, Cal.	2/5/48
Hesseman, Howard	Lebanon, Ore.	2/27/40
Heston, Charlton	Evanston, Ill.	10/4/23
Hewitt, Christopher	Sussex, England	4/5/-
Higgins, Joel	Bloomington, Ill.	9/28/43
Hildegarde	Adell, Wis.	2/1/06
Hill, Arthur	Melfort, Sask.	8/1/22
Hill, Benny	Southampton, England	1/21/25
Hill, George Roy	Minneapolis, Minn.	12/20/22
Hiller, Wendy	Stockport, England	8/15/12
Hillerman, John	Denison, Tex.	12/30/32
Hines, Gregory	New York, N.Y.	2/14/46
Hines, Jerome	Hollywood, Cal.	11/8/21
Hingle, Pat	Miami, Fla.	7/19/23
Hirsch, Judd	Bronx, N.Y.	3/15/35
Hirt, Al	New Orleans, La.	11/7/22
Ho, Don	Kakaako, Oahu, Ha.	8/13/30
Hoffman, Dustin	Los Angeles, Cal.	8/8/37
Hogan, Paul	New South Wales, Australia.	1941
Holbrook, Hal	Cleveland, Oh.	2/17/25
Holder, Geoffrey	Trinidad	8/1/30
Holliday, Polly	Jasper, Ala.	7/2/37

Name	Birthplace	Born	Name	Birthplace	Born
Holliman, Earl	Delhi, La.	9/11/28	Jones, Jack	Hollywood, Cal.	1/14/38
Holloway, Sterling	Cedartown, Ga.	1/4/05	Jones, James Earl	Tate Co., Miss.	1/17/31
Holm, Celeste	New York, N.Y.	4/29/19	Jones, Jennifer	Tulsa, Okla.	3/2/19
Hooks, Jan	Decatur, Ga.	4/23/57	Jones, Shirley	Smithton, Pa.	3/31/34
Hooks, Robert	Washington, D.C.	4/18/37	Jones, Tom	Pontypridd, Wales	6/7/40
Hope, Bob	London, England	5/29/03	Jones, Tommy Lee	San Saba, Tex.	9/15/46
Hopkins, Anthony	Wales	12/31/37	Jordan, Richard	New York, N.Y.	7/19/38
Hopkins, Telma	Louisville, Ky.	10/28/48	Jourdan, Louis	Marseilles, France	6/19/21
Hopper, Dennis	Dodge City, Kan.	5/17/36	Julia, Raul	San Juan, P.R.	3/9/40
Horne, Lena	Brooklyn, N.Y.	6/30/17	Jump, Gordon	Dayton, Oh.	4/1/32
Horne, Marilyn	Bradford, Pa.	1/16/34	Jurado, Katy	Guadalajara, Mexico	1/16/24
Horowitz, Vladimir	Kiev, Russia	10/1/04			
Horsley, Lee	Muleshoe, Tex.	5/15/55	Kahn, Madeline	Boston, Mass.	9/29/42
Horton, Robert	Los Angeles, Cal.	7/29/24	Kanaly, Steve	Burbank, Cal.	3/14/46
Hoskins, Bob	Suffolk, England	10/26/42	Kane, Carol	Cleveland, Oh.	6/18/52
Houston, Whitney	E. Orange, N.J.	8/9/63	Kaplan, Gabe	Brooklyn, N.Y.	3/31/45
Howard, Ken	El Centro, Cal.	3/28/44	Karlen, John	New York, N.Y.	5/28/33
Howard, Ron	Duncan, Okla.	3/1/54	Karras, Alex	Gary, Ind.	7/15/35
Howell, C. Thomas	Los Angeles, Cal.	12/7/66	Kasem, Casey	Detroit, Mich.	1933
Howes, Sally Ann	London, England	7/20/30	Katt, William	Los Angeles, Cal.	2/16/51
Hughes, Barnard	Bedford Hills, N.Y.	7/16/15	Kavner, Julie	Los Angeles, Cal.	9/7/51
Hulce, Tom	White Water, Wis.	1953	Kazan, Elia	Istanbul, Turkey	9/7/09
Humperdinck, Engelbert	Madras, India	5/3/36	Kazan, Lainie	New York, N.Y.	5/15/42
Hunt, Linda	Morristown, N.J.	4/2/45	Keach, Stacy	Savannah, Ga.	6/2/41
Hunter, Holly	Conyers, Ga.	1959	Keaton, Diane	Santa Ana, Cal.	1/5/46
Hunter, Kim	Detroit, Mich.	11/12/22	Keaton, Michael	Pittsburgh, Pa.	9/9/51
Hunter, Ross	Cleveland, Oh.	5/6/21	Keel, Howard	Gillespie, Ill.	4/13/17
Hunter, Tab	New York, N.Y.	7/11/31	Keeler, Ruby	Halifax, N.S.	8/25/09
Hurt, John	Chesterfield, England	1/22/40	Keeshan, Bob	Lynbrook, N.Y.	6/27/27
Hurt, Mary Beth	Marshalltown, Ia.	9/26/48	Keitel, Harvey	Brooklyn, N.Y.	1947
Hurt, William	Washington, D.C.	3/20/50	Keith, Brian	Bayonne, N.J.	11/14/21
Hussey, Olivia	Buenos Aires, Argentina	4/17/51	Keith, David	Knoxville, Tenn.	5/8/54
Hussey, Ruth	Providence, R.I.	10/30/14	Kellerman, Sally	Long Beach, Cal.	6/2/37
Huston, Anjelica	Ireland	1952	Kelley, DeForest	Atlanta, Ga.	1/20/20
Hutchinson, Josephine	Seattle, Wash.	10/12/-	Kelly, Gene	Pittsburgh, Pa.	8/23/12
Hutton, Betty	Battle Creek, Mich.	2/26/21	Kelly, Jack	Astoria, N.Y.	9/16/27
Hutton, Lauren	Charleston, S.C.	11/17/43	Kelly, Nancy	Lowell, Mass.	3/25/21
Hutton, Timothy	Malibu, Cal.	8/16/61	Kennedy, Arthur	Worcester, Mass.	2/17/14
Hyde-White, Wilfrid	Gloucester, England	5/12/03	Kennedy, George	New York, N.Y.	2/18/26
Hyman, Earle	Rocky Mount, N.C.	10/11/26	Kennedy, Jayne	Washington, D.C.	11/27/51
			Kennedy, Tom	Louisville, Ky.	2/26/27
Ian, Janis	New York, N.Y.	4/7/50	Kent, Allegra	Los Angeles, Cal.	8/11/37
Idol, Billy	London, England	11/30/55	Kercheval, Ken	Wolcottville, Ind.	7/15/35
Iglesias, Julio	Madrid, Spain	9/23/43	Kerns, Joanna	San Francisco, Cal.	2/12/55
Ireland, Jill	London, England	4/24/36	Kerr, Deborah	Helensburgh, Scotland	9/30/21
Ireland, John	Vancouver, B.C.	1/30/14	Kerr, John	New York, N.Y.	11/15/31
Irons, Jeremy	Cowes, England	9/19/48	Khan, Chaka	Great Lakes, Ill.	3/23/53
Irving, Amy	Palo Alto, Cal.	9/10/53	Kidder, Margot	Yellowknife, N.W.T.	10/17/48
Irving, George S.	Springfield, Mass.	11/1/22	Kiley, Richard	Chicago, Ill.	3/31/22
Ives, Burl	Hunt Township, Ill.	6/14/09	King, Alan	Brooklyn, N.Y.	12/26/27
Ivey, Judith	El Paso, Tex.	9/4/51	King, B. B.	Itta Bena, Miss.	9/16/25
			King, Carole	Brooklyn, N.Y.	2/9/42
Jackson, Anne	Allegheny, Pa.	9/3/25	King, Perry	Alliance, Oh.	4/30/48
Jackson, Glenda	Liverpool, England	5/9/36	Kingsley, Ben	Yorkshire, England	12/31/43
Jackson, Janet	Gary, Ind.	5/16/66	Kinski, Klaus	Sopot, Poland	10/8/26
Jackson, Jermaine	Gary, Ind.	12/11/54	Kinski, Nastassia	Berlin, W. Germany	1/24/60
Jackson, La Toya	Gary, Ind.	1/29/56	Kirby, Durward	Covington, Ky.	8/24/12
Jackson, Kate	Birmingham, Ala.	10/29/48	Kirkland, Gelsey	Bethlehem, Pa.	12/29/52
Jackson, Michael	Gary, Ind.	8/29/58	Kirsten, Dorothy	Montclair, N.J.	7/6/19
Jackson, Victoria	Miami, Fla.	8/2/59	Kitt, Eartha	North, S.C.	1/26/28
Jacobi, Derek	London, England	10/22/38	Klein, Robert	New York, N.Y.	2/8/42
Jaeckel, Richard	Long Beach, N.Y.	10/10/26	Klemperer, Werner	Cologne, Germany	3/22/19
Jagger, Dean	Lima, Oh.	11/7/03	Kline, Kevin	St. Louis, Mo.	10/24/47
Jagger, Mick	Dartford, England	7/26/43	Klugman, Jack	Philadelphia, Pa.	4/27/22
James, Dennis	Jersey City, N.J.	8/24/17	Knight, Gladys	Atlanta, Ga.	5/28/44
James, John	Minneapolis, Minn.	4/18/56	Knotts, Don	Morgantown, W. Va.	7/21/24
Janis, Conrad	New York, N.Y.	2/11/28	Knox, Alexander	Strathroy, Ont.	1/16/07
Jarreau, Al	Milwaukee, Wis	3/12/40	Kopell, Bernie	New York, N.Y.	6/21/33
Jeffreys, Anne	Goldsboro, N.C.	1/26/23	Korman, Harvey	Chicago, Ill.	2/15/27
Jenner, Bruce	Mt. Kisco, N.Y.	10/28/49	Kotero, Apollonia	Santa Monica, Cal.	8/2/60
Jennings, Waylon	Littlefield, Tex.	6/15/37	Kotto, Yaphet	New York, N.Y.	11/15/44
Jett, Joan	Philadelphia, Pa.	9/22/60	Kramer, Stanley	New York, N.Y.	9/29/13
Jewison, Norman	Toronto, Ont.	7/21/26	Kramer, Stepfanie	Los Angeles, Cal.	8/6/56
Jillian, Ann	Cambridge, Mass.	1/29/50	Kristofferson, Kris	Brownsville, Tex.	6/22/36
Joel, Billy	Bronx, N.Y.	5/9/49	Kubelik, Rafael	Bychori, Czechoslovakia	6/29/14
John, Elton	Middlesex, England	3/25/47	Kubrick, Stanley	Bronx, N.Y.	7/26/28
Johns, Glynis	Durban, S. Africa	10/5/23	Kulp, Nancy	Harrisburg, Pa.	8/28/21
Johnson, Anne-Marie	Los Angeles, Cal.	7/18/-	Kurtz, Swoosie	Omaha, Neb.	9/6/44
Johnson, Arte	Benton Harbor, Mich.	1/20/29			
Johnson, Ben	Foeaker, Okla.	6/13/18	LaBelle, Patti	Philadelphia, Pa.	10/4/44
Johnson, Don	Flatt Creek, Mo.	12/15/49	Ladd, Cheryl	Huron, S.D.	7/2/51
Johnson, Van	Newport, R.I.	8/25/16	Ladd, Diane	Meridian, Miss.	11/29/32
Jones, Allan	Scranton, Pa.	10/14/07	Lahti, Christine	Detroit, Mich.	4/5/50
Jones, Charlie	Ft. Smith, Ark.	11/9/30	Laine, Cleo	Middlesex, England	10/28/27
Jones, Dean	Morgan City, Ala.	1/25/35	Laine, Frankie	Chicago, Ill.	3/30/13
Jones, George	Saratoga, Tex.	9/12/31	Lamarr, Hedy	Vienna, Austria	11/9/13
Jones, Grace	Spanishtown, Jamaica	5/19/52	Lamas, Lorenzo	Santa Monica, Cal.	1/20/58
Jones, Grandpa	Niagara, Ky.	10/20/13	Lamb, Gil	Minneapolis, Minn.	6/14/06
Jones, Henry	Philadelphia, Pa.	8/1/12	Lamour, Dorothy	New Orleans, La.	12/10/14

Name	Birthplace	Born
Lancaster, Burt	New York, N.Y.	11/2/13
Landau, Martin	New York, N.Y.	6/20/34
Landesberg, Steve	New York, N.Y.	11/23/45
Landis, John	Chicago, Ill.	8/3/50
Landon, Michael	Forest Hills, N.Y.	10/21/36
Lane, Abbe	Brooklyn, N.Y.	12/14/32
Lane, Diane	New York, N.Y.	1/22/63
Lane, Priscilla	Indianola, Ia.	6/12/17
Lang, K.D.	Consort, Alberta	1962
Lang, Stephen	New York, N.Y.	7/11/52
Lange, Hope	Redding Ridge, Conn.	11/28/31
Lange, Jessica	Cloquet, Minn.	4/20/49
Langella, Frank	Bayonne, N.J.	1/1/40
Langford, Frances	Lakeland, Fla.	4/4/13
Lansbury, Angela	London, England	10/16/25
Lansing, Robert	San Diego, Cal.	6/5/28
Laredo, Ruth	Detroit, Mich.	11/20/37
Larroquette, John	New Orleans, La.	11/25/47
Lasser, Louise	New York, N.Y.	4/11/39
Lauper, Cyndi	New York, N.Y.	6/20/53
Laurie, Piper	Detroit, Mich.	1/22/32
Lauter, Ed	Long Beach, N.Y.	10/30/40
Lavin, Linda	Portland, Me.	10/15/37
Lawrence, Carol	Melrose Park, Ill.	9/5/34
Lawrence, Steve	Brooklyn, N.Y.	7/8/35
Lawrence, Vicki	Inglewood, Cal.	3/26/49
Leach, Robin	London, England	8/29/41
Leachman, Cloris	Des Moines, Ia.	4/4/26
Lean, David	Croydon, England	3/25/08
Lear, Norman	New Haven, Conn.	7/27/22
Learned, Michael	Washington, D.C.	4/9/39
LeBon, Simon	Bushey, England	10/27/58
Lederer, Francis	Prague, Czechoslovakia	11/6/06
Lee, Brenda	Atlanta, Ga.	12/11/44
Lee, Christopher	London, England	5/27/22
Lee, Michele	Los Angeles, Cal.	6/24/42
Lee, Peggy	Jamestown, N.D.	5/26/20
Le Gallienne, Eva	London, England	1/11/99
Legrand, Michel	Paris, France	2/24/32
Leibman, Ron	New York, N.Y.	10/11/37
Leifer, Carol	E. Williston, N.Y.	1956
Leigh, Janet	Merced, Cal.	7/6/27
Leinsdorf, Erich	Vienna, Austria	2/4/12
Lemmon, Chris	Los Angeles, Cal.	1/22/54
Lemmon, Jack	Boston, Mass.	2/8/25
Lennon, Julian	Liverpool, England	4/8/63
Lennon Sisters		
Dianne	Los Angeles, Cal.	12/1/39
Janet	Culver City, Cal.	11/15/46
Kathy	Santa Monica, Cal.	8/22/42
Peggy	Los Angeles, Cal.	4/8/41
Leno, Jay	New Rochelle, N.Y.	4/28/50
Leonard, Sheldon	New York, N.Y.	2/22/07
Leontovich, Eugenie	Moscow, Russia	3/21/00
Leslie, Joan	Detroit, Mich.	1/26/25
Lester, Jerry	Chicago, Ill.	1911
Letterman, David	Indianapolis, Ind.	4/12/47
Levine, James	Cincinnati, Oh.	6/23/43
Lewis, Dawnn	New York, N.Y.	3/9/71
Lewis, Emmanuel	New York, N.Y.	—
Lewis, Huey	New York, N.Y.	1952
Lewis, Jerry	Newark, N.J.	3/16/26
Lewis, Jerry Lee	Ferriday, La.	9/29/35
Lewis, Shari	New York, N.Y.	1/17/34
Light, Judith	Trenton, N.J.	2/9/49
Lightfoot, Gordon	Orillia, Ont.	11/17/38
Linden, Hal	New York, N.Y.	3/20/31
Lindfors, Viveca	Uppsala, Sweden	12/29/20
Linkletter, Art	Saskatchewan, Canada	7/17/12
Linn-Baker, Mark	St. Louis, Mo.	6/17/53
Lithgow, John	Rochester, N.Y.	10/19/45
Little, Cleavon	Chickasha, Okla.	6/1/39
Little, Rich	Ottawa, Ont.	11/26/38
Little Richard	Macon, Ga.	12/5/32
Lloyd, Christopher	Stamford, Conn.	10/22/38
Lloyd, Emily	England	9/29/70
Locke, Sondra	Shelbyville, Tenn.	5/28/47
Lockhart, June	New York, N.Y.	6/25/25
Locklear, Heather	Los Angeles, Cal.	9/25/61
Lockwood, Margaret	Karachi, India	9/15/16
Loggia, Robert	New York, N.Y.	1/3/30
Loggins, Kenny	Everett, Wash.	1/17/47
Lollobrigida, Gina	Subiaco, Italy	7/4/28
Lom, Herbert	Prague, Czechoslovakia	1/9/17
London, Julie	Santa Rosa, Cal.	9/26/26
Long, Shelley	Ft. Wayne, Ind.	8/23/49
Lopez, Priscilla	New York, N.Y.	2/26/48
Lopez, Trini	Dallas, Tex.	5/15/37
Lord, Jack	New York, N.Y.	—
Loren, Sophia	Rome, Italy	9/20/34
Loring, Gloria	New York, N.Y.	12/10/46
Loudon, Dorothy	Boston, Mass.	9/17/33
Louise, Tina	New York, N.Y.	2/11/34
Lovitz, Jon	Tarzana, Cal.	7/21/57
Lowe, Rob	Charlottesville, Va.	3/17/64
Loy, Myrna	Helena, Mon.	8/2/05
Lucas, George	Modesto, Cal.	– 5/14/44
Lucci, Susan	Westchester Co., N.Y.	12/23/49
Luckinbill, Laurence	Ft. Smith, Ark.	11/21/34
Ludwig, Christa	Berlin, Germany	3/16/28
Luke, Keye	Canton, China	1904
Lumet, Sidney	Philadelphia, Pa.	6/25/24
Lund, John	Rochester, N.Y.	2/6/13
Lupino, Ida	London, England	2/4/18
LuPone, Patti	Northport, N.Y.	4/21/49
Lynley, Carol	New York, N.Y.	2/13/42
Lynn, Jeffrey	Auburn, Mass.	2/16/-
Lynn, Loretta	Butcher Hollow, Ky.	4/14/-
Maazel, Lorin	Paris, France	3/6/30
MacArthur, James	Los Angeles, Cal.	12/8/37
MacCorkindale, Simon	Cambridge, England	2/12/53
MacGraw, Ali	Pound Ridge, N.Y.	4/1/39
MacKenzie, Gisele	Winnipeg, Man.	1/10/27
MacLaine, Shirley	Richmond, Va.	4/24/34
MacLeod, Gavin	Mt. Kisco, N.Y.	2/28/30
MacMurray, Fred	Kankakee, Ill.	8/30/08
MacNee, Patrick	London, England	2/6/22
MacNeil, Cornell	Minneapolis, Minn.	9/24/22
Macchio, Ralph	Long Island, N.Y.	11/4/62
Macy, Bill	Revere, Mass.	5/18/22
Madden, John	Austin, Minn.	4/10/36
Madonna (Ciccone)	Bay City, Mich.	8/16/58
Majors, Lee	Wyandotte, Mich.	4/23/40
Makarova, Natalia	Leningrad, USSR	11/21/40
Malbin, Elaine	New York, N.Y.	5/24/32
Malden, Karl	Chicago, Ill.	3/22/13
Malfitano, Catherine	New York, N.Y.	4/18/48
Malkovich, John	Christopher, Ill.	12/9/53
Malle, Louis	Thumeries, France	10/30/32
Malone, Dorothy	Chicago, Ill.	1/30/25
Manchester, Melissa	Bronx, N.Y.	2/15/51
Mancini, Henry	Cleveland, Oh.	4/16/24
Mandel, Howie	Toronto, Ont.	11/29/-
Mandrell, Barbara	Houston, Tex.	12/25/48
Mangione, Chuck	Rochester, N.Y.	11/29/40
Manilow, Barry	New York, N.Y.	6/17/46
Mann, Herbie	New York, N.Y.	4/16/30
Manoff, Dinah	New York, N.Y.	1/25/58
Marceau, Marcel	Strasbourg, France	3/22/23
Marchand, Nancy	Buffalo, N.Y.	6/19/28
Margolin, Janet	New York, N.Y.	7/25/43
Marin, Cheech	Los Angeles, Cal.	7/13/46
Markova, Alicia	London, England	12/1/10
Marriner, Neville	Lincoln, England	4/15/24
Marsh, Jean	London, England	7/1/34
Marshall, E. G.	Owatonna, Minn.	6/18/10
Marshall, Penny	New York, N.Y.	10/15/43
Marshall, Peter	Huntington, W.Va.	3/30/27
Martin, Dean	Steubenville, Oh.	6/17/17
Martin, Dick	Detroit, Mich.	1/30/23
Martin, Mary	Weatherford, Tex.	12/1/13
Martin, Pamela Sue	Westport, Conn.	1/5/54
Martin, Steve	Waco, Tex.	1945
Martin, Tony	San Francisco, Cal.	12/25/13
Martins, Peter	Copenhagen, Denmark	10/27/46
Mason, Jackie	Sheboygan, Wis.	6/9/31
Mason, Marsha	St. Louis, Mo.	4/3/42
Mason, Pamela	London, England	3/10/22
Mastrantonio, Mary Eliz.	Lombard, Ill.	11/17/58
Mastroianni, Marcello	Rome, Italy	9/28/24
Matheson, Tim	Glendale, Cal.	12/31/47
Mathis, Johnny	San Francisco, Cal.	9/30/35
Matthau, Walter	New York, N.Y.	10/1/20
Mature, Victor	Louisville, Ky.	1/29/16
May, Elaine	Philadelphia, Pa.	4/21/32
Mayfield, Curtis	Chicago, Ill.	6/3/42
Mayo, Virginia	St. Louis, Mo.	11/30/20
Mazurki, Mike	Austria	12/25/09
Mazursky, Paul	Brooklyn, N.Y.	4/25/30
McArdle, Andrea	Philadelphia, Pa.	11/5/63
McBride, Patricia	Teaneck, N.J.	8/23/42
McCallum, David	Glasgow, Scotland	9/19/33
McCambridge, Mercedes	Joliet, Ill.	3/17/18
McCarthy, Andrew	New York, N.Y.	1963
McCarthy, Kevin	Seattle, Wash.	2/15/14

Name	Birthplace	Born	Name	Birthplace	Born
McCartney, Paul	Liverpool, England	6/18/42	Moran, Erin	Los Angeles, Cal.	10/18/61
McClanahan, Rue	Healdton, Okla.	2/21/36	Moreau, Jeanne	Paris, France	1/23/28
McClure, Doug	Glendale, Cal.	5/11/35	Moreno, Rita	Humacao, P.R.	12/11/31
McClurg, Edie	Kansas City, MD.	7/23/-	Morgan, Dennis	Prentice, Wis.	12/10/10
McCoo, Marilyn	Jersey City, N.J.	9/30/43	Morgan, Harry	Detroit, Mich.	4/10/15
McCord, Kent	Los Angeles, Cal.	9/26/42	Morgan, Henry	New York, N.Y.	3/31/15
McCrea, Joel	Los Angeles, Cal.	11/5/05	Morgan, Jane	Boston, Mass.	1920
McDowall, Roddy	London, England	9/28/28	Morgan, Jaye P.	Mancos, Col.	12/3/31
McDowell, Malcolm	Leeds, England	6/13/43	Moriarty, Michael	Detroit, Mich.	4/5/41
McEntire, Reba	McAlester, Okla.	3/28/55	Morini, Erika	Vienna, Austria	1/5/10
McFarland, Spanky	Dallas, Tex.	10/2/28	Morita, Pat	Isleton, Cal.	6/28/30
McGavin, Darren	Spokane, Wash.	5/7/22	Morley, Robert	Wiltshire, England	5/26/08
McGillis, Kelly	Newport, Cal.	1957	Morris, Greg	Cleveland, Oh.	9/27/34
McGoohan, Patrick	New York, N.Y.	3/19/28	Morris, Howard	New York, N.Y.	9/4/25
McGovern, Elizabeth	Evanston, Ill.	7/18/61	Morse, Robert	Newton, Mass.	5/18/31
McGovern, Maureen	Youngstown, Oh.	7/27/49	Moses, William	Los Angeles, Cal.	11/17/59
McGuire, Al	New York, N.Y.	9/7/31	Mulgrew, Kate	Dubuque, Ia.	4/29/55
McGuire, Dorothy	Omaha, Neb.	6/14/19	Mulhare, Edward	Ireland	4/8/23
McIntire, John	Spokane, Wash.	6/27/07	Mull, Martin	Chicago, Ill.	8/18/43
McKechnie, Donna	Pontiac, Mich.	11/16/42	Mulligan, Richard	New York, N.Y.	11/13/32
McKee, Lonette	Detroit, Mich.	1954	Munsel, Patrice	Spokane, Wash.	5/14/25
McKellen, Ian	Burnley, England	5/25/39	Murphy, Ben	Jonesboro, Ark.	3/6/42
McKeon, Nancy	Westbury, N.Y.	4/4/66	Murphy, Eddie	Brooklyn, N.Y.	4/3/61
McLean, Don	New Rochelle, N.Y.	10/2/45	Murphy, George	New Haven, Conn.	7/4/02
McLerie, Allyn	Grand Mere, Que.	12/1/26	Murphy, Michael	Los Angeles, Cal.	5/5/38
McMahon, Ed	Detroit, Mich.	3/6/23	Murray, Anne	Springhill, Nova Scotia	6/20/45
McNair, Barbara	Racine, Wis.	3/4/39	Murray, Arthur	New York, N.Y.	4/4/95
McNichol, Jimmy	Los Angeles, Cal.	7/2/61	Murray, Bill	Evanston, Ill.	9/21/50
McNichol, Kristy	Los Angeles, Cal.	9/11/62	Murray, Don	Hollywood, Cal.	7/31/29
McQueen, Butterfly	Tampa, Fla.	1/7/11	Murray, Kathryn	Jersey City, N.J.	9/15/06
McRaney, Gerald	Collins, Miss.	8/19/47	Musante, Tony	Bridgeport, Conn.	6/30/36
Meadows, Audrey	Wu Chang, China	2/8/24	Musburger, Brent	Portland, Ore.	5/26/39
Meadows, Jayne	Wu Chang, China	9/27/20	Muti, Riccardo	Naples, Italy	7/28/41
Meara, Anne	New York, N.Y.	9/20/29	Nabors, Jim	Sylacauga, Ala.	6/12/33
Mehta, Zubin	Bombay, India	4/29/36	Nash, Graham	Blackpool, England	2/2/42
Melanie	New York, N.Y.	2/3/47	Natwick, Mildred	Baltimore, Md.	6/19/08
Mendes, Sergio	Nitero, Brazil	2/11/41	Neal, Patricia	Packard, Ky.	1/20/26
Menuhin, Yehudi	New York, N.Y.	4/22/16	Neff, Hildegarde	Ulm, Germany	12/28/25
Mercer, Marian	Akron, Oh.	11/26/35	Neill, Sam	New Zealand	1948
Mercouri, Melina	Athens, Greece	10/18/25	Nelligan, Kate	London, Ontario	3/16/51
Meredith, Burgess	Cleveland, Oh.	11/16/08	Nelson, Barry	San Francisco, Cal.	4/16/20
Merrick, David	Hong Kong	11/27/12	Nelson, Craig T.	Spokane, Wash.	4/4/46
Merrill, Dina	New York, N.Y.	12/9/25	Nelson, Ed	New Orleans, La.	12/21/28
Merrill, Gary	Hartford, Conn.	8/2/15	Nelson, Gene	Seattle, Wash.	3/24/20
Merrill, Robert	Brooklyn, N.Y.	6/4/19	Nelson, Harriet (Hilliard)	Des Moines, Ia.	7/18/14
Messina, Jim	Maywood, Cal.	12/5/47	Nelson, Judd	Portland, Me.	1959
Meyers, Ari	San Juan, Puerto Rico	4/6/69	Nelson, Tracy	Santa Monica, Cal.	10/25/63
Michaels, Al	New York, N.Y.	11/12/44	Nelson, Willie	Abbott, Tex.	4/30/33
Midler, Bette	Paterson, N.J.	12/1/45	Nero, Peter	New York, N.Y.	5/22/34
Milano, Alyssa	New York, N.Y.	12/19/73	Newhart, Bob	Oak Park, Ill.	9/29/29
Miles, Sarah	Ingatestone, England	12/31/41	Newley, Anthony	Hackney, England	9/24/31
Miles, Vera	near Boise City, Okla.	8/23/30	Newman, Laraine	Los Angeles, Cal.	3/2/52
Miller, Ann	Houston, Tex.	4/12/19	Newman, Paul	Cleveland, Oh.	1/26/25
Miller, Dennis	Pittsburgh, Pa.	11/3/53	Newman, Phyllis	Jersey City, N.J.	3/19/35
Miller, Mitch	Rochester, N.Y.	7/4/11	Newman, Randy	Los Angeles, Cal.	11/28/43
Miller, Roger	Ft. Worth, Tex.	1/2/36	Newton, Wayne	Norfolk, Va.	4/3/42
Mills, Donna	Chicago, Ill.	12/11/43	Newton-John, Olivia	Cambridge, England	9/26/48
Mills, Hayley	London, England	4/18/46	Nichols, Mike	Berlin, Germany	11/6/31
Mills, John	Suffolk, England	2/22/08	Nicholson, Jack	Neptune, N.J.	4/28/37
Mills, Juliet	London, England	11/21/41	Nicks, Stevie	California	5/26/48
Milner, Martin	Detroit, Mich.	12/28/27	Nielsen, Leslie	Regina, Sask.	2/11/26
Milnes, Sherrill	Downers Grove, Ill.	1/10/35	Nilsson, Birgit	Karup, Sweden	5/17/18
Milsap, Ronnie	Robinsville, N.C.	1/16/43	Nimoy, Leonard	Boston, Mass.	3/26/31
Milstein, Nathan	Odessa, Russia	12/31/04	Noble, James	Dallas, Tex.	3/5/22
Mimieux, Yvette	Hollywood, Cal.	1/8/39	Nolte, Nick	Omaha, Neb.	2/8/40
Minnelli, Liza	Los Angeles, Cal.	3/12/46	Norman, Jessye	Augusta, Ga.	9/15/45
Mitchell, Cameron	Dallastown, Pa.	4/11/18	Norris, Chuck	Ryan, Okla.	1939
Mitchell, James	Sacramento, Cal.	2/29/20	North, Sheree	Los Angeles, Cal.	1/17/33
Mitchell, Joni	McLeod, Alta.	11/7/43	Novak, Kim	Chicago, Ill.	2/13/33
Mitchum, Robert	Bridgeport, Conn.	8/6/17	Novello, Don	Ashabula, Oh.	1/1/43
Moffat, Donald	Plymouth, England	12/26/30	Nureyev, Rudolf	Russia	3/17/38
Moffo, Anna	Wayne, Pa.	6/27/27			
Molinaro, Al	Kenosha, Wis.	6/24/19	Oates, John	New York, N.Y.	4/7/48
Moll, Richard	Pasadena, Cal.	1/13/43	O'Brian, Hugh	Rochester, N.Y.	4/19/30
Montalban, Ricardo	Mexico City, Mexico	11/25/20	O'Brien, Margaret	San Diego, Cal.	1/15/37
Montand, Yves	Monsumagno, Italy	10/13/21	Ocean, Billy	Trinidad	1/21/52
Montgomery, Elizabeth	Hollywood, Cal.	4/15/33	O'Connell, Helen	Lima, Oh.	5/23/20
Montgomery, George	Brady, Mon.	8/29/16	O'Connor, Carroll	New York, N.Y.	8/2/24
Moody, Ron	London, England	1/8/24	O'Connor, Donald	Chicago, Ill.	8/28/25
Moore, Clayton	Chicago, Ill.	9/14/14	Odetta	Birmingham, Ala.	12/31/30
Moore, Constance	Sioux City, Ia.	1/18/22	O'Hara, Maureen	Dublin, Ireland	8/17/20
Moore, Demi	Roswell, N.M.	11/11/62	O'Herlihy, Dan	Wexford, Ireland	5/1/19
Moore, Dudley	London, England	4/19/35	O'Keefe, Michael	Paulland, N.J.	1955
Moore, Garry	Baltimore, Md.	1/31/15	Olin, Ken	Chicago, Ill.	7/30/54
Moore, Mary Tyler	Brooklyn, N.Y.	12/29/37	Olmos, Edward James	E. Los Angeles, Cal.	2/24/47
Moore, Melba	New York, N.Y.	10/29/45	Olsen, Merlin	Logan, Ut.	9/15/40
Moore, Roger	London, England	10/14/27	O'Neal, Patrick	Ocala, Fla.	9/26/27
Moore, Terry	Los Angeles, Cal.	1/1/29	O'Neal, Ryan	Los Angeles, Cal.	4/20/41

Name	Birthplace	Born
O'Neal, Tatum	Los Angeles, Cal.	11/5/63
O'Neill, Jennifer	Brazil.	2/20/47
Ontkean, Michael	Vancouver, B.C.	1/24/46
Opatoshu, David	New York, N.Y.	1/30/18
Orbach, Jerry	New York, N.Y.	10/20/35
Orlando, Tony	New York, N.Y.	4/3/44
Osbourne, Ozzy	Birmingham, England.	12/3/48
O'Shea, Milo	Ireland.	1926
Osmond, Donny	Ogden, Ut.	12/9/57
Osmond, Marie	Ogden, Ut.	10/13/59
O'Sullivan, Maureen	Boyle, Ireland	5/17/11
O'Toole, Annette	Houston, Tex.	4/1/52
O'Toole, Peter	Connemara, Ireland	8/2/32
Owens, Buck	Sherman, Tex.	8/12/29
Owens, Gary	Mitchell, S.D.	5/10/36
Ozawa, Seiji	Shenyang, China	9/1/35
Paar, Jack	Canton, Oh.	5/1/18
Pacino, Al	New York, N.Y.	4/25/40
Page, LaWanda	Cleveland, Oh.	10/19/20
Page, Patti	Claremore, Okla.	11/8/27
Paige, Janis	Tacoma, Wash.	9/16/22
Palance, Jack	Lattimer, Pa.	2/18/20
Palin, Michael	England	1943
Palmer, Betsy	East Chicago, Ind.	11/1/29
Papas, Irene	Greece.	3/9/26
Papp, Joseph	Brooklyn, N.Y.	6/22/21
Parker, Alan	London, England	2/14/44
Parker, Eleanor	Cedarville, Oh.	6/26/22
Parker, Fess	Ft. Worth, Tex.	8/16/25
Parker, Jameson	Baltimore, Md.	11/18/47
Parker, Jean	Deer Lodge, Mon.	8/11/12
Parks, Bert	Atlanta, Ga.	12/30/14
Parsons, Estelle	Lynn, Mass.	11/20/27
Parton, Dolly	Sevierville, Tenn.	1/19/46
Pasternak, Joseph	Hungary	9/19/01
Patane, Giuseppe	Napoli, Italy	1/1/32
Patinkin, Mandy	Chicago, Ill.	11/30/52
Pavarotti, Luciano	Modena, Italy	10/12/35
Paycheck, Johnny	Greenfield, Oh.	5/31/41
Payne, John	Roanoke, Va.	5/23/12
Pearl, Minnie	Centerville, Tenn.	10/25/12
Peck, Gregory	La Jolla, Cal.	4/5/16
Pendergrass, Teddy	Philadelphia, Pa.	3/26/50
Penn, Arthur	Philadelphia, Pa.	9/27/22
Penn, Sean	Burbank, Cal.	8/17/60
Penny, Joe	London, England	9/14/56
Peppard, George	Detroit, Mich.	10/1/28
Perkins, Anthony	New York, N.Y.	4/4/32
Perlman, Itzhak	Tel Aviv, Israel	8/31/45
Perlman, Rhea	Brooklyn, N.Y.	3/31/48
Perlman, Ron	New York, N.Y.	4/13/-
Perrine, Valerie	Galveston, Tex.	9/3/43
Persoff, Nehemiah	Jerusalem, Palestine.	8/14/20
Peters, Bernadette	New York, N.Y.	2/28/48
Peters, Brock	New York, N.Y.	7/2/27
Peters, Jean	Canton, Oh.	10/15/26
Peters, Roberta	New York, N.Y.	5/4/30
Petit, Pascale	Paris, France	2/27/38
Pfeiffer, Michelle	Santa Ana, Cal.	4/29/57
Phillips, MacKenzie	Alexandria, Va.	11/10/59
Phillips, Michelle	Long Beach, Cal.	6/4/44
Phoenix, River	Madras, Ore.	8/23/70
Pickett, Cindy	Norman, Okla.	4/18/47
Picon, Molly	New York, N.Y.	6/1/98
Pinchot, Bronson	New York, N.Y.	5/20/59
Piscopo, Joe	Passaic, N.J.	6/17/51
Pleasence, Donald	Worksop, England	10/5/19
Pleshette, Suzanne	New York, N.Y.	1/31/37
Plowright, Joan	Brigg, England	10/28/29
Plummer, Amanda	New York, N.Y.	3/23/57
Plummer, Christopher	Toronto, Ont.	12/13/29
Poitier, Sidney	Miami, Fla.	2/20/27
Polanski, Roman	Paris, France	8/18/33
Ponti, Carlo	Milan, Italy.	12/11/13
Porizkova, Paulina.	Czechoslovakia.	4/9/65
Post, Markie	Palo Alto, Cal.	11/4/50
Poston, Tom	Columbus, Oh.	10/17/27
Potts, Annie	Nashville, Tenn.	10/28/-
Powell, Jane	Portland, Ore.	4/1/28
Powers, Stefanie	Hollywood, Cal.	11/2/42
Prentiss, Paula	San Antonio, Tex.	3/4/39
Presley, Priscilla	New York, N.Y.	5/24/45
Preston, Billy	Houston, Tex.	9/9/46
Previn, Andre	Berlin, Germany	4/6/29
Price, Leontyne	Laurel, Miss.	2/10/27
Price, Ray	Perryville, Tex.	1/12/26
Price, Vincent	St. Louis, Mo.	5/27/11
Pride, Charlie	Sledge, Miss.	3/18/39

Name	Birthplace	Born
Prince	Minneapolis, Minn.	6/7/58
Principal, Victoria	Japan	1/3/45
Prosky, Robert.	Philadelphia, Pa.	12/13/30
Prowse, Juliet	Bombay, India.	9/25/37
Pryor, Richard	Peoria, Ill.	12/1/40
Pulliam, Keshia Knight	Newark, N.J.	4/9/79
Pyle, Denver	Bethune, Col.	5/11/20
Quaid, Dennis	Houston, Tex.	4/9/54
Quaid, Randy	Houston, Tex.	10/1/50
Quayle, Anthony	Lancashire, England	9/7/13
Quinlan, Kathleen	Pasadena, Cal.	11/19/54
Quinn, Anthony	Chihuahua, Mexico	4/21/15
Quinn, Martha	Albany, N.Y.	5/11/59
Rabb, Ellis	Memphis, Tenn.	6/20/30
Rabbitt, Eddie	Brooklyn, N.Y.	11/27/41
Rachins, Alan	Cambridge, Mass.	10/10/-
Rae, Charlotte	Milwaukee, Wis.	4/22/26
Raffin, Deborah	Los Angeles, Cal.	3/13/53
Rainer, Luise.	Vienna, Austria	1/12/09
Raitt, John	Santa Ana, Cal.	1/19/17
Ralston, Esther	Bar Harbor, Me.	9/17/02
Ralston, Vera Hruba	Prague, Czechoslovakia.	6/12/19
Rambo, Dack	Delano, Cal.	11/13/41
Rampal, Jean-Pierre	Marseilles, France	1/7/22
Randall, Tony	Tulsa, Okla.	2/26/20
Randolph, John	New York, N.Y.	6/1/15
Rashad, Phylicia.	Houston, Tex.	6/17/48
Ratzenberger, John.	Bridgeport, Conn.	4/6/47
Rawls, Lou	Chicago, Ill.	12/1/36
Ray, Aldo	Pen Argyl, Pa.	9/25/26
Ray, Gene Anthony	New York, N.Y.	5/24/63
Ray, Johnnie	Dallas, Ore.	1/10/27
Rayburn, Gene	Christopher, Ill.	12/22/17
Raye, Martha	Butte, Mon.	8/27/16
Raymond, Gene	New York, N.Y.	8/13/08
Reddy, Helen	Melbourne, Australia.	10/25/41
Redford, Robert	Santa Monica, Cal.	8/18/37
Redgrave, Lynn	London, England	3/8/43
Redgrave, Vanessa	London, England	1/30/37
Reed, Jerry	Atlanta, Ga.	3/20/37
Reed, Oliver	London, England	2/13/38
Reed, Rex	Ft. Worth, Tex.	10/2/38
Reed, Robert	Highland Park, Ill.	10/19/32
Reese, Della	Detroit, Mich.	7/6/31
Reeve, Christopher	New York, N.Y.	9/25/52
Reeves, Dell	Sparta, N.C.	7/14/33
Reid, Kate	London, England	11/4/30
Reid, Tim	Norfolk, Va.	12/19/44
Reilly, Charles Nelson	New York, N.Y.	1/13/31
Reiner, Carl	Bronx, N.Y.	3/20/22
Reiner, Rob	Bronx, N.Y.	3/6/45
Reinhold, Judge	Wilmington, Del.	1956
Reinking, Ann	Seattle, Wash.	11/10/50
Remick, Lee	Quincy, Mass.	12/14/35
Resnik, Regina	New York, N.Y.	8/30/24
Reynolds, Burt	Waycross, Ga.	2/11/36
Reynolds, Debbie	El Paso, Tex.	4/1/32
Reynolds, Marjorie	Buhl, Ida.	8/12/21
Rhue, Madlyn	Washington, D.C.	10/3/34
Rich, Charlie	Forest City, Ark.	12/14/32
Richards, Keith	Kent, England.	12/18/43
Richardson, Tony	Shipley, England	6/5/28
Richie, Lionel.	Tuskegee, Ala.	6/20/50
Rickles, Don	New York, N.Y.	5/8/26
Riegert, Peter	New York, N.Y.	1948
Rigg, Diana.	Doncaster, England	7/20/38
Ringwald, Molly	Rosewood, Cal.	2/14/68
Ritter, John.	Burbank, Cal.	9/17/48
Rivera, Chita	Washington, D.C.	1/23/33
Rivers, Joan	Brooklyn, N.Y.	6/8/33
Robards, Jason Jr.	Chicago, Ill.	7/26/22
Robbins, Jerome	New York, N.Y.	10/11/18
Roberts, Doris	St. Louis, Mo.	11/4/30
Roberts, Eric	Biloxi, Miss.	4/18/56
Roberts, Pernell	Waycross, Ga.	5/18/30
Roberts, Tony	New York, N.Y.	10/22/39
Robertson, Cliff	La Jolla, Cal.	9/9/25
Robertson, Dale	Harrah, Okla.	7/14/23
Robinson, Charles.	Houston, Tex.	11/9/-
Robinson, Smokey	Detroit, Mich.	2/19/40
Roche, Eugene	Boston, Mass.	9/22/28
Rodgers, Jimmie	Camas, Wash.	1933
Rodrigues, Percy	Montreal, Que.	6/13/24
Rodriquez, Johnny	Sabinal, Tex.	12/10/51
Rogers, Chas. (Buddy)	Olathe, Kan.	8/13/04
Rogers, Fred.	Latrobe, Pa.	3/20/28
Rogers, Ginger	Independence, Mo.	7/16/11

Name	Birthplace	Born	Name	Birthplace	Born
Rogers, Kenny	Houston, Tex.	8/21/38	Shackelford, Ted	Oklahoma City, Okla.	6/23/46
Rogers, Mimi	Coral Gables, Fla.	1/27/-	Shandling, Garry	Tucson, Ariz.	1950
Rogers, Roy	Cincinnati, Oh.	11/5/12	Shankar, Ravi	India	4/7/20
Rogers, Wayne	Birmingham, Ala.	4/7/33	Sharif, Omar	Alexandria, Egypt.	4/10/32
Roland, Gilbert	Juarez, Mexico	12/11/05	Shatner, William	Montreal, Que.	3/22/31
Rolle, Esther	Pompano Beach, Fla.	11/8/33	Shearer, Moira	Scotland	1/17/26
Rollins, Howard	Baltimore, Md.	10/17/50	Sheedy, Ally	New York, N.Y.	6/12/62
Romero, Cesar	New York, N.Y.	2/15/07	Sheen, Charlie	Santa Monica, Cal.	1966
Ronstadt, Linda	Tucson, Ariz.	7/15/46	Sheen, Martin	Dayton, Oh.	8/3/40
Rooney, Mickey	Brooklyn, N.Y.	9/23/20	Sheldon, Jack	Jacksonville, Fla.	11/30/31
Rose Marie	New York, N.Y.	8/15/25	Shelley, Carole	London, England	8/16/39
Ross, Diana	Detroit, Mich.	3/26/44	Shepard, Sam	Ft. Sheridan, Ill.	11/5/43
Ross, Katharine	Hollywood, Cal.	1/29/43	Shepherd, Cybill	Memphis, Tenn.	2/18/50
Ross, Marion	Albert Lea, Minn.	10/25/28	Shera, Mark	Bayonne, N.J.	7/10/49
Rosselini, Isabella	Rome, Italy	1952	Shields, Brooke	New York, N.Y.	5/31/65
Rostropovich, Mstislav	Baku, USSR.	3/12/27	Shire, Talia	New York, N.Y.	4/25/46
Roth, David Lee	Bloomington, Ind.	10/10/55	Shirley, Ann	New York, N.Y.	4/17/18
Rourke, Mickey	Miami, Fla.	1956	Shore, Dinah	Winchester, Tenn.	3/1/17
Rowlands, Gena	Cambria, Wis.	6/19/34	Short, Bobby	Danville, Ill.	9/15/24
Rubinstein, John	Los Angeles, Cal.	12/8/46	Short, Martin	Hamilton, Ont.	3/26/51
Rudolf, Max	Frankfurt, Germany	6/15/02	Shull, Richard B.	Evanston, Ill.	2/24/29
Rule, Janice	Norwood, Oh.	8/15/31	Sidney, Sylvia	New York, N.Y.	8/8/10
Rush, Barbara	Denver, Col.	1/4/30	Siepi, Cesare	Milan, Italy	2/10/23
Russell, Jane	Bemidji, Minn.	6/21/21	Sikking, James B.	Los Angeles, Cal.	3/5/34
Russell, Ken	Southampton, England.	7/3/27	Sills, Beverly	Brooklyn, N.Y.	5/25/29
Russell, Kurt	Springfield, Mass.	3/17/51	Silver, Ron	New York, N.Y.	7/2/46
Russell, Mark	Buffalo, N.Y.	8/23/32	Simmons, Gene	Haifa, Israel	8/25/49
Russell, Nipsey	Atlanta, Ga.	10/13/24	Simmons, Jean	London, England	1/31/29
Russell, Theresa	San Diego, Cal.	1957	Simon, Carly	New York, N.Y.	6/25/45
Rutherford, Ann	Toronto, Ont.	11/2/20	Simon, Paul	Newark, N.J.	11/5/42
Ruttan, Susan	Oregon City, Ore.	9/16/50	Simone, Nina	Tyron, N.C.	2/21/33
Ryan, Peggy	Long Beach, Cal.	8/28/24	Sinatra, Frank	Hoboken, N.J.	12/12/15
Ryan, Roz	Detroit, Mich.	7/7/51	Sinatra, Nancy	Jersey City, N.J.	6/8/40
Rydell, Bobby	Philadelphia, Pa.	4/26/42	Singer, Lori	Corpus Christie, Tex.	11/6/62
			Singer, Marc	Vancouver, B.C.	1/29/-
Sahl, Mort	Montreal, Que.	5/11/27	Siskel, Gene	Chicago, Ill.	1/26/46
Saint, Eva Marie	Newark, N.J.	7/4/24	Skelton, Red (Richard)	Vincennes, Ind.	7/18/13
St. James, Susan	Los Angeles, Cal.	8/14/46	Skerritt, Tom	Detroit, Mich.	8/25/33
St. John, Jill	Los Angeles, Cal.	8/19/40	Slater, Helen	Massapequa, N.Y.	12/14/63
Sainte-Marie, Buffy	Maine	2/20/41	Slezak, Erika	Hollywood, Cal.	8/5/46
Sajak, Pat	Chicago, Ill.	10/26/47	Slick, Grace	Chicago, Ill.	10/30/39
Saks, Gene	New York, N.Y.	11/8/21	Smirnoff, Yakov	Odessa, USSR.	1/24/51
Sales, Soupy	Franklinton, N.C.	1/8/26	Smith, Allison	New York, N.Y.	12/9/69
Samms, Emma	London, England	8/28/60	Smith, Alexis	Penticton, B.C.	6/8/21
Sanderson, William	Memphis, Tenn.	1/10/48	Smith, Buffalo Bob	Buffalo, N.Y.	11/27/17
Sandy, Gary	Dayton, Oh.	12/25/45	Smith, Connie	Elkhart, Ind.	8/14/41
Sanford, Isabel	New York, N.Y.	8/29/17	Smith, Jaclyn	Houston, Tex.	10/26/47
Santana, Carlos	Mexico	7/20/47	Smith, Keely	Norfolk, Va.	3/9/35
Sarandon, Chris	Beckley, W.Va.	7/24/42	Smith, Maggie	Ilford, England.	12/28/34
Sarandon, Susan	New York, N.Y.	10/4/46	Smith, Roger	South Gate, Cal.	12/18/32
Sarnoff, Dorothy	New York, N.Y.	5/25/17	Smits, Jimmy	New York, N.Y.	7/9/58
Sarrazin, Michael	Quebec City, Que.	5/22/40	Smothers, Dick	New York, N.Y.	11/20/39
Savalas, Telly	Garden City, N.Y.	1/21/24	Smothers, Tom	New York, N.Y.	2/2/37
Saxon, John	Brooklyn, N.Y.	8/5/35	Snodgress, Carrie	Park Ridge, Ill.	10/27/46
Sayles, John	Schenectady, N.Y.	9/28/50	Snow, Hank	Nova Scotia, Canada	5/9/14
Scaggs, Boz	Dallas, Tex.	6/8/44	Snyder, Tom	Milwaukee, Wis.	5/12/36
Schallert, William	Los Angeles, Cal.	7/6/22	Solti, Georg	Budapest, Hungary.	10/21/12
Scheider, Roy	Orange, N.J.	11/10/32	Somers, Suzanne	San Bruno, Cal.	10/16/46
Schell, Maria	Vienna, Austria	1/15/26	Somes, Michael	nr. Stroud, England.	9/28/17
Schell, Maximilian	Vienna, Austria	12/8/30	Sommer, Elke	Berlin, Germany	11/5/41
Schell, Ronnie	Richmond, Cal.	12/23/31	Sorvino, Paul	New York, N.Y.	1939
Schenkel, Chris	Bippus, Ind.	8/21/23	Sothern, Ann	Valley City, N.D.	1/22/09
Schnabel, Stefan	Berlin, Germany	2/2/12	Soul, David	Chicago, Ill.	8/28/43
Schneider, Alexander	Vilna, Poland	10/21/08	Spacek, Sissy	Quitman, Tex.	12/25/49
Schneider, John	Mt. Kisco, N.Y.	4/8/54	Spano, Joe	San Francisco, Cal.	7/7/46
Schreiber, Avery	Chicago, Ill.	4/9/35	Spelling, Aaron	Dallas, Tex.	4/22/28
Schroder, Ricky	Staten Island, N.Y.	4/3/70	Spielberg, Steven	Cincinnati, Oh.	12/18/47
Schwarzenegger, Arnold	Graz, Austria	7/30/47	Springfield, Dusty	London, England	4/16/39
Schwarzkopf, Elisabeth	Jarotschin, Poland	12/9/15	Springfield, Rick	Sydney, Australia.	8/23/49
Scofield, Paul	Hurst, Pierpont, England.	1/21/22	Springsteen, Bruce	Freehold, N.J.	9/23/49
Scolari, Peter	New Rochelle, Ill.	9/12/54	Stack, Robert	Los Angeles, Cal.	1/13/19
Scorsese, Martin	New York, N.Y.	11/17/42	Stafford, Jo	Coalinga, Cal.	11/12/18
Scott, George C.	Wise, Va.	10/18/27	Stahl, Richard	Detroit, Mich.	1/4/32
Scott, Lizabeth	Scranton, Pa.	9/29/22	Stallone, Sylvester	New York, N.Y.	7/6/46
Scott, Martha	Jamesport, Mo.	9/22/14	Stamos, John	Cypress, Cal.	8/19/63
Scotto, Renata	Savona, Italy	2/24/35	Stamp, Terence	Stepney, England.	7/22/39
Scully, Vin	New York, N.Y.	11/29/27	Stander, Lionel	New York, N.Y.	1/11/08
Sebastian, John	New York, N.Y.	3/17/44	Stang, Arnold	New York, N.Y.	9/28/25
Sedaka, Neil	New York, N.Y.	3/13/39	Stanley, Kim	Tularosa, N.M.	2/11/25
Seeger, Pete	New York, N.Y.	5/3/19	Stanton, Harry Dean	Kentucky	7/14/26
Segal, George	Great Neck, N.Y.	2/13/34	Stanwyck, Barbara	Brooklyn, N.Y.	7/16/07
Segal, Vivienne	Philadelphia, Pa.	4/19/97	Stapleton, Jean	New York, N.Y.	1/19/23
Seinfeld, Jerry	New York, N.Y.	1954	Stapleton, Maureen	Troy, N.Y.	6/21/25
Sellecca, Connie	New York, N.Y.	5/25/55	Starr, Kay	Dougherty, Okla.	7/21/22
Selleck, Tom	Detroit, Mich.	1/29/45	Starr, Ringo	Liverpool, England	7/7/40
Serkin, Rudolf	Eger, Austria	3/28/03	Steber, Eleanor	Wheeling, W. Va.	7/17/14
Severinsen, Doc	Arlington, Ore.	7/7/27	Steenburgen, Mary	Little Rock, Ark.	1953
Seymour, Jane	Middlesex, England.	2/15/51	Steiger, Rod	W. Hampton, N.Y.	4/14/25

Name	Birthplace	Born
Steinberg, David	Winnipeg, Man.	8/9/42
Stephens, James	Mt. Kisco, N.Y.	5/18/51
Sterling, Jan	New York, N.Y.	4/3/23
Sterling, Robert	New Castle, Pa.	11/13/17
Stern, Isaac	Kreminiecz, Russia	7/21/20
Sternhagen, Frances	Washington, D.C.	1/13/30
Stevens, Andrew	Memphis, Tenn.	6/10/55
Stevens, Cat	London, England	7/21/48
Stevens, Connie	Brooklyn, N.Y.	8/8/38
Stevens, Kaye	E. Cleveland, Oh.	7/21/35
Stevens, Rise	New York, N.Y.	6/11/13
Stevens, Stella	Yazoo City, Miss.	10/1/36
Stevenson, McLean	Normal, Ill.	11/14/29
Stevenson, Parker	Philadelphia, Pa.	6/4/52
Stewart, James	Indiana, Pa.	5/20/08
Stewart, Rod	London, England	1/10/45
Stickney, Dorothy	Dickinson, N.D.	6/21/00
Stiers, David Ogden	Peoria, Ill.	10/31/42
Stiller, Jerry	New York, N.Y.	6/8/29
Stills, Stephen	Dallas, Tex.	1/3/45
Sting (G. Sumner)	Newcastle, England	10/2/51
Stockwell, Dean	Hollywood, Cal.	3/5/36
Stookey, Paul	Baltimore, Md.	12/30/37
Storch, Larry	New York, N.Y.	1/8/23
Storm, Gale	Bloomington, Tex.	4/5/22
Straight, Beatrice	Old Westbury, N.Y.	8/2/18
Strasberg, Susan	New York, N.Y.	5/22/38
Strasser, Robin	New York, N.Y.	5/7/45
Stratas, Teresa	Toronto, Ont.	5/26/38
Strauss, Peter	New York, N.Y.	2/20/47
Streep, Meryl	Summit, N.J.	6/22/49
Streisand, Barbra	Brooklyn, N.Y.	4/24/42
Stritch, Elaine	Detroit, Mich.	2/2/26
Struthers, Sally	Portland, Ore.	7/28/48
Stuarti, Enzo	Rome, Italy	3/3/25
Sullivan, Barry	New York, N.Y.	8/29/12
Sullivan, Susan	New York, N.Y.	11/18/44
Sullivan, Tom	Boston, Mass.	3/27/47
Sumac, Yma	Ichocan, Peru	9/10/27
Summer, Donna	Boston, Mass.	12/31/48
Sutherland, Donald	St. John, New Brunswick	7/17/34
Sutherland, Joan	Sydney, Australia	11/7/26
Swayze, Patrick	Houston, Tex.	8/18/54
Swenson, Inga	Omaha, Neb.	12/29/34
Swit, Loretta	Passaic, N.J.	11/4/37
Mr. T (Lawrence Tero)	Chicago, Ill.	5/21/52
Talbot, Lyle	Pittsburgh, Pa.	2/8/02
Tallchief, Maria	Fairfax, Okla.	1/24/25
Tambor, Jeffrey	San Francisco, Cal.	7/8/-
Tandy, Jessica	London, England	6/7/09
Tarkenton, Fran	Richmond, Va.	2/3/40
Tayback, Vic	New York, N.Y.	1/6/29
Taylor, Elizabeth	London, England	2/27/32
Taylor, James	Boston, Mass.	3/12/48
Taylor, Rod	Sydney, Australia	1/11/30
Te Kanawa, Kiri	Gisborne, New Zealand	3/6/44
Tebaldi, Renata	Pesaro, Italy	2/1/22
Temple, Shirley	Santa Monica, Cal.	4/23/28
Tennille, Toni	Montgomery, Ala.	5/8/43
Terry-Thomas	London, England	7/14/11
Tharp, Twyla	Portland, Ind.	7/1/41
Thaxter, Phyllis	Portland, Me.	11/20/19
Thicke, Alan	Kirkland Lake, Ont.	3/1/47
Thomas, B.J.	Hugo, Okla.	8/7/42
Thomas, Betty	St. Louis, Mo.	7/27/48
Thomas, Danny	Deerfield, Mich.	1/6/14
Thomas, Heather	Greenwich, Conn.	9/8/57
Thomas, Marlo	Detroit, Mich.	11/21/43
Thomas, Philip Michael	Columbus, Oh.	5/26/49
Thomas, Richard	New York, N.Y.	6/13/51
Thompson, Jack	Sydney, Australia	8/31/40
Thompson, Lea	Rochester, Minn.	5/31/61
Thompson, Sada	Des Moines, Ia.	9/27/29
Thulin, Ingrid	Sweden	1/27/29
Tiegs, Cheryl	Minnesota	9/27/47
Tierney, Gene	Brooklyn, N.Y.	11/20/20
Tiffany	Norwalk, Cal.	1972
Tillis, Mel	Tampa, Fla.	8/8/32
Tiny Tim	New York, N.Y.	4/12/23
Todd, Richard	Dublin, Ireland	6/11/19
Tomlin, Lily	Detroit, Mich.	9/1/39
Tomlinson, David	Scotland	5/7/17
Toomey, Regis	Pittsburgh, Pa.	8/13/02
Torme, Mel	Chicago, Ill.	9/13/25
Torn, Rip	Temple, Tex.	2/6/31
Tracy, Arthur	Russia	6/25/03
Travanti, Daniel J.	Kenosha, Wis.	3/7/40
Travers, Mary	Louisville, Ky.	11/9/36

Name	Birthplace	Born
Travis, Randy	Marshville, N.C.	1959
Travolta, John	Englewood, N.J.	2/18/54
Trebek, Alex	Sudbury, Ont.	7/22/40
Trevor, Claire	New York, N.Y.	3/8/09
Troyanos, Tatiana	New York, N.Y.	9/12/38
Tucker, Michael	Baltimore, Md.	2/6/44
Tucker, Tanya	Seminole, Tex.	10/10/58
Tune, Tommy	Wichita Falls, Tex.	2/28/39
Turner, Ike	Clarksdale, Miss.	11/5/39
Turner, Kathleen	Springfield, Mo.	6/19/54
Turner, Lana	Wallace, Ida.	2/8/20
Turner, Tina	Nutbush, Tenn.	11/26/39
Tushingham, Rita	Liverpool, England	3/14/40
Twiggy (Leslie Hornby)	London, England	9/19/49
Twitty, Conway	Friar's Point, Miss.	9/1/33
Tyson, Cicely	New York, N.Y.	12/19/33
Uecker, Bob	Milwaukee, Wis.	1/26/35
Uggams, Leslie	New York, N.Y.	5/25/43
Ullman, Tracey	Slough, England	1960
Ullmann, Liv	Tokyo, Japan	12/16/38
Urich, Robert	Toronto, Oh.	12/19/46
Ustinov, Peter	London, England	4/16/21
Vaccaro, Brenda	Brooklyn, N.Y.	11/18/39
Vale, Jerry	New York, N.Y.	7/8/31
Valente, Caterina	Paris, France	1/14/31
Valentine, Karen	Santa Rosa, Cal.	5/25/47
Valli, Frankie	Newark, N.J.	5/3/37
Van Ark, Joan	New York, N.Y.	6/16/43
Van Cleef, Lee	Somerville, N.J.	1/9/25
Van Doren, Mamie	Rowena, S.D.	2/6/33
Van Dyke, Dick	West Plains, Mo.	12/13/25
Van Dyke, Jerry	Danville, Ill.	7/27/32
Van Fleet, Jo	Oakland, Cal.	12/30/19
Van Pallandt, Nina	Copenhagen, Denmark	7/15/32
Van Patten, Dick	New York, N.Y.	12/9/28
Vaughan, Sarah	Newark, N.J.	3/27/24
Vaughn, Robert	New York, N.Y.	11/22/32
Venuta, Benay	San Francisco, Cal.	1/27/11
Verdon, Gwen	Los Angeles, Cal.	1/13/25
Vereen, Ben	Miami, Fla.	10/10/46
Verrett, Shirley	New Orleans, La.	5/31/31
Vickers, Jon	Prince Albert, Sask.	10/26/26
Vigoda, Abe	New York, N.Y.	2/24/21
Villella, Edward	Long Island, N.Y.	10/1/36
Vincent, Jan-Michael	Denver, Col.	7/15/44
Vinson, Helen	Beaumont, Tex.	9/17/07
Vinton, Bobby	Canonsburg, Pa.	4/16/35
Vitale, Dick	E. Rutherford, N.J.	6/9/40
Voight, Jon	Yonkers, N.Y.	12/29/38
Von Stade, Frederica	Somerville, N.J.	6/1/45
Von Sydow, Max	Lund, Sweden	4/10/29
Waggoner, Lyle	Kansas City, Kan.	4/13/35
Wagner, Lindsay	Los Angeles, Cal.	6/22/49
Wagner, Robert	Detroit, Mich.	2/10/30
Wagoner, Porter	West Plains, Mo.	8/12/27
Wahl, Ken	Chicago, Ill.	1956
Wain, Bea	Bronx, N.Y.	4/30/17
Waite, Ralph	White Plains, N.Y.	6/22/29
Walden, Robert	New York, N.Y.	9/25/43
Walken, Christopher	New York, N.Y.	3/31/43
Walker, Clint	Hartford, Ill.	5/30/27
Walker, Nancy	Philadelphia, Pa.	5/10/21
Wallach, Eli	Brooklyn, N.Y.	12/7/15
Walston, Ray	Laurel, Miss.	12/2/14
Walter, Jessica	New York, N.Y.	1/31/44
Wanamaker, Sam	Chicago, Ill.	6/14/19
Ward, Rachel	London, England	1957
Ward, Simon	London, England	10/19/41
Warden, Jack	Newark, N.J.	9/18/20
Warfield, William	W. Helena, Ark.	1/22/20
Warner, Malcolm-Jamal	Jersey City, N.J.	8/18/70
Warren, Lesley Ann	New York, N.Y.	8/16/46
Warren, Michael	So. Bend, Ind.	3/5/46
Warrick, Ruth	St. Joseph, Mo.	6/29/16
Warwick, Dionne	E. Orange, N.J.	12/12/41
Washington, Denzel	Mt. Vernon, N.Y.	12/28/54
Waterston, Sam	Cambridge, Mass.	11/15/40
Watkins, Carlene	Hartford, Conn.	6/4/52
Watts, Andre	Nuremberg, Germany	6/20/46
Wayne, David	Traverse City, Mich.	1/30/14
Waxman, Al	Toronto, Ont.	3/2/35
Weaver, Dennis	Joplin, Mo.	6/4/24
Weaver, Fritz	Pittsburgh, Pa.	1/19/26
Weaver, Sigourney	New York, N.Y.	10/8/49
Weir, Peter	Sydney, Australia	8/8/44
Weitz, Bruce	Norwalk, Conn.	5/27/43
Welch, Raquel	Chicago, Ill.	9/5/40

Name	Birthplace	Born	Name	Birthplace	Born
Weld, Tuesday	New York, N.Y.	8/27/43	Winkler, Henry	New York, N.Y.	10/30/45
Welk, Lawrence	nr. Strasburg, N.D.	3/11/03	Winters, Jonathan	Dayton, Oh.	11/11/25
Wells, Kitty	Nashville, Tenn.	8/30/19	Winters, Shelley	St. Louis, Mo.	8/18/22
Wendt, George	Chicago, Ill.	10/17/48	Winwood, Steve	Birmingham, England.	5/12/48
Weston, Jack	Cleveland, Oh.	8/21/24	Wiseman, Joseph	Montreal, Que.	5/15/18
Whelchel, Lisa	Ft. Worth, Tex.	5/29/63	Withers, Jane	Atlanta, Ga.	4/12/26
White, Barry	Galveston, Tex.	9/12/44	Wonder, Stevie	Saginaw, Mich.	5/13/50
White, Betty	Oak Park, Ill.	1/17/22	Woodard, Alfre	Tulsa, Okla.	11/2/53
White, Jesse	Buffalo, N.Y.	1/3/19	Woods, James	Vernal, N.J.	4/18/47
White, Vanna	N. Myrtle Beach, S.C.	2/18/57	Woodward, Edward	Croyden, England	6/1/30
Whiting, Margaret	Detroit, Mich.	7/22/24	Woodward, Joanne	Thomasville, Ga.	2/27/30
Whitmore, James	White Plains, N.Y.	10/1/21	Wopat, Tom	Lodi, Wis.	9/9/51
Widmark, Richard	Sunrise, Minn.	12/26/14	Worth, Irene	Nebraska	6/23/16
Wiest, Dianne	Kansas City, Mo.	3/28/48	Wray, Fay	Alberta, Canada	9/10/07
Wilde, Cornel	New York, N.Y.	10/13/15	Wright, Martha	Seattle, Wash.	3/23/26
Wilder, Billy	Vienna, Austria	6/22/06	Wright, Max	Detroit, Mich.	8/2/-
Wilder, Gene	Milwaukee, Wis.	6/11/35	Wright, Steven	New York, N.Y.	12/6/55
Williams, Andy	Wall Lake, Ia.	12/3/30	Wright, Teresa	New York, N.Y.	10/27/18
Williams, Billy Dee	New York, N.Y.	4/6/37	Wrightson, Earl	Baltimore, Md.	1/1/16
Williams, Cindy	Van Nuys, Cal.	8/22/47	Wyatt, Jane	Campgaw, N.J.	8/10/11
Williams, Esther	Los Angeles, Cal.	8/8/23	Wyman, Jane	St. Joseph, Mo.	1/4/14
Williams, Hal	Columbus, Oh.	12/14/38	Wynette, Tammy	Red Bay, Ala.	5/5/42
Williams Jr., Hank	Shreveport, La.	5/26/49	Yarborough, Glenn	Milwaukee, Wis.	1/12/30
Williams, Joe	Cordele, Ga.	12/12/18	Yarrow, Peter	New York, N.Y.	5/31/38
Williams, JoBeth	Houston, Tex.	1953	York, Michael	Fulmer, England	3/27/42
Williams, Paul	Omaha, Neb.	9/19/40	York, Susannah	London, England	1/9/42
Williams, Robin	Chicago, Ill.	7/21/52	Yothers, Tina	Whittier, Cal.	9/5/73
Williams, Roger	Omaha, Neb.	1926	Young, Alan	Northumberland, England	11/19/19
Williams, Treat	Rowayton, Conn.	12/1/51	Young, Burt	New York, N.Y.	4/30/40
Williamson, Nicol	Hamilton, Scotland	9/14/38	Young, Loretta	Salt Lake City, Ut.	1/6/13
Willis, Bruce	Penns Grove, N.J.	3/19/55	Young, Neil	Toronto, Ont.	11/12/45
Wilson, Demond	Valdosta, Ga.	10/13/46	Young, Robert	Chicago, Ill.	2/22/07
Wilson, Dolores	Philadelphia, Pa.	1929	Youngman, Henny	Liverpool, England	1/12/06
Wilson, Elizabeth	Grand Rapids, Mich.	4/4/25	Zadora, Pia	Hoboken, N.J.	1957
Wilson, Flip	Jersey City, N.J.	12/8/33	Zappa, Frank	Baltimore, Md.	12/21/40
Wilson, Nancy	Chillicothe, Oh.	2/20/37	Zeffirelli, Franco	Florence, Italy.	2/12/23
Windom, William	New York, N.Y.	9/28/23	Zimbalist, Efrem Jr.	New York, N.Y.	11/30/23
Winfield, Paul	Los Angeles, Cal.	5/22/41	Zimbalist, Stephanie	New York, N.Y.	10/6/56
Winfrey, Oprah	Kosciusko, Miss.	1/29/54	Zmed, Adrian	Chicago, Ill.	3/14/54
Winger, Debra	Cleveland, Oh.	5/16/55	Zukerman, Pinchas	Tel Aviv, Israel	7/16/48

Entertainment Personalities of the Past

(as of July 15, 1989)

Born	Died	Name	Born	Died	Name	Born	Died	Name
1895	1974	Abbott, Bud	1890	1952	Banks, Leslie	1895	1973	Blackmer, Sidney
1872	1953	Adams, Maude	1890	1955	Bara, Theda	1908	1989	Blanc, Mel
1855	1926	Adler, Jacob P.	1810	1891	Barnum, Phineas T.	1882	1951	Blaney, Charles E.
1903	1984	Adler, Luther	1912	1978	Barrie, Wendy	1900	1943	Bledsoe, Jules
1898	1933	Adoree, Renee	1879	1959	Barrymore, Ethel	1928	1972	Blocker, Dan
1902	1986	Aherne, Brian	1882	1942	Barrymore, John	1909	1979	Blondell, Joan
1909	1964	Albertson, Frank	1878	1954	Barrymore, Lionel	1888	1959	Biore, Eric
1907	1981	Albertson, Jack	1848	1905	Barrymore, Maurice	1901	1975	Blue, Ben
1885	1952	Alda, Frances	1897	1963	Barthelmess, Richard	1899	1957	Bogart, Humphrey
1894	1956	Allen, Fred	1890	1962	Barton, James	1880	1965	Boland, Mary
1906	1964	Allen, Gracie	1914	1984	Basehart, Richard	1895	1969	Boles, John
1883	1950	Allgood, Sara	1904	1984	Basie, Count	1904	1987	Bolger, Ray
1886	1954	Anderson, John Murray	1873	1951	Bauer, Harold	1903	1960	Bond, Ward
1915	1967	Andrews, Laverne	1923	1985	Baxter, Anne	1892	1981	Bondi, Beulah
1876	1958	Anglin, Margaret	1889	1951	Baxter, Warner	1917	1981	Boone, Richard
1887	1933	Arbuckle, Fatty (Roscoe)	1880	1928	Bayes, Nora	1833	1893	Booth, Edwin
1900	1976	Arlen, Richard	1904	1965	Beatty, Clyde	1796	1852	Booth, Junius Brutus
1868	1946	Arliss, George	1902	1962	Beavers, Louise	1894	1953	Bordoni, Irene
1888	1945	Armetta, Henry	1884	1946	Beery, Noah	1888	1960	Bori, Lucrezia
1900	1971	Armstrong, Louis	1889	1949	Beery, Wallace	1905	1965	Bow, Clara
1917	1986	Arnaz, Desi	1901	1970	Begley, Ed	1874	1946	Bowes, Maj. Edward
1890	1956	Arnold, Edward	1854	1931	Belasco, David	1928	1977	Boyd, Stephen
1905	1974	Arquette, Cliff	1949	1982	Belushi, John	1898	1972	Boyd, William
1899	1987	Astaire, Fred	1906	1968	Benaderet, Bea	1899	1978	Boyer, Charles
1906	1987	Astor, Mary	1906	1964	Bendix, William	1893	1939	Brady, Alice
1885	1946	Atwill, Lionel	1904	1965	Bennett, Constance	1871	1936	Breese, Edmund
1845	1930	Auer, Leopold	1943	1987	Bennett, Michael	1898	1964	Brendel, El
1905	1967	Auer, Mischa	1873	1944	Bennett, Richard	1894	1974	Brennan, Walter
1900	1972	Austin, Gene	1894	1974	Benny, Jack	1904	1979	Brent, George
1898	1940	Ayres, Agnes	1924	1970	Benzell, Mimi	1875	1948	Brian, Donald
			1899	1966	Berg, Gertrude	1891	1951	Brice, Fanny
1913	1989	Backus, Jim	1903	1978	Bergen, Edgar	1891	1959	Broderick, Helen
1864	1922	Bacon, Frank	1915	1982	Bergman, Ingrid	1904	1951	Bromberg, J. Edward
1892	1968	Bainter, Fay	1895	1976	Berkeley, Busby	1892	1973	Brown, Joe E.
1895	1957	Baker, Belle	1863	1927	Bernard, Sam	1926	1966	Bruce, Lenny
1906	1975	Baker, Josephine	1923	1986	Bernardi, Herschel	1895	1953	Bruce, Nigel
1904	1983	Balanchine, George	1844	1923	Bernhardt, Sarah	1910	1982	Bruce, Virginia
1911	1989	Ball, Lucille	1893	1943	Bernie, Ben	1920	1985	Brynner, Yul
1882	1956	Bancroft, George	1889	1967	Bickford, Charles	1903	1979	Buchanan, Edgar
1903	1968	Bankhead, Tallulah	1911	1960	Bjoerling, Jussi	1891	1957	Buchanan, Jack

Born	Died	Name	Born	Died	Name	Born	Died	Name
1885	1957	Buck, Gene	1916	1944	Cregar, Laird	1898	1985	Fetchit, Stepin
1938	1982	Buono, Victor	1880	1942	Crews, Laura Hope	1894	1979	Fiedler, Arthur
1885	1970	Burke, Billie	1880	1974	Crisp, Donald	1918	1973	Field, Betty
1911	1967	Burnette, Smiley	1942	1973	Croce, Jim	1898	1979	Fields, Gracie
1896	1956	Burns, Bob	1910	1960	Cromwell, Richard	1867	1941	Fields, Lew
1902	1971	Burns, David	1903	1977	Crosby, Bing	1879	1946	Fields, W.C.
1882	1941	Burr, Henry	1897	1975	Cross, Milton	1931	1978	Fields, Totie
1925	1984	Burton, Richard	1910	1986	Crothers, Scatman	1916	1977	Finch, Peter
1897	1946	Busch, Mae	1878	1968	Currie, Finlay	1865	1932	Fiske, Minnie Maddern
1883	1966	Bushman, Francis X.	1816	1876	Cushman, Charlotte	1888	1961	Fitzgerald, Barry
1896	1946	Butterworth, Charles				1895	1962	Flagstad, Kirsten
1893	1971	Byington, Spring	1914	1978	Dailey, Dan	1900	1971	Flippen, Jay C.
			1899	1981	Chief Dan George	1909	1959	Flynn, Errol
1904	1972	Cabot, Bruce	1923	1965	Dandridge, Dorothy	1925	1974	Flynn, Joe
1918	1977	Cabot, Sebastian	1869	1941	Danforth, William	1880	1942	Fokine, Michel
1899	1986	Cagney, James	1894	1963	Daniell, Henry	1910	1968	Foley, Red
1895	1956	Calhern, Louis	1901	1971	Daniels, Bebe	1905	1982	Fonda, Henry
1923	1977	Callas, Maria	1860	1935	Daniels, Lew	1920	1978	Fontaine, Frank
1853	1942	Calve, Emma	1936	1973	Darin, Bobby	1887	1983	Fontanne, Lynn
1933	1976	Cambridge, Godfrey	1921	1965	Darnell, Linda	1853	1937	Forbes-Robertson, J.
1865	1940	Campbell, Mrs. Patrick	1879	1967	Darwell, Jane	1895	1973	Ford, John
1892	1964	Cantor, Eddie	1909	1986	Da Silva, Howard	1901	1976	Ford, Paul
1878	1947	Carey, Harry	1866	1949	Davenport, Harry	1899	1966	Ford, Wallace
1950	1983	Carpenter, Karen	1907	1961	Davis, Joan	1806	1872	Forrest, Edwin
1906	1988	Carradine, John	1931	1955	Dean, James	1927	1987	Fosse, Bob
1880	1961	Carrillo, Leo	1905	1968	Dekker, Albert	1901	1970	Foster, Preston
1892	1972	Carroll, Leo G.	1908	1983	Del Rio, Dolores	1857	1928	Foy, Eddie
1905	1965	Carroll, Nancy	1892	1983	Demarest, William	1903	1968	Francis, Kay
1910	1963	Carson, Jack	1881	1959	DeMille, Cecil B.	1887	1966	Frawley, William
1862	1937	Carter, Mrs. Leslie	1891	1967	Denny, Reginald	1885	1938	Frederick, Pauline
1873	1921	Caruso, Enrico	1901	1974	DeSica, Vittorio	1870	1955	Friganza, Trixie
1876	1973	Casals, Pablo	1905	1977	Devine, Andy	1890	1958	Frisco, Joe
1929	1989	Cassavetes, John	1942	1972	De Wilde, Brandon	1860	1915	Frohman, Charles
1927	1976	Cassidy, Jack	1907	1974	De Wolfe, Billy	1851	1940	Frohman, Daniel
1893	1969	Castle, Irene	1865	1950	De Wolfe, Elsie	1885	1947	Fyffe, Will
1887	1918	Castle, Vernon	1920	1985	Diamond, Selma			
1889	1960	Catlett, Walter	1879	1947	Digges, Dudley	1901	1960	Gable, Clark
1887	1950	Cavanaugh, Hobart	1901	1966	Disney, Walt	1889	1963	Galli-Curci, Amelita
1873	1938	Chaliapin, Feodor	1894	1949	Dix, Richard	1877	1967	Garden, Mary
1919	1980	Champion, Gower	1856	1924	Dockstader, Lew	1913	1952	Garfield, John
1918	1961	Chandler, Jeff	1892	1941	Dolly, Jennie	1922	1969	Garland, Judy
1883	1930	Chaney, Lon	1892	1970	Dolly, Rosie	1939	1984	Gaye, Marvin
1905	1973	Chaney Jr., Lon	1905	1958	Donat, Robert	1906	1984	Gaynor, Janet
1942	1981	Chapin, Harry	1889	1972	Donlevy, Brian	1902	1978	Geer, Will
1889	1977	Chaplin, Charles	1901	1981	Douglas, Melvyn	1900	1954	George, Gladys
1893	1940	Chase, Charlie	1907	1959	Douglas, Paul	1892	1962	Gibson, Hoot
1893	1961	Chatterton, Ruth	—	1980	Dragonette, Jessica	1890	1957	Gigli, Beniamino
1888	1972	Chevalier, Maurice	1889	1956	Draper, Ruth	1894	1971	Gilbert, Billy
1888	1960	Clark, Bobby	1881	1965	Dresser, Louise	1895	1936	Gilbert, John
1914	1968	Clark, Fred	1869	1934	Dressler, Marie	1855	1937	Gillette, William
1887	1950	Clayton, Lou	1820	1897	Drew, Mrs. John	1867	1943	Gillmore, Frank
1920	1966	Clift, Montgomery	1853	1927	Drew, John (son)	1879	1939	Gilpin, Charles
1932	1963	Cline, Patsy	1909	1951	Duchin, Eddy	1897	1987	Gingold, Hermione
1898	1937	Clive, Colin	1890	1974	Dumbrille, Douglass	1898	1968	Gish, Dorothy
1892	1967	Clyde, Andy	1889	1965	Dumont, Margaret	1916	1987	Gleason, Jackie
1911	1976	Cobb, Lee J.	1878	1927	Duncan, Isadora	1886	1959	Gleason, James
1877	1961	Coburn, Charles	1905	1967	Dunn, James	1884	1938	Gluck, Alma
1887	1934	Cody, Lew	1935	1973	Dunn, Michael	1903	1983	Godfrey, Arthur
1878	1942	Cohan, George M.	1893	1980	Durante, Jimmy	1874	1955	Golden, John
1919	1965	Cole, Nat (King)	1907	1968	Duryea, Dan	1882	1974	Goldwyn, Samuel
1878	1955	Collier, Constance	1858	1924	Duse, Eleanora	1915	1969	Gorcey, Leo
1890	1965	Collins, Ray				1884	1940	Gordon, C. Henry
1891	1958	Colman, Ronald	1894	1929	Eagels, Jeanne	1896	1985	Gordon, Ruth
1908	1934	Columbo, Russ	1896	1930	Eames, Clare	1899	1982	Gosden, Freeman (Amos)
1907	1944	Compton, Betty	1865	1952	Eames, Emma	1869	1944	Gottschalk, Ferdinand
1887	1940	Connolly, Walter	1901	1967	Eddy, Nelson	1829	1869	Gottschalk, Louis
1917	1982	Conried, Hans	1897	1971	Edwards, Cliff	1916	1973	Grable, Betty
1855	1909	Conried, Henrich	1879	1945	Edwards, Gus	1925	1981	Grahame, Gloria
1914	1975	Conte, Richard	1899	1974	Ellington, Duke	1904	1986	Grant, Cary
1914	1984	Coogan, Jackie	1941	1974	Elliot, Cass	1915	1987	Greene, Lorne
1935	1964	Cooke, Sam	1871	1940	Elliott, Maxine	1879	1954	Greenstreet, Sydney
1901	1961	Cooper, Gary	1891	1967	Elman, Mischa	1893	1978	Greenwood, Charlotte
1888	1971	Cooper, Gladys	1881	1951	Errol, Leon	1874	1948	Griffith, David Wark
1896	1973	Cooper, Melville	1903	1967	Erwin, Stuart	1912	1980	Griffith, Hugh
1914	1968	Corey, Wendell	1888	1976	Evans, Edith	1912	1967	Guthrie, Woody
1893	1974	Cornell, Katherine	1901	1989	Evans, Maurice	1875	1959	Gwenn, Edmund
1890	1972	Correll, Charles (Andy)	1913	1967	Evelyn, Judith			
1905	1979	Costello, Dolores				1888	1942	Hackett, Charles
1904	1957	Costello, Helene	1883	1939	Fairbanks, Douglas	1902	1958	Hackett, Raymond
1908	1959	Costello, Lou	1914	1970	Farmer, Frances	1903	1943	Haines, Robert T.
1877	1950	Costello, Maurice	1870	1929	Farnum, Dustin	1892	1950	Hale, Alan
1899	1973	Coward, Noel	1876	1953	Farnum, William	1925	1981	Haley, Bill
1890	1950	Cowl, Jane	1882	1967	Farrar, Geraldine	1899	1979	Haley, Jack
1924	1973	Cox, Wally	1904	1971	Farrell, Glenda	1902	1985	Hamilton, Margaret
1908	1983	Crabbe, Buster	1868	1940	Faversham, William	1847	1919	Hammerstein, Oscar
1847	1924	Crabtree, Lotta	1861	1939	Fawcett, George	1879	1955	Hampden, Walter
1928	1978	Crane, Bob	1897	1961	Fay, Frank	1924	1964	Haney, Carol
1911	1986	Crawford, Broderick	1895	1962	Fazenda, Louise	1893	1964	Hardwicke, Cedric
1908	1977	Crawford, Joan	1933	1982	Feldman, Marty	1892	1957	Hardy, Oliver

Born	Died	Name
1883	1939	Hare, T.E. (Ernie)
1911	1937	Harlow, Jean
1872	1946	Harned, Virginia
1844	1911	Harrigan, Edward
1870	1946	Hart, William S.
1907	1955	Hartman, Grace
1928	1973	Harvey, Laurence
1910	1973	Hawkins, Jack
1890	1973	Hayakawa, Sessue
1885	1969	Hayes, Gabby
1918	1980	Haymes, Dick
1902	1971	Hayward, Leland
1917	1975	Hayward, Susan
1918	1987	Hayworth, Rita
1896	1937	Healy, Ted
1910	1971	Heflin, Van
1901	1987	Heifetz, Jascha
1873	1918	Held, Anna
1942	1970	Hendrix, Jimi
1910	1969	Henie, Sonja
1879	1942	Herbert, Henry
1887	1951	Herbert, Hugh
1886	1956	Hersholt, Jean
1895	1942	Hibbard, Edna
1899	1980	Hitchcock, Alfred
1914	1955	Hodiak, John
1894	1973	Holden, Fay
1918	1981	Holden, William
1922	1965	Holliday, Judy
1936	1959	Holly, Buddy
1888	1951	Holt, Jack
1918	1973	Holt, Tim
1871	1947	Homer, Louise
1898	1978	Homolka, Oscar
1902	1972	Hopkins, Miriam
1858	1935	Hopper, DeWolf
1874	1959	Hopper, Edna Wallace
1915	1970	Hopper, William
1886	1970	Horton, Edward Everett
1874	1926	Houdini, Harry
1902	1988	Houseman, John
1881	1965	Howard, Eugene
1867	1961	Howard, Joe
1890	1943	Howard, Leslie
1885	1955	Howard, Tom
1916	1988	Howard, Trevor
1885	1949	Howard, Willie
1925	1985	Hudson, Rock
1890	1977	Hull, Henry
1886	1957	Hull, Josephine
1895	1958	Humphrey, Doris
1895	1945	Hunter, Glenn
1927	1969	Hunter, Jeffrey
1901	1962	Husing, Ted
1906	1987	Huston, John
1884	1950	Huston, Walter
1892	1950	Ingram, Rex
1895	1969	Ingram, Rex
1895	1980	Iturbi, Jose
1838	1905	Irving, Henry
1871	1944	Irving, Isabel
1872	1914	Irving, Laurence
1875	1942	Jackson, Joe
1911	1972	Jackson, Mahalia
1891	1984	Jaffe, Sam
1916	1983	James, Harry
1889	1956	Janis, Elsie
1886	1950	Jannings, Emil
1930	1980	Janssen, David
1829	1905	Jefferson, Joseph
1859	1923	Jefferson, Thomas
1900	1974	Jenkins, Allen
1898	1981	Jessel, George
1862	1930	Jewett, Henry
1892	1962	Johnson, Chic
1878	1952	Johnson, Edward
1886	1950	Jolson, Al
1889	1942	Jones, Buck
1933	1983	Jones, Carolyn
1911	1965	Jones, Spike
1943	1970	Joplin, Janis
1896	1988	Jordan, Jim
1897	1961	Jordan, Marian
1902	1982	Jory, Victor
1905	1981	Joslyn, Allyn
1910	1966	Kane, Helen

Born	Died	Name
1887	1969	Karloff, Boris
1893	1970	Karns, Roscoe
1913	1987	Kaye, Danny
1910	1987	Kaye, Sammy
1811	1868	Kean, Charles
1806	1880	Kean, Mrs. Charles
1787	1833	Kean, Edmund
1895	1966	Keaton, Buster
1830	1873	Keene, Laura
1841	1893	Keene, Thomas W.
1899	1960	Keith, Ian
1894	1973	Kellaway, Cecil
1898	1979	Kelly, Emmett
1929	1982	Kelly, Grace
1910	1981	Kelly, Patsy
1899	1956	Kelly, Paul
1873	1939	Kelly, Walter C.
1907	1968	Kelton, Pert
1823	1895	Kemble, Agnes
1775	1854	Kemble, Charles
1809	1893	Kemble, Fannie
1848	1935	Kendal, Madge
1843	1917	Kendal, William H.
1926	1959	Kendall, Kay
1890	1948	Kennedy, Edgar
1886	1945	Kent, William
1880	1947	Kerrigan, J. Warren
1886	1956	Kibbee, Guy
1902	1966	Kiepura, Jan
1888	1964	Kilbride, Percy
1863	1933	Kilgour, Joseph
1894	1944	King, Charles
1897	1971	King, Dennis
1923	1986	Knight, Ted
1901	1980	Kostelanetz, Andre
1919	1962	Kovacs, Ernie
1885	1974	Kruger, Otto
1913	1964	Ladd, Alan
1895	1967	Lahr, Bert
1919	1973	Lake, Veronica
1925	1982	Lamas, Fernando
1902	1986	Lanchester, Elsa
1919	1948	Landis, Carole
1904	1972	Landis, Jessie Royce
1884	1944	Langdon, Harry
1853	1929	Langtry, Lillie
1921	1959	Lanza, Mario
1870	1950	Lauder, Harry
1899	1962	Laughton, Charles
1890	1965	Laurel, Stan
1923	1984	Lawford, Peter
1898	1952	Lawrence, Gertrude
1890	1929	Lawrence, Margaret
1940	1973	Lee, Bruce
1907	1952	Lee, Canada
1914	1970	Lee, Gypsy Rose
1848	1929	Lehmann, Lilli
1888	1976	Lehmann, Lotte
1896	1950	Lehr, Lew
1913	1967	Leigh, Vivien
1852	1908	Leighton, Margaret
1922	1976	Leighton, Margaret
1894	1931	Leitzel, Lillian
1940	1980	Lennon, John
1898	1981	Lenya, Lotte
1870	1941	Leonard, Eddie
1900	1987	LeRoy Mervyn
1906	1972	Levant, Oscar
1905	1980	Levene, Sam
1881	1955	Levy, Ethel
1902	1971	Lewis, Joe E.
1892	1971	Lewis, Ted
1874	1944	Lhevinne, Josef
1919	1987	Liberace
1889	1952	Lincoln, Elmo
1820	1887	Lind, Jenny
1894	1989	Lillie, Beatrice
1889	1968	Lindsay, Howard
1869	1952	Lipman, Clara
1893	1971	Lloyd, Harold
1870	1922	Lloyd, Marie
1891	1957	Lockhart, Gene
1913	1969	Logan, Ella
1909	1942	Lombard, Carole
1902	1977	Lombardo, Guy
1927	1974	Long, Richard
1903	1983	Loo, Richard
1895	1975	Lopez, Vincent

Born	Died	Name
1888	1968	Lorne, Marion
1904	1964	Lorre, Peter
1912	1962	Lovejoy, Frank
1890	1971	Lowe, Edmund
1892	1947	Lubitsch, Ernst
1882	1956	Lugosi, Bela
1894	1971	Lukas, Paul
1892	1977	Lunt, Alfred
1853	1932	Lupino, George
1893	1942	Lupino, Stanley
1897	1957	Lyman, Abe
1926	1982	Lynde, Paul
1926	1971	Lynn, Diana
1885	1954	Lytell, Bert
1867	1936	Lytton, Henry
1903	1965	MacDonald, Jeanette
1902	1969	MacLane, Barton
1921	1986	MacRae, Gordon
1909	1973	Macready, George
1861	1946	Macy, George Carleton
1908	1973	Magnani, Anna
1896	1967	Mahoney, Will
1890	1975	Main, Marjorie
1933	1967	Mansfield, Jayne
1854	1907	Mansfield, Richard
1905	1980	Mantovani, Annunzio
1897	1975	March, Fredric
1945	1981	Marley, Bob
1865	1950	Marlowe, Julia
1890	1966	Marshall, Herbert
1864	1943	Marshall, Tully
1920	1981	Martin, Ross
1885	1969	Martinelli, Giovanni
1924	1987	Marvin, Lee
1888	1964	Marx, Arthur (Harpo)
1890	1977	Marx, Julius (Groucho)
1887	1961	Marx, Leonard (Chico)
1909	1984	Mason, James
1896	1983	Massey, Raymond
1862	1951	Maude, Cyril
1879	1948	May, Edna
1885	1957	Mayer, Louis B.
1895	1973	Maynard, Ken
1884	1945	McCormack, John
1907	1962	McCormick, Myron
1888	1931	McCoy, Bessie
1891	1978	McCoy, Tim
1895	1952	McDaniel, Hattie
1924	1965	McDonald, Marie
1913	1975	McGiver, John
1899	1981	McHugh, Frank
1879	1949	McIntyre, Frank J.
1857	1937	McIntyre, James
1879	1937	McKinley, Mabel
1883	1959	McLaglen, Victor
1907	1971	McMahon, Horace
1930	1980	McQueen, Steve
1920	1980	Medford, Kay
1880	1946	Meek, Donald
1879	1936	Meighan, Thomas
1861	1931	Melba, Nellie
1890	1973	Melchior, Lauritz
1904	1961	Melton, James
1890	1963	Menjou, Adolphe
1902	1966	Menken, Helen
1908	1984	Merman, Ethel
1905	1986	Milland, Ray
1904	1944	Miller, Glenn
1860	1926	Miller, Henry
1898	1936	Miller, Marilyn
1895	1927	Mills, Florence
1939	1976	Mineo, Sal
1903	1955	Minnevitch, Borrah
1913	1955	Miranda, Carmen
1892	1962	Mitchell, Thomas
1880	1940	Mix, Tom
1845	1909	Modjeska, Helena
1926	1962	Monroe, Marilyn
1911	1973	Monroe, Vaughn
1875	1964	Monteux, Pierre
1917	1951	Montez, Maria
1904	1981	Montgomery, Robert
1901	1947	Moore, Grace
1876	1962	Moore, Victor
1906	1974	Moorehead, Agnes
1882	1949	Moran, George
1884	1952	Moran, Polly
1890	1949	Morgan, Frank

Born	Died	Name	Born	Died	Name	Born	Died	Name
1900	1941	Morgan, Helen	1872	1935	Powers, Eugene	1858	1935	Sembrich, Marcella
1888	1956	Morgan, Ralph	1905	1986	Preminger, Otto	1884	1960	Sennett, Mack
1901	1970	Morris, Chester	1935	1977	Presley, Elvis	1881	1951	Shattuck, Arthur
1849	1925	Morris, Clara	1918	1987	Preston, Robert	1860	1929	Shaw, Mary
1914	1959	Morris, Wayne	1911	1978	Prima, Louis	1927	1978	Shaw, Robert
1943	1971	Morrison, Jim	1856	1919	Primrose, George	1891	1972	Shawn, Ted
1932	1982	Morrow, Vic	1954	1977	Prinze, Freddie	1868	1949	Shean, Al
1915	1977	Mostel, Zero	1879	1956	Prouty, Jed	1902	1983	Shearer, Norma
1897	1969	Mowbray, Alan	1871	1942	Pryor, Arthur	1915	1967	Sheridan, Ann
1895	1967	Muni, Paul				1885	1934	Sherman, Lowell
1894	1953	Munn, Frank	1946	1989	Radner, Gilda	1918	1970	Shriner, Herb
1915	1970	Munshin, Jules	1895	1980	Raft, George	1875	1953	Shubert, Lee
1924	1971	Murphy, Audie	1890	1967	Rains, Claude	1755	1831	Siddons, Mrs. Sarah
1885	1965	Murray, Mae	1889	1916	Rambeau, Marjorie	1921	1985	Signoret, Simone
			1900	1947	Rankin, Arthur	1882	1930	Sills, Milton
1896	1970	Nagel, Conrad	1892	1967	Rathbone, Basil	1912	1985	Silvers, Phil
1900	1973	Naish, J. Carroll	1897	1960	Ratoff, Gregory	1900	1976	Sim, Alastair
1898	1961	Naldi, Nita	1883	1953	Rawlinson, Herbert	1891	1934	Skelly, Hal
1888	1950	Nash, Florence	1891	1943	Ray, Charles	1858	1942	Skinner, Otis
1865	1945	Nash, George	1941	1967	Redding, Otis	1863	1948	Smith, C. Aubrey
1879	1945	Nazimova, Alla	1908	1985	Redgrave, Michael	1907	1986	Smith, Kate
1846	1905	Neilson, Ada	1921	1986	Reed, Donna	1917	1979	Soo, Jack
1848	1880	Neilson, Adelaide	1914	1959	Reeves, George	1826	1881	Sothern, Edward A.
1868	1957	Neilson-Terry, Julia	1923	1964	Reeves, Jim	1859	1933	Sothern, Edward H.
1906	1975	Nelson, Ozzie	1860	1916	Rehan, Ada	1884	1957	Sothern, Harry
1940	1985	Nelson, Rick	1892	1923	Reid, Wallace	1854	1932	Sousa, John Philip
1885	1967	Nesbit, Evelyn	1873	1943	Reinhardt, Max	1884	1957	Sparks, Ned
1870	1951	Nethersole, Olga	1909	1971	Rennie, Michael	1876	1948	Speaks, Oley
1910	1983	Niven, David	1902	1983	Richardson, Ralph	1890	1970	Spitalny, Phil
1874	1948	Niblo, Fred	1870	1940	Richman, Charles	1873	1937	Standing, Guy
1890	1950	Nijinsky, Vaslav	1895	1972	Richman, Harry	1900	1941	Stephenson, James
1893	1974	Nilsson, Anna Q.	1921	1985	Riddle, Nelson	1883	1939	Sterling, Ford
1902	1985	Nolan, Lloyd	1872	1961	Ring, Blanche	1882	1928	Stevens, Emily A.
1898	1930	Normand, Mabel	1898	1977	Ritchard, Cyril	1934	1970	Stevens, Inger
1879	1959	Norworth, Jack	1907	1974	Ritter, Tex	1882	1977	Stokowski, Leopold
1899	1968	Novarro, Ramon	1905	1969	Ritter, Thelma	1873	1959	Stone, Fred
1893	1951	Novello, Ivor	1901	1965	Ritz, Al	1879	1953	Stone, Lewis
			1906	1986	Ritz, Harry	1904	1980	Stone, Milburn
1903	1978	Oakie, Jack	1903	1985	Ritz, Jimmy	1898	1959	Sturges, Preston
1860	1926	Oakley, Annie	1925	1982	Robbins, Marty	1911	1960	Sullavan, Margaret
1928	1982	Oates, Warren	1898	1976	Robeson, Paul	1902	1974	Sullivan, Ed
1911	1979	Oberon, Merle	1878	1949	Robinson, Bill	1903	1956	Sullivan, Francis L.
1915	1985	O'Brien, Edmond	1893	1973	Robinson, Edward G.	1892	1946	Summerville, Slim
1899	1983	O'Brien, Pat	1865	1942	Robson, May	1899	1983	Swanson, Gloria
1908	1981	O'Connell, Arthur	1905	1977	Rochester (E. Anderson)	1904	1969	Swarthout, Gladys
1898	1943	O'Connell, Hugh	1897	1933	Rodgers, Jimmy			
1880	1959	O'Connor, Una	1894	1958	Rodzinsky, Artur	1893	1957	Talmadge, Norma
1878	1945	O'Hara, Fiske	1879	1935	Rogers, Will	1899	1972	Tamiroff, Akim
1908	1968	O'Keefe, Dennis	1880	1962	Rooney, Pat	1878	1947	Tanguay, Eva
1880	1938	Oland, Warner	1899	1966	Rose, Billy	1899	1934	Tashman, Lilyan
1860	1932	Olcott, Chauncey	1910	1980	Roth, Lillian	1885	1966	Taylor, Deems
1883	1942	Oliver, Edna May	1922	1987	Rowan, Dan	1899	1958	Taylor, Estelle
1907	1989	Olivier, Laurence	1887	1982	Rubinstein, Artur	1887	1946	Taylor, Laurette
1892	1963	Olsen, Ole	1878	1953	Ruffo, Titta	1911	1969	Taylor, Robert
1849	1920	O'Neill, James	1886	1970	Ruggles, Charles	1878	1938	Tearle, Conway
1936	1988	Orbison, Roy	1864	1936	Russell, Annie	1884	1953	Tearle, Godfrey
1899	1985	Ormandy, Eugene	1924	1961	Russell, Gail	1892	1937	Tell, Alma
1876	1949	Ouspenskaya, Maria	1861	1922	Russell, Lillian	1864	1942	Tempest, Marie
1887	1972	Owen, Reginald	1911	1976	Russell, Rosalind	1910	1963	Templeton, Alec
			1892	1972	Rutherford, Margaret	1847	1928	Terry, Ellen
1860	1941	Paderewski, Ignace	1903	1973	Ryan, Irene	1871	1940	Tetrazzini, Luisa
1924	1987	Page, Geraldine	1909	1973	Ryan, Robert	1899	1936	Thalberg, Irving
1889	1954	Pailette, Eugene				1857	1914	Thomas, Brandon
1914	1986	Palmer, Lilli	1924	1963	Sabu (Dastagir)	1892	1960	Thomas, John Charles
1894	1958	Pangborn, Franklin	1877	1968	St. Denis, Ruth	1882	1976	Thorndike, Sybil
1914	1975	Parks, Larry	1884	1955	Sakall, S.Z.			(Three Stooges)
1881	1940	Pasternack, Josef A.	1885	1936	Sale (Chic), Charles	1902	1975	Fine, Larry
1837	1908	Pastor, Tony	1906	1972	Sanders, George	1906	1952	Howard, Curly
1843	1919	Patti, Adelina	1934	1973	Sands, Diana	1897	1975	Howard, Moe
1840	1889	Patti, Carlotta	1896	1960	Savo, Jimmy	1869	1936	Thurston, Howard
1885	1931	Pavlova, Anna	1879	1954	Scheff, Fritzi	1896	1960	Tibbett, Lawrence
1900	1973	Paxinou, Katina	1892	1930	Schenck, Joe	1887	1940	Tinney, Frank
1904	1984	Peerce, Jan	1895	1964	Schildkraut, Joseph	1909	1958	Todd, Michael
1885	1950	Pemberton, Brock	1865	1930	Schildkraut, Rudolph	1874	1947	Toler, Sidney
1899	1967	Pendleton, Nat	1889	1965	Schipa, Tito	1905	1968	Tone, Franchot
1905	1941	Penner, Joe	1882	1951	Schnabel, Artur	1867	1957	Toscanini, Arturo
1892	1937	Perkins, Osgood	1938	1982	Schneider, Romy	1898	1968	Tracy, Lee
1893	1956	Peters, Brandon	1910	1949	Schumann, Henrietta	1900	1967	Tracy, Spencer
1915	1963	Piaf, Edith	1861	1936	Schumann-Heink, E.	1903	1972	Traubel, Helen
1893	1979	Pickford, Mary	1866	1945	Scott, Cyril	1894	1975	Treacher, Arthur
1897	1984	Pidgeon, Walter	1920	1981	Scott, Hazel	1853	1917	Tree, Herbert Beerbohm
1892	1957	Pinza, Ezio	1898	1987	Scott, Randolph	1890	1973	Truex, Ernest
1898	1963	Pitts, Zasu	1914	1965	Scott, Zachary	1932	1984	Truffaut, Francois
1904	1976	Pons, Lily	1843	1896	Scott-Siddons, Mrs.	1919	1986	Tucker, Forrest
1897	1981	Ponselle, Rosa	1938	1979	Seberg, Jean	1915	1975	Tucker, Richard
1904	1963	Powell, Dick	1892	1974	Seeley, Blossom	1884	1966	Tucker, Sophie
1912	1982	Powell, Eleanor	1893	1987	Segovia, Andres	1874	1940	Turpin, Ben
1892	1984	Powell, William	1925	1980	Sellers, Peter	1908	1959	Twelvetrees, Helen
1913	1958	Power, Tyrone	1902	1965	Selznick, David O.			

Born	Died	Name	Born	Died	Name	Born	Died	Name
1894	1970	Ulric, Lenore	1876	1958	Warner, H. B.	1905	1975	Wills, Bob
1933	1975	Ure, Mary	1878	1964	Warwick, Robert	1903	1978	Wills, Chill
			1924	1963	Washington, Dinah	1894	1953	Wilson, Dooley
1895	1926	Valentino, Rudolph	1900	1977	Waters, Ethel	1917	1972	Wilson, Marie
1901	1986	Vallee, Rudy	1867	1945	Watson, Billy	1884	1969	Winninger, Charles
1870	1950	Van, Billy B.	1907	1979	Wayne, John	1904	1959	Withers, Grant
1911	1979	Vance, Vivian	1891	1966	Webb, Clifton	1881	1931	Wolheim, Louis
1893	1943	Veidt, Conrad	1920	1982	Webb, Jack	1907	1961	Wong, Anna May
1926	1981	Vera-Ellen	1867	1942	Weber, Joe	1938	1981	Wood, Natalie
1885	1957	Von Stroheim, Erich	1905	1973	Webster, Margaret	1892	1978	Wood, Peggy
1906	1981	Von Zell, Harry	1915	1985	Welles, Orson	1888	1963	Woolley, Monty
			1896	1975	Wellman, William	1881	1956	Wycherly, Margaret
1887	1969	Walburn, Raymond	1922	1984	Werner, Oskar	1902	1981	Wyler, William
1874	1946	Waldron, Charles D.	1892	1980	West, Mae	1886	1966	Wynn, Ed
1904	1966	Walker, June	1895	1968	Wheeler, Bert	1916	1986	Wynn, Keenan
1914	1951	Walker, Robert	1889	1938	White, Pearl			
1898	1983	Wallenstein, Alfred	1891	1967	Whiteman, Paul	1890	1960	Young, Clara Kimball
1887	1980	Walsh, Raoul	1865	1948	Whitty, May	1917	1978	Young, Gig
1876	1962	Walter, Bruno	1912	1979	Wilding, Michael	1887	1953	Young, Roland
1878	1936	Walthall, Henry B.	1895	1948	William, Warren			
1872	1952	Ward, Fannie	1877	1922	Williams, Bert	1902	1979	Zanuck, Darryl F.
1866	1951	Warfield, David	1867	1918	Williams, Evan	1869	1932	Ziegfeld, Florenz
1900	1984	Waring, Fred	1923	1953	Williams, Hank	1873	1976	Zukor, Adolph

Original Names of Selected Entertainers

Edie Adams: Elizabeth Edith Enke
Eddie Albert: Edward Albert Heimberger
Alan Alda: Alphonso D'Abruzzo
Jane Alexander: Jane Quigley
Fred Allen: John Sullivan
Woody Allen: Allen Konigsberg
Julie Andrews: Julia Wells
Eve Arden: Eunice Quedens
Beatrice Arthur: Bernice Frankel
Jean Arthur: Gladys Greene
Fred Astaire: Frederick Austerlitz

Lauren Bacall: Betty Joan Perske
Anne Bancroft: Anna Maria Italiano
Brigitte Bardot: Camille Javal
Gene Barry: Eugene Klass
Orson Bean: Dallas Burrows
Pat Benatar: Patricia Andrejewski
Robbie Benson: Robert Segal
Tony Bennett: Anthony Benedetto
Busby Berkeley: William Berkeley Enos
Jack Benny: Benjamin Kubelsky
Joey Bishop: Joseph Gottlieb
Robert Blake: Michael Gubitosi
Victor Borge: Borge Rosenbaum
David Bowie: David Robert Jones
Boy George: George Alan O'Dowd
Fanny Brice: Fanny Borach
Morgan Brittany: Suzanne Cupito
Charles Bronson: Charles Buchinski
Albert Brooks: Albert Einstein
Mel Brooks: Melvin Kaminsky
George Burns: Nathan Birnbaum
Ellen Burstyn: Edna Gilhooley
Richard Burton: Richard Jenkins
Red Buttons: Aaron Chwatt
Nicolas Cage: Nicholas Coppola
Michael Caine: Maurice Micklewhite
Maria Callas: Maria Kalogeropoulos
Vikki Carr: Florencia Casillas
Diahann Carroll: Carol Diahann Johnson
Cyd Charisse: Tula Finklea
Ray Charles: Ray Charles Robinson
Cher: Cherilyn Sarkisian
Patsy Cline: Virginia Patterson Hensley
Lee J. Cobb: Leo Jacoby
Claudette Colbert: Lily Chauchoin
Michael Connors: Kreker Ohanian
Robert Conrad: Conrad Robert Falk
Alice Cooper: Vincent Furnier
Howard Cosell: Howard Cohen
Elvis Costello: Declan Patrick McManus
Lou Costello: Louis Cristillo
Joan Crawford: Lucille Le Sueur
Michael Crawford: Michael Dumbell-Smith
Tony Curtis: Bernard Schwartz

Vic Damone: Vito Farinola
Rodney Dangerfield: Jacob Cohen
Bobby Darin: Walden Waldo Cassotto
Doris Day: Doris von Kappelhoff

Yvonne De Carlo: Peggy Middleton
Sandra Dee: Alexandra Zuck
John Denver: Henry John Deutschendorf Jr.
Bo Derek: Cathleen Collins
John Derek: Derek Harris
Angie Dickinson: Angeline Brown
Phyllis Diller: Phyllis Driver
Diana Dors: Diana Fluck
Melvyn Douglas: Melvyn Hesselberg
Bob Dylan: Robert Zimmerman

Sheena Easton: Sheena Shirley Orr
Barbara Eden: Barbara Huffman
Ron Ely: Ronald Pierce
Chad Everett: Raymond Cramton
Tom Ewell: S. Yewell Tompkins

Douglas Fairbanks: Douglas Ullman
Morgan Fairchild: Patsy McClenny
Alice Faye: Ann Leppert
Stepin Fetchit: Lincoln Perry
W.C. Fields: William Claude Dukenfield
Peter Finch: William Mitchell
Barry Fitzgerald: William Joseph Shields
Joan Fontaine: Joan de Havilland
John Ford: Sean O'Fearna
John Forsythe: John Freund
Redd Foxx : John Sanford
Anthony Franciosa: Anthony Papaleo
Arlene Francis: Arlene Kazanjian
Connie Francis: Concetta Franconero

Greta Garbo: Greta Gustafsson
Vincent Gardenia: Vincent Scognamiglio
John Garfield: Julius Garfinkle
Judy Garland: Frances Gumm
James Garner: James Baumgardner
Crystal Gayle: Brenda Gayle Webb
Eydie Gorme: Edith Gormezano
Stewart Granger: James Stewart
Cary Grant: Archibald Leach
Lee Grant: Lyova Rosenthal
Joel Grey: Joe Katz

Buddy Hackett: Leonard Hacker
Jean Harlow: Harlean Carpentier
Rex Harrison: Reginald Carey
Laurence Harvey: Larushka Skikne
Helen Hayes: Helen Brown
Susan Hayward: Edythe Marriner
Rita Hayworth: Margarita Cansino
Pee-Wee Herman: Paul Rubenfeld
Barbara Hershey: Barbara Herzstine
William Holden: William Beedle
Judy Holliday: Judith Tuvim
Harry Houdini: Ehrich Weiss
Leslie Howard: Leslie Stainer
Moe Howard: Moses Horowitz
Rock Hudson: Roy Scherer Jr. (later Fitzgerald)
Engelbert Humperdinck: Arnold Dorsey
Kim Hunter: Janet Cole

Mary Beth Hurt: Mary Supinger
Betty Hutton: Betty Thornberg

David Janssen: David Meyer
Elton John: Reginald Dwight
Don Johnson: Donald Wayne
Jennifer Jones: Phyllis Isley
Tom Jones: Thomas Woodward
Louis Jourdan: Louis Gendre

Boris Karloff: William Henry Pratt
Danny Kaye: David Kaminsky
Diane Keaton: Diane Hall
Michael Keaton: Michael Douglas
Howard Keel: Harold Leek
Chaka Khan: Yvette Stevens
Carole King: Carole Klein
Ben Kingsley: Krishna Banji
Nastassja Kinski: Nastassja Naksyznyski
Ted Knight: Tadeus Wladyslaw Konopka

Cheryl Ladd: Cheryl Stoppelmoor
Veronica Lake: Constance Ockleman
Dorothy Lamour: Mary Kaumeyer
Michael Landon: Eugene Orowitz
Mario Lanza: Alfredo Cocozza
Stan Laurel: Arthur Jefferson
Steve Lawrence: Sidney Leibowitz
Brenda Lee: Brenda Mae Tarpley
Bruce Lee: Lee Yuen Kam
Gypsy Rose Lee: Rose Louise Hovick
Michelle Lee: Michelle Dusiak
Peggy Lee: Norma Egstrom
Janet Leigh: Jeanette Morrison
Vivien Leigh: Vivien Hartley
Huey Lewis: Hugh Cregg
Jerry Lewis: Joseph Levitch
Hal Linden: Harold Lipshitz
Carole Lombard: Jane Peters
Jack Lord: John Joseph Ryan
Sophia Loren: Sophia Scicoloni
Peter Lorre: Laszio Lowenstein
Myrna Loy: Myrna Williams
Bela Lugosi: Bela Ferenc Blasko

Moms Mabley: Loretta Mary Aitken
Shirley MacLaine: Shirley Beaty
Madonna: Madonna Louise Ciccone
Lee Majors: Harvey Lee Yeary 2d
Karl Malden: Malden Sekulovich
Jayne Mansfield: Vera Jane Palmer
Fredric March: Frederick Bickel
Peter Marshall: Pierre LaCock
Dean Martin: Dino Crocetti
Ethel Merman: Ethel Zimmerman
Ray Milland: Reginald Truscott-Jones
Ann Miller: Lucille Collier
Joni Mitchell: Roberta Joan Anderson
Marilyn Monroe: Norma Jean Mortenson, (later) Baker
Yves Montand: Ivo Levi
Ron Moody: Ronald Moodnick
Demi Moore: Demi Guynes
Garry Moore: Thomas Garrison Morfit
Rita Moreno: Rosita Alverio
Harry Morgan: Harry Bratsburg
Paul Muni: Muni Weisenfreund

Mike Nichols: Michael Igor Peschowsky
Sheree North: Dawn Bethel
Hugh O'Brian: Hugh Krampke
Maureen O'Hara: Maureen Fitzsimmons

Patti Page: Clara Ann Fowler
Jack Palance: Walter Palanuik
Lilli Palmer: Lilli Peiser
Bert Parks: Bert Jacobson
Minnie Pearl: Sarah Ophelia Cannon
Bernadette Peters: Bernadette Lazzaro
Edith Piaf: Edith Gassion
Slim Pickens: Louis Lindley
Mary Pickford: Gladys Smith
Stephanie Powers: Stefania Federkiewcz
Paula Prentiss: Paula Ragusa
Robert Preston: Robert Preston Meservey
Prince: Prince Rogers Nelson

Tony Randall: Leonard Rosenberg
Martha Raye: Margaret O'Reed
Donna Reed: Donna Belle Mullenger
Della Reese: Delloreese Patricia Early
Joan Rivers: Joan Sandra Molinsky
Edward G. Robinson: Emmanuel Goldenberg
Ginger Rogers: Virginia McMath
Roy Rogers: Leonard Slye
Mickey Rooney: Joe Yule Jr.
Lillian Russell: Helen Leonard

Susan St. James: Susan Miller
Soupy Sales: Milton Hines
Susan Sarandon: Susan Tomaling
Randolph Scott: George Randolph Crane
Jane Seymour: Joyce Frankenberg
Omar Sharif: Michael Shalhoub
Martin Sheen: Ramon Estevez
Beverly Sills: Belle Silverman
Talia Shire: Talia Coppola
Phil Silvers: Philip Silversmith
Suzanne Somers: Suzanne Mahoney
Ann Sothern: Harriette Lake
Barbara Stanwyck: Ruby Stevens
Jean Stapleton: Jeanne Murray
Ringo Starr: Richard Starkey
Connie Stevens: Concetta Ingolia
Sting: George Sumner
Donna Summers: LaDonna Gaines

Robert Taylor: Spangler Arlington Brugh
Danny Thomas: Amos Jacobs
Sophie Tucker: Sophia Kalish
Tina Turner: Annie Mae Bullock
Conway Twitty: Harold Lloyd Jenkins
Rudolph Valentino: Rudolpho D'Antonguolla
Frankie Valli: Frank Castelluccio

David Wayne: Wayne McMeekan
John Wayne: Marion Morrison
Clifton Webb: Webb Parmalee Hollenbeck
Raquel Welch: Raquel Tejada
Gene Wilder: Jerome Silberman
Shelly Winters: Shirley Schrift
Stevie Wonder: Stevland Morris
Natalie Wood: Natasha Gurdin
Jane Wyman: Sarah Jane Fulks
Gig Young: Byron Barr

Personal Consumption Expenditures for Entertainment: 1970 to 1987

Source: U.S. Bureau of Economic Analysis

(In billions of dollars, except percent. Represents market value of purchases of goods and services by individuals and nonprofit institutions)

Type of Product or Service	1970	1975	1980	1981	1982	1983	1984	1985	1986	1987
Percent of total personal consumption	6.7	6.9	6.6	6.7	6.7	6.8	6.9	7.1	7.2	7.4
Books and maps	2.9	3.6	5.6	6.2	6.6	7.2	7.8	8.1	8.6	9.7
Magazines, newspapers, and sheet music	4.1	6.4	10.4	11.0	11.4	12.0	12.7	13.2	13.9	15.8
Radio and television receivers, records, and musical instruments	8.5	13.5	19.9	22.0	24.5	28.2	31.5	37.0	38.9	41.2
Admissions to specified spectator amusements	3.3	4.3	6.5	6.9	7.8	8.6	9.5	9.5	10.2	11.1
Motion picture theaters	1.6	2.2	2.7	2.9	3.3	3.6	3.9	3.6	3.8	4.1
Legitimate theaters and opera, and entertainments of nonprofit institutions[1]	.5	.8	1.8	2.0	2.1	2.4	2.7	3.0	3.4	3.7
Spectator sports	1.1	1.3	2.0	2.0	2.3	2.6	2.9	2.9	3.1	3.3
Other[2]	5.1	9.7	19.4	23.4	26.0	30.0	33.1	38.9	44.1	49.3

(1) Except athletic. (2) Consists of net receipts of lotteries and expenditures for purchase of pets and pet care services, cable TV, film processing, photographic studios, sporting and recreation camps, and recreational services, not elsewhere classified.

WEIGHTS AND MEASURES

Source: National Institute of Standards and Technology, U.S. Commerce Department

The International System of Units

Two systems of weights and measures exist side by side in the United States today, with roughly equal but separate legislative sanction: the U.S. Customary System and the International (Metric) System. Throughout U.S. history, the Customary System (inherited from, but now different from, the British Imperial System) has been, as its name implies, customarily used; a plethora of federal and state legislation has given it, through implication, standing as our primary weights and measures system. However, the Metric System (incorporated in the scientists' new SI or Systeme International d'Unites) is the only system that has ever received specific legislative sanction by Congress. The "Law of 1866" reads:

It shall be lawful throughout the United States of America to employ the weights and measures of the metric system; and no contract or dealing, or pleading in any court, shall be deemed invalid or liable to objection because the weights or measures expressed or referred to therein are weights or measures of the metric system.

Over the last 100 years, the Metric System has seen slow, steadily increasing use in the United States. In science and also in the pharmaceutical industry, the use of metrics has for many years been predominant; today, the manufacturing industry is steadily increasing its use of the metric system largely motivated by the automotive industry, which is now predominantly metric.

On Feb. 10, 1964, the National Bureau of Standards issued the following bulletin:

Henceforth it shall be the policy of the National Bureau of Standards to use the units of the International System (SI), as adopted by the 11th General Conference on Weights and Measures (October 1960), except when the use of these units would obviously impair communication or reduce the usefulness of a report.

What had been the Metric System became the International System (SI), a more complete scientific system.

Seven units have been adopted to serve as the base for the International System as follows: length—meter; mass—kilogram; time—second; electric current—ampere; thermodynamic temperature—kelvin; amount of substance—mole; and luminous intensity—candela.

Prefixes

The following prefixes, in combination with the basic unit names, provide the multiples and submultiples in the International System. For example, the unit name "meter," with the prefix "kilo" added, produces "kilometer," meaning "1,000 meters."

Prefix	Symbol	Multiples	Equivalent	Prefix	Symbol	Submultiples	Equivalent
exa	E	10^{18}	quintillionfold	deci	d	10^{-1}	tenth part
peta	P	10^{15}	quadrillionfold	centi	c	10^{-2}	hundredth part
tera	T	10^{12}	trillionfold	milli	m	10^{-3}	thousandth part
giga	G	10^{9}	billionfold	micro	μ	10^{-6}	millionth part
mega	M	10^{6}	millionfold	nano	n	10^{-9}	billionth part
kilo	k	10^{3}	thousandfold	pico	p	10^{-12}	trillionth part
hecto	h	10^{2}	hundredfold	femto	f	10^{-15}	quadrillionth part
deka	da	10	tenfold	atto	a	10^{-18}	quintillionth part

Tables of Metric Weights and Measures

Linear Measure

10 millimeters (mm)	= 1 centimeter (cm)
10 centimeters	= 1 decimeter (dm) = 100 millimeters
10 decimeters	= 1 meter (m) = 1,000 millimeters
10 meters	= 1 dekameter (dam)
10 dekameters	= 1 hectometer (hm) = 100 meters
10 hectometers	= 1 kilometer (km) = 1,000 meters

Area Measure

100 square millimeters (mm²)	= 1 square centimeter (cm²)
10,000 square centimeters	= 1 square meter (m²) = 1,000,000 square millimeters
100 square meters	= 1 are (a)
100 ares	= 1 hectare (ha) = 10,000 square meters
100 hectares	= 1 square kilometer (km²) = 1,000,000 square meters

Fluid Volume Measure

10 milliliters (mL)	= 1 centiliter (cL)
10 centiliters	= 1 deciliter (dL) = 100 milliliters
10 deciliters	= 1 liter (L) = 1,000 milliliters
10 liters	= 1 dekaliter (daL)
10 dekaliters	= 1 hectoliter (hL) = 100 liters
10 hectoliters	= 1 kiloliter (kL) = 1,000 liters

Cubic Measure

1,000 cubic millimeters (mm³)	= 1 cubic centimeter (cm³)
1,000 cubic centimeters	= 1 cubic decimeter (dm³) = 1,000,000 cubic millimeters
1,000 cubic decimeters	= 1 cubic meter (m³) = 1 stere = 1,000,000 cubic centimeters = 1,000,000,000 cubic millimeters

Weight

10 milligrams (mg)	= 1 centigram (cg)
10 centigrams	= 1 decigram (dg) = 100 milligrams
10 decigrams	= 1 gram (g) = 1,000 milligrams
10 grams	= 1 dekagram (dag)
10 dekagrams	= 1 hectogram (hg) = 100 grams
10 hectograms	= 1 kilogram (kg) = 1,000 grams
1,000 kilograms	= 1 metric ton (t)

Table of U.S. Customary Weights and Measures

Linear Measure

12 inches (in)	= 1 foot (ft)
3 feet	= 1 yard (yd)
5 ½ yards	= 1 rod (rd), pole, or perch (16 ½ feet)
40 rods	= 1 furlong (fur) = 220 yards = 660 feet
8 furlongs	= 1 statute mile (mi) = 1,760 yards = 5,280 feet
3 miles	= 1 league = 5,280 yards = 15,840 feet
6076.11549 feet	= 1 International Nautical Mile

Liquid Measure

When necessary to distinguish the liquid pint or quart from the dry pint or quart, the word "liquid" or the abbreviation "liq" should be used in combination with the name or abbreviation of the liquid unit.

4 gills	= 1 pint (pt) = 28.875 cubic inches
2 pints	= 1 quart (qt) = 57.75 cubic inches
4 quarts	= 1 gallon (gal) = 231 cubic inches = 8 pints = 32 gills

Area Measure

Squares and cubes of units are sometimes abbreviated by using "superior" figures. For example. ft² means square foot. and ft³ means cubic foot.

144 square inches	= 1 square foot (ft²)
9 square feet	= 1 square yard (yd²) = 1,296 square inches
30 ¼ square yards	= 1 square rod (rd²) = 272 ¼ square feet
160 square rods	= 1 acre = 4,840 square yards = 43,560 square feet
640 acres	= 1 square mile (mi²)
1 mile square	= 1 section (of land)
6 miles square	= 1 township = 36 sections = 36 square miles

Cubic Measure

1 cubic foot (ft³)	= 1,728 cubic inches (in³)
27 cubic feet	= 1 cubic yard (yd³)

Gunter's or Surveyors' Chain Measure

7.92 inches (in)	= 1 link
100 links	= 1 chain (ch) = 4 rods = 66 feet
80 chains	= 1 survey mile (mi) = 320 rods = 5,280 feet

Troy Weight

24 grains	= 1 pennyweight (dwt)
20 pennyweights	= 1 ounce troy (oz t) = 480 grains
12 ounces troy	= 1 pound troy (lb t) = 240 pennyweights = 5,760 grains

Dry Measure

When necessary to distinguish the dry pint or quart from the liquid pint or quart, the word "dry" should be used in combination with the name or abbreviation of the dry unit.

2 pints (pt)	= 1 quart (qt) = 67.2006 cubic inches
8 quarts	= 1 peck (pk) = 537.605 cubic inches = 16 pints
4 pecks	= 1 bushel (bu) = 2,150.42 cubic inches = 32 quarts

Avoirdupois Weight

When necessary to distinguish the avoirdupois ounce or pound from the troy ounce or pound. the word "avoirdupois" or the abbreviation "avdp" should be used in combination with the name or abbreviation of the avoirdupois unit.

(The "grain" is the same in avoirdupois and troy weight.)

27 ¹¹/₃₂ grains	= 1 dram (dr)
16 drams	= 1 ounce (oz) = 437 ½ grains
16 ounces	= 1 pound (lb) = 256 drams = 7,000 grains
100 pounds	= 1 hundredweight (cwt)ᵃ
20 hundredweights	= 1 ton = 2,000 poundsᵃ

In "gross" or "long" measure. the following values are recognized.

112 pounds	= 1 gross or long hundredweightᵃ
20 gross or long hundredweights	= 1 gross or long ton = 2,240 poundsᵃ

ᵃWhen the terms "hundredweight" and "ton" are used unmodified. they are commonly understood to mean the 100-pound hundredweight and the 2,000-pound ton, respectively: these units may be designated "net" or "short" when necessary to distinguish them from the corresponding units in gross or long measure.

Tables of Equivalents

In this table it is necessary to distinguish between the "international" and the "survey" foot. The international foot, defined in 1959 as exactly equal to 0.3048 meter. is shorter than the old survey foot by exactly 2 parts in one million. The survey foot is still used in data expressed in feet in geodetic surveys within the U.S. In this table the survey foot is italicized.

When the name of a unit is enclosed in brackets thus. [1 hand], this indicates (1) that the unit is not in general current use in the United States, or (2) that the unit is believed to be based on "custom and usage" rather than on formal definition.

Equivalents involving decimals are. in most instances. rounded off to the third decimal place except where they are exact. in which cases these exact equivalents are so designated.

Lengths

1 angstrom (A)	0.1 nanometer (exactly) 0.000 1 micrometer (exactly) 0.000 000 1 millimeter (exactly) 0.000 000 004 inch
1 cable's length	120 fathoms (exactly) 720 *feet* (exactly) 219 meters
1 centimeter (cm)	0.3937 inch
1 chain (ch) (Gunter's or surveyors)	66 *feet* (exactly) 20.1168 meters
1 chain (engineers)	100 feet 30.48 meters (exactly)
1 decimeter (dm)	3.937 inches
1 degree (geographical)	364,566.929 *feet* 69.047 miles (avg.) 111.123 kilometers (avg.)
-of latitude	68.708 miles at equator 69.403 miles at poles
-of longitude	69.171 miles at equator
1 dekameter (dam)	32.808 feet
1 fathom	6 *feet* (exactly) 1.8288 meters (exactly)
1 foot (ft)	0.3048 meters (exactly)
1 furlong (fur)	10 chains (surveyors) (exactly) 660 *feet* (exactly) ⅛ statute mile (exactly) 201.168 meters
[1 hand] (height measure for horses from ground to top of shoulders)	4 inches
1 inch (in)	2.54 centimeters (exactly)
1 kilometer (km)	0.621 mile 3,281.5 feet

1 league (land)	3 survey miles (exactly) 4.828 kilometers
1 link (Gunter's or surveyors)	7.92 inches (exactly) 0.201 meter
1 link engineers	1 foot 0.305 meter
1 meter (m)	39.37 inches 1.094 yards
1 micrometer (μm) [the Greek letter mu]	0.001 millimeter (exactly) 0.000 039 37 inch
1 mil	0.001 inch (exactly) 0.025 4 millimeter (exactly)
1 mile (mi) (statute or land)	5,280 *feet* (exactly) 1.609 kilometers
1 international nautical mile (nmi)	1.852 kilometers (exactly) 1.150779 survey miles 6,076.11549 feet
1 millimeter (mm)	0.039 37 inch
1 nanometer (nm)	0.001 micrometer (exactly) 0.000 000 039 37 inch
1 pica (typography)	12 points
1 point (typography)	0.013 837 inch (exactly) 0.351 millimeter
1 rod (rd). pole. or perch	16 ½ *feet* (exactly) 5.029 meters
1 yard (yd)	0.9144 meter (exactly)

Areas or Surfaces

1 acre	43,560 square *feet* (exactly) 4,840 square yards 0.405 hectare
1 are (a)	119.599 square yards 0.025 acre

1 bolt (cloth measure):	
length	100 yards (on modern looms)
width	{ 42 inches (usually, for cotton) 60 inches (usually, for wool)
1 hectare (ha)	2.471 acres
[1 square (building)]	100 square feet
1 square centimeter (cm²)	0.155 square inch
1 square decimeter (dm²)	15.500 square inches
1 square foot (ft²)	929.030 square centimeters
1 square inch (in²)	6.4516 square centimeters (exactly)
1 square kilometer (km²)	{ 247.104 acres 0.386 square mile
1 square meter (m²)	{ 1.196 square yards 10.764 square feet
1 square mile (mi²)	258.999 hectares
1 square millimeter (mm²)	0.002 square inch
1 square rod (rd²) sq. pole, or sq. perch	25.293 square meters
1 square yard (yd²)	0.836 square meter

Capacities or Volumes

1 barrel (bbl) liquid . . . . 31 to 42 gallons°

"There are a variety of "barrels," established by law or usage. For example: federal taxes on fermented liquors are based on a barrel of 31 gallons: many state laws fix the "barrel for liquids" as 31 ½ gallons; one state fixes a 36-gallon barrel for cistern measurement; federal law recognizes a 40-gallon barrel for "proof spirits"; by custom, 42 gallons comprise a barrel of crude oil or petroleum products for statistical purposes, and this equivalent is recognized "for liquids" by 4 states.

1 barrel (bbl), standard, for fruits. vegetables. and other dry com- modities except dry cranberries	{ 7,056 cubic inches 105 dry quarts 3.281 bushels, struck measure
1 barrel (bbl), standard, cranberry	{ 5,826 cubic inches 86⁴⁵⁄₆₄ dry quarts 2.709 bushels, struck measure
1 board foot (lumber measure) . .	a foot-square board 1 inch thick
1 bushel (bu) (U.S.) (struck measure)	{ 2,150.42 cubic inches (exactly) 35.239 liters
[1 bushel, heaped (U.S.)]	{ 2,747.715 cubic inches 1.278 bushels, struck measure°
"Frequently recognized as 1¼ bushels, struck measure.	
[1 bushel (bu) (British Imperial) (struck measure)]	{ 1.032 U.S. bushels struck measure 2,219.36 cubic inches
1 cord (cd) firewood	128 cubic feet (exactly)
1 cubic centimeter (cm³)	0.061 cubic inch
1 cubic decimeter (dm³)	61.024 cubic inches
1 cubic inch (in³)	{ 0.554 fluid ounce 4.433 fluid drams 16.387 cubic centimeters
1 cubic foot (ft³).	{ 7.481 gallons 28.317 cubic decimeters
1 cubic meter (m³)	1.308 cubic yards
1 cubic yard (yd³)	0.765 cubic meter
1 cup, measuring	{ 8 fluid ounces (exactly) 1½ liquid pint (exactly)
[1 dram. fluid (fl dr) (British)]	{ 0.961 U.S. fluid dram 0.217 cubic inch 3.552 milliliters
1 dekaliter (daL)	{ 2.642 gallons 1.135 pecks
1 gallon (gal) (U.S.)	{ 231 cubic inches (exactly) 3.785 liters 0.833 British gallon 128 U.S. fluid ounces (exactly)
[1 gallon (gal) British Imperial]	{ 277.42 cubic inches 1.201 U.S. gallons 4.546 liters 160 British fluid ounces (exactly)
1 gill (gi)	{ 7.219 cubic inches 4 fluid ounces (exactly) 0.118 liter
1 hectoliter (hL)	{ 26.418 gallons 2.838 bushels
1 liter (L) (1 cubic decimeter exactly)	{ 1.057 liquid quarts 0.908 dry quart 61.025 cubic inches

1 milliliter (mL) (1 cu cm exactly)	{ 0.271 fluid dram 16.231 minims 0.061 cubic inch
1 ounce, liquid (U.S.)	{ 1.805 cubic inches 29.573 milliliters 1.041 British fluid ounces
[1 ounce, fluid (fl oz) (British)]	{ 0.961 U.S. fluid ounce 1.734 cubic inches 28.412 milliliters
1 peck (pk)	8.810 liters
1 pint (pt). dry	{ 33.600 cubic inches 0.551 liter
1 pint (pt). liquid	{ 28.875 cubic inches (exactly) 0.473 liter
1 quart (qt) dry (U.S.) . . .	{ 67.201 cubic inches 1.101 liters 0.969 British quart
1 quart (qt) liquid (U.S.)	{ 57.75 cubic in (exactly) 0.946 liter 0.833 British quart
[1 quart (qt) (British)]	{ 69.354 cubic inches 1.032 U.S. dry quarts 1.201 U.S. liquid quarts
1 tablespoon	{ 3 teaspoons (exactly) 4 fluid drams ½ fluid ounce (exactly)
1 teaspoon	{ ⅓ tablespoon (exactly) 1⅓ fluid drams°

"The equivalent "1 teaspoon—1⅓ fluid drams" has been found by the bureau to correspond more closely with the actual capacities of "measuring" and silver teaspoons than the equivalent "1 teaspoon—1 fluid dram" which is given by many dictionaries.

Weights or Masses

1 assay ton°° (AT) . . . . 29.167 grams

°°Used in assaying. The assay ton bears the same relation to the milligram that a ton of 2,000 pounds avoirdupois bears to the ounce troy; hence the weight in milligrams of precious metal obtained from one assay ton of ore gives directly the number of troy ounces to the net ton.

1 bale (cotton measure)	{ 500 pounds in U.S. 750 pounds in Egypt
1 carat (c)	{ 200 milligrams (exactly) 3.086 grains
1 dram avoirdupois (dr avdp) gamma. see microgram	{ 27¹¹⁄₃₂ (=27.344) grains 1.772 grams
1 grain	64.799 milligrams
1 gram.	{ 15.432 grains 0.035 ounce. avoirdupois
1 hundredweight. gross or long°° (gross cwt)	{ 112 pounds (exactly) 50.802 kilograms
1 hundredweight. net or short	{ 100 pounds (exactly) 45.359 kilograms
1 kilogram (kg)	2.205 pounds
1 microgram (μg [The Greek letter mu in combination with the letter g])	0.000001 gram (exactly)
1 milligram (mg)	0.015 grain
1 ounce. avoirdupois (oz avdp)	{ 437.5 grains (exactly) 0.911 troy ounce 28.350 grams
1 ounce. troy (oz t)	{ 480 grains (exactly) 1.097 avoirdupois ounces 31.103 grams
1 pennyweight (dwt)	1.555 grams
1 pound. avoirdupois (lb avdp)	{ 7,000 grains (exactly) 1.215 troy pounds 453.592 37 grams (exactly)
1 pound. troy (lb t) . . .	{ 5,760 grains (exactly) 0.823 avoirdupois pound 373.242 grams
1 ton, gross or long°° (gross ton)	{ 2,240 pounds (exactly) 1.12 net tons (exactly) 1.016 metric tons

°°The gross or long ton and hundredweight are used commercially in the United States to only a limited extent. usually in restricted industrial fields. These units are the same as British "ton" and "hundredweight."

1 ton. metric (t)	{ 2,204.623 pounds 0.984 gross ton 1.102 net tons
1 ton. net or short (sh ton) . .	{ 2,000 pounds (exactly)° 0.893 gross ton 0.907 metric ton

Tables of Interrelation of Units of Measurement

Units of length and area of the international and survey measures are included in the following tables. Units unique to the survey measure are italicized. See p. 414, Tables of Equivalents, 1st para.

1 international foot	= 0.999 998 survey foot (exactly)
1 survey foot	= 1200/3937 meter (exactly)
1 international foot	= 12 × 0.0254 meter (exactly)

Bold face type indicates exact values

Units of Length

Units	Inches	Links	Feet	Yards	Rods	Chains	Miles	cm	Meters
1 inch=	1	0.126 263	0.083 333	0.027 778	0.005 051	0.001 263	0.000 016	2.54	0.025 4
1 link=	7.92	1	0.66	0.22	0.04	0.01	0.000 125	20.117	0.201 168
1 foot=	12	1.515 152	1	0.333 333	0.060 606	0.015 152	0.000 189	30.48	0.304 8
1 yard=	36	4.545 45	3	1	0.181 818	0.045 455	0.000 568	91.44	0.914 4
1 rod=	198	25	16.5	5.5	1	0.25	0.003 125	502.92	5.029 2
1 chain=	792	100	66	22	4	1	0.012 5	2011.68	20.116 8
1 mile=	63 360	8000	5280	1760	320	80	1	160 934.4	1609.344
1 cm=	0.3937	0.049 710	0.032 808	0.010 936	0.001 988	0.000 497	0.000 006	1	0.01
1 meter=	39.37	4.970 960	3.280 840	1.093 613	0.198 838	0.049 710	0.000 621	100	1

Units of Area

Units	Sq. inches	Sq. links	Sq. feet	Sq. yards	Sq. rods	Sq. chains
1 sq. inch=	1	.015 942 3	0.006 944	0.000 771 605	0.000 025 5	0.000 001 594
1 sq. link=	62.726 4	1	0.435 6	0.0484	0.0016	0.000 1
1 sq. foot=	144	2.295 684	1	0.111 111 1	0.003 673 09	0.000 229 568
1 sq. yard=	1296	20.661 16	9	1	0.033 057 85	0.002 066 12
1 sq. rod=	39 204	625	272.25	30.25	1	0.062 5
1 sq. chain=	627 264	10 000	4 356	484	16	1
1 acre=	6 272 640	100 000	43 560	4 840	160	10
1 sq. mile=	4 014 489 600	64 000 000	27 878 400	3 097 600	102 400	6400
1 sq. cm=	0.155 000 3	0.002 471 05	0.001 076	0.000 119 599	0.000 003 954	0.000 000 247
1 sq. meter=	1550.003	24.710 44	10.763 91	1.195 990	0.039 536 70	0.002 471 044
1 hectare=	15 500 031	247 104	107 639.1	11 959.90	395.367 0	24.710 44

Units	Acres	Sq. miles	Sq. cm	Sq. meters	Hectares
1 sq. inch=	0.000 000 159 423	0.000 000 000 249 10	6.451 6	0.000 645 16	0.000 000 065
1 sq. link=	0.000 01	0.000 000 015 625	404.685 642 24	0.040 468 56	0.000 004 047
1 sq. foot=	0.000 022 956 84	0.000 000 035 870 06	929.034 1	0.092 903 41	0.000 009 290
1 sq. yard=	0.000 206 611 6	0.000 000 322 830 6	8 361.273 6	0.836 127 36	0.000 083 613
1 sq. rod=	0.006 25	0.000 009 765 625	252 929.5	25.292 95	0.002 529 295
1 sq. chain=	0.1	0.000 156 25	4 046 873	404.687 3	0.040 468 73
1 acre=	1	0.001 562 5	40 468 73	4 046.873	0.404 687 3
1 sq. mile=	640	1	25 899 881 103	2 589 988.11	258.998 811 034
1 sq. cm=	0.000 000 024 711	0.000 000 000 038 610	1	0.000 1	0.000 000 01
1 sq. meter=	0.000 247 104 4	0.000 000 386 102 2	10 000	1	0.0001
1 hectare=	2.471 044	0.003 861 006	100 000 000	10 000	1

Units of Mass Not Greater than Pounds and Kilograms

Units	Grains	Pennyweights	Avdp drams	Avdp ounces
1 grain=	1	0.041 666 67	0.036 571 43	0.002 285 71
1 pennyweight=	24	1	0.877 714 3	0.054 857 14
1 dram avdp=	27.343 75	1.139 323	1	0.062 5
1 ounce avdp=	437.5	18.229 17	16	1
1 ounce troy=	480	20	17.554 29	1.097 143
1 pound troy=	5760	240	210.651 4	13.165 71
1 pound avdp=	7000	291.666 7	256	16
1 milligram=	0.015 432	0.000 643 015	0.000 564 383	0.000 035 274
1 gram=	15.432 36	0.643 014 9	0.564 383 4	0.035 273 96
1 kilogram=	15 432.36	643.014 9	564.383 4	35.273 96

Units	Troy ounces	Troy pounds	Avdp pounds	Milligrams	Grams	Kilograms
1 grain=	0.002 083 33	0.000 173 611	0.000 142 857	64.798 91	0.064 798 91	0.000 064 799
1 pennyw't.=	0.05	0.004 166 667	0.003 428 571	1555.173 84	1.555 173 84	0.001 555 174
1 dram avdp=	0.056 966 15	0.004 747 179	0.003 906 25	1771.845 195	1.771 845 195	0.001 771 845
1 oz avdp=	0.911 458 3	0.075 954 86	0.062 5	28 349.523 125	28.349 523 125	0.028 349 52
1 oz troy=	1	0.083 333 333	0.068 571 43	31 103.476 8	31.103 476 8	0.031 103 48
1 lb troy=	12	1	0.822 857 1	373 241.721 6	373.241 721 6	0.373 241 722
1 lb avdp=	14.583 33	1.215 278	1	453 592.37	453.592 37	0.453 592 37
1 milligram=	0.000 032 151	0.000 002 679	0.000 002 205	1	0.001	0.000 001
1 gram=	0.032 150 75	0.002 679 229	0.002 204 623	1000	1	0.001
1 kilogram=	32.150 75	2.679 229	2.204 623	1 000 000	1000	1

Units of Mass Not Less than Avoirdupois Ounces

Units	Avdp oz	Avdp lb	Short cwt	Short tons	Long tons	Kilograms	Metric tons
1 oz av=	1	0.0625	0.000 625	0.000 031 25	0.000 027 902	0.028 349 523	0.000 028 350
1 lb av=	16	1	0.01	0.000 5	0.000 446 429	0.453 592 37	0.000 453 592
1 sh cwt=	1 600	100	1	0.05	0.044 642 86	45.359 237	0.045 359 237
1 sh ton=	32 000	2000	20	1	0.892 857 1	907.184 74	0.907 184 74
1 long ton=	35 840	2240	22.4	1.12	1	1016.046 908 8	1.016 046 909
1 kg=	35.273 96	2.204 623	0.022 046 23	0.001 102 311	0.000 984 207	1	0.001
1 metric ton=	35 273.96	2 204.623	22.046 23	1.102 311	0.984 206 5	1000	1

Units of Volume

Units	Cubic inches	Cubic feet	Cubic yards	Cubic cm	Cubic dm	Cubic meters
1 cubic inch =	1	0.000 578 704	0.000 021 433	16.387 064	0.016 387	0.000 016 387
1 cubic foot =	1728	1	0.037 037 04	28 316.846 592	28.316 847	0.028 316 847
1 cubic yard =	46 656	27	1	764 554.857 984	764.554 858	0.764 554 858
1 cubic cm =	0.061 023 74	0.000 035 315	0.000 001 308	1	0.001	0.000 001
1 cubic dm =	61.023 74	0.035 314 67	0.001 307 951	1 000	1	0.001
1 cubic meter =	61 023.74	35.314 67	1.307 951	1 000 000	1000	1

Units of Capacity (Liquid Measure)

Units	Minims	Fluid drams	Fluid ounces	Gills	Liquid pt
1 minim =	1	0.016 666 7	0.002 083 33	0.000 520 833	0.000 130 208
1 fluid dram =	60	1	0.125	0.031 25	0.007 812 5
1 fluid ounce =	480	8	1	0.25	0.062 5
1 gill =	1920	32	4	1	0.25
1 liquid pint =	7680	128	16	4	1
1 liquid quart =	15 360	256	32	8	2
1 gallon =	61 440	1024	128	32	8
1 cubic inch =	265.974	4.432 900	0.554 112 6	0.138 528 1	0.034 632 03
1 cubic foot =	459 603.1	7 660.052	957.506 5	239.376 6	59.844 16
1 milliliter =	16.230 73	0.270 512 18	0.033 814 02	0.008 453 506	.002 113 376
1 liter =	16 230.73	270.512 18	33.814 02	8.453 506	2.113 376

Units	Liquid quarts	Gallons	Cubic inches	Cubic feet	Liters
1 minim =	0.000 065 104 17	0.000 016 276 04	0.003 759 766	0.000 002 175 790	0.000 061 611 52
1 flu. dram =	0.003 906 25	0.000 976 562 5	0.225 585 9	0.000 130 547 4	0.003 696 691
1 fluid oz =	0.031 25	0.007 812 5	1.804 687 5	0.001 044 379	0.029 573 53
1 gill =	0.125	0.031 25	7.218 75	0.004 177 517	0.118 294 118
1 liquid pt =	0.5	0.125	28.875	0.016 710 07	0.473 176 473
1 liquid qt =	1	0.25	57.75	0.033 420 14	0.946 352 946
1 gallon =	4	1	231	0.133 680 6	3.785 411 784
1 cubic in. =	0.017 316 02	0.004 329 004	1	0.000 578 703 7	0.016 387 064
1 cubic foot =	29.922 08	7.480 519	1728	1	28.316 846 592
1 liter =	1.056 688	0.264 172 05	61.023 74	0.035 314 67	1

Units of Capacity (Dry Measure)

Units	Dry pints	Dry quarts	Pecks	Bushels	Cubic in.	Liters
1 dry pint =	1	0.5	0.062 5	0.015 625	33.600 312 5	0.550 610 47
1 dry quart =	2	1	0.125	0.031 25	67.200 625	1.101 220 9
1 peck =	16	8	1	0.25	537.605	8.809 767 5
1 bushel =	64	32	4	1	2150.42	35.239 07
1 cubic inch =	0.029 761 6	0.014 880 8	0.001 860 10	0.000 465 025	1	0.016 387 06
1 liter =	1.816 166	0.908 083	0.113 510 37	0.028 377 59	61.023 74	1

Miscellaneous Measures

Caliber—the diameter of a gun bore. In the U.S., caliber is traditionally expressed in hundredths of inches, eg. .22 or .30. In Britain, caliber is often expressed in thousandths of inches, eg. .270 or .465. Now, it is commonly expressed in millimeters, eg. the 7.62 mm. M14 rifle and the 5.56 mm. M16 rifle. Heavier weapons' caliber has long been expressed in millimeters, eg. the 81 mm. mortar, the 105 mm. howitzer (light), the 155 mm. howitzer (medium or heavy).

Naval guns' caliber refers to the barrel length as a multiple of the bore diameter. A 5-inch, 50-caliber naval gun has a 5-inch bore and a barrel length of 250 inches.

Carat, karat—a measure of the amount of alloy per 24 parts in gold. Thus 24-carat gold is pure; 18-carat gold is one-fourth alloy.

Decibel (dB)—a measure of the relative loudness or intensity of sound. A 20-decibel sound is 10 times louder than a 10-decibel sound; 30 decibels is 100 times louder; 40 decibels is 1,000 times louder, etc. One decibel is the smallest difference between sounds detectable by the human ear. A 140-decibel sound is painful.

10 decibels	– a light whisper
20	– quiet conversation
30	– normal conversation
40	– light traffic
50	– typewriter, loud conversation
60	– noisy office
70	– normal traffic, quiet train
80	– rock music, subway
90	– heavy traffic, thunder
100	– jet plane at takeoff

Em—a printer's measure designating the square width of any given type size. Thus, an em of 10-point type is 10 points. An en is half an em.

Gauge—a measure of shotgun bore diameter. Gauge numbers originally referred to the number of lead balls of the gun barrel diameter in a pound. Thus, a 16 gauge shotgun's bore was smaller than a 12-gauge shotgun's. Today, an international agreement assigns millimeter measures to each gauge, eg:

Gauge	Bore diameter in mm
6	23.34
10	19.67
12	18.52
14	17.60
16	16.81
20	15.90

Horsepower—the power needed to lift 550 pounds one foot in one second, or to lift 33,000 pounds one foot in one minute. Equivalent to 746 watts or 2,546.0756 Btu/h.

Quire—25 sheets of paper

Ream—500 sheets of paper

Electrical Units

The **watt** is the unit of power (electrical, mechanical, thermal, etc.). Electrical power is given by the product of the voltage and the current.

Energy is sold by the **joule**, but in common practice the billing of electrical energy is expressed in terms of the kilowatt-hour, which is 3,600,000 joules or 3.6 megajoules.

The **horsepower** is a non-metric unit sometimes used in mechanics. It is equal to 746 watts.

The **ohm** is the unit of electrical resistance and represents the physical property of a conductor which offers a resistance to the flow of electricity, permitting just 1 ampere to flow at 1 volt of pressure.

Compound Interest

Compounded Annually

Principal $100	Period	4%	5%	6%	7%	8%	9%	10%	12%	14%	16%
	1 day	0.011	0.014	0.016	0.019	0.022	0.025	0.027	0.033	0.038	0.044
	1 week	0.077	0.096	0.115	0.134	0.153	0.173	0.192	0.230	0.268	0.307
	6 mos.	2.00	2.50	3.00	3.50	4.00	4.50	5.00	6.00	7.00	8.00
	1 year	4.00	5.00	6.00	7.00	8.00	9.00	10.00	12.00	14.00	16.00
	2 years	8.16	10.25	12.36	14.49	16.64	18.81	21.00	25.44	29.96	34.56
	3 years	12.49	15.76	19.10	22.50	25.97	29.50	33.10	40.49	48.15	56.09
	4 years	16.99	21.55	26.25	31.08	36.05	41.16	46.41	57.35	68.90	81.06
	5 years	21.67	27.63	33.82	40.26	46.93	53.86	61.05	76.23	92.54	110.03
	6 years	26.53	34.01	41.85	50.07	58.69	67.71	77.16	97.38	119.50	143.64
	7 years	31.59	40.71	50.36	60.58	71.38	82.80	94.87	121.07	150.23	182.62
	8 years	36.86	47.75	59.38	71.82	85.09	99.26	114.36	147.60	185.26	227.84
	9 years	42.33	55.13	68.95	83.85	99.90	117.19	135.79	177.31	225.19	280.30
	10 years	48.02	62.89	79.08	96.72	115.89	136.74	159.37	210.58	270.72	341.14
	12 years	60.10	79.59	101.22	125.22	151.82	181.27	213.84	289.60	381.79	493.60
	15 years	80.09	107.89	139.66	175.90	217.22	264.25	317.72	447.36	613.79	826.55
	20 years	119.11	165.33	220.71	286.97	366.10	460.44	572.75	864.63	1,274.35	1,846.08

Ancient Measures

Biblical			Greek			Roman		
Cubit	=	21.8 inches	Cubit	=	18.3 inches	Cubit	=	17.5 inches
Omer	=	0.45 peck	Stadion	=	607.2 or 622 feet	Stadium	=	202 yards
		3.964 liters	Obolos	=	715.38 milligrams	As, libra,	=	325.971 grams,
Ephah	=	10 omers	Drachma	=	4.2923 grams	pondus		.71864 pounds
Shekel	=	0.497 ounce	Mina	=	0.9463 pounds			
		14.1 grams	Talent	=	60 mina			

Weight of Water

1	cubic inch	.0360 pound	1	imperial gallon	10.0 pounds
12	cubic inches	.433 pound	11.2	imperial gallons	112.0 pounds
1	cubic foot	62.4 pounds	224	imperial gallons	2240.0 pounds
1	cubic foot	7.48052 U.S. gal	1	U.S. gallon	8.33 pounds
1.8	cubic feet	112.0 pounds	13.45	U.S. gallons	112.0 pounds
35.96	cubic feet	2240.0 pounds	269.0	U.S. gallons	2240.0 pounds

Density of Gases and Vapors

at 0°C and 760 mmHg

Source: National Bureau of Standards (kilograms per cubic meter)

Gas	Wgt.	Gas	Wgt.	Gas	Wgt.
Acetylene	1.171	Ethylene	1.260	Methyl fluoride	1.545
Air	1.293	Fluorine	1.696	Mono methylamine	1.38
Ammonia	.759	Helium	.178	Neon	.900
Argon	1.784	Hydrogen	.090	Nitric oxide	1.341
Arsene	3.48	Hydrogen bromide	3.50	Nitrogen	1.250
Butane-iso.	2.60	Hydrogen chloride	1.639	Nitrosyl chloride	2.99
Butane-n	2.519	Hydrogen iodide	5.724	Nitrous oxide	1.997
Carbon dioxide	1.977	Hydrogen selenide	3.66	Oxygen	1.429
Carbon monoxide	1.250	Hydrogen sulfide	1.539	Phosphine	1.48
Carbon oxysulfide	2.72	Krypton	3.745	Propane	2.020
Chlorine	3.214	Methane	.717	Silicon tetrafluoride	4.67
Chlorine monoxide	3.89	Methyl chloride	2.25	Sulfur dioxide	2.927
Ethane	1.356	Methyl ether	2.091	Xenon	5.897

Temperature Conversion Table

The numbers in bold face type refer to the temperature either in degrees Celsius or Fahrenheit which are to be converted. If converting from degrees Fahrenheit to Celsius, the equivalent will be found in the column on the left, while if converting from degrees Celsius to Fahrenheit the answer will be found in the column on the right.

For temperatures not shown. To convert Fahrenheit to Celsius subtract 32 degrees and multiply by 5, divide by 9; to convert Celsius to Fahrenheit. multiply by 9, divide by 5 and add 32 degrees.

Celsius		Fahrenheit	Celsius		Fahrenheit	Celsius		Fahrenheit
− 273.2	− 459.7		− 17.8	0	32	35.0	95	203
− 184	− 300		− 12.2	10	50	36.7	98	208.4
− 169	− 273	− 459.4	− 6.67	20	68	37.8	100	212
− 157	− 250	− 418	− 1.11	30	86	43	110	230
− 129	− 200	− 328	4.44	40	104	49	120	248
− 101	− 150	− 238	10.0	50	122	54	130	266
− 73.3	− 100	− 148	15.6	60	140	60	140	284
− 45.6	− 50	− 58	21.1	70	158	66	150	302
− 40.0	− 40	− 40	23.9	75	167	93	200	392
− 34.4	− 30	− 22	26.7	80	176	121	250	482
− 28.9	− 20	− 4	29.4	85	185	149	300	572
− 23.3	− 10	14	32.2	90	194			

Boiling and Freezing Points of Water

Water boils at 212°F at sea level. For every 550 feet above sea level, boiling point of water is lower by about 1°F. Methyl alcohol boils at 148°F. Average human oral temperature. 98.6°F. Water freezes at 32°F. Although "Centigrade" is still frequently used, the International Committee on Weights and Measures and the National Bureau of Standards have recommended since 1948 that this scale be called "Celsius."

Breaking the Sound Barrier; Speed of Sound

The prefix Mach is used to describe supersonic speed. It derives from Ernst Mach, a Czech-born German physicist, who contributed to the study of sound. When a plane moves at the speed of sound it is Mach 1. When twice the speed of sound it is Mach 2. When it is near but below the speed of sound its speed can be designated at less than Mach 1, for example, Mach .90. Mach is defined as "in jet propulsion, the ratio of the velocity of a rocket or a jet to the velocity of sound in the medium being considered."

When a plane passes the sound barrier—flying faster than sound travels—listeners in the area hear thunderclaps, but pilots do not hear them.

Sound is produced by vibrations of an object and is transmitted by alternate increase and decrease in pressures that radiate outward through a material media of molecules —somewhat like waves spreading out on a pond after a rock has been tossed into it.

The frequency of sound is determined by the number of times the vibrating waves undulate per second, and is measured in cycles per second. The slower the cycle of waves, the lower the frequency. As frequencies increase, the sound is higher in pitch.

Sound is audible to human beings only if the frequency falls within a certain range. The human ear is usually not sensitive to frequencies of less than 20 vibrations per second, or more than about 20,000 vibrations per second—although this range varies among individuals. Anything at a pitch higher than the human ear can hear is termed ultrasonic.

Intensity or loudness is the strength of the pressure of these radiating waves, and is measured in decibels. The human ear responds to intensity in a range from zero to 120 decibels. Any sound with pressure over 120 decibels is painful.

The speed of sound is generally placed at 1,088 feet per second at sea level at 32°F. It varies in other temperatures and in different media. Sound travels faster in water than in air, and even faster in iron and steel. If in air it travels a mile in 5 seconds, it does a mile under water in 1 second, and through iron in ⅓ of a second. It travels through ice cold vapor at approximately 4,708 feet per second, ice-cold water, 4,938; granite, 12,960; hardwood, 12,620; brick, 11,960; glass, 16,410 to 19,690; silver, 8,658; gold, 5,717.

Colors of the Spectrum

Color, an electromagnetic wave phenomenon, is a sensation produced through the excitation of the retina of the eye by rays of light. The colors of the spectrum may be produced by viewing a light beam refracted by passage through a prism, which breaks the light into its wave lenghts.

Customarily, the primary colors of the spectrum are thought of as those 6 monochromatic colors that occupy relatively large areas of the spectrum: red, orange, yellow, green, blue, and violet. However, Sir Isaac Newton named a 7th, indigo, situated between blue and violet on the spectrum. Aubert estimated (1865) the solar spectrum to contain approximately 1,000 distinguishable hues of which according to Rood (1881) 2 million tints and shades can be distinguished; Luckiesh stated (1915) that 55 distinctly different hues have been seen in a single spectrum.

Many physicists recognize only 3 primary colors: red, yellow, and blue (Mayer, 1775); red, green, and violet (Thomas Young, 1801); red, green, and blue (Clerk Maxwell, 1860).

The color sensation of black is due to complete lack of stimulation of the retina, that of white to complete stimulation. The infra-red and ultra-violet rays, below the red (long) end of the spectrum and above the violet (short) end respectively, are invisible to the naked eye. Heat is the principal effect of the infra-red rays and chemical action that of the ultra-violet rays.

Common Fractions Reduced to Decimals

8ths	16ths	32ds	64ths		8ths	16ths	32ds	64ths		8ths	16ths	32ds	64ths	
			1	.015625				23	.359375				45	.703125
		1	2	.03125	3	6	12	24	.375			23	46	.71875
			3	.046875				25	.390625				47	.734375
	1	2	4	.0625				26	.40625	6	12	24	48	.75
			5	.078125			13						49	.765625
		3	6	.09375		7	14	27	.421875			25	50	.78125
			7	.109375				28	.4375				51	.796875
1	2	4	8	.125			15	29	.453125		13	26	52	.8125
			9	.140625				30	.46875				53	.828125
		5	10	.15625	4	8	16	31	.484375			27	54	.84375
			11	.171875				32	.5				55	.859375
	3	6	12	.1875			17	33	.515625	7	14	28	56	.875
			13	.203125				34	.53125				57	.890625
		7	14	.21875		9	18	35	.546875			29	58	.90625
			15	.234375				36	.5625				59	.921875
2	4	8	16	.25			19	37	.578125		15	30	60	.9375
			17	.265625				38	.59375				61	.953125
		9	18	.28125	5	10	20	39	.609375			31	62	.96875
			19	.296875				40	.625				63	.984375
	5	10	20	.3125			21	41	.640625	8	16	32	64	1.
			21	.328125				42	.65625					
		11	22	.34375		11	22	43	.671875					
								44	.6875					

Spirits Measures

Pony	0.5 jigger	
Shot	{ 0.666 jigger	
	{ 1.0 ounce	
Jigger	1.5 shot	
Pint	{ 16 shots	
	{ 0.625 fifth	
Fifth	{ 25.6 shots	
	{ 1.6 pints	
	{ 0.8 quart	
	{ 0.75706 liter	

Quart	{ 32 shots	
	{ 1.25 fifth	
Magnum	{ 2 quarts	
	{ 2.49797 bottles (wine)	

For champagne and brandy only:

Jeroboam	{ 6.4 pints	
	{ 1.6 magnum	
	{ 0.8 gallon	

For champagne only:

Rehoboam	3 magnums
Methuselah	4 magnums
Salmanazar	6 magnums
Balthazar	8 magnums
Nebuchadnezzar	10 magnums

Wine bottle (standard):

	{ 0.800633 quart
	{ 0.7576778 liter

Mathematical Formulas

To find the CIRCUMFERENCE of a:

Circle — Multiply the diameter by 3.14159265 (usually 3.1416).

To find the AREA of a:

Circle — Multiply the square of the diameter by .785398 (usually .7854).

Rectangle — Multiply the length of the base by the height.

Sphere (surface) — Multiply the square of the radius by 3.1416 and multiply by 4.

Square — Square the length of one side.

Trapezoid — Add the two parallel sides, multiply by the height and divide by 2.

Triangle — Multiply the base by the height and divide by 2.

To find the VOLUME of a:

Cone — Multiply the square of the radius of the base by 3.1416, multiply by the height, and divide by 3.

Cube — Cube the length of one edge.

Cylinder — Multiply the square of the radius of the base by 3.1416 and multiply by the height.

Pyramid — Multiply the area of the base by the height and

divide by 3.

Rectangular Prism — Multiply the length by the width by the height.

Sphere — Multiply the cube of the radius by 3.1416, multiply by 4 and divide by 3.

Playing Cards and Dice Chances

Poker Hands

Hand	Number possible	Odds against
Royal flush	4	649,739 to 1
Other straight flush	36	72,192 to 1
Four of a kind	624	4,164 to 1
Full house	3,744	693 to 1
Flush	5,108	508 to 1
Straight	10,200	254 to 1
Three of a kind	54,912	46 to 1
Two pairs	123,552	20 to 1
One pair	1,098,240	4 to 3 (1.37 to 1)
Nothing	1,302,540	1 to 1
Total	**2,598,960**	

Dice
(Probabilities of consecutive winning plays)

No. consecutive wins	By 7, 11 or point	No. consecutive wins	By 7, 11 or point
1	244 in 495	6	1 in 70
2	6 in 25	7	1 in 141
3	3 in 25	8	1 in 287
4	1 in 17	9	1 in 582
5	1 in 34		

Dice
(probabilities on 2 dice)

Total	Odds against (Single toss)	Total	Odds against (Single toss)
2	35 to 1	8	31 to 5
3	17 to 1	9	8 to 1
4	11 to 1	10	11 to 1
5	8 to 1	11	17 to 1
6	31 to 5	12	35 to 1
7	5 to 1		

Pinochle Auction
(Odds against finding in "widow" of 3 cards)

Open places	Odds against	Open places	Odds against
1	5 to 1	4	3 to 2 for
2	2 to 1	5	2 to 1 for
3	Even		

Bridge

The odds—against suit distribution in a hand of 4-4-3-2 are about 4 to 1, against 5-4-2-2 about 8 to 1, against 6-4-2-1 about 20 to 1, against 7-4-1-1 about 254 to 1, against 8-4-1-0 about 2,211 to 1, and against 13-0-0-0 about 158,753,389,899 to 1.

Measures of Force and Pressure

Dyne = force necessary to accelerate a 1-gram mass 1 centimeter per second squared = 0.000072 poundal

Poundal = force necessary to accelerate a 1-pound mass 1 foot per second squared = 13,825.5 dynes = 0.138255 newtons

Newton = force needed to accelerate a 1-kilogram mass 1 meter per second squared

Pascal (pressure) = 1 newton per square meter = 0.020885 pound per square foot

Atmosphere (air pressure at sea level) = 2,116.102 pounds per square foot = 14.6952 pounds per square inch = 1.0332 kilograms per square centimeter = 101,323 newtons per square meter.

Large Numbers

U.S.	Number of zeros	French British, German	U.S.	Number of zeros	French British, German
million	6	million	sextillion	21	1,000 trillion
billion	9	milliard	septillion	24	quadrillion
trillion	12	billion	octillion	27	1,000 quadrillion
quadrillion	15	1,000 billion	nonillion	30	quintillion
quintillion	18	trillion	decillion	33	1,000 quintillion

Roman Numerals

I	–	1	VI	–	6	XI	–	11	L	–	50	CD	–	400	$\overline{\text{X}}$	–	10.000
II	–	2	VII	–	7	XIX	–	19	LX	–	60	D	–	500	$\overline{\text{L}}$	–	50.000
III	–	3	VIII	–	8	XX	–	20	XC	–	90	CM	–	900	$\overline{\text{C}}$	–	100.000
IV	–	4	IX	–	9	XXX	–	30	C	–	100	M	–	1.000	$\overline{\text{D}}$	–	500.000
V	–	5	X	–	10	XL	–	40	CC	–	200	$\overline{\text{V}}$	–	5.000	$\overline{\text{M}}$	–	1.000.000

UNITED STATES FACTS
Superlative U.S. Statistics
Source: U.S. Geological Survey, U.S. Bureau of the Census

Area for 50 states and D. of C.	Total	3,618,770 sq. mi.
	Land 3,539,289 sq. mi.—Water 79,481 sq. mi.	
Largest state	Alaska	591,004 sq. mi.
Smallest state	Rhode Island	1,212 sq. mi.
Largest county (excludes Alaska)	San Bernardino County, California	20,064 sq. mi.
Smallest county	Kalawo, Hawaii	14 sq. mi.
Northernmost city	Barrow, Alaska	71°17'N.
Northernmost point	Point Barrow, Alaska	71°23'N.
Southernmost city	Hilo, Hawaii	19°43'N.
Southernmost settlement	Naalehu, Hawaii	19°03'N.
Southernmost point	Ka Lae (South Cape), Island of Hawaii	18°55'N. (155°41'W.)
Easternmost city	Eastport, Maine	66°59'02"W.
Easternmost settlement	Lubec, Maine	66°58'49"W.
Easternmost point	Quoddy Head, Maine	66°57'W.
Westernmost city	Unalaska, Alaska	166°32'W.
Westernmost settlement	Adak, Alaska	176°39'W.
Westernmost point	Cape Wrangell, Alaska	172°27'E.
Highest settlement	Climax, Colorado	11,560 ft.
Lowest settlement	Calipatria, California	−185 ft.
Highest point on Atlantic coast	Cadillac Mountain, Mount Desert Is., Maine	1,530 ft.
Oldest national park	Yellowstone National Park (1872), Wyoming,	
	Montana, Idaho	3,468 sq. mi.
Largest national park	Wrangell-St. Elias, Alaska	13,018 sq. mi.
Largest national monument	Death Valley, California, Nevada	3,231 sq. mi.
Highest waterfall	Yosemite Falls—Total in three sections	2,425 ft.
	Upper Yosemite Fall	1,430 ft.
	Cascades in middle section	675 ft.
	Lower Yosemite Fall	320 ft.
Longest river	Mississippi-Missouri	3,710 mi.
Highest mountain	Mount McKinley, Alaska	20,320 ft.
Lowest point	Death Valley, California	−282 ft.
Deepest lake	Crater Lake, Oregon	1,932 ft.
Rainiest spot	Mt. Waialeale, Hawaii	Annual aver. rainfall 460 inches
Largest gorge	Grand Canyon, Colorado River, Arizona	277 miles long, 600 ft.
		to 18 miles wide, 1 mile deep
Deepest gorge	Hell's Canyon, Snake River, Idaho-Oregon	7,900 ft.
Strongest surface wind	Mount Washington, New Hampshire recorded 1934	231 mph
Biggest dam	New Cornelia Tailings, Ten Mile Wash,	
	Arizona	274,026,000 cu. yds. material used
Tallest building	Sears Tower, Chicago, Illinois	1,454 ft.
Largest building	Boeing 747 Manufacturing Plant, Everett,	
	Washington	205,600,000 cu. ft.; covers 47 acres.
Tallest structure	TV tower, Blanchard, North Dakota	2,063 ft.
Longest bridge span	Verrazano-Narrows, New York	4,260 ft.
Highest bridge	Royal Gorge, Colorado	1,053 ft. above water
Deepest well	Gas well, Washita County, Oklahoma	31,441 ft.

The 48 Contiguous States

Area for 48 states	Total	3,021,295 sq. mi.
	Land 2,962,031 sq. mi.—Water 59,264 sq. mi.	
Largest state	Texas	266,807 sq. mi
Northernmost city	International Falls, Minnesota	48°36'N.
Northernmost settlement	Angle Inlet, Minnesota	49°21'N.
Northernmost point	Northwest Angle, Minnesota	49°23'N.
Southernmost city	Key West, Florida	24°33'N.
Southernmost mainland city	Florida City, Florida	25°27'N.
Southernmost point	Key West, Florida	24°33'N.
Westernmost town	La Push, Washington	124°38'W.
Westernmost point	Cape Alava, Washington	124°44'W.
Highest mountain	Mount Whitney, California	14,494 ft.

Note to users: The distinction between cities and towns varies from state to state. In this table the U.S. Bureau of the Census usage was followed.

Geodetic Datum of North America

In July 1986, the National Oceanic and Atmospheric Administration's National Geodetic Survey (NGS) completed the readjustment and redefinition of the North American Datum. Rapid advances in economic growth and scientific exploration in the United States after World War II resulted in an increasing need for accurate coordinate information. To facilitate the use of satellite surveying and navigation systems, the new datum was redefined using the Geodetic Reference System 1980 as the reference ellipsoid because this model more closely approximates the true size and shape of the Earth. The readjustment of the datum resulted in position changes of as much as 330 feet in the Continental United States and as much as 1/4 mile in Hawaii, the Aleutian Islands, Puerto Rico, and the Virgin Islands.

Statistical Information about the U.S.

In the *Statistical Abstract of the United States* the Bureau of the Census, U.S. Dept. of Commerce, annually publishes a summary of social, political, and economic information. A book of almost 1,000 pages, it presents in 31 sections comprehensive data on population, housing, health, education, employment, income, prices, business, banking, energy, science, defense, trade, government finance, foreign country comparison, and other subjects. Special features include sections on State Rankings and Metropolitan Statistical Areas and a new section with telephone contacts. The book is prepared under the direction of Glenn W. King, Chief, Statistical Compendia Staff, Bureau of the Census. Supplements to the *Statistical Abstract* are *County and City Data Book, 1988; Historical Statistics of the United States, Colonial Times to 1970;* and *State and Metropolitan Area Data Book, 1986* (1990 forthcoming). Information concerning these and other publications may be obtained from the Supt. of Documents, Government Printing Office, Wash., D.C. 20402, or from the U.S. Bureau of the Census, Data User Services Division, Wash., D.C. 20233.

Highest and Lowest Altitudes in the U.S. and Territories

Source: U.S. Geological Survey (Minus sign means below sea level; elevations are in feet.)

State	Highest Point Name	County	Elev.	Lowest Point Name	County	Elev.
Alabama	Cheaha Mountain	Cleburne	2,407	Gulf of Mexico		Sea level
Alaska	Mount McKinley		20,320	Pacific Ocean		Sea level
Arizona	Humphreys Peak	Coconino	12,633	Colorado R.	Yuma	70
Arkansas	Magazine Mountain	Logan	2,753	Ouachita R.	Ashley/Union	55
California	Mount Whitney	Inyo-Tulare	14,494	Death Valley	Inyo	−282
Colorado	Mount Elbert	Lake	14,433	Arkansas R.	Prowers	3,350
Connecticut	Mount Frissell	Litchfield	2,380	L.I. Sound		Sea level
Delaware	On Ebright Road	New Castle	442	Atlantic Ocean		Sea level
Dist. of Col.	Tenleytown	N. W. part	410	Potomac R.		1
Florida	Sec. 30, T 6N, R 20W	Walton	345	Atlantic Ocean		Sea level
Georgia	Brasstown Bald	Towns-Union	4,784	Atlantic Ocean		Sea level
Guam	Mount Lamlam	Agat District	1,332	Pacific Ocean		Sea level
Hawaii	Mauna Kea	Hawaii	13,796	Pacific Ocean		Sea level
Idaho	Borah Peak	Custer	12,662	Snake R.	Nez Perce	710
Illinois	Charles Mound	Jo Daviess	1,235	Mississippi R.	Alexander	279
Indiana	Franklin Township	Wayne	1,257	Ohio R.	Posey	320
Iowa	Sec. 29, T 100N, R 41W	Osceola	1,670	Mississippi R.	Lee	480
Kansas	Mount Sunflower	Wallace	4,039	Coffeyville E.	Coffey	679
Kentucky	Black Mountain	Harlan	4,139	Mississippi R.	Fulton	257
Louisiana	Driskill Mountain	Bienville	535	Spanish Fort		−8
Maine	Mount Katahdin	Piscataquis	5,267	Atlantic Ocean		Sea level
Maryland	Backbone Mountain	Garrett	3,360	Atlantic Ocean		Sea level
Massachusetts	Mount Greylock	Berkshire	3,487	Atlantic Ocean		Sea level
Michigan	Mount Arvon	Baraga	1,979	Lake Erie	Monroe	571
Minnesota	Eagle Mountain	Cook	2,301	Lake Superior		600
Mississippi	Woodall Mountain	Tishomingo	806	Gulf of Mexico		Sea level
Missouri	Taum Sauk Mt.	Iron	1,772	St. Francis R.	Dunklin	230
Montana	Granite Peak	Park	12,799	Kootenai R.	Lincoln	1,800
Nebraska	Johnson Township	Kimball	5,426	S.E. cor. State	Richardson	840
Nevada	Boundary Peak	Esmeralda	13,140	Mount Manchester		479
New Hamp.	Mt. Washington	Coos	6,288	Atlantic Ocean	Rockingham	Sea level
New Jersey	High Point	Sussex	1,803	Atlantic Ocean		Sea level
New Mexico	Wheeler Peak	Taos	13,161	Red Bluff Res.	Eddy	2,842
New York	Mount Marcy	Essex	5,344	Atlantic Ocean		Sea level
North Carolina	Mount Mitchell	Yancey	6,684	Atlantic Ocean		Sea level
North Dakota	White Butte	Slope	3,506	Red R.	Pembina	750
Ohio	Campbell Hill	Logan	1,549	Ohio R.	Hamilton	455
Oklahoma	Black Mesa	Cimarron	4,973	Little R.	McCurtain	289
Oregon	Mount Hood	Clackamas-Hood R.	11,239	Pacific Ocean		Sea level
Pennsylvania	Mt. Davis	Somerset	3,213	Delaware R.	Delaware	Sea level
Puerto Rico	Cerro de Punta	Ponce District	4,390	Atlantic Ocean		Sea level
Rhode Island	Jerimoth Hill	Providence	812	Atlantic Ocean		Sea level
Samoa	Lata Mountain	Tau Island	3,160	Pacific Ocean		Sea level
South Carolina	Sassafras Mountain	Pickens	3,560	Atlantic Ocean		Sea level
South Dakota	Harney Peak	Pennington	7,242	Big Stone Lake	Roberts	966
Tennessee	Clingmans Dome	Sevier	6,643	Mississippi R.	Shelby	178
Texas	Guadalupe Peak	Culberson	8,749	Gulf of Mexico		Sea level
Utah	Kings Peak	Duchesne	13,528	Beaverdam Wash.	Washington	2,000
Vermont	Mount Mansfield	Lamoille	4,393	Lake Champlain	Franklin	95
Virginia	Mount Rogers	Grayson-Smyth	5,729	Atlantic Ocean		Sea level
Virgin Islands	Crown Mountain	St. Thomas Island	1,556	Atlantic Ocean		Sea level
Washington	Mount Rainier	Pierce	14,410	Pacific Ocean		Sea level
West Virginia	Spruce Knob	Pendleton	4,861	Potomac R.	Jefferson	240
Wisconsin	Timms Hill	Price	1,951	Lake Michigan		579
Wyoming	Gannett Peak	Fremont	13,804	B. Fourche R.	Crook	3,099

U.S. Coastline by States

Source: NOAA, U.S. Commerce Department
(statute miles)

State	Coastline[1]	Shoreline[2]	State	Coastline[1]	Shoreline[2]
Atlantic coast	**2,069**	**28,673**	**Gulf coast**	**1,631**	**17,141**
Connecticut	0	618	Alabama	53	607
Delaware	28	381	Florida	770	5,095
Florida	580	3,331	Louisiana	397	7,721
Georgia	100	2,344	Mississippi	44	359
Maine	228	3,478	Texas	367	3,359
Maryland	31	3,190			
Massachusetts	192	1,519	**Pacific coast**	**7,623**	**40,298**
New Hampshire	13	131	Alaska	5,580	31,383
New Jersey	130	1,792	California	840	3,427
New York	127	1,850	Hawaii	750	1,052
North Carolina	301	3,375	Oregon	296	1,410
Pennsylvania	0	89	Washington	157	3,026
Rhode Island	40	384			
South Carolina	187	2,876	**Arctic coast, Alaska**	**1,060**	**2,521**
Virginia	112	3,315	**United States**	**12,383**	**88,633**

(1) Figures are lengths of general outline of seacoast. Measurements were made with a unit measure of 30 minutes of latitude on charts as near the scale of 1:1,200,000 as possible. Coastline of sounds and bays is included to a point where they narrow to width of unit measure, and includes the distance across at such point. (2) Figures obtained in 1939-40 with a recording instrument on the largest-scale charts and maps then available. Shoreline of outer coast, offshore islands, sounds, bays, rivers, and creeks is included to the head of tidewater or to a point where tidal waters narrow to a width of 100 feet.

States: Settled, Capitals, Entry into Union, Area, Rank

The original 13 states—The 13 colonies that seceded from Great Britain and fought the War of Independence (American Revolution) became the 13 original states. They were: Delaware, Pennsylvania, New Jersey, Georgia, Connecticut, Massachusetts, Maryland, South Carolina, New Hampshire, Virginia, New York, North Carolina, and Rhode Island. The order for the original 13 states is the order in which they ratified the Constitution.

State	Settled*	Capital	Entered Union Date	Order	Extent in miles Long (approx. mean)	Wide	Area in square miles Land	Inland Water	Total	Rank in area
Ala.	1702	Montgomery	Dec. 14, 1819	22	330	190	50,767	938	51,705	29
Alas.	1784	Juneau	Jan. 3, 1959	49	(a)1,480	810	570,833	20,171	591,004	1
Ariz.	1776	Phoenix	Feb. 14, 1912	48	400	310	113,508	492	114,000	6
Ark.	1686	Little Rock	June 15, 1836	25	260	240	52,078	1,109	53,187	27
Cal.	1769	Sacramento	Sept. 9, 1850	31	770	250	156,299	2,407	158,706	3
Col.	1858	Denver	Aug. 1, 1876	38	380	280	103,595	496	104,091	8
Conn.	1634	Hartford	Jan. 9, 1788	5	110	70	4,872	147	5,018	48
Del.	1638	Dover	Dec. 7, 1787	1	100	30	1,932	112	2,045	49
D.C.		Washington			...	...	63	6	69	51
Fla.	1565	Tallahassee	Mar. 3, 1845	27	500	160	54,153	4,511	58,664	22
Ga.	1733	Atlanta	Jan. 2, 1788	4	300	230	58,056	854	58,910	21
Ha.	1820	Honolulu	Aug. 21, 1959	50	...	...	6,425	46	6,471	47
Ida.	1842	Boise	July 3, 1890	43	570	300	82,412	1,153	83,564	13
Ill.	1720	Springfield	Dec. 3, 1818	21	390	210	55,645	700	56,345	24
Ind.	1733	Indianapolis.	Dec. 11, 1816	19	270	140	35,932	253	36,185	38
Ia.	1788	Des Moines	Dec. 28, 1846	29	310	200	55,965	310	56,275	25
Kan.	1727	Topeka	Jan. 29, 1861	34	400	210	81,778	499	82,277	14
Ky.	1774	Frankfort	June 1, 1792	15	380	140	39,669	740	40,410	37
La.	1699	Baton Rouge	Apr. 30, 1812	18	380	130	44,521	3,230	47,752	31
Me.	1624	Augusta	Mar. 15, 1820	23	320	190	30,995	2,270	33,265	39
Md.	1634	Annapolis	Apr. 28, 1788	7	250	90	9,837	623	10,460	42
Mass.	1620	Boston	Feb. 6, 1788	6	190	50	7,824	460	8,284	45
Mich.	1668	Lansing	Jan. 26, 1837	26	490	240	56,954	1,573	58,527	23
Minn.	1805	St. Paul	May 11, 1858	32	400	250	79,548	4,854	84,402	12
Miss.	1699	Jackson	Dec. 10, 1817	20	340	170	47,233	457	47,689	32
Mo.	1735	Jefferson City	Aug. 10, 1821	24	300	240	68,945	752	69,697	19
Mon.	1809	Helena	Nov. 8, 1889	41	630	280	145,388	1,658	147,046	4
Neb.	1823	Lincoln	Mar. 1, 1867	37	430	210	76,644	711	77,355	15
Nev.	1849	Carson City	Oct. 31, 1864	36	490	320	109,894	667	110,561	7
N.H.	1623	Concord	June 21, 1788	9	190	70	8,993	286	9,279	44
N.J.	1664	Trenton	Dec. 18, 1787	3	150	70	7,468	319	7,787	46
N.M.	1610	Santa Fe	Jan. 6, 1912	47	370	343	121,335	258	121,593	5
N.Y.	1614	Albany	July 26, 1788	11	330	283	47,377	1,731	49,108	30
N.C.	1660	Raleigh	Nov. 21, 1789	12	500	150	48,843	3,826	52,669	28
N.D.	1812	Bismarck	Nov. 2, 1889	39	340	211	69,300	1,403	70,702	17
Oh.	1788	Columbus	Mar. 1, 1803	17	220	220	41,004	325	41,330	35
Okla.	1889	Oklahoma City	Nov. 16, 1907	46	400	220	68,655	1,301	69,956	18
Ore.	1811	Salem	Feb. 14, 1859	33	360	261	96,184	889	97,073	10
Pa.	1682	Harrisburg	Dec. 12, 1787	2	283	160	44,888	420	45,308	33
R.I.	1636	Providence	May 29, 1790	13	40	30	1,055	158	1,212	50
S.C.	1670	Columbia	May 23, 1788	8	260	200	30,203	909	31,113	40
S.D.	1859	Pierre	Nov. 2, 1889	40	380	210	75,952	1,164	77,116	16
Tenn.	1769	Nashville	June 1, 1796	16	440	120	41,155	989	42,144	34
Tex.	1682	Austin	Dec. 29, 1845	28	790	660	262,017	4,790	266,807	2
Ut.	1847	Salt Lake City	Jan. 4, 1896	45	350	270	82,073	2,826	84,899	11
Vt.	1724	Montpelier	Mar. 4, 1791	14	160	80	9,273	341	9,614	43
Va.	1607	Richmond	June 25, 1788	10	430	200	39,704	1,063	40,767	36
Wash.	1811	Olympia	Nov. 11, 1889	42	360	240	66,511	1,627	68,139	20
W.Va.	1727	Charleston	June 20, 1863	35	240	130	24,119	112	24,232	41
Wis.	1766	Madison	May 29, 1848	30	310	260	54,426	1,727	56,153	26
Wy.	1834	Cheyenne	July 10, 1890	44	360	280	96,989	820	97,809	9

*First European permanent settlement. (a) Aleutian Islands and Alexander Archipelago are not considered in these lengths.

The Continental Divide

The Continental Divide: watershed, created by mountain ranges or table-lands of the Rocky Mountains, from which the drainage is easterly or westerly; the easterly flowing waters reaching the Atlantic Ocean chiefly through the Gulf of Mexico, and the westerly flowing waters reaching the Pacific Ocean through the Columbia River, or through the Colorado River, which flows into the Gulf of California.

The location and route of the Continental Divide across the United States may briefly be described as follows:

Beginning at point of crossing the United States-Mexican boundary, near long. 108°45'W., the Divide, in a northerly direction, crosses New Mexico along the western edge of the Rio Grande drainage basin, entering Colorado near long. 106°41'W.

Thence by a very irregular route northerly across Colorado along the western summits of the Rio Grande and of the Arkansas, the South Platte, and the North Platte River basins, and across Rocky Mountain National Park, entering Wyoming near long. 106°52'W.

Thence in a northwesterly direction, forming the western rims of the North Platte, Big Horn, and Yellowstone River basins, crossing the southwestern portion of Yellowstone National Park.

Thence in a westerly and then a northerly direction forming the common boundary of Idaho and Montana, to a point on said boundary near long. 114°00'W.

Thence northeasterly and northwesterly through Montana and the Glacier National Park, entering Canada near long. 114°04'W.

Chronological List of Territories

Source: National Archives and Records Service

Name of territory	Date of Organic Act	Organic Act effective	Admission as state	Yrs. terr.
Northwest Territory(a)	July 13, 1787	No fixed date.	Mar. 1, 1803(b)	16
Territory southwest of River Ohio	May 26, 1790	No fixed date.	June 1, 1796(c)	6
Mississippi	Apr. 7, 1798	When president acted.	Dec. 10, 1817	19
Indiana	May 7, 1800	July 4, 1800	Dec. 11, 1816	16
Orleans	Mar. 26, 1804	Oct. 1, 1804	Apr. 30, 1812(d)	7
Michigan	Jan. 11, 1805	June 30, 1805	Jan. 26, 1837	31
Louisiana-Missouri(e)	Mar. 3, 1805	July 4, 1805	Aug. 10, 1821	16
Illinois	Feb. 3, 1809	Mar. 1, 1809	Dec. 3, 1818	9
Alabama	Mar. 3, 1817	When Miss. became a state	Dec. 14, 1819	2
Arkansas	Mar. 2, 1819	July 4, 1819	June 15, 1836	17
Florida	Mar. 30, 1822	No fixed date.	Mar. 3, 1845	23
Wisconsin	Apr. 20, 1836	July 3, 1836	May 29, 1848	12
Iowa	June 12, 1838	July 3, 1838	Dec. 28, 1846	7
Oregon	Aug. 14, 1848	Date of act.	Feb. 14, 1859	10
Minnesota	Mar. 3, 1849	Date of act	May 11, 1858	9
New Mexico	Sept. 9, 1850	On president's proclamation	Jan. 6, 1912	61
Utah	Sept. 9, 1850	Date of act.	Jan. 4, 1896	44
Washington	Mar. 2, 1853	Date of act.	Nov. 11, 1889	36
Nebraska	May 30, 1854	Date of act.	Mar. 1, 1867	12
Kansas	May 30, 1854	Date of act.	Jan. 29, 1861	6
Colorado	Feb. 28, 1861	Date of act.	Aug. 1, 1876	15
Nevada	Mar. 2, 1861	Date of act	Oct. 31, 1864	3
Dakota	Mar. 2, 1861	Date of act.	Nov. 2, 1889	28
Arizona	Feb. 24, 1863	Date of act.	Feb. 14, 1912	49
Idaho	Mar. 3, 1863	Date of act.	July 3, 1890	27
Montana	May 26, 1864	Date of act.	Nov. 8, 1889	25
Wyoming	July 25, 1868	When officers were qualified	July 10, 1890	22
Alaska(f)	May 17, 1884	No fixed date.	Jan. 3, 1959	75
Oklahoma	May 2, 1890	Date of act.	Nov. 16, 1907	17
Hawaii	Apr. 30, 1900	June 14, 1900	Aug. 21, 1959	59

(a) Included Ohio, Indiana, Illinois, Michigan, Wisconsin, eastern Minnesota; (b) as the state of Ohio; (c) as the state of Tennessee; (d) as the state of Louisiana; (e) organic act for Missouri Territory of June 4, 1812, became effective Dec. 7, 1812; (f) Although the May 17, 1884 act actually constituted Alaska as a district, it was often referred to as a territory, and unofficially administered as such. The Territory of Alaska was legally and formally organized by an act of Aug. 24, 1912.

Geographic Centers, U.S. and Each State

Source: U.S. Geological Survey

United States, including Alaska and Hawaii — South Dakota; Butte County, W of Castle Rock, Approx. lat. 44°58'N. long. 103°46'W.
Contiguous U.S. (48 states) — Near Lebanon, Smith Co., Kansas, lat. 39°50'N. long. 98°35'W.
North American continent — The geographic center is in Pierce County, North Dakota, 6 miles W of Balta, latitude 48°10', longitude 100°10'W.

State-county, locality

Alabama—Chilton, 12 miles SW of Clanton.
Alaska—lat. 63°50'N. long. 152°W. Approx. 60 mi. NW of Mt. McKinley.
Arizona—Yavapai, 55 miles ESE of Prescott.
Arkansas—Pulaski, 12 miles NW of Little Rock.
California—Madera, 38 miles E of Madera.
Colorado—Park, 30 miles NW of Pikes Peak.
Connecticut—Hartford, at East Berlin.
Delaware—Kent, 11 miles S of Dover.
District of Columbia—Near 4th and L Sts., NW.
Florida—Hernando, 12 miles NNW of Brooksville.
Georgia—Twiggs, 18 miles SE of Macon.
Hawaii—Hawaii, 20°15'N, 156°20'W, off Maui Island.
Idaho—Custer, at Custer, SW of Challis.
Illinois—Logan, 28 miles NE of Springfield.
Indiana—Boone, 14 miles NNW of Indianapolis.
Iowa—Story, 5 miles NE of Ames.
Kansas—Barton, 15 miles NE of Great Bend.
Kentucky—Marion, 3 miles NNW of Lebanon.
Louisiana—Avoyelles, 3 miles SE of Marksville.
Maine—Piscataquis, 18 miles north of Dover.
Maryland—Prince Georges, 4.5 miles NW of Davidsonville.

Massachusetts—Worcester, north part of city.
Michigan—Wexford, 5 miles NNW of Cadillac.
Minnesota—Crow Wing, 10 miles SW of Brainerd.
Mississippi—Leake, 9 miles WNW of Carthage.
Missouri—Miller, 20 miles SW of Jefferson City.
Montana—Fergus, 11 miles west of Lewistown.
Nebraska—Custer, 10 miles NW of Broken Bow.
Nevada—Lander, 26 miles SE of Austin.
New Hampshire—Belknap, 3 miles E of Ashland.
New Jersey—Mercer, 5 miles SE of Trenton.
New Mexico—Torrance, 12 miles SSW of Willard.
New York—Madison, 12 miles S of Oneida and 26 miles SW of Utica.
North Carolina—Chatham, 10 miles NW of Sanford.
North Dakota—Sheridan, 5 miles SW of McClusky.
Ohio—Delaware, 25 miles NNE of Columbus.
Oklahoma—Oklahoma, 8 miles N of Oklahoma City.
Oregon—Crook, 25 miles SSE of Prineville.
Pennsylvania—Centre, 2.5 miles SW of Bellefonte.
Rhode Island—Kent, 1 mile SW of Crompton.
South Carolina—Richland, 13 miles SE of Columbia.
South Dakota—Hughes, 8 miles NE of Pierre.
Tennessee—Rutherford, 5 mi. NE of Murfreesboro.
Texas—McCulloch, 15 miles NE of Brady.
Utah—Sanpete, 3 miles N of Manti.
Vermont—Washington, 3 miles E of Roxbury.
Virginia—Buckingham, 5 miles SW of Buckingham.
Washington—Chelan, 10 mi. WSW of Wenatchee.
West Virginia—Braxton, 4 miles E of Sutton.
Wisconsin—Wood, 9 miles SE of Marshfield.
Wyoming—Fremont, 58 miles ENE of Lander.

There is no generally accepted definition of geographic center, and no satisfactory method for determining it. The geographic center of an area may be defined as the center of gravity of the surface, or that point on which the surface of the area would balance if it were a plane of uniform thickness.

No marked or monumented point has been established by any government agency as the geographic center of either the 50 states, the contiguous United States, or the North American continent. A monument was erected in Lebanon, Kan., contiguous U.S. center, by a group of citizens. A cairn in Rugby, N.D. marks the center of the North American continent.

International Boundary Lines of the U.S.

The length of the northern boundary of the contiguous U.S. — the U.S.-Canadian border, excluding Alaska — is 3,987 miles according to the U.S. Geological Survey, Dept. of the Interior. The length of the Alaskan-Canadian border is 1,538 miles. The length of the U.S.-Mexican border, from the Gulf of Mexico to the Pacific Ocean, is approximately 1,933 miles (1963 boundary agreement).

Origin of the Names of U.S. States

Source: State officials, the Smithsonian Institution, and the Topographic Division, U.S. Geological Survey.

Alabama—Indian for tribal town, later a tribe (Alabamas or Alibamons) of the Creek confederacy.

Alaska—Russian version of Aleutian (Eskimo) word, alakshak, for "peninsula," "great lands," or "land that is not an island."

Arizona—Spanish version of Pima Indian word for "little spring place," or Aztec arizuma, meaning "silver-bearing."

Arkansas—French variant of Quapaw, a Siouan people meaning "downstream people."

California—Bestowed by the Spanish conquistadors (possibly by Cortez). It was the name of an imaginary island, an earthly paradise, in "Las Serges de Esplandian," a Spanish romance written by Montalvo in 1510. Baja California (Lower California, in Mexico) was first visited by Spanish in 1533. The present U.S. state was called Alta (Upper) California.

Colorado—Spanish, red, first applied to Colorado River.

Connecticut—From Mohican and other Algonquin words meaning "long river place."

Delaware—Named for Lord De La Warr, early governor of Virginia; first applied to river, then to Indian tribe (Lenni-Lenape), and the state.

District of Columbia—For Columbus, 1791.

Florida—Named by Ponce de Leon on Pascua Florida, "Flowery Easter," on Easter Sunday, 1513.

Georgia—For King George II of England by James Oglethorpe, colonial administrator, 1732.

Hawaii—Possibly derived from native word for homeland, Hawaiki or Owhyhee.

Idaho—A coined name with an invented Indian meaning: "gem of the mountains;" originally suggested for the Pike's Peak mining territory (Colorado), then applied to the new mining territory of the Pacific Northwest. Another theory suggests Idaho may be a Kiowa Apache term for the Comanche.

Illinois—French for Illini or land of Illini, Algonquin word meaning men or warriors.

Indiana—Means "land of the Indians."

Iowa—Indian word variously translated as "one who puts to sleep" or "beautiful land."

Kansas—Sioux word for "south wind people."

Kentucky—Indian word variously translated as "dark and bloody ground," "meadow land" and "land of tomorrow."

Louisiana—Part of territory called Louisiana by Sieur de La Salle for French King Louis XIV.

Maine—From Maine, ancient French province. Also: descriptive, referring to the mainland as distinct from the many coastal islands.

Maryland—For Queen Henrietta Maria, wife of Charles I of England.

Massachusetts—From Indian tribe named after "large hill place" identified by Capt. John Smith as being near Milton, Mass.

Michigan—From Chippewa words mici gama meaning "great water," after the lake of the same name.

Minnesota—From Dakota Sioux word meaning "cloudy water" or "sky-tinted water" of the Minnesota River.

Mississippi—Probably Chippewa; mici zibi, "great river" or "gathering-in of all the waters." Also: Algonquin word, "Messipi."

Missouri—Algonquin Indian tribe named after Missouri River, meaning "muddy water."

Montana—Latin or Spanish for "mountainous."

Nebraska—From Omaha or Otos Indian word meaning "broad water" or "flat river," describing the Platte River.

Nevada—Spanish, meaning snow-clad.

New Hampshire—Named 1629 by Capt. John Mason of Plymouth Council for his home county in England.

New Jersey—The Duke of York, 1664, gave a patent to John Berkeley and Sir George Carteret to be called Nova Caesaria, or New Jersey, after England's Isle of Jersey.

New Mexico—Spaniards in Mexico applied term to land north and west of Rio Grande in the 16th century.

New York—For Duke of York and Albany who received patent to New Netherland from his brother Charles II and sent an expedition to capture it, 1664.

North Carolina—In 1619 Charles I gave a large patent to Sir Robert Heath to be called Province of Carolana, from Carolus, Latin name for Charles. A new patent was granted by Charles II to Earl of Clarendon and others. Divided into North and South Carolina, 1710.

North Dakota—Dakota is Sioux for friend or ally.

Ohio—Iroquois word for "fine or good river."

Oklahoma—Choctaw coined word meaning red man, proposed by Rev. Allen Wright, Choctaw-speaking Indian.

Oregon—Origin unknown. One theory holds that the name may have been derived from that of the Wisconsin River shown on a 1715 French map as "Ouaricon-sint."

Pennsylvania—William Penn, the Quaker, who was made full proprietor by King Charles II in 1681, suggested Sylvania, or woodland, for his tract. The king's government owed Penn's father, Admiral William Penn, £16,000, and the land was granted as partial settlement. Charles II added the Penn to Sylvania, against the desires of the modest proprietor, in honor of the admiral.

Puerto Rico—Spanish for Rich Port.

Rhode Island—Exact origin is unknown. One theory notes that Giovanni de Verrazano recorded an island about the size of Rhodes in the Mediterranean in 1524, but others believe the state was named Roode Eylandt by Adriaen Block, Dutch explorer, because of its red clay.

South Carolina—See North Carolina.

South Dakota—See North Dakota.

Tennessee—Tanasi was the name of Cherokee villages on the Little Tennessee River. From 1784 to 1788 this was the State of Franklin, or Frankland.

Texas—Variant of word used by Caddo and other Indians meaning friends or allies, and applied to them by the Spanish in eastern Texas. Also written texias, tejas, teyas.

Utah—From a Navajo word meaning upper, or higher up, as applied to a Shoshone tribe called Ute. Spanish form is Yutta, English Uta or Utah. Proposed name Deseret, "land of honeybees," from Book of Mormon, was rejected by Congress.

Vermont—From French words vert (green) and mont (mountain). The Green Mountains were said to have been named by Samuel de Champlain. The Green Mountain Boys were Gen. Stark's men in the Revolution. When the state was formed, 1777, Dr. Thomas Young suggested combining vert and mont into Vermont.

Virginia—Named by Sir Walter Raleigh, who fitted out the expedition of 1584, in honor of Queen Elizabeth, the Virgin Queen of England.

Washington—Named after George Washington. When the bill creating the Territory of Columbia was introduced in the 32d Congress, the name was changed to Washington because of the existence of the District of Columbia.

West Virginia—So named when western counties of Virginia refused to secede from the United States, 1863.

Wisconsin—An Indian name, spelled Ouisconsin and Mesconsing by early chroniclers. Believed to mean "grassy place" in Chippewa. Congress made it Wisconsin.

Wyoming—The word was taken from Wyoming Valley, Pa., which was the site of an Indian massacre and became widely known by Campbell's poem, "Gertrude of Wyoming." In Algonquin it means "large prairie place."

Territorial Sea of the U.S.

According to a December 27, 1988 proclamation by Pres. Ronald Reagan: "The territorial sea of the United States henceforth extends to 12 nautical miles from the baselines of the United States determined in accordance with international law. In accordance with international law, as reflected in the applicable provisions of the 1982 United Nations Convention on the Law of the Sea, within the territorial sea of the United States, the ships of all countries enjoy the right of innocent passage and the ships and aircraft of all countries enjoy the right of transit passage through international straits."

Accession of Territory by the U.S.

Source: U.S. Bureau of the Census

	Acquisi-tion date	Gross Area (Land and water) Sq. mi.		Acquisi-tion date	Gross Area (Land and water) Sq. mi.		Acquisi-tion date	Gross Area (Land and water) Sq. mi.
Total U.S.	(x)	3,623,434	Gadsden Purchase .	1853	29,640	Virgin Islands of		
United States.	(x)	3,618,770	Alaska	1867	591,004	the U.S.	1917	132
Territory in 1790[1] . . .	(x)	891,364	Hawaii	1898	6,471	Pacific Islands,		
Louisiana Purchase	1803	831,321	Other areas:			Trust Territory		
Purchase of Florida	1819	69,866	Puerto Rico	[2]1898	3,515	of the[5]	1947	533
Texas	1845	384,958	Guam	[3]1898	209	No. Mariana Islands[5]	1947	184
Oregon	1846	283,439	American Samoa. .	[4]1899	77	All other[6]	(x)	14
Mexican Cession . .	1848	530,706						

(x) Not applicable. (1) Includes that part of drainage basin of Red River of the North, south of 49th parallel, sometimes considered part of Louisiana Purchase. (2) Ceded by Spain in 1898, ratified in 1899, and became Commonwealth of Puerto Rico by Act of Congress on July 25, 1952. (3) Acquired 1898; ratified 1899. (4) Acquired 1899; ratified 1900. (5) Land area only. (6) Comprises the following islands with gross areas as indicated, in sq. mi.: Midway (2), Wake (3), Palmyra (4), Navassa (2), Baker, Howland, and Jarvis (combined area, 3), Johnston Atoll (combined area, less than .5), and Kingman Reef (less than .5). Excludes Canton and Enderbury Islands (combined area 27 sq. mi.), which are considered to be under the jurisdiction of Kiribati since 1979, and Swan Islands (1 sq. mi.), which were returned to Honduras in 1972.

Public Lands of the U. S.

Source: Bureau of Land Management, U.S. Interior Department

Disposition of Public Lands 1781 to 1988

Disposition by methods not elsewhere classified[1]	Acres	Granted to states for:	Acres
Granted or sold to homesteaders	303,500,000	Support of common schools	77,630,000
Granted to railroad corporations	287,500,000	Reclamation of swampland	64,920,000
Granted to veterans as military bounties. .	94,400,000	Construction of railroads	37,130,000
Confirmed as private land claims[2]	61,000,000	Support of misc. institutions[6]	21,700,000
Sold under timber and stone law[3].	34,000,000	Purposes not elsewhere classified[7] . . .	117,600,000
Granted or sold under timber culture law[4] . .	13,900,000	Canals and rivers	6,100,000
Sold under desert land law[5]	10,900,000	Construction of wagon roads	3,400,000
	10,700,000	**Total granted to states**	**328,480,000**

(1) Chiefly public, private, and preemption sales, but includes mineral entries, scrip locations, sales of townsites and townlots. (2) The Government has confirmed title to lands claimed under valid grants made by foreign governments prior to the acquisition of the public domain by the United States. (3) The law provided for the sale of lands valuable for timber or stone and unfit for cultivation. (4) The law provided for the granting of public lands to settlers on condition that they plant and cultivate trees on the lands granted. (5) The law provided for the sale of arid agricultural public lands to settlers who irrigate them and bring them under cultivation. (6) Universities, hospitals, asylums, etc. (7) For construction of various public improvements (individual items not specified in the granting act) reclamation of desert lands, construction of water reservoirs, etc.

Public Lands Administered by Federal Agencies

Agency (Acres, Sept. 30, 1987)	Public domain	Acquired	Total
Forest Service	161,038,854.3	28,341,223.5	189,380,077.8
Bureau of Land Management.	268,093,335.0	2,324,840.0	270,418,175.0
Bureau of Reclamation	3,533,817.5	1,969,275.9	5,503,093.4
Fish and Wildlife Service	486,827,455.7	18,024,330.9	504,851,786.6
National Park Service	64,325,741.0	8,517,114.8	72,842,855.8
Bureau of Indian Affairs	2,554,358.7	193,079.6	2,747,438.3
Tennessee Valley Authority.	0	1,040,231.3	1,040,231.3
Corps of Engineers	604,971.2	4,869,200.0	5,474,171.2
U.S. Army.	3,187,901.0	6,495,173.0	9,683,074.0
U.S. Navy	618,005.6	1,743,750.2	2,361,755.8
U.S. Air Force	6,858,510.0	1,255,022.0	8,113,532.0
Department of Energy	1,465,862.4	700,478.8	2,166,341.2
Total, all agencies (incl. those not shown) . .	660,976,655.8	63,089,515.1	724,066,170.9

National Parks, Other Areas Administered by Nat'l Park Service

Figures given are date area initially protected by Congress or presidential proclamation, date given current designation, and gross area in acres 12/31/88.

National Parks

Acadia, Me. (1916/1929) 41,409. Includes Mount Desert Island, half of Isle au Haut, Schoodic Point on mainland. Highest elevation on Eastern seaboard.

Arches, Ut. (1929/1971) 73,379. Contains giant red sandstone arches and other products of erosion.

Badlands, S.D. (1929/1978) 243,244; eroded prairie, bison, bighorn and antelope. Contains animal fossils of 40 million years ago.

Big Bend, Tex. (1935/1944) 802,541. Rio Grande, Chisos Mts.

Biscayne, Fla. (1968/1980) 173,039. Aquatic park encompasses chain of islands south of Miami.

Bryce Canyon, Ut. (1923/1928) 35,835. Spectacularly colorful, unusual display of erosion effects.

Canyonlands, Ut. (1964) 337,570. At junction of Colorado and Green rivers, extensive evidence of prehistoric Indians.

Capitol Reef, Ut. (1937/1971) 241,904. A 60-mile uplift of sandstone cliffs dissected by high-walled gorges.

Carlsbad Caverns, N.M. (1923/1930) 46,755. Largest known caverns; not yet fully explored.

Channel Islands, Cal. (1938/1980) 249,354. Seal lion breeding place, nesting sea birds, unique plants.

Crater Lake, Ore. (1902) 183,224. Extraordinary blue lake in crater of extinct volcano encircled by lava walls 500 to 2,000 feet high.

Denali, Alas. (1917/1980) 4,716,726. Name changed from Mt. McKinley NP. Contains highest mountain in U.S.; wildlife.

Everglades, Fla. (1934) 1,398,938. Largest remaining subtropical wilderness in continental U.S.

Gates of the Arctic, Alas. (1978/1980) 7,523,888. Vast wilderness in north central region.

Glacier, Mon. (1910) 1,013,572. Superb Rocky Mt. scenery, numerous glaciers and glacial lakes. Part of Waterton-Glacier Intl. Peace Park established by U.S. and Canada in 1932.

Glacier Bay, Alas. (1925/1980) 3,225,284. Great tidewater glaciers that move down mountain sides and break up into the sea; much wildlife.

Grand Canyon, Ariz. (1908/1919) 1,218,375. Most spectacular part of Colorado River's greatest canyon.

Grand Teton, Wy. (1929) 309,994. Most impressive part of the Teton Mountains, winter feeding ground of largest American elk herd.

Great Basin, Nev. (1922/1986) 76,109. Wide basins and high mountain ranges.

Great Smoky Mountains, N.C.-Tenn. (1926/1934) 520,269. Largest eastern mountain range, magnificent forests.

Guadalupe Mountains, Tex. (1966/1972) 86,416. Extensive Permian limestone fossil reef; tremendous earth fault.

Haleakala, Ha. (1916/1960) 28,655. Dormant volcano on Maui with large colorful craters.

Hawaii Volcanoes, Ha. (1916/1961) 229,177. Contains Kilauea and Mauna Loa, active volcanoes.

Hot Springs, Ark. (1832/1921) 5,839. Government supervised bath houses use waters of 45 of the 47 natural hot springs.

Isle Royale, Mich. (1931) 571,790. Largest island in Lake Superior, noted for its wilderness area and wildlife.

Katmai, Alas. (1918/1980) 3,716,000. Valley of Ten Thousand Smokes, scene of 1912 volcanic eruption.

Kenai Fjords, Alas. (1978/1980) 669,541. Abundant mountain goats, marine mammals, birdlife; the Harding Icefield, one of the major icecaps in U.S.

Kings Canyon, Cal. (1890/1940) 461,901. Mountain wilderness, dominated by Kings River Canyons and High Sierra; contains giant sequoias.

Kobuk Valley, Alas. (1978/1980) 1,750,421. Broad river is core of native culture.

Lake Clark, Alas. (1978/1980) 2,636,839. Across Cook Inlet from Anchorage. A scenic wilderness rich in fish and wildlife.

Lassen Volcanic, Cal. (1907/1916) 106,372. Contains Lassen Peak, recently active volcano, and other volcanic phenomena.

Mammoth Cave, Ky. (1926/1941) 52,419. 144 miles of surveyed underground passages, beautiful natural formations, river 300 feet below surface.

Mesa Verde, Col. (1906) 52,085. Most notable and best preserved prehistoric cliff dwellings in the United States.

Mount Rainier, Wash. (1899) 235,404. Greatest single-peak glacial system in the lower 48 states.

North Cascades, Wash. (1968) 504,781. Spectacular mountainous region with many glaciers, lakes.

Olympic, Wash. (1909/1938) 921,942. Mountain wilderness containing finest remnant of Pacific Northwest rain forest, active glaciers, Pacific shoreline, rare elk.

Petrified Forest, Ariz. (1906/1962) 93,533. Extensive petrified wood and Indian artifacts. Contains part of Painted Desert.

Redwood, Cal. (1968) 110,132. Forty miles of Pacific coastline, groves of ancient redwoods and world's tallest trees.

Rocky Mountain, Col. (1915) 265,200. On the continental divide, includes 107 named peaks over 11,000 feet.

Samoa, American Samoa (1988) 8,000. Features the only paleotropical rain forest.

Sequoia, Cal. (1890) 402,482. Groves of giant sequoias, highest mountain in contiguous United States — Mount Whitney (14,494 feet). World's largest tree.

Shenandoah, Va. (1926/1935) 195,382. Portion of the Blue Ridge Mountains; overlooks Shenandoah Valley; Skyline Drive.

Theodore Roosevelt, N.D. (1947/1978) 70,416. Contains part of T.R.'s ranch and scenic badlands.

Virgin Islands, V.I. (1956) 14,689. Covers 75% of St. John Island, lush growth, lovely beaches, Indian relics, evidence of colonial Danes.

Voyageurs, Minn. (1971/1975) 218,036. Abundant lakes, forests, wildlife, canoeing, boating.

Wind Cave, S.D. (1903) 28,292. Limestone caverns in Black Hills. Extensive wildlife includes a herd of bison.

Wrangell-St. Elias, Alas. (1978/1980) 8,331,604. Largest area in park system, most peaks over 16,000 feet, abundant wildlife; day's drive east of Anchorage.

Yellowstone, Ida., Mon., Wy., (1872) 2,219,791. Oldest national park. World's greatest geyser area has about 3,000 geysers and hot springs; spectacular falls and impressive canyons of the Yellowstone River; grizzly bear, moose, and bison.

Yosemite, Cal. (1890) 761,170. Yosemite Valley, the nation's highest waterfall, 3 groves of sequoias, and mountainous.

Zion, Ut. (1909/1919) 146,598. Unusual shapes and landscapes have resulted from erosion and faulting; Zion Canyon, with sheer walls ranging up to 2,500 feet, is readily accessible.

National Historical Parks

Appomattox Court House, Va. (1930/1954) 1,325. Where Lee surrendered to Grant.

Boston, Mass. (1974) 41. Includes Faneuil Hall, Old North Church, Bunker Hill, Paul Revere House.

Chaco Culture, N.M. (1907/1980) 33,974. Ruins of pueblos built by prehistoric Indians.

Chesapeake and Ohio Canal, Md.-W.Va.-D.C. (1961/1971) 20,781. 184 mile historic canal; D.C. to Cumberland, Md.

Colonial, Va. (1930/1936) 9,327. Includes most of Jamestown Island, site of first successful English colony; Yorktown, site of Cornwallis' surrender to George Washington; and the Colonial Parkway.

Cumberland Gap, Ky.-Tenn.-Va. (1940) 20,274. Mountain pass of the Wilderness Road which carried the first great migration of pioneers into America's interior.

George Rogers Clark, Vincennes, Ind. (1966) 26. Commemorates American defeat of British in west during Revolution.

Harpers Ferry, Md., W. Va. (1944/1963) 2,239. At the confluence of the Shenandoah and Potomac rivers, the site of John Brown's 1859 raid on the Army arsenal.

Independence, Pa. (1948/1956) 45. Contains several properties in Philadelphia associated with the Revolutionary War and the founding of the U.S. Includes Independence Hall.

Jean Laffite (and preserve), La. (1939/1978) 20,020. Includes Chalmette, site of 1814 Battle of New Orleans; French Quarter.

Kalaupapa, Ha. (1980) 10,779. Molokai's former leper colony site and other historic areas.

Kaloko-Honokohau, Ha. (1978) 1,161. Culture center has 234 historic features and grave of first king, Kamehameha.

Klondike Gold Rush, Alas.-Wash. (1976) 13,191. Alaskan Trails in 1898 Gold Rush. Museum in Seattle.

Lowell, Mass. (1978) 136. Seven mills, canal, 19th C. structures, park to show planned city of Industrial Revolution.

Lyndon B. Johnson, Tex. (1969/1980) 1,571. President's birthplace, boyhood home, ranch.

Minute Man, Mass. (1959) 750. Where the colonial Minute Men battled the British, April 19, 1775. Also contains Nathaniel Hawthorne's home.

Morristown, N.J. (1933) 1,671. Sites of important military encampments during the Revolutionary War; Washington's headquarters 1777, 1779-80.

Natchez, Miss. (1988) 80. Mansions, townhouses, and villas concerning history of Natchez, Miss.

Nez Perce, Ida. (1965) 2,109. Illustrates the history and culture of the Nez Perce Indian country. 20 separate sites.

Pu'uhonua o Honaunau, Ha. (1955/1978) 182. Until 1819, a sanctuary for Hawaiians vanquished in battle, and those guilty of crimes or breaking taboos.

San Antonio Missions, Tex. (1978/1983) 493. Four of finest Spanish missions in U.S., 18th C. irrigation system.

San Francisco Maritime (1988) 50. Artifacts, photographs, and historic vessels related to the development of the Pacific Coast.

San Juan Island, Wash. (1966) 1,752. Commemorates peaceful relations of the U.S., Canada and Great Britain since the 1872 boundary disputes.

Saratoga, N.Y. (1938) 3,393. Scene of a major battle which became a turning point in the War of Independence.

Sitka, Alas. (1910/1972) 107. Scene of last major resistance of the Tlingit Indians to the Russians, 1804.

Valley Forge, Pa. (1976) 3,468. Continental Army campsite in 1777-78 winter.

War in the Pacific, Guam (1978) 1,960. Scenic park memorial for WWII combatants in Pacific.

Women's Rights, N.Y. (1980) 6. Seneca Falls site where Susan B. Anthony, Elizabeth Cady Stanton began rights movement in 1848.

Zuni-Cibola, N. Mex. (1988) 800. Historical, archeological, and cultural site associated with the Zuni Tribe over its 1700-year cultural continuum.

National Battlefields

Antietam, Md. (1890/1978) 3,244. Battle ended first Confederate invasion of North, Sept. 17, 1862.

Big Hole, Mon. (1910/1963) 656. Site of major battle with Nez Perce Indians.

Cowpens, S.C. (1929/1972) 842. Revolutionary War battlefield.

Fort Donelson, Tenn. (1928/1985) 537. Site of first major Union victory.

Fort Necessity, Pa. (1931/1961) 903. First battle of French and Indian War.

Monocacy, Md. (1934/1976) 1,647. Civil War battle in defense of Wash., D.C., July 9, 1864.

Moores Creek, N.C. (1926/1980) 87. Pre-Revolutionary War battle.

Petersburg, Va. (1926/1962) 2,735. Scene of 10-month Union campaign 1864-65.

(continued)

Stones River, Tenn. (1927/1960) 331. Civil War battle leading to Sherman's "March to the Sea."

Tupelo, Miss. (1929/1961) 1. Crucial battle over Sherman's supply line.

Wilson's Creek, Mo. (1960/1970) 1,750. Civil War battle for control of Missouri.

National Battlefield Parks

Kennesaw Mountain, Ga. (1917/1935) 2,885. Two major battles of Atlanta campaign in Civil War.

Manassas, Va. (1940) 5,114. Two battles of Bull Run in Civil War, 1861 and 1862.

Richmond, Va. (1936) 769. Site of battles defending Confederate capital.

National Battlefield Site

Brices Cross Roads, Miss. (1929) 1. Civil War battlefield.

National Military Parks

Chickamauga and Chattanooga, Ga.-Tenn. (1890) 8,106. Four Civil War battlefields.

Fredericksburg and Spotsylvania County, Va. (1927) 5,907. Sites of several major Civil War battles and campaigns.

Gettysburg, Pa. (1895) 3,896. Site of decisive Confederate defeat in North. Gettysburg Address.

Guilford Courthouse, N.C. (1917) 220. Revolutionary War battle site.

Horseshoe Bend, Ala. (1956) 2,040. On Tallapoosa River, where Gen. Andrew Jackson broke the power of the Creek Indian Confederacy.

Kings Mountain, S.C. (1931) 3,945. Revolutionary War battle.

Pea Ridge, Ark. (1956) 4,300. Civil War battle.

Shiloh, Tenn. (1894) 3,838. Major Civil War battle; site includes some well-preserved Indian burial mounds.

Vicksburg, Miss. (1899) 1,620. Union victory gave North control of the Mississippi and split the Confederacy in two.

National Memorials

Arkansas Post, Ark. (1960) 389. First permanent French settlement in the lower Mississippi River valley.

Arlington House, the Robert E. Lee Memorial, Va. (1925/1972) 28. Lee's home overlooking the Potomac.

Chamizal, El Paso, Tex. (1966/1974) 55. Commemorates 1963 settlement of 99-year border dispute with Mexico.

Coronado, Ariz. (1941/1952) 4,750. Commemorates first European exploration of the Southwest.

DeSoto, Fla. (1948) 27. Commemorates 16th-century Spanish explorations.

Federal Hall, N.Y. (1939/1955) 0.45. First seat of U.S. government under the Constitution.

Fort Caroline, Fla. (1950) 138. On St. Johns River, overlooks site of second attempt by French Huguenots to colonize North America.

Fort Clatsop, Ore. (1958) 125. Lewis and Clark encampment 1805-06.

General Grant, N.Y. (1958) 0.76. Tombs of Pres. and wife.

Hamilton Grange, N.Y. (1962) 0.11. Home of Alexander Hamilton.

John F. Kennedy Center for the Performing Arts, D.C. (1958/1964) 18.

Johnstown Flood, Pa. (1964) 164. Commemorates tragic flood of 1889.

Lincoln Boyhood, Ind. (1962) 200. Lincoln grew up here.

Lincoln Memorial, D.C. (1911) 110.

Lyndon B. Johnson Grove on the Potomac, D.C. (1973) 17.

Mount Rushmore, S.D. (1925) 1,278. World famous sculpture of 4 presidents.

Roger Williams, R.I. (1965) 5. Memorial to founder of Rhode Island.

Thaddeus Kosciuszko, Pa. (1972) 0.02. Memorial to Polish hero of American Revolution.

Theodore Roosevelt Island, D.C. (1932) 89.

Thomas Jefferson Memorial, D.C. (1934) 18.

USS Arizona, Ha. (1980) .00. Memorializes American losses at Pearl Harbor.

Washington Monument, D.C. (1848) 106.

Wright Brothers, N.C. (1927/1953) 431. Site of first powered flight.

National Historic Sites

Abraham Lincoln Birthplace, Hodgenville, Ky. (1916/1959) 117.

Adams, Quincy, Mass. (1946/1952) 10. Home of Presidents John Adams, John Quincy Adams, and celebrated descendants.

Allegheny Portage Railroad, Pa. (1964) 1,247. Part of the Pennsylvania Canal system.

Andersonville, Andersonville, Ga. (1970) 476. Noted Civil War prison.

Andrew Johnson, Greeneville, Tenn. (1935/1963) 17. Home of the President.

Bent's Old Fort, Col. (1960) 800. Old West fur-trading post.

Boston African American (1980) Pre-Civil War black history structures.

Carl Sandburg Home, N.C. (1968/1972) 264. Poet's home.

Charles Pinckney, S.C. (1988)

Christiansted, St. Croix; V.I. (1952/1961) 27. Commemorates Danish colony.

Clara Barton, Md. (1974) 9. Home of founder of American Red Cross.

Edgar Allan Poe, Pa. (1978/1980) 1. Poet's home.

Edison, West Orange, N.J. (1955/1962) 21. Home and laboratory.

Eisenhower, Gettysburg, Pa. (1967/1969) 690. Home of 34th president.

Eleanor Roosevelt, Hyde Park, N.Y. (1977) 181. Personal retreat.

Eugene O'Neill, Danville, Cal. (1976) 13. Playwright's home.

Ford's Theatre, Washington, D.C. (1866/1970) 0.29. Includes theater, now restored, where Lincoln was assassinated, house where he died, and Lincoln Museum.

Fort Bowie, Ariz. (1964/1972) 1,000. Focal point of operations against Geronimo and the Apaches.

Fort Davis, Tex. (1961/1963) 460. Frontier outpost battled Comanches and Apaches.

Fort Laramie, Wy. (1938/1960) 833. Military post on Oregon Trail.

Fort Larned, Kan. (1964/1966) 718. Military post on Santa Fe Trail.

Fort Point, San Francisco, Cal. (1970) 29. Largest West Coast fortification.

Fort Raleigh, N.C. (1941) 157. First English settlement.

Fort Scott, Kan. (1965/1978) 17. Commemorates U.S. frontier of 1840-50.

Fort Smith, Ark. (1961) 75. Active post from 1817 to 1890.

Fort Union Trading Post, Mon., N.D. (1966) 442. Principal fur-trading post on upper Missouri, 1829-1867.

Fort Vancouver, Wash. (1948/1961) 209. Hdqts. for Hudson's Bay Company in 1825. Early military and political seat.

Frederick Douglass Home, D.C. (1962/1988) 9. Home of nation's leading black spokesman.

Frederick Law Olmsted, Mass. (1979) 2. Home of famous park planner (1822-1903).

Friendship Hill, Pa. (1978) 675. Home of Albert Gallatin, Jefferson's Sec'y of Treasury. Not open to public.

Golden Spike, Utah (1957) 2,735. Commemorates completion of first transcontinental railroad in 1869.

Grant-Kohrs Ranch, Mon. (1972) 1,499. Ranch house and part of 19th century ranch.

Hampton, Md. (1948) 62. 18th-century Georgian mansion.

Harry S Truman, Mo. (1983). 0.78. Home of Pres. Truman after 1919.

Herbert Hoover, West Branch, Ia. (1965) 187. Birthplace and boyhood home of 31st president.

Home of Franklin D. Roosevelt, Hyde Park, N.Y. (1944) 290. Birthplace, home and "Summer White House".

Hopewell Furnace, Pa. (1938/1985) 848. 19th-century iron making village.

Hubbell Trading Post, Ariz. (1965) 160. Indian trading post.

James A. Garfield, Mentor, Oh. (1980) 8. President's home.

Jefferson National Expansion, Mo. (1935/1954) 191. Commemorates westward expansion.

Jimmy Carter, Ga. (1987) 70. Birthplace and home of 39th president.

John Fitzgerald Kennedy, Brookline, Mass. (1967) 0.09. Birthplace and childhood home of the President.

John Muir, Martinez, Cal. (1964) 339. Home of early conservationist and writer.

Knife River Indian Villages, N.D. (1974) 1,293. Remnants of 5 Hidatsa villages.

Lincoln Home, Springfield, Ill. (1971) 12. Lincoln's residence when he was elected President, 1860.

Longfellow, Cambridge, Mass. (1972) 2. Longfellow's home, 1837-82, and Washington's hq. during Boston Siege, 1775-76.

Maggie L. Walker, Va. (1978) 1. Richmond home of black leader and 1903 founder of bank.

Martin Luther King, Jr., Atlanta, Ga. (1980) 23. Birthplace, grave.

Martin Van Buren, N.Y. (1974) 40. Lindenwald, home of 8th president, near Kinderhook.

Ninety Six, S.C. (1976) 989. Colonial trading village.

Palo Alto Battlefield, Tex. (1978) 50. One of 2 Mexican War battles fought in U.S.

Pennsylvania Avenue, D.C. (1965) NA. Includes area between Capitol and White House, Ford's Theatre.

Puukohola Heiau, Ha. (1972) 80. Ruins of temple built by King Kamehameha.

Sagamore Hill, Oyster Bay, N.Y. (1962) 83. Home of President Theodore Roosevelt from 1885 until his death in 1919.

Saint-Gaudens, Cornish, N.H. (1964/1977) 148. Home, studio and gardens of American sculptor Augustus Saint-Gaudens.

Saint Paul's Church, N.Y. (1943/1978) 6. Eighteenth Century site of John Peter Zenger's "freedom of press" trial.

Salem Maritime, Mass. (1938) 9. Only port never seized from the patriots by the British. Major fishing and whaling port.

San Juan, P.R. (1949) 75. 16th-century Spanish fortifications.

Saugus Iron Works, Mass. (1968) 9. Reconstructed 17th-century colonial ironworks.

Springfield Armory, Mass. (1974) 55. Small arms manufacturing center for nearly 200 years.

Steamtown, Pa. (1986) 42. Railyard, roadhouse and repair shops of former Delaware, Lackawanna and Western Railroad.

Theodore Roosevelt Birthplace, N.Y., N.Y. (1962) 0.11.

Theodore Roosevelt Inaugural, Buffalo, N.Y. (1966) 1. Wilcox House where he took oath of office, 1901.

Thomas Stone, Md. (1978) 328. Home of signer of Declaration, built in 1771. Not open to public.

Tuskegee Institute, Ala. (1974) 74. College founded by Booker T. Washington in 1881 for blacks, includes student-made brick buildings.

Vanderbilt Mansion, Hyde Park, N.Y. (1940) 212. Mansion of 19th-century financier.

Whitman Mission, Wash. (1936/1963) 98. Site where Dr. and Mrs. Marcus Whitman ministered to the Indians until slain by them in 1847.

William Howard Taft, Cincinnati, Oh. (1969) 3. Birthplace and early home of the 27th president.

National Monuments

Name	State	Year	Acreage
Agate Fossil Beds	Neb.	1965	3,055
Alibates Flint Quarries	N.M.-Tex.	1965	1,371
Aniakchak	Alas.	1978	137,176
Aztec Ruins	N.M.	1923	319
Bandelier	N.M.	1916	32,737
Black Canyon of the Gunnison	Col.	1933	20,766
Booker T. Washington	Va.	1956	224
Buck Island Reef	V.I.	1961	880
Cabrillo	Cal.	1913	144
Canyon de Chelly	Ariz.	1931	83,840
Cape Krusenstern	Alas.	1978	659,807
Capulin Volcano	N.M.	1916	793
Casa Grande Ruins	Ariz.	1892	473
Castillo de San Marcos	Fla.	1924	20
Castle Clinton	N.Y.	1946	1
Cedar Breaks	Ut.	1933	6,155
Chiricahua	Ariz.	1924	11,985
Colorado	Col.	1911	20,454
Congaree Swamp	S.C.	1976	22,200
Craters of the Moon	Ida.	1924	53,545
Custer Battlefield	Mon.	1879	765
Death Valley	Cal.-Nev.	1933	2,067,628
Devils Postpile	Cal.	1911	798
Devils Tower	Wy.	1906	1,347
Dinosaur	Col.-Ut.	1915	211,142
Effigy Mounds	Ia.	1949	1,481
El Malpais	N.M.	1987	114,716
El Morro	N.M.	1906	1,279
Florissant Fossil Beds**	Col.	1969	5,998
Fort Frederica	Ga.	1936	216
Fort Jefferson	Fla.	1935	64,700
Fort Matanzas	Fla.	1924	228
Fort McHenry National Monument and Historic Shrine	Md.	1925	43
Fort Pulaski	Ga.	1924	5,623
Fort Stanwix	N.Y.	1935	16
Fort Sumter	S.C.	1948	197
Fort Union	N.M.	1954	721
Fossil Butte	Wy.	1972	8,198
G. Washington Birthplace	Va.	1930	538
George Washington Carver	Mo.	1943	210
Gila Cliff Dwellings	N.M.	1907	533
Grand Portage	Minn.	1951	710
Great Sand Dunes	Col.	1932	38,662
Hagerman Fossil Beds	Ida.	1988	4,394
Hohokam Pima*	Ariz.	1972	1,690
Homestead Nat'l. Monument of America	Neb.	1936	195
Hovenweep	Col.-Ut.	1923	785
Jewel Cave	S.D.	1908	1,274
John Day Fossil Beds	Ore.	1974	14,014

Name	State	Year	Acreage
Joshua Tree	Cal.	1936	559,955
Lava Beds	Cal.	1925	46,560
Montezuma Castle	Ariz.	1906	858
Mound City Group	Oh.	1923	270
Muir Woods	Cal.	1908	554
Natural Bridges	Ut.	1908	7,636
Navajo	Ariz.	1909	360
Ocmulgee	Ga.	1934	683
Oregon Caves	Ore.	1909	488
Organ Pipe Cactus	Ariz.	1937	330,689
Pecos	N.M.	1965	365
Pinnacles	Cal.	1908	16,265
Poverty Point	La.	1988	880
Pipe Spring	Ariz.	1923	40
Pipestone	Minn.	1937	282
Rainbow Bridge	Ut.	1910	160
Russell Cave	Ala.	1961	310
Saguaro	Ariz.	1933	83,574
Salinas	N.M.	1909	1,077
Scotts Bluff	Neb.	1919	2,997
Statue of Liberty	N.J.-N.Y.	1924	58
Sunset Crater	Ariz.	1930	3,040
Timpanogos Cave	Ut.	1922	250
Tonto	Ariz.	1907	1,120
Tumacacori	Ariz.	1908	17
Tuzigoot	Ariz.	1939	801
Walnut Canyon	Ariz.	1915	2,249
White Sands	N.M.	1933	143,733
Wupatki	Ariz.	1924	35,253
Yucca House*	Col.	1919	10

National Preserves

Name	State	Year	Acreage
Aniakchak	Alas.	1978	465,603
Bering Land Bridge	Alas.	1978	2,784,960
Big Cypress	Fla.	1974	570,000
Big Thicket	Tex.	1974	85,733
City of Rocks	Ida.	1988	N.A.
Denali	Alas.	1917	1,311,365
Gates of the Arctic	Alas.	1978	948,629
Glacier Bay	Alas.	1925	57,884
Katmai	Alas.	1918	374,000
Lake Clark	Alas.	1978	1,407,293
Noatak	Alas.	1978	6,574,481
Timucuan Ecological & Historic Preserve	Fla.	1988	35,000
Wrangell-St. Elias	Alas.	1978	4,856,720
Yukon-Charley Rivers	Alas.	1978	2,523,509

National Seashores

Name	State	Year	Acreage
Assateague Island	Md.-Va.	1965	39,631
Canaveral	Fla.	1975	57,662
Cape Cod	Mass.	1961	43,557
Cape Hatteras	N.C.	1937	30,319
Cape Lookout**	N.C.	1966	28,415
Cumberland Island	Ga.	1972	36,415
Fire Island	N.Y.	1964	19,579
Gulf Islands	Fla.-Miss.	1971	139,775
Padre Island	Tex.	1962	130,697
Point Reyes	Cal.	1962	71,047

National Parkways

Name	State	Year	Acreage
Blue Ridge	Va.-N.C.	1936	85,955
George Washington Memorial	Va.-Md.	1930	7,131
John D. Rockefeller Jr. Mem.	Wy.	1972	23,777
Natchez Trace	Ala.-Miss.-Tenn.	1938	51,756

National Lakeshores

Name	State	Year	Acreage
Apostle Islands	Wis.	1970	69,372
Indiana Dunes	Ind.	1966	13,832
Pictured Rocks	Mich.	1966	72,899
Sleeping Bear Dunes	Mich.	1970	71,132

National Rivers

Name	State	Year	Acreage
Buffalo	Ark.	1972	94,219
New River Gorge	W.Va.	1978	62,663
Ozark	Mo.	1964	80,788
Mississippi Natl. R. and Recreation	Minn.	1988	50,000

(continued)

Name	State	Year	Acreage
National Scenic Rivers and Riverways			
Alagnak Wild	Alas.	1980	24,038
Big South Fork	Ky.-Tenn.	1976	122,960
Bluestone	W.Va.	1988	N.A.
Delaware	N.Y.-N.J.-Pa.	1978	1,973
Lower Saint Croix	Minn.-Wis.	1972	9,475
Missouri Natl. Recreational River.	Neb.	1978	0
Obed Wild	Tenn.	1976	5,077
Rio Grande	Tex.	1978	9,600
Saint Croix	Minn.-Wis.	1968	67,434
Upper Delaware	N.Y.-N.J.	1978	75,000
Parks (no other classification)			
Catoctin Mountain	Md.	1954	5,770
Constitution Gardens	D.C.	1978	52
Fort Washington	Md.	1930	341
Greenbelt	Md.	1950	1,176
Perry's Victory	Oh.	1936	25
Piscataway	Md.	1961	4,263
Prince William Forest	Va.	1948	18,572
Rock Creek	D.C.	1890	1,754
Vietnam Veterans	D.C.	1980	2
Wolf Trap Farm Park for the Performing Arts	Va.	1966	130
National Recreation Areas			
Amistad	Tex.	1965	57,292
Bighorn Canyon	Mon.-Wy.	1966	120,296
Chattahoochee R.	Ga.	1978	9,265
Chickasaw	Okla.	1902	9,522

Name	State	Year	Acreage
Coulee Dam	Wash.	1946	100,390
Curecanti	Col.	1965	42,114
Cuyahoga Valley	Oh.	1974	32,460
Delaware Water Gap	N.J.-Pa.	1965	66,652
Gateway	N.Y.-N.J.	1972	26,311
Gauley R.	W.Va.	1988	N.A.
Glen Canyon	Ariz.-Ut.	1958	1,236,880
Golden Gate	Cal.	1972	73,080
Lake Chelan	Wash.	1968	61,889
Lake Mead	Ariz.-Nev.	1936	1,495,666
Lake Meredith	Tex.	1965	44,978
Ross Lake	Wash.	1968	117,574
Santa Monica Mts.	Cal.	1978	150,050
Whiskeytown	Cal.	1965	42,503
National Mall	D.C.	1933	146
National Scenic Trails			
Appalachian	Me. to Ga.	1968	161,208
Natchez Trace	Ga.-Ala.-Tenn.	1983	10,995
Potomac Heritage	Md.-D.C.-Va.-Pa.	1983	***
International Historic Sites			
Saint Croix Island	Me.	1949	35

*Not open to the public. **No federal facilities. ***Undetermined.

Visitors to National Parks in 1988

Source: National Park Service

The following national parks and historical parks had more than 1 million visitors in 1988:

Park	Visitors	Park	Visitors
Great Smoky Mountains, TN/NC	8,770,781	Glacier, MT	1,817,733
National Capital Parks, D.C.	8,088,040	Mammoth Cave, KY	1,735,610
Independence, PA	5,362,893	Chesapeake and Ohio Canal	1,728,981
Acadia, ME	4,502,283	Haleakala, HI	1,314,683
Valley Forge, PA	4,202,511	Mount Rainier, WA	1,255,618
Grand Canyon, AZ	3,859,886	Grand Teton, WY	1,232,691
Yosemite, CA	3,216,681	Hot Springs, AR	1,185,772
Olympic, WA	2,959,122	Badlands, SD	1,110,040
Rocky Mountain, CO	2,544,211	Sequoia, CA	1,031,129
Boston, MA	2,183,824	Jean Lafitte, LA	1,023,819
Yellowstone, MT/WY	2,182,113	Everglades, FL	1,023,812
Zion, UT	1,948,332	Kings Canyon, CA	1,007,695
Shenandoah, VA	1,937,155	Minute Man, MA	1,001,990

Attendance at all areas administered by the National Park Service in 1988 was 282,555,336 persons.

National Recreation Areas Administered by Forest Service

Allegheny	Pa.	1984	23,063
Arapaho	Col.	1978	34,928
Flaming Gorge	Ut.-Wyo.	1968	201,114
Hell's Canyon	Ida.-Ore.	1975	538,115
Mount Baker	Wash.	1984	8,473
Mount Rogers	Va.	1966	154,770
Oregon Dunes	Ore.	1972	31,566
Rattlesnake	Mon.	1980	61,000
Sawtooth	Ida.	1972	756,019
Spruce Knob-Seneca Rocks	W. Va.	1965	100,000
Whiskeytown Shasta-Trinity	Cal.	1965	203,587
White Rocks	Vt.	1984	36,400

Recreational Use of Public Lands Administered by Bureau of Land Management

Source: U.S. Bureau of Land Management

(In thousands. For year ending Sept. 30.)

Year and State	Number of visits	Total	Type of Recreation Use (visitor hours) Land-based recreation activities Motorized travel — Off road vehicle travel	Other motorized travel	Non-motorized travel	Site based — Camping	Hunting	Water-based recreation activities Fishing	Boating	Snow- and ice-based recreational activity, winter sports
1983	56,270	334,010	24,397	35,534	12,237	84,066	92,974	20,290	16,869	2,917
1984	59,228	271,373	21,348	25,433	9,579	73,032	73,898	14,263	11,184	2,894
1985	51,739	244,612	36,995	24,053	10,047	65,397	51,842	14,254	11,710	5,023
1986	54,253	284,142	49,688	25,866	14,397	95,196	35,570	18,227	15,891	6,025
1987	56,427	514,716[1]	123,325	34,325	19,172	195,315	57,624	22,932	15,140	3,259

(1) Increase due to an estimated longer length of stay per visit, especially in California.

Federal Indian Reservations[1]

Source: Bureau of Indian Affairs, U.S. Interior Department (data as of 1988)
The total American Indian population according to the 1980 Census is 1.534 million.

State	No of Reser.	Tribally-owned acreage[2]	Individually-owned acreage	No. of persons[3]	Average (%) unempl. rate[4]	Major tribes and/or nations
Alabama	1	230	0	1,480	30	Poarch Creek
Alaska	1[5]	86,773	884,100	91,106	47	Aleut, Eskimo, Athapascan[6], Haida, Tlingit, Tsimpshian
Arizona.	20	19,766,911	256,927	165,385	48	Navajo, Apache, Papago, Hopi, Yavapai, Pima
California. . . .	83	513,005	67,175	28,815	38	Hoopa, Paiute, Yurok, Karok, Mission Bands
Colorado.	2	785,411	2,964	10,467	17	Ute
Connecticut . . .	1	1,201	0	80	0	Mashantucket Pequot
Florida	4	153,840	0	2,062	28	Seminole, Miccosukee[7]
Idaho	4	464,077	327,301	10,607	45	Shoshone, Bannock, Nez Perce
Iowa	1	4,164	0	737	31	Sac and Fox[8]
Kansas	4	7,620	22,058	2,321	17	Potawatomi, Kickapoo, Iowa
Louisiana.	3	567	0	936	41	Chitimacha, Coushatta, Tunica-Biloxi
Maine.	3	212,699	0	2,859	32	Passamaquoddy, Penobscot, Maliseet
Michigan	8	12,433	9,224	12,723	47	Chippewa, Potawatomi, Ottawa
Minnesota . . .	14	714,271	51,011	19,863	58	Chippewa, Sioux
Mississippi . . .	1	17,715	19	4,832	26	Choctaw
Montana	7	2,327,347	2,881,339	34,001	50	Blackfeet, Crow, Sioux, Assiniboine, Cheyenne
Nebraska	3	21,657	43,186	3,690	46	Omaha, Winnebago, Santee Sioux
Nevada	22	1,147,163	78,566	9,075	37	Paiute, Shoshone, Washoe
New Mexico . . .	24	7,174,491	675,968	126,346	37	Zuni, Apache, Navajo
New York	8	87,058	0	12,314	51	Seneca, Mohawk, Onondaga, Oneida[9]
North Carolina. .	1	56,461	0	6,110	40	Cherokee
North Dakota . .	3	217,049	634,950	23,629	57	Sioux, Chippewa, Mandan, Arikara, Hidatsa
Oklahoma	1[10]	94,488	1,018,738	231,952	21	Cherokee, Creek, Choctaw, Chickasaw, Osage, Cheyenne, Arapahoe, Kiowa, Comanche
Oregon.	6	643,561	135,052	10,231	37	Warm Springs, Wasco, Paiute, Umatilla, Siletz
Rhode Island. . .	1	1,800	0	2,058	45	Narragansett
South Dakota . .	9	2,660,995	2,421,092	58,201	74	Sioux
Texas.	3	4,574	0	1,320	12	Alabama-Coushatta, Tiwa, Kickapoo
Utah	4	2,298,302	33,343	9,010	23	Ute, Goshute, Southern Paiute
Washington . . .	27	2,102,097	467,785	40,893	53	Yakima, Lummi, Quinault
Wisconsin . . .	11	337,330	80,671	21,037	40	Chippewa, Oneida, Winnebago
Wyoming.	1	1,793,420	93,842	4,935	46	Shoshone, Arapahoe

(1) As of 1988 the federal government recognized and acknowledged that it had a special relationship with, and a trust responsibility for, 307 federally recognized Indian entities in the continental U.S., plus some 200 tribal entities in Alaska. The term "Indian entities" encompasses Indian tribes, bands, villages, groups, pueblos, Eskimos, and Aleuts, eligible for federal services and classified in the following 3 categories: (a) Officially approved Indian organizations pursuant to federal statutory authority (Indian Reorganization Act; Oklahoma Indian Welfare Act and Alaska Native Act.) (b) Officially approved Indian organizations outside of specified federal statutory authority. (c) Traditional Indian organizations recognized without formal federal approval of organizational structure. Some reservation boundaries transcend state boundaries (e.g., Navaho which is in Arizona, New Mexico, and Utah). For statistical convenience under "Number of Reservations," such reservations are counted in the state where population is predominant and/or tribal headquarters is located.
(2) The acreages refer only to Indian lands which are either owned by the tribes or individual Indians, and held in trust by the U.S. government. Many of these parcels are located off reservations. Not all lands within reservation boundaries are necessarily trust lands. Many parcels are privately-owned by tribes, individual Indians, and non-Indians. Also, some internal lands are the property of various governmental agencies.
(3) Number of Indians living on or adjacent to federally recognized reservations comprising the BIA service population.
(4) Unemployment rate of Indian work force consisting of all those 16 years old and over who are able and actively seeking work.
(5) Alaskan Indian Affairs are carried out under the Alaska Native Claims Settlement Act (Dec. 18, 1971). The Act provided for the establishment of regional and village corporations to conduct business for profit and non-profit purposes. There are 13 such regional corporations, each one with organized village corporations. The Annette Island Reservation remains the only federally recognized reservation in Alaska in the sense of specific reservation boundaries, trust lands, etc.
(6) Aleuts and Eskimos are racially and linguistically related. Athapascans are related to the Navaho and Apache Indians.
(7) "Seminole" means "runaways" and these Indians from various tribes were originally refugees from whites in the Carolinas and Georgia. Later joined by runaway slaves, the Seminole were united by their hostility to the United States. Formal peace with the Seminoles in Florida was not achieved until 1934. The Miccosukee are a branch of the Seminole; they retain their Indian religion and have not made formal peace with the United States.
(8) Once two tribes, the Sac and Fox formed a political alliance in 1734.
(9) These 4 tribes along with the Cayuga and Tuscarora made up the Iroquois League, which ruled large portions of New York, New England and Pennsylvania and ranged into the Midwest and South. The Onondaga, who traditionally provide the president of the league, maintain that they are a foreign nation within New York and the United States.
(10) Indian land status in Oklahoma is unique and there are no reservations except for Osage in the sense that the term is used elsewhere in the U.S. Likewise, many of the Oklahoma tribes are unique in their high degree of assimilation to the white culture.

BIOGRAPHIES OF U.S. PRESIDENTS

George Washington (1789-1797)

George Washington, first president, was born Feb. 22, 1732 (Feb. 11, 1731, old style), the son of Augustine Washington and Mary Ball, at Wakefield on Pope's Creek, Westmoreland Co., Va. His early childhood was spent on the Ferry farm, near Fredericksburg. His father died when George was 11. He studied mathematics and surveying and when 16 went to live with his half brother Lawrence, who built and named Mount Vernon. George surveyed the lands of William Fairfax in the Shenandoah Valley, keeping a diary. He accompanied Lawrence to Barbados, West Indies, contracted small pox, and was deeply scarred. Lawrence died in 1752 and George acquired his property by inheritance. He valued land and when he died owned 70,000 acres in Virginia and 40,000 acres in what is now West Virginia.

Washington's military service began in 1753 when Gov. Dinwiddie of Virginia sent him on missions deep into Ohio country. He clashed with the French and had to surrender Fort Necessity July 3, 1754. He was an aide to Braddock and at his side when the army was ambushed and defeated on a march to Ft. Duquesne, July 9, 1755. He helped take Fort Duquesne from the French in 1758.

After his marriage to Martha Dandridge Custis, a widow, in 1759, Washington managed his family estate at Mount Vernon. Although not at first for independence, he opposed British exactions and took charge of the Virginia troops before war broke out. He was made commander-in-chief by the Continental Congress June 15, 1775.

The successful issue of a war filled with hardships was due to his leadership. He was resourceful, a stern disciplinarian, and the one strong, dependable force for unity. He favored a federal government and became chairman of the Constitutional Convention of 1787. He helped get the Constitution ratified and was unanimously elected president by the electoral college and inaugurated, Apr. 30, 1789, on the balcony of New York's Federal Hall.

He was reelected 1792, but refused to consider a 3d term and retired to Mount Vernon. He suffered acute laryngitis after a ride in snow and rain around his estate, was bled profusely, and died Dec. 14, 1799.

John Adams (1797-1801)

John Adams, 2d president, Federalist, was born in Braintree (Quincy), Mass., Oct. 30, 1735 (Oct. 19, o. s.), the son of John Adams, a farmer, and Susanna Boylston. He was a great-grandson of Henry Adams who came from England in 1636. He was graduated from Harvard, 1755, taught school, studied law. In 1765 he argued against taxation without representation before the royal governor. In 1770 he defended in court the British soldiers who fired on civilians in the "Boston Massacre." He was a delegate to the first Continental Congress, and signed the Declaration of Independence. He was a commissioner to France, 1778, with Benjamin Franklin and Arthur Lee; won recognition of the U.S. by The Hague, 1782; was first American minister to England, 1785-1788, and was elected vice president, 1788 and 1792.

In 1796 Adams was chosen president by the electors. Intense antagonism to America by France caused agitation for war, led by Alexander Hamilton. Adams, breaking with Hamilton, opposed war.

To fight alien influence and muzzle criticism Adams supported the Alien and Sedition laws of 1798, which led to his defeat for reelection. He died July 4, 1826, on the same day as Jefferson (the 50th anniversary of the Declaration of Independence).

Thomas Jefferson (1801-1809)

Thomas Jefferson, 3d president, was born Apr. 13, 1743 (Apr. 2, o. s.), at Shadwell, Va., the son of Peter Jefferson, a civil engineer of Welsh descent who raised tobacco, and Jane Randolph. His father died when he was 14, leaving him 2,750 acres and his slaves. Jefferson attended the College of William and Mary, 1760-1762, read classics in Greek and Latin and played the violin. In 1769 he was elected to the House of Burgesses. In 1770 he began building Monticello, near Charlottesville. He was a member of the Virginia Committee of Correspondence and the Continental Congress. Named a member of the committee to draw up a Declaration of Independence, he wrote the basic draft. He was a member of the Virginia House of Delegates, 1776-79, elected governor to succeed Patrick Henry, 1779, reelected June 1781, resigned June 1781, amid charges of ineffectual military preparation. During his term he wrote the statute on religious freedom. In the Continental Congress, 1783, he drew up an ordinance for the Northwest Territory, forbidding slavery after 1800; its terms were put into the Ordinance of 1787. He was sent to Paris with Benjamin Franklin and John Adams to negotiate commercial treaties, 1784; made minister to France, 1785.

Washington appointed him secretary of state, 1789. Jefferson's strong faith in the consent of the governed, as opposed to executive control favored by Hamilton, secretary of the treasury, often led to conflict: Dec. 31, 1793, he resigned. He was the Democrat Republican candidate for president in 1796; beaten by John Adams, he became vice president. In 1800, Jefferson and Aaron Burr received equal electoral college votes for president. The House of Representatives elected Jefferson. Major events of his administration were the Louisiana Purchase, 1803, and the Lewis and Clark Expedition. He established the Univ. of Virginia and designed its buildings. He died July 4, 1826, on the same day as John Adams.

James Madison (1809-1817)

James Madison, 4th president, Democrat Republican, was born Mar. 16, 1751 (Mar. 5, 1750, o. s.) at Port Conway, King George Co., Va., eldest son of James Madison and Eleanor Rose Conway. Madison was graduated from Princeton, 1771; studied theology, 1772; sat in the Virginia Constitutional Convention, 1776. He was a member of the Continental Congress. He was chief recorder at the Constitutional Convention in 1787, and supported ratification in the Federalist Papers, written with Alexander Hamilton and John Jay. He was elected to the House of Representatives in 1789, helped frame the Bill of Rights and fought the Alien and Sedition Acts. He became Jefferson's secretary of state, 1801.

Elected president in 1808, Madison was a "strict constructionist," opposed to the free interpretation of the Constitution by the Federalists. He was reelected in 1812 by the votes of the agrarian South and recently admitted western states. Caught between British and French maritime restrictions, the U.S. drifted into war, declared June 18, 1812. The war ended in a stalemate. He retired in 1817 to his estate at Montpelier. There he edited his famous papers on the Constitutional Convention. He became rector of the Univ. of Virginia, 1826. He died June 28, 1836.

James Monroe (1817-1825)

James Monroe, 5th president, Democrat Republican, was born Apr. 28, 1758, in Westmoreland Co., Va., the son of Spence Monroe and Eliza Jones, who were of Scottish and Welsh descent, respectively. He attended the College of William and Mary, fought in the 3d Virginia Regiment at White Plains, Brandywine, Monmouth, and was wounded at Trenton. He studied law with Thomas Jefferson, 1780, was a member of the Virginia House of Delegates and of Congress, 1783-86. He opposed ratification of the Constitution because it lacked a bill of rights; was U.S. senator, 1790; minister to France, 1794-96; governor of Virginia, 1799-1802, and 1811. Jefferson sent him to France as minister, 1803. He helped Robert Livingston negotiate the Louisiana Purchase, 1803. He ran against Madison for president in 1808. He was elected to the Virginia Assembly, 1810-1811; was secretary of state under Madison, 1811-1817.

In 1816 Monroe was elected president; in 1820 reelected with all but one electoral college vote. Monroe's administration became the "Era of Good Feeling." He obtained Florida from Spain; settled boundaries with Canada, and eliminated border forts. He supported the anti-slavery position that led to the Missouri Compromise. His most significant contribution was the "Monroe Doctrine," which became a cornerstone of U.S. foreign policy. Monroe retired to Oak Hill, Va. Financial problems forced him to sell his property. He moved to New York City to live with a daughter. He died there July 4, 1831.

John Quincy Adams (1825-1829)

John Quincy Adams, 6th president, independent Federalist, was born July 11, 1767, at Braintree (Quincy), Mass., the son of John and Abigail Adams. His father was the 2d president. He was educated in Paris, Leyden, and Harvard, graduating in 1787. He served as American minister in various European capitals, and helped draft the War of 1812 peace treaty. He was U.S. Senator, 1803-08. President Monroe made him secretary of state, 1817, and he negotiated the cession of the Floridas from Spain, supported exclusion of slavery in the Missouri Compromise, and helped formulate the Monroe Doctrine. In 1824 he was elected president by the House after he failed to win an electoral college majority. His expansion of executive powers was strongly opposed and he was beaten in 1828 by Jackson. In 1831 he entered Congress and served 17 years with distinction. He opposed slavery, the annexation of Texas, and the Mexican War. He helped establish the Smithsonian Institution. He had a stroke in the House and died in the Speaker's Room, Feb. 23, 1848.

Andrew Jackson (1829-1837)

Andrew Jackson, 7th president, was a Jeffersonian-Republican, later a Democrat. He was born in the Waxhaws district, New Lancaster Co., S.C., Mar. 15, 1767, the posthumous son of Andrew Jackson and Elizabeth Hutchinson, who were Irish immigrants. At 13, he joined the militia in the Revolution and was captured.

He read law in Salisbury, N.C., moved to Nashville, Tenn., speculated in land, married, and practiced law. In 1796 he helped draft the constitution of Tennessee and for a year occupied its one seat in Congress. He was in the Senate in 1797, and again in 1823. He defeated the Creek Indians at Horseshoe Bend, Ala., 1814. With 6,000 backwoods fighters he defeated Packenham's 12,000 British troops at the Chalmette, outside New Orleans, Jan. 8, 1815. In 1818 he briefly invaded Spanish Florida to quell Seminoles and outlaws who harassed frontier settlements. In 1824 he ran for president against John Quincy Adams and had the most popular and electoral votes but not a majority; the election was decided by the House, which chose Adams. In 1828 he defeated Adams, carrying the West and South. He was a noisy debater and a duelist and introduced rotation in office called the "spoils system." Suspicious of privilege, he ruined the Bank of the United States by depositing federal funds with state banks. Though "Let the people rule" was his slogan, he at times supported strict constructionist policies against the expansionist West. He killed the congressional caucus for nominating presidential candidates and substituted the national convention, 1832. When South Carolina refused to collect imports under his protective tariff he ordered army and naval forces to Charleston. Jackson recognized the Republic of Texas, 1836. He died at the Hermitage, June 8, 1845.

Martin Van Buren (1837-1841)

Martin Van Buren, 8th president, Democrat, was born Dec. 5, 1782, at Kinderhook, N.Y., the son of Abraham Van Buren, a Dutch farmer, and Mary Hoes. He was surrogate of Columbia County, N.Y., state senator and attorney general. He was U.S. senator 1821, reelected, 1827, elected governor of New York, 1828. He helped swing eastern support to Jackson in 1828 and was his secretary of state 1829-31. In 1832 he was elected vice president. He was a consummate politician, known as "the little magician," and influenced Jackson's policies. In 1836 he defeated William Henry Harrison for president and took office as the Panic of 1837 initiated a 5-year nationwide depression. He inaugurated the independent treasury system. His refusal to spend land revenues led to his defeat by Harrison in 1840. He lost the Democratic nomination in 1844 to Polk. In 1848 he ran for president on the Free Soil ticket and lost. He died July 24, 1862, at Kinderhook.

William Henry Harrison (1841)

William Henry Harrison, 9th president, Whig, who served only 31 days, was born in Berkeley, Charles City Co., Va., Feb. 9, 1773, the 3d son of Benjamin Harrison, signer of the Declaration of Independence. He attended Hampden Sydney College. He was secretary of the Northwest Territory, 1798; its delegate in Congress, 1799; first governor of Indiana Territory, 1800; and superintendent of Indian affairs. With 900 men he routed Tecumseh's Indians at Tippecanoe, Nov. 7, 1811. A major general, he defeated British and Indians at Battle of the Thames, Oct. 5, 1813. He served in Congress, 1816-19; Senate, 1825-28. In 1840, when 68, he was elected president with a "log cabin and hard cider" slogan. He caught pneumonia during the inauguration and died Apr. 4, 1841.

John Tyler (1841-1845)

John Tyler, 10th president, independent Whig, was born Mar. 29, 1790, in Greenway, Charles City Co., Va., son of John Tyler and Mary Armistead. His father was governor of Virginia, 1808-11. Tyler was graduated from William and Mary, 1807; member of the House of Delegates, 1811; in congress, 1816-21; in Virginia legislature, 1823-25; governor of Virginia, 1825-26; U.S. senator, 1827-36. In 1840 he was elected vice president and, on Harrison's death, succeeded him. He favored pre-emption, allowing settlers to get government land; rejected a national bank bill and thus alienated most Whig supporters; refused to honor the spoils system. He signed the resolution annexing Texas, Mar. 1, 1845. He accepted renomination, 1844, but withdrew before election. In 1861, he chaired an unsuccessful Washington conference called to avert civil war. After its failure he supported secession, sat in the provisional Confederate Congress, became a member of the Confederate House, but died in Richmond, Jan. 18, 1862, before it met.

James Knox Polk (1845-1849)

James Knox Polk, 11th president, Democrat, was born in Mecklenburg Co., N.C., Nov. 2, 1795, the son of Samuel Polk, farmer and surveyor of Scotch-Irish descent, and Jane Knox. He graduated from the Univ. of North Carolina, 1818; member of the Tennessee state legislature, 1823-25. He served in Congress 1825-39 and as speaker 1835-39. He was governor of Tennessee 1839-41, but was defeated 1841 and 1843. In 1844, when both Clay and Van Buren announced opposition to annexing Texas, the Democrats made Polk the first dark horse nominee because he demanded control of all Oregon and annexation of Texas. Polk re-established the independent treasury system originated by Van Buren. His expansionist policy was opposed by Clay, Webster, Calhoun; he sent troops under Zachary Taylor to the Mexican border and, when Mexicans attacked, declared war existed. The Mexican war ended with the annexation of California and much of the Southwest as part of America's "manifest destiny." He compromised on the Oregon boundary ("54-40 or fight!") by accepting the 49th parallel and giving Vancouver to the British. Polk died in Nashville, June 15, 1849.

Zachary Taylor (1849-1850)

Zachary Taylor, 12th president, Whig, who served only 16 months, was born Nov. 24, 1784, in Orange Co., Va., the son of Richard Taylor, later collector of the port of Louisville, Ky., and Sarah Strother. Taylor was commissioned first lieutenant, 1808; fought in the War of 1812; the Black Hawk War, 1832; and the second Seminole War, 1837. He was called Old Rough and Ready. He settled on a plantation near Baton Rouge, La. In 1845 Polk sent him with an army to the Rio Grande. When the Mexicans attacked him, Polk declared war. Taylor was successful at Palo Alto and Resaca de la Palma, 1846; occupied Monterrey. Polk made him major general but sent many of his troops to Gen. Winfield Scott. Outnumbered 4-1, he defeated Santa Anna at Buena Vista, 1847. A national hero, he received the Whig nomination in 1848, and was elected president. He resumed the spoils system and though once a slave-holder worked to have California admitted as a free state. He died in office July 9, 1850.

Millard Fillmore (1850-1853)

Millard Fillmore, 13th president, Whig, was born Jan. 7, 1800, in Cayuga Co., N.Y., the son of Nathaniel Fillmore and Phoebe Millard. He taught school and studied law; admitted to the bar, 1823. He was a member of the state assembly, 1829-32; in Congress, 1833-35 and again 1837-43. He opposed the entrance of Texas as slave territory and voted for a protective tariff. In 1844 he was defeated for governor of New York. In 1848 he was elected vice president and succeeded as president July 10, 1850, after Taylor's death. Fillmore favored the Compromise of 1850 and signed the Fugitive Slave Law. His policies pleased neither expansionists nor slave-holders and he was not renominated in 1852. In 1856 he was nominated by the American (Know-Nothing) party and accepted by the Whigs, but defeated by Buchanan. He died in Buffalo, Mar. 8, 1874.

Franklin Pierce (1853-1857)

Franklin Pierce, 14th president, Democrat, was born in Hillsboro, N. H., Nov. 23, 1804, the son of Benjamin Pierce, veteran of the Revolution and governor of New Hampshire, 1827. He graduated from Bowdoin, 1824. A lawyer, he served in the state legislature 1829-33; in Congress, supporting Jackson, 1833-37; U.S. senator, 1837-42. He enlisted in the Mexican War, became brigadier general under Gen. Winfield Scott. In 1852 Pierce was nominated on the 49th ballot over Lewis Cass, Stephen A. Douglas, and James Buchanan, and defeated Gen. Scott, Whig. Though against slavery, Pierce was influenced by pro-slavery Southerners. He ignored the Ostend Manifesto that the U.S. either buy or take Cuba. He approved the Kansas-Nebraska Act, leaving slavery to popular vote ("squatter sovereignty"), 1854. He signed a reciprocity treaty with Canada and approved the Gadsden Purchase from Mexico, 1853. Denied renomination by the Democrats, he spent most of his remaining years in Concord, N.H., where he died Oct. 8, 1869.

James Buchanan (1857-1861)

James Buchanan, 15th president, Federalist, later Democrat, was born of Scottish descent near Mercersburg, Pa., Apr. 23, 1791. He graduated from Dickinson, 1809; was a volunteer in the War of 1812; member, Pennsylvania legislature, 1814-16, Congress, 1820-31; Jackson's minister to Russia, 1831-33; U.S. senator 1834-45. As Polk's secretary of state, 1845-49, he ended the Oregon dispute with Britain, supported the Mexican War and annexation of Texas. As minister to Britain, 1853, he signed the Ostend Manifesto. Nominated by Democrats, he was elected, 1856, over John C. Fremont (Republican) and Millard Fillmore (American Know-Nothing and Whig tickets). On slavery he favored popular sovereignty and choice by state constitutions; he accepted the pro-slavery Dred Scott decision as binding. He denied the right of states to secede. A strict constructionist, he desired to keep peace and found no authority for using force. He died at Wheatland, near Lancaster, Pa., June 1, 1868.

Abraham Lincoln (1861-1865)

Abraham Lincoln, 16th president, Republican, was born Feb. 12, 1809, in a log cabin on a farm then in Hardin Co., Ky., now in Larue. He was the son of Thomas Lincoln, a carpenter, and Nancy Hanks.

The Lincolns moved to Spencer Co., Ind., near Gentryville, when Abe was 7. When his mother died his father married Mrs. Sarah Bush Johnston, 1819; she had a favorable influence on Abe. In 1830 the family moved to Macon Co., Ill. Lincoln lost election to the Illinois General Assembly, 1832, but later won 4 times, beginning in 1834. He enlisted in the militia for the Black Hawk War, 1832. In New Salem he ran a store, surveyed land, and was postmaster.

In 1837 Lincoln was admitted to the bar and became partner in a Springfield, Ill., law office. He was elected to Congress, 1847-49. He opposed the Mexican War. He supported Zachary Taylor, 1848. He opposed the Kansas-Nebraska Act and extension of slavery, 1854. He failed, in his bid for the Senate, 1855. He supported John C. Fremont, 1856.

In 1858 Lincoln had Republican support in the Illinois legislature for the Senate but was defeated by Stephen A. Douglas, Dem., who had sponsored the Kansas-Nebraska Act.

Lincoln was nominated for president by the Republican party on an anti-slavery platform, 1860. He ran against Douglas, a northern Democrat; John C. Breckinridge, southern pro-slavery Democrat; John Bell, Constitutional Union party. When he won the election, South Carolina seceded from the Union Dec. 20, 1860, followed in 1861 by 10 Southern states.

The Civil War erupted when Fort Sumter was attacked Apr. 12, 1861. On Sept. 22, 1862, 5 days after the battle of Antietam, he announced that slaves in territory then in rebellion would be free Jan. 1, 1863, date of the Emancipation Proclamation, His speeches, including his Gettysburg and Inaugural addresses, are remembered for their eloquence.

Lincoln was reelected, 1864, over Gen. George B. McClellan, Democrat. Lee surrendered Apr. 9, 1865. On Apr. 14, Lincoln was shot by actor John Wilkes Booth in Ford's Theatre, Washington. He died the next day.

Andrew Johnson (1865-1869)

Andrew Johnson, 17th president, Democrat, was born in Raleigh, N.C., Dec. 29, 1808, the son of Jacob Johnson, porter at an inn and church sexton, and Mary McDonough. He was apprenticed to a tailor but ran away and eventually settled in Greeneville, Tenn. He became an alderman, 1828; mayor, 1830; state representative and senator, 1835-43; member of Congress, 1843-53; governor of Tennessee, 1853-57; U.S. senator, 1857-62. He supported John C. Breckinridge against Lincoln in 1860. He had held slaves, but opposed secession and tried to prevent his home state, Tennessee, from seceding. In Mar. 1862, Lincoln appointed him military governor of occupied Tennessee. In 1864 he was nominated for vice president with Lincoln on the National Union ticket to win Democratic support. He succeeded Lincoln as president Apr. 15, 1865. In a controversy with Congress over the president's power over the South, he proclaimed, May 26, 1865, an amnesty to all Confederates except certain leaders if they would ratify the 13th Amendment abolishing slavery. States doing so added anti-Negro provisions that enraged Congress, which restored military control over the South. When Johnson removed Edwin M. Stanton, secretary of war, without notifying the Senate, thus repudiating the Tenure of Office Act, the House impeached him for this and other reasons. He was tried by the Senate, and acquitted by only one vote, May 26, 1868. He returned to the Senate in 1875. Johnson died July 31, 1875.

Ulysses Simpson Grant (1869-1877)

Ulysses S. Grant, 18th president, Republican, was born at Point Pleasant, Oh., Apr. 27, 1822, son of Jesse R. Grant, a tanner, and Hannah Simpson. The next year the family moved to Georgetown, Oh. Grant was named Hiram Ulysses, but on entering West Point, 1839, his name was entered as Ulysses Simpson and he adopted it. He was graduated in 1843; served under Gens. Taylor and Scott in the Mexican War; resigned, 1854; worked in St. Louis until 1860, then went to Galena, Ill. With the start of the Civil War, he was named colonel of the 21st Illinois Vols., 1861, then brigadier general; took Forts Henry and Donelson; fought at Shiloh, took Vicksburg. After his victory at Chattanooga, Lincoln placed him in command of the Union Armies. He accepted Lee's surrender at Appomattox, Apr., 1865. President Johnson appointed Grant secretary of war when he suspended Stanton, but Grant was not confirmed. He was nominated for president by the Republicans in 1868 and elected over Horatio Seymour, Democrat. The 15th Amendment, amnesty bill, and civil service reform were events of his administration. The Liberal Republicans and Democrats opposed him with Horace Greeley, 1872, but he

was reelected. An attempt by the Stalwarts (Old Guard) to nominate him in 1880 failed. In 1884 the collapse of Grant & Ward, investment house, left him penniless. He wrote his personal memoirs while ill with cancer and completed them 4 days before his death at Mt. McGregor, N.Y., July 23, 1885. The book realized over $450,000.

Rutherford Birchard Hayes (1877-1881)

Rutherford B. Hayes, 19th president, Republican, was born in Delaware, Oh., Oct. 4, 1822, the posthumous son of Rutherford Hayes, a farmer, and Sophia Birchard. He was raised by his uncle Sardis Birchard. He graduated from Kenyon College, 1842, and Harvard Law School, 1845. He practiced law in Lower Sandusky, Oh., now Fremont; was city solicitor of Cincinnati, 1858-61. In the Civil War, he was major of the 23d Ohio Vols., was wounded several times, and rose to the rank of brevet major general, 1864. He served in Congress 1864-67, supporting Reconstruction and Johnson's impeachment. He was elected governor of Ohio, 1867 and 1869; beaten in the race for Congress, 1872; reelected governor, 1875. In 1876 he was nominated for president and believed he had lost the election to Samuel J. Tilden, Democrat. But a few Southern states submitted 2 different sets of electoral votes and the result was in dispute. An electoral commission, appointed by Congress, 8 Republicans and 7 Democrats, awarded all disputed votes to Hayes allowing him to become president by one electoral vote. Hayes, keeping a promise to southerners, withdrew troops from areas still occupied in the South, ending the era of Reconstruction. He proceeded to reform the civil service, alienating political spoilsmen. He advocated repeal of the Tenure of Office Act. He supported sound money and specie payments. Hayes died in Fremont, Oh., Jan. 17, 1893.

James Abram Garfield (1881-1881)

James A. Garfield, 20th president, Republican, was born Nov. 19, 1831, in Orange, Cuyahoga Co., Oh., the son of Abram Garfield and Eliza Ballou. His father died in 1833. He worked as a canal bargeman, farmer, and carpenter; attended Western Reserve Eclectic, later Hiram College, and was graduated from Williams in 1856. He taught at Hiram, and later became principal. He was in the Ohio senate in 1859. Anti-slavery and anti-secession, he volunteered for the war, became colonel of the 42d Ohio Infantry and brigadier in 1862. He fought at Shiloh, was chief of staff for Rosecrans and was made major general for gallantry at Chickamauga. He entered Congress as a radical Republican in 1863; supported specie payment as against paper money (greenbacks). On the electoral commission in 1877 he voted for Hayes against Tilden on strict party lines. He was senator-elect in 1880 when he became the Republican nominee for president. He was chosen as a compromise over Gen. Grant, James G. Blaine, and John Sherman. This alienated the Grant following but Garfield was elected. On July 2, 1881, Garfield was shot by mentally disturbed office-seeker, Charles J. Guiteau, while entering a railroad station in Washington. He died Sept. 19, 1881, at Elberon, N.J.

Chester Alan Arthur (1881-1885)

Chester A. Arthur, 21st president, Republican, was born at Fairfield, Vt., Oct. 5, 1829, the son of the Rev. William Arthur, from County Antrim, Ireland, and Malvina Stone. He graduated from Union College, 1848, taught school at Pownall, Vt., studied law in New York. In 1853 he argued in a fugitive slave case that slaves transported through N.Y. State were thereby freed. He was made collector of the Port of New York, 1871. President Hayes, reforming the civil service, forced Arthur to resign, 1879. This made the New York machine stalwarts enemies of Hayes. Arthur and the stalwarts tried to nominate Grant for a 3d term in 1880. When Garfield was nominated, Arthur received 2d place in the interests of harmony. When Garfield died, Arthur became president. He supported civil service reform and the tariff of 1883. He was defeated for renomination by James G. Blaine. He died in New York City Nov. 18, 1886.

Grover Cleveland (1885-1889) (1893-1897)

(According to a ruling of the State Dept., Grover Cleveland is both the 22d and the 24th president, because his 2 terms were not consecutive. By individuals, he is only the 22d.)

Grover Cleveland, 22d and 24th president, Democrat, was born in Caldwell, N.J. Mar. 18, 1837, the son of Richard F. Cleveland, a Presbyterian minister, and Ann Neale. He was named Stephen Grover, but dropped the Stephen. He clerked in Clinton and Buffalo, N.Y., taught at the N.Y. City Institution for the Blind; was admitted to the bar in Buffalo, 1859; became assistant district attorney, 1863; sheriff, 1871; mayor, 1881; governor of New York, 1882. He was an independent, honest administrator who hated corruption. He was nominated for president over Tammany Hall opposition, 1884, and defeated Republican James G. Blaine. He enlarged the civil service, vetoed many pension raids on the Treasury. In 1888 he was defeated by Benjamin Harrison, although his popular vote was larger. Reelected over Harrison in 1892, he faced a money crisis brought about by lowering of the gold reserve, circulation of paper and exorbitant silver purchases under the Sherman Act; obtained a repeal of the latter and a reduced tariff. A severe depression and labor troubles racked his administration but he refused to interfere in business matters and rejected Jacob Coxey's demand for unemployment relief. He broke the Pullman strike, 1894. In 1896, the Democrats repudiated his administration and chose silverite William Jennings Bryan as their candidate. Cleveland died in Princeton, N.J., June 24, 1908.

Benjamin Harrison (1889-1893)

Benjamin Harrison, 23d president, Republican, was born at North Bend, Oh., Aug. 20, 1833. His great-grandfather, Benjamin Harrison, was a signer of the Declaration of Independence; his grandfather, William Henry Harrison, was 9th President; his father, John Scott Harrison, was a member of Congress. His mother was Elizabeth F. Irwin. He attended school on his father's farm; graduated from Miami Univ. at Oxford, Oh., 1852; admitted to the bar, 1853, and practiced in Indianapolis. In the Civil War, he rose to the rank of brevet brigadier general, fought at Kennesaw Mountain, Peachtree Creek, Nashville, and in the Atlanta campaign. He failed to be elected governor of Indiana, 1876; but became senator, 1881. In 1888 he defeated Cleveland for president despite having fewer popular votes. He expanded the pension list, signed the McKinley high tariff bill, the Sherman Antitrust Act, and the Sherman Silver Purchase Act. During his administration, 6 states were admitted to the union. He was defeated for reelection, 1892. He represented Venezuela in a boundary arbitration with Great Britain in Paris, 1899. He died in Indianapolis, Mar. 13, 1901.

William McKinley (1897-1901)

William McKinley, 25th president, Republican, was born in Niles, Oh., Jan. 29, 1843, the son of William McKinley, an ironmaker, and Nancy Allison. McKinley attended school in Poland, Oh., and Allegheny College, Meadville, Pa., and enlisted for the Civil War at 18 in the 23d Ohio, in which Rutherford B. Hayes was a major. He rose to captain and in 1865 was made brevet major. He studied law in the Albany, N.Y., law school; opened an office in Canton, Oh., in 1867, and campaigned for Grant and Hayes. He served in the House of Representatives, 1877-83, 1885-91, and led the fight for passage of the McKinley Tarriff, 1890. Defeated for reelection on the issue in 1890, he was governor of Ohio, 1892-96. He had support for president in the convention that nominated Benjamin Harrison in 1892. In 1896 he was elected president on a protective tariff, sound money (gold standard) platform over William Jennings Bryan, Democratic proponent of free silver. McKinley was reluctant to intervene in Cuba but the loss of the battleship Maine at Havana crystallized opinion. He demanded Spain's withdrawal from Cuba; Spain made some concessions but Congress announced state of war as of Apr. 21. He was reelected in the 1900 campaign, defeating Bryan's anti-imperialist arguments with the promise of a "full dinner pail." McKinley was respected for his conciliatory nature, but conservative on business issues. On Sept. 6, 1901, while welcoming citizens at the Pan-American Exposition, Buffalo, N.Y., he was shot by Leon Czolgosz, an anarchist. He died Sept. 14.

Theodore Roosevelt (1901-1909)

Theodore Roosevelt, 26th president, Republican, was born in N.Y. City, Oct. 27, 1858, the son of Theodore Roosevelt, a glass importer, and Martha Bulloch. He was a 5th cousin of Franklin D. Roosevelt and an uncle of Eleanor Roosevelt. Roosevelt graduated from Harvard, 1880; attended Columbia Law School briefly; sat in the N.Y. State Assembly, 1882-84; ranched in North Dakota, 1884-86; failed election as mayor of N.Y. City, 1886; member of U.S. Civil Service Commission, 1889; president, N.Y. Police Board, 1895, supporting the merit system; assistant secretary of the Navy under McKinley, 1897-98. In the war with Spain, he organized the 1st U.S. Volunteer Cavalry (Rough Riders) as lieutenant colonel; led the charge up Kettle Hill at San Juan. Elected New York governor, 1898-1900, he fought the spoils system and achieved taxation of corporation franchises. Nominated for vice president, 1900, he became nation's youngest president when McKinley died. As president he fought corruption of politics by big business; dissolved Northern Securities Co. and others for violating, anti-trust laws; intervened in coal strike on behalf of the public, 1902; obtained Elkins Law forbidding rebates to favored corporations, 1903; Hepburn Law regulating railroad rates, 1906; Pure Food and Drugs Act, 1906, Reclamation Act and employers' liability laws. He organized conservation, mediated the peace between Japan and Russia, 1905; won the Nobel Peace Prize. He was the first to use the Hague Court of International Arbitration. By recognizing the new Republic of Panama he made Panama Canal possible. He was reelected in 1904.

In 1908 he obtained the nomination of William H. Taft, who was elected. Feeling that Taft had abandoned his policies, Roosevelt unsuccessfully sought the nomination in 1912. He bolted the party and ran on the Progressive "Bull Moose", ticket against Taft and Woodrow Wilson, splitting the Republicans and insuring Wilson's election. He was shot during the campaign but recovered. In 1916 he supported Charles E. Hughes, Republican. A strong friend of Britain, he fought American isolation in World War I. He wrote some 40 books on many topics; his *Winning of the West* is best known. He died Jan. 6, 1919, at Sagamore Hill, Oyster Bay, N.Y.

William Howard Taft (1909-1913)

William Howard Taft, 27th president, Republican, was born in Cincinnati, Oh., Sept. 15, 1857, the son of Alphonso Taft and Louisa Maria Torrey. His father was secretary of war and attorney general in Grant's cabinet; minister to Austria and Russia under Arthur. Taft was graduated from Yale, 1878; Cincinnati Law School, 1880; became law reporter for Cincinnati newspapers; was assistant prosecuting attorney, 1881-83; assistant county solicitor, 1885; judge, superior court, 1887; U.S. solicitor-general, 1890; federal circuit judge, 1892. In 1900 he became head of the U.S. Philippines Commission and was first civil governor of the Philippines, 1901-04; secretary of war, 1904; provisional governor of Cuba, 1906. He was groomed for president by Roosevelt and elected over Bryan, 1908. His administration dissolved Standard Oil and tobacco trusts; instituted Dept. of Labor; drafted direct election of senators and income tax amendments. His tariff and conservation policies angered progressives; though renominated he was opposed by Roosevelt; the result was Democrat Woodrow Wilson's election. Taft, with some reservations, supported the League of Nations. He was professor of constitutional law, Yale, 1913-21; chief justice of the U.S. Supreme Court, 1921-30; illness forced him to resign. He died in Washington, Mar. 8, 1930.

Woodrow Wilson (1913-1921)

Woodrow Wilson, 28th president, Democrat, was born at Staunton, Va., Dec. 28, 1856, as Thomas Woodrow Wilson, son of a Presbyterian minister, the Rev. Joseph Ruggles Wilson and Janet (Jessie) Woodrow. In his youth Wilson lived in Augusta, Ga., Columbia, S.C., and Wilmington, N.C. He attended Davidson College, 1873-74; was graduated from Princeton, A.B., 1879; A.M., 1882; read law at the Univ. of Virginia, 1881; practiced law, Atlanta, 1882-83; Ph.D., Johns Hopkins, 1886. He taught at Bryn Mawr, 1885-88; at Wesleyan, 1888-90; was professor of jurisprudence and political economy at Princeton, 1890-1910; president of Princeton, 1902-1910; governor of New Jersey, 1911-13. In 1912 he was nominated for president with the aid of William Jennings Bryan, who sought to block James "Champ" Clark and Tammany Hall. Wilson won the election because the Republican vote for Taft was split by the Progressives under Roosevelt.

Wilson protected American interests in revolutionary Mexico and fought for American rights on the high seas. His sharp warnings to Germany led to the resignation of his secretary of state, Bryan, a pacifist. In 1916 he was reelected with a slim margin with the slogan, "He kept us out of war." Wilson's attempts to mediate in the war failed. After 4 American ships had been sunk by the Germans, he secured a declaration of war against Germany on Apr. 6, 1917.

Wilson proposed peace Jan. 8, 1918, on the basis of his "Fourteen Points," a state paper with worldwide influence. His doctrine of self-determination continues to play a major role in territorial disputes. The Germans accepted his terms and an armistice, Nov. 11.

Wilson went to Paris to help negotiate the peace treaty, the crux of which he considered the League of Nations. The Senate demanded reservations that would not make the U.S. subordinate to the votes of other nations in case of war. Wilson refused to consider any reservations and toured the country to get support. He suffered a stroke, Oct., 1919. An invalid for months, he clung to his executive powers while his wife and doctor sought to shield him from affairs which would tire him.

He was awarded the 1919 Nobel Peace Prize, but the treaty embodying the League of Nations was rejected by the Senate, 1920. He died in Washington, Feb. 3, 1924.

Warren Gamaliel Harding (1921-1923)

Warren Gamaliel Harding, 29th president, Republican, was born near Corsica, now Blooming Grove, Oh., Nov. 2, 1865, the son of Dr. George Tyron Harding, a physician, and Phoebe Elizabeth Dickerson. He attended Ohio Central College. He was state senator, 1900-04; lieutenant governor, 1904-06; defeated for governor, 1910; chosen U.S. senator, 1915. He supported Taft, opposed federal control of food and fuel; voted for anti-strike legislation, woman's suffrage, and the Volstead prohibition enforcement act over President Wilson's veto; and opposed the League of Nations. In 1920 he was nominated for president and defeated James M. Cox in the election. The Republicans capitalized on war weariness and fear that Wilson's League of Nations would curtail U.S. sovereignty. Harding stressed a return to "normalcy"; worked for tariff revision and repeal of excess profits law and high income taxes. Two Harding appointees, Albert B. Fall (interior) and Harry Daugherty (attorney general), became involved in the Teapot Dome scandal that embittered Harding's last days. He called the International Conference on Limitation of Armaments, 1921-22. Returning from a trip to Alaska he became ill and died in San Francisco, Aug. 2, 1923.

Calvin Coolidge (1923-1929)

Calvin Coolidge, 30th president, Republican, was born in Plymouth, Vt., July 4, 1872, the son of John Calvin Coolidge, a storekeeper, and Victoria J. Moor, and named John Calvin Coolidge. Coolidge graduated from Amherst in 1895. He entered Republican state politics and served as mayor of Northampton, Mass., state senator, lieutenant governor, and, in 1919, governor. In Sept., 1919, Coolidge attained national prominence by calling out the state guard in the Boston police strike. He declared: "There is no right to strike against the public safety by anybody, anywhere, anytime." This brought his name before the Republican convention of 1920, where he was nominated for vice president. He succeeded to the presidency on Harding's death. He opposed the League of Nations; approved the World Court; vetoed the soldiers' bonus bill, which was passed over his veto. In 1924 he was elected by a huge majority. He reduced the national debt by $2 billion in 3 years. He twice vetoed the McNary-Haugen farm bill, which would have provided relief to financially hard-pressed farmers. With Republicans eager to renominate him he announced, Aug. 2, 1927: "I do not choose to run for president in 1928." He died in Northampton, Jan. 5, 1933.

Herbert Clark Hoover (1929-1933)

Herbert C. Hoover, 31st president, Republican, was born at West Branch, Ia., Aug. 10, 1874, son of Jesse Clark Hoover, a blacksmith, and Hulda Randall Minthorn. Hoover grew up in Indian Territory (now Oklahoma) and Oregon; won his A.B. in engineering at Stanford, 1891. He worked briefly with U.S. Geological Survey and western mines; then was a mining engineer in Australia, Asia, Europe, Africa, U.S. While chief engineer, imperial mines, China, he directed food relief for victims of Boxer Rebellion, 1900. He directed

American Relief Committee, London, 1914-15; U.S. Comm. for Relief in Belgium, 1915-1919; was U.S. Food Administrator, 1917-1919; American Relief Administrator, 1918-1923, feeding children in defeated nations; Russian Relief, 1918-1923. He was secy. of commerce, 1921-28. He was elected president over Alfred E. Smith, 1928. In 1929 the stock market crashed and the economy collapsed. During the depression, Hoover opposed federal aid to the unemployed. He was defeated in the 1932 election by Franklin D. Roosevelt. President Truman made him coordinator of European Food Program, 1947, chairman of the Commission for Reorganization of the Executive Branch, 1947-49. He founded the Hoover Institution on War, Revolution, and Peace at Stanford Univ. He died in N.Y. City, Oct. 20, 1964.

Franklin Delano Roosevelt (1933-1945)

Franklin D. Roosevelt, 32d president, Democrat, was born near Hyde Park, N.Y., Jan. 30, 1882, the son of James Roosevelt and Sara Delano. He graduated from Harvard, 1904; attended Columbia Law School; was admitted to the bar. He went to the N.Y. Senate, 1910 and 1913. In 1913 President Wilson made him assistant secretary of the navy.

Roosevelt ran for vice president, 1920, with James Cox and was defeated. From 1920 to 1928 he was a N.Y. lawyer and vice president of Fidelity & Deposit Co. In Aug., 1921, polio paralyzed his legs. He learned to walk with leg braces and a cane.

Roosevelt was elected governor of New York, 1928 and 1930. In 1932, W. G. McAdoo, pledged to John N. Garner, threw his votes to Roosevelt, who was nominated. The depression and the promise to repeal prohibition insured his election. He asked emergency powers, proclaimed the New Deal, and put into effect a vast number of administrative changes. Foremost was the use of public funds for relief and public works, resulting in deficit financing. He greatly expanded the controls of the central government over business, and by an excess profits tax and progressive income taxes produced a redistribution of earnings on an unprecedented scale. The Wagner Act gave labor many advantages in organizing and collective bargaining. He was the last president inaugurated on Mar. 4 (1933) and the first inaugurated on Jan. 20 (1937).

Roosevelt was the first president to use radio for "fireside chats." When the Supreme Court nullified some New Deal laws, he sought power to "pack" the court with additional justices, but Congress refused to give him the authority. He was the first president to break the "no 3d term" tradition (1940) and was elected to a 4th term, 1944, despite failing health. He was openly hostile to fascist governments before World War II and launched a lend-lease program on behalf of the Allies. He wrote the principles of fair dealing into the Atlantic Charter, Aug. 14, 1941 (with Winston Churchill), and urged the Four Freedoms (freedom of speech, of worship, from want, from fear) Jan. 6, 1941. When Japan attacked Pearl Harbor, Dec. 7, 1941, the U.S. entered the war. He conferred with allied heads of state at Casablanca, Jan., 1943; Quebec, Aug., 1943; Teheran, Nov.-Dec., 1943; Cairo, Dec., 1943; Yalta, Feb., 1945. He died at Warm Springs, Ga., Apr. 12, 1945.

Harry S. Truman (1945-1953)

Harry S. Truman, 33d president, Democrat, was born at Lamar, Mo., May 8, 1884, the son of John Anderson Truman and Martha Ellen Young. A family disagreement on whether his middle name was Shippe or Solomon, after names of 2 grandfathers, resulted in his using only the middle initial S. He attended public schools in Independence, Mo., worked for the Kansas City Star, 1901, and as railroad timekeeper, and helper in Kansas City banks up to 1905. He ran his family's farm, 1906-17. He was commissioned a first lieutenant and took part in the Vosges, Meuse-Argonne, and St. Mihiel actions in World War I. After the war he ran a haberdashery, became judge of Jackson Co. Court, 1922-24; attended Kansas City School of Law, 1923-25.

Truman was elected U.S. senator in 1934; reelected 1940. In 1944 with Roosevelt's backing he was nominated for vice president and elected. On Roosevelt's death Truman became president. In 1948 he was elected president.

Truman authorized the first uses of the atomic bomb (Hiroshima and Nagasaki, Aug. 6 and 9, 1945), bringing World War II to a rapid end. He was responsible for creating NATO, the Marshall Plan, and what came to be called the Truman Doctrine (to aid nations such as Greece and Turkey, threatened by Russian or other communist takeover). He broke a Russian blockade of West Berlin with a massive airlift, 1948-49. When communist North Korea invaded South Korea, June, 1950, he won UN approval for a "police action" and sent in forces under Gen. Douglas MacArthur. When MacArthur opposed his policy of limited objectives, Truman removed him from command.

Truman was responsible for higher minimum-wage, increased social-security, and aid-for-housing laws. Truman died Dec. 26, 1972, in Kansas City, Mo.

Dwight David Eisenhower (1953-1961)

Dwight D. Eisenhower, 34th president, Republican, was born Oct. 14, 1890, at Denison, Tex., the son of David Jacob Eisenhower and Ida Elizabeth Stover. The next year, the family moved to Abilene, Kan. He graduated from West Point, 1915. He was on the American military mission to the Philippines, 1935-39 and during 4 of those years on the staff of Gen. Douglas MacArthur. He was made commander of Allied forces landing in North Africa, 1942, full general, 1943. He became supreme Allied commander in Europe, 1943, and as such led the Normandy invasion June 6, 1944. He was given the rank of general of the army Dec. 20, 1944, made permanent in 1946. On May 7, 1945, he received the surrender of the Germans at Rheims. He returned to the U.S. to serve as chief of staff, 1945-1948. In 1948, Eisenhower published *Crusade in Europe*, his war memoirs, which quickly became a best seller. From 1948 to 1953, he was president of Columbia Univ., but took leave of absence in 1950, to command NATO forces.

Eisenhower resigned from the army and was nominated for president by the Republicans, 1952. He defeated Adlai E. Stevenson in the election. He again defeated Stevenson, 1956. He called himself a moderate, favored "free market system" vs. government price and wage controls; kept government out of labor disputes; reorganized defense establishment; promoted missile programs. He continued foreign aid; sped end of Korean fighting; endorsed Taiwan and SE Asia defense treaties; backed UN in condemning Anglo-French raid on Egypt; advocated "open skies" policy of mutual inspection to USSR. He sent U.S. troops into Little Rock, Ark., Sept., 1957, during the segregation crisis and ordered Marines into Lebanon July-Aug., 1958.

During his retirement at his farm near Gettysburg, Pa., Eisenhower took up the role of elder statesman, counseling his 3 successors in the White House. He died Mar. 28, 1969, in Washington.

John Fitzgerald Kennedy (1961-1963)

John F. Kennedy, 35th president, Democrat, was born May 29, 1917, in Brookline, Mass., the son of Joseph P. Kennedy, financier, who later became ambassador to Great Britain, and Rose Fitzgerald. He entered Harvard, attended the London School of Economics briefly in 1935, received a B.S., from Harvard, 1940. He served in the Navy, 1941-1945, commanded a PT boat in the Solomons and won the Navy and Marine Corps Medal. He wrote *Profiles in Courage*, which won a Pulitzer prize. He served as representative in Congress, 1947-1953; was elected to the Senate in 1952, reelected 1958. He nearly won the vice presidential nomination in 1956.

In 1960, Kennedy won the Democratic nomination for president and defeated Richard M. Nixon, Republican. He was the first Roman Catholic president.

In Apr. 1961, Kennedy's new administration suffered a severe setback when an invasion force of anti-Castro Cubans, trained and directed by the U.S. Central Intelligence Agency, failed to establish a beachhead at the Bay of Pigs in Cuba.

Kennedy's most important act was his successful demand Oct. 22, 1962, that the Soviet Union dismantle its missile bases in Cuba. He established a quarantine of arms shipments to Cuba and continued surveillance by air. He defied Soviet attempts to force the Allies out of Berlin. He made the steel industry rescind a price rise. He backed civil rights, a mental health program, arbitration of railroad disputes, and expanded medical care for the aged. Astronaut flights and satellite orbiting were greatly developed during his administration.

On Nov. 22, 1963, Kennedy was assassinated in Dallas, Tex.

Lyndon Baines Johnson (1963-1969)

Lyndon B. Johnson, 36th president, Democrat, was born near Stonewall, Tex., Aug. 27, 1908, son of Sam Ealy Johnson and Rebekah Baines. He received a B.S. degree at Southwest Texas State Teachers College, 1930, attended Georgetown Univ. Law School, Washington, 1935. He taught public speaking in Houston, 1930-32; served as secretary to Rep. R. M. Kleberg, 1932-35. In 1937 Johnson won a contest to fill the vacancy caused by the death of a representative and in 1938 was elected to the full term, after which he returned for 4 terms. He was elected U.S. senator in 1948 and reelected in 1954. He became Democratic leader, 1953. Johnson was Texas' favorite son for the Democratic presidential nomination in 1956 and had strong support in the 1960 convention, where the nominee, John F. Kennedy, asked him to run for vice president. His campaigning helped overcome religious bias against Kennedy in the South.

Johnson became president on the death of Kennedy. Johnson worked hard for welfare legislation, signed civil rights, anti-proverty, and tax reduction laws, and averted strikes on railroads. He was elected to a full term, 1964. The war in Vietnam overshadowed other developments during his administration.

In face of increasing division in the nation and his own party over his handling of the war, Johnson announced that he would not seek another term, Mar. 31, 1968.

Retiring to his ranch near Johnson City, Tex., Johnson wrote his memoirs and oversaw the construction of the Lyndon Baines Johnson Library. He died Jan. 22, 1973.

Richard Milhous Nixon (1969-1974)

Richard M. Nixon, 37th president, Republican, was the only president to resign without completing an elected term. He was born in Yorba Linda, Cal., Jan. 9, 1913, the son of Francis Anthony Nixon and Hannah Milhous. Nixon graduated from Whittier College, 1934; Duke Univ. Law School, 1937. After practicing law in Whittier and serving briefly in the Office of Price Administration in 1942, he entered the navy, and served in the South Pacific.

Nixon was elected to the House of Representatives in 1946 and 1948. He achieved prominence as the House Un-American Activities Committee member who forced the showdown that resulted in the Alger Hiss perjury conviction. In 1950 Nixon was elected to the Senate.

He was elected vice president in the Eisenhower landslides of 1952 and 1956. With Eisenhower's endorsement, Nixon won the Republican nomination in 1960. He was defeated by Democrat John F. Kennedy, returned to Cal. and was defeated in his race for governor, 1962.

In 1968, he won the presidential nomination and went on to defeat Democrat Hubert H. Humphrey.

Nixon was the first U.S. president to visit China and Russia (1972). He and his foreign affairs advisor, Henry A. Kissinger, achieved a detente with China. Nixon appointed 4 Supreme Court justices, including the chief justice, thus altering the court's balance in favor of a more conservative view.

Reelected 1972, Nixon secured a cease-fire agreement in Vietnam and completed the withdrawal of U.S. troops.

Nixon's 2d term was cut short by a series of scandals beginning with the burglary of Democratic party national headquarters in the Watergate office complex on June 17, 1972. Nixon denied any White House involvement in the Watergate break-in. On July 16, 1973, a White House aide, under questioning by a Senate committee, revealed that most of Nixon's office conversations and phone calls had been recorded. Nixon claimed executive privilege to keep the tapes secret and the courts and Congress sought the tapes for criminal proceedings against former White House aides and for a House inquiry into possible impeachment.

On Oct. 10, 1973, Nixon fired the Watergate special prosecutor and the attorney general resigned in protest. The public outcry which followed caused Nixon to appoint a new special prosecutor and to turn over to the courts a number of subpoenaed tape recordings. Public reaction also brought the initiation of a formal inquiry into impeachment.

On July 24, 1974, the Supreme Court ruled that Nixon's claim of executive privilege must fall before the special prosecutor's subpoenas of tapes relevant to criminal trial proceedings. That same day, the House Judiciary Committee opened debate on impeachment. On July 30, the committee recommended House adoption of 3 articles of impeachment charging Nixon with obstruction of justice, abuse of power, and contempt of Congress.

On Aug. 5, Nixon released transcripts of conversations held 6 days after the Watergate break-in showing that Nixon had known of, approved, and directed Watergate cover-up activities. Nixon resigned from office Aug. 9.

Gerald Rudolph Ford (1974-1977)

Gerald R. Ford, 38th president, Republican, was born July 14, 1913, in Omaha, Neb., son of Leslie King and Dorothy Gardner, and was named Leslie Jr. When he was 2, his parents were divorced and his mother moved with the boy to Grand Rapids, Mich. There she met and married Gerald R. Ford, who formally adopted the boy and gave him his own name.

He graduated from the Univ. of Michigan, 1935 and Yale Law School, 1941.

He began practicing law in Grand Rapids, but in 1942 joined the navy and served in the Pacific, leaving the service in 1946 as a lieutenant commander.

He entered congress in 1949 and spent 25 years in the House, 8 of them as Republican leader.

On Oct. 12, 1973, after Vice President Spiro T. Agnew resigned, Ford was nominated by President Nixon to replace him. It was the first use of the procedures set out in the 25th Amendment.

When Nixon resigned Aug. 9, 1974, Ford became president, the first to serve without being chosen in a national election. On Sept. 8 he pardoned Nixon for any federal crimes he might have committed as president. Ford vetoed 48 bills in his first 21 months in office, saying most would prove too costly. He visited China. In 1976, he was defeated in the election by Democrat Jimmy Carter.

Jimmy (James Earl) Carter (1977-1981)

Jimmy (James Earl) Carter, 39th president, Democrat, was the first president from the Deep South since before the Civil War. He was born Oct. 1, 1924, at Plains, Ga., where his parents, James and Lillian Gordy Carter, had a farm and several businesses.

He attended Georgia Tech, and graduated from the U.S. Naval Academy. He entered the Navy's nuclear submarine program as an aide to Adm. Hyman Rickover, and studied nuclear physics at Union College.

His father died in 1953 and Carter left the Navy to take over the family businesses — peanut-raising, warehousing, and cotton-ginning. He was elected to the Georgia state senate, was defeated for governor, 1966, but elected in 1970.

Carter won the Democratic nomination and defeated President Gerald R. Ford in the election of 1976. He played a major role in the peace negotiations between Israel and Egypt. In Nov. 1979, Iranian student militants attacked the U.S. embassy in Teheran and held members of the embassy staff hostage.

Carter was widely criticized for the poor state of the economy and high inflation. He was also viewed as weak in his handling of foreign policy. He reacted to the Soviet invasion of Afghanistan by imposing a grain embargo and boycotting the Moscow Olympic games. His failure to obtain the release of the remaining 52 hostages held in Iran plagued Carter to the end of his term. He was defeated by Ronald Reagan in the 1980 election. Carter finally succeeded in obtaining the release of the hostages on Inauguration Day, as the new president was taking the oath of office.

Ronald Wilson Reagan (1981-1989)

Ronald Wilson Reagan, 40th president, Republican, was born Feb. 6, 1911, in Tampico, Ill., the son of John Edward Reagan and Nellie Wilson. Reagan graduated from Eureka (Ill.) College in 1932. Following his graduation, he worked as a sports announcer in Des Moines, Ia.

Reagan began a successful career as a film actor in 1937, and starred in numerous movies, and later television, until the 1960s. He was a captain in the Army Air Force during World War II.

He served as president of the Screen Actors Guild from 1947 to 1952, and in 1959.

Once a liberal Democrat, Reagan became active in Republican politics during the 1964 presidential campaign of Barry Goldwater. He was elected governor of California in 1966, and reelected in 1970.

In 1980, he gained the Republican nomination and won a landslide victory over Jimmy Carter. He was easily reelected in 1984. Reagan, at 73, was the oldest man ever elected president.

Reagan successfully forged a bipartisan coalition in Congress which led to enactment of an economic program which included the largest budget and tax cuts in U.S. history, and a Social Security reform bill designed to insure the long-term solvency of the system. In 1986, he signed into law a revolutionary tax-reform bill. He was shot in an assassination attempt in 1981, and had major surgery in 1985 and 1987.

In 1983, Reagan sent a task force to lead the invasion of Grenada, and joined 3 European nations in maintaining a peacekeeping force in Beirut, Lebanon. His opposition to international terrorism led to the U.S. bombing of Lybian military installations in 1986. He strongly supported El Salvador, the Nicaraguan contras, and other anti-communist governments and forces throughout the world. Aid was sent to the rebels fighting Soviet troops in Afghanistan. When the Iran/Iraq war threatened freedom of the seas, U.S. Navy ships were sent to the Persian Gulf.

Reagan held summit meetings with Soviet leader Gorbachev in 1985 in Geneva, 1986 in Iceland, 1987 in Washington, D.C. where an historic treaty eliminating short and medium-range missiles from Europe was signed, and 1988 in Moscow where Reagan criticized the Soviet record on human rights, and met with Soviet dissidents.

Reagan faced a major crisis in 1986-1987, when it was revealed that the U.S. had sold weapons to Iran in exchange for the release of U.S. hostages being held in Lebanon; and that subsequently some of the money was diverted to the Nicaraguan contras. The scandal led to the resignation of leading White House aides; some were indicted and convicted of criminal charges.

As Reagan left office, the nation was experiencing its 6th consecutive year of economic prosperity. Along with the strong economy, the nation enjoyed low unemployment, energy costs, and inflation. Reagan, however, was unable to control the high budget deficits which plagued him throughout his administration.

George Herbert Walker Bush (1989-   )

George Herbert Walker Bush, 41st president, Republican, was born June 12, 1924, in Milton, Mass., the son of Prescott Bush, U.S. senator from Connecticut, and Dorothy Walker. He served as a U.S. Navy pilot in World War II, earning the Distinguished Flying Cross and three Air Medals for service in the Pacific. After graduating from Yale Univ. (1948), he settled in Texas where, in 1953, he helped found an oil company.

After losing a bid for a U.S. Senate seat in Texas, 1964, he was elected to the House of Representatives in 1966 and 1968. He lost a 2d U.S. Senate race in 1970. He served as U.S. ambassador to the United Nations, 1971-73, headed the U.S. Liaison Office in Beijing, 1974-75, and was director of the Central Intelligence Agency, 1976-77.

Following an unsuccessful bid for the 1980 Republican presidential nomination, Bush was chosen by Ronald Reagan as his vice presidential running mate. He served as U.S. vice president, 1981-89.

In 1988, he gained the Republican presidential nomination and defeated Democrat Michael Dukakis in the election. Calling on Americans "to make kinder the face of the nation and gentler the face of the world," Bush took office faced with the ongoing U.S. budget and trade deficits as well as the rescue of insolvent U.S. savings and loan institutions.

He presented a sweeping arms-control plan that challenged the Soviet Union to hasten the reduction of their superiority in conventional forces in Europe.

UNITED STATES HISTORY

1492
Christopher Columbus and crew sighted land Oct. 12 in the present-day Bahamas.

1497
John Cabot explored northeast coast to Delaware.

1513
Juan Ponce de Leon explored Florida coast.

1524
Giovanni da Verrazano led French expedition along coast from Carolina north to Nova Scotia; entered New York harbor.

1539
Hernando de Soto landed in Florida May 28; crossed Mississippi River, 1541.

1540
Francisco Vazquez de Coronado explored Southwest north of Rio Grande. Hernando de Alarcon reached Colorado River, Don Garcia Lopez de Cardenas reached Grand Canyon. Others explored California coast.

1565
St. Augustine, Fla. founded by Pedro Menendez. Razed by Francis Drake 1586.

1579
Francis Drake claimed California for Britain. Metal plate, found 1936, thought to be left by Drake, termed probable hoax 1979.

1607
Capt. John Smith and 105 cavaliers in 3 ships landed on Virginia coast, started first permanent English settlement in New World at Jamestown, May 13.

1609
Henry Hudson, English explorer of Northwest Passage, employed by Dutch, sailed into New York harbor in Sept., and up Hudson to Albany. The same year, Samuel de Champlain explored Lake Champlain just to the north. Spaniards settled Santa Fe, N.M.

1619
House of Burgesses, first representative assembly in New World, elected July 30 at Jamestown, Va.
First black laborers — indentured servants — in English N. American colonies, landed by Dutch at Jamestown in Aug. Chattel slavery legally recognized, 1650.

1620
Plymouth Pilgrims, Puritan separatists from Church of England, some living in Holland, left Plymouth, England Sept. 15 on Mayflower. Original destination Virginia, they reached Cape Cod Nov. 19, explored coast; 103 passengers landed Dec. 21 (Dec. 11 Old Style) at Plymouth. Mayflower Compact was agreement to have a government and abide by its laws. Half of colony died during harsh winter.

1624
Dutch left 8 men from ship New Netherland on Manhattan Island in May. Rest sailed to Albany.

1626
Peter Minuit bought Manhattan for Dutch from Man-a-hat-a Indians May 6 for trinkets valued at $24.

1634
Maryland founded as Catholic colony with religious tolerance.

1636
Harvard College founded Oct. 28, now oldest in U.S., Grammar school, compulsory education established at Boston.
Roger Williams founded Providence, R.I., June, as a democratically ruled colony with separation of church and state. Charter was granted, 1644.

1654
First Jews arrived in New Amsterdam.

1660
British Parliament passed Navigation Act, regulating colonial commerce to suit English needs.

1664
Three hundred British troops Sept. 8 seized New Netherland from Dutch, who yield peacefully. Charles II granted province of New Netherland and city of New Amsterdam to brother, Duke of York; both renamed New York. The Dutch recaptured the colony Aug. 9, 1673, but ceded it to Britain Nov. 10, 1674.

1676
Nathaniel Bacon led planters against autocratic British Gov. Berkeley, burned Jamestown, Va. Bacon died, 23 followers executed.
Bloody Indian war in New England ended Aug. 12. King Philip, Wampanoag chief, and many Narragansett Indians killed.

1682
Robert Cavelier, Sieur de La Salle, claimed lower Mississippi River country for France, called it Louisiana Apr. 9. Had French outposts built in Illinois and Texas, 1684. Killed during mutiny Mar. 19, 1687.

1683
William Penn signed treaty with Delaware Indians and made payment for Pennsylvania lands.

1692
Witchcraft delusion at Salem (now Danvers) Mass. inspired by preaching; 19 persons executed.

1696
Capt. William Kidd, American hired by British to fight pirates and take booty, becomes pirate. Arrested and sent to England, where he was hanged 1701.

1699
French settlements made in Mississippi, Louisiana.

1704
Indians attacked Deerfield, Mass. Feb. 28-29, killed 40, carried off 100.
Boston News Letter, first regular newspaper, started by John Campbell, postmaster. (Publick Occurences was suppressed after one issue 1690.)

1709
British-Colonial troops captured French fort, Port Royal, Nova Scotia, in Queen Anne's War 1701-13. France yielded Nova Scotia by treaty 1713.

1712
Slaves revolted in New York Apr. 6. Six committed suicide, 21 were executed. Second rising, 1741; 13 slaves hanged, 13 burned, 71 deported.

1716
First theater in colonies opened in Williamsburg, Va.

1728
Pennsylvania Gazette founded by Samuel Keimer in Philadelphia. Benjamin Franklin bought interest 1729.

1732
Benjamin Franklin published first Poor Richard's Almanac; published annually to 1757.

1735
Freedom of the press recognized in New York by acquittal of John Peter Zenger, editor of Weekly Journal, on charge of libeling British Gov. Cosby by criticizing his conduct in office.

1740-41
Capt. Vitus Bering, Dane employed by Russians, reached Alaska.

1744
King George's War pitted British and colonials vs. French. Colonials captured Louisburg, Cape Breton Is. June 17, 1745. Returned to France 1748 by Treaty of Aix-la-Chapelle.

1752
Benjamin Franklin, flying kite in thunderstorm, proved

lghtning is electricity **June 15**; invented lightning rod.

1754

French and Indian War (in Europe called 7 Years War, started 1756) began when French occupied Ft. Duquesne (Pittsburgh). British moved Acadian French from Nova Scotia to Louisiana **Oct. 1755**. British captured Quebec **Sept. 18, 1759** in battles in which French Gen. Montcalm and British Gen. Wolfe were killed. Peace signed **Feb. 10 1763**. French lost Canada and American Midwest. British tightened colonial administration in North America.

1764

Sugar Act placed duties on lumber, foodstuffs, molasses and rum in colonies.

1765

Stamp Act required revenue stamps to help defray cost of royal troops. Nine colonies, led by New York and Massachusetts at Stamp Act Congress in New York **Oct. 7-25, 1765**, adopted Declaration of Rights opposing taxation without representation in Parliament and trial without jury by admiralty courts. **Stamp Act** repealed **Mar. 17, 1766**.

1767

Townshend Acts levied taxes on glass, painter's lead, paper, and tea. In 1770 all duties except on tea were repealed.

1770

British troops fired **Mar. 5** into Boston mob, killed 5 including **Crispus Attucks**, a black man, reportedly leader of group; later called **Boston Massacre**.

1773

East India Co. tea ships turned back at Boston, New York, Philadelphia in May. Cargo ship burned at Annapolis **Oct. 14**, cargo thrown overboard at **Boston Tea Party Dec. 16**.

1774

"Intolerable Acts" of Parliament curtailed Massachusetts self-rule; barred use of Boston harbor till tea was paid for.

First Continental Congress held in Philadelphia **Sept. 5-Oct. 26**; protested British measures, called for civil disobedience.

Rhode Island abolished slavery.

1775

Patrick Henry addressed Virginia convention, **Mar. 23** said "Give me liberty or give me death."

Paul Revere and **William Dawes** on night of **Apr. 18** rode to alert patriots that British were on way to Concord to destroy arms. At Lexington, Mass. **Apr. 19** Minutemen lost 8 killed. On return from Concord British took 273 casualties.

Col. Ethan Allen (joined by Col. Benedict Arnold) captured **Ft. Ticonderoga, N.Y. May 10**; also Crown Point. Colonials headed for Bunker Hill, fortified Breed's Hill, Charlestown, Mass., repulsed British under Gen. William Howe twice before retreating **June 17**; British casualties 1,000; called Battle of Bunker Hill. Continental Congress **June 15** named George Washington commander-in-chief.

1776

France and Spain each agreed **May 2** to provide one million livres in arms to Americans.

In Continental Congress **June 7**, Richard Henry Lee (Va.) moved "that these united colonies are and of right ought to be free and independent states." Resolution adopted July 2. **Declaration of Independence** approved **July 4**.

Col. Moultrie's batteries at **Charleston, S.C.** repulsed British sea attack **June 28**.

Washington, with 10,000 men, lost **Battle of Long Island Aug. 27**, evacuated New York.

Nathan Hale executed as spy by British **Sept. 22**.

Brig. Gen. Arnold's Lake Champlain fleet was defeated at Valcour **Oct. 11**, but British returned to Canada. Howe failed to destroy Washington's army at White Plains **Oct. 28**. Hessians captured **Ft. Washington, Manhattan**, and 3,000 men **Nov. 16**; Ft. Lee, N.J. **Nov. 18**.

Washington in Pennsylvania, recrossed **Delaware River Dec. 25-26**, defeated 1,400 Hessians at Trenton, N.J. **Dec. 26**.

1777

Washington defeated Lord Cornwallis at **Princeton Jan.**

3. Continental Congress adopted Stars and Stripes. *See Flag article.*

Maj. Gen. John Burgoyne with 8,000 from Canada captured **Ft. Ticonderoga July 6**. Americans beat back Burgoyne at Bemis Heights **Oct. 7** and cut off British escape route. Burgoyne surrendered 5,000 men at **Saratoga N.Y. Oct. 17**.

Marquis de Lafayette, aged 20, made major general.

Articles of Confederation and Perpetual Union adopted by Continental Congress **Nov. 15**

France recognized independence of 13 colonies **Dec. 17**.

1778

France signed treaty of aid with U.S. **Feb. 6**. Sent fleet; British evacuated Philadelphia in consequence **June 18**.

1779

John Paul Jones on the *Bonhomme Richard* defeated *Serapis* in British North Sea waters **Sept. 23**.

1780

Charleston, S.C. fell to the British **May 12**, but a British force was defeated near **Kings Mountain, N.C. Oct. 7** by militiamen.

Benedict Arnold found to be a traitor **Sept. 23**. Arnold escaped, made brigadier general in British army.

1781

Bank of North America incorporated in Philadelphia May 26.

Cornwallis, sapped by patriot victories, retired to Yorktown, Va. Adm. De Grasse landed 3,000 French and stopped British fleet in Hampton Roads. Washington and Rochambeau joined forces, arrived near Williamsburg **Sept. 26**. When siege of Cornwallis began **Oct. 6**, British had 6,000, Americans 8,846, French 7,800. **Cornwallis** surrendered **Oct. 19**.

1782

New British cabinet agreed in March to recognize U.S. independence. Preliminary agreement signed in Paris **Nov. 30**.

1783

Massachusetts Supreme Court outlawed slavery in that state, noting the words in the state Bill of Rights "all men are born free and equal."

Britain, U.S. signed peace treaty **Sept. 3** (Congress ratified it **Jan. 14, 1784**).

Washington ordered army disbanded **Nov. 3**, bade farewell to his officers at Fraunces Tavern, N.Y. City **Dec. 4**.

Noah Webster published *American Spelling Book*, great bestseller.

1784

First successful daily newspaper, **Pennsylvania Packet & General Advertiser**, published **Sept. 21**.

1786

Delegates from 5 states at **Annapolis, Md. Sept. 11-14** asked Congress to call convention in Philadelphia to write practical constitution for the 13 states.

1787

Shays's Rebellion, of debt-ridden farmers in Massachusetts, failed **Jan. 25**.

Northwest Ordinance adopted **July 13** by Continental Congress. Determined government of Northwest Territory north of Ohio River, west of New York; 60,000 inhabitants could get statehood. Guaranteed freedom of religion, support for schools, no slavery.

Constitutional convention opened at Philadelphia **May 25** with George Washington presiding. Constitution adopted by delegates **Sept. 17**; ratification by 9th state, New Hampshire, **June 21, 1788**, meant adoption; declared in effect **Mar. 4, 1789**.

1789

George Washington chosen president by all electors voting (73 eligible, 69 voting, 4 absent); John Adams, vice president, 34 votes. **Feb. 4**, First Congress met at Federal Hall, N.Y. City; regular sessions began **Apr. 6**. Washington inaugurated there **Apr. 30**. Supreme Court created by Federal Judiciary Act **Sept. 24**.

1790

Congress met in Phila. **Dec. 6**, new temporary Capital.

1791
Bill of Rights went into effect Dec. 15.

1792
Gen. "Mad" Anthony Wayne made commander in Ohio-Indiana area, trained "American Legion"; established string of forts. Routed Indians at Fallen Timbers on Maumee River Aug. 20, 1794, checked British at Fort Miami, Ohio.

1793
Eli Whitney invented cotton gin, reviving southern slavery.

1794
Whiskey Rebellion, west Pennsylvania farmers protesting liquor tax of 1791, was suppressed by 15,000 militiamen Sept. 1794. Alexander Hamilton used incident to establish authority of the new federal government in enforcing its laws.

1795
U.S. bought peace from Algiers and Tunis by paying $800,000, supplying a frigate and annual tribute of $25,000 Nov. 28.
Gen. Wayne signed peace with Indians at Fort Greenville.
Univ. of North Carolina became first operating state university.

1796
Washington's Farewell Address as president delivered Sept. 19. Gave strong warnings against permanent alliances with foreign powers, big public debt, large military establishment and devices of "small, artful, enterprising minority" to control or change government.

1797
U.S. frigate United States launched at Philadelphia July 10; Constellation at Baltimore Sept. 7; Constitution (Old Ironsides) at Boston Sept. 20.

1798
War with France threatened over French raids on U.S. shipping and rejection of U.S. diplomats. Congress voided all treaties with France, ordered Navy to capture French armed ships. Navy (45 ships) and 365 privateers captured 84 French ships. USS Constellation took French warship Insurgente 1799. Napoleon stopped French raids after becoming First Consul.

1801
Tripoli declared war June 10 against U.S., which refused added tribute to commerce-raiding Arab corsairs. Land and naval campaigns forced Tripoli to conclude peace June 4, 1805.

1803
Supreme Court, in Marbury v. Madison case, for the first time overturned a U.S. law Feb. 24.
Napoleon, who had recovered Louisiana from Spain by secret treaty, sold all of Louisiana, stretching to Canadian border, to U.S., for $11,250,000 in bonds, plus $3,750,000 indemnities to American citizens with claims against France. U.S. took title Dec. 20. Purchases doubled U.S. area.

1804
Lewis and Clark expedition ordered by Pres. Jefferson to explore what is now northwest U.S. Started from St. Louis May 14; ended Sept. 23, 1806. Sacagawea, an Indian woman, served as guide.
Vice Pres. Aaron Burr, after long political rivalry, shot Alexander Hamilton in a duel July 11 in Weehawken, N.J.; Hamilton died the next day.

1807
Robert Fulton made first practical steamboat trip; left N.Y. City Aug. 17, reached Albany, 150 mi., in 32 hrs.

1808
Slave importation outlawed. Some 250,000 slaves were illegally imported 1808-1860.

1811
William Henry Harrison, governor of Indiana, defeated Indians under the Prophet, in battle of Tippecanoe Nov. 7.
Cumberland Road begun at Cumberland, Md.; became important route to West.

1812
War of 1812 had 3 main causes: Britain seized U.S. ships trading with France; Britain seized 4,000 naturalized U.S. sailors by 1810; Britain armed Indians who raided western border. U.S. stopped trade with Europe 1807 and 1809. Trade with Britain only was stopped, 1810.
Unaware that Britain had raised the blockade 2 days before, Congress declared war June 18 by a small majority. The West favored war, New England opposed it. The British were handicapped by war with France.
U.S. naval victories in 1812 included: USS Essex captured Alert Aug. 13; USS Constitution destroyed Guerriere Aug. 19; USS Wasp took Frolic Oct. 18; USS United States defeated Macedonian off Azores Oct. 25; Constitution beat Java Dec. 29. British captured Detroit Aug. 16.

1813
Oliver H. Perry defeated British fleet at Battle of Lake Erie, Sept. 10. U.S. victory at Battle of the Thames, Ont., Oct. 5, broke Indian allies of Britain, and made Detroit frontier safe for U.S. But Americans failed in Canadian invasion attempts. York (Toronto) and Buffalo were burned.

1814
British landed in Maryland in August, defeated U.S. force Aug. 24, burned Capitol and White House. Maryland militia stopped British advance Sept. 12. Bombardment of Ft. McHenry, Baltimore, for 25 hours, Sept. 13-14, by British fleet failed; Francis Scott Key wrote words to Star Spangled Banner.
U.S. won naval Battle of Lake Champlain Sept. 11. Peace treaty signed at Ghent Dec. 24.

1815
Some 5,300 British, unaware of peace treaty, attacked U.S. entrenchments near New Orleans, Jan. 8. British had over 2,000 casualties, Americans lost 71.
U.S. flotilla finally ended piracy by Algiers, Tunis, Tripoli by Aug. 6.

1816
Second Bank of the U.S. chartered.

1817
Rush-Bagot treaty signed Apr. 28-29; limited U.S., British armaments on the Great Lakes.

1819
Spain cedes Florida to U.S. Feb. 22.
American steamship Savannah made first part steam-powered, part sail-powered crossing of Atlantic, Savannah, Ga. to Liverpool, Eng., 29 days.

1820
Henry Clay's Missouri Compromise bill passed by Congress May 3. Slavery was allowed in Missouri, but not elsewhere west of the Mississippi River north of 36° 30′ latitude (the southern line of Missouri). Repealed 1854.

1821
Emma Willard founded Troy Female Seminary, first U.S. women's college.

1823
Monroe Doctrine enunciated Dec. 2, opposing European intervention in the Americas.

1824
Pawtucket, R.I. weavers strike in first such action by women.

1825
Erie Canal opened; first boat left Buffalo Oct. 26, reached N.Y. City Nov. 4. Canal cost $7 million but cut travel time one-third, shipping costs nine-tenths; opened Great Lakes area, made N.Y. City chief Atlantic port.
John Stevens, of Hoboken, N.J., built and operated first experimental steam locomotive in U.S.

1828
South Carolina Dec. 19 declared the right of state nullification of federal laws, opposing the "Tariff of Abominations."
Noah Webster published his American Dictionary of the English Language.
Baltimore & Ohio 1st U.S. passenger RR, was begun July 4.

1830
Mormon church organized by Joseph Smith in Fayette, N.Y. Apr. 6.

1831
Nat Turner, black slave in Virginia, led local slave rebellion, killed 57 whites in Aug. Troops called in, Turner captured, tried, and hanged.

1832
Black Hawk War (Ill.-Wis.) Apr.-Sept. pushed Sauk and Fox Indians west across Mississippi.

South Carolina convention passed Ordinance of Nullification in Nov. against permanent tariff, threatening to withdraw from the Union. Congress Feb. 1833 passed a compromise tariff act, whereupon South Carolina repealed its act.

1833
Oberlin College, first in U.S. to adopt coeducation; refused to bar students on account of race, 1835.

1835
Texas proclaimed right to secede from Mexico; Sam Houston put in command of Texas army, Nov. 2-4.

Gold discovered on Cherokee land in Georgia. Indians forced to cede lands Dec. 20 and to cross Mississippi.

1836
Texans besieged in Alamo in San Antonio by Mexicans under Santa Anna Feb. 23-Mar. 6; entire garrison killed. Texas independence declared, Mar. 2. At San Jacinto Apr. 21 Sam Houston and Texans defeated Mexicans.

Marcus Whitman, H.H. Spaulding and wives reached Fort Walla Walla on Columbia River, Oregon. First white women to cross plains.

Seminole Indians in Florida under Osceola began attacks Nov. 1, protesting forced removal. The unpopular 8-year war ended Aug. 14, 1842; Indians were sent to Oklahoma. War cost the U.S. 1,500 soldiers.

1841
First emigrant wagon train for California, 47 persons, left Independence, Mo. May 1, reached Cal. Nov. 4.

Brook Farm commune set up by New England transcendentalist intellectuals. Lasts to 1846.

1842
Webster-Ashburton Treaty signed Aug. 9, fixing the U.S.-Canada border in Maine and Minnesota.

First use of anesthetic (sulphuric ether gas).

Settlement of Oregon begins via Oregon Trail.

1844
First message over first telegraph line sent May 24 by inventor Samuel F.B. Morse from Washington to Baltimore: "What hath God wrought!"

1845
Texas Congress voted for annexation to U.S. July 4. U.S. Congress admits Texas to Union Dec. 29.

1846
Mexican War. Pres. James K. Polk ordered Gen. Zachary Taylor to seize disputed Texan land settled by Mexicans. After border clash, U.S. declared war May 13; Mexico May 23. Northern Whigs opposed war, southerners backed it.

Bear flag of Republic of California raised by American settlers at Sonoma June 14.

About 12,000 U.S. troops took Vera Cruz Mar. 27, 1847. Mexico City Sept. 14, 1847. By treaty, Feb. 1848, Mexico ceded claims to Texas, California, Arizona, New Mexico, Nevada, Utah, part of Colorado. U.S. assumed $3 million American claims and paid Mexico $15 million.

Treaty with Great Britain June 15 set boundary in Oregon territory at 49th parallel (extension of existing line). Expansionists had used slogan "54° 40' or fight."

Mormons, after violent clashes with settlers over polygamy, left Nauvoo, Ill. for West under Brigham Young, settled July 1847 at Salt Lake City, Utah.

Elias Howe invented sewing machine.

1847
First adhesive U.S. postage stamps on sale July 1; Benjamin Franklin 5¢, Washington 10¢.

Ralph Waldo Emerson published first book of poems; Henry Wadsworth Longfellow published Evangeline.

1848
Gold discovered Jan. 24 in California; 80,000 prospectors emigrate in 1849.

Lucretia Mott and Elizabeth Cady Stanton lead Seneca Falls, N.Y. Women's Rights Convention July 19-20.

1850
Sen. Henry Clay's Compromise of 1850 admitted California as 31st state Sept. 9, slavery forbidden; made Utah and New Mexico territories without decision on slavery; made Fugitive Slave Law more harsh; ended District of Columbia slave trade.

1851
Herman Melville's Moby Dick, Nathaniel Hawthorne's House of the Seven Gables published.

1852
Uncle Tom's Cabin, by Harriet Beecher Stowe, published.

1853
Commodore Matthew C. Perry, U.S.N., received by Lord of Toda, Japan July 14; negotiated treaty to open Japan to U.S. ships.

1854
Republican party formed at Ripon, Wis. Feb. 28. Opposed Kansas-Nebraska Act (became law May 30) which left issue of slavery to vote of settlers.

Henry David Thoreau published Walden.

1855
Walt Whitman published Leaves of Grass.

First railroad train crossed Mississippi on the river's first bridge, Rock Island, Ill.-Davenport, Ia. Apr. 21.

1856
Republican party's first nominee for president, John C. Fremont, defeated. Abraham Lincoln made 50 speeches for him.

Lawrence, Kan. sacked May 21 by slavery party; abolitionist John Brown led anti-slavery men against Missourians at Osawatomie, Kan. Aug. 30

1857
Dred Scott decision by U.S. Supreme Court Mar. 6 held, 6-3, that a slave did not become free when taken into a free state. Congress could not bar slavery from a territory, and blacks could not be citizens.

1858
First Atlantic cable completed by Cyrus W. Field Aug. 5; cable failed Sept. 1.

Lincoln-Douglas debates in Illinois Aug. 21-Oct. 15.

1859
First commercially productive oil well, drilled near Titusville, Pa., by Edwin L. Drake Aug. 27.

Abolitionist John Brown with 21 men seized U.S. Armory at Harpers Ferry (then Va.) Oct. 16. U.S. Marines captured raiders, killing several. Brown was hanged for treason by Virginia Dec. 2.

1860
New England shoe-workers, 20,000, strike, win higher wages.

Abraham Lincoln, Republican, elected president in 4-way race.

First Pony Express between Sacramento, Cal. and St. Joseph, Mo. started Apr. 3; service ended Oct. 24, 1861 when first transcontinental telegraph line was completed.

1861
Seven southern states set up Confederate States of America Feb. 8, with Jefferson Davis as president. Civil War began as Confederates fired on Ft. Sumter in Charleston, S.C. Apr. 12; they captured it Apr. 14.

President Lincoln called for 75,000 volunteers Apr. 15. By May, 11 states had seceded. Lincoln blockaded southern ports Apr. 19, cutting off vital exports, aid.

Confederates repelled Union forces at first Battle of Bull Run July 21.

First transcontinental telegraph was put in operation.

1862
Homestead Act was approved May 20; it granted free

family farms to settlers.

Land Grant Act approved **July 7**, providing for public land sale to benefit agricultural education; eventually led to establishment of state university systems.

Union forces were victorious in western campaigns, took New Orleans. Battles in East were inconclusive.

1863

Lincoln issued **Emancipation Proclamation Jan. 1**, freeing "all slaves in areas still in rebellion."

The entire **Mississippi River** was in Union hands by **July 4**. Union forces won a major victory at **Gettysburg, Pa. July 1-July 4**. Lincoln read his Gettysburg Address **Nov. 19**.

Draft riots in N.Y. City killed about 1,000, including blacks who were hanged by mobs **July 13-16**. Rioters protested provision allowing money payment in place of service. Such payments were ended 1864.

1864

Gen. **Sherman marched through Georgia**, taking Atlanta **Sept. 1**, Savannah **Dec. 22**.

Sand Creek massacre of Cheyenne and Arapaho Indians **Nov. 29** in a raid by 900 cavalrymen who killed 150-500 men, women, and children; 9 soldiers died. The tribes were awaiting surrender terms when attacked.

1865

Robert E. Lee surrendered 27,800 Confederate troops to Grant at Appomattox Court House, Va. **Apr. 9**. J.E. Johnston surrendered 31,200 to Sherman at Durham Station, N.C. **Apr. 18**. Last rebel troops surrendered **May 26**.

President **Lincoln was shot Apr. 14** by John Wilkes Booth in Ford's Theater, Washington; died the following morning. Booth was reported dead **Apr. 26**. Four co-conspirators were hanged **July 7**.

Thirteenth Amendment, abolishing slavery, took effect **Dec. 18**.

1866

First post of the **Grand Army of the Republic** formed **Apr. 6**; was a major national political force for years. Last encampment, **Aug. 31, 1949**, attended by 6 of the 16 surviving veterans.

Ku Klux Klan formed secretly in South to terrorize blacks who voted. Disbanded **1869-71**. A second Klan was organized 1915.

Congress took control of southern Reconstruction, backed freedmen's rights.

1867

Alaska sold to U.S. by Russia for $7.2 million **Mar. 30** through efforts of Sec. of State William H. Seward.

Horatio Alger published first book, *Ragged Dick*.

The **Grange** was organized **Dec 4**, to protect farmer interests.

1868

The **World Almanac**, a publication of the *New York World*, appeared for the first time.

Pres. **Andrew Johnson** tried to remove Edwin M. Stanton, secretary of war; was impeached by House **Feb. 24** for violation of Tenure of Office Act; acquitted by Senate **March-May**. Stanton resigned.

1869

Financial "**Black Friday**" in New York **Sept. 24**; caused by attempt to "corner" gold.

Transcontinental railroad completed; golden spike driven at Promontory, Utah **May 10** marking the junction of Central Pacific and Union Pacific.

Knights of Labor formed in Philadelphia. By **1886**, it had 700,000 members nationally.

Woman suffrage law passed in Territory of Wyoming **Dec. 10**.

1871

Great fire destroyed Chicago Oct. 8-11; loss est. at $196 million.

1872

Amnesty Act restored civil rights to citizens of the South **May 22** except for 500 Confederate leaders.

Congress founded first national park — **Yellowstone** in Wyoming.

1873

First U.S. **postal card** issued **May 1**.

Banks failed, panic began in **Sept.** Depression lasted 5 years.

"**Boss**" **William Tweed** of N.Y. City convicted of stealing public funds. He died in jail in **1878**.

Bellevue Hospital in N.Y. City started the first **school of nursing**.

1875

Congress passed **Civil Rights Act Mar. 1** giving equal rights to blacks in public accommodations and jury duty. Act invalidated in 1883 by Supreme Court.

First **Kentucky Derby** held **May 17** at Churchill Downs, Louisville, Ky.

1876

Samuel J. Tilden, Democrat, received majority of popular votes for president over **Rutherford B. Hayes**, Republican, but 22 electoral votes were in dispute; issue left to Congress. Hayes given presidency in **Feb., 1877** after Republicans agree to end Reconstruction of South.

Col. **George A. Custer** and 264 soldiers of the 7th Cavalry killed **June 25** in "last stand," Battle of the Little Big Horn, Mont., in Sioux Indian War.

Mark Twain published *Tom Sawyer*.

1877

Molly Maguires, Irish terrorist society in Scranton, Pa. mining areas, broken up by hanging of 11 leaders for murders of mine officials and police.

Pres. Hayes sent troops in violent national **railroad strike**.

1878

First commercial **telephone** exchange opened, New Haven, Conn. **Jan. 28**.

1879

F.W. Woolworth opened his first five-and-ten store in Utica, N.Y. **Feb. 22**.

Henry George published *Progress & Poverty*, advocating single tax on land.

1881

Pres. **James A. Garfield shot** in Washington, D.C. **July 2**; died **Sept. 19**.

Booker T. Washington founded Tuskegee Institute for blacks.

Helen Hunt Jackson published *A Century of Dishonor* about mistreatment of Indians.

1883

Pendleton Act, passed **Jan. 16**, reformed federal civil service.

Brooklyn Bridge opened **May 24**.

1886

Haymarket riot and bombing, evening of **May 4**, followed bitter labor battles for 8-hour day in Chicago; 7 police and 4 workers died, 66 wounded. Eight anarchists found guilty. Gov. John P. Altgeld denounced trial as unfair.

Geronimo, Apache Indian, finally surrendered **Sept. 4**.

American Federation of Labor (AFL) formed **Dec. 8** by 25 craft unions.

1888

Great blizzard in eastern U.S. **Mar. 11-14**; 400 deaths.

1889

Johnstown, Pa. **flood May 31**; 2,200 lives lost.

1890

First execution by **electrocution**: William Kemmler **Aug. 6** at Auburn Prison, Auburn, N.Y., for murder.

Battle of **Wounded Knee**, S.D. **Dec. 29**, the last major conflict between Indians and U.S. troops. About 200 Indian men, women, and children, and 29 soldiers were killed.

Castle Garden closed as N.Y. immigration depot; **Ellis Island** opened **Dec. 31**, closed 1954.

Sherman Antitrust Act begins federal effort to curb monopolies.

Jacob Riis published *How the Other Half Lives*, about city slums.

1892

Homestead, Pa., strike at Carnegie steel mills; 7 guards and 11 strikers and spectators shot to death **July 6**; setback for unions.

1893

Financial panic began, led to 4-year depression.

1894

Thomas A. Edison's kinetoscope (motion pictures) (invented 1887) given first public showing Apr. 14.

Jacob S. Coxey led 500 unemployed from the Midwest into Washington, D.C. Apr. 29. Coxey was arrested for trespassing on Capitol grounds.

1896

William Jennings Bryan delivered "Cross of Gold" into Washington, D.C. Apr. 29. Coxey was arrested for trespassing on Capitol grounds.

Supreme Court, in Plessy v. Ferguson, approved racial segregation under the "separate but equal" doctrine.

1898

U.S. battleship Maine blown up Feb. 15 at Havana, 260 killed.

U.S. blockaded Cuba Apr. 22 in aid of independence forces. U.S. declared war on Spain. Apr. 24, destroyed Spanish fleet in Philippines May 1, took Guam June 20.

Puerto Rico taken by U.S. July 25-Aug. 12. Spain agreed Dec. 10 to cede Philippines, Puerto Rico, and Guam, and approved independence for Cuba.

U.S. annexed independent republic of Hawaii.

1899

Filipino insurgents, unable to get recognition of independence from U.S., started guerrilla war Feb. 4. Crushed with capture May 23, 1901 of leader, Emilio Aguinaldo.

U.S. declared Open Door Policy to make China an open international market and to preserve its integrity as a nation.

John Dewey published School and Society, backing progressive education.

1900

Carry Nation, Kansas anti-saloon agitator, began raiding with hatchet.

U.S. helped suppress "Boxers" in Peking.

1901

Pres. William McKinley was shot Sept. 6 by an anarchist, Leon Czolgosz; died Sept. 14.

1903

Treaty between U.S. and Colombia to have U.S. dig Panama Canal signed Jan. 22, rejected by Colombia. Panama declared independence with U.S. support Nov. 3; recognized by Pres. Theodore Roosevelt Nov. 6. U.S., Panama signed canal treaty Nov. 18.

Wisconsin set first direct primary voting system May 23.

First automobile trip across U.S. from San Francisco to New York May 23-Aug. 1.

First successful flight in heavier-than-air mechanically propelled airplane by Orville Wright Dec. 17 near Kitty Hawk, N.C., 120 ft. in 12 seconds. Fourth flight same day by Wilbur Wright, 852 ft. in 59 seconds. Improved plane patented May 22, 1906.

Jack London published Call of the Wild.

Great Train Robbery, pioneering film, produced.

1904

Ida Tarbell published muckraking History of Standard Oil.

1905

First Rotary Club of businessmen founded in Chicago.

1906

San Francisco earthquake and fire Apr. 18-19 left 503 dead, $350 million damages.

Pure Food and Drug Act and Meat Inspection Act both passed June 30.

1907

Financial panic and depression started Mar. 13.

First round-world cruise of U.S. "Great White Fleet"; 16 battleships, 12,000 men.

1909

Adm. Robert E. Peary reached North Pole Apr. 6 on 6th attempt, accompanied by Matthew Henson, a black man, and 4 Eskimos.

National Conference on the Negro convened May 30, leading to founding of the National Association for the Advancement of Colored People.

1910

Boy Scouts of America founded Feb. 8.

1911

Supreme Court dissolved Standard Oil Co.

First transcontinental airplane flight (with numerous stops) by C.P. Rodgers, New York to Pasadena, Sept. 17-Nov. 5; time in air 82 hrs., 4 min.

1912

Amer. Girl Guides founded Mar. 12; name changed in 1913 to Girl Scouts.

U.S. sent marines Aug. 14 to Nicaragua, which was in default of loans to U.S. and Europe.

1913

N.Y. Armory Show brought modern art to U.S. Feb. 17.

U.S. blockaded Mexico in support of revolutionaries.

Charles Beard published his Economic Interpretation of the Constitution.

Federal Reserve System was authorized Dec. 23, in a major reform of U.S. banking and finance.

1914

Ford Motor Co. raised basic wage rates from $2.40 for 9-hr. day to $5 for 8-hr. day Jan. 5.

When U.S. sailors were arrested at Tampico Apr. 9, Atlantic fleet was sent to Veracruz, occupied city.

Pres. Wilson proclaimed U.S. neutrality in the European war Aug. 4.

The Clayton Antitrust Act was passed Oct. 15, strengthening federal anti-monopoly powers.

1915

First telephone talk, New York to San Francisco, Jan. 25 by Alexander Graham Bell and Thomas A. Watson.

British ship Lusitania sunk May 7 by German submarine; 128 American passengers lost (Germany had warned passengers in advance). As a result of U.S. campaign, Germany issued apology and promise of payments Oct. 5. Pres. Wilson asked for a military fund increase Dec. 7.

U.S. troops landed in Haiti July 28. Haiti became a virtual U.S. protectorate under Sept. 16 treaty.

1916

Gen. John J. Pershing entered Mexico to pursue Francisco (Pancho) Villa, who had raided U.S. border areas. Forces withdrawn Feb. 5, 1917.

Rural Credits Act passed July 17, followed by Warehouse Act. Aug. 11; both provided financial aid to farmers.

Bomb exploded during San Francisco Preparedness Day parade July 22, killed 10. Thomas J. Mooney, labor organizer, and Warren K. Billings, shoe worker, were convicted; both pardoned in 1939.

U.S. bought Virgin Islands from Denmark Aug. 4.

Jeanette Rankin, 1st U.S. Congresswoman (R-Montana) elected.

U.S. established military government in the Dominican Republic Nov. 29.

Trade and loans to European Allies soared during the year.

John Dewey published Democracy and Education.

Carl Sandburg published Chicago Poems.

1917

Germany, suffering from British blockade, declared almost unrestricted submarine warfare Jan. 31. U.S. cut diplomatic ties with Germany Feb. 3, and formally declared war Apr. 6.

Conscription law was passed May 18. First U.S. troops arrived in Europe June 26.

The 18th (Prohibition) Amendment to the Constitution was submitted to the states by Congress Dec. 18. On Jan. 16, 1919, the 36th state (Nevada) ratified it. Franklin D. Roosevelt, as 1932 presidential candidate, endorsed repeal; 21st Amendment repealed 18th; ratification completed Dec. 5, 1933.

1918

Over one million **American troops** were in Europe by July. War ended **Nov. 11.**

Influenza epidemic killed an estimated 20 million worldwide, 548,000 in U.S.

1919

First transatlantic flight, by U.S. Navy seaplane, left Rockaway, N.Y. **May 8,** stopped at Newfoundland, Azores, Lisbon **May 27.**

Boston police strike Sept. 9; National Guard breaks strike.

Sherwood Anderson published *Winesburg, Ohio.*

About 250 **alien radicals** were deported **Dec. 22.**

1920

In national **Red Scare,** some 2,700 Communists, anarchists, and other radicals were arrested **Jan.-May.**

Senate refused Mar. 19 to ratify the **League of Nations** Covenant.

Nicola Sacco, 29, shoe factory employee and radical agitator, and **Bartolomeo Vanzetti,** 32, fish peddler and anarchist, accused of killing 2 men in Mass. payroll holdup **Apr. 15.** Found guilty **1921.** A 6-year worldwide campaign for release on grounds of want of conclusive evidence and prejudice failed. Both were executed **Aug. 23, 1927.** Vindicated July 19, 1977 by proclamation of Mass. Gov. Dukakis.

First regular licensed **radio broadcasting** begun **Aug. 20.**

19th Amendment ratified **Aug. 26,** giving women right to vote.

League of Women Voters founded.

Wall St., N.Y. City, **bomb** explosion killed 30, injured 100, did $2 million damage **Sept. 16.**

Sinclair Lewis' *Main Street,* F. Scott Fitzgerald's *This Side of Paradise* published.

1921

Congress sharply curbed **immigration,** set national quota system **May 19.**

Joint Congressional resolution declaring **peace with Germany,** Austria, and Hungary signed **July 2** by Pres. Harding; treaties were signed in **Aug.**

Limitation of Armaments Conference met in Washington **Nov. 12 to Feb. 6, 1922.** Major powers agreed to curtail naval construction, outlaw poison gas, restrict submarine attack on merchantmen, respect integrity of China.

Ku Klux Klan began revival with violence against blacks in North, South, and Midwest.

1922

Violence during **coal-mine strike** at Herrin, Ill., **June 22-23** cost 36 lives, 21 of them non-union miners.

Reader's Digest founded.

1923

First **sound-on-film motion picture,** "Phonofilm" was shown by Lee de Forest at Rivoli Theater, N.Y. City, beginning in **April.**

1924

Law approved by Congress **June 15** making all **Indians citizens.**

Nellie Tayloe Ross elected governor of Wyoming **Nov. 9** after death of her husband **Oct. 2;** installed **Jan. 5, 1925,** first woman governor. **Miriam (Ma) Ferguson** was elected governor of Texas **Nov. 9;** installed **Jan. 20, 1925.**

George Gershwin wrote *Rhapsody in Blue.*

1925

John T. Scopes found guilty of having taught evolution in Dayton, Tenn. high school, fined $100 and costs **July 24.**

1926

Dr. Robert H. Goddard demonstrated practicality of rockets **Mar. 16** at Auburn, Mass. with first liquid fuel rocket; rocket traveled 184 ft. in 2.5 secs.

Air Commerce Act passed, providing federal aid for airlines and airports.

1927

About 1,000 **marines** landed in China **Mar. 5** to protect property in civil war.

Capt. **Charles A. Lindbergh** left Roosevelt Field, N.Y. **May 20** alone in plane Spirit of St. Louis on first New York-Paris nonstop flight. Reached Le Bourget airfield **May 21,** 3,610 miles in 33½ hours.

The Jazz Singer, with **Al Jolson,** demonstrated part-talking pictures in N.Y. City **Oct. 6.**

Show Boat opened in New York **Dec. 27.**

O. E. Rolvaag published *Giants in the Earth.*

1929

"St. Valentine's Day massacre" in Chicago **Feb. 14;** gangsters killed 7 rivals.

Farm price stability aided by **Agricultural Marketing Act,** passed **June 15.**

Albert B. Fall, former sec. of the interior, was convicted of accepting a bribe of $100,000 in the leasing of the **Elk Hills (Teapot Dome)** naval oil reserve; sentenced **Nov. 1** to $100,000 fine and year in prison.

Stock Market crash Oct. 29 marked end of postwar prosperity as stock prices plummeted. Stock losses for 1929-31 estimated at $50 billion; worst American depression began.

Thomas Wolfe published *Look Homeward, Angel.* William Faulkner published *The Sound and the Fury.*

1930

London Naval Reduction Treaty signed by U.S., Britain, Italy, France, and Japan **Apr. 22;** in effect **Jan. 1, 1931;** expired **Dec. 31, 1936.**

Hawley-Smoot Tariff signed; rate hikes slash world trade.

1931

Empire State Building opened in N.Y. City **May 1.**

Pearl Buck published *The Good Earth.*

1932

Reconstruction Finance Corp. established **Jan. 22** to stimulate banking and business. Unemployment at 12 million.

Charles Lindbergh Jr. kidnaped Mar. 1, found dead **May 12.**

Bonus March on Washington **May 29** by World War I veterans demanding Congress pay their bonus in full.

1933

FDR named **Frances Perkins** U.S. Secy of Labor; 1st woman in U.S. Cabinet.

All banks in the U.S. were ordered closed by Pres. Roosevelt **Mar. 6.**

In the **"100 days"** special session, **Mar. 9—June 16,** Congress passed **New Deal** social and economic measures.

Gold standard dropped by U.S.; announced by Pres. Roosevelt **Apr. 19,** ratified by Congress **June 5.**

Prohibition ended in the U.S. as 36th state ratified 21st Amendment **Dec. 5.**

U.S. foreswore armed intervention in **Western Hemisphere** nations **Dec. 26.**

1934

U.S. troops pull out of Haiti **Aug. 6.**

1935

Comedian **Will Rogers** and aviator **Wiley Post** killed **Aug. 15** in Alaska plane crash.

Social Security Act passed by Congress **Aug. 14.**

Huey Long, Senator from Louisiana and national political leader, was assassinated **Sept. 8.**

Porgy and Bess, George Gershwin opera on American theme, opened **Oct. 10** in N.Y. City.

Committee for Industrial Organization (CIO) formed to expand industrial unionism **Nov. 9.**

1936

Boulder Dam completed.

Margaret Mitchell published *Gone With the Wind.*

1937

Amelia Earhart Putnam, aviator, and co-pilot Fred Noonan lost **July 2** near Howland Is. in the Pacific.

Pres. Roosevelt asked for 6 additional Supreme Court justices; "packing" plan defeated.

Auto, steel labor unions won first big contracts.

1938

Naval Expansion Act passed **May 17.**

National minimum wage enacted **June 28.**

Orson Welles radio dramatization of *War of the Worlds* caused nationwide scare **Oct. 30.**

1939
Pres. Roosevelt asked **defense budget hike** Jan. 5, 12.

N.Y. World's Fair opened Apr. 30, closed Oct. 31; reopened May 11, 1940, and finally closed Oct. 21.

Einstein alerts FDR to A-bomb opportunity in Aug. 2 letter.

U.S. **declares its neutrality** in European war Sept. 5.

Roosevelt proclaimed a limited **national emergency** Sept. 8, an unlimited emergency May 27, 1941. Both ended by Pres. Truman Apr. 28, 1952.

John Steinbeck published *Grapes of Wrath.*

1940
U.S. okayed sale of **surplus war material** to Britain June 3; announced transfer of 50 overaged destroyers Sept. 3.

First **peacetime draft** approved Sept. 14.

Richard Wright published *Native Son.*

1941
The **Four Freedoms** termed essential by Pres. Roosevelt in speech to Congress Jan. 6: freedom of speech and religion, freedom from want and fear.

Lend-Lease Act signed Mar. 11, providing $7 billion in military credits for Britain. Lend-Lease for USSR approved in Nov.

U.S. occupied **Iceland** July 7.

The **Atlantic Charter,** 8-point declaration of principles, issued by Roosevelt and Winston Churchill Aug. 14.

Japan attacked **Pearl Harbor,** Hawaii, 7:55 a.m. Dec. 7, 19 ships sunk or damaged, 2,300 dead. U.S. declared war on Japan Dec. 8, on Germany and Italy Dec. 11 after those countries declared war.

1942
Federal government forcibly moved 110,000 **Japanese-Americans** (including 75,000 U.S. citizens) from West Coast to detention camps. Exclusion lasted 3 years.

Battle of **Midway** June 4-7 was Japan's first major defeat.

Marines landed on **Guadalcanal** Aug. 7; last Japanese not expelled until Feb. 9, 1943.

U.S., Britain invaded North Africa Nov. 8.

First **nuclear chain reaction** (fission of uranium isotope U-235) produced at Univ. of Chicago, under physicists Arthur Compton, Enrico Fermi, others Dec. 2.

1943
All war contractors barred from **racial discrimination** May 27.

Pres. Roosevelt signed June 10 the pay-as-you-go income tax bill. Starting July 1 wage and salary earners were subject to a **paycheck withholding** tax.

Race riot in Detroit June 21; 34 dead, 700 injured. Riot in Harlem section of N.Y. City; 6 killed.

U.S. troops invaded Italy Sept. 9.

Marines advanced in **Gilbert Is.** in Nov.

1944
U.S., Allied forces invaded Europe at **Normandy** June 6.

G.I. Bill of Rights signed June 22, providing veterans benefits.

U.S. forces landed on **Leyte,** Philippines Oct. 20.

1945
Yalta Conference met in the Crimea, USSR, Feb. 3-11. Roosevelt, Churchill, and Stalin agreed Russia would enter war against Japan.

Marines landed on **Iwo Jima** Feb. 19; U.S. forces invaded **Okinawa** Apr. 1.

Pres. **Roosevelt,** 63, **died** of cerebral hemorrhage in Warm Springs, Ga. Apr. 12; V.P. **Harry S. Truman** became pres.

Germany surrendered May 7.

First **atomic bomb,** produced at Los Alamos, N.M., exploded at Alamogordo, N.M. July 16. Bomb dropped on **Hiroshima** Aug. 6, on **Nagasaki** Aug. 9. Japan surrendered Aug. 15.

U.S. forces entered **Korea** south of 38th parallel to displace Japanese Sept. 8.

Gen. **Douglas MacArthur** took over supervision of Japan Sept. 9.

1946
Strike by 400,000 **mine workers** began Apr. 1; other industries followed.

Philippines given independence by U.S. July 4.

1947
Truman Doctrine: Pres. Truman asked Congress to aid Greece and Turkey to combat Communist terrorism Mar. 12. Approved May 15.

United Nations Security Council voted unanimously Apr. 2 to place under U.S. **trusteeship** the Pacific islands formerly mandated to Japan.

Jackie Robinson on Brooklyn Dodgers Apr. 11, broke the color barrier in major league baseball.

Taft-Hartley Labor Act curbing strikes was vetoed by Truman June 20; Congress overrode the veto.

Proposals later known as the **Marshall Plan,** under which the U.S. would extend aid to European countries, were made by Sec. of State George C. Marshall June 5. Congress authorized some $12 billion in next 4 years.

1948
USSR began a land **blockade of Berlin's** Allied sectors Apr. 1. This blockade and Western counter-blockade were lifted Sept. 30, 1949, after British and U.S. planes had lifted 2,343,315 tons of food and coal into the city.

Organization of American States founded Apr. 30.

Alger Hiss, former State Dept. official, indicted Dec. 15 for perjury, after denying he had passed secret documents to Whittaker Chambers for transmission to a communist spy ring. His second trial ended in conviction Jan. 21, 1950, and a sentence of 5 years in prison.

Kinsey Report on Sexuality in the Human Male published.

1949
U.S. troops withdrawn from **Korea** June 29.

North Atlantic Treaty Organization (**NATO**) established Aug. 24 by U.S., Canada, and 10 West European nations, agreeing that an armed attack against one or more of them would be considered an attack against all.

Mrs. I. Toguri D'Aquino (**Tokyo Rose** of Japanese wartime broadcasts) was sentenced Oct. 7 to 10 years in prison for treason. Paroled 1956, pardoned 1977.

Eleven leaders of **U.S. Communist party** convicted Oct. 14, after 9-month trial in N.Y. City, of advocating violent overthrow of U.S. government. Ten defendants sentenced to 5 years in prison each and the 11th to 3 years. Supreme Court upheld the convictions June 4, 1951.

1950
U.S. **Jan 14** recalled all consular officials from China after the latter seized the American consulate general in Peking.

Masked bandits robbed **Brink's Inc.,** Boston express office, Jan. 17 of $2.8 million, of which $1.2 million was in cash. Case solved 1956, 8 sentenced to life.

Pres. Truman authorized production of **H-bomb** Jan. 31.

United Nations asked for troops to restore Korea peace June 25.

Truman ordered Air Force and Navy to **Korea** June 27 after North Korea invaded South. Truman approved ground forces, air strikes against North June 30.

U.S. sent 35 military advisers to **South Vietnam** June 27, and agreed to provide military and economic aid to anti-Communist government.

Army seized all **railroads** Aug. 27 on Truman's order to prevent a general strike; roads returned to owners in 1952.

U.S. forces landed at **Inchon** Sept. 15; UN force took Pyongyang Oct. 20, reached China border Nov. 20, China sent troops across border Nov. 26.

Two members of a **Puerto Rican nationalist** movement tried to kill Pres. Truman **Nov. 1.** (see Assassinations)

U.S. **Dec. 8** banned shipments to **Communist China** and to Asiatic ports trading with it.

1951

Sen. **Estes Kefauver** led Senate investigation into organized crime. Preliminary report **Feb. 28** said gambling take was over $20 billion a year.

Julius Rosenberg, his wife, Ethel, and Morton Sobell, all U.S. citizens, were found guilty **Mar. 29** of conspiracy to commit wartime espionage. Rosenbergs sentenced to death, Sobell to 30 years. Rosenbergs **executed June 19, 1953.** Sobell released **Jan. 14, 1969.**

Gen. **Douglas MacArthur** was removed from his Korea command **Apr. 11** for unauthorized policy statements.

Korea cease-fire talks began in July; lasted 2 years. **Fighting ended July 27, 1953.**

Tariff concessions by the U.S. to the Soviet Union, Communist China, and all communist-dominated lands were suspended **Aug. 1.**

The U.S., **Australia,** and **New Zealand** signed a mutual security pact **Sept. 1.**

Transcontinental television inaugurated **Sept. 4** with Pres. Truman's address at the Japanese Peace Treaty Conference in San Francisco.

Japanese Peace Treaty signed in San Francisco **Sept. 8** by U.S., Japan, and 47 other nations.

J.D. Salinger published *Catcher in the Rye.*

1952

U.S. seizure of nation's steel mills was ordered by Pres. Truman **Apr. 8** to avert a strike. Ruled illegal by Supreme Court **June 2.**

Peace contract between West Germany, U.S., Great Britain, and France was signed **May 26.**

The last racial and ethnic barriers to naturalization were removed, **June 26-27,** with the passage of the **Immigration and Naturalization Act of 1952.**

First **hydrogen device** explosion **Nov. 1** at Eniwetok Atoll in Pacific.

1953

Pres. Eisenhower announced **May 8** that U.S. had given France $60 million for **Indochina War.** More aid was announced in **Sept.** In **1954** it was reported that three fourths of the war's costs were met by U.S.

1954

Nautilus, first atomic-powered submarine, was launched at Groton, Conn. **Jan. 21.**

Five members of Congress were wounded in the House **Mar. 1** by 4 **Puerto Rican independence supporters** who fired at random from a spectators' gallery.

Sen. **Joseph McCarthy** led televised hearings **Apr. 22-June 17** into alleged Communist influence in the Army.

Racial segregation in public schools was unanimously ruled unconstitutional by the Supreme Court **May 17,** as a violation of the 14th Amendment clause guaranteeing equal protection of the laws.

Southeast Asia Treaty Organization **(SEATO)** formed by collective defense pact signed in Manila **Sept. 8** by the U.S., Britain, France, Australia, New Zealand, Philippines, Pakistan, and Thailand.

Condemnation of **Sen. Joseph R. McCarthy (R., Wis.)** voted by Senate, 67-22 **Dec. 2** for contempt of a Senate elections subcommittee, for abuse of its members, and for insults to the Senate during his Army investigation hearings.

1955

U.S. agreed **Feb. 12** to help train **South Vietnamese** army.

Supreme Court ordered **"all deliberate speed"** in integration of public schools **May 31.**

A **summit meeting** of leaders of U.S., Britain, France, and USSR took place **July 18-23** in Geneva, Switzerland.

Rosa Parks refused **Dec. 1** to give her seat to a white man on a bus in Montgomery, Ala. Bus segregation ordinance declared unconstitutional by a federal court following boycott and NAACP protest.

Merger of America's 2 largest labor organizations was effected **Dec. 5** under the name American Federation of Labor and Congress of Industrial Organizations. The merged **AFL-CIO** had a membership estimated at 15 million.

1956

Massive resistance to Supreme Court desegregation rulings was called for **Mar. 12** by 101 Southern congressmen.

Federal-Aid **Highway Act** signed **June 29,** inaugurating interstate highway system.

First transatlantic **telephone cable** went into operation **Sept. 25.**

1957

Congress approved first **civil rights bill** for blacks since Reconstruction **Apr. 29,** to protect voting rights.

National Guardsmen, called out by Arkansas Gov. Orval Faubus **Sept. 4,** barred 9 black students from entering previously all-white Central High School in **Little Rock.** Faubus complied **Sept. 21** with a federal court order to remove the National Guardsmen. The blacks entered school **Sept. 23** but were ordered to withdraw by local authorities because of fear of mob violence. Pres. Eisenhower sent federal troops **Sept. 24** to enforce the court's order.

Jack Kerouac published *On the Road.*

1958

First U.S. earth satellite to go into orbit, **Explorer I,** launched by Army **Jan. 31** at Cape Canaveral, Fla.; discovered Van Allen radiation belt.

Five thousand U.S. Marines sent to **Lebanon** to protect elected government from threatened overthrow **July-Oct.**

First domestic jet airline passenger service in U.S. opened by National Airlines **Dec. 10** between N.Y. and Miami.

1959

Alaska admitted as 49th state **Jan. 3;** Hawaii admitted **Aug. 21.**

St. Lawrence Seaway opened **Apr. 25.**

The **George Washington,** first U.S. ballistic-missile submarine, launched at Groton, Conn. **June 9.**

N.S. Savannah, world's first atomic-powered merchant ship, launched **July 21** at Camden, N.J.

Soviet Premier **Khrushchev** paid unprecedented visit to U.S. **Sept. 15-27,** made transcontinental tour.

1960

Sit-ins began **Feb. 1** when 4 black college students in Greensboro, N.C. refused to move from a Woolworth lunch counter when denied service. By **Sept. 1961** more than 70,000 students, whites and blacks, had participated in sit-ins.

U.S. launched first **weather satellite,** Tiros I, **Apr. 1.**

Congress approved a strong **voting rights act Apr. 21.**

A **U-2 reconnaissance plane** of the U.S. was shot down in the Soviet Union **May 1.** The incident led to cancellation of an imminent Paris summit conference.

Mobs attacked U.S. embassy in **Panama Sept. 17** in dispute over flying of U.S. and Panamanian flags.

U.S. announced **Dec. 15** it backed rightist group in **Laos,** which took power the next day.

1961

The U.S. severed diplomatic and consular relations with **Cuba Jan. 3,** after disputes over nationalizations of U.S. firms, U.S. military presence at Guantanamo base, etc.

Invasion of Cuba's **"Bay of Pigs" Apr. 17** by Cuban exiles trained, armed, and directed by the U.S., attempting to overthrow the regime of Premier Fidel Castro, was repulsed.

Commander Alan B. Shepard Jr. was rocketed from Cape Canaveral, Fla., 116.5 mi. above the earth in a Mercury capsule **May 5** in the first U.S. manned sub-orbital space flight.

1962

Lt. Col. John H. Glenn Jr. became the first American in orbit **Feb. 20** when he circled the earth 3 times in the Mercury capsule **Friendship 7.**

Pres. Kennedy said **Feb. 14** U.S. military advisers in Vietnam would fire if fired upon.

Supreme Court **Mar. 26** backed **one-man one-vote** apportionment of seats in state legislatures.

First U.S. **communications** satellite launched in **July.**

James Meredith became first black student at Univ. of Mississippi **Oct. 1** after 3,000 troops put down riots.

A Soviet **offensive missile buildup** in Cuba was revealed **Oct. 22** by Pres. Kennedy, who ordered a naval and air quarantine on shipment of offensive military equipment to the island. Kennedy and Soviet Premier Khrushchev reached agreement **Oct. 28** on a formula to end the crisis. Kennedy announced **Nov. 2** that Soviet missile bases in Cuba were being dismantled.

Rachel Carson's *Silent Spring* launched environmentalist movement.

1963

Supreme Court ruled **Mar. 18** that all **criminal defendants** must have counsel and that illegally acquired evidence was not admissible in state as well as federal courts.

Supreme Court ruled, 8-1, **June 17** that laws requiring **recitation of the Lord's Prayer** or Bible verses in public schools were unconstitutional.

A limited **nuclear test-ban treaty** was agreed upon **July 25** by the U.S., Soviet Union and Britain, barring all nuclear tests except underground.

Washington demonstration by 200,000 persons **Aug. 28** in support of **black demands** for equal rights. Highlight was speech in which Dr. Martin Luther King said: "I have a dream that this nation will rise up and live out the true meaning of its creed. 'We hold these truths to be self-evident: that all men are created equal.' "

South Vietnam Pres. **Ngo Dinh Diem assassinated Nov. 2;** U.S. had earlier withdrawn support.

Pres. **John F. Kennedy was shot** and fatally wounded by an assassin **Nov. 22** as he rode in a motorcade through downtown Dallas, Tex. Vice Pres. Lyndon B. Johnson was inaugurated president shortly after in Dallas. Lee Harvey Oswald was arrested and charged with the murder. Oswald was shot and fatally wounded **Nov. 24** by Jack Ruby, 52, a Dallas nightclub owner, who was convicted of murder **Mar. 14, 1964** and sentenced to death. Ruby died of natural causes **Jan. 3, 1967** while awaiting retrial.

U.S. troops in **Vietnam** totalled over 15,000 by year-end; aid to South Vietnam was over $500 million in **1963.**

1964

Panama suspended relations with U.S. **Jan. 9** after riots. U.S. offered **Dec. 18** to negotiate a new canal treaty.

Supreme Court ordered **Feb. 17** that **congressional districts** have equal populations.

U.S. reported **May 27** it was sending military planes to **Laos.**

Omnibus **civil rights bill** passed **June 29** banning discrimination in voting, jobs, public accommodations, etc.

Three civil rights workers were reported missing in Mississippi **June 22;** found buried **Aug. 4.** Twenty-one white men were arrested. On **Oct. 20, 1967,** an all-white federal jury convicted 7 of conspiracy in the slayings.

U.S. Congress **Aug. 7** passed **Tonkin Resolution,** authorizing presidential action in Vietnam, after North Vietnam boats reportedly attacked 2 U.S. destroyers **Aug. 2.**

Congress approved War on Poverty bill **Aug. 11.**

The **Warren Commission** released **Sept. 27** a report concluding that Lee Harvey Oswald was solely responsible for the Kennedy assassination.

1965

Pres. Johnson in **Feb.** ordered continuous **bombing of** North Vietnam below 20th parallel.

Some 14,000 U.S. troops sent to **Dominican Republic** during civil war **Apr. 28.** All troops withdrawn by next year.

New **Voting Rights Act** signed **Aug. 6.**

Los Angeles riot by blacks living in **Watts** area resulted in death of 34 persons and property damage est. at $200 mil-

lion **Aug. 11-16.**

Water Quality Act passed **Sept. 21** to meet pollution, shortage problems.

National origins quota system of **immigration** abolished **Oct. 3.**

Electric power failure blacked out most of northeastern U.S., parts of 2 Canadian provinces the night of **Nov. 9-10.**

U.S. forces in S. Vietnam reached 184,300 by year-end.

1966

U.S. forces began firing into **Cambodia May 1.**

Bombing of Hanoi area of North Vietnam by U.S. planes began **June 29.** By Dec. 31, 385,300 U.S. troops were stationed in South Vietnam, plus 60,000 offshore and 33,000 in Thailand.

Medicare, government program to pay part of the medical expenses of citizens over 65, began July 1.

Edward Brooke (R. Mass.) elected **Nov. 8** as first black U.S. senator in 85 years.

1967

Black representative **Adam Clayton Powell** (D. N.Y.) was denied **Mar. 1** his seat in Congress because of charges he misused gvt. funds. Reelected in 1968, he was seated, but fined $25,000 and stripped of his 22 years' seniority.

Pres. Johnson and Soviet Premier Aleksei Kosygin met **June 23 and 25** at Glassboro State College in N.J.; agreed not to let any crisis push them into war.

Black riots in **Newark, N.J. July 12-17** killed 26, injured 1,500; over 1,000 arrested. In Detroit, Mich., **July 23-30** at least 40 died; 2,000 injured, 5,000 left homeless by rioting, looting, burning in city's black ghetto. Quelled by 4,700 federal paratroopers and 8,000 National Guardsmen.

Thurgood Marshall sworn in **Oct. 2** as first black U.S. Supreme Court Justice. Carl B. Stokes (D. Cleveland) and Richard G. Hatcher (D. Gary, Ind.) were elected first black mayors of major U.S. cities **Nov. 7.**

By **December** 475,000 U.S. troops were in **South Vietnam,** all North Vietnam was subject to bombing. Protests against the war mounted in U.S. during year.

1968

USS Pueblo and 83-man crew seized in Sea of Japan **Jan. 23** by North Koreans; 82 men released **Dec. 22.**

"Tet offensive": Communist troops attacked Saigon, 30 province capitals **Jan. 30,** suffer heavy casualties.

Pres. Johnson **curbed bombing** of North Vietnam **Mar. 31.** Peace talks began in Paris **May 10.** All bombing of North halted **Oct. 31.**

Martin Luther King Jr., 39, **assassinated Apr. 4** in Memphis, Tenn. James Earl Ray, an escaped convict, pleaded guilty to the slaying, was sentenced to 99 years.

Sen. **Robert F. Kennedy** (D. N.Y.) 42, **shot June 5** in Hotel Ambassador, Los Angeles, after celebrating presidential primary victories. Died **June 6.** Sirhan Bishara Sirhan, Jordanian, convicted of murder.

Rep. **Shirley Chisholm** (D., N.Y.) became the first black woman elected to Congress.

1969

Expanded four-party **Vietnam peace talks** began **Jan. 18.** U.S. force peaked at 543,400 in April. Withdrawal started **July 8.** Pres. Nixon set Vietnamization policy **Nov. 3.**

A car driven by **Sen. Edward M. Kennedy** (D, Mass.) plunged off a bridge into a tidal pool on Chappaquiddick Is., Martha's Vineyard, Mass. **July 18.** The body of Mary Jo Kopechne, a 28-year-old secretary, was found drowned in the car.

U.S. astronaut **Neil A. Armstrong,** 38, commander of the Apollo 11 mission, became the first man to **set foot on the moon July 20.** Air Force Col. Edwin E. Aldrin Jr. accompanied Armstrong.

Anti-Vietnam War **demonstrations reached peak** in U.S.; some 250,000 marched in Washington, D.C. **Nov. 15.**

Massacre of hundreds of civilians at **Mylai, South Vietnam** in 1968 incident was reported **Nov. 16.**

1970

United Mine Workers official **Joseph A. Yablonski**, his wife, and their daughter were found shot **Jan. 5** in their Clarksville, Pa. home. UMW chief W. A. (Tony) Boyle was later convicted of the killing.

A federal jury **Feb. 18** found the "Chicago 7" innocent of conspiring to incite riots during the 1968 Democratic National Convention. However, 5 were convicted of crossing state lines with intent to incite riots.

Millions of Americans participated in anti-pollution demonstrations **Apr. 22** to mark the first **Earth Day**.

U.S. and South Vietnamese forces crossed **Cambodian** borders **Apr. 30** to get at enemy bases. Four students were killed **May 4 at Kent St.** Univ. in Ohio by National Guardsmen during a protest against the war.

Two **women generals**, the first in U.S. history, were named by Pres. Nixon **May 15**.

A **postal reform** measure was signed **Aug. 12**, creating an independent U.S. Postal Service, thus relinquishing governmental control of the U.S. mails after almost 2 centuries.

1971

Charles Manson, 36, and 3 of his followers were found guilty **Jan. 26** of first-degree murder in the 1969 slaying of actress Sharon Tate and 6 others.

U.S. air and artillery forces aided a 44-day incursion by South Vietnam forces into **Laos** starting **Feb. 8**.

A Constitutional Amendment lowering the **voting age** to 18 in all elections was approved in the Senate by a vote of 94-0 **Mar. 10**. The proposed 26th Amendment got House approval by a 400-19 vote **Mar. 23**. Thirty-eighth state ratified **June 30**.

A court-martial jury **Mar. 29**, convicted **Lt. William L. Calley Jr.** of premeditated murder of 22 South Vietnamese at Mylai on **Mar. 16, 1968**. He was sentenced to life imprisonment **Mar. 31**. Sentence was reduced to 20 years **Aug. 20**.

Publication of classified **Pentagon papers** on the U.S. involvement in Vietnam was begun **June 13** by the New York Times. In a 6-3 vote, the U.S. Supreme Court **June 30** upheld the right of the Times and the Washington Post to publish the documents under the protection of the First Amendment.

U.S. bombers struck massively in North Vietnam for 5 days starting **Dec. 26**, in retaliation for alleged violations of agreements reached prior to the 1968 bombing halt. U.S. forces at year-end were down to 140,000.

1972

Pres. Nixon arrived in Peking **Feb. 21** for an 8-day visit to China, which he called a "journey for peace." The unprecedented visit ended with a joint communique pledging that both powers would work for "a normalization of relations."

By a vote of 84 to 8, the Senate approved **Mar. 22** a Constitutional Amendment banning **discrimination against women** because of their sex and sent the measure to the states for ratification.

North Vietnamese forces launched the biggest attacks in 4 years across the demilitarized zone **Mar. 30**. The U.S. responded **Apr. 15** by resumption of bombing of Hanoi and Haiphong after a 4-year lull.

Nixon announced **May 8** the mining of **North Vietnam** ports. Last U.S. combat troops left **Aug. 11**.

Alabama Gov. George C. **Wallace**, campaigning at a Laurel, Md. shopping center **May 15**, **was shot** and seriously wounded as he greeted a large crowd. Arthur H. Bremer, 21, was sentenced **Aug. 4** to 63 years for shooting Wallace and 3 bystanders.

In the first visit of a U.S. president to Moscow, Nixon arrived **May 22** for a week of summit talks with Kremlin leaders which culminated in a landmark **strategic arms pact.**

Five men were arrested **June 17** for breaking into the offices of the Democratic National Committee in the **Watergate** office complex in Washington, D.C.

The White House announced **July 8** that the U.S. would sell to the USSR at least $750 million of **American wheat**, corn, and other grains over a period of 3 years.

1973

Five of seven defendants in the **Watergate** break-in trial pleaded guilty **Jan. 11 and 15**, and the other 2 were convicted **Jan. 30**.

The Supreme Court ruled 7-2, **Jan. 22**, that a state may not prevent a woman from having an **abortion** during the **first 6 months of pregnancy**, invalidating abortion laws in Texas and Georgia, and, by implication, overturning restrictive abortion laws in 44 other states.

Four-party **Vietnam peace pacts** were signed in Paris **Jan. 27**, and North Vietnam released some 590 U.S. prisoners by **Apr. 1**. Last U.S. troops left **Mar. 29**.

The end of the military draft was announced **Jan. 27**.

China and the U.S. agreed **Feb. 22** to set up permanent liaison offices in each other's country.

Top **Nixon** aides H.R. Haldeman, John D. Ehrlichman, and John W. Dean, and Attorney General Richard Kleindienst **resigned Apr. 30** amid charges of White House efforts to obstruct justice in the Watergate case.

The Senate Armed Services Committee **July 16** began a probe into allegations that the U.S. Air Force had made 3,500 secret B-52 raids into **Cambodia** in 1969 and 1970.

John Dean, former Nixon counsel, told Senate hearings **June 25** that Nixon, his staff and campaign aides, and the Justice Department all had conspired to cover up Watergate facts. Nixon refused **July 23** to release **tapes** of relevant White House conversations. Some tapes were turned over to the court **Nov. 26**.

The U.S. officially ceased bombing in **Cambodia** at midnight **Aug. 14** in accord with a June Congressional action.

Vice Pres. **Spiro T. Agnew Oct. 10** resigned and pleaded "nolo contendere" (no contest) to charges of tax evasion on payments made to him by Maryland contractors when he was governor of that state. Gerald Rudolph Ford **Oct. 12** became first appointed vice president under the 25th Amendment; sworn in **Dec. 6**.

A total ban on **oil exports** to the U.S. was imposed by Arab oil-producing nations **Oct. 19-21** after the outbreak of an Arab-Israeli war. The ban was lifted **Mar. 18, 1974**.

Atty. Gen. Elliot **Richardson** resigned, and his deputy William D. Ruckelshaus and Watergate Special Prosecutor Archibald Cox were fired by Pres. Nixon **Oct. 20** when Cox threatened to secure a judicial ruling that Nixon was violating a court order to turn tapes over to Watergate case Judge John Sirica.

Leon Jaworski, conservative Texas Democrat, was named **Nov. 1** by the Nixon administration to be special prosecutor to succeed Archibald Cox.

Congress overrode **Nov. 7** Nixon's veto of the **war powers** bill which curbed the president's power to commit armed forces to hostilities abroad without Congressional approval.

1974

Impeachment hearings were opened **May 9** against Nixon by the House Judiciary Committee.

John D. Ehrlichman and 3 White House **"plumbers"** were found guilty **July 12** of conspiring to violate the civil rights of Dr. Lewis Fielding, formerly psychiatrist to Pentagon Papers leaker Daniel Ellsberg, by breaking into his Beverly Hills, Cal. office.

The U.S. Supreme Court ruled, 8-0, **July 24** that Nixon had to turn over 64 **tapes** of White House conversations sought by Watergate Special Prosecutor Leon Jaworski.

The House Judiciary Committee, in televised hearings **July 24-30**, recommended 3 **articles of impeachment** against Nixon. The first, voted 27-11 **July 27**, charged Nixon with taking part in a criminal conspiracy to obstruct justice in the Watergate cover-up. The second, voted 28-10 **July 29**, charged he "repeatedly" failed to carry out his constitutional oath in a series of alleged abuses of power. The third, voted 27-17 **July 30**, accused him of unconstitutional defiance of committee subpoenas. The House of Representatives voted without debate **Aug. 20**, by 412-3, to accept the committee report, which included the recommended impeachment articles.

Nixon resigned Aug. 9. His support began eroding Aug. 5 when he released 3 tapes, admitting he originated plans to have the FBI stop its probe of the Watergate break-in for political as well as national security reasons. Vice President **Gerald R. Ford** was sworn in as the 38th U.S. president on **Aug. 9.**

An **unconditional pardon** to ex-Pres. Nixon for all federal crimes that he "committed or may have committed" while president was issued by Pres. Gerald Ford **Sept. 8.**

1975

Found guilty of **Watergate** cover-up charges **Jan. 1** were ex-Atty. Gen. John N. Mitchell, ex-presidential advisers H.R. Haldeman and John D. Ehrlichman.

U.S. civilians were evacuated from **Saigon Apr. 29** as communist forces completed takeover of South Vietnam.

U.S. merchant ship **Mayaguez** and crew of 39 seized by Cambodian forces in Gulf of Siam **May 12.** In rescue operation, U.S. Marines attacked Tang Is., planes bombed air base; Cambodia surrendered ship and crew; U.S. losses were 15 killed in battle and 23 dead in a helicopter crash.

Congress voted $405 million for South **Vietnam** refugees **May 16;** 140,000 were flown to the U.S.

Illegal **CIA operations,** including records on 300,000 persons and groups, and infiltration of agents into black, anti-war and political movements, were described by a "blue-ribbon" panel headed by Vice Pres. Rockefeller **June 10.**

FBI agents captured **Patricia (Patty) Hearst,** kidnapped Feb. 4, 1974, in San Francisco **Sept. 18** with others. She was indicted for bank robbery; a San Francisco jury convicted her **Mar. 20, 1976.**

1976

Payments abroad of $22 million in bribes by Lockheed Aircraft Corp. to sell its planes were revealed **Feb. 4** by a Senate subcommittee. Lockheed admitted payments in Japan, Turkey, Italy, and Holland.

The U.S. celebrated its **Bicentennial July 4,** marking the 200th anniversary of its independence with festivals, parades, and N.Y. City's Operation Sail, a gathering of tall ships from around the world viewed by 6 million persons.

A mystery ailment **"legionnaire's disease"** killed 29 persons who attended an American Legion convention **July 21-24** in Philadelphia. The cause was found to be a bacterium, it was reported **June 18, 1977.**

The **Viking II** lander set down on **Mars' Utopia Plains Sept. 3,** following the successful landing by Viking I **July 20.**

1977

Pres. Jimmy Carter **Jan. 27** pardoned most Vietnam War draft evaders, who numbered some 10,000.

Convicted murderer **Gary Gilmore** was executed by a Utah firing squad **Jan. 17,** in the first exercise of capital punishment anywhere in the U.S. since 1967. Gilmore had opposed all attempts to delay the execution.

Carter signed an act **Aug. 4** creating a new Cabinet-level **Energy Department.**

1978

Sen. **Hubert H. Humphrey** (D., Minn.), 66, lost a battle with cancer **Jan. 13,** after 32 years of public service, including 4 years as vice-president of the United States.

U.S. Senate voted **Apr. 18** to turn over the **Panama Canal** to Panama on Dec. 31, 1999, by a vote of 68-32, ending several months of heated debate; an earlier vote **(Mar. 16)** had given approval to a treaty guaranteeing the area's neutrality after the year 2000.

California voters **June 6** approved (by a 65% majority) the **Proposition 13** initiative to cut property taxes in the state by 57%, thus severely limiting government spending.

The U.S. Supreme Court **June 28** voted 5-4 not to allow a firm quota system in affirmative action plans; the Court did uphold programs that were more "flexible" in nature.

The **House Select Committee on Assassinations** opened hearings **Sept. 6** into assassinations of Pres. Kennedy and Martin Luther King Jr.; the committee recessed **Dec. 30** after concluding conspiracies likely in both cases, but with no further hard evidence for further prosecutions.

Congress passed the **Humphrey-Hawkins "full employment" Bill Oct. 15,** which set national goal of reducing unemployment to 4% by 1983, while reducing inflation to 3% in same period; Pres. Carter signed bill, **Oct. 27.**

1979

A major accident occurred, **Mar. 28,** at a nuclear reactor on **Three Mile Island** near Middletown, Pa. Radioactive gases escaped through the plant's venting system and a large hydrogen gas bubble formed in the top of the reactor containment vessel.

In the worst disaster in U.S. aviation history, an American Airlines **DC-10** jetliner lost its left engine and crashed shortly after takeoff in Chicago, **May 25,** killing 275 people.

Pope John Paul II, Oct. 1-6, visited the U.S. and reaffirmed traditional Roman Catholic teachings.

The federal government announced, **Nov. 1,** a $1.5 billion loan-guarantee plan to aid the nation's 3d largest automaker, **Chrysler Corp.,** which had reported a loss of $460.6 million for the 3d quarter of 1979.

Some 90 people, including 63 Americans, were taken hostage, **Nov. 3,** at the American embassy in Teheran, Iran, by militant student followers of Ayatollah Khomeini who demanded the return of former Shah Mohammad Reza Pahlavi, who was undergoing medical treatment in New York City.

1980

Citing "an extremely serious threat to peace," Pres. Carter announced, **Jan. 4,** a series of **punitive measures against the USSR,** most notably an embargo on the sale of grain and high technology, in retaliation for the Soviet invasion of Afghanistan. At Carter's request, the U.S. Olympic Committee voted, **Apr. 12,** not to attend the Moscow Summer Olympics.

Eight Americans were killed and 5 wounded, **Apr. 24,** in an ill-fated attempt to **rescue the hostages** held by Iranian **militants** at the U.S. Embassy in Teheran.

In Washington, Mt. **St. Helens erupted, May 18,** in a violent blast estimated to be 500 times as powerful as the Hiroshima atomic bomb. The blast, followed by others on **May 25** and June 12, left about 60 dead, and economic losses estimated at nearly $3 billion.

In a sweeping victory, **Nov. 4, Ronald Wilson Reagan** was elected 40th President of the United States, defeating incumbent Jimmy Carter. The stunning GOP victory extended to the U.S. Congress where Republicans gained control of the Senate and wrested 33 House seats from the Democrats.

Former Beatle **John Lennon** was shot and killed, **Dec. 8,** outside his apartment building in New York City, by Mark David Chapman, a former psychiatric patient.

1981

Minutes after the inauguration of Pres. Ronald Reagan, **Jan. 20,** the 52 Americans who had been held **hostage in Iran** for 444 days were flown to freedom following an agreement in which the U.S. agreed to return to Iran $8 billion in frozen assets.

President Reagan was **shot** in the chest by John W. Hinckley, Jr., a would-be assassin, **Mar. 30,** in Washington, D.C., as he walked to his limousine following an address at the Washington Hilton.

The world's first reusable spacecraft, the **Space Shuttle Columbia,** was sent into space, **Apr. 12,** and completed its successful mission 2 days later.

Both houses of Congress passed, **July 29,** President Reagan's **tax-cut legislation.** The bill, the largest tax cut in the nation's history, was expected to reduce taxes by $37.6 billion in fiscal year 1982, and would save taxpayers $750 billion over the next 5 years.

Federal air traffic controllers, Aug. 3, began an illegal nationwide strike after their union rejected the government's final offer for a new contract. Most of the 13,000 striking controllers defied the back-to-work order, and were dismissed by President Reagan on **Aug. 5.**

In a 99-0 vote, the Senate confirmed, **Sept. 21,** the appointment of **Sandra Day O'Connor** as an associate justice of the U.S. Supreme Court. She was the first woman appointed to that body.

President Reagan ordered sanctions against the new Polish military government, Dec. 23, in response to the imposition of martial law in that country.

1982

The 13-year-old lawsuit against AT&T by the Justice Dept. was settled Jan. 8. AT&T agreed to give up the 22 Bell System companies but, in return, was allowed to expand into previously prohibited areas inc. data processing, telephone and computer equipment sales, and computer communication devices.

On Mar. 2, the Senate voted 57-37 for a bill that virtually eliminated busing for the purposes of racial integration.

On June 12, in N.Y.'s Central Park, hundreds of thousands demonstrated against nuclear arms.

The Equal Rights Amendment was defeated after a 10-year struggle for ratification.

The elections on Nov. 2 resulted in gains for the Democrats—the margin in the new House was 269-166. In the Senate elections, Democrats won 20 out of 33 seats, but were still the minority, 54-46.

The highest unemployment rate since 1940, 10.4%, was reported on Nov. 5. The rate for Nov. reached 10.8%, with over 11 million unemployed.

Leonid Brezhnev, 75, general secretary of the central committee of the Communist Party and the Soviet Union, died of a heart attack on Nov. 10.

Lech Walesa, former leader of Solidarity, the Polish labor union, was freed Nov. 13, after 11 months of internment following the imposition of martial law and the outlawing of Solidarity. The Polish government declared Walesa "no longer a threat to internal security." Pres. Reagan lifted the U.S. embargo on sales of oil and gas equipment to the Soviet Union.

The Space Shuttle Columbia completed its first operational flight on Nov. 16.

A retired dentist, Dr. Barney B. Clark, 61, became the first recipient of a permanent artificial heart during a 7½ hour operation in Salt Lake City on Dec. 2. The heart was designed by Dr. Robert Jarvik, also on the surgical team.

On Dec. 16, Anne M. Gorsuch, administrator of the Environmental Protection Agency, became the first Cabinet level official to be cited for contempt by the House when she declined to submit certain documents requested by a House subcommittee.

1983

On Mar. 14, for the first time in its 23-year history, the Organization of Petroleum Exporting Countries (OPEC) agreed to cut the prices of its crude oil. The decision in London reflected falling worldwide demand for OPEC products.

On Apr. 20, Pres. Reagan signed a compromise, bipartisan bill designed to rescue the Social Security System from bankruptcy.

The National Commission on Excellence in Education issued its report on Apr. 26. The report labelled U.S. elementary and secondary education "mediocre," and recommended that: schools put more emphasis on English, math, social studies, and computer science; the school day be lengthened; teachers be rewarded for merit rather than seniority; and college admissions standards be raised.

In an 8-1 decision, the U.S. Supreme Court held, May 24, that the Internal Revenue Service could deny tax exemptions to private schools that practiced racial discrimination.

Sally Ride became the first American woman to travel in space, June 18, when the space shuttle Challenger was launched from Cape Canaveral, Fla.

The Soviet Union shot a South Korean airliner out of the sky on Sept. 1, killing all 269 people aboard. The attack occurred in Soviet air space, and the plane crashed into the Sea of Japan. The USSR charged that the plane, which carried 240 passengers and a crew of 29, had been on a spying mission. Most of the noncommunist world, led by Pres. Reagan, responded with condemnation.

The Big 3 auto companies reported, Oct. 4, that sales had increased 16.7 percent during the 1983 model year. It was the biggest gain from the previous year since 1978.

On Oct. 23, 241 U.S. Marines and sailors, members of the multinational peacekeeping force in Lebanon, were killed when a TNT-laden suicide terrorist blew up Marine headquarters at Beirut Intl. Airport. Almost simultaneously, a second truck bomb blew up a French paratroop barracks two miles away, killing more than 40.

U.S. Marines and Rangers and a small force from 6 Caribbean nations invaded the island of Grenada on Oct. 25, in response to a request from the Organization of Eastern Caribbean States. After a few days, Grenadian militia and Cuban "construction workers" were overcome, hundreds of U.S. citizens evacuated safely, and the hard-line Marxist regime deposed. The U.S. Congress applied the War Powers Resolution, requiring U.S. troops to leave Grenada by Dec. 24.

1984

In his State of the Union address, Jan. 25, Pres. Reagan called for budget cuts of $100 billion over 3 years, but opposed increased taxes.

Soviet leader Yuri V. Andropov, 69, died in Moscow, Feb. 9, after a long illness.

On Feb. 26, as the position of Pres. Amin Gemayel of Lebanon deteriorated and his army crumbled, Pres. Reagan removed U.S. Marines from Beirut and placed them on U.S. ships offshore.

The space shuttle Challenger was launched on its 4th trip into space, Feb. 3. On Feb. 7, Navy Capt. Bruce McCandless, followed by Army Lt. Colonel Robert Stewart, became the first humans to fly free of a spacecraft.

During March, the U.S. Senate rejected 2 Constitutional amendments that would have permitted prayer in the public schools.

The Central Intelligence Agency (CIA) acknowledged in April that it had participated in the mining of Nicaraguan harbors. This touched off a controversy in Congress, and the Senate, Apr. 10, adopted a nonbinding resolution condemning U.S. participation in the mining.

From Apr. 26 to May 1, Pres. Reagan visited China for the first time, holding a series of discussions with Chinese leaders.

On May 7, American veterans of the Vietnam war reached an out-of-court settlement with 7 chemical companies in their class-action suit relating to the herbicide Agent Orange.

A federal judge in Salt Lake City held, May 10, that the U.S. government had been negligent in its above-ground testing of nuclear weapons in Nevada from 1951 to 1962.

Jose Napoleon Duarte, the candidate of the Christian Democratic Party and a political moderate, was elected president of strife-torn El Salvador, May 7.

An undamaged Mayan tomb was discovered by archaeologists, May 15.

On June 6, former vice president Walter Mondale claimed victory in his struggle with Sen. Gary Hart for the Democratic presidental nomination. In a historic move, July 12, Mondale chose a woman, Rep. Geraldine Ferraro (N.Y.) to run with him as candidate for vice president.

A report written by Italian State Prosecutor Antonio Albano and made public in June, linked the Bulgarian secret service to the plot to assassinate Pope John Paul II in 1981.

Pres. Reagan, Aug. 11, signed a law prohibiting public high schools from barring students who wished to assemble for religious or political activities outside of school hours.

Pres. Ronald Reagan and Vice Pres. George Bush were renominated, Aug. 23, at the Republican National convention.

Indira Gandhi, the prime minister of India, was slain by 2 of her own bodyguards in New Delhi, Oct. 31. Her assassins were reportedly members of the Sikh religious minority, who had been in violent confrontation with the Gandhi government for months.

1985

On **Feb. 16,** Israeli troops completed their withdrawal from the Sidon area of Lebanon, in the first phase of a long-awaited 3-stage pullout.

Konstantin Chernenko, 73, president of the Soviet Union and general secretary of the Soviet Communist Party, died **Mar. 10.** He was succeeded by **Mikhail Gorbachev as the new party secretary.** The USSR's 4th leader in 3 years, Gorbachev, 54, was the youngest member of the Politburo.

The **war** between **Iran and Iraq** took a new turn in **mid-March** when planes from each side bombed civilian-occupied areas in each other's territory.

The controversial MX missile survived critical votes in the Senate and House. **The Senate,** on **Mar. 19** and **21,** voted to **authorize the missiles** and then to **appropriate $1.5 million** for the construction of 21 missiles. **The House** gave its endorsement **Mar. 26** and **28.**

E.F. Hutton, one of the nation's largest brokerage companies, **pleaded guilty, May 2,** to 2,000 **federal charges** related to the manipulation of its checking accounts. The company agreed to pay $2 million in fines and to pay back up to $8 million to banks it had defrauded.

On **June 14, Shiite Muslim extremists seized** an airplane flying from Athens to Rome; 153 persons were aboard, including 104 Americans. One American was killed, more than 100 others freed, and 39 American men were kept hostage until their release on **June 30.**

The government of **South Africa declared a state of emergency** in July. The U.S. Senate had voted, **July 11,** to impose **economic sanctions** on South Africa in protest against its policy of apartheid. Violence, building for a year, had resulted in up to 500 deaths, almost all the victims black.

"Live Aid," a 17-hour rock concert broadcast **July 13** on radio and TV from London and Phila. to 152 countries, raised $70 million for the starving peoples of Africa.

On **Oct. 7, 5 hijackers seized an Italian cruise ship, the Achille Lauro,** in the open sea as it approached Port Said, Egypt. Some 400 persons were aboard, including about 340 crew. The hijackers, members of the Palestine Liberation Front, a faction broken from the PLO, demanded the release of 50 Palestinians held by Israel. On **Oct. 9,** Egypt said the hijackers had surrendered to a PLO representative and would be given safe conduct from Egypt. Italy then announced that Leon Klinghoffer, a 69-year-old, wheelchair-bound American, had been shot to death and thrown overboard. On **Oct. 10,** Egyptian Pres. Hosni Mubarek said the hijackers were in the hands of the PLO. However, they did not actually leave Egypt until that evening. The Reagan administration ordered the Egyptian plane intercepted in international air space, and Navy F-14 fighter jets forced the plane to land in Sicily.

In November, for the first time in 6 years, the leaders of the U.S. and the Soviet Union met at a **summit conference.** In Geneva, Switzerland, **Pres. Reagan and Mikhail Gorbachev,** the general secretary of the Soviet Communist Party, talked privately for 5 hours, **Nov. 19 and 20.** No substantive agreements were reached, but Pres. Reagan called the talks a "fresh start."

Arab gunmen seized an **Egyptian jetliner** en route from Athens to Cairo, **Nov. 23.** Of the 98 persons aboard, 60 were killed.

Congress passed a compromise **Gramm-Rudman bill, Dec. 11,** that was a last-ditch effort to end the huge federal deficit. Signed by Pres. Reagan **Dec. 12,** it was expected to require an initial $11.7 billion reduction in the fiscal 1986 budget deficit, then 4 reductions in equal amounts until a balanced budget was achieved in 1991.

Palestinian terrorists killed 20 civilians at airports in Rome and Vienna, Dec. 27. Both attacks were at ticket counters of El Al, Israel's national airline.

The **biggest corporate merger yet,** outside the oil industry, was announced **Dec. 11,** when General Electric Corp. agreed to buy RCA Corp. for $6.28 billion.

1986

On **Jan. 20,** for the 1st time, the U.S. officially observed **Martin Luther King Day.**

Moments after liftoff, **Jan. 28,** the space shuttle *Challenger* exploded, killing 6 astronauts and Christa McAuliffe, a New Hampshire teacher. Subsequent investigations found that NASA had abandoned "good judgment and common sense" regarding safety problems that caused the explosion.

The 20-year rule of **Pres. Ferdinand Marcos of the Philippines ended in Feb.,** when he fled into exile in Hawaii. His successor: Corazon Aquino, widow of opposition leader Benigno Aquino, murdered in 1983 on return from exile in the U.S.

Jean-Claude Duvalier, Haiti's head, fled into exile in France in Feb., ending 28 years of his family's dictatorship.

Soviet dissident **Anatoly Schcharansky was freed in Feb.** after 8 years in prison.

U.S. warplanes struck targets in Tripoli and Benghazi, Libya, Apr. 14—retaliation against the Libyan bombing of a W. Berlin disco that killed 2, injured 200, Apr. 5. On Jan. 7, Pres. Reagan had said that the U.S. had aborted 26 "terrorist missions" in 1985. In an executive order, he banned trade with and travel to Libya, ordering Americans out. A 2nd executive order, **Jan. 8,** had frozen all Libyan government assets in the U.S. and U.S. bank branches abroad.

After 3 days, Soviet authorities reported a **major accident at the Chernobyl, Ukraine nuclear power plant, Apr. 28.** The resultant radiation cloud killed 23; 40,000 were evacuated.

U.S. officials said, **June 12, that AIDS cases and deaths would increase tenfold in the next 5 years.** At that time, the government had recorded 21,517 cases, 11,713 deaths. An anti-viral drug, azidothymidine (AZT) was found to improve the health of some AIDS patient, but was not a cure.

Because of the mounting **abuse of illegal drugs** in the U.S., specifically **cocaine as "crack,"** Congress passed anti-drug laws and the U.S. joined Bolivia in raids against cocaine processing hideouts.

The Supreme Court, **July 7,** found a key provision of the **Gramm-Rudman "balanced budget" law unconstitutional.**

The U.S., via Congress's **Sept.** override of Pres. Reagan's veto, joined other nations in imposing **economic sanctions** on So. Africa, pressuring the Botha gvt. to end apartheid.

The U.S. Senate confirmed, **Sept. 17,** Pres. Reagan's nomination of **William Rehnquist as chief justice,** Antonin Scalia as associate justice of the Supreme Court.

Sept. terrorist attacks: bombers struck in **Paris,** killing 8, injuring 170; an airplane hijacking in **Karachi, Pakistan** killed 21, injured 100; 2 terrorists entered a synagogue in **Istanbul, Turkey,** killed 20 and wounded 3.

Congress passed, in late **Sept.,** the comprehensive **Tax Reform Law.** In effect in 1987, it simplified the system, drastically changing tax brackets, deductions, and more.

The U.S. and USSR reached tentative agreement on a world-wide ban of medium-range missiles, Sept. 18. But hopes of reducing strategic long-range missiles ended in Iceland in Oct., when Gorbachev called for a limit on the development of "Star Wars," and Reagan refused it.

One day before the 1986 Congressional elections, it was reported that the U.S. had sent spare parts and ammunition to Iran. Over the next months it was revealed that **additional arms sales had been made to Iran, and profits diverted to a fund for Nicaraguan contras.** This brought on the worst crisis in the Reagan administration.

In the Congressional races, **Nov. 4, Democrats won a 55-45 Senate majority,** after 6 yrs. of a Republican majority, and **enlarged their House majority by 5, to 258-177.**

The most scandalous year in Wall Street history ended with **Ivan Boesky's** agreeing, **Nov. 14,** to plead guilty to an unspecified criminal count, pay a $100 million fine, and return profits; he was barred for life from trading securities.

1987

Pres. Reagan produced the nation's first **trillion-dollar budget**, Jan. 5.

The stock market continued its phenomenal rise. The **Dow closed at 2002.25, Jan. 8**, its first finish above 2000. The Dow advanced for 13 consecutive trading days, another record; Jan. 20; the average soared 51.60 points, **Jan. 22**, a one-day record. At month's end, the cumulative advance was more than 250 points, yet another record.

Condom ads became prominent in the U.S. media in Jan., reflecting concern for "safe sex" to prevent AIDS.

USSR General Secy. **Mikhail Gorbachev, Jan. 27**, signaled a new era of **"glasnost"** (openness), proposing economic and social reforms. The Communist Party Central Committee, **Jan. 28**, gave a general endorsement to Gorbachev's proposals, including allowing more than one candidate to seek a party office and changing the way in which members of the ruling Politburo and Secretariat were chosen.

Gorbachev called for, **June 25**, and the Supreme Soviet passed a law embodying, **June 30**, "a radical reorganization of economic management."

The **Tower Commission Report, Feb. 27**, found **Pres. Reagan** confused and uninformed; and further faulted White House Chief of Staff Donald Regan; former Natl. Security Adviser Robert McFarlane; his successor Adm. John Poindexter; and CIA Director William Casey. Casey had resigned, Feb. 2, on doctors' discovery of a brain tumor; McFarlane attempted suicide, Feb. 9; Regan resigned, Feb. 27.

An **Iraqi warplane missile killed 37 sailors** on the frigate U.S.S. Stark in the Persian Gulf, May 27. Iraq called it an accident. The Stark's officers were found negligent, June 14. The U.S. escorted Kuwaiti oil tankers to the Gulf, reflagging them for the U.S.

For the first time since the 1820's, a British prime minister won a 3d consecutive term, as **Margaret Thatcher** swept to victory, June 11.

Pres. Reagan, Aug. 4, and the **presidents of 5 Central American countries** both presented plans for peace in the region. The presidents of Nicaragua, El Salvador, Honduras, Costa Rica, and Guatemala signed their own preliminary peace agreement, Aug. 8.

Public hearings by the Senate and House committees investigating the **Iran-contra affair** went on from May-Aug. Former CIA Director Casey died, May 6, 5 months after brain surgery; Lt. Col. Oliver North, a media sensation, said he had believed all his activities authorized by his superiors; Poindexter said his own purpose had been "to provide some future deniability for the president . . ."; Shultz said Casey, McFarlane, and Poindexter had lied to him and deceived Pres. Reagan. Pres. Reagan, Aug. 12, said he had been "stubborn in pursuit of a policy that went astray," but again denied knowing of the funds' diversion to the contras.

Wall Street crashed, Oct. 19, the Dow plummeting a record 508 points—22.6 percent—after a record high of 2722.42, Aug. 25; a 200-point drop by Oct., called a correction by most; and drops of 91.55, Oct. 6; 95.46, Oct. 14; and 108.36, Oct. 16.

The Senate, Oct. 23, rejected Pres. Reagan's nomination of Robert Bork to the Supreme Court. The Judiciary Committee, Oct. 15, had found Bork unfit, due to insensitivity to individual rights and liberties. The 58-42 vote was the biggest margin of rejection for the position in history.

Deng Xiaoping, 83, stepped down as China's top leader, Nov. 1. Premier Zhao Ziyang, his protege, was elected General Secy of the party, Nov. 2.

Pres. Reagan and Soviet leader **Gorbachev** met in Wash., **Dec. 8**, and signed an unprecedented agreement calling for the dismantling of all 1,752 U.S. and 859 Soviet missiles with a 300-3,400-mile range. The leaders agreed to meet in Moscow in 1988.

Violent protests by Palestinians broke out in territories occupied by Israel in Dec., with more than 20 killed.

1988

Federal grand juries in Miami and Tampa returned indictments, **Feb. 4**, against Gen. Manuel Noriega, the effective ruler of Panama, charging that he had protected and otherwise assisted the Medellin drug cartel, linked to 80 percent of the cocaine smuggled into the U.S. Attempts by the U.S. to oust Noriega plunged Panama into political and economic turmoil.

Pakistan and Afghanistan signed agreements in Geneva, **Apr. 14**, providing for the withdrawal of Soviet troops between May 15, 1988 and Feb. 15, 1989; the establishment of a nonaligned Afghan state; and the repatriation of millions of Afghan refugees.

Nearly **1.4 million illegal aliens** met the May 4 deadline for applying for amnesty under a U.S. Immigration and Naturalization Service policy. It was estimated that more than half the applications were in Calif., and that, nationwide, about 71 percent of the aliens had entered the U.S. from Mexico.

Congress approved, in June, the greatest expansion ever of **Medicare** benefits, by protecting the elderly and disabled against "catastrophic" medical costs. Beneficiaries would bear the cost, estimated at more than $32 billion in 5 years.

Much of the U.S. suffered the worst **drought** in more than 50 years, during the spring, with the northern Great Plains and Southeast especially hard-hit. The Agriculture Dept. attributed the drought to a division of the jet stream, which pushed precipitation to the north and south of the affected areas. By June 23, one-half of the nation's agricultural counties had been designated disaster areas.

The **"greenhouse effect"** was taking place, according to congressional testimony by NASA scientist James Hansen, **June 23**. Hansen said that the Earth had been warmer during the first 5 months of 1988 than at any time since records had been kept; he warned of an "increasing tendency" to drought, along with the possible melting of polar and glacial ice, and the subsequent rise in sea levels and flooding of coastal areas.

A missile, fired from the U.S. Navy warship *Vincennes*, in the Persian Gulf, **struck and destroyed a commercial Iranian airliner, July 3**, killing all 290 persons on the plane. Navy personnel had mistaken the airliner for an Iranian F-14 jet fighter. Although the Pentagon first said that the plane was outside its designated commercial air corridor, headed directly for the *Vincennes*, and descending, this was subsequently disproven.

The **Soviet Communist Party, July 1**, declared support for **perestroika** (restructuring), the centerpiece of the reform movement of Soviet leader Mikhail Gorbachev. The Party also approved competitive elections, 10-year limits on the tenure of elected government and party officials, and the principle of glasnost. On **Oct. 1**, the Supreme Soviet unanimously confirmed Gorbachev as president. The government revealed, **Oct. 27**, that it had experienced huge budget deficits for years.

In a policy reversal, **Iran, July 18**, accepted a U.N. proposal to end the war with Iraq in the Persian Gulf. A cease-fire went into effect, Aug. 20.

King Hussein of Jordan announced, **July 31**, his country's renunciation of all claims to the Israeli-occupied West Bank, and its support for an independent Palestinian state.

Fire destroyed about 4 million acres of forest land throughout the west, including Alaska, during the late summer. Property damage was also considerable.

Failures at nuclear-power plants posed problems across the U.S., according to congressional testimony, starting **Sept. 30**. Problems cited including aging equipment, poor management and training, and lax safety standards.

George Bush, vice president under Ronald Reagan, was elected 41st U.S. president, **Nov. 8**. Bush defeated the Democratic nominee, Gov. Michael Dukakis (Mass.), by 54 to 46 percent of the popular vote, and 426 electoral votes to Dukakis's 112. **Sen. Dan Quayle** (Ind.) was the successful vice presidential nominee; Sen. Lloyd Bentsen (Tex.) was the Democratic nominee for v.p. Democrats continued to control both houses of Congress.

Declaration of Independence

The Declaration of Independence was adopted by the Continental Congress in Philadelphia, on July 4, 1776. John Hancock was president of the Congress and Charles Thomson was secretary. A copy of the Declaration, engrossed on parchment, was signed by members of Congress on and after Aug. 2, 1776. On Jan. 18, 1777, Congress ordered that "an authenticated copy, with the names of the members of Congress subscribing the same, be sent to each of the United States, and that they be desired to have the same put upon record." Authenticated copies were printed in broadside form in Baltimore, where the Continental Congress was then in session. The following text is that of the original printed by John Dunlap at Philadelphia for the Continental Congress.

IN CONGRESS, July 4, 1776.

A DECLARATION

By the REPRESENTATIVES of the

UNITED STATES OF AMERICA,

In GENERAL CONGRESS assembled

When in the Course of human Events, it becomes necessary for one People to dissolve the Political Bands which have connected them with another, and to assume among the Powers of the Earth, the separate and equal Station to which the Laws of Nature and of Nature's God entitle them, a decent Respect to the Opinions of Mankind requires that they should declare the causes which impel them to the Separation.

We hold these Truths to be self-evident, that all Men are created equal, that they are endowed by their Creator with certain unalienable Rights, that among these are Life, Liberty, and the Pursuit of Happiness—That to secure these Rights, Governments are instituted among Men, deriving their just Powers from the Consent of the Governed, that whenever any Form of Government becomes destructive of these Ends, it is the Right of the People to alter or to abolish it, and to institute new Government, laying its Foundation on such Principles, and organizing its Powers in such Form, as to them shall seem most likely to effect their Safety and Happiness. Prudence, indeed, will dictate that Governments long established should not be changed for light and transient Causes; and accordingly all Experience hath shewn, that Mankind are more disposed to suffer, while Evils are sufferable, than to right themselves by abolishing the Forms to which they are accustomed. But when a long Train of Abuses and Usurpations, pursuing invariably the same Object, evinces a Design to reduce them under absolute Despotism, it is their Right, it is their Duty, to throw off such Government, and to provide new Guards for their future Security. Such has been the patient Sufferance of these Colonies; and such is now the Necessity which constrains them to alter their former Systems of Government. The History of the present King of Great-Britain is a History of repeated Injuries and Usurpations, all having in direct Object the Establishment of an absolute Tyranny over these States. To prove this, let Facts be submitted to a candid World.

He has refused his Assent to Laws, the most wholesome and necessary for the public Good.

He has forbidden his Governors to pass Laws of immediate and pressing Importance, unless suspended in their Operation till his Assent should be obtained; and when so suspended, he has utterly neglected to attend to them.

He has refused to pass other Laws for the Accommodation of large Districts of People, unless those People would relinquish the Right of Representation in the Legislature, a Right inestimable to them, and formidable to Tyrants only.

He has called together Legislative Bodies at Places unusual, uncomfortable, and distant from the Depository of their Public Records, for the sole Purpose of fatiguing them into Compliance with his Measures.

He has dissolved Representative Houses repeatedly, for opposing with manly Firmness his Invasions on the Rights of the People.

He has refused for a long Time, after such Dissolutions, to cause others to be elected; whereby the Legislative Powers, incapable of Annihilation, have returned to the People at large for their exercise; the State remaining in the mean time exposed to all the Dangers of Invasion from without, and Convulsions within.

He has endeavoured to prevent the Population of these States; for that Purpose obstructing the Laws for Naturalization of Foreigners; refusing to pass others to encourage their Migrations hither, and raising the Conditions of new Appropriations of Lands.

He has obstructed the Administration of Justice, by refusing his Assent to Laws for establishing Judiciary Powers.

He has made Judges dependent on his Will alone, for the Tenure of their Offices, and the Amount and payment of their Salaries.

He has erected a Multitude of new Offices, and sent hither Swarms of Officers to harrass our People, and eat out their Substance.

He has kept among us, in Times of Peace, Standing Armies, without the consent of our Legislatures.

He has affected to render the Military independent of, and superior to the Civil Power.

He has combined with others to subject us to a Jurisdiction foreign to our Constitution, and unacknowledged by our Laws; giving his Assent to their Acts of pretended Legislation:

For quartering large Bodies of Armed Troops among us:

For protecting them, by a mock Trial, from Punishment for any Murders which they should commit on the Inhabitants of these States:

For cutting off our Trade with all Parts of the World:

For imposing Taxes on us without our Consent:

For depriving us, in many Cases, of the Benefits of Trial by Jury:

For transporting us beyond Seas to be tried for pretended Offences:

For abolishing the free System of English Laws in a neighbouring Province, establishing therein an arbitrary Government, and enlarging its Boundaries, so as to render it at once an Example and fit Instrument for introducing the same absolute Rule into these Colonies:

For taking away our Charters, abolishing our most valuable Laws, and altering fundamentally the Forms of our Governments:

For suspending our own Legislatures, and declaring themselves invested with Power to legislate for us in all Cases whatsoever.

He has abdicated Government here, by declaring us out of his Protection and waging War against us.

He has plundered our Seas, ravaged our Coasts, burnt our towns, and destroyed the Lives of our People.

He is, at this Time, transporting large Armies of foreign Mercenaries to complete the works of Death, Desolation, and Tyranny, already begun with circumstances of Cruelty and Perfidy, scarcely paralleled in the most barbarous Ages, and totally unworthy the Head of a civilized Nation.

He has constrained our fellow Citizens taken Captive on the high Seas to bear Arms against their Country, to become the Executioners of their Friends and Brethren, or to fall themselves by their Hands.

He has excited domestic Insurrections amongst us, and has endeavoured to bring on the Inhabitants of our Frontiers, the merciless Indian Savages, whose known Rule of Warfare, is an undistinguished Destruction, of all Ages, Sexes and Conditions.

In every stage of these Oppressions we have Petitioned for Redress in the most humble Terms: Our repeated Petitions have been answered only by repeated Injury. A Prince, whose Character is thus marked by every act which may define a Tyrant, is unfit to be the Ruler of a free People.

Nor have we been wanting in Attentions to our British Brethren. We have warned them from Time to Time of Attempts by their Legislature to extend an unwarrantable Jurisdiction over us. We have reminded them of the Circumstances of our Emigration and Settlement here. We have appealed to their native Justice and Magnanimity, and we have conjured them by the Ties of our common Kindred to disavow these Usurpations, which, would inevitably interrupt our Connections and Correspondence. They too have been deaf to the Voice of Justice and of Consanguinity. We must, therefore, acquiesce in the Necessity, which denounces our Separation, and hold them, as we hold the rest of Mankind, Enemies in War, in Peace, Friends.

We, therefore, the Representatives of the UNITED STATES OF AMERICA, in General Congress, Assembled, appealing to the Supreme Judge of the World for the Rectitude of our Intentions, do, in the Name, and by Authority of the good People of these Colonies, solemnly Publish and Declare, That these United Colonies are, and of Right ought to be, Free and Independent States; that they are absolved from all Allegiance to the British Crown, and that all political Connection between them and the State of Great-Britain, is and ought to be totally dissolved; and that as Free and Independent States, they have full Power to levy War, conclude Peace, contract Alliances, establish Commerce, and to do all other Acts and Things which Independent States may of right do. And for the support of this declaration, with a firm Reliance on the Protection of divine Providence, we mutually pledge to each other our lives, our Fortunes, and our sacred Honor.

JOHN HANCOCK, President

Attest.
CHARLES THOMSON, Secretary.

Signers of the Declaration of Independence

Delegate and state	Vocation	Birthplace	Born	Died
Adams, John (Mass.)	Lawyer	Braintree (Quincy), Mass.	Oct. 30, 1735	July 4, 1826
Adams, Samuel (Mass.)	Political leader	Boston, Mass.	Sept. 27, 1722	Oct. 2, 1803
Bartlett, Josiah (N.H.)	Physician, judge	Amesbury, Mass.	Nov. 21, 1729	May 19, 1795
Braxton, Carter (Va.)	Farmer	Newington Plantation, Va.	Sept. 10, 1736	Oct. 10, 1797
Carroll, Chas. of Carrollton (Md.)	Lawyer	Annapolis, Md.	Sept. 19, 1737	Nov. 14, 1832
Chase, Samuel (Md.)	Judge	Princess Anne, Md.	Apr. 17, 1741	June 19, 1811
Clark, Abraham (N.J.)	Surveyor	Roselle, N.J.	Feb. 15, 1726	Sept. 15, 1794
Clymer, George (Pa.)	Merchant	Philadelphia, Pa.	Mar. 16, 1739	Jan. 23, 1813
Ellery, William (R.I.)	Lawyer	Newport, R.I.	Dec. 22, 1727	Feb. 15, 1820
Floyd, William (N.Y.)	Soldier	Brookhaven, N.Y.	Dec. 17, 1734	Aug. 4, 1821
Franklin, Benjamin (Pa.)	Printer, publisher.	Boston, Mass.	Jan. 17, 1706	Apr. 17, 1790
Gerry, Elbridge (Mass.)	Merchant	Marblehead, Mass.	July 17, 1744	Nov. 23, 1814
Gwinnett, Button (Ga.)	Merchant	Down Hatherly, England.	c. 1735	May 19, 1777
Hall, Lyman (Ga.)	Physician	Wallingford, Conn.	Apr. 12, 1724	Oct. 19, 1790
Hancock, John (Mass.)	Merchant	Braintree (Quincy), Mass.	Jan. 12, 1737	Oct. 8, 1793
Harrison, Benjamin (Va.)	Farmer	Berkeley, Va.	Apr. 5, 1726	Apr. 24, 1791
Hart, John (N.J.)	Farmer	Stonington, Conn.	c. 1711	May 11, 1779
Hewes, Joseph (N.C.)	Merchant	Princeton, N.J.	Jan. 23, 1730	Nov. 10, 1779
Heyward, Thos. Jr. (S.C.)	Lawyer, farmer.	St. Luke's Parish, S.C.	July 28, 1746	Mar. 6, 1809
Hooper, William (N.C.)	Lawyer	Boston, Mass.	June 28, 1742	Oct. 14, 1790
Hopkins, Stephen (R.I.)	Judge, educator	Providence, R.I.	Mar. 7, 1707	July 13, 1785
Hopkinson, Francis (N.J.)	Judge, author.	Philadelphia, Pa.	Sept. 21, 1737	May 9, 1791
Huntington, Samuel (Conn.)	Judge	Windham County, Conn.	July 3, 1731	Jan. 5, 1796
Jefferson, Thomas (Va.)	Lawyer	Shadwell, Va.	Apr. 13, 1743	July 4, 1826
Lee, Francis Lightfoot (Va.)	Farmer	Westmoreland County, Va.	Oct. 14, 1734	Jan. 11, 1797
Lee, Richard Henry (Va.)	Farmer	Westmoreland County, Va.	Jan. 20, 1732	June 19, 1794
Lewis, Francis (N.Y.)	Merchant	Llandaff, Wales	Mar., 1713	Dec. 31, 1802
Livingston, Philip (N.Y.)	Merchant	Albany, N.Y.	Jan. 15, 1716	June 12, 1778
Lynch, Thomas Jr. (S.C.)	Farmer	Winyah, S.C.	Aug. 5, 1749	(at sea) 1779
McKean, Thomas (Del.)	Lawyer	New London, Pa.	Mar. 19, 1734	June 24, 1817
Middleton, Arthur (S.C.)	Farmer	Charleston, S.C.	June 26, 1742	Jan. 1, 1787
Morris, Lewis (N.Y.)	Farmer	Morrisania (Bronx County), N.Y.	Apr. 8, 1726	Jan. 22, 1798
Morris, Robert (Pa.)	Merchant	Liverpool, England.	Jan. 20, 1734	May 9, 1806
Morton, John (Pa.)	Judge	Ridley, Pa.	1724	Apr., 1777
Nelson, Thos. Jr. (Va.)	Farmer	Yorktown, Va.	Dec. 26, 1738	Jan. 4, 1789
Paca, William (Md.)	Judge	Abingdon, Md.	Oct. 31, 1740	Oct. 23, 1799
Paine, Robert Treat (Mass.)	Judge	Boston, Mass.	Mar. 11, 1731	May 12, 1814
Penn, John (N.C.)	Lawyer	Near Port Royal, Va.	May 17, 1741	Sept. 14, 1788
Read, George (Del.)	Judge	Near North East, Md.	Sept. 18, 1733	Sept. 21, 1798
Rodney, Caesar (Del.)	Judge	Dover, Del.	Oct. 7, 1728	June 29, 1784
Ross, George (Pa.)	Judge	New Castle, Del.	May 10, 1730	July 14, 1779
Rush, Benjamin (Pa.)	Physician	Byberry, Pa. (Philadelphia).	Dec. 24, 1745	Apr. 19, 1813
Rutledge, Edward (S.C.)	Lawyer	Charleston, S.C.	Nov. 23, 1749	Jan. 23, 1800
Sherman, Roger (Conn.)	Lawyer	Newton, Mass.	Apr. 19, 1721	July 23, 1793
Smith, James (Pa.)	Lawyer.	Dublin, Ireland	c. 1719	July 11, 1806
Stockton, Richard (N.J.)	Lawyer	Near Princeton, N.J.	Oct. 1, 1730	Feb. 28, 1781
Stone, Thomas (Md.)	Lawyer	Charles County, Md.	1743	Oct. 5, 1787
Taylor, George (Pa.)	Ironmaster	Ireland.	1716	Feb. 23, 1781
Thornton, Matthew (N.H.)	Physician	Ireland.	1714	June 24, 1803
Walton, George (Ga.)	Judge	Prince Edward County, Va.	1741	Feb. 2, 1804
Whipple, William (N.H.)	Merchant, judge.	Kittery, Me.	Jan. 14, 1730	Nov. 28, 1785
Williams, William (Conn.)	Merchant	Lebanon, Conn.	Apr. 23, 1731	Aug. 2, 1811
Wilson, James (Pa.)	Judge	Carskerdo, Scotland	Sept. 14, 1742	Aug. 28, 1798
Witherspoon, John (N.J.)	Clergyman, educator	Gifford, Scotland	Feb. 5, 1723	Nov. 15, 1794
Wolcott, Oliver (Conn.)	Judge	Windsor, Conn.	Dec. 1, 1726	Dec. 1, 1797
Wythe, George (Va.)	Lawyer	Elizabeth City Co. (Hampton), Va.	1726	June 8, 1806

Constitution of the United States
The Original 7 Articles

PREAMBLE

We, the people of the United States, in order to form a more perfect Union, establish justice, insure domestic tranquility, provide for the common defense, promote the general welfare, and secure the blessings of liberty to ourselves and our posterity do ordain and establish this Constitution for the United States of America.

ARTICLE I.

Section 1—Legislative powers; in whom vested:

All legislative powers herein granted shall be vested in a Congress of the United States, which shall consist of a Senate and House of Representatives.

Section 2—House of Representatives, how and by whom chosen. Qualifications of a Representative. Representatives and direct taxes, how apportioned. Enumeration. Vacancies to be filled. Power of choosing officers, and of impeachment.

1. The House of Representatives shall be composed of members chosen every second year by the people of the several States, and the electors in each State shall have the qualifications requisite for electors of the most numerous branch of the State Legislature.

2. No person shall be a Representative who shall not have attained to the age of twenty-five years, and been seven years a citizen of the United States, and who shall not, when elected, be an inhabitant of that State in which he shall be chosen.

3. *(Representatives and direct taxes shall be apportioned among the several States which may be included within this Union, according to their respective numbers, which shall be determined by adding to the whole number of free persons, including those bound to service for a term of years, and excluding Indians not taxed, three-fifths of all other persons.) (The previous sentence was superseded by Amendment XIV, section 2.)* The actual enumeration shall be made within three years after the first meeting of the Congress of the United States, and within every subsequent term of ten years, in such manner as they shall by law direct. The number of Representatives shall not exceed one for every thirty thousand, but each State shall have at least one Representative; and until such enumeration shall be made, the State of New Hampshire shall be entitled to choose three, Massachusetts eight, Rhode Island and Providence Plantations one, Connecticut five, New York six, New Jersey four, Pennsylvania eight, Delaware one, Maryland six, Virginia ten, North Carolina five, South Carolina five, and Georgia three.

4. When vacancies happen in the representation from any State, the Executive Authority thereof shall issue writs of election to fill such vacancies.

5. The House of Representatives shall choose their Speaker and other officers; and shall have the sole power of impeachment.

Section 3—Senators, how and by whom chosen. How classified. Qualifications of a Senator. President of the Senate, his right to vote. President pro tem., and other officers of the Senate, how chosen. Power to try impeachments. When President is tried, Chief Justice to preside. Sentence.

1. The Senate of the United States shall be composed of two Senators from each State, *(chosen by the Legislature thereof), (The preceding five words were superseded by Amendment XVII, section 1.)* for six years; and each Senator shall have one vote.

2. Immediately after they shall be assembled in consequence of the first election, they shall be divided as equally as may be into three classes. The seats of the Senators of the first class shall be vacated at the expiration of the second year, of the second class at the expiration of the fourth year, and of the third class at the expiration of the sixth year, so that one-third may be chosen every second year; *(and if vacancies happen by resignation, or otherwise, during the recess of the Legislature of any State, the Executive thereof may make temporary appointments until the next meeting of the Legislature, which shall then fill such vacancies.) (The words*

in parentheses were superseded by Amendment XVII, section 2.)

3. No person shall be a Senator who shall not have attained to the age of thirty years, and been nine years a citizen of the United States, and who shall not, when elected, be an inhabitant of that State for which he shall be chosen.

4. The Vice President of the United States shall be President of the Senate, but shall have no vote, unless they be equally divided.

5. The Senate shall choose their other officers, and also a President pro tempore, in the absence of the Vice President, or when he shall exercise the office of President of the United States.

6. The Senate shall have the sole power to try all impeachments. When sitting for that purpose, they shall be on oath or affirmation. When the President of the United States is tried, the Chief Justice shall preside: and no person shall be convicted without the concurrence of two-thirds of the members present.

7. Judgment in cases of impeachment shall not extend further than to removal from office, and disqualification to hold and enjoy any office of honor, trust or profit under the United States: but the party convicted shall nevertheless be liable and subject to indictment, trial, judgment and punishment, according to law.

Section 4—Times, etc., of holding elections, how prescribed. One session each year.

1. The times, places and manner of holding elections for Senators and Representatives, shall be prescribed in each State by the Legislature thereof; but the Congress may at any time by law make or alter such regulations, except as to the places of choosing Senators.

2. The Congress shall assemble at least once in every year, and such meeting shall *(be on the first Monday in December.) (The words in parentheses were superseded by Amendment XX, section 2).* unless they shall by law appoint a different day.

Section 5—Membership, quorum, adjournments, rules. Power to punish or expel. Journal. Time of adjournments, how limited, etc.

1. Each House shall be the judge of the elections, returns and qualifications of its own members, and a majority of each shall constitute a quorum to do business; but a smaller number may adjourn from day to day, and may be authorized to compel the attendance of absent members, in such manner, and under such penalties as each House may provide.

2. Each House may determine the rules of its proceedings, punish its members for disorderly behavior, and, with the concurrence of two-thirds, expel a member.

3. Each House shall keep a journal of its proceedings, and from time to time publish the same, excepting such parts as may in their judgment require secrecy; and the yeas and nays of the members of either House on any question shall, at the desire of one-fifth of those present, be entered on the journal.

4. Neither House, during the session of Congress, shall, without the consent of the other, adjourn for more than three days, nor to any other place than that in which the two Houses shall be sitting.

Section 6—Compensation, privileges, disqualifications in certain cases.

1. The Senators and Representatives shall receive a compensation for their services, to be ascertained by law, and paid out of the Treasury of the United States. They shall in all cases, except treason, felony and breach of the peace, be privileged from arrest during their attendance at the session of their respective Houses, and in going to and returning from the same; and for any speech or debate in either House, they shall not be questioned in any other place.

2. No Senator or Representative shall, during the time for which he was elected, be appointed to any civil office under the authority of the United States, which shall have been created, or the emoluments whereof shall have been increased during such time; and no person holding any office under the United States, shall be a member of either House

during his continuance in office.

Section 7—House to originate all revenue bills. Veto. Bill may be passed by two-thirds of each House, notwithstanding, etc. Bill, not returned in ten days, to become a law. Provisions as to orders, concurrent resolutions, etc.

1. All bills for raising revenue shall originate in the House of Representatives; but the Senate may propose or concur with amendments as on other bills.

2. Every bill which shall have passed the House of Representatives and the Senate, shall, before it becomes a law, be presented to the President of the United States; if he approves he shall sign it, but if not he shall return it, with his objections to that House in which it shall have originated, who shall enter the objections at large on their journal, and proceed to reconsider it. If after such reconsideration two-thirds of that House shall agree to pass the bill, it shall be sent, together with the objections, to the other House, by which it shall likewise be reconsidered, and if approved by two-thirds of that House, it shall become a law. But in all such cases the votes of both Houses shall be determined by yeas and nays, and the names of the persons voting for and against the bill shall be entered on the journal of each House respectively. If any bill shall not be returned by the President within ten days (Sundays excepted) after it shall have been presented to him, the same shall be a law, in like manner as if he had signed it, unless the Congress by their adjournment prevent its return, in which case it shall not be a law.

3. Every order, resolution, or vote to which the concurrence of the Senate and House of Representatives may be necessary (except on a question of adjournment) shall be presented to the President of the United States; and before the same shall take effect, shall be approved by him, or being disapproved by him, shall be repassed by two-thirds of the Senate and House of Representatives, according to the rules and limitations prescribed in the case of a bill.

Section 8—Powers of Congress.

The Congress shall have power

1. To lay and collect taxes, duties, imposts and excises, to pay the debts and provide for the common defense and general welfare of the United States; but all duties, imposts and excises shall be uniform throughout the United States;

2. To borrow money on the credit of the United States;

3. To regulate commerce with foreign nations, and among the several States, and with the Indian tribes;

4. To establish a uniform rule of naturalization, and uniform laws on the subject of bankruptcies throughout the United States;

5. To coin money, regulate the value thereof, and of foreign coin, and fix the standard of weights and measures;

6. To provide for the punishment of counterfeiting the securities and current coin of the United States;

7. To establish post-offices and post-roads;

8. To promote the progress of science and useful arts, by securing for limited times to authors and inventors the exclusive right to their respective writings and discoveries;

9. To constitute tribunals inferior to the Supreme Court;

10. To define and punish piracies and felonies committed on the high seas, and offenses against the law of nations;

11. To declare war, grant letters of marque and reprisal, and make rules concerning captures on land and water;

12. To raise and support armies, but no appropriation of money to that use shall be for a longer term than two years;

13. To provide and maintain a navy;

14. To make rules for the government and regulation of the land and naval forces;

15. To provide for calling forth the militia to execute the laws of the Union, suppress insurrections and repel invasions;

16. To provide for organizing, arming, and disciplining the militia, and for governing such part of them as may be employed in the service of the United States, reserving to the States respectively, the appointment of the officers, and the authority of training the militia according to the discipline prescribed by Congress;

17. To exercise exclusive legislation in all cases whatsoever, over such district (not exceeding ten miles square) as may, by cession of particular States, and the acceptance of Congress, become the seat of the Government of the United States, and to exercise like authority over all places purchased by the consent of the Legislature of the State in which the same shall be, for the erection of forts, magazines, arsenals, dockyards, and other needful buildings;—And

18. To make all laws which shall be necessary and proper for carrying into execution the foregoing powers, and all other powers vested by this Constitution in the Government of the United States, or in any department or officer thereof.

Section 9—Provision as to migration or importation of certain persons. Habeas corpus, bills of attainder, etc. Taxes, how apportioned. No export duty. No commercial preference. Money, how drawn from Treasury, etc. No titular nobility. Officers not to receive presents, etc.

1. The migration or importation of such persons as any of the States now existing shall think proper to admit, shall not be prohibited by the Congress prior to the year one thousand eight hundred and eight, but a tax or duty may be imposed on such importation, not exceeding ten dollars for each person.

2. The privilege of the writ of habeas corpus shall not be suspended, unless when in cases of rebellion or invasion the public safety may require it.

3. No bill of attainder or ex post facto law shall be passed.

4. No capitation, or other direct, tax shall be laid, unless in proportion to the census or enumeration herein before directed to be taken. *(Modified by Amendment XVI.)*

5. No tax or duty shall be laid on articles exported from any State.

6. No preference shall be given by any regulation of commerce or revenue to the ports of one State over those of another: nor shall vessels bound to, or from, one State, be obliged to enter, clear, or pay duties in another.

7. No money shall be drawn from the Treasury, but in consequence of appropriations made by law; and a regular statement and account of the receipts and expenditures of all public money shall be published from time to time.

8. No title of nobility shall be granted by the United States: and no person holding any office of profit or trust under them, shall, without the consent of the Congress, accept of any present, emolument, office, or title, of any kind whatever, from any king, prince, or foreign state.

Section 10—States prohibited from the exercise of certain powers.

1. No State shall enter into any treaty, alliance, or confederation; grant letters of marque and reprisal; coin money; emit bills of credit; make anything but gold and silver coin a tender in payment of debts; pass any bill of attainder, ex post facto law, or law impairing the obligation of contracts, or grant any title of nobility.

2. No State shall, without the consent of the Congress, lay any imposts or duties on imports or exports, except what may be absolutely necessary for executing its inspection laws: and the net produce of all duties and imposts, laid by any State on imports or exports, shall be for the use of the Treasury of the United States; and all such laws shall be subject to the revision and control of the Congress.

3. No State shall, without the consent of Congress, lay any duty of tonnage, keep troops, or ships of war in time of peace, enter into any agreement or compact with another State, or with a foreign power, or engage in war, unless actually invaded, or in such imminent danger as will not admit of delay.

ARTICLE II.

Section 1—President: his term of office. Electors of President; number and how appointed. Electors to vote on same day. Qualification of President. On whom his duties devolve in case of his removal, death, etc. President's compensation. His oath of office.

1. The Executive power shall be vested in a President of the United States of America. He shall hold his office during the term of four years, and together with the Vice President, chosen for the same term, be elected as follows

2. Each State shall appoint, in such manner as the Legis-

lature thereof may direct, a number of electors, equal to the whole number of Senators and Representatives to which the State may be entitled in the Congress: but no Senator or Representative, or person holding an office of trust or profit under the United States, shall be appointed an elector.

(The electors shall meet in their respective States, and vote by ballot for two persons, of whom at least shall not be an inhabitant of the same State with themselves. And they shall make a list of all the persons voted for, and of the number of votes for each; which list they shall sign and certify, and transmit sealed to the seat of the Government of the United States, directed to the President of the Senate. The President of the Senate shall, in the presence of the Senate and House of Representatives, open all the certificates, and the votes shall then be counted. The person having the greatest number of votes shall be the President, if such number be a majority of the whole number of electors appointed; and if there be more than one who have such majority, and have an equal number of votes, then the House of Representatives shall immediately choose by ballot one of them for President; and if no person have a majority, then from the five highest on the list the said House shall in like manner choose the President. But in choosing the President, the votes shall be taken by States, the representation from each State having one vote; a quorum for this purpose shall consist of a member or members from two-thirds of the States, and a majority of all the States shall be necessary to a choice. In every case, after the choice of the President, the person having the greatest number of votes of the electors shall be the Vice President. But if there should remain two or more who have equal votes, the Senate shall choose from them by ballot the Vice President.)

(This clause was superseded by Amendment XII.)

3. The Congress may determine the time of choosing the electors, and the day on which they shall give their votes; which day shall be the same throughout the United States.

4. No person except a natural born citizen, or a citizen of the United States, at the time of the adoption of this Constitution, shall be eligible to the office of President; neither shall any person be eligible to that office who shall not have attained to the age of thirty-five years, and been fourteen years a resident within the United States.

(For qualification of the Vice President, see Amendment XII.)

5. In case of the removal of the President from office, or of his death, resignation, or inability to discharge the powers and duties of the said office, the same shall devolve on the Vice President, and the Congress may by law provide for the case of removal, death, resignation or inability, both of the President and Vice President, declaring what officer shall then act as President, and such officer shall act accordingly, until the disability be removed, or a President shall be elected.

(This clause has been modified by Amendments XX and XXV.)

6. The President shall, at stated times, receive for his services, a compensation, which shall neither be increased nor diminished during the period for which he shall have been elected, and he shall not receive within that period any other emolument from the United States, or any of them.

7. Before he enter on the execution of his office, he shall take the following oath or affirmation:

"I do solemnly swear (or affirm) that I will faithfully execute the office of President of the United States, and will to the best of my ability, preserve, protect and defend the Constitution of the United States."

Section 2—President to be Commander-in-Chief. He may require opinions of cabinet officers, etc., may pardon. Treaty-making power. Nomination of certain officers. When President may fill vacancies.

1. The President shall be Commander-in-Chief of the Army and Navy of the United States, and of the militia of the several States, when called into the actual service of the United States; he may require the opinion, in writing, of the principal officer in each of the executive departments, upon any subject relating to the duties of their respective offices, and he shall have power to grant reprieves and pardons for offenses against the United States, except in cases of impeachment.

2. He shall have power, by and with the advice and con-

sent of the Senate, to make treaties, provided two-thirds of the Senators present concur; and he shall nominate, and by and with the advice and consent of the Senate, shall appoint ambassadors, other public ministers and consuls, judges of the Supreme Court, and all other officers of the United States, whose appointments are not herein otherwise provided for, and which shall be established by law: but the Congress may by law vest the appointment of such inferior officers, as they think proper, in the President alone, in the courts of law, or in the heads of departments.

3. The President shall have power to fill up all vacancies that may happen during the recess of the Senate, by granting commissions, which shall expire at the end of their next session.

Section 3—President shall communicate to Congress. He may convene and adjourn Congress, in case of disagreement, etc. Shall receive ambassadors, execute laws, and commission officers.

He shall from time to time give to the Congress information of the state of the Union, and recommend to their consideration such measures as he shall judge necessary and expedient; he may, on extraordinary occasions, convene both Houses, or either of them, and in case of disagreement between them, with respect to the time of adjournment, he may adjourn them to such time as he shall think proper; he shall receive ambassadors and other public ministers; he shall take care that the laws be faithfully executed, and shall commission all the officers of the United States.

Section 4—All civil offices forfeited for certain crimes.

The President, Vice President, and all civil officers of the United States, shall be removed from office on impeachment for, and conviction of, treason, bribery, or other high crimes and misdemeanors.

ARTICLE III.

Section 1—Judicial powers, Tenure. Compensation.

The judicial power of the United States, shall be vested in one Supreme Court, and in such inferior courts as the Congress may from time to time ordain and establish. The judges, both of the Supreme and inferior courts, shall hold their offices during good behavior, and shall at stated times, receive for their services, a compensation, which shall not be diminished during their continuance in office.

Section 2—Judicial power; to what cases it extends. Original jurisdiction of Supreme Court; appellate jurisdiction. Trial by jury, etc. Trial, where.

1. The judicial power shall extend to all cases, in law and equity, arising under this Constitution, the laws of the United States, and treaties made, or which shall be made, under their authority; to all cases affecting ambassadors, other public ministers and consuls; to all cases of admiralty and maritime jurisdiction; to controversies to which the United States shall be a party; to controversies between two or more States; between a State and citizens of another State; between citizens of different States, between citizens of the same State claiming lands under grants of different States, and between a State, or the citizens thereof, and foreign states, citizens or subjects.

(This section is modified by Amendment XI.)

2. In all cases affecting ambassadors, other public ministers and consuls, and those in which a State shall be party, the Supreme Court shall have original jurisdiction. In all the other cases before mentioned, the Supreme Court shall have appellate jurisdiction, both as to law and fact, with such exceptions, and under such regulations as the Congress shall make.

3. The trial of all crimes, except in cases of impeachment, shall be by jury; and such trial shall be held in the State where the said crimes shall have been committed; but when not committed within any State, the trial shall be at such place or places as the Congress may by law have directed.

Section 3—Treason Defined, Proof of, Punishment of.

1. Treason against the United States, shall consist only in levying war against them, or in adhering to their enemies,

giving them aid and comfort. No person shall be convicted of treason unless on the testimony of two witnesses to the same overt act, or on confession in open court.

2. The Congress shall have power to declare the punishment of treason, but no attainder of treason shall work corruption of blood, or forfeiture except during the life of the person attainted.

ARTICLE IV.

Section 1—Each State to give credit to the public acts, etc., of every other State.

Full faith and credit shall be given in each State to the public acts, records, and judicial proceedings of every other State. And the Congress may by general laws prescribe the manner in which such acts, records and proceedings shall be proved, and the effect thereof.

Section 2—Privileges of citizens of each State. Fugitives from justice to be delivered up. Persons held to service having escaped, to be delivered up.

1. The citizens of each State shall be entitled to all privileges and immunities of citizens in the several States.

2. A person charged in any State with treason, felony, or other crime, who shall flee from justice, and be found in another State, shall on demand of the Executive authority of the State from which he fled, be delivered up, to be removed to the State having jurisdiction of the crime.

(3. No person held to service or labor in one State, under the laws thereof, escaping into another, shall in consequence of any law or regulation therein, be discharged from such service or labor, but shall be delivered up on claim of the party to whom such service or labor may be due.) (This clause was superseded by Amendment XIII.)

Section 3—Admission of new States. Power of Congress over territory and other property.

1. New States may be admitted by the Congress into this Union; but no new State shall be formed or erected within the jurisdiction of any other State; nor any State be formed by the junction of two or more States, or parts of States, without the consent of the Legislatures of the States concerned as well as of the Congress.

2. The Congress shall have power to dispose of and make all needful rules and regulations respecting the territory or other property belonging to the United States; and nothing in this Constitution shall be so construed as to prejudice any claims of the United States, or of any particular State.

Section 4—Republican form of government guaranteed. Each state to be protected.

The United States shall guarantee to every State in this Union a Republican form of government, and shall protect each of them against invasion; and on application of the Legislature, or of the Executive (when the Legislature cannot be convened) against domestic violence.

ARTICLE V.

Constitution: how amended; proviso.

The Congress, whenever two-thirds of both Houses shall deem it necessary, shall propose amendments to this Constitution, or, on the application of the Legislatures of two-thirds of the several States, shall call a convention for proposing amendments, which, in either case, shall be valid to all intents and purposes, as part of this Constitution, when ratified by the Legislatures of three-fourths of the several States, or by conventions in three-fourths thereof, as the one or the other mode of ratification may be proposed by the Congress: provided that no amendment which may be made prior to the year one thousand eight hundred and eight shall in any manner affect the first and fourth clauses in the Ninth Section of the First Article; and that no State, without its consent, shall be deprived of its equal suffrage in the Senate.

ARTICLE VI.

Certain debts, etc., declared valid. Supremacy of Constitution, treaties, and laws of the United States. Oath to support Constitution, by whom taken. No religious test.

1. All debts contracted and engagements entered into, before the adoption of this Constitution, shall be as valid against the United States under this Constitution, as under the Confederation.

2. This Constitution, and the laws of the United States which shall be made in pursuance thereof; and all treaties made, or which shall be made, under the authority of the United States, shall be the supreme law of the land; and the judges in every State shall be bound thereby, any thing in the Constitution or laws of any State to the contrary notwithstanding.

3. The Senators and Representatives before mentioned, and the members of the several State Legislatures, and all executive and judicial officers, both of the United States and of the several States, shall be bound by oath or affirmation, to support this Constitution; but no religious test shall ever be required as a qualification to any office or public trust under the United States.

ARTICLE VII.

What ratification shall establish Constitution.

The ratification of the Conventions of nine States, shall be sufficient for the establishment of this Constitution between the States so ratifying the same.

Done in convention by the unanimous consent of the States present the Seventeenth day of September in the year of our Lord one thousand seven hundred and eighty seven, and of the independence of the United States of America the Twelfth. In witness whereof we have hereunto subscribed our names.

George Washington, President and deputy from Virginia.

New Hampshire—John Langdon, Nicholas Gilman.

Massachusetts—Nathaniel Gorham, Rufus King.

Connecticut—Wm. Saml. Johnson, Roger Sherman.

New York—Alexander Hamilton.

New Jersey—Wil: Livingston, David Brearley, Wm. Paterson, Jona: Dayton.

Pennsylvania—B. Franklin, Thomas Mifflin, Robt. Morris, Geo. Clymer, Thos. FitzSimons, Jared Ingersoll, James Wilson, Gouv. Morris.

Delaware—Geo: Read, Gunning Bedford Jun., John Dickinson, Richard Bassett, Jaco: Broom.

Maryland—James McHenry, Daniel of Saint Thomas' Jenifer, Danl. Carroll.

Virginia—John Blair, James Madison Jr.

North Carolina—Wm. Blount, Rich'd. Dobbs Spaight, Hugh Williamson.

South Carolina—J. Rutledge, Charles Cotesworth Pinckney, Charles Pinckney, Pierce Butler.

Georgia—William Few, Abr. Baldwin.

Attest: William Jackson, Secretary.

Ten Original Amendments: The Bill of Rights
In force Dec. 15, 1791

(The First Congress, at its first session in the City of New York, Sept. 25, 1789, submitted to the states 12 amendments to clarify certain individual and state rights not named in the Constitution. They are generally called the Bill of Rights.

(Influential in framing these amendments was the Declaration of Rights of Virginia, written by George Mason (1725-1792) in 1776. Mason, a Virginia delegate to the Constitutional Convention, did not sign the Constitution and opposed its ratification on the ground that it did not sufficiently oppose slavery or safeguard individual rights.

(In the preamble to the resolution offering the proposed amendments, Congress said: "The conventions of a number of the States having at the time of their adopting the Constitution, expressed a desire, in order to prevent misconstruction or abuse of its powers, that further declaratory and restrictive clauses should be added, and as extending the ground of public confidence in the government will best insure the beneficent ends of its institution, be it resolved," etc.

(Ten of these amendments now commonly known as one to 10 inclusive, but originally 3 to 12 inclusive, were ratified by the states as follows: New Jersey, Nov. 20, 1789; Maryland, Dec. 19, 1789; North Carolina, Dec. 22, 1789; South Carolina, Jan. 19, 1790; New Hampshire, Jan 25, 1790; Delaware, Jan 28, 1790; New York, Feb. 27, 1790; Pennsylvania, Mar. 10, 1790; Rhode

Island, June 7, 1790; Vermont, Nov 3, 1791; Virginia, Dec. 15, 1791; Massachusetts, Mar. 2, 1939; Georgia, Mar. 18, 1939; Connecticut, Apr. 19, 1939. These original 10 ratified amendments follow as Amendments I to X inclusive.

(Of the two original proposed amendments which were not ratified by the necessary number of states, the first related to apportionment of Representatives; the second, to compensation of members. See p. 465.)

AMENDMENT I.
Religious establishment prohibited. Freedom of speech, of the press, and right to petition.

Congress shall make no law respecting an establishment of religion, or prohibiting the free exercise thereof; or abridging the freedom of speech, or of the press; or the right of the people peaceably to assemble, and to petition the Government for a redress of grievances.

AMENDMENT II.
Right to keep and bear arms.

A well-regulated militia, being necessary to the security of a free State, the right of the people to keep and bear arms, shall not be infringed.

AMENDMENT III.
Conditions for quarters for soldiers.

No soldier shall, in time of peace be quartered in any house, without the consent of the owner, nor in time of war, but in a manner to be prescribed by law.

AMENDMENT IV.
Right of search and seizure regulated.

The right of the people to be secure in their persons, houses, papers, and effects, against unreasonable searches and seizures, shall not be violated, and no warrants shall issue, but upon probable cause, supported by oath or affirmation, and particularly describing the place to be searched, and the persons or things to be seized.

AMENDMENT V.
Provisions concerning prosecution. Trial and punishment—private property not to be taken for public use without compensation.

No person shall be held to answer for a capital, or otherwise infamous crime, unless on a presentment or indictment of a Grand Jury, except in cases arising in the land or naval forces, or in the militia, when in actual service in time of war or public danger; nor shall any person be subject for the same offense to be twice put in jeopardy of life or limb; nor shall be compelled in any criminal case to be a witness against himself, nor be deprived of life, liberty, or property, without due process of law; nor shall private property be taken for public use without just compensation.

AMENDMENT VI.
Right to speedy trial, witnesses, etc.

In all criminal prosecutions, the accused shall enjoy the right to a speedy and public trial, by an impartial jury of the State and district wherein the crime shall have been committed, which district shall have been previously ascertained by law, and to be informed of the nature and cause of the accusation; to be confronted with the witnesses against him; to have compulsory process for obtaining witnesses in his favor, and to have the assistance of counsel for his defense.

AMENDMENT VII.
Right of trial by jury.

In suits at common law, where the value in controversy shall exceed twenty dollars, the right of trial by jury shall be preserved, and no fact tried by a jury shall be otherwise reexamined in any court of the United States, than according to the rules of the common law.

AMENDMENT VIII.
Excessive bail or fines and cruel punishment prohibited.

Excessive bail shall not be required, nor excessive fines imposed, nor cruel and unusual punishments inflicted.

AMENDMENT IX.
Rule of construction of Constitution.

The enumeration in the Constitution, of certain rights, shall not be construed to deny or disparage others retained by the people.

AMENDMENT X.
Rights of States under Constitution.

The powers not delegated to the United States by the Constitution, nor prohibited by it to the States, are reserved to the States respectively, or to the people.

Amendments Since the Bill of Rights

AMENDMENT XI.
Judicial powers construed.

The judicial power of the United States shall not be construed to extend to any suit in law or equity, commenced or prosecuted against one of the United States by citizens of another State, or by citizens or subjects of any foreign state.

(This amendment was proposed to the Legislatures of the several States by the Third Congress on March 4, 1794, and was declared to have been ratified in a message from the President to Congress, dated Jan. 8, 1798.

(It was on Jan 5, 1798, that Secretary of State Pickering received from 12 of the States authenticated ratifications, and informed President John Adams of that fact.

(As a result of later research in the Department of State, it is now established that Amendment XI became part of the Constitution on Feb. 7, 1795, for on that date it had been ratified by 12 States as follows:

(1. New York, Mar. 27, 1794. 2. Rhode Island, Mar. 31, 1794. 3. Connecticut, May 8, 1794. 4. New Hampshire, June 16, 1794. 5. Massachusetts, June 26, 1794. 6. Vermont, between Oct 9, 1794, and Nov. 9, 1794. 7. Virginia, Nov. 18, 1794. 8. Georgia, Nov. 29, 1794. 9. Kentucky, Dec. 7, 1794. 10. Maryland, Dec. 26, 1794. 11. Delaware, Jan 23, 1795. 12. North Carolina, Feb. 7, 1795.

(On June 1, 1796, more than a year after Amendment XI had become a part of the Constitution (but before anyone was officially aware of this), Tennessee had been admitted as a State; but not until Oct. 16, 1797, was a certified copy of the resolution of Congress proposing the amendment sent to the Governor of Tennessee (John Sevier) by Secretary of State Pickering, whose office was then at Trenton, New Jersey, because of the epidemic of yellow fever at Philadelphia; it seems, however, that the Legislature of Tennessee took no action on Amendment XI, owing doubtless to the fact that public announcement of its adoption was made soon thereafter.

(Besides the necessary 12 States, one other, South Carolina, ratified Amendment XI, but this action was not taken until Dec. 4, 1797; the two remaining States, New Jersey and Pennsylvania, failed to ratify.)

AMENDMENT XII.
Manner of choosing President and Vice-President.

(Proposed by Congress Dec. 9, 1803; ratification completed June 15, 1804.)

The Electors shall meet in their respective States and vote by ballot for President and Vice-President, one of whom, at least, shall not be an inhabitant of the same State with themselves; they shall name in their ballots the person voted for as President, and in distinct ballots the person voted for as Vice-President, and they shall make distinct lists of all persons voted for as President, and of all persons voted for as Vice-President, and of the number of votes for each, which lists they shall sign and certify, and transmit sealed to the seat of the Government of the United States, directed to the President of the Senate; the President of the Senate shall, in the presence of the Senate and House of Representatives, open all the certificates and the votes shall then be counted;—The person having the greatest number of votes for President, shall be the President, if such number be a majority of the whole number of Electors appointed; and if no person have such majority, then from the persons having the highest numbers not exceeding three on the list of those voted for as President, the House of Representatives shall choose immediately, by ballot, the President. But in choosing the President, the votes shall be taken by States, the representation from each State having one vote; a quorum for this purpose shall consist of a member or members from two-thirds of the States, and a majority of all the States shall be necessary to a choice. *(And if the House of Representatives shall not choose a President whenever the right of choice, shall devolve upon them, before the fourth day of March next following, then the Vice-President shall act as President, as in the case of the death or other constitutional disability of the President.) (The words in parentheses were superseded by Amendment XX, section 3.)* The person having the greatest number of votes as Vice-President, shall be the Vice-President, if such number be a majority of the whole number of Electors appointed, and if no person have a majority, then from the two highest numbers on the list, the Senate shall choose the Vice-President; a quorum for the purpose shall consist of two-thirds of the whole number of Senators, and a majority of the whole number shall be necessary to a choice. But no person constitutionally ineligible to the office of President shall be eligible to that of Vice-President of the United States.

THE RECONSTRUCTION AMENDMENTS

(Amendments XIII, XIV, and XV are commonly known as the Reconstruction Amendments, inasmuch as they followed the Civil War, and were drafted by Republicans who were bent on imposing their own policy of reconstruction on the South. Post-bellum legislatures there—Mississippi, South Carolina, Georgia, for example—had set up laws which, it was charged, were contrived to perpetuate Negro slavery under other names.)

AMENDMENT XIII.

Slavery abolished.

(Proposed by Congress Jan. 31, 1865; ratification completed Dec. 18, 1865. The amendment, when first proposed by a resolution in Congress, was passed by the Senate, 38 to 6, on Apr. 8, 1864, but was defeated in the House, 95 to 66 on June 15, 1864. On reconsideration by the House, on Jan. 31, 1865, the resolution passed, 119 to 56. It was approved by President Lincoln on Feb. 1, 1865, although the Supreme Court had decided in 1798 that the President has nothing to do with the proposing of amendments to the Constitution, or their adoption.)

1. Neither slavery nor involuntary servitude, except as a punishment for crime whereof the party shall have been duly convicted, shall exist within the United States or any place subject to their jurisdiction.

2. Congress shall have power to enforce this article by appropriate legislation.

AMENDMENT XIV.

Citizenship rights not to be abridged.

(The following amendment was proposed to the Legislatures of the several states by the 39th Congress, June 13, 1866, and was declared to have been ratified in a proclamation by the Secretary of State, July 28, 1868.

(The 14th amendment was adopted only by virtue of ratification subsequent to earlier rejections. Newly constituted legislatures in both North Carolina and South Carolina (respectively July 4 and 9, 1868), ratified the proposed amendment, although earlier legislatures had rejected the proposal. The Secretary of State issued a proclamation, which, though doubtful as to the effect of attempted withdrawals by Ohio and New Jersey, entertained no doubt as to the validity of the ratification by North and South Carolina. The following day (July 21, 1868), Congress passed a resolution which declared the 14th Amendment to be a part of the Constitution and directed the Secretary of State so to promulgate it. The Secretary waited, however, until the newly constituted Legislature of Georgia had ratified the amendment, subsequent to an earlier rejection, before the promulgation of the ratification of the new amendment.)

1. All persons born or naturalized in the United States, and subject to the jurisdiction thereof, are citizens of the United States and of the State wherein they reside. No State shall make or enforce any law which shall abridge the privileges or immunities of citizens of the United States; nor shall

any State deprive any person of life, liberty, or property, without due process of law; nor deny to any person within its jurisdiction the equal protection of the laws.

2. Representatives shall be apportioned among the several States according to their respective numbers, counting the whole number of persons in each State, excluding Indians not taxed. But when the right to vote at any election for the choice of Electors for President and Vice-President of the United States, Representatives in Congress, the executive and judicial officers of a State, or the members of the Legislature thereof, is denied to any of the male inhabitants of such State, being twenty-one years of age, and, citizens of the United States, or in any way abridged, except for participation in rebellion, or other crime, the basis of representation therein shall be reduced in the proportion which the number of such male citizens shall bear to the whole number of male citizens twenty-one years of age in such State.

3. No person shall be a Senator or Representative in Congress, or Elector of President and Vice-President, or hold any office, civil or military, under the United States, or under any State, who, having previously taken an oath, as a member of Congress, or as an officer of the United States, or as a member of any State Legislature, or as an executive or judicial officer of any State, to support the Constitution of the United States, shall have engaged in insurrection or rebellion against the same, or given aid or comfort to the enemies thereof. But Congress may by a vote of two-thirds of each House, remove such disability.

4. The validity of the public debt of the United States, authorized by law, including debts incurred for payment of pensions and bounties for services in suppressing insurrection or rebellion, shall not be questioned. But neither the United States nor any State shall assume or pay any debt or obligation incurred in aid of insurrection or rebellion against the United States, or any claim for the loss or emancipation of any slave; but all such debts, obligations and claims, shall be held illegal and void.

5. The Congress shall have power to enforce, by appropriate legislation, the provisions of this article.

AMENDMENT XV.

Race no bar to voting rights.

(The following amendment was proposed to the legislatures of the several States by the 40th Congress, Feb. 26, 1869, and was declared to have been ratified in a proclamation by the Secretary of State, Mar. 30, 1870.)

1. The right of citizens of the United States to vote shall not be denied or abridged by the United States or by any State on account of race, color, or previous condition of servitude.

2. The Congress shall have power to enforce this article by appropriate legislation.

AMENDMENT XVI.

Income taxes authorized.

(Proposed by Congress July 12, 1909; ratification declared by the Secretary of State Feb. 25, 1913.)

The Congress shall have power to lay and collect taxes on incomes, from whatever source derived, without apportionment among the several States, and without regard to any census or enumeration.

AMENDMENT XVII.

United States Senators to be elected by direct popular vote.

(Proposed by Congress May 13, 1912; ratification declared by the Secretary of State May 31, 1913.)

1. The Senate of the United States shall be composed of two Senators from each State, elected by the people thereof, for six years; and each Senator shall have one vote. The electors in each State shall have the qualifications requisite for electors of the most numerous branch of the State Legislatures.

2. When vacancies happen in the representation of any State in the Senate, the executive authority of such State shall issue writs of election to fill such vacancies: Provided, That the Legislature of any State may empower the Executive thereof to make temporary appointments until the peo-

ple fill the vacancies by election as the Legislature may direct.

3. This amendment shall not be so construed as to affect the election or term of any Senator chosen before it becomes valid as part of the Constitution.

AMENDMENT XVIII.

Liquor prohibition amendment.

(Proposed by Congress Dec. 18, 1917; ratification completed Jan. 16, 1919. Repealed by Amendment XXI, effective Dec. 5, 1933.)

(1. After one year from the ratification of this article the manufacture, sale, or transportation of intoxicating liquors within, the importation thereof into, or the exportation thereof from the United States and all territory subject to the jurisdiction thereof for beverage purposes is hereby prohibited.

(2. The Congress and the several States shall have concurrent power to enforce this article by appropriate legislation.

(3. This article shall be inoperative unless it shall have been ratified as an amendment to the Constitution by the Legislatures of the several States, as provided in the Constitution, within seven years from the date of the submission hereof to the States by the Congress.)

(The total vote in the Senates of the various States was 1,310 for, 237 against—84.6% dry. In the lower houses of the States the vote was 3,782 for, 1,035 against—78.5% dry.

(The amendment ultimately was adopted by all the States except Connecticut and Rhode Island.)

AMENDMENT XIX.

Giving nationwide suffrage to women.

(Proposed by Congress June 4, 1919; ratification certified by Secretary of State Aug. 26, 1920.)

1. The right of citizens of the United States to vote shall not be denied or abridged by the United States or by any State on account of sex.

2. Congress shall have power to enforce this Article by appropriate legislation.

AMENDMENT XX.

Terms of President and Vice President to begin on Jan. 20; those of Senators, Representatives, Jan. 3.

(Proposed by Congress Mar. 2, 1932; ratification completed Jan. 23, 1933.)

1. The terms of the President and Vice President shall end at noon on the 20th day of January, and the terms of Senators and Representatives at noon on the 3rd day of January, of the years in which such terms would have ended if this article had not been ratified; and the terms of their successors shall then begin.

2. The Congress shall assemble at least once in every year, and such meeting shall begin at noon on the 3rd day of January, unless they shall by law appoint a different day.

3. If, at the time fixed for the beginning of the term of the President, the President elect shall have died, the Vice President elect shall become President. If a President shall not have been chosen before the time fixed for the beginning of his term, or if the President elect shall have failed to qualify, then the Vice President elect shall act as President until a President shall have qualified; and the Congress may by law provide for the case wherein neither a President elect nor a Vice President elect shall have qualified, declaring who shall then act as President, or the manner in which one who is to act shall be selected, and such person shall act accordingly until a President or Vice President shall have qualified.

4. The Congress may by law provide for the case of the death of any of the persons from whom the House of Representatives may choose a President whenever the right of choice shall have devolved upon them, and for the case of the death of any of the persons from whom the Senate may choose a Vice President whenever the right of choice shall have devolved upon them.

5. Sections 1 and 2 shall take effect on the 15th day of October following the ratification of this article (Oct., 1933).

6. This article shall be inoperative unless it shall have been ratified as an amendment to the Constitution by the Legislatures of three-fourths of the several States within seven years from the date of its submission.

AMENDMENT XXI.

Repeal of Amendment XVIII.

(Proposed by Congress Feb. 20, 1933; ratification completed Dec. 5, 1933.)

1. The eighteenth article of amendment to the Constitution of the United States is hereby repealed.

2. The transportation or importation into any State, Territory, or Possession of the United States for delivery or use therein of intoxicating liquors, in violation of the laws thereof, is hereby prohibited.

3. This article shall be inoperative unless it shall have been ratified as an amendment to the Constitution by conventions in the several States, as provided in the Constitution, within seven years from the date of the submission hereof to the States by the Congress.

AMENDMENT XXII.

Limiting Presidential terms of office.

(Proposed by Congress Mar. 24, 1947; ratification completed Feb. 27, 1951.)

1. No person shall be elected to the office of the President more than twice, and no person who has held the office of President, or acted as President, for more than two years of a term to which some other person was elected President shall be elected to the office of the President more than once. But this Article shall not apply to any person holding the office of President when this Article was proposed by the Congress, and shall not prevent any person who may be holding the office of President, or acting as President, during the term within which this Article becomes operative from holding the office of President or acting as President during the remainder of such term.

2. This article shall be inoperative unless it shall have been ratified as an amendment to the Constitution by the Legislatures of three-fourths of the several States within seven years from the date of its submission to the States by the Congress.

AMENDMENT XXIII.

Presidential vote for District of Columbia.

(Proposed by Congress June 16, 1960; ratification completed Mar. 29, 1961.)

1. The District constituting the seat of Government of the United States shall appoint in such manner as the Congress may direct:

A number of electors of President and Vice President equal to the whole number of Senators and Representatives in Congress to which the District would be entitled if it were a State, but in no event more than the least populous State; they shall be in addition to those appointed by the States, but they shall be considered, for the purposes of the election of President and Vice President, to be electors appointed by a State; and they shall meet in the District and perform such duties as provided by the twelfth article of amendment.

2. The Congress shall have power to enforce this article by appropriate legislation.

AMENDMENT XXIV.

Barring poll tax in federal elections.

(Proposed by Congress Aug. 27, 1962; ratification completed Jan. 23, 1964.)

1. The right of citizens of the United States to vote in any primary or other election for President or Vice President, for electors for President or Vice President, or for Senator or Representative in Congress, shall not be denied or abridged by the United States or any State by reason of failure to pay any poll tax or other tax.

2. The Congress shall have power to enforce this article by appropriate legislation.

AMENDMENT XXV.

Presidential disability and succession.

(Proposed by Congress July 6, 1965; ratification completed Feb. 10, 1967.)

1. In case of the removal of the President from office or of his death or resignation, the Vice President shall become President.

2. Whenever there is a vacancy in the office of the Vice President, the President shall nominate a Vice President who shall take office upon confirmation by a majority vote of both houses of Congress.

3. Whenever the President transmits to the President pro tempore of the Senate and the Speaker of the House of Representatives his written declaration that he is unable to discharge the powers and duties of his office, and until he transmits to them a written declaration to the contrary, such powers and duties shall be discharged by the Vice President as Acting President.

4. Whenever the Vice President and a majority of either the principal officers of the executive departments or of such other body as Congress may by law provide, transmit to the President pro tempore of the Senate and the Speaker of the House of Representatives their written declaration that the President is unable to discharge the powers and duties of his office, the Vice President shall immediately assume the powers and duties of the office as Acting President.

Thereafter, when the President transmits to the President pro tempore of the Senate and the Speaker of the House of Representatives his written declaration that no inability exists, he shall resume the powers and duties of his office unless the Vice President and a majority of either the principal officers of the executive department or of such other body as Congress may by law provide, transmit within four days to the President pro tempore of the Senate and the Speaker of the House of Representatives their written declaration that the President is unable to discharge the powers and duties of his office. Thereupon Congress shall decide the issue, assembling within forty-eight hours for that purpose if not in session. If the Congress, within twenty-one days after receipt of the latter written declaration, or, if Congress is not in session, within twenty-one days after Congress is required to assemble, determines by two-thirds vote of both houses that the President is unable to discharge the powers and duties of his office, the Vice President shall continue to discharge the same as Acting President; otherwise, the President shall resume the powers and duties of his office.

AMENDMENT XXVI.

Lowering voting age to 18 years.

(Proposed by Congress Mar. 23, 1971; ratification completed July 1, 1971.)

1. The right of citizens of the United States, who are 18 years of age or older, to vote shall not be denied or abridged by the United States or any state on account of age.

2. The Congress shall have the power to enforce this article by appropriate legislation.

PROPOSED AMENDMENT RELATING TO CONGRESSIONAL PAY

(Proposed by the first Congress Sept. 25, 1789 as one of the 12 amendments to the Constitution, the 10 that were accepted became the Bill of Rights; ratified as of May 1989 by 32 states: Maryland, North Carolina, South Carolina, Delaware, Vermont, Virginia 1789-1791; Ohio 1873; Wyoming 1978; Maine 1983; Colorado 1984; South Dakota, New Hampshire, Arizona, Tennessee, Oklahoma 1985; New Mexico, Indiana, Utah 1986; Montana, Connecticut, Wisconsin, Arkansas 1987; Georgia, W. Virginia, Louisiana 1988; Iowa, Idaho, Nevada, Alaska, Oregon, Minnesota, Texas 1989. An additional 6 ratifications are needed to attain the requisite three-quarters of the States.)

No law, varying the compensation for the services of the Senators and Representatives, shall take effect, until an election of Representatives shall have intervened.

Origin of the Constitution

The War of Independence was conducted by delegates from the original 13 states, called the Congress of the United States of America and generally known as the Continental Congress. In 1777 the Congress submitted to the legislatures of the states the Articles of Confederation and Perpetual Union, which were ratified by New Hampshire, Massachusetts, Rhode Island, Connecticut, New York, New Jersey, Pennsylvania, Delaware, Virginia, North Carolina, South Carolina, and Georgia, and finally, in 1781, by Maryland.

The first article of the instrument read: "The stile of this confederacy shall be the United States of America." This did not signify a sovereign nation, because the states delegated only those powers they could not handle individually, such as power to wage war, establish a uniform currency, make treaties with foreign nations and contract debts for general expenses (such as paying the army). Taxes for the payment of such debts were levied by the individual states. The president under the Articles signed himself "President of the United States in Congress assembled," but here the United States were considered in the plural, a cooperating group. Canada was invited to join the union on equal terms but did not act.

When the war was won it became evident that a stronger federal union was needed to protect the mutual interests of the states. The Congress left the initiative to the legislatures. Virginia in Jan. 1786 appointed commissioners to meet with representatives of other states, with the result that delegates from Virginia, Delaware, New York, New Jersey, and Pennsylvania met at Annapolis. Alexander Hamilton prepared for their call by asking delegates from all states to meet in Philadelphia in May 1787 "to render the Constitution of the Federal government adequate to the exigencies of the union." Congress endorsed the plan Feb. 21, 1787. Delegates were appointed by all states except Rhode Island.

The convention met May 14, 1787. George Washington was chosen president (presiding officer). The states certified 65 delegates, but 10 did not attend. The work was done by 55, not all of whom were present at all sessions. Of the 55 attending delegates, 16 failed to sign, and 39 actually signed Sept. 17, 1787, some with reservations. Some historians have said 74 delegates (9 more than the 65 actually certified) were named and 19 failed to attend. These 9 additional persons refused the appointment, were never delegates and never counted as absentees. Washington sent the Constitution to Congress with a covering letter and that body, Sept. 28, 1787, ordered it sent to the legislatures, "in order to be submitted to a convention of delegates chosen in each state by the people thereof."

The Constitution was ratified by votes of state conventions as follows: Delaware, Dec. 7, 1787, unanimous; Pennsylvania, Dec. 12, 1787, 43 to 23; New Jersey, Dec. 18, 1787, unanimous; Georgia, Jan 2, 1788, unanimous; Connecticut, Jan. 9, 1788, 128 to 40; Massachusetts, Feb. 6, 1788, 187 to 168; Maryland, Apr. 28, 1788, 63 to 11; South Carolina, May 23, 1788, 149 to 73; New Hampshire, June 21, 1788, 57 to 46; Virginia, June 25, 1788, 89 to 79; New York, July 26, 1788, 30 to 27. Nine states were needed to establish the operation of the Constitution "between the states so ratifying the same" and New Hampshire was the 9th state. The government did not declare the Constitution in effect until the first Wednesday in Mar. 1789 which was Mar. 4. After that North Carolina ratified it Nov. 21, 1789, 194 to 77; and Rhode Island, May 29, 1790, 34 to 32. Vermont in convention ratified it Jan. 10, 1791, and by act of Congress approved Feb. 18, 1791, was admitted into the Union as the 14th state, Mar. 4, 1791.

On Sept. 17, 1987, the nation began a four-year celebration of the 200th anniversary of the signing of the Constitution of the United States.

As of April 1987, 32 states have voted to issue convention calls to hold a second constitutional convention. Convention bills are pending before 11 more state legislatures, while bills to rescind previous calls are under consideration in four states. When the total reaches 34, the Constitution stipulates that a convention must be held. The convention drive began in the mid 1970s to bring about the consideration of an amendment requiring a balanced federal budget.

The Continental Congress: Meetings, Presidents

Meeting places	Dates of meetings		Congress presidents	Date elected
Philadelphia	Sept. 5 to Oct. 26, 1774		Peyton Randolph, Va. (1)	Sept. 5, 1774
"			Henry Middleton, S.C.	Oct. 22, 1774
Philadelphia	May 10, 1775 to Dec. 12, 1776		Peyton Randolph, Va.	May 10, 1775
"			John Hancock, Mass.	May 24, 1775
Baltimore	Dec. 20, 1776 to Mar. 4, 1777		"	
Philadelphia	Mar. 5 to Sept. 18, 1777		"	
Lancaster, Pa.	Sept. 27, 1777 (one day)		"	
York, Pa.	Sept. 30, 1777 to June 27, 1778		Henry Laurens, S.C.	Nov. 1, 1777(4)
Philadelphia	July 2, 1778 to June 21, 1783		John Jay, N.Y.	Dec. 10, 1778
"	"		Samuel Huntington, Conn.	Sept. 28, 1779
"	"		Thomas McKean, Del.	July 10, 1781
"	"		John Hanson, Md. (2)	Nov. 5, 1781
"	"		Elias Boudinot, N.J.	Nov. 4, 1782
"	"		Thomas Mifflin, Pa.	Nov. 3, 1783
Princeton, N.J.	June 30 to Nov. 4, 1783			
Annapolis, Md.	Nov. 26, 1783 to June 3, 1784		Richard Henry Lee, Va.	Nov. 30, 1784
Trenton, N.J.	Nov. 1 to Dec. 24, 1784			
New York City	Jan. 11 to Nov. 4, 1785		John Hancock, Mass. (3)	Nov. 23, 1785
"	Nov. 7, 1785 to Nov. 3, 1786		Nathaniel Gorham, Mass.	June 6, 1786
"	Nov. 6, 1786 to Oct. 30, 1787		Arthur St. Clair, Pa.	Feb. 2, 1787
"	Nov. 5, 1787 to Oct. 21, 1788		Cyrus Griffin, Va.	Jan. 22, 1788
"	Nov. 3, 1788 to Mar. 2, 1789			

(1) Resigned Oct. 22, 1774. (2) Titled "President of the United States in Congress Assembled," John Hanson is considered by some to be the first U.S. President as he was the first to serve under the Articles of Confederation. He was, however, little more than presiding officer of the Congress, which retained full executive power. He could be considered the head of government, but not head of state. (3) Resigned May 29, 1786, without serving, because of illness. (4) Articles of Confederation agreed upon, Nov. 15, 1777; last ratification from Maryland, Mar. 1, 1781.

Patrick Henry's Speech to the Virginia Convention

The following is an excerpt from Patrick Henry's speech to the Virginia Convention on Mar. 23, 1775:

Gentlemen may cry, peace, peace—but there is no peace. The war is actually begun! The next gale that sweeps from the north will bring to our ears the clash of resounding arms! Our brethren are already in the field! Why stand we here idle? What is it that gentlemen wish? What would they have? Is life so dear, or peace so sweet, as to be purchased at the price of chains and slavery? Forbid it, Almighty God! I know not what course others may take; but as for me, give me liberty, or give me death!

Common Sense

The following is an excerpt from Thomas Paine's *Common Sense*. Paine adopted the doctrine of separation from Britain after the battles of Lexington and Concord, and published his pamphlet in Jan. 1776.

The cause of America is in great measure the cause of all mankind. Many circumstances hath, and will arise, which are not local, but universal, and through which principles of all Lovers of Mankind are affected, and in the Event of which, their Affections are interested. The laying a Country desolate with Fire and Sword, declaring war against natural rights of all Mankind, and extirpating the Defenders thereof from the Face of the Earth, is the Concern of every Man to whom Nature hath given the Power of feeling; . . . It is repugnant to reason, to the universal order of things, to all examples from former ages, to suppose, that this continent can longer remain subject to any external power . . .

The last cord is now broken, the people of England are presenting addresses against us. There are injuries which nature cannot forgive; she would cease to be nature if she did . . .

O ye that love mankind! Ye that dare oppose, not only the tyranny, but the tyrant, stand forth! Every spot of the old world is overrun with oppression. Freedom hath been hunted round the globe. Asia, and Africa, have long expelled her—Europe regards her like a stranger, and England hath given her warning to depart. O! Receive the fugitive, and prepare in time an asylum for mankind.

Law on Succession to the Presidency

If by reason of death, resignation, removal from office, inability, or failure to qualify there is neither a president nor vice president to discharge the powers and duties of the office of president, then the speaker of the House of Representatives shall upon his resignation as speaker and as representative, act as president. The same rule shall apply in the case of the death, resignation, removal from office, or inability of an individual acting as president.

If at the time when a speaker is to begin the discharge of the powers and duties of the office of president there is no speaker, or the speaker fails to qualify as acting president, then the president pro tempore of the Senate, upon his resignation as president pro tempore and as senator, shall act as president.

An individual acting as president shall continue to act until the expiration of the then current presidential term, except that (1) if his discharge of the powers and duties of the office is founded in whole or in part in the failure of both the president-elect and the vice president-elect to qualify, then he shall act only until a president or vice president qualifies, and (2) if his discharge of the powers and duties of the office is founded in whole or in part on the inability of the president or vice president, then he shall act only until the removal of the disability of one of such individuals.

If, by reason of death, resignation, removal from office, or failure to qualify, there is no president pro tempore to act as president, then the officer of the United States who is highest on the following list, and who is not under any disability to discharge the powers and duties of president shall act as president; the secretaries of state, treasury, defense, attorney general; secretaries of interior, agriculture, commerce, labor, health and human services, housing and urban development, transportation, energy, education.

(*Legislation approved July 18, 1947; amended Sept. 9, 1965, Oct. 15, 1966, Aug. 4, 1977, and Sept. 27, 1979. (See also Constitutional Amendment XXV.)*)

How the Declaration of Independence Was Adopted

On June 7, 1776, Richard Henry Lee, who had issued the first call for a congress of the colonies, introduced in the Continental Congress at Philadelphia a resolution declaring "that these United Colonies are, and of right ought to be, free and independent states, that they are absolved from all allegiance to the British Crown, and that all political connection between them and the state of Great Britain is, and ought to be, totally dissolved."

The resolution, seconded by John Adams on behalf of the Massachusetts delegation, came up again June 10 when a committee of 5, headed by Thomas Jefferson, was appointed to express the purpose of the resolution in a declaration of independence. The others on the committee were John Adams, Benjamin Franklin, Robert R. Livingston, and Roger Sherman.

Drafting the Declaration was assigned to Jefferson, who worked on a portable desk of his own construction in a room at Market and 7th Sts. The committee reported the result June 28, 1776. The members of the Congress suggested a number of changes, which Jefferson called "deplorable." They didn't approve Jefferson's arraignment of the British people and King George III for encouraging and fostering the slave trade, which Jefferson called "an execrable commerce." They made 86 changes, eliminating 480 words and leaving 1,337. In the final form capitalization was erratic. Jefferson had written that men were endowed with "inalienable" rights; in the final copy it came out as "unalienable" and has been thus ever since.

The Lee-Adams resolution of independence was adopted by 12 yeas July 2 — the actual date of the act of independence. The Declaration, which explains the act, was adopted July 4, in the evening.

After the Declaration was adopted, July 4, 1776, it was turned over to John Dunlap, printer, to be printed on broadsides. The original copy was lost and one of his broadsides was attached to a page in the journal of the Congress. It was read aloud July 8 in Philadelphia, Easton, Pa., and Trenton, N.J. On July 9 at 6 p.m. it was read by order of Gen. George Washington to the troops assembled on the Common in New York City (City Hall Park).

The Continental Congress of July 19, 1776, adopted the following resolution:

"Resolved, That the Declaration passed on the 4th, be fairly engrossed on parchment with the title and stile of 'The Unanimous Declaration of the thirteen United States of America' and that the same, when engrossed, be signed by every member of Congress."

Not all delegates who signed the engrossed Declaration were present on July 4. Robert Morris (Pa.), William Williams (Conn.) and Samuel Chase (Md.) signed on Aug. 2, Oliver Wolcott (Conn.), George Wythe (Va.), Richard Henry Lee (Va.) and Elbridge Gerry (Mass.) signed in August and September, Matthew Thornton (N. H.) joined the Congress Nov. 4 and signed later. Thomas McKean (Del.) rejoined Washington's Army before signing and said later that he signed in 1781.

Charles Carroll of Carrollton was appointed a delegate by Maryland on July 4, 1776, presented his credentials July 18, and signed the engrossed Declaration Aug. 2. Born Sept. 19, 1737, he was 95 years old and the last surviving signer when he died Nov. 14, 1832.

Two Pennsylvania delegates who did not support the Declaration on July 4 were replaced.

The 4 New York delegates did not have authority from their state to vote on July 4. On July 9 the New York state convention authorized its delegates to approve the Declaration and the Congress was so notified on July 15, 1776. The 4 signed the Declaration on Aug. 2.

The original engrossed Declaration is preserved in the National Archives Building in Washington.

The Liberty Bell: Its History and Significance

The Liberty Bell, in Independence Hall, Philadelphia, is an object of great reverence to Americans because of its association with the historic events of the War of Independence.

The original Province bell, ordered to commemorate the 50th anniversary of the Commonwealth of Pennsylvania, was cast by Thomas Lister, Whitechapel, London, and reached Philadelphia in Aug. 1752. It bore an inscription from Leviticus XXV, 10: "Proclaim liberty throughout all the land until all the inhabitants thereof."

The bell was cracked by a stroke of its clapper in Sept. 1752 while it hung on a truss in the State House yard for testing. Pass & Stow, Philadelphia founders, recast the bell, adding 1 1/2 ounces of copper to a pound of the original metal to reduce brittleness. It was found that the bell contained too much copper, injuring its tone, so Pass & Stow recast it again, this time successfully.

In June 1753 the bell was hung in the wooden steeple of the State House, erected on top of the brick tower. In use while the Continental Congress was in session in the State House, it rang out in defiance of British tax and trade restrictions, and proclaimed the Boston Tea Party and the first public reading of the Declaration of Independence.

On Sept. 18, 1777, when the British Army was about to occupy Philadelphia, the bell was moved in a baggage train of the American Army to Allentown, Pa. where it was hidden in the Zion Reformed Church until June 27, 1778. It was moved back to Philadelphia after the British left.

In July 1781 the wooden steeple became insecure and had to be taken down. The bell was lowered into the brick section of the tower. Here it was hanging in July, 1835, when it cracked while tolling for the funeral of John Marshall, chief justice of the United States. Because of its association with the War of Independence it was not recast but remained mute in this location until 1846, the year of the Mexican War, when it was placed on exhibition in the Declaration Chamber of Independence Hall.

In 1876, when many thousands of Americans visited Philadelphia for the Centennial Exposition, it was placed in its old walnut frame in the tower hallway. In 1877 it was hung from the ceiling of the tower by a chain of 13 links. It was returned again to the Declaration Chamber and in 1896 taken back to the tower hall, where it occupied a glass case. In 1915 the case was removed so that the public might touch it. On Jan. 1, 1976, just after midnight to mark the opening of the Bicentennial Year, the bell was moved to a new glass and steel pavilion behind Independence Hall for easier viewing by the larger number of visitors expected during the year.

The measurements of the bell follow: circumference around the lip, 12 ft.; circumference around the crown, 7 ft. 6 in.; lip to the crown, 3 ft.; height over the crown, 2 ft. 3 in.; thickness at lip, 3 in.; thickness at crown, 1 1/4 in.; weight, 2080 lbs.; length of clapper, 3 ft. 2 in.; cost, £60 14s 5d.

Confederate States and Secession

The American Civil War, 1861-65, grew out of sectional disputes over the continued existence of slavery in the South and the contention of Southern legislators that the states retained many sovereign rights, including the right to secede from the Union.

The war was not fought by state against state but by one federal regime against another, the Confederate government in Richmond assuming control over the economic, political, and military life of the South, under protest from Georgia and South Carolina.

South Carolina voted an ordinance of secession from the Union, repealing its 1788 ratification of the U.S. Constitution on Dec. 20, 1860, to take effect Dec. 24. Other states seceded in 1861. Their votes in conventions were:

Mississippi, Jan. 9, 84-15; Florida, Jan. 10, 62-7; Alabama, Jan. 11; 61-39; Georgia, Jan. 19, 208-89; Louisiana, Jan. 26, 113-17; Texas, Feb. 1, 166-7, ratified by popular vote Feb. 23 (for 34,794, against 11,325); Virginia, Apr. 17, 88-55, ratified by popular vote May 23 (for 128,884; against 32,134); Arkansas, May 6, 69-1; Tennessee, May 7, ratified by popular vote June 8 (for 104,019, against 47,238); North Carolina, May 21.

Missouri Unionists stopped secession in conventions Feb. 28 and Mar. 9. The legislature condemned secession Mar. 7. Under the protection of Confederate troops, secessionist members of the legislature adopted a resolution of secession at Neosho, Oct. 31. The Confederate Congress seated the secessionists' representatives.

Kentucky did not secede and its government remained Unionist. In a part occupied by Confederate troops, Kentuckians approved secession and the Confederate Congress admitted their representatives.

The Maryland legislature voted against secession Apr. 27, 53-13. Delaware did not secede. Western Virginia held conventions at Wheeling, named a pro-Union governor June 11, 1861; admitted to Union as West Virginia June 20, 1863; its constitution provided for gradual abolition of slavery.

Confederate Government

Forty-two delegates from South Carolina, Georgia, Alabama, Mississippi, Louisiana, and Florida met in convention at Montgomery, Ala., Feb. 4, 1861. They adopted a provisional constitution of the Confederate States of America, and elected Jefferson Davis (Miss.) provisional president, and Alexander H. Stephens (Ga.) provisional vice president.

A permanent constitution was adopted Mar. 11; it abolished the African slave trade. The Congress moved to Richmond, Va. July 20. Davis was elected president in October, and was inaugurated Feb. 22, 1862.

The Congress adopted a flag, consisting of a red field with a white stripe, and a blue jack with a circle of white stars. Later the more popular flag was the red field with blue diagonal cross bars that held 13 white stars. The stars represented the 11 states actually in the Confederacy plus Kentucky and Missouri.

(See also Civil War, U.S., in Index)

Lincoln's Address at Gettysburg, 1863

Fourscore and seven years ago our fathers brought forth on this continent a new nation, conceived in liberty and dedicated to the proposition that all men are created equal.

Now we are engaged in a great civil war, testing whether that nation or any nation so conceived and so dedicated can long endure. We are met on a great battle field of that war. We have come to dedicate a portion of that field, as a final resting-place for those who here gave their lives that that nation might live. It is altogether fitting and proper that we should do this.

But, in a larger sense, we can not dedicate — we can not consecrate — we can not hallow — this ground. The brave men, living and dead, who struggled here, have consecrated it, far above our poor power to add or detract. The world will little note, nor long remember, what we say here, but it can never forget what they did here. It is for us the living, rather, to be dedicated here to the unfinished work which they who fought here have thus far so nobly advanced. It is rather for us to be here dedicated to the great task remaining before us — that from these honored dead we take increased devotion to that cause for which they gave the last full measure of devotion — that we here highly resolve that these dead shall not have died in vain — that this nation, under God, shall have a new birth of freedom — and that government of the people, by the people, for the people, shall not perish from the earth.

Origin of the United States National Motto

In God We Trust, designated as the U. S. National Motto by Congress in 1956, originated during the Civil War as an inscription for U. S. coins, although it was used by Francis Scott Key in a slightly different form when he wrote The Star Spangled Banner in 1814. On Nov. 13, 1861, when Union morale had been shaken by battlefield defeats, the Rev. M. R. Watkinson, of Ridleyville, Pa., wrote to Secy. of the Treasury Salmon P. Chase. "From my heart I have felt our national shame in disowning God as not the least of our present national disasters," the minister wrote, suggesting "recognition of the Almighty God in some form on our coins." Secy. Chase ordered designs prepared with the inscription *In God We Trust* and backed coinage legislation which authorized use of this slogan. It first appeared on some U. S. coins in 1864, disappeared and reappeared on various coins until 1955, when Congress ordered it placed on all paper money and all coins.

The National Anthem — The Star-Spangled Banner

The Star-Spangled Banner was ordered played by the military and naval services by President Woodrow Wilson in 1916. It was designated the National Anthem by Act of Congress, Mar. 3, 1931. It was written by Francis Scott Key, of Georgetown, D. C., during the bombardment of Fort McHenry, Baltimore, Md., Sept. 13-14, 1814. Key was a lawyer, a graduate of St. John's College, Annapolis, and a volunteer in a light artillery company. When a friend, Dr. Beanes, a physician of Upper Marlborough, Md., was taken aboard Admiral Cockburn's British squadron for interfering with ground troops, Key and J. S. Skinner, carrying a note from President Madison, went to the fleet under a flag of truce on a cartel ship to ask Beanes' release. Admiral Cockburn consented, but as the fleet was about to sail up the Patapsco to bombard Fort McHenry he detained them, first on H. M. S. Surprise, and then on a supply ship.

Key witnessed the bombardment from his own vessel. It began at 7 a.m., Sept. 13, 1814, and lasted, with intermissions, for 25 hours. The British fired over 1,500 shells, each weighing as much as 220 lbs. They were unable to approach closely because the Americans had sunk 22 vessels in the channel. Only four Americans were killed and 24 wounded. A British bomb-ship was disabled.

During the bombardment Key wrote a stanza on the back of an envelope. Next day at Indian Queen Inn, Baltimore, he wrote out the poem and gave it to his brother-in-law, Judge J. H. Nicholson. Nicholson suggested the tune, Anacreon in Heaven, and had the poem printed on broadsides, of which two survive. On Sept. 20 it appeared in the "Baltimore American." Later Key made 3 copies; one is in the Library of Congress and one in the Pennsylvania Historical Society.

The copy that Key wrote in his hotel Sept. 14, 1814, remained in the Nicholson family for 93 years. In 1907 it was sold to Henry Walters of Baltimore. In 1934 it was bought at auction in New York from the Walters estate by the Walters Art Gallery, Baltimore, for $26,400. The Walters Gallery in 1953 sold the manuscript to the Maryland Historical Society for the same price.

The flag that Key saw during the bombardment is preserved in the Smithsonian Institution, Washington. It is 30 by 42 ft., and has 15 alternate red and white stripes and 15 stars, for the original 13 states plus Kentucky and Vermont.

It was made by Mary Young Pickersgill. The Baltimore Flag House, a museum, occupies her premises, which were restored in 1953.

The Star-Spangled Banner

I

Oh, say can you see by the dawn's early light
  What so proudly we hailed at the twilight's last gleaming?
Whose broad stripes and bright stars thru the perilous fight,
  O'er the ramparts we watched were so gallantly streaming?
And the rocket's red glare, the bombs bursting in air,
  Gave proof through the night that our flag was still there.
Oh, say does that star-spangled banner yet wave
  O'er the land of the free and the home of the brave?

II

On the shore, dimly seen through the mists of the deep,
  Where the foe's haughty host in dread silence reposes,
What is that which the breeze, o'er the towering steep,
  As it fitfully blows, half conceals, half discloses?
Now it catches the gleam of the morning's first beam,
  In full glory reflected now shines in the stream:

'Tis the star-spangled banner! Oh long may it wave
  O'er the land of the free and the home of the brave!

III

And where is that band who so vauntingly swore
  That the havoc of war and the battle's confusion,
A home and a country should leave us no more!
  Their blood has washed out their foul footsteps' pollution.
No refuge could save the hireling and slave
  From the terror of flight, or the gloom of the grave:
And the star-spangled banner in triumph doth wave
  O'er the land of the free and the home of the brave!

IV

Oh! thus be it ever, when freemen shall stand
  Between their loved home and the war's desolation!
Blest with victory and peace, may the heav'n rescued land
  Praise the Power that hath made and preserved us a nation.
Then conquer we must, when our cause it is just,
  And this be our motto: "In God is our trust."
And the star-spangled banner in triumph shall wave
  O'er the land of the free and the home of the brave!

Statue of Liberty National Monument

Since 1886, the Statue of Liberty Enlightening the World has stood as a symbol of freedom in New York harbor. It also commemorates French-American friendship as given by the people of France, designed by Frederic Auguste Bartholdi (1834-1904). A $2.5 million building housing the American Museum of Immigration was opened by Pres. Nixon Sept. 26, 1972, at the base of the statue. It houses a permanent exhibition of photos, posters, and artifacts tracing the history of American immigration. The Monument is administered by the National Park Service.

Nearby Ellis Island, gateway to America for more than 12 million immigrants between 1892 and 1954, was proclaimed part of the National Monument in 1965 by Pres. Johnson.

Edouard de Laboulaye, French historian and admirer of American political institutions, suggested that the French present a monument to the United States, the latter to provide pedestal and site. Bartholdi visualized a colossal statue at the entrance of New York harbor, welcoming the peoples of the world with the torch of liberty.

On Washington's birthday, Feb. 22, 1877, Congress approved the use of a site on Bedloe's Island suggested by Bartholdi. This island of 12 acres had been owned in the 17th century by a Walloon named Isaac Bedloe. It was called Bedloe's until Aug. 3, 1956, when Pres. Eisenhower approved a resolution of Congress changing the name to Liberty Island.

The statue was finished May 21, 1884, and formally presented to U.S. Minister Morton July 4, 1884, by Ferdinand de Lesseps, head of the Franco-American Union, promoter of the Panama Canal, and builder of the Suez Canal.

On Aug. 5, 1884, the Americans laid the cornerstone for the pedestal. This was to be built on the foundations of Fort Wood, which had been erected by the Government in 1811. The American committee had raised $125,000, but this was found to be inadequate. Joseph Pulitzer, owner of the New York World, appealed on Mar. 16, 1885, for general donations. By Aug. 11, 1885, he had raised $100,000.

The statue arrived dismantled, in 214 packing cases, from Rouen, France, in June, 1885. The last rivet of the statue was driven Oct. 28, 1886, when Pres. Grover Cleveland dedicated the monument.

The statue weighs 450,000 lbs. or 225 tons. The copper sheeting weighs 200,000 lbs. There are 167 steps from the land level to the top of the pedestal, 168 steps inside the statue to the head, and 54 rungs on the ladder leading to the arm that holds the torch.

Two years of restoration work was completed before the statue's centennial celebration on July 4, 1986. Among other repairs, the multi-million dollar project included replacing the 1,600 wrought iron bands that hold its copper skin to its frame, replacing its torch, and installing an elevator.

A four-day extravaganza of concerts, tall ships, ethnic festivals, and fireworks celebrated the 100th anniversary. The festivities included Chief Justice Warren E. Burger's swearing-in of 5,000 new citizens on Liberty Island, while 20,000 others across the country were simultaneously sworn in through a satellite telecast.

The ceremonies were followed by others on Oct. 28, 1986, the statue's 100th birthday.

Dimensions of the Statue	Ft.	In.
Height from base to torch (45.3 meters)	151	1
Foundation of pedestal to torch (91.5 meters)	305	1
Heel to top of head	111	1
Length of hand	16	5
Index finger	8	0
Circumference at second joint	3	6
Size of finger nail	13x10 in.	
Head from chin to cranium	17	3
Head thickness from ear to ear	10	0
Distance across the eye	2	6
Length of nose	4	6
Right arm, length	42	0
Right arm, greatest thickness	12	0
Thickness of waist	35	0
Width of mouth	3	0
Tablet, length	23	7
Tablet, width	13	7
Tablet, thickness	2	0

Emma Lazarus' Famous Poem

A poem by Emma Lazarus is graven on a tablet within the pedestal on which the statue stands.

The New Colossus

Not like the brazen giant of Greek fame,
  With conquering limbs astride from land to land;
Here at our sea-washed, sunset gates shall stand
A mighty woman with a torch, whose flame
Is the imprisoned lightning, and her name
Mother of Exiles. From her beacon-hand
Glows world-wide welcome; her mild eyes command
The air-bridged harbor that twin cities frame.
"Keep ancient lands, your storied pomp!" cries she
With silent lips. "Give me your tired, your poor,
Your huddled masses yearning to breathe free,
The wretched refuse of your teeming shore.
Send these, the homeless, tempest-tost to me,
I lift my lamp beside the golden door!"

Forms of Address for Persons of Rank and Public Office

In these examples John Smith is used as a representative American name. The salutation Dear Sir or Dear Madam is always permissible when addressing a person not known to the writer. Female equivalents should be substituted where appropriate.

President of the United States

Address: The President, The White House, Washington, DC 20500. Also, The President and Mrs. ___.
Salutation: Dear Sir or Mr. President or Dear Mr. President. More intimately: My dear Mr. President. Also: Dear Mr. President and Mrs. ___

The vice president takes the same forms.

Cabinet Officers

Address: Mr. John Smith, Secretary of State, Washington, D.C. or The Hon. John Smith. Similar addresses for other members of the cabinet. Also: Secretary and Mrs. John Smith.
Salutation: Dear Sir, or Dear Mr. Secretary. Also: Dear Mr. and Mrs. Smith.

The Bench

Address: The Hon. John Smith, Chief Justice of the United States. The Hon. John Smith, Associate Justice of the Supreme Court of the United States. The Hon. John Smith, Associate Judge, U.S. District Court.
Salutation: Dear Sir, or Dear Mr. Chief Justice. Dear Mr. Justice. Dear Judge Smith.

Members of Congress

Address: The Hon. John Smith, United States Senate, Washington, DC 20510, or Sen. John Smith, etc. Also The Hon. John Smith, House of Representatives, Washington, DC 20515, or Rep. John Smith, etc.
Salutation: Dear Mr. Senator or Dear Mr. Smith; for Representative, Dear Mr. Smith.

Officers of Armed Forces

Address: Careful attention should be given to the precise rank, thus: General of the Army John Smith. Fleet Admiral John Smith. The rules for Air Force are same as Army.
Salutation: Dear Sir, or Dear General. All general officers, whatever rank, are entitled to be addressed as generals. Likewise a lieutenant colonel is addressed as colonel and first and second lieutenants are addressed as lieutenant.

Warrant officers and flight officers are addressed as Mister. Chaplains are addressed as Chaplain. A Catholic chaplain may be addressed as Father. Cadets of the United States Military Academy and Air Force Academy are addressed as Cadet. Noncommissioned officers are addressed by their titles.

Ambassador, Governor, Mayor

Address: The Hon. John Smith, followed by his or her title. They can be addressed either at their embassy, or at the Department of State, Washington, D.C. An ambassador from a foreign nation may be addressed as His or Her Excellency. An American is not to be so addressed.
Salutation: Dear Mr. or Madam Ambassador. An ambassador from a foreign nation may be called Your Excellency.

Governors and mayors are often addressed as The Hon. Jane Smith, Governor of ___, or The Hon. John Smith, Mayor of ___; also Governor John Smith, State House, Albany, N.Y., or Mayor Jane Smith, City Hall, Erie, Pa.

The Clergy

Address: His Holiness, the Pope, or His Holiness Pope (name), State of Vatican City, Italy.
Salutation: Your Holiness or Most Holy Father.
Also: His Eminence, John, Cardinal Smith; salutation: Your Eminence. An archbishop or a bishop is addressed The Most Reverend, and the salutation is Your Excellency. A monsignor who is a papal chamberlain is The Very Reverend Monsignor and the salutation is Dear Sir or Very Reverend Monsignor; a monsignor who is a domestic prelate is The Right Reverend Monsignor and salutation is Right Reverend Monsignor. A priest is addressed Reverend John Smith. A brother of an order is addressed Brother ―. A sister takes the same form.

A bishop of the Episcopal Church is The Right Reverend John Smith; salutation is Right Reverend Sir, or Dear Bishop Smith. If a clergyman is a doctor of divinity, he is addressed: The Reverend John Smith, D.D., and the salutation is Reverend Sir, or Dear Dr. Smith. When a clergyman does not have the degree the salutation is Dear Mr. Smith.

A bishop of the Methodist Church is addressed Bishop John Smith with titles following.

Royalty and Nobility

An emperor is to be addressed in a letter as Sir, or Your Imperial Majesty.

A king or queen is addressed as His Majesty (Name), King of (Name), or Her Majesty (Name), Queen of (Name). Salutation: Sir, or Madam, or May it please Your Majesty.

Princes and princesses and other persons of royal blood are addressed as His (or Her) Royal Highness, and saluted with May it please Your Royal Highness.

A duke or marquis is My Lord Duke (or Marquis), a duke is His (or Your) Grace.

The Mayflower Compact

The threat of James I to "harry them out of the land" sent a little band of religious dissenters from England to Holland in 1608. They were known as "Separatists" because they wished to cut all ties with the Established Church. In 1620, some of them, known now as the Pilgrims, joined with a larger group in England to set sail on the *Mayflower* for the New World. A joint stock company financed their venture.

In November, they sighted Cape Cod and decided to land an exploring party at Plymouth Harbor. However, a rebellious group picked up at Southhampton and London troubled the Pilgrim leaders, and to control their actions forty-one of the Pilgrims drew up the "Mayflower Compact," which was signed before going ashore. The voluntary agreement to govern themselves was America's first written constitution.

In the name of God, Amen. We, whose names are underwritten, the Loyal Subjects of our dread Sovereign Lord, King *James*, by the Grace of God, of *Great Britain, France and Ireland*, King, *Defender of the Faith*, etc.

Having undertaken for the Glory of God, and Advancement of the Christian Faith, and the Honour of our King and Country, a voyage to plant the first colony in the northern Parts of Virginia; do by these Presents, solemnly and mutually in the Presence of God and one of another, covenant and combine ouselves together into a civil Body Politick, for our better Ordering and Preservation, and Further-

ance of the Ends aforesaid; And by Virtue hereof to enact, constitute, and frame, such just and equal Laws, Ordinances, Acts, Constitutions and Offices, from time to time, as shall be thought meet and convenient for the General good of the Colony; unto which we promise all due Submission and Obedience.

In Witness whereof we have hereunto subscribed our names at *Cape Cod* the eleventh of *November*, in the Reign of our Sovereign Lord, King *James* of *England, France* and *Ireland*, the eighteenth, and of *Scotland* the fifty-fourth. *Anno Domini, 1620.*

The Great Seal of the U.S.

On July 4, 1776, the Continental Congress appointed a committee consisting of Benjamin Franklin, John Adams and Thomas Jefferson "to bring in a device for a seal of the United States of America." After many delays, a verbal description of a design by William Barton was finally approved by Congress on June 20, 1782. The seal shows an American bald eagle with a ribbon in its mouth bearing the device *E pluribus unum* (One out of many). In its talons are the arrows of war and an olive branch of peace. On the reverse side it shows an unfinished pyramid with an eye (the eye of Providence) above it.

The American's Creed

William Tyler Page, Clerk of the U.S. House of Representatives, wrote "The American's Creed" in 1917.
It was accepted by the House on behalf of the American people on April 3, 1918.

"I believe in the United States of America as a government of the people, by the people, for the people; whose just powers are derived from the consent of the governed; a democracy in a republic; a sovereign Nation of many sovereign States; a perfect union, one and inseparable; established upon those principles of freedom, equality, justice, and humanity for which American patriots sacrificed their lives and fortunes.

"I therefore believe it is my duty to my country to love it, to support its Constitution, to obey its laws, to respect its flag, and to defend it against all enemies."

Code of Etiquette for Display and Use of the U.S. Flag

Although the Stars and Stripes originated in 1777, it was not until 146 years later that there was a serious attempt to establish a uniform code of etiquette for the U.S. flag. The War Department issued Feb. 15, 1923, a circular on the rules of flag usage. These were adopted almost in their entirety June 14, 1923, by a conference of 68 patriotic organizations in Washington. Finally, on June 22, 1942, a joint resolution of Congress, amended by Public Law 94-344 July 7, 1976, codified "existing rules and customs pertaining to the display and use of the flag..."

When to Display the Flag—The flag should be displayed on all days, especially on legal holidays and other special occasions, on official buildings when in use, in or near polling places on election days, and in or near schools when in session. A citizen may fly the flag at any time he wishes. It is customary to display the flag only from sunrise to sunset on buildings and on stationary flagstaffs in the open. However, it may be displayed at night on special occasions, preferably lighted. In Washington, the flag now flies over the White House both day and night. It flies over the Senate wing of the Capitol when the Senate is in session and over the House wing when that body is in session. It flies day and night over the east and west fronts of the Capitol, without floodlights at night but receiving light from the illuminated Capitol Dome. It flies 24 hours a day at several other places, including the Fort McHenry Nat'l Monument in Baltimore, where it inspired Francis Scott Key to write The Star Spangled Banner.

How to Fly the Flag—The flag should be hoisted briskly and lowered ceremoniously, and should never be allowed to touch the ground or the floor. When hung over a sidewalk from a rope extending from a building to a pole, the union should be away from the building. When hung over the center of a street it should have the union to the north in an east-west street and to the east in a north-south street. No other flag may be flown above or, if on the same level, to the right of the U.S. flag, except that at the United Nations Headquarters the UN flag may be placed above flags of all member nations and other national flags may be flown with equal prominence or honor with the flag of the U.S. At services by Navy chaplains at sea, the church pennant may be flown above the flag.

When two flags are placed against a wall with crossed staffs, the U.S. flag should be at right—its own right, and its staff should be in front of the staff of the other flag; when a number of flags are grouped and displayed from staffs, it should be at the center and highest point of the group.

Church and Platform Use—In an auditorium, the flag may be displayed flat, above and behind the speaker. When displayed from a staff in a church or public auditorium, the flag should hold the position of superior prominence, in advance of the audience, and in the position of honor at the clergyman's or speaker's right as he faces the audience. Any other flag so displayed should be placed on the left of the clergyman or speaker or to the right of the audience.

When the flag is displayed horizontally or vertically against a wall, the stars should be uppermost and at the observer's left.

How to Dispose of Worn Flags—The flag, when it is in such condition that it is no longer a fitting emblem for display, should be destroyed in a dignified way, preferably by burning.

When to Salute the Flag—All persons present should face the flag, stand at attention and salute on the following occasions: (1) When the flag is passing in a parade or in a review, (2) During the ceremony of hoisting or lowering, (3) When the National Anthem is played, and (4) During the Pledge of Allegiance. Those present in uniform should render the military salute. When not in uniform, men should remove the hat with the right hand holding it at the left shoulder, the hand being over the heart. Men without hats should salute in the same manner. Aliens should stand at attention. Women should salute by placing the right hand over the heart.

On Memorial Day, the flag should fly at half-staff until noon, then be raised to the peak.

As provided by Presidential proclamation the flag should fly at half-staff for 30 days from the day of death of a president or former president; for 10 days from the day of death of a vice president, chief justice or retired chief justice of the U.S., or speaker of the House of Representatives; from day of death until burial of an associate justice of the Supreme Court, cabinet member, former vice president, or Senate president pro tempore, majority or minority Senate leader, or majority or minority House leader; for a U.S. senator, representative, territorial delegate, or the resident commissioner of Puerto Rico, on day of death and the following day within the metropolitan area of the District of Columbia and from day of death until burial within the decedent's state, congressional district, territory or commonwealth; and for the death of the governor of a state, territory, or possession of the U.S., from day of death until burial within that state, territory, or possession.

When used to cover a casket, the flag should be placed so that the union is at the head and over the left shoulder. It should not be lowered into the grave nor touch the ground.

Prohibited Uses of the Flag—The flag should not be dipped to any person or thing. (An exception—customarily, ships salute by dipping their colors.) It should never be displayed with the union down save as a distress signal. It should never be carried flat or horizontally, but always aloft and free.

It should not be displayed on a float, motor car or boat except from a staff.

It should never be used as a covering for a ceiling, nor have placed upon it any word, design, or drawing. It should never be used as a receptacle for carrying anything. It should not be used to cover a statue or a monument.

The flag should never be used for advertising purposes, nor be embroidered on such articles as cushions or handkerchiefs, printed or otherwise impressed on boxes or anything that is designed for temporary use and discard; or used as a costume or athletic uniform. Advertising signs should not be fastened to its staff or halyard.

The flag should never be used as drapery of any sort, never festooned, drawn back, nor up, in folds, but always allowed to fall free. Bunting of blue, white and red always arranged with the blue above and the white in the middle, should be used for covering a speaker's desk, draping the front of a platform, and for decoration in general.

An Act of Congress approved Feb. 8, 1917, provided certain penalties for the desecration, mutilation or improper use of the flag within the District of Columbia. A 1968 federal law provided penalties of up to a year's imprisonment or a $1,000 fine or both, for publicly burning or otherwise desecrating any flag of the United States. In addition, many states have laws against flag desecration. In 1989, the Supreme Court ruled that no laws could prohibit political protesters from burning the flag. The decision had the effect of declaring unconstitutional the flag desecration laws of 48 states, as well as a similar Federal statute, in cases of peaceful political expression.

Pledge of Allegiance to the Flag

I pledge allegiance to the flag of the United States of America and to the republic for which it stands, one nation under God, indivisible, with liberty and justice for all.

This, the current official version of the Pledge of Allegiance, has developed from the original pledge, which was first published in the Sept. 8, 1892, issue of the Youth's Companion, a weekly magazine then published in Boston. The original pledge contained the phrase "my flag," which was changed more than 30 years later to "flag of the United States of America." An act of Congress in 1954 added the words "under God."

The authorship of the pledge had been in dispute for many years. The Youth's Companion stated in 1917 that the original draft was written by James B. Upham, an executive of the magazine who died in 1910. A leaflet circulated by the magazine later named Upham as the originator of the draft "afterwards condensed and perfected by him and his associates of the Companion force."

Francis Bellamy, a former member of the Youth's Companion editorial staff, publicly claimed authorship of the pledge in 1923. The United States Flag Assn., acting on the advice of a committee named to study the controversy, upheld in 1939 the claim of Bellamy, who had died 8 years earlier. The Library of Congress issued in 1957 a report attributing the authorship to Bellamy.

The Flag of the U.S.—The Stars and Stripes

The 50-star flag of the United States was raised for the first time officially at 12:01 a.m. on July 4, 1960, at Fort McHenry National Monument in Baltimore, Md. The 50th star had been added for Hawaii; a year earlier the 49th, for Alaska. Before that, no star had been added since 1912, when N.M. and Ariz. were admitted to the Union.

The true history of the Stars and Stripes has become so cluttered by a volume of myth and tradition that the facts are difficult, and in some cases impossible, to establish. For example, it is not certain who designed the Stars and Stripes, who made the first such flag, or even whether it ever flew in any sea fight or land battle of the American Revolution.

One thing all agree on is that the Stars and Stripes originated as the result of a resolution offered by the Marine Committee of the Second Continental Congress at Philadelphia and adopted June 14, 1777. It read:

Resolved: that the flag of the United States be thirteen stripes, alternate red and white; that the union be thirteen stars, white in a blue field, representing a new constellation.

Congress gave no hint as to the designer of the flag, no instructions as to the arrangement of the stars, and no information on its appropriate uses. Historians have been unable to find the original flag law.

The resolution establishing the flag was not even published until Sept. 2, 1777. Despite repeated requests, Washington did not get the flags until 1783, after the Revolutionary War was over. And there is no certainty that they were the Stars and Stripes.

Early Flags

Although it was never officially adopted by the Continental Congress, many historians consider the first flag of the U.S. to have been the Grand Union (sometimes called Great Union) flag. This was a modification of the British Meteor flag, which had the red cross of St. George and the white cross of St. Andrew combined in the blue canton. For the Grand Union flag, 6 horizontal stripes were imposed on the red field, dividing it into 13 alternate red and white stripes. On Jan. 1, 1776, when the Continental Army came into formal existence, this flag was unfurled on Prospect Hill, Somerville, Mass. Washington wrote that "we hoisted the Union Flag in compliment to the United Colonies."

One of several flags about which controversy has raged for years is at Easton, Pa. Containing the devices of the national flag in reversed order, this has been in the public library at Easton for over 150 years. Some contend that this flag was actually the first Stars and Stripes, first displayed on July 8, 1776. This flag has 13 red and white stripes in the canton, 13 white stars centered in a blue field.

A flag was hastily improvised from garments by the defenders of Fort Schuyler at Rome, N.Y., Aug. 3-22, 1777. Historians believe it was the Grand Union Flag.

The Sons of Liberty had a flag of 9 red and white stripes, to signify 9 colonies, when they met in New York in 1765 to oppose the Stamp Tax. By 1775, the flag had grown to 13 red and white stripes, with a rattlesnake on it.

At Concord, Apr. 19, 1775, the minute men from Bedford, Mass., are said to have carried a flag having a silver arm with sword on a red field.

At Cambridge, Mass., the Sons of Liberty used a plain red flag with a green pine tree on it.

In June 1775, Washington went from Philadelphia to Boston to take command of the army, escorted to New York by the Philadelphia Light Horse Troop. It carried a yellow flag which had an elaborate coat of arms — the shield charged with 13 knots, the motto "For These We Strive" — and a canton of 13 blue and silver stripes.

In Feb., 1776, Col. Christopher Gadsden, member of the Continental Congress, gave the S. Carolina Provincial Congress a flag "such as is to be used by the commander-in-chief of the American Navy." It had a yellow field, with a rattlesnake about to strike and the words "Don't Tread on Me."

At the battle of Bennington, Aug. 16, 1777, patriots used a flag of 7 white and 6 red stripes with a blue canton extending down 9 stripes and showing an arch of 11 white stars over the figure 76 and a star in each of the upper corners. The stars are seven-pointed. This flag is preserved in the Historical Museum at Bennington, Vt.

At the Battle of Cowpens, Jan. 17, 1781, the 3d Maryland Regt. is said to have carried a flag of 13 red and white stripes, with a blue canton containing 12 stars in a circle around one star.

Who Designed the Flag? No one knows for a certainty. Francis Hopkinson, designer of a naval flag, declared he also had designed the flag and in 1781 asked Congress to reimburse him for his services. Congress did not do so. Dumas Malone of Columbia Univ. wrote: "This talented man . . . designed the American flag."

Who Called the Flag Old Glory? — The flag is said to have been named Old Glory by William Driver, a sea captain of Salem, Mass. One legend has it that when he raised the flag on his brig, the Charles Doggett, in 1824, he said: "I name thee Old Glory." But his daughter, who presented the flag to the Smithsonian Institution, said he named it at his 21st birthday celebration Mar. 17, 1824, when his mother presented the homemade flag to him.

The Betsy Ross Legend — The widely publicized legend that Mrs. Betsy Ross made the first Stars and Stripes in June 1776, at the request of a committee composed of George Washington, Robert Morris, and George Ross, an uncle, was first made public in 1870, by a grandson of Mrs. Ross. Historians have been unable to find a historical record of such a meeting or committee.

Adding New Stars

The flag of 1777 was used until 1795. Then, on the admission of Vermont and Kentucky to the Union, Congress passed and Pres. Washington signed an act that after May 1, 1795, the flag should have 15 stripes, alternate red and white, and 15 white stars on a blue field in the union.

When new states were admitted it became evident that the flag would become burdened with stripes. Congress thereupon ordered that after July 4, 1818, the flag should have 13 stripes, symbolizing the 13 original states; that the union have 20 stars, and that whenever a new state was admitted a new star should be added on the July 4 following admission. No law designates the permanent arrangement of the stars. However, since 1912 when a new state has been admitted, the new design has been announced by executive order. No star is specifically identified with any state.

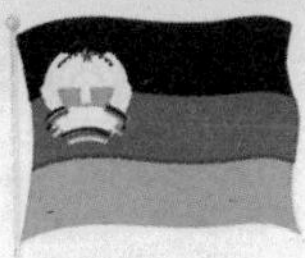

AFGHANISTAN

ALBANIA

ALGERIA

ANGOLA

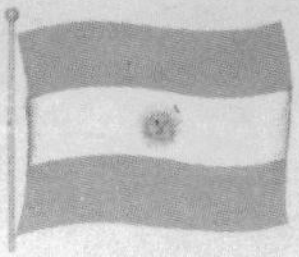

ARGENTINA

AUSTRALIA

AUSTRIA

BAHAMAS

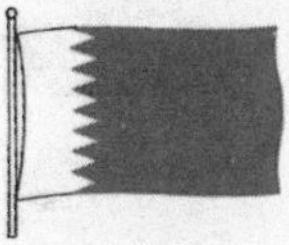

BAHRAIN

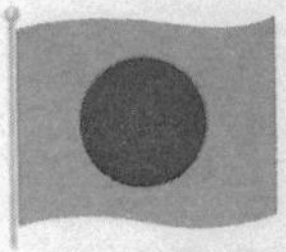

BANGLADESH

BARBADOS

BELGIUM

BELIZE

BENIN

BHUTAN

BOLIVIA

BOTSWANA

BRAZIL

BRUNEI

BULGARIA

BURKINA FASO

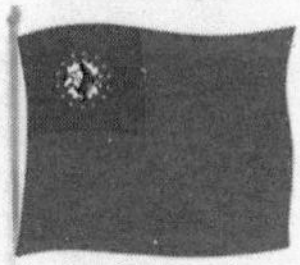

BURMA
(Myanmar)

BURUNDI

CAMBODIA
(Kampuchea)

CAMEROON

CANADA

CAPE VERDE

CENTRAL AFRICAN
REPUBLIC

CHAD

CHILE

CHINA

COLOMBIA

COMOROS

CONGO

COSTA RICA

CUBA

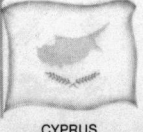

CYPRUS

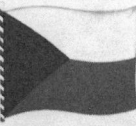

CZECHOSLOVAKIA

DENMARK

DJIBOUTI

F2

DOMINICA	 DOMINICAN REPUBLIC	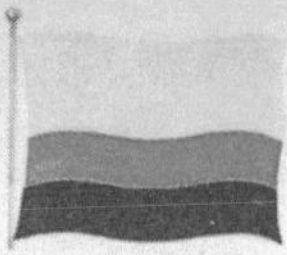 ECUADOR	 EGYPT	 EL SALVADOR
 EQUATORIAL GUINEA	 ETHIOPIA	 FIJI	 FINLAND	 FRANCE
 GABON	 GAMBIA	 GERMANY (EAST)	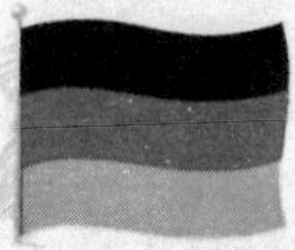 GERMANY (WEST)	 GHANA
 GREECE	 GRENADA	 GUATEMALA	 GUINEA	 GUINEA-BISSAU
 GUYANA	 HAITI	 HONDURAS	 HUNGARY	 ICELAND
 INDIA	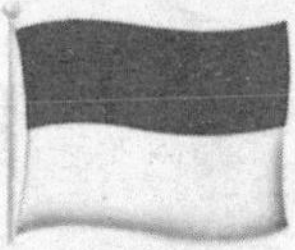 INDONESIA	 IRAN	 IRAQ	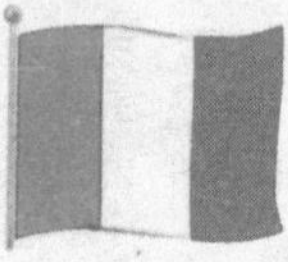 IRELAND
 ISRAEL	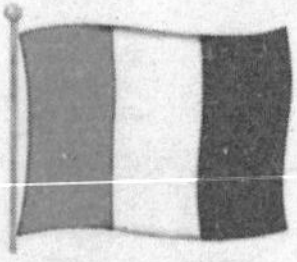 ITALY	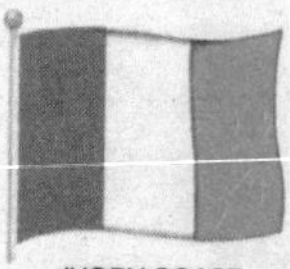 IVORY COAST	 JAMAICA	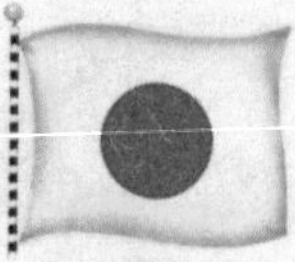 JAPAN
 JORDAN	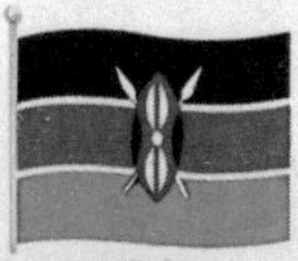 KENYA	 KOREA (NORTH)	 KOREA (SOUTH)	 KUWAIT

LAOS

LEBANON

LESOTHO

LIBERIA

LIBYA

LIECHTENSTEIN

LUXEMBOURG

MADAGASCAR

MALAWI

MALAYSIA

MALI

MALTA

MAURITANIA

MAURITIUS

MEXICO

MONACO

MONGOLIA

MOROCCO

MOZAMBIQUE

NEPAL

NETHERLANDS

NEW ZEALAND

NICARAGUA

NIGER

NIGERIA

NORWAY

OMAN

PAKISTAN

PANAMA

PAPUA-NEW GUINEA

PARAGUAY

PERU

PHILIPPINES

POLAND

PORTUGAL

QATAR

ROMANIA

RWANDA

SAINT LUCIA

ST. VINCENT AND
THE GRENADINES

F4

SAN MARINO

SAO TOME
AND PRINCIPE

SAUDI ARABIA

SENEGAL

SIERRA LEONE

SINGAPORE

SOLOMON ISLANDS

SOMALIA

SOUTH AFRICA

SPAIN

SRI LANKA

SUDAN

SURINAME

SWAZILAND

SWEDEN

SWITZERLAND

SYRIA

TAIWAN

TANZANIA

THAILAND

TOGO

TRINIDAD AND TOBAGO

TUNISIA

TURKEY

UGANDA

UNION OF SOVIET
SOCIALIST REPUBLICS

UNITED ARAB EMIRATES

UNITED KINGDOM

UNITED STATES

URUGUAY

VATICAN CITY

VENEZUELA

VIETNAM

WESTERN SAMOA

YEMEN

PEOPLE'S DEMOCRATIC
REPUBLIC OF YEMEN

YUGOSLAVIA

ZAIRE

ZAMBIA

ZIMBABWE

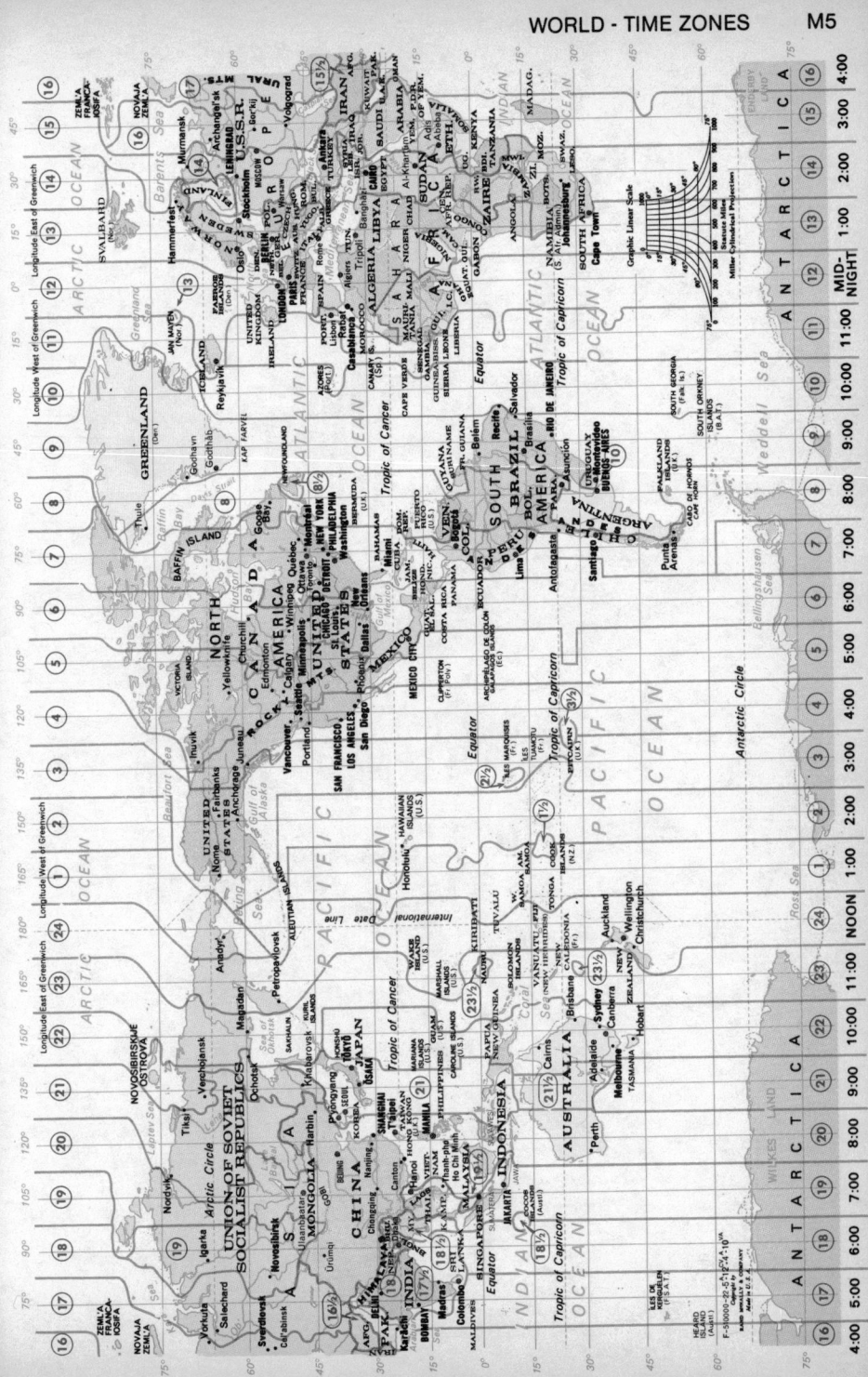

Kilometres
Miles

200   400   600 Km.

200   400   600 Mi.

NORWEGIAN SEA

ATLANTIC OCEAN

NORTH SEA

Baltic Sea

MEDITERRANEAN SEA

BLACK SEA

CASPIAN SEA

Barents Sea

URAL MOUNTAINS

URAL-SKIJEGORY

UNION OF SOVIET SOCIALIST REPUBLICS

MOSCOW
LENINGRAD

FINLAND
SWEDEN
NORWAY
DENMARK
IRELAND
UNITED KINGDOM
LONDON
FRANCE
PARIS
SPAIN
PORTUGAL
Lisbon
Madrid
ITALY
Rome
POLAND
Warsaw
CZECH
AUSTRIA
HUNGARY
Budapest
YUGOSLAVIA
ROMANIA
Bucharest
BULGARIA
Sofija
GREECE
Athens
TURKEY
Ankara
ASIA MINOR
CYPRUS
SYRIA
IRAQ
Baghdad
IRAN
TEHRAN
MOROCCO
Rabat
ALGERIA
TUNISIA
Tunis
Algiers
ATLAS MOUNTAINS
CAUCASUS
Baku
Tbilisi
CRETE
CORSE
SARDEGNA
SICILIA

National capitals are shown
with a solid underscore.
Secondary capitals are shown
with a dashed underscore.
PARIS   National capital
Tallinn   Secondary capital

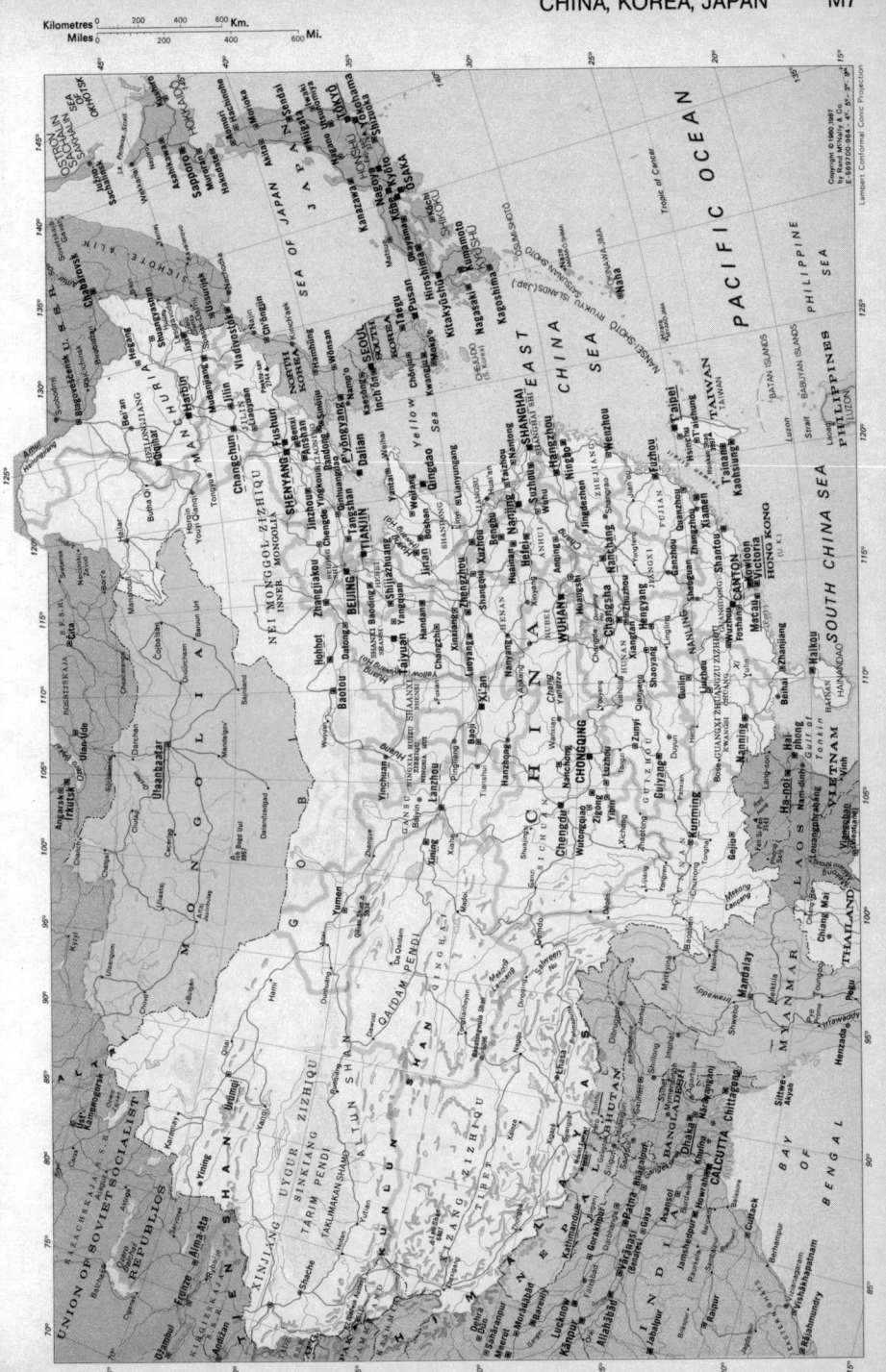

Kilometres 0   200   400   600 Km.
Miles 0   200   400   600 Mi.

Lambert Conformal Conic Projection

PACIFIC OCEAN

PHILIPPINE SEA

SOUTH CHINA SEA

INDIAN OCEAN

CELEBES SEA

BANDA SEA

ARAFURA SEA

TIMOR SEA

JAVA SEA — LAUT JAWA

LAUT MALUKU

BAY OF BENGAL

ANDAMAN SEA

Gulf of Tonkin

Gulf of Thailand

Strait of Malacca

GREATER SUNDA ISLANDS

LESSER SUNDA ISLANDS

INDONESIA

MALAYSIA

MYANMAR

THAILAND

VIETNAM

LAOS

KAMPUCHEA

CHINA

TAIWAN

PHILIPPINES

PAPUA NEW GUINEA

NEW GUINEA

AUSTRALIA

BORNEO — KALIMANTAN

SUMATERA

SULAWESI — CELEBES

MINDANAO

LUZON

PALAWAN

HALMAHERA

TRUST TERRITORY OF THE PACIFIC ISLANDS (U.S. Admin.)

MARIANA ISLANDS

CAROLINE ISLANDS

GUAM (U.S.)

Tropic of Cancer

Equator

YANGON

MANDALAY

MOULMEIN

BANGKOK

Chiang Mai

HA-NOI

Hai-phong

Da-nang

Hue

THANH PHO HO CHI MINH (SAIGON)

Phnum Penh

KUALA LUMPUR

SINGAPORE

JAKARTA

BANDUNG

SURABAYA

Semarang

Yogyakarta

Surakarta

MEDAN

Palembang

Padang

Pontianak

Banjarmasin

Balikpapan

Samarinda

Ujung Pandang

Manado

MANILA

Quezon City

Cebu

Davao

Baguio

VICTORIA HONG KONG (U.K.)

Macau (Port.)

CANTON — Kowloon

GUANGDONG

GUANGXI

YUNNAN

HAINAN — HAINANDAO

Haikou

KAOHSIUNG — Tainan — TAIWAN

CHRISTMAS ISLAND (Aust.)

NICOBAR ISLANDS (India)

ANDAMAN ISLANDS (India)

Port Blair

Chittagong

Sittwe (Akyab)

INDIA

BANGLADESH

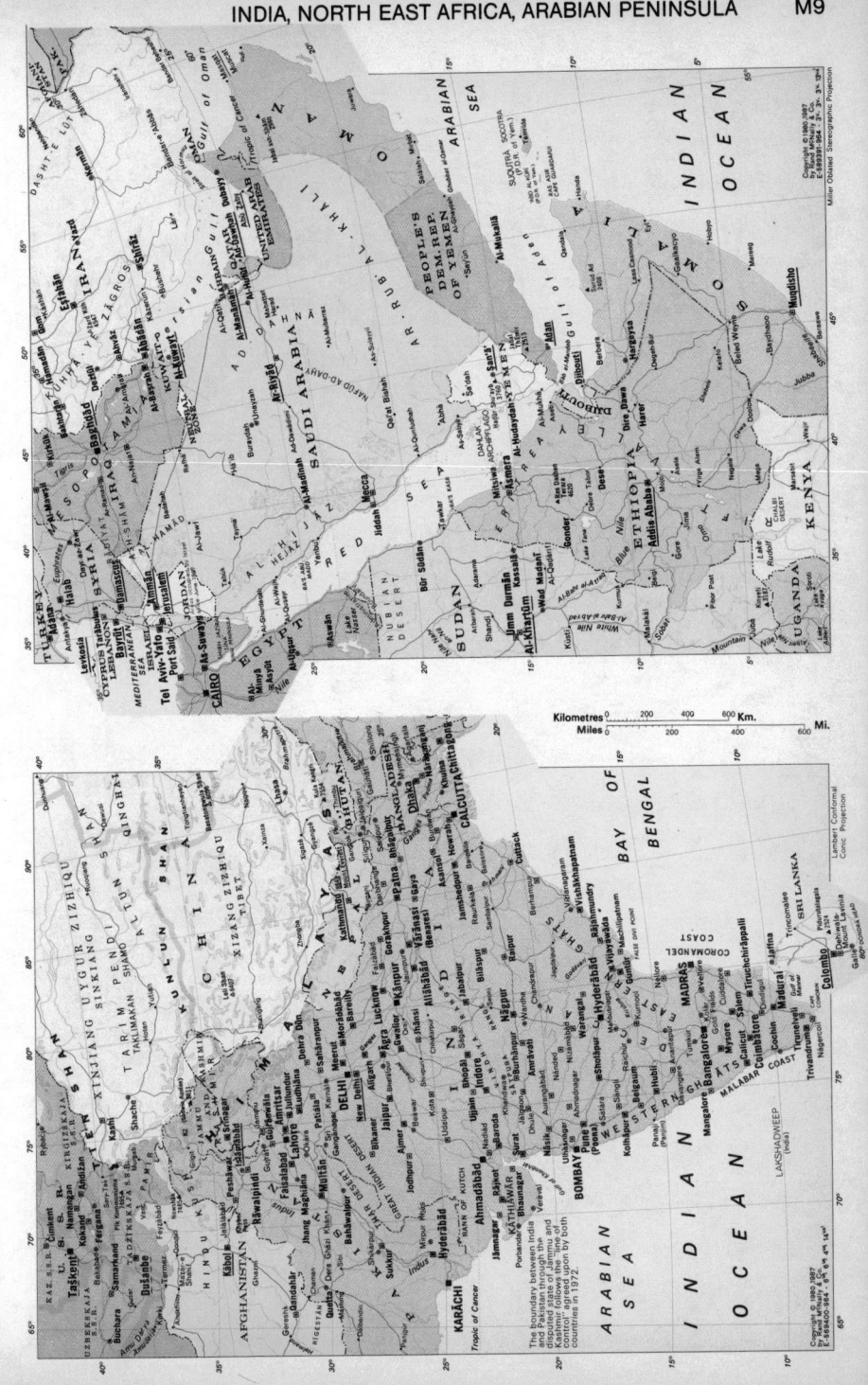

Kilometres 0   200   400   600 Km.
Miles 0   200   400   600 Mi.

MEDITERRANEAN SEA

ATLANTIC OCEAN

Gulf of Guinea

SPAIN · ITALY · GREECE · TURKEY · SYRIA · IRAQ · JORDAN · ISRAEL · LEBANON · CYPRUS · SAUDI ARABIA · EGYPT · LIBYA · TUNISIA · ALGERIA · MOROCCO · WESTERN SAHARA · MAURITANIA · MALI · NIGER · CHAD · SUDAN · ETHIOPIA · KENYA · UGANDA · ZAIRE · CENTRAL AFRICAN REPUBLIC · CAMEROON · NIGERIA · BENIN · TOGO · GHANA · IVORY COAST · BURKINA FASO · GUINEA · SENEGAL · GAMBIA · GUINEA-BISSAU · SIERRA LEONE · LIBERIA · SAO TOME AND PRINCIPE · EQUATORIAL GUINEA · GABON

SAHARA · SUDAN · LIBYAN DESERT · NUBIAN DESERT · ARABIAN DESERT · TIBESTI · FAZZAN

CAIRO · Alexandria · Tripoli · Banghāzī · Tunis · Algiers · Casablanca · Rabat · Marrakech · Dakar · Nouakchott · Bamako · Niamey · Lagos · Ibadan · Accra · Abidjan · Conakry · Freetown · Monrovia · Khartūm · Al-Khartūm · Addis Ababa · Tamanrasset

Tropic of Cancer

Western Sahara has been occupied by Morocco

Copyright © 1980, 1987
Rand McNally & Co.
R-5-88300-564 - 41 6° 9° 7 yrs

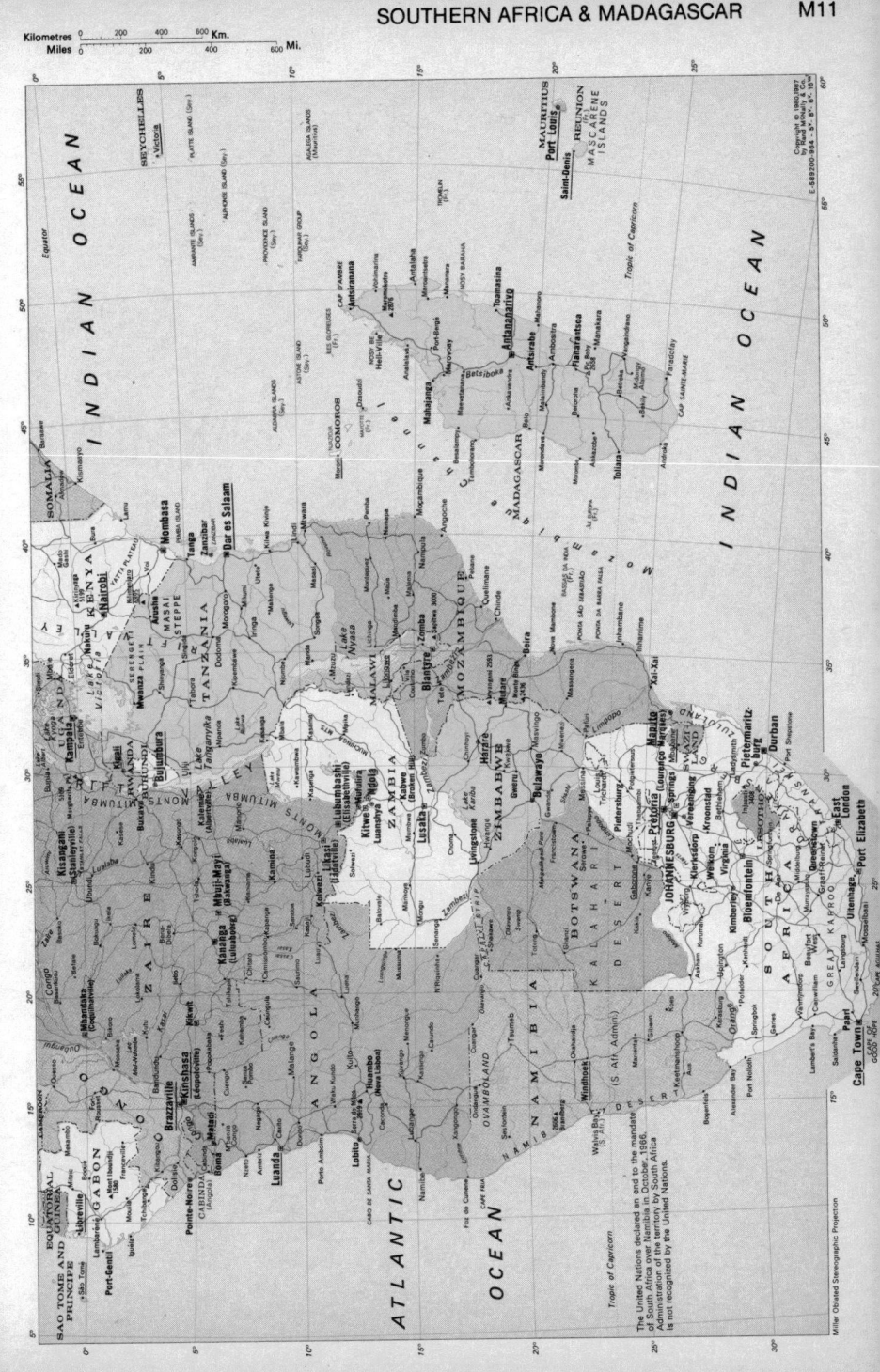

Kilometres 0 200 400 600 Km.
Miles 0   200   400   600 Mi.

Copyright © 1960, 1967
Replaces edition of
E 420200-964 • 6 • 2 • 6 • 84 ° 84 M
Lambert Conformal Conic Projection

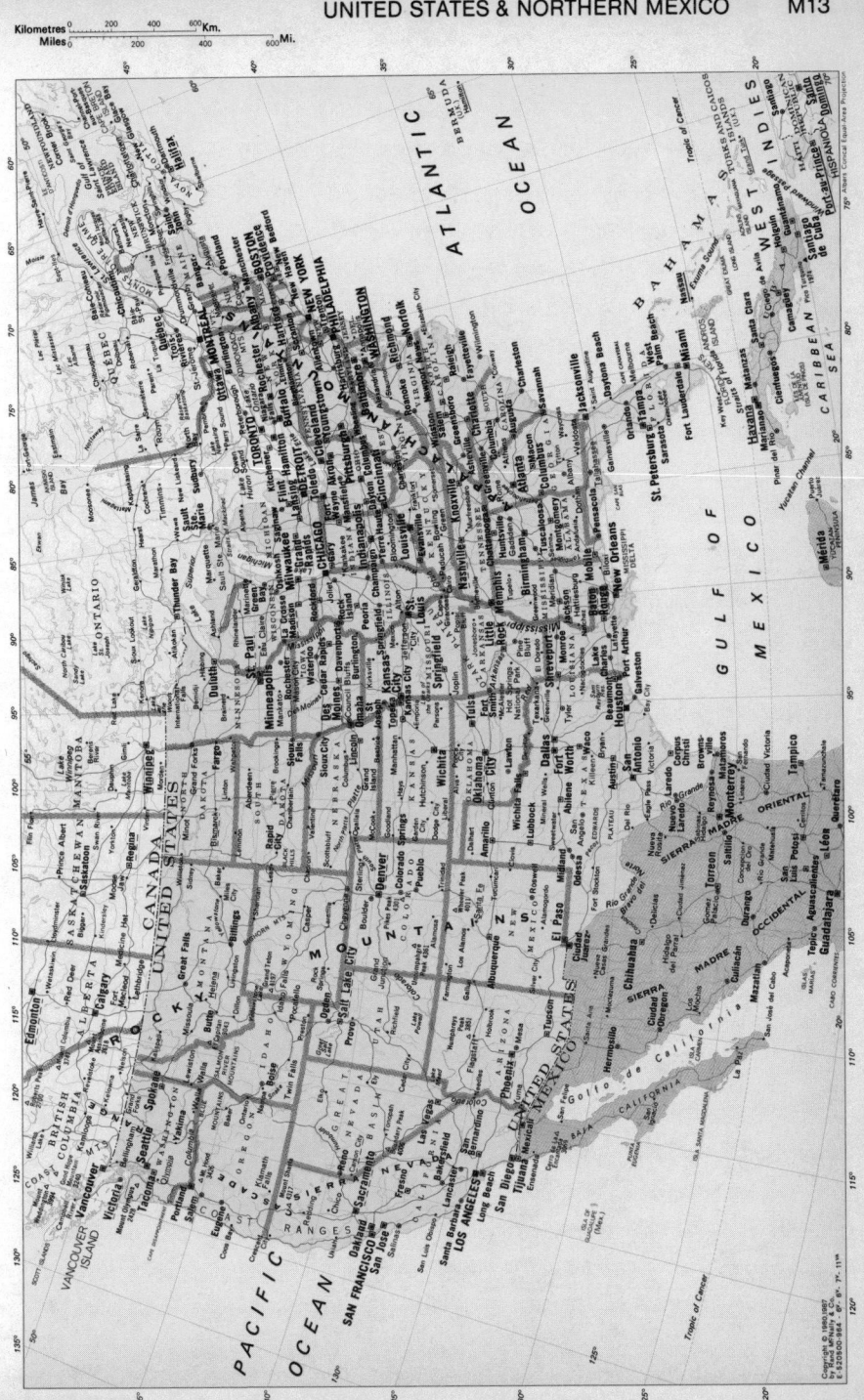

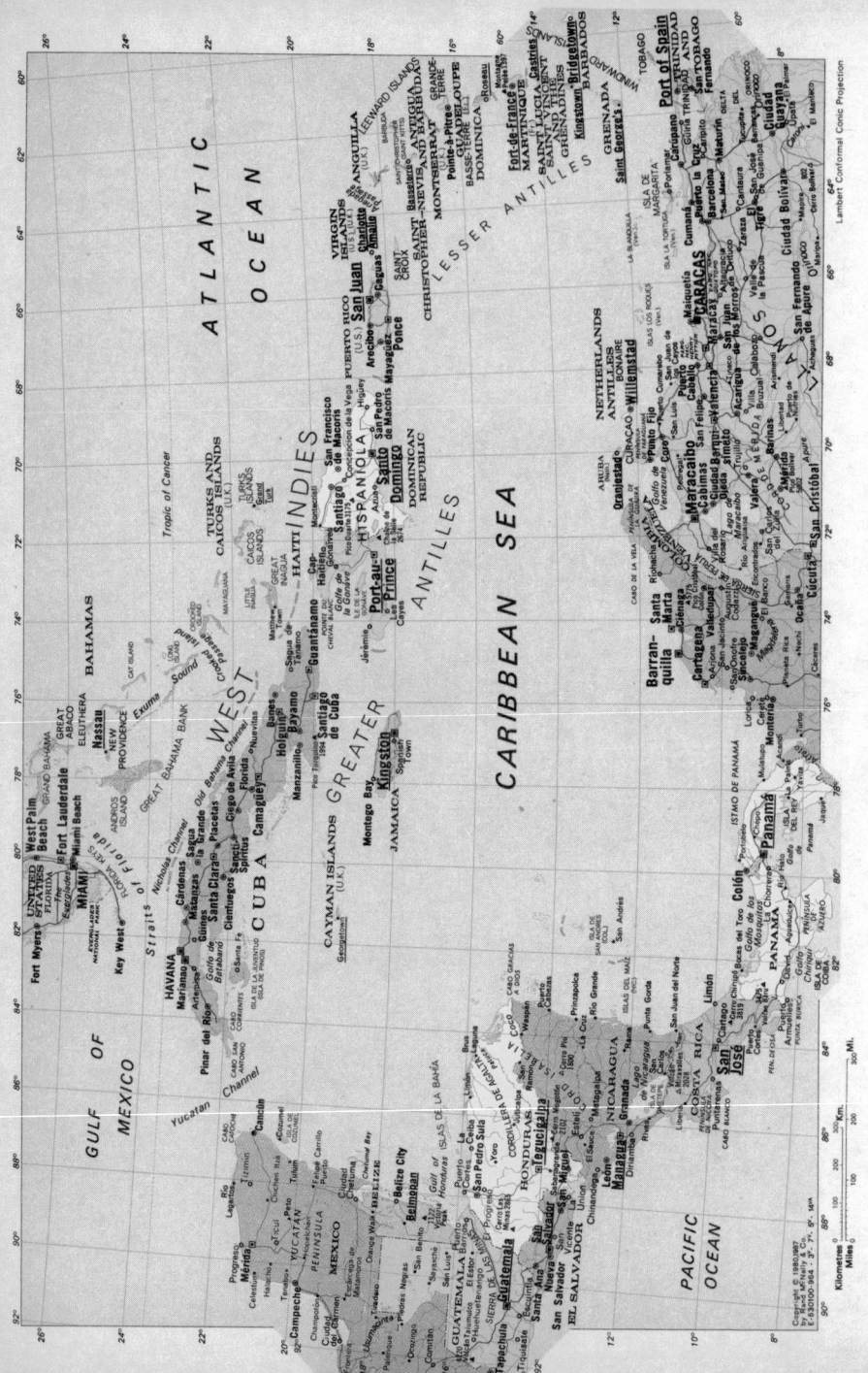

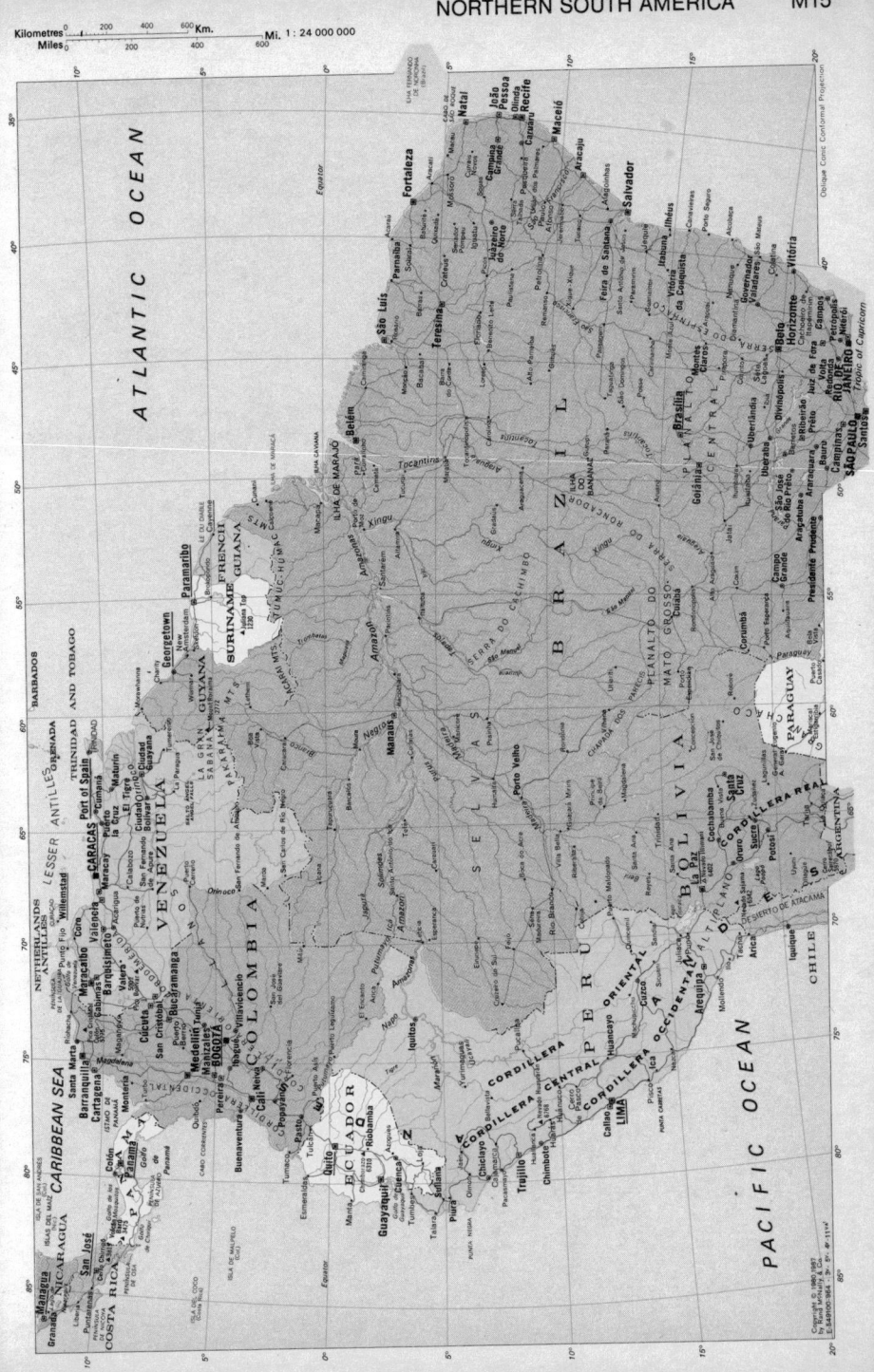

Kilometres 0 200 400 600 Km.   Mi. 1 : 24 000 000
Miles 0 200 400 600

ATLANTIC OCEAN

PACIFIC OCEAN

CARIBBEAN SEA

BRAZIL

VENEZUELA

COLOMBIA

PERU

BOLIVIA

ECUADOR

GUYANA

SURINAME

FRENCH GUIANA

PARAGUAY

CHILE

ARGENTINA

NICARAGUA

COSTA RICA

PANAMA

TRINIDAD AND TOBAGO

BARBADOS

GRENADA

LESSER ANTILLES

NETHERLANDS ANTILLES

Equator

Tropic of Capricorn

CARACAS

BOGOTÁ

LIMA

Quito

Paramaribo

Georgetown

Brasília

RIO DE JANEIRO

SÃO PAULO

La Paz

Sucre

Managua

San José

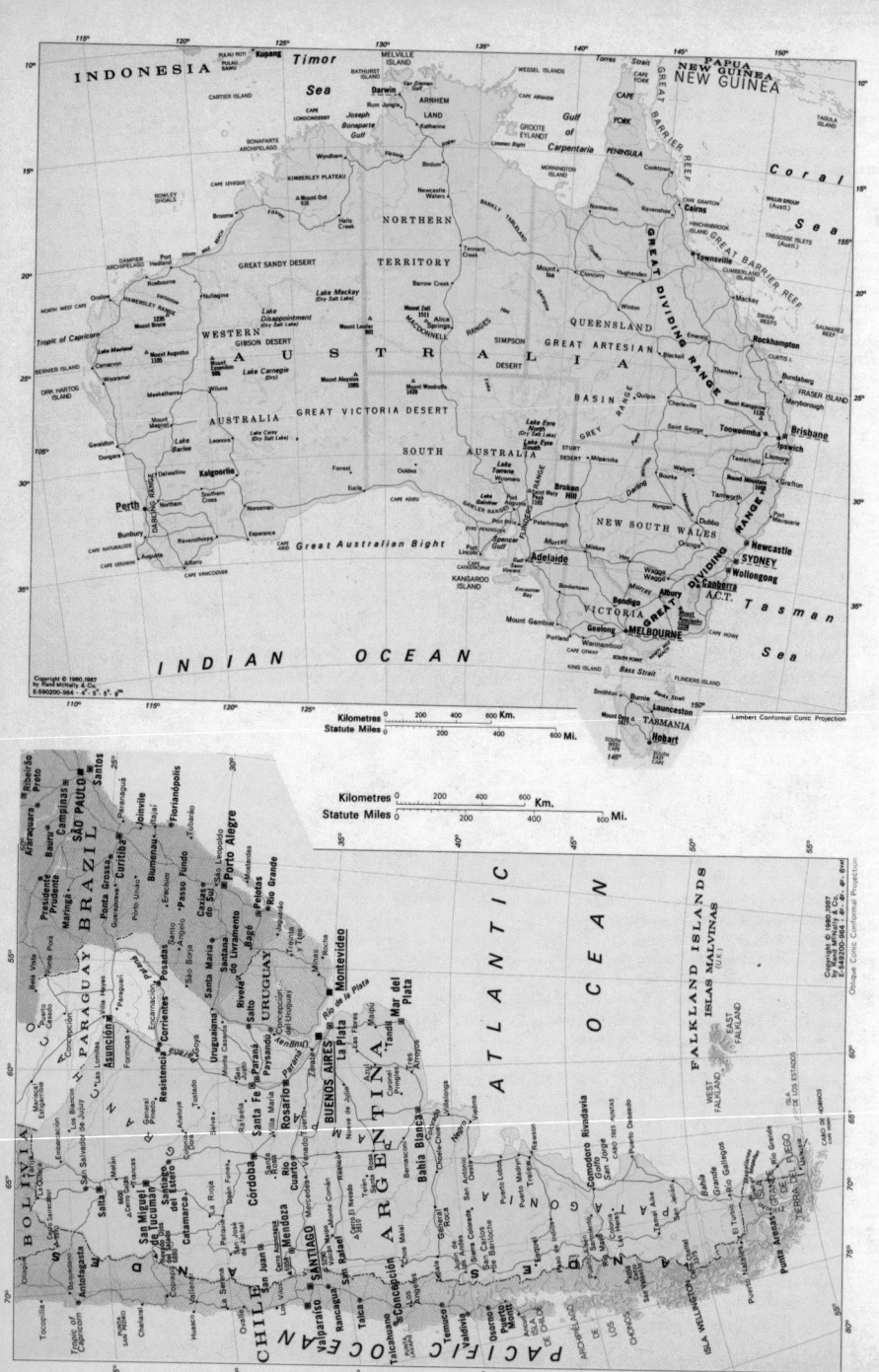

Prehistory: Our Ancestors Take Over

Homo sapiens. The precise origins of *homo sapiens*, the species to which all humans belong, are subject to broad speculation based on a small number of fossils, genetic and anatomical studies, and the geological record. But most scientists agree that we evolved from ape-like primate ancestors in a process that began millions of years ago.

Current theories say the first hominid (human-like primate) was *Ramapithecus*, who emerged 12 million years ago. Its remains have been found in Asia, Europe, and Africa. Further development was apparently limited to Africa, where 2 lines of hominids appeared some 5 or 6 million years ago. One was *Australopithecus*, a tool-maker and social animal, who lived from perhaps 4 to 3 million years ago, and then apparently became extinct.

The 2nd was a human line, *Homo habilus,* a large-brained specimen that walked upright and had a dextrous hand. *Homo habillus* lived in semi-permanent camps and had a food-gathering and sharing economy.

Homo erectus, our nearest ancestor, appeared in Africa perhaps 1.75 million years ago, and began spreading into Asia and Europe soon after. It had a fairly large brain and a skeletal structure similar to ours. *Homo erectus* learned to control fire, and probably had primitive language skills. The final brain development to *Homo sapiens* and then to our sub-species *Homo sapiens sapiens* occurred between 500,000 and 50,000 years ago, either in one place — probably Africa — or virtually simultaneously and independently in different places in Africa, Europe, and Asia. There is no question that all modern races are members of the same species, *Homo sapiens sapiens.*

The spread of mankind into the remaining habitable continents probably took place during the last ice age up to 100,000 years ago: to the Americas across a land bridge from Asia, and to Australia across the Timor Straits.

Earliest cultures. A variety of cultural modes — in tool-making, diet, shelter, and possibly social arrangements and spiritual expression, arose as early mankind adapted to different geographic and climatic zones.

Three basic tool-making traditions are recognized by archeologists as arising and often coexisting from one million years ago to the near past: the *chopper tradition,* found largely in E. Asia, with crude chopping tools and simple flake tools; the *flake tradition,* found in Africa and W. Europe, with a variety of small cutting and flaking tools, and the *biface tradition,* found in all of Africa, W. and S. Europe, and S. Asia, producing pointed hand axes chipped on both faces. Later biface sites yield more refined axes and a variety of other tools, weapons, and ornaments using bone, antler, and wood as well as stone.

Only sketchy evidence remains for the different stages in man's increasing control over the environment. Traces of 400,000-year-old covered wood shelters have been found at Nice, France. Scraping tools at Neanderthal sites (200,000-30,000 BC in Europe, N. Africa, the Middle East and Central Asia) suggest the treatment of skins for clothing. Sites from all parts of the world show seasonal migration patterns and exploitation of a wide range of plant and animal food sources.

Painting and decoration, for which there is evidence at the Nice site, flourished along with stone and ivory sculpture after 30,000 years ago; 60 caves in France and 30 in Spain show remarkable examples of wall painting. Other examples have been found in Africa. Proto-religious rites are suggested by these works, and by evidence of ritual cannibalism by Peking Man, 500,000 BC, and of ritual burial with medicinal plants and flowers by Neanderthals at Shanidar in Iraq.

The Neolithic Revolution. Sometime after 10,000 BC, among widely separated human communities, a series of dramatic technological and social changes occurred that are summed up as the Neolithic Revolution. The cultivation of previously wild plants encouraged the growth of permanent settlements. Animals were domesticated as a work force and food source. The manufacture of pottery and cloth began. These techniques permitted a huge increase in world population and in human control over the earth.

No region can safely claim priority as the "inventor" of these techniques. Dispersed sites in Cen. and S. America, S.E. Europe, and the Middle East show roughly contemporaneous (10-8,000 BC) evidence of one or another "neolithic" trait. Dates near 6-3,000 BC have been given for E. and S. Asian, W. European, and sub-Saharan African neolithic remains. The variety of crops — field grains, rice, maize, and roots, and the varying mix of other traits suggest that the revolution occurred independently in all these regions.

History Begins: 4000 - 1000 BC

Near Eastern cradle. If history began with writing, the first chapter opened in Mesopotamia, the Tigris-Euphrates river valley. Clay tablets with pictographs were used by the Sumerians to keep records after 4000 BC. A cuneiform (wedge shaped) script evolved by 3000 BC as a full syllabic alphabet. Neighboring peoples adapted the script to their own language.

Sumerian life centered, from 4000 BC, on large cities (Eridu, Ur, Uruk, Nippur, Kish, Lagash) organized around temples and priestly bureaucracies, with the surrounding plains watered by vast irrigation works and worked with traction plows. Sailboats, wheeled vehicles, potters wheels, and kilns were used. Copper was smelted and tempered in Sumeria from c4000 BC and bronze was produced not long after. Ores, as well as precious stones and metals were obtained through long-distance ship and caravan trade. Iron was used from c2000 BC. Improved ironworking, developed partly by the **Hittites,** became widespread by 1200 BC.

Sumerian political primacy passed among cities and their kingly dynasties. Semitic-speaking peoples, with cultures derived from the Sumerian, founded a succession of dynasties that ruled in Mesopotamia and neighboring areas for most of 1800 years; among them the **Akkadians** (first under Sargon c2350 BC), the Amorites (whose laws, codified by **Hammurabi,** c1792-1750 BC, have Biblical parallels), and the Assyrians, with interludes of rule by the Hittites, Kassites, and Mitanni, all possibly Indo-Europeans. The political and cultural center of gravity shifted northwest with each successive empire.

Mesopotamian learning, maintained by scribes and preserved by successive rulers in vast libraries, was not abstract or theoretical. Algebraic and geometric problems could be solved on a practical basis in construction, commerce, or administration. Systematic lists of astronomical phenomena, plants, animals and stones were kept; medical texts listed ailments and their herbal cures.

The Sumerians worshipped anthropomorphic gods representing natural forces — Anu, god of heaven; Enlil (Ea), god of water. Epic poetry related these and other gods in a hierarchy. Sacrifices were made at **ziggurats** — huge stepped temples. Gods were thought to control all events, which could be foretold using oracular materials. This religious pattern persisted into the first millenium BC.

The Syria-Palestine area, site of some of the earliest urban remains (Jericho, 7000 BC), and of the recently uncovered **Ebla** civilization (fl. 2500 BC), experienced Egyptian cultural and political influence along with Mesopotamian. The **Phoenician** coast was an active commercial center. A phonetic alphabet was invented here before 1600 BC. It became the ancestor of all European, Middle Eastern, Indian, S.E.

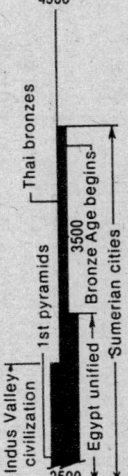

2500 BC

Ebla civilization

Bronze-age Minoan civilization emerges on Crete

Egyptian literature begins

Peruvian neolithic ceremonial centers

Phonetic alphabet invented before 1600

1750 — Hammurabi

Aryans invade India

Mt. Sinai revelations to Moses

Chinese Shang dynasty

Mexican Olmec civilization established

1000 BC

Asian, Ethiopian, and Korean alphabets.

Regional commerce and diplomacy were aided by the use of Akkadian as a *lingua franca*, later replaced by Aramaic.

Egypt. Agricultural villages along the Nile were united by 3300 BC into two kingdoms, Upper and Lower Egypt, unified under the Pharaoh Menes c3100 BC; Nubia to the south was added 2600 BC. A national bureaucracy supervised construction of canals and monuments (**pyramids** starting 2700 BC). Brilliant First Dynasty achievements in architecture, sculpture and painting, set the standards and forms for all subsequent Egyptian civilization and are still admired. Hieroglyphic **writing** appeared by 3400 BC, recording a sophisticated literature including romantic and philosophical modes after 2300 BC.

An ordered hierarchy of gods, including totemistic animal elements, was served by a powerful priesthood in Memphis. The pharaoh was identified with the falcon god Horus. Later trends were the belief in an afterlife, and the quasi-monotheistic reforms of **Akhenaton** (c1379-1362 BC).

After a period of conquest by Semitic Hyksos from Asia (c1700-1500 BC), the New Kingdom established an empire in Syria. Egypt became increasingly embroiled in Asiatic wars and diplomacy. Eventually it was conquered by Persia in 525 BC, and it faded away as an independent culture.

India. An urban civilization with a so-far-undeciphered writing system stretched across the Indus Valley and along the Arabian Sea c3000-1500 BC. Major sites are Harappa and **Mohenjo-Daro** in Pakistan, well-planned geometric cities with underground sewers and vast granaries. The entire region (600,000 sq. mi.) may have been ruled as a single state. Bronze was used, and arts and crafts were highly developed. Religious life apparently took the form of fertility cults.

Indus civilization was probably in decline when it was destroyed by **Aryan invaders** from the northwest, speaking an Indo-European language from which all the languages of Pakistan, north India and Bangladesh descend. Led by a warrior aristocracy whose legendary deeds are recorded in the **Rig Veda**, the Aryans spread east and south, bringing their pantheon of sky gods, elaborate priestly (Brahmin) ritual, and the beginnings of the caste system; local customs and beliefs were assimilated by the conquerors.

Europe. On Crete, the bronze-age **Minoan** civilization emerged c2500 BC. A prosperous economy and richly decorative art (e.g. at Knossos palace) was supported by seaborne commerce. Mycenae and other cities in Greece and Asia Minor (e.g. **Troy**) preserved elements of the culture to c1100 BC. Cretan Linear A script, c2000-1700 BC, is undeciphered; Linear B, c1300-1200 BC, records a Greek dialect.

Possible connection between Minoan-Mycenaean monumental stonework, and the great megalithic monuments and tombs of W. Europe, Iberia, and Malta (c4000-1500 BC) is unclear.

China. Proto-Chinese neolithic cultures had long covered northern and southeastern China when the first large political state was organized in the north by the **Shang dynasty** c1500 BC. Shang kings called themselves Sons of Heaven, and presided over a cult of human and animal sacrifice to ancestors and nature gods. The Chou dynasty, starting c1100 BC, expanded the area of the Son of Heaven's dominion, but feudal states exercised most temporal power.

A writing system with 2,000 different characters was already in use under the Shang, with **pictographs** later supplemented by phonetic characters. The system, with modifications, is still in use, despite changes in spoken Chinese.

Technical advances allowed urban specialists to create fine ceramic and jade products, and bronze casting after 1500 BC was the most advanced in the world.

Bronze artifacts have recently been discovered in northern Thailand dating to 3600 BC, hundreds of years before similar Middle Eastern finds.

Americas. Olmecs settled on the Gulf coast of Mexico, 1500 BC, and soon developed the first civilization in the Western Hemisphere. Temple cities and huge stone sculpture date to 1200 BC. A rudimentary calendar and writing system existed. Olmec religion, centering on a jaguar god, and art forms influenced all later Meso-American cultures.

Neolithic ceremonial centers were built on the Peruvian desert coast, c2000 BC.

Classical Era of Old World Civilizations

Greece. After a period of decline during the Dorian Greek invasions (1200-1000 BC), Greece and the Aegean area developed a unique civilization. Drawing upon Mycenaean traditions, Mesopotamian learning (weights and measures, lunisolar calendar, astronomy, musical scales), the Phoenician alphabet (modified for Greek), and Egyptian art, the revived **Greek city-states** saw a rich elaboration of intellectual life. Long-range commerce was aided by metal coinage (introduced by the Lydians in Asia Minor before 700 BC); colonies were founded around the Mediterranean and Black Sea shores (Cumae in Italy 760 BC, Massalia in France c600 BC).

Philosophy, starting with Ionian speculation on the nature of matter and the universe (Thales c634-546), and including mathematical speculation (Pythagoras c580-c500), culminated in Athens in the rationalist idealism of **Plato** (c428-347) and **Socrates** (c470-399); the latter was executed for alleged impiety. Aristotle (384-322) united all fields of study in his system. The arts were highly valued. Architecture culminated in the **Parthenon** in Athens (438, sculpture by Phidias); poetry and drama (Aeschylus 525-456) thrived. Male beauty and strength, a chief artistic theme, were enhanced at the gymnasium and the national games at Olympia.

Ruled by local tyrants or oligarchies, the Greeks were never politically united, but managed to resist inclusion in the Persian Empire (Darius defeated at Marathon 490 BC, Xerxes at Salamis, Plataea 479 BC). Local warfare was common; the **Peloponnesian Wars**, 431-404 BC, ended in Sparta's victory over Athens. Greek political power waned, but classical Greek cultural forms spread throughout the ancient world from the Atlantic to India.

Hebrews. Nomadic Hebrew tribes entered Canaan before 1200 BC, settling among other Semitic peoples speaking the same language. They brought from the desert a **monotheistic faith** said to have been revealed to Abraham in Canaan c1800 BC and to Moses at Mt. Sinai c1250 BC, after the Hebrews' escape from bondage in Egypt. David (ruled 1000-961 BC) and Solomon (ruled 961-922 BC) united the Hebrews in a kingdom that briefly dominated the area. Phoenicians to the north established colonies

Paleontology: The History of Life

All dates are approximate, and are subject to change based on new fossil finds or new dating techniques; but the sequence of events is generally accepted. Dates are in years before the present.

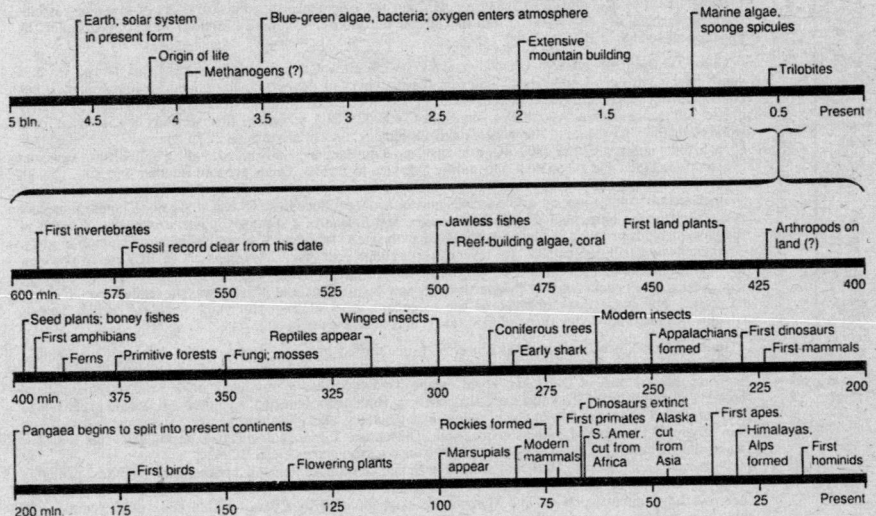

Ancient Near Eastern Civilizations 4000 B.C.-500 B.C.

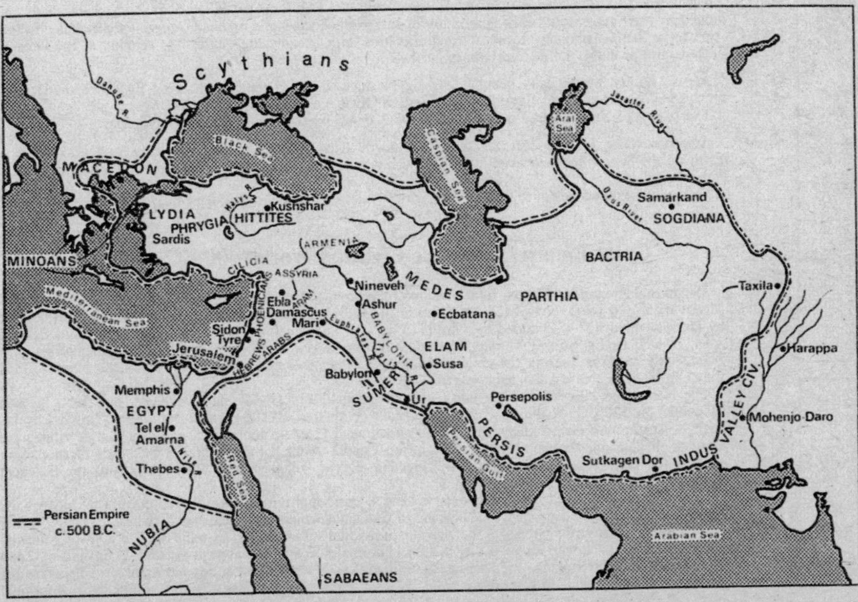

1000 BC

Chavin dynasty begins in Peru

Hebrew kingdom divided

Chou dynasty begins in China

Carthage established

800

Nubia begins rule of Egypt

Metal coins in Asia Minor

Isaiah d.

Zoroaster b.

Pythagoras b.

600

Indian Buddhism, Jainism begin

Confucius b.

Siddarta b.

Aeschylus b.

Socrates b.

Plato b.

Parthenon

Peloponnesian Wars

400 BC

around the E. and W. Mediterranean (**Carthage** c814 BC) and sailed into the Atlantic.

A temple in Jerusalem became the national religious center, with sacrifices performed by a hereditary priesthood. Polytheistic influences, especially of the fertility cult of Baal, were opposed by **prophets** (Elijah, Amos, Isaiah).

Divided into **two kingdoms** after Solomon, the Hebrews were unable to resist the revived Assyrian empire, which conquered Israel, the northern kingdom in 722 BC. Judah, the southern kingdom, was conquered in 586 BC by the Babylonians under Nebuchadnezzar II. But with the fixing of most of the Biblical canon by the mid-fourth century BC, and the emergence of rabbis, arbiters of law and custom, Judaism successfully survived the loss of Hebrew autonomy. A Jewish kingdom was revived under the Hasmoneans (168-42 BC).

China. During the **Eastern Chou** dynasty (770-256 BC), Chinese culture spread east to the sea and south to the Yangtze. Large feudal states on the periphery of the empire contended for pre-eminence, but continued to recognize the Son of Heaven (king), who retained a purely ritual role enriched with courtly music and dance. In the Age of Warring States (403-221 BC), when the first sections of the **Great Wall** were built, the Ch'in state in the West gained supremacy, and finally united all of China.

Iron tools entered China c500 BC, and casting techniques were advanced, aiding agriculture. Peasants owned their land, and owed civil and military service to nobles. Cities grew in number and size, though barter remained the chief trade medium.

Intellectual ferment among noble scribes and officials produced the Classical Age of Chinese literature and philosophy. **Confucius** (551-479 BC) urged a restoration of a supposedly harmonious social order of the past through proper conduct in accordance with one's station and through filial and ceremonial piety. The *Analects*, attributed to him, are revered throughout East Asia. **Mencius** (d. 289 BC) added the view that the Mandate of Heaven can be removed from an unjust dynasty. The Legalists sought to curb the supposed natural wickedness of people through new institutions and harsh laws; they aided the Ch'in rise to power. The Naturalists emphasized the balance of opposites — yin, yang — in the world. **Taoists** sought mystical knowledge through meditation and disengagement.

India. The political and cultural center of India shifted from the Indus to the Ganges River Valley. Buddhism, Jainism, and mystical revisions of orthodox Vedism all developed around 500-300 BC. The *Upanishads*, last part of the *Veda*, urged escape from the illusory physical world. Vedism remained the preserve of the priestly Brahmin caste. In contrast, **Buddhism**, founded by Siddarta Gautama (c563-c483 BC), appealed to merchants in the growing urban centers, and took hold at first (and most lastingly) on the geographic fringes of Indian civilization. The classic Indian epics were composed in this era: The *Ramayana* around 300 BC, the *Mahabharata* over a period starting 400 BC.

Northern India was divided into a large number of monarchies and aristocratic republics, probably derived from tribal groupings, when the Magadha kingdom was formed in Bihar c542 BC. It soon became the dominant power. The **Maurya dynasty**, founded by Chandragupta c321 BC, expanded the kingdom, uniting most of N. India in a centralized bureaucratic empire. The third Mauryan king, **Asoka** (ruled c274-236) conquered most of the subcontinent: he converted to Buddhism, and inscribed its tenets on pillars throughout India. He downplayed the caste system and tried to end expensive sacrificial rites.

Before its final decline in India, Buddhism developed the popular worship of heavenly Bodhisatvas (enlightened beings), and produced a refined architecture (stupa—shrine—at Sanchi 100 AD) and sculpture (Gandhara reliefs 1-400 AD).

Persia. Aryan peoples (Persians, Medes) dominated the area of present Iran by the beginning of the first millenium BC. The prophet **Zoroaster** (born c628 BC) introduced a dualistic religion in which the forces of good (Ahura Mazda, Lord of Wisdom) and evil (Ahiram) battle for dominance; individuals are judged by their actions and earn damnation or salvation. Zoroaster's hymns (*Gathas*) are included in the *Avesta*, the Zoroastrian scriptures. A version of this faith became the established religion of the Persian Empire, and probably influenced later monotheistic religions.

Africa. Nubia, periodically occupied by Egypt since the third millenium, ruled Egypt c750-661, and survived as an independent Egyptianized kingdom (**Kush**; capital Meroe) for 1,000 years.

The Iron Age Nok culture flourished c500 BC-200 AD on the Benue Plateau of **Nigeria.**

Americas. The Chavin culture controlled north Peru from 900-200 BC. Its ceremonial centers, featuring the jaguar god, survived long after. Chavin architecture, ceramics, and textiles influenced other Peruvian cultures.

Mayan civilization began to develop in Central America in the 5th century BC.

Great Empires Unite the Civilized World: 400 BC - 400 AD

Persia and Alexander. Cyrus, ruler of a small kingdom in Persia from 559 BC, united the Persians and Medes within 10 years, conquered Asia Minor and Babylonia in another 10. His son Cambyses followed by **Darius** (ruled 522-486) added vast lands to the east and north as far as the Indus Valley and Central Asia, as well as Egypt and Thrace. The whole empire was ruled by an international bureaucracy and army, with Persians holding the chief positions. The resources and styles of all the subject civilizations were exploited to create a rich syncretic art.

The Hellenized kingdom of Macedon, which under Phillip II dominated Greece, passed to his son **Alexander** in 336 BC. Within 13 years, Alexander conquered all the Persian dominions. Imbued by his tutor Aristotle with Greek ideals, Alexander encouraged Greek colonization, and Greek-style cities were founded throughout the empire (e.g. Alexandria, Egypt). After his death in 323 BC, wars of succession divided the empire into three parts — Macedon, Egypt (ruled by the **Ptolemies**), and the **Seleucid** Empire.

In the ensuing 300 years (the **Hellenistic Era**), a cosmopolitan Greek-oriented culture permeated the ancient world from W. Europe to the borders of India, absorbing native elites everywhere.

Hellenistic philosophy stressed the private individual's search for happiness. The Cynics followed Diogenes (c372-287), who stressed satisfaction of animal needs and contempt for social convention. Zeno (c335-c263) and the Stoics exalted reason, identified it with virtue, and counseled an ascetic disregard for misfortune. The Epicureans tried to build lives of moderate pleasure without political or emotional

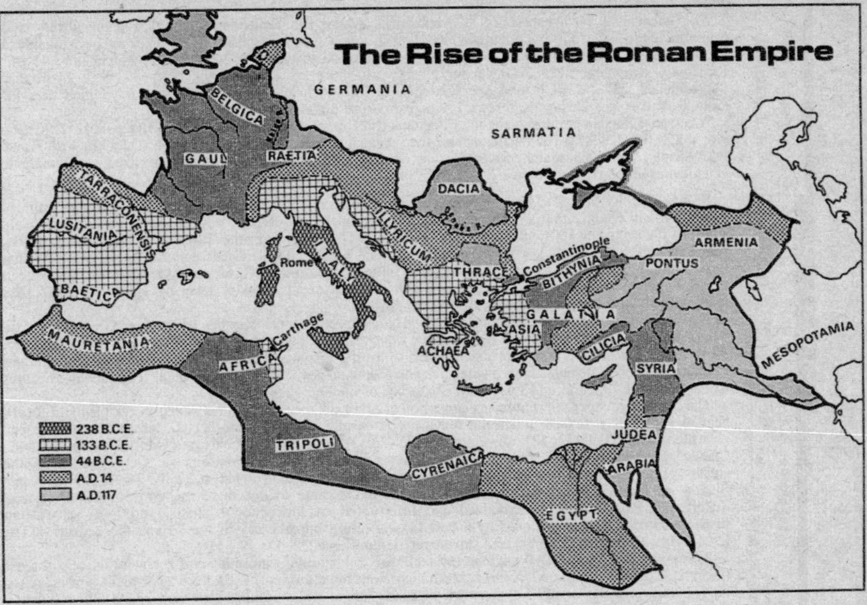

The Rise of the Roman Empire

GERMANIA

SARMATIA

BELGICA

GAUL
RAETIA

DACIA

TARRACONENSIS

LUSITANIA

ILLYRICUM

ARMENIA

THRACE
Constantinople
BITHYNIA
PONTUS

BAETICA

Rome
ITALY

GALATIA

ASIA

MESOPOTAMIA

ACHAEA

CILICIA

MAURETANIA

Carthage

AFRICA

SYRIA

JUDEA

ARABIA

	238 B.C.E.
	133 B.C.E.
	44 B.C.E.
	A.D.14
	A.D.117

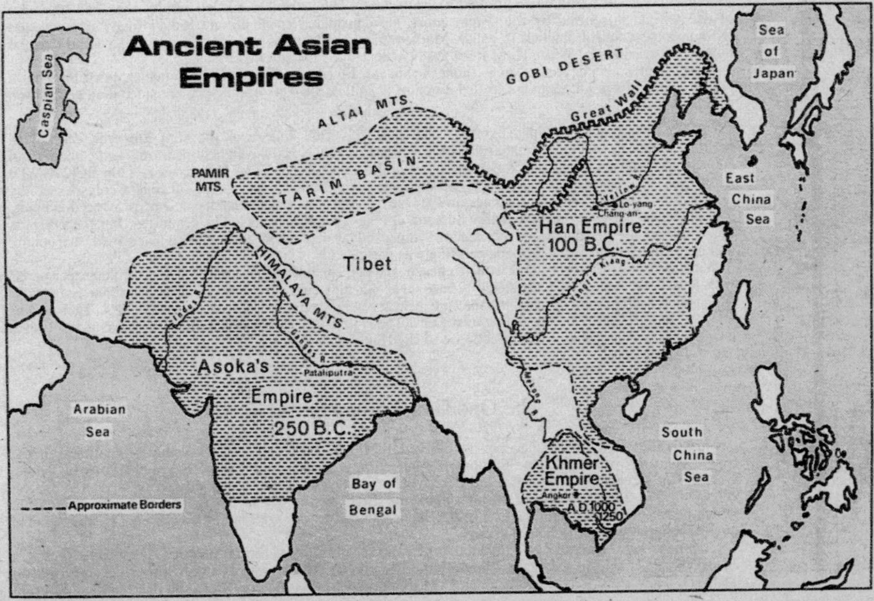

TRIPOLI

CYRENAICA

EGYPT

Ancient Asian Empires

Caspian Sea

GOBI DESERT

Sea of Japan

ALTAI MTS.

Great Wall

PAMIR MTS.

TARIM BASIN

East China Sea

HIMALAYA MTS.

Tibet

Han Empire 100 B.C.

Lo-yang
Chang-an

Asoka's Empire 250 B.C.

Patahputra

Arabian Sea

Bay of Bengal

South China Sea

Khmer Empire
Angkor
A.D.1000

- - - Approximate Borders

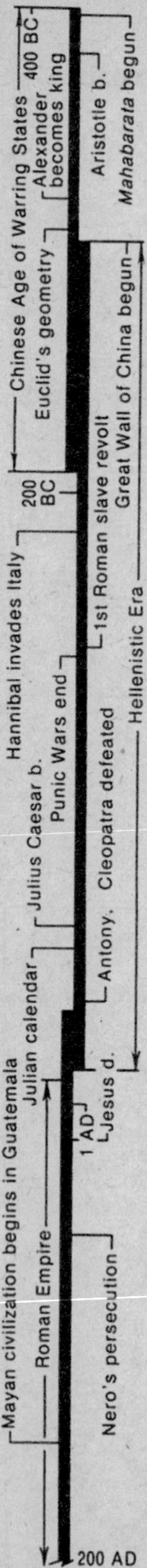
400 BC
Chinese Age of Warring States
Alexander becomes king
Aristotle b.
Mahabarata begun
Euclid's geometry
Great Wall of China begun
1st Roman slave revolt
200 BC
Hellenistic Era
Hannibal invades Italy
Julius Caesar b.
Punic Wars end
Antony, Cleopatra defeated
Julian calendar
1 AD
Jesus d.
Mayan civilization begins in Guatemala
Roman Empire
Nero's persecution
200 AD

involvement. Hellenistic arts imitated life realistically, especially in sculpture and literature (comedies of Menander, 342-292).

The sciences thrived, especially at Alexandria, where the Ptolemies financed a great library and museum. Fields of study included mathematics (**Euclid's** geometry, c300 BC; Menelaus' non-Euclidean geometry, c100 AD); astronomy (heliocentric theory of Aristarchus, 310-230 BC; Julian calendar 45 BC; Ptolemy's *Almagest*, c150 AD); geography (world map of Eratosthenes, 276-194 BC); hydraulics (**Archimedes**, 287-212 BC); medicine (Galen, 130-200 AD), and chemistry. Inventors refined uses for siphons, valves, gears, springs, screws, levers, cams, and pulleys.

A restored Persian empire under the **Parthians** (N. Iranian tribesmen) controlled the eastern Hellenistic world 250 BC-229 AD. The Parthians and the succeeding Sassanian dynasty (229-651) fought with Rome periodically. The **Sassanians** revived Zoroastrianism as a state religion, and patronized a nationalistic artistic and scholarly renaissance.

Rome. The city of Rome was founded, according to legend, by Romulus in 753 BC. Through military expansion and colonization, and by granting citizenship to conquered tribes, the city annexed all of Italy south of the Po in the 100-year period before 268 BC. The Latin and other Italic tribes were annexed first, followed by the Etruscans (a civilized people north of Rome) and the Greek colonies in the south. With a large standing army and reserve forces of several hundred thousand, Rome was able to defeat Carthage in the 3 **Punic Wars**, 264-241, 218-201, 149-146 (despite the invasion of Italy by Hannibal, 218), thus gaining Sicily and territory in Spain and North Africa.

New provinces were added in the East, as Rome exploited local disputes to conquer Greece and Asia Minor in the 2d century BC, and Egypt in the first (after the defeat and suicide of **Antony and Cleopatra**, 30 BC). All the Mediterranean civilized world up to the disputed Parthian border was now Roman, and remained so for 500 years. Less civilized regions were added to the Empire: Gaul (conquered by Julius Caesar, 56-49 BC), Britain (43 AD) and Dacia NE of the Danube (117 AD).

The original aristocratic republican government, with democratic features added in the fifth and fourth centuries BC, deteriorated under the pressures of empire and class conflict (**Gracchus** brothers, social reformers, murdered 133, 121; slave revolts 135, 73). After a series of civil wars (Marius vs. Sulla 88-82, Caesar vs. Pompey 49-45, triumvirate vs. Caesar's assassins 44-43, Antony vs. Octavian 32-30), the empire came under the rule of a deified monarch (first emperor, **Augustus,** 27 BC-14 AD). Provincials (nearly all granted citizenship by Caracalla, 212 AD) came to dominate the army and civil service. Traditional Roman law, systematized and interpreted by independent jurists, and local self-rule in provincial cities were supplanted by a vast tax-collecting bureaucracy in the 3d and 4th centuries. The legal rights of women, children, and slaves were strengthened.

Roman innovations in **civil engineering** included water mills, windmills, and rotary mills, and the use of cement that hardened under water. Monumental architecture (baths, theaters, apartment houses) relied on the arch and the dome. The network of roads (some still standing) stretched 53,000 miles, passing through mountain tunnels as long as 3.5 miles. Aqueducts brought water to cities, underground sewers removed waste.

Roman art and literature were derivative of Greek models. Innovations were made in sculpture (naturalistic busts and equestrian statues), decorative wall painting (as at Pompeii), satire (Juvenal, 60-127), history (Tacitus 56-120), prose romance (Petronius, d. 66 AD). Violence and torture dominated mass public amusements, which were supported by the state.

India. The **Gupta** monarchs reunited N. India c320 AD. Their peaceful and prosperous reign saw a revival of Hindu religious thought and Brahmin power. The old Vedic traditions were combined with devotion to a plethora of indigenous deities (who were seen as manifestations of Vedic gods). **Caste lines** were reinforced, and Buddhism gradually disappeared. The art (often erotic), architecture, and literature of the period, patronized by the Gupta court, are considered to be among India's finest achievements (Kalidasa, poet and dramatist, fl. c400). Mathematical innovations included the use of zero and decimal numbers. Invasions by White Huns from the NW destroyed the empire c550.

Rich cultures also developed in S. India in this era. Emotional Tamil religious poetry aided the Hindu revival. The Pallava kingdom controlled much of S. India c350-880, and helped spread Indian civilization to S.E. Asia.

China. The Ch'in ruler Shih Huang Ti (ruled 221-210 BC), known as the First Emperor, centralized political authority in China, standardized the written language, laws, weights, measures, and coinage, and conducted a census, but tried to destroy most philosophical texts. The **Han dynasty** (206 BC-220 AD) instituted the Mandarin bureaucracy, which lasted for 2,000 years. Local officials were selected by examination in the Confucian classics and trained at the imperial university and at provincial schools. The invention of **paper** facilitated this bureaucratic system. Agriculture was promoted, but the peasants bore most of the tax burden. Irrigation was improved; water clocks and sundials were used; astronomy and mathematics thrived; landscape painting was perfected.

With the expansion south and west (to nearly the present borders of today's China), trade was opened with India, S.E. Asia, and the Middle East, over sea and caravan routes. Indian missionaries brought Mahayana Buddhism to China by the first century AD, and spawned a variety of sects. Taoism was revived, and merged with popular superstitions. Taoist and Buddhist monasteries and convents multiplied in the turbulent centuries after the collapse of the Han dynasty.

The One God Triumphs: 1-750 AD

Christianity. Religions indigenous to particular Middle Eastern nations became international in the first 3 centuries of the Roman Empire. Roman citizens worshipped **Isis** of Egypt, **Mithras** of Persia, **Demeter** of Greece, and the great mother **Cybele** of Phrygia. Their cults centered on mysteries (secret ceremonies) and the promise of an afterlife, symbolized by the death and rebirth of the god. Judaism, which had begun as the national cult of Judea, also spread by emigration and conversion. It was the only ancient religion west of India to survive.

Christians, who emerged as a distinct sect in the second half of the 1st century AD, revered **Jesus,** a Jewish preacher said to have been killed by the Romans at the request of Jewish authorities in Jerusalem c30 AD. They considered him the Savior (Messiah, or Christ) who rose from the dead and could grant eternal life to the faithful, despite their sinfulness. They believed he was an incarnation of the one god worshipped by the Jews, and that he would return soon to pass final judgment on the world. The missionary activities of such early leaders as **Paul of Tarsus** spread the faith, at first mostly among Jews or among quasi-Jews attracted by the Pauline rejection of such difficult Jewish laws as circumcision. Intermittent persecution, as in Rome under Nero in 64 AD, on grounds of suspected disloyalty, failed to disrupt the Christian communities. Each congregation, generally urban and of plebeian character, was tightly organized under a leader (bishop) elders (presbyters or priests), and assistants (deacons). Stories about Jesus (the Gospels) and the early church (Acts) were written down in the late first and early 2d centuries, and circulated along with letters of Paul. An authoritative canon of these writings was not fixed until the 4th century.

A school for priests was established at Alexandria in the second century. Its teachers (**Origen** c182-251) helped define Christian doctrine and promote the faith in Greek-style philosophical works. Pagan Neoplatonism was given Christian coloration in the works of Church Fathers such as Augustine (354-430). Christian hermits, often drawn from the lower classes, began to associate in monasteries, first in Egypt (St. Pachomius c290-345), then in other eastern lands, then in the West (**St. Benedict's rule,** 529). Popular devotion to saints, especially Mary, mother of Jesus, spread.

Under **Constantine** (ruled 306-337), Christianity became in effect the established religion of the Empire. Pagan temples were expropriated, state funds were used to build huge churches and support the hierarchy, and laws were adjusted in accordance with Christian notions. Pagan worship was banned by the end of the fourth century, and severe restrictions were placed on Judaism.

The newly established church was rocked by doctrinal disputes, often exacerbated by regional rivalries both within and outside the Empire. Chief heresies (as defined by church councils backed by imperial authority) were **Arianism,** which denied the divinity of Jesus; **Donatism,** which rejected the convergence of church and state and denied the validity of sacraments performed by sinful clergy; and the **Monophysite** position denying the dual nature of Christ.

Judaism. First century Judaism embraced several sects, including: the **Sadducees,** mostly drawn from the Temple priesthood, who were culturally Hellenized; the **Pharisees,** who upheld the full range of traditional customs and practices as of equal weight to literal scriptural law, and elaborated synagogue worship; and the **Essenes,** an ascetic, millenarian sect. Messianic fervor led to repeated, unsuccessful rebellions against Rome (66-70, 135). As a result, the Temple was destroyed, and the population decimated.

To avoid the dissolution of the faith, a program of codification of law was begun at the academy of Yavneh. The work continued for some 500 years in Palestine and Babylonia, ending in the final redaction of the **Talmud** (c600), a huge collection of legal and moral debates, rulings, liturgy, Biblical exegesis, and legendary materials.

Islam. The earliest Arab civilization emerged by the end of the 2d millenium BC in the watered highlands of Yemen. Seaborne and caravan trade in frankincense and myrrh connected the area with the Nile and Fertile Crescent. The Minaean, Sabean (Sheba), and Himyarite states successively held sway. By Mohammed's time (7th century AD), the region was a province of Sassanian Persia. In the North, the **Nabataean kingdom** at Petra and the kingdom of Palmyra were first Aramaicized and then Romanized, and finally absorbed like neighboring Judea into the Roman Empire. Nomads shared the central region with a few trading towns and oases. Wars between tribes and raids on settled communities were common, and were celebrated in a poetic tradition that by the 6th century helped establish a classic literary Arabic.

In 611 **Mohammed,** a wealthy 40-year-old Arab of Mecca, had a revelation from Allah, the one true god, calling on him to repudiate pagan idolatry. Drawing on elements of Judaism and Christianity, and eventually incorporating some Arab pagan traditions (such as reverence for the black stone at the kaaba shrine in Mecca), Mohammed's teachings, recorded in the **Koran,** forged a new religion, Islam (submission to Allah). Opposed by the leaders of Mecca, Mohammed made a *hejira* (migration) to Medina to the north in 622, the beginning of the Moslem lunar calendar. He and his followers defeated the Meccans in 624 in the first *jihad* (holy war), and by his death (632), nearly all the Arabian peninsula accepted his religious and secular leadership.

Under the first two **caliphs** (successors) Abu Bakr (632-34) and Oman (634-44), Moslem rule was confirmed over Arabia. Raiding parties into Byzantine and Persian border areas developed into campaigns of conquest against the two empires, which had been weakened by wars and by disaffection among subject peoples (including Coptic and Syriac Christians opposed to the Byzantine orthodox church). Syria, Palestine, Egypt, Iraq, and Persia all fell to the inspired Arab armies. The Arabs at first remained a distinct minority, using non-Moslems in the new administrative system, and tolerating Christians, Jews, and Zoroastrians as self-governing "Peoples of the Book," whose taxes supported the empire.

Disputes over the succession, and puritan reaction to the wealth and refinement that empire brought to the ruling strata, led to the growth of schismatic movements. The followers of Mohammed's son-in-law Ali (assassinated 661) and his descendants became the founders of the more mystical **Shi'ite** sect, still the largest non-orthodox Moslem sect. The Karijites, puritanical, militant, and egalitarian, persist as a minor sect to the present.

Under the **Ummayad** caliphs (661-750), the boundaries of Islam were extended across N. Africa and into Spain. Arab armies in the West were stopped at Tours in 732 by the Frank **Charles Martel.** Asia Minor, the Indus Valley, and Transoxiana were conquered in the East. The vast majority of the subject population gradually converted to Islam, encouraged by tax and career privileges. The Arab language supplanted the local tongues in the central and western areas, but Arab soldiers and rulers in the East eventually became assimilated to the indigenous languages.

New Peoples Enter History: 400-900

Barbarian invasions. Germanic tribes infiltrated S and E from their Baltic homeland during the 1st millenium BC, reaching S. Germany by 100 BC and the Black Sea by 214 AD. Organized into large federated tribes under elected kings, most resisted Roman domination and raided the empire in time of civil war (Goths took Dacia 214, raided Thrace 251-269). German troops and commanders came to dominate the Roman armies by the end of the 4th century. **Huns,** invaders from Asia, entered Europe 372, driving more Germans into the western empire. Emperor Valens allowed Visigoths to cross

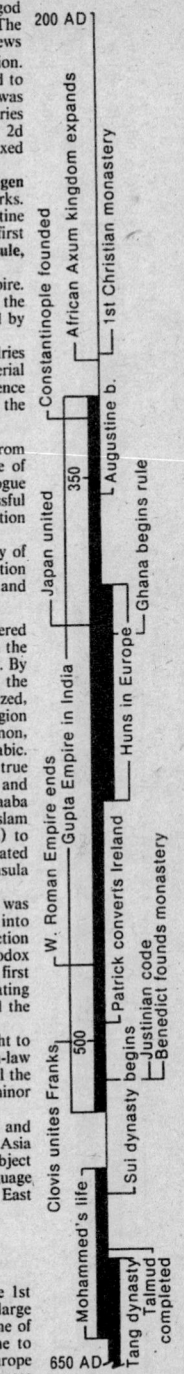

200 AD

African Axum kingdom expands

Constantinople founded

1st Christian monastery

Japan united

350

Augustine b.

Ghana begins rule

Gupta Empire in India

Huns in Europe

W. Roman Empire ends

Patrick converts Ireland

500

Justinian code

Benedict founds monastery

Clovis unites Franks

Sui dynasty begins

Mohammed's life

Tang dynasty

Talmud completed

650 AD

Greek replaces Latin in Byzantium

Slav-Turk Bulgarian Empire begins

Chinese poet Li Po b.

Nara period begins, Japan

Baghdad founded

Charlemagne rules

Viking explorations, raids

Arab-Moslem golden age

Vietnam independent

650

750

850

950

the Danube 376. Huns under Attila (d. 453) raided Gaul, Italy, Balkans. The western empire, weakened by overtaxation and social stagnation, was overrun in the 5th century. Gaul was effectively lost 406-7, Spain 409, Britain 410, Africa 429-39. Rome was sacked 410 by Visigoths under Alaric, 455 by Vandals. The last western emperor, Romulus Augustulus, was deposed 476 by the Germanic chief Odoacer.

Celts. Celtic cultures, which in pre-Roman times covered most of W. Europe, were confined almost entirely to the British Isles after the Germanic invasions. **St. Patrick** completed the conversion of Ireland (c457-92). A strong monastic tradition took hold. Irish monastic missionaries in Scotland, England, and the continent (Columba c521-597; Columban c543-615) helped restore Christianity after the Germanic invasions. The monasteries became renowned centers of classic and Christian learning, and presided over the recording of a Christianized Celtic mythology, elaborated by secular writers and bards. An intricate decorative art style developed, especially in book illumination (Lindisfarne Gospels, c700, Book of Kells, 8th century).

Successor states. The Visigoth kingdom in Spain (from 419) and much of France (to 507) saw a continuation of much Roman administration, language, and law (Breviary of Alaric 506), until its destruction by the Moslems, 711. The Vandal kingdom in Africa, from 429, was conquered by the Byzantines, 533. Italy was ruled in succession by an Ostrogothic kingdom under Byzantine suzerainty 489-554, direct Byzantine government, and the German Lombards (568-774). The latter divided the peninsula with the Byzantines and the papacy under the dynamic reformer Pope Gregory the Great (590-604) and his successors.

King Clovis (ruled 481-511) united the Franks on both sides of the Rhine, and after his conversion to orthodox Christianity, defeated the Arian Burgundians (after 500) and Visigoths (507) with the support of the native clergy and the papacy. Under the **Merovingian** kings a feudal system emerged: power was fragmented among hierarchies of military landowners. Social stratification, which in late Roman times had acquired legal, hereditary sanction, was reinforced. The Carolingians (747-987) expanded the kingdom and restored central power. **Charlemagne** (ruled 768-814) conquered nearly all the Germanic lands, including Lombard Italy, and was crowned Emperor by Pope Leo III in Rome in 800. A centuries-long decline in commerce and the arts was reversed under Charlemagne's patronage. He welcomed Jews to his kingdom, which became a center of Jewish learning (Rashi 1040-1105). He sponsored the "Carolingian Renaissance" of learning under the Anglo-Latin scholar Alcuin (c732-804), who reformed church liturgy.

Byzantine Empire. Under Diocletian (ruled 284-305) the empire had been divided into 2 parts to facilitate administration and defense. Constantine founded **Constantinople**, 330, (at old Byzantium) as a fully Christian city. Commerce and taxation financed a sumptuous, orientalized court, a class of hereditary bureaucratic families, and magnificent urban construction (Hagia Sophia, 532-37). The city's fortifications and naval innovations (Greek fire) repelled assaults by Goths, Huns, Slavs, Bulgars, Avars, Arabs, and Scandinavians. Greek replaced Latin as the official language by c700. Byzantine art, a solemn, sacral, and stylized variation of late classical styles (mosaics at S. Vitale, Ravenna, 526-48) was a starting point for medieval art in E. and W. Europe.

Justinian (ruled 527-65) reconquered parts of Spain, N. Africa, and Italy, codified Roman law (*codex Justinianus*, 529, was medieval Europe's chief legal text), closed the Platonic Academy at Athens and ordered all pagans to convert. Lombards in Italy, Arabs in Africa retook most of his conquests. The Isaurian dynasty from Anatolia (from 717) and the Macedonian dynasty (867-1054) restored military and commercial power. The Iconoclast controversy (726-843) over the permissibility of images, helped alienate the Eastern Church from the papacy.

Arab Empire. Baghdad, founded 762, became the seat of the **Abbasid** Caliphate (founded 750), while Ummayads continued to rule in Spain. A brilliant cosmopolitan civilization emerged, inaugurating an Arab-Moslem golden age. Arab lyric poetry revived; Greek, Syriac, Persian, and Sanskrit books were translated into Arabic, often by Syriac Christians and Jews, whose theology and Talmudic law, respectively, influenced Islam. The arts and music flourished at the court of **Harun al-Rashid** (786-809), celebrated in *The Arabian Nights*. The sciences, medicine, and mathematics were pursued at Baghdad, Cordova, and Cairo (founded 969). Science and Aristotelian philosophy culminated in the systems of Avicenna (980-1037), Averroes (1126-98), and Maimonides (1135-1204), a Jew; all influenced later Christian scholarship and theology. The Islamic ban on images encouraged a sinuous, geometric decorative tradition, applied to architecture and illumination. A gradual loss of Arab control in Persia (from 874) led to the capture of Baghdad by Persians, 945. By the next century, Spain and N. Africa were ruled by Berbers, while Turks prevailed in Asia Minor and the Levant. The loss of political power by the caliphs allowed for the growth of non-orthodox trends, especially the mystical **Sufi** tradition (theologian Ghazali, 1058-1111).

Africa. Immigrants from Saba in S. Arabia helped set up the **Axum** kingdom in Ethiopia in the 2d century (their language, Ge'ez, is preserved by the Ethiopian Church). In the 4th century, when the kingdom became Christianized, it defeated Kushite Meroe and expanded into Yemen. Axum was the center of a vast ivory trade; it controlled the Red Sea coast until c1100. Arab conquest in Egypt cut Axum's political and economic ties with Byzantium.

The Iron Age entered W. Africa by the end of the 1st millenium BC. **Ghana,** the first known sub-Saharan state, ruled in the upper Senegal-Niger region c400-1240, controlling the trade of gold from mines in the S to trans-Sahara caravan routes to the N. The **Bantu** peoples, probably of W. African origin, began to spread E and S perhaps 2000 years ago, displacing the Pygmies and Bushmen of central and southern Africa over a 1,500-year period.

Japan. The advanced Neolithic Yayoi period, when irrigation, rice farming, and iron and bronze casting techniques were introduced from China or Korea, persisted to c400 AD. The myriad Japanese states were then united by the **Yamato** clan, under an emperor who acted as the chief priest of the animistic **Shinto** cult. Japanese political and military intervention in Korea by the 6th century quickened a Chinese cultural invasion, bringing Buddhism, the Chinese language (which long remained a literary and governmental medium), Chinese ideographs and Buddhist styles in painting, sculpture, literature, and architecture (7th c. Horyu-ji temple at Nara). The Taika Reforms, 646, tried to centralize Japan according to Chinese bureaucratic and Buddhist philosophical values, but failed to curb traditional Japanese decentralization. A nativist reaction against the Buddhist **Nara period** (710-94) ushered in the

Heian period (794-1185) centered at the new capital, Kyoto. Japanese elegance and simplicity modified Chinese styles in architecture, scroll painting, and literature; the writing system was also simplified. The courtly novel *Tale of Genji* (1010-20) testifies to the enhanced role of women.

Southeast Asia. The historic peoples of southeast Asia began arriving some 2500 years ago from China and Tibet, displacing scattered aborigines. Their agriculture relied on rice and tubers (yams), which they may have introduced to Africa. Indian cultural influences were strongest; literacy and Hindu and Buddhist ideas followed the southern India-China trade route. From the southern tip of Indochina, the kingdom of **Funan** (1st-7th centuries) traded as far west as Persia. It was absorbed by Chenla, itself conquered by the **Khmer Empire** (600-1300). The Khmers, under Hindu god-kings (Suryavarman II, 1113-c1150), built the monumental Angkor Wat temple center for the royal phallic cult. The **Nam-Viet** kingdom in Annam, dominated by China and Chinese culture for 1,000 years, emerged in the 10th century, growing at the expense of the Khmers, who also lost ground in the NW to the new, highly-organized **Thai** kingdom. On Sumatra, the **Srivijaya** Empire at Palembang controlled vital sea lanes (7th to 10th centuries). A Buddhist dynasty, the Sailendras, ruled central **Java** (8th-9th centuries), building at Borobudur one of the largest stupas in the world.

China. The short-lived Sui dynasty (581-618) ushered in a period of commercial, artistic, and scientific achievement in China, continuing under the **T'ang** dynasty (618-906). Such inventions as the magnetic compass, gunpowder, the abacus, and printing were introduced or perfected. Medical innovations included cataract surgery. The state, from the cosmopolitan capital, Ch'ang-an, supervised foreign trade which exchanged Chinese silks, porcelains, and art works for spices, ivory, etc., over Central Asian caravan routes and sea routes reaching Africa. A golden age of poetry bequeathed tens of thousands of works to later generations (Tu Fu 712-70, Li Po 701-62). Landscape painting flourished. Commercial and industrial expansion continued under the **Northern Sung** dynasty (960-1126), facilitated by paper money and credit notes. But commerce never achieved respectability; government monopolies expropriated successful merchants. The population, long stable at 50 million, doubled in 200 years with the introduction of early-ripening rice and the double harvest. In art, native Chinese styles were revived.

Americas. An Indian empire stretched from the Valley of Mexico to Guatemala, 300-600, centering on the huge city **Teotihuacan** (founded 100 BC). To the S, in Guatemala, a high **Mayan** civilization developed, 150-900, around hundreds of rural ceremonial centers. The Mayans improved on Olmec writing and the calendar, and pursued astronomy and mathematics (using the idea of zero). In S. America, a widespread pre-Inca culture grew from **Tiahuanaco** near Lake Titicaca (Gateway of the Sun, c700).

Christian Europe Regroups and Expands: 900-1300

Scandinavians. Pagan Danish and Norse (**Viking**) adventurers, traders, and pirates raided the coasts of the British Isles (Dublin founded c831), France, and even the Mediterranean for over 200 years beginning in the late 8th century. Inland settlement in the W was limited to Great Britain (King Canute, 994-1035) and Normandy, settled under Rollo, 911, as a fief of France. Other Vikings reached Iceland (874), Greenland (c986), and probably N. America (Leif Eriksson c1000). Norse traders (**Varangians**) developed Russian river commerce from the 8th-11th centuries, and helped set up a state at Kiev in the late 9th century. Conversion to Christianity occurred during the 10th century, reaching Sweden 100 years later. Eleventh century Norman bands conquered S. Italy and Sicily. Duke **William of Normandy** conquered England, 1066, bringing continental feudalism and the French language, essential elements in later English civilization.

East Europe. Slavs inhabited areas of E. Central Europe in prehistoric times, and reached most of their present limits by c850. The first Slavic states were in the Balkans (Slav-Turk **Bulgarian Empire**, 680-1018) and Moravia (628). Missions of St. Cyril (whose Greek-based Cyrillic alphabet is still used by S. and E. Slavs) converted Moravia, 863. The Eastern Slavs, part-civilized under the overlordship of the Turkish-Jewish **Khazar** trading empire (7th-10th centuries), gravitated toward Constantinople by the 9th century. The **Kievan** state adopted Eastern Christianity under Prince Vladimir, 989. King Boleslav I (992-1025) began **Poland's** long history of eastern conquest. The Magyars (**Hungarians**) in Europe since 896, accepted Latin Christianity, 1001.

Germany. The German kingdom that emerged after the breakup of Charlemagne's Empire remained a confederation of largely autonomous states. The Saxon **Otto I**, king from 936, established the **Holy Roman Empire** of Germany and Italy in alliance with Pope John XII, who crowned him emperor, 962; he defeated the Magyars, 955. Imperial power was greatest under the **Hohenstaufens** (1138-1254), despite the growing opposition of the papacy, which ruled central Italy, and the Lombard League cities. **Frederick II** (1194-1250) improved administration, patronized the arts; after his death German influence was removed from Italy.

Christian Spain. From its northern mountain redoubts, Christian rule slowly migrated south through the 11th century, when Moslem unity collapsed. After the capture of **Toledo** (1085), the kingdoms of Portugal, Castile, and Aragon undertook repeated crusades of reconquest, finally completed in 1492. Elements of Islamic civilization persisted in recaptured areas, influencing all W. Europe.

Crusades. Pope Urban II called, 1095, for a crusade to restore Asia Minor to Byzantium and conquer the Holy Land from the Turks. Some 10 crusades (to 1291) succeeded only in founding 4 temporary Frankish states in the Levant. The 4th crusade sacked Constantinople, 1204. In Rhineland (1096), England (1290), France (1306), Jews were massacred or expelled, and wars were launched against Christian heretics (**Albigensian** crusade in France, 1229). Trade in eastern luxuries expanded, led by the Venetian naval empire.

Economy. The agricultural base of European life benefitted from improvements in **plow design** c1000, and by draining of lowlands and clearing of forests, leading to a rural population increase. Towns grew in N. Italy, Flanders, and N. Germany (Hanseatic League). Improvements in **loom design** permitted factory textile production. Guilds dominated urban trades from the 12th century. Banking (centered in Italy, 12th-15th century) facilitated long-distance trade.

The Church. The split between the Eastern and Western churches was formalized in 1054. W. and

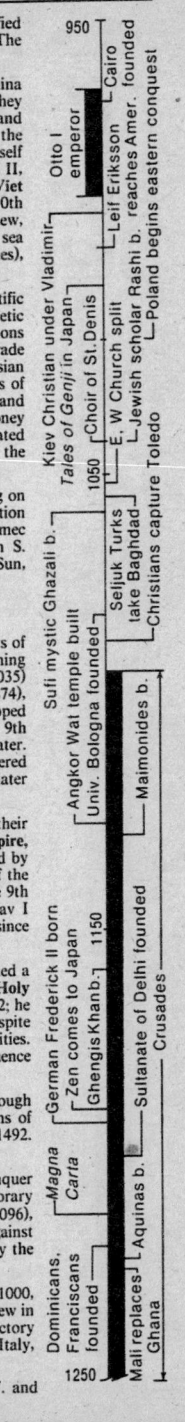

950
Cairo founded
Otto I emperor
Leif Eriksson reaches Amer.
Kiev Christian under Vladimir
Tales of Genji in Japan
Choir of St. Denis
E. W Church split
Jewish scholar Rashi b.
Poland begins eastern conquest
1050
Christians capture Toledo
Sufi mystic Ghazali b.
Seljuk Turks take Baghdad
Angkor Wat temple built
Univ. Bologna founded
Maimonides b.
German Frederick II born
Zen comes to Japan
Ghengis Khan b.
1150
Sultanate of Delhi founded
Crusades
Magna Carta
Aquinas b.
Dominicans, Franciscans founded
Mali replaces Ghana
1250

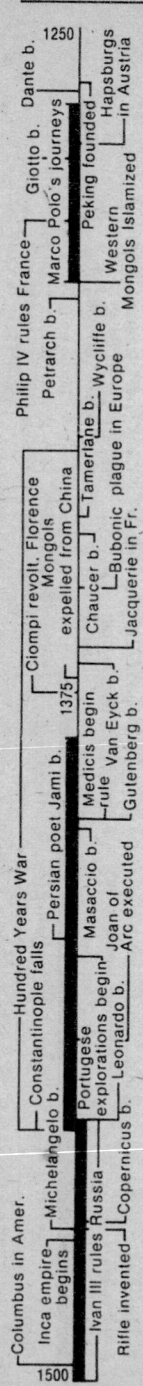

Central Europe was divided into 500 bishoprics under one united hierarchy, but conflicts between secular and church authorities were frequent (German **Investiture Controversy**, 1075-1122). Clerical power was first strengthened through the international monastic reform begun at Cluny, 910. Popular religious enthusiasm often expressed itself in heretical movements (Waldensians from 1173), but was channelled by the **Dominican** (1215) and **Franciscan** (1223) friars into the religious mainstream.

Arts. Romanesque architecture (11th-12th centuries) expanded on late Roman models, using the rounded arch and massed stone to support enlarged basilicas. Painting and sculpture followed Byzantine models. The literature of **chivalry** was exemplified by the epic (Chanson de Roland, c1100) and by courtly love poems of the troubadours of Provence and minnesingers of Germany. **Gothic architecture** emerged in France (choir of St. Denis, c1040) and spread as French cultural influence predominated in Europe. Rib vaulting and pointed arches were used to combine soaring heights with delicacy, and freed walls for display of stained glass. Exteriors were covered with painted relief sculpture and elaborate architectural detail.

Learning. Law, medicine, and philosophy were advanced at independent **universities** (Bologna, late 11th century), originally corporations of students and masters. Twelfth century translations of Greek classics, especially Aristotle, encouraged an analytic approach. Scholastic philosophy, from Anselm (1033-1109) to Aquinas (1225-74) attempted to reconcile reason and revelation.

Apogee of Central Asian Power; Islam Grows: 1250-1500

Turks. Turkic peoples, of Central Asian ancestry, were a military threat to the Byzantine and Persian Empires from the 6th century. After several waves of invasions, during which most of the Turks adopted Islam, the **Seljuk Turks** took Baghdad, 1055. They ruled Persia, Iraq, and, after 1071, Asia Minor, where massive numbers of Turks settled. The empire was divided in the 12th century into smaller states ruled by Seljuks, Kurds (**Saladin** c1137-93), and Mamelukes (a military caste of former Turk, Kurd, and Circassian slaves), which governed Egypt and the Middle East until the Ottoman era (c1290-1922).

Osman I (ruled c1290-1326) and succeeding sultans united Anatolian Turkish warriors in a militaristic state that waged holy war against Byzantium and Balkan Christians. Most of the Balkans had been subdued, and Anatolia united, when **Constantinople fell**, 1453. By the mid-16th century, Hungary, the Middle East, and North Africa had been conquered. The Turkish advance was stopped at Vienna, 1529, and at the naval battle of Lepanto, 1571, by Spain, Venice, and the papacy.

The Ottoman state was governed in accordance with orthodox Moslem law. Greek, Armenian, and Jewish communities were segregated, and ruled by religious leaders responsible for taxation; they dominated trade. State offices and most army ranks were filled by slaves through a system of child conscription among Christians.

India. Mahmud of Ghazni (971-1030) led repeated Turkish raids into N. India. Turkish power was consolidated in 1206 with the start of the **Sultanate at Delhi.** Centralization of state power under the early Delhi sultans went far beyond traditional Indian practice. Moslem rule of most of the subcontinent lasted until the British conquest some 600 years later.

Mongols. Genghis Khan (c1162-1227) first united the feuding Mongol tribes, and built their armies into an effective offensive force around a core of highly mobile cavalry. He and his immediate successors created the largest land empire in history; by 1279 it stretched from the east coast of Asia to the Danube, from the Siberian steppes to the Arabian Sea. East-West trade and contacts were facilitated (Marco Polo c1254-1324). The western Mongols were Islamized by 1295; successor states soon lost their Mongol character by assimilation. They were briefly reunited under the Turk Tamerlane (1336-1405).

Kublai Khan ruled China from his new capital Peking (founded 1264). Naval campaigns against Japan (1274, 1281) and Java (1293) were defeated, the latter by the Hindu-Buddhist maritime kingdom of Majapahit. The **Yuan** dynasty made use of Mongols and other foreigners (including Europeans) in official posts, and tolerated the return of Nestorian Christianity (suppressed 841-45) and the spread of Islam in the South and West. A native reaction expelled the Mongols, 1367-68.

Russia. The Kievan state in Russia, weakened by the decline of Byzantium and the rise of the Catholic Polish-Lithuanian state, was overrun by the Mongols, 1238-40. Only the northern trading republic of Novgorod remained independent. The grand dukes of Moscow emerged as leaders of a coalition of princes that eventually defeated the Mongols, by 1481. With the fall of Constantinople, the **Tsars** (Caesars) at Moscow (from Ivan III, ruled 1462-1505) set up an independent Russian Orthodox Church. Commerce failed to revive. The isolated Russian state remained agrarian, with the peasant class falling into serfdom.

Persia. A revival of Persian literature, using the Arab alphabet and literary forms, began in the 10th century (epic of Firdausi, 935-1020). An art revival, influenced by Chinese styles, began in the 12th. Persian cultural and political forms, and often the Persian language, were used for centuries by Turkish and Mongol elites from the Balkans to India. Persian mystics from Rumi (1207-73) to Jami (1414-92) promoted **Sufism** in their poetry.

Africa. Two Berber dynasties, imbued with Islamic militance, emerged from the Sahara to carve out empires from the Sahel to central Spain — the **Almoravids**, c1050-1140, and the fanatical **Almohads**, c1125-1269. The Ghanaian empire was replaced in the upper Niger by Mali, c1230-c1340, whose Moslem rulers imported Egyptians to help make Timbuktu a center of commerce (in gold, leather, slaves) and learning. The Songhay empire (to 1590) replaced Mali. To the S, forest kingdoms produced refined art works (Ife terra cotta, **Benin** bronzes). Other Moslem states in Nigeria (Hausas) and Chad originated in the 11th century, and continued in some form until the 19th century European conquest. Less developed Bantu kingdoms existed across central Africa.

Some 40 Moslem Arab-Persian trading colonies and city-states were established all along the E. African coast from the 10th century (Kilwa, Mogadishu). The interchange with Bantu peoples produced the **Swahili** language and culture. Gold, palm oil, and slaves were brought from the interior, stimulating the growth of the Monamatapa kingdom of the Zambezi (15th century). The Christian Ethiopian empire (from 13th century) continued the traditions of Axum.

Southeast Asia. Islam was introduced into Malaya and the Indonesian islands by Arab, Persian, and

Indian traders. Coastal Moslem cities and states (starting before 1300), enriched by trade, soon dominated the interior. Chief among these was the **Malacca** state, on the Malay peninsula, c1400-1511.

Arts and Statecraft Thrive in Europe: 1350-1600

Italian Renaissance & humanism. Distinctive Italian achievements in the arts in the late Middle Ages (Dante, 1265-1321, Giotto, 1276-1337) led to the vigorous new styles of the Renaissance (14th-16th centuries). Patronized by the rulers of the quarreling petty states of Italy (Medicis in Florence and the papacy, c1400-1737), the plastic arts perfected realistic techniques, including **perspective** (Masaccio, 1401-28, Leonardo 1452-1519). Classical motifs were used in architecture and increased talent and expense were put into secular buildings. The Florentine dialect was refined as a national literary language (Petrarch, 1304-74). Greek refugees from the E strengthened the respect of humanist scholars for the classic sources (Bruni 1370-1444). Soon an international movement aided by the spread of **printing** (Gutenberg c1400-1468), **humanism** was optimistic about the power of human reason (Erasmus of Rotterdam, 1466-1536, Thomas More's *Utopia*, 1516) and valued individual effort in the arts and in politics (Machiavelli, 1469-1527).

France. The French monarchy, strengthened in its repeated struggles with powerful nobles (Burgundy, Flanders, Aquitaine) by alliances with the growing commercial towns, consolidated bureaucratic control under Philip IV (ruled 1285-1314) and extended French influence into Germany and Italy (popes at Avignon, France, 1309-1417). The **Hundred Years War**, 1337-1453, ended English dynastic claims in France (battles of Crécy, 1346, Poitiers, 1356; Joan of Arc executed, 1431). A French Renaissance, dating from royal invasions of Italy, 1494, 1499, was encouraged at the court of Francis I (ruled 1515-47), who centralized taxation and law. French vernacular literature consciously asserted its independence (La Pleiade, 1549).

England. The evolution of England's unique political institutions began with the Magna Carta, 1215, by which King John guaranteed the privileges of nobles and church against the monarchy and assured jury trial. After the Wars of the Roses (1455-85), the **Tudor dynasty** reasserted royal prerogatives (Henry VIII, ruled 1509-47), but the trend toward independent departments and ministerial government also continued. English trade (wool exports from c1340) was protected by the nation's growing maritime power (**Spanish Armada** destroyed, 1588).
English replaced French and Latin in the late 14th century in law and literature (Chaucer, 1340-1400) and English translation of the Bible began (Wycliffe, 1380s). Elizabeth I (ruled 1558-1603) presided over a confident flowering of poetry (Spenser, 1552-99), drama (**Shakespeare**, 1564-1616), and music.

German Empire. From among a welter of minor feudal states, church lands, and independent cities, the **Hapsburgs** assembled a far-flung territorial domain, based in Austria from 1276. The family held the title Holy Roman Emperor from 1452 to the Empire's dissolution in 1806, but failed to centralize its domains, leaving Germany disunited for centuries. Resistance to Turkish expansion brought Hungary under Austrian control from the 16th century. The Netherlands, Luxembourg, and Burgundy were added in 1477, curbing French expansion.
The Flemish painting tradition of naturalism, technical proficiency, and bourgeois subject matter began in the 15th century (Jan Van Eyck, 1366-1440), the earliest northern manifestation of the Renaissance. **Durer** (1471-1528) typified the merging of late Gothic and Italian trends in 16th century German art. Imposing civic architecture flourished in the prosperous commercial cities.

Spain. Despite the unification of Castile and Aragon in 1479, the 2 countries retained separate governments, and the nobility, especially in Aragon and Catalonia, retained many privileges. Spanish lands in Italy (Naples, Sicily) and the Netherlands entangled the country in European wars through the mid-17th century, while explorers, traders, and conquerors built up a Spanish empire in the Americas and the Philippines.
From the late 15th century, a **golden age** of literature and art produced works of social satire (plays of Lope de Vega, 1562-1635; Cervantes, 1547-1616), as well as spiritual intensity (El Greco, 1541-1614; Velazquez, 1599-1660).

Black Death. The bubonic plague reached Europe from the E in 1348, killing as much as half the population by 1350. Labor scarcity forced a rise in wages and brought greater freedom to the peasantry, making possible **peasant uprisings** (Jacquerie in France, 1358, Wat Tyler's rebellion in England, 1381). In the *ciompi* revolt, 1378, Florentine wage earners demanded a say in economic and political power.

Explorations. Organized European maritime exploration began, seeking to evade the Venice-Ottoman monopoly of eastern trade and to promote Christianity. Expeditions from Portugal beginning 1418 explored the west coast of Africa, until **Vasco da Gama** rounded the Cape of Good Hope in 1497 and reached India. A Portuguese trading empire was consolidated by the seizure of Goa, 1510, and Malacca, 1551. Japan was reached in 1542. Spanish voyages (**Columbus**, 1492-1504) uncovered a new world, which Spain hastened to subdue. Navigation schools in Spain and Portugal, the development of large sailing ships (carracks), and the invention of the rifle, c1475, aided European penetration.

Mughals and Safavids. East of the Ottoman empire, two Moslem dynasties ruled unchallenged in the 16th and 17th centuries. The Mughal empire in India, founded by Persianized Turkish invaders from the NW under Babur, dates from their 1526 conquest of Delhi. The dynasty ruled most of India for over 200 years, surviving nominally until 1857. **Akbar** (ruled 1556-1605) consolidated administration at his glorious court, where Urdu (Persian-influenced Hindi) developed. Trade relations with Europe increased. Under Shah Jahan (1629-58), a secularized art fusing Hindu and Moslem elements flourished in miniature painting and architecture (**Taj Mahal**). Sikhism, founded c1519, combined elements of both faiths. Suppression of Hindus and Shi'ite Moslems in S India in the late 17th century weakened the empire.
Fanatical devotion to the Shi'ite sect characterized the Safavids of Persia, 1502-1736, and led to hostilities with the Sunni Ottomans for over a century. The prosperity and strength of the empire are evidenced by the mosques at its capital, **Isfahan**. The dynasty enhanced Iranian national consciousness.

China. The Ming emperors, 1368-1644, the last native dynasty in China, wielded unprecedented personal power, while the Confucian bureaucracy began to suffer from inertia. European trade (Portugese

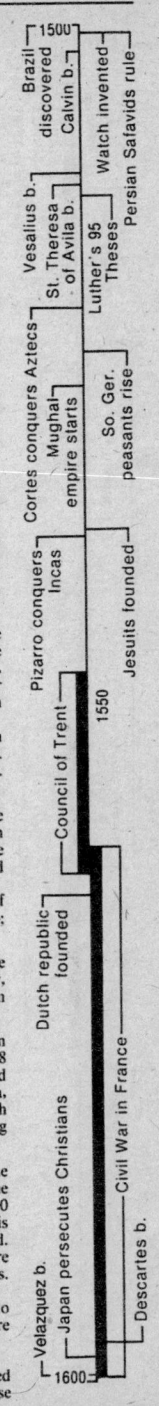

1500 — Brazil discovered
Calvin b.
Vesalius b.
St. Theresa of Avila b.
Watch invented
Luther's 95 Theses
Persian Safavids rule
Aztecs
Cortes conquers Aztecs
So. Ger. peasants rise
Mughal empire starts
Pizarro conquers Incas
Jesuits founded
1550
Council of Trent
Dutch republic founded
Civil War in France
Japan persecutes Christians
Velazquez b.
Descartes b.
1600

Timeline (left margin):
1600 — Jamestown founded · French settle Canada · Bank of Amsterdam · Tokugawa Ieyasu shogun · Thirty Years War · Kepler d. · Galileo d. · Plymouth founded · Van Dyck d. · Manchus rule 1640 · English Revolution · Charles I killed · Fronde · Royal Soc. founded · Mazarin d. · Rembrandt d. · Bernini d. · Spinoza d. · Princesse de Cleves — 1680

monopoly through **Macao** from 1557) was strictly controlled. Jesuit scholars and scientists (Matteo Ricci 1552-1610) introduced some Western science; their writings familiarized the West with China. Chinese technological inventiveness declined from this era, but the arts thrived, especially painting and ceramics.

Japan. After the decline of the first hereditary shogunate (chief generalship) at Kamakura (1185-1333), fragmentation of power accelerated, as did the consequent social mobility. Under Kamakura and the Ashikaga shogunate, 1338-1573, the daimyos (lords) and samurai (warriors) grew more powerful and promoted a martial ideology. Japanese pirates and traders plied the China coast. Popular Buddhist movements included the nationalist Nichiren sect (from c1250) and **Zen** (brought from China, 1191), which stressed meditation and a disciplined esthetic (tea ceremony, landscape gardening, judo, Noh drama).

Reformed Europe Expands Overseas: 1500-1700

Reformation begun. Theological debate and protests against real and perceived clerical corruption existed in the medieval Christian world, expressed by such dissenters as Wycliffe (c1320-84) and his followers, the Lollards, in England, and **Huss** (burned as a heretic, 1415) in Bohemia.

Luther (1483-1546) preached that only faith could lead to salvation, without the mediation of clergy or good works. He attacked the authority of the Pope, rejected priestly celibacy, and recommended individual study of the Bible (which he translated, c1525). His 95 Theses (1517) led to his excommunication (1520). **Calvin** (1509-64) said God's elect were predestined for salvation; good conduct and success were signs of election. Calvin in Geneva and Knox (1505-72) in Scotland erected theocratic states.

Henry VIII asserted English national authority and secular power by breaking away from the Catholic church, 1534. Monastic property was confiscated, and some Protestant doctrines given official sanction.

Religious wars. A century and a half of religious wars began with a South German peasant uprising, 1524, repressed with Luther's support. Radical sects—democratic, pacifist, millennarian—arose (Anabaptists ruled Muenster, 1534-35), and were suppressed violently. Civil war in France from 1562 between **Huguenots** (Protestant nobles and merchants) and Catholics ended with the 1598 Edict of Nantes tolerating Protestants (revoked 1685). Hapsburg attempts to restore Catholicism in Germany were resisted in 25 years of fighting; the 1555 Peace of Augsburg guarantee of religious independence to local princes and cities was confirmed only after the **Thirty Years War**, 1618-48, when much of Germany was devastated by local and foreign armies (Sweden, France).

A Catholic Reformation, or **counter-reformation,** met the Protestant challenge, clearly defining an official theology at the Council of Trent, 1545-63. The **Jesuit** order, founded 1534 by Loyola (1491-1556), helped reconvert large areas of Poland, Hungary, and S. Germany and sent missionaries to the New World, India, and China, while the Inquisition helped suppress heresy in Catholic countries. A revival of piety appeared in the devotional literature (Theresa of Avila, 1515-82) and the grandiose Baroque art (Bernini, 1598-1680) of Roman Catholic countries.

Scientific Revolution. The late nominalist thinkers (Ockham, c1300-49) of Paris and Oxford challenged Aristotelian orthodoxy, allowing for a freer scientific approach. But metaphysical values, such as the Neoplatonic faith in an orderly, mathematical cosmos, still motivated and directed subsequent inquiry. **Copernicus** (1473-1543) promoted the heliocentric theory, which was confirmed when Kepler (1571-1630) discovered the mathematical laws describing the orbits of the planets. The Christian-Aristotelian belief that heavens and earth were fundamentally different collapsed when Galileo (1564-1642) discovered moving sunspots, irregular moon topography, and moons around Jupiter. He and Newton (1642-1727) developed a mechanics that unified cosmic and earthly phenomena. To meet the needs of the new physics, Newton and Leibnitz (1646-1716) invented calculus. Descartes (1596-1650) invented analytic geometry.

An explosion of observational science included the discovery of blood circulation (Harvey, 1578-1657) and microscopic life (Leeuwenhoek, 1632-1723), and advances in anatomy (Vesalius, 1514-64, dissected corpses) and chemistry (Boyle, 1627-91). Scientific research institutes were founded: Florence, 1657, London (**Royal Society**), 1660, Paris, 1666. Inventions proliferated (Savery's steam engine, 1696).

Arts. Mannerist trends of the high Renaissance (Michelangelo, 1475-1564) exploited virtuosity, grace, novelty, and exotic subjects and poses. The notion of artistic genius was promoted, in contrast to the anonymous medieval artisan. Private connoisseurs entered the art market. These trends were elaborated in the 17th century **Baroque** era, on a grander scale. Dynamic movement in painting and sculpture was emphasized by sharp lighting effects, use of rich materials (colored marble, gilt), realistic details. Curved facades, broken lines, rich, deep-cut detail, and ceiling decoration characterized Baroque architecture, especially in Germany. Monarchs, princes, and prelates, usually Catholic, used Baroque art to enhance and embellish their authority, as in royal portraits by Velazquez (1599-1660) and Van Dyck (1599-1641).

National styles emerged. In France, a taste for rectilinear order and serenity (Poussin, 1594-1665), linked to the new rational philosophy, was expressed in classical forms. The influence of **classical values** in French literature (tragedies of Racine, 1639-99) gave rise to the "battle of the Ancients and Moderns." New trends included the essay (Montaigne, 1533-92) and novel (*Princesse de Cleves*, La Fayette, 1678).

Dutch painting of the 17th century was unique in its wide social distribution. The Flemish tradition of undemonstrative realism reached its peak in Rembrandt (1606-69) and Vermeer (1632-75).

Economy. European economic expansion was stimulated by the new trade with the East, New World gold and silver, and a doubling of population (50 mln. in 1450, 100 mln. in 1600). New business and financial techniques were developed and refined, such as joint-stock companies, insurance, and letters of credit and exchange. The Bank of Amsterdam, 1609, and the Bank of England, 1694, broke the old monopoly of private banking families. The rise of a business mentality was typified by the spread of clock towers in cities in the 14th century. By the mid-15th century, portable clocks were available; the first watch was invented in 1502.

By 1650, most governments had adopted the **mercantile system,** in which they sought to amass metallic wealth by protecting their merchants' foreign and colonial trade monopolies. The rise in prices and the new coin-based economy undermined the craft guild and feudal manorial systems. Expanding industries, such as clothweaving and mining, benefitted from technical advances. Coal replaced disappearing wood as the chief fuel; it was used to fuel new 16th century blast furnaces making cast iron.

New World. The **Aztecs** united much of the Mesoamerican culture area in a militarist empire by 1519, from their capital, Tenochtitlan (pop. 300,000), which was the center of a cult requiring enormous levels of ritual human sacrifice. Most of the civilized areas of S. America were ruled by the centralized **Inca Empire** (1476-1534), stretching 2,000 miles from Ecuador to N.W. Argentina. Lavish and sophisticated traditions in pottery, weaving, sculpture, and architecture were maintained in both regions.

These empires, beset by revolts, fell in 2 short campaigns to gold-seeking Spanish forces based in the Antilles and Panama. **Cortes** took Mexico, 1519-21; **Pizarro** Peru, 1531-35. From these centers, land and sea expeditions claimed most of N. and S. America for Spain. The Indian high cultures did not survive the impact of Christian missionaries and the new upper class of whites and mestizos. In turn, New World silver, and such Indian products as potatoes, tobacco, corn, peanuts, chocolate, and rubber exercised a major economic influence on Europe. While the Spanish administration intermittently concerned itself with the welfare of Indians, the population remained impoverished at most levels, despite the growth of a distinct South American civilization. European diseases reduced the native population.

Brazil, which the Portuguese discovered in 1500 and settled after 1530, and the Caribbean colonies of several European nations developed a plantation economy where sugar cane, tobacco, cotton, coffee, rice, indigo, and lumber were grown commercially by slaves. From the early 16th to the late 19th centuries, some 10 million Africans were transported to **slavery** in the New World.

Netherlands. The urban, Calvinist northern provinces of the Netherlands rebelled against Hapsburg Spain, 1568, and founded an oligarchic mercantile republic. Their strategic control of the Baltic grain market enabled them to exploit Mediterranean food shortages. Religious refugees — French and Belgian Protestants, Iberian Jews — added to the cosmopolitan commercial talent pool. After Spain absorbed Portugal in 1580, the Dutch seized Portuguese possessions and created a vast, though generally short-lived commercial empire in Brazil, the Antilles, Africa, India, Ceylon, Malacca, Indonesia, and Taiwan, and challenged or supplanted Portuguese traders in China and Japan.

England. Anglicanism became firmly established under Elizabeth I after a brief Catholic interlude under "Bloody Mary," 1553-58. But religious and political conflicts led to a rebellion by Parliament, 1642. Roundheads (Puritans) defeated Cavaliers (Royalists); Charles I was beheaded, 1649. The new **Commonwealth** was ruled as a military dictatorship by Cromwell, who also brutally crushed an Irish rebellion, 1649-51. Conflicts within the Puritan camp (democratic Levelers defeated 1649) aided the Stuart restoration, 1660, but Parliament was permanently strengthened and the peaceful "**Glorious Revolution**", 1688, advanced political and religious liberties (writings of Locke, 1632-1704). British privateers (Drake, 1540-96) challenged Spanish control of the New World, and penetrated Asian trade routes (Madras taken, 1639). N. American colonies (Jamestown, 1607, Plymouth, 1620) provided an outlet for religious dissenters.

France. Emerging from the religious civil wars in 1628, France regained military and commercial great power status under the ministries of **Richelieu** (1624-42), Mazarin (1643-61), and Colbert (1662-83). Under Louis XIV (ruled 1643-1715) royal absolutism triumphed over nobles and local *parlements* (defeat of Fronde, 1648-53). Permanent colonies were founded in Canada (1608), the Caribbean (1626), and India (1674).

Sweden. Sweden seceded from the Scandinavian Union in 1523. The thinly-populated agrarian state (with copper, iron, and timber exports) was united by the Vasa kings, whose conquests by the mid-17th century made Sweden the dominant Baltic power. The empire collapsed in the Great Northern War (1700-21).

Poland. After the union with Lithuania in 1447, Poland ruled vast territories from the Baltic to the Black Sea, resisting German and Turkish incursions. Catholic nobles failed to gain the loyalty of the Orthodox Christian peasantry in the East; commerce and trades were practiced by German and Jewish immigrants. The bloody 1648-49 cossack uprising began the kingdom's dismemberment.

China. A new dynasty, the **Manchus**, invaded from the NE and seized power in 1644, and expanded Chinese control to its greatest extent in Central and Southeast Asia. Trade and diplomatic contact with Europe grew, carefully controlled by China. New crops (sweet potato, maize, peanut) allowed an economic and population growth (300 million pop. in 1800). Traditional arts and literature were pursued with increased sophistication (*Dream of the Red Chamber*, novel, mid-18th century).

Japan. Tokugawa Ieyasu, shogun from 1603, finally unified and pacified feudal Japan. Hereditary daimyos and samurai monopolized government office and the professions. An urban merchant class grew, literacy spread, and a cultural renaissance occurred (haiku of Basho, 1644-94). Fear of European domination led to persecution of Christian converts from 1597, and stringent isolation from outside contact from 1640.

Philosophy, Industry, and Revolution: 1700-1800

Science and Reason. Faith in human reason and science as the source of truth and a means to improve the physical and social environment, espoused since the Renaissance (Francis Bacon, 1561-1626), was bolstered by scientific discoveries in spite of theological opposition (**Galileo's forced retraction**, 1633). Descartes applied the logical method of mathematics to discover "self-evident" scientific and philosophical truths, while Newton emphasized induction from experimental observation.

The challenge of reason to traditional religious and political values and institutions began with **Spinoza** (1632-77), who interpreted the Bible historically and called for political and intellectual freedom.

French philosophes assumed leadership of the "**Enlightenment**" in the 18th century. Montesquieu (1689-1755) used British history to support his notions of limited government. Voltaire's (1694-1778) diaries and novels of exotic travel illustrated the intellectual trends toward secular ethics and relativism. Rousseau's (1712-1778) radical concepts of the **social contract** and of the inherent goodness of the common man gave impetus to anti-monarchical republicanism. The *Encyclopedia*, 1751-72, edited by Diderot and d'Alembert, designed as a monument to reason, was largely devoted to practical technology.

In England, ideals of political and religious liberty were connected with empiricist philosophy and science in the followers of Locke. But the extreme **empiricism of Hume** (1711-76) and Berkeley

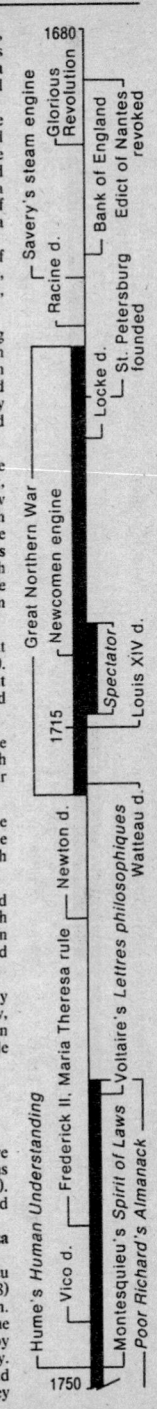

1680

Savery's steam engine

Glorious Revolution

Racine d.

Bank of England

Edict of Nantes revoked

Locke d.

St. Petersburg founded

Great Northern War

Newcomen engine

1715

Spectator

Louis XIV d.

Newton d.

Watteau d.

Maria Theresa rule

Frederick II,

Voltaire's Lettres philosophiques

Hume's Human Understanding

Vico d.

Montesquieu's Spirit of Laws

Poor Richard's Almanack

1750

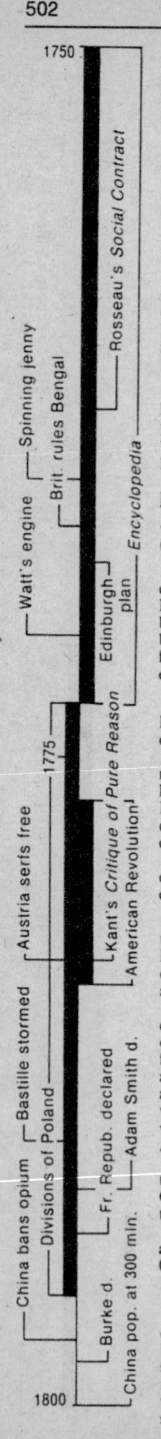

(1685-1753) posed limits to the identification of reason with absolute truth, as did the evolutionary approach to law and politics of Burke (1729-97) and the utilitarianism of Bentham (1748-1832). Adam Smith (1723-90) and other **physiocrats** called for a rationalization of economic activity by removing artificial barriers to a supposedly natural free exchange of goods.

Despite the political disunity and backwardness of most of Germany, German writers participated in the new philosophical trends popularized by Wolff (1679-1754). **Kant's** (1724-1804) **idealism,** unifying an empirical epistemology with *a priori* moral and logical concepts, directed German thought away from skepticism. Italian contributions included work on electricity by Galvani (1737-98) and Volta (1745-1827), the pioneer **historiography** of Vico (1668-1744), and writings on penal reform by Beccaria (1738-94). The American Franklin (1706-90) was celebrated in Europe for his varied achievements.

The growth of the **press** (*Spectator,* 1711-14) and the wide distribution of realistic but sentimental **novels** attested to the increase of a large bourgeois public.

Arts. Rococo art, characterized by extravagant decorative effects, asymmetries copied from organic models, and artificial pastoral subjects, was favored by the continental aristocracy for most of the century (Watteau, 1684-1721), and had musical analogies in the ornamentalized polyphony of late Baroque. The **Neoclassical** art after 1750, associated with the new scientific archeology, was more streamlined, and infused with the supposed moral and geometric rectitude of the Roman Republic (David, 1748-1825). In England, **town planning** on a grand scale began (Edinburgh, 1767).

Industrial Revolution in England. Agricultural improvements, such as the sowing drill (1701) and livestock breeding, were implemented on the large fields provided by enclosure of common lands by private owners. Profits from agriculture and from colonial and foreign trade (1800 volume, £ 54 million) were channelled through hundreds of banks and the **Stock Exchange** (founded 1773) into new industrial processes.

The Newcomen steam pump (1712) aided coal mining. Coal fueled the new efficient steam engines patented by Watt in 1769, and coke-smelting produced cheap, sturdy iron for machinery by the 1730s. The **flying shuttle** (1733) and **spinning jenny** (1764) were used in the large new cotton textile factories, where women and children were much of the work force. Goods were transported cheaply over **canals** (2,000 miles built 1760-1800).

American Revolution. The British colonies in N. America attracted a mass immigration of religious dissenters and poor people throughout the 17th and 18th centuries, coming from all parts of the British Isles, Germany, the Netherlands, and other countries. The population reached 3 million whites and blacks by the 1770s. The small native population was decimated by European diseases and wars with and between the various colonies. British attempts to control colonial trade, and to tax the colonists to pay for the costs of colonial administration and defense clashed with traditions of local self government, and eventually provoked the colonies to rebellion. (*See American Revolution in Index.*)

Central and East Europe. The monarchs of the three states that dominated eastern Europe — Austria, Prussia, and Russia — accepted the advice and legitimation of philosophes in creating more modern, centralized institutions in their kingdoms, enlarged by the division of Poland (1772-95).

Under **Frederick II** (ruled 1740-86) Prussia, with its efficient modern army, doubled in size. State monopolies and tariff protection fostered industry, and some legal reforms were introduced. Austria's heterogeneous realms were legally unified under **Maria Theresa** (ruled 1740-80) and **Joseph II** (1780-90). Reforms in education, law, and religion were enacted, and the Austrian serfs were freed (1781). With its defeat in the Seven Years' War in 1763, Austria lost Silesia and ceased its active role in Germany, but was compensated by expansion to the E and S (Hungary, Slavonia, 1699, Galicia, 1772).

Russia, whose borders continued to expand in all directions, adopted some Western bureaucratic and economic policies under **Peter I** (ruled 1682-1725) and **Catherine II** (ruled 1762-96). Trade and cultural contacts with the West multiplied from the new Baltic Sea capital, St. Petersburg (founded ¿703).

French Revolution. The growing French middle class lacked political power, and resented aristocratic tax privileges, especially in light of liberal political ideals popularized by the American Revolution. Peasants lacked adequate land and were burdened with feudal obligations to nobles. Wars with Britain drained the treasury, finally forcing the king to call the **Estates-General** in 1789 (first time since 1614), in an atmosphere of food riots (poor crop in 1788).

Aristocratic resistance to absolutism was soon overshadowed by the reformist Third Estate (middle class), which proclaimed itself the **National Constituent Assembly** June 17 and took the "Tennis Court oath" on June 20 to secure a constitution. The storming of the **Bastille** July 14 by Parisian artisans was followed by looting and seizure of aristocratic property throughout France. Assembly reforms included abolition of class and regional privileges, a Declaration of Rights, suffrage by taxpayers (75% of males), and the **Civil Constitution of the Clergy** providing for election and loyalty oaths for priests. A republic was declared Sept. 22, 1792, in spite of royalist pressure from Austria and Prussia, which had declared war in April (joined by Britain the next year). Louis XVI was beheaded Jan. 21, 1793. Queen Marie Antoinette was beheaded Oct. 16, 1793.

Royalist uprisings in La Vendee and the S and military reverses led to a **reign of terror** in which tens of thousands of opponents of the Revolution and criminals were executed. Radical reforms in the **Convention** period (Sept. 1793-Oct. 1795) included the abolition of colonial slavery, economic measures to aid the poor, support of public education, and a short-lived de-Christianization.

Division among radicals (execution of Hebert, March 1794, Danton, April, and Robespierre, July) aided the ascendance of a moderate **Directory,** which consolidated military victories. **Napoleon Bonaparte** (1769-1821), a popular young general, exploited political divisions and participated in a coup Nov. 9, 1799, making himself first consul (dictator).

India. Sikh and Hindu rebels (Rajputs, Marathas) and Afghans destroyed the power of the Mughals during the 18th century. After France's defeat in the Seven Years War, 1763, Britain was the chief European trade power in India. Its control of inland **Bengal and Bihar** was recognized by the Mughal shah in 1765, who granted the **British East India Co.** (under Clive, 1727-74) the right to collect land revenue there. Despite objections from Parliament (1784 India Act) the company's involvement in local wars and politics led to repeated acquisitions of new territory. The company exported Indian textiles, sugar, and indigo.

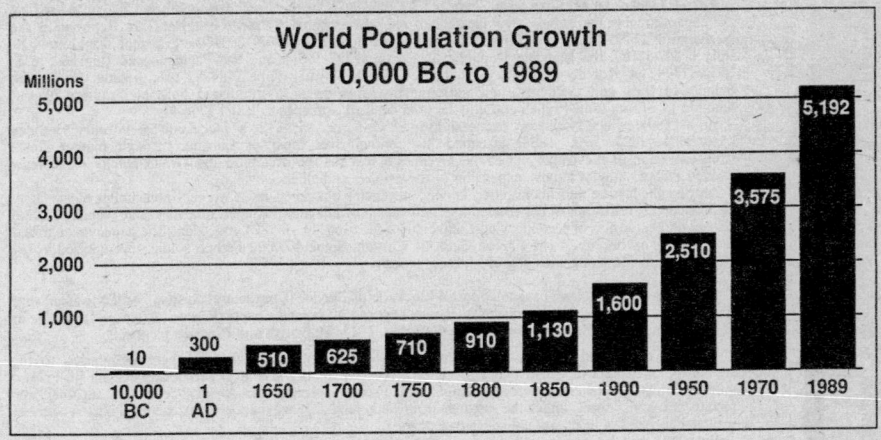

World Population Growth
10,000 BC to 1989

Millions

5,000	
4,000	
3,000	
2,000	
1,000	

5,192

3,575

2,510

1,600

1,130

910

710

625

510

300

10

| 10,000 BC | 1 AD | 1650 | 1700 | 1750 | 1800 | 1850 | 1900 | 1950 | 1970 | 1989 |

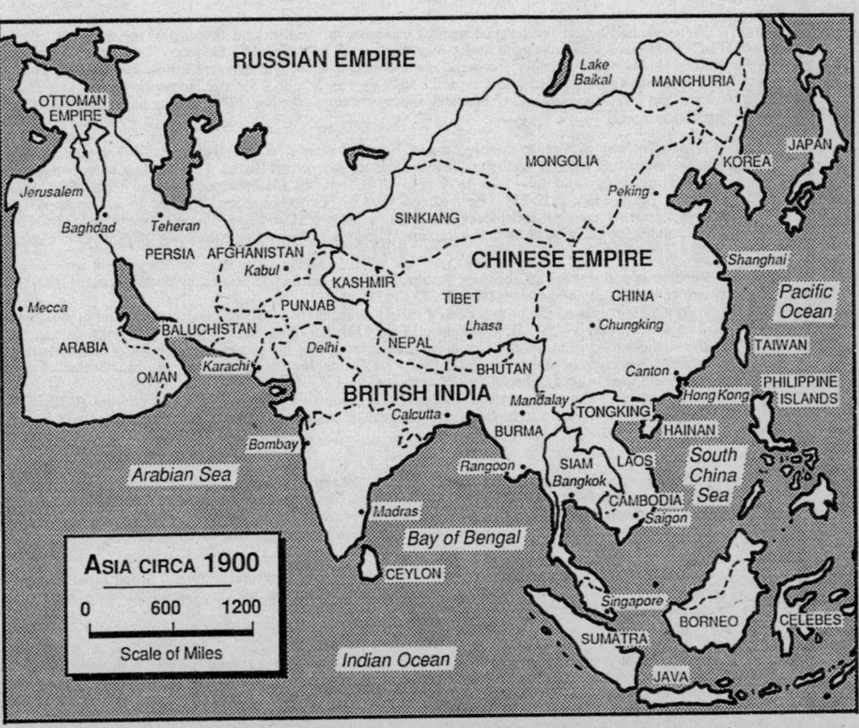

RUSSIAN EMPIRE

OTTOMAN EMPIRE

Lake Baikal

MANCHURIA

JAPAN

MONGOLIA

KOREA

Jerusalem

Peking

SINKIANG

Baghdad   Teheran

PERSIA   AFGHANISTAN

CHINESE EMPIRE

Shanghai

Kabul

KASHMIR

Mecca

PUNJAB

TIBET

CHINA

Pacific Ocean

BALUCHISTAN

Lhasa

Chungking

TAIWAN

ARABIA

Delhi

NEPAL

OMAN

Karachi

BHUTAN

Canton

Hong Kong

PHILIPPINE ISLANDS

BRITISH INDIA

Mandalay

TONGKING

Calcutta

HAINAN

Bombay

BURMA

South China Sea

Arabian Sea

Rangoon

SIAM   LAOS

Bangkok

CAMBODIA

Madras

Saigon

Bay of Bengal

CEYLON

ASIA CIRCA 1900

| 0 | 600 | 1200 |

Scale of Miles

Singapore

BORNEO

CELEBES

SUMATRA

Indian Ocean

JAVA

Change Gathers Steam: 1800-1840

French ideals and empire spread. Inspired by the ideals of the French Revolution, and supported by the expanding French armies, new republican regimes arose near France: the **Batavian** Republic in the Netherlands (1795-1806), the **Helvetic** Republic in Switzerland (1798-1803), the **Cisalpine** Republic in N. Italy (1797-1805), the **Ligurian** Republic in Genoa (1797-1805), and the **Parthenopean** Republic in S. Italy (1799). A Roman Republic existed briefly in 1798 after Pope Pius VI was arrested by French troops. In Italy and Germany, new nationalist sentiments were stimulated both in imitation of and reaction to France (anti-French and anti-Jacobin peasant uprisings in Italy, 1796-9).

From 1804, when Napoleon declared himself emperor, to 1812, a succession of military victories (Austerlitz, 1805, Jena, 1806) extended his control over most of Europe, through puppet states (**Confederation of the Rhine** united W. German states for the first time and **Grand Duchy of Warsaw** revived Polish national hopes), expansion of the empire, and alliances.

Among the lasting reforms initiated under Napoleon's absolutist reign were: establishment of the Bank of France, centralization of tax collection, codification of law along Roman models (*Code Napoleon*), and reform and extension of secondary and university education. In an 1801 concordat, the papacy recognized the effective autonomy of the French Catholic Church. Some 400,000 French soldiers were killed in the Napoleonic Wars, along with 600,000 foreign troops.

Last gasp of old regime. France's coastal blockade of Europe (**Continental System**) failed to neutralize Britain. The disastrous 1812 invasion of Russia exposed Napoleon's overextension. After an 1814 exile at Elba, Napoleon's armies were defeated at **Waterloo**, 1815, by British and Prussian troops.

At the **Congress of Vienna**, the monarchs and princes of Europe redrew their boundaries, to the advantage of Prussia (in Saxony and the Ruhr), Austria (in Illyria and Venetia), and Russia (in Poland and Finland). British conquest of Dutch and French colonies (S. Africa, Ceylon, Mauritius) was recognized, and France, under the restored Bourbons, retained its expanded 1792 borders. The settlement brought 50 years of international peace to Europe.

But the Congress was unable to check the advance of liberal ideals and of nationalism among the smaller European nations. The 1825 **Decembrist uprising** by liberal officers in Russia was easily suppressed. But an independence movement in Greece, stirred by commercial prosperity and a cultural revival, succeeded in expelling Ottoman rule by 1831, with the aid of Britain, France, and Russia.

A constitutional monarchy was secured in France by an **1830 revolution**; Louis Philippe became king. The revolutionary contagion spread to **Belgium**, which gained its independence from the Dutch monarchy, 1830; to **Poland**, whose rebellion was defeated by Russia, 1830-31; and to Germany.

Romanticism. A new style in intellectual and artistic life began to replace Neo-classicism and Rococo after the mid-18th century. By the early 19th, this style, Romanticism, had prevailed in the European world.

Rousseau had begun the reaction against excessive rationalism and skepticism; in education (*Emile*, 1762) he stressed subjective spontaneity over regularized instruction. In Germany, Lessing (1729-81) and Herder (1744-1803) favorably compared the German folk song to classical forms, and began a cult of Shakespeare, whose passion and "natural" wisdom was a model for the Romantic *Sturm und Drang* (storm and stress) period. **Goethe's** *Sorrows of Young Werther* (1774) set the model for the tragic, passionate genius.

A new interest in **Gothic architecture** in England after 1760 (Walpole, 1717-97) spread through Europe, associated with an aesthetic Christian and mystic revival (Blake, 1757-1827). Celtic, Norse, and German mythology and folk tales were revived or imitated (Macpherson's Ossian translation, 1762, Grimm's *Fairy Tales*, 1812-22). The medieval revival (Scott's *Ivanhoe*, 1819) led to a new interest in history, stressing national differences and organic growth (Carlyle, 1795-1881; Michelet, 1798-1874), corresponding to theories of natural evolution (Lamarck's *Philosophie zoologique*, 1809, Lyell's *Geology*, 1830-33).

Revolution and war fed an obsession with freedom and conflict, expressed by poets (**Byron**, 1788-1824, **Hugo**, 1802-85) and philosophers (**Hegel**, 1770-1831).

Wild gardens replaced the formal French variety, and painters favored rural, stormy, and mountainous landscapes (**Turner**, 1775-1851; **Constable**, 1776-1837). Clothing became freer, with wigs, hoops, and ruffles discarded. Originality and genius were expected in the life as well as the work of inspired artists (Murger's *Scenes from Bohemian Life*, 1847-49). Exotic locales and themes (as in "Gothic" horror stories) were used in art and literature (Delacroix, 1798-1863, Poe, 1809-49).

Music exhibited the new dramatic style and a breakdown of classical forms (Beethoven, 1770-1827). The use of folk melodies and modes aided the growth of distinct national traditions (Glinka in Russia, 1804-57).

Latin America. Haiti, under the former slave **Toussaint L'Ouverture,** was the first Latin American independent state, 1800. All the mainland Spanish colonies won their independence 1810-24, under such leaders as **Bolivar** (1783-1830). Brazil became an independent empire under the Portuguese prince regent, 1822. A new class of military officers divided power with large landholders and the church.

United States. Heavy immigration and exploitation of ample natural resources fueled rapid economic growth. The spread of the franchise, public education, and antislavery sentiment were signs of a widespread democratic ethic.

China. Failure to keep pace with Western arms technology exposed China to greater European influence, and hampered efforts to bar imports of opium, which had damaged Chinese society and drained wealth overseas. In the **Opium War**, 1839-42, Britain forced China to expand trade opportunities and to cede Hong Kong.

Timeline (left margin):

1800

Haiti indep.

Mill b. — Hugo b. — Dix b.

Napoleon emperor — Lamarck's *Philosophie Zoologique*

Congress of Vienna

1815 — S. Amer. colonies win indep. — Scott's *Ivanhoe*

Brazil indep. — Byron d. — Grimm's *Fairy Tales* — Decembrist uprising

Greek indep. movement — Blake d. — Volta d. — Beethoven d.

1830 — Belgian indep. — Brit. Emp. slavery banned

1st Eng. reform bill — 1st Brit. Factory Act.

Brook Farm, Mass. — Opium War — Telegraph perfected by Morse

1845

Triumph of Progress: 1840-80

Idea of Progress. As a result of the cumulative scientific, economic, and political changes of the preceding eras, the idea took hold among literate people in the West that continuing growth and improvement was the usual state of human and natural life.

Darwin's statement of the **theory of evolution** and survival of the fittest (*Origin of Species*, 1859), defended by intellectuals and scientists against theological objections, was taken as confirmation that progress was the natural direction of life. The controversy helped define popular ideas of the dedicated scientist and ever-expanding human knowledge of and control over the world (Foucault's demonstration of earth's rotation, 1851, Pasteur's germ theory, 1861).

Liberals following Ricardo (1772-1823) in their faith that unrestrained competition would bring continuous economic expansion sought to adjust political life to the new social realities, and believed that unregulated competition of ideas would yield truth (Mill, 1806-73). In England, successive reform bills (1832, 1867, 1884) gave representation to the new industrial towns, and extended the franchise to the middle and lower classes and to Catholics, Dissenters, and Jews. On both sides of the Atlantic, reformists tried to improve conditions for the mentally ill (Dix, 1802-87), women (Anthony, 1820-1906), and prisoners. Slavery was barred in the British Empire, 1833; the United States, 1865; and Brazil, 1888.

Socialist theories based on ideas of human perfectibility or historical progress were widely disseminated. Utopian socialists like Saint-Simon (1760-1825) envisaged an orderly, just society directed by a technocratic elite. A model factory town, New Lanark, Scotland, was set up by utopian Robert Owen (1771-1858), and utopian communal experiments were tried in the U.S. (Brook Farm, Mass., 1841-7). Bakunin's (1814-76) anarchism represented the opposite utopian extreme of total freedom. Marx (1818-83) posited the inevitable triumph of socialism in the industrial countries through a historical process of class conflict.

Spread of industry. The technical processes and managerial innovations of the English industrial revolution spread to Europe (especially Germany) and the U.S., causing an explosion of industrial production, demand for raw materials, and competition for markets. Inventors, both trained and self-educated, provided the means for larger-scale production (Bessemer steel, 1856, sewing machine, 1846). Many inventions were shown at the 1851 London Great Exhibition at the Crystal Palace, whose theme was universal prosperity.

Local specialization and long-distance trade were aided by a revolution in transportation and communication. Railroads were first introduced in the 1820s in England and the U.S. Over 150,000 miles of track had been laid worldwide by 1880, with another 100,000 miles laid in the next decade. Steamships were improved (*Savannah* crossed Atlantic, 1819). The telegraph, perfected by 1844 (Morse), connected the Old and New Worlds by cable in 1866, and quickened the pace of international commerce and politics. The first commercial telephone exchange went into operation in the U.S. in 1878.

The new class of industrial workers, uprooted from their rural homes, lacked job security, and suffered from dangerous overcrowded conditions at work and at home. Many responded by organizing trade unions (legalized in England, 1824; France, 1884). The U.S. Knights of Labor had 700,000 members by 1886. The First International, 1864-76, tried to unite workers internationally around a Marxist program. The quasi-Socialist Paris Commune uprising, 1871, was violently suppressed. Factory Acts to reduce child labor and regulate conditions were passed (1833-50 in England). Social security measures were introduced by the Bismarck regime in Germany, 1883-89.

Revolutions of 1848. Among the causes of the continent-wide revolutions were an international collapse of credit and resulting unemployment, bad harvests in 1845-7, and a cholera epidemic. The new urban proletariat and expanding bourgeoisie demanded a greater political role. Republics were proclaimed in France, Rome, and Venice. Nationalist feelings reached fever pitch in the Hapsburg empire, as Hungary declared independence under Kossuth, a Slav Congress demanded equality, and Piedmont tried to drive Austria from Lombardy. A national liberal assembly at Frankfurt called for German unification.

But riots fueled bourgeois fears of socialism (Marx and Engels' 1848 *Communist Manifesto*) and peasants remained conservative. The old establishment — The Papacy, the Hapsburgs (using Croats and Romanians against Hungary), the Russian army — was able to rout the revolutionaries by 1849. The French Republic succumbed to a renewed monarchy by 1852 (Emperor Napoleon III).

Great nations unified. Using the "blood and iron" tactics of Bismarck from 1862, Prussia controlled N. Germany by 1867 (war with Denmark, 1864, Austria, 1866). After defeating France in 1870 (loss of Alsace-Lorraine), it won the allegiance of S. German states. A new **German Empire** was proclaimed, 1871. Italy, inspired by Mazzini (1805-72) and Garibaldi (1807-82), was unified by the reformed Piedmont kingdom through uprisings, plebiscites, and war.

The U.S., its area expanded after the 1846-47 Mexican War, defeated a secession attempt by slave states, 1861-65. The Canadian provinces were united in an autonomous **Dominion of Canada**, 1867. Control in **India** was removed from the East India Co. and centralized under British administration after the 1857-58 Sepoy rebellion, laying the groundwork for the modern Indian State. Queen Victoria was named Empress of India, 1876.

Europe dominates Asia. The Ottoman Empire began to collapse in the face of Balkan nationalisms and European imperial incursions in N. Africa (Suez Canal, 1869). The Turks had lost control of most of both regions by 1882. Russia completed its expansion south by 1884 (despite the temporary setback of the Crimean War with Turkey, Britain, and France, 1853-56) taking Turkestan, all the Caucasus, and Chinese areas in the East and sponsoring Balkan Slavs against the Turks. A succession of reformist and reactionary regimes presided over a slow modernization (serfs freed, 1861). Persian independence suffered as Russia and British India competed for influence.

China was forced to sign a series of unequal treaties with European powers and Japan. Overpopulation and an inefficient dynasty brought misery and caused rebellions (Taiping, Moslems) leaving tens of millions dead. Japan was forced by the U.S. (Commodore Perry's visits, 1853-54) and Europe to end its isolation. The Meiji restoration, 1868, gave power to a Westernizing oligarchy. Intensified empire-building gave Burma to Britain, 1824-86, and Indo-China to France, 1862-95. Christian missionary activity followed imperial and trade expansion in Asia.

Respectability. The fine arts were expected to reflect and encourage the progress of morals and —

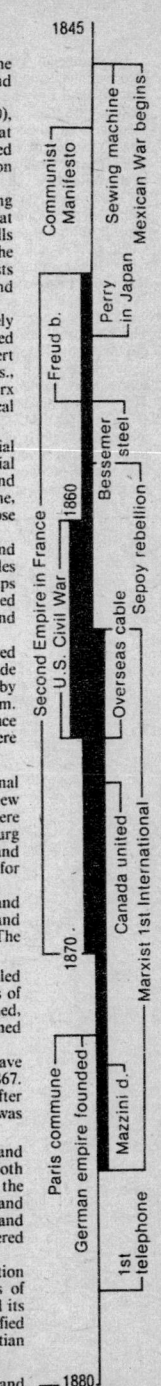

1845

Communist Manifesto
Freud b.
Sewing machine
Perry in Japan
Mexican War begins

Second Empire in France
U.S. Civil War
1860
Bessemer steel
Overseas cable
Sepoy rebellion

1870
Canada united
Marxist 1st International

Paris commune
German empire founded
Mazzini d.
1st telephone

1880

The Seven Wonders of the World

These ancient works of art and architecture were considered awe-inspiring in splendor and/or size by the Greek and Roman world of the Alexandrian epoch and later. Classical writers disagreed as to which works made up the list of Wonders, but the following were usually included:

The Pyramids of Egypt: The only surviving Wonder, these monumental structures of masonry located on the west bank of the Nile River above Cairo were built from 3000 to 1800 B.C. as royal tombs. Three—Khufu, Khafra, and Menkaura—were often grouped as the first Wonder of the World. The largest, **The Great Pyramid of Khufu,** or Cheops, is a solid mass of limestone blocks covering 13 acres. It is estimated to contain 2.3 million blocks of stone, the stones themselves averaging 2½ tons and some weighing 30 tons. Its construction reputedly took 100,000 laborers 20 years.

The Hanging Gardens of Babylon: These gardens were laid out on a brick terrace about 400 feet square and 75 feet above the ground. To irrigate the trees, shrubs, and flowers, screws were turned to lift water from the Euphrates River. The gardens were probably built by King Nebuchandnezzar II around 600 B.C. **The Walls of Babylon,** long, thick, and made of colorfully glazed brick, were considered by some to be among the Seven Wonders.

The Statue of Zeus (Jupiter) at Olympia: This statue of the king of the gods showed him seated on a throne. His flesh was made of ivory, his robe and ornaments of gold. Reputedly 40 feet high, the statue was made by Phidias and was placed in the great temple of Zeus in the sacred grove of Olympia around 457 B.C.

The Colossus of Rhodes: A bronze statue of the sun god Helios, the Colossus was worked on for 12 years in the early 200's B.C. by the sculptor Chares. It was probably 120 feet high. A symbol of the city of Rhodes at its height, the statue stood on a promontory overlooking the harbor.

The Temple of Artemis (Diana) at Ephesus: This largest and most complex temple of ancient times was built around 550 B.C. and was made of marble except for its tile-covered wooden roof. It was begun in honor of a non-Hellenic goddess who later became identified with the Greek goddess of the same name. Ephesus was one of the greatest of the Ionian cities.

The Mausoleum at Halicarnassus: The source of our word "mausoleum," this marble tomb was built in what is now southeastern Turkey by Artemisia for her husband Mausolus, an official of the Persian Empire who died in 353 B.C. About 135 feet high, it was adorned with the works of 4 sculptors.

The Pharos (Lighthouse) of Alexandria: This sculpture was designed around 270 B.C., during the reign of King Ptolemy II, by the Greek architect Sostratos. Estimates of its height range from 200 to 600 feet.

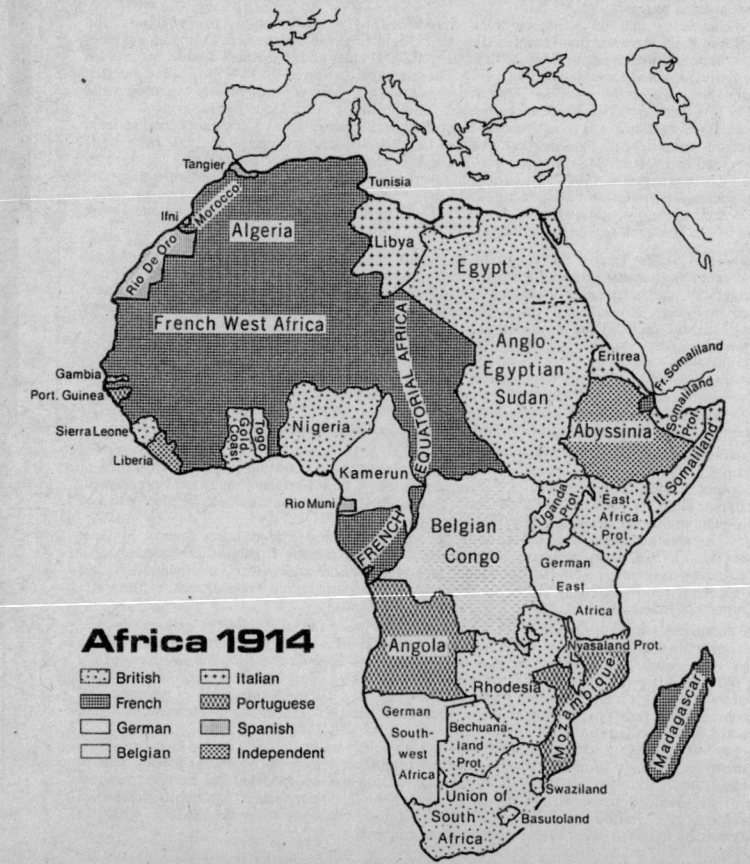

manners among the different classes. "Victorian" prudery, exaggerated delicacy, and familial piety were heralded by **Bowdler's** expurgated edition of Shakespeare (1818). Government-supported mass education inculcated a work ethic as a means to escape poverty (Horatio Alger, 1832-99).

The official **Beaux Arts** school in Paris set an international style of imposing public buildings (Paris Opera, 1861-74, Vienna Opera, 1861-69) and uplifting statues (Bartholdi's *Statue of Liberty*, 1885). Realist painting, influenced by photography (Daguerre, 1837), appealed to a new mass audience with social or historical narrative (Wilkie, 1785-1841, Poynter, 1836-1919) or with serious religious, moral, or social messages (pre-Raphaelites, Millet's *Angelus*, 1858) often drawn from ordinary life. The **Impressionists** (Pissarro, 1830-1903, Renoir, 1841-1919) rejected the central role of serious subject matter in favor of a colorful and sensual depiction of a moment, but their sunny, placid depictions of bourgeois scenes kept them within the respectable consensus.

Realistic **novelists** presented the full panorama of social classes and personalities, but retained sentimentality and moral judgment (Dickens, 1812-70, Eliot, 1819-80, Tolstoy, 1828-1910, Balzac, 1799-1850).

Veneer of Stability: 1880-1900

Imperialism triumphant. The vast **African** interior, visited by European explorers (Barth, 1821-65, Livingstone, 1813-73) was conquered by the European powers in rapid, competitive thrusts from their coastal bases after 1880, mostly for domestic political and international strategic reasons. W. African Moslem kingdoms (Fulani), Arab slave traders (Zanzibar), and Bantu military confederations (Zulu) were alike subdued. Only Christian Ethiopia (defeat of Italy, 1896) and Liberia resisted successfully. France (W. Africa) and Britain ("Cape to Cairo," Boer War, 1899-1902) were the major beneficiaries. The ideology of "the white man's burden" (Kipling, *Barrack Room Ballads*, 1892) or of a "civilizing mission" (France) justified the conquests.

West European foreign capital investments soared to nearly $40 billion by 1914, but most was in E. Europe (France, Germany) the Americas (Britain) and the white colonies. The foundation of the modern interdependent world economy was laid, with cartels dominating raw material trade.

An industrious world. Industrial and technological proficiency characterized the 2 new great powers — Germany and the U.S. Coal and iron deposits enabled Germany to reach second or third place status in iron, steel, and shipbuilding in the 1900s. German electrical and chemical industries were world leaders. The U.S. post-civil war boom (interrupted by "panics," 1884, 1893, 1896) was shaped by massive immigration from S. and E. Europe from 1880, government subsidy of railroads, and huge private monopolies (Standard Oil, 1870, U.S. Steel, 1901). The **Spanish-American War**, 1898 (Philippine rebellion, 1899-1901) and the Open Door policy in China (1899) made the U.S. a world power.

England led in **urbanization** (72% by 1890), with **London** the world capital of finance, insurance, and shipping. Electric subways (London, 1890), sewer systems (Paris, 1850s), parks, and bargain department stores helped improve living standards for most of the urban population of the industrial world.

Asians assimilate. Asian reaction to European economic, military, and religious incursions took the form of imitation of Western techniques and adoption of Western ideas of progress and freedom. The Chinese "self-strengthening" movement of the 1860s and 70s included rail, port, and arsenal improvements and metal and textile mills. Reformers like **K'ang Yu-wei** (1858-1927) won liberalizing reforms in 1898, right after the European and Japanese "scramble for concessions."

A universal education system in Japan and importation of foreign industrial, scientific, and military experts aided Japan's unprecedented rapid modernization after 1868, under the authoritarian Meiji regime. Japan's victory in the **Sino-Japanese War**, 1894-95, put Formosa and Korea in its power.

In India, the British alliance with the remaining princely states masked reform sentiment among the Westernized urban elite; higher education had been conducted largely in English for 50 years. The **Indian National Congress**, founded in 1885, demanded a larger government role for Indians.

"Fin-de-siecle" sophistication. **Naturalist** writers pushed realism to its extreme limits, adopting a quasi-scientific attitude and writing about formerly taboo subjects like sex, crime, extreme poverty, and corruption (Flaubert, 1821-80, Zola, 1840-1902, Hardy, 1840-1928). Unseen or repressed psychological motivations were explored in the clinical and theoretical works of **Freud** (1856-1939) and in the fiction of Dostoevsky (1821-81), James (1843-1916), Schnitzler (1862-1931) and others.

A contempt for bourgeois life or a desire to shock a complacent audience was shared by the French **symbolist** poets (Verlaine, 1844-96, Rimbaud, 1854-91), neo-pagan English writers (Swinburne, 1837-1909), continental dramatists (Ibsen, 1828-1906) and satirists (Wilde, 1854-1900). **Nietzsche** (1844-1900) was influential in his elitism and pessimism.

Post-impressionist art neglected long-cherished conventions of representation (Cezanne, 1839-1906) and showed a willingness to learn from primitive and non-European art (Gauguin, 1848-1903, Japanese prints).

Racism. Gobineau (1816-82) gave a pseudo-biological foundation to modern racist theories, which spread in the latter 19th century along with **Social Darwinism**, the belief that societies are and should be organized as a struggle for survival of the fittest. The Medieval period was interpreted as an era of natural Germanic rule (Chamberlain, 1855-1927) and notions of superiority were associated with German national aspirations (Treitschke, 1834-96). **Anti-Semitism**, with a new racist rationale, became a significant political force in Germany (Anti-Semitic Petition, 1880), Austria (Lueger, 1844-1910), and France (Dreyfus case, 1894-1906).

Last Respite: 1900-1909

Alliances. While the peace of Europe (and its dependencies) continued to hold (1907 **Hague Conference** extended the rules of war and international arbitration procedures), imperial rivalries, protectionist trade practices (in Germany and France), and the escalating arms race (British *Dreadnought* battleship launched, Germany widens Kiel canal, 1906) exacerbated minor disputes (German-French Moroccan "crises", 1905, 1911).

Security was sought through alliances: **Triple Alliance** (Germany, Austria-Hungary, Italy) renewed

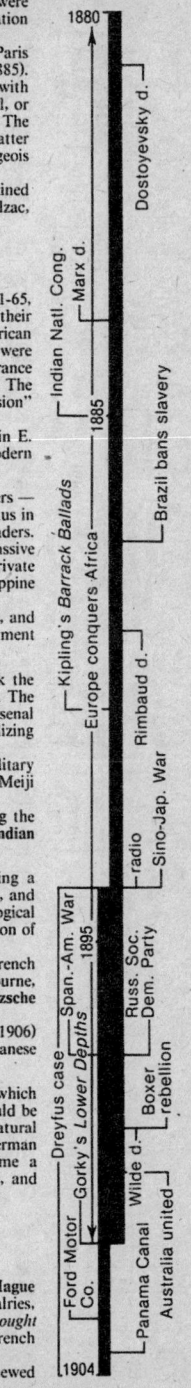

1880

Dostoevsky d.

Marx d.

Indian Natl. Cong.

1885

Brazil bans slavery

Kipling's *Barrack Room Ballads*

Europe conquers Africa

Rimbaud d.

radio

Sino-Jap. War

Span.-Am. War

1895

Russ. Soc. Dem. Party

Dreyfus case

Gorky's *Lower Depths*

Boxer rebellion

Ford Motor Co.

Wilde d.

Panama Canal

Australia united

1904

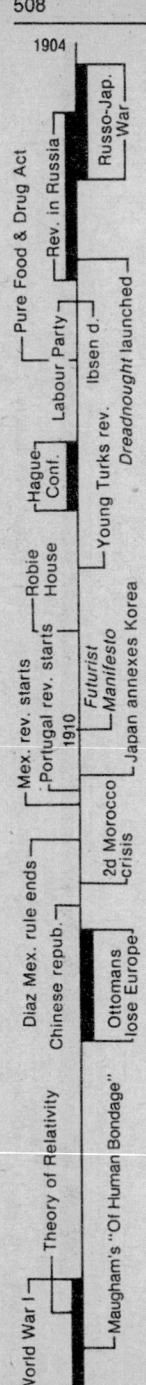

1904

Russo-Jap. War
Rev. in Russia
Pure Food & Drug Act
Labour Party
Ibsen d.
Dreadnought launched
Hague Conf.
Young Turks rev.
Robie House
Futurist Manifesto
Japan annexes Korea
Mex. rev. starts
Portugal rev. starts
1910
2d Morocco crisis
Diaz Mex. rule ends
Chinese repub.
Ottomans lose Europe
Theory of Relativity
Maugham's "Of Human Bondage"
World War I
1916

1902, 1907; Anglo-Japanese Alliance, 1902; Franco-Russian Alliance, 1899; **Entente Cordiale** (Britain, France) 1904; Anglo-Russian Treaty, 1907; German-Ottoman friendship.

Ottomans decline. The inefficient, corrupt Ottoman government was unable to resist further loss of territory. Nearly all European lands were lost in 1912 to Serbia, Greece, Montenegro, and Bulgaria. Italy took Libya and the Dodecanese islands the same year, and Britain took Kuwait, 1899, and the Sinai, 1906. The **Young Turk** revolution in 1908 forced the sultan to restore a constitution, introduced some social reform, industrialization, and secularization.

British Empire. British trade and cultural influence remained dominant in the empire, but constitutional reforms presaged its eventual dissolution: the colonies of **Australia** were united in 1901 under a self-governing commonwealth. **New Zealand** acquired dominion status in 1907. The old Boer republics joined Cape Colony and Natal in the self-governing **Union of South Africa** in 1910.
The 1909 Indian Councils Act enhanced the role of elected province legislatures in **India**. The Moslem League, founded 1906, sought separate communal representation.

East Asia. Japan exploited its growing industrial power to expand its empire. Victory in the 1904-05 war against Russia (naval battle of Tsushima, 1905) assured Japan's domination of **Korea** (annexed 1910) and Manchuria (took Port Arthur 1905).
In China, central authority began to crumble (empress died, 1908). Reforms (Confucian exam system ended 1905, modernization of the army, building of railroads) were inadequate and secret societies of reformers and nationalists, inspired by the Westernized **Sun Yat-sen** (1866-1925) fomented periodic uprisings in the south.
Siam, whose independence had been guaranteed by Britain and France in 1896, was split into spheres of influence by those countries in 1907.

Russia. The population of the Russian Empire approached 150 million in 1900. Reforms in education, law, and local institutions (*zemstvos*), and an industrial boom starting in the 1880s (oil, railroads) created the beginnings of a modern state, despite the autocratic tsarist regime. Liberals (1903 Union of Liberation), Socialists (Social Democrats founded 1898, Bolsheviks split off 1903), and populists (Social Revolutionaries founded 1901) were periodically repressed, and national minorities persecuted (anti-Jewish pogroms, 1903, 1905-6).
An industrial crisis after 1900 and harvest failures aggravated poverty in the urban proletariat, and the 1904-05 defeat by Japan (which checked Russia's Asian expansion) sparked the revolution of 1905-06. A **Duma** (parliament) was created, and an agricultural reform (under Stolypin, prime minister 1906-11) created a large class of landowning peasants (kulaks).

The world shrinks. Developments in transportation and communication, and mass population movements helped create an awareness of an interdependent world. Early **automobiles** (Daimler, Benz, 1885) were experimental, or designed as luxuries. Assembly-line mass production (Ford Motor Co., 1903) made the invention practicable, and by 1910 nearly 500,000 motor vehicles were registered in the U.S. alone. **Heavier-than-air flights** began in 1903 in the U.S. (Wright brothers), preceded by glider, balloon, and model plane advances in several countries. Trade was advanced by improvements in **ship design** (gyrocompass, 1907), speed (Lusitania crossed Atlantic in 5 days, 1907), and reach (Panama Canal begun, 1904).
The first transatlantic **radio** telegraphic transmission occurred in 1901, 6 years after Marconi discovered radio. Radio transmission of human speech had been made in 1900. Telegraphic transmission of photos was achieved in 1904, lending immediacy to news reports. **Phonographs,** popularized by Caruso's recordings (starting 1902) made for quick international spread of musical styles (ragtime). **Motion pictures,** perfected in the 1890s (Dickson, Lumiere brothers), became a popular and artistic medium after 1900; newsreels appeared in 1909.
Emigration from crowded European centers soared in the decade: 9 million migrated to the U.S., and millions more went to Siberia, Canada, Argentina, Australia, South Africa, and Algeria. Some 70 million Europeans emigrated in the century before 1914. Several million Chinese, Indians, and Japanese migrated to Southeast Asia, where their urban skills often enabled them to take a predominant economic role.

Social reform. The social and economic problems of the poor were kept in the public eye by realist fiction writers (Dreiser's *Sister Carrie,* 1900; Gorky's *Lower Depths,* 1902; Sinclair's *Jungle,* 1906), journalists (U.S. muckrakers — Steffens, Tarbell) and artists (Ashcan school). Frequent labor strikes and occasional assassinations by anarchists or radicals (Austrian Empress, 1898; King Umberto I of Italy, 1900; U.S. Pres. McKinley, 1901; Russian Interior Minister Plehve, 1904; Portugal's King Carlos, 1908) added to social tension and fear of revolution.
But democratic reformism prevailed. In Germany, Bernstein's (1850-1932) **revisionist** Marxism, downgrading revolution, was accepted by the powerful Social Democrats and trade unions. The British Fabian Society (the Webbs, Shaw) and the Labour Party (founded 1906) worked for reforms such as social security and union rights (1906), while women's suffragists grew more militant. U.S. **progressives** fought big business (Pure Food and Drug Act, 1906). In France, the 10-hour work day (1904) and separation of church and state (1905) were reform victories, as was universal suffrage in Austria (1907).

Arts. An unprecedented period of experimentation, centered in France, produced several new **painting** styles: fauvism exploited bold color areas (Matisse, *Woman with Hat,* 1905); expressionism reflected powerful inner emotions (the Brücke group, 1905); cubism combined several views of an object on one flat surface (Picasso's *Demoiselles,* 1906-07); futurism tried to depict speed and motion (Italian Futurist Manifesto, 1910). **Architects** explored new uses of steel structures, with facades either neo-classical (Adler and Sullivan in U.S.); curvilinear Art Nouveau (Gaudi's Casa Mila, 1905-10); or functionally streamlined (Wright's Robie House, 1909).
Music and **Dance** shared the experimental spirit. Ruth St. Denis (1877-1968) and Isadora Duncan (1878-1927) pioneered modern dance, while Diaghilev in Paris revitalized classic ballet from 1909. Composers explored atonal music (Debussy, 1862-1918) and dissonance (Schönberg, 1874-1951), or revolutionized classical forms (Stravinsky, 1882-1971), often showing jazz or folk music influences.

War and Revolution: 1910-1919

War threatens. Germany under Wilhelm II sought a political and imperial role consonant with its industrial strength, challenging Britain's world supremacy and threatening France, still resenting the loss of Alsace-Lorraine. Austria wanted to curb an expanded Serbia (after 1912) and the threat it posed to its own Slav lands. Russia feared Austrian and German political and economic aims in the Balkans and Turkey. An accelerated arms race resulted: the German standing army rose to over 2 million men by 1914. Russia and France had over a million each, Austria and the British Empire nearly a million each. Dozens of enormous battleships were built by the powers after 1906.

The **assassination of Austrian Archduke Ferdinand** by a Serbian, June 28, 1914, was the pretext for war. The system of alliances made the conflict Europe-wide; Germany's invasion of Belgium to outflank France forced Britain to enter the war. Patriotic fervor was nearly unanimous among all classes in most countries.

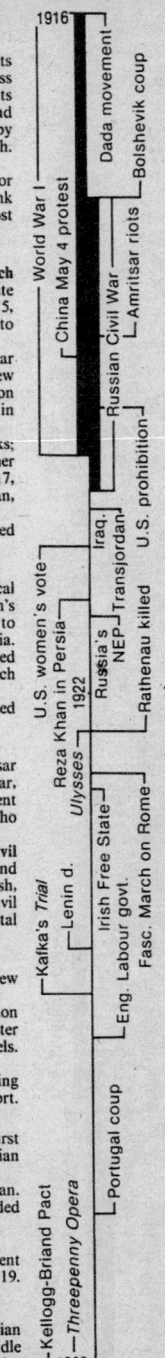

World War I. German forces were stopped in France in one month. The rival armies dug **trench networks.** Artillery and improved machine guns prevented either side from any lasting advance despite repeated assaults (600,000 dead at **Verdun,** Feb.-July 1916). Poison gas, used by Germany in 1915, proved ineffective. Over one million U.S. troops tipped the balance after mid-1917, forcing Germany to sue for peace.

In the East, the Russian armies were thrown back (battle of **Tannenberg,** Aug. 20, 1914) and the war grew unpopular. An allied attempt to relieve Russia through Turkey failed (**Gallipoli** 1916). The new Bolshevik regime signed the capitulatory Brest-Litovsk peace in March, 1918. Italy entered the war on the allied side, Apr. 1915, but was pushed back by Oct. 1917. A renewed offensive with Allied aid in Oct.-Nov. 1918 forced Austria to surrender.

The British Navy successfully blockaded Germany, which responded with submarine U-boat attacks; **unrestricted submarine warfare** against neutrals after Jan. 1917 helped bring the U.S. into the war. Other battlefields included Palestine and Mesopotamia, both of which Britain wrested from the Turks in 1917, and the African and Pacific colonies of Germany, most of which fell to Britain, France, Australia, Japan, and South Africa.

From 1916, the civilian population and economy of both sides were mobilized to an unprecedented degree. Over 10 million soldiers died (May 1917 French mutiny crushed).

Settlement. At the **Versailles conference** (Jan.-June 1919) and in subsequent negotiations and local wars (Russian-Polish War 1920), the map of Europe was redrawn with a nod to U.S. Pres. Wilson's principle of self-determination. Austria and Hungary were separated and much of their land was given to Yugoslavia (formerly Serbia), Romania, Italy, and the newly independent Poland and Czechoslovakia. Germany lost territory in the West, North, and East, while Finland and the Baltic states were detached from Russia. Turkey lost nearly all its Arab lands to British-sponsored Arab states or to direct French and British rule.

A huge **reparations** burden and partial demilitarization were imposed on Germany. Wilson obtained approval for a League of Nations, but the U.S. Senate refused to allow the U.S. to join.

Russian revolution. Military defeats and high casualties caused a contagious lack of confidence in Tsar Nicholas, who was forced to abdicate, Mar. 1917. A liberal provisional government failed to end the war, and massive desertions, riots, and fighting between factions followed. A moderate socialist government under Kerensky was overthrown in a violent **coup by the Bolsheviks** in Petrograd under Lenin, who disbanded the elected Constituent Assembly, Nov. 1917.

The Bolsheviks brutally suppressed all opposition and ended the war with Germany, Mar. 1918. **Civil war** broke out in the summer between the Red Army, including the Bolsheviks and their supporters, and monarchists, anarchists, nationalities (Ukrainians, Georgians, Poles) and others. Small U.S., British, French and Japanese units also opposed the Bolsheviks, 1918-19 (Japan in Vladivostok to 1922). The civil war, anarchy, and pogroms devastated the country until the 1920 Red Army victory. The wartime total monopoly of political, economic, and police power by the Communist Party leadership was retained.

Other European revolutions. An unpopular monarchy in **Portugal** was overthrown in 1910. The new republic took severe anti-clerical measures, 1911.

After a century of Home Rule agitation, during which **Ireland** was devastated by famine (one million dead, 1846-47) and emigration, republican militants staged an unsuccessful uprising in Dublin, Easter 1916. The execution of the leaders and mass arrests by the British won popular support for the rebels. The Irish Free State, comprising all but the 6 northern counties, achieved dominion status in 1922.

In the aftermath of the world war, radical revolutions were attempted in Germany (**Spartacist** uprising Jan. 1919), **Hungary** (Kun regime 1919), and elsewhere. All were suppressed or failed for lack of support.

Chinese revolution. The Manchu Dynasty was overthrown and a republic proclaimed, Oct. 1911. First president Sun Yat-sen resigned in favor of strongman Yuan Shih-k'ai. Sun organized the parliamentarian **Kuomintang** party.

Students launched protests May 4, 1919 against League of Nations concessions in China to Japan. Nationalist, liberal, and socialist ideas and political groups spread. The **Communist Party** was founded 1921. A communist regime took power in Mongolia with Soviet support in 1921.

India restive. Indian objections to British rule erupted in nationalist riots as well as in the non-violent tactics of Gandhi (1869-1948). Nearly 400 unarmed demonstrators were shot at **Amritsar,** Apr. 1919. Britain approved limited self-rule that year.

Mexican revolution. Under the long Diaz dictatorship (1876-1911) the economy advanced, but Indian and mestizo lands were confiscated, and concessions to foreigners (mostly U.S.) damaged the middle class. A **revolution in 1910** led to civil wars and U.S. intervention (1914, 1916-17). Land reform and a more democratic constitution (1917) were achieved.

The Aftermath of War: 1920-29

U.S. Easy credit, technological ingenuity, and war-related industrial decline in Europe caused a long economic boom, in which ownership of the new products — autos, phones, radios — became democratized. Prosperity, an increase in women workers, women's suffrage (1920) and drastic change in fashion (flappers, mannish bob for women, clean-shaven men), created a wide perception of social change, despite prohibition of alcoholic beverages (1919-33). Union membership and strikes increased. Fear of radicals led to Palmer raids (1919-20) and Sacco/Vanzetti case (1921-27).

Europe sorts itself out. Germany's liberal **Weimar constitution** (1919) could not guarantee a stable government in the face of rightist violence (Rathenau assassinated 1922) and Communist refusal to cooperate with Socialists. Reparations and allied occupation of the Rhineland caused staggering inflation which destroyed middle class savings, but economic expansion resumed after mid-decade, aided by U.S. loans. A sophisticated, innovative culture developed in architecture and design (Bauhaus, 1919-28), film (Lang, *M*, 1931), painting (Grosz), music (Weill, *Threepenny Opera*, 1928), theater (Brecht, *A Man's a Man*, 1926), criticism (Benjamin), philosophy (Jung), and fashion. This culture was considered decadent and socially disruptive by rightists.

England elected its first labor governments (Jan. 1924, June 1929). A 10-day general strike in support of coal miners failed, May 1926. In **Italy**, strikes, political chaos and violence by small Fascist bands culminated in the Oct. 1922 Fascist March on Rome, which established Mussolini's dictatorship. Strikes were outlawed (1926), and Italian influence was pressed in the Balkans (Albania a protectorate 1926). A conservative dictatorship was also established in **Portugal** in a 1926 military coup.

Czechoslovakia, the only stable democracy to emerge from the war in Central or East Europe, faced opposition from Germans (in the Sudetenland), Ruthenians, and some Slovaks. As the industrial heartland of the old Hapsburg empire, it remained fairly prosperous. With French backing, it formed the Little Entente with Yugoslavia (1920) and **Romania** (1921) to block Austrian or Hungarian irredentism. Hungary remained dominated by the landholding classes and expansionist feeling. Croats and Slovenes in Yugoslavia demanded a federal state until King Alexander proclaimed a dictatorship (1929). Poland faced nationality problems as well (Germans, Ukrainians, Jews); Pilsudski ruled as dictator from 1926. The Baltic states were threatened by traditionally dominant ethnic Germans and by Soviet-supported communists.

An economic collapse and famine in **Russia**, 1921-22, claimed 5 million lives. The New Economic Policy (1921) allowed land ownership by peasants and some private commerce and industry. Stalin was absolute ruler within 4 years of Lenin's 1924 death. He inaugurated a brutal collectivization program 1929-32, and used foreign communist parties for Soviet state advantage.

Internationalism. Revulsion against World War I led to pacifist agitation, the Kellogg-Briand Pact renouncing aggressive war (1928), and **naval disarmament** pacts (Washington, 1922, London, 1930). But the League of Nations was able to arbitrate only minor disputes (Greece-Bulgaria, 1925).

Middle East. Mustafa Kemal (Ataturk) led **Turkish** nationalists in resisting Italian, French, and Greek military advances, 1919-23. The sultanate was abolished 1922, and elaborate reforms passed, including secularization of law and adoption of the Latin alphabet. Ethnic conflict led to persecution of **Armenians** (over 1 million dead in 1915, 1 million expelled). Greeks (forced Greek-Turk population exchange, 1923), and Kurds (1925 uprising).

With evacuation of the Turks from **Arab** lands, the puritanical Wahabi dynasty of eastern Arabia conquered present Saudi Arabia, 1919-25. British, French, and Arab dynastic and nationalist maneuvering resulted in the creation of two more Arab monarchies in 1921: Iraq and Transjordan (both under British control), and two French mandates: Syria and Lebanon. Jewish immigration into British-mandated **Palestine**, inspired by the Zionist movement, was resisted by Arabs, at times violently (1921, 1929 massacres).

Reza Khan ruled **Persia** after his 1921 coup (shah from 1925), centralized control, and created the trappings of a modern state.

China. The Kuomintang under **Chiang Kai-shek** (1887-1975) subdued the warlords by 1928. The Communists were brutally suppressed after their alliance with the Kuomintang was broken in 1927. Relative peace thereafter allowed for industrial and financial improvements, with some Russian, British, and U.S. cooperation.

Arts. Nearly all bounds of subject matter, style, and attitude were broken in the arts of the period. Abstract art first took inspiration from natural forms or narrative themes (Kandinsky from 1911), then worked free of any representational aims (Malevich's suprematism, 1915-19, Mondrian's geometric style from 1917). The **Dada** movement from 1916 mocked artistic pretension with absurd collages and constructions (Arp, Tzara, from 1916). Paradox, illusion, and psychological taboos were exploited by **surrealists** by the latter 1920s (Dali, Magritte). Architectural schools celebrated industrial values, whether vigorous abstract constructivism (Tatlin, *Monument to 3rd International*, 1919) or the machined, streamlined **Bauhaus** style, which was extended to many design fields (Helvetica type face). Prose writers explored revolutionary narrative modes related to dreams (Kafka's *Trial*, 1925), internal monologue (Joyce's *Ulysses*, 1922), and word play (Stein's *Making of Americans*, 1925). Poets and novelists wrote of modern alienation (Eliot's *Waste Land*, 1922) and aimlessness (Lost Generation).

Sciences. Scientific specialization prevailed by the 20th century. Advances in knowledge and technological aptitude increased with the geometric increase in the number of practitioners. Physicists challenged common-sense views of causality, observation, and a mechanistic universe, putting science further beyond popular grasp (Einstein's general theory of relativity, 1915; Bohr's quantum mechanics, 1913; Heisenberg's uncertainty principle, 1927).

Timeline (left margin):

1928

- India salt march
- Stock market crash
- Smoot-Hawley Tariff
- Alfonso leaves Spain
- Japan seizes Manchuria
- Gandhi's fast

1933

- Hitler dictator
- International Style
- FDR in office
- Hitler takes Rhineland
- Nuremberg Laws
- Long March in China
- Fr. Popular Front
- Italy takes Ethiopia
- Japan invades China
- Civil War in Spain

1938

Rise of the Totalitarians: 1930-39

Depression. A worldwide financial panic and economic depression began with the Oct. 1929 U.S. stock market crash and the May 1931 failure of the Austrian Credit-Anstalt. A credit crunch caused international bankruptcies and **unemployment:** 12 million jobless by 1932 in the U.S., 5.6 million in Germany, 2.7 million in England. Governments responded with **tariff restrictions** (Smoot-Hawley Act 1930; Ottawa Imperial Conference, 1932) which dried up world trade. Government public works programs were vitiated by deflationary budget balancing.

Germany. Years of agitation by violent extremists was brought to a head by the Depression. Nazi leader **Hitler** was named chancellor by Pres. Hindenburg Jan. 1933, and given dictatorial power by the Reichstag in Mar. Opposition parties were disbanded, strikes banned, and all aspects of economic, cultural, and religious life brought under central government and Nazi party control and manipulated by sophisticated propaganda. Severe persecution of Jews began (**Nuremberg Laws** Sept. 1935). Many Jews, political opponents and others were sent to concentration camps (Dachau, 1933) where thousands died or were killed. Public works, renewed conscription (1935), arms production, and a 4-year plan (1936) ended unemployment.

Hitler's expansionism started with reincorporation of the Saar (1935), occupation of the **Rhineland** (Mar. 1936), and annexation of Austria (Mar. 1938). At **Munich**, Sept. 1938, an indecisive Britain and France sanctioned German dismemberment of Czechoslovakia.

Russia. Urbanization and education advanced. Rapid industrialization was achieved through successive **5-year-plans** starting 1928, using severe labor discipline and mass forced labor. Industry was financed by a decline in living standards and exploitation of agriculture, which was almost totally collectivized by the early 1930s (*kolkhoz,* collective farm; *sovkhoz,* state farm, often in newly-worked lands). Successive **purges** increased the role of professionals and management at the expense of workers. Millions perished in a series of man-made disasters: elimination of kulaks (peasant land-owners), 1929-34; severe famine, 1932-33; party purges (Great Purge, 1936-38); suppression of nationalities; and poor conditions in labor camps.

Spain. An industrial revolution during World War I created an urban proletariat, which was attracted to socialism and anarchism; Catalan nationalists challenged central authority. The 5 years after King Alfonso left Spain, Apr. 1931, were dominated by tension between intermittent leftist and anti-clerical governments and clericals, monarchists and other rightists. Anarchist and communist rebellions were crushed, but a July, 1936, extreme right rebellion led by Gen. Francisco Franco and aided by Nazi Germany and Fascist Italy succeeded, after a 3-year **civil war** (over 1 million dead in battles and atrocities). The war polarized international public opinion.

Italy. Despite propaganda for the ideal of the Corporate State, few domestic reforms were attempted. An entente with Hungary and Austria, Mar. 1934, a pact with Germany and Japan, Nov. 1937, and intervention by 50-75,000 troops in Spain, 1936-39, sealed Italy's identification with the fascist bloc (anti-Semitic laws after Mar. 1938). Ethiopia was conquered, 1935-37, and **Albania** annexed, Jan. 1939, in conscious imitation of ancient Rome.

East Europe. Repressive regimes fought for power against an active opposition (liberals, socialists, communists, peasants, Nazis). Minority groups and Jews were restricted within national boundaries that did not coincide with ethnic population patterns. In the destruction of **Czechoslovakia, Hungary** occupied southern Slovakia (Mar. 1938) and Ruthenia (Mar. 1939), and a pro-Nazi regime took power in the rest of Slovakia. Other boundary disputes (e.g. Poland-Lithuania, Yugoslavia-Bulgaria, Romania-Hungary) doomed attempts to build joint fronts against Germany or Russia. Economic depression was severe.

East Asia. After a period of liberalism in **Japan,** nativist militarists dominated the government with peasant support. Manchuria was seized, Sept. 1931-Feb. 1932, and a puppet state set up (Manchukuo). Adjacent Jehol (inner Mongolia) was occupied in 1933. China proper was invaded July 1937; large areas were conquered by Oct. 1938.

In China Communist forces left Kuomintang-besieged strongholds in the South in a Long March (1934-35) to the North. The Kuomintang-Communist civil war was suspended Jan. 1937 in the face of threatening Japan.

The democracies. The Roosevelt Administration, in office Mar. 1933, embarked on an extensive program of social reform and economic stimulation, including protection for labor unions (heavy industries organized), social security, public works, wages and hours laws, assistance to farmers. Isolationist sentiment (1937 Neutrality Act) prevented U.S. intervention in Europe, but military expenditures were increased in 1939.

French political instability and polarization prevented resolution of economic and international security questions. The **Popular Front** government under Blum (June 1936-Apr. 1938) passed social reforms (40-hour week) and raised arms spending. National coalition governments ruled Britain from Aug. 1931, brought some economic recovery, but failed to define a consistent foreign policy until Chamberlain's government (from May 1937), which practiced deliberate **appeasement** of Germany and Italy.

India. Twenty years of agitation for autonomy and then for independence (Gandhi's **salt march,** 1930) achieved some constitutional reform (extended provincial powers, 1935) despite Moslem-Hindu strife. Social issues assumed prominence with peasant uprisings (1921), strikes (1928), Gandhi's efforts for untouchables (1932 "fast unto death"), and social and agrarian reform by the provinces after 1937.

Arts. The streamlined, geometric design motifs of Art Deco (from 1925) prevailed through the 1930s. Abstract art flourished (Moore sculptures from 1931) alongside a new realism related to social and political concerns (**Socialist Realism** the official Soviet style from 1934; Mexican muralists Rivera, 1886-1957, and Orozco, 1883-1949), which was also expressed in fiction and poetry (Steinbeck's *Grapes of Wrath,* 1939; Sandburg's *The People, Yes,* 1936). Modern architecture (*International Style,* 1932) was unchallenged in its use of man-made materials (concrete, glass), lack of decoration, and monumentality (Rockefeller Center, 1929-40). U.S.-made films captured a world-wide audience with their larger-than-life fantasies (*Gone with the Wind,* 1939).

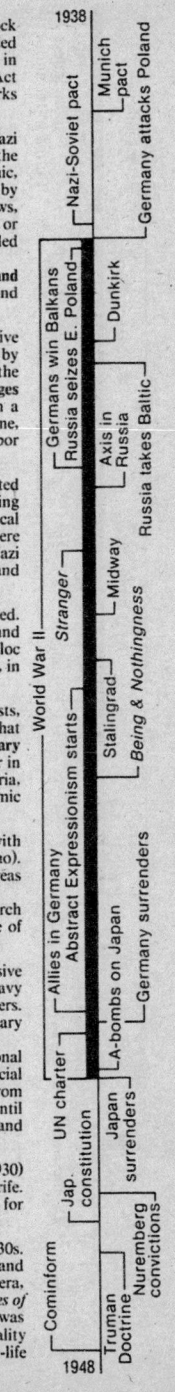

War, Hot and Cold: 1940-49

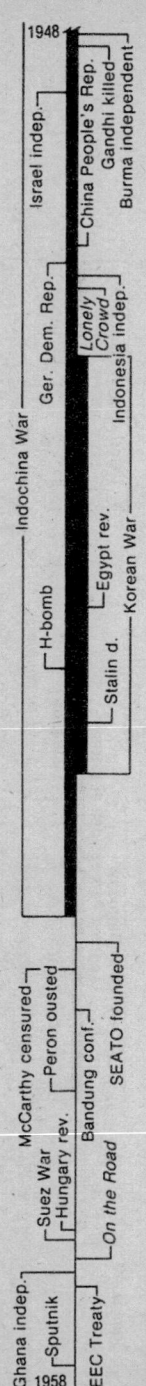

War in Europe. The Nazi-Soviet non-aggression pact (Aug. '39) freed Germany to attack Poland (Sept.). Britain and France, who had guaranteed Polish independence, declared war on Germany. Russia seized East Poland (Sept.), attacked Finland (Nov.) and took the Baltic states (July '40). Mobile German forces staged "blitzkrieg" attacks Apr.-June, '40, conquering neutral Denmark, Norway, and the low countries and defeating France; 350,000 British and French troops were evacuated at **Dunkirk** (May). The Battle of Britain, June-Dec. '40, denied Germany air superiority, German-Italian campaigns won the Balkans by Apr. '41. Three million Axis troops **invaded Russia** June '41, marching through the Ukraine to the Caucasus, and through White Russia and the Baltic republics to Moscow and Leningrad.

Russian winter counterthrusts, '41-'42 and '42-'43 stopped the German advance (Stalingrad Sept. '42-Feb. '43). With British and U.S. Lend-Lease aid and sustaining great casualties, the Russians drove the Axis from all E. Europe and the Balkans in the next 2 years. Invasions of N. Africa (Nov. '42), Italy (Sept. '43), and Normandy (June '44) brought U.S., British, Free French and allied troops to Germany by spring '45. Germany surrendered May 7, 1945.

War in Asia-Pacific. Japan occupied Indochina Sept. '40, dominated Thailand Dec. '41, attacked Hawaii, the Philippines, Hong Kong, Malaya Dec. 7, 1941. Indonesia was attacked Jan. '42, Burma conquered Mar. 42. Battle of **Midway** (June '42) turned back the Japanese advance. "Island-hopping" battles (Guadalcanal Aug. '42-Jan. '43, **Leyte Gulf** Oct. '44, Iwo Jima Feb.-Mar. '45, Okinawa Apr. '45) and massive bombing raids on Japan from June '44 wore out Japanese defenses. Two U.S. atom bombs, dropped Aug. 6 and 9, forced Japan to surrender Aug. 14, 1945.

Atrocities. The war brought 20th-century cruelty to its peak. Nazi murder camps (Auschwitz) systematically killed 6 million Jews. Gypsies, political opponents, sick and retarded people, and others deemed undesirable were murdered by the Nazis, as were vast numbers of Slavs, especially leaders.

Civilian deaths. German bombs killed 70,000 English civilians. Some 100,000 Chinese civilians were killed by Japanese forces in the capture of Nanking. Severe retaliation by the Soviet army, E. European partisans, Free French and others took a heavy toll. U.S. and British bombing of Germany killed hundreds of thousands, as did U.S. bombing of Japan (80-200,000 at Hiroshima alone). Some 45 million people lost their lives in the war.

Settlement. The United Nations charter was signed in San Francisco June 26, 1945 by 50 nations. The International Tribunal at Nuremberg convicted 22 German leaders for war crimes Sept. '46. 23 Japanese leaders were convicted Nov. '48. Postwar border changes included large gains in territory for the USSR, losses for Germany, a shift westward in Polish borders, and minor losses for Italy. Communist regimes, supported by Soviet troops, took power in most of E. Europe, including Soviet-occupied Germany (GDR proclaimed Oct. '49). Japan lost all overseas lands.

Recovery. Basic political and social changes were imposed on Japan and W. Germany by the western allies (Japan constitution Nov. '46, W. German basic law May '49). U.S. Marshall Plan aid ($12 billion '47-'51) spurred W. European economic recovery after a period of severe inflation and strikes in Europe and the U.S. The British Labour Party introduced a national health service and nationalized basic industries in 1946.

Cold War. Western fears of further Soviet advances (Cominform formed Oct. '47, Czechoslovakia coup, Feb. '48, Berlin blockade Apr.'48-Sept. '49) led to formation of NATO. Civil War in Greece and Soviet pressure on Turkey led to U.S. aid under the Truman Doctrine (Mar. '47). Other anti-communist security pacts were the Org. of American States (Apr. '48) and Southeast Asia Treaty Org. (Sept. '54). A new wave of Soviet purges and repression intensified in the last years of Stalin's rule, extending to E. Europe (Slansky trial in Czechoslovakia, 1951). Only Yugoslavia resisted Soviet control (expelled by Cominform, June '48; U.S. aid, June '49).

China, Korea. Communist forces emerged from World War II strengthened by the Soviet takeover of industrial Manchuria. In 4 years of fighting, the Kuomintang was driven from the mainland; the People's Republic was proclaimed Oct. 1, 1949. Korea was divided by Russian and U.S. occupation forces. Separate republics were proclaimed in the 2 zones Aug.-Sept. '48.

India. India and Pakistan became independent dominions Aug. 15, 1947. Millions of Hindu and Moslem refugees were created by the partition; riots, 1946-47, took hundreds of thousands of lives; Gandhi himself was assassinated Jan. '48. Burma became completely independent Jan. '48; Ceylon took dominion status in Feb.

Middle East. The UN approved partition of Palestine into Jewish and Arab states. Israel was proclaimed May 14, 1948. Arabs rejected partition, but failed to defeat Israel in war, May '48-July '49. Immigration from Europe and the Middle East swelled Israel's Jewish population. British and French forces left Lebanon and Syria, 1946. Transjordan occupied most of Arab Palestine.

Southeast Asia. Communists and others fought against restoration of French rule in Indochina from 1946; a non-communist government was recognized by France Mar. '49, but fighting continued. Both Indonesia and the Philippines became independent, the former in 1949 after 4 years of war with Netherlands, the latter in 1946. Philippine economic and military ties with the U.S. remained strong; a communist-led peasant rising was checked in '48.

Arts. New York became the center of the world art market; abstract expressionism was the chief mode (Pollock from '43, de Kooning from '47). Literature and philosophy explored existentialism (Camus' *Stranger*, 1942, Sartre's *Being and Nothingness*, 1943). Non-western attempts to revive or create regional styles (Senghor's Negritude, Mishima's novels) only confirmed the emergence of a universal culture. Radio and phonograph records spread American popular music (swing, bebop) around the world.

The American Decade: 1950-59

Polite decolonization. The peaceful decline of European political and military power in Asia and Africa accelerated in the 1950s. Nearly all of N. Africa was freed by 1956, but France fought a bitter war to retain Algeria, with its large European minority, until 1962. **Ghana**, independent 1957, led a parade of new black African nations (over 2 dozen by 1962) which altered the political character of the UN. Ethnic disputes often exploded in the new nations after decolonization (UN troops in Cyprus 1964; **Nigeria** civil war 1967-70). Leaders of the new states, mostly sharing socialist ideologies, tried to create an Afro-Asian bloc (Bandung Conf. 1955), but Western economic influence and U.S. political ties remained strong (Baghdad Pact, 1955).

Trade. World trade volume soared, in an atmosphere of monetary stability assured by international accords (**Bretton Woods** 1944). In Europe, economic integration advanced (**European Economic Community** 1957, European Free Trade Association 1960). Comecon (1949) coordinated the economies of Soviet-bloc countries.

U.S. Economic growth produced an abundance of consumer goods (9.3 million motor vehicles sold, 1955). Suburban housing tracts changed life patterns for middle and working classes (Levittown 1946-51). **Eisenhower's** landslide election victories (1952, 1956) reflected consensus politics. Censure of McCarthy (Dec. '54) curbed the political abuse of anti-communism. A system of alliances and military bases bolstered U.S. influence on all continents. Trade and payments surpluses were balanced by overseas investments and foreign aid ($50 billion, 1950-59).

USSR. In the "thaw" after Stalin's death in 1953, relations with the West improved (evacuation of Vienna, Geneva summit conf., both 1955). Repression of scientific and cultural life eased, and many prisoners were freed or rehabilitated culminating in **de-Stalinization** (1956). Khrushchev's leadership aimed at consumer sector growth, but farm production lagged, despite the virgin lands program (from 1954). The 1956 Hungarian revolution, the 1960 U-2 spy plane episode, and other incidents renewed East-West tension and domestic curbs.

East Europe. Resentment of Russian domination and Stalinist repression combined with nationalist, economic and religious factors to produce periodic violence. East Berlin workers rioted in 1953, Polish workers rioted in Poznan, June 1956, and a broad-based revolution broke out in Hungary, Oct. 1956. All were suppressed by Soviet force or threats (at least 7,000 dead in Hungary). But Poland was allowed to restore private ownership of farms, and a degree of personal and economic freedom returned to Hungary. Yugoslavia experimented with worker self-management and a market economy.

Korea. The 1945 division of Korea left industry in the North, which was organized into a militant regime and armed by Russia. The South was politically disunited. Over 60,000 North Korean troops invaded the South June 25, 1950. The U.S., backed by the UN Security Council, sent troops. UN troops reached the Chinese border in Nov. Some 200,000 Chinese troops crossed the Yalu River and drove back UN forces. Cease-fire in July 1951 found the opposing forces near the original 38th parallel border. After 2 years of sporadic fighting, an armistice was signed July 27, 1953. U.S. troops remained in the South, and U.S. economic and military aid continued. The war stimulated rapid economic recovery in Japan.

China. Starting in 1952, industry, agriculture, and social institutions were forcibly collectivized. As many as several million people were executed as Kuomintang supporters or as class and political enemies. The Great Leap Forward, 1958-60, unsuccessfully tried to force the pace of development by substituting labor for investment.

Indochina. Ho's forces, aided by Russia and the new Chinese Communist government, fought French and pro-French Vietnamese forces to a standstill, and captured the strategic Dienbienphu camp in May, 1954. The Geneva Agreements divided Vietnam in half pending elections (never held), and recognized Laos and Cambodia as independent, The U.S. aided the anti-Communist Republic of Vietnam in the South.

Middle East. Arab revolutions placed leftist, militantly nationalist regimes in power in Egypt (1952) and Iraq (1958). But Arab unity attempts failed (United Arab Republic joined Egypt, Syria, Yemen 1958-61). Arab refusal to recognize Israel (Arab League economic blockade began Sept. 1951) led to a permanent state of war, with repeated incidents (Gaza, 1955). Israel occupied Sinai, Britain and France took the Suez Canal, Oct. 1956, but were replaced by the UN Emergency Force. The Mossadegh government in Iran nationalized the British-owned oil industry May 1951, but was overthrown in a U.S.-aided coup Aug. 1953.

Latin America. Dictator Juan Peron, in office 1946, enforced land reform, some nationalization, welfare state measures, and curbs on the Roman Catholic Church, but crushed opposition. A Sept. 1955 coup deposed Peron. The 1952 revolution in Bolivia brought land reform, nationalization of tin mines, and improvement in the status of Indians, who nevertheless remained poor. The Batista regime in Cuba was overthrown, Jan. 1959, by Fidel Castro, who imposed a communist dictatorship, aligned Cuba with Russia, improved education and health care. A U.S.-backed anti-Castro invasion (Bay of Pigs, Apr. 1961) was crushed. Self-government advanced in the British Caribbean.

Technology. Large outlays on research and development in the U.S. and USSR focussed on military applications (H-bomb in U.S. 1952, USSR 1953, Britain 1957, intercontinental missiles late 1950s). Soviet launching of the Sputnik satellite, Oct. 1957, spurred increases in U.S. science education funds (National Defense Education Act).

Literature and letters. Alienation from social and literary conventions reached an extreme in the theater of the absurd (Beckett's *Waiting for Godot* 1952), the "new novel" (Robbe-Grillet's *Voyeur* 1955), and avant-garde film (Antonioni's *L'Avventura* 1960). U.S. Beatniks (Kerouac's *On the Road* 1957) and others rejected the supposed conformism of Americans (Riesman's *Lonely Crowd* 1950).

1958

Castro in Cuba

Sino-Soviet split begins

Man in Space

Berlin Wall

Algeria indep.

Silent Spring

March on Wash.

Feminine Mystique

JFK killed

Diem deposed

Tonkin Gulf res.

Indonesia coup

China Cult. Rev.

GATT

Mideast War

U.S. in Vietnam

1968

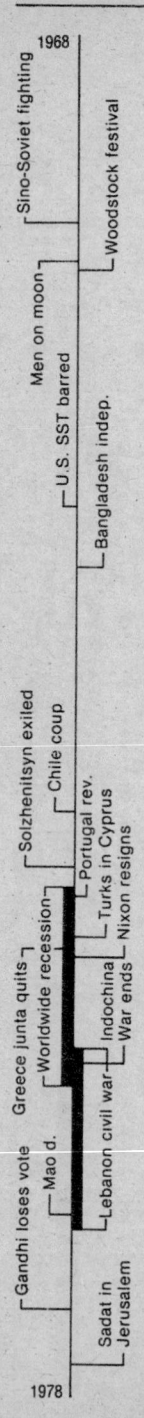

Rising Expectations: 1960-69

Economic boom. The longest sustained economic boom on record spanned almost the entire decade in the capitalist world; the closely-watched GNP figure doubled in the U.S. 1960-70, fueled by Vietnam War-related budget deficits. The **General Agreement on Tariffs and Trade,** 1967, stimulated West European prosperity, which spread to peripheral areas (Spain, Italy, E. Germany). Japan became a top economic power ($20 billion exports 1970). Foreign investment aided the industrialization of Brazil. Soviet 1965 economic reform attempts (decentralization, material incentives) were limited; but growth continued.

Reform and radicalization. A series of political and social reform movements took root in the U.S., later spreading to other countries with the help of ubiquitous U.S. film and television programs and heavy overseas travel (2.2 million U.S. passports issued 1970). Blacks agitated peaceably and with partial success against segregation and poverty (1963 March on Washington, 1964 **Civil Rights Act**); but some urban ghettos erupted in extensive riots (Watts, 1965; Detroit, 1967; King assassination, Apr. 4, 1968). New concern for the poor (Harrington's *Other America,* 1963) led to Pres. Johnson's **"Great Society"** programs (Medicare, Water Quality Act, Higher Education Act, all 1965). Concern with the environment surged (Carson's *Silent Spring,* 1962). **Feminism** revived as a cultural and political movement (Friedan's *Feminine Mystique,* 1963, National Organization for Women founded 1966) and a movement for homosexual rights emerged (Stonewall riot, in NYC, 1969).

Opposition to U.S. involvement in Vietnam, especially among university students (**Moratorium** protest Nov. '69) turned violent (Weatherman Chicago riots Oct. '69). New Left and Marxist theories became popular, and membership in radical groups swelled (Students for a Democratic Society, Black Panthers). Maoist groups, especially in Europe, called for total transformation of society. In France, students sparked a nationwide strike affecting 10 million workers May-June '68, but an electoral reaction barred revolutionary change.

Arts and styles. The boundary between fine and popular arts were blurred by Pop Art (Warhol) and rock musicals (Hair, 1968). Informality and exaggeration prevailed in fashion (beards, miniskirts). A non-political "counterculture" developed, rejecting traditional bourgeois life goals and personal habits, and use of marijuana and hallucinogens spread (Woodstock festival Aug. '69). Indian influence was felt in music (Beatles), religion (Ram Dass), and fashion.

Science. Achievements in space (men on moon July '69) and electronics (lasers, integrated circuits) encouraged a faith in scientific solutions to problems in agriculture ("green revolution"), medicine (heart transplants 1967) and other areas. The harmful effects of science, it was believed, could be controlled (1963 nuclear weapon test ban treaty, 1968 non-proliferation treaty).

China. Mao's revolutionary militance caused disputes with Russia under "revisionist" Khrushchev, starting 1960. The two powers exchanged fire in 1969 border disputes. China used force to capture areas disputed with India, 1962. The "Great Proletarian Cultural Revolution" tried to impose a utopian egalitarian program in China and spread revolution abroad; political struggle, often violent, convulsed China 1965-68.

Indochina. Communist-led guerrillas aided by N. Vietnam fought from 1960 against the S. Vietnam government of Ngo Dinh Diem (killed 1963). The U.S. military role increased after the 1964 Tonkin Gulf incident. U.S. forces peaked at 543,400, Apr. '69. Massive numbers of N. Viet troops also fought. Laotian and Cambodian neutrality were threatened by communist insurgencies, with N. Vietnamese aid, and U.S. intrigues.

Third World. A bloc of authoritarian leftist regimes among the newly independent nations emerged in political opposition to the U.S.-led Western alliance, and came to dominate the conference of nonaligned nations (Belgrade 1961, Cairo 1964, Lusaka 1970). Soviet political ties and military bases were established in Cuba, Egypt, Algeria, Guinea, and other countries, whose leaders were regarded as revolutionary heros by opposition groups in pro-Western or colonial countries. Some leaders were ousted in coups by pro-Western groups—Zaire's Lumumba (killed 1961), Ghana's Nkrumah (exiled 1966), and Indonesia's Sukarno (effectively ousted 1965 after a Communist coup failed).

Middle East. Arab-Israeli tension erupted into a brief war June 1967. Israel emerged as a major regional power. Military shipments before and after the war brought much of the Arab world into the Soviet political sphere. Most Arab states broke U.S. diplomatic ties, while Communist countries cut their ties to Israel. Intra-Arab disputes continued: Egypt and Saudi Arabia supported rival factions in a bloody Yemen civil war 1962-70; Lebanese troops fought Palestinian commandos in 1969.

East Europe. To stop the large-scale exodus of citizens, E. German authorities built a fortified wall across Berlin Aug. '61. Soviet sway in the Balkans was weakened by Albania's support of China (USSR broke ties Dec. '61) and Romania's assertion of industrial and foreign policy autonomy in 1964. Liberalization in Czechoslovakia, spring 1968, was crushed by troops of 5 Warsaw Pact countries. West German treaties with Russia and Poland, 1970, facilitated the transfer of German technology and confirmed post-war boundaries.

Disillusionment: 1970-79

U.S.: Caution and neoconservatism. A relatively sluggish economy, energy and resource shortages (natural gas crunch 1975, gasoline shortage 1979), and environmental problems contributed to a "limits of growth" philosophy. Suspicion of science and technology killed or delayed major projects (supersonic transport dropped 1971, DNA recombination curbed 1976, Seabrook A-plant protests 1977-78) and was fed by the Three Mile Island nuclear reactor accident in Mar. '79.

Mistrust of big government weakened support for government reform plans among liberals. School busing and racial quotas were opposed (Bakke decision June '78); the Equal Rights Amendment for women languished; civil rights for homosexuals were opposed (Dade County referendum June '77).

Completion of communist forces' takeover of So. Vietnam (evacuation of U.S. civilians Apr. '75), revelations of Central Intelligence Agency misdeeds (Rockefeller Commission report June '75), and the **Watergate** scandals (Nixon quit Aug. '74) reduced faith in U.S. moral and material capacity to influence world affairs. Revelations of Soviet crimes (Solzhenitsyn's *Gulag Archipelago* from 1974) and Russian intervention in Africa aided a revival of anti-Communist sentiment.

Economy sluggish. The 1960s boom faltered in the 1970s; a severe recession in the U.S. and Europe 1974-75 followed a huge oil price hike Dec. '73. Monetary instability (U.S. cut ties to gold Aug. '71), the decline of the dollar, and protectionist moves by industrial countries (1977-78) threatened trade. Business investment and spending for research declined. Severe inflation plagued many countries (25% in Britain, 1975; 18% in U.S., 1979).

China picks up pieces. After the 1976 deaths of Mao and Chou, a power struggle for the leadership succession was won by pragmatists. A nationwide purge of orthodox Maoists was carried out, and the "Gang of Four", led by Mao's widow Chiang Ching, was arrested.

The new leaders freed over 100,000 political prisoners, and reduced public adulation of Mao. Political and trade ties were expanded with Japan, Europe, and the U.S. in the late 1970's, as relations worsened with Russia, Cuba, and Vietnam (4-week invasion by China in 1979). Ideological guidelines in industry, science, education, and the armed forces, which the ruling faction said had caused chaos and decline, were reversed (bonuses to workers, Dec. '77; exams for college entrance, Oct. '77). Severe restrictions on cultural expression were eased (Beethoven ban lifted Mar. '77).

Europe. European unity moves (EEC-EFTA trade accord 1972) faltered as economic problems appeared (Britain floated pound 1972; France floated franc 1974). Germany and Switzerland curbed guest workers from S. Europe. Greece and Turkey quarreled over Cyprus (Turks intervened 1974) and Aegean oil rights.

All of non-Communist Europe was under democratic rule after free elections were held in Spain June '76, 7 months after the death of Franco. The conservative, colonialist regime in Portugal was overthrown Apr. '74. In Greece, the 7-year-old military dictatorship yielded power in 1974. Northern Europe, though ruled mostly by Socialists (Swedish Socialists unseated 1976, after 44 years in power), turned conservative. The British Labour government imposed wage curbs 1975, and suspended nationalization schemes. Terrorism in Germany (1972 Munich Olympics killings) led to laws curbing some civil liberties. French "new philosophers" rejected leftist ideologies, and the shaky Socialist-Communist coalition lost a 1978 election bid.

Religion back in politics. The improvement in Moslem countries' political fortunes by the 1950s (with the exception of Central Asia under Soviet and Chinese rule), and the growth of Arab oil wealth, was followed by a resurgence of traditional piety. Libyan dictator Qaddafi mixed strict Islamic laws with socialism in his militant ideology and called for an eventual Moslem return to Spain and Sicily. The illegal Moslem Brotherhood in Egypt was accused of violence, while extreme Moslem groups bombed theaters, 1977, to protest secular values.

In Turkey, the National Salvation Party was the first Islamic group to share power (1974) since secularization in the 1920s. Religious authorities, such as Ayatollah Ruholla Khomeini, led the Iranian revolution and religiously motivated Moslems took part in the insurrection in Saudi Arabia that briefly seized the Grand Mosque in Mecca in 1979. Moslem puritan opposition to Pakistan Pres. Bhutto helped lead to his overthrow July '77. However, Moslem solidarity could not prevent Pakistan's eastern province (Bangladesh) from declaring independence, Dec. '71, after a bloody civil war.

Moslem and Hindu resentment against coerced sterilization in India helped defeat the Gandhi government, which was replaced Mar. '77 by a coalition including religious Hindu parties and led by devout Hindu Desai. Moslems in the southern Philippines, aided by Libya, conducted a long rebellion against central rule from 1973.

Evangelical Protestant groups grew in numbers and prosperity in the U.S. ("born again" Pres. Carter elected 1976), and the Catholic charismatic movement obtained respectability. A revival of interest in Orthodox Christianity occurred among Russian intellectuals (Solzhenitsyn). The secularist Israeli Labor party, after decades of rule, was ousted in 1977 by conservatives led by Begin, an observant Jew; religious militants founded settlements on the disputed West Bank, part of Biblically-promised Israel. U.S. Reform Judaism revived many previously discarded traditional practices.

The Buddhist Soka Gakkai movement launched the Komeito party in Japan, 1964, which became a major opposition party in 1972 and 1976 elections.

Old-fashioned religious wars raged intermittently in N. Ireland (Catholic vs. Protestant, 1969-   ) and Lebanon (Christian vs. Moslem, 1975-   ), while religious militancy complicated the Israel-Arab dispute (1973 Israel-Arab war). In spite of a 1979 peace treaty between Egypt and Israel which looked forward to a resolution of the Palestinian issue, increased religious militancy on the West Bank made such a resolution seem unlikely.

Latin America. Repressive conservative regimes strengthened their hold on most of the continent, with the violent coup against the elected Allende government in Chile, Sept. '73, the 1976 military coup in Argentina, and coups against reformist regimes in Bolivia, 1971 and 1979, and Peru, 1976. In Central America, increasing liberal and leftist militancy led to the ouster of the Somoza regime of Nicaragua in 1979 and civil conflict in El Salvador.

Indochina. Communist victory in Vietnam, Cambodia, and Laos by May '75 did not bring peace. Attempts at radical social reorganization left over one million dead in Cambodia during 1975-78 and caused hundreds of thousands of ethnic Chinese and others to flee Vietnam ("boat people," 1979). The Vietnamese invasion of Cambodia swelled the refugee population and contributed to widespread starvation in that devastated country.

Russian expansion. Soviet influence, checked in some countries (troops ousted by Egypt 1972) was projected further afield, often with the use of Cuban troops (Angola 1975-89, Ethiopia 1977-88), and aided by a growing navy, merchant fleet, and international banking ability. Detente with the West — 1972 Berlin pact, 1972 strategic arms pact (SALT) — gave way to a more antagonistic relationship in the late 1970s, exacerbated by the Soviet invasion of Afghanistan in 1979.

Africa. The last remaining European colonies were granted independence (Spanish Sahara 1976, Djibouti 1977) and, after 10 years of civil war and many negotiation sessions, a black government took over Zimbabwe (Rhodesia) in 1979; white domination remained in S. Africa. Great power involvement in local wars (Russia in Angola, Ethiopia; France in Chad, Zaire, Mauritania) and the use of tens of thousands of Cuban troops was denounced by some African leaders as neocolonialism. Ethnic or tribal clashes made Africa the chief world locus of sustained warfare in the late 1970s.

Arts. Traditional modes in painting, architecture, and music, pursued in relative obscurity for much of the 20th century, returned to popular and critical attention in the 1970s. The pictorial emphasis in neorealist and photorealist painting, the return of many architects to detail, decoration, and traditional natural materials, and the concern with ordered structure in musical composition were, ironically, novel experiences for artistic consumers after the exhaustion of experimental possibilities. However, these more conservative styles coexisted with modernist works in an atmosphere of variety and tolerance.

1980-1985

Rise of terrorism. Following the overthrow of the Shah, Iranian militants, with the support of Ayatollah Kohmeini, held 52 Americans hostage in Iran for 444 days, 1980-81; a TNT-laden suicide terrorist blew up Marine headquarters in Beirut, killing 241 Americans, while a truck bomb blew up a French paratroop barracks, killing 58, 1983; 1985 saw almost 700 terrorist attacks worldwide, including attacks in London, Paris, Rome, Vienna.

Assassinations included Egypt's Pres. Anwar el-Sadat by Moslem extremists (1981); India's Prime Minister Indira Gandhi by Sikh extremists (1984).

Anti-nuclear movement. Western Europe saw widespread anti-nuclear protests from the early 1980s. The U.S. nuclear freeze movement began in 1981; more than 500,000 people demonstrated in New York's Central Park (1982).

U.S.: Economic recession, recovery. Double-digit inflation, high unemployment, and a severe drop in industrial output strongly influenced Pres. Jimmy Carter's defeat and the election of former Calif. Gov. Ronald Reagan as U.S. President, 1980. With Reagan's supply-side economic program, interest rates and inflation decreased by 1983. The recovery was largely responsible for Reagan's landslide re-election, 1984, but that year the **deficit** was over $200 billion, and U.S. debt had doubled under Reagan to $2 trillion.

Technological advances, problems. From 1982-1985, 5 people were implanted with artificial hearts. Only 2 did not suffer strokes and other setbacks and these 2 died.

U.S.S.R. 1980-85 were troublesome years, with 3 consecutive heads of state dying in office (Brezhnev,'82; Andropov, '84; Chernenko,'85); a sluggish domestic economy, dissent dealt with harshly (Nobel Peace Prize winner Sakharov's exile to Gorky, 1980); emigration restricted for Jews, others. With the invasion of Afghanistan (Dec.'79), U.S. Pres. Carter embargoed grain sales, led a boycott of Moscow Olympics (1980); Pres. Reagan lifted the embargo (1981), but **mutual mistrust** and **recrimination** continued, climaxing with 1983 Soviet shooting down of an unarmed South Korean commercial airliner, killing 260, and U.S.-led worldwide condemnation. Soviets led most Eastern European nations in a boycott of Los Angeles Olympics (1984). In 1985, the economy improved slightly; Chernenko's successor, Mikhail Gorbachev, met with Pres. Reagan.

Poland. 17,000 Polish workers, embittered by food shortages, insufficient housing and public transport, went on strike (Aug.'80); they were joined by 120,000 other workers, and won the right to strike, to form independent trade unions, the release of political prisoners, and the end of government censorship. The unions formed a national body headed by Lech Walesa by 1981, 1 million of 2.9 million Polish Communist Party members joined the 9.5-million-member **Solidarity.** But the union's call (Dec.'81) for a referendum on establishing a non-Communist government brought martial law, detention of Walesa; the U.S. imposed economic sanctions. In 1982, Parliament dissolved the unions, Walesa was released as a "private person, " martial law was ended. Walesa was awarded the Nobel Peace Prize. (Oct.'83).

The Middle East. This area remained the most militarily unstable in the world, with sharp divisions on economic, political, racial, and religious issues. In **Iran**, the revolution (1979-80) and violent political upheavals afterward, brought virtual civil war. A dispute with Iraq over the Shatt al-Arab waterway became open warfare, Sept.'80, with no end in sight in 1985.

Libya's support for international terrorism caused the U.S. to close their diplomatic mission in Washington (May '81). American jets shot down 2 Libyan warplanes off Libya after being fired on (Aug.'81). Pres. Reagan embargoed Libyan oil (Mar.'82). The U.S. accused **Muammar al-Qaddafi** of aiding terrorists in Dec.'85 Rome and Vienna airport attacks.

Israel affirmed all of Jerusalem as its capital (July'80); destroyed an Iraqi atomic reactor (1981); invaded Lebanon (1982), bringing the PLO to agree to withdraw peacefully. Christian militia killed more than 600 Palestinians at refugee camps in West Beirut (1982). Israeli withdrawal from **Lebanon** began in Feb.'85 and ended in June'85, as Lebanon continued to be torn with military and political conflict between rival factions.

Central America. In **Nicaragua**, the leftist Sandinista National Liberation Front, in power after the 1979 civil war, faced increasing problems because of Nicaragua's military aid to leftist guerrillas in El Salvador and the U.S. backing of antigovernment forces, or **"contras,"** based in Honduras and Costa Rica. The U.S. CIA admitted to directing the mining of Nicaraguan ports (1984). In 1985, the House rejected Pres. Reagan's request for military aid to the contras, but okayed $26 million in humanitarian aid. In **El Salvador**, a military coup (Oct.'79) failed to halt extreme right-wing violence and left-wing activity. Archbishop Oscar Romero was assassinated (Mar.'80), allegedly by rightists, and from Jan. to June, 1980 some 4,000 civilians reportedly were killed. U.S. support for the government was based on a declared commitment to land reform and human rights. From 1981, right-wing activity was increasingly directed not just against the left but against the junta, which received increasing U.S. military and economic aid. In 1984, the newly elected Pres. José Napoleón Duarte issued more humane codes of conduct to the Army, investigated alleged human rights abuses, and disbanded the military police's intelligence unit; the U.S. then approved $126 million in military aid.

Africa. 1980-85 marked the rapid decline of the economies of virtually all of Africa's 61 countries, due to accelerating desertification, the world economic recession, heavy indebtedness to overseas creditors, rapid population growth, and political instability. In 1981, 60 million Africans, almost one-fifth of the population, faced prolonged hunger. In 1983, a large part of the continent experienced one of the worst droughts ever, and by year's end, 150 million faced near-**famine**; 2 of 5 Africans in 24 countries were affected. In Nov.'85, the U.S. and many Western nations rushed assistance. Economic hardship fueled political unrest, influencing many political coups and attempted coups.

South Africa. Anti-apartheid sentiment gathered force. In 1981, the U.N. General Assembly voted against allowing South Africa to reoccupy the seat it was denied in 1974. In South Africa, anti-apartheid demonstrations grew, as did a violent response from the police. From 1983, **anti-apartheid protests** increased in the U.S. and Europe. South African white voters approved a constitution (Nov.'83) that for the first time gave "Coloureds" and Asians a limited voice, while still excluding Blacks—70% of the population. Bishop Desmond Tutu, a South African black, was awarded the Nobel Peace Price (Oct.'84). The South African government declared a state of emergency in July'85; Pres. Reagan imposed economic sanctions, Aug.'85; in Sept., 11 Western European nations imposed sanctions.

China. From 1980-85 the new leadership of the Chinese Communist Party, under Chairman Deng Xiaoping, pursued far-reaching changes in political and economic institutions and expanded China's commercial and technical ties to the industrialized world. A major effort was made to increase the role of market forces in stimulating urban economic development.

Japan. Relations with the U.S., Western Europe, and the Assn. of Southeast Asian Nations, 1980-85, were dominated by trade imbalances favoring Japan. Japanese automakers heeded U.S. criticism, agreeing to voluntary restraints (1984), but postponed negotiations over tariff reduction on imports. In 1984, Japan had achieved a record annual trade surplus, with U.S. exports of $60 billion. Pres. Reagan pressed for increased imports, and Japan reduced tariffs on 1,790 items.

In history's worst industrial accident, methyl isocyanate, a deadly gas, leaked from a Union Carbide plant at Bhopal, **India** (Dec.'84), killing more than 2,500.

Britain. In 1980, the British economy had its worst **recession** since the 1930s. A 13-week strike in the nationalized steel industry ended with a 15.5% wage rise. Prime Minister Margaret Thatcher trusted the British economy to the discipline of market forces, while unemployment continued to rise and black and white inner-city youths rioted (1981). The Natl. Union of Mineworkers year-long strike (1984-85) ended with the Natl. Coal Board's plan to close 20 "uneconomic" pits.

France elected its first socialist president, Francois Mitterand, in May '81; in Sept.'81 the government nationalized 5 major industries and most private banks. Italy elected its first socialist premier, Bettino Craxi, in June '83. **Greece** was reintegrated into the military wing of NATO in Oct.'80, and became the 10th full member of the European Community in Jan.'81.

HISTORICAL FIGURES

Ancient Greeks and Latins

Greeks

Aeschines, orator, 389-314BC.
Aeschylus, dramatist, 525-456BC.
Aesop, fableist, c620-c560BC.
Alcibiades, politician, 450-404BC.
Anacreon, poet, c582-c485BC.
Anaxagoras, philosopher, c500-428BC.
Anaximander, philosopher, 611-546BC.
Antiphon, speechwriter, c480-411BC.
Apollonius, mathematician, c265-170BC.
Archimedes, math. c287-212BC.
Aristophanes, dramatist, c448-380BC.
Aristotle, philosopher, 384-322BC.
Athenaeus, scholar, fl.c200.
Callicrates, architect, fl.5th cent.BC.
Callimachus, poet, c305-240BC.
Cratinus, comic dramatist, 520-421BC.
Democritus, philosopher, c460-370BC.
Demosthenes, orator, 384-322BC.
Diodorus, historian, fl.20BC.
Diogenes, philosopher, c372-c287BC.

Dionysius, historian, d.c7BC.
Empedocles, philosopher, c490-430BC.
Epicharmus, dramatist, c530-440BC.
Epictetus, philosopher, c55-c135.
Epicurus, philosopher, 341-270BC.
Eratosthenes, scientist, c276-194BC.
Euclid, mathematician, fl.c300BC.
Euripides, dramatist, c484-406BC.
Galen, physician, c129-199.
Heraclitus, philosopher, c535-c475BC.
Herodotus, historian, c484-420BC.
Hesiod, poet, 8th cent. BC.
Hippocrates, physician, c460-377BC.
Homer, poet, believed lived c850BC.
Isocrates, orator, 436-338BC.
Menander, dramatist, 342-292BC.
Phidias, sculptor, c500-435BC.
Pindar, poet, c518-c438BC.
Plato, philosopher, c428-c347BC.
Plutarch, biographer, c46-120.

Polybius, historian, c200-c118BC.
Praxiteles, sculptor, 400-330BC.
Pythagoras, phil., math., c580-c500BC.
Sappho, poet, c610-c580BC.
Simonides, poet, 556-c468BC.
Socrates, philosopher, c470-399BC.
Solon, statesman, 640-560BC.
Sophocles, dramatist, C496-406BC.
Strabo, geographer, c63BC-AD24.
Thales, philosopher, c634-c546BC.
Themistocles, politician, c524-c460BC.
Theocritus, poet, c310-250BC.
Theophrastus, phil. c372-c287BC.
Thucydides, historian, fl.5th cent.BC.
Timon, philosopher, c320-c230BC.
Xenophon, historian, c434-c355BC.
Zeno, philosopher, c495-c430BC.

Latins

Ammianus, historian, c330-395.
Apuleius, satirist, c124-c170.
Boethius, scholar, c480-524
Caesar, Julius, general, 100-44BC.
Catilina, politician, c108-62BC.
Cato(Elder), statesman, 234-149BC.
Catullus, poet, c84-54BC.
Cicero, orator, 106-43BC.
Claudian, poet, c370-c404.
Ennius, poet, 239-170BC.
Gellius, author, c130-c165.
Horace, poet, 65-8BC.

Juvenal, satirist, c60-c127.
Livy, historian, 59BC-AD17.
Lucan, poet, 39-65.
Lucilius, poet, c180-c102BC.
Lucretius, poet, c99-c55BC.
Martial, epigrammatist, c38-c103.
Nepos, historian, c100-c25BC.
Ovid, poet, 43BC-AD17.
Persius, satirist, 34-62.
Plautus, dramatist, c254-c184BC.
Pliny, scholar, 23-79.
Pliny(Younger), author, 62-113.

Quintilian, rhetorician, c35-c97.
Sallust, historian, 86-34BC.
Seneca, philosopher, 4BC-AD65.
Silius, poet, c25-101.
Statius, poet, c45-c96.
Suetonius, biographer, c69-c122.
Tacitus, historian, c56-c120.
Terence, dramatist, 185-159BC.
Tibullus, poet, c55-c19BC.
Virgil, poet, 70-19BC.
Vitruvius, architect, fl.1st cent.BC.

Rulers of England and Great Britain

Name	England	Began	Died	Age	Rgd
	Saxons and Danes				
Egbert	King of Wessex, won allegiance of all English	829	839	—	10
Ethelwulf	Son, King of Wessex, Sussex, Kent, Essex	839	858	—	19
Ethelbald	Son of Ethelwulf, displaced father in Wessex	858	860	—	2
Ethelbert	2d son of Ethelwulf, united Kent and Wessex	860	866	—	6
Ethelred I	3d son, King of Wessex, fought Danes	866	871	—	5
Alfred	The Great, 4th son, defeated Danes, fortified London	871	899	52	28
Edward	The Elder, Alfred's son, united English, claimed Scotland	899	924	55	25
Athelstan	The Glorious, Edward's son, King of Mercia, Wessex	924	940	45	16
Edmund I	3d son of Edward, King of Wessex, Mercia	940	946	25	6
Edred	4th son of Edward	946	955	32	9
Edwy	The Fair, eldest son of Edmund, King of Wessex	955	959	18	3
Edgar	The Peaceful, 2d son of Edmund, ruled all English	959	975	32	17
Edward	The Martyr, eldest son of Edgar, murdered by stepmother	975	978	17	4
Ethelred II	The Unready, 2d son of Edgar, married Emma of Normandy	978	1016	48	37
Edmund II	Ironside, son of Ethelred II, King of London	1016	1016	27	0
Canute	The Dane, gave Wessex to Edmund, married Emma	1016	1035	40	19
Harold I	Harefoot, natural son of Canute	1035	1040	—	5
Hardecanute	Son of Canute by Emma, Danish King	1040	1042	24	2
Edward	The Confessor, son of Ethelred II (Canonized 1161)	1042	1066	62	24
Harold II	Edward's brother-in-law, last Saxon King	1066	1066	44	0
	House of Normandy				
William I	The Conqueror, defeated Harold at Hastings	1066	1087	60	21
William II	Rufus, 3d son of William I, killed by arrow	1087	1100	43	13
Henry I	Beauclerc, youngest son of William I	1100	1135	67	35
	House of Blois				
Stephen	Son of Adela, daughter of William I, and Count of Blois	1135	1154	50	19
	House of Plantagenet				
Henry II	Son of Geoffrey Plantagenet (Angevin) by Matilda, dau. of Henry I	1154	1189	56	35
Richard I	Coeur de Lion, son of Henry II, crusader	1189	1199	42	10
John	Lackland, son of Henry II, signed Magna Carta, 1215	1199	1216	50	17
Henry III	Son of John, acceded at 9, under regency until 1227	1216	1272	65	56
Edward I	Longshanks, son of Henry III	1272	1307	68	35
Edward II	Son of Edward I, deposed by Parliament, 1327	1307	1327	43	20
Edward III	Of Windsor, son of Edward II	1327	1377	65	50
Richard II	Grandson of Edw. III, minor until 1389, deposed 1399	1377	1400	33	22
	House of Lancaster				
Henry IV	Son of John of Gaunt, Duke of Lancaster, son of Edw. III	1399	1413	47	13
Henry V	Son of Henry IV, victor of Agincourt	1413	1422	34	9
Henry VI	Son of Henry V, deposed 1461, died in Tower	1422	1471	49	39

Name		Began	Died	Age	Rgd
House of York					
Edward IV	Great-great-grandson of Edward III, son of Duke of York	1461	1483	41	22
Edward V	Son of Edward IV, murdered in Tower of London	1483	1483	13	0
Richard III	Crookback, bro. of Edward IV, fell at Bosworth Field	1483	1485	35	2
House of Tudor					
Henry VII	Son of Edmund Tudor, Earl of Richmond, whose father had married the widow of Henry V; descended from Edward III through his mother, Margaret Beaufort via John of Gaunt. By marriage with dau. of Edward IV he united Lancaster and York	1485	1509	53	24
Henry VIII	Son of Henry VII by Elizabeth, dau. of Edward IV.	1509	1547	56	38
Edward VI	Son of Henry VIII, by Jane Seymour, his 3d queen. Ruled under regents. Was forced to name Lady Jane Grey his successor. Council of State proclaimed her queen July 10, 1553. Mary Tudor won Council, was proclaimed queen July 19, 1553. Mary had Lady Jane Grey beheaded for treason, Feb., 1554	1547	1553	16	6
Mary I	Daughter of Henry VIII, by Catherine of Aragon	1553	1558	43	5
Elizabeth I	Daughter of Henry VIII, by Anne Boleyn	1558	1603	69	44

Great Britain
House of Stuart

Name		Began	Died	Age	Rgd
James I	James VI of Scotland, son of Mary, Queen of Scots. *First to call himself King of Great Britain. This became official with the Act of Union, 1707*	1603	1625	59	22
Charles I	Only surviving son of James I; beheaded Jan. 30, 1649	1625	1649	48	24

Commonwealth, 1649-1660
Council of State, 1649; Protectorate, 1653

Name		Began	Died	Age	Rgd
The Cromwells	Oliver Cromwell, Lord Protector	1653	1658	59	—
	Richard Cromwell, son, Lord Protector, resigned May 25, 1659	1658	1712	86	—

House of Stuart (Restored)

Name		Began	Died	Age	Rgd
Charles II	Eldest son of Charles I, died without issue	1660	1685	55	25
James II	2d son of Charles I. Deposed 1688. Interregnum Dec. 11, 1688, to Feb. 13, 1689	1685	1701	68	3
William III	Son of William, Prince of Orange, by Mary, dau. of Charles I	1689	1702	51	13
and Mary II	Eldest daughter of James II and wife of William III		1694	33	6
Anne	2d daughter of James II	1702	1714	49	12

House of Hanover

Name		Began	Died	Age	Rgd
George I	Son of Elector of Hanover, by Sophia, grand-dau. of James I	1714	1727	67	13
George II	Only son of George I, married Caroline of Brandenburg	1727	1760	77	33
George III	Grandson of George II, married Charlotte of Mecklenburg	1760	1820	81	59
George IV	Eldest son of George III, Prince Regent, from Feb., 1811	1820	1830	67	10
William IV	3d son of George III, married Adelaide of Saxe-Meiningen	1830	1837	71	7
Victoria	Dau. of Edward, 4th son of George III; married (1840) Prince Albert of Saxe-Coburg and Gotha, who became Prince Consort	1837	1901	81	63

House of Saxe-Coburg and Gotha

Name		Began	Died	Age	Rgd
Edward VII	Eldest son of Victoria, married Alexandra, Princess of Denmark	1901	1910	68	9

House of Windsor
Name Adopted July 17, 1917

Name		Began	Died	Age	Rgd
George V	2d son of Edward VII, married Princess Mary of Teck	1910	1936	70	25
Edward VIII	Eldest son of George V; acceded Jan. 20, 1936, abdicated Dec. 11	1936	1972	77	1
George VI	2d son of George V; married Lady Elizabeth Bowes-Lyon	1936	1952	56	15
Elizabeth II	Elder daughter of George VI, acceded Feb. 6, 1952	1952	—	—	—

Rulers of Scotland

Kenneth I MacAlpin was the first Scot to rule both Scots and Picts, 846 AD.

Duncan I was the first general ruler, 1034. Macbeth seized the kingdom 1040, was slain by Duncan's son, Malcolm III MacDuncan (Canmore), 1057.

Malcolm married Margaret, Saxon princess who had fled from the Normans. Queen Margaret introduced English language and English monastic customs. She was canonized, 1250. Her son Edgar, 1097, moved the court to Edinburgh. His brothers Alexander I and David I succeeded. Malcolm IV, the Maiden, 1153, grandson of David I, was followed by his brother, William the Lion, 1165, whose son was Alexander II, 1214. The latter's son, Alexander III, 1249, defeated the Norse and regained the Hebrides. When he died, 1286, his granddaughter, Margaret, child of Eric of Norway and grandniece of Edward I of England, known as the Maid of Norway, was chosen ruler, but died 1290, aged 8.

John Baliol, 1292-1296. (Interregnum, 10 years).

Robert Bruce (The Bruce), 1306-1329, victor at Bannockburn, 1314.

David II, only son of Robert Bruce, ruled 1329-1371.

Robert II, 1371-1390, grandson of Robert Bruce, son of Walter, the Steward of Scotland, was called The Steward, first of the so-called Stuart line.

Robert III, son of Robert II, 1390-1406.

James I, son of Robert III, 1406-1437.

James II, son of James I, 1437-1460.

James III, eldest son of James II, 1460-1488.

James IV, eldest son of James III, 1488-1513.

James V, eldest son of James IV, 1513-1542.

Mary, daughter of James V, born 1542, became queen when one week old; was crowned 1543. Married, 1558, Francis, son of Henry II of France, who became king 1559, died 1560. Mary ruled Scots 1561 until abdication, 1567. She also married (2) Henry Stewart, Lord Darnley, and (3) James, Earl of Bothwell. Imprisoned by Elizabeth I, Mary was beheaded 1587.

James VI, 1566-1625, son of Mary and Lord Darnley, became King of England on death of Elizabeth in 1603. Although the thrones were thus united, the legislative union of Scotland and England was not effected until the Act of Union, May 1, 1707.

Prime Ministers of Great Britain

(W = Whig; T = Tory; Cl = Coalition; P = Peelite; L = Liberal; C = Conservative; La = Labour)

Sir Robert Walpole (W)	1721-1742	Earl Russell (L)	1865-1866
Earl of Wilmington (W)	1742-1743	Earl of Derby (C)	1866-1868
Henry Pelham (W)	1743-1754	Benjamin Disraeli (C)	1868
Duke of Newcastle (W)	1754-1756	William E. Gladstone (L)	1868-1874
Duke of Devonshire (W)	1756-1757	Benjamin Disraeli (C)	1874-1880
Duke of Newcastle (W)	1757-1762	William E. Gladstone (L)	1880-1885
Earl of Bute (T)	1762-1763	Marquess of Salisbury (C)	1885-1886
George Grenville (W)	1763-1765	William E. Gladstone (L)	1886
Marquess of Rockingham (W)	1765-1766	Marquess of Salisbury (C).	1886-1892
William Pitt the Elder		William E. Gladstone (L)	1892-1894
(Earl of Chatham) (W)	1766-1768	Earl of Rosebery (L)	1894-1895
Duke of Grafton (W)	1768-1770	Marquess of Salisbury (C)	1895-1902
Frederick North (Lord North) (T)	1770-1782	Arthur J. Balfour (C)	1902-1905
Marquess of Rockingham (W)	1782	Sir Henry Campbell-Bannerman (L)	1905-1908
Earl of Shelburne (W)	1782-1783	Herbert H. Asquith (L)	1908-1915
Duke of Portland (Cl)	1783	Herbert H. Asquith (Cl)	1915-1916
William Pitt the Younger (T)	1783-1801	David Lloyd George (Cl)	1916-1922
Henry Addington (T)	1801-1804	Andrew Bonar Law (C)	1922-1923
William Pitt the Younger (T)	1804-1806	Stanley Baldwin (C)	1923-1924
William Wyndham Grenville,		James Ramsay MacDonald (La)	1924
Baron Grenville (W)	1806-1807	Stanley Baldwin (C)	1924-1929
Duke of Portland (T)	1807-1809	James Ramsay MacDonald (La)	1929-1931
Spencer Perceval (T)	1809-1812	James Ramsay MacDonald (Cl)	1931-1935
Earl of Liverpool (T).	1812-1827	Stanley Baldwin (Cl).	1935-1937
George Canning (T)	1827	Neville Chamberlain (Cl)	1937-1940
Viscount Goderich (T).	1827-1828	Winston Churchill (Cl)	1940-1945
Duke of Wellington (T)	1828-1830	Winston Churchill (C).	1945
Earl Grey (W)	1830-1834	Clement Attlee (La)	1945-1951
Viscount Melbourne (W)	1834	Sir Winston Churchill (C).	1951-1955
Sir Robert Peel (T).	1834-1835	Sir Anthony Eden (C)	1955-1957
Viscount Melbourne (W)	1835-1841	Harold Macmillan (C)	1957-1963
Sir Robert Peel (T).	1841-1846	Sir Alec Douglas-Home (C)	1963-1964
Lord John Russell (later Earl) (W)	1846-1852	Harold Wilson (La)	1964-1970
Earl of Derby (T)	1852	Edward Heath (C)	1970-1974
Earl of Aberdeen (P).	1852-1855	Harold Wilson (La)	1974-1976
Viscount Palmerston (L).	1855-1858	James Callaghan (La)	1976-1979
Earl of Derby (C)	1858-1859	Margaret Thatcher (C).	1979-
Viscount Palmerston (L).	1859-1865		

Prime Ministers of Canada

Canada is a constitutional monarchy with a parliamentary system of government. It is also a federal state. Canada's offical head of state is the King or Queen of England, represented by a resident Governor-General. However, in practice the nation is governed by the Prime Minister, leader of the party that commands the support of a majority of the House of Commons, dominant chamber of Canada's bicameral Parliament.

Name	Party	Term	Name	Party	Term
Sir John A. MacDonald	Conservative	1867-1873			1926-1930
		1878-1891			1935-1948
Alexander Mackenzie	Liberal	1873-1878	R. B. Bennett	Conservative	1930-1935
Sir John J. C. Abbott	Conservative	1891-1892	Louis St. Laurent	Liberal	1948-1957
Sir John S. D. Thompson	Conservative	1892-1894	John G. Diefenbaker	Prog. Cons.	1957-1963
Sir Mackenzie Bowell	Conservative	1894-1896	Lester B. Pearson	Liberal	1963-1968
Sir Charles Tupper.	Conservative	1896	Pierre Elliott Trudeau	Liberal	1968-1979
Sir Wilfrid Laurier	Liberal	1896-1911	Joe Clark	Prog. Cons.	1979-1980
Sir Robert L. Borden	Cons. Union.	1911-1920	Pierre Elliott Trudeau	Liberal	1980-1984
Arthur Meighen	Cons. Union.	1920-1921	John Turner	Liberal	1984
W.L. Mackenzie King	Liberal	1921-1926[1]	Brian Mulroney	Prog. Cons.	1984-

(1) King's term was interrupted from June 26-Sept. 25, 1926, when Arthur Meighen again served as prime minister.

Rulers of France: Kings, Queens, Presidents

Caesar to Charlemagne

Julius Caesar subdued the Gauls, native tribes of Gaul (France) 57 to 52 BC. The Romans ruled 500 years. The Franks, a Teutonic tribe, reached the Somme from the East ca. 250 AD. By the 5th century the Merovingian Franks ousted the Romans. In 451 AD, with the help of Visigoths, Burgundians and others, they defeated Attila and the Huns at Chalons-sur-Marne.

Childeric I became leader of the Merovingians 458 AD. His son Clovis I (Chlodwig, Ludwig, Louis), crowned 481, founded the dynasty. After defeating the Alemanni (Germans) 496, he was baptized a Christian and made Paris his capital. His line ruled until Childeric III was deposed, 751.

The West Merovingians were called Neustrians, the eastern Austrasians. Pepin of Herstal (687-714) major domus, or head of the palace, of Austrasia, took over Neustria as dux (leader) of

the Franks. Pepin's son, Charles, called Martel (the Hammer) defeated the Saracens at Tours-Poitiers, 732; was succeeded by his son, Pepin the Short, 741, who deposed Childeric III and ruled as king until 768.

His son, Charlemagne, or Charles the Great (742-814) became king of the Franks, 768, with his brother Carloman, who died 771. He ruled France, Germany, parts of Italy, Spain, Austria, and enforced Christianity. Crowned Emperor of the Romans by Pope Leo III in St. Peter's, Rome, Dec. 25, 800 AD. Succeeded by son, Louis I the Pious, 814. At death, 840, Louis left empire to sons, Lothair (Roman emperor); Pepin I (king of Aquitaine); Louis II (of Germany); Charles the Bald (France). They quarreled and by the peace of Verdun, 843, divided the empire.

(continued)

AD Name, year of accession

The Carolingians

843   Charles I (the Bald), Roman Emperor, 875
877   Louis II (the Stammerer), son
879   Louis III (died 882) and Carloman, brothers
885   Charles II (the Fat), Roman Emperor, 881
888   Eudes (Odo) elected by nobles
898   Charles III (the Simple), son of Louis II, defeated by
922   Robert, brother of Eudes, killed in war
923   Rudolph (Raoul) Duke of Burgundy
936   Louis IV, son of Charles III
954   Lothair, son, aged 13, defeated by Capet
986   Louis V (the Sluggard), left no heirs

The Capets

987   Hugh Capet, son of Hugh the Great
996   Robert II (the Wise), his son
1031   Henry I, his son
1060   Philip I (the Fair), son
1108   Louis VI (the Fat), son
1137   Louis VII (the Younger), son
1180   Philip II (Augustus), son, crowned at Reims
1223   Louis VIII (the Lion), son
1226   Louis IX, son, crusader; Louis IX (1214-1270) reigned 44 years, arbitrated disputes with English King Henry III; led crusades, 1248 (captured in Egypt 1250) and 1270, when he died of plague in Tunis. Canonized 1297 as St. Louis.
1270   Philip III (the Hardy), son
1285   Philip IV (the Fair), son, king at 17
1314   Louis X (the Headstrong), son. His posthumous son, John I, lived only 7 days
1316   Philip V (the Tall), brother of Louis X
1322   Charles IV (the Fair), brother of Louis X

House of Valois

1328   Philip VI (of Valois), grandson of Philip III
1350   John II (the Good), his son, retired to England
1364   Charles V (the Wise), son
1380   Charles VI (the Beloved), son
1422   Charles VII (the Victorious), son. In 1429 Joan of Arc (Jeanne d'Arc) promised Charles to oust the English, who occupied northern France. Joan won at Orleans and Patay and had Charles crowned at Reims July 17, 1429. Joan was captured May 24, 1430, and executed May 30, 1431, at Rouen for heresy. Charles ordered her rehabilitation, effected 1455.
1461   Louis XI (the Cruel), son, civil reformer
1483   Charles VIII (the Affable), son
1498   Louis XII, great-grandson of Charles V
1515   Francis I, of Angouleme, nephew, son-in-law. Francis I (1494-1547) reigned 32 years, fought 4 big wars, was patron of the arts, aided Cellini, del Sarto, Leonardo da Vinci, Rabelais, embellished Fontainebleau.
1547   Henry II, son, killed at a joust in a tournament. He was the husband of Catherine de Medicis (1519-1589) and the lover of Diane de Poitiers (1499-1566). Catherine was born in Florence, daughter of Lorenzo de Medicis. By her marriage to Henry II she became the mother of Francis II, Charles IX, Henry III and Queen Margaret (Reine Margot) wife of Henry IV. She persuaded Charles IX to order the massacre of Huguenots on the Feast of St. Bartholomew, Aug. 24, 1572, the day her daughter was married to Henry of Navarre.
1559   Francis II, son. In 1548, Mary, Queen of Scots since infancy, was betrothed to Francis, aged 4. They were married 1558. Francis died 1560, aged 16; Mary ruled Scotland, abdicated 1567.
1560   Charles IX, brother
1574   Henry III, brother, assassinated

House of Bourbon

1589   Henry IV, of Navarre, assassinated. Henry IV made enemies when he gave tolerance to Protestants by Edict of Nantes, 1598. He was grandson of Queen Margaret of Navarre, literary patron. He married Margaret of Valois, daughter of Henry II and Catherine de Medicis; was divorced; in 1600 married Marie de Medicis, who became Regent of France, 1610-17 for her son, Louis XIII, but was exiled by Richelieu, 1631.

1610   Louis XIII (the Just), son. Louis XIII (1601-1643) married Anne of Austria. His ministers were Cardinals Richelieu and Mazarin.
1643   Louis XIV (The Grand Monarch), son. Louis XIV was king 72 years. He exhausted a prosperous country in wars for thrones and territory. By revoking the Edict of Nantes (1685) he caused the emigration of the Huguenots. He said: "I am the state."
1715   Louis XV, great-grandson. Louis XV married a Polish princess; lost Canada to the English. His favorites, Mme. Pompadour and Mme. Du Barry, influenced policies. Noted for saying "After me, the deluge".
1774   Louis XVI, grandson; married Marie Antoinette, daughter of Empress Maria Therese of Austria. King and queen beheaded by Revolution, 1793. Their son, called Louis XVII, died in prison, never ruled.

First Republic

1792   National Convention of the French Revolution
1795   Directory, under Barras and others
1799   Consulate, Napoleon Bonaparte, first consul. Elected consul for life, 1802.

First Empire

1804   Napoleon I, emperor. Josephine (de Beauharnais) empress, 1804-09; Marie Louise, empress, 1810-1814. Her son, Francis (1811-1832), titular King of Rome, later Duke de Reichstadt and "Napoleon II," never ruled. Napoleon abdicated 1814, died 1821.

Bourbons Restored

1814   Louis XVIII king; brother of Louis XVI.
1824   Charles X, brother; reactionary; deposed by the July Revolution, 1830.

House of Orleans

1830   Louis-Philippe, the "citizen king."

Second Republic

1848   Louis Napoleon Bonaparte, president, nephew of Napoleon I. He became:

Second Empire

1852   Napoleon III, emperor; Eugenie (de Montijo) empress. Lost Franco-Prussian war, deposed 1870. Son, Prince Imperial (1856-79), died in Zulu War. Eugenie died 1920.

Third Republic—Presidents

1871   Thiers, Louis Adolphe (1797-1877)
1873   MacMahon, Marshal Patrice M. de (1808-1893)
1879   Grevy, Paul J. (1807-1891)
1887   Sadi-Carnot, M. (1837-1894), assassinated
1894   Casimir-Perier, Jean P. P. (1847-1907)
1895   Faure, Francois Felix (1841-1899)
1899   Loubet, Emile (1838-1929)
1906   Fallieres, C. Armand (1841-1931)
1913   Poincare, Raymond (1860-1934)
1920   Deschanel, Paul (1856-1922)
1920   Millerand, Alexandre (1859-1943)
1924   Doumergue, Gaston (1863-1937)
1931   Doumer, Paul (1857-1932), assassinated
1932   Lebrun, Albert (1871-1950), resigned 1940
1940   **Vichy govt.** under German armistice: Henri Philippe Petain (1856-1951) Chief of State, 1940-1944. **Provisional govt.** after liberation: Charles de Gaulle (1890-1970) Oct. 1944-Jan. 21, 1946; Felix Gouin (1884-1977) Jan. 23, 1946; Georges Bidault (1899-1983) June 24, 1946.

Fourth Republic—Presidents

1947   Auriol, Vincent (1884-1966)
1954   Coty, Rene (1882-1962)

Fifth Republic—Presidents

1959   de Gaulle, Charles Andre J. M. (1890-1970)
1969   Pompidou, Georges (1911-1974)
1974   Giscard d'Estaing, Valery (1926-   )
1981   Mitterrand, Francois (1916-   )

Rulers of Middle Europe; Rise and Fall of Dynasties

Carolingian Dynasty

Charles the Great, or Charlemagne, ruled France, Italy, and Middle Europe; established Ostmark (later Austria); crowned Roman emperor by pope in Rome, 800 AD; died 814.

Louis I (Ludwig) the Pious, son; crowned by Charlemagne 814, d. 840.

Louis II, the German, son; succeeded to East Francia (Germany) 843-876.

Charles the Fat, son; inherited East Francia and West Francia (France) 876, reunited empire, crowned emperor by pope, 881, deposed 887.

Arnulf, nephew, 887-899. Partition of empire.

Louis the Child, 899-911, last direct descendant of Charle-magne.

Conrad I, duke of Franconia, first elected German king, 911-918, founded House of Franconia.

Saxon Dynasty; First Reich

Henry I, the Fowler, duke of Saxony, 919-936.

Otto I, the Great, 936-973, son; crowned Holy Roman Em-peror by pope, 962.

Otto II, 973-983, son; failed to oust Greeks and Arabs from Sicily.

Otto III, 983-1002, son; crowned emperor at 16.

Henry II, the Saint, duke of Bavaria, 1002-1024, great-grand-son of Otto the Great.

House of Franconia

Conrad II, 1024-1039, elected king of Germany.

Henry III, the Black, 1039-1056, son; deposed 3 popes; an-nexed Burgundy.

Henry IV, 1056-1106, son; regency by his mother, Agnes of Poitou. Banned by Pope Gregory VII, he did penance at Canossa.

Henry V, 1106-1125, son; last of Salic House.

Lothair, duke of Saxony, 1125-1137. Crowned emperor in Rome, 1134.

House of Hohenstaufen

Conrad III, duke of Swabia, 1138-1152. In 2d Crusade.

Frederick I, Barbarossa, 1152-1190; Conrad's nephew.

Henry VI, 1190-1196, took lower Italy from Normans. Son be-came king of Sicily.

Philip of Swabia, 1197-1208, brother.

Otto IV, or House of Welf, 1198-1215; deposed.

Frederick II, 1215-1250, son of Henry VI; king of Sicily; crowned king of Jerusalem; in 5th Crusade.

Conrad IV, 1250-1254, son; lost lower Italy to Charles of An-jou.

Conradin (1252-1268) son, king of Jerusalem and Sicily, be-headed. Last Hohenstaufen.

Interregnum, 1254-1273, Rise of the Electors.

Transition

Rudolph I of Hapsburg, 1273-1291, defeated King Ottocar II of Bohemia. Bequeathed duchy of Austria to eldest son, Albert.

Adolph of Nassau, 1292-1298, killed in war with Albert of Aus-tria.

Albert I, king of Germany, 1298-1308, son of Rudolph.

Henry VII, of Luxemburg, 1308-1313, crowned emperor in Rome. Seized Bohemia, 1310.

Louis IV of Bavaria (Wittelsbach), 1314-1347. Also elected was Frederick of Austria, 1314-1330 (Hapsburg). Abolition of papal sanction for election of Holy Roman Emperor.

Charles IV, of Luxemburg, 1347-1378, grandson of Henry VII, German emperor and king of Bohemia, Lombardy, Burgundy; took Mark of Brandenburg.

Wenceslaus, 1378-1400, deposed.

Rupert, Duke of Palatine, 1400-1410.

Hungary

Stephen I, house of Arpad, 997-1038. Crowned king 1000; converted Magyars; canonized 1083. After several centuries of feuds Charles Robert of Anjou became Charles I, 1308-1342.

Louis I, the Great, son, 1342-1382; joint ruler of Poland with Casimir III, 1370. Defeated Turks.

Mary, daughter, 1382-1395, ruled with husband. Sigismund of Luxemburg, 1387-1437, also king of Bohemia. As bro. of Wen-ceslaus he succeeded Rupert as Holy Roman Emperor, 1410.

Albert II, 1438-1439, son-in-law of Sigismund; also Roman emperor. (see under Hapsburg.)

Ulaszlo I of Poland, 1440-1444.

Ladislaus V, posthumous son of Albert II, 1444-1457. John Hunyadi (Hunyadi Janos) governor (1446-1452), fought Turks, Czechs; died 1456.

Matthias I (Corvinus) son of Hunyadi, 1458-1490. Shared rule of Bohemia, captured Vienna, 1485, annexed Austria, Styria, Ca-rinthia.

Ladislas II (king of Bohemia), 1490-1516.

Louis II, son, aged 10, 1516-1526. Wars with Suleiman, Turk. In 1527 Hungary was split between Ferdinand I, Archduke of

Austria, bro.-in-law of Louis II, and John Zapolya of Transylvania. After Turkish invasion, 1547, Hungary was split between Ferdi-nand, Prince John Sigismund (Transylvania) and the Turks.

House of Hapsburg

Albert V of Austria, Hapsburg, crowned king of Hungary, Jan. 1438, Roman emperor, March, 1438, as Albert II; died 1439.

Frederick III, cousin, 1440-1493. Fought Turks.

Maximilian I, son, 1493-1519. Assumed title of Holy Roman Emperor (German), 1493.

Charles V, grandson, 1519-1556. King of Spain with mother co-regent; crowned Roman emperor at Aix, 1520. Confronted Luther at Worms; attempted church reform and religious concili-ation; abdicated 1556.

Ferdinand I, king of Bohemia, 1526, of Hungary, 1527; dis-puted. German king, 1531. Crowned Roman emperor on abdica-tion of brother Charles V, 1556.

Maximilian II, son, 1564-1576.

Rudolph II, son, 1576-1612.

Matthias, brother, 1612-1619, king of Bohemia and Hungary.

Ferdinand II of Styria, king of Bohemia, 1617, of Hungary, 1618, Roman emperor, 1619. Bohemian Protestants deposed him, elected Frederick V of Palatine, starting Thirty Years War.

Ferdinand III, son, king of Hungary, 1625, Bohemia, 1627, Ro-man emperor, 1637. Peace of Westphalia, 1648, ended war. Le-opold I, 1658-1705; Joseph I, 1705-1711; Charles VI, 1711-1740.

Maria Theresa, daughter, 1740-1780, Archduchess of Austria, queen of Hungary; ousted pretender, Charles VII, crowned 1742; in 1745 obtained election of her husband Francis I as Roman emperor and co-regent (d. 1765). Fought Seven Years' War with Frederick II (the Great) of Prussia. Mother of Marie Antoinette, Queen of France.

Joseph II, son 1765-1790, Roman emperor, reformer; powers restricted by Empress Maria Theresa until her death, 1780. First partition of Poland. Leopold II, 1790-1792.

Francis II, son, 1792-1835. Fought Napoleon. Proclaimed first hereditary emperor of Austria, 1804. Forced to abdicate as Ro-man emperor, 1806; last use of title. Ferdinand I, son, 1835-1848, abdicated during revolution.

Austro-Hungarian Monarchy

Francis Joseph I, nephew, 1848-1916, emperor of Austria, king of Hungary. Dual monarchy of Austria-Hungary formed, 1867. After assassination of heir, Archduke Francis Ferdinand, June 28, 1914, Austrian diplomacy precipitated World War I.

Charles I, grand-nephew, 1916-1918, last emperor of Austria and king of Hungary. Abdicated Nov. 11-13, 1918, died 1922.

Rulers of Prussia

Nucleus of Prussia was the Mark of Brandenburg. First mar-grave was Albert the Bear (Albrecht), 1134-1170. First Hohen-zollern margrave was Frederick, burgrave of Nuremberg, 1417-1440.

Frederick William, 1640-1688, the Great Elector. Son, Freder-ick III, 1688-1713, was crowned King Frederick of Prussia, 1701.

Frederick William I, son, 1713-1740.

Frederick II, the Great, son, 1740-1786, annexed Silesia part of Austria.

Frederick William II, nephew, 1786-1797.

Frederick William III, son, 1797-1840. Napoleonic wars.

Frederick William IV, son, 1840-1861. Uprising of 1848 and first parliament and constitution.

Second and Third Reich

William I, 1861-1888, brother. Annexation of Schleswig and Hanover; Franco-Prussian war, 1870-71, proclamation of Ger-man Reich, Jan. 18, 1871, at Versailles; William, German em-peror (Deutscher Kaiser), Bismarck, chancellor.

Frederick III, son, 1888.

William II, son, 1888-1918. Led Germany in World War I, abdi-cated as German emperor and king of Prussia, Nov. 9, 1918. Died in exile in Netherlands June 4, 1941. Minor rulers of Ba-varia, Saxony, Wurttemberg also abdicated.

Germany proclaimed a republic at Weimar, July 1, 1919. Pres-idents: Frederick Ebert, 1919-1925, Paul von Hindenburg-Be-neckendorff, 1925, reelected 1932, d. Aug. 2, 1934. Adolf Hitler, chancellor, chosen successor as Leader-Chancellor (Fuehrer & Reichskanzler) of Third Reich. Annexed Austria, March, 1938. Precipitated World War II, 1939-1945. Committed suicide April 30, 1945.

Rulers of Poland

House of Piasts

Miesko I, 962?-992; Poland Christianized 966. Expansion un-der 3 Boleslavs: I, 992-1025, son, crowned king 1024; II,

1058-1079, great-grandson, exiled after killing bishop Stanislav who became chief patron saint of Poland: III, 1106-1138, nephew, divided Poland among 4 sons eldest suzerain.

(continued)

1138-1306, feudal division. 1226 founding in Prussia of military order Teutonic Knights. 1226 invasion by Tartars/Mongols.

Vladislav I, 1306-1333, reunited most Polish territories, crowned king 1320. Casimir III the Great, 1333-1370, son, developed economic, cultural life, foreign policy.

House of Anjou

Louis I, 1370-1382, nephew/identical with Louis I of Hungary. Jadwiga, 1384-1399, daughter, married 1386 Jagiello, Grand Duke of Lituania.

House of Jagelloneans

Vladislav II, 1386-1434, Christianized Lituania, founded personal union between Poland & Lituania. Defeated 1410 Teutonic Knights at Grunwald.

Vladislav III, 1434-1444, son, simultaneously king of Hungary. Fought Turks, killed 1444 in battle of Varna.

Casimir IV, 1446-1492, brother, competed with Hapsburgs, put son Vladislav on throne of Bohemia, later also of Hungary.

Sigismund I, 1506-1548, brother, patronized science & arts, his & son's reign "Golden Age."

Sigismund II, 1548-1572, son, established 1569 real union of Poland and Lituania (lasted until 1795).

Elective kings

Polish nobles proclaimed 1572 Poland a Republic headed by king to be elected by whole nobility.

Stephen Batory, 1576-1586, duke of Transylvania, married Ann, sister of Sigismund II August. Fought Russians.

Sigismund III Vasa, 1587-1632, nephew of Sigismund II. 1592-1598 also king of Sweden. His generals fought Russians, Turks.

Vladislav II Vasa, 1632-1648, son. Fought Russians.

John II Casimir Vasa, 1648-1668, brother. Fought Cossacks, Swedes, Russians, Turks, Tartars (the "Deluge"). Abdicated 1668.

John III Sobieski, 1674-1696. Won Vienna from Turks, 1683.

Stanislav II, 1764-1795, last king. Encouraged reforms; 1791 1st modern Constitution in Europe. 1772, 1793, 1795 Poland partitioned among Russia, Prussia, Austria. Unsuccessful insurrection against foreign invasion 1794 under Kosciuszko, Amer-Polish gen.

1795-1918 Poland under foreign rule

1807-1815 Grand Duchy of Warsaw created by Napoleon I, Frederick August of Saxony grand duke.

1815 Congress of Vienna proclaimed part of Poland "Kingdom" in personal union with Russia.

Polish uprisings: 1830 against Russia, 1846, 1848 against Austria, 1863 against Russia—all repressed.

1918-1939 Second Republic

1918-1922 Head of State Jozef Pilsudski. Presidents: Gabriel Narutowicz 1933, assassinated. Stanislav Wojsiechowski 1922-1926, had to abdicate after Pilsudski's coup d'état. Ignacy Mosciecki, 1926-1939, ruled with Pilsudski as (until 1935) virtual dictator.

1939-1945 Poland under foreign occupation

Nazi aggression Sept. 1939. Polish govt.-in-exile, first in France, then in England. Vladislav Raczkiewicz pres., Gen. Vladislav Sikorski, then Stanislav Mikolajczyk, prime ministers. Polish Committee of Natl. Liberation proclaimed at Lublin July 1944, transformed into govt. Jan. 1, 1945.

Rulers of Denmark, Sweden, Norway

Denmark

Earliest rulers invaded Britain; King Canute, who ruled in London 1016-1035, was most famous. The Valdemars furnished kings until the 15th century. In 1282 the Danes won the first national assembly, Danehof, from King Erik V.

Most redoubtable medieval character was Margaret, daughter of Valdemar IV, born 1353, married at 10 to King Haakon VI of Norway. In 1376 she had her first infant son Olaf made king of Denmark. After his death, 1387, she was regent of Denmark and Norway. In 1388 Sweden accepted her as sovereign. In 1389 she made her grand-nephew, Duke Erik of Pomerania, titular king of Denmark, Sweden, and Norway, with herself as regent. In 1397 she effected the Union of Kalmar of the three kingdoms and had Erik VII crowned. In 1439 the three kingdoms deposed him and elected, 1440, Christopher of Bavaria king (Christopher III). On his death, 1448, the union broke up.

Succeeding rulers were unable to enforce their claims as rulers of Sweden until 1520, when Christian II conquered Sweden. He was thrown out 1522, and in 1523 Gustavus Vasa united Sweden. Denmark continued to dominate Norway until the Napoleonic wars, when Frederick VI, 1808-1839, joined the Napoleonic cause after Britain had destroyed the Danish fleet, 1807. In 1814 he was forced to cede Norway to Sweden and Helgoland to Britain, receiving Lauenburg. Successors Christian VIII, 1839; Frederick VII, 1848; Christian IX, 1863; Frederick VIII, 1906; Christian X, 1912; Frederick IX, 1947; Margrethe II, 1972.

Sweden

Early kings ruled at Uppsala, but did not dominate the country. Sverker, c1130-c1156, united the Swedes and Goths. In 1435 Sweden obtained the Riksdag, or parliament. After the Union of Kalmar, 1397, the Danes either ruled or harried the country until Christian II of Denmark conquered it anew, 1520. This led to a rising under Gustavus Vasa, who ruled Sweden 1523-1560, and established an independent kingdom. Charles IX, 1599-1611, crowned 1604, conquered Moscow. Gustavus II Adolphus, 1611-1632, was called the Lion of the North. Later rulers: Christina, 1632; Charles X, Gustavus 1654; Charles XI, 1660; Charles XII (invader of Russia and Poland, defeated at Poltava, June 28, 1709), 1697; Ulrika Eleanora, sister, elected queen 1718; Frederick I (of Hesse), her husband, 1720; Adolphus Frederick, 1751; Gustavus III, 1771; Gustavus IV Adolphus, 1792; Charles XIII, 1809. (Union with Norway began 1814.) Charles XIV John, 1818. He was Jean Bernadotte, Napoleon's Prince of Ponte Corvo, elected 1810 to succeed Charles XIII. He founded the present dynasty: Oscar I, 1844; Charles XV, 1859; Oscar II, 1872; Gustavus V, 1907; Gustav VI Adolf, 1950; Carl XVI Gustaf, 1973.

Norway

Overcoming many rivals, Harald Haarfager, 872-930, conquered Norway, Orkneys, and Shetlands; Olaf I, great-grandson, 995-1000, brought Christianity into Norway, Iceland, and Greenland. In 1035 Magnus the Good also became king of Denmark. Haakon V, 1299-1319, had married his daughter to Erik of Sweden. Their son, Magnus, became ruler of Norway and Sweden at 6. His son, Haakon VI, married Margaret of Denmark; their son Olaf IV became king of Norway and Denmark, followed by Margaret's regency and the Union of Kalmar, 1397.

In 1450 Norway became subservient to Denmark. Christian IV, 1588-1648, founded Christiania, now Oslo. After Napoleonic wars, when Denmark ceded Norway to Sweden, a strong nationalist movement forced recognition of Norway as an independent kingdom united with Sweden under the Swedish kings, 1814-1905. In 1905 the union was dissolved and Prince Carl of Denmark became Haakon VII. He died Sept. 21, 1957, aged 85; succeeded by son, Olav V, b. July 2, 1903.

Rulers of the Netherlands and Belgium

The Netherlands (Holland)

William Frederick, Prince of Orange, led a revolt against French rule, 1813, and was crowned King of the Netherlands, 1815. Belgium seceded Oct. 4, 1830, after a revolt, and formed a separate government. The change was ratified by the two kingdoms by treaty Apr. 19, 1839.

Succession: William II, son, 1840; William III, son, 1849; Wilhelmina, daughter of William III and his 2d wife Princess Emma of Waldeck, 1890; Wilhelmina abdicated, Sept. 4, 1948, in favor of daughter, Juliana. Juliana abdicated Apr. 30, 1980, in favor of daughter, Beatrix.

Belgium

A national congress elected Prince Leopold of Saxe-Coburg King; he took the throne July 21, 1831, as Leopold I. Succession: Leopold II, son 1865; Albert I, nephew of Leopold II, 1909; Leopold III, son of Albert, 1934; Prince Charles, Regent 1944; Leopold returned 1950, yielded powers to son Baudouin, Prince Royal, Aug. 6, 1950, abdicated July 16, 1951. Baudouin I took throne July 17, 1951.

For political history prior to 1830 see articles on the Netherlands and Belgium.

Roman Rulers

From Romulus to the end of the Empire in the West. Rulers of the Roman Empire in the East sat in Constantinople and for a brief period in Nicaea, until the capture of Constantinople by the Turks in 1453, when Byzantium was succeeded by the Ottoman Empire.

BC	Name	AD	Name	AD	Name
	The Kingdom	98	Trajanus	324	Constantinus I (the Great)
753	Romulus (Quirinus)	117	Hadrianus	337	Constantinus II, Constans I,
716	Numa Pompilius	138	Antoninus Pius		Constantius II
673	Tullus Hostilius	161	Marcus Aurelius and Lucius Verus	340	Constantius II and Constans I
640	Ancus Marcius	169	Marcus Aurelius (alone)	350	Constantius II
616	L. Tarquinius Priscus	180	Commodus	361	Julianus II (the Apostate)
578	Servius Tullius	193	Pertinax; Julianus I	363	Jovianus
534	L. Tarquinius Superbus	193	Septimius Severus		**West (Rome) and East**
	The Republic	211	Caracalla and Geta		**(Constantinople)**
509	Consulate established	212	Caracalla (alone)	364	Valentinianus I (West) and Valens
509	Quaestorship instituted	217	Macrinus		(East)
498	Dictatorship introduced	218	Elagabalus (Heliogabalus)	367	Valentinianus I with
494	Plebeian Tribunate created	222	Alexander Severus		Gratianus (West) and Valens (East)
494	Plebeian Aedileship created	235	Maximinus I (the Thracian)	375	Gratianus with Valentinianus
444	Consular Tribunate organized	238	Gordianus I and Gordianus II;		II (West) and Valens (East)
435	Censorship instituted		Pupienus and Balbinus	378	Gratianus with Valentinianus II
366	Praetorship established	238	Gordianus III		(West) Theodosius I (East)
366	Curule Aedileship created	244	Philippus (the Arabian)	383	Valentinianus II (West) and
362	Military Tribunate elected	249	Decius		Theodosius I (East)
326	Proconsulate introduced	251	Gallus and Volusianus	394	Theodosius I (the Great)
311	Naval Duumvirate elected	253	Aemilianus	395	Honorius (West) and Arcadius
217	Dictatorship of Fabius Maximus	253	Valerianus and Gallienus		(East)
133	Tribunate of Tiberius Gracchus	258	Gallienus (alone)	408	Honorius (West) and Theodosius II
123	Tribunate of Gaius Gracchus	268	Claudius Gothicus		(East)
82	Dictatorship of Sulla	270	Quintillus	423	Valentinianus III (West) and
60	First Triumvirate formed	270	Aurelianus		Theodosius II (East)
	(Caesar, Pompeius, Crassus)	275	Tacitus	450	Valentinianus III (West)
46	Dictatorship of Caesar	276	Florianus		and Marcianus (East)
43	Second Triumvirate formed	276	Probus	455	Maximus (West), Avitus
	(Octavianus, Antonius, Lepidus)	282	Carus		(West); Marcianus (East)
	The Empire	283	Carinus and Numerianus	456	Avitus (West), Marcianus (East)
27	Augustus (Gaius Julius	284	Diocletianus	457	Majorianus (West), Leo I (East)
	Caesar Octavianus)	286	Diocletianus and Maximianus	461	Severus II (West), Leo I (East)
14	Tiberius I	305	Galerius and Constantius I	467	Anthemius (West), Leo I (East)
37	Gaius Caesar (Caligula)	306	Galerius, Maximinus II, Severus I	472	Olybrius (West), Leo I (East)
41	Claudius I	307	Galerius, Maximinus	473	Glycerius (West), Leo I (East)
54	Nero		II, Constantinus I, Licinius,	474	Julius Nepos (West), Leo II (East)
68	Galba		Maxentius	475	Romulus Augustulus (West) and
69	Galba; Otho, Vitellius	311	Maximinus II, Constantinus I,		Zeno (East)
69	Vespasianus		Licinius, Maxentius	476	End of Empire in West; Odovacar,
79	Titus	314	Maximinus II, Constantinus I,		King, drops title of Emperor;
81	Domitianus		Licinius		murdered by King Theodoric of
96	Nerva	314	Constantinus I and Licinius		Ostrogoths 493 AD

Rulers of Modern Italy

After the fall of Napoleon in 1814, the Congress of Vienna, 1815, restored Italy as a political patchwork, comprising the Kingdom of Naples and Sicily, the Papal States, and smaller units. Piedmont and Genoa were awarded to Sardinia, ruled by King Victor Emmanuel I of Savoy.

United Italy emerged under the leadership of Camillo, Count di Cavour (1810-1861), Sardinian prime minister. Agitation was led by Giuseppe Mazzini (1805-1872) and Giuseppe Garibaldi (1807-1882), soldier, Victor Emmanuel I abdicated 1821. After a brief regency for a brother, Charles Albert was King 1831-1849, abdicating when defeated by the Austrians at Novara. Succeeded by Victor Emmanuel II, 1849-1861.

In 1859 France forced Austria to cede Lombardy to Sardinia, which gave rights to Savoy and Nice to France. In 1860 Garibaldi led 1,000 volunteers in a spectacular campaign, took Sicily and expelled the King of Naples. In 1860 the House of Savoy annexed Tuscany, Parma, Modena, Romagna, the Two Sicilies, the Marches, and Umbria. Victor Emmanuel assumed the title of King of Italy at Turin Mar. 17, 1861. In 1866 he allied with Prussia in the Austro-Prussian War, with Prussia's victory received Venetia. On Sept. 20, 1870, his troops under Gen. Raffaele Cadorna entered Rome and took over the Papal States, ending the temporal power of the Roman Catholic Church.

Succession: Umberto I; 1878, assassinated 1900; Victor Emmanuel III, 1900, abdicated 1946, died 1947; Umberto II, 1946, ruled a month. In 1921 Benito Mussolini (1883-1945) formed the Fascist party and became prime minister Oct. 31, 1922. He made the King Emperor of Ethiopia, 1937; entered World War II as ally of Hitler. He was deposed July 25, 1943.

At a plebiscite June 2, 1946, Italy voted for a repub- lic; Premier Alcide de Gasperi became chief of state June 13, 1946. On June 28, 1946, the Constituent Assembly elected Enrico de Nicola, Liberal, provisional president. Successive presidents: Luigi Einaudi, elected May 11, 1948, Giovanni Gronchi, Apr. 29, 1955; Antonio Segni, May 6, 1962; Giuseppe Saragat, Dec. 28, 1964; Giovanni Leone, Dec. 29, 1971; Alessandro Pertini, July 9, 1978; Francesco Cossiga, July 9, 1985.

Rulers of Spain

From 8th to 11th centuries Spain was dominated by the Moors (Arabs and Berbers). The Christian reconquest established small kingdoms (Asturias, Aragon, Castile, Catalonia, Leon, Navarre, and Valencia). In 1474 Isabella (Isabel), b. 1451, became Queen of Castile & Leon. Her husband, Ferdinand, b. 1452, inherited Aragon 1479, with Catalonia, Valencia, and the Balearic Islands, became Ferdinand V of Castile. By Isabella's request Pope Sixtus IV established the Inquisition, 1478. Last Moorish kingdom, Granada, fell 1492. Columbus opened New World of colonies, 1492. Isabella died 1504, succeeded by her daughter, Juana "the Mad," but Ferdinand ruled until his death 1516.

Charles I, b. 1500, son of Juana and grandson of Ferdinand and Isabella, and of Maximilian I of Hapsburg; succeeded later as Holy Roman Emperor, Charles V, 1520; abdicated 1556. Philip II, son, 1556-1598, inherited only Spanish throne; conquered Portugal, fought Turks, persecuted non-Catholics, sent Armada against England. Was briefly married to Mary I of England, 1554-1558. Succession: Philip III, 1598-1621; Philip IV, 1621-1665; Charles II, 1665-1700, left Spain to Philip of Anjou, grandson of Louis XIV, who as Philip V, 1700-1746, founded Bourbon dynasty. Ferdinand VI, 1746-1759; Charles III, 1759-1788; Charles IV, 1788-1808, abdicated.

Napoleon now dominated politics and made his brother Joseph King of Spain 1808, but the Spanish ousted him in 1813. Ferdinand VII, 1808, 1814-1833, lost American colonies; succeeded by daughter Isabella II, aged 3, with wife Maria Christina of Naples regent

until 1843. Isabella deposed by revolution 1868. Elected king by the Cortes, Amadeo of Savoy, 1870; abdicated 1873. First republic, 1873-74. Alphonso XII, son of Isabella, 1875-85. His posthumous son was Alphonso XIII, with his mother, Queen Maria Christina regent; Spanish-American war, Spain lost Cuba, gave up Puerto Rico, Philippines, Sulu Is., Marianas. Alphonso took throne 1902, aged 16, married British Princess Victoria Eugenia of Battenberg. The dictatorship of Primo de Rivera, 1923-30, precipitated the revolution of 1931. Alphonso agreed to leave without formal abdication. The monarchy was abolished and the second republic established, with socialist backing. Presidents were Niceto Alcala Zamora, to 1936, when Manuel Azaña was chosen.

In July, 1936, the army in Morocco revolted against the government and General Francisco Franco led the troops into Spain. The revolution succeeded by Feb., 1939, when Azaña resigned. Franco became chief of state, with provisions that if he was incapacitated the Regency Council by two-thirds may propose a king to the Cortes, which must have a two-thirds majority to elect him.

Alphonso XIII died in Rome Feb. 28, 1941, aged 54. His property and citizenship had been restored.

A succession law restoring the monarchy was approved in a 1947 referendum. Prince Juan Carlos, son of the pretender to the throne, was designated by Franco and the Cortes in 1969 as the future king and chief of state. Upon Franco's death, Nov. 20, 1975, Juan Carlos was proclaimed king, Nov. 22, 1975.

Leaders in the South American Wars of Liberation

Simon Bolivar (1783-1830), Jose Francisco de San Martin (1778-1850), and Francisco Antonio Gabriel Miranda (1750-1816), are among the heroes of the early 19th century struggles of South American nations to free themselves from Spain. All three, and their contemporaries, operated in periods of factional strife, during which soldiers and civilians suffered.

Miranda, a Venezuelan, who had served with the French in the American Revolution and commanded parts of the French Revolutionary armies in the Netherlands, attempted to start a revolt in Venezuela in 1806 and failed. In 1810, with British and American backing, he returned and was briefly a dictator, until the British withdrew their support. In 1812 he was overcome by the royalists in Venezuela and taken prisoner, dying in a Spanish prison in 1816.

San Martin was born in Argentina and during 1789-1811 served in campaigns of the Spanish armies in Europe and Africa. He first joined the independence movement in Argentina in 1812 and then in 1817 invaded Chile with 4,000 men over the mountain passes. Here he and Gen. Bernardo O'Higgins (1778-1842) defeated the Spaniards at Chacabuco, 1817, and O'Higgins was named Liberator and became first director of Chile, 1817-23. In 1821 San Martin occupied Lima and Callao, Peru, and became protector of Peru.

Bolivar, the greatest leader of South American liberation from Spain, was born in Venezuela, the son of an aristocratic family. He first served under Miranda in 1812 and in 1813 captured Caracas, where he was

named Liberator. Forced out next year by civil strife, he led a campaign that captured Bogota in 1814. In 1817 he was again in control of Venezuela and was named dictator. He organized Nueva Granada with the help of General Francisco de Paula Santander (1792-1840). By joining Nueva Granada, Venezuela, and the present terrain of Panama and Ecuador, the republic of Colombia was formed with Bolivar president. After numerous setbacks he decisively defeated the Spaniards in the second battle of Carabobo, Venezuela, June 24, 1821.

In May, 1822, Gen. Antonio Jose de Sucre, Bolivar's lieutenant, took Quito. Bolivar went to Guayaquil to confer with San Martin, who resigned as protector of Peru and withdrew from politics. With a new army of Colombians and Peruvians Bolivar defeated the Spaniards in a battle at Junin in 1824 and cleared Peru.

De Sucre organized Charcas (Upper Peru) as Republica Bolivar (now Bolivia) and acted as president in place of Bolivar, who wrote its constitution. De Sucre defeated the Spanish faction of Peru at Ayacucho, Dec. 19, 1824.

Continued civil strife finally caused the Colombian federation to break apart. Santander turned against Bolivar, but the latter defeated him and banished him. In 1828 Bolivar gave up the presidency he had held precariously for 14 years. He became ill from tuberculosis and died Dec. 17, 1830. He is buried in the national pantheon in Caracas.

Rulers of Russia; Premiers of the USSR

First ruler to consolidate Slavic tribes was Rurik, leader of the Russians who established himself at Novgorod, 862 A.D. He and his immediate successors had Scandinavian affiliations. They moved to Kiev after 972 AD and ruled as Dukes of Kiev. In 988 Vladimir was converted and adopted the Byzantine Greek Orthodox service, later modified by Slav influences. Important as organizer and lawgiver was Yaroslav, 1019-1054, whose daughters married kings of Norway, Hungary, and France. His grandson, Vladimir II (Monomakh), 1113-1125, was progenitor of several rulers, but in 1169 Andrew Bogolubski overthrew Kiev and began the line known as Grand Dukes of Vladimir.

Of the Grand Dukes of Vladimir, Alexander Nevsky, 1246-1263, had a son, Daniel, first to be called Duke of Muscovy (Moscow) who ruled 1294-1303. His successors became Grand Dukes of Muscovy. After Dmitri III Donskoi defeated the Tartars in 1380, they also became Grand Dukes of all Russia. Independence of the Tartars and considerable territorial expansion were achieved under Ivan III, 1462-1505.

Tsars of Muscovy—Ivan III was referred to in church ritual as Tsar. He married Sofia, niece of the last Byzantine emperor. His successor, Basil III, died in 1533 when Basil's son Ivan was only 3. He became Ivan IV, "the Terrible"; crowned 1547 as Tsar of all the Russias, ruled till 1584. Under the weak rule of his son, Feodor I, 1584-1598, Boris Godunov had control. The dynasty died, and after years of tribal strife and intervention by Polish and Swedish armies, the Russians united under 17-year-old Michael Romanov, distantly related to the first wife of Ivan IV. He ruled 1613-1645 and established the Romanov line. Fourth ruler after Michael was Peter I.

Tsars, or Emperors of Russia (Romanovs)—Peter I, 1682-1725, known as Peter the Great, took title of Emperor in 1721. His successors and dates of accession were: Catherine, his widow, 1725; Peter II, his grandson, 1727-1730; Anne, Duchess of Courland, 1730, daughter of Peter the Great's brother, Tsar Ivan V; Ivan VI, 1740-1741, greatgrandson of Ivan V, child, kept in prison and murdered 1764; Elizabeth, daughter of Peter I, 1741; Peter III, grandson of Peter I, 1761, deposed 1762 for his consort, Catherine

II, former princess of Anhalt Zerbst (Germany) who is known as Catherine the Great, 1762-1796; Paul I, her son, 1796, killed 1801; Alexander I, son of Paul, 1801-1825, defeated Napoleon; Nicholas I, his brother, 1825; Alexander II, son of Nicholas, 1855, assassinated 1881 by terrorists; Alexander III, son, 1881-1894.

Nicholas II, son, 1894-1917, last Tsar of Russia, was forced to abdicate by the Revolution that followed losses to Germany in WWI. The Tsar, the Empress, the Tsesarevich (Crown Prince) and the Tsar's 4 daughters were murdered by the Bolsheviks in Ekaterinburg, July 16, 1918.

Provisional Government—Prince Georgi Lvov and Alexander Kerensky, premiers, 1917.

Union of Soviet Socialist Republics

Bolshevik Revolution, Nov. 7, 1917, displaced Kerensky; council of People's Commissars formed, Lenin (Vladimir Ilyich Ulyanov), premier. Lenin died Jan. 21, 1924. Aleksei Rykov (executed 1938) and V. M. Molotov held the office, but actual ruler was Joseph Stalin (Joseph Vissarionovich Djugashvili), general secretary of the Central Committee of the Communist Party. Stalin became president of the Council of Ministers (premier) May 7, 1941, died Mar. 5, 1953. Succeeded by Georgi M. Malenkov, as head of the Council and premier and Nikita S. Khrushchev, first secretary of the Central Committee. Malenkov resigned Feb. 8, 1955, became deputy premier, was dropped July 3, 1957. Marshal Nikolai A. Bulganin became premier Feb. 8, 1955; was demoted and Khrushchev became premier Mar. 27 1958. Khrushchev was ousted Oct. 14-15, 1964, replaced by Leonid I. Brezhnev as first secretary of the party and by Aleksei N. Kosygin as premier. On June 16, 1977, Brezhnev took office as president. Brezhnev died Nov. 10, 1982; 2 days later the Central Committee unanimously elected former KGB head Yuri V. Andropov president. Andropov died Feb. 9, 1984; on Feb. 13, Konstantin U. Chernenko was chosen by Central Committee to succeed Andropov as its general secretary. Chernenko died Mar. 10, 1985. On Mar. 11, he was succeeded as general secretary by Mikhail Gorbachev, who replaced Andre Gromyko as president on Oct. 1, 1988.

Governments of China

(Until 221 BC and frequently thereafter, China was not a unified state. Where dynastic dates overlap, the rulers or events referred to appeared in different areas of China.)

Hsia	c1994BC	- c1523BC	ture; capital: Sian)	618	- 906
Shang	c1523	- c1028	Five Dynasties (Yellow River basin)	902	- 960
Western Chou	c1027	- 770	Ten Kingdoms (southern China)	907	- 979
Eastern Chou	770	- 256	Liao (Khitan Mongols; capital: Peking)	947	- 1125
Warring States	403	- 222			
Ch'in (first unified empire)	221	- 206	Sung	960	- 1279
Han	202BC	- 220AD	Northern Sung (reunified central and southern China)	960	- 1126
Western Han (expanded Chinese state beyond the Yellow and Yangtze River valleys)	202BC	- 9AD	Western Hsai (non-Chinese rulers in northwest)	990	- 1227
Hsin (Wang Mang, usurper)	9AD	- 23AD	Chin (Tartars; drove Sung out of central China)	1115	- 1234
Eastern Han (expanded Chinese state into Indo-China and Turkestan)	25	- 220	Yuan (Mongols; Kublai Khan made Peking his capital in 1267)	1271	- 1368
Three Kingdoms (Wei, Shu, Wu)	220	- 265	Ming (China reunified under Chinese rule; capital: Nanking, then Peking in 1420)	1368	- 1644
Chin (western)	265	- 317			
(eastern)	317	- 420			
Northern Dynasties (followed several short-lived governments by Turks, Mongols, etc.)	386	- 581	Ch'ing (Manchus, descendents of Tartars)	1644	- 1911
Southern Dynasties (capital: Nanking)	420	- 589	Republic (disunity; provincial rulers, warlords)	1912	- 1949
Sui (reunified China)	581	- 618	People's Republic of China (Nationalist China established on Taiwan)	1949	- —
Tang (a golden age of Chinese cul-					

Leaders Since 1949

Mao Zedong	Chairman, Central People's Administrative Council, Communist Party (CPC), 1949-1976	Hua Guofeng	Premier, 1976-1980; CPC Chairman, 1976-1981
		Zhao Ziyong	Premier, 1980-; CPC Chairman, 1987-
Zhou Enlai	Premier, foreign minister, 1949-1976	Hu Yaobang	CPC Chairman, 1981-1987
Deng Xiaoping	Vice Premier, 1949-1976; 1977-1987	Li Xiannian	President, 1983-1988
Liu Shaoqi	President, 1959-1969	Yong Shang-Kun	President, 1988-
		Li Peng	Premier, 1988-

Chronological List of Popes

Source: Annuario Pontificio. Table lists year of accession of each Pope.

The Roman Catholic Church names the Apostle Peter as founder of the Church in Rome. He arrived there c. 42, was martyred there c. 67, and raised to sainthood.

The Pope's temporal title is: Sovereign of the State of Vatican City.

The Pope's spiritual titles are: Bishop of Rome, Vicar of Jesus Christ, Successor of St. Peter, Prince of the Apostles, Supreme Pontiff of the Universal Church, Patriarch of the West, Primate of Italy, Archbishop and Metropolitan of the Roman Province.

Anti-Popes are in *Italics*. Anti-Popes were illegitimate claimants of or pretenders to the papal throne.

Year	Name of Pope	Year	Name of Pope	Year	Name of Pope	Year	Name of Pope
See above.	St. Peter	615	St. Deusdedit	974	Benedict VII	1305	Clement V
67	St. Linus		or Adeodatus	983	John XIV	1316	John XXII
76	St. Anacletus	619	Boniface V	985	John XV	*1328*	*Nicholas V*
	or Cletus	625	Honorius I	996	Gregory V	1334	Benedict XII
88	St. Clement I	640	Severinus	*997*	*John XVI*	1342	Clement VI
97	St. Evaristus	640	John IV	999	Sylvester II	1352	Innocent VI
105	St. Alexander I	642	Theodore I	1003	John XVII	1362	Bl. Urban V
115	St. Sixtus I	649	St. Martin I, Martyr	1004	John XVIII	1370	Gregory XI
125	St. Telesphorus	654	St. Eugene I	1009	Sergius IV	1378	Urban VI
136	St. Hyginus	657	St. Vitalian	1012	Benedict VIII	*1378*	*Clement VII*
140	St. Pius I	672	Adeodatus II	*1012*	*Gregory*	1389	Boniface IX
155	St. Anicetus	676	Donus	1024	John XIX	*1394*	*Benedict XIII*
166	St. Soter	678	St. Agatho	1032	Benedict IX	1404	Innocent VII
175	St. Eleutherius	682	St. Leo II	1045	Sylvester III	1406	Gregory XII
189	St. Victor I	684	St. Benedict II	1045	Benedict IX	*1409*	*Alexander V*
199	St. Zephyrinus	685	John V	1045	Gregory VI	*1410*	*John XXIII*
217	St. Callistus I	686	Conon	1046	Clement II	1417	Martin V
217	*St. Hippolytus*	*687*	*Theodore*	1047	Benedict IX	1431	Eugene IV
222	St. Urban I	*687*	*Paschal*	1048	Damasus II	*1439*	*Felix V*
230	St. Pontian	687	St. Sergius I	1049	St. Leo IX	1447	Nicholas V
235	St. Anterus	701	John VI	1055	Victor II	1455	Callistus III
236	St. Fabian	705	John VII	1057	Stephen IX (X)	1458	Pius II
251	St. Cornelius	708	Sisinnius	*1058*	*Benedict X*	1464	Paul II
251	*Novatian*	708	Constantine	1059	Nicholas II	1471	Sixtus IV
253	St. Lucius I	715	St. Gregory II	1061	Alexander II	1484	Innocent VIII
254	St. Stephen I	731	St. Gregory III	*1061*	*Honorius II*	1492	Alexander VI
257	St. Sixtus II	741	St. Zachary	1073	St. Gregory VII	1503	Pius III
259	St. Dionysius	752	Stephen II (III)	*1080*	*Clement III*	1503	Julius II
269	St. Felix I	757	St. Paul I	1086	Bl. Victor III	1513	Leo X
275	St. Eutychian	*767*	*Constantine*	1088	Bl. Urban II	1522	Adrian VI
283	St. Caius	*768*	*Philip*	1099	Paschal II	1523	Clement VII
296	St. Marcellinus	768	Stephen III (IV)	*1100*	*Theodoric*	1534	Paul III
308	St. Marcellus I	772	Adrian I	*1102*	*Albert*	1550	Julius III
309	St. Eusebius	795	St. Leo III	*1105*	*Sylvester IV*	1555	Marcellus II
311	St. Melchiades	816	Stephen IV (V)	1118	Gelasius II	1555	Paul IV
314	St. Sylvester I	817	St. Paschal I	*1118*	*Gregory VIII*	1559	Pius IV
336	St. Marcus	824	Eugene II	1119	Callistus II	1566	St. Pius V
337	St. Julius I	827	Valentine	1124	Honorius II	1572	Gregory XIII
352	Liberius	827	Gregory IV	*1124*	*Celestine II*	1585	Sixtus V
355	*Felix II*	*844*	*John*	1130	Innocent II	1590	Urban VII
366	St. Damasus I	844	Sergius II	*1130*	*Anacletus II*	1590	Gregory XIV
366	*Ursinus*	847	St. Leo IV	1138	Victor IV	1591	Innocent IX
384	St. Siricius	855	Benedict III	1143	Celestine II	1592	Clement VIII
399	St. Anastasius I	*855*	*Anastasius*	1144	Lucius II	1605	Leo XI
401	St. Innocent I	858	St. Nicholas I	1145	Bl. Eugene III	1605	Paul V
417	St. Zosimus	867	Adrian II	1153	Anastasius IV	1621	Gregory XV
418	St. Boniface I	872	John VIII	1154	Adrian IV	1623	Urban VIII
418	*Eulalius*	882	Marinus I	1159	Alexander III	1644	Innocent X
422	St. Celestine I	884	St. Adrian III	*1159*	*Victor IV*	1655	Alexander VII
432	St. Sixtus III	885	Stephen V (VI)	*1164*	*Paschal III*	1667	Clement IX
440	St. Leo I	891	Formosus	*1168*	*Callistus III*	1670	Clement X
461	St. Hilary	896	Boniface VI	1179	Innocent III	1676	Bl. Innocent XI
468	St. Simplicius	896	Stephen VI (VII)	1181	Lucius III	1689	Alexander VIII
483	St. Felix III (II)	897	Romanus	1185	Urban III	1691	Innocent XII
492	St. Gelasius I	897	Theodore II	1187	Gregory VIII	1700	Clement XI
496	Anastasius II	898	John IX	1187	Clement III	1721	Innocent XIII
498	St. Symmachus	900	Benedict IV	1191	Celestine III	1724	Benedict XIII
498	*Lawrence*	903	Leo V	1198	Innocent III	1730	Clement XII
	(501-505)	*903*	*Christopher*	1216	Honorius III	1740	Benedict XIV
514	St. Hormisdas	904	Sergius III	1227	Gregory IX	1758	Clement XIII
523	St. John I, Martyr	911	Anastasius III	1241	Celestine IV	1769	Clement XIV
526	St. Felix IV (III)	913	Landus	1243	Innocent IV	1775	Pius VI
530	Boniface II	914	John X	1254	Alexander IV	1800	Pius VII
530	*Dioscorus*	928	Leo VI	1261	Urban IV	1823	Leo XII
533	John II	928	Stephen VII (VIII)	1265	Clement IV	1829	Pius VIII
535	St. Agapitus I	931	John XI	1271	Bl. Gregory X	1831	Gregory XVI
536	St. Silverius, Martyr	936	Leo VII	1276	Bl. Innocent V	1846	Pius IX
537	Vigilius	939	Stephen VIII (IX)	1276	Adrian V	1878	Leo XIII
556	Pelagius I	942	Marinus II	1276	John XXI	1903	St. Pius X
561	John III	946	Agapitus II	1277	Nicholas III	1914	Benedict XV
575	Benedict I	955	John XII	1281	Martin IV	1922	Pius XI
579	Pelagius II	963	Leo VIII	1285	Honorius IV	1939	Pius XII
590	St. Gregory I	964	Benedict V	1288	Nicholas IV	1958	John XXIII
604	Sabinian	965	John XIII	1294	St. Celestine V	1963	Paul VI
607	Boniface III	973	Benedict VI	1294	Boniface VIII	1978	John Paul I
608	St. Boniface IV	*974*	*Boniface VII*	1303	Bl. Benedict XI	1978	John Paul II

WORLD FACTS

Early Explorers of the Western Hemisphere

The first men to discover the New World or Western Hemisphere are believed to have walked across a "land bridge" from Siberia to Alaska, an isthmus since broken by the Bering Strait. From Alaska, these ancestors of the Indians spread through North, Central, and South America. Anthropologists have placed these crossings at between 18,000 and 14,000 B.C.; but evidence found in 1967 near Puebla, Mex., indicates mankind reached there as early as 35,000-40,000 years ago.

At first, these people were hunters using flint weapons and tools. In Mexico, about 7000-6000 B.C., they founded farming cultures, developing corn, squash, etc. Eventually, they created complex civilizations — Olmec, Toltec, Aztec, and Maya and, in South America, Inca. Carbon-14 tests show men lived about 8000 B.C. near what are now Front Royal, Va., Kanawha, W. Va., and Dutchess Quarry, N.Y. The Hopewell Culture, based on farming, flourished about 1000 B.C.; remains of it are seen today in large mounds in Ohio and other states.

Norsemen (Norwegian Vikings sailing out of Iceland and Greenland) are credited by most scholars with being the first Europeans to discover America, with at least 5 voyages around 1000 A.D. to areas they called Helluland, Markland, Vinland—possibly Labrador, Nova Scotia or Newfoundland, and New England.

Christopher Columbus, most famous of the explorers, was born at Genoa, Italy, but made his discoveries sailing for the Spanish rulers Ferdinand and Isabella. Dates of his voyages, places he discovered, and other information follow:

1492—First voyage. Left Palos, Spain, Aug. 3 with 88 men (est.). Discovered San Salvador (Guanahani or Watling Is., Bahamas) Oct. 12. Also Cuba, Hispaniola (Haiti-Dominican Republic); built Fort La Navidad on latter.

1493—Second voyage, first part, Sept. 25, with 17 ships, 1,500 men. Dominica (Lesser Antilles) Nov. 3; Guadeloupe, Montserrat, Antigua, San Martin, Santa Cruz, Puerto Rico, Virgin Islands. Settled Isabela on Hispaniola. **Second part** (Columbus having remained in Western Hemisphere), Jamaica, Isle of Pines, La Mona Is.

1498—Third voyage. Left Spain May 30, 1498, 6 ships. Discovered Trinidad. Saw South American continent Aug. 1, 1498, but called it Isla Sancta (Holy Island). Entered Gulf of Paria and landed, first time on continental soil. At mouth of Orinoco Aug. 14 he decided this was the mainland.

1502—Fourth voyage, 4 caravels, 150 men. St. Lucia, Guanaja off Honduras; Cape Gracias a Dios, Honduras; San Juan River, Costa Rica; Almirante, Portobelo, and Laguna de Chiriqui, Panama.

Year	Explorer	Nationality and employer	Discovery or exploration
1497	John Cabot	Italian-English	Newfoundland or Nova Scotia
1498	John and Sebastian Cabot	Italian-English	Labrador to Hatteras
1499	Alonso de Ojeda	Spanish	South American coast, Venezuela
1500, Feb.	Vicente y Pinzon	Spanish	South American coast, Amazon River
1500, Apr.	Pedro Alvarez Cabral	Portuguese	Brazil (for Portugal)
1500-02	Gaspar Corte-Real	Portuguese	Labrador
1501	Rodrigo de Bastidas	Spanish	Central America
1513	Vasco Nunez de Balboa	Spanish	Pacific Ocean
1513	Juan Ponce de Leon	Spanish	Florida
1515	Juan de Solis	Spanish	Rio de la Plata
1519	Alonso de Pineda	Spanish	Mouth of Mississippi River
1519	Hernando Cortes	Spanish	Mexico
1520	Ferdinand Magellan	Portuguese-Spanish	Straits of Magellan, Tierra del Fuego
1524	Giovanni da Verrazano	Italian-French	Atlantic coast-New York harbor
1532	Francisco Pizarro	Spanish	Peru
1534	Jacques Cartier	French	Canada, Gulf of St. Lawrence
1536	Pedro de Mendoza	Spanish	Buenos Aires
1536	A.N. Cabeza de Vaca	Spanish	Texas coast and interior
1539	Francisco de Ulloa	Spanish	California coast
1539-41	Hernando de Soto	Spanish	Mississippi River near Memphis
1539	Marcos de Niza	Italian-Spanish	Southwest (now U.S.)
1540	Francisco V. de Coronado	Spanish	Southwest (now U.S.)
1540	Hernando Alarcon	Spanish	Colorado River
1540	Garcia de L. Cardenas	Spanish	Grand Canyon of the Colorado
1541	Francisco de Orellana	Spanish	Amazon River
1542	Juan Rodriguez Cabrillo	Portuguese-Spanish	San Diego harbor
1565	Pedro Menendez de Aviles	Spanish	St. Augustine
1576	Martin Frobisher	English	Frobisher's Bay, Canada
1577-80	Francis Drake	English	California coast
1582	Antonio de Espejo	Spanish	Southwest (named New Mexico)
1584	Amadas & Barlow (for Raleigh)	English	Virginia
1585-87	Sir Walter Raleigh's men	English	Roanoke Is., N.C.
1595	Sir Walter Raleigh	English	Orinoco River
1603-09	Samuel de Champlain	French	Canadian interior, Lake Champlain
1607	Capt. John Smith	English	Atlantic coast
1609-10	Henry Hudson	English-Dutch	Hudson River, Hudson Bay
1634	Jean Nicolet	French	Lake Michigan; Wisconsin
1673	Jacques Marquette, Louis Jolliet	French	Mississippi S to Arkansas
1682	Sieur de La Salle	French	Mississippi S to Gulf of Mexico
1789	Alexander Mackenzie	Canadian	Canadian Northwest

Arctic Exploration

Early Explorers

1587 — John Davis (England). Davis Strait to Sanderson's Hope, 72° 12' N.

1596 — Willem Barents and Jacob van Heemskerck (Hol-

land). Discovered Bear Island, touched northwest tip of Spitsbergen, 79° 49' N, rounded Novaya Zemlya, wintered at Ice Haven.

1607 — Henry Hudson (England). North along Greenland's east coast to Cape Hold-with-Hope, 73° 30', then north of Spitsbergen to 80° 23'. Returning he discovered Hudson's Touches (Jan Mayen).

1616 — William Baffin and Robert Bylot (England). Baffin Bay to Smith Sound.

1728 — Vitus Bering (Russia). Proved Asia and America were separated by sailing through strait.

1733-40 — Great Northern Expedition (Russia). Surveyed Siberian Arctic coast.

1741 — Vitus Bering (Russia). Sighted Alaska from sea, named Mount St. Elias. His lieutenant, Chirikof, discovered coast.

1771 — Samuel Hearne (Hudson's Bay Co.). Overland from Prince of Wales Fort (Churchill) on Hudson Bay to mouth of Coppermine River.

1778 — James Cook (Britain). Through Bering Strait to Icy Cape, Alaska, and North Cape, Siberia.

1789 — Alexander Mackenzie (North West Co., Britain). Montreal to mouth of Mackenzie River.

1806 — William Scoresby (Britain). N. of Spitsbergen to 81° 30'.

1820-3 — Ferdinand von Wrangel (Russia). Completed a survey of Siberian Arctic coast. His exploration joined that of James Cook at North Cape, confirming separation of the continents.

1845 — Sir John Franklin (Britain) was one of many to seek the Northwest Passage—an ocean route connecting the Atlantic and Pacific via the Arctic. His 2 ships (the Erebus and Terror) were last seen entering Lancaster Sound July 26.

1881 — The steamer *Jeanette* on an expedition led by Lt. Cmdr. George W. DeLong was trapped in ice and crushed, June 1881. DeLong and 11 crewmen died; 12 others survived.

1888 — Fridtjof Nansen (Norway) crossed Greenland's icecap, 1893-96 — Nansen in Fram drifted from New Siberian Is. to Spitsbergen; tried polar dash in 1895, reached Franz Josef Land.

1897 — Salomon A. Andree (Sweden) and 2 others started in balloon from Danes, Is., Spitsbergen, July 11, to drift across pole to America, and disappeared. Over 33 years later, Aug. 6, 1930, their frozen bodies were found on White Is., 82° 57' N 29° 52' E.

1903-06 — Roald Amundsen (Norway) first sailed Northwest Passage.

Discovery of North Pole

Robert E. Peary explored Greenland's coast 1891-92, tried for North Pole 1893. In 1900 he reached northern limit of Greenland and 83° 50' N; in 1902 he reached 84° 06' N; in 1906 he went from Ellesmere Is. to 87° 06' N. He sailed in the *Roosevelt*, July, 1908, to winter off Cape Sheridan, Grant Land. The dash for the North Pole began Mar. 1 from Cape Columbia, Ellesmere Land. Peary reached the pole, 90° N, Apr. 6, 1909.

Peary had several supporting groups carrying supplies until the last group turned back at 87° 47' N. Peary, Matthew

Henson, and 4 Eskimos proceeded with dog teams and sleds. They crossed the pole several times, finally built an igloo at 90°, remained 36 hours. Started south Apr. 7 at 4 p.m. for Cape Columbia. The Eskimos were Coqueeh, Ootah, Eginwah, and Seegloo.

1914 — Donald MacMillan (U.S.). Northwest. 200 miles, from Axel Heiberg Island to seek Peary's Crocker Land.

1915-17 — Vihjalmur Stefansson (Canada) discovered Borden, Brock, Meighen, and Lougheed Islands.

1918-20 — Roald Amundsen sailed Northeast Passage.

1925 — Amundsen and Lincoln Ellsworth (U.S.) reached 87° 44' N in attempt to fly to North Pole from Spitsbergen.

1926 — Richard E. Byrd and Floyd Bennett (U.S.) first over North Pole by air, May 9.

1926 — Amundsen, Ellsworth, and Umberto Nobile (Italy) flew from Spitsbergen over North Pole May 12, to Teller, Alaska, in dirigible *Norge*.

1928 — Nobile crossed North Pole in airship May 24, crashed May 25. Amundsen lost while trying to effect rescue by plane.

North Pole Exploration Records

On Aug. 3, 1958, the *Nautilus*, under Comdr. William R. Anderson, became the first ship to cross the North Pole beneath the Arctic ice.

The nuclear-powered U.S. submarine *Seadragon*, Comdr. George P. Steele 2d, made the first east-west underwater transit through the Northwest Passage during August, 1960. It sailed from Portsmouth N.H., headed between Greenland and Labrador through Baffin Bay, then west through Lancaster Sound and McClure Strait to the Beaufort Sea. Traveling submerged for the most part, the submarine made 850 miles from Baffin Bay to the Beaufort Sea in 6 days.

On Aug. 16, 1977, the Soviet nuclear icebreaker *Arktika* reached the North Pole and became the first surface ship to break through the Arctic ice pack to the top of the world.

On April 30, 1978, Naomi Uemura, a Japanese explorer, became the first man to reach the North Pole alone by dog sled. During the 54-day, 600-mile trek over the frozen Arctic, Uemura survived attacks by a marauding polar bear.

In April, 1982, Sir Ranulph Fiennes and Charles Burton, British explorers, reached the North Pole and became the first to circle the earth from pole to pole. They had reached the South Pole 16 months earlier. The 52,000-mile trek took 3 years, involved 23 people, and cost an estimated $18 million. The expedition was also the first to travel down the Scott Glacier and the first to journey up the Yukon and through the Northwest Passage in a single season.

On May 2, 1986, 6 American and Canadian explorers reached the North Pole assisted only by dogs. They became the first to reach the Pole without mechanical assistance since Robert E. Peary planted a flag there in 1909. The explorers, Americans Will Steger, Paul Schurke, Anne Bancroft, and Geoff Carroll, and Canadians Brent Boddy and Richard Weber completed the 500-mile journey in 56 days.

Antarctic Exploration

Early History

Antarctica has been approached since 1773-75, when Capt. James Cook (Britain) reached 71° 10' S. Many sea and landmarks bear names of early explorers. Bellingshausen (Russia) discovered Peter I and Alexander I Islands, 1819-21. Nathaniel Palmer (U.S.) discovered Palmer Peninsula, 60° W, 1820, without realizing that this was a continent. James Weddell (Britain) found Weddell Sea, 74° 15' S, 1823.

First to announce existence of the continent of Antarctica was Charles Wilkes (U.S.), who followed the coast for 1,500 mi., 1840. Adelie Coast, 140° E, was found by Dumont d'Urville (France), 1840. Ross Ice Shelf was found by James Clark Ross (Britain), 1841-42.

1895 — Leonard Kristensen (Norway) landed a party on the coast of Victoria Land. They were the first ashore on the main continental mass. C.E. Borchgrevink, a member of that party, returned in 1899 with a British expedition, first to

winter on Antarctica.

1902-04 — Robert F. Scott (Britain) discovered Edward VII Peninsula. He reached 82° 17' S, 146° 33' E from McMurdo Sound.

1908-09 — Ernest Shackleton (Britain) introduced the use of Manchurian ponies in Antarctic sledging. He reached 88° 23' S, discovering a route on to the plateau by way of the Beardmore Glacier and pioneering the way to the pole.

Discovery of South Pole

1911 — Roald Amundsen (Norway) with 4 men and dog teams reached the pole Dec. 14.

1912 — Capt. Scott reached the pole from Ross Island Jan. 18, with 4 companions. They found Amundsen's tent. None of Scott's party survived. They were found Nov. 12.

1928 — First man to use an airplane over Antarctica was Hubert Wilkins (Britain).

1929 — Richard E. Byrd (U.S.) established Little America on Bay of Whales. On 1,600-mi. airplane flight begun Nov. 28 he crossed South Pole Nov. 29 with 3 others.

1934-35 — Byrd led 2d expedition to Little America, explored 450,000 sq. mi., wintered alone at weather station, 80° 08' S.

1934-37 — John Rymill led British Graham Land expedition; discovered that Palmer Peninsula is part of Antarctic mainland.

1935 — Lincoln Ellsworth (U.S.) flew south along Palmer Peninsula's east coast, then crossed continent to Little America, making 4 landings on unprepared terrain in bad weather.

1939-41 — U.S. Antarctic Service built West Base on Ross Ice Shelf under Paul Siple, and East Base on Palmer Peninsula under Richard Black. U.S. Navy plane flights discovered about 150,000 sq. miles of new land.

1940 — Byrd charted most of coast between Ross Sea and Palmer Peninsula.

1946-47 — U.S. Navy undertook Operation High-jump under Byrd. Expedition included 13 ships and 4,000 men. Airplanes photomapped coastline and penetrated beyond pole.

1946-48 — Ronne Antarctic Research Expedition, Comdr. Finn Ronne, USNR, determined the Antarctic to be only one continent with no strait between Weddell Sea and Ross Sea; discovered 250,000 sq. miles of land by flights to 79° S Lat., and made 14,000 aerial photographs over 450,000 sq. miles of land. Mrs. Ronne and Mrs. H. Darlington were the first women to winter on Antarctica.

1955-57 — U.S. Navy's Operation Deep Freeze led by Adm. Byrd. Supporting U.S. scientific efforts for the International Geophysical Year, the operation was commanded by Rear Adm. George Dufek. It established 5 coastal stations fronting the Indian, Pacific, and Atlantic oceans and also 3 interior stations; explored more than 1,000,000 sq. miles in Wilkes Land.

1957-58 — During the International Geophysical year, July, 1957, through Dec. 1958, scientists from 12 countries conducted ambitious programs of Antarctic research. A network of some 60 stations on the continent and sub-Arctic islands studied oceanography, glaciology, meteorology, seismology, geomagnetism, the ionosphere, cosmic rays, aurora, and airglow.

Dr. V.E. Fuchs led a 12-man Trans-Antarctic Expedition on the first land crossing of Antarctica. Starting from the Weddell Sea, they reached Scott Station Mar. 2, 1958, after traveling 2,158 miles in 98 days.

1958 — A group of 5 U.S. scientists led by Edward C. Thiel, seismologist, moving by tractor from Ellsworth Station on Weddell Sea, identified a huge mountain range, 5,000 ft. above the ice sheet and 9,000 ft. above sea level. The range, originally seen by a Navy plane, was named the Dufek Massif, for Rear Adm. George Dufek.

1959 — Twelve nations — Argentina, Australia, Belgium, Chile, France, Japan, New Zealand, Norway, South Africa, the Soviet Union, the United Kingdom, and the U.S. — signed a treaty suspending any territorial claims for 30 years and reserving the continent for research.

1961-62 — Scientists discovered a trough, the Bentley Trench, running from Ross Ice Shelf, Pacific, into Marie Byrd Land, around the end of the Ellsworth Mtns., toward the Weddell Sea.

1962 — First nuclear power plant began operation at McMurdo Sound.

1963 — On Feb. 22 a U.S. plane made the longest nonstop flight ever made in the S. Pole area, covering 3,600 miles in 10 hours. The flight was from McMurdo Station south past the geographical S. Pole to Shackleton Mtns., southeast to the "Area of Inaccessibility" and back to McMurdo Station.

1964 — A British survey team was landed by helicopter on Cook Island, the first recorded visit since its discovery in 1775.

1964 — New Zealanders completed one of the last and most important surveys when they mapped the mountain area from Cape Adare west some 400 miles to Pennell Glacier.

1989 — Two Americans, Victoria Murden and Shirley Metz, became the first women to reach the South Pole overland when they arrived with 9 others on Jan. 17, 1989. The 51-day trek on skis covered 740 miles.

Volcanoes

More than 75 per cent of the world's 850 active volcanoes lie within the "Ring of Fire," a zone running along the west coast of the Americas from Chile to Alaska and down the east coast of Asia from Siberia to New Zealand. Twenty per cent of these volcanoes are located in Indonesia. Other prominent groupings are located in Japan, the Aleutian Islands, and Central America. Almost all active regions are found at the boundaries of the large moving plates which comprise the earth's surface. The "Ring of Fire" marks then boundary between the plates underlying the Pacific Ocean and those underlying the surrounding continents. Other active regions, such as the Mediterranean Sea and Iceland, are located on plate boundaries.

Major Historical Eruptions

Approximately 7,000 years ago, Mazama, a 9,900-feet-high volcano in southern Oregon, erupted violently, ejecting ash and lava. The ash spread over the entire northwestern United States and as far away as Saskatchewan, Canada. During the eruption, the top of the mountain collapsed, leaving a caldera 6 miles across and about a half mile deep, which filled with rain water to form what is now called Crater Lake.

In 79 A.D., Vesuvio, or Vesuvius, a 4,190 feet volcano overlooking Naples Bay became active after several centuries of quiescence. On Aug. 24 of that year, a heated mud and ash flow swept down the mountain engulfing the cities of Pompeii, Herculaneum, and Stabiae with debris over 60 feet deep. About 10 percent of the population of the 3 towns was killed.

The largest eruptions in recent centuries have been in Indonesia. In 1883, an eruption similar to the Mazama eruption occurred on the island of Krakatau. On August 27, the 2,640-feet-high peak of the volcano collapsed to 1,000 feet below sea level, leaving only a small portion of the island standing above the sea. Ash from the eruption colored sunsets around the world for 2 years. A tsunami ("tidal wave") generated by the collapse killed 36,000 people in nearby Java and Sumatra and eventually reached England. A similar, but even more powerful, eruption had taken place 68 years earlier at Tambora volcano on the Indonesian island of Sumbawa.

Notable Active Volcanoes

Name, latest activity	Location	Feet	Name, latest activity	Location	Feet
Africa			**Antarctica**		
Cameroon (1982)	Cameroon	13,354	Erebus (1988)	Ross Island	12,450
Nyirangongo (1977)	Zaire	11,400	Big Ben (1960)	Heard Island	9,007
Nyamuragira (1988)	Zaire	10,028	Deception Island (1970)	South Shetland	
Karthala (1977)	Comoro Is.	8,000		Islands	1,890
Piton de la Fournaise (1988)	Reunion Is.	5,981			
Erta-Ale (1973)	Ethiopia	1,650		*(continued)*	

Name, latest activity	Location	Feet
Asia-Oceania		
Klyuchevskaya (1985)	USSR	15,584
Kerinci (1987)	Sumatra	12,467
Rindjani (1966)	Indonesia	12,224
Semeru (1988)	Java	12,060
Slamet (1988)	Java	11,247
Raung (1982)	Java	10,932
Shiveluch (1964)	USSR	10,771
Agung (1964)	Bali	10,308
On-Take (1980)	Japan	10,049
Mayon (1988)	Philippines	9,991
Merapi (1988)	Java	9,551
Bezymianny (1986)	USSR	9,514
Marapi (1988)	Sumatra	9,485
Ruapehu (1989)	New Zealand	9,175
Asama (1988)	Japan	8,300
Niigata Yakeyama (1987)	Japan	8,111
Yake Dake (1963)	Japan	8,064
Alaid (1972)	Kuril Is.	7,662
Ulawun (1989)	New Britain	7,532
Ngauruhoe (1975)	New Zealand	7,515
Chokai (1974)	Japan	7,300
Galunggung (1982)	Java	7,113
Amburombu (1969)	Indonesia	7,051
Azuma (1978)	Japan	6,700
Tangkuban Prahu (1967)	Java	6,637
Sangeang Api (1988)	Indonesia	6,351
Nasu (1977)	Japan	6,210
Tiatia (1973)	Kuril Islands	6,013
Manam (1988)	Papua New Guinea	6,000
Soputan (1984)	Indonesia	5,994
Siau (1976)	Indonesia	5,853
Kelud (1967)	Java	5,679
Batur (1968)	Bali	5,636
Ternate (1963)	Indonesia	5,627
Kirisima (1982)	Japan	5,577
Keli Mutu (1968)	Indonesia	5,460
Akita Komaga take (1970)	Japan	5,449
Gamkonora (1981)	Indonesia	5,364
Aso (1989)	Japan	5,223
Lewotobi Laki-Laki (1968)	Indonesia	5,217
Lokon-Empung (1988)	Indonesia	5,187
Bulusan (1988)	Philippines	5,115
Sarycheva (1976)	Kuril Islands	4,960
Me-akan (1966)	Japan	4,931
Karkar (1981)	Papua New Guinea	4,920
Karymsky (1985)	USSR	4,869
Lopevi (1982)	New Hebrides	4,755
Ambrym (1979)	New Hebrides	4,376
Awu (1968)	Indonesia	4,350
Sakurajima (1989)	Japan	3,668
Langila (1989)	New Britain	3,586
Dukono (1971)	Indonesia	3,566
Suwanosezima (1988)	Japan	2,640
Oshima (1988)	Japan	2,550
Usu (1978)	Japan	2,400
Pagan (1988)	Mariana Is.	1,870
White Island (1989)	New Zealand	1,075
Taal (1988)	Philippines	984
Central America—Caribbean		
Acatenango (1972)	Guatemala	12,992
Fuego (1988)	Guatemala	12,582
Tacana (1988)	Guatemala	12,400
Santiaguito (Santa Maria) (1989)	Guatemala	12,362
Irazu (1988)	Costa Rica	11,260
Poas (1989)	Costa Rica	8,930
Pacaya (1989)	Guatemala	8,346
Izalco (1966)	El Salvador	7,749
San Miguel (1986)	El Salvador	6,994
Rincon de la Vieja (1987)	Costa Rica	6,234
El Viejo (San Cristobal) (1987)	Nicaragua	5,840
Ometepe (Concepcion) (1986)	Nicaragua	5,106
Arenal (1989)	Costa Rica	5,092
Momotombo (1982)	Nicaragua	4,199
Soufriere (1979)	St. Vincent	4,048
Telica (1987)	Nicaragua	3,409
South America		
Guallatiri (1987)	Chile	19,882
Lascar (1989)	Chile	19,652
Cotopaxi (1975)	Ecuador	19,347
Tupungatito (1986)	Chile	18,504
Sangay (1988)	Ecuador	17,159
Guagua Pichincha (1988)	Ecuador	15,696
Purace (1977)	Colombia	15,604
Llaima (1988)	Chile	10,239
Villarica (1984)	Chile	9,318
Hudson (1973)	Chile	8,580
Alcedo (1970)	Galapagos Is.	3,599
Ruiz (1989)	Colombia	...
Mid-Pacific		
Mauna Loa (1987)	Hawaii	13,680
Kilauea (1989)	Hawaii	4,077
Mid-Atlantic Ridge		
Beerenberg (1985)	Jan Mayen Is.	7,470
Hekla (1981)	Iceland	4,892
Leirhnukur (1975)	Iceland	2,145
Krafla (1984)	Iceland	2,145
Surtsey (1967)	Iceland	568
Europe		
Etna (1989)	Italy	11,053
Stromboli (1989)	Italy	3,038
North America		
Colima (1988)	Mexico	14,003
Redoubt (1966)	Alaska	10,197
Iliamna (1978)	Alaska	10,092
Shishaldin (1987)	Aleutian Is.	9,387
Mt. St. Helens (1986)	Washington	8,300+
Veniaminof (1987)	Alaska	8,225
Pavlof (1988)	Aleutian Is.	8,215
El Chichon (1983)	Mexico	7,300
Makushin (1987)	Aleutian Is.	6,680
Pogromni (1964)	Alaska	6,568
Trident 1963	Alaska	6,010
Great Sitkin (1974)	Aleutian Is.	5,710
Cleveland (1987)	Aleutian Is.	5,675
Gareloi (1982)	Aleutian Is.	5,334
Korovin (1987)	Aleutian Is.	4,852
Akutan (1988)	Aleutian Is.	4,275
Kiska (1969)	Aleutian Is.	4,275
Augustine (1988)	Alaska	4,025
Okmok (1988)	Aleutian Is.	3,519
Seguam (1977)	Alaska	3,458

Notable Volcanic Eruptions

Date	Volcano	Deaths
79 A.D.	Mt. Vesuvius, Italy	16,000
1169	Mt. Etna, Sicily	15,000
1631	Mt. Vesuvius, Italy	4,000
1669	Mt. Etna, Sicily	20,000
1772	Mt. Papandayan, Java	3,000
1792	Mt. Unzen-Dake, Japan	10,400
1815	Tamboro, Java	12,000
Aug. 26-28, 1883	Krakatau, Indonesia	35,000
Apr. 8, 1902	Santa Maria, Guatemala	1,000
May 8, 1902	Mt. Pelée, Martinique	30,000
1911	Mt. Taal, Philippines	1,400
1919	Mt. Kelud, Java	5,000
Jan. 18-21, 1951	Mt. Lamington, New Guinea	3,000
Apr. 26, 1966	Mt. Kelud, Java	1,000
May 18, 1980	Mt. St. Helens, U.S.	60
Nov. 13, 1985	Nevado del Ruiz, Colombia	22,940
Aug. 24, 1986	NW Cameroon	1,700+

Mountains

Height of Mount Everest

Mt. Everest was considered to be 29,002 ft. tall when Edmund Hillary and Tenzing Norgay scaled it in 1953. This triangulation figure had been accepted since 1850. In 1954 the Surveyor General of the Republic of India set the height at 29,028 ft., plus or minus 10 ft. because of snow. The National Geographic Society accepts the new figure, but many mountaineering groups still use 29,002 ft.

In 1987, new calculations based on satellite measurements indicate that the Himalayan peak K-2 rose 29,064 feet above sea level and that Mt. Everest is 800 feet higher. The National Geographic Society has not yet accepted the revised figure.

United States, Canada, Mexico

Name	Place	Feet	Name	Place	Feet	Name	Place	Feet
McKinley	Alas	20,320	Alverstone	Alas-Yukon	14,565	Princeton	Col	14,197
Logan	Yukon	19,850	Browne Tower	Alas	14,530	Crestone Needle	Col	14,197
Citlaltepec (Orizaba)	Mexico	18,700	Whitney	Cal	14,494	Yale	Col	14,196
St. Elias	Alas-Yukon	18,008	Elbert	Col	14,433	Bross	Col	14,172
Popocatepetl	Mexico	17,887	Massive	Col	14,421	Kit Carson	Col	14,165
Foraker	Alas	17,400	Harvard	Col	14,420	Wrangell	Alas	14,163
Iztaccihuatl	Mexico	17,343	Rainier	Wash	14,410	Shasta	Cal	14,162
Lucania	Yukon	17,147	Williamson	Cal	14,375	Sill	Cal	14,162
King	Can	16,971	Blanca Peak	Col	14,345	El Diente	Col	14,159
Steele	Can	16,644	La Plata	Col	14,336	Maroon	Col	14,156
Bona	Alas	16,550	Uncompahgre	Col	14,309	Tabeguache	Col	14,155
Blackburn	Alas	16,390	Crestone	Col	14,294	Oxford	Col	14,153
Kennedy	Alas	16,286	Lincoln	Col	14,286	Sneffels	Col	14,150
Sanford	Alas	16,237	Grays Peak	Col	14,270	Point Success	Wash	14,150
South Buttress	Alas	15,885	Antero	Col	14,269	Democrat	Col	14,148
Wood	Yukon	15,885	Torreys	Col	14,267	Capitol	Col	14,130
Vancouver	Alas-Yukon	15,700	Castle	Col	14,265	Liberty Cap	Wash	14,112
Churchill	Alas	15,638	Quandary	Col	14,265	Pikes Peak	Col	14,110
Fairweather	Alas-Yukon	15,300	Evans	Col	14,264	Snowmass	Col	14,092
Zinantecatl (Toluca)	Mexico	15,016	Longs Peak	Col	14,256	Windom	Col	14,087
Hubbard	Alas-Yukon	15,015	McArthur	Yukon	14,253	Russell	Cal	14,086
Bear	Alas	14,831	Wilson	Col	14,246	Eolus	Col	14,084
Walsh	Yukon	14,780	White	Cal	14,246	Columbia	Col	14,073
East Buttress	Alas	14,730	North Palisade	Cal	14,242	Augusta	Alas-Yukon	14,070
Matlalcueyetl	Mexico	14,636	Shavano	Col	14,229	Missouri	Col	14,067
Hunter	Alas	14,573	Belford	Col	14,197	Humboldt	Col	14,064

South America

Peak, Country	Feet	Peak, Country	Feet	Peak, Country	Feet
Aconcagua, Argentina	22,834	Laudo, Argentina	20,997	Polleras, Argentina	20,456
Ojos del Salado, Arg.-Chile	22,572	Ancohuma, Bolivia	20,958	Pular, Chile	20,423
Bonete, Argentina	22,546	Ausangate, Peru	20,945	Chani, Argentina	20,341
Tupungato, Argentina-Chile	22,310	Toro, Argentina-Chile	20,932	Aucanquilcha, Chile	20,295
Pissis, Argentina	22,241	Illampu, Bolivia	20,873	Juncal, Argentina-Chile	20,276
Mercedario, Argentina	22,211	Tres Cruces, Argentina-Chile	20,853	Negro, Argentina	20,184
Huascaran, Peru	22,205	Huandoy, Peru	20,852	Quela, Argentina	20,128
Llullaillaco, Argentina-Chile	22,057	Parinacota, Bolivia-Chile	20,768	Condoriri, Bolivia	20,095
El Libertador, Argentina	22,047	Tortolas, Argentina-Chile	20,745	Palermo, Argentina	20,079
Cachi, Argentina	22,047	Ampato, Peru	20,702	Solimana, Peru	20,068
Yerupaja, Peru	21,709	Condor, Argentina	20,669	San Juan, Argentina-Chile	20,049
Galan, Argentina	21,654	Salcantay, Peru	20,574	Sierra Nevada, Arg.-Chile	20,023
El Muerto, Argentina-Chile	21,457	Chimborazo, Ecuador	20,561	Antofalla, Argentina	20,013
Sajama, Bolivia	21,391	Huancarhuas, Peru	20,531	Marmolejo, Argentina-Chile	20,013
Nacimiento, Argentina	21,302	Famatina, Argentina	20,505	Chachani, Peru	19,931
Illimani, Bolivia	21,201	Pumasillo, Peru	20,492	Licancabur, Argentina-Chile	19,425
Coropuna, Peru	21,083	Solo, Argentina	20,492		

The highest point in the West Indies is in the Dominican Republic, Pico Duarte (10,417 ft.)

Africa, Australia, and Oceania

Peak, country	Feet	Peak, country	Feet	Peak, country	Feet
Kilimanjaro, Tanzania	19,340	Meru, Tanzania	14,979	Toubkal, Morocco	13,661
Kenya, Kenya	17,058	Wilhelm, Papua New Guinea	14,793	Kinabalu, Malaysia	13,455
Margherita Pk., Uganda-Zaire	16,763	Karisimbi, Zaire-Rwanda	14,787	Kerinci, Sumatra	12,467
Jaja, New Guinea	16,500	Elgon, Kenya-Uganda	14,178	Cook, New Zealand	12,349
Trikora, New Guinea	15,585	Batu, Ethiopia	14,131	Teide, Canary Islands	12,198
Mandala, New Guinea	15,420	Guna, Ethiopia	13,881	Semeru, Java	12,060
Ras Dashan, Ethiopia	15,158	Gughe, Ethiopia	13,780	Kosciusko, Australia	7,310

Europe

Peak, country	Feet	Peak, county	Feet	Peak, country	Feet
Alps		Liskamm, It., Switz.	14,852	Nadelhorn, Switz.	14,196
Mont Blanc, Fr. It.	15,771	Weisshorn, Switz.	14,780	Grand Combin, Switz.	14,154
Monte Rosa (highest peak of group), Switz.	15,203	Taschhorn, Switz.	14,733	Lenzpitze, Switz.	14,088
		Matterhorn, It., Switz.	14,690	Finsteraarhorn, Switz.	14,022
Dom, Switz.	14,911	Dent Blanche, Switz.	14,293	Castor, Switz.	13,865

Peak, country	Feet
Zinalrothorn, Switz.	13,849
Hohberghorn, Switz.	13,842
Alphubel, Switz.	13,799
Rimpfischhorn, Switz.	13,776
Aletschorn, Switz.	13,763
Strahlhorn, Switz.	13,747
Dent D'Herens, Switz.	13,686
Breithorn, It., Switz.	13,665
Bishorn, Switz.	13,645
Jungfrau, Switz.	13,642
Ecrins, Fr.	13,461
Monch, Switz.	13,448
Pollux, Switz.	13,422
Schreckhorn, Switz.	13,379
Ober Gabelhorn, Switz.	13,330
Gran Paradiso, It.	13,323
Bernina, It., Switz.	13,284
Fiescherhorn, Switz.	13,283

Peak, county	Feet
Grunhorn, Switz.	13,266
Lauteraarhorn, Switz.	13,261
Durrenhorn, Switz.	13,238
Allalinhorn, Switz.	13,213
Weissmies, Switz.	13,199
Lagginhorn, Switz.	13,156
Zupo, Switz.	13,120
Fletschhorn, Switz.	13,110
Adlerhorn, Switz.	13,081
Gletscherhorn, Switz.	13,068
Schalihorn, Switz.	13,040
Scserscen, Switz.	13,028
Eiger, Switz.	13,025
Jagerhorn, Switz.	13,024
Rottalhorn, Switz.	13,022

Peak, country	Feet
Pyrenees	
Aneto, Sp.	11,168
Posets, Sp.	11,073
Perdido, Sp.	11,007
Vignemale, Fr., Sp.	10,820
Long, Sp.	10,479
Estats, Sp.	10,304
Montcalm, Sp.	10,105
Caucasus (Europe-Asia)	
El'brus, USSR	18,510
Shkara, USSR	17,064
Dykh Tau, USSR	17,054
Kashtan Tau, USSR	16,877
Dzhangi Tau, USSR	16,565
Kazbek, USSR	16,558

Asia

Peak	Country	Feet
Everest	Nepal-Tibet.	29,028
K2 (Godwin Austen)	Kashmir	28,250
Kanchenjunga	India-Nepal	28,208
Lhotse I (Everest)	Nepal-Tibet.	27,923
Makalu I	Nepal-Tibet.	27,824
Lhotse II (Everest)	Nepal-Tibet.	27,560
Dhaulagiri	Nepal	26,810
Manaslu I	Nepal	26,760
Cho Oyu	Nepal-Tibet.	26,750
Nanga Parbat	Kashmir	26,660
Annapurna I	Nepal	26,504
Gasherbrum	Kashmir	26,470
Broad	Kashmir	26,400
Gosainthan	Tibet.	26,287
Annapurna II	Nepal	26,041
Gyachung Kang	Nepal-Tibet.	25,910
Disteghil Sar	Kashmir	25,868
Himalchuli	Nepal	25,801
Nuptse (Everest)	Nepal-Tibet.	25,726
Masherbrum	Kashmir	25,660
Nanda Devi	India	25,645
Rakaposhi	Kashmir	25,550
Kamet	India-Tibet	25,447
Namcha Barwa	Tibet.	25,445
Gurla Mandhata	Tibet.	25,355
Ulugh Muz Tagh	Sinkiang-Tibet.	25,340

Peak	Country	Feet
Kungur	Sinkiang	25,325
Tirich Mir	Pakistan	25,230
Makalu II	Nepal-Tibet.	25,120
Minya Konka	China	24,900
Kula Gangri	Bhutan-Tibet	24,784
Changtzu (Everest)	Nepal-Tibet.	24,780
Muz Tagh Ata	Sinkiang	24,757
Skyang Kangri	Kashmir	24,750
Communism Peak	USSR	24,590
Jongsang Peak	India-Nepal	24,472
Pobedy Peak	Sinkiang-USSR	24,406
Sia Kangri	Kashmir	24,350
Haramosh Peak	Pakistan	24,270
Istoro Nal	Pakistan	24,240
Tent Peak	India-Nepal	24,165
Chomo Lhari	Bhutan-Tibet	24,040
Chamlang	Nepal	24,012
Kabru	India-Nepal	24,002
Alung Gangri	Tibet.	24,000
Baltoro Kangri	Kashmir	23,990
Mussu Shan	Sinkiang	23,890
Mana	India	23,860
Baruntse	Nepal	23,688
Nepal Peak	India-Nepal	23,500
Amne Machin	China	23,490
Gauri Sankar	Nepal-Tibet.	23,440

Peak	Country	Feet
Badrinath	India	23,420
Nunkun	Kashmir	23,410
Lenina Peak	USSR	23,405
Pyramid	India-Nepal	23,400
Api	Nepal	23,399
Pauhunri	India-Tibet	23,385
Trisul	India	23,360
Kangto	India-Tibet	23,260
Nyenchhen Thanglha	Tibet.	23,255
Trisuli	India	23,210
Pumori	Nepal-Tibet.	23,190
Dunagiri	India	23,184
Lombo Kangra	Tibet.	23,165
Saipal	Nepal	23,100
Macha Pucchare	Nepal	22,958
Numbar	Nepal	22,817
Kanjiroba	Nepal	22,580
Ama Dablam	Nepal	22,350
Cho Polu	Nepal	22,093
Lingtren	Nepal-Tibet.	21,972
Khumbutse	Nepal-Tibet.	21,785
Hlako Gangri	Tibet.	21,266
Mt. Grosvenor	China	21,190
Thagchhab Gangri	Tibet.	20,970
Damavand	Iran	18,606
Ararat	Turkey	16,804

Antarctica

Peak	Feet	Peak	Feet	Peak	Feet	Peak	Feet
Vinson Massif	16,864	Andrew Jackson	13,750	Shear	13,100	Campbell	12,434
Tyree	16,290	Sidley	13,720	Odishaw	13,008	Don Pedro Christophersen	12,355
Shinn	15,750	Ostenso	13,710	Donaldson	12,894	Lysaght	12,326
Gardner	15,375	Minto	13,668	Ray	12,808	Huggins	12,247
Epperly	15,100	Miller	13,650	Sellery	12,779	Sabine	12,200
Kirkpatrick	14,855	Long Gables	13,620	Waterman	12,730	Astor	12,175
Elizabeth	14,698	Dickerson	13,517	Anne	12,703	Mohl	12,172
Markham	14,290	Giovinetto	13,412	Press	12,566	Frankes	12,064
Bell	14,117	Wade	13,400	Falla	12,549	Jones	12,040
Mackellar	14,098	Fisher	13,386	Rucker	12,520	Gjelsvik	12,008
Anderson	13,957	Fridtjof Nansen	13,350	Goldthwait	12,510	Coman	12,000
Bentley	13,934	Wexler	13,202	Morris	12,500		
Kaplan	13,878	Lister	13,200	Erebus	12,450		

Ocean Areas and Average Depths

Four major bodies of water are recognized by geographers and mapmakers. They are: the Pacific, Atlantic, Indian, and Arctic oceans. The Atlantic and Pacific oceans are considered divided at the equator into the No. and So. Atlantic; the No. and So. Pacific. The Arctic Ocean is the name for waters north of the continental land masses in the region of the Arctic Circle.

	Sq. miles	Avg. depth in feet		Sq. miles	Avg. depth in feet
Pacific Ocean	64,186,300	12,925	Hudson Bay	281,900	305
Atlantic Ocean	33,420,000	11,730	East China Sea	256,600	620
Indian Ocean	28,350,500	12,598	Andaman Sea	218,100	3,667
Arctic Ocean	5,105,700	3,407	Black Sea	196,100	3,906
South China Sea	1,148,500	4,802	Red Sea	174,900	1,764
Caribbean Sea	971,400	8,448	North Sea	164,900	308
Mediterranean Sea	969,100	4,926	Baltic Sea	147,500	180
Bering Sea	873,000	4,893	Yellow Sea	113,500	121
Gulf of Mexico	582,100	5,297	Persian Gulf	88,800	328
Sea of Okhotsk	537,500	3,192	Gulf of California	59,100	2,375
Sea of Japan	391,100	5,468			

How Deep Is the Ocean?

Principal ocean depths. **Source:** Defense Mapping Agency Hydrographic/Topographic Center

Name of area	Location	Meters	Depth Fathoms	Feet
Pacific Ocean				
Mariana Trench	11°22'N 142°36'E	10,924	5,973	35,840
Tonga Trench	23°16'S 174°44'W	10,800	5,906	35,433
Philippine Trench	10°38'N 126°36'E	10,057	5,499	32,995
Kermadec Trench	31°53'S 177°21'W	10,047	5,494	32,963
Bonin Trench	24°30'N 143°24'E	9,994	5,464	32,788
Kuril Trench	44°15'N 150°34'E	9,750	5,331	31,988
Izu Trench	31°05'N 142°10'E	9,695	5,301	31,808
New Britain Trench	06°19'S 153°45'E	8,940	4,888	29,331
Yap Trench	08°33'N 138°02'E	8,527	4,663	27,976
Japan Trench	36°08'N 142°43'E	8,412	4,600	27,599
Peru-Chile Trench	23°18'S 71°14'W	8,064	4,409	26,457
Palau Trench	07°52'N 134°56'E	8,054	4,404	26,424
Aleutian Trench	50°51'N 177°11'E	7,679	4,199	25,194
New Hebrides Trench	20°36'S 168°37'E	7,570	4,139	24,836
North Ryukyu Trench	24°00'N 126°48'E	7,181	3,927	23,560
Mid. America Trench	14°02'N 93°39'W	6,662	3,643	21,857
Atlantic Ocean				
Puerto Rico Trench	19°55'N 65°27'W	8,605	4,705	28,232
So. Sandwich Trench	55°42'S 25°56'E	8,325	4,552	27,313
Romanche Gap	0°13'S 18°26'W	7,728	4,226	25,354
Cayman Trench	19°12'N 80°00'W	7,535	4,120	24,721
Brazil Basin	09°10'S 23°02'W	6,119	3,346	20,076
Indian Ocean				
Java Trench	10°19'S 109°58'E	7,125	3,896	23,376
Ob' Trench	09°45'S 67°18'E	6,874	3,759	22,553
Diamantina Trench	35°50'S 105°14'E	6,602	3,610	21,660
Vema Trench	09°08'S 67°15'E	6,402	3,501	21,004
Agulhas Basin	45°20'S 26°50'E	6,195	3,387	20,325
Arctic Ocean				
Eurasia Basin	82°23'N 19°31'E	5,450	2,980	17,881
Mediterranean Sea				
Ionian Basin	36°32'N 21°06'E	5,150	2,816	16,896

Note: Deeper depths have been reported in some of the above areas. However, they are not official unless confirmed by research vessels.

Principal World Rivers

Source: U.S. Geological Survey (length in miles)

River	Outflow	Lgth	River	Outflow	Lgth	River	Outflow	Lgth
Albany	James Bay	610	Indus	Arabian Sea	1,800	Red River of N.	Lake Winnipeg	545
Amazon	Atlantic Ocean	4,000	Irrawaddy	Bay of Bengal	1,337	Rhine	North Sea	820
Amu	Aral Sea	1,578	Japura	Amazon River	1,750	Rhone	Gulf of Lions	505
Amur	Tatar Strait	2,744	Jordan	Dead Sea	200	Rio de la Plata	Atlantic Ocean	150
Angara	Yenisey River	1,151	Kootenay	Columbia River	485	Rio Grande	Gulf of Mexico	1,760
Arkansas	Mississippi	1,459	Lena	Laptev Sea	2,734	Rio Roosevelt	Aripuana	400
Back	Arctic Ocean	605	Loire	Bay of Biscay	634	Saguenay	St. Lawrence R.	434
Brahmaputra	Bay of Bengal	1,800	Mackenzie	Arctic Ocean	2,635	St. John	Bay of Fundy	418
Bug, Southern	Dnieper River	532	Madeira	Amazon River	2,013	St. Lawrence	Gulf of St. Law.	800
Bug, Western	Wisla River	481	Magdalena	Caribbean Sea	956	Salween	Andaman Sea	1,500
Canadian	Arkansas River	906	Marne	Seine River	326	Sao Francisco	Atlantic Ocean	1,988
Chang Jiang	E. China Sea	3,964	Mekong	S. China Sea	2,600	Saskatchewan	Lake Winnipeg	1,205
Churchill, Man.	Hudson Bay	1,000	Meuse	North Sea	580	Seine	English Chan.	496
Churchill, Que.	Atlantic Ocean	532	Mississippi	Gulf of Mexico	2,340	Shannon	Atlantic Ocean	230
Colorado	Gulf of Calif.	1,450	Missouri	Mississippi	2,540	Snake	Columbia River	1,038
Columbia	Pacific Ocean	1,243	Murray-Darling	Indian Ocean	2,310	Sungari	Amur River	1,150
Congo	Atlantic Ocean	2,900	Negro	Amazon	1,400	Syr	Aral Sea	1,370
Danube	Black Sea	1,776	Nelson	Hudson Bay	1,410	Tajo, Tagus	Atlantic Ocean	626
Dnieper	Black Sea	1,420	Niger	Gulf of Guinea	2,590	Tennessee	Ohio River	652
Dniester	Black Sea	877	Nile	Mediterranean	4,160	Thames	North Sea	236
Don	Sea of Azov	1,224	Ob-Irtysh	Gulf of Ob	3,362	Tiber	Tyrrhenian Sea	252
Drava	Danube River	447	Oder	Baltic Sea	567	Tigris	Shatt al-Arab	1,180
Dvina, North	White Sea	824	Ohio	Mississippi	1,310	Tisza	Danube River	600
Dvina, West	Gulf of Riga	634	Orange	Atlantic Ocean	1,300	Tocantins	Para River	1,677
Ebro	Mediterranean	565	Orinoco	Atantic Ocean	1,600	Ural	Caspian Sea	1,575
Elbe	North Sea	724	Ottawa	St. Lawrence R.	790	Uruguay	Rio de la Plata	1,000
Euphrates	Shatt al-Arab	1,700	Paraguay	Parana River	1,584	Volga	Caspian Sea	2,194
Fraser	Str. of Georgia	850	Parana	Rio de la Plata	2,485	Weser	North Sea	454
Gambia	Atlantic Ocean	700	Peace	Slave River	1,210	Wisla	Bay of Danzig	675
Ganges	Bay of Bengal	1,560	Pilcomayo	Paraguay River	1,000	Yellow (See Huang)		
Garonne	Bay of Biscay	357	Po	Adriatic Sea	405	Yenisey	Kara Sea	2,543
Hsi	S. China Sea	1,200	Purus	Amazon River	2,100	Yukon	Bering Sea	1,979
Huang	Yellow Sea	2,903	Red	Mississippi	1,290	Zambezi	Indian Ocean	1,700

Major Rivers in North America

Source: U.S. Geological Survey

River	Source or Upper Limit of Length	Outflow	Miles
Alabama	Gilmer County, Ga.	Mobile River	729
Albany	Lake St. Joseph, Ontario	James Bay	610
Allegheny	Potter County, Pa.	Ohio River	325
Altamaha-Ocmulgee	Junction of Yellow and South Rivers, Newton County, Ga.	Atlantic Ocean	392
Apalachicola-Chattahoochee	Towns County, Ga.	Gulf of Mexico	524
Arkansas	Lake County, Col.	Mississippi River	1,459
Assiniboine	Eastern Saskatchewan	Red River	450
Attawapiskat	Attawapiskat, Ontario	James Bay	465
Big Black (Miss.)	Webster County, Miss.	Mississippi River	330
Black (N.W.T.)	Contwoyto Lake	Chantrey Inlet	600
Brazos	Junction of Salt and Double Mountain Forks, Stonewall County, Tex.	Gulf of Mexico	923
Canadian	Las Animas County, Col.	Arkansas River	906
Cedar (Iowa)	Dodge County, Minn.	Iowa River	329
Cheyenne	Junction of Antelope Creek and Dry Fork, Converse County, Wyo.	Missouri River	290
Churchill	Methy Lake, Saskatchewan	Hudson Bay	1,000
Cimarron	Colfax County, N.M.	Arkansas River	600
Colorado (Ariz.)	Rocky Mountain National Park, Col. (90 miles in Mexico)	Gulf of Cal.	1,450
Colorado (Texas)	West Texas	Matagorda Bay	862
Columbia	Columbia Lake, British Columbia	Pacific Ocean, bet. Ore. and Wash.	1,243
Columbia, Upper	Columbia Lake, British Columbia	To mouth of Snake River	890
Connecticut	Third Connecticut Lake, N.H.	L.I. Sound, Conn.	407
Coppermine (N.W.T.)	Lac de Gras	Coronation Gulf (Arctic Ocean)	525
Cumberland	Letcher County, Ky.	Ohio River	720
Delaware	Schoharie County, N.Y.	Liston Point, Delaware Bay	390
Fraser	Near Mount Robson (on Continental Divide)	Strait of Georgia	850
Gila	Catron County, N.M.	Colorado River	649
Green (Ut.-Wyo.)	Junction of Wells and Trail Creeks, Sublette County, Wyo.	Colorado River	730
Hamilton (Lab.)	Lake Ashuanipi	Atlantic Ocean	532
Hudson	Henderson Lake, Essex County, N.Y.	Upper N.Y. Bay	306
Illinois	St. Joseph County, Ind.	Mississippi River	420
James (N.D.-S.D.)	Wells County, N.D.	Missouri River	710
James (Va.)	Junction of Jackson and Cowpasture Rivers, Botetourt County, Va.	Hampton Roads	340
Kanawha-New	Junction of North and South Forks of New River, N.C.	Ohio River	352
Kentucky	Junction of North and Middle Forks, Lee County, Ky.	Ohio River	259
Klamath	Lake Ewauna, Klamath Falls, Ore.	Pacific Ocean	250
Koyukuk	Endicott Mountains, Alaska	Yukon River	470
Kuskokwim	Alaska Range	Kuskokwim Bay	724
Liard	Southern Yukon, Alaska	Mackenzie River	693
Little Missouri	Crook County, Wyo.	Missouri River	560
Mackenzie	Great Slave Lake, N.W.T.	Arctic Ocean	2,635
Milk	Junction of North and South Forks, Alberta	Missouri River	625
Minnesota	Big Stone Lake, Minn.	Mississippi River	332
Mississippi	Lake Itasca, Minn.	Mouth of Southwest Pass	2,340
Mississippi, Upper	Lake Itasca, Minn.	To mouth of Missouri River	1,171
Mississippi-Missouri-Red Rock	Source of Red Rock, Beaverhead Co., Mon.	Mouth of Southwest Pass	3,710
Missouri	Junction of Jefferson, Madison, and Gallatin rivers, Madison County, Mon.	Mississippi River	2,315
Missouri-Red Rock	Source of Red Rock, Beaverhead Co., Mon.	Mississippi River	2,540
Mobile-Alabama-Coosa	Gilmer County, Ga.	Mobile Bay	774
Nelson (Manitoba)	Lake Winnipeg	Hudson Bay	410
Neosho	Morris County, Kan.	Arkansas River, Okla.	460
Niobrara	Niobrara County, Wyo.	Missouri River, Neb.	431
North Canadian	Union County, N.M.	Canadian River, Okla.	800
North Platte	Junction of Grizzly and Little Grizzly creeks, Jackson County, Col.	Platte River, Neb.	618
Ohio	Junction of Allegheny and Monongahela rivers, Pittsburgh, Pa.	Mississippi River	1,310
Ohio-Allegheny	Potter County, Pa.	Mississippi River	1,306
Osage	East-central Kansas	Missouri River	500
Ottawa	Lake Capimitchigama	St. Lawrence River	790
Ouachita	Polk County, Ark.	Red River	605
Peace	Stikine Mountains, B.C.	Slave River	1,210
Pearl	Neshoba County, Miss.	Gulf of Mexico	411
Pecos	Mora County, N.M.	Rio Grande	926
Pee Dee-Yadkin	Watauga County, N.C.	Winyah Bay	435
Pend Oreille-Clark Fork	Near Butte, Mon.	Columbia River	531
Platte	Junction of North and South Platte Rivers, Neb.	Missouri River	310
Porcupine	Ogilvie Mountains, Alaska	Yukon River, Alaska	569
Potomac	Garrett County, Md.	Chesapeake Bay	383
Powder	Junction of South and Middle Forks, Wyo.	Yellowstone River	375
Red (Okla.-Tex.-La.)	Curry County, N.M.	Mississippi River	1,290
Red River of the North	Junction of Otter Tail and Bois de Sioux Rivers, Wilkin County, Minn.	Lake Winnipeg	545
Republican	Junction of North Fork and Arikaree River, Neb.	Kansas River	445
Rio Grande	San Juan County, Col.	Gulf of Mexico	1,760

River	Source or Upper Limit of Length	Outflow	Miles
Roanoke	Junction of North and South Forks, Montgomery County, Va.	Albemarle Sound	380
Rock (Ill.-Wis.)	Dodge County, Wis.	Mississippi River	300
Sabine	Junction of South and Caddo Forks, Hunt County, Tex.	Sabine Lake	380
Sacramento	Siskiyou County, Cal.	Suisun Bay	377
St. Francis	Iron County, Mo.	Mississippi River	425
St. Lawrence	Lake Ontario	Gulf of St. Lawrence (Atlantic Ocean)	800
Salmon (Idaho)	Custer County, Ida.	Snake River	420
San Joaquin	Junction of South and Middle Forks, Madera County, Cal.	Suisun Bay	350
San Juan	Silver Lake, Archuleta County, Col.	Colorado River	360
Santee-Wateree-Catawba	McDowell County, N.C.	Atlantic Ocean	538
Saskatchewan, North	Rocky Mountains	Lake Winnipeg	800
Saskatchewan, South	Rocky Mountains	Lake Winnipeg	865
Savannah	Junction of Seneca and Tugaloo rivers, Anderson County, S.C.	Atlantic Ocean, Ga.-S.C.	314
Severn (Ontario)	Sandy Lake	Hudson Bay	610
Smoky Hill	Cheyenne County, Col.	Kansas River, Kan.	540
Snake	Teton County, Wyo.	Columbia River, Wash.	1,038
South Platte	Junction of South and Middle Forks, Park County, Col.	Platte River	424
Susitna	Alaska Range	Cook Inlet	313
Susquehanna	Otsego Lake, Otsego County, N.Y.	Chesapeake Bay	444
Tallahatchie	Tippah County, Miss.	Yazoo River	301
Tanana	Wrangell Mountains, Alaska	Yukon River	659
Tennessee	Junction of French Broad and Holston Rivers	Ohio River	652
Tennessee-French Broad	Transylvania County, N.C.	Ohio River	883
Tombigbee	Prentiss County, Miss.	Mobile River	525
Trinity	North of Dallas, Tex.	Galveston Bay	360
Wabash	Darke County, Oh.	Ohio River	512
Washita	Hemphill County, Tex.	Red River, Okla.	500
White (Ark.-Mo.)	Madison County, Ark.	Mississippi River	722
Willamette	Douglas County, Ore.	Columbia River	309
Wind-Bighorn	Junction of Wind and Little Wind Rivers, Fremont Co., Wyo. (Source of Wind R. is Togwotee Pass, Teton Co., Wyo.)	Yellowstone River	336
Wisconsin	LeVieux Desert, Vilas County, Wis.	Mississippi River	430
Yellowstone	Park County, Wyo.	Missouri River	692
Yukon	Coast Mountains of British Columbia	Bering Sea	1,979

Flows of Largest U.S. Rivers

Source: U.S. Geological Survey. Discharges in cubic feet per second (ft³/s). Ranked according to average discharge at mouth. 1951-80 (shorter records for some Alaskan streams). Data have been rounded to no more than 3 significant figures.

River	Average discharge	Length[a] (miles)	Drainage area (sq. mi.)	Name, location of source stream at headwater	Maximum discharge at a downstream gauging station
Mississippi	593,000[b]	2,340[c]	1,150,000[d]	Mississippi R., Clearwater Co., Minn.	2,080,000
St. Lawrence (-Great Lakes)	348,000	1,900	396,000 (U.S.-Canada)	North R., Lake Co., Minn.	[c]352,000
Ohio	281,000	1,310	203,000	Allegheny R., Potter Co., Pa.	1,850,000
Columbia	265,000	1,240	258,000 (U.S.-Canada)	Columbia R., B.C., Canada	1,240,000
Yukon	225,000	1,980	328,000 (U.S.-Canada)	McNeil R., Yukon Terr., Canada	1,100,000
Missouri	76,200	2,540	529,000 (U.S.-Canada)	Red Rock Creek, Beaverhead Co., Mont.	892,000
Tennessee	68,000	886	40,900	Courthouse Creek, Transylvania Co., N.C.	500,000
Mobile (-Alabama)	67,200	774	44,600	Tickanetley Creek, Gilmer Co., Ga.	——
Kuskokwim	67,000	724	48,000	South Fork Kuskokwim R. at terminus of unnamed glacier, Alaska	392,000
Copper	59,000	286	24,400	Copper R. at terminus of Copper Glacier, Alaska	380,000
Atchafalaya (-Red)	58,000	1,420	95,100	Tierra Blanca Creek, Curry Co., N. M.	781,000
Snake	56,900	1,040	108,000	Snake R., Teton Co., Wyo.	409,000
Red	56,000	1,290	93,200	Tierra Blanca Creek, Curry Co., N. M.	233,000
Stikine	56,000	379	20,000 (U.S.-Canada)	Stikine R., B. C., Canada	300,000
Susitna	51,000	313	20,000	Susitna R. at terminus of Susitna Glacier, Alaska	312,000
Tanana	41,000	659	44,500	Nabesna R. at terminus of Nabesna Glacier, Alaska	186,000
Arkansas	41,000	1,460	161,000	E. Fork Arkansas R., Lake Co., Col.	536,000
Susquehanna	38,200	447	27,200	Hayden Creek, Otsego Co., N.Y.	1,130,000
Willamette	37,400	309	11,400	Middle Fork Willamette R., Douglas Co., Ore.	500,000
Nushagak	36,000	285	13,400	Nushagak R., Alaska	89,200

(a) From source to mouth; because river lengths and methods of measurement may change from time to time, the length figures given are subject to revision; (b) includes about 167,000 ft³/s diverted from the Mississippi into the Atchafalaya River but excludes the flow of the Red River; (c) the length from the source of the Missouri River to the Mississippi River and thence to the Gulf of Mexico is about 3,710 miles; (d) excluding the drainage areas of the Red and Atchafalaya rivers; (e) drainage area at gaging station, 299,000 mi²; average discharge at that station, 1959-80, 252,000 ft³/s; (f) continuation of Red River; data on average discharge, length, and drainage area include the Red River but exclude about 167,000 ft³/s diverted from the Mississippi into the Atchafalaya River.

Some streams that are widely known for their length, their location, or for their large flows in flood, have too small an average flow to qualify for this list.

Important Islands and Their Areas

Figure in parentheses shows rank among the world's 10 largest islands; some islands have not been surveyed accurately; in such cases estimated areas are shown.

Location-Ownership
Area in square miles

Arctic Ocean

Canadian
Axel Heiberg	16,671
Baffin (5)	195,928
Banks	27,038
Bathurst	6,194
Devon	21,331
Ellesmere (10)	75,767
Melville	16,274
Prince of Wales	12,872
Somerset	9,570
Southampton	15,913
Victoria (9)	83,896

USSR
Franz Josef Land	8,000
Novaya Zemlya (two is.)	35,000
Wrangel	2,800

Norwegian
Svalbard	23,940
Nordaustlandet	5,410
Spitsbergen	15,060

Atlantic Ocean
Anticosti, Canada	3,066
Ascension, UK	34
Azores, Portugal	888
Faial	67
Sao Miguel	291
Bahamas	5,353
Bermuda Is., UK	20
Block, Rhode Island	10
Canary Is., Spain	2,808
Fuerteventura	668
Gran Canaria	592
Tenerife	795
Cape Breton, Canada	3,981
Cape Verde Is.	1,750
Faeroe Is., Denmark	540
Falkland Is., UK	4,700
Fernando de Noronha Archipelago, Brazil	7
Greenland, Denmark (1)	840,000
Iceland	39,769
Long Island, N.Y.	1,396
Bioko Is. Equatorial Guinea	785
Madeira Is., Portugal	307
Marajo, Brazil	15,528
Martha's Vineyard, Mass.	91
Mount Desert, Me.	108
Nantucket, Mass.	46
Newfoundland, Canada	42,030
Prince Edward, Canada	2,184
St. Helena, UK	47
South Georgia, UK	1,450
Tierra del Fuego, Chile and Argentina	18,800
Tristan da Cunha, UK	40

British Isles
Great Britain, mainland (8)	84,200
Channel Islands	75
Guernsey	24
Jersey	45
Sark	2
Hebrides	2,744
Ireland	32,599
Irish Republic	27,136
Northern Ireland	5,463
Man	227
Orkney Is.	390
Scilly Is.	6
Shetland Is.	567
Skye	670
Wight	147

Baltic Sea
Aland Is., Finland	581
Bornholm, Denmark	227
Gotland, Sweden	1,164

Caribbean Sea
Antigua	108
Aruba, Netherlands	75
Barbados	166
Cuba	44,218
Isle of Youth	1,182
Curacao, Netherlands	171
Dominica	290
Guadeloupe, France	687
Hispaniola, Haiti and Dominican Republic	29,530
Jamaica	4,244
Martinique, France	425
Puerto Rico, U.S.	3,515
Tobago	116
Trinidad	1,864
Virgin Is., UK	59
Virgin Is., U.S.	132

Indian Ocean
Andaman Is., India	2,500
Madagascar (4)	226,658
Mauritius	720
Pemba, Tanzania	380
Reunion, France	969
Seychelles	171
Sri Lanka	25,332
Zanzibar, Tanzania	640

Persian Gulf
Bahrain	258

Mediterranean Sea
Balearic Is., Spain	1,936
Corfu, Greece	229
Corsica, France	3,369
Crete, Greece	3,186
Cyprus	3,572
Elba, Italy	86
Euboea, Greece	1,409
Malta	122
Rhodes, Greece	542
Sardinia, Italy	9,262
Sicily, Italy	9,822

Pacific Ocean
Aleutian Is., U.S.	6,821
Adak	289
Amchitka	121
Attu	388
Kanaga	135
Kiska	110
Tanaga	209
Umnak	675
Unalaska	1,064
Unimak	1,600
Canton, Kiribati*	4
Caroline Is., U.S. trust terr.	472
Christmas, Kiribati*	94
Diomede, Big, USSR	11
Diomede, Little, U.S.	2
Easter, Chile	69
Fiji	7,056
Vanua Levu	2,242
Viti Levu	4,109
Funafuti, Tuvalu*	2
Galapagos Is., Ecuador	3,043
Guadalcanal, UK	2,500
Guam	209
Hainan, China	13,000
Hawaiian Is., U.S.	6,450
Hawaii	4,037
Oahu	593
Hong Kong, UK	29
Japan	145,809
Hokkaido	30,144
Honshu (7)	87,805
Iwo Jima	8
Kyushu	14,114
Okinawa	459
Shikoku	7,049
Kodiak, U.S.	3,670
Marquesas Is., France	492
Marshall Is., U.S. trust terr.	70
Bikini*	2
Nauru	8
New Caledonia, France	6,530
New Guinea (2)	306,000
New Zealand	103,883
Chatham	372
North	44,035
South	58,305
Stewart	674
Northern Mariana Is.	184
Philippines	115,831
Leyte	2,787
Luzon	40,880
Mindanao	36,775
Mindoro	3,790
Negros	4,907
Palawan	4,554
Panay	4,446
Samar	5,050
Quemoy	56
Sakhalin, USSR	29,500
Samoa Is.	1,177
American Samoa	77
Tutuila	52
Samoa (Western)	1,133
Savaii	670
Upolu	429
Santa Catalina, U.S.	72
Tahiti, France	402
Taiwan	13,823
Tasmania, Australia	26,178
Tonga Is.	270
Vancouver, Canada	12,079
Vanuatu	5,700

East Indies
Bali, Indonesia	2,147
Borneo, Indonesia-Malaysia, UK (3)	280,100
Celebes, Indonesia	69,000
Java, Indonesia	48,900
Madura, Indonesia	2,113
Moluccas, Indonesia	28,766
New Britain, Papua New Guinea	14,093
New Ireland, Papua New Guinea	3,707
Sumatra, Indonesia (6)	165,000
Timor	11,570

*Atolls: Bikini (lagoon area, 230 sq. mi., land area 2 sq. mi.), U.S. Trust Territory of the Pacific Islands; Canton (lagoon 20 sq. mi., land 4 sq. mi.), Kiribati; Christmas (lagoon 140 sq. mi., land 94 sq. mi.), Kiribati; Funafuti (lagoon 84 sq. mi., land 2 sq. mi.), Tuvalu. **Australia**, often called an island, is a continent. Its mainland area is 2,939,975 sq. mi.

Islands in minor waters; Manhattan (22 sq mi.) Staten (59 sq. mi.) and Governors (173 acres), all in New York Harbor, U.S.; Isle Royale (209 sq. mi.), Lake Superior, U.S.; Manitoulin (1,068 sq. mi.), Lake Huron, Canada; Pinang (110 sq. mi.), Strait of Malacca, Malaysia; Singapore (239 sq. mi.), Singapore Strait, Singapore.

Lakes of the World

Source: U.S. Geological Survey

A lake is a body of water surrounded by land. Although some lakes are called seas, they are lakes by definition. The Caspian Sea is bounded by the Soviet Union and Iran and is fed by eight rivers.

Name	Continent	Area sq. mi.	Length mi.	Depth feet	Elev. feet
Caspian Sea	Asia-Europe	143,244	760	3,363	−92
Superior	North America	31,700	350	1,330	600
Victoria	Africa	26,828	250	270	3,720
Aral Sea	Asia	24,904	280	220	174
Huron	North America	23,000	206	750	579
Michigan	North America	22,300	307	923	579
Tanganyika	Africa	12,700	420	4,823	2,534
Baykal	Asia	12,162	395	5,315	1,493
Great Bear	North America	12,096	192	1,463	512
Malawi	Africa	11,150	360	2,280	1,550
Great Slave	North America	11,031	298	2,015	513
Erie	North America	9,910	241	210	570
Winnipeg	North America	9,417	266	60	713
Ontario	North America	7,550	193	802	245
Balkhash	Asia	7,115	376	85	1,115
Ladoga	Europe	6,835	124	738	13
Chad	Africa	6,300	175	24	787
Maracaibo	South America	5,217	133	115	Sea level
Onega	Europe	3,710	145	328	108
Eyre	Australia	3,600	90	4	−52
Volta	Africa	3,276	250		
Titicaca	South America	3,200	122	922	12,500
Nicaragua	North America	3,100	102	230	102
Athabasca	North America	3,064	208	407	700
Reindeer	North America	2,568	143	720	1,106
Turkana	Africa	2,473	154	240	1,230
Issyk Kul	Asia	2,355	115	2,303	5,279
Torrens	Australia	2,230	130	....	92
Vanern	Europe	2,156	91	328	144
Nettilling	North America	2,140	67	....	95
Winnipegosis	North America	2,075	141	38	830
Albert	Africa	2,075	100	168	2,030
Kariba	Africa	2,050	175	390	1,590
Nipigon	North America	1,872	72	540	1,050
Gairdner	Australia	1,840	90	....	112
Urmia	Asia	1,815	90	49	4,180
Manitoba	North America	1,799	140	12	813

The Great Lakes

Source: National Ocean Service, U.S. Commerce Department

The Great Lakes form the largest body of fresh water in the world and with their connecting waterways are the largest inland water transportation unit. Draining the great North Central basin of the U.S., they enable shipping to reach the Atlantic via their outlet, the St. Lawrence R., and also the Gulf of Mexico via the Illinois Waterway, from Lake Michigan to the Mississippi R. A third outlet connects with the Hudson R. and thence the Atlantic via the N. Y. State Barge Canal System. Traffic on the Illinois Waterway and the N.Y. State Barge Canal System is limited to recreational boating and small shipping vessels.

Only one of the lakes, Lake Michigan, is wholly in the United States; the others are shared with Canada. Ships carrying grain, lumber and iron ore move from the shores of Lake Superior to Whitefish Bay at the east end of the lake,

thence through the Soo (Sault Ste. Marie) locks, through the St. Mary's River and into Lake Huron. To reach the steel mills at Gary, and Port of Indiana and South Chicago, Ill., ore ships move west from Lake Huron to Lake Michigan through the Straits of Mackinac.

Lake Huron discharges its waters into Lake Erie through a narrow waterway, the St. Clair R., Lake St. Clair (both included in the drainage basin figures) and the Detroit R. Lake St. Clair, a marshy basin, is 26 miles long and 24 miles wide at its maximum. A ship channel has been dredged through the lake.

Lake Superior is 600 feet above mean water level at Point-au-Pere, Quebec, on the International Great Lakes Datum (1955). From Duluth, Minn., to the eastern end of Lake Ontario is 1,156 mi.

	Superior	Michigan	Huron	Erie	Ontario
Length in miles	350	307	206	241	193
Breadth in miles	160	118	183	57	53
Deepest soundings in feet	1,330	923	750	210	802
Volume of water in cubic miles	2,900	1,180	850	116	393
Area (sq. miles) water surface—U.S.	20,600	22,300	9,100	4,980	3,560
Canada	11,100	.....	13,900	4,930	3,990
Area (sq. miles) entire drainage basin—U.S.	16,900	45,600	16,200	18,000	15,200
Canada	32,400	.....	35,500	4,720	12,100
Total Area (sq. miles) U.S. and Canada	**81,000**	**67,900**	**74,700**	**32,630**	**34,850**
Mean surface above mean water level at Point-au-Pere, Quebec, aver. level in feet (1900-1988)	600.61	578.35	578.35	570.52	244.73
Latitude, North	46° 25'	41° 37'	43° 00'	41° 23'	43° 11'
	49° 00'	46° 06'	46° 17'	42° 52'	44° 15'
Longitude, West	84° 22'	84° 45'	79° 43'	78° 51'	76° 03'
	92° 06'	88° 02'	84° 45'	83° 29'	79° 53'
National boundary line in miles	282.8	None	260.8	251.5	174.6
United States shore line (mainland only) miles	863	1,400	580	431	300

Large U.S. Lakes

Source: U.S. Geological Survey

Natural U.S. lakes (excluding the Great Lakes) with areas of 100 sq. mi.

Lake	State	Area (sq. mi.)	Lake	State	Area (sq. mi.)
Lake of the Woods	Minn., Ontario, Manitoba	1,697	Flathead	Mon.	197
Great Salt[1]	Ut.	1,361[2]	Tahoe	Cal., Nev.	193
Iliamna	Alas.	1,000	Leech	Minn.	176
Okeechobee	Fla.	700	Pyramid[1]	Nev.	168[2]
Pontchartrain[1]	La.	625	Pend Oreille	Ida.	148
Becharof	Alas.	458	Ugashik (upper and lower)	Alas.	147
Red Lake (upper and lower)	Minn.	451	Upper Klamath	Ore.	142
Champlain	N.Y., Vt., Quebec	435	Utah	Ut.	140
St. Clair	Mich., Ontario	432	Bear (including Mud Lake)	Ida., Ut.	136
Salton Sea[1]	Cal.	374[2]	Yellowstone	Wyo.	134
Rainy	Minn., Ontario	360	Moosehead	Me.	117
Teshekpuk	Alas.	315	Tustumena	Alas.	117
Naknek	Alas.	242	Clark	Alas.	110
Winnebago	Wis.	215	Winnibigoshish	Minn.	109
Mille Lacs	Minn.	207	Dall	Alas.	100

(1) Salty. (2) Variable.

Famous Waterfalls

Source: National Geographic Society, Washington, D.C.

The earth has thousands of waterfalls, some of considerable magnitude. Their importance is determined not only by height but volume of flow, steadiness of flow, crest width, whether the water drops sheerly or over a sloping surface, and in one leap or a succession of leaps. A series of low falls flowing over a considerable distance is known as a cascade.

Sete Quedas or Guaira is the world's greatest waterfall when its mean annual flow (estimated at 470,000 cusecs, cubic feet per second) is combined with height. A greater volume of water passes over Boyoma Falls (Stanley Falls), though not one of its seven cataracts, spread over nearly 60 miles of the Congo River, exceeds 10 feet.

Estimated mean annual flow, in cusecs, of other major waterfalls are: Niagara, 212,200; Paulo Afonso, 100,000; Urubupunga, 97,000; Iguazu, 61,000; Patos-Maribondo, 53,000; Victoria, 35,400; and Kaieteur, 23,400.

Height = total drop in feet in one or more leaps. † = falls of more than one leap; * = falls that diminish greatly seasonally; ** = falls that reduce to a trickle or are dry for part of each year. If river names not shown, they are same as the falls. R. = river; L. = lake; (C) = cascade type.

Name and location	Ht.
Africa	
Angola	
Duque de Braganca,	
Lucala R.	344
Ruacana, Cuene R.	406
Ethiopia	
Dal Verme,	
Dorya R.	98
Fincha	508
Tesissat, Blue Nile R.	140
Lesotho	
*Maletsunyane	630
Zimbabwe-Zambia	
*Victoria, Zambezi R.	343
South Africa	
*Augrabies, Orange R.	480
Howick, Umgeni R.	364
† Tugela	2,014
Highest fall	597
Tanzania-Zambia	
*Kalambo	726
Uganda	
Kabalega (Murchison) Victoria	
Nile R.	130
Asia	
India—*Cauvery	330
*Gokak, Ghataprabha R.	170
*Jog (Gersoppa), Sharavathi R.	830
Japan	
*Kegon, Daiya R.	330
Laos	
Khon Cataracts,	
Mekong R. (C)	70
Australasia	
Australia	
New South Wales	
Wentworth	614
Highest fall	360
Wollomombi	1,100

Name and location	Ht.
Queensland	
Coomera	210
Tully	885
† Wallaman, Stony Cr.	1,137
Highest fall	937
New Zealand	
Bowen	540
Helena	890
Stirling	505
† Sutherland, Arthur R.	1,904
Highest fall	815
Europe	
Austria—† Gastein	492
Highest fall	280
† *Golling, Schwarzbach R.	250
† Krimml	1,312
France—*Gavarnie	1,385
Great Britain—Scotland	
Glomach	370
Wales	
Cain	150
Rhaiadr	240
Iceland—Detti	144
† Gull, Hvita R.	105
Italy—Frua, Toce R. (C).	470
Norway	
Mardalsfossen (Northern)	1,535
† Mardalsfossen (Southern).	2,149
† **Skjeggedal, Nybuai R.	1,378
**Skykje	984
Vetti, Morka-Koldedola R.	900
Voring, Bjoreio R.	597
Sweden	
† Handol	427
† Tannforsen, Are R.	120
Switzerland	
† Diesbach	394
Giessbach (C)	984
Handegg, Aare R.	150
Iffigen	120
Pissevache, Salanfe R.	213

Name and location	Ht.
† Reichenbach	656
Rhine	79
† Simmen	459
Staubbach	984
† Trummelbach	1,312
North America	
Canada	
Alberta	
Panther, Nigel Cr.	600
British Columbia	
† Della	1,443
† Takakkaw, Daly Glacier.	1,200
Northwest Territories	
Virginia, S. Nahanni R.	294
Quebec	
Montmorency	274
Canada—United States	
Niagara: American	182
Horseshoe	173
United States	
California	
*Feather, Fall R.	640
Yosemite National Park	
*Bridalveil	620
*Illilouette	370
*Nevada, Merced R.	594
**Ribbon	1,612
**Silver Strand, Meadow Br.	1,170
*Vernal, Merced R.	317
† **Yosemite	2,425
Yosemite (upper)	1,430
Yosemite (lower)	320
Yosemite (middle) (C)	675
Colorado	
† Seven, South Cheyenne Cr.	300
Hawaii	
Akaka, Kolekole Str.	442
Idaho	
**Shoshone, Snake R.	212
Twin, Snake R.	120
Kentucky	

Name and location	Ht.	Name and location	Ht.	Name and location	Ht.
Kentucky		**Snoqualmie.	268	Urubupunga, Parana R.	40
Cumberland.	68	Wisconsin		Brazil-Paraguay	
Maryland		*Big Manitou, Black R. (C).	165	Sete Quedas	
*Great, Potomac R. (C)	71	Wyoming		Parana R.	130
Minnesota		Yellowstone Natl. Pk. Tower . . .	132	Colombia	
**Minnehaha.	53	*Yellowstone (upper).	109	Catarata de Candelas,	
New Jersey		*Yellowstone (lower).	308	Cusiana R.	984
Passaic.	70	**Mexico**		*Tequendama, Bogota R.	427
New York		El Salto	218	Ecuador	
*Taughannock	215	**Juanacatlan, Santiago R.	72	*Agoyan, Pastaza R.	200
Oregon				Guyana	
† Multnomah	620	**South America**		Kaieteur, Potaro R.	741
Highest fall.	542			Great, Kamarang R.	1,600
Tennessee		**Argentina-Brazil**		† Marina, Ipobe R.	500
Fall Creek.	256	Iguazu	230	Highest fall	300
Washington		**Brazil**		Venezuela—	
Mt. Rainier Natl. Park		Glass	1,325	† *Angel.	3,212
Narada, Paradise R.	168	Patos-Maribondo, Grande R. . . .	115	Highest fall	2,648
Sluiskin, Paradise R.	300	Paulo Afonso, Sao Francisco R. . .	275	Cuquenan.	2,000
Palouse	197				

Notable Deserts of the World

Arabian (Eastern), 70,000 sq. mi. in Egypt between the Nile river and Red Sea, extending southward into Sudan.

Atacama, 600 mi. long area rich in nitrate and copper deposits in N. Chile.

Chihuahuan, 140,000 sq. mi. in Tex., N.M., Ariz., and Mexico.

Death Valley, 3,300 sq. mi. in E. Cal. and SW Nev. Contains lowest point below sea level (282 ft.) in Western Hemisphere.

Gibson, 120,000 sq. mi. in the interior of W. Australia.

Gobi, 500,000 sq. mi. in Mongolia and China.

Great Sandy, 150,000 sq. mi. in W. Australia.

Great Victoria, 150,000 sq. mi. in W. and S. Australia.

Kalahari, 225,000 sq. mi. in southern Africa.

Kara-Kum, 120,000 sq. mi. in Turkmen SSR.

Kavir (Dasht-e Kavir), great salt waste in central Iran some 400 mi. long.

Kyzyl Kum, 100,000 sq. mi. in Kazakh and Uzbek SSRs.

Libyan, 450,000 sq. mi. in the Sahara extending from Lybia through SW Egypt into Sudan.

Lut (Dasht-e Lut), 20,000 sq. mi. in E. Iran.

Mojave, 15,000 sq. mi. in S. Cal.

Nafud (An Nafud), 40,000 sq. mi. near Jawf in Saudi Arabia.

Namib, long narrow area extending 800 miles along SW coast of Africa.

Nubian, 100,000 sq. mi. in the Sahara in NE Sudan.

Painted Desert, section of high plateau in N. Ariz. extending 150 mi.

Rub al Khali (Empty Quarter), 250,000 sq. mi. in the south Arabian Peninsula.

Sahara, 3,500,000 sq. mi. in N. Africa extending westward to the Atlantic. Largest desert in the world.

Simpson, 40,000 sq. mi. in central Australia.

Sonoran, 70,000 sq. mi. in SW Ariz. and SE Cal. extending into Mexico.

Syrian, 100,000 sq. mi. arid wasteland extending over much of N. Saudi Arabia, E. Jordan, S. Syria, and W. Iraq.

Taklimakan, 140,000 sq. mi. in Sinkiang Province, China.

Thar (Great Indian), 100,000 sq. mi. arid area extending 400 mi. along India-Pakistan border.

Area and Population of the World

Source: Rand McNally & Co.

Continent	Area (1,000 sq. mi.)	% of Earth	Population (est., thousands)						% World Total, 1989
			1650	1750	1850	1900	1950	1989	
North America	9,400	16.2	5,000	5,000	39,000	106,000	219,000	420,100	8.1
South America	6,900	11.9	8,000	7,000	20,000	38,000	111,000	287,500	5.5
Europe	3,800	6.6	100,000	140,000	265,000	400,000	530,000	685,400	13.2
Asia	17,400	30.1	335,000	476,000	754,000	932,000	1,418,000	3,130,600	60.3
Africa	11,700	20.2	100,000	95,000	95,000	118,000	199,000	642,100	12.4
Oceania, incl.									
Australia	3,300	5.7	2,000	2,000	2,000	6,000	13,000	26,300	0.5
Antarctica	5,400	9.3	Uninhabited						
World	57,900	—	550,000	725,000	1,175,000	1,600,000	2,490,000	5,192,000	—

Highest and Lowest Continental Altitudes

Source: National Geographic Society, Washington, D.C.

Continent	Highest point	Feet elevation	Lowest point	Feet below sea level
Asia	Mount Everest, Nepal-Tibet	29,028	Dead Sea, Israel-Jordan	1,312
South America . .	Mount Aconcagua, Argentina	22,834	Valdes Peninsula, Argentina	131
North America . .	Mount McKinley, Alaska	20,320	Death Valley, California.	282
Africa	Kilimanjaro, Tanzania	19,340	Lake Assal, Djibouti.	512
Europe	Mount El'brus, USSR	18,510	Caspian Sea, USSR	92
Antarctica.	Vinson Massif	16,864	Unknown	. . .
Australia	Mount Kosciusko, New South Wales	7,310	Lake Eyre, South Australia.	52

DISASTERS
Some Notable Shipwrecks Since 1850
(Figures indicate estimated lives lost; as of mid-1989)

1854, Mar.—City of Glasgow; British steamer missing in North Atlantic; 480.

1854, Sept. 27—Arctic; U.S. (Collins Line) steamer sunk in collision with French steamer Vesta near Cape Race; 285-351.

1856, Jan. 23—Pacific; U.S. (Collins Line) steamer missing in North Atlantic; 186-286.

1858, Sept. 23—Austria; German steamer destroyed by fire in North Atlantic; 471.

1863, Apr. 27—Anglo-Saxon; British steamer wrecked at Cape Race; 238.

1865, Apr. 27—Sultana; a Mississippi River steamer blew up near Memphis, Tenn; 1,450.

1869, Oct. 27—Stonewall; steamer burned on Mississippi River below Cairo, Ill.; 200.

1870, Jan. 25—City of Boston; British (Inman Line) steamer vanished between New York and Liverpool; 177.

1870, Oct 19—Cambria; British steamer wrecked off northern Ireland; 196.

1872, Nov. 7—Mary Celeste; U.S. half-brig sailed from New York for Genoa; found abandoned in Atlantic 4 weeks later in mystery of sea; crew never heard from; loss of life unknown.

1873, Jan. 22—Northfleet; British steamer foundered off Dungeness, England; 300.

1873, Apr. 1—Atlantic; British (White Star) steamer wrecked off Nova Scotia; 585.

1873, Nov. 23—Ville du Havre; French steamer, sunk after collision with British sailing ship Loch Earn; 226.

1875, May 7—Schiller; German steamer wrecked off Scilly Isles; 312.

1875, Nov. 4—Pacific; U.S. steamer sunk after collision off Cape Flattery; 236.

1878, Sept. 3—Princess Alice; British steamer sank after collision in Thames River; 700.

1878, Dec. 18—Byzantin; French steamer sank after Dardanelles collision; 210.

1881, May 24—Victoria; steamer capsized in Thames River, Canada; 200.

1883, Jan. 19—Cimbria; German steamer sunk in collision with British steamer Sultan in North Sea; 389.

1887, Nov. 15—Wah Yeung; British steamer burned at sea; 400.

1890, Feb. 17—Duburg; British steamer wrecked, China Sea; 400.

1890, Sept. 19—Ertogrul; Turkish frigate foundered off Japan; 540.

1891, Mar. 17—Utopia; British steamer sank in collision with British ironclad Anson off Gibraltar; 562.

1895, Jan. 30—Elbe; German steamer sunk in collision with British steamer Craithie in North Sea; 332.

1895, Mar. 11—Reina Regenta; Spanish cruiser foundered near Gibraltar; 400.

1898, Feb. 15—Maine; U.S. battleship blown up in Havana Harbor; 260.

1898, July 4—La Bourgogne; French steamer sunk in collision with British sailing ship Cromartyshire off Nova Scotia; 549.

1898, Nov. 26—Portland; U.S. steamer wrecked off Cape Cod; 157.

1904, June 15—General Slocum; excursion steamer burned in East River, New York City; 1,030.

1904, June 28—Norge; Danish steamer wrecked on Rockall Island, Scotland; 620.

1906, Aug. 4—Sirio; Italian steamer wrecked off Cape Palos, Spain; 350.

1908, Mar. 23—Matsu Maru; Japanese steamer sank in collision near Hakodate, Japan; 300.

1909, Aug. 1—Waratah; British steamer, Sydney to London, vanished; 300.

1910, Feb. 9—General Chanzy; French steamer wrecked off Minorca, Spain; 200.

1911, Sept. 25—Liberté; French battleship exploded at Toulon; 285.

1912, Mar. 5—Principe de Asturias; Spanish steamer wrecked off Spain; 500.

1912, Apr. 14-15—Titanic; British (White Star) steamer hit iceberg in North Atlantic; 1,503.

1912, Sept. 28—Kichemaru; Japanese steamer sank off Japanese coast; 1,000.

1914, May 29—Empress of Ireland; British (Canadian Pacific) steamer sunk in collision with Norwegian collier in St. Lawrence River; 1,014.

1915, May 7—Lusitania; British (Cunard Line) steamer torpedoed and sunk by German submarine off Ireland; 1,198.

1915, July 24—Eastland; excursion steamer capsized in Chicago River; 812.

1916, Feb. 26—Provence; French cruiser sank in Mediterranean; 3,100.

1916, Mar. 3—Principe de Asturias; Spanish steamer wrecked near Santos, Brazil; 558.

1916, Aug. 29—Hsin Yu; Chinese steamer sank off Chinese coast; 1,000.

1917, Dec. 6—Mont Blanc, Imo; French ammunition ship and Belgian steamer collided in Halifax Harbor; 1,600.

1918, Apr. 25—Kiang-Kwan Chinese steamer sank in collision off Hankow; 500.

1918, July 12—Kawachi; Japanese battleship blew up in Tokayama Bay; 500.

1918, Oct. 25—Princess Sophia; Canadian steamer sank off Alaskan coast; 398.

1919, Jan. 17—Chaonia; French steamer lost in Straits of Messina, Italy; 460.

1919, Sept. 9—Valbanera; Spanish steamer lost off Florida coast; 500.

1921, Mar. 18—Hong Kong; steamer wrecked in South China Sea; 1,000.

1922, Aug. 26—Niitaka; Japanese cruiser sank in storm off Kamchatka, USSR; 300.

1927, Oct. 25—Principessa Mafalda; Italian steamer blew up, sank off Porto Seguro, Brazil; 314.

1928, Nov. 12—Vestris; British steamer sank in gale off Virginia; 113.

1934, Sept. 8—Morro Castle; U.S. steamer, Havana to New York, burned off Asbury Park, N.J.; 134.

1939, May 23—Squalus; U.S. submarine sank off Portsmouth, N.H.; 26.

1939, June 1—Thetis; British submarine, sank in Liverpool Bay; 99.

1942, Feb. 18—Truxtun and Pollux; U.S. destroyer and cargo ship ran aground, sank off Newfoundland; 204.

1942, Oct. 2—Curacao; British cruiser sank after collision with liner Queen Mary; 338.

1944, Dec. 17-18—3 U.S. Third Fleet destroyers sank during typhoon in Philippine Sea; 790.

1947, Jan. 19—Himera; Greek steamer hit a mine off Athens; 392.

1947, Apr. 16—Grandcamp; French freighter exploded in Texas City, Tex., Harbor, starting fires; 510.

1948, Nov.—Chinese army evacuation ship exploded and sunk off S. Manchuria; 6,000.

1948, Dec. 3—Kiangya; Chinese refugee ship wrecked in explosion S. of Shanghai; 1,100+.

1949, Sept. 17—Noronic; Canadian Great Lakes Cruiser burned at Toronto dock; 130.

1952, Apr. 26—Hobson and Wasp; U.S. destroyer and aircraft carrier collided in Atlantic; 176.

1953, Jan. 31—Princess Victoria; British ferry sank in storm off northern Irish coast; 134.

1954, Sept. 26—Toya Maru; Japanese ferry sank in Tsugaru Strait, Japan; 1,172.

1956, July 26—Andrea Doria and Stockholm; Italian liner and Swedish liner collided off Nantucket; 51.

1957, July 14—Eshghabad; Soviet ship ran aground in Caspian Sea; 270.

1961, July 8—Save; Portuguese ship ran aground off Mozambique; 259.

1962, Apr. 8—Dara; British liner exploded and sunk in Persian Gulf; 236.

1963, Apr. 10—Thresher; U.S. Navy atomic submarine sank in North Atlantic; 129.

1964, Feb. 10—Voyager, Melbourne; Australian destroyer sank after collision with Australian aircraft carrier Melbourne off New South Wales; 82.

1965, Nov. 13—Yarmouth Castle; Panamanian registered cruise ship burned and sank off Nassau; 90.

1967, July 29—Forrestal; U.S. aircraft carrier caught fire off N. Vietnam; 134.

1968, Jan. 25—Dakar; Israeli submarine vanished in Mediterranean Sea; 69.

1968, Jan. 27—Minerve; French submarine vanished in Mediterranean; 52.

1968, late May—Scorpion; U.S. nuclear submarine sank in Atlantic near Azores; 99 (located Oct. 31).

1969, June 2—Evans; U.S. destroyer cut in half by Australian carrier Melbourne, S. China Sea; 74.

1970, Mar. 4—Eurydice; French submarine sank in Mediterranean near Toulon; 57.

1970, Dec. 15—Namyong-Ho; South Korean ferry sank in Korea Strait; 308.

1974, May 1— Motor launch capsized off Bangladesh; 250.

1974, Sept. 26— Soviet destroyer burned and sank in Black Sea; 200+.

1976, Oct. 20—George Prince and Frosta; ferryboat and Norwegian tanker collided on Mississippi R. at Luling, La.; 77.

1976, Dec. 25—Patria; Egyptian liner caught fire and sank in the Red Sea; c. 100.

1977, Jan. 11—Grand Zenith; Panamanian-registered tanker sank off Cape Cod, Mass.; 38.

1979, Aug. 14—23 yachts competing in Fastnet yacht race sunk or abandoned during storm in S. Irish Sea; 18.

1981, Jan. 27—Tamponas II; Indonesian passenger ship caught fire and sank in Java Sea; 580.

1981, May 26—Nimitz; U.S. Marine combat jet crashed on deck of U.S. aircraft carrier; 14.

1983, Feb. 12—Marine Electric; coal freighter sank during storm off Chincoteague, Va.; 33.

1983, May 25—10th of Ramadan; Nile steamer caught fire and sank in L. Nassar; 357.

1986, Aug. 31—Admiral Nakhimov; Soviet passenger ship and Pyotr Vasev, Soviet freighter, collided in the Black Sea; 398.

1987, Mar. 6—British ferry capsized off Zeebrugge, Belgium; 188.

1987, Dec. 20—Philippine ferry Dona Paz and oil tanker Victor collided in the Tablas Strait; 3,000+.

1988, Aug. 6—Indian ferry capsized on Ganges R.; 400+.

1989, Apr. 7—Soviet submarine caught fire and sank off Norway; 42.

1989, Apr. 19—USS Iowa; U.S. battleship; explosion in gun turret; 47.

Major Earthquakes

Magnitude of earthquakes (Mag.), distinct from deaths or damage caused, is measured on the Richter scale, on which each higher number represents a tenfold increase in energy measured in ground motion. Adopted in 1935, the scale has been applied in the following table to earthquakes as far back as reliable seismograms are available.

Date		Place	Deaths	Mag.	Date		Place	Deaths	Mag.
526	May 20	Syria, Antioch.	250,000	N.A.	1957	Dec. 13	Western Iran	2,000	7.1
856	....	Greece, Corinth	45,000	"	1960	Feb. 29	Morocco, Agadir	12,000	5.8
1057	....	China, Chihli	25,000	"	1960	May 21-30	Southern Chile	5,000	8.3
1268	....	Asia Minor, Cilicia	60,000	"	1962	Sept. 1	Northwestern Iran	12,230	7.1
1290	Sept. 27	China, Chihli	100,000	"	1963	July 26	Yugoslavia, Skopje	1,100	6.0
1293	May 20	Japan, Kamakura	30,000	"	1964	Mar. 27	Alaska.	131	8.4
1531	Jan. 26	Portugal, Lisbon	30,000	"	1966	Aug. 19	Eastern Turkey.	2,520	6.9
1556	Jan. 24	China, Shaanxi	830,000	"	1968	Aug. 31	Northeastern Iran	12,000	7.4
1667	Nov.	Caucasia, Shemaka	80,000	"	1970	Jan. 5	Yunnan Province, China.	10,000	7.7
1693	Jan. 11	Italy, Catania	60,000	"	1970	Mar. 28	Western Turkey	1,086	7.4
1730	Dec. 30	Japan, Hokkaido	137,000	"	1970	May 31	Northern Peru	66,794	7.7
1737	Oct. 11	India, Calcutta	300,000	"	1971	Feb. 9	San Fernando Valley, Cal.	65	6.6
1755	June 7	Northern Persia	40,000	"					
1755	Nov. 1	Portugal, Lisbon	60,000	8.75*	1972	Apr. 10	Southern Iran	5,057	6.9
1783	Feb. 4	Italy, Calabria.	30,000	N.A.	1972	Dec. 23	Nicaragua.	5,000	6.2
1797	Feb. 4	Ecuador, Quito	41,000	"	1974	Dec. 28	Pakistan (9 towns)	5,200	6.3
1811-12		New Madrid, Mo. (series)	—	8.7*	1975	Sept. 6	Turkey (Lice, etc.)	2,312	6.8
1822	Sept. 5	Asia Minor, Aleppo.	22,000	"	1976	Feb. 4	Guatemala	22,778	7.5
1828	Dec. 28	Japan, Echigo	30,000	"	1976	May 6	Northeast Italy	946	6.5
1868	Aug. 13-15	Peru and Ecuador	40,000	"	1976	June 26	New Guinea, Irian Jaya	443	7.1
1875	May 16	Venezuela, Colombia	16,000	"	1976	July 28	China, Tangshan	242,000	8.2
1886	Aug. 31	Charleston, S.C.	60	6.6	1976	Aug. 17	Philippines, Mindanao	8,000	7.8
1896	June 15	Japan, sea wave.	27,120	N.A.	1976	Nov. 24	Eastern Turkey.	4,000	7.9
1906	Apr. 18-19	San Francisco, Cal.	503	8.3	1977	Mar. 4	Romania, Bucharest, etc.	1,541	7.5
1906	Aug. 16	Chile, Valparaiso	20,000	8.6	1977	Aug. 19	Indonesia	200	8.0
1908	Dec. 28	Italy, Messina.	83,000	7.5	1977	Nov. 23	Northwestern Argentina	100	8.2
1915	Jan. 13	Italy, Avezzano.	29,980	7.5	1978	June 12	Japan, Se—	21	7.5
1920	Dec. 16	China, Gansu	100,000	8.6	1978	Sept. 16	Northeast Iran	25,000	7.7
1923	Sept. 1	Japan, Yokohama	200,000	8.3	1979	Sept. 12	Indonesia	100	8.1
1927	May 22	China, Nan-Shan.	200,000	8.3	1979	Dec. 12	Colombia, Ecuador	800	7.9
1932	Dec. 26	China, Gansu	70,000	7.6	1980	Oct. 10	Northwestern Algeria	4,500	7.3
1933	Mar. 2	Japan	2,990	8.9	1980	Nov. 23	Southern Italy	4,800	7.2
1933	Mar. 10	Long Beach, Cal.	115	6.2	1982	Dec. 13	North Yemen	2,800	6.0
1934	Jan. 15	India, Bihar-Nepal	10,700	8.4	1983	Mar. 31	Southern Colombia	250	5.5
1935	May 31	India, Quetta	50,000	7.5	1983	May 26	N. Honshu, Japan.	81	7.7
1939	Jan. 24	Chile, Chillan	28,000	8.3	1983	Oct. 30	Eastern Turkey.	1,300	7.1
1939	Dec. 26	Turkey, Erzincan	30,000	7.9	1985	Mar. 3	Chile.	146	7.8
1946	Dec. 21	Japan, Honshu	2,000	8.4	1985	Sept. 19, 21	Mexico City	4,200+	8.1
1948	June 28	Japan, Fukui	5,131	7.3	1987	Mar. 5-6	NE Ecuador	4,000+	7.3
1949	Aug. 5	Ecuador, Pelileo	6,000	6.8	1988	Aug. 20	India/Nepal border.	1,000+	6.5
1950	Aug. 15	India, Assam	1,530	8.7	1988	Nov. 6	China/Burma border	1,000	7.3
1953	Mar. 18	NW Turkey	1,200	7.2	1988	Dec. 7	NW Armenia	55,000+	6.8
1956	June 10-17	N. Afghanistan	2,000	7.7					
1957	July 2	Northern Iran	2,500	7.4	(*) estimated from earthquake intensity. (N.A.) not available.				

Some Recent Earthquakes

Source: Scientific Event Alert Network, Smithsonian Institution

Attached is a list of recent earthquakes. Magnitude of earthquakes is measured on the Richter scale, on which each higher number represents a tenfold increase in energy measured in ground motion. The United States Geological Survey reported that there were 61 significant earthquakes in 1988, 15 fewer than in 1987. A quake is considered significant if it has a magnitude of 6.5 on the Richter scale or if it causes casualities or considerable damage.

Date	Place	Magnitude	Date	Place	Magnitude
Mar. 10, 1989	Malawi	6.2	Dec. 3	Pasadna, Cal.	5.0
Feb. 14	Solomon Islands	6.5	Nov. 17	Samar Island, Philippines	6.6
Feb. 10	Indonesia	6.8	Nov. 6	China/Burma	7.3
Jan. 22	Tadzhikistan, USSR	5.3	Nov. 2	Guatemala	6.2
Jan. 10	Indonesia	6.5	Oct. 16	Ionian Sea	5.8
Dec. 7, 1988	Armenia, USSR	6.8	Aug. 20	Nepal	6.5

Date	Place	Magnitude	Date	Place	Magnitude
Aug. 11	Iran	6.1	July 20	Taiwan	5.9
Aug. 10	Solomon Islands	7.4	July 5	Papua New Guinea	6.7
Aug. 6	Burma, India	7.1	June 3	New Zealand	6.5
July 25	Aru Islands, Indonesia	6.8	May 30	N. Australia	6.5
July 23	Papua New Guinea	6.7			

Some Notable Tornadoes In U.S. Since 1925

Date			Place	Deaths	Date			Place	Deaths
1925	Mar.	18	Mo., Ill. Ind.	689	1958	June	4	Northwestern Wisconsin	30
1927	Apr.	12	Rock Springs, Tex.	74	1959	Feb.	10	St. Louis, Mo.	21
1927	May	9	Arkansas, Poplar Bluff, Mo.	92	1960	May	5, 6	SE Oklahoma, Arkansas	30
1927	Sept.	29	St. Louis, Mo.	90	1965	Apr.	11	Ind., Ill., Oh., Mich., Wis.	271
1930	May	6	Hill, Navarro, Ellis Co., Tex.	41	1966	Mar.	3	Jackson, Miss.	57
1932	Mar.	21	Ala. (series of tornadoes)	268	1966	Mar.	3	Mississippi, Alabama	61
1936	Apr.	5	Miss., Ga.	455	1967	Apr.	21	Ill., Mich.	33
1936	Apr.	6	Gainesville, Ga.	203	1968	May	15	Midwest	71
1938	Sept.	29	Charleston, S.C.	32	1969	Jan.	23	Mississippi	32
1942	Mar.	16	Central to NE Miss.	75	1971	Feb.	21	Mississippi delta	110
1942	Apr.	27	Rogers & Mayes Co., Okla.	52	1973	May	26-27	South, Midwest (series)	47
1944	June	23	Oh., Pa., W. Va., Md.	150	1974	Apr.	3-4	Ala., Ga., Tenn., Ky., Oh.	350
1945	Apr.	12	Okla.-Ark.	102	1977	Apr.	4	Ala., Miss., Ga.	22
1947	Apr.	9	Tex., Okla. & Kan.	169	1979	Apr.	10	Tex., Okla.	60
1948	Mar.	19	Bunker Hill & Gillespie, Ill.	33	1980	June	3	Grand Island, Neb. (series)	4
1949	Jan.	3	La. & Ark.	58	1982	Mar.	2-4	South, Midwest (series)	17
1952	Mar.	21	Ark., Mo., Tenn. (series)	208	1982	May	29	So. Ill.	10
1953	May	11	Waco, Tex.	114	1983	May	18-22	Tex.	12
1953	June	8	Mich., Oh.	142	1984	Mar.	28	N. Carolina; S. Carolina	67
1953	June	9	Worcester and vicinity, Mass.	90	1984	Apr.	21-22	Mississippi	15
1953	Dec.	5	Vicksburg, Miss.	38	1984	Apr.	26	Series Okla to Minn.	17
1955	May	25	Kan., Mo., Okla., Tex.	115	1985	May	31	N.Y., Pa., Oh., Ont. (series)	90
1957	May	20	Kan., Mo.	48	1987	May	22	Saragosa, Tex.	29

Hurricanes, Typhoons, Blizzards, Other Storms

Names of hurricanes and typhoons in italics—H.—hurricane; T.—typhoon

Date	Location	Deaths	Date	Location	Deaths
1888 Mar. 11-14	Blizzard, Eastern U.S.	400	1966 Sept. 24-30	H. *Inez*, Carib., Fla., Mex.	293
1900 Aug.-Sept.	H., Galveston, Tex.	6,000	1967 July 9	T. *Billie*, SW Japan	347
1906 Sept. 21	H., La., Miss.	350	1967 Sept. 5-23	H. *Beulah*, Carib., Mex., Tex.	54
1906 Sept. 18	Typhoon, Hong Kong	10,000	1967 Dec. 12-20	Blizzard, Southwest, U.S.	51
1926 Sept. 11-22	H., Fla., Ala.	243	1968 Nov. 18-28	T. *Nina*, Philippines	63
1926 Oct. 20	H., Cuba	600	1969 Aug. 17-18	H. *Camille*, Miss., La.	256
1928 Sept. 6-20	H., So. Fla.	1,836	1970 July 30-		
1930 Sept. 3	H., Dominican Rep.	2,000	Aug. 5	H. *Celia*, Cuba, Fla., Tex.	31
1938 Sept. 21	H., Long, Island N.Y., New England	600	1970 Aug. 20-21	H. *Dorothy*, Martinique	42
1940 Nov. 11-12	Blizzard, U.S. NE, Midwest	144	1970 Sept. 15	T. *Georgia*, Philippines	300
1942 Oct. 15-16	H., Bengal, India	40,000	1970 Oct. 14	T. *Sening*, Philippines	583
1944 Sept. 9-16	H., N.C. to New Eng.	46	1970 Oct. 15	T. *Titang*, Philippines	526
1952 Oct. 22	Typhoon, Philippines	0,300	1970 Nov. 13	Cyclone, Bangladesh	300,000
1954 Aug. 30	H. *Carol*, Northeast U.S.	68	1971 Aug. 1	T. *Rose*, Hong Kong	130
1954 Oct. 5-18	H. *Hazel*, Eastern, U.S., Haiti	347	1972 June 19-29	H. *Agnes*, Fla. to N.Y.	118
1955 Aug. 12-13	H. *Connie*, Carolinas, Va., Md.	43	1972 Dec. 3	T. *Theresa*, Philippines	169
1955 Aug. 7-21	H. *Diane*, Eastern U.S.	400	1973 June-Aug.	Monsoon rains in India	1,217
1955 Sept. 19	H. *Hilda*, Mexico	200	1974 June 11	Storm Dinah, Luzon Is., Philip.	71
1955 Sept. 22-28	H. *Janet*, Caribbean	500	1974 July 11	T. *Gilda*, Japan, S. Korea	108
1956 Feb. 1-29	Blizzard, Western Europe	1,000	1974 Sept. 19-20	H. *Fifi*, Honduras	2,000
1957 June 25-30	H. *Audrey*, Tex. to Ala.	390	1974 Dec. 25	Cyclone leveled Darwin, Aus.	50
1958 Feb. 15-16	Blizzard, NE U.S.	171	1975 Sept. 13-27	H. *Eloise*, Caribbean, NE U.S.	71
1959 Sept. 17-19	T. *Sarah*, Japan, S. Korea	2,000	1976 May 20	T. *Olga*, floods, Philippines	215
1959 Sept. 26-27	T. *Vera*, Honshu, Japan	4,466	1977 July 25, 31	T. *Thelma*, T. *Vera*, Taiwan	39
1960 Sept. 4-12	H. *Donna*, Caribbean, E. U.S.	148	1978 Oct. 27	H. *Rita*, Philippines	c. 400
1961 Sept. 11-14	H. *Carla*, Tex.	46	1979 Aug. 30-		
1961 Oct. 31	H. *Hattie*, Br. Honduras	400	Sept. 7	H. *David*, Caribbean, East. U.S.	1,100
1963 May 28-29	Windstorm, Bangladesh	22,000	1980 Aug. 4-11	H. *Allen*, Caribbean, Texas	272
1963 Oct. 4-8	H. *Flora*, Caribbean	6,000	1981 Nov. 25	H. *Irma*, Luzon Is., Philippines	176
1964 Oct. 4	H. *Hilda*, La., Miss., Ga.	38	1983 June	Monsoon rains in India	900
1964 June 30	T. *Winnie*, N. Philippines	107	1983 Aug. 18	H. *Alicia*. southern Texas	17
1964 Sept. 5	T. *Ruby*, Hong Kong and China	735	1984 Sept. 2	T. *Ike*, southern Philippines	1,363
1965 May 11-12	Windstorm, Bangladesh	17,000	1985 May 25	Cyclone, Bangladesh.	10,000
1965 June 1-2	Windstorm, Bangladesh	30,000	1985 Oct. 26-		
1965 Sept. 7-12	H. *Betsy*, Fla., Miss., La.	74	Nov. 6	H. *Juan*, SE U.S.	97
1965 Dec. 15	Windstorm, Bangladesh	10,000	1987 Nov. 25	T. *Nina*, Philippines	650
1966 June 4-10	H. *Alma*, Honduras, SE U.S.	51			

Floods, Tidal Waves

Date		Location	Deaths	Date		Location	Deaths
1228	....	Holland	100,000	1911	....	Chang Jiang River, China.	100,000
1642	....	China	300,000	1913	Mar. 25-27	Ohio, Indiana.	732
1887	....	Huang He River, China	900,000	1915	Aug. 17	Galveston, Tex.	275
1889	May 31	Johnstown, Pa.	2,200	1928	Mar. 13	Collapse of St. Francis Dam, Saugus, Cal.	450
1900	Sept. 8	Galveston, Tex.	5,000	1928	Sept. 13	Lake Okeechobee, Fla.	2,000
1903	June 15	Heppner, Ore.	325				

Date		Location	Deaths	Date		Location	Deaths
1931	Aug.	Huang He River, China	3,700,000	1972	Feb. 26	Buffalo Creek, W. Va.	118
1937	Jan. 22	Ohio, Miss. Valleys	250	1972	June 9	Rapid City, S.D.	236
1939	....	Northern China	200,000	1972	Aug. 7	Luzon Is., Philippines	454
1946	Apr. 1	Hawaii, Alaska	159	1973	Aug. 19-31	Pakistan	1,500
1947	....	Honshu Island, Japan	1,900	1974	Mar. 29	Tubaro, Brazil	1,000
1951	Aug.	Manchuria	1,800	1974	Aug. 12	Monty-Long, Bangladesh	2,500
1953	Jan. 31	Western Europe	2,000	1976	June 5	Teton Dam collapse, Ida.	11
1954	Aug. 17	Farahzad, Iran	2,000	1976	July 31	Big Thompson Canyon, Col.	139
1955	Oct. 7-12	India, Pakistan	1,700	1976	Nov. 17	East Java, Indonesia	136
1959	Nov. 1	Western Mexico	2,000	1977	July 19-20	Johnstown, Pa.	68
1959	Dec. 2	Frejus, France	412	1978	June-Sept.	Northern India	1,200
1960	Oct. 10	Bangladesh	6,000	1979	Jan.-Feb.	Brazil	204
1960	Oct. 31	Bangladesh	4,000	1979	July 17	Lomblem Is., Indonesia	539
1962	Feb. 17	German North Sea coast.	343	1979	Aug. 11	Morvi, India	5,000-15,000
1962	Sept. 27	Barcelona, Spain	445	1980	Feb. 13-22	So. Cal., Ariz.	26
1963	Oct. 9	Dam collapse, Vaiont, Italy	1,800	1981	Apr.	Northern China	550
1966	Nov. 3-4	Florence, Venice, Italy	113	1981	July	Sichuan, Hubei Prov., China	1,300
1967	Jan. 18-24	Eastern Brazil	894	1982	Jan. 23	Nr. Lima, Peru	600
1967	Mar. 19	Rio de Janeiro, Brazil	436	1982	May 12	Guangdong, China	430
1967	Nov. 26	Lisbon, Portugal	464	1982	June 6	So. Conn.	12
1968	Aug. 7-14	Gujarat State, India	1,000	1982	Sept. 17-21	El Salvador, Guatemala	1,300+
1968	Oct. 7	Northeastern India	780	1982	Dec. 2-9	Ill., Mo., Ark.	22
1969	Jan. 18-26	So. Cal.	100	1983	Feb.-Mar.	Cal. coast	13
1969	Mar. 17	Mundau Valley, Alagoas, Brazil	218	1983	Apr. 6-12	Ala., La., Miss., Tenn.	15
1969	Aug. 20-22	Western Virginia	189	1984	May 27	Tulsa, Okla.	13
1969	Sept. 15	South Korea	250	1984	Aug-Sept.	S. Korea	200+
1969	Oct. 1-8	Tunisia	500	1985	July 19	Northern Italy, dam burst	361
1970	May 20	Central Romania	160	1987	Aug.-Sept.	Northern Bangladesh	1,000+
1970	July 22	Himalayas, India	500	1988	Sept.	Northern India	1,000+
1971	Feb. 26	Rio de Janeiro, Brazil	130				

Fires

Date		Location	Deaths	Date		Location	Deaths
1835	Dec. 16	New York City, 500 bldgs. destroyed	—	1963	May 4	Diourbel, Senegal, theater.	64
1845	May	Canton, China, theater	1,670	1963	Nov. 18	Surfside Hotel, Atlantic City, N.J.	25
1871	Oct. 8	Chicago, $196 million loss.	250	1963	Nov. 23	Fitchville, Oh., rest home	63
1871	Oct. 8	Peshtigo, Wis., forest fire	1,182	1963	Dec. 29	Roosevelt Hotel, Jacksonville, Fla.	22
1872	Nov. 9	Boston, 800 bldgs. destroyed	—	1964	May 8	Manila, apartment bldg	30
1876	Dec. 5	Brooklyn (N.Y.), theater	295	1964	Dec. 18	Fountaintown, Ind., nursing home.	20
1877	June 20	St. John, N. B., Canada	100	1965	Mar. 1	LaSalle, Canada, apartment	28
1881	Dec. 8	Ring Theater, Vienna	850	1966	Mar. 11	Numata, Japan, 2 ski resorts	31
1887	May 25	Opera Comique, Paris	200	1966	Aug. 13	Melbourne, Australia, hotel	29
1887	Sept. 4	Exeter, England, theater.	200	1966	Sept. 12	Anchorage, Alaska, hotel	14
1894	Sept. 1	Minn., forest fire	413	1966	Oct. 17	N. Y. City bldg. (firemen)	12
1897	May 4	Paris, charity bazaar	150	1966	Dec. 7	Erzurum, Turkey, barracks	68
1900	June 30	Hoboken, N. J., docks	326	1967	Feb. 7	Montgomery, Ala., restaurant.	25
1902	Sept. 20	Birmingham, Ala., church	115	1967	May 22	Brussels, Belgium, store.	322
1903	Dec. 30	Iroquois Theater, Chicago	602	1967	July 16	Jay, Fla., state prison	37
1908	Jan. 13	Rhoads Theater, Boyertown, Pa.	170	1968	Feb. 26	Shrewsbury, England, hospital.	22
1908	Mar. 4	Collinwood, Oh., school	176	1968	May 11	Vijayawada, India, wedding hall.	58
1911	Mar. 25	Triangle factory, N. Y. City	145	1968	Nov. 18	Glasgow, Scotland, factory.	24
1913	Oct. 14	Mid Glamorgan, Wales, colliery.	439	1969	Jan. 26	Victoria Hotel, Dunnville, Ont.	13
1918	Apr. 13	Norman Okla., state hospital	38	1969	Dec. 2	Notre Dame, Can., nursing home.	54
1918	Oct. 12	Cloquet, Minn., forest fire	400	1970	Jan. 9	Marietta, Oh., nursing home.	27
1919	June 20	Mayaguez Theater, San Juan.	150	1970	Mar. 20	Seattle, Wash., hotel	19
1923	May 17	Camden, S. C., school.	76	1970	Nov. 1	Grenoble, France, dance hall	145
1924	Dec. 24	Hobart, Okla., school	35	1970	Dec. 20	Tucson, Arizona, hotel	28
1929	May 15	Cleveland, Oh., clinic.	125	1971	Mar. 6	Burghoezli, Switzerland, psychiatric clinic	28
1930	Apr. 21	Columbus, Oh., penitentiary.	320	1971	Apr. 20	Hotel, Bangkok, Thailand	24
1931	July 24	Pittsburgh, Pa., home for aged	48	1971	Oct. 19	Honesdale, Pa., nursing home	15
1934	Dec. 11	Hotel Kerns, Lansing, Mich.	34	1971	Dec. 25	Hotel, Seoul, So. Korea	162
1938	May 16	Atlanta, Ga., Terminal Hotel.	35	1972	May 13	Osaka, Japan, nightclub	116
1940	Apr. 23	Natchez, Miss., dance hall.	198	1972	July 5	Sherborne, England, hospital	30
1942	Nov. 28	Cocoanut Grove, Boston	491	1973	Feb. 6	Paris, France, school.	21
1942		St. John's, Newfoundland, hostel.	100	1973	Nov. 6	Fukui, Japan, train	28
1943	Sept. 7	Gulf Hotel, Houston	55	1973	Nov. 29	Kumamoto, Japan, department store.	107
1944	July 6	Ringling Circus, Hartford.	168	1973	Dec. 2	Seoul, Korea, theater	50
1946	June 5	LaSalle Hotel, Chicago	61	1974	Feb. 1	Sao Paulo, Brazil, bank building	189
1946	Dec. 7	Winecoff Hotel, Atlanta	119	1974	June 30	Port Chester, N. Y., discotheque	24
1946	Dec. 12	New York, ice plant, tenement	37	1974	Nov. 3	Seoul, So. Korea, hotel discotheque	88
1949	Apr. 5	Effingham, Ill., hospital	77	1975	Dec. 12	Mina, Saudi Arabia, tent city.	138
1950	Jan. 7	Davenport, Ia., Mercy Hospital	41	1976	Oct. 24	Bronx, N.Y., social club	25
1953	Mar. 29	Largo, Fla., nursing home	35	1977	Feb. 25	Moscow, Rossiya hotel	45
1953	Apr. 16	Chicago, metalworking plant	35	1977	May 28	Southgate, Ky., nightclub	164
1957	Feb. 17	Warrenton, Mo., home for aged.	72	1977	June 9	Abidjan, Ivory Coast, nightclub	41
1958	Mar. 19	New York City, loft building	24	1977	June 26	Columbia, Tenn., jail	42
1958	Dec. 1	Chicago, parochial school	95	1977	Nov. 14	Manila, PI, hotel.	47
1958	Dec. 16	Bogota, Colombia, store.	83	1978	Jan. 28	Kansas City, Coates House Hotel	16
1959	June 23	Stalheim, Norway, resort hotel	34	1979	July 14	Saragossa, Spain, hotel	80
1960	Mar. 12	Pusan, Korea, chemical plant	68	1979	Dec. 31	Chapais, Quebec, social club	42
1960	July 14	Guatemala City, mental hospital	225	1980	May 20	Kingston, Jamaica, nursing home.	157
1960	Nov. 13	Amude, Syria, movie theater	152	1980	Nov. 21	MGM Grand Hotel, Las Vegas	84
1961	Jan. 6	Thomas Hotel, San Francisco.	20	1980	Dec. 4	Stouffer Inn, Harrison, N.Y.	26
1961	Dec. 8	Hartford, Conn., hospital.	16	1981	Jan. 9	Keansburg, N.J., boarding home	30
1961	Dec. 17	Niteroi, Brazil, circus.	323				

Date			Location	Deaths
1981	Feb.	10	Las Vegas Hilton	8
1981	Feb.	14	Dublin, Ireland, discotheque	44
1982	Sept.	4	Los Angeles, apartment house . . .	24
1982	Nov.	8	Biloxi, Miss., county jail	29
1983	Feb.	13	Turin, Italy, movie theater	64
1983	Dec.	17	Madrid, Spain, discotheque	83
1984	May	11	Great Adventure Amusement Park,	

Date			Location	Deaths
			N.J.	8
1985	Apr.	21	Tabaco, Philippines, movie theater .	44
1985	Apr.	26	Buenos Aires, Argentina hospital . .	79
1985	May	11	Bradford, England, soccer stadium. .	53
1986	Dec.	31	Puerto Rico, Dupont Plaza Hotel . .	96
1987	May 6-			
	June 2		Northern China forest fire	193
1987	Nov.	17	London, England subway	30

Explosions

Date			Location	Deaths
1910	Oct.	1	Los Angeles Times Bldg., ...	21
1913	Mar.	7	Dynamite, Baltimore harbor	55
1915	Sept.	27	Gasoline tank car, Ardmore, Okla. . .	47
1917	Apr.	10	Munitions plant, Eddystone, Pa.. . .	133
1917	Dec.	6	Halifax Harbor, Canada	1,654
1918	May	18	Chemical plant, Oakdale, Pa.. . . .	193
1918	July	2	Explosives, Split Rock, N.Y.	50
1918	Oct.	4	Shell plant, Morgan Station, N.J.. . .	64
1919	May	22	Food plant, Cedar Rapids, Ia.. . . .	44
1920	Sept.	16	Wall Street, New York, bomb.	30
1924	Jan.	3	Food plant, Pekin, Ill.	42
1928	April	13	Dance hall, West Plains, Mo.	40
1937	Mar.	18	New London, Tex., school.	413
1940	Sept.	12	Hercules Powder, Kenvil, N.J.. . . .	55
1942	June	5	Ordnance plant, Elwood, Ill.	49
1944	Apr.	14	Bombay, India, harbor	700
1944	July	17	Port Chicago, Cal., pier	322
1944	Oct.	21	Liquid gas tank, Cleveland	135
1947	Apr.	16	Texas City, Tex., pier.	561
1948	July	28	Farben works, Ludwigshafen, Ger. .	184
1950	May	19	Munitions barges, S. Amboy, N. J. .	30
1956	Aug.	7	Dynamite trucks, Cali, Colombia . .	1,100
1958	Apr.	18	Sunken munitions ship, Okinawa . .	40
1958	May	22	Nike missiles, Leonardo, N.J.	10
1959	Apr.	10	World War II bomb, Philippines . . .	38
1959	June	28	Rail tank cars, Meldrin, Ga.	25
1959	Aug.	7	Dynamite truck, Roseburg, Ore. . . .	13
1959	Nov.	2	Jamuri Bazar, India, explosives . . .	46
1959	Dec.	13	Dortmund, Ger., 2 apt. bldgs.. . . .	26
1960	Mar.	4	Belgian munitions ship, Havana. . .	100
1960	Oct.	25	Gas, Windsor, Ont., store	11
1962	Jan.	16	Gas pipeline, Edson, Alberta, Canada.	8
1962	Oct.	3	Telephone Co. office, N. Y. City . . .	23
1963	Jan.	2	Packing plant, Terre Haute, Ind. . .	16
1963	Mar.	9	Dynamite plant, S. Africa	45
1963	Aug.	13	Explosives dump, Gauhiti, India . . .	32
1963	Oct.	31	State Fair Coliseum, Indianapolis. .	73

Date			Location	Deaths
1964	July	23	Bone, Algeria, harbor munitions. . .	100
1965	Mar.	4	Gas pipeline, Natchitoches, La.. . .	17
1965	Aug.	9	Missile silo, Searcy, Ark..	53
1965	Oct.	21	Bridge, Tila Bund, Pakistan	80
1965	Oct.	30	Cartagena, Colombia	48
1965	Nov.	24	Armory, Keokuk, Ia.	20
1966	Oct.	13	Chemical plant, La Salle, Que. . . .	11
1967	Feb.	17	Chemical plant, Hawthorne, N.J.. . .	11
1967	Dec.	25	Apartment bldg., Moscow	20
1968	Apr.	6	Sports store, Richmond, Ind.	43
1970	Apr.	8	Subway construction, Osaka, Japan	73
1971	June	24	Tunnel, Sylmar, Cal.	17
1971	June	28	School, fireworks, Pueblo, Mex. . .	13
1971	Oct.	21	Shopping center, Glasgow, Scot. . .	20
1973	Feb.	10	Liquified gas tank, Staten Is., N.Y. .	40
1975	Dec.	27	Chasnala, India, mine	431
1976	Apr.	13	Lapua, Finland, munitions works . .	45
1977	Nov.	11	Freight train, Iri, S. Korea	57
1977	Dec.	22	Grain elevator, Westwego, La. . . .	35
1978	Feb.	24	Derailed tank car, Waverly, Tenn. . .	12
1978	July	11	Propylene tank truck, Spanish	
			coastal campsite.	150
1980	Oct.	23	School, Ortuella, Spain	64
1981	Feb.	11	Sewer system, Louisville, Ky.	0
1982	Apr.	7	Tanker truck, tunnel, Oakland, Cal. .	7
1982	Apr.	25	Antiques exhibition, Todi, Italy. . . .	33
1982	Nov.	2	Salang Tunnel, Afghanistan .	1,000-3,000
1984	Feb.	25	Oil pipeline, Cubatao, Brazil.	508
1984	June	21	Naval supply depot, Severomorsk,	
			USSR	200+
1984	Nov.	19	Gas storage area, NE Mexico City . .	334
1984	Dec.	5	Coal mine, Taipei, Taiwan	94
1985	June	25	Fireworks factory, Hallett, Okla. . .	21
1988	July	6	Oil rig, North Sea.	167
1989	June	3	Gas pipeline, between Ufa, Asha,	
			USSR	650+

Notable Nuclear Accidents

Oct. 7, 1957 — A fire in the Windscale plutonium production reactor north of Liverpool, England spread radioactive material throughout the countryside. In 1983, the British government said that 39 people probably died of cancer as a result.

1957 — A chemical explosion in Kasli, USSR, in tanks containing nuclear waste, spread radioactive material and forced a major evacuation.

Jan. 3, 1961 — An experimental reactor at a federal installation near Idaho Falls, Id. killed three workers—the only deaths in U.S. reactor operations. The plant had high radiation levels but damage was contained.

Oct. 5, 1966 — A sodium cooling system malfunction caused a partial core meltdown at the Enrico Fermi demonstration breeder reactor near Detroit, Mich. Radiation was contained.

Jan. 21, 1969 — A coolant malfunction from an experimental underground reactor at Lucens Vad, Switzerland resulted in the release of a large amount of radiation into a cavern, which was then sealed.

Nov. 19, 1971 — The water-storage space at the Northern States Power Co.'s reactor in Monticello, Minn. filled to capacity and spilled over, dumping about 50,000 gallons of radioactive waste water into the Mississippi River. Some was taken into the St. Paul water system.

Mar. 22, 1975 — A technician checking for air leaks with a lighted candle caused a $100 million fire at the Brown's Ferry reactor in Decatur, Ala. The fire burned out electrical controls, lowering the cooling water to dangerous levels.

Mar. 28, 1979 — The worst commercial nuclear accident in the U.S. occured as equipment failures and human mistakes led to a loss of coolant, and partial core meltdown at the Three Mile Island reactor in Middletown, Pa.

Aug. 7, 1979 — Highly enriched uranium was released from a top-secret nuclear fuel plant near Erwin, Tenn. About 1,000 people were contaminated with up to 5 times as much radiation as would normally be received in a year.

Feb. 11, 1981 — Eight workers were contaminated when over 100,000 gallons of radioactive coolant leaked into the containment building of the TVA's Sequoyah 1 plant in Tennessee.

Apr. 25, 1981 — Some 100 workers were exposed to radioactive material during repairs of a nuclear plant at Tsuruga, Japan.

Jan. 25, 1982 — A steam-generator pipe broke at the Rochester Gas & Electric Co's Ginna plant near Rochester, N.Y. Small amounts of radioactive steam escaped into the air.

Jan. 6, 1986 — A cylinder of nuclear material burst after being improperly heated at a Kerr-McGee plant at Gore, Okla. One worker died and 100 were hospitalized.

Apr., 1986 — A serious accident at the Chernobyl nuclear plant about 60 miles from Kiev in the Soviet Union spewed clouds of radiation that spread over several European nations.

Some Notable Aircraft Disasters Since 1937

Date			Aircraft	Site of accident	Deaths
1937	May	6	German zeppelin Hindenburg	Burned at mooring, Lakehurst, N.J.	36
1944	Aug.	23	U.S. Air Force B-24	Hit school, Freckelton, England	76[1]
1945	July	28	U.S. Army B-25.	Hit Empire State bldg., N.Y.C.	14[1]
1947	May	30	Eastern Air Lines DC-4	Crashed near Port Deposit, Md.	53
1952	Dec.	20	U.S. Air Force C-124	Fell, burned, Moses Lake, Wash.	87
1953	Mar.	3	Canadian Pacific Comet Jet	Karachi, Pakistan	11[2]
1953	June	18	U.S. Air Force C-124	Crashed, burned near Tokyo	129
1955	Nov.	1	United Air Lines DC-6B	Exploded, crashed near Longmont, Col.	44[3]
1956	June	20	Venezuelan Super-Constellation	Crashed in Atlantic off Asbury Park, N.J.	74
1956	June	30	TWA Super-Const., United DC-7	Collided over Grand Canyon, Arizona	128
1960	Dec.	16	United DC-8 jet, TWA Super-Const.	Collided over N.Y. City.	134[4]
1962	Mar.	16	Flying Tiger Super-Const.	Vanished in Western Pacific	107
1962	June	3	Air France Boeing 707 jet	Crashed on takeoff from Paris	130
1962	June	22	Air France Boeing 707 jet	Crashed in storm, Guadeloupe, W.I.	113
1963	June	3	Chartered Northw. Airlines DC-7	Crashed in Pacific off British Columbia.	101
1963	Nov.	29	Trans-Canada Airlines DC-8F	Crashed after takeoff from Montreal	118
1965	May	20	Pakistani Boeing 720-B	Crashed at Cairo, Egypt, airport	121
1966	Jan.	24	Air India Boeing 707 jetliner	Crashed on Mont Blanc, France-Italy	117
1966	Feb.	4	All-Nippon Boeing 727	Plunged into Tokyo Bay	133
1966	Mar.	5	BOAC Boeing 707 jetliner	Crashed on Mount Fuji, Japan	124
1966	Dec.	24	U.S. military-chartered CL-44.	Crashed into village in So. Vietnam.	129[1]
1967	Apr.	20	Swiss Britannia turboprop	Crashed at Nicosia, Cyprus	126
1967	July	19	Piedmont Boeing 727, Cessna 310	Collided in air, Hendersonville, N.C.	82
1968	Apr.	20	S. African Airways Boeing 707	Crashed on takeoff, Windhoek, SW Africa.	122
1968	May	3	Braniff International Electra	Crashed in storm near Dawson, Tex.	85
1969	Mar.	16	Venezuelan DC-9	Crashed after takeoff from Maracaibo, Venezuela	155[5]
1969	Dec.	8	Olympia Airways DC-6B	Crashed near Athens in storm	93
1970	Feb.	15	Dominican DC-9	Crashed into sea on takeoff from Santo Domingo	102
1970	July	3	British chartered jetliner	Crashed near Barcelona, Spain.	112
1970	July	5	Air Canada DC-8.	Crashed near Toronto International Airport	108
1970	Aug.	9	Peruvian turbojet	Crashed after takeoff from Cuzco, Peru.	101[1]
1970	Nov.	14	Southern Airways DC-9	Crashed in mountains near Huntington, W. Va.	75[6]
1971	July	30	All-Nippon Boeing 727 and Japanese Air Force F-86	Collided over Morioka, Japan.	162[7]
1971	Sept.	4	Alaska Airlines Boeing 727	Crashed into mountain near Juneau, Alaska	111
1972	Aug.	14	E. German Ilyushin-62	Crashed on take-off East Berlin.	156
1972	Oct.	13	Aeroflot Ilyushin-62	E. German airline crashed near Moscow	176
1972	Dec.	3	Chartered Spanish airliner	Crashed on take-off, Canary Islands	155
1972	Dec.	29	Eastern Airlines Lockheed Tristar	Crashed on approach to Miami Int'l. Airport.	101
1973	Jan.	22	Chartered Boeing 707	Burst into flames during landing, Kano Airport, Nigeria.	176
1973	Feb.	21	Libyan jetliner.	Shot down by Israeli fighter planes over Sinai.	108
1973	Apr.	10	British Vanguard turboprop	Crashed during snowstorm at Basel, Switzerland	104
1973	June	3	Soviet Supersonic TU-144	Crashed near Goussainville, France	14[8]
1973	July	11	Brazilian Boeing 707	Crashed on approach to Orly Airport, Paris.	122
1973	July	31	Delta Airlines jetliner.	Crashed, landing in fog at Logan Airport, Boston.	89
1973	Dec.	23	French Caravelle jet	Crashed in Morocco.	106
1974	Mar.	3	Turkish DC-10 jet	Crashed at Ermenonville near Paris	346
1974	Apr.	23	Pan American 707 jet.	Crashed in Bali, Indonesia.	107
1974	Dec.	1	TWA-727.	Crashed in storm, Upperville, Va.	92
1974	Dec.	4	Dutch-chartered DC-8.	Crashed in storm near Colombo, Sri Lanka	191
1975	Apr.	4	Air Force Galaxy C-5B	Crashed near Saigon, So. Vietnam, after takeoff with load of orphans	172
1975	June	24	Eastern Airlines 727 jet	Crashed in storm, JFK Airport, N.Y. City.	113
1975	Aug.	3	Chartered 707	Hit mountainside, Agadir, Morocco	188
1976	Sept.	10	British Airways Trident, Yugoslav DC-9	Collided near Zagreb, Yugoslavia	176
1976	Sept.	19	Turkish 727	Hit mountain, southern Turkey	155
1976	Oct.	13	Bolivian 707 cargo jet	Crashed in Santa Cruz, Bolivia	100[9]
1977	Jan.	13	Aeroflot TU-104	Exploded and crashed at Alma-Ata, Central Asia.	90
1977	Mar.	27	KLM 747, Pan American 747	Collided on runway, Tenerife, Canary Islands.	582
1977	Nov.	19	TAP Boeing 727	Crashed on Madeira	130
1977	Dec.	4	Malaysian Boeing 737	Hijacked, then exploded in mid-air over Straits of Johore	100
1977	Dec.	13	U.S. DC-3.	Crashed after takeoff at Evansville, Ind.	29[10]
1978	Jan.	1	Air India 747	Exploded, crashed into sea off Bombay	213
1978	Sept.	25	Boeing 727, Cessna 172	Collided in air, San Diego, Cal.	150
1978	Nov.	15	Chartered DC-8	Crashed near Colombo, Sri Lanka	183
1979	May	25	American Airlines DC-10	Crashed after takeoff at O'Hare Intl. Airport, Chicago	275[11]
1979	Aug.	17	Two Soviet Aeroflot jetliners	Collided over Ukraine	173
1979	Oct.	31	Western Airlines DC-10	Mexico City Airport.	74
1979	Nov.	26	Pakistani Boeing 707	Crashed near Jidda, Saudi Arabia	156
1979	Nov.	28	New Zealand DC-10.	Crashed into mountain in Antarctica	257
1980	Mar.	14	Polish Ilyushin 62	Crashed making emergency landing, Warsaw	87[12]
1980	Aug.	19	Saudi Arabian Tristar	Burned after emergency landing, Riyadh	301
1981	Dec.	1	Yugoslavian DC-9	Crashed into mountain in Corsica	174
1982	Jan.	13	Air Florida Boeing 737.	Crashed into Potomac River after takeoff	78
1982	July	9	Pan-Am Boeing 727	Crashed after takeoff in Kenner, La.	153[13]
1982	Sept.	11	U.S. Army CH-47 Chinook helicopter	Crashed during air show in Mannheim, W. Germany	46
1983	Sept.	1	S. Korean Boeing 747	Shot down after violating Soviet airspace	269
1983	Nov.	27	Colombian Boeing 747	Crashed near Barajas Airport, Madrid	183
1985	Feb.	19	Spanish Boeing 727	Crashed into Mt. Oiz, Spain	148
1985	June	23	Air-India Boeing 747	Crashed into Atlantic Ocean S. of Ireland	329
1985	Aug.	2	Delta Air Lines jumbo jet	Crashed at Dallas-Ft. Worth Intl. Airport.	133
1985	Aug.	12	Japan Air Lines Boeing 747.	Crashed into Mt. Ogura, Japan.	520[14]
1985	Dec.	12	Arrow Air DC 8.	Crashed after takeoff in Gander, Newfoundland	256[15]
1986	Mar.	31	Mexican Boeing 727.	Crashed NW of Mexico City	166
1986	Aug.	31	Aeromexico DC-9	Collided with Piper PA-28 over Cerritos, Cal.	82[16]

Date		Aircraft	Site of accident	Deaths
1987	May 9	Ilyushin 62M	Crashed after takeoff in Warsaw, Poland	183
1987	Aug. 16	Northwest Airlines MD-82	Crashed after takeoff in Romulus, Mich.	156
1988	July 3	Iranian A300 Airbus	Shot down by U.S. Navy warship *Vincennes* over Persian Gulf	290
1988	Dec. 21	Pan Am Boeing 747	Exploded and crashed in Lockerbie, Scotland. . . .	270[17]
1989	Feb. 8	Boeing 707	Crashed into mountain in Azores Islands off Portugal. . . .	144
1989	June 7	Suriname DC-8.	Crashed near Paramaribo Airport, Suriname	168

(1) Including those on the ground and in buildings. (2) First fatal crash of commercial jet plane. (3) Caused by bomb planted by John G. Graham in insurance plot to kill his mother, a passenger. (4) Including all 128 aboard the planes and 6 on ground. (5) Killed 84 on plane and 71 on ground. (6) Including 43 Marshall U. football players and coaches. (7) Airliner-fighter crash, pilot of fighter parachuted to safety, was arrested for negligence. (8) First supersonic plane crash killed 6 crewmen and 8 on the ground; there were no passengers. (9) Crew of 3 killed; 97, mostly children, killed on ground. (10) Including U. of Evansville basketball team. (11) Highest death toll in U.S. aviation history. (12) Including 22 members of U.S. boxing team. (13) Including 8 on ground. (14) Worst single-plane disaster. (15) Incl. 248 members of U.S. 101st Airborne Division. (16) Incl. 15 on the ground. (17) Incl. 11 on the ground.

Major U.S. Railroad Wrecks

Date		Location	Deaths	Date		Location	Deaths
1876	Dec. 29	Ashtabula, Oh.	92	1925	June 16	Hackettstown, N. J.	50
1880	Aug. 11	Mays Landing, N. J.	40	1925	Oct. 27	Victoria, Miss.	21
1887	Aug. 10	Chatsworth, Ill.	81	1926	Sept. 5	Waco, Col.	30
1888	Oct. 10	Mud Run, Pa.	55	1928	Aug. 24	I.R.T. subway, Times Sq., N. Y.	18
1896	July 30	Atlantic City, N. J.	60	1938	June 19	Saugus, Mont.	47
1903	Dec. 23	Laurel Run, Pa.	53	1939	Aug. 12	Harney, Nev.	24
1904	Aug. 7	Eden, Col.	96	1940	Apr. 19	Little Falls, N. Y.	31
1904	Sept. 24	New Market Tenn.	56	1940	July 31	Cuyahoga Falls, Oh.	43
1906	Mar. 16	Florence, Col.	35	1943	Aug. 29	Wayland, N. J.	27
1906	Oct. 28	Atlantic City, N. J.	40	1943	Sept. 6	Frankford Junction, Philadelphia, Pa.	79
1906	Dec. 30	Washington, D. C.	53	1943	Dec. 16	Between Rennert and Buie, N. C.. .	72
1907	Jan. 2	Volland, Kan.	33	1944	July 6	High Bluff, Tenn.	35
1907	Jan. 19	Fowler, Ind.	29	1944	Aug. 4	Near Stockton, Ga..	47
1907	Feb. 16	New York, N.Y.	22	1944	Sept. 14	Dewey, Ind.	29
1907	Feb. 23	Colton, Cal.	26	1944	Dec. 31	Bagley, Utah	50
1907	July 20	Salem, Mich.	33	1945	Aug. 9	Michigan, N. D.	34
1910	Mar. 1	Wellington, Wash.	96	1946	Apr. 25	Naperville, Ill.	45
1910	Mar. 21	Green Mountain, Ia.	55	1947	Feb. 18	Gallitzin, Pa..	24
1911	Aug. 25	Manchester, N. Y.	29	1950	Feb. 17	Rockville Centre, N. Y..	31
1912	July 4	East Corning, N. Y.	39	1950	Sept. 11	Coshocton, Oh..	33
1912	July 5	Ligonier, Pa..	23	1950	Nov. 22	Richmond Hill, N. Y.	79
1914	Aug. 5	Tipton Ford, Mo.	43	1951	Feb. 6	Woodbridge, N. J.	84
1914	Sept. 15	Lebanon, Mo.	28	1951	Nov. 12	Wyuta, Wyo.	17
1916	Mar. 29	Amherst, Oh.	27	1951	Nov. 25	Woodstock, Ala.	17
1917	Sept. 28	Kellyville, Okla.	23	1953	Mar. 27	Conneaut, Oh.	21
1917	Dec. 20	Shepherdsville, Ky.	46	1956	Jan. 22	Los Angeles, Cal..	30
1918	June 22	Ivanhoe, Ind.	68	1956	Feb. 28	Swampscott, Mass.	13
1918	July 9	Nashville, Tenn.	101	1956	Sept. 5	Springer, N. M.	20
1918	Nov. 1	Brooklyn, N. Y.	97	1957	June 11	Vroman, Col.	12
1919	Jan. 12	South Byron, N. Y.	22	1958	Sept. 15	Elizabethport, N. J.	48
1919	July 1	Dunkirk, N. Y.	12	1960	Mar. 14	Bakersfield, Cal.	14
1919	Dec. 20	Onawa, Maine	23	1962	July 28	Steelton, Pa.	19
1921	Feb. 27	Porter, Ind.	37	1966	Dec. 28	Everett, Mass.	13
1921	Dec. 5	Woodmont, Pa.	27	1971	June 10	Salem, Ill.	11
1922	Aug. 5	Sulphur Spring, Mo.	34	1972	Oct. 30	Chicago, Ill.	45
1922	Dec. 13	Humble, Tex.	22	1977	Feb. 4	Chicago, Ill., elevated train	11
1923	Sept. 27	Lockett, Wy.	31	1987	Jan. 4	Essex, Md.	16

World's worst train wreck occurred Dec. 12, 1917, Modane, France, passenger train derailed, 543 killed.

Principal U.S. Mine Disasters Since 1900

Source: Bureau of Mines, U.S. Interior Department

Note: Prior to 1968, only disasters with losses of 60 or more lives are listed; since 1968, all disasters in which 5 or more people were killed are listed. Only fatalities to mining company employees are included. All bituminous-coal mines unless otherwise noted.

Date		Location	Deaths	Date		Location	Deaths
1900	May 1	Scofield, Ut.	100	1913	Oct. 22	Dawson, N.M.	263
1902	May 19	Coal Creek, Tenn.	184	1914	Apr. 28	Eccles, W. Va.	181
1902	July 10	Johnstown, Pa.	112	1915	Mar. 2	Layland, W. Va.	112
1903	June 30	Hanna, Wy.	169	1917	Apr. 27	Hastings, Col.	121
1904	Jan. 25	Cheswick, Pa.	179	1917[2]	June 8	Butte, Mon.	163
1905	Feb. 20	Virginia City, Ala.	112	1917	Aug. 4	Clay, Ky.	62
1907	Jan. 29	Stuart W. Va.	84	1919[1]	June 5	Wilkes-Barre, Pa.	92
1907	Dec. 6	Monongah, W. Va.	361	1922	Nov. 6	Spangler, Pa.	77
1907	Dec. 19	Jacobs Creek, Pa.	239	1922	Nov. 22	Dolomite, Ala.	90
1908	Nov. 28	Marianna, Pa.	154	1923	Feb. 8	Dawson, N.M.	120
1909	Jan. 12	Switchback, W. Va.	67	1923	Aug. 14	Kemmerer, Wy.	99
1909	Nov. 13	Cherry, Ill.	259	1924	Mar. 8	Castle Gate, Ut.	171
1910	Jan. 31	Primero, Col.	75	1924	Apr. 28	Benwood, W. Va.	119
1910	May 5	Palos, Ala.	90	1926	Jan. 13	Wilburton, Okla.	91
1910	Nov. 8	Delagua, Col.	79	1926[2]	Nov. 3	Ishpeming, Mich.	51
1911	Apr. 7	Throop, Pa.	72	1927	Apr. 30	Everettville, W. Va.	97
1911	Apr. 8	Littleton, Ala.	128	1928	May 19	Mather, Pa.	195
1911	Dec. 9	Briceville, Tenn.	84	1929	Dec. 17	McAlester, Okla.	61
1912	Mar. 20	McCurtain, Okla.	73	1930	Nov. 5	Millfield, Oh.	79
1912	Mar. 26	Jed, W. Va.	83	1940	Jan. 10	Bartley, W. Va.	91
1913	Apr. 23	Finleyville, Pa.	96	1940	Mar. 16	St. Clairsville, Oh.	72

Date		Location	Deaths	Date		Location	Deaths
1940	July 15	Portage, Pa.	63	1976	Mar. 9, 11	Oven Fork, Ky.	26
1943	Feb. 27	Washoe, Mon.	74	1977	Mar. 1	Tower City, Pa.	9
1944	July 5	Belmont, Oh.	66	1981	Apr. 15	Redstone, Col.	15
1947	Mar. 25	Centralia, Ill.	111	1981	Dec. 7	Topmost, Ky.	8
1951	Dec. 21	West Frankfort, Ill.	119	1981	Dec. 8	nr. Chattanooga, Tenn.	13
1968³	Mar. 6	Calumet, La.	21	1982	Jan. 20	Floyd County, Ky.	7
1968	Nov. 20	Farmington, W. Va.	78	1983	June 21	McClure, Va	7
1970	Dec. 30	Hyden, Ky.	38	1984	Dec. 19	Huntington, Ut.	27
1972²	May 2	Kellogg, Ida	91				

(1) Anthracite mine. (2) Metal mine. (3) Nonmetal mine.
World's worst mine disaster killed 1,549 workers in Honkeiko Colliery in Manchuria Apr. 25, 1942.

Record Oil Spills

As a rule, the number of tons can be multiplied by 7 to estimate the number of barrels spilled; the exact number of barrels in a ton varies with the type of oil. Each barrel contains 42 gallons.

Name, place	Date	Cause	Tons
Ixtoc I oil well, southern Gulf of Mexico	June 3, 1979	Blowout.	600,000
Nowruz oil field, Persian Gulf.	Feb., 1983	Blowout.	600,000 (est.)
Atlantic Empress & Aegean Captain, off Trinidad & Tobago	July 19, 1979	Collision.	300,000
Castillo de Bellver, off Cape Town, South Africa.	Aug. 6, 1983	Fire.	250,000
Amoco Cadiz, near Portsall, France.	March 16, 1978	Grounding.	223,000
Torrey Canyon, off Land's End, England	March 18, 1967	Grounding.	119,000
Sea Star, Gulf of Oman.	Dec. 19, 1972	Collision.	115,000
Urquiola, La Coruna, Spain.	May 12, 1976.	Grounding.	100,000
Hawaiian Patriot, northern Pacific	Feb. 25, 1977.	Fire.	99,000
Othello, Tralhavet Bay, Sweden.	March 20, 1970	Collision.	60,000-100,000

Other Notable Oil Spills

Name, place	Date	Cause	Gallons
World Glory, off South Africa.	June 13, 1968	Hull failure.	13,524,000
Burmah Agate, Galveston Bay, Tex..	Nov. 1, 1979	Collision.	10,700,000
Exxon Valdez, Prince William Sound, Alas..	Mar. 24, 1989	Grounding.	10,080,000
Keo, off Massachusetts.	Nov. 5, 1969	Hull failure.	8,820,000
Storage tank, Sewaren, N.J..	Nov. 4, 1969	Tank rupture.	8,400,000
Ekofisk oil field, North Sea.	Apr. 22, 1977.	Well blowout.	8,200,000
Argo Merchant, Nantucket, Mass..	Dec. 15, 1976	Grounding.	7,700,000
Pipeline, West Delta, La..	Oct. 15, 1967.	Dragging anchor.	6,720,000
Tanker off Japan.	Nov. 30, 1971	Ship broke in half.	6,258,000
Storage tank, Monongahela River.	Jan. 2, 1988	Tank rupture.	3,800,000

Historic Assassinations Since 1865

1865—Apr. 14. U. S. Pres. Abraham Lincoln, shot by John Wilkes Booth in Washington, D. C.; died Apr. 15.

1881—Mar. 13. Alexander II, of Russia—July 2. U. S. Pres. James A. Garfield, shot by Charles J. Guiteau, Washington D.C.; died Sept. 19.

1900—July 29. Umberto I, king of Italy.

1901—Sept. 6. U. S. Pres. William McKinley in Buffalo, N. Y., died Sept. 14. Leon Czolgosz executed for the crime Oct. 29.

1913—Feb. 23. Mexican Pres. Francisco I, Madero and Vice Pres. Jose Pino Suarez.—Mar. 18. George, king of Greece.

1914—June 28. Archduke Francis Ferdinand of Austria-Hungary and his wife in Sarajevo, Bosnia (later part of Yugoslavia), by Gavrilo Princip.

1916—Dec. 30. Grigori Rasputin, politically powerful Russian monk.

1918—July 12. Grand Duke Michael of Russia, at Perm.—July 16. Nicholas II, abdicated as czar of Russia; his wife, the Czarina Alexandra, their son, Czarevitch Alexis, and their daughters, Grand Duchesses Olga, Tatiana, Marie, Anastasia, and 4 members of their household were executed by Bolsheviks at Ekaterinburg.

1920—May 20. Mexican Pres. Gen. Venustiano Carranza in Tlaxcalantongo.

1922—Aug. 22. Michael Collins, Irish revolutionary.—Dec. 16. Polish President Gabriel Narutowicz in Warsaw by an anarchist.

1923—July 20. Gen. Francisco "Pancho" Villa, ex-rebel leader, in Parral, Mexico.

1928—July 17. Gen. Alvaro Obregon, president-elect of Mexico, in San Angel, Mexico.

1933—Feb. 15. In Miami, Fla. Joseph Zangara, anarchist, shot at Pres.-elect Franklin D. Roosevelt, but a woman seized his arm, and the bullet fatally wounded Mayor Anton J. Cermak, of Chicago, who died Mar. 6. Zangara was electrocuted on Mar. 20, 1933.

1934—July 25. In Vienna, Austrian Chancellor Engelbert Dollfuss by Nazis.

1935—Sept. 8. U. S. Sen. Huey P. Long, shot in Baton Rouge, La., by Dr. Carl Austin Weiss, who was slain by Long's bodyguards.

1940—Aug. 20. Leon Trotsky (Lev Bronstein), 63, exiled Russian war minister, near Mexico City. Killer identified as Ramon Mercador del Rio, a Spaniard, served 20 years in Mexican prison.

1948—Jan. 30. Mohandas K. Gandhi, 78, shot in New Delhi, India, by Nathuran Vinayak Godse.—Sept. 17. Count Folke Bernadotte, UN mediator for Palestine, ambushed in Jerusalem.

1951—July 20. King Abdullah ibn Hussein of Jordan.

1956—Sept. 21. Pres. Anastasio Somoza of Nicaragua, in Leon; died Sept. 29.

1957—July 26. Pres. Carlos Castillo Armas of Guatemala, in Guatemala City by one of his own guards.

1958—July 14. King Faisal of Iraq; his uncle, Crown Prince Abdul Illah, and July 15, Premier Nuri as-Said, by rebels in Baghdad.

1959—Sept. 25. Prime Minister Solomon Bandaranaike of Ceylon, by Buddhist monk in Colombo.

1961—Jan. 17. Ex-Premier Patrice Lumumba of the Congo, in Katanga Province—May 30. Dominican dictator Rafael Leonidas Trujillo Molina shot to death by assassins near Ciudad Trujillo.

1963—June 12. Medgar W. Evers, NAACP's Mississippi field secretary, in Jackson, Miss.—Nov. 2. Pres. Ngo Dinh Diem of the Republic of Vietnam and his brother, Ngo Dinh Nhu, in a military coup.—Nov. 22. U. S. Pres. John F. Kennedy fatally shot in Dallas, Tex.; accused Lee Harvey Oswald murdered by Jack Ruby while awaiting trial.

1965—Jan. 21. Iranian premier Hassan Ali Mansour fatally wounded by assassin in Teheran; 4 executed.—Feb. 21. Malcolm X, black nationalist, fatally shot in N. Y. City.

1966—Sept. 6. Prime Minister Hendrik F. Verwoerd of South Africa stabbed to death in parliament at Capetown.

1968—Apr. 4. Rev. Dr. Martin Luther King Jr. fatally shot in Memphis, Tenn. by James Earl Ray.—June 5. Sen. Robert F. Kennedy (D-N. Y.) fatally shot in Los Angeles; Sirhan Sirhan, resident alien, convicted of murder.

1971—Nov. 28. Jordan Prime Minister Wasfi Tal, in Cairo, by Palestinian guerrillas.

1973—Mar. 2. U. S. Ambassador Cleo A. Noel Jr., U. S. Charge d'Affaires George C. Moore and Belgian Charge d'Affaires Guy Eid killed by Palestinian guerrillas in Khartoum, Sudan.

1974—Aug. 15. Mrs. Park Chung Hee, wife of president of So. Korea, hit by bullet meant for her husband.—Aug. 19. U. S. Ambassador to Cyprus, Rodger P. Davies, killed by sniper's bullet in Nicosia.

1975—Feb. 11. Pres. Richard Ratsimandrava, of Madagascar, shot in Tananarive.—Mar. 25. King Faisal of Saudi Arabia shot by nephew Prince Musad Abdel Aziz, in royal palace, Riyadh.—Aug. 15. Bangladesh Pres. Sheik Mujibur Rahman killed in coup.

1976—Feb. 13. Nigerian head of state, Gen. Murtala Ramat Mohammed, slain by self-styled "young revolutionaries."

1977—Mar. 16. Kamal Jumblat, Lebanese Druse chieftain, was shot near Beirut.—Mar. 18. Congo Pres. Marien Ngouabi shot in Brazzaville.

1978—July 9. Former Iraqi Premier Abdul Razak Al-Naif shot in London.

1979—Feb. 14. U.S. Ambassador Adolph Dubs shot and killed by Afghan Moslem extremists in Kabul.—Aug. 27. Lord Mountbatten, WW2 hero, and 2 others were killed when a bomb exploded on his fishing boat off the coast of Co. Sligo, Ire. The IRA claimed responsibility. —Oct. 26. So. Korean President Park Chung Hee and 6 bodyguards fatally shot by Kim Jae Kyu, head of Korean CIA, and 5 aides in Seoul.

1980—Apr. 12. Liberian President William R. Tolbert slain in military coup.—Sept. 17. Former Nicaraguan President Anastasio Somoza Debayle and 2 others shot in Paraguay.

1981—Oct. 6. Egyptian President Anwar El-Sadat fatally shot by a band of commandos while reviewing a military parade in Cairo.

1982—Sept. 14. Lebanese President-elect Bishir Gemayel killed by bomb in east Beirut.

1983—Aug. 21. Philippine opposition political leader Benigno Aquino Jr. fatally shot by a gunman at Manila International Airport.—Oct. 9. Four S. Korea cabinet ministers and 15 others killed by bomb blast in Rangoon, Burma.

1984—Oct. 31. Indian Prime Minister Indira Gandhi shot and killed by 2 of her bodyguards, who were members of the minority Sikh sect, in New Delhi.

1986—Feb. 28. Swedish Premier Olof Palme shot and killed by a gunman in Stockholm.

1988—June 1. Lebanese Premier Rashid Karami killed when a bomb exploded aboard a helicopter in which he was traveling. —Apr. 16. PLO military chief Khalil Wazir (Abu Jihad) was gunned down by Israeli commandos in Tunisia.

Assassination Attempts

1910—Aug. 6. N. Y. City Mayor William J. Gaynor shot and seriously wounded by discharged city employee.

1912—Oct. 14. Former U. S. President Theodore Roosevelt shot and seriously wounded by demented man in Milwaukee, Wis.

1950—Nov. 1. In an attempt to assassinate President Truman, 2 members of a Puerto Rican nationalist movement—Griselio Torresola and Oscar Collazo—tried to shoot their way into Blair House. Torresola was killed, and a guard, Pvt. Leslie Coffelt was fatally shot. Collazo was convicted Mar. 7, 1951 for the murder of Coffelt.

1970—Nov. 27. Pope Paul VI unharmed by knife-wielding assailant who attempted to attack him in Manila airport.

1972—May 15. Alabama Gov. George Wallace shot in Laurel, Md. by Arthur Bremer; seriously crippled.

1972—Dec. 7. Mrs. Ferdinand E. Marcos, wife of the Philippine president, was stabbed and seriously injured in Pasay City, Philippines.

1975—Sept. 5. Pres. Gerald R. Ford was unharmed when a Secret Service agent grabbed a pistol aimed at him by Lynette (Squeaky) Fromme, a Charles Manson follower, in Sacramento.

1975—Sept. 22. Pres. Gerald R. Ford escaped unharmed when Sara Jane Moore, a political activist, fired a revolver at him.

1980—Apr. 14. Indian Prime Minister Indira Gandhi was unharmed when a man threw a knife at her in New Delhi.

1980—May 29. Civil rights leader Vernon E. Jordan Jr. shot and wounded in Ft. Wayne, Ind.

1981—Jan. 16. Irish political activist Bernadette Devlin McAliskey and her husband were shot and seriously wounded by 3 members of a protestant paramilitary group in Co. Tyrone, Ire.

1981—Mar. 30. Pres. Ronald Reagan, Press Secy. James Brady, Secret Service agent Timothy J. McCarthy, and Washington, D.C. policeman Thomas Delahanty were shot and seriously wounded by John W. Hinckley Jr. in Washington, D.C.

1981—May 13. Pope John Paul II and 2 bystanders were shot and wounded by Mehmet Ali Agca, an escaped Turkish murderer, in St. Peter's Square, Rome.

1982—May 12. Pope John Paul II was unharmed when a man with a knife was overpowered by guards, in Fatima, Portugal.

1982—June 3. Israel's ambassador to Britain Shlomo Argov was shot and seriously wounded by Arab terrorists in London.

1986—Sept. 7. Chile President Gen. Augusto Pinochet Ugarte escaped unharmed when his motorcade was attacked by rebels using rockets, bazookas, grenades, and rifles.

Notable Kidnapings

Edward A. Cudahy Jr., 16, in Omaha, Neb., Dec. 18, 1900. Returned Dec. 20 after $25,000 paid. Pat Crowe confessed.

Robert Franks, 13, in Chicago, May 22, 1924, by 2 youths, Richard Loeb and Nathan Leopold, who killed boy. Demand for $10,000 ignored. Loeb died in prison, Leopold paroled 1958.

Charles A. Lindbergh Jr., 20 mos. old, in Hopewell, N.J., Mar. 1, 1932; found dead May 12. Ransom of $50,000 was paid to man identified as Bruno Richard Hauptmann, 35, paroled German convict who entered U.S. illegally. Hauptmann was convicted after spectacular trial at Flemington, and electrocuted in Trenton, N.J. prison, Apr. 3, 1936.

William A. Hamm Jr., 39, in St. Paul, June 15, 1933. $100,000 paid. Alvin Karpis given life, paroled in 1969.

Charles F. Urschel, in Oklahoma City, July 22, 1933. Released July 31 after $200,000 paid. George (Machine Gun) Kelly and 5 others given life.

Brooke L. Hart, 22, in San Jose, Cal. Thomas Thurmond and John Holmes arrested after demanding $40,000 ransom. When Hart's body was found in San Francisco Bay, Nov. 26, 1933, a mob attacked the jail at San Jose and lynched the 2 kidnapers.

George Weyerhaeuser, 9, in Tacoma, Wash., May 24, 1935. Returned home June 1 after $200,000 paid. Kidnapers given 20 to 60 years.

Charles Mattson, 10, in Tacoma, Wash., **Dec. 27, 1936.** Found dead Jan. 11, 1937. Kidnaper asked $28,000, failed to contact.

Arthur Fried, in White Plains, N.Y., **Dec. 4, 1937.** Body not found. Two kidnapers executed.

Robert C. Greenlease, 6, taken from Kansas City, Mo. school **Sept. 28, 1953,** and held for $600,000. Body found Oct. 7. Mrs. Bonnie Brown Heady and Carl A. Hall pleaded guilty and were executed.

Peter Weinberger, 32 days old, Westbury, N.Y., **July 4, 1956,** for $2,000 ransom, not paid. Child found dead. Angelo John LaMarca, 31, convicted, executed.

Cynthia Ruotolo, 6 wks old, taken from carriage in front of Hamden, Conn. store **Sept. 1, 1956.** Body found in lake.

Lee Crary, 8 in Everett, Wash., **Sept. 22, 1957,** $10,000 ransom, not paid. He escaped after 3 days, led police to George E. Collins, who was convicted.

Eric Peugeot, 4, taken from playground at St. Cloud golf course, Paris, **Apr. 12, 1960.** Released unharmed 3 days later after payment of undisclosed sum. Two sentenced to prison.

Frank Sinatra Jr., 19, from hotel room in Lake Tahoe, Cal., **Dec. 8, 1963.** Released **Dec. 11** after his father paid $240,000 ransom. Three men sentenced to prison; most of ransom recovered.

Barbara Jane Mackle, 20, abducted **Dec. 17, 1968,** from Atlanta, Ga., motel, was found unharmed 3 days later, buried in a coffin-like wooden box 18 inches underground, after her father had paid $500,000 ransom; Gary Steven Krist sentenced to life, Ruth Eisenmann-Schier to 7 years; most of ransom recovered.

Anne Katherine Jenkins, 22, abducted **May 10, 1969,** from her Baltimore apartment, freed 3 days later after father paid $10,000 ransom.

Mrs. Roy Fuchs, 35, and 3 children held hostage 2 hours, **May 14, 1969,** in Long Island, N. Y., released after her husband, a bank manager, paid kidnapers $129,000 in bank funds; 4 men arrested, ransom recovered.

C. Burke Elbrick, U.S. ambassador to Brazil, kidnaped by revolutionaries in Rio de Janeiro **Sept. 4, 1969;** released 3 days later after Brazil yielded to kidnaper's demands to publish manifesto and release 15 political prisoners.

Patrick Dolan, 18, found shot to death near Sao Paulo, Brazil, **Nov. 5, 1969,** after he was kidnaped and $12,500 paid.

Sean M. Holly, U.S. diplomat, in Guatemala **Mar. 6, 1970;** freed 2 days later upon release of 3 terrorists from prison.

Lt. Col. Donald J. Crowley, U.S. air attache, in Dominican Republic **Mar. 24, 1970;** released after government allowed 20 prisoners to leave the country.

Count Karl von Spreti, W. German ambassador to Guatemala. **Mar. 31, 1970;** slain after Guatemala refused demands for $700,000 and release of 22 prisoners.

Pedro Eugenio Aramburu, former Argentine president, by terrorists **May 29, 1970;** body found July 17.

Ehrenfried von Holleben, W. German ambassador to Brazil, by terrorists **June 11, 1970;** freed after release of 40 prisoners.

Daniel A. Mitrione, U.S. diplomat, **July 31, 1970,** by terrorists in Montevideo, Uruguay; body found Aug. 10 after government rejected demands for release of all political prisoners.

James R. Cross, British trade commissioner, **Oct. 5, 1970,** by French Canadian separatists in Quebec; freed Dec. 3 after 3 kidnapers and relatives flown to Cuba by government.

Pierre Laporte, Quebec Labor Minister, by separatists **Oct. 10, 1970;** body found Oct. 18.

Giovanni E. Bucher, Swiss ambassador **Dec. 7, 1970,** by revolutionaries in Rio de Janeiro; freed Jan. 16, 1971, after Brazil released 70 political prisoners.

Geoffrey Jackson, British ambassador, in Montevideo, **Jan. 8, 1971,** by Tupamaro terrorists. Held as ransom for release of imprisoned terrorists; released Sept. 9; prisoners escaped.

Ephraim Elrom, Israel consul general in Istanbul, **May 17, 1971.** Held as ransom for imprisoned terrorists; found dead May 23.

Mrs. Virginia Piper, 49 abducted **July 27, 1972,** from her home in suburban Minneapolis; found unharmed near Duluth 2 days later after her husband paid $1 million ransom to the kidnapers.

Victor E. Samuelson, Exxon executive, **Dec. 6, 1973,** in Campana, Argentina, by Marxist guerrillas, freed Apr. 29, 1974, after payment of record $14.2 million ransom.

J. Paul Getty 3d, 17, grandson of the U.S. oil mogul, released **Dec. 15, 1973,** in southern Italy after $2.8 million ransom paid.

Patricia (Patty) Hearst, 19, taken from her Berkeley, Cal., apartment **Feb. 4, 1974.** Symbionese Liberation Army demanded her father, Randolph A. Hearst, publisher, give millions to poor. She was identified by FBI as taking part in a San Francisco bank holdup, **Apr. 15.** FBI. **Sept. 18, 1975,** captured Patricia and others in San Francisco; they were indicted on various charges. Patricia for bank robbery. Convicted, **Mar. 20, 1976.** She was released from prison under executive clemency, **Feb. 1, 1979.** In 1978, William and Emily Harris were sentenced to 10 years to life for the Hearst kidnapping. Both were paroled in 1983.

J. Reginald Murphy, 40, an editor of *Atlanta* (Ga.) *Constitution,* kidnaped **Feb. 20, 1974,** freed **Feb. 22** after payment of $700,000 ransom by the newspaper. Police arrested William A. H. Williams, a contractor; most of the money was recovered.

J. Guadalupe Zuno Hernandez, 83, father-in-law of Mexican President Luis Echeverria Alvarez, seized by 4 terrorists **Aug. 28, 1974;** government refused to negotiate; he was released Sept. 8.

E. B. Reville, Hepzibah, Ga., banker, and wife Jean, kidnaped **Sept. 30, 1974.** Ransom of $30,000 paid. He was found alive; Mrs. Reville was found dead in car trunk Oct. 2.

Jack Teich, Kings Point, N.Y., steel executive, seized **Nov. 12, 1974;** released Nov. 19 after payment of $750,000.

William F. Niehous, a U.S. businessman, was abducted from his suburban Caracas, Venezuela home, **Feb. 27, 1976.** He was rescued by police **June 29, 1979,** ending more than 3 years of captivity.

Hanns-Martin Schleyer, a West German industrialist, was kidnaped in Cologne, **Sept. 5, 1977** by armed terrorists. Schleyer was found dead, **Oct. 19,** in an abandoned car shortly after 3 jailed terrorist leaders of the Baader-Meinhof gang were found dead in their prison cells near Stuttgart, West Germany.

Aldo Moro, former Italian premier, kidnaped in Rome, **Mar. 16, 1978,** by left-wing terrorists. Five of his bodyguards killed during abduction. Moro's bullet-ridden body was found in a parked car, May 9, in Rome. Six members of the Red Brigades arrested, charged, June 5, with complicity in the kidnaping.

James L. Dozier, a U.S. Army general, kidnaped from his apartment in Verona, Italy, **Dec. 17, 1981,** by members of the Red Brigades terrorist organization. He was rescued, **Jan. 28, 1982.**

Enrique Camarena Salazar, and **Alfredo Zavala Avelar**, U.S. Drug Enforcement Agency employees were kidnaped in Guadalajara, Mexico, Feb. 7, 1985. Their bodies were found Mar. 6.

UNITED STATES POPULATION

Changing Population Patterns

By C.L. Kincannon

Deputy Director, U.S. Bureau of the Census

On January 1, 1989, the estimated resident population of the United States was 247.1 million, a 9.1 percent increase over the April 1, 1980 census count of 226.5 million. The growth of 20.6 million was attributable to a natural increase of 14.7 million (32.6 million births less 18.0 million deaths) and a net immigration of 5.9 million.

Changes in **age structure** during the 1980s reflect past trends in childbearing: the low birth rate in the 2 decades ending in 1945, the higher birth rate during the "baby boom" (1946-1964), and the lower birth rate subsequently. From 1980 to July 1, 1988, the population 18 to 24 years old declined 11.2 percent while the population 25 to 44 years old increased 25.9 percent. The elderly population (65 years and over) rose 18.9 percent and increased from 11.3 percent to 12.4 percent of the total population. The median age (the age at which half the population is younger and half is older) rose from 30.0 to 32.3. The elderly percentage and the median age in 1988 were the highest in the nation's history.

The South and West accounted for 16.8 million, or 87 percent, of the **nation's population growth** from 1980 to 1988 and increased their share of the population from 52.3 to 55.1 percent. The share of the population residing in the North (Northeast and Midwest regions) dropped below 50 percent in 1975. During the 1980 to 1988 period, the South and West added 8.1 million population through net migration while the North lost 2.5 million population through net migration. California, Texas, and Florida together accounted for 9.8 million, or 51 percent, of national growth from 1980 to 1988. The highest growth rates were in Nevada (31.7 percent), Alaska (30.5 percent), and Arizona (28.4 percent) while Michigan, Iowa, West Virginia, and the District of Columbia lost population. In 1988, 11.5 percent of the nation's population resided in California. This is the highest concentration in any one state since 1870 when 11.4 percent resided in New York. California's population in 1988 (28.3 million) exceeded the combined population of the 21 least populous states.

In 1987, the nation's 37 **metropolitan areas** with at least 1 million population had 119 million residents, or 48.9 percent of the national population. Altogether, 187.1 million persons, or 76.9 percent, lived in the nation's 282 designated metropolitan areas. From 1980 to 1987, the population in metropolitan areas increased 8.5 percent, about twice the 4.1 percent increase in nonmetropolitan territory. During the 1970s, the growth rate was higher in nonmetropolitan territory than in metropolitan areas. The growth rates in metropolitan areas by size category were similar in the 1980 to 1987 period. In the 1970s, the metropolitan growth rate was lowest in the largest areas (those with 5 million or more population). For nonmetropolitan counties, the growth rate was highest in both periods in counties with 15 percent or more of their resident workers commuting to metropolitan areas. The New York City metropolitan area had 18.1 million residents in 1987, followed by Los Angeles (13.5 million) and Chicago (8.1 million) metropolitan areas. Among metropolitan areas with at least 1 million population, the highest growth rates in the 1980 to 1987 period were in Phoenix (29.8 percent), Dallas-Ft. Worth (27.1 percent), and Atlanta (24.3 percent).

In 1987, only 5 million persons lived on **farms,** down from 15.6 million in 1960 and 32 million in 1920. The 1987 figure represented only 2 percent of the nation's population compared to 8.7 percent in 1960 and 30.2 percent in 1920.

Based on data from the *Current Population Survey,* there were 91.1 million **households** (occupied housing units) in the U.S. in March 1988, up 12.7 percent from the March 1980 estimate of 80.8 million. The more rapid growth rate in households than in population reflects changes in age structure, which in turn reflect the changes in childbearing noted

earlier. The average number of persons per household dropped from 3.33 in 1964 to 2.76 in 1980 and to a record low of 2.64 in 1988. Most of the decline is attributable to the decline in the average number of children (under 18 years), which dropped from 1.23 in 1964 (at the end of the baby boom) to 0.79 in 1980 and 0.70 in 1988. There were 21.9 million 1-person households in 1988, up from 18.3 million in 1980 and 10.9 million in 1970. Households with 5 or more persons numbered 9.6 million in 1988, down from 10.4 million in 1980 and 13.3 million in 1970. From 1980 to 1988, the number of married-couple families increased from 49.1 million to 51.8 million, and the number of female-householder families (no spouse present) rose from 8.7 million to 10.6 million. (Families have at least two members, including at least one relative of the householder.)

Today's **young adults** are less likely to have married or to be maintaining their own households than in the past. The median age at first marriage for females rose from 20.3 in 1960 to 22.0 in 1980 and 23.6 in 1988. The corresponding figures for males are 22.8, 24.7, and 25.9. In 1988, 54.4 percent of persons 18 to 24 years old lived with one or both parents, up from 48.4 percent in 1980 and 43.0 percent in 1960. Among **children under 18 years,** 72.7 percent lived with both parents in 1988, down from 76.7 percent in 1980 and 87.7 percent in 1960. The decline reflects changing marital patterns: the number of divorced persons per 1,000 married persons with spouse present was 133 in 1988, up from 100 in 1980 and 35 in 1960.

The **educational level** of the population continues to rise. Among persons 25 years and over in 1988, 76.2 percent had completed 4 years of high school (or more education), up from 68.6 percent in 1980 and 24.5 percent in 1940; 20.3 percent had completed 4 or more years of college, compared to 17.0 percent in 1980 and 4.6 percent in 1940. In 1988, 24.0 percent of males and 17.0 percent of females had completed 4 or more years of college. The differences by sex is likely to narrow in the future, reflecting the educational experience of young adults. For example, among persons 25 to 29 years in 1988, the figures were 23.4 percent for males and 21.9 percent for females.

Income and Poverty

In 1987, median family income was $30,850, 1.0 percent higher than in 1986 after adjusting for inflation. This represents the fifth consecutive year real median family income has increased, putting it at a level comparable to that of 1973, an earlier all-time high. The number of persons below the poverty level was 32.5 million in 1987, not significantly different from the 32.4 million in 1986. The poverty rate was 13.5 percent in 1987, not significantly different from the 13.6 percent in 1986. Real per capita income in 1987, $12,290, was at an all time high, increasing 1.6 percent over its 1986 level.

A report on "Household Wealth and Asset Ownership," found the median net worth of households to be $32,670 in 1984. Two-thirds of households reported homeownership with median home equity of $40,600. Householders 55 to 64 reported median wealth of $73,660 compared with $5,760 for those under 35 years and $55,180 for those aged 75 and over. After taxes, household incomes averaged $23,680 in 1986, up 2.6 percent after adjustment for inflation. Households paid an average of $7,650 in the four types of taxes covered by the census study. The proportions of pretax income paid were 14 percent for Federal income taxes, 6 percent for FICA payroll taxes (Social Security), 4 percent for state income taxes, and about 2 percent for property taxes.

Among the 29.1 million married couples having both partners as wage earners in 1983, 5.3 million wives earned more than their husbands. The average earnings of married couples was $37,170 rising to $49,030 if both husband and wife worked full time.

Benefits

About 89 percent of U.S. households, 80.9 million, received at least one noncash benefit in 1987. That was up 1.1 million since 1986. About 16 percent of all households received means-tested noncash benefits; their median income was $8,920. About 7 percent received food stamps, while 21 percent of households with school-age children received free or reduced-price lunches. Of the 8.3 million households with Medicaid coverage, 25 percent had a householder 65 or older and 41 percent had a female householder with no husband present. About one out of every four households with children under age 19 received a means-tested benefit. There were 8.5 million such households in 1987.

1990 Bicentennial Census

The Census Bureau is well along with plans to take the 21st decennial census in 1990. This count will mark the 200th anniversary of the first census in 1790 when George Washington was president and the young United States had just under 4 million residents. Census workers in 1990 are expected to count about 250 million people and 106 million housing units.

In the spring of 1988, the Census Bureau conducted three "dress rehearsal" censuses—in St. Louis, central Missouri, and eastern Washington—as a final check of its equipment, procedures, questionnaires, and statistical processing methods. Census Bureau workers in the field and at headquarters also began preparing a nationwide mailing list of most residential addresses, since the 1990 count (as in 1970 and 1980) largely will be taken by the mail-out/mail-back technique.

In the 1990 census, the processing of the returned questionnaires will be speeded up with the use of more automation and computers to hasten the release of final totals for people and housing. Even so, the Census Bureau will hire a "census army" of some 480,000 temporary employees between fall 1989 and fall 1990.

The Census Bureau and the U.S. Geological Survey are participating in a joint effort that will produce and maintain a nationwide set of maps and related graphic and digital products needed to support both the Census Bureau's decennial and economic censuses and the Geological Survey's national mapping program. The agencies completed the initial cartographic data base in early 1988, and the Census Bureau used this automated file to produce maps for its field operations for the 1990 census.

Processing and tabulating of the more than 106 million questionnaires will occur in 7 processing centers between April and October 1990 in order to report the count for each state to the President by Dec. 31, 1990, as required by law. These counts are for reapportioning seats in the House of Representatives, called for by the Constitution. By Apr. 1, 1991, one year after "Census Day" (Apr. 1, 1990), the Census Bureau will make available to state officials the small-area counts needed to carry out redrawing state and local election district and legislative boundaries.

Further information about the 1990 census is available from the 1990 Census Promotional Office, Bureau of the Census, Washington, D.C. 20233.

1990 Census: Minority Survey

In July 1989, the U.S. Bureau of the Census agreed to conduct a random survey of 150,000 homes along with 1990 census. The results could lead to the first adjustment in the census for any undercounting of racial, ethnic, and other groups. The agreement was the direct result of a suit filed by civic and civil rights groups and state, county, and local governments, led by New York City and State, along with Chicago, Los Angeles, Houston, the state of California, and Dade County, Fla. The Commerce Dept. did not commit itself to adjusting the 1990 tally, only to performing the subsequent national survey. By comparing the results from that random survey, officials hope to determine who was counted correctly, who was counted improperly, and who was not counted at all.

Resident Population by Sex, Race, Residence, and Median Age: 1790 to 1988

Source: U.S. Bureau of the Census (thousands, except as indicated)

Date	Sex		Race				Residence		Median Age (years)		
	Male	Female	White	Black Number	Percent	Other	Urban	Rural	All races	White	Black
Conterminous U.S.[1]											
1790 (Aug. 2)...	NA	NA	3,172	757	19.3	NA	202	3,728	NA	NA	NA
1810 (Aug. 6)...	NA	NA	5,862	1,378	19.0	NA	525	6,714	NA	16.0	NA
1820 (Aug. 7)...	4,897	4,742	7,867	1,772	18.4	NA	693	8,945	16.7	16.5	17.2
1840 (June 1)...	8,689	8,381	14,196	2,874	16.8	NA	1,845	15,224	17.8	17.9	17.3
1860 (June 1)...	16,085	15,358	26,923	4,442	14.1	79	6,217	25,227	19.4	19.7	17.7
1870 (June 1)...	19,494	19,065	33,589	4,880	12.7	89	9,902	28,656	20.2	20.4	18.5
1880 (June 1)...	25,519	24,637	43,403	6,581	13.1	172	14,130	36,026	20.9	21.4	18.0
1890 (June 1)...	32,237	30,711	55,101	7,489	11.9	358	22,106	40,841	22.0	22.5	17.8
1900 (June 1)...	38,816	37,178	66,809	8,834	11.6	351	30,160	45,835	22.9	23.4	19.4
1920 (Jan. 1)...	53,900	51,810	94,821	10,463	9.9	427	54,158	51,553	25.3	25.6	22.3
1930 (Apr. 1)...	62,137	60,638	110,287	11,891	9.7	597	68,955	53,820	26.4	26.9	23.5
1940 (Apr. 1)...	66,062	65,608	118,215	12,866	9.8	589	74,424	57,246	29.0	29.5	25.3
United States											
1950 (Apr. 1)...	75,187	76,139	135,150	15,045	9.9	1,131	96,847	54,479	30.2	30.7	26.2
1960 (Apr. 1)...	88,331	90,992	158,832	18,872	10.5	1,620	125,269	54,054	29.5	30.3	23.5
1970 (Apr. 1)[2]..	98,926	104,309	178,098	22,581	11.1	2,557	149,325	53,887	28.0	28.9	22.4
1980 (Apr. 1)[3]..	110,053	116,493	194,713	26,683	11.8	5,150	167,051	59,495	30.0	30.9	24.9
1983 (July 1, est)	113,119	120,365	199,849	28,056	12.0	6,379	NA	NA	30.8	31.8	26.0
1984 (July 1, est)	115,022	121,455	201,290	28,457	12.0	6,730	NA	NA	31.2	32.1	26.3
1985 (July 1, est)	116,160	122,576	202,769	28,870	12.1	7,097	NA	NA	31.5	32.4	26.6
1986 (July 1, est)	117,370	123,737	204,326	29,303	12.2	7,478	NA	NA	31.7	32.7	26.9
1987 (July 1, est)	118,539	124,880	205,827	29,748	12.2	7,845	NA	NA	32.3	33.0	27.2
1988 (July 1, est)	119,738	126,069	207,377	30,202	12.3	8,228	NA	NA	32.3	NA	NA

(NA) Not available. (1) Excludes Alaska and Hawaii. (2) The revised 1970 resident population count is 203,302,031, which incorporates changes due to errors found after tabulations were completed. The race and sex data shown here reflect the official 1970 census count while the residence data come from the tabulated count. (3) The race data shown for April 1, 1980 have been modified.

U.S. Population by Official

(Members of the Armed Forces overseas or

State	1790	1800	1810	1820	1830	1840	1850	1860	1870	1880
Ala. . .	....	1,250	9,046	127,901	309,527	590,756	771,623	964,201	996,992	1,262,505
Alas. .	....	....	....	....	....	....	....	....	....	33,426
Ariz. .	....	....	....	....	....	....	....	....	9,658	40,440
Ark. . .	....	....	1,062	14,273	30,388	97,574	209,897	435,450	484,471	802,525
Cal. . .	....	....	....	....	....	....	92,597	379,994	560,247	864,694
Col. . .	....	....	....	....	....	....	....	34,277	39,864	194,327
Conn. .	237,946	251,002	261,942	275,248	297,675	309,978	370,792	460,147	537,454	622,700
Del. . .	59,096	64,273	72,674	72,749	76,748	78,085	91,532	112,216	125,015	146,608
D.C. . .	....	8,144	15,471	23,336	30,261	33,745	51,687	75,080	131,700	177,624
Fla. . .	....	....	....	....	34,730	54,477	87,445	140,424	187,748	269,493
Ga. . .	82,548	162,686	252,433	340,989	516,823	691,392	906,185	1,057,286	1,184,109	1,542,180
Ha. . .	....	....	....	....	....	....	....	....	....	....
Ida. . .	....	....	....	....	....	....	....	....	14,999	32,610
Ill. . .	....	....	12,282	55,211	157,445	476,183	851,470	1,711,951	2,539,891	3,077,871
Ind. . .	....	5,641	24,520	147,178	343,031	685,866	988,416	1,350,428	1,680,637	1,978,301
Ia. . .	....	....	....	....	....	43,112	192,214	674,913	1,194,020	1,624,615
Kan. . .	....	....	....	....	....	....	....	107,206	364,399	996,096
Ky. . .	73,677	220,955	406,511	564,317	687,917	779,828	982,405	1,155,684	1,321,011	1,648,690
La. . .	....	....	76,556	153,407	215,739	352,411	517,762	708,002	726,915	939,946
Me. . .	96,540	151,719	228,705	298,335	399,455	501,793	583,169	628,279	626,915	648,936
Md. . .	319,728	341,548	380,546	407,350	447,040	470,019	583,034	687,049	780,894	934,943
Mass. .	378,787	422,845	472,040	523,287	610,408	737,699	994,514	1,231,066	1,457,351	1,783,085
Mich. .	....	....	4,762	8,896	31,639	212,267	397,654	749,113	1,184,059	1,636,937
Minn. .	....	....	....	....	....	....	6,077	172,023	439,706	780,773
Miss. .	....	7,600	31,306	75,448	136,621	375,651	606,526	791,305	827,922	1,131,597
Mo. . .	....	....	19,783	66,586	140,455	383,702	682,044	1,182,012	1,721,295	2,168,380
Mon. .	....	....	....	....	....	....	....	....	20,595	39,159
Neb. . .	....	....	....	....	....	....	....	28,841	122,993	452,402
Nev. . .	....	....	....	....	....	....	....	6,857	42,491	62,266
N.H. . .	141,885	183,858	214,460	244,161	269,328	284,574	317,976	326,073	318,300	346,991
N.J. . .	184,139	211,149	245,562	277,575	320,823	373,306	489,555	672,035	906,096	1,131,116
N.M. .	....	....	....	....	....	....	61,547	93,516	91,874	119,565
N.Y. . .	340,120	589,051	959,049	1,372,812	1,918,608	2,428,921	3,097,394	3,880,735	4,382,759	5,082,871
N.C. . .	393,751	478,103	555,500	638,829	737,987	753,419	869,039	992,622	1,071,361	1,399,750
N.D. . .	....	....	....	....	....	....	....	....	*2,405	36,909
Oh. . .	....	45,365	230,760	581,434	937,903	1,519,467	1,980,329	2,339,511	2,665,260	3,198,062
Okla. .	....	....	....	....	....	....	....	....	....	....
Ore. . .	....	....	....	....	....	....	12,093	52,465	90,923	174,768
Pa. . .	434,373	602,365	810,091	1,049,458	1,348,233	1,724,033	2,311,786	2,906,215	3,521,951	4,282,891
R.I. . .	68,825	69,122	76,931	83,059	97,199	108,830	147,545	174,620	217,353	276,531
S.C. . .	249,073	345,591	415,115	502,741	581,185	594,398	668,507	703,708	705,606	995,577
S.D. . .	....	....	....	....	....	....	....	*4,837	*11,776	98,268
Tenn. .	35,691	105,602	261,727	422,823	681,904	829,210	1,002,717	1,109,801	1,258,520	1,542,359
Tex. . .	....	....	....	....	....	....	212,592	604,215	818,579	1,591,749
Ut. . .	....	....	....	....	....	....	11,380	40,273	86,786	143,963
Vt. . .	85,425	154,465	217,895	235,981	280,652	291,948	314,120	315,098	330,551	332,286
Va. . .	691,737	807,557	877,683	938,261	1,044,054	1,025,227	1,119,348	1,219,630	1,225,163	1,512,565
Wash. .	....	....	....	....	....	....	1,201	11,594	23,955	75,116
W. Va. .	55,873	78,592	105,469	136,808	176,924	224,537	302,313	376,688	442,014	618,457
Wis. . .	....	....	....	....	....	30,945	305,391	775,881	1,054,670	1,315,497
Wy. . .	....	....	....	....	....	....	....	....	9,118	20,789
U.S. . .	3,929,214	5,308,483	7,239,881	9,638,453	12,860,702	17,063,353¹	23,191,876	31,443,321¹	38,558,371	50,189,209

Note: Where possible, population shown is that of 1980 area of state.
*1860 figure is for Dakota Territory; 1870 figures are for parts of Dakota Territory. (1) U.S. total includes persons (5,318 in 1830 and 6,100 in 1840) on public ships in the service of the United States not credited to any region, division, or state.

Density of Population by States

(Per square mile, land area only)

State	1920	1960	1980	1988	State	1920	1960	1980	1988	State	1920	1960	1980	1988
Ala. . .	45.8	64.2	76.6	80.8	La. . .	39.6	72.2	94.5	99.0	Oh. . .	141.4	236.6	263.3	264.7
Alas.*	0.1	0.4	0.7	0.9	Me. . .	25.7	31.3	36.3	38.9	Okla. .	29.2	33.8	44.1	47.2
Ariz. .	2.9	11.5	23.9	30.7	Md. . .	145.8	313.5	428.7	469.9	Ore. . .	8.2	18.4	27.4	28.8
Ark. . .	33.4	34.2	43.9	46.0	Mass. .	479.2	657.3	733.3	752.7	Pa. . .	194.5	251.4	264.3	267.4
Cal. . .	22.0	100.4	151.4	181.2	Mich. .	63.8	137.7	162.6	162.2	R.I. . .	566.4	819.3	897.8	940.9
Col. . .	9.1	16.9	27.9	31.9	Minn. .	29.5	43.1	51.2	54.1	S.C. . .	55.2	78.7	103.4	114.9
Conn. .	286.4	520.6	637.8	663.6	Miss. .	38.6	46.0	53.4	55.5	S.D. . .	8.3	9.0	9.1	9.4
Del. . .	113.5	225.2	307.6	341.7	Mo. . .	49.5	62.6	71.3	74.6	Tenn. .	56.1	86.2	111.6	118.9
D.C. . .	7,292.9	12,523.9	10,132.3	9,792.0	Mon. .	3.8	4.6	5.4	5.5	Tex. . .	17.8	36.4	54.3	64.3
Fla. . .	17.7	91.5	180.0	227.8	Neb. . .	16.9	18.4	20.5	20.9	Ut. . .	5.5	10.8	17.8	20.6
Ga. . .	49.3	67.8	94.1	109.2	Nev. . .	.7	2.6	7.3	9.6	Vt. . .	38.6	42.0	55.2	60.1
Ha.*	39.9	98.5	150.1	170.9	N.H. . .	49.1	67.2	102.4	120.7	Va. . .	57.4	99.6	134.7	151.5
Ida. . .	5.2	8.1	11.5	12.2	N.J. . .	420.0	805.5	986.2	1,033.9	Wash. .	20.3	42.8	62.1	69.9
Ill. . .	115.7	180.4	205.3	208.7	N.M. .	2.9	7.8	10.7	12.4	W. Va. .	60.9	77.2	80.8	77.8
Ind. . .	81.3	128.8	152.8	154.6	N.Y. . .	217.9	350.6	370.6	378.0	Wis. . .	47.6	72.6	86.5	89.2
Ia. . .	43.2	49.2	52.1	50.6	N.C. . .	52.5	93.2	120.4	132.9	Wy. . .	2.0	3.4	4.9	4.9
Kan. . .	21.6	26.6	28.9	30.5	N.D. . .	9.2	9.1	9.4	9.6					
Ky. . .	60.1	76.2	92.3	93.9						U.S. .	*29.9	50.6	64.0	69.5

*For purposes of comparison, Alaska and Hawaii included in above tabulation for 1920, even though not states then.

Census from 1790 to 1980

other U.S. nationals overseas are not included.

1890	1900	1910	1920	1930	1940	1950	1960	1970	1980[1]
1,513,401	1,828,697	2,138,093	2,348,174	2,646,248	2,832,961	3,061,743	3,266,740	3,444,354	3,894,025
32,052	63,592	64,356	55,036	59,278	72,524	128,643	226,167	302,583	401,851
88,243	122,931	204,354	334,162	435,573	499,261	749,587	1,302,161	1,775,399	2,716,546
1,128,211	1,311,564	1,574,449	1,752,204	1,854,482	1,949,387	1,909,511	1,786,272	1,923,322	2,286,357
1,213,398	1,485,053	2,377,549	3,426,861	5,677,251	6,907,387	10,586,223	15,717,204	19,971,069	23,667,764
413,249	539,700	799,024	939,629	1,035,791	1,123,296	1,325,089	1,753,947	2,209,596	2,889,735
746,258	908,420	1,114,756	1,380,631	1,606,903	1,709,242	2,007,280	2,535,234	3,032,217	3,107,564
168,493	184,735	202,322	223,003	238,380	266,505	318,085	446,292	548,104	594,338
230,392	278,718	331,069	437,571	486,869	663,091	802,178	763,956	756,668	638,432
391,422	528,542	752,619	968,470	1,468,211	1,897,414	2,771,305	4,951,560	6,791,418	[2]9,746,961
1,837,353	2,216,331	2,609,121	2,895,832	2,908,506	3,123,723	3,444,578	3,943,116	4,587,930	5,462,982
....	154,001	191,874	255,881	368,300	422,770	499,794	632,772	769,913	964,691
88,548	161,772	325,594	431,866	445,032	524,873	588,637	667,191	713,015	944,127
3,826,352	4,821,550	5,638,591	6,485,280	7,630,654	7,897,241	8,712,176	10,081,158	11,110,285	11,427,409
2,192,404	2,516,462	2,700,876	2,930,390	3,238,503	3,427,796	3,934,224	4,662,498	5,195,392	5,490,214
1,912,297	2,231,853	2,224,771	2,404,021	2,470,939	2,538,268	2,621,073	2,757,537	2,825,368	2,913,808
1,428,108	1,470,495	1,690,949	1,769,257	1,880,999	1,801,028	1,905,299	2,178,611	2,249,071	2,364,236
1,858,635	2,147,174	2,289,905	2,416,630	2,614,589	2,845,627	2,944,806	3,038,156	3,220,711	3,660,324
1,118,588	1,381,625	1,656,388	1,798,509	2,101,593	2,363,880	2,683,516	3,257,022	3,644,637	4,206,116
661,086	694,466	742,371	768,014	797,423	847,226	913,774	969,265	993,722	1,125,043
1,042,390	1,188,044	1,295,346	1,449,661	1,631,526	1,821,244	2,343,001	3,100,689	3,923,897	4,216,933
2,238,947	2,805,346	3,366,416	3,852,356	4,249,614	4,316,721	4,690,514	5,148,578	5,689,170	5,737,093
2,093,890	2,420,982	2,810,173	3,668,412	4,842,325	5,256,106	6,371,766	7,823,194	8,881,826	9,262,044
1,310,283	1,751,394	2,075,708	2,387,125	2,563,953	2,792,300	2,982,483	3,413,864	3,806,103	4,075,970
1,289,600	1,551,270	1,797,114	1,790,618	2,009,821	2,183,796	2,178,914	2,178,141	2,216,994	2,520,770
2,679,185	3,106,665	3,293,335	3,404,055	3,629,367	3,784,664	3,954,653	4,319,813	4,677,623	4,916,766
142,924	243,329	376,053	548,889	537,606	559,456	591,024	674,767	694,409	786,690
1,062,656	1,066,300	1,192,214	1,296,372	1,377,963	1,315,834	1,325,510	1,411,330	1,485,333	1,569,825
47,355	42,335	81,875	77,407	91,058	110,247	160,083	285,278	488,738	800,508
376,530	411,588	430,572	443,083	465,293	491,524	533,242	606,921	737,681	920,610
1,444,933	1,883,669	2,537,167	3,155,900	4,041,334	4,160,165	4,835,329	6,066,782	7,171,112	7,365,011
160,282	195,310	327,301	360,350	423,317	531,818	681,187	951,023	1,017,055	1,303,302
6,003,174	7,268,894	9,113,614	10,385,227	12,588,066	13,479,142	14,830,192	16,782,304	18,241,391	17,558,165
1,617,949	1,893,810	2,206,287	2,559,123	3,170,276	3,571,623	4,061,929	4,556,155	5,084,411	5,880,095
190,983	319,146	577,056	646,872	680,845	641,935	619,636	632,446	617,792	652,717
3,672,329	4,157,545	4,767,121	5,759,394	6,646,697	6,907,612	7,946,627	9,706,397	10,657,423	10,797,603
258,657	790,391	1,657,155	2,028,283	2,396,040	2,336,434	2,233,351	2,328,284	2,559,463	3,025,487
317,704	413,536	672,765	783,389	953,786	1,089,684	1,521,341	1,768,687	2,091,533	2,633,156
5,258,113	6,302,115	7,665,111	8,720,017	9,631,350	9,900,180	10,498,012	11,319,366	11,800,766	11,864,720
345,506	428,556	542,610	604,397	687,497	713,346	791,896	859,488	949,723	947,154
348,600	401,570	583,888	636,547	692,849	642,961	652,740	680,514	666,257	690,768
1,767,518	2,020,616	2,184,789	2,337,885	2,616,556	2,915,841	3,291,718	3,567,089	3,926,018	4,591,023
2,235,527	3,048,710	3,896,542	4,663,228	5,824,715	6,414,824	7,711,194	9,579,677	11,198,655	14,225,513
210,779	276,749	373,351	449,396	507,847	550,310	688,862	890,627	1,059,273	1,461,037
332,422	343,641	355,956	352,428	359,611	359,231	377,747	389,881	444,732	511,456
1,655,980	1,854,184	2,061,612	2,309,187	2,421,851	2,677,773	3,318,680	3,966,949	4,651,448	5,346,797
357,232	518,103	1,141,990	1,356,621	1,563,396	1,736,191	2,378,963	2,853,214	3,413,244	4,132,353
762,794	958,800	1,221,119	1,463,701	1,729,205	1,901,974	2,005,552	1,860,421	1,744,237	1,950,186
1,693,330	2,069,042	2,333,860	2,632,067	2,939,006	3,137,587	3,434,575	3,951,777	4,417,821	4,705,642
62,555	92,531	145,965	194,402	225,565	250,742	290,529	330,066	332,416	469,557
62,979,766	76,212,168	92,228,496	106,021,537	123,202,624	132,164,569	151,325,798	179,323,175	203,302,031	226,542,203

(1) Updated, April 1989. (2) According to 1986 estimates, Florida has passed Illinois in population.

U.S. Center of Population, 1790-1980

Center of Population is that point which may be considered as center of population gravity of the U.S. or that point upon which the U.S. would balance if it were a rigid plane without weight and the population distributed thereon with each individual being assumed to have equal weight and to exert an influence on a central point proportional to his distance from that point.

Year	N. Lat. ° ′ ″			W.Long. ° ′ ″			Approximate location
1790	39	16	30	76	11	12	23 miles east of Baltimore, Md.
1800	39	16	6	76	56	30	18 miles west of Baltimore, Md.
1810	39	11	30	77	37	12	40 miles northwest by west of Washington, D.C. (in Va.)
1820	39	5	42	78	33	0	16 miles east of Moorefield, W. Va.[1]
1830	38	57	54	79	16	54	19 miles west-southwest of Moorefield, W. Va.[1]
1840	39	2	0	80	18	0	16 miles south of Clarksburg, W. Va.[1]
1850	38	59	0	81	19	0	23 miles southeast of Parkersburg, W. Va.[1]
1860	39	0	24	82	48	48	20 miles south by east of Chillicothe, Oh.
1870	39	12	0	83	35	42	48 miles east by north of Cincinnati, Oh.
1880	39	4	8	84	39	40	8 miles west by south of Cincinnati, Oh. (in Ky.)
1890	39	11	56	85	32	53	20 miles east of Columbus, Ind.
1900	39	9	36	85	48	54	6 miles southeast of Columbus, Ind.
1910	39	10	12	86	32	20	In the city of Bloomington, Ind.
1920	39	10	21	86	43	15	8 miles south-southeast of Spencer, Owen County, Ind.
1930	39	3	45	87	8	6	3 miles northeast of Linton, Greene County, Ind.
1940	38	56	54	87	22	35	2 miles southeast by east of Carlisle, Haddon township, Sullivan Co., Ind.
1950 (Inc. Alaska & Hawaii)	38	48	15	88	22	8	3 miles northeast of Louisville, Clay County, Ill.
1960	38	35	58	89	12	35	6 1/2 miles northwest of Centralia, Clinton Co., Ill.
1970	38	27	47	89	42	22	5 miles east southeast of Mascoutah, St. Clair County, Ill.
1980	38	8	13	90	34	26	1/4 mile west of De Soto, Jefferson Co., Mo.

(1) West Virginia was set off from Virginia Dec. 31, 1862, and admitted as a state June 20, 1863.

Projections of the Total Population by Sex and Age: 1990 to 2000

Source: U.S. Bureau of the Census (thousands)

Sex and age	Lowest series[1]			Middle series			Highest series		
	1990	1995	2000	1990	1995	2000	1990	1995	2000
Total population	248,656	255,259	259,576	250,410	260,138	268,266	251,897	265,151	278,228
Male									
Under 5 years old	9,163	8,376	7,647	9,426	9,118	8,661	9,700	9,889	9,960
5–17 years old	23,247	24,303	23,779	23,377	24,787	25,027	23,475	25,284	26,501
18–24 years old	13,065	12,063	12,505	13,216	12,290	12,770	13,332	12,522	13,118
25–44 years old	40,598	40,958	39,409	40,863	41,683	40,607	41,050	42,259	41,686
45–64 years old	22,444	25,222	29,361	22,509	25,441	29,853	22,566	25,648	30,305
65 years old and over. .	12,814	13,645	13,930	12,853	13,803	14,273	12,911	14,088	14,927
Female									
Under 5 years old	8,731	7,975	7,275	8,982	8,681	8,237	9,244	9,508	9,470
5–17 years old	22,133	23,132	22,607	22,253	23,587	23,788	22,344	24,053	25,176
18–24 years old	12,800	11,795	12,223	12,924	11,991	12,461	13,020	12,183	12,752
25–44 years old	40,739	41,050	39,560	40,960	41,617	40,453	41,113	42,080	41,316
45–64 years old	24,281	27,022	31,233	24,341	27,180	31,528	24,390	27,339	31,863
65 years old and over. .	18,641	19,699	20,048	18,706	19,961	20,608	18,754	20,198	21,155

(1) For the series shown the following assumptions were made about fertility (ultimate lifetime births per woman), mortality (life expectancy in 2080), and immigration (yearly net immigration). Lowest series: 1.6 births per woman, 85.9 years, and 250,000 net immigration. Middle series: 1.9 births per woman, 81.0 years, and 450,000 net immigration. Highest series: 2.3 births per woman, 77.4 years, and 750,000 net immigration. Zero migration series: 1.9 births per woman and 81.0 years.

U.S. Area and Population: 1790 to 1980

Source: U.S. Bureau of the Census

	Area (square miles)			Population			
Census date	Gross	Land	Water	Number	Per sq. mile of land	Increase over preceding census Number	%
1980 (Apr. 1).	3,618,770	3,539,289	79,481	226,542,203	64.0	23,240,172	11.4
1970 (Apr. 1).	3,618,770	3,536,855	81,915	203,302,031	57.5	23,978,856	13.4
1960 (Apr. 1).	3,618,770	3,540,911	77,859	179,323,175	50.6	27,997,377	18.5
1950 (Apr. 1).	3,618,770	3,552,206	66,564	151,325,798	42.6	19,161,229	14.5
1940 (Apr. 1).	3,618,770	3,554,608	64,162	132,164,569	37.2	8,961,945	7.3
1930 (Apr. 1).	3,618,770	3,551,608	67,162	123,202,624	34.7	17,181,087	16.2
1920 (Jan. 1).	3,618,770	3,546,931	71,839	106,021,537	29.9	13,793,041	15.0
1910 (Apr. 15).	3,618,770	3,547,045	71,725	92,228,496	26.0	16,016,328	21.0
1900 (June 1)	3,618,770	3,547,314	71,456	76,212,168	21.5	13,232,402	21.0
1890 (June 1)	3,612,299	3,540,705	71,594	62,979,766	17.8	12,790,557	25.5
1880 (June 1)	3,612,299	3,540,705	71,594	50,189,209	14.2	11,630,838	30.2
1870 (June 1)	3,612,299	3,540,705	71,594	38,558,371	10.9	7,115,050	22.6
1860 (June 1)	3,021,295	2,969,640	51,655	31,443,321	10.6	8,251,445	35.6
1850 (June 1)	2,991,655	2,940,042	51,613	23,191,876	7.9	6,122,423	35.9
1840 (June 1)	1,792,552	1,749,462	43,090	17,069,453	9.8	4,203,433	32.7
1830 (June 1)	1,792,552	1,749,462	43,090	12,866,020	7.4	3,227,567	33.5
1820 (June 1)	1,792,552	1,749,462	43,090	9,638,453	5.5	2,398,572	33.1
1810 (Aug. 6)	1,722,685	1,681,828	40,857	7,239,881	4.3	1,931,398	36.4
1800 (Aug. 4)	891,364	864,746	26,618	5,308,483	6.1	1,379,269	35.1
1790 (Aug. 2)	891,364	864,746	26,618	3,929,214	4.5	—	—

NOTE: Percent changes are computed on basis of change in population since preceding census date, and period covered therefore is not always exactly 10 years.

Population density figures given for various years represent the area within the boundaries of the United States which was under the jurisdiction on date in question, including in some cases considerable areas not organized or settled and not covered by the census. In 1870, for example, Alaska was not covered by the census.

Revised figure of 39,818,449 for the 1870 population includes adjustments for undernumeration in the Southern states. On the basis of the revised figure, the population increased by 8,375,128, or 26.6 percent between 1860 and 1870, and by 10,370,760, or 26.1 percent between 1870 and 1880.

Congressional Apportionment

	1980	1970		1980	1970		1980	1970		1980	1970		1980	1970
Ala..	7	7	Ida..	2	2	Minn..	8	8	N. D..	1	1	Vt..	1	1
Alas..	1	1	Ill...	22	24	Miss..	5	5	Oh...	21	23	Va..	10	10
Ariz..	5	4	Ind...	10	11	Mo...	9	10	Okla..	6	6	Wash..	8	7
Ark..	4	4	Ia...	6	6	Mon...	2	2	Ore...	5	4	W. Va..	4	4
Cal..	45	43	Kan..	5	5	Neb...	3	3	Pa...	23	25	Wis...	9	9
Col..	6	5	Ky...	7	7	Nev...	2	1	R. I..	2	2	Wy...	1	1
Conn..	6	6	La...	8	8	N. H...	2	2	S. C..	6	6			
Del..	1	1	Me...	2	2	N. J...	14	15	S. D..	1	2	Totals.	435	435
Fla..	19	15	Md...	8	8	N. M...	3	2	Tenn..	9	8			
Ga..	10	10	Mass..	11	12	N. Y...	34	39	Tex...	27	24			
Ha...	2	2	Mich..	18	19	N. C...	11	11	Ut....	3	2			

The primary reason the Constitution provided for a census of the population every 10 years was to give a basis for apportionment of representatives among the states. This apportionment largely determines the number of electoral votes allotted to each state.

The number of representatives of each state in Congress is determined by the state's population, but each state is entitled to one representative regardless of population. A Congressional apportionment has been made after each decennial census except that of 1920.

Under provisions of a law that became effective Nov. 15, 1941, apportionment of representatives is made by the method of equal proportions. In the application of this method, the apportionment is made so that the average population per representative has the least possible variation between one state and any other. The first House of Representatives, in 1789, had 65 members, as provided by the Constitution. As the population grew, the number of representatives was increased, but the total membership has been fixed at 435 since the apportionment based on the 1910 census.

Percent Distribution of the Population by Age

Source: U.S. Bureau of the Census

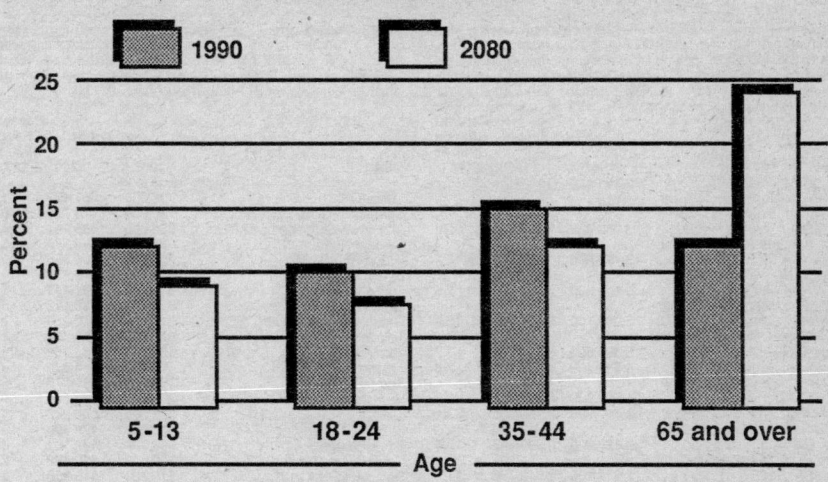

U.S. Population Abroad, by Selected Country: 1988

Source: U.S. Dept. of State

(In thousands. As of May 1. Data compiled as part of noncombatant personnel evacuation requirements report)

Country	Total[1]	Resident U.S. citizen	U.S. tourists	Country	Total[1]	Resident U.S. citizen	U.S. tourists
Total[2]	4,006.7	2,174.6	1,041.4	Japan	121.0	41.7	9.6
Australia	92.7	68.7	21.0	Mexico	601.8	396.0	203.1
Belgium	19.8	13.9	4.0	Netherlands	48.8	34.5	4.3
Brazil	52.7	40.4	11.2	Panama	40.3	11.3	0.4
Canada	447.3	235.1	209.9	Philippines	273.4	156.3	3.9
Colombia	21.4	19.9	1.2	Portugal	25.0	15.7	6.4
Costa Rica	26.0	17.1	7.4	Saudi Arabia	25.9	21.6	0.3
Dominican Republic	77.5	63.2	13.0	South Africa	26.5	9.4	16.5
France	132.2	43.5	86.2	South Korea	68.4	10.0	26.6
Greece	69.6	54.4	9.8	Spain	110.4	60.1	30.3
Hong Kong	22.2	14.5	6.6	Switzerland	32.3	24.1	7.5
Ireland	34.1	30.0	4.0	United Kingdom	284.8	158.8	80.1
Israel	121.8	60.9	60.0	Venezuela	22.3	20.6	1.3
Italy	174.0	86.4	58.2	West Germany	491.1	134.1	21.2

(1) Includes Dept. of Defense noncombatant employees, other U.S. government employees, and dependents of U.S. military and civilian employees, not shown separately. (2) Includes other countries not shown separately.

Estimated Population of American Colonies: 1630-1780

Source: U.S. Bureau of the Census (thousands)

Colony	1780	1770	1750	1740	1720	1700	1690	1670	1650	1630
Total	2,780.4	2,148.1	1,170.8	905.6	466.2	250.9	210.4	111.9	50.4	4.6
Maine (counties)	49.1	31.3	...	...	...	...	...	...	1.0	0.4
New Hampshire	87.8	62.4	27.5	23.3	9.4	5.0	4.2	1.8	1.3	0.5
Vermont	47.6	10.0	...	...	...	...	...	...	...	...
Plymouth and Massachusetts	268.6	235.3	188.0	151.6	91.0	55.9	56.9	35.3	15.6	0.9
Rhode Island	52.9	58.2	33.2	25.3	11.7	5.9	4.2	2.2	0.8	...
Connecticut	206.7	183.9	111.3	89.6	58.8	26.0	21.6	12.6	4.1	...
New York	210.5	162.9	76.7	63.7	36.9	19.1	13.9	5.8	4.1	0.4
New Jersey	139.6	117.4	71.4	51.4	29.8	14.0	8.0	1.0	...	...
Pennsylvania	327.3	240.1	119.7	85.6	31.0	18.0	11.4	...	...	...
Delaware	45.4	35.5	28.7	19.9	5.4	2.5	1.5	0.7	0.2	...
Maryland	245.5	202.6	141.1	116.1	66.1	29.6	24.0	13.2	4.5	...
Virginia	538.0	447.0	231.0	180.4	87.8	58.6	53.0	35.3	18.7	2.5
North Carolina	270.1	197.2	73.0	51.8	21.3	10.7	7.6	3.8	...	...
South Carolina	180.0	124.2	64.0	45.0	17.0	5.7	3.9	0.2	...	...
Georgia	56.1	23.4	5.2	2.0	...	...	...	...	...	...
Kentucky	45.0	15.7	...	...	...	...	...	...	...	...
Tennessee	10.0	1.0	...	...	...	...	...	...	...	...

Metropolitan Statistical Areas: 1980–1987

Source: U.S. Bureau of the Census
(MSAs over 297,000 listed by 1987 population)

By current standards, an area qualifies for recognition as a Metropolitan Statistical Area (MSA) in one of two ways: if there is a city of at least 50,000 population; or a Census Bureau-defined urbanized area of at least 50,000 with a total metropolitan population of at least 100,000 (75,000 in New England). In addition to the county containing the main city, an MSA also includes other counties having strong economic and social ties to the central county. If an area has more than one million population and meets certain other specified requirements, it is termed a Consolidated Metropolitan Statistical Area (CMSA). MSAs are defined by the Office of Management and Budget as of June 30, 1988.

MSA	Population 1987 (estimate)	Population 1980	Percent Change 1980 to 1987
New York-Northern New Jersey-Long Island, NY-NJ-CT CMSA	18,053,800	17,539,532	2.9
Los Angeles-Anaheim-Riverside, CA CMSA	13,470,900	11,497,549	17.2
Chicago-Gary-Lake County, IL-IN-WI CMSA	8,146,900	7,937,290	2.6
San Francisco-Oakland-San Jose, CA CMSA	5,953,100	5,367,900	10.9
Philadelphia-Wilmington-Trenton, PA-NJ-DE-MD CMSA	5,890,600	5,680,509	3.7
Detroit-Ann Arbor, MI CMSA	4,629,400	4,752,764	-2.6
Boston-Lawrence-Salem, MA-NH CMSA	4,092,900	3,971,792	3.0
Dallas-Fort Worth, TX CMSA	3,724,900	2,930,568	27.1
Houston-Galveston-Brazoria, TX CMSA	3,626,300	3,099,942	17.0
Miami-Fort Lauderdale, FL CMSA	2,954,100	2,643,766	11.7
Cleveland-Akron-Lorain, OH CMSA	2,766,900	2,834,062	-2.4
Atlanta, GA	2,656,800	2,138,136	24.3
St. Louis, MO-IL	2,458,100	2,376,968	3.4
Seattle-Tacoma, WA CMSA	2,340,600	2,093,285	11.8
Minneapolis-St. Paul, MN-WI	2,335,600	2,137,133	9.3
Baltimore, MD	2,302,900	2,199,497	4.7
Pittsburgh-Beaver Valley, PA CMSA	2,296,400	2,423,311	-5.2
San Diego, CA	2,285,900	1,861,846	22.8
Tampa-St. Petersburg-Clearwater, FL	1,965,100	1,613,600	21.8
Phoenix, AZ	1,959,600	1,509,175	29.8
Denver-Boulder, CO CMSA	1,861,300	1,618,461	15.0
Cincinnati-Hamilton, OH-KY-IN CMSA	1,714,600	1,660,257	3.3
Milwaukee-Racine, WI CMSA	1,562,100	1,570,152	-0.5
Kansas City, MO-KS	1,546,400	1,433,464	7.9
Portland-Vancouver, OR-WA CMSA	1,383,400	1,297,977	6.6
Norfolk-Virginia Beach-Newport News, VA	1,346,100	1,160,311	16.0
Sacramento, CA	1,336,500	1,099,814	21.5
New Orleans, LA	1,321,000	1,256,668	5.1
Columbus, OH	1,320,100	1,243,827	6.1
San Antonio, TX	1,306,700	1,072,125	21.9
Indianapolis, IN	1,228,600	1,166,575	5.3
Buffalo-Niagara Falls, NY CMSA	1,174,500	1,242,826	-5.5
Providence-Pawtucket-Fall River, RI-MA CMSA	1,117,700	1,083,139	3.2
Charlotte-Gastonia-Rock Hill, NC-SC	1,091,000	971,447	12.3
Hartford-New Britain-Middletown, CT CMSA	1,057,500	1,013,508	4.3
Salt Lake City-Ogden, UT	1,054,500	910,222	15.9
Rochester, NY	979,100	971,230	0.8
Oklahoma City, OK	975,000	860,969	13.2
Memphis, TN-AK-MI	971,900	913,472	6.4
Louisville, KY-IN	966,500	956,426	1.1
Nashville, TN	956,200	850,505	12.4
Dayton-Springfield, OH	938,800	942,083	-0.4
Orlando, FL	934,700	699,904	33.5
Birmingham, AL	916,900	883,993	3.7
Greensboro-Winston-Salem-High Point, NC	915,700	851,444	7.5
Jacksonville, FL	878,200	722,252	21.6
Albany-Schenectady-Troy, NY	846,400	835,880	1.3
Honolulu, HA	830,600	762,565	8.9
Richmond-Petersburg, VA	825,300	761,311	8.4
West Palm Beach-Boca Raton-Delray Beach, FL	790,100	576,758	37.0
Austin, TX	738,000	536,688	37.5
Tulsa, OK	733,000	657,173	11.5
Scranton-Wilkes-Barre, PA	730,900	728,796	0.3
Allentown-Bethlehem, PA-NJ	666,000	635,481	4.8
Raleigh-Durham, NC	665,400	560,775	18.7
Grand Rapids, MI	657,000	601,680	9.2
Syracuse, NY	647,000	642,971	0.6
Tucson, AZ	619,400	531,443	16.5
Omaha, NE-IA	616,400	585,122	5.3
Greenville-Spartanburg, SC	611,900	570,210	7.3
Toledo, OH	611,000	616,864	-1.0
Las Vegas, NV	599,900	463,087	29.5
Fresno, CA	597,400	514,621	16.1
Knoxville, TN	594,000	565,970	5.0
Harrisburg-Lebanon-Carlisle, PA	583,700	556,242	4.9
El Paso, TX	572,800	479,899	19.4
Baton Rouge, LA	538,300	494,151	8.9
New Haven-Meriden, CT	519,000	500,462	3.7
Springfield, MA	516,700	515,259	0.3
Little Rock-North Little Rock, AK	511,500	474,463	7.8
Bakersfield, CA	504,500	403,089	25.2
Youngstown-Warren, OH	502,500	531,350	-5.4
Charleston, SC	502,100	430,346	16.7
Albuquerque, NM	486,200	420,261	15.7
Mobile, AL	483,000	443,536	8.9
Wichita, KS	474,700	442,401	7.3
Columbia, SC	451,400	409,953	10.1
Stockton, CA	443,500	347,342	27.7
Johnson City-Kingsport-Bristol, TN-VA	442,600	433,638	2.1
Flint, MI	435,100	450,449	-3.4
Chattanooga, TN-GA	431,500	426,443	1.2
Lansing-East Lansing, MI	427,800	419,750	1.9
Worcester, MA	410,200	402,918	1.8
Saginaw-Bay City-Midland, MI	404,400	421,518	-4.1
Lancaster, PA	403,700	362,346	11.4
York, PA	403,600	381,255	5.9
Canton, OH	397,100	404,421	-1.8
Jackson, MI	395,900	362,038	9.4
Augusta, GA-SC	392,500	345,923	13.5
Colorado Springs, CO	389,900	309,424	26.0
Lakeland-Winter Haven, FL	387,000	321,652	20.3
Des Moines, IA	385,100	367,561	4.8
McAllen-Edinburg-Mission, TX	378,600	283,323	33.6
Melbourne-Titusville-Palm Bay, FL	374,900	272,959	37.3
Beaumont-Port Arthur, TX	371,100	373,211	-0.6
Davenport-Rock Island-Moline, IA-IL	366,600	384,749	-4.7
Fort Wayne, IN	364,400	354,156	2.9
Shreveport, LA	363,800	333,158	9.2
Corpus Christi, TX	360,300	326,228	10.4
Spokane, WA	355,300	341,835	3.9
Madison, WI	347,400	323,545	7.4
Pensacola, FL	343,900	289,782	18.7
Salinas-Seaside-Monterey, CA	343,100	290,444	18.1
Lexington-Fayette, KY	341,500	317,548	7.6
Santa Barbara-Santa Maria-Lompoc, CA	340,900	298,694	14.1
Peoria, IL	338,500	365,864	-7.5
Daytona Beach, FL	331,900	258,762	28.3
Modesto, CA	327,400	265,900	23.1
Reading, PA	324,300	312,509	3.8
Huntington-Ashland, W.VA-KY-OH	323,400	336,410	-3.9
Utica-Rome, NY	313,900	320,180	-2.0
Appleton-Oshkosh-Neenah, WI	309,100	291,369	6.1
Atlantic City, NJ	302,700	276,385	9.5
Montgomery, AL	297,400	272,687	9.1

Population of U.S. Cities

Source: U.S. Bureau of the Census (100 most populated cities ranked by July 1, 1986 estimates)

Rank	City	1986	1980	1970	1960	1950	1900	1850
1	New York, N.Y.	7,262,700	7,071,639	7,895,563	7,781,984	7,891,957	3,437,202	696,115
2	Los Angeles, Cal.	3,259,340	2,966,850	2,811,801	2,479,015	1,970,358	102,479	1,610
3	Chicago, Ill.	3,009,530	3,005,072	3,369,357	3,550,404	3,620,962	1,698,575	29,963
4	Houston, Tex.	1,728,910	1,595,138	1,233,535	938,219	596,163	44,633	2,396
5	Philadelphia, Pa.	1,642,900	1,688,210	1,949,996	2,002,512	2,071,605	1,293,697	121,376
6	Detroit, Mich.	1,086,220	1,203,339	1,514,063	1,670,144	1,849,568	285,704	21,019
7	San Diego, Cal.	1,015,190	875,538	697,471	573,224	334,387	17,700	...
8	Dallas, Tex.	1,003,520	904,078	844,401	679,684	434,462	42,638	...
9	San Antonio, Tex.	914,350	785,880	654,153	587,718	408,442	53,321	3,488
10	Phoenix, Ariz.	894,070	789,704	584,303	439,170	106,818	5,544	...
11	Baltimore, Md.	752,800	786,775	905,787	939,024	949,708	508,957	169,054
12	San Francisco, Cal.	749,000	678,974	715,674	740,316	775,357	342,782	34,776
13	Indianapolis, Ind.	719,820	700,807	736,856	476,258	427,173	169,164	8,091
14	San Jose, Cal.	712,080	629,442	459,913	204,196	95,280	21,500	...
15	Memphis, Tenn.	652,640	646,356	623,988	497,524	396,000	102,320	8,841
16	Washington, D.C.	626,000	638,333	756,668	763,956	802,178	278,718	40,001
17	Jacksonville, Fla.	609,860	540,920	504,265	201,030	204,517	28,429	1,045
18	Milwaukee, Wis.	605,090	636,212	717,372	741,324	637,392	285,315	20,061
19	Boston, Mass.	573,600	562,994	641,071	697,197	801,444	560,892	136,881
20	Columbus, Oh.	566,030	564,871	540,025	471,316	375,901	125,560	17,882
21	New Orleans, La.	554,500	557,515	593,471	627,525	570,445	287,104	116,375
22	Cleveland, Oh.	535,830	573,822	750,879	876,050	914,808	381,768	17,034
23	Denver, Col.	505,000	492,365	514,678	493,887	415,786	133,859	...
24	El Paso, Tex.	491,800	425,259	322,261	276,687	130,485	15,906	...
25	Seattle, Wash.	486,200	493,846	530,831	557,087	467,591	80,671	...
26	Nashville-Davidson, Tenn.	473,670	455,651	426,029	170,874	174,307	80,865	10,165
27	Austin, Tex.	466,550	345,496	253,539	186,545	132,459	22,258	629
28	Oklahoma City, Okla.	446,120	403,213	368,164	324,253	243,504	10,037	...
29	Kansas City, Mo.	441,170	448,159	507,330	475,539	456,622	163,752	...
30	Fort Worth, Tex.	429,550	385,164	393,455	356,268	278,778	26,688	...
31	St. Louis, Mo.	426,300	453,085	622,236	750,026	856,796	575,238	77,860
32	Atlanta, Ga.	421,910	425,022	495,039	487,455	331,314	89,872	2,572
33	Long Beach, Cal.	396,280	361,334	358,879	344,168	250,767	2,252	...
34	Portland, Ore.	387,870	366,383	379,967	372,676	373,628	90,426	...
35	Pittsburgh, Pa.	387,490	423,938	520,089	604,332	676,806	321,616	46,601
36	Miami, Fla.	373,940	346,865	334,859	291,688	249,276	1,681	...
37	Tulsa, Okla.	373,750	360,919	330,350	261,685	182,740	1,390	...
38	Honolulu, Ha.	372,330	762,874	630,528	294,194	248,034	39,306	...
39	Cincinnati, Oh.	369,750	385,457	453,514	502,550	503,998	325,902	115,435
40	Albuquerque, N.M.	366,750	331,767	244,501	201,189	96,815	6,238	...
41	Tucson, Ariz.	358,850	330,537	262,933	212,892	45,454	7,531	...
42	Oakland, Cal.	356,960	339,337	361,561	367,548	384,575	66,960	...
43	Minneapolis, Minn.	356,840	370,951	434,400	482,872	521,718	202,718	...
44	Charlotte, N.C.	352,070	314,447	241,420	201,564	134,042	18,091	1,065
45	Omaha, Neb.	349,270	314,255	346,929	301,598	251,117	102,555	...
46	Toledo, Oh.	340,680	354,635	383,062	318,003	303,616	131,822	3,829
47	Virginia Beach, Va.	333,400	262,199	172,106	8,091	5,390	...	...
48	Buffalo, N.Y.	324,820	357,870	462,768	532,759	580,132	352,387	42,261
49	Sacramento, Cal.	323,550	275,741	257,105	191,667	137,572	29,282	6,820
50	Newark, N.J.	316,240	329,248	381,930	405,220	438,776	246,070	38,894
51	Wichita, Kan.	288,870	279,272	276,554	254,698	168,279	24,671	...
52	Louisville, Ky.	286,470	298,451	361,706	390,639	369,129	204,731	43,194
53	Fresno, Cal.	284,660	218,202	165,655	133,929	91,669	12,470	...
54	Tampa, Fla.	277,580	271,523	277,714	274,970	124,681	15,839	...
55	Birmingham, Ala.	277,510	284,413	300,910	340,887	326,037	38,415	...
56	Norfolk, Va.	274,800	266,979	307,951	304,869	213,513	46,624	14,326
57	Colorado Springs, Col.	272,660	215,150	135,517	70,194	45,472	21,085	...
58	Corpus Christi, Tex.	263,900	231,999	204,525	167,690	108,287	4,703	...
59	St. Paul, Minn.	263,680	270,230	309,866	313,411	311,349	163,065	1,112
60	Mesa, Ariz.	251,430	152,453	63,049	33,772	16,790	722	...
61	Arlington, Tex.	249,770	160,113	90,229	44,775	7,692	1,079	...
62	Baton Rouge, La.	241,130	346,029	165,921	152,419	125,629	11,269	3,905
63	Anaheim, Cal.	240,730	219,311	166,408	104,184	14,556	1,456	...
64	St. Petersburg, Fla.	239,410	238,647	216,159	181,298	96,738	1,575	...
65	Santa Ana, Cal.	236,780	203,713	155,710	100,350	45,533	4,933	...
66	Rochester, N.Y.	235,970	241,741	295,011	318,611	332,488	162,608	36,403
67	Anchorage, Alas.	235,000	174,431	48,081	44,237	11,254	...	...
68	Akron, Oh.	222,060	237,177	275,425	290,351	274,605	42,728	3,266
69	Shreveport, La.	220,380	205,820	182,064	164,372	127,206	16,013	1,728
70	Jersey City, N.J.	219,480	223,532	260,350	276,101	299,017	206,433	6,856
71	Aurora, Col.	217,990	158,588	74,974	48,548	11,421	202	...
72	Richmond, Va.	217,700	219,214	249,332	219,958	230,310	85,050	27,570
73	Lexington-Fayette, Ky.	212,900	204,165	108,137	62,810	55,534	26,369	8,159
74	Jackson, Miss.	208,420	202,895	153,968	144,422	98,271	7,816	1,881
75	Mobile, Ala.	203,260	200,452	190,026	194,856	129,009	38,469	20,515
76	Riverside, Cal.	196,750	170,876	140,089	84,332	46,764	7,973	...
77	Montgomery, Ala.	194,290	177,857	133,386	134,393	106,525	30,346	8,728
78	Des Moines, Ia.	192,060	191,003	201,404	208,982	177,965	62,139	...
79	Las Vegas, Nev.	191,510	164,674	125,787	64,405	24,624	...	...
80	Grand Rapids, Mich.	186,530	181,843	197,649	177,313	176,515	87,565	2,686
81	Lubbock, Tex.	186,400	173,979	149,101	126,691	71,747	...	...
82	Yonkers, N.Y.	186,080	195,351	204,297	190,634	152,798	47,931	...
83	Huntington Beach, Cal.	183,620	170,505	115,960	11,492	5,237	...	...
84	Stockton, Cal.	183,430	149,779	109,963	86,321	70,853	17,506	...

(continued)

Rank	City	1986	1980	1970	1960	1950	1900	1850
85	Lincoln, Neb.	183,050	171,932	149,518	128,521	98,884	40,169	...
86	Little Rock, Ark.	181,030	158,461	132,483	107,813	102,213	38,307	2,167
87	Raleigh, NC	180,430	150,255	122,830	93,931	65,679	13,643	4,518
88	Columbus, Ga.	180,180	169,441	155,028	116,779	79,611	17,614	9,621
89	Dayton, Oh.	178,920	203,371	243,023	262,332	243,872	85,333	10,977
90	Greensboro, N.C.	176,650	170,279	144,076	119,574	74,389	10,035	...
91	Garland, Tex.	176,510	138,857	81,437	38,501	10,571	819	...
92	Madison, Wis.	175,830	170,616	171,809	126,706	96,056	19,164	1,525
93	Knoxville, Tenn.	173,210	175,030	174,587	111,827	124,769	32,637	2,076
94	Fort Wayne, Ind.	172,900	172,196	178,269	161,776	133,607	45,115	4,282
95	Spokane, Wash.	172,890	171,300	170,516	181,608	161,721	36,848	...
96	Amarillo, Tex.	165,850	149,230	127,010	137,969	74,246	1,442	...
97	Huntsville, Ala.	163,420	142,513	139,282	72,365	16,437	8,068	2,863
98	Chattanooga, Tenn.	162,170	169,565	119,923	130,009	131,041	30,154	...
99	Kansas City, Kans.	162,070	161,087	168,213	121,901	129,553	51,418	...
100	Hialeah, Fla.	161,760	145,254	102,452	66,972	19,676	...	...

City Population by Race and Hispanic Origin

Source: U.S. Bureau of the Census

This table presents a summary of the final 1980 census population estimates (data are based on sample tabulations) for cities over 250,000, classified by race and Hispanic origin.

	Total	White	Black	Am. Indian Eskimos Aleut.	Asian & Pacific Islander	Race N.E.C.[1]	Hispanic Origin[2]
Albuquerque, NM	331,767	275,758	7,691	7,163	3,755	37,400	112,030
Atlanta, GA	425,022	138,235	283,158	610	2,001	1,018	5,750
Austin, TX	345,544	263,618	42,108	1,516	4,127	34,175	64,945
Baltimore, MD	786,775	346,692	430,934	2,170	4,898	2,081	7,804
Birmingham, AL	284,413	124,767	158,200	220	933	293	2,054
Boston, MA	562,994	396,635	126,438	1,455	16,298	22,168	36,430
Buffalo, NY	357,870	253,507	95,622	2,084	1,335	5,322	8,926
Charlotte, NC	314,447	212,293	97,896	1,162	2,393	703	3,091
Chicago, IL	3,005,078	1,512,411	1,197,174	6,804	73,745	214,944	423,357
Cincinnati, OH	385,457	251,332	130,490	567	2,332	736	3,263
Cleveland, OH	573,822	309,299	251,084	1,282	3,372	8,785	17,896
Columbus, OH	564,866	431,966	124,689	1,024	5,410	1,777	5,300
Dallas, TX	904,074	558,443	265,105	3,878	9,163	67,485	110,511
Denver, CO	492,365	375,628	59,095	4,318	8,934	44,390	92,257
Detroit, MI	1,203,339	420,529	758,468	3,846	7,614	12,882	28,466
El Paso, TX	425,259	306,510	13,641	1,563	3,995	99,550	265,997
Fort Worth, TX	385,166	266,638	87,635	1,841	2,954	26,098	48,568
Honolulu, HI (County)	762,565	262,604	17,203	2,445	463,117	17,196	54,619
Houston, TX	1,595,167	981,563	439,604	3,945	35,448	134,607	280,691
Indianapolis, IN	700,719	540,496	152,590	1,356	4,539	1,738	6,430
Jacksonville, FL	540,920	394,661	137,150	1,950	5,485	1,674	9,879
Kansas City, MO	448,154	313,835	122,336	2,115	3,591	6,277	14,643
Long Beach, CA	361,334	272,272	40,463	3,531	22,025	23,043	50,450
Los Angeles, CA	2,966,850	1,842,050	504,301	19,296	206,536	394,667	815,305
Louisville, KY	298,455	212,052	84,254	408	1,327	414	2,049
Memphis, TN	646,356	334,363	307,573	680	2,864	876	5,730
Miami, FL	346,865	225,200	87,018	334	2,050	32,263	194,185
Milwaukee, WI	636,212	468,064	147,055	5,348	4,451	11,294	26,487
Minneapolis, MN	370,951	325,415	28,469	9,198	5,358	2,511	4,762
Nashville-Davidson, TN	455,663	345,766	105,869	743	2,418	867	3,257
New Orleans, LA	557,515	238,192	308,039	623	7,458	3,203	19,215
New York, NY	7,071,639	4,348,605	1,788,377	13,400	245,759	675,498	1,406,389
Newark, NJ	329,248	107,465	191,968	923	2,421	26,471	61,322
Norfolk, VA	266,979	163,052	93,977	822	7,075	2,053	5,792
Oakland, CA	339,337	131,127	159,351	2,754	28,053	18,052	32,133
Oklahoma City, OK	403,243	323,665	58,550	11,199	4,610	5,219	11,767
Omaha, NE	314,267	268,995	37,889	1,839	2,381	3,163	7,354
Philadelphia, PA	1,688,210	988,337	638,788	2,799	19,950	38,336	64,323
Phoenix, AZ	789,704	673,488	37,747	11,645	8,429	58,395	116,875
Pittsburgh, PA	423,938	318,287	101,549	584	2,818	700	3,370
Portland, OR	366,423	319,220	28,034	3,374	12,980	2,815	7,541
Sacramento, CA	275,741	187,992	36,842	3,506	24,558	22,843	38,905
St. Louis, MO	453,085	242,988	206,170	679	2,214	1,034	5,380
St. Paul, MN	270,230	245,795	13,018	2,558	5,345	3,514	7,553
San Antonio, TX	785,809	621,679	57,566	2,375	5,821	98,368	421,808
San Diego, CA	875,538	674,268	77,508	5,833	61,655	56,274	129,953
San Francisco, CA	678,974	402,131	86,190	3,566	149,269	37,818	84,194
San Jose, CA	629,442	470,458	28,792	5,801	53,205	71,186	140,318
Seattle, WA	493,846	396,275	46,565	6,821	38,936	5,249	12,744
Tampa, FL	271,523	202,507	63,578	607	1,894	2,937	35,781
Toledo, OH	354,635	284,104	61,855	989	2,005	5,682	10,984
Tucson, AZ	330,537	274,750	11,587	4,578	3,427	36,195	82,106
Tulsa, OK	360,919	298,926	42,845	13,816	2,962	2,370	6,291
Virginia Beach, VA	262,199	227,454	26,266	630	6,489	1,360	5,269
Washington, DC	638,333	174,705	448,370	1,014	6,883	7,361	17,777
Wichita, KS	279,272	236,549	30,263	2,942	4,525	4,993	9,455

(1) Not elsewhere classified.
(2) Persons of Hispanic origin may be of any race.

Population by State: 1988

Source: U.S. Bureau of the Census (1988 estimates)
(in thousands)

1988 rank	State	1988 Population	Percent change 1980-88	1988 rank	State	1988 Population	Percent change 1980-88	1988 rank	State	1988 Population	Percent change 1980-88
1	Cal.	28,314	19.6	18	Wash.	4,648	12.5	35	Utah	1,690	15.7
2	N.Y.	17,909	2.0	19	Md.	4,622	9.6	36	Neb.	1,602	2.1
3	Tex.	16,841	18.4	20	La.	4,408	4.8	37	N.M.	1,507	15.6
4	Fla.	12,335	26.6	21	Minn.	4,307	5.7	38	Me.	1,205	7.2
5	Pa.	12,001	1.2	22	Ala.	4,102	5.4	39	Ha.	1,098	13.8
6	Ill.	11,614	1.6	23	Ky.	3,727	1.8	40	N.H.	1,085	17.9
7	Oh.	10,855	0.5	24	Ariz.	3,489	28.4	41	Nev.	1,054	31.7
8	Mich.	9,240	-0.2	25	S.C.	3,470	11.2	42	Id.	1,003	6.2
9	N.J.	7,721	4.8	26	Colo.	3,301	14.2	43	R.I.	993	4.8
10	N.C.	6,489	10.3	27	Okla.	3,242	7.2	44	Mont.	805	2.3
11	Ga.	6,342	16.1	28	Conn.	3,233	4.0	45	S.D.	713	3.2
12	Va.	6,015	12.5	29	Ia.	2,834	-2.7	46	N.D.	667	2.2
13	Mass.	5,889	2.7	30	Ore.	2,767	5.1	47	Del.	660	11.1
14	Ind.	5,556	1.2	31	Miss.	2,620	3.9	48	D. of C.	617	-3.4
15	Mo.	5,141	4.6	32	Kan.	2,495	5.6	49	Vt.	557	9.0
16	Tenn.	4,895	6.6	33	Ark.	2,395	4.7	50	Alas.	524	30.5
17	Wis.	4,855	3.2	34	W.Va.	1,876	-3.8	51	Wyo.	479	2.1

Foreign-Born Population in Twelve Metropolitan Areas of the United States: 1980

Source: U.S. Bureau of the Census

Country of origin	New York City	Chicago	Los Angeles	Philadelphia	Houston	Detroit	Dallas	San Diego	Phoenix	San Antonio	San Francisco	Washington DC
Number of foreign-born persons....	1,946,800	744,930	1,664,793	242,658	220,861	282,766	124,697	235,593	82,536	76,944	509,352	249,994
Percent of population foreign-born .	21.3	10.5	22.3	5.1	7.6	6.5	4.2	12.7	5.5	7.2	15.7	8.2
Europe......	37.7	40.9	13.0	54.8	11.7	47.9	16.4	18.5	30.6	13.8	23.8	26.9
Austria	1.6	1.2	0.4	1.6	0.3	1.2	0.4	0.4	0.9	0.3	0.6	0.8
Czechoslovakia .	1.0	1.4	0.3	0.8	0.3	0.9	0.4	0.3	0.7	0.3	0.4	0.6
France	0.8	0.5	0.5	0.9	0.7	0.7	0.9	0.7	1.4	0.8	1.1	1.8
Germany.....	4.3	6.0	2.1	9.4	2.6	6.3	5.0	3.7	7.2	5.8	4.2	6.2
Greece......	2.4	3.2	0.4	2.5	0.7	2.1	0.5	0.5	0.8	0.2	0.8	1.9
Hungary	1.3	0.9	0.7	1.6	0.3	1.6	0.4	0.4	1.2	0.2	0.5	0.7
Ireland	2.7	2.0	0.3	3.8	0.2	1.0	0.4	0.5	0.9	0.5	1.2	0.7
Italy	10.5	6.0	1.3	14.9	0.7	8.0	0.7	2.0	3.4	0.6	3.3	2.4
Netherlands ...	0.2	0.5	0.5	0.5	0.5	0.6	0.5	0.7	0.9	0.2	0.8	0.6
Poland	4.6	8.4	1.0	4.7	0.5	7.6	0.6	0.7	1.8	0.5	0.6	1.1
Portugal	0.5	0.1	0.2	0.9	0.1	*	*	0.8	0.1	0.1	1.4	0.6
Sweden	0.2	0.9	0.2	0.3	0.1	0.3	0.2	0.5	0.5	0.1	0.6	0.3
United Kingdom .	2.5	2.5	2.8	7.8	3.2	8.1	4.6	4.7	6.4	3.0	4.1	5.2
England	1.6	1.6	1.9	4.6	2.2	4.4	3.4	3.2	4.3	2.3	2.8	3.6
Northern Ireland....	0.1	0.1	0.1	0.5	*	0.2	0.1	0.1	0.1	0.1	0.1	0.1
Scotland....	0.6	0.6	0.5	2.1	0.4	3.0	0.6	1.0	1.4	0.3	0.7	0.7
Wales	*	*	*	0.2	0.1	0.2	0.1	0.1	0.1	*	0.1	0.1
Yugoslavia....	1.3	3.0	0.6	1.0	0.2	3.7	0.2	0.5	1.1	0.1	0.5	0.3
U.S.S.R.	4.9	3.3	2.1	8.9	0.7	3.5	0.9	0.9	2.1	0.5	1.9	1.8
Asia	13.1	17.2	20.4	16.7	21.7	18.3	21.2	27.4	12.7	9.7	42.3	32.0
China.......	3.3	1.2	2.0	1.4	2.1	0.9	1.5	1.0	1.6	0.5	11.0	2.8
India.......	1.4	2.9	0.6	2.8	3.5	2.2	2.4	0.4	0.8	0.6	1.3	3.6
Japan.......	0.9	0.8	2.0	0.9	1.1	0.6	1.5	2.8	1.5	1.7	2.7	1.6
Korea.......	1.2	2.3	3.0	3.4	1.4	1.1	2.0	0.9	1.6	1.1	1.8	5.9
Philippines	1.3	4.3	4.4	2.1	1.9	2.0	1.8	13.0	1.3	1.7	13.2	3.6
Vietnam	0.2	0.6	1.7	1.4	5.3	0.4	3.8	3.3	1.6	1.5	2.2	3.6
North and Central America....	27.4	28.7	54.8	9.5	51.0	23.1	48.5	44.9	44.6	69.4	21.9	17.4
Canada......	1.2	2.2	3.4	3.2	2.3	19.9	3.8	5.9	10.8	1.6	4.1	3.3
Mexico......	0.4	21.6	41.9	0.6	42.4	1.7	40.0	36.9	31.9	64.9	11.0	0.9
West Indies ...	22.6	3.2	2.7	4.8	3.8	1.2	2.8	0.9	0.8	1.3	1.0	8.4
Cuba.......	2.8	1.9	2.1	1.2	2.0	0.3	2.0	0.3	0.3	0.7	0.6	2.0
Dominican Republic ..	6.6	0.1	*	0.3	0.1	0.1	0.1	0.1	0.1	0.1	*	0.5
Jamaica.....	5.1	0.6	0.2	1.7	0.5	0.4	0.2	0.2	0.1	0.2	0.2	2.8
South America.	8.8	2.5	3.5	2.5	3.9	1.0	2.4	1.7	1.9	1.0	2.5	9.6
North Africa ..	0.6	0.3	0.6	0.5	0.5	0.4	0.6	0.3	0.3	0.3	0.5	1.3
Other Africa ..	0.7	0.8	0.5	1.1	1.7	0.5	1.5	0.5	0.6	0.3	0.6	3.8
All other countries ...	0.2	0.2	0.5	0.3	0.3	0.2	0.5	1.0	0.6	0.3	1.6	0.8
Country not reported ...	6.5	6.2	4.7	5.6	8.5	5.0	7.9	4.8	6.6	4.8	4.9	6.4

Note: * indicates amount less or rounds than 0.1 percent.

Immigration by Country of Last Residence 1820-1988

Source: U.S. Immigration and Naturalization Service

(thousands)

Country	Total 1820-1988	Total 1961-1970	Total 1971-1980	1983[10]	1984	1985	1986	1987	1988[12]	Percent 1820-1988	Percent 1961-1970	Percent 1971-1980
All countries*..	54,367	3,321.7	4,493.3	559.8	543.9	570.0	601.7	601.5	643.0	100.0	100.0	100.0
Europe	36,876	1,123.5	800.4	58.9	69.9	69.5	69.2	68.0	64.8	67.8	33.8	17.8
Austria[1]	4,331	20.6	9.5	0.4	2.4	1.9	2.0	2.4	0.5	—	.6	0.2
Hungary.......	—	5.4	6.6	0.6	0.5	0.6	0.6	—	1.2	8.0	.2	0.1
Belgium.......	210	9.2	5.3	0.5	0.8	0.8	0.8	0.9	0.6	0.4	.3	0.1
Czechoslovakia ..	147	3.3	6.0	0.9	0.7	0.7	0.6	0.7	1.5	0.3	.1	0.1
Denmark	371	9.2	4.4	0.5	0.5	0.5	0.5	0.5	0.6	0.7	.3	0.1
Finland	36	4.2	2.9	0.3	0.2	0.2	0.3	0.3	—	0.1	.1	0.1
France	779	45.2	25.1	2.1	3.3	3.5	3.9	3.8	2.5	1.4	1.4	0.6
Germany[1]	7,058	190.8	74.4	7.2	9.4	10.2	9.9	9.9	6.6	13.0	5.7	1.7
Great Britain[2]....	5,095	214.5	137.4	14.8	16.5	15.6	16.0	15.9	13.2	9.4	6.5	3.1
Greece	694	86.0	92.4	3.0	3.3	3.5	3.5	4.1	2.5	1.3	2.6	2.1
Ireland.......	4,707	33.0	11.5	1.1	1.1	1.3	1.8	3.0	5.1	8.7	1.0	0.3
Italy	5,346	214.1	129.4	3.2	6.3	6.4	5.7	4.7	2.9	9.8	6.4	2.9
Netherlands	371	30.6	10.5	1.2	1.3	1.2	1.3	1.3	1.2	0.7	.9	0.2
Norway[11]	859	15.5	3.9	0.4	0.4	0.4	0.4	0.4	—	1.6	.5	0.1
Poland[1]	578	53.5	37.2	6.4	7.2	7.4	6.5	5.8	9.5	1.1	1.6	0.8
Portugal.......	493	76.1	101.7	3.2	3.8	3.8	4.0	3.2	0.9	0.9	2.3	2.3
Spain	280	44.7	39.1	1.5	2.2	2.3	2.2	2.1	1.5	0.5	1.3	0.9
Sweden[11]	1,130	17.1	6.5	0.9	1.1	1.2	1.2	1.2	1.2	2.1	.5	0.1
Switzerland......	357	18.5	8.2	0.7	0.8	1.0	0.9	0.1	0.8	0.7	.6	0.2
USSR[1,3]	3,426	2.5	39.0	5.2	3.3	1.5	1.0	1.1	2.9	6.3	.1	0.9
Yugoslavia	131	20.4	30.5	1.4	1.4	1.5	1.9	+1.8	1.9	0.2	.6	0.7
Other Europe....	334	9.1	18.9	3.4	3.4	4.0	4.4	4.0	1.5	0.6	.2	0.2
Asia	5,406	427.6	1,588.2	277.7	247.8	255.2	258.5	248.3	264.5	9.9	12.9	35.2
China[5]........	785	34.8	124.3	42.5	29.1	33.1	16.5	18.6	28.7	1.4	1.0	2.8
Hong Kong	270	75.0	113.5	5.9	12.3	10.8	9.9	8.8	8.6	0.5	2.3	2.5
India	399	27.2	164.1	25.5	23.6	24.5	24.8	26.4	26.3	0.7	.8	3.7
Iran	152	10.3	45.1	11.2	11.1	12.3	12.0	10.3	15.2	0.3	.3	1.0
Israel	125	29.6	37.7	3.2	4.1	4.3	5.1	4.8	3.6	0.2	.9	0.8
Japan.........	450	40.0	49.8	4.1	4.5	4.6	4.4	4.7	4.5	0.8	1.2	1.1
Jordan	67	11.7	27.5	2.7	2.2	2.7	2.8	2.8	3.2	0.1	.4	0.6
Korea	578	34.5	267.6	33.3	32.5	34.8	35.2	35.4	34.7	1.1	1.0	6.0
Lebanon	88	15.2	41.3	2.9	3.0	2.5	3.0	3.0	4.9	0.2	.5	0.9
Philippines	874	98.4	355.0	41.5	40.7	53.1	61.5	58.3	50.7	1.6	3.0	7.9
Turkey	406	10.1	13.4	2.3	1.7	1.7	2.0	2.1	1.6	0.7	.3	0.3
Vietnam........	443	4.3	172.8	37.6	25.8	20.4	15.0	13.1	25.8	0.8	1.1	3.8
Other Asia	656	36.5	176.1	65.0	50.9	50.4	66.3	60.0	2.2	1.2	1.1	3.8
America	11,340	1,716.4	1,982.5	204.6	208.1	225.5	254.1	265.0	291.0	20.9	51.7	44.3
Argentina	116	49.7	29.9	2.0	2.3	1.9	2.3	2.2	2.4	0.2	1.5	0.7
Brazil	79	29.3	17.8	1.5	2.2	2.6	2.7	2.7	2.7	0.1	.9	0.4
Canada........	4,249	413.3	169.9	11.4	15.7	16.4	16.1	16.7	11.8	7.8	12.4	3.8
Colombia......	251	72.0	77.3	9.7	10.9	11.8	11.2	11.5	10.3	0.5	2.2	1.7
Cuba	679	208.5	264.9	9.0	5.7	17.1	30.8	27.4	17.6	1.2	6.3	5.9
Dominican Rep. ..	434	93.3	148.1	22.1	23.2	23.9	26.2	24.9	27.2	0.8	2.8	3.3
Ecuador.......	134	36.8	50.1	4.2	4.2	4.6	4.5	4.7	4.7	0.2	1.1	1.1
El Salvador.....	132	15.0	34.4	8.6	8.8	10.1	10.9	10.6	12.0	0.2	.5	0.8
Guatemala	83	15.9	25.9	4.1	4.0	4.4	5.3	5.8	5.7	0.1	.5	0.6
Haiti	201	34.5	56.3	8.4	9.6	9.9	12.4	14.6	34.8	0.4	1.0	1.3
Honduras	70	15.7	17.4	3.6	3.4	3.7	4.6	4.8	4.3	0.1	.5	0.4
Mexico	2,805	453.9	640.3	59.1	57.8	61.3	66.8	72.5	95.0	5.2	13.7	14.3
Panama........	80	19.4	23.5	2.5	3.2	3.2	3.1	2.8	2.5	0.1	.6	0.5
Peru.........	94	19.1	29.2	4.4	4.3	4.1	4.8	5.8	5.9	0.2	.6	0.6
West Indies	1,284	133.9	271.8	33.8	29.9	28.5	29.2	48.3	112.4	2.4	4.0	6.1
Other America ...	704	106.1	125.7	20.2	22.9	22.0	23.2	9.7	0.8	1.3	3.1	2.8
Africa	282	29.0	80.8	15.1	13.6	15.2	15.5	15.7	18.9	0.5	.9	1.8
Australia and New Zealand.	140	19.6	23.8	1.9	2.3	2.5	2.4	2.3	2.0	0.3	.6	0.5
Other Oceania....	28	5.6	17.6	1.6	1.9	2.1	1.9	2.1	0.8	0.1	.1	0.4
Unknown or Not Reported	295	—	—	—	—	0.3	—	0.6	0.1	0.5	—	—

* Figures may not add to total due to rounding. (1) 1938-1945, Austria included with Germany; 1899-1919, Poland included with Austria-Hungary, Germany, and USSR. (2) Beginning 1952, includes data for United Kingdom not specified, formerly included with "Other Europe". (3) Europe and Asia. (4) Beginning 1957, includes Taiwan. (5) Prior to 1951, included with "Other Asia". (6) Prior to 1951, Philippines included with "All other". (7) Prior to 1953, data for Vietnam not available. (8) Prior to 1951, included with "Other America". (9) Prior to 1951, included with "West Indies". (10) Data on immigration by country of last residence for 1980-1983 are not available; data based on country of birth. (11) Norway and Sweden were combined from 1820-1868. (12) First full year with Immigration Reform and Control Act of 1986 in effect.

Poverty by Family Status, Sex, and Race

Source: U.S. Bureau of the Census, Current Population Reports
By thousands

	1987 No.[1]	1987 %[2]	1986 No.[1]	1986 %[2]	1984 No.[1]	1984 %[2]	1978 No.[1]	1978 %[2]
Total poor	32,546	13.5	32,370	13.6	22,700	14.4	24,497	11.4
In families	24,979	12.1	24,754	12.0	26,458	13.1	19,062	10.0
Head	7,059	10.8	7,023	10.9	7,277	11.6	5,280	9.1
Related children	12,435	20.0	12,257	19.8	12,929	21.0	9,722	15.7
Other relatives	5,485	6.9	5,475	6.9	6,251	8.0	4,509	5.7
Unrelated individuals	6,843	20.8	6,846	21.6	6,609	21.8	5,435	22.1
In families with a female householder, no husband present	12,076	38.3	11,944	38.3	11,831	38.4	9,269	35.6
Head	3,636	34.3	3,613	34.6	3,498	34.5	2,654	31.4
Related children	7,074	54.7	6,943	54.4	6,772	54.0	5,687	50.6
Other relatives	1,366	17.0	1,388	17.5	1,562	19.1	928	14.6
Unrelated female individuals	4,167	23.7	4,311	25.1	4,035	24.4	3,611	26.0
All other	12,903	7.4	12,811	7.3	14,627	8.5	9,793	5.9
Head	3,423	6.3	3,410	6.3	3,780	7.2	2,626	5.3
Related children	5,361	10.9	5,313	10.8	6,157	12.5	4,035	7.9
Other relatives	4,119	5.8	4,087	5.8	4,690	6.7	3,131	4.8
Unrelated male individuals	2,677	17.5	2,536	17.5	2,575	18.7	1,824	17.1
Total white poor	21,409	10.5	22,138	11.0	22,955	11.5	16,259	8.7
In families	15,804	9.1	16,393	9.4	17,299	10.1	12,050	7.3
Head	4,592	8.2	4,811	8.6	4,925	9.1	3,523	6.9
Female	1,930	26.7	2,041	28.2	1,878	27.1	1,391	23.5
Related children	7,550	15.0	7,714	15.3	8,086	16.1	5,674	11.0
Other relatives	3,662	5.4	3,868	5.7	4,289	6.4	2,852	4.5
Unrelated individuals	5,118	18.2	5,198	19.2	5,181	19.9	4,209	19.8
Total black poor	9,683	33.1	8,983	31.1	9,490	33.8	7,625	30.6
In families	7,952	31.8	7,401	29.7	8,104	33.2	6,493	29.5
Head	2,149	29.9	1,987	28.0	2,094	30.9	1,622	27.5
Female	1,593	51.8	1,488	50.1	1,533	51.7	1,208	50.6
Related children	4,297	45.1	4,039	42.7	4,320	46.2	3,781	41.2
Other relatives	1,506	18.1	1,375	16.5	1,691	20.5	1,094	15.7
Unrelated individuals	1,511	38.3	1,431	38.5	1,255	35.8	1,132	38.6

(1) Beginning in 1979, total includes members of unrelated subfamilies not shown separately. For earlier years, unrelated subfamily members are included in the "in family" category. (2) Percent of total population in that general category who fell below poverty level. For example, of all black female heads of households in 1978, 50.6% were poor.

Poverty Level by Family Size 1986, 1987
By thousands

	1986	1987		1986	1987
1 persons	$ 5,572	$ 5,778	3 persons	$ 8,737	$ 9,056
Under 65 years	5,701	5,909	4 persons	11,203	11,611
65 years and over	5,255	5,447	5 persons	13,259	13,737
2 persons	7,138	7,397	6 persons	14,986	15,509
Householder under 65 years	7,372	7,641	7 persons	17,049	17,649
Householder 65 years and over	6,630	6,872	8 persons	18,791	19,515
			9 persons or more	22,497	23,105

Income Distribution by Population Fifths

Families, 1987 Race	Top income of each fifth					Percent distribution of total income					
	Lowest	Second	Third	Fourth	Top 5%	Lowest fifth	Second fifth	Third fifth	Fourth fifth	Highest fifth	Top 5%
Total	$14,450	$25,100	$36,600	$52,910	$86,300	4.6	10.8	16.9	24.1	43.7	16.9
White	16,057	27,000	38,200	54,280	88,472	5.1	11.2	17.0	23.8	42.9	16.7
Black and other	7,514	15,500	25,500	41,338	69,901	3.2	8.5	15.3	24.8	48.3	18.4
Black	6,800	13,801	22,590	36,652	62,000	3.3	8.7	15.5	25.1	47.4	17.4
Region											
Northeast	$16,308	$28,070	$40,100	$57,260	$94,624	4.7	11.1	17.0	23.9	43.3	16.5
Midwest	15,001	25,665	36,300	51,350	80,943	4.9	11.4	17.4	24.2	42.2	16.0
South	12,833	22,555	34,200	49,777	81,129	4.3	10.5	16.7	24.3	44.4	17.1
West	15,606	26,120	38,200	55,406	91,467	4.8	10.7	16.5	23.7	44.2	17.7

Persons Below Poverty Level, 1960-1987

Year	Number Below Poverty Level (mil.)				Percent Below Poverty Level				Average income cutoffs for non-farm family of 4[3] at poverty level
	All races[1]	White	Black	Spanish origin[2]	All races[1]	White	Black	Spanish origin[2]	
1960	39.9	28.3	NA	NA	22.2	17.8	NA	NA	$3,022
1965	33.2	22.5	NA	NA	17.3	13.3	NA	NA	3,223
1970	25.4	17.5	7.5	NA	12.6	9.9	33.5	NA	3,968
1975	25.9	17.8	7.5	3.0	12.3	9.7	31.3	26.9	5,500
1980[4]	29.3	19.7	8.6	3.5	13.0	10.2	32.5	25.7	8,414
1986[4]	32.4	22.2	9.0	5.1	13.6	11.0	31.1	27.3	11,203
1987[4]	32.5	21.4	9.7	5.5	13.5	10.5	33.1	28.2	11,611

NA = Not Available. (1) Includes other races not shown separately. (2) Persons of Spanish origin may be of any race. (3) Beginning in 1981, income cutoffs for nonfarm families are applied to both farm and nonfarm families. (4) Data based on revised poverty definition.

Poverty Rate

The poverty rate is the proportion of the population whose income falls below the government's official poverty level, which is adjusted each year to take account of inflation.

The national poverty rate was higher in 1986 than in any year from 1969 through 1980. The rate reached a peak of 15.2 percent in 1983.

Aid to Families with Dependent Children

Source: Office of Research and Statistics, Social Security Administration

FY 1988 State	Total Assistance Payments[1]	Average Monthly Caseload	Average Monthly Recipients	Average Monthly Children	Average Payment per Family	Average Payment per Person
Alabama	$62,145,301	45,425	131,403	93,122	$114.01	$39.41
Alaska	53,719,155	7,543	19,506	12,632	593.47	229.50
Arizona	103,272,770	32,113	93,810	65,498	267.99	91.74
Arkansas	53,328,663	23,442	68,519	48,550	189.58	64.86
California	4,090,963,327	587,279	1,718,552	1,152,124	580.50	198.37
Colorado	125,110,995	32,909	94,468	63,262	316.81	110.36
Connecticut	218,421,953	37,440	106,792	72,586	486.15	170.44
Delaware	24,210,031	7,555	19,640	13,391	267.04	102.73
Dist. of Col.	76,217,791	18,522	49,285	38,654	342.91	128.87
Florida	318,066,700	110,627	307,053	219,274	239.59	86.32
Georgia	265,837,033	87,832	251,095	176,146	252.22	88.23
Guam	3,286,355	1,279	4,526	3,219	214.14	60.52
Hawaii	77,233,519	13,385	41,240	27,120	480.85	156.07
Idaho	19,315,950	6,430	17,396	11,791	250.34	92.53
Illinois	814,778,451	220,071	671,237	456,691	308.53	101.15
Indiana	167,271,960	52,975	151,517	102,734	263.13	92.00
Iowa	154,978,187	37,082	104,065	66,365	348.28	124.10
Kansas	97,278,395	23,996	70,447	46,745	337.82	115.07
Kentucky	142,916,705	58,340	155,201	104,031	204.14	76.74
Louisiana	182,154,892	90,847	272,442	191,439	167.09	55.72
Maine	79,847,174	18,002	51,396	32,365	369.63	129.46
Maryland	250,242,267	63,334	175,424	116,078	329.26	118.88
Massachusetts	557,868,171	86,708	234,772	151,928	536.16	198.02
Michigan	1,231,396,991	213,163	646,087	416,208	481.40	158.83
Minnesota	337,811,251	54,696	163,483	104,402	514.68	172.20
Mississippi	85,311,301	59,682	179,730	128,117	119.12	39.56
Missouri	214,728,871	67,778	203,649	133,665	264.01	87.87
Montana	41,411,246	9,544	28,383	18,079	361.58	121.58
Nebraska	56,317,248	14,677	42,685	29,013	319.76	109.95
Nevada	20,413,125	6,234	17,294	11,926	272.88	98.37
New Hampshire	21,057,770	4,312	11,212	7,482	406.95	156.51
New Jersey	458,736,032	107,063	313,172	214,083	357.06	122.07
New Mexico	56,153,522	20,753	59,002	40,289	225.49	79.31
New York	2,140,122,504	340,890	1,010,780	668,390	523.17	176.44
North Carolina	205,618,868	70,586	182,842	124,124	242.75	93.71
North Dakota	21,904,905	5,219	14,471	9,580	349.74	126.14
Ohio	805,344,095	225,541	647,730	418,902	297.56	103.61
Oklahoma	118,454,513	35,454	101,979	70,004	278.43	96.80
Oregon	128,077,428	30,684	83,794	55,832	347.84	127.37
Pennsylvania	746,771,373	179,329	538,040	355,582	347.02	115.66
Puerto Rico	66,744,831	54,857	177,360	120,669	101.39	31.36
Rhode Island	81,585,512	15,104	41,993	27,485	450.13	161.90
South Carolina	91,191,517	40,874	116,758	82,806	185.92	65.09
South Dakota	21,038,706	6,495	18,554	12,966	269.96	94.49
Tennessee	125,367,446	67,531	185,757	125,780	154.70	56.24
Texas	344,140,822	169,403	507,703	355,825	169.29	56.49
Utah	61,282,309	14,890	43,775	28,021	342.98	116.66
Vermont	40,188,072	7,141	20,170	12,687	468.97	166.04
Virgin Islands	2,320,902	989	3,510	2,626	195.66	55.10
Virginia	168,611,096	54,749	144,630	97,996	256.64	97.15
Washington	401,366,560	75,546	211,486	135,944	442.74	158.15
West Virginia	106,873,023	37,401	110,798	67,646	238.12	80.38
Wisconsin	505,878,638	89,109	269,581	174,141	473.09	156.38
Wyoming	18,650,838	5,122	13,505	8,995	303.45	115.08
U.S. Total	**$16,663,337,060**	**3,747,949**	**10,919,695**	**7,325,008**	**$370.50**	**$127.17**

(1) Total assistance payments include basic, up, grant diversions, and home repairs.

Welfare Recipients and Payments, 1955-1988

Category		1955, Dec.	1965, Dec.	1970, Dec.	1975, Dec.[1]	1980, Dec.	1985, Dec.	1988, Dec.
Old age:	Recipients	2,538,000	2,087,000	2,082,000	2,307,105	1,807,776	1,504,469	1,433,420
	Total amt.	$127,003,000	$131,674,000	$161,642,000	$209,777,000	$221,303,000	$247,133,000	$269,817,000
	Avg. amt.	$50.05	$63.10	$77.65	$90.93	$128.20	$164.26	$188.23
Blind:	Recipients	104,000	85,100	81,000	74,489	78,401	82,220	82,864
	Total amt.	$5,803,000	$6,922,000	$8,446,000	$10,918,000	$16,381,000	$22,555,000	$25,385,000
	Avg. amt.	$55.55	$81.35	$104.35	$146.57	$213.23	$274.32	$306.34
Disabled:	Recipients	241,000	557,000	935,000	1,932,681	2,255,840	2,551,332	2,947,585
	Total amt.	$11,750,000	$37,035,000	$91,325,000	$272,800,000	$444,322,000	$665,774,000	$866,231,000
	Avg. amt.	$48.75	$66.50	$97.65	$141.15	$197.90	$260.95	$293.87

(1) Administration of the public assistance programs of Old-age Assistance, Aid to the Blind, and Aid to the Disabled was transferred to the Social Security Administration by Public Law 92-603 effective 1/1/74. (2) Thousands. (3) Millions.

Characteristics of Persons Receiving Benefits from Major Assistance Programs

Using data from the *Survey of Income and Program Participation*, the Bureau of the Census issued a report in April 1989 to examine the attachment of persons (noninstitutional population of the U.S.) to the welfare system over a 32-month period (1983-1986). The program participation data refer to the following programs: Aid to Families with Dependent Children; General Assistance; Supplemental Security Income; Medicaid; Federal food stamps; and Federal and State rent assistance.

The report showed that the percentage of persons who participated in at least one of the major assistance programs was 18.3 percent. Over the entire 32-month period, 15.0 percent of the population received at least part of their income (money income plus the value of any food stamps received) from cash assistance or food stamps. The percentage that received all of their income from these two sources was 2.1 percent.

Gender and Poverty

Females were more likely than males to be recipients of welfare assistance. While 20.5 percent of females of all ages received assistance at some time during the 32-month period, the comparable figure for males was 15.8 percent. The difference between the sexes in receipt of welfare assistance reflects differences in the likelihood of being in poverty. In 1986, the poverty rate for females was 15.2 percent, and the rate for males was 11.8 percent.

The difference in poverty status is partly due to family relationship factors. Women are more likely than men to live in a family in which no spouse is present, and the poverty rate among persons in such families is higher than the rate among persons in married-couple families or among unrelated individuals. Data from another Census Bureau report, *Measuring the Effect of Benefits and Taxes on Income and Poverty: 1986*, show that 39.1 million persons lived in a family with no spouse present, and 23.2 million of these persons were

females. The poverty rate for persons in families with no spouse present was 34.6 percent compared to 7.1 percent for persons in married-couple families and 21.6 percent for unrelated individuals. The poverty rate was especially high, 39.1 percent, among persons living in a family with a female householder, no spouse present.

Race

There was a strong association between race and hispanic origin (Mexican, Puerto Rican, Cuban, Central or South American, or some other Spanish origin) and the likelihood of receiving welfare assistance. The percentage of persons who received assistance at some time during the period was 13.9 percent among whites, 48.5 percent among blacks, and 34.2 percent among hispanics. Over the entire 32-month period, the percentage of persons who received half or more of their income from cash assistance and/or food stamps was 4.1 percent among whites, 21.2 percent among blacks, and 14.3 percent among hispanics. The differences among whites, blacks, and hispanics reflect differences in poverty status and in the factors that help determine poverty status. The 1986 report showed that the poverty rates among the three groups were 11.0 percent (white), 31.1 percent (black), and 27.3 percent (hispanic). The report also showed that 73.5 percent of all whites lived in married-couple families, compared with 47.0 percent of all blacks and 66.8 percent for hispanics.

Age

When classified by age, the population group with the strongest dependence on welfare assistance was the very young. The percentage of children under 6 years of age who received welfare assistance during some part of the 32-month period was 30.1 percent. The proportion of persons under 18 years was 26.6 percent. The rate for persons 65 years and over was 17.9 percent.

Public Aid Recipients as Percent of Population, by State: 1980 and 1987

Source: Social Security Admin.

State	1980 %	1987 %	State	1980 %	1987 %	State	1980 %	1987 %
Alabama	8.1	6.5	Louisiana	8.3	8.8	Ohio	6.0	7.5
Alaska	4.6	4.3	Maine	7.4	6.5	Oklahoma	5.2	4.8
Arizona	3.0	3.5	Maryland	6.1	5.1	Oregon	4.9	4.0
Arkansas	7.2	5.9	Massachusetts	8.3	5.9	Pennsylvania	6.7	6.1
California	8.8	8.8	Michigan	8.9	8.5	Rhode Island	7.2	6.0
Colorado	3.7	3.7	Minnesota	4.2	4.6	South Carolina	7.6	6.3
Connecticut	5.2	4.3	Mississippi	11.4	11.1	South Dakota	4.2	3.9
Delaware	6.6	4.3	Missouri	5.9	5.5	Tennessee	6.4	6.4
Dist. of Col.	15.5	11.2	Montana	3.4	4.5	Texas	4.0	4.5
Florida	4.4	4.1	Nebraska	3.2	3.8	Utah	3.2	3.2
Georgia	6.9	6.4	Nevada	2.3	2.6	Vermont	6.4	5.6
Hawaii	7.3	4.9	New Hampshire	3.0	1.7	Virginia	4.6	4.0
Idaho	3.1	2.7	New Jersey	7.4	5.6	Washington	4.9	5.8
Illinois	7.0	7.5	New Mexico	6.1	5.7	West Virginia	6.0	8.2
Indiana	3.7	3.6	New York	8.4	8.0	Wisconsin	6.1	7.7
Iowa	4.6	5.0	North Carolina	5.8	5.0	Wyoming	1.9	3.2
Kansas	3.8	3.8	North Dakota	3.0	3.1			
Kentucky	7.2	7.0				U.S.	6.5	6.2

U.S. Places of 5,000 or More Population—With ZIP and Area Codes

Source: U.S. Bureau of the Census; U.S. Postal Service; N.Y. Telephone Co.

The listings below show the official urban population of the United States. "Urban population" is defined as all persons living in (a) places of 5,000 inhabitants or more, incorporated as cities, villages, boroughs (except Alaska), and towns (except in New England, New York, New Jersey, Pennsylvania and Wisconsin), but excluding those persons living in the rural portions of extended cities; (b) unincorporated places of 5,000 inhabitants or more; and (c) other territory, incorporated or unincorporated, included in urbanized areas.

The non-urban portion of an extended city contains one or more areas, each at least 5 square miles in extent and with a population density of less than 100 persons per square mile. The area or areas constitute at least 25 percent of the legal city's land area of a total of 25 square miles or more.

In New England, New York, New Jersey, Pennsylvania, and Wisconsin, minor civil divisions called "towns" often include rural areas and one or more urban areas. Only the urban areas of these "towns" are included here, except in the case of New England where entire town populations, which may include some rural population, are shown; these towns are indicated by italics. Boroughs in Alaska may contain one or more urban areas which are included here. Population in Hawaii is counted by county subdivisions.

(u) means place is unincorporated.

The ZIP Code of each place appears before the name of that place, if it is obtainable. Telephone Area Code appears in parentheses after the name of the state or, if a state has more than one number, after the name of the place.

CAUTION—Where an asterisk (*) appears before the ZIP Code, ask your local postmaster for the correct ZIP Code for a specific address within the place listed.

ZIP code	Place	1980	1970
	Alabama (205)		
35007	Alabaster.	7,079	2,642
35950	Albertville.	12,039	9,963
35010	Alexander City.	13,807	12,358
36420	Andalusia.	10,415	10,092
36201	Anniston.	29,135	31,533
35016	Arab.	6,053	4,399
35611	Athens.	14,558	14,360
36502	Atmore.	8,789	8,293
35954	Attalla.	7,737	7,510
36830	Auburn.	28,471	22,767
36507	Bay Minette.	7,455	6,727
35020	Bessemer.	31,729	33,428
*35203	Birmingham.	284,413	300,910
35957	Boaz.	7,151	5,635
36426	Brewton.	6,680	6,747
35020	Brighton.	5,308	2,277
35215	Center Point(u).	23,317	15,675
36611	Chickasaw.	7,402	8,447
35044	Childersburg.	5,084	4,831
35045	Clanton.	5,832	5,868
35055	Cullman.	13,084	12,601
35601	Decatur.	42,002	38,044
36732	Demopolis.	7,678	7,651
36301	Dothan.	48,750	36,733
36330	Enterprise.	18,033	15,591
36027	Eufaula.	12,097	9,102
35064	Fairfield.	13,242	14,369
36532	Fairhope.	7,286	5,720
35555	Fayette.	5,287	4,568
35630	Florence.	37,029	34,031
35214	Forestdale(u).	10,814	6,091
35967	Fort Payne.	11,485	8,435
36360	Fort Rucker(u).	8,932	14,242
35068	Fultondale.	6,217	5,163
*35901	Gadsden.	47,565	53,928
35071	Gardendale.	8,005	6,537
36037	Greenville.	7,807	8,033
35976	Guntersville.	7,041	6,491
35565	Haleyville.	5,306	4,190
35640	Hartselle.	8,858	7,355
35209	Homewood.	21,271	21,245
35226	Hoover.	18,996	688
35020	Hueytown.	13,452	7,095
*35804	Huntsville.	142,513	139,282
35210	Irondale.	6,521	3,166
36545	Jackson.	6,073	5,957
36265	Jacksonville.	9,735	7,715
35501	Jasper.	11,894	10,798
36863	Lanett.	8,922	6,908
35094	Leeds.	8,638	6,991
35228	Midfield.	6,182	6,621
*36601	Mobile.	200,452	190,026
36460	Monroeville.	5,674	4,846
*36104	Montgomery.	177,857	133,386
35223	Mountain Brook.	17,400	19,474
35660	Muscle Shoals.	8,911	6,907
35476	Northport.	14,291	9,435
36801	Opelika.	21,896	19,027
36467	Opp.	7,204	6,493
36203	Oxford.	8,939	4,361
36360	Ozark.	13,188	13,555
35124	Pelham.	6,759	931
35125	Pell City.	6,616	5,602
36867	Phenix City.	26,928	25,281
36272	Piedmont.	5,544	5,063
35127	Pleasant Grove.	7,102	5,090
36067	Prattville.	18,647	13,116
36610	Prichard.	39,541	41,578
35901	Rainbow City.	6,299	3,099
35809	Redstone Arsenal(u).	5,728	....
36274	Roanoke.	5,809	5,251
35653	Russellville.	8,195	7,814
36201	Saks(u).	11,118	....
36571	Saraland.	9,833	7,840
35768	Scottsboro.	14,758	9,324
36701	Selma.	26,684	27,379
36701	Selmont-West Selmont(u).	5,255	2,270
35660	Sheffield.	11,903	13,115
35901	Southside.	5,141	983
35150	Sylacauga.	12,708	12,255
35160	Talladega.	19,128	17,662
35217	Tarrant City.	8,148	6,835
36582	Theodore(u).	6,392	....
36619	Tillman's Corner(u).	15,941	....
36081	Troy.	13,124	11,482
35401	Tuscaloosa.	75,143	65,773
35674	Tuscumbia.	9,137	8,828
36083	Tuskegee.	12,716	11,028
35216	Vestavia Hills.	15,733	12,250
36201	West End-Cobb(u).	5,189	5,515
	Alaska (907)		
*99502	Anchorage.	174,431	48,081
99702	Eielson AFB(u).	5,232	6,149
99701	Fairbanks.	22,645	14,771
99801	Juneau.	19,528	6,050
99611	Kenai Peninsula borough.	25,282	16,586
99901	Ketchikan.	7,198	6,994
99835	Sitka.	7,803	3,370
	Arizona (602)		
85321	Ajo(u).	5,189	5,881
85220	Apache Junction.	9,935	2,443
85323	Avondale.	8,134	6,626
85603	Bisbee.	7,154	8,328
86430	Bullhead City-Riviera(u).	10,364	....
85222	Casa Grande.	14,971	10,536
85224	Chandler.	29,673	13,763
85228	Coolidge.	6,851	5,314
85707	Davis-Monthan AFB(u).	6,279	....
85607	Douglas.	13,058	12,462
85205	Dreamland-VeldaRose(u).	5,969	....
85231	Eloy.	6,240	5,381
86001	Flagstaff.	34,641	26,117
85613	Fort Huachuca(u).	NA	6,659
85234	Gilbert.	5,717	1,971
*85301	Glendale.	96,988	36,228
85501	Globe.	6,886	7,333
85614	Green Valley(u).	7,999	....
86025	Holbrook.	5,785	4,759
86401	Kingman.	9,257	7,312
86403	Lake Havasu City.	15,737	4,111
85301	Luke(u).	NA	5,047
*85201	Mesa.	152,404	63,049
85621	Nogales.	15,683	8,946
86040	Page(u).	NA	1,439
85253	Paradise Valley.	10,832	6,637
85345	Peoria.	12,171	4,792
*85026	Phoenix.	789,704	584,303
86301	Prescott.	19,865	13,631
85546	Safford.	7,010	5,493

ZIP code	Place		1980	1970
85631	San Manuel(u)		5,443	....
*85251	Scottsdale		88,622	67,823
85635	Sierra Vista		25,968	6,689
85713	South Tucson		6,554	6,220
85351	Sun City(u)		40,505	13,670
*85282	Tempe		106,919	63,550
86045	Tuba City(u)		5,045	....
*85726	Tucson		330,537	262,933
85364	West Yuma(u)		NA	5,552
86047	Winslow		7,921	8,066
85364	Yuma		42,481	29,007

Arkansas (501)

ZIP code	Place	1980	1970
71923	Arkadelphia	10,005	9,841
72501	Batesville	8,447	7,209
72015	Benton	17,437	16,499
72712	Bentonville	8,756	5,508
72315	Blytheville	24,314	24,752
71701	Camden	15,356	15,147
72830	Clarksville	5,237	4,616
72032	Conway	20,375	15,510
71635	Crossett	6,706	6,191
71639	Dumas	6,091	4,600
71730	El Dorado	26,685	25,283
72701	Fayetteville	36,604	30,729
71742	Fordyce	5,175	4,837
72335	Forrest City	13,803	12,521
72901	Fort Smith	71,384	62,802
72601	Harrison	9,567	7,239
72342	Helena	9,598	10,415
71801	Hope	10,290	8,830
71901	Hot Springs	35,166	35,631
72076	Jacksonville	27,589	19,832
72401	Jonesboro	31,530	27,050
*72201	Little Rock	159,159	132,483
71753	Magnolia	11,909	11,303
72104	Malvern	10,163	8,739
72360	Marianna	6,220	6,196
71654	McGehee	5,671	4,683
71953	Mena	5,154	4,530
71655	Monticello	8,259	5,085
72110	Morrilton	7,355	6,814
72653	Mountain Home	7,447	3,936
72112	Newport	8,339	7,725
*72114	North Little Rock	64,388	60,040
72370	Osceola	8,881	7,892
72450	Paragould	15,214	10,639
71601	Pine Bluff	56,576	57,389
72455	Pocahontas	5,995	4,544
72756	Rogers	17,429	11,050
72801	Russellville	14,518	11,750
72143	Searcy	13,612	9,040
72116	Sherwood	10,423	2,754
72761	Siloam Springs	7,940	6,009
72764	Springdale	23,458	16,783
72160	Stuttgart	10,941	10,477
55022	Texarkana	21,459	21,682
72472	Trumann	6,395	6,023
72956	Van Buren	12,020	8,373
71671	Warren	7,646	6,433
72390	West Helena	11,367	11,007
72301	West Memphis	28,138	26,070
72396	Wynne	7,927	6,696

California

ZIP code	Place		1980	1970
94501	Alameda	(415)	63,852	70,968
94507	Alamo(u)	(415)	8,505	14,059
94706	Albany	(415)	15,130	15,561
*91802	Alhambra	(818)	64,767	62,125
90249	Alondra Park(u)	(213)	12,096	12,193
92001	Alpine(u)	(619)	5,368	1,570
91001	Altadena(u)	(818)	40,510	42,415
95116	Alum Rock(u)	(408)	17,471	18,355
94590	American Canyon(u)	(707)	5,712	....
*92803	Anaheim	(714)	219,494	166,408
96007	Anderson	(916)	7,381	5,492
94509	Antioch	(415)	43,559	28,060
92307	Apple Valley(u)	(619)	14,305	6,702
95003	Aptos(u)	(408)	7,039	8,704
91006	Arcadia	(818)	45,993	45,138
95521	Arcata	(707)	12,849	8,985
95825	Arden-Arcade(u)	(916)	87,570	82,492
93420	Arroyo Grande	(805)	11,290	7,454
90701	Artesia	(213)	14,301	14,757
93203	Arvin	(805)	6,863	5,199
94577	Ashland(u)	(415)	13,893	14,810
93422	Atascadero	(805)	15,930	10,290
94025	Atherton	(415)	7,797	8,085
95301	Atwater	(209)	17,530	11,640
95603	Auburn	(916)	7,540	6,570
92505	August(u)	(714)	6,350	6,293
91746	Avocado Heights(u)	(818)	11,721	9,810
91702	Azusa	(818)	29,380	25,217
*93302	Bakersfield	(805)	105,611	69,515
91706	Baldwin Park	(818)	50,554	47,285

ZIP code	Place		1980	1970
92220	Banning	(714)	14,020	12,034
92311	Barstow	(619)	17,690	17,442
93402	Baywood-Los Osos(u)	(805)	10,933	3,487
95903	Beale AFB East(u)	(916)	6,329	7,029
92223	Beaumont	(714)	6,818	5,484
90201	Bell	(213)	25,450	21,836
90706	Bellflower	(213)	53,441	52,334
90201	Bell Gardens	(213)	34,117	29,308
94002	Belmont	(415)	24,505	23,538
94510	Benicia	(707)	15,376	7,349
95005	Ben Lomond(u)	(408)	7,238	2,793
*94704	Berkeley	(415)	103,328	114,091
90213	Beverly Hills	(213)	32,646	33,416
92314	Big Bear(u)	(714)	11,151	5,268
92316	Bloomington(u)	(714)	6,674	11,957
92225	Blythe	(619)	6,805	7,047
92002	Bonita(u)	(619)	6,257	....
95006	Boulder Creek(u)	(408)	5,662	1,806
92227	Brawley	(619)	14,946	13,746
92621	Brea	(714)	27,913	18,447
95605	Broderick-Bryte(u)	(916)	10,194	12,782
*90620	Buena Park	(714)	64,165	63,646
*91505	Burbank	(818)	84,625	88,871
94010	Burlingame	(415)	26,173	27,320
92231	Calexico	(619)	14,412	10,625
93725	Calwa(u)	(209)	6,640	5,191
93010	Camarillo	(805)	37,732	19,219
93010	Camarillo Heights(u)	(805)	6,341	5,892
95682	Cameron Park(u)	(916)	5,607	....
95008	Campbell	(408)	26,843	23,797
91351	Canyon Country(u)	(805)	15,728	....
92055	Camp Pendleton South(u)	(714)	7,952	13,692
92624	Capistrano Beach(u)	(714)	6,168	4,149
95010	Capitola	(408)	9,095	5,080
92007	Cardiff-by-the-Sea(u)	(619)	10,054	5,724
92008	Carlsbad	(619)	35,490	14,944
95608	Carmichael(u)	(916)	43,108	37,625
93013	Carpinteria	(805)	10,835	6,982
90744	Carson	(213)	81,221	71,150
92077	Casa De Oro-Mt. Helix(u)	(619)	19,651	....
92010	Castle Park-Otay(u)	(619)	21,049	15,445
94546	Castro Valley(u)	(415)	44,011	44,760
95307	Ceres	(209)	13,281	6,029
90701	Cerritos	(213)	52,756	15,856
91724	Charter Oak(u)	(818)	6,840	....
94541	Cherryland(u)	(415)	9,425	9,969
92223	Cherry Valley(u)	(714)	5,012	3,165
95926	Chico	(916)	26,716	19,580
95926	Chico North(u)	(916)	11,739	6,656
95926	Chico West(u)	(916)	6,378	4,787
91710	Chino	(714)	40,165	20,411
93610	Chowchilla	(209)	5,122	4,349
*92010	Chula Vista	(619)	83,927	67,901
95610	Citrus(u)	(916)	12,450	....
95610	Citrus Heights(u)	(916)	85,911	21,760
91711	Claremont	(714)	31,028	24,776
93612	Clovis	(209)	33,021	13,856
92236	Coachella	(619)	9,129	8,353
93210	Coalinga	(209)	6,593	6,161
92324	Colton	(714)	27,419	20,016
90022	Commerce	(213)	10,509	10,635
*90220	Compton	(213)	81,350	78,547
*94520	Concord	(415)	103,763	85,164
93212	Corcoran	(209)	6,454	5,249
91720	Corona	(714)	37,791	27,519
92118	Coronado	(619)	18,790	20,020
94925	Corte Madera	(415)	8,074	8,464
*92626	Costa Mesa	(714)	82,291	72,660
	Country Club(u)	(209)	9,585	....
*91722	Covina	(818)	32,746	30,395
92325	Crestline(u)	(714)	6,715	....
90201	Cudahy	(213)	18,275	16,998
90230	Culver City	(213)	38,139	34,451
95014	Cupertino	(408)	34,297	17,895
90630	Cypress	(714)	40,738	31,569
*94017	Daly City	(415)	78,519	66,922
94526	Danville(u)	(415)	26,446	....
92629	Dana Point(u)	(714)	10,602	4,745
95616	Davis	(916)	36,640	23,488
90250	Del Aire(u)	(213)	6,487	11,930
93215	Delano	(805)	16,491	14,559
92014	Del Mar	(619)	5,017	3,956
92240	Desert Hot Springs	(619)	5,941	2,738
91765	Diamond Bar(u)	(714)	28,045	10,576
93618	Dinuba	(209)	9,907	7,917
95620	Dixon	(916)	7,541	4,432
*90241	Downey	(213)	82,602	88,573
91010	Duarte	(818)	16,766	14,981
94566	Dublin(u)	(415)	13,496	13,641
90220	East Compton(u)	(213)	6,435	5,853
92343	East Hemet(u)	(714)	14,712	8,598
90638	East La Mirada(u)	(213)	9,688	12,339
90022	East Los Angeles(u)	(213)	110,017	104,881
94303	East Palo Alto(u)	(415)	18,191	18,727
93257	East Porterville(u)	(209)	5,218	4,042
92508	Edgemont(u)	(714)	5,215	....
93523	Edwards AFB(u)	(805)	8,554	10,331
*92020	El Cajon	(619)	73,892	52,273
92243	El Centro	(619)	23,996	19,272
94530	El Cerrito	(415)	22,731	25,190
95624	Elk Grove(u)	(916)	10,959	3,721

ZIP code	Place		1980	1970
*91734	El Monte	(818)	79,494	69,892
93446	El Paso de Robles	(213)	9,163	7,168
93030	El Rio(u)	(805)	5,674	6,173
90245	El Segundo	(213)	13,752	15,620
94803	El Sobrante(u)	(415)	10,535	....
92630	El Toro(u)	(714)	38,153	8,654
92709	El Toro Station(u)	(714)	7,632	6,970
92024	Encinitas(u)	(619)	10,796	5,375
*92025	Escondido	(619)	62,480	36,792
95501	Eureka	(707)	24,153	24,337
93221	Exeter	(209)	5,619	4,475
94930	Fairfax	(415)	7,391	7,661
94533	Fairfield	(707)	58,099	44,146
95628	Fair Oaks(u)	(916)	20,235	11,256
92028	Fallbrook(u)	(619)	14,041	6,945
93223	Farmersville	(209)	5,544	3,456
93015	Fillmore	(805)	9,602	6,285
90001	Florence-Graham(u)	(213)	48,662	42,900
95828	Florin(u)	(916)	16,523	9,646
95630	Folsom	(916)	11,003	5,810
92335	Fontana	(714)	36,804	20,673
95841	Foothill Farms(u)	(916)	13,700	....
95437	Fort Bragg	(707)	5,019	4,455
95540	Fortuna	(707)	7,591	4,203
94404	Foster City	(415)	23,287	9,522
92708	Fountain Valley	(714)	55,080	31,886
95019	Freedom(u)	(408)	6,416	5,563
*94536	Fremont	(415)	131,945	100,869
*93706	Fresno	(209)	217,491	165,655
*92631	Fullerton	(714)	102,246	85,987
95632	Galt	(209)	5,514	3,200
*90247	Gardena	(213)	45,165	41,021
95205	Garden Acres(u)	(213)	7,361	7,870
*92640	Garden Grove	(714)	123,351	121,155
92392	George AFB(u)	(619)	7,407	7,404
95020	Gilroy	(408)	21,641	12,684
92509	Glen Avon(u)	(714)	8,444	5,759
*91209	Glendale	(818)	139,060	132,664
91740	Glendora	(818)	38,500	32,143
92324	Grand Terrace	(714)	8,498	5,901
95945	Grass Valley	(916)	6,697	5,149
93308	Greenacres(u)	(805)	5,381	2,116
93433	Grover City	(805)	8,827	5,939
91745	Hacienda Heights	(818)	49,422	35,969
94019	Half Moon Bay	(415)	7,282	4,023
93230	Hanford	(209)	20,958	15,179
90716	Hawaiian Gardens	(213)	10,548	9,052
90250	Hawthorne	(213)	56,437	53,304
*94544	Hayward	(415)	93,585	93,058
95448	Healdsburg	(707)	7,217	5,438
92343	Hemet	(714)	22,531	12,252
94547	Hercules	(415)	5,963	252
90254	Hermosa Beach	(213)	18,070	17,412
92345	Hesperia(u)	(619)	13,540	4,592
92346	Highland(u)	(714)	10,908	12,669
94010	Hillsborough	(415)	10,372	8,753
95023	Hollister	(408)	11,488	7,663
91720	Home Gardens(u)	(714)	5,783	5,116
*92647	Huntington Beach	(714)	170,505	115,960
90255	Huntington Park	(213)	45,932	33,744
92032	Imperial Beach	(619)	22,689	20,244
92201	Indio	(619)	21,611	14,459
*90306	Inglewood	(213)	94,162	89,985
*92711	Irvine	(714)	62,134	7,381
94707	Kensington(u)	(415)	5,342	5,823
93930	King City	(408)	5,495	3,717
93631	Kingsburg	(209)	5,115	3,843
91011	La Canada-Flintridge	(818)	20,153	20,714
91214	La Crescenta-Montrose(u)	(818)	16,531	19,620
90045	Ladera Heights(u)	(213)	6,647	6,079
94549	Lafayette	(415)	20,837	20,484
*92651	Laguna Beach	(714)	17,858	14,550
92653	Laguna Hills(u)	(714)	33,600	13,676
92677	Laguna Niguel(u)	(714)	12,237	4,644
90631	La Habra	(213)	45,232	41,350
92352	Lake Arrowhead(u)	(714)	6,272	2,682
92040	Lakeside(u)	(619)	23,921	11,991
92330	Lake Elsinore	(714)	5,982	3,530
*90714	Lakewood	(213)	74,511	83,025
92041	La Mesa	(619)	50,342	39,178
90638	La Mirada	(213)	40,986	30,808
93241	Lamont(u)	(805)	9,616	7,007
93534	Lancaster	(805)	48,027	32,728
90624	La Palma	(213)	15,663	9,687
91747	La Puente	(818)	30,882	31,092
	La Riviera(u)	(916)	10,906	....
94939	Larkspur	(415)	11,064	10,487
91750	La Verne	(714)	23,508	12,965
90260	Lawndale	(213)	23,460	24,825
92045	Lemon Grove	(619)	20,780	19,794
93245	Lemoore	(209)	8,832	4,219
93245	Lemoore Station(u)	(209)	5,860	9,210
90304	Lennox(u)	(213)	18,445	16,121
92024	Leucadia(u)	(619)	9,478	....
95207	Lincoln Village(u)	(916)	7,067	6,112
95901	Linda(u)	(916)	10,225	7,112
93247	Lindsay	(209)	6,936	5,206
95062	Live Oak(u) (Santa Cruz)	(916)	11,482	6,443
94550	Livermore	(415)	48,349	37,703
95334	Livingston	(209)	5,326	2,588
95240	Lodi	(209)	35,221	26,691
92354	Loma Linda	(714)	10,694	7,651
90717	Lomita	(213)	17,191	19,784
93436	Lompoc	(805)	26,267	25,284
*90801	Long Beach	(213)	361,498	358,879
90720	Los Alamitos	(213)	11,529	11,346
94022	Los Altos	(415)	25,769	25,062
94022	Los Altos Hills	(415)	7,421	6,871
*90052	Los Angeles	(213)	2,968,528	2,811,801
93635	Los Banos	(209)	10,341	9,188
95030	Los Gatos	(408)	26,593	22,613
94903	Lucas Valley-Marinwood(u)	(415)	6,409	....
90262	Lynwood	(213)	48,289	43,354
93640	Madera	(209)	21,732	16,044
90266	Manhattan Beach	(213)	31,542	35,352
95336	Manteca	(209)	24,925	13,845
93933	Marina	(408)	20,647	8,343
90291	Marina Del Rey(u)	(213)	8,065	....
94553	Martinez	(415)	22,582	16,506
95901	Marysville	(916)	9,898	9,353
95655	Mather AFB(u)	(916)	5,245	7,027
91016	Mayflower Village(u)	(818)	5,617	....
90270	Maywood	(213)	21,810	16,996
93250	Mc Farland	(805)	5,151	4,177
95521	McKinleyville(u)	(707)	7,772	....
93023	Meiners Oaks-Mira Monte(u)	(805)	9,512	7,025
93640	Mendota	(209)	5,038	2,705
94025	Menlo Park	(415)	26,438	26,826
95340	Merced	(209)	36,423	22,670
94030	Millbrae	(415)	20,058	20,920
94941	Mill Valley	(415)	12,967	12,942
95035	Milpitas	(408)	37,820	26,561
91752	Mira Loma(u)	(714)	8,707	8,482
92675	Mission Viejo(u)	(714)	48,384	11,933
*95350	Modesto	(209)	106,963	61,712
91016	Monrovia	(818)	30,531	30,562
91763	Montclair	(714)	22,628	22,546
90640	Montebello	(213)	52,929	42,807
93940	Monterey	(408)	27,558	26,302
91754	Monterey Park	(818)	54,338	49,166
94556	Moraga	(415)	15,014	14,205
95037	Morgan Hill	(408)	17,060	5,579
93442	Morro Bay	(805)	9,064	7,109
*94042	Mountain View	(415)	58,655	54,132
92405	Muscoy(u)	(714)	6,188	7,091
94558	Napa	(707)	50,879	36,103
92050	National City	(619)	48,772	43,184
94560	Newark	(415)	32,126	27,153
91321	Newhall(u)	(805)	12,029	9,651
*92660	Newport Beach	(714)	63,475	49,582
93444	Nipomo(u)	(805)	5,247	3,642
91760	Norco	(714)	19,732	14,511
95603	North Auburn(u)	(916)	7,619	....
94025	North Fair Oaks(u)	(415)	10,294	9,740
95660	North Highlands(u)	(916)	37,825	31,854
90650	Norwalk	(213)	84,901	90,164
94947	Novato	(415)	43,916	31,006
95361	Oakdale	(209)	8,474	6,594
*94615	Oakland	(415)	339,337	361,561
92054	Oceanside	(619)	76,698	40,494
93308	Oildale(u)	(805)	23,382	20,879
93023	Ojai	(805)	6,816	5,591
95961	Olivehurst(u)	(916)	8,929	8,100
*91761	Ontario	(714)	88,820	64,118
95060	Opal Cliffs(u)	(408)	5,041	5,425
92667	Orange	(714)	91,450	77,365
95662	Orangevale(u)	(916)	20,585	16,493
94563	Orinda (u)	(415)	16,825	6,790
95965	Oroville	(916)	8,683	7,536
93030	Oxnard	(805)	108,195	71,225
94044	Pacifica	(415)	36,866	36,020
93950	Pacific Grove	(408)	15,755	13,505
93550	Palmdale	(805)	12,277	8,511
92260	Palm Desert	(619)	11,801	6,171
92262	Palm Springs	(619)	32,359	20,936
94302	Palo Alto	(415)	55,225	56,040
90274	Palos Verdes Estates	(213)	14,376	13,631
95969	Paradise	(916)	22,571	14,539
90723	Paramount	(213)	36,407	34,734
95823	Parkway-Sacramento So.(u)	(916)	26,815	28,574
*91109	Pasadena	(818)	118,072	112,951
92370	Perris	(714)	6,740	4,228
94952	Petaluma	(707)	33,834	24,870
90660	Pico Rivera	(213)	53,387	54,170
94611	Piedmont	(415)	10,498	10,917
94564	Pinole	(415)	14,253	13,266
93449	Pismo Beach	(805)	5,364	4,043
94565	Pittsburg	(415)	33,465	21,423
92670	Placentia	(714)	35,041	21,948
95667	Placerville	(916)	6,739	5,416
94523	Pleasant Hill	(415)	25,547	24,610
94566	Pleasanton	(415)	35,160	18,328
*91766	Pomona	(714)	92,742	87,384
93257	Porterville	(209)	19,707	12,602
93041	Port Hueneme	(805)	17,803	14,295
92064	Poway	(619)	32,263	9,422
93534	Quartz Hill(u)	(213)	7,421	4,935
92065	Ramona(u)	(619)	8,173	3,554
95670	Rancho Cordova(u)	(916)	42,881	30,451
91730	Rancho Cucamonga	(714)	55,250	19,484

ZIP code	Place		1980	1970
92270	Rancho Mirage	(619)	6,281	2,767
90274	Rancho Palos Verdes	(213)	35,227	33,285
96080	Red Bluff	(916)	9,490	7,676
96001	Redding	(916)	42,103	16,659
92373	Redlands	(714)	43,619	36,355
*90277	Redondo Beach	(213)	57,102	57,451
*94064	Redwood City	(415)	54,965	55,686
93654	Reedley	(209)	11,071	8,131
92376	Rialto	(714)	37,862	28,370
*94802	Richmond	(415)	74,676	79,043
93555	Ridgecrest	(619)	15,929	7,629
95003	Rio Del Mar(u)	(408)	7,067	....
95673	Rio Linda(u)	(916)	7,359	7,524
95367	Riverbank	(209)	5,695	3,949
*92502	Riverside	(714)	170,591	140,089
95677	Rocklin	(916)	7,344	3,039
94572	Rodeo(u)	(415)	8,286	5,356
94928	Rohnert Park	(707)	22,965	6,133
90274	Rolling Hills Estates	(213)	9,412	6,735
95401	Roseland(u)	(707)	7,915	5,105
91770	Rosemead	(818)	42,604	40,972
95826	Rosemont(u)	(916)	18,888	....
95678	Roseville	(916)	24,347	18,221
90720	Rossmoor(u)	(213)	10,457	12,922
91745	Rowland Heights(u)	(818)	28,252	16,881
92509	Rubidoux(u)	(714)	16,763	13,969
*95813	Sacramento	(916)	275,741	257,105
93901	Salinas	(408)	80,479	58,896
94960	San Anselmo	(415)	12,067	13,031
*92403	San Bernardino	(714)	118,794	106,869
94066	San Bruno	(415)	35,417	36,254
....	San Buenaventura (see Ventura)	(805)		
94070	San Carlos	(415)	24,710	26,053
92672	San Clemente	(714)	27,325	17,063
*92109	San Diego	(619)	875,538	697,471
91773	San Dimas	(714)	24,014	15,692
*91340	San Fernando	(818)	17,731	16,571
94101	San Francisco	(415)	678,974	715,674
91776	San Gabriel	(818)	30,072	29,336
93657	Sanger	(209)	12,558	10,088
92383	San Jacinto	(714)	7,098	4,385
*95101	San Jose	(408)	629,400	459,913
92375	San Juan Capistrano	(714)	18,959	3,781
94577	San Leandro	(415)	63,952	68,698
94580	San Lorenzo(u)	(415)	20,545	24,633
93401	San Luis Obispo	(805)	34,252	28,036
92069	San Marcos	(619)	17,479	3,896
91108	San Marino	(818)	13,307	14,177
*94402	San Mateo	(415)	77,640	78,991
94806	San Pablo	(415)	19,750	21,461
*94901	San Rafael	(415)	44,700	38,977
94583	San Ramon(u)	(415)	22,356	4,084
*92711	Santa Ana	(714)	204,023	155,710
93102	Santa Barbara	(805)	74,542	70,215
*95050	Santa Clara	(408)	87,700	86,118
95060	Santa Cruz	(408)	41,483	32,076
90670	Santa Fe Springs	(213)	14,559	14,750
93454	Santa Maria	(805)	39,685	32,749
*90406	Santa Monica	(213)	88,314	88,289
93060	Santa Paula	(805)	20,658	18,001
*95402	Santa Rosa	(707)	82,658	50,006
92071	Santee(u)	(619)	47,080	21,107
95070	Saratoga	(408)	29,261	26,810
91350	Saugus-Bouquet Canyon(u)	(805)	16,283	....
94965	Sausalito	(415)	7,090	6,158
95066	Scotts Valley	(408)	6,891	3,621
90740	Seal Beach	(213)	25,975	24,441
93955	Seaside	(408)	36,567	36,883
95472	Sebastopol	(707)	5,500	3,993
93662	Selma	(209)	10,942	7,459
93263	Shafter	(805)	7,010	5,327
91024	Sierra Madre	(818)	10,837	12,140
90806	Signal Hill	(213)	5,734	5,588
93065	Simi Valley	(805)	77,500	59,832
92075	Solana Beach(u)	(619)	13,047	5,023
93960	Soledad	(408)	5,928	4,222
95476	Sonoma	(707)	6,054	4,259
95073	Soquel(u)	(408)	6,212	5,795
91733	South El Monte	(213)	16,623	13,443
90280	South Gate	(213)	66,784	56,909
92677	South Laguna(u)	(714)	6,013	2,566
95705	South Lake Tahoe	(916)	20,681	12,921
95350	South Modesto(u)	(209)	12,492	7,889
95965	South Oroville(u)	(916)	7,246	4,111
91030	South Pasadena	(818)	22,681	22,979
94080	South San Francisco	(415)	49,393	46,646
91770	South San Gabriel(u)	(213)	5,421	5,051
91744	South San Jose Hills(u)	(213)	16,049	12,386
90605	South Whittier(u)	(213)	43,815	46,641
95991	South Yuba(u)	(916)	7,530	5,352
*92077	Spring Valley(u)	(619)	40,191	29,742
94305	Stanford(u)	(415)	11,045	8,691
90680	Stanton	(714)	21,144	18,186
*95204	Stockton	(209)	148,283	109,963
94585	Suisun City	(707)	11,087	2,917
92381	Sun City(u)	(714)	8,460	5,519
92388	Sunnymead(u)	(714)	11,554	6,708
*94086	Sunnyvale	(408)	106,618	95,976
96130	Susanville	(916)	6,520	6,608

ZIP code	Place		1980	1970
93268	Taft	(805)	5,316	4,285
94806	Tara Hills-Montalvin Manor(u)	(415)	9,471	....
94941	Tamalpais-Homestead Valley(u)	(415)	8,511	....
91780	Temple City	(818)	28,972	31,034
*91360	Thousand Oaks	(805)	77,797	35,873
94920	Tiburon	(415)	6,685	6,209
*90510	Torrance	(213)	131,497	134,968
95396	Tracy	(209)	18,428	14,724
93274	Tulare	(209)	22,530	16,235
95380	Turlock	(209)	26,291	13,992
92680	Tustin	(714)	32,248	22,313
92705	Tustin-Foothills(u)	(714)	26,174	26,699
92277	Twentynine Palms	(619)	7,465	5,667
92278	Twentynine Palms Base(u)	(619)	7,079	5,647
95482	Ukiah	(707)	12,035	10,095
94587	Union City	(415)	39,406	14,724
91786	Upland	(714)	47,647	32,551
95688	Vacaville	(707)	43,367	21,690
91355	Valencia(u)	(805)	12,163	4,243
91744	Valinda(u)	(818)	18,700	18,837
94590	Vallejo	(707)	80,188	71,710
92343	Valle Vista(u)	(714)	5,474	....
93437	Vandenberg AFB(u)	(805)	8,136	13,193
93436	Vandenberg Village(u)	(805)	5,839	....
*93001	Ventura	(805)	73,774	57,964
92392	Victorville	(619)	14,220	10,845
90043	View Park-Windsor Hills(u)	(213)	12,101	12,268
92667	Villa Park	(714)	7,137	2,723
94553	Vine Hill-Pacheco(u)	(415)	6,129	....
93277	Visalia	(209)	49,729	27,130
92083	Vista	(619)	35,834	24,688
91789	Walnut	(714)	9,978	5,992
*94596	Walnut Creek	(415)	54,033	39,844
94596	Walnut Creek West(u)	(415)	5,893	8,330
90255	Walnut Park(u)	(213)	11,811	8,925
93280	Wasco	(805)	9,613	8,269
95076	Watsonville	(408)	23,662	14,719
90044	West Athens(u)	(213)	8,531	13,311
90502	West Carson(u)	(213)	17,997	15,501
90247	West Compton(u)	(213)	5,907	5,748
*91793	West Covina	(818)	80,292	68,034
90069	West Hollywood	(213)	35,754	34,622
92683	Westminster	(714)	71,133	60,076
95351	West Modesto(u)	(209)	NA	6,135
90047	Westmont(u)	(213)	27,916	29,310
94565	West Pittsburg(u)	(415)	8,773	5,969
91746	West Puente Valley(u)	(818)	20,445	20,733
95691	West Sacramento(u)	(916)	10,875	12,002
*90606	West Whittier-Los Nietos(u)	(213)	20,962	20,845
90605	Whittier	(213)	68,558	72,863
90222	Willowbrook(u)	(213)	30,845	28,705
93286	Woodlake	(209)	5,375	3,371
95695	Woodland	(916)	30,235	20,677
94062	Woodside	(415)	5,291	4,734
92686	Yorba Linda	(714)	28,254	11,856
96097	Yreka City	(916)	5,916	5,394
95991	Yuba City	(916)	18,736	13,986
92399	Yucaipa(u)	(714)	23,345	19,284
92284	Yucca Valley(u)	(619)	8,294	3,893

Colorado

ZIP code	Place		1980	1970
80840	Air Force Academy	(719)	8,655	....
81101	Alamosa	(719)	6,830	6,985
80401	Applewood(u)	(303)	12,040	8,214
*80001	Arvada	(303)	84,576	49,844
80010	Aurora	(303)	158,588	74,974
*80302	Boulder	(303)	76,685	66,870
80601	Brighton	(303)	12,773	8,309
80020	Broomfield	(303)	20,730	7,261
81212	Canon City	(719)	13,037	9,206
....	Castlewood	(303)	16,413	....
80110	Cherry Hills Village	(303)	5,127	4,605
81220	Cimarron Hills	(303)	6,597	....
81520	Clifton	(303)	5,223	....
*80901	Colorado Springs	(719)	215,105	135,517
80120	Columbine	(303)	23,523	....
80022	Commerce City	(303)	16,234	17,407
81321	Cortez	(303)	7,095	6,032
81625	Craig	(303)	8,133	4,205
*80202	Denver	(303)	492,686	514,678
80022	Derby(u)	(303)	8,578	10,206
81301	Durango	(303)	11,649	10,333
80110	Englewood	(303)	30,021	33,695
80620	Evans	(303)	5,063	2,570
80439	Evergreen	(303)	6,376	2,321
80221	Federal Heights	(303)	7,846	1,502
80913	Fort Carson(u)	(303)	13,219	19,399
*80521	Fort Collins	(303)	64,632	43,337
80701	Fort Morgan	(303)	8,768	7,594
80017	Fountain	(719)	8,324	3,515
80401	Golden	(303)	12,237	9,817
81501	Grand Junction	(303)	27,956	20,170
80631	Greeley	(303)	53,006	38,902
80110	Greenwood Village	(303)	5,729	3,095
80501	Gunbarrel	(303)	5,172	....
81230	Gunnison	(303)	5,785	4,613

ZIP code	Place		1980	1970
.....	Ken Caryl	(303)	10,661	.....
80026	Lafayette	(303)	8,985	3,498
81050	La Junta	(719)	8,338	8,205
80215	Lakewood	(303)	113,808	92,743
81052	Lamar	(719)	7,713	7,797
80120	Littleton	(303)	28,631	26,466
80120	Littleton Southeast(u)	(303)	33,029	22,899
80501	Longmont	(303)	42,942	23,209
80027	Louisville	(303)	5,593	2,409
80537	Loveland	(303)	30,215	16,220
81401	Montrose	(303)	8,722	6,496
80233	Northglenn	(303)	29,847	27,785
*81003	Pueblo	(719)	101,686	97,774
80911	Security-Widefield(u)	(719)	18,768	15,297
80110	Sheridan	(719)	5,377	4,787
80221	Sherrelwood(u)	(303)	17,629	18,868
80122	Southglenn	(303)	37,787	.....
80477	Steamboat Springs	(303)	5,098	2,340
80751	Sterling	(303)	11,385	10,636
80906	Stratmoor	(719)	5,519	.....
80229	Thornton	(303)	40,343	13,326
81082	Trinidad	(719)	9,663	9,901
80229	Welby(u)	(303)	9,668	6,875
80030	Westminster	(303)	50,211	19,512
80221	Westminster East(u)	(303)	6,002	7,576
80033	Wheat Ridge	(303)	30,293	29,778

Connecticut (203)

See Note on Page 564

ZIP code	Place		1980	1970
06401	Ansonia		19,039	21,160
06001	Avon		11,201	8,352
06037	Berlin		15,121	14,149
06801	Bethel		16,004	10,945
06002	Bloomfield		18,608	18,301
06405	Branford		23,363	20,444
*05602	Bridgeport		142,546	156,542
06010	Bristol		57,370	55,487
06804	Brookfield		12,872	9,688
06013	Burlington		5,660	4,070
06234	Brooklyn		5,691	4,965
06019	Canton		7,635	6,868
06410	Cheshire		21,788	19,051
06413	Clinton		11,195	10,267
06415	Colchester		7,761	6,603
06340	Conning Towers-Nautilus Park(u)		9,665	9,791
06238	Coventry		8,895	8,140
06416	Cromwell		10,265	7,400
06810	Danbury		60,470	50,781
06820	Darien		18,892	20,336
06418	Derby		12,346	12,599
06422	Durham		5,143	4,489
06423	East Haddam		5,621	4,676
06424	East Hampton		8,572	7,078
06108	East Hartford		52,563	57,583
06512	East Haven		25,028	25,120
06333	East Lyme		13,870	11,399
06425	Easton		5,962	4,885
06016	East Windsor		8,925	8,513
06029	Ellington		9,711	7,707
06082	Enfield		42,695	46,189
06426	Essex		5,078	4,911
06430	Fairfield		54,849	56,487
06032	Farmington		16,407	14,390
06033	Glastonbury		24,327	20,651
06035	Granby		7,956	6,150
06830	Greenwich		59,578	59,755
06351	Griswold		8,967	7,763
06340	Groton		41,062	38,244
06340	Groton Borough		10,086	8,933
06437	Guilford		17,375	12,033
06438	Haddam		6,383	4,934
06514	Hamden		51,071	49,357
*06101	Hartford		136,392	158,017
06082	Hazardville(u)		5,436	.....
06248	Hebron		5,453	3,815
06037	Kensington(u)		7,502	.....
06239	Killingly		14,519	13,573
06339	Ledyard		13,735	14,837
06759	Litchfield		7,605	7,399
06443	Madison		14,031	9,768
06040	Manchester		49,761	47,994
06250	Mansfield		20,634	19,994
06450	Meriden		57,118	55,959
06762	Middlebury		5,995	5,542
06457	Middletown		39,040	36,924
06460	Milford		50,898	50,858
06468	Monroe		14,010	12,047
06353	Montville		16,455	15,662
06770	Naugatuck		26,456	23,034
*06050	New Britain		73,840	83,441
06840	New Canaan		17,931	17,451
06810	New Fairfield		11,260	6,991
*06510	New Haven		126,089	137,707
06111	Newington		28,841	26,037
06320	New London		28,842	31,630
06776	New Milford		19,420	14,601

ZIP code	Place		1980	1970
06470	Newtown		19,107	16,942
06471	North Branford		11,554	10,778
06473	North Haven		22,080	22,194
06856	Norwalk		77,767	79,288
06360	Norwich		38,074	41,739
06779	Oakville(u)		8,737	.....
06371	Old Lyme		6,159	4,964
06475	Old Saybrook		9,287	8,468
06477	Orange		13,237	13,524
06483	Oxford		6,634	4,480
02891	Pawcatuck(u)		5,216	5,255
06374	Plainfield		12,774	11,957
06062	Plainville		16,401	16,733
06782	Plymouth		10,732	10,321
06480	Portland		8,383	8,812
06712	Prospect		6,807	6,543
06260	Putnam		6,855	6,918
.....	Putnam		8,580	8,598
06875	Redding		7,272	5,590
06877	Ridgefield Center(u)		6,066	5,878
.....	Ridgefield		20,120	18,188
06067	Rocky Hill		14,559	11,103
06483	Seymour		13,434	12,776
06484	Shelton		31,314	27,165
06082	Sherwood Manor(u)		6,303	.....
06070	Simsbury		21,161	17,475
06071	Somers		8,473	6,893
06488	Southbury		14,156	7,852
06489	Southington		36,879	30,946
06074	South Windsor		17,198	15,553
06082	Southwood Acres(u)		9,779	.....
06075	Stafford		9,268	8,680
*06904	Stamford		102,466	108,798
06378	Stonington		16,220	15,940
06268	Storrs(u)		11,394	10,691
06430	Stratfield-Brooklawn(u)		8,890	.....
06497	Stratford		50,541	49,775
06078	Suffield		9,294	8,634
06786	Terryville(u)		5,234	.....
06787	Thomaston		6,272	6,233
06277	Thompson		8,141	7,580
06084	Tolland		9,694	7,857
06790	Torrington		30,987	31,952
06611	Trumbull		32,989	31,394
06066	Vernon		27,974	27,237
06492	Wallingford		37,274	35,714
*06701	Waterbury		103,266	108,033
06385	Waterford		17,843	17,227
06795	Watertown		19,489	18,610
06498	Westbrook		5,216	3,820
06107	West Hartford		61,301	68,031
06516	West Haven		53,184	52,851
06880	Weston		8,284	7,417
06880	Westport		25,290	27,318
06109	Wethersfield		26,013	26,662
06226	Willimantic		14,652	14,402
06897	Wilton		15,351	13,572
06094	Winchester		10,841	11,106
06280	Windham		21,062	19,626
06095	Windsor		25,204	22,502
06096	Windsor Locks		12,190	15,080
06098	Winsted		8,092	8,954
06716	Wolcott		13,008	12,495
06525	Woodbridge		7,761	7,673
06798	Woodbury		6,942	5,869
06281	Woodstock		5,117	4,311

Delaware (302)

ZIP code	Place		1980	1970
19713	Brookside(u)		15,255	7,856
19703	Claymont(u)		10,022	6,584
19901	Dover		23,507	17,488
19802	Edgemoor(u)		7,397	.....
19805	Elsmere		6,493	8,415
19963	Milford		5,366	5,314
*19711	Newark		25,247	21,298
19973	Seaford		5,256	5,537
19804	Stanton(u)		5,495	.....
19808	Talleyville(u)		6,880	.....
*19899	Wilmington		70,195	80,386
19720	Wilmington Manor —Chelsea—Leedom		9,233	10,134

District of Columbia (202)

ZIP code	Place		1980	1970
*20013	Washington		638,432	756,66i

Florida

ZIP code	Place		1980	1970
*32701	Altamonte Springs	(305)	21,105	4,391
32703	Apopka	(407)	6,019	4,045
33821	Arcadia	(813)	6,002	5,658
32233	Atlantic Beach	(904)	7,847	6,132
33823	Auburndale	(813)	6,501	5,396
.....	Aventura(u)	(305)	10,162	.....
33825	Avon Park	(813)	8,026	6,712
32807	Azalea Park(u)	(305)	8,304	7,367
33830	Bartow	(813)	14,780	12,891
.....	Bay Crest(u)	(813)	5,927	.....

ZIP code	Place		1980	1970
.....	Bayonet Point(u)	(813)	16,455	....
33504	Bay Pines(u)	(813)	5,757	....
33505	Bayshore Gardens(u).	(813)	14,945	9,255
33589	Beacon Square(u)	(813)	6,513	2,927
32073	Bellair-Meadowbrook Terrace(u).	(904)	12,144	....
33430	Belle Glade	(407)	16,535	15,949
32506	Belieview(u)	(904)	15,439	916
32661	Beverly Hills(u)	(904)	5,024	....
*33448	Boca Raton	(407)	49,447	28,506
33959	Bonita Springs(u)	(813)	5,435	1,932
*33435	Boynton Beach	(407)	35,624	18,115
*34206	Bradenton	(813)	30,228	21,040
33511	Brandon(u).	(813)	41,826	12,749
32525	Brent(u)	(904)	21,872	....
33314	Broadview Park(u)	(305)	6,022	6,049
33313	Broadview-Pompano Park(u)	(305)	5,256	....
*34601	Brooksville	(904)	5,582	4,060
33311	Browardale(u)	(305)	7,571	17,444
33142	Browns Village(u)	(305)	NA	23,442
33142	Brownsville(u)	(305)	18,058	....
33054	Bunche Park(u)	(305)	NA	5,773
32401	Callaway	(904)	7,154	3,240
32920	Cape Canaveral.	(407)	5,733	4,258
33904	Cape Coral	(813)	32,103	11,470
33055	Carol City(u)	(305)	47,349	27,361
32707	Casselberry	(305)	15,037	9,438
33401	Century Village(u).	(305)	10,619	2,679
32324	Chattahoochee	(904)	5,332	7,944
*34615	Clearwater City	(813)	85,170	52,074
32711	Clermont	(904)	5,461	3,661
33440	Clewiston	(813)	5,219	3,896
32922	Cocoa	(407)	16,096	16,110
32931	Cocoa Beach	(407)	10,926	9,952
32922	Cocoa West(u)	(305)	6,432	5,779
33066	Coconut Creek	(305)	6,288	1,359
33060	Collier City(u)	(305)	7135	....
33064	Collier Manor-Cresthaven(u)	(305)	7,045	7,202
33801	Combee Settlement(u).	(813)	5,400	4,963
32809	Conway(u)	(305)	23,940	8,642
33314	Cooper City	(305)	10,140	2,535
33134	Coral Gables	(305)	43,241	42,494
33065	Coral Springs	(305)	37,349	1,489
.....	Coral Terrace(u)	(305)	22,702	....
32536	Crestview	(904)	7,617	7,952
33803	Crystal Lake(u)	(813)	6,827	6,227
33157	Cutler(u)	(305)	15,593	....
33157	Cutler Ridge(u)	(305)	20,886	17,441
33880	Cypress Gardens(u)	(813)	8,043	3,757
.....	Cypress Lake(u)	(813)	8,721	....
33004	Dania	(305)	11,796	9,013
33314	Davie.	(305)	20,515	5,859
*32015	Daytona Beach	(904)	54,176	45,327
33441	Deerfield Beach.	(305)	39,193	16,662
32433	DeFuniak Springs	(904)	5,563	4,966
32720	De Land	(904)	15,354	11,641
*33444	Delray Beach	(407)	34,329	19,915
32725	Del Rio(u)	(813)	7,409	....
32725	Deltona(u)	(407)	15,710	4,868
*34698	Dunedin	(813)	30,203	17,639
33610	East Lake-Orient Park (u)	(813)	5,612	5,697
33940	East Naples(u)	(813)	12,127	6,152
32032	Edgewater	(904)	6,726	3,348
32542	Eglin AFB(u)	(904)	7,574	7,769
33614	Egypt Lake(u)	(813)	11,932	7,556
34680	Elfers(u)	(813)	11,396	....
*34223	Englewood(u)	(813)	10,242	5,108
32504	Ensley(u).	(904)	14,422	....
32726	Eustis.	(904)	9,453	6,722
32804	Fairview Shores(u)	(305)	10,174	....
32034	Fernandina Beach	(904)	7,224	6,955
32730	Fern Park(u).	(305)	8,890	....
32504	Ferry Pass(u)	(904)	16,910	....
33030	Florida City	(305)	6,174	5,133
32751	Forest City(u)	(305)	6,819	....
*33319	Fort Lauderdale.	(305)	153,256	139,590
33841	Fort Meade	(813)	5,546	4,374
*33901	Fort Myers.	(813)	36,638	27,351
33931	Fort Myers Beach(u)	(813)	5,753	4,305
*34950	Fort Pierce.	(407)	33,802	29,721
33452	Fort Pierce NW(u)	(407)	5,929	3,269
32548	Fort Walton Beach	(904)	20,829	19,994
*32601	Gainesville.	(904)	81,371	64,510
33801	Gibsonia(u)	(813)	5,011	....
32960	Gifford(u)	(305)	6,240	5,772
.....	Gladeview(u)	(305)	18,919	....
33143	Glenvar Heights(u)	(305)	13,216	....
33055	Golden Glades(u).	(305)	23,154	....
32733	Goldenrod(u)	(305)	13,681	....
32560	Gonzalez(u)	(904)	6,084	....
32503	Goulding(u)	(904)	5,352	....
33170	Goulds(u)	(305)	7,078	6,690
33463	Greenacres City.	(407)	8,780	1,731
32561	Gulf Breeze	(904)	5,478	4,190
33581	Gulf Gate Estates(u)	(813)	9,248	5,874
33707	Gulfport	(813)	11,180	9,976
33844	Haines City	(813)	10,799	8,956
33009	Hallandale.	(305)	36,517	23,849
*33010	Hialeah.	(305)	145,254	102,452

ZIP code	Place		1980	1970
33455	Hobe Sound(u)	(407)	6,822	2,029
32805	Holden Heights(u).	(305)	13,840	6,206
34690	Holiday(u)	(813)	18,392	....
32017	Holly Hill	(904)	9,953	8,191
*33022	Hollywood	(305)	117,188	106,873
33030	Homestead	(305)	20,668	13,674
33030	Homestead Base(u)	(305)	7,594	8,257
34667	Hudson(u)	(813)	5,799	2,278
33934	Immokalee(u)	(813)	11,038	3,764
32937	Indian Harbour Beach	(407)	5,967	5,371
33880	Inwood(u)	(813)	6,668	....
33162	Ives Estates(u)	(305)	12,623	....
*32201	Jacksonville.	(904)	540,920	504,265
32250	Jacksonville Beach.	(904)	15,462	12,779
33568	Jasmine Estates(u)	(813)	11,995	2,967
*34957	Jensen Beach(u)	(407)	6,639	....
33458	Jupiter	(407)	9,868	3,136
.....	Kendale Lakes(u)	(305)	32,769	....
33156	Kendall(u)	(305)	73,758	35,497
.....	Kendall Green(u)	(305)	6,768	....
33149	Key Biscayne(u).	(305)	6,313	....
33037	Key Largo(u)	(305)	7,447	2,866
33040	Key West	(305)	24,292	29,312
32303	Killearn(u)	(904)	8,700	....
.....	Kings Point(u)	(305)	8,724	....
32741	Kissimmee	(305)	15,487	7,119
33618	Lake Carroll(u)	(305)	13,012	5,577
32055	Lake City.	(904)	9,257	10,575
*33802	Lakeland.	(813)	47,406	42,803
33801	Lakeland Highlands(u)	(813)	10,426	....
.....	Lake Lorraine(u)	(904)	5,427	....
33054	Lake Lucerne(u)	(305)	9,762	....
33612	Lake Magdalene(u)	(813)	13,331	9,266
33403	Lake Park	(407)	6,909	6,993
.....	Lakeside(u)	(904)	10,534	....
33853	Lake Wales	(813)	8,466	8,240
33460	Lake Worth	(407)	27,048	23,714
33460	Lantana	(407)	8,048	7,126
*34640	Largo.	(813)	57,958	24,230
33313	Lauderdale Lakes.	(305)	25,426	10,577
33313	Lauderhill	(305)	37,271	8,465
34272	Laurel(u)	(813)	6,368	....
33717	Lealman(u)	(813)	19,873	....
32748	Leesburg.	(904)	13,191	11,869
*33936	Lehigh Acres(u)	(813)	9,604	4,394
33033	Leisure City(u)	(305)	17,905	....
33614	Leto(u)	(904)	9,003	8,458
33064	Lighthouse Point	(305)	11,488	9,071
.....	Lindgren Acres(u)	(305)	11,986	....
32060	Live Oak	(904)	6,732	6,830
32810	Lockhart(u)	(305)	10,571	5,809
34228	Longboat Key	(813)	8,221	2,850
*32750	Longwood	(407)	10,029	3,203
33549	Lutz(u)	(813)	5,555	....
32444	Lynn Haven	(904)	6,239	4,044
32751	Maitland	(305)	8,763	7,157
33550	Mango-Seffner(u)	(813)	6,493	....
33050	Marathon(u)	(305)	7,568	4,397
33063	Margate	(305)	35,900	8,867
32446	Marianna	(904)	7,074	7,282
*32901	Melbourne	(407)	46,536	40,236
33314	Melrose Park(u)	(904)	5,725	6,111
33561	Memphis(u)	(813)	5,501	3,207
32952	Merritt Island(u)	(407)	30,708	29,233
*33152	Miami.	(305)	346,681	334,859
33139	Miami Beach.	(305)	96,298	87,072
33023	Miami Gardens —Utopia-Carver(u)	(305)	9,025	....
33014	Miami Lakes(u)	(305)	9,809	....
33153	Miami Shores.	(305)	9,244	9,425
33166	Miami Springs.	(305)	12,350	13,279
32570	Milton.	(904)	7,206	5,360
32754	Mims(u)	(407)	7,583	8,309
33023	Miramar	(305)	32,813	23,997
32757	Mount Dora	(904)	5,883	4,646
32506	Myrtle Grove(u)	(904)	14,238	16,186
*33962	Naples	(813)	17,581	12,042
33940	Naples Park(u)	(813)	5,438	1,522
33032	Naranja-Princeton(u)	(305)	10,381	....
32233	Neptune Beach	(904)	5,248	4,281
*34652	New Port Richey	(813)	11,196	6,098
33552	New Port Richey East(u).	(813)	6,627	2,758
32069	New Smyrna Beach	(904)	13,557	10,580
32578	Niceville	(904)	8,543	4,155
33169	Norland(u)	(305)	19,471	....
33308	North Andrews Gardens(u)	(305)	8,967	7,082
33903	North Fort Myers(u)	(813)	22,808	8,798
33068	North Lauderdale.	(305)	18,653	1,213
33161	North Miami	(305)	42,566	34,767
33160	North Miami Beach	(305)	36,481	30,544
33940	North Naples(u)	(813)	7,950	3,201
33408	North Palm Beach	(407)	11,344	9,035
33596	North Port	(813)	6,205	2,244
33169	Norwood(u)	(305)	NA	14,973
33308	Oakland Park	(305)	22,944	16,261
33860	Oak Ridge(u)	(813)	15,477	....
32670	Ocala.	(904)	37,170	22,583
32548	Ocean City(u)	(904)	5,582	5,267
32761	Ocoee	(407)	7,803	3,937
33163	Ojus(u)	(305)	17,344	....
33165	Olympia Heights(u)	(305)	33,112	....

ZIP code	Place		1980	1970
33558	Oneco(u)	(813)	6,417	3,246
33054	Opa-Locka	(305)	14,460	11,902
33054	Opa-Locka North(u)	(305)	5,721	....
32073	Orange Park	(904)	8,766	5,019
32820	Orlando	(407)	128,394	99,006
32811	Orlovista(u)	(305)	6,474	....
32074	Ormond Beach	(904)	21,438	14,063
32074	Ormond By-The-Sea(u)	(904)	7,665	6,002
32570	Pace(u)	(904)	5,006	1,776
33476	Pahokee	(407)	6,346	5,663
32077	Palatka	(904)	10,175	9,444
33505	Palma Sola(u)	(813)	5,297	1,745
32905	Palm Bay	(407)	18,560	7,176
33480	Palm Beach	(407)	9,729	9,086
33403	Palm Beach Gardens	(407)	14,407	6,102
34221	Palmetto	(813)	8,637	7,422
33157	Palmetto Estates(u)	(305)	11,116	....
*34683	Palm Harbor(u)	(813)	5,215	....
33619	Palm River-Clair Mel(u)	(813)	14,447	8,536
33460	Palm Springs	(407)	8,166	4,340
33012	Palm Springs North(u)	(407)	5,838	....
32401	Panama City	(904)	33,346	32,096
33866	Pembroke Park	(305)	5,326	2,949
33023	Pembroke Pines	(305)	35,776	15,496
*32502	Pensacola	(904)	57,619	59,507
33157	Perrine(u)	(305)	16,129	10,257
32347	Perry	(904)	8,254	7,701
32809	Pine Castle(u)	(305)	9,992	....
32808	Pine Hills(u)	(305)	35,771	13,882
*34665	Pinellas Park	(813)	32,811	22,287
33168	Pinewood(u)	(305)	16,216	....
33566	Plant City	(813)	17,064	15,451
33314	Plantation	(813)	48,653	23,523
*33067	Pompano Beach	(305)	52,618	38,587
33064	Pompano Beach Highlands(u)	(305)	16,154	5,014
33950	Port Charlotte(u)	(813)	25,730	10,769
32019	Port Orange	(904)	18,756	3,781
34952	Port St. Lucie	(407)	14,690	330
*33950	Punta Gorda	(813)	6,797	3,879
32351	Quincy	(904)	8,591	8,334
33156	Richmond Heights(u)	(305)	8,577	6,663
33312	Riverland (u)	(305)	5,919	5,512
33404	Riviera Beach	(407)	26,596	21,401
33314	Rock Island(u)	(813)	5,022	....
32955	Rockledge	(407)	11,877	10,523
33570	Ruskin(u)	(813)	5,117	2,414
34695	Safety Harbor	(813)	6,461	3,103
32084	St. Augustine	(904)	11,985	12,352
32769	St. Cloud	(305)	7,840	5,041
*33702	St. Petersburg	(813)	238,647	216,159
33706	St. Petersburg Beach	(813)	9,354	8,024
33508	Samoset(u)	(813)	5,747	4,070
33432	Sandalfoot Cove(u)	(305)	5,299	....
32771	Sanford	(407)	23,176	17,393
*34236	Sarasota	(813)	48,868	40,237
33577	Sarasota Springs(u)	(813)	13,860	4,405
32937	Satellite Beach	(407)	9,163	6,558
	Scott Lake(u)	(305)	14,154	....
*33870	Sebring	(813)	8,736	7,223
33578	Siesta Key(u)	(813)	7,010	4,460
32809	Sky Lake(u)	(305)	6,602	....
32703	South Apopka(u)	(305)	5,687	2,293
33505	South Bradenton(u)	(813)	14,297	....
32021	South Daytona	(904)	9,608	4,979
33579	Southgate(u)	(813)	7,322	6,885
33143	South Miami	(305)	10,895	11,780
33157	South Miami Heights(u)	(305)	23,559	10,395
32937	South Patrick Shores(u)	(305)	9,816	10,313
33595	South Venice(u)	(813)	8,075	4,680
32401	Springfield	(904)	7,220	5,949
32091	Starke	(904)	5,306	4,848
*34994	Stuart	(407)	9,467	4,820
33586	Sun City Center(u)	(813)	5,605	2,143
33160	Sunny Isles(u)	(305)	12,564	....
33304	Sunrise	(305)	39,681	7,403
33139	Sunset(u)	(813)	13,531	....
33144	Sweetwater	(305)	8,067	3,357
33614	Sweetwater Creek(u)	(813)	NA	19,453
*32303	Tallahassee	(904)	81,548	72,624
33313	Tamarac	(305)	29,142	5,193
33144	Tamiami(u)	(305)	17,607	....
*33625	Tampa	(813)	271,577	277,714
	Tanglewood(u)	(813)	8,229	....
*34689	Tarpon Springs	(813)	13,251	7,118
33617	Temple Terrace	(813)	11,097	7,347
33905	Tice(u)	(813)	6,645	7,254
32780	Titusville	(407)	31,910	30,515
32505	Town 'n' Country(u)	(904)	37,834	....
33707	Treasure Island	(813)	6,316	6,120
32807	Union Park(u)	(305)	19,175	2,595
33620	University (Hillsborough)(u)	(813)	24,514	10,039
32580	Valparaiso	(904)	6,142	6,504
*34285	Venice	(813)	12,153	6,648
33595	Venice Gardens(u)	(813)	6,568	....
32960	Vero Beach	(407)	16,176	11,908
32960	Vero Beach South(u)	(407)	12,636	7,330
33901	Villas(u)	(813)	8,724	....
32507	Warrington(u)	(904)	15,792	15,848

ZIP code	Place		1980	1970
33314	Washington Park(u)	(305)	7,240	....
32703	Wekiva Springs(u)	(305)	13,386	....
33505	West Bradenton(u)	(813)	NA	6,162
33155	Westchester(u)	(305)	29,272	....
32446	West End(u)	(904)	NA	5,289
32138	West Little River(u)	(305)	32,492	....
32901	West Melbourne	(407)	5,078	3,050
33144	West Miami	(305)	6,076	5,494
*33404	West Palm Beach	(407)	62,530	57,375
32505	West Pensacola(u)	(904)	24,371	20,924
33168	Westview(u)	(305)	9,102	....
33880	West Winter Haven(u)	(813)	NA	7,716
33165	Westwood Lakes(u)	(305)	11,478	12,811
33305	Wilton Manors	(305)	12,742	10,948
33803	Winston(u)	(813)	9,315	4,505
32787	Winter Garden	(407)	6,789	5,153
33880	Winter Haven	(813)	21,119	16,136
32789	Winter Park	(407)	22,314	21,895
32708	Winter Springs	(407)	10,475	1,161
32548	Wright(u)	(904)	13,011	....
33599	Zephyrhills	(813)	5,742	3,369

Georgia

ZIP code	Place		1980	1970
31620	Adel	(912)	5,592	4,972
*31701	Albany	(912)	74,425	72,623
31709	Americus	(912)	16,120	16,091
*30601	Athens	(404)	42,549	44,342
*30304	Atlanta	(404)	425,022	495,039
*30901	Augusta	(404)	47,532	59,864
31717	Bainbridge	(912)	10,553	10,887
30032	Belvedere Park(u)	(404)	17,766	....
31723	Blakely	(912)	5,880	5,267
31520	Brunswick	(912)	17,605	19,585
30518	Buford	(404)	6,578	4,640
31728	Cairo	(912)	8,777	8,061
30701	Calhoun	(404)	5,335	4,748
31730	Camilla	(912)	5,414	4,987
30032	Candler-McAfee(u)	(404)	27,306	....
30117	Carrollton	(404)	14,078	13,520
30120	Cartersville	(404)	9,247	10,138
30125	Cedartown	(404)	8,619	9,253
30341	Chamblee	(404)	7,137	9,127
31014	Cochran	(912)	5,121	5,161
30337	College Park	(404)	24,632	18,203
*31902	Columbus	(404)	169,441	155,028
30027	Conley(u)	(404)	6,033	....
30207	Conyers	(404)	6,567	4,809
31015	Cordele	(912)	11,184	10,733
30209	Covington	(404)	10,586	10,267
30720	Dalton	(404)	20,581	18,872
31742	Dawson	(912)	5,699	5,383
*30030	Decatur	(404)	18,404	21,943
31520	Dock Junction(u)	(912)	6,189	6,009
30340	Doraville	(404)	7,414	9,157
31533	Douglas	(912)	10,980	10,195
30134	Douglasville	(404)	7,641	5,472
30333	Druid Hills(u)	(404)	12,700	....
31021	Dublin	(912)	16,083	15,143
30338	Dunwoody(u)	(404)	17,768	....
31023	Eastman	(912)	5,330	5,416
30344	East Point	(404)	37,486	39,315
30635	Elberton	(404)	5,686	6,438
30060	Fair Oaks(u)	(404)	8,458	....
30535	Fairview(u)	(404)	6,558	....
31750	Fitzgerald	(912)	10,187	8,187
30050	Forest Park	(404)	18,782	19,994
31905	Fort Benning South(u)	(404)	15,074	27,495
30905	Fort Gordon(u)	(404)	14,069	15,589
30741	Fort Oglethorpe	(404)	5,443	3,869
31313	Fort Stewart(u)	(912)	15,031	4,467
31030	Fort Valley	(912)	9,000	9,251
30501	Gainesville	(404)	15,280	15,459
31408	Garden City	(912)	6,895	5,790
30316	Gresham Park(u)	(404)	6,232	....
30223	Griffin	(404)	20,728	22,734
30354	Hapeville	(404)	6,166	9,567
31313	Hinesville	(912)	11,309	4,115
31545	Jesup	(912)	9,418	9,091
30144	Kennesaw	(404)	5,095	3,548
30728	La Fayette	(404)	6,517	6,044
30240	La Grange	(404)	24,204	23,301
30245	Lawrenceville	(404)	8,928	5,207
30057	Lithia Springs(u)	(404)	9,145	....
30059	Mableton(u)	(404)	25,111	....
*31201	Macon	(912)	116,860	122,423
30060	Marietta	(404)	30,821	27,216
30907	Martinez(u)	(404)	16,472	....
31034	Midway-Hardwick(u)	(912)	8,977	14,047
31061	Milledgeville	(404)	12,176	11,601
30655	Monroe	(404)	8,854	8,071
31768	Moultrie	(912)	15,105	14,400
30075	Mountain Park(u)	(404)	9,425	268
30263	Newnan	(404)	11,449	11,205
30319	North Atlanta(u)	(404)	30,521	....
30033	North Decatur(u)	(404)	11,830	....
30033	North Druid Hills(u)	(404)	12,438	....
30032	Panthersville(u)	(404)	11,366	....
30269	Peachtree City	(404)	6,429	793
31069	Perry	(912)	9,453	7,771
31643	Quitman	(912)	5,188	4,818

ZIP code	Place		1980	1970
*30274	Riverdale	(404)	7,121	2,521
30161	Rome	(404)	28,915	30,759
30075	Roswell	(404)	23,337	5,430
31522	St. Simons(u)	(912)	6,566	5,346
31082	Sandersville	(912)	6,137	5,546
30328	Sandy Springs(u)	(404)	46,877	
*31401	Savannah	(912)	141,654	118,349
30079	Scottdale(u)	(404)	8,770	
30080	Smyrna	(404)	20,312	19,157
30278	Snellville	(404)	8,514	1,990
30901	South Augusta(u)	(404)	51,072	
30458	Statesboro	(912)	14,866	14,616
30401	Swainsboro	(912)	7,602	7,325
31791	Sylvester	(912)	5,860	4,226
30286	Thomaston	(404)	9,682	10,024
31792	Thomasville	(912)	18,463	18,155
30824	Thomson	(404)	7,001	6,503
31794	Tifton	(912)	13,749	12,179
30577	Toccoa	(404)	8,869	6,971
30084	Tucker(u)	(404)	25,399	
31601	Valdosta	(912)	37,596	32,303
30474	Vidalia	(912)	10,393	9,507
31093	Warner Robins	(912)	39,893	33,491
31501	Waycross	(912)	19,371	18,996
30830	Waynesboro	(404)	5,760	5,530
30901	West Augusta(u)	(404)	24,242	
31410	Wilmington Island(u)	(912)	7,546	3,284
30680	Winder	(404)	6,705	6,605

Hawaii (808)

See Note on Page 564

96706	Ewa		190,037	132,299
96720	Hilo		37,017	28,412
*96815	Honolulu		365,048	324,871
96732	Kahului		13,026	8,287
96749	Keaau-Mountain View		7,055	3,802
96752	Kekaha-Waimea		5,256	4,159
96753	Kihei		6,035	1,636
......	Koolauloa		14,195	10,562
......	Koolaupoko		109,373	92,219
96790	Kula		5,077	2,124
96761	Lahaina		10,284	5,524
96768	Makawao-Paia		10,361	5,788
......	North Kona		13,748	4,832
96781	Papaikou-Wailea		5,261	5,503
......	South Kona		5,914	4,004
96786	Wahiawa		41,562	37,329
96791	Waialua		9,849	9,171
96792	Waianae		32,810	24,077
96703	Wailua-Anahola		6,030	3,599
96793	Wailuku		10,674	9,084

Idaho (208)

83221	Blackfoot		10,065	8,716
*83708	Boise City		102,249	74,990
83318	Burley		8,761	8,279
83605	Caldwell		17,699	14,219
83201	Chubbuck		7,052	2,924
83814	Coeur D'Alene		19,913	16,228
83401	Idaho Falls		39,739	35,776
83338	Jerome		6,891	4,183
83501	Lewiston		27,986	26,068
83642	Meridian		6,658	2,616
83843	Moscow		16,513	14,146
83647	Mountain Home		7,540	6,451
83648	Mountain Home AFB(u)		6,403	6,038
83651	Nampa		25,112	20,768
83661	Payette		5,448	4,521
83201	Pocatello		46,340	40,036
83854	Post Falls		5,736	2,371
83440	Rexburg		11,559	8,272
83350	Rupert		5,476	4,563
83301	Twin Falls		26,209	21,914

Illinois

60101	Addison	(312)	29,826	24,482
60102	Algonquin	(312)	5,834	3,515
60658	Alsip	(312)	17,134	11,608
62002	Alton	(618)	34,171	39,700
62906	Anna	(618)	5,408	4,766
*60004	Arlington Heights	(312)	66,116	65,058
*60507	Aurora	(312)	81,293	74,389
60010	Barrington	(312)	9,029	8,581
60103	Bartlett	(312)	13,254	3,501
61607	Bartonville	(309)	6,110	7,221
60510	Batavia	(312)	12,574	9,060
62618	Beardstown	(217)	6,338	6,222
*62220	Belleville	(618)	42,150	41,223
60104	Bellwood	(312)	19,811	22,096
61008	Belvidere	(815)	15,176	14,061
60106	Bensenville	(312)	16,106	12,956
62812	Benton	(618)	7,778	6,833
60162	Berkeley	(312)	5,467	6,152
60402	Berwyn	(312)	46,849	52,502
62010	Bethalto	(618)	8,630	7,074
60108	Bloomingdale	(312)	12,656	2,974
61701	Bloomington	(309)	44,189	39,992
60406	Blue Island	(312)	21,855	22,629
60439	Bolingbrook	(312)	37,261	7,651
60538	Boulder Hill(u)	(312)	9,333	
60914	Bourbonnais	(815)	13,280	5,909
60915	Bradley	(815)	11,015	9,881
60455	Bridgeview	(312)	14,155	12,506
60153	Broadview	(312)	8,618	9,623
60513	Brookfield	(312)	19,395	20,284
60090	Buffalo Grove	(312)	22,230	12,333
60459	Burbank	(312)	28,462	26,726
*62206	Cahokia	(618)	18,904	20,649
62914	Cairo	(618)	5,931	6,277
60409	Calumet City	(312)	39,673	33,107
60643	Calumet Park	(312)	8,788	10,069
61520	Canton	(309)	14,626	14,217
62901	Carbondale	(618)	26,414	22,816
62626	Carlinville	(217)	5,439	5,675
62821	Carmi	(618)	6,107	6,033
60187	Carol Stream	(312)	15,472	4,434
60110	Carpentersville	(312)	23,272	24,059
60013	Cary	(312)	6,640	4,358
62801	Centralia	(618)	15,126	15,966
62206	Centreville	(618)	9,747	11,378
61820	Champaign	(217)	58,267	56,837
61920	Charleston	(217)	19,355	16,421
62629	Chatham	(217)	5,597	2,788
62233	Chester	(618)	8,027	5,310
*60607	Chicago	(312)	3,005,072	3,369,357
60411	Chicago Heights	(312)	37,026	40,900
60415	Chicago Ridge	(312)	13,473	9,187
61523	Chillicothe	(309)	6,176	6,052
60650	Cicero	(312)	61,232	67,058
60514	Clarendon Hills	(312)	6,857	6,750
61727	Clinton	(217)	8,014	7,581
62234	Collinsville	(618)	19,475	18,224
60477	Country Club Hills	(312)	14,676	6,920
60525	Countryside	(312)	6,242	2,864
60435	Crest Hill	(815)	9,252	7,460
60445	Crestwood	(312)	10,712	5,770
60417	Crete	(312)	5,417	4,656
61611	Creve Coeur	(309)	6,851	6,440
60014	Crystal Lake	(815)	18,590	14,541
61832	Danville	(217)	38,985	42,570
60559	Darien	(312)	14,968	7,789
*62521	Decatur	(217)	93,939	90,397
60015	Deerfield	(312)	17,432	18,876
60115	De Kalb	(815)	33,157	32,949
*60016	Des Plaines	(312)	53,568	57,239
61021	Dixon	(815)	15,710	18,147
60419	Dolton	(312)	24,766	25,990
60515	Downers Grove	(312)	42,691	32,544
62832	Du Quoin	(618)	6,594	6,691
62024	East Alton	(618)	7,096	7,309
60411	East Chicago Heights	(312)	5,347	5,000
61244	East Moline	(309)	20,907	20,956
61611	East Peoria	(309)	22,385	18,671
*62201	East St. Louis	(618)	55,200	70,169
62025	Edwardsville	(618)	12,460	11,070
62401	Effingham	(217)	11,270	9,458
62930	Eldorado	(618)	5,198	3,876
60120	Elgin	(312)	63,668	55,691
60007	Elk Grove Village	(312)	28,679	20,346
60126	Elmhurst	(312)	44,251	46,392
60635	Elmwood Park	(312)	24,016	26,160
*60204	Evanston	(312)	73,706	80,113
60642	Evergreen Park	(312)	22,260	25,921
62837	Fairfield	(618)	5,944	5,897
62208	Fairview Heights	(618)	12,414	10,050
62839	Flora	(618)	5,379	5,283
60422	Flossmoor	(312)	8,423	7,846
60130	Forest Park	(312)	15,177	15,472
60020	Fox Lake	(312)	6,831	4,511
60131	Franklin Park	(312)	17,507	20,348
61032	Freeport	(815)	26,406	27,736
60030	Gages Lake-Wildwood(u)	(312)	5,848	5,337
61401	Galesburg	(309)	35,305	36,290
61254	Geneseo	(309)	6,373	5,840
60134	Geneva	(312)	9,881	9,049
62034	Glen Carbon	(618)	5,197	1,897
60022	Glencoe	(312)	9,200	10,542
60137	Glendale Heights	(618)	23,251	11,406
60137	Glen Ellyn	(312)	23,691	21,909
60025	Glenview	(312)	30,842	24,880
60425	Glenwood	(312)	10,538	7,416
62040	Granite City	(618)	36,815	40,685
60030	Grayslake	(312)	5,260	4,907
62246	Greenville	(618)	5,271	4,631
60031	Gurnee	(312)	7,179	2,738
60103	Hanover Park	(312)	28,719	11,735
62946	Harrisburg	(618)	9,322	9,535
60033	Harvard	(815)	5,126	5,177
60426	Harvey	(312)	35,810	34,636
60656	Harwood Heights	(312)	8,228	9,060
60429	Hazel Crest	(312)	13,973	10,329
62948	Herrin	(618)	10,708	9,623
60457	Hickory Hills	(312)	13,778	13,176
62249	Highland	(618)	7,122	5,981

ZIP code	Place		1980	1970
60035	Highland Park	(312)	30,599	32,263
60040	Highwood	(312)	5,455	4,973
60162	Hillside	(312)	8,279	8,888
60521	Hinsdale	(312)	16,726	15,918
60172	Hoffman Estates	(312)	38,258	22,238
60456	Hometown	(312)	5,324	6,729
60430	Homewood	(312)	19,724	18,871
60942	Hoopeston	(217)	6,411	6,461
60143	Itasca	(312)	7,948	4,638
62650	Jacksonville	(217)	20,284	20,553
62052	Jerseyville	(618)	7,506	7,446
*60431	Joliet	(815)	77,956	78,827
60458	Justice	(312)	10,552	9,473
60901	Kankakee	(815)	29,633	30,944
61443	Kewanee	(309)	14,508	15,762
60525	La Grange	(312)	15,693	17,814
60525	La Grange Park	(312)	13,359	15,459
60045	Lake Forest	(312)	15,245	15,642
60102	Lake in the Hills	(312)	5,651	3,240
60047	Lake Zurich	(312)	8,225	4,082
60438	Lansing	(312)	29,039	25,805
61301	La Salle	(815)	10,347	10,736
62439	Lawrenceville	(618)	5,652	5,863
60439	Lemont	(312)	5,640	5,080
60048	Libertyville	(312)	16,520	11,684
62656	Lincoln	(217)	16,327	17,582
60645	Lincolnwood	(312)	11,921	12,929
60046	Lindenhurst	(312)	6,220	3,141
60532	Lisle	(312)	13,638	5,329
62056	Litchfield	(217)	7,204	7,190
60441	Lockport	(815)	9,192	9,861
60148	Lombard	(312)	36,879	34,043
61111	Loves Park	(815)	13,192	12,390
60534	Lyons	(312)	9,925	11,124
61455	Macomb	(309)	19,632	19,643
62060	Madison	(618)	5,301	7,042
62959	Marion	(618)	14,031	11,724
60426	Markham	(312)	15,172	15,987
60443	Matteson	(312)	10,223	4,741
61938	Mattoon	(217)	19,293	19,681
60153	Maywood	(312)	27,998	29,019
*60160	Melrose Park	(312)	20,735	22,716
61342	Mendota	(815)	7,134	6,902
62960	Metropolis	(618)	7,171	6,940
60445	Midlothian	(312)	14,274	14,422
61264	Milan	(309)	6,371	4,873
61265	Moline	(309)	46,407	46,237
61462	Monmouth	(309)	10,706	11,022
60450	Morris	(815)	8,833	8,194
61550	Morton	(309)	14,178	10,811
60053	Morton Grove	(312)	23,747	26,369
62863	Mount Carmel	(618)	8,908	8,096
60056	Mount Prospect	(312)	52,634	34,995
62864	Mount Vernon	(618)	16,995	16,270
60060	Mundelein	(312)	17,053	16,128
62966	Murphysboro	(618)	9,866	10,013
60540	Naperville	(312)	42,601	22,794
60451	New Lenox	(815)	5,792	2,855
60648	Niles	(312)	30,363	31,432
61761	Normal	(309)	35,672	26,396
60656	Norridge	(312)	16,483	17,113
60542	North Aurora	(312)	5,205	4,833
60062	Northbrook	(312)	30,735	25,422
60064	North Chicago	(312)	38,774	47,275
60164	Northlake	(312)	12,166	14,191
61111	North Park(u)	(815)	15,806	15,679
60546	North Riverside	(312)	6,764	8,097
60521	Oak Brook	(312)	6,676	4,164
60452	Oak Forest	(312)	25,040	19,271
*60454	Oak Lawn	(312)	60,590	60,305
*60301	Oak Park	(312)	54,887	62,511
62269	O'Fallon	(618)	12,173	7,268
62450	Olney	(618)	9,026	8,974
60462	Orland Park	(312)	23,045	6,391
61350	Ottawa	(815)	18,166	18,716
60067	Palatine	(312)	32,176	26,050
60463	Palos Heights	(312)	11,096	8,544
60465	Palos Hills	(312)	16,654	6,629
62557	Pana	(217)	6,040	6,326
61944	Paris	(217)	9,885	9,971
60466	Park Forest	(312)	26,222	30,638
60466	Park Forest South	(312)	6,245	1,748
60068	Park Ridge	(312)	38,704	42,614
61554	Pekin	(309)	33,967	31,375
*61601	Peoria	(309)	124,160	126,963
61614	Peoria Heights	(309)	7,453	7,943
61354	Peru	(815)	10,886	11,772
61764	Pontiac	(815)	11,227	10,595
61356	Princeton	(815)	7,342	6,959
60070	Prospect Heights	(312)	11,823	13,333
62301	Quincy	(217)	42,352	45,288
61866	Rantoul	(217)	20,161	25,562
60471	Richton Park	(312)	9,403	2,558
60627	Riverdale	(312)	13,233	15,806
60305	River Forest	(312)	12,392	13,402
60171	River Grove	(312)	10,368	11,465
60546	Riverside	(312)	9,236	10,357
60472	Robbins	(312)	8,119	9,641
62454	Robinson	(618)	7,285	7,178
61068	Rochelle	(815)	8,982	8,594
61071	Rock Falls	(815)	10,624	10,287
*61125	Rockford	(815)	139,712	147,370
61201	Rock Island	(309)	46,821	50,166
60008	Rolling Meadows	(312)	20,167	19,178
60441	Romeoville	(815)	15,519	12,888
60172	Roselle	(312)	17,034	6,207
62024	Rosewood Heights(u)	(618)	5,085	3,391
60073	Round Lake Beach	(312)	12,921	5,717
60174	St. Charles	(312)	17,492	12,945
62881	Salem	(618)	7,813	6,187
60548	Sandwich	(815)	5,356	5,056
60411	Sauk Village	(312)	10,906	7,479
60172	Schaumburg	(312)	53,355	18,531
60176	Schiller Park	(312)	11,458	12,712
62225	Scott AFB(u)	(618)	6,648	7,871
62565	Shelbyville	(217)	5,259	4,887
61282	Silvis	(309)	7,130	5,907
60076	Skokie	(312)	60,278	68,322
60177	South Elgin	(312)	5,970	4,289
60473	South Holland	(312)	24,977	23,931
*62703	Springfield	(217)	100,054	91,753
61362	Spring Valley	(815)	5,822	5,605
60475	Steger	(312)	9,269	8,104
61081	Sterling	(815)	16,273	16,113
60402	Stickney	(312)	5,893	6,601
60103	Streamwood	(312)	23,456	18,176
61364	Streator	(815)	14,795	15,600
60501	Summit	(312)	10,110	11,569
62881	Swansea	(618)	5,529	5,432
60178	Sycamore	(815)	9,219	7,843
62568	Taylorville	(217)	11,386	10,644
60477	Tinley Park	(312)	26,178	12,572
61801	Urbana	(217)	35,978	33,976
62471	Vandalia	(618)	5,338	5,160
60061	Vernon Hills	(312)	9,827	1,056
60181	Villa Park	(312)	23,155	25,891
60555	Warrenville	(312)	7,519	3,281
61571	Washington	(309)	10,364	6,790
62204	Washington Park	(618)	8,223	9,524
60970	Watseka	(815)	5,543	5,294
60084	Wauconda	(312)	5,688	5,460
60085	Waukegan	(312)	67,653	65,134
60153	Westchester	(312)	17,730	20,033
60185	West Chicago	(312)	12,550	9,988
60558	Western Springs	(312)	12,876	13,029
62896	West Frankfort	(618)	9,437	8,854
60559	Westmont	(312)	17,353	8,832
61604	West Peoria(u)	(309)	5,219	6,873
60187	Wheaton	(312)	43,043	31,138
60090	Wheeling	(312)	23,266	13,243
60091	Wilmette	(312)	28,221	32,134
60093	Winnetka	(312)	12,772	14,131
60096	Winthrop Harbor	(312)	5,427	4,794
60097	Wonder Lake(u)	(815)	5,917	4,806
60191	Wood Dale	(312)	11,251	8,831
60515	Woodridge	(312)	21,763	11,028
62095	Wood River	(618)	12,446	13,186
60098	Woodstock	(815)	11,725	10,226
60482	Worth	(312)	11,592	11,999
60099	Zion	(312)	17,865	17,268

Indiana

ZIP code	Place		1980	1970
46001	Alexandria	(317)	6,028	5,600
46011	Anderson	(317)	64,695	70,787
46703	Angola	(219)	5,486	5,117
46706	Auburn	(219)	8,122	7,388
47421	Bedford	(812)	14,410	13,087
46107	Beech Grove	(317)	13,196	13,559
47401	Bloomington	(812)	52,667	43,262
46714	Bluffton	(219)	8,705	8,297
47601	Boonville	(812)	6,300	5,736
47834	Brazil	(812)	7,852	8,163
46112	Brownsburg	(317)	6,242	5,751
46032	Carmel	(317)	18,272	6,691
46303	Cedar Lake	(219)	8,754	7,589
47111	Charlestown	(812)	5,596	5,933
46304	Chesterton	(219)	8,531	6,177
47130	Clarksville	(812)	15,164	13,298
47842	Clinton	(317)	5,267	5,340
46725	Columbia City	(219)	5,091	4,911
47201	Columbus	(812)	30,292	26,457
47331	Connersville	(317)	17,023	17,604
47933	Crawfordsville	(317)	13,325	13,842
46307	Crown Point	(219)	16,455	10,931
46733	Decatur	(219)	8,649	8,445
46514	Dunlap(u)	(219)	5,397	....
46311	Dyer	(219)	9,555	4,906
46312	East Chicago	(219)	39,786	46,982
46514	Elkhart	(219)	41,305	43,152
46036	Elwood	(317)	10,867	11,196
*47708	Evansville	(812)	130,496	138,764
*46802	Fort Wayne	(219)	172,391	178,269
46041	Frankfort	(317)	15,168	14,956
46131	Franklin	(317)	11,563	11,477
*46401	Gary	(219)	151,968	175,415
46526	Goshen	(219)	19,665	17,871
46135	Greencastle	(317)	8,403	8,852

ZIP code	Place		1980	1970
46140	Greenfield	(317)	11,288	9,986
47240	Greensburg	(812)	9,254	8,620
46142	Greenwood	(317)	19,327	11,869
46319	Griffith	(219)	17,026	18,168
*46320	Hammond	(219)	93,714	107,983
47348	Hartford City	(317)	7,622	8,207
46322	Highland	(219)	25,935	24,947
46342	Hobart	(219)	22,987	21,485
47542	Huntingburg	(812)	5,376	4,794
46750	Huntington	(219)	16,202	16,217
*46206	Indianapolis	(317)	700,807	736,856
47546	Jasper	(812)	9,097	8,641
47130	Jeffersonville	(812)	21,220	20,008
46755	Kendallville	(219)	7,299	6,838
46901	Kokomo	(317)	47,808	44,042
*47901	Lafayette	(317)	43,011	44,955
46405	Lake Station	(219)	15,087	9,858
46350	La Porte	(219)	21,796	22,140
46226	Lawrence	(317)	25,591	16,353
46052	Lebanon	(317)	11,456	9,766
47441	Linton	(812)	6,315	5,450
46947	Logansport	(219)	17,731	19,255
46356	Lowell	(219)	5,827	3,839
47250	Madison	(812)	12,472	13,081
46952	Marion	(317)	35,874	39,607
46151	Martinsville	(317)	11,311	9,723
46410	Merrillville	(219)	27,677	15,918
46360	Michigan City	(219)	36,850	39,369
46544	Mishawaka	(219)	40,224	36,060
47960	Monticello	(219)	5,162	4,869
46158	Mooresville	(317)	5,349	5,800
47620	Mount Vernon	(812)	7,656	6,770
*47302	Muncie	(317)	77,216	69,082
46321	Munster	(219)	20,671	16,514
47150	New Albany	(812)	37,103	38,402
47362	New Castle	(317)	20,056	21,215
46774	New Haven	(219)	6,714	5,346
46060	Noblesville	(317)	12,253	7,548
46962	North Manchester	(219)	5,998	5,791
47265	North Vernon	(812)	5,768	4,582
47130	Oak Park(u)	(812)	5,871	—
46970	Peru	(317)	13,764	14,139
46168	Plainfield	(317)	9,191	8,211
46563	Plymouth	(219)	7,693	7,661
46368	Portage	(219)	27,409	19,127
47371	Portland	(219)	7,074	7,115
47670	Princeton	(812)	8,976	7,431
47374	Richmond	(317)	41,349	43,999
46975	Rochester	(219)	5,050	4,631
46173	Rushville	(317)	6,113	6,686
47167	Salem	(812)	5,290	5,041
46375	Schererville	(219)	13,209	3,663
47170	Scottsburg	(812)	5,068	4,791
47274	Seymour	(812)	15,050	13,352
47176	Shelbyville	(317)	14,989	15,094
*46624	South Bend	(219)	109,727	125,580
46383	South Haven(u)	(219)	6,679	—
46224	Speedway	(317)	12,641	14,523
47586	Tell City	(812)	8,704	7,933
*47808	Terre Haute	(812)	61,125	70,335
46072	Tipton	(317)	5,004	5,313
46383	Valparaiso	(219)	22,247	20,020
47591	Vincennes	(812)	20,857	19,867
46992	Wabash	(219)	12,985	13,379
46580	Warsaw	(219)	10,647	7,506
47501	Washington	(812)	11,325	11,358
47906	West Lafayette	(317)	21,247	19,157
46394	Whiting	(219)	5,630	7,054
47394	Winchester	(317)	5,659	5,493

Iowa

ZIP code	Place		1980	1970
50511	Algona	(515)	6,289	6,032
50009	Altoona	(515)	5,764	2,883
50010	Ames	(515)	45,775	39,505
50021	Ankeny	(515)	15,429	9,151
50022	Atlantic	(712)	7,789	7,306
52722	Bettendorf	(319)	27,381	22,126
50036	Boone	(515)	12,602	12,468
52601	Burlington	(319)	29,529	32,366
51401	Carroll	(712)	9,705	8,716
50613	Cedar Falls	(319)	36,322	29,597
*52401	Cedar Rapids	(319)	110,243	110,642
52544	Centerville	(515)	6,558	6,531
50049	Chariton	(515)	5,116	5,009
50616	Charles City	(515)	8,778	9,268
51012	Cherokee	(712)	7,004	7,272
51632	Clarinda	(712)	5,458	5,420
50428	Clear Lake City	(515)	7,458	6,430
52732	Clinton	(319)	32,828	34,719
50053	Clive	(515)	5,906	3,005
52240	Coralville	(319)	7,687	6,130
51501	Council Bluffs	(712)	56,449	60,348
50801	Creston	(515)	8,429	8,234
*52802	Davenport	(319)	103,264	98,469
52101	Decorah	(319)	7,991	7,237
51442	Denison	(712)	6,675	6,218
*50318	Des Moines	(515)	191,003	201,404
52001	Dubuque	(319)	62,374	62,309
51334	Estherville	(712)	7,518	8,108
52556	Fairfield	(515)	9,428	~8,715
50501	Fort Dodge	(515)	29,423	31,263
52627	Fort Madison	(319)	13,520	13,996
51534	Glenwood	(712)	5,280	4,421
50112	Grinnell	(515)	8,868	8,402
51537	Harlan	(712)	5,357	5,049
50644	Independence	(319)	6,392	5,910
50125	Indianola	(515)	10,843	8,852
52240	Iowa City	(319)	50,508	46,850
50126	Iowa Falls	(515)	6,174	6,454
52632	Keokuk	(319)	13,536	14,631
50138	Knoxville	(515)	8,143	7,755
51031	Le Mars	(712)	8,276	8,159
52060	Maquoketa	(319)	6,313	5,677
52302	Marion	(319)	19,474	18,028
50158	Marshalltown	(515)	26,938	26,219
50401	Mason City	(515)	30,144	30,379
52641	Mount Pleasant	(319)	7,322	7,007
52761	Muscatine	(319)	23,467	22,405
50201	Nevada	(515)	5,912	4,952
50208	Newton	(515)	15,292	15,619
50662	Oelwein	(319)	7,564	7,735
52577	Oskaloosa	(515)	10,629	11,224
52501	Ottumwa	(515)	27,381	29,610
50219	Pella	(515)	8,349	6,668
50220	Perry	(515)	7,053	6,906
51566	Red Oak	(712)	6,810	6,210
51201	Sheldon	(712)	5,003	4,535
51601	Shenandoah	(712)	6,274	5,968
*51101	Sioux City	(712)	82,003	85,925
51301	Spencer	(712)	11,726	10,278
50588	Storm Lake	(712)	8,814	8,591
50322	Urbandale	(515)	17,869	14,434
52349	Vinton	(319)	5,040	4,845
52353	Washington	(319)	6,584	6,317
*50701	Waterloo	(319)	75,985	75,533
50677	Waverly	(319)	8,444	7,205
50595	Webster City	(515)	8,572	8,488
50265	West Des Moines	(515)	21,894	16,441
50311	Windsor Heights	(515)	5,632	6,303

Kansas

ZIP code	Place		1980	1970
67410	Abilene	(913)	6,572	6,661
67005	Arkansas City	(316)	13,201	13,216
66002	Atchison	(913)	11,407	12,565
67010	Augusta	(316)	6,968	5,977
67012	Bonner Springs	(913)	6,266	3,884
66720	Chanute	(316)	10,506	10,341
67337	Coffeyville	(316)	15,185	15,116
67701	Colby	(913)	5,544	4,658
66901	Concordia	(913)	6,847	7,221
67037	Derby	(316)	9,786	7,947
67801	Dodge City	(316)	18,001	14,127
67042	El Dorado	(316)	11,551	12,308
66801	Emporia	(316)	25,287	23,327
66442	Fort Riley North(u)	(913)	16,086	12,469
66701	Fort Scott	(316)	8,893	8,967
67846	Garden City	(316)	18,256	14,790
67735	Goodland	(913)	5,708	5,510
67530	Great Bend	(316)	16,608	16,133
67601	Hays	(913)	16,301	15,396
67060	Haysville	(316)	8,006	6,531
67501	Hutchinson	(316)	40,284	36,885
67301	Independence	(316)	10,598	10,347
66749	Iola	(316)	6,938	6,493
66441	Junction City	(913)	19,305	19,018
*66110	Kansas City	(913)	161,148	168,213
66043	Lansing	(913)	5,307	3,797
66044	Lawrence	(913)	52,738	45,698
66048	Leavenworth	(913)	33,656	25,147
66206	Leawood	(913)	13,360	10,645
66215	Lenexa	(913)	18,639	5,549
67901	Liberal	(316)	14,911	13,862
67460	McPherson	(316)	11,753	10,851
66502	Manhattan	(913)	32,644	27,575
66203	Merriam	(913)	10,794	10,955
66222	Mission	(913)	8,643	8,125
67114	Newton	(316)	16,332	15,439
66061	Olathe	(913)	37,258	17,917
66067	Ottawa	(913)	11,016	11,036
66204	Overland Park	(913)	81,784	77,934
67357	Parsons	(316)	12,898	13,015
66762	Pittsburg	(316)	18,770	20,171
66208	Prairie Village	(913)	24,657	28,378
67124	Pratt	(316)	6,885	6,736
66203	Roeland Park	(913)	7,962	9,760
67665	Russell	(913)	5,427	5,371
67401	Salina	(913)	41,843	37,714
*66203	Shawnee	(913)	29,653	20,946
*66603	Topeka	(913)	118,690	125,011
67152	Wellington	(316)	8,212	8,072
*67202	Wichita	(316)	279,838	276,554
67156	Winfield	(316)	10,736	11,405

Kentucky

ZIP code	Place		1980	1970
41101	Ashland	(606)	27,064	29,245
40004	Bardstown	(502)	6,155	5,816

ZIP code	Place		1980	1970
41073	Bellevue	(606)	7,678	8,847
40403	Berea	(606)	8,226	6,956
42101	Bowling Green	(502)	40,450	36,705
40218	Buechel(u)	(502)	6,912	5,359
42718	Campbellsville	(502)	8,715	7,598
42330	Central City	(502)	5,250	5,450
40701	Corbin	(606)	8,075	7,474
*41011	Covington	(606)	49,585	52,535
41031	Cynthiana	(606)	5,881	6,356
40422	Danville	(606)	12,942	11,542
41074	Dayton	(606)	6,979	8,751
41017	Edgewood	(606)	7,243	4,139
42701	Elizabethtown	(502)	15,380	11,748
41018	Elsmere	(606)	7,203	5,161
41018	Erlanger	(606)	14,466	12,676
40118	Fairdale(u)	(502)	7,315	----
40291	Fern Creek(u)	(502)	16,866	----
41139	Flatwoods	(606)	8,354	7,380
41042	Florence	(606)	15,586	11,661
42223	Fort Campbell North(u)	(502)	17,211	13,616
40121	Fort Knox(u)	(502)	31,035	37,608
41017	Fort Mitchell	(606)	7,294	6,982
41075	Fort Thomas	(606)	16,012	16,338
40601	Frankfort	(502)	25,973	21,902
42134	Franklin	(502)	7,738	6,553
40324	Georgetown	(502)	10,972	8,629
42141	Glasgow	(502)	12,958	11,301
40330	Harrodsburg	(606)	7,265	6,741
41701	Hazard	(606)	5,429	5,459
42420	Henderson	(502)	24,834	22,976
40228	Highview(u)	(502)	13,286	----
40229	Hillview	(502)	5,196	----
42240	Hopkinsville	(502)	27,318	21,395
41051	Independence	(606)	7,998	1,715
40299	Jeffersontown	(502)	15,795	9,701
40342	Lawrenceburg	(502)	5,167	3,579
40033	Lebanon	(502)	6,590	5,528
*40511	Lexington-Fayette	(606)	204,165	108,137
*40201	Louisville	(502)	298,694	361,706
42431	Madisonville	(502)	16,979	15,332
42066	Mayfield	(502)	10,705	10,724
41056	Maysville	(606)	7,983	7,411
40965	Middlesborough	(606)	12,251	11,878
42633	Monticello	(606)	5,677	3,618
40351	Morehead	(606)	7,789	7,191
40353	Mount Sterling	(606)	5,820	5,083
42071	Murray	(502)	14,248	13,537
40218	Newburg(u)	(502)	24,612	----
*41071	Newport	(606)	21,587	25,998
40356	Nicholasville	(606)	10,400	5,829
40219	Okolona(u)	(502)	20,039	17,643
42301	Owensboro	(502)	54,450	50,329
42001	Paducah	(502)	29,315	31,627
40361	Paris	(606)	7,935	7,823
40258	Pleasure Ridge Park(u)	(502)	27,332	28,566
42445	Princeton	(502)	7,073	6,292
40160	Radcliff	(502)	14,656	8,426
40475	Richmond	(606)	21,705	16,861
42276	Russellville	(502)	7,520	6,456
40207	St. Matthews	(502)	13,519	13,152
40065	Shelbyville	(502)	5,308	4,182
40216	Shively	(502)	16,645	19,139
42501	Somerset	(606)	10,649	10,436
40272	Valley Station(u)	(502)	24,474	24,471
40383	Versailles	(606)	6,427	5,679
41101	Westwood(u)	(606)	5,973	777
40769	Williamsburg	(606)	5,560	3,687
40391	Winchester	(606)	15,216	13,402

Louisiana

ZIP code	Place		1980	1970
70510	Abbeville	(318)	12,391	10,996
71301	Alexandria	(318)	51,565	41,811
70032	Arabi(u)	(504)	10,248	----
70094	Avondale(u)	(504)	6,699	----
70714	Baker	(504)	12,865	8,281
71220	Bastrop	(318)	15,527	14,713
*70821	Baton Rouge	(504)	220,394	165,921
70360	Bayou Cane(u)	(504)	15,723	9,077
70380	Bayou Vista(u)	(504)	5,805	5,121
70037	Belle Chasse(u)	(504)	5,412	----
70427	Bogalusa	(504)	16,976	18,412
71010	Bossier City	(318)	49,969	43,769
70517	Breaux Bridge	(318)	5,922	4,942
	Broadmoor(u)	(504)	7,051	----
71291	Brownsville-Bawcomville(u)	(318)	7,252	----
71322	Bunkie	(318)	5,364	5,395
70043	Chalmette(u)	(504)	33,847	----
71291	Claiborne(u)	(318)	6,278	----
70433	Covington	(504)	7,892	7,170
70526	Crowley	(318)	16,036	16,104
70345	Cut Off(u)	(504)	5,049	----
70726	Denham Springs	(504)	8,412	6,752
70634	De Ridder	(318)	10,337	8,030
70346	Donaldsonville	(504)	7,901	7,367
70072	Estelle(u)	(504)	12,724	----
70535	Eunice	(318)	12,479	11,390
70538	Franklin	(318)	9,584	9,325
70354	Galliano(u)	(504)	5,159	----
70737	Gonzales	(504)	7,287	4,512
70053	Gretna	(504)	20,615	24,875
70401	Hammond	(504)	15,226	12,487
70123	Harahan	(504)	11,384	13,037
70058	Harvey(u)	(504)	22,709	6,347
70360	Houma	(504)	32,602	30,922
70544	Jeanerette	(318)	6,511	6,322
70121	Jefferson(u)	(504)	15,550	16,489
70546	Jennings	(318)	12,401	11,783
71251	Jonesboro	(318)	5,061	5,072
70548	Kaplan	(318)	5,016	5,540
70062	Kenner	(504)	66,382	29,858
70445	Lacombe(u)	(504)	5,146	----
70501	Lafayette	(318)	80,584	68,908
70601	Lake Charles	(318)	75,051	77,998
71254	Lake Providence	(318)	6,361	6,183
70068	Laplace(u)	(504)	16,112	5,953
70373	Larose(u)	(504)	5,234	4,267
71446	Leesville	(318)	9,054	8,928
70123	Little Farms(u)	(504)	NA	15,713
70448	Mandeville	(504)	6,076	2,571
71052	Mansfield	(318)	6,485	6,432
71351	Marksville	(318)	5,113	4,519
70072	Marrero(u)	(504)	36,548	29,015
*70004	Metairie	(504)	164,160	136,477
71055	Minden	(318)	15,074	13,996
71201	Monroe	(318)	57,597	56,374
70380	Morgan City	(504)	16,114	16,586
70601	Moss Bluff(u)	(318)	7,004	----
71457	Natchitoches	(318)	16,664	15,974
70560	New Iberia	(318)	32,766	30,147
*70113	New Orleans	(318)	557,927	593,471
71463	Oakdale	(318)	7,155	7,301
70570	Opelousas	(318)	18,903	20,387
71360	Pineville	(318)	12,034	8,951
70764	Plaquemine	(504)	7,521	7,739
70454	Ponchatoula	(504)	5,469	4,545
70767	Port Allen	(504)	6,114	5,728
70085	Poydras(u)	(504)	5,722	----
70601	Prien(u)	(318)	6,224	----
70394	Raceland(u)	(504)	6,302	4,880
70578	Rayne	(318)	9,066	9,510
70084	Reserve(u)	(504)	7,288	6,381
70123	River Ridge(u)	(504)	17,146	----
71270	Ruston	(318)	20,585	17,365
70582	St. Martinville	(318)	7,965	7,153
70807	Scotlandville(u)	(504)	15,113	22,599
*71102	Shreveport	(318)	206,989	182,064
70458	Slidell	(504)	26,718	16,101
71459	South Fort Polk(u)	(318)	12,498	15,600
71075	Springhill	(318)	6,516	6,496
70663	Sulphur	(318)	19,709	14,959
71282	Tallulah	(318)	11,341	9,643
71285	Terrytown(u)	(318)	23,548	13,382
70301	Thibodaux	(318)	15,810	15,028
70053	Timberlane(u)	(504)	11,579	----
71373	Vidalia	(318)	5,936	5,538
70586	Ville Platte	(318)	9,201	9,692
70092	Violet(u)	(504)	11,678	----
70094	Waggaman(u)	(504)	9,004	----
70669	Westlake	(318)	5,246	4,082
71291	West Monroe	(318)	14,993	14,868
70094	Westwego	(504)	12,663	11,402
71483	Winnfield	(318)	7,311	7,142
71295	Winnsboro	(318)	5,921	5,349
70791	Zachary	(504)	7,297	4,964

Maine (207)

See Note Page 564

ZIP code	Place	1980	1970
04210	Auburn	23,128	24,151
04330	Augusta	21,819	21,945
04401	Bangor	31,643	33,168
04530	Bath	10,246	9,679
04915	Belfast	6,243	5,957
04005	Biddeford	19,638	19,983
04412	Brewer	9,017	9,300
04011	Brunswick Center(u)	10,990	10,867
04011	Brunswick	17,366	16,195
04093	Buxton	5,775	3,135
04107	Cape Elizabeth	7,838	7,873
04736	Caribou	9,916	10,419
04021	Cumberland	5,284	4,096
04605	Ellsworth	5,179	4,603
04937	Fairfield	6,113	5,684
04105	Falmouth	6,853	6,291
04938	Farmington	6,730	5,657
04032	Freeport	5,863	4,781
04345	Gardiner	6,485	6,685
04038	Gorham	10,101	7,839
04444	Hampden	5,250	4,693
04730	Houlton Center(u)	5,730	6,760
04730	Houlton	6,766	8,111
04239	Jay	5,080	3,954
04043	Kennebunk	6,621	5,646
03904	Kittery Center(u)	5,465	7,363
03904	Kittery	9,314	11,028
04240	Lewiston	40,481	41,779

ZIP code	Place	1980	1970
04750	Limestone	8,719	10,360
04457	Lincoln	5,066	4,759
04250	Lisbon	8,769	6,544
04750	Loring(u)	6,572	7,881
04756	Madawaska	5,282	5,585
04462	Millinocket Center(u)	7,567	7,558
04462	Millinocket	7,567	7,742
04062	North Windham(u)	5,492	....
04963	Oakland	5,162	3,535
04064	Old Orchard Beach Ctr.(u).	6,023	5,273
04064	Old Orchard Beach	6,291	5,404
04468	Old Town	8,422	8,741
04473	Orono Center(u)	9,891	9,146
04473	Orono	10,578	9,989
*04101	Portland	61,572	65,116
04769	Presque Isle	11,172	11,452
04841	Rockland	7,919	8,505
04276	Rumford Compact(u)	6,256	6,198
04276	Rumford	8,240	9,363
04072	Saco	12,921	11,678
04073	Sanford Center(u)	10,268	10,457
04073	Sanford	18,020	15,812
04074	Scarborough	11,347	7,845
04976	Skowhegan Center(u)	6,517	6,571
04976	Skowhegan	8,098	7,601
04106	South Portland	22,712	23,267
04084	Standish	5,946	3,122
04086	Topsham	6,431	5,022
04901	Waterville	17,779	18,192
04090	Wells	8,211	4,448
04092	Westbrook	14,976	14,444
04082	Windham	11,282	6,593
04901	Winslow Center(u)	5,903	5,389
04901	Winslow	8,057	7,299
04364	Winthrop	5,889	4,335
04096	Yarmouth	6,585	4,854
03909	York	8,465	5,690

Maryland (301)

ZIP code	Place	1980	1970
21001	Aberdeen	11,533	7,403
21005	Aberdeen Proving Ground(u)	5,772	7,403
20783	Adelphi(u)	12,530	....
20331	Andrews AFB(u)	10,064	6,418
*21401	Annapolis	31,740	30,095
21227	Arbutus(u)	20,163	22,745
21012	Arnold(u)	12,285	....
20906	Aspen Hill(u)	47,455	16,887
*21233	Baltimore	786,741	905,787
21014	Bel Air	7,814	6,307
21050	Bel Air North(u)	5,043	....
21014	Bel Air South(u)	8,461	....
20705	Beltsville(u)	12,760	8,912
*20815	Bethesda(u)	63,022	71,621
20710	Bladensburg	7,691	7,977
*20715	Bowie	33,695	35,028
21225	Brooklyn Park(u)	11,508	....
20818	Cabin John-Brookmont(u)	5,135	....
20619	California(u)	5,770	....
21613	Cambridge	11,703	11,595
20748	Camp Springs(u)	16,118	22,776
21401	Cape St. Clair(u)	6,022	....
20743	Carmody Hills-Pepper Mill(u)	5,571	6,245
21234	Carney(u)	21,488	....
21228	Catonsville(u)	33,208	54,812
20785	Cheverly	5,751	6,808
20815	Chevy Chase(u)	12,232	16,424
20783	Chillum(u)	32,775	35,656
20735	Clinton(u)	16,438	....
20904	Cloverly(u)	5,153	....
21030	Cockeysville(u)	17,013	....
20904	Colesville(u)	14,359	9,455
20740	College Park	23,614	26,156
*21044	Columbia(u)	52,518	8,815
20743	Coral Hills(u)	11,602	9,058
21114	Crofton(u)	12,009	4,478
21502	Cumberland	25,933	29,724
20747	District Heights	6,799	7,846
20785	Dodge Park(u)	5,275	....
21222	Dundalk(u)	71,293	85,377
21601	Easton	7,536	6,809
20737	East Riverdale(u)	14,117	....
21219	Edgemere(u)	9,078	10,352
21040	Edgewood	19,455	8,551
21921	Elkton	6,468	5,362
21043	Ellicott City(u)	21,784	9,435
21221	Essex(u)	39,614	38,193
20904	Fairland(u)	5,154	....
21047	Fallston(u)	5,572	....
21061	Ferndale(u)	14,314	9,929
20747	Forestville(u)	16,401	16,188
20755	Fort Meade(u)	14,083	16,699
21701	Frederick	27,557	23,641
....	Friendly(u)	8,848	....
21532	Frostburg	7,715	7,327
*20877	Gaithersburg	26,424	8,344
20874	Germantown(u)	9,721	....

ZIP code	Place	1980	1970
....	Glassmanor(u)	7,751	....
21061	Glen Burnie(u)	37,263	38,608
20769	Glenn Dale(u)	5,106	....
20771	Goddard(u)	6,147	....
20770	Greenbelt	16,000	18,199
21122	Green Haven(u)	6,577	....
21740	Hagerstown	34,132	35,862
21740	Halfway(u)	8,659	6,106
21204	Hampton(u)	5,220	....
21078	Havre De Grace	8,763	9,791
20903	Hillandale(u)	9,686	....
20748	Hillcrest Heights.	17,021	24,037
*20780	Hyattsville	12,709	14,998
21085	Joppatowne(u)	11,348	9,092
20785	Kentland(u)	8,596	9,649
20772	Kettering(u)	6,972	....
21122	Lake Shore(u)	10,181	....
20785	Landover(u)	5,374	5,597
20787	Langley Park(u)	14,038	11,564
20706	Lanham-Seabrook(u)	15,814	13,244
21227	Lansdowne-Baltimore Highlands(u)	16,759	17,770
20772	Largo(u)	5,557	....
*20707	Laurel	12,103	10,525
21502	La Vale-Narrows Park(u)	5,523	3,971
20653	Lexington Pk.(u)	10,361	9,136
21090	Linthicum(u)	7,457	9,775
21207	Lochearn(u)	26,908	....
21037	Londontowne(u)	6,052	3,864
21093	Lutherville-Timonium(u)	17,854	24,055
20748	Marlow Heights(u)	5,824	....
20707	Maryland City(u)	6,949	7,102
....	Mays Chapel(u)	5,213	....
21220	Middle River(u)	26,756	19,935
....	Milford Mill(u)	20,354	....
20879	Montgomery Village(u)	18,725	....
20822	Mount Rainier	7,361	8,180
21402	Naval Academy(u)	5,367	....
20784	New Carrollton	12,632	14,870
20815	North Bethesda(u)	22,671	....
20895	North Kensington(u)	9,039	....
20707	North Laurel(u)	6,093	....
21113	Odenton(u)	13,270	5,989
20832	Olney(u)	13,026	2,138
21206	Overlea(u)	12,965	13,124
21117	Owings Mills(u)	9,526	7,360
20745	Oxon Hill(u)	36,267	11,974
20785	Palmer Park(u)	7,986	8,172
21234	Parkville	35,159	33,589
21122	Pasadena(u)	7,439	....
21128	Perry Hall(u)	13,455	5,446
21208	Pikesville(u)	22,555	25,395
20854	Potomac(u)	40,402	....
21227	Pumphrey(u)	5,666	6,425
20878	Quince Orchard(u)	5,107	....
21133	Randallstown(u)	25,927	33,683
....	Redland(u)	10,759	....
21136	Reisterstown(u)	19,385	12,568
21122	Riviera Beach(u)	8,812	7,464
*20850	Rockville	43,811	42,739
21237	Rosedale(u)	19,956	19,417
21221	Rossville(u)	8,646	....
20601	St. Charles(u)	13,921	....
21801	Salisbury	16,429	15,252
20743	Seat Pleasant	5,217	7,217
21207	Security(u)	29,453	....
21144	Severn(u)	20,147	....
21146	Severna Park	21,253	16,358
*20907	Silver Spring(u)	72,893	77,411
21061	South Gate(u)	24,185	9,356
20895	South Kensington(u)	9,344	10,289
20707	South Laurel(u)	18,034	13,345
20746	Suitland-Silver Hills(u)	32,164	30,355
20912	Takoma Park	16,231	18,507
....	Tantallon(u)	9,945	....
20748	Temple Hills(u)	6,630	....
21204	Towson(u)	51,083	77,768
20601	Waldorf(u)	9,782	7,368
20743	Walker Mill(u)	10,651	7,103
21157	Westminster	8,808	7,207
20902	Wheaton Glenmont(u)	48,598	66,280
20903	White Oak(u)	13,700	19,769
20695	White Plains(u)	5,167	....
21207	Woodlawn(u)	5,306	....

Massachusetts

See Note on Page 564

ZIP code	Place		1980	1970
02351	Abington	(617)	13,517	12,334
01720	Acton	(508)	17,544	14,770
02743	Acushnet	(508)	8,704	7,767
01220	Adams Center(u)	(413)	6,857	11,256
....	Adams	(413)	10,381	11,772
01001	Agawam	(413)	26,271	21,717
01913	Amesbury Center(u)	(508)	12,236	10,088
....	Amesbury	(508)	13,971	11,388
01002	Amherst Center	(413)	17,773	17,926
....	Amherst	(413)	33,229	26,331
01810	Andover	(508)	26,370	23,695
02174	Arlington	(617)	48,219	53,524
01721	Ashland	(508)	9,165	8,882

ZIP code	Place		1980	1970
01331	Athol Center(u)	(617)	8,708	9,723
......	Athol	(508)	10,634	11,185
02703	Attleboro	(508)	34,196	32,907
01501	Auburn	(508)	14,845	15,347
02322	Avon	(508)	5,026	5,295
*01432	Ayer	(508)	6,993	8,325
02630	Barnstable	(508)	30,898	19,842
01730	Bedford	(617)	13,067	13,513
01007	Belchertown	(413)	8,339	5,936
02019	Bellingham	(508)	14,300	13,967
02178	Belmont	(617)	26,100	28,285
01915	Beverly	(508)	37,655	38,348
01821	Billerica	(508)	36,727	31,648
01504	Blackstone	(508)	6,570	6,566
*02109	Boston	(617)	562,994	641,071
02532	Bourne	(508)	13,874	12,636
01921	Boxford	(508)	5,374	4,032
02184	Braintree	(617)	36,337	35,050
02631	Brewster	(508)	5,226	1,790
02324	Bridgewater	(508)	17,202	12,911
*02403	Brockton	(508)	95,172	89,040
02146	Brookline	(617)	55,062	58,689
01803	Burlington	(617)	23,486	21,980
*02138	Cambridge	(617)	95,322	100,361
02021	Canton	(617)	18,182	17,100
02330	Carver	(508)	6,988	2,420
01507	Charlton	(508)	6,719	4,654
02633	Chatham	(508)	6,071	4,554
01824	Chelmsford	(508)	31,174	31,432
02150	Chelsea	(617)	25,431	30,625
*01021	Chicopee	(413)	55,112	66,676
01510	Clinton	(508)	12,771	13,383
01778	Cochituate(u)	(617)	6,126	
02025	Cohasset	(617)	7,174	6,954
01742	Concord	(508)	16,293	16,148
01226	Dalton	(413)	6,797	7,505
01923	Danvers	(508)	24,100	26,151
02714	Dartmouth	(508)	23,966	18,800
02026	Dedham	(617)	25,298	26,938
02638	Dennis	(508)	12,360	6,454
02715	Dighton	(508)	5,352	4,667
01826	Dracut	(508)	21,249	18,214
01570	Dudley	(508)	8,717	8,087
02332	Duxbury	(617)	11,807	7,636
02333	East Bridgewater	(508)	9,945	8,347
02536	East Falmouth(u)	(617)	5,181	2,971
01027	Easthampton	(413)	15,580	13,012
01028	East Longmeadow	(413)	12,905	13,029
02334	Easton	(508)	16,623	12,157
02149	Everett	(617)	37,195	42,485
02719	Fairhaven	(508)	15,759	16,332
*02722	Fall River	(508)	92,574	96,898
*02540	Falmouth Center(u)	(508)	5,720	5,806
......	Falmouth	(508)	23,640	15,942
01420	Fitchburg	(508)	39,580	43,343
01433	Fort Devens(u)	(617)	9,546	12,915
02035	Foxborough	(508)	14,148	14,218
01701	Framingham	(508)	65,113	64,048
02038	Franklin Center(u)	(508)	9,296	8,863
......	Franklin	(508)	18,217	17,830
02702	Freetown	(508)	7,058	4,270
01440	Gardner	(508)	17,900	19,748
01833	Georgetown	(508)	5,687	5,290
01930	Gloucester	(508)	27,768	27,941
01519	Grafton	(508)	11,238	11,659
01033	Granby	(413)	5,380	5,473
01230	Great Barrington	(413)	7,405	7,537
01301	Greenfield Center(u)	(413)	14,198	14,642
......	Greenfield	(413)	18,436	18,116
01450	Groton	(508)	6,154	5,109
01834	Groveland	(508)	5,040	5,382
02338	Halifax	(617)	5,513	3,537
01936	Hamilton	(508)	6,960	6,373
02339	Hanover	(617)	11,358	10,107
02341	Hanson	(617)	8,508	7,148
01451	Harvard	(508)	12,170	12,494
02645	Harwich	(508)	8,971	5,892
01830	Haverhill	(508)	46,865	46,120
02043	Hingham	(617)	20,339	18,845
02343	Holbrook	(617)	11,140	11,775
01520	Holden	(508)	13,336	12,564
01746	Holliston	(508)	12,622	12,069
01040	Holyoke	(413)	44,678	50,112
01748	Hopkinton	(508)	7,114	5,981
01749	Hudson Center(u)	(508)	14,156	14,283
......	Hudson	(508)	16,408	16,084
02045	Hull	(617)	9,714	9,961
02601	Hyannis(u)	(617)	9,118	6,847
01938	Ipswich(u)	(508)	NA	5,022
......	Ipswich	(508)	11,158	10,750
02364	Kingston	(617)	7,362	5,999
02346	Lakeville	(508)	5,931	4,376
01523	Lancaster	(508)	6,334	6,095
*01842	Lawrence	(508)	63,175	66,915
01238	Lee	(413)	6,247	6,426
01524	Leicester	(508)	9,446	9,140
01240	Lenox	(413)	6,523	5,804
01453	Leominster	(508)	34,508	32,939
02173	Lexington	(617)	29,479	31,886
01773	Lincoln	(617)	7,098	7,567
01460	Littleton	(508)	6,970	6,380
01106	Longmeadow	(413)	16,301	15,630
*01853	Lowell	(508)	92,418	94,239
01056	Ludlow	(413)	18,150	17,580
01462	Lunenburg	(508)	6,405	7,419
*01901	Lynn	(617)	78,471	90,294
01940	Lynnfield	(617)	11,267	10,826
02148	Malden	(617)	53,386	56,127
01944	Manchester	(508)	5,424	5,151
02048	Mansfield	(508)	13,453	9,939
01945	Marblehead	(617)	20,126	21,295
01752	Marlborough	(508)	30,508	27,936
02050	Marshfield	(617)	20,916	15,223
02739	Mattapoisett	(508)	5,597	4,500
01754	Maynard	(508)	9,590	9,710
02052	Medfield	(508)	10,220	9,821
02155	Medford	(617)	58,076	64,397
02053	Medway	(508)	8,447	7,938
02176	Melrose	(617)	30,055	33,180
01844	Methuen	(508)	36,701	35,456
02346	Middleborough Center(u)	(508)	7,012	6,259
......	Middleborough	(508)	16,404	13,607
01757	Milford Center(u)	(508)	NA	13,740
......	Milford	(508)	23,390	19,352
01527	Millbury	(508)	11,808	11,987
02054	Millis	(508)	6,908	5,686
02186	Milton	(617)	25,860	27,190
01057	Monson	(413)	7,315	7,355
01351	Montague	(413)	8,011	8,451
02554	Nantucket	(508)	5,087	3,774
01760	Natick	(508)	29,461	31,057
02192	Needham	(617)	27,901	29,748
*02741	New Bedford	(508)	98,478	101,777
01950	Newburyport	(508)	15,900	15,807
02158	Newton	(617)	83,622	91,263
02056	Norfolk	(508)	6,363	4,656
01247	North Adams	(413)	18,063	19,195
01002	North Amherst(u)	(413)	5,616	2,854
01060	Northampton	(413)	29,286	29,664
01845	North Andover	(508)	20,129	16,284
*02760	North Attleborough	(508)	21,095	18,665
01532	Northborough	(508)	10,568	9,218
01534	Northbridge	(508)	12,246	11,795
01864	North Reading	(508)	11,455	11,264
02060	North Scituate(u)	(617)	5,221	5,507
02766	Norton	(508)	12,690	9,487
02061	Norwell	(617)	9,182	7,796
02062	Norwood	(617)	29,711	30,815
01364	Orange	(508)	6,844	6,104
02653	Orleans	(508)	5,306	3,055
01253	Otis(u)	(413)	NA	5,596
01540	Oxford Center(u)	(508)	6,369	6,109
......	Oxford	(508)	11,680	10,345
01069	Palmer	(413)	11,389	11,680
01960	Peabody	(508)	45,976	48,080
02359	Pembroke	(617)	13,487	11,193
01463	Pepperell	(508)	8,061	5,887
01866	Pinehurst(u)	(617)	6,588	
01201	Pittsfield	(413)	51,974	57,020
02762	Plainville	(508)	5,857	4,953
*02360	Plymouth Center(u)	(508)	7,232	6,940
......	Plymouth	(508)	35,913	18,606
02169	Quincy	(617)	84,743	87,966
02368	Randolph	(617)	28,218	27,035
02767	Raynham	(508)	9,085	6,705
01867	Reading	(617)	22,678	22,539
02769	Rehoboth	(508)	7,570	6,512
02151	Revere	(617)	42,423	43,159
02370	Rockland	(617)	15,695	15,674
01966	Rockport	(508)	6,345	5,636
01970	Salem	(508)	38,276	40,556
01950	Salisbury	(508)	5,973	4,179
02563	Sandwich	(508)	8,727	5,239
01906	Saugus	(617)	24,746	25,110
02066	Scituate	(617)	17,317	16,973
02771	Seekonk	(508)	12,269	11,116
02067	Sharon	(617)	13,601	12,367
01464	Shirley	(508)	5,124	4,909
01545	Shrewsbury	(508)	22,674	19,196
02725	Somerset	(508)	18,813	18,088
02143	Somerville	(617)	77,372	88,779
01772	Southborough	(508)	6,193	5,798
01550	Southbridge Center(u)	(508)	12,882	14,261
......	Southbridge	(508)	16,665	17,057
01075	South Hadley	(413)	16,399	17,033
01077	Southwick	(413)	7,382	6,330
02664	South Yarmouth(u)	(617)	7,525	5,380
01562	Spencer Center	(617)	6,350	5,895
......	Spencer	(508)	10,774	8,779
*01101	Springfield	(413)	152,319	163,905
01564	Sterling	(508)	5,440	4,247
02180	Stoneham	(617)	21,424	20,725
02072	Stoughton	(617)	26,710	23,459
01775	Stow	(508)	5,144	3,984
01566	Sturbridge	(508)	5,976	4,878
01776	Sudbury	(508)	14,027	13,506
01527	Sutton	(508)	5,855	4,590
01907	Swampscott	(617)	13,837	13,578
02777	Swansea	(508)	15,461	12,640
02780	Taunton	(508)	45,001	43,756

ZIP code	Place		1980	1970
01468	Templeton	(508)	6,070	5,863
01876	Tewksbury	(508)	24,635	22,755
01983	Topsfield	(508)	5,709	5,225
01469	Townsend	(508)	7,201	4,281
01376	Turners Falls(u)	(413)	NA	5,168
01879	Tyngsborough	(508)	5,683	4,204
01569	Uxbridge	(508)	8,374	8,253
01880	Wakefield	(617)	24,895	25,402
02081	Walpole	(508)	18,859	18,149
02154	Waltham	(617)	58,200	61,582
01082	Ware Center(u)	(413)	6,806	6,509
....	Ware	(413)	8,953	8,187
02571	Wareham	(508)	18,457	11,492
02172	Watertown	(617)	34,384	39,307
01778	Wayland	(508)	12,170	13,461
01570	Webster Center(u)	(508)	11,175	12,432
....	Webster	(508)	14,480	14,917
02181	Wellesley	(617)	27,209	28,051
01581	Westborough	(508)	13,619	12,594
01583	West Boylston	(508)	6,204	6,369
02379	West Bridgewater	(508)	6,359	6,070
01742	West Concord(u)	(617)	5,331	....
01085	Westfield	(413)	36,465	31,433
01886	Westford	(508)	13,434	10,368
01473	Westminster	(508)	5,139	4,273
02193	Weston	(617)	11,169	10,870
02790	Westport	(508)	13,763	9,791
01089	West Springfield	(413)	27,042	28,461
02090	Westwood	(617)	13,212	12,570
02188	Weymouth	(617)	55,601	54,610
01588	Whitinsville(u)	(508)	5,379	5,210
02382	Whitman	(617)	13,534	13,059
01095	Wilbraham	(413)	12,053	11,984
01267	Williamstown	(413)	8,741	8,454
01887	Wilmington	(508)	17,471	17,102
01475	Winchendon	(508)	7,019	6,635
01890	Winchester	(617)	20,701	22,269
02152	Winthrop	(617)	19,294	20,335
01801	Woburn	(617)	36,626	37,406
*01613	Worcester	(508)	161,799	176,572
02093	Wrentham	(508)	7,580	7,315
02675	Yarmouth	(508)	18,449	12,033

Michigan

ZIP code	Place		1980	1970
49221	Adrian	(517)	21,276	20,382
49224	Albion	(517)	11,059	12,112
48101	Allen Park	(313)	34,196	40,747
48801	Alma	(517)	9,652	9,611
49707	Alpena	(517)	12,214	13,805
*48106	Ann Arbor	(313)	107,969	100,035
48063	Avon(u).	(313)	40,779	....
*49016	Battle Creek	(616)	35,724	38,931
48706	Bay City	(517)	41,593	49,449
48505	Beecher(u)	(313)	17,178	....
48809	Belding	(616)	5,634	5,121
49022	Benton Harbor	(616)	14,707	16,481
49022	Benton Heights(u).	(616)	6,787	....
48072	Berkley	(313)	18,637	21,879
48009	Beverly Hills	(313)	11,598	13,598
49307	Big Rapids	(616)	14,361	11,995
*48012	Birmingham	(313)	21,689	26,170
48013	Bloomfield(u)	(313)	42,876	....
48107	Buchanan	(616)	5,142	4,645
*48502	Burton	(313)	29,976	32,540
49601	Cadillac	(616)	10,199	9,990
48724	Carrollton(u)	(517)	7,482	7,300
48015	Center Line	(313)	9,293	10,379
48813	Charlotte	(517)	8,251	8,244
49721	Cheboygan	(616)	5,106	5,553
48017	Clawson	(313)	15,103	17,617
48043	Clinton(u)	(313)	72,400	1,677
49036	Coldwater	(517)	9,461	9,155
49321	Comstock Park(u)	(616)	5,506	5,766
49508	Cutlerville(u)	(616)	8,256	6,267
48423	Davison	(313)	6,087	5,259
*48120	Dearborn	(313)	90,660	104,199
48127	Dearborn Heights	(313)	67,706	80,069
*48233	Detroit	(313)	1,203,368	1,514,063
49047	Dowagiac	(616)	6,307	6,583
48021	East Detroit	(313)	38,280	45,920
49506	East Grand Rapids	(616)	10,914	12,565
48823	East Lansing	(517)	48,309	47,540
49001	Eastwood(u)	(517)	7,186	9,682
48229	Ecorse	(313)	14,447	17,515
49829	Escanaba	(906)	14,355	15,368
49022	Fair Plain(u)	(616)	8,289	3,680
48024	Farmington	(313)	11,022	10,329
48024	Farmington Hills	(313)	58,056	48,694
48430	Fenton	(313)	8,098	8,284
48220	Ferndale	(313)	26,227	30,850
48134	Flat Rock	(313)	6,853	5,643
*48502	Flint	(313)	159,611	193,317
48433	Flushing	(313)	8,624	7,190
48026	Fraser	(313)	14,560	11,868
48135	Garden City	(313)	35,640	41,864
48439	Grand Blanc	(313)	6,848	5,132
49417	Grand Haven	(616)	11,763	11,844
48837	Grand Ledge	(517)	6,920	6,032
*49501	Grand Rapids	(616)	181,843	197,649
49418	Grandville	(616)	12,412	10,764
48838	Greenville	(616)	8,019	7,493
48138	Grosse Ile(u).	(313)	9,320	8,306
48236	Grosse Pointe	(313)	5,901	6,637
48236	Grosse Pointe Farms	(313)	10,551	11,701
48236	Grosse Pointe Park	(313)	13,562	15,641
48236	Grosse Pointe Woods	(313)	18,886	21,878
48212	Hamtramck	(313)	21,300	26,783
49930	Hancock	(906)	5,122	4,820
48236	Harper Woods	(313)	16,361	20,186
48625	Harrison(u).	(517)	23,649	....
48840	Haslett(u)	(517)	7,025	....
49058	Hastings	(616)	6,418	6,501
48030	Hazel Park	(313)	20,914	23,784
48203	Highland Park	(313)	27,909	35,444
49242	Hillsdale	(517)	7,432	7,728
49423	Holland	(616)	26,281	26,479
48842	Holt(u)	(517)	10,097	6,980
49931	Houghton	(906)	7,512	6,067
48843	Howell	(517)	6,976	5,224
48070	Huntington Woods	(313)	6,937	8,536
48141	Inkster	(313)	35,190	38,595
48846	Ionia	(616)	5,920	6,361
49801	Iron Mountain	(906)	8,341	8,702
49938	Ironwood	(906)	7,741	8,711
49849	Ishpeming	(906)	7,538	8,245
*49201	Jackson	(517)	39,739	45,484
49428	Jenison(u)	(616)	16,330	11,266
*49001	Kalamazoo	(616)	79,722	85,555
49508	Kentwood	(616)	30,438	20,310
49801	Kingsford	(906)	5,290	5,276
49843	K.I. Sawyer(u)	(906)	7,345	8,224
49015	Lakeview(u)	(517)	13,345	11,391
48144	Lambertville(u)	(313)	6,341	5,711
*48924	Lansing	(517)	130,414	131,403
48446	Lapeer	(313)	6,225	6,314
48146	Lincoln Park	(313)	45,105	52,984
*48150	Livonia	(313)	104,814	110,109
49431	Ludington	(616)	8,937	9,021
48071	Madison Heights	(313)	35,375	38,599
49660	Manistee	(616)	7,665	7,723
49855	Marquette	(906)	23,288	21,967
49068	Marshall	(616)	7,201	7,253
48040	Marysville	(313)	7,345	5,610
48854	Mason	(517)	6,019	5,468
48122	Melvindale	(313)	12,322	13,862
49858	Menominee	(906)	10,099	10,748
49254	Michigan Center(u)	(517)	5,244	....
48640	Midland	(517)	37,269	35,176
48042	Milford	(313)	5,041	4,699
48161	Monroe	(313)	23,531	23,894
48043	Mount Clemens	(313)	18,991	20,476
48858	Mount Pleasant	(517)	23,746	20,524
*49440	Muskegon	(616)	40,823	44,631
49444	Muskegon Heights	(616)	14,611	17,304
49866	Negaunee	(906)	5,189	5,248
48047	New Baltimore	(313)	5,439	4,132
49120	Niles	(616)	13,115	12,988
....	Northview(u)		11,662	....
48167	Northville	(313)	5,698	5,400
49441	Norton Shores.	(616)	22,025	22,271
48050	Novi	(313)	22,525	9,668
48237	Oak Park	(313)	31,537	36,762
48864	Okemos(u).	(517)	8,882	7,770
48867	Owosso	(517)	16,455	17,179
49770	Petoskey	(616)	6,097	6,342
48170	Plymouth	(313)	9,986	11,758
*48053	Pontiac	(313)	76,715	85,279
49081	Portage	(616)	38,157	33,590
48060	Port Huron	(313)	33,981	35,794
48239	Redford(u)	(313)	58,441	....
48218	River Rouge	(313)	12,912	15,947
48192	Riverview	(313)	14,569	11,342
48063	Rochester	(313)	7,203	7,054
48174	Romulus	(313)	24,857	22,879
48066	Roseville	(313)	54,311	60,529
*48068	Royal Oak	(313)	70,893	86,238
*48605	Saginaw	(517)	77,508	91,849
*48083	St. Clair Shores	(313)	76,210	88,093
48879	St. Johns	(517)	7,376	6,672
49085	St. Joseph	(616)	9,622	11,042
48176	Saline	(313)	6,483	4,811
49783	Sault Ste. Marie	(906)	14,448	15,136
*48075	Southfield	(313)	75,568	69,285
48198	Southgate	(313)	32,058	33,909
49090	South Haven	(616)	5,943	6,471
48178	South Lyon	(313)	5,214	2,675
49015	Springfield	(517)	5,917	3,994
*48078	Sterling Heights	(313)	108,999	61,365
49091	Sturgis	(616)	9,468	9,295
48473	Swartz Creek	(313)	5,013	4,928
48180	Taylor	(313)	77,568	70,020
49286	Tecumseh	(517)	7,320	7,120
49093	Three Rivers	(616)	7,015	7,355
49684	Traverse City	(616)	15,516	18,048
48183	Trenton	(313)	22,762	24,127
48084	Troy	(313)	67,102	39,419
48087	Utica	(313)	5,282	3,504
49504	Walker	(616)	15,088	11,492

ZIP code	Place		1980	1970
*48089	Warren	(313)	161,134	179,260
48095	Waterford(u)	(313)	64,250	....
48184	Wayne	(313)	21,159	21,054
48033	West Bloomfield(u)	(313)	41,962	....
48185	Westland	(313)	84,603	86,749
49007	Westwood(u)	(616)	8,519	9,143
48019	White Lake-Seven Harbors(u)	(313)	7,557	....
48096	Wixom	(313)	6,705	2,010
48183	Woodhaven	(313)	10,902	3,566
48753	Wurtsmith(u)	(517)	5,166	6,932
*48192	Wyandotte	(313)	34,006	41,061
49509	Wyoming	(616)	59,616	56,560
48197	Ypsilanti	(313)	24,031	29,538

Minnesota

ZIP code	Place		1980	1970
56007	Albert Lea	(507)	19,190	19,418
56308	Alexandria	(612)	7,608	6,973
55303	Andover	(612)	9,387	....
55303	Anoka	(612)	15,634	13,298
55124	Apple Valley	(612)	21,818	8,502
55112	Arden Hills	(612)	8,012	5,149
55912	Austin	(507)	23,020	26,210
56601	Bemidji	(218)	10,949	11,490
55433	Blaine	(612)	28,558	20,573
55420	Bloomington	(612)	81,831	81,970
56401	Brainerd	(218)	11,489	11,667
55429	Brooklyn Center	(612)	31,230	35,173
55429	Brooklyn Park	(612)	43,332	26,230
55337	Burnsville	(612)	35,674	19,940
55316	Champlin	(612)	9,006	2,275
55317	Chanhassen	(612)	6,359	4,879
55318	Chaska	(612)	8,346	4,352
55719	Chisholm	(218)	5,930	5,913
55720	Cloquet	(218)	11,142	8,699
55421	Columbia Heights	(612)	20,029	23,997
55433	Coon Rapids	(612)	35,826	30,505
55016	Cottage Grove	(612)	18,994	13,419
56716	Crookston	(218)	8,628	8,312
55428	Crystal	(612)	25,543	30,925
56501	Detroit Lakes	(218)	7,106	5,797
*55806	Duluth	(218)	92,811	100,578
55121	Eagan	(612)	20,532	10,398
55005	East Bethel	(612)	6,626	2,586
56721	East Grand Forks	(218)	8,537	7,607
55343	Eden Prairie	(612)	16,263	6,938
55435	Edina	(612)	46,073	44,046
55330	Elk River	(612)	6,785	2,252
55734	Eveleth	(218)	5,042	4,721
56031	Fairmont	(507)	11,506	10,751
55113	Falcon Heights	(507)	5,291	5,530
55021	Faribault	(507)	16,241	16,595
56537	Fergus Falls	(218)	12,519	12,443
55421	Fridley	(612)	30,228	29,233
55416	Golden Valley	(612)	22,775	24,246
55744	Grand Rapids	(218)	7,934	7,247
*55303	Ham Lake	(612)	7,832	3,327
55033	Hastings	(612)	12,827	12,195
55811	Hermantown	(218)	6,759	....
55746	Hibbing	(218)	21,193	16,104
55343	Hopkins	(612)	15,336	13,428
55350	Hutchinson	(612)	9,244	8,031
56649	International Falls	(218)	5,611	6,439
55075	Inver Grove Heights	(612)	17,171	12,148
55042	Lake Elmo	(612)	5,296	3,565
55044	Lakeville	(612)	14,790	7,556
55355	Litchfield	(612)	5,904	5,262
55110	Little Canada	(612)	7,102	3,481
56345	Little Falls	(612)	7,250	7,467
56001	Mankato	(507)	28,646	30,895
55369	Maple Grove	(612)	20,525	6,275
55109	Maplewood	(612)	26,990	25,186
56258	Marshall	(507)	11,161	9,886
55118	Mendota Heights	(612)	7,288	6,565
*55101	Minneapolis	(612)	370,951	434,400
55343	Minnetonka	(612)	38,683	35,776
56265	Montevideo	(612)	5,845	5,661
56560	Moorhead	(218)	29,998	29,687
56267	Morris	(612)	5,367	5,366
55364	Mound	(612)	9,280	7,572
55112	Mounds View	(612)	12,593	10,599
55112	New Brighton	(612)	23,269	19,507
54428	New Hope	(612)	23,087	23,180
56073	New Ulm	(507)	13,755	13,051
55057	Northfield	(507)	12,562	10,235
56001	North Mankato	(507)	9,145	7,347
55109	North St. Paul	(612)	11,921	11,950
55119	Oakdale	(612)	12,123	7,795
55323	Orono	(612)	6,845	6,787
55060	Owatonna	(507)	18,632	15,341
55427	Plymouth	(612)	31,615	18,077
55372	Prior Lake	(612)	7,284	1,114
55303	Ramsey	(612)	10,093	....
55066	Red Wing	(612)	13,736	10,441
56283	Redwood Falls	(507)	5,210	4,774
55423	Richfield	(612)	37,851	47,231
55422	Robbinsdale	(612)	14,422	16,845
55901	Rochester	(507)	57,906	53,766
55068	Rosemount	(612)	5,083	1,337
55113	Roseville	(612)	35,820	34,438
55418	St. Anthony	(612)	7,981	9,239
56301	St. Cloud	(612)	42,566	39,691
55426	St. Louis Park	(612)	42,931	48,883
*55101	St. Paul	(612)	270,230	309,866
56082	St. Peter	(507)	9,056	8,339
56379	Sauk Rapids	(612)	5,793	5,051
55379	Shakopee	(612)	9,941	6,876
55126	Shoreview	(612)	17,300	10,978
55075	South St. Paul	(612)	21,235	25,016
55432	Spring Lake Park	(612)	6,477	6,417
55082	Stillwater	(612)	12,290	10,191
56701	Thief River Falls	(218)	9,105	8,618
55110	Vadnais Heights	(612)	5,111	3,411
55792	Virginia	(218)	11,056	12,450
56093	Waseca	(507)	8,219	6,789
55118	West St. Paul	(612)	18,527	18,802
55110	White Bear Lake	(612)	22,538	23,313
56201	Willmar	(612)	15,895	12,869
55987	Winona	(507)	25,075	26,438
55119	Woodbury	(612)	10,297	6,184
56187	Worthington	(507)	10,243	9,916

Mississippi (601)

ZIP code	Place	1980	1970
39730	Aberdeen	7,184	6,507
38821	Amory	7,307	7,236
38606	Batesville	5,162	3,796
39520	Bay St. Louis	7,850	6,752
*39530	Biloxi	49,311	48,486
38829	Booneville	6,199	5,895
39042	Brandon	9,626	2,685
39601	Brookhaven	10,800	10,700
39046	Canton	11,116	10,503
38614	Clarksdale	21,137	21,673
38732	Cleveland	14,524	13,327
39056	Clinton	14,660	7,289
39429	Columbia	7,733	7,587
39701	Columbus	27,503	25,795
38834	Corinth	13,180	11,581
39532	D'Iberville(u)	13,369	7,288
39552	Escatawpa(u)	5,367	1,579
39074	Forest	5,229	4,085
39553	Gautier(u)	8,917	2,087
38701	Greenville	40,613	39,648
38930	Greenwood	20,115	22,400
38901	Grenada	11,508	9,944
39501	Gulfport	39,676	40,791
39401	Hattiesburg	40,829	38,277
38635	Holly Springs	7,285	5,728
38751	Indianola	8,050	8,947
*39205	Jackson	202,895	153,968
39090	Kosciusko	7,415	7,266
39440	Laurel	21,897	24,145
38756	Leland	6,667	6,000
39560	Long Beach	14,199	6,170
39339	Louisville	7,323	6,626
39648	McComb	12,331	11,851
39301	Meridian	46,577	45,083
39563	Moss Point	18,998	19,321
39120	Natchez	22,209	19,704
38652	New Albany	7,072	6,426
39501	North Gulfport(u)	6,660	6,996
39564	Ocean Springs	14,504	9,160
39567	Orange Grove(u)	13,476	....
38655	Oxford	9,882	8,519
39567	Pascagoula	29,318	27,264
39571	Pass Christian	5,014	2,979
39208	Pearl	18,602	9,623
39465	Petal	8,476	6,986
39350	Philadelphia	6,434	6,274
39466	Picayune	10,361	9,760
39157	Ridgeland	5,461	1,650
38668	Senatobia	5,013	4,247
38671	Southaven(u)	16,071	8,931
39759	Starkville	16,139	11,369
38801	Tupelo	23,905	20,471
39180	Vicksburg	25,434	25,478
39367	Waynesboro	5,349	4,368
39773	West Point	8,811	8,714
38967	Winona	6,177	5,521
39194	Yazoo City	12,092	11,688

Missouri

ZIP code	Place		1980	1970
63123	Affton(u)	(314)	23,181	24,264
63010	Arnold	(314)	19,141	17,381
65605	Aurora	(417)	6,437	5,359
63011	Ballwin	(314)	12,750	10,656
63042	Bellefontaine Neighbors	(314)	12,082	14,084
64012	Belton	(816)	12,708	12,270
63134	Berkeley	(314)	15,922	19,743
63031	Black Jack	(314)	5,293	4,145
64015	Blue Springs	(816)	25,936	6,779
65613	Bolivar	(417)	5,919	4,769
65233	Boonville	(816)	6,959	7,514
63114	Breckenridge Hills	(314)	5,666	7,011
63144	Brentwood	(314)	8,209	11,248
63044	Bridgeton	(314)	18,445	19,992

ZIP code	Place		1980	1970
64628	Brookfield	(816)	5,555	5,491
63701	Cape Girardeau	(314)	34,361	31,282
64836	Carthage	(417)	11,104	11,035
63830	Caruthersville	(314)	7,958	7,350
63834	Charleston	(314)	5,230	5,131
64601	Chillicothe	(816)	9,089	9,519
63105	Clayton	(314)	14,306	16,100
64735	Clinton	(816)	8,366	7,504
65201	Columbia	(314)	62,061	58,812
63128	Concord(u)	(314)	20,896	21,217
63126	Crestwood	(314)	12,815	15,123
63141	Creve Coeur	(314)	11,743	8,967
63136	Dellwood	(314)	6,200	7,137
63020	De Soto	(314)	5,993	5,984
63131	Des Peres	(314)	7,953	5,333
63841	Dexter	(314)	7,043	6,024
63011	Ellisville	(314)	6,233	4,681
64024	Excelsior Springs	(816)	10,424	9,411
63640	Farmington	(314)	8,270	6,590
63135	Ferguson	(314)	24,549	28,759
63028	Festus	(314)	7,574	7,530
*63033	Florissant	(314)	55,721	65,908
65473	Fort Leonard Wood(u)	(314)	21,262	33,799
65251	Fulton	(314)	11,046	12,248
64118	Gladstone	(816)	24,990	23,422
63122	Glendale	(314)	6,035	6,981
64030	Grandview	(816)	24,561	17,456
63401	Hannibal	(314)	18,811	18,609
64701	Harrisonville	(816)	6,372	5,052
*63042	Hazelwood	(314)	13,098	14,082
*64051	Independence	(816)	111,797	111,630
63755	Jackson	(314)	7,827	5,896
65101	Jefferson City	(314)	33,619	32,407
63136	Jennings	(314)	16,934	19,379
64801	Joplin	(417)	39,126	39,256
*64108	Kansas City	(816)	448,028	507,330
63857	Kennett	(314)	10,145	10,090
63501	Kirksville	(816)	17,167	15,560
63122	Kirkwood	(314)	27,739	31,679
63124	Ladue	(314)	9,369	10,306
65536	Lebanon	(417)	9,507	8,616
64063	Lee's Summit	(816)	28,741	16,230
63125	Lemay(u)	(314)	35,424	40,529
64067	Lexington	(816)	5,063	5,388
64068	Liberty	(816)	16,251	13,704
63552	Macon	(816)	5,680	5,301
63863	Malden	(314)	6,096	5,374
63011	Manchester	(314)	6,351	5,031
63143	Maplewood	(314)	10,960	12,785
65340	Marshall	(816)	12,781	12,051
63043	Maryland Heights(u)	(314)	5,676	8,805
64468	Maryville	(816)	9,558	9,970
65265	Mexico	(314)	12,276	11,807
65270	Moberly	(816)	13,418	12,988
65708	Monett	(417)	6,148	5,937
63026	Murphy(u)	(314)	8,121	....
64850	Neosho	(417)	9,493	7,517
64772	Nevada	(417)	9,044	9,736
63121	Normandy	(314)	5,174	6,236
63121	Northwoods	(314)	5,831	4,607
63366	O'Fallon	(314)	8,654	7,018
63124	Olivette	(314)	7,952	9,156
63114	Overland	(314)	19,620	24,819
63775	Perryville	(314)	7,343	5,149
63120	Pine Lawn	(314)	6,570	5,745
63901	Poplar Bluff	(314)	17,139	16,653
64133	Raytown	(816)	31,831	33,306
64085	Richmond	(816)	5,499	4,948
63117	Richmond Heights	(314)	11,516	13,802
63124	Rock Hill	(314)	5,702	6,815
65401	Rolla	(314)	13,303	13,571
63074	St. Ann	(314)	15,523	18,215
63301	St. Charles	(314)	37,379	31,834
63114	St. John	(314)	7,854	8,960
*64501	St. Joseph	(816)	76,691	72,748
*63155	St. Louis	(314)	452,801	622,236
63376	St. Peters	(314)	15,700	486
63126	Sappington(u)	(314)	11,388	10,603
65301	Sedalia	(816)	20,927	22,847
63119	Shrewsbury	(314)	5,077	5,896
63801	Sikeston	(314)	17,431	14,699
63138	Spanish Lake(u)	(314)	20,632	15,647
*65801	Springfield	(417)	133,116	120,096
63080	Sullivan	(314)	5,461	5,111
64683	Trenton	(816)	6,811	6,063
63084	Union	(314)	5,506	5,183
63130	University City	(314)	42,690	47,527
64093	Warrensburg	(816)	13,807	13,125
63090	Washington	(314)	9,251	8,499
64870	Webb City	(417)	7,309	6,923
63119	Webster Groves	(314)	23,097	27,457
65775	West Plains	(417)	7,741	6,893

Montana (406)

59711	Anaconda-Deer Lodge County		12,518	9,771
*59101	Billings		66,813	61,581
59101	Billings Heights(u)		8,480	....

59715	Bozeman		21,645	18,670
59701	Butte-Silver Bow		37,205	23,368
59330	Glendive		5,978	6,305
*59401	Great Falls		56,884	60,091
59501	Havre		10,891	10,558
59601	Helena		23,938	22,730
59901	Kalispell		10,689	10,526
59044	Laurel		5,481	4,454
59457	Lewistown		7,104	6,437
59047	Livingston		6,994	6,883
59402	Malmstrom AFB(u)		6,675	8,374
59301	Miles City		9,602	9,023
59801	Missoula		33,351	29,497
59801	Missoula South(u)		5,557	4,886
59801	Orchard Homes(u)		10,837	....
59270	Sidney		5,726	4,543

Nebraska

69301	Alliance	(308)	9,920	6,862
68310	Beatrice	(402)	12,891	12,389
68005	Bellevue	(402)	21,813	21,953
68008	Blair	(402)	6,418	6,106
69337	Chadron	(308)	5,933	5,921
68601	Columbus	(402)	17,328	15,471
68355	Falls City	(402)	5,374	5,444
68025	Fremont	(402)	23,979	22,962
69341	Gering	(308)	5,760	5,639
68801	Grand Island	(308)	33,180	32,358
68901	Hastings	(402)	23,045	23,580
68949	Holdrege	(308)	5,624	5,635
68847	Kearney	(308)	21,158	19,181
68128	La Vista	(402)	9,588	4,858
68850	Lexington	(308)	6,898	5,654
*68501	Lincoln	(402)	171,932	149,518
69001	McCook	(308)	8,404	8,285
68410	Nebraska City	(402)	7,127	7,441
68701	Norfolk	(402)	19,449	16,607
69101	North Platte	(308)	24,509	19,447
68113	Offutt AFB West(u)	(402)	8,787	8,445
69153	Ogallala	(308)	5,638	4,976
*68108	Omaha	(402)	313,939	346,929
68046	Papillion	(402)	6,399	5,606
68048	Plattsmouth	(402)	6,295	6,371
68127	Ralston	(402)	5,143	4,731
69361	Scottsbluff	(308)	14,156	14,507
68434	Seward	(402)	5,713	5,294
69162	Sidney	(308)	6,010	6,403
68776	South Sioux City	(402)	9,339	7,920
68787	Wayne	(402)	5,240	5,379
68467	York	(402)	7,723	6,778

Nevada (702)

89005	Boulder City		9,590	5,223
89701	Carson City		32,022	15,468
89112	East Las Vegas(u)		6,449	6,501
89801	Elko		8,758	7,621
89015	Henderson		24,363	16,395
89450	Incline Village-Crystal Bay(u)		6,225	....
*89114	Las Vegas		164,674	125,787
89110	Nellis AFB(u)		6,205	6,449
89030	North Las Vegas		42,739	46,067
89109	Paradise(u)		84,818	24,477
*89501	Reno		100,756	72,863
89431	Sparks		40,780	24,187
89110	Sunrise Manor(u)		44,155	9,684
89431	Sun Valley(u)		8,822	2,414
89109	Vegas Creek(u)		NA	8,970
89101	Winchester(u)		19,728	13,981

New Hampshire (603)

See note on page 564

03031	Amherst		8,243	4,605
03102	Bedford		9,481	5,859
03570	Berlin		13,084	15,256
03743	Claremont		14,557	14,221
03301	Concord		30,400	30,022
03818	Conway		7,158	4,865
03038	Derry		12,248	6,090
	Derry Compact(u)		18,875	11,712
03820	Dover		22,377	20,850
03824	Durham Compact(u)		6,448	7,221
	Durham		10,652	8,869
03833	Exeter Compact(u)		6,947	6,439
	Exeter		11,024	8,892
03235	Franklin		7,901	7,292
03045	Goffstown		11,315	9,284
03842	Hampton Compact(u)		6,779	5,407
	Hampton		10,493	8,011
03755	Hanover Compact(u)		6,861	6,147
	Hanover		9,119	8,494
03106	Hooksett		7,303	5,564
03061	Hudson		14,022	10,638
03431	Keene		21,449	20,467
03246	Laconia		15,575	14,888
03766	Lebanon		11,134	9,725

ZIP code	Place	1980	1970
03561	*Littleton*	5,558	5,290
03053	*Londonderry*	13,598	5,346
*03101	*Manchester*	90,936	87,754
03054	*Merrimack*	15,406	8,595
03055	*Milford*	8,685	6,622
03060	*Nashua*	67,865	55,820
03773	*Newport*	6,229	5,899
03076	*Pelham*	8,609	5,408
03865	*Plaistow*	5,609	4,712
03801	*Portsmouth*	26,254	25,717
03077	*Raymond*	5,453	3,003
03867	*Rochester*	21,560	17,938
03079	*Salem*	24,124	20,142
03874	*Seabrook*	5,917	3,053
03878	*Somersworth*	10,350	9,026
03087	*Windham*	5,664	3,008

New Jersey

ZIP code	Place		1980	1970
07747	Aberdeen(u)	(201)	17,235	....
08609	Absecon	(609)	6,859	6,094
07401	Allendale	(201)	5,901	6,240
07712	Asbury Park	(201)	17,015	16,533
*08401	Atlantic City	(609)	40,199	47,859
08106	Audubon	(609)	9,533	10,802
08007	Barrington	(609)	7,418	8,409
07002	Bayonne	(201)	65,047	72,743
08722	Beachwood	(201)	7,687	4,390
07109	Belleville	(201)	35,367	37,629
08031	Bellmawr	(609)	13,721	15,618
07719	Belmar	(201)	6,771	5,782
07621	Bergenfield	(201)	25,568	29,000
07922	Berkeley Hts. Twp.	(201)	12,549	13,078
08009	Berlin	(609)	5,786	4,997
07924	Bernardsville	(201)	6,715	6,652
08012	Blackwood(u)	(609)	5,219	....
07003	Bloomfield	(201)	47,792	52,029
07403	Bloomingdale	(201)	7,867	7,797
07603	Bogota	(201)	8,344	8,960
07005	Boonton	(201)	8,620	9,261
08805	Bound Brook	(201)	9,710	10,450
08723	Brick Twp	(201)	53,629	35,057
08302	Bridgeton	(609)	18,795	20,435
08203	Brigantine	(609)	8,318	6,741
08015	Browns Mills(u)	(609)	10,568	7,144
07828	Budd Lake	(201)	6,523	....
08016	Burlington	(609)	10,246	12,010
07405	Butler	(201)	7,616	7,051
07006	Caldwell	(201)	7,624	8,677
*08101	Camden	(609)	84,910	102,551
08701	Candlewood(u)	(201)	6,750	5,629
07072	Carlstadt	(201)	6,166	6,724
08069	Carney's Point	(609)	7,574	....
07008	Carteret	(201)	20,598	23,137
07009	Cedar Grove Twp.	(201)	12,600	15,582
07928	Chatham	(201)	8,537	9,566
*08002	Cherry Hill Twp.	(609)	68,785	64,395
08077	Cinnaminson Twp.	(609)	16,072	16,962
07066	Clark Twp.	(201)	16,699	18,829
08312	Clayton	(609)	6,013	5,193
08021	Clementon	(609)	5,764	4,492
07010	Cliffside Park	(201)	21,464	18,891
07721	Cliffwood-Cliffwood Beach(u)	(201)	NA	7,056
*07015	Clifton	(201)	74,388	82,437
07624	Closter	(201)	8,164	8,604
08108	Collingswood	(609)	15,838	17,422
07016	Cranford Twp.	(201)	24,573	27,391
07626	Cresskill	(201)	7,609	8,298
	Crestwood Village	(201)	7,965	....
08075	Delran Twp.	(609)	14,811	10,065
07834	Denville Twp.	(201)	14,380	14,045
08096	Deptford Twp.	(609)	23,473	24,232
07801	Dover.	(201)	14,681	15,039
07628	Dumont	(201)	18,334	20,155
08812	Dunellen	(201)	6,593	7,072
08816	East Brunswick Twp.	(201)	37,711	34,166
07936	East Hanover	(201)	9,319	....
*07019	East Orange	(201)	77,878	75,471
07073	East Rutherford	(201)	7,849	8,536
08520	East Windsor Twp.	(609)	21,041	11,736
07724	Eatontown	(201)	12,703	14,619
08010	Edgewater Park	(609)	9,273	....
08817	Edison Twp.	(201)	70,193	67,120
*07201	Elizabeth	(201)	106,201	112,654
07407	Elmwood Park	(201)	18,377	20,511
07630	Emerson	(201)	7,793	8,428
*07631	Englewood	(201)	23,701	24,985
07632	Englewood Cliffs	(201)	5,698	5,938
08053	Evesham Twp.	(609)	21,659	13,477
08618	Ewing Twp.	(609)	34,842	32,831
07006	Fairfield	(201)	7,987	6,731
07701	Fair Haven	(201)	5,679	6,142
07410	Fair Lawn	(201)	32,229	38,040
07022	Fairview	(201)	10,519	10,698
07023	Fanwood	(201)	7,767	8,920
08518	Florence-Roebling(u)	(609)	7,677	7,551
07932	Florham Park	(201)	9,359	9,373
08640	Fort Dix(u)	(609)	14,297	26,290
07024	Fort Lee	(201)	32,449	30,631
07417	Franklin Lakes	(201)	8,769	7,550
07728	Freehold	(201)	10,020	10,545
07026	Garfield	(201)	26,803	30,797
08753	Gilford Park	(201)	6,528	4,007
08028	Glassboro	(609)	14,574	12,938
08029	Glendora	(609)	5,632	....
07028	Glen Ridge	(201)	7,855	8,518
07452	Glen Rock	(201)	11,497	13,011
08030	Gloucester City	(609)	13,121	14,707
	Gordon's Corner	(201)	6,320	....
*07093	Guttenberg	(201)	7,340	5,754
*07602	Hackensack	(201)	36,039	36,008
07840	Hackettstown	(201)	8,850	9,472
08108	Haddon Twp.	(609)	15,875	18,192
08033	Haddonfield	(609)	12,337	13,118
08035	Haddon Heights	(609)	8,361	9,365
07508	Haledon	(201)	6,607	6,767
08650	Hamilton Twp. (Mercer)	(609)	82,801	79,609
08037	Hammonton	(609)	12,298	11,464
07981	Hanover Twp.	(201)	11,846	10,700
07029	Harrison	(201)	12,242	11,811
07604	Hasbrouck Heights	(201)	12,166	13,651
07506	Hawthorne	(201)	18,200	19,173
07730	Hazlet Twp.	(201)	23,013	22,239
08904	Highland Park	(201)	13,396	14,385
07732	Highlands	(201)	5,187	3,916
07642	Hillsdale	(201)	10,495	11,768
07205	Hillside Twp.	(201)	21,440	21,636
07030	Hoboken	(201)	42,460	45,380
08753	Holiday City-Berkeley	(201)	9,019	....
07843	Hopatcong	(201)	15,531	9,052
08560	Hopewell Twp. (Mercer)	(609)	10,893	10,030
07111	Irvington	(201)	61,493	59,743
08527	Jackson Twp.	(201)	25,644	18,276
*07303	Jersey City	(201)	223,532	260,350
07734	Keansburg	(201)	10,613	9,720
07032	Kearny	(201)	35,735	37,585
08824	Kendall Park(u)	(201)	7,419	7,412
07033	Kenilworth	(201)	8,221	9,165
07735	Keyport	(201)	7,413	7,205
07405	Kinnelon	(201)	7,770	7,600
07034	Lake Hiawatha(u)	(201)	NA	11,389
07871	Lake Mohawk(u)	(201)	8,498	6,262
07054	Lake Parsippany(u)	(201)	NA	7,488
08701	Lakewood(u)	(201)	22,863	17,874
08879	Laurence Harbor(u).	(201)	6,737	6,715
07605	Leonia	(201)	8,027	8,847
07035	Lincoln Park	(201)	8,806	9,034
07036	Linden	(201)	37,836	41,409
08021	Lindenwold	(609)	18,196	12,199
08221	Linwood	(609)	6,144	6,159
07424	Little Falls Twp.	(201)	11,496	11,727
07643	Little Ferry	(201)	9,399	9,064
07739	Little Silver	(201)	5,548	6,010
07039	Livingston Twp.	(201)	28,040	30,127
07644	Lodi	(201)	23,956	25,163
07740	Long Branch	(201)	29,819	31,774
07071	Lyndhurst Twp.	(201)	20,326	22,729
07940	Madison	(201)	15,357	16,710
08859	Madison Park	(201)	7,447	....
07430	Mahwah Twp.	(201)	12,127	10,800
08736	Manasquan	(201)	5,354	4,971
08835	Manville	(201)	11,278	13,029
08052	Maple Shade Twp.	(609)	20,525	16,464
07040	Maplewood Twp.	(201)	22,950	24,932
08402	Margate City.	(609)	9,179	10,576
07746	Marlboro Twp.	(201)	17,560	12,273
08053	Marlton(u)	(609)	9,411	10,180
07747	Matawan	(201)	8,837	9,136
07607	Maywood	(201)	9,895	11,087
08641	McGuire AFB(u).	(609)	7,853	10,933
08619	Mercerville-Hamilton Sq.(u)	(609)	25,446	24,465
08840	Metuchen	(201)	13,762	16,031
08846	Middlesex	(201)	13,480	15,038
07748	Middletown Twp.	(201)	61,615	54,623
07432	Midland park.	(201)	7,381	8,159
07041	Milburn Twp.	(201)	19,543	21,089
08850	Milltown	(201)	7,136	6,470
08332	Millville	(609)	24,815	21,366
08094	Monroe Twp. (Gloucester)	(609)	21,639	14,071
*07042	Montclair	(201)	38,321	44,043
07645	Montvale	(201)	7,327	7,327
07045	Montville Twp.	(201)	14,290	11,846
08057	Moorestown-Lenola(u)	(609)	13,695	14,179
07950	Morris Plains	(201)	5,305	5,540
07960	Morristown	(201)	16,614	17,662
07092	Mountainside	(201)	7,118	7,520
08060	Mount Holly Twp.	(609)	10,818	12,713
07753	Neptune Twp.	(201)	28,366	27,863
07753	Neptune City	(201)	5,276	5,502
*07102	Newark	(201)	329,248	381,930
*08901	New Brunswick	(201)	41,442	41,885
08511	New Hanover	(201)	14,248	27,410
07646	New Milford	(201)	16,876	19,149
07974	New Providence	(201)	12,426	13,796
07860	Newton	(201)	7,748	7,297
07032	North Arlington	(201)	16,587	18,096
07047	North Bergen Twp.	(201)	47,019	47,751
08902	North Brunswick Twp.	(201)	22,220	16,691
07006	North Caldwell	(201)	5,832	6,733
08225	Northfield	(609)	7,795	8,646

ZIP code	Place		1980	1970
07508	North Haledon	(201)	8,177	7,614
07060	North Plainfield	(201)	19,108	21,796
07647	Northvale	(201)	5,046	5,177
07110	Nutley	(201)	28,998	31,913
07755	Oakhurst(u)	(201)	NA	5,558
07436	Oakland	(201)	13,443	14,420
08226	Ocean City	(609)	13,949	10,575
07757	Oceanport	(201)	5,888	7,503
08758	Ocean Twp	(609)	23,570	....
08857	Old Bridge	(201)	21,815	25,176
08857	Old Bridge Twp	(201)	51,515	48,715
07649	Oradell	(201)	8,658	8,903
*07050	Orange	(201)	31,136	32,566
07650	Palisades Park	(201)	13,732	13,351
08065	Palmyra	(609)	7,085	6,969
07652	Paramus	(201)	26,474	28,381
07656	Park Ridge	(201)	8,515	8,709
07054	Parsippany-Troy Hills	(201)	49,868	....
*07055	Passaic	(201)	52,463	55,124
*07510	Paterson	(201)	137,970	144,824
08066	Paulsboro	(609)	6,944	8,084
08110	Pennsauken Twp	(609)	33,775	36,394
08069	Penns Grove	(609)	5,760	5,727
08070	Pennsville Center(u)	(609)	12,467	-11,014
07440	Pequannock Twp	(201)	13,776	14,350
*08861	Perth Amboy	(201)	38,951	38,798
08865	Phillipsburg	(201)	16,647	17,849
08021	Pine Hill	(201)	8,684	5,132
08854	Piscataway Twp	(201)	42,223	36,418
08071	Pitman	(609)	9,744	10,257
*07061	Plainfield	(201)	45,555	46,862
08232	Pleasantville	(609)	13,435	14,007
08742	Point Pleasant	(201)	17,747	15,968
08742	Point Pleasant Beach	(201)	5,415	4,882
07442	Pompton Lakes	(201)	10,660	11,397
08540	Princeton	(201)	12,035	12,311
08540	Princeton North(u)	(609)	NA	5,488
07508	Prospect Park	(201)	5,142	5,176
*07065	Rahway	(201)	26,723	29,114
08057	Ramblewood(u)	(609)	6,475	5,556
07446	Ramsey	(201)	12,899	12,571
07869	Randolph Twp	(201)	17,828	13,296
08869	Raritan	(201)	6,128	6,691
07701	Red Bank	(201)	12,031	12,847
07657	Ridgefield	(201)	10,294	11,308
07660	Ridgefield Park	(201)	12,738	13,990
*07451	Ridgewood	(201)	25,208	27,547
07456	Ringwood	(201)	12,625	10,393
07661	River Edge	(201)	11,111	12,850
08075	Riverside Twp	(609)	7,941	8,591
07675	River Vale	(201)	9,489	....
07726	Robertsville	(201)	8,461	....
07662	Rochelle Park Twp	(201)	5,603	6,380
07866	Rockaway	(201)	6,852	6,383
07068	Roseland	(201)	5,330	4,453
07203	Roselle	(201)	20,641	22,585
07204	Roselle Park	(201)	13,377	14,277
07760	Rumson	(201)	7,623	7,421
08078	Runnemede	(609)	9,461	10,475
*07070	Rutherford	(201)	19,068	20,802
07662	Saddle Brook Twp	(201)	14,084	15,910
08079	Salem	(609)	6,959	7,648
08872	Sayreville	(201)	29,969	32,508
07076	Scotch Plains Twp	(201)	20,774	22,279
07094	Secaucus	(201)	13,719	13,228
08753	Silverton	(201)	7,236	....
08083	Somerdale	(609)	5,900	6,510
08873	Somerset	(201)	21,731	....
08244	Somers Point	(609)	10,330	7,919
08876	Somerville	(201)	11,973	13,652
08879	South Amboy	(201)	8,322	9,338
07079	South Orange Vill. Twp.	(201)	15,864	....
07080	South Plainfield	(201)	20,521	21,142
08882	South River	(201)	14,361	15,428
07871	Sparta Twp	(201)	13,333	10,819
08884	Spotswood	(201)	7,840	7,891
07081	Springfield Twp	(201)	13,955	15,740
07762	Spring Lake Heights	(201)	5,424	4,602
08084	Stratford	(609)	8,005	9,801
07747	Strathmore(u)	(201)	NA	7,674
07876	Succasunna-Kenvil	(201)	10,931	....
07901	Summit	(201)	21,071	23,620
07666	Teaneck Twp	(201)	39,007	42,355
07670	Tenafly	(201)	13,552	14,827
07724	Tinton Falls	(201)	7,740	8,395
*08753	Toms River(u)	(201)	7,465	7,303
07512	Totowa	(201)	11,448	11,580
*08608	Trenton	(609)	92,124	104,786
08520	Twin Rivers	(609)	7,742	....
07083	Union Twp	(201)	50,184	53,077
07735	Union Beach	(201)	6,354	6,472
07087	Union City	(201)	55,593	57,305
07458	Upper Saddle River	(201)	7,958	7,949
08406	Ventnor City	(609)	11,704	10,385
07044	Verona	(201)	14,166	15,067
08251	Villas	(609)	5,909	3,155
08360	Vineland	(609)	53,753	47,399
07463	Waldwick	(201)	10,802	-12,313
07057	Wallington	(201)	10,741	10,284
07465	Wanaque	(201)	10,025	8,636
07882	Washington	(201)	6,429	5,943
07675	Washington Twp. (Bergen)	(201)	9,550	10,577
07060	Watchung	(201)	5,290	4,750
07470	Wayne Twp	(201)	46,474	49,141
07087	Weehawken Twp	(201)	13,168	13,383
07006	West Caldwell	(201)	11,407	11,913
*07091	Westfield	(201)	30,447	33,720
07728	West Freehold	(201)	9,929	....
07764	West Long Branch	(201)	7,380	6,845
07480	West Milford Twp	(201)	22,750	17,304
07093	West New York	(201)	39,194	40,627
07052	West Orange	(201)	39,510	43,715
07424	West Paterson	(201)	11,293	11,692
07675	Westwood	(201)	10,714	11,105
07885	Wharton	(201)	5,485	5,535
08610	White Horse	(609)	10,098	....
07886	White Meadow Lake(u)	(201)	8,429	8,499
08094	Williamstown	(609)	5,768	4,075
08046	Willingboro Twp	(609)	39,912	43,386
08095	Winslow Twp	(609)	20,034	11,202
07095	Woodbridge Twp	(201)	90,074	98,944
08096	Woodbury	(609)	10,353	12,408
07675	Woodcliff Lake	(201)	5,644	5,506
07075	Wood-Ridge	(201)	7,929	8,311
07481	Wyckoff Twp	(201)	15,500	16,039
08620	Yardville-Groveville	(609)	9,414	....
.....	Yorketown	(201)	5,330	....

New Mexico (505)

ZIP code	Place		1980	1970
88310	Alamogordo		24,024	23,035
*87101	Albuquerque		332,920	244,501
88210	Artesia		10,385	10,315
87410	Aztec		5,512	3,354
87002	Belen		5,617	4,823
88101	Cannon(u)		NA	5,461
88220	Carlsbad		25,496	21,297
88101	Clovis		31,194	28,495
88030	Deming		9,964	8,343
87532	Espanola		6,803	4,528
87401	Farmington		30,729	21,979
87301	Gallup		18,167	14,596
87020	Grants		11,451	8,768
88240	Hobbs		28,794	26,025
88330	Holloman AFB(u)		7,245	8,001
88001	Las Cruces		45,086	37,857
87701	Las Vegas		14,322	7,528
87544	Los Alamos(u)		11,039	11,310
88260	Lovington		9,727	8,915
87107	North Valley(u)		13,006	10,366
87114	Paradise Hills		5,096	....
88130	Portales		9,940	10,554
87740	Raton		8,225	6,962
87124	Rio Rancho Estates		9,985	....
88201	Roswell		39,676	33,908
87115	Sandia(u)		5,288	6,867
87501	Santa Fe		49,160	41,167
87420	Shiprock		7,237	....
88061	Silver City		9,887	8,557
87801	Socorro		7,576	5,849
87105	South Valley(u)		38,916	29,389
87901	Truth or Consequences		5,219	4,656
88401	Tucumcari		6,765	7,189
87544	White Rock		6,560	3,861
87327	Zuni Pueblo		5,551	3,958

New York

ZIP code	Place		1980	1970
*12207	Albany	(518)	101,727	115,781
11507	Albertson(u)	(516)	5,561	6,825
11701	Amityville	(516)	9,076	9,794
12010	Amsterdam	(518)	21,872	25,524
12603	Arlington(u)	(914)	11,305	11,203
13021	Auburn	(315)	32,548	34,599
*11702	Babylon	(516)	12,388	12,897
11510	Baldwin(u)	(516)	31,630	34,525
13027	Baldwinsville	(315)	6,446	6,298
14020	Batavia	(716)	16,703	17,338
14810	Bath	(607)	6,042	6,053
13088	Bayberry-Lynelle Meadows(u)	(315)	14,813	....
11705	Bayport(u)	(516)	9,282	8,232
11706	Bay Shore(u)	(516)	10,784	11,119
11709	Bayville	(516)	7,034	6,147
12508	Beacon	(914)	12,937	13,255
11710	Bellmore(u)	(516)	18,106	18,431
11714	Bethpage(u)	(516)	16,840	18,555
*13902	Binghamton	(607)	55,860	64,123
10913	Blauvelt(u)	(914)	NA	5,426
11716	Bohemia(u)	(516)	9,308	8,926
11717	Brentwood(u)	(516)	44,321	28,327
10510	Briarcliff Manor	(914)	7,115	6,521
14610	Brighton (u)	(716)	35,776	....
14420	Brockport	(716)	9,776	7,878
10708	Bronxville	(914)	6,267	6,674
*14240	Buffalo	(716)	357,870	462,768
14424	Canandaigua	(716)	10,419	10,488

ZIP code	Place		1980	1970
13617	Canton	(315)	7,055	6,398
11514	Carle Place(u)	(516)	5,470	6,326
11516	Cedarhurst	(516)	6,162	6,941
11720	Centereach(u)	(516)	30,136	9,427
11934	Center Moriches(u)	(516)	5,703	3,802
11721	Centerport(u)	(516)	6,576	....
11722	Central Islip(u)	(516)	19,734	36,391
14225	Cheektowaga(u)	(716)	92,145	....
12065	Clifton Park	(518)	23,989	14,867
12043	Cobleskill	(518)	5,272	4,368
12047	Cohoes	(518)	18,144	18,653
11724	Cold Spring Harbor(u)	(516)	5,336	5,509
12205	Colonie	(518)	8,869	8,701
11725	Commack(u)	(516)	34,719	24,138
10920	Congers(u)	(914)	7,123	5,928
11726	Copiague(u)	(516)	20,132	19,632
11727	Coram(u)	(516)	24,752	....
14830	Corning	(607)	12,953	15,792
13045	Cortland	(607)	20,138	19,621
10520	Croton-on-Hudson	(914)	6,889	7,523
11729	Deer Park(u)	(516)	30,394	32,274
12054	Delmar(u)	(518)	8,423	....
14043	Depew	(716)	19,819	22,158
13214	DeWitt(u)	(315)	9,024	10,032
11746	Dix Hills(u)	(516)	26,693	10,050
10522	Dobbs Ferry	(914)	10,053	10,353
14048	Dunkirk	(716)	15,310	16,855
14052	East Aurora	(716)	6,803	7,033
10709	Eastchester(u)	(914)	20,305	23,750
11735	East Farmingdale(u)	(516)	5,522	....
12302	East Glenville(u)	(518)	6,537	5,898
11746	East Half Hollow Hills(u)	(516)	NA	9,691
11576	East Hills	(516)	7,160	8,624
11730	East Islip(u)	(516)	13,852	6,861
11758	East Massapequa(u)	(516)	13,987	15,926
11554	East Meadow(u)	(516)	39,317	46,290
11743	East Neck(u)	(516)	NA	5,221
11731	East Northport(u)	(516)	20,187	12,392
11772	East Patchogue(u)	(516)	18,139	6,092
14445	East Rochester	(716)	7,596	8,347
11518	East Rockaway	(516)	10,917	11,795
13902	East Vestal(u)	(607)	NA	10,472
*14901	Elmira	(607)	35,327	39,945
11003	Elmont(u)	(516)	27,592	29,363
11731	Elwood(u)	(516)	11,847	15,031
13760	Endicott	(607)	14,457	16,556
13760	Endwell(u)	(607)	13,745	15,999
13219	Fairmount(u)	(315)	13,415	15,317
14450	Fairport	(716)	5,970	6,474
12601	Fairview(u)	(914)	5,852	8,517
11735	Farmingdale	(516)	7,946	9,297
11738	Farmingville(u)	(516)	13,398	....
*11001	Floral Park	(516)	16,805	18,466
11768	Fort Salonga(u)	(516)	9,550	....
11010	Franklin Square(u)	(516)	29,051	32,156
14063	Fredonia	(716)	11,126	10,326
11520	Freeport	(516)	38,272	40,374
13069	Fulton	(315)	13,312	14,003
11530	Garden City	(516)	22,927	25,373
11040	Garden City Park(u)	(516)	7,712	7,488
14624	Gates-North Gates(u)	(716)	15,244	....
14454	Geneseo	(716)	6,746	5,714
14456	Geneva	(315)	15,133	16,793
11542	Glen Cove	(516)	24,618	25,770
12801	Glens Falls	(518)	15,897	17,222
12801	Glens Falls North(u)	(518)	6,956	NA
12078	Gloversville	(518)	17,836	19,677
*11022	Great Neck	(516)	9,168	10,798
11020	Great Neck Plaza	(516)	5,604	6,043
14616	Greece(u)	(716)	16,177	....
11740	Greenlawn(u)	(516)	13,869	8,493
12083	Greenville(u)	(518)	8,706	....
11746	Half Hollow Hills(u)	(516)	NA	12,081
14075	Hamburg	(716)	10,582	10,215
11946	Hampton Bays(u)	(516)	7,256	1,862
14221	Harris Hill(u)	(716)	5,087	....
10528	Harrison	(914)	23,046	21,544
10530	Hartsdale(u)	(914)	10,216	12,226
10706	Hastings-on-Hudson	(914)	8,573	9,479
11787	Hauppauge(u)	(516)	20,960	13,957
10927	Haverstraw	(914)	8,800	8,198
10532	Hawthorne(u)	(914)	5,010	....
*11551	Hempstead	(516)	40,404	39,411
13350	Herkimer	(315)	8,383	8,960
11040	Herricks(u)	(516)	8,123	9,112
11557	Hewlett(u)	(516)	6,986	6,796
*11802	Hicksville(u)	(516)	43,245	49,820
10977	Hillcrest(u)	(914)	5,733	5,357
11741	Holbrook(u)	(516)	24,382	....
11742	Holtsville(u)	(516)	13,515	....
14843	Hornell	(607)	10,234	12,144
14845	Horseheads(u)	(607)	7,348	7,989
12534	Hudson	(518)	7,986	8,940
12839	Hudson Falls	(518)	7,419	7,917
11743	Huntington(u)	(516)	21,727	12,601
11746	Huntington Station(u)	(516)	28,769	28,817
13357	Ilion	(315)	9,450	9,808
11696	Inwood(u)	(516)	8,228	8,433
14617	Irondequoit(u)	(716)	57,648	....
10533	Irvington	(914)	5,774	5,878
11751	Islip(u)	(516)	13,438	7,692
11752	Islip Terrace(u)	(516)	5,588	....
14850	Ithaca	(607)	28,732	26,226
14701	Jamestown	(716)	35,775	39,795
10535	Jefferson Valley-Yorktown(u)	(914)	13,380	9,008
11753	Jericho(u)	(516)	12,739	14,010
13790	Johnson City	(607)	17,126	18,025
12095	Johnstown	(518)	9,360	10,045
14217	Kenmore	(716)	18,474	20,980
11754	Kings Park(u)	(516)	16,131	5,555
11024	Kings Point	(516)	5,234	5,614
12401	Kingston	(914)	24,481	25,544
14218	Lackawanna	(716)	22,701	28,657
10512	Lake Carmel(u)	(914)	7,295	4,796
11755	Lake Grove	(516)	9,692	8,133
11779	Lake Ronkonkoma(u)	(516)	38,336	7,284
11552	Lakeview(u)	(516)	5,276	5,471
14086	Lancaster	(716)	13,056	13,365
10538	Larchmont	(914)	6,308	7,203
12110	Latham(u)	(518)	11,182	9,661
11559	Lawrence	(516)	6,175	6,566
11756	Levittown(u)	(516)	57,045	65,440
11757	Lindenhurst	(516)	26,919	28,359
13365	Little Falls	(315)	6,156	7,629
11561	Long Beach	(516)	34,073	33,127
12211	Loudonville(u)	(518)	11,480	9,299
11563	Lynbrook	(516)	20,424	23,151
13208	Lyncourt(u)	(315)	5,129	....
10541	Mahopac(u)	(914)	7,681	5,265
12953	Malone	(518)	7,668	8,048
11565	Malverne	(516)	9,262	10,036
10543	Mamaroneck	(914)	17,616	18,909
11030	Manhasset(u)	(516)	8,485	8,541
13104	Manlius	(315)	5,241	4,295
11050	Manorhaven	(516)	5,384	5,488
11758	Massapequa(u)	(516)	24,454	26,821
11762	Massapequa Park	(516)	19,779	22,112
13662	Massena	(315)	12,851	14,042
11950	Mastic(u)	(516)	10,413	....
11951	Mastic Beach(u)	(516)	8,318	4,870
13211	Mattydale(u)	(315)	7,511	8,292
12118	Mechanicville	(518)	5,500	6,247
11763	Medford(u)	(516)	20,418	....
14103	Medina	(716)	6,392	6,415
11746	Melville(u)	(516)	8,139	6,641
11566	Merrick(u)	(516)	24,478	25,904
11953	Middle Island(u)	(516)	5,703	....
10940	Middletown	(914)	21,454	22,607
11764	Miller Place(u)	(516)	7,877	....
11501	Mineola	(516)	20,757	21,845
10950	Monroe	(914)	5,996	4,439
10952	Monsey(u)	(914)	12,380	8,797
12701	Monticello	(914)	6,306	5,991
10549	Mt. Kisco	(914)	8,025	8,172
11766	Mount Sinai(u)	(516)	6,591	....
*10551	Mount Vernon	(914)	66,713	72,788
12590	Myers Corner(u)	(914)	5,180	2,826
10954	Nanuet(u)	(914)	12,578	10,447
11767	Nesconset(u)	(516)	10,706	10,048
14513	Newark	(315)	10,017	11,644
12550	Newburgh	(914)	23,438	26,219
11590	New Cassel(u)	(516)	9,635	8,721
10956	New City(u)	(914)	35,859	27,344
11040	New Hyde Park	(516)	9,801	10,116
*10802	New Rochelle	(914)	70,794	75,385
*12550	New Windsor Center(u)	(914)	7,812	8,803
*10001	New York	(212)	7,071,639	7,895,563
*10451	Bronx	(212)	1,168,972	1,471,701
*11201	Brooklyn	(718)	2,230,936	2,602,102
*10001	Manhattan	(212)	1,428,285	1,539,233
*(Q)	Queens	(718)	1,891,325	1,987,174

(Q) There are 4 P.O.s for Queens: 11101 for L.I. City; 11690 Far Rockaway; 11351 Flushing; and 11431 Jamaica.

ZIP code	Place		1980	1970
*10314	Staten Island	(718)	352,121	295,443
*14301	Niagara(u)	(716)	9,648	....
14302	Niagara Falls	(716)	71,384	85,615
12309	Niskayuna(u)	(518)	5,223	6,186
11701	North Amityville(u)	(516)	13,140	11,936
11703	North Babylon(u)	(516)	19,019	39,526
11706	North Bay Shore(u)	(516)	35,020	....
11710	North Bellmore(u)	(516)	20,630	22,893
11713	North Bellport(u)	(516)	7,432	5,903
11752	North Great River(u)	(516)	11,416	12,080
11757	North Lindenhurst(u)	(516)	11,511	11,117
11758	North Massapequa(u)	(516)	21,385	23,123
11566	North Merrick(u)	(516)	12,848	13,650
11040	North New Hyde Park(u)	(516)	15,114	18,154
11772	North Patchogue(u)	(516)	7,126	5,232
11768	Northport(u)	(516)	7,651	7,494
13212	North Syracuse	(315)	7,970	8,687
10591	North Tarrytown(u)	(914)	7,994	8,334
14120	North Tonawanda	(716)	35,760	36,012
11580	North Valley Stream(u)	(516)	14,530	14,881
11793	North Wantagh(u)	(516)	12,677	15,053
13815	Norwich	(607)	8,082	8,843
10960	Nyack	(914)	6,428	6,659
11769	Oakdale(u)	(516)	8,090	7,334

ZIP code	Census Division		1980	1970
11572	Oceanside(u)	(516)	33,639	35,372
13669	Ogdensburg	(315)	12,375	14,554
11804	Old Bethpage(u)	(516)	6,215	7,084
14760	Olean	(716)	18,207	19,169
13421	Oneida	(315)	10,810	11,658
13820	Oneonta	(607)	14,933	16,030
12550	Orange Lake(u)	(914)	5,120	4,348
10562	Ossining	(914)	20,196	21,659
13126	Oswego	(315)	19,793	20,913
11771	Oyster Bay(u)	(516)	6,497	6,822
11772	Patchogue	(516)	11,291	11,582
10965	Pearl River(u)	(914)	15,893	17,146
10566	Peekskill	(914)	18,236	19,283
10803	Pelham	(914)	6,848	2,076
10803	Pelham Manor	(914)	6,130	6,673
14527	Penn Yan	(315)	5,242	5,293
13212	Pitcher Hill		6,063	....
11714	Plainedge(u)	(516)	9,629	10,759
11803	Plainview(u)	(516)	28,037	31,695
12901	Plattsburgh	(518)	21,057	18,715
12903	Plattsburgh AFB(u)	(518)	5,905	7,078
10570	Pleasantville	(914)	6,749	7,110
10573	Port Chester	(914)	23,565	25,803
11777	Port Jefferson	(516)	6,731	5,515
11776	Port Jefferson Station(u)	(516)	17,009	7,403
12771	Port Jervis	(914)	8,699	8,852
11050	Port Washington(u)	(516)	14,521	15,923
13676	Potsdam	(315)	10,635	10,303
*12601	Poughkeepsie	(914)	29,757	32,029
12603	Red Oaks Mill(u)	(914)	5,236	3,919
12144	Rensselaer	(518)	9,047	10,136
11961	Ridge(u)	(516)	8,977	....
11901	Riverhead(u)	(516)	6,339	7,585
11901	Riverside-Flanders(u)	(516)	5,400	....
*14603	Rochester	(716)	241,741	295,011
*11570	Rockville Centre	(516)	25,412	27,444
11778	Rocky Point(u)	(516)	7,012	....
12205	Roessleville(u)	(518)	11,685	5,476
13440	Rome	(315)	43,826	50,148
11575	Roosevelt(u)	(516)	14,109	15,008
11577	Roslyn Heights(u)	(516)	6,546	7,242
12303	Rotterdam(u)	(518)	22,933	25,214
10580	Rye	(914)	15,083	15,869
11780	St. James(u)	(516)	12,122	10,500
14779	Salamanca	(716)	6,890	7,877
12983	Saranac Lake	(518)	5,578	6,086
12866	Saratoga Springs	(518)	23,906	18,845
11782	Sayville(u)	(516)	12,013	11,680
10583	Scarsdale	(914)	17,650	19,229
*12301	Schenectady	(518)	67,972	77,958
10940	Scotchtown(u)	(914)	7,352	2,119
12302	Scotia	(518)	7,280	7,370
11579	Sea Cliff	(516)	5,364	5,890
11783	Seaford(u)	(516)	16,117	17,379
11784	Selden(u)	(516)	17,259	11,613
13148	Seneca Falls	(315)	7,466	7,794
11733	Setauket-East Setauket(u)	(516)	10,176	6,857
11967	Shirley(u)	(516)	18,072	6,280
11787	Smithtown(u)	(516)	30,906	....
13209	Solvay	(315)	7,140	8,280
11789	South Beach(u)	(516)	8,071	....
11735	South Farmingdale(u)	(516)	16,439	20,464
14850	South Hill(u)	(607)	5,276	....
11746	South Huntington(u)	(516)	14,854	9,115
14904	Southport(u)	(607)	8,329	8,685
11581	South Valley Stream(u)	(516)	5,462	6,595
11590	South Westbury(u)	(516)	9,732	10,978
10977	Spring Valley	(914)	20,537	18,112
11790	Stony Brook(u)	(516)	16,155	6,391
10980	Stony Point(u)	(914)	8,686	8,270
10901	Suffern(u)	(914)	10,794	8,273
11791	Syosset(u)	(516)	9,818	10,084
*13201	Syracuse	(315)	170,105	197,297
10983	Tappan(u)	(914)	8,267	7,424
10591	Tarrytown	(914)	10,648	11,115
10594	Thornwood(u)	(914)	7,197	6,874
14150	Tonawanda	(716)	18,693	21,898
*12180	Troy	(518)	56,638	62,918
10707	Tuckahoe	(914)	6,076	6,236
11553	Uniondale(u)	(516)	20,016	22,077
*13503	Utica	(315)	75,632	91,373
10989	Valley Cottage(u)	(914)	8,214	6,007
*11580	Valley Stream	(516)	35,769	40,413
13850	Vestal	(607)	27,238	26,909
10901	Viola(u)	(914)	5,340	5,136
12586	Walden	(914)	5,659	5,277
11793	Wantagh(u)	(516)	19,817	21,783
12590	Wappingers Falls	(914)	5,110	5,607
13165	Waterloo	(315)	5,303	5,418
13601	Watertown	(315)	27,861	30,787
12189	Watervliet	(518)	11,354	12,404
14580	Webster	(716)	5,499	5,037
14895	Wellsville	(716)	5,769	5,815
11758	West Amityville(u)	(516)	6,623	6,424
11704	West Babylon(u)	(516)	41,699	12,893
11706	West Bay Shore(u)	(516)	5,118	....
11590	Westbury	(516)	13,871	15,362
14905	West Elmira(u)	(607)	5,485	5,901
12801	West Glens Falls(u)	(518)	5,331	3,363
10993	West Haverstraw	(914)	9,181	8,558
11552	West Hempstead(u)	(516)	18,536	20,375
11743	West Hills(u)	(516)	6,071	....
11795	West Islip(u)	(516)	29,533	17,374
12203	Westmere(u)	(518)	6,881	6,364
10994	West Nyack(u)	(914)	8,553	5,510
10996	West Point(u)	(914)	8,105	....
11796	West Sayville(u)	(516)	8,185	7,386
14224	West Seneca(u)	(716)	51,210	....
13219	Westvale(u)	(315)	6,169	7,253
*10602	White Plains	(914)	46,999	50,346
14221	Williamsville	(716)	6,017	6,878
11596	Williston Park	(516)	8,216	9,154
11797	Woodbury(u)	(516)	7,043	....
11598	Woodmere(u)	(516)	17,205	19,831
11798	Wyandanch(u)	(516)	13,215	15,716
*10701	Yonkers	(914)	195,351	204,297
10598	Yorktown Heights(u)	(914)	7,696	6,805

North Carolina

ZIP code	Census Division		1980	1970
28001	Albemarle	(704)	15,110	11,126
27263	Archdale	(919)	5,326	4,874
27203	Asheboro	(919)	15,252	10,797
*28801	Asheville	(704)	54,022	57,820
28303	Bonnie Doone(u)	(919)	5,950	....
28607	Boone	(704)	10,191	8,754
28712	Brevard	(704)	5,323	5,243
27215	Burlington	(919)	37,266	35,930
28542	Camp Le Jeune(u)	(919)	30,764	34,549
27510	Carrboro	(919)	7,517	5,058
27511	Cary	(919)	21,612	7,640
27514	Chapel Hill	(919)	32,421	26,199
*28202	Charlotte	(704)	315,474	241,420
27012	Clemmons(u)	(919)	7,401	....
28328	Clinton	(919)	7,552	7,157
28025	Concord	(704)	16,942	18,464
28334	Dunn	(919)	8,962	8,302
*27701	Durham	(919)	101,149	95,438
28379	East Rockingham(u)	(919)	5,190	2,858
27288	Eden	(919)	15,672	15,871
27932	Edenton	(919)	5,264	4,956
27909	Elizabeth City	(919)	13,784	14,381
28728	Enka(u)	(704)	5,567	....
*28302	Fayetteville	(919)	59,507	53,510
28043	Forest City	(704)	7,688	7,179
28307	Fort Bragg(u)	(919)	37,834	46,995
27529	Garner	(919)	9,556	4,923
28052	Gastonia	(704)	47,218	47,322
27530	Goldsboro	(919)	31,871	26,960
27253	Graham	(919)	8,415	8,172
*27420	Greensboro	(919)	155,642	144,076
27834	Greenville	(919)	35,740	29,063
28532	Havelock	(919)	17,718	3,012
27536	Henderson	(919)	13,522	13,896
28739	Hendersonville	(704)	6,862	6,443
28601	Hickory	(704)	20,757	20,569
*27260	High Point	(919)	63,479	63,229
28348	Hope Mills	(919)	5,412	1,866
28540	Jacksonville	(919)	18,237	16,289
28081	Kannapolis(u)	(704)	34,564	36,293
27284	Kernersville	(919)	5,875	4,815
27021	King(u)	(919)	8,757	1,033
....	Kings Grant(u)	(919)	6,652	....
28086	Kings Mountain	(704)	9,080	8,465
28501	Kinston	(919)	25,234	23,020
28352	Laurinburg	(919)	11,480	8,859
28645	Lenoir	(704)	13,748	14,705
27292	Lexington	(704)	15,711	17,205
28358	Lumberton	(919)	18,340	16,961
28212	Mint Hill	(704)	9,830	....
28110	Monroe	(704)	12,639	11,282
28115	Mooresville	(704)	8,575	8,808
28655	Morganton	(704)	13,763	13,625
27030	Mount Airy	(919)	6,862	7,325
28560	New Bern	(919)	14,557	14,660
27604	New Hope (Wake)(u)	(919)	6,768	....
....	New Hope (Wayne)(u)	(919)	6,685	....
28540	New River Station(u)	(919)	5,401	....
28658	Newton	(704)	7,624	7,857
28012	North Belmont(u)	(704)	10,762	10,672
27565	Oxford	(919)	7,709	7,178
....	Piney Green-White Oak(u)	(919)	6,058	....
*27611	Raleigh	(919)	149,771	122,830
27320	Reidsville	(919)	12,492	13,636
27870	Roanoke Rapids	(919)	14,702	13,508
28379	Rockingham	(919)	8,300	5,852
27801	Rocky Mount	(919)	41,526	34,284
27573	Roxboro	(919)	7,532	5,370
28601	St. Stephens(u)	(704)	10,797	....
28144	Salisbury	(704)	22,677	22,515
27330	Sanford	(919)	14,773	11,716
28150	Shelby	(704)	15,310	16,328
27577	Smithfield	(919)	7,288	6,677
28387	Southern Pines	(919)	8,620	5,937
28390	Spring Lake	(919)	6,273	3,968
27045	Stanleyville(u)	(919)	5,039	2,362
28677	Statesville	(704)	18,622	20,007
28778	Swannanoa(u)	(704)	5,586	1,966
27886	Tarboro	(919)	8,741	9,425
27360	Thomasville	(919)	14,144	15,230

ZIP code	Place		1980	1970
27370	Trinity(u)	(919)	6,726	....
27889	Washington	(919)	8,418	8,961
28786	Waynesville	(704)	6,765	6,488
28025	West Concord(u)	(704)	5,859	5,347
28472	Whiteville	(919)	5,565	4,195
27892	Williamston	(919)	6,159	6,570
28401	Wilmington	(919)	44,000	46,169
27893	Wilson	(919)	34,424	29,347
*27102	Winston-Salem	(919)	131,885	133,683

North Dakota (701)

58501	Bismarck		44,485	34,703
58301	Devils Lake		7,442	7,078
58601	Dickinson		15,924	12,405
58102	Fargo		61,308	53,365
58237	Grafton		5,293	5,946
58201	Grand Forks		43,765	39,008
58201	Grand Forks AFB(u)		9,390	10,474
58401	Jamestown		16,280	15,385
58554	Mandan		15,513	11,093
58701	Minot		32,843	32,290
58701	Minot AFB(u)		9,880	12,077
58072	Valley City		7,774	7,843
58075	Wahpeton		9,064	7,076
58078	West Fargo		10,099	5,161
58801	Williston		13,336	11,280

Ohio

45810	Ada	(419)	5,669	5,309
*44309	Akron	(216)	237,177	275,425
44601	Alliance	(216)	24,315	26,547
44001	Amherst	(216)	10,638	9,902
44805	Ashland	(419)	20,326	19,872
44004	Ashtabula	(216)	23,449	24,313
45701	Athens	(614)	19,743	24,168
44202	Aurora	(216)	8,177	6,549
44515	Austintown(u)	(216)	33,636	29,393
44011	Avon	(216)	7,241	7,214
44012	Avon Lake	(216)	13,222	12,261
44203	Barberton	(216)	29,751	33,052
44140	Bay Village	(216)	17,846	18,163
44122	Beachwood	(216)	9,983	9,631
45385	Beavercreek	(513)	31,589	...
44146	Bedford	(216)	15,056	17,552
44146	Bedford Heights	(216)	13,214	13,063
43906	Bellaire	(614)	8,241	9,655
45305	Bellbrook	(513)	5,174	1,268
43311	Bellefontaine	(513)	11,888	11,255
44811	Bellevue	(419)	8,187	8,604
45714	Belpre	(614)	7,193	7,189
44017	Berea	(216)	19,567	22,465
43209	Bexley	(614)	13,405	14,888
43004	Blacklick Estates(u)	(614)	11,223	8,351
45242	Blue Ash	(513)	9,510	8,324
44512	Boardman(u)	(216)	39,161	30,852
43402	Bowling Green	(419)	25,728	14,656
44141	Brecksville	(216)	10,132	9,137
45231	Brentwood(u)	(513)	5,508	...
45211	Bridgetown(u)	(513)	11,460	13,352
44141	Broadview Heights	(216)	10,920	11,463
44144	Brooklyn	(216)	12,342	13,142
44142	Brook Park	(216)	26,195	30,774
44212	Brunswick	(216)	27,689	15,852
43506	Bryan	(419)	7,879	7,008
44820	Bucyrus	(419)	13,433	13,111
43725	Cambridge	(614)	13,573	13,656
44405	Campbell	(216)	11,619	12,577
44406	Canfield	(216)	5,535	4,997
*44711	Canton	(216)	93,077	110,053
45822	Celina	(419)	9,137	8,072
45459	Centerville	(513)	18,886	10,333
45211	Cheviot	(513)	9,888	11,135
45601	Chillicothe	(614)	23,420	24,842
*45234	Cincinnati	(513)	385,409	453,514
43113	Circleville	(614)	11,700	11,687
*44101	Cleveland	(216)	573,822	750,879
44118	Cleveland Heights	(216)	56,438	60,767
43410	Clyde	(419)	5,489	5,503
*43216	Columbus	(614)	565,032	540,025
44030	Conneaut	(216)	13,835	14,552
44410	Cortland	(216)	5,011	2,525
43812	Coshocton	(614)	13,405	13,747
45238	Covedale(u)	(513)	5,830	6,639
44827	Crestline	(419)	5,406	5,965
*44222	Cuyahoga Falls	(216)	43,710	49,815
*45401	Dayton	(513)	193,536	243,023
45236	Deer Park	(513)	6,745	7,415
43512	Defiance	(419)	16,810	16,281
43015	Delaware	(614)	18,780	15,008
45238	Delhi Hills(u)	(513)	27,647	....
45833	Delphos	(419)	7,314	7,608
44622	Dover	(216)	11,526	11,516
44112	East Cleveland	(216)	36,957	39,600
44094	Eastlake	(216)	22,104	19,690
43920	East Liverpool	(216)	16,687	20,020
44413	East Palestine	(216)	5,306	5,604
45320	Eaton	(513)	6,839	6,020
*44035	Elyria	(216)	57,504	53,427
45322	Englewood	(513)	11,329	7,885
44117	Euclid	(216)	59,999	71,552
45324	Fairborn	(513)	29,702	32,267
45014	Fairfield	(513)	30,777	14,680
44313	Fairlawn	(216)	6,100	6,102
44126	Fairview Park	(216)	19,311	21,699
45840	Findlay	(419)	35,594	35,800
45505	Forest Park	(513)	18,566	15,139
45426	Fort McKinley(u)	(513)	10,161	11,536
44830	Fostoria	(419)	15,743	16,037
45005	Franklin	(513)	10,711	10,075
43420	Fremont	(419)	17,834	18,490
43230	Gahanna	(614)	18,001	12,400
44833	Galion	(419)	12,391	13,123
45631	Gallipolis	(614)	5,576	7,490
44125	Garfield Heights	(216)	33,380	41,417
44041	Geneva	(216)	6,655	6,449
45327	Germantown	(513)	5,015	4,088
44420	Girard	(216)	12,517	14,119
43212	Grandview Heights	(614)	7,420	8,460
45123	Greenfield	(513)	5,150	4,780
45331	Greenville	(513)	12,999	12,380
45239	Groesbeck(u)	(513)	9,594	....
43123	Grove City	(614)	16,793	13,911
*45012	Hamilton	(513)	63,189	67,865
45030	Harrison	(513)	5,855	4,408
43055	Heath	(614)	6,969	6,768
44124	Highland Heights	(216)	5,739	5,926
43026	Hilliard	(614)	8,131	8,369
45133	Hillsboro	(513)	6,356	5,584
44484	Howland(u)	(216)	7,441	....
44425	Hubbard	(216)	9,245	8,583
45424	Huber Heights(u)	(513)	31,731	18,943
43081	Huber Ridge(u)	(614)	5,835	...
44839	Huron	(419)	7,123	6,896
44131	Independence	(216)	8,165	7,034
45638	Ironton	(614)	14,290	15,030
45640	Jackson	(614)	6,675	6,843
44240	Kent	(216)	26,164	28,183
43326	Kenton	(419)	8,605	8,315
45236	Kenwood(u)	(513)	9,928	15,789
45429	Kettering	(513)	61,186	71,864
44094	Kirtland	(216)	5,969	5,530
44107	Lakewood	(216)	61,963	70,173
43130	Lancaster	(614)	34,953	32,911
45036	Lebanon	(513)	9,636	7,934
*45802	Lima	(419)	47,827	53,734
45215	Lincoln Heights	(513)	5,259	6,099
43228	Lincoln Village(u)	(614)	10,548	11,215
43138	Logan	(614)	6,557	6,269
43140	London	(614)	6,958	6,481
*44052	Lorain	(216)	75,416	78,185
44641	Louisville	(216)	7,996	6,298
45140	Loveland	(513)	9,106	7,126
44124	Lyndhurst	(216)	18,092	19,749
44056	Macedonia	(216)	6,571	6,375
45243	Madeira	(513)	9,341	6,713
*44901	Mansfield	(419)	53,927	55,047
44137	Maple Heights	(216)	29,735	34,093
45750	Marietta	(614)	16,467	16,861
43302	Marion	(614)	37,040	38,646
43935	Martins Ferry	(614)	9,331	10,757
43040	Marysville	(513)	7,414	5,744
45040	Mason	(513)	8,692	5,677
44646	Massillon	(216)	30,557	32,539
43537	Maumee	(419)	15,747	15,937
44124	Mayfield Heights	(216)	21,550	22,139
44256	Medina	(216)	15,268	10,913
44060	Mentor	(216)	42,065	36,912
44060	Mentor-on-the-Lake	(216)	7,919	6,517
45342	Miamisburg	(513)	15,304	14,797
44130	Middleburg Heights	(216)	16,218	12,367
45042	Middletown	(513)	43,719	48,767
45042	Middletown South(u)	(513)	5,260	....
45150	Milford	(513)	5,232	4,828
45239	Monfort Heights(u)	(513)	9,745	....
45242	Montgomery	(513)	10,084	5,683
45439	Moraine	(513)	5,325	4,898
45231	Mount Healthy	(513)	7,562	7,446
43050	Mount Vernon	(614)	14,380	13,373
43545	Napoleon	(419)	8,614	7,791
43055	Newark	(614)	41,200	41,836
45344	New Carlisle	(513)	6,498	6,112
43764	New Lexington	(614)	5,179	4,921
44663	New Philadelphia	(216)	16,883	15,184
44446	Niles	(216)	23,088	21,581
45239	Northbrook(u)	(513)	8,357	....
44720	North Canton	(216)	14,228	15,228
45239	North College Hill	(513)	10,990	12,363
44057	North Madison(u)	(216)	8,741	6,882
44070	North Olmsted	(216)	36,486	34,861
45502	Northridge(u) (Clark)	(513)	5,559	12
45414	Northridge(u) (Montgomery)	(513)	9,720	10,084
44039	North Ridgeville	(216)	21,522	13,152
44133	North Royalton	(216)	17,671	12,807
....	Northview(u)	(513)	9,973	....
43619	Northwood	(419)	5,495	4,222

ZIP code	Place		1980	1970
44203	Norton	(216)	12,242	12,308
44857	Norwalk	(419)	14,358	13,386
45212	Norwood	(513)	26,342	30,420
45873	Oakwood	(419)	9,372	10,095
44074	Oberlin	(216)	8,660	8,761
44138	Olmsted Falls	(216)	5,868	2,504
43616	Oregon	(419)	18,675	16,563
44667	Orrville	(216)	7,511	7,408
45431	Overlook-Page Manor(u)	(513)	14,825	19,719
45056	Oxford	(513)	17,655	15,868
44077	Painesville	(216)	16,391	16,536
45344	Park Layne(u)	(513)	5,372	....
44129	Parma	(216)	92,548	100,216
44130	Parma Heights	(216)	23,112	27,192
44124	Pepper Pike	(216)	6,177	5,382
44646	Perry Heights(u)	(216)	9,206	....
43551	Perrysburg	(419)	10,215	7,693
45356	Piqua	(513)	20,480	20,741
45069	Pisgah(u)	(513)	15,660	....
44319	Portage Lakes(u)	(216)	11,310	....
43452	Port Clinton	(419)	7,223	7,202
45662	Portsmouth	(614)	25,943	27,633
44266	Ravenna	(216)	11,987	11,780
45215	Reading	(513)	12,879	14,617
43068	Reynoldsburg	(614)	20,661	13,921
44143	Richmond Heights	(213)	10,095	9,220
44270	Rittman	(216)	6,063	6,308
44116	Rocky River	(216)	21,084	22,958
43460	Rossford	(419)	5,978	5,302
45217	St. Bernard	(513)	5,396	6,131
43950	St. Clairsville	(614)	5,452	4,754
45885	St. Marys	(419)	8,414	7,699
44460	Salem	(216)	12,869	14,186
44870	Sandusky	(419)	31,360	32,674
44870	Sandusky South(u)	(419)	6,548	8,501
44672	Sebring	(216)	5,078	4,954
44131	Seven Hills	(216)	13,650	12,700
44120	Shaker Heights	(216)	32,487	36,306
45241	Sharonville	(513)	10,108	11,393
44054	Sheffield Lake	(216)	10,484	8,734
44875	Shelby	(419)	9,703	9,847
45365	Sidney	(513)	17,657	16,332
45236	Silverton	(513)	6,172	6,588
44139	Solon	(216)	14,341	11,147
44121	South Euclid	(216)	25,713	29,579
45246	Springdale	(216)	10,111	8,127
*45501	Springfield	(513)	72,563	81,941
43952	Steubenville	(614)	26,400	30,771
44224	Stow	(216)	25,303	20,061
44240	Streetsboro	(216)	9,055	7,966
44136	Strongsville	(216)	28,577	15,182
44471	Struthers	(216)	13,624	15,343
43560	Sylvania	(419)	15,527	12,031
44278	Tallmadge	(216)	15,269	15,274
45243	The Village of Indian Hill	(513)	5,521	5,651
44883	Tiffin	(419)	19,549	21,596
45371	Tipp City	(513)	5,595	5,090
*43601	Toledo	(419)	354,635	383,062
43964	Toronto	(614)	6,934	7,705
45067	Trenton	(513)	6,401	5,278
45426	Trotwood	(513)	7,802	6,997
45373	Troy	(513)	19,086	17,186
44087	Twinsburg	(216)	7,632	6,432
44683	Uhrichsville	(614)	6,130	5,731
45322	Union	(513)	5,219	3,654
44118	University Heights	(216)	15,401	17,055
43221	Upper Arlington	(614)	35,648	38,727
43351	Upper Sandusky	(419)	5,967	5,645
43078	Urbana	(513)	10,762	11,237
45377	Vandalia	(513)	13,161	10,796
45891	Van Wert	(419)	11,035	11,320
44089	Vermilion	(216)	11,012	9,872
44281	Wadsworth	(216)	15,166	13,142
45895	Wapakoneta	(419)	8,402	7,324
*44481	Warren	(216)	56,629	63,494
44122	Warrensville Heights	(216)	16,565	18,925
43160	Washington C.H.	(614)	12,682	12,495
43567	Wauseon	(419)	6,173	4,932
45692	Wellston	(614)	6,016	5,410
43968	Wellsville	(216)	5,095	5,891
45449	West Carrollton	(513)	13,148	10,748
43081	Westerville	(614)	23,414	12,530
44145	Westlake	(216)	19,483	15,689
43213	Whitehall	(614)	21,299	25,263
45239	White Oak(u)	(513)	9,563	....
44092	Wickliffe	(216)	16,790	20,632
44890	Willard	(419)	5,674	5,510
44094	Willoughby	(216)	19,329	18,634
44094	Willoughby Hills	(216)	8,612	5,969
44094	Willowick	(216)	17,834	21,237
45177	Wilmington	(513)	10,431	10,051
45459	Woodbourne-Hyde Park(u)	(513)	8,826	....
44691	Wooster	(216)	19,289	18,703
43085	Worthington	(614)	15,016	15,326
45215	Wyoming	(513)	8,282	9,089
45385	Xenia	(513)	24,653	25,373
*44501	Youngstown	(216)	115,511	140,909
43701	Zanesville	(614)	28,655	33,045

Oklahoma

ZIP code	Place		1980	1970
74820	Ada	(405)	15,902	14,859
73521	Altus	(405)	23,101	23,302
73717	Alva	(405)	6,416	7,440
73005	Anadarko	(405)	6,378	6,682
73401	Ardmore	(405)	23,689	20,881
74003	Bartlesville	(918)	34,568	29,683
73008	Bethany	(405)	22,038	22,694
74008	Bixby	(918)	6,969	3,973
74631	Blackwell	(405)	8,400	8,645
74012	Broken Arrow	(918)	35,761	11,018
73018	Chickasha	(405)	15,828	14,194
73020	Choctaw	(405)	7,520	4,750
74017	Claremore	(918)	12,085	9,084
73601	Clinton	(405)	8,796	8,513
74023	Cushing	(918)	7,720	7,529
73115	Del City	(405)	28,523	27,133
73533	Duncan	(405)	22,517	19,718
74701	Durant	(405)	11,972	11,118
73034	Edmond	(405)	34,637	16,633
73644	Elk City	(405)	9,579	7,323
73036	El Reno	(405)	15,486	14,510
73701	Enid	(405)	50,363	44,986
73503	Fort Sill(u)	(405)	15,924	21,217
73542	Frederick	(405)	6,153	6,132
73044	Guthrie	(405)	10,312	9,575
73942	Guymon	(405)	8,492	7,674
74437	Henryetta	(918)	6,432	6,430
74848	Holdenville	(405)	5,469	5,181
74743	Hugo	(405)	7,172	6,585
74745	Idabel	(405)	7,622	5,946
74037	Jenks	(918)	5,876	2,685
73501	Lawton	(405)	80,054	74,470
73055	Marlow	(405)	5,017	3,995
74501	McAlester	(918)	17,255	18,802
74354	Miami	(918)	14,237	13,880
73110	Midwest City	(405)	49,559	48,212
73060	Moore	(405)	35,063	18,761
74401	Muskogee	(918)	40,011	37,331
73064	Mustang	(405)	7,496	2,637
73069	Norman	(405)	68,020	52,117
*73125	Oklahoma City	(405)	404,014	368,164
74447	Okmulgee	(918)	16,263	15,180
74055	Owasso	(918)	6,149	3,491
73075	Pauls Valley	(405)	5,664	5,769
73077	Perry	(405)	5,796	5,341
74601	Ponca City	(405)	26,238	25,940
74953	Poteau	(918)	7,089	5,500
74361	Pryor Creek	(918)	8,483	7,057
74955	Sallisaw	(918)	6,403	4,888
74063	Sand Springs	(918)	13,121	10,565
74066	Sapulpa	(918)	15,853	15,159
74868	Seminole	(405)	8,590	7,878
74801	Shawnee	(405)	26,506	25,075
74074	Stillwater	(405)	38,268	31,126
73086	Sulphur	(405)	5,516	5,158
74464	Tahlequah	(918)	9,708	9,254
74873	Tecumseh	(405)	5,123	4,451
73120	The Village	(405)	11,114	13,695
*74101	Tulsa	(918)	360,919	330,350
74156	Turley(u)	(918)	6,336	....
74301	Vinita	(918)	6,740	5,847
74467	Wagoner	(918)	6,191	4,959
73132	Warr Acres	(405)	9,940	9,887
73096	Weatherford	(405)	9,640	7,959
74884	Wewoka	(405)	5,472	5,284
73801	Woodward	(405)	13,781	9,563
73099	Yukon	(405)	17,112	8,411

Oregon (503)

ZIP code	Place	1980	1970
97321	Albany	26,511	18,181
97005	Aloha(u)	28,353	....
97601	Altamont(u)	19,805	15,746
97520	Ashland	14,943	12,342
97103	Astoria	9,998	10,244
97814	Baker	9,471	9,354
97005	Beaverton	31,926	18,577
97701	Bend	17,263	13,710
97013	Canby	7,659	3,813
97225	Cedar Hills(u)	9,619	....
	Centennial(u)	22,118	....
97502	Central Point	6,357	4,004
97420	Coos Bay	14,424	13,466
97330	Corvallis	40,960	35,056
97424	Cottage Grove	7,148	6,004
	Cully(u)	10,569	....
97338	Dallas	8,530	6,361
97266	Errol Heights(u)	10,487	....
*97401	Eugene	105,664	79,028
97116	Forest Grove	11,499	8,275
97301	Four Corners(u)	11,331	5,823
97223	Garden Home-Whitford(u)	6,926	....
97027	Gladstone	9,500	6,254
97526	Grants Pass	14,997	12,455
97030	Gresham	33,005	10,030
97303	Hayesville(u)	9,213	5,518
97230	Hazelwood(u)	25,541	....
97838	Hermiston	9,408	4,893

ZIP code	Place		1980	1970
97123	Hillsboro	(503)	27,664	14,675
97303	Keizer(u)		18,592	11,405
97601	Klamath Falls		16,661	15,775
97850	La Grande		11,354	9,645
97034	Lake Oswego		22,527	14,615
97355	Lebanon		10,413	6,636
97367	Lincoln City		5,469	4,198
97128	McMinnville		14,080	10,125
97501	Medford		39,746	28,973
97223	Metzger(u)		5,544	....
97862	Milton-Freewater		5,086	4,105
97222	Milwaukie		17,931	16,444
97361	Monmouth		5,594	5,237
97132	Newberg		10,394	6,507
97365	Newport		7,519	5,188
97459	North Bend		9,779	8,553
.....	North Springfield(u)		6,140	....
97268	Oak Grove(u)		11,640	....
97914	Ontario		8,814	6,523
97045	Oregon City		14,673	9,176
97220	Parkrose(u)		21,108	....
97801	Pendleton		14,521	13,197
*97208	Portland		368,148	379,967
97236	Powellhurst(u)		20,132	....
97754	Prineville		5,276	4,101
97225	Raleigh Hills(u)		6,517	....
97756	Redmond		6,452	3,721
97404	River Road(u)		10,370	....
97470	Roseburg		16,644	14,461
97051	St. Helens		7,064	6,212
*97301	Salem		89,091	68,725
97401	Santa Clara(u).		14,288	....
97138	Seaside		5,193	4,402
97381	Silverton		5,168	4,301
97477	Springfield		41,621	26,874
97386	Sweet Home		6,921	3,799
97058	The Dalles		10,820	10,423
97223	Tigard		14,799	6,499
97060	Troutdale		5,908	1,661
97062	Tualatin		7,483	750
97068	West Linn		11,358	7,091
97225	West Slope(u)		5,364	....
97501	White City(u)		5,445	....
97233	Wilkes-Rockwood(u)		23,216	....
97071	Woodburn		11,196	7,495

Pennsylvania

ZIP code	Place		1980	1970
19001	Abington Township(u)	(215)	59,084	63,625
15001	Aliquippa	(412)	17,094	22,277
*18101	Allentown	(215)	103,758	109,871
*16603	Altoona	(814)	57,078	63,115
19002	Ambler	(215)	6,628	7,800
15003	Ambridge	(412)	9,575	11,324
18403	Archbald	(717)	6,295	6,118
19003	Ardmore(u)	(215)	NA	5,131
15068	Arnold	(412)	6,853	8,174
19014	Aston Township(u)	(215)	14,530	13,704
15202	Avalon	(412)	6,240	7,010
15005	Baden	(412)	5,318	5,536
19004	Bala-Cynwyd(u)	(215)	NA	6,483
15234	Baldwin	(412)	24,714	26,729
18013	Bangor	(215)	5,006	5,425
15009	Beaver	(412)	5,441	6,100
15010	Beaver Falls	(412)	12,525	14,635
16823	Bellefonte	(814)	6,300	6,828
15202	Bellevue	(412)	10,128	11,586
19020	Bensalem Township(u)	(215)	52,399	33,038
18603	Berwick	(717)	12,189	12,274
15102	Bethel Park	(412)	34,755	34,758
*18016	Bethlehem	(215)	70,419	72,686
18447	Blakely	(717)	7,438	6,391
17815	Bloomsburg	(717)	11,717	11,652
15104	Braddock	(412)	5,634	8,795
16701	Bradford	(814)	11,211	12,672
15227	Brentwood	(412)	11,859	13,732
15017	Bridgeville	(412)	6,154	6,717
19007	Bristol	(215)	10,867	12,085
19007	Bristol Twp(u)	(215)	58,733	67,498
19015	Brookhaven	(215)	7,912	7,370
16001	Butler	(412)	17,026	18,691
15419	California	(412)	5,703	6,635
17011	Camp Hill	(717)	8,422	9,931
15317	Canonsburg	(412)	10,459	11,439
18407	Carbondale	(717)	11,255	12,478
17013	Carlisle	(717)	18,314	18,079
15106	Carnegie	(412)	10,099	10,864
15108	Carnot-Moon(u)	(412)	11,102	13,093
15234	Castle Shannon	(412)	10,164	12,036
18032	Catasauqua	(215)	7,944	5,702
17201	Chambersburg	(717)	16,174	17,315
15022	Charleroi	(412)	5,717	6,723
19012	Cheltenham Twp(u).	(215)	35,509	40,238
*19013	Chester	(215)	45,794	56,331
19013	Chester Twp(u)	(215)	5,687	5,708
15025	Clairton	(412)	12,188	15,051
16214	Clarion	(814)	6,198	6,095
18411	Clarks Summit	(717)	5,272	5,376

ZIP code	Place		1980	1970
16830	Clearfield	(814)	7,580	8,176
19018	Clifton Heights	(215)	7,320	8,348
19320	Coatesville	(215)	10,698	12,331
19023	Collingdale	(215)	9,539	10,605
17512	Columbia	(717)	10,466	11,237
15425	Connellsville	(412)	10,319	11,643
19428	Conshohocken	(215)	8,591	10,195
15108	Coraopolis	(412)	7,308	8,435
16407	Corry	(814)	7,149	7,435
15026	Crafton	(412)	7,623	8,233
17821	Danville	(717)	5,239	6,176
19023	Darby	(215)	11,513	13,729
19036	Darby Twp(u)	(215)	12,264	.....
19333	Devon-Berwyn(u)	(215)	5,246	....
18519	Dickson City	(717)	6,699	7,698
15033	Donora	(412)	7,524	8,825
15216	Dormont	(412)	11,275	12,856
19335	Downingtown	(215)	7,650	7,437
18901	Doylestown	(215)	8,717	8,270
15801	Du Bois.	(814)	9,290	10,112
18512	Dunmore	(717)	16,781	18,168
15110	Duquesne	(412)	10,094	11,410
18642	Duryea	(717)	5,415	5,264
19401	East Norriton(u)	(215)	12,711	....
18042	Easton	(215)	26,027	29,450
18301	East Stroudsburg	(717)	8,039	7,894
15005	Economy	(412)	9,538	7,176
16412	Edinboro	(814)	6,324	4,871
18704	Edwardsville	(717)	5,729	5,633
17022	Elizabethtown	(717)	8,233	8,072
16117	Ellwood City	(412)	9,998	10,857
18049	Emmaus	(215)	11,001	11,511
17522	Ephrata	(717)	11,095	9,662
*16501	Erie	(814)	119,123	129,265
18643	Exeter	(717)	5,493	4,670
19054	Falls Twp(u)	(215)	36,083	35,830
16121	Farrell	(412)	8,645	11,000
19032	Folcroft	(215)	8,231	9,610
15221	Forest Hills	(412)	8,198	9,561
18704	Forty Fort	(717)	5,590	6,114
15238	Fox Chapel	(412)	5,049	4,684
17931	Frackville	(717)	5,308	5,445
16323	Franklin	(814)	8,146	8,629
15143	Franklin Park	(412)	6,135	5,310
18052	Fullerton(u)	(215)	8,055	7,908
17325	Gettysburg	(717)	7,194	7,275
15045	Glassport	(412)	6,242	7,450
19036	Glenolden	(215)	7,633	8,697
15601	Greensburg	(412)	17,558	17,077
15220	Green Tree	(412)	5,722	6,441
16125	Greenville	(412)	7,730	8,704
16127	Grove City	(412)	8,162	8,312
17331	Hanover	(717)	14,890	15,623
*17105	Harrisburg	(717)	53,264	68,061
19040	Hatboro	(215)	7,579	8,880
19083	Haverford Twp(u)	(215)	52,349	55,132
18201	Hazleton	(717)	27,318	30,426
18055	Hellertown	(215)	6,025	6,615
17033	Hershey(u)	(717)	13,249	7,407
18042	Highland Park (Northampton)(u)	(215)	5,922	5,500
16648	Hollidaysburg	(814)	5,892	6,262
16001	Homeacre-Lyndora(u)	(412)	8,333	8,415
15120	Homestead	(412)	5,092	6,309
18431	Honesdale	(717)	5,128	5,224
19044	Horsham(u)	(215)	9,900	....
17036	Hummelstown	(717)	6,159	4,723
16652	Huntingdon	(814)	7,042	6,987
15701	Indiana	(412)	16,051	16,100
15644	Jeannette	(412)	13,106	15,209
15344	Jefferson	(412)	8,643	8,512
18229	Jim Thorpe	(717)	5,263	5,456
*15901	Johnstown	(814)	35,496	42,476
15108	Kennedy Twp(u)	(412)	7,159	6,859
18704	Kingston	(717)	15,681	18,325
16201	Kittanning	(412)	5,432	6,231
*17604	Lancaster	(717)	54,725	57,690
19446	Lansdale	(215)	16,526	18,451
19050	Lansdowne	(215)	11,891	14,090
15650	Latrobe	(412)	10,799	11,749
17042	Lebanon	(717)	25,711	28,572
18235	Lehighton	(215)	5,826	6,095
17837	Lewisburg	(717)	5,407	5,718
17044	Lewistown	(717)	9,830	11,098
17543	Lititz	(717)	7,590	7,072
17745	Lock Haven	(717)	9,617	11,427
15068	Lower Burrell	(412)	13,200	13,654
19003	Lower Merion Twp(u)	(215)	59,651	63,392
19006	Lower Moreland Twp(u)	(215)	12,472	11,746
19047	Lower Southampton Twp(u).	(215)	18,305	17,576
19008	Marple Twp(u)	(215)	23,642	25,040
15237	McCandless Twp(u)	(412)	26,250	22,404
*15134	McKeesport	(412)	31,012	37,977
15136	McKees Rocks	(412)	8,742	11,901
17948	Mahanoy City	(717)	6,167	7,257
17545	Manheim	(717)	5,015	5,434
16335	Meadville	(814)	15,544	16,573
17055	Mechanicsburg	(717)	9,487	9,385
*19063	Media	(215)	6,119	6,444
17057	Middletown (Dauphin)	(717)	10,122	9,080
18017	Middletown (Northampton)(u)	(215)	5,801	....

ZIP code	Place		1980	1970
.....	Middletown Twp (Delaware)(u)	(215)	12,463	12,878
17551	Millersville	(717)	7,668	6,396
17847	Milton	(717)	6,730	7,723
17954	Minersville	(717)	5,635	6,012
15061	Monaca	(412)	7,661	7,486
15062	Monessen	(412)	11,928	15,216
15063	Monongahela	(412)	5,950	7,113
15146	Monroeville	(412)	30,977	29,011
17754	Montoursville	(717)	5,403	5,985
18507	Moosic	(717)	6,068	4,646
19067	Morrisville	(215)	9,845	11,309
17851	Mount Carmel	(717)	8,190	9,317
17552	Mount Joy	(717)	5,680	5,041
15666	Mount Pleasant	(412)	5,354	5,895
15228	Mount Lebanon(u)	(412)	34,414	39,157
15120	Munhall	(412)	14,535	16,574
15668	Murrysville	(412)	16,036	12,661
18634	Nanticoke	(717)	13,044	14,638
18064	Nazareth	(215)	5,443	5,815
.....	Nether Providence Twp(u)	(215)	12,730	13,644
15066	New Brighton	(412)	7,364	7,637
*16101	New Castle	(412)	33,621	38,559
17070	New Cumberland	(717)	8,051	9,803
15068	New Kensington	(412)	17,660	20,312
*19401	Norristown	(215)	34,684	38,169
18067	Northampton	(215)	8,240	8,389
15104	North Braddock	(412)	8,711	10,838
15137	North Versailles(u)	(412)	13,294	.....
16421	Northwest Harbor-Creek(u)	(814)	7,485	.....
19074	Norwood	(215)	6,647	7,229
15139	Oakmont	(412)	7,039	7,550
16301	Oil City	(814)	13,881	15,033
18518	Old Forge	(717)	9,304	9,522
18447	Olyphant	(717)	5,204	5,422
18071	Palmerton	(215)	5,455	5,620
17078	Palmyra	(717)	7,228	7,615
19301	Paoli(u)	(215)	6,698	5,835
17331	Parkville(u)	(717)	5,009	5,120
15235	Penn Hills(u)	(412)	57,632	.....
18944	Perkasie	(215)	5,241	5,451
*19104	Philadelphia	(215)	1,688,210	1,949,996
19460	Phoenixville	(215)	14,165	14,823
*15219	Pittsburgh	(412)	423,959	520,089
*18640	Pittston	(717)	9,930	11,113
18705	Plains(u)	(717)	5,455	6,606
15236	Pleasant Hills	(412)	9,604	10,409
15239	Plum	(412)	25,390	21,932
18651	Plymouth	(717)	7,605	9,536
19462	Plymouth Twp(u)	(215)	17,168	16,876
15133	Port Vue	(412)	5,316	5,862
19464	Pottstown	(215)	22,729	25,355
17901	Pottsville	(717)	18,195	19,715
19076	Prospect Park	(215)	6,593	7,250
15767	Punxsutawney	(814)	7,479	7,792
18951	Quakertown	(215)	8,867	7,276
19087	Radnor Twp(u)	(215)	27,676	27,459
*19603	Reading	(215)	78,686	87,643
17356	Red Lion	(717)	5,824	5,645
18954	Richboro(u)	(215)	5,141	.....
15853	Ridgway	(814)	5,604	6,022
19078	Ridley Park	(215)	7,889	9,025
19033	Ridley Twp(u)	(215)	33,771	39,085
15237	Ross Twp(u)	(412)	35,102	32,892
15857	St. Marys	(814)	6,417	7,470
18840	Sayre	(717)	6,951	7,473
17972	Schuylkill Haven	(717)	5,977	6,125
15683	Scottdale	(412)	5,833	5,818
15106	Scott Twp(u)	(412)	20,413	21,856
*18503	Scranton	(717)	88,117	102,696
17870	Selinsgrove	(717)	5,227	5,116
15116	Shaler Twp(u)	(412)	33,712	33,369
17872	Shamokin	(717)	10,357	11,719
16146	Sharon	(412)	19,057	22,653
19079	Sharon Hill	(215)	6,221	7,464
16150	Sharpsville	(412)	5,375	6,126
17976	Shenandoah	(717)	7,589	8,287
19607	Shillington	(215)	5,601	6,249
17404	Shiloh(u)	(717)	5,315	.....
17257	Shippensburg	(717)	5,261	6,536
15501	Somerset	(814)	6,474	6,269
18964	Souderton	(215)	6,657	6,366
17701	South Williamsport	(717)	6,581	7,153
19064	Springfield(u)	(215)	25,326	.....
19118	Springfield Twp(u)	(215)	20,344	22,394
16801	State College	(814)	36,130	32,833
17113	Steelton	(717)	6,484	8,556
15136	Stowe Twp(u)	(412)	9,202	10,119
18360	Stroudsburg	(717)	5,148	5,451
16323	Sugar Creek	(814)	5,954	5,944
17801	Sunbury	(717)	12,292	13,025
19081	Swarthmore	(215)	5,950	6,156
17111	Swatara Twp(u)	(717)	18,796	17,178
15218	Swissvale	(412)	11,345	13,819
18704	Swoyersville	(717)	5,795	6,786
18252	Tamaqua	(717)	8,843	9,246
15084	Tarentum	(412)	6,419	7,379
18517	Taylor	(717)	7,246	6,977
16354	Titusville	(814)	6,884	7,331

ZIP code	Place		1980	1970
19401	Trooper(u)	(215)	7,370	.....
15145	Turtle Creek	(412)	6,959	8,308
16686	Tyrone	(814)	6,346	7,072
15401	Uniontown	(412)	14,510	16,282
19061	Upper Chichester Twp(u)	(215)	14,377	11,414
19082	Upper Darby(u)	(215)	84,054	95,910
19034	Upper Dublin Twp(u)	(215)	22,348	19,449
19406	Upper Merion Twp(u)	(215)	26,138	23,699
19090	Upper Moreland Twp(u)	(215)	25,874	24,866
19063	Upper Providence Twp(u)	(215)	9,477	9,234
15241	Upper St. Clair(u)	(412)	19,023	.....
19006	Upper Southampton Twp(u)	(215)	15,806	13,936
15690	Vandergrift	(412)	6,823	7,889
19974	Warminster(u)	(215)	35,543	.....
16365	Warren	(814)	12,146	12,998
15301	Washington	(412)	18,363	19,827
17268	Waynesboro	(717)	9,726	10,011
.....	Weigelstown(u)	(717)	5,213	.....
*19380	West Chester	(215)	17,435	19,301
19380	West Goshen(u)	(215)	7,998	.....
15122	West Mifflin	(412)	26,322	28,070
19401	West Norriton(u)	(215)	14,034	.....
15905	Westmont	(814)	6,113	6,673
18643	West Pittston	(717)	5,980	7,074
15229	West View	(412)	7,648	8,312
18052	Whitehall	(215)	15,143	16,450
19428	Whitemarsh Twp(u)	(215)	15,101	15,886
15131	White Oak	(412)	9,480	9,304
*18701	Wilkes-Barre	(717)	51,551	58,856
15221	Wilkinsburg	(412)	23,669	26,780
15145	Wilkins Twp(u)	(412)	8,472	8,749
17701	Williamsport	(717)	33,401	37,918
15025	Wilson	(412)	7,564	8,406
15963	Windber	(814)	5,585	6,332
19610	Wyomissing	(215)	6,551	7,136
19050	Yeadon	(215)	11,727	12,136
*17405	York	(717)	44,619	50,335

Rhode Island (401)

See Note on Page 564

ZIP code	Place	1980	1970
02806	Barrington	16,174	17,554
02809	Bristol	20,128	17,860
02830	Burrillville	13,164	10,087
02863	Central Falls	16,995	18,716
02816	Coventry	27,065	22,947
02910	Cranston	71,992	74,287
02864	Cumberland	27,069	26,605
02864	Cumberland Hill(u)	5,421	.....
02818	East Greenwich	10,211	9,577
02914	East Providence	50,980	48,207
02814	Glocester	7,550	5,160
02828	Greenville(u)	7,576	.....
02833	Hopkinton	6,406	5,392
02919	Johnston	24,907	22,037
02881	Kingston(u)	5,479	5,601
02865	Lincoln	16,949	16,182
02840	Middletown	17,216	29,290
02882	Narragansett	12,088	7,138
02840	Newport	29,259	34,562
02843	Newport East(u)	11,030	10,285
02852	North Kingstown	21,938	29,793
02908	North Providence	29,188	24,337
02876	North Smithfield	9,972	9,349
*02860	Pawtucket	71,204	76,984
02871	Portsmouth	14,257	12,521
*02904	Providence	156,804	179,116
02857	Scituate	8,405	7,489
02917	Smithfield	16,886	13,468
02879	South Kingstown	20,414	16,913
02878	Tiverton	13,526	12,559
02864	Valley Falls(u)	10,892	.....
*02880	Wakefield-Peacedale(u)	6,474	6,331
02885	Warren	10,640	10,523
*02887	Warwick	87,123	83,694
02891	Westerly	18,580	17,248
02891	Westerly Center(u)	14,093	13,654
02893	West Warwick	27,026	24,323
02895	Woonsocket	45,914	46,820

South Carolina (803)

ZIP code	Place	1980	1970
29620	Abbeville	5,863	5,515
29801	Aiken	14,978	13,436
29621	Anderson	27,546	27,556
29407	Avondale-Moorland(u)	5,255	5,236
29812	Barnwell	5,572	4,439
29902	Beaufort	8,634	9,434
29627	Belton	5,312	5,257
29841	Belvedere(u)	6,859	.....
29512	Bennettsville	8,774	7,468
29611	Berea(u)	13,164	7,186
.....	Brookdale(u)	6,123	.....
29020	Camden	7,462	8,532
29209	Capitol View(u)	9,962	.....
29033	Cayce	11,701	9,967
*29401	Charleston	69,779	66,945
29404	Charleston Base(u)	NA	6,238

ZIP code	Place	1980	1970
29408	Charleston Yard(u)	NA	13,565
29520	Cheraw	5,654	5,627
29706	Chester	6,820	7,045
29631	Clemson	8,118	6,690
29325	Clinton	8,596	8,138
*29201	Columbia	101,229	113,542
29526	Conway	10,240	8,151
29532	Darlington	7,989	6,990
29204	Dentsville(u)	13,579	....
29536	Dillon	7,042	6,391
29405	Dorchester Terrace-Brentwood(u)	7,862	....
29601	Dunean(u)	5,146	1,266
29640	Easley	14,264	11,175
29501	Florence	29,842	25,997
29206	Forest Acres	6,062	6,808
29340	Gaffney	13,453	13,131
29605	Gantt(u)	13,719	11,386
29440	Georgetown	10,144	10,449
29445	Goose Creek	17,811	3,825
*29602	Greenville	58,242	61,436
29203	Greenview(u)	5,515	....
29646	Greenwood	21,613	21,069
29651	Greer	10,525	10,642
29410	Hanahan	13,224	9,118
29550	Hartsville	7,631	8,017
29928	Hilton Head Island(u)	11,344	....
29621	Homeland Park(u)	6,720	....
29412	James Island(u)	24,124	....
29456	Ladson(u)	13,246	....
29560	Lake City	5,636	6,247
29720	Lancaster	9,703	9,186
29902	Laurel Bay(u)	5,238	....
29360	Laurens	10,587	10,298
29571	Marion	7,700	7,435
29662	Mauldin	8,143	3,797
29464	Mount Pleasant	14,464	6,879
29574	Mullins	6,068	6,006
29577	Myrtle Beach	18,758	9,035
29108	Newberry	9,866	9,218
29841	North Augusta	13,593	12,883
29406	North Charleston	62,479	21,211
....	North Trenholm(u)	10,962	....
29565	Oak Grove(u)	7,092	....
29115	Orangeburg	14,933	13,252
29905	Parris Island(u)	7,752	8,868
29483	Pinehurst-Sheppard Park(u)	6,956	1,711
29730	Rock Hill	35,327	33,846
29407	St. Andrews (Charleston)(u)	9,908	9,202
29210	St. Andrews (Richland)(u)	20,245	....
29609	Sans Souci(u)	8,393	....
29678	Seneca	7,436	6,573
....	Seven Oaks(u)	16,604	....
29152	Shaw AFB(u)	6,939	5,819
29681	Simpsonville	9,037	3,308
....	South Sumter(u)	7,096	....
*29301	Spartanburg	43,826	44,546
29483	Summerville	6,492	3,839
29150	Sumter	24,921	24,555
29687	Taylors(u)	15,801	6,831
29379	Union	10,523	10,775
29205	Valencia Heights(u)	5,328	....
29607	Wade-Hampton(u)	20,180	17,152
29488	Walterboro	6,036	6,257
29405	Wando Woods(u)	5,266	....
29611	Welcome(u)	6,922	....
29169	West Columbia	10,409	7,838
29206	Woodfield(u)	9,588	....
29388	Woodruff	5,171	4,690
29745	York	6,412	5,081

South Dakota (605)

ZIP code	Place	1980	1970
57401	Aberdeen	25,851	26,476
57006	Brookings	14,951	13,717
57350	Huron	13,000	14,299
57042	Madison	6,210	6,315
57301	Mitchell	13,916	13,425
57501	Pierre	11,973	9,699
57701	Rapid City	46,492	43,836
*57101	Sioux Falls	81,343	72,488
57785	Sturgis	5,184	4,536
57069	Vermillion	9,582	9,128
57201	Watertown	15,649	13,388
57078	Yankton	12,011	11,919

Tennessee

ZIP code	Place	Area	1980	1970
37701	Alcoa	(615)	6,870	7,739
37303	Athens	(615)	12,080	11,790
38134	Bartlett	(901)	17,170	1,150
37660	Bloomingdale(u)	(615)	12,088	3,120
38008	Bolivar	(901)	6,597	6,674
37027	Brentwood	(615)	9,431	4,099
37620	Bristol	(615)	23,986	20,064
38012	Brownsville	(901)	9,307	7,011
*37401	Chattanooga	(615)	169,514	119,923
37040	Clarksville	(615)	54,777	31,719
37311	Cleveland	(615)	26,415	21,446
37716	Clinton	(615)	5,245	4,794
38017	Collierville	(901)	7,839	3,651
37663	Colonial Heights(u)	(615)	6,744	3,027
38401	Columbia	(615)	26,571	21,471
37922	Concord (Knox)(u)	(615)	8,569	....
38501	Cookeville	(615)	20,350	14,403
38019	Covington	(901)	6,065	5,801
38555	Crossville	(615)	6,394	5,381
37321	Dayton	(615)	5,233	4,361
37055	Dickson	(615)	7,040	5,665
38024	Dyersburg	(901)	15,856	14,523
37801	Eagleton Village(u)	(615)	5,331	5,345
37412	East Ridge	(615)	21,236	21,799
37643	Elizabethton	(615)	12,431	12,269
37334	Fayetteville	(615)	7,559	7,691
37064	Franklin	(615)	12,407	9,497
37066	Gallatin	(615)	17,191	13,253
38138	Germantown	(901)	21,482	3,474
37072	Goodlettsville	(615)	8,327	6,168
37075	Greater Hendersonville(u)	(615)	25,029	11,996
37743	Greeneville	(615)	14,097	13,722
37918	Halls(u)	(615)	10,363	....
37748	Harriman	(615)	8,303	8,734
37341	Harrison(u)	(615)	6,206	....
37075	Hendersonville	(615)	26,561	412
38343	Humboldt	(901)	10,209	10,066
38301	Jackson	(901)	49,258	39,996
37760	Jefferson City	(615)	5,612	5,124
37601	Johnson City	(615)	39,753	33,770
*37662	Kingsport	(615)	32,027	31,938
*37901	Knoxville	(615)	175,045	174,587
37766	La Follette	(615)	8,176	6,902
37086	LaVergne	(615)	5,495	5,220
38464	Lawrenceburg	(615)	10,175	8,889
37087	Lebanon	(615)	11,872	12,492
37771	Lenoir City	(615)	5,180	5,324
37091	Lewisburg	(615)	8,760	7,207
38351	Lexington	(901)	5,934	5,024
37665	Lynn Garden(u)	(615)	7,213	....
38201	McKenzie	(901)	5,405	4,873
37110	McMinnville	(615)	10,683	10,662
37355	Manchester	(615)	7,250	6,208
38237	Martin	(901)	8,898	7,781
37701	Maryville	(615)	17,480	13,808
*38101	Memphis	(901)	646,174	623,988
37343	Middle Valley(u)	(615)	11,420	....
38358	Milan	(901)	8,083	7,313
38053	Millington	(901)	20,236	21,177
37814	Morristown	(615)	19,570	20,318
37130	Murfreesboro	(615)	32,845	26,360
*37202	Nashville-Davidson	(615)	455,651	**426,029
37821	Newport	(615)	7,580	7,328
37830	Oak Ridge	(615)	27,662	28,319
38242	Paris	(901)	10,728	9,892
37849	Powell(u)	(615)	7,220	....
38478	Pulaski	(615)	7,184	6,989
37415	Red Bank White Oak	(615)	13,129	12,715
38063	Ripley	(901)	6,366	4,794
37854	Rockwood	(615)	5,687	5,259
38372	Savannah	(901)	6,992	5,576
37160	Shelbyville	(615)	13,530	12,262
37377	Signal Mountain	(615)	5,818	4,839
37167	Smyrna	(615)	8,839	5,698
37379	Soddy-Daisy	(615)	8,388	7,569
37172	Springfield	(615)	10,814	9,720
37363	Summit (Hamilton)(u)	(615)	8,345	....
37388	Tullahoma	(615)	15,800	15,311
38261	Union City	(901)	10,436	11,925
37398	Winchester	(615)	5,821	5,256

**Comprises the Metropolitan Government of Nashville and Davidson County.

Texas

ZIP code	Place	Area	1980	1970
*79604	Abilene	(915)	98,315	89,653
75001	Addison	(214)	5,553	593
78516	Alamo	(512)	5,831	4,291
78209	Alamo Heights	(512)	6,252	6,933
77039	Aldine(u)	(713)	12,623	....
78332	Alice	(512)	20,961	20,121
75002	Allen	(214)	8,314	1,940
79830	Alpine	(915)	5,465	5,971
77511	Alvin	(713)	16,515	10,671
*79105	Amarillo	(806)	149,230	127,010
79714	Andrews	(915)	11,061	8,625
77515	Angleton	(409)	13,929	9,906
78336	Aransas Pass	(512)	7,173	5,813
*76010	Arlington	(817)	160,113	90,229
75751	Athens	(214)	10,197	9,582
75551	Atlanta	(214)	6,272	5,007
*78710	Austin	(512)	345,890	253,539
76020	Azle	(817)	5,822	4,493
75149	Balch Springs	(214)	13,746	10,464
77414	Bay City	(409)	17,837	13,445
77520	Baytown	(713)	56,923	43,980
*77704	Beaumont	(409)	118,102	117,548
76021	Bedford	(817)	20,821	10,049
78102	Beeville	(512)	14,574	13,506
77401	Bellaire	(713)	14,950	19,009

ZIP code	Place	1980	1970	ZIP code	Place	1980	1970
76704	Bellmead (817)	7,569	7,698	77562	Highlands (713)	6,467	3,462
76513	Belton (817)	10,660	8,696	76645	Hillsboro (817)	7,397	7,224
76126	Benbrook (817)	13,579	8,169	77563	Hitchcock (713)	6,103	5,565
79720	Big Spring (915)	24,804	28,735	78861	Hondo (512)	6,057	5,487
75418	Bonham (214)	7,338	7,698	*77013	Houston (713)	1,595,138	1,233,535
79007	Borger (806)	15,837	14,195	77338	Humble (713)	6,729	3,272
76230	Bowie (817)	5,610	5,185	77340	Huntsville (409)	23,936	17,610
76825	Brady (915)	5,969	5,557	76053	Hurst (817)	31,420	27,215
76024	Breckenridge (817)	6,921	5,944	78362	Ingleside (512)	5,436	3,763
77833	Brenham (409)	10,966	8,922	76367	Iowa Park (817)	6,184	5,796
77611	Bridge City (713)	7,667	8,164	*75061	Irving (214)	109,943	97,260
79316	Brownfield (806)	10,387	9,647	77029	Jacinto City (713)	8,953	9,563
78520	Brownsville (512)	84,997	52,522	75766	Jacksonville (214)	12,264	9,734
76801	Brownwood (915)	19,203	17,368	75951	Jasper (409)	6,959	6,251
77801	Bryan (409)	44,337	33,719	77450	Katy (713)	5,660	2,923
76354	Burkburnett (817)	10,668	9,230	79745	Kermit (915)	8,015	7,884
76028	Burleson (817)	11,734	7,713	78028	Kerrville (512)	15,276	12,672
76520	Cameron (817)	5,721	5,546	75662	Kilgore (214)	11,331	9,495
79015	Canyon (806)	10,724	8,333	76541	Killeen (817)	46,296	35,507
78834	Carrizo Springs (512)	6,886	5,374	78363	Kingsville (512)	28,808	28,915
75006	Carrollton (214)	40,591	13,855	....	Kingwood (713)	16,261	....
75633	Carthage (214)	6,447	5,392	78219	Kirby (512)	6,435	3,238
75104	Cedar Hill (214)	6,849	2,610	78236	Lackland AFB(u) (512)	14,459	19,141
75935	Center (409)	5,827	4,989	77566	Lake Jackson (409)	19,102	13,376
....	Champions(u) (713)	14,692	....	77568	La Marque (409)	15,372	16,131
77530	Channelview(u) (713)	17,471	....	79631	Lamesa (806)	11,790	11,559
79201	Childress (817)	5,817	5,408	76550	Lampasas (512)	6,165	5,922
76031	Cleburne (817)	19,218	16,015	75146	Lancaster (214)	14,807	10,522
77327	Cleveland (713)	5,977	5,627	77571	La Porte (713)	14,062	7,149
77015	Clover Leaf(u) (713)	17,317	....	78040	Laredo (512)	91,449	69,024
77531	Clute (409)	9,577	6,023	77573	League City (713)	16,578	10,818
76834	Coleman (915)	5,960	5,608	78238	Leon Valley (512)	9,088	2,487
77840	College Station (409)	37,272	17,676	79336	Levelland (806)	13,809	11,445
76034	Colleyville (817)	6,700	3,342	75067	Lewisville (214)	24,273	9,264
79512	Colorado City (915)	5,405	5,227	77575	Liberty (713)	7,945	5,591
75428	Commerce (214)	8,136	9,534	79339	Littlefield (806)	7,409	6,738
77301	Conroe (409)	18,034	11,969	78233	Live Oak (512)	8,183	2,779
78109	Converse (512)	5,150	1,383	78644	Lockhart (512)	7,953	6,489
76522	Copperas Cove (817)	19,469	10,818	75601	Longview (214)	62,762	45,547
*78408	Corpus Christi (512)	232,134	204,525	*79408	Lubbock (806)	173,873	149,101
75110	Corsicana (214)	21,712	19,972	75901	Lufkin (409)	28,562	23,049
75835	Crockett (713)	7,405	6,616	78648	Luling (512)	5,039	4,719
76036	Crowley (817)	5,852	2,662	78501	McAllen (512)	67,042	37,636
78839	Crystal City (512)	8,334	8,104	75069	McKinney (214)	16,249	15,193
77954	Cuero (512)	7,124	6,956	77063	Mansfield (817)	8,092	3,658
79022	Dalhart (806)	6,854	5,705	76661	Marlin (817)	7,099	6,351
*75260	Dallas (214)	904,599	844,401	75670	Marshall (214)	24,921	22,937
77536	Deer Park (713)	22,648	12,773	76368	Mathis (512)	5,667	5,351
78840	Del Rio (512)	30,034	21,330	78570	Mercedes (512)	11,851	9,355
75020	Denison (214)	23,884	24,923	75149	Mesquite (214)	67,053	55,131
76201	Denton (817)	48,063	39,874	76667	Mexia (817)	7,094	5,943
75115	De Soto (214)	15,538	6,617	79701	Midland (915)	70,525	59,463
77539	Dickinson (713)	7,505	10,776	76067	Mineral Wells (817)	14,468	18,411
79027	Dimmitt (806)	5,019	4,327	78572	Mission (512)	22,653	13,043
78537	Donna (512)	9,952	7,365	77459	Missouri City (713)	24,423	4,136
79029	Dumas (806)	12,194	9,771	79756	Monahans (915)	8,397	8,333
75116	Duncanville (214)	27,781	14,105	75455	Mount Pleasant (214)	11,003	9,459
78852	Eagle Pass (512)	21,407	15,364	75961	Nacogdoches (409)	27,149	22,544
78539	Edinburg (512)	24,075	17,163	77868	Navasota (409)	5,971	5,111
77957	Edna (512)	5,650	5,332	77627	Nederland (409)	16,855	16,810
77437	El Campo (619)	10,462	9,332	78130	New Braunfels (512)	22,402	17,859
*79910	El Paso (915)	425,259	322,261	76118	North Richland Hills (817)	30,592	16,514
78543	Elsa (512)	5,061	4,400	*79760	Odessa (915)	90,027	78,380
75119	Ennis (214)	12,110	11,046	77630	Orange (409)	23,628	24,457
76039	Euless (817)	24,002	19,316	75801	Palestine (214)	15,948	14,525
76140	Everman (817)	5,387	4,570	79065	Pampa (806)	21,396	21,726
78355	Falfurrias (512)	6,103	6,355	75460	Paris (214)	25,498	23,441
75234	Farmers Branch (214)	24,863	27,492	*77501	Pasadena (713)	112,560	89,957
76119	Forest Hill (817)	11,684	8,236	77581	Pearland (713)	13,248	6,444
79906	Fort Bliss(u) (915)	12,687	13,288	78061	Pearsall (512)	7,383	5,545
76544	Fort Hood(u) (817)	31,250	32,597	79772	Pecos (915)	12,855	12,682
79735	Fort Stockton (915)	8,688	8,283	79070	Perryton (806)	7,991	7,810
*76101	Fort Worth (817)	385,164	393,455	78577	Pharr (512)	21,381	15,829
78624	Fredericksburg (512)	6,412	5,326	79072	Plainview (806)	22,187	19,096
77541	Freeport (409)	13,444	11,997	75075	Plano (214)	72,331	17,872
77546	Friendswood (713)	10,719	5,675	78064	Pleasanton (512)	6,346	5,407
76240	Gainesville (817)	14,081	13,830	77640	Port Arthur (409)	61,195	57,371
77547	Galena Park (713)	9,879	10,479	78374	Portland (512)	12,023	7,302
77550	Galveston (409)	61,902	61,809	77979	Port Lavaca (512)	10,911	10,491
*75040	Garland (214)	138,857	81,437	77651	Port Neches (713)	13,944	10,894
76528	Gatesville (817)	6,078	4,683	78580	Raymondville (512)	9,493	7,987
78626	Georgetown (512)	9,468	6,395	75080	Richardson (214)	72,496	48,405
75644	Gilmer (214)	5,167	4,196	76118	Richland Hills (817)	7,977	8,865
75647	Gladewater (214)	6,548	5,574	77469	Richmond (713)	9,692	5,777
78629	Gonzales (512)	7,152	5,854	78582	Rio Grande City(u) (512)	8,930	5,676
76046	Graham (817)	9,055	7,477	77019	River Oaks (817)	6,890	8,193
75050	Grand Prairie (214)	71,462	50,904	76701	Robinson (817)	6,074	3,807
76051	Grapevine (817)	11,801	7,049	78380	Robstown (512)	12,100	11,217
75401	Greenville (214)	22,161	22,043	76567	Rockdale (512)	5,611	4,655
77619	Groves (409)	17,090	18,067	75087	Rockwall (214)	5,939	3,121
76117	Haltom City (817)	29,014	28,127	77471	Rosenberg (713)	17,840	12,098
76541	Harker Heights (817)	7,345	4,216	78664	Round Rock (512)	12,740	2,811
78550	Harlingen (512)	43,543	33,503	75088	Rowlett (214)	7,522	2,243
77859	Hearne (713)	5,418	4,982	76179	Saginaw (817)	5,736	2,382
75652	Henderson (214)	11,473	10,187	76901	San Angelo (915)	73,240	63,884
79045	Hereford (806)	15,853	13,414	*78284	San Antonio (512)	785,940	654,153
76643	Hewitt (817)	5,247	569	78586	San Benito (512)	17,988	15,176
75205	Highland Park (214)	8,909	10,133	78384	San Diego (512)	5,225	4,490
				78589	San Juan (512)	7,608	5,070
				78666	San Marcos (512)	23,420	18,860
				77550	Santa Fe (713)	5,413	....

ZIP code	Place		1980	1970
78154	Schertz	(512)	7,262	4,061
75159	Seagoville	(214)	7,304	4,390
78155	Seguin	(512)	17,854	15,934
79360	Seminole	(915)	6,080	5,007
75090	Sherman	(214)	30,413	29,061
77656	Silsbee	(713)	7,684	7,271
78387	Sinton	(512)	6,044	5,563
79364	Slaton	(806)	6,804	6,583
79549	Snyder	(915)	12,705	11,171
77587	South Houston	(713)	13,293	11,527
76401	Stephenville	(817)	11,881	9,277
77478	Sugar Land	(713)	8,826	3,318
75482	Sulphur Springs	(214)	12,804	10,642
79556	Sweetwater	(915)	12,242	12,020
76574	Taylor	(512)	10,619	9,616
76501	Temple	(817)	42,354	33,431
75160	Terrell	(214)	13,269	14,182
75501	Texarkana	(214)	31,271	30,497
77590	Texas City	(409)	41,201	38,908
75056	The Colony	(214)	11,586	....
77380	The Woodlands	(713)	8,443	....
79088	Tulia	(806)	5,033	5,294
75701	Tyler	(214)	70,508	57,770
78148	Universal City	(512)	10,720	7,613
76308	University Park	(214)	22,254	23,498
78801	Uvalde	(512)	14,178	10,764
76384	Vernon	(817)	12,695	11,454
77901	Victoria	(512)	50,695	41,349
77662	Vidor	(713)	11,834	9,738
*76701	Waco	(817)	101,261	95,326
76148	Watauga	(817)	10,284	3,778
75165	Waxahachie	(214)	14,624	13,452
76086	Weatherford	(817)	12,049	11,750
78596	Weslaco	(512)	19,331	15,313
77005	West University Place	(713)	12,010	13,317
77488	Wharton	(713)	9,033	7,881
76108	White Settlement	(817)	13,508	13,449
*76307	Wichita Falls	(817)	94,201	96,265
78239	Windcrest	(512)	5,332	3,371
76710	Woodway	(817)	7,091	4,819
77995	Yoakum	(512)	6,148	5,755

Utah (801)

		1980	1970
84003	American Fork	12,417	7,713
84118	Bennion(u)	9,632	....
84010	Bountiful	32,877	27,751
84302	Brigham City	15,596	14,007
84720	Cedar City	10,972	8,946
84014	Centerville	8,069	3,268
84015	Clearfield	17,982	13,316
84015	Clinton	5,777	1,768
84121	Cottonwood(u)	11,554	8,431
84121	Cottonwood Heights(u)	22,665	....
84020	Draper	5,530	....
84109	East Millcreek(u)	24,150	26,579
84106	Granite Park(u)	5,554	9,573
84117	Holladay(u)	22,189	23,014
84037	Kaysville	9,811	6,192
84118	Kearns(u)	21,353	17,247
84041	Layton	22,862	13,603
84043	Lehi	6,848	4,659
84321	Logan	26,844	22,333
84044	Magna(u)	13,138	5,509
84047	Midvale	10,144	7,840
84532	Moab	5,333	4,793
84117	Mount Olympus(u)	6,068	5,909
84107	Murray	25,750	21,206
84404	North Ogden	9,309	5,257
84054	North Salt Lake	5,548	2,143
*84401	Ogden	64,407	69,478
84057	Orem	52,399	25,729
84651	Payson	8,246	4,501
84062	Pleasant Grove	10,669	5,327
84501	Price	9,086	6,218
84601	Provo	74,111	53,131
84701	Richfield	5,482	4,471
84065	Riverton	7,032	2,820
84067	Roy	19,694	14,356
84770	St. George	11,350	7,097
*84101	Salt Lake City	163,034	175,885
84070	Sandy City	52,210	6,438
84121	South Cottonwood(u)	11,117	....
84065	South Jordan	7,492	2,942
84403	South Ogden	11,366	9,991
84115	South Salt Lake	10,413	7,810
84660	Spanish Fork	9,825	7,284
84663	Springville	12,101	8,790
84015	Sunset	5,733	6,268
84107	Taylorsville(u)	17,448	....
84074	Tooele	14,335	12,539
84047	Union-East Midvale(u)	9,665	....
84010	Val Verda(u)	6,422	....
84078	Vernal	6,600	3,908
84403	Washington Terrace	8,212	7,241
84084	West Jordan	27,325	4,221
84119	West Valley(u)	72,299	....
84070	White City(u)	7,180	6,402

Vermont (802)

See Note on Page 564

		1980	1970
05641	Barre	9,824	10,209
.....	Barre	7,090	6,509
05201	Bennington	15,815	14,586
.....	Bennington(u)	9,349	7,950
05301	Brattleboro Center(u)	8,596	9,055
.....	Brattleboro	11,886	12,239
05401	Burlington	37,712	38,633
05446	Colchester	12,629	8,776
05451	Essex	14,392	10,951
05452	Essex Junction	7,033	6,511
05753	Middlebury	7,574	6,532
05602	Montpelier	8,241	8,609
05701	Rutland	18,436	19,293
05478	St. Albans	7,308	8,082
05819	St. Johnsbury	7,938	8,409
05401	South Burlington	10,679	10,032
05156	Springfield Center(u)	5,603	5,632
.....	Springfield	10,190	10,063
05404	Winooski	6,318	7,309

Virginia

			1980	1970
*22313	Alexandria	(703)	103,217	110,927
*22003	Annandale(u)	(703)	49,524	27,405
*22210	Arlington(u)	(703)	152,599	174,284
22041	Bailey's Crossroads(u)	(703)	12,564	7,295
24523	Bedford	(703)	5,991	6,011
22307	Belle Haven(u)	(703)	6,520	....
23234	Bellwood(u)	(804)	6,439	....
23234	Bensley(u)	(804)	5,299	....
24060	Blacksburg	(703)	30,638	9,384
24605	Bluefield	(703)	5,946	5,286
23235	Bon Air(u)	(804)	16,224	10,771
24201	Bristol	(703)	19,042	14,857
24416	Buena Vista	(703)	6,717	6,425
22015	Burke(u)	(703)	33,835	....
24018	Cave Spring(u)	(703)	21,682	....
22020	Centreville(u)	(703)	7,473	....
23227	Chamberlayne(u)	(804)	5,136	....
22021	Chantilly(u)	(703)	12,259	....
*22906	Charlottesville	(804)	45,010	38,880
*23320	Chesapeake	(804)	114,226	89,580
23831	Chester(u)	(804)	11,728	5,556
24073	Christiansburg	(703)	10,345	7,857
24422	Clifton Forge	(703)	5,046	5,501
24078	Collinsville(u)	(703)	7,517	6,015
23834	Colonial Heights	(804)	16,509	15,097
24426	Covington	(703)	9,063	10,060
22701	Culpeper	(703)	6,621	6,056
22191	Dale City(u)	(703)	33,127	13,857
24541	Danville	(804)	45,642	46,391
23228	Dumbarton(u)	(804)	8,149	....
22027	Dunn Loring(u)	(703)	6,077	....
23222	East Highland Park(u)	(804)	11,797	....
22030	Fairfax	(703)	19,390	22,727
*22046	Falls Church	(703)	9,515	10,772
23901	Farmville	(804)	6,067	4,331
22060	Fort Belvoir(u)	(703)	7,726	14,591
22308	Fort Hunt(u)	(703)	14,294	10,415
23801	Fort Lee(u)	(804)	9,784	12,435
22310	Franconia(u)	(703)	8,476	....
23851	Franklin	(804)	7,308	6,880
22401	Fredericksburg	(703)	15,322	14,450
22630	Front Royal	(703)	11,126	8,211
24333	Galax	(703)	6,524	6,278
23060	Glen Allen(u)	(804)	6,202	....
23062	Gloucester Point(u)	(804)	5,841	....
23306	Groveton(u)	(703)	18,860	11,761
*23660	Hampton	(804)	122,617	120,779
22801	Harrisonburg	(703)	19,671	14,605
*22070	Herndon	(703)	11,449	4,301
23075	Highland Springs(u)	(804)	12,146	7,345
24019	Hollins(u)	(703)	12,187	....
23860	Hopewell	(804)	23,397	23,471
22303	Huntington(u)	(703)	5,813	5,559
23306	Hybla Valley(u)	(703)	15,533	....
22043	Idylwood(u)	(703)	11,982	....
22042	Jefferson(u)	(804)	24,342	25,432
22041	Lake Barcroft(u)	(703)	8,725	11,605
22191	Lake Ridge(u)	(703)	11,072	....
23228	Lakeside(u)	(804)	12,289	11,137
23060	Laurel(u)	(804)	10,569	....
22075	Leesburg	(703)	8,357	4,821
24450	Lexington	(703)	7,292	7,597
22312	Lincolnia(u)	(703)	10,350	10,355
22079	Lorton(u)	(703)	5,813	....
*24505	Lynchburg	(804)	66,743	54,083
24572	Madison Heights(u)	(804)	14,146	....
22110	Manassas	(703)	15,438	9,164
22110	Manassas Park	(703)	6,524	6,844
22030	Mantua(u)	(703)	6,523	6,911
24354	Marion	(703)	7,287	8,158
24112	Martinsville	(703)	18,149	19,653
22101	McLean(u)	(703)	35,664	17,698
23111	Mechanicsville(u)	(804)	9,269	5,189
22116	Merrifield(u)	(703)	7,525	....

ZIP code	Place		1980	1970
23231	Montrose(u)	(804)	5,349	....
22121	Mount Vernon(u)	(703)	24,058	....
22122	Newington(u)	(703)	8,313	....
*23607	Newport News	(804)	144,903	138,177
*23501	Norfolk	(804)	266,979	307,951
22151	North Springfield(u)	(703)	9,538	8,631
22124	Oakton(u)	(703)	19,150	....
23803	Petersburg	(804)	41,055	36,103
22043	Pimmit Hills(u)	(703)	6,658	....
23662	Poquoson	(804)	8,726	5,441
*23705	Portsmouth	(804)	104,577	110,963
24301	Pulaski	(703)	10,106	10,279
22134	Quantico Station(u)	(703)	7,121	6,213
24141	Radford	(703)	13,225	11,596
22090	Reston(u)	(703)	36,407	5,723
24641	Richlands	(703)	5,796	4,843
*23232	Richmond	(804)	219,214	249,332
*24001	Roanoke	(703)	100,427	92,115
22310	Rose Hill(u)	(703)	11,926	14,492
24153	Salem	(703)	23,958	21,982
22044	Seven Corners(u)	(703)	6,058	5,590
24592	South Boston	(804)	7,093	6,889
*22150	Springfield	(703)	21,435	11,613
24401	Staunton	(703)	21,857	24,504
22170	Sterling Park(u)	(703)	16,080	8,321
23434	Suffolk	(804)	47,621	9,858
22170	Sugarland Run(u)	(703)	6,258	....
24502	Timberlake(u)	(804)	9,697	....
23229	Tuckahoe(u)	(804)	39,868	....
22101	Tysons Corner(u)	(703)	10,065	....
22180	Vienna	(703)	15,469	17,146
24179	Vinton	(703)	8,027	6,347
*23458	Virginia Beach	(804)	262,199	172,106
22980	Waynesboro	(703)	15,329	16,707
22110	West Gate(u)	(703)	7,119	....
22152	West Springfield(u)	(703)	25,012	14,143
23185	Williamsburg	(804)	9,870	9,069
22601	Winchester	(703)	20,217	14,643
24592	Wolf Trap(u)	(804)	9,875	....
22191	Woodbridge(u)	(703)	24,004	25,412
24382	Wytheville	(703)	7,135	6,069

Washington

98520	Aberdeen	(206)	18,739	18,489
98036	Alderwood Manor(u)	(206)	16,524	....
98221	Anacortes	(206)	9,013	7,701
98002	Auburn	(206)	26,417	21,653
*98009	Bellevue	(206)	73,903	61,196
98225	Bellingham	(206)	45,794	39,375
98390	Bonney Lake	(206)	5,328	2,700
98011	Bothell	(206)	7,943	5,420
	Boulevard Park(u)	(206)	8,382	....
98310	Bremerton	(206)	36,208	35,307
98178	Bryn Mawr-Skyway(u)	(206)	11,754	....
98166	Burien(u)	(206)	23,189	....
98607	Camas	(206)	5,681	5,790
98055	Cascade-Fairwood(u)	(206)	16,939	....
98531	Centralia	(206)	10,809	10,054
98532	Chehalis	(206)	6,100	5,727
99004	Cheney	(509)	7,630	6,358
99403	Clarkston	(509)	6,903	6,312
99324	College Place	(509)	5,771	4,510
98188	Des Moines	(206)	7,378	3,951
99213	Dishman(u)	(509)	10,169	9,079
	Dumas Bay-Twin Lakes(u)..	(206)	14,535	....
98004	Eastgate(u)	(206)	8,341	....
	East Renton Highlands(u)	(206)	12,033	....
98801	East Wenatchee Bench(u)	(509)	11,410	2,446
98020	Edmonds	(206)	27,526	23,684
98926	Ellensburg	(509)	11,752	13,568
98022	Enumclaw	(206)	5,427	4,703
98823	Ephrata	(509)	5,359	5,255
99210	Esperance(u)	(509)	11,120	....
*98201	Everett	(206)	54,413	53,622
99011	Fairchild AFB(u)	(509)	5,353	6,754
98201	Fairmont-Intercity(u)	(206)	6,997	....
98055	Fairwood(u)	(206)	5,337	....
98466	Fircrest	(206)	5,477	5,651
98433	Fort Lewis(u)	(206)	23,761	38,054
98930	Grandview	(509)	5,615	3,605
98660	Hazel Dell(u)	(206)	15,386	....
98550	Hoquiam	(206)	9,719	10,466
98011	Inglewood(u)	(206)	12,467	....
98027	Issaquah	(206)	5,536	4,313
98033	Juanita(u)	(206)	17,232	....
98626	Kelso	(206)	11,129	10,296
98028	Kenmore(u)	(206)	7,281	....
99336	Kennewick	(509)	34,397	15,212
98031	Kent	(206)	22,961	17,711
98033	Kingsgate(u)	(206)	12,652	....
98033	Kirkland	(206)	18,785	14,970
98503	Lacey	(206)	13,940	9,696
98155	Lake Forest North(u)	(206)	7,995	....
	Lakeland North(u)	(206)	11,451	....
	Lakeland South(u)	(206)	5,225	....

....	Lake Stickney(u)	(206)	6,135	....
98499	Lakes District(u)	(206)	54,533	48,195
98632	Longview	(206)	31,052	28,373
98036	Lynnwood	(206)	21,937	17,381
....	Martha Lake(u)	(206)	7,022	....
98270	Marysville	(206)	5,080	4,343
98438	McChord AFB(u)	(206)	5,746	6,515
98040	Mercer Island	(206)	21,522	19,047
98837	Moses Lake	(509)	10,629	10,310
98043	Mountlake Terrace	(206)	16,534	16,600
98273	Mount Vernon	(206)	13,009	8,804
98006	Newport Hills(u)	(206)	12,245	....
98155	North City-Ridgecrest(u)	(206)	13,551	....
....	North Hill(u)	(206)	10,170	....
98270	North Marysville(u)	(206)	15,159	....
98277	Oak Harbor	(206)	12,271	9,167
*98501	Olympia	(206)	27,447	23,296
99214	Opportunity(u)	(509)	21,241	16,604
98662	Orchards(u)	(206)	8,828	....
98444	Parkland(u)	(206)	23,355	21,012
99301	Pasco	(509)	18,428	13,920
98362	Port Angeles	(206)	17,311	16,367
98368	Port Townsend	(206)	6,067	5,241
....	Poverty Bay(u)	(206)	8,353	....
99163	Pullman	(509)	23,579	20,509
98371	Puyallup	(206)	18,251	14,742
98052	Redmond	(206)	23,318	11,020
98055	Renton	(206)	31,031	25,878
99352	Richland	(509)	33,578	26,290
98160	Richmond Beach-Innis Arden(u)	(206)	6,700	....
98113	Richmond Highlands(u)	(206)	24,463	....
98188	Riverton(u)	(206)	14,182	....
98033	Rose Hill(u)	(206)	7,616	....
*98109	Seattle	(206)	493,846	530,831
98284	Sedro Woolley	(206)	6,110	4,598
98584	Shelton	(206)	7,629	6,515
98155	Sheridan Beach(u)	(206)	6,873	....
98201	Silver Lake-Fircrest(u)	(206)	10,299	....
98290	Snohomish	(206)	5,294	5,174
98387	Spanaway(u)	(206)	8,868	5,768
*99210	Spokane	(509)	171,300	170,516
98944	Sunnyside	(509)	9,225	6,751
*98402	Tacoma	(206)	158,501	154,407
96501	Tanglewilde-Thompson Place(u)		5,910	3,423
98948	Toppenish	(509)	6,517	5,744
99258	Town and Country(u)	(509)	5,578	6,484
98502	Tumwater	(206)	6,705	5,373
98406	University Place(u)	(206)	20,381	13,230
....	Valley Ridge(u)	(206)	17,961	....
*98660	Vancouver	(206)	42,834	41,859
99037	Veradale(u)	(509)	7,256	....
99362	Walla Walla	(509)	25,618	23,619
98801	Wenatchee	(509)	17,257	16,912
98003	West Federal Way(u)	(206)	16,872	....
99301	West Pasco(u)	(509)	6,210	....
98166	White Center-Shorewood(u)	(206)	19,362	....
*98901	Yakima	(509)	49,826	45,588
98188	Zenith-Saltwater(u)	(206)	8,982	....

West Virginia (304)

25801	Beckley		20,492	19,884
24701	Bluefield		16,060	15,921
26330	Bridgeport		6,604	4,777
26201	Buckhannon		6,820	7,261
*25301	Charleston		63,968	71,505
26301	Clarksburg		22,371	24,864
25064	Dunbar		9,285	9,151
26241	Elkins		8,536	8,287
26554	Fairmont		23,863	26,093
26354	Grafton		6,845	6,433
*25701	Huntington		63,684	74,315
26726	Keyser		6,569	6,586
25401	Martinsburg		13,063	14,626
26505	Morgantown		27,605	29,431
26041	Moundsville		12,419	13,560
26155	New Martinsville		7,109	6,528
25143	Nitro		8,074	8,019
25901	Oak Hill		7,120	4,738
26101	Parkersburg		39,946	44,208
25550	Point Pleasant		5,682	6,122
24740	Princeton		7,538	7,253
25177	St. Albans		12,402	14,356
25303	South Charleston		15,968	16,333
26105	Vienna		11,618	11,549
26062	Weirton		25,371	27,131
26452	Weston		6,250	7,323
26003	Wheeling		43,070	48,188
25661	Williamson		5,219	5,831

Wisconsin

54301	Allouez(u)	(414)	14,882	13,753
54409	Antigo	(715)	8,653	9,005
54911	Appleton	(414)	58,913	56,377
54806	Ashland	(715)	9,115	9,615

ZIP code	Place		1980	1970
54304	Ashwaubenon	(414)	14,486	9,323
53913	Baraboo	(608)	8,081	7,931
53916	Beaver Dam	(414)	14,149	14,265
53511	Beloit	(608)	35,207	35,729
53511	Beloit North(u)	(608)	5,457	....
54923	Berlin	(414)	5,478	5,338
53005	Brookfield	(414)	34,035	31,761
53209	Brown Deer	(414)	12,921	12,582
53105	Burlington	(414)	8,385	7,479
53012	Cedarburg	(414)	9,005	7,697
54729	Chippewa Falls	(715)	11,845	12,351
53110	Cudahy	(414)	19,547	22,078
53115	Delavan	(414)	5,684	5,526
54115	De Pere	(414)	14,892	13,309
54701	Eau Claire	(715)	51,509	44,619
53122	Elm Grove	(414)	6,735	7,201
54935	Fond Du Lac	(414)	35,863	35,515
53538	Fort Atkinson	(414)	9,785	9,164
53217	Fox Point	(414)	7,649	7,939
53132	Franklin	(414)	16,871	12,247
53022	Germantown	(414)	10,729	6,974
53209	Glendale	(414)	13,882	13,426
53024	Grafton	(414)	8,381	5,998
54305	Green Bay	(414)	87,899	87,809
53129	Greendale	(414)	16,928	15,089
53220	Greenfield	(414)	31,353	24,424
53130	Hales Corners	(414)	7,110	7,771
53027	Hartford	(414)	7,159	6,499
53029	Hartland	(414)	5,559	2,763
54303	Howard	(414)	8,240	4,911
54016	Hudson	(715)	5,434	5,049
53545	Janesville	(608)	51,071	46,426
53549	Jefferson	(414)	5,647	5,429
54130	Kaukauna	(414)	11,310	11,308
53140	Kenosha	(414)	77,685	78,805
54136	Kimberly	(414)	5,881	6,131
54601	La Crosse	(608)	48,347	50,286
53147	Lake Geneva	(414)	5,612	4,890
54140	Little Chute	(414)	7,907	5,522
53701	Madison	(608)	170,616	171,809
54220	Manitowoc	(414)	32,547	33,430
54143	Marinette	(715)	11,965	12,696
54449	Marshfield	(715)	18,290	15,619
54952	Menasha	(414)	14,728	14,836
53051	Menomonee Falls	(414)	27,845	31,697
54751	Menomonie	(715)	12,769	11,112
53092	Mequon	(414)	16,193	12,150
54452	Merrill	(715)	9,578	9,502
53562	Middleton	(608)	11,851	8,246
53203	Milwaukee	(414)	636,297	717,372
53716	Monona	(608)	8,809	10,420
53566	Monroe	(608)	10,027	8,654
53150	Muskego	(414)	15,277	11,573
54956	Neenah	(414)	23,272	22,902
53151	New Berlin	(414)	30,529	26,910
54961	New London	(414)	6,210	5,801
53154	Oak Creek	(414)	16,932	13,928
53066	Oconomowoc	(414)	9,909	8,741

ZIP code	Place		1980	1970
54650	Onalaska	(608)	9,249	4,909
54901	Oshkosh	(414)	49,678	53,082
53818	Platteville	(608)	9,580	9,599
54467	Plover	(715)	5,310	....
53073	Plymouth	(414)	6,027	5,810
53901	Portage	(608)	7,896	7,821
53074	Port Washington	(414)	8,612	8,752
53821	Prairie du Chien	(608)	5,859	5,540
53401	Racine	(414)	85,725	95,162
53959	Reedsburg	(608)	5,038	4,585
54501	Rhinelander	(715)	7,873	8,218
54868	Rice Lake	(715)	7,691	7,278
54971	Ripon	(414)	7,111	7,053
54022	River Falls	(715)	9,019	7,238
53207	St. Francis	(414)	10,095	10,489
54166	Shawano	(715)	7,013	6,488
53081	Sheboygan	(414)	48,085	48,484
53085	Sheboygan Falls	(414)	5,253	4,771
53211	Shorewood	(414)	14,327	15,576
53172	South Milwaukee	(414)	21,069	23,297
54656	Sparta	(608)	6,934	6,258
54481	Stevens Point	(715)	22,970	23,479
53589	Stoughton	(608)	7,589	6,096
54235	Sturgeon Bay	(414)	8,847	6,776
53590	Sun Prairie	(608)	12,931	9,935
54880	Superior	(715)	29,571	32,237
54660	Tomah	(608)	7,204	5,647
54241	Two Rivers	(414)	13,354	13,732
53094	Watertown	(414)	18,113	15,683
53186	Waukesha	(414)	50,365	39,695
53963	Waupun	(414)	8,132	7,946
54401	Wausau	(715)	32,426	32,806
54401	Wausau West Rib Mt.(u)	(715)	6,005	....
53213	Wauwatosa	(414)	51,308	58,676
53214	West Allis	(414)	63,982	71,649
53095	West Bend	(414)	21,484	16,555
54476	Weston(u)	(715)	8,775	3,375
53217	Whitefish Bay	(414)	14,930	17,402
53190	Whitewater	(414)	11,520	12,038
54494	Wisconsin Rapids	(715)	17,995	18,587

Wyoming (307)

ZIP code	Place		1980	1970
82601	Casper		51,016	39,361
82001	Cheyenne		47,283	41,254
82414	Cody		6,599	5,161
82633	Douglas		6,030	2,677
82930	Evanston		6,265	4,462
82716	Gillette		12,134	7,194
82335	Green River		12,807	4,196
82520	Lander		7,125	
82070	Laramie		24,410	23,143
82435	Powell		5,310	4,807
82301	Rawlins		11,547	7,855
82501	Riverton		9,562	7,995
82901	Rock Springs		19,458	11,657
82801	Sheridan		15,146	10,856
82240	Torrington		5,441	4,237
82201	Wheatland		5,816	2,498
82401	Worland		6,391	5,055

Census and Areas of Counties and States

Source: U.S. Bureau of the Census
With names of county seats or court houses

Population figures listed below are final counts in the 1980 census, conducted on Apr. 1, 1980, and updated in April 1989, for all counties and states. Figures are subject to change pending the outcome of various lawsuits dealing with the census counts.

Alabama

(67 counties, 50,767 sq. mi. land; pop., 3,894,025)

County	Pop.	County seat or court house	Land area sq. mi.
Autauga	32,259	Prattville	597
Baldwin	78,440	Bay Minette	1,589
Barbour	24,756	Clayton	884
Bibb	15,723	Centreville	625
Blount	36,459	Oneonta	643
Bullock	10,596	Union Springs	625
Butler	21,680	Greenville	779
Calhoun	116,936	Anniston	611
Chambers	39,191	Lafayette	596
Cherokee	18,760	Centre	553
Chilton	30,612	Clanton	695
Choctaw	16,839	Butler	909
Clarke	27,702	Grove Hill	1,230
Clay	13,703	Ashland	605
Cleburne	12,595	Heflin	561
Coffee	38,533	Elba	680
Colbert	54,519	Tuscumbia	589
Conecuh	15,884	Evergreen	854
Coosa	11,377	Rockford	657
Covington	36,850	Andalusia	1,038
Crenshaw	14,110	Luverne	611
Cullman	61,642	Cullman	738
Dale	47,821	Ozark	561
Dallas	53,981	Selma	975
De Kalb	53,658	Fort Payne	778

County	Pop.	County seat or court house	Land area sq. mi.
Elmore	43,390	Wetumpka	622
Escambia	38,392	Brewton	951
Etowah	103,057	Gadsden	542
Fayette	18,809	Fayette	630
Franklin	28,350	Russellville	643
Geneva	24,253	Geneva	578
Greene	11,021	Eutaw	631
Hale	15,604	Greensboro	661
Henry	15,302	Abbeville	557
Houston	74,632	Dothan	577
Jackson	51,407	Scottsboro	1,070
Jefferson	671,371	Birmingham	1,119
Lamar	16,453	Vernon	605
Lauderdale	80,504	Florence	661
Lawrence	30,170	Moulton	693
Lee	76,283	Opelika	609
Limestone	46,005	Athens	559
Lowndes	13,253	Hayneville	714
Macon	26,829	Tuskegee	614
Madison	196,966	Huntsville	806
Marengo	25,047	Linden	982
Marion	30,041	Hamilton	743
Marshall	65,622	Guntersville	567
Mobile	364,379	Mobile	1,238
Monroe	22,651	Monroeville	1,019
Montgomery	197,038	Montgomery	793
Morgan	90,231	Decatur	575
Perry	15,012	Marion	718
Pickens	21,481	Carrollton	890
Pike	28,050	Troy	672
Randolph	20,075	Wedowee	584

County	Pop.	County Seat or court house	Land area sq. mi.
Russell	47,356	Phenix City	634
St. Clair	41,205	Ashville & Pell City	646
Shelby	66,298	Columbiana	800
Sumter	16,908	Livingston	907
Talladega	73,826	Talladega	753
Tallapoosa	38,766	Dadeville	701
Tuscaloosa	137,473	Tuscaloosa	1,336
Walker	68,660	Jasper	804
Washington	16,821	Chatom	1,081
Wilcox	14,755	Camden	883
Winston	21,953	Double Springs	613

Alaska

(23 divisions, 570,833 sq. mi. land; pop., 401,851)

Census area	Pop.	Land area sq. mi.
Aleutian Islands	7,768	10,890
Anchorage Borough	173,017	1,732

Census division	Pop.	Land area sq. mi.
Bethel	10,999	36,104
Bristol Bay Borough	1,094	531
Dillingham	4,616	46,042
Fairbanks North Star Borough	53,983	7,404
Haines Borough	1,680	2,374
Juneau Borough	19,528	2,626
Kenai Peninsula Borough	25,282	16,056
Ketchikan Gateway Borough	11,316	1,242
Kobuk	4,831	31,593
Kodiak Island Borough	9,939	4,796
Matanuska-Susitna Borough	17,766	24,502
Nome	6,537	23,871
North Slope Borough	4,199	90,955
Prince of Wales-Outer Ketchikan	3,822	7,660
Sitka Borough	7,803	2,938
Skagway-Yakutat-Angoon	3,478	13,239
Southeast Fairbanks	5,770	24,169
Valdez-Cordova	8,348	39,229
Wade Hampton	4,665	17,816
Wrangell-Petersburg	6,167	5,965
Yukon-Koyukuk	7,873	159,099

Arizona

(15 counties, 113,508 sq. mi. land; pop. 2,716,546)

County	Pop.	County seat or court house	Land area sq. mi.
Apache	52,083	Saint Johns	11,211
Cochise	86,717	Bisbee	6,218
Coconino	74,947	Flagstaff	18,608
Gila	37,080	Globe	4,752
Graham	22,862	Safford	4,630
Greenlee	11,406	Clifton	1,837
La Paz	12,487	Parker	4,430
Maricopa	1,509,175	Phoenix	9,127
Mohave	55,693	Kingman	13,285
Navajo	67,709	Holbrook	9,955
Pima	531,263	Tucson	9,187
Pinal	90,918	Florence	5,343
Santa Cruz	20,459	Nogales	1,238
Yavapai	68,145	Prescott	8,123
Yuma	88,762	Yuma	9,994

Arkansas

(75 counties, 52,078 sq. mi. land; pop. 2,286,357)

County	Pop.	County seat or court house	Land area sq. mi.
Arkansas	24,175	DeWitt & Stuttgart	1,006
Ashley	26,538	Hamburg	934
Baxter	27,409	Mountain Home	546
Benton	78,115	Bentonville	843
Boone	26,067	Harrison	584
Bradley	13,803	Warren	654
Calhoun	6,079	Hampton	628
Carroll	16,203	Berryville and Eureka Sp.	634
Chicot	17,793	Lake Village	649
Clark	23,326	Arkadelphia	867
Clay	20,616	Corning; Piggott	641
Cleburne	16,909	Heber Springs	551
Cleveland	7,868	Rison	599
Columbia	26,644	Magnolia	767
Conway	19,505	Morrilton	558
Craighead	63,218	Jonesboro and Lake City	713
Crawford	36,892	Van Buren	594
Crittenden	49,097	Marion	599
Cross	20,434	Wynne	622
Dallas	10,515	Fordyce	668
Desha	19,760	Arkansas City	746
Drew	17,910	Monticello	831
Faulkner	46,192	Conway	645
Franklin	14,705	Charleston and Ozark	609
Fulton	9,975	Salem	616
Garland	69,916	Hot Spgs. Nat'l Pk.	657
Grant	13,008	Sheridan	633
Greene	30,744	Paragould	579
Hempstead	23,635	Hope	725
Hot Spring	26,819	Malvern	615
Howard	13,459	Nashville	574
Independence	30,147	Batesville	763
Izard	10,768	Melbourne	581
Jackson	21,646	Newport	633
Jefferson	90,718	Pine Bluff	882
Johnson	17,423	Clarksville	676
Lafayette	10,213	Lewisville	518
Lawrence	18,447	Walnut Ridge	589
Lee	15,539	Marianna	602
Lincoln	13,369	Star City	562
Little River	13,952	Ashdown	516
Logan	20,144	Booneville & Paris	717
Lonoke	34,518	Lonoke	783
Madison	11,373	Huntsville	837
Marion	11,334	Yellville	587
Miller	37,766	Texarkana	619
Mississippi	59,517	Blytheville and Osceola	896
Monroe	14,052	Clarendon	609
Montgomery	7,771	Mount Ida	774
Nevada	11,097	Prescott	620
Newton	7,756	Jasper	823
Ouachita	30,541	Camden	737
Perry	7,266	Perryville	550
Phillips	34,772	Helena	685
Pike	10,373	Murfreesboro	598
Poinsett	27,032	Harrisburg	762
Polk	17,007	Mena	860
Pope	38,964	Russellville	820
Prairie	10,140	Des Arc and De Valls Bluff	656
Pulaski	340,597	Little Rock	767
Randolph	16,834	Pocahontas	656
St. Francis	30,858	Forrest City	638
Saline	53,156	Benton	725
Scott	9,685	Waldron	896
Searcy	8,847	Marshall	668
Sebastian	94,930	Fort Smith; Greenwood	535
Sevier	14,060	De Queen	560
Sharp	14,607	Ash Flat	606
Stone	9,022	Mountain View	606
Union	49,988	El Dorado	1,053
Van Buren	13,357	Clinton	709
Washington	99,735	Fayetteville	951
White	50,835	Searcy	1,040
Woodruff	11,222	Augusta	592
Yell	17,026	Danville and Dardanelle	930

California

(58 counties, 156,299 sq. mi. land; pop. 23,667,764)

County	Pop.	County seat or court house	Land area sq. mi.
Alameda	1,105,379	Oakland	736
Alpine	1,097	Markleeville	738
Amador	19,314	Jackson	589
Butte	143,851	Oroville	1,646
Calaveras	20,710	San Andreas	1,021
Colusa	12,791	Colusa	1,152
Contra Costa	656,331	Martinez	730
Del Norte	18,217	Crescent City	1,007
El Dorado	85,812	Placerville	1,715
Fresno	515,013	Fresno	5,978
Glenn	21,350	Willows	1,319
Humboldt	108,525	Eureka	3,579
Imperial	92,110	El Centro	4,173
Inyo	17,895	Independence	10,223
Kern	403,089	Bakersfield	8,130
Kings	73,738	Hanford	1,392
Lake	36,366	Lakeport	1,262
Lassen	21,661	Susanville	4,553
Los Angeles	7,477,238	Los Angeles	4,070
Madera	63,116	Madera	2,145
Marin	222,592	San Rafael	523
Mariposa	11,108	Mariposa	1,456
Mendocino	66,738	Ukiah	3,512
Merced	134,558	Merced	1,944
Modoc	8,610	Alturas	4,064
Mono	8,577	Bridgeport	3,018
Monterey	290,444	Salinas	3,303
Napa	99,199	Napa	744
Nevada	51,645	Nevada City	960
Orange	1,932,921	Santa Ana	798
Placer	117,247	Auburn	1,416
Plumas	17,340	Quincy	2,573
Riverside	663,199	Riverside	7,214
Sacramento	783,381	Sacramento	971
San Benito	25,005	Hollister	1,388
San Bernardino	893,157	San Bernardino	20,064
San Diego	1,861,846	San Diego	4,212
San Francisco	678,974	San Francisco	46
San Joaquin	347,342	Stockton	1,415
San Luis Obispo	155,345	San Luis Obispo	3,308
San Mateo	588,164	Redwood City	447
Santa Barbara	298,660	Santa Barbara	2,748
Santa Clara	1,295,071	San Jose	1,293
Santa Cruz	188,141	Santa Cruz	446
Shasta	115,613	Redding	3,786
Sierra	3,073	Downieville	959
Siskiyou	39,732	Yreka	6,281
Solano	235,203	Fairfield	834
Sonoma	299,827	Santa Rosa	1,604
Stanislaus	265,902	Modesto	1,506
Sutter	52,246	Yuba City	602
Tehama	38,888	Red Bluff	2,953
Trinity	11,858	Weaverville	3,190

County	Pop.	County seat or court house	Land area sq. mi.
Tulare	245,751	Visalia	4,808
Tuolumne	33,920	Sonora	2,234
Ventura	529,899	Ventura	1,862
Yolo	113,374	Woodland	1,014
Yuba	49,733	Marysville	640

Colorado
(63 counties, 103,595 sq. mi. land; pop. 2,889,735)

County	Pop.	County seat or court house	Land area sq. mi.
Adams	245,944	Brighton	1,235
Alamosa	11,799	Alamosa	719
Arapahoe	293,300	Littleton	800
Archuleta	3,664	Pagosa Springs	1,353
Baca	5,419	Springfield	2,554
Bent	5,945	Las Animas	1,517
Boulder	189,625	Boulder	742
Chaffee	13,227	Salida	1,008
Cheyenne	2,153	Cheyenne Wells	1,783
Clear Creek	7,308	Georgetown	396
Conejos	7,794	Conejos	1,284
Costilla	3,071	San Luis	1,227
Crowley	2,988	Ordway	790
Custer	1,528	Westcliffe	740
Delta	21,225	Delta	1,141
Denver	492,686	Denver	111
Dolores	1,658	Dove Creek	1,064
Douglas	25,153	Castle Rock	841
Eagle	13,171	Eagle	1,690
Elbert	6,850	Kiowa	1,851
El Paso	309,424	Colorado Springs	2,129
Fremont	28,676	Canon City	1,538
Garfield	22,514	Glenwood Springs	2,952
Gilpin	2,441	Central City	149
Grand	7,475	Hot Sulphur Springs	1,854
Gunnison	10,689	Gunnison	3,238
Hinsdale	408	Lake City	1,115
Huerfano	6,440	Walsenburg	1,584
Jackson	1,863	Walden	1,614
Jefferson	371,741	Golden	768
Kiowa	1,936	Eads	1,758
Kit Carson	7,599	Burlington	2,160
Lake	8,830	Leadville	379
La Plata	27,195	Durango	1,692
Larimer	149,184	Fort Collins	2,604
Las Animas	14,897	Trinidad	4,771
Lincoln	4,663	Hugo	2,586
Logan	19,800	Sterling	1,818
Mesa	81,530	Grand Junction	3,309
Mineral	804	Creede	877
Moffat	13,133	Craig	4,732
Montezuma	16,510	Cortez	2,038
Montrose	24,352	Montrose	2,240
Morgan	22,513	Fort Morgan	1,276
Otero	22,567	LaJunta	1,247
Ouray	1,925	Ouray	542
Park	5,333	Fairplay	2,192
Phillips	4,542	Holyoke	688
Pitkin	10,338	Aspen	968
Prowers	13,070	Lamar	1,629
Pueblo	125,972	Pueblo	2,377
Rio Blanco	6,255	Meeker	3,222
Rio Grande	10,511	Del Norte	913
Routt	13,404	Steamboat Springs	2,367
Saguache	3,935	Saguache	3,167
San Juan	833	Silverton	388
San Miguel	3,192	Telluride	1,287
Sedgwick	3,266	Julesburg	540
Summit	8,848	Breckenridge	607
Teller	8,034	Cripple Creek	559
Washington	5,304	Akron	2,520
Weld	123,438	Greeley	3,990
Yuma	9,682	Wray	2,365

Connecticut
(8 counties, 4,872 sq. mi. land; pop. 3,107,564)

County	Pop.	County seat or court house	Land area sq. mi.
Fairfield	807,143	Bridgeport	632
Hartford	807,766	Hartford	739
Litchfield	156,769	Litchfield	921
Middlesex	129,017	Middletown	373
New Haven	761,325	New Haven	610
New London	238,409	Norwich	669
Tolland	114,823	Rockville	412
Windham	92,312	Putnam	515

Delaware
(3 counties, 1,932 sq. mi. land; pop. 594,338)

County	Pop.	County seat or court house	Land area sq. mi.
Kent	98,219	Dover	595
New Castle	399,002	Wilmington	396
Sussex	98,004	Georgetown	942

District of Columbia
(63 sq. mi. land; pop. 638,432)

Florida
(67 counties, 54,153 sq. mi. land; pop. 9,746,961)

County	Pop.	County seat or court house	Land area sq. mi.
Alachua	151,369	Gainesville	901
Baker	15,289	Macclenny	585
Bay	97,740	Panama City	758
Bradford	20,023	Starke	293
Brevard	272,959	Titusville	995
Broward	1,018,257	Fort Lauderdale	1,211
Calhoun	9,294	Blountstown	568
Charlotte	59,115	Punta Gorda	690
Citrus	54,703	Inverness	629
Clay	67,052	Green Cove Spgs.	592
Collier	85,791	Naples	1,994
Columbia	35,399	Lake City	796
Dade	1,625,509	Miami	1,955
De Soto	19,039	Arcadia	636
Dixie	7,751	Cross City	701
Duval	570,981	Jacksonville	776
Escambia	233,794	Pensacola	660
Flagler	10,913	Bunnell	491
Franklin	7,661	Apalachicola	545
Gadsden	41,674	Quincy	518
Gilchrist	5,767	Trenton	354
Glades	5,992	Moore Haven	763
Gulf	10,658	Port St. Joe	559
Hamilton	8,761	Jasper	517
Hardee	20,357	Wauchula	637
Hendry	18,599	La Belle	1,163
Hernando	44,469	Brooksville	477
Highlands	47,526	Sebring	1,029
Hillsborough	646,939	Tampa	1,053
Holmes	14,723	Bonifay	488
Indian River	59,896	Vero Beach	497
Jackson	39,154	Marianna	942
Jefferson	10,703	Monticello	609
Lafayette	4,035	Mayo	545
Lake	104,870	Tavares	954
Lee	205,266	Fort Myers	803
Leon	148,655	Tallahassee	676
Levy	19,870	Bronson	1,100
Liberty	4,260	Bristol	837
Madison	14,894	Madison	710
Manatee	148,445	Bradenton	747
Marion	122,488	Ocala	1,610
Martin	64,014	Stuart	555
Monroe	63,098	Key West	1,034
Nassau	32,894	Fernandina Beach	649
Okaloosa	109,920	Crestview	936
Okeechobee	20,264	Okeechobee	770
Orange	470,865	Orlando	910
Osceola	49,287	Kissimmee	1,350
Palm Beach	576,758	West Palm Beach	1,993
Pasco	193,661	Dade City	738
Pinellas	728,409	Clearwater	280
Polk	321,652	Bartow	1,823
Putnam	50,549	Palatka	733
St. Johns	51,303	Saint Augustine	617
St. Lucie	87,182	Fort Pierce	581
Santa Rosa	55,988	Milton	1,024
Sarasota	202,251	Sarasota	573
Seminole	179,752	Sanford	298
Sumter	24,272	Bushnell	561
Suwannee	22,287	Live Oak	690
Taylor	16,532	Perry	1,058
Union	10,166	Lake Butler	246
Volusia	258,762	De Land	1,113
Wakulla	10,887	Crawfordville	601
Walton	21,300	De Funiak Springs	1,066
Washington	14,509	Chipley	590

Georgia
(159 counties, 58,056 sq. mi. land; pop. 5,462,982)

County	Pop.	County seat or court house	Land area sq. mi.
Appling	15,565	Baxley	510
Atkinson	6,141	Pearson	344
Bacon	9,379	Alma	286
Baker	3,808	Newton	347
Baldwin	34,686	Milledgeville	257
Banks	8,702	Homer	234
Barrow	21,293	Winder	163
Bartow	40,760	Cartersville	456
Ben Hill	16,000	Fitzgerald	254
Berrien	13,525	Nashville	456
Bibb	151,085	Macon	253
Bleckley	10,767	Cochran	219
Brantley	8,701	Nahunta	445
Brooks	15,255	Quitman	491
Bryan	10,175	Pembroke	441
Bulloch	35,785	Statesboro	678
Burke	19,349	Waynesboro	833
Butts	13,665	Jackson	187
Calhoun	5,717	Morgan	284
Camden	13,371	Woodbine	649
Candler	7,518	Metter	248
Carroll	56,346	Carrollton	501
Catoosa	36,991	Ringgold	162
Charlton	7,343	Folkston	780
Chatham	202,226	Savannah	443
Chattahoochee	21,732	Cusseta	250
Chattooga	21,856	Summerville	313
Cherokee	51,699	Canton	424
Clarke	74,498	Athens	122
Clay	3,553	Fort Gaines	196
Clayton	150,357	Jonesboro	148
Clinch	6,660	Homerville	821
Cobb	297,694	Marietta	343
Coffee	26,894	Douglas	602
Colquitt	35,376	Moultrie	557

County	Pop.	County seat or court house	Land area sq. mi.
Columbia	40,118	Appling	290
Cook	13,490	Adel	233
Coweta	39,268	Newnan	444
Crawford	7,684	Knoxville	328
Crisp	19,489	Cordele	275
Dade	12,318	Trenton	176
Dawson	4,774	Dawsonville	210
Decatur	25,495	Bainbridge	586
De Kalb	483,024	Decatur	270
Dodge	16,955	Eastman	504
Dooly	10,826	Vienna	397
Dougherty	100,710	Albany	330
Douglas	54,573	Douglasville	203
Early	13,158	Blakely	516
Echols	2,297	Statenville	421
Effingham	18,327	Springfield	482
Elbert	18,758	Elberton	367
Emanuel	20,795	Swainsboro	688
Evans	8,428	Claxton	186
Fannin	14,748	Blue Ridge	384
Fayette	29,043	Fayetteville	199
Floyd	79,800	Rome	519
Forsyth	27,958	Cumming	226
Franklin	15,185	Carnesville	264
Fulton	589,904	Atlanta	534
Gilmer	11,110	Ellijay	427
Glascock	2,382	Gibson	144
Glynn	54,981	Brunswick	412
Gordon	30,070	Calhoun	355
Grady	19,845	Cairo	459
Greene	11,391	Greensboro	389
Gwinnett	166,808	Lawrenceville	435
Habersham	25,020	Clarkesville	278
Hall	75,649	Gainesville	379
Hancock	9,466	Sparta	470
Haralson	18,422	Buchanan	283
Harris	15,464	Hamilton	464
Hart	18,585	Hartwell	230
Heard	6,520	Franklin	292
Henry	36,309	McDonough	321
Houston	77,605	Perry	380
Irwin	8,988	Ocilla	362
Jackson	25,343	Jefferson	342
Jasper	7,553	Monticello	371
Jeff Davis	11,473	Hazlehurst	335
Jefferson	18,403	Louisville	529
Jenkins	8,841	Millen	353
Johnson	8,660	Wrightsville	306
Jones	16,579	Gray	394
Lamar	12,215	Barnesville	186
Lanier	5,654	Lakeland	194
Laurens	36,990	Dublin	816
Lee	11,684	Leesburg	358
Liberty	37,583	Hinesville	517
Lincoln	6,949	Lincolnton	196
Long	4,524	Ludowici	402
Lowndes	67,972	Valdosta	507
Lumpkin	10,762	Dahlonega	287
McDuffie	18,546	Thomson	256
McIntosh	8,046	Darien	425
Macon	14,003	Oglethorpe	404
Madison	17,747	Danielsville	285
Marion	5,297	Buena Vista	366
Meriwether	21,229	Greenville	506
Miller	7,038	Colquitt	284
Mitchell	21,114	Camilla	512
Monroe	14,610	Forsyth	397
Montgomery	7,011	Mount Vernon	246
Morgan	11,572	Madison	349
Murray	19,685	Chatsworth	345
Muscogee	170,108	Columbus	218
Newton	34,666	Covington	277
Oconee	12,427	Watkinsville	186
Oglethorpe	8,929	Lexington	442
Paulding	26,042	Dallas	312
Peach	19,151	Fort Valley	152
Pickens	11,652	Jasper	232
Pierce	11,897	Blackshear	344
Pike	8,937	Zebulon	219
Polk	32,382	Cedartown	311
Pulaski	8,950	Hawkinsville	249
Putnam	10,295	Eatonton	344
Quitman	2,357	Georgetown	146
Rabun	10,466	Clayton	370
Randolph	9,599	Cuthbert	431
Richmond	181,629	Augusta	326
Rockdale	36,570	Conyers	132
Schley	3,433	Ellaville	169
Screven	14,043	Sylvania	655
Seminole	9,057	Donalsonville	225
Spalding	47,899	Griffin	199
Stephens	21,761	Toccoa	177
Stewart	5,896	Lumpkin	452
Sumter	29,360	Americus	489
Talbot	6,536	Talbotton	395
Taliaferro	2,032	Crawfordville	196
Tattnall	18,134	Reidsville	484
Taylor	7,902	Butler	382
Telfair	11,445	McRae	444
Terrell	12,017	Dawson	337
Thomas	38,098	Thomasville	551
Tift	32,862	Tifton	268
Toombs	22,592	Lyons	371
Towns	5,638	Hiawassee	165
Treutlen	6,087	Soperton	202
Troup	50,003	La Grange	414
Turner	9,510	Ashburn	289
Twiggs	9,354	Jeffersonville	362
Union	9,390	Blairsville	320
Upson	25,998	Thomaston	326
Walker	56,470	La Fayette	446
Walton	31,211	Monroe	330
Ware	37,180	Waycross	907
Warren	6,583	Warrenton	286
Washington	18,842	Sandersville	684
Wayne	20,750	Jesup	647
Webster	2,341	Preston	210
Wheeler	5,155	Alamo	299
White	10,120	Cleveland	242
Whitfield	65,775	Dalton	291
Wilcox	7,682	Abbeville	382
Wilkes	10,951	Washington	470
Wilkinson	10,368	Irwinton	451
Worth	18,064	Sylvester	575

Hawaii

(4 counties, 6,645 sq. mi. land; pop. 964,691)

County	Pop.	County seat or court house	Land area sq. mi.
Hawaii	92,053	Hilo	4,034
Honolulu	762,874	Honolulu	596
Kauai	39,082	Lihue	620
Maui*	70,991	Wailuku	1,175

*Includes population of Kalawao County (146).

Idaho

(44 counties, 82,412 sq. mi. land; pop. 944,127)

County	Pop.	County seat or court house	Land area sq. mi.
Ada	173,125	Boise	1,052
Adams	3,347	Council	1,362
Bannock	65,421	Pocatello	1,112
Bear Lake	6,931	Paris	990
Benewah	8,292	Saint Maries	784
Bingham	36,489	Blackfoot	2,096
Blaine	9,841	Hailey	2,634
Boise	2,999	Idaho City	1,901
Bonner	24,163	Sandpoint	1,726
Bonneville	65,980	Idaho Falls	1,840
Boundary	7,289	Bonners Ferry	1,268
Butte	3,342	Arco	2,236
Camas	818	Fairfield	1,071
Canyon	83,756	Caldwell	584
Caribou	8,695	Soda Springs	1,763
Cassia	19,427	Burley	2,560
Clark	798	Dubois	1,763
Clearwater	10,390	Orofino	2,236
Custer	3,385	Challis	4,927
Elmore	21,565	Mountain Home	3,071
Franklin	8,895	Preston	664
Fremont	10,813	Saint Anthony	1,852
Gem	11,972	Emmett	558
Gooding	11,874	Gooding	728
Idaho	14,769	Grangeville	8,497
Jefferson	15,304	Rigby	1,093
Jerome	14,840	Jerome	601
Kootenai	59,770	Coeur d'Alene	1,240
Latah	28,749	Moscow	1,077
Lemhi	7,460	Salmon	4,564
Lewis	4,118	Nezperce	478
Lincoln	3,436	Shoshone	1,205
Madison	19,480	Rexburg	468
Minidoka	19,718	Rupert	757
Nez Perce	33,220	Lewiston	845
Oneida	3,258	Malad City	1,200
Owyhee	8,272	Murphy	7,643
Payette	15,825	Payette	405
Power	6,844	American Falls	1,403
Shoshone	19,226	Wallace	2,641
Teton	2,897	Driggs	448
Twin Falls	52,927	Twin Falls	1,944
Valley	5,604	Cascade	3,670
Washington	8,803	Weiser	1,454

Illinois

(102 counties, 55,645 sq. mi. land; pop. 11,427,409)

County	Pop.	County seat or court house	Land area sq. mi.
Adams	71,622	Quincy	852
Alexander	12,264	Cairo	236
Bond	16,224	Greenville	377
Boone	28,630	Belvidere	282
Brown	5,411	Mount Sterling	306
Bureau	39,114	Princeton	869
Calhoun	5,867	Hardin	250
Carroll	18,779	Mount Carroll	444
Cass	15,084	Virginia	374
Champaign	168,392	Urbana	998
Christian	36,446	Taylorville	710
Clark	16,913	Marshall	506
Clay	15,283	Louisville	469
Clinton	32,617	Carlyle	472
Coles	52,992	Charleston	509

County	Pop.	County seat or court house	Land area sq. mi.
Cook	5,253,628	Chicago	958
Crawford	20,818	Robinson	446
Cumberland	11,062	Toledo	346
De Kalb	74,628	Sycamore	634
De Witt	18,108	Clinton	397
Douglas	19,774	Tuscola	417
Du Page	658,858	Wheaton	337
Edgar	21,725	Paris	623
Edwards	7,961	Albion	223
Effingham	30,944	Effingham	478
Fayette	22,167	Vandalia	709
Ford	15,265	Paxton	486
Franklin	43,201	Benton	414
Fulton	43,687	Lewiston	871
Gallatin	7,590	Shawneetown	325
Greene	16,661	Carrollton	543
Grundy	30,582	Morris	423
Hamilton	9,172	McLeansboro	436
Hancock	23,877	Carthage	796
Hardin	5,383	Elizabethtown	181
Henderson	9,114	Oquawka	373
Henry	57,968	Cambridge	824
Iroquois	32,976	Watseka	1,118
Jackson	61,649	Murphysboro	590
Jasper	11,318	Newton	496
Jefferson	36,558	Mount Vernon	570
Jersey	20,538	Jerseyville	373
Jo Daviess	23,520	Galena	603
Johnson	9,624	Vienna	346
Kane	278,405	Geneva	524
Kankakee	102,926	Kankakee	679
Kendall	37,202	Yorkville	322
Knox	61,607	Galesburg	720
Lake	440,388	Waukegan	454
La Salle	109,139	Ottawa	1,139
Lawrence	17,807	Lawrenceville	374
Lee	36,328	Dixon	725
Livingston	41,381	Pontiac	1,046
Logan	31,802	Lincoln	619
McDonough	37,236	Macomb	590
McHenry	147,724	Woodstock	606
McLean	119,149	Bloomington	1,185
Macon	131,375	Decatur	581
Macoupin	49,384	Carlinville	865
Madison	247,661	Edwardsville	728
Marion	43,523	Salem	573
Marshall	14,479	Lacon	388
Mason	19,492	Havana	536
Massac	14,990	Metropolis	241
Menard	11,700	Petersburg	315
Mercer	19,286	Aledo	559
Monroe	20,117	Waterloo	388
Montgomery	31,686	Hillsboro	705
Morgan	37,502	Jacksonville	568
Moultrie	14,546	Sullivan	325
Ogle	46,338	Oregon	759
Peoria	200,466	Peoria	621
Perry	21,714	Pinckneyville	443
Piatt	16,581	Monticello	439
Pike	18,896	Pittsfield	830
Pope	4,404	Golconda	374
Pulaski	8,840	Mound City	203
Putnam	6,085	Hennepin	160
Randolph	35,566	Chester	583
Richland	17,587	Olney	360
Rock Island	166,759	Rock Island	423
St. Clair	265,469	Belleville	672
Saline	27,360	Harrisburg	385
Sangamon	176,070	Springfield	866
Schuyler	8,365	Rushville	436
Scott	6,142	Winchester	251
Shelby	23,923	Shelbyville	747
Stark	7,389	Toulon	288
Stephenson	49,536	Freeport	564
Tazewell	132,078	Pekin	650
Union	16,651	Jonesboro	414
Vermilion	95,222	Danville	900
Wabash	13,713	Mt. Carmel	224
Warren	21,943	Monmouth	543
Washington	15,472	Nashville	563
Wayne	18,059	Fairfield	715
White	17,864	Carmi	497
Whiteside	65,970	Morrison	682
Will	324,460	Joliet	844
Williamson	56,538	Marion	427
Winnebago	250,884	Rockford	516
Woodford	33,320	Eureka	527

Indiana
(92 counties, 35,932 sq. mi. land; pop. 5,490,214)

County	Pop.	County seat or court house	Land area sq. mi.
Adams	29,619	Decatur	340
Allen	294,335	Fort Wayne	659
Bartholomew	65,088	Columbus	409
Benton	10,218	Fowler	407
Blackford	15,570	Hartford City	166
Boone	36,446	Lebanon	423
Brown	12,377	Nashville	312
Carroll	19,722	Delphi	372
Cass	40,936	Logansport	414
Clark	88,838	Jeffersonville	376
Clay	24,862	Brazil	360
Clinton	31,545	Frankfort	405
Crawford	9,820	English	307
Daviess	27,836	Washington	432
Dearborn	34,291	Lawrenceburg	307
Decatur	23,841	Greensburg	373
DeKalb	33,606	Auburn	364
Delaware	128,587	Muncie	392
Dubois	34,238	Jasper	429
Elkhart	137,330	Goshen	466
Fayette	28,272	Connersville	215
Floyd	61,205	New Albany	150
Fountain	19,033	Covington	398
Franklin	19,612	Brookville	385
Fulton	19,335	Rochester	369
Gibson	33,156	Princeton	490
Grant	80,934	Marion	415
Greene	30,416	Bloomfield	546
Hamilton	82,381	Noblesville	398
Hancock	43,939	Greenfield	307
Harrison	27,276	Corydon	486
Hendricks	69,804	Danville	409
Henry	53,336	New Castle	394
Howard	86,896	Kokomo	293
Huntington	35,596	Huntington	366
Jackson	36,523	Brownstown	513
Jasper	26,138	Rensselaer	561
Jay	23,239	Portland	384
Jefferson	30,419	Madison	363
Jennings	22,854	Vernon	378
Johnson	77,240	Franklin	321
Knox	41,838	Vincennes	520
Kosciusko	59,555	Warsaw	540
Lagrange	25,550	Lagrange	380
Lake	522,917	Crown Point	501
La Porte	108,632	La Porte	600
Lawrence	42,472	Bedford	452
Madison	139,336	Anderson	453
Marion	765,233	Indianapolis	396
Marshall	39,155	Plymouth	444
Martin	11,001	Shoals	339
Miami	39,820	Peru	369
Monroe	98,787	Bloomington	385
Montgomery	35,501	Crawfordsville	505
Morgan	51,999	Martinsville	409
Newton	14,844	Kentland	401
Noble	35,443	Albion	413
Ohio	5,114	Rising Sun	87
Orange	18,677	Paoli	408
Owen	15,840	Spencer	386
Parke	16,372	Rockville	444
Perry	19,346	Cannelton	382
Pike	13,465	Petersburg	341
Porter	119,816	Valparaiso	418
Posey	26,414	Mount Vernon	409
Pulaski	13,258	Winamac	435
Putnam	29,163	Greencastle	482
Randolph	29,997	Winchester	454
Ripley	24,398	Versailles	447
Rush	19,604	Rushville	408
St. Joseph	241,617	South Bend	459
Scott	20,422	Scottsburg	191
Shelby	39,887	Shelbyville	413
Spencer	19,361	Rockport	400
Starke	21,997	Knox	309
Steuben	24,694	Angola	308
Sullivan	21,107	Sullivan	452
Switzerland	7,153	Vevay	223
Tippecanoe	121,702	Lafayette	502
Tipton	16,819	Tipton	260
Union	6,860	Liberty	162
Vanderburgh	167,515	Evansville	236
Vermillion	18,229	Newport	260
Vigo	112,385	Terre Haute	405
Wabash	36,640	Wabash	398
Warren	8,976	Williamsport	366
Warrick	41,474	Boonville	391
Washington	21,932	Salem	516
Wayne	76,058	Richmond	404
Wells	25,401	Bluffton	370
White	23,867	Monticello	506
Whitley	26,215	Columbia City	336

Iowa
(99 counties; 55,965 sq. mi. land; pop. 2,913,808)

County	Pop.	County seat or court house	Land area sq. mi.
Adair	9,509	Greenfield	570
Adams	5,731	Corning	425
Allamakee	15,108	Waukon	633
Appanoose	15,511	Centerville	498
Audubon	8,559	Audubon	444
Benton	23,649	Vinton	718
Black Hawk	137,961	Waterloo	573
Boone	26,184	Boone	573
Bremer	24,820	Waverly	439
Buchanan	22,900	Independence	572
Buena Vista	20,774	Storm Lake	575
Butler	17,668	Allison	582
Calhoun	13,542	Rockwell City	571

County	Pop.	County seat or court house	Land area sq. mi.
Carroll.	22,951	Carroll.	570
Cass.	16,932	Atlantic.	565
Cedar.	18,635	Tipton.	582
Cerro Gordo	48,458	Mason City	569
Cherokee.	16,238	Cherokee.	577
Chickasaw	15,437	New Hampton	505
Clarke.	8,612	Osceola.	431
Clay.	19,576	Spencer.	569
Clayton.	21,098	Elkader.	779
Clinton.	57,122	Clinton.	695
Crawford	18,935	Denison.	714
Dallas.	29,513	Adel.	591
Davis.	9,104	Bloomfield.	504
Decatur.	9,794	Leon.	535
Delaware.	18,933	Manchester.	578
Des Moines.	46,203	Burlington.	414
Dickinson	15,629	Spirit Lake.	381
Dubuque.	93,745	Dubuque.	607
Emmet.	13,336	Estherville.	394
Fayette.	25,488	West Union	731
Floyd.	19,597	Charles City.	501
Franklin.	13,036	Hampton.	583
Fremont.	9,401	Sidney.	515
Greene.	12,119	Jefferson	571
Grundy.	14,366	Grundy Center.	501
Guthrie.	11,983	Guthrie Center.	590
Hamilton.	17,862	Webster City.	576
Hancock.	13,833	Garner.	571
Hardin.	21,776	Eldora.	569
Harrison.	16,348	Logan.	697
Henry.	18,890	Mount Pleasant.	436
Howard.	11,114	Cresco.	473
Humboldt.	12,246	Dakota City.	436
Ida.	8,908	Ida Grove.	432
Iowa.	15,429	Marengo.	587
Jackson.	22,503	Maquoketa.	638
Jasper.	36,425	Newton.	731
Jefferson.	16,316	Fairfield.	440
Johnson.	81,717	Iowa City.	614
Jones.	20,401	Anamosa.	576
Keokuk.	12,921	Sigourney.	580
Kossuth.	21,891	Algona.	974
Lee.	43,106	Fort Madison and Keokuk	522
Linn.	169,775	Cedar Rapids.	724
Louisa.	12,055	Wapello.	402
Lucas.	10,313	Chariton.	432
Lyon.	12,896	Rock Rapids.	588
Madison.	12,597	Winterset.	563
Mahaska.	22,507	Oskaloosa.	571
Marion.	29,669	Knoxville.	560
Marshall.	41,652	Marshalltown.	573
Mills.	13,406	Glenwood.	439
Mitchell.	12,329	Osage.	470
Monona.	11,692	Onawa.	697
Monroe.	9,209	Albia.	434
Montgomery.	13,413	Red Oak.	424
Muscatine.	40,436	Muscatine.	442
O'Brien.	16,972	Primghar.	574
Osceola.	8,371	Sibley.	399
Page.	19,063	Clarinda.	535
Palo Alto	12,721	Emmetsburg.	562
Plymouth	24,743	Le Mars.	864
Pocahontas.	11,369	Pocahontas.	577
Polk.	303,170	Des Moines.	582
Pottawattamie.	86,500	Council Bluffs.	953
Poweshiek.	19,306	Montezuma.	585
Ringgold.	6,112	Mount Ayr.	535
Sac.	14,118	Sac City.	576
Scott.	160,022	Davenport.	459
Shelby.	15,043	Harlan.	591
Sioux.	30,813	Orange City.	769
Story.	72,326	Nevada.	574
Tama.	19,533	Toledo.	721
Taylor.	8,353	Bedford.	537
Union.	13,858	Creston.	426
Van Buren.	8,626	Keosauqua.	484
Wapello.	40,241	Ottumwa.	434
Warren.	34,878	Indianola.	573
Washington.	20,141	Washington.	570
Wayne.	8,199	Corydon.	526
Webster.	45,953	Fort Dodge.	718
Winnebago.	13,010	Forest City.	401
Winneshiek.	21,876	Decorah.	690
Woodbury.	100,884	Sioux City.	873
Worth.	9,075	Northwood.	401
Wright.	16,319	Clarion.	579

Kansas

(105 counties, 81,778 sq. mi. land; pop. 2,364,236)

Allen.	15,654	Iola.	505
Anderson.	8,749	Garnett.	584
Atchison.	18,397	Atchison.	431
Barber.	6,548	Medicine Lodge.	1,136
Barton.	31,343	Great Bend.	895
Bourbon.	15,969	Fort Scott.	638
Brown.	11,955	Hiawatha.	572
Butler.	44,782	El Dorado.	1,443

Chase.	3,309	Cottonwood Falls.	777
Chautauqua.	5,016	Sedan.	644
Cherokee.	22,304	Columbus.	590
Cheyenne.	3,678	Saint Francis.	1,021
Clark.	2,599	Ashland.	975
Clay.	9,802	Clay Center.	632
Cloud.	12,494	Concordia.	718
Coffey.	9,370	Burlington.	615
Comanche.	2,554	Coldwater.	789
Cowley.	36,824	Winfield.	1,128
Crawford.	37,916	Girard.	595
Decatur.	4,509	Oberlin.	894
Dickinson.	20,175	Abilene.	852
Doniphan.	9,268	Troy.	388
Douglas.	67,640	Lawrence.	461
Edwards.	4,271	Kinsley.	620
Elk.	3,918	Howard.	650
Ellis.	26,098	Hays.	900
Ellsworth.	6,640	Ellsworth.	717
Finney.	23,825	Garden City.	1,302
Ford.	24,315	Dodge City.	1,099
Franklin.	21,813	Ottawa.	577
Geary.	29,852	Junction City.	377
Gove.	3,726	Gove.	1,072
Graham.	3,995	Hill City.	898
Grant.	6,977	Ulysses.	575
Gray.	5,138	Cimarron.	868
Greeley.	1,845	Tribune.	778
Greenwood.	8,764	Eureka.	1,135
Hamilton.	2,514	Syracuse.	998
Harper.	7,778	Anthony.	802
Harvey.	30,531	Newton.	540
Haskell.	3,814	Sublette.	578
Hodgeman.	2,269	Jetmore.	860
Jackson.	11,644	Holton.	658
Jefferson.	15,207	Oskaloosa.	535
Jewell.	5,241	Mankato.	910
Johnson.	270,269	Olathe.	478
Kearny.	3,435	Lakin.	868
Kingman.	8,960	Kingman.	865
Kiowa.	4,046	Greensburg.	723
Labette.	25,682	Oswego.	653
Lane.	2,472	Dighton.	717
Leavenworth.	54,809	Leavenworth.	463
Lincoln.	4,145	Lincoln.	720
Linn.	8,234	Mound City.	601
Logan.	3,478	Oakley.	1,073
Lyon.	35,108	Emporia.	844
McPherson.	26,855	McPherson.	900
Marion.	13,522	Marion.	944
Marshall.	12,720	Marysville.	878
Meade.	4,788	Meade.	979
Miami.	21,618	Paola.	590
Mitchell.	8,117	Beloit.	717
Montgomery.	42,281	Independence.	646
Morris.	6,419	Council Grove.	693
Morton.	3,454	Elkhart.	731
Nemaha.	11,211	Seneca.	719
Neosho.	18,967	Erie.	576
Ness.	4,498	Ness City.	1,074
Norton.	6,689	Norton.	873
Osage.	15,319	Lyndon.	695
Osborne.	5,959	Osborne.	882
Ottawa.	5,971	Minneapolis.	721
Pawnee.	8,065	Larned.	755
Phillips.	7,406	Phillipsburg.	887
Pottawatomie.	14,782	Westmoreland.	828
Pratt.	10,275	Pratt.	735
Rawlins.	4,105	Atwood.	1,069
Reno.	64,983	Hutchinson.	1,259
Republic.	7,569	Belleville.	719
Rice.	11,900	Lyons.	728
Riley.	63,505	Manhattan.	593
Rooks.	7,006	Stockton.	888
Rush.	4,516	LaCrosse.	718
Russell.	8,868	Russell.	869
Saline.	48,905	Salina.	721
Scott.	5,782	Scott City.	718
Sedgwick.	367,088	Wichita.	1,007
Seward.	17,071	Liberal.	640
Shawnee.	154,916	Topeka.	549
Sheridan.	3,544	Hoxie.	896
Sherman.	7,759	Goodland.	1,057
Smith.	5,947	Smith Center.	897
Stafford.	5,539	Saint John.	788
Stanton.	2,339	Johnson.	681
Stevens.	4,736	Hugoton.	727
Sumner.	24,928	Wellington.	1,183
Thomas.	8,451	Colby.	1,075
Trego.	4,165	Wakeeney.	890
Wabaunsee.	6,867	Alma.	797
Wallace.	2,045	Sharon Springs.	914
Washington.	8,543	Washington.	898
Wichita.	3,041	Leoti.	719
Wilson.	12,128	Fredonia.	575
Woodson.	4,600	Yates Center.	498
Wyandotte.	172,335	Kansas City.	149

Kentucky

(120 counties, 39,669 sq. mi. land; pop. 3,660,324)

Adair.	15,233	Columbia.	407

County	Pop.	County seat or court house	Land area sq. mi.
Allen.	14,128	Scottsville	338
Anderson.	12,567	Lawrenceburg	204
Ballard	6,798	Wickliffe	254
Barren.	34,009	Glasgow	482
Bath	10,025	Owingsville	277
Bell	34,330	Pineville	361
Boone	45,842	Burlington	246
Bourbon.	19,405	Paris	292
Boyd.	55,513	Catlettsburg.	160
Boyle	25,066	Danville	182
Bracken.	7,738	Brooksville	203
Breathitt.	17,004	Jackson	495
Breckinridge	16,861	Hardinsburg	565
Bullitt	43,346	Shepherdsville	300
Butler	11,064	Morgantown.	431
Caldwell	13,473	Princeton	347
Calloway	30,031	Murray	386
Campbell	83,317	Alexandria.	152
Carlisle	5,487	Bardwell.	191
Carroll.	9,270	Carrollton	130
Carter	25,060	Grayson	407
Casey.	14,818	Liberty	445
Christian	66,878	Hopkinsville	722
Clark	28,322	Winchester	255
Clay	22,752	Manchester	471
Clinton	9,321	Albany	196
Crittenden	9,207	Marion	360
Cumberland	7,289	Burkesville	304
Daviess	85,949	Owensboro	463
Edmonson	9,962	Brownsville	302
Elliott	6,908	Sandy Hook	234
Estill	14,495	Irvine.	256
Fayette	204,165	Lexington	285
Fleming	12,323	Flemingsburg	351
Floyd	48,764	Prestonsburg	393
Franklin	41,830	Frankfort.	212
Fulton	8,971	Hickman.	211
Gallatin	4,842	Warsaw.	99
Garrard	10,853	Lancaster	232
Grant	13,308	Williamstown	259
Graves	34,049	Mayfield	557
Grayson	20,854	Leitchfield	493
Green	11,043	Greensburg	289
Greenup	39,132	Greenup	347
Hancock	7,742	Hawesville	189
Hardin	88,911	Elizabethtown	629
Harlan	41,889	Harlan.	468
Harrison	15,166	Cynthiana	310
Hart	15,402	Munfordville	412
Henderson	40,849	Henderson	438
Henry	12,740	New Castle	291
Hickman	6,065	Clinton.	245
Hopkins	46,174	Madisonville	552
Jackson	11,996	McKee.	346
Jefferson	684,638	Louisville.	386
Jessamine	26,065	Nicholasville.	174
Johnson	24,432	Paintsville	264
Kenton	137,058	Independence.	163
Knott	17,940	Hindman.	352
Knox.	30,239	Barbourville	388
Larue	11,983	Hodgenville	263
Laurel	38,982	London.	434
Lawrence	14,121	Louisa	420
Lee	7,754	Beattyville	211
Leslie	14,882	Hyden.	402
Letcher	30,687	Whitesburg	339
Lewis	14,545	Vanceburg	484
Lincoln	19,053	Stanford	337
Livingston.	9,219	Smithland	312
Logan	24,138	Russellville	556
Lyon.	6,490	Eddyville	209
McCracken	61,310	Paducah	251
McCreary	15,634	Whitley City	427
McLean	10,090	Calhoun	256
Madison	53,352	Richmond	443
Magoffin	13,515	Salyersville	310
Marion	17,910	Lebanon	347
Marshall	25,637	Benton.	304
Martin	13,925	Inez	230
Mason	17,760	Maysville	241
Meade	22,854	Brandenburg	306
Menifee	5,117	Frenchburg	203
Mercer	19,011	Harrodsburg	250
Metcalfe	9,484	Edmonton.	291
Monroe	12,353	Tompkinsville	331
Montgomery	20,046	Mount Sterling	199
Morgan	12,103	West Liberty	382
Muhlenberg	32,238	Greenville	478
Nelson	27,584	Bardstown.	424
Nicholas	7,157	Carlisle	197
Ohio	21,765	Hartford	596
Oldham	28,094	La Grange	190
Owen	8,924	Owenton	354
Owsley	5,709	Booneville	198
Pendleton	10,989	Falmouth	281
Perry	33,763	Hazard.	341
Pike	81,123	Pikeville	785
Powell	11,101	Stanton	180
Pulaski	45,803	Somerset	660
Robertson	2,270	Mount Olivet	100
Rockcastle	13,973	Mount Vernon.	318
Rowan	19,049	Morehead	282
Russell	13,708	Jamestown	250
Scott	21,813	Georgetown.	286
Shelby	23,328	Shelbyville	385
Simpson	14,673	Franklin	236
Spencer	5,929	Taylorsville	192
Taylor	21,178	Campbellsville	270
Todd.	11,874	Elkton	377
Trigg.	9,384	Cadiz	421
Trimble	6,253	Bedford	148
Union	17,821	Morganfield	341
Warren	71,828	Bowling Green	548
Washington	10,764	Springfield	301
Wayne	17,022	Monticello	446
Webster	14,832	Dixon.	336
Whitley	33,396	Williamsburg	443
Wolfe	6,698	Campton	223
Woodford	17,778	Versailles	192

Louisiana

(64 parishes, 44,521 sq. mi land; pop. 4,206,116)

County	Pop.	County seat or court house	Land area sq. mi.
Acadia	56,427	Crowley	657
Allen.	21,408	Oberlin.	765
Ascension	50,068	Donaldsville	296
Assumption	22,084	Napoleonville	342
Avoyelles	41,393	Marksville	846
Beauregard	29,692	De Ridder	1,163
Bienville	16,387	Arcadia	816
Bossier	80,721	Benton	845
Caddo	252,437	Shreveport	894
Calcasieu	167,048	Lake Charles	1,082
Caldwell	10,761	Columbia	541
Cameron	9,336	Cameron	1,417
Catahoula	12,287	Harrisonburg	732
Claiborne	17,095	Homer.	765
Concordia	22,981	Vidalia	717
De Soto	25,664	Mansfield	880
East Baton Rouge	366,164	Baton Rouge	458
East Carroll	11,772	Lake Providence	426
East Feliciana	19,015	Clinton	455
Evangeline	33,343	Ville Platte	667
Franklin	24,141	Winnsboro	635
Grant	16,703	Colfax	653
Iberia	63,752	New Iberia	589
Iberville	32,159	Plaquemine	638
Jackson	17,321	Jonesboro	579
Jefferson	454,592	Gretna	348
Jefferson Davis	32,168	Jennings	655
Lafayette	150,017	Lafayette	270
Lafourche	82,483	Thibodaux	1,141
La Salle	17,004	Jena	638
Lincoln	39,763	Ruston	472
Livingston	58,655	Livingston	661
Madison	15,682	Tallulah	631
Morehouse	34,803	Bastrop	807
Natchitoches	39,863	Natchitoches	1,264
Orleans	557,927	New Orleans	199
Ouachita	139,241	Monroe	627
Plaquemines	26,049	Pointe a la Hache	1,035
Pointe Coupee	24,045	New Roads	566
Rapides	135,282	Alexandria	1,341
Red River	10,433	Coushatta	394
Richland	22,187	Rayville	563
Sabine	25,280	Many.	855
St. Bernard	64,097	Chalmette	486
St. Charles	37,259	Hahnville	286
St. Helena	9,827	Greensburg	409
St. James	21,495	Convent	248
St. John The Baptist	31,924	Edgard.	213
St. Landry	84,128	Opelousas	936
St. Martin	40,214	Saint Martinville	749
St. Mary.	64,395	Franklin	613
St. Tammany	110,554	Covington	873
Tangipahoa	80,698	Amite	783
Tensas	8,525	Saint Joseph	623
Terrebonne	94,393	Houma.	1,367
Union	21,167	Farmerville	884
Vermilion	48,458	Abbeville	1,205
Vernon	53,475	Leesville	1,332
Washington	44,207	Franklinton	676
Webster	43,631	Minden.	602
West Baton Rouge	19,086	Port Allen	194
West Carroll	12,922	Oak Grove	360
West Feliciana	12,186	Saint Francisville	406
Winn	17,253	Winnfield.	953

Maine

(16 counties, 30,995 sq. mi land; pop. 1,125,043)

County	Pop.	County seat or court house	Land area sq. mi.
Androscoggin	99,509	Auburn.	477
Aroostook	91,344	Houlton	6,721
Cumberland	215,789	Portland	876
Franklin	27,447	Farmington	1,699
Hancock	41,781	Ellsworth	1,537
Kennebec	109,889	Augusta	876
Knox.	32,941	Rockland	370
Lincoln	25,691	Wiscasset	458
Oxford	49,043	South Paris	2,053

County	Pop.	County seat or court house	Land area sq. mi.
Penobscot	137,015	Bangor	3,430
Piscataquis	17,634	Dover-Foxcroft	3,986
Sagadahoc	28,795	Bath	257
Somerset	45,049	Skowhegan	3,930
Waldo	28,414	Belfast	730
Washington	34,963	Machias	2,586
York	139,739	Alfred	1,008

Maryland
(23 cos., 1 ind. city, 9,837 sq. mi. land; pop. 4,216,933)

County	Pop.	County seat	Land area sq. mi.
Allegany	80,548	Cumberland	421
Anne Arundel	370,775	Annapolis	418
Baltimore	655,615	Towson	598
Calvert	34,638	Prince Frederick	213
Caroline	23,143	Denton	321
Carroll	96,356	Westminster	452
Cecil	60,430	Elkton	360
Charles	72,751	La Plata	452
Dorchester	30,623	Cambridge	593
Frederick	114,263	Frederick	663
Garrett	26,490	Oakland	657
Harford	145,930	Bel Air	448
Howard	118,572	Ellicott City	251
Kent	16,695	Chestertown	278
Montgomery	579,053	Rockville	495
Prince Georges	665,071	Upper Marlboro	487
Queen Annes	25,508	Centreville	372
St. Mary's	59,895	Leonardtown	373
Somerset	19,188	Princess Anne	338
Talbot	25,604	Easton	259
Washington	113,086	Hagerstown	455
Wicomico	64,540	Salisbury	379
Worcester	30,889	Snow Hill	475
Independent City			
Baltimore	786,775		80

Massachusetts
(14 counties; 7,824 sq. mi. land; pop. 5,737,093)

County	Pop.	County seat	Land area sq. mi.
Barnstable	147,925	Barnstable	400
Berkshire	145,110	Pittsfield	929
Bristol	474,641	Taunton	557
Dukes	8,942	Edgartown	102
Essex	633,688	Salem	495
Franklin	64,317	Greenfield	702
Hampden	443,018	Springfield	618
Hampshire	138,813	Northampton	528
Middlesex	1,367,034	Cambridge	822
Nantucket	5,087	Nantucket	47
Norfolk	606,587	Dedham	400
Plymouth	405,437	Plymouth	655
Suffolk	650,142	Boston	57
Worcester	646,352	Worcester	1,513

Michigan
(83 counties; 56,954 sq. mi. land; pop. 9,262,044)

County	Pop.	County seat	Land area sq. mi.
Alcona	9,740	Harrisville	679
Alger	9,225	Munising	912
Allegan	81,555	Allegan	832
Alpena	32,315	Alpena	567
Antrim	16,194	Bellaire	480
Arenac	14,706	Standish	367
Baraga	8,484	L'Anse	901
Barry	45,781	Hastings	560
Bay	119,881	Bay City	447
Benzie	11,205	Beulah	322
Berrien	171,276	Saint Joseph	576
Branch	40,188	Coldwater	508
Calhoun	141,579	Marshall	712
Cass	49,499	Cassopolis	496
Charlevoix	19,907	Charlevoix	421
Cheboygan	20,649	Cheboygan	720
Chippewa	29,029	Sault Sainte Marie	1,590
Clare	23,822	Harrison	570
Clinton	55,893	Saint Johns	573
Crawford	9,465	Grayling	559
Delta	38,947	Escanaba	1,173
Dickinson	25,341	Iron Mountain	770
Eaton	88,337	Charlotte	579
Emmet	22,992	Petoskey	468
Genesee	450,449	Flint	642
Gladwin	19,957	Gladwin	505
Gogebic	19,686	Bessemer	1,105
Grand Traverse	54,899	Traverse City	466
Gratiot	40,448	Ithaca	570
Hillsdale	42,071	Hillsdale	603
Houghton	37,872	Houghton	1,014
Huron	36,459	Bad Axe	830
Ingham	272,437	Mason	560
Ionia	51,815	Ionia	577
Iosco	28,349	Tawas City	577
Iron	13,635	Crystal Falls	1,163
Isabella	54,110	Mount Pleasant	577
Jackson	151,495	Jackson	705
Kalamazoo	212,378	Kalamazoo	562
Kalkaska	10,952	Kalkaska	563
Kent	444,506	Grand Rapids	862
Keweenaw	1,963	Eagle River	543
Lake	7,711	Baldwin	568
Lapeer	70,038	Lapeer	658
Leelanau	14,007	Leland	341
Lenawee	89,948	Adrian	753
Livingston	100,289	Howell	574
Luce	6,659	Newberry	904
Mackinac	10,178	Saint Ignace	1,025
Macomb	694,600	Mount Clemens	482
Manistee	23,019	Manistee	543
Marquette	74,101	Marquette	1,821
Mason	26,365	Ludington	494
Mecosta	36,961	Big Rapids	560
Menominee	26,201	Menominee	1,045
Midland	73,578	Midland	525
Missaukee	10,009	Lake City	565
Monroe	134,659	Monroe	557
Montcalm	47,555	Stanton	713
Montmorency	7,492	Atlanta	550
Muskegon	157,589	Muskegon	507
Newaygo	34,917	White Cloud	847
Oakland	1,011,793	Pontiac	875
Oceana	22,002	Hart	541
Ogemaw	16,436	West Branch	570
Ontonagon	9,861	Ontonagon	1,311
Osceola	18,928	Reed City	569
Oscoda	6,858	Mio	568
Otsego	14,993	Gaylord	516
Ottawa	157,174	Grand Haven	567
Presque Isle	14,267	Rogers City	656
Roscommon	16,374	Roscommon	528
Saginaw	228,059	Saginaw	815
St. Clair	138,802	Port Huron	734
St. Joseph	56,083	Centreville	503
Sanilac	40,789	Sandusky	964
Schoolcraft	8,575	Manistique	1,173
Shiawassee	71,140	Corunna	540
Tuscola	56,961	Caro	812
Van Buren	66,814	Paw Paw	611
Washtenaw	264,740	Ann Arbor	710
Wayne	2,337,843	Detroit	615
Wexford	25,102	Cadillac	566

Minnesota
(87 counties; 79,548 sq. mi. land; pop., 4,075,970)

County	Pop.	County seat	Land area sq. mi.
Aitkin	13,404	Aitkin	1,834
Anoka	195,998	Anoka	430
Becker	29,336	Detroit Lakes	1,312
Beltrami	30,982	Bemidji	2,507
Benton	25,187	Foley	408
Big Stone	7,716	Ortonville	497
Blue Earth	52,314	Mankato	749
Brown	28,645	New Ulm	610
Carlton	29,936	Carlton	864
Carver	37,046	Chaska	351
Cass	21,050	Walker	2,033
Chippewa	14,941	Montevideo	584
Chisago	25,717	Center City	417
Clay	49,327	Moorhead	1,049
Clearwater	8,761	Bagley	999
Cook	4,092	Grand Marais	1,412
Cottonwood	14,854	Windom	640
Crow Wing	41,722	Brainerd	1,008
Dakota	194,111	Hastings	574
Dodge	14,773	Mantorville	439
Douglas	27,839	Alexandria	643
Faribault	19,714	Blue Earth	714
Fillmore	21,930	Preston	862
Freeborn	36,329	Albert Lea	705
Goodhue	38,749	Red Wing	763
Grant	7,711	Elbow Lake	547
Hennepin	941,411	Minneapolis	541
Houston	19,617	Caledonia	564
Hubbard	14,098	Park Rapids	936
Isanti	23,600	Cambridge	440
Itasca	43,006	Grand Rapids	2,661
Jackson	13,690	Jackson	699
Kanabec	12,161	Mora	527
Kandiyohi	36,763	Willmar	784
Kittson	6,672	Hallock	1,104
Koochiching	17,571	International Falls	3,108
Lac qui Parle	10,592	Madison	772
Lake	13,043	Two Harbors	2,053
Lake of the Woods	3,764	Baudette	1,296
Le Sueur	23,434	Le Center	446
Lincoln	8,207	Ivanhoe	538
Lyon	25,207	Marshall	714
McLeod	29,657	Glencoe	489
Mahnomen	5,535	Mahnomen	559
Marshall	13,027	Warren	1,760
Martin	24,687	Fairmont	706
Meeker	20,594	Litchfield	624
Mille Lacs	18,430	Milaca	578
Morrison	29,311	Little Falls	1,124
Mower	40,390	Austin	711
Murray	11,507	Slayton	702
Nicollet	26,929	Saint Peter	440
Nobles	21,840	Worthington	714
Norman	9,379	Ada	877
Olmsted	91,971	Rochester	655
Otter Tail	51,937	Fergus Falls	1,973

County	Pop.	County seat or court house	Land area sq. mi.
Pennington	15,258	Thief River Falls	618
Pine	19,871	Pine City	1,421
Pipestone	11,690	Pipestone	466
Polk	34,844	Crookston	1,982
Pope	11,657	Glenwood	668
Ramsey	459,784	Saint Paul	154
Red Lake	5,471	Red Lake Falls	433
Redwood	19,341	Redwood Falls	882
Renville	20,401	Olivia	984
Rice	46,087	Faribault	501
Rock	10,703	Luverne	483
Roseau	12,574	Roseau	1,677
St. Louis	222,229	Duluth	6,125
Scott	43,784	Shakopee	357
Sherburne	29,908	Elk River	435
Sibley	15,448	Gaylord	593
Stearns	108,161	Saint Cloud	1,338
Steele	30,328	Owatonna	431
Stevens	11,322	Morris	560
Swift	12,920	Benson	743
Todd	24,991	Long Prairie	941
Traverse	5,542	Wheaton	575
Wabasha	19,335	Wabasha	537
Wadena	14,192	Wadena	538
Waseca	18,448	Waseca	422
Washington	113,571	Stillwater	390
Watonwan	12,361	Saint James	435
Wilkin	8,382	Breckenridge	751
Winona	46,256	Winona	630
Wright	58,962	Buffalo	672
Yellow Medicine	13,653	Granite Falls	758

Mississippi
(82 counties, 47,233 sq. mi. land; pop. 2,520,770)

County	Pop.	County seat or court house	Land area sq. mi.
Adams	38,071	Natchez	456
Alcorn	33,036	Corinth	401
Amite	13,369	Liberty	732
Attala	19,865	Kosciusko	737
Benton	8,153	Ashland	407
Bolivar	45,965	Cleveland & Rosedale	892
Calhoun	15,664	Pittsboro	573
Carroll	9,776	Carrollton & Vaiden	634
Chickasaw	17,851	Houston & Okolona	503
Choctaw	8,996	Ackerman	420
Claiborne	12,279	Port Gibson	494
Clarke	16,945	Quitman	692
Clay	21,082	West Point	415
Coahoma	36,918	Clarksdale	559
Copiah	26,503	Hazlehurst	779
Covington	15,927	Collins	416
De Soto	53,930	Hernando	483
Forrest	66,018	Hattiesburg	469
Franklin	8,208	Meadville	566
George	15,297	Lucedale	483
Greene	9,827	Leakesville	718
Grenada	21,115	Grenada	421
Hancock	24,496	Bay Saint Louis	478
Harrison	157,665	Gulfport	581
Hinds	250,998	Jackson & Raymond	875
Holmes	22,970	Lexington	759
Humphreys	13,931	Belzoni	430
Issaquena	2,513	Mayersville	406
Itawamba	20,518	Fulton	540
Jackson	118,015	Pascagoula	731
Jasper	17,265	Bat Springs & Paulding	678
Jefferson	9,181	Fayette	523
Jefferson Davis	13,846	Prentiss	409
Jones	61,912	Ellisville & Laurel	696
Kemper	10,148	De Kalb	766
Lafayette	31,030	Oxford	669
Lamar	23,821	Purvis	499
Lauderdale	77,285	Meridian	705
Lawrence	12,518	Monticello	435
Leake	18,790	Carthage	584
Lee	57,061	Tupelo	451
Leflore	41,525	Greenwood	605
Lincoln	30,174	Brookhaven	587
Lowndes	57,304	Columbus	517
Madison	41,613	Canton	718
Marion	25,708	Columbia	548
Marshall	29,296	Holly Springs	709
Monroe	36,404	Aberdeen	772
Montgomery	13,366	Winona	408
Neshoba	23,789	Philadelphia	572
Newton	19,967	Decatur	580
Noxubee	13,212	Macon	698
Oktibbeha	36,018	Starkville	459
Panola	28,164	Batesville & Sardis	694
Pearl River	33,795	Poplarville	818
Perry	9,864	New Augusta	651
Pike	36,173	Magnolia	410
Pontotoc	20,918	Pontotoc	499
Prentiss	24,025	Booneville	418
Quitman	12,636	Marks	406
Rankin	69,427	Brandon	782
Scott	24,556	Forest	610
Sharkey	7,964	Rolling Fork	435
Simpson	23,441	Mendenhall	591
Smith	15,077	Raleigh	635
Stone	9,716	Wiggins	446
Sunflower	34,844	Indianola	706
Tallahatchie	17,157	Charleston & Sumner	651
Tate	20,119	Senatobia	406
Tippah	18,739	Ripley	458
Tishomingo	18,434	Iuka	434
Tunica	9,652	Tunica	460
Union	21,741	New Albany	416
Walthall	13,761	Tylertown	404
Warren	51,627	Vicksburg	596
Washington	72,344	Greenville	733
Wayne	19,135	Waynesboro	813
Webster	10,300	Walthall	424
Wilkinson	10,021	Woodville	678
Winston	19,474	Louisville	610
Yalobusha	13,183	Coffeeville & Water Valley	478
Yazoo	27,349	Yazoo City	933

Missouri
(114 cos., 1 ind. city, 68,945 sq. mi. land; pop. 4,916,766)

County	Pop.	County seat or court house	Land area sq. mi.
Adair	24,870	Kirksville	567
Andrew	13,980	Savannah	435
Atchison	8,605	Rockport	542
Audrain	26,458	Mexico	697
Barry	24,408	Cassville	773
Barton	11,292	Lamar	596
Bates	15,873	Butler	849
Benton	12,183	Warsaw	729
Bollinger	10,301	Marble Hill	621
Boone	100,376	Columbia	687
Buchanan	87,888	Saint Joseph	409
Butler	37,693	Poplar Bluff	698
Caldwell	8,660	Kingston	430
Callaway	32,252	Fulton	842
Camden	19,963	Camdenton	641
Cape Girardeau	58,837	Jackson	577
Carroll	12,131	Carrollton	695
Carter	5,532	Van Buren	509
Cass	51,029	Harrisonville	701
Cedar	11,894	Stockton	470
Chariton	10,489	Keytesville	758
Christian	22,402	Ozark	564
Clark	8,493	Kahoka	507
Clay	136,488	Liberty	403
Clinton	15,916	Plattsburg	423
Cole	56,663	Jefferson City	392
Cooper	14,643	Boonville	567
Crawford	18,300	Steelville	744
Dade	7,383	Greenfield	491
Dallas	12,096	Buffalo	543
Daviess	8,905	Gallatin	568
De Kalb	8,222	Maysville	425
Dent	14,517	Salem	755
Douglas	11,594	Ava	814
Dunklin	36,320	Kennett	547
Franklin	71,129	Union	922
Gasconade	13,181	Hermann	521
Gentry	7,887	Albany	493
Greene	185,302	Springfield	677
Grundy	11,959	Trenton	437
Harrison	9,890	Bethany	725
Henry	19,672	Clinton	729
Hickory	6,367	Hermitage	379
Holt	6,882	Oregon	457
Howard	10,008	Fayette	465
Howell	28,807	West Plains	928
Iron	11,084	Ironton	552
Jackson	629,180	Independence	611
Jasper	86,958	Carthage	641
Jefferson	146,814	Hillsboro	661
Johnson	39,059	Warrensburg	834
Knox	5,508	Edina	507
Laclede	24,323	Lebanon	768
Lafayette	29,931	Lexington	632
Lawrence	28,973	Mount Vernon	613
Lewis	10,901	Monticello	509
Lincoln	22,193	Troy	627
Linn	15,495	Linneus	620
Livingston	15,739	Chillicothe	537
McDonald	14,917	Pineville	540
Macon	16,313	Macon	797
Madison	10,725	Fredericktown	497
Maries	7,551	Vienna	528
Marion	28,638	Palmyra	438
Mercer	4,685	Princeton	454
Miller	18,539	Tuscumbia	593
Mississippi	15,726	Charleston	410
Moniteau	12,068	California	417
Monroe	9,716	Paris	670
Montgomery	11,537	Montgomery City	540
Morgan	13,807	Versailles	594
New Madrid	22,945	New Madrid	658
Newton	40,555	Neosho	627
Nodaway	21,996	Maryville	875
Oregon	10,238	Alton	792
Osage	12,014	Linn	606
Ozark	7,961	Gainesville	731
Pemiscot	24,987	Caruthersville	517
Perry	16,784	Perryville	473

County	Pop.	County seat or court house	Land area sq. mi.
Pettis	36,378	Sedalia	686
Phelps	33,633	Rolla	674
Pike	17,568	Bowling Green	673
Platte	46,341	Platte City	421
Polk	18,822	Bolivar	636
Pulaski	42,011	Waynesville	550
Putnam	6,092	Unionville	520
Ralls	8,984	New London	482
Randolph	25,460	Huntsville	477
Ray	21,378	Richmond	568
Reynolds	7,230	Centerville	809
Ripley	12,458	Doniphan	631
St. Charles	143,455	St. Charles	558
St. Clair	8,622	Osceola	699
St. Francois	42,600	Farmington	451
St. Louis	974,180	Clayton	506
Ste. Genevieve	15,180	Ste. Genevieve	504
Saline	24,913	Marshall	755
Schuyler	4,979	Lancaster	309
Scotland	5,415	Memphis	438
Scott	39,647	Benton	423
Shannon	7,885	Eminence	1,004
Shelby	7,826	Shelbyville	501
Stoddard	29,009	Bloomfield	815
Stone	15,587	Galena	451
Sullivan	7,434	Milan	651
Taney	20,467	Forsyth	608
Texas	21,070	Houston	1,180
Vernon	19,806	Nevada	837
Warren	14,900	Warrenton	429
Washington	17,983	Potosi	762
Wayne	11,277	Greenville	762
Webster	20,414	Marshfield	594
Worth	3,008	Grant City	266
Wright	16,188	Hartville	682
Independent City			
St. Louis	452,801	.....	61

Montana

(56 counties, 145,388 sq. mi. land; pop., 786,690)

County	Pop.	County seat	Land area sq. mi.
Beaverhead	8,186	Dillon	5,529
Big Horn	11,096	Hardin	4,983
Blaine	6,999	Chinook	4,257
Broadwater	3,267	Townsend	1,189
Carbon	8,099	Red Lodge	2,056
Carter	1,799	Ekalaka	3,342
Cascade	80,696	Great Falls	2,699
Chouteau	6,092	Fort Benton	3,987
Custer	13,109	Miles City	3,776
Daniels	2,835	Scobey	1,427
Dawson	11,805	Glendive	2,374
Deer Lodge	12,518	Anaconda	740
Fallon	3,763	Baker	1,623
Fergus	13,076	Lewistown	4,340
Flathead	51,966	Kalispell	5,112
Gallatin	42,865	Bozeman	2,510
Garfield	1,656	Jordan	4,491
Glacier	10,628	Cut Bank	2,994
Golden Valley	1,026	Ryegate	1,172
Granite	2,700	Philipsburg	1,729
Hill	17,985	Havre	2,897
Jefferson	7,029	Boulder	1,657
Judith Basin	2,646	Stanford	1,871
Lake	19,056	Polson	1,445
Lewis & Clark	43,039	Helena	3,461
Liberty	2,329	Chester	1,426
Lincoln	17,752	Libby	3,616
McCone	2,702	Circle	2,626
Madison	5,448	Virginia City	3,590
Meagher	2,154	White Sulphur Springs	2,392
Mineral	3,675	Superior	1,216
Missoula	76,016	Missoula	2,582
Musselshell	4,428	Roundup	1,871
Park	12,869	Livingston	1,665
Petroleum	655	Winnett	1,652
Phillips	5,367	Malta	5,130
Pondera	6,731	Conrad	1,632
Powder River	2,520	Broadus	3,288
Powell	6,958	Deer Lodge	2,326
Prairie	1,836	Terry	1,732
Ravalli	22,493	Hamilton	2,384
Richland	12,243	Sidney	2,081
Roosevelt	10,467	Wolf Point	2,357
Rosebud	9,899	Forsyth	5,019
Sanders	8,675	Thompson Falls	2,749
Sheridan	5,414	Plentywood	1,681
Silver Bow	38,092	Butte	718
Stillwater	5,598	Columbus	1,793
Sweet Grass	3,216	Big Timber	1,903
Teton	6,491	Choteau	2,275
Toole	5,559	Shelby	1,931
Treasure	981	Hysham	975
Valley	10,250	Glasgow	4,936
Wheatland	2,359	Harlowton	1,419
Wibaux	1,476	Wibaux	888
Yellowstone	108,035	Billings	2,624

Nebraska

(93 counties, 76,644 sq. mi. land; pop., 1,569,825)

County	Pop.	County seat	Land area sq. mi.
Adams	30,656	Hastings	564
Antelope	8,675	Neligh	859
Arthur	513	Arthur	711
Banner	918	Harrisburg	747
Blaine	867	Brewster	714
Boone	7,391	Albion	687
Box Butte	13,696	Alliance	1,077
Boyd	3,331	Butte	532
Brown	4,377	Ainsworth	1,214
Buffalo	34,797	Kearney	945
Burt	8,813	Tekamah	486
Butler	9,330	David City	584
Cass	20,297	Plattsmouth	557
Cedar	10,852	Hartington	740
Chase	4,758	Imperial	894
Cherry	6,758	Valentine	5,961
Cheyenne	10,057	Sidney	1,196
Clay	8,106	Clay Center	574
Colfax	9,890	Schuyler	410
Cuming	11,664	West Point	575
Custer	13,877	Broken Bow	2,571
Dakota	16,573	Dakota City	258
Dawes	9,609	Chadron	1,397
Dawson	22,162	Lexington	982
Deuel	2,462	Chappell	437
Dixon	7,137	Ponca	474
Dodge	35,847	Fremont	534
Douglas	397,884	Omaha	333
Dundy	2,861	Benkelman	920
Fillmore	7,920	Geneva	576
Franklin	4,377	Franklin	576
Frontier	3,647	Stockville	976
Furnas	6,486	Beaver City	721
Gage	24,456	Beatrice	858
Garden	2,802	Oshkosh	1,680
Garfield	2,363	Burwell	570
Gosper	2,140	Elwood	461
Grant	877	Hyannis	775
Greeley	3,462	Greeley	570
Hall	47,690	Grand Island	537
Hamilton	9,301	Aurora	543
Harlan	4,292	Alma	555
Hayes	1,356	Hayes Center	713
Hitchcock	4,079	Trenton	709
Holt	13,552	O'Neill	2,406
Hooker	990	Mullen	721
Howard	6,773	Saint Paul	564
Jefferson	9,817	Fairbury	575
Johnson	5,285	Tecumseh	377
Kearney	7,053	Minden	516
Keith	9,364	Ogallala	1,039
Keya Paha	1,301	Springview	769
Kimball	4,882	Kimball	952
Knox	11,457	Center	1,105
Lancaster	192,884	Lincoln	839
Lincoln	36,455	North Platte	2,525
Logan	983	Stapleton	571
Loup	859	Taylor	574
McPherson	593	Tryon	859
Madison	31,382	Madison	575
Merrick	8,945	Central City	478
Morrill	6,085	Bridgeport	1,405
Nance	4,740	Fullerton	439
Nemaha	8,367	Auburn	409
Nuckolls	6,726	Nelson	576
Otoe	15,183	Nebraska City	615
Pawnee	3,937	Pawnee City	433
Perkins	3,637	Grant	885
Phelps	9,769	Holdrege	540
Pierce	8,481	Pierce	575
Platte	28,852	Columbus	669
Polk	6,320	Osceola	437
Red Willow	12,615	McCook	718
Richardson	11,315	Falls City	553
Rock	2,383	Bassett	1,003
Saline	13,131	Wilber	575
Sarpy	86,015	Papillion	238
Saunders	18,716	Wahoo	753
Scotts Bluff	38,344	Gering	725
Seward	15,789	Seward	575
Sheridan	7,544	Rushville	2,453
Sherman	4,226	Loup City	564
Sioux	1,845	Harrison	2,070
Stanton	6,549	Stanton	431
Thayer	7,582	Hebron	575
Thomas	973	Thedford	713
Thurston	7,186	Pender	391
Valley	5,633	Ord	567
Washington	15,508	Blair	386
Wayne	9,858	Wayne	443
Webster	4,858	Red Cloud	575
Wheeler	1,060	Bartlett	575
York	14,798	York	576

Nevada

(16 cos., 1 ind. city, 109,894 sq. mi. land; pop., 800,508)

County	Pop.	County seat	Land area sq. mi.
Churchill	13,917	Fallon	4,990
Clark	461,816	Las Vegas	7,881

County	Pop.	County seat or court house	Land area sq. mi.
Douglas	19,421	Minden	708
Elko	17,269	Elko	17,135
Esmeralda	777	Goldfield	3,587
Eureka	1,198	Eureka	4,175
Humboldt	9,449	Winnemucca	9,698
Lander	4,082	Battle Mountain	5,515
Lincoln	3,732	Pioche	10,635
Lyon	13,594	Yerington	2,007
Mineral	6,217	Hawthorne	3,744
Nye	9,048	Tonopah	18,155
Pershing	3,408	Lovelock	6,036
Storey	1,459	Virginia City	264
Washoe	193,623	Reno	6,317
White Pine	8,167	Ely	8,902
Independent City			
Carson City	32,022	Carson City	146

New Hampshire
(10 counties, 8,993 sq. mi. land; pop., 920,610)

County	Pop.	County seat	Land area
Belknap	42,884	Laconia	404
Carroll	27,931	Ossipee	933
Cheshire	62,116	Keene	711
Coos	35,147	Lancaster	1,804
Grafton	65,806	Woodsville	1,719
Hillsborough	276,608	Nashua	876
Merrimack	98,302	Concord	936
Rockingham	190,345	Exeter	699
Strafford	85,408	Dover	370
Sullivan	36,063	Newport	540

New Jersey
(21 counties, 7,468 sq. mi. land; pop., 7,365,011)

County	Pop.	County seat	Land area
Atlantic	194,119	Mays Landing	568
Bergen	845,385	Hackensack	237
Burlington	362,542	Mount Holly	808
Camden	471,650	Camden	223
Cape May	82,266	Cape May Court House	263
Cumberland	132,866	Bridgeton	498
Essex	851,304	Newark	127
Gloucester	199,917	Woodbury	327
Hudson	556,972	Jersey City	46
Hunterdon	87,361	Flemington	426
Mercer	307,863	Trenton	227
Middlesex	595,893	New Brunswick	316
Monmouth	503,173	Freehold	472
Morris	407,630	Morristown	470
Ocean	346,038	Toms River	641
Passaic	447,585	Paterson	187
Salem	64,676	Salem	338
Somerset	203,129	Somerville	305
Sussex	116,119	Newton	526
Union	504,094	Elizabeth	103
Warren	84,429	Belvidere	359

New Mexico
(33 counties, 121,335 sq. mi. land; pop., 1,303,302)

County	Pop.	County seat	Land area
Bernalillo	420,261	Albuquerque	1,169
Catron	2,720	Reserve	6,929
Chaves	51,103	Roswell	6,066
Cibola	30,347	Grants	4,468
Colfax	13,706	Raton	3,762
Curry	42,019	Clovis	1,408
De Baca	2,454	Fort Sumner	2,323
Dona Ana	96,340	Las Cruces	3,819
Eddy	47,855	Carlsbad	4,184
Grant	26,204	Silver City	3,969
Guadalupe	4,496	Santa Rosa	3,032
Harding	1,090	Mosquero	2,122
Hidalgo	6,049	Lordsburg	3,445
Lea	55,634	Lovington	4,389
Lincoln	10,997	Carrizozo	4,832
Los Alamos	17,599	Los Alamos	109
Luna	15,585	Deming	2,965
McKinley	56,536	Gallup	5,442
Mora	4,205	Mora	1,930
Otero	44,665	Alamogordo	6,626
Quay	10,577	Tucumcari	2,874
Rio Arriba	29,282	Tierra Amarilla	5,856
Roosevelt	15,695	Portales	2,453
Sandoval	34,400	Bernalillo	3,707
San Juan	80,833	Aztec	5,521
San Miguel	22,751	Las Vegas	4,709
Santa Fe	75,519	Santa Fe	1,905
Sierra	8,454	Truth or Consequences	4,178
Socorro	12,969	Socorro	6,625
Taos	18,862	Taos	2,204
Terrance	7,491	Estancia	3,335
Union	4,725	Clayton	3,830
Valencia	60,853	Los Lunas	5,616

New York
(62 counties, 47,377 sq. mi. land; pop., 17,558,165)

County	Pop.	County seat	Land area
Albany	285,909	Albany	524
Allegany	51,742	Belmont	1,032
Bronx	1,168,972	Bronx	42
Broome	213,648	Binghamton	712
Cattaraugus	85,697	Little Valley	1,306
Cayuga	79,894	Auburn	695
Chautauqua	146,925	Mayville	1,064
Chemung	97,656	Elmira	411
Chenango	49,344	Norwich	897
Clinton	80,750	Plattsburgh	1,043
Columbia	59,487	Hudson	638
Cortland	48,820	Cortland	500
Delaware	46,824	Delhi	1,440
Dutchess	245,055	Poughkeepsie	804
Erie	1,015,472	Buffalo	1,046
Essex	36,176	Elizabethtown	1,806
Franklin	44,929	Malone	1,642
Fulton	55,153	Johnstown	497
Genesee	59,400	Batavia	495
Greene	40,861	Catskill	648
Hamilton	5,034	Lake Pleasant	1,721
Herkimer	66,714	Herkimer	1,416
Jefferson	88,151	Watertown	1,273
Kings	2,231,028	Brooklyn	70
Lewis	25,035	Lowville	1,283
Livingston	57,006	Geneseo	633
Madison	65,150	Wampsville	656
Monroe	702,238	Rochester	663
Montgomery	53,439	Fonda	404
Nassau	1,321,582	Mineola	287
New York	1,428,285	New York	22
Niagara	227,354	Lockport	526
Oneida	253,940	Utica	1,219
Onondaga	463,920	Syracuse	784
Ontario	88,909	Canandaigua	644
Orange	259,603	Goshen	826
Orleans	38,496	Albion	391
Oswego	113,901	Oswego	954
Otsego	59,075	Cooperstown	1,004
Putnam	77,193	Carmel	231
Queens	1,891,325	Jamaica	109
Rensselaer	151,966	Troy	655
Richmond	352,029	Saint George	59
Rockland	259,530	New City	175
St. Lawrence	114,347	Canton	2,728
Saratoga	153,759	Ballston Spa	810
Schenectady	149,946	Schenectady	206
Schoharie	29,710	Schoharie	624
Schuyler	17,686	Watkins Glen	329
Seneca	33,733	Ovid & Waterloo	327
Steuben	89,217	Bath	1,396
Suffolk	1,284,231	Riverhead	911
Sullivan	65,155	Monticello	976
Tioga	49,812	Owego	519
Tompkins	87,085	Ithaca	477
Ulster	158,158	Kingston	1,131
Warren	54,854	Lake George	882
Washington	54,795	Hudson Falls	836
Wayne	84,581	Lyons	605
Westchester	866,599	White Plains	438
Wyoming	39,895	Warsaw	595
Yates	21,459	Penn Yan	339

North Carolina
(100 counties, 48,843 sq. mi. land; pop., 5,880,095)

County	Pop.	County seat	Land area
Alamance	99,136	Graham	433
Alexander	24,999	Taylorsville	259
Alleghany	9,587	Sparta	235
Anson	25,562	Wadesboro	533
Ashe	22,325	Jefferson	426
Avery	14,409	Newland	247
Beaufort	40,266	Washington	826
Bertie	21,024	Windsor	701
Bladen	30,448	Elizabethtown	879
Brunswick	35,767	Southport	860
Buncombe	160,934	Asheville	659
Burke	72,504	Morganton	504
Cabarrus	85,895	Concord	364
Caldwell	67,746	Lenoir	471
Camden	5,829	Camden	240
Carteret	41,092	Beaufort	526
Caswell	20,705	Yanceyville	428
Catawba	105,208	Newton	396
Chatham	33,415	Pittsboro	708
Cherokee	18,933	Murphy	452
Chowan	12,558	Edenton	182
Clay	6,619	Hayesville	214
Cleveland	83,435	Shelby	468
Columbus	51,037	Whiteville	938
Craven	71,043	New Bern	701
Cumberland	247,160	Fayetteville	657
Currituck	11,089	Currituck	256
Dare	13,377	Manteo	391
Davidson	113,162	Lexington	548
Davie	24,599	Mocksville	267
Duplin	40,952	Kenansville	819
Durham	152,235	Durham	298
Edgecombe	55,988	Tarboro	506
Forsyth	243,704	Winston-Salem	412
Franklin	30,055	Louisburg	494
Gaston	162,568	Gastonia	357
Gates	8,875	Gatesville	338
Graham	7,217	Robbinsville	289
Granville	33,995	Oxford	534
Greene	16,117	Snow Hill	266

County	Pop.	County seat or court house	Land area sq. mi.
Guilford	317,154	Greensboro	651
Halifax	55,076	Halifax	724
Harnett	59,570	Lillington	601
Haywood	46,495	Waynesville	555
Henderson	58,580	Hendersonville	374
Hertford	23,368	Winton	356
Hoke	20,383	Raeford	391
Hyde	5,873	Swanquarter	624
Iredell	82,538	Statesville	574
Jackson	25,811	Sylva	491
Johnston	70,599	Smithfield	795
Jones	9,705	Trenton	470
Lee	36,718	Sanford	259
Lenoir	59,819	Kinston	402
Lincoln	42,372	Lincolnton	298
McDowell	35,135	Marion	437
Macon	20,178	Franklin	517
Madison	16,827	Marshall	451
Martin	25,948	Williamston	461
Mecklenburg	404,270	Charlotte	528
Mitchell	14,428	Bakersville	222
Montgomery	22,469	Troy	490
Moore	50,505	Carthage	701
Nash	67,153	Nashville	540
New Hanover	103,471	Wilmington	185
Northampton	22,195	Jackson	538
Onslow	112,784	Jacksonville	763
Orange	77,055	Hillsboro	400
Pamlico	10,398	Bayboro	341
Pasquotank	28,462	Elizabeth City	228
Pender	22,262	Burgaw	875
Perquimans	9,486	Hertford	246
Person	29,164	Roxboro	398
Pitt	83,651	Greenville	657
Polk	12,984	Columbus	238
Randolph	91,300	Asheboro	789
Richmond	45,161	Rockingham	477
Robeson	101,577	Lumberton	949
Rockingham	83,426	Wentworth	569
Rowan	99,186	Salisbury	519
Rutherford	53,787	Rutherfordton	568
Sampson	49,687	Clinton	947
Scotland	32,273	Laurinburg	319
Stanly	48,517	Albemarle	396
Stokes	33,086	Danbury	452
Surry	59,449	Dobson	539
Swain	10,283	Bryson City	526
Transylvania	23,417	Brevard	378
Tyrrell	3,975	Columbia	407
Union	70,436	Monroe	639
Vance	36,748	Henderson	249
Wake	301,429	Raleigh	854
Warren	16,232	Warrenton	427
Washington	14,801	Plymouth	332
Watauga	31,678	Boone	314
Wayne	97,054	Goldsboro	554
Wilkes	58,657	Wilkesboro	752
Wilson	63,132	Wilson	374
Yadkin	28,439	Yadkinville	336
Yancey	14,934	Burnsville	314

North Dakota

(53 counties, 69,300 sq. mi. land; pop., 652,717)

County	Pop.	County seat or court house	Land area sq. mi.
Adams	3,584	Hettinger	988
Barnes	13,960	Valley City	1,498
Benson	7,944	Minnewaukan	1,412
Billings	1,138	Medora	1,152
Bottineau	9,338	Bottineau	1,668
Bowman	4,229	Bowman	1,162
Burke	3,822	Bowbells	1,118
Burleigh	54,811	Bismarck	1,618
Cass	88,247	Fargo	1,767
Cavalier	7,636	Langdon	1,507
Dickey	7,207	Ellendale	1,139
Divide	3,494	Crosby	1,288
Dunn	4,627	Manning	1,993
Eddy	3,554	New Rockford	634
Emmons	5,877	Linton	1,499
Foster	4,611	Carrington	640
Golden Valley	2,391	Beach	1,003
Grand Forks	66,100	Grand Forks	1,440
Grant	4,274	Carson	1,660
Griggs	3,714	Cooperstown	708
Hettinger	4,275	Mott	1,133
Kidder	3,833	Steele	1,362
La Moure	6,473	La Moure	1,150
Logan	3,493	Napoleon	1,000
McHenry	7,858	Towner	1,987
McIntosh	4,800	Ashley	984
McKenzie	7,132	Watford City	2,754
McLean	12,288	Washburn	2,065
Mercer	9,378	Stanton	1,044
Morton	25,177	Mandan	1,921
Mountrail	7,679	Stanley	1,837
Nelson	5,233	Lakota	991
Oliver	2,495	Center	723
Pembina	10,399	Cavalier	1,120
Pierce	6,166	Rugby	1,037
Ramsey	13,048	Devils Lake	1,241
Ransom	6,698	Lisbon	862
Renville	3,608	Mohall	874
Richland	19,207	Wahpeton	1,436
Rolette	12,177	Rolla	914
Sargent	5,512	Forman	857
Sheridan	2,819	McClusky	989
Sioux	3,620	Fort Yates	1,099
Slope	1,157	Amidon	1,219
Stark	23,697	Dickinson	1,338
Steele	3,106	Finley	713
Stutsman	24,154	Jamestown	2,263
Towner	4,052	Cando	1,035
Traill	9,624	Hillsboro	861
Walsh	15,371	Grafton	1,290
Ward	58,392	Minot	2,041
Wells	6,979	Fessenden	1,288
Williams	22,237	Williston	2,074

Ohio

(88 counties, 41,004 sq. mi. land; pop., 10,797,603)

County	Pop.	County seat or court house	Land area sq. mi.
Adams	24,328	West Union	586
Allen	112,241	Lima	405
Ashland	46,178	Ashland	424
Ashtabula	104,215	Jefferson	703
Athens	56,399	Athens	508
Auglaize	42,554	Wapakoneta	398
Belmont	82,569	Saint Clairsville	537
Brown	31,920	Georgetown	493
Butler	258,787	Hamilton	470
Carroll	25,598	Carrollton	393
Champaign	33,649	Urbana	429
Clark	150,236	Springfield	398
Clermont	128,483	Batavia	456
Clinton	34,603	Wilmington	410
Columbiana	113,572	Lisbon	534
Coshocton	36,024	Coshocton	566
Crawford	50,075	Bucyrus	403
Cuyahoga	1,498,295	Cleveland	459
Darke	55,096	Greenville	600
Defiance	39,987	Defiance	414
Delaware	53,840	Delaware	443
Erie	79,655	Sandusky	264
Fairfield	93,678	Lancaster	506
Fayette	27,467	Washington C. H.	405
Franklin	869,126	Columbus	543
Fulton	37,751	Wauseon	407
Gallia	30,098	Gallipolis	471
Geauga	74,474	Chardon	408
Greene	129,769	Xenia	416
Guernsey	42,024	Cambridge	522
Hamilton	873,203	Cincinnati	412
Hancock	64,581	Findlay	532
Hardin	32,719	Kenton	471
Harrison	18,152	Cadiz	400
Henry	28,383	Napoleon	415
Highland	33,477	Hillsboro	553
Hocking	24,304	Logan	423
Holmes	29,416	Millersburg	424
Huron	54,608	Norwalk	494
Jackson	30,592	Jackson	420
Jefferson	91,564	Steubenville	410
Knox	46,309	Mount Vernon	529
Lake	212,801	Painesville	231
Lawrence	63,849	Ironton	457
Licking	120,981	Newark	686
Logan	39,155	Bellefontaine	458
Lorain	274,909	Elyria	495
Lucas	471,741	Toledo	341
Madison	33,004	London	467
Mahoning	289,487	Youngstown	417
Marion	67,974	Marion	403
Medina	113,150	Medina	422
Meigs	23,641	Pomeroy	432
Mercer	38,334	Celina	457
Miami	90,381	Troy	410
Monroe	17,382	Woodsfield	457
Montgomery	571,697	Dayton	458
Morgan	14,241	McConnelsville	420
Morrow	26,480	Mount Gilead	406
Muskingum	83,340	Zanesville	654
Noble	11,310	Caldwell	399
Ottawa	40,076	Port Clinton	253
Paulding	21,302	Paulding	419
Perry	31,032	New Lexington	412
Pickaway	43,662	Circleville	503
Pike	22,802	Waverly	443
Portage	135,856	Ravenna	486
Preble	38,223	Eaton	426
Putnam	32,991	Ottawa	484
Richland	131,205	Mansfield	497
Ross	65,004	Chillicothe	692
Sandusky	63,267	Fremont	409
Scioto	84,545	Portsmouth	613
Seneca	61,901	Tiffin	553
Shelby	43,089	Sidney	409
Stark	378,823	Canton	574
Summit	524,472	Akron	412
Trumbull	241,863	Warren	612
Tuscarawas	84,614	New Philadelphia	570

County	Pop.	County seat or court house	Land area sq. mi.
Union	29,536	Marysville	437
Van Wert	30,458	Van Wert	410
Vinton	11,584	McArthur	414
Warren	99,276	Lebanon	403
Washington	64,266	Marietta	640
Wayne	97,408	Wooster	557
Williams	36,369	Bryan	422
Wood	107,372	Bowling Green	619
Wyandot	22,651	Upper Sandusky	406

Oklahoma

(77 counties, 68,655 sq. mi. land; pop., 3,025,487)

County	Pop.	County seat	Land area
Adair	18,575	Stillwell	577
Alfalfa	7,077	Cherokee	864
Atoka	12,748	Atoka	980
Beaver	6,806	Beaver	1,808
Beckham	19,243	Sayre	904
Blaine	13,443	Watonga	920
Bryan	30,535	Durant	902
Caddo	30,905	Anadarko	1,286
Canadian	56,452	El Reno	901
Carter	43,610	Ardmore	828
Cherokee	30,684	Tahlequah	748
Choctaw	17,203	Hugo	762
Cimarron	3,648	Boise City	1,842
Cleveland	133,173	Norman	529
Coal	6,041	Coalgate	520
Comanche	112,456	Lawton	1,076
Cotton	7,338	Walters	656
Craig	15,014	Vinita	763
Creek	59,210	Sapulpa	930
Custer	25,995	Arapaho	981
Delaware	23,946	Jay	720
Dewey	5,922	Taloga	1,007
Ellis	5,596	Arnett	1,232
Garfield	62,820	Enid	1,060
Garvin	27,856	Pauls Valley	813
Grady	39,490	Chickasha	1,106
Grant	6,518	Medford	1,004
Greer	6,877	Mangum	638
Harmon	4,519	Hollis	537
Harper	4,715	Buffalo	1,039
Haskell	11,010	Stigler	570
Hughes	14,338	Holdenville	806
Jackson	30,356	Altus	817
Jefferson	8,294	Waurika	769
Johnston	10,356	Tishomingo	639
Kay	49,852	Newkirk	921
Kingfisher	14,187	Kingfisher	906
Kiowa	12,711	Hobart	1,019
Latimer	9,840	Wilburton	728
Le Flore	40,698	Poteau	1,585
Lincoln	26,601	Chandler	964
Logan	26,881	Guthrie	748
Love	7,469	Marietta	519
McClain	20,291	Purcell	582
McCurtain	36,151	Idabel	1,826
McIntosh	15,495	Eufaula	599
Major	8,772	Fairview	958
Marshall	10,550	Madill	372
Mayes	32,261	Pryor	644
Murray	12,147	Sulphur	420
Muskogee	67,033	Muskogee	815
Noble	11,573	Perry	736
Nowata	11,486	Nowata	540
Okfuskee	11,125	Okemah	628
Oklahoma	568,933	Oklahoma City	708
Okmulgee	39,169	Okmulgee	698
Osage	39,327	Pawhuska	2,265
Ottawa	32,870	Miami	465
Pawnee	15,310	Pawnee	551
Payne	62,435	Stillwater	691
Pittsburg	40,524	McAlester	1,251
Pontotoc	32,598	Ada	717
Pottawatomie	55,239	Shawnee	783
Pushmataha	11,773	Antlers	1,417
Roger Mills	4,799	Cheyenne	1,146
Rogers	46,436	Claremore	683
Seminole	27,465	Wewoka	639
Sequoyah	30,749	Sallisaw	678
Stephens	43,419	Duncan	884
Texas	17,727	Guymon	2,040
Tillman	12,398	Frederick	904
Tulsa	470,593	Tulsa	572
Wagoner	41,801	Wagoner	559
Washington	48,113	Bartlesville	423
Washita	13,798	Cordell	1,006
Woods	10,923	Alva	1,291
Woodward	21,172	Woodward	1,242

Oregon

(36 counties, 96,184 sq. mi. land; pop., 2,633,156)

County	Pop.	County seat	Land area
Baker	16,134	Baker	3,072
Benton	68,211	Corvallis	679
Clackamas	241,911	Oregon City	1,870
Clatsop	32,489	Astoria	805
Columbia	35,646	Saint Helens	651
Coos	64,047	Coquille	1,606
Crook	13,091	Prineville	2,984
Curry	16,992	Gold Beach	1,629
Deschutes	62,142	Bend	3,025
Douglas	93,748	Roseburg	5,044
Gilliam	2,057	Condon	1,213
Grant	8,210	Canyon City	4,525
Harney	8,314	Burns	10,174
Hood River	15,835	Hood River	521
Jackson	132,456	Medford	2,787
Jefferson	11,599	Madras	1,789
Josephine	58,820	Grants Pass	1,640
Klamath	59,117	Klamath Falls	5,954
Lake	7,532	Lakeview	8,251
Lane	275,226	Eugene	4,562
Lincoln	35,264	Newport	980
Linn	89,495	Albany	2,296
Malheur	26,896	Vale	9,861
Marion	204,692	Salem	1,184
Morrow	7,519	Heppner	2,044
Multnomah	562,647	Portland	431
Polk	45,203	Dallas	741
Sherman	2,172	Moro	827
Tillamook	21,164	Tillamook	1,101
Umatilla	58,861	Pendleton	3,218
Union	23,921	La Grande	2,035
Wallowa	7,273	Enterprise	3,150
Wasco	21,732	The Dalles	2,384
Washington	245,860	Hillsboro	725
Wheeler	1,513	Fossil	1,713
Yamhill	55,332	McMinnville	715

Pennsylvania

(67 counties, 44,888 sq. mi. land; pop., 11,864,720)

County	Pop.	County seat	Land area
Adams	68,292	Gettysburg	521
Allegheny	1,450,195	Pittsburgh	727
Armstrong	77,768	Kittanning	646
Beaver	204,441	Beaver	436
Bedford	46,784	Bedford	1,017
Berks	312,509	Reading	861
Blair	136,621	Hollidaysburg	527
Bradford	62,919	Towanda	1,152
Bucks	479,180	Doylestown	610
Butler	147,912	Butler	789
Cambria	183,263	Ebensburg	691
Cameron	6,674	Emporium	398
Carbon	53,285	Jim Thorpe	384
Centre	112,760	Bellefonte	1,106
Chester	316,660	West Chester	758
Clarion	43,362	Clarion	607
Clearfield	83,578	Clearfield	1,149
Clinton	38,971	Lock Haven	891
Columbia	61,967	Bloomsburg	486
Crawford	88,869	Meadville	1,011
Cumberland	179,625	Carlisle	547
Dauphin	232,317	Harrisburg	528
Delaware	555,029	Media	184
Elk	38,338	Ridgeway	830
Erie	279,780	Erie	804
Fayette	160,395	Uniontown	794
Forest	5,072	Tionesta	428
Franklin	113,629	Chambersburg	774
Fulton	12,842	McConnellsburg	438
Greene	40,355	Waynesburg	577
Huntingdon	44,253	Huntingdon	877
Indiana	92,281	Indiana	829
Jefferson	48,303	Brookville	657
Juniata	19,188	Mifflintown	392
Lackawanna	227,908	Scranton	461
Lancaster	362,346	Lancaster	952
Lawrence	107,150	New Castle	363
Lebanon	109,829	Lebanon	363
Lehigh	273,582	Allentown	348
Luzerne	343,079	Wilkes-Barre	891
Lycoming	118,416	Williamsport	1,237
McKean	50,635	Smethport	979
Mercer	128,299	Mercer	672
Mifflin	46,908	Lewistown	413
Monroe	69,409	Stroudsburg	609
Montgomery	643,371	Norristown	486
Montour	16,675	Danville	131
Northampton	225,418	Easton	376
Northumberland	100,381	Sunbury	461
Perry	35,718	New Bloomfield	557
Philadelphia	1,688,210	Philadelphia	136
Pike	18,271	Milford	550
Potter	17,726	Coudersport	1,081
Schuylkill	160,630	Pottsville	782
Snyder	33,584	Middleburg	329
Somerset	81,243	Somerset	1,073
Sullivan	6,349	Laporte	451
Susquehanna	37,876	Montrose	826
Tioga	40,973	Wellsboro	1,131
Union	32,870	Lewisburg	317
Venango	64,444	Franklin	679
Warren	47,449	Warren	885
Washington	217,074	Washington	858
Wayne	35,237	Honesdale	731
Westmoreland	392,184	Greensburg	1,033
Wyoming	26,433	Tunkhannock	399
York	312,963	York	906

County	Pop.	County seat or court house	Land area sq. mi.

Rhode Island
(5 counties, 1,055 sq. mi. land; pop., 947,154)

County	Pop.	Seat	Area
Bristol	46,942	Bristol	26
Kent	154,163	East Greenwich	172
Newport	81,383	Newport	107
Providence	571,349	Providence	416
Washington	93,317	West Kingston	333

South Carolina
(46 counties, 30,203 sq. mi. land; pop., 3,120,729)

County	Pop.	Seat	Area
Abbeville	22,627	Abbeville	508
Aiken	105,630	Aiken	1,092
Allendale	10,700	Allendale	413
Anderson	133,235	Anderson	718
Bamberg	18,118	Bamberg	395
Barnwell	19,868	Barnwell	558
Beaufort	65,364	Beaufort	579
Berkeley	94,745	Moncks Corner	1,108
Calhoun	12,206	Saint Matthews	380
Charleston	276,556	Charleston	938
Cherokee	40,983	Gaffney	396
Chester	30,148	Chester	580
Chesterfield	38,161	Chesterfield	802
Clarendon	27,464	Manning	602
Colleton	31,676	Walterboro	1,052
Darlington	62,717	Darlington	563
Dillon	31,083	Dillon	406
Dorchester	59,045	Saint George	575
Edgefield	17,528	Edgefield	490
Fairfield	20,700	Winnsboro	685
Florence	110,163	Florence	804
Georgetown	42,461	Georgetown	822
Greenville	287,895	Greenville	795
Greenwood	55,859	Greenwood	451
Hampton	18,159	Hampton	561
Horry	101,419	Conway	1,143
Jasper	14,504	Ridgeland	655
Kershaw	39,015	Camden	723
Lancaster	53,361	Lancaster	552
Laurens	52,214	Laurens	712
Lee	18,929	Bishopville	411
Lexington	140,353	Lexington	707
McCormick	7,797	McCormick	350
Marion	34,179	Marion	493
Marlboro	31,634	Bennettsville	483
Newberry	31,111	Newberry	634
Oconee	48,611	Walhalla	629
Orangeburg	82,276	Orangeburg	1,111
Pickens	79,292	Pickens	499
Richland	269,600	Columbia	762
Saluda	16,136	Saluda	456
Spartanburg	203,023	Spartanburg	814
Sumter	88,243	Sumter	665
Union	30,764	Union	515
Williamsburg	38,226	Kingstree	934
York	106,720	York	685

South Dakota
(67 counties, 75,952 sq. mi. land; pop., 690,768)

County	Pop.	Seat	Area
Aurora	3,628	Plankinton	707
Beadle	19,195	Huron	1,259
Bennett	3,236	Martin	1,182
Bon Homme	8,059	Tyndall	552
Brookings	24,332	Brookings	795
Brown	36,962	Aberdeen	1,722
Brule	5,245	Chamberlain	815
Buffalo	1,795	Gannvalley	475
Butte	8,372	Belle Fourche	2,251
Campbell	2,243	Mound City	732
Charles Mix	9,680	Lake Andes	1,090
Clark	4,894	Clark	953
Clay	13,135	Vermillion	409
Codington	20,885	Watertown	694
Corson	5,196	McIntosh	2,467
Custer	6,000	Custer	1,559
Davison	17,820	Mitchell	436
Day	8,133	Webster	1,022
Deuel	5,289	Clear Lake	631
Dewey	5,366	Timber Lake	2,310
Douglas	4,181	Armour	434
Edmunds	5,159	Ipswich	1,149
Fall River	8,439	Hot Springs	1,740
Faulk	3,327	Faulkton	1,004
Grant	9,013	Milbank	681
Gregory	6,015	Burke	1,013
Haakon	2,794	Philip	1,822
Hamlin	5,261	Hayti	512
Hand	4,948	Miller	1,437
Hanson	3,415	Alexandria	433
Harding	1,700	Buffalo	2,678
Hughes	14,220	Pierre	757
Hutchinson	9,350	Olivet	816
Hyde	2,069	Highmore	860
Jackson	3,437	Kadoka	1,872
Jerauld	2,929	Wessington Spgs.	530
Jones	1,463	Murdo	971
Kingsbury	6,679	De Smet	824
Lake	10,724	Madison	560
Lawrence	18,339	Deadwood	800
Lincoln	13,942	Canton	578
Lyman	3,864	Kennebec	1,679
McCook	6,444	Salem	576
McPherson	4,027	Leola	1,148
Marshall	5,404	Britton	848
Meade	20,717	Sturgis	3,481
Mellette	2,249	White River	1,311
Miner	3,739	Howard	570
Minnehaha	109,435	Sioux Falls	810
Moody	6,692	Flandreau	520
Pennington	70,133	Rapid City	2,783
Perkins	4,700	Bison	2,884
Potter	3,674	Gettysburg	869
Roberts	10,911	Sisseton	1,102
Sanborn	3,213	Woonsocket	569
Shannon	11,323	(Attached to Fall River)	2,094
Spink	9,201	Redfield	1,505
Stanley	2,533	Fort Pierre	1,431
Sully	1,990	Onida	972
Todd	7,328	(Attached to Tripp)	1,388
Tripp	7,268	Winner	1,618
Turner	9,255	Parker	617
Union	10,938	Elk Point	453
Walworth	7,011	Selby	707
Washabaugh	—	(Attached to Jackson)	—
Yankton	18,952	Yankton	518
Ziebach	2,308	Dupree	1,969

Tennessee
(95 counties, 41,155 sq. mi. land; pop., 4,591,023)

County	Pop.	Seat	Area
Anderson	67,346	Clinton	339
Bedford	27,916	Shelbyville	475
Benton	14,901	Camden	392
Bledsoe	9,478	Pikeville	407
Blount	77,770	Maryville	558
Bradley	67,547	Cleveland	327
Campbell	34,841	Jacksboro	479
Cannon	10,234	Woodbury	266
Carroll	28,285	Huntingdon	600
Carter	50,205	Elizabethton	341
Cheatham	21,616	Ashland City	304
Chester	12,727	Henderson	289
Claiborne	24,595	Tazewell	432
Clay	7,676	Celina	227
Cocke	28,792	Newport	432
Coffee	38,311	Manchester	428
Crockett	14,941	Alamo	266
Cumberland	28,676	Crossville	682
Davidson	477,811	Nashville	501
Decatur	10,857	Decaturville	330
De Kalb	13,589	Smithville	291
Dickson	30,037	Charlotte	491
Dyer	34,663	Dyersburg	520
Fayette	25,305	Somerville	705
Fentress	14,826	Jamestown	498
Franklin	31,983	Winchester	543
Gibson	49,467	Trenton	602
Giles	24,625	Pulaski	610
Grainger	16,751	Rutledge	273
Greene	54,406	Greeneville	619
Grundy	13,787	Altamont	361
Hamblen	49,300	Morristown	156
Hamilton	287,643	Chattanooga	539
Hancock	6,887	Sneedville	223
Hardeman	23,873	Bolivar	670
Hardin	22,280	Savannah	578
Hawkins	43,751	Rogersville	486
Haywood	20,318	Brownsville	534
Henderson	21,390	Lexington	520
Henry	28,656	Paris	560
Hickman	15,151	Centerville	610
Houston	6,871	Erin	200
Humphreys	15,957	Waverly	528
Jackson	9,398	Gainesboro	308
Jefferson	31,284	Dandridge	265
Johnson	13,745	Mountain City	297
Knox	319,694	Knoxville	506
Lake	7,455	Tiptonville	169
Lauderdale	24,555	Ripley	474
Lawrence	34,110	Lawrenceburg	617
Lewis	9,700	Hohenwald	282
Lincoln	26,483	Fayetteville	571
Loudon	28,553	Loudon	235
McMinn	41,878	Athens	429
McNairy	22,525	Selmer	562
Macon	15,700	Lafayette	307
Madison	74,546	Jackson	558
Marion	24,416	Jasper	512
Marshall	19,698	Lewisburg	376
Maury	51,095	Columbia	616
Meigs	7,431	Decatur	189
Monroe	28,700	Madisonville	648
Montgomery	83,342	Clarksville	539
Moore	4,510	Lynchburg	129
Morgan	16,604	Wartburg	523
Obion	32,781	Union City	550
Overton	17,575	Livingston	433
Perry	6,111	Linden	412
Pickett	4,358	Byrdstown	159

County	Pop.	County seat or court house	Land area sq. mi.
Polk	13,602	Benton	438
Putnam	47,601	Cookeville	399
Rhea	24,235	Dayton	309
Roane	48,425	Kingston	357
Robertson	37,021	Springfield	476
Rutherford	84,058	Murfreesboro	606
Scott	19,259	Huntsville	528
Sequatchie	8,605	Dunlap	266
Sevier	41,418	Sevierville	590
Shelby	777,113	Memphis	772
Smith	14,935	Carthage	313
Stewart	8,665	Dover	454
Sullivan	143,968	Blountville	415
Sumner	85,790	Gallatin	529
Tipton	32,747	Covington	454
Trousdale	6,137	Hartsville	114
Unicoi	16,362	Erwin	186
Union	11,707	Maynardville	218
Van Buren	4,728	Spencer	273
Warren	32,653	McMinnville	431
Washington	88,755	Jonesboro	326
Wayne	13,946	Waynesboro	734
Weakley	32,896	Dresden	581
White	19,567	Sparta	373
Williamson	58,108	Franklin	584
Wilson	56,064	Lebanon	570

Texas

(254 counties, 262,017 sq. mi. land; pop., 14,225,513)

County	Pop.	County seat or court house	Land area sq. mi.
Anderson	38,381	Palestine	1,077
Andrews	13,323	Andrews	1,501
Angelina	64,172	Lufkin	807
Aransas	14,260	Rockport	280
Archer	7,266	Archer City	907
Armstrong	1,994	Claude	909
Atascosa	25,055	Jourdanton	1,218
Austin	17,726	Bellville	656
Bailey	8,168	Muleshoe	826
Bandera	7,084	Bandera	793
Bastrop	24,726	Bastrop	895
Baylor	4,919	Seymour	862
Bee	26,030	Beeville	880
Bell	157,820	Belton	1,055
Bexar	988,971	San Antonio	1,248
Blanco	4,681	Johnson City	714
Borden	859	Gail	900
Bosque	13,401	Meridian	989
Bowie	75,301	Boston	891
Brazoria	169,587	Angleton	1,407
Brazos	93,588	Bryan	589
Brewster	7,573	Alpine	6,169
Briscoe	2,579	Silverton	887
Brooks	8,428	Falfurrias	942
Brown	33,057	Brownwood	936
Burleson	12,313	Caldwell	669
Burnet	17,803	Burnet	994
Caldwell	23,637	Lockhart	546
Calhoun	19,574	Port Lavaca	540
Callahan	10,992	Baird	899
Cameron	209,680	Brownsville	906
Camp	9,275	Pittsburg	203
Carson	6,672	Panhandle	924
Cass	29,430	Linden	937
Castro	10,556	Dimmitt	899
Chambers	18,538	Anahuac	616
Cherokee	38,127	Rusk	1,052
Childress	6,950	Childress	707
Clay	9,582	Henrietta	1,086
Cochran	4,825	Morton	775
Coke	3,196	Robert Lee	908
Coleman	10,439	Coleman	1,277
Collin	144,490	McKinney	851
Collingsworth	4,648	Wellington	909
Colorado	18,823	Columbus	965
Comal	36,446	New Braunfels	555
Comanche	12,617	Comanche	930
Concho	2,915	Paint Rock	992
Cooke	27,656	Gainesville	893
Coryell	56,767	Gatesville	1,057
Cottle	2,947	Paducah	895
Crane	4,600	Crane	782
Crockett	4,608	Ozona	2,806
Crosby	8,859	Crosbyton	899
Culberson	3,315	Van Horn	3,815
Dallam	6,531	Dalhart	1,505
Dallas	1,556,419	Dallas	880
Dawson	16,184	Lamesa	903
Deaf Smith	21,165	Hereford	1,497
Delta	4,839	Cooper	278
Denton	143,126	Denton	911
Dewitt	18,903	Cuero	910
Dickens	3,539	Dickens	907
Dimmit	11,367	Carrizo Springs	1,307
Donley	4,075	Clarendon	929
Duval	12,517	San Diego	1,795
Eastland	19,480	Eastland	924
Ector	115,374	Odessa	903
Edwards	2,033	Rocksprings	2,121
Ellis	59,743	Waxahachie	939
El Paso	479,899	El Paso	1,014
Erath	22,560	Stephenville	1,080
Falls	17,946	Marlin	770
Fannin	24,285	Bonham	895
Fayette	18,832	La Grange	950
Fisher	5,891	Roby	897
Floyd	9,834	Floydada	992
Foard	2,158	Crowell	703
Fort Bend	130,962	Richmond	876
Franklin	6,893	Mount Vernon	294
Freestone	14,830	Fairfield	888
Frio	13,785	Pearsall	1,133
Gaines	13,150	Seminole	1,504
Galveston	195,738	Galveston	399
Garza	5,336	Post	895
Gillespie	13,532	Fredericksburg	1,061
Glasscock	1,304	Garden City	900
Goliad	5,193	Goliad	859
Gonzales	16,949	Gonzales	1,068
Gray	26,386	Pampa	921
Grayson	89,796	Sherman	934
Gregg	99,495	Longview	273
Grimes	13,580	Anderson	799
Guadalupe	46,708	Seguin	713
Hale	37,592	Plainview	1,005
Hall	5,594	Memphis	877
Hamilton	8,297	Hamilton	836
Hansford	6,209	Spearman	921
Hardeman	6,368	Quanah	688
Hardin	40,721	Kountze	898
Harris	2,409,544	Houston	1,734
Harrison	52,265	Marshall	908
Hartley	3,967	Channing	1,462
Haskell	7,725	Haskell	901
Hays	40,594	San Marcos	678
Hemphill	5,304	Canadian	903
Henderson	42,606	Athens	888
Hidalgo	283,323	Edinburg	1,569
Hill	25,024	Hillsboro	968
Hockley	23,230	Levelland	908
Hood	17,714	Granbury	425
Hopkins	25,247	Sulphur Springs	789
Houston	22,299	Crockett	1,234
Howard	33,142	Big Spring	901
Hudspeth	2,728	Sierra Blanca	4,567
Hunt	55,248	Greenville	840
Hutchinson	26,304	Stinnett	872
Irion	1,386	Mertzon	1,052
Jack	7,408	Jacksboro	920
Jackson	13,352	Edna	844
Jasper	30,781	Jasper	921
Jeff Davis	1,647	Fort Davis	2,257
Jefferson	248,652	Beaumont	937
Jim Hogg	5,168	Hebbronville	1,136
Jim Wells	36,498	Alice	867
Johnson	67,649	Cleburne	730
Jones	17,268	Anson	931
Karnes	13,593	Karnes City	753
Kaufman	39,038	Kaufman	788
Kendall	10,635	Boerne	663
Kenedy	543	Sarita	1,389
Kent	1,145	Jayton	878
Kerr	28,780	Kerrville	1,107
Kimble	4,063	Junction	1,250
King	425	Guthrie	914
Kinney	2,279	Brackettville	1,359
Kleberg	33,358	Kingsville	853
Knox	5,329	Benjamin	845
Lamar	42,156	Paris	919
Lamb	18,669	Littlefield	1,013
Lampasas	12,005	Lampasas	714
La Salle	5,514	Cotulla	1,517
Lavaca	19,004	Hallettsville	971
Lee	10,952	Giddings	631
Leon	9,594	Centerville	1,079
Liberty	47,088	Liberty	1,174
Limestone	20,224	Groesbeck	930
Lipscomb	3,766	Lipscomb	933
Live Oak	9,606	George West	1,057
Llano	10,144	Llano	939
Loving	91	Mentone	670
Lubbock	211,651	Lubbock	900
Lynn	8,605	Tahoka	888
McCulloch	8,735	Brady	1,071
McLennan	170,755	Waco	1,031
McMullen	789	Tilden	1,163
Madison	10,649	Madisonville	472
Marion	10,360	Jefferson	385
Martin	4,684	Staton	914
Mason	3,683	Mason	934
Matagorda	37,828	Bay City	1,127
Maverick	31,398	Eagle Pass	1,287
Medina	23,164	Hondo	1,331
Menard	2,346	Menard	902
Midland	82,636	Midland	902
Milam	22,732	Cameron	1,019
Mills	4,477	Goldthwaite	748
Mitchell	9,088	Colorado City	912
Montague	17,410	Montague	928
Montgomery	127,222	Conroe	1,047

County	Pop.	County seat or court house	Land area sq. mi.
Moore	10,575	Dumas	905
Morris	14,629	Daingerfield	256
Motley	1,950	Matador	959
Nacogdoches	46,786	Nacogdoches	939
Navarro	35,323	Corsicana	1,068
Newton	13,254	Newton	935
Nolan	17,359	Sweetwater	915
Nueces	268,215	Corpus Christi	847
Ochiltree	9,588	Perryton	919
Oldham	2,283	Vega	1,485
Orange	83,838	Orange	362
Palo Pinto	24,062	Palo Pinto	949
Panola	20,724	Carthage	812
Parker	44,609	Weatherford	902
Parmer	11,038	Farwell	885
Pecos	14,618	Fort Stockton	4,777
Polk	24,407	Livingston	1,061
Potter	98,637	Amarillo	902
Presidio	5,188	Marfa	3,857
Rains	4,839	Emory	243
Randall	75,062	Canyon	917
Reagan	4,135	Big Lake	1,173
Real	2,469	Leakey	697
Red River	16,101	Clarksville	1,054
Reeves	15,801	Pecos	2,626
Refugio	9,289	Refugio	771
Roberts	1,187	Miami	915
Robertson	14,653	Franklin	864
Rockwall	14,528	Rockwall	128
Runnels	11,872	Ballinger	1,056
Rusk	41,382	Henderson	932
Sabine	8,702	Hemphill	486
San Augustine	8,785	San Augustine	524
San Jacinto	11,434	Coldspring	572
San Patricio	58,013	Sinton	693
San Saba	5,841	San Saba	1,136
Schleicher	2,820	Eldorado	1,309
Scurry	18,192	Snyder	900
Shackelford	3,915	Albany	915
Shelby	23,084	Center	791
Sherman	3,174	Stratford	923
Smith	128,366	Tyler	932
Somervell	4,154	Glen Rose	188
Starr	27,266	Rio Grande City	1,226
Stephens	9,926	Breckenridge	894
Sterling	1,206	Sterling City	923
Stonewall	2,406	Aspermont	925
Sutton	5,130	Sonora	1,455
Swisher	9,723	Tulia	902
Tarrant	860,880	Fort Worth	868
Taylor	110,932	Abilene	917
Terrell	1,595	Sanderson	2,357
Terry	14,581	Brownfield	887
Throckmorton	2,053	Throckmorton	912
Titus	21,442	Mount Pleasant	412
Tom Green	84,784	San Angelo	1,515
Travis	419,335	Austin	989
Trinity	9,450	Groveton	692
Tyler	16,223	Woodville	922
Upshur	28,595	Gilmer	587
Upton	4,619	Rankin	1,243
Uvalde	22,441	Uvalde	1,564
Val Verde	35,910	Del Rio	3,150
Van Zandt	31,426	Canton	855
Victoria	68,807	Victoria	887
Walker	41,789	Huntsville	786
Waller	19,798	Hempstead	514
Ward	13,976	Monahans	836
Washington	21,998	Brenham	610
Webb	99,258	Laredo	3,362
Wharton	40,242	Wharton	1,086
Wheeler	7,137	Wheeler	904
Wichita	121,082	Wichita Falls	606
Wilbarger	15,931	Vernon	947
Willacy	17,495	Raymondville	589
Williamson	76,521	Georgetown	1,137
Wilson	16,756	Floresville	807
Winkler	9,944	Kermit	840
Wise	26,525	Decatur	902
Wood	24,697	Quitman	689
Yoakum	8,299	Plains	800
Young	19,001	Graham	919
Zapata	6,628	Zapata	999
Zavala	11,666	Crystal City	1,298

Utah

(29 counties, 82,073 sq. mi. land; pop. 1,461,037)

County	Pop.	County seat	Land area
Beaver	4,378	Beaver	2,586
Box Elder	33,222	Brigham City	5,614
Cache	57,176	Logan	1,171
Carbon	22,179	Price	1,479
Daggett	769	Manila	699
Davis	146,540	Farmington	299
Duchesne	12,565	Duchesne	3,233
Emery	11,451	Castle Dale	4,449
Garfield	3,673	Panguitch	5,148
Grand	8,241	Moab	3,689
Iron	17,349	Parowan	3,301
Juab	5,530	Nephi	3,396
Kane	4,024	Kanab	3,898
Millard	8,970	Fillmore	6,818
Morgan	4,917	Morgan	603
Piute	1,329	Junction	759
Rich	2,100	Randolph	1,034
Salt Lake	619,066	Salt Lake City	756
San Juan	12,253	Monticello	7,725
Sanpete	14,620	Manti	1,587
Sevier	14,727	Richfield	1,910
Summit	10,198	Coalville	1,865
Tooele	26,033	Tooele	6,919
Uintah	20,506	Vernal	4,479
Utah	218,106	Provo	2,018
Wasatch	8,523	Heber City	1,191
Washington	26,065	Saint George	2,422
Wayne	1,911	Loa	2,461
Weber	144,616	Ogden	566

Vermont

(14 counties, 9,273 sq. mi. land; pop. 511,456)

County	Pop.	County seat	Land area
Addison	29,406	Middlebury	773
Bennington	33,345	Bennington	677
Caledonia	25,808	Saint Johnsbury	651
Chittenden	115,534	Burlington	540
Essex	6,313	Guildhall	666
Franklin	34,788	Saint Albans	649
Grand Isle	4,613	North Hero	89
Lamoille	16,767	Hyde Park	461
Orange	22,739	Chelsea	690
Orleans	23,440	Newport	697
Rutland	58,347	Rutland	932
Washington	52,393	Montpelier	690
Windham	36,933	Newfane	787
Windsor	51,030	Woodstock	972

Virginia

(95 cos., 41 ind. cities, 39,704 sq. mi. land; pop. 5,346,797)

County	Pop.	County seat	Land area
Accomack	31,268	Accomac	476
Albemarle	50,689	Charlottesville	725
Alleghany	14,333	Covington	446
Amelia	8,405	Amelia, C.H.	357
Amherst	29,122	Amherst	479
Appomattox	11,971	Appomattox	336
Arlington	152,599	Arlington	26
Augusta	53,732	Staunton	989
Bath	5,860	Warm Springs	538
Bedford	34,927	Bedford	747
Bland	6,349	Bland	359
Botetourt	23,270	Fincastle	545
Brunswick	15,632	Lawrenceville	563
Buchanan	37,989	Grundy	504
Buckingham	11,751	Buckingham	583
Campbell	45,424	Rustburg	505
Caroline	17,904	Bowling Green	535
Carroll	27,270	Hillsville	478
Charles City	6,692	Charles City	181
Charlotte	12,266	Charlotte Courthouse	477
Chesterfield	141,372	Chesterfield	434
Clarke	9,965	Berryville	178
Craig	3,948	New Castle	330
Culpeper	22,620	Culpeper	382
Cumberland	7,881	Cumberland	300
Dickenson	19,806	Clintwood	331
Dinwiddie	22,602	Dinwiddie	507
Essex	8,864	Tappahannock	263
Fairfax	596,901	Fairfax	394
Fauquier	35,889	Warrenton	651
Floyd	11,563	Floyd	381
Fluvanna	10,244	Palmyra	290
Franklin	35,740	Rocky Mount	683
Frederick	34,150	Winchester	415
Giles	17,810	Pearisburg	362
Gloucester	20,107	Gloucester	225
Goochland	11,761	Goochland	281
Grayson	16,579	Independence	446
Greene	7,625	Stanardsville	157
Greensville	10,903	Emporia	300
Halifax	30,418	Halifax	816
Hanover	50,398	Hanover	467
Henrico	180,735	Richmond	238
Henry	57,654	Martinsville	382
Highland	2,937	Monterey	416
Isle of Wight	21,603	Isle of Wight	319
James City	22,763	Williamsburg	153
King and Queen	5,968	King and Queen	317
King George	10,543	King George	180
King William	9,327	King William	278
Lancaster	10,129	Lancaster	133
Lee	25,956	Jonesville	437
Loudoun	57,427	Leesburg	521
Louisa	17,825	Louisa	497
Lunenburg	12,124	Lunenburg	432
Madison	10,232	Madison	322
Mathews	7,995	Mathews	87
Mecklenburg	29,444	Boydton	616
Middlesex	7,719	Saluda	134
Montgomery	63,516	Christiansburg	390
Nelson	12,204	Lovingston	474
New Kent	8,781	New Kent	213

County	Pop.	County seat or court house	Land area sq. mi.
Northampton	14,625	Eastville	226
Northumberland	9,828	Heathsville	185
Nottoway	14,666	Nottoway	316
Orange	17,827	Orange	342
Page	19,401	Luray	313
Patrick	17,585	Stuart	481
Pittsylvania	66,147	Chatham	995
Powhatan	13,062	Powhatan	261
Prince Edward	16,456	Farmville	354
Prince George	25,733	Prince George	266
Prince William	144,703	Manassas	339
Pulaski	35,229	Pulaski	318
Rappahannock	6,093	Washington	267
Richmond	6,952	Warsaw	193
Roanoke	72,945	Salem	251
Rockbridge	17,911	Lexington	603
Rockingham	57,038	Harrisonburg	865
Russell	31,761	Lebanon	479
Scott	25,068	Gate City	535
Shenandoah	27,559	Woodstock	512
Smyth	33,345	Marion	452
Southampton	18,731	Courtland	603
Spotsylvania	34,435	Spotsylvania	404
Stafford	40,470	Stafford	271
Surry	6,046	Surry	281
Sussex	10,874	Sussex	491
Tazewell	50,511	Tazewell	520
Warren	21,200	Front Royal	217
Washington	46,487	Abingdon	562
Westmoreland	14,041	Montross	227
Wise	43,863	Wise	405
Wythe	25,522	Wytheville	465
York	35,463	Yorktown	113

Independent cities

City	Pop.	Land area sq. mi.
Alexandria	103,217	15
Bedford	5,991	7
Bristol	19,042	12
Buena Vista	6,717	3
Charlottesville	45,010	10
Chesapeake	114,226	340
Clifton Forge	5,046	3
Colonial Heights	16,509	8
Covington	9,063	4
Danville	45,642	17
Emporia	4,840	2
Fairfax	19,390	6
Falls Church	9,515	2
I,1 Franklin	7,308	4
Fredericksburg	15,322	6
Galax	6,524	8
Hampton	122,617	51
Harrisonburg	19,671	6
Hopewell	23,397	10
Lexington	7,292	2
Lynchburg	66,743	50
Manassas	15,438	8
Manassas Park	6,524	2
Martinsville	18,149	11
Newport News	144,903	65
Norfolk	266,979	53
Norton	4,757	7
Petersburg	41,055	23
Poquoson	8,726	17
Portsmouth	104,577	30
Radford	13,225	7
Richmond	219,214	60
Roanoke	100,427	43
Salem	23,958	14
South Boston	7,093	6
Staunton	21,857	9
Suffolk	47,621	409
Virginia Beach	262,199	256
Waynesboro	15,329	8
Williamsburg	9,870	5
Winchester	20,217	9

Washington

(39 counties, 66,511 sq. mi. land; pop. 4,132,353)

County	Pop.	County seat or court house	Land area sq. mi.
Adams	13,267	Ritzville	1,921
Asotin	16,823	Asotin	635
Benton	109,444	Prosser	1,715
Chelan	45,061	Wenatchee	2,916
Clallam	51,648	Port Angeles	1,753
Clark	192,227	Vancouver	627
Columbia	4,057	Dayton	865
Cowlitz	79,548	Kelso	1,140
Douglas	22,144	Waterville	1,817
Ferry	5,811	Republic	2,200
Franklin	35,025	Pasco	1,243
Garfield	2,468	Pomeroy	706
Grant	48,522	Ephrata	2,660
Grays Harbor	66,314	Montesano	1,918
Island	44,048	Coupeville	212
Jefferson	15,965	Port Townsend	1,805
King	1,269,898	Seattle	2,128
Kitsap	146,609	Port Orchard	393
Kittitas	24,877	Ellensburg	2,308
Klickitat	15,822	Goldendale	1,880
Lewis	55,279	Chehalis	2,409
Lincoln	9,604	Davenport	2,310
Mason	31,184	Shelton	961
Okanogan	30,663	Okanogan	5,281
Pacific	17,237	South Bend	908
Pend Oreille	8,580	Newport	1,400
Pierce	485,667	Tacoma	1,675
San Juan	7,838	Friday Harbor	179
Skagit	64,138	Mount Vernon	1,735
Skamania	7,919	Stevenson	1,672
Snohomish	337,016	Everett	2,098
Spokane	341,835	Spokane	1,762
Stevens	28,979	Colville	2,470
Thurston	124,264	Olympia	727
Wahkiakum	3,832	Cathlamet	261
Walla Walla	47,435	Walla Walla	1,261
Whatcom	106,701	Bellingham	2,125
Whitman	40,103	Colfax	2,151
Yakima	172,508	Yakima	4,287

West Virginia

(55 counties, 24,119 sq. mi. land; pop. 1,950,186)

County	Pop.	County seat or court house	Land area sq. mi.
Barbour	16,639	Philippi	343
Berkeley	46,775	Martinsburg	321
Boone	30,447	Madison	503
Braxton	13,894	Sutton	513
Brooke	31,117	Wellsburg	90
Cabell	106,835	Huntington	282
Calhoun	8,250	Grantsville	280
Clay	11,265	Clay	346
Doddridge	7,433	West Union	321
Fayette	57,863	Fayetteville	667
Gilmer	8,334	Glenville	340
Grant	10,210	Petersburg	480
Greenbrier	37,665	Lewisburg	1,025
Hampshire	14,867	Romney	644
Hancock	41,053	New Cumberland	84
Hardy	10,030	Moorefield	585
Harrison	77,710	Clarksburg	417
Jackson	25,794	Ripley	464
Jefferson	30,302	Charles Town	209
Kanawha	231,414	Charleston	901
Lewis	18,813	Weston	389
Lincoln	23,675	Hamlin	439
Logan	50,679	Logan	456
McDowell	49,899	Welch	535
Marion	65,789	Fairmont	312
Marshall	41,608	Moundsville	305
Mason	27,045	Point Pleasant	433
Mercer	73,870	Princeton	420
Mineral	27,234	Keyser	329
Mingo	37,336	Williamson	424
Monongalia	75,024	Morgantown	363
Monroe	12,873	Union	473
Morgan	10,711	Berkeley Springs	230
Nicholas	26,126	Summersville	650
Ohio	61,389	Wheeling	106
Pendleton	7,910	Franklin	698
Pleasants	8,236	St. Marys	131
Pocahontas	9,919	Marlinton	942
Preston	30,460	Kingwood	651
Putnam	38,181	Winfield	346
Raleigh	86,821	Beckley	608
Randolph	28,734	Elkins	1,040
Ritchie	11,442	Harrisville	454
Roane	15,952	Spencer	484
Summers	15,875	Hinton	353
Taylor	16,584	Grafton	174
Tucker	8,675	Parsons	421
Tyler	11,320	Middlebourne	258
Upshur	23,427	Buckhannon	355
Wayne	46,021	Wayne	508
Webster	12,245	Webster Springs	556
Wetzel	21,874	New Martinsville	359
Wirt	4,922	Elizabeth	235
Wood	93,627	Parkersburg	367
Wyoming	35,993	Pineville	502

Wisconsin

(72 counties, 54,426 sq. mi. land; pop. 4,705,642)

County	Pop.	County seat or court house	Land area sq. mi.
Adams	13,457	Friendship	648
Ashland	16,783	Ashland	1,048
Barron	38,730	Barron	865
Bayfield	13,822	Washburn	1,462
Brown	175,280	Green Bay	524
Buffalo	14,309	Alma	699
Burnett	12,340	Grantsburg	818
Calumet	30,867	Chilton	326
Chippewa	51,702	Chippewa Falls	1,017
Clark	32,910	Neillsville	1,218
Columbia	43,222	Portage	771
Crawford	16,556	Prairie du Chien	566
Dane	323,545	Madison	1,205
Dodge	74,747	Juneau	887
Door	25,029	Sturgeon Bay	492
Douglas	44,421	Superior	1,305
Dunn	34,314	Menomonie	853
Eau Claire	78,805	Eau Claire	638
Florence	4,172	Florence	486

County	Pop.	County seat or court house	Land area sq. mi.
Fond Du Lac	88,952	Fond du Lac	725
Forest	9,044	Crandon	1,011
Grant	51,736	Lancaster	1,144
Green	30,012	Monroe	583
Green Lake	18,370	Green Lake	357
Iowa	19,802	Dodgeville	760
Iron	6,730	Hurley	751
Jackson	16,831	Black River Falls	998
Jefferson	66,152	Jefferson	562
Juneau	21,037	Mauston	774
Kenosha	123,137	Kenosha	273
Kewaunee	19,539	Kewaunee	343
La Crosse	91,056	La Crosse	457
Lafayette	17,412	Darlington	634
Langlade	19,978	Antigo	873
Lincoln	26,311	Merrill	886
Manitowoc	82,918	Manitowoc	589
Marathon	111,270	Wausau	1,559
Marinette	39,314	Marinette	1,395
Marquette	11,672	Montello	455
Menominee	3,373	Keshena	359
Milwaukee	964,988	Milwaukee	241
Monroe	35,074	Sparta	904
Oconto	28,947	Oconto	1,002
Oneida	31,216	Rhinelander	1,130
Outagamie	128,730	Appleton	642
Ozaukee	66,981	Port Washington	235
Pepin	7,477	Durand	231
Pierce	31,149	Ellsworth	577
Polk	32,351	Balsam Lake	919
Portage	57,420	Stevens Point	810
Price	15,788	Phillips	1,256
Racine	173,132	Racine	335
Richland	17,476	Richland Center	585
Rock	139,420	Janesville	723
Rusk	15,589	Ladysmith	913
St. Croix	43,872	Hudson	723
Sauk	43,469	Baraboo	838
Sawyer	12,843	Hayward	1,255
Shawano	35,928	Shawano	897
Sheboygan	100,935	Sheboygan	515
Taylor	18,817	Medford	975
Trempealeau	26,158	Whitehall	736
Vernon	25,642	Viroqua	808
Vilas	16,535	Eagle River	867
Walworth	71,507	Elkhorn	556
Washburn	13,174	Shell Lake	815
Washington	84,848	West Bend	430
Waukesha	280,203	Waukesha	554
Waupaca	42,831	Waupaca	754
Waushara	18,526	Wautoma	628
Winnebago	131,772	Oshkosh	449
Wood	72,799	Wisconsin Rapids	801

Wyoming

(23 counties, 96,989 sq. mi. land; pop., 469,557)

County	Pop.	County seat	Land area sq. mi.
Albany	29,062	Laramie	4,268
Big Horn	11,896	Basin	3,139
Campbell	24,367	Gillette	4,796
Carbon	21,896	Rawlins	7,877
Converse	14,069	Douglas	4,271
Crook	5,308	Sundance	2,855
Fremont	40,251	Lander	9,181
Goshen	12,040	Torrington	2,186
Hot Springs	5,710	Thermopolis	2,005
Johnson	6,700	Buffalo	4,166
Laramie	68,649	Cheyenne	2,684
Lincoln	12,177	Kemmerer	4,070
Natrona	71,856	Casper	5,347
Niobrara	2,924	Lusk	2,684
Park	21,639	Cody	6,936
Platte	11,975	Wheatland	2,023
Sheridan	25,048	Sheridan	2,532
Sublette	4,548	Pinedale	4,872
Sweetwater	41,723	Green River	10,352
Teton	9,355	Jackson	4,011
Uinta	13,021	Evanston	2,085
Washakie	9,496	Worland	2,243
Weston	7,106	Newcastle	2,402

Population of Outlying Areas

Source: U.S. Bureau of the Census
Population figures are final counts from the census conducted on Apr. 1, 1980.

Puerto Rico

ZIP code	Municipios	Pop.	Land area sq. mile
00601	Adjuntas	18,786	67
00602	Aguada	31,567	31
00603	Aguadilla	54,606	37
00607	Aguas Buenas	22,429	30
00609	Aibonito	22,167	31
00610	Anasco	23,274	40
00612	Arecibo	86,766	127
00615	Arroyo	17,014	15
00617	Barceloneta	18,942	24
00618	Barranquitas	21,639	34
00619	Bayamon	196,206	45
00623	Cabo Rojo	34,045	72
00625	Caguas	117,959	59
00627	Camuy	24,884	47
00629	Canovanas	31,880	33
00630	Carolina	165,954	48
00632	Catano	26,243	6
00633	Cayey	41,099	52
00635	Ceiba	14,944	27
00638	Ciales	16,211	67
00639	Cidra	28,365	36
00640	Coamo	30,822	78
00642	Comerio	18,212	29
00643	Corozal	28,221	43
00645	Culebra	1,265	13
00646	Dorado	25,511	24
00648	Fajardo	32,087	31
00650	Florida	7,232	10
00653	Guanica	18,799	37
00654	Guayama	40,183	65
00656	Guayanilla	21,050	42
00657	Guaynabo	80,742	27
00658	Gurabo	23,574	28
00659	Hatillo	28,958	42
00660	Hormigueros	14,030	11
00661	Humacao	46,134	45
00662	Isabela	37,435	56
00664	Jayuya	14,722	44
00665	Juana Diaz	43,505	61
00666	Juncos	25,397	27
00667	Lajas	21,236	60
00669	Lares	26,743	62
00670	Las Marias	8,747	46
00671	Las Piedras	22,412	34
00672	Loiza	20,867	21
00673	Luquillo	14,895	26
00701	Manati	36,562	46
00706	Maricao	6,737	37
00707	Maunabo	11,813	21
00708	Mayaguez	96,193	77
00716	Moca	29,185	50
00717	Morovis	21,142	39
00718	Naguabo	20,617	52
00719	Naranjito	23,633	20
00720	Orocovis	19,332	64
00723	Patillas	17,774	47
00724	Penuelas	19,116	45
00731	Ponce	189,046	117
00742	Quebradillas	19,728	23
00743	Rincon	11,788	14
00745	Rio Grande	34,283	62
00747	Sabana Grande	20,207	36
00751	Salinas	26,438	71
00753	San German	32,922	54
*00936	San Juan	434,849	47
00754	San Lorenzo	32,428	53
00755	San Sebastian	35,690	71
00757	Santa Isabel	19,854	35
00758	Toa Alta	31,910	28
00759	Toa Baja	78,246	24
00760	Trujillo Alto	51,389	21
00761	Utuado	34,505	115
00762	Vega Alta	28,696	28
00763	Vega Baja	47,115	48
00765	Vieques	7,662	53
00766	Villalba	20,734	37
00767	Yabucoa	31,425	55
00768	Yauco	37,742	69
	Total	3,196,520	3,459

ZIP code	Area	Pop.	Land area sq. mile
American Samoa			
96799	American Samoa	32,297	77
Guam			
96910	Agana	896	1
	Agana Hts.	3,284	1
96915	Agat	3,999	10
	Asan	2,034	6
96913	Barrigada	7,756	9
	Chalan-Pago-Ordot	3,120	6
96912	Dededo	23,644	30
96916	Inarajan	2,059	19
	Mangilao	6,840	10
96916	Merizo	1,663	6
	Mongmong-Toto-Maite	5,245	2
	Piti	2,866	7
96915	Santa Rita	9,183	17
	Sinajana	2,485	1
	Talofofo	2,006	17
96911	Tamuning	13,580	6
	Umatac	732	6
	Yigo	10,359	35
96914	Yona	4,228	20
	Total	105,979	209
Virgin Islands			
	St. Croix	49,725	80
	St. John	2,472	20
	St. Thomas	44,372	32
00801	Charlotte Amalie	11,671	
00820	Christiansted	2,904	
00840	Frederiksted	1,046	
	Total	96,569	132

Trust Territory of Pacific Islands

Area	Pop.	Land area sq. mile
Kosrae	NA	42
Marshall Islands	NA	70
Palau	NA	192
Ponape	NA	176
Truk	NA	49
Yap	NA	46
Total	NA	533
No. Mariana Islands	16,758	184

RELIGIOUS INFORMATION

Census of Religious Groups in the U.S.

Source: *1989 Yearbook of American and Canadian Churches*

The 1989 Yearbook of American and Canadian Churches reported a total of 143,830,806 members of religious groups in the U.S.—58.6 percent of the population; membership rose 0.72 percent from the previous year.

Comparisons of membership statistics from group to group are not necessarily meaningful. Membership definitions vary —e.g., Roman Catholics count members from infancy, but some Protestant groups count only "adult" members, usually 13 years or older; some groups compile data carefully, but others estimate; not all groups report annually.

The number of churches appear in parentheses. Asterisk (*) indicates church declines to publish membership figures; (**) indicates figures date from 1979 or earlier.

Group	Members	Group	Members
Adventist churches:		The Episcopal Church in the U.S.A. (7,387) . . .	2,462,300
Advent Christian Ch. (352)	19,946	American Ethical Union (Ethical Culture	
Primitive Advent Christian Ch. (10)	546	Movement) (21).	3,500
Seventh-day Adventists (4,096)	675,702	Evangelical Church of North America (155) . . .	17,417
American Rescue Workers (20)	2,700	Evangelical Congregational Church (155)	33,275
Anglican Orthodox Church (40)	6,000	The Evangelical Covenant Church of	
Baha'i Faith (1,700)	110,000	America (575)	86,741
Baptist churches:		Evangelical Free Church of America (880)	95,722
Amer. Baptist Assn. (1,705)	250,000	**Evangelical associations:**	
Amer. Baptist Chs. in U.S.A. (5,833)	1,568,778	Apostolic Christian Chs. of America (80)	11,300
Baptist General Conference (762).	131,480	Apostolic Christian Ch. (Nazarean) (48)	2,799
Baptist Missionary Assn. of America (1,347) . . .	227,638	Christian Congregation (1,456)	106,831
Conservative Baptist Assn. of America (1,140) .	225,000	**Friends:**	
Duck River (and Kindred) Assn. of Baptists		Evangelical Friends Alliance (217)	24,095
(85)	**8,632	Friends General Conference (505)	31,600
Free Will Baptists (2,524)	200,387	Friends United Meeting (532)	55,616
Gen. Assn. of Regular Baptist Chs. (1,571) . . .	300,839	Grace Gospel Fellowship (52)	4,500
Natl. Baptist Convention of America (11,398) . .	**2,668,799	**Independent Fundamental Churches of**	
Natl. Baptist Convention, U.S.A. (26,000).	**5,500,000	America (1,019).	120,446
Natl. Primitive Baptist Convention (606)	**250,000	Jehovah's Witnesses (8,547)	773,219
No. Amer. Baptist Conference (253)	42,150	**Jewish organizations:**	
Seventh Day Baptist General Conference (81) . .	5,149	Union of Amer. Hebrew Congregations (Re-	
Southern Baptist Convention (37,238).	14,722,617	form) (822)	1,300,000
Brethren (German Baptists):		Union of Orthodox Jewish Congregations of	
Brethren Ch. (Ashland, Ohio) (122)	14,229	America (1,000).	1,000,000
Fellowship of Grace Brethren (312).	41,767	United Synagogue of America (Conservative)	
Brethren, River:		(850)	2,000,000
Brethren in Christ Ch. (186)	16,877	**Latter-day Saints:**	
Buddhist Churches of America (100)	100,000	Ch. of Jesus Christ (Bickertonites) (60).	2,668
		Ch. of Jesus Christ of Latter-day Saints (Mormon)	
Christadelphians (850)	**15,800	(8,682)	4,000,000
The Christian and Missionary Alliance (1,785). .	244,296	Reorganized Ch. of Jesus Christ of Latter Day	
Christian Catholic Church (6)	2,500	Saints (1,097).	191,618
Christian Church (Disciples of Christ) (4,195). . .	1,086,668	**Lutheran churches:**	
Christian Churches and Churches of Christ		Ch. of the Lutheran Brethren of America (104) .	11,360
(5,614)	1,071,995	Ch. of the Lutheran Confession (67)	8,717
Christian Methodist Episcopal Church (2,340). .	718,922	Evangelical Luthern Church in America (11,133)	5,288,230
Christian Nation Church U.S.A. (5)	200	Evangelical Lutheran Synod (123)	21,454
Christian Union (114)	6,000	Assn. of Free Lutheran Congregations (186). . .	26,509
Churches of Christ (13,364).	1,623,754	Latvian Evangelical Lutheran Church of America	
Churches of Christ in Christian Union (260) . . .	11,037	(57).	13,588
Churches of God:		Lutheran Ch.-Missouri Synod (5,912)	2,614,375
Chs. of God, General Conference (348)	34,028	Protestant Conference (Lutheran) (7).	1,004
Ch. of God (Anderson, Ind.) (2,314).	198,552	Wisconsin Evangelical Lutheran Synod	
Ch. of God (Seventh Day), Denver, Col. (135). .	6,478	(1,187).	418,791
Church of Christ, Scientist (3,000)	*	**Mennonite churches:**	
Church of God by Faith (105)	**4,500	Beachy Amish Mennonite Chs. (97).	6,524
Church of the Nazarene (5,080)	543,762	Evangelical Mennonite Ch. (26)	3,879
Conservative Congregational Christian Con-		General Conference of Mennonite Brethren	
ference (175)	29,429	Chs. (128)	17,065
Eastern Orthodox churches:		The General Conference Mennonite Ch. (214) .	34,889
Albanian Orth. Diocese of America (2)	953	Hutterian Brethren (77).	3,988
American Carpatho-Russian Orth. Greek		Mennonite Ch. (1,007).	92,902
Catholic Ch. (70)	**100,000	Old Order Amish Ch. (722)	64,980
Antiochian Orth. Christian Archdiocese of No.		Old Order (Wisler) Mennonite Ch. (36).	9,731
Amer. (150)	280,000	**Methodist churches:**	
Diocese of the Armenian Ch. of America (66) . .	**450,000	African Methodist Episcopal Ch. (6,200)	2,210,000
Bulgarian Eastern Orth. Ch. (13)	**86,000	African Methodist Episcopal Zion Ch. (6,060). . .	1,220,260
Coptic Orthodox Ch. (28).	115,000	Evangelical Methodist Ch. (130).	8,282
Greek Orth. Archdiocese of N. and S.		Free Methodist Ch. of North America (1,072) . .	73,225
America (535).	**1,950,000	Fundamental Methodist Ch. (13)	733
Orthodox Ch. in America (440)	**1,000,000	Primitive Methodist Ch., U.S.A. (84)	8,487
Patriarchal Parishes of the Russian Orth. Ch.		Reformed Methodist Union Episcopal Ch. (18) .	3,800
in the U.S.A. (38)	9,780	Southern Methodist Ch. (150)	7,231
Romanian Orth. Episcopate of America (34). . .	60,000	United Methodist Ch. (37,750)	9,124,575
Serbian Eastern Orth. Ch. (68)	67,000	**Moravian churches:**	
Syrian Orth. Ch. of Antioch (Archdiocese of		Moravian Ch. (Unitas Fratrum), Northern	
the U.S.A. and Canada) (28)	30,000	Province (102)	31,986
Ukrainian Orth. Ch. of America (Ecumenical		Moravian Ch. in America (Unitas Fratrum),	
Patriarchate) (27).	5,000	Southern Province (55)	21,675
Ukrainian Orthodox Church in the U.S.A. (107) .	**87,745	Unity of the Brethren (26)	3,495

Moslems . . . . 6,000,000+
New Apostolic Church of North America (487) .   36,241
North American Old Roman Catholic Church
(133).   62,611
Old Catholic churches:
  Christ Catholic Ch. (10).   1,365
Pentecostal churches:
  Apostolic Faith (Portland, Ore.) (45)   4,100
  Assemblies of God (11,004)   2,160,667
  Bible Church of Christ (6)   6,405
  Bible Way Church of Our Lord Jesus Christ
    World Wide (350). **30,000
  Church of God (Cleveland, Tenn.) (5,346)   505,775
  Church of God of Prophecy (2,085).   74,588
  Congregational Holiness Ch. (174).   8,347
  Gen. Council, Christian Ch. of No. Amer. (104) .   13,500
  Intl. Ch. of the Foursquare Gospel (1,290) . . .   192,327
  Open Bible Standard Chs. (281)   46,000
  Pentecostal Assemblies of the World (550) . . .   **4,500
  Pentecostal Church of God (1,166)   88,616
  Pentecostal Free-Will Baptist Ch. (130)   10,700
  United Pentecostal Ch. Intl. (3,410)   500,000
Polish Natl. Catholic Church of America (162). .   **282,411
Presbyterian churches:
  Associate Reformed Presbyterian Ch. (Gen.
    Synod) (179)   37,585
  Cumberland Presbyterian Ch. (759)   91,646
  Evangelical Presbyterian Ch. (120)   33,000

Orthodox Presbyterian Ch. (168)   19,094
Presbyterian Ch. in America (924)   190,960
Presbyterian Ch. (U.S.A.) (11,531)   2,967,781
Reformed Presbyterian Ch. in No. Amer. (70) . .   5,114
Reformed churches:
  Christian Reformed Ch. in N. America (682) . . .   225,951
  Hungarian Reformed Ch. in America (31)   12,500
  Protestant Reformed Chs. in America (21). . . .   4,544
  Reformed Ch. in America (925)   338,348
  Reformed Ch. in the U.S. (34)   3,778
The Roman Catholic Church (23,552).   53,496,862
The Salvation Army (1,097).   434,002
The Schwenkfelder Church (5).   2,666
Social Brethren (40) **1,784
Natl. Spiritualist Assn. of Churches (142).   5,558
Gen. Convention, The Swedenborgian
  Church (50)   2,423
Unitarian Universalist Assn. (956)   173,167
United Brethren:
  Ch. of the United Brethren in Christ (256)   26,869
  United Christian Ch. (12)   420
United Church of Christ (6,395).   1,662,568
Universal Fellowship of Metropolitan
  Community Chs. (230).   34,000
Vedanta Society (13)   2,500
Volunteers of America (607) **36,634
The Wesleyan Church (3,217).   185,641

Religious Population of the U.S.

Source: *1989 Yearbook of American and Canadian Churches*

(Membership in thousands, except as indicated)

Religious Body	1960	1965	1970	1975	1980	1987	1988	Number of churches 1988
Total	114,449	124,682	131,045	131,013	134,817	142,780	143,830	349,381
Members as percent of population	64	64	63	61	59	58.7	58.6	
Buddhists	20	92	100	60	60	100	100	100
Eastern Churches	2,699	3,172	3,850	3,696	3,823	3,980	3,973	1,682
Jews	5,367	5,600	5,870	6,115	5,920	5,814	5,944	3,416
Old Catholic, Polish National Catholic, Armenian Churches	590	484	848	846	924	829	829	428
Protestants	42,105	46,246	48,125	48,882	50,450	79,991	79,296	319,073
Roman Catholics	63,669	69,088	71,173	71,043	73,479	52,893	53,497	23,552
Miscellaneous	—	—	449	372	161	192	192	1,130

Estimated Religious Population of the World, 1988

Source: *The 1989 Encyclopaedia Britannica Book of the Year*

Religionists	Africa	East Asia	Europe	Latin America	Northern America	Oceania	South Asia	U.S.S.R.	World	%
Christians	282,526,720	81,585,730	412,312,390	402,245,550	232,557,080	21,431,200	132,198,760	104,663,010	1,669,520,440	32.9
Roman Catholics	106,487,220	9,503,860	260,457,890	377,753,520	94,274,950	7,557,820	90,524,300	5,283,800	951,843,360	18.8
Protestants	74,678,880	35,328,490	73,330,350	14,502,350	93,637,200	7,570,210	29,234,900	9,198,600	337,480,980	6.6
Orthodox	25,363,450	87,810	35,861,140	718,760	5,871,470	508,670	3,198,740	90,164,310	161,774,350	3.2
Anglicans	23,282,850	341,230	32,696,030	1,228,900	7,262,000	5,236,620	293,010	300	70,340,940	1.4
Other Christians	52,714,320	36,324,340	9,966,980	8,042,020	31,511,460	557,880	8,947,810	16,000	148,080,810	2.9
Moslems	253,153,340	23,446,260	8,760,660	664,820	2,689,480	98,480	559,621,790	32,120,380	880,552,210	17.4
Nonreligious	1,556,150	664,128,370	53,058,960	13,772,620	22,785,380	2,909,630	22,916,140	85,682,390	886,759,660	17.1
Hindus	1,424,610	10,460	594,640	683,660	855,800	305,920	659,619,440	1,100	663,495,450	13.1
Buddhists	11,750	154,432,950	222,400	483,020	186,560	15,120	156,194,080	290,290	311,836,170	6.1
Atheists	245,530	140,189,970	18,452,730	2,687,590	1,116,880	516,080	5,515,660	60,986,970	229,711,410	4.5
Chinese folk religionists	8,780	164,156,970	47,650	51,540	103,840	12,830	7,896,520	100	172,278,230	3.4
New Religionists	13,920	43,145,100	34,530	382,170	1,126,150	7,290	67,202,200	200	111,911,560	2.2
Tribal religionists	66,268,630	687,230	150	1,151,840	54,790	77,270	23,800,660	0	92,040,570	1.8
Jews	237,610	1,650	1,447,140	1,003,770	8,117,900	86,460	4,206,190	3,068,620	18,169,340	0.3
Sikhs	22,890	920	217,760	6,050	150,340	6,670	16,782,710	50	17,187,390	0.3
Shamanists	900	12,171,470	500	300	110	110	8,000	200,250	12,381,640	0.2
Confucians	450	6,164,410	1,010	500	18,980	110	2,500	200	6,188,160	0.1
Baha'is	1,210,650	52,600	73,910	596,540	319,890	61,460	2,371,740	5,100	4,691,890	0.1
Jains	45,020	570	9,930	2,020	1,960	820	3,495,350	20	3,555,690	0.1
Shintoists	50	3,376,040	330	610	1,290	410	200	100	3,379,030	0.1
Other religionists	66,600	65,500	323,860	6,812,590	674,950	26,730	244,250	7,000	8,221,480	0.2
Total Pop.	606,793,600	1,293,616,200	495,558,390	430,495,190	270,761,380	25,556,590	1,622,076,190	287,025,780	5,071,883,320	100.0

Headquarters, Leaders of U.S. Religious Groups

Year organized in parentheses. See Associations and Societies section for religious organizations.

Adventist churches:

Advent Christian Church (1854) — Pres., Rev. Donald E. Wrigley; sec., Rev. Marshall Tidwell, 1002 Grove Ave. SW, Lenoir, NC 28645.

Primitive Advent Christian Church — Pres., Donald Young; sec.-treas., Hugh W. Good, 395 Frame Rd., Elkview, WV 25071.

Seventh-day Adventists (1863) — Pres., Neal C. Wilson; sec., G. Ralph Thompson, 6840 Eastern Ave. NW, Wash., DC 20012.

Baptist churches:

American Baptist Assn. (1905) — Pres., Ken Ashlock; sec.-treas., D.S. Madden, P.O. Box 1050, Texarkana, AR-TX 75504.

American Baptist Churches in the U.S.A. (1907) — Pres., Harold Davis; gen. sec., Daniel E. Weiss, P.O. Box 851, Valley Forge, PA 19482.

Baptist General Conference (1879) — Pres., Dr. Robert S. Ricker, 2002 S. Arlington Heights Rd., Arlington Heights, IL 60005.

Baptist Missionary Assn. of America (formerly North American Baptist Assn.) (1950) — Pres., Rev. Gary D. Divine, rec. sec., Rev. Ralph Cottrell, P.O. Box 1203, Van, TX 75790.

Conservative Baptist Assn. of America (1947) — Gen. Dir., Dr. Tim Blanchard, Box 66, Wheaton, IL 60189.

Free Will Baptists (1727) — Mod., Rev. Ralph Hampton; exec. sec., Dr. Melvin Worthington, P.O. Box 1088, Nashville, TN 37202.

General Assn. of General Baptists (1823) — Mod., Rev. Dean Trivitt; clerk, Rev. Edwin Runyon, 801 Kendall, Poplar Bluff, MO 63901.

General Assn. of Regular Baptist Churches (1932) — Chpsn., Dr. David Nettleton; sec., Dr. John White, 1300 N. Meacham Rd., Schaumburg, IL 60173.

Natl. Baptist Convention, U.S.A. (1880) — Pres., Dr. T.J. Jemison; gen. sec., W. Franklyn Richardson, 52 S. 6th Ave., Mt. Vernon, NY 10550.

North American Baptist Conference (1865) — Mod., Rev. Harvey Mehlhaff; exec. dir., Dr. John Binder, 1 S. 210 Summit Ave., Oakbrook Terrace, IL 60181.

Southern Baptist Convention (1845) — Pres., C. Jerry Vines; rec. sec., Martin B. Bradley, 127 9th Ave. N., Nashville, TN 37234.

Brethren in Christ Church (1798) — Mod., Bishop John A. Byers; gen. sec., Dr. R. Donald Shafer, P.O. Box 245, Upland, CA 91785.

Brethren (German Baptists):

Brethren Church (Ashland, Oh.) (1882) — Mod., Dr. Dale Stoffer, sec., Norma Waters, RR 1, Box 421, McGaheysville, VA 22840.

Buddhist Churches of America (1899) — Bishop, Rt. Rev. Seigen H. Yamaoka; exec. asst., Rev. Seikan Fukuma, 1710 Octavia St., San Francisco, CA 94109.

The Christian and Missionary Alliance (1887) — Pres., David L. Rambo; sec., Elwood N. Nielsen, 350 N. Highland Ave., Nyack, NY 10960.

Christian Church (Disciples of Christ) (1809) — Gen. minister and pres., John O. Humbert; v.p. for communication, Carolyn W. Day, 222 S. Downey Ave., Box 1986, Indianapolis, IN 46206.

Christian Methodist Episcopal Church (1870) — Exec. sec., Dr. W. Clyde Williams, 2805 Shoreland Dr., Atlanta, GA 30331, sec., Rev. Edgar L. Wade, P.O. Box 3403, Memphis, TN 38101.

Churches of Christ in Christian Union (1909) — Gen. supt., Rev. Robert Kline; gen. sec., Rev. Robert Barth, P.O. Box 188, Alma, GA 31510.

Grace Brethren Church, Fellowship of (1882) — Mod., Dr. John Davies; sec., Rev. Kenneth Koontz, 605 Turnbull St., Delona, FL 32725.

Churches of God:

Churches of God, General Conference (1825) — Pres., Pastor Larry G. White; journalizing sec., Rev. Harry G. Cadamore, 157 N. Second St., W. Newton, PA 15089.

Church of God (Anderson, Ind.) (1880) — Chpsn., Samuel G. Hines; exec. sec., Edward L. Foggs, Box 2420, Anderson, IN 46018.

Church of Christ, Scientist (1879) — Pres., Pearline B. Thompson; clk., Mrs. Virginia S. Harris, The First Church of Christ, Scientist, 175 Huntington Ave., Boston, MA 02115.

Church of the Nazarene (1908) — Gen. sec., B. Edgar Johnson, 6401 The Paseo, Kansas City, MO 64131.

National Association of Congregational Christian Churches (1955) — Mod., Rev. Cliff Schutger; exec. sec., J. Fred Rennebohm, Box 1620, Oak Creek, WI 53154.

Eastern Orthodox churches:

Antiochian Orthodox Christian Archdiocese of North America (formerly Syrian Antiochian Orthodox Archdiocese) (1894) — Primate, Metropolitan Archbishop Philip (Saliba); aux., Archbishop Michael (Shaheen), Bishop Antoun (Khouri), 358 Mountain Rd., Englewood, NJ 07631.

Diocese of the Armenian Church of America (1889) — Primate, Eastern Diocese, Archbishop Torkom Manoogian; sec., Edward Onanian, 13010 Hathaway Dr., Wheaton, MD 20906; Western Diocese, Primate, His Eminence Archbishop Vatche Hovsepian, 1201 N. Vine St., Hollywood, CA 90038.

Coptic Orthodox Ch. — Archpriest Fr. Gabriel Abdelsayed, 427 West Side Ave., Jersey City, NJ 07304.

Greek Orthodox Archdiocese of North and South America (1864) — Pres., Archbishop Iakovos; sec., Peter Kourides, 8-10 E. 79th St., N.Y., NY 10021.

Orthodox Church in America (formerly Russian Orthodox Greek Catholic Church of North America) (1792) — Primate, Metropolitan Theodosius; chancellor, V. Rev. Robert S. Kondratick, P.O. Box 675, Syosset, NY 11791.

Romanian Orthodox Episcopate of America (1929) — Archbishop Victorin (Urache); sec., Rev. Fr. Felix Dubneae, 3355 Ridgewood Rd., Akron, OH 44313.

Serbian Orthodox Church for the U.S.A. and Canada — Bishops, Rt. Rev. Bishop Firmilian, Rt. Rev. Bishop Chrysostom; Bishop Christopher; St. Sava Monastery, Box 519, Libertyville, IL 60048.

Syrian Orthodox Church of Antioch, Archdiocese of the U.S.A. and Canada (1957) — Primate, Archbishop Mar-Athanasius Y. Samuel; gen. sec., Very Rev. Chorepiscopus John Meno, 45 Fairmount Ave., Hackensack, NJ 07601.

Ukrainian Orthodox Church in America (Ecumenical Patriarchate) (1928) — Primate, Rev. Bishop Vsevolod; sec., Rt. Rev. Ivan Tkaczuk, 90-34 139th St., Jamaica, NY 11435.

Ukrainian Orthodox Church of the U.S.A. (1919) — Metropolitan, Most Rev. Mstyslav S. Skrypnyk, Box 495, South Bound Brook, NJ 08880.

The Episcopal Church (1789) — Presiding bishop and primate, Most Rev. Edmond L. Browning; sec., Rt. Rev. Herbert A. Donovan Jr., Box 6120, Little Rock, AR 72216.

The Evangelical Covenant Church (1885) — Pres., Dr. Paul E. Larsen; sec., Rev. Timothy C. Ek, 5101 N. Francisco Ave., Chicago, IL 60625.

Friends:

Evangelical Friends Alliance (1965) — Mid-America YM, Ed Key, 2018 Maple, Wichita, KS 67213.

Friends General Conference (1900) — Gen. sec., Meredith Walton, 1520B Race St., Phila., PA 19102.

Friends United Meeting (formerly Five Years Meeting of Friends) (1902) — Presiding clerk, Paul Enyart, 101 Quaker Hill Dr., Richmond, IN 47374.

Independent Fundamental Churches of America (1930) — Natl. Exec. Dir., Dr. Richard Gregory, 2684 Meadow Ridge Dr., Bryon Ctr., MI 49315.

Jehovah's Witnesses (1879) — Pres., Frederick W. Franz, 25 Columbia Heights, Brooklyn, NY 11201.

Jewish congregations:

Union of American Hebrew Congregations (Reform) — Pres., Rabbi Alexander M. Schindler, 838 5th Ave., N.Y., NY 10021.

Union of Orthodox Jewish Congregations of America — Pres., Sidney Kwestel, 45 W. 36th St., N.Y., NY 10018.

United Synagogue of America (Conservative) — Pres., Franklin D. Kreutzer, 155 5th Ave., N.Y., NY 10010.

Latter-day Saints:

The Church of Jesus Christ of Latter-day Saints (Mormon) (1830) — Pres., Ezra Taft Benson, 50 E. North Temple St., Salt Lake City, UT 84150.

Reorganized Church of Jesus Christ of Latter Day Saints (1830) — Pres., Wallace B. Smith; sec., W. Grant McMurray, The Auditorium, P.O. Box 1059, Independence, MO 64051.

Lutheran churches:

Church of the Lutheran Brethren of America (1900) — Pres., Rev. Robert M. Overgard Sr.; sec., Rev. Richard Vettrus, 707 Crestview Dr., W. Union, IA 52175.

Church of the Lutheran Confession (1961) — Pres., Rev. Daniel Fleischer; sec., Rev. Paul F. Nolting, 620 E. 50th St., Loveland, CO 80537.

Evangelical Lutheran Church in America (1987) — Bishop, Rev. Dr. Herbert W. Chilstrom; sec., Rev. Dr. Lowell G. Almen, 8765 W. Higgins Rd., Chicago, IL 60631.

Evangelical Lutheran Synod (1853) — Pres., Rev. George Orrvick; sec., Rev. Alf Merseth, 106 13th St. S., Northwood, IA 50459.

Assn. of Free Lutheran Congregations (1962) — Pres. Rev. Richard Snipstead; sec., Rev. Ronald Knutson, 402 W. 11th St., Canton, SD 57013.

Lutheran Church — Missouri Synod (1847) — Pres., Dr. Ralph A. Bohlmann; sec., Dr. Walter L. Rosin, 1333 S. Kirkwood, St. Louis, MO 63122.

Wisconsin Evangelical Lutheran Synod (1850) — Pres., Rev. Carl H. Mischke; sec., Prof. David Worgull, 1270 N. Dobson, Chandler, AZ 85224.

Mennonite churches:
The General Conference of Mennonite Brethren Churches (1860) — Chpsn., Herb Brandt; sec., Roland Reimer, 8000 W. 21st St., Wichita, KS 67212.

Mennonite Church (1690) — Mod., George R. Brunk, II, 421 S. Second St. Ste. 600, Elkhart, IN 46516.

Methodist churches:
African Methodist Episcopal Zion Church (1796) — Sr. Bishop, William Milton Smith; sec., Bd. of Bishops, Bishop John Henry Miller, Sr., 8605 Caswell Court, Raleigh, NC 27612.

Free Methodist Church of North America (1860) — Bishops R.F. Andrews, D. Bastian, G.E. Bates, D.M. Foster, N. Nzeyimana, C.E. Van Valin; gen. conf. sec., Melvin J. Spencer, 901 College Ave., Winona Lake, IN 46590.

The United Methodist Church (1968) — Sec., Gen. Conference, Faith Richardson, 168 Mt. Vernon St., Newtonville, MA 02160.

Universal Fellowship of Metropolitan Community Churches — Mod., Rev. Elder Troy D. Perry; clerk, Rev. Elder Nancy L. Wilson, 5300 Santa Monica Blvd., Los Angeles, CA 90029.

Moravian Church (Unitas Fratrum) (1740) **Northern Province** — Pres., Dr. Gordon L. Sommers, 1021 Center St., P.O. Box 1245, Bethlehem, PA 18016. **Southern Province** — Pres., Rev. Graham H. Rights, 459 S. Church St., Winston-Salem, NC 27108.

Pentecostal churches:
Assemblies of God (1914) — Gen. supt., G. Raymond Carlson; gen. sec., Joseph R. Flower, 1445 Boonville Ave., Springfield, MO 65802.

Bible Way Church of Our Lord Jesus Christ World Wide (1927) — Presiding bishop, Smallwood E. Williams; gen. sec., Bishop Edward William, 5118 Clarendon Rd., Brooklyn, NY 11226.

Gen. Council, Christian Church of No. America (1948) — Gen. overseer; Rev. Guy BonGiovanni; gen. sec.-treas., Rev. Richard A. Tedesco, Rt. 18 & Rutledge Rd., Box 141-A, RD #1, Transfer, PA 16154.

The Church of God (1903) — Gen. overseer, Bishop Voy M. Bullen; gen. sec.-treas., Marie Powell, Box 13036, 1207 Willow Brook, Huntsville, AL 35802.

Church of God (Cleveland, Tenn.) (1886) — Gen. overseer, Raymond Crowley; gen. sec.-treas., John Nichols, P.O. Box 2430, Cleveland, TN 37320.

International Church of the Foursquare Gospel (1927) — Pres., Dr. John R. Holland; sec., Rev. John W. Bowers, 1100 Glendale Blvd., Los Angeles, CA 90026.

National Gay Pentecostal Alliance (1980) — Pres., Rev. Wm. H. Carey, P.O. Box 1391, Schenectady, NY 12301.

Open Bible Standard Churches (1919) — Gen. supt., Ray E. Smith; sec.-treas., Patrick L. Bowlin, 2020 Bell Ave., Des Moines, IA 50315.

Pentecostal Church of God (1919) — Gen. supt., Dr. James D. Gee; gen. sec.-treas., Dr. Ronald R. Minor, 4901 Pennsylvania, P.O. Box 850, Joplin, MO 64802.

Pentecostal Free Will Baptist Church (1959) — Gen. supt., Rev. Don Sauls; gen. sec., Rev. J.T. Hammond, Box 1568, Dunn, NC 28334.

United Pentecostal Church International (1945) — Gen. supt., Rev. Nathaniel A. Urshan; gen. sec.-treas., Rev. C. M. Becton, 8855 Dunn Rd., Hazelwood, MO 63042.

Presbyterian churches:
Cumberland Presbyterian Church (1810) — Mod., Beverly St. John; stated clerk, Robert Prosser, 1978 Union Ave., Memphis, TN 38104.

Evangelical Presbyterian Church (1981) — Mod., Richard Heidtman; stated clerk, Rev. L. Edward Davis, 26049 Five Mile Rd., Detroit, MI 48239.

The Orthodox Presbyterian Church (1936) — Mod., Mark T. Bube; stated clerk, John P. Galbraith, 2345 Willow Brook Dr., Huntingdon Valley, PA 19006.

Presbyterian Church in America (1973) — Mod., Dr. D. James Kennedy; stated clerk, Dr. Paul R. Gilchrist, 1852 Century Pl., Atlanta, GA 30345.

Presbyterian Church (U.S.A.) (1983) — Mod., C. Kenneth Hall; stated clerk, Rev. James E. Andrews, 100 Witherspoon St., Louisville, KY 40202.

Reformed Presbyterian Church of No. America (1871) — Mod., Dr. John H. White; clerk, Rev. Paul M. Martin, 1117 E. Devonshire, Phoenix, AZ 85014.

Reformed churches:
Christian Reformed Church in North America (1857) — Stated clerk, Rev. Leonard J. Hofman, 2850 Kalamazoo Ave., SE, Grand Rapids, MI 49560.

Reformed Church in America (1628) — Pres., Wilbur T. Washington; gen. sec., Edwin G. Mulder, 475 Riverside Dr., N.Y., NY 10115.

Reformed Episcopal Church (1873) — Pres., and Presid. Bishop, Rev. William H. S. Jerden Jr; sec., Rev. Roger F. Spence, 6300 Greenwood Pkwy., 203, Sagamore Hills, OH 44067.

Roman Catholic Church — National Conference of Catholic Bishops. Pres., Archbishop John L. May; sec., Archbishop Eugene Marino, 1312 Massachusetts Ave. NW, Wash., DC 20005.

The Salvation Army (1880) — Natl. Cmdr. Commissioner Andrew S. Miller; natl. chief sec., Col. Harold E. Shoults, 799 Bloomfield Ave., Verona, NJ 07044.

Sikh (1972) — Chief adm., Siri Singh Sahib, Harbhajan Singh Khalsa Yogiji; sec. gen., Mukhia Sardarni Sahiba, Sardarni Premka Kaur Khalsa, 1649 S. Robertson Blvd., Los Angeles, CA 90035.

Unitarian Universalist Assn. (1961) — Pres., Rev. William Schulz; sec., Barry Johnson-Fay, 25 Beacon St., Boston, MA 02108.

United Brethren in Christ (1789) — Chpsn., Bishop C. Ray Miller; 302 Lake St., Huntington, IN 46750.

United Church of Christ (1957) — Pres., Rev. Avery D. Post; sec., Rev. Carol Joyce Brun, 105 Madison Ave., N.Y., NY 10016.

Volunteers of America (1896) — Pres., Raymond C. Tremont; 3813 N. Causeway Blvd., Metairie, LA 70002.

The Wesleyan Church (1968) — Gen. supt., Rev. J. Stevan Manley; gen. sec., Rev. Robert W. Wilson, 10880 State Rt. 170, Negley, OH.

Church/Synagogue Attendance and Membership, 1988

Source: 1989 Yearbook of American & Canadian Churches

Four adults out of every ten (42%) Americans attended church or synagogue in a typical week in 1988, according to a Gallup survey reported in the Yearbook. Church attendance was found to have remained constant since 1969, after having declined from a high of 49 percent in 1955 and 1958. Two-thirds of U.S. adults (65%) said they were members of a church or synagogue, in the same survey. The highest figure for membership —76%— occurred in 1947; the 1988 percentage was the lowest recorded.

Church/Synagogue Attendance

1988	42%	1967	43%
1987	40	1962	46
1985	42	1958	49**
1983	40	1957	47
1982	41	1955	49**
1981	41	1954	46
1979	40	1950	39
1972	40	1940	37*
1969	42	1939	41

*Low point. **High point.

Church/Synagogue Membership

1988	65*
1987	69
1985	71
1983	69
1982	67
1979	68
1976	71
1965	73
1952	73
1947	76**
1944	75
1940	72
1937	73

Jewish Holy Days, Festivals, and Fasts

	1989 (5749-50)		1990 (5750-51)		1991 (5751-52)		1992 (5752-53)		1993 (5753-54)	
Tu B'Shvat	Jan. 21	Sat.	Feb. 10	Sat.	Jan. 30	Wed.	Jan. 20	Mon.	Feb. 6	Sat.
Ta'anis Esther (Fast of Esther)	Mar. 20	Mon.	Mar. 8	Thu.*	Feb. 27	Wed.	Mar. 18	Wed.	Mar. 4	Thu.*
Purim	Mar. 21	Tue.	Mar. 11	Sun.	Feb. 28	Thu.	Mar. 19	Thu.	Mar. 7	Sun.
Passover	Apr. 20	Thu.	Apr. 10	Tue.	Mar. 30	Sat.	Apr. 18	Sat.	Apr. 6	Tue.
	Apr. 27	Thu.	Apr. 17	Tue.	Apr. 6	Sat	Apr. 25	Sat.	Apr. 13	Tue.
Lag B'Omer	May 23	Tue.	May 13	Sun.	May 2	Thu.	May 21	Thu.	May 9	Sun.
Shavuot	June 9	Fri.	May 30	Wed.	May 19	Sun.	June 7	Sun.	May 26	Wed.
	June 10	Sat.	May 31	Thu.	May 20	Mon.	June 8	Mon.	May 27	Thu.
Fast of the 17th Day of Tammuz	July 20	Thu.	July 10	Tue.	June 30	Sun.*	July 19	Sun.*	July 6	Tue.
Fast of the 9th Day of Ac	Aug. 10	Thu.	July 31	Tue.	July 21	Sun.*	Aug. 9	Sun.*	July 27	Tue.
Rosh Hashanah	Sept. 30	Sat.	Sept. 20	Thu.	Sept. 9	Mon.	Sept. 28	Mon.	Sept. 16	Thu.
	Oct. 1	Sun.	Sept. 21	Fri.	Sept. 10	Tue.	Sept. 29	Tue.	Sept. 17	Fri.
Fast of Gedalya	Oct. 2	Mon.	Sept. 23	Sun.*	Sept. 11	Wed.	Sept. 30	Wed.	Sept. 19	Sun.*
Yom Kippur	Oct. 9	Mon.	Sept. 29	Sat.	Sept. 18	Wed.	Oct. 7	Wed.	Sept. 25	Sat.
Sukkot	Oct. 14	Sat.	Oct. 4	Thu.	Sept. 23	Mo.n	Oct. 12	Mon.	Sept. 30	Thu.
	Oct. 20	Fri.	Oct. 10	Wed.	Sept. 29	Sun.	Oct. 18	Sun.	Oct. 6	Wed.
Shmini Atzeret	Oct. 21	Sat.	Oct. 11	Thu.	Sept. 30	Mon.	Oct. 19	Mon.	Oct. 7	Thu.
	Oct. 22	Sun.	Oct. 12	Fri.	Oct. 1	Tue.	Oct. 20	Tue.	Oct. 8	Fri.
Chanukah	Dec. 23	Sat.	Dec. 12	Wed.	Dec. 2	Mon.	Dec. 20	Sun.	Dec. 9	Thu.
	Dec. 30	Sat.	Dec. 19	Wed.	Dec. 9	Mon.	Dec. 27	Sun.	Dec. 16	Thu.
Fast of the 10th of Tevet	Jan. 7	Sun.	Dec. 27	Thu.	Dec. 17	Tue.	Jan. 3	Sun.	Dec. 24	Fri.
	1990						1993			

The months of the Jewish year are: 1) Tishri; 2) Cheshvan (also Marcheshvan); 3) Kislev; 4) Tebet (also Tebeth); 5) Shebat (also Shebhat); 6) Adar; 6a) Adar Sheni (II) added in leap years; 7) Nisan; 8) Iyar; 9) Sivan; 10) Tammuz; 11) Av (also Abh); 12) Elul. All Jewish holy days, etc., begin at sunset on the day previous. *Date changed to avoid Sabbath.

Greek Orthodox Church Calendar, 1990

Date		Holy Days	Date		Holy Days
Jan.	1	Circumcision of Jesus Christ; feast day of St. Basil	May	21	Feast day of Sts. Constantine and Helen
			June	3	Sunday of Pentecost
Jan.	6	Epiphany: Baptism of Jesus Christ - Sanctification of the Waters	June	29	Feast day of Sts. Peter and Paul
			June	30	Feast day of the Twelve Apostles of Jesus Christ
Jan.	7	Feast day of St. John the Baptist			
Jan.	30	Feast day of the Three Hierarchs: St. Basil the Great, St. Gregory the Theologian, and St. John Chrysostom	Aug.	6	Transfiguration of Jesus Christ
			Aug.	15	Dormition of the Virgin Mary
			Aug.	29	Beheading of St. John the Baptist
Feb.	2	Presentation of Jesus Christ in the Temple	Sept.	1	Beginning of the Church Year
Feb.	26	Easter Lent begins	Sept.	14	Adoration of the Holy Cross
Mar.	4	Sunday of Orthodoxy (1st. Sunday of Lent)	Oct.	23	Feast day of St. James
Mar.	25	Annunciation of the Virgin Mary	Oct.	26	Feast day of St. Demetrios the Martyr
Apr.	8	Palm Sunday	Nov.	15	Christmas Lent begins
Apr.	8-15	Holy Week	Nov.	21	Presentation of the Virgin Mary
Apr.	13	Holy (Good) Friday: Burial of Jesus Christ	Nov.	30	Feast day of St. Andrew the Apostle
Apr.	15	Easter Sunday: Resurrection of Jesus Christ	Dec.	6	Feast day of St. Nicholas, Bishop of Myra
Apr.	23	Feast of St. George	Dec.	25	Christmas Day; Nativity of Jesus Christ
May	24	Ascension of Jesus Christ			

Islamic (Moslem) Calendar 1989-1990 (1410-1411)

The Islamic Calendar is a lunar reckoning from the year of the *hegira*, 622 A.D., when Muhammed moved from Mecca to Medina. It runs in cycles of 30 years, of which the 2d, 5th, 7th, 10th, 13th, 16th, 18th, 21st, 24th, 26th, and 29th years are leap years; 1410 is the 30th year, 1411 the 31st year of the cycle. Common years have 354 days, leap years 355, the extra day being added to the last month, Zu'lhijjah. Except for this case, the 12 months beginning with Muharram have alternately 30 and 29 days.

Year	Name of month	Month begins	Year	Name of month	Month begins
1410	Muharram (New Year)	Aug. 4, 1989	1410	Shawwai	Apr. 27, 1990
1410	Safar	Sept. 3, 1989	1410	Zu'lkadah	May 26, 1990
1410	Rabia I	Oct. 2, 1989	1410	Zu'lhijjah	June 25, 1990
1410	Rabia II	Nov. 1, 1989	1411	Muharram (New Year)	July 24, 1990
1410	Jumada I	Nov. 30, 1989	1411	Safar	Aug. 23, 1990
1410	Jumada II	Dec. 30, 1989	1411	Rabia I	Sept. 21, 1990
1410	Rajab	Jan. 28, 1990	1411	Rabia II	Oct. 21, 1990
1410	Shaban	Feb. 27, 1990	1411	Jamada I	Nov. 19, 1990
1410	Ramadan	Mar. 28, 1990			

Episcopal Church Calendar and Liturgical Colors

White—from Christmas Day through the First Sunday after Epiphany; Maundy Thursday (as an alternative to crimson at the Eucharist); from the Vigil of Easter to the Day of Pentecost (Whitsunday); Trinity Sunday; Feasts of the Lord (except Holy Cross Day); the Confession of St. Peter; the Conversion of St. Paul; St. Joseph; St. Mary Magdalene; St. Mary the Virgin; St. Michael and All Angels; All Saint's Day; St. John the Evangelist; memorials of other saints who were not martyred; Independence Day and Thanksgiving Day; weddings and funerals. **Red.**—the Day of Pentecost; Holy Cross Day; feasts of apostles and evangelists (except those listed above); feasts and memorials of martyrs (including Holy Innocents' Day). **Violet**—Advent and Lent. **Crimson** (dark red)—Holy Week. **Green**—the seasons after Epiphany and after Pentecost. **Black**—optional alternative for funerals. Alternative colors used in some churches: **Blue**—Advent; **Lenten White**—Ash Wednesday to Palm Sunday.   *(continued)*

In the Episcopal Church the days of fasting are Ash Wednesday and Good Friday. Other days of special devotion (abstinence) are the 40 days of Lent and all Fridays of the year, except those in Christmas and Easter seasons and any Feasts of the Lord which occur on a Friday or during Lent. Ember Days (optional) are days of prayer for the Church's ministry. They fall on the Wednesday, Friday, and Saturday after the first Sunday in Lent, the Day of Pentecost, Holy Cross Day, and the Third Sunday of Advent. Rogation Days (also optional) are the three days before Ascension Day, and are days of prayer for God's blessing on the crops, on commerce and industry, and for the conservation of the earth's resources.

Days, etc.	1987	1988	1989	1990	1991	1992
Golden Number	12	13	14	15	16	17
Sunday Letter	D	CB	A	G	F	ED
Sundays after Epiphany	8	6	5	8	5	8
Ash Wednesday	Mar. 4	Feb. 17	Feb. 8	Feb. 28	Feb. 13	Mar. 4
First Sunday in Lent	Mar. 8	Feb. 21	Feb. 12	Mar. 4	Feb. 17	Mar. 8
Passion/Palm Sunday	Apr. 12	Mar. 27	Mar. 19	Apr. 8	Mar. 24	Apr. 12
Good Friday	Apr. 17	Apr. 1	Mar. 24	Apr. 13	Mar. 29	Apr. 17
Easter Day	Apr. 19	Apr. 3	Mar. 26	Apr. 15	Mar. 31	Apr. 19
Ascension Day	May 28	May 12	May 4	May 24	May 9	May 28
The Day of Pentecost	June 7	May 22	May 14	June 3	May 19	June 7
Trinity Sunday	June 14	May 29	May 21	June 10	May 26	June 14
Numbered Proper of 2 Pentecost	#7	#5	#3	#6	#4	#7
First Sunday of Advent	Nov. 29	Nov. 27	Dec. 3	Dec. 2	Dec. 1	Nov. 29

Ash Wednesday and Easter Sunday

Year	Ash Wed.	Easter Sunday	Year	Ash Wed.	Easter Sunday	Year	Ash Wed.	Easter Sunday	Year	Ash Wed.	Easter Sunday
1901	Feb. 20	Apr. 7	1951	Feb. 7	Mar. 25	2001	Feb. 28	Apr. 15	2051	Feb. 15	Apr. 2
1902	Feb. 12	Mar. 30	1952	Feb. 27	Apr. 13	2002	Feb. 13	Mar. 31	2052	Mar. 6	Apr. 21
1903	Feb. 25	Apr. 12	1953	Feb. 18	Apr. 5	2003	Mar. 5	Apr. 20	2053	Feb. 19	Apr. 6
1904	Feb. 17	Apr. 3	1954	Mar. 3	Apr. 18	2004	Feb. 25	Apr. 11	2054	Feb. 11	Mar. 29
1905	Mar. 8	Apr. 23	1955	Feb. 23	Apr. 10	2005	Feb. 9	Mar. 27	2055	Mar. 3	Apr. 18
1906	Feb. 28	Apr. 15	1956	Feb. 15	Apr. 1	2006	Mar. 1	Apr. 16	2056	Feb. 16	Apr. 2
1907	Feb. 13	Mar. 31	1957	Mar. 6	Apr. 21	2007	Feb. 21	Apr. 8	2057	Mar. 7	Apr. 22
1908	Mar. 4	Apr. 19	1958	Feb. 19	Apr. 6	2008	Feb. 6	Mar. 23	2058	Feb. 27	Apr. 14
1909	Feb. 24	Apr. 11	1959	Feb. 11	Mar. 29	2009	Feb. 25	Apr. 12	2059	Feb. 12	Mar. 30
1910	Feb. 9	Mar. 27	1960	Mar. 2	Apr. 17	2010	Feb. 17	Apr. 4	2060	Mar. 3	Apr. 18
1911	Mar. 1	Apr. 16	1961	Feb. 15	Apr. 2	2011	Mar. 9	Apr. 24	2061	Feb. 23	Apr. 10
1912	Feb. 21	Apr. 7	1962	Mar. 7	Apr. 22	2012	Feb. 22	Apr. 8	2062	Feb. 8	Mar. 26
1913	Feb. 5	Mar. 23	1963	Feb. 27	Apr. 14	2013	Feb. 13	Mar. 31	2063	Feb. 28	Apr. 15
1914	Feb. 25	Apr. 12	1964	Feb. 12	Mar. 29	2014	Mar. 5	Apr. 20	2064	Feb. 20	Apr. 6
1915	Feb. 17	Apr. 4	1965	Mar. 3	Apr. 18	2015	Feb. 18	Apr. 5	2065	Feb. 11	Mar. 29
1916	Mar. 8	Apr. 23	1966	Feb. 23	Apr. 10	2016	Feb. 10	Mar. 27	2066	Feb. 24	Apr. 11
1917	Feb. 21	Apr. 8	1967	Feb. 8	Mar. 26	2017	Mar. 1	Apr. 16	2067	Feb. 16	Apr. 3
1918	Feb. 13	Mar. 31	1968	Feb. 28	Apr. 14	2018	Feb. 14	Apr. 1	2068	Mar. 7	Apr. 22
1919	Mar. 5	Apr. 20	1969	Feb. 19	Apr. 6	2019	Mar. 6	Apr. 21	2069	Feb. 27	Apr. 14
1920	Feb. 18	Apr. 4	1970	Feb. 11	Mar. 29	2020	Feb. 26	Apr. 12	2070	Feb. 12	Mar. 30
1921	Feb. 9	Mar. 27	1971	Feb. 24	Apr. 11	2021	Feb. 17	Apr. 4	2071	Mar. 4	Apr. 19
1922	Mar. 1	Apr. 16	1972	Feb. 16	Apr. 2	2022	Mar. 2	Apr. 17	2072	Feb. 24	Apr. 10
1923	Feb. 14	Apr. 1	1973	Mar. 7	Apr. 22	2023	Feb. 22	Apr. 9	2073	Feb. 8	Mar. 26
1924	Mar. 5	Apr. 20	1974	Feb. 27	Apr. 14	2024	Feb. 14	Mar. 31	2074	Feb. 28	Apr. 15
1925	Feb. 25	Apr. 12	1975	Feb. 12	Mar. 30	2025	Mar. 5	Apr. 20	2075	Feb. 20	Apr. 7
1926	Feb. 17	Apr. 4	1976	Mar. 3	Apr. 18	2026	Feb. 18	Apr. 5	2076	Mar. 4	Apr. 19
1927	Mar. 2	Apr. 17	1977	Feb. 23	Apr. 10	2027	Feb. 10	Mar. 28	2077	Feb. 24	Apr. 11
1928	Feb. 22	Apr. 8	1978	Feb. 8	Mar. 26	2028	Mar. 1	Apr. 16	2078	Feb. 16	Apr. 3
1929	Feb. 13	Mar. 31	1979	Feb. 28	Apr. 15	2029	Feb. 14	Apr. 1	2079	Mar. 8	Apr. 23
1930	Mar. 5	Apr. 20	1980	Feb. 20	Apr. 6	2030	Mar. 6	Apr. 21	2080	Feb. 21	Apr. 7
1931	Feb. 18	Apr. 5	1981	Mar. 4	Apr. 19	2031	Feb. 26	Apr. 13	2081	Feb. 12	Mar. 30
1932	Feb. 10	Mar. 27	1982	Feb. 24	Apr. 11	2032	Feb. 11	Mar. 28	2082	Mar. 4	Apr. 19
1933	Mar. 1	Apr. 16	1983	Feb. 16	Apr. 3	2033	Mar. 2	Apr. 17	2083	Feb. 17	Apr. 4
1934	Feb. 14	Apr. 1	1984	Mar. 7	Apr. 22	2034	Feb. 22	Apr. 9	2084	Mar. 9	Apr. 26
1935	Mar. 6	Apr. 21	1985	Feb. 20	Apr. 7	2035	Feb. 7	Mar. 25	2085	Feb. 28	Apr. 15
1936	Feb. 26	Apr. 12	1986	Feb. 12	Mar. 30	2036	Feb. 27	Apr. 13	2086	Feb. 13	Mar. 31
1937	Feb. 10	Mar. 28	1987	Mar. 4	Apr. 19	2037	Feb. 18	Apr. 5	2087	Mar. 5	Apr. 20
1938	Mar. 2	Apr. 17	1988	Feb. 17	Apr. 3	2038	Mar. 10	Apr. 25	2088	Feb. 25	Apr. 11
1939	Feb. 22	Apr. 9	1989	Feb. 8	Mar. 26	2039	Feb. 23	Apr. 10	2089	Feb. 16	Apr. 3
1940	Feb. 7	Mar. 24	1990	Feb. 28	Apr. 15	2040	Feb. 15	Apr. 1	2090	Mar. 1	Apr. 16
1941	Feb. 26	Apr. 13	1991	Feb. 13	Mar. 31	2041	Mar. 6	Apr. 21	2091	Feb. 21	Apr. 8
1942	Feb. 18	Apr. 5	1992	Mar. 4	Apr. 19	2042	Feb. 19	Apr. 6	2092	Feb. 13	Mar. 30
1943	Mar. 10	Apr. 25	1993	Feb. 24	Apr. 11	2043	Feb. 11	Mar. 29	2093	Feb. 25	Apr. 12
1944	Feb. 23	Apr. 9	1994	Feb. 16	Apr. 3	2044	Mar. 2	Apr. 17	2094	Feb. 17	Apr. 4
1945	Feb. 14	Apr. 1	1995	Mar. 1	Apr. 16	2045	Feb. 22	Apr. 9	2095	Mar. 9	Apr. 24
1946	Mar. 6	Apr. 21	1996	Feb. 21	Apr. 7	2046	Feb. 7	Mar. 25	2096	Feb. 29	Apr. 15
1947	Feb. 19	Apr. 6	1997	Feb. 12	Mar. 30	2047	Feb. 27	Apr. 14	2097	Feb. 13	Mar. 31
1948	Feb. 11	Mar. 28	1998	Feb. 25	Apr. 12	2048	Feb. 19	Apr. 5	2098	Mar. 5	Apr. 20
1949	Mar. 2	Apr. 17	1999	Feb. 17	Apr. 4	2049	Mar. 3	Apr. 18	2099	Feb. 25	Apr. 12
1950	Feb. 22	Apr. 9	2000	Mar. 8	Apr. 23	2050	Feb. 23	Apr. 10	2100	Feb. 10	Mar. 28

The Ten Commandments

According to Judeo-Christian tradition, as related in the Bible, the Ten Commandments were revealed by God to Moses, and form the basic moral component of God's covenant with Israel. The Ten Commandments appear in two different places in the Old Testament—Exodus 20:1-17 and Deuterotomy 5:6-21—the phrasing similar but not identical. Most Protestant, Anglican, and Orthodox Christians enumerate the commandments differently from Roman Catholics and Lutherans. Jewish tradition considers the introduction, "I am the Lord . . ." to be the first commandment and makes the prohibition against "other gods" and idolatry the second.

Abridged Text of the Ten Commandments in Exodus 20:1-17

I. I am the Lord your God, who brought you out of the land of Egypt, out of the house of bondage. You shall have no other gods before me.
II. You shall not make for yourself a graven image. You shall not bow down to them or serve them.
III. You shall not take the name of the Lord your God in vain.
IV. Remember the sabbath day, to keep it holy.
V. Honor your father and your mother.
VI. You shall not kill.
VII. You shall not commit adultery.
VIII. You shall not steal.
IX. You shall not bear false witness against your neighbor.
X. You shall not covet.

Books of the Bible

Old Testament—Standard Protestant English Versions

Genesis	II Chronicles	Daniel
Exodus	Ezra	Hosea
Leviticus	Nehemiah	Joel
Numbers	Esther	Amos
Deuteronomy	Job	Obadiah
Joshua	Psalms	Jonah
Judges	Proverbs	Micah
Ruth	Ecclesiastes	Nahum
I Samuel	Song of Solomon	Habakkuk
II Samuel	Isaiah	Zephaniah
I Kings	Jeremiah	Haggai
II Kings	Lamentations	Zechariah
I Chronicles	Ezekiel	Malachi

New Testament—Standard Protestant English Versions

Matthew	Ephesians	Hebrews
Mark	Phillippians	James
Luke	Colossians	I Peter
John	I Thessalonians	II Peter
Acts	II Thessalonians	I John
Romans	I Timothy	II John
I Corinthians	II Timothy	III John
II Corinthians	Titus	Jude
Galatians	Philemon	Revelation

Catholic Versions

All the Catholic books of the Bible (Old Testament and New Testament) have the same names as Protestant Versions. A Catholic Version (and Pre-Reformation Bibles) simply has the books **Tobit, Judith, Wisdom, Sirach (Ecclesiasticus), Baruch, I Maccabees,** and **II Maccabees** as part of the Old Testament. The Old Testament books that a Catholic Bible includes and a Protestant Bible does not are called "Deuterocanonical Books."

Roman Catholic Hierarchy

Source: U.S. Catholic Conference; Mid-year, 1989

Supreme Pontiff

At the head of the Roman Catholic Church is the Supreme Pontiff, Pope John Paul II, Karol Wojtyla, born at Wadowice (Krakow), Poland, May 18, 1920; ordained priest Nov. 1, 1946; promoted to Archbishop of Krakow Jan. 13, 1964; proclaimed Cardinal June 26, 1967; elected pope as successor of Pope John Paul I Oct. 16, 1978; solemn commencement as pope Oct. 22, 1978.

College of Cardinals

Members of the Sacred College of Cardinals are chosen by the Pope to be his chief assistants and advisors in the administration of the church. Among their duties is the election of the Pope when the Holy See becomes vacant. The title of cardinal is a high honor, but it does not represent any increase in the powers of holy orders.

In its present form, the College of Cardinals dates from the 12th century. The first cardinals, from about the 6th century, were deacons and priests of the leading churches of Rome, and bishops of neighboring diocese. The title of cardinal was limited to members of the college in 1567. The number of cardinals was set at 70 in 1586 by Pope Sixtus V. From 1959 Pope John XXIII began to increase the number. However, the number of cardinals eligible to participate in papal elections was limited to 120. There were lay cardinals until 1918, when the Code of Canon Law specified that all cardinals must be priests. Pope John XXIII in 1962 established that all cardinals must be bishops. The first age limits were set in 1971 by Pope Paul VI, who decreed that at age 80 cardinals must retire from curial departments and offices and from participation in papal elections. They continue as members of the college, with all rights and privileges.

U.S. Cardinals

Name	Office	Born	Named Cardinal
Aponte Martinez, Luis	Archbishop of San Juan	1922	1973
Baum, William	Prefect of Congregation for Seminaries and Institutes of Study	1926	1976
Bernardin, Joseph	Archbishop of Chicago	1928	1983
Carberry, John*	Archbishop emeritus of St. Louis	1904	1969
Hickey, James	Archbishop of Washington	1920	1988
Krol, John	Archbishop emeritus of Philadelphia	1910	1967
Law, Bernard F.	Archbishop of Boston	1931	1985
O'Connor, John J	Archbishop of New York	1920	1985
Szoka, Edmund	Archbishop of Detroit	1927	1988

*Asterisk indicates cardinals ineligible to take part in papal elections.

The Major World Religions

Buddhism

Founded: About 525 BC, reportedly near Benares, India.
Founder: Gautama Siddhartha (ca. 563-480), the Buddha, who achieved enlightenment through intense meditation.
Sacred Texts: The *Tripitaka*, a collection of the Buddha's teachings, rules of monastic life, and philosophical commentaries on the teachings; also a vast body of Buddhist teachings and commentaries, many of which are called *sutras*.
Organization: The basic institution is the *sangha* or monastic order through which the traditions are passed to each generation. Monastic life tends to be democratic and anti-authoritarian. Large lay organizations have developed in some sects.
Practice: Varies widely according to the sect and ranges from austere meditation to magical chanting and elaborate temple rites. Many practices, such as exorcism of devils, reflect pre-Buddhist beliefs.
Divisions: A wide variety of sects grouped into 3 primary branches: Theravada (sole survivor of the ancient Hinayana schools) which emphasizes the importance of pure thought and deed; Mahayana, which includes Zen and Soka-gakkai, ranges from philosophical schools to belief in the saving grace of higher beings or ritual practices, and to practical meditative disciplines; and Tantrism, an unusual combination of belief in ritual magic and sophisticated philosophy.
Location: Throughout Asia, from Ceylon to Japan. Zen and Soka-gakkai have several thousand adherents in the U.S.
Beliefs: Life is misery and decay, and there is no ultimate reality in it or behind it. The cycle of endless birth and rebirth continues because of desire and attachment to the unreal "self". Right meditation and deeds will end the cycle and achieve Nirvana, the Void, nothingness.

Hinduism

Founded: Ca. 1500 BC by Aryan invaders of India where their Vedic religion intermixed with the practices and beliefs of the natives.
Sacred texts: The *Veda*, including the *Upanishads*, a collection of rituals and mythological and philosophical commentaries; a vast number of epic stories about gods, heroes and saints, including the *Bhagavadgita*, a part of the *Mahabharata*, and the *Ramayana;* and a great variety of other literature.
Organization: None, strictly speaking. Generally, rituals should be performed or assisted by Brahmins, the priestly caste, but in practice simpler rituals can be performed by anyone. Brahmins are the final judges of ritual purity, the vital element in Hindu life. Temples and religious organizations are usually presided over by Brahmins.
Practice: A variety of private rituals, primarily passage rites (eg. initiation, marriage, death, etc.) and daily devotions, and a similar variety of public rites in temples. Of the latter, the *puja*, a ceremonial dinner for a god, is the most common.
Divisions: There is no concept of orthodoxy in Hinduism, which presents a bewildering variety of sects, most of them devoted to the worship of one of the many gods. The 3 major living traditions are those devoted to the gods Vishnu and Shiva and to the goddess Shakti; each of them divided into further sub-sects. Numerous folk beliefs and practices, often in amalgamation with the above groups, exist side-by-side with sophisticated philosophical schools and exotic cults.
Location: Confined to India, except for the missionary work of Vedanta, the Krishna Consciousness society, and individual *gurus* (teachers) in the West.
Beliefs: There is only one divine principle; the many gods are only aspects of that unity. Life in all its forms is an aspect of the divine, but it appears as a separation from the divine, a meaningless cycle of birth and rebirth (*samsara*) determined by the purity or impurity of past deeds (*karma*). To improve one's *karma* or escape *samsara* by pure acts, thought, and/or devotion is the aim of every Hindu.

Islam

Founded: 622 AD in Medina, Arabian peninsula.
Founder: Mohammed (ca. 570-632), the Prophet.
Sacred texts: *Koran*, the words of God. *Hadith*, collections of the sayings of the Prophet.
Organization: Theoretically the state and religious community are one, administered by a caliph. In practice, Islam is a loose collection of congregations united by a very conservative tradition. Islam is basically egalitarian and non-authoritarian.
Practice: Every Moslem has 5 duties: to make the profession of faith ("There is no god but Allah ..."), pray 5 times a day, give a regular portion of his goods to charity, fast during the day in the month of Ramadan, and make at least one pilgrimage to Mecca if possible.
Divisions: The 2 major sects of Islam are the Sunni (orthodox) and the Shi'ah. The Shi'ah believe in 12 *imams*, perfect teachers, who still guide the faithful from Paradise. Shi'ah practice tends toward the ecstatic, while the Sunni is staid and simple. The Shi'ah sect affirms man's free will; the Sunni is deterministic. The mystic tradition in Islam is Sufism. A Sufi adept believes he has acquired a special inner knowledge direct from Allah.
Location: From the west coast of Africa to the Philipines across a broad band that includes Tanzania, southern USSR and western China, India, Malaysia and Indonesia. Islam claims over 2 million adherents in the U.S.
Beliefs: Strictly monotheistic. God is creator of the universe, omnipotent, just, and merciful. Man is God's highest creation, but limited and commits sins. He is misled by Satan, an evil spirit. God revealed the *Koran* to Mohammed to guide men to the truth. Those who repent and sincerely submit to God return to a state of sinlessness. In the end, the sinless go to Paradise, a place of physical and spiritual pleasure, and the wicked burn in Hell.

Judaism

Founded: About 1300 BCE.
Founder: Abrahm is regarded as the founding patriarch, but the Torah of Moses is the basic source of the teachings.
Sacred Texts: The five books of Moses constitute the written Torah. Special sanctity is also assigned other writings of the Hebrew Bible—the teachings of oral Torah are recorded in the Talmud, the Midrash, and various commentaries.
Organization: Originally theocratic, Judaism has evolved a congregational polity. The basic institution is the local synagogue, operated by the congregation and led by a rabbi of their choice. Chief Rabbis in France and Great Britain have authority only over those who accept it; in Israel, the 2 Chief Rabbis have civil authority in family law.
Practice: Among traditional practitioners, almost all areas of life are governed by strict religious discipline. Sabbath and holidays are marked by special observances, and attendance at public worship is regarded as especially important then. The chief annual observances are Passover, celebrating the liberation of the Israelites from Egypt and marked by the ritual Seder meal in the home, and the 10 days from Rosh Hashana (New Year) to Yom Kippur (Day of Atonement), a period of fasting and penitence.
Divisions: Judaism is an unbroken spectrum from ultra conservative to ultra liberal, largely reflecting different points of view regarding the binding character of the prohibitions and duties—particularly the dietary and Sabbath observations—prescribed in the daily life of the Jew.
Location: Almost worldwide, with concentrations in Israel and the U.S.
Beliefs: Strictly monotheistic. God is the creator and absolute ruler of the universe. Men are free to choose to rebel against God's rule. God established a particular relationship with the Hebrew people: by obeying a divine law God gave them they would be a special witness to God's mercy and justice. The emphasis in Judaism is on ethical behavior (and, among the traditional, careful ritual obedience) as the true worship of God.

Major Christian Denominations:
Italics indicate that area which, generally speaking, most

Denomination	Origins	Organization	Authority	Special rites
Baptists	In radical Reformation objections to infant baptism, demands for church-state separation; John Smyth, English Separatist in 1609; Roger Williams, 1638, Providence, R.I.	Congregational, *i.e.,* each local church is autonomous.	Scripture; some Baptists, particularly in the South, interpret the Bible literally.	Baptism, after about age 12, by total immersion; Lord's Supper.
Church of Christ (Disciples)	Among evangelical Presbyterians in Ky. (1804) and Penn. (1809), in distress over Protestant factionalism and decline of fervor. Organized 1832.	Congregational.	*"Where the Scriptures speak, we speak; where the Scriptures are silent, we are silent."*	Adult baptism, Lord's Supper (weekly).
Episcopalians	Henry VIII separated English Catholic Church from Rome, 1534, for political reasons. Protestant Episcopal Church in U.S. founded 1789.	*Bishops, in apostolic succession, are elected by diocesan representatives; part of Anglican Communion, symbolically headed by Archbishop of Canterbury.*	Scripture as interpreted by tradition, esp. 39 Articles (1563); not dogmatic. Tri-annual convention of bishops, priests, and laymen.	Infant baptism, Holy Communion, others. Sacrament is symbolic, but has real spiritual effect.
Lutherans	Martin Luther in Wittenberg, Germany, 1517, objected to Catholic doctrine of salvation by merit and sale of indulgences; break complete by 1519.	Varies from congregational to episcopal; in U.S. a combination of regional synods and congregational polities is most common.	*Scripture, and tradition as spelled out in Augsburg Confession (1530) and other creeds. These confessions of faith are binding although interpretations vary.*	Infant baptism, Lord's Supper. Christ's true body and blood present "in, with, and under the bread and wine."
Methodists	Rev. John Wesley began movement, 1738, within Church of England. First U.S. denomination Baltimore, 1784.	Conference and superintendent system. *In United Methodist Church, general superintendents are bishops—not a priestly order, only an office—who are elected for life.*	Scripture as interpreted by tradition, reason, and experience.	Baptism of infants or adults, Lord's Supper commanded. Other rites, inc. marriage, ordination, solemnize personal commitments.
Mormons	In visions of the Angel Moroni by Joseph Smith, 1827, in New York, in which he received a new revelation on golden tablets: *The Book of Mormon.*	Theocratic; all male adults in priesthood which culminates in Council of 12 Apostles and 1st Presidency (1st President, 2 counselors).	*The Bible, Book of Mormon and other revelations to Smith, and certain pronouncements of the 1st Presidency.*	Adult baptism, laying on of hands (which confers the gift of the Holy Spirit), Lord's Supper. Temple rites: baptism for the dead, marriage for eternity, others.
Orthodox	Original Christian proselytizing in 1st century; broke with Rome, 1054, after centuries of doctrinal disputes and diverging traditions.	Synods of bishops in autonomous, usually national, churches elect a patriarch, archbishop or metropolitan. These men, as a group, are the heads of the church.	Scripture, tradition, and the first 7 church councils up to Nicaea II in 787. Bishops in council have authority in doctrine and policy.	Seven sacraments: infant baptism and anointing, Eucharist (both bread and wine), ordination, penance, anointing of the sick, marriage.
Pentecostal	In Topeka, Kansas (1901), and Los Angeles (1906) in reaction to loss of evangelical fervor among Methodists and other denominations.	Originally a movement, not a formal organization, Pentecostalism now has a variety of organized forms and continues also as a movement.	Scripture, individual charismatic leaders, the teachings of the Holy Spirit.	Spirit baptism, esp. as shown in "speaking in tongues"; healing and sometimes exorcism; adult baptism, Lord's Supper.
Presbyterians	In Calvinist Reformation in 1500s; differed with Lutherans over sacraments, church government. John Knox founded Scotch Presbyterian church about 1560.	*Highly structured representational system of ministers and laypersons (presbyters) in local, regional and national bodies. (synods).*	Scripture.	Infant baptism, Lord's Supper; bread and wine symbolize Christ's spiritual presence.
Roman Catholics	Traditionally, by Jesus who named St. Peter the 1st Vicar; historically, in early Christian proselytizing and the conversion of imperial Rome in the 4th century.	Hierarchy with supreme power vested in Pope elected by cardinals. Councils of Bishops advise on matters of doctrine and policy.	*The Pope, when speaking for the whole church in matters of faith and morals, and tradition, which is partly recorded in scripture and expressed in church councils.*	Seven sacraments: baptism, contrition and penance, confirmation, Eucharist, marriage, ordination, and anointing of the sick (unction).
United Church of Christ	*By ecumenical union, 1957, of Congregationalists and Evangelical & Reformed, representing both Calvinist and Lutheran traditions.*	Congregational; a General Synod, representative of all congregations, sets general policy.	Scripture.	Infant baptism, Lord's Supper.

How Do They Differ?

distinguishes that denomination from any other.

Practice	Ethics	Doctrine	Other	Denomination
Worship style varies from staid to evangelistic. Extensive missionary activity.	Usually opposed to alcohol and tobacco; sometimes tends toward a perfectionist ethical standard.	*No creed; true church is of believers only, who are all equal.*	Since no authority can stand between the believer and God, the Baptists are strong supporters of church-state separation.	Baptists
Tries to avoid any rite or doctrine not explicitly part of the 1st century church. Some congregations may reject instrumental music.	Some tendency toward perfectionism; increasing interest in social action programs.	Simple New Testament faith; avoids any elaboration not firmly based on Scripture.	Highly tolerant in doctrinal and religious matters; strongly supportive of scholarly education.	Church of Christ (Disciples)
Formal, based on *Book of Common Prayer* (1549); services range from austerely simple to highly elaborate.	Tolerant; sometimes permissive; some social action programs.	*Apostles' Creed* is basic; otherwise, considerable variation ranges from rationalist and liberal to acceptance of most Roman Catholic dogma.	Strongly ecumenical, holding talks with all other branches of Christendom.	Episcopalians
Relatively simple formal liturgy with emphasis on the sermon.	Generally, conservative in personal and social ethics; doctrine of "2 kingdoms" (worldly and holy) supports conservatism in secular affairs.	Salvation by faith alone through grace. Lutheranism has made major contributions to Protestant theology.	Though still somewhat divided along ethnic lines (German, Swede, etc.), main divisions are between funamentalists and liberals.	Lutherans
Worship style varies widely by denomination, local church, geography.	Originally pietist and perfectionist; always strong social activist elements	No distinctive theological development; 25 Articles abriged from Church of England's 39 not binding.	In 1968, United Methodist Church joined pioneer English- and German-speaking groups. UMs leaders in ecumenical movement.	Methodists
Staid service with hymns, sermon. Secret temple ceremonies may be more elaborate. Strong missionary activity.	Temperance; strict tithing. Combine a strong work ethic with communal self-reliance.	God is a material being; he created the universe out of pre-existing matter; all persons can be saved and many will become divine. Most other beliefs are traditionally Christian.	Mormons regard mainline churches as apostate, corrupt. Reorganized Church (founded 1860) rejects most Mormon doctrine and practice except Book of Mormon.	Mormons
Elaborate liturgy, usually in the vernacular, though extremely traditional. The liturgy is the essence of Orthodoxy. Veneration of icons.	Tolerant; very little social action; divorce and remarriage permitted in some cases. Priests need not be celibate; bishops are.	Emphasis on Christ's resurrection, rather than crucifixion; the Holy Spirit proceeds from God the Father only.	Orthodox Church in America, orginally under Patriarch of Moscow, was granted autonomy in 1970. Greek Orthodox do not recognize this autonomy.	Orthodox
Loosely structured service with rousing hymns and sermons, culminating in spirit baptism.	Usually, emphasis on perfectionism with varying degrees of tolerance.	Simple traditional beliefs, usually Protestant, with emphasis on the immediate presence of God in the Holy Spirit	Once confined to lower-class "holy rollers," Pentecostalism now appears in mainline churches and has established middle-class congregations.	Pentecostal
A simple, sober service in which the sermon is central.	Traditionally, a tendency toward strictness with firm church- and self-discipline; otherwise tolerant.	Emphasizes the sovereignty and justice of God; no longer doctrinaire.	While traces of belief in predestination (that God has foreordained salvation for the "elect") remain, this idea is no longer a central element in Presbyterianism.	Presbyterians
Relatively elaborate ritual; wide variety of public and private rites, eg., rosary recitation, processions, novenas.	Theoretically very strict; tolerant in practice on most issues. Divorce and remarriage not accepted. Celibate clergy, except in Eastern rite.	Highly elaborated. Salvation by merit gained through faith. Unusual development of doctrines surrounding Mary. Dogmatic.	Roman Catholicism is presently in a period of relatively rapid change as a result of Vatican Councils I and II.	Roman Catholics
Usually simple services with emphasis on the sermon.	Tolerant; some social action emphasis.	Standard Protestant; *Statement of Faith* (1959) is not binding.	The 2 main churches in the 1957 union represented earlier unions with small groups of almost every Protestant denomination.	United Church of Christ

STATES AND OTHER AREAS OF THE U.S.

Sources: Population: Commerce Dept., Bureau of the Census (July, 1988 provisional estimates, inc. armed forces personnel in each state but excluding such personnel stationed overseas); area: Bureau of the Census, Geography Division; forested land: Agriculture Dept., Forest Service; lumber production: Bureau of the Census, Industry Division; mineral production: Interior Dept., Bureau of Mines (preliminary); commercial fishing: Commerce Dept., Natl. Marine Fisheries Service; value of construction: McGraw-Hill Information Systems Co., F.W. Dodge Division; per capita income (estimate): Commerce Dept., Bureau of Economic Analysis; unemployment: Labor Dept., Bureau of Labor Statistics; finance: Federal Deposit Insurance Corp., U.S. League of Savings Institutions; federal employees: Labor Dept., Office of Personnel Management; energy: Energy Dept., Energy Information Administration; education: Education Dept., National Education Assn. Other information from sources in individual states, usually Commerce Dept.

Alabama

Heart of Dixie, Camellia State

People. Population (1988): 4,102,000; **rank:** 22. **Pop. density:** 79.3 per sq. mi. **Urban** (1985): 60%. **Racial distrib.** (1985): 73.8% White; 26.2% Black; Hispanic 18,300. **Net change** (1980-88): +209,000; 5.4%.

Geography. Total area: 51,705 sq. mi.; **rank:** 29. **Land area:** 50,708 sq. mi. **Acres forested land:** 21,361,100. **Location:** in the east south central U.S., extending N-S from Tenn. to the Gulf of Mexico; east of the Mississippi River. **Climate:** long, hot summers; mild winters; generally abundant rainfall. **Topography:** coastal plains inc. Prairie Black Belt give way to hills, broken terrain; highest elevation, 2,407 ft. **Capital:** Montgomery.

Economy. Principal industries: pulp and paper, chemicals, electronics, apparel, textiles, primary metals, lumber and wood, food processing, fabricated metals, automotive tires. **Principal manufactured goods** (1987-1988): electronics, cast iron and plastic pipe, fabricated steel prods., ships, paper products, chemicals, steel, mobile homes, fabrics, poultry processing. **Agriculture:** Chief crops (1987-88): peanuts, cotton, soybeans, hay, corn, wheat, potatoes, pecans, sweet potatoes, cottonseed, catfish. **Livestock** (1987): 1.67 mln. cattle; 345,000 hogs/pigs; 16.3 mln. poultry. **Timber/lumber** (1987): pine, hardwoods; 2.1 bln. bd. ft. **Nonfuel Minerals** (1988): $452 mln., mostly cement, clays, lime, sand & gravel, stone. **Commercial fishing** (1988): $39.7 mln. **Chief ports:** Mobile. **Value of construction** (1988): $3.5 bln. **Employment distribution** (1988): 19% manuf.; 17% trade; 16% serv. **Per capita income** (1988): $12,604. **Unemployment** (1987): 7.2%. **Tourism** (1987): tourists spent $3.6 bln. **Sales Tax** (1988): 4%.

Finance. FDIC-insured commercial banks & trust companies (1987): 228. **Deposits:** $23.4 bln. **Savings institutions:** 36. **Assets:** $9.0 bln.

Federal government. No. federal civilian employees (Mar. 1988): 49,757. **Avg. salary:** $28,245. **Notable federal facilities:** George C. Marshall NASA Space Center, Huntsville; Gunter & Maxwell AFB, Montgomery; Ft. Rucker, Ozark; Ft. McClellan, Anniston; Natl. Fertilizer Development Center, Muscle Shoals; Navy Station & U.S. Corps of Engineers, Mobile; Redstone Arsenal, Huntsville.

Energy. Electricity production (1988, mwh, by source): Hydroelectric: 5.4 mln. Mineral: 49.2 mln. Nuclear: 13.0 mln.

Education. Expenditure per pupil, public schools (1987): $2,573. **Avg. salary, public school teachers** (1988-1989): $25,190.

State data. Motto: We dare defend our rights. **Flower:** Camellia. **Bird:** Yellowhammer. **Tree:** Southern Pine. **Song:** Alabama. **Entered union** Dec. 14, 1819; **rank,** 22d. **State fair** at: Birmingham; early Oct.

History. First Europeans were Spanish explorers in the early 1500s. The French made the first permanent settlement, on Mobile Bay, 1701-02; later, English settled in the northern areas. France ceded the entire region to England at the end of the French and Indian War, 1763, but Spanish Florida claimed the Mobile Bay area until U. S. troops took it, 1813. Gen. Andrew Jackson broke the power of the Creek Indians, 1814, and they were removed to Oklahoma. The Confederate States were organized Feb. 4, 1861, at Montgomery, the first capital.

Tourist attractions. Jefferson Davis' "first White House" of the Confederacy; Ivy Green, Helen Keller's birthplace, Tuscumbia; statue of Vulcan, Birmingham; George Washington Carver Museum, Tuskegee Univ.; W.C. Handy Home & Museum, Florence; Alabama Space and Rocket Center, Huntsville; Alabama Shakespeare Festival, Montgomery; Moundville State Monument, Moundville; Pike Pioneer Museum, Troy; 28 hunting areas, 24 public lakes, 82 campgrounds, 21 state parks.

At Russell Cave National Monument, near Bridgeport: a detailed record of occupancy by humans from about 10,000 BC to 1650 AD.

Famous Alabamians include Hank Aaron, Tallulah Bankhead, Hugo L. Black, Paul "Bear" Bryant, George Washington Carver, Nat King Cole, William C. Handy, Helen Keller, Harper Lee, Joe Louis, Willie Mays, John Hunt Morgan, Jesse Owens, George Wallace, Booker T. Washington, Hank Williams.

Alabama Business Council. 468 S. Perry St., P.O. Box 76, Montgomery, AL 36195; 1-800-248-5033.

Toll-free travel information. 1-800-392-8096; 1-800-ALABAMA out of state.

Alaska

Unofficial nickname: "The Last Frontier"

People. Population (1988): 524,000; **rank:** 49. **Pop. density:** 0.89 per sq. mi., **Urban** (1980): 64.3%. **Net change** (1980-88): +123,000; 30.5%.

Geography. Total area: 586,412 sq. mi.; **rank:** 1. **Land area:** 586,412 sq. mi. **Acres forested land:** 119,145,000. **Location:** NW corner of North America, bordered on east by Canada. **Climate:** SE, SW, and central regions, moist and mild; far north extremely dry. Extended summer days, winter nights, throughout. **Topography:** includes Pacific and Arctic mountain systems, central plateau, and Arctic slope. Mt. McKinley, 20,320 ft., is the highest point in North America. **Capital:** Juneau.

Economy. Principal industries: oil, gas, tourism, commercial fishing. **Principal manufactured goods:** fish products, lumber and pulp, furs. **Agriculture** (1988): Chief crops: barley, hay, greenhouse nursery prods., potatoes, lettuce, milk. **Livestock** (1988): 9,500 cattle; 2,400 sheep; 6,000 poultry; 23,000 reindeer. **Timber/lumber** (1988): spruce, yellow cedar, hemlock. **Nonfuel minerals** (1988): $174 mln.; gold, sand & gravel, crushed and broken stone. **Commercial fishing** (1988): $1.3 bln. **Chief ports:** Anchorage, Dutch Harbor, Kodiak, Seward, Skagway, Juneau, Sitka, Valdez, Wrangell. **International airports at:** Anchorage, Fairbanks, Ketchikan, Juneau. **Value of construction** (1988): $800 mln. **Employment distribution:** 29.3% gvt.; 19.7% trade; 18.3% serv.; 8.7% transp. **Per capita income** (1988): $19,514. **Unemployment** (1988): 9.3%. **Tourism** (1987-88): $500 mln.

Finance. Commerical bank deposits, per capita (1985): $7,475. **Savings institutions:** 6. **Assets:** $796 mln.

Federal government. No. federal civilian employees (Mar. 1988): 11,786. **Avg. salary:** $32,396.

Energy. Electricity production (1988, mwh, by source): Hydroelectric: 935,000. Mineral: 3.3 mln.

Education. Expenditure per pupil, public schools (1987): $8,010. **Avg. salary, public school teachers** (1988-89.): $41,693.

State data. Motto: North to the future. **Flower:** Forget-Me-Not. **Bird:** Willow Ptarmigan. **Tree:** Sitka Spruce. **Song:** Alaska's Flag. **Entered union:** Jan. 3, 1959; rank, 49th. **State fair at:** Palmer; late Aug.—early Sept.

History. Vitus Bering, a Danish explorer working for Russia, was the first European to land in Alaska, 1741. Alexander Baranov, first governor of Russian America, set up headquarters at Archangel, near present Sitka, in 1799. Secretary of State William H. Seward in 1867 bought Alaska from Russia for $7.2 million, a bargain some called "Seward's Folly." In 1896 gold was discovered and the famed Gold Rush was on.

Tourist attractions. Portage Glacier, Mendenhall Glacier, Glacier Bay National Park, Katmai National Park & Preserve, Denali National Park, one of North America's great wildlife sanctuaries, Pribilof Islands fur seal rookeries, restored St. Michael's Russian Orthodox Cathedral, Sitka.

Famous Alaskans include Tom Bodett, Susan Butcher, Ernest Gruening, Sydney Laurence, Libby Riddles, Jefferson "Soapy" Smith.

Tourist information. Alaska Division of Tourism, P.O. Box E, Juneau, AK 99811-0800.

Arizona

Grand Canyon State

People. Population (1988): 3,489,000; **rank:** 25. **Pop. density:** 30.6 per sq. mi. **Urban** (1980): 83.8% **Racial distrib.** (1985): 91.6% White; 2.0% Black; 6.6% Other (includes American Indians); Hispanic 533,200. **Net change** (1980-88): +771,000; 28.4%.

Geography. Total area: 114,000 sq. mi.; **rank:** 6. **Land area:** 113,508 sq. mi. **Acres forested land:** 18,493,900. **Location:** in the southwestern U.S. **Climate:** clear and dry in the southern regions and northern plateau; high central areas have heavy winter snows. **Topography:** Colorado plateau in the N, containing the Grand Canyon; Mexican Highlands running diagonally NW to SE; Sonoran Desert in the SW. **Capital:** Phoenix.

Economy. Principal industries: manufacturing, tourism, mining, agriculture. **Principal manufactured goods:** electronics, printing and publishing, foods, primary and fabricated metals, aircraft and missiles, apparel. **Agriculture: Chief crops:** cotton, sorghum, barley, corn, wheat, sugar beets, citrus fruits. **Livestock** (1988): 972,000 mln. cattle; 130,000 hogs/pigs; 284,000 sheep; 310,000 poultry. **Timber/lumber** (1987): pine, fir, spruce; 407 mln. bd. ft. **Nonfuel Minerals** (1988): $2.8 bln.; copper, molybdenum, gold, silver. **International airports at:** Phoenix, Tucson, Yuma. **Value of construction** (1988): $5.2 bln. **Employment distribution** (1986): 24.3% services; 24.2% trade; 16.9% gvt.; 13.7% manuf. **Per capita income** (1988): $14,887. **Unemployment** (1988): 6.3%. **Tourism** (1985): tourists spent $5.6 bln. **Sales tax:** 5.0% (Maricopa, Pinal Countries, 5.5%).

Finance. FDIC-insured commercial bank & trust companies (1987): 54. **Deposits:** $23.8 bln. **Savings institutions:** 12. **Assets:** $24.1 bln.

Federal government: No. federal civilian employees (Mar. 1988): 27,513. **Avg. salary:** $25,996. **Notable federal facilities:** Williams, Luke, Davis-Monthan AF bases; Ft. Huachuca Army Base; Yuma Proving Grounds.

Energy. Electricity production (1988, mwh, by source): Hydroelectric: 7.8 mln.; Mineral: 30.8; Nuclear: 22.9

Education. Expenditure per pupil, public schools (1987): $3,544. **Avg. salary, public school teachers** (1988-89): $28,684.

State data. Motto: Ditat Deus (God enriches). **Flower:** Blossom of the Saguaro cactus. **Bird:** Cactus wren. **Tree:**

Paloverde. **Song:** Arizona. **Entered union** Feb. 14, 1912; rank, 48th. **State fair at:** Phoenix; late Oct.–early Nov.

History. Marcos de Niza, a Franciscan, and Estevan, a black slave, explored the area, 1539. Eusebio Francisco Kino, Jesuit missionary, taught Indians Christianity and farming, 1690-1711, left a chain of missions. Spain ceded Arizona to Mexico, 1821. The U. S. took over at the end of the Mexican War, 1848. The area below the Gila River was obtained from Mexico in the Gadsden Purchase, 1854. Long Apache wars did not end until 1886, with Geronimo's surrender.

Tourist attractions. The Grand Canyon of the Colorado, an immense, vari-colored fissure 217 mi. long, 4 to 13 mi. wide at the brim, 4,000 to 5,500 ft. deep; the Painted Desert, extending for 30 mi. along U.S. 66; the Petrified Forest; Canyon Diablo, 225 ft. deep and 500 ft. wide; Meteor Crater, 4,150 ft. across, 570 ft. deep, made by a prehistoric meteor. Also, London Bridge at Lake Havasu City.

Famous Arizonans include Cochise, Geronimo, Barry Goldwater, Zane Grey, Carl Hayden, George W. P. Hunt, Helen Jacobs, Percival Lowell, Sandra Day O'Connor, William H. Pickering, John J. Rhodes, Morris Udall, Stewart Udall, Frank Lloyd Wright.

Tourist information. Phoenix & Valley of the Sun Visitor and Convention Bureau, 1-602-254-6500.

Arkansas

Land of Opportunity

People. Population (1988): 2,395,000; **rank:** 33. **Pop. density:** 45.0 per sq. mi. **Urban** (1980): 51.5%. **Racial distrib.** (1985): 83.4% White; 16.6% Black; Hispanic 13,500. **Net change** (1980-88): +108,000; 4.7%.

Geography. Total area: 53,187 sq. mi.; **rank:** 27. **Land area:** 52,078 sq. mi. **Acres forested land:** 18,281,500. **Location:** in the west south-central U.S. **Climate:** long, hot summers, mild winters; generally abundant rainfall. **Topography:** eastern delta and prairie, southern lowland forests, and the northwestern highlands, which include the Ozark Plateaus. **Capital:** Little Rock.

Economy. Principal industries: manufacturing, agriculture, tourism, mining, forestry. **Principal manufactured goods:** food prods., chemicals, lumber, paper, electric meters, furniture, home appliances, auto complements, transformers, apparel, fertilizers, machinery, petroleum prods. **Agriculture: Chief crops:** soybeans, rice, cotton, hay, wheat, sorghum, tomatoes, strawberries, peaches. **Livestock** (1987): 1.85 mln. cattle; 465,000 hogs/pigs; 8.77 mln. poultry. **Timber/lumber** (1987): oak, hickory, gum, cypress, pine; 1.5 bln. bd. ft. **Nonfuel Minerals** (1988): $321 mln.; abrasives, bauxite, bromine. **Commercial fishing** (1986): $7.3 mln. **Chief ports:** Little Rock, Pine Bluff, Osceola, Helena, Fort Smith, Van Buren, Camden, Dardanelle. **Value of construction** (1988): $1.3 bln. **Employment distribution** (1988): 22% manuf.; 18.7% trade; 15.6% serv.; 4.3% agric. **Per capita income** (1988): $12,172. **Unemployment** (1988): 7.7% **Tourism** (1987): travelers spent $2 bln.

Finance. FDIC-insured commercial banks & trust companies (1987): 256. **Deposits:** $15.9 bln. **Savings institutions:** 37. **Assets:** $6.8 bln.

Federal government: No. federal civilian employees (Mar. 1988): 12,310. **Avg. salary:** $24,954. **Notable federal facilities:** Nat'l. Center for Toxicological Research, Jefferson; Pine Bluff Arsenal.

Energy. Electricity production (1987, mwh, by source): Hydroelectric: 2.8 mln.; Mineral: 22.1 mln.; Nuclear: 8.9 mln.

Education. Expenditure per pupil, public schools (1987): $2,733. **Avg. salary, public school teachers** (1988-89 est.): $21,692.

State data. Motto: Regnat Populus (The people rule). **Flower:** Apple Blossom. **Bird:** Mockingbird. **Tree:** Pine. **Song:** Arkansas. **Entered union:** June 15, 1836; rank, 25th. **State fair at:** Little Rock; late Sept.- early Oct.

History. First European explorers were de Soto, 1541, Jolliet, 1673; La Salle, 1682. First settlement was by the French under Henri de Tonty, 1686, at Arkansas Post. In 1762 the area was ceded by France to Spain, then back again in 1800, and was part of the Louisiana Purchase by the U.S. in 1803. Arkansas seceded from the Union in 1861, only after the Civil War began, and more than 10,000 Arkansans fought on the Union side.

Tourist attractions. 6 natl. parks & 40 state parks, inc. Hot Springs National Park, water ranging from 95° to 147°F. Eureka Springs, resort since 1880s; Blanchard Caverns, near Mountain View, are among the nation's largest; Crater of Diamonds, near Murfreesboro, only U.S. diamond mine; Buffalo Natl. River; Mid-America Museum, Ozark Folk Center.

Famous Arkansans include Dee Brown, Johnny Cash, Hattie Caraway, "Dizzy" Dean, Orval Faubus, James W. Fulbright, Douglas MacArthur, John L. McClellan, James S. McDonnel, Dick Powell, Winthrop Rockefeller, Mary Steenburgen, Edward Durell Stone, Archibald Yell.

Chamber of Commerce. One Spring Bldg., Little Rock, AR 72201.

Toll-free travel information. 1-800-643-8383 out of state; 800-482-8999 in Arkansas.

California
Golden State

People. Population (1988): 28,314,000; **rank:** 1. **Pop. density:** 178.4 per sq. mi. **Urban** (1985): 91.3%. **Racial distrib.** (1985): 85.6% White; 7.8% Black; 6.6% Other (includes American Indians, Asian Americans, and Pacific Islanders); Hispanic 5.9%. **Net change** (1980-1988): +4,646,000; 19.6%.

Geography. Total area 158,706 sq. mi.; **rank:** 3. **Land area:** 156,299 sq. mi. **Acres forested land:** 40,152,100. **Location:** on western coast of the U.S. **Climate:** moderate temperatures and rainfall along the coast; extremes in the interior. **Topography:** long mountainous coastline; central valley; Sierra Nevada on the east; desert basins of the southern interior; rugged mountains of the north. **Capital:** Sacramento.

Economy. Principal industries: agriculture, manufacturing, services, trade. **Principal manufactured goods:** foods, primary and fabricated metals, machinery, electric and electronic equipment, transportation equipment. **Agriculture: Chief crops:** grapes, cotton, flowers, oranges, nursery products, hay, tomatoes, lettuce, strawberries, almonds, broccoli, walnuts, sugar beets, peaches, potatoes. **Livestock** (1988): 4.7 mln. cattle & calves; 0.9 mln. hogs/pigs; 0.9 mln. sheep; 270.1 mln. poultry. **Timber/lumber** (1987): fir, pine, redwood, oak; 5.1 bln. bd. ft. **Nonfuel Minerals:** (1988): leading state in U.S., with value of $2.85 bln.; mostly asbestos, boron minerals, cement, diatomite, calcined gypsum, construction sand & gravel. **Commercial fishing** (1986): $199.3 mln. **Chief ports:** Long Beach, San Diego, Oakland, San Francisco, Sacramento, Stockton. **International airports at:** Los Angeles, San Francisco, San Jose. **Value of construction** (1988): $39.1 bln. **Employment distribution** (1988): 25.6% serv.; 23.7% trade; 17.8% manuf.; 15.9% gvt. **Per capita income** (1988): $18,855. **Unemployment** (1988): 5.3% **Tourism** (1988): $36.9 bln. **Sales tax:** 6-7%.

Finance. FDIC-insured commercial banks & trust companies (1987): 484. **Deposits:** $241 bln. **Savings institutions:** 207. **Assets:** $346.4 bln.

Federal government. No. federal civilian employees (Mar. 1988): 211,989. **Avg. salary:** $27,587. **Notable federal facilities:** Vandenberg, Beale, Travis, McClellan AF bases, San Francisco Mint.

Energy. Electricity production (1988, mwh, by source): Hydroelectric: 23.5 mln.; Mineral: 61.5 mln.; Nuclear: 30.9 mln.

Education. Expenditure per pupil, public schools (1987): $3,728. **Avg. salary, public school teachers** (1988-89 est.): $35,285.

State Data. Motto: Eureka (I have found it). **Flower:** Golden poppy. **Bird:** California valley quail. **Tree:** California redwood. **Song:** I Love You, California. **Entered Union** Sept. 9, 1850; rank, 31st. **State fair** at: Sacramento; late Aug.—early Sept.

History. First European explorers were Cabrillo, 1542, and Drake, 1579. First settlement was the Spanish Alta California mission at San Diego, 1769, first in a string founded by Franciscan Father Junipero Serra. U. S. traders and settlers arrived in the 19th century and staged the abortive Bear Flag Revolt, 1846; the Mexican War began later in 1846 and U.S. forces occupied California; Mexico ceded the province to the U.S., 1848, the same year the Gold Rush began.

Tourist attractions. Scenic regions are Yosemite Valley; Lassen and Sequoia-Kings Canyon national parks; Lake Tahoe; the Mojave and Colorado deserts; San Francisco Bay; and Monterey Peninsula. Oldest living things on earth are believed to be a stand of Bristlecone pines in the Inyo National Forest, est. to be 4,600 years old. The world's tallest tree, the Howard Libbey redwood, 362 ft. with a girth of 44 ft., stands on Redwood Creek, Humboldt County.

Also, RMS Queen Mary, Spruce Goose, both Long Beach; Palomar Observatory; Disneyland; J. Paul Getty Museum, Malibu; Tournament of Roses and Rose Bowl.

Famous Californians include Luther Burbank, John C. Fremont, Bret Harte, Wm. R. Hearst, Jack London, Aimee Semple McPherson, John Muir, Richard M. Nixon, William Saroyan, Junipero Serra, Leland Stanford, John Steinbeck, Earl Warren.

Chamber of Commerce: 1027 10th, Sacramento, CA 95814.

Toll-free travel information. 1-800-862-2543, x T100.

Colorado
Centennial State

People. Population (1988): 3,301,000; **rank:** 26. **Pop. density:** 31.7 per sq. mi. **Urban** (1980): 80.6%. **Racial distrib.** (1985): 96.3% White; 3.7% Black; Hispanic 383,500. **Net change** (1980-88): +411,000; 14.2%.

Geography. Total area: 104,091 sq. mi.; **rank:** 8. **Land area:** 103,595 sq. mi. **Acres forested land:** 22,271,000. **Location:** in west central U.S. **Climate:** low relative humidity, abundant sunshine, wide daily, seasonal temperatures ranges; alpine conditions in the high mountains. **Topography:** eastern dry high plains; hilly to mountainous central plateau; western Rocky Mountains of high ranges alternating with broad valleys and deep, narrow canyons. **Capital:** Denver.

Economy. Principal industries: manufacturing, government, tourism, agriculture, aerospace, electronics equipment. **Principal manufactured goods:** computer equipment, instruments, foods, machinery, aerospace products. **Agriculture: Chief crops:** corn, wheat, hay, sugar beets, barley, potatoes, apples, peaches, pears, dry edible beans, sorghum, onions, oats. **Livestock** (1988): 2.8 mln. cattle; 220,000 hogs/pigs; 825,000 sheep; 4.0 mln. poultry. **Timber/lumber** (1987): oak, ponderosa pine, Douglas fir; 135 mln. bd. ft. **Nonfuel Minerals** (1988): $375 mln.; gold, construction sand & gravel, crushed stone. **International airports at:** Denver. **Value of construction** (1988): $2.7 bln. **Employment distribution** (1987 est.): 26.7% serv.; 20.8% trade; 17.0% gvt.; 10.0% manuf. **Per capita income** (1988): $16,417. **Unemployment** (1988): 6.4%. **Tourism** (1988): $5.6 bln. **Sales Tax:** 3%.

Finance. FDIC-insured commercial banks & trust companies (1987): 471. **Deposits:** $21.6 bln. **Savings institutions:** 38. **Assets:** $14.8 bln.

Federal government. No. federal civilian employees (Mar. 1988): 36,006. **Avg. salary:** $28,328. **Notable federal facilities:** U.S. Air Force Academy; U.S. Mint; Ft. Carson, Lowry AFB; Solar Energy Research Institute; U.S. Rail Transport. Test Center; N. Amer. Aerospace Defense Command; Consolidated Space Operations Center; U.S. Documents Center, Fitzsimons Army Medical Center, Federal Center.

Energy. Electricity production (1988, mwh, by source): Hydroelectric: 1.7 mln.; Mineral: 28.5 min. Nuclear: 0.6 mln.

Education. Expenditures per pupil, public schools (1987): $4,147. **Avg. salary, public school teachers** (1988-89): $29,558.

State data. Motto: Nil Sine Numine (Nothing without Providence). **Flower:** Rocky Mountain columbine. **Bird:** Lark bunting. **Tree:** Colorado blue spruce. **Song:** Where the Columbines Grow. Entered union Aug. 1, 1876; rank 38th. **State fair at:** Pueblo; last week in Aug.

History. Early civilization centered around Mesa Verde 2,000 years ago. The U.S. acquired eastern Colorado in the Louisiana Purchase, 1803; Lt. Zebulon M. Pike explored the area, 1806, discovering the peak that bears his name. After the Mexican War, 1846-48, U.S. immigrants settled in the east, former Mexicans in the south.

Tourist attractions. 310 or more sunshine days per year; more than 1,000 peaks of 2 or more miles; Rocky Mountain National Park; Garden of the Gods; Great Sand Dunes, Dinosaur, Black Canyon of the Gunnison, and Colorado national monuments; Pikes Peak and Mt. Evans highways; Mesa Verde National Park (Ancient Anasazi Indian cliff dwellings); 35 major ski areas; the Grand Mesa tableland comprises Grand Mesa Forest, 659,584 acres, with 200 lakes stocked with trout. Mining towns of Central City, Silverton, Cripple Creek; Burlington's Old Town; Bent's Fort, outside La Junta; Georgetown Loop Historic Mining Railroad Park, Cumbres & Toltec Scenic Railroad.

Famous Coloradans include Frederick Bonfils, Molly Brown, William N. Byers, M. Scott Carpenter, Jack Dempsey, Mamie Eisenhower, Douglas Fairbanks, Scott Hamilton, "Baby Doe" Tabor, Lowell Thomas, Byron R. White, Paul Whiteman.

Toll-free travel information. 1-800-433-2656.

Connecticut
Constitution State, Nutmeg State

People. Population (1988): 3,233,000; **rank:** 28. **Pop. density:** 644.3 per sq. mi. **Urban** (1980): 78.8% **Racial distrib.** (1985): 92.3% White; 7.7% Black; Hispanic 139,200. **Net change** (1980-88): +126,000; 4.0%.

Geography. Total area: 5,018 sq. mi.; **rank:** 48. **Land area:** 4,872 sq. mi. **Acres forested land:** 1,860,800. **Location:** New England state in the northeastern corner of the U.S. **Climate:** moderate; winters avg. slightly below freezing, warm, humid summers. **Topography:** western upland, the Berkshires, in the NW, highest elevations; narrow central lowland N-S; hilly eastern upland drained by rivers. **Capital:** Hartford.

Economy. Principal industries: manufacturing, retail trade, government, services. **Principal manufactured goods:** aircraft engines and parts, submarines, copper, helicopters, bearings, instruments, electrical equipment. **Agriculture:** Chief crops: tobacco, hay, apples, potatoes, nursery stock. **Livestock** (1967): 60,000 cattle; 9,000 hogs/pigs; 6,000 sheep; 6.2 mln. poultry. **Timber/lumber:** oak, birch, beech, maple. **Nonfuel Minerals** (1988): $135 mln; crushed stone; construction sand & gravel. **Commercial fishing** (1988): $17.4 mln. **Chief ports:** New Haven, Bridgeport, New London. **International airports at:** Windsor Locks. **Value of construction** (1988): $4.4 mln. **Employment distribution:** 24.4% manuf.; 23% serv. **Per capita income** (1988): $22,761. **Unemployment** (1988): 3.0%. **Tourism** (1985): out-of-state visitors spent $2.5 bln. **Sales tax:** 7.5%.

Finance. FDIC-insured commercial banks & trust companies (1987): 59. **Deposits:** $26.7 bln. **Savings institutions:** 88. **Assets:** $43.5 bln.

Federal Government. No. federal civilian employees (Mar. 1988): 9,468. **Avg. salary:** $28,652. **Notable federal facilities:** U.S. Coast Guard Academy; U.S. Navy Submarine Base.

Energy. Electricity production (1988, mwh, by source): Hydroelectric: 324,000; Mineral: 13.6 mln.; Nuclear: 22.3 mln.

Education. Expenditures per pupil, public schools (1987): $5,435. **Avg. salary, public school teachers** (1988-89): $37,339.

State data. Motto: Qui Transtulit Sustinet (He who transplanted still sustains). **Flower:** Mountain laurel. **Bird:** American robin. **Tree:** White oak. **Song:** Yankee Doodle Dandy. Fifth of the 13 original states to ratify the Constitution, Jan. 9, 1788.

History. Adriaen Block, Dutch explorer, was the first European visitor, 1614. By 1634, settlers from Plymouth Bay started colonies along the Connecticut River and in 1637 defeated the Pequot Indians. In the Revolution, Connecticut men fought in most major campaigns and turned back British raids on Danbury and other towns, while Connecticut privateers captured British merchant ships.

Tourist attractions. Mark Twain House, Hartford; Yale University's Art Gallery, Peabody Museum, all in New Haven; Mystic Seaport; Mystic Marine Life Aquarium; P.T. Barnum Museum, Bridgeport; Gillette Castle, Hadlyme; U.S.S. Nautilus Memorial, Groton (1st nuclear-powered submarine).

Famous "Nutmeggers" include Ethan Allen, Phineas T. Barnum, Samuel Colt, Jonathan Edwards, Nathan Hale, Katharine Hepburn, Isaac Hull, J. Pierpont Morgan, Israel Putnam, Harriet Beecher Stowe, Mark Twain, Noah Webster, Eli Whitney.

Tourist information. State Dept. of Economic Development, 210 Washington St., Hartford, CT 06106.

Toll-free travel information. 1-800-243-1685 out of state; 800-842-7492 in Connecticut.

Delaware
First State, Diamond State

People. Population (1988): 660,000; **rank:** 47. **Pop. density:** 322.7 per sq. mi. **Urban** (1980): 70.6%. **Racial distrib.** (1985): 82.9% White; 17.1% Black; Hispanic 10,000. **Net change** (1980-88): +66.000; 11.1%.

Geography. Total area: 2,045 sq. mi.; **rank:** 49. **Land area:** 1,932 sq. mi. **Acres forested land:** 391,800. **Location:** occupies the Delmarva Peninsula on the Atlantic coastal plain. **Climate:** moderate. **Topography:** Piedmont plateau to the N, sloping to a near sea-level plain. **Capital:** Dover.

Economy. Principal industries: chemistry, agriculture, finance, poultry, shellfish, tourism, auto assembly, food processing, transportation equipment. **Principal manufactured goods:** nylon, apparel, luggage, foods, autos, processed meats and vegetables, railroad and aircraft equipment. **Agriculture:** Chief crops: soybeans, potatoes, corn, mushrooms, lima beans, green peas, barley, cucumbers, snap beans, watermelons, apples. **Livestock** (1988): 29,000 cattle; 217.5 mln. broilers. **Nonfuel Minerals** (1988): $4 mln; construction sand & gravel, magnesium compounds, greensand marl. **Commercial fishing** (1988): $3.2 mln. **Chief ports:** Wilmington. **International airports at:** Philadelphia/Wilmington. **Value of construction** (1988): $813.4 mln. **Employment distribution** (1988): 78.9% non-manufacturing; 21.1% manuf. **Per capita income** (1988): $17,699. **Unemployment** (1988): 3.2%. **Tourism** (1985): out-of-state visitors spent $666 mln.

Finance. FDIC-insured commercial banks & trust companies (1987): 42. **Deposits:** $16.4 bln. **Savings institutions:** 6. **Assets:** $1.9 bln.

Federal government. No. federal civilian employees (Mar. 1988): 2,987. **Avg. salary:** $26,186. **Notable federal facilities:** Dover Air Force Base, Federal Wildlife Refuge, Bombay Hook.

Energy. Electricity production (1988, mwh, by source): Mineral: 9.0 mln.

Education. Expenditure per pupil, public schools (1987): $4,825. **Avg. salary, public school teachers** (1988-89): $31,605.

State data. Motto: Liberty and independence. **Flower:** Peach blossom. **Bird:** Blue hen chicken. **Tree:** American holly. **Song:** Our Delaware. First of original 13 states to ratify the Constitution, Dec. 7, 1787. **State fair** at: Harrington; end of July.

History. The Dutch first settled in Delaware near present Lewes, 1631, but were wiped out by Indians. Swedes settled at present Wilmington, 1638; Dutch settled anew, 1651, near New Castle and seized the Swedish settlement, 1655, only to lose all Delaware and New Netherland to the British, 1664.

Tourist attractions. Ft. Christina Monument, the site of founding of New Sweden; John Dickinson "Penman of the Revolution" home, Dover; Henry Francis du Pont Winterthur Museum; Hagley Museum, Wilmington; Rehoboth Beach, "nation's summer capitol," Rehoboth; Dover Downs Intl. Speedway, Dover; Old Swedes (Trinity Parish) Church, erected 1698, is the oldest Protestant church in the U.S. still in use.

Famous Delawareans include Thomas F. Bayard, Henry Seidel Canby, E. I. du Pont, John P. Marquand, Howard Pyle, Caesar Rodney.

Chamber of Commerce. One Commerce Center, Wilmington, DE 19801.

Toll-free travel information. 1-800-441-8846.

Florida
Sunshine State

People. Population (1988): 12,335,000; **rank:** 4. **Pop. density:** 210.3 per sq. mi. **Urban** (1980): 84.3%. **Racial distrib.** (1985): 86.1% White; 13.9% Black; Hispanic 1.1 mln. **Net change** (1980-88): +2,588,000; 26.6%.

Geography. Total area: 58,664 sq. mi.; **rank:** 22. **Land area:** 54,153 sq. mi. **Acres forested land:** 17,039,700. **Location:** peninsula jutting southward 500 mi. bet. the Atlantic and the Gulf of Mexico. **Climate:** subtropical N of Bradenton-Lake Okeechobee-Vero Beach line; tropical S of line. **Topography:** land is flat or rolling; highest point is 345 ft. in the NW. **Capital:** Tallahassee.

Economy. Principal industries: services, trade, gvt., manufacturing, tourism. **Principal manufactured goods:** electric & electronic equip., transp. equipment; food; printing & publishing; machinery. **Agriculture: Chief crops:** citrus fruits, vegetables, potatoes, melons, strawberries, sugar cane. **Livestock** (1987): 1.97 mln. cattle; 150,000 hogs/pigs; 7,360 sheep; 13.5 mln. poultry. **Timber/lumber** (1987): pine, cypress, cedar; 597 mln. bd. ft. **Nonfuel Minerals** (1988): $1.5 bln.; mostly cement, phosphate rock, crushed stone. **Commercial fishing** (1988): $169.6 mln. **Chief ports:** Pensacola, Tampa, Miami, Port Everglades, Jacksonville, St. Petersburg, Canaveral. **International airports at:** Miami, Tampa, Jacksonville, Orlando, Ft. Lauderdale, W. Palm Beach. **Value of construction** (1988): $18.9 bln. **Per capita income** (1988): $16,546. **Unemployment** (1988): 5.0% **Tourism** (1988): out-of-state visitors spent $24.3 bln. **Sales tax:** 6%.

Finance. FDIC-insured commercial banks & trust companies (1987): 417. **Deposits:** $87.2 bln. **Savings institutions:** 157. **Assets:** $83.8 bln.

Federal government. No. federal civilian employees (Mar. 1988): 59,315. **Avg. salary:** $27,669. **Notable federal facilities:** John F. Kennedy Space Center, NASA-Kennedy Space Center's Spaceport USA; Eglin Air Force Base.

Energy. Electricity production (1988, mwh, by source): Hydroelectric: 209,000; Mineral: 97.7 mln.; Nuclear: 26.2 mln.

Education. Expenditure per pupil, public schools (1987): $3,794. **Avg. salary, public school teachers** (1988-89): $26,648.

State data. Motto: In God we trust. **Flower:** Orange blossom. **Bird:** Mockingbird. **Tree:** Sabal palmetto palm. **Song:** Old Folks at Home. **Entered union** Mar. 3, 1845; rank, 27th. **State fair** at: Tampa; early to mid-Feb.

History. First European to see Florida was Ponce de Leon, 1513. France established a colony, Fort Caroline, on the St. Johns River, 1564; Spain settled St. Augustine, 1565, and Spanish troops massacred most of the French. Britain's Francis Drake burned St. Augustine, 1586. Britain

held the area briefly, 1763-83, returning it to Spain. After Andrew Jackson led a U.S. invasion, 1818, Spain ceded Florida to the U.S., 1819. The Seminole War, 1835-42, resulted in removal of most Indians to Oklahoma. Florida seceded from the Union, 1861, was readmitted, 1868.

Tourist attractions. Miami, with a variety of luxury hotels at Miami Beach; St. Augustine, oldest city in U.S.; Walt Disney World's Magic Kingdom and EPCOT; Spaceport U.S.A.

Everglades National Park, 3d largest of U.S. national parks, preserves the beauty of the vast Everglades swamp. Castillo de San Marcos, St. Augustine, is a national monument. Also, the Ringling Museum of Art, and the Ringling Museum of the Circus, both in Sarasota; Sea World, and Circus World, Orlando; Busch Gardens, Tampa.

Famous Floridians include Henry M. Flagler, James Weldon Johnson, MacKinlay Kantor, Henry B. Plant, Marjorie Kinnan Rawlings, Joseph W. Stilwell, Charles P. Summerall.

Tourist information. Florida Division of Tourism, 126 Van Buren St., Tallahassee, FL 32399-2000, 1-904-487-1462.

Georgia
Empire State of the South, Peach State

People. Population (1988): 6,342,000; **rank:** 11. **Pop. density:** 107.7 per sq. mi. **Urban** (1980): 62.4%. **Racial distrib.** (1985): 73.0% White; 27.0% Black; Hispanic 47,700. **Net** (1980-88): +879,000; 16.1%.

Geography. Total area: 58,910 sq. mi.; **rank:** 21. **Land area:** 58,056 sq. mi. **Acres forested land:** 25,256,000. **Location:** South Atlantic state. **Climate:** maritime tropical air masses dominate in summer; continental polar air masses in winter; east central area drier. **Topography:** most southerly of the Blue Ridge Mtns. cover NE and N central; central Piedmont extends to the fall line of rivers; coastal plain levels to the coast flatlands. **Capital:** Atlanta.

Economy. Principal industries: manufacturing, forestry, agriculture, chemicals. **Principal manufactured goods** (1988): textiles, apparel, food, electric, electronic machinery, transportation equipment, lumber, paper. **Agriculture Chief crops:** peanuts, corn, soybeans, tobacco, corn, cotton. **Livestock** (1988): 1.5 mln. cattle; 1.2 mln. hogs/pigs; 8,726 sheep; **Timber/lumber** (1987): pine, hardwood; 2.5 bln. bd. ft. **Nonfuel Minerals** (1988): $1.3 bln.; clays, crushed stone. **Commercial fishing** (1988): $21.5 mln. **Chief ports:** Savannah, Brunswick. **International airports at:** Atlanta. **Value of construction** (1988): $8.3 bln. **Employment distribution:** 25% trade; 19% serv.; 17% gvt. **Per capita income** (1988): $14,980. **Unemployment** (1988): 5.8% **Tourism** (1988): tourists spent $8.6 bln.

Finance. FDIC-insured commercial banks & trust companies (1987): 369. **Deposits:** $39.0 bln. **Savings institutions:** 69. **Assets:** $18.2 bln.

Federal government. No. federal civilian employees (Mar. 1988): 67,066. **Avg. salary:** $26,473. **Notable federal facilities:** Dobbins AFB; Fts. Benning, Gordon, McPherson; Fed. Law Enforcement Training Ctr., Glynco, Warner Robins AFB; Centers for Disease Control, Atlanta.

Energy. Electricity production (1987, mwh, by source): Hydroelectric: 2.0 mln.; Mineral: 64.9 mln.; Nuclear: 15.2 mln.

Education. Expenditure per pupil, public schools (1987): $3,374. **Avg. salary, public school teachers** (1988-89): $28,038.

State data. Motto: Wisdom, justice and moderation. **Flower:** Cherokee rose. **Bird:** Brown thrasher. **Tree:** Live oak. **Song:** Georgia On My Mind. **Fourth** of the 13 original states to ratify the Constitution, Jan. 2, 1788.

History. Gen. James Oglethorpe established the first settlements, 1733, for poor and religiously-persecuted Englishmen. Oglethorpe defeated a Spanish army from Florida at Bloody Marsh, 1742. In the Revolution, Georgians seized the Savannah armory, 1775, and sent the munitions to the Continental Army; they fought seesaw campaigns with Cornwallis' British troops, twice liberating Augusta and forcing final evacuation by the British from Savannah, 1782.

Tourist attractions. The Little White House in Warm Springs where Pres. Franklin D. Roosevelt died Apr. 12, 1945, 2,500-acre Callaway Gardens, Jekyll Island State Park, the restored 1850s farming community of Westville; Alpine Helen, tiny mountain town converted to Alpine Village. Dahlonega, site of America's first gold rush; Air Force Museum, Robins AFB; Underground Atlanta, Six Flags Over Georgia, Stone Mountain, Martin Luther King, Jr. Natl. Historic Site, Jimmy Carter Library & Museum, Atlanta; historic riverfront, Savannah; Georgia's Golden Isles; Andersonville Natl. Historic Site.

Okefenokee in the SE is one of the largest swamps in the U.S., a wetland wilderness and peat bog covering 660 sq. mi. A large part of it is a National Wildlife Refuge, a home for wild birds, alligators, bear, deer, many rare plants.

Famous Georgians include Hank Aaron, Griffin Bell, James Bowie, Erskine Caldwell, Jimmy Carter, Ray Charles, Lucius D. Clay, Ty Cobb, John C. Fremont, Joel Chandler Harris, Gladys Knight, Juliette Gordon Low, Martin Luther King Jr., Sidney Lanier, Margaret Mitchell, Flannery O'Connor, Jackie Robinson, Joseph Wheeler.

Chamber of Commerce. 235 International Blvd., Atlanta, GA 30303.

Toll-free travel information. 1-800-VISIT GA.

Hawaii
The Aloha State

People. Population (1988): 1,098,000; **rank:** 39. **Pop. density:** 169.7 per sq. mi. **Urban** (1980): 86.5%. **Racial distrib.** (1985): 24.5% Caucasian; 23.2% Japanese; 11.3% Filipino; 20% Hawaiian and part-Hawaiian. **Net change** (1980-88): +134,000; 13.8%.

Geography. Total area: 6,471 sq. mi.; **rank:** 47. **Land area:** 6,425 sq. mi. **Acres forested land:** 1,986,000. **Location:** Hawaiian Islands lie in the North Pacific, 2,397 mi. SW from San Francisco. **Climate:** subtropical, with wide variations in rainfall; Waialeale, on Kauai, wettest spot in U.S. (annual rainfall 444 in.) **Topography:** islands are tops of a chain of submerged volcanic mountains; active volcanoes: Mauna Loa, Kilauea. **Capital:** Honolulu.

Economy. Principal industries: tourism, defense and other government, sugar refining, pineapple and diversified agriculture, aquaculture, fishing, motion pictures. **Principal manufactured goods:** sugar, canned pineapple, clothing, foods, printing and publishing. **Agriculture: Chief crops:** sugar, pineapples, macadamia nuts, fruits, coffee, vegetables, melons, and floriculture. **Livestock** (1987): 199,000 cattle and calves; 47,000 hogs/pigs; 1.21 mln. chickens. **Nonfuel Minerals** (1988): $78 mln.; mostly crushed stone & cement. **Commercial fishing** (1988): $39.8 mln. **Chief ports:** Honolulu, Nawiliwili, Barbers Point, Kahului, Hilo. **International airports at:** Honolulu. **Value of construction** (1988): $1.7 bln. **Employment distribution** (1988): 24% trade; 24.5% serv.; 19.3% gvt. **Per capita income** (1988): $16,898. **Unemployment** (1988): 3.2%. **Tourism** (1987): visitors spent $6.6 bln. **General excise tax:** 4%.

Finance. FDIC-insured commercial banks & trust companies: (1987): 22. **Deposits:** $9.8 bln. **Savings institutions:** 6. **Assets:** $5.5 bln.

Federal government. No. federal civilian employees (Mar. 1988): 22,883. **Avg. salary:** $28,591. **Notable federal facilities:** Pearl Harbor Naval Shipyard; Hickam AFB; Schofield Barracks.

Energy. Electricity production (1988, mwh, by source): Hydroelectric: 14,000; Mineral: 7.6 mln.

Education. Expenditure per pupil, public schools (1987): $3,787. **Avg. Salary, public school teachers** (1988-89): $30,778.

State data. Motto: The life of the land is perpetuated in righteousness. **Flower:** Yellow Hibiscus. **Bird:** Hawaiian

goose. **Tree:** Candlenut. **Song:** Hawaii Ponoi. **Entered union** Aug. 21, 1959; **rank,** 50th. **State fair at:** Honolulu; late May–mid-June.

History. Polynesians from islands 2,000 mi. to the south settled the Hawaiian Islands, probably between 300 A.D. and 600 A.D. First European visitor was British Capt. James Cook, 1778. Missionaries arrived, 1820, taught religion, reading and writing. King Kamehameha III and his chiefs created the first Constitution and a Legislature which set up a public school system. Sugar production began in 1835 and it became the dominant industry. In 1893, Queen Liliuokalani was deposed, followed, 1894, by a republic headed by Sanford B. Dole. Annexation by the U.S. came in 1898.

Tourist attractions. Hawaii Volcanoes, Haleakala National Parks; Polynesian Cultural Center, Waikiki Beach, Nuuanu Pali, Bishop Museum, Waimea Canyon, Wailua River State Park, Honolulu Academy of Arts.

Famous Islanders include Bernice Pauahi Bishop, John A. Burns, Father Damien de Veuster, Daniel K. Inouye, Duke Kahanamoku, King Kamehameha the Great, Queen Kaahumanu, Queen Liliuokalani, Ellison Onizuka.

Chamber of Commerce. Dillingham Bldg., 735 Bishop St., Honolulu, HI 96813.

Idaho
Gem State

People. Population (1988): 1,003,000; **rank:** 42. **Pop. density:** 12.0 per sq. mi. **Urban** (1980): 54.0%. **Racial distrib.** (1980): 95.5% White; 0.3% Black; Hispanic 41,800. **Net change** (1980-88): +59,000; 6.2%.

Geography. Total area: 83,564 sq. mi.; **rank:** 13. **Land area:** 82,412 sq. mi. **Acres forested land:** 21,726,600. **Location:** Pacific Northwest-Mountain state bordering on British Columbia. **Climate:** tempered by Pacific westerly winds; drier, colder, continental clime in SE; altitude an important factor. **Topography:** Snake R. plains in the S; central region of mountains, canyons, gorges (Hells Canyon, 7,000 ft., deepest in N.A.); subalpine northern region. **Capital:** Boise.

Economy. Principal industries: agriculture, manufacturing, tourism, lumber, mining, electronics. **Principal manufactured goods:** processed foods, lumber and wood products, chemical products, primary metals, fabricated metal products, machinery, electronic components. **Agriculture: Chief crops:** potatoes, peas, sugar beets, alfalfa seed, wheat, hops, barley, plums and prunes, mint, onions, corn, cherries, apples, hay. **Livestock:** 1.89 mln. cattle; 120,000 hogs/pigs; 383,000 sheep; 1.27 mln. poultry. **Timber/lumber** (1987): yellow, white pine; Douglas fir; white spruce; 2.2 bln. bd. ft. **Nonfuel Minerals** (1988): $339 mln.; phosphate rock, silver, gold, sand & gravel. **Chief ports:** Lewiston. **Value of construction** (1988) $846.3 mln. **Employment distribution:** 21% trade; 15% serv., 14% manuf.; 10% agric. **Per capita income** (1988): $12,657. **Unemployment** (1988): 5.8%. **Tourism** (1982): travellers spent $1.2 bln.

Finance. FDIC-insured commercial banks & trust companies (1987): 24. **Deposits:** $5.9 bln. **Savings institutions:** 7. **Assets:** $929 mln.

Federal government. No. federal civilian employees (Mar. 1988): 6,946. **Avg. salary:** $27,764. **Notable federal facilities:** Ida. Nat'l. Engineering Lab, Idaho Falls; Nat'l. Reactor Testing Sta., Upper Snake River Plains.

Energy. Electricity production (1988, mwh, by source): Hydroelectric: 6.8 mln.

Education. Expenditure per pupil, public schools (1987): $2,585. **Avg. salary, public school teachers** (1988-89): $22,860.

State data. Motto: Esto Perpetua (It is perpetual). **Flower:** Syringa. **Bird:** Mountain bluebird. **Tree:** White pine. **Song:** Here We Have Idaho. **Entered union** July 3, 1890; **rank,** 43d. **State fair at:** Boise, late Aug.; and Blackfoot, early Sept.

History. Exploration of the Idaho area began with Lewis and Clark, 1805-06. Next came fur traders, setting up posts, 1809-34, and missionaries, establishing missions, 1830s-1850s. Mormons made their first permanent settlement at Franklin, 1860. Idaho's Gold Rush began that same year, and brought thousands of permanent settlers. Strangest of the Indian Wars was the 1,300-mi. trek in 1877 of Chief Joseph and the Nez Perce tribe, pursued by troops that caught them a few miles short of the Canadian border. In 1890, Idaho adopted a progressive Constitution and became a state.

Tourist attractions. Hells Canyon, deepest gorge in N.A.; Craters of the Moon; Sun Valley, year-round resort in the Sawtooth Mtns.; Crystal Falls Cave; Shoshone Falls; Lava Hot Springs; Lake Pend Oreille; Lake Coeur d'Alene; Sawtooth Natl. Recreation Area; River of No Return Wilderness Area.

Famous Idahoans include William E. Borah, Frank Church, Fred T. Dubois, Chief Joseph, Sacagawea.

Tourist information. Department of Commerce, Room 108, State House, Boise, ID 83720.

Illinois

The Prairie State

People. Population (1988): 11,614,000; **rank:** 6. **Pop. density:** 206.1 per sq. mi. **Urban** (1980): 83.3%. **Racial distrib.** (1985): 84.6% White; 15.4% Black; Hispanic 754,900. **Net change** (1980-88): +187,000; 1.6%.

Geography. Total area: 56,345 sq. mi.; **rank:** 24. **Land area:** 55,645 sq. mi. **Acres forested land:** 3,810,400. **Location:** east-north central state; western, southern, and eastern boundaries formed by Mississippi, Ohio, and Wabash Rivers, respectively. **Climate:** temperate; typically cold, snowy winters, hot summers. **Topography:** prairie and fertile plains throughout; open hills in the southern region. **Capital:** Springfield.

Economy. Principal industries: manufacturing, wholesale and retail trade, finance, insurance, foods, agriculture. **Principal manufactured goods:** machinery, electric and electronic equipment, primary and fabricated metals, chemical products, printing and publishing. **Agriculture:** Chief crops: corn, soybeans, wheat, oats, hay. **Livestock** (1987): 2.25 mln. cattle; 5.3 mln. hogs/pigs; 119,000 sheep; 3.27 mln. poultry. **Timber/lumber** (1987): oak, hickory, maple, cottonwood; 107 mln. bd. ft. **Nonfuel Minerals** (1988): $549 mln.; mostly crushed stone, cement, construction & industrial sand & gravel. **Commercial fishing** (1988): $330,000. **Chief ports:** Chicago. **International airports at:** Chicago. **Value of construction** (1988): $10.1 bln. **Employment distribution** (1987): 25.0% trade; 23.6% serv.; 19.0% manuf. **Per capita income** (1988): $17,611. **Unemployment** (1988) 6.8%. **Tourism** (1987): out-of-state visitors spent $10.5 bln. **Sales tax:** 5%.

Finance. FDIC-insured commercial banks & trust companies (1987): 1,219. **Deposits:** $134.7 bln. **Savings institutions:** 264. **Assets:** $68.9 bln.

Federal government. No. federal civilian employees (Mar. 1988): 54,152. **Avg. salary:** $27,713. **Notable federal facilities:** Fermi Nat'l. Accelerator Lab; Argonne Nat'l. Lab; Ft. Sheridan; Rock Island; Great Lakes, Naval Training Station, Scott AFB.

Energy. Electricity production (1988, mwh, by source): Hydroelectric: 48,000; Mineral: 54.1 mln.; Nuclear: 69.2 mln.

Education. Expenditure per pupil, public schools (1987): $4,106. **Avg. salary, public school teachers** (1988-89): $31,195.

State data. Motto: State sovereignty—national union. **Flower:** Native violet. **Bird:** Cardinal. **Tree:** White oak. **Song:** Illinois. **Entered union** Dec. 3, 1818; **rank,** 21st. **State fair** at: Springfield; early Aug.

History. Fur traders were the first Europeans in Illinois, followed shortly, 1673, by Jolliet and Marquette, and, 1680, La Salle, who built a fort near present Peoria. First settlements were French, at Fort St. Louis on the Illinois River, 1692, and Kaskaskia, 1700. France ceded the area to Britain, 1763; Amer. Gen. George Rogers Clark, 1778, took Kaskaskia from the British without a shot. Defeat of

Indian tribes in Black Hawk War, 1832, and railroads in 1850s, inspired imchange.

Tourist attractions: Chicago museums, parks; Lincoln shrines at Springfield, New Salem, Sangamon; Cahokia Mounds, E. St. Louis; Starved Rock State Park; Crab Orchard Wildlife Refuge; Mormon settlement at Nauvoo; Fts. Kaskaskia, Chartres, Massac (parks); Shawnee Natl. Forest, Southern Illinois; Illinois State Museum, Springfield; Dickson Mounds Museum, btwn. Havana & Lewistown.

Famous Illinoisans include Jane Addams, Saul Bellow, Jack Benny, Ray Bradbury, Gwendolyn Brooks, William Jennings Bryan, St. Francis Xavier Cabrini, Clarence Darrow, Stephen A. Douglas, James T. Farrell, Betty Friedan, Ulysses S. Grant, Ernest Hemingway, Wild Bill Hickock, Abraham Lincoln, Vachel Lindsay, Edgar Lee Masters, Ronald Reagan, Carl Sandburg, Adlai Stevenson, Frank Lloyd Wright.

Tourist information. Illinois Dept. of Commerce and Community Affairs, 620 E. Adams St., Springfield, IL 62701.

Toll-free literature on Illinois events. 1-800-223-0121.

Indiana

Hoosier State

People. Population (1988): 5,556,000; **rank:** 14. **Pop. density:** 153.5 per sq. mi. **Urban** (1980): 64.2%. **Racial distrib.** (1985): 92.0 White; 8.0% Black; Hispanic 182,600. **Net change** (1980-88): +66,000; 1.2%.

Geography. Total area: 36,185 sq. mi.; **rank:** 38. **Land area:** 35,932 sq. mi. **Acres forested land:** 3,942,900. **Location:** east north-central state; Lake Michigan on northern border. **Climate:** 4 distinct seasons with a temperate climate. **Topography:** hilly southern region; fertile rolling plains of central region; flat, heavily glaciated north; dunes along Lake Michigan shore. **Capital:** Indianapolis.

Economy. Principal industries: manufacturing, wholesale and retail trade, agriculture, government, services. **Principal manufactured goods:** primary and fabricated metals, transportation equipment, electrical and electronic equipment, non-electrical machinery, plastics, chemical products, foods. **Agriculture:** Chief crops (1986): corn, sorghum, oats, wheat, rye, soybeans, hay. **Livestock** (1986): 1.5 mln. cattle; 4.2 mln. hogs/pigs; 91,000 sheep; 28 mln. chickens. **Timber/lumber** (1987): oak, tulip, beech, sycamore; 397 mln. bd. ft. **Nonfuel Minerals** (1988): $385 mln.; mostly crushed stone, abrasives, cement, construction sand & gravel. **Commercial fishing** (1987): $1.7 mln. **Chief ports:** Burns Harbor, Portage; Southwind Maritime, Mt. Vernon; Clark Maritime, Jeffersonville. **International airports at:** Indianapolis. **Value of construction** (1988): $5.1 bln. **Employment distribution** (1986): 27.1% manuf.; 23.6% trade; 19.2% serv. **Per capita income** (1988): $14,721. **Unemployment** (1988): 5.3%. **Tourism** (1985): tourists spent $3 bln. **Sales tax:** 5%, with exemptions.

Finance. FDIC-insured commercial banks & trust companies (1987): 355. **Deposits:** $40.7 bln. **Savings institutions:** 117. **Assets:** $14.1 bln.

Federal government. No. federal civilian employees (Mar. 1988): 26,079. **Avg. salary:** $25,774. **Notable federal facilities:** Naval Avionics Ctr.; Ft. Benjamin Harrison; Grissom AFB; Navy Weapons Support Ctr., Crane.

Energy. Electricity production (1988 mwh, by source): Hydroelectric: 441,000; Mineral: 83.5 mln.

Education. Expenditure per pupil, public schools (1987): $3,558. **Avg. salary, public school teachers** (1988-89): $28,664.

State data. Motto: Crossroads of America. **Flower:** Peony. **Bird:** Cardinal. **Tree:** Tulip poplar. **Song:** On the Banks of the Wabash, Far Away. **Entered union** Dec. 11, 1816; **rank,** 19th. **State fair** at: Indianapolis; mid-Aug.

History. Pre-historic Indian Mound Builders of 1,000 years ago were the earliest known inhabitants. A French trading post was built, 1731-32, at Vincennes and La Salle visited the present South Bend area, 1679 and 1681.

France ceded the area to Britain, 1763. During the Revolution, American Gen. George Rogers Clark captured Vincennes, 1778, and defeated British forces 1779; at war's end Britain ceded the area to the U.S. Miami Indians defeated U.S. troops twice, 1790, but were beaten, 1794, at Fallen Timbers by Gen. Anthony Wayne. At Tippecanoe, 1811, Gen. William H. Harrison defeated Tecumseh's Indian confederation. ·

Tourist attractions. Lincoln Boyhood, George Rogers Clark memorials; Wyandotte Cave; Vincennes, Tippecanoe sites; Indiana Dunes; Hoosier Nat'l. Forest; Benjamin Harrison Home.

Famous "Hoosiers" include Larry Bird, Ambrose Burnside, Hoagy Carmichael, Jim Davis, James Dean, Eugene V. Debs, Theodore Dreiser, Paul Dresser, Gil Hodges, David Letterman, Jane Pauley, Cole Porter, Gene Stratton Porter, Ernie Pyle, James Whitcomb Riley, Oscar Robertson, Red Skelton, Booth Tarkington, Lew Wallace, Wendell L. Willkie, Wilbur Wright.

Chamber of Commerce. One North Capital, Suite 200, Indianapolis, IN 46204.

Toll-free travel information. 1-800-2-WANDER.

Iowa

Hawkeye State

People. Population (1988): 2,834,000; **rank:** 29. **Pop. density:** 50.4 per sq. mi. **Urban** (1980): 58.6%. **Racial distrib.** (1985): 98.4% White; 1.6% Black; 0.5% Hispanic 25,800. **Net change** (1980-88): —80,000; —2.7%.

Geography. Total area: 56,275 sq. mi.; **rank:** 25. **Land area:** 55,965 sq. mi. **Acres forested land:** 1,561,300. **Location:** Midwest state bordered by Mississippi R. on the E and Missouri R. on the W. **Climate:** humid, continental. **Topography:** Watershed from NW to SE; soil especially rich and land level in the N central counties. **Capital:** Des Moines.

Economy. Principal industries: insurance, manufacturing, agriculture. **Principal manufactured goods:** tires, farm machinery, electronic products, appliances, office furniture, chemicals, fertilizers, auto accessories. **Agriculture: Chief crops:** silage and grain corn, soybeans, oats, hay. **Livestock** (1988): 4.8 mln. cattle; 13.9 mln. hogs/pigs; 415,000 sheep; 3 mln. poultry. **Timber/lumber** (1987): red cedar; 45 mln. bd. ft. **Nonfuel Minerals** (1988): $314 mln.; mostly crushed stone, portland cement, construction sand & gravel. **Value of construction** (1988): 1.6 bln. **Employment distribution** (1988): 25.5% trade; 22.1% serv; 19.7% manuf.; 18.8% gvt. **Per capita income** (1988): $14,764. **Unemployment** (1988): 4.5%. **Tourism** (1986): tourists spent $2 bln. **Sales tax:** 4%.

Finance. FDIC-insured commercial banks & trust companies (1987): 614. **Deposits:** $26.0 bln. **Savings institutions:** 54. **Assets:** $9.5 bln.

Federal government. No. federal civilian employees (Mar. 1988): 7,852. **Avg. salary:** $26,225.

Energy. Electricity production (1988, mwh, by source): Hydroelectric: 698,000; Mineral: 23.1 mln.; Nuclear: 3.2 mln.

Education. Expenditure per pupil, public schools (1987): $3,808. **Avg. salary, public school teachers** (1988-89): $25,884.

State data. Motto: Our liberties we prize and our rights we will maintain. **Flower:** Wild rose. **Bird:** Eastern goldfinch. **Tree:** Oak. **Rock:** Geode. **Entered union** Dec. 28, 1846; **rank,** 29th. **State fair at:** Des Moines; mid-to-late Aug.

History. A thousand years ago several groups of prehistoric Indian Mound Builders dwelt on Iowa's fertile plains. Marquette and Jolliet gave France its claim to the area, 1673. It became U.S. territory through the 1803 Louisiana Purchase. Indian tribes were moved into the area from states further east, but by mid-19th century were forced to move on to Kansas. Before and during the Civil War, Iowans strongly supported Abraham Lincoln and became traditional Republicans.

Tourist attractions. Herbert Hoover birthplace and library, West Branch; Effigy Mounds Nat'l. Monument, Marquette, a pre-historic Indian burial site; Amana colonies; Davenport Municipal Art Gallery's collection of Grant Wood's paintings and memorabilia; Living History Farms, Des Moines; Adventureland, Altoona; Boone & Scenic Valley Railroad, Boone; Greyhound Parks in Dubuque, Council Bluffs & Waterloo; Prairie Meadows horse racing, Altoona.

Famous Iowans include James A. Van Allen, Marquis Childs, Buffalo Bill Cody, Mamie Dowd Eisenhower, George Gallup, Susan Glaspell, James Norman Hall, Harry Hansen, Herbert Hoover, Glenn Miller, Billy Sunday, Carl Van Vechten, Henry Wallace, John Wayne, Meredith Willson, Grant Wood.

Tourist information. Bureau of Tourism & Visitors, Iowa Dept. of Economic Development, 200 E. Grand Ave. Des Moines, IA 50309.

Toll-free travel information. 1-800-345-IOWA.

Kansas

Sunflower State

People. Population (1988): 2,495,000; **rank:** 32. **Pop. density:** 30.3 per sq. mi. **Urban** (1980): 66.7%. **Racial distrib.** (1985): 94.4% White; 5.6% Black; Hispanic 69,900. **Net change** (1980-88): +131,000; 5.6%.

Geography. Total area: 82,277 sq. mi.; **rank:** 14. **Land area:** 81,778 sq. mi. **Acres forested land:** 1,344,400. **Location:** West North Central state, with Missouri R. on E. **Climate:** temperate but continental, with great extremes bet. summer and winter. **Topography:** hilly Osage Plains in the E; central region level prairie and hills; high plains in the W. **Capital:** Topeka.

Economy. Principal industries: agriculture, machinery, mining, aerospace. **Principal manufactured goods:** processed foods, aircraft, petroleum products, farm machinery. **Agriculture: Chief crops:** wheat, sorghum, corn, hay. **Livestock** (1988): 5.86 mln. cattle; 1.45 mln. hogs/pigs; 277,000 sheep; 2.1 mln. poultry. **Timber/lumber:** oak, walnut. **Nonfuel Minerals** (1988): $308 mln.; cement, salt, crushed stone. **Chief ports:** Kansas City. **International airports at:** Wichita. **Value of construction** (1988): $2.1 bln. **Employment distribution** (1988): 25.0% trade; 20.5% serv.; 19.9% gvt.; 17.1% manuf. **Per capita income** (1988): $15,905. **Unemployment** (1988): 4.8%. **Tourism** (1985): out-of-state visitors spent $1.9 bln. **Sales tax:** 6.25% maximum.

Finance. FDIC-insured commercial banks & trust companies (1987): 613. **Deposits:** $21.5 bln. **Savings institutions:** 55. **Assets:** $20.5 bln.

Federal government. No. federal civilian employees (Mar. 1988): 15,712. **Avg. salary:** $25,780. **Notable federal facilities:** McConnell AFB; Fts. Riley, Leavenworth.

Energy. Electricity production (1988, mwh, by source): Hydroelectric: 12,000; Mineral: 24.7 mln; Nuclear: 6.7 mln.

Education. Expenditure per pupil, public schools (1987): $3,933. **Avg. salary, public school teachers** (1988-89): $27,401.

State data. Motto: Ad Astra per Aspera (To the stars through difficulties). **Flower:** Native sunflower. **Bird:** Western meadowlark. **Tree:** Cottonwood. **Song:** Home on the Range. **Entered union** Jan. 29, 1861; **rank,** 34th. **State fair at:** Hutchinson; 2d week of Sept.

History. Coronado marched through the Kansas area, 1541; French explorers came next. The U.S. took over in the Louisiana Purchase, 1803. In the pre-war North-South struggle over slavery, so much violence swept the area it was called Bleeding Kansas. Railroad construction after the war made Abilene and Dodge City terminals of large cattle drives from Texas.

Tourist attractions. Eisenhower Center and "Place of Meditation," Abilene; Agricultural Hall of Fame and National Ctr., Bonner Springs, displays farm equipment; Dodge City-Boot Hill & Frontier Town; Cowtown-historic frontier town, Wichita; Ft. Scott & Ft. Larned-restored

1800s cavalry forts. Kansas Cosmosphere and Space Discovery Center, Hutchinson.

Famous Kansans include Thomas Hart Benton, John Brown, Walter P. Chrysler, John Steuart Curry, Amelia Earhart, Dwight D. Eisenhower, Ron Evans, Wild Bill Hickok, Cyrus Holliday, William Inge, Walter Johnson, Alf Landon, Carry Nation, Gordon Parks, Jim Ryun, William Allen White.

Tourist information. Kansas Dept. of Commerce, Travel and Tourism Div., 400 SW 8th St., 5th Fl., Topeka, KS 66603; 1-913-296-2009.

Toll-free travel information. 1-800-2KANSAS in state.

Kentucky

Bluegrass State

People. Population (1988): 3,727,000 **rank:** 23. **Pop. density:** 92.2 per sq. mi. **Urban** (1980): 50.9% **Racial Distrib.** (1985): 92.9% White; 7.1% Black; Hispanic 14,300. **Net change** (1980-88): +66,000; 1.8%.

Geography. Total area: 40,410 sq. mi.; **rank:** 37. **Land area:** 39,669 sq. mi. **Acres forested land:** 12,160,800. **Location:** east south central state, bordered on N by Illinois, Indiana, Ohio; on E by West Virginia and Virginia; in S by Tennessee; on W by Missouri. **Climate:** moderate, with plentiful rainfall. **Topography:** mountainous in E; rounded hills of the Knobs in the N; Bluegrass, heart of state; wooded rocky hillsides of the Pennyroyal; Western Coal Field; the fertile Purchase the SW. **Capital:** Frankfort.

Economy. Principal industries: manufacturing, coal mining, construction, agriculture. **Principal manufactured goods:** nonelectrical machinery, food products, electrical & electronic products, apparel, primary metals, chemicals and allied prods. **Agriculture: Chief crops** (1986): tobacco, soybeans, corn. **Livestock** (1987): 2.5 mln. cattle; 880,000 hogs/pigs; 32,000 sheep; 1.8 mln. chickens; 1985 receipts for horse & mule sales, $450 mln. **Timber/ lumber** (1987): hardwoods, pines; 419 mln. bd. ft. **Nonfuel Minerals** (1988): $304 mln.; mostly crushed stone. **Chief ports:** Paducah, Louisville, Covington, Owensboro, Ashland, Henderson County, Lyon County, Hickman-Fulton County. **International airports at:** Covington. **Value of construction** (1988): $3.2 bln. **Employment distribution:** 23.8% trade; 20.4% manuf.; 19.7% serv.; 18.4% gvt. **Per capita income** (1988): $12,795. **Unemployment** (1988): 7.9%. **Tourism** (1988): tourists spent $4.2 bln. **Sales tax:** 5%.

Finance. FDIC-insured commercial banks & trust companies (1987): 331. **Deposits:** $26.5 bln. **Savings institutions:** 67. **Assets:** $7.5 bln.

Federal government. No. federal civilian employees (Mar. 1988): 27,178. **Avg. salary:** $24,234. **Notable federal facilities:** U.S. Gold Bullion Depository, Fort Knox; Federal Correctional Institution, Lexington.

Energy. Electricity production (1988, mwh, by source): Hydroelectric: 2.4 mln.; Mineral: 74.0 mln.

Education. Expenditure per pupil, public schools (1987): $2,733. **Avg. salary, public school teachers** (1988-89): $24,920.

State data. Motto: United we stand, divided we fall. **Flower:** Goldenrod. **Bird:** Cardinal. **Tree:** Kentucky coffee tree. **Song:** My Old Kentucky Home. **Entered union** June 1, 1792; **rank,** 15th. **State fair at:** Louisville.

History. Kentucky was the first area west of the Alleghenies settled by American pioneers; first permanent settlement, Harrodsburg, 1774. Daniel Boone blazed the Wilderness Trail through the Cumberland Gap and founded Fort Boonesborough, 1775. Indian attacks, spurred by the British, were unceasing until, during the Revolution, Gen. George Rogers Clark captured British forts in Indiana and Illinois, 1778. In 1792, after Virginia dropped its claims to the region, Kentucky became the 15th state.

Tourist attractions. Kentucky Derby and accompanying festivities, Louisville; Land Between the Lakes Nat'l. Recreation Area encompassing Kentucky Lake and Lake Barkley; Mammoth Cave National Park with 300 mi. of explored passageways, 200-ft. high rooms, blind fish, and Echo River, 360 ft. below ground; Shaker Village of Pleasant Hill, Harrodsburg; Lincoln birthplace, Hodgenville; My Old Kentucky Home, Bardstown; Cumberland Gap Natl. Historical Park, Middlesboro; Kentucky Horse Park, Lexington.

Famous Kentuckians include Muhammad Ali, John James Audubon, Alben Barkley, Daniel Boone, Louis D. Brandeis, John C. Breckinridge, Kit Carson, Albert B. "Happy" Chandler, Cassius Marcellus Clay, Henry Clay, Jefferson Davis, "Casey" Jones, Abraham Lincoln, Mary Todd Lincoln, Thomas Hunt Morgan, Carry Nation, Col. Harland Sanders, Diane Sawyer, Jesse Stuart, Adlai Stevenson, Zachary Taylor, Robert Penn Warren, Whitney Young, Jr.

Chamber of Commerce. 452 Versailles Rd., P.O. Box 817, Frankfort, KY 40602.

Toll-free travel information. 1-800-225-TRIP in U.S., Ontario & Quebec, Canada.

Louisiana

Pelican State

People. Population (1988): 4,408,000; **rank:** 20. **Pop. density:** 92.3 per sq. mi. **Urban** (1980): 68.7%. **Racial distrib.** (1985): 70.0% White; 30.0% Black; Hispanic 98,400. **Net change** (1980-88): +202,000; 4.8%.

Geography. Total area: 47,752 sq. mi.; **rank:** 31. **Land area:** 44,521 sq. mi. **Acres forested land:** 14,558,100. **Location:** south central Gulf Coast state. **Climate:** subtropical, affected by continental weather patterns. **Topography:** lowlands of marshes and Mississippi R. flood plain; Red R. Valley lowlands; upland hills in the Florida Parishes; average elevation, 100 ft. **Capital:** Baton Rouge.

Economy. Principal industries: wholesale and retail trade, government, manufacturing, construction, transportation, mining. **Principal manufactured goods:** chemical products, foods, transportation equipment, electronic equipment, apparel, petroleum products. **Agriculture: Chief crops:** soybean, sugarcane, rice, corn, cotton, sweet potatoes, melons, pecans. **Livestock** (1987): 573,000 cattle; 154,000 hogs/pigs; 21,000 sheep; 600,000 poultry. **Timber/lumber** (1987): pines, hardwoods, oak; 776 mln. bd. ft. **Nonfuel Minerals** (1988): $433 mln., mostly salt, sand & gravel, sulfur. **Commercial fishing** (1988): $317.3 mln. **Chief ports:** New Orleans, Baton Rouge, Lake Charles, S. Louisiana Port Commission at La Place. **International airports at:** New Orleans. **Value of construction** (1988): $2.7 bln. **Employment distribution** (1985): 23.8% trade; 21.5% gvt.; 21.3% serv.; 10.9% manuf. **Per capita income** (1988): $12,193. **Unemployment** (1988): 10.9%. **Tourism** (1988): out-of-state visitors spent $4.4 bln. **Sales tax:** .04%.

Finance. FDIC-insured commercial banks & trust companies (1987): 298. **Deposits:** $31.7 bln. **Savings institutions:** 98. **Assets:** $16.2 bln.

Federal government. No. federal civilian employees (Mar. 1988): 20,928. **Avg. salary:** $25,925. **Notable federal facilities:** Barksdale, England, Ft. Polk military bases; Strategic Petroleum Reserve, New Orleans; Michoud Assembly Plant, New Orleans; U.S. Public Service Hospital, Carville.

Energy. Electricity production (1988, mwh, by source): Hydroelectric: 2.1 mln.; Mineral: 43.0 mln.; Nuclear: 13.8 mln.

Education. Expenditure per pupil, public schools (1987): $3,069. **Avg. salary, public school teachers** (1988-89): $22,470.

State data. Motto: Union, justice and confidence. **Flower:** Magnolia. **Bird:** Eastern brown pelican. **Tree:** Cypress. **Song:** Give Me Louisiana. **Entered union** Apr. 30, 1812; **rank,** 18th. **State fair at:** Shreveport; Oct.

History. The area was first visited, 1530, by Cabeza de Vaca and Panfilo de Narvaez. The region was claimed for France by LaSalle, 1682. First permanent settlement was by French at Biloxi, now in Mississippi, 1699. France ceded the region to Spain, 1762, took it back, 1800, and sold it to the U.S., 1803, in the Louisiana Purchase. During the Revolution, Spanish Louisiana aided the Americans. Admitted to statehood, 1812, Louisiana was the scene of the Battle of New Orleans, 1815.

Louisiana Creoles are descendants of early French and/or Spanish settlers. About 4,000 Acadians, French settlers in Nova Scotia, Canada, were forcibly transported by the British to Louisiana in 1755 (an event commemorated in Longfellow's *Evangeline*) and settled near Bayou Teche; their descendants became known as Cajuns. Another group, the Islenos, were descendants of Canary Islanders brought to Louisiana by a Spanish governor in 1770. Traces of Spanish and French survive in local dialects.

Tourist attractions. Mardi Gras, French Quarter, Superdome, Dixieland jazz, all New Orleans; Battle of New Orleans site; Longfellow-Evangeline Memorial Park; Kent House Museum, Alexandria; Hodges Gardens, Natchilotches.

Famous Louisianans include Louis Armstrong, Pierre Beauregard, Judah P. Benjamin, Braxton Bragg, Grace King, Huey Long, Leonidas K. Polk, Henry Miller Shreve, Edward D. White Jr.

Tourist Information. State Dept. of Culture, Recreation & Tourism, P.O. Box 94291, Baton Rouge, LA 70804-9291.

Toll-free travel information. 1-800-33-GUMBO.

Maine

Pine Tree State

People. Population (1988): 1,205,000; **rank:** 38. **Pop. density:** 36.2 per sq. mi. **Urban** (1980): 47.5% **Racial distrib.** (1980): 98.3% White; 0.3% Black; Hispanic; 4,400. **Net change** (1980-88): +81,000; 7.2%.

Geography. Total area: 33,265 sq. mi.; **rank:** 39. **Land area:** 33,215 sq. mi. **Acres forested land:** 17,718,300. **Location:** New England state at northeastern tip of U.S. **Climate:** Southern interior and coastal, influenced by air masses from the S and W; northern clime harsher, avg. +100 in. snow in winter. **Topography:** Appalachian Mtns. extend through state; western borders have rugged terrain; long sand beaches on southern coast; northern coast mainly rocky promontories, peninsulas, fjords. **Capital:** Augusta.

Economy. Principal industries: manufacturing, services, trade, government, finance, insurance, real estate, construction. **Principal manufactured goods:** paper and wood products, leather goods. **Agriculture: Chief crops:** potatoes, apples, hay, blueberries. **Livestock** (1986): 135,000 cattle; 79,000 hogs/pigs; 17,000 sheep; 4.9 mln. poultry. **Timber/lumber** (1987): pine, spruce, fir; 769 mln. bd ft. **Nonfuel Minerals** (1988): $62 mln.; construction sand & gravel, cement, crushed stone, dimension stone. **Commercial fishing** (1988): $123.9 mln. **Chief ports:** Searsport, Portland, Eastport. **International airports at:** Portland, Bangor. **Value of construction** (1988): $1.2 bln. **Employment distribution** (1987): 24.3% trade; 21.4% serv.; 20.1% manuf.; 18.9% gvt. **Per capita income** (1988): $14,976. **Unemployment** (1988): 3.8% **Tourism** (1988): $2 bln. **Sales tax:** 5%.

Finance. FDIC-insured commercial banks & trust companies (1987): 22. **Deposits:** $5.2 bln. **Savings institutions:** 35. **Assets:** $7.2 bln.

Federal government. No. federal civilian employees (Mar. 1988): 13,092. **Avg. salary:** $25,622. **Notable federal facilities:** Kittery Naval Shipyard; Brunswick Naval Air Station; Loring Air Force Base.

Energy. Electricity production (1988, mwh, by source): Hydroelectric: 1.6 mln.; Mineral: 2.9 mln.; Nuclear: 5.0 mln.

Education. Expenditure per pupil, public schools (1987): $3,850. **Avg. salary, public school teachers** (1988-89): $24,933.

State data. Motto: Dirigo (I direct). **Flower:** White pine cone and tassel. **Bird:** Chickadee. **Tree:** Eastern white pine. **Song:** State of Maine Song. **Entered union:** Mar. 15, 1820; **rank,** 23d.

History. Maine's rocky coast was explored by the Cabots, 1498-99. French settlers arrived, 1604, at the St. Croix River; English, 1607, on the Kennebec. In 1691, Maine was made part of Massachusetts. In the Revolution, a Maine regiment fought at Bunker Hill; a British fleet destroyed Falmouth (now Portland), 1775, but the British ship Margaretta was captured near Machiasport. In 1820, Maine broke off from Massachusetts, became a separate state.

Tourist attractions. Acadia Nat'l. Park, Bar Harbor, on Mt. Desert Is.; Funtown, Saco; Bath Iron Works and Marine Museum; Boothbay (Harbor) Railway Museum; Portland Art Museum; Sugarloaf/USA Ski Area; Ogunquit, Portland, York.

Famous "Down Easters" include James G. Blaine, Cyrus H.K. Curtis, Hannibal Hamlin, Longfellow, Sir Hiram and Hudson Maxim, Edna St. Vincent Millay, Kate Douglas Wiggin, Ben Ames Williams.

Chamber of Commerce and Industry. 126 Sewall St., Augusta, ME 04330.

Toll-free travel information. 1-800-533-9595, winter only, out of state only; 1-207-289-2423 year round.

Maryland

Old Line State, Free State

People. Population (1988): 4,622,000; **rank:** 19 **Pop. density:** 441.9 per sq. mi. **Urban** (1980): 80.3% **Racial distrib.** (1985): 75.8% White; 24.2% Black; Hispanic 71,400. **Net change** (1980-88): +405,000; 9.6%.

Geography. Total area: 10,460 sq. mi.; **rank:** 42. **Land area:** 9,837 sq. mi. **Acres forested land:** 2,653,200. **Location:** Middle Atlantic state stretching from the Ocean to the Allegheny Mtns. **Climate:** continental in the west; humid subtropical in the east. **Topography:** Eastern Shore of coastal plain and Maryland Main of coastal plain, piedmont plateau, and the Blue Ridge, separated by the Chesapeake Bay. **Capital:** Annapolis.

Economy. Principal industries: manufacturing, tourism. **Principal manufactured goods:** electric and electronic equipment; food and kindred products; chemicals and allied products. **Agriculture: Chief crops** (1987): corn, soybeans, tobacco. **Livestock** (1988): 329,000 cattle; 220,000 hogs/pigs; 22,000 sheep; 3.74 mln. poultry. **Timber/lumber:** hardwoods. **Nonfuel Minerals** (1988): $377 mln.; crushed stone, sand & gravel, Portland cement. **Commercial fishing** (1988): $44.1 mln. **Chief ports:** Baltimore. **International airports at:** Baltimore. **Value of construction** (1988): 6.8 bln. **Employment distribution** (1987): 26.0% serv.; 26.9% trade; 18.6% gvt. **Per capita income** (1988): $19,314. **Unemployment** (1988): 4.5%. **Tourism** (1987): tourists spent $5.2 bln. **Sales tax:** 5%.

Finance. FDIC-insured commercial banks & trust companies (1987): 93. **Deposits:** $30.0 bln. **Savings institutions:** 98. **Assets:** $22.3 bln.

Federal government. No. federal civilian employees (Mar. 1988): 103,734. **Avg. salary:** $31,624. **Notable federal facilities:** U.S. Naval Academy, Annapolis; Natl. Agric. Research Cen.; Ft. George C. Meade, Aberdeen Proving Ground; Goddard Space Flight Center.

Energy. Electricity production (1988, mwh, by source): Hydroelectric: 1.3 mln.; Mineral: 27.3 mln.; Nuclear: 11.7 mln.

Education. Expenditure per pupil, public schools (1987): $4,777. **Avg. salary, public school teachers** (1988-89): $33,700.

State data. Motto: Fatti Maschii, Parole Femine (Manly deeds, womanly words). **Flower:** Black-eyed susan. **Bird:** Baltimore oriole. **Tree:** White oak. **Song:** Maryland, My Maryland. **Seventh** of the original 13 states to ratify Constitution, Apr. 28, 1788. **State fair** at: Timonium; late Aug.-early Sept.

History. Capt. John Smith first explored Maryland, 1608. William Claiborne set up a trading post on Kent Is. in Chesapeake Bay, 1631. Britain granted land to Cecilius Calvert, Lord Baltimore, 1632; his brother led 200 settlers to St. Marys River, 1634. The bravery of Maryland troops in the Revolution, as at the Battle of Long Island, won the state its nickname, The Old Line State. In the War of 1812, when a British fleet tried to take Fort McHenry, Marylander Francis Scott Key, 1814, wrote *The Star-Spangled Banner.*

Tourist Attractions. Racing events include the Preakness, at Pimlico track, Baltimore; the International at Laurel Race Course; the Maryland Million at Pimlico. Also Annapolis yacht races; Ocean City summer resort; restored Ft. McHenry, Baltimore, near which Francis Scott Key wrote *The Star-Spangled Banner;* Antietam Battlefield, 1862, near Hagerstown; South Mountain Battlefield, 1862; Edgar Allan Poe house, Baltimore; The State House, Annapolis, 1772, the oldest still in use in the U.S.; Montgomery & Prince George's County gateway to Washington, D.C.

Famous Marylanders include Benjamin Banneker, Francis Scott Key, H.L. Mencken, William Pinkney, Upton Sinclair, Roger B. Taney, Charles Willson Peale.

Chamber of Commerce. 60 West St., Suite 405, Annapolis, MD 21401.

Toll-free travel information. 1-800-543-1036.

Massachusetts
Bay State, Old Colony

People. Population (1988): 5,889,000; **rank:** 13. **Pop. density:** 710.8 per sq. mi. **Urban** (1980): 83.8% **Racial distrib.** (1985): 96.5% White; 3.5% Black; Hispanic 154,100. **Net change** (1980-88): +152,000; 2.7%.

Geography. Total area: 8,284 sq. mi.; **rank:** 45. **Land area:** 7,824 sq. mi. **Acres forested land:** 2,952,300. **Location:** New England state along Atlantic seaboard. **Climate:** temperate, with colder and drier clime in western region. **Topography:** jagged indented coast from Rhode Island around Cape Cod; flat land yields to stony upland pastures near central region and gentle hilly country in west; except in west, land is rocky, sandy, and not fertile. **Capital:** Boston.

Economy. Principal industries: services, trade, manufacturing. **Principal manufactured goods** (1988): electric and electronic equipment, machinery, printing and publishing, instruments, fabricated metal products. **Agriculture: Chief crops:** cranberries, greenhouse, nursery, vegetables. **Livestock** (1983): 120,000 cattle; 50,000 hogs/pigs; 8,000 sheep; 125,000 horses, ponies; 3.6 mln. poultry. **Timber/lumber** (1987): white pine, oak, other hard woods; 99 mln. bd. ft. **Nonfuel Minerals** (1988): $192 mln.; mostly construction sand & gravel, crushed stone. **Commercial fishing** (1988): $274.0 mln. **Chief ports:** Boston, Fall River, New Bedford, Salem, Gloucester. **International airport at:** Boston. **Value of construction** (1988): $7.5 bln. **Employment distribution** (1988): 28.4% serv.; 22.8% trade; 18.8% manuf. **Per capita income** (1988): $20,701. **Unemployment** (1988): 3.3%. **Tourism** (1987): out-of-state visitors spent $12.9 bln. **Sales tax:** 5%.

Finance. FDIC-insured commercial banks & trust companies (1987): 107. **Deposits:** $66.9 bln. **Savings institutions:** 359. **Assets:** $63.7 bln.

Federal government. No. federal civilian employees (Mar. 1988): 31,733. **Avg. salary:** $27,162. **Notable federal facilities:** Ft. Devens; U.S. Customs House, John Fitzgerald Kennedy Federal Bldg., Boston; Q.M. Laboratory, Natick.

Energy. Electricity production (1988, mwh, by source): Hydroelectric: 150,000; Mineral: 33.3 mln.; Nuclear: 1.1 mln.

Education. Expenditure per pupil, public schools (1987): $5,145. **Avg. salary, public school teachers** (1988-89): $31,670.

State data. Motto: Ense Petit Placidam Sub Libertate Quietem (By the sword we seek peace, but peace only under liberty). **Flower:** Mayflower. **Bird:** Chickadee. **Tree:** American elm. **Song:** All Hail to Massachusetts. Sixth of the original 13 states to ratify Constitution, Feb. 6, 1788.

History. Pilgrims settled in Plymouth, 1620; the following year they gave thanks for their survival with the first Thanksgiving Day. Indian opposition reached a high point in King Philip's War, 1675-76, won by the colonists. Demonstrations against British restrictions set off the "Boston Massacre," 1770, and Boston "tea party," 1773. First bloodshed of the Revolution was at Lexington, 1775.

Tourist attractions. Cape Cod—Plymouth Rock, Plymouth Plantation, Mayflower II, Provincetown artists colony; Boston—Freedom Trail, Museum of Fine Arts, Children's Museum, Museum of Science, New England Aquarium, JFK Library, Boston Ballet, Boston Pops, Boston Symphony Orchestra; Berkshires—Tanglewood, Jacob's Pillow Dance Festival, Hancock Shaker Village, Berkshire Scenic Railroad; Old Sturbridge Village.

Famous "Bay Staters" include John Adams, John Quincy Adams, Samuel Adams, Louisa May Alcott, Horatio Alger, Clara Barton, Emily Dickinson, Emerson, Hancock, Hawthorne, Oliver W. Holmes, Winslow Homer, Elias Howe, John Fitzgerald Kennedy, Samuel F.B. Morse, Poe, Revere, Sargent, Thoreau, Whistler, Whittier.

Tourist information. Massachusetts Office of Travel & Tourism, 100 Cambridge St., 13th Floor, Boston, MA 02202.

Toll-free travel information. 1-800-624-MASS.

Michigan
Great Lake State, Wolverine State

People. Population (1988): 9,240,000; **rank:** 8. **Pop. density:** 157.9 per sq. mi. **Urban** (1980): 70.7%. **Racial distrib.** (1985): 86.5% White; 13.5% Black; Hispanic 155,200. **Net change** (1980-88): −0.2%.

Geography. Total area: 58,527 sq. mi.; **rank:** 23. **Land area:** 56,954 sq. mi. **Acres forested land:** 19,270,400. **Location:** east north central state bordering on 4 of the 5 Great Lakes, divided into an Upper and Lower Peninsula by the Straits of Mackinac, which link lakes Michigan and Huron. **Climate:** well-defined seasons tempered by the Great Lakes. **Topography:** low rolling hills give way to northern tableland of hilly belts in Lower Peninsula; Upper Peninsula is level in the east, with swampy areas; western region is higher and more rugged. **Capital:** Lansing.

Economy. Principal industries: manufacturing, services, tourism, agriculture, mining. **Principal manufactured goods:** transportation equipment, machinery, fabricated metals, primary metals, food prods., rubber & plastics. **Agriculture: Chief crops:** corn, winter wheat, soybeans, dry beans, oats, hay, sugar beets, honey, asparagus, sweet corn, apples, cherries, grapes, peaches, blueberries, flowers. **Livestock** (1986): 1.4 mln. cattle; 1.2 mln. hogs/pigs; 108,000 sheep; 8.9 mln. poultry. **Timber/lumber** (1987): maple, oak, aspen; 345 mln. bd. ft. **Nonfuel Minerals** (1988): $1.55 bln.; iron ore, Portland cement, crushed stone, sand & gravel. **Commercial fishing** (1988): $9.6 mln. **Chief ports:** Detroit, Saginaw River, Escanaba, Muskegon, Saulte Ste. Marie, Port Huron. **International airports at:** Detroit, Grand Rapids, Saginaw, Sault St. Marie. **Value of construction** (1988): $8.8 bln. **Employment distribution** (1988): 22% manuf.; 20% serv.; **Per capita income** (1988): $16,387. **Unemployment** (1988): 7.6%. **Tourism** (1988): out-of-state visitors spent $8.9 bln. **Sales tax:** 4%.

Finance. FDIC-insured commercial banks & trust companies (1987): 345. **Deposits:** $64.7 bln. **Savings institutions:** 51. **Assets:** $37.2 bln.

Federal government. No. federal civilian employees (Mar. 1988): 27,423. **Avg. salary:** $27,532. **Notable federal facilities:** Isle Royal, Sleeping Bear Dunes national parks.

Energy. Electricity production (1988, mwh, by source): Hydroelectric: 483,000 mln; Mineral: 70.6 mln.; Nuclear: 17.8 mln.

Education. Expenditure per pupil, public schools (1987): $4,353. **Avg. salary, public school teachers** (1988-89): $34,419.

State data. Motto: Si Quaeris Peninsulam Amoenam Circumspice (If you seek a pleasant peninsula, look about you). **Flower:** Apple blossom. **Bird:** Robin. **Tree:** White pine. **Song:** Michigan, My Michigan. **Entered union** Jan. 26, 1837; rank, 26th. **State fair** at: Detroit, late Aug.-early Sept.; Upper Peninsula (Escanaba) mid-Aug.

History. French fur traders and missionaries visited the region, 1616, set up a mission at Sault Ste. Marie, 1641, and a settlement there, 1668. The whole region went to Britain, 1763. Anthony Wayne defeated their Indian allies at Fallen Timbers, Ohio, 1794. The British returned, 1812, seized Ft. Mackinac and Detroit. Oliver H. Perry's Lake Erie victory and William H. Harrison's troops, who carried the war to the Thames River in Canada, 1813, freed Michigan once more.

Tourist attractions. Henry Ford Museum, Greenfield Village, reconstruction of a typical 19th cent. American village, both in Dearborn; Michigan Space Ctr., Jackson; Tahquamenon (*Hiawatha*) Falls; DeZwaan windmill and Tulip Festival, Holland; "Soo Locks," St. Marys Falls Ship Canal, Sault Ste. Marie.

Famous Michiganians include Ralph Bunche, Gerald R. Ford, Paul de Kruif, Edna Ferber, Henry Ford, Aretha Franklin, Edgar Guest, Lee Iacocca, Robert Ingersoll, Magic Johnson, Will Kellogg, Ring Lardner, Elmore Leonard, Charles Lindbergh, Joe Louis, Madonna, Pontiac, Diana Ross, Tom Selleck, Lily Tomlin, Stewart Edward White.

Chamber of Commerce: 200 N. Washington Sq., Suite 400, Lansing, MI 48933.

Toll-free travel information. 1-800-543-2937.

Minnesota

North Star State, Gopher State

People. Population (1988): 4,307,000; **rank:** 21. **Pop. density:** 51.0 per sq. mi. **Urban** (1980): 66.9%. **Racial distrib.** (1985): 98.5% White; 1.5% Black; Hispanic 33,500. **Net change** (1980-88): +231,000; 5.7%.

Geography. Total area: 84,402 sq. mi.; **rank:** 12. **Land area:** 79,548 sq. mi. **Acres forested land:** 16,709,200. **Location:** north central state bounded on the E by Wisconsin and Lake Superior, on the N by Canada, on the W by the Dakotas, and on the S by Iowa. **Climate:** northern part of state lies in the moist Great Lakes storm belt; the western border lies at the edge of the semi-arid Great Plains. **Topography:** central hill and lake region covering approx. half the state; to the NE, rocky ridges and deep lakes; to the NW, flat plain; to the S, rolling plains and deep river valleys. **Capital:** St. Paul.

Economy. Principal industries: agri business, forest products, mining, manufacturing, tourism. **Principal manufactured goods:** food processing, non-electrical machinery, chemicals, paper, electric and electronic equipment, printing and publishing, instruments, fabricated metal products. **Agriculture: Chief crops:** corn, soybeans, wheat, sugar beets, sunflowers, barley. **Livestock** (1988): 2.9 mln. cattle; 4.7 mln. hogs/pigs; 263,000 sheep; 11.7 mln. poultry. **Timber/lumber** (1987): needleleaves and hardwoods; 152 mln. bd. ft. **Nonfuel Minerals** (1988): 1.39 bln.; mostly iron ore. **Commercial fishing:** $97,000. **Chief ports:** Duluth, St. Paul, Minneapolis. **International airports at:** Minneapolis-St. Paul. **Value of construction** (1988): $4.8 bln. **Employment distribution** (1988): 25.1% trade; 24.3% serv.; 19.5% manuf.; 15.9% gvt. **Per capita income** (1988): $16,787. **Unemployment** (1988): 4.0%. **Tourism** (1987): out-of-state visitors spent $3.6 bln. **Sales tax:** 6%.

Finance. FDIC-insured commercial banks & trust companies (1987): 733. **Deposits:** $41.2 bln. **Savings institutions:** 36. **Assets:** $16.3 bln.

Federal government. No. federal civilian employees (Mar. 1988): 14,307. **Avg. salary:** $27,873.

Energy. Electricity production (1988, mwh, by source): Hydroelectric: 532,000; Mineral: 25.4 mln.; Nuclear: 12.3 mln.

Education. Expenditure per pupil, public schools (1987): $4,180. **Avg. salary, public school teachers** (1988-89): $31,500.

State data. Motto: L'Etoile du Nord (The star of the north). **Flower:** Pink and white lady's-slipper. **Bird:** Common loon. **Tree:** Red pine. **Song:** Hail! Minnesota. **Entered union** May 11, 1858; rank, 32d. **State fair** at: Saint Paul; late Aug. to early Sept.

History. Fur traders and missionaries from French Canada opened the region in the 17th century. Britain took over the area east of the Mississippi, 1763. The U.S. took over that portion after the Revolution and in 1803 bought the western area as part of the Louisiana Purchase. The U.S. built present Ft. Snelling, 1820, bought lands from the Indians, 1837. Sioux Indians staged a bloody uprising, 1862, and were driven from the state.

Tourist attractions. Minnehaha Falls, Minneapolis, inspiration for Longfellow's *Hiawatha;* over 10,000 lakes; 64 state parks; 20 historical sites; Minneapolis Aquatennial; Ordway Theater, St. Paul; Guthrie Theater, Minneapolis; professional baseball, football, hockey. Voyageurs Nat'l. Park, a water wilderness along the Canadian border; Mayo Clinic, Rochester; St. Paul Winter Carnival.

Famous Minnesotans include F. Scott Fitzgerald, Cass Gilbert, Hubert Humphrey, Sister Elizabeth Kenny, Sinclair Lewis, Paul Manship, E. G. Marshall, William and Charles Mayo, Walter F. Mondale, Charles Schulz, Harold Stassen, Thorstein Veblen.

Tourist Information. Minnesota Office of Tourism, 375 Jackson St., 250 Skyway Level, St. Paul, MN 55101.

Toll-free travel information. 1-800-328-1461.

Mississippi

Magnolia State

People. Population (1988): 2,620,000; **rank:** 31. **Pop. density:** 54.9 per sq. mi. **Urban** (1980): 47.3%. **Racial distrib.** (1985): 63.7% White; 36.3% Black; Hispanic 11,700. **Net change** (1980-88): +99,000; 3.9%.

Geography. Total area: 47,689 sq. mi.; **rank:** 32. **Land area:** 47,233 sq. mi. **Acres forested land:** 16,715,600. **Location:** south central state bordered on the W by the Mississippi R. and on the S by the Gulf of Mexico. **Climate:** semi-tropical, with abundant rainfall, long growing season, and extreme temperatures unusual. **Topography:** low, fertile delta bet. the Yazoo and Mississippi rivers; loess bluffs stretching around delta border; sandy Gulf coastal terraces followed by piney woods and prairie; rugged, high sandy hills in extreme NE followed by black prairie belt. Pontotoc Ridge, and flatwoods into the north central highlands. **Capital:** Jackson.

Economy. Principal industries: manufacturing, food processing, seafood, government, wholesale and retail trade, agriculture. **Principal manufactured goods:** apparel, lumber and wood products, foods and kindred products, electrical machinery and equipment, transportation equip. **Agriculture: Chief crops:** cotton, soybeans, catfish, rice. **Livestock** (1986): 1.4 mln. cattle; 210,000 hogs/pigs; 4,500 sheep; 335.7 mln. broilers. **Timber/lumber** (1987): pine, oak, hardwoods; 2.1 bln. bd. ft. **Nonfuel Minerals** (1988): $121 mln., mostly construction sand & gravel. **Commercial fishing** (1988): $61.2 mln. **Chief ports:** Pascagoula, Vicksburg, Gulfport, Natchez, Greenville. **Value of construction** (1988): $1.5 bln. **Employment distribution** (1987): 22.1% manuf.; 18.5% gvt.; 17.9% trade; 13.4% serv. **Per capita income** (1988): $10,992. **Unemployment** (1988): 8.4%. **Tourism** (1986): out-of-state visitors spent $1.3 bln. **Sales tax:** 6%.

Finance. FDIC-insured commercial banks & trust companies (1987): 138. **Deposits:** $15.1 bln. **Savings institutions:** 44. **Assets:** $5.8 bln.

Federal government. No. federal civilian employees (Mar. 1988): 17,702. **Avg. salary:** $26,717. **Notable federal facilities:** Columbus, Keesler AF bases; Meridian Naval Air Station, NASA/NOAA International Earth Sciences Center.

Energy. Electricity production (1988, mwh, by source): Mineral 15.5 mln; Nuclear 9.6 mln.

Education. Expenditure per pupil, public schools (1987): $2,350. **Avg. salary, public school teachers** (1988-89): $22,036.

State data. Motto: Virtute et Armis (By valor and arms). **Flower:** Magnolia. **Bird:** Mockingbird. **Tree:** Magnolia. **Song:** Go, Mississippi! **Entered union** Dec. 10, 1817; rank, 20th. **State fair at:** Jackson; Fall.

History. De Soto explored the area, 1540, discovered the Mississippi River, 1541. La Salle traced the river from Illinois to its mouth and claimed the entire valley for France, 1682. First settlement was the French Ft. Maurepas, near Ocean Springs, 1699. The area was ceded to Britain, 1763; American settlers followed. During the Revolution, Spain seized part of the area and refused to leave even after the U.S. acquired title at the end of the Revolution, finally moving out, 1798. Mississippi seceded 1861. Union forces captured Corinth and Vicksburg and destroyed Jackson and much of Meridian.

Tourist attractions. Vicksburg National Military Park and Cemetery, other Civil War sites; Natchez Trace; Indian mounds; estate pilgrimage at Natchez; Mardi Gras and blessing of the shrimp fleet, June, both in Biloxi.

Famous Mississippians include Dana Andrews, William Faulkner, L.Q.C. Lamar, Elvis Presley, Leontyne Price, Charlie Pride, Eudora Welty.

Chamber of Commerce. P.O. Box 1849, Jackson, MS 39205.

Toll-free travel information. 1-800-962-2346; 1-800-647-2290 out of state.

Missouri

Show Me State

People. Population (1988): 5,141,000; **rank:** 15. **Pop. density:** 73.8 per sq. mi. **Urban** (1980): 68.1%. **Racial distrib.** (1985): 89.1% White; 10.9% Black; Hispanic 48,300. **Net change** (1980-88): +224,000; 4.6%.

Geography. Total area: 69,697 sq. mi.; **rank:** 19. **Land area:** 68,945 sq. mi. **Acres forested land:** 12,876,000. **Location:** West North central state near the geographic center of the conterminous U.S.; bordered on the E by the Mississippi R., on the NW by the Missouri R. **Climate:** continental, susceptible to cold Canadian air, moist, warm Gulf air, and drier SW air. **Topography:** Rolling hills, open, fertile plains, and well-watered prairie N of the Missouri R.; south of the river land is rough and hilly with deep, narrow valleys; alluvial plain in the SE; low elevation in the west. **Capital:** Jefferson City.

Economy. Principal industries: agriculture, manufacturing, aerospace, tourism. **Principal manufactured goods:** transportation equipment, food and related products, electrical and electronic equipment, chemicals. **Agriculture: Chief crops:** soybeans, corn, wheat, cotton. **Livestock** (1987): 4.6 mln. cattle; 2.9 mln. hogs/pigs; 110,000 sheep; 8 mln. chickens, 13.5 mln. turkeys. **Timber/lumber** (1987): oak, hickory; 383 mln. bd. ft. **Nonfuel Minerals** (1988): $969 mln., mostly lead, crushed stone, Portland cement. **Chief ports:** St. Louis, Kansas City. **International airports at:** St. Louis, Kansas City. **Value of construction** (1988): $4.2 bln. **Employment distribution** (1987): 24% trade; 23% serv.; 19% manuf.; 16% gvt. **Per capita income** (1988): $15,492. **Unemployment** (1988): 5.7%. **Tourism** (1987): total travelers spent $5 bln. **Sales tax:** 4.225%.

Finance. FDIC-insured commercial banks & trust companies (1987): 610. **Deposits:** $43.9 bln. **Savings institutions:** 82. **Assets:** $24.0 bln.

Federal government. No. federal civilian employees (Mar. 1988): 46,031. **Avg. salary:** $26,465. **Notable federal facilities:** Federal Reserve banks, St. Louis, Kansas City; Ft. Leonard Wood, Rolla; Jefferson Barracks, St. Louis; Whiteman AFB, Knob Noster.

Energy. Electricity production (1988 mwh, by source): Hydroelectric: 1.5 mln.; Mineral: 49.3 mln; Nuclear: 8.9 mln.

Education. Expenditure per pupil, public schools (1987): $3,472. **Avg. salary, public school teachers** (1988-89): $25,981.

State data. Motto: Salus Populi Suprema Lex Esto (The welfare of the people shall be the supreme law).

Flower: Hawthorn. **Bird:** Bluebird. **Tree:** Dogwood. **Song:** Missouri Waltz. **Entered union** Aug. 10, 1821; rank, 24th. **State fair at:** Sedalia; 3d week in Aug.

History. DeSoto visited the area, 1541. French hunters and lead miners made the first settlement, c. 1735, at Ste. Genevieve. The U.S. acquired Missouri as part of the Louisiana Purchase, 1803. The fur trade and the Santa Fe Trail provided prosperity; St. Louis became the "jump-off" point for pioneers on their way West. Pro- and anti-slavery forces battled each other there during the Civil War.

Tourist attractions. Mark Twain Area, Hannibal; Pony Express Museum, St. Joseph; Harry S. Truman Library, Independence; Gateway Arch, St. Louis; Silver Dollar City, Branson Worlds of Fun, Kansas City; Lake of the Ozarks, Churchill Memorial, Fulton.

Famous Missourians include Josephine Baker, Thomas Hart Benton, George Caleb Bingham, Gen. Omar Bradley, George Washington Carver, Walter Cronkite, Dale Carnegie, Walt Disney, T.S. Eliot, Betty Grable, Jesse James, J. C. Penney, John J. Pershing, Joseph Pulitzer, Ginger Rogers, Bess Truman, Harry S. Truman, Mark Twain, Tennessee Williams.

Chamber of Commerce. 400 E. High St., P.O. Box 149, Jefferson City, MO 65101.

Toll-free travel information. 1-800-877-1234.

Montana

Treasure State

People. Population (1988): 805,000; **rank:** 44. **Pop. density:** 5.47 per sq. mi. **Urban** (1980): 52.9%. **Racial distrib.** (1980): 94.0% White; 0.2% Black; Hispanic 10,800. **Net change** (1980-88): +18,000; 2.3%.

Geography. Total area: 147,046 sq. mi.; **rank:** 4. **Land area:** 145,388 sq. mi. **Acres forested land:** 22,559,300. **Location:** Mountain state bounded on the E by the Dakotas, on the S by Wyoming, on the S/SW by Idaho, and on the N by Canada. **Climate:** colder, continental climate with low humidity. **Topography:** Rocky Mtns. in western third of the state; eastern two-thirds gently rolling northern Great Plains. **Capital:** Helena.

Economy. Principal industries: manufacturing, agriculture, mining, tourism. **Principal manufactured goods:** lumber and wood products, petroleum products, primary metals and minerals, farm machinery, processed foods. **Agriculture: Chief crops:** wheat, barley, sugar beets, hay, oats. **Livestock** (1988): 2.35 mln. cattle; 230,000 hogs/pigs; 538,000 sheep; 990,000 poultry. **Timber/lumber** (1987): Douglas fir, pines, larch; 1.8 bln. bd. ft. **Nonfuel Minerals** (1988): $572 mln. mostly metallics. **International airports at:** Great Falls, Billings, Kalispell, Missoula. **Value of construction** (1988): $499.6 mln. **Employment distribution** (1987): 25.7% serv.; 21.4% trade; 16.1% govt.; 7.9% agric; 5.8% manuf. **Per capita income** (1988): $12,670. **Unemployment** (1988): 6.8%. **Tourism** (1987): non-resident visitors spent $500 mln.

Finance. FDIC-insured commercial banks & trust companies (1987): 169. **Deposits:** $6.1 bln. **Savings institutions:** 11. **Assets:** $1.2 bln.

Federal government. No. federal civilian employees (Mar. 1988): 8,124. **Avg. salary:** $27,616. **Notable federal facilities:** Malmstrom AFB; Ft. Peck, Hungry Horse, Libby, Yellowtail dams, numerous missile silos.

Energy. Electricity production (1988, mwh, by source): Hydroelectric: 8.3 mln; Mineral: 16.5 mln.

Education. Expenditure per pupil, public schools (1987): $4,194. **Avg. salary, public school teachers** (1988-89): $24,414.

State data. Motto: Oro y Plata (Gold and silver). **Flower:** Bitterroot. **Bird:** Western meadowlark. **Tree:** Ponderosa pine. **Song:** Montana. **Entered union** Nov. 8, 1889; rank, 41st. **State fair at:** Great Falls; late July to early Aug.

History. French explorers visited the region, 1742. The U.S. acquired the area partly through the Louisiana Purchase, 1803, and partly through the explorations of Lewis and Clark, 1805-06. Fur traders and missionaries established posts in the early 19th century. Indian uprisings reached their peak with the Battle of the Little Big Horn, 1876. Mining activity and the coming of the Northern Pacific Railway, 1883, brought population growth.

Tourist attractions. Glacier Natl. Park, on the Continental Divide, is a scenic and recreational wonderland, with 60 glaciers, 200 lakes, and many trout streams. Yellowstone Natl. Park, the largest & oldest national park, has 3 of 5 entrances in Montana, with 2,221,000 acres of scenic beauty, inc. geysers, mountains, canyons, streams, lakes, forests, waterfalls.

Also, Museum of the Plains Indian, Blackfeet Reservation near Browning; Custer Battlefield National Cemetery; Flathead Lake, in the NW, Lewis and Clark Caverns State Park, near Whitehall; 7 Indian reservations, covering over 5 million acres.

Famous Montanans include Gary Cooper, Marcus Daly, Chet Huntley, Will James, Myrna Loy, Mike Mansfield, Brent Musberger, Jeannette Rankin, Charles M. Russell, Lester Thurow.

Chamber of Commerce. 2030 11th Ave., P.O. Box 1730, Helena, MT 59624.

Toll-free travel information. 1-800-541-1447.

1862 Homestead Act; struggles followed between homesteaders and ranchers.

Tourist attractions. Architecturally unique, 400' tall state capitol, Lincoln; Stuhr Museum of the Prairie Pioneer, Grand Island; Museum of the Fur Trade, Chadron; State Museum (Elephant Hall), Lincoln; Joslyn Art Museum, Omaha; Strategic Air Command Museum, Bellevue; Boys Town, founded by Fr. Flanagan, west of Omaha; Arbor Lodge State Park, Nebraska City; Buffalo Bill Ranch State Historical Park, North Platte; Pioneer Village, Minden; Oregon Trail landmarks, Scotts Bluff National Monument, Chimney Rock Historic Site, Ft. Robinson.

Famous Nebraskans include Fred Astaire, Charles W. and William Jennings Bryan, Johnny Carson, Willa Cather, William F. "Buffalo Bill" Cody, Loren Eiseley, Rev. Edward J. Flanagan, Henry Fonda, Gerald R. Ford, Rollin Kirby, Harold Lloyd, Wright Morris, J. Sterling Morton, John Neidhardt, George Norris, Gen. John J. Pershing, Chief Red Cloud, Mari Sandoz, Malcolm X, Roscoe Pound.

Chamber of Commerce. 1320 Lincoln Mall, Box 95128, Lincoln, NE 68501.

Toll-free travel information. 1-800-742-7595; 1-800-228-4307 out of state.

Nebraska
Cornhusker State

People. Population (1988): 1,602,000; **rank:** 36. **Pop. density:** 20.7 per sq. mi. **Urban** (1980): 62.9%. **Racial distrib.** (1985): 96.7% White; 3.3% Black; Hispanic 29,900. **Net change** (1980-88): +32,000; 2.1%.

Geography. Total area: 77,355 sq. mi.; **rank:** 15. **Land area:** 76,644 sq. mi. **Acres forested land:** 1,029,100. **Location:** West North Central state with the Missouri R. for a NE/E border. **Climate:** continental semi-arid. **Topography:** till plains of the central lowland in the eastern third rising to the Great Plains and hill country of the north central and NW. **Capital:** Lincoln.

Economy. Principal industries: agriculture, food processing, manufacturing. **Principal manufactured goods:** foods, machinery, electric and electronic equipment, primary and fabricated metal products, transportation equipment, instruments & related prod. **Agriculture: Chief crops:** corn, sorghum, soybeans, hay, wheat, beans, oats, potatoes, sugar beets. **Livestock** (1988): 5.5 mln. cattle; 4.0 mln. hogs/pigs; 180,000 sheep; 4.5 mln. poultry. **Nonfuel Minerals** (1988): $94 mln.; mostly Portland cement, crushed stone, construction sand & gravel. **Chief ports:** Omaha, Sioux City, Brownville, Blair, Plattsmouth, Nebraska City. **Value of construction** (1988): $1.0 bln. **Employment distribution** (1988): 25.8% trade; 23.0% serv.; 20.1% gvt.; 13.8% manuf.; 8.8% agric. **Per capita income** (1988): $15,184. **Unemployment** (1988): 3.6%. **Tourism** (1988): traveler expenditures $3.6 bln. **Sales tax:** 4%, + some local sales taxes of .5-1.5%.

Finance. FDIC-insured commercial banks & trust companies (1987): 437. **Deposits:** $14.5 bln. **Savings institutions:** 24. **Assets:** $11.4 bln.

Federal government. No. federal civilian employees (Mar. 1988): 9,005. **Avg. salary:** $26,662. **Notable federal facilities:** Strategic Air Command Base, Omaha.

Energy. Electricity production (1988, mwh, by source): Hydroelectric: 1.4 mln.; Mineral: 12.5 mln.; Nuclear: 6.8 mln.

Education. Expenditure per pupil, public schools (1987): $3,758. **Avg. salary, public school teachers** (1988-89): $24,203.

State data. Motto: Equality before the law. **Flower:** Goldenrod. **Bird:** Western meadowlark. **Tree:** Cottonwood. **Song:** Beautiful Nebraska. **Entered union** Mar. 1, 1867; **rank,** 37th. **State fair** at: Lincoln; Aug. 31-Sept. 9, 1990.

History. Spanish and French explorers and fur traders visited the area prior to the Louisiana Purchase, 1803. Lewis and Clark passed through, 1804-06. First permanent settlement was Bellevue, near Omaha, 1823. Many Civil War veterans settled under free land terms of the

Nevada
Sagebrush State, Battle Born State, Silver State

People. Population (1988): 1,054,000; **rank:** 41. **Pop. density:** 9.5 per sq. mi. **Urban** (1980): 85.3%. **Racial distrib.** (1985): 93.4% White; 6.6% Black; Hispanic 69,700. **Net change** (1980-88): +254,000; 31.7%.

Geography. Total area: 110,561 sq. mi.; **rank:** 7. **Land area:** 109,894 sq. mi. **Acres forested land:** 7,683,300. **Location:** Mountain state bordered on N by Oregon and Idaho, on E by Utah and Arizona, on SE by Arizona, and on SW/W by California. **Climate:** semi-arid. **Topography:** rugged N-S mountain ranges; highest elevation, Boundary Peak, 13,140 ft.; southern area is within the Mojave Desert; lowest elevation, Colorado R. Canyon, 470 ft. **Capital:** Carson City.

Economy. Principal industries: gaming, tourism, mining, manufacturing, government, agriculture, warehousing, trucking. **Principal manufactured goods:** gaming devices, electronics, chemicals, stone-clay-glass products. **Agriculture: Chief crops:** alfalfa, potatoes, hay, barley, wheat, cotton. **Livestock** (1988): 500,000 cattle; 16,000 hogs/pigs; 96,000 sheep; 18,000 poultry. **Timber/lumber:** piñon, juniper, other pines. **Nonfuel Minerals** (1988): $1.87 bln.; mostly gold, silver, barite, construction sand & gravel. **International airports** at Las Vegas, Reno. **Value of construction** (1988): $2.3 bln. **Employment distribution** (1988): 42% serv.; 20% trade; 12% gvt. **Per capita income** (1988): $17,440. **Unemployment** (1988): 5.2%. **Tourism** (1984): out-of-state travelers spent $6.5 bln. **Sales tax:** 5.75-6%.

Finance. FDIC-insured commercial banks & trust companies (1987): 18. **Deposits:** $6.1 bln. **Savings institutions:** 5. **Assets:** $4.6 bln.

Federal government. No. federal civilian employees (Mar. 1988): 6,497. **Avg. salary:** $28,444. **Notable federal facilities:** Nevada Test Site; Hawthorne Munitions Plant, Nellis Air Force Base & Gunnery Range.

Energy. Electricity production (1988, mwh, by source): Hydroelectric: 2.1 mln.; Mineral: 18.2 mln.

Education. Expenditure per pupil, public schools (1987): $3,573. **Avg. salary, public school teachers** (1988-89): $28,840.

State data. Motto: All for our country. **Flower:** Sagebrush. **Bird:** Mountain bluebird. **Trees:** Single-leaf pinon and bristlecone pine. **Song:** Home Means Nevada. **Entered union** Oct. 31, 1864; **rank,** 36th. **State fair** at Reno; early Sept.

History. Nevada was first explored by Spaniards in 1776. Hudson's Bay Co. trappers explored the north and central region, 1825; trader Jedediah Smith crossed the state, 1826 and 1827. The area was acquired by the U.S., in 1848, at the end of the Mexican War. First settlement, Mormon Station, now Genoa, was est. 1849. In the early 20th century, Nevada adopted progressive measures such as the initiative, referendum, recall, and woman suffrage.

Tourist attractions. Legalized casino gambling provided the impetus for the development of resort facilities at Lake Tahoe, Reno, Las Vegas, and elsewhere. Ghost towns, rodeos, mountain climbing, skiing, golfing, trout fishing, water sports and hunting important. Notable are Hoover Dam, Lake Mead Natl. Recreation Area, Lake Tahoe, Great Basin Natl. Park, Valley of Fire State Park & Virginia City. Annual events inc. Helldorado Days & Rodeo, Las Vegas; Reno Rodeo; Basque Festival, Elko; Nevada Day, Carson City; Cowboy Poetry Gathering, Elko.

Famous Nevadans include Walter Van Tilburg Clark, Sarah Winnemucca Hopkins, Paul Laxalt, John William Mackay, Pat McCarran, Dat So La Lee, Key Pittman, William Morris Stewart.

Tourist Information. Commission on Economic Development, Capitol Complex, Carson City, NV 89710.

Toll-free travel information. 1-800-638-2328.

New Hampshire
Granite State

People. Population (1988): 1,085,000; **rank:** 40. **Pop. density:** 116.9 per sq. mi. **Urban** (1980): 52.2%. **Racial distrib.** (1980): 98.8% White; 0.4% Black; Hispanic 5,700. **Net change** (1980-88): +165,000; 17.9%.

Geography. Total area: 9,279 sq. mi.; **rank:** 44. **Land area:** 8,993 sq. mi. **Acres forested land:** 5,013,500. **Location:** New England state bounded on S by Massachusetts, on W by Vermont, on N/NW by Canada, on E by Maine and the Atlantic O. **Climate:** highly varied, due to its nearness to high mountains and ocean. **Topography:** low, rolling coast followed by countless hills and mountains rising out of a central plateau. **Capital:** Concord.

Economy. Principal industries: manufacturing, tourism, agriculture, trade, mining. **Principal manufactured goods:** machinery, electrical & electronic products, plastics, fabricated metal products, leather goods. **Agriculture: Chief crops:** dairy products, nursery and greenhouse products, hay, vegetables, fruit, maple syrup & sugar prods. **Livestock** (1987): 55,000 cattle; 9,000 hogs/pigs; 12,000 sheep; 365,000 poultry. **Timber/lumber** (1987): white pine, hemlock, oak, birch; 175 mln. bd. ft. **Nonfuel Minerals** (1988): $48 mln.; mostly construction sand & gravel, crushed & dimension stone. **Commercial fishing** (1988): $8.8 mln. **Chief ports:** Portsmouth, Hampton, Rye. **Value of construction** (1989): $1.9 bln. **Employment distribution** (1988): 22.5% manuf.; 25.7% trade; 22.4% serv; 12.9% gvt. **Per capita income** (1988): $19,016. **Unemployment** (1988): 2.4%. **Tourism** (1988): out-of-state visitors spent $2.2 bln.

Finance. FDIC-insured **commercial banks & trust companies** (1987): 60. **Deposits:** $6.9 bln. **Savings institutions:** 39. **Assets:** $8.7 bln.

Federal government. No. federal civilian employees (Mar. 1988): 3,617. **Avg. salary:** $28,833.

Energy. Electricity production (1988, mwh, by source): Hydroelectric: 968,000; Mineral: 6.0 mln.

Education. Expenditure per pupil, public schools (1987): $3,933. **Avg. salary, public school teachers** (1988-89): $26,703.

State Data. Motto: Live free or die. **Flower:** Purple lilac. **Bird:** Purple finch. **Tree:** White birch. **Song:** Old New Hampshire. Ninth of the original 13 states to ratify the Constitution, June 21, 1788.

History. First explorers to visit the New Hampshire area were England's Martin Pring, 1603, and Champlain, 1605. First settlement was Odiorne's Point (now port of Rye), 1623. Indian raids were halted, 1759, by Robert Rogers' Rangers. Before the Revolution, New Hampshire men seized a British fort at Portsmouth, 1774, and drove the royal governor out, 1775. Three regiments served in the Continental Army and scores of privateers raided British shipping.

Tourist attractions. Mt. Washington, highest peak in Northeast, hub of network of trails; Lake Winnipesaukee; White Mt. Natl. Forest; Crawford, Franconia, Pinkham notches in White Mt. region—Franconia famous for the Old Man of the Mountains, described by Hawthorne as the Great Stone Face; the Flume, a spectacular gorge; the aerial tramway on Cannon Mt; Strawbery Banke, Portsmouth; Shaker Village, Canterbury.

Famous New Hampshirites include Salmon P. Chase, Ralph Adams Cram, Mary Baker Eddy, Daniel Chester French, Robert Frost, Horace Greeley, Sarah Buell Hale, Franklin Pierce, Augustus Saint-Gaudens, Daniel Webster.

Tourist Information. Department of Resources and Economic Development, Office of Vacation Travel, P.O. Box 856, Concord, NH 03301.

Toll-free travel information. 1-800-258-3608 in northeast.

New Jersey
Garden State

People. Population (1988): 7,721,000; **rank:** 9. **Pop. density:** 991.5 per sq. mi. **Urban** (1980): 89.0%. **Racial distrib.** (1985): 86.4% White; 13.6% Black; Hispanic 573,200. **Net change** (1980-88): +356,000; 4.8%.

Geography. Total area: 7,787 sq. mi.; **rank:** 46. **Land area:** 7,468 sq. mi. **Acres forested land:** 1,928,400. **Location:** Middle Atlantic state bounded on the N and E by New York and the Atlantic O., on the S and W by Delaware and Pennsylvania. **Climate:** moderate, with marked difference bet. NW and SE extremities. **Topography:** Appalachian Valley in the NW also has highest elevation, High Pt., 1,801 ft.; Appalachian Highlands, flat-topped NE-SW mountain ranges; Piedmont Plateau, low plains broken by high ridges (Palisades) rising 400-500 ft.; Coastal Plain, covering three-fifths of state in SE, gradually rises from sea level to gentle slopes. **Capital:** Trenton.

Economy. Principal industries: services, trade, manufacturing. **Principal manufactured goods:** chemicals, electronic and electrical equipment, non-electrical machinery, fabricated metals. **Agriculture: Chief crops:** hay, corn, soybeans, tomatoes, blueberries, peaches, cranberries. **Livestock** (1987): 77,500 cattle; 32,000 hogs/pigs; 12,600 sheep; 2.1 mln. poultry. **Timber/lumber** (1987): pine, cedar, mixed hardwoods; 8 mln. bd. ft. **Nonfuel Minerals** (1988): $266.8 mln.; mostly crushed stone, construction sand & gravel. **Commercial fishing** (1988): $71.9 mln. **Chief ports:** Newark, Elizabeth, Hoboken, Camden. **International airports at:** Newark. **Value of construction** (1988): $8.4 bln. **Employment distribution** (1988): 24.7% serv.; 24.0% trade; 18.3% manuf.; 15.1% gvt. **Per capita income** (1988): $21,882. **Unemployment** (1988): 3.8%. **Tourism** (1987): tourists spent $11.4 bln. **Sales tax:** 6%.

Finance. FDIC-insured **commercial banks & trust companies** (1987): 125. **Deposits:** $59.6. **Savings institutions:** 174. **Assets:** $67.6 bln.

Federal government. No. federal civilian employees (Mar. 1988): 38,120. **Avg. salary:** $28,690. **Notable federal facilities:** McGuire AFB Fort Dix; Fort Monmouth; Picatinny Arsenal; Lakewood Naval Air Station, Lakehurst Naval Air Engineering Center.

Energy. Electricity production (1988, mwh, by source): Mineral: 16.7 mln.; Nuclear: 23.9 mln.

Education. Expenditure per pupil, public schools (1987): $5,953. **Avg. salary, public school teachers** (1988-89): $32,923.

State Data. Motto: Liberty and prosperity. **Flower:** Purple violet. **Bird:** Eastern goldfinch. **Tree:** Red oak. Third of the original 13 states to ratify the Constitution, Dec. 18, 1787. **State fair:** usually Sept.

History. The Lenni Lenape (Delaware) Indians had mostly peaceful relations with European colonists who arrived after the explorers Verrazano, 1524, and Hudson, 1609. The Dutch were first; when the British took New

Netherland, 1664, the area between the Delaware and Hudson Rivers was given to Lord John Berkeley and Sir George Carteret. New Jersey was the scene of nearly 100 battles, large and small, during the Revolution, including Trenton, 1776, Princeton, 1777, Monmouth, 1778.

Tourist attractions. 127 miles of beaches; Miss America Pageant and hotel-casinos, Atlantic City; Grover Cleveland birthplace, Caldwell. Cape May Historic District; Edison Labs, W. Orange; Great Adventure amusement park; Liberty State Park; Meadowlands Sports Complex; Pine Barrens wilderness area; Princeton University; numerous Revolutionary War historical sites.

Famous New Jerseyans include Count Basie, Aaron Burr, Grover Cleveland, James Fenimore Cooper, Stephen Crane, Thomas Edison, Albert Einstein, Alexander Hamilton, Joyce Kilmer, Gen. George McClellan, Thomas Paine, Molly Pitcher, Paul Robeson, Walter Schirra, Frank Sinatra, Bruce Springsteen, Walt Whitman, Woodrow Wilson.

Chamber of Commerce. 50 Commerce St., Newark, NJ 07102.

Toll-free travel information. 1-800-JERSEY-7.

New Mexico

Land of Enchantment

People. Population (1988): 1,507,000; **rank:** 37. **Pop. density:** 12.4 per sq. mi. **Urban** (1980): 72.1%. **Racial distrib.** (1985): 89.0% White; 2.0% Black; 9.0% Other (includes American Indians); Hispanic 550,600. **Net change** (1980-88): +204,000; +15.6%.

Geography. Total area: 121,593 sq. mi.; **rank:** 5. **Land area:** 121,335 sq. mi. **Acres forested land:** 18,059,800. **Location:** southwestern state bounded by Colorado on the N, Oklahoma, Texas, and Mexico on the E and S, and Arizona on the W. **Climate:** dry, with temperatures rising or falling 5°F with every 1,000 ft. elevation. **Topography:** eastern third, Great Plains; central third Rocky Mtns. (85% of the state is over 4,000 ft. elevation); western third high plateau. **Capital:** Santa Fe.

Economy. Principal industries: extractive industries, tourism, agriculture. **Principal manufactured goods:** foods, electrical machinery, apparel, lumber, printing, transportation equipment. **Agriculture:** Chief **crops:** wheat, hay, sorghum, grain, onions, cotton, corn. **Livestock:** 1.72 mln. cattle; 72,000 hogs/pigs; 578,000 sheep; 1.21 mln. poultry. **Timber/lumber** (1987): Ponderosa pine, Douglas fir; 193 mln. bd. ft. **Nonfuel Minerals** (1988): $1.0 bln.; copper, potash, construction sand & gravel. **International airports at:** Albuquerque. **Value of construction** (1988): $1.4 bln. **Employment distribution:** 22.3% serv.; 18.0% agric.; 10% manuf.; 26.2% gvt. **Per capita income** (1988): $12,481. **Unemployment** (1988): 7.8%. **Tourism** (1987): out-of-state visitors spent $2.0 bln. **Sales tax:** 4¾%.

Finance. FDIC-insured commercial banks & trust companies (1987): 94. **Deposits:** $8.5 bln. **Savings institutions:** 25. **Assets:** $6.0 bln.

Federal government. No. federal civilian employees (Mar. 1988): 22,990. **Avg. salary:** $26,894. **Notable federal facilities:** Kirtland, Cannon, Holloman AF bases; Los Alamos Scientific Laboratory; White Sands Missile Range.

Energy. Electricity production (1988, mwh, by source): Hydroelectric: 100,000; Mineral: 26.3 mln.

Education. Expenditure per pupil, public schools (1987): $3,558. **Avg. salary, public school teachers** (1988-89): $25,205.

State data. Motto: Crescit Eundo (It grows as it goes). **Flower:** Yucca. **Bird:** Roadrunner. **Tree:** Pinon. **Song:** O, Fair New Mexico, and Asi Es Nuevo Mexico. **Entered the** Jan. 6, 1912; rank, 47th. **State fair** at: Albuquerque; mid-Sept.

History. Franciscan Marcos de Niza and a black slave Estevan explored the area, 1539, seeking gold. First settlements were at San Juan Pueblo, 1598, and Santa Fe, 1610. Settlers alternately traded and fought with the Apaches, Comanches, and Navajos. Trade on the Santa Fe Trail to Missouri started 1821. The Mexican War was declared May, 1846, Gen. Stephen Kearny took Santa Fe, August. In the 1870s, cattlemen staged the famed Lincoln County War in which Billy (the Kid) Bonney played a leading role. Pancho Villa raided Columbus, 1916.

Tourist Attractions. Carlsbad Caverns, a national park, has caverns on 3 levels and the largest natural cave "room" in the world, 1,500 by 300 ft., 300 ft. high; White Sands Natl. Monument, the largest gypsum deposit in the world.

Pueblo ruins from 100 AD, Chaco Canyon; Acoma, the "sky city," built atop a 357-ft. mesa; 19 Pueblo, 4 Navajo, and 2 Apache reservations. Also, ghost towns, dude ranches, skiing, hunting, and fishing.

Famous New Mexicans include Billy (the Kid) Bonney, Kit Carson, Peter Hurd, Archbishop Jean Baptiste Lamy, Nancy Lopez, Bill Mauldin, Georgia O'Keeffe, Kim Stanley, Al Unser, Bobby Unser, Lew Wallace.

Tourist information. New Mexico Travel Division, Joseph M. Montoya Bldg., 1100 St. Francis Dr., Santa Fe, N.M. 87503.

Toll-free travel information. 1-800-545-2040.

New York

Empire State

People. Population (1988): 17,909,000; **rank:** 2. **Pop. density:** 364.7 per sq. mi. **Urban** (1980): 84.6%. **Racial distrib.** (1985): 84.6% White; 15.4% Black; Hispanic: 1.9 mln. **Net change** (1980-88): +351,000; 2.0%.

Geography. Total area: 49,108 sq. mi.; **rank:** 30. **Land area:** 47,377 sq. mi. **Acres forested land:** 17,218,400. **Location:** Middle Atlantic state, bordered by the New England states, Atlantic Ocean, New Jersey and Pennsylvania, Lakes Ontario and Erie, and Canada. **Climate:** variable; the SE region moderated by the ocean. **Topography:** highest and most rugged mountains in the NE Adirondack upland; St. Lawrence-Champlain lowlands extend from Lake Ontario NE along the Canadian border; Hudson-Mohawk lowland follows the flows of the rivers N and W, 10-30 mi. wide; Atlantic coastal plain in the SE; Appalachian Highlands, covering half the state westward from the Hudson Valley, include the Catskill Mtns., Finger Lakes; plateau of Erie-Ontario lowlands. **Capital:** Albany.

Economy. Principal industries: manufacturing, finance, communications, tourism, transportation, services. **Principal manufactured goods:** books and periodicals, clothing and apparel, pharmaceuticals, machinery, instruments, toys and sporting goods, electronic equipment, automotive and aircraft components. **Agriculture:** Chief **crops:** apples, cabbage, cauliflower, celery, cherries, grapes, corn, peas, snap beans, sweet corn. **Products:** milk, cheese, maple syrup, wine. **Livestock** (1987): 1.9 mln. cattle; 124,000 hogs/pigs; 64,000 sheep; 10.9 mln. poultry. **Timber/lumber** (1987): saw log production; 321 mln. bd. ft. **Nonfuel Minerals** (1988): $675 mln.; mostly crushed stone, cement, construction sand & gravel, zinc. **Commercial fishing** (1988): $54.2 mln. **Chief ports:** New York, Buffalo, Albany. **International airports at:** New York, Buffalo, Syracuse, Massena, Ogdensburg, Watertown, Niagara Falls, Newburgh, Sullivan county. **Value of construction** (1988): $13.7 bln. **Employment distribution:** 1.3% agric.; 21% manuf.; 33% serv.; 19% trade. **Per capita income** (1988): $19,299. **Unemployment** (1988): 4.2%. **Tourism** (1987): tourists spent $17.4 bln. **Sales tax:** 4%.

Finance. FDIC-insured commercial banks & trust companies (1987): 200. **Deposits:** $468.8 bln. **Savings institutions:** 167. **Assets:** $161 bln.

Federal government. No. federal civilian employees (Mar. 1988): 68,819. **Avg. salary:** $26,876. **Notable federal facilities:** West Point Military Academy; Merchant Marine Academy; Ft. Drum; Griffiss, Plattsburgh AF bases; Watervliet Arsenal.

Energy. Electricity production (1988, mwh, by source): Hydroelectric: 24.0 mln.; Mineral: 76.6 mln.; Nuclear: 24.2 mln.

Education: Expenditure per pupil, public schools (1987): $6,497. **Avg. salary, public school teachers** (1988-89): $36,500.

State data. Motto: Excelsior (Ever upward). **Flower:** Rose. **Bird:** Bluebird. **Tree:** Sugar maple. **Song:** I Love New York. **Eleventh** of the original 13 states to ratify the Constitution, July 26, 1788. **State fair at:** Syracuse, late Aug.-early Sept.

History. In 1609 Henry Hudson discovered the river that bears his name and Champlain explored the lake, far upstate, which was named for him. Dutch built posts near Albany 1614 and 1624; in 1626 they settled Manhattan. A British fleet seized New Netherland, 1664. Ninety-two of the 300 or more engagements of the Revolution were fought in New York, including the Battle of Bemis Heights-Saratoga, a turning point of the war.

Tourist attractions. New York City; Adirondack and Catskill mtns.; Finger Lakes, Great Lakes; Long Island beaches; Thousand Islands; Niagara Falls; Saratoga Springs racing and spas; Philipsburg Manor, Sunnyside, the restored home of Washington Irving, The Dutch Church of Sleepy Hollow, all in North Tarrytown; Corning Glass Center and Steuben factory, Corning; Fenimore House, National Baseball Hall of Fame and Museum, both in Cooperstown; Ft. Ticonderoga overlooking lakes George and Champlain; Albany's Empire State Plaza, Lake Placid Olympic Village.

The Franklin D. Roosevelt National Historic Site, Hyde Park, includes the graves of Pres. and Mrs. Roosevelt, the family home since 1867, the Roosevelt Library. Sagamore Hill, Oyster Bay, the Theodore Roosevelt estate, includes his home.

Famous New Yorkers include Susan B. Anthony, Peter Cooper, George Eastman, Millard Fillmore, Julia Ward Howe, Charles Evans Hughes, Henry and William James, Herman Melville, Franklin Delano Roosevelt, Theodore Roosevelt, Alfred E. Smith, Elizabeth Cady Stanton, Martin Van Buren, Walt Whitman.

Tourist information: N.Y. State Dept. of Economic Development, 1 Commerce Plaza, Albany, NY 12245.

Toll-free travel information. 1-800-CALLNYS, from the 48 contiguous states; 1-518-474-4116 from other areas and Canada.

North Carolina

Tar Heel State, Old North State

People. Population (1988): 6,489,000; **rank:** 10. **Pop. density:** 123.2 per sq. mi. **Urban** (1980): 42.9%. **Racial distrib.** (1985): 77.5% White; 22.5% Black; Hispanic: 38,900. **Net change** (1980-88): +607,000; 10.3%.

Geography. Total area: 52,669 sq. mi.; **rank:** 28. **Land area:** 48,843 sq. mi. **Acres forested land:** 20,043,300. **Location:** South Atlantic state bounded by Virginia, South Carolina, Georgia, Tennessee, and the Atlantic O. **Climate:** sub-tropical in SE, medium-continental in mountain region; tempered by the Gulf Stream and the mountains in W. **Topography:** coastal plain and tidewater, two-fifths of state, extending to the fall line of the rivers; piedmont plateau, another two-fifths, 200 mi. wide of gentle to rugged hills; southern Appalachian Mtns. contains the Blue Ridge and Great Smoky mtns. **Capital:** Raleigh.

Economy. Principal industries: manufacturing, agriculture, tobacco, tourism. **Principal manufactured goods:** textiles, tobacco products, electrical/electronic equip., chemicals, furniture, food products, non-electrical machinery. **Agriculture:** Chief crops: tobacco, soybeans, corn, peanuts, small sweet potatoes, feed grains, vegetables, fruits. **Livestock** (1987): 950,000 cattle; 2.6 mln. hogs/pigs; 20.9 mln. chickens. **Timber/lumber** (1987): yellow pine, oak, hickory, poplar, maple. 1.7 bln. bd. ft. **Nonfuel Minerals** (1988): Total $523 mln., mostly clay, sand & gravel, crushed stone. **Commercial fishing** (1988): $75.8 mln. **Chief ports:** Morehead City, Wilmington. **Value of construction** (1988): $7.6 bln. **Employment distribution** (1988): 29.2% manuf.; 22.9% trade; 17.6% serv.; 15.3% gvt. **Per capita income** (1988):

$14,128. **Unemployment** (1988): 3.6%. **Tourism** (1988): out-of-state visitors spent $6.2 bln. **Sales tax:** 5.0%.

Finance. FDIC-insured commercial banks & trust companies (1987): 65. **Deposits:** $41.0 bln. **Savings institutions:** 137. **Assets:** $20.2 bln.

Federal government. No. federal civilian employees (Mar. 1988): 28,915. **Avg. salary:** $25,553. **Notable federal facilities:** Ft. Bragg; Camp LeJeune Marine Base; U.S. EPA Research and Development Labs, Cherry Point Marine Corps Air Station; Natl. Humanities Center; Natl. Inst. of Environmental Health Science; Natl. Center for Health Statistics Lab, Research Triangle Park.

Energy. Electricity production (1988, mwh, by source): Hydroelectric: 2.9 mln.; Mineral: 46.4 mln.; Nuclear: 29.2 mln.

Education. Expenditure per pupil, public schools (1987): $3,129. **Avg. salary, public school teachers** (1988-89): $25,650.

State data. Motto: Esse Quam Videri (To be rather than to seem). **Flower:** Dogwood. **Bird:** Cardinal. **Tree:** Pine. **Song:** The Old North State. **Twelfth** of the original 13 states to ratify the Constitution, Nov. 21, 1789. **State fair at:** Raleigh; mid-Oct.

History. The first English colony in America was the first of 2 established by Sir Walter Raleigh on Roanoke Is., 1585 and 1587. The first group returned to England; the second, the "Lost Colony," disappeared without trace. Permanent settlers came from Virginia, c. 1660. Roused by British repressions, the colonists drove out the royal governor, 1775; the province's congress was the first to vote for independence; ten regiments were furnished to the Continental Army. Cornwallis' forces were defeated at Kings Mountain, 1780, and forced out after Guilford Courthouse, 1781.

Tourist attractions. Cape Hatteras and Cape Lookout national seashores; Great Smoky Mtns. (half in Tennessee); Guilford Courthouse and Moore's Creek parks, 66 Revolutionary battle sites; Bennett Place, NW of Durham, where Gen. Joseph Johnston surrendered the last Confederate army to Gen. Wm. Sherman; Ft. Raleigh, Roanoke Is., where Virginia Dare, first child of English parents in the New World, was born Aug. 18, 1587; Wright Brothers National Memorial, Kitty Hawk; N.C. Zoo, Asheboro; N. Carolina Symphony, Raleigh.

Famous North Carolinians include Richard J. Gatling, Billy Graham, Andrew Jackson, Andrew Johnson, Wm. Rufus King, Dolley Madison, Edward R. Murrow, James K. Polk, Enos Slaughter, Moses Waddel, Thomas Wolfe.

Tourist information. Division of Travel & Tourism Development, P.O. Box 25249, Raleigh, NC 27611.

Toll-free travel information. 1-800-VISITNC.

North Dakota

Peace Garden State

People. Population (1988): 667,000; **rank:** 46. **Pop. density:** 9.4 per sq. mi. **Urban** (1980): 48.8%. **Racial distrib.** (1980): 95.8% White; 0.39% Black; Hispanic (1980): 3,700. **Net change** (1980-88): +14,000; 2.2%.

Geography. Total area: 70,702 sq. mi.; **rank:** 17. **Land area:** 69,300 sq. mi. **Acres forested land:** 421,800. **Location:** West North Central state, situated exactly in the middle of North America, bounded on the N by Canada, on the E by Minnesota, on the S by South Dakota, on the W by Montana. **Climate:** continental, with a wide range of temperature and moderate rainfall. **Topography:** Central Lowland in the E comprises the flat Red River Valley and the Rolling Drift Prairie; Missouri Plateau of the Great Plains on the W. **Capital:** Bismarck.

Economy. Principal industries: agriculture, mining, tourism, manufacturing. **Principal manufactured goods:** farm equipment, processed foods. **Agriculture:** Chief crops: spring wheat, durum, barley, rye, flaxseed, oats, potatoes, dried edible beans, honey, soybeans, sugarbeets, sunflowers, hay. **Livestock** (1987): 2.0 mln. cattle; 285,000 hogs/pigs; 180,000 sheep; 1.4 mln. poultry. **Nonfuel Minerals** (1988): $26 mln. mostly lime, construction sand & gravel, crushed stone. **International airports at:** Fargo, Grand Forks, Bismarck, Minot. **Value of construction** (1988): $445.3 mln. **Employment distribution:** 21.9% trade; 20.4% gvt.; 18.6% serv.; 17.2% agric. **Per capita income** (1988): $12,720. **Unemployment** (1988): 4.8%. **Tourism** (1986): out-of-state visitors spent $11.4 mln. **Sales tax:** 6.5%-7.5%.

Finance. FDIC-insured commercial banks & trust companies (1987): 176. **Deposits:** $6.1 bln. **Savings institutions:** 6. **Assets:** $4.2 bln.

Federal government. No. federal civilian employees (Mar. 1988): 5,443. **Avg. salary:** $25,388. **Notable federal facilities:** Strategic Air Command bases at Minot, Grand Forks; Northern Prairie Wildlife Research Center; Garrison Dam; Theodore Roosevelt Natl. Park; Grand Forks Energy Research Center; Ft. Union Natl. Historic Site.

Energy. Electricity production (1988, mwh, by source): Hydroelectric: 1.9 mln.; Mineral: 25.5 mln.

Education. Expenditure per pupil, public schools, (1987): $3,437. **Avg. salary, public school teachers** (1988-89): $22,249.

State data. Motto: Liberty and union, now and forever, one and inseparable. **Flower:** Wild prairie rose. **Bird:** Western Meadowlark. **Tree:** American elm. **Song:** North Dakota Hymn. **Entered union** Nov. 2, 1889; rank, 39th. **State fair** at: Minot; 3d week in July.

History. Pierre La Verendrye was the first French fur trader in the area, 1738, followed later by the English. The U.S. acquired half the territory in the Louisiana Purchase, 1803. Lewis and Clark built Ft. Mandan, spent the winter of 1804-05 there. In 1818, American ownership of the other half was confirmed by agreement with Britain. First permanent settlement was at Pembina, 1812. Missouri River steamboats reached the area, 1832; the first railroad, 1873, bringing many homesteaders. The state was first to hold a presidential primary, 1912.

Tourist attractions. North Dakota Heritage Center, state capitol grounds; Bonanzaville, Fargo, restored pioneer town; Ft. Union Trading Post Natl. Historic Site, built 1829; Lake Sakakawea, 180 miles of fishing, boating, 1,600 miles of shoreline. Interntl. Peace Garden, 2,200-acre tract extending across the border into Manitoba; 65,000-acre Theodore Roosevelt National Park, Badlands, contains the president's Elkhorn Ranch; Ft. Abraham Lincoln State Park and Museum, S of Mandan.

Famous North Dakotans include Maxwell Anderson, Angie Dickinson, John Bernard Flannagan; Louis L'Amour, Peggy Lee, Eric Sevareid, Vilhjalmur Stefansson, Lawrence Welk.

Chamber of Commerce. P.O. Box 2467, Fargo, ND 58108.

Toll-free travel information. 1-800-437-2077.

Ohio

Buckeye State

People. Population (1988): 10,855,000; **rank:** 7. **Pop. density:** 262.6 per sq. mi. **Urban** (1980): 73.3%. **Racial distrib.** (1985): 89.4% White; 10.6% Black; Hispanic (1980): 107,700. **Net change** (1980-88): +57,000; 0.5%.

Geography. Total area: 41,330 sq. mi.; **rank:** 35. **Land area:** 41,004 sq. mi. **Acres forested land:** 6,146,600. **Location:** East North Central state bounded on the N by Michigan and Lake Erie; on the E and S by Pennsylvania, West Virginia; and Kentucky; on the W by Indiana. **Climate:** temperate but variable; weather subject to much precipitation. **Topography:** generally rolling plain; Allegheny plateau in E; Lake [Erie] plains extend southward; central plains in the W. **Capital:** Columbus.

Economy. Principal industries: manufacturing, trade, services. **Principal manufactured goods:** transportation equipment, machinery, primary and fabricated metal products. **Agriculture:** Chief crops: corn, hay, winter wheat, oats, soybeans. **Livestock** (1985): 1.8 mln. cattle; 2.0 mln. hogs/pigs; 275,000 sheep; 22.0 mln. poultry. **Timber/lumber** (1987): oak, ash, maple, walnut, beech. 303

mln. bd. ft. **Nonfuel Minerals** (1988): $730 mln.; mostly crushed stone, construction sand & gravel, lime, Portland cement. **Commercial fishing** (1988): $1.1 mln. **Chief ports:** Toledo, Conneaut, Cleveland, Ashtabula. **International airports at:** Cleveland, Cincinnati, Columbus, Dayton. **Value of construction** (1988): $9.5 bln. **Employment distribution** (1988): 25.6% manuf.; 24.2% trade; 21.8% serv.; 15.2% gvt. **Per capita income** (1988): $15,485. **Unemployment** (1988): 6.0%. **Tourism** (1982): travelers spent nearly $5.4 bln.

Finance. FDIC-insured commercial banks & trust companies (1987): 308. **Deposits:** $70.4 bln. **Savings institutions:** 231. **Assets:** $58.8.

Federal government. No. federal civilian employees (Mar. 1988): 53,805. **Avg. salary:** $29,279. **Notable federal facilities:** Wright Patterson AF base; Defense Construction Supply Center; Lewis Research Ctr.; Portsmouth Gaseous Diffusion Plant; Mound Laboratory.

Energy. Electricity production (1988, mwh, by source): Hydroelectric: 176,000; Mineral: 115.0 mln.; Nuclear: 8.5.

Education. Expenditure per pupil, public schools (1987): $3,671. **Avg. salary, public school teachers** (1988-89): $29,152.

State data. Motto: With God, all things are possible. **Flower:** Scarlet carnation. **Bird:** Cardinal. **Tree:** Buckeye. **Song:** Beautiful Ohio. **Entered union** Mar. 1, 1803; rank, 17th. **State fair** at: Columbus; mid-Aug.

History. LaSalle visited the Ohio area, 1669. American fur-traders arrived, beginning 1685; the French and Indians sought to drive them out. During the Revolution, Virginians defeated the Indians, 1774, but hostilities were renewed, 1777. The region became U.S. territory after the Revolution. First organized settlement was at Marietta, 1788. Indian warfare ended with Anthony Wayne's victory at Fallen Timbers, 1794. In the War of 1812, Oliver H. Perry's victory on Lake Erie and William H. Harrison's invasion of Canada, 1813, ended British incursions.

Tourist attractions. Mound City Group National Monuments, a group of 24 prehistoric Indian burial mounds; Neil Armstrong Air and Space Museum, Wapakoneta; Air Force Museum, Dayton; Pro Football Hall of Fame, Canton; King's Island amusement park, King's Island; Cedar Point amusement park, Sandusky. birthplaces, homes, and memorials to Ohio's 8 U.S. presidents: Wm. Henry Harrison, Grant, Garfield, Hayes, McKinley, Harding, Taft, Benjamin Harrison; Lake Erie Islands, Sandusky; Amish Region, Tuscarawas/Holmes counties; German Village, Columbus; Sea World, Aurora; Jack Nicklaus Sports Center, Mason; Bob Evans Farm, Rio Grande.

Famous Ohioans include Sherwood Anderson, Neil Armstrong, George Bellows, Ambrose Bierce, Clarence Darrow, Paul Laurence Dunbar, Thomas Edison, Clark Gable, John Glenn, Bob Hope, Jack Nicklaus, Jesse Owens, Eddie Rickenbacker, John D. Rockefeller Sr. and Jr., Pete Rose, Gen. Wm. Sherman, Harriet Beecher Stowe, Charles Taft, Robert A. Taft, William H. Taft, James Thurber, Orville Wright.

Chamber of Commerce. 35 E. Gay St., Columbus, OH 43215.

Toll-free travel information. 1-800-BUCKEYE.

Oklahoma

Sooner State

People. Population (1988): 3,242,000; **rank:** 27. **Pop. density:** 46.4 per sq. mi. **Urban** (1980): 67.3%. **Racial distrib.** (1985): 85.6% White; 6.9% Black; 6.3% Amer. Ind; Hispanic 69,800. **Net change** (1980-88): +217,000; 7.2%.

Geography. Total area: 69,919 sq. mi.; **rank:** 18. **Land area:** 68,782 sq. mi. **Acres forested land:** 8,513,300. **Location:** West South Central state bounded on the N by Colorado and Kansas; on the E by Missouri and Arkansas; on the S and W by Texas and New Mexico. **Climate:** temperate; southern humid belt merging with colder non-continental; humid eastern and dry western zones. **Topography:** high plains predominate the W, hills and small mountains in the E; the east central region is dominated by the Arkansas R. Basin, and the Red R. Plains, in the S. **Capital:** Oklahoma City.

Economy. Principal industries: manufacturing, mineral and energy exploration and production, agriculture, printing & publishing. **Principal manufactured goods:** non-electrical machinery, fabricated metal products, petroleum. **Agriculture: Chief crops:** wheat, hay, peanuts, grain sorghum, soybeans, corn, pecans, oats, barley, rye. **Livestock** (1987): 5.2 mln. cattle; 220,000 hogs/pigs; 105,000 sheep; 4.5 mln. poultry. **Timber/lumber** (1987): pine, oaks, hickory; 309 mln. bd. ft. **Nonfuel Minerals** (1988): $215 mln.; mostly crushed stone, Portland cement, sand & gravel. **Chief ports:** Catoosa, Muskogee. **International airports at:** Oklahoma City, Tulsa. **Value of construction** (1988): $1.7 bln. **Employment distribution** (1987): 24.3% trade; 22.5% gvt.; 21.0% serv.; 14.0% manuf. **Per capita income** (1988): $13,269. **Unemployment** (1988): 6.7%. **Tourism** (1987): tourists spent $2.9 bln.

Finance. FDIC-insured commercial banks & trust companies (1987): 520. **Deposits:** $25.4 bln. **Savings institutions:** 53. **Assets:** $10.2 bln.

Federal government. No. federal civilian employees (Mar. 1988): 36,640. **Avg. salary:** $26,183. **Notable federal facilities:** Federal Aviation Agency and Tinker AFB, both Oklahoma City; Ft. Sill, Lawton; Altus AFB, Altus; Vance AFB, Enid.

Energy. Electricity production (1988, mwh, by source): Hydroelectric: 2.1 mln.; Mineral: 42.0 mln.

Education. Expenditure per pupil, public schools (1987): $3,099. **Avg. salary, public school teachers** (1988-89): $22,000.

State data. Motto: Labor Omnia Vincit (Labor conquers all things). **Flower:** Mistletoe. **Bird:** Scissortailed flycatcher. **Tree:** Redbud. **Song:** Oklahoma! **Entered union** Nov. 16, 1907; rank, 46th. **State fair** at: Oklahoma City; last week of Sept.

History. Part of the Louisiana Purchase, 1803, Oklahoma was known as Indian Territory (but was not given territorial government) after it became the home of the "Five Civilized Tribes"—Cherokee, Choctaw, Chickasaw, Creek, and Seminole—1828-1846. The land was also used by Comanche, Osage, and other Plains Indians. As white settlers pressed west, land was opened for homesteading by runs and lottery, the first run taking place Apr. 22, 1889. The most famous run was to the Cherokee Outlet, 1893.

Tourist attractions. Will Rogers Memorial, Claremore; National Cowboy Hall of Fame, Oklahoma City; restored Ft. Gibson Stockade, near Muskogee, the Army's largest outpost in Indian lands; Indian pow-wows; rodeos; fishing; hunting; Ouachita National Forest; Enterprise Square, museum devoted to American economic system.

Famous Oklahomans include Carl Albert, L. Gordon Cooper, Woody Guthrie, Gen. Patrick J. Hurley, Karl Jansky, Mickey Mantle, Carry Nation, Wiley Post, Oral Roberts, Will Rogers, Maria Tallchief, Jim Thorpe.

Chamber of Commerce. 4020 N. Lincoln Blvd., Oklahoma City, OK 73105.

Toll-free travel information. 1-800-652-6552.

volcanic peaks E of the valley; plateau E of Cascades, remaining two-thirds of state. **Capital:** Salem.

Economy. Principal industries: manufacturing, agriculture, forestry, tourism, high technology. **Principal manufactured goods:** lumber & wood products, foods, machinery, fabricated metals, paper, printing & publishing, primary metals. **Agriculture: Chief crops:** hay, wheat, potatoes, rye grass seed, pears, onions, cherries, mint oil, strawberries, fall fescue seed. **Livestock** (1987): 1.4 mln. cattle; 100,000 hogs/pigs; 490,000 sheep; 22.6 mln. poultry. **Timber/lumber** (1987): Douglas fir, hemlock, ponderosa pine; 8.5 bln. bd. ft. **Nonfuel Minerals** (1988): $169 mln.; mostly crushed stone, construction sand & gravel. **Commercial fishing** (1988): $97.7 mln. **Chief ports:** Portland, Astoria, Newport, Coos Bay. **International airports at:** Portland. **Value of construction** (1988): $2.2 bln. **Employment distribution** (1985): 25.2% trade; 20.8% serv.; 19.4% manuf.; 19.2% gvt. **Per capita income** (1988): $14,982. **Unemployment** (1988): 5.8%. **Tourism** (1985): travel expenditures, $2.6 bln.

Finance: FDIC-insured commercial banks & trust companies (1987): 59. **Deposits:** $14.5 bln. **Savings institutions:** 17. **Assets:** $9.7 bln.

Federal government. No. federal civilian employees (Mar. 1988): 18,535. **Avg. salary:** $28,457. **Notable federal facilities:** Bonneville Power Administration.

Energy. Electricity production (1988, mwh, by source): Hydroelectric: 34.7 mln.; Nuclear: 6.3 mln.

Education. Expenditure per pupil, public schools (1987): $4,337. **Avg. salary, public school teachers** (1988-89): $29,500.

State data. Motto: The union. **Flower:** Oregon grape. **Bird:** Western meadowlark. **Tree:** Douglas fir. **Song:** Oregon, My Oregon. **Entered union** Feb. 14, 1859; rank, 33d. **State fair** at: Salem; late Aug. to early Sept.

History. American Capt. Robert Gray discovered and sailed into the Columbia River, 1792; Lewis and Clark, traveling overland, wintered at its mouth 1805-06; fur traders followed. Settlers arrived in the Willamette Valley, 1834. In 1843 the first large wave of settlers arrived via the Oregon Trail. Early in the 20th century, the "Oregon System," reforms which included the initiative, referendum, recall, direct primary, and woman suffrage, was adopted.

Tourist attractions. John Day Fossil Beds National Monument; Columbia River Gorge; Mt. Hood & Timberline Lodge; Crater Lake National Park; Oregon Dunes National Recreation Area; Ft. Clatsop National Memorial; Oregon Caves National Monument; Shakespearean Festival, Ashland; High Desert Museum, Bend. Also, skiing, fishing; Annual Albany Timber Carnival, Pendelton Round-Up, Portland Rose Festival.

Famous Oregonians include Ernest Bloch, Ernest Haycox, Chief Joseph, Edwin Markham, Tom McCall, Dr. John McLoughlin, Joaquin Miller, Linus Pauling, John Reed, Alberto Salazar, Mary Decker Slaney, William Simon U'Ren.

Tourist Information: Economic Development Department, 595 Cottage St. NE, Salem, OR 97310.

Toll-free travel information. 1-800-233-3306; 1-800-547-7842 out of state.

Oregon

Beaver State

People. Population (1988): 2,767,000; **rank:** 30. **Pop. density:** 28.5 per sq. mi. **Urban** (1980): 67.9%. **Racial distrib.** (1985): 98.5% White; 1.5% Black; Hispanic: 76,000. **Net change** (1980-88): +133,000; 5.1%.

Geography. Total area: 97,073 sq. mi.; **rank:** 10. **Land area:** 96,184 sq. mi. **Acres forested land:** 29,810,000. **Location:** Pacific state, bounded on N by Washington; on E by Idaho; on S by Nevada and California; on W by the Pacific. **Climate:** coastal mild and humid climate; continental dryness and extreme temperatures in the interior. **Topography:** Coast Range of rugged mountains; fertile Willamette R. Valley to E and S; Cascade Mtn. Range of

Pennsylvania

Keystone State

People. Population (1988): 12,001,000; **rank:** 5. **Pop. density:** 264.9 per sq. mi. **Urban** (1980): 69.3%. **Racial distrib.** (1985): 90.7% White; 9.3% Black; Hispanic: 158,500. **Net change** (1980-88): +137,000; 1.2%.

Geography. Total area: 45,308 sq. mi.; **rank:** 33. **Land area:** 44,888 sq. mi. **Acres forested land:** 16,825,900. **Location:** Middle Atlantic state, bordered on the E by the Delaware R., on the S by the Mason-Dixon Line; on the W by West Virginia and Ohio; on the N/NE by Lake Erie and New York. **Climate:** continental with wide fluctuations in seasonal temperatures. **Topography:** Allegheny Mtns. run SW to NE, with Piedmont and Coast Plain in the SE triangle; Allegheny Front a diagonal spine across the state's center; N and W rugged plateau falls to Lake Erie Lowland. **Capital:** Harrisburg.

Economy. Principal industries: steel, travel, health, apparel, machinery, food & agriculture. **Principal manufactured goods:** primary metals, foods, fabricated metal products, non-electrical machinery, electrical machinery. **Agriculture: Chief crops:** corn, hay, mushrooms, apples, potatoes, winter wheat, oats, vegetables, tobacco, grapes. **Livestock** (1985): 1.96 mln. cattle; 800,000 hogs/pigs; 88,000 sheep; 22.5 mln. poultry. **Timber/lumber** (1987): pine, oak, maple; 605 mln. bd. ft. **Nonfuel Minerals** (1988): $1.0 bln.; mostly crushed stone, cement, lime, construction sand & gravel. **Commercial fishing** (1988): $277,000. **Chief ports:** Philadelphia, Pittsburgh, Erie. **International airports at:** Philadelphia, Pittsburgh, Erie, Harrisburg. **Value of construction** (1988): $9.9 bln. **Employment distribution** (1986): 24.4% serv.; 23.9% trade; 23.3% manuf.; 14.9% gvt. **Per capita income** (1988): $16,168 **Unemployment** (1988): 5.1%. **Tourism** (1985): out-of-state visitors spent $8.9 bln.

Finance. FDIC-insured commercial banks & trust companies (1987): 299. **Deposits:** $109.1 bln. **Savings institutions:** 235. **Assets:** $64.7 bln.

Federal government. No. federal civilian employees (Mar. 1988): 88,629. **Avg. salary:** $25,551. **Notable federal facilities:** Army War College, Carlisle; Ships Control Ctr., Mechanicsburg; New Cumberland Army Depot; Philadelphia Navy Yard, Philadelphia.

Energy. Electricity production (1988, mwh, by source): Hydroelectric: 705,000 Mineral: 114.4 mln. Nuclear: 37.9 mln.

Education. Expenditure per pupil, public schools (1987): $4,616. **Avg. salary, public school teachers** (1988-89): $30,720.

State data. Motto: Virtue, liberty and independence. **Flower:** Mountain laurel. **Bird:** Ruffed grouse. **Tree:** Hemlock. **Second** of the original 13 states to ratify the Constitution, Dec. 12, 1787. **State fair** at: Harrisburg; 2d week in Jan.

History. First settlers were Swedish, 1643, on Tinicum Is. In 1655 the Dutch seized the settlement but lost it to the British, 1664. The region was given by Charles II to William Penn, 1681, Philadelphia (brotherly love) was the capital of the colonies during most of the Revolution, and of the U.S., 1790-1800. Philadelphia was taken by the British, 1777; Washington's troops encamped at Valley Forge in the bitter winter of 1777-78. The Declaration of Independence, 1776, and the Constitution, 1787, were signed in Philadelphia.

Tourist attractions. Independence Hall & Natl. Historic Park, Franklin Institute Science Museum, Philadelphia Museum of Art, all in Philadelphia; Valley Forge Natl. Historic Park, Gettysburg Natl. Military Park; Pennsylvania Dutch Country; Hershey; Dusquesne Incline, Carnegie Institute, Heinz Hall, all in Pittsburgh; year 'round outdoor sports in Pocono Mtns., Pine Creek River Gorge, Alleghenies, Laurel Highlands & Presque Isle State Park.

Famous Pennsylvanians include Marian Anderson, Maxwell Anderson, James Buchanan, Andrew Carnegie, Stephen Foster, Benjamin Franklin, George C. Marshall, Andrew W. Mellon, Robert E. Peary, Mary Roberts Rinehart, Betsy Ross.

Chamber of Commerce. 222 N. 3d St., Harrisburg, PA 17101.

Toll-free travel information. 1-800-VISITPA.

Rhode Island

Little Rhody, Ocean State

People. Population (1988): 993,000; **rank:** 43. **Pop. density:** 819.3 per sq. mi. **Urban** (1980): 87.0% **Racial distrib.** (1985): 96.5% White; 3.5% Black; Hispanic: 19,700. **Net change** (1980-88): +46,000; 4.8%.

Geography. Total area: 1,212 sq. mi.; **rank:** 50. **Land area:** 1,055 sq. mi. **Acres forested land:** 404,200. **Location:** New England state. **Climate:** invigorating and changeable. **Topography:** eastern lowlands of Narragansett Basin; western uplands of flat and rolling hills. **Capital:** Providence.

Economy. Principal industries: manufacturing, services. **Principal manufactured goods:** costume jewelry, machinery, textiles, electronics, silverware. **Agriculture: Chief crops:** nursery prods., turf, potatoes, apples. **Livestock:** 7,000 cattle; 6,400 hogs/pigs; 6,500 sheep; 430,000 poultry. **Timber/lumber:** oak, chestnut. **Nonfuel Minerals** (1988): $17 mln.; construction sand & gravel, crushed stone. **Commercial fishing** (1988): $69.4 mln. **Chief ports:** Providence, Quonset Point, Newport, Tiverton. **Value of construction** (1988): $1.1 bln. **Employment distribution** (1988): 25.0% manuf.; 25.4% serv.; 22.8% trade. **Per capita income** (1988): $16,793. **Unemployment** (1988): 3.1%. **Tourism** (1987): visitors spent $1.1 bln. **Sales tax:** 6%.

Finance. FDIC-insured commercial banks & trust companies (1987): 15. **Deposits:** $9.0 bln. **Savings institutions:** 10. **Assets:** $8.3 bln.

Federal government. No. federal civilian employees (Mar. 1988): 5,925. **Avg. salary:** $27,955. **Notable federal facilities:** Naval War College; Naval Underwater Systems Center.

Energy. Electricity production (1988, mwh, by source): Mineral: 764,000.

Education. Expenditure per pupil, public schools (1987): $4,985. **Avg. salary, public school teachers** (1988-89): $34,233.

State data. Motto: Hope. **Flower:** Violet. **Bird:** Rhode Island red. **Tree:** Red maple. **Song:** Rhode Island. **Thirteenth** of original 13 states to ratify the Constitution, May 29, 1790. **State fair** at: E. Greenwich; mid-Aug.

History. Rhode Island is distinguished for its battle for freedom of conscience and action, begun by Roger Williams, founder of Providence, who was exiled from Massachusetts Bay Colony in 1636, and Anne Hutchinson, exiled in 1638. Rhode Island gave protection to Quakers in 1657 and to Jews from Holland in 1658.

The colonists broke the power of the Narragansett Indians in the Great Swamp Fight, 1675, the decisive battle in King Philip's War. British trade restrictions angered the colonists and they burned the British revenue cutter Gaspee, 1772. The colony declared its independence May 4, 1776. Gen. John Sullivan and Lafayette won a partial victory, 1778, but failed to oust the British.

Tourist attractions. Newport mansions; summer resorts and water sports; various yachting races inc. Newport to Bermuda. Touro Synagogue, Newport, 1763; first Baptist Church in America, Providence, 1638; Gilbert Stuart birthplace, Saunderstown; Narragansett Indian Fall Festival.

Famous Rhode Islanders include Ambrose Burnside, George M. Cohan, Nelson Eddy, Jabez Gorham, Nathanael Greene, Christopher and Oliver La Farge, Matthew C. and Oliver Perry, Gilbert Stuart.

Chamber of Commerce. 30 Exchange Terr., Providence, RI 02908.

Toll-free travel information. 1-800-556-2484.

South Carolina

Palmetto State

People. Population (1988): 3,470,000. **rank:** 25, **Pop. density:** 111.5 per sq. mi. **Urban** (1980): 54.1%. **Racial distrib.** (1985): 69.5% White; 30.5% Black; Hispanic: 20,100. **Net change** (1980-88): +348,000; 11.2%.

Geography. Total area: 31,113 sq. mi.; **rank:** 40. **Land area:** 30,203 sq. mi. **Acres forested land:** 12,249,400. **Location:** south Atlantic coast state, bordered by North Carolina on the N; Georgia on the SW and W; the Atlantic O. on the E, SE and S. **Climate:** humid sub-tropical. **Topo- graphy:** Blue Ridge province in NW has highest peaks; piedmont lies between the mountains and the fall line; coastal plain covers two-thirds of the state. **Capital:** Columbia.

Economy: Principal industries: tourism, agriculture, manufacturing. **Principal manufactured goods:** textiles, chemicals and allied products, machinery & fabricated metal products, apparel and related products. **Agriculture: Chief crops:** tobacco, soybeans, corn, cotton, peaches, hay. **Livestock** (1988): 620,000 cattle; 400,000 hogs/pigs; 8.1 mln. poultry. **Timber/lumber** (1987): pine, oak; 1.3 bln. **Nonfuel Minerals** (1988): $393 mln.; mostly crushed stone, Portland cement, clay. **Commercial fishing** (1987): $21.1 mln. **Chief ports:** Charleston, Georgetown, Port Royal. **International airports at:** Charleston. **Value of construction** (1988): $3.7 bln. **Employment distribution** (1987): 26.8% manuf.; 18.3% gvt.; 17.3% serv. **Per capita income** (1988): $12,764. **Unemployment** (1988): 4.5%. **Tourism** (1987): $4.3 bln. **Sales tax:** 5%.

Finance. FDIC-insured commercial banks & trust companies (1987): 73. **Deposits:** $13.2 bln. **Savings institutions:** 49. **Assets:** $10.9 bln.

Federal government: No. federal civilian employees (Mar. 1988): 25,611. **Avg. Salary:** $25,619. **Notable federal facilities:** Polaris Submarine Base; Barnwell Nuclear Power Plant; Ft. Jackson; Parris Island; Savannah River Plant.

Energy. Electricity production (1988, mwh, by source): Hydroelectric: 631,000; Mineral: 23.8 mln.; Nuclear: 40.8 mln.

Education. Expenditure per pupil, public schools (1987): $3,237. **Avg. salary, public school teachers** (1988-89): $25,060.

State data. Motto: Dum Spiro Spero (While I breathe, I hope). **Flower:** Yellow jessamine. **Bird:** Carolina wren. **Tree:** Palmetto. **Song:** Carolina. Eighth of the original 13 states to ratify the Constitution, May 23, 1788. **State fair at:** Columbia; mid-Oct.

History. The first English colonists settled, 1670, on the Ashley River, moved to the site of Charleston, 1680. The colonists seized the government, 1775, and the royal governor fled. The British took Charleston, 1780, but were defeated at Kings Mountain that year, and at Cowpens and Eutaw Springs, 1781. In the 1830s, South Carolinians, angered by federal protective tariffs, adopted the Nullification Doctrine, holding a state can void an act of Congress. The state was the first to secede and, in 1861, Confederate troops fired on and forced the surrender of U. S. troops at Ft. Sumter, in Charleston Harbor, launching the Civil War.

Tourist attractions. Restored historic Charleston harbor area and Charleston gardens: Middleton Place, Magnolia, Cypress; other gardens at Brookgreen, Edisto, Glencairn; state parks; coastal islands; shore resorts such as Myrtle Beach and Hilton Head Island; fishing and quail hunting; Ft. Sumter National Monument, in Charleston Harbor; Charleston Museum, est. 1773, is the oldest museum in the U.S.; South Carolina State Museum, one of largest museums in South, Columbia.

Famous South Carolinians include Charles Bolden, James F. Byrnes, John C. Calhoun, DuBose Heyward, Ernest F. Hollings, Andrew Jackson, Jesse Jackson, James Longstreet, Francis Marion, Ronald McNair, Charles Pinckney, John Rutledge, Thomas Sumter, Strom Thurmond.

Chamber of Commerce. 1301 Gervais St., Suite 520, No. Carolina National Bank Tower, Columbia, SC 29201.

South Dakota

Coyote State, Sunshine State

People. Population (1988): 713,000; **rank:** 45. **Pop. density:** 9.2 per sq. mi. **Urban** (1980): 46.4%. **Racial distrib.** (1980): 92.6% White; 0.31% Black; 7.1% Other (includes American Indians); Hispanic, 3,700. **Net change** (1980-88): +22,000; 3.2%.

Geography. Total area: 77,116 sq. mi.; **rank:** 16. **Land area:** 75,952 sq. mi. **Acres forested land:** 1,702,000. **Location:** West North Central state bounded on the N by North Dakota; on the E by Minnesota and Iowa; on the S by Nebraska; on the W by Wyoming and Montana. **Cli-**

mate: characterized by extremes of temperature, persistent winds, low precipitation and humidity. **Topography:** Prairie Plains in the E; rolling hills of the Great Plains in the W; the Black Hills, rising 3,500 ft. in the SW corner. **Capital:** Pierre.

Economy: Principal industries: agriculture, services, manufacturing. **Principal manufactured goods** (1985): food & kindred prods., machinery, electric & electronic equipment. **Agriculture: Chief crops** (1988): corn, oats, wheat, sunflowers, rye, flaxseed, sorghum. **Livestock** (1988): 3.5 mln. cattle; 1.8 mln. hogs/ pigs; 590,000 sheep. **Timber/lumber** (1988): ponderosa pine; 186 mln. bd. ft. **Nonfuel Minerals** (1988): $298 mln.; mostly gold, Portland cement. **Value of construction** (1988): $425.1 mln. **Employment distribution** (1988): 24.6% serv.; 11.7% manuf. **Per capita income** (1988): $12,475. **Unemployment** (1988): 3.9%. **Tourism** (1986): travellers spent $520 mln. **Sales tax:** 4%.

Finance. FDIC-insured commercial banks & trust companies (1987): 135. **Deposits:** $8.1 bln. **Savings institutions:** 12. **Assets:** $1.4 bln.

Federal government. No. federal civilian employees (Mar. 1988): 6,720. **Avg. salary:** $25,241. **Notable federal facilities:** Bureau of Indian Affairs, Ellsworth AFB, Corp of Engineers, Nat'l Park Service.

Energy. Electricity production (1988, mwh, by source): Hydroelectric: 5.3 mln.; Mineral: 2.6 mln.

Education. Expenditures per pupil, public schools (1987): $3,097. **Avg. salary, public school teachers** (1988-89): $20,480.

State data. Motto: Under God, the people rule. **Flower:** Pasque flower. **Bird:** Ringnecked pheasant. **Tree:** Black Hills spruce. **Song:** Hail, South Dakota. **Entered union** Nov. 2, 1889; rank, 40th. **State fair at:** Huron; late Aug.-early Sept.

History. Les Verendryes explored the region, 1742-43. Lewis and Clark passed through the area, 1804 and 1806. First white American settlement was at Fort Pierre, 1817. Gold was discovered, 1874, on the Sioux Reservation; miners rushed in. The U.S. first tried to stop them, then relaxed its opposition. The Sioux relinquished the land, 1877, and the "great Dakota Boom" began, 1879. A new Indian uprising came in 1890, climaxed by the massacre of Indian families at Wounded Knee.

Tourist attractions. Black Hills; Mt. Rushmore, with colossal likeness of the faces of U.S. Presidents Washington, Jefferson, Lincoln & T. Roosevelt carved by sculptor Gutzon Borglum. Needles Highway; Harney Peak, at 7,242 ft. the tallest peak between the Rockies and the Alps; Deadwood, an 1876 Gold Rush town; Custer State Park's buffalo and burro herds; Jewel Cave, the 4th largest cave in the world; Badlands Natl. Park's "moonscape"; "Great Lakes of So. Dakota"; Ft. Sisseton, restored 1864 army frontier post; Great Plains Zoo & Museum; Corn Palace in Mitchell.

Famous South Dakotans include Sparky Anderson, Catherine Bach, Tom Brokaw, "Calamity Jane", Mary Hart, Crazy Horse, Myron Floren, Alvin H. Hansen, Cheryl Ladd, Dr. Ernest O. Lawrence, George McGovern, Billy Mills, Pat O'Brien, Sitting Bull.

Tourist information. South Dakota Tourism, Capitol Lake Plaza, Pierre, SD 57501.

Toll-free travel information. 1-800-952-2217; 1-800-843-1930 out of state.

Tennessee

Volunteer State

People. Population (1988): 4,895,000; **rank:** 16. **Pop. density:** 116.1 per sq. mi. **Urban** (1980): 60.4%. **Racial distrib.** (1985): 83.8% White; 16.2% Black; Hispanic: 18,200. **Net change** (1980-88): +304,000; 6.6%.

Geography. Total area: 42,144 sq. mi.; **rank:** 34. **Land area:** 41,155 sq. mi. **Acres forested land:** 13,160,500. **Location:** East South Central state bounded on the N by Kentucky and Virginia; on the E by North Carolina; on the S by Georgia, Alabama, and Mississippi; on the W by Arkansas and Missouri. **Climate:** humid continental to the N; humid sub-tropical to the S. **Topography:** rugged country in the E; the Great Smoky Mtns. of the Unakas; low ridges of the Appalachian Valley; the flat Cumberland Plateau; slightly rolling terrain and knobs of the Interior Low Plateau, the largest region; Eastern Gulf Coastal Plain to the W, is laced with meandering streams; Mississippi Alluvial Plain, a narrow strip of swamp and flood plain in the extreme W. **Capital:** Nashville.

Economy. Principal industries: trade, services, construction; transp., commun., public utilities; finance, ins., real estate. **Principal manufactured goods:** chemicals & allied prods.; food & kindred prods.; nonelectrical machinery; electric/electronic equip.; apparel; fabr. metal prods.; transp. equip.; rubber/misc. plastic prods.; paper & allied prods., printing and publishing. **Agriculture: Chief crops:** soybeans, tobacco, wheat, cotton, corn. **Livestock** (1987): 2.4 mln. cattle; 770,000 hogs/pigs; 13,000 sheep; 3.5 mln. poultry. **Timber/lumber** (1987): red oak, white oak, yellow poplar, hickory; 696 mln. bd. ft. **Nonfuel Minerals** (1988): $592 mln.; mostly clay, sand and gravel, crushed stone. **Chief ports:** Memphis, Nashville, Chattanooga, Knoxville. **International airports at:** Memphis, Nashville. **Value of construction** (1988): $4.8 bln. **Employment distribution** (1988): 24.6% manuf.; 23.6% trade; 20.8% serv.; 15.8% gvt. **Per capita income** (1988): $13,659. **Unemployment** (1988): 5.8%. **Tourism** (1988): out-of-state visitors spent $3.3 bln. **Sales tax:** 5½%.

Finance. FDIC-insured commercial banks & trust companies (1987): 283. **Deposit:** $32.3 bln. **Savings institutions:** 63. **Assets:** $11.3 bln.

Federal government. No. federal civilian employees (Mar. 1988): 46,263. **Avg. salary:** $28,421. **Notable federal facilities:** Tennessee Valley Authority; Oak Ridge Nat'l. Laboratories.

Energy: Electricity production (1988, mwh, by source): Hydroelectric: 4.6 mln.; Mineral: 51.3 mln.

Education. Expenditures per pupil, public schools (1987): $2,827. **Avg. salary, public school teachers** (1988-89): $25,619.

State data. Motto: Agriculture and commerce. **Flower:** Iris. **Bird:** Mockingbird. **Tree:** Tulip poplar. **Song:** The Tennessee Waltz. **Entered union** June 1, 1796; rank, 16th. **State fair** at: Nashville; mid-Sept.

History. Spanish explorers first visited the area, 1541. English traders crossed the Great Smokies from the east while France's Marquette and Jolliet sailed down the Mississippi on the west, 1673. First permanent settlement was by Virginians on the Watauga River, 1769. During the Revolution, the colonists helped win the Battle of Kings Mountain, N.C., 1780, and joined other eastern campaigns. The state seceded from the Union 1861, and saw many engagements of the Civil War, but 30,000 soldiers fought for the Union.

Tourist attractions. Natural wonders include Reelfoot Lake, the reservoir basin of the Mississippi R. formed by the 1811 earthquake; Lookout Mountain, Chattanooga; Fall Creek Falls, 256 ft. high; Great Smoky Mountains National Park; Lost Sea, Sweetwater; Cherokee Natl. Forest.

Also, the Hermitage, 13 mi. E of Nashville, home of Andrew Jackson; the homes of presidents Polk and Andrew Johnson; American Museum of Science, Oak Ridge; the Parthenon, Nashville, a replica of the Parthenon of Athens; the Grand Old Opry, Nashville, Opryland, USA, theme park, Nashville; Graceland, home of Elvis Presley, Memphis; Alex Haley Home & Museum, Henning; Casey Jones Home & Museum, Jackson.

Famous Tennesseans include Davy Crockett, David Farragut, William C. Handy, Sam Houston, Cordell Hull, Grace Moore, Dinah Shore, Alvin York.

Tourist information. Dept. of Tourist Development, 5th Floor, Rachel Jackson Bldg., Nashville, TN 37219.

Texas

Lone Star State

People. Population (1988): 16,841,000; **rank:** 3. **Pop. density:** 63.1 per sq. mi. **Urban** (1980): 79.6%. **Racial distrib.** (1985): 88.2% White; 11.8% Black; Hispanic 3.7 mln. **Net change** (1980-88): +2,612,000; 18.4%.

Geography: Total area: 266,807 sq. mi.; **rank:** 2. **Land area:** 262,017 sq. mi. **Acres forested land:** 23,279,300. **Location:** Southwestern state, bounded on the SE by the Gulf of Mexico; on the SW by Mexico, separated by the Rio Grande; surrounding states are Louisiana, Arkansas, Oklahoma, New Mexico. **Climate:** extremely varied; driest region is the Trans-Pecos; wettest is the NE. **Topography:** Gulf Coast Plain in the S and SE; North Central Plains slope upward with some hills; the Great Plains extend over the Panhandle, are broken by low mountains; the Trans-Pecos is the southern extension of the Rockies. **Capital:** Austin.

Economy. Principal industries: trade, services, manufacturing. **Principal manufactured goods:** machinery, transportation equipment, foods, refined petroleum, apparel. **Agriculture: Chief crops:** cotton, grain sorghum, grains, vegetables, citrus and other fruits, pecans, peanuts. **Livestock** (1985): 14.1 mln. cattle; 415,000 hogs/pigs; 1.81 mln. sheep; 17.4 mln. poultry. **Timber/lumber** (1987): pine, cypress; 1.2 bln. bd. ft. **Nonfuel Minerals** (1988): $1.49 bln.; mostly cement, stone, sand & gravel. **Commercial fishing** (1988): $175.8 mln. **Chief ports:** Houston, Galveston, Brownsville, Beaumont, Port Arthur, Corpus Christi. **Major international airports at:** Houston, Dallas/Ft. Worth, San Antonio. **Value of construction** (1988) $12.5 bln. **Employment distribution** (1987): 25.0% trade; 22.4% serv.; 18.0% gvt.; 14.3% manuf. **Per capita income** (1988): $14,640. **Unemployment** (1988): 7.3%. **Tourism** (1986): out-of-state visitors spent $17.3 bln. **Sales tax:** 6%, + optional 1% local, 1% transit.

Finance. FDIC-insured commercial banks & trust companies (1987): 1,972. **Deposits:** $165.0 bln. **Savings institutions:** 279. **Assets:** $100.1 bln.

Federal government. No. federal civilian employees (Mar. 1988): 120,238. **Avg. salary:** $25,789. **Notable federal facilities:** Fort Hood (Killeen); Kelly AFB, and Ft. Sam Houston, both San Antonio.

Energy. Electricity production (1988, mwh, by source): Hydroelectric: 1.2 mln.; Mineral: 215.2 mln. Nuclear: 3.7 mln.

Education. Expenditures per pupil, public schools (1987): $3,409 **Avg. salary, public school teachers** (1988-89): $26,513.

State data. Motto: Friendship. **Flower:** Bluebonnet. **Bird:** Mockingbird. **Tree:** Pecan. **Song:** Texas, Our Texas. **Entered union** Dec. 29, 1845; rank, 28th. **State fair** at: Dallas; mid-Oct.

History. Pineda sailed along the Texas coast, 1519; Cabeza de Vaca and Coronado visited the interior, 1541. Spaniards made the first settlement at Ysleta, near El Paso, 1682. Americans moved into the land early in the 19th century. Mexico, of which Texas was a part, won independence from Spain, 1821; Santa Anna became dictator, 1835. Texans rebelled; Santa Anna wiped out defenders of the Alamo, 1836. Sam Houston's Texans defeated Santa Anna at San Jacinto and independence was proclaimed the same year. In 1845, Texas was admitted to the Union.

Tourist attractions. Padre Island National Seashore; Big Bend, Guadalupe Mtns. national parks; The Alamo; Ft. Davis; Six Flags Amusement Park. Named for Pres. Lyndon B. Johnson are a state park, a natl. historic site marking his birthplace, boyhood home, and ranch, all near Johnson City, and a library in Austin.

Famous Texans include Stephen F. Austin, James Bowie, Carol Burnett, J. Frank Dobie, Dwight D. Eisenhower, Sam Houston, Howard Hughes, Lyndon B. Johnson, Mary Martin, Chester Nimitz, Katharine Ann Porter, Sam Rayburn.

Chamber of Commerce. 206 W. 13th, Austin, TX 78701.

Utah

Beehive State

People. Population (1988): 1,690,000; **rank:** 35. **Pop. density:** 19.9 per sq. mi. **Urban** (1980): 84.4%. **Racial distrib.** (1985): 97.1% White; Hispanic 70,600. **Net change** (1980-88): +229,000; 15.7%.

Geography. Total area: 84,899 sq. mi.; **rank:** 11. **Land area:** 82,073 sq. mi. **Acres forested land:** 15,557,400. **Location:** Middle Rocky Mountain state; its southeastern corner touches Colorado, New Mexico, and Arizona, and is the only spot in the U.S. where 4 states join. **Climate:** arid; ranging from warm desert in SW to alpine in NE. **Topography:** high Colorado plateau is cut by brilliantly-colored canyons of the SE; broad, flat, desert-like Great Basin of the W; the Great Salt Lake and Bonneville Salt Flats to the NW; Middle Rockies in the NE run E-W; valleys and plateaus of the Wasatch Front. **Capital:** Salt Lake City.

Economy. Principal industries: manufacturing, tourism, trade, services, mining, transportation, education. **Principal manufactured goods:** guided missiles and parts, electronic components, food products, fabricated metals, steel, electrical and transportation equipment. **Agriculture:** Chief crops: hay, wheat, apples, barley, alfalfa seed, corn, potatoes, cherries, onions. **Livestock:** 855,000 cattle; 34,000 hogs/pigs; 600,000 sheep; 3.8 mln. poultry. **Timber/lumber:** aspen, spruce, pine. **Nonfuel Minerals** (1988): $990 mln.; copper, gold, magnesium. **International airports at:** Salt Lake City. **Value of construction** (1988): $1.4 bln. **Employment distribution:** (1988) 23.7% serv.; 23.6% trade; 21.6% govt; 15.0% mfg. **Per capita income** (1988): $12,013. **Unemployment** (1988): 4.9%. **Tourism** (1986): travellers spent $2.0 bln. **Sales tax:** 6.25%.

Finance. FDIC-insured commercial banks & trust companies (1987): 61. **Deposits:** $9.1 bln. **Savings institutions:** 13. **Assets:** $7.1 bln.

Federal government. No. federal civilian employees (Mar. 1988): 32,219. **Avg. salary:** $25,366. **Notable federal facilities:** Hill AFB; Tooele Army Depot, IRS Western Service Center.

Energy. Electricity production (1988, mwh, by source): Hydroelectric: 593,000 mln.; Mineral: 28.9 mln.

Education. Expenditures per pupil, public schools (1987): $2,415. **Avg. salary, public school teachers** (1988-89): $23,023.

State data. Motto: Industry. **Flower:** Sego lily. **Bird:** Seagull. **Tree:** Blue spruce. **Song:** Utah, We Love Thee. **Entered union** Jan. 4, 1896; **rank,** 45th. **State fair** at: Salt Lake City; Sept.

History. Spanish Franciscans visited the area, 1776, the first white men to do so. American fur traders followed. Permanent settlement began with the arrival of the Mormons, 1847. They made the arid land bloom and created a prosperous economy, organized the State of Deseret, 1849, and asked admission to the Union. This was not achieved until 1896, after a long period of controversy over the Mormon Church's doctrine of polygamy, which it discontinued in 1890.

Tourist attractions. Temple Square, Mormon Church hdqtrs., Salt Lake City; Great Salt Lake; fishing streams, lakes and reservoirs, numerous winter sports; campgrounds. Natural wonders may be seen at Zion, Canyonlands, Bryce Canyon, Arches, and Capitol Reef national parks; Dinosaur, Rainbow Bridge, Timpanogos Cave, and Natural Bridges national monuments. Also Lake Powell and Flaming Gorge reservoirs.

Famous Utahans include Maude Adams, Ezra Taft Benson, John Moses Browning, Mariner Eccles, Philo Farnsworth, James Fletcher, David M. Kennedy, J. Willard Marriott, Osmond Family, Merlin Olsen, Ivy Baker Priest, George Romney, Brigham Young, Loretta Young.

Tourist information. Utah Travel Council, Council Hall, Salt Lake City, UT 84114.

Vermont

Green Mountain State

People. Population (1988): 557,000; **rank:** 48. **Pop. density:** 57.9 per sq. mi. **Urban** (1980): 33.8%. **Racial distrib.** (1980): 99.0% White; 0.22% Black; Hispanic 3,700. **Net change** (1980-88): +46,000; 9.0%.

Geography. Total area: 9,614 sq. mi.; **rank:** 43. **Land area:** 9,273 sq. mi. **Acres forested land:** 4,511,700. **Location:** northern New England state. **Climate:** temperate, with considerable temperature extremes; heavy snowfall in mountains. **Topography:** Green Mtns. N-S backbone 20-36 mi. wide; avg. altitude 1,000 ft. **Capital:** Montpelier.

Economy. Principal industries: manufacturing, tourism, agriculture, trade; finance, insurance, real estate, government. **Principal manufactured goods:** machine tools, furniture, scales, books, computer components, fishing rods. **Agriculture:** Chief crops: dairy products, apples, maple syrup, silage corn, hay. **Livestock** (1988): 320,000 cattle; 5,100 hogs/ pigs; 20,456 sheep; 406,000 poultry. **Timber/lumber** (1987): pine, spruce, fir, hemlock; 143 mln. bd. ft. **Nonfuel Minerals** (1988): $73. mln.; mostly dimension stone, crashed stone, construction sand & gravel. **International airports at:** Burlington. **Value of construction** (1988): $702.7 mln. **Employment distribution** (1988): 24% serv.; 24% trade; 20% manuf. **Per capita income** (1988): $15,382. **Unemployment** (1988): 2.8%. **Tourism** (1986): visitors spent $1.2 bln.

Finance. FDIC-insured commercial banks & trust companies (1987): 25. **Deposits:** $4.2 bln. **Savings institutions:** 9. **Assets** $ 1.9 bln.

Federal government. No. federal civilian employees (Mar. 1988): 2,450. **Avg. salary:** $26,248.

Energy. Electricity production (1987, mwh, by source): Hydroelectric: 809,000; Mineral: 26,000; Nuclear: 4.1 mln.

Education. Expenditures per pupil, public schools (1988): $4,399. **Avg. salary, public school teachers** (1988-89): $26,861.

State data. Motto: Freedom and unity. **Flower:** Red clover. **Bird:** Hermit thrush. **Tree:** Sugar maple. **Song:** Hail, Vermont. **Entered union** Mar. 4, 1791; **rank,** 14th. **State fair** at: Rutland; early Sept.

History. Champlain explored the lake that bears his name, 1609. First American settlement was Ft. Dummer, 1724, near Brattleboro. Ethan Allen and the Green Mountain Boys captured Ft. Ticonderoga, 1775; John Stark defeated part of Burgoyne's forces near Bennington, 1777. In the War of 1812, Thomas MacDonough defeated a British fleet on Champlain off Plattsburgh, 1814.

Tourist attractions. Year-round outdoor sports, esp. hiking, camping and skiing; there are over 56 ski areas in the state. Popular are the Shelburne Museum; Rock of Ages Tourist Center, Graniteville; Vermont Marble Exhibit, Proctor; Bennington Battleground; Pres. Coolidge homestead, Plymouth; Maple Grove Maple Museum, St. Johnsbury.

Famous Vermonters include Ethan Allen, Chester A. Arthur, Calvin Coolidge, Adm. George Dewey, John Dewey, Stephen A. Douglas, Dorothy Canfield Fisher, James Fisk.

Tourist Information. Vermont Travel Division, 134 State St., Montpelier, VT 05602.

Virginia

Old Dominion

People. Population (1988): 6,015,000; **rank:** 12. **Pop. density:** 147.5 per sq. mi. **Urban** (1980): 66.0% **Racial distrib.** (1985): 81.0% White; 19.0% Black; Hispanic 87,000. **Net change** (1980-88): +668,000; 12.5%.

Geography. Total area: 40,767 sq. mi.; **rank:** 36. **Land area:** 39,704 sq. mi. **Acres forested land:** 16,417,400. **Location:** South Atlantic state bounded by the Atlantic O. on the E and surrounded by North Carolina, Tennessee, Kentucky, West Virginia, and Maryland. **Climate:** mild and equable. **Topography:** mountain and valley region in the

W, including the Blue Ridge Mtns.; rolling piedmont plateau; tidewater, or coastal plain, including the eastern shore. **Capital:** Richmond.

Economy. Principal industries: services, trade, government, manufacturing, tourism, agriculture. **Principal manufactured goods:** textiles, transportation equipment, electric & electronic equipment, food processing, chemicals. **Agriculture: Chief crops** (1987): tobacco, soybeans, peanuts, winterwheat, corn, far grain, tomatoes. **Livestock** (1988): 1.70 mln. cattle; 420,000 hogs/pigs; 140,000 sheep; 5.26 mln. poultry. **Timber/lumber** (1987): pine and hardwoods; 1.0 bln. bd. ft. **Nonfuel Minerals** (1988): $473 mln.; mostly crushed stone. **Commercial fishing** (1988): $104.3 mln. **Chief ports:** Hampton Roads, Richmond, Alexandria. **International airports at:** Norfolk, Dulles, Richmond, Newport News. **Value of construction** (1988): $9.9 bln. **Employment distribution** (1987): 23% serv.; 23% trade; 20% gvt.; 16% manuf. **Per capita income** (1988): $17,640. **Unemployment** (1988): 3.9%. **Tourism** (1987): out-of-state visitors spent $4.4 bln. **Sales tax:** 4.5%.

Finance. FDIC-insured commercial banks & trust companies (1987): 171. **Deposits:** $41.2 bln. **Savings institutions:** 66. **Assets:** $25.6 bln.

Federal government. No. federal civilian employees (Mar. 1988): 135,915. **Avg. salary:** $29,851. **Notable federal facilities:** Pentagon; Naval Sta., Norfolk; Naval Air Sta., Norfolk, Virginia Beach; Naval Shipyard, Portsmouth; Marine Corps Base, Quantico; Langley AFB; NASA at Langley.

Energy. Electricity production (1988, mwh, by source): Mineral: 24.4 mln.; Nuclear: 21.0 mln.

Education. Expenditures per pupil, public schools (1987): $3,780. **Avg. salary, public school teachers** (1988-89): $29,056.

State data. Motto: Sic Semper Tyrannis (Thus always to tyrants). **Flower:** Dogwood. **Bird:** Cardinal. **Tree:** Dogwood. **Song:** Carry Me Back to Old Virginia. **Tenth** of the original 13 states to ratify the Constitution, June 25, 1788. **State fair** at: Richmond; late Sept.-early Oct.

History. English settlers founded Jamestown, 1607. Virginians took over much of the government from royal Gov. Dunmore in 1775, forcing him to flee. Virginians under George Rogers Clark freed the Ohio-Indiana-Illinois area of British forces. Benedict Arnold burned Richmond and Petersburg for the British, 1781. That same year, Britain's Cornwallis was trapped at Yorktown and surrendered.

Tourist attractions. Colonial Williamsburg; Busch Gardens; Wolf Trap Farm, near Falls Church; Arlington National Cemetery; Mt. Vernon, home of George Washington; Jamestown Festival Park; Yorktown; Jefferson's Monticello, Charlottesville; Robert E. Lee's birthplace, Stratford Hall, and grave, at Lexington; Appomattox; Shenandoah National Park; Blue Ridge Parkway; Virginia Beach.

Famous Virginians include Richard E. Byrd, James B. Cabell, William Henry Harrison, Patrick Henry, Thomas Jefferson, Joseph E. Johnston, Robert E. Lee, Meriwether Lewis and William Clark, James Madison, James Monroe, John Marshall, Edgar Allan Poe, Walter Reed, Zachary Taylor, John Tyler, Booker T. Washington, George Washington, Woodrow Wilson.

Chamber of Commerce: 9th South Fifth St., Richmond, VA 23219.

Toll-free travel information. 1-800-VISITVA.

Washington

Evergreen State

People. Population (1988): 4,648,000; **rank:** 18. **Pop. density:** 68.2 per sq. mi. **Urban** (1980): 73.5%. **Racial distrib.** (1985): 97.2% White; 2.8% Black; Hispanic 142,000. **Net change** (1980-88): +516,000; 12.5%.

Geography. Total area: 68,139 sq. mi.; **rank:** 20. **Land area:** 66,511 sq. mi. **Acres forested land:** 23,181,000. **Location:** northwestern coastal state bordered by Canada on the N; Idaho on the E; Oregon on the S; and the

Pacific O. on the W. **Climate:** mild, dominated by the Pacific O. and protected by the Rockies. **Topography:** Olympic Mtns. on NW peninsula; open land along coast to Columbia R.; flat terrain of Puget Sound Lowland; Cascade Mtns. region's high peaks to the E; Columbia Basin in central portion; highlands to the NE; mountains to the SE. **Capital:** Olympia.

Economy. Principal industries: aerospace, forest products, food products, primary metals, agriculture. **Principal manufactured goods:** aircraft, pulp and paper, lumber and plywood, aluminum, processed fruits and vegetables. **Agriculture: Chief crops:** wheat, apples, hay, potatoes, barley, nursery/greenhouse products, hops, corn, pears. **Livestock** (1986): 1.3 mln. cattle; 50,000 hogs/pigs; 59,000 sheep; 5.7 mln. poultry. **Timber/lumber** (1987): Douglas fir, hemlock, cedar, pine; 4.9 bln. bd. ft. **Nonfuel Minerals** (1988): $387 mln.; mostly construction sand & gravel, crushed stone, Portland cement. **Commercial fishing** (1988): $172.3 mln. **Chief ports:** Seattle, Tacoma, Vancouver, Kelso-Longview. **International airports at:** Seattle/Tacoma, Spokane, Boeing Field. **Value of construction** (1988): $5.0 bln. **Employment distribution** (1984): 24.4% trade; 20.7% serv.; 18.3% gvt.; 17.3% manuf. **Per capita income** (1988): $16,569. **Unemployment** (1986): 6.2%. **Tourism** (1986): $3.4 bln. **Sales tax:** 6.5%.

Finance. FDIC-insured commercial banks & trust companies (1987): 94. **Deposits:** $26.9 bln. **Savings institutions:** 48. **Assets:** $26.5 bln.

Federal government. No. federal civilian employees (Mar. 1988): 47,956. **Avg. salary:** $28,287. **Notable federal facilities:** Bonneville Power Admin.; Ft. Lewis; McChord AFB; Hanford Nuclear Reservation; Bremerton Naval Shipyards.

Energy. Electricity production (1988, mwh, by source): Hydroelectric: 68.4 mln.; Mineral: 8.8 mln.; Nuclear: 6.0 mln.

Education. Expenditures per pupil, public schools (1987): $3,964. **Avg. salary, public school teachers** (1988-89): $29,176.

State data. Motto. Alki (By and by). **Flower:** Western rhododendron. **Bird:** Willow goldfinch. **Tree:** Western hemlock. **Song:** Washington, My Home. **Entered union** Nov. 11, 1889; rank, 42d.

History. Spain's Bruno Hezeta sailed the coast, 1775. American Capt. Robert Gray sailed up the Columbia River, 1792. Canadian fur traders set up Spokane House, 1810; Americans under John Jacob Astor established a post at Fort Okanogan, 1811. Missionary Marcus Whitman settled near Walla Walla, 1836. Final agreement on the border of Washington and Canada was made with Britain, 1846, and gold was discovered in the state's northeast, 1855, bringing new settlers.

Tourist attractions. Mt. Rainier, Olympic and North Cascades National Parks; Mt. St. Helens; Pacific beaches; Puget Sound; wineries; Indian cultures; year-round outdoor recreation: Seattle Waterfront, Seattle Center, Space Needle, San Juan Islands, Grand Coulee Dam, Spokane's Riverfront Park.

Famous Washingtonians include Bing Crosby, William O. Douglas, Henry M. Jackson, Gary Larson, Mary McCarthy, Edward R. Murrow, Theodore Roethke, Marcus Whitman, Minoru Yamasaki.

Local Chambers of Commerce. P.O. Box 658, Olympia, WA 98507.

Toll-free travel information. 1-800-544-1800.

West Virginia

Mountain State

People. Population (1988): 1,876,000. **rank:** 34. **Pop. density:** 77.4 per sq. mi. **Urban** (1980): 36.2. **Racial distrib.** (1985): 96.7% White; 3.3% Black; Hispanic (1980): 7,900. **Net change** (1980-88): −73,000; −3.8%.

Geography. Total area: 24,232 sq. mi.; **rank:** 41. **Land area:** 24,119 sq. mi. **Acres forested land:** 11,668,600. **Location:** South Atlantic state bounded on the N by Ohio,

Pennsylvania, Maryland; on the S and W by Virginia, Kentucky, Ohio; on the E by Maryland and Virginia. **Climate:** humid continental climate except for marine modification in the lower panhandle. **Topography:** ranging from hilly to mountainous; Allegheny Plateau in the W, covers two-thirds of the state; mountains here are the highest in the state, over 4,000 ft. **Capital:** Charleston.

Economy. Principal industries: mining, mineral and chemical production, primary metals and stone, clay, and glass prods., timber, tourism. **Principal manufactured goods:** machinery, plastic and hardwood prods., fabricated metals, basic organic and inorganic chemicals, aluminum, steel. **Agriculture: Chief crops:** apples, peaches, hay, tobacco, corn, wheat, oats, barley. **Chief products:** milk, eggs, honey. **Livestock** (1986): 560,000 cattle; 37,000 hogs/pigs; 90,000 sheep; 670,000 chickens. **Timber/ lumber** (1987): oak, yellow poplar, hickory, walnut, cherry; 372 mln. bd. ft. **Nonfuel Minerals** (1988): $148 mln.; mostly crushed stone. **Chief port:** Huntington. **Value of construction** (1988): $788.5 mln. **Employment distribution** (1986): 23% trade; 21.6% gvt.; 20.3% serv.; 15% manuf. **Per capita income** (1988): $11,658. **Unemployment** (1988): 9.9%. **Tourism** (1986): travel-related expenditures were $1.6 bln. **Sales tax:** 5%.

Finance. FDIC-insured commercial banks & trust companies (1987): 213. **Deposits:** $12.8 bln. **Savings institutions:** 18. **Assets:** $2.0 bln.

Federal government. No. federal civilian employees (Mar. 1988): 9,907. **Avg. salary:** $26,425. **Notable federal facilities:** National Radio Astronomy Observatory, Green Bank; Bureau of Public Debt. Bldg., Parkersburg; Natl. Park, Harper's Ferry; Correctional Institution for Women, Alderson.

Energy. Electricity production (1988, mwh, by source): Hydroelectric: 298,000; Mineral: 81.0 mln.

Education. Expenditures per pupil, public schools (1987): $3,784. **Avg. salary, public school teachers** (1988-89): $21,904.

State Data. Motto: Montani Semper Liberi (Mountaineers are always free) **Flower:** Big rhododendron. **Bird:** Cardinal. **Tree:** Sugar maple. **Songs:** The West Virginia Hills; This Is My West Virginia; West Virginia, My Home, Sweet Home. **Entered union** June 20, 1863; rank, 35th. **State fair** at: Lewisburg (Fairlea), late Aug.

History. Early explorers included George Washington, 1753, and Daniel Boone. The area became part of Virginia and often objected to rule by the eastern part of the state. When Virginia seceded, 1861, the Wheeling Conventions repudiated the act and created a new state, Kanawha, subsequently changed to West Virginia. It was admitted to the Union as such, 1863.

Tourist attractions. Harpers Ferry National Historic Park has been restored to its condition in 1859, when John Brown seized the U.S. Armory.

Also Science and Cultural Center, Charleston; White Sulphur and Berkeley Springs mineral water spas; Monongahela Natl. Forest; state parks and forests; trout fishing; turkey, deer, and bear hunting; white water rafting, paddleboat tours, skiing; glass tours at Fentonglass in Williamstown, Viking Glass in New Martinsville, Blenk Glass in Milton; Sternwheel Regatta, Charleston; Mountain State Forest Festival.

Famous West Virginians include Newton D. Baker, Pearl Buck, John W. Davis, Thomas "Stonewall" Jackson, Don Knotts, Dwight Whitney Morrow, Michael Owens, Cyrus Vance, Col. Charles "Chuck" Yeager.

Tourist information. Dept. of Commerce, State Capitol, Charleston WV 25305.

Toll-free travel information. 1-800-CALLW.VA.

Wisconsin
Badger State

People. Population (1988): 4,855,000; **rank:** 17. **Pop. density:** 86.5 per sq. mi. **Urban** (1980): 64.2%. **Racial distrib.** (1985): 95.7% White; 4.3% Black; Hispanic 66,300. **Net change** (1980-88): +149,000; 3.2%.

Geography. Total area: 56,153 sq. mi.; **rank:** 26. **Land area:** 54,426 sq. mi. **Acres forested land:** 14,907,700. **Location:** North central state, bounded on the N by Lake Superior and Upper Michigan; on the E by Lake Michigan; on the S by Illinois; on the W by the St. Croix and Mississippi rivers. **Climate:** long, cold winters and short, warm summers tempered by the Great Lakes. **Topography:** narrow Lake Superior Lowland plain met by Northern Highland which slopes gently to the sandy crescent Central Plain; Western Upland in the SW; 3 broad parallel limestone ridges running N-S are separated by wide and shallow lowlands in the SE. **Capital:** Madison.

Economy. Principal industries: manufacturing, trade, services, government, transportation, communications, agriculture, tourism. **Principal manufactured goods:** machinery, foods, fabricated metals, transportation equipment, paper and wood products. **Agriculture: Chief crops:** corn, beans, beets, peas, hay, oats, cabbage, cranberries. **Chief products:** milk, butter, cheese. **Livestock** (1988): 4.2 mln. cattle, 1.3 mln. hogs/pigs; 78,000 sheep; 9.8 mln. poultry. **Timber/lumber** (1987): maple, birch, oak, evergreens; 415 mln. bd. ft. **Nonfuel Minerals** (1988): $231 mln.; mostly crushed stone, construction & industrial sand & gravel, lime. **Commercial fishing** (1988): $5.6 mln. **Chief ports:** Superior, Ashland, Milwaukee, Green Bay, Kewaunee, Pt. Washington, Manitowoc, Sheboygan, Marinette, Kenosha. **International airports at:** Milwaukee. **Value of construction** (1988): $3.9 bln. **Employment distribution** (1988): 27.8% trade; 25.6% manuf; 22.0% serv.; 15.7% gvt. **Per capita income** (1988): $15,444. **Unemployment** (1988): 4.3%. **Tourism** (1987): out-of-state visitors spent $5.0 bln. **Sales tax:** 5%.

Finance. FDIC-insured commercial banks & trust companies (1987): 566. **Deposits:** $34.1 bln. **Savings institutions:** 77. **Assets:** $16.6 bln.

Federal government. No. federal civilian employees (Mar. 1988): 12,193. **Avg. salary:** $25,924. **Notable federal facilities:** Ft. McCoy.

Energy. Electricity production (1988, mwh, by source): Hydroelectric: 1.2 mln.; Mineral: 32.1 mln.; Nuclear: 11.5 mln.

Education. Expenditures per pupil, public schools (1987): $4,523. **Avg. salary, public school teachers** (1988-89): $31,046.

State data. Motto: Forward. **Flower:** Wood violet. **Bird:** Robin. **Tree:** Sugar maple. **Song:** On, Wisconsin! **Entered union** May 29, 1848; rank, 30th. **State fair** at: West Allis; mid-Aug.

History. Jean Nicolet was the first European to see the Wisconsin area, arriving in Green Bay, 1634; French missionaries and fur traders followed. The British took over, 1763. The U.S. won the land after the Revolution but the British were not ousted until after the War of 1812. Lead miners came next, then farmers. Railroads were started in 1851, serving growing wheat harvests and iron mines.

Tourist attractions. Old Wade House and Carriage Museum, Greenbush; Villa Louis, Prairie du Chien; Circus World Museum, Baraboo; Wisconsin Dells; Old World Wisconsin, Eagle; Door County peninsula; Chequamegon and Nicolet national forests; Lake Winnebago; numerous lakes for water sports, ice boating and fishing; skiing and hunting.

Famous Wisconsinites include Edna Ferber, King Camp Gillette, Harry Houdini, Robert LaFollette, Alfred Lunt, Georgia O'Keeffe, Spencer Tracy, Thorstein Veblen, Orson Welles, Thornton Wilder, Frank Lloyd Wright.

Tourist information. Wisconsin Dept. of Development, Division of Tourism, 123 W. Washington Ave., Madison, WI 53702.

Toll-free travel information. 1-800-372-2737.

Wyoming
Equality State

People. Population (1988) 479,000; **rank:** 50. **Pop. density:** 4.9 per sq. mi. **Urban** (1980): 62.7%. **Racial distrib.** (1980): 95.0% White; 0.71% Black; Hispanic (1980): 26,500. **Net change** (1980-88): +10,000; 2.1%.

Geography. Total area: 97,809 sq. mi.; **rank:** 9. **Land area:** 96,989 sq. mi. **Acres forested land:** 10,028,300. **Location:** Mountain state lying in the high western plateaus of the Great Plains. **Climate:** semi-desert conditions throughout; true desert in the Big Horn and Great Divide basins. **Topography:** the eastern Great Plains rise to the foothills of the Rocky Mtns.; the Continental Divide crosses the state from the NW to the SE. **Capital:** Cheyenne.

Economy. Principal industries: mineral extraction, tourism and recreation, agriculture. **Principal manufactured goods:** refined petroleum products, foods, wood products, stone, clay and glass products. **Agriculture: Chief crops:** wheat, beans, barley, oats, sugar beets, hay. **Livestock** (1988): 1.3 mln. cattle; 20,000 hogs/pigs; 865,000 sheep. **Timber/lumber** (1987): aspen, yellow pine; 318 mln. bd. ft. **Nonfuel Minerals** (1988): $755 mln.; mostly Portland cement, crushed stone. **International airports at:** Casper. **Value of construction** (1988): $451.6 mln. **Employment distribution** (1985): 30% serv.; 25% trade; 13% mining. **Per capita income** (1988): $13,718. **Unemployment** (1988): 6.3%. **Tourism** (1986): out-of-state visitors spent $850 mln.

Finance. FDIC-insured commercial banks & trust companies: 106. **Deposits:** $3.9 bln. **Savings institutions:** 11. **Assets:** $1.2 bln.

Federal government. No. federal civilian employees (Mar. 1988): 4,804. **Avg. salary:** $27,151. **Notable federal facilities:** Warren AFB.

Energy. Electricity production (1986, mwh, by source): Hydroelectric: 789,000; Mineral: 38.4 mln.

Education. Expenditures per pupil, public schools (1987): $5,201. **Avg. salary, public school teachers** (1988-89): $27,685.

State data. Motto: Equal Rights. **Flower:** Indian paintbrush. **Bird:** Meadowlark. **Tree:** Cottonwood. **Song:** Wyoming. **Entered union** July 10, 1890; rank, 44th. **State fair at:** Douglas; late Aug.

History. Francis Francois and Louis Verendrye were the first Europeans, 1743. John Colter, American, was first to traverse Yellowstone Park, 1807-08. Trappers and fur traders followed in the 1820s. Forts Laramie and Bridger became important stops on the pioneer trail to the West Coast. Indian wars followed massacres of army detachments in 1854 and 1866. Population grew after the Union Pacific crossed the state, 1869. Women won the vote, for the first time in the U.S., from the Territorial Legislature, 1869.

Tourist attractions. Yellowstone National Park, 3,472 sq. mi. in the NW corner of Wyoming and the adjoining edges of Montana and Idaho, the oldest U.S. national park, est. 1872, has some 10,000 geysers, hot springs, mud volcanoes, fossil forests, a volcanic glass (obsidian) mountain, the 1,000-ft.-deep canyon and 308-ft.-high waterfall of the Yellowstone River, and a wide variety of animals living free in their natural habitat.

Also, Grand Teton National Park, with mountains 13,000 ft. high; National Elk Refuge, covering 25,000 acres; Devils Tower, a columnar rock of igneous origin 1,280 ft. high; Fort Laramie and surrounding areas of pioneer trails; Buffalo Bill Museum, Cody; Cheyenne Frontier Days Celebration, last full week in July, the state's largest rodeo, and world's largest purse.

Famous Wyomingites include James Bridger, Buffalo Bill Cody, Nellie Tayloe Ross.

Tourist information. Travel Commission, Etchepare Circle, Cheyenne, WY 82002.

Toll-free travel information. 1-800-CALLWYO.

District of Columbia

Area: 67 sq. mi. **Population:** (1988): 617,000. **Motto:** Justitia omnibus, Justice for all. **Flower:** American beauty rose. **Tree:** Scarlet oak. **Bird:** Wood thrush. The city of Washington is coextensive with the District of Columbia.

The District of Columbia is the seat of the federal government of the United States. It lies on the west central edge of Maryland on the Potomac River, opposite Virginia.

Its area was originally 100 sq. mi. taken from the sovereignty of Maryland and Virginia. Virginia's portion south of the Potomac was given back to that state in 1846.

The 23d Amendment, ratified in 1961, granted residents the right to vote for president and vice president for the first time and gave them 3 members in the Electoral College. The first such votes were cast in Nov. 1964.

Congress, which has legislative authority over the District under the Constitution, established in 1878 a government of 3 commissioners appointed by the president. The Reorganization Plan of 1967 substituted a single commissioner (also called mayor), assistant, and 9-member City Council. Funds were still appropriated by Congress; residents had no vote in local government, except to elect school board members.

In Sept. 1970, Congress approved legislation giving the District one delegate to the House of Representatives. The delegate could vote in committee but not on the House floor. The first was elected 1971.

In May 1974 voters approved a charter giving them the right to elect their own mayor and a 13-member city council; the first took office Jan. 2, 1975. The district won the right to levy its own taxes but Congress retained power to veto council actions, and approve the city's annual budget.

Proposals for a "federal town" for the deliberations of the Continental Congress were made in 1783, 4 years before the adoption of the Constitution that gave the Confederation a national government. Rivalry between northern and southern delegates over the site appeared in the First Congress, 1789. John Adams, presiding officer of the Senate, cast the deciding vote of that body for Germantown, Pa. In 1790 Congress compromised by making Philadelphia the temporary capital for 10 years. The Virginia members of the House wanted a capital on the eastern bank of the Potomac; they were defeated by the Northerners, while the Southerners defeated the Northern attempt to have the nation assume the war debts of the 13 original states, the Assumption Bill fathered by Alexander Hamilton. Hamilton and Jefferson arranged a compromise: the Virginia men voted for the Assumption Bill, and the Northerners conceded the capital to the Potomac. President Washington chose the site in Oct. 1790 and persuaded landowners to sell their holdings to the government at £25, then about $66, an acre. The capital was named Washington.

Washington appointed Pierre Charles L'Enfant, a French engineer who had come over with Lafayette, to plan the capital on an area not over 10 mi. square. The L'Enfant plan, for streets 100 to 110 feet wide and one avenue 400 feet wide and a mile long, seemed grandiose and foolhardy. But Washington endorsed it. When L'Enfant ordered a wealthy landowner to remove his new manor house because it obstructed a vista, and demolished it when the owner refused, Washington stepped in and dismissed the architect. The official map and design of the city was completed by Benjamin Banneker, a distinguished black architect and astronomer, and Andrew Ellicott.

On Sept. 18, 1793, Pres. Washington laid the cornerstone of the north wing of the Capitol. On June 3, 1800, Pres. John Adams moved to Washington and on June 10, Philadelphia ceased to be the temporary capital. The City of Washington was incorporated in 1802; the District of Columbia was created as a municipal corporation in 1871, embracing Washington, Georgetown, and Washington County.

Outlying U.S. Areas

Commonwealth of Puerto Rico

(Estado Libre Asociado de Puerto Rico)

People. Population (1986): 3,286,000. **Pop. density:** 956.6 per sq. mi. **Urban** (1980): 66.8%. **Racial distribution** (1980): 99.9% Hispanic. **Net migration** (1985): −27,691.

Geography. Total area: 3,435 sq. mi. **Land area:** 3,421 sq. mi. **Location:** island lying between the Atlantic to the N and the Caribbean to the S; it is easternmost of the West Indies group called the Greater Antilles, of which Cuba, Hispaniola, and Jamaica are the larger islands. **Climate:** mild, with a mean temperature of 77°. **Topography:** mountainous throughout three-fourths of its rectangular area, surrounded by a broken coastal plain; highest peak is Cerro de Punta, 4,389 ft. **Capital:** San Juan.

Economy. Principal industries: manufacturing. **Principal manufactured goods:** pharmaceuticals; chemicals, machinery and metals, electric machinery and equipment, petroleum refining, food products, apparel. **Agriculture: Chief crops:** coffee; plantains; bananas; yams; taniers; pineapples; pidgeon peas; peppers; pumpkins; coriander; lettuce; tobacco. **Livestock** (1985): 579,810 cattle; 210,013 pigs; 7.4 mln. poultry. **Nonfuel Minerals** (1987): $111.6 mln., mostly cement. **Commercial fishing** (1984): $7.9 mln. **Chief ports/river shipping:** San Juan, Ponce, Mayaguez, Guayanillá, Guánica, Yabucoa, Aguirre. **Major airports at:** San Juan, Ponce, Mayaguez, Aguadilla. **Value of construction** (1987): $2.5 bln. **Employment distribution:** 24% gvt.; 18% manuf.; 19% trade; 20% serv. **Per capita income** (1985): $4,301. **Unemployment** (1988): 15%. **Tourism** (1987): Out-of-area visitors spent $1 bln.

Finance. No. FDIC-insured commercial banks & trust companies (1987): 14. **Deposits:** $9.7 bln. **No. savings institutions** (1987): 10. **Assets:** $6.2 bln.

Federal government. No. federal civilian employees (1985): 9,989. **Notable federal facilities:** U.S. Naval Station at Roosevelt Roads; U.S. Army Salinas Training Area and Ft. Allen; Sabana SECA Communications Center (U.S. Navy); Ft. Buchanan.

Energy Production (1985): Steam and gas: 11,938 mln. kwh; Other: 209 mln. kwh.

Education. No. schools (1985): 1,782 public, 818 private elem. and second.; 69 higher ed. **Avg. salary, public school teachers** (1985): $12,000.

Misc. Data. Motto. Joannes Est Nomen Eius (John is his name). **Flower:** Maga. **Bird:** Reinita. **Tree:** Ceiba. **National anthem:** La Borinqueña.

History: Puerto Rico (or Borinquen, after the original Arawak Indian name Boriquen), was discovered by Columbus, Nov. 19, 1493. Ponce de Leon conquered it for Spain, 1509, and established the first settlement at Caparra, across the bay from San Juan.

Sugar cane was introduced, 1515, and slaves were imported 3 years later. Gold mining petered out, 1570. Spaniards fought off a series of British and Dutch attacks; slavery was abolished, 1873. Under the treaty of Paris, Puerto Rico was ceded to the U.S. after the Spanish-American War, 1898. In 1952 the people voted in favor of Commonwealth status.

The Commonwealth of Puerto Rico is a self-governing part of the U.S. with a primary Hispanic culture. Puerto Ricans are U.S. citizens and about 2.0 million now live on the mainland, although since 1974 there has also been a reverse migration flow.

The current commonwealth political status of Puerto Rico gives the island's citizens virtually the same control over their internal affairs as the fifty states of the U.S. However, they do not vote in national elections, although they do vote in national primary elections.

Puerto Rico is represented in Congress solely by a resident commissioner who has a voice but no vote, except in committees.

No federal income tax is collected from residents on income earned from local sources in Puerto Rico.

Puerto Rico's famous "Operation Bootstrap," begun in the late 1940s, succeeded in changing the island from "The Poorhouse of the Caribbean" to an area with the highest per capita income in Latin America. This pioneering program encouraged manufacturing and the development of the tourist trade by selective tax exemption, low-interest loans, and other incentives. Despite the marked success of Puerto Rico's development efforts over an extended period of time, per capita income in Puerto Rico is low in comparison to that of the U.S. In calendar year 1985, the transfer payments from the U.S. government to individuals and governments in Puerto Rico totalled $3.2 bln., or 22% of the Gross Domestic Product of $14.8 bln.

General tourist attractions: Ponce Museum of Art; forts El Morro and San Cristobal; Old Walled City of San Juan; Arecibo Observatory; Cordillera Central and state parks; El Yunque Rain Forest; San Juan Cathedral; Porta Coeli Chapel and Museum of Religious Art, Interamerican Univ., San Germán; Condado Convention Center; Casa Blanca, Ponce de León family home, Puerto Rican Family Museum of 16th and 17 centuries and the Fine Arts Center in San Juan.

Cultural facilities, festivals, etc.: Festival Casals classical music concerts, mid-June; Puerto Rico Symphony Orchestra at Music Conservatory; Botanical Garden and Museum of Anthropology, Art, and History at the University of Puerto Rico; Institute of Puerto Rican Culture, at the Dominican Convent, and many popular festivals throughout the island.

Famous Puerto Ricans include: José Celso Barbosa, Julia de Burgos, Pablo Casals, Orlando Cepeda, Roberto Clemente, José de Diego, José Feliciano, Luis A. Ferré, José Ferrer, Doña Felisa Rincón de Gautier, Commodore Diego E. Hernández, Rafael Hernández (El Jibarito), Raúl Julia, Luis Muñoz Marín, René Marqués, Luis Palés Matos, Concha Meléndez, Rita Moreno, Adm. Horacio Rivero, Rafael Hernández Colón, Marta Casals Istomier, Miguel Hernándo Agosto.

Chamber of Commerce: 100 Tetuán P.O.Box. S-3789, San Juan, PR 00904; Ponce & South: El Señorial Bldg., Ponce, PR 00731.

Guam

Where America's Day Begins

People. Population (1987): 127,675. **Pop. density:** 589 per sq. mi. **Urban** (1980): 39.5%. **Major ethnic groups** (1987): Chamorro 48.8%, Filipino 25.2%, stateside immigrants 20%, remainder Micronesians. Native Guamanians, ethnically called Chamorros, are basically of Indonesian stock, with a mixture of Spanish and Filipino. In addition to the offical language, they speak the native Chamorro.

Geography. Total area: 209 sq. mi. land, 30 mi. long and 4 to 8.5 mi. wide. **Location:** largest and southernmost of the Mariana Islands in the West Pacific, 3,700 mi. W of Hawaii. **Climate:** tropical, with temperatures from 70° to 90°F; avg. annual rainfall, about 70 in. **Topography:** coralline limestone plateau in the N; southern chain of low volcanic mountains sloping gently to the W, more steeply to coastal cliffs on the E; general elevation, 500 ft.; highest pt., Mt. Lamlam, 1,334 ft. **Capital:** Agana.

Economy. Principal industries: construction, light manufacturing, tourism, banking, defense. **Principal manufactured goods:** textiles, foods. **Agriculture: Chief crops:** cabbages, eggplants, cucumber, long beans, tomatoes, bananas, coconuts, watermelon, yams, canteloupe, papayas, maize, sweet potatoes. **Livestock** (1984): 2,000 cattle; 14,000 hogs/pigs. **Chief ports:** Apra Harbor. **International airports at:** Tamuning. **Value of construction** (1980): $80.60 mln. **Employment distribution** (1987): 61.3% private sector; 38.7% gvt. **Per capita income** (1986): $7,116. **Unemployment** (1987): 3%. **Tourism** (1980): visitors' receipts $117.9 mln.

Finance. Notable industries: insurance, real estate, finance. **No. banks:** 13; **No. savings and loan assns.:** 2.

Federal government. No. federal employees (1980): 6,600. **Notable federal facilities:** Andersen AFB; other naval and air bases.

Education. No. public schools: 37 elementary; 19 secondary; 2 higher education. **Avg. salary, public school teachers** (1979): $12,684.

Misc. Data. Flower: Puti Tai Nobio (Bougainvillea). **Bird:** Toto (Fruit dove). **Tree:** Ifit (Intsiabijuga). **Song:** Stand Ye Guamanians.

History. Magellan arrived in the Marianas Mar. 6, 1521. They were colonized in 1668 by Spanish missionaries who renamed them the Mariana Islands in honor of Maria Anna, queen of Spain. When Spain ceded Guam to the U.S., it sold the other Marianas to Germany. Japan obtained a League of Nations mandate over the German islands in 1919; in Dec. 1941 it seized Guam; the island was retaken by the U.S. in July 1944.

Guam is a self-governing organized unincorporated U.S. territory. Under the jurisdiction of the Interior Department, it is administered under the Organic Act of 1950, which provides for a governor and a 21-member unicameral legislature, elected biennially by the residents who are American citizens but do not vote for president.

Beginning in Nov., 1970, Guamanians elected their own governor, previously appointed by the U.S. president. He took office in Jan. 1971. In 1972 a U.S. law gave Guam one delegate to the U.S. House of Representatives; the delegate may vote in committee but not on the House floor.

General tourist attractions. annual mid-Aug. Merizo Water Festival; Tarzan Falls; beaches; water sports, duty-free port shopping.

Virgin Islands

St. John, St. Croix, St. Thomas

People. Population (1988): 106,000 (52,400, St. Croix; 50,860, St. Thomas; 2,740, St. John). **Pop. density:** 814.47 per sq. mi. **Urban** (1980): 39%. **Racial distribution:** 15% White; 85% Black. **Major ethnic groups:** West Indian, French, Hispanic.

Geography. Total area: 133 sq. mi.; **Land area:** 136 sq. mi. **Location:** 3 larger and 50 smaller islands and cays in the S and W of the V.I. group (British V.I. colony to the N and E) which is situated 70 mi. E of Puerto Rico, located W of the Anegada Passage, a major channel connecting the Atlantic O. and the Caribbean Sea. **Climate:** subtropical; the sun tempered by gentle trade winds; humidity is low; average temperature, 78° F. **Topography:** St. Thomas is mainly a ridge of hills running E and W, and has little tillable land; St. Croix rises abruptly in the N but slopes to the S to flatlands and lagoons; St. John has steep, lofty hills and valleys with little level tillable land. **Capital:** Charlotte Amalie, St. Thomas.

Economy. Principal industries: tourism, rum, petroleum refining, watch industry, textiles, electronics. **Principal manufactured goods:** rum, textiles, pharmaceuticals, perfumes. **Gross Domestic Product** (1987): $1.246 bln. **Agriculture:** Chief crops: truck garden produce. **Minerals:** sand, gravel. **Chief ports:** Cruz Bay, St. John; Frederiksted and Christiansted, St. Croix; Charlotte Amalie, St. Thomas. **International airports on:** St. Thomas, St. Croix. **Value of construction** (1987): $167.0 mln. **Per capita income** (1987): $7,465. **Unemployment** (1987): 3.3%. **Tourism** (1988): $662.8. **No. banks** (1985): 8.

Education (1987): **No. public schools:** 34 elem. and second.; 1 college. **Avg. starting salary, public school teachers:** $18,001.

Misc. data. Flower: Yellow elder or yellow trumpet, local designation Ginger Thomas. **Bird:** Yellow breast. **Song:** Virgin Islands March.

History. The islands were discovered by Columbus in 1493. Spanish forces, 1555, defeated the Caribes and claimed the territory; by 1596 the native population was annihilated. First permanent settlement in the U.S. territory, 1672, by the Danes; U.S. purchased the islands, 1917, for defense purposes.

The Virgin Islands has a republican form of government, headed by a governor and lieut. governor elected, since 1970, by popular vote for 4-year terms. There is a 15-member unicameral legislature, elected by popular vote. Residents of the V.I. have been U.S. citizens since 1927. Since 1973 they have elected a delegate to the U.S. House of Representatives, who may vote in committee but not in the House.

General tourist attractions. Magens Bay, St. Thomas; duty-free shopping; Virgin Islands National Park, 14,488 acres on St. John of lush growth, beaches, Indian relics, and evidence of colonial Danes.

Tourist information. Dept. of Economic Development & Agriculture, St. Thomas, P.O. Box 6400, St. Thomas, VI 00801; St. Croix, P.O. Box 4535, Christiansted, St. Croix 00820.

American Samoa

Capital: Pago Pago, Island of Tutuila. **Area:** 77 sq. mi. **Population:** (1988) 47,450. **Motto:** Samoa Muamua le Atua (In Samoa, God Is First). **Song:** Amerika Samoa. **Flower:** Paogo (Ula-fala). **Plant:** Ava.

Blessed with spectacular scenery and delightful South Seas climate, American Samoa is the most southerly of all lands under U. S. sovereignty. It is an unincorporated territory consisting of 6 small islands of the Samoan group: **Tutuila, Aunu'u, Manu'a Group (Ta'u, Olosega and Ofu)**, and **Rose**. Also administered as part of American Samoa is **Swain's Island**, 210 mi. to the NW, acquired by the U.S. in 1925. The islands are 2,300 mi. SW of Honolulu.

American Samoa became U. S. territory in Feb., 1900 by a treaty with the United Kingdom and Germany in 1899. The islands were ceded by local chiefs in April, 1900 and July, 1904, and became U.S territories. The U.S. acquired commercial rights pursuant to the convention 1899, a tripartite agreement among Great Britain, Germany, and the U.S.

Samoa (Western), comprising the larger islands of the Samoan group, was a New Zealand mandate and UN Trusteeship until it became an independent nation Jan. 1, 1962 (see Index.)

Tutuila and Annu'u have an area of 53 sq. mi. Ta'u has an area of 17 sq. mi., and the islets of Ofu and Olosega, 5 sq. mi. with a population of a few thousand. Swain's Island has nearly 2 sq. mi. and a population of about 100.

About 70% of the land is bush. Chief products and exports are fish products, copra, and handicrafts. Taro, bread-fruit, yams, coconuts, pineapples, oranges, and bananas are also produced.

From 1900-1951, American Samoa was under the jurisdiction of the U.S. Navy. Since 1951, it has been under the Interior Dept. On Jan. 3, 1978, the first popularly elected Samoan governor and lieutenant governor were inaugurated. Previously, the governor was appointed by the Secretary of the Interior. American Samoa has a bicameral legislature and elects its own member of Congress, who can introduce legislation and vote in committee, but not in the House.

The American Samoans are of Polynesian origin. They are nationals of the U.S.; 20,000 live in Hawaii, 65,000 in California and Washington.

Minor Caribbean Islands

Quita Sueño Bank, Roncador and Serrana, lie in the Caribbean between Nicaragua and Jamaica. They are uninhabited. U.S. claim to the islands was relinquished in a treaty with Colombia, which entered into force on Sept. 17, 1981.

Navassa lies between Jamaica and Haiti, covers about 2 sq. mi., is reserved by the U.S. for a lighthouse and is uninhabited. It is administered by the U.S. Coast Guard.

Wake, Midway, Other Islands

Wake Island, and its sister islands, **Wilkes** and **Peale,** lie in the Pacific Ocean on the direct route from Hawaii to Hong Kong, about 2,300 mi. W of Hawaii and 1,290 mi. E of Guam. The group is 4.5 mi. long, 1.5 mi. wide, and totals less than 3 sq. mi.

The U.S. flag was hoisted over Wake Island, July 4, 1898, formal possession taken Jan. 17, 1899; Wake has been administered by the U.S. Air Force since 1972. The population consists of a number of USAF personnel.

The **Midway Islands,** acquired in 1867, consist of 2, **Sand** and **Eastern,** in the North Pacific, 1,150 mi. NW of Hawaii, with area of about 3 sq. mi., administered by the U.S. Navy. There is no indigenous population; it is currently populated with several U.S. military personnel.

Johnston Atoll, SW of Hawaii, area 1 sq. mi. is operated by The Defense Nuclear Agency, and **Kingman Reef,** S of Hawaii, is under Navy control.

Howland, Jarvis, and **Baker Islands,** 1,500-1,650 miles southwest of the Hawaiian group, uninhabited since World War II, are under the Interior Dept.

Palmyra is an atoll about 1,000 miles south of Hawaii, 4 sq. mi. Privately owned, it is under the Interior Dept.

Islands Under Trusteeship

The Trust Territory of the Pacific Islands was established in 1947, as the only strategic trusteeship of the 11 trusteeships established by the U.N. The territory has a heterogeneous population of about 140,000 people scattered among more than 2,100 islands and atolls in 3 major archipelagos: the Carolines, the Marshalls, and the Marianas. The entire geographic area is sometimes referred to as "Micronesia," meaning "little islands." The area of the Trust Territory covered some 3 million sq. miles of the Pacific Ocean, slightly larger than the continental U.S. However, its islands constituted a land area of only 715.8 sq. miles—half the size of Rhode Island. It formerly contained 4 political jurisdictions: The Commonwealth of the Northern Mariana Islands (CNMI), the Federated States of Micronesia (FSM), the Republic of the Marshall Islands (RMI), and the Republic of Palau (RP). As of Oct. 21, 1986, the RMI entered into free association with the U.S., as did the FSM effective Nov. 3, 1986. The CNMI became a commonwealth of the U.S., also effective Nov. 3. Only the RP remains under trusteeship.

Commonwealth of the Northern Mariana Islands

Located in the perpetually warm climes between Guam and the Tropic of Cancer, the 16 islands of the Northern Marianas form a 300-mile-long archipelago, comprising a total land area of 183.5 sq. miles. The native population, estimated at 20,000, is concentrated on the 3 largest of the 6 inhabited islands: **Saipan,** the seat of government and commerce (16,532), **Rota** (1,484), and **Tinian** (1,012).

The people of the Northern Marianas are predominantly of Chamorro cultural extraction, although numbers of Carolinians and immigrants from other areas of E. Asia and Micronesia have also settled in the islands. Pursuant to the Covenant of 1975, which established the Northern Marianas as a commonwealth in political union with the U.S., most natives and many domiciliaries of these islands achieved U.S. citizenship on Nov. 13, 1986, when the U.S. terminated its administration of the U.N. trusteeship as it affected the Northern Marianas. From July 18, 1947, the U.S. had administered the Northern Marianas under a trusteeship agreement with the U.N. Security Council. English is among the several languages commonly spoken.

The Northern Mariana Islands has been self-governing since 1978, when both a constitution drafted and adopted by the people became effective, and a bicameral legislature with offices of governor and lieutenant governor was inaugurated. Commercial activity has increased steadily in the last few years, with 1,600 establishments operated in 1985, mostly in tourism, construction, and light industry. In 1986, more than 150,000 tourists visited, an increase of 10% over previous years. An agreement with the U.S. for 1986-1992 entitles the Northern Marianna Islands to $228 million for capital development, government operations and special programs.

Federated States of Micronesia

The Federated States of Micronesia extends across the 1,800-mile-long Caroline Island archipelago. The 4 states of the FSM are Pohnpei, Kosrae, Truk, and Yap. Each state consists of several islands, except for Kosrae, a single island. The capital of the FSM is Pohnpei. Populations are: Pohnpei, 26,000; Truk, 43,000; Kosrae, 6,000; Yap, 10,200. Pohnpei is 2,900 miles SW of Honolulu and 1,000 miles SE of Guam. The islands vary geologically from high, mountainous islands to low, coral atolls. The FSM lies between the equator and 9 degrees N and 138 degrees and 168 degrees E. Average year-round temperature is 80 degrees. Pohnpei gets the highest annual rainfall, averaging up to 250 inches.

The cultures of the FSM are very diverse. Several languages, each with dialects, are spoken throughout: Yapese, Ulithian, Woleaian, Ponapean, Nukuoran, Kapingamarangi, Trukese, and Kosraean. Each state has a constitution and government, headed by a governor. The status of free association recognizes that the FSM is a sovereign-self-governing state, with the U.S. responsible for defense and also extending agreed-upon amounts of economic and service assistance. Each of the state's constitutions recognizes a role for traditional leaders and customs.

Republic of the Marshall Islands

The Republic of the Marshall Islands consists of 2 island/atoll chains, the Ratak (sunrise) Chain, and the Ralik (sunset) Chain, totalling 31 atolls. Each atoll is a cluster of several small islands circling a lagoon. Total land area is 70 sq. miles. The capital is **Majuro,** 2,000 miles SW of Honolulu and 1,300 SE of Guam. Population is 35,000, 12,000 in Majuro. Average year-round temperature is 81 degrees.

Marshallese culture revolves around the complex clan system. Land is owned by each clan and passed down over the generations. In the late 1970's, the U.S. embarked upon an ambitious Capital Improvement Program, with a goal of building a major infrastructure (airport, dock, roads, water-power-sewer system) in Majuro. Funding was completed in 1985.

The Marshall Islands' Constitution includes both American and British concepts. The executive branch is the Nitijela (parliament) and is consulted by a Council of Iroij (local chiefs). The Nitijela elects the President from among its own members. The status of free association recognizes that the Marshall Islands is a sovereign, self-governing state, with the U.S. responsible for defense, and for extending agreed-upon amounts of economic and service assistance. A subsidiary agreement allows the U.S. continued use of Kwajalein Missile Range for 30 years. Another subsidiary agreement provides for settlement of all claims arising out of the nuclear testing programs conducted by the U.S. at Bikini and Enewetak Atolls from 1946 to 1958.

Republic of Palau

Palau consists of more than 200 islands in the Caroline chain, of which 8 are permanently inhabited. The Palau archipelago stretches over 400 miles. The capital of Palau, Koror, lies 4,450 miles SW of Honolulu and 720 miles S of Guam. Population of Palau is approximately 14,000, 8,100 in Koror. Average year-round temperature is 80 degrees, average annual rainfall 150 inches.

Until 1979, a High Commissioner appointed by the U.S. president, himself appointed a district administrator for Palau to oversee programs and administration there. In support of the evolving political status, the U.S. recognized the Constitution of Palau and the establishment of the Government of Palau. The Constitution became effective in 1980. The President and Vice President are elected by popular vote. A Council of Chiefs advises the President on matters concerning traditional law and custom. Palau has a bicameral national legislature composed of a House of Delegates and a Senate.

Projected State Population: 1990-2010

Source: U.S. Bureau of the Census

(Total population in thousands by state, 1990 to 2010; absolute change and percent change for 1990 to 2000, and 2000 to 2010)

U.S. total	1990	2000	2010	1990-2000 Change	%	2000-2010 Change	%
U.S. total	249,891	267,747	282,055	17,856	7.1	14,308	5.3
Alabama	4,181	4,410	4,609	229	5.5	199	4.5
Alaska	576	687	765	111	19.3	78	11.4
Arizona	3,752	4,618	5,319	866	23.1	701	15.2
Arkansas	2,427	2,529	2,624	102	4.2	95	3.8
California	29,126	33,500	37,347	4,374	15.0	3,847	11.5
Colorado	3,434	3,813	4,098	379	11.0	285	7.5
Connecticut	3,279	3,445	3,532	166	5.1	87	2.5
Delaware	666	734	790	68	10.2	56	7.6
District of Columbia	614	634	672	20	3.3	38	6.0
Florida	12,818	15,415	17,530	2,597	20.3	2,115	13.7
Georgia	6,663	7,957	9,045	1,294	19.4	1,088	13.7
Hawaii	1,141	1,345	1,559	204	17.9	214	15.9
Idaho	1,017	1,047	1,079	30	2.9	32	3.1
Illinois	11,612	11,580	11,495	-32	-0.3	-85	-0.7
Indiana	5,550	5,502	5,409	-48	-0.9	-93	-1.7
Iowa	2,758	2,549	2,382	-209	-7.6	-167	-6.6
Kansas	2,492	2,529	2,564	37	1.5	35	1.4
Kentucky	3,745	3,733	3,710	-12	-0.3	-23	-0.6
Louisiana	4,513	4,516	4,545	3	0.1	29	0.6
Maine	1,212	1,271	1,308	59	4.9	37	2.9
Maryland	4,729	5,274	5,688	545	11.5	414	7.8
Massachusetts	5,860	6,087	6,255	207	3.5	168	2.8
Michigan	9,293	9,250	9,097	-43	-0.5	-153	-1.7
Minnesota	4,324	4,490	4,578	166	3.8	88	2.0
Mississippi	2,699	2,877	3,028	178	6.6	151	5.2
Missouri	5,192	5,383	5,521	191	3.7	138	2.6
Montana	805	794	794	-11	-1.4	0	0.0
Nebraska	1,588	1,556	1,529	-32	-2.0	-27	-1.7
Nevada	1,076	1,303	1,484	227	21.1	181	13.9
New Hampshire	1,142	1,333	1,455	191	16.7	122	9.2
New Jersey	7,899	8,546	8,980	647	8.2	434	5.1
New Mexico	1,632	1,968	2,248	336	20.6	280	14.2
New York	17,773	17,986	18,139	213	1.2	153	0.9
North Carolina	6,690	7,483	8,154	793	11.9	671	9.0
North Dakota	660	629	611	-31	-4.7	-18	-2.9
Ohio	10,791	10,629	10,397	-162	-1.5	-232	-2.2
Oklahoma	3,285	3,376	3,511	91	2.8	135	4.0
Oregon	2,766	2,877	2,991	111	4.0	114	4.0
Pennsylvania	11,827	11,503	11,134	-324	-2.7	-369	-3.2
Rhode Island	1,002	1,049	1,085	47	4.7	36	3.4
South Carolina	3,549	3,906	4,205	357	10.1	299	7.7
South Dakota	708	714	722	6	0.8	8	1.1
Tennessee	4,972	5,266	5,500	294	5.9	234	4.4
Texas	17,712	20,211	22,281	2,499	14.1	2,070	10.2
Utah	1,776	1,991	2,171	215	12.1	180	9.0
Vermont	562	591	608	29	5.2	17	2.9
Virginia	6,157	6,877	7,410	720	11.7	533	7.8
Washington	4,657	4,991	5,282	334	7.2	291	5.8
West Virginia	1,856	1,722	1,617	-134	-7.2	-105	-6.1
Wisconsin	4,808	4,784	4,713	-24	-0.5	-71	-1.5
Wyoming	502	489	487	-13	-2.6	-2	-0.4

Note: Numbers may not add to totals due to rounding.

Changes in State Taxes

Source: National Conference of State Legislatures

Total increase or decrease in state taxes in millions of dollars for fiscal 1990, and change as a percent of state tax revenue in 1988. Figures do not include continuation of temporary tax increases that otherwise would have expired in 1990. There was no change in nine states.

State	Change	Pct.	State	Change	Pct.
Alaska	242	19.3	Nevada	54	4.6
Arizona	92	2.4	New Hampshire	16	2.7
Arkansas	9	0.4	New Mexico	17	0.9
Colorado	71	2.6	New York	-569	-2.2
Connecticut	802	18.3	North Carolina	236	3.4
Florida	78	0.7	North Dakota	84	13.2
Georgia	687	11.9	Ohio	165	1.7
Hawaii	-174	-8.5	Oklahoma	3	0.1
Idaho	-3	-0.3	Oregon	57	2.7
Illinois	1,078	9.8	Rhode Island	70	6.1
Iowa	-7	-0.2	South Carolina	20	0.6
Kansas	11	0.4	South Dakota	-2	-0.4
Louisiana	-66	-1.7	Tennessee	125	3.2
Maine	-11	-0.7	Texas	-278	-2.0
Maryland	-37	-0.6	Vermont	29	4.7
Massachusetts	494	5.8	Virginia	-173	-28.0
Michigan	10	0.1	Washington	48	0.8
Mississippi	17	0.8	West Virginia	327	18.8
Missouri	99	2.2	Wisconsin	-209	-3.5
Montana	19	2.7	Wyoming	8	1.4
Nebraska	17	1.3			

CITIES OF THE U.S. [1]

Sources: Bureau of the Census: population (1986 estimates); population growth (1970-1980); population over 65 and under 35 (1980). Geography Division, Bureau of the Census: population density (1980); area (1980). Bureau of Labor Statistics: employment (Jan. 1989). Bureau of Economic Analysis: per capita personal income (MSA, 1987).

Akron, Ohio

Population: 222,060; **Pop. density:** 4,312 per sq. mi.; **Pop. growth:** −13.9%; **Pop. over 65:** 13.5%; **Pop. under 35:** 57.1%. **Area:** 55 sq. mi. **Employment:** 101,353 employed, 8.7% unemployed; **Per capita income:** $15,115.

Transportation: Akron-Canton airport; major trucking industry; Conrail; metro transit system. **Communications:** 1 TV, and 7 radio stations; 2 public broadcast outlets. **Medical facilities:** 11 hospitals; specialized children's treatment center. **Educational facilities:** Univ. of Arkon and 12 others; 68 public schools. **Further information:** Akron Regional Development Board or Akron-Summit Convention and Visitors Bureau, both One Cascade Plaza, Akron, OH 44308.

Albuquerque, New Mexico

Population: 366,750; **Pop. density:** 3,492 per sq. mi.; **Pop. growth:** 35.7%; **Pop. over 65:** 8.4%; **Pop. under 35:** 61.6%. **Area:** 95 sq. mi. **Employment:** 200,774 employed, 5.0% unemployed; **Per capita income:** $14,305.

Transportation: 1 international airport; 2 railroads; 2 bus lines. **Communications:** 5 TV, 21 radio stations; 3 cable TV systems. **Medical facilities:** 9 major hospitals. **Educational facilities:** 2 universities. **Further information:** Convention & Visitors Bureau, 625 Silver S.W., Albuquerque, NM 87125.

Amarillo, Texas

Population: 165,850; **Pop. density:** 1,863 per sq. mi.; **Pop. growth:** 17.5%; **Pop. over 65:** 10.1%; **Pop. under 35:** 60.1%. **Area:** 80 sq. mi. **Employment:** 76,698 employed, 6.5% (Mar.) unemployed; **Per capita income:** $14,153.

Transportation: 2 railroads; 4 bus lines; city transit system; 1 airport with 6 airlines. **Communications:** 5 TV stations; 15 radio stations. **Medical facilities:** 9 hospitals; Amarillo Medical Ctr. **Educational facilities:** 47 public schools; Amarillo Jr. College. **Further information:** Chamber of Commerce, P.O. Box 9480, Amarillo, TX 79105.

Anaheim, California

Population: 240,730; **Pop. density:** 5,349 per sq. mi.; **Pop. growth:** 31.6%; **Pop. over 65:** 7.7%; **Pop. under 35:** 60.7%. **Area:** 41 sq. mi. **Employment:** 155,200 employed, 3.4% unemployed; **Per capita income:** $21,444.

Transportation: John Wayne, Fullerton, and Long Beach Municipal airports; 4 railroads; Greyhound buses. **Communications:** 12 TV channels, one CATV; 4 radio stations. **Medical facilities:** 6 general hospitals. **Educational facilities:** 3 colleges, 5 junior colleges; 62 elementary, 8 junior high, 8 high schools. **Further information:** Chamber of Commerce, 100 South Anaheim Blvd., Suite 300, Anaheim, CA 92805.

Anchorage, Alaska

Population: 235,000; **Pop. density:** 100 per sq. mi.; **Pop. growth:** 259.5%; **Pop. over 65:** 2.0%; **Pop. under 35:** 70.2%. **Area:** 1,732 sq. mi.. **Employment:** 102,359 employed, 7.5% unemployed; **Per capita income:** $21,102.

Transportation: Anchorage International Airport, 5 other airports. **Communications:** 5 TV, 11 radio stations. **Medical facilities:** 3 hospitals. **Educational facilities:** Univ. of Alaska, Anchorage Comm. College, Alaska Pacific Univ. **Further information:** Chamber of Commerce, 415 F St., Anchorage, AK 99501.

Arlington, Texas

Population: 249,770; **Pop. density:** 2,024 per sq. mi.; **Pop. growth:** 77.5%; **Pop. over 65:** 4.5%; **Pop. under 35:** 67.3%. **Area:** 79 sq. mi.; **Employment:** 115,253 employed, 5.2% unemployed; **Per capita income:** $15,890.

Transportation: Dallas/Ft. Worth airport is 20 minutes away; 12 railway lines; intracity transport system in planning stage. **Communications:** 9 TV stations; 39 radio stations. **Medical facilities:** almost 1,000 beds in hospital network. **Educational facilities:** 47 public schools; Univ. of Texas at Arlington. **Further information:** Chamber of Commerce, 316 W. Main St., Arlington, TX 76010.

Atlanta, Georgia

Population: 421,910; **Pop. density:** 3,244 per sq. mi.; **Pop. growth:** −14.1%; **Pop. over 65:** 11.5%; **Pop. under 35:** 60.7%. **Area:** 131 sq. mi.. **Employment:** 217,536 employed, 6.9% unemployed; **Per capita income:** $17,293.

Transportation: 1 international airport; 7 railroad lines, 2 systems; 2 bus terminals; rapid rail under construction; 6 legs of 3 interstate highways intersecting downtown interchange. **Communications:** 9 TV, 41 radio stations; 21 cable TV companies. **Medical facilities:** 60 hospitals; VA hospital; Natl. Centers for Disease Control; Natl. Cancer Center. **Educational facilities:** 30 colleges, universities, seminaries, junior colleges. **Further information:** Chamber of Commerce, 235 International Blvd., Atlanta, GA 30303.

Aurora, Colorado

Population: 217,990; **Pop. density:** 2,652 per sq. mi.; **Pop. growth:** 111.5%; **Pop. over 65:** 4.3%; **Pop. under 35:** 67.3%. **Area:** 60 sq. mi. **Employment:** 102,496 employed, 6.3% unemployed; **Per capita income:** $17,214.

Transportation: 1 international airport; 4 railroads; 2 bus lines; city bus system. **Further information:** ECO Aurora, Inc., 1470 S. Havana, Ste. 708, Aurora, CO 80012.

Austin, Texas

Population: 466,550; **Pop. density:** 2,978 per sq. mi.; **Pop. growth:** 36.3%; **Pop. over 65:** 7.5%; **Pop. under 35:** 69%. **Area:** 116 sq. mi. **Employment:** 253,162 employed, 6.1% unemployed; **Per capita income:** $15,027.

Transportation: 1 international airport; 4 railroads. **Communications:** 5 TV, 18 radio stations. **Medical facilities:** 15 hospitals. **Educational facilities:** 10 universities and colleges. **Further information:** Chamber of Commerce, P.O. Box 1967, Austin, TX 78767.

Baltimore, Maryland

Population: 752,800; **Pop. density:** 9,835 per sq. mi.; **Pop. growth:** −13.1%; **Pop. over 65:** 12.8%; **Pop. under 35%:** 56.9%. **Area:** 80 sq. mi.. **Employment:** 318,708 employed, 6.7% unemployed; **Per capita income:** $17,776.

Transportation: 1 major airport; 3 railroads, bus system; subway system; 2 underwater tunnels. **Communications:** 6 TV stations; 33 radio stations. **Medical facilities:** 29 hospitals; 2 major medical centers. **Educational facilities:** 189 public schools; over 30 universities and colleges; major public library system. **Further information:** Greater

(1) Based on 1986 estimates, the 100 most populated cities.

Baltimore Committee, Suite 900, Two Hopkins Plaza, Baltimore, MD 21202.

Baton Rouge, Louisiana

Population: 241,130; **Pop. density:** 5,673 per sq. mi.; **Pop. growth:** 32.2%; **Pop. over 65:** 8.7%; **Pop. under 35:** 64.0%. **Area:** 61 sq. mi.. **Employment:** 107,139 employed; 9.7% unemployed; **Per capita income:** $12,734.

Transportation: 1 airport with 5 airlines; 3 bus lines; 4 railroad trunk lines; Port of Greater Baton Rouge is one of largest in U.S. **Communications:** 4 TV, 13 radio stations. **Medical facilities:** 7 hospitals. **Educational facilities:** 97 public schools; Louisiana St. Univ., center of 8-campus system; Southern Univ. **Further information:** Chamber of Commerce, P.O. Box 3217, Baton Rouge, LA 70821.

Birmingham, Alabama

Population: 277,510; **Pop. density:** 2,872 per sq. mi.; **Pop. growth:** −5.5%; **Pop. over 65%;** 13.9%; **Pop. under 35:** 57.5%. **Area:** 99 sq. mi.. **Employment:** 120,798 employed, 8.8% unemployed; **Per capita income:** $13,722.

Transportation: 1 airport; 5 major rail freight lines, Amtrak; 2 bus lines; 75 truck line terminals; 3 interstate highways. **Communications:** 3 TV, 16 radio stations; 1 educational TV, 1 educational radio station. **Medical facilities:** Univ. of Alabama in Birmingham Medical Center; VA hospital with organ transplant program; 15 other hospitals. **Educational facilities:** 1 university, 3 colleges, 2 junior colleges. **Further information:** Chamber of Commerce, 2027 First Ave. N., Birmingham, AL 35202.

Boston, Massachusetts

Population: 573,600; **Pop. density:** 11,979 per sq. mi.; **Pop. growth:** −12.2%; **Pop. over 65:** 12.7%; **Pop. under 35:** 60.4%. **Area:** 46 sq. mi.. **Employment:** 290,514 employed, 3.5% unemployed; **Per capita income:** $20,239.

Transportation: 1 major airport; 2 railroads; city rail and subway system; 2 underwater tunnels. **Communications:** 8 TV stations; 33 radio stations. **Medical facilities:** numerous hospitals; 8 major medical research centers. **Educational facilities:** 28 universities and colleges; major public library system. **Further information:** Chamber of Commerce, Federal Reserve Bank, 600 Atlantic Ave., 13th Fl., Boston, MA 02106.

Buffalo, New York

Population: 324,820; **Pop. density:** 8,520 per sq. mi.; **Pop. growth:** −22.7%; **Pop. over 65:** 15.0%; **Pop. under 35:** 55.3%. **Area:** 42 sq. mi.. **Employment:** 132,463 employed, 9.9% unemployed; **Per capita income:** $15,349.

Transportation: 1 international airport; 6 major railroads, metro rail system; direct highway & rail to all of Canada; water service to Great Lakes-St. Lawrence seaways system, overseas, and Atlantic seaboard. **Communications:** 5 TV, 23 AM & FM radio stations, 5 cable systems. **Medical facilities:** 21 hospitals. **Educational facilities:** 2 universities; 9 colleges, 78 public schools. **Further information:** Greater Buffalo Chamber of Commerce, 107 Delaware Ave., Buffalo, NY 14202.

Charlotte, North Carolina

Population: 352,070; **Pop. density:** 2,278 per sq. mi.; **Pop. growth:** 30.2%; **Pop. over 65:** 8.6%; **Pop. under 35:** 60.4%. **Area:** 138 sq. mi. **Employment:** 214,576 employed, 3.4% unemployed; **Per capita income:** $15,267.

Transportation: Charlotte/Douglas Airport; 2 major railway lines; 3 bus lines; 150 trucking firms. **Communications:** 6 TV, 12 radio stations. **Medical facilities:** 7 hospitals, 1 medical center. **Educational facilities:** 2 universities, 5 colleges. **Further information:** Chamber of Commerce, P.O. Box 32785, Charlotte, NC 28232.

Chattanooga, Tennessee

Population: 162,170; **Pop. density:** 1,370 per sq. mi.; **Pop. growth:** 41.4%; **Pop. over 65:** 12.7%; **Pop. under 35:** 57.3%. **Area:** 124 sq. mi. **Employment:** 77,790 employed, 6.1% unemployed; **Per capita income:** $13,429.

Transportation: Lovell Field airport, 4 airlines; 2 bus lines and local service; 2 railroads. **Communications:** 5 TV stations; cable TV; 22 radio stations. **Medical facilities:** 17 hospitals. **Educational facilities:** 53 public schools; 2 universities; 3 junior colleges, 4 colleges. **Further information:** Partners for Economic Progress, Civic Forum, 1001 Market St., Chattanooga, TN 37402.

Chicago, Illinois

Population: 3,009,530; **Pop. density:** 13,180 per sq. mi.; **Pop. growth:** −10.8%; **Pop. over 65:** 11.4%; **Pop. under 35:** 58.5%. **Area:** 228 sq. mi. **Employment:** 1,306,506 employed, 7.0% unemployed; **Per capita income:** $17,733.

Transportation: 3 airports; major railroad system; major trucking industry. **Communications:** 9 TV stations; 31 radio stations. **Medical facilities:** over 123 hospitals. **Educational facilities:** 95 institutions of higher learning; major public library system. **Further information:** Association of Commerce and Industry, 200 N. LaSalle St., Chicago, IL 60601.

Cincinnati, Ohio

Population: 369,750; **Pop. density:** 4,941 per sq. mi.; **Pop. growth:** −15.0%; **Pop. over 65:** 14.5%; **Pop. under 35:** 58.5%. **Area:** 78 sq. mi.. **Employment:** 189,430 employed, 6.2% unemployed; **Per capita income:** $15,472.

Transportation: 1 international airport; 3 railroads; 1 bus system. **Communications:** 6 TV, 5 cable TV systems; 24 radio stations. **Medical facilities:** 32 hospitals; Children's Hospital Medical Center; VA hospital. **Educational facilities:** 3 universities; 4 4-year colleges, 8 technical & 2-year colleges; major public library system. **Further information:** Chamber of Commerce, 120 W. 5th St., Cincinnati, OH 45202.

Cleveland, Ohio

Population: 535,830; **Pop. density:** 7,264 per sq. mi.; **Pop. growth:** −23.6%; **Pop. over 65:** 13.0%; **Pop. under 35:** 56.7%. **Area:** 79 sq. mi.. **Employment:** 221,243 employed, 9.2% unemployed; **Per capita income:** $16,898.

Transportation: Hopkin's Intl. airport; rail service; major port; rapid transit system. **Communications:** 7 TV stations; 20 radio stations. **Medical facilities:** numerous hospitals; major medical research center. **Educational facilities:** 23 universities and colleges; major public library system. **Further information:** Convention & Visitor's Bureau, 1301 E. 6th Street, Cleveland, OH 44114.

Colorado Springs, Colorado

Population: 272,660; **Pop. density:** 2,088 per sq. mi.; **Pop. growth:** 58.8%; **Pop. over 65:** 8.3%; **Pop. under 35:** 62.3%. **Area:** 103 sq. mi. **Employment:** 129,850 employed, 8.3% unemployed; **Per capita income:** $14,615.

Transportation: Municipal airport served by 9 air lines; Denver & Rio Grande, Santa Fe, Burlington railroads; Greyhound, Continental Trailways buses. **Communications:** 9 TV, 15 radio stations. **Medical facilities:** 9 hospitals, 1,418 beds. **Educational facilities:** Univ. of Colorado at Colo. Springs, U.S. Air Force Acad., Pikes Peak Comm. College. **Further information:** Chamber of Commerce, P.O. Drawer B, Colorado Springs, CO 80901.

Columbus, Georgia

Population: 180,180; **Pop. density:** 779 per sq. mi.; **Pop. growth:** 9.3%; **Pop. over 65:** 8.9%; **Pop. under 35:** 61.5%. **Area:** 218 sq. mi. **Employment:** 72,437 employed, 5.8% unemployed; **Per capita income:** $12,261.

Transportation: Metropolitan airport; metro bus system; 2 bus lines; 2 railroads. Communications: 5 TV stations, 11 radio stations. Medical facilities: 5 hospitals. Educational facilities: 53 public schools;ᵀ1 college. Further information: Chamber of Commerce, P.O. Box 1200, Columbus, GA 31902.

Columbus, Ohio

Population: 566,030; Pop. density: 3,121 per sq. mi.; Pop. growth: 4.6%; Pop. over 65: 8.9%; Pop. under 35: 64.4%. Area: 181 sq. mi.. Employment: 314,335 employed, 5.9% unemployed; Per capita income: $15,308.

Transportation: 2 airports; 3 railroads; 4 intercity bus lines; major highway system. Communications: 5 TV stations; 19 radio stations. Medical facilities: 22 hospitals. Educational facilities: 12 universities and colleges; major public library system. Further information: Chamber of Commerce, P.O. Box 1527, Columbus, OH 43216.

Corpus Christi, Texas

Population: 263,900; Pop. density: 2,230 per sq. mi.; Pop. growth: 13.4%; Pop. over 65: 8.2%; Pop. under 35: 63.2%. Area: 104 sq. mi. Employment: 105,510 employed, 8.6% unemployed; Per capita income: $11,990.

Transportation: 5 airlines; 2 bus lines, metro bus system; 3 freight railroads. Communications: 6 TV stations; 17 radio stations. Medical facilities: 10 hospitals including a children's center. Educational facilities: 54 public schools; Del Mar Coll., Corpus Christi State Univ. Further information: Chamber of Commerce, PO Box 640, Corpus Christi, TX 78403.

Dallas, Texas

Population: 1,003,520; Pop. density: 2,715 per sq. mi.; Pop. growth: 7%; Pop. over 65: 9.5%; Pop. under 35: 61.1%. Area: 333 sq. mi.. Employment: 598,251 employed, 6.8% unemployed; Per capita income: $17,748.

Transportation: 1 international airport; 6 railroads; major transit system. Communications: 9 TV stations; 38 radio stations. Medical facilities: 42 hospitals; major medical center. Educational facilities: 37 universities and colleges; major public library system; 186 public schools. Further information: Chamber of Commerce, 1507 Pacific Ave., Dallas, TX 75201.

Dayton, Ohio

Population: 178,920; Pop. density: 4,236 per sq. mi.; Pop, growth: -16.3%; Pop. over 65: 11.8%; Pop. under 35: 59.8%. Area: 48 sq. mi. Employment: 82,119 employed, 8.4% unemployed; Per capita income: $15,066.

Transportation: 1 international airport; 9 airlines, 3 railroads; 4 bus lines; countywide Dayton Regional Transit Authority. Communications: 5 TV, 8 radio stations. Medical facilities: 14 hospitals including VA facility. Educational facilities: Univ. of Dayton, Wright St. Univ.. Further information: Chamber of Commerce, Suite 1980, Kettering Tower, Dayton Oh 45423.

Denver, Colorado

Population: 505,000; Pop. density: 4,435 per sq. mi.; Pop. growth: -4.3%; Pop. over 65: 12.6%; Pop. under 35: 58.9%. Area: 111 sq. mi. Employment: 242,939 employed, 7.4% unemployed; Per capita income: $17,214.

Transportation: 1 international airport; 5 major rail freight lines, Amtrak; 2 bus lines; 3 interstate highways intersect city. Communications: 7 TV, 35 radio stations. Medical facilities: 34 hospitals. Educational facilities: 2 universities; 3 colleges. Further information: Chamber of Commerce, 1301 Welton St., Denver, CO 80204.

Des Moines, Iowa

Population: 192,060; Pop. density: 2,890 per sq. mi.; Pop. growth: -5.2%; Pop. over 65: 12.5; Pop. under

35: 58.4%. Area: 66 sq. mi.. Employment: 118,543 employed, 4.4% unemployed; Per capita income: $16,173.

Transportation: 1 international airport; 3 bus lines; 4 railroads; metro bus system. Communications: 5 TV, 18 radio stations; CATV. Medical facilities: 8 hospitals with 2,700 beds. Educational facilities: Drake Univ.; 2 Bible colleges. Further information: Chamber of Commerce, 8th & High Sts., Des Moines, IA 50309.

Detroit, Michigan

Population: 1,086,220; Pop. density: 8,848 per sq. mi.; Pop. growth: -20.5%; Pop. over 65: 11.7%; Pop. under 35: 59.5%. Area: 136 sq. mi.. Employment: 416,874 employed, 10.9% unemployed; Per capita income: $17,241.

Transportation: 1 international airport; 10 railroads; major international port; public transit system. Communications: 9 TV stations, 37 radio stations. Medical facilities: 28 hospitals, major medical center. Educational facilities: 13 universities and colleges; major public library system. Further information: Chamber of Commerce, 150 Michigan Avenue, Detroit, MI 48226.

El Paso, Texas

Population: 491,800; Pop. density: 1,779 per sq. mi.; Pop. growth: 32.0%; Pop. over 65: 6.9%; Pop. under 35: 65%. Area: 239 sq. mi. Employment: 196,227 employed, 10.9% unemployed; Per capita income: $9,484.

Transportation: International airport; 5 major rail lines; 8 bus lines; 9 major highways; gateway to Mexico. Communications: 6 TV, 23 radio stations. Medical facilities: 16 hospitals; 1 medical school; 1 nursing school; 1 cancer treatment center. Educational facilities: 2 colleges and universities. Further information: Convention and Visitors Bureau, 5 Civic Center Plaza, El Paso, TX 79901.

Fort Wayne, Indiana

Population: 172,900; Pop. density: 3,274 per sq. mi.; Pop. growth: -3.4%; Pop. over 65: 11.9%; Pop. under 35: 60.5%. Area: 52 sq. mi. Employment: 91,783 employed, 4.9% unemployed; Per capita income: $15,281.

Transportation: 1 airport, 6 airlines; 3 railroads; 5 bus lines. Communications: 5 TV stations; 10 radio stations. Medical facilities: 3 major hospitals; Veteran's Admin. hospital. Educational facilities: 81 public schools; Indiana Univ.-Purdue Univ. Further information: Chamber of Commerce, 826 Ewing Street, Fort Wayne, IN 46802.

Fort Worth, Texas

Population: 429,550; Pop. density: 1,604 per sq. mi.; Pop. growth: -2.1%; Pop. over 65: 11.8%; Pop. under 35: 58.5%. Area: 240 sq. mi. Employment: 237,995 employed, 7.8% unemployed; Per capita income: $15,890.

Transportation: Dallas/Fort Worth airport; 8 major railroads, Amtrak; 41 motor carriers; local bus service; 2 transcontinental, 3 intrastate bus lines. Communications: 9 TV, 37 radio stations. Medical facilities: 35 hospitals; 2 children's hospitals; 4 government hospitals. Educational facilities: 8 colleges & universities. Further information: Chamber of Commerce, 700 Throckmorton, Fort Worth, TX 76102.

Fresno, California

Population: 284,660; Pop. density: 3,356 per sq. mi.; Pop. growth: 31.7%; Pop. over 65: 10.9%; Pop. under 35: 62.5%. Area: 65 sq. mi. Employment: 118,227 employed, 9.7% unemployed; Per capita income: $14,545.

Transportation: 7 airlines; Amtrak; freeways connect to all major areas in state; U.S. port of entry. Communications: one public, 6 commercial TV stations, 5 CATV services; 18 commercial, 2 public radio stations. Medical facilities: 6 general hospitals including a VA facility. Educational facilities: Cal. State-Fresno, Pacific Coll., Frenso City Coll. (oldest jr. coll. in Cal.). Further information: Chamber of Commerce, P.O. Box 1469, Fresno, CA 93721.

Garland, Texas

Population: 176,510; **Pop. density:** 2,493 per sq. mi.; **Pop. growth:** 70.5%; **Pop. over 65:** 4.1%; **Pop. under 35:** 33.7%. **Area:** 56 sq. mi. **Employment:** 94,283 employed, 4.5% unemployed; **Per capita income:** $17,748.

Transportation: 35 miles from Dallas/Ft. Worth airport; 2 railroads. **Communications:** 3 TV stations (from Dallas) plus 1 local station. **Medical facilities:** total of 333 hospital beds. **Educational facilities:** 48 public schools; 2 universities, 2 junior colleges. **Further information:** Chamber of Commerce, P.O. Box 460939, Garland, TX 75046.

Grand Rapids, Michigan

Population: 186,530; **Pop. density:** 4,190 per sq. mi.; **Pop. growth:** −8.0%; **Pop. over 65:** 13.4%; **Pop. under 35:** 60.5%. **Area:** 43.4 sq. mi. **Employment:** 97,060 employed, 6.9% unemployed; **Per capita income:** $15,257.

Transportation: 4 railroads; 1 international airport; 3 bus lines. **Communications:** 6 TV stations; 20 radio stations. **Medical facilities:** 12 hospitals. **Educational facilities:** 119 public schools; 8 colleges. **Further information:** Chamber of Commerce, 17 Fountain St., NW, Grand Rapids, MI 49503.

Greensboro, North Carolina

Population: 176,650; **Pop. density:** 2,581 per sq. mi.; **Pop. growth:** 8.0%; **Pop. over 65:** 9.8%; **Pop. under 35:** 57%. **Area:** 60 sq. mi.; **Employment:** 91,984 employed, 4.6% unemployed; **Per capita income:** $15,396.

Transportation: 1 regional airport; 2 railroads; Trailways/Greyhound bus service. **Communications:** all cable TV stations; 11 radio stations. **Medical facilities:** 4 hospitals. **Educational facilities:** 38 public schools; U.N.C.-Greensboro, N.C. A&T State Univ., Guilford College. **Further information:** Chamber of Commerce, P.O. Box 3246, Greensboro, NC 27402.

Honolulu, Hawaii

Population: 372,330; **Pop. density:** 1,280 per sq. mi.; **Pop. growth:** 20.9%; **Pop. over 65:** 7.4%; **Pop. under 35:** 62.4%. **Area:** 596 sq. mi. **Employment:** 367,729 employed, 3.0% unemployed; **Per capita income:** $16,412.

Transportation: 1 major airport; large, active port for passengers and cargo. **Communications:** 5 TV stations; 23 radio stations. **Medical facilities:** 43 hospitals. **Educational facilities:** 230 public schools (state); 146 private schools (state); 1 university (9 campus centers); major public library system. **Further information:** Visitors Bureau, 2270 Kalakaua Avenue, Honolulu, HI 96815.

Houston, Texas

Population: 1,728,910; **Pop. density:** 2,869 per sq. mi.; **Pop. growth:** 29.3%; **Pop. over 65:** 6.9%; **Pop. under 35:** 64.4%. **Area:** 556 sq. mi. **Employment:** 893,169 employed; 7.0% unemployed; **Per capita income:** $15,200.

Transportation: 2 commercial airports; 5 railroads; major bus transit system; major international port. **Communications:** 9 TV stations; 45 radio stations. **Medical facilities:** 59 hospitals; major medical center. **Educational facilities:** 27 universities and colleges; 7th largest U.S. public school system; major public library system. **Further information:** Chamber of Commerce, 1100 Milam, Houston, TX 77002.

Huntington Beach, California

Population: 183,620; **Pop. density:** 6,315 per sq. mi.; **Pop. growth:** 47%. **Area:** 27 sq. mi. **Employment:** 122,859 employed, 3.0% unemployed; **Per capita income:** $21,444.

Transportation: 1 airport; 1 railroad; 2 bus lines. **Communications:** 1 TV station; cable TV. **Medical facilities:** 2 hospitals. **Educational facilities:** 45 public schools; 1 junior college. **Further information:** Chamber of Commerce, Seacliff Village, 2213 Main #32, Huntington Beach, CA 92648.

Huntsville, Alabama

Population: 163,420; **Pop. density:** 1,256 per sq. mi.; **Pop. growth:** 2.3%; **Pop. over 65:** 7.0%; **Pop. under 35:** 59%.; **Area:** 114 sq. mi.; **Employment:** 92,959 employed, 5.4% unemployed; **Per capita income:** $15,082.

Transportation: Huntsville-Madison County Airport; 2 railroads. **Communications:** 5 TV, 13 radio stations. **Medical facilities:** 4 hospitals. **Educational facilities:** 38 public schools; Univ. of Alabama, Oakwood College, Alabama Agricultural & Mechanical Univ. **Further information:** Huntsville/Madison County Chamber of Commerce, P.O. Box 408, Huntsville, AL 35804.

Indianapolis, Indiana

Population: 719,820; **Pop. density:** 1,991 per sq. mi.; **Pop. growth:** −4.9%; **Pop. over 65:** 10.3%; **Pop. under 35:** 59.4%. **Area:** 352 sq. mi.. **Employment:** 382,193 employed, 4.3% unemployed; **Per capita income:** $15,809.

Transportation: 1 international airport; 6 railroads; 3 interstate bus lines. **Communications:** 7 TV stations; 27 radio stations. **Medical facilities:** 17 hospitals; major medical center. **Educational facilities:** 6 universities and colleges; major public library system. **Further information:** Chamber of Commerce, 320 N. Meridian Street, Indianapolis, IN 46204.

Jackson, Mississippi

Population: 208,420; **Pop. density:** 1,914 per sq. mi.; **Pop. growth:** 31.8%; **Pop. over 65:** 9.9%; **Pop. under 35:** 59.3%. **Area:** 106.2 sq. mi.. **Employment:** 100,381 employed, 5.9% unemployed; **Per capita income:** $12,591.

Transportation: 6 airlines; 2 bus lines; Ill. Central Gulf railroad. **Communications:** 5 TV, 25 radio stations. **Medical facilities:** 12 hospitals including a VA facility. **Educational facilities:** Jackson St. Univ.; Belhaven, Millsaps, Mississippi, Tougaloo, and Wesley colleges. **Further information:** Chamber of Commerce, P.O. Box 22548, Jackson, MS 39225.

Jacksonville, Florida

Population: 609,860; **Pop. density:** 712 per sq. mi.; **Pop. growth:** 7.3%; **Pop. over 65:** 9.6%; **Pop. under 35:** 60.0%. **Area:** 760 sq. mi.. **Employment:** 304,318 employed, 6.4% unemployed; **Per capita income:** $14,611.

Transportation: 1 international airport; 3 railroads; 2 interstate bus lines. **Communications:** 6 TV stations; 21 radio stations. **Medical facilities:** 14 hospitals. **Educational facilities:** 5 universities and colleges; major public library system. **Further information:** Chamber of Commerce, 3 Independent Drive, P.O. Box 329, Jacksonville, FL 32201.

Jersey City, New Jersey

Population: 219,480; **Pop. density:** 16,934 per sq. mi.; **Pop. growth:** −14.1%; **Pop. over 65:** 11.8%; **Pop. under 35:** 57.6%. **Area:** 13.2 sq. mi. **Employment:** 92,716 employed, 8.3% unemployed; **Per capita income:** $15,521.

Transportation: bus and subway system. **Medical facilities:** 10 hospitals. **Educational facilities:** 3 colleges. **Further information:** Chamber of Commerce & Industry of Hudson County, 911 Bergen Ave., Jersey City, NJ 07303.

Kansas City, Kansas

Population: 162,070; **Pop. density:** 1,500 per sq. mi.; **Pop. growth:** −4.2%; **Pop. over 65:** 11.7%; **Pop. under 35:** 57.1%. **Area:** 107 sq. mi. **Employment:** 76,739 employed, 8.4% unemployed; **Per capita income:** $16,309.

Transportation: 1 airport, 11 airlines; 9 railroads; bus system. **Communications:** 4 TV stations; 32 radio stations. **Medical facilities:** 3 hospitals, medical center. **Edu-**

cational facilities: 50 public schools; 1 junior college, Univ. of Kansas Medical Ctr. Further information: Chamber of Commerce, P.O. Box 1310, Kansas City, KS 66117.

Kansas City, Missouri

Population: 441,170; Pop. density: 1,418 per sq. mi.; Pop. growth: −11.7%; Pop. over 65: 12.3%; Pop. under 35: 57.1%. Area: 316 sq. mi. Employment: 235,796 employed, 6.8% unemployed; Per capita income: $16,309.

Transportation: 1 international airport; a major rail center; 191 trunk lines; several barge companies. Communications: 6 TV, 14 AM, 18 FM radio stations. Medical facilities: 41 hospitals; 18 clinics. Educational facilities: 13 colleges & universities. Further information: Chamber of Commerce, 600 Boatmen's Center, 920 Main St., Kansas City, MO 64105.

Knoxville, Tennessee

Population: 173,210; Pop. density: 2,273 per sq. mi.; Pop. growth: .25%; Pop. over 65: 13.8%; Pop. under 35: 57.8%. Area: 77 sq. mi. Employment: 79,625 employed, 6.2% unemployed; Per capita income: $13,144.

Transportation: 13 airlines, 2 bus lines, 61 motor freight carriers; 2 railroads. Communications: 5 TV, 16 radio stations. Medical facilities: 8 hospitals. Educational facilities: 85 public schools; Univ. of Tennessee, Knoxville College. Further information: Chamber of Commerce, P.O. Box 2688, Knoxville, TN 37901.

Las Vegas, Nevada

Population: 191,510; Pop. density: 2,994 per sq. mi.; Pop. growth: 30.9%; Pop. over 65: 8.3%; Pop. under 35: 58.4%. Area: 55 sq. mi. Employment: 118,367 employed, 5.9% unemployed; Per capita income: $15,944.

Transportation: 1 international airport; 2 railroads; bus system. Communications: 6 TV and 24 radio stations. Medical facilities: 8 hospitals. Educational facilities: 116 public schools; Clark Comm. College; Univ. of Nevada. Further information: Chamber of Commerce, 2301 E. Sahara Ave., Las Vegas, NV, 89104.

Lexington–Fayette, Kentucky

Population: 212,900; Pop. density: 719 per sq. mi.; Pop. growth: 88.8%; Pop. over 65: 8.6%; Pop. under 35: 63.3%. Area: 284 sq. mi. Employment: 124,469 employed, 4.1% unemployed; Per capita income: $14,953.

Transportation: 8 airlines, 2 railroads; city buses. Communications: 5 TV stations, CATV; 9 radio stations. Medical facilities: 4 general, 5 specialized hospitals. Educational facilities: Univ. of Kentucky, Transylvania Univ., Lexington Baptist College. Further information: Chamber of Commerce, 330 East Main, Lexington, KY 40507.

Lincoln, Nebraska

Population: 183,050; Pop. density: 2,866 per sq. mi.; Pop. growth: 15.0%; Pop. over 65: 10.3%; Pop. under 35: 63.9%. Area: 60 sq. mi. Employment: 110,382 employed, 2.4% unemployed; Per capita income: $14,373.

Transportation: 7 airlines serve Lincoln Municipal Airport; Greyhound, Trailways buses; Amtrak. Communications: 1 TV, 11 radio stations; CATV. Medical facilities: 4 hospitals including a VA facility. Educational facilities: 3 colleges; 6 business, professional, or technical schools. Further information: Chamber of Commerce, 1221 N St., Lincoln, NE 68508.

Little Rock, Arkansas

Population: 181,030; Pop. density: 1,996 per sq. mi.; Pop. growth: 19.6%; Pop. over 65: 11.0%; Pop. under 35: 60.8%. Area: 79 sq. mi. Employment: 90,632 employed, 5.4% unemployed; Per capita income: $13,966.

Transportation: 1 airport, 7 airlines; 3 railroads; 2 bus lines. Communications: 6 TV stations, 30 radio stations.

Medical facilities: 15 hospitals; veterans' medical center. Educational facilities: 36 public schools; 7 colleges and universities; Univ. of Arkansas. Further information: Chamber of Commerce, One Spring St., Little Rock, AR 72201.

Long Beach, California

Population: 396,280; Pop. density: 7,256 per sq. mi.; Pop. growth: 0.7%; Pop. over 65: 14.0%; Pop. under 35: 56.6%. Area: 50 sq. mi.. Employment: 186,829 employed, 4.3% unemployed; Per capita income: $17,863.

Transportation: 1 airport; 3 railroads; major international port; 6 bus lines. Communications: 1 cable TV station; 2 AM, 6 FM radio stations. Medical facilities: 10 hospitals. Educational facilities: 78 public schools; 1 university; 1 college. Further information: Chamber of Commerce, 330 Golden Shore, Long Beach, CA 90802.

Los Angeles, California

Population: 3,259,340; Pop. density: 6,380 per sq. mi.; Pop. growth: +5.5%; Pop. over 65: 10.6%; Pop. under 35: 58.1%. Area: 465 sq. mi.. Employment: 1,600,568 employed, 5.0% unemployed; Per capita income: $17,863.

Transportation: 1 major airport; 4 railroads; major bus carrier service; major freeway system. Communications: 19 TV stations; 71 radio stations. Medical facilities: 822 hospitals and clinics; 409 nursing homes. Educational facilities: 11 universities and colleges; 1,642 public schools; 800 private schools; 61 public libraries. Further information: Chamber of Commerce, P.O. Box 3696, Terminal Annex, Los Angeles, CA 90051.

Louisville, Kentucky

Population: 286,470; Pop. density: 4,974 per sq. mi.; Pop. growth: −17.5%; Pop. over 65: 15.3%; Pop. under 35: 54.1%. Area: 60 sq. mi. Employment: 130,310 employed, 6.5% unemployed. Per capita income: $14,599.

Transportation: 2 municipal airports; 1 terminal, 6 trunk-line railroads; 3 bus lines; 125 inter-city truck lines; 5 barge lines. Communications: 4 TV, 20 radio stations, 2 educational, 1 cable. Medical facilities: 21 hospitals. Educational facilities: 10 colleges & universities, 9 business colleges & technical schools. Further information: Chamber of Commerce, One Riverfront Plaza, Louisville, KY 40202.

Lubbock, Texas

Population: 186,400; Pop. density: 1,933 per sq. mi.; Pop. growth: 16.7%; Pop. over 65: 7.8%; Pop. under 35: 66.9%. Area: 90 sq. mi. Employment: 89,994 employed, 5.5% unemployed; Per capita income: $12,750.

Transportation: Lubbock International Airport; 2 railroads, bus line. Communications: 5 TV, 18 radio stations. Medical facilities: 7 hospitals. Educational facilities: 51 public schools; Texas Tech Univ., South Plains College, Lubbock Christian College. Further information: Chamber of Commerce, P.O. Box 561, Lubbock, TX 79408.

Madison, Wisconsin

Population: 175,830; Pop. density: 3,165 per sq. mi.; Pop. growth: −.7%; Pop. over 65: 8.7%; Pop. under 35: 65.1%. Area: 60 sq. mi. Employment: 111,653 employed, 2.7% unemployed; Per capita income: $16,895.

Transportation: 1 airport, 9 airlines; 2 railroads; bus system. Communications: 4 TV stations; 19 radio stations. Medical facilities: 6 hospitals. Educational facilities: 41 public schools; 4 colleges and universities; Univ. of Wisconsin. Further information: Chamber of Commerce, P.O. Box 71, Madison, WI 53701.

Memphis, Tennessee

Population: 652,640; Pop. density: 2,448 per sq. mi.; Pop. growth: 3.6%; Pop. over 65: 10.4%; Pop. under

35: 60.5%. **Area:** 264 sq. mi.. **Employment:** 318,308 employed, 5.7% unemployed; **Per capita income:** $14,271.

Transportation: 1 major airport; 6 railroads; bus system. **Communications:** 6 TV stations; 26 radio stations. **Medical facilities:** 20 hospitals. **Educational facilities:** 10 universities and colleges; 149 private schools; 76 private schools. **Further information:** Chamber of Commerce, 555 Beale St., Box 224, Memphis TN 38101.

Mesa, Arizona

Population: 251,430; **Pop. density:** 2,242 per sq. mi.; **Pop. growth:** 141.8%; **Pop. over 65:** 11.2%; **Pop. under 35:** 62.4%. **Area:** 68 sq. mi. **Employment:** 97,437 employed, 4.5% unemployed; **Per capita income:** $16,077.

Transportation: Falcon Field Memorial and Sky Harbor Intl. airports; 2 railroads; trolley and bus lines. **Medical facilities:** 4 major hospitals. **Educational facilities:** 49 public schools; Mesa Community College; Ariz. State Univ. **Further information:** Convention and Visitor's Bureau, 120 N. Center, Mesa, AZ 85201.

Miami, Florida

Population: 373,940; **Pop. density:** 11,256 per sq. mi.; **Pop. growth:** 3.6%; **Pop. over 65:** 17.0%; **Pop. under 35:** 46.5%. **Area:** 34 sq. mi.. **Employment:** 186,808 employed; 7.8% unemployed; **Per capita income:** $15,689.

Transportation: 1 international airport; 2 passenger railroads, 1 all-freight; 2 bus lines; 65 truck lines. **Communications:** 6 commercial, 5 educational TV stations; 31 radio stations. **Medical facilities:** 41 hospitals, 39 nursing homes; VA Hospital. **Educational facilities:** 6 colleges & universities. **Further information:** Metro-Dade Department of Tourism, 234 W. Flagler St., Miami, FL 33130.

Milwaukee, Wisconsin

Population: 605,090; **Pop. density:** 6,627 per sq. mi.; **Pop. growth:** −11.3%; **Pop. over 65:** 12.5%; **Pop. under 35:** 59.8%. **Area:** 96 sq. mi.. **Employment:** 306,046 employed, 4.5% unemployed; **Per capita income:** $16,686.

Transportation: 1 international airport; 2 railroads; major port; 4 bus lines. **Communications:** 7 TV stations; 33 radio stations. **Medical facilities:** 29 hospitals; major medical center. **Educational facilities:** 12 universities and colleges; major public school and library system. **Further information:** Association of Commerce, 756 N. Milwaukee Street, Milwaukee, WI 53202.

Minneapolis, Minnesota

Population: 356,840; **Pop. density:** 6,744 per sq. mi.; **Pop. growth:** −14.6%; **Pop. over 65:** 15.4%; **Pop. under 35:** 59.4%. **Area:** 55 sq. mi.. **Employment:** 208,205 employed; 3.7% unemployed; **Per capita income:** $18,277.

Transportation: 1 international airport; 6 railroads; mass transit systems; 5 major barge lines. **Communications:** 6 TV, 39 radio stations. **Medical facilities:** 36 hospitals, including leading heart hospital at Univ. of Minnesota. **Educational facilities:** 48 public school districts; 13 colleges and universities. **Further information:** Chamber of Commerce, 15 S. 5th St., Minneapolis, MN 55402.

Mobile, Alabama

Population: 203,260; **Pop. density:** 1,630 per sq. mi.; **Pop. growth:** 5.5%; **Pop. over 65:** 11.1%; **Pop. under 35:** 59.3%. **Area:** 123 sq. mi. **Employment:** 85,276 employed, 10.5% unemployed; **Per capita income:** $11,566.

Transportation: 4 railroads, 4 major airlines, 55 truck lines; leading river system. **Communications:** 5 TV, 12 radio stations; CATV. **Medical facilities:** 6 hospitals. **Educational facilities:** Univ. of South Alabama; Spring Hill, Mobile colleges. **Further information:** Chamber of Commerce, P.O. Box 2187, Mobile, AL 36652.

Mon[...]

Population: 19[...]
Pop. growth: 3[...]
35: 60.7%. **Are**[...]
ployed, 7.0% [...]

Transport[...]
bus line; In[...]
River is na[...]
TV, 14 ra[...]
hospitals.[...]
cilities: 5 co[...]
Chamber of Con[...]
36192.

Nashville-Davidson[...]

Population: 473,670; **Pop. density**[...]
Pop. growth: 7.0%; **Pop. over 65:** 11.0[...]
35: 58.7%. **Area:** 480 sq. mi.. **Employment:** 2[...]
ployed, 4.2% unemployed; **Per capita income:** $15[...]

Transportation: 1 airport, 9 airlines; 2 railroads; 3 bus lines. **Communications:** 7 TV, 30 radio stations. **Medical facilities:** 17 hospitals; 2 medical schools; VA Hospital, speech-hearing center. **Educational facilities:** 16 colleges & universities. **Further information:** Chamber of Commerce, 161 4th Ave., Nashville, TN 37219.

Newark, New Jersey

Population: 316,240; **Pop. density:** 13,718 per sq. mi.; **Pop. growth:** −13.8%; **Pop. over 65:** 8.8%; **Pop. under 35:** 61.6%. **Area:** 24 sq. mi. **Employment:** 116,581 employed, 9.2% unemployed; **Per capita income:** $21,061.

Transportation: 1 international airport; 2 railroads; bus system; 2 subways. **Communications:** 3 TV, 5 radio stations. **Medical facilities:** 6 hospitals. **Educational facilities:** 5 universities and colleges; 71 public schools. **Further information:** Chamber of Commerce, 50 Park Pl., Newark, NJ 07102.

New Orleans, Louisiana

Population: 554,500; **Pop. density:** 2,802 per sq. mi.; **Pop. growth:** −6%; **Pop. over 65:** 11.7%; **Pop. under 35:** 60.1%. **Area:** 199 sq. mi.. **Employment:** 204,637 employed, 10.3% unemployed; **Per capita income:** $13,130.

Transportation: 2 airports; major railroad center; major international port. **Communications:** 2 TV stations; 28 radio stations. **Medical facilities:** numerous hospitals; major medical research center. **Educational facilities:** 13 universities and colleges; major public library system. **Further information:** Chamber of Commerce, 301 Camp Street, New Orleans, LA 70130.

New York City, New York

Population: 7,262,700; **Pop. density:** 23,494 per sq. mi.; **Pop. growth:** −10.4%; **Pop. over 65:** 13.5%; **Pop. under 35:** 53.7%. **Area:** 301 sq. mi. **Employment:** 3,079,542 employed, 5.7% unemployed; **Per capita income:** $19,185.

Transportation: 2 airports; 4 heliports; 2 rail terminals; 40 bus carriers; major subway network; ferry system; 4 underwater tunnels. **Communications:** 17 TV stations, 117 radio stations. **Medical facilities:** 100 hospitals; 5 medical research centers. **Educational facilities:** 94 universities and colleges; 976 public schools, 914 private schools; 201 public libraries. **Further information:** Convention and Visitors Bureau, 2 Columbus Circle, New York, NY 10019.

Norfolk, Virginia

Population: 274,800; **Pop. density:** 5,037 per sq. mi.; **Pop. growth:** −13.3%; **Pop. over 65:** 9.2%; **Pop. under 35:** 68.6%. **Area:** 53 sq. mi.. **Employment:** 89,058 employed, 6.0% unemployed; **Per capita income:** $14,462.

Transportation: 1 international airport; 4 major railroad systems in area. **Communications:** 7 TV, 38 radio stations. **Medical facilities:** 11 hospitals, 1 medical school. **Educational facilities:** 53 public schools; 2 universities, 1

...ation: Hampton Roads Chamber
...k St., Norfolk, VA 23510.

...kland, California

...6,960; **Pop. density:** 6,284 per sq. mi.;
...6.2%; **Pop. over 65:** 13.2%; **Pop. under**
...a: 54 sq. mi.. **Employment:** 179,019 em-
...unemployed; **Per capita income:** $19,896.

...tation: 1 international airport; western termi-
...ailroads; underground, underwater 75-mile sub-
...nmunications: 1 TV, 3 radio stations. **Medical**
...s. 8 hospitals, including Children's Hospital Medi-
...enter, VA hospital. **Educational facilities:** 94 public
...ols; 3 colleges and universities. **Further information:**
...amber of Commerce, 1939 Harrison St., Ste. 400,
...akland, CA 94612.

Oklahoma City, Oklahoma

Population: 446,120; **Pop. density:** 667 per sq. mi.;
Pop. growth: 9.5%; **Pop. over 65:** 11.3%; **Pop. under**
35: 58.2%. **Area.** 604 sq. mi.. **Employment:** 217,735 employed, 5.5% unemployed; **Per capita income:** $13,021.

Transportation: 1 international airport; 3 railroads; public transit system; 5 major bus lines. **Communications:** 8
TV, 24 radio stations; cable TV. **Medical facilities:** 22
hospitals. **Educational facilities:** 87 public schools; 14
colleges and universities. **Further information:** Chamber
of Commerce, One Santa Fe Plaza, Oklahoma City, OK
73102.

Omaha, Nebraska

Population: 349,270; **Pop. density:** 3,453 per sq. mi.;
Pop. growth: −9.5%; **Pop. over 65:** 12.2%; **Pop. under**
35: 41.9%. **Area:** 91 sq. mi.. **Employment:** 171,989 employed, 4.2% unemployed; **Per capita income:** $15,033.

Transportation: 9 major airlines; major rail center, with
5 major railroads; intercity bus line. **Communications:** 6
TV, 17 radio stations. **Medical facilities:** 17 hospitals; 2
medical, 1 dental, 6 nursing schools; institute for cancer
research. **Educational facilities:** 114 public schools; 3
universities, 6 colleges. **Further information:** Chamber of
Commerce, 1301 Harney St., Omaha, NE 68102.

Philadelphia, Pennsylvania

Population: 1,642,900; **Pop. density:** 12,413 per sq.
mi.; **Pop. growth:** −13.4%; **Pop. over 65:** 14.1%; **Pop.
under 35:** 54.4%. **Area:** 136 sq. mi.. **Employment:**
711,073 employed, 5.1% unemployed; **Per capita income:** $17,294.

Transportation: 1 major airport; 3 railroads; biggest
freshwater port in world; subway, el, rail commuter, bus,
and streetcar system. **Communications:** 6 TV stations;
53 radio stations. **Medical facilities:** 124 hospitals. **Educational facilities:** 88 degree-granting institutions; major
public library system. **Further information:** Office of City
Representative, 1660 Municipal Services Bldg., Philadelphia, PA 19107.

Phoenix, Arizona

Population: 894,070; **Pop. density:** 2,438 per sq. mi.;
Pop. growth: 35.1%; **Pop. over 65:** 9.3%; **Pop. under
35:** 60.4%. **Area:** 324 sq. mi.. **Employment:** 542,456 employed, 5.0% unemployed; **Per capita income:** $16,077.

Transportation: 1 major airport; 2 railroads; 2 transcontinental bus lines; public transit system. **Communications:** 9 TV stations; 34 radio stations. **Medical facilities:**
34 hospitals, 1 medical research center. **Educational facilities:** 8 universities and colleges; 6 community colleges;
major public library system. **Further information:** Chamber of Commerce, 34 W. Monroe, Suite 900, Phoenix, AZ
85003.

Pittsburgh, Pennsylvania

Population: 387,490; **Pop. density:** 7,707 per sq. mi.;
Pop. growth: −18%; **Pop. over 65:** 16.0%; **Pop. under**
35: 52.9%. **Area:** 55 sq. mi.. **Employment:** 165,338 employed, 4.7% unemployed; **Per capita income:** $15,419.

Transportation: 1 international airport; 20 railroads; 2
bus lines; trolley/subway system. **Communications:** 6
TV, 25 radio stations. **Medical facilities:** 32 hospitals; VA
installation. **Educational facilities:** 86 public schools; 3
universities; 6 colleges. **Further information:** Chamber of
Commerce, 3 Gateway Ctr., Pittsburgh, PA 15222.

Portland, Oregon

Population: 387,870; **Pop. density:** 3,557 per sq. mi.;
Pop. growth: −3.6%; **Pop. over 65:** 10.9%; **Pop. under
35:** 58.9%. **Area:** 103 sq. mi.. **Employment:** 195,913 employed, 5.8% unemployed; **Per capita income:** $15,732.

Transportation: 1 international airport; 3 major rail
freight lines; Amtrak; 2 bus lines; 27-mi. frontage freshwater port; mass transit system. **Communications:** 5 TV, 27
radio stations. **Medical facilities:** 32 hospitals; Oregon
Health Sciences University Hospital; VA hospital. **Educational facilities:** 11 colleges and universities; 4 community colleges. **Further information:** Chamber of Commerce, 221 N.W. Second Ave., Portland, OR 97209.

Raleigh, North Carolina

Population: 180,430; **Pop. density:** 2,793 per sq. mi.;
Pop. growth: 22.3%; **Pop. over 65:** 8.3%; **Pop. under
35:** 62.8%. **Area:** 54 sq. mi. **Employment:** 112,415 employed, 3.4% unemployed; **Per capita income:** $16,613.

Transportation: Raleigh-Durham airport, 15 airlines; 3
railroads; 1 bus line. **Communications:** 6 TV stations; 13
radio stations. **Medical facilities:** 11 hospitals. **Educational facilities:** 4 colleges and universities; 3 junior colleges; 78 public schools. **Further information:** Chamber
of Commerce, 800 S. Salisbury St., P.O. Box 2978, Raleigh, NC 27602.

Richmond, Virginia

Population: 217,700; **Pop. density:** 3,650 per sq. mi.;
Pop. growth: −12.1%; **Pop. over 65:** 14.1%; **Pop. under 35:** 56.9%. **Area:** 60 sq. mi. **Employment:** 108,584
employed, 4.9% unemployed; **Per capita income:**
$17,446.

Transportation: Richmond International airport; 4 railroads, 3 intercity bus lines; deepwater terminal accessible
to ocean-going ships. **Communications:** 7 TV, 28 radio
stations. **Medical facilities:** Medical Coll. of Virginia renowned for heart and kidney transplants; 19 other hospitals including VA facility. **Educational facilities:** 181 public schools; 9 colleges and universities. **Further
information:** Chamber of Commerce, P.O. Box 12324,
Richmond, VA 23241.

Riverside, California

Population: 196,750; **Pop. density:** 2,406 per sq. mi.;
Pop. growth: 22.0%; **Pop. over 65:** 8.8%; **Pop. under
35:** 62.8%. **Area:** 71 sq. mi.. **Employment:** 115,005 employed, 6.4% unemployed; **Per capita income:** $15,075.

Communications: 11 TV, 13 radio stations. **Educational facilities:** Univ. of Cal.- Riverside, Cal. Baptist. **Further information:** Chamber of Commerce, 4261 Main St.,
Riverside, CA 92501.

Rochester, New York

Population: 235,970; **Pop. density:** 7,068 per sq. mi.;
Pop. growth: −18.1%; **Pop. over 65:** 14.0%; **Pop. under 35:** 60.0%. **Area:** 34 sq. mi.. **Employment:** 111,811
employed, 6.5% unemployed; **Per capita income:**
$16,913.

Transportation: Amtrak; Greyhound, Trailways, Blue
Bird bus lines; Monroe Co. airport with 8 major airlines;
Rochester Transit Service; Port of Rochester; some 75
motor freight firms. **Communications:** 5 TV, 18 radio stations. **Medical facilities:** 8 general hospitals including
Strong Memorial. **Educational facilities:** 8 private and 2
public 4-year colleges; 3 community colleges. **Further in-**

formation: Chamber of Commerce, 55 St. Paul St., Rochester, NY 14604.

Sacramento, California

Population: 323,550; **Pop. density:** 2,872 per sq. mi.; **Pop. growth:** 10.7%; **Pop. over 65:** 9.6%; **Pop. under 35:** 59%. **Area:** 96 sq. mi.. **Employment:** 160,477 employed, 6.2% unemployed; **Per capita income:** $16,300.

Transportation: metropolitan airport; 2 mainline transcontinental rail carriers; bus and light rail system. **Communications:** 7 TV, 22 radio stations. **Medical facilities:** 15 hospitals. **Educational facilities:** 3 universities, 4 community colleges. **Further information:** Chamber of Commerce, 917 7th St., P.O. Box 1017, Sacramento, CA 95805.

St. Louis, Missouri

Population: 426,300; **Pop. density:** 7,427 per sq. mi.; **Pop. growth:** −27.2%; **Pop. over 65:** 17.6%; **Pop. under 35:** 54%. **Area:** 61 sq. mi.. **Employment:** 179,055 employed, 8.4% unemployed; **Per capita income:** $16,706.

Transportation: 1 international airport; 3d largest rail center in U.S.; 17 trunk line railroads; 2d largest inland port in U.S.; 14 bus lines; 350 motor freight lines, 14 barge lines. **Communications:** 6 TV, 35 radio stations. **Medical facilities:** 65 hospitals. **Educational facilities:** 5 universities, 26 colleges and seminaries. **Further information:** Regional Commerce and Growth Assoc., Ten Broadway, St. Louis, MO 63102.

St. Paul, Minnesota

Population: 263,680; **Pop. density:** 5,196 per sq. mi.; **Pop. growth:** −12.8%; **Pop. over 65:** 15.0%; **Pop. under 35:** 41.5%. **Area:** 52 sq. mi.. **Employment:** 142,463 employed, 4.1% unemployed; **Per capita income:** $18,277.

Transportation: 1 international airport; 5 major rail lines; 3 interstate bus lines; 10 barge lines. **Communications:** 5 TV, 36 radio stations. **Medical facilities:** 12 private hospitals; community hospital and research center. **Educational facilities:** 1 university; 5 colleges; 51 public schools. **Further information:** Chamber of Commerce, 600 N. Central Tower, 445 Minnesota St., St. Paul, MN 55101.

St. Petersburg, Florida

Population: 239,410; **Pop. density:** 4,186 per sq. mi.; **Pop. growth:** 10.4%; **Pop. over 65:** 25.8%; **Pop. under 35:** 43.7%. **Area:** 57 sq. mi.. **Employment:** 128,139 employed, 5.9% unemployed; **Per capita income:** $15,435.

Transportation: 1 international airport; bus system; 2 full-service ports. **Communications:** 9 TV, 49 radio stations. **Medical facilities:** 9 hospitals. **Educational facilities:** 106 public schools; 7 colleges. **Further information:** Chamber of Commerce, P.O. Box 1371, St. Petersburg, FL 33731.

Salt Lake City, Utah

Population: 164,844; **Pop. density:** 2,168 per sq. mi.; **Pop. growth:** −7.3%; **Pop. over 65:** 14.7%; **Pop. under 35:** 67.2%. **Area:** 75 sq. mi.. **Employment:** 94,170 employed, 4.4% unemployed; **Per capita income:** $12,343.

Transportation: 1 international airport, 9 airlines; 3 railroads; mass transit system. **Communications:** 6 TV stations; 27 radio stations. **Medical facilities:** 13 hospitals; 5 emergency care centers. **Educational facilities:** 47 public schools (Salt Lake); Univ. of Utah, Salt Lake Community College. **Further information:** Chamber of Commerce, 175 E. 400 South, Ste. 600, Salt Lake City, UT 84111.

San Antonio, Texas

Population: 914,350; **Pop. density:** 2,988 per sq. mi.; **Pop. growth:** 20%; **Pop. over 65:** 9.5%; **Pop. under 35:** 62.1%. **Area:** 263 sq. mi.. **Employment:** 400,983 employed, 8.6% unemployed; **Per capita income:** $12,921.

Transportation: 1 major airport; 4 railroads; 5 bus lines. **Communications:** 6 TV, 28 radio stations. **Medical facilities:** 26 hospitals; major medical center. **Educational facilities:** 15 universities and colleges; major public library system. **Further information:** Chamber of Commerce, 602 E. Commerce, P.O. Box 1628, San Antonio, TX 78296.

San Diego, California

Population: 1,015,190; **Pop. density:** 2,736 per sq. mi.; **Pop. growth:** 25.5%; **Pop. over 65:** 9.7%; **Pop. under 35:** 62.1%. **Area:** 320 sq. mi.. **Employment:** 519,626 employed, 4.1% unemployed; **Per capita income:** $16,633.

Transportation: 1 major airport; 1 railroad; major freeway system; bus system. **Communications:** 7 TV, 27 radio stations. **Medical facilities:** 18 hospitals; 2 major medical research centers. **Educational facilities:** 8 universities and colleges; major public library system. **Further information:** Chamber of Commerce, 110 West "C," Suite 1600, San Diego, CA 92101.

San Francisco, California

Population: 749,000; **Pop. density:** 14,760 per sq. mi.; **Pop. growth:** −5.1%; **Pop. over 65:** 15.4%; **Pop. under 35:** 51.7%. **Area:** 46 sq. mi.. **Employment:** 388,349 employed, 4.3% unemployed; **Per capita income:** $24,593.

Transportation: 1 major airport; intra-city railway system; 2 railway transit systems; bus and railroad service; ferry system; 1 underwater tunnel. **Communications:** 7 TV stations; 27 radio stations. **Medical facilities:** 23 hospitals; 1 major medical center. **Educational facilities:** 4 universities and colleges; major public library system. **Further information:** Chamber of Commerce, 465 California Street, San Francisco, CA 94104.

San Jose, California

Population: 712,080; **Pop. density:** 3,984 per sq. mi.; **Pop. growth:** 36.9%; **Pop. over 65:** 6.2%; **Pop. under 35:** 64.7%. **Area:** 158 sq. mi.. **Employment:** 380,437 employed, 4.7% unemployed; **Per capita income:** $21,510.

Transportation: 1 international airport; 2 railroads; bus system. **Communications:** 4 TV stations; 14 radio stations. **Medical facilities:** 6 hospitals. **Educational facilities:** 3 universities and colleges; major public library system. **Further information:** Chamber of Commerce, One Paseo de San Antonio, San Jose, CA 95113.

Santa Ana, California

Population: 236,780, **Pop. density:** 7,544 per sq. mi.; **Pop. growth:** 30.8%; **Pop. over 65:** 7.4%; **Pop. under 35:** 66.9%. **Area:** 27 sq. mi.. **Employment:** 130,602 employed, 4.0% unemployed (county); **Per capita income:** $21,444.

Transportation: John Wayne airport; 5 major freeways including main Los Angeles-San Diego artery; Amtrak. **Communications:** $27 mln. installation of CATV system. **Medical facilities:** 4 hospitals with 561 beds. **Educational facilities:** 1 university, 1 community college. **Further information:** Chamber of Commerce, 600 W. Santa Ana Blvd., P.O. Box 205, Santa Ana, CA 92702.

Seattle, Washington

Population: 486,200; **Pop. density:** 5,879 per sq. mi.; **Pop. growth:** −7.0%; **Pop. over 65:** 15.4%; **Pop. under 35:** 54.9%. **Area:** 84 sq. mi.. **Employment:** 311,949 employed, 5.2% unemployed; **Per capita income:** $18,610.

Transportation: 1 international airport; 3 railroads; ferries serve Puget Sound, Alaska, Canada. **Communications:** 7 TV, 23 AM & 19 FM radio stations. **Medical facilities:** 27 hospitals. **Educational facilities:** 4 colleges; 11 community colleges. **Further information:** Chamber of Commerce, 215 Columbia St., Seattle, WA 98104.

Shreveport, Louisiana

Population: 220,380; **Pop. density:** 2,572 per sq. mi.; **Pop. growth:** 13%; **Pop. over 65:** 11.7%; **Pop. under 35:** 59.4%. **Area:** 80 sq. mi.. **Employment:** 88,032 employed, 11.0% unemployed; **Per capita income:** $12,574.

Transportation: 6 air lines service Shreveport Regional airport; 2 bus lines. **Communications:** 4 TV, 17 radio stations; CATV. **Medical facilities:** 11 hospitals with over 3,000 beds. **Educational facilities:** La. Tech., Northwestern St., and Grambling univs.; Centenary Coll., Bossier Parish Comm. College, Louisiana St. Univ. **Further information:** Chamber of Commerce, P.O. Box 20074, Shreveport, LA 71120.

Spokane, Washington

Population: 172,890; **Pop. density:** 3,313 per sq. mi.; **Pop. growth:** .5; **Pop. over 65:** 15.3%; **Pop. under 35:** 59.2%. **Area:** 52 sq. mi. **Employment:** 79,574 employed, 7.0% unemployed; **Per capita income:** $13,656.

Transportation: 1 international airport with 9 airlines; 2 railroads; bus system. **Communications:** 8 TV and 17 radio stations. **Medical facilities:** 6 major hospitals. **Educational facilities:** 8 colleges and universities; 14 public school districts, 11 high schools. **Further information:** Chamber of Commerce, W. 1020 Riverside Ave., P.O. Box 2147, Spokane, WA 99210.

Stockton, California

Population: 183,430; **Pop. density:** 3,744 per sq. mi.; **Pop. growth:** 36.2%; **Pop. over 65:** 11.0%; **Pop. under 35:** 58.0%. **Area:** 40 sq. mi. **Employment:** 75,276 employed, 10.8% unemployed; **Per capita income:** $13,774.

Transportation: 1 airport, 2 airlines; 7 railroads; 2 bus lines, city bus system. **Communications:** 5 TV stations. **Medical facilities:** 4 hospitals; regional burn center. **Educational facilities:** 45 public schools; 4 colleges and universities. **Further information:** Chamber of Commerce, 445 W. Weber Ave., Suite 220, Stockton, CA 95203.

Tampa, Florida

Population: 277,580; **Pop. density:** 3,232 per sq. mi.; **Pop. growth:** -2.2%; **Pop. over 65:** 14.8%; **Pop. under 35:** 54%. **Area:** 84 sq. mi. **Employment:** 170,288 employed, 6.1% unemployed; **Per capita income:** $15,435.

Transportation: 1 international airport; Port of Tampa, 140 steamship lines; 2 bus lines. **Communications:** 7 TV, 27 radio stations. **Medical facilities:** 19 hospitals. **Educational facilities:** 131 public schools; 4 colleges and universities. **Further information:** Chamber of Commerce, 801 E. Kennedy Blvd., P.O. Box 420, Tampa, FL 33601.

Toledo, Ohio

Population: 340,680; **Pop. density:** 4,221 per sq. mi.; **Pop. growth:** -7.4%; **Pop. over 65;** 12.5%; **Pop. under 35:** 58.5%. **Area:** 84 sq. mi.. **Employment:** 162,011 employed, 8.0% unemployed; **Per capita income:** $15,103.

Transportation: 10 major airlines; 9 railroads; 100 motor freight lines; 2 interstate bus lines. **Communications:** 5 TV, 17 radio stations; 4 cablevision company. **Medical facilities:** 9 major hospital complexes. **Educational facilities:** 7 colleges and universities. **Further information:** Office of Tourism and Conventions, 218 Huron, Toledo, OH 43604.

Tucson, Arizona

Population: 358,850; **Pop. density:** 3,338 per sq. mi.; **Pop. growth:** 25.7%; **Pop. over 65:** 11.7%; **Pop. under 35:** 60.7%. **Area:** 99 sq. mi. **Employment:** 194,195 employed, 4.7% unemployed; **Per capita income:** $13,845.

Transportation: 1 international airport; 3 railroads; bus system. **Communications:** 7 TV, 23 radio stations. **Medical facilities:** 12 hospitals. **Educational facilities:** 1 university, 1 college; 157 public schools. **Further information:** Chamber of Commerce, P.O. Box 991, Tucson, AZ 85702.

Tulsa, Oklahoma

Population: 373,750; **Pop. density:** 1,940 per sq. mi.; **Pop. growth:** 9.3%; **Pop. over 65:** 10.8%; **Pop. under 35:** 58.1%. **Area:** 185.6 sq. mi. **Employment:** 182,313 employed, 6.3% unemployed; **Per capita income:** $14,085.

Transportation: 1 international airport; 4 rail lines; 2 regional bus lines, 2 national bus lines. **Communications:** 7 TV, 21 radio stations. **Medical facilities:** 6 hospitals. **Educational facilities:** 89 public schools; 6 colleges and universities. **Further information:** Chamber of Commerce, 616 S. Boston Ave., Tulsa, OK 74119.

Virginia Beach, Virginia

Population: 333,400; **Pop. density:** 1,028 per sq. mi.; **Pop. growth:** 52.3%; **Pop. over 65:** 4.5%; **Pop. under 35:** 66.0%. **Area:** 255 sq. mi. **Employment:** 153,580 employed, 3.7% unemployed; **Per capita income:** $14,462.

Transportation: 10 airlines serve Norfolk/Virginia Beach Airport; Greyhound, Trailways buses. **Communications:** 6 TV, 39 radio stations. **Medical facilities:** 2 hospitals. **Educational facilities:** 59 public schools; 1 university. **Further information:** Chamber of Commerce, 4512 Virginia Beach Blvd., Virginia Beach, VA 23462.

Washington, District of Columbia

Population: 626,000; **Pop. density:** 10,121 per sq. mi.; **Pop. growth:** -15.7%; **Pop. over 65:** 11.6%; **Pop. under 35:** 56.9%. **Area:** 63 sq. mi.. **Employment:** 312,701 employed, 5.3% unemployed; **Per capita income:** $21,539.

Transportation: 2 airports; rail transit system; extensive local bus service; long distance rail and bus service. **Communications:** 8 TV stations; 40 radio stations. **Medical facilities:** 43 hospitals; major medical research center. **Educational facilities:** 6 universities and colleges; 24 public libraries. **Further information:** Convention and Visitors Association, 1575 I Street NW, Suite 250, Washington, DC 20005.

Wichita, Kansas

Population: 288,870; **Pop. density:** 2,765 per sq. mi.; **Pop. growth:** 1.0%; **Pop. over 65:** 10.6%; **Pop. under 35:** 59.9%. **Area:** 101 sq. mi. **Employment:** 157,934 employed, 5.3% unemployed; **Per capita income:** $15,937.

Transportation: 1 airport; 4 major rail freight lines; 2 bus lines. **Communications:** 5 TV stations; 16 radio stations. **Medical facilities:** 5 hospitals; speech & hearing rehabilitation center. **Educational facilities:** 101 public schools; Wichita St. Univ.; Butler County Comm. College. **Further information:** Chamber of Commerce, 350 W. Douglas, Wichita, KS 67202.

Yonkers, New York

Population: 186,080; **Pop. density:** 10,852 per sq. mi.; **Pop. growth:** -4%. **Pop. over 65:** 14.8%. **Area:** 18 sq. mi.. **Employment:** 101,313 employed, 5.0% unemployed; **Per capita income:** $19,185.

Transportation: intracity bus system; rail service. **Communications:** see New York City. **Medical facilities:** St. Joseph's Medical Center, St. John's Riverside Hospital, Yonkers General Hospital. **Educational facilities:** Elizabeth Seton, Mercy, Sarah Lawrence colleges. **Further information:** Chamber of Commerce, 480 N. Broadway, Yonkers, NY 10701.

Washington, Capital of the U.S.

Arlington National Cemetery

Arlington National Cemetery, on the former Custis estate in Virginia, is the site of the **Tomb of the Unknown Soldier** and the final resting place of John Fitzgerald Kennedy, president of the United States, who was buried there Nov. 25, 1963. A torch burns day and night over his grave. The remains of his brother Sen. Robert F. Kennedy (N.Y.) were interred on June 8, 1968, in an area adjacent. Many other famous Americans are also buried at Arlington, as well as 175,000 American soldiers from every major war.

Arlington House, The Robert E. Lee Memorial

On a hilltop above the cemetery, stands Arlington House, the Robert E. Lee Memorial, which from 1955 to 1972 was officially called the Custis-Lee Mansion.

U.S. Marine Corps War Memorial (Iwo Jima)

North of the National Cemetery, approximately 350 yards, stands the bronze statue of the raising of the United States flag on Mt. Suribachi during WWII, executed by Felix de Weldon from the photograph by Joe Rosenthal, and presented to the nation by members and friends of the U.S. Marine Corps.

Vietnam War Memorial

Dedicated on November 13, 1982, it is a symbol of the U.S.' honor and recognition of the men and women who served in the armed forces in the Vietnam War. It is inscribed with the names of the more than 58,000 who gave their lives or remain missing.

The Capitol

The United States Capitol was originally designed by Dr. William Thornton, an amateur architect, who submitted a plan in the spring of 1793 that won him $500 and a city lot.

The south, or House wing, was completed in 1807 under the direction of Benjamin H. Latrobe.

The present Senate and House wings and the iron dome were designed and constructed by Thomas U. Walter, the 4th architect of the Capitol, between 1851-1863.

The present cast iron dome at its greatest exterior measures 135 ft. 5 in., and it is topped by the bronze Statue of Freedom that stands $19\frac{1}{2}$ ft. and weighs 14,985 pounds. On its base are the words "E Pluribus Unum" (Out of Many One).

The Capitol is normally open from 9 a.m. to 4:30 p.m. Tours through the Capitol, including the House and Senate galleries, are conducted from 9 a.m. to 4 p.m. without charge.

Folger Shakespeare Library

The Folger Shakespeare Library on Capitol Hill, Washington, D. C., is a research institution devoted to the advancement of learning in the background of Anglo-American civilization in the 16th and 17th centuries, and in most aspects of the continental Renaissance. It has the largest collection of Shakespeareana in the world, with 79 copies of the First Folio.

Library of Congress

Established by and for Congress in 1800, the Library of Congress has extended its services over the years to other government agencies and other libraries, to scholars, and to the general public, and it now serves as the national library. It contains over 80 million items in 470 languages.

The library's exhibit halls are open to the public. Guided tours are given every hour from 9 a.m. through 4 p.m. Monday through Friday.

Thomas Jefferson Memorial

Dedicated in 1943, The Thomas Jefferson Memorial stands on the south shore of the Tidal Basin in West Potomac park. It is a circular stone structure, with Vermont marble on the exterior and Georgia white marble inside and combines architectural elements of the dome of the Pantheon in Rome and the rotunda designed by Jefferson for the University of Virginia.

The memorial is open daily from 8 a.m. to midnight. An elevator and curb ramps for the handicapped are in service.

Lincoln Memorial

The Lincoln Memorial in West Potomac Park, on the axis of the Capitol and the Washington Monument, consists of a large marble hall enclosing a heroic statue of Abraham Lincoln in meditation sitting on a large armchair. It was dedicated on Memorial Day, May 30, 1922. The Memorial was designed by Henry Bacon. The statue was made by Daniel Chester French and sculpted by the Piccirilli family. Murals and ornamentation on the bronze ceiling beams are by Jules Guerin.

The memorial is open daily from 8 a.m. to midnight. An elevator for the handicapped is in service.

John F. Kennedy Center

John F. Kennedy Center for the Performing Arts, designated by Congress as the National Cultural Center and the official memorial in Washington to President Kennedy, opened September 8, 1971. Tours are available daily between 10:00 a.m. and 1:00 p.m.

Mount Vernon

Mount Vernon on the south bank of the Potomac R., 16 miles below Washington, D. C., is part of a large tract of land in northern Virginia.

The present house is an enlargement of one apparently built on the site of an earlier one by Augustine Washington, who lived there 1735-1738. His son Lawrence came there in 1743, when he renamed the plantation Mount Vernon in honor of Admiral Vernon under whom he had served in the West Indies. Lawrence Washington died in 1752 and was succeeded as proprietor of Mount Vernon by his half-brother, George Washington.

National Arboretum

The National Arboretum, one of Washington's great showplaces, occupies 444 acres in the northeastern section of the city. The National Herb Garden and National Bonsai Collection are special attractions in the nation's only federally-supported gardens.

The Arboretum is open every day of the year except Christmas.

National Archives

The Declaration of Independence, the Constitution of the United States, and the Bill of Rights are on permanent display in the National Archives Exhibition Hall. They are sealed in glass-and-bronze cases. The National Archives also holds the permanently valuable federal records of the United States government.

National Gallery of Art

The National Gallery of Art, situated in an area bounded by Constitution Avenue and the Mall, between Third and Seventh Streets, was established by Joint Resolution of Congress Mar. 24, 1937, and opened Mar. 17, 1941.

Normally open daily from 10 a.m. to 5 p.m.; noon to 9 p.m. Sunday. Summer, 10 a.m. to 9 p.m., noon to 9 p.m. on Sunday.

The Pentagon

The Pentagon, headquarters of the Department of Defense, is one of the world's largest office buildings. Situated in Arlington, Va., it houses more than 23,000 employees in offices that occupy 3,707,745 square feet.

Tours are available Monday through Friday (excluding federal holidays), from 9 a.m. to 3:30 p.m.

Smithsonian Institution

The Smithsonian Institution, established in 1846, the world's largest museum complex, is comprised of 14 museums and the National Zoo. It holds some 100 million artifacts and specimens in its trust "for the increase and diffusion of knowledge among men." Nine museums are located on the National Mall between the Washington Monument and the Capitol; 4 other museums and the zoo are elsewhere in Washington, and the Cooper-Hewitt Museum in New York City. The National Air and Space Museum, National Museum of Natural History, and the National Portrait Gallery are some of the more popular museums. They are open daily, except Dec. 25, from 10 a.m. to 5:30 p.m. unless otherwise noted.

Washington Monument

The Washington Monument, dedicated in 1885, is a tapering shaft or obelisk of white marble, 555 ft., 5-1/8 inches in height and 55 ft., 1-1/2 inches square at base. Eight small windows, 2 on each side, are located at the 500-ft. level, where points of interest are indicated.

Open daily except Dec. 25, 9 a.m. to 5 p.m., 8 a.m. to 12 p.m. in summer.

The White House

The White House, the president's residence, stands on 18 acres on the south side of Pennsylvania Avenue, between the Treasury and the Executive Office Building.

The walls are of sandstone, quarried at Aquia Creek, Va. The exterior walls were painted, causing the building to be termed the "White House." On Aug. 24, 1814, during Madison's administration, the house was burned by the British. James Hoban rebuilt it by Oct. 1817.

The White House is normally open from 10 a.m. to 12 noon, Tuesday through Saturday, Jun. 1 through Labor Day, and 8 a.m. to noon. Only the public rooms on the ground floor and state floor may be visited.

Projected Job Growth in Metropolitan Areas: 1985-2000

Source: National Planning Association

Following are the top 30 metro area for employment growth:

City	Year 2000 job totals	1985-2000 increase	City	Year 2000 job Totals	1985-2000 increase
			Denver	1,283,700	354,800
Los Angeles	5,306,000	1,032,000	Minneapolis-St. Paul	1,652,800	352,000
Boston	3,056,800	754,700	Detroit	2,177,300	328,500
Anaheim	1,849,900	701,500	Nassau-Suffolk, NY	1,498,500	318,500
San Jose	1,453,600	539,200	Orlando	773,700	308,600
Phoenix	1,453,700	537,000	Fort Lauderdale	796,400	299,400
Washington	2,622,100	509,000	Miami	1,198,400	284,100
Houston	2,191,500	497,700	Oakland	1,149,000	277,700
Chicago	3,627,700	493,500	Seattle	1,202,500	268,400
Dallas	1,853,700	485,000	Baltimore	1,445,800	249,000
Atlanta	1,875,900	462,700	Middlesex Cty., NJ	736,000	206,100
San Diego	1,438,200	422,400	Riverside, CA	816,500	200,500
Tampa	1,245,400	421,500	West Palm Beach	534,200	196,400
Philadelphia	2,700,000	406,100	Newark	1,232,300	195,300
New York	4,700,800	383,600	Hartford	844,800	190,200
San Francisco	1,435,700	360,400	United States	140.1 mil.	26.1 mil

Percentage of the U.S. Population Living in Metropolitan Areas: 1987

Source: U.S. Bureau of the Census

New Jersey	100.0	Hawaii	76.7	Kansas	52.8		
California	95.7	Arizona	76.2	New Mexico	48.4		
Maryland	92.9	Virginia	71.7	Nebraska	47.2		
Connecticut	92.6	Louisiana	69.0	Kentucky	45.8		
Rhode Island	92.6	Oregon	67.6	Iowa	43.1		
Florida	90.8	Indiana	68.0	Alaska	42.4		
Massachusetts	90.7	Alabama	67.2	Arkansas	39.5		
New York	90.5	Tennessee	67.0	North Dakota	38.0		
Pennsylvania	84.7	Wisconsin	66.5	West Virginia	36.3		
Nevada	82.6	Minnesota	66.2	Maine	36.1		
Illinois	82.5	Delaware	66.0	Mississippi	30.3		
Colorado	81.7	Missouri	66.0	Wyoming	29.0		
Washington	81.2	Georgia	64.6	South Dakota	28.7		
Texas	81.0	South Carolina	60.4	Montana	24.2		
Michigan	80.2	Oklahoma	58.8	Vermont	23.1		
Ohio	78.9	New Hampshire	56.3	Idaho	19.6		
Utah	77.2	North Carolina	55.3				

As of July 1, 1987, 48.9 percent of all Americans live in the 37 metropolitan areas with populations of 1 million or more.

Nearly 86 percent of the nation's population growth since 1980 occurred in the 282 officially designated metropolitan areas, reversing a trend in the 1970s of nonurban regions growing faster. According to the Census Bureau, the pattern of the 1980s represents a return to the dominance of metropolitan areas that has been common since the 1920s and 1930s.

Reflecting the nation's overall population trend, metropolitan area growth has tended to flow to the South and West in recent years. The population loss experienced in the Northeast in the 1970s stopped in this decade, while the Midwest has continued to have a net outward migration in recent years.

Notable Tall Buildings in North American Cities

Height from sidewalk to roof, including penthouse and tower if enclosed as integral part of structure; actual number of stories beginning at street level. Asterisks (*) denote buildings still under construction Jan. 1990.

City	Hgt. ft.	Stories
Akron, Oh.		
First National Tower	330	28
National City Center.	301	23
Albany, N.Y.		
Erastus Corning II Tower	589	44
State Office Building	388	34
Agency (4 bldgs.), So. Mall.	310	23
Atlanta, Ga.		
IBM Tower, 1179 W. Peachtree	828	52
*191 Peachtree	770	54
Westin Peachtree Plaza	723	71
Georgia Pacific Tower	697	51
Southern Bell Telephone.	677	47
Promenade II.	617	40
First Atlanta Bank, 2 Peachtree	556	44
Marriott Marquis	554	52
Concourse Tower, 1001 Hammond Dr.	570	32
Equitable Building, 100 Peachtree	453	34
101 Marietta Tower, 101 Marietta St.	446	36
*Bell South Enterprises	428	28
Atlanta Plaza I	425	32
Park Place, 2660 Peachtree	420	40
Club Towers Apts.	410	38
First American Bank.	409	32
Peachtree Summit.	406	31
North Avenue Tower, 310 North Ave.	403	26
Tower Place, 3361 Piedmont Road	401	29
Peachtree Place, 999 Peachtree	396	30
Richard B. Russell, Federal Bldg.	383	26
Atlanta Hilton Hotel	383	32
Peachtree Center, Harris Bldg.	382	31
AT&T Long Line Bldg.	380	...
Marquis One	378	30
Marquis Two, 275 Peachtree.	378	30
Trust Company Bank	377	28
Coastal States Insurance.	377	27
Peachtree Center Cain Building	376	30
Peachtree Center Building	374	31
One Georgia Center	371	29
The Campanile, 1145 Peachtree	367	25
Riverwood Tower	362	26
Austin, Tex.		
One American Center, 600 Congress.	395	32
One Congress Plaza, 111 Congress	391	30
First RepublicBank Tower, 515 Congress	328	26
Baltimore, Md.		
U.S. Fidelity & Guaranty Co.	529	40
Maryland National Bank Bldg.	509	34
6 St. Paul Place	493	37
World Trade Center Bldg.	395	32
Tremont Plaza Hotel	395	37
250 W. Pratt St.	360	26
Harbor Court.	356	28
Blaustein Bldg.	342	30
Union Trust Tower.	335	24
Central Savings Bank Bldg.	330	28
Charles Center South.	330	26
Baton Rouge, La.		
State Capitol.	460	34
American Bank Bldg.	315	24
Birmingham, Ala.		
South Trust Tower.	454	34
First Natl. Southern Natural Bldg.	390	30
South Central Bell Hdqts. Bldg.	390	30
City Federal Bldg.	325	27
Boston, Mass.		
John Hancock Tower	790	60
Prudential Center	750	52
Boston Co. Bldg., Court St.	605	41
Federal Reserve Bldg.	604	32
International Place, 100 Oliver St.	600	46
First National Bank of Boston	591	37
One Financial Center	590	46
Shawmut Bank Bldg.	520	38
Exchange Place, 53 State St.	510	39

City	Hgt. ft.	Stories
Sixty State St.	509	38
One Post Office Sq.	507	40
One Beacon St.	507	40
New England Merch. Bank Bldg.	500	40
U.S. Custom House	496	32
John Hancock Bldg.	495	26
State St. Bank Bldg.	477	34
125 High St.	455	30
One Hundred Summer St.	450	33
McCormack Bldg.	401	22
Keystone Custodian Funds.	400	32
Saltonstall Office Bldg.	396	22
Devonshire, 250 Wash. St.	396	40
Harbor Towers (2 bldgs.).	396	40
Westin Hotel, Copley Place	395	36
Federal Center.	393	28
75 State St.	390	31
John F. Kennedy Bldg.	387	24
Marriott Hotel, Copley Place	383	39
101 Federal St.	382	31
Longfellow Towers (2 bldgs.)	380	38
Buffalo, N.Y.		
Marine Midland Center	529	40
City Hall	378	32
Rand Bldg., not incl. 40-ft. beacon.	351	29
Main Place Tower	350	26
Calgary, Alta.		
Petro-Canada Tower #2.	689	52
Calgary Tower.	626	...
First Canadian Centre.	547	44
Scotia Centre	504	38
Nova Sq., 801 7th Ave. SW	500	37
Petro-Canada Tower #1.	469	33
Two Bow Valley Square	468	39
Fifth & Fifth Bldg.	460	35
Home Oil Tower.	463	34
Shell Tower	460	34
Dome Oil Tower.	449	33
Four Bow Valley Square	441	37
Esso Plaza (twin towers)	435	34
Oxford Square.	421	33
Family Life Bldg.	410	33
Pan Canadian Bldg., 150 9th Ave. SW	410	28
Norcen Tower.	408	33
Alberta Stock Exchange Bldg.	407	33
Western Centre	385	40
Calgary Place	385	30
Three Bow Valley Square	382	33
Charlotte, N.C.		
One First Union Center	580	42
NCNB Plaza	503	40
Two First Union Center.	433	32
Wachovia Center	420	32
Charlotte Plaza	388	27
First Citizens Plaza	320	23
Chicago, Ill.		
Sears Tower (world's tallest).	1,454	110
Amoco	1,136	80
John Hancock Center.	1,127	100
311 S. Wacker.	970	65
Two Prudential Plaza	901	64
AT&T Corporate Center	891	60
900 N. Michigan.	871	66
Water Tower Place	859	74
First Natl. Bank	852	60
Three First National Plaza	775	57
Olympia Centre	727	63
Leo Burnett Bldg.	700	46
600 N. Lakeshore Dr.	697	75
IBM Plaza	695	52
One Magnificent Mile	673	58
Daley Center.	662	31
1,000 Lake Shore Plaza	648	55
Lake Point Tower	645	70
Board of Trade, incl. 81 ft. statue	605	44
Prudential Bldg., 130 E. Randolph.	601	41
Antenna tower, 311 ft., makes total.	912	...
CNA Plaza	600	44

City	Hgt. ft.	Stories	City	Hgt. ft.	Stories
Huron Apts.	599	56	One Lincoln Plaza	579	45
Marina City Apts., 2 buildings	588	61	Olympia York, 1999 Bryan St.	562	37
Mid Continental Plaza, 55 E. Monroe	580	50	Reunion Tower	560	50
Associates Center	575	41	Southland Life Tower	550	42
Pittsfield, 55 E. Washington St.	572	38	Maxus Energy, 717 N. Harwood St.	550	34
Onterie Center	570	58	2001 Bryan St.	512	40
Kemper Insurance Bldg.	555	45	San Jacinto Tower	456	33
Newberry Plaza, State & Oak	553	56	Republic Bank Bldg., not incl. 150-ft.		
One South Wacker Dr.	550	40	ornamental tower	452	36
Harbor Point	550	54	Stouffer Hotel	451	29
Madison Plaza	551	45	Skyway Tower	448	31
190 S. LaSalle	550	40	One Main Place	445	34
LaSalle Natl. Bank, 135 S. LaSalle St.	535	44	1600 Pacific Bldg.	434	31
One LaSalle Street	530	49	Mercantile Natl. Bank Bldg., not		
111 E. Chestnut St.	529	56	incl. 115-ft. weather beacon	430	31
Chicago Mercantile Exchange (2 Bldgs)	525	40	Magnolia Bldg.	430	31
River Plaza, Rush & Hubbard	524	56	Mart Hotel	400	29
35 E. Wacker Drive	523	40	Complex Union Tower	400	33
United Ins. Bldg., 1 E. Wacker Dr.	522	41	One Dallas Centre	386	30
Lincoln Tower, 75 E. Wacker Dr.	519	42	Southwestern Bell Toll Bldg.	372	22
Quaker Tower	518	35	**Dayton, Oh.**		
Carbide & Carbon, 230 N. Mich.	503	37			
Walton Colonnade	500	44	Kettering Tower, 2d & Main	405	30
Xerox Center	500	40	Mead World Hqtrs, 10 W. 2d St.	365	28
One Financial Place	498	40	Centre City Office Bldg, 40 S. Main St.	297	20
LaSalle-Wacker, 221 N. LaSalle St.	491	41	**Denver, Col.**		
Amer. Nat'l. Bank, 33 N. LaSalle St.	479	40			
Bankers, 105 W. Adams St.	476	41	Republic Plaza	714	56
Brunswick Bldg.	475	37	Mountain Bell Center	709	54
310 Center	475	37	United Bank of Denver	698	52
American Furniture Mart	474	24	1999 Broadway	544	43
333 Wacker Dr.	472	36	Arco Tower	527	41
Sheraton Hotel, 505 N. Mich. Ave.	471	42	Anaconda Tower	507	40
Playboy Bldg., 919 N. Mich. Ave.	468	37	Amoco Bldg., 17th Ave. & Broadway	448	36
Cincinnati, Oh.			17th Street Plaza	438	35
			Stellar Plaza	437	31
Carew Tower	568	49	First Interstate Tower North	434	32
Central Trust Tower	504	33	One Denver Place	428	34
Dubois Tower, 5th & Walnut	423	32	Brooks Towers, 1020 15th St.	420	42
Netherland Plaza	372	31	Tabor Center, #1	408	32
Central Trust Center	355	27	Manville Plaza	404	29
Atrium Two	350	30	Colorado Nat'l. Bank, 17th & Curtis	389	26
Star Bank Center	351	26	First Interstate Tower South	385	28
Clarion North Tower	350	33	Security Life Bldg.	384	33
Cinn. Commerce Center	346	29	Mellon Financial Center	374	31
Cleveland, Oh.			Dominion Plaza	368	30
			Lincoln Center	366	30
Tower City	708	52	Denver Natl. Bank Plaza	363	29
BP America	658	46	Bank Western	357	27
Tower at Erieview	529	40	Colorado State Bank	352	26
One Cleveland Center	450	31	**Des Moines, Ia.**		
Justice Center, 1250 Ontario	420	26			
Federal Bldg.	419	32	Principal Financial Group Bldg.	630	44
National City Center	410	35	Ruan Center	457	36
Ameritrust	383	29	Financial Center, 7th & Walnut	345	25
Eaton Center	360	28	Marriott Hotel, 700 Grand Ave.	340	33
Ohio-Bell Hqs.	360	22	Plaza, 3d & Walnut	340	25
Columbus, Oh.			**Detroit, Mich.**		
James A. Rhodes (State Office Tower)	624	41	Westin Hotel	720	71
LeVeque Tower, 50 W. Broad	555	47	Penobscot Bldg.	557	47
*Ohio Bureau of Worker's Compensation			Guardian	485	40
& Ind. Comm.	530	33	Renaissance Center (4 bldgs.)	479	39
Huntington Center, 41 S. High St.	512	37	Book Tower	472	35
State Office Tower	503	33-	Prudential 4000 Town Center	448	32
Gilmore-Riffe Bldg.	503	32	3000 Town Center Dr.	443	32
One Nationwide Plaza	482	40	Cadillac Tower	437	40
One Riverside Plaza	456	31	David Stott	436	38
Borden Bldg., 180 E. Broad	438	34	ANR Bldg.	430	32
*Three Nationwide Plaza	408	27	Fisher	420	28
One Columbus	366	26	J. L. Hudson Bldg.	397	28
Columbus Center, 100 E. Broad	357	24	McNamara Federal Office Bldg.	393	27
Capitol Square	348	26	American Center	374	27
Ohio Bell Bldg., 150 E. Gay St.	346	26	Top of Troy Bldg.	374	27
Dallas, Tex.			Comerica Bldg., 211 N. Fort	370	28
			Edison Plaza	365	25
First RepublicBank Plaza, 901 Main St.	939	73	David Broderick Tower	358	34
Momentum Place	787	61	Buhl, 535 Griswold	350	26
Texas Commerce Tower	738	55	**Edmonton, Alta.**		
Allied Bank Tower	721	60			
Renaissance Tower	710	56	Manulife Place, 10170-101 St.	479	39
Trammell Crow Tower	686	50	Royal Trust Tower	476	30
Arco Tower, 1601 Bryan St.	660	49	AGT Tower, 10020-100 St.	441	34
First City Center	655	49	CCB Tower, 10124-103 Ave.	410	34
Thanksgiving Tower, 1600 Pacific Ave.	645	50	Principal Plaza, 10303 Jasper Ave.	370	30
First National Bank	625	52	Scotia Place, 10060 Jasper Ave.	366	30
Republic Bank Tower	598	50	CN Tower, 1004-104 Ave.	365	26
SW Bell Admin. Tower	580	37	Phipps McKinnon	359	21

City	Hgt. ft.	Stories	City	Hgt. ft.	Stories
Fort Wayne, Ind.			Phoenix Tower.	434	34
One Summit Square, 911 S. Calhoun . . .	442	27	Gulf Bldg.	428	37
Ft. Wayne Natl. Bank	339	26	The Spires	426	41
Fort Worth, Tex.			Central Tower (4 Oaks Place)	420	30
City Center Tower II.	546	38	First City Natl. Bank	410	32
1st United Tower	536	40	Houston Lighting & Power	410	27
Continental Plaza	525	40	Niels Esperson Bldg.	409	31
1st City Bank Tower.	475	33	Hyatt Regency Houston	401	34
Texas American Bank.	454	37	**Indianapolis, Ind.**		
Texas Bldg.	380	30	Bank One Tower	728	51
Hamilton, Ont.			AUL Tower	533	38
Century Twenty One	418	43	Market Tower	515	32
Stelco Tower.	339	25	Indiana Natl. Bank Tower	504	35
Harrisburg, Pa.			Riley Towers (2 bldgs.)	427	30
State Office Tower #2	334	21	300 N. Meridian Bldg.	408	28
333 Market St. (incl. tower).	327	19	First Indiana Plaza.	396	31
Hartford, Conn.			City-County Bldg.	375	28
Cutter Financial Center	878	59	Indiana Bell Telephone	321	20
One Allen Place	801	46	**Jacksonville, Fla.**		
*Society Center	700	45	Barnett Tower	631	43
City Place	535	38	Independent Life & Acccident Ins. Co...	535	37
Travelers Ins. Co. Bldg..	527	34	Southern Bell	447	32
Goodwin Square.	522	30	Gulf Life Tower	435	27
Hartford Plaza	420	22	American Heritage Ins. Bldg..	357	23
Hartford Natl. Bank & Trust	360	26	Blue Cross-Blue Shield	350	22
One Commercial Plaza	349	27	**Kansas City, Mo.**		
Bushnell Tower	349	27	One Kansas City Place	626	42
One Financial Plaza, 755 Main.	335	26	AT&T Town Pavilion.	590	38
Honolulu, Hi.			Hyatt Regency.	504	40
Ala Moana Hotel.	396	38	Kansas City Power and Light Bldg. . . .	476	32
Pacific Tower.	350	30	City Hall	443	29
Franklin Towers	350	41	Federal Office Bldg.	413	35
Honolulu Tower	350	40	Commerce Tower	402	32
Discovery Bay	350	42	City Center Sq.	402	30
Hyatt Regency Waikiki	350	39	Southwest Bell Telephone Bldg.	394	27
Maile Court Hotel	350	43	Pershing Road Associates	352	28
Regency Tower, 2525 Date St.	350	42	**Las Vegas, Nev.**		
Pearlridge Square.	350	43	Fitzgerald Casino-Hotel.	400	34
Yacht Harbor Towers	350	43	Landmark Hotel	356	31
Canterbury Place	350	40	Las Vegas Hilton	345	30
Royal Iolani.	350	38	**Lexington, Ky.**		
Island Colony	350	44	Lexington Financial Center	410	30
Century Center	350	41	Kincaid Tower	333	22
Pacific Beach Hotel	350	43	**Little Rock, Ark.**		
Hawaiian Monarch Hotel	350	43	TCBY Towers	546	40
Waikiki Hobron.	350	43	First Commercial Bank	454	30
Honolulu Tower 2	350	40	Worthen Bank & Trust	375	24
Tapa Tower, 2005 Kalia Rd.	350	36	First South Bldg.	365	25
Executive Center, 1088 Bishop St. . . .	350	41	Tower Bldg.	350	18
1001 Bishop	350	28	Union National Bank.	331	21
Houston, Tex.			**Los Angeles, Cal.**		
Texas Commerce Tower	1,002	75	Library Tower	1,017	73
Allied Bank Plaza, 1000 Louisiana. . . .	992	71	First Interstate Bank.	858	62
Transco Tower.	901	64	Wells Fargo Tower	750	53
RepublicBank Center	780	56	Security Pacific Natl. Bank	735	55
Heritage Plaza, 1111 Bagby	762	53	*Mitsui Fudoson.	716	52
InterFirst Plaza	744	55	Atlantic Richfield Tower.	699	52
1600 Smith St.	729	54	Bank of America Tower.	699	52
Gulf Tower, 1301 McKinney	725	52	444 S. Flower St.	625	48
One Shell Plaza			AT&T Bldg.	620	42
(not incl. 285 ft. TV tower)	714	50	California Plaza	578	42
Four Allen Center	692	50	Century Plaza Towers (2 bldgs.).	571	44
Capital Natl. Bank Plaza	685	50	IBM Tower	560	44
One Houston Center	678	47	Citicorp Plaza	534	42
First City Tower	662	47	1999 Ave. of the Stars	533	38
1100 Milam Bldg.	651	47	*Manulife Tower	517	37
San Felipe Plaza.	620	45	*865 S. Figueroa St.	517	35
Exxon Bldg.	606	44	Union Bank Square	516	41
The America Tower	577	42	MCA-Getty	506	36
Marathon Oil Tower	572	41	WTC Bldg.	496	36
Two Houston Center	570	40	Fox Plaza	492	36
Dresser Tower.	550	40	ARCO Center	462	32
1415 Louisiana Tower.	550	44	City Hall	454	28
Pennzoil, 700 Milam (2 bldgs.)	523	36	Equitable Life Bldg.	454	34
Two Allen Center	521	36	Transamerica Center	452	32
Entex Bldg.	518	35	Mutual Benefit Life Ins. Bldg..	435	31
Huntington	506	34	Warner Center Plaza III	415	25
Tenneco Bldg.	502	33	Broadway Plaza	414	33
Conoco Tower	465	32	1900 Ave. of Stars	398	27
One Allen Center	452	34	1 Wilshire Bldg.	395	28
Summit Tower West	441	31	The Evian.	390	31
Coastal Tower	441	31	400 S. Hope St.	375	26
Four Leafs Towers (2 bldgs.)	439	40			

City	Hgt. ft.	Stories
Westin Bonaventure Hotel	367	35
Beaudry Center	365	26
Cal. Fed. Savings & Loan Bldg.	363	28
Wilshire-Glendon	363	26
Century City Office Bldg.	363	26
Home Savings Tower	356	25
Louisville, Ky.		
First Natl. Bank	512	40
Citizen's Plaza	420	30
Humana Bldg.	350	27
Meindinger Tower	338	26
Brown & Williamson Tower	338	26
Memphis, Tenn.		
100 N. Main Bldg.	430	37
Commerce Square	396	31
Sterick Bldg.	365	31
Clark, 5100 Poplar	365	32
Morgan Keegan Tower, 50 Front St.	341	23
First Natl. Bank Bldg.	332	25
Miami, Fla.		
Southeast Financial Center	764	55
Centrust Tower	562	35
Metro-Dade Administration Bldg.	510	30
Florida National Tower	484	35
One Biscayne Corp.	456	40
Amerifirst Bldg.	375	32
Hotel Inter-Continental Miami	366	35
Venitia, 1635 Bayshore Dr.	365	42
Dade County Court House	357	28
Milwaukee, Wis.		
First Wis. Center & Office Tower	625	42
100 E. Wise	576	37
Milwaukee Center	422	28
Faison Bldg.	417	34
411 Bldg.	385	30
Northwestern Mutual Insurance	359	19
City Hall	350	9
Allen-Bradley Co.	333	17
Hyatt Regency	320	22
Minneapolis, Minn.		
IDS Center	775	57
Norwest	772	57
Multifoods Tower	668	52
Piper Jaffray Tower	579	42
Pillsbury Center, 200 S. 6th St.	561	42
Opus, 150 S. 5th.	503	36
Plaza VII, 45 S. 7th	475	36
Lincoln Centre, 333 S. 7th	454	32
Foshay Tower, not including 163-ft. antenna tower.	447	32
Marriott Hotel	440	32
Northwestern Bell	416	26
Hennepin County Government Center	403	24
First Natl. Bank Bldg.	366	28
100 South Fifth.	356	25
Municipal Building	355	14
100 Washington Square	340	22
Montreal, Que.		
Place Victoria	624	47
Place Ville Marie	616	42
Canadian Imperial Bank of Commerce	604	43
Le Complexe Desjardins		
La Tour du Sud	498	40
La Tour du L'Est.	428	32
La Tour du Nord	355	27
La Tour Laurier	425	36
C.I.L. House	429	32
Chateau Champlain Hotel	420	38
Port Royal Apts.	400	33
Royal Bank Tower	397	22
Sun Life Bldg.	390	26
Banque Canadienne National	390	32
Nashville, Tenn.		
Third National Financial Center	490	30
American General Center	452	31
Landmark Center	409	30
James K. Polk State Office Bldg.	392	32
Stouffer Hotel	385	35
First American N.A. Bank.	354	28
One Nashville Plaza.	346	23

City	Hgt. ft.	Stories
Newark, N.J.		
Natl. Newark & Essex Bldg.	465	36
Raymond-Commerce.	448	37
Park Plaza Bldg.	400	26
Prudential Plaza	370	24
Public Service Elec. & Gas.	360	26
Prudential Ins. Co., 753 Broad St.	360	26
AT&T Bldg.	359	31
Gateway 1	355	28
New Orleans, La.		
One Shell Square	697	51
Place St. Charles	645	53
Plaza Tower	531	45
Energy Centre	530	39
LL&E Tower, 901 Poydras	481	36
Sheraton Hotel.	478	47
Marriott Hotel	450	42
Texaco Bldg.	442	33
Canal Place One	439	32
1010 Common.	438	31
Int'l. Trade Mart Bldg.	407	33
225 Baronne St.	362	28
One Poydras Plaza	360	28
Hyatt-Regency Hotel, Poydras Plaza	360	25
Hibernia Bank Bldg.	355	23
New York, N.Y.		
World Trade Center (2 towers)	1,350	110
Empire State, 34th St. & 5th Ave.	1,250	102
TV tower, 164 ft., makes total	1,414	...
Chrysler, Lexington Ave. & 43d St.	1,046	77
40 Wall Tower	927	71
Citicorp Center.	914	46
G.E. Bldg., Rockefeller Center	850	70
American International	826	67
Chase Manhattan Plaza	813	60
Pan Am Bldg., 200 Park Ave.	808	59
Cityspire	802	72
Woolworth, 233 Broadway	792	60
1 Worldwide Plaza	778	47
1 Penn Plaza.	764	57
Carnegie Tower	756	59
Exxon, 1251 Ave. of Americas	750	54
Equitable Center Tower West	750	58
*60 Wall St.	745	51
1 Liberty Plaza.	743	50
Citibank.	741	57
World Financial Center, Tower C	739	54
One Astor Plaza	730	54
9 W. 57 St.	725	50
Marine Midland	724	52
Metropolitan Tower, 146 W. 57th St.	716	66
Union Carbide Bldg., 270 Park Ave.	707	52
General Motors Bldg.	705	50
Metropolitan Life, 1 Madison Ave.	700	57
500 5th Ave.	697	58
Chem. Bank, N.Y. Trust Bldg.	687	50
55 Water St.	687	53
1585 Broadway	685	42
Chanin, Lexington Ave. & 42d St.	680	56
15 Columbus Circle	679	44
McGraw Hill, 1221 Ave. of Am.	674	51
Citicorp (Queens)	673	50
Lincoln, 60 E. 42d Street	673	53
1633 Broadway	670	48
Trump Tower, 725 5th Ave.	664	68
599 Lexington Ave.	653	47
Museum Tower Apts.	650	58
712 5th Ave.	650	56
American Brands, 245 Park Ave.	648	47
A. T. & T. Tower, 570 Madison Ave.	648	37
World Financial Center Tower B.	645	50
General Electric, 570 Lexington	640	50
Irving Trust, 1 Wall St.	640	50
345 Park Ave.	634	44
Grace Plaza, 1114 Ave. of Am.	630	50
1 New York Plaza.	630	50
Home Insurance Co. Bldg.	630	44
N.Y. Telephone, 1095 Ave. of Am.	630	40
Central Park Place	628	56
888 7th Ave.	628	42
1 Hammarskjold Plaza	628	50
Waldorf-Astoria, 301 Park Ave.	625	47
Burlington House, 1345 Ave. of Am.	625	50
Olympic Tower, 645 5th Ave.	620	51
10 E. 40th St.	620	48
101 Park Ave.	618	50

City	Hgt. ft.	Stories
750 7th Ave.	615	35
New York Life, 51 Madison Ave.	615	40
17 State St.	610	41
Penney Bldg., 1301 Ave. of Am.	609	46
IBM, 590 Madison Ave.	603	41
780 3rd Ave.	600	50
560 Lexington Ave.	600	22
Celanese Bldg., 1211 Ave. of Am.	592	45
U.S. Court House, 505 Pearl St.	590	37
Federal Bldg., Foley Square	587	41
Time & Life, 1271 Ave. of Am.	587	47
Cooper Bregstein Bldg., 1250 Bway.	580	40
1185 Ave. of Americas	580	42
Municipal, Park Row & Centre St.	580	34
520 Madison Ave.	577	42
1 Madison Square Plaza	576	42
World Financial Center Tower A	575	42
One Financial Sq.	575	37
Park Ave. Plaza	575	44
Westvaco Bldg. 299 Park Ave.	574	42
Marriott Marquis Hotel	574	42
Socony Mobil Bldg., East 42d St.	572	45
Sperry Rand Bldg., 1290 Ave. of Am.	570	43
600 3d Ave.	570	42
Helmsley Bldg., 230 Park Ave.	565	35
1 Bankers Trust Plaza	565	40
Palace Hotel, Madison & 51st St.	563	51
30 Broad St.	562	48
Park Ave Tower	561	36
Sherry-Netherland, 5th Ave. & 59th St.	560	40
Continental Can, 633 3d Ave.	557	39
Sperry & Hutchinson, 330 Madison	555	39
Continental Corp., 180 Maiden Lane	555	41
Galleria, 117 E. 57th St.	552	57
Interchem Bldg., 1133 Ave. of Am.	552	45
151 E. 44th St.	550	44
N.Y. Telephone, 323 Bway.	550	45
919 3d Ave.	550	47
Burroughs Bldg., 605 3d Ave.	550	44
Bankers Trust, 33 E. 48 St.	547	41
Transportation Bldg., 225 Bway.	546	45
Equitable, 120 Broadway	545	42
1 Brooklyn Bridge Plaza	540	42
Paine Webber, 1285 Ave. of Am.	540	42
Ritz Tower, Park Ave. & 57th St.	540	41
Bankers Trust, 6 Wall St.	540	39
1166 Ave. of Americas	540	44
1700 Broadway	533	41
Downtown Athletic Club, 19 West St.	530	45
Nelson Towers, 7th Ave. & 34th St.	525	45
767 3d Ave.	525	39
Hotel Pierre, 5th Ave. & 61st St.	525	44
House of Seagram, 375 Park Ave.	525	38
7 World Trade Center.	525	44
Random House, 825 3d Ave.	522	40
3 Park Ave.	522	42
North American Plywood, 800 3d Ave.	520	41
Du Mont Bldg., 515 Madison Ave.	520	42
26 Broadway.	520	31
Newsweek Bldg., 444 Madison Ave.	518	43
Sterling Drug Bldg., 90 Park Ave.	515	41
First National City Bank.	515	41
Bank of New York, 48 Wall St.	513	32
Navarre, 512 7th Ave.	513	43
Williamsburgh Savings Bank, Bklyn.	512	42
ITT—American, 437 Madison Ave.	512	40
International, Rockefeller Center	512	41
1407 Broadway Realty Corp.	512	44
United Nations, 405 E. 42 St.	505	39

Oakland, Cal.

City	Hgt. ft.	Stories
Ordway Bldg., 2150 Valdez St.	404	28
Kaiser Bldg.	390	28
Lake Merritt Plaza.	371	27
Raymond Kaiser Engineer Bldg.	336	25
Clorox Bldg.	330	24

Oklahoma City, Okla.

City	Hgt. ft.	Stories
Liberty Tower	500	36
First National Center	493	33
City Place	440	32
First Oklahoma Tower	425	31
Kerr-McGee Center	393	30
Mid America Tower	362	19
Citizens Plaza	321	22

Omaha, Neb.

City	Hgt. ft.	Stories
Woodmen Tower	469	30
Northwestern Bell Telephone Hdqrs.	334	16

City	Hgt. ft.	Stories
Masonic Manor	320	22
First Natl. Center	320	22

Orlando, Fla.

City	Hgt. ft.	Stories
Sun Bank Center Tower	441	31
First F.A. Bldg.	409	28

Ottawa, Ont.

City	Hgt. ft.	Stories
Place de Ville, Tower C	368	29
R.H. Coats Bldg.	326	27

Philadelphia, Pa.

City	Hgt. ft.	Stories
One Liberty Place	945	61
Mellon Bank Center	880	54
Two Liberty Place	825	58
Bell Atlantic Tower	725	53
Blue Cross Tower	700	50
1919 Market St.	700	50
Commerce Sq., #1	559	41
City Hall Tower, incl. 37-ft. statue of Wm. Penn.	548	7
1818 Market St.	500	40
Provident Mutual Life.	491	40
Fidelity Mutual Life Ins. Bldg.	492	38
Phila. Saving Fund Society	492	39
Central Penn Natl. Bank	490	36
Centre Square (2 towers)	490/416	38/32
Industrial Valley Bank	482	32
Philadelphia National Bank	475	25
Two Mellon Plaza	450	30
2000 Market St.	435	29
Two Logan Square	435	34
Fidelity Bank Bldg.	405	30
2 Girard Plaza	404	30
One Logan Square	400	32
Lewis Tower, 15th & Locust	400	33
1500 Locust St.	390	44
Philadelphia Electric Co.	384	27
INA Annex	383	27
Academy House, 1420 Locust St.	377	37
Penn Mutual Life.	375	20
The Drake, 15th & Spruce	375	33
Medical Tower, 255 So. 17th.	364	33
State Bldg., 1400 Spring Garden	351	18
United Engineers, 17th & Ludlow	344	20
Packard, 15th & Chestnut	340	25
Inquirer Building	340	18

Phoenix, Ariz.

City	Hgt. ft.	Stories
Valley National Bank	483	40
Arizona Bank Downtown	407	31
Phoenix Plaza	397	25
First Interstate Bank Plaza	372	27
Phoenix Center	361	28
Citibank Plaza	356	27
One Renaissance Sq.	347	26
Two Renaissance Sq.	347	26
Merabank Tower	341	26

Pittsburgh, Pa.

City	Hgt. ft.	Stories
USX Towers	841	64
One Mellon Bank Center	725	54
One PPG Place	635	40
Fifth Avenue Place	616	32
One Oxford Centre	615	46
Gulf, 7th Ave. and Grant St.	582	44
University of Pittsburgh	535	42
Mellon Bank Bldg.	520	41
1 Oliver Plaza	511	39
Grant, Grant St. at 3rd Ave.	485	40
Koppers, 7th Ave. and Grant.	475	34
Equibank Bldg.	445	34
CNG Tower	430	32
Pittsburgh National Bldg.	424	30
Alcoa Bldg., 425 Sixth Ave.	410	30
Liberty Tower	358	29
Westinghouse Bldg.	355	23
Oliver, 535 Smithfield St.	347	25
Gateway Bldg. No. 3	344	24
Centre City Tower.	341	26
Federal Bldg., 1000 Liberty Ave.	340	23
Bell Telephone, 416 7th Ave.	339	21
Hilton Hotel.	333	22
Frick, 437 Grant St.	330	20

Portland, Ore.

City	Hgt. ft.	Stories
First Interstate Tower	546	41
U.S. Bancorp Tower.	536	39
Koin Tower Plaza	509	35

City	Hgt. ft.	Stories
Standard Insurance Center.	367	27
Pacwest Center.	356	31

Providence, R.I.

City	Hgt. ft.	Stories
Fleet National Bank.	420	26
Rhode Island Hospital Trust Tower.	410	30
40 Westminster Bldg.	301	24

Richmond, Va.

City	Hgt. ft.	Stories
James Monroe Bldg.	450	29
City Hall (incl. penthouse)	425	17
United Virginia Bank Bldg.	400	24
Federal Reserve Bank	393	26
First & Merchants Natl. Bank.	333	25

Rochester, N.Y.

City	Hgt. ft.	Stories
Xerox Tower.	443	30
Lincoln First Tower.	390	26
Eastman Kodak Bldg.	360	19

St. Louis, Mo.

City	Hgt. ft.	Stories
Gateway Arch.	630	...
Metropolitan Square Tower	591	42
S.W. Bell Telephone Bldg.	587	44
Mercantile Center Tower.	550	37
Centerre Plaza.	433	31
Laclede Gas. Bldg., 8th & Olive	400	31
S.W. Bell Telephone Bldg.	398	31
Civil Courts.	387	13
Queeny Tower.	321	24
Counsel Tower.	320	30

St. Paul, Minn.

City	Hgt. ft.	Stories
First Natl. Bank Bldg., incl. 100-ft. sign.	517	32
Minn. World Trade Center	471	36
Galtier Plaza's Jackson Tower.	440	46
Osborn Bldg., 320 Wabasha.	368	20
Kellogg Square Apts.	366	32
Northwestern Bell Telephone (2 bldgs.).	340	16
Pointe of St. Paul	340	34
American National Bank Bldg.	335	25
North Central Tower, 445 Minn.	328	27
Amhoist/Park Tower.	324	26

Salt Lake City, Ut.

City	Hgt. ft.	Stories
L.D.S. Church Office Bldg.	420	30
Beneficial Life Tower	351	21
Amer. Towers (2 bldgs.)	324	27

San Antonio, Tex.

City	Hgt. ft.	Stories
Marriott Rivercenter.	656	38
Tower of the Americas	622	
NBC Plaza.	444	32
Tower Life.	404	30
Interfirst Plaza.	387	28
Nix Professional Bldg.	375	23

San Diego, Cal.

City	Hgt. ft.	Stories
Symphony Tower.	499	34
First Interstate Bank.	398	23
Union Bank.	388	27
First National Bank	379	27
The Meridan.	375	27
Imperial Bank	355	24
Executive Complex	350	25
Wells Fargo Bldg.	348	20
Great American Bldg.	339	24

San Francisco, Cal.

City	Hgt. ft.	Stories
Transamerica Pyramid.	853	48
Bank of America.	778	52
101 California St.	600	48
5 Fremont Center.	600	43
Embarcadero Center, No. 4	570	45
Security Pacific Bank.	569	45
One Market Plaza, Spear St.	565	43
Wells Fargo Bldg.	561	43
Standard Oil, 575 Market St.	551	39
One Sansome-Citicorp.	550	39
Shaklee Bldg., 444 Market.	537	38
Aetna Life	529	38
First & Market Bldg.	529	38
Metropolitan Life.	524	38
Crocker National Bank	500	38
Hilton Hotel.	493	46
Pacific Gas & Electric.	492	34
Union Bank.	487	37
Pacific Insurance.	476	34

City	Hgt. ft.	Stories
Bechtel Bldg., Fremont St.	475	33
333 Market Bldg.	474	33
Hartford Bldg.	465	33
Mutual Benefit Life.	438	32
Russ Bldg.	435	31
Pacific Telephone Bldg.	435	26
Pacific Gateway.	416	30
Embarcadero Center, No. 3	412	31
Embarcadero Center, No. 2	412	31
595 Market Bldg.	410	31
101 Montgomery St.	405	28
Cal. State Automobile Assn.	399	29
Alcoa Bldg.	398	27
St. Francis Hotel.	395	32
Shell Bldg.	386	29
Del Monte	378	28
Pacific 3-Apparel Mart	376	30
Meridien Hotel	374	34

Seattle, Wash.

City	Hgt. ft.	Stories
Columbia Seafirst Center.	954	76
Two Union Square.	740	56
Washington Mutual Tower	730	55
*AT&T Gateway Tower.	722	62
1001 4th Pl.	609	50
Space Needle	605	...
Pacific First Center	580	44
First Interstate Center.	574	48
Seafirst 5th Ave. Plaza	543	42
Bank of Cal., 900 4th Ave.	536	42
Rainier Bank Tower, 4th & Univ.	514	42
Smith Tower.	500	42
Key Tower.	493	40
Federal Office Bldg.	487	37
Pacific Northwest Bell.	466	33
One Union Square.	456	38
1111 3d Ave. Bldg.	454	35
Washington Plaza Second Tower	448	44
Westin Bldg., 2001 6th Ave.	409	34
Westin Hotel.	397	40
Financial Center.	389	30
Daon Bldg., 840 Olive Way.	381	19
Sheraton Seattle Hotel.	371	34
Sixth & Pike Bldg.	365	29
Fourth & Blanchard Bldg.	360	24
Crown Plaza Hotel.	352	33

Tampa, Fla.

City	Hgt. ft.	Stories
Barnett Plaza.	577	42
Tampa City Center.	537	39
First Financial Tower.	458	36
NCNB Plaza.	454	33

Toledo, Oh.

City	Hgt. ft.	Stories
Owens-Illinois Corp. Headquarters.	411	32
Owens-Corning Fiberglas Tower.	400	30
Ohio Citizens Bank Bldg.	368	27
Toledo Govt. Center.	327	22

Toronto, Ont.

City	Hgt. ft.	Stories
CN Tower, World's tallest self-supporting structure	1,821	...
First Canadian Place.	952	72
Scotia Plaza.	886	68
*Canada Trust Tower.	846	52
BCE Place (2 towers).	790/705	53/43
Commerce Court West.	784	57
Toronto-Dominion Tower (TD Centre).	758	56
Royal Trust Tower (TD Centre).	600	46
Royal Bank Plaza—South Tower.	589	41
Manulife Centre.	545	53
IBM Tower TD Centre.	520	36
Two Bloor West.	486	34
Exchange Tower.	480	36
Commerce Court North.	476	34
Simpson Tower.	473	33
Cadillac-Fairview Bldg., 10 Queen St.	465	36
*Palace Place.	455	46
Palace Pier.	452	46
Continental Bank Bldg.	450	35
Sheraton Centre.	443	43
Hudson's Bay Centre.	442	35
Old Toronto Exchange Bldg.	436	31
Leaside Towers (2 bldgs.)	423	44
Commercial Union Tower (TD Centre).	420	32
Maple Leaf Mills Tower.	419	30
Plaza 2 Hotel.	415	41
Sun Life Bldg., 150 King St.	410	28
Royal York Hotel.	399	27

City	Hgt. ft.	Stories	City	Hgt. ft.	Stories
Tulsa, Okla.			**Vancouver, B.C.**		
Bank of Oklahoma Tower	667	52	Royal Centre	460	34
City of Faith Clinic Tower	648	60	Canada Trust Tower, 1055 Melville	454	35
Mid-Continent Tower	530	36	Scotiabank Tower	451	36
1st National Tower	516	41	Park Place	450	35
4th Natl. Bank of Tulsa	412	33	200 Granville Square	438	30
320 South Boston Bldg.	400	24	T-D Bank Tower	432	30
Cities Service Bldg.	388	28	Harbour Centre	428	21
Univ. Club Tower	377	32	**Winston-Salem, N.C.**		
City of Faith Hospital	348	30	Wachovia Bldg.	410	30
Philtower	343	24	Reynolds Bldg.	315	21

Other Notable Tall Buildings in U.S.

Cape Canaveral, Fla., Vehicle Assembly Bldg., 40 (552); Allentown, Pa., Power & Light Bldg., 23 (320); Amarillo, Tex., American Natl. Bank, 33 (374); Bethlehem, Pa., Martin Tower, 21 (332); Charleston, W. Va., Kanawha Valley Bldg., 20 (384); Frankfort, Ky., Capital Plaza Office Tower, 28 (338); Galveston, Tex., American National Ins., 20 (358); Knoxville, Tenn., United American Bank, 30 (400); Lincoln, Neb., State Capitol (432); Mobile, Ala., First Natl. Bank, 33 (420); Niagara Falls, Ont., Skylon, (520); Shreveport La., Commercial National Tower, 24 (365); Springfield, Mass., Valley Bank Tower, 29 (370); Tallahassee, Fla., State Capitol Tower, 22 (345).

Some Notable Foreign Structures

Structure	Hgt. ft.	Stories	Structure	Hgt. ft.	Stories
Moscow State Univ (incl. spire)	994	32	Shinjuku Nomura, Tokyo	666	53
Eiffel Tower, Paris	984	-	Overseas-Chinese Banking Corp., Singa-		
Palace of Science & Culture, Warsaw	790	42	pore	660	52
M.L.C. Centre, Sydney	786	70	Shinjuku Sumitomo, Tokyo	656	52
Maine Montparnasse, Paris	751	64	Parque Central Torre Oficinas, Caracas	656	56
Ikebukuro Office Tower, Tokyo	742	60	Ukraine Hotel, Moscow	650	60
Carlton Centre, Johannesburg	722	50	Ulm Cathedral, W. Germany	530	-
Shinjuku Center, Tokyo	709	55	Cologne Cathedral, W. Germany	515	-
Shinjuku Mitsui, Tokyo	696	55			

Notable Bridges in North America

Source: State Highway Engineers: Canadian Civil Engineering — ASCE

Asterisk (*) designates railroad bridge. Span of a bridge is distance (in feet) between its supports.

Year	Bridge	Location	Longest span	Year	Bridge	Location	Longest span
	Suspension			1958	Mississippi R.	New Orleans, La.	1,575
				1936	Transbay	San Fran. Bay	1,400
1964	Verrazano-Narrows	New York, N.Y.	4,260	1968	W. 17th St.	Huntington, W. Va.	1,312
1937	Golden Gate	San Fran. Bay, Cal.	4,200	1968	Mississippi R.	Baton Rouge, La.	1,235
1957	Mackinac	Sts. of Mackinac	3,800	1955	Tappan Zee	Hudson River	1,212
1931	Geo. Washington	Hudson River, N.Y.-		1930	Longview, Wash.	Columbia River	1,200
		N.J.	3,500	1909	Queensboro	East R., N.Y.C.	1,182
1950	Tacoma Narrows	Washington	2,800	1927	Carquinez Strait	California	1,100
1936	Transbay	San Fran. Bay, Cal.	2,310	1958	Parallel Span	"	1,100
1939	Bronx-Whitestone	East R., N.Y.C.	2,300	1930	Jacques Cartier	Montreal, P.Q.	1,097
1970	Pierre Laporte	Quebec	2,190	1968	Isaiah D. Hart	Jacksonville, Fla.	1,088
1951	Del. Memorial	Wilmington, Del.	2,150	1957	*Richmond	San Fran. Bay, Cal.	1,070
1968	Del. Mem. (new)	Wilmington, Del.	2,150	1929	Grace Memorial	Charleston, S.C.	1,050
1957	Walt Whitman	Phila., Pa.	2,000	1963	Newburgh-Beacon	Hudson, R., N.Y.	1,000
1929	Ambassador	Detroit-Canada	1,850	1982	Yeager	Charleston, W. Va.	947
1961	Throgs Neck	Long Is. Sound	1,800	1975	Caruthersville, Mo.	Mississippi R.	920
1926	Benjamin Franklin	Philadelphia	1,750	1977	Saint Marys	Saint Marys, W. Va.	900
1924	Bear Mt., N.Y.	Hudson River	1,632	1969	Silver Memorial	Pt. Pleasant, W. Va.	900
1952	*Wm. Preston Lane			1987	Carl Perkins	Ohio River/So. Ports-	
	Mem.	Sandy Point, Md.	1,600			mouth, Ky.	900
1903	Williamsburg	East R., N.Y.C.	1,600	1940	Natchez	Mississippi R.	875
1969	Newport	Narragansett Bay, R.I.	1,600	1938	Blue Water	Pt. Huron, Mich.	871
1883	Brooklyn	East R., N.Y.C.	1,595	1972	Vicksburg	Mississippi River	870
1939	Lion's Gate	Burrard Inlet, B.C.	1,550	1954	Sunshine Skyway	St. Petersburg, Fla.	864
1930	Mid-Hudson, N.Y.	Poughkeepsie	1,500	1972	N. Fork American R.	Auburn, Cal.	862
1964	Vincent Thomas	Los Angeles Harbor	1,500	1940	*Baton Rouge	Mississippi R.	848
1909	Manhattan	East R., N.Y.C.	1,470	1899	*Cornwall	St. Lawrence R.	843
1936	Triboro	East R., N.Y.C.	1,380	1940	Greenville	Mississippi R.	840
1931	St. Johns	Portland, Ore.	1,207	1961	Helena, Ark.	Mississippi R.	840
1929	Mount Hope	Rhode Island	1,200	1963	Brent Spence	Covington, Ky.	831
1960	Ogdensburg, N.Y.	St. Lawrence R.	1,150	1963	Cincinnati, Oh.	Ohio River	830
1939	Deer Isle	Maine	1,080	1963	Mississippi, R.	Donaldsonville, La.	825
1931	Maysville (Ky.)	Ohio River	1,060	1930	*Vicksburg	Mississippi R.	825
1867	Cincinnati	Ohio River	1,057	1929	Louisville	Ohio River	820
1971	Dent.	Clearwater Co., Ida.	1,050	1961	Campbellton-Cross	New Brunswick-	
1900	Miampimi	Mexico	1,030		Point	Quebec	815
1849	Wheeling, W. Va.	Ohio River	1,010	1950	Maurice J. Tobin	Boston, Mass.	800
	Cantilever			1935	Rip Van Winkle	Catskill, N.Y.	800
1917	Quebec	Quebec	1,800	1938	Cairo	Ohio River, Ill.-Ky.	800
1981	Ravenswood	W. Va.	1,723	1932	Washington Mem.	Seattle, Wash.	800
1974	Commodore Barry	Chester, Pa.	1,622	1936	McCullough	Coos Bay, Ore.	793

Year	Bridge	Location	Longest span
1935	⁴Huey P Long	New Orleans	790
1916	*Memphis (Harahan)	Mississippi R.	790
1892	*Memphis	Mississippi R.	790
1949	Memphis-Arkansas	Mississippi R.	790
1904	*Mingo Jct., W. Va.	Ohio River	769
1910	*Beaver, Pa.	Ohio River	767
1966	⁵S.N. Pearman	Charleston, S.C.	760
1940	Owensboro	Ohio River	750
1928	Outerbridge, N.Y.-N.J.	Arthur Kill	750
1910	*P&LE	Beaver, Pa.	750

Simple Truss

Year	Bridge	Location	Longest span
1976	Chester	Chester, W. Va.	745
1917	*Metropolis	Ohio River	720
1929	Irvin S. Cobb	Ohio River-Ill.-Ky.	716
1922	*Tanana River	Nenana, Alaska	700
1933	*Henderson	Ohio River-Ind.-Ky.	665
1967	I-77, Ohio River	Williamstown, W. Va.	650
1917	⁴MacArthur, Ill.-Mo.	St. Louis	647
1919	Louisville	Ohio River	644
1933	Atchafalaya	Morgan City, La.	608
1924	*Castleton	Hudson River	598
1937	Delaware R.	Easton, Pa.	550
1889	*Cincinnati	Ohio River	542
1951	Allegheny River	Allegheny Co., Pa.	533
1914	Pittsburgh	Allegheny R.	531
1930	*Martinez	California	528
1951	Rankin	Pittsburgh, Pa.	525
1913	Old Brownsville	Brownsville, Pa.	520
1906	Donora-Webster	Donora-Webster, Pa.	515
1909	Hulton	Pittsburgh, Pa.	505
1967	Tanana River	Alaska	500

Steel Truss

Year	Bridge	Location	Longest span
1973	Atchafalaya R.	Krotz Springs, La.	780
1972	Atchafalaya R.	Simmesport, La.	720
1975	I-24	Tenn R., Ky.	720
1938	US-62, Ky.	Green River	700
1952	US-62, Ky.	Cumberland River	700
1940	Jamestown	Jamestown, R.I.	640
1940	Greenville	Mississippi R., Ark.	640
1949	Memphis	Mississippi R., Ark.	621
1978	Atchafalaya R.	Morgan City, La.	607
1938	US-22	Delaware River, N.J.	540
1955	Interstate (I-5)	Columbia River, Ore.-Wash.	531
1910	⁴McKinley, St. Louis	Mississippi River	517
1972	Mississippi River	Muscatine, Ia.	512
1896	Newport	Ohio River, Ky.	511
1970	Lake Koocanusa	Lincoln Co., Mon.	500
1931	US-60	Cumberland R., Ky.	500
1958	Lake Oahe	Mobridge, S.D.	500
1958	Lake Oahe	Gettysburg, S.D.	500

Continuous Truss

Year	Bridge	Location	Longest span
1966	Columbia R. (Astoria)	Ore.-Wash.	1,232
1977	Francis Scott Key	Baltimore, Md.	1,200
1943	Dubuque, Ia.	Mississippi R.	845
1956	⁶Earl C. Clements	Ohio R., Ill-Ky.	825
1953	John E. Mathews	Jacksonville, Fla.	810
1940	Gov. Nice Mem.	Potomac River, Md.	800
1957	Kingston-Rhinecliff	Hudson R., N.Y.	800
1986	Rochester-Monaca	Rochester-Monaca, Pa.	780
1918	*Sciotoville	Ohio River	775
1981	Sewickley	Sewickley, Pa.	750
1984	13th St. Bridge, Ohio R.	Ashland, Ky.	740
1959	Monaca-E. Rochester	Monaca-East Rochester, Pa.	730
1976	Betsy Ross	Philadelphia, Pa.	729
1929	Madison-Milton	Ohio River	727
1970	Vanport	Vanport, Pa.	715
1966	⁴Matthew E. Welsh	Mauckport	707
1962	Champlain	Montreal, P.Q.	707
1973	Girard Point	Philadelphia, Pa.	700
1954	Pa. Tpk., Delaware R.	Philadephia, Pa.	682
1949	George Platt	Philadelphia, Pa.	680
1938	Port Arthur-Orange	Texas.	680
1929	*Cincinnati	Ohio River	675
1928	Cape Girardeau, Mo.	Mississippi R.	672
1946	Chester, Ill.	Mississippi R.	670
1970	Gulfgate	Port Arthur, Tex.	664
1930	Quincy, Ill.	Mississippi R.	628
1961	Shippingport	Shippingport, Pa.	620
1959	US 181, over harbor	Corpus Christi, Tex.	620
1934	Bourne	Cape Cod Canal	616
1935	Sagamore	Cape Cod Canal	616
1965	Clarion R. (I-80)	Clarion Co., Pa.	612

Year	Bridge	Location	Longest span
1975	Donora-Monesson	Donora-Monesson, Pa.	608
1957	Blatnik	Duluth, Minn.	600
1965	Rio Grande Gorge	Taos, N.M.	600
1941	Columbia River	Kettle Falls, Wash.	600
1954	Columbia River	Umatilla, Ore.	600
1954	Columbia River	The Dalles, Ore.	576
1962	W. Br. Feather River	Oroville, Cal.	576
1967	Glenwood	Pittsburgh, Pa.	567
1936	Meredosia	Illinois River	567
1936	Mark Twain Mem.	Hannibal, Mo.	562
1957	Mackinac	Mackinac Straits, Mich.	560
1937	Homestead	Pittsburgh	553
1961	Ship Canal	Seattle, Wash.	552
1932	Pulaski Skyway	Passaic R., N.J.	550
1973	I-95, Thames River	New London, Conn.	540
1966	Emlenton	Emlenton, Pa.	540

Continuous Box and Plate Girder

Year	Bridge	Location	Longest span
1988	Piney Creek-US19	Beckley, W. Va.	1,760
1973	Danville-US119	Danville, W. Va.	1,545
1983	Mississippi R.	Luling, La.	1,222
1974	Dunbar-S. Charleston	South Charleston, W. Va.	842
1988	Beaver Creek-I-64	Beckley, W. Va.	764
1967	San Mateo-Hayward No. 2	San Fran. Bay, Cal.	750
1977	Intracoastal Canal	Gibbstown, La.	750
1976	Intracoastal Canal	Forked Is., La.	750
1963	Gunnison River	Gunnison, Col.	720
1969	*San Diego-Coronado	San Diego Bay, Cal.	660
1973	Ship Channel (I-610)	Houston, Tex.	630
1981	Douglas	Juneau, Alaska	620
1976	Wax L. Outlet	Calumet, La.	618
1975	S. Charleston-I-64	South Charleston, W. Va.	612
1981	Glenn Jackson (I-205)	Columbia R., Ore.-Wash.	600
1967	Poplar St.	St. Louis, Mo.	600
1982	Illinois R.	Pekin, Ill.	550
1982	I-440	Arkansas R.	540
1977	US-64, Tennessee R.	Savannah, Tenn.	525
1988	Mon City	Monongahela, Pa.	520
1965	McDonald-Cartier	Ottawa, Ont.	520
1972	Sitka Harbor	Sitka, Alaska	450
1986	Veterans	Pittsburgh, Pa.	440
1986	SR 76, Cumberland R.	Dover, Tenn.	440
1985	SR 20, Tennessee R.	Perryville, Tenn.	440
1970	Willamette R., I-205	West Linn, Ore.	430
1974	I-430	Arkansas R.	430
1985	I-435	Missouri R., Ks.-Mo.	425
1984	US-36	Missouri R., Ks.-Mo.	425
1972	I-635, Kansas City	Missouri R., Kan.-Mo.	425
1985	FAU 3456, Tennessee R.	Chattanooga, Tenn.	420
1967	I-24, Tennessee R.	Marion Co., Tenn.	420
1978	Snake River	Clarkston, Wash.	420
1976	35th St. Bridge, Kanawha	Charleston, W. Va.	415
1986	SR 1, Tennessee R.	New Johnsonville, Tenn.	411
1979	Arkansas R.	Clarksville, Ark.	410
1975	Yukon River	Alaska	410
1973	Intracoastal Waterway	Corpus Christi, Tex.	400
1972	I-75, Tennessee River	Loudon Co., Tenn.	400
1941	Susquehanna	Susquehanna R., Md.	400
1987	Clairton-Glassport	Clairton-Glassport, Pa	400

Continuous Plate

Year	Bridge	Location	Longest span
1982	Houston Ship Chan	Texas.	750
1971	W. Atchafalaya	Henderson, La.	573
1981	Illinois 23	Illinois R., Ill.	510
1968	Trinity R.	Dallas, Tex.	480
1978	San Joaquin R.	Antioch, Cal.	460
1977	Thomas Johnson Mem.	Solomons, Md.	451
1975	I-129	Missouri R., Ia.	450
1967	Mississippi River	LaCrescent, Minn.	450
1966	I-480	Missouri R., Ia.-Neb.	425
1970	I-435	Missouri R., Mo.	425
1972	I-80	Missouri R., Ia.-Neb.	425
1971	St. Croix River	Hudson, Wisc.	390
1968	Lafayette St.	St. Paul, Minn.	362
1967	San Mateo Creek	Hillsborough, Cal.	360
1961	Whiskey Creek	Shasta Co., Cal.	350
1964	Lexington Ave.	St. Paul, Minn.	340

I-Beam Girder

Year	Bridge	Location	Longest span
1980	Shreveport Int.	Louisiana	438
1941	US-31E	Rolling Fork R., Ky.	340
1948	US-27	Licking River, Ky.	316
1947	US-31E	Green River, Ky.	316

Year	Bridge	Location	Longest span	Year	Bridge	Location	Longest span
1941	US-62............	Rolling Fork, Ky....	240	1945	*Harry S. Truman	Kansas City	427
1942	Licking River	Owingsville, Ky....	240	1955	Roosevelt Island....	East River, N.Y.C....	418
1954	Fuller Warren	Jacksonville, Fla. ...	224	1980	US-17, James R.....	Isle of Wight, Co., Va..	415
				1932	*M-K-T R.R........	Missouri R........	414
	Steel Arch			1969	Wilm'gtn Mem.....	Wilmington, N.C. ...	408
1977	New River Gorge ...	Fayetteville, W. Va. ..	1,700	1930	Aerial...........	Duluth, Minn.......	386
1931	Bayonne, N.J.......	Kill Van Kull	1,652	1941	Main St..........	Jacksonville, Fla. ...	386
1973	Fremont	Portland, Ore......	1,255	1962	Burlington	Ontario...........	370
1964	Port Mann	British Columbia....	1,200	1941	Acosta	St. Johns R., Fla. ...	365
1916	*Hell Gate	East R., N.Y.C.....	1,038	1922	*Cincinnati	Ohio River	365
1959	Glen Canyon.......	Colorado River	1,028	1967	SR-156, James R....	Prince George Co., Va.	364
1967	Trois-Rivieres	St. Lawrence R., P.Q.	1,100	1964	Red R...........	Alexandria, La.	360
1962	Lewiston-Queenston .	Niagara River, Ont. .	1,000	1957	Industrial Canal ...	New Orleans, La....	360
1976	Perrine	Twin Falls, Ida.....	993	1950	Red R...........	Moncla, La........	360
1941	Rainbow	Niagara Falls	984	1936	Tribo	Harlem River, N.Y.C.	344
1986	Moundsville Bridge, Ohio			1961	*Corpus Christi Harbor	Corpus Christi, Tex...	344
	R...............	Moundsville, W. Va..	912	1939	U.S. 1&9, Passaic R. .	Newark, N.J.......	333
1984	I-255	Mississippi R., Mo. ..	909	1929	Carlton	Bath-Woolwich, Me. .	328
1972	[10]I-40, Mississippi R....	Memphis, Tenn. ...	900	1930	*Martinez........	California.........	328
1970	Lake Quinsigamond. .	Worcester, Mass. ..	849	1950	St. Andrews Bay....	Panama City, Fla. ...	327
1966	Charles Braga	Somerset, Mass....	840	1929	*Penn-Lehigh	Newark Bay	322
1936	Henry Hudson	Harlem River, N.Y.C.	840	1920	*Chattanooga	Tennessee R.......	310
1967	Lincoln Trail	Ohio R., Ind.-Ky....	825				
1978	I-57, Cairo, Ill.	Mississippi R.......	821		**Bascule**		
1961	Sherman Minton	Louisville, Ky.	800	1969	E. Pearl River	Slidell, La........	482
1936	French King	Conn. R. (Rt. 2, Mass.)	782	1955	Chehalis R........	Aberdeen, Wash. ..	340
1978	I-470 Bridge, Ohio R..	Wheeling, W. Va. ...	780	1917	SR-8, Tennessee River.	Chattanooga, Tenn...	306
1930	West End.........	Pittsburgh	780	1940	Lorain, Ohio	Black River	300
1976	I-471, Ohio R......	Newport, Ky.......	760	1968	Elizabeth River.....	Chesapeake, Va. ...	280
				1913	Broadway	Portland, Ore......	278
	Concrete Arch			1982	Columbus Drive	Chicago R.........	269
1971	Selah Creek (twin) ..	Selah, Wash.......	549	1954	Fuller Warren	St. Johns R., Fla. ...	267
1968	Cowlitz River.......	Mossyrock, Wash. ..	520	1958	Morrison	Portland, Ore......	262
1931	Westinghouse	Pittsburgh	460	1926	Burnside	Portland, Ore......	252
1923	Cappelen..........	Minneapolis	400	1977	Curtis Creek	Baltimore, Md.....	251
1973	Elwha River	Port Angeles, Wash. .	380				
					Swing Bridges		
	Twin Concrete Trestle			1926	[4]Fort Madison	Mississippi R.......	525
1979	I-55/I-10	Manchae, La.....	181,157	1930	Rigolets Pass	New Orleans, La....	400
1969	L. Pontchartrain Cswy.	Mandeville, La.....	126,720	1950	Douglass Memorial ..	Wash. D.C........	386
1972	Atchafalaya Flwy. ...	Baton Rouge, La. ..	93,984	1916	Keokuk Municipal ...	Mississippi R., La. ..	377
1963	[9]L. Pontchartrain.....	Slidell, La........	28,547	1945	Lord Delaware.....	Mattaponi River, Va. .	252
				1957	Eltham	Pamunkey River, Va. .	237
	Concrete Slab Dam						
1927	Conowingo Dam.....	Maryland........	4,611		**Swing Span**		
1952	SR-4, Roanoke R...	Mecklenburg Co., Va.	2,785	1908	*Willamette R......	Portland, Ore......	521
1936	Hoover Dam.......	Boulder City, Nev....	1,324	1903	*East Omaha	Missouri R........	519
				1952	US-17............	York River, Va.	500
	Drawbridges			1897	*Duluth, Minn......	St. Louis Bay	486
	Vertical Lift			1899	*C.M.&N.R.R.......	Chicago..........	474
1937	Marine Parkway	Jamaica Bay, N.Y.C. .	590	1913	Rt. 82, Conn-R.....	E. Haddam, Ct.....	465
1959	*Arthur Kill	N.Y.-N.J.........	558	1914	*Coos Bay	Oregon..........	458
1935	*Cape Cod Canal	Massachusetts	544				
1960	*Delair, N.J........	Delaware River	542		**Floating Pontoon**		
1931	Burlington, N.J......	Delaware R.......	534	1963	Evergreen Pt.	Seattle, Wash.....	7,518
1968	Second Narrows	Vancouver, B.C.....	493	1940	Lacey V. Murrow ...	Seattle...........	6,561
1912	*A-S-B Fratt	Kansas City	428	1961	Hood Canal	Pt. Gamble, Wash...	6,471
				1989	3rd Lake Washington		
					Bridge...........	Seattle, Wash.....	6,130

(1) The Transbay Bridge has 2 spans of 2,310 ft. each. (2) A second bridge in parallel was completed in 1973. (3) The Richmond Bridge has twin spans, 1,070 ft. each. (4) Railroad and vehicular bridge. (5) Two spans each 760 ft. (6) Two spans each 707 ft. (7) Two spans each 660 ft. (8) Two spans each 825 ft. (9) Total length of bridge. (10) Two spans each 900 ft.

Notable International Bridges

Angostura, suspension type, span 2,336 feet, 1967 at Ciudad Bolivar, Venezuela. Total length, 5,507.

Bendorf Bridge on the Rhine River, 5 mi. n. of Coblenz, completed 1965, is a 3-span cement girder bridge, 3,378 ft. overall length, 101 ft. wide, with the main span 682 ft.

Bosporus Bridge linking Europe and Asia opened at Istanbul in 1973, at 3,524 ft. is the fifth longest suspension bridge in the world.

Gladesville Bridge at Sydney, Australia, has the longest concrete arch in the world (1,000 ft. span).

Humber Bridge, with a suspension span of 4,626 ft., the longest in the world, crosses the Humber estuary 5 miles west of the city of Kingston upon Hull, England. Unique in a large suspension bridge are the towers of reinforced concrete instead of steel.

Second Narrow's Bridge, Canada's longest railway lift span connecting Vancouver and North Vancouver over Burrard Inlet.

Oland Island Bridge in Sweden was completed in 1972. It is 19,882 feet long, Europe's longest.

Oosterscheldebrug, opened Dec. 15, 1965, is a 3.125-mile causeway for automobiles over a sea arm in Zeeland, the Netherlands. It completes a direct connection between Flushing and Rotterdam.

Rio-Niteroi, Guanabara Bay, Brazil, completed in 1972, is world's longest continuous box and plate girder bridge, 8 miles, 3,363 feet long, with a center span of 984 feet and a span on each side of 656 feet.

Tagus River Bridge near Lisbon, Portugal, has a 3,323-ft. main span. Opened Aug. 6, 1966, it was named Salazar Bridge for the former premier.

Zoo Bridge across the Rhine at Cologne, with steel box girders, has a main span of 850 ft.

Oldest Bridge in Continuous Use

Completed in 1841, the 178 ft. long, wood truss (with orthotropic steel deck) covered bridge spans the Housatonic River on Rt. 128 in West Cornwall, Connecticut.

Underwater Vehicular Tunnels in North America

(3,000 feet in length or more)

Name	Location	Waterway	Lgth. Ft.
Bart Trans-Bay Tubes (Rapid Transit)	San Francisco, Cal.	S.F. Bay	3.6 miles
Brooklyn-Battery	New York, N.Y.	East River	9,117
Holland Tunnel	New York, N.Y.	Hudson River	8,557
Lincoln Tunnel	New York, N.Y.	Hudson River	8,216
Thimble Shoal Channel	Newport News, Va.	Chesapeake Bay	8,187
Chesapeake Channel	Northampton Co., Va.	Chesapeake Bay	7,941
Baltimore Harbor Tunnel	Baltimore, Md.	Patapsco River	7,650
Hampton Roads	Newport News, Va.	Hampton Roads	7,479
Fort McHenry Tunnel (2)	Baltimore, Md.	Baltimore Harbor	7,200
Queens Midtown	New York, N.Y.	East River	6,414
Sumner Tunnel	Boston, Mass.	Boston Harbor	5,650
Louis-Hippolyte Lafontaine Tunnel	Montreal, Que.	St. Lawrence River	5,280
Detroit-Windsor	Detroit, Mich.	Detroit River	5,135
Callahan Tunnel	Boston, Mass.	Boston Harbor	5,046
Midtown Tunnel	Norfolk, Va.	Elizabeth River	4,194
Baytown Tunnel	Baytown, Tex.	Houston Ship Channel	4,111
Posey Tube	Oakland, Cal.	Oakland Estuary	3,500
Downtown Tunnel	Norfolk, Va.	Elizabeth River	3,350
Webster St.	Alameda, Cal.	Oakland Estuary	3,350
Bankhead Tunnel	Mobile, Ala.	Mobile River	3,109
I-10 Twin Tunnel	Mobile, Ala.	Mobile River	3,000

Land Vehicular Tunnels in U.S.

(over 2,000 feet in length.)

Name	Location	Lgth. Ft.	Name	Location	Lgth. Ft.
			Fort Pitt	Pittsburgh, Pa.	3,560
E. Johnson Memorial	I-70, Col.	8,959	Mall Tunnel	Dist. of Columbia	3,400
Eisenhower Memorial	I-70, Col.	8,941	Caldecott	Oakland, Cal.	3,371
Allegheny (twin)	Penna. Turnpike	6,072	Cody No. 1	U.S. 14, 16, 20, Wyo.	3,202
Liberty Tubes	Pittsburgh, Pa.	5,920	Kalihi	Honolulu, Ha.	2,780
Zion Natl. Park	Rte. 9, Utah.	5,766	Memorial	W. Va. Tpke. (I-77)	2,669
East River Mt. (twin)	Interstate 77, W. Va.-Va.	5,412	Ft. Cronkhite	Sausalito, Cal.	2,690
Tuscarora (twin)	Penna. Turnpike	5,400	Cross-Town	178 St. N.Y.C.	2,414
Kittatinny (twin)	Penna. Turnpike	4,660	F.D. Roosevelt Dr.	81-89 Sts. N.Y.C.	2,400
Blue Mountain (twin)	Penna. Turnpike	4,435	Dewey Sq.	Boston, Mass.	2,400
Lehigh	Penna. Turnpike	4,379	Battery Park	N.Y.C.	2,300
Wawona	Yosemite Natl. Park	4,233	Battery St.	Seattle, Wash.	2,140
Big Walker Mt.	Route I-77, Va.	4,229	Big Oak Flat	Yosemite Natl. Park	2,083
Squirrel Hill	Pittsburgh, Pa.	4,225			

World's Longest Railway Tunnels

Source: Railway Directory & Year Book. Tunnels over 5 miles in length.

Tunnel	Date	Miles	Operating railway	Country
Seikan	1985	33.5	Japanese National	Japan
Dai-shimizu	1979	14	Japanese National	Japan
Simplon No. 1 and 2	1906, 1922	12	Swiss Fed. & Italian St.	Switz.-Italy
Kanmon	1975	12	Japanese National	Japan
Apennine	1934	11	Italian State	Italy
Rokko	1972	10	Japanese National	Japan
Mt. MacDonald	1989	9.1	Canadian Pacific	Canada
Gotthard	1882	9	Swiss Federal	Switzerland
Lotschberg	1913	9	Bern-Lotschberg-Simplon	Switzerland
Hokuriku	1962	9	Japanese National	Japan
Mont Cenis (Frejus)	1871	8	Italian State	France-Italy
Shin-Shimizu	1961	8	Japanese National	Japan
Aki	1975	8	Japanese National	Japan
Cascade	1929	8	Burlington Northern	U.S.
Flathead	1970	8	Burlington Northern	U.S.
Keijo	1970	7	Japanese National	Japan
Lierasen	1973	7	Norwegian State	Norway
Santa Lucia	1977	6	Italian State	Italy
Arlberg	1884	6	Austrian Federal	Austria
Moffat	1928	6	Denver & Rio Grande Western	U.S.
Shimizu	1931	6	Japanese National	Japan

ASSOCIATIONS AND SOCIETIES

Source: World Almanac questionnaire

Arranged according to key words in titles. Founding year of organization in parentheses; last figure after ZIP code indicates membership.

Aaron Burr Assn. (1946), 2064 Faculty Dr., Winston-Salem, NC 27106; 400.

Abortion Federation, Natl. (1977), 1436 U St. NW, Suite 103, Washington, DC 20009; 300 organizations.

Accountants, Amer. Institute of Certified Public (1887), 1211 Ave. of the Americas, N.Y., NY 10036; 250,000.

Accountants, Natl. Assn. of (1919), 10 Paragon Dr., Box 433, Montvale, NJ 07645; 95,000.

Accountants, Natl. Society of Public (1945), 1010 N. Fairfax St., Alexandria, VA 22314.

Accountants for Cooperatives, Natl. Soc. of (1936), 6320 Augusta Dr., Springfield, VA 22150; 1,708.

Acoustical Society of America (1929), 500 Sunnyside Blvd., Woodbury, NY 11797; 6,500.

Actors' Equity Assn. (1913), 165 W. 46 St., N.Y., NY 10036.

Actors' Fund of America (1882), 1501 Broadway, N.Y., NY 10036; 3,500.

Actuaries, American Academy of (1965), 1720 I St. NW, Wash., DC 20006; 9,500.

Actuaries, Society of (1949), 475 N. Martingale Rd., Suite 800, Schaumburg, IL 60173-2226; 12,000.

Adirondack Mountain Club (1922), RD 3, Box 3055, Lake George, NY 12845; 16,000.

Advertisers, Assn. of Natl. (1910), 155 E. 44th St., 33d fl., N.Y., NY 10017; 300 cos.

Advertising Agencies, Amer. Assn. of (1917), 666 Third Ave., N.Y., NY 10017; 765 agencies.

Aeronautic Assn. of USA, Natl. (1905), 1763 R Street, NW, Wash., DC 20009; 7,500.

Aeronautics and Astronautics, Amer. Institute of (1963), 1633 Broadway, N.Y., NY 10019; 38,000.

Aerospace Industries Assn. of America (1919), 1725 De Sales St. NW, Wash., DC 20036; 48 cos.

Aerospace Medical Assn. (1929), 320 S. Henry St., Alexandria, VA 22314-3524; 4,600.

Afro-American Life and History, Assn. for the Study of (1915), 1401 14th St. NW, Wash., DC 20005; 1,800.

Aging Assn., Amer. (1970), 42d & Dewey Ave., Omaha, NE 68105; 400.

Agricultural Chemicals Assn., Natl. (1933), 1155 15th St. NW, Wash., DC 20005; 125 cos.

Agricultural Economics Assn., Amer. (1910), 80 Heady Hall, Iowa State Univ., Ames, IA 50011; 4,618.

Agricultural History Society (1919), Room 1232, 1301 New York Ave. NW, Wash., DC 20005-4788; 1,400.

Agronomy, Amer. Society of (1907), 677 S. Segoe Rd., Madison, WI 53711; 12,284.

Aircraft Assn., Experimental (1953), EAA Aviation Center, Oshkosh, WI 54901; 125,000.

Aircraft Owners and Pilots Assn. (1939), 421 Aviation Way, Frederick, MD 21701; 264,000.

Air Force Assn. (1946), 1501 Lee Hwy., Arlington, VA 22209; 220,000.

Air Force Sergeants Assn. (1961), P.O. Box 31050, Temple Hills, MD 20748.

Air Line Employees Assn. (1951), 5600 S. Central Ave., Chicago, IL 60638.

Air Line Pilots Assn. (1931), 1625 Massachusetts Ave. NW, Wash., DC 20036; 41,000.

Air Pollution Control Assn. (1907), P.O. Box 2861, Pittsburgh, PA 15230; 8,500.

Air Transport Assn. of America (1936), 1709 New York Ave. NW, Wash., DC 20006; 27 airlines.

Al-Anon Family Groups (1950), P.O. Box 862, Midtown Sta., N.Y., NY 10018; 24,918.

Alcohol Problems, Amer. Council on (1964), 3426 Bridgeland Dr., Bridgeton, MO 63044.

Alcoholics Anonymous (1935), 468 Park Ave. So., N.Y., NY 10016; 1 mln.+.

Alcoholism, Natl. Council on (1944), 12 W. 21st St., N.Y., NY 10010; 184 affiliates.

All-Terrain Vehicle Owners Assn., Natl. (1972), P.O. Box 1272, Bensalem, PA 19020; 2,514.

Allergy and Immunology, Amer. Academy of (1943), 611 E. Wells St., Milwaukee, WI 53202; 4,000.

Alpine Club, Amer. (1902), 113 E. 90th St., N.Y., NY 10028.

Altrusa Intl. (1917), 332 S. Michigan Ave., Chicago, IL 60604.

Alzheimer's Disease and Related Disorders Assn. (1980), 70 E. Lake St., Chicago, IL 60601-5997; 170 chapters.

Amer. Feder. of Labor & Congress of Industrial Organizations (AFL-CIO) (1955, by merging Amer. Feder. of Labor es-

tab. 1881 and Congress of Industrial Organizations estab. 1935), 815 16th St. NW, Wash., DC 20006; 15,000,000.

Amer. Indian Affairs, Assn. on (1923), 95 Madison Ave., N.Y., NY 10016; 10,500.

American Legion, The (1919), 700 N. Pennsylvania St., Indianapolis, IN 46204; 2.9 mln. American Legion Auxiliary (1921), 777 N. Meridian St., Indianapolis, IN 46204; 1 mln.

Amer. States, Organization of (1890), 17th & Constitution Ave. NW, Wash., DC 20006; 32 countries.

Amer. Veterans of World War II, Korea & Vietnam (AMVETS), (1944), 4647 Forbes Blvd., Lanham, MD 20706; 200,000. AMVETS Auxiliary (1946), 4647 Forbes Blvd., Lanham, MD 20706; 20,000.

Amideast (Amer. Mideast Educational & Training Services) (1951), 1100 17th St. NW, Suite 300, Wash., DC 20036.

Amnesty Intl. USA (1961), 322 Eighth Ave., N.Y., NY 10001.

Amputation Foundation, Natl. (1919), 12-45 150th St., Whitestone, NY 11357; 2,000.

Anderson, Inc., Historical (1973), P.O. Box 268, Anderson, TX 77830; 250.

Andersonville, Natl. Soc. of (1975), P.O. Box 65, Andersonville, GA 31711; 155.

Animal Protection Institute of America (1968), 6130 Freeport Blvd., Sacramento, CA 95822; 180,000.

Animal Welfare Institute (1951), P.O. Box 3650, Wash., DC 20007; 8,000.

Animals, Amer. Society for Prevention of Cruelty to (ASPCA) (1866), 441 E. 92d St., N.Y., NY 10128; 300,000.

Animals, Friends of (1957), One Pine St., Neptune, NJ 07753; 125,000.

Animals, The Fund for (1967), 200 W. 57th St., N.Y., NY 10019; 175,000.

Antelopes, Grand United Order of (1925), 162 Fourth Ave., E. Orange, NJ 01017; 499.

Anthropological Assn., Amer. (1902), 1703 New Hampshire Ave. NW, Wash., DC 20009; 10,000.

Antiquarian Society, Amer. (1812), 185 Salisbury St., Worcester, MA 01609; 522.

Anti-Vivisection Society, Amer. (1883), Suite 204, Noble Plaza, 801 Old York Rd., Jenkintown, PA 19046; 10,000+.

Appalachian Mountain Club (1876), 5 Joy St., Boston, MA 02108; 34,000.

Appalachian Trail Conference (1925), P.O. Box 807, Harpers Ferry, WV 25425; 22,000.

Appraisers, Amer. Society of (1936), 535 Herndon Pkwy., #150, Herndon, VA 22070; 5,600.

Arab Americans, Natl. Assn. of (1972), 2033 M St. NW, Wash., DC 20036.

Arbitration Assn., Amer. (1926), 140 W. 51st St., N.Y., NY 10020-1203; 6,523.

Arboriculture, Intl. Society of (1924), 5 Lincoln Sq., Urbana, IL 61801; 4,500.

Archaeological Institute of America (1879), 675 Commonwealth Ave., Boston, MA 02215; 7,500.

Archaeology, Institute of Nautical (1976), P.O. Drawer HG, College Station, TX 77841; 800.

Archery, Assn., Natl. (1879), 1750 E. Boulder St., Colorado Springs, CO 80909; 3,500.

Architects, Amer. Institute of (1857), 1735 New York Ave. NW, Wash., DC 20006; 51,000.

Architectural Historians, Society of (1940), 1232 Pine Street, Phila., PA 19107-5944; 3,500.

Armed Forces Communications and Electronics Assn. (1946), 4400 Fair Lakes Ct., Fairfax, VA 22033; 37,000.

Army, Assn. of the United States (1950), 2425 Wilson Blvd., Arlington, VA 22201; 160,000.

Arts, Amer. Council for the (1960), 1285 Avenue of the Americas, N.Y., NY 10019; 3,000.

Arts, Amer. Federation of (1909), 41 E. 65th St., N.Y., NY 10021; 1,100.

Arts and Letters, Amer. Academy and Institute of (1898), 633 W. 155th St., N.Y., NY 10032; 246.

Arts and Letters, Natl. Society of (1944), 3299 K. St. NW, Washington, DC 20007; 1,700.

Arts & Sciences, Amer. Academy of (1780), 136 Irving St., Cambridge, MA 02138; 3,200.

Assistance League, Natl. (1949), 5627 Fernwood Ave., Los Angeles, CA 90038; 17,000.

Association Executives, American Society of (1920), 1575 Eye St. NW, Wash., DC 20005; 18,000.

Astrologers, Amer. Federation of (1938), 6536 S. Rural Rd., Tempe, AZ 85283; 4,500.

Astronautical Society, Amer. (1953), 6212 Old Keene Mill Ct., Springfield, VA 22152; 1,500.

Astronomical Society, Amer. (1899), 2000 Florida Ave., NW, Suite 300, Wash., DC 20009; 4,700.

Ataxia Foundation, Natl. (1957), 600 Twelve Oaks Cntr., 15500 Wayzata Blvd., Wayzata MN 55391; 1,400.

Atheist Assn. (1925), Box 2832, San Diego, CA 92112.

Atheists, Amer. (1963), P.O. Box 2117, Austin, TX 78768.

Athetic Assn., Natl. Jr. College (1949), 1825 Austin Bluffs Pkwy., Colorado Springs, CO 80918; 556.

Athletic Assn., Natl. Scholastic (1985), 6991 Simson St., Oakland, CA 94605-2226.

Athletic Associations, Natl. Federation of State H. S. (1920), 11724 Plaza Circle, Box 20626, Kansas City, MO 64195.

Athletic Union of the U.S., Amateur (1888), 3400 W. 86th St., Box 68207, Indianapolis, IN 46268.

Athletics Congress/USA, The (1979), 200 S. Capital Ave., Suite 140, Indianapolis, IN 46225; 125,000.

Auctioneers Assn., Natl. (1949), 8880 Ballentine, Overland Park, KS 66214; 5,800.

Audubon Society, Natl. (1905), 950 Third Ave., N.Y., NY 10022; 550,000.

Authors League of America (1912), 234 W. 44th St., N.Y., NY 10036; 14,500.

Autism, Natl. Society for Children and Adults with, (1965), 1234 Massachusetts Ave. NW, Wash., DC 20005; 6,000.

Autograph Collectors Club, Universal (1965), P.O. Box 6181, Wash., DC 20044-6181; 2,447.

Automobile Assn., Amer. (1902), 8111 Gatehouse Rd., Falls Church, VA 22047; 28 million+.

Automobile Club, Natl. (1924), One Market Plaza, San Francisco, CA 94105; 316,000.

Automobile Club of America, Antique (1935), 501 W. Governor Rd., Hershey, PA 17033; 53,000.

Automobile Dealers Assn., Natl. (1917), 8400 Westpark Dr., McLean, VA 22102; 20,000.

Automobile License Plate Collectors' Assn. (1954), P.O. Box 712, Weston, W. VA 26452; 2,110.

Automotive Booster Clubs Intl. (1921), 501 W. Algonquin Rd., Arlington Heights, IL 60005; 2,918.

Automotive Hall of Fame (1939), 3225 Cook Rd., Midland, MI 48640; 2,465.

Avon Collectors, Inc., Natl. Assn. of (1971), P.O. Box 68, W. Newton, IN 46183; 100 clubs.

B-24 Liberator Club, Intl. (1968), P.O. Box 15-2424, San Diego, CA 92115; 10,000.

Badminton Assn., U.S. (1936), 501 W. Sixth Street, Papillion, NE 68046; 1,650.

Bald-Headed Men of America (1973), P.O. Box 1466, Morehead Pl., Morehead City, N.C. 28557-1466; approx. 20,000.

Ball Players of Amer., Assn. of Professional (1924), 12062 Valley View St., #211, Garden Grove, CA 92645; 56,000.

Band & Choral Directors Hall of Fame, Natl. (1985), 519 N. Halifax Ave., Daytona Beach, FL 32018.

Bankers Assn., Amer. (1875), 1120 Connecticut Ave. NW, Wash., DC 20036.

Bankers Assn. of America, Independent (1930), 1625 Massachusetts Ave. NW, Suite 202, Wash. DC 20036; 7,000 banks.

Banks, Natl. Assn. of Mutual Savings (1920), 200 Park Ave., N.Y., NY 10166; 435 banks.

Bar Assn., Federal (1920), 1815 H St. NW, Wash., DC 20006; 15,000.

Barbershop Quartet Singing in Amer., Soc. for Preservation & Encouragement of (1938), 6315 Third Ave., Kenosha, WI 53140-5199; 38,000.

Baseball Congress, Amer. Amateur (1935), 215 E. Green St., Marshall, WI 49068; 10,000 teams.

Baseball Congress, Natl. (1931), P.O. Box 1420, Wichita, KS 67213.

Baseball Players of America, Assn. of Pro. (1924), 12062 Valley View St., Garden Grove, CA 92645.

Baseball Research, Society for Amer. (1971), P.O. Box 10033, Kansas City, MO 64111; 7,000.

Basketball Assn., Natl. (1946), 645 Fifth Ave., N.Y., NY 10022.

Battleship Assn., Amer. (1964), P.O. Box 11247, San Diego, CA 92111; 1,700.

Beer Can Collectors of America (1970), 747 Merus Ct., Fenton, MO 63026-2092; 4,000.

Beta Gamma Sigma (1913), 605 Old Ballas Rd., Suite 200, St. Louis, MO 63141; 260,000.

Beta Sigma Phi (1931), P.O. Box 8500, Kansas City, MO 64114; 250,000.

Bible Society, Amer. (1816), 1865 Broadway, N.Y., NY 10023; 500,000.

Biblical Literature, Society of (1880), 819 Houston Mill Rd. NE, Atlanta, GA 30329.

Bibliographical Society of America (1904), P.O. Box 397, Grand Central Sta., N.Y., NY 10163; 1,325.

Big Brothers/Big Sisters of America (1903), 230 No. 13th St., Philadelphia, PA 19107; 80,000.

Biochemistry and Molecular Biology, Amer. Society for (1906), 9650 Rockville Pike, Bethesda, MD 20814; 7,500.

Birding Assn., Amer. (1969), 618 Lavaca, Austin, TX 78701.

Blind, Amer. Council of the (1961) 1010 Vermont Ave. NW, Suite 1100, Wash., DC 20005; 20,000.

Blind, Amer. Foundation for the (1921), 15 W. 16th St., N.Y., NY 10011.

Blind, Natl. Federation of the (1940), 655 15th St. NW, Suite 300, Washington, DC 20005.

Blindness, Natl. Society to Prevent (1908), 79 Madison Ave., N.Y., NY 10016.

Blindness, Research to Prevent (1960), 598 Madison Ave., N.Y., NY 10022; 3,300.

Blue Cross Assn. (1948), 676 St. Clair, Chicago, IL 60611.

Blue Shield Plans, Natl. Assn. of (1946), 676 St. Clair, Chicago, IL 60611; 69 plans.

Blueberry Council, No. Amer. (1965), P.O. Box 166, Marmora, NJ 08223; 35 members, 18 assoc., 6 contributing.

Bluebird Society, No. Amer. (1978), 2 Countryside, Silver Spring, MD 20906; 5,500.

B'nai B'rith Intl. (1843), 1640 Rhode Island Ave. NW, Wash., DC 20036; 500,000.

Boat Assn., Amer. Power (1903), 17640 E. Nine Mile Rd., E. Detroit, MI 48021; 5,000.

Boat Club, Chris Craft Antique (1973), 217 S. Adams St., Tallahassee, FL 32302; 1,300.

Boat Owners Assn. of the U.S. (1966), 880 S. Pickett St., Alexandria, VA 22304; 300,000.

Bodybuilders Assn., Amer. (1981), 6991 Simson St., Oakland, CA 94605-2226; 854.

Bookplate Collectors and Designers, Amer. Soc. of (1922), 605 N. Stoneman Ave. #F, Alhambra, CA 91801; 200.

Booksellers Assn., Amer. (1900), 122 E. 42d St., N.Y., NY 10168; 5,557.

Botanical Gardens & Arboreta, Amer. Assn. of (1940), P.O. Box 206, Swarthmore, PA 19081; 1,600.

Bottle Clubs, Federation of Historical (1969), 5001 Queen Ave. N., Minneapolis, MN 55430; 120 clubs.

Bowling Congress, Amer. (1895), 5301 S. 76th St., Greendale, WI 53129; 3.3 mln.

Boys' Brigades of America, United (1893), P.O. Box 8406, Baltimore, MD 21234; 200.

Boys' Clubs of America (1906), 771 First Ave., N.Y., NY 10017; 1.2 mln.

Boy Scouts of America (1910), 1325 Walnut Hill Lane, Irving, TX 75015-2079; 5.2 mln.

Bread for the World (1974), 802 Rhode Island Ave. NE, Washington, DC 20018; 40,000.

Bridge, Tunnel and Turnpike Assn., Intl. (1932), 2120 L St., Suite 305, Wash., DC 20037; 225.

Brith Sholom (1905), 3939 Conshohocken Ave., Philadelphia, PA 19131; 5,000.

Broadcasters, Natl. Assn. of (1922), 1771 N St. NW, Wash., DC 20036; 6,170 radio & TV stations.

Burroughs Bibliophiles, The (1960), 454 Elaine Dr., Pittsburgh, PA 15236; 148.

Bus Assn., Amer. (1928), 1015 15th St. NW, Suite 250, Wash., DC 20005; 3,000.

Business Bureaus, Council of Better (1970), 4200 Wilson Blvd., Arlington, VA 22203.

Business Clubs, Natl. Assn. of Amer. (1922), 3315 No. Main St., High Point, NC 27262; 7,000.

Business Communication, Assn. for (1935), Univ. of Illinois, 100 English Bldg., 608 S. Wright St., Urbana, IL 61801; 2,500.

Business Communicators, Intl. Assn. of (1970), One Hallidie Pl., Suite 600, San Francisco, CA 94920; 11,000.

Business Education Assn., Natl. (1946), 1906 Association Dr., Reston, VA 22091; 18,000.

Business Real Estate & Law Assn., Amer. (1923), Dept. of Legal Studies, Univ. of Georgia, Athens, GA 30602; 1,200.

Business-Professional Advertising Assn. (1922), 100 Metroplex Dr., Edison, NJ 08817; 4,500.

Button Society, Natl. (1938), 2733 Juno Pl., Akron, OH 44313; 2,300.

Byron Society, The (1971 England, 1973 in U.S.), 259 New Jersey Ave., Collingswood, NJ 08108; 300.

CARE (Cooperative For American Relief Everywhere) (1945), 660 First Ave., N.Y., NY 10016.

CB Radio Patrol of Amer., Federation of Police (1977), 1100 NE 125th St., N. Miami, FL 33161; 35,000.

CLU & CHFC, Amer. Soc. of (1928), 270 Bryn Mawr Ave., Bryn Mawr, PA 19010; 32,000.

CORE (Congress of Racial Equality) (1942), 1484 Flatbush Ave., Brooklyn, NY 11210; 150,000.

CPCU, The Society of (1944), 720 Providence Rd., Malvern, PA 19355; 18,000.

Campers & Hikers Assn., Natl. (1954), 4804 Transit Rd., Bld. 2, Depew, NY 14043; 24,000 families.

Camp Fire (1910), 4601 Madison Ave., Kansas City, MO 64112; 550,000.

Campers & Hikers Assn., Inc. (1954), 7172 Transit Rd., Buffalo, NY 14221; 30,000.

Camping Assn., Amer. (1910), Bradford Woods, Martinsville, IN 46151; 5,400.

Cancer Council, United (1959), 650 E. Carmel Dr., Suite 340, Carmel, IN 46032; 50 agencies.

Cancer Society, Amer. (1913), 90 Park Ave., N.Y., NY 10017; 257.

Canoe Assn., U.S. (1968), 606 Ross St., Middletown, OH 45044; 1,300.

Carillonneurs in North America, Guild of (1936), 3718 Settle Rd., Cincinnati, OH 45227; 483.

Carnegie Hero Fund Commission (1904), 2307 Oliver Bldg., Pittsburgh, PA 15222.

Cartoonists Society, Natl. (1946), 9 Ebony Ct., Brooklyn, NY 11229; 450.

Cat Fanciers' Assn. (1906), 1309 Allaire Ave., Ocean, NJ 07712; 600 member clubs.

Catholic Bishops, Natl. Conference of/U.S. Cath. Conference (1966), 1312 Massachusetts Ave. NW, Wash., DC 20005.

Catholic Charities, USA (1910), 1319 F St. NW, Wash., DC 20004; 3,350.

Catholic Church Extension Society of the U.S.A. (1905), 35 E. Wacker Dr., Chicago, IL 60601.

Catholic Daughters of the Americas (1903), 10 W. 71st St., N.Y., NY 10023; 150,000.

Catholic Educational Assn., Natl. (1908), 1077-30th St. NW, Suite 100, Wash, DC 20007; 15,000.

Catholic Historical Soc., Amer. (1884), 263 S. Fourth St., Philadelphia, PA 19106; 800.

Catholic Library Assn. (1921), 461 W. Lancaster Ave., Haverford, PA 19041; 1,518.

Catholic Press Assn. of U.S. and Canada (1911), 119 N. Park Ave., Rockville Centre, NY 11570; 600.

Catholic Rural Life Conference, Natl. (1923), 4625 NW Beaver Dr., Des Moines, IA 50310; 3,000.

Catholic War Veterans of the U.S.A. (1935), 419 North Lee Street, Alexandria, VA 22314; 30,000.

Celiac Sprue Assn./USA (1986), 2313 Rocklyn Dr., Suite 1, Des Moines, IA 50322; 1,800.

Cemetery Assn., Amer. (1887), 5201 Leesburg Pike, Falls Church, VA 22041; 2,300.

Ceramic Society, Amer. (1899), 757 Brooksedge Plaza Dr., Westerville, OH 43081; 12,785.

Cerebral Palsy Assns., United (1949), 66 E. 34th St., N.Y., NY 10016.

Chamber of Commerce of the U.S.A. (1912), 1615 H St. NW, Wash., DC 20062; 200,000.

Chamber Music Players, Amateur (1948), 545 Eighth Ave., N.Y., NY 10018; 4,000.

Chaplain's Intl. Assn. (1962), U.S. Box 4266, Norton Air Force Base, CA 92409; 700.

Chaplains Assn. of the U.S.A., The Military (1925), P.O. Box 645, Riverdale, MD 20737-0645; 1,550.

Checker Federation, Amer., (1948), 3475 Belmont Ave., Baton Rouge, LA 70808; 1,000.

Chemical Manufacturers Assn. (1872), 2501 M St. NW, Wash., DC 20037; 171 companies.

Chemical Society, Amer. (1876), 1155 16th St. NW, Wash., DC 20036; 135,000.

Chemistry, Amer. Assn. for Clinical (1948), 1725 K St. NW, Wash., DC 20006; 6,247.

Chemists, Amer. Institute of (1923), 7315 Wisconsin Ave., Bethesda, Md. 20814; 7,000

Chemists, Amer. Society of Brewing (1934), 3340 Pilot Knob Rd., St. Paul MN 55121; 760.

Chemists, Amer. Assn. of Cereal (1915), 3340 Pilot Knob Rd., St. Paul, MN 55121; 3,523.

Chess Federation, U.S. (1939), 186 Rte. 9W, New Windsor, NY 11550; 54,000.

Chess League of Amer., Correspondence (1897), P.O. Box 416, Warrenville, IL 60555; 1,000.

Child Welfare League of America (1920), 440 First St. NW, Wash., DC 20001; 500 agencies.

Childbirth Without Pain Education Assn. (1959), 20134 Snowden, Detroit, MI 48235; 3,000.

Childhood Education Intl., Assn. for (1892), 11141 Georgia Ave., Suite 200, Wheaton, MD 20902; 14,000.

Children of the Amer. Revolution, Natl. Society of the (1895), 1776 D St. NW, Wash., DC 20006; 10,000.

Children's Aid Society (1853), 105 E. 22d St., N.Y., NY 10010; 1,207.

Children's Book Council (1945), 67 Irving Pl., N.Y., NY 10003; 65 publishing houses.

Chiropractic Assn., Amer. (1930), 1916 Wilson Blvd., Arlington, VA 22201; 20,000.

Chiropractors Assn., Intl. (1926), 1901 L St. NW, Wash., DC 20036; 7,000.

Christian Endeavor, Intl. Society of (1881), 1221 E. Broad St., Columbus, OH 43216.

Christian Laity Counseling Board (1970), 5901 Plainfield Dr., Charlotte, NC 28215; 38 min.

Christians and Jews, Natl. Conference of (1928), 71 Fifth Ave., N.Y., NY 10003; 100,000.

Church Business Administration, Natl. Assn. of (1956), Suite 324, 7001 Grapevine Hwy., Ft. Worth, TX 76180; 1,500.

Church Federation, Ecumenical (1982), 13014-270, N. Dalembary, Tampa, FL 33618-2808.

Churches, U.S. Conference for the World Council of (1948), 475 Riverside Dr., N.Y., NY 10115; 27 churches.

Church Women United (1941), The Interchurch Center, 475 Riverside Dr., Rm. 812, N.Y., NY 10115.

Cincinnati, Society of the (1783), 2118 Massachusetts Ave. NW, Wash., DC 20008; 3,305.

Circulation Managers Assn., Intl. (1889), 11600 Sunrise Valley Dr., Reston, VA 22091; 1,536.

Circus Fans Assn. of America (1926), P.O. Box 3187, Flint, MI 48502; 2,300.

Cities, Natl. League of (1924), 1301 Pennsylvania Ave. NW, Wash., DC 20004; 15,000 cities.

Citizens Band Radio Patrol (1977), 1100 NE 125th St., N. Miami, FL 33161; 35,000.

City Management Assn., Intl. (1914), 1120 G St. NW, Wash., DC 20005; 7,240.

Civic League, Natl. (1894), 1601 Grant St., Suite 250, Denver, CO 80203; 1,500.

Civil Air Patrol, (1941), Bldg. 714, Maxwell AFB, AL 36112-5572; 73,000.

Civil Engineers, Amer. Society of (1852), 345 E. 47th St., N.Y., NY 10017; 104,000.

Civil Liberties Union, Amer. (1920), 132 W. 43rd St., N.Y. NY 10036; 250,000.

Civil War Round Table of New York (1951), P.O. Box 3485, N.Y., NY 10185; 150+.

Civic League, Natl. (1894), 55 West 44th St., N.Y., NY 10036; 3,000.

Civitan Internatl. (1920), 1401 52nd St. S., Birmingham, AL 35213-1903; 35,000.

Classical League, Amer. (1919), Miami Univ., Oxford, OH 45056; 3,500.

Clergy, Academy of Parish (1968), 12604 Britton Dr., Cleveland, OH 44120; 401.

Clinical Pastoral Education, Assn. for (1967), 1549 Clairmont Rd., Decatur, GA 30033; 4,366.

Clinical Pathologists, Amer. Society of (1922), 2100 W. Harrison St., Chicago, IL 60612; 34,000.

Coal Association, Natl. (1917), 1130 17th St. NW, Wash., DC 20036; 175 corporate members.

College Athletic Assn., Natl. Junior (1949), P.O. Box 7305, Colorado Springs, CO 80933-7305; 570 schools.

College Athletic Conference, Eastern (1938), 1311 Craigville Beach Rd., P.O. Box 3, Centerville, MA 02632.

College Board, The (1900), 45 Columbus Ave., N.Y., NY 10023; 2,600 institutions.

College Music Society (1958), 1444 Fifteenth St., Boulder, CO 80302; 6,000.

College Physical Education Assn. for Men, Natl. (1897), 108 Cooke Hall, Univ. of Minnesota, Minneapolis, MN 55455.

College Placement Council (1956), 62 Highland Ave., Bethlehem, PA 18017; 2,850.

Colleges, Amer. Assn. of Community and Jr. (1920), One Dupont Circle NW, Suite 410, Wash., DC 20036.

Colleges, Assn. of Amer. (1914), 1818 R St. NW, Wash., DC 20009; 615 institutions.

Colleges and Universities, Assn. of Intl. (1973), I301 S. Noland Rd., Independence, MO 64055; 11,780.

Collegiate Athletic Assn., Natl. (1906), 6299 Nall, Mission, KS 66202; 983.

Collegiate Body-Building Assn., Natl. (1983), 6991 Simson St., Oakland, CA 94605; 683.

Collegiate Schools of Business, Amer. Assembly of (1916), 605 Old Ballas Rd., St. Louis, MO 63141-7077; 800+ schools.

Colonial Dames of Amer. (1899), 421 E. 61 St., N.Y., NY 10021; 2,049.

Colonial Dames XVII Century, Natl. Society (1915), 1300 New Hampshire Ave. NW, Wash., DC 20036; 13,000.

Colonial Wars, General Society of (1892), 840 Woodbine Ave., Glendale, OH 45246; 4,250.

Commercial Collectors Assn., Amer. (1969), 4040 W. 70th St., Minneapolis, MN 55435; 3,159.

Commercial Law League of America (1895), 222 W. Adams St., Chicago, IL 60606; 5,200.

Commercial Travelers of America, Order of United (1888), 632 N. Park St., Columbus, OH 43215; 186,000.

Common Cause (1970), 2030 M St. NW, Wash., DC 20036.

Communication, Intl. Training In (1938), 2519 Woodland Dr., Anaheim, CA 92801; 20,000.

Communication Administration, Assn. for (1971), 5105 Backlick Rd., Annadale, VA 22003; 700.

Communities, Federation of Egalitarian (1976), E. Wind Community, Rt. 6, Box 2, Tecumseh, MO 65760; 200.

Community Cultural Center Assoc., Amer. (1978), 19 Foothills Dr., Pompton Plains, NJ 07444.

Composers/USA, Natl. Assn. of (1932), P.O. Box 49652, Barrington Sta., Los Angeles, CA 90049; 500.

Composers, Authors & Publishers, Amer. Society of (ASCAP) (1914), One Lincoln Plaza, N.Y., NY 10023; 24,000.

Computing Machinery, Assn. for (1947), 11 W. 42nd St., N.Y., NY 10036; 55,000.

Concrete Institute, Amer. (1904), 22400 W. Seven Mile Rd., Detroit, MI 48219; 20,000.

Conscientious Objection, Central Committee for (1948), 2208 South St., Phila., PA 19146.

Conservation Corps Alumni, Natl. Assn. of Civilian (1977), 7245 Arlington Blvd., Falls Church, VA 22042; 12,300.

Conservation Engineers, Assn. of (1961), Missouri Dept. of Conservation, P.O. Box 180, Jefferson City, MO 65076.

Constantian Society, The (1970), 123 Orr Rd., Pittsburgh, PA 15241; 500.

Construction Industry Manufacturers Assn. (1911), 111 E. Wisconsin Ave., Milwaukee, WI 53202; 160 companies.

Construction Specifications Institute (1948), 601 Madison St., Alexandria, VA 22314-1791; 19,200.

Consumer Credit Assn., Intl. (1912), 243 N. Lindbergh, St. Louis, MO 63141; 20,000.

Consumer Federation of America (1968), 1314 14th St. NW, Wash., DC 20005; 200+.

Consumer Interests, Amer. Council on (1953), 240 Stanley Hall, Univ. of Missouri, Columbia, MO 65211; 1,800.

Consumer Protection Institute (1970), 5901 Plainfield Dr., Charlotte, NC 28215.

Consumers League, Natl. (1899), 815 15th St. NW, Suite 516, Wash., DC 20005; 12,000.

Consumers Union of the U.S. (1936), 256 Washington St., Mount Vernon, NY 10553; 291,000.

Contraception, Assn. for Voluntary Surgical (1943), 122 E. 42nd St., New York, NY 10168; 2,500.

Contract Bridge League, Amer. (1937), 2200 Democrat Rd., Memphis, TN 38132; 190,000.

Contract Management Assn., Natl. (1959), 6728 Old McLean Village Dr., McLean, VA 22101; 20,176.

Contractors of Amer., General (1918), 1957 E St. NW, Wash., DC 20036; 30,000.

Cooperative Business Assn., Natl. (1916), 1401 New York Ave. NW, #1100, Wash., DC 20005; 180 organizations, 50 indvls.

Cooperative League of the U.S.A. (1916), 1401 New York Ave. NW, #1100, Wash., DC 20005; 176 co-ops.

Correctional Assn., Amer. (1870), 4321 Hartwick Rd., Suite L-208, College Park, MD 20740; 22,000.

Correctional Officers, Amer. Assn. of (1980), P.O. Box 7051, Marquette, MI 49855; 8,000.

Cosmetology Assn., Natl. (1921), 3510 Olive St., St. Louis, MO 63103; 48,000.

Cosmopolitan Intl. (1919), 7341 W. 80th, Overland Park, KS 66204; 3,100.

Cotton Council of America, Natl. (1938), 1918 North Parkway, Memphis, TN 38112; 297 delegates.

Counseling and Development, Amer. Assn. for (1952), 5999 Stevenson Ave., Alexandria, VA 22304; 57,084.

Counselors and Family Therapists, Natl. Academy of (1974), 55 Morris Ave., Springfield, NJ 07081-1422; 535.

Country Music Assn. (1958), P.O. Box 22299, Nashville, TN 37202; 8,000+.

Creative Children and Adults, Natl. Assn. for (1974), 8080 Springvalley Dr., Cincinnati, OH 45236; 700.

Credit Assn., International (1912), 243 N. Lindberg, St. Louis, MO 63141; 13,500.

Credit Management, Nat. Assn. of (1896), 8815 Centre Park Dr., Columbia, MD 21045.

Credit Union Natl. Assn. (1934), P.O.Box 431, Madison, WI 53701; 14,000 institutions.

Crime and Delinquency, Natl. Council on (1907), 77 Maiden Lane, 4th fl., San Francisco, CA 94606; 1,500.

Criminal Investigators Assn., Intl. (1970), P.O. Box 15350, Chevy Chase, MD 20815; 1,000.

Criminology, Amer. Society of (1941), 1314 Kinnear Rd., Suite 212, Columbus, OH 43212; 2,180.

Crop Science Society of America (1955), 677 S. Segoe Rd., Madison, WI 53711; 5,510.

Cross-Examination Debate Assn. (1971), California State Univ.-Northridge, Northridge, CA 91330.

Cryptogram Assn., Amer. (1929) 4 Hawthorne Dr., Cherry Hill, NJ 08003; 1,100.

Customs Brokers & Forwarders Assn. of Amer. (1897), 1 World Trade Center, Suite 1153, N.Y., NY 10048; 552.

Cyprus, Sovereign Order of (1192, 1964 in U.S.), 853 Seventh Ave., N.Y., NY 10019; 474.

Dairy Council, Natl. (1915), 6300 N. River Rd., Rosemont, IL 60018.

Dairy and Food Industries Supply Assn. (1911), 6245 Executive Blvd., Rockville, MD 20852; 760.

Dairylea Cooperative (1907), 831 James St., Syracuse, NY13203; 3,000.

Daughters of the American Revolution, Natl. Society, (1890), 1776 D St. NW, Wash., DC 20006; 206,517.

Daughters of the Confederacy, United (1894), 328 N. Blvd., Richmond, VA 23220-4057; 26,000.

Daughters of 1812, Natl. Society, U.S. (1892), 1461 Rhode Island Ave. NW, Wash., DC 20005; 4,700.

Daughters of Union Veterans of the Civil War (1885), 503 S. Walnut St., Springfield, IL 62704; 5,000.

Deaf, Alexander Graham Bell Assn. for the (1890), 3417 Volta Pl. NW, Wash., DC 20007; 5,000.

Deaf, Natl. Assn. of the (1880), 814 Thayer Ave., Silver Spring, MD 20910; 18,000.

Defense Preparedness Assn., Amer. (1919), 1700 N. Moore St., Arlington, VA 22209; 45,000.

Delta Kappa Gamma Society Intl. (1929), P.O. Box 1589, Austin, TX 78767; 164,000.

Deltiologists of America (1960), P.O. Box 8, Norwood, PA 19074; 1,200.

Democratic Natl. Committee, (1792), 430 So. Capitol St. SE, Wash., DC 20003; 380.

DeMolay, Intl. Council, Order of (1919), 10200 N. Executive Hills Blvd., Kansas City, MO 64153; 2 mln.

Dental Assn., Amer. (1859), 211 E. Chicago Ave., Chicago, IL 60611; 136,415.

Descendants of the Colonial Clergy, Society of the (1933), 30 Leewood Rd., Wellesley, MA 02181; 1,400.

Descendants of the Signers of the Declaration of Independence (1907), 1300 Locust St., Phila., PA 19107; 937.

Descendants of Washington's Army at Valley Forge, Society of (1976), P.O. Box 915, Valley Forge, PA 19482-0915.

Diabetes Assn., Amer. (1940), 1660 Duke St., Alexandria, VA 22314; 225,000.

Dialect Society, Amer. (1889), c/o Allan Metcalf, English Dept., MacMurray College, Jacksonville, IL 62650; 500.

Dietetic Assn., Amer. (1917), 208 S. LaSalle St., #1100, Chicago, IL 60604-1003; 57,000.

Direct Marketing Assn. (1917), 6 E. 43d St., N.Y., NY 10017.

Directors Guild of America (1936), 7950 Sunset Blvd., Los Angeles, CA 90046; 7,800.

Disabled Amer. Veterans (1920), 3725 Alexandria Pike, Cold Spring, KY 41076; 1.09 mln.

Disc Sports, U.S. (1982), P.O. Box 88, Lake Katrine, NY 12449; 5,000.

Dogs on Stamps Study Unit, Amer. Topical Assn. (1979), 3208 Hana Rd., Edison, NJ 08817; 250.

Dowsers, Amer. Society of (1961), Brainerd St., Danville, VT 05828; 3,500.

Dozenal Society of America (1944), Math Dept., Nassau Community College, Garden City, NY 11530; 144.

Dracula Society, Count (1962), 334 W. 54th St., Los Angeles, CA 90037; 1,000.

Drug, Chemical and Allied Trades Assn. (1890), 2 Roosevelt Ave., Syosset, NY 11791; 1,000.

Ducks Unlimited (1937), One Waterfowl Way at Gilmer Rd., Long Grove, IL 60014; 640,000.

Dutch Settlers Soc. of Albany (1927), 6 DeLucia Terr., Albany, NY 12211; 300.

Eagles, Fraternal Order of (1898), 12660 West Capitol Dr., Brookfield, WI 53055; 1.1 mln.

Earth, Friends of the (1969), 530 7th St. SE, Washington, DC 20003; 20,000.

Easter Seal Society, Natl. (1919), 70 E. Lake St., Chicago, IL 60601.

Eastern Star, Order of the (1876), 1618 New Hampshire Ave. NW, Wash., DC 20009.

Economic Assn., Amer. (1885), 1313 21st Ave. So., Nashville, TN 37212; 19,500.

Economic Development, Committee for (1942), 1700 K St., NW, Suite 700, Washington, DC 20006; 365.

Edison Electric Institute (1933), 1111 19th St. NW, Wash., DC 20036; 180 corporations.

Education, Amer. Assn. for Adult and Continuing (1982), 1201 16th St. NW, Suite 230, Wash., DC 20036; 3,500.

Education, Amer. Council on (1918), One Dupont Circle NW, #800, Wash., DC 20036; 1,600 schools.

Education, Amer. Soc. for Engineering (1893), 11 Dupont Circle NW, Suite 200, Washington, DC 20036; 10,000+.

Education, Council for Advancement & Support of (1974), 11 Dupont Circle NW, Wash., DC 20036; 2,500 schools.

Education, Council for Basic (1956), 725 15th St. NW, Wash., DC 20005; 10,000.

Education, Institute of Intl. (1919), 809 United Nations Plaza, N.Y., NY 10017.

Education, Natl. Committee for Citizens in (1973), 10840 Little Patuxent Pwky., Suite 301, Columbia, MD 21044.

Education, Natl. Society for the Study of (1901), 5835 Kimbark Ave., Chicago, IL 60637; 2,400.

Education Assn., Natl. (1857), 1201 16th St. NW, Wash., DC 20036; 1.9 mln.

Education Society, Comparative and Intl. (1956), Univ. of S. California, Univ. Park, Los Angeles, CA 90089; 2,500.

Education of Young Children, Natl. Assn. for the (1926), 1834 Connecticut Ave. NW, Wash., DC 20009; 86,000.

Educational Exchange, Council on Intl. (1947), 205 E. 42d St., N.Y., NY 10017; 200 organizations.

Educational Research Assn., Amer. (1916), 1230 17th St. NW, Wash., DC 20036; 14,000+.

8th Air Force Historical Society (1975), P.O. Box 727, Oldsmar, FL 34677; 15,000.

88th Infantry Division Assn., Inc. (1948), P.O. Box 925, Havertown, PA 19083; 5,152.

Electrical and Electronics Engineers, Institute of (1884), 345 E. 47th St., N.Y., NY 10017; 300,000.

Electrical Manufacturers Assn., Natl. (1926), 2101 L St. NW, Wash., DC 20037; 560 companies.

Electrochemical Society (1902), 10 S. Main St., Pennington, NJ 08534-2896; 5,893.

Electronic Industries Assn. (1924), 1722 Eye St. NW, Wash., DC 20006; 1,000 companies.

Electronics Sales & Service Dealers Assn., Natl. (1973), 2708 W. Berry, Ft. Worth, TX 76109; 1,800.

Electronics Technicians, Intl. Society of Certified (1970), 2708 W. Berry, Ft. Worth, TX 76109; 1,400.

Electroplaters' and Surface Finishers' Society, Amer. (1909), 12644 Research Pkwy, Orlando, FL 32826-3298; 8,600.

Elks of the U.S.A., Benevolent and Protective Order of (1868), 2750 Lakeview Ave., Chicago, IL 60614; 1.5 mln.

Energy Research Institute, Clean (1974), 1251 Memorial Dr., 219 MacArthur Engineering Bldg., Coral Gables, FL 33146.

Energy, Intl. Assn. for Hydrogen (1974), P.O. Box 24866, Coral Gables, FL 33124; 1,500.

Engine and Boat Manufacturers, Natl. Assn. of (1904), 401 N. Michigan Ave., Chicago, IL 60611.

Engineering, Natl. Academy of (1964), 2101 Constitution Ave. NW, Wash., DC 20418; 1,535.

Engineering, Soc. for the Advancement of Material & Process (1944), P.O. Box 2459, Covina, CA 91722; 10,000.

Engineering Societies, Amer. Assn. of (1979), 345 E. 47th St., N.Y., NY 10017; 38 societies.

Engineering Society of N. America, Illuminating (1906), 345 E. 47th St., N.Y., NY 10017; 10,000.

Engineering Trustees, United (1904), 345 E. 47th St., N.Y., NY 10017.

Engineers, Amer. Inst. of Chemical (1908), 345 E. 47th St., N.Y., N.Y. 10003; 52,000.

Engineers, Amer. Institute of Mining, Metallurgical and Petroleum (1871), 345 E. 47th St., N.Y., NY 10017.

Engineers, Amer. Soc. of Agricultural (1907), 2950 Niles Rd., St. Joseph, MI 49085-9659; 10,000.

Engineers, Amer. Soc. of Civil (1852), 345 E. 47th St., N.Y., NY 10017; 100,000.

Engineers, Amer. Soc. of Naval (1888), 1452 Duke St., Alexandria, VA 22314; 8,100.

Engineers, Amer. Soc. of Plumbing (1964), 3617 Thousand Oaks Blvd., #210, Westlake Vlge, CA 91362-3625; 4,500.

Engineers, Amer. Soc. of Safety (1911), 1800 E. Oakton St., Des Plaines, IL 60018; 21,000.

Engineers, Assn. of Conservation (1961), Missouri Conservation Dept., P.O. Box 180, Jefferson City, MO 65102; 200.

Engineers, Assn. of Energy (1977), 4025 Pleasantdale Rd., Suite 420, Atlanta, GA 30340; 6,200.

Engineers, Inst. of Industrial (1948), 25 Technology Park, Atlanta, GA 30092; 43,000.

Engineers, Inst. of Transportation (1930), Suite 410, 525 School St. NW, Wash., DC 20024, 7,700.

Engineers, Natl. Society of Professional (1934), 1420 King St., Alexandria, VA 22314; 75,000.

Engineers, Soc. of Fire Protection (1951), 60 Batterymarch St., Boston, MA 02110; 3,450.

Engineers, Soc. of Logistics (1966), 125 W. Park Loop, Suite 201, Huntsville, AL 35806; 10,000.

Engineers, Soc. of Manufacturing (1932), One SME Drive, P.O. Box 930, Dearborn, MI 48121; 80,000.

Engineers, Society of Mining (1871), 8307 Shaffer Pkwy., Littleton, CO 80127; 23,058.

Engineers, Society of Plastics (1942), 14 Fairfield Dr., Brookfield Ctr., CT 06805; 25,000.

Engineers, Society of Tribologists & Lubrication (1944), 838 Busse Hwy., Park Ridge, IL 60068; 4,100.

English Assn., College (1939), English Dept., Nazareth College, 4245 East Ave., Rochester, NY 14610; 1,400.

English-Speaking Union of the U.S. (1920), 16 E. 69th St., N.Y., NY 10021; 27,000.

Entomological Society of America (1889), 9301 Annapolis Rd., Lanham, MD 20706.

Environmental Health Assn., Natl. (1937), 720 S. Colorado Blvd., Suite 970, Denver, CO 80222; 5,000.

Epigraphic Society, Inc., The (1974), 6625 Bamburgh Dr,, San Diego, CA 92117; 980.

Esperanto League for North America (1932), P.O. Box 1129, El Cerrito, CA 94530; 850.

Evangelism Crusades, Intl. (1959), 14617 Victory Blvd., Van Nuys, CA 91411.

Exchange Club, Natl. (1911), 3050 Central Ave., Toledo, OH 43606-1757; 45,000.

Executive Management Services Corp. (1973), P.O. Box 58, Atlantic Beach, NY 11509.

Experiment in Internatl. Living (1932), Kipling Rd., Brattleboro, VT 05301; 60,000.

Fairs & Expositions, Intl. Assn. of (1919), P.O. Box 985, Springfield, MO 65801; 1,500.

Family Life, Natl. Alliance for, Inc. (1973), Ste. 4, 225 Jericho Tpk., Floral Park, NY 11001; 499.

Family Relations, Natl. Council on (1938), 1910 W. Country Rd. B, Suite 147, St. Paul, MN 55113; 4,000.

Family Service Assn. of America (1911), 11700 W. Lake Park Dr., Park Pl, Milwaukee, WI 53224.

Farm Bureau Federation, Amer. (1919), 225 Touhy Ave., Park Ridge, IL 60068; 3.6 mln. families.

Farmers of America, Future (1928), 5632 Mt. Vernon Memorial Hwy., Alexandria, VA 22309-0160; 404,900.

Farmers' Educational and Co-Operative Union of America (1902), 10065 E. Harvard Ave., Denver, CO 80231; 250,000.

Fat Americans, Natl. Assn. to Aid (NAAFA) (1969), P.O. Box 43, Bellerose, NY 11426; 1,200.

Federal Employees, Natl. Federation of (1917), 1016 16th St. NW, Wash., DC 20036; 150,000.

Federal Employees Veterans Assn. (1954), Leslie Harris, 1024 E. Cliveden St., Phila., PA 19119; 4,562.

Feminists for Life of America (1972), 811 E. 47th St., Kansas City, MO 64110; 2,000.

Fencers League of America, Amateur (1893), 601 Curtis St., Albany, CA 94706; 8,000.

Film Library Assn., Educational (1943), 45 John St., Suite 301, N.Y., NY 10038; 1,600.

Financial Analysts Federation (1945), #5 Boar's Head Lane, Charlottesville, VA 22901; 17,000.

Financial Executives Institute (1931), 10 Madison Ave., P.O. Box 1938, Morristown, NJ 07960, 13,200.

Financiers, Intl. Soc. of (1979), P.O. Box 18508, Asheville, NC 28814; 600+.

Fire Chiefs, Intl. Assn. of (1873), 1329 18th St. NW, Wash., DC 20036; 9,500.

Fire Marshals Assn. of No. America (1906), Capital Gallery, 1110 Vermont Ave., NW, Wash., DC 20005; 1,300.

Fire Protection Assn., Natl. (1896), Batterymarch Park, Quincy MA 02269; 38,000.

Fish Assn., Intl. Game (1939), 3000 E. Las Olas Blvd., Ft. Lauderdale, FL 33316; 25,000.

Fisheries Institute, Natl. (1945), 2000 M St., Washington, DC 20036; 1,250.

Fishes, Soc. for the Protection of Old (1967), School of Fisheries, Univ. of Washington, Seattle, WA 98195; 250.

Fishing Institute, Sport (1949), 1010 Massachusetts Ave. NW, Suite 100, Wash., DC 20006; 15,000.

Fishing Tackle Manufacturers Assn., Amer. (1933), 2625 Clearbrook Dr., Arlington Heights, IL 60005; 550 organizations.

Florida Tobacco & Candy Assn. (1976), 217 S. Adams St., Tallahassee, FL 32302; 35.

Fly Fishers, Fed. of (1965), Box 1088, W. Yellowstone, MT 59758; 12,000.

Flying Disc Fed., World (1985), Gnejsvägen 24, 85240; Sundsvall, Sweden; 14,200.

Food Brokers Assn., Natl. (1904), 1010 Massachusetts Ave. NW, Wash., DC 20001; 2,150 companies.

Food Institute, Amer. Frozen (1942), 1764 Old Meadow Ln., Suite 350, McLean, VA 22102; 500 firms.

Food Society, Living (1983), 11015 Cumpston St., N. Hollywood, CA 91601; 1,800.

Footwear Industries Assn., Amer. (1871), 3700 Market St., Philadelphia, PA 19104; 180.

Foreign Relations, Council on (1921), 58 E. 68th St., N.Y., NY 10021; 2,510.

Foreign Student Affairs, Natl. Assn. for (1948), 1860 19th St. NW, Wash., DC 20009; 5,500.

Foreign Study, Amer. Institute for (1964), 102 Greenwich Ave., Greenwich, CT 06830; 300,000.

Foreign Trade Council, Inc., Natl. (1914), 1625 K St. NW, Washington, DC 20002; 550+ companies.

Forensic Sciences, Amer. Academy of (1948), 218 E. Cache La Poudre, Colorado Springs, CO 80903; 3,140.

Forest Council (1932), 1250 Connecticut Ave. NW, Suite 320, Washington, DC 20036.

Forest History Society (1946), 701 Vickers Ave., Durham, NC 27701.

Forest Products Assn., Natl. (1902), 1250 Connecticut Ave. NW, Wash., DC 20036; 700 companies.

Forest Products Research Society (1947), 2801 Marshall Ct., Madison, WI 53705; 3,600.

Foresters, Society of Amer. (1900), 5400 Grosvenor La., Bethesda, MD 20814; 19,500.

Forestry Assn., Amer. (1875), 1516 P St. NW, Wash., DC 20005; 30,000.

Fortean Organization, Intl. (1965), P.O. Box 367, Arlington, VA 22210; 700.

Founders and Patriots of Amer., The Order of the (1896), 3813 Acapulco Ct., Irving, TX 75062; 1,250.

Foundrymen's Society, Amer. (1896), Golf & Wolf Rds., Des Plaines, IL 60016; 13,255.

4-H Clubs (1901-1905), Extension Service, U.S. Dept of Agriculture, Wash., DC 20250; 5.8 mln.

Franklin D. Roosevelt Philatelic Society (1963), 154 Laguna Ct., St. Augustine Shores, FL 32086; 696.

Frederick A. Cook Society, The (1977), Sullivan County Historical Society, Hurleyville, NY 14747; 100.

Freedom, Young Americans for (1960), Box 1002, Woodland Rd. Sterling, VA 22170; 80,000.

Freedom of Information Center (1958), 20 Walter Williams Hall, Univ. of Missouri, Columbia, MO 65211.

Freedoms Foundation at Valley Forge (1969), Valley Forge, PA 19481; 6,000.

Friedreich's Ataxia Group in America (1969), P.O. Box 11116, Oakland, CA 94611; 2,100+.

French Institute (1911), 22 E. 60th St., N.Y., NY 10022.

Friendship and Good Will, Intl. Soc. of (1978), P.O. Box 2637, Gastonia, NC 28053-2637.

Frisbee Assn., Intl. (1967), 900 E. El Monte, San Gabriel, CA 91776; 110,000.

Funeral and Memorial Societies, Continental Assn. of (1963), 2001 S. St. NW, Suite 530, Washington, DC 20009.

GASP (Group Against Smokers' Pollution) (1971), P.O. Box 632, College Park, MD 20740; 200 chapters.

Gamblers Anonymous (1957), 3255 Wilshire Blvd., #610, Los Angeles, CA 90010; 12,000.

Garden Club of Amer. (1913), 598 Madison Ave., N.Y., NY 10022; 15,000.

Garden Clubs, Natl. Council of State (1929), 4401 Magnolia Ave., St. Louis, MO 63110; 308,623.

Garden Clubs of America, Men's (1932), 5560 Merle Hay Rd., Johnston, IA 50131; 9,500.

Gas Appliance Manufacturers Assn. (1935), 1901 N. Ft. Myer Dr., Arlington, VA 22209; 240 companies.

Gas Assn., Amer. (1918), 1515 Wilson Blvd., Arlington, VA 22209; 300 companies; 3,000 individuals.

Gay and Lesbian Task Force, Natl. (1973), 1517 U St. NW, Washington, DC 20009; 15,000.

Genealogical Society, Natl. (1903), 4527 17th St. N., Arlington, VA 22207; 9,500.

Genetic Assn., Amer. (1903), P.O. Box 39, Buckeystown, MD 21717; 3,000.

Geographers, Assn. of Amer. (1904), 1710 16th St. NW, Wash., DC 20009-3198; 6,300.

Geographic Education, Natl. Council for (1915), Dept. of Geography, IUPA, Indiana, PA 15701; 3,360.

Geographic Society, Natl. (1888), 1145 17 St. NW, Wash., DC 20036; 10 mln.

Geographical Society, Amer. (1851), 156 Fifth Ave., Suite 600, N.Y., NY 10010-7002; 1,300.

Geolinguistics, Amer. Society of (1965), University of Rhode Island, Kingston, RI 02892; 70.

Geological Institute, Amer. (1948), 4220 King St., Alexandria, VA 22302; 19 societies.

Geological Society of America (1888), 3300 Penrose Pl., P.O. Box 9140, Boulder, CO 80301; 16,987.

Geologists, Assn. of Engineering (1957), 3479 Rainbow Dr., Palo Alto, CA 94306; 3,500.

Geologists, Amer. Assn. of Petroleum (1917), 1444 S. Boulder, Tulsa, OK 74119; 38,000.

Geophysicists, Society of Exploration (1930), P.O. Box 702740, 8801 S. Yale, Tulsa OK 74170-2740; 16,766.

George S. Patton, Jr. Historical Society (1970), 11307 Vela Dr., San Diego, CA 92126.

Geriatrics Society, Amer. (1942), 770 Lexington Ave., Suite 400, N.Y., NY 10021; 6,000.

Gideons Intl. (1899), 2900 Lebanon Rd., Nashville, TN 37214; 140,000.

Gifted & Talented Club, Natl. (1987), 4049 Ross Park Dr., San Jose, CA 95118; 200.

Gifted Children, Amer. Assn. for (1946), 15 Gramercy Park, N.Y., NY 10003.

Gifted Children, Natl. Assn. for (1954), 4175 Lovell Rd., Suite 140, Circle Pines, MN 55014; 6,500.

Girls Clubs of America (1945), 30 E. 33d St., N.Y., NY 10016; 250,000+.

Girl Scouts of the U.S.A. (1912), 830 Third Ave., N.Y., NY 10022; 2.9 mln.

Gladiolus Council, No. Amer. (1945), 9338 Manzanita Dr., Sun City, AZ 85373; 1,275.

Gold Star Mothers, Amer. (1929), 2128 Leroy Pl. NW, Wash., DC 20008; 4,000.

Golf Association, U.S. (1894), Liberty Corner Rd., Far Hills, NJ 07931; 6,187 clubs.

Goose Island Bird & Girl Watching Society (1960), 301 Arthur Ave., Park Ridge, IL 60068; 876.

Gospel Music Assn. (1964), 38 Music Square W., Nashville, TN 37203; 3,000.

Governing Boards, Assn. of (1922), 1 Dupont Circle, Ste. 400, Washington, DC 20036; 1,107.

Government Finance Officers Assn. (1906), 180 N. Michigan Ave., Suite 800, Chicago, IL 60601; 11,000.

Gov't. Funding of Soc. Serv., Greater Wash. Organizations for (1981), 6612 Virginia View Ct. NW, Wash., DC 20816.

Graduate Schools in the U.S., Council of (1961), One Dupont Circle NW, Wash., DC 20036; 365 institutions.

Grandmother Clubs of America, Natl. Federation of (1934), 203 N. Wabash Ave., Chicago, IL 60601; 10,000.

Grange, Natl. (1867), 1616 H St. NW, Wash., DC 20006.

Graphic Artists, Society of Amer. (1915), 32 Union Sq., East, N.Y., NY 10003; 203.

Graphic Arts, Amer. Institute of (1914), 1059 Third Ave., N.Y., NY 10021; 2,200.

Gray Panthers (1970), 311 S. Juniper St., Suite 601, Phila., PA 19107; 80,000.

Greek-Amer. War Veterans in America, Natl. Legion of (1938), 739 W. 186th St., N.Y., NY 10033; 11.

Green Mountain Club, The (1910), 43 State St., Box 889, Montpelier, VT 05601; 5,250.

Grocers, Natl. Assn. of (1893), 1825 Samuel Morse Dr., Reston, VA 22090.

Grocery Manufacturers of America (1908), 1010 Wisconsin Ave., Wash., DC 20007; 140 companies.

Guide Dog Foundation for the Blind (1946), 371 Jericho Tpke., Smithtown, NY 11787; 1,500.

Gyro Intl. (1912), 1096 Mentor Ave., Painesville, OH 44077.

HIAS (Hebrew Immigrant Aid Society) (1881), 200 Park Ave. S, N.Y., NY 10003; 5,000.

Hadassah, the Women's Zionist Organization of America (1912), 50 W. 58th St., N.Y., NY 10019; 385,000.

Hairdressers and Cosmetologists Assn., Natl. (1921), 3510 Olive St., St. Louis, MO 63103; 50,406.

Handball Assn., U.S. (1951), 930 N. Benton Ave., Tucson, AZ 85711; 10,000.

Handgun, Intl. Metallic Silhouette Assn. (1976), Box 1609, 1409 Benton, Idaho Falls, ID 83401; 45,672.

Handicapped, Federation of the (1935), 211 W. 14th St., N.Y., NY 10011; 650.

Handicapped, Natl. Assn. of the Physically (1958), 76 Elm St., London, OH 43140; 700.

Hang Gliding Assn., U.S. (1971), P.O. Box 500, Pearblossom, CA 93553; 7,000.

Health Council, Natl. (1920), 350 Fifth Ave., Suite 1118, N.Y., NY 10017; 90 natl. organizations.

Health Insurance Institute (1956), 1850 K St. NW, Wash., DC; 325 companies.

Health, Physical Education, Recreation and Dance, Amer. Alliance for (1885), 1900 Association Dr., Reston, VA 22091.

Hearing Aid Society, Natl. (1951), 20361 Middlebelt Rd., Livonia, MI 48152; 2,500.

Hearing and Speech Action, Natl. Assn. for (1910), 10801 Rockville Pike, Rockville, MD 20852; 3,500.

Heart Assn., Amer. (1924), 7320 Greenville Ave., Dallas TX 75231; 144,000.

Hearts, Mended (1951), 7320 Greenville Ave., Dallas TX 75231; 18,000.

Heating, Refrigerating & Air Conditioning Engineers, Amer. Soc. of (1894), 1791 Tullie Circle NE, Atlanta, GA 30329.

Helicopter Assn. Intl. (1948), 1619 Duke St., Alexandria, VA 22314; 1,100.

Helicopter Society, Amer. (1943), 217 N. Washington St., Alexandria VA 22314; 8,000+.

Hemispheric Affairs, Council on (1975), 1612 20th St. NW, Wash., DC 20009; 2,400.

High School Assns., Natl. Federation of State (1920), 11724 Plaza Circle, Kansas City, MO 64195; 51.

High Twelve Internatl. (1921), 11155-B2 South Towne Square, St. Louis, MO 63123; 25,000.

Hiking Society, Amer. (1977), 1015 31st St. NW, Wash., DC 20007-4490; 4,500.

Historians, Organization of Amer. (1907), 112 N. Bryan St., Bloomington, IN 47408; 8,500.

Historical Assn., Amer. (1884), 400 A St. SE, Wash., DC 20003; 13,500.

Historic Preservation, Natl. Trust for (1949), 1785 Massachusetts Ave. NW, Wash., DC 20036; 140,000.

Hockey Assn. of the U.S., Amateur (1937), 2997 Broadmoor Valley Rd., Colorado Springs, CO 80906; 300,000.

Holy Cross of Jerusalem, Order of (1965), 853 Seventh Ave., N.Y., NY 10019; 2,225.

Home Builders, Natl. Assn. of (1942), 15th & M Sts. NW, Wash., DC 20005; 104,000+ firms.

Home Economics Assn., Amer. (1909), 2010 Massachusetts Ave. NW, Wash., DC 20036; 27,000.

Homemakers of America, Future (1945), 1910 Association Dr., Reston, VA 22091; 300,000.

Homemakers Council, Natl. Extension (1936), 4089 Snake Island Rd., Sturgeon Bay, WI 54235; 456,000.

Hospital Marketing and Public Relations of the Amer. Hospital, Amer. Soc. for (1964), 840 N. Lake Shore Dr., 9E, Chicago, IL 60611; 3,100.

Horatio Alger Soc. (1961), 4907 Allison Dr., Lansing, MI 48910; 300.

Horse Council, American (1969), 1700 K St. NW, #300, Washington, DC 20006; 2,100.

Horse Protection Assn., Amer. (1966), 1000 29th St. NW, Suite T-100, Wash., DC 20007; 10,000.

Horse Show Assn. of America Ltd., Natl. (1883), 680 5th Ave., #1602, N.Y., NY 10019.

Horse Shows Assn., Amer. (1917), 220 E. 42 St., N.Y., NY 10017-5806; 45,000.

Hospital Association, Amer. (1899), 840 N. Lake Shore Dr., Chicago, IL 60611; 40,000.

Hospital Marketing and Public Relations, Amer. Society for (1964), 840 N. Lake Shore Dr., Chicago, IL 60611; 3,167.

Hotel & Motel Assn., Amer. (1910), 888 Seventh Ave., N.Y., NY 10106; 10,000.

Human Rights and Social Justice, Americans for (1977), P.O. Box 6258, Ft. Worth, TX 76115.

Humane Society of the U.S. (1954), 2100 L St. NW, Wash., DC 20037; 930,000+.

Humanics, American (1949), 4601 Madison Ave., Kansas City, MO 64112; 2,000.

Hydrogen Energy, Intl. Assn. for (1975), P.O. Box 248266, Coral Gables, FL 33124; 2,000.

Idaho, U.S.S. (BB-42) Assn. (1957), P.O. Box 11247, San Diego, CA 92111; 750.

Identification, Intl. Assn. for (1916), P.O. Box 2309, Alameda, CA 94501-2370; 2,350.

Illustrators, Society of (1901), 128 E. 63 St., N.Y., NY 10021; 975.

Indian Rights Assn. (1882), 1505 Race St., Phila., PA 19102.

Industrial Democracy, League for (1905), 181 Hudson St., N.Y., NY 10013; 1,500.

Industrial Designers Society of America (1965), 1142-E Walker Rd., Great Falls, VA 22066; 2,030.

Industrial Engineers, Amer. Institute of (1948), 25 Technology Park, Norcross, GA 30092; 35,000.

Industrial Health Foundation (1935), 34 Penn Circle West, Pittsburgh, PA 15206; 170 companies.

Industrial Security, Amer. Soc. for (1955), 1655 N. Ft. Myer Dr., Suite 1200, Arlington, VA 22209; 23,000.

Information, Freedom of, Center (1958), P.O. Box 858, Columbia, MO 65205.

Information Industry Assn. (1968), 555 New Jersey Ave. NW, Suite 800, Wash., DC 20001; 600 companies.

Information Managers, Associated (1981), 10005 Rhode Island Ave., College Park, MD 20740; 600.

Insurance Assn., Amer. (1964), 1025 Connecticut Ave. NW, Wash., DC 20036; 171 companies.

Intelligence Officers, Assn. of Former (1975), 6723 Whittier Ave., Suite 303A, McLean, VA 22101; 3,500.

Intercollegiate Athletics, Natl. Assn. of (1940), 1221 Baltimore Ave., Kansas City, MO 64105; 482 schools.

Interior Designers, Amer. Society of (1975), 1430 Broadway, N.Y., NY 10018; 26,000.

International Interculture Programs, AFS (1947), 313 E. 43rd St., N.Y., NY 10017; 100,000.

Intertel, Inc. (1966), P.O. Box 150580, Lakewood, CO 80215; 2,200.

Inventors, Amer. Assn. of (1891), 2020 Pennsylvania Ave. NW, Wash., DC 20006; 5,727.

Investment Clubs, Natl. Assn. of (1951), 1515 E. Eleven Mile Rd., Royal Oak, MI 48067; 65,000.

Investors, Natl. Assn. of (1951), 1515 E. Eleven Mile Rd., Royal Oak, MI 48067; 136,000.

Irish-American Cultural Inst. (1962), 2115 Summit Ave., St. Paul, MN 55105.

Iron Castings Society (1897), 455 State St., Des Plaines, IL 60016; 200 firms.

Iron and Steel Engineers, Assn. of (1907), Three Gateway Center, Suite 2350, Pittsburgh, PA 15222; 11,856.

Iron and Steel Institute, Amer. (1908), 1133 15th St. NW, Wash., DC 20005-2701; 1,200.

Italian Historical Society of America (1949), 111 Columbia Heights, Bklyn., NY 11201.

Italy-America Chamber of Commerce (1887), 350 Fifth Ave., N.Y., NY 10118; 850.

Izaak Walton League of America, The (1922), 1401 Wilson Blvd., Level B, Arlington, VA 22209; 48,000.

JAPOS Study Group (1974), 154 Laguna Ct., St. Augustine Shores, FL 32086-7031; 250+.

Jamestown Society (1936), P.O. Box 14523, Richmond, VA 23221; 2,605.

Jane Austen Society of N. Amer. (1979), P.O. Box 252, Wayne, PA 19087; 2,400.

Japanese Amer. Citizens League (1929), 1765 Sutter St., San Francisco, CA 94115; 26,000.

Jaycees, U.S. (1915), 4 W. 21st St., Tulsa, OK 74114.

Jewish Appeal, United (1939), 99 Park Avenue, N.Y., NY 10016.

Jewish Book Council (1943), 15 E. 26th St., N.Y., NY 10010.

Jewish Committee, Amer. (1906), 165 E. 56th St., N.Y., NY 10022; 50,000.

Jewish Congress, Amer. (1918), 15 E. 84th St., N.Y., NY 10028; 50,000.

Jewish Federations, Council of (1932), 730 Broadway, N.Y., NY 10003; 200 agencies.

Jewish Historical Society, Amer. (1892), 2 Thornton Rd., Waltham, MA 02154; 3,100.

Jewish War Veterans of the U.S.A. (1896), 1811 R St. NW, Wash., DC 20009; 100,000.

Jewish Welfare Bd. Natl. (1917), 15 E. 26th St., N.Y., NY 10010.

Jewish Women, Natl. Council of (1893), 53 W. 23rd St., N.Y., NY 10010; 100,000.

Job's Daughters, Internatl. Order of (1921), 2515 St. Mary's Ave., Omaha, NE 68105; 36,000.

Jockey Club (1894), 380 Madison Ave., N.Y., NY 10017; 90.

John Birch Society (1958), 395 Concord Ave., Belmont, MA 02178; 25,000.

John Pelham Historical Assn. (1982), 7 Carmel Terr., Hampton, VA 23666; 125.

Joseph Diseases Foundation, Intl. (1977), P.O. Box 2550, Livermore, CA 94550; 3,800.

Journalists, Society of Professional (Sigma Delta Chi) (1909), 53 W. Jackson Blvd., Suite 731, Chicago, IL 60604.

Journalists and Authors, Amer. Society of (1948), 1501 Broadway, Suite 1907, N.Y., NY 10036; 750+.

Judaism, Amer. Council for (1943), 298 Fifth Ave., N.Y., NY 10001; 20,000.

Judicature Society, Amer. (1913), 25 E. Washington, Chicago, IL 60602; 20,000.

Juggler's Assn., Intl. (1947), P.O. Box 29, Kenmore, NY 14217; 3,100.

Junior Achievement (1919), 550 Summer St., Stamford, CT 06901; 300,000.

Junior Auxiliaries, Natl. Assn. of (1941), 845 S. Main, Greenville, MS 38701; 8,650.
Junior Colleges, Amer. Assn. of Community and (1920), One Dupont Circle NW, Wash., DC 20036; 900.
Junior Leagues, Assn. of (1921), 660 First Ave., N.Y., NY 10016; 189,000.

Kennel Club, Amer. (1884), 51 Madison Ave., N.Y., NY 10010; 450 clubs.
Kidney Fund, Amer. (1971), 6110 Executive Blvd., #1010, Rockville, MD 20852.
Kiwanis Intl. (1915), 3636 Woodview, Indianapolis, IN 46268.
Knights of Columbus (1882), One Columbus Plaza, New Haven, CT 06507; 1.4 mln.
Knights of Pythias (1864), 2785 E. Desert Inn Rd., #150, Las Vegas, NV 89121; 96,000.
Knights Templar U.S.A., Grand Encampment (1816), 14 E. Jackson Blvd., Suite 1700, Chicago, IL 60604; 300,000.

La Leche League Intl. (1956), 9616 Minneapolis Ave., Franklin Park, IL 60131; 34,000.
Lambs, The (1874), 3 W. 51st St., N.Y., NY 10019; 175.
Landscape Architects, Amer. Society of (1899), 1733 Connecticut Ave., NW, Wash., DC 20009; 7,000.
Law, Amer. Society of International (1906), 2223 Massachusetts Ave. NW, Washington, DC 20008; 4,300.
Law Enforcement Officers Assn., Amer. (1966), 1000 Connecticut Ave. NW, Suite 9, Wash., DC 20036; 50,000.
Law Libraries, Amer. Assn. of (1920), 53 W. Jackson Blvd., Chicago, IL 60604; 4,500.
Law and Social Policy, Center for (1969), 1751 N St. NW, Wash., DC 20036.
Learned Societies, Amer. Council of (1919), 228 E. 45th St., N.Y., NY 10017; 45 societies.
Lefthanders, League of (1975), P.O. Box 89, New Milford, NJ 07646; 1,200.
Lefthanders Intl. (1975), P.O. Box 8249, N. Topeka, Topeka, KS 66608; 24,000.
Legal Administrators, Assn. of (1971), 175 E. Hawthorn Pkwy. #325, Vernon Hills, IL 60061-1428; 6,700.
Legion of Valor of the U.S.A. (1890), 92 Oak Leaf Lane, Chapel Hill, NC 27516; 700.
Leif Ericson Society (1962), Box 301, Chicago, IL 60690-0301; 1,200.
Leprosy Missions, Amer. (1906), One Broadway, Elmwood Park, NJ 07407.
Leukemia Society of America (1949), 733 Third Ave., N.Y., NY 10017; 2,000 natl. & chapter trustees.
Lewis and Clark Trail Heritage Foundation, Inc. (1969), P.O. Box 3443, Great Falls, MT 59403; 1,400.
Lewis Carroll Society of N. America (1974), 617 Rockford Rd., Silver Spring, MD 20902; 350.
Liberty Lobby (1955), 300 Independence Ave. SE, Wash., DC 20003; 25,000.
Libraries Assn., Special (1909), 1700 18th St., NW, Wash., DC 20009; 12,500.
Library Administration & Management Assn. (1957), 50 E. Huron St., Chicago, IL 60611; 5,074.
Library Assn., Amer. (1876), 50 E. Huron St., Chicago, IL 60611; 45,145.
Library Assn., Medical (1898), 6 N. Michigan Ave., Suite 300, Chicago, IL 60602; 5,000+.
Life, Americans United for (1971), 343 N. Dearborn, Chicago, IL 60604.
Life Insurance, Amer. Council of (1975), 1001 Pennsylvania Ave., NW, Wash., DC 20004; 612 firms.
Life Office Management Assn. (1924), 5770 Powers Ferry Rd., Atlanta, GA 30327; 700+companies.
Life Underwriters, Amer. Soc. of Certified (1929), 270 Bryn Mawr Ave., Byrn Mawr, PA 19010; 28,000.
Life Underwriters, Natl. Assn. of (1890), 1922 F St. NW, Wash., DC 20006; 135,000.
Lighter-Than-Air Society (1952), 1800 Triplett Blvd., Akron, OH 44306; 1,200.
Lions Clubs, Intl. Assn. of (1917), 300 22d St., Oak Brook, IL 60570; 1,350,000.
Litchfield Institute, The (1984), 26 Hillside Ave., Bristol, CT 06010-6819; 52.
Literacy Volunteers of America (1962), 5795 Widewaters Parkway, Syracuse, NY 13214; 60,000.
Little League Baseball (1939), P.O. Box 3485, S. Williamsport, PA 17701; 16,450 leagues.
Little People of America (1957), P.O. Box 9897, Washington, DC 20016; 4,000.
London Club (1975), Rt. One, Bay Springs, KS 66050; 400.
Longwave Club of America (1974), 45 Wildflower Rd., Levittown, PA 19057; 536.

Lung Assn., Amer. (1904), 1740 Broadway, N.Y., NY 10019.
Lutheran Education Assn. (1942), 7400 Augusta St., River Forest, IL 60305; 3,750.

Magazine Publishers Assn. (1919), 575 Lexington Ave., N.Y., NY 10021; 42 publishers.
Magicians, Intl. Brotherhood of (1926), 103 N. Main St., Bluffton, OH 45817; 12,000.
Magicians, Society of Amateur (1988), 325 Maple St., Lynn, MA 01904; 2,400.
Magicians, Society of Amer. (1902), 1333 Cory St., Yellow Springs, OH 45387; 5,500.
Male Nurse Assn., Natl. (1971), Rush Univ., 1725 W. Harrison St., Chicago, IL 60612; 1,400.
Management Assn., Amer. (1923), 135 W. 50th St., N.Y., NY 10020; 75,000.
Management Consultants, Institute of (1968), 230 Park Ave., Suite 544, N.Y., NY 10169; 2,144.
Management Consulting Firms, Assn. of (1929), 230 Park Ave., N.Y., NY 10169; 53 firms.
Manufacturers, Natl. Assn. of (1897), 1776 F St. NW, Wash., DC 20006; 13,000 companies.
Manufacturers' Agents Natl. Assn. (1947), P.O. Box 3467, Laguna Hills, CA 92654; 10,000.
March of Dimes Birth Defects Foundation (1938), 1275 Mamaroneck Ave., White Plains, NY 10605.
Marijuana Laws, Natl. Organization for the Reform of (NORML) (1970), 2001 S St., #640, Wash., DC 20009; 5,000.
Marine Corps League (1923), 956 N. Monroe St., P.O. Box 11100, Arlington, VA 22201; 29,000.
Marine Manufacturers Assn., Natl. (1904), 401 N. Michigan Ave., Chicago, IL 60611; 1,650 companies.
Marine Technology Society (1963), 1825 K St. NW, Suite 203, Wash., DC 20006; 2,200.
Marketing Assn., Amer. (1937), 250 S. Wacker Dr., Chicago, IL 60606; 50,000.
Mary Stuart Society (1982), 6 St. John's Pl., N.Y., NY 10014.
Masonic Relief Assn. of U.S. and Canada (1885), 32613 Seidel Dr., Burlington, WS 53105; 14,700.
Masonic Service Assn. of the U.S. (1919), 8120 Fenton St., Silver Spring, MD 20910; 43 Grand Lodges.
Masons, Ancient and Accepted Scottish Rite, Southern Jurisdiction, Supreme Council (1801), 1733 16th St. NW, Wash., DC 20009; 592,753.
Masons, Supreme Council 33°, Ancient and Accepted Scottish Rite, Northern Masonic Jurisdiction (1813), 33 Marrett Rd., Lexington, MA 02173; 435,497.
Masons, Royal Arch, General Grand Chapter (1797), 1084 New Circle Rd. NE, Lexington, KY 40505; 298,744.
Mathematical Assn. of America (1915), 1529 Eighteenth Street, NW, Wash., DC 20036; 26,000.
Mathematical Society, Amer. (1888), 201 Charles St., Providence, RI 02940; 22,600.
Mathematical Statistics, Institute of (1935), 3401 Investment Blvd., #7, Hayward, CA 94545; 3,800.
Mathematics, Society for Industrial and Applied (1952), 117 S. 17th St., Phila., PA 19103-5052; 5,500.
Mayflower Descendants, General Society of (1897), 4 Winslow St., Plymouth, MA 02360; 25,000.
Mayors, U.S. Conference of (1933), 1620 Eye St. NW, Wash., DC 20006; over 30,000.
Mechanical Engineers, Amer. Society of (1880), 345 E. 47th St., N.Y., NY 10017; 120,000.
Mechanics, Amer. Academy of (1969), Dept. of Civil Engineering, Northwestern Univ., Evanston, IL 60201; 1,200.
Medical Assn., Amer. (1847), 535 N. Dearborn St., Chicago, IL 60610; 290,000.
Medical Assn., Natl. (1895), 1012 Tenth St. NW, Wash., DC 20001; 16,000.
Medical Record Assn., Amer. (1928), 875 N. Michigan Ave., Chicago, IL 60611; 28,000.
Medical Technologists, Amer. College of (1942), 5606 Lane, Raytown, MO 64133; 368.
Medieval Academy of America (1926), 1430 Massachusetts Ave., Cambridge, MA 02138; 3,600.
Mensa, Amer. (1960), 2626 E. 14th St., Brooklyn, NY 11235.
Mental Health Assn., Natl. (1909), 1021 Prince St., Alexandria, VA 22314; 1 mln.
Mental Health Program Directors, Natl. Assn. of State (1963), 1101 King St., Suite 160, Alexandria, VA 22314; 55.
Mentally Ill, Natl. Alliance for the (1979), 2102 Wilson Blvd., Suite 302, Arlington, VA 22201; 75,000.
Merchant Marine Library Assn., Amer. (1921), One World Trade Center, Suite 1365, N.Y., NY 10048.
Merchant Marine Veterans, Amer. (1983), 905 Cape Coral Pkwy., Cape Coral, FL 33904; 1,734.
Merchant Marine Veterans of WWII, U.S. (1944), 6475 Pacific Coast Hwy., Suite 396, Long Beach, CA 90803; 5,940.

Merchants Assn., Natl. Retail (1911), 100 W. 31st St., N.Y., NY 10001; 45,000.

Metal Finishers, Natl. Assn. of (1950), 111 E. Wacker Dr., Chicago, IL 60601; 1,000.

Metallurgy Institute, Amer. Powder (1959), 105 College Rd. East, Princeton, NJ 08540; 2,600.

Metal Powder Industries Federation, (1943), 105 College Rd. East, Princeton, NJ 08540; 260 cos.

Metals, Amer. Society for (ASM Internatl.) (1913), Metals Park, OH 44073; 53,000.

Meteorological Society, Amer. (1919), 45 Beacon St., Boston, MA 02108; 10,200.

Metric Assn., U.S. (1916), 10245 Andasol Ave., Northridge, CA 91325; 3,000.

Microbiology, Amer. Society for (1899), 1913 Eye St. NW, Wash. DC 20006; 34,500.

Mideast Educational and Training Services, America-, (1951), 1100 17th Street, NW, Wash., DC 20036.

Military Order of the Loyal Legion of the U.S.A. (1865), 1805 Pine St., Phila., PA 19103; 1,200.

Military Order of the Purple Heart of the USA (1932), 5413-B Backlick Rd., Springfield, VA 22151; 18,000.

Military Order of the World Wars (1920), 435 N. Lee St., Alexandria, VA 22314; 17,000.

Mining and Metallurgical Society of America (1908), 275 Madison Ave., N.Y., NY 10016; 295.

Ministerial Assn., Amer. (1929), 2210 Wilshire Blvd., Suite 582, Santa Monica, CA 90403; 2,500+.

Model Railroad Assn., Natl. (1935), 4121 Cromwell Rd., Chattanooga, TN 37421; 22,597.

Modern Language Assn. of America (1883), 10 Astor Pl., N.Y., NY 10003; 27,500.

Modern Language Teachers Assns., Natl. Federation of (1916), Gannon Univ., Erie, PA 16541; 7,200.

Moose, Loyal Order of (1888), Mooseheart, IL 60539; 1.8 mln.

Mothers, American (1935), 301 Park Ave., N.Y., NY 10022.

Mothers-in-Law Club Intl. (1970), 420 Adelberg Ln., Cedarhurst, NY 11516; 5,000.

Mothers of Twins Clubs, Natl. Organization of (1960), 12404 Princess Jeanne NE, Albuquerque, NM 87112-4640; 10,750+.

Motion Picture Arts & Sciences, Academy of (1927), 8949 Wilshire Blvd., Beverly Hills, CA 90211; 5,000.

Motion Pictures, Natl. Board of Review of (1909), P.O. Box 589, Lenox Hill Sta., N.Y., NY 10021.

Motion Picture & Television Engineers, Society of (1916), 595 West Hartsdale Ave., White Plains, NY 10607; 9,500.

Motor Vehicle Administrators, Amer. Assn. of (1933), 4200 Wilson Blvd.; Suite 600, Arlington, VA 22203; 1,000.

Motor Vehicle Manufacturers Assn. (1900), 7430 2nd Ave., Suite 300, Detroit, MI 48202; 17 companies.

Motorcyclist Assn., American (1924), 33 Collegeview Rd., Westerville, OH 43081; 160,000.

Multiple Sclerosis Society, Natl. (1945), 205 E. 42d St., N.Y., NY 10017; 360,000.

Municipal Finance Officers Assn. (1906), 180 N. Michigan Ave., Suite 800, Chicago, IL 60601.

Municipal League, Natl. (1894), 55 W. 44th St., N.Y., NY 10036; 3,000.

Muscular Dystrophy Assn. (1950), 810 Seventh Ave., N.Y., NY 10019; 2 mln. volunteers.

Museums, Amer. Assn. of (1906), 1055 Thomas Jefferson St. NW, Wash., DC 20007; 8,780.

Music Center, Amer. (1939), 250 W. 54th St., Suite 300, N.Y., NY 10019; 1,400.

Music Council, Natl. (1940), 40 W. 37th St., N.Y., NY 10018; 50 organizations.

Music Educators Natl. Conference (1907), 1902 Association Dr., Reston, VA 22090; 54,069.

Music Scholarship Assn., Amer. (1956), 1826 Carew Tower, Cincinnati, OH 45202; 15,000.

Music Teachers Natl. Assn. (1876), 617 Vine St., Suite 1432, Cincinnati, OH 45202-2439; 22,000+.

Musicological Society, Amer. (1934), 201 S. 34th St., Phila., PA 19104, 3,500.

Music Publishers' Assn., Natl. (1917), 205 E. 42nd St., N.Y., NY 10017; 300.

Muzzle Loading Rifle Assn., Natl. (1933), P.O. Box 67, Friendship, IN 47021; 25,000.

NAACP (Natl. Assn. for the Advancement of Colored People) (1909), 4805 Mt. Hope Drive, Baltimore, MD 21215.

Na'amat USA, Women's Labor Zionist Organization (1925), 200 Madison Ave., N.Y., NY 10016; 50,000.

Narcolepsy and Cataplexy Foundation of Amer. (1975), 1410 York Ave., Suite 2D, N.Y. NY 10021; 3,991.

Narcolepsy Assoc., Amer. (1975), P.O. Box 1187, San Carlos, CA 94070; 4,000.

National Guard Assn. of the U.S. (1878), One Massachusetts Ave. NW, Wash., DC 20001; 54,000.

Naturalists, Assn. of Interpretive (1961), 6700 Needwood Rd., Derwood, MD 20855; 1,100.

Nature Conservancy (1951), 1815 N. Lynn St., Arlington, VA 22209; 436,407.

Naturist Society, The (1980), 456 N. Main St., Oshkosh, WI 54901; 15,000.

Navajo Code Talkers Assn. (1971), Box 1182, Window Rock, AZ 86515; 475.

Naval Engineers, Amer. Society of (1888), 1452 Duke St., Alexandria, VA 22314; 7,500.

Naval Institute, U.S. (1873), U.S. Naval Academy, Annapolis, MD 21402; 110,000.

Naval Reserve Assn. (1954), 1619 King St., Alexandria, VA 22314; 24,500.

Navigation, Institute of (1945), 1026 16th St. NW, Suite 104, Wash., DC 20036; 3,000.

Navy Club of the U.S.A. Auxiliary (1941), 418 W. Pontiac St., Ft. Wayne, IN 46807; 1,000.

Navy League of the U.S. (1902); 2300 Wilson Blvd., Arlington, VA 22201; 70,000.

Needlework Guild of America (1885), 1007-B St. Road, Southhampton, PA 18966; 3,000 directors.

Negro College Fund, United (1944), 500 E. 62d St., N.Y., NY 10021; 42 institutions.

Neurofibromatosis Foundation, Natl. (1978), 141 Fifth Ave., N.Y., NY 10010; 27,000.

Newspaper Editors, Amer. Society of (1922), 11600 Sunrise Valley Dr., Reston, VA 22091; 1,000.

Newspaper Marketing Assn., Intl. (1930), 11600 Sunrise Valley Dr., Reston, VA 22091; 1,300+.

Newspaper Publishers Assn., Amer. (1887), 11600 Sunrise Valley Dr., Reston, VA 22091; 1,400 newspapers.

Ninety-Nines (Intl. Organization of Women Pilots) (1929), P.O. Box 59965; Will Rogers Airport, Oklahoma City, OK 73159; 6,600.

Nobel Anniversary Committee, Amer. (1941), 1 Morningside Dr., Westport, CT 06880; 1,000.

Non-Commissioned Officers Assn. (1960), 10635 IH 35 No., San Antonio, TX 78233; 151,416.

Northern Cross Society (1983), Route One, Big Springs, KS 66050; 150+.

Notaries, Amer. Society of (1965), 918 16th St. NW, Wash., DC 20006; 25,224.

Nuclear Society, Amer. (1954), 555 N. Kensington Ave., La Grange Park, IL 60525; 15,000.

Numismatic Assn., Amer.- (1891), 818 N. Cascade Ave., Colorado Springs, CO 80903; 34,000.

Numismatic Society, Amer. (1858), Broadway at 155th St., N.Y., NY 10032; 2,223.

Nurses' Assn., Amer. (1896), 2420 Pershing Rd., Kansas City, MO 64108.

Nursing, Amer. Assembly of Men in (1971), Rush Univ., 600 S. Paulina, #474-H, Chicago, IL 60612; 280.

Nursing, Natl. League for (1952), 10 Columbus Circle, N.Y., NY 10019; 15,000.

Nutrition, Amer. Institute of (1928), 9650 Rockville Pike, Bethesda, MD 20814; 2,774.

ORT Federation, Amer. (Org. for Rehabilitation through Training) (1925), 817 Broadway, N.Y., NY 10014; 20,000.

Odd Fellows, Sovereign Grand Lodge Independent Order of (1819), 422 N. Trade St., Winston Salem, NC 27101.

Old Crows, Assn. of (1964), 2300 9th St. S., Arlington, VA 22204; 18,000.

Olympic Committee, U.S. (1921), 1750 E. Boulder St., Colorado Springs, CO 80909; 70 organizations.

Opthalmology, Amer. Academy of (1979), 655 Beach St., San Francisco, CA 94109; 16,250.

Optical Society of America (1916), 1816 Jefferson Pl. NW, Wash., DC 20036; 10,900.

Optimist Intl. (1919), 4494 Lindell Blvd., St. Louis, MO 63108.

Optometric Assn., Amer. (1898), 243 N. Lindbergh Blvd., St. Louis, MO 63141; 27,000.

Oral and Maxillofacial Surgeons, Amer. Assn. of (1918), 9700 W. Bryn Mawr Ave., Rosemont, IL 60018; 5,302.

Organists, Amer. Guild of (1896), 815 Second Ave., Suite 318, N.Y., NY 10017; 22,000.

Oriental Society, Amer. (1842), 329 Sterling Memorial Library, Yale Sta., New Haven, CT 06520; 1,350.

Ornithologists' Union, Amer. (1883), c/o National Museum of Natural History, Smithsonian, Wash., DC 20560; 4,000.

Ortho Missions (1934), 14526 Haynes St., #4, Van Nuys, CA 91411; 1,600.

Osteopathic Assn., Amer. (1887), 212 E. Ohio St., Chicago, IL 60611; 23,292.

Ostomy Assn., United (1962), 36 Executive Park, Suite 120, Irving, CA 92714, 44,231.

Outlaw and Lawman History, Natl. Assn. for (1974), Univ. of Wyoming, Box 3334, Laramie, WY 82071; 470.

Overeaters Anonymous (1960), 4025 Spencer St., #203, Torrance, CA 90503; 120,000.

Over-the-Counter Cos., Natl. Assn. of (1973), 1735 K St. NW, Washington, DC 20006; 500+.

PTA (Natl. Congress of Parents and Teachers), Natl. (1897), 700 N. Rush St., Chicago, IL 60611; 6.1 mln.

Paleontological Research Institution (1932), 1259 Trumansburg Rd., Ithaca, NY 14850; 700+.

Paper Converters Assn. (1934), 1133 15th St. NW, Wash., DC 20005.

Paper Industry, Technical Assn. of the Pulp and (1916), P.O. Box 105113, Atlanta, GA 30348; 28,000.

Paper Institute, Amer. (1964), 260 Madison Ave., N.Y., NY 10016; 166 companies.

Parasitologists, Amer. Society of (1924), 1041 New Hampshire St., Box 368, Lawrence, KS 66044; 1,491.

Parents Without Partners (1958), 7910 Woodmont Ave. NW, Wash., DC 20814; 210,000.

Parkinson's Disease Foundation (1957), 650 W. 168th St., N.Y., NY 10032; 50,000+.

Parliamentarians, Amer. Institute of (1958), 124 W. Washington Blvd., Ft. Wayne, IN 46802; 1,300.

Parliamentarians, Natl. Assn. of (1930), 6601 Winchester, Kansas City, MO 64133-4600; 4,200.

Parliamentary Law, Intl. Organization of Professionals in (1977), 3611 Victoria Ave., Los Angeles, CA 90016; 300.

Pasta Assn., Natl. (1904), 1901 N. Ft. Myer Dr., Suite 1000, Arlington, VA 22209; 100 member companies.

Pathologists, Amer. Assn. of (1976), 9650 Rockville Pike, Bethesda, MD 20814; 2,350.

Patriotism, Natl. Committee for Responsible (1967), P.O. Box 665, Grand Central Sta., N.Y., NY 10163; 150.

Pearl Harbor History Associates (1982), P.O. Box 205, Sperryville, VA 22740-0205; 350.

Pearl Harbor Survivors Assn. (1958), 3215 Albert St., Orlando, FL 32806.

PEN Amer. Center (1922), 568 Broadway, N.Y., NY 10012.

PEN Women, Natl. League of Amer. (1897), 1300 17th St. NW, Wash., DC 20036-1973; 5,000.

Pen Friends, Intl. (1967), P.O. Box 290065, Homecrest Station, Brooklyn, NY 11229–0001; 200,000.

Pennsylvania Society of New York (1899), 80 N. Main St., Sellersville, PA 18960; 1,896.

Pension Actuaries, Amer. Society of (1966), 2029 K St. NW, Wash., DC 20006; 2,500.

Pension Plan, Committee for a Natl. (1979), P.O. Box 27851, Las Vegas, NV 89126; 2,000.

P.E.O. (Philanthropic Educational Organization) Sisterhood (1869), 3700 Grand Ave., Des Moines, IA 50312; 240,000.

Personnel Administration, Amer. Society for (1948), 606 N. Washington St., Alexandria, VA 22314; 40,000.

Petroleum Equipment Inst. (1951), 3739 E. 31st St., Tulsa, OK 74135; 1,200 member companies.

Petroleum Institute, Amer. (1919), 1220 L St. NW, Wash., DC 20005; 200+ corporations.

Petroleum Landmen, Amer. Assn. of (1955), 777 Main St., Suite 1470, Fort Worth, TX 76102; 11,200.

Pharmaceutical Assn., Amer. (1852), 2215 Constitution Ave. NW, Wash., DC 20037; 50,000.

Phi Delta Kappa (1906), 8th & Union, Box 789, Bloomington, IN 47401-0789; 132,000.

Philatelic Pages & Panels, Amer. Soc. for (1984), 1138 Princeton Dr., Richardson, TX 75081-3615; 679.

Philatelic Society, Amer. (1886), P.O. Box 8000, State College, PA 16803; 57,800.

Philatelians, Society of (1972), 154 Laguna Ct., St. Augustine Shores, FL 32086; 300+.

Philological Assn., Amer. (1869), ⸢Dept. of Classics, Fordham Univ., Bronx, NY 10458; 2,500.

Philosophical Assn., Amer. (1900), Univ. of Delaware, Newark, DE 19716; 7,600.

Philosophical Enquiry, Intl. Society for (1974), 304 Lexington Blvd., Carmel, IN 46032; 430.

Philosophical Society, Amer. (1743), 104 S. 5th St., Phila., PA 19106; 650.

Photogrammetry and Remote Sensing, Amer. Society of (1934), 210 Little Falls St., Falls Church, VA 22046; 8,753.

Photographers of America, Professional (1880), 1090 Executive Way, Des Plaines, IL 60018; 15,000.

Photographic Society of Amer. (1937), 3000 United Founders Blvd. #103, Oklahoma City, OK 73112; 10,000+.

Physical Therapy Assn., Amer. (1921), 1111 N. Fairfax St., Alexandria, VA 22314; 48,000.

Physicians, Amer. Academy of Family (1947), 8880 Ward Pkwy., Kansas City, MO 64114; 65,000.

Physics, Amer. Inst. of (1931), 335 E. 45th St., N.Y., NY 10017-3483.

Physiological Society, Amer. (1887), 9650 Rockville Pike, Bethesda, MD 20814; 6,700.

Phytopathological Soc., The Amer. (1908), 3340 Pilot Knob Rd., St. Paul, MN 55121; 4,300+.

Pilgrim Society (1820), 75 Court St., Plymouth, MA 02360-3891; 900.

Pilgrims of the U.S. (1903), 80 Broadway, N.Y., NY 10005.

Pilot Club Intl. (1921), 244 College St., Macon, GA 31213-0599; 21,000.

Planetary Society (1980), 65 N. Catalina, Pasadena, CA 91106; 125,000.

Planned Parenthood Federation of America (1916), 810 Seventh Ave., N.Y., NY 10019; 187 affiliates.

Planning Assn., Amer. (1909), 1776 Massachusetts Ave. NW, Wash., DC 20036; 23,250.

Plastic Modelers Society, Intl. (1965), 1615 Calvert, Lincoln, NE 68502; 6,000.

Plastics Industry, Society of (1937), 1275 K St. NW, Suite 400, Washington, DC 20005; 2,099.

Platform Assn., Intl. (1831), Box 250, Winnetka, IL 60093; 8,000.

Podiatric Medical Assn., Amer. (1912), 20 Chevy Chase Circle NW, Wash., DC 20015; 8,416.

Poetry Day Committee, Natl. (1947), 1110 N. Venetian Dr., Miami, FL 33139; 17,500.

Poetry Society of America (1910), 15 Gramercy Park, N.Y., NY 10003; 1,605.

Poets, Academy of Amer. (1934), 177 E. 87th St., N.Y., NY 10121; 2,000.

Polar Society, Amer. (1934), 98-20 62d Dr., Apt. 7H, Rego Park, NY 11374; 2,143.

Police, Internatl. Assn. of Chiefs of (1893), 1110 N. Glebe Rd., Suite 200, Arlington, VA 22201; 14,500.

Police Officers Assn., Natl. (1967), 1316 Gardiner Lane, Louisville, KY 40213; 6,000.

Polish Army Veterans Assn. of America (1921), 19 Irving Pl., N.Y., NY 10003; 9,762.

Polish Cultural Society of America (1940), P.O. Box 31, Wall Street P.O., N.Y., NY 10005; 110,114.

Polish Genealogical Society of CT (1984), 8 Lyle Rd., New Britain, CT 06053.

Polish Legion of American Veterans (1921), 3024 N. Laramie Ave., Chicago, IL 60641; 15,000.

Political Items Collectors, Amer. (1945), P.O. Box 340339, San Antonio, TX 78234; 2,500.

Political Science, Academy of (1880), 475 Riverside Dr., Suite 1274, N.Y., NY 10115-0012; 10,000.

Political Science Assn., Amer. (1903), 1527 New Hampshire Ave. NW, Wash., DC 20036; 13,000.

Political & Social Science, Amer. Academy of (1889), 3937 Chestnut St., Phila., PA 19104; 10,000.

Pollution Control, Internatl. Assn. for (1970), 444 N. Capital St. NW, Wash. DC 20001; 500.

Polo Assn., U.S. (1890), 4059 Iron Works Pike, Lexington, KY, 40511; 2,210.

Population Assn. of America (1931), 1429 Duke St., Alexandria, VA 22314-3402.

Portuguese Continental Union of the U.S.A. (1925), 899 Boylston St., Boston, MA 02115; 8,000.

Postmasters of the U.S., Natl. Assn. of (1898), 4212 King St., Arlington, VA 22302; 3,000.

Postmasters of the U.S., Natl. League of (1904), 1023 N. Royal St., Alexandria, VA 22003; 22,300.

Poultry Science Assn. (1908), 309 W. Clark St., Champaign, IL 61820; 3,500.

Power Boat Assn., Amer. (1903), 17640 E. Nine Mile Rd., E. Detroit, MI 48021; 6,352.

Precancel Collectors, Natl. Assn. of (1950), 5121 Park Blvd., Wildwood, NJ 08260; 7,500+.

Press, Associated (1848), 50 Rockefeller Plaza, N.Y., NY 10020; 1,365 newspapers & 3,600 broadcast stations.

Press Club, Natl. (1908), 529 14th St. NW, Wash., DC 20045.

Press Intl., United (1907), 1400 I St. NW, Wash. DC 20005.

Press and Radio Club (1948), P.O. Box 7023, Montgomery, AL 36107; 737.

Press Women, Natl. Federation of (1937), 1105 Main St., Box 99, Blue Springs, MO 64015; 5,000.

Printing Industries of America (1887), 1730 N. Lynn St., Arlington, VA 22209; 12,900 companies.

Prisoners of War, Amer. Ex- (1949), 3201 E. Pioneer Pkwy. #40, Arlington, TX 76010-5396; 33,000.

Procrastinator Club of America (1956), 1111 Broad–Locust Bldg., Phila., PA 19102; 5,600.

Propeller Club of the U.S. (1927), 1030 15th St. NW, Suite 430, Wash., DC 20005; 14,000.

Psychiatric Assn., Amer. (1844), 1400 K St. NW, Wash., DC 20005; 35,000.

Psychical Research, Amer. Society for (1885), 5 W. 73d St., N.Y., NY 10023; 1,800.

Psychoanalytic Assn., Amer. (1911), 309 E. 49th St., N.Y., NY 10017; 3,020.

Psychological Assn., Amer. (1892), 1200 17th St. NW, Wash., DC 20036; 60,000.

Psychological Assn. for Psychoanalysis, Natl. (1948), 150 W. 13th St., N.Y., NY 10011; 306.

Psychological Minorities, Society for the Aid of (1953), 42-25 Hampton St., Elmhurst, NY 11373; 523.

Psychotherapy Assn., Amer. Group (1942), 25 E. 21st St., N.Y., NY 10010; 3,400.

Psoriasis Foundation, Natl (1968), 6443 SW Beaverton Hwy., #210, Portland, OR 97221; 14,000.

Public Administration, Amer. Soc. for (1939), 1120 G St. NW, Wash, DC 20005; 14,800.

Public Health Assn., Amer. (1972), 1015 15th St. NW, Wash., DC 20005; 30,000.

Public Relations Soc. of Amer. (1947), 33 Irving Pl. N.Y., NY 10003.

Publishers, Assn. of Amer. (1970), One Park Ave., N.Y., NY 10016; 330 publishing houses.

Puppeteers of Amer. (1937), 5 Cricklewood Path, Pasadena, CA 91107; 2,400.

Quality Control, Amer. Society for (1946), 310 W. Wisconsin Ave., Milwaukee, WI 53203; 60,000.

Quota Internatl. (1919), 1828 L St. NW, Wash., DC 20036.

Rabbinical Alliance of America (1944), 3 W. 16th St. N.Y., NY 10011.

Rabbinical Assembly (1900), 3080 Broadway, N.Y., NY 10027; 1,170.

Rabbis, Central Conference of Amer. (1889), 21 E. 40th St., N.Y., NY 10016; 1,500.

Radio, Natl. Assn. of Business and Educational (1965), 1501 Duke St., Suite 200, Alexandria, VA 22314; 4,873.

Radio Union, Intl. Amateur (1925), P.O. Box AAA, Newington, CT 06111; 126 societies.

Radio and TV Society, Intl. (1939), 420 Lexington Ave., N.Y., NY 10170; 1,700.

Radio Relay League, Amer. (1914), 225 Main St., Newington, CT 06111; 158,000.

Railroad Club of Chicago, The (1934), 506 5th St., Wilmette, IL 60091; 100.

Railroad Passengers, Natl. Assn. of (1967), 236 Massachusetts Ave. NE, Suite 603, Wash., DC 20002; 12,659.

Railroads, Assn. of Amer. (1934), 50 F St. NW, Wash., DC 20001; 113.

Railway Historical Society, Natl. (1935), P.O. Box 58153, Phila., PA 19102; 15,000.

Railway Progress Institute (1908), 700 N. Fairfax St., Suite 601, Alexandria, VA 22314-2098; 130 companies.

Rainbow Walkers (1982), 4370 Fairlawn Dr., Lake Canada, CA 91011; 1,444.

Range Management, Society for (1946), 2760 W. 5th Ave., Denver, CO 80204; 5,500.

Rape, Feminist Alliance Against (1974), P.O. Box 21033, Wash., DC 20009.

Reading Assn., Intl. (1956), P.O. Box 8139, 800 Barksdale Rd., Newark, DE 19714-8139; 84,000.

Real Estate Appraisers, Natl. Assn. of (1967), 853 Broadway, N.Y., NY 10003; 1,000.

Real Estate Institute, Intl. (1975), 8383 E. Evans Rd., Scottsdale, AZ 85260; 6,000.

Rebekah Assemblies, Intl. Assn. of (1851), 422 N. Trade St., Suite "R" Winston-Salem, NC 27101; 227,857.

Reconciliation, Fellowship of (1915), 523 N. Broadway, Nyack, NY 10960; 35,000.

Records Managers & Administrators, Assn. of (1975), 4200 Somerset Dr., Suite 215, Prairie Village, KS 66208; 10,000.

Recreation and Park Assn., Natl. (1965), 3101 Park Ctr. Dr., 12th Fl., Alexandria, VA 22302; 20,727.

Red Cross, American National (1881), 18th & D Sts. NW, Wash., DC 20006; 1.2 mln. volunteers.

Red Men, Improved Order of (1765), 1525 West Avenue, Waco, TX 76707; 40,000.

Redwoods League, Save-the- (1918), 114 Sansome St., Rm. 605, San Francisco, CA 94104; 45,000.

Reed Organ Society, Inc. (1981), The Musical Museum, Deansboro, NY 13328; 700.

Regional Plan Assn. (1929), 1040 Ave. of the Americas, N.Y., NY 10018; 1,200.

Rehabilitation Assn., Natl. (1925), 633 S. Washington St., Alexandria, VA 22314; 16,000.

Religion, Amer. Academy of (1909), 501 Hall of Languages, Syracuse Univ., Syracuse, NY 13244-1170; 5,600.

Religion, Freedom from, Foundation (1978), P.O. Box 750, Madison, WI 53701; 3,000.

Remodeling Industry, Natl. Assn. of the (1956), 1901 N. Moore St., Suite 808, Arlington, VA 22209.

Renaissance Society of America (1954), 1161 Amsterdam Ave., N.Y., NY 10027; 3,000.

Reserve Officers Assn. of the U.S. (1922), One Constitution Ave., NE, Wash., DC 20002; 125,000.

Restaurant Assn., Natl. (1919), 1200 17th St. NW, Wash., DC 20036; 15,000.

Retarded Citizens of the U.S., Assn. for (1950), 2501 Ave. J, Arlington, TX 76006; 160,000.

Retired Credit Union People, Natl. Assn. for (1978), 5910 Mineral Pt. Rd., Madison, WI 53705; 101,000.

Retired Federal Employees, Natl. Assn. of (1921), 1533 New Hampshire Ave. NW, Wash., DC 20036; 490,000.

Retired Officers Assn. (1929), 201 N. Washington St., Alexandria, VA 22314-2529; 360,000.

Retired Persons, Amer. Assn. of (1958), 1909 K St. NW, Wash., DC 20049; 18 mln.

Retired Teachers Assn., Natl. (1947), 1909 K St. NW, Wash., DC 20049; 540,000.

Retreads (of World War I & II) (1947), 40-07 154th St., Flushing, NY 11354; 1,000.

Revolver Assn., U.S. (1900), 96 W. Union St., Ashland, MA 01721; 1,400.

Reye's Syndrome Foundation, Natl. (1974), 426 N. Lewis, Bryan, OH 43506; 10,000.

Richard III Society (1969), P.O. Box 13787, New Orleans, LA 70185; 700.

Rifle Assn., Natl. (1871), 1600 Rhode Island Ave. NW, Wash., DC 20036; 3 mln.

Road & Transportation Builders' Assn., Amer. (1902), 525 School St. SW, Wash., DC 20024; 4,500.

Rodeo Cowboys Assn., Professional (1936), 101 Pro Rodeo Dr., Colorado Springs, CO 80919; 8,790.

Roller Skating, U.S. Amateur Confederation of (1937), 1500 S. 70th St., Lincoln, NE 68506; 23,000.

Roller Skating Rink Operators Assn. (1937), 7700 A St., Lincoln, NE 68510; 1,200 rinks.

Rose Society, Amer. (1899), P.O. Box 30,000, Shreveport, LA 71130; 17,782.

Rotary Intl. (1905), 1560 Sherman Ave., Evanston, IL 60201-3698; 1.1 mln.

Running and Fitness Assn., Amer. (1968), 9310 Old Georgetown Rd., Bethesda, MD 20814; 23,000.

Ruritan Natl. (1928), Ruritan Natl. Rd., Dublin, VA 24084.

Safety and Fairness Everywhere, Natl. Assn. Taunting (1980), P.O. Box 5743WA, Montecito, CA 93150; 12,000.

Safety Council, Natl. (1913), 444 N. Michigan Ave., Chicago, IL 60611; 12,500.

Sailors, Tin Can (1976), Battleship Cove, Fall River, MA 02721; 10,300.

St. Andrew the Apostle, The Soc. of (1983), Route 3, Sylvester, WV 25193; 450.

St. Dennis of Zante, Sovereign Greek Order of (1096; 1953 in U.S.), 739 W. 186th St., N.Y., NY 10033; 91.

St. George the Martyr, Knightly Assn. of (1980), State Route #3, Sylvester, WV 25193; 10,000.

St. Luke, Physician of Amer., Order of (1952), 2210 Wilshire Blvd., Santa Monica, CA 90403; 300+.

St. Paul, Natl. Guild of (1937), 601 Hill 'n Dale, Lexington, KY 40503; 13,652.

Salespersons, Natl. Assn. of Professional (1970), P.O. Box 76461, Atlanta, GA 30358; 35,000.

Salt Institute (1914), 206 N. Washington St., Alexandria, VA, 22314; 12.

Sane Nuclear Policy, Committee for a (1957), 711 G St. SE, Wash., DC 20003; 130,000.

Savings Institutions, Natl. Council of (1983), 1101 15th St. NW, Wash., DC 20005; 550 members.

Savings & Loan League, Natl. (1943), 1101 15th St. NW, Wash., DC 20005; 300 associations.

School Administrators, Amer. Assn. of (1865), 1801 N. Moore St., Arlington, VA 22209; 18,889.

School Boards Assn., Natl. (1940), 1680 Duke St., Alexandria, VA 22314.

School Counselor Assn., Amer. (1953), 5999 Stevenson Ave., Alexandria, VA 22304; 12,500.

Schools of Art, Natl. Assn. of (also: School of Art and Design, School of Dance, Music, and Theater) (1944), 11250 Roger Bacon Dr., #5, Reston, VA 22090.

Schools & Colleges, Amer. Council on (1927), 13014 Dale Mabry Hwy., Ste. 270-B, Tampa, FL 33180-2808; 137.

Science, Amer. Assn. for the Advancement of (1848), 1333 H St. NW, Wash., DC 20005; 132,000.

Science Fiction Society, World (1939), P.O. Box 1270, Kendall Sq. Sta., Cambridge, MA 02142; 5,000.

Science Service (1921), 1719 N St. NW, Wash., DC 20036.

Science Teachers Assn., Natl. (1944), 1742 Connecticut Ave. NW, Wash., DC 20009; 50,000.

Science Writers, Natl. Assn. of (1934), P.O. Box 294, Greenlawn, NY 11740; 1,500.

Sciences, Natl. Academy of (1863), 2101 Constitution Ave. NW, Wash., DC 20418; 1,816.

Scientists, Federation of American (1945), 307 Massachusetts Ave. NE, Wash., DC 20002; 5,000.

Scientists of America Foundation, Young (1979), P.O. Box 9066, Phoenix, AZ 85068; 250 chapters.

Screen Actors Guild (1933), 7065 Hollywood Blvd. Hollywood, CA 90028; 73,000.

Screen Printing Assn. Intl. (1948), 10015 Main St., Fairfax, VA 22031; 3,000 companies.

Sculpture Soc., Natl. (1893), 15 E. 26th St., N.Y., NY 10010.

Seamen's Service, United (1942), One World Trade Ctr., Suite 1365, N.Y., NY 10048.

2d Air Division Assn. (1947), 1 Jeffrey's Neck Rd., Ipswich, MA 01938; 6,000.

Secondary School Principals, Natl. Assn. of (1916), 1904 Association Dr., Reston, VA 22091; 41,000.

Secretaries, Natl. Assn. of Legal (1950), 2250 E73, #550, Tulsa, OK 74136-6865; 17,000.

Secularists of America, United (1947), 1301 E. Ventura Blvd. #36, Oxnard, CA 93030.

Securities Industry Assn. (1972), 120 Broadway, N.Y., NY 10271; 580 firms.

Semantics, Institute of General (1938), Office of the Director, 3029 Eastern Ave., Baltimore, MD 21224; 500.

Separation of Church & State, Americans United for (1947), 8120 Fenton St., Silver Spring, MD 20910; 50,000.

Sertoma Internatl. (1912), 1912 E. Meyer Blvd., Kansas City, MO 64132; 35,000.

Sex Information & Education Council of the U.S. (SIECUS) (1964), New York University, 32 Washington Place, N.Y., NY 10003; 3,000.

Shakespeare Assn. of America (1972), Box 6328, Vanderbilt Sta. B, Nashville, TN 37235; 812.

Sheet Metal & Air Conditioning Contractor's Natl. Assn., The (1943), 8224 Old Courthouse Rd., Vienna, VA 22182.

Shipbuilders Council of America (1921), 1110 Vermont Ave. NW, Wash., DC 20005; 53 organizations.

Ships in Bottles Assn. of Amer. (1983), P.O. Box 550, Coronado, CA 92118; 350.

Shoe Retailers Assn., Natl. (1913), 1414 Ave. of the Americas, N.Y., NY 10016; 4,000.

Shore & Beach Preservation Assn., Amer. (1926), 3000 Citrus Circle, Suite 230, Walnut Creek, CA 94598; 1,000.

Shrine, Ancient Arabic Order of the Nobles of the Mystic (1872), 2900 Rocky Pt. Dr., Tampa, FL 33607; 799,000.

Shut-Ins, Natl. Society for (1970), P.O. Box 1392, Reading, PA 19603; 65.

Sierra Club (1892), 730 Polk St., San Francisco, CA 94109; 440,000.

Signalmen, Society of (1971), P.O. Box 11247, San Diego, CA 92111; 850.

Silurians, Soc. of the (1924), 164 Lexington Ave., N.Y., NY 10016; 500.

Skating Union of the U.S., Amateur (1928), 1033 Shady Lane, Glen Ellyn, IL 60137; 2,400.

Skeet Shooting Assn., Natl. (1946), P.O. Box 680007, San Antonio, TX 78268; 15,800.

Ski Assn., U.S. (1904), 1750 E. Boulder St., Colorado Springs, CO 80909; 23,244.

Small Business, Amer. Federation of (1938), 407 S. Dearborn St., Chicago, IL 60605; 25,000.

Small Business United, Natl. (1937), 1155 15th St. NW, Suite 710, Wash., DC 20005; 25,000.

Smoking & Health, Natl. Clearinghouse for (1965), Center for Disease Control, 1600 Clifton Road NE, Atlanta, GA 30333.

Soaring Society of America (1932), P.O. Box 66071, Los Angeles, CA 90066-0071; 16,000.

Soccer Federation, U.S. (1913), Viscount Hotel, 40 JFK Intl. Airport, Jamaica, NY 11430; 700,000.

Social Biology, Society for the Study of (1926), Medical Dept., Brookhaven Natl. Laboratory, Upton, NY 11973; 415.

Social Sciences, Natl. Institute of (1899), c/o Mr. J. Sinclair Armstrong, 30 Rockefeller Plaza, N.Y., NY 10112; 800.

Social Work Education, Council on (1952), 1744 R St. NW, Wash. DC 20009; 3,500.

Social Workers, Natl. Assn. of (1955), 7981 Eastern Ave., Silver Spring, MD 20910; 112,000.

Socialists of America, Democratic (1981), 15 Dutch St., Suite 500, N.Y., NY 10038; 6,000.

Sociological Assn., Amer. (1905), 1722 N St. NW, Wash., DC 20036; 12,300.

Softball Assn. of America, Amateur (1933), 2801 N.E. 50th St., Oklahoma City, OK 73111; 220,000 teams.

Softball League, Cinderella (1958), P.O. Box 1411, Corning, NY 14830.

Soft Drink Assn., Natl. (1919), 1101 16th St. NW, Wash., DC 20036; 1,100.

Soil Conservation Society of America (1945), 7515 N.E. Ankeny Rd., Ankeny, IA 50021; 12,000.

Soil Science Society of America (1936), 677 S. Segoe Rd., Madison, WI 53711; 6,084.

Sojourners, Natl. (1919), 8301 E. Boulevard Dr., Alexandria, VA 22308; 9,500.

Soldier's, Sailor's and Airmen's Club (1919), 283 Lexington Ave., N.Y., NY 10016; 2,054.

Songwriters Guild of America, The (1931), 276 Fifth Ave., N.Y., NY 10001; 5,000.

Sons of the Amer. Legion (1932), Box 1055, Indianapolis, IN 46206; 99,116.

Sons of the American Revolution, Natl. Society of (1889), 1000 S. 4th, Louisville, KY 40203; 24,000.

Sons of Confederate Veterans (1896), Southern Station, Box 5164, Hattiesburg, MS 39406; 8,500.

Sons of the Desert (1965), P.O. Box 8341, Universal City, CA 91608; 6,000.

Sons of Italy in America, Supreme Lodge Order (1905), 219 E. St., NE, Wash. DC 20002; 100,000.

Sons of Norway (1895), 1455 W. Lake St., Minneapolis, MN 55408; 105,000.

Sons of Poland, Assn. of the (1903), 591 Summit Ave., Rm. 702, Jersey City, NJ 07306; 10,000.

Sons of the Revolution in the State of New York/ Fraunces Tavern Museum (1876), 54 Pearl St., N.Y., NY 10004; 1,350.

Sons of St. Patrick, Society of the Friendly (1784), 80 Wall St., N.Y., NY 10005; 1,400.

Sons of Sherman's March to the Sea (1966), 1725 Farmers Ave., Tempe, AZ 85281; 660.

Sons of Union Veterans of the Civil War (1881), P.O. Box 3024, Gettysburg, PA 17325-0024; 3,570.

Soroptimist Intl. of the Americas (1921), 1616 Walnut St., Phila., PA 19103; 50,000.

Southern Christian Leadership Conference (1957), 334 Auburn Ave. NE, Atlanta, GA 30303; 1 mln.

Space Education Assoc., U.S. (1973), 746 Turnpike Rd., Elizabethtown, PA 17022-1161; 1,000.

Speech Communication Assn. (1914), 5105 Backlick Rd., Annandale, VA 22003; 6,700.

Speech-Language-Hearing Assn., Amer. (1925), 10801 Rockville Pike, Rockville, MD 20852; 55,000.

Speleological Society, Natl. (1941), 2813 Cave Ave., Huntsville, AL 35810; 8,100.

Spiritist Assn., Basilio (1917), 269 W. 23rd St., N.Y., NY 10011.

Spiritual Awareness, Assn. for (1985), P.O. Box 224, Clarence, MO 63437; 2,000.

Sports Car Club of America (1944), 9033 E. Easter Pl., Englewood, CO 80112; 51,081.

Sports Club, Indoor (1930), 1145 Highland St., Napoleon, OH 43545.

Sportscasters Assn., Amer. (1980), 5 Beekman St., N.Y., NY 10038; 500.

Standards Institute, Amer. Natl. (1918), 1430 Broadway, N.Y., NY 10018; 1,000.

State Communities Aid Assn. (1872), 151 Chestnut St., Albany, NY 12210; 95.

State Governments, Council of (1933), P.O. Box 11910, Iron Works Pike, Lexington, KY 40578; 50 states.

State & Local History, Amer. Assn. for (1940), 172 Second Ave. N., Nashville, TN 37201; 6,000.

Statistical Assn., Amer. (1839), 1429 Duke St., Alexandria, VA 22314-3402; 15,103.

Steamship Historical Society of America (1935), H.C. Hall Bldg., 345 Blackstone Blvd., Providence, RI 02906; 3,364.

Steel Construction, Amer. Institute of (1921), 400 N. Michigan Ave., Chicago, IL 60611-4185; 2,600+.

Stock Car Auto Racing, Natl. Assn. for (NASCAR) (1948), 1801 Speedway Blvd., Daytona Beach, FL 32015; 17,000.

Stock Exchange, Amer. (1911), 86 Trinity Pl., N.Y., NY 10006; 871.

Stock Exchange, N.Y. (1792), 11 Wall St., N.Y., NY 10005.

Stock Exchange, Phila. (1790), 1900 Market St., Phila., PA 19103; 505.

Structural Stability Research Council (1944), Fritz Engineering Laboratory No. 13, Lehigh Univ., Bethlehem, PA 18015.

Student Assn., U.S. (1947), 1012 14th St. NW, Suite 403, Wash., DC 20005.

Student Councils, Natl. Assn. of (1931), 1904 Association Dr., Reston, VA 22091; 200,000.

Stuttering Project, Natl. (1977), 4601 Irving St., San Francisco, CA 94122-1020; 4,200.

Sudden Infant Death Syndrome Foundation, Natl. (1962), 8200 Professional Pl., Landover, MD 20785-2264.

Sugar Brokers Assn., Natl. (1903), 1 World Trade Center, N.Y., NY 10047; 100.

Sunbathing Assn., Amer. (1931), 1703 N. Main St., Kissimmee, FL 32743-3396; 30,000.

Sunday League (1933), 279 Highland Ave., Newark, NJ 07104; 25,000.

Surgeons, College of (1913), 55 E. Erie St., Chicago IL 60611; 49,950.

Surgeons, Intl. College of (1935), 1516 N. Lake Shore Dr., Chicago IL 60610; 14,000.

Surgeons of the U.S., Assn. of Military (1903), 10605 Concord St., #306, Kensington, MD 20895; 15,000.

Surveying & Mapping, Amer. Congress on (1941), 210 Little Falls, Falls Church, VA 22046; 10,800.

Symphony Orchestra League, Amer. (1942), 777 14th St. NW, Wash., DC 20005; 870 orchestras.

Systems Management, Assn. for (1947), 24587 Bagley Rd., Cleveland, OH 44138; 9,000.

Table Tennis Assn., U.S. (1933), Olympic Complex, 1750 E. Boulder, Colorado Springs, CO 80909; 5,500.

Tailhook Assn., The (1968), P.O. Box 40, Bonita, CA 92002-0040; 14,211.

Tall Buildings and Urban Habitat, Council on (1969), Bldg. 13, Lehigh Univ., Bethlehem, PA 18015; 1,200.

Tax Accountants, Natl. Assn. of Enrolled Federal (1960), 6108 N. Harding Ave., Chicago, IL 60659-3108; 450.

Tax Administrators, Federation of (1937), 444 N. Capitol St. NW, Wash., DC 20001.

Tax Assn., Natl.–Tax Institute of America (1907), 5310 E. Main St., Suite 104, Columbus, OH 43213; 1,900.

Tax Foundation, Inc. (1937), 1 Thomas Circle NW, Suite 500, Wash., DC 20005; 568 corporations.

Tax Free America (1986), 11015 Cumpston St., N. Hollywood, CA 91601; 400,000.

Taxpayers Union, Natl. (1969), 713 Maryland Ave., NE, Washington, DC 20002; 150,000.

Tea Assn. of the U.S.A. (1899), 230 Park Ave., N.Y., NY 10169; 179.

Teachers Assn., Amer. String (1954), UGA Sta. Box 2066, Athens, GA 30612; 6,400+.

Teachers of English, Natl. Council of (1911), 1111 Kenyon Rd., Urbana, IL 61801; 115,000.

Teachers of English to Speakers of Other Languages (1967), 1600 Cameron St., Suite 300, Alexandria, VA 22314; 30,000+.

Teachers of French, Amer. Assn. of (1927), 57 E. Armory Ave., Champaign, IL 61820; 11,000.

Teachers of German, American Assn. of (1926), 112 Haddontowne Court #104, Cherry Hill, NJ 08034; 6,200.

Teachers of Mathematics, Natl. Council of (1920), 1906 Association Dr., Reston, VA 22091; 74,000.

Teachers of Singing, Natl. Assn. of (1944), 2800 Univ. Blvd. N, J.U. Sta., Jacksonville, FL 32211; 4,600.

Teachers of Spanish & Portuguese, Amer. Assn. of (1917), P.O. Box 6349, Lee Hall 218, Mississippi State Univ., Mississippi State, MS 39762-6349; 13,000.

Telephone Pioneers of Amer. (1911), 22 Cortland, St., 25th fl., N.Y., NY 10007; 780,000.

Television Arts & Sciences, Natl. Academy of (1947), 111 W. 57th St., Suite 1020, N.Y., NY 10019.

Television Bureau of Advertising (1954), 485 Lexington Ave., N.Y., NY 10017.

Television & Radio Artists, Amer. Federation of (1937), 1350 Ave. of the Americas, N.Y., NY 10019; 66,000.

Telluride Assn. (1911), 217 West Ave., Ithaca, NY 14850.

Tennis Assn., U.S. (1881), 1212 Ave. of Americas, N.Y., NY 10036.

Terraplane Club, Hudson-Essex (1959), 100 E. Cross St., Ypsilanti, MI 48198; 2,850.

Tesla Memorial Soc., Inc. (1979), 453 Martin Rd., Lackawanna, NY 14218; 1,500.

Testing & Materials, Amer. Society for (1898), 1916 Race St., Phila., PA 19103; 32,000.

Texas State Genealogical Society (1960), 2507 Tannehill, Houston, TX 77008-3052; 1,000.

Textile Assn., Northern (1854), 230 Congress St., Boston, MA 02110; 100+.

Textile Manufacturers Institute, Amer. (1949), 1101 Connecticut Ave. NW, Suite 300, Wash., DC 20036.

Theatre Organ Society, Amer. (1955), P.O. Box 3043, Olivenhain, CA 92024; 6,000.

Theodore Roosevelt Assn. (1919), P.O. Box 720, Oyster Bay, NY 11771; 1,500.

Theological Library Assn., Amer. (1947), 5600 S. Woodlawn Ave., Chicago, IL 60637; 502.

Theological Schools in the U.S. and Canada, Assn. of (1918), 42 E. National Rd., Vandalia, OH 45377; 204.

Theosophical Society in America, The (1886), 1926 N. Main St., Wheaton, IL 60187; 5,700.

Thoreau Society (1941), 156 Belknap St., Concord, MA 01742; 1,400.

Thoroughbred Racing Assns. (1942), 3000 Marcus Ave., Lake Success, NY 11042; 51 racing associations.

Titanic Historical Society (1963), P.O. Box 51053, Indian Orchard, MA 01151-0053; 4,122.

Toastmasters Intl. (1924), 2200 N. Grand Ave., Santa Ana,, CA 92711; 150,000.

Topical Assn., Amer. (1949), P.O. Box 630, Johnstown, PA 15907; 7,000.

Torch Clubs, Internatl. Assn. of (1924), 435 N. Michigan Ave., #1717, Chicago, IL 60611; 3,375.

Toy Manufacturers of America (1916), 200 Fifth Ave., N.Y., NY 10010; 240.

Traffic and Transportation, Amer. Society of (1946), 1816 Norris Pl. #4, Louisville, KY 40205; 2,400.

Trail Association, North Country (1980), 2780 Mundy Ave., White Cloud, MI 49349; 200.

Transit Assn., Amer. Public (1974), 1225 Connecticut Ave. NW, Wash., DC 20036; 888.

Translators Assn., Amer. (1959), 109 Croton Ave., Ossining, NY 10562; 2,800+.

Transportation and Logistics, Inc., Amer. Society of (1946), P.O. Box 33095, Louisville, KY 40232; 1,900.

Trapshooting Assn., Amateur (1923), 601 W. National Rd. Vandalia, OH 45377; 100,000+.

Travel Agents, Amer. Society of (1931), 1101 King St., Alexandria, VA 22314; 19,135.

Travel Industry Assn. of America (1941), 1133 21st St. NW, Wash., DC 20036; 1,700.

Travelers Protective Assn. of America (1890), 3755 Lindell Blvd., St. Louis, MO 63108; 179,222.

Triple Nine Society (1979), 2119 College St., Cedar Falls, IA 50613; 700.

Trucking Assn., Amer. (1933), 2200 Mill Rd., Alexandria, VA 22314.

True Sisters, United Order (1846), 212 Fifth Ave., N.Y., NY 10010; 8,500.

Tuberous Sclerosis Assn. of Amer. (1970), P.O. Box 44, Rockland, MA 02370; 2,500.

UFOs, Natl. Investigation Committee on (1957), 14617 Victory Blvd., Suite 4, Van Nuys, CA 91411.

UNICEF, U.S. Committee for (1947), 331 E. 38th St., N.Y., NY 10016.

USO (United Service Organizations) (1941), 601 Indiana Ave., NW, Wash., DC 20004.

Underwriters, Amer. Soc. of Chartered Life (1927), 270 Bryn Mawr Ave., Bryn Mawr, PA 19010; 30,000.

Underwriters, Soc. of Chartered Property and Casualty (1944), Kahler Hall, 720 Providence Rd., Malvern, PA 19355.

Uniformed Services Society of Military Widows, Natl. Assn. for (1968), 5535 Hempstead Way, Springfield, VA 22151; 55,000.

United Nations Assn. of the U.S.A. (1923, as League of Nations Assn.) 300 E. 42d St., N.Y., NY 10017; 31,500.

U.S., Amer. Assn. for Study of the, in World Affairs (1948), 3613 Annandale Rd., Annandale, VA 22003; 1,500.

United Way of America (1918), 801 N. Fairfax St., Alexandria, VA 22309; 1,200.

Universities, Assn. of Amer. (1900), One Dupont Circle NW, Wash., DC 20036; 56 institutions.

Universities & Colleges, Assn. of Governing Bds. of (1921), One Dupont Circle NW, Suite 400, Wash., DC 20036.

University Extension Assn., Natl. (1915), One Dupont Circle, Suite 360, NW, Wash., DC 20036; 1,200.

University Foundation, Intl. (1973), 1301 S. Noland Rd., Independence, MO 64055; 11,575.

University Professors, Amer. Assn. of (1915), 1012 14th St. NW, Wash., DC 20005; 41,000.

University Professors for Academic Order (1970), 635 SW 4th St., Corvallis, OR 97333; 500.

University Women, Amer. Assn. of (1881), 2401 Virginia Ave. NW, Wash., DC 20037; 140,000.

Urban Coalition, Natl. (1967), 1120 G St. NW, Suite 900, Wash., DC 20005; 42 affiliates.

Urban League, Natl. (1910), 500 E. 62d St., N.Y., NY 10020.

Utility Commissioners, Natl. Assn. of Regulatory (1889), 1102 Interstate Commerce Commission Bldg., 12th & Constitution NW, Wash., DC 20044-0684; 96 agencies.

Vampire Research Center (1972), P.O. Box 252, Elmhurst, NY 11373; 120.

Variety Clubs Intl. (1928), 1560 Bdway., N.Y., NY 10036.

VASA Order of America (1896), 65 Bryant Rd., Cranston, R.I. 02910; 32,000.

Ventriloquists, No. American Assn. of (1944), 800 W. Littleton Blvd., Box 420, Littleton, CO 80120; 1,700.

Veterans Assn., Blinded (1945), 477 H St. NW, Wash., DC 20001; 6,800.

Veterans Assn., China-Burma-India (1947), 750 N. Lincoln Memorial Dr., Milwaukee, WI 53201; 3,221 +.

Veterans Committee, Amer. (1944), 1735 De Sales St. NW, Suite 402, Wash., DC 20817; 25,000.

Veterans of Foreign Wars of the U.S. (1899) **& Ladies Auxiliary** (1914), 406 W. 34th St., Kansas City, MO 64111.

Veterans of the Vietnam War (1980), 2090 Bald Mountain Rd., Wilkes-Barre, PA 18702-9609; 30,000.

Veterans of World War I (1958), 941 N. Capitol St. NE, Room 1201-C, Wash., DC 20421; 150,000.

Veterans of WWII, Submarine, (1955), 6523 San Joaquin St., Sacramento, CA 95820; 7,979.

Veterinary Medical Assn., Amer. (1863), 930 N. Meacham Rd., Schaumburg, IL 60196; 43,000.

Victorian Society in America (1966), 219 S. Sixth St., Phila., PA 19106; 4,088.

Volleyball Assn., U.S. (1928), 1750 E. Boulder St., Colorado Springs, CO 80909; 45,000.

Walking Society, American (1980), Viana House, Box 3432, Palm Beach, FL 33480; 2.7 mln.

War Mothers, Amer. (1917), 2615 Woodley Pl. NW, Wash., DC 20008; 4,000.

Warrant and Warrant Officers' Assn., Chief, U.S. Coast Guard (1929), c/o Fort McNair Yacht Basin, 200 V Street, SW, Wash., DC 20024; 3,346.

Washington, DC Area Trucking Assn. (1933), 2200 Mill Rd., Alexandria, VA 22314; 130 companies.

Watch & Clock Collectors, Natl. Assn. of (1943), 514 Poplar St., Columbia, PA 17512-2124; 32,140.

Watercolor Soc., American (1866), 47 Fifth Ave., N.Y., NY 10003; 517.

Water Pollution Control Admin., Assn. of State and Interstate (1961), 444 N. Capital St. NW, #330, Washington, DC 20001.

Water Pollution Control Federation (1928), 2626 Pennsylvania Ave. NW, Wash., DC 20037; 30,000.

Water Resources Assn., Amer. (1964), 5410 Grosvenor Ln., Suite 220, Bethesda, MD 20814-2192; 3,200.

Water Ski Assn., Amer. (1939), 799 Overlook Dr. SE, Winter Haven, FL 33884; 20,000.

Water Well Assn., Natl. (1948), 6375 Riverside Drive, Dublin, OH 43017; 17,000.

Water Works Assn., Amer. (1881), 6666 W. Quincy Ave., Denver, CO 80235; 36,500.

Watts Family Assn. (1969), 12401 Burton St., N. Hollywood, CA 91605; 12 branches.

Weather Modification Assn. (1950), P.O. Box 8116, Fresno, CA 93747; 200.

Welding Society, Amer. (1919), 550 NW LeJeune Rd., Miami, FL 33126; 35,000.

Wheelchair Athletic Assn., Natl. (1956), 3617 Betty Dr., Suite 5, Colorado Springs, CO 80917; 2,000.

Widows, Society of Military (1968), 5535 Hemstead Way, Springfield, VA 22151; 2,000.

Wilderness Society (1935), 1400 Eye St. NW, Wash., DC 20005; 212,000.

Wild Horse Organized Assistance (WHOA!) (1971), 140 Greenstone Dr., Reno, NV 89512; 10,000.

Wildlife, Defenders of (1947), 1244 19th St. NW, Wash., DC 20036; 80,000.

Wildlife Federation, Natl. (1936), 1400 16th St. NW, Wash., DC 20036; 5.1 mln.

Wildlife Foundation, No. Amer. (1911), 102 Wilmot Rd., #410, Deerfield, IL 60015.

Wildlife Fund, World (1961), 1255 23rd St. NW, Wash., DC 20037; 230,000.

Wildlife Management Institute (1911), 1101-14th St., Suite 725, NW, Wash., DC 20005.

William Penn Assn. (1886), 709 Brighton Rd., Pittsburgh, PA 15233; 90,000.

Wireless Pioneers, Society of (1968), 146 Coleen St., Livermore, CA 94550; 5,233.

Wizard of Oz Club, Intl. (1957), Box 95, Kinderhook, IL 62345; 2,500.

Women, Natl. Assn. of Bank (1920), 500 No. Michigan Ave., Suite 1400, Chicago, IL 60611; 30,000.

Women, Natl. Organization for (NOW) (1966), 1401 New York Ave. NW, Wash., DC 20005; 150,000.

Women Artists, Natl. Assn. of (1889), 41 Union Sq., N.Y., NY 10003; 675.

Women Engineers, Society of (1950), 345 E. 47th St., N.Y., NY 10017; 14,000.

Women in Communications (1909), 3724 Executive Center Dr., #165, Austin, TX 78731; 10,000.

Women in Radio and TV, Inc. (1951), 1321 Connecticut Ave. NW, Washington, DC 20036; 3,000.

Women Geographers, Society of (1925); 1619 New Hampshire Ave. NW, Wash., DC 20009; 500.

Women Marines Assn. (1960), P.O. Box 387, Quantico, VA 22134; 3,009.

Women Strike for Peace (1961), 145 S. 13th St., Rm. 706, Phila., PA 19107; 8,000.

Women of the U.S., Natl. Council of (1888), 777 U.N. Plaza, N.Y., NY 10017; 28 organizations.

Women Voters of the U.S., League of (1920), 1730 M St. NW, Wash., DC 20036; 120,000.

Women World War Veterans (1919), 237 Madison Ave., N.Y., NY 10016; 35,000.

Women's Army Corps Veterans Assn. (1947), Hwy. 21, Anniston, AL 36206; 3,500.

Women's Association, American Business (1949), 9100 Ward Parkway, P.O. Box 8728, Kansas City, MO 64114; 100,000.

Women's Christian Temperance Union, Natl. (1874), 1730 Chicago Ave., Evanston, IL 60201; 200,000.

Women's Clubs, General Federation of (1890), 1734 N St. NW, Wash. DC, 20036.

Women's Clubs, National Federation of Business & Professional (1919), 2012 Massachusetts Ave. NW, Wash., DC 20036.

Women's Educational & Industrial Union (1877), 356 Boylston St., Boston, MA 02116; 2,000.

Women's Intl. League for Peace & Freedom (1915), 1213 Race St., Phila., PA 19107; 15,000.

Women's Legal Defense Fund (1971), 2000 P St. NW, Suite 400, Washington, DC 20036; 1,900.

Women's Overseas Service League (1921), P.O. Box 39058, Friendship Station, Washington, DC 20016; 1,450.

Woodmen of America, Modern (1883), Mississippi River at 17th St., Rock Island, IL 61201; 600,000.

Woodmen of the World Life Insurance Soc. (1890), 1700 Farnam St., Omaha, NE 68102; 900,000.

Wool Growers Association, National (1865), 1301 Pennsylvania Ave., NW, Room 300, Wash., DC. 20004; 24 state assns.

Workmen's Circle (1900), 45 E. 33d St., N.Y., NY 10016.

World Federalist Assn. (1969), 418 7th St. SE, Washington, DC 20003; 9,874.

World Future Society (1966), 4916 St. Elmo Ave., Bethesda, MD 20814; 30,000.

World Health, Amer. Assn. for (1953), 2001 S St., NW, Suite 530, Washington, DC 20009; 500.

World Peace, Intl Assn. of Educators for (1969), P.O. Box 3282, Mastin Lake Sta., Huntsville, AL 35810-0282; 18,500.

World's Fair Collectors Soc. (1968), P.O. Box 20806, Sarasota, FL 34238-3806; 350.

Writers Guild of America, West (1933), 8955 Beverly Blvd., W. Hollywood, CA 90048; 19,500.

Yeoman F. Natl. (1936), 223 El Camino Real, Vallejo, CA 94590; 800.

Young Men's Christian Assns. of the U.S.A. (1851), 101 N. Wacker Dr., Chicago, IL 60606; 13 mln.

YM-YMHAs of Greater New York, Associated (1957), 130 E. 59th St., N.Y., NY 10020; 55,100.

Young Women's Christian Assn. of the U.S.A. (1906), 726 Broadway, N.Y., NY 10003; 1.6 mln.

Youth Hostels, American (1934), P.O. Box 37613, Wash., DC 20013; 100,000.

Zero Population Growth (1968), 1400 16th St. NW, Suite 320, Wash., DC 20036; 25,000.

Ziegfeld Club (1936), 593 Park Ave., N.Y., NY 10021; 303.

Zionist Organization of America (1897), 4 E. 34th St., N.Y., NY 10016; 140,000.

Zoological Parks & Aquariums, Amer. Assn. of (1924), Oglebay Park, Wheeling, WV 26003; 5,300.

Zoologists, Amer. Society of (1890), 104 Sirius Circle, Thousand Oaks, CA 91360; 4,000.

NATIONS OF THE WORLD

As of mid-1989

The nations of the world are listed in alphabetical order. Initials in the following articles include UN (United Nations), OAS (Org. of American States), NATO (North Atlantic Treaty Org.), EC (European Communities or Common Market), OAU (Org. of African Unity), ILO (Intl. Labor Org.), FAO (Food & Agricultural Org.), WHO (World Health Org.), IMF (Intl. Monetary Fund), GATT (General Agreements on Tarriffs & Trade). **Sources:** U.S. Dept. of State; U.S. Census Bureau; The World Factbook; International Monetary Fund; UN Statistical Yearbook; UN Demographic Yearbook; International Iron and Steel Institute; The Statesman's Year-Book; Encyclopaedia Britannica. All embassy addresses are Wash., DC; area codes (202), unless otherwise noted. Literacy rates are usually based on the ability to read and write on a lower elementary school level. The concept of literacy is changing in the industrialized countries, where literacy is defined as the ability to read instructions necessary for a job or a license. By these standards, illiteracy may be more common than present rates suggest.

See special color section for maps and flags.

Afghanistan

Republic of Afghanistan

De Afghanistan Jamhuriat

People: Population (1989 est.): 16,592,000. **Pop. density:** 65 per sq. mi. **Ethnic groups:** Pushtun 50%; Tajik 25%; Uzbek 9%; Hazara 9%. **Languages:** Pushtu, Dari Persian (spoken by Tajiks, Hazaras), Uzbek (Turkic). **Religions:** Sunni Moslem 74%, Shi'a Moslem 25%.

Geography: Area: 251,773 sq. mi., about the size of Texas. **Location:** Between Soviet Central Asia and the Indian subcontinent. **Neighbors:** Pakistan on E, S, Iran on W, USSR on N; the NE tip touches China. **Topography:** The country is landlocked and mountainous, much of it over 4,000 ft. above sea level. The Hindu Kush Mts. tower 16,000 ft. above Kabul and reach a height of 25,000 ft. to the E. Trade with Pakistan flows through the 35-mile long Khyber Pass. The climate is dry, with extreme temperatures, and large desert regions, though mountain rivers produce intermittent fertile valleys. **Capital:** Kabul. **Cities** (1987 est.): Kabul 1.2 mln.

Government: Type: Communist, backed by Soviet force. **Head of state, and President of the Revolutionary Council:** Pres. Mohammad Najibullah; in office: Nov. 30, 1987. **Head of Government:** Prime Min. Soltan Ali Keshtmand; in office: Feb. 21, 1989. **Head of Communist Party:** Secy. Gen. Mohammad Najibullah; in office: May 4, 1986. **Local divisions:** 29 provinces, each under a governor. **Defense:** 7.7% of GNP (1984).

Economy: Industries: Textiles, carpets, cement. **Chief crops:** Nuts, wheat, fruits. **Minerals:** Copper, coal, zinc, iron. **Other resources:** Wool, hides, karacul pelts. **Arable land:** 13%. **Livestock** (1986): cattle: 3.7 mln.; sheep: 20 mln. **Electricity prod.** (1986): 1.3 bln. kwh. **Labor force:** cannot be estimated due to war.

Finance: Currency: Afghani (Mar. 1989: 50.60 = $1 US). **Gross national product** (1985): $3.3 bln. **Imports** (1987): $996 mln.; partners: USSR 30%, Jap. 10%. **Exports** (1987): $512 mln.; partners: USSR 86%. **International reserves less gold** (Feb. 1989): $260 mln. **Gold:** 965,000 oz t.

Transport: Motor vehicles: in use (1982): 30,000 passenger cars, 35,000 comm. vehicles. **Civil aviation** (1987): 174 mln. passenger-km; 8.0 mln. net ton-km.

Communications: Television sets: 20,000 in use (1986); **Radios:** 150,000 in use (1986). **Telephones in use** (1985): 31,000. **Daily newspaper circ.** (1987): 6 per 1,000 pop.

Health: Life expectancy at birth (1986): 42.5 male; 40.8 female. **Births** (per 1,000 pop. 1987): 47.5. **Deaths** (per 1,000 pop. 1987): 22.5. **Natural increase** (1987): 2.5%. **Hospital beds:** 6,875. **Physicians:** 1,215 (1982). **Infant mortality** (per 1,000 live births 1987): 175.

Education (1987): **Literacy:** 12%. Over 88% of adults have no formal schooling.

Major International Organizations: UN (World Bank, IMF) **Embassy:** 2341 Wyoming Ave. NW, 20008; 234-3770.

Afghanistan, occupying a favored invasion route since antiquity, has been variously known as Ariana or Bactria (in ancient times) and Khorasan (in the Middle Ages). Foreign empires alternated rule with local emirs and kings until the 18th century, when a unified kingdom was established. In 1973, a military coup ushered in a republic.

Pro-Soviet leftists took power in a bloody 1978 coup, and concluded an economic and military treaty with the USSR.

Late in Dec. 1979, the USSR began a massive military airlift into Kabul. The three-month old regime of Hafizullah Amin ended with a Soviet backed coup, Dec. 27th. He was replaced by Babrak Karmal, a more pro-Soviet leader. Soviet troops, estimated at between 60,000-100,000, fanned out over Afghanistan, fighting rebels. Fighting continued for 8 years as the Soviets found themselves engaged in a long, protracted guerrilla war.

An UN-mediated agreement was signed Apr. 14, 1988 providing for the withdrawal of Soviet troops from Afghanistan, creation of a neutral Afghan state, and repatriation of millions of Afghan refugees. The U.S. and USSR pledged to serve as guarantors of the agreement. Afghan rebels rejected the pact and vowed to continue fighting while the "Soviets and their puppets" remained in Afghanistan.

The Soviets disclosed that during the war some 15,000 soldiers were killed. They completed their troop withdrawal Feb. 15, 1989 as Afghan rebels and the government began a civil war; the rebels elected a government-in-exile Feb. 23. (*See Chronology*).

Albania

Peoples Socialist Republic of Albania

Republika Popullore Socialiste e Shqipërisë

People: Population (1989 est.): 3,201,000. **Pop. density:** 288 per sq. mi. **Urban** (1984): 33%. **Ethnic groups:** Albanians (Gegs in N, Tosks in S) 96%, Greeks 2.5%. **Languages:** Albanian (Tosk is official dialect), Greek. **Religions:** officially atheist; (historically) mostly Moslems. All public worship and religious institutions were outlawed in 1967.

Geography: Area: 11,100 sq. mi., slightly larger than Maryland. **Location:** On SE coast of Adriatic Sea. **Neighbors:** Greece on S, Yugoslavia on N, E. **Topography:** Apart from a narrow coastal plain, Albania consists of hills and mountains covered with scrub forest, cut by small E-W rivers. **Capital:** Tirana. **Cities** (1986 est.): Tirana 272,000; Durres 127,000; Vlore 90,000.

Government: Type: Communist. **Head of state:** Pres. Ramiz Alia, b. Oct. 18, 1925; in office: Nov. 22, 1982. **Head of government:** Premier Adil Carcani; in office: Jan. 18, 1982. **Head of Communist Party:** Ramiz Alia; in office: Apr. 13, 1985. **Local divisions:** 26 districts. **Defense:** 5.3% of GNP (1986).

Economy: Industries: Chem. fertilizers, textiles. **Chief crops:** Corn, wheat, cotton, potatoes, tobacco, fruits. **Minerals:** Chromium, coal, oil. **Other resources:** Forests. **Arable land:** 21%. **Livestock** (1986): 610,000 cattle; 1.2 mln. sheep. **Electricity prod.** (1986): 4.9 bln. kwh. **Labor force:** 50% agric; 50% ind. & comm.

Finance: Currency: Lek (Nov. 1989: 5.95 = $1 US). **Gross national product** (1986 est.) $2.8 bln. **Per capita income** (1985): $900. **Imports** (1985): $335 mln.; partners: Czech., Yugoslavia, Rom. **Exports** (1985): $345 mln.; partners: Czech., Yugoslavia, N. Korea, Italy.

Chief ports: Durres, Vlone.

Communications: Television sets: 187,000 in use (1985). **Radios:** 210,000 in use (1986). **Daily newspaper circ.** (1985): 52 per 1,000 pop.

Health: Life expectancy at birth (1985): 70.4 yrs. **Births** (per 1,000 pop. 1985): 27.0. **Deaths** (per 1,000 pop. 1985): 6.0.

Natural increase 2.0%. **Hospital beds** 17,600 (1982): 70. **Physicians** (1983): 4,967 doctors & dentists. **Infant mortality** (per 1,000 live births 1982): 44.0.

Major International Organizations: UN (FAO, WHO).

Education (1986): **Literacy:** 75%. Free and compulsory ages 7-15.

Ancient Illyria was conquered by Romans, Slavs, and Turks (15th century); the latter Islamized the population. Independent Albania was proclaimed in 1912, republic was formed in 1920. Self-styled King Zog I ruled 1925-39, until Italy invaded.

Communist partisans took over in 1944, allied Albania with USSR, then broke with USSR in 1960 over de-Stalinization. Strong political alliance with China followed, leading to several billion dollars in aid, which was curtailed after 1974. China cut off aid in 1978 when Albania attacked its policies after the death of Chinese ruler Mao Tse-tung.

Large-scale purges of officials occurred during the 1970s. Enver Hoxha, the nation's ruler for 4 decades, died Apr. 11, 1985.

Algeria

Democratic and Popular Republic of Algeria

al-Jumhuriya al-Jazāiriya ad-Dimuqratiya ash-Shabiya

People: Population (1989 est.): 25,063,000. **Age distrib.** (%): 0–14: 43.9; 15–59: 50.3; 60+: 5.8. **Pop. density:** 27 per sq. mi. **Urban** (1987): 49%. **Ethnic groups:** Arabs 75%, Berbers 25%. **Languages:** Arabic (official), Berber (indigenous language), French. **Religions:** Sunni Moslem (state religion).

Geography: Area: 918,497 sq. mi., more than 3 times the size of Texas. **Location:** In NW Africa, from Mediterranean Sea into Sahara Desert. **Neighbors:** Morocco on W, Mauritania, Mali, Niger on S, Libya, Tunisia on E. **Topography:** The Tell, located on the coast, comprises fertile plains 50-100 miles wide, with a moderate climate and adequate rain. Two major chains of the Atlas Mts., running roughly E-W, and reaching 7,000 ft., enclose a dry plateau region. Below lies the Sahara, mostly desert with major mineral resources. **Capital:** Algiers (El Djazair). **Cities** (1987 est.): El Djazair 1,483,000; Wahran 590,000; Qacentina 483,000.

Government: Type: Republic. **Head of state:** Pres. Chadli Benjedid; b. Apr. 14, 1929; in office: Feb. 9, 1979. **Head of government:** Premier Kasdi Merbah; in office: Nov. 5, 1988. **Local divisions:** 48 wilayaat (provinces). **Defense:** 2.5% of GDP (1985).

Economy: Industries: Oil, light industry, autos, textiles, iron & steel. **Chief crops:** Grains, wine-grapes, potatoes, dates, tomatoes, oranges. **Minerals:** Mercury, iron, zinc, lead. **Crude oil reserves** (1987): 4.8 bln. bbls. **Other resources:** Cork trees. **Arable land:** 17%; **Livestock** (1986): cattle: 1.7 mln. sheep: 3 mln. **Electricity prod.** (1986): 12.4 bln. kwh. **Crude steel prod.** (1986): 1.4 mln. metric tons **Labor force:** 22% agric.; 32% ind. and commerce; 33% government, & services.

Finance: Currency: Dinar (Mar. 1989: 7.06 = $1 US). **Gross national product** (1986): $58.0 bln. **Per capita income** (1986): $2,645. **Imports** (1987): $7.4 bln.; partners: EEC 64%. **Exports** (1986): $7.8 bln.; partners: EEC 74%. **National budget** (1987): $21.3 bln. **International reserves less gold** (Mar. 1989): $646 mln. **Gold:** 5.58 mln. oz t. **Consumer prices** (change in 1988): 5.9%.

Transport: Motor vehicles: in use (1986): 712,000 passenger cars, 471,000 comm. vehicles. **Chief ports:** El Djazair.

Communications: Television sets: 1.5 mln. in use (1986). **Radios:** 3.2 mln. in use (1986). **Telephones in use** (1986): 819,000. **Daily newspaper circ.** (1986): 23 per 1,000 pop.

Health: Life expectancy at birth (1984): 56.7 male; 58.9 female. **Births** (per 1,000 pop. 1987): 34.6. **Deaths** (per 1,000 pop. 1987): 7.0. **Natural increase** (1987): 2.7%. **Hospital beds** (1987): 63,000. **Physicians** (1987): 17,760. **Infant mortality** (per 1,000 live births 1986): 82.4

Education (1987): **Literacy:** 52%. **School:** Free and compulsory to age 16; Attendance: 94% primary, 47% secondary.

Major International Organizations: UN (FAO, IMF, WHO), OAU, Arab League, OPEC.

Embassy: 2118 Kalorama Rd. NW, 20008; 328-5300.

Earliest known inhabitants were ancestors of Berbers, followed by Phoenicians, Romans, Vandals, and, finally, Arabs. Turkey ruled 1518 to 1830, when France took control.

Large-scale European immigration and French cultural inroads did not prevent an Arab nationalist movement from launching guerilla war. Peace, and French withdrawal, was negotiated with French Pres. Charles de Gaulle. One million Europeans left.

Ahmed Ben Bella was the victor of infighting, and ruled 1962-65, when an army coup installed Col. Houari Boumedienne as leader.

In 1967, Algeria declared war with Israel, broke with U.S., and moved toward eventual military and political ties with the USSR. Some 500 died in riots protesting economic hardship in 1988. In 1989, voters approved a new constitution which cleared the way for a multiparty system and guaranteed "fundamental rights and freedoms" of Algerians.

Andorra

Principality of Andorra

Principat d'Andorra

People: Population (1989 est.): 56,000. **Age distrib.** (%): 0–14: 19.0; 14–59: 68.5; 60+: 12.5. **Pop. density:** 302 per sq. mi. **Ethnic groups:** Catalan 61%, Spanish 30%, Andorran 6%, French 3%. **Languages:** Catalan (official), Spanish, French. **Religion:** Roman Catholic.

Geography: Area: 185 sq. mi., half the size of New York City. **Location:** In Pyrenees Mtns. **Neighbors:** Spain on S, France on N. **Topography:** High mountains and narrow valleys over the country. **Capital:** Andorra la Vella.

Government: Type: Co-principality. **Head of state:** Co-princes are the president of France and the Roman Catholic bishop of Urgel in Spain. **Local divisions:** 7 parishes.

Economy: Industries: Tourism, tobacco products. **Labor force:** 20% agric.; 80% ind. and commerce; services; government.

Finance: Currency: French franc, Spanish peseta.

Communications: Television sets: 4,000 in use (1986). **Radios:** 8,000 in use (1986). **Telephones in use** (1982): 17,719.

Health: Births (per 1,000 pop. 1987): 11.1. **Deaths** (per 1,000 pop. 1987): 3.7. **Natural increase** (1987): 0.7%.

Education (1987): **Literacy:** 99%. School compulsory to age 16.

The present political status, with joint sovereignty by France and the bishop of Urgel, dates from 1278.

Tourism, especially skiing, is the economic mainstay. A free port, allowing for an active trading center, draws some 10 million tourists annually. The ensuing economic prosperity accompanied by Andorra's virtual law-free status, has given rise to calls for reform.

Angola

People's Republic of Angola

República Popular de Angola

People: Population (1989 est.): 8,971,000. **Pop. density:** 18 per sq. mi. **Ethnic groups:** Ovimbundu 38%, Kimbundu 25%; Bakongo 15%, Lunda-Chokwe 8%; Nganguela 6%. **Languages:** Portuguese (official), various Bantu languages. **Religions:** Roman Catholic 68%, Protestant 20%, animist.

Geography: Area: 481,353 sq. mi., larger than Texas and California combined. **Location:** In SW Africa on Atlantic coast. **Neighbors:** Namibia (SW Africa) on S, Zambia on E, Zaire on N; Cabinda, an enclave separated from rest of country by short Atlantic coast of Zaire, borders Congo Republic. **Topography:** Most of Angola consists of a plateau elevated 3,000 to 5,000 feet above sea level, rising from a narrow coastal strip. There is also a temperate highland area in the west-central region, a desert in the S, and a tropical rain forest covering Cabinda. **Capital:** Luanda (1988 est.): 1.1 mln.

Government: Type: Marxist people's republic, one-party rule. **Head of state:** Pres. Jose Eduardo dos Santos b. Aug. 28, 1942; in office: Sept. 20, 1979. **Local divisions:** 18 provinces. **Defense:** 14.3% of GNP (1984).

Economy: Industries: Food processing, textiles, mining, tires, petroleum. **Chief crops:** Coffee, bananas. **Minerals:** Iron, diamonds (over 2 mln. carats a year), copper, phosphates, oil. **Crude oil reserves** (1987): 1.9 bln. bbls. **Arable land:** 3%. **Fish catch** (1986): 58,000 metric tons. **Electricity prod.** (1986): 851 mln.kwh. **Labor force:** 75% agric., 15% industry.

Finance: Currency: Kwanza (Nov. 1988: 29.90 = $1 US). **Gross domestic product** (1985): $4.5 bln. **Imports** (1986): $1.1 bln.; partners: Portugal 9%, Fra. 12%; U.S. 9.2%. **Exports** (1986): $1.4 bln.; partners: U.S. 38%.

Transport: Motor vehicles: in use (1984): 56,000 passenger cars, 29,000 comm. vehicles. **Chief ports:** Cabinda, Lobito, Luanda.

Communications: Radios: 400,000 in use (1986). **Telephones in use** (1987): 40,000. **Daily newspaper circ.** (1984): 13 per 1,000 pop.

Health: Life expectancy at birth (1987): 41.0 male; 44.0 female. **Births** (per 1,000 pop. 1986): 47.3. **Deaths** (per 1,000 pop. 1986): 21.9. **Natural increase** (1986): 2.5%. **Hospital beds** (1986): 13,000. **Physicians** (1986): 655. **Infant mortality** (per 1,000 live births 1986): 200.

Education (1987): **Literacy:** 30%.

Major International Organizations: UN (ILO, WHO), OAU.

From the early centuries AD to 1500, Bantu tribes penetrated most of the region. Portuguese came in 1583, allied with the Bakongo kingdom in the north, and developed the slave trade. Large-scale colonization did not begin until the 20th century, when 400,000 Portuguese immigrated.

A guerrilla war begun in 1961 lasted until 1974, when Portugal offered independence. Violence between the National Front, based in Zaire, the Soviet-backed Popular Movement, and the National Union, aided by the U.S. and S. Africa, killed thousands of blacks, drove most whites to emigrate, and completed economic ruin. Cuban troops and Soviet aid helped the Popular Movement win most of the country after independence Nov. 11, 1975, igniting a Civil War.

S. African troops crossed the southern Angolan border June 7, 1981, killing more than 300 civilians and occupying several towns. The S. Africans withdrew in Sept.

Jonas Savimbi, leader of the National Union for Total Independence of Angola (UNITA), a rebel group fighting to overthrow the government, visited the U.S. in 1986 and was favorably received by the Reagan administration.

An agreement was signed Dec. 1988 between Angola, Cuba, and S. Africa on a timetable for withdrawal of Cuban troops (1991), and for the independence of Namibia. The 14-year war ended June 22, 1989, as the government and the rebels agreed to a cease fire.

Antigua and Barbuda

People: Population (1989 est.) 86,000. **Urban:** (1985) 34%. **Ethnic groups:** Mostly African. **Language:** English (official). **Religion:** Predominantly Church of England.

Geography: Area: 171 sq. mi. **Location:** Eastern Caribbean. **Neighbors:** approx. 30 mi. north of Guadeloupe. **Capital:** St. John's, (1988 est.) 27,000.

Government: Type: Constitutional monarchy with British-style parliament. **Head of State:** Queen Elizabeth II; represented by Sir Wilfred E. Jacobs. **Head of Government:** Prime Min. Vere Cornwall Bird; b. Dec. 7, 1910; in office Nov. 1, 1981.

Economy: Industries: manufacturing, tourists (195,000 in 1984). **Arable Land:** 18%.

Finance: Currency: East Caribbean dollar (Jan. 1989): 2.70 = $1 U.S. **Gross national product** (1986): $188 mln.

Health: infant mortality (per 1,000 live births 1985): 31.5.

Education (1988): **Literacy:** 90%.

Major International Organizations: UN, Commonwealth of Nations.

Embassy: 2400 International Dr., NW 20008; 362-5122.

Antigua was discovered by Columbus in 1493. The British colonized it in 1632.

The British associated state of Antigua achieved independence as Antigua and Barbuda on Nov. 1, 1981. The government maintains close relations with the U.S., United Kingdom, and Venezuela.

Argentina

Argentine Republic

República Argentina

People: Population (1989 est.): 32,617,000. **Age distrib.** (%): 0–14: 31.1; 15–59: 56.6; 60+: 12.3. **Pop. density:** 30 per sq. mi. **Urban** (1986): 80%. **Ethnic groups:** Europeans 97% (Spanish, Italian), Indians, Mestizos, Arabs. **Languages:** Spanish (official), English, Italian, German, French. **Religions:** Roman Catholic 92%.

Geography: Area: 1,065,189 sq. mi., 4 times the size of Texas, second largest in S. America. **Location:** Occupies most of southern S. America. **Neighbors:** Chile on W, Bolivia, Paraguay on N, Brazil, Uruguay on NE. **Topography:** The mountains in W: the Andean, Central, Misiones, and Southern. Aconcagua is the highest peak in the Western hemisphere, alt. 22,834 ft. E of the Andes are heavily wooded plains, called the Gran Chaco in the N, and the fertile, treeless Pampas in the central region. Patagonia, in the S, is bleak and arid. Rio de la Plata, 170 by 140 mi., is mostly fresh water, from 2,485-mi. Parana and 1,000-mi. Uruguay rivers. **Capital:** Buenos Aires. (The Senate has approved the moving of the capital to the Patagonia Region). **Cities** (1982 est.): Buenos Aires 2,908,000; Cordoba 969,000; Rosario 750,455; Mendoza 597,000; San Miguel de Tucuman 497,000.

Government: Type: Republic. **Head of state:** Pres. Carlos Saúl Menem; b. July 2, 1930; in office: July 1, 1989. **Local divisions:** 22 provinces, 1 natl. terr. and 1 federal dist., under military governors. **Defense:** 3.3% of GNP (1985).

Economy: Industries: Meat processing, flour milling, chemicals, textiles, machinery, autos. **Chief crops:** Grains, corn, grapes, linseed, sugar, tobacco, rice, soybeans, citrus fruits. **Minerals:** Oil, lead, zinc, iron, copper, uranium. **Crude oil reserves** (1987): 2.1 bln. bbls. **Arable land:** 13%. **Livestock** (1986): cattle: 54 mln.; sheep: 26 mln; pigs: 4 mln. **Fish catch** (1987): 420,000 metric tons. **Electricity prod.** (1986): 42.7 bln. kwh. **Crude steel prod.** (1987): 3.6 mln. metric tons. **Labor force:** 19% agric.; 36% ind. and comm.; 20% services.

Finance: Currency: Austral (June 1989: 150 = $1 US). **Gross national product** (1986): $72.9 bln. **Per capita income** (1978 est.): $2,331. **Imports** (1987): $5.8 bln.; partners: U.S. 18%, W. Ger. 9%, Braz. 16%, Jap. 7%. **Exports** (1987): $6.3 bln.; partners: USSR 13%, Neth. 9%, U.S. 12%. **Tourists** (1986): receipts: $545 mln. **National budget** (1986): $31.3 bln. expenditures. **International reserves less gold** (Jan. 1989): $3.3 bln. **Gold:** 4.37 mln. oz t. **Consumer prices** (change in 1988): 343%.

Transport: Railway traffic (1986): 10.7 bln. passenger-km; 9.5 bln. net ton-km. **Motor vehicles:** in use (1986): 3.8 mln. passenger cars, 1.4 mln. comm. vehicles. **Civil aviation:** (1986) 6.6 mln. passenger-km; 538 mln. net ton-km. **Chief ports:** Buenos Aires, Bahia Blanca, La Plata.

Communications: Television sets: 5.9 mln. in use (1986). **Radios:** 19 mln. in use (1985). **Telephones in use** (1986): 3.2 mln. **Daily newspaper circ.** (1986): 88 per 1,000 pop.

Health: Life expectancy at birth (1983): 66.8 male; 73.2 female. **Births** (per 1,000 pop. 1987): 20.7. **Deaths** (per 1,000 pop. 1987): 8.6 **Natural increase** (1987): 1.2%. **Hospital beds** (1980): 150,010. **Physicians** (1986): 79,000. **Infant mortality** (per 1,000 live births 1988): 35.3.

Education (1988): **Literacy:** 92%. **School attendence:** 21.5% through secondary school.

Major International Organizations: UN (WHO, IMF, FAO), OAS.

Embassy: 1600 New Hampshire Ave. NW 20009; 939-6400.

Nomadic Indians roamed the Pampas when Spaniards arrived, 1515-1516, led by Juan Diaz de Solis. Nearly all the Indians were killed by the late 19th century. The colonists won independence, 1810-1819, and a long period of disorders ended in a strong centralized government.

Large-scale Italian, German, and Spanish immigration in the decades after 1880 spurred modernization, making Argentina the most prosperous, educated, and industrialized of the major Latin American nations. Social reforms were enacted in the 1920s, but military coups prevailed 1930-46, until the election of Gen. Juan Peron as president.

Peron, with his wife Eva Duarte effected labor reforms, but also suppressed speech and press freedoms, closed religious schools, and ran the country into debt. A 1955 coup exiled Peron, who was followed by a series of military and civilian regimes. Peron returned in 1973, and was once more elected president. He died 10 months later, succeeded by his wife, Isabel, who had been elected vice president, and who became the first woman head of state in the Western hemisphere.

A military junta seized Mrs. Peron in 1976 amid charges of corruption. Under a continuing state of siege, the army battled guerrillas and leftists, killed 5,000 people, and jailed and tortured others. On Dec. 9, 1985, after a trial of 5 months and nearly 1,000 witnesses, 5 former junta members, including ex-presidents Jorge Videla and Gen. Roberto Eduardo Viola, were found guilty of murder and human rights abuses.

A severe worsening in economic conditions placed extreme pressure on the military government.

Argentine troops seized control of the British-held Falkland Islands on Apr. 2, 1982. Both countries had claimed sovereignty over the islands, located 250 miles off the Argentine coast, since 1833. The British dispatched a task force and declared a total air and sea blockade around the Falklands. Fighting began May 1; several hundred lost their lives as the result of the destruction of a British destroyer and the sinking of an Argentine cruiser.

British troops landed in force on East Falkland Island May 21. By June 2, the British had surrounded Stanley, the capital city and Argentine stronghold. The Argentine troops surrendered, June 14; Argentine President Leopoldo Galtieri resigned June 17.

Democratic rule returned to Argentina in 1983 as Raul Alfonsin's Radical Civic Union gained an absolute majority in the presidential electoral college and Congress. In 1989 the nation was plagued by severe financial problems as inflation reached crisis levels; over 6,000%. The hyperinflation sparked a week of looting and rioting in several cities; the government declared a 30-day state of siege May 29. (*See Chronology*).

Australia
Commonwealth of Australia

People: Population (1989 est.): 16,090,000. **Age distrib. (%):** 0–14: 22.6; 15–59; 62.2; ; 59 +: 15.2. **dop. density:** 5.4 per sq. mi. **Urban** (1984): 85%. **Ethnic groups:** European 93%, Asian 5%, aborigines (including mixed) 1.5%. **Languages:** English, aboriginal languages. **Religions:** Anglican 26%, other Protestant 25%, Roman Catholic 25%.

Geography: Area: 2,966,200 sq. mi., almost as large as the continental U.S. **Location:** SE of Asia, Indian O. is W and S, Pacific O. (Coral, Tasman seas) is E; they meet N of Australia in Timor and Arafura seas: Tasmania lies 150 mi. S of Victoria state, across Bass Strait. **Neighbors:** Nearest are Indonesia, Papua New Guinea on N, Solomons, Fiji, and New Zealand on E. **Topography:** An island continent. The Great Dividing Range along the E coast has Mt. Kosciusko, 7,310 ft. The W plateau rises to 2,000 ft., with arid areas in the Great Sandy and Great Victoria deserts. The NW part of Western Australia and Northern Terr. are arid and hot. The NE has heavy rainfall and Cape York Peninsula has jungles. The Murray R. rises in New South Wales and flows 1,600 mi. to the Indian O. **Capital:** Canberra. **Cities** (1987 est.): Sydney 3,500,000; Melbourne 3,000,000; Brisbane 1,200,000; Adelaide 993,000; Perth 1,100,000.

Government: Type: Democratic, federal state system. **Head of state:** Queen Elizabeth II, represented by Gov.-Gen. Ninian Martin Stephen; in office: July 29, 1982. **Head of government:** Prime Min. Robert James Lee Hawke; b. Dec. 9, 1929; in office: Mar. 11, 1983. **Local divisions:** 6 states, 2 territories. **Defense:** 2.7% of GNP (1988).

Economy: Industries: Iron, steel, textiles, electrical equip., chemicals, autos, aircraft, ships, machinery. **Chief crops:** Wheat (a leading export), barley, oats, corn, hay, sugar, wine, fruit, vegetables. **Minerals:** Coal, copper, iron, lead, tin, uranium, zinc. **Crude oil reserves** (1987): 1.6 bln. bbls. **Other resources:** Wool (30% of world output). **Arable land:** 9%. **Livestock** (1987): cattle: 21 mln.; sheep: 154 mln.; pigs: 2.4 mln. **Fish catch** (1987): 156,000 metric tons. **Electricity prod.** (1987): 130 bln. kwh. **Crude steel prod.** (1987): 6.1 mln. metric tons. **Labor force:** 6% agric.; 22% services; 34% trade & manuf.

Finance: Currency: Dollar (June 1989: 1.29 = $1.00 US). **Gross national product** (1988): $220 bln. **Per capita income** (1988): $14,458. **Imports** (1988): $36.0 bln; partners: U.S. 21%,

Jap. 20%, UK 7%. **Exports** (1988): $32.9 bln.; partners: Jap. 27%, U.S. 11%, NZ 5%. **Tourists** (1986): $1.3 bln. receipts. **National budget** (1989): $65 bln. expenditures. **International reserves less gold** (Mar. 1989): $12.8 bln. **Gold:** 7.93 mln. oz t. **Consumer prices** (change in 1988): 7.2%.

Transport: Railway traffic (1986): 48 bln. net ton-km. **Motor vehicles:** in use (1986): 8.7 mln. passenger cars, 1.2 mln. comm. vehicles. **Civil aviation** (1987): 22.7 mln. passenger-km.; 2.0 bln. freight ton-km. **Chief ports:** Sydney, Melbourne, Newcastle, Port Kembla, Fremantle, Geelong.

Communications: Television sets: 6.5 mln. (1985). **Radios:** 20 mln. (1985). **Telephones in use** (1985): 8.7 mln. **Daily newspaper circ.** (1982): 426 per 1,000 pop.

Health: Life expectancy at birth (1986): 72.3 male; 78.8 female. **Births** (per 1,000 pop. 1987): 15.2. **Deaths** (per 1,000 pop. 1987): 7.5. **Natural increase** (1987): .7%. **Hospital beds** (1986): 87,000. **Physicians** (1982): 27,500. **Infant mortality** (per 1,000 live births 1989): 8.1.

Education (1989): **Literacy:** 99%. **School:** compulsory to age 15; attendance 94%.

Major International Organizations: UN and all its specialized agencies, OECD, Commonwealth of Nations.

Embassy: 1601 Massachusetts Ave NW 20036; 797-3000.

Capt. James Cook explored the E coast in 1770, when the continent was inhabited by a variety of different tribes. Within decades, Britain had claimed the entire continent, which became a penal colony until immigration increased in the 1850s. The commonwealth was proclaimed Jan. 1, 1901. Northern Terr. was granted limited self-rule July 1, 1978. Their capitals and 1987 population estimates:

	Area (sq. mi.)	Population
New South Wales, Sydney	309,500	5,581,300
Victoria, Melbourne	87,900	4,188,300
Queensland, Brisbane	666,990	2,616,300
South Aust., Adelaide	379,900	1,378,900
Western Aust., Perth	975,100	1,458,700
Tasmania, Hobart	26,200	448,600
Aust. Capital Terr., Canberra	900	267,600
Northern Terr., Darwin	519,800	150,300

Australia's racially discriminatory immigration policies were abandoned in 1973, after 3 million Europeans (half British) had entered since 1945. The 50,000 aborigines and 150,000 part-aborigines are mostly detribalized, but there are several preserves in the Northern Territory. They remain economically disadvantaged.

On Jan. 26, 1988, some 15,000 aborigines demonstrated in Sydney to protest discrimination while the rest of the nation celebrated the 200th anniversary of the landing of the first European settlers.

Australia's agricultural success made it among the top exporters of beef, lamb, wool, and wheat. Major mineral deposits have been developed as well, largely for exports. Industrialization has been completed.

Australia harbors many plant and animal species not found elsewhere, including the kangaroo, koala bear, platypus, dingo (wild dog), Tasmanian devil (racoon-like marsupial), wombat (bear-like marsupial), and barking and frilled lizards.

Australian External Territories

Norfolk Is., area 13½ sq. mi., pop. (1985) 1,800, was taken over, 1914. The soil is very fertile, suitable for citrus fruits, bananas, and coffee. Many of the inhabitants are descendants of the Bounty mutineers, moved to Norfolk 1856 from Pitcairn Is. Australia offered the island limited home rule, 1978.

Coral Sea Is. Territory, 1 sq. mi., is administered from Norfolk Is.

Territory of Ashmore and Cartier Is., area 2 sq. mi., in the Indian O. came under Australian authority 1934 and are administered as part of Northern Territory. **Heard** and **McDonald Is.** are administered by the Dept. of Science.

Cocos (Keeling) Is., 27 small coral islands in the Indian O. 1,750 mi. NW of Australia. Pop. (1981) 569, area: 5½ sq. mi. The residents voted to become part of Australia, Apr. 1984.

Christmas Is., 52 sq. mi., pop. 3,000 (1983), 230 mi. S of Java, was transferred by Britain in 1958. It has phosphate deposits.

Australian Antarctic Territory was claimed by Australia in 1933, including 2,472,000 sq. mi. of territory S of 60th parallel S Lat. and between 160th-45th meridians E Long.

Austria

Republic of Austria

Republik Österreich

People: Population (1989 est.): 7,555,000. **Age distrib. (%):** 0–14: 17.7; 15–59: 62.1; 60+: 20.2. **Pop. density:** 233 per sq. mi. **Urban** (1986): 55.0%. **Ethnic groups:** German 98%, Slovene, Croatian. **Languages:** German 98%. **Religions:** Roman Catholic 85%.

Geography: Area: 32,374 sq. mi., slightly smaller than Maine. **Location:** In S Central Europe. **Neighbors:** Switzerland, Liechtenstein on W, W. Germany, Czechoslovakia on N, Hungary on E, Yugoslavia, Italy on S. **Topography:** Austria is primarily mountainous, with the Alps and foothills covering the western and southern provinces. The eastern provinces and Vienna are located in the Danube River Basin. **Capital:** Vienna. **Cities** (1987 cen.): Vienna 1,500,000.

Government: Type: Parliamentary democracy. **Head of state:** Pres. Kurt Waldheim; b. Dec. 21, 1918; in office: June 8, 1986. **Head of government:** Chancellor Franz Vranitzky; b. Oct. 4, 1937; in office: June 16, 1986. **Local divisions:** 9 lander (states), each with a legislature. **Defense:** 1.3% of GNP (1986).

Economy: Industries: Steel, machinery, autos, electrical and optical equip., glassware, sport goods, paper, textiles, chemicals, cement. **Chief crops:** Grains, potatoes, beets. **Minerals:** Iron ore, oil, magnesite. **Crude oil reserves** (1985): 116 mln. bbls. **Other resources:** Forests, hydro power. **Arable land:** 18.3%. **Livestock:** (1986): Cattle: 2.6 mln.; pigs: 3.8 mln. **Electricity prod.** (1986): 46.4 bln. kwh. **Crude steel prod.** (1987): 4.3 mln. metric tons. **Labor force:** 8% agric.; 35% ind. & comm.; 56% service.

Finance: Currency: Schilling (June 1989: 14.13 = $1 US). **Gross national product** (1986): $94.7 bln. **Per capita income** (1986): $12,521. **Imports** (1988): $36.0 bln.; partners: W. Ger. 44%, It. 9%, Switz. 5%. **Exports** (1988): $31.0 bln.; partners: W. Ger. 33%, It. 9%, Switz. 7%. **Tourists** (1985): receipts: $6.0 bln. **National budget** (1984): $20.3 bln. expenditures. **International reserves less gold** (Mar. 1989): $7.0 bln. **Gold:** 21.15 mln. oz t. **Consumer prices** (change in 1988): 1.9%.

Transport: Railway traffic (1986): 7.3 bln. passenger-km; 11.2 bln. net ton-km. **Motor vehicles:** in use (1987): 2.6 mln. passenger cars, 212,000 comm. **Civil aviation** (1986): 1.3 bln. passenger-km; 23.4 mln. freight ton-km.

Communications: Television sets: 2.6 mln. (1987). **Radios:** 2.6 mln. (1987). **Telephones in use** (1987): 3.8 mln. **Daily newspaper circ.** (1985): 312 per 1,000 pop.

Health: Life expectancy at birth (1981): 69.3 male; 76.4 female. **Births** (per 1,000 pop. 1986): 11.5. **Deaths** (per 1,000 pop. 1986): 11.5. **Natural increase** (1986): –.0%. **Hospital beds** (1986): 83,021. **Physicians** (1986): 21,676. **Infant mortality** (per 1,000 live births 1987): 10.6.

Education (1987): Literacy: 99%. School years compulsory 9; attendance 95%.

Major International Organizations: UN and all of its specialized agencies, EFTA, OECD.

Embassy: 2343 Massachusetts Ave. NW 20008; 483-4474.

Rome conquered Austrian lands from Celtic tribes around 15 BC. In 788 the territory was incorporated into Charlemagne's empire. By 1300, the House of Hapsburg had gained control; they added vast territories in all parts of Europe to their realm in the next few hundred years.

Austrian dominance of Germany was undermined in the 18th century and ended by Prussia by 1866. But the Congress of Vienna, 1815, confirmed Austrian control of a large empire in southeast Europe consisting of Germans, Hungarians, Slavs, Italians, and others.

The dual Austro-Hungarian monarchy was established in 1867, giving autonomy to Hungary and almost 50 years of peace.

World War I, started after the June 28, 1914 assassination of Archduke Franz Ferdinand, the Hapsburg heir, by a Serbian nationalist, destroyed the empire. By 1918 Austria was reduced to a small republic, with the borders it has today:

Nazi Germany invaded Austria Mar. 13, 1938. The republic was reestablished in 1945, under Allied occupation. Full independence and neutrality were restored in 1955.

Austria produces most of its food, as well as an array of industrial products. A large part of Austria's economy is controlled by state enterprises. Socialists have shared or alternated power with the conservative People's Party.

Economic agreements with the Common Market give Austria access to a free-trade area encompassing most of West Europe.

An international panel of historians issued a report in 1988 which concluded that Pres. Kurt Waldheim knew of war crimes in Greece and Yugoslavia while serving in the German army during WW 2, did nothing to stop them, and later covered up his war record. The panel found no evidence that Waldheim committed war crimes.

The Bahamas

The Commonwealth of the Bahamas

People: Population (1989 est.): 247,000. **Age distrib. (%):** 0–14: 38.0; 15–59: 56.3; 60+: 5.7. **Pop. density:** 45 per sq. mi. **Urban** (1987): 75%. **Ethnic groups:** black 85%, white (British, Canadian, U.S.) 15%. **Languages:** English. **Religions:** Baptist 29%, Anglican 23%, Roman Catholic 22%.

Geography: Area: 5,380 sq. mi., about the size of Connecticut. **Location:** In Atlantic O., E of Florida. **Neighbors:** Nearest are U.S. on W, Cuba on S. **Topography:** Nearly 700 islands (30 inhabited) and over 2,000 islets in the western Atlantic extend 760 mi. NW to SE. **Capital:** Nassau. **Cities:** (1985 est.) New Providence 135,437; Freeport 16,000.

Government: Type: Independent commonwealth. **Head of state:** Queen Elizabeth II, represented by Gov.-Gen. Henry Taylor, in office: June 25, 1988. **Head of government:** Prime Min. Lynden Oscar Pindling; b. Mar. 22, 1930; in office: Jan. 16, 1967. **Local divisions:** 18 districts.

Economy: Industries: Tourism (70% of GNP), rum, banking, pharmaceuticals. **Chief crops:** Fruits, vegetables. **Minerals:** Salt. **Other resources:** Lobsters. **Arable land:** 2%. **Electricity prod.** (1986): 885 mln. kwh. **Labor force:** 5% agric.; 25% tourism, 30% government.

Finance: Currency: Dollar (June 1988: 1 = $1 US). **Gross national product** (1986): $1.7 bln. **Per capita income** (1986): $7,598. **Imports** (1987): $1.7 bln.; partners: U.S. 74%, EC 30%. **Exports** (1987): $733 mln. (not incl. oil); partners: U.S. 41%, U.K. 7%. **Tourists** (1987): $1.0 bln. **National budget** (1987): $404 mln. expenditures. **International reserves less gold** (Mar. 1989): $175 mln. **Consumer prices** (change in 1988): 4.1%.

Transport: Motor vehicles: in use (1984): 88,000 passenger cars, 5,600 comm. vehicles. **Chief ports:** Nassau, Freeport.

Communications: Radios: 120,000 in use (1986). **Television sets** (1986): 40,000. **Telephones in use** (1986): 108,000. **Daily newspaper circ.** (1986): 118 per 1,000 pop.

Health: Life expectancy at birth (1987): 64.0 male; 70 female. **Births** (per 1,000 pop. 1987): 16.7. **Deaths** (per 1,000 pop. 1987): 5.0. **Natural increase** (1987): 1.1%. **Infant mortality** (per 1,000 live births 1987): 29.8.

Education (1988): Literacy: 93%; School compulsory through age 14.

Major International Organizations: UN (World Bank, IMF, WHO), OAS.

Embassy: 600 New Hampshire Ave. NW 20037; 338-3940.

Christopher Columbus first set foot in the New World on San Salvador (Watling I.) in 1492, when Arawak Indians inhabited the islands. British settlement began in 1647; the islands became a British colony in 1783. Internal self-government was granted in 1964; full independence within the Commonwealth was attained July 10, 1973.

International banking and investment management has become a major industry alongside tourism, despite controversy over financial irregularities.

Bahrain

State of Bahrain

Dawlat al-Bahrayn

People: Population (1989 est.): 483,000. **Age distrib. (%):** 0–14: 33.4; 15–59: 62.8; 60+: 3.8. **Pop. density:** 1,872 per sq. mi. **Urban** (1986): 82%. **Ethnic groups:** Bahraini 63%, Asian

13%, other Arab 10%, Iranian 6%. **Languages:** Arabic (official), Persian. **Religions:** Sunni Moslem 30%, Shi'ah Moslem 70%.

Geography: Area: 258 sq. mi., smaller than New York City. **Location:** In Persian Gulf. **Neighbors:** Nearest are Saudi Arabia on W. Qatar on E. **Topography:** Bahrain Island, and several adjacent, smaller islands, are flat, hot and humid, with little rain. **Capital:** Manama. **Cities** (1987 est.): Manama 146,000.

Government: Type: Traditional monarchy. **Head of state:** Amir Isa bin Sulman al-Khalifa; b. July 3, 1933; in office: Nov. 2, 1961. **Head of government:** Prime Min. Kahlifa ibn Sulman al-Khalifa; b. 1935; in office: Jan. 19, 1970. **Local divisions:** 6 towns and cities. **Defense:** 4.0% of GNP (1985).

Economy: Industries: Oil products, aluminum smelting. **Chief crops:** Fruits, vegetables. **Minerals:** Oil, gas. **Crude oil reserves** (1985): 173 mln. bbls. **Arable land:** 5%. **Electricity prod.** (1986): 6.8 bln. kwh. **Labor force:** 4% agric.; 84% ind. and commerce; 5% services; 3% gov.

Finance: Currency: Dinar (Mar. 1989: 1.00 = $2.66 US). **Gross national product** (1987): $4.6 bln. **Per capita income** (1982 est.): $11,900. **Imports** (1987): $2.6 bln.; partners: Sau. Ar. 60%, UK 6%, U.S. 9%. **Exports** (1987): $2.3 bln.; partners: UAE 18%, Jap. 12%, Sing. 10%, U.S. 6%. **National Budget** (1987): $2.6 bln. expenditures. **International reserves less gold** (Mar. 1989): $1.1 bln. **Gold:** 150,000 oz t. **Consumer prices** (change in 1988): −0.3%.

Transport: Motor vehicles: in use (1986): 81,000 passenger cars, 24,000 comm. vehicles. **Chief ports:** Sitra.

Communications: Television sets: 114,000 in use (1986). **Radios:** 200,000 in use (1986). **Telephones in use** (1986): 119,000.

Health: Life Expectancy at Birth (1986): 65.0 male; 68.4 female. **Births** (per 1,000 pop. 1986): 36.8. **Deaths** (per 1,000 pop. 1986): 5.8. **Natural Increase** (1986): 3.1. Medical services are free.

Education (1987): **Literacy:** 74%.

Major International Organizations: UN (GATT, IMF, WHO), Arab League.

Embassy: 3502 International Dr. NW 20008; 342-0741.

Long ruled by the Khalifa family, Bahrain was a British protectorate from 1861 to 1971, when it regained independence.

Pearls, shrimp, fruits, and vegetables were the mainstays of the economy until oil was discovered in 1932. By the 1970s, oil reserves were depleted; international banking thrived.

Bahrain took part in the 1973-74 Arab oil embargo against the U.S. and other nations. The government bought controlling interest in the oil industry in 1975.

Saudi Arabia has built a 15-mile causeway linking Bahrain with the Arab mainland.

Bangladesh

People's Republic of Bangladesh

Gama Prajãtantri Bangladesh

People: Population (1989 est.): 112,757,000. **Age distrib.** (%): 0-14: 44.3; 15-59: 50.4; 60+: 5.3. **Pop. density:** 2,028 per sq. mi. **Urban** (1985): 20%. **Ethnic groups:** Bengali 98%, Bihari, tribesmen. **Languages:** Bengali (official), English. **Religions:** Moslem 83%, Hindu 16%.

Geography: Area: 55,598 sq. mi. slightly smaller than Wisconsin. **Location:** In S Asia, on N bend of Bay of Bengal. **Neighbors:** India nearly surrounds country on W, N, E; Burma on SE. **Topography:** The country is mostly a low plain cut by the Ganges and Brahmaputra rivers and their delta. The land is alluvial and marshy along the coast, with hills only in the extreme SE and NE. A tropical monsoon climate prevails, among the rainiest in the world. **Capital:** Dhaka. **Cities** (1987 est.): Dhaka (met.) 3.4 mln.; Chittagong (met.) 1.4 mln.; Khulna (met.) 646,000.

Government: Type: Islamic republic. **Head of state:** Pres. Hossain Mohammad Ershad; b. Feb. 1, 1930, in office: Dec. 11, 1983. **Head of Government:** Prime Min. Moudud Ahmed, in office: Mar. 27, 1988. **Local divisions:** 20 districts. **Defense:** 1.7% of GNP (1985).

Economy: Industries: Cement, jute, textiles, fertilizers, petroleum products. **Chief crops:** Jute (most of world output), rice, tea. **Minerals:** Natural gas, offshore oil, coal. **Livestock** (1986): cattle: 23 mln.; goats: 10.7 mln. **Fish catch** (1986): 763,000 metric tons. **Electricity prod.** (1986): 5.1 bln. kwh. **Labor force:** 74% agric; 11% ind.; 15% services.

Finance: Currency: Taka (Mar. 1989: 32.27 = $1 US). **Gross national product** (1986): $16.0 bln. **Per capita income** (1986) $113. **Imports** (1987): $2.6 bln.; partners: Jap. 13%, U.S. 13%. **Exports** (1988): $1.2 bln.; partners: U.S. 31%, It. 9%; Pak 5%. **Tourists** (1986): $14.6 mln. receipts. **International reserves less gold** (Mar. 1989): $1.0 bln. **Gold:** 74,000 oz t. **Consumer prices** (change in 1988): 9.3%.

Transport: Railway traffic (1986): 6.0 bln. passenger-km; 612 mln. net ton-km. **Motor vehicles:** in use (1986): 40,000 passenger cars, 24,000 comm. vehicles. **Chief ports:** Chittagong, Khulna.

Communications: Radios: 775,000 (1985). **Television sets:** 368,000 (1986). **Telephones in use** (1986): 163,000. **Daily newspaper circ.** (1986) 6 per 1,000 pop.

Health: Life expectancy at birth (1987): 50.5 male; 49.6 female. **Births** (per 1,000 pop. 1987): 42.1. **Deaths** (per 1,000 pop. 1987): 15.9. **Natural increase** (1987): 2.6%. **Hospital beds** (1985): 31,900. **Physicians** (1985): 16,294. **Infant mortality** (per 1,000 live births 1987): 120.

Education (1985): **Literacy:** 33%. **Attendance:** 24% primary school; 4% secondary school.

Major International Organizations: UN (GATT, IMF, WHO).

Embassy: 2201 Wisconsin Ave. NW 20007; 342-8372.

Moslem invaders conquered the formerly Hindu area in the 12th century. British rule lasted from the 18th century to 1947, when East Bengal became part of Pakistan.

Charging West Pakistani domination, the Awami League, based in the East, won National Assembly control in 1971. Assembly sessions were postponed; riots broke out. Pakistani troops attacked Mar. 25; Bangladesh independence was proclaimed the next day. In the ensuing civil war, one million died and 10 million fled to India.

War between India and Pakistan broke out Dec. 3, 1971. Pakistan surrendered in the East Dec. 15. Sheik Mujibur Rahman became prime minister. The country moved into the Indian and Soviet orbits, in response to U.S. support of Pakistan, and much of the economy was nationalized.

In 1974, the government took emergency powers to curb widespread violence; Mujibur was assassinated and a series of coups followed.

Chronic destitution among the densely crowded population has been worsened by the decline of jute as a major world commodity.

On May 30, 1981, Pres. Ziaur Rahman was shot and killed in an unsuccessful coup attempt by army rivals. Vice President Abdus Sattar assumed the presidency but was ousted in a coup led by army chief of staff Gen. H.M. Ershad, Mar. 1982. Ershad declared Bangladesh an Islamic Republic in 1988. Bangladesh remains one of the world's poorest countries.

In 1988, monsoon rains brought devastation to Bangladesh: over 2,000 died, 30 million were made homeless, and damages were nearly $2 billion.

Barbados

People: Population (1989 est.): 256,000 **Age distrib.** (%): 0-14: 27.3%; 15-59: 59.6; 60+: 12.9. **Pop. density:** 1,542 per sq. mi. **Urban** (1985): 42%. **Ethnic groups:** African 80%, mixed 16%, Caucasian 4%. **Languages:** English. **Religions:** Anglican 70%, Methodist 9%, Roman Catholic 4%.

Geography: Area: 166 sq. mi. **Location:** In Atlantic, farthest E of W. Indies. **Neighbors:** Nearest are Trinidad, Grenada on SW. **Topography:** The island lies alone in the Atlantic almost completely surrounded by coral reefs. Highest point is Mt. Hilaby, 1,115 ft. **Capital:** Bridgetown. **Cities** (1982 est.): Bridgetown 7,600.

Government: Type: Independent sovereign state within the Commonwealth. **Head of state:** Queen Elizabeth II, represented by Gov.-Gen. Hugh Springer. **Head of government:** Prime Min. Erskine Sandiford; b. Mar. 24, 1937; in office: June 1, 1987. **Local divisions:** 11 parishes and Bridgetown.

Economy: Industries: Rum, molasses, tourism. **Chief crops:** Sugar, corn. **Minerals:** Lime. **Other resources:** Fish. **Arable land:** 76%. **Electricity prod.** (1987): 425 mln. kwh. **Labor force:** 6.9% agric.; 12.7% ind. and comm.; 80.9% services and government.

Finance: Currency: Dollar (June 1989: 2.01 = $1 US). **Gross national product** (1986): $1.3 bln. **Per capita income** (1982): $3,040. **Imports** (1988): $582 mln.; partners: U.S. 32%, CARACOM 12%. **Exports** (1988): $173 mln.; partners: U.S.

26%, CARACOM 30%. **Tourists** (1986): $326 mln. receipts. **National budget** (1987): $470 mln. expenditures. **International reserves less gold** (Mar. 1989): $150 mln. **Consumer prices** (change in 1988): 4.7%.

Transport: Motor vehicles: in use (1986): 32,000 passenger cars; 5,200 comm. vehicles. **Chief ports:** Bridgetown.

Communications: Television sets: 62,000 in use (1987). **Radios:** 335,000 in use (1966). **Telephones in use** (1986): 90,000. **Daily newspaper circ.** (1987): 156 per 1,000 pop.

Health: Life expectancy at birth (1987): male: 70.0; female: 75.4. **Births** (per 1,000 pop. 1987): 15.1. **Deaths** (per 1,000 pop. 1987): 8.1. **Natural increase** (1987): .7%. **Hospital beds** (1984): 2,143. **Physicians** (1984): 213. **Infant mortality** (per 1,000 live births 1985): 14.

Education (1987): **Literacy:** 99%. **Years compulsory:** 9.

Major international Organizations: UN (FAO, GATT, ILO, IMF, WHO), OAS.

Embassy: 2144 Wyoming Ave. NW 20008; 387-7374.

Barbados was probably named by Portuguese sailors in reference to bearded fig trees. An English ship visited in 1605, and British settlers arrived on the uninhabited island in 1627. Slaves worked the sugar plantations, but were freed in 1834.

Self-rule came gradually, with full independence proclaimed Nov. 30, 1966. British traditions have remained.

Belgium

Kingdom of Belgium

Koninkrijk België (Dutch)
Royaume de Belgique (French)

People: Population (1989 est.): 9,897,000. **Age distrib. (%):** 0–14: 19.3; 15–59: 61.5; 60+: 19.2. **Pop. density:** 840 per sq. mi. **Urban** (1980): 73%. **Ethnic groups:** Fleming 55%, Walloon 33%. **Languages:** Flemish (Dutch) 57%, French 33%, legally bilingual 10%, German 1%. **Religions:** Roman Catholic 75%.

Geography: Area: 11,779 sq. mi., slightly larger than Maryland. **Location:** in NW Europe, on N. Sea. **Neighbors:** France on W, S, Luxembourg on SE, W. Germany on E, Netherlands on N. **Topography:** Mostly flat, the country is trisected by the Scheldt and Meuse, major commercial rivers. The land becomes hilly and forested in the SE (Ardennes) region. **Capital:** Brussels. **Cities** (1987 est.): Brussels (met.) 973,196; Antwerp (met.) 479,000; Ghent 233,000; Charleroi 209,000; Liege 200,000.

Government: Type: Parliamentary democracy under a constitutional monarch. **Head of state:** King Baudouin; b. Sept. 7, 1930; in office: July 17, 1951. **Head of government:** Premier Wilfried Martens; b. Apr. 19, 1936; in office: Dec. 17, 1981. **Local divisions:** 9 provinces; 3 regions; 3 cultural communities. **Defense:** 3.3% of GNP (1985).

Economy: Industries: Steel, glassware, diamond cutting, textiles, chemicals. **Chief crops:** Grains, fruits, potatoes, sugar beets. **Minerals:** Coal, coke. **Other resources:** Forests. **Arable land** (incl. Lux.): 26.5%. **Livestock** (1986): cattle: 2.9 mln; pigs: 5.7 mln. **Fish catch** (1986): 34,000 metric tons. **Electricity prod.** (1986): 57.4 bln. kwh. **Crude steel prod.** (1987): 9.8 mln. metric tons. **Labor force:** 2% agric.; 26% ind. & comm.; 37% services & transportation; 23% public service.

Finance: Currency: Franc (June 1989: 42.06 = $1 US). **Gross national product** (1986): $111 bln. **Per capita income** (1986): $10,475. *Note:* the following trade and tourist data includes Luxembourg. **Imports** (1987): $83.2 bln.; partners: W. Ger. 23%, Neth. 17%, France 11%, UK 8%, U.S. 5%. **Exports** (1987): $84.0 bln.; partners: W. Ger. 19%, France 18%, Neth. 15%, UK 6%. **Tourists** (1986): receipts: $2.2 bln. **National budget** (1987): $43.5 bln. expenditures. **International reserves less gold** (Mar. 1989): $10.3 bln. **Gold:** 29.58 mln. oz t. **Consumer prices** (change in 1988): 1.2%.

Transport: Railway traffic (1987): 6.0 bln. passenger-km; 7.2 bln. net ton-km. **Motor vehicles:** in use (1987): 3.4 mln. passenger cars, 296,000 comm. **Civil aviation** (1986): 5.5 bln. passenger-km; 594 mln. freight ton-km. **Chief ports:** Antwerp, Zeebrugge, Ghent.

Communications: Television sets: 2.9 mln. licensed (1986). **Radios:** 4.6 mln. licensed (1986); **Telephones in use** (1986): 4.3 mln. **Daily newspaper circ.** (1986): 260 per 1,000 pop.

Health: Life expectancy at birth (1985): 70.1 male; 76.7 female. **Births** (per 1,000 pop. 1987): 11.9. **Deaths** (per 1,000 pop. 1987): 11.3. **Natural increase** (1987) .0%. **Hospital beds** (1984): 90,720. **Physicians:** 29,776. **Infant mortality** (per 1,000 live births 1985): 10.

Education (1987): **Literacy:** 98%. School compulsory to age 16.

Major International Organizations: UN and all of its specialized agencies, NATO, EC, OECD.

Embassy: 330 Garfield St. NW 20008; 333-6900

Belgium derives its name from the Belgae, the first recorded inhabitants, probably Celts. The land was conquered by Julius Caesar, and was ruled for 1800 years by conquerors, including Rome, the Franks, Burgundy, Spain, Austria, and France. After 1815, Belgium was made a part of the Netherlands, but it became an independent constitutional monarchy in 1830.

Belgian neutrality was violated by Germany in both world wars. King Leopold III surrendered to Germany, May 28, 1940. After the war, he was forced by political pressure to abdicate in favor of his son, King Baudouin.

The Flemings of northern Belgium speak Dutch while French is the language of the Walloons in the south. The language difference has been a perennial source of controversy and led to antagonism between the 2 groups. Parliament has passed measures aimed at transferring power from the central government to 3 regions—Wallonia, Flanders, and Brussels.

Belgium lives by its foreign trade; about 50% of its entire production is sold abroad.

Belize

People: Population (1989 est.): 179,400. **Age distrib. (%):** 0–14: 44.9; 15–59: 47.8; 60+: 7.3. **Pop. density:** 20 per sq. mi. **Ethnic groups:** African, Mestizo, Amerindian, Creole. **Languages:** English (official), Spanish, native Creole dialects. **Religions:** Roman Catholic 60%, Protestant 40%.

Geography: Area: 8,867 sq. mi. **Location:** eastern coast of Central America. **Neighbors:** Mexico on N., Guatemala on W. and S. **Capital:** Belmopan. **Cities:** (1987 est.): Belize City 40,000.

Government: Type: Parliamentary. **Head of State:** Gov. Gen. Minita Gordon. **Head of government:** Prime Min. Manual Esquivel; b. 1940; in office: Dec. 17, 1984. **Local divisions:** 6 districts.

Economy: Sugar is the main export.

Finance: Currency: Belize dollar (Mar. 1989) 2 = $1 U.S. **Gross national product** (1986): 200 mln. **Per capita income** (1984): $1,000. **Imports** (1988) $176 mln.; partners: U.S. 55%, UK 8%. **Exports:** (1988): 120 mln.; partners: U.S. 46%, UK 31%. **National Budget** (1986): $106 mln. expenditures.

Health: life expectancy (1987) male: 66.0; female: 71.0. **Births** (per 1,000 pop. 1986): 36.1. **Deaths** (per 1,000 pop. 1986): 4.1. **Hospital beds** (1986): 583; **Physicians** (1986): 73. **Infant mortality** (per 1,000 live births, 1985): 54.

Education: (1987) **Literacy:** 90%.; **Years compulsory:** 9; attendance 55%.

Major International Organizations: UN (IMF, World Bank), Commonwealth of Nations.

Embassy: 3400 International Dr., NW 20005; 363-4505.

Belize (formerly called British Honduras), Great Britain's last colony on the American mainland, achieved independence on Sept. 21, 1981. Guatemala claims territorial sovereignty over the country and has refused to recognize Belize's independence. British troops in Belize guarantee security.

Benin

People's Republic of Benin

République Populaire du Benin

People: Population (1989 est.): 4,551,000. **Age distrib. (%):** 0–14: 46.5; 15–59: 49.0; 60+: 4.5. **Pop. density:** 104 per sq. mi. **Urban** (1985): 20%. **Ethnic groups:** Fon, Adja, Bariba, Yoruba. **Languages:** French (official), local dialects. **Religions:** Mainly animist with Christian, Moslem minorities.

Geography: Area: 43,483 sq. mi., slightly smaller than Pennsylvania. **Location:** in W Africa on Gulf of Guinea. **Neighbors:** Togo on W, Burkina Faso, Niger on N, Nigeria on E. **Topography:** most of Benin is flat and covered with dense vegetation.

The coast is hot, humid, and rainy. **Capital:** Porto-Novo. **Cities** (1984 est.): Cotonou 330,000.

Government: Type: Marxist-Leninist. **Head of state:** Pres. Mathieu Kerekou; b. Sept. 2, 1933; in office: Oct. 27, 1972. **Local divisions:** 6 provinces, 84 districts. **Defense:** 2.6% of GNP (1984).

Economy: Chief crops: Palm products, peanuts, cotton, coffee, tobacco. **Minerals:** Oil. **Arable land:** 16%. **Livestock** (1986): sheep: 1.1 mln.; goats: 1.1 mln. **Fish catch** (1987): 23,000 metric tons. **Electricity prod.** (1986): 124 mln. kwh. **Labor force:** 60% agric; 30% serv. & comm.

Finance: Currency: CFA franc (Mar. 1989: 319 = $1 US). **Gross national product** (1987): $1.4 bln. **Per capita income** (1987): $374. **Imports** (1984): $225 mln.; partners: Fr. 27%, UK 13%, W. Ger. 6%, Neth. 6%. **Exports** (1984): $172 mln.; partners: Neth. 28%, Jap. 27%, Fr. 24%. **National Budget** (1987): $159 bln. expenditures. **International reserves less gold** (Feb. 1989): $4.2 mln.

Transport: Railway traffic (1985): 137 mln. passenger-km; 176 mln. net ton-km. **Chief ports:** Cotonou.

Communications: Radios: 290,000 in use (1985). **Televisions:** 17,000 (1985). **Daily newspaper circ.** (1986): 3 per 1,000 pop.

Health: Life expectancy at birth (1984): 47.0 male; 51.0 female. **Births** (per 1,000 pop. 1985): 47. **Deaths** (per 1,000 pop. 1985): 16. **Natural increase** (1985): 3.1%. **Hospital beds** (1982): 4,902. **Physicians** (1982): 204. **Infant mortality** (per 1,000 live births 1985): 143.

Education (1987): **Literacy:** 28%. Years compulsory 6; attendance 43%.

Major International Organizations: UN (GATT, IMF, WHO), OAU.

Embassy: 2737 Cathedral Ave. NW 20008; 232-6656.

The Kingdom of Abomey, rising to power in wars with neighboring kingdoms in the 17th century, came under French domination in the late 19th century, and was incorporated into French West Africa by 1904.

Under the name Dahomey, the country became independent Aug. 1, 1960. The name was changed to Benin in 1975. In the fifth coup since independence Col. Ahmed Kerekou took power in 1972; two years later he declared a socialist state with a "Marxist-Leninist" philosophy. The economy relies on the development of agriculturally-based industries.

Bhutan
Kingdom of Bhutan
Druk-Yul

People: Population (1989 est.): 1,538,000. **Age distrib.** (%): 0–14: 39.8; 15–59: 53.8; over 60: 6.4 **Pop. density:** 84 per sq. mi. **Ethnic groups:** Ngalops and Sharchops 70%. Nepalese 25%, Lepcha (indigenous), Indians. **Languages:** Dzongkha (official), Nepali, English. **Religions:** Buddhist (state religion) 75%, Hindu 25%.

Geography: Area: 18,147 sq. mi., the size of Vermont and New Hampshire combined. **Location:** In eastern Himalayan Mts. **Neighbors:** India on W (Sikkim) and S, China on N. **Topography:** Bhutan is comprised of very high mountains in the N, fertile valleys in the center, and thick forests in the Duar Plain in the S. **Capital:** Thimphu. **City** (1987 est.): Thimphu 20,000.

Government: Type: Monarchy. **Head of state:** King Jigme Singye Wangchuk; b. Nov. 11, 1955; in office: July 21, 1972. **Local divisions:** 18 districts.

Economy: Industries: Handicrafts. **Chief crops:** Rice, corn, wheat. **Other resources:** Timber. **Arable land:** 2%. **Labor force:** 95% agric.

Finance: Currency: Ngultrum (Jan. 1989: 14 = 1 US) (Indian Rupee also used). **Gross national product** (1986): $200 mln. **Per capita income** (1985): $120. **Tourism** (1986): 2.2 mln. **Imports** (1986): $72.6 mln.; partners India 99%. **Exports** (1986): $22.2 mln.; partners India 99%.

Communications: Radios: 12,500 in use (1987). **Telephones in use** (1987): 2,000.

Health: Life expectancy at birth (1987): 48.1 male; 46.8 female. **Births** (per 1,000 pop. 1987): 37.5 **Deaths** (per 1,000 pop. 1987): 17.0 **Natural increase** (1987): 2.0%. **Hospital beds** (1985): 857. **Physicians** (1985): 70. **Infant mortality** (per 1,000 live births 1985): 122.

Education (1987): **Literacy:** 12%. School attendance: 21%.
Major International Organizations: UN (IMF, World Bank).

The region came under Tibetan rule in the 16th century. British influence grew in the 19th century. A monarchy, set up in 1907, became a British protectorate by a 1910 treaty. The country became independent in 1949, with India guiding foreign relations and supplying aid.

Links to India have been strengthened by airline service and a road network. Most of the population engages in subsistence agriculture.

Bolivia
Republic of Bolivia
República de Bolivia

People: Population (1989 est.): 6,876,000. **Age distrib.** (%): 0–14: 43; 15–59: 51.8; 60+: 5.2. **Pop. density:** 16 per sq. mi. **Urban** (1987): 49%. **Ethnic groups:** Quechua 30%, Aymara 25%, mixed 30%, European 14%. **Languages:** Spanish, Quechua, Aymara (all official). **Religions:** Roman Catholic 95%.

Geography: Area: 424,165 sq. mi., the size of Texas and California combined. **Location:** In central Andes Mtns. **Neighbors:** Peru, Chile on W, Argentina, Paraguay on S, Brazil on E and N. **Topography:** The great central plateau, at an altitude of 12,000 ft., over 500 mi. long, lies between two great cordilleras having 3 of the highest peaks in S. America. Lake Titicaca, on Peruvian border, is highest lake in world on which steamboats ply (12,506 ft.). The E central region has semitropical forests; the llanos, or Amazon-Chaco lowlands are in E. **Capitals:** Sucre, (legal), La Paz (de facto). **Cities** (1986 est.): La Paz 955,000; Santa Cruz 419,000; Cochabamba 304,000.

Government: Type: Republic. **Head of state:** Pres. Victor Paz Estenssoro; b. Oct. 2, 1907; in office: Aug. 6, 1985. **Local divisions:** 9 departments, 94 provinces.

Economy: Industry: Textiles, food processing, mining, clothing. **Chief crops:** Potatoes, sugar, coffee, barley, cocoa, rice, corn, bananas, citrus. **Minerals:** Antimony, tin, tungsten, silver, zinc, oil, gas, iron. **Crude oil reserves** (1985): 157 mln. bbls. **Other resources:** rubber, cinchona bark. **Arable land:** 37%. **Livestock** (1986): cattle: 6 mln.; sheep: 9.5 mln.; pigs: 1.1 mln. **Electricity prod.** (1986): 2.0 bln. kwh. **Labor force:** 47% agric., 19% ind. & comm, 34% serv. & govt.

Finance: Currency: Peso (Mar. 1989: 2,520 = $1 US). **Gross national product** (1986): $3.7 bln. **Per capita income** (1985): $536. **Imports** (1988): $604 mln.; partners: U.S. 22%, Jap. 7%, Arg. 14%, Braz. 22%. **Exports** (1988): $601 mln.; partners: Arg. 53%, U.S. 14%. **National budget** (1986): $669 mln. revenues; $4.7 bln. expenditures. **International reserves less gold** (Mar. 1988): $108.8 mln. **Gold:** 894,000 oz t. **Consumer prices** (change in 1988): 16%.

Transport: Railway traffic (1987): 790 mln. passenger-km; 521 mln. net ton-miles. **Motor vehicles:** in use (1985): 43,000 passenger cars, 36,000 comm. vehicles. **Civil aviation** (1987): 912 mln. passenger-km.; 26.9 mln. freight ton-km.

Communications: Television sets (1987). **Radios:** 3.4 mln. in use (1985). **Telephones in use** (1986): 182,000. **Daily newspaper circ.** (1984): 40 per 1,000 pop.

Health: Life expectancy at birth (1985): 48.6 male; 53.0 female. **Births** (per 1,000 pop. 1985): 42.0. **Deaths** (per 1,000 pop. 1985): 15. **Natural increase** (1985): 2.9%. **Hospital beds** (1983): 10,789. **Physicians** (1984): 4,032. **Infant mortality** (per 1,000 live births 1986): 123.

Education (1986): **Literacy:** 75%. **Years compulsory:** ages 7-14; attendance 82%.

Major International Organizations: UN (IMF, FAO, WHO), OAS.

Embassy: 3014 Massachusetts Ave. NW 20008; 483-4410.

The Incas conquered the region from earlier Indian inhabitants in the 13th century. Spanish rule began in the 1530s, and lasted until Aug. 6, 1825. The country is named after Simon Bolivar, independence fighter.

In a series of wars, Bolivia lost its Pacific coast to Chile, the oilbearing Chaco to Paraguay, and rubber-growing areas to Brazil, 1879-1935.

Economic unrest, especially among the militant mine workers, has contributed to continuing political instability. A reformist government under Victor Paz Estenssoro, 1951-64, nationalized tin mines and attempted to improve conditions for the Indian majority, but was overthrown by a military junta. A series of coups and countercoups continued through 1981, until the military junta elected Gen. Villa as president.

In July 1982, the military junta assumed power amid a growing economic crisis and foreign debt difficulties. The junta resigned in October and allowed the Congress, elected democratically in 1980, to take power.

In 1988, U.S. pressure on the government to reduce the country's output of coca, the raw material for cocaine, led to clashes between police and coca growers and increased anti-U.S. feeling among Bolivians.

Botswana
Republic of Botswana

People: Population (1989 est.): 1,220,000. **Age distrib. (%):** 0–14: 48.1; 15–59: 46.1; 60+: 5.8. **Pop. density:** 5 per sq. mi. **Urban** (1986): 21%. **Ethnic groups:** Batswana, 95%. **Languages:** English (official), Setswana (national). **Religions:** indigenous beliefs (majority), Christian 15%.

Geography: Area: 231,804 sq. mi., slightly smaller than Texas. **Location:** In southern Africa. **Neighbors:** Namibia (S.W. Africa) on N and W, S. Africa on S, Zimbabwe on NE; Botswana claims border with Zambia on N. **Topography:** The Kalahari Desert, supporting nomadic Bushmen and wildlife, spreads over SW; there are swamplands and farming areas in N, and rolling plains in E where livestock are grazed. **Capital:** Gaborone. **Cities** (1986): Gaborone 96,000.

Government: Type: Republic, parliamentary democracy. **Head of state:** Pres. Quett Masire; b. 1925; in office: July 13, 1980. **Local divisions:** 10 district councils and 4 town councils. **Defense:** 4.1% of national budget (1988).

Economy: Industries: Livestock processing, mining. **Chief crops:** Corn, sorghum, peanuts. **Minerals:** Copper, coal, nickel, diamonds. **Other resources:** Big game. **Arable land:** 2%. **Electricity prod.** (1986): 533 mln. kwh. **Labor force:** 70% agric.

Finance: Currency: Pula (Mar. 1989: 1.00 = $.48 US). **Gross national product** (1986): $930 mln. **Imports** (1986): $765 mln.; partners: S. Africa 88%. **Exports** (1986): $959 mln.; partners: Europe 67%, U.S. 17%, S. Africa 7%. **National budget** (1987): $395 mln. **International reserves less gold** (Mar. 1989): $1.6 bln. **Consumer prices** (change in 1987): 9.8%

Transport: Railway traffic (1984): 1.0 bln. net ton km. **Motor vehicles:** in use (1986): 16,000 passenger cars, 24,000 comm. vehicles.

Communications: Radios: 77,000 in use (1985). **Daily newspaper circ.** (1986): 22 per 1,000 pop.

Health: Life expectancy at birth (1986): male: 54.7; female: 61.4. **Births** (male: 54.7; female: 61.4. per 1,000 pop. 1986): 45.6. **Deaths** (per 1,000 pop. 1986): 11. **Natural increase** (1986): 3.4%. **Hospital beds** (1985): 2,367. **Physicians** (1985): 155. **Infant mortality** (per 1,000 live births 1985): 63.

Education (1987): Literacy: 35% (in English).

Major International Organizations: UN (GATT, IMF, WHO), OAU, Commonwealth of Nations.

Embassy: 4301 Connecticut Ave. NW 20008; 244-4990.

First inhabited by bushmen, then by Bantus, the region became the British protectorate of Bechuanaland in 1886, halting encroachment by Boers and Germans from the south and southwest. The country became fully independent Sept. 30, 1966, changing its name to Botswana.

Cattle-raising and mining (diamonds, copper, nickel) have contributed to the country's economic growth. The economy is closely tied to S. Africa.

Brazil
Federative Republic of Brazil
República Federativa do Brasil

People: Population (1989 est.): 153,992,000. **Age distrib. (%):** 0–14: 36.4; 15–59: 57.0; 60+: 6.6. **Pop. density:** 47 per sq. mi. **Urban** (1987): 76%. **Ethnic groups:** Portuguese, Africans, and mulattoes make up the vast majority; Italians, Germans, Japanese, Indians, Jews, Arabs. **Languages:** Portuguese (official), English. **Religions:** Roman Catholic 89%.

Geography: Area: 3,286,470 sq. mi., larger than contiguous 48 U.S. states; largest country in S. America. **Location:** Occupies eastern half of S. America. **Neighbors:** French Guiana, Suriname, Guyana, Venezuela on N, Colombia, Peru, Bolivia, Paraguay, Argentina on W, Uruguay on S. **Topography:** Brazil's Atlantic coastline stretches 4,603 miles. In N is the heavily-wooded Amazon basin covering half the country. Its network of rivers navigable for 15,814 mi. The Amazon itself flows 2,093 miles in Brazil, all navigable. The NE region is semiarid scrubland, heavily settled and poor. The S central region, favored by climate and resources, has almost half of the population, produces 75% of farm goods and 80% of industrial output. The narrow coastal belt includes most of the major cities. Almost the entire country has a tropical or semitropical climate. **Capital:** Brasilia. **Cities** (1985 est.): Sao Paulo 10.1 mln.; Rio de Janeiro 5.6 mln.; Belo Horizonte 2.1 mln.; Fortaleza 1.9 mln.; Salvador 1.8 mln.; Porto Alegre 2.6 mln.

Government: Type: Federative republic. **Head of state:** Pres. Jose Sarney; b. Apr. 30, 1930; in office: Apr. 22, 1985. **Local divisions:** 23 states, with individual constitutions and elected governments; 3 territories, federal district. **Defense:** 0.8% of GNP (1985).

Economy: Industries: Steel, autos, textiles, ships, appliances, petrochemicals, machinery. **Chief crops:** Coffee (largest grower), cotton, soybeans, sugar, cocoa, rice, corn, fruits. **Minerals:** Chromium, iron, manganese, columbium, titanium, diamonds, gold, nickel, gem stones, coal, tin, tungsten, bauxite, oil. **Crude oil reserves** (1987): 2.3 bln. bbls. **Arable land:** 8%. **Livestock** (1986): cattle: 128 mln.; pigs: 33 mln.; sheep: 18 mln. **Fish catch** (1984): 946,000 metric tons. **Electricity prod.** (1986): 175.7 bln. kwh. **Crude steel prod.** (1987): 22.2 mln. metric tons. **Labor force:** 40% services, 35% agric.; 25% ind.

Finance: Currency: New Cruzado (June 1989: 1.12 = $1 US). **Gross national product** (1986): $250 bln. **Per capita income** (1978): $1,523. **Imports** (1987): $16.5 bln.; partners: U.S. 21%, Iraq 13%. **Exports** (1987): $26.2 bln.; partners: U.S. 26%, EC 27%. **Tourists** (1986): receipts: $1.5 bln. **International reserves less gold** (Jan. 1989): $5.9 bln. **Gold:** 2.2 mln. oz t. **Consumer prices** (change in 1988): 692%.

Transport: Railway traffic (1985): 16.3 bln. passenger-km; 99 bln. net ton-km. **Motor vehicles:** in use (1986): 10 mln. passenger cars, 1.1 mln. **Civil aviation** (1986): 24.4 bln. passenger-km: 1.2 bln. freight ton-km: **Chief ports:** Santos, Rio de Janeiro, Vitoria, Salvador, Rio Grande, Recife.

Communications: Television sets: 36 mln. in use (1987). **Radios:** 50 mln. in use (1986). **Telephones in use** (1986): 12 mln. **Daily newspaper circ.** (1986): 62 per 1,000 pop.

Health: Life expectancy at birth (1987): 62.3 male; 67.6 female. **Births** (per 1,000 pop. 1985): 30.6. **Deaths** (per 1,000 pop. 1985): 8.4. **Natural increase** (1985): 2.2%. **Hospital beds** (1985): 538,000. **Physicians** (1980): 97,100. **Infant mortality** (per 1,000 live births 1986): 70.

Education (1987): Literacy: 76%.

Major International Organizations: UN and most of its specialized agencies, OAS.

Embassy: 3006 Massachusetts Ave. NW 20008; 797-0200.

Pedro Alvares Cabral, a Portuguese navigator, is generally credited as the first European to reach Brazil, in 1500. The country was thinly settled by various Indian tribes. Only a few have survived to the present, mostly in the Amazon basin.

In the next centuries, Portuguese colonists gradually pushed inland, bringing along large numbers of African slaves. Slavery was not abolished until 1888.

The King of Portugal, fleeing before Napoleon's army, moved the seat of government to Brazil in 1808. Brazil thereupon became a kingdom under Dom Joao VI. After his return to Portugal, his son Pedro proclaimed the independence of Brazil, Sept. 7, 1822, and was acclaimed emperor. The second emperor, Dom Pedro II, was deposed in 1889, and a republic proclaimed, called the United States of Brazil. In 1967 the country was renamed the Federative Republic of Brazil.

A military junta took control in 1930; dictatorial power was assumed by Getulio Vargas, who alternated with military coups until finally forced out by the military in 1954. A democratic regime prevailed 1956-64, during which time the capital was moved from Rio de Janeiro to Brasilia in the interior.

The next 5 presidents were all military leaders. Censorship was imposed, and much of the opposition was suppressed amid charges of torture. In 1974 elections, the official opposition party made gains in the chamber of deputies; some relaxation of censorship occurred.

Since 1930, successive governments have pursued industrial and agricultural growth and the development of interior areas. Exploiting vast mineral resources, fertile soil in several regions, and a huge labor force, Brazil became the leading industrial power of Latin America by the 1970s, while agricultural output soared. Democratic elections were held in 1985 as the nation returned to civilian rule.

However, income maldistribution, inflation and government land policies have all led to severe economic recession. Foreign debt is among the largest in the world.

Brazil unveiled a comprehensive environmental program for the Amazon region in 1989, amid an international outcry by environmentalists and others concerned about the ongoing destruction of the Amazon ecosystem. The Amazon rain forest was considered a global resource because of its impact on world weather patterns.

Brunei Darussalam

State of Brunei Darussalam

Negara Brunei Darussalam

People: Population (1989 est.): 267,000. **Pop. Density:** 119 per sq. mi. **Ethnic groups:** Malay 65%, Chinese 20%. **Language:** Malay (official), English, Chinese. **Religion:** Moslem 64%, Buddhist 14%, Christian 10%.

Geography: Area: 2,226 sq. mi.; smaller than Delaware. **Location:** on the north coast of the island of Borneo; it is surrounded on its landward side by the Malaysian state of Sarawak. **Capital:** Bandar Seri Begawan. **Cities** (1982 est.): Bandar Seri Begawan 51,000.

Government: Type: Independent sultanate. **Head of Government:** Sultan Sir Muda Hassanal Bolkiah Mu'izzadin Waddaulah; in office: Jan. 1, 1984.

Economy: Industries: petroleum (about 90% of revenue is derived from oil exports). **Chief crops:** rice, bananas, cassava.

Finance: Currency: Brunei dollar (Dec. 1988: 2.04 = $1). **Gross domestic product** (1986): $3.5 bln. **Per capita income** (1987): $20,000.

Communications: Television sets: 48,000 (1986). **Radios:** 74,000 (1986). **Telephones:** 35,000 (1986).

Education (1987): **Literacy:** 95% among young.

Health: Life expectancy at birth: (1987): 74 yrs. **Infant Mortality** (per 1,000 live births 1985): 12.1.

Major International Organizations: UN and some of its specialized agencies.

The Sultanate of Brunei was a powerful state in the early 16th century with authority over all of the island of Borneo as well as parts of the Sulu Islands and the Philippines. In 1888, a treaty was signed which placed the state under the protection of Great Britain.

Brunei became a fully sovereign and independent state on Jan. 1, 1984.

The Sultan of Brunei donated $10 million to the Nicaraguan *contras* in 1987; the subsequent misplacement of the funds generated much media attention in the U.S.

Bulgaria

People's Republic of Bulgaria

Narodna Republika Bulgaria

People: Population (1989 est.): 9,037,000. **Age distrib. (%):** 0–14: 20.8; 15–59: 60.9; 60+: 18.3. **Pop. density:** 203 per sq. mi. **Urban** (1987): 65%. **Ethnic groups:** Bulgarian 85%, Turk 8.5%. **Languages:** Bulgarian, Turkish, Greek. **Religions:** Government promotes atheism; background of people is 85% Orthodox.

Geography: Area: 44,365 sq. mi., about the size of Ohio. **Location:** In eastern Balkan Peninsula on Black Sea. **Neighbors:** Romania on N, Yugoslavia on W, Greece, Turkey on S. **Topography:** The Stara Planina (Balkan) Mts. stretch E-W across the center of the country, with the Danubian plain on N, the Rhodope Mts. on SW, and Thracian Plain on SE. **Capital:** Sofia. **Cities** (1987 est.): Sofia 1,119,000; Plovdiv 346,000; Varna 303,000.

Government: Type: Communist. **Head of state:** Pres. Todor Zhivkov; b. Sept. 7, 1911; in office: July 7, 1971. **Head of gov-**

ernment: Premier Georgy Atanasov; in office: Mar. 21, 1986. **Head of Communist Party:** First Sec. Todor Zhivkov; in office: Jan. 1954. **Local divisions:** 9 administrative counties. **Defense:** 3.8% of GNP (1985).

Economy: Industries: Chemicals, machinery, metals, textiles, fur, leather goods, vehicles, wine, processed food. **Chief crops:** Grains, fruit, corn, potatoes, tobacco. **Minerals:** Lead, bauxite, coal, oil, zinc. **Arable land:** 38%. **Livestock** (1986): cattle: 1.7 mln.; pigs: 4.0 mln.; sheep: 9.7 mln. **Fish catch** (1986): 138,000 metric tons. **Electricity prod.** (1986): 45 bln. kwh. **Crude steel prod.** (1987): 3.0 mln. metric tons. **Labor force:** 22% agric.; 43% ind. & comm.

Finance: Currency: Lev (Dec. 1988: 1.00 = $.84 US). **Gross National Product** (1985): $25 bln. **Per capita income** (1985): $2,806. **Imports** (1985): $14.0 bln.; partners: USSR 56%, E. Ger. 6%, W. Ger. 5%. **Exports** (1985): $13.7 bln.; partners: USSR 61%, E. Ger. 6%. **Tourists** (1986): revenues $345 mln. **National budget** (1983): $16.7 bln. expenditures.

Transport: Railway traffic (1986): 8.9 bln. passenger-km; 18 bln. net ton-km. **Motor vehicles:** in use (1985) 1 mln. passenger cars, 587,000 commercial. **Civil aviation** (1986): 2.9 bln. passenger km; 43 mln. freight ton km. **Chief ports:** Burgas, Varna.

Communications: Television sets: 1.6 mln. licensed (1986). **Radios:** 2.1 mln. licensed (1986). **Telephones** in use (1986): 1.9 mln. **Daily newspaper circ.** (1986): 316 per 1,000 pop.

Health: Life expectancy at birth (1984): 68 male; 74 female. **Births** (per 1,000 pop. 1986): 13.4. **Deaths** (per 1,000 pop. 1986): 11.6. **Hospital beds** (1986): 84,300. **Physicians:** 25,000. **Infant mortality** (per 1,000 live births 1986): 16.1

Education (1987): **Literacy:** 95%. **Years compulsory:** ages 7-16.

Major International Organizations: UN, Warsaw Pact.

Embassy: 1621-22d St. NW 20008; 387-7970.

Bulgaria was settled by Slavs in the 6th century. Turkic Bulgars arrived in the 7th century, merged with the Slavs, became Christians by the 9th century, and set up powerful empires in the 10th and 12th centuries. The Ottomans prevailed in 1396 and remained for 500 years.

A revolt in 1876 led to an independent kingdom in 1908. Bulgaria expanded after the first Balkan War but lost its Aegean coastline in World War I, when it sided with Germany. Bulgaria joined the Axis in World War II, but withdrew in 1944. Communists took power with Soviet aid; the monarchy was abolished Sept. 8, 1946.

Burkina Faso

People: Population (1989 est.): 7,704,000. **Pop. density:** 72 per sq. mi. **Urban** (1986): 8%. **Ethnic groups:** Voltaic groups (Mossi, Bobo), Mande. **Languages:** French (official), Sudanic tribal languages. **Religions:** animist 65%, Moslems 25%, Christian 10%.

Geography: Area: 105,869 sq. mi., the size of Colorado. **Location:** In W. Africa, S of the Sahara. **Neighbors:** Mali on NW, Niger on NE, Benin, Togo, Ghana, Côte d' Ivoire on S. **Topography:** Landlocked Burkina Faso is in the savannah region of W. Africa. The N is arid, hot, and thinly populated. **Capital:** Ouagadougou. **Cities** (1986): Ouagadougou 366,000; Bobo-Dioulasso 202,000.

Government: Type: Military. **Head of state:** Pres. Blaise Compaore; in office: Oct. 15, 1987. **Local divisions:** 30 provinces. **Defense:** 2.7% of GNP (1984).

Economy: Chief crops: Millet, sorghum, rice, peanuts, grain. **Minerals:** Manganese, gold, limestone. **Arable land:** 10%. **Electricity prod.** (1986): 159 mln. kwh. **Labor force:** 83% agric.; 12% industry.

Finance: Currency: CFA franc (Mar. 1989: 319 = $1 US). **Gross national product** (1986): $1.2 bln. **Per capita income** (1983): $150. **Imports** (1987): $434 mln.; partners: EC, Côte d' Ivoire. **Exports** (1987): $310 mln.; partners: Côte d' Ivoire, EC, China. **International reserves less gold** (Jan. 1989): $320 mln. **Gold:** 11,000 oz t. **Consumer prices** (change in 1988): 4.2%.

Transport: Motor vehicles: in use (1983): 21,000 passenger cars, 6,600 comm. vehicles.

Communications: Television sets: 41,000 in use (1986). **Radios:** 311,000 in use (1986). **Telephones** in use (1986): 16,000. **Daily newspaper circ.** (1987): 1 per 1,000 pop.

Health: Life expectancy at birth (1984): 42 yrs. **Births** (per 1,000 pop. 1985): 48. **Deaths** (per 1,000 pop. 1985): 22. **Natural increase** (1985): 2.6%. **Hospital beds** (1984): 5,580. **Physi-**

cians (1984): 180. **Infant mortality** (per 1,000 live births 1985): 176.

  Education (1986): **Literacy:** 8%. Only 8% attend school.
  Major International Organizations: UN and many of its specialized agencies, OAU.
  Embassy: 2340 Massachusetts Ave. NW 20008; 332-5577.

  The Mossi tribe entered the area in the 11th to 13th centuries. Their kingdoms ruled until defeated by the Mali and Songhai empires.

  French control came by 1896, but Upper Volta (name changed to Burkina Faso on Aug. 4, 1984), was not finally established as a separate territory until 1947. Full independence came Aug. 5, 1960, and a pro-French government was elected. A 1982 coup established the current regime.

  Several hundred thousand farm workers migrate each year to Cote D'Ivoire and Ghana. Burkina Faso is heavily dependent on foreign aid.

Burma

Socialist Republic of the Union of Burma

Pyidaungsu Socialist Thammada Myanma Naingngandaw

(See Myanmar)

Burundi

Republic of Burundi

Republika y'Uburundi

  People: Population (1989 est.): 5,233,000. **Age distrib. (%):** 0–14: 44.3; 15–59: 49.6; 60+: 6.1. **Pop. density:** 486 per sq. mi. **Urban** (1986): 8%. **Ethnic groups:** Hutu 85%, Tutsi 14%, Twa (pygmy) 1%. **Languages:** French, Rundi (both official). **Religions:** Christian 67%, traditional African 32%.
  Geography: Area: 10,759 sq. mi., the size of Maryland. **Location:** In central Africa. **Neighbors:** Rwanda on N, Zaire on W, Tanzania on E. **Topography:** Much of the country is grassy highland, with mountains reaching 8,900 ft. The southernmost source of the White Nile is located in Burundi. Lake Tanganyika is the second deepest lake in the world. **Capital:** Bujumbura. **Cities** (1986 est.): Bujumbura 272,000.
  Government: Type: Republic. **Head of state and head of government:** Pres. Adrien Sibomana; in office: Oct. 19, 1988. **Local divisions:** 15 provinces. **Defense** (1985): 3.2% of GNP.
  Economy: Chief crops: Coffee (87% of exports), cotton, tea. **Minerals:** Nickel. **Arable land:** 50%. **Fish catch** (1985): 14,000 metric tons. **Electricity prod.** (1986): 44 mln. kwh. **Labor force:** 93% agric.
  Finance: Currency: Franc (Apr. 1989: 155 = $1 US). **Gross national product** (1986): $1.3 bln. **Per capita income** (1986): $239. **Imports** (1986): $202 mln.; partners: Belg.-Lux. 20%; W. Ger. 12%. **Exports** (1986): $168 mln; partners: W. Ger. 55%, Belg. 10%. **Tourism** (1986): $35 mln. receipts. **National budget** (1986): $203 mln. expenditures. **International reserves less gold** (Mar. 1989): $116.7 mln. **Gold:** 17,000 oz t. **Consumer prices** (change in 1988): 8.6%.
  Transport: Motor vehicles: in use (1986): 9,000 passenger cars, 6,000 comm. vehicles.
  Communications: Radios: 230,000 in use (1986). **Telephones in use** (1986): 7,000.
  Health: Life expectancy at birth (1987): 46.9 male; 50.2 female. **Births** (per 1,000 pop. 1987): 45.7. **Deaths** (per 1,000 pop. 1987): 17.4. **Natural increase** (1987): 2.8%. **Hospital beds** (1985): 5,506. **Physicians** (1985): 178. **Infant mortality** (per 1,000 live births 1988): 122.
  Education (1988): **Literacy:** 30%.
  Major International Organizations: UN (GATT, IMF, WHO), OAU.
  Embassy: 2233 Wisconsin Ave. NW 20007; 342-2574.

  The pygmy Twa were the first inhabitants, followed by Bantu Hutus, who were conquered in the 16th century by the tall Tutsi (Watusi), probably from Ethiopia. Under German control in 1899, the area fell to Belgium in 1916, which exercised successively a

League of Nations mandate and UN trusteeship over Ruanda-Urundi (now 2 countries).

  Independence came in 1962, and the monarchy was overthrown in 1966. An unsuccessful Hutu rebellion in 1972-73 left 10,000 Tutsi and 150,000 Hutu dead. Over 100,000 Hutu fled to Tanzania and Zaire. Burundi is pledged to ethnic reconciliation, but remains one of the poorest and most densely populated countries in Africa.

Cambodia

State of Cambodia

  People: Population (1989 est.): 6,855,000. **Pop. density:** 98 per sq. mi. **Urban** (1985): 10%. **Ethnic groups:** Khmers 90%, Vietnamese 4%, Chinese 5%. **Languages:** Khmer (official), French. **Religions:** Theravada Buddhism 95%.
  Geography: Area: 69,898 sq. mi., the size of Missouri. **Location:** In Indochina Peninsula. **Neighbors:** Thailand on W, N, Laos on NE, Vietnam on E. **Topography:** The central area, formed by the Mekong R. basin and Tonle Sap lake, is level. Hills and mountains are in SE, a long escarpment separates the country from Thailand on NW. 75% of the area is forested. **Capital:** Phnom Penh. **Cities** (1987 est.): Phnom Penh 300,000.
  Government: Type: No single authority controls the whole country. Vietnamese-installed government controls Phnom Penh. **Head of State:** Pres., People's Revolutionary Party Heng Samrin; in office: Jan. 7, 1979. **Head of Government:** Premier Hun Sen; in office: Jan. 14, 1985. **Local divisions:** 20 provinces.
  Economy: Industries: Rice milling, wood & rubber. **Chief crops:** Rice, sugar. **Minerals:** Iron, copper, manganese. **Other resources:** Forests, rubber, kapok. **Arable land:** 16%. **Livestock** (1986): cattle: 1.5 mln. pigs: 1.2 mln. **Fish catch** (1986): 70,000 metric tons. **Electricity prod.** (1986): 142.00 mln. kwh.
  Finance: Currency: Riel (Jan. 1989: 100 = $1 US). **Per capita income** (1984): $100. **Imports** (1983): $30 mln. **Exports** (1983): $10 mln.
  Transport: Railway traffic (1986): 54 mln. passenger-miles; 10 mln. net ton-miles. **Motor vehicles:** in use (1981): 700 passenger cars, (1981) 700 trucks. **Chief ports** (1986): Kompong Som.
  Communications: Television sets: 30,000 in use (1987). **Radios:** 200,000 in use (1986). **Telephones in use** (1981): 7,000.
  Health: Life expectancy at birth (1987): 46.5 male; 49.4 female. **Births** (per 1,000 pop. 1987): 41.8. **Deaths** (per 1,000 pop. 1987): 16.9. **Natural increase** (1987): 2.4. **Infant Mortality** (per 1,000 live births 1987): 133.
  Education (1987): **Literacy:** 48%.
  Major International Organizations: UN.

  Early kingdoms dating from that of Funan in the 1st century AD culminated in the great Khmer empire which flourished from the 9th century to the 13th, encompassing present-day Thailand, Cambodia, Laos, and southern Vietnam. The peripheral areas were lost to invading Siamese and Vietnamese, and France established a protectorate in 1863. Independence came in 1953.

  Prince Norodom Sihanouk, king 1941-1955 and head of state from 1960, tried to maintain neutrality. Relations with the U.S. were broken in 1965, after South Vietnam planes attacked Vietcong forces within Cambodia. Relations were restored in 1969, after Sihanouk charged Viet communists with arming Cambodian insurgents.

  In 1970, pro-U.S. premier Lon Nol seized power, demanding removal of 40,000 North Viet troops; the monarchy was abolished. Sihanouk formed a government-in-exile in Peking, and open war began between the government and the Khmer Rouge. The U.S. provided heavy military and economic aid.

  Khmer Rouge forces captured Phnom Penh April 17, 1975. Over 100,000 people had died in 5 years of fighting. The new government evacuated all cities and towns, and shuffled the rural population, sending virtually the entire population to clear jungle, forest, and scrub, which covered half the country. Over one million people were killed in executions and enforced hardships.

  Severe border fighting broke out with Vietnam in 1978; developed into a full-fledged Vietnamese invasion. The Vietnamese-backed Kampuchean National United Front for National Salvation, a Cambodian rebel movement, announced, Jan. 8, 1979, the formation of a government one day after the Vietnamese capture of Phnom Pehn. Thousands of refugees flowed into Thailand. Widespread starvation was reported; by Sept., when the UN confirmed diplomatic recognition to the ousted Pol Pot government, international food assistance was allowed to aid the famine-stricken country.

On Jan. 10, 1983, Vietnam launched an offensive against rebel forces in the west. They overran a refugee camp, Jan. 31, driving 30,000 residents into Thailand. In March, Vietnam launched a major offensive against camps on the Cambodian-Thailand border, engaged Khmer Rouge guerrillas, and crossed the border instigating clashes with Thai troops. By Feb. 1985, Vietnamese forces had overrun all major Khmer Rouge bases. Vietnam announced that it would withdraw all its troops by Sept. 1989 (See Chronology).

Cameroon
Republic of Cameroon

People: Population (1989 est.): 10,874,000. **Age distrib. (%): 0–14:** 44.6; **15–59:** 49.8; **60 +:** 5.6. **Pop. density:** 58 per sq. mi. **Urban** (1988): 40%. **Ethnic groups:** Some 200 tribes; largest are Bamileke 30%, Fulani 7%. **Languages:** English, French (both official), 24 African groups. **Religions:** Animist 51%, Moslem 16%, Christian 33%.

Geography; Area: 185,568 sq. mi., somewhat larger than California. **Location:** Between W and central Africa. **Neighbors:** Nigeria on NW, Chad, Central African Republic on E, Congo, Gabon, Equatorial Guinea on S. **Topography:** A low coastal plain with rain forests is in S; plateaus in center lead to forested mountains in W, including Mt. Cameroon, 13,000 ft.; grasslands in N lead to marshes around Lake Chad. **Capital:** Yaounde. **Cities** (1988 est.): Douala 852,000; Yaounde 700,000.

Government: Type: Independent republic. **Head of state:** Pres. Paul Biya; b. Feb. 13, 1933; in office: Nov. 6, 1982. **Local divisions:** 10 provinces. **Defense:** 6.5% of budget (1987).

Economy: Industries: Aluminum processing, oil prod., palm products. **Chief crops:** Cocoa, coffee, cotton. **Crude oil reserves** (1985): 531 mln. bbls. **Other resources:** Timber. **Arable land:** 14%. **Livestock** (1986): cattle: 4.3 mln.; sheep: 2.5 mln.; pigs: 1.1 mln. **Fish catch** (1986): 83,000 metric tons. **Electricity prod.** (1986): 4.2 bln. kwh. **Labor force:** 70% agric., 13% ind. and commerce.

Finance: Currency: CFA franc (Mar. 1989: 319 = $1 US). **Gross national product** (1986): $11.7 bln. **Per capita income** (1986): $1,171. **Imports** (1986): 1.7 bln.; partners: Fr. 42%, W. Ger. 10%. **Exports** (1986): $782,000; partners: Fr. 21%, U.S. 16%, Neth. 28%. **National budget** (1986): $1.6 bln. **International reserves less gold** (Jan. 1989): $148 mln. **Gold:** 30,000 oz t. **Consumer prices** (change in 1988): 8.6%.

Transport: Railway traffic (1986): 432 mln. passenger-km; 756 mln. net ton-km. **Motor vehicles:** in use (1985): 72,000 passenger cars, 41,000 comm. vehicles. **Chief ports:** Douala.

Communications: Radios: 800,000 in use (1986). **Telephones in use** (1984): 49,000. **Daily newspaper circ.** (1986): 6 per 1,000 pop.

Health: Life expectancy at birth (1987): 49.0 male; 52.0 female. **Births** (per 1,000 pop. 1985): 44. **Deaths** (per 1,000 pop. 1985): 17. **Natural increase** (1985): 2.8%. **Hospital beds** (1981): 24,541. **Physicians** (1982): 604. **Infant mortality** (per 1,000 live births 1985): 113.

Education (1988): **Literacy:** 65%. About 70% attend school.

Major International Organizations: UN, OAU, EC (Associate).

Embassy: 2349 Massachusetts Ave. NW 20008; 265-8790.

Portuguese sailors were the first Europeans to reach Cameroon, in the 15th century. The European and American slave trade was very active in the area. German control lasted from 1884 to 1916, when France and Britain divided the territory, later receiving League of Nations mandates and UN trusteeships. French Cameroon became independent Jan. 1, 1960; one part of British Cameroon joined Nigeria in 1961, the other part joined Cameroon. Stability has allowed for development of roads, railways, agriculture, and petroleum production. Some 3,000 died in 1986 as a result of clouds of toxic gas of volcanic origin emanating from Lake Nyos.

Canada

People: Population (1989 est.): 25,334,000. **Age distrib. (%): 0–14:** 21.4; **15–59:** 63.6; **60 +:** 15.0. **Pop. density:** 6 per sq. mi. **Urban** (1985): 75.9%. **Ethnic groups:** British Isles origin

47%; French 27%. other European 23%. **Language:** English, French (both official). **Religion:** Roman Catholic 46%, Protestant 41%.

Geography: Area: 3,851,790 sq. mi., the 2d largest country in land size, Canada stretches 3,223 miles from east to west and extends southward from the North Pole to the U.S. border. Its seacoast includes 36,356 miles of mainland and 115,133 miles of islands, including the Arctic islands almost from Greenland to near the Alaskan border. Climate, while generally temperate, varies from freezing winter cold to blistering summer heat. **Capitol:** Ottawa. **Cities** (met. 1986 est.): Montreal 2,921,000; Toronto 3,427,000; Vancouver 1,380,000; Ottawa-Hull 819,000; Winnipeg 625,000; Edmonton 785,000, Calgary 671,000, Quebec 603,000.

Government: Type: Confederation with parliamentary democracy. **Head of state:** Queen Elizabeth II, represented by Gov.-Gen. Jeanne Sauve; in office: May 14, 1985. **Head of government:** Prime Min. Brian Mulroney; born: Mar. 20, 1939; in office: Sept. 4, 1984. **Local divisions:** 10 provinces, 2 territories. **Defense:** 2% of GNP (1986).

Economy: Minerals: Nickel, zinc, copper, gold, lead, molybdenum, potash, silver. **Crude oil reserves** (1987): 4.8 bln. bbls. **Arable land:** 5%. **Livestock** (1986): cattle: 11.4 mln.; pigs: 10.7 mln.; sheep: 722,000. **Fish catch** (1986): 1.1 mln. metric tons. **Electricity prod.** (1986): 448 bln. kwh. **Crude steel prod.** (1987): 14.7 mln. metric tons. **Labor force:** 4% agric.; 52% ind. & comm., 28% services.

Finance: Currency: Dollar (June 1989: 1.20 = $1 US). **Gross national product** (1986): $367 bln. **Per capita income** (1984 est.) $13,000. **Imports** (1987): $92.7 bln.; partners: U.S. 69%, EC 8%, Jap. 5%. **Exports** (1987): $98.1 bln.; partners: U.S. 78%, EC 9%, Jap. 5%. **Tourists** (1986): receipts: $3.8 bln. **National budget** (1987-88): Can $122 bln. expenditures. **International reserves less gold** (Mar. 1989): $15.4 bln. **Gold:** 17.0 mln. oz t. **Consumer prices** (change in 1988): 4.0%.

Transport: Railway traffic (1986): 2.0 bln. passenger-km; 236 bln. net ton-km. **Motor vehicles:** in use (1986): 11.1 mln. passenger cars, 3 mln. comm. **Civil aviation** (1987): 48.2 bln. passenger-km: 1.2 bln. net ton-km.

Communications: Television sets: 15.7 mln. in use (1987). **Radios:** 28 mln. in use (1985). **Telephones in use** (1987): 19.5 mln. **Daily newspaper circ.** (1987): 211 per 1,000 pop.

Health: Life expectancy at birth (1987): 69 male; 76 female. **Births** (per 1,000 pop. 1986): 14.8. **Deaths** (per 1,000 pop. 1986): 7.3. **Natural increase** (1986): .7%. **Hospital beds** (1987): 150,000. **Physicians** (1987): 52,000. **Infant mortality** (per 1,000 live births 1985): 8.

Education (1987): **Literacy:** 99%.

Major International Organizations: UN and all of its specialized agencies, NATO, OECD, Commonwealth of Nations.

Embassy: 1746 Massachusetts Ave. NW 20036; 785-1400.

French explorer Jacques Cartier, who discovered the Gulf of St. Lawrence in 1534, is generally regarded as the founder of Canada. But English seaman John Cabot sighted Newfoundland 37 years earlier, in 1497, and Vikings are believed to have reached the Atlantic coast centuries before either explorer.

Canadian settlement was pioneered by the French who established Quebec City (1608) and Montreal (1642) and declared New France a colony in 1663.

Britain, as part of its American expansion, acquired Acadia (later Nova Scotia) in 1717, and through military victory over French forces in Canada (an extension of a European conflict between the 2 powers), captured Quebec (1759) and obtained control of the rest of New France in 1763. The French, through the Quebec Act of 1774, retained the rights to their own language, religion, and civil law.

The British presence in Canada increased during the American Revolution when many colonials, proudly calling themselves United Empire Loyalists, moved north to Canada.

Fur traders and explorers led Canadians westward across the continent. Sir Alexander Mackenzie reached the Pacific in 1793 and scrawled on a rock by the ocean, "from Canada by land."

In Upper and Lower Canada (later called Ontario and Quebec) and in the Maritimes, legislative assemblies appeared in the 18th century and reformers called for responsible government. But the War of 1812 intervened. The war, a conflict between Great Britain and the United States fought mainly in Upper Canada, ended in a stalemate in 1814.

In 1837 political agitation for more democratic government culminated in rebellions in Upper and Lower Canada. Britain sent Lord Durham to investigate and, in a famous report (1839), he recommended union of the 2 parts into one colony called Canada. The union lasted until Confederation, July 1, 1867, when proclamation of the British North America (BNA) Act launched the Dominion of Canada, consisting of Ontario, Quebec, and the former colonies of Nova Scotia and New Brunswick.

Since 1840 the Canadian colonies had held the right to internal self-government. The BNA act, which became the country's written constitution, established a federal system of government on the model of a British parliament and cabinet structure under the crown. Canada was proclaimed a self-governing Dominion within the British Empire in 1931.

In 1982 Canada severed its last formal legislative link with Britain by obtaining the right to amend its constitution (the British North America Act of 1867).

The Meech Lake Agreement was signed June 3, 1987. The historic accord, subject to ratification by Parliament and the provincial legislatures, assured constitutional protection for Quebec's efforts to preserve its French language and culture. Parliament ratified a controversial free-trade arrangement with the U.S. on Dec. 30, 1988.

Canadian Provinces

	Sq. mi.	Population, 1986 cen.
Alberta	248,390	2,375,278
British Columbia	358,971	2,889,207
Manitoba	211,723	1,071,232
New Brunswick	27,834	710,422
Newfoundland	143,510	568,349
Nova Scotia	20,402	873,119
Ontario	344,090	9,113,515
Prince Edward Island	2,185	126,646
Quebec	523,859	6,540,276
Saskatchewan	220,348	1,010,198
Territories		
Northwest Territories	1,271,442	52,238
Yukon	184,931	23,504

Cape Verde
Republic of Cape Verde
Republica de Cabo Verde

People: Population (1989 est.): 337,000. **Age distrib.** (%): 0–14: 45.6; 15–59: 47.7; 60+: 6.7. **Pop. density:** 337 per sq. mi. **Urban** (1980): 26.2%. **Ethnic groups:** Creole (mulatto) 71%, African 28%, European 1%. **Languages:** Portuguese (official), Crioulo. **Religions:** 80% Roman Catholic.

Geography: Area: 1,557 sq. mi., a bit larger than Rhode Island. **Location:** In Atlantic O., off western tip of Africa. **Neighbors:** Nearest are Mauritania, Senegal. **Topography:** Cape Verde Islands are 15 in number, volcanic in origin (active crater on Fogo). The landscape is eroded and stark, with vegetation mostly in interior valleys. **Capital:** Praia. **Cities** (1986 est.): Mindelo 40,000; Praia 50,000.

Government: Type: Republic. **Head of state:** Pres. Aristide Pereira; b. Nov. 17, 1923; in office: July 5, 1975. **Head of government:** Prime Min. Pedro Pires, b. Apr. 29, 1934; in office: July 5, 1975. **Local divisions:** 14 administrative districts.

Economy: Chief crops: Bananas, coffee, sugarcane, corn, beans. **Minerals:** Salt. **Other resources:** Fish. **Arable land:** 10%. **Electricity prod.** (1987): 30.8 mln. kwh.

Finance: Currency: Escudo (Dec. 1988: 76.86 = $1 US). **Gross national product** (1985): $140 mln. **Per capita income** (1984): $350. **Imports** (1981): $104 mln.; partners: Port. 33%, Neth. 12%. **Exports** (1981): $6 mln.; partners: Port. 32%, Ang. 21%.

Transport: Motor vehicles: in use (1981): 4,000 passenger cars, 1,343 comm. vehicles. **Chief ports:** Mindelo, Praia.

Communications: Radios: 47,000 licensed (1985). **Telephones in use** (1985): 4,300.

Health: Life expectancy at birth (1985): 60.3 male, 64.0 female. **Births** (per 1,000 pop. 1987): 32.1. **Deaths** (per 1,000 pop. 1987): 7.7. **Natural increase** (1987): 2.4%. **Hospital beds** (1980): 632. **Physicians** (1980): 51. **Infant mortality** (per 1,000 live births 1985): 89.

Education (1986): **Literacy:** 37%.
Major International Organizations: UN (GATT, IMF, WHO), OAU.
Embassy: 3415 Massachusetts Ave. NW 20007; 965-6820.

The uninhabited Cape Verdes were discovered by the Portuguese in 1456 or 1460. The first Portuguese colonists landed in 1462; African slaves were brought soon after, and most Cape Verdeans descend from both groups. Cape Verde independence came July 5, 1975. The islands have suffered from repeated extreme droughts and famines. Emphasis is placed on the development of agriculture and on fishing.

Central African Republic
Republique Centrafricaine

People: Population (1989 est.): 2,999,000. **Pop. density:** 12 per sq. mi. **Urban** (1986): 44%. **Ethnic groups:** Banda 27%, Baya 34%, Mandja 21%, Sara 10%. **Languages:** French (official), local dialects. **Religions:** Protestant 25%, Roman Catholic 25%, traditional 24%.

Geography: Area: 240,534 sq. mi., slightly smaller than Texas. **Location:** In central Africa. **Neighbors:** Chad on N, Cameroon on W, Congo, Zaire on S, Sudan on E. **Topography:** Mostly rolling plateau, average altitude 2,000 ft., with rivers draining S to the Congo and N to Lake Chad. Open, well-watered savanna covers most of the area, with an arid area in NE, and tropical rainforest in SW. **Capital:** Bangui. **Cities** (1985 est.): Bangui (met.) 473,000.

Government: Type: Republic. (under military rule). **Head of state:** Gen. Andre Kolingba; in office: Sept. 1, 1981. **Local divisions:** 14 prefectures. **Defense:** 2% of GNP (1984).

Economy: Industries: Textiles, light manuf., mining. **Chief crops:** Cotton, coffee, peanuts, corn, sorghum. **Minerals:** Diamonds (chief export), uranium, iron. **Other resources:** Timber. **Arable land:** 3%. **Electricity prod.** (1986): 61 mln. kwh. **Labor force:** 86% agric.

Finance: Currency: CFA franc (Mar. 1989: 319 = $1 US). **Gross national product** (1986): $770 mln. **Per capita income** (1982): $310. **Imports** (1984): $139 mln.; partners: Fr. 52%. **Exports** (1984): $145 mln.; partners: Fr. 17%, Bel.-Lux. 42%. **International reserves less gold** (Jan. 1989): $95.4 mln. **Gold:** 11,000 oz t.

Transport: Motor vehicles: in use (1984): 43,000 passenger cars, 3,861 comm. vehicles.

Communications: Radios: 135,000 in use (1986). **Telephones** (1986): 7,000.

Health: Life expectancy at birth (1983): 44 years. **Births** (per 1,000 pop. 1985): 47. **Deaths** (per 1,000 pop. 1985): 19%. **Natural increase** (1985): 2.8%. **Hospital beds** (1984): 3,774. **Physicians** (1984): 112. **Infant mortality** (per 1,000 live births 1986): 134.

Education (1983): **Literacy:** 20%. **Attendance:** primary school 64%; secondary school 11%.

Major International Organizations: UN (GATT, IMF, WHO), OAU.
Embassy: 1618 22d St. NW 20008; 483-7800.

Various Bantu tribes migrated through the region for centuries before French control was asserted in the late 19th century, when the region was named Ubangi-Shari. Complete independence was attained Aug. 13, 1960.

All political parties were dissolved in 1960, and the country became a center for Chinese political influence in Africa. Relations with China were severed after 1965. Elizabeth Domitien, premier 1975-76, was the first woman to hold that post in an African country. Pres. Jean-Bedel Bokassa, who seized power in a 1965 military coup, proclaimed himself constitutional emperor of the renamed Central African Empire Dec. 1976.

Emp. Bokassa's rule was characterized by virtually unchecked ruthless and cruel authority, and human rights violations. Bokassa was ousted in a bloodless coup aided by the French government, Sept. 20, 1979, and replaced by his cousin David Dacko, former president from 1960 to 1965. In 1981, the political situation deteriorated amid strikes and economic crisis. Gen. Kolingba replaced Dacko as head of state in a bloodless coup.

Chad

Republic of Chad

République du Tchad

People: Population (1989 est.): 5,714,000. **Age distrib.** (%): 0–14: 42.5; 15–59: 51.7; 60+: 5.8. **Pop. density:** 11 per sq. mi. **Urban** (1986): 23%. **Ethnic groups:** 200 distinct groups. **Languages:** French, Arabic, (both official), some 100 other languages. **Religions:** Moslem 44%, animist 23%, Christian 33%.

Geography: Area: 495,755 sq. mi., four-fifths the size of Alaska. **Location:** In central N. Africa. **Neighbors:** Libya on N, Niger, Nigeria, Cameroon on W, Central African Republic on S, Sudan on E. **Topography:** Southern wooded savanna, steppe, and desert, part of the Sahara, in the N. Southern rivers flow N to Lake Chad, surrounded by marshland. **Capital:** N'Djamena. **Cities** (1986 est.): N'Djamena 511,000.

Government: Type: Republic. **Head of state:** Pres. Hissen Habre; b. 1942; in office: June 19, 1982. **Local divisions:** 14 prefectures. **Defense:** 1.9% of GNP (1985).

Economy: Chief crops: Cotton. **Minerals:** Uranium. **Arable land:** 2%. **Fish catch** (1986): 110,000 metric tons. **Electricity prod.** (1986): 65 mln. kwh. **Labor force:** 81% agric.

Finance: Currency: CFA franc (Mar. 1989: 319 = $1 US). **Gross national product** (1986): $811 mln. **Per capita income** (1986): $158. **Imports** (1987): $732 mln.; partners: Fr. 47%. **Exports** (1987): $221 mln.; partners Fra, EDEAC countries. **International reserves less gold** (Jan. 1989): $60.7 mln. **Gold:** 11,000 oz t.

Transport: Motor vehicles: in use (1982): 7,000 passenger cars, 5,000 comm. vehicles.

Communications: Radios: 100,000 in use (1986). **Telephones in use** (1984): 4,500.

Health: Life expectancy at birth (1984): 43.0 male; 45.0 female. **Births** (per 1,000 pop. 1985): 51. **Deaths** (per 1,000 pop. 1985): 28. **Natural increase** (1985): 2.3%. **Hospital beds** (1980): 3,500. **Physicians** (1980): 94. **Infant mortality** (per 1,000 live births 1985): 140.

Education (1980): **Literacy:** 17%.

Major International Organizations: UN, (GATT, IMF, WHO), OAU, EEC.

Embassy: 2002 R St. NW 20009; 462-4009.

Chad was the site of paleolithic and neolithic cultures before the Sahara Desert formed. A succession of kingdoms and Arab slave traders dominated Chad until France took control around 1900. Independence came Aug. 11, 1960.

Northern Moslem rebels, have fought animist and Christian southern government and French troops from 1966, despite numerous cease-fires and peace pacts.

Libyan troops entered the country at the request of the Chad government, December 1980. On Jan. 6, 1981 Libya and Chad announced their intention to unite. France together with several African nations condemned the agreement as a menace to African security. The Libyan troops were withdrawn from Chad in November 1981.

Rebel forces, led by Hissen Habre, captured the capital and forced Pres. Oueddei to flee the country in June 1982.

In 1983, France sent some 3,000 troops to Chad to assist Habre in opposing Libyan-backed rebels. France and Libya agreed to a simultaneous withdrawal of troops from Chad in September 1984 but Libyan forces remained in the north until Mar. 1987 when Chad forces drove them from their last major stronghold. Libyan troops abandoned almost $1 billion of military equipment during their retreat.

Chile

Republic of Chile

República de Chile

People: Population (1989 est.): 12,866,000. **Age distrib.** (%): 0–14: 31.1; 15–59: 60.6; 60+: 8.3. **Pop. density:** 44 per sq. mi. **Urban** (1988): 83%. **Ethnic groups:** Mestizo 66%, Spanish 25%, Indian 5%. **Languages:** Spanish. **Religions:** Roman Catholic 89%, Protestant 11%.

Geography: Area: 292,257 sq. mi., larger than Texas. **Location:** Occupies western coast of southern S. America. **Neigh-** bors: Peru on N, Bolivia on NE, Argentina on E. **Topography:** Andes Mtns. are on E border including some of the world's highest peaks; on W is 2,650-mile Pacific Coast. Width varies between 100 and 250 miles. In N is Atacama Desert, in center are agricultural regions, in S are forests and grazing lands. **Capital:** Santiago. **Cities** (1987 metro est.) Santiago 4,858,000.

Government: Type: Republic. **Head of state:** Pres. Augusto Pinochet Ugarte; b. Nov. 25, 1915; in office: Sept. 11, 1973. **Local divisions:** 12 regions and Santiago region. **Defense:** 3.6% of GNP (1988).

Economy: Industries: Steel, textiles, wood products. **Chief crops:** Grain, onions, beans, potatoes, peas, fruits, grapes. **Minerals:** Copper (27% world resources and 40% of export revenues), molybdenum, nitrates, iodine (half world output), iron, coal, oil, gas, gold, cobalt, zinc, manganese, borate, mica, mercury, salt, sulphur, marble, onyx. **Crude oil reserves** (1985): 224 mln. bbls. **Other resources:** Water, forests. **Arable land:** 7%. **Livestock** (1986): pigs: 1.1 mln. **Fish catch** (1986): 5.6 mln. metric tons. **Electricity prod.** (1986): 13.9 bln. kwh. **Crude steel prod.** (1984): 684,000 metric tons. **Labor force:** 21% agric., forestry, fishing; 32% ind & comm., 28% serv.

Finance: Currency: Peso (June 1989: 251 = $1 US). **Gross national product** (1987): $18.4 bln. **Per capita income** (1979): $1,950. **Imports** (1987): $4.0 bln.; partners: U.S. 19%, Braz. 9%. **Exports** (1987): $5.0 bln.; partners: W. Ger. 10%, Jap. 11%, U.S. 22%. **Tourists** (1986): $172 mln. receipts. **National budget** (1988): $5.7 bln. expenditures. **International reserves less gold** (Mar. 1989): $3.3 bln. **Gold:** 1.53 mln. oz. t. **Consumer prices** (change in 1988): 14.7%

Transport: Railway traffic (1986): 1.2 bln. passenger-km; 2.4 bln. net ton-km. **Motor vehicles:** in use (1986): 638,000 passenger cars, 263,000 comm. vehicles. **Civil aviation** (1986): 1.9 bln. passenger-km; 137 mln. net ton-km. **Chief ports:** Valparaiso, Arica, Antofagasta.

Communications: Television sets: 2.3 mln. in use (1987). **Radios:** 17 mln. in use (1986). **Telephones in use** (1986): 795,000.

Health: Life expectancy at birth (1983): 63.8 male; 70.4 female. **Births** (per 1,000 pop. 1986): 22.1. **Deaths** (per 1,000 pop. 1986): 5.9. **Natural increase** (1986): 1.6%. **Hospital beds** (1986): 33,000. **Physicians** (1985): 12,334. **Infant mortality** (per 1,000 live births 1986): 18.

Education (1988): **Literacy:** 92%. Compulsory ages 6-14.

Major International Organizations: UN and all of its specialized agencies, OAS.

Embassy: 1732 Massachusetts Ave. NW 20036; 785-1746.

Northern Chile was under Inca rule before the Spanish conquest, 1536-40. The southern Araucanian Indians resisted until the late 19th century. Independence was gained 1810-18, under Jose de San Martin and Bernardo O'Higgins; the latter, as supreme director 1817-23, sought social and economic reforms until deposed. Chile defeated Peru and Bolivia in 1836-39 and 1879-84, gaining mineral-rich northern land.

Eduardo Frei Montalva came into office in 1964, instituting social programs and gradual nationalization of foreign-owned mining companies. In 1970, Salvador Allende Gossens, a Marxist, became president with a third of the national vote.

The Allende government furthered nationalizations, and improved conditions for the poor. But illegal and violent actions by extremist supporters of the government, the regime's failure to attain majority support, and poorly planned socialist economic programs led to political and financial chaos.

A military junta seized power Sept. 11, 1973, and said Allende killed himself. The junta named a mostly military cabinet, and announced plans to "exterminate Marxism."

Repression continued during the 1980s with little sign of any political liberalization. In a plebiscite held Oct. 5, 1988, voters rejected junta-candidate Gen. Pinochet who, if victorious, would have governed Chile until 1997. Pinochet accepted the rejection and called for presidential elections in Dec. 1989.

Tierra del Fuego is the largest (18,800 sq. mi.) island in the archipelago of the same name at the southern tip of South America, an area of majestic mountains, tortuous channels, and high winds. It was discovered 1520 by Magellan and named the Land of Fire because of its many Indian bonfires. Part of the island is in Chile, part in Argentina. Punta Arenas, on a mainland peninsula, is a center of sheep-raising and the world's southernmost city (pop. 67,600); Puerto Williams, pop. 949, is the southernmost settlement.

China

People's Republic of China

Zhonghua Renmin Gonghe Guo

People: Population (1989 est.): 1,069,628,000. **Pop. density:** 288 per sq. mi. **Urban** (1987): 46%. **Ethnic groups:** Han Chinese 94%, Mongol, Korean, Manchu, others. **Languages:** Mandarin Chinese (official), Yue, Wu Minbei, Minnan, Xiang, Gan. **Religions:** officially atheist; Confucianism, Buddhism, Taoism are traditional.

Geography: Area: 3,705,390 sq. mi., slightly larger than the conterminous U.S. **Location:** Occupies most of the habitable mainland of E. Asia. **Neighbors:** Mongolia on N, USSR on NE and NW, Afghanistan, Pakistan on W, India, Nepal, Bhutan, Burma, Laos, Vietnam on S, N. Korea on NE. **Topography:** Two-thirds of the vast territory is mountainous or desert, and only one-tenth is cultivated. Rolling topography rises to high elevations in the N in the Daxinganlingshanmai separating Manchuria and Mongolia; the Tienshan in Xinjiang; the Himalayan and Kunlunshanmai in the SW and in Tibet. Length is 1,860 mi. from N to S, width E to W is more than 2,000 mi. The eastern half of China is one of the best-watered lands in the world. Three great river systems, the Changjiang, the Huanghe, and the Xijiang provide water for vast farmlands. **Capital:** Beijing. **Cities** (1987 est.): Shanghai 7 mln.; Beijing 5.9 mln.; Tianjin 5.4 mln.; Canton 3.3 mln.; Shenyang 4.2 mln.; Wuhan 3.4 mln.; Chengdu 2.6 mln.

Government: Type: Communist Party led state. **Head of state:** Pres. Yang Shangkun; in office: Apr. 8, 1988. **Head of government:** Premier Li Peng; in office: Apr. 9, 1988. **Gen. Secy. of Communist Party:** Jiang Zemin; b. 1926; in office June 24, 1989. **Local divisions:** 22 provinces, 5 autonomous regions, and 3 cities. **Defense:** 6.7% of GNP (1985).

Economy: Industries: Iron and steel, textiles, agriculture implements, trucks. **Chief crops:** Grain, rice, cotton, tea. **Minerals:** Tungsten, antimony, coal, iron, lead, manganese, mercury, molybdenum, tin. **Crude oil reserves** (1987): 18.5 bln. bbls. **Other resources:** Silk. **Arable land:** 11%. **Livestock** (1986): cattle: 66.9 mln.; pigs: 328 mln.; sheep: 66 mln. **Fish catch** (1986): 8 mln. metric tons. **Electricity prod.** (1987): 898 bln. kwh. **Crude steel prod.** (1987): 56.0 mln. metric tons. **Labor force:** 68% agric.; 18% ind. & comm.

Finance: Currency: Yuan (Mar. 1989): 3.72 = $1 US). **Gross national product** (1987): $270 bln. **Per capita income** (1986): $258. **Imports** (1988): $55.2 bln.; partners: Jap. 35%, U.S. 14%, Hong Kong 11%. **Exports** (1988): $47.5 bln.; partners: Hong Kong 26%, Jap. 22%, U.S. 9%. **Tourism** (1987): $1.8 bln. receipts. **National budget** (1987): $66.1 bln. expenditures. **International reserves less gold** (Feb. 1989): 18.2 bln. **Gold:** 12.7 mln. oz t. **Consumer prices** (change in 1988): 20.7%.

Transport: Railway traffic (1987): 284 passenger-km., 974 bln. net ton-km. **Motor vehicles:** in use (1986): 794,000 passenger cars, 2.2 mln. comm. vehicles. **Civil aviation** (1987): 18.6 bln. passenger km, 660 mln. net ton-km. **Chief ports:** Shanghai, Tianjin, Luda.

Communications: Television sets: 92 mln. in use (1987). **Radios:** 253 mln. in use (1987). **Telephones** (1986): 7 mln.; **Daily newspaper circ.** (1986): 50 per 1,000 pop.

Health: Life expectancy at birth (1987): 67.8 male; 70.7 female. **Births** (per 1,000 pop. 1987): 21.0. **Deaths** (per 1,000 pop. 1987): 6.6. **Natural increase** (1987): 1.4%. **Infant Mortality** (per 1,000 live births 1987): 33. **Hospital beds** (1987): 2.6 mln. **Physicians** (1987): 1.4 mln.

Education (1987): **Literacy:** 70%. Years compulsory 9; first grade enrollment 93%.

Major International Organizations: UN (IMF, FAO, WHO).

Embassy: 2300 Conn. Ave. NW 20008; 328-2520.

History. Remains of various man-like creatures who lived as early as several hundred thousand years ago have been found in many parts of China. Neolithic agricultural settlements dotted the Huanghe basin from about 5,000 BC. Their language, religion, and art were the sources of later Chinese civilization.

Bronze metallurgy reached a peak and Chinese pictographic writing, similar to today's, was in use in the more developed culture of the Shang Dynasty (c. 1500 BC-c. 1000 BC) which ruled much of North China.

A succession of dynasties and interdynastic warring kingdoms ruled China for the next 3,000 years. They expanded Chinese

political and cultural domination to the south and west, and developed a brilliant technologically and culturally advanced society. Rule by foreigners (Mongols in the Yuan Dynasty, 1271-1368, and Manchus in the Ch'ing Dynasty, 1644-1911) did not alter the underlying culture.

A period of relative stagnation left China vulnerable to internal and external pressures in the 19th century. Rebellions left tens of millions dead, and Russia, Japan, Britain, and other powers exercised political and economic control in large parts of the country. China became a republic Jan. 1, 1912, following the Wuchang Uprising inspired by Dr. Sun Yat-sen.

For a period of 50 years, 1894-1945, China was involved in conflicts with Japan. In 1895, China ceded Korea, Taiwan, and other areas. On Sept. 18, 1931, Japan seized the Northeastern Provinces (Manchuria) and set up a puppet state called Manchukuo. The border province of Jehol was cut off as a buffer state in 1933. Japan invaded China proper July 7, 1937. After its defeat in World War II, Japan gave up all seized land.

Following World War II, internal disturbances arose involving the Kuomintang, communists, and other factions. China came under domination of communist armies, 1949-1950. The Kuomintang government moved to Taiwan, 90 mi. off the mainland, Dec. 8, 1949.

The People's Republic of China was proclaimed in Peking Sept. 21, 1949, by the Chinese People's Political Consultative Conference under Mao Zedong.

China and the USSR signed a 30-year treaty of "friendship, alliance and mutual assistance," Feb. 15, 1950.

The U.S. refused recognition of the new regime. On Nov. 26, 1950, the People's Republic sent armies into Korea against U.S. troops and forced a stalemate.

By the 1960s, relations with the USSR deteriorated, with disagreements on borders, ideology and leadership of world communism. The USSR cancelled aid accords, and China, with Albania, launched anti-Soviet propaganda drives. High level talks have been held with the USSR to seek improved trade and cultural contracts; little progress was reported.

On Oct. 25, 1971, the UN General Assembly ousted the Taiwan government from the UN and seated the People's Republic in its place. The U.S. had supported the mainland's admission but opposed Taiwan's expulsion.

U.S. Pres. Nixon visited China Feb. 21-28, 1972, on invitation from Premier Zhou Enlai, ending years of antipathy between the 2 nations. China and the U.S. opened liaison offices in each other's capitals, May-June 1973. The U.S., Dec. 15, 1978, formally recognized the People's Republic of China as the sole legal government of China; diplomatic relations between the 2 nations were established, Jan. 1, 1979.

In a continuing "reassessment" of the policies of Mao Zedong, Mao's widow, Jiang Quing, and other Gang of Four members were convicted of "committing crimes during the 'Cultural Revolution,'" Jan. 25, 1981.

Internal developments. After an initial period of consolidation, 1949-52, industry, agriculture, and social and economic institutions were forcibly molded according to Maoist ideals. However, frequent drastic changes in policy and violent factionalism interfered with economic development.

In 1957, Mao Tse-tung admitted an estimated 800,000 people had been executed 1949-54; opponents claimed much higher figures.

The Great Leap Forward, 1958-60, tried to force the pace of economic development through intensive labor on huge new rural communes, and through emphasis on ideological purity and enthusiasm. The program caused resistance and was largely abandoned. Serious food shortages developed, and the government was forced to buy grain from the West.

The Great Proletarian Cultural Revolution, 1965, was an attempt to oppose pragmatism and bureaucratic power and instruct a new generation in revolutionary principles. Massive purges took place. A program of forcibly relocating millions of urban teenagers into the countryside was launched.

By 1968 the movement had run its course; many purged officials returned to office in subsequent years, and reforms in education and industry that had placed ideology above expertise were gradually weakened.

In the mid-1970s, factional and ideological fighting increased, and emerged into the open after the 1976 deaths of Mao and Premier Zhou Enlai. Mao's widow and 3 other leading leftists were purged and placed under arrest, after reportedly trying to seize power. Their opponents said the "gang of four" had used severe repression and mass torture, had sparked local fighting and had disrupted production. The new ruling group modified Maoist policies in education, culture, and industry, and sought better ties with non-communist countries.

Relations with Vietnam deteriorated in 1978 as China charged persecution of ethnic Chinese. In retaliation for Vietnam's invasion of Cambodia, China attacked 4 Vietnamese border provinces Feb. 17, 1979; heavy border fighting ensued.

Sweeping reforms of the central bureaucracy were announced March 1982. By the mid 1980's, China had enacted far-reaching economic reforms highlighted by the departure from rigid central planning and the stressing of market-oriented socialism.

Some 100,000 students and workers staged a march in Beijing to demand democratic reforms, May 4, 1989. The demonstrations continued during a visit to Beijing by Soviet leader Mikhail Gorbachev May 15-18. It was the first Sino-Soviet summit since 1959. A million people gathered in Beijing to demand democratic reforms and the removal of Deng and other leaders. There were protests in at least 20 other Chinese cities. Martial law was imposed, May 20, but was mostly ignored by the protesters.

Chinese army troops entered Beijing, June 3-4, and crushed the pro-democracy protests. Tanks and armored personnel carriers attacked Tiananmen Square, outside the Great Hall of the People, which was the main scene of the demonstrations and hunger strikes. It was estimated that 5,000 died, 10,000 were injured, and hundreds of students and workers arrested. (See Chronology).

Manchuria. Home of the Manchus, rulers of China 1644-1911, Manchuria has accommodated millions of Chinese settlers in the 20th century. Under Japanese rule 1931-45, the area became industrialized. China no longer uses the name Manchuria for the region, which is divided into the 3 NE provinces of Heilongjiang, Jilin, and Liaoning.

Guandong is the southernmost part of Manchuria. Russia in 1898 forced China to lease it Guandong, and built Port Arthur (Lushun) and the port of Dairen (Luda). Japan seized Port Arthur in 1905. It was turned over to the USSR by the 1945 Yalta agreement, but finally returned to China in 1950.

Inner Mongolia was organized by the People's Republic in 1947. Its boundaries have undergone frequent changes, reaching its greatest extent (and restored in 1979) in 1956, with an area of 454,000 sq. mi., allegedly in order to dilute the minority Mongol population. Chinese settlers outnumber the Mongols more than 10 to 1. Pop. (1986 est.): 20.0 mln. Capital: Hohhot.

Xinjiang Uygur Autonomous Region, in Central Asia, is 633,802 sq. mi., pop. (1983 est.): 13.6 mln. (75% Uygurs, a Turkic Moslem group, with a heavy Chinese increase in recent years). Capital: Urumqi. It is China's richest region in strategic minerals. Some Uygurs have fled to the USSR, claiming national oppression.

Tibet, 470,000 sq. mi., is a thinly populated region of high plateaus and massive mountains, the Himalayas on the S, the Kunluns on the N. High passes connect with India and Nepal; roads lead into China proper. Capital: Lhasa. Average altitude is 15,000 ft. Jiachan, 15,870 ft., is believed to be the highest inhabited town on earth. Agriculture is primitive. Pop. (1986 est.): 1.9 mln. (of whom 500,000 are Chinese). Another 4 million Tibetans form the majority of the population of vast adjacent areas that have long been incorporated into China.

China ruled all of Tibet from the 18th century, but independence came in 1911. China reasserted control in 1951, and a communist government was installed in 1953, revising the theocratic Lamaist Buddhist rule. Serfdom was abolished, but all land remained collectivized.

A Tibetan uprising within China in 1956 spread to Tibet in 1959. The rebellion was crushed with Chinese troops, and Buddhism was almost totally suppressed. The Dalai Lama and 100,000 Tibetans fled to India.

Colombia
Republic of Colombia
República de Colombia

People: Population (1989 est.): 31,821,000. **Age distrib.** (%): 0–14: 36.1; 15–59: 57.9; 60+: 6.0. **Pop. density:** 72 per sq. mi. **Urban** (1983): 65.4%. **Ethnic groups:** Mestizo 58%, Caucasian 20%, Mulatto 14%. **Languages:** Spanish. **Religions:** Roman Catholic 95%.

Geography: Area: 439,735 sq. mi., about the size of Texas, and New Mexico combined. **Location:** At the NW corner of S. America. **Neighbors:** Panama on NW, Ecuador, Peru on S, Brazil, Venezuela on E. **Topography:** Three ranges of Andes, the Western, Central, and Eastern Cordilleras, run through the country from N to S. The eastern range consists mostly of high table lands, densely populated. The Magdalena R. rises in Andes, flows N to Carribean, through a rich alluvial plain. Sparsely-settled plains in E are drained by Orinoco and Amazon systems. **Capital:** Bogota. **Cities** (1985 cen.): Bogota 3,967,000; Medellin 1,664,000; Cali 1,450,000; Barranquilla 924,000.

Government: Type: Republic. **Head of state:** Pres. Virgilio Barco Vargas; b. Sept. 17, 1921; in office: Aug. 7, 1986. **Local divisions:** 23 departments, 8 national territories, and special district of Bogota. **Defense:** 2.1% of GNP (1985).

Economy: Industries: Textiles, processed goods, hides, steel, cement, chemicals. **Chief crops:** Coffee (50% of exports), rice, corn, cotton, sugar, bananas. **Minerals:** Oil, gas, emeralds (90% world output), gold, copper, lead, coal, iron, nickel, salt. **Crude oil reserves** (1987): 1.6 bln. bbls. **Other resources:** Rubber, balsam, dye-woods, copaiba, hydro power. **Arable land:** 5%. **Livestock** (1986): cattle: 23.5 mln.; pigs: 2.4 mln.; sheep: 1.9 mln. **Fish catch** (1987): 80,000 metric tons. **Electricity prod.** (1986): 29.5 bln. kwh. **Crude steel prod.** (1986): 500,000 metric tons. **Labor force:** 26% agric.; 21% ind.; 53% services.

Finance: Currency: Peso (June 1989: 363 = $1 US). **Gross national product** (1986): $31.0 bln. **Per capita income** (1981): $1,112. **Imports** (1987): $4.3 bln.; partners: U.S. 34%, EEC 14%, Jap. 11%. **Exports** (1987): $46 bln.; partners: U.S. 30%, EEC 38%. **Tourists** (1986): $220 mln. receipts. **National budget** (1987): $5.6 bln. **International reserves less gold** (Mar. 1989): $3.2 bln. **Gold** 707,000 oz t. **Consumer prices** (change in 1988): 28.1.

Transport: Railway traffic (1986): 180 mln. passenger-km; 696 mln. net ton-km. **Motor vehicles:** in use (1986): 840,000 passenger cars, 391,000. **Civil aviation** (1986): 1.9 bln. passenger-km; 252 mln. net ton-km. **Chief ports:** Buena Ventura, Santa Marta, Barranquilla, Cartagena.

Communications: Television sets: 5.5 mln. in use (1987). **Radios:** 7.9 mln. in use (1987). **Telephones in use** (1986): 2.2 mln. **Daily newspaper circ.** (1987): 61 per 1,000 pop.

Health: Life expectancy at birth (1985): 61.4 male; 66 female. **Births** (per 1,000 pop. 1985): 31. **Deaths** (per 1,000 pop. 1985): 7.7. **Natural increase** (1985): 2.3%. **Hospital beds** (1982): 26,880. **Physicians** (1983): 21,778. **Infant mortality** (per 1,000 live births 1985): 62%.

Education (1986): **Literacy:** 80%. Only 28% finish primary school.

Major International Organizations: UN (World Bank, GATT), OAS.

Embassy: 2118 Leroy Pl. NW, 20008; 387-8338.

Spain subdued the local Indian kingdoms (Funza, Tunja) by the 1530s, and ruled Colombia and neighboring areas as New Granada for 300 years. Independence was won by 1819. Venezuela and Ecuador broke away in 1829-30, and Panama withdrew in 1903.

One of the Latin American democracies, Colombia is plagued by rural and urban violence, though scaled down from "La Violencia" of 1948-58, which claimed 200,000 lives. Attempts at land and social reform, and progress in industrialization have not yet succeeded in reducing massive social problems aggravated by a very high birth rate.   (See Chronology).

Comoros

Federal Islamic Republic of the Comoros

Jumhurīyat al-Qumur al-Itthādīyah al-Islāmīyah

People: Population (1989 est.): 459,000. **Pop. density:** 547 per sq. mi. **Ethnic groups:** Arabs, Africans, East Indians. **Languages:** Shaafi Islam, (a Swahili dialect), French (official), Malagasy. **Religions:** Islam (official), Roman Catholic.

Geography: Area: 838 sq. mi., half the size of Delaware. **Location:** 3 islands (Grande Comore, Anjouan, and Moheli) in the Mozambique Channel between NW Madagascar and SE Africa. **Neighbors:** Nearest are Mozambique on W, Madagascar on E. **Topography:** The islands are of volcanic origin, with an active volcano on Grand Comoro. **Capital:** Moroni. **Cities** (1988 est.): Moroni (met.) 28,000.

Government: Type: Republic. **Head of state:** Pres. Ahmed Abdallah Abderemane; b. 1919; in office: May 23, 1978. **Local divisions:** each of the 3 main islands is a prefecture.

Economy: Industries: Perfume. **Chief crops:** Vanilla, copra, perfume plants, fruits. **Arable land:** 35%. **Electricity prod.** (1986): 5 mln. kwh. **Labor force:** 87% agric.

Finance: Currency: CFA franc (Mar. 1989: 319 = $1 US). **Gross national product** (1986): $210 mln. **Per capita income** (1986): $340. **Imports** (1986): $38 mln.; partners: Fr. 51%, Ken. 10%. **Exports** (1986): $20 mln.; partners: Fr. 43%, U.S. 40%.

Transport: Chief ports: Dzaoudzi.

Communications: Radios: 100,000 in use (1987). **Telephones in use** (1981): 3,000.

Health: Life expectancy at birth (1987): 53.0 male; 57.0 female. **Births** (per 1,000 pop. 1987): 47. **Deaths** (per 1,000 pop. 1987): 14. **Natural increase** (1987): 3.3%. **Infant mortality** (per 1,000 live births 1987): 96.0.

Education: (1988): **Literacy:** 15%; less than 20% attend secondary school.

Major International Organizations: UN (IMF, World Bank); OAU.

Embassy: 336 E. 45th St., New York, NY 10017; (212) 972-8010.

The islands were controlled by Moslem sultans until the French acquired them 1841-1909. A 1974 referendum favored independence, with only the Christian island of Mayotte preferring association with France. The French National Assembly decided to allow each of the islands to decide its own fate. The Comoro Chamber of Deputies declared independence July 6, 1975. In a referendum in 1976, Mayotte voted to remain French. A leftist regime that seized power in 1975 was deposed in a pro-French 1978 coup.

Congo

People's Republic of the Congo

République Populaire du Congo

People: Population (1989 est.): 2,031,000. **Pop. density:** 15 per sq. mi. **Urban** (1986): 51%. **Ethnic groups:** Bakongo 45%, Bateke 20%, others. **Languages:** French (official), Bantu dialects. **Religions:** Christians 47% (two-thirds Roman Catholic), animists 47%, Moslem 2%.

Geography: Area: 132,046 sq. mi., slightly smaller than Montana. **Location:** In western central Africa. **Neighbors:** Gabon, Cameroon on W, Central African Republic on N, Zaire on E, Angola (Cabinda) on SW. **Topography:** Much of the Congo is covered by thick forests. A coastal plain leads to the fertile Niari Valley. The center is a plateau; the Congo R. basin consists of flood plains in the lower and savanna in the upper portion. **Capital:** Brazzaville. **Cities** (1984 est.): Brazzaville (met.) 595,000; Pointe-Noire 297,000; Loubomo 35,000.

Government: Type: People's republic. **Head of state:** Pres. Denis Sassou-Nguesso; b. 1943; in office: Feb. 8, 1979. **Head of government:** Prime Min. Ange Edouard Poungui; in office: Aug. 12, 1984. **Local divisions:** 9 regions and capital district. **Defense:** 2.5% of GNP (1985).

Economy: Chief crops: Palm oil and kernels, cocoa, coffee, tobacco. **Minerals:** Oil, potash, natural gas, lead, copper, zinc. **Crude oil reserves** (1985): 798 mln. bbls. **Arable land:** 2%.

Fish catch (1986): 29,000 metric tons. **Electricity prod.** (1986): 262 mln. kwh. **Labor force:** 90% agric.

Finance: Currency: CFA franc (Mar. 1989: 319 = $1 US). **Gross national product** (1986): $2.0 bln. **Per capita income** (1988): $1,100. **Imports** (1986): $630 mln.; partners: Fr. 39%. **Exports** (1986): $650 mln.; partners: U.S. 60%, Sp. 13%. **Tourist receipts** (1986): $7 mln. **International reserves less gold** (Jan. 1989): $1.8 mln. **Gold:** 11,000 oz t. **Consumer prices** (change in 1988): 2.8%.

Transport: Railway traffic (1985): 432 mln. passenger-km; 516 mln. net ton-km. **Motor vehicles:** in use (1982): 41,000 passenger cars, 79,000 comm. vehicles. **Chief ports:** Pointe-Noire, Brazzaville.

Communications: Television sets: 5,500 in use (1987). **Radios:** 200,000 in use (1986). **Telephones in use** (1986): 18,000.

Health: Life expectancy at birth (1986): 44.9 male; 48.1 female. **Births** (per 1,000 pop. 1985): 44.5. **Deaths** (per 1,000 pop. 1985): 17.1. **Natural increase** (1985): 2.7%. **Hospital beds** (1978): 6,876. **Physicians** (1980): 278. **Infant mortality** (per 1,000 live births 1985): 110.

Education (1988): **Literacy:** 50%+. Years compulsory 10; attendance 80%.

Major International Organizations: UN (GATT, IMF, WHO), OAU.

Embassy: 4891 Colorado Ave. NW 20011; 726-5500.

The Loango Kingdom flourished in the 15th century, as did the Anzico Kingdom of the Batekes; by the late 17th century they had become weakened. France established control by 1885. Independence came Aug. 15, 1960.

After a 1963 coup sparked by trade unions, the country adopted a Marxist-Leninist stance, with the USSR and China vying for influence. Tribal divisions remain strong. France remains a dominant trade partner and source of technical assistance, and French-owned private enterprise retained a major economic role. However, the government of Pres. Sassou-Nguesso favored a strengthening of relations with the USSR, a socialist constitution was adopted, 1979.

Costa Rica

Republic of Costa Rica

República de Costa Rica

People: Population (1989 est.): 2,922,000. **Age distrib. (%):** 0–14: 35; 15–49: 51.8; 50+: 13.2. **Pop. density:** 149 per sq. mi. **Urban** (1986): 50%. **Ethnic groups:** Spanish (with Mestizo minority). **Language:** Spanish (official). **Religions:** Roman Catholic 95%.

Geography: Area: 19,575 sq. mi., smaller than W. Virginia. **Location:** In central America. **Neighbors:** Nicaragua on N, Panama on S. **Topography:** Lowlands by the Caribbean are tropical. The interior plateau, with an altitude of about 4,000 ft., is temperate. **Capital:** San Jose. **Cities** (1988 met. est.): San Jose 890,000.

Government: Type: Democratic republic. **Head of state:** Pres. Oscar Arias Sanchez; b. Sept. 13 1941; in office May 8, 1986. **Local divisions:** 7 provinces and 80 cantons.

Economy: Industries: Fiberglass, aluminum, textiles, fertilizers, roofing, cement. **Chief crops:** Coffee (chief export), bananas, sugar, cocoa, cotton, hemp. **Minerals:** Gold, salt, sulphur, iron. **Other resources:** Fish, forests. **Arable land:** 12%. **Livestock** (1986): cattle: 2.4. mln. **Fish catch** (1986): 20,000 metric tons. **Electricity prod.** (1986): 2.7 bln. kwh. **Labor force:** 32% agric.; 25% ind. & comm.; 38% service and government.

Finance: Currency: Colone (Mar. 1989: 80 = $1 US). **Gross national product** (1988): $4.2 bln. **Per capita income** (1987): $1,584. **Imports** (1988): $1.4 bln.; partners: U.S. 38%, CACM 10%, Jap. 10%. **Exports** (1988): $1.3 bln.; partners: U.S. 41%, CACM 18%. **Tourists** (1986): receipts: $133 mln. **National budget** (1987): $791 mln. expenditures. **International reserves less gold** (Mar. 1989): $697 mln. **Gold:** 23,000 oz t. **Consumer prices** (change in 1988): 20.8%.

Transport: Motor vehicles: in use (1986): 113,000 passenger cars, 72,000 comm. vehicles. **Civil aviation** (1986): 558 mln. passenger-km; 29 mln. net ton-km. **Chief ports:** Limon, Puntarenas, Golfito.

Communications: Television sets: 470,000 in use (1987). **Radios:** 200,000 in use (1986). **Telephones in use** (1986): 343,000. **Daily newspaper circ.** (1986): 78 per 1,000 pop.

Health: Life expectancy at birth (1988): 67.5 male; 71.9 female. **Births** (per 1,000 pop. 1985): 31. **Deaths** (per 1,000 pop. 1985): 4. **Natural increase** (1985): 2.7%. **Hospital beds** (1982): 7,700. **Physicians** (1982): 1,929. **Infant mortality** (per 1,000 live births 1988): 15.2.

Education (1989): **Literacy:** 93%. Years compulsory 6; attendance 99%.

Major International Organizations: UN (FAO, ILO, IMF, WHO), OAS.

Embassy: 1825 Connecticut Ave. NW, 20009; 234-2945.

Guaymi Indians inhabited the area when Spaniards arrived, 1502. Independence came in 1821. Costa Rica seceded from the Central American Federation in 1838. Since the civil war of 1948-49, there has been little violent social conflict, and free political institutions have been preserved.

Costa Rica, though still a largely agricultural country, has achieved a relatively high standard of living and social services, and land ownership is widespread.

Côte d'Ivoire

Ivory Coast

République de la Côte d'Ivoire

People: Population (1989 est.): 11,798,000. **Age distrib.** (%): 0–14: 45.1; 15–59: 50.2; 60+: 4.7. **Pop. density:** 94 per sq. mi. **Urban** (1986): 47%. **Ethnic groups:** Baule 23%, Bete 18%, Senufo 15%, Malinke 11%, over 60 tribes. **Languages:** French (official), tribal languages. **Religions:** Moslem 25%, Christian 12%, indigenous 63%.

Geography: Area: 124,503 sq. mi., slightly larger than New Mexico. **Location:** On S. coast of W. Africa. **Neighbors:** Liberia, Guinea on W, Mali, Burkina Faso on N, Ghana on E. **Topography:** Forests cover the W half of the country, and range from a coastal strip to halfway to the N on the E. A sparse inland plain leads to low mountains in NW. **Capital:** Abidjan. **Cities** (1985 est.): Abidjan 1,850,000 (met.)

Government: Type: Republic. **Head of state:** Pres. Felix Houphouet-Boigny; b. Oct. 18, 1905; in office: Aug. 7, 1960. **Local divisions:** 34 departments.

Economy: Chief crops: Coffee, cocoa. **Minerals:** Diamonds, manganese. **Other resources:** Timber, rubber, petroleum. **Arable land:** 9%. **Livestock** (1986): goats: 1.4 mln.; sheep: 1.5 mln.; cattle: 881,000. **Fish catch** (1986): 97,000 metric tons. **Electricity prod.** (1986): 2.1 bln. kwh. **Labor force:** 85% agric., forestry.

Finance: Currency: CFA franc (Mar. 1989: 319 = $1 US). **Gross national product** (1986): $9.3 bln. **Per capita income** (1986): $921. **Imports** (1987): $4.6 bln.; partners: Fr. 31%, Jap. 5%, U.S. 5%. **Exports** (1987): $6.2 bln.; partners: Fr. 14%, Neth. 19%, U.S. 11%, It. 8%. **Tourists** (1986): $70 mln receipts; **International reserves less gold** (Jan. 1989): $10.4 mln. **Gold:** 45,000 oz t. **Consumer prices** (changed in 1988): 4.4%.

Transport: Railway traffic (1987): 857 mln. passenger-km; 530 mln. net ton-km. **Motor vehicles:** in use (1984): 182,000 passenger cars, 52,000 comm. vehicles. **Chief ports:** Abidjan, Sassandra.

Communications: Television sets: 625,000 in use (1987). **Radios:** 1.2 mln. in use (1986). **Telephones in use** (1981): 88,000. **Daily newspaper circ.** (1986): 12 per 1,000 pop.

Health: Life expectancy at birth (1983): 46.9 male; 50.2 female. **Births** (per 1,000 pop. 1985): 48.0. **Deaths** (per 1,000 pop. 1985): 12.0. **Natural increase** (1985): 3.6%. **Hospital beds** (1982): 10,062. **Physicians** (1982): 502. **Infant mortality** (per 1,000 live births 1987): 121.

Education (1988): **Literacy:** 35%. **Years compulsory:** none; attendance 75%.

Major International Organizations: UN and all of its specialized agencies, OAU.

Embassy: 2424 Massachusetts Ave. NW 20008; 483-2400.

A French protectorate from 1842, Côte D'Ivoire became independent in 1960. It is the most prosperous of tropical African nations, due to diversification of agriculture for export, close ties to France, and encouragement of foreign investment. About 20% of the population are workers from neighboring countries. Côte D'Ivoire, which officially changed its name from Ivory Coast in Oct. 1985, is a leader of the pro-Western bloc in Africa.

Cuba

Republic of Cuba

República de Cuba

People: Population (1989 est.): 10,587,000. **Age distrib.** (%): 0-under 15: 24.8; 15–59: 63.6; 60+: 11.6. **Pop. density:** 239 per sq. mi. **Urban** (1987): 71%. **Ethnic groups:** Spanish, African. **Languages:** Spanish. **Religions:** Roman Catholic 42%, none 49%.

Geography: Area: 44,218 sq. mi., nearly as large as Pennsylvania. **Location:** Westernmost of West Indies. **Neighbors:** Bahamas, U.S., on N, Mexico on W, Jamaica on S, Haiti on E. **Topography:** The coastline is about 2,500 miles. The N coast is steep and rocky, the S coast low and marshy. Low hills and fertile valleys cover more than half the country. Sierra Maestra, in the E is the highest of 3 mountain ranges. **Capital:** Havana. **Cities** (1987 est.): Havana 2,036,000; Santiago de Cuba 364,000; Camaguey 265,000.

Government: Type: Communist state. **Head of state:** Pres. Fidel Castro Ruz; b. Aug. 13, 1926; in office: Dec. 3, 1976 (formerly Prime Min. since Feb. 16, 1959). **Local divisions:** 14 provinces, 169 municipal assemblies. **Defense:** 5.4% of GNP (1985).

Economy: Industries: Texiles, wood products, cement, chemicals, cigars. **Chief crops:** Sugar (75% of exports), tobacco, coffee, pineapples, bananas, citrus fruit, coconuts. **Minerals:** Cobalt, nickel, iron, copper, manganese, salt. **Other resources:** Forests. **Arable land:** 29%. **Livestock** (1986): cattle: 6.5 mln.; pigs: 2.4 mln. **Fish catch** (1985): 221,000 metric tons. **Electricity prod.** (1986): 14.0 bln. kwh. **Crude steel prod.** (1985): 412,000 metric tons. **Labor force:** 25% agric.; 47% ind. & comm.; 28% services & govt.

Finance: Currency: Peso (Dec. 1988: .76 = $1 US). **Gross national product** (1984): $26.9 bln. **Per capita income** (1983): $1,590. **Imports** (1985): $8.6 bln.; partners: USSR 67%. **Exports** (1985): $6.5 bln.; partners: USSR 72%. **Tourists** (1986): Revenues: 130 mln.

Transport: Railway traffic (1986): 2.2 bln. passenger-km; 2.4 bln. net ton-km. **Motor vehicles:** in use (1985): 200,000 passenger cars, 164,000 comm. vehicles. **Civil aviation** (1986): 2.6 bln. passenger-km.; 33 mln. net ton-km. **Chief ports:** Havana, Matanzas, Cienfuegos, Santiago de Cuba.

Communications: Television sets: 2.0 mln. in use (1987). **Radios:** 3.2 mln. in use (1986). **Telephones in use** (1986): 543,000. **Daily newspaper circ.** (1986): 126 per 1,000 pop.

Health: Life expectancy at birth: (1980): 71.0 male; 74.0 female. **Births** (per 1,000 pop. 1987): 17.4. **Deaths** (per 1,000 pop. 1987): 6.3. **Natural increase** (1987): 1.1%. **Hospital beds** (1986): 56,000. **Physicians** (1986): 25,418. **Infant mortality** (per 1,000 live births 1987): 13.3.

Education (1985): **Literacy:** 96%. 92% of those between ages 6-14 attend school.

Major International Organizations: UN (GATT, WHO).

Some 50,000 Indians lived in Cuba when it was discovered by Columbus in 1492. Its name derives from the Indian Cubanacan. Except for British occupation of Havana, 1762-63, Cuba remained Spanish until 1898. A slave-based sugar plantation economy developed from the 18th century, aided by early mechanization of milling. Sugar remains the chief product and chief export despite government attempts to diversify.

A ten-year uprising ended in 1878 with guarantees of rights by Spain, which Spain failed to carry out. A full-scale movement under Jose Marti began Feb. 24, 1895.

The U.S. declared war on Spain in April, 1898, after the sinking of the U.S.S. Maine in Havana harbor, and defeated it in the short Spanish-American War. Spain gave up all claims to Cuba. U.S. troops withdrew in 1902, but under 1903 and 1934 agreements, the U.S. leases a site at Guantanamo Bay in the SE as a naval base. U.S. and other foreign investments acquired a dominant role in the economy. In 1952, former president Fulgencio Batista seized control and established a dictatorship, which grew increasingly harsh and corrupt. Former student leader Fidel Castro assembled a rebel band in 1956; guerrilla fighting intensified in 1958. Batista fled Jan. 1, 1959, and in the resulting political vacuum Castro took power, becoming premier Feb. 16.

The government began a program of sweeping economic and social changes, without restoring promised liberties. Opponents were imprisoned and some were executed. Some 700,000 Cubans emigrated in the years after the Castro takeover, mostly to the U.S.

Cattle and tobacco lands were nationalized, while a system of cooperatives was instituted. By the end of 1960 all banks and industrial companies had been nationalized, including over $1 billion worth of U.S.-owned properties, mostly without compensation.

Poor sugar crops resulted in collectivization of farms, stringent labor controls, and rationing, despite continued aid from the USSR and other communist countries.

The U.S. imposed an export embargo in 1962, severely damaging the economy. In 1961, some 1,400 Cubans, trained and backed by the U.S. Central Intelligence Agency, unsuccessfully tried to invade and overthrow the regime.

In the fall of 1962, the U.S. learned that the USSR had brought nuclear missiles to Cuba. After an Oct. 22 warning from Pres. Kennedy, the missiles were removed.

In 1977, Cuba and the U.S. signed agreements to exchange diplomats, without restoring full ties, and to regulate offshore fishing. In 1978, and again in 1980, the U.S. agreed to accept political prisoners released by Cuba some of whom, it was later discovered, were criminals and mental patients. A 1987 agreement provided for 20,000 Cubans to immigrate to the U.S. each year; Cuba agreed to take back some 2,500 jailed in the U.S. since the 1980 Mariel boat lift.

In 1975-78, Cuba sent troops to aid one faction in the Angola Civil War. Cuban troops or advisers are stationed in several African countries. This presence, along with Cuba's involvement in Central America and the Caribbean, has contributed to poor relations with the U.S. In Dec. 1988, Cuba agreed to a peace accord in which Cuban troops would withdraw from Angola by July 1991.

In 1983, 24 Cubans died and over 700 were captured, later repatriated, as a result of the U.S.-led invasion of Grenada.

Soviet leader Gorbachev visited Cuba Apr. 2-5, 1989; Cuba had been critical of the social and economic reforms that Gorbachev had brought to the USSR.

Cyprus

Republic of Cyprus

Kypriaki Dimokratia (Greek)

Kibris Cumhuriyeti (Turkish)

People: Population (1989 est.): 696,000. **Age distrib. (%):** 0–14: 25.4; 15–59: 60.4; 60+: 14.2. **Pop. density:** 194 per sq. mi. **Urban** (1982): 53%. **Ethnic groups:** Greeks 78%, Turks 18.7%, Armenians, Maronites. **Languages:** Greek, Turkish (both official), English. **Religions:** Orthodox 77%, Moslems 18%.

Geography: Area: 3,572 sq. mi., smaller than Connecticut. **Location:** In eastern Mediterranean Sea, off Turkish coast. **Neighbors:** Nearest are Turkey on N, Syria, Lebanon on E. **Topography:** Two mountain ranges run E-W, separated by a wide, fertile plain. **Capital:** Nicosia. **Cities** (1984 est.): Nicosia 124,300.

Government: Type: Republic. **Head of state:** Pres. George Vassiliou; b. May 21, 1931; in office: Feb. 28, 1988. **Local divisions:** 6 districts. **Defense:** 11% of govt. budget (1984).

Economy: Industries: Wine, clothing, construction, chemicals. **Chief crops:** Grains, grapes, carobs, citrus fruits, potatoes, olives. **Minerals:** Copper, pyrites, asbetos, gypsum, umber. **Arable land:** 47%. **Electricity prod.** (1987): 1.5 mln. kwh. **Labor force:** 21% agric.; 20% ind., 18% comm., 19% serv.

Finance: Currency: Pound (Mar. 1989: 1.00 = $2.03 US). **GNP** (1985): $2.3 bln. **Per capita income** (1985): $4,400. **Imports** (1988): $1.8 bln.; partners: UK 13%, Itl. 12%. **Exports** (1988): $767 mln.; partners: UK 21%, Sau. Ar. 5%. **Tourists** (1985): receipts: $298 mln. **National budget** (1985): $623 mln. revenues; $734 mln. expenditures. **International reserves less gold** (Mar. 1989): $841 mln. **Gold:** 459,000 oz. t. **Consumer prices** (change in 1988): 3.4%.

Transport: Motor vehicles: in use (1986): 126,000 passenger cars, 54,000 comm. vehicles. **Civil aviation** (1984): 1.1 bln. passenger-km; 26 mln. net ton-km. **Chief ports:** Famagusta, Limassol.

Communications: Television sets: 88,000 (1987). **Radios:** 171,000 (1987). **Telephones in use** (1986): 153,000. **Daily newspaper circ.** (1987): 157 per 1,000 pop.

Health: Life expectancy at birth (1988): 72.3 male; 77.0 female. **Births** (per 1,000 pop. 1985): 21. **Deaths** (per 1,000 pop.

1985): 8. **Natural increase** (1985): 1.3%. **Hospital beds** (1987): 4,256. **Physicians** (1987): 1,195. **Infant mortality** (per 1,000 live births 1988): 12.

Education (1988): **Literacy:** 99%. **Years compulsory:** 9; attendance 99%.

Major International Organizations: UN (GATT, IMF, WHO), Commonwealth of Nations, EC (Assoc.).

Embassy: 2211 R St. NW, 20008; 462-5772.

Agitation for enosis (union) with Greece increased after World War II, with the Turkish minority opposed, and broke into violence in 1955-56. In 1959, Britain, Greece, Turkey, and Cypriot leaders approved a plan for an independent republic, with constitutional guarantees for the Turkish minority and permanent division of offices on an ethnic basis. Greek and Turkish Communal Chambers dealt with religion, education, and other matters.

Archbishop Makarios, formerly the leader of the enosis movement, was elected president, and full independence became final Aug. 16, 1960. Makarios was re-elected in 1968 and 1973.

Further communal strife led the United Nations to send a peace-keeping force in 1964; its mandate has been repeatedly renewed.

The Cypriot National Guard, led by officers from the army of Greece, seized the government July 15, 1974, and named Nikos Sampson, an advocate of union with Greece, president. Makarios fled the country. On July 20, Turkey invaded the island; Greece mobilized its forces but did not intervene. A cease-fire was arranged July 22. On the 23d, Sampson turned over the presidency to Glafkos Clerides (on the same day, Greece's military junta resigned). A peace conference collapsed Aug. 14; fighting resumed. By Aug. 16 Turkish forces had occupied the NE 40% of the island, despite the presence of UN peace forces. Makarios resumed the presidency in Dec., until his death, 1977.

Turkish Cypriots voted overwhelmingly, June 8, 1975, to form a separate Turkish Cypriot federated state. A president and assembly were elected in 1976. Some 200,000 Greeks have been expelled from the Turkish-controlled area, replaced by thousands of Turks, some from the mainland.

Turkish Republic of Northern Cyprus

A declaration of independence was announced by Turkish-Cypriot leader Rauf Denktash, Nov. 15, 1983. The new state is not internationally recognized although it does have trade relations with some countries. TRNC contains 1,295 sq mi., pop. (1988 est.): 165,000, 99% Turkish.

Czechoslovakia

Czechoslovak Socialist Republic

Československá Socialistická Republika

People: Population (1989 est.): 15,661,000. **Age distrib. (%):** 0–14: 24.2; 15–59: 59.3; 60+: 16.5. **Pop. density:** 317 per sq. mi. **Urban** (1985): 73%. **Ethnic groups:** Czechs 64%, Slovaks 31%, Hungarian, German, Ukrainian, Polish. **Languages:** Czech, Slovak (both official). **Religions:** Roman Catholic 65%.

Geography: Area: 49,365 sq. mi., the size of New York. **Location:** In E central Europe. **Neighbors:** Poland, E. Germany on N, W. Germany on W. Austria, Hungary on S, USSR on E. **Topography:** Bohemia, in W, is a plateau surrounded by mountains; Moravia is hilly, Slovakia, in E, has mountains (Carpathians) in N, fertile Danube plain in S. Vltava (Moldau) and Labe (Elbe) rivers flow N from Bohemia to G. **Capital:** Prague. **Cities** (1987 est.): Prague 1.2 mln.; Brno 385,000; Bratislava 413,000; Ostrava 327,000.

Government: Type: Communist. **Head of state:** Pres. Gustav Husak; b. Jan 10, 1913; in office: May 29, 1975; **Head of government:** Prime Min. Ladislav Adamec; in office: Oct. 11, 1988. **Head of Communist Party:** Gen. Sec. Milos Jakes; in office: Dec. 17, 1987. **Local divisions:** Czech and Slovak republics each have an assembly. **Defense:** 5.8% of GNP (1986).

Economy: Industries: Machinery, oil products, iron and steel, glass, chemicals, motor vehicles, cement. **Chief crops:** Wheat, sugar beets, potatoes, rye, corn, barley. **Minerals:** coke, coal, iron. **Arable land:** 40%. **Livestock:** (1987): cattle: 5 mln.; pigs: 6.6 mln.; sheep: 1 mln. **Electricity prod.** (1986): 83.0 bln. kwh. **Crude steel prod.** (1987): 15.4 mln. metric tons. **Labor force:** 14% agric.; 64% ind., comm.; 22% service, govt.

Finance: Currency: Koruna (Jan. 1989: 5.43 = $1 US). **Gross national product** (1986): $142.5 bln. **Per capita income** (1984): $8,300. **Imports** (1985): $18.1 bln.; partners: USSR 46%, E. Ger. 10%, Pol. 6%, W. Ger. 5%. **Exports** (1985): $18.0 bln.; partners: USSR 41%, E. Ger. 9%, Pol. 7%, Hung. 5%.

Transport: Railway traffic (1986): 19.8 bln. passenger-km; 69 bln. net ton-km. **Motor vehicles:** in use (1985): 2.6 mln. passenger cars, 425,000 comm. **Civil aviation** (1985): 1.1 bln. passenger-km; 60 mln. net ton-km.

Communications: Television sets: 4.3 mln. (1986). **Radios:** 4.2 mln. (1985). **Telephones in use** (1986): 3.5 mln. **Daily newspaper circ.** (1986): 280 per 1,000 pop.

Health: Life expectancy at birth (1985): 67.2 male; 74.4 female. **Births** (per 1,000 pop. 1986): 14.2. **Deaths** (per 1,000 pop. 1986): 11.9. **Natural increase** (1986): .2%. **Hospital beds** (1987): 122,000; **Physicians** (1987): 48,414. **Infant mortality** (per 1,000 live births 1985): 15.6.

Education (1987): **Literacy:** 99%.

Major International Organizations: UN (GATT, WHO), Warsaw Pact.

Embassy: 3900 Linnean Ave. NW 20008; 263-6315.

Bohemia, Moravia and Slovakia were part of the Great Moravian Empire in the 9th century. Later, Slovakia was overrun by Magyars, while Bohemia and Moravia became part of the Holy Roman Empire. Under the kings of Bohemia, Prague in the 14th century was the cultural center of Central Europe. Bohemia and Hungary became part of Austria-Hungary.

In 1914-1918 Thomas G. Masaryk and Eduard Benes formed a provisional government with the support of Slovak leaders including Milan Stefanik. They proclaimed the Republic of Czechoslovakia Oct. 28, 1918.

By 1938 Nazi Germany had worked up disaffection among German-speaking citizens in Sudetenland and demanded its cession. Prime Min. Neville Chamberlain of Britain, with the acquiescence of France, signed with Hitler at Munich, Sept. 30, 1938, an agreement to the cession, with a guarantee of peace by Hitler and Mussolini. Germany occupied Sudetenland Oct. 1-2.

Hitler on Mar. 15, 1939, dissolved Czechoslovakia, made protectorates of Bohemia and Moravia, and supported the autonomy of Slovakia, which was proclaimed independent Mar. 14, 1939.

Soviet troops with some Czechoslovak contingents entered eastern Czechoslovakia in 1944 and reached Prague in May 1945; Benes returned as president. In May 1946 elections, the Communist Party won 38% of the votes, and Benes accepted Klement Gottwald, a communist, as prime minister.

In February, 1948, the communists seized power in advance of scheduled elections. In May 1948 a new constitution was approved. Benes refused to sign it. On May 30 the voters were offered a one-slate ballot and the communists won full control. Benes resigned June 7 and Gottwald became president. A harsh Stalinist period followed, with complete and violent suppression of all opposition.

In Jan. 1968 a liberalization movement spread explosively through Czechoslovakia. Antonin Novotny, long the Stalinist boss of the nation, was deposed as party leader and succeeded by Alexander Dubcek, a Slovak, who declared he intended to make communism democratic. On Mar. 22 Novotny resigned as president and was succeeded by Gen. Ludvik Svoboda. On Apr. 6, Premier Joseph Lenart resigned and was succeeded by Oldrich Cernik, whose new cabinet was pledged to carry out democratization and economic reforms.

In July 1968 the USSR and 4 Warsaw Pact nations demanded an end to liberalization. On Aug. 20, the Russian, Polish, East German, Hungarian, and Bulgarian armies invaded Czechoslovakia.

Despite demonstrations and riots by students and workers, press censorship was imposed, liberal leaders were ousted from office and promises of loyalty to Soviet policies were made by some old-line Communist Party leaders.

On Apr. 17, 1969, Dubcek resigned as leader of the Communist Party and was succeeded by Gustav Husak. In Jan. 1970, Premier Cernik was ousted. Censorship was tightened and the Communist Party expelled a third of its members. In 1973, amnesty was offered to some of the 40,000 who fled the country after the 1968 invasion, but repressive policies continue to remain in force.

More than 700 leading Czechoslovak intellectuals and former party leaders signed a human rights manifesto in 1977, called Charter 77, prompting a renewed crackdown by the regime.

Czechoslovakia has long been an industrial and technological leader of the eastern European countries, though its relative standing has declined in recent years because of the government's rejection of economic reforms. The adoption of Soviet-style political and economic reforms was announced in 1988.

Denmark
Kingdom of Denmark
Kongeriget Danmark

People: Population (1989 est.): 5,074,000. **Age distrib. (%):** 0-14: 17.6; 15-59: 62.0; 60+: 20.4. **Pop. density:** 305 per sq. mi. **Urban** (1986): 84%. **Ethnic groups:** Almost all Scandinavian. **Languages:** Danish. **Religions:** Evangelical Lutheran 90%.

Geography: Area: 16,633 sq. mi., the size of Massachusetts and New Hampshire combined. **Location:** In northern Europe, separating the North and Baltic seas. **Neighbors:** W. Germany on S., Norway on NW, Sweden on NE. **Topography:** Denmark consists of the Jutland Peninsula and about 500 islands, 100 inhabited. The land is flat or gently rolling, and is almost all in productive use. **Capital:** Copenhagen. **Cities** (1987): Copenhagen 622,000.

Government: Type: Constitutional monarchy. **Head of state:** Queen Margrethe II; b. Apr. 16, 1940; in office: Jan. 14, 1972. **Head of government:** Prime Min. Poul Schluter; b. 1929; in office: Sept. 10, 1982. **Local divisions:** 14 counties and one city (Copenhagen). **Defense:** 2.3% of GNP (1988).

Economy: Industries: Machinery, textiles, furniture, electronics. **Chief crops:** Dairy products. **Crude oil reserves** (1985): 533 mln. bbls. **Arable land:** 62%. **Livestock** (1987): cattle: 2.3 mln.; pigs: 9.2 mln. **Fish catch** (1987): 1.5 mln. metric tons. **Electricity prod.** (1986): 30.7 bln. kwh. **Crude steel prod.** (1985): 560,000 metric tons. **Labor force:** 8.2% agric.; 50% ind. & comm.; 13% serv.

Finance: Currency: Krone (June 1989: 7.82 = $1 US). **Gross national product** (1987): $101.3 bln. **Per capita income** (1988): $19,750. **Imports** (1987): $25.4 bln.; partners: W. Ger. 24%, Swed. 12%, UK 9%, Neth. 5%. **Exports** (1987): $26.6 bln.; partners: W. Ger. 15%, EC 42%, U.S. 8%. **Tourists** (1986): $1.7 bln. receipts. **National budget** (1980): $23 bln. expenditures. **International reserves less gold** (Mar. 1989): $8.3 bln. **Gold:** 2.0 mln. oz t. **Consumer prices** (change in 1988): 4.6%.

Transport: Railway traffic (1986): 4.5 bln. passenger-km; 1.7 bln. net ton-km. **Motor vehicles:** in use (1986): 1.5 mln. passenger cars, 282,000 comm. **Civil aviation** (1987): 7.3 bln. passenger-km; 826 mln. net ton-km. **Chief ports:** Copenhagen, Alborg, Arhus, Odense.

Communications: Television sets: 1.9 mln. licensed (1987). **Radios:** 2 mln. licensed (1986). **Telephones in use** (1986): 4.0 mln. **Daily newspaper circ.** (1986): 367 per 1,000 pop.

Health: Life expectancy at birth (1986): 71.5 male; 77.5 female. **Births** (per 1,000 pop. 1987): 11.0. **Deaths** (per 1,000 pop. 1987): 11.3. **Hospital beds** (1986): 35,000. **Physicians** (1986): 12,975. **Infant mortality** (per 1,000 live births 1985): 7.8.

Education (1986): **Literacy:** 99%. Years compulsory 9; attendance 100%.

Major International Organizations: UN and all of its specialized agencies, OECD, EC.

Embassy: 3200 Whitehaven St. NW 20008; 234-4300.

The origin of Copenhagen dates back to ancient times, when the fishing and trading place named Havn (port) grew up on a cluster of islets, but Bishop Absalon (1128-1201) is regarded as the actual founder of the city.

Danes formed a large component of the Viking raiders in the early Middle Ages. The Danish kingdom was a major north European power until the 17th century, when it lost its land in southern Sweden. Norway was separated in 1815, and Schleswig-Holstein in 1864. Northern Schleswig was returned in 1920.

The **Faeroe Islands** in the N. Atlantic, about 300 mi. NE of the Shetlands, and 850 mi. from Denmark proper, 18 inhabited, have an area of 540 sq. mi. and pop. (1987) of 46,000. They are self-governing in most matters.

Greenland

(Kalaallit Nunaat)

Greenland, a huge island between the N. Atlantic and the Polar Sea, is separated from the North American continent by Davis Strait and Baffin Bay. Its total area is 840,000 sq. mi., 84% of which is ice-capped. Most of the island is a lofty plateau 9,000 to 10,000 ft. in altitude. The average thickness of the cap is 1,000 ft. The population (1987 est.) is 54,000. Under the 1953 Danish constitution the colony became an integral part of the realm with representatives in the Folketing. The Danish parliament, 1978, approved home rule for Greenland, effective May 1, 1979. Accepting home rule the islanders elected a socialist-dominated legislature, Apr. 4th. With home rule, Greenlandic place names came into official use. The technically-correct name for Greenland is now Kalaallit Nunaat; its capital is Nuuk, rather than Gothab. Fish is the principal export.

Djibouti

Republic of Djibouti

Jumhouriyya Djibouti

People: Population (1989 est.): **327,000. Pop. density:** 38 per sq. mi. **Ethnic groups:** Issa (Somali) 60%; Afar 35%; European 5%. **Languages:** French, Arabic (both official); Somali, Saho-Afar, Arabic. **Religions:** Sunni Moslem 94%.

Geography: Area: 8,494 sq. mi., about the size of New Hampshire. **Location:** On E coast of Africa, separated from Arabian Peninsula by the strategically vital strait of Bab el-Mandeb. **Neighbors:** Ethiopia on N (Eritrea) and W, Somalia on S. **Topography:** The territory, divided into a low coastal plain, mountains behind, and an interior plateau, is arid, sandy, and desolate. The climate is generally hot and dry. **Capital:** Djibouti. **Cities** (1982): Djibouti (met.) 200,000.

Government: Type: Republic. **Head of state:** Pres. Hassan Gouled Aptidon b. 1916; in office: June 24, 1977; **Head of government:** Prem. Barkat Gourad Hamadou; in office: Sept. 30, 1978. **Local divisions:** 5 cercles (districts).

Economy: Minerals: Salt. **Electricity prod.** (1986): 140 mln. kwh.

Finance: Currency Franc (Mar. 1989: 172=$1 US). **Gross national product** (1986): $344 mln. **Per capita income** (1982): $400. **Imports** (1986): $197 mln.; partners: Fr. 47%, Jap. 8%, UK 8%. **Exports** (1986): $96 mln.; partners: Fr. 87%.

Transport: Motor vehicles: in use (1985): 12,000 passenger cars, 950 commercial vehicles. **Chief ports:** Djibouti.

Communications: Television sets: 14,000 in use (1987). **Radios:** 32,000 in use (1986). **Telephones in use** (1986): 8,200.

Health: Life expectancy at birth (1988): 50 years. **Births** (per 1,000 pop. 1985): 49.2. **Deaths** (per 1,000 pop. 1985): 18.3. **Natural increase** (1985): 3.0%. **Infant mortality** (per 1,000 live births 1988): 114.

Education (1988): **Literacy:** 20%.

Major International Organizations: UN, OAU, Arab League. **Embassy:** 866 United Nations Plaza, New York, NY 10017; (212) 753-3163.

France gained control of the territory in stages between 1862 and 1900.

Ethiopia and Somalia have renounced their claims to the area, but each has accused the other of trying to gain control. There were clashes between Afars (ethnically related to Ethiopians) and Issas (related to Somalis) in 1976. Immigrants from both countries continued to enter the country up to independence, which came June 27, 1977.

Unemployment is high and there are few natural resources. French aid is the mainstay of the economy and some 5,000 French troops are present.

Dominica

Commonwealth of Dominica

People: Population (1989 est.): **76,000. Pop. density:** 262 per sq. mi. **Ethnic groups:** nearly all African or mulatto, Caribs.

Languages: English (official), French patois. **Religions:** mainly Roman Catholic.

Geography: Area: 290 sq. mi., about one-fourth the size of Rhode Island. **Location:** In Eastern Caribbean, most northerly Windward Is. **Neighbors:** Guadeloupe to N, Martinique to S. **Topography:** Mountainous, a central ridge running from N to S, terminating in cliffs; volcanic in origin, with numerous thermal springs; rich deep topsoil on leeward side, red tropical clay on windward coast. **Capital** (1983 est.) Roseau 18,000.

Government: Type: Parliamentary democracy; republic within Commonwealth. **Head of state:** Pres. Clarence Augustus Seignoret; in office: 1984. **Head of government:** Prime Min. Mary Eugenia Charles; b. 1919; in office: July 21, 1980. **Local divisions:** 10 parishes.

Economy: Industries: Agriculture, tourism. **Chief crops:** Bananas, citrus fruits, coconuts. **Minerals:** Pumice. **Other resources:** Forests. **Arable land:** 23%. **Electricity prod.** (1987): 16 mln. kwh. **Labor force:** 40% agric.; 32% ind & comm.; 28% services.

Finance: Currency: East Caribbean dollar (May 1989: 2.70 = $1 US). **Gross domestic product** (1986): $102 mln. **Imports** (1986): $63 mln.; partners: UK 12%, U.S. 27%, Can. 7%. **Exports** (1986): $35 mln.; partners: UK 47%. **Tourists** (1986): $10 mln. receipts. **Consumer prices** (change in 1987): 4.8%.

Transport: Chief ports: Roseau.

Communications: Telephones in use (1985): 6,000.

Health: Life expectancy at birth (1987): 73.0 male; 79.0 female. **Births** (per 1,000 pop. 1985): 19. **Deaths** (per 1,000 pop. 1985): 6. **Natural increase** (1985): 1.3%. **Hospital beds** (1986): 312. **Physicians** (1986): 27. **Infant mortality** (per 1,000 live births 1985): 20.

Education: **Literacy:** 80%.

Major International Organizations: UN, OAS.

A British colony since 1805, Dominica was granted self government in 1967. Independence was achieved Nov. 3, 1978.

Hurricane David struck, Aug. 30, 1979, devastating the island and destroying the banana plantations, Dominica's economic mainstay. Coups were attempted in 1980 and 1981.

Dominica took a leading role in the instigation of the 1983 invasion of Grenada.

Dominican Republic

República Dominicana

People: Population (1989 est.): **7,307,000. Age distrib. (%):** 0–14: 40.7; 15–59: 54.6; 60+: 4.7. **Pop. density:** 388 per sq. mi. **Urban** (1986): 55%. **Ethnic groups:** Caucasian 16%, mixed 73%, black 11%. **Languages:** Spanish. **Religions:** Roman Catholic 95%.

Geography: Area: 18,816 sq. mi., the size of Vermont and New Hampshire combined. **Location:** In West Indies, sharing I. of Hispaniola with Haiti. **Neighbors:** Haiti on W. **Topography:** The Cordillera Central range crosses the center of the country, rising to over 10,000 ft., highest in the Caribbean. The Cibao valley to the N is major agricultural area. **Capital:** Santo Domingo. **Cities** (1987 est.): Santo Domingo 1,700,000; Santiago de Los Caballeros 422,000.

Government: Type: Representative democracy. **Head of state:** Pres. Joaquin Balaguer; in office: Aug. 16, 1986. **Local divisions:** 29 provinces and Santo Domingo. **Defense:** 1.5% of GDP. (1986).

Economy: Industries: Sugar refining, cement, pharmaceuticals. **Chief crops:** sugar, cocoa, coffee, tobacco, rice. **Minerals:** Nickel, gold, silver. **Other resources:** Timber. **Arable land:** 30%. **Livestock.** (1986): cattle: 1.9 mln. **Electricity prod.** (1986): 3.8 bln. kwh. **Labor force:** 45% agric.; 21% ind. & comm.; 34% serv. & govt.

Finance: Currency: Peso (Mar. 1989: 6.50 = $1 US). **Gross national product** (1986): $5.5 bln. **Per capita income** (1980): $1,221. **Imports** (1987): $1.8 bln.; partners: U.S. 35%, Venez. 21%, Mex. 11%. **Exports** (1987): $720 mln.; partners: U.S. 64%, Swit. 5%, Neth. 4%. **Tourists** (1986): $463 mln. receipts. **National budget** (1986): $781 mln. expenditures. **International reserves less gold** (Mar. 1989): $182 mln. **Gold:** 18,000 oz t. **Consumer prices** (change in 1987): 15.9%

Transport: Motor vehicles: in use (1984): 101,000 passenger cars, 55,000 comm. vehicles. **Chief ports:** Santo Domingo, San Pedro de Macoris, Puerto Plata.

Communications: Television sets: 425,000 in use (1987). **Radios:** 800,000 in use (1986). **Telephones in use** (1987): 425,000. **Daily newspaper circ.** (1987): 44 per 1,000 pop.

Health: Life expectancy at birth (1985): 60.7 male; 64.6 female. **Births** (per 1,000 pop. 1985): 34. **Deaths** (per 1,000 pop. 1985): 9. **Natural increase** (1985): 2.5%. **Hospital beds** (1980): 8,953. **Physicians** (1984): 3,555. **Infant mortality** (per 1,000 live births 1985): 74.

Education (1987): **Literacy:** 68%. Years compulsory 6; attendance 60%.

Major International Organizations: UN (World Bank, IMF, GATT), OAS.

Embassy: 1712 22d St. NW 20008; 332-6280.

Carib and Arawak Indians inhabited the island of Hispaniola when Columbus landed in 1492. The city of Santo Domingo, founded 1496, is the oldest settlement by Europeans in the hemisphere and has the supposed ashes of Columbus in an elaborate tomb in its ancient cathedral.

The western third of the island was ceded to France in 1697. Santo Domingo itself was ceded to France in 1795. Haitian leader Toussaint L'Ouverture seized it, 1801. Spain returned intermittently 1803-21, as several native republics came and went. Haiti ruled again, 1822-44, and Spanish occupation occurred 1861-63.

The country was occupied by U.S. Marines from 1916 to 1924, when a constitutionally elected government was installed.

In 1930, Gen. Rafael Leonidas Trujillo Molina was elected president. Trujillo ruled brutally until his assassination in 1961. Pres. Joaquin Balaguer, appointed by Trujillo in 1960, resigned under pressure in 1962. Juan Bosch, elected president in the first free elections in 38 years, was overthrown in 1963.

On April 24, 1965, a revolt was launched by followers of Bosch and others, including a few communists. Four days later U.S. Marines intervened against the pro-Bosch forces. Token units were later sent by 5 So. American countries as a peacekeeping force.

A provisional government supervised a June 1966 election, in which Balaguer defeated Bosch by a 3-2 margin; there were some charges of election fraud. The Inter-American Peace Force completed its departure Sept. 20, 1966.

Continued depressed world prices have affected the main export commodity, sugar.

Ecuador
Republic of Ecuador
República del Ecuador

People: Population (1989 est.): 10,490,000. **Age distrib.** (%): 0–14: 41.3; 15–64: 55.0; 65+: 3.7. **Pop. density:** 95 per sq. mi. **Urban** (1987): 52% **Ethnic groups:** Indians 25%, Mestizo 55%, Spanish 10%, African 10%. **Languages:** Spanish (official), Quechuan, Jivaroan. **Religions:** Roman Catholic 95%.

Geography: Area: 109,483 sq. mi., the size of Colorado. **Location:** In NW S. America, on Pacific coast, astride Equator. **Neighbors:** Colombia to N, Peru to E and to S. **Topography:** Two ranges of Andes run N and S, splitting the country into 3 zones: hot, humid lowlands on the coast; temperate highlands between the ranges, and rainy, tropical lowlands to the E. **Capital:** Quito. **Cities** (1987 est.): Guayaquil 1,500,000; Quito 1,200,000.

Government: Type: Republic. **Head of state:** Pres. Rodrigo Borja Cevallos; in office: Aug. 10, 1988. **Local divisions:** 20 provinces. **Defense:** 1.6% of GNP (1984).

Economy: Industries: Food processing, wood prods., textiles. **Chief crops:** Bananas (largest exporter), coffee, rice, sugar, corn. **Minerals:** Oil, copper, iron, lead, silver, sulphur. **Crude oil reserves** (1987): 1.2 bln. bbls. **Other resources:** Rubber, bark. **Arable land:** 9%. **Livestock** (1986): cattle: 3.7 mln.; pigs: 4.9 mln.; sheep: 2.3 mln. **Fish catch** (1986): 268,000 metric tons. **Electricity prod.** (1986): 5.3 bln. kwh. **Labor force:** 34% agric., 12% ind., 35% services.

Finance: Currency: Sucre (June 1989: 500 = $1 US). **Gross national product** (1985): $12.1 bln. **Per capita income** (1985): $1,299. **Imports** (1988): $1.7 bln.; partners: U.S. 32%, EC 16%, Jap. 13%. **Exports** (1988): $2.0 bln.; partners: U.S. 64%. **Tourism** (1986): $135 mln. receipts. **National budget** (1986): $1.2 bln. **International reserves less gold** (Mar. 1989): $397 mln. **Gold:** 414,000 oz t. **Consumer prices** (change in 1988): 58.2%.

Transport: Railway traffic (1986) 43 mln. passenger-km; 11 mln. net ton-km. **Motor vehicles:** in use (1986): 256,000 passenger cars, 36,000 comm. vehicles. **Civil aviation** (1984): 893 mln. passenger-km; 42.6 mln. net ton-km. **Chief ports:** Guayaquil, Manta, Esmeraldas, Puerto Bolivar.

Communications: Television sets: 600,000 in use (1987). **Radios:** 1.9 mln. in use (1986). **Telephones in use** (1986): 351,000. **Daily newspaper circ.** (1985): 57 per 1,000 pop.

Health: Life expectancy at birth (1981): 59.8 male, 63.6 female. **Births** (per 1,000 pop. 1985): 36.0. **Deaths** (per 1,000 pop. 1985): 8.0. **Natural increase** (1985): 2.9%. **Hospital beds** (1984): 15,455. **Physicians** (1984): 11,000. **Infant mortality** (per 1,000 live births 1985): 63.

Education (1986): **Literacy:** 90%. Attendance through 6th grade—76% urban, 33% rural.

Major International Organizations: UN (IMF, WHO), OAS, OPEC.

Embassy: 2535 15th St. NW 20009; 234-7200.

Spain conquered the region, which was the northern Inca empire, in 1633. Liberation forces defeated the Spanish May 24, 1822, near Quito. Ecuador became part of the Great Colombia Republic but seceded, May 13, 1830.

Ecuador had been ruled by civilian and military dictatorships since 1968. A peaceful transfer of power from the military junta to the democratic civilian government took place, 1979.

Since 1972, the economy has revolved around its petroleum exports, which have declined since 1982 causing severe economic problems. Ecuador suspended interest payments for 1987 on its estimated $8.2 billion foreign debt following a Mar. 5-6 earthquake which left 20,000 homeless, and destroyed a stretch of the country's main oil pipeline.

Ecuador and Peru have long disputed their Amazon Valley boundary.

The **Galapagos Islands**, 600 mi. to the W, are the home of huge tortoises and other unusual animals.

Egypt
Arab Republic of Egypt
Jumhūriyah Misr al-Arabiya

People: Population (1989 est.): 54,779,000. **Age distrib** (%) 0-14: 41.8; 15-59: 52.7; 60+: 5.5. **Pop. density:** 141 per sq. mi. **Urban** (1986): 44%. **Ethnic groups:** Eastern Hamitic stock 90%, Bedouin, Nubian. **Languages:** Arabic (official), English. **Religions:** 94% Sunni Moslem.

Geography: Area: 386,650 sq. mi, about the size of Texas, Oklahoma, and Arkansas combined. **Location:** NE corner of Africa. **Neighbors:** Libya on W, Sudan on S, Israel on E. **Topography:** Almost entirely desolate and barren, with hills and mountains in E and along Nile. The Nile Valley, where most of the people live, stretches 550 miles. **Capital:** Cairo. **Cities** (1986 est.): Cairo 6,305,000; Alexandria 2,800,000; al-Jizah 1,600,000.

Government: Type: Republic. **Head of state:** Pres. Hosni Mubarak; b. 1929; in office: Oct. 14, 1981. **Head of Government:** Atef Sedki in office: Nov. 10, 1986. **Local divisions:** 26 governorates. **Defense:** 8.2% of GNP (1987).

Economy: Industries: Textiles, chemicals, petrochemicals, food processing, cement. **Chief crops:** Cotton (one of largest producers), rice, beans, fruits, grains, vegetables, sugar, corn. **Minerals:** Oil, phosphates, gypsum, iron, manganese, limestone. **Crude oil reserves** (1987): 4 bln. bbls. **Arable land:** 4%. **Livestock** (1986): cattle: 2.7 mln.; sheep: 2.5 mln. **Fish catch** (1986): 138,000 metric tons. **Electricity prod.** (1986): 40.6 bln. kwh. **Labor force:** 41% agric.; 22% services; 14% industry.

Finance: Currency: Pound (June 1989: 2.55 = $1 US). **Gross national product** (1986): $30.0 bln. **Per capita income** (1983): $686. **Imports** (1987): $11.9 bln.; partners: U.S. 19%, W. Ger. 10%, It. 8%, France 8%. **Exports** (1987): $4.3 bln.; partners: It. 22%, Isr. 14%. **Tourists** (1985): $990 mln. receipts. **National budget** (1987): $12.2 bln. expenditures. **International reserves less gold** (Jan. 1989): $1.2 bln. **Gold:** 2.43 mln. oz t. **Consumer prices** (change in 1988): 17.7%.

Transport: Railway traffic (1986): 28.3 bln. passenger-km; 8.6 bln. net ton-km. **Motor vehicles:** in use (1986): 757,000 passenger cars, 354,000 comm. vehicles. **Civil aviation** (1986): 4.0 bln. passenger-km, 111 mln. freight ton-km. **Chief ports:** Alexandria, Port Said, Suez.

Communications: Television sets: 2 mln. in use (1986). **Radios:** 15 mln. in use (1986). **Telephones in use** (1986): 1.3 mln. **Daily newspaper circ.** (1986): 88 per 1,000 pop.

Health: Life expectancy at birth (1986): 59.0 male; 62.1 female. **Births** (per 1,000 pop. 1985): 40. **Deaths** (per 1,000 pop. 1985): 11. **Natural increase** (1985): 2.9%. **Hospital beds** (1984): 85,350. **Physicians** (1984): 73,300. **Infant mortality** (per 1,000 live births 1986): 102.

Education (1988): Literacy: 44%. Compulsory ages 6-12.

Major International Organizations: UN (IMF, World Bank, GATT), OAU.

Embassy: 2310 Decatur Pl. NW 20008; 232-5400.

Archeological records of ancient Egyptian civilization date back to 4000 BC. A unified kingdom arose around 3200 BC, and extended its way south into Nubia and north as far as Syria. A high culture of rulers and priests was built on an economic base of serfdom, fertile soil, and annual flooding of the Nile banks.

Imperial decline facilitated conquest by Asian invaders (Hyksos, Assyrians). The last native dynasty fell in 341 BC to the Persians, who were in turn replaced by Greeks (Alexander and the Ptolemies), Romans, Byzantines, and Arabs, who introduced Islam and the Arabic language. The ancient Egyptian language is preserved only in the liturgy of the Coptic Christians.

Egypt was ruled as part of larger Islamic empires for several centuries. The Mamluks, a military caste of Caucasian origin, ruled Egypt from 1250 until defeat by the Ottoman Turks in 1517. Under Turkish sultans the khedive as hereditary viceroy had wide authority. Britain intervened in 1882 and took control of administration, though nominal allegiance to the Ottoman Empire continued until 1914.

The country was a British protectorate from 1914 to 1922. A 1936 treaty strengthened Egyptian autonomy, but Britain retained bases in Egypt and a condominium over the Sudan. Britain fought German and Italian armies from Egypt, 1940-42, but Egypt did not declare war against Germany until 1945. In 1951 Egypt abrogated the 1936 treaty. The Sudan became independent in 1956.

The uprising of July 23, 1952, led by the Society of Free Officers, named Maj. Gen. Mohammed Naguib commander in chief and forced King Farouk to abdicate. When the republic was proclaimed June 18, 1953, Naguib became its first president and premier. Lt. Col. Gamal Abdel Nasser removed Naguib and became premier in 1954. In 1956, he was voted president. Nasser died in 1970 and was replaced by Vice Pres. Anwar Sadat.

A series of decrees in July, 1961, nationalized about 90% of industry. Economic liberalization was begun, 1974, with more emphasis on private domestic and foreign investment.

The Aswan High Dam, completed 1971, provides irrigation for more than a million acres of land. Artesian wells, drilled in the Western Desert, reclaimed 43,000 acres, 1960-66.

When the state of Israel was proclaimed in 1948, Egypt joined other Arab nations invading Israel and was defeated.

After terrorist raids across its border, Israel invaded Egypt's Sinai Peninsula, Oct. 29, 1956. Egypt rejected a cease-fire demand by Britain and France; on Oct. 31 the 2 nations dropped bombs and on Nov. 5-6 landed forces. Egypt and Israel accepted a UN cease-fire; fighting ended Nov. 7.

A UN Emergency Force guarded the 117-mile long border between Egypt and Israel until May 19, 1967, when it was withdrawn at Nasser's demand. Egyptian troops entered the Gaza Strip and the heights of Sharm el Sheikh and 3 days later closed the Strait of Tiran to all Israeli shipping. Full-scale war broke out June 5 and before it ended under a UN cease-fire June 10, Israel had captured Gaza and the Sinai Peninsula, controlled the east bank of the Suez Canal and reopened the gulf.

Sporadic fighting with Israel broke out late in 1968 and continued almost daily, 1969-70. Military and economic aid was received from the USSR. Israel and Egypt agreed, Aug. 7, 1970, to a cease-fire and peace negotiations proposed by the U.S. Negotiations failed to achieve results, but the cease-fire continued.

In a surprise attack Oct. 6, 1973, Egyptian forces crossed the Suez Canal into the Sinai. (At the same time, Syrian forces attacked Israelis on the Golan Heights.) Egypt was supplied by a USSR military airlift; the U.S. responded with an airlift to Israel. Israel counter-attacked, crossed the canal, surrounded Suez City. A UN cease-fire took effect Oct. 24.

A disengagement agreement was signed Jan. 18, 1974. Under it, Israeli forces withdrew from the canal's W bank; limited numbers of Egyptian forces occupied a strip along the E bank. A second accord was signed in 1975, with Israel yielding Sinai oil fields. Pres. Sadat's surprise visit to Jerusalem, Nov. 1977,

opened the prospect of peace with Israel, but worsened relations with Libya (border clashes, July 1977). On Mar. 26, 1979, Egypt and Israel signed a formal peace treaty, ending 30 years of war, and establishing diplomatic relations. Israel returned control of the Sinai to Egypt in April 1982.

Tension between Moslem fundamentalists and Christians in 1981 caused street riots and culminated in a nationwide security crackdown in Sept. Pres Sadat was assassinated on Oct. 6.

Relations with the U.S. were strained in 1985 because of the U.S. interception of an Egyptian airliner carrying the hijackers of the *Achille Lauro.*

The Suez Canal, 103 mi. long, links the Mediterranean and Red seas. It was built by a French corporation 1859-69, but Britain obtained controlling interest in 1875. The last British troops were removed June 13, 1956. On July 26, Egypt nationalized the canal.

Egypt had barred Israeli ships and cargoes destined for Israel since 1948, and closed the canal to all shipping after the 1967 Arab-Israeli War. The canal was reopened in 1975.

El Salvador
Republic of El Salvador
República de El Salvador

People: Population (1989 est.): 5,548,000. **Age distrib. (%):** 0–14: 45.3; 15–59: 51; 60+: 4.7. **Pop. density:** 671 per sq. mi. **Urban** (1986): 42%. **Ethnic groups:** Mestizo 89%, Indian 10%. **Languages:** Spanish, Nahuatl (among some Indians). **Religions:** Roman Catholicism prevails.

Geography: Area: 8,260 sq. mi., the size of Massachusetts. **Location:** In Central America. **Neighbors:** Guatemala on W, Honduras on N. **Topography:** A hot Pacific coastal plain in the south rises to a cooler plateau and valley region, densely populated. The N is mountainous, including many volcanoes. **Capital:** San Salvador. **Cities** (1987 est.): San Salvador 1.4 mln.

Government: Type: Republic. **Head of state:** Pres., Alfredo Cristiani; b. Nov. 22, 1947; in office: June 1, 1989. **Local divisions:** 14 departments. **Defense:** 5.5% of GNP (1985).

Economy: Industries: Food and beverages, textiles, petroleum products. **Chief crops:** Coffee (21% of GNP), cotton, corn, sugar. **Other resources:** Rubber, forests. **Arable land:** 35%. **Livestock** (1986): cattle: 1 mln.; pigs: 400,000. **Electricity prod.** (1986): 1.7 bln. kwh. **Labor force:** 50% agric.; 22% ind.; 27% services.

Finance: Currency: Colon (Mar. 1989: 5.00 = $1 US). **Gross national product** (1986): $4.0 bln. **Per capita income** (1986): $700. **Imports** (1987): $1.9 bln.; partners: U.S. 39%, CACM 22%. **Exports** (1987): $1.1 bln.; partners: U.S. 49%, CACM 23%. **National budget** (1986): $740 mln. expenditures. **International reserves less gold** (Mar. 1989): $154 mln. **Gold:** 469,000 oz t. **Consumer prices** (change in 1987): 24.9%.

Transport: Railway traffic (1986): 4.9 mln. passenger-km; 24 mln. net ton-km. **Motor vehicles:** in use (1985): 136,000 passenger cars, 19,000 comm. vehicles. **Chief ports:** La Unión, Acajutla.

Communications: Television sets: 425,000 in use (1987). **Radios:** 1.2 mln. in use (1986). **Telephones in use** (1986): 126,000. **Daily newspaper circ.** (1986): 52 per 1,000 pop.

Health: Life expectancy at birth (1985): 62.6 male; 66.3 female. **Births** (per 1,000 pop. 1987): 37. **Deaths** (per 1,000 pop. 1987): 10. **Natural increase** (1987): 2.7%. **Hospital beds** (1985): 6,525. **Physicians** (1985): 1,592. **Infant mortality** (per 1,000 live births 1985): 71.

Education (1987): Literacy: 62% (urban areas); 40% (rural areas). Years compulsory 6; attendance 82%.

Major International Organizations: UN (IMF, WHO, ILO), OAS, CACM.

Embassy: 2308 California St. NW 20008; 265-3480.

El Salvador became independent of Spain in 1821, and of the Central American Federation in 1839.

A fight with Honduras in 1969 over the presence of 300,000 Salvadorean workers left 2,000 dead. Clashes were renewed 1970 and 1974.

A military coup overthrew the Romero government, 1979, but the ruling military-civilian junta failed to quell the civil war which has resulted in some 50,000 deaths. Some 10,000 leftists insurgents, armed by Cuba and Nicaragua, control about 25% of the country, mostly in the east. Extreme right-wing death squads organized to eliminate suspected leftists were blamed for over 1,000 deaths in 1983. The Reagan administration has staunchly supported the government with military aid.

Voters turned out in large numbers in the May 1984 presidential election. Christian Democrat Jose Napoleon Duarte, a moderate, was victorious with 54% of the vote. Duarte was diagnosed as having terminal cancer in 1988.

Lefist guerrillas continued their offensive in 1989 as the civil war entered its 9th year.

Equatorial Guinea

Republic of Equatorial Guinea

República de Guinea Ecuatorial

People: Population (1989 est.): 389,000. **Age distrib. (%):** 0–14: 38.1; 15–59: 55.2; 60+: 6.7. **Pop. density:** 35 per sq. mi. **Ethnic groups:** Fangs 80%, Bubi 15%. **Languages:** Spanish (official), Fang, English. **Religions:** Mostly Roman Catholic.

Geography: Area: 10,832 sq. mi., the size of Maryland. **Location:** Bioko Is. off W. Africa coast in Gulf of Guinea, and Rio Muni, mainland enclave. **Neighbors:** Gabon on S, Cameroon on E, N. **Topography:** Bioko Is. consists of 2 volcanic mountains and a connecting valley. Rio Muni, with over 90% of the area, has a coastal plain and low hills beyond. **Capital:** Malabo. **Cities** (1989 est.): Malabo 38,000.

Government: Type: Unitary Republic. **Head of state:** Pres., Supreme Military Council Teodoro Obiang Nguema Mbasogo; b. June 5, 1942; in office: Oct. 10, 1979. **Head of government:** Prime Min. Cristino Seriche Bioko. **Local divisions:** 6 provinces.

Economy: Chief crops: Cocoa, coffee, bananas, sweet potatoes. **Other resources:** Timber. **Arable land:** 8%. **Electricity prod.** (1986): 17 mln. kwh. **Labor force:** agric. 50%; public sector 40%.

Finance: Currency: Bipkwele (Mar. 1989: 319 = $1 US). **Gross national product** (1987): $130 mln. **Per capita income** (1987): $300. **Imports** (1987): $50 mln.; partners: Spain 54%, China 17%. **Exports** (1987): $39 mln.; partners: Sp. 40%, Neth. 28%, W. Ger. 23%.

Transport: Chief ports: Malabo, Bata.

Communications: Radios: 90,000 in use (1984).

Health: Life expectancy at birth (1988): 44.0 male; 48.0 female. **Births** (per 1,000 pop. 1985): 42.2 **Deaths** (per 1,000 pop. 1985): 17.6. **Natural increase** (1985): 2.4% **Hospital beds** (1982): 3,200. **Infant mortality** (per 1,000 live births 1986): 142.

Education (1989): Literacy: 55%. About 65% attend primary school.

Major International Organizations: UN (IMF, World Bank), OAU.

Embassy: 801 2d Ave., New York, NY 10017; (212) 599-1523.

Fernando Po (now Bioko) Island was discovered by Portugal in the late 15th century and ceded to Spain in 1778. Independence came Oct. 12, 1968. Riots occurred in 1969 over disputes between the island and the more backward Rio Muni province on the mainland. Masie Nguema Biyogo, himself from the mainland, became president for life in 1972.

Masie's 11-year reign was one of the most brutal in Africa, resulting in a bankrupted nation. Most of the nation's 7,000 Europeans emigrated. In 1976, 45,000 Nigerian workers were evacuated amid charges of a reign of terror. Masie was ousted in a military coup, Aug., 1979.

The nation is heavily dependent on external aid.

Ethiopia

People's Democratic Republic of Ethiopia

Ye Etiyop'iya Hezbawi Dimokrasiyawi Republek

People: Population (1989 est.): 47,709,000. **Age distrib. (%):** 0–14: 46.5; 15–59: 47.3; 60+: 6.2. **Pop. density:** 101 per sq. mi. **Urban** (1988): 11%. **Ethnic groups:** Oromo 40%, Amhara 25%, Tigre 12%, Sidama 9%. **Languages:** Amharic (official), Tigre (Semitic languages); Galla (Hamitic), Arabic, others. **Religions:** Orthodox Christian 40%, Moslem 40%.

Geography: Area: 471,776 sq. mi., four-fifths the size of Alaska. **Location:** In E. Africa. **Neighbors:** Sudan on W, Kenya

on S. Somalia, Djibouti on E. **Topography:** A high central plateau, between 6,000 and 10,000 ft. high, rises to higher mountains near the Great Rift Valley, cutting in from the SW. The Blue Nile and other rivers cross the plateau, which descends to plains on both W and SE. **Capital:** Addis Ababa. **Cities** (1984 est.): Addis Ababa 1,412,000.

Government: Type: Unitary single-party People's Republic. **Head of state:** Pres. Mengistu Haile Mariam; b. 1937; in office: Feb. 11, 1977. **Head of Government:** Prime Min. Fikre Selassie Wogderess. **Local divisions:** 24 administrative zones, 5 autonomous regions. **Defense:** 9% of GNP (1986).

Economy: Industries: Food processing, cement, textiles. **Chief crops:** Coffee (61% export earnings), grains. **Minerals:** Platinum, gold, copper, potash. **Arible Land:** 13%. **Livestock** (1986): cattle: 26.3 mln.; sheep: 23.5 mln. **Electricity prod.** (1986): 722 mln. kwh. **Labor force:** 80% agric.

Finance: Currency: Birr (Mar. 1989: 2.07 = $1 US). **Gross national product** (1986): $5.4 bln. **Per capita income** (1986): $121. **Imports** (1986): $976 mln.; partners: USSR 22%, U.S. 15%, Italy 10%, Jap. 6%, W.Ger. 10%. **Exports** (1986): $487 mln.; partners: U.S. 20%, W. Ger. 18%, Italy 7%. **National budget** (1986): $2.0 bln. expenditures. **International reserves less gold** (Mar. 1989): $78 mln. **Gold:** 209,000 oz t. **Consumer prices** (change in 1987): −2.4%.

Transport: Railway traffic (1986): 350 mln. passenger-km; 125 mln. net ton-km. **Motor vehicles:** in use (1985): 41,300 passenger cars, 19,000 comm. vehicles. **Civil aviation** (1983): 762 mln. passenger-km; 27.1 mln. net ton-km. **Chief ports:** Masewa, Aseb.

Communications: Television sets: 70,000 in use (1987), **Radios:** 2 mln. in use (1986). **Telephones in use** (1986): 132,000. **Daily newspaper circ.** (1986): 1 per 1,000 pop.

Health: Life expectancy at birth (1985): 41.3 male; 44.5 female. **Births** (per 1,000 pop. 1985): 49.2. **Deaths** (per 1,000 pop. 1985): 21.5. **Natural increase** (1985): 4.7%. **Hospital beds** (1984): 11,307. **Physicians** (1984): 539. **Infant mortality** (per 1,000 live births 1985): 168.

Education (1985): Literacy: 18%.

Major International Organizations: UN (IMF, WHO), OAU.

Embassy: 2134 Kalorama Rd. NW 20008; 234-2281.

Ethiopian culture was influenced by Egypt and Greece. The ancient monarchy was invaded by Italy in 1880, but maintained its independence until another Italian invasion in 1936. British forces freed the country in 1941.

The last emperor, Haile Selassie I, established a parliament and judiciary system in 1931, but barred all political parties.

A series of droughts since 1972 have killed hundreds of thousands. An army mutiny, strikes, and student demonstrations led to the dethronement of Selassie in 1974. The ruling junta pledged to form a one-party socialist state, and instituted a successful land reform; opposition was violently suppressed. The influence of the Coptic Church, embraced in 330 AD, was curbed, and the monarchy was abolished in 1975.

The regime, torn by bloody coups, faced uprisings by tribal and political groups in part aided by Sudan and Somalia. Ties with the U.S., once a major arms and aid source, deteriorated, while cooperation accords were signed with the USSR in 1977. In 1978, Soviet advisors and Cuban troops helped defeat Somalia forces. Ethiopia and Somalia signed a peace agreement in 1988.

A world-wide relief effort began in 1984, as an extended drought caused millions to face starvation and death. In 1988, victories by Eritean guerrillas forced the government to curtail the work of foreign aid workers in drought-stricken regions. Foreign relief officials expressed the fear that suspension of their operations would lead to the starvation death of hundreds of thousands.

Fiji

Dominion of Fiji

People: Population (1989 est.): 758,000. **Age distrib. (%):** 0–14: 38.2; 15–59: 56.9; 60+: 4.9. **Pop. density:** 107 per sq. mi. **Urban** (1986): 39%. **Ethnic groups:** Indian 48%, Fijian (Melanesian-Polynesian) 46%, Europeans 2%. **Languages:** English (official), Fijian, Hindustani. **Religions:** Christian 52%, Hindu 38%, Moslem 8%.

Geography: Area: 7,056 sq. mi., the size of Massachusetts. **Location:** In western S. Pacific O. **Neighbors:** Nearest are Solomons on NW, Tonga on E. **Topography:** 322 islands (106 inhabited), many mountainous, with tropical forests and large fertile areas. Viti Levu, the largest island, has over half the total land area. **Capital:** Suva. **Cities** (1986 est.): Suva 69,000.

Government: Type: Republic. **Head of state:** Pres. Penaia Ganilau; in office: Dec. 5, 1987. **Head of government:** Prime Min. Kamisese Mara; b. May 13, 1920; in office: Oct. 10, 1970. **Local divisions:** 4 divisions.

Economy: Industries: Sugar refining, light industry, tourism. **Chief crops:** Sugar, bananas, ginger. **Minerals:** Gold. **Other resources:** Timber. **Arable land:** 12%. **Electricity prod.** (1986): 402 mln. kwh. **Labor force:** 44% agric.

Finance: Currency: Dollar (Mar. 1989: 1.00 = $.69 US). **Gross national product** (1986): $1.0 bln. **Per capita income** (1984): $1,086. **Imports** (1988): $462 mln.; partners: Austrai. 29%, Jap. 12%, N.Z. 16%. **Exports** (1988): $307 mln.; partners: UK 42%, Aust. 18%. **Tourists** (1987): $145 mln. receipts. **National budget** (1986): $402 mln. expenditures. **International reserves less gold** (Mar. 1989): $216 mln. **Gold:** 10,000 oz t. **Consumer prices** (change in 1986): 2.0%.

Transport: Motor vehicles: in use (1987): 34,000 passenger cars, 24,000 comm. vehicles. **Civil aviation** (1986): 509 mln. passenger-km; 6.4 mln. net ton-km. **Chief ports:** Suva, Lautoka.

Communications: Radios: 400,000 in use (1987). **Telephones in use** (1986): 58,000. **Daily newspaper circ.** (1985): 76 per 1,000 pop.

Health: Life expectancy at birth (1987): 68.0 male; 72.4 female. **Births** (per 1,000 pop. 1987): 28.0. **Deaths** (per 1,000 pop. 1987): 5.2. **Natural increase** (1987): 2.2%. **Hospital beds** (1986): 1,736. **Physicians** (1986): 385. **Infant mortality** (per 1,000 live births 1987): 19.

Education (1985): **Literacy:** 80%. 95% attend school.

Major International Organizations: UN (IMF, WHO), Commonwealth of Nations.

Embassy: 2233 Wisconsin Ave. NW 20007; 337-8320.

A British colony since 1874, Fiji became an independent parliamentary democracy Oct. 10, 1970.

Cultural differences between the majority Indian community, descendants of contract laborers brought to the islands in the 19th century, and the less modernized native Fijians, who by law own 83% of the land in communal villages, have led to political polarization.

The discovery of copper on Viti Levu along with increased sugar production bode well for the economy.

In 1987, a military coup ousted the government; order was restored May 21 when a compromise was reached granting Lt. Col. Sitiveni Rabuka, the coup's leader, increased power. Rabuka staged a second coup Sept. 25 and in Oct. declared Fiji a republic. A civilian government was restored to power in Dec.

Finland

Republic of Finland

Suomen Tasavalta

People: Population (1989 est.): 4,990,000. **Age distrib. (%):** 0–14: 19.3; 15–59: 62.9; 60+: 17.8. **Pop. density:** 38 per sq. mi. **Urban** (1988): 61%. **Ethnic groups:** Finns 94%, Swedes, Lapps. **Languages:** Finnish, Swedish (both official). **Religions:** Lutheran 90%.

Geography: Area: 130,119 sq. mi., slightly smaller than Montana. **Location:** In northern Europe. **Neighbors:** Norway on W, Sweden on W, USSR on E. **Topography:** South and central Finland are mostly flat areas with low hills and many lakes. The N has mountainous areas, 3,000–4,000 ft. **Capital:** Helsinki. **Cities** (1988 est.). Helsinki 487,000; Tampere 170,000; Turku 160,000.

Government: Type: Constitutional republic. **Head of state:** Pres. Mauno Koivisto; b. Nov. 25, 1923; in office: Jan. 27, 1982. **Head of government:** Prime Min. Harri Holkeri. b. Jan. 6, 1937; in office: Apr. 30, 1987. **Local divisions:** 12 laanit (provinces). **Defense:** 1.5% of GNP (1985).

Economy: Industries: Machinery, metal, shipbuilding, textiles, clothing. **Chief crops:** Grains, potatoes, dairy prods. **Minerals:** Copper, iron, zinc. **Other resources:** Forests (40% of exports). **Arable land:** 8%. **Livestock** (1987): cattle; 1.5 mln. pigs: 1.3 mln. **Fish catch** (1987): 160,000 metric tons. **Electricity prod.** (1986): 45.5 bln. kwh. **Crude steel prod.** (1987): 2.6 mln. metric tons. **Labor force:** 11% agric.; 46% ind. & comm.; 28% services.

Finance: Currency: Markkaa (June 1989: 4.48 = $1 US). **Gross national product** (1987): $96.9 bln. **Per capita income** (1986): $11,900. **Imports** (1988): $21.1 bln.; partners: USSR 14%, Swed. 12%, W. Ger. 18%, UK 7%. **Exports** (1988): $19.9 bln.; partners: USSR 15%, Swed. 13%, UK 11%, W. Ger. 11%. **Tourists** (1985): $501 mln. receipts. **National budget** (1985): $18.6 bln. expenditures. **International reserves less gold** (Mar. 1989): $6.4 bln. **Gold** 1.9 mln. oz t. **Consumer prices** (change in 1988): 5.1%.

Transport: Railway traffic (1987): 3.1 bln. passenger-km; 7.4 bln. net ton-km. **Motor vehicles:** in use (1987): 1.6 mln. passenger cars, 196,000 comm. vehicles; **Civil aviation** (1986): 2.9 bln. passenger-km; 92 mln. freight ton-km. **Chief ports:** Helsinki, Turku.

Communications: Television sets: 1.8 mln. licensed (1987). **Radios:** 2.5 mln. in use (1986). **Telephones in use** (1986): 3.0 mln. **Daily newspaper circ.** (1986): 543 per 1,000 pop.

Health: Life expectancy at birth (1986): 70.4 male; 78.8 female. **Births** (per 1,000 pop. 1986): 12.3. **Deaths** (per 1,000 pop. 1986): 9.6. **Natural increase** (1986): .02%. **Hospital beds** (1985): 61,082. **Physicians** (1986): 10,193. **Infant mortality** (per 1,000 live births 1986): 5.8.

Education (1988): **Literacy:** 99%. **Years compulsory** 9; attendance 99%.

Major International Organizations: UN (IMF, GATT), EFTA, OECD.

Embassy: 3216 New Mexico Ave. NW 20016; 363-2430.

The early Finns probably migrated from the Ural area at about the beginning of the Christian era. Swedish settlers brought the country into Sweden, 1154 to 1809, when Finland became an autonomous grand duchy of the Russian Empire. Russian exactions created a strong national spirit; on Dec. 6, 1917, Finland declared its independence and in 1919 became a republic. On Nov. 30, 1939, the Soviet Union invaded, and the Finns were forced to cede 16,173 sq. mi., including the Karelian Isthmus, Viipuri, and an area on Lake Ladoga. After World War II, in which Finland tried to recover its lost territory, further cessions were exacted. In 1948, Finland signed a treaty of mutual assistance with the USSR. In 1956 Russia returned Porkkala, which had been ceded as a military base.

Finland is an integral member of the Nordic group of five countries and maintains good relations with the Soviet Union.

Aland, constituting an autonomous department, is a group of small islands, 572 sq. mi., in the Gulf of Bothnia, 25 mi. from Sweden, 15 mi. from Finland. Mariehamn is the principal port.

France

French Republic

République Française

People: Population (1989 est.): 55,813,000. **Age distrib. (%):** 0–14: 20.5; 15–60: 60.8; 60+: 18.7. **Pop. density:** 252 per sq. mi. **Urban** (1985): 77.2%. **Ethnic groups:** A mixture of various European and Mediterranean groups. **Languages:** French; minorities speak Breton, Alsatian German, Flemish, Italian, Basque, Catalan. **Religions:** Mostly Roman Catholic.

Geography: Area: 220,668 sq. mi., four-fifths the size of Texas. **Location:** In western Europe, between Atlantic O. and Mediterranean Sea. **Neighbors:** Spain on S, Italy, Switzerland, W. Germany on E, Luxembourg, Belgium on N. **Topography:** A wide plain covers more than half of the country, in N and W, drained to W by Seine, Loire, Garonne rivers. The Massif Central is a mountainous plateau in center. In E are Alps (Mt. Blanc is tallest in W. Europe, 15,771 ft.), the lower Jura range, and the forested Vosges. The Rhone flows from Lake Geneva to Mediterranean. Pyrenees are in SW, on border with Spain. **Capital:** Paris. **Cities** (1982 cen.): Paris 2,188,918; Marseille 878,689; Lyon 418,476; Toulouse 354,289; Nice 338,486; Nantes 247,227; Strasbourg 252,264; Bordeaux 211,197.

Government: Type: Republic. **Head of state:** Pres. François Mitterrand; b. Oct. 26, 1916; in office: May 21, 1981. **Head of government:** Prime Min. Michel Rocard; b. Aug. 23, 1930; in office: May 10, 1988. **Local divisions:** 22 administrative regions containing 95 departments. **Defense:** 19% of govt. budget. (1987).

Economy: Industries: Steel, chemicals, autos, textiles, wine, perfume, aircraft, electronic equipment. **Chief crops:** Grains, corn, rice, fruits, vegetables. France is largest food producer, exporter, in W. Eur. **Minerals:** Bauxite, iron, coal. **Crude oil reserves** (1985): 221 mln. bbls. **Other resources:** Forests. **Arable land:** 34%. **Livestock** (1986): cattle: 22.3 mln.; pigs: 12.5 mln.; sheep: 12.0 mln. **Fish catch** (1986): 850,000 metric tons. **Electricity prod.** (1985): 326 bln. kwh. **Crude steel prod.** (1987): 17.7 mln. metric tons. **Labor force:** 9% agric.; 45% ind. & comm.; 46% services.

Finance: Currency: Franc (June 1989: 6.81 = $1 US). **Gross national product** (1986): $724 mln. **Per capita income** (1986): $13,046. **Imports** (1988): $178 bln.; partners: EC 51%. **Exports** (1988): $167 bln.; partners: EC 50%, U.S. 9%. **Tourists** (1985) receipts: $7.9 bln. **National budget** (1987): $164 bln. expenditures. **International reserves less gold** (Feb. 1989): $25.0 bln. **Gold:** 81.85 mln. oz t. **Consumer prices** (change in 1988): 2.7%.

Transport: Railway traffic (1985): 60.7 bln. passenger-km; 58.4 bln. net ton-km. **Motor vehicles:** in use (1986): 21.2 mln. passenger cars, 3.4 mln. **Civil aviation** (1987): 44.0 bln. passenger-km; 3.4 bln net ton-km. **Chief ports:** Marseille, LeHavre, Nantes, Bordeaux, Rouen.

Communications: Television sets: 18.1 mln. in use (1987). **Radios:** 58 mln. in use (1987). **Telephones in use** (1987): 33 mln. **Daily newspaper circ.** (1986): 205 per 1,000 pop.

Health: Life expectancy at birth (1986): 71.3 male; 79.5 female. **Births** (per 1,000 pop. 1987): 13.8. **Deaths** (per 1,000 pop. 1987): 9.5. **Natural increase** (1987): .4%. **Hospital beds** (1986): 722,378. **Physicians** (1986): 138,000. **Infant mortality** (per 1,000 live births 1986): 8.2.

Education (1987): **Literacy:** 99%. **Years compulsory** 10; 17.7% of natl. budget.

Major International Organizations: UN and most of its specialized agencies, OECD, EC, NATO.

Embassy: 4101 Reservoir Rd. NW 20007; 944-6000.

Celtic Gaul was conquered by Julius Caesar 58-51 BC; Romans ruled for 500 years. Under Charlemagne, Frankish rule extended over much of Europe. After his death France emerged as one of the successor kingdoms.

The monarchy was overthrown by the French Revolution (1789-93) and succeeded by the First Republic; followed by the First Empire under Napoleon (1804-15), a monarchy (1814-48), the Second Republic (1848-52), the Second Empire (1852-70), the Third Republic (1871-1946), the Fourth Republic (1946-58), and the Fifth Republic (1958 to present).

France suffered severe losses in manpower and wealth in the first World War, 1914-18, when it was invaded by Germany. By the Treaty of Versailles, France exacted return of Alsace and Lorraine, French provinces seized by Germany in 1871. Germany invaded France again in May, 1940, and signed an armistice with a government based in Vichy. After France was liberated by the Allies Sept. 1944, Gen. Charles de Gaulle became head of the provisional government, serving until 1946.

De Gaulle again became premier in 1958, during a crisis over Algeria, and obtained voter approval for a new constitution, ushering in the Fifth Republic. Using strong executive powers, he promoted French economic and technological advances in the context of the European Economic Community, and guarded French foreign policy independence.

France had withdrawn from Indochina in 1954, and from Morocco and Tunisia in 1956. Most of its remaining African territories were freed 1958-62, but France retained strong economic and political ties.

In 1966, France withdrew all its troops from the integrated military command of NATO, though 60,000 remained stationed in Germany. France continued to attend political meetings of NATO.

In May 1968 rebellious students in Paris and other centers rioted, battled police, and were joined by workers who launched nationwide strikes. The government awarded pay increases to the strikers May 26. In elections to the Assembly in June, de Gaulle's backers won a landslide victory. Nevertheless, he resigned from office in April, 1969, after losing a nationwide referendum on constitutional reform. De Gaulle's policies were largely continued after his death in 1970.

On May 10, 1981, France elected François Mitterrand, a Socialist candidate, president in a stunning victory over Valéry Giscard d'Estaing. In September, the government nationalized 5 major industries and most private banks. In 1986, France began a privatization program in which some 80 state-owned companies would be sold. Mitterrand was elected to a 2d 7-year term in 1988.

France supported Chad in its war with Libya.

Agents of France's external security service were responsible for the July 10, 1985 sinking of the *Rainbow Warrior*, flagship of the Greenpeace environmental movement, in the port of Auckland, New Zealand.

In 1989, the nation celebrated the bicentennial of the French Revolution. World leaders joined in the celebration at the opening of the Opera Bastille July 13, the eve of the anniversary of the storming of the famed prison.

The island of **Corsica**, in the Mediterranean W of Italy and N of Sardinia, is an official region of France comprising 2 departments. Area: 3,369 sq. mi.; pop. (1986 est.): 248,000. The capital is Ajaccio, birthplace of Napoleon.

Overseas Departments

French Guiana is on the NE coast of South America with Suriname on the W and Brazil on the E and S. Its area is 43,740 sq. mi.; pop. (1988): 92,038. Guiana sends one senator and one deputy to the French Parliament. Guiana is administered by a prefect and has a Council General of 16 elected members; capital is Cayenne.

The famous penal colony, Devil's Island, was phased out between 1938 and 1951.

Immense forests of rich timber cover 90% of the land. Placer gold mining is the most important industry. Exports are shrimp, timber, and machinery.

Guadeloupe, in the West Indies' Leeward Islands, consists of 2 large islands, Basse-Terre and Grande-Terre, separated by the Salt River, plus Marie Galante and the Saintes group to the S and to the N, Desirade, St. Barthelemy, and over half of St. Martin (the Netherlands portion is St. Maarten). A French possession since 1635, the department is represented in the French Parliament by 2 senators and 3 deputies; administration consists of a prefect (governor) and an elected general and regional councils.

Area of the islands is 660 sq. mi.; pop. (1988 est.) 340,000, mainly descendants of slaves; capital is Basse-Terre on Basse-Terre Is. The land is fertile; sugar, rum, and bananas are exported; tourism is an important industry.

Martinique, the northernmost of the Windward Islands, in the West Indies, has been a possession since 1635, and a department since March, 1946. It is represented in the French Parliament by 2 senators and 3 deputies. The island was the birthplace of Napoleon's Empress Josephine.

It has an area of 425 sq. mi.; pop. (1988 est.) 336,000, mostly descendants of slaves. The capital is Fort-de-France (pop. 1988: 117,000). It is a popular tourist stop. The chief exports are rum, bananas, and petroleum products.

Mayotte, formerly part of Comoros, voted in 1976 to become an overseas department of France. An island NW of Madagascar, area is 144 sq. mi., pop. (1988 est.) 77,000.

Reunion is a volcanic island in the Indian O. about 420 mi. E of Madagascar, and has belonged to France since 1665. Area, 969 sq. mi.; pop. (1988 est.) 575,000, 30% of French extraction. Capital: Saint-Denis. The chief export is sugar. It elects 3 deputies, 2 senators to the French Parliament.

St. Pierre and Miquelon, formerly an Overseas Territory, made the transition to department status in 1976. It consists of 2 groups of rocky islands near the SW coast of Newfoundland, inhabited by fishermen. The exports are chiefly fish products. The St. Pierre group has an area of 10 sq. mi.; Miquelon, 83 sq. mi. Total pop. (1987 est.), 6,300. The capital is St. Pierre. A deputy and a senator are elected to the French Parliament.

Overseas Territories

French Polynesia Overseas Territory, comprises 130 islands widely scattered among 5 archipelagos in the South Pacific; administered by a governor. Territorial Assembly and a Council with headquarters at Papeete, Tahiti, one of the **Society Islands** (which include the **Windward** and **Leeward** islands). A deputy and a senator are elected to the French Parliament.

Other groups are the **Marquesas Islands**, the **Tuamotu Archipelago**, including the **Gambier Islands**, and the **Austral Islands**.

Total area of the islands administered from Tahiti is 1,544 sq. mi.; pop. (1987 est.), 185,000, more than half on Tahiti. Tahiti is picturesque and mountainous with a productive coastline bearing coconut, banana and orange trees, sugar cane and vanilla.

Tahiti was visited by Capt. James Cook in 1769 and by Capt. Bligh in the Bounty, 1788-89. Its beauty impressed Herman Melville, Paul Gauguin, and Charles Darwin.

French Southern and Antarctic Lands Overseas Territory, comprises Adelie Land, on Antarctica, and 4 island groups in the Indian O. Adelie, discovered 1840, has a research station, a coastline of 185 mi. and tapers 1,240 mi. inland to the South Pole. The U.S. does not recognize national claims in Antarctica. There are 2 huge glaciers, Ninnis, 22 mi. wide, 99 mi. long, and Mentz, 11 mi. wide, 140 mi. long. The Indian O. groups are:

Kerguelen Archipelago, discovered 1772, one large and 300 small islands. The chief is 87 mi. long, 74 mi. wide, and has Mt. Ross, 6,429 ft. tall. Principal research station is Port-aux-Francais. Seals often weigh 2 tons; there are blue whales, coal, peat, semi-precious stones. Crozet Archipelago, discovered 1772, covers 195 sq. mi. Eastern Island rises to 6,560 ft. Saint Paul, in southern Indian O., has warm springs with earth at places heating to 120° to 390° F. Amsterdam is nearby; both produce cod and rock lobster.

New Caledonia and its dependencies, an overseas territory, are a group of islands in the Pacific O. about 1,115 mi. E of Australia and approx. the same distance NW of New Zealand. Dependencies are the Loyalty Islands, the Isle of Pines, Huon Islands and the Chesterfield Islands.

New Caledonia, the largest, has 6,530 sq. mi. Total area of the territory is 8,548 sq. mi.; population (1988 est.) 156,000. The group was acquired by France in 1853.

The territory is administered by a governor and government council. There is a popularly elected Territorial Assembly. A deputy and a senator are elected to the French Parliament. Capital: Noumea.

Mining is the chief industry. New Caledonia is one of the world's largest nickel producers. Other minerals found are chrome, iron, cobalt, manganese, silver, gold, lead, and copper. Agricultural products include coffee, copra, cotton, manioc (cassava), corn, tobacco, bananas and pineapples.

In 1987, New Caledonian voters chose by referendum to remain within the French Republic. There were clashes between French and Melanesians (Kanaks) in 1988.

Wallis and Futuna Islands, 2 archipelagos raised to status of overseas territory July 29, 1961, are in the SW Pacific S of the Equator between Fiji and Samoa. The islands have a total area of 106 sq. mi. and population (1987 est.) of 14,800. Alofi, an island attached to Futuna, is uninhabited. Capital: Mata-Utu. Chief products are copra, yams, taro roots, bananas. A senator and a deputy are elected to the French Parliament.

Gabon
Gabonese Republic
République Gabonaise

People: Population (1989 est.): 1,110,000. Pop. density: 11 per sq. mi. Urban (1985): 40%. Ethnic groups: Fangs 25%, Bapounon 10%, others. Languages: French (official), Bantu dialects. Religions: Tribal beliefs, Christian minority.

Geography: Area: 103,346 sq. mi., the size of Colorado. Location: On Atlantic coast of central Africa. Neighbors: Equatorial Guinea, Cameroon on N, Congo on E, S. Topography: Heavily forested, the country consists of coastal lowlands plateaus in N, E, and S, mountains in N, SE, and center. The Ogooue R. system covers most of Gabon. Capital: Libreville. Cities (1987 est.): Libreville 352,000.

Government: Type: Republic. Head of state: Pres. Omar Bongo; b. Dec. 30, 1935; in office: Dec. 2, 1967. Head of government: Prime Min. Leon Mebiame, b. Sept. 1, 1934; in office: Apr. 16, 1975. Local divisions: 44 prefectures. Defense: 2.1% of GNP (1985).

Economy: Industries: Oil products. Chief crops: Cocoa, coffee, rice, peanuts, palm products, cassava, bananas. Minerals: Manganese, uranium, oil, iron, gas. Crude oil reserves (1985): 623 mln. bbls. Other resources: Timber. Arable land: 2%. Electricity prod. (1986): 981 mln. kwh. Labor force: 65% agric.; 30% ind. & comm.

Finance: Currency: CFA franc (Mar. 1989: 319 = $1 US). Gross national product (1986) $3.3 bln. Per capita income (1983): $2,613. Imports (1987): $785 mln.; partners: Fr. 51%, U.S. 14%. Exports (1986): $1.9 bln.; partners: Fr. 26%, U.S. 32%. Tourists receipts (1986): $4 mln. National budget (1987): $1.2 bln. International reserves less gold (Jan. 1989):

$31 mln. Gold: 13,000 oz t. Consumer prices (change in 1987): −.09%.

Transport: Motor vehicles: in use (1985): 16,000 passenger cars, 10,000 comm. vehicles. Civil aviation (1986): 905 mln. passengers carried. Chief ports Port-Gentil, Owendo, Mayumba.

Communications: Television sets: 37,000 licensed (1987). Radios: 145,000 licensed (1986). Telephones in use (1984): 11,600.

Health: Life expectancy at birth (1985): 48.0 male; 51.4 female. Births (per 1,000 pop. 1985): 33.7. Deaths (per 1,000 pop. 1985): 19.9. Natural increase (1985): 1.3%. Hospital beds (1985): 4,617. Physicians (1985): 265. Infant mortality (per 1,000 live births 1988): 159.

Education (1988): Literacy: 70%. Compulsory to age 16; attendance: 100% primary, 14% secondary.

Major International Organizations: UN (World Bank), OAU, OPEC.

Embassy: 2034 20th St NW 20009; 797-1000.

France established control over the region in the second half of the 19th century. Gabon became independent Aug. 17, 1960. It is one of the most prosperous black African countries, thanks to abundant natural resources, foreign private investment, and government development programs.

The Gambia
Republic of The Gambia

People: Population (1989 est.): 840,000. Age distrib. (%): 0–14: 45.9; 15–59: 54.4; 60+: 3.8. Pop. density: 192 per sq. mi. Urban (1985): 21%. Ethnic groups: Mandinka 42%, Fula 16%, Wolof 16%, others. Languages: English (official), Mandinka, Wolof. Religions: Moslem 90%.

Geography: Area: 4,361 sq. mi., smaller than Connecticut. Location: On Atlantic coast near western tip of Africa. Neighbors: Surrounded on 3 sides by Senegal. Topography: A narrow strip of land on each side of the lower Gambia. Capital: Banjul. Cities (1986 est.): Banjul 40,000.

Government: Type: Republic. Head of state: Pres. Dawda Kairaba Jawara; b. May 16, 1924; in office: Apr. 24, 1970 (prime min. from June 12, 1962). Local divisions: 5 divisions and Banjul.

Economy: Industries: Tourism. Chief crops: Peanuts (main export), rice. Arable land: 28%. Fish catch (1986): 11,000 metric tons. Electricity prod. (1986): 63 mln. kwh. Labor force: 75% agric.; 18% ind. & comm.

Finance: Currency: Dalasi (Mar. 1989: 1.00 = $1.39 US). Gross national product (1986): $180 mln. Per capita income (1985): $255. Imports (1986): $99 mln.; partners: Fra. 15%, UK 11%, China 5%. Exports (1986): $35 mln.; partners: EEC 40%. Tourists (1985): 65,000. National budget (1985): $57 mln. expenditures. International reserves less gold (Mar. 1988): $15.5 mln. Consumer prices (change in 1987): 23.5%.

Transport: Motor vehicles: in use (1986): 5,200 passenger cars, 720 comm. vehicles. Chief ports: Banjul.

Communications: Radios: 110,000 in use (1986). Telephones in use (1985): 3,500.

Health: Life expectancy at birth (1985): 40.9 male; 44.1 female. Births (per 1,000 pop. 1985): 47.5. Deaths (per 1,000 pop. 1985): 21.7. Natural increase (1985): 2.5%. Hospital beds (1980): 635. Physicians (1980): 65. Infant mortality (per 100,000 live births 1986): 217.

Education (1986): Literacy: 12%.

Major International Organizations: UN (GATT, IMF, WHO), OAU.

Embassy: 19 E. 42 St., New York, NY 10017.

The tribes of Gambia were at one time associated with the West African empires of Ghana, Mali, and Songhay. The area became Britain's first African possession in 1588.

Independence came Feb. 18, 1965; republic status within the Commonwealth was achieved in 1970. Gambia is one of the only functioning democracies in Africa. The country suffered from severe famine in 1977-78.

Gambia has a treaty with Senegal to form a confederation of the 2 countries under the name of Senegambia. However, each country will retain its sovereignty.

Germany

Now comprises 2 nations: Federal Republic of Germany (West Germany), German Democratic Republic (East Germany).

Germany, prior to World War II, was a central European nation composed of numerous states which had a common language and traditions and which had been united in one country since 1871; since World War II it has been split in 2 parts.

History and government. Germanic tribes were defeated by Julius Caesar, 55 and 53 BC, but Roman expansion N of the Rhine was stopped in 9 AD. Charlemagne, ruler of the Franks, consolidated Saxon, Bavarian, Rhenish, Frankish, and other lands; after him the eastern part became the German Empire. The Thirty Years' War, 1618-1648, split Germany into small principalities and kingdoms. After Napoleon, Austria contended with Prussia for dominance, but lost the Seven Weeks' War to Prussia, 1866. Otto von Bismarck, Prussian chancellor, formed the North German Confederation, 1867.

In 1870 Bismarck maneuvered Napoleon III into declaring war. After the quick defeat of France, Bismarck formed the **German Empire** and on Jan. 18, 1871, in Versailles, proclaimed King Wilhelm I of Prussia German emperor (Deutscher kaiser).

The German Empire reached its peak before World War I in 1914, with 208,780 sq. mi., plus a colonial empire. After that war Germany ceded Alsace-Lorraine to France; West Prussia and Posen (Poznan) province to Poland; part of Schleswig to Denmark; lost all of its colonies and the ports of Memel and Danzig.

Republic of Germany, 1919-1933, adopted the Weimar constitution; met reparation payments and elected Friedrich Ebert and Gen. Paul von Hindenburg presidents.

Third Reich, 1933-1945, Adolf Hitler led the National Socialist German Workers' (Nazi) party after World War I. In 1923 he attempted to unseat the Bavarian government and was imprisoned. Pres. von Hindenburg named Hitler chancellor Jan. 30, 1933; on Aug. 3, 1934, the day after Hindenburg's death, the cabinet joined the offices of president and chancellor and made Hitler fuehrer (leader). Hitler abolished freedom of speech and assembly, and began a long series of persecutions climaxed by the murder of millions of Jews and opponents.

Hitler repudiated the Versailles treaty and reparations agreements. He remilitarized the Rhineland 1936 and annexed Austria (Anschluss, 1938). At Munich he made an agreement with Neville Chamberlain, British prime minister, which permitted Hitler to annex part of Czechoslovakia. He signed a non-aggression treaty with the USSR, 1939. He declared war on Poland Sept. 1, 1939, precipitating World War II.

With total defeat near, Hitler committed suicide in Berlin Apr. 1945. The victorious Allies voided all acts and annexations of Hitler's Reich.

Postwar changes. The zones of occupation administered by the Allied Powers and later relinquished gave the USSR Saxony, Saxony-Anhalt, Thuringia, and Mecklenburg, and the former Prussian provinces of Saxony and Brandenburg.

The territory E of the Oder-Neisse line within 1937 boundaries comprising the provinces of Silesia, Pomerania, and the southern part of East Prussia, totaling about 41,220 sq. mi., was taken by Poland. Northern East Prussia was taken by the USSR.

The Western Allies ended the state of war with Germany in 1951. The USSR did so in 1955.

There was also created the area of Greater Berlin, within but not part of the Soviet zone, administered by the 4 occupying powers under the Allied Command. In 1948 the USSR withdrew, established its single command in East Berlin, and cut off supplies. The Allies utilized a gigantic airlift to bring food to West Berlin, 1948-1949. In Aug. 1961 the East Germans built a wall dividing Berlin, after over 3 million E. Germans had emigrated.

Geography: Area: 41,768 sq. mi., the size of Virginia. **Location:** In E. Central Europe. **Neighbors:** W. Germany on W, Czechoslovakia on S, Poland on E. **Topography:** E. Germany lies mostly on the North German plains, with lakes in N, Harz Mtns., Elbe Valley, and sandy soil of Bradenburg in center, and highlands in S. **Capital:** East Berlin. **Cities** (1987 est.): East Berlin 1,236,000; Leipzig 553,000; Dresden 520,000.

Government: Type: Communist. **Head of state:** Chmn. Erich Honecker; b. Aug. 25, 1912; in office: Oct. 29, 1976. **Head of government:** Prime Min. Willi Stoph; b. July 9, 1914; in office: Oct. 29, 1976. **Head of Communist Party:** Sec.-Gen. Erich Honecker; in office: May 3, 1971. **Local divisions:** 14 districts. **Defense:** 6.4% of GNP (1985).

Economy: Industries: Steel, chemicals, electrical prods., textiles, machinery. **Chief crops:** Grains, potatoes, sugarbeets. **Minerals:** Potash, lignite, uranium, coal. **Arable land:** 47%. **Livestock** (1986): cattle: 5.8 mln.; pigs: 12.9 mln.; sheep: 2.5 mln. **Fish catch** (1986): 247,000 metric tons. **Electricity prod.** (1986): 118 bln. kwh. **Crude steel prod.** (1987): 8.2 min metric tons. **Labor force:** 10% agric.; 42.5% ind. & construction.

Finance: Currency: Mark (Jan. 1989: 1.86 = $1 US). **Gross national product** (1986): $185 bln. (excl. service sector) **Per capita income** (1987): $10,000. **Imports:** (1985): $22.2 bln.; partners: USSR, E. Europe. **Exports** (1985): $23.9 bln.; partners: USSR, E. Europe. **Tourists** (1983): 933,000. **National budget** (1984): $78 bln.

Transport: Railway traffic (1986): 22.4 bln. passenger-km; 58 bln. net ton-km. **Motor vehicles:** in use (1986): 3.4 min. passenger cars, 425,000 comm. vehicles. **Civil aviation** (1986): 2.6 bln. passenger-km; 71 mln. freight ton-km. **Chief ports:** Rostack, Wismar, Stralsund.

Communications: Television sets: 6.1 mln. licensed (1987). **Radios:** 6.6 min. licensed (1986). **Telephones in use** (1986): 3.6 mln. **Daily newspaper circ.** (1986): 559 per 1,000 pop.

Health: Life expectancy at birth (1987): 68.8 male; 74.7 female. **Births** (per 1,000 pop. 1986): 13.4. **Deaths** (per 1,000 pop. 1986): 13.4. **Natural increase** (1987): 0.0%. **Hospital beds** (1987): 169,000. **Physicians** (1987): 39,000. **Infant mortality** (per 1,000 live births 1986): 13.1.

Education (1987): Literacy: 99%. **Years compulsory:** 10.

Major International Organizations: UN (IMF, GATT), Warsaw Pact.

Embassy: 1717 Massachusetts Ave. NW 20036; 232-3134.

The German Democratic Republic was proclaimed in the Soviet sector of Berlin Oct. 7, 1949. It was proclaimed fully sovereign in 1954, but Soviet troops remain on grounds of security and the 4-power Potsdam agreement.

Coincident with the entrance of W. Germany into the European Defense community in 1952, the East German government decreed a prohibited zone 3 miles deep along its 600-mile border with W. Germany and cut Berlin's telephone system in two. Berlin was further divided by erection of a fortified wall in 1961, but the exodus of refugees to the West continued, though on a smaller scale.

E. Germany suffered severe economic problems until the mid-1960s. A "new economic system" was introduced, easing the former central planning controls and allowing factories to make profits provided they were reinvested in operations or redistributed to workers as bonuses. By the early 1970s, the economy was highly industrialized. In May 1972 the few remaining private firms were ordered sold to the government. The nation was credited with the highest standard of living among Warsaw Pact countries. But growth slowed in the late 1970s, due to shortages of natural resources and labor, and a huge debt to lenders in the West.

The government has firmly resisted following the USSR's policy of *glasnost.*

East Germany

German Democratic Republic

Deutsche Demokratische Republik

People: Population (1989 est.): 16,736,000. **Age distrib.** (%): 0–14: 19.2; 15–59: 61.5; 60+: 19.3. **Pop. density:** 400 per sq. mi. **Urban** (1986): 76.6%. **Ethnic groups:** German 99%. **Languages:** German. **Religions:** Protestant 47%, Roman Catholic 7%; none 45%.

West Germany

Federal Republic of Germany

Bundesrepublik Deutschland

People: Population (1989 est.): 60,162,000. **Age distrib.** (%): 0–14: 14.7; 15–59: 64.7; 60+: 20.6. **Pop. density:** 626 per sq. mi. **Urban** (1985): 86% **Ethnic groups:** German 93%. **Languages:** German. **Religions:** Protestant 44%, Roman Catholic 45%.

Geography: Area: 95,975 sq. mi. (incl. W. Berlin), the size of Wyoming. **Location:** In central Europe. **Neighbors:** Denmark on N, Netherlands, Belgium, Luxembourg, France on W, Switzerland, Austria on S, Czechoslovakia, E. Germany on E. **Topography:** West Germany is flat in N, hilly in center and W, and mountainous in Bavaria. Chief rivers are Elbe, Weser, Ems, Rhine, and Main, all flowing toward North Sea, and Danube, flowing toward Black Sea. **Capital:** Bonn. **Cities** (1987 est.): Berlin 1.8 mln.; Hamburg 1.6 mln.; Munich 1.3 mln.; Cologne 919,000; Essen 622,000; Frankfurt 598,000; Dortmund 575,000; Dusseldorf 593,000; Stuttgart 561,000.

Government: Type: Federal republic. **Head of state:** Pres. Richard von Weizsacker; b. Apr. 15, 1920; in office: May 23, 1984. **Head of government:** Chan. Helmut Kohl; b. Apr. 3, 1930; in office: Oct. 1, 1982. **Local divisions:** West Berlin and 10 laender (states) with substantial powers. **Defense:** 3.2% of GNP (1985).

Economy: Industries: Steel, ships, autos, machinery, coal, chemicals. **Chief crops:** Grains, potatoes, sugar beets. **Minerals:** Coal, potash, lignite, iron. **Crude oil reserves** (1985): 289 mln. bbls. **Arable land:** 30%. **Livestock** (1986): cattle: 15.6 mln.; pigs: 24.3 mln.; sheep: 1.2 mln. **Fish catch** (1986): 305,000 metric tons. **Electricity prod.** (1986): 406 bln. kwh. **Crude steel prod.** (1987): 36.2 mln. metric tons. **Labor force:** 6% agric.; 42% ind. & comm.; 42% service.

Finance: Currency: Mark (June 1989: 1.94 = $1 US). **Gross national product** (1986): $898 bln. **Per capita income** (1986): $10,680. **Imports** (1988): $250 bln.; partners: Neth. 12%, Fr. 11%, It. 8%, Belg. 7%. **Exports** (1988): $323 bln.; partners: Fr. 14%, Neth. 8%, Belg. 7%, It. 8%. **Tourists** (1986): receipts $7.8 bln. **National budget** (1986): $151 bln. **International reserves less gold** (Mar. 1988): $73 bln. **Gold:** 95.18 mln. oz t. **Consumer prices** (change in 1988): 1.2%.

Transport: Railway traffic (1987): 46 bln. passenger-km; 60 bln. net ton-km. **Motor vehicles:** in use (1987): 27.9 mln. passenger cars, 1.3 mln. comm. **Civil aviation** (1987): 31.7 bln. passenger-km; 3.3 bln. freight ton-km. **Chief ports:** Hamburg, Bremen, Lubeck.

Communications: Television sets: 23.3 mln. in use (1987). **Radios:** 26 mln. in use (1987). **Telephones in use** (1987): 40.2 mln. **Daily newspaper circ.** (1987): 417 per 1,000 pop.

Health: Life expectancy at birth (1985): 67.2 male; 73.4 female. **Births** (per 1,000 pop. 1987): 10.5 **Deaths** (per 1,000 pop. 1987): 11.2 **Natural increase** (1987): −.7%. **Hospital beds** (1987): 674,000. **Physicians** (1987): 165,000. **Infant mortality** (per 1,000 live births 1986): 8.6.

Education (1987): **Literacy:** 99%. **Years compulsory:** 10; attendance 100%.

Major International Organizations: UN and all of its specialized agencies, EC, OECD, NATO.

Embassy: 4645 Reservoir Rd. NW 20007; 298-4000.

The Federal Republic of Germany was proclaimed May 23, 1949, in Bonn, after a constitution had been drawn up by a consultative assembly formed by representatives of the 11 laender (states) in the French, British, and American zones. Later reorganized into 9 units, the laender numbered 10 with the addition of the Saar, 1957. Berlin also was granted land (state) status, but the 1945 occupation agreements placed restrictions on it.

The occupying powers, the U.S., Britain, and France, restored the civil status, Sept. 21, 1949. The U. S. resumed diplomatic relations July 2, 1951. The powers lifted controls and the republic became fully independent May 5, 1955.

Dr. Konrad Adenauer, Christian Democrat, was made chancellor Sept. 15, 1949, re-elected 1953, 1957, 1961. Willy Brandt, heading a coalition of Social Democrats and Free Democrats, became chancellor Oct. 21, 1969.

In 1970 Brandt signed friendship treaties with the USSR and Poland. In 1971, the U.S., Britain, France, and the USSR signed an agreement on Western access to West Berlin. In 1972 the Bundestag approved the USSR and Polish treaties and East and West Germany signed their first formal treaty, implementing the agreement easing access to West Berlin. In 1973 a West Germany-Czechoslovakia pact normalized relations and nullified the 1938 "Munich Agreement."

In May 1974 Brandt resigned, saying he took full responsibility for "negligence" for allowing an East German spy to become a member of his staff.

West Germany has experienced economic growth since the 1950s. The country leads Europe in provisions for worker participation in the management of industry.

The NATO decision to deploy medium-range nuclear missiles in Western Europe sparked a demonstration by some 400,000 protesters in 1983. In 1989, Chancellor Kohl's call for early negotiations with the Soviets on reducing short-range missiles caused a rift with the NATO allies, especially the U.S. and GT. Britain.

Helgoland, an island of 130 acres in the North Sea, was taken from Denmark by a British Naval Force in 1807 and later ceded to Germany to become a part of Schleswig-Holstein province in return for rights in East Africa. The heavily fortified island was surrendered to UK, May 23, 1945, demilitarized in 1947, and returned to W. Germany, Mar 1, 1952. It is a free port.

Ghana

Republic of Ghana

People: Population (1988 est.): 13,754,000. **Age distrib.** (%): 0–14: 46.6; 15-59: 48.9; 60+: 4.5. **Pop. density:** 160 per sq. mi. **Urban** (1984): 31%. **Ethnic groups:** Akan 44%, Moshi-Dagomba 16%, Ewe 13%, Ga 8%, others. **Languages:** English (official), 50 tribal languages. **Religions:** Christian 24%, traditional beliefs 38%, Moslem 24%.

Geography: Area: 92,098 sq. mi., slightly smaller than Oregon. **Location:** On southern coast of W. Africa. **Neighbors:** Ivory Coast on W, Burkina Faso on N, Togo on E. **Topography:** Most of Ghana consists of low fertile plains and scrubland, cut by rivers and by the artificial Lake Volta. **Capital:** Accra. **Cities** (1988 est.): Accra 949,000.

Government: Type: Military. **Head of government:** Pres. Jerry Rawlings; b. 1947; in office: Dec. 31, 1981. **Local divisions:** 10 regions.

Economy: Industries: Aluminum, light industry. **Chief crops:** Cocoa (70% of exports), coffee. **Minerals:** Gold, manganese, industrial diamonds, bauxite. **Crude oil reserves** (1980): 7 mln. bbls. **Other resources:** Timber, rubber. **Arable land:** 12%. **Fish catch** (1985): 254,000 metric tons. **Electricity prod.** (1986): 3.6 bln. kwh. **Labor force:** 60% agric.; 10% ind.

Finance: Currency: Cedi (Mar. 1989: 1.00 = $.03 US). **Gross national product** (1986): $5.1 bln. **Per capita income** (1980): $420. **Imports** (1987): $988 mln.; partners: UK 18%, W. Ger. 12%, Nigeria 12%. **Exports** (1987): $977 mln.; partners: UK 16%, U.S. 16%, Neth. 9%, W. Ger. 9%. **International reserves less gold** (Mar. 1989): 221 mln. **Gold:** 217,000 oz t. **Consumer prices** (change in 1988): 39.8%.

Transport: Railway traffic (1985): 201 mln. passenger-km; 73 mln. net ton-km. **Motor vehicles:** in use (1985): 52,000 passenger cars, 24,000 comm. vehicles. **Civil aviation** (1986): 298 mln. passenger-km; 6.9 mln. freight ton-km. **Chief ports:** Tema, Takoradi.

Communications: Television sets: 175,000 in use (1987). **Radios:** 3.0 mln. in use (1986). **Telephones in use** (1986): 72,000.

Health: Life expectancy at birth (1985): 50.3 male; 53.7 female. **Births** (per 1,000 pop. 1985): 47.0. **Deaths** (per 1,000 pop. 1985): 14.6. **Natural increase** (1985): 3.2%. **Physicians** (1984): 1,900. **Infant mortality** (per 1,000 live births 1985): 98.

Education (1983): **Literacy:** 30%.

Major International Organizations: UN and all of its specialized agencies, OAU.

Embassy: 2460 16th St. NW 20009; 462-0761.

Named for an African empire along the Niger River, 400-1240 AD, Ghana was ruled by Britain for 113 years as the Gold Coast. The UN in 1956 approved merger with the British Togoland trust territory. Independence came March 6, 1957. Republic status within the Commonwealth was attained in 1960.

Pres. Kwame Nkrumah built hospitals and schools, promoted development projects like the Volta R. hydroelectric and aluminum plants, but ran the country into debt, jailed opponents, and was accused of corruption. A 1964 referendum gave Nkrumah dictatorial powers and set up a one-party socialist state.

Nkrumah was overthrown in 1966 by a police-army coup, which expelled Chinese and East German teachers and technicians. Elections were held in 1969, but 4 further coups occurred in 1972, 1978, 1979, and 1981. The 1979 and 1981 coups were led by Flight Lieut. Jerry Rawlings.

Greece

Hellenic Republic

Elliniki Dimokratia

People: Population (1989 est.): 10,048,000. **Age distrib.** (%): 0–14: 20.5; 15–59: 61.1; 60+: 20.4. **Pop. density:** 196 per sq. mi. **Urban** (1985): 58.0%. **Ethnic groups:** Greeks 98.5%. **Languages:** Greek, others. **Religions:** Greek Orthodox 97%.

Geography: Area: 51,146 sq. mi., the size of Alabama. **Location:** Occupies southern end of Balkan Peninsula in SE Europe. **Neighbors:** Albania, Yugoslavia, Bulgaria on N, Turkey on E. **Topography:** About 75% of Greece is non-arable, with mountains in all areas. Pindus Mts. run through the country N to S. The heavily indented coastline is 9,385 mi. long. Of over 2,000 islands, only 169 are inhabited, among them Crete, Rhodes, Milos, Kerkira (Corfu), Chios, Lesbos, Samos, Euboea, Delos, Mykonos. **Capital:** Athens. **Cities** (1981 est.): Athens (met.) 3,016,457; Thessaloniki (met.) 800,000; Patras 120,000.

Government: Type: Presidential parliamentary republic. **Head of state:** Pres. Christos Sartzetakis; in office: Mar. 30, 1985. **Head of government:** Prime Min. Andreas Papandreou; b. Feb. 5, 1919, in office: Oct. 21, 1981. **Local divisions:** 51 prefectures. **Defense:** 5% of GDP (1985).

Economy: Industries: Textiles, chemicals, metals, wine, food processng, cement. **Chief crops:** Grains, corn, rice, cotton, tobacco, olives, citrus fruits, raisins, figs. **Minerals:** Bauxite, lignite, oil, manganese. **Crude oil reserves** (1985): 35 mln. bbls. **Arable land:** 30%. **Livestock** (1986): sheep: 10.1 mln.; goats: 5.6 mln. **Fish catch** (1986): 102,000 metric tons. **Electricity prod.** (1986): 29.5 bln. kwh. **Crude steel prod.** (1987): 900,000 metric tons. **Labor force:** 28% agric.; 29% ind., 42% service.

Finance: Currency: Drachma (June 1989: 170.00 = $1 US). **Gross national product** (1984): $36.6 bln. **Per capita income** (1984): $3,260. **Imports** (1987): $13.1 bln.; partners: W. Ger. 22%, It. 12%, Fr. 7%. **Exports** (1987): $6.5 bln.; partners: W. Ger. 25%, It. 18%, U.S. 8%. **Tourists** (1986): $1.3 bln. receipts. **National budget** (1986): $12.4 bln. expenditures. **International reserves less gold** (Mar. 1989): $3.3 bln. **Gold:** 3.3 mln. oz t. **Consumer prices** (change in 1988): 13.5%.

Transport: Railway traffic (1986): 1.6 bln. passenger-km; 708 mln. net ton-km. **Motor vehicles:** in use (1987): 1.4 mln. passenger cars, 680,000 comm. vehicles. **Civil aviation** (1986): 6.3 bln. passenger-km; 101 mln. freight ton-km. **Chief ports:** Piraeus, Thessaloniki, Patrai.

Communications: Television sets: 1.7 mln. in use (1986). **Radios:** 4 mln. in use (1986). **Telephones in use** (1987): 3.5 mln. **Daily newspaper circ.** (1986): 88 per 1,000 pop.

Health: Life expectancy at birth (1985): 72 male; 75 female. **Births** (per 1,000 pop. 1987): 10.6. **Deaths** (per 1,000 pop. 1987): 9.5. **Natural increase** (1987): .1%. **Hospital beds** (1986): 52,000. **Physicians** (1986): 29,000. **Infant mortality** (per 1,000 live births 1986): 12.2.

Education (1985): **Literacy:** men 96%, women 89%. **Years compulsory:** 9.

Major International Organizations: UN (GATT, IMF, WHO, ILO), EC, NATO, OECD.

Embassy: 2221 Massachusetts Ave. NW 20008; 667-3168.

The achievements of ancient Greece in art, architecture, science, mathematics, philosophy, drama, literature, and democracy became legacies for succeeding ages. Greece reached the height of its glory and power, particularly in the Athenian city-state, in the 5th century BC.

Greece fell under Roman rule in the 2d and 1st centuries BC. In the 4th century AD it became part of the Byzantine Empire and, after the fall of Constantinople to the Turks in 1453, part of the Ottoman Empire.

Greece won its war of independence from Turkey 1821-1829, and became a kingdom. A republic was established 1924; the monarchy was restored, 1935, and George II, King of the Hellenes, resumed the throne. In Oct., 1940, Greece rejected an ultimatum from Italy. Nazi support resulted in its defeat and occupation by Germans, Italians, and Bulgarians. By the end of 1944 the invaders withdrew. Communist resistance forces were defeated by Royalist and British troops. A plebiscite recalled King George II. He died Apr. 1, 1947, was succeeded by his brother, Paul I.

Communists waged guerrilla war 1947-49 against the government but were defeated with the aid of the U.S.

A period of reconstruction and rapid development followed, mainly with conservative governments under Premier Constantine Karamanlis. The Center Union led by George Papandreou won elections in 1963 and 1964. King Constantine, who acceded in 1964, forced Papandreou to resign. A period of political maneuvers ended in the military takeover of April 21, 1967, by Col. George Papadopoulos. King Constantine tried to reverse the consolidation of the harsh dictatorship Dec. 13, 1967, but failed and fled to Italy. Papadopoulos was ousted Nov. 25, 1973.

Greek army officers serving in the National Guard of Cyprus staged a coup on the island July 15, 1974. Turkey invaded Cyprus a week later, precipitating the collapse of the Greek junta, which was implicated in the Cyprus coup.

The military turned the government over to Karamanlis, who named a civilian cabinet, freed political prisoners, and sought to solve the Cyprus crisis. In Nov. 1974 elections his party won a large parliamentary majority, reduced by socialist gains in 1977. A Dec. 1974 referendum resulted in the proclamation of a republic.

Greece was reintegrated into the military wing of NATO in October 1980, and it became the 10th full member of the European Community on Jan. 1, 1981.

The 1981 victory of the Panhellenic Socialist Movement (Pasok) of Andreas Papandreou has brought about substantial changes in the internal and external policies that Greece has pursued for the past 5 decades. Greece has been victimized in the 1980s by incidents of international terrorism.

A scandal centered on George Kostokas, a banker and publisher, led to the arrest or investigation of about a dozen leading Socialists, implicated Papandreou, and led to the defeat of the Socialists at the polls in 1989 (*See Chronology*).

Grenada

State of Grenada

People: Population (1989 est.): 87,000. **Pop. density:** 654 per sq. mi. **Ethnic groups:** Mostly African descent. **Languages:** English (official), French-African patois. **Religions:** Roman Catholic 64%, Anglican 22%.

Geography: Area: 133 sq. mi., twice the size of Washington, D.C. **Location:** 90 mi. N. of Venezuela. **Topography:** Main island is mountainous; country includes Carriacou and Petit Martinique islands. **Capital:** St. George's. **Cities** (1980 est.): St. George's 7,500.

Government: Type: Independent state. **Head of state:** Queen Elizabeth II, represented by Gov.-Gen. Paul Scoon, b. July 4, 1935; in office: Sept. 30, 1978. **Head of government:** Prime Minister: Herbert Blaize; b. Feb. 26, 1918; in office: Dec. 4, 1984. **Local divisions:** 6 parishes and one dependency.

Economy: Industries: Rum. **Chief crops:** Nutmegs, bananas, cocoa, mace. **Arable land:** 41%. **Electricity prod.** (1986): 24.00 mln. kwh. **Labor force:** 33% agric.; 31% services.

Finance: Currency: East Caribbean dollar (Apr. 1989: 2.70 = $1 US). **Gross national product** (1986): $103 mln. **Per capita income** (1977): $500. **Imports** (1987): $89 mln.; partners: UK 19%, Trin./Tob. 25%. U.S. 17%. **Exports** (1987): $32 mln.; partners: UK 35%, CARICOM countries 38%. **Tourists** (1987): $27 mln. receipts. **National budget** (1987): $83.8 mln. expenditures. **International reserves less gold** (Jan. 1989): $17 mln.

Transport: Motor vehicles: in use (1981): 4,700 passenger cars, 1,000 comm. vehicles. **Chief ports:** Saint George's.

Communications: Radios: 50,000 in use (1986). **Telephones in use** (1987): 6,000.

Health: Life expectancy at birth (1985): 66.5 male; 72.5 female. **Births** (per 1,000 pop. 1986): 32.5. **Deaths** (per 1,000 pop. 1986): 7.2. **Natural increase** (1986): 2.5%. **Infant mortality** (per 1,000 live births 1987): 16.7.

Education (1987): **Literacy:** 95%; **Years compulsory:** 6.

Major International Organizations: UN (IMF, WHO), OAS.

Embassy: 1701 New Hampshire Ave. NW 20009; 265-2561.

Columbus sighted the island 1498. First European settlers were French, 1650. The island was held alternately by France and England until final British occupation, 1784. Grenada became fully independent Feb. 7, 1974 during a general strike. It is the smallest independent nation in the Western Hemisphere. The U.S. has criticized the government for following Soviet and Cuban policies.

On Oct. 14, 1983, a military coup ousted Prime Minister Maurice Bishop, who was put under house arrest, later freed by supporters, rearrested, and, finally, on Oct. 19, executed. U.S. forces, with a token force from 6 area nations, invaded Grenada, Oct. 25. Resistance from the Grenadian army and Cuban advisors was quickly overcome as most of the population welcomed the invading forces as liberators. U.S. troops left Grenada in June 1985.

Guatemala
Republic of Guatemala
República de Guatemala

People: Population (1989 est.): 9,412,000. **Age distrib. (%):** 0–14: 45.9; 15–59: 49.4; 60+: 4.7. **Pop. density:** 233 per sq. mi. **Urban** (1986): 33%. **Ethnic groups:** Maya 55%, Mestizos 44%. **Languages:** Spanish, Indian dialects. **Religions:** Mostly Roman Catholics.

Geography: Area: 42,042 sq. mi., the size of Tennessee. **Location:** In Central America. **Neighbors:** Mexico N, W; El Salvador on S, Honduras, Belize on E. **Topography:** The central highland and mountain areas are bordered by the narrow Pacific coast and the lowlands and fertile river valleys on the Caribbean. There are numerous volcanoes in S, more than half a dozen over 11,000 ft. **Capital:** Guatemala City. **Cities** (1986 est.): Guatemala City 1,800,000.

Government: Type: Republic. **Head of state:** Pres. Marco Vinicio Cerezo Arevalo; b. Dec. 26, 1942; in office: Jan. 14, 1986. **Local divisions:** Guatemala City and 22 departments. **Defense:** 2.2% of GNP (1986).

Economy: Industries: Prepared foods, tires, textiles. **Chief crops:** Coffee (one third of exports), sugar, bananas, cotton, corn. **Minerals:** Oil, nickel. **Crude oil reserves** (1985): 500 mln. bbls. **Other resources:** Rare woods, fish, chicle. **Arable land:** 16%. **Electricity prod.** (1986): 2.2 bln. kwh. **Labor force:** 50% agric.; 27% ind. & comm., 12% services.

Finance: Currency: Quetzal (Apr. 1989: 2.70 = $1 US). **Gross national product** (1986): $7.6 bln. **Per capita income** (1985): $1,000. **Imports** (1987): $1.4 bln.; partners: U.S. 33%, CACM 8%. **Exports** (1987): $1.0 bln.; partners: U.S. 34%, CACM 20%. **Tourism** (1986): $77 mln. **National budget** (1986): $1.7 bln. expenditures. **International reserves less gold** (Mar. 1989): $187 mln. **Gold:** 523,000 oz t. **Consumer prices** (change in 1987): 12.3%.

Transport: Motor vehicles: in use (1983): 188,000 passenger cars, 58,000 comm. vehicles. **Civil aviation** (1986) 136 mln. passenger-km; 7 mln. freight ton-km. **Chief ports:** Puerto Barrios, San Jose.

Communications: Television sets: 300,000 in use (1986). **Radios:** 500,000 in use (1986). **Telephones in use** (1985): 128,000. **Daily newspaper circ.** (1983): 30 per 1,000 pop.

Health: Life expectancy at birth (1987): 58.0 male; 62.0 female. **Births** (per 1,000 pop. 1987): 36.5. **Deaths** (per 1,000 pop. 1987): 9.5. **Natural increase** (1987): 2.7% **Health: Physicians** (1984) 3,500. **Infant mortality** (per 1,000 live births 1987): 66.

Education (1987): **Literacy:** 48%. **Years compulsory:** 6; **Attendance:** 35%.

Major International Organizations: UN (IMF, World Bank), OAS.

Embassy: 2220 R St. NW 20008; 745-4952.

The old Mayan Indian empire flourished in what is today Guatemala for over 1,000 years before the Spanish.

Guatemala was a Spanish colony 1524-1821; briefly a part of Mexico and then of the U.S. of Central America, the republic was established in 1839.

Since 1945 when a liberal government was elected to replace the long-term dictatorship of Jorge Ubico, the country has seen a swing toward socialism, an armed revolt, renewed attempts at social reform, a military coup, and, in 1986, civilian rule. The Guerrilla Army of the Poor, an insurgent group founded 1975, led a military offensive by attacking army posts and succeeded in incorporating segments of the large Indian population in its struggle against the government.

Dissident army officers seized power, Mar. 23, 1982, denouncing the Mar. 7 Presidential election as fraudulent and pledging to restore "authentic democracy" to the nation. Political violence has caused some 200,000 Guatemalans to seek refuge

in Mexico. A second military coup occurred Oct. 8, 1983. The nation returned to civilian rule in 1986. A military coup was thwarted May, 1989.

Guinea
Republic of Guinea
République de Guinée

People: Population (1989 est.): 6,147,000. **Pop. density:** 64 per sq. mi. **Urban** (1986): 26%. **Ethnic groups:** Foulah 40%, Malinké 25%, Soussous 10%, 15 other tribes. **Languages:** French (official), tribal languages. **Religions:** Moslem 85%, Christian 10%.

Geography: Area: 94,964 sq. mi., slightly smaller than Oregon. **Location:** On Atlantic coast of W. Africa. **Neighbors:** Guinea-Bissau, Senegal, Mali on N, Côte d'Ivoire on E, Liberia on S. **Topography:** A narrow coastal belt leads to the mountainous middle region, the source of the Gambia, Senegal, and Niger rivers. Upper Guinea, farther inland, is a cooler upland. The SE is forested. **Capital:** Conakry. **Cities** (1983 est.): Conakry 656,000; Labe 273,000; N'Zerekore 250,000; Kankan 278,000.

Government: Type: Republic under Military Committee For National Recovery. **Head of state:** Pres. Brig. Gen. Lansana Conte; b. 1944; in office: Apr. 5, 1984. **Local divisions:** 33 districts. **Defense:** 3.2% of GNP (1985).

Economy: Chief crops: Bananas, pineapples, rice, corn, palm nuts, coffee, honey. **Minerals:** Bauxite, iron, diamonds. **Arable land:** 6%. **Electricity prod.** (1986) 236 mln. kwh. **Labor force:** 82% agric.; 11% ind. & comm.

Finance: Currency: Franc (Jan. 1989: 299 = $1 US). **Gross national product** (1985): $1.9 bln. **Per capita income** (1984): $305. **Imports** (1984): $403 mln.; partners: Fr. 36% USSR 11%, U.S. 6% It. 6%. **Exports** (1984): $537 mln.; partners: U.S. 18%, Fr. 13%, W. Ger. 12%, USSR 12%. **National budget** (1982): 140 mln.

Transport: Motor vehicles: in use (1982): 10,000 passenger cars, 10,000 comm. vehicles. **Chief ports:** Conakry.

Communications: Radios: 200,000 in use (1986).

Health: Life expectancy at birth (1985): 38.7 male; 41.8 female. **Births** (per 1,000 pop. 1985): 46.8. **Deaths** (per 1,000 pop. 1985): 23.5. **Natural increase** (1985): 2.3%. **Physicians** (1980): 301. **Infant mortality** (per 1,000 live births 1985): 159.

Education (1983): **Literacy:** 48%. **Years compulsory:** 8; attendance: 34% primary, 15% secondary.

Major International Organizations: UN and most specialized agencies, OAU.

Embassy: 2112 Leroy Pl. NW 20008; 483-9420.

Part of the ancient West African empires, Guinea fell under French control 1849-98. Under Sekou Toure, it opted for full independence in 1958, and France withdrew all aid.

Toure turned to communist nations for support, and set up a militant one-party state. Western firms, as well as the Soviet government, have invested in Guinea's vast bauxite mines.

Thousands of opponents were jailed in the 1970s, in the aftermath of an unsuccessful Portuguese invasion. Many were tortured and killed.

The military took control of the government in a bloodless coup after the March 1984 death of Toure.

Guinea-Bissau
Republic of Guinea-Bissau
Republica da Guiné-Bissau

People: Population (1989 est.): 929,000. **Pop. density:** 66 per sq. mi. **Ethnic groups:** Balanta 27%, Fula 23%, Manjaca 11%, Mandinka 12%. **Languages:** Portuguese (official), Criolo, tribal languages. **Religion:** Traditional 65%, Moslem 30%, Christian 4%.

Geography: Area: 13,948 sq. mi. about the size of Connecticut and New Hampshire combined. **Location:** On Atlantic coast of W. Africa. **Neighbors:** Senegal on N, Guinea on E, S. **Topography:** A swampy coastal plain covers most of the country; to the east is a low savanna region. **Capital:** Bissau. **Cities** (1979): Bissau 109,500.

Government: Type: Republic. **Head of government:** Gen. Joao Bernardo Vieira; b. 1939; in office: Nov. 14,1980. **Local divisions:** 8 regions. **Defense:** 8.4% of GNP (1984).

Economy: Chief crops: Peanuts, cotton, rice. **Minerals:** Bauxite. **Arable land:** 10%. **Electricity prod.** (1986): 28 mln. kwh. **Labor force:** 90% agric.

Finance: Currency: Peso (Jan. 1989: 649 = $1 US). **Gross national product** (1986): $150 mln. **Per capita income** (1985): $185. **Imports** (1986): $63 mln.; partners: Port. 20%, It. 15%, Fr. 6%. **Exports** (1987): $16 mln.; partners: Port. 65%. **National Budget** (1987): $40 mln. expenditures.

Communications: Radios: 26,000 receivers (1986). **Daily newspaper circ.** (1984): 7 per 1,000 pop.

Health: Life expectancy at birth (1985): 42 years. **Births** (per 1,000 pop. 1985): 39. **Deaths** (per 1,000 pop. 1985): 20. **Natural increase** (1985): 1.9%. **Infant mortality** (per 1,000 live births 1989): 137.

Education (1989): Literacy 19%. **Years compulsory:** 4.

Major International Organizations: UN, OAU.

Embassy: 211 E 43d St., New York, NY 10017; (212) 611-3977.

Portuguese mariners explored the area in the mid-15th century; the slave trade flourished in the 17th and 18th centuries, and colonization began in the 19th.

Beginning in the 1960s, an independence movement waged a guerrilla war and formed a government in the interior that achieved international support. Full independence came Sept. 10, 1974, after the Portuguese regime was overthrown.

The November 1980 coup gave Joao Bernardo Vieira absolute power.

Guyana
Co-operative Republic of Guyana

People: Population (1989 est.): 779,000. **Age distrib. (%):** 0–14: 37.5; 5–59: 56.5; 60+: 6.0. **Pop. density:** 9.2 per sq. mi. **Urban** (1983): 32%. **Ethnic groups:** East Indians 51%, African and mixed 43%. **Languages:** English (official), Amerindian dialects. **Religions:** Christian 57%, Hindu 34%.

Geography: Area: 83,000 sq. mi., the size of Idaho. **Location:** On N coast of S. America. **Neighbors:** Venezuela on W, Brazil on S, Suriname on E. **Topography:** Dense tropical forests cover much of the land, although a flat coastal area up to 40 mi. wide, where 90% of the population lives, provides rich alluvial soil for agriculture. A grassy savanna divides the 2 zones. **Capital:** Georgetown. **Cities** (1985 est.): Georgetown 170,000.

Government: Type: Republic within the Commonwealth of Nations. **Head of state:** President Hugh Desmond Hoyte; b. Mar. 9, 1929; in office: Aug. 6, 1985. **Head of Government:** Prime Min. Hamilton Green; in office: Aug. 6, 1985. **Local divisions:** 10 regions. **Defense:** 8.9% of GDP (1985).

Economy: Industries: Cigarettes, rum, clothing, furniture, drugs. **Chief crops:** Sugar, rice, citrus and other fruits. **Minerals:** Bauxite, diamonds. **Other resources:** Timber, shrimp. **Arable land:** 2%. **Electricity prod.** (1986): 500 bln. kwh. **Labor force:** 33% agric.; 45% ind. & comm.; 22% services.

Finance: Currency: Dollar (Mar. 1989: 10.00 = $1 US). **Gross national product** (1986): $400 mln. **Per capita income** (1983): $457. **Imports** (1986): $242 mln.; partners: U.S. 21%, CARICOM 33%. **Exports** (1986): $242 mln.; partners: UK 28%, U.S. 18%, CARICOM 17%. **National budget** (1987): $1.5 bln. **International reserves less gold** (Feb. 1989): $4.0 mln. **Consumer prices** (change in 1987): 28.7%.

Transport: Motor vehicles: in use (1985): 25,000 passenger cars, 7,000 comm. vehicles. **Chief ports:** Georgetown.

Communications: Radios: 350,000 in use (1986). **Telephones in use** (1986): 33,000. **Daily newspaper circ.** (1986): 99 per 1,000 pop.

Health: Life expectancy at birth (1985): 70 years. **Births** (per 1,000 pop. 1985): 28.0. **Deaths** (per 1,000 pop. 1985): 7.0. **Natural increase** (1985): 2.1% **Health** (1987): 142 doctors, 213 health facilities. **Infant mortality** (per 1,000 live births 1985): 32.

Education (1985): Literacy: 86%. **Years compulsory:** ages 5-14.

Major International Organizations: UN (GATT, ILO, IMF, World Bank), CARICOM, Commonwealth of Nations.

Embassy: 2490 Tracy Pl. NW 20008; 265-6900.

Guyana became a Dutch possession in the 17th century, but sovereignty passed to Britain in 1815. Indentured servants from India soon outnumbered African slaves. Ethnic tension has affected political life.

Guyana became independent May 26, 1966. A Venezuelan claim to the western half of Guyana was suspended in 1970 but renewed in 1982. The Suriname border is also disputed. The government has nationalized most of the economy which has remained severely depressed.

The Port Kaituma ambush of U.S. Rep. Leo J. Ryan and others investigating mistreatment of American followers of the Rev. Jim Jones' People's Temple cult, triggered a mass suicide-execution of 911 cultists in the Guyana jungle, Nov. 18, 1978.

Haiti
Republic of Haiti
Républiqe d'Haiti

People: Population (1989 est.): 6,216,000. **Age distrib. (%):** 4–14: 39.2; 15–59: 52.5; 60+: 8.3. **Pop. density:** 580 per sq. mi. **Urban** (1986): 29%. **Ethnic groups:** African descent 95%. **Languages:** French, Creole (both official). **Religions:** Roman Catholics 80%, Protestants 10%; Voodoo widely practiced.

Geography: Area: 10,714 sq. mi., the size of Maryland. **Location:** In West Indies, occupies western third of I. of Hispaniola. **Neighbors:** Dominican Republic on E, Cuba on W. **Topography:** About two-thirds of Haiti is mountainous. Much of the rest is semiarid. Coastal areas are warm and moist. **Capital:** Port-au-Prince. **Cities** (1987 est.): Port-au-Prince 472,000.

Government: Type: Military. **Head of state:** Gen. Prosper Avril; in office: Sept. 17, 1988. **Local divisions:** 26 provinces, 1 federal dist. **Defense:** 1.6% of GNP (1985).

Economy: Industries: Sugar refining, textiles. **Chief crops:** Coffee, sugar, bananas, cocoa, tobacco, rice. **Minerals:** Bauxite. **Other resources:** Timber. **Arable land:** 32%. **Livestock** (1986): cattle: 1.3 mln.; goats: 1.1 mln. **Electricity prod.** (1986): 332 mln. kwh. **Labor force:** 75% agric.; 18% ind. & comm.; 7% services.

Finance: Currency: Gourde (Apr. 1989: 5.00 = $1 US). **Gross national product** (1986): $1.8 bln. **Per capita income** (1983): $300. **Imports** (1987): $400 mln.; partners: U.S. 45%. **Exports** (1987): $166 mln.; partners: U.S. 52%. **Tourists** (1986): receipts $58 mln. **National budget** (1987): $258 mln. expenditures. **International reserves less gold** (Mar. 1989): $10 mln. **Gold:** 18,000 oz t. **Consumer prices** (change in 1987): −11.5%.

Transport: Motor vehicles: in use (1985): 34,000 passenger cars, 11,000 comm. vehicles. **Chief ports:** Port-au-Prince, Les Cayes.

Communications: Television sets: 25,000 in use (1986). **Radios:** 200,000 in use (1986). **Telephones in use** (1986): 82,000 **Daily newspaper circ.** (1985): 4 per 1,000 pop.

Health: Life expectancy at birth (1985): 51.2 male; 54.4 female. **Births** (per 1,000 pop. 1985): 35.6. **Deaths** (per 1,000 pop. 1985): 13.0. **Natural increase** (1985): 2.2%. **Hospital beds** (1982): 3,600. **Physicians** (1985): 803. **Infant mortality rate** (per 1,000 live births, 1985): 107.

Education (1987): **Literacy:** 23%. **Years compulsory:** 6; attendance 20%.

Major International Organizations: UN and some of its specialized agencies, OAS.

Embassy: 2311 Massachusetts Ave. NW 20008; 332-4090.

Haiti, visited by Columbus, 1492, and a French colony from 1677, attained its independence, 1804, following the rebellion led by former slave Toussaint L'Ouverture. Following a period of political violence, the U.S. occupied the country 1915-34.

Dr. Francois Duvalier was voted president in 1957; in 1964 he was named president for life. Upon his death in 1971, he was succeeded by his son, Jean-Claude. Drought in 1975-77 brought famine, and Hurricane Allen in 1980 destroyed most of the rice, bean, and coffee crops.

Haiti is the poorest nation in the Western hemisphere; unemployment was estimated at 50% in 1987.

Following several weeks of unrest, President Jean Claude Duvalier fled Haiti aboard a U.S. Air Force jet Feb. 7, 1986, ending the 28-year dictatorship by the Duvalier family. A military-civilian council headed by Gen. Henri Namphy assumed control. In 1987, voters approved a new constitution.

The Jan. 17, 1988 elections led to Leslie Manigat being named president; opposition leaders charged widespread fraud. Gen. Namphy seized control, June 20, and named himself president of a military government. Namphy was ousted by a military coup in Sept.

Honduras
Republic of Honduras
Republica de Honduras

People: Population (1989 est.): 5,106,000. **Age distrib.** (%): 0–14: 46.9; 15–59: 48.6; 60+: 4.5. **Pop. density:** 117 per sq. mi. **Urban** (1986): 40.0%. **Ethnic groups:** Mestizo 90%, Indian 7%. **Languages:** Spanish, Indian dialects. **Religions:** Roman Catholic, small Protestant minority.

Geography: Area: 43,277 sq. mi., slightly larger than Tennessee. **Location:** In Central America. **Neighbors:** Guatemala on W, El Salvador, Nicaragua on S. **Topography:** The Caribbean coast is 500 mi. long. Pacific coast, on Gulf of Fonseca, is 40 mi. long. Honduras is mountainous, with wide fertile valleys and rich forests. **Capital:** Tegucigalpa. **Cities** (1986 est.) Tegucigalpa 604,000; San Pedro Sula 399,000.

Government: Type: Democratic constitutional republic. **Head of State:** Pres. Jose Azcona Hoyo; b. 1927; in office: Jan. 27, 1986. **Local divisions:** 18 departments. **Defense:** 3.8% of GNP (1985).

Economy: Industries: Clothing, textiles, cement, wood prods, cigars. **Chief crops:** Bananas (chief export), coffee, corn, beans. **Minerals:** Gold, silver, copper, lead, zinc, iron, antimony, coal. **Other resources:** Timber. **Arable land:** 16%. **Livestock** (1985): cattle: 2.3 mln. **Electricity prod.** (1986): 1.4 bln. kwh. **Labor force:** 62% agric.; 20% services; 9% manuf.

Finance: Currency: Lempira (Apr. 1989): 2.00 = $1 US). **Gross national product** (1986): $3.3 bln. **Per capita income** (1985): $815. **Imports** (1987): $1.7 bln.; partners: U.S. 39%, Jap. 8%. **Exports** (1987): $1.5 bln.; partners: U.S. 48%, Europe 34%. **Tourists** (1986): $26 mln. receipts. **National budget** (1984): $805 mln. revenues; $1.3 bln. expenditures. **International reserves less gold** (Mar. 1989): $59.4 mln. **Gold:** 16,000 oz t. **Consumer prices** (change in 1988): 4.5%.

Transport: Motor vehicles: in use (1985) 66,000 passenger cars, 18,000 comm. vehicles. **Civil aviation** (1983): 348 mln. passenger-km; 2.3 mln. freight ton-km. **Chief ports:** Puerto Cortes, La Ceiba.

Communications: Television sets: 140,000 in use (1987). **Radios:** 300,000 in use (1986). **Telephones in use** (1987): 50,000. **Daily newspaper circ.** (1984): 58 per 1,000 pop.

Health: Life expectancy at birth (1984): 58.7 yrs. **Births** (per 1,000 pop. 1985): 41. **Deaths** (per 1,000 pop. 1985): 8. **Natural increase** (1985): 3.3%. **Hospital beds** (1986): 5,600. **Physicians** (1986): 2,087. **Infant mortality** (per 1,000 live births 1985): 73.

Education (1987): **Literacy:** 56%. **Years compulsory:** 6; attendance 70%.

Major International Organizations: UN, (IMF, WHO, ILO), OAS.

Embassy: 4301 Connecticut Ave. NW 20008; 966-7700.

Mayan civilization flourished in Honduras in the 1st millenium AD. Columbus arrived in 1502. Honduras became independent after freeing itself from Spain, 1821 and from the Fed. of Central America, 1838.

Gen. Oswaldo Lopez Arellano, president for most of the period 1963-75 by virtue of one election and 2 coups, was ousted by the army in 1975 over charges of pervasive bribery by United Brands Co. of the U.S.

The government has resumed land distribution, raised minimum wages, and started a literacy campaign. An elected civilian government took power in 1982, the country's first in 10 years.

The U.S. has provided military aid and advisors to help withstand pressures from Nicaragua and help block arms shipments from Nicaragua to rebel forces in El Salvador. Some 3,200 U.S. troops were sent to Honduras after the Honduran border was violated by Nicaraguan forces, Mar. 1988.

Hungary
Hungarian People's Republic
Magyar Népköztársaság

People: Population (1989 est.): 10,571,000. **Age distrib.** (%): 0–14: 21.1; 15–59: 60.4; 60+: 18.5. **Pop. density:** 293 per sq. mi. **Urban** (1988): 58%. **Ethnic groups:** Magyar 92%, German 2.5%, Gypsy 3%. **Languages:** Hungarian (Magyar). **Religions:** Roman Catholic 67%, Protestant 25%.

Geography: Area: 35,919 sq. mi., slightly smaller than Indiana. **Location:** In East Central Europe. **Neighbors:** Czechoslovakia on N, Austria on W, Yugoslavia on S, Romania, USSR on E. **Topography:** The Danube R. forms the Czech border in the NW, then swings S to bisect the country. The eastern half of Hungary is mainly a great fertile plain, the Alfold; the W and N are hilly. **Capital:** Budapest. **Cities** (1988 est.): Budapest 2,104,000; Miskolc 209,000; Debrecen 217,000.

Government: Type: Communist. **Head of state:** Bruno Ferenc Straub; in office: June 29, 1988. **Head of government:** Prime Min. Miklos Nemeth; in office: June 29, 1988. **Head of Hungary Socialist Workers Party:** Karoly Grosz; b. 1930; in office: May 22, 1988. **Local divisions:** 19 counties, 5 cities with county status. **Defense:** 4.4% of GNP (1985).

Economy: Industries: Iron and steel, machinery, pharmaceuticals, vehicles, communications equip., milling, distilling. **Chief crops:** Grains, vegetables, fruits, grapes. **Minerals:** Bauxite, natural gas. **Arable land:** 57%. **Livestock** (1987): cattle: 1.7 mln.; pigs: 8.2 mln.; sheep: 2.4 mln. **Electricity prod.** (1986): 27.2 bln. kwh. **Crude steel prod.** (1987): 3.5 mln. metric tons. **Labor force:** 20% agric.; 31% ind.; 40% services.

Finance: Currency: Forint (Mar. 1989: 57 = $1 US). **Gross national product** (1986): $83.8 bln. **Per capita income** (1982): $4,180. **Imports** (1988): $9.3 bln.; partners: USSR 29%, W. Ger. 11%, E. Ger. 7%, Czech. 5%. **Exports** (1988): $9.9 bln.; partners: USSR 34%, E. Ger. 6%, W. Ger. 9%, Czech. 6%. **National budget** (1983): $13.4 bln. **Tourists** (1987): $831 mln. receipts. **Consumer prices** (change in 1988): 15.6%.

Transport: Railway traffic (1986): 11.2 bln. passenger-km; 22.0 bln. net ton-km. **Motor vehicles:** in use (1987): 1.6 mln. passenger cars, 201,000 comm. vehicles. **Civil aviation** (1987): 1.2 bln. Passenger-km; 15.8 mln. net freight-km.

Communications: Television sets: 2.9 mln. (1986). **Radios:** 5.5 mln. (1985). **Telephones in use** (1987): 1.6 mln. **Daily newspaper circ.** (1986): 236 per 1,000 pop.

Health: Life expectancy at birth (1987): 65.3 male; 73.2 female. **Births** (per 1,000 pop. 1987): 11.8. **Deaths** (per 1,000 pop. 1987): 13.4 **Natural increase** (1987): −1%. **Hospital beds** (1987): 104,000. **Physicians** (1987): 31,000. **infant mortality** (per 1,000 live births 1987): 17.4.

Education (1985): **Literacy:** 98%. **Years compulsory:** to age 16; attendance 99%.

Major International Organizations: UN (IMF, World Bank, GATT), Warsaw Pact.

Embassy: 3910 Shoemaker St. NW 20008; 362-6730.

Earliest settlers, chiefly Slav and Germanic, were overrun by Magyars from the east. Stephen I (997-1038) was made king by Pope Sylvester II in 1000 AD. The country suffered repeated Turkish invasions in the 15th-17th centuries. After the defeats of the Turks, 1686-1697, Austria dominated, but Hungary obtained concessions until it regained internal independence in 1867, with the emperor of Austria as king of Hungary in a dual monarchy with a single diplomatic service. Defeated with the Central Powers in 1918, Hungary lost Transylvania to Romania, Croatia and Bacska to Yugoslavia, Slovakia and Carpatho-Ruthenia to Czechoslovakia, all of which had large Hungarian minorities. A republic under Michael Karolyi and a bolshevist revolt under Bela Kun were followed by a vote for a monarchy in 1920 with Admiral Nicholas Horthy as regent.

Hungary joined Germany in World War II, and was allowed to annex most of its lost territories. Russian troops captured the country, 1944-1945. By terms of an armistice with the Allied powers Hungary agreed to give up territory acquired by the 1938 dismemberment of Czechoslovakia and to return to its borders of 1937.

A republic was declared Feb. 1, 1946; Zoltan Tildy was elected president. In 1947 the communists forced Tildy out. Premier Imre Nagy, in office since mid-1953, was ousted for his moderate policy of favoring agriculture and consumer production, April 18, 1955.

In 1956, popular demands for the ousting of Erno Gero, Communist Party secretary, and for formation of a government by Nagy, resulted in the latter's appointment Oct. 23; demonstrations against communist rule developed into open revolt. Gero called in Soviet forces. On Nov. 4 Soviet forces launched a massive attack against Budapest with 200,000 troops, 2,500 tanks and armored cars.

About 200,000 persons fled the country. In the spring of 1963 the regime freed many anti-communists and captives from the revolution in a sweeping amnesty. Nagy was executed by the Russians. In 1989, Nagy was exhumed from an unmarked grave and reburied. In Mar. 1987, some 2,000 marched in Budapest calling for democracy.

Soviet troops are stationed in Hungary. Hungarian troops participated in the 1968 Warsaw Pact invasion of Czechoslovakia.

Major economic reforms were launched early in 1968, switching from a central planning system to one in which market forces and profit control much of production. Hungary has embraced *glasnost*; the media comments freely on most topics. In 1989 parliament passed legislation legalizing freedom of assembly and association. President Bush visited Hungary in 1989. (*See Chronology*).

Iceland

Republic of Iceland

Lýoveldio Island

People: Population (1989 est.): 251,000. **Age distrib.** (%): 0–14: 25.5; 15–59: 60.1; 60+: 14.4. **Pop. density:** 6 per sq. mi. **Urban** (1987): 90% **Ethnic groups:** Homogeneous, descendants of Norwegians, Celts. **Language:** Icelandic (Islenska). **Religion:** Evangelical Lutheran 95%.

Geography: Area: 39,769 sq. mi., the size of Virginia. **Location:** At N end of Atlantic O. **Neighbors:** Nearest is Greenland. **Topography:** Iceland is of recent volcanic origin. Three-quarters of the surface is wasteland: glaciers, lakes, a lava desert. There are geysers and hot springs, and the climate is moderated by the Gulf Stream. **Capital:** Reykjavik. **Cities** (1986 est.): Reykjavik 89,000.

Government: Type: Constitutional republic. **Head of state:** Pres. Vigdis Finnbogadottir; b. Apr. 15, 1930; in office: Aug. 1, 1980. **Head of government:** Prime Min. Steingrimur Hermannsson; in office: Sept. 28, 1988. **Local divisions:** 23 counties.

Economy: Industries: Fish products (some 80% of exports), aluminum. **Chief crops:** Potatoes, turnips, hay. **Arable land:** 0.5%. **Livestock** (1985): lamb: 14,000 metric tons. **Fish catch** (1986): 1,600,000 metric tons. **Electricity prod.** (1986): 4.4 bln. kwh. **Labor force:** 11% agric.; 55% comm. & services, 14% fisheries .

Finance: Currency: Kronur (Mar. 1989: 53.23 = $1 US). **Gross national product** (1986): $3.2 bln. **Per capita income** (1984): $10,216. **Imports** (1988): $1.5 bln.; partners: W. Ger. 15%, UK 9%, Den. 10%. **Exports** (1988): $1.4 bln.; partners: U.S. 88%, UK 19%. **Tourists** (1987): receipts: $139 mln. **National budget** (1985): $704 mln. expenditures. **International reserves less gold** (Mar. 1989): $392 mln. **Gold:** 49,000 oz t. **Consumer prices** (change in 1988): 24.7%.

Transport: Motor vehicles: in use (1986): 100,000 passenger cars, 12,000 comm. vehicles. **Civil aviation** (1987): 2.7 bln. passenger-km ; 281 mln. freight ton-km . **Chief ports:** Reykjavik.

Communications: Television sets: 71,000 in use (1987). **Radios:** 79,000 licensed (1987). **Telephones in use** (1986): 102,000. **Daily newspaper circ.** (1986): 415 per 1,000 pop.

Health: Life expectancy at birth (1985): 73.5 male; 79.5 female. **Births** (per 1,000 pop. 1987): 16.9 **Deaths** (per 1,000 pop. 1987): 6.9. **Natural increase** (1987): 1.0%. **Hospital beds** (1985): 2,678. **Physicians** (1985): 574. **Infant mortality** per (1,000 live births 1987): 3.4.

Education (1986): **Literacy:** 99%. **Years compulsory:** 8; **Attendance:** 99%.

Major International Organizations: UN (GATT), NATO, OECD.

Embassy: 2022 Connecticut Ave. NW 20008; 235-6653.

Iceland was an independent republic from 930 to 1262, when it joined with Norway. Its language has maintained its purity for

1,000 years. Danish rule lasted from 1380-1918; the last ties with the Danish crown were severed in 1941. The Althing, or assembly, is the world's oldest surviving parliament.

India

Republic of India

Bharat

People: Population (1989 est.): 833,422,000. **Age distrib.** (%): 0–14: 36.8; 15–59: 56.4; 60+: 5.8. **Pop. density:** 658 per sq. mi. **Urban** (1985): 26%. **Ethnic groups:** Indo-Aryan groups 72%, Dravidians 25%, Mongoloids 3%. **Languages:** 16 languages, including Hindi (official) and English (associate official). **Religions:** Hindu 83%, Moslem 11%, Christian 3%, Sikh 2%.

Geography: Area: 1,266,595 sq. mi., one third the size of the U.S. **Location:** Occupies most of the Indian subcontinent in S. Asia. **Neighbors:** Pakistan on W, China, Nepal, Bhutan on N, Burma, Bangladesh on E. **Topography:** The Himalaya Mts., highest in world, stretch across India's northern borders. Below, the Ganges Plain is wide, fertile, and among the most densely populated regions of the world. The area below includes the Deccan Peninsula. Close to one quarter the area is forested. The climate varies from tropical heat in S to near-Arctic cold in N. Rajasthan Desert is in NW; NE Assam Hills get 400 in. of rain a year. **Capital:** New Delhi. **Cities** (1988 est.): Calcutta 9.9 mln.; Bombay (met.) 8.7 mln.; New Delhi 7.2 mln.; Madras 4.9 mln.; Bangalore 3.9 mln.; Hyderabad 2.8 mln.; Ahmedabad 2.3 mln.

Government: Type: Federal republic. **Head of state:** Pres. Ramaswamy Venkataraman; b. Dec. 4, 1910; in office: July 25, 1987. **Head of government:** Prime Min. Rajiv Gandhi, b. Aug. 20, 1944; in office: Oct. 31, 1984. **Local divisions:** 25 states, 6 union territories. **Defense:** 3.8% of GNP (1985).

Economy: Industries: Textiles, steel, processed foods, cement, machinery, chemicals, fertilizers, consumer appliances, autos. **Chief crops:** Rice, grains, coffee, sugar cane, spices, tea, cashews, cotton, copra, coir, juta, linseed. **Minerals:** Chromium, coal, iron, manganese, mica salt, bauxite, gypsum, oil. **Crude oil reserves** (1987): 4.3 bln. bbls. **Other resources:** Rubber, timber. **Arable land:** 57%. **Livestock** (1985): cattle: 185 mln.; pigs: 9 mln.; sheep: 54.4 mln. **Fish catch** (1987): 2.9 mln. metric tons. **Electricity prod.** (1987): 198 bln. kwh. **Crude steel prod.** (1987): 13.1 mln. metric tons. **Labor force:** 70% agric.; 19% ind. & comm.

Finance: Currency: Rupee (June 1989: 16.31 = $1 US). **Gross national product** (1988): $246 bln. **Imports** (1987): $16.7 bln.; partners: Jap. 12%, U.S. 12%, W. Ger. 10%, UK 8%. **Exports** (1987): $11.3 bln.; partners: U.S. 18%, USSR 15%, UK 6%, Jap. 9%. **Tourists** (1986): receipts: $1.4 bln. **National budget** (1988): $56 bln. expenditures. **International reserves less gold** (Jan. 1989): $4.9 bln. **Gold:** 10.4 mln. oz. t. **Consumer prices** (change in 1988): 9.0%.

Transport: Railway traffic (1987): 258 bln. passenger-km; 217 bln. net ton-km. **Motor vehicles:** in use (1985): 1.5 mln. passenger cars, 952,000 comm. **Civil aviation** (1987): 17.1 bln. passenger-km; 671 mln. freight ton-km. **Chief ports:** Calcutta, Bombay, Madras, Cochin, Vishakhapatnam.

Communications: Television sets: 9.3 mln. (1987). **Radios:** 50 mln. (1986). **Telephones in use** (1986): 4.0 mln. **Daily newspaper circ.** (1986): 16 per. 1,000 pop.

Health: Life expectancy at birth (1987): 56.7 male; 57.6 female. **Births** (per 1,000 pop. 1986): 29.6. **Deaths** (per 1,000 pop. 1986): 11.5. **Natural increase** (1987): 1.8%. **Hospital beds** (1984): 599,000. **Physicians** (1984): 284,000. **Infant mortality** (per 1,000 live births 1987): 96.0.

Education (1988): **Literacy:** 36%. **Years Compulsory:** to age 14.

Major International Organizations: UN (IMF, World Bank). **Embassy:** 2107 Massachusetts Ave. NW 20008; 939-7000.

India has one of the oldest civilizations in the world. Excavations trace the Indus Valley civilization back for at least 5,000 years. Paintings in the mountain caves of Ajanta, richly carved temples, the Taj Mahal in Agra, and the Kutab Minar in Delhi are among relics of the past.

Aryan tribes, speaking Sanskrit, invaded from the NW around 1500 BC, and merged with the earlier inhabitants to create classical Indian civilization.

Asoka ruled most of the Indian subcontinent in the 3d century BC, and established Buddhism. But Hinduism revived and eventually predominated. During the Gupta kingdom, 4th-6th century AD, science, literature, and the arts enjoyed a "golden age."

Arab invaders established a Moslem foothold in the W in the 8th century, and Turkish Moslems gained control of North India by 1200. The Mogul emperors ruled 1526-1857.

Vasco de Gama established Portuguese trading posts 1498-1503. The Dutch followed. The British East India Co. sent Capt. William Hawkins, 1609, to get concessions from the Mogul emperor for spices and textiles. Operating as the East India Co. the British gained control of most of India. The British parliament assumed political direction; under Lord Bentinck, 1828-35, rule by rajahs was curbed. After the Sepoy troops mutinied, 1857-58, the British supported the native rulers.

Nationalism grew rapidly after World War I. The Indian National Congress and the Moslem League demanded constitutional reform. A leader emerged in Mohandas K. Gandhi (called Mahatma, or Great Soul), born Oct. 2, 1869, assassinated Jan. 30, 1948. He advocated self-rule, non-violence, removal of untouchability. In 1930 he launched "civil disobedience," including boycott of British goods and rejection of taxes without representation.

In 1935 Britain gave India a constitution providing a bicameral federal congress. Mohammed Ali Jinnah, head of the Moslem League, sought creation of a Moslem nation, Pakistan.

The British government partitioned British India into the dominions of India and Pakistan. Aug. 15, 1947, was designated Indian Independence Day. India became a self-governing member of the Commonwealth and a member of the UN. It became a democratic republic, Jan. 26, 1950.

More than 12 million Hindu & Moslem refugees crossed the India-Pakistan borders in a mass transferral of some of the 2 peoples during 1947; about 200,000 were killed in communal fighting.

After Pakistan troops began attacks on Bengali separatists in East Pakistan, Mar. 25, 1971, some 10 million refugees fled into India. India and Pakistan went to war Dec. 3, 1971, on both the East and West fronts. Pakistan troops in the East surrendered Dec. 16; Pakistan agreed to a cease-fire in the west Dec. 17.

India and Pakistan agreed to withdraw troops from their borders and seek peaceful solutions. In Aug. 1973 India released 93,000 Pakistanis held prisoner since 1971. The 2 countries resumed full relations in 1976.

In 2 days of carnage, the Bengali population of the village of Mandai, Tripura State, 700 people, were massacred in a raid by indigenous tribal residents of the area, June 8-9, 1980. A similar year-long campaign against Bengali immigrants had been going on in Assam State.

Prime Min. Mrs. Indira Gandhi, named Jan. 19, 1966, was the 2d successor to Jawaharlal Nehru, India's prime minister from 1947 to his death, May 27, 1964.

Long the dominant power in India's politics, the Congress Party lost some of its near monopoly by 1967. The party split into New and Old Congress parties in 1969. Mrs. Gandhi's New Congress party won control of the House.

Threatened with adverse court rulings in a voting law case, an opposition protest campaign and strikes, Gandhi invoked emergency provisions of the constitution June, 1975. Thousands of opponents were arrested and press censorship imposed. Measures to control prices, protect small farmers, and improve productivity were adopted.

The emergency, especially enforcement of coercive birth control measures in some areas, and the prominent extra-constitutional role of Indira Gandhi's son Sanjay, was widely resented. Opposition parties, united in the Janata coalition, scored massive victories in federal and state parliamentary elections in 1977, turning the New Congress Party from power.

Indira Gandhi became prime minister for the second time, Jan. 14, 1980. Gandhi was assassinated by 2 of her Sikh bodyguards Oct. 31, 1984. Widespread rioting followed. Thousands of Sikhs were killed and some 50,000 left homeless. The assassination was in response to the government supression of a Sikh uprising in Punjab in June 1984 which included an assault on the Golden Temple, the holiest Sikh shrine. Rajiv, her son, replaced her as prime minister.

On Dec. 3, 1984, methyl isocyanate, a deadly gas, escaped from a tank owned by the Union Carbide Corp. at Bhopal and killed over 2,500, in history's worst industrial accident. In 1989, the Indian Supreme Court ordered Union Carbide to pay $470 million to victims of the gas leak.

Sikhs ignited several violent clashes during the 1980s. The government's May 1987 decision to bring the state of Punjab under the rule of the central government led to violence. Many died during a government siege of the Golden Temple at Amritsar, May 1988.

As India's population passed 800 mln., government officials expressed alarm that the failure to control the birth rate would lead to disaster.

Sikkim, bordered by Tibet, Bhutan and Nepal, formerly British protected, became a protectorate of India in 1950. Area, 2,740 sq. mi.; pop. 1981 cen. 315,000; capital, Gangtok. In Sept. 1974 India's parliament voted to make Sikkim an associate Indian state, absorbing it into India.

Kashmir, a predominantly Moslem region in the NW, has been in dispute between India and Pakistan since 1947. A cease-fire was negotiated by the UN Jan. 1, 1949; it gave Pakistan control of one-third of the area, in the west and northwest, and India the remaining two-thirds, the Indian state of Jammu and Kashmir, which enjoys internal autonomy. Repeated clashes broke out along the line.

There were also clashes in April 1965 along the Assam-East Pakistan border and in the **Rann** (swamp) **of Kutch** area along the West Pakistan-Gujarat border near the Arabian Sea. An international arbitration commission on Feb. 19, 1968, awarded 90% of the Rann to India, 10% to Pakistan.

France, 1952-54, peacefully yielded to India its 5 colonies, former French India, comprising Pondicherry, Karikal, Mahe, Yanaon (which became Pondicherry Union Territory, area 185 sq. mi., pop. 1981, 604,136) and Chandernagor (which was incorporated into the state of West Bengal).

Goa, 1,429 sq. mi., pop., 1981, 1 mln., which had been ruled by Portugal since 1505 AD, was taken by India by military action Dec. 18, 1961, together with 2 other Portuguese enclaves, **Daman** and **Diu,** located near Bombay. They became states of India in 1987.

Indonesia
Republic of Indonesia
Republik Indonesia

People: Population (1989 est.): 187,726,000. **Age distrib.** (%): 0-14: 39.2; 15-59: 56.5; 60+: 5.3. **Pop. density:** 255 per sq. mi. **Urban** (1985): 25%. **Ethnic groups:** Malay, Chinese, Irianese. **Languages:** Bahasa Indonesian (Malay) (official), Javanese, other Austronesian languages. **Religions:** Moslem 88%.

Geography: Area: 735,268 sq. mi. **Location:** Archipelago SE of Asia along the Equator. **Neighbors:** Malaysia on N, Papua New Guinea on E. **Topography:** Indonesia comprises 13,500 islands, including Java (one of the most densely populated areas in the world with 1,500 persons to the sq. mi.), Sumatra, Kalimantan (most of Borneo), Sulawesi (Celebes), and West Irian (Irian Jaya, the W. half of New Guinea). Also: Bangka, Billiton, Madura, Bali, Timor. The mountains and plateaus on the major islands have a cooler climate than the tropical lowlands. **Capital:** Jakarta. **Cities** (1985 est.): Jakarta 7,800,000; Surabaja 2,345,000; Bandung 1,613,000; Medan 1,110,000.

Government: Type: Independent Republic. **Head of state:** Pres. Suharto; b. June 8, 1921; in office: Mar. 6, 1967. **Local divisions:** 28 provinces, 282 regencies. **Defense:** 2.5% of GNP (1985).

Economy: Industries: Food processing, textiles, light industry. **Chief crops:** Rice, coffee, sugar. **Minerals:** Nickel, tin, oil, bauxite, copper, natural gas. **Crude oil reserves** (1987): 8.4 bln. bbls. **Other resources:** Rubber. **Arable land:** 11%. **Livestock** (1986): cattle: 6.4 mln.; sheep: 5.1 mln. **Fish catch** (1985): 2.2 mln. metric tons. **Electricity prod.** (1986): 29.8 bln. kwh. **Labor force:** 66% agric.; 23% ind. & comm.; 10% services.

Finance: Currency: Rupiah (June 1989: 1,756 = $1 US). **Gross national product** (1986): $85 bln. **Per capita income** (1982): $560. **Imports** (1987): $12.8 bln.; partners: Jap. 30%, U.S. 12%, Sing. 9%. **Exports** (1987): $17.1 bln.; partners: Jap. 47%, U.S. 20%, Sing. 10%. **Tourists** (1986): $590 mln. receipts. **National budget** (1986): $13.8 bln. **International reserves less gold** (Feb. 1989): $4.7 bln. **Gold:** 3.10 mln. oz t. **Consumer prices** (change in 1988): 8.0%.

Transport: Railway traffic (1987): 6.5 bln. passenger-km; 1.4 bln. net ton-km. **Motor vehicles:** in use (1986): 1.0 mln. passenger cars, 1.1 mln. comm. **Civil aviation** (1986): 9.1 bln. passen-

ger-km; 226 mln. freight ton-km. **Chief ports:** Jakarta, Surabaja, Medan, Palembang, Semarang.
Communications: Television sets: 8.9 mln. in use (1986). **Radios:** 32 mln. in use (1985). **Telephones in use** (1986): 763,000.
Health: Life expectancy at birth (1986): male: 53.9; female 56.7 years. **Births** (per 1,000 pop. 1986): 29.8. **Deaths** (per 1,000 pop. 1986): 11.7. **Natural increase** (1986) 1.8%. **Hospital beds** (1985): 106,000. **Physicians** (1985): 18,447. **Infant mortality** (per 1,000 live births 1987): 75.0.
Education (1984): **Literacy:** 72%. 86% attend primary school; 15% secondary school.
Major International Organizations: UN and all of its specialized agencies, ASEAN, OPEC.
Embassy: 2020 Massachusetts Ave. NW 20036; 393-1745.

Hindu and Buddhist civilization from India reached the peoples of Indonesia nearly 2,000 years ago, taking root especially in Java. Islam spread along the maritime trade routes in the 15th century, and became predominant by the 16th century. The Dutch replaced the Portuguese as the most important European trade power in the area in the 17th century. They secured territorial control over Java by 1750. The outer islands were not finally subdued until the early 20th century, when the full area of present-day Indonesia was united under one rule for the first time.

Following Japanese occupation, 1942-45, nationalists led by Sukarno and Hatta proclaimed a republic. The Netherlands ceded sovereignty Dec. 27, 1949, after 4 years of fighting. West Irian, on New Guinea, remained under Dutch control.

After the Dutch in 1957 rejected proposals for new negotiations over West Irian, Indonesia stepped up the seizure of Dutch property. A U.S. mediator's plan was adopted in 1962. In 1963 the UN turned the area over to Indonesia, which promised a plebiscite. In 1969, voting by tribal chiefs favored staying in Indonesia, despite an uprising and widespread opposition.

Sukarno suspended Parliament in 1960, and was named president for life in 1963. Russian-armed Indonesian troops staged raids in 1964 and 1965 into Malaysia, whose formation Sukarno had opposed.

Indonesia's popular, pro-Peking Communist Party tried to seize control in 1965; the army smashed the coup, later intimated that Sukarno had played a role in it. In parts of Java, communists seized several districts before being defeated; over 300,000 communists were executed.

Gen. Suharto, head of the army, was named president in 1968, reelected 1973, 1978, and 1988. A coalition of his supporters won a strong majority in House elections in 1971. Moslem opposition parties made gains in 1977 elections but lost ground in the 1982 elections. The military retains a predominant political role.

In 1966 Indonesia and Malaysia signed an agreement ending hostility. After ties with Peking were cut in 1967, there were riots against the economically important ethnic Chinese minority. Riots against Chinese and Japanese also occurred in 1974. Indonesia and China agreed to begin bilateral trade talks in 1985.

Oil export earnings, and political stability have made Indonesia's economy stable.

Iran
Islamic Republic of Iran
Jomhori-e-Islami-e-Irân

People: Population (1989 est.): 51,005,000. **Age distrib. (%):** 0-14: 44.4; 15-59: 50.3; 60+: 5.2. **Pop. density:** 80 per sq. mi. **Urban** (1980): 50%. **Ethnic groups:** Persian 63%, Turkomans & Baluchis 19%, Kurds 3%, Arabs 4%. **Languages:** Persian, Turk, Kurdish, Arabic, English, French. **Religions:** Shi'a Moslem 93%.
Geography: Area: 636,293 sq. mi. slightly larger than Alaska. **Location:** Between the Middle East and S. Asia. **Neighbors:** Turkey, Iraq on W, USSR of N (Armenia, Azerbaijan, Turkmenistan), Afghanistan, Pakistan on E. **Topography:** Interior highlands and plains are surrounded by high mountains, up to 18,000 ft. Large salt deserts cover much of the area, but there are many oases and forest areas. Most of the population inhabits the N and NW. **Capital:** Teheran. **Cities** (1986 cen.): Teheran 6,022,000; Esfahan 1,001,000; Mashhad 1,466,000; Tabriz 994,000; Shiraz 848,000.

Government: Type: Islamic republic. **Religious head:** Hojatolislam Ali Khamenei; b. 1939; in office: June 4, 1989. **Head of state:** Pres. Hashemi Rafsanjani; in office: July 28, 1989. **Local divisions:** 24 provinces. **Defense:** 7.2% of GNP (1984).
Economy: Industries: Petrochemicals, cement, sugar refining, carpets. **Chief crops:** Grains, rice, fruits, sugar beets, cotton, grapes. **Minerals:** Chromium, oil, gas. **Crude oil reserves** (1987): 36.5 bln. bbls. **Other resources:** Gums, wool, silk, caviar. **Arable land:** 9%. **Livestock** (1986): cattle: 8.3 mln.; sheep: 34.5 mln. **Electricity prod.** (1986): 36.8 bln. kwh. **Crude steel prod.** (1987) 1.2 mln. metric tons. **Labor force:** 40% agric.; 33% ind. & comm; 27% services.
Finance: Currency: Rial (Mar. 1989: 71.45 = $1 US). **Gross national product** (1986): $75 bln. **Per capita income** (1986): $1,667. **Imports** (1987): $9.5 bln.; partners: W. Ger. 16%, Jap. 13%, UK 6%. **Exports** (1987): $8.3 bln.; partners: Jap. 16%, It. 10%. **National budget** (1983): $33.3 bln. expenditures.
Transport: Motor vehicles: in use (1983): 2.1 mln. passenger cars, 313,000 comm. vehicles. **Chief ports:** Bandar Abbas.
Communications: Television sets: 2.1 mln. in use (1987). **Radios:** 10 mln. in use (1987). **Telephones in use** (1986): 1.8 mln. **Daily newspaper circ.** (1986): 13 per 1,000 pop.
Health: Life expectancy at birth (1985): 58.0 male; 58.3 female. **Births** (per 1,000 pop. 1985): 43. **Deaths** (per 1,000 pop. 1985): 12. **Natural increase** (1985): 3.1%. **Hospital beds** (1986): 70,152. **Physicians** (1986): 15,945. **Infant mortality** (per 1,000 live births 1986): 110.
Education (1986): **Literacy:** 48%.
Major International Organizations: UN (IMF, WHO), OPEC.

Iran was once called Persia. The Iranians, who supplanted an earlier agricultural civilization, came from the E during the 2d millenium BC; they were an Indo-European group related to the Aryans of India.

In 549 BC Cyrus the Great united the Medes and Persians in the Persian Empire, conquered Babylonia in 538 BC, restored Jerusalem to the Jews. Alexander the Great conquered Persia in 333 BC, but Persians regained their independence in the next century under the Parthians, themselves succeeded by Sassanian Persians in 226 AD. Arabs brought Islam to Persia in the 7th century, replacing the indigenous Zoroastrian faith. After Persian political and cultural autonomy was reasserted in the 9th century, the arts and sciences flourished for several centuries.

Turks and Mongols ruled Persia in turn from the 11th century to 1502, when a native dynasty reasserted full independence. The British and Russian empires vied for influence in the 19th century, and Afghanistan was severed from Iran by Britain in 1857.

The previous dynasty was founded by Reza Khan, a military leader, in 1925. He abdicated as shah in 1941, and was succeeded by his son, Mohammad Reza Pahlavi.

Parliament, under Premier Mohammed Mossadegh, nationalized the oil industry in 1951, leading to a British blockade. Mossadegh was overthrown in 1953; the shah assumed control. Under his rule, Iran underwent economic and social change but political opposition was not tolerated.

Conservative Moslem protests led to 1978 violence. Martial law in 12 cities was declared Sept. 8. A military government was appointed Nov. 6 to deal with striking oil workers. Prime Min. Shahpur Bakhtiar was designated by the shah to head a regency council in his absence. The shah left Iran Jan. 16, 1979.

Exiled religious leader Ayatollah Ruhollah Khomeini named a provisional government council in preparation for his return to Iran, Jan. 31. Clashes between Khomeini's supporters and government troops culminated in a rout of Iran's elite Imperial Guard Feb. 11, leading to the fall of Bakhtiar's government.

The Iranian revolution was marked by revolts among the ethnic minorities and by a continuing struggle between the clerical forces and westernized intellectuals and liberals. The Islamic Constitution established final authority to be vested in a Faghi, the Ayatollah Khomeini.

Iranian militants seized the U.S. embassy, Nov. 4, 1979, and took hostages including 62 Americans. The militants vowed to stay in the embassy until the deposed shah was returned to Iran. Despite international condemnations and U.S. efforts, including an abortive Apr., 1980, rescue attempt, the crisis continued. The U.S. broke diplomatic relations with Iran, Apr. 7th. The shah died in Egypt, July 27th. The hostage drama finally ended Jan. 21, 1981 when an accord, involving the release of frozen Iranian assets, was reached.

The ruling Islamic Party, increasingly dissatisfied with President Abolhassan Bani-Sadr, declared him unfit for office. In the weeks following Bani-Sadr's dismissal, June 22, 1981, a new wave of executions began. The political upheavals have brought Iran to almost total isolation from other countries.

A dispute over the Shatt al-Arab waterway that divides the two countries brought Iran and Iraq, Sept. 22, 1980, into open warfare. Iranian planes attacked Iranian air fields including Teheran airport. Iranian planes bombed Iraqi bases. Iraqi troops occupied Iranian territory including the port city of Khorramshahr in October. Iranian troops recaptured the city and drove Iraqi troops back across the border, May 1982. Iraq, and later Iran, attacked several oil tankers in the Persian Gulf during 1984. Saudi Arabian war planes shot down 2 Iranian jets, June 5, which they felt were threatening Saudi shipping. In Aug. 1988, Iran agreed to accept a UN resolution calling for a cease fire.

In Nov. 1986, senior U.S. officials secretly visited Iran and exchanged arms for Iran's help in obtaining the release of U.S. hostages held by terrorists in Lebanon. The exchange sparked a major scandal in the Reagan administration.

A U.S. Navy warship shot down an Iranian commercial airliner, July 3, 1988, after mistaking it for an F-14 fighter jet; all 290 aboard the plane died.

In 1989, Ayatollah Khomeini offered a $1 million reward for the killing of Salman Rushdie, author of *The Satanic Verses*, a novel perceived as blasphemous to Islam. Khomeini died following a long illness, June 4, 1989.

Iraq
Republic of Iraq
al Jumhouriya al 'Iraqia

People: Population (1989 est.): 17,610,000. **Age distrib. (%):** 0–14: 45.3; 15–59: 49.6; 60+: 5.1. **Pop. density:** 104 per sq. mi. **Urban** (1986): 72%. **Ethnic groups:** Arabs, 75% Kurds, 15% Turks. **Languages:** Arabic (official), Kurdish, others. **Religions:** Moslem 95% (Shiites 60%, Sunnis 35%), Christian 5%.

Geography: Area: 167,924 sq. mi., larger than California. **Location:** In the Middle East, occupying most of historic Mesopotamia. **Neighbors:** Jordan, Syria on W, Turkey on N, Iran on E, Kuwait, Saudi Arabia on S. **Topography:** Mostly an alluvial plain, including the Tigris and Euphrates rivers, descending from mountains in N to desert in SW. Persian Gulf region is marshland. **Capital:** Baghdad. **Cities** (1985 est.): Baghdad (met.) 3,400,000.

Government: Type: Ruling council. **Head of state:** Pres. Saddam Hussein At-Takriti, b. 1935 in office: July 16, 1979. **Local divisions:** 18 provinces. **Defense:** 42% of GNP (1984).

Economy: Industries: Textiles, petrochemicals, oil refining, cement. **Chief crops:** Grains, rice, dates, cotton. **Minerals:** Oil, gas. **Crude oil reserves** (1987): 40 bln. bbls. **Other resources:** Wool, hides. **Arable land:** 13%. **Livestock** (1986): cattle: 1.5 mln.; sheep 8.5 mln; goats: 2.3 mln. **Electricity prod.** (1986): 22.5 bln. kwh. **Labor force:** 50% agric.

Finance: Currency: Dinar (Mar. 1989: 1.00 = $3.21 US). **Gross national product** (1985): $35 bln. **Per capita income** (1984): $1,740. **Imports** (1987): $7.4 bln.; partners: W. Ger. 16%, Jap. 14%, Fr. 7%. **Exports** (1987): $9.0 bln.; partners: It. 13%, Tur. 11%, Braz. 22%, Jap. 6%.

Transport: Railway traffic (1986): 1.0 bln. passenger-km; 1.2 bln. net ton-km. **Motor vehicles:** in use (1986): 491,000 passenger cars, 246,700 comm. vehicles. **Civil aviation** (1985): 1.2 bln. passenger-km; 52.0 mln. freight ton-km. **Chief ports:** Basra.

Communications: Television sets: 605,000 in use (1987). **Radios:** 2.8 mln. in use (1986). **Telephones in use** (1985): 886,000. **Daily newspaper circ.** (1987): 21 per 1,000 pop.

Health: Life expectancy at birth (1986): 61.0 male; 64.5 female. **Births** (per 1,000 pop. 1986): 45.1. **Deaths** (per 1,000 pop. 1986): 8.6. **Natural increase** (1986): 3.6%. **Hospital beds** (1984): 26,657. **Physicians** (1984): 4,428. **Infant mortality** (per 1,000 live births 1986): 63.3.

Major International Organizations: UN (IMF, ILO), Arab League, OPEC.

Education (1987): **Literacy:** 70%. Compulsory age 6 to grade 6.

The Tigris-Euphrates valley, formerly called Mesopotamia, was the site of one of the earliest civilizations in the world. The Sumerian city-states of 3,000 BC originated the culture later developed by the Semitic Akkadians, Babylonians, and Assyrians.

Mesopotamia ceased to be a separate entity after the conquests of the Persians, Greeks, and Arabs. The latter founded Baghdad, from where the caliph ruled a vast empire in the 8th and 9th centuries. Mongol and Turkish conquests led to a decline in population, the economy, cultural life, and the irrigation system.

Britain secured a League of Nations mandate over Iraq after World War I. Independence under a king came in 1932. A leftist, pan-Arab revolution established a republic in 1958, which oriented foreign policy toward the USSR. Most industry has been nationalized, and large land holdings broken up.

A local faction of the international Baath Arab Socialist party has ruled by decree since 1968. Russia and Iraq signed an aid pact in 1972, and arms were sent along with several thousand advisers. The 1978 execution of 21 communists and a shift of trade to the West signalled a more neutral policy, straining relations with the USSR. In the 1973 Arab-Israeli war Iraq sent forces to aid Syria. Within a month of assuming power, Saddam Hussein instituted a bloody purge in the wake of a reported coup attempt against the new regime.

Years of battling with the Kurdish minority resulted in total defeat for the Kurds in 1975, when Iran withdrew support. Kurdish rebels continued their war, 1979; fighting led to Iraqi bombing of Kurdish villages in Iran, causing relations with Iran to deteriorate.

After skirmishing intermittently for 10 months over the sovereignty of the disputed Shatt al-Arab waterway that divides the two countries, Iraq and Iran, Sept. 22, 1980, entered into open warfare when Iraqi fighter-bombers attacked 10 Iranian airfields, including Teheran airport, and Iranian planes retaliated with strikes on 2 Iraqi bases. In the following days, there was heavy ground fighting around Abadan and the adjacent port of Khorramshahr as Iraq pressed its attack on Iran's oil-rich province of Khuzistan. In May 1982, Iraqi troops were driven back across the border. A fierce border war continued through 1988 with both sides suffering heavy casualties.

Israeli airplanes destroyed a nuclear reactor near Baghdad on June 7, 1981, claiming that it could be used to produce nuclear weapons.

Iraq and Iran expanded their war to the Persian Gulf in Apr. 1984. Several attacks on oil tankers were reported. An Iraqi warplane launched a missile attack on the U.S.S. *Stark*, a U.S. Navy frigate on patrol in the Persian Gulf, May 17, 1987; 37 U.S. sailors died. Iraq apologized for the attack claiming it was inadvertent.

The bloody war with Iran ended Aug. 1988, when Iraq accepted a UN resolution calling for a ceasefire.

Ireland

People: Population (1989 est.): 3,734,000. **Age distrib. (%):** 0–14: 30.5; 15–59: 54.5; 60+:15.0. **Pop. density:** 137 per sq. mi. **Urban** (1985): 57%. **Ethnic groups:** Celtic, English minority. **Languages:** English predominates, Irish (Gaelic) spoken by minority. **Religions:** Roman Catholic 95%, Anglican 3%.

Geography: Area: 27,137 sq. mi. slightly larger than W. Va. **Location:** In the Atlantic O. just W of Great Britain. **Neighbors:** United Kingdom (Northern Ireland). **Topography:** Ireland consists of a central plateau surrounded by isolated groups of hills and mountains. The coastline is heavily indented by the Atlantic O. **Capital:** Dublin. **Cities** (1986 est.): Dublin 502,000; Cork (met.) 133,000.

Government: Type: Parliamentary republic. **Head of State:** Pres. Patrick J. Hillery; b. May 2, 1923; in office: Dec. 3, 1976. **Head of government:** Prime Min. Charles Haughey; in office: Mar. 10, 1987. **Local divisions:** 26 counties. **Defense:** 1.3% of GNP (1988).

Economy: Industries: Food processing, metals, textiles, chemicals, brewing, electrical and non-electrical machinery, tourism. **Chief crops:** Potatoes, grain, sugar beets, fruits, vegetables. **Minerals:** Zinc, lead, silver, gas. **Arable land:** 14%. **Livestock** (1987): cattle: 6.7 mln.; pigs: 994,000; sheep: 2.7 mln. **Fish catch** (1985): 179,000 metric tons. **Electricity prod.** (1986): 12.6 bln. kwh. **Crude steel prod.** (1985): 203,000 metric tons. **Labor force:** 15% agric.; 27% ind. 38% services.

Finance: Currency: Pound (June 1989: 0.75 = $1 US). **Gross national product** (1988): $28.6 bln. **Per capita income** (1988): $6,200. **Imports** (1988): $15.5 bln.; partners: UK 42%, U.S. 17%, W. Ger. 8%, Fr. 5%. **Exports** (1988): $18.7 bln.; partners: UK 33%, Fr. 9%, W. Ger. 9%. **Tourists** (1986); receipts: $634 mln. **National budget** (1986): $8.6 bln. expenditures. **International reserves less gold** (Mar. 1989): $4.2 bln. **Gold:** 359,000 oz. t. **Consumer prices** (change in 1988): 2.2%.

Transport: Railway traffic (1986): 1.0 bln. passenger-km; 574 mln. net ton-km. **Motor vehicles:** in use (1986): 711,000 passenger cars, 106,000 comm. vehicles. **Civil aviation:** (1986): 2.4 bln. passenger-km; 79 mln. freight ton-km. **Chief ports:** Dublin, Cork.

Communications: Television sets: 795,000 receivers (1987). **Radios:** 2 mln. receivers (1986). **Telephones in use** (1985): 942,000. **Daily newspaper circ.** (1986): 200 per 1,000 pop.

Health: Life expectancy at birth (1988): 70.1 male; 75.6 female. **Births** (per 1,000 pop. 1987): 16.6. **Deaths** (per 1,000 pop. 1987): 8.8. **Natural increase** (1987): .7%. **Hospital beds** (1984): 32,000. **Physicians** (1984): 4,250 infant mortality (per 1,000 live births 1988): 8.8

Education (1988): **Literacy:** 99%. **Years compulsory:** 9; attendance 91%.

Major International Organizations: UN (GATT, IMF, World Bank), EC, OECD.

Embassy: 2234 Massachusetts Ave. NW 20008; 462-3939.

Celtic tribes invaded the islands about the 4th century BC; their Gaelic culture and literature flourished and spread to Scotland and elsewhere in the 5th century AD, the same century in which St. Patrick converted the Irish to Christianity. Invasions by Norsemen began in the 8th century, ended with defeat of the Danes by the Irish King Brian Boru in 1014. English invasions started in the 12th century; for over 700 years the Anglo-Irish struggle continued with bitter rebellions and savage repressions.

The Easter Monday Rebellion (1916) failed but was followed by guerrilla warfare and harsh reprisals by British troops, the "Black and Tans." The Dail Eireann, or Irish parliament, reaffirmed independence in Jan. 1919. The British offered dominion status to Ulster (6 counties) and southern Ireland (26 counties) Dec. 1921. The constitution of the Irish Free State, a British dominion, was adopted Dec. 11, 1922. Northern Ireland remained part of the United Kingdom.

A new constitution adopted by plebiscite came into operation Dec. 29, 1937. It declared the name of the state Eire in the Irish language (Ireland in the English) and declared it a sovereign democratic state.

On Dec. 21, 1948, an Irish law declared the country a republic rather than a dominion and withdrew it from the Commonwealth. The British Parliament recognized both actions, 1949, but reasserted its claim to incorporate the 6 northeastern counties in the United Kingdom. This claim has not been recognized by Ireland. *(See United Kingdom — Northern Ireland.)*

Irish governments have favored peaceful unification of all Ireland. Ireland cooperated with England against terrorist groups.

Ireland has suffered economic hardship in the 1980's; unemployment reached 16% in 1988.

Israel
State of Israel
Medinat Israel

People: Population (1989 est.): 4,477,000. **Age distrib. (%):** 0–14: 32.4; 15–59: 55.3; 60+: 13.3. **Pop. density:** 570 per sq. mi. **Urban** (1986): 89%. **Ethnic groups:** Jewish 83%, Arab 16%. **Languages:** Hebrew and Arabic (official), Yiddish, various European and West Asian languages. **Religions:** Jewish 83%, Moslem 13%.

Geography: Area: 7,847 sq. mi. about the size of New Jersey. **Location:** On eastern end of Mediterranean Sea. **Neighbors:** Lebanon on N, Syria, Jordan on E, Egypt on W. **Topography:** The Mediterranean coastal plain is fertile and well-watered. In the center is the Judean Plateau. A triangular-shaped semi-desert region, the Negev, extends from south of Beersheba to an apex at the head of the Gulf of Aqaba. The eastern border drops sharply into the Jordan Rift Valley, including Lake Tiberias (Sea of Galilee) and the Dead Sea, which is 1,296 ft. below sea level, lowest point on the earth's surface. **Capital:** Jerusalem. Most countries maintain their embassy in Tel Aviv. **Cities** (1986 est.): Jerusalem 457,000; Tel Aviv-Yafo 322,000; Haifa 224,000.

Government: Type: Parliamentary democracy. **Head of state:** Pres. Chaim Herzog; b. Sept. 17, 1918; in office: May 5,

1983. **Head of government:** Prime Min. Yitzhak Shamir; b. 1915; in office: Oct. 20, 1986. **Local divisions:** 6 administrative districts. **Defense:** 13.9% of GNP (1985).

Economy: Industries: Diamond cutting, textiles, electronics, machinery, food processing. **Chief crops:** Citrus fruit, vegetables. **Minerals:** Potash, copper, phosphates, manganese, sulphur. **Crude oil reserves** (1987): 700,000 mln. bbls. **Arable land:** 21%. **Livestock** (1986): cattle: 310,000; sheep: 281,000. **Fish catch** (1987): 22,000 metric tons. **Electricity prod.** (1986): 16.3 bln. kwh. **Labor force:** 6% agric.; 23% ind., 30% public services.

Finance: Currency: Shekel (May 1989: 1.82 = $1 US). **GNP** (1986): $25.9 bln. **Per capita income** (1986): $5,995. **Imports** (1988): $14.3 bln.; partners: U.S. 16%, W. Ger. 13%, UK 9%. **Exports** (1988): $9.6 bln.; partners: U.S. 34%, W. Ger. 5%, UK 7%. **Tourists** (1987): receipts $1.3 bln. **National budget** (1985): $23 bln. expenditures. **International reserves less gold** (Jan. 1989): $5.6 bln. **Gold:** 1.01 mln. oz t. **Consumer prices** (change in 1988): 16.3%.

Transport: Railway traffic (1987): 173 mln. passenger-km; 983 mln. net ton-km. **Motor vehicles:** in use (1986): 648,000 passenger cars, 129,000 comm. vehicles. **Civil aviation** (1987): 7.2 mln. passenger-km; 648 mln. freight ton-km. **Chief ports:** Haifa, Ashdod, Eilat.

Communications: Television sets: 620,000 in use (1986). **Radios:** 700,000 (1986). **Telephones in use** (1986): 1.7 mln. **Daily newspaper circ.** (1986): 263 per 1,000 pop.

Health: Life expectancy at birth (1985) Jewish pop. only 73.5 male; 77.0 female. **Births** (per 1,000 pop. 1987): 22.7. **Deaths** (per 1,000 pop. 1987): 6.7%. **Natural increase** (1987): 1.6%. **Hospital beds** (1986): 27,399. **Physicians** (1986): 9,500. Infant mortality (per 1,000 live births 1986): 11.2.

Education (1987): **Literacy:** 88% (Jewish), 70% (Arab).

Major International Organizations: UN (GATT).

Embassy: 3541 International Dr. NW 20008; 364-5500.

Occupying the SW corner of the ancient Fertile Crescent, Israel contains some of the oldest known evidence of agriculture and of primitive town life. A more advanced civilization emerged in the 3d millenium BC. The Hebrews probably arrived early in the 2d millenium BC. Under King David and his successors (c.1000 BC-597 BC), Judaism was developed and secured. After conquest by Babylonians, Persians, and Greeks, an independent Jewish kingdom was revived, 168 BC, but Rome took effective control in the next century, suppressed Jewish revolts in 70 AD and 135 AD, and renamed Judea Palestine, after the earlier coastal inhabitants, the Philistines.

Arab invaders conquered Palestine in 636. The Arabic language and Islam prevailed within a few centuries, but a Jewish minority remained. The land was ruled from the 11th century as a part of non-Arab empires by Seljuks, Mamluks, and Ottomans (with a crusader interval, 1098-1291).

After 4 centuries of Ottoman rule, during which the population declined to a low of 350,000 (1785), the land was taken in 1917 by Britain, which in the Balfour Declaration that year pledged to support a Jewish national homeland there, as foreseen by the Zionists. In 1920 a British Palestine Mandate was recognized; in 1922 the land east of the Jordan was detached.

Jewish immigration, begun in the late 19th century, swelled in the 1930s with refugees from the Nazis; heavy Arab immigration from Syria and Lebanon also occurred. Arab opposition to Jewish immigration turned violent in 1920, 1921, 1929, and 1936. The UN General Assembly voted in 1947 to partition Palestine into an Arab and a Jewish state. Britain withdrew in May 1948.

Israel was declared an independent state May 14, 1948; the Arabs rejected partition. Egypt, Jordan, Syria, Lebanon, Iraq, and Saudi Arabia invaded, but failed to destroy the Jewish state, which gained territory. Separate armistices with the Arab nations were signed in 1949; Jordan occupied the West Bank, Egypt occupied Gaza, but neither granted Palestinian autonomy. No peace settlement was obtained, and the Arab nations continued policies of economic boycott, blockade in the Suez Canal, and support of guerrillas. Several hundred thousand Arabs left the area of Jewish control; an equal number of Jews left the Arab countries for Israel 1949-53.

After persistent terrorist raids, Israel invaded Egypt's Sinai, Oct. 29, 1956, aided briefly by British and French forces. A UN cease-fire was arranged Nov. 6.

An uneasy truce between Israel and the Arab countries, supervised by a UN Emergency Force, prevailed until May 19, 1967, when the UN force withdrew at the demand of Egypt's Pres. Nasser. Egyptian forces reoccupied the Gaza Strip and closed the Gulf of Aqaba to Israeli shipping. In a 6-day war that started June 5, the Israelis took the Gaza Strip, occupied the Sinai Peninsula to the Suez Canal, and captured Old Jerusalem, Syria's Golan Heights, and Jordan's West Bank. The fighting was halted June 10 by UN-arranged cease-fire agreements.

Egypt and Syria attacked Israel, Oct. 6, 1973 (Yom Kippur, most solemn day on the Jewish calendar). Egypt and Syria were supplied by massive USSR military airlifts; the U.S. responded with an airlift to Israel. Israel counter-attacked, driving the Syrians back, and crossed the Suez Canal.

A cease fire took effect Oct. 24; a UN peace-keeping force went to the area. A disengagement agreement was signed Jan. 18, 1974. Israel withdrew from the canal's W bank. A second withdrawal was completed in 1976; Israel returned the Sinai to Egypt in 1982.

Israel and Syria agreed to disengage June 1; Israel completed withdrawing from its salient (and a small part of the land taken in the 1967 war) June 25.

In the wake of the war, Golda Meir, long Israel's premier, resigned; severe inflation gripped the nation. Palestinian guerrillas staged massacres, killing scores of civilians 1974-75. Israel aided Christian forces in the 1975-76 Lebanese civil war.

Israeli forces raided Entebbe, Uganda, July 3, 1976, and rescued 103 hostages seized by Arab and German terrorists.

In 1977, the conservative opposition, led by Menachem Begin, was voted into office for the first time. Egypt's Pres. Sadat visited Jerusalem Nov. 1977 and on Mar. 26, 1979. Egypt and Israel signed a formal peace treaty, ending 30 years of war, and establishing diplomatic relations.

Israel invaded S. Lebanon, March 1978, following a Lebanon-based terrorist attack in Israel. Israel withdrew in favor of a 6,000-man UN force, but continued to aid Christian militiamen.

A 5-day occupation of Israeli forces in southern Lebanon took place April 1980, in retaliation to the Palestinian raid on a kibbutz earlier that month. Violence on the Israeli-occupied West Bank rose in 1982 when Israel announced plans to build new Jewish settlements.

Israel affirmed the entire city of Jerusalem as its capital, July, 1980, encompassing the annexed Arab East Jerusalem.

Israel shot down, Apr. 28, 1981, two Syrian helicopters Israel claimed were attacking Lebanese Christian militia forces in the Beirut-Zahle area of Lebanon. Syria responded by installing Soviet-built surface-to-air missiles in Lebanon. Both the U.S. and Israel were unable to persuade Syria to withdraw the missiles, and Israel threatened to destroy them.

On June 7, 1981, Israeli jets destroyed an Iraqi atomic reactor near Baghdad that, Israel claimed, would have enabled Iraq to manufacture nuclear weapons.

In a close election, June 30, 1981, Prime Min. Menachem Begin was able to assemble a narrow coalition, he survived a no confidence motion in the Knesset by one vote, May 1982. He retired Oct. 1983.

Israeli jets bombed Palestine Liberation Organization (PLO) strongholds in Lebanon April, May 1982. In reaction to the wounding of the Israeli ambassador to Great Britain, Israeli forces in a coordinated land, sea, and air attack invaded Lebanon, June 6, to destroy PLO strongholds in that country. Israeli and Syrian forces engaged in the Bekka Valley, June 9, but quickly agreed to a truce. Israeli forces encircled Beirut June 14. Following massive Israeli bombing of West Beirut, the PLO agreed to evacuate the city.

Israeli troops entered West Beirut after newly-elected Lebanese president Bashir Gemayel was assassinated on Sept. 14. Israel received widespread condemnation when Lebenese Christian forces, Sept. 16, entered 2 West Beirut refugee camps and slaughtered hundreds of Palestinian refugees. Israeli troops withdrew from Lebanon in June 1986.

In 1989, violence continued over the Israeli military occupation of the West Bank and Gaza Strip; protesters and Israeli troops clashed frequently. (See Chronology.)

Italy

Italian Republic

Repubblica Italiana

People: Population (1989 est.): 57,439,000. **Age distrib.** (%): 0–14: 19.9; 15–59: 61.3; 60+: 18.8. **Pop. density:** 493 per sq. mi. **Urban** (1987): 67%. **Ethnic groups:** Italians, small minorities of Germans, Slovenes, Albanians. **Languages:** Italian. **Religions:** Predominantly Roman Catholic.

Geography: Area: 116,303 sq. mi., about the size of Florida and Georgia combined. **Location:** In S Europe, jutting into Mediterranean S. **Neighbors:** France on W, Switzerland, Austria on N, Yugoslavia on E. **Topography:** Occupies a long boot-shaped peninsula, extending SE from the Alps into the Mediterranean, with the islands of Sicily and Sardinia offshore. The alluvial Po Valley drains most of N. The rest of the country is rugged and mountainous, except for intermittent coastal plains, like the Campania, S of Rome. Apennine Mts. run down through center of peninsula. **Capital:** Rome. **Cities** (1987 est.): Rome 2.8 mln.; Milan 1.4 mln.; Naples 1.2 mln.; Turin 1.0 mln.

Government: Type: Republic. **Head of state:** Pres. Francesco Cossiga; b. July 26, 1929; in office: July 9, 1985; **Head of government:** vacant. **Local divisions:** 20 regions with some autonomy, 95 provinces. **Defense:** 2.5% of GNP (1986).

Economy: Industries: Steel, machinery, autos, textiles, shoes, machine tools, chemicals. **Chief crops:** Grapes, olives, citrus fruits, vegetables, wheat, rice. **Minerals:** Mercury, potash, gas, marble, sulphur, coal. **Crude oil reserves** (1987): 951 mln. bbls. **Arable land:** 41%. **Livestock** (1986): cattle: 8.9 mln.; pigs: 9.1 mln.; sheep: 9.6 mln. **Fish catch** (1986): 414,000 metric tons. **Electricity prod.** (1986): 188 bln. kwh. **Crude steel prod.** (1987): 22.8 mln. metric tons. **Labor force:** 10% agric.; 30% ind. and comm.; 49% services and govt.

Finance: Currency: Lira (June 1989: 1,454 = $1 US). **Gross national product** (1986): $368 bln. **Per capita income** (1986): $6,447. **Imports** (1988): $138 bln.; partners: W. Ger. 20%, Fr. 15%, U.S. 7%. **Exports** (1988): $128 bln.; partners: W. Ger. 16%, Fr. 15%, U.S. 10%, UK 6%. **Tourists** (1985): receipts $8.7 bln. **National budget** (1983): $173 bln. expenditures. **International reserves less gold** (Apr. 1989): $37 bln. **Gold:** 66.67 mln. oz t. **Consumer prices** (change in 1988): 5.3%.

Transport: Railway traffic (1986): 40 bln. passenger-km; 17.5 bln. net ton-km. **Motor vehicles:** in use (1985): 22.3 mln. passenger cars, 1.9 mln. comm. **Civil aviation** (1986): 13.9 bln. passenger-km; 859 mln. freight ton-km. **Chief ports:** Genoa, Venice, Trieste, Taranto, Naples, La Spezia.

Communications: Television sets: 15.0 mln. in use (1986). **Radios:** 14 mln. in use (1986). **Telephones** in use (1986): 26.8 mln. **Daily newspaper circ.** (1985): 109 per 1,000 pop.

Health: Life expectancy at birth (1983): 73.0 male; 79.1 female. **Births** (per 1,000 pop. 1986): 9.7. **Deaths** (per 1,000 pop. 1986): 9.2. **Natural increase** (1986): .0%. **Hospital beds** (1986): 470,579. **Physicians** (1985): 237,579. **Infant mortality** (per 1,000 live births 1985): 12.

Education (1985): **Literacy:** 97%. **Years compulsory:** 8.

Major International Organizations: UN and all of its specialized agencies, NATO, OECD, EC.

Embassy: 1601 Fuller St. NW 20009; 328-5500.

Rome emerged as the major power in Italy after 500 BC, dominating the more civilized Etruscans to the N and Greeks to the S. Under the Empire, which lasted until the 5th century AD, Rome ruled most of Western Europe, the Balkans, the Near East, and North Africa. In 1988, archeologists unearthed evidence showing Rome as a dynamic society in the 6th and 7th centuries B.C.

After the Germanic invasions, lasting several centuries, a high civilization arose in the city-states of the N, culminating in the Renaissance. But German, French, Spanish, and Austrian intervention prevented the unification of the country. In 1859 Lombardy came under the crown of King Victor Emmanuel II of Sardinia. By plebiscite in 1860, Parma, Modena, Romagna, and Tuscany joined, followed by Sicily and Naples, and by the Marches and Umbria. The first Italian parliament declared Victor Emmanuel king of Italy Mar. 17, 1861. Mantua and Venetia were added in 1866 as an outcome of the Austro-Prussian war. The Papal States were taken by Italian troops Sept. 20, 1870, on the withdrawal of the French garrison. The states were annexed to the kingdom by plebiscite. Italy recognized the State of Vatican City as independent Feb. 11, 1929.

Fascism appeared in Italy Mar. 23, 1919, led by Benito Mussolini, who took over the government at the invitation of the king Oct. 28, 1922. Mussolini acquired dictatorial powers. He made war on Ethiopia and proclaimed Victor Emmanuel III emperor, defied the sanctions of the League of Nations, joined the Berlin-Tokyo axis, sent troops to fight for Franco against the Republic of Spain and joined Germany in World War II.

After Fascism was overthrown in 1943, Italy declared war on Germany and Japan and contributed to the Allied victory. It surrendered conquered lands and lost its colonies. Mussolini was killed by partisans Apr. 28, 1945.

Victor Emmanuel III abdicated May 9, 1946; his son Humbert II was king until June 10, when Italy became a republic after a referendum, June 2-3.

Reorganization of the Fascist party is forbidden. The cabinet normally represents a coalition of the Christian Democrats, largest of Italy's many parties, and one or 2 other parties.

The Vatican agreed in 1976 to revise its 1929 concordat with the state, depriving Roman Catholicism of its status as state religion. In 1974 Italians voted by a 3-to-2 margin to retain a 3-year-old law permitting divorce, which was opposed by the church.

Italy has enjoyed an extraordinary growth in industry and living standards since World War II, in part due to membership in the Common Market. Italy joined the European Monetary System, 1980. A wave of left-wing political violence began in the late 1970s with kidnappings and assassinations and continued through the 1980s. Christian Dem. leader and former Prime Min. Moro was murdered May 1978 by Red Brigade terrorists.

The Cabinet of Prime Min. Arnaldo Forlani resigned, May 26, 1981, in the wake of revelations that numerous high-ranking officials were members of an illegally secret Masonic lodge. The June 1983 elections saw Bettino Craxi chosen the nation's first Socialist premier. Craxi's government faced a severe crisis as the result of a chain of events sparked by the Oct. 17, 1985 hijacking of the Italian cruise ship *Achille Lauro* and the subsequent U.S. downing on Italian soil of an Egyptian aircraft carrying the 4 hijackers and Abul Abbas, a PLO leader suspected of planning the hijacking. Craxi's release of Abbas and refusal to turn the 4 hijackers over to the U.S. caused an internal crisis that almost saw his government fall. Craxi ended the longest tenure of an Italian leader since World War II by resigning Mar. 1987.

Sicily, 9,926 sq. mi., pop. (1987) 5,112,000, is an island 180 by 120 mi., seat of a region that embraces the island of **Pantelleria,** 32 sq. mi., and the **Lipari** group, 44 sq. mi., 63 14,000, including 2 active volcanoes: **Vulcano,** 1,637 ft. and **Stromboli,** 3,038 ft. From prehistoric times Sicily has been settled by various peoples; a Greek state had its capital at Syracuse. Rome took Sicily from Carthage 215 BC. **Mt. Etna,** 11,053 ft. active volcano, is tallest peak.

Sardinia, 9,301 sq. mi., pop. (1986) 1,638,000, lies in the Mediterranean, 115 mi. W of Italy and 7-½ mi. S of Corsica. It is 160 mi. long, 68 mi. wide, and mountainous, with mining of coal, zinc, lead, copper. In 1720 Sardinia was added to the possessions of the Dukes of Savoy in Piedmont and Savoy to form the Kingdom of Sardinia. Giuseppe Garibaldi is buried on the nearby isle of Caprera. **Elba,** 86 sq. mi., lies 6 mi. W of Tuscany. Napoleon I lived in exile on Elba 1814-1815.

Trieste. An agreement, signed Oct. 5, 1954, by Italy and Yugoslavia, confirmed, Nov. 10, 1975, gave Italy provisional administration over the northern section and the seaport of Trieste, and Yugoslavia the part of Istrian peninsula it has occupied.

Jamaica

People: Population (1989 est.): 2,362,000. **Age distrib.** (%): 0-14: 36.7; 15-59: 52.8; 60+: 8.5. **Pop. density:** 556 per sq. mi. **Urban** (1989): 48%. **Ethnic groups:** African 76%, mixed 15%, Chinese, Caucasians, East Indians. **Languages:** English, Jamaican Creole. **Religions:** Protestant 70%.

Geography: Area: 4,232 sq. mi., slightly smaller than Connecticut. **Location:** In West Indies. **Neighbors:** Nearest are Cuba on N, Haiti on E. **Topography:** The country is four-fifths covered by mountains. **Capital:** Kingston. **Cities** (1984 est.): St. Andrews 393,100, Kingston 100,000.

Government: Type: Independent state. **Head of state:** Queen Elizabeth II, represented by Gov.-Gen. Florizel A. Glasspole; b. Sept. 25, 1909; in office: Mar. 2, 1973. **Head of government:** Prime Min. Michael N. Manley; in office: Feb. 9, 1989. **Local divisions:** 14 parishes; Kingston and St. Andrew corporate area. **Defense:** 1.1% of GDP (1986).

Economy: Industries: Rum, molasses, cement, paper, tourism. **Chief crops:** Sugar cane, coffee, bananas, coconuts, citrus fruits. **Minerals:** Bauxite, limestone, gypsum. **Arable land:** 24%. **Livestock** (1986): cattle: 290,000; goats: 420,000. **Electricity prod.** (1986): 1.5 bln. kwh. **Labor force:** 35% agric.; 19% services; 13% manuf.

Finance: Currency: Dollar (Apr. 1989: 5.48 = $1 US). **Gross national product** (1986): $2.0 bln. **Per capita income** (1981): $1,340. **Imports** (1988): $1.4 bln.; partners: U.S. 44%, UK 17%.

Exports (1988): $755 mln.; partners: U.S. 33%, UK 17%, Can. 16%. **Tourists** (1987): receipts: $551 mln. **National budget** (1986): $584 mln. **International reserves less gold** (Feb. 1989): $99 mln. **Consumer prices** (change in 1988): 8.3%.

Transport: Railway traffic (1985): 40 mln. passenger-km; 129 mln. net ton-km. **Motor vehicles:** in use (1987): 42,000 passenger cars, 20,000 comm. vehicles. **Civil aviation** (1987): 2.1 bln. passenger km.; 2.6 mln. freight ton-km. **Chief ports:** Kingston, Montego Bay.

Communications: Television sets: 387,000 in use (1987). **Radios:** 910,000 in use (1986). **Telephones in use** (1987): 152,000. **Daily newspaper circ.** (1987): 36 per 1,000 pop.

Health: Life expectancy at birth (1985): 61.8 male; 72.6 female. **Births** (per 1,000 pop. 1987): 22.2. **Deaths** (per 1,000 pop. 1987): 5.3. **Natural increase** (1987): 1.6%. **Hospital beds** (1987): 5,463. **Physicians** (1987): 330. **Infant mortality** (per 1,000 live births 1987): 18.0.

Education (1987): **Literacy:** 73%. Compulsory to age 14.

Major International Organizations: UN (World Bank, GATT), OAS.

Embassy: 1850 K St. NW 20006; 452-0660.

Jamaica was visited by Columbus, 1494, and ruled by Spain (under whom Arawak Indians died out) until seized by Britain, 1655. Jamaica won independence Aug. 6, 1962.

In 1974 Jamaica sought an increase in taxes paid by U.S. and Canadian companies which mine bauxite on the island. The socialist government acquired 50% ownership of the companies' Jamaican interests in 1976, and was reelected that year. Rudimentary welfare state measures were passed, but unemployment increased. Relations with the U.S. improved greatly in the 1980s following the election of Edward Seaga.

Jamaica took part in the October 1983 invasion of Grenada.

Hurricane Gilbert struck Jamaica Sept. 12, 1988, killing some 45 and causing extensive damage including half the nation's houses.

Japan

Nippon

People: Population (1989 est.): 123,231,000. **Age distrib.** (%): 0-14: 20.0; 15-59: 64.0; 60+: 16.0. **Pop. density:** 844 per sq. mi. **Urban** (1985): 76.7%. **Language:** Japanese. **Ethnic groups:** Japanese 99.4%, Korean 0.5%. **Religions:** Buddhism, Shintoism shared by large majority.

Geography: Area: 145,856 sq. mi., slightly smaller than California. **Location:** Archipelago off E. coast of Asia. **Neighbors:** USSR on N, S. Korea on W. **Topography:** Japan consists of 4 main islands: Honshu ("mainland"), 87,805 sq. mi.; Hokkaido, 30,144 sq. mi.; Kyushu, 14,114 sq. mi.; and Shikoku, 7,049 sq. mi. The coast, deeply indented, measures 16,654 mi. The northern islands are a continuation of the Sakhalin Mts. The Kunlun range of China continues into southern islands, the ranges meeting in the Japanese Alps. In a vast transverse fissure crossing Honshu E-W rises a group of volcanoes, mostly extinct or inactive, including 12,388 ft. Fuji-San (Fujiyama) near Tokyo. **Capital:** Tokyo. **Cities** (1987 est.): Tokyo 8.3 mln.; Osaka 2.6 mln.; Yokohama 3.0 mln.; Nagoya 2.1 mln.; Kyoto 1.4 mln.; Kobe 1.4 mln.; Sapporo 1.5 mln.; Kitakyushu 1 mln.; Kawasaki 1.1 mln; Fukuoka 1.1 mln.

Government: Type: Parliamentary democracy. **Head of state:** Emp. Akihito; b. Dec. 23, 1933; in office: Jan. 7, 1989. **Head of government:** Prime Min. Toshiki Kaifu; b. Jan. 2, 1931; in office: Aug. 9, 1989. **Local divisions:** 47 prefectures. **Defense:** Less than 1% of GNP (1985).

Economy: Industries: Electrical & electronic equip., autos, machinery, chemicals. **Chief crops:** Rice, grains, vegetables, fruits. **Minerals:** negligible. **Crude oil reserves** (1985): 26 mln. bbls. **Arable land:** 13%. **Livestock** (1986): cattle: 4.6 mln.; pigs: 10.3 mln. **Fish catch** (1986): 12.6 mln. metric tons. **Electricity prod.** (1986): 601 bln. kwh. **Crude steel prod.** (1987): 98.5 mln. metric tons. **Labor force:** 9% agric.; 34% manuf; 53% services & trade.

Finance: Currency: Yen (May 1989: 142 = $1 US). **Gross national product** (1986): $1.9 trl. **Per capita income** (1984): $10,266. **Imports** (1988): $187 bln.; partners: U.S. 20%, Middle East 26%, SE Asia 22%, EC 6%. **Exports** (1988): $264 bln.; partners: U.S. 37%, EC 12%, SE Asia 23%. **Tourists** (1986): $1.4 bln. receipts. **National budget** (1989): $470 bln. expenditures. **International reserves less gold** (Mar. 1989): $98 bln. **Gold:** 24.23 mln. oz. t. **Consumer prices** (change in 1988): 0.7%.

Transport: Railway traffic (1986): 334 bln. passenger-km; 20 bln. net ton-km. **Motor vehicles:** in use (1987): 28.6 mln. passenger cars, 19.1 mln. **Civil aviation** (1986): 70.9 bln. passenger-km; 3.6 bln. freight ton-km. **Chief ports:** Yokohama, Tokyo, Kobe, Osaka, Nagoya, Chiba, Kawasaki, Hakodate.

Communications: Television sets: 31.5 mln. in use (1987). **Radios:** 94 mln. in use (1986). **Telephones in use** (1985): 66.6 mln. **Daily newspaper circ.** (1987): 569 per 1,000 pop.

Health: Life expectancy at birth (1987): 75.2 male; 80.9 female. **Births** (per 1,000 pop. 1987): 11.2 **Deaths** (per 1,000 pop. 1987): 6.1. **Natural increase** (1987): .05%. **Hospital beds** (1987): 1.5 mln. **Physicians** (1987): 183,000. **Infant mortality** (per 1,000 live births 1987): 4.9.

Education (1987): **Literacy:** 99%. Most attend school for 12 years.

Major International Organizations: UN (IMF, GATT, ILO), OECD.

Embassy: 2520 Massachusetts Ave. NW 20008; 939-6700.

According to Japanese legend, the empire was founded by Emperor Jimmu, 660 BC, but earliest records of a unified Japan date from 1,000 years later. Chinese influence was strong in the formation of Japanese civilization. Buddhism was introduced before the 6th century.

A feudal system, with locally powerful noble families and their samurai warrior retainers, dominated from 1192. Central power was held by successive families of shoguns (military dictators), 1192-1867, until recovered by the Emperor Meiji, 1868. The Portuguese and Dutch had minor trade with Japan in the 16th and 17th centuries; U.S. Commodore Matthew C. Perry opened it to U.S. trade in a treaty ratified 1854. Japan fought China, 1894-95, gaining Taiwan. After war with Russia, 1904-05, Russia ceded S half of Sakhalin and gave concessions in China. Japan annexed Korea 1910. In World War I Japan ousted Germany from Shantung, took over German Pacific islands. Japan took Manchuria 1931, started war with China 1932. Japan launched war against the U.S. by attack on Pearl Harbor Dec. 7, 1941. Japan surrendered Aug. 14, 1945.

In a new constitution adopted May 3, 1947, Japan renounced the right to wage war; the emperor gave up claims to divinity; the Diet became the sole law-making authority.

The U.S. and 48 other non-communist nations signed a peace treaty and the U.S. a bilateral defense agreement with Japan, in San Francisco Sept. 8, 1951, restoring Japan's sovereignty as of April 28, 1952. Japan signed separate treaties with China, 1952; India, 1952; a declaration with USSR ending a technical state of war, 1956. In Dec. 1965 Japan and South Korea agreed to resume diplomatic relations.

On June 26, 1968, the U.S. returned to Japanese control the Bonin Is., the Volcano Is. (including Iwo Jima) and Marcus Is. On May 15, 1972, Okinawa, the other Ryukyu Is. and the Daito Is. were returned to Japan by the U.S.; it was agreed the U.S. would continue to maintain military bases on Okinawa. Japan and the USSR have failed to resolve disputed claims of sovereignty over 4 of the Kurile Is. and over offshore fishing rights.

In 1972, Japan and China resumed diplomatic relations.

Industrialization was begun in the late 19th century. After World War II, Japan emerged as one of the most powerful economies in the world, and as a leader in technology.

The U.S. and EC member nations have criticized Japan for its restrictive policy on imports which has given Japan a substantial trade surplus.

In Apr. 1987, the U.S. imposed 100% tariffs on Japanese electronics imports in retaliation for what the U.S. considered various unfair trade practices.

The Recruit scandal, the nation's worst political scandal since World War II, which involved illegal political donations and stock trading, led to the resignation of Premier Noboru Takeshita in May 1989. A few months later the government was again rocked by scandal. (*See Chronology*).

Jordan
Hashemite Kingdom of Jordan
al Mamlaka al Urduniya al Hashemiyah

Population (1989 est.): 3,031,000. **Age distrib.** (%): 0–14: 48.1; 15–59: 46.9; 60+: 4.0. **Pop. density:** 80 per sq. mi. **Urban** (1986): 70%. **Ethnic groups:** Arab 98%. **Languages:** Arabic (official), English. **Religions:** Sunni Moslem 93.6%, Christian 5%.

Geography: Area: 37,737 sq. mi., slightly larger than Indiana. **Location:** In W Asia. **Neighbors:** Israel on W, Saudi Arabia on S, Iraq on E, Syria on N. **Topography:** About 88% of Jordan is arid. Fertile areas are in W. Only port is on short Aqaba Gulf coast. Country shares Dead Sea (1,296 ft. below sea level) with Israel. **Capital:** Amman. **Cities** (1986 est.): Amman 833,000; az-Zarqa 285,000; Irbid 150,000.

Government: Type: Constitutional monarchy. **Head of state:** King Hussein I; b. Nov. 14, 1935; in office: Aug. 11, 1952. **Head of government:** Prime Min. Field Marshal Sharif Zeid bin Shaker; in office: Apr. 27, 1989. **Local divisions:** 8 governorates. **Defense:** 12% of GNP (1985).

Economy: Industries: Textiles, cement, food processing. **Chief crops:** Grains, olives, vegetables, fruits. **Minerals:** Phosphate, potash. **Arable land:** 5%. **Electricity prod.** (1986): 2.8 bln. kwh. **Labor force:** 20% agric. 20% manuf. & mining.

Finance: Currency: Dinar (Mar. 1989: 0.52 = $1 US). **Gross national product** (1986): $4.3 bln. **Imports** (1987): $2.7 bln.; partners: Saudi Ar. 6%, U.S. 11%, Jap. 8%. **Exports** (1987): $930 mln.; partners: Saudi Ar. 12%, Ind. 13%, Iraq. 18%. **Tourists** (1986): receipts: $534 mln. **National budget** (1985): $2.2 bln. revenues: $1.68 bln. expenditures. **International reserves less gold** (Mar. 1989): $74 mln. **Gold:** 1.0 mln. oz t. **Consumer prices** (change in 1987): −0.3%.

Transport: Motor vehicles: in use (1986): 158,000 passenger cars, 158,000 comm. vehicles. **Civil aviation** (1987): 3.5 bln. passenger-km; 165 mln. freight ton-km. **Chief ports:** Aqaba.

Communications: Television sets: 240,000 in use (1986). **Radios:** 700,000 in use (1986). **Telephones in use** (1986): 177,000. **Daily newspaper circ.** (1987): 68 per 1,000 pop.

Health: Life expectancy at birth (1986): 65.0 male; 68.8 female. **Births** (per 1,000 pop. 1986): 34.7. **Deaths** (per 1,000 pop. 1986): 5.8. **Natural increase** (1986): 2.8%. **Hospital beds** (1986): 5,246. **Physicians** (1986): 3,114. **Infant mortality** (per 1,000 live births 1985): 51.

Education (1980): **Literacy:** 31%.

Major International Organizations: UN (WHO, IMF), Arab League.

Embassy: 3504 International Dr. NW 20008; 966-2664.

From ancient times to 1922 the lands to the E of the Jordan were culturally and politically united with the lands to the W. Arabs conquered the area in the 7th century; the Ottomans took control in the 16th. Britain's 1920 Palestine Mandate covered both sides of the Jordan. In 1921, Abdullah, son of the ruler of Hejaz in Arabia, was installed by Britain as emir of an autonomous Transjordan, covering two-thirds of Palestine. An independent kingdom was proclaimed, 1946.

During the 1948 Arab-Israeli war the West Bank and old city of Jerusalem were added to the kingdom, which changed its name to Jordan. All these territories were lost to Israel in the 1967 war, which swelled the number of Arab refugees on the East Bank. A 1974 Arab summit conference designated the Palestine Liberation Organization as the sole representative of Arabs on the West Bank. Jordan accepted the move, and was granted an annual subsidy by Arab oil states.

In 1988 Jordan cut legal and administrative ties with the Israeli-occupied West Bank. In Apr. 1989, riots broke out over price increases imposed under an agreement with the International Monetary Fund.

Kenya
Republic of Kenya
Jamhuri ya Kenya

People: Population (1989 est.): 23,727,000. **Age distrib.** (%): 0–14: 52.3; 15–59: 43.2; 60+: 4.5. **Pop. density:** 105 per sq. mi. **Urban** (1986): 20%. **Ethnic groups:** Kikuyu 21%, Luo 13%, Luhya 14%, Kelenjin 11%, Kamba 11%, others, including Asians, Arabs, Europeans. **Languages:** Swahili (official), English. **Religions:** Protestant 38%, Roman Catholic 26%, Moslem 6%, others.

Geography: Area: 224,960 sq. mi., slightly smaller than Texas. **Location:** On Indian O. coast of E. Africa. **Neighbors:** Uganda on W, Tanzania on S, Somalia on E, Ethopia, Sudan on N. **Topography:** The northern three-fifths of Kenya is arid. To the S, a low coastal area and a plateau varying from 3,000 to 10,000 ft. The Great Rift Valley enters the country N-S, flanked by high mountains. **Capital:** Nairobi. **Cities** (1987 est.): Nairobi 959,000; Mombasa 401,000.

Government: Type: Republic. Head of state: Pres. Daniel arap Moi, b. Sept., 1924; in office: Aug. 22, 1978. **Local divisions:** Nairobi and 7 provinces. **Defense:** 4.8% of GDP (1985).

Economy: Industries: Tourism, light industry, petroleum prods. **Chief crops:** Coffee, corn, tea, cereals, cotton, sisal. **Minerals:** Gold, limestone, diatomite, salt, barytes, magnesite, felspar, sapphires, fluospar, garnets. **Other resources:** Timber, hides. **Arable land:** 4%. **Livestock** (1986): cattle: 12.5 mln. **Fish catch** (1986): 102,000 metric tons. **Electricity prod.** (1986): 1.9 bln. kwh. **Labor force:** 21% agric.; 21% ind. and commerce; 13% services; 40% public sector.

Finance: Currency: Shilling (Mar. 1989: 18.88 = $1 US). **Gross national product** (1986): $6.7 bln. **Per capita income** (1986): $322. **Imports** (1987): $1.7 bln.; partners: UK 14%, W. Ger. 11%, Jap. 11%, Fra. 11%. **Exports** (1987): $961 mln.; partners: W. Ger. 11%, UK 18%, Ugan. 9%. **Tourists** (1987) receipts: $355 mln. **National budget** (1986): $2 bln. **International reserves less gold** (Mar. 1989): $265 mln. **Gold:** 80,000 oz t. **Consumer prices** (change in 1988): 8.3%.

Transport: Motor vehicles: in use (1985): 126,000 passenger cars, 103,000 comm. vehicles. **Civil Aviation** (1987): 1.0 bln. passenger-km; 136 mln. freight ton-km. **Chief ports:** Mombasa.

Communications: Television sets: 192,000 in use (1987). **Radios:** 2.1 mln. in use (1986). **Telephones in use** (1986): 291,000. **Daily newspaper circ.** (1986): 16 per 1,000 pop.

Health: Life expectancy at birth (1983): 56.3 male; 60.0 female. **Births** (per 1,000 pop. 1985): 55.1. **Deaths** (per 1,000 pop. 1985): 14.0. **Natural increase** (1985): 4.1%. **Hospital beds** (1985): 30,886. **Physicians** (1985): 2,752. **Infant mortality** (per 1,000 live births 1985): 83.

Education (1988): **Literacy:** 50%. 86% attend primary school.

Major International Organizations: UN and all of its specialized agencies, OAU, Commonwealth of Nations.

Embassy: 2249 R St. NW 20008; 387-6101.

Arab colonies exported spices and slaves from the Kenya coast as early as the 8th century. Britain obtained control in the 19th century. Kenya won independence Dec. 12, 1963, 4 years after the end of the violent Mau Mau uprising.

Kenya has shown steady growth in industry and agriculture under a modified private enterprise system, and has had a relatively free political life. But stability was shaken in 1974-5, with opposition charges of corruption and oppression.

In 1968 ties with Somalia were restored after 4 years of skirmishes. Tanzania closed its Kenya border in 1977 in a dispute over the collapse of the East African Community.

Kenya has close ties to the West.

Kiribati

Republic of Kiribati

People: Population (1989 est.): 65,000. **Pop. density:** 244 per sq. mi. **Ethnic groups:** nearly all Micronesian, some Polynesians. **Languages:** Gilbertese and English (official). **Religions:** evenly divided between Protestant and Roman Catholic.

Geography: Area: 266 sq. mi., slightly smaller than New York City. **Location:** 33 Micronesian islands (the Gilbert, Line and Phoenix groups) in the mid-Pacific scattered in a 2-mln. sq. mi. chain around the point where the International Date Line cuts the Equator. **Neighbors:** Nearest are Nauru to SW, Tuvalu and Tokelau Is. to S. **Topography:** except Banaba (Ocean) I., all are low-lying, with soil of coral sand and rock fragments, subject to erratic rainfall. **Capital** (1985): Tarawa 21,000.

Government: Type: Republic. Head of state and of government: Pres. Ieremia Tabai, b. Dec. 16, 1950; in office: July 12, 1979.

Economy: Industries: Copra. **Chief crops:** Coconuts, breadfruit, pandanus, bananas, paw paw. **Other resources:** Fish. **Electricity prod.** (1986): 8 mln. kwh.

Finance: Currency: Australian dollar. **Gross national product** (1986): $21 mln.

Transport: Chief port: Tarawa.

Communications: Radios: 10,000 in use (1986). **Telephones in use** (1984): 1,400.

Health: Hospital beds (1983): 263; **Physicians:** 19.

Education: Literacy (1985): 90%.

A British protectorate since 1892, the Gilbert and Ellice Islands colony was completed with the inclusion of the Phoenix Islands, 1937. Self-rule was granted 1971; the Ellice Islands separated from the colony 1975 and became independent Tuvalu, 1978. Kiribati (pronounced *Kiribass*) independence was attained July 12, 1979. Under a Treaty of Friendship the U.S. relinquished its claims to several of the Line and Phoenix islands, including Christmas, Canton, and Enderbury.

Tarawa Atoll was the scene of some of the bloodiest fighting in the Pacific during WW II.

North Korea

Democratic People's Republic of Korea

Chosun Minchu-chui Inmin Konghwa-guk

People: Population (1989 est.): 21,964,000. **Pop. density:** 471 per sq. mi. **Urban** (1985): 62%. **Ethnic groups:** Korean. **Languages:** Korean. **Religions:** activities almost nonexistent; traditionally Buddhism, Confucianism, Chondokyo.

Geography: Area: 46,540 sq. mi., slightly smaller than Mississippi. **Location:** In northern E. Asia. **Neighbors:** China, USSR on N, S. Korea on S. **Topography:** Mountains and hills cover nearly all the country, with narrow valleys and small plains in between. The N and the E coast are the most rugged areas. **Capital:** Pyongyang. **Cities** (1981 est.): Pyongyang 1,283,000.

Government: Type: Communist state. **Head of state:** Pres. Kim Il-Sung; b. Apr. 15, 1912; in office: Dec. 28, 1972. **Head of government:** Premier Yong Hyong Muk; in office: Dec. 12, 1988. **Head of Communist Party:** Gen. Sec. Kim Il-Sung; in office: 1945. **Local divisions:** 9 provinces, 4 municipalities. **Defense** (1985): 22.2% of GNP.

Economy: Industries: Textiles, petrochemicals, food processing. **Chief crops:** Corn, potatoes, fruits, vegetables, rice. **Minerals:** Coal, lead tungsten, graphite, magnesite, iron, copper, gold, phosphate, salt, fluorspar. **Arable land:** 19%. **Livestock** (1986): cattle: 1.1 mln; pigs: 2.9 mln. **Fish catch** (1986): 1.7 mln. metric tons. **Crude steel prod.** (1987) 6.1 mln. metric tons. **Electricity prod.** (1986): 41 bln. kwh. **Labor force:** 48% agric.

Finance: Currency: Won (Jan. 1989): 0.97 = $1 US). **Gross national product** (1986): $17.4 bln. **Imports** (1986): $2.0 bln.; partners: China 17%, USSR 36%, Jap. 13%. **Exports** (1985): $1.3 bln.; partners: USSR 43% China 13%, Jap. 15%.

Communications: Television sets: 1 mln. in use (1984). **Radios:** 4.1 mln. in use (1984).

Transport: Chief ports: Chonglin, Hamhung, Nampo.

Health: Life expectancy at birth (1984): 65 male; 72 female. **Births** (per 1,000 pop. 1985): 30. **Deaths** (per 1,000 pop. 1985): 7. **Natural increase** (1985): 2.3%. **Hospital beds** (1982): 244,000. **Physicians** (1982): 45,000. **Infant mortality** (per 1,000 live births, 1985): 30.

Education (1986): **Literacy:** 99%. **Years compulsory:** 11.

The Democratic People's Republic of Korea was founded May 1, 1948, in the zone occupied by Russian troops after World War II. Its armies tried to conquer the south, 1950. After 3 years of fighting with Chinese and U.S. intervention, a cease-fire was proclaimed.

Industry, begun by the Japanese during their 1910-45 occupation, and nationalized in the 1940s, had grown substantially, using N. Korea's abundant mineral and hydroelectric resources.

Two N. Korean Army officers were sentenced to death by Burmese authorities after they confessed to the October 9, 1983 bombing which killed 17, including 4 S. Korean cabinet ministers, in Rangoon.

South Korea

Republic of Korea

Taehan Min'guk

People: Population (1989 est.): 45,243,000. **Age distrib. (%):** 0–14: 30.6; 15–59: 52.7; 60+: 6.7. **Pop. density:** 1,189 per sq. mi. **Urban** (1985): 65%. **Ethnic groups:** Korean. **Languages:** Korean. **Religions:** Buddhism, Confucianism, Christian.

Geography: Area: 38,025 sq. mi., slightly larger than Indiana. **Location:** In Northern E. Asia. **Neighbors:** N. Korea on N. **Topography:** The country is mountainous, with a rugged east coast. The western and southern coasts are deeply indented, with many islands and harbors. **Capital:** Seoul. **Cities** (1985 cen.): Seoul 9,600,000; Pusan 3,500,000; Taegu 2,000,000.

Government: Type: Republic, with power centralized in a strong executive. **Head of state:** Pres. Roh Tae Woo; b. 1932; in office: Feb. 25, 1988. **Head of government:** Prime Min. Kang Young Hoon; in office: Dec. 5, 1988. **Local divisions:** 9 provinces and Seoul, Pusan, Inchon, and Taegu. **Defense:** 5.5% of GNP (1986).

Economy: Industries: Electronics, ships, textiles, clothing, motor vehicles. **Chief crops:** Rice, barley, vegetables, wheat. **Minerals:** Tungsten, coal, graphite. **Arable land:** 22%. **Livestock** (1986): cattle: 2.8 mln.; pigs: 3.3 mln. **Fish catch:** (1987): 3.3 mln. metric tons. **Electricity prod.** (1986): 65.0 bln. kwh. **Crude steel prod.** (1987): 16.7 mln. metric tons. **Labor force:** 30% agric.; 21% manuf. & mining; 47% services.

Finance: Currency: Won (Mar. 1989: 671 = $1 US). **Gross national product** (1987): $118.6 bln. **Per capita income** (1986): $2,180. **Imports** (1988): $51 bln.; partners: Jap. 33%, U.S. 21%. **Exports** (1988): $60 bln.; partners: U.S. 40%, Jap. 15%. **Tourists** (1986): receipts: $1.5 bln. **National budget** (1987): $18.0 bln. expenditures. **International reserves less gold** (Mar. 1989): $14.0 bln. **Gold:** 320,000 oz t. **Consumer prices** (change in 1988): 7.1%.

Transport: Railway traffic (1986): 21.6 bln. passenger-km; 11.6 bln. net ton-km. **Motor vehicles:** in use (1987): 845,000 passenger cars, 748,000 comm. vehicles. **Civil aviation** (1986): 13.4 bln. passenger-km; 1.4 bln. freight ton-km. **Chief ports:** Pusan, Inchon.

Communications: Television sets: 8.6 mln. in use (1987). **Radios:** 38.2 mln. in use (1986). **Telephones in use** (1987): 9.2 mln. **Daily newspaper circ.** (1986): 24 per 1,000 pop.

Health: Life expectancy at birth (1987): 65.6 male; 71.8 female. **Births** (per 1,000 pop. 1987): 19.4. **Deaths** (per 1,000 pop. 1987): 6.3. **Natural increase** (1987): 1.3%. **Hospital beds** (1987): 85,000. **Physicians** (1987): 38,000. **Infant mortality** (per 1,000 live births 1987): 25.0.

Education (1987): Literacy: 92%. **Attendance:** High school 90%, college 14%.

Embassy: 2320 Massachusetts Ave. NW 20008; 939-5600.

Korea, once called the Hermit Kingdom, has a recorded history since the 1st century BC. It was united in a kingdom under the Silla Dynasty, 668 AD. It was at times associated with the Chinese empire; the treaty that concluded the Sino-Japanese war of 1894-95 recognized Korea's complete independence. In 1910 Japan forcibly annexed Korea as Chosun.

At the Potsdam conference, July, 1945, the 38th parallel was designated as the line dividing the Soviet and the American occupation. Russian troops entered Korea Aug. 10, 1945, U.S. troops entered Sept. 8, 1945. The Soviet military organized socialists and communists and blocked efforts to let the Koreans unite their country. *(See Index for Korean War.)*

The South Koreans formed the Republic of Korea in May 1948 with Seoul as the capital. Dr. Syngman Rhee was chosen president but a movement spearheaded by college students forced his resignation Apr. 26, 1960.

In an army coup May 16, 1961, Gen. Park Chung Hee became chairman of the ruling junta. He was elected president, 1963; a 1972 referendum allowed him to be reelected for 6 year terms unlimited times. Park was assassinated by the chief of the Korean CIA, Oct. 26, 1979. The calm of the new government was halted by the rise of Gen. Chun Doo Hwan, head of the military intelligence, who reinstated martial law, and reverted South Korea to the police state it was under Park.

North Korean raids across the border tapered off in 1971, but incidents occurred in 1973 and 1974. In July 1972 South and North Korea agreed on a common goal of reunifying the 2 na-

tions by peaceful means. But there had been no sign of a thaw in relations between the two regimes until 1985 when they agreed to discuss economic issues. In 1988, radical students demanding reunification clashed with police.

A Korean Air Lines passenger airliner was shot down by a Soviet jet fighter, Sept. 1, 1983, after it strayed into Soviet airspace; all 269 people aboard died.

On June 10, 1987, middle class office workers, shopkeepers, and business executives joined students in antigovernment protests in Seoul. They were protesting President Chun's decision to choose his successor and not allow the next president to be chosen by direct vote of the people. Following weeks of rioting and violence, Chun, July 1, agreed to permit election of the next president by direct popular vote and other constitutional reforms. In Dec., Roh Tae Woo was elected president.

Kuwait

State of Kuwait

Dowlat al-Kuwait

People: Population (1989 est.): 1,967,000. **Age distrib. (%):** 0–14: 40.2; 15–59: 57.6; 60+: 2.3. **Pop. density:** 285 per sq. mi. **Urban** (1986): 90%. **Ethnic groups:** Kuwaiti 39%, other Arab 39%, Iranians, Indians, Pakistanis. **Languages:** Arabic, others. **Religions:** Moslem 85%.

Geography: Area: 6,880 sq. mi., slightly smaller than New Jersey. **Location:** In Middle East, at N end of Persian Gulf. **Neighbors:** Iraq on N, Saudi Arabia on S. **Topography:** The country is flat, very dry, and extremely hot. **Capital:** Kuwait. **Cities** (1985 est.): Hawalli 145,000; as-Salimiyah 153,000.

Government: Type: Constitutional monarchy. **Head of state:** Emir Shaikh Jabir al-Ahmad al-Jabir as-Sabah; b. 1928; in office: Jan. 1, 1978. **Head of government:** Prime Min. Shaikh Saad Abdulla as-Salim as-Sabah; in office: Feb. 8, 1978. **Local divisions:** 4 governorates. **Defense:** 6.3% of GNP (1985).

Economy: Type: Industries: Oil products. **Minerals:** Oil, gas. **Crude oil reserves** (1987): 94 bln. bbls. **Cultivated land:** 1%. **Electricity prod.** (1986): 16.3 bln. kwh. **Labor force:** social services 45%; construction 20%.

Finance: Currency: Dinar (May 1989: 1.00 = $3.36 US). **Gross national product** (1986): $17.3 bln. **Per capita income** (1975): $11,431. **Imports** (1987): $5.2 bln.; partners: Jap. 21%, U.S. 9%. **Exports** (1987): $8.3 bln.; partners: Jap. 16%, It. 10%. **Tourists** (1986): $86 mln. receipts. **National budget** (1986): $11.1 bln. expenditures. **International reserves less gold** (Mar. 1989): $1.6 bln. **Gold:** 2.53 mln. oz t. **Consumer prices** (change in 1988): 1.1%.

Transport: Motor vehicles: in use (1987): 420,000 passenger cars, 114,000 comm. vehicles. **Civil aviation** (1986): 3.7 bln. passenger-km; 343 mln. freight ton-km. **Chief ports:** Mina al-Ahmadi.

Communications: Television sets: 700,000 in use (1987). **Radios:** 500,000 in use (1986). **Telephones in use** (1986): 450,000. **Daily newspaper circ.** (1986): 253 per 1,000 pop.

Health: Life expectancy at birth (1986): 70.3 male; 73.0 female. **Births** (per 1,000 pop. 1986): 29.5. **Deaths** (per 1,000 pop. 1986): 2.4. **Natural increase** (1986): 2.7%. **Hospital beds** (1986): 5,523 plus 232 clinics and health centers. **Physician** (1986): 2,308. **Infant mortality** (per 1,000 live births 1987): 26.1.

Education (1987): Literacy: 71%. **Years compulsory:** 8.

Major International Organizations: UN (World Bank, IMF, GATT), Arab League, OPEC.

Embassy: 2940 Tilden St. NW 20008; 966-0702.

Kuwait is ruled by the Al-Sabah dynasty, founded 1759. Britain ran foreign relations and defense from 1899 until independence in 1961. The majority of the population is non-Kuwaiti, with many Palestinians, and cannot vote.

Oil, first exported in 1946, is the fiscal mainstay, providing most of Kuwait's income. Oil pays for free medical care, education, and social security. There are no taxes, except customs duties.

Kuwaiti oil tankers have come under frequent attack by Iran because of Kuwait's support of Iraq in the Iran-Iraq War. In July 1987, U.S. Navy warships began escorting Kuwaiti tankers in the Persian Gulf.

In 1988, a Kuwaiti Airways jet was hijacked by pro-Iranian Shiite Moslem terrorists who demanded the release of 17 Shiite terrorists. The ordeal lasted 16 days as Kuwait refused to release the terrorists.

Laos

Lao People's Democratic Republic

Sathalanalat Paxathipatai Paxaxōn Lao

People: Population (1989 est.): 3,923,000. **Pop. density:** 42 per sq. mi. **Urban** (1987): 15%. **Ethnic groups:** Lao 48%, Mon-Khmer tribes 25%, Thai 14%, Meo and Yao 13%, others. **Languages:** Lao (official), French. **Religions:** Buddhists 50%, tribal 50%.

Geography: Area: 91,428 sq. mi., slightly larger than Utah. **Location:** In Indochina Peninsula in SE Asia. **Neighbors:** Burma, China on N, Vietnam on E, Cambodia on S, Thailand on W. **Topography:** Landlocked, dominated by jungle. High mountains along the eastern border are the source of the E-W rivers slicing across the country to the Mekong R., which defines most of the western border. **Capital:** Vientiane. **Cities** (1984 est.); Vientiane 120,000.

Government: Type: Communist. **Head of state:** Pres. Phoumi Vongvichit in office: Oct. 31, 1986. **Head of government:** Prime Min. Kaysone Phomvihan; b. Dec. 13, 1920; in office: Dec. 2, 1975. **Local divisions:** 17 provinces. **Armed forces: Defense:** 10.5% of GNP (1984).

Economy: Industries: Wood products. **Chief crops:** Rice, corn, tobacco, cotton, opium, citrus fruits, coffee. **Minerals:** Tin. **Other resources:** Forests. **Arable land:** 4%. **Livestock** (1986): pigs: 1.5 mln. **Fish catch** (1986): 20,000 metric tons. **Electricity prod.** (1986): 900 mln. kwh. **Labor force:** 85% agric.; 6% ind.

Finance: Currency: New kip (Jan. 1989): 350 = $1 US). **Gross national product** (1987): $500 mln. **Per capita income** (1985 est.): $500. **Imports** (1986): $205 mln.; partners: Thai. 34%, Jap. 20%, Sing. 17%. **Exports** (1986): $58 mln.; partners: Chi. 45%.

Transport: Motor vehicles: in use (1987): 15,800 passenger cars, 3,000 comm. vehicles. **Civil Aviation** (1985): 9 mln. passenger km; 100,000 net ton-km.

Communications: Radios: 367,000 in use (1987).

Health: Life expectancy at birth (1987): 50.3 male; 53.3 female. **Births** (per 1,000 pop. 1987): 42.7. **Deaths** (per 1,000 pop. 1987): 14.1. **Natural increase** (1987): 2.8%. **Hospital beds** (1985): 11,650. **Physicians** (1985): 1,430. **Infant mortality** (per 1,000 live births, 1987): 111.

Education: (1986): **Literacy:** 41%.

Major International Organizations: UN (FAO, IMF, WHO). **Embassy:** 2222 S St. NW 20008; 332-6416.

Laos became a French protectorate in 1893, but regained independence as a constitutional monarchy July 19, 1949.

Conflicts among neutralist, communist and conservative factions created a chaotic political situation. Armed conflict increased after 1960.

The 3 factions formed a coalition government in June 1962, with neutralist Prince Souvanna Phouma as premier. A 14-nation conference in Geneva signed agreements, 1962, guaranteeing neutrality and independence. By 1964 the Pathet Lao had withdrawn from the coalition, and, with aid from N. Vietnamese troops, renewed sporadic attacks. U.S. planes bombed the Ho Chi Minh trail, supply line from N. Vietnam to communist forces in Laos and S. Vietnam. An estimated 2.75 million tons of bombs were dropped on Laos during the fighting.

In 1970 the U.S. stepped up air support and military aid. After Pathet Lao military gains, Souvanna Phouma in May 1975 ordered government troops to cease fighting; the Pathet Lao took control. A Lao People's Democratic Republic was proclaimed Dec. 3, 1975; it is strongly influenced by Vietnam.

Lebanon

Republic of Lebanon

al-Jumhouriya al-Lubnaniya

People: Population (1989 est.): 2,852,000. **Age distrib. (%):** 0–14: 37.0; 15–59: 55.1; 60+: 7.9. **Pop. density:** 710 per sq. mi. **Urban** (1986): 81%. **Ethnic groups:** Lebanese 82%, Armenians

5%, Palestinian 9%. **Languages:** Arabic (official), French, Armenian. **Religions:** Moslem 57%; Christian 42%.

Geography: Area: 4,015 sq. mi., smaller than Connecticut. **Location:** On Eastern end of Mediterranean Sea. **Neighbors:** Syria on E. Israel on S. **Topography:** There is a narrow coastal strip, and 2 mountain ranges running N-S enclosing the fertile Beqaa Valley. The Litani R. runs S through the valley, turning W to empty into the Mediterranean. **Capital:** Beirut. **Cities** (1985 est.): Beirut 1,500,000; Tripoli 500,000.

Government: Type: Republic. **Head of state:** vacant. **Head of government:** Prime Min. Michel Aoun in office: Sept. 23, 1988. **Local divisions:** 4 provinces. **Defense:** 18% of govt. budget (1984).

Economy: Industries: Trade, food products, textiles, cement, oil products. **Chief crops:** Fruits, olives, tobacco, grapes, vegetables, grains. **Minerals:** Iron. **Arable land:** 29%. **Livestock** (1986): goats: 460,000; sheep: 137,000. **Electricity prod.** (1986): 2.2 bln. kwh. **Labor force:** 17% agric.; 75% ind., comm., services.

Finance: Currency: Pound (Mar. 1989: 540 = $1 US). **Gross national product** (1983): $3.0 bln. **Per capita income** (1983): $1,150. **imports** (1987): $1.8 bln.; partners: It. 15%, Fr. 10%, U.S. 9%, Saudi Ar. 6%. **Exports** (1987): $591 mln.; partners: Saudi Ar. 33%, Syria 8%, Jor. 6%, Kuw. 8%. **National budget** (1988): $202 mln. **International reserves less gold** (Mar. 1989): $960 mln. **Gold:** 9.22 mln. oz t.

Transport: Railway traffic (1982): 5.3 mln. passenger-km; 42 mln. net ton-km. **Motor vehicles:** in use (1982): 460,000 passenger cars, 21,000 comm. vehicles. **Civil aviation** (1984): 830 mln. passenger-km; 19 mln. freight ton-km. **Chief ports:** Beirut, Tripoli, Sidon.

Communications: Television sets: 500,000 in use (1987). **Radios:** 2.0 mln. in use (1987). **Telephones:** in use (1987): 150,000. **Daily newspaper circ.** (1986): 211 per 1,000 pop.

Health: Life expectancy at birth (1985): 65.0 male; 68.9 female. **Births** (per 1,000 pop. 1986): 30.4 **Deaths** (per 1,000 pop. 1986): 7.7. **Natural increase** (1986): 2.2%. **Hospital beds** (1982): 11,400. **Physicians** (1986): 3,500. **Infant mortality** (per 1,000 live births 1988): 48.

Education: (1988): **Literacy:** 75%. **Years compulsory:** 5; attendance 93%.

Major International Organizations: UN (IMF, ILO, WHO). **Embassy:** 2560 28th St. NW 20008; 939-6300.

Formed from 5 former Turkish Empire districts, Lebanon became an independent state Sept. 1, 1920, administered under French mandate 1920-41. French troops withdrew in 1946.

Under the 1943 National Covenant, all public positions were divided among the various religious communities, with Christians in the majority. By the 1970s, Moslems became the majority, and demanded a larger political and economic role.

U.S. Marines intervened, May-Oct. 1958, during a Syrian-aided revolt. Lebanon's efforts to restrain Palestinian commandos caused armed clashes in 1969. Continued raids against Israeli civilians, 1970-75, brought Israeli attacks against guerrilla camps and villages. Israeli troops occupied S. Lebanon, March 1978, and again in Apr. 1980.

An estimated 60,000 were killed and billions of dollars in damage inflicted in a 1975-76 civil war. Palestinian units and leftist Moslems fought against the Maronite militia, the Phalange, and other Christians. Several Arab countries provided political and arms support to the various factions, while Israel aided Christian forces. Up to 15,000 Syrian troops intervened in 1976, and fought Palestinian groups. Arab League troops from several nations tried to impose a cease-fire.

Clashes between Syrian troops and Christian forces erupted, Apr. 1, 1981, near Zahle, Lebanon, bringing to an end the cease-fire that had been in place. By Apr. 22, fighting had broken out not only between Syrians and Christians, but also between two Moslem factions. Israeli commandos attacked Palestinian positions at Tyre and Tulin. In July, Israeli air raids on Beirut killed or wounded some 800 persons. A cease-fire between Israel and the Palestinians was concluded July 24, but hostilities continued.

Israeli forces invaded Lebanon June 6, 1982, in a coordinated land, sea, and air attack aimed at crushing strongholds of the Palestine Liberation Organization (PLO). Israeli and Syrian forces engaged in the Bekka Valley. By June 14, Israeli troops had encircled Beirut. On Aug. 21, the PLO evacuated west Beirut following massive Israeli bombings of the city. The withdrawal was supervised by U.S., French, and Italian troops. Israeli troops withdrew from Lebanon in June 1985.

Israeli troops entered west Beirut following the Sept. 14 assassination of newly-elected Lebanese Pres. Bashir Gemayel. On Sept. 16, Lebanese Christian troops entered 2 refugee camps and massacred hundreds of Palestinian refugees.

In 1983, terrorist bombings became a way of life in Beirut as some 50 people were killed in an explosion at the U.S. Embassy, Apr. 18; 241 U.S. servicemen and 58 French soldiers died in separate Moslem suicide attacks, Oct. 23.

PLO leader Yasir Arafat and PLO dissidents backed by Syria fought a 6-week battle in Tripoli until negotiations allowed Arafat and some 4,000 followers to evacuate the city.

On Apr. 26, 1984, pro-Syrian Rashid Karami was appointed premier. The appointment failed to end virtual civil war in Beirut between Christian forces, and Druse and Shiite Moslem militias. There was heavy fighting between Shiite militiamen and Palestinian guerrillas in May 1985. In June, Beirut Airport was the scene of a hostage crisis where Shiite terrorists held U.S. citizens for 17 days. Fierce artillery duels between Christian east Beirut and Moslem west Beirut, Mar.-Apr., 1989, left some 200 dead and 700 wounded.

Kidnapping of foreign nationals by Islamic militants has become common in the 1980s. U.S., British, French, and Soviet citizens have been victims.

Premier Karami was assassinated June 1, 1987, when a bomb exploded aboard a helicopter in which he was traveling.

Lesotho

Kingdom of Lesotho

People: Population (1989 est.): 1,681,000. **Age distrib. (%):** 0–14: 42.3; 15–59: 52.2; 60+: 5.7. **Pop. density:** 143 per sq. mi. **Ethnic groups:** Sotho 99%. **Languages:** English, Sesotho (official). **Religions:** Roman Catholic 38%, Protestant 42%.

Geography: Area: 11,716 sq. mi., slightly larger than Maryland. **Location:** In Southern Africa. **Neighbors:** Completely surrounded by Republic of South Africa. **Topography:** Landlocked and mountainous, with altitudes ranging from 5,000 to 11,000 ft. **Capital:** Maseru. **Cities** (1984 est.): Maseru 80,250.

Government: Type: Constitutional monarchy. **Head of state:** King Moshoeshoe II, b. May 2, 1938; in office: Mar. 12, 1960. **Head of government:** Gen. Justin Lekhanya; b. Apr. 7, 1938; in office: Jan. 20, 1986. **Local divisions:** 10 districts. **Defense:** 6.5% of GNP (1984).

Economy: Industries: Diamond polishing, food processing. **Chief crops:** Corn, grains, peas, beans. **Other resources:** Wool, mohair. **Arable land:** 10%. **Electricity prod.** (1986): 1 mln. kwh. **Labor force:** 31% agric.; 8% ind. and comm., 45% services.

Finance: Currency: Maloti (Mar. 1989: 1.00 = $.39 US). **Gross national product** (1986): $660 mln. **Per capita income** (1984): $520. **Imports** (1985): $326 mln.; partners: Mostly So. Afr. **Exports** (1985): $21 mln.; partners: Mostly So. Afr. **National budget** (1987): $163 mln.

Transport: Motor vehicles: in use (1982): 5,000 passenger cars, 11,000 comm. vehicles.

Communications: Radios: 100,000 in use (1986). **Daily newspaper circ.** (1985): 28 per 1,000 pop.

Health: Life expectancy at birth (1985): 54.2 yrs. **Births** (per 1,000 pop. 1985): 41.7. **Deaths** (per 1,000 pop. 1985): 16.4. **Natural increase** (1985): 2.5%. **Hospital beds** (1982): 2,300. **Physicians** (1982): 114. **Infant mortality** (per 1,000 live births 1985): 98.

Education (1987): **Literacy:** 59%.

Major International Organizations: UN (IMF, UNESCO, WHO), OAU.

Embassy: 1430 K St. NW 20005; 628-4833.

Lesotho (once called Basutoland) became a British protectorate in 1868 when Chief Moshesh sought protection against the Boers. Independence came Oct. 4, 1966. Elections were suspended in 1970. Over 50% of Lesotho's GNP is provided by citizens working in S. Africa. Livestock raising is the chief industry; diamonds are the chief export.

S. Africa imposed a blockade, Jan. 1, 1986, because of Lesotho's giving sanctuary to rebel groups fighting to overthrow the S. African Government. The blockade sparked a Jan. 20 military coup, and was lifted, Jan. 25, when the new leaders agreed to expel the rebels.

Liberia

Republic of Liberia

People: Population (1989 est.): 2,544,000. **Age distrib. (%):** 0–14: 46.8; 15–59: 48.3; 60+: 4.9. **Pop. density:** 66 per sq. mi. **Urban** (1985): 39.5%. **Ethnic groups:** Americo-Liberians 5%, indigenous tribes 95% **Languages:** English (official), tribal dialects. **Religions:** Moslem 20%, Christian 10%, traditional beliefs 70%.

Geography: Area: 38,250 sq. mi., slightly smaller than Pennsylvania. **Location:** On SW coast of W. Africa. **Neighbors:** Sierra Leone on W, Guinea on N, Côte d'Ivoire on E. **Topography:** Marshy Atlantic coastline rises to low mountains and plateaus in the forested interior; 6 major rivers flow in parallel courses to the ocean. **Capital:** Monrovia. **Cities** (1987 est.): Monrovia 400,000.

Government: Type: Civilian republic. **Head of state:** Pres. Samuel K. Doe; in office: Apr. 12, 1980. **Local divisions:** 13 counties. **Defense:** 2.7% of GDP (1985).

Economy: Industries: Food processing, mining. **Chief crops:** Rice, cassava, coffee, cocoa, sugar. **Minerals:** Iron, diamonds, gold. **Other resources:** Rubber, timber. **Arable land:** 4%. **Fish catch** (1986): 11,500 metric tons. **Electricity prod.** (1986): 655 mln. kwh. **Labor force:** 82% agric.

Finance: Currency: Dollar (May 1989: 1.00 = $1 US). **Gross national product** (1986): $1.0 bln. **Per capita income** (1982): $400. **Imports** (1987): $308 mln.; partners: U.S. 27%, W. Ger. 10%, Jap. 6%, Neth. 7%. **Exports** (1987): $382 mln.; partners: W. Ger. 31%, U.S. 17%, It. 14%, Fr. 9%. **National budget** (1988): $240 mln. **International reserves less gold** (Feb. 1989): $44,000. **Consumer prices** (change in 1988): 12.2%.

Transport: Motor vehicles: in use (1984): 12,000 passenger cars, 8,000 comm. vehicles. **Chief ports:** Monrovia, Buchanan, Greenville.

Communications: Television sets: 43,000 in use (1987). **Radios:** 500,000 in use (1986): **Telephones in use** (1985): 7,500. **Daily newspaper circ.** (1985): 12 per 1,000 pop.

Health: Lne expectancy at birth (1984): 54 yrs.; **Births** (per 1,000 pop. 1985): 48.7. **Deaths** (per 1,000 pop. 1985): 17.2. **Natural increase** (1985): 3.1%. **Hospital beds** (1981): 3,000. **Physicians** (1981): 236. **Infant mortality** (per 1,000 live births 1985): 127.

Education (1987): **Literacy:** 25%; 35% attend primary school.

Major International Organizations: UN and most specialized agencies, OAU.

Embassy: 5201 16th St. NW 20011; 723-9437.

Liberia was founded in 1822 by U.S. black freedmen who settled at Monrovia with the aid of colonization societies. It became a republic July 26, 1847, with a constitution modeled on that of the U.S. Descendants of freedmen dominated politics.

Charging rampant corruption, an Army Redemption Council of enlisted men staged a bloody predawn coup, April 12, 1980, in which Pres. Tolbert was killed and replaced as head of state by Sgt. Samuel Doe. Doe was chosen president in a disputed election, and survived a subsequent coup, in 1985.

Libya

Socialist People's Libyan Arab Jamahiriya

al-Jamahiriyah al-Arabiya al-Libya al-Shabiya al-Ishtirakiya

People: Population: (1989 est.): 4,271,000. **Age distrib. (%):** 0–14: 45.0; 15–59: 51.2; 60+: 3.8. **Pop. density:** 6 per sq. mi. **Urban** (1985): 64%. **Ethnic groups:** Arab-Berber 97%. **Languages:** Arabic. **Religions:** Sunni Moslem 97%.

Geography: Area: 679,359 sq. mi., larger than Alaska. **Location:** On Mediterranean coast of N. Africa. **Neighbors:** Tunisia, Algeria on W, Niger, Chad on S, Sudan, Egypt on E. **Topography:** Desert and semidesert regions cover 92% of the land, with low mountains in N, higher mountains in S, a narrow coastal zone. **Capital:** Tripoli. **Cities** (1982 est.): Tripoli 820,000.

Government: Type: Islamic Arabic Socialist "Mass-State." **Head of state:** Col. Muammar al-Qaddafi; b. Sept. 1942; in office: Sept. 1969. **Head of government:** Premier Umar Mustafa al-Muntasir; in office: Mar. 1, 1987. **Local divisions:** 10 regions. **Defense:** 17.8% of GNP (1984).

Economy: Industries: Carpets, textiles, petroleum. **Chief crops:** Dates, olives, citrus and other fruits, grapes, wheat. **Minerals:** Gypsum, oil, gas. **Crude oil reserves** (1987): 22 bln. bbls. **Arable land:** 2%. **Livestock** (1986): sheep: 4.8 mln.; goats: 1.5 mln. **Electricity prod.** (1986): 12.6 bln. kwh. **Labor force:** 18% agric.; 31% ind.; 27% services; 24% govt.

Finance: Currency: Dinar (Feb. 1989: 1.00 = $3.36 US). **Gross domestic product** (1986): $20 bln. **Per capita income** (1984): $7,000. **Imports** (1987): $4.8 bln.; partners: It. 30%, W. Ger. 11%, Fr. 6%, Jap. 8%. **Exports** (1987): $5.7 bln.; partners: It. 24%, W. Ger. 10%, Sp. 7%. **International reserves less gold** (Mar. 1988): $5.5 bln. **Gold:** 3.6 mln. oz t.

Transport: Motor vehicles: in use (1982): 415,000 passenger cars, 334,000 comm. vehicles. **Chief ports:** Tripoli, Benghazi.

Communications: Television sets: 235,000 licensed (1987). **Radios:** 500,000 (1986). **Daily newspaper circ.** (1986): 10 per 1,000 pop.

Health: Life expectancy at birth (1985): 56.1 male; 59.4 female. **Births** (per 1,000 pop. 1985): 46. **Deaths** (per 1,000 pop. 1985): 11.2. **Natural increase** (1985): 3.4%. **Hospital beds** (1982): 16,051. **Physicians** (1982): 5,200. **Infant mortality** (per 1,000 live births 1985): 84.

Education (1985): Literacy: 60%. **Years compulsory:** 7; **Attendance:** 90%.

Major International Organizations: UN, Arab League, OAU, OPEC.

First settled by Berbers, Libya was ruled by Carthage, Rome, and Vandals, the Ottomans, Italy from 1912, and Britain and France after WW II. It became an independent constitutional monarchy Jan. 2, 1952. In 1969 a junta lead by Col. Muammar al-Qaddafi seized power.

In the mid-1970s, Libya helped arm violent revolutionary groups in Egypt and Sudan, and had aided terrorists of various nationalities. The USSR sold Libya advanced arms, and established close political ties.

Libya and Egypt fought several air and land battles along their border in July, 1977. Chad charged Libya with military occupation of its uranium-rich northern region in 1977. Libya's 1979 offensive into the Aouzou Strip was repulsed by Chadian forces. Libyan forces withdrew from Chad, Nov. 1981 but returned. Libyan troops were driven from their last major stronghold by Chad forces in 1987, leaving over $1 billion in military equipment behind.

Widespread nationalization, arrests, imposition of currency regulations, wholesale conscription of civil servants into the army, and the fall in crude oil prices have hurt the economy.

On May 6, 1981, the U.S., citing "a wide range of Libyan provocations and misconduct," closed the Libyan mission in Wash. In August, 2 Libyan jets were shot down by U.S. Navy planes taking part in naval exercises in the Gulf of Sidra which Libya claims as its territory.

The U.S. has accused Libya of masterminding numerous international terrorist actions, including the Dec. 1985 attacks on the Rome and Vienna airports.

On Jan. 7, 1986, the U.S. imposed economic sanctions against Libya, ordered all Americans to leave that country and froze all Libyan assets in the U.S. The U.S. commenced flight operations over the Gulf of Sidra, Jan. 27, and a U.S. Navy task force began conducting exercises in the Gulf, Mar. 23. When Libya fired antiaircraft missiles at American warplanes, the U.S. responded by sinking 2 Libyan ships and bombing a missile installation in Libya. The U.S. withdrew from the Gulf, Mar. 27.

The U.S. accused Libyan leader Qaddafi of having ordered the April 5 bombing of a West Berlin discotheque which killed 2, including a U.S. serviceman. After failing to get their European allies to join them in imposing economic sanctions against Libya, the U.S. sent warplanes to attack terrorist-related targets in Tripoli and Benghazi, Libya, Apr. 14.

At the economic summit of the 7 major industrial democracies in Tokyo, May 4–6, a joint statement was issued which condemned terrorism and singled out Libya as a target for action.

Liechtenstein

Principality of Liechtenstein

Fürstentum Liechtenstein

People: Population: (1989 est.): 30,000. **Age distrib. (%):** 0–14: 20.1; 15–59: 66.3; 60+: 11.6. **Pop. density:** 483 per sq. mi. **Ethnic groups:** Alemannic 95%, Italian 5%. **Languages:** German (official), Alemannic dialect. **Religions:** Roman Catholic 87%, Protestant 8%.

Geography: Area: 62 sq. mi., the size of Washington, D.C. **Location:** In the Alps. **Neighbors:** Switzerland on W, Austria on E. **Topography:** The Rhine Valley occupies one-third of the country, the Alps cover the rest. **Capital:** Vaduz. **Cities** (1986 cen.): Vaduz 4,920.

Government: Type: Hereditary constitutional monarchy. **Head of state:** Prince Franz Josef II; b. Aug. 16, 1906; in office: Mar. 30, 1938. **Head of government:** Hans Brunhart; b. Mar. 28, 1945; in office: Apr. 26, 1978. **Local divisions:** 2 districts, 11 communities.

Economy: Industries: Machines, instruments, chemicals, furniture, ceramics. **Arable land:** 25%. **Labor force:** 54% industry, trade and building; 41% services; 4% agric., fishing, forestry.

Finance: Currency: Swiss Franc. **Gross National Product** (1986): $450 mln. **Tourists** (1986): 76,000.

Communications: Radios: 9,000 in use (1986). **Telephones in use** (1986): 26,000. **Daily newspaper circ.** (1987): 546 per 1,000 pop.

Health: Births (per 1,000 pop. 1986): 12.8. **Deaths** (per 1,000 pop. 1986): 6.7. **Natural increase** (1986): .6%. **Infant mortality** (per 1,000 live births 1987): 15.4.

Education (1989): Literacy: 100%. **Years compulsory:** 9; attendance: 100%.

Liechtenstein became sovereign in 1866. Austria administered Liechtenstein's ports up to 1920; Switzerland has administered its postal services since 1921. Liechtenstein is united with Switzerland by a customs and monetary union. Taxes are low; many international corporations have headquarters there. Foreign workers comprise a third of the population.

The 1986 general elections were the first in which women were allowed to vote.

Luxembourg

Grand Duchy of Luxembourg

Grand-Duché de Luxembourg

People: Population: (1989 est.): 369,000. **Age distrib. (%):** 0–14: 17.3; 15–59: 64.5; 60+: 18.2. **Pop. density:** 369 per sq. mi. **Urban** (1985): 81%. **Ethnic groups:** Mixture of French and Germans predominate. **Languages:** French, German, Luxembourgian. **Religions:** Roman Catholic 97%.

Geography: Area: 998 sq. mi., smaller than Rhode Island. **Location:** In W. Europe. **Neighbors:** Belgium on W, France on S, W. Germany on E. **Topography:** Heavy forests (Ardennes) cover N, S is a low, open plateau. **Capital:** Luxembourg. **Cities** (1986 est.): Luxembourg 86,000.

Government: Type: Constitutional monarchy. **Head of state:** Grand Duke Jean; b. Jan. 5, 1921; in office: Nov. 12, 1964. **Head of government:** Prime Min. Jacques Santer; in office: July 21, 1984. **Local divisions:** 3 districts, 12 cantons. **Defense:** 0.8% of GNP (1985).

Economy: Industries: Steel, chemicals, beer, tires, tobacco, metal products, cement. **Chief crops:** Corn, wine. **Minerals:** Iron. **Arable land:** 25%. **Electricity prod.** (1986): 1.0 bln. kwh. **Crude steel prod.** (1984): 3.9 mln. metric tons. **Labor force:** 1% agric.; 42% ind. & comm.; 45% services.

Finance: Currency: Franc (Mar. 1989: 39.62 = $1 US). **Gross national product** (1986): $5.8 bln. **Per capita income** (1981): $10,444. **Note:** trade and tourist data included in Belgian statistics. **Consumer prices** (change in 1987): −0.1%.

Transport: Railway traffic (1986): 276 mln. passenger-km; 600 mln. net ton-km. **Motor vehicles:** in use (1986): 156,000 passenger cars, 13,000 comm. vehicles.

Communications: Television sets: 91,000 in use (1987). **Radios:** 227,000 in use (1987). **Telephones in use** (1987): 91,000. **Daily newspaper circ.** (1986): 365 per 1,000 pop.

Health: Life expectancy at birth (1987): 70.6 male; 77.9 female. **Births** (per 1,000 pop. 1987): 11.4. **Deaths** (per 1,000 pop. 1987): 10.8. **Hospital beds** (1986): 4,616. **Physicians** (1986): 686. **Infant mortality** (per 1,000 live births 1987): 10.

Education (1983): **Literacy:** 100%. **Years compulsory** 9; attendance 100%.

Major International Organizations: UN, OECD, EC, NATO.
Embassy: 2200 Massachusetts Ave. NW 20008; 265-4171.

Luxembourg, founded about 963, was ruled by Burgundy, Spain, Austria, and France from 1448 to 1815. It left the Germanic Confederation in 1866. Overrun by Germany in 2 world wars, Luxembourg ended its neutrality in 1948, when a customs union with Belgium and Netherlands was adopted.

Madagascar
Democratic Republic of Madagascar
Repoblika Demokratika Malagasy

People: Population (1989 est.): 11,148,000. **Pop. density:** 49 per sq. mi. **Urban** (1985): 21.8%. **Ethnic groups:** 18 Malayan-Indonesian tribes (Merina 26%), with Arab and African presence. **Languages:** Malagasy (official), French. **Religions:** animists 52%, Christian 41%, Moslem 7%.

Geography: Area: 226,657 sq. mi., slightly smaller than Texas. **Location:** In the Indian O., off the SE coast of Africa. **Neighbors:** Comoro Is., Mozambique (across Mozambique Channel). **Topography:** Humid coastal strip in the E, fertile valleys in the mountainous center plateau region, and a wider coastal strip on the W. **Capital:** Antananarivo. **Cities** (1985 est.): Antananarivo 650,000.

Government: Type: Republic, strong presidential authority. **Head of state:** Pres. Didier Ratsiraka; b. Nov. 4, 1936; in office: June 15, 1975. **Head of government:** Prime Min. Victor Ramahatra; in office: Feb. 12, 1988. **Local divisions:** 6 provinces. **Defense:** 9% of govt. budget (1987).

Economy: Industries: Light industry. **Chief crops:** Coffee (over 50% of exports), cloves, vanilla, rice, sugar, sisal, tobacco, peanuts. **Minerals:** Chromium, graphite, coal, bauxite. **Arable land:** 5%. **Livestock** (1986): cattle: 10.4 mln.; pigs: 1.3 mln. **Fish catch** (1986): 63,000 metric tons. **Electricity prod.** (1986): 420 mln. kwh. **Labor force:** 90% agric.

Finance: Currency: Franc (Mar. 1989: 1,596 = $1 US). **Gross national product** (1986): $2.6 bln. **Per capita income** (1986): $255. **Imports** (1986): $438 mln.; partners: Fr. 32%, U.S. 15%. **Exports** (1986): $326 mln.; partners: Fr. 34%, U.S. 14%. **Tourists** (1986): $5.6 mln. receipts. **National budget** (1986): $770 mln. **International reserves less gold** (June 1987): $156 mln. **Consumer prices** (change in 1987): 15.0%.

Transport: Railway traffic (1986): 208 mln. passenger-km; 208 mln. net ton-km. **Motor vehicles:** in use (1986): 21,000 passenger cars, 14,000 comm. vehicles. **Civil aviation:** (1987): 422 mln. passenger-km; 38 mln. freight ton-km. **Chief ports:** Tamatave, Diego-Suarez, Majunga, Tulear.

Communications: Television sets: 100,000 in use (1987). **Radios:** 2 mln. in use (1986). **Telephones in use** (1987): 43,000.

Health: Life expectancy at birth (1984): 46 years. **Births** (per 1,000 pop. 1985): 45. **Deaths** (per 1,000 pop. 1985): 17. **Natural increase** (1985): 2.8%. **Hospital beds** (1982): 20,800. **Physicians** (1982): 940. **Infant mortality** (per 1,000 live births 1985): 101.

Education (1987): **Literacy:** 53%. **Years compulsory:** 5; attendance 83%.

Major International Organizations: UN (GATT, WHO, IMF), OAU.
Embassy: 2374 Massachusetts Ave. NW 20008; 265-5525.

Madagascar was settled 2,000 years ago by Malayan-Indonesian people, whose descendants still predominate. A unified kingdom ruled the 18th and 19th centuries. The island became a French protectorate, 1885, and a colony 1896. Independence came June 26, 1960.

Discontent with inflation and French domination led to a coup in 1972. The new regime nationalized French-owned financial interests, closed French bases and a U.S. space tracking station, and obtained Chinese aid. The government conducted a program of arrests, expulsion of foreigners, and repression of strikes, 1979.

Malawi
Republic of Malawi

People: Population (1989 est.): 8,063,000. **Age distrib. (%):** 0–14: 47.8; 15–59: 48.0; 60+: 4.2. **Pop. density:** 176 per sq. mi. **Urban** (1987): 12%. **Ethnic groups:** Chewa, 90%, Nyanja, Lomwe, other Bantu tribes. **Languages:** English, Chichewa (both official). **Religions:** Christian 75%, Moslem 20%.

Geography: Area: 45,747 sq. mi., the size of Pennsylvania. **Location:** In SE Africa. **Neighbors:** Zambia on W, Mozambique on SE, Tanzania on N. **Topography:** Malawi stretches 560 mi. N-S along Lake Malawi (Lake Nyasa), most of which belongs to Malawi. High plateaus and mountains line the Rift Valley the length of the nation. **Capital:** Lilongwe. **Cities** (1987 est.): Blantyre 402,000; Lilongwe 220,000.

Government: Type: Republic. **Head of state:** Pres. Hastings Kamuzu Banda, b. May 14, 1906; in office: July 6, 1966. **Local divisions:** 24 administrative districts. **Defense:** 1.7% of GNP (1984).

Economy: Industries: Textiles, sugar, farm implements. **Chief crops:** Tea, tobacco, sugar, coffee. **Other resources:** Rubber. **Arable land:** 20%. **Fish catch** (1986): 72 metric tons. **Electricity prod.** (1986): 467 mln. kwh. **Labor force:** 51% agric.; 18% ind. and comm.; 20% govt.; 17% services.

Finance: Currency: Kwacha (Mar. 1989: 2.63 = $1 US). **Gross national product** (1986): $1.1 bln. **Imports** (1988): $402 mln.; partners: So. Afr. 29%, UK 24%, Jap. 6%. **Exports** (1988): $292 mln.; partners: UK 27%, S. Afr. 8%., W. Ger. 10%. **National budget** (1987): $360 mln. **International reserves less gold** (Mar. 1989): $131 mln. **Gold:** 13,000 oz t. **Consumer prices** (change in 1988): 25.0%.

Transport: Railway traffic (1987): 102 mln. passenger-km; 98 mln. net ton-km. **Motor vehicles:** in use (1986): 15,000 passenger cars, 15,000 comm. vehicles. **Civil aviation** (1986) 119 mln. passenger-km; 1.0 mln. freight ton-km.

Communications: Radios: 1 mln. in use (1986). **Telephones in use** (1986): 44,000. **Daily newspaper circ.** (1985): 5 per 1,000 pop.

Health: Life expectancy at birth (1985): 44.0 male; 46.0 female. **Births** (per 1,000 pop. 1985): 54.0. **Deaths** (per 1,000 pop. 1985): 21.0. **Natural increase** (1985): 3.3%. **Hospital beds** (1984): 6,596. **Infant mortality** (per 1,000 live births 1985): 170.

Education (1989): **Literacy:** 25%. About 45% attend school.
Major International Organizations: UN (World Bank, IMF), OAU, Commonwealth of Nations.
Embassy: 2408 Massachusetts Ave. NW 20008; 797-1007.

Bantus came in the 16th century, Arab slavers in the 19th. The area became the British protectorate Nyasaland, in 1891. It became independent July 6, 1964, and a republic in 1966. It has a pro-West foreign policy and cooperates economically with S. Africa.

Malaysia

People: Population (1989 est.): 16,901,000. **Age distrib. (%):** 0–14: 37.8; 15–59: 56.5; 60+: 5.7. **Pop. density:** 132 per sq. mi. **Urban** (1985): 38%. **Ethnic groups:** Malays 59%, Chinese 32%, Indian 9%. **Languages:** Malay (official), English, Chinese, Indian languages. **Religions:** Moslem, Hindu, Buddhist, Confucian, Taoist, local religions.

Geography: Area: 127,316 sq. mi., slightly larger than New Mexico. **Location:** On the SE tip of Asia, plus the N. coast of the island of Borneo. **Neighbors:** Thailand on N, Indonesia on S. **Topography:** Most of W. Malaysia is covered by tropical jungle, including the central mountain range that runs N-S through the peninsula. The western coast is marshy, the eastern, sandy. E. Malaysia has a wide, swampy coastal plain, with interior jungles and mountains. **Capital:** Kuala Lumpur. **Cities** (1986 est.): Kuala Lumpur 1 mln.

Government: Type: Federal parliamentary democracy with a constitutional monarch. **Head of state:** Paramount Ruler Sultan Azlan Shah; in office: Apr. 26, 1989. **Head of government:** Prime Min. Datuk Seri Mahathir bin Mohamad; b. Dec. 20, 1925; in office: July 16, 1981. **Local divisions:** 13 states and capital. **Defense:** 4.2% of GNP (1987).

Economy: Industries: Rubber goods, steel, electronics. **Chief crops:** Palm oil, copra, rice, pepper. **Minerals:** Tin (35% world output), iron. **Crude oil reserves** (1987): 3.2 bln. bbls. **Other resources:** Rubber (35% world output). **Arable land:** 13%. **Livestock** (1966): pigs: 2.1 mln. **Fish catch** (1986): 571,000 metric tons. **Electricity prod.** (1986): 10.7 bln. kwh. **Labor force:** 21% agric.; 22% manuf.; 11% tourism & trade.

Finance: Currency: Ringgit (Mar. 1989: 2.69 = $1 US). **Gross national product** (1987): $28.4 bln. **Imports** (1987): $12.1 bln.; partners: Jap. 21%, U.S. 18%, Sing. 14%. **Exports** (1987): $18.0 bln.; partners: Jap. 20%, U.S. 17% Sing. 19%, Neth. 6%. **Tourists** (1986): $612 mln. receipts. **National budget** (1988): $10.8 bln. **International reserves less gold** (Mar. 1989): $6.0 bln. **Gold:** 2.35 mln. oz t. **Consumer prices** (change in 1988): 2.0%.

Transport: Railway traffic (incl. Singapore) (1986): 1.3 bln. passenger-km; 1.1 bln. net ton-km. **Motor vehicles:** in use (1986): 1.4 mln. passenger cars, 330,000 comm. vehicles. **Civil aviation:** (1987): 7.6 bln. passenger-km; 354 mln. metric ton-km. **Chief ports:** George Town, Kelang, Melaka, Kuching.

Communications: Television sets: 1.6 mln. in use (1987). **Radios:** 2 mln. in use (1985). **Telephones in use** (1987): 1.3 mln. **Daily newspaper circ.** (1985): 133 per 1,000 pop.

Health: Life expectancy at birth (1987): 68.0 male; 72.7 female. **Births** (per 1,000 pop. 1987): 29.5. **Deaths** (per 1,000 pop. 1987): 5.0. **Natural increase** (1987): 2.4%. **Hospital beds** (1986): 33,000. **Physicians** (1986): 5,300. **Infant mortality** (per 1,000 live births 1988): 25.0.

Education (1989): **Literacy:** 80%; 96% attend primary school, 48% attend secondary.

Major International Organizations: UN (World Bank, IMF, GATT), ASEAN.

Embassy: 2401 Massachusetts Ave. NW 20008; 328-2700.

European traders appeared in the 16th century; Britain established control in 1867. Malaysia was created Sept. 16, 1963. It included Malaya (which had become independent in 1957 after the suppression of Communist rebels), plus the formerly-British Singapore, Sabah (N Borneo), and Sarawak (NW Borneo). Singapore was separated in 1965, in order to end tensions between Chinese, the majority in Singapore, and Malays in control of the Malaysian government.

A monarch is elected by a council of hereditary rulers of the Malayan states every 5 years.

Abundant natural resources have assured prosperity, and foreign investment has aided industrialization.

Maldives
Republic of Maldives
Divehi Jumhuriya

People: Population (1989 est.): 202,000. **Age distrib.** (%): 0-14: 44.4; 15-59: 51.7; 60+: 3.9. **Pop. density:** 1,756 per sq. mi. **Urban** (1985): 26%. **Ethnic groups:** Sinhalese, Dravidian, Arab mixture. **Languages:** Divehi (Sinhalese dialect). **Religions:** Sunni Moslem.

Geography: Area: 115 sq. mi., twice the size of Washington, D.C. **Location:** In the Indian O. SW of India. **Neighbors:** Nearest is India on N. **Topography:** 19 atolls with 1,087 islands, about 200 inhabited. None of the islands are over 5 sq. mi. in area, and all are nearly flat. **Capital:** Male. **Cities** (1985 est.): Male 46,334.

Government: Type: Republic. **Head of state:** Pres. Maumoon Abdul Gayoom; b. Dec. 29, 1939; in office: Nov. 11, 1978.

Local divisions: 19 atolls, each with an elected committee and a government-appointed chief.

Economy: Industries: Fish processing, tourism. **Chief crops:** Coconuts, fruit, millet. **Other resources:** Shells. **Arable land:** 10%. **Fish catch** (1986): 45,000 metric tons. **Electricity prod.** (1986): 13.0 mln. kwh. **Labor force:** 80% fishing, agriculture, & manufacturing.

Finance: Currency: Rufiyaa (Mar. 1989: 8.41 = $1 US). **Gross national product** (1966): $60 mln. **Per capita income** (1985): $470. **Imports** (1986): $64 mln.; partners: Sing., Jap., Sri Lan. **Exports** (1986): $31 mln.; partners: Jap., Europe. **Tourists** (1986): $42 mln. receipts.

Transport: Chief ports: Male Atoll.

Communications: Radios: 21,000 in use (1987). **Telephones in use** (1985): 3,000.

Health: Life expectancy at birth (1987): 58.0 male; 59.0 female. **Births** (per 1,000 pop. 1987): 42.8. **Deaths** (per 1,000 pop. 1987): 10.4. **Natural increase** (1987): 3.2%. **Infant morality** (per 1,000 live births 1987): 77.0.

Education (1987): **Literacy:** 82%. (claimed by govt.). Only 6% of those aged 11-15 attend school.

Major International Organizations: UN.

The islands had been a British protectorate since 1887. The country became independent July 26, 1965. Long a sultanate, the Maldives became a republic in 1968. Natural resources and tourism are being developed; however, it remains one of the world's poorest countries.

Mali
Republic of Mali
République du Mali

People: Population (1989 est.): 8,460,000. **Age distrib.** (%): 0-14: 46.0; 15-59: 49.4; 60+: 4.6. **Pop. density:** 17 per sq. mi. **Urban** (1985): 20.8%. **Ethnic groups:** Mande (Bambara, Malinke, Sarakolle) 50%, Peul 17%, Voltaic 12%, Songhai 6%, Tuareg, Moors. **Languages:** French (official), Bambara. **Religions:** Moslem 90%.

Geography: Area: 478,764 sq. mi., about the size of Texas and California combined. **Location:** In the interior of W. Africa. **Neighbors:** Mauritania, Senegal on W, Guinea, Côte d'Ivoire, Burkina Faso on S, Niger on E, Algeria on N. **Topography:** A landlocked grassy plain in the upper basins of the Senegal and Niger rivers, extending N into the Sahara. **Capital:** Bamako. **Cities** (1986 est.): Bamako (met.) 800,000.

Government: Type: Republic. **Head of state:** Pres. Moussa Traore; b. Sept. 25, 1936; in office: Dec. 6, 1968. **Local divisions:** 7 regions and a capital district. **Defense:** 3% of GDP (1986).

Economy: Chief crops: Millet, rice, peanuts, cotton. **Other resources:** Bauxite, iron, gold. **Arable land:** 2%. **Livestock** (1986): sheep: 5.5 mln.; cattle: 4.6 mln. **Fish catch** (1986): 61,000 metric tons. **Electricity prod.** (1986): 170 mln. kwh. **Labor force:** 73% agric.; 12% ind. & comm.; 16% services.

Finance: Currency: Franc (Mar. 1989: 319 = $1 US). **Gross national product** (1986): $1.3 bln. **Per capita income** (1984): $190. **Imports** (1987): $493 mln.; partners: Fr. 22%, Ivory Coast 25%. **Exports** (1987): $260 mln.; partners: Belg.-Lux. 25%, Fr. 15%. **Tourists** (1986): $16 mln. receipts. **International reserves less gold** (Feb. 1989): $36.0 mln. **Gold:** 19,000 oz t.

Transport: Railway traffic (1987): 772 mln. passenger-km; 429 mln. net ton-km. **Motor vehicles:** in use (1987): 29,000 passenger cars, 7,500 comm. vehicles.

Communications: Radios: 300,000 in use (1986). **Telephones in use** (1984): 9,500.

Health: Life expectancy at birth (1985): 40.4 male; 43.6 female. **Births** (per 1,000 pop. 1985): 50.2. **Deaths** (per 1,000 pop. 1985): 22.4. **Natural increase** (1985): 2.7%. **Hospital beds** (1983): 4,215. **Physicians** (1983): 283. **Infant mortality** (per 1,000 live births 1985): 173.

Education (1984): **Literacy:** 10%. **Attendance:** 28% under 15 attend school.

Major International Organizations: UN and all of its specialized agencies, OAU, EC.

Embassy: 2130 R St. NW 20008; 332-2250.

Until the 15th century the area was part of the great Mali Empire. Timbuktu was a center of Islamic study. French rule was secured, 1898. The Sudanese Rep. and Senegal became independent as the Mali Federation June 20, 1960, but Senegal withdrew, and the Sudanese Rep. was renamed Mali.

Mali signed economic agreements with France and, in 1963, with Senegal. In 1968, a coup ended the socialist regime. Famine struck in 1973-74, killing as many as 100,000 people. Drought conditions returned in the 1980s.

Malta

Repubblika Ta' Malta

People: Population (1989 est.): 358,000. **Age distrib. (%):** 0–14: 23.9; 15–59: 61.6; 60+: 14.5. **Pop. density:** 2,934 per sq. mi. **Ethnic groups:** Italian, Arab, French. **Languages:** Maltese, English both official. **Religions:** Mainly Roman Catholic.

Geography: Area: 122 sq. mi., twice the size of Washington, D.C. **Location:** In center of Mediterranean Sea. **Neighbors:** Nearest is Italy on N. **Topography:** Island of Malta is 95 sq. mi.; other islands in the group: Gozo, 26 sq. mi., Comino, 1 sq. mi. The coastline is heavily indented. Low hills cover the interior. **Capital:** Valletta. **Cities** (1986 est.): Birkirkara 20,000, Qormi 18,000.

Government: Type: Republic. **Head of state:** Pres. Paul Xuerub; in office: Feb. 15, 1987. **Head of government:** Prime Min. Eddie Fenech Adami; b. Feb. 7, 1934; in office: May 12, 1987. **Local Divisions:** 13 electoral districts.

Economy: Industries: Textiles, tourism. **Chief crops:** Potatoes, onions, beans. **Arable land:** 41%. **Electricity prod.** (1986): 825 mln. kwh. **Labor force:** 35% ind. & comm.; 30% services; 22% gov.

Finance: Currency: Pound (Mar. 1989: 1.00 = $2.88 US). **Gross national product** (1988): $1.6 bln. **Per capita income** (1986): $4,750. **Imports** (1987): $1.1 bln.; partners: UK 18%, It. 23%, W. Ger. 14%, U.S. 7%. **Exports** (1987): $605 mln.; partners: W. Ger. 31%, UK 20%, Libya 8%. **Tourists** (1985): receipts: $149 mln. **National budget** (1986): $890 mln. expenditures. **International reserves less gold** (Mar. 1989): 1.3 bln. **Gold:** 466,000 oz t. **Consumer prices** (change in 1988): 0.9% .

Transport: Motor vehicles: in use (1986): 85,000 passenger cars, 18,000 comm. vehicles. **Civil aviation** (1986): 744 mln. passenger-km; 4.4 mln. freight ton-km. **Chief ports:** Valletta.

Communications: Television sets: 123,000 licensed (1987). **Radios:** 92,000 in use (1986). **Telephones in use** (1986): 140,000.

Health: Life expectancy at birth (1987): 72.5 male; 77.0 female. **Births** (per 1,000 pop. 1987): 15.4. **Deaths** (per 1,000 pop. 1987): 8.4. **Natural increase** (1987): .7%. **Hospital beds** (1984): 3,142. **Physicians** (1984): 413. **Infant mortality** (per 1,000 live births 1988): 10.1.

Education (1988): **Literacy:** 90%. **Compulsory:** until age 16. **Major International Organizations:** UN (GATT, WHO, IMF), Commonwealth of Nations.

Embassy: 2017 Connecticut Ave. NW 20008; 462-3611.

Malta was ruled by Phoenicians, Romans, Arabs, Normans, the Knights of Malta, France, and Britain (since 1814). It became independent Sept. 21, 1964. Malta became a republic in 1974. The withdrawal of the last of its sailors, Apr. 1, 1979, ended 179 years of British military presence on the island.

With Malta's approval, Egyptian commandos stormed a hijacked EgyptAir passenger plane at Valletta airport Nov. 23, 1985; 57 died in the battle.

Malta is democratic but nonaligned.

Mauritania

Islamic Republic of Mauritania
République Islamique de Mauritanie

People: Population (1989 est.): 1,804,000. **Age distrib. (%):** 0–14: 46.4; 15–59: 49.0; 60+: 4.6. **Pop. density:** 4.5 per sq. mi. **Urban** (1983): 6%. **Ethnic groups:** Arab-Berber 80%, Negroes 20%. **Languages:** French (official), Hassanya Arabic (national), Toucouleur, Fula, Sarakole, Wolof. **Religion:** Nearly 100% Moslem.

Geography: Area: 397,954 sq. mi., the size of Texas and California combined. **Location:** In W. Africa. **Neighbors:** Morocco on N, Algeria, Mali on E, Senegal on S. **Topography:** The fertile

Senegal R. valley in the S gives way to a wide central region of sandy plains and scrub trees. The N is arid and extends into the Sahara. **Capital:** Nouakchott. **Cities** (1987 est.): Nouakchott 400,000; Nouadhibou 70,000; Kaedi 22,000.

Government: Type: Military republic. **Head of Government:** President & Premier Maaouya Ould Sidi Ahmed Taya; in office: Apr. 25, 1981. **Local divisions:** 12 regions, one district. **Defense:** 20% of GNP (1986).

Economy: Chief crops: Dates, grain. **Industries:** iron mining. **Minerals:** Iron, ore, gypsum. **Livestock** (1986): sheep: 3.0 mln.; goats: 3.9 mln.; cattle: 1.0 mln. **Fish catch** (1985): 60,000 metric tons. **Electricity prod.** (1986): 74 mln. kwh. **Labor force:** 47% agric., 14% ind. & comm., 29% services.

Finance: Currency: Ouguiya (Mar. 1989: 78 = $1 US). **Gross national product** (1986): $600 mln. **Per capita income** (1986): $450. **Imports** (1987): $235 mln.; partners: Fr. 29%, Sp. 9%. **Exports** (1987): $428 mln.; partners: Fr. 21%, It. 26%, Jap. 20%. **International reserves less gold** (Feb. 1989): $43 mln. **Gold:** 12,000 oz t. **Consumer prices** (change in 1986): 7%.

Transport: Motor vehicles: in use (1985): 15,000 passenger cars, 2,000 comm. vehicles. **Chief ports:** Nouakchott, Nouadhibou.

Communications: Radios: 200,000 in use (1986).

Health: Life expectancy at birth (1987): 44.0 male; 47.0 female. **Births** (per 1,000 pop. 1985): 47.0. **Deaths** (per 1,000 pop. 1985): 27. **Natural increase** (1985): 2.0%. **Hospital beds** (1984): 1,325. **Physicians** (1984): 170. **Infant mortality** (per 1,000 live births 1985): 138.

Education (1987): **Literacy:** 17%. **Attendance:** 41% in primary school, 10% in secondary school.

Major International Organizations: UN (GATT, IMF, WHO), OAU, Arab League.

Embassy: 2129 Leroy Pl. NW 20008; 232-5700.

Mauritania became independent Nov. 28, 1960. It annexed the south of former Spanish Sahara in 1976. Saharan guerrillas stepped up attacks in 1977; 8,000 Moroccan troops and French bomber raids aided the government. Mauritania signed a peace treaty with the Polsario Front, 1980, resumed diplomatic relations with Algeria while breaking a defense treaty with Morocco, and renounced sovereignty over its share of former Spanish Sahara. Morocco annexed the territory.

Famine struck repeatedly during the 1980s.

Mauritius

People: Population (1989 est.): 1,047,900. **Age distrib. (%):** 0–14: 36.3; 15–59: 57.2; 60+: 6.4. **Pop. density:** 1,325 per sq. mi. **Urban** (1987): 41%. **Ethnic groups:** Indo-Mauritian 68%, Creole 27%, others. **Languages:** English (official), French, Creole. **Religions:** Hindu 51%, Christian 30%, Moslem 16%.

Geography: Area: 790 sq. mi., about the size of Rhode Island. **Location:** In the Indian O., 500 mi. E of Madagascar. **Neighbors:** Nearest is Madagascar on W. **Topography:** A volcanic island nearly surrounded by coral reefs. A central plateau is encircled by mountain peaks. **Capital:** Port Louis. **Cities** (1986 est.): Port Louis 155,000.

Government: Type: Parliamentary democracy. **Head of state:** Queen Elizabeth II, represented by Gov.-Gen. Sir Veerasamy Ringadoo; in office: Jan. 17, 1986. **Head of government:** Prime Min. Aneerood Jugnauth; in office: June 12, 1982. **Local divisions:** 9 administrative divisions.

Economy: Industries: Tourism. **Chief crops:** Sugar cane, tea. **Arable land:** 58%. **Electricity prod.** (1986): 378 mln. kwh. **Labor force:** 20% agric. & fishing; 38% manuf.; 19% govt. services.

Finance: Currency: Rupee (Mar. 1989: 15.02 = $1 US). **Gross national product** (1987): $1.4 bln. **Per capita income** (1987): $1,400. **Imports** (1986): $684 mln.; partners: UK 9%, Fr. 12%, So. Afr. 9%. **Exports** (1986): $676 mln.; partners: UK 50%, Fr. 22%, U.S. 8%. **Tourists** (1986): $88 mln. receipts. **National budget** (1985): $310 mln. **International reserves less gold** (Feb. 1989): $449 mln. **Gold:** 61,000 oz t. **Consumer prices** (change in 1988): 9.2%.

Transport: Motor vehicles: in use (1986): 33,000 passenger cars, 11,000 comm. vehicles. **Chief ports:** Port Louis.

Communications: Television sets: 128,000 in use (1987). **Radios:** 200,000 in use (1986). **Telephones in use** (1986): 64,000. **Daily newspaper circ.** (1987): 75 per 1,000 pop.

Health: Life expectancy at birth (1988): 64.4 male; 71.2 female. **Births** (per 1,000 pop. 1986): 18.0. **Deaths** (per 1,000

pop. 1986): 6.6. **Natural increase** (1986): 1.1%. **Hospital beds** (1986): 2,811. **Physicians** (1986): 760. **Infant mortality** (per 1,000 live births 1987): 26.3.

Education (1988): **Literacy:** 94%. **Attendance:** almost all children attend school.

Major International Organizations: UN and all of its specialized agencies, OAU, Commonwealth of Nations.

Embassy: 4301 Connecticut Ave. NW 20008; 244-1491.

Mauritius was uninhabited when settled in 1638 by the Dutch, who introduced sugar cane. France took over in 1721, bringing African slaves. Britain ruled from 1810 to Mar. 12, 1968, bringing Indian workers for the sugar plantations.

The economy suffered in the 1980s because of low world sugar prices.

Mexico
United Mexican States
Estados Unidos Mexicanos

People: Population (1989 est.): 88,087,000. **Age distrib. (%):** 0–14: 37.5; 15–59: 57.0; 60+: 5.5. **Pop. density:** 115 per sq. mi. **Urban** (1986): 70%. **Ethnic groups:** Mestizo 60%, American Indian 29%, Caucasian 9%. **Languages:** Spanish. **Religions:** Roman Catholic 97%.

Geography: Area: 761,604 sq. mi., three times the size of Texas. **Location:** In southern N. America. **Neighbors:** U.S. on N, Guatemala, Belize on S. **Topography:** The Sierra Madre Occidental Mts. run NW-SE near the west coast; the Sierra Madre Oriental Mts., run near the Gulf of Mexico. They join S of Mexico City. Between the 2 ranges lies the dry central plateau, 5,000 to 8,000 ft. alt., rising toward the S, with temperate vegetation. Coastal lowlands are tropical. About 45% of land is arid. **Capital:** Mexico City. **Cities** (1985 est.): Mexico City (metro) 18 mln.; Guadalajara (metro) 3 mln.; Monterrey (metro) 2.7 mln.

Government: Type: Federal republic. **Head of state:** Pres. Carlos Salinas de Gortari; b. Apr. 3, 1948; in office: Dec. 1, 1988. **Local divisions:** Federal district and 31 states. **Defense:** 0.6% of GNP (1985).

Economy: Industries: Steel, chemicals, electric goods, textiles, rubber, petroleum, tourism. **Chief crops:** Cotton, coffee, sugar cane, vegetables, corn. **Minerals:** Silver, lead, zinc, gold, oil, natural gas. **Crude oil reserves** (1987): 54 bln. bbls. **Arable land:** 13%. **Livestock** (1986): cattle: 31.1 mln.; pigs: 19 mln.; sheep: 8.4 mln. **Fish catch** (1986): 1.3 mln. metric tons. **Electricity prod.** (1986): 90.4 bln. kwh. **Crude steel prod.** (1987): 7.4 mln. metric tons. **Labor force:** 26% agric.; 13% manuf; 31% services; 14% comm.

Finance: Currency: Peso (May 1989: 2,272 = $1 US). **Gross national product** (1987): $126 bln. **Per capita income** (1984): $2,082. **Imports** (1987): $12.7 bln.; partners: U.S. 64%, EC 11%. **Exports** (1987): $20.6 bln.; partners: U.S. 64%, EC 10%. **Tourists** (1986): receipts: $2.9 bln. **National budget** (1985): $86.5 bln. expenditures. **International reserves less gold** (Jan. 1989): $5.2 bln. **Gold:** 2.5 mln. oz t. **Consumer prices** (change in 1988): 114.2%.

Transport: Railway traffic (1988): 4.0 bln. passenger-km; 40.8 bln. net ton-km. **Motor vehicles:** in use (1985): 5.0 mln. passenger cars, 2.1 mln. comm. **Civil aviation** (1986): 16.8 bln. passenger-km; 159 mln. freight ton-km. **Chief ports:** Veracruz, Tampico, Mazatlan, Coatzacoalcos.

Communications: Television sets: 9.5 mln. in use (1987). **Radios:** 25 mln. in use (1986). **Telephones in use** (1988): 8.8 mln. **Daily newspaper circ.** (1986): 142 per 1,000 pop.

Health: Life expectancy at birth (1988): 65.9 male; 72.3 female. **Births** (per 1,000 pop. 1987): 32.0 **Deaths** (per 1,000 pop. 1987): 5.1 **Natural increase** (1987): 2.6%. **Hospital beds** (1984): 72,000. **Physicians** (1980): 53,053. **Infant mortality** (per 1,000 live births 1985): 42.

Education (1988): **Literacy:** 88%. **Years compulsory:** 10. **Major International Organizations:** UN (IMF, GATT), OAS. **Embassy:** 2829 16th St. NW 20009; 234-6000.

Mexico was the site of advanced Indian civilizations. The Mayas, an agricultural people, moved up from Yucatan, built immense stone pyramids, invented a calendar. The Toltecs were overcome by the Aztecs, who founded Tenochtitlan 1325 AD, now Mexico City. Hernando Cortes, Spanish conquistador, destroyed the Aztec empire, 1519-1521.

After 3 centuries of Spanish rule the people rose, under Fr. Miguel Hidalgo y Costilla, 1810, Fr. Morelos y Payon, 1812, and Gen. Agustin Iturbide, who made independence effective Sept. 27, 1821, but made himself emperor as Agustin I. A republic was declared in 1823.

Mexican territory extended into the present American Southwest and California until Texas revolted and established a republic in 1836; the Mexican legislature refused recognition but was unable to enforce its authority there. After numerous clashes, the U.S.-Mexican War, 1846-48, resulted in the loss by Mexico of the lands north of the Rio Grande.

French arms supported an Austrian archduke on the throne of Mexico as Maximilian I, 1864-67, but pressure from the U.S. forced France to withdraw. A dictatorial rule by Porfirio Diaz, president 1877-80, 1884-1911, led to fighting by rival forces until the new constitution of Feb. 5, 1917 provided social reform. Since then Mexico has developed large-scale programs of social security, labor protection, and school improvement. A constitutional provision requires management to share profits with labor.

The Institutional Revolutionary Party has been dominant in politics since 1929. Radical opposition, including some guerrilla activity, has been contained by strong measures.

The presidency of Luis Echeverria, 1970-76, was marked by a more leftist foreign policy and domestic rhetoric. Some land redistribution begun in 1976 was reversed under the succeeding administration.

Some gains in agriculture, industry, and social services have been achieved. The land is rich, but the rugged topography and lack of sufficient rainfall are major obstacles. Crops and farm prices are controlled, as are export and import. Economic prospects brightened with the discovery of vast oil reserves, perhaps the world's greatest. But much of the work force is jobless or underemployed.

Inflation and the drop in world oil prices caused economic problems in the 1980s. The peso was devalued and private banks were nationalized to restore financial stability.

Many thousands died when a disastrous earthquake struck Mexico City, Sept. 19, 1985.

The U.S. has been critical of Mexico for its failure to combat the production of illegal drugs.

In 1988, amid charges of election fraud, Carlos Salinas de Gortari was elected president.

Monaco
Principality of Monaco

People: Population (1989 est.): 29,000. **Age distrib. (%):** 0–14: 12.7; 15–59: 56.3 60+: 30.7. **Pop. density:** 28,072 per sq. mi. **Ethnic groups:** French 47%, Italian 16%, Monegasque 16%. **Languages:** French (official). **Religions:** Predominantly Roman Catholic.

Geography: Area: 0.6 sq. mi. **Location:** On the NW Mediterranean coast. **Neighbors:** France to W, N, E. **Topography:** Monaco-Ville sits atop a high promontory, the rest of the principality rises from the port up the hillside. **Capital:** Monaco-Ville (1985 est.): 1,700.

Government: Type: Constitutional monarchy. **Head of state:** Prince Rainier III; b. May 31, 1923; in office: May 9, 1949. **Head of government:** Min. of State Jean Ausseil; in office: Sept. 1985.

Economy: Industries: Tourism, gambling, chemicals, precision instruments, plastics.

Finance: Currency: French franc or Monégasque franc.

Transport: Chief ports: La Condamine.

Communications: Television sets: 17,000 in use (1984). **Telephones in use** (1984): 18,000.

Health: Births (per 1,000 pop. 1985): 7. **Deaths** (per 1,000 pop. 1985): 10. **Natural increase** (1985): −.3%. **Infant mortality** (per 1,000 live births 1970): 9.3.

Education (1988): **Literacy:** 99%. **Years compulsory:** 10; attendance 99%.

An independent principality for over 300 years, Monaco has belonged to the House of Grimaldi since 1297 except during the French Revolution. It was placed under the protectorate of Sardinia in 1815, and under that of France, 1861. The Prince of Monaco was an absolute ruler until a 1911 constitution.

Monaco's fame as a tourist resort is widespread. It is noted for its mild climate and magnificent scenery. The area has been extended by land reclamation.

Mongolia

Mongolian People's Republic

Bügd Nayramdakh Mongol Ard Uls

People: Population (1989 est.): 2,093,000. **Pop. density:** 3 per sq. mi. **Urban** (1986): 52%. **Ethnic groups:** Mongol 90%. **Languages:** Khalkha Mongolian (official, written in Cyrillic letters since 1941), Russian, Chinese. **Religions:** curbed by govt., traditionally Lama Buddhism.

Geography: Area: 604,247 sq. mi., more than twice the size of Texas. **Location:** In E Central Asia. **Neighbors:** USSR on N, China on S. **Topography:** Mostly a high plateau with mountains, salt lakes, and vast grasslands. Arid lands in the S are part of the Gobi Desert. **Capital:** Ulaanbaatar. **Cities** (1985 est.): Ulaanbaatar 488,000, Darhan 69,000.

Government: Type: Communist state. **Head of state:** Chmn. Zhambyn Batmunkh; b. May 10, 1926; in office: Aug. 23, 1984. **Head of government:** Premier Dumaagiyn Sodnom; in office: Aug. 23, 1984. **Local divisions:** 18 provinces, 3 autonomous municipalities. **Defense:** 11.5% of GNP (1984).

Economy: Industries: Food processing, textiles, chemicals, cement. **Chief crops:** Grain. **Minerals:** Coal, tungsten, copper, molybdenum, gold, tin. **Arable land:** 1%. **Livestock** (1986): sheep: 13.5 mln.; cattle 2.4 mln. **Electricity prod.** (1986): 2.8 bln. kwh. **Labor force:** 52% agric.; 10% manuf.

Finance: Currency: Tugrik (Jan. 1989: 3.36 = $1 US). **Gross national product** (1985): $1.6 bln. **Per capita income** (1984): $1,000. **Imports** (1985): $1 bln.; partners: USSR 91%. **Exports** (1985): $660 mln.; partners: USSR 80%.

Transport: Railway traffic (1985): 436 mln. passenger-km; 5.9 bln. net ton-km.

Communications: Television sets: 88,000 in use (1986). **Radios:** 194,000 in use (1986). **Telephones in use** (1986): 49,000. **Daily newspaper circ.** (1985): 91 per 1,000 pop.

Health: Life expectancy at birth (1986): 61.1 male; 65.2 female. **Births** (per 1,000 pop. 1985): 35. **Deaths** (per 1,000 pop. 1985): 10. **Natural increase** (1985): 2.5%. **Hospital beds** (1986): 21,200. **Physicians** (1986): 4,400. **Infant mortality** (per 1,000 live births 1986): 47.

Major International Organizations: UN (ILO, WHO).

Education (1985): **Literacy:** 89%. **Years compulsory:** 7 in major population centers.

One of the world's oldest countries, Mongolia reached the zenith of its power in the 13th century when Genghis Khan and his successors conquered all of China and extended their influence as far W as Hungary and Poland. In later centuries, the empire dissolved and Mongolia came under the suzerainty of China.

With the advent of the 1911 Chinese revolution, Mongolia, with Russian backing, declared its independence. A Mongolian Communist regime was established July 11, 1921.

Mongolia has been changed from a nomadic culture to one of settled agriculture and growing industries with aid from the USSR and East European nations.

Mongolia has sided with the Russians in the Sino-Soviet dispute. A Mongolian-Soviet mutual assistance pact was signed Jan. 15, 1966, and some 60,000 Soviet troops are based in the country.

Morocco

Kingdom of Morocco

al-Mamlaka al-Maghrebia

People: Population (1989 est.): 25,380,000. **Age distrib.** (%): 0–14: 46.4; 15–59: 49.2; 60+: 4.2. **Pop. density:** 147 per sq. mi. **Urban** (1986): 44%. **Ethnic groups:** Arab-Berber 99%. **Languages:** Arabic (official), with Berber, French, Spanish minorities. **Religions:** Sunni Moslems 99%.

Geography: Area: 172,413 sq. mi., larger than California. **Location:** on NW coast of Africa. **Neighbors:** W. Sahara on S, Algeria on E. **Topography:** Consists of 5 natural regions: mountain ranges (Riff in the N, Middle Atlas, Upper Atlas, and Anti-Atlas); rich plains in the W; alluvial plains in SW; well-cultivated plateaus in the center; a pre-Sahara arid zone extending from SE. **Capital:** Rabat. **Cities** (1984): Casablanca 2,600,000; Rabat 556,000, Fes 852,000.

Government: Type: Constitutional monarchy. **Head of state:** King Hassan II; b. July 9, 1929; in office: Mar. 3, 1961. **Head of government:** Prime Min. Azzedine Laraki; in office: Sept. 30, 1986. **Local divisions:** 2 prefectures, 36 provinces. **Defense:** 6.5% of GNP (1985).

Economy: Industries: Carpets, clothing, leather goods, tourism. **Chief crops:** Grain, fruits, dates, grapes. **Minerals:** Antimony, cobalt, manganese, phosphates, lead, oil, coal. **Crude oil reserves** (1980): 100 mln. bbls. **Arable land:** 18%. **Livestock** (1986): cattle: 3.3 mln.; sheep; 12 mln.; goats: 4.5 mln. **Fish catch** (1986): 591,000 metric tons. **Electricity prod.** (1986): 6.9 bln. kwh. **Labor force:** 50% agric., 26% services; 15% ind.

Finance: Currency: Dirham (Mar. 1989: 8.74 = $1 US). **Gross national product** (1986): $13.1 bln. **Per capita income** (1984): $630. **Imports** (1987): $4.2 bln.; partners: Fr. 25%, Sp. 7%, Saudi Ar. 15%. **Exports** (1987): $2.8 bln.; partners: Fr. 22%, W. Ger. 7%, Sp. 7%, It. 5%. **Tourists** (1986): $800 mln. receipts. **National budget** (1985): $6.8 bln. expenditures. **International reserves less gold** (Mar. 1989): $577 mln. **Gold:** 704,000 oz t. **Consumer prices** (change in 1988): 2.4%.

Transport: Railway traffic (1986): 1.9 bln. passenger-km; 4.9 bln. net ton-km. **Motor vehicles:** in use (1986): 527,000 passenger cars, 247,000 comm. vehicles. **Civil aviation** (1987): 2.2 bln. passenger-km; 50.9 mln. freight ton-km. **Chief ports:** Tangier, Casablanca, Kenitra.

Communications: Television sets: 1.2 mln. in use (1987). **Radios:** 3.0 mln. in use (1986). **Telephones in use** (1986): 325,000. **Daily newspaper circ.** (1986): 12 per 1,000 pop.

Health: Life expectancy at birth (1985): 56.1 male; 59.4 female. **Births** (per 1,000 pop. 1985): 44.1. **Deaths** (per 1,000 pop. 1985): 11.7. **Natural increase** (1985): 3.2%. **Hospital beds** (1986): 25,000. **Physicians** (1986): 3,945. **Infant mortality** (per 1,000 live births 1985): 93.

Education (1980): **Literacy:** 70%.

Major International Organizations: UN (ILO, IMF, WHO), OAU, Arab League.

Embassy: 1601 21st St. NW 20009; 462-7979.

Berbers were the original inhabitants, followed by Carthaginians and Romans. Arabs conquered in 683. In the 11th and 12th centuries, a Berber empire ruled all NW Africa and most of Spain from Morocco.

Part of Morocco came under Spanish rule in the 19th century; France controlled the rest in the early 20th. Tribal uprisings lasted from 1911 to 1933. The country became independent Mar. 2, 1956. Tangier, an internationalized seaport, was turned over to Morocco, 1956. Ifni, a Spanish enclave, was ceded in 1969.

Morocco annexed over 70,000 sq. mi. of phosphate-rich land Apr. 14, 1976, two-thirds of former Spanish Sahara, with the remainder annexed by Mauritania. Spain had withdrawn in February. Polisario, a guerrilla movement, proclaimed the region independent Feb. 27, and launched attacks on Algerian support. Morocco accepted U.S. military and economic aid. When Mauritania signed a treaty with the Polisario Front, and gave up its portion of the former Spanish Sahara, Morocco occupied the area, 1980. Morocco accused Algeria of instigating Polisario attacks.

After years of bitter fighting, Morocco controls the main urban areas, but the Polisario Front's guerrillas move freely in the vast, sparsely populated deserts.

Mozambique

People's Republic of Mozambique

República Popular de Moçambique

People: Population (1989 est.): 15,259,000. **Age distrib.** (%): 0–14: 45.3; 15–59: 50.6; 60+: 4.1. **Pop. density:** 49 per sq. mi. **Ethnic groups:** Bantu tribes. **Languages:** Portuguese (official), Bantu languages predominate. **Religions:** Traditional beliefs 60%, Christian 30%, Moslem 10%.

Geography: Area: 309,494 sq. mi., about the size of Texas. **Location:** On SE coast of Africa. **Neighbors:** Tanzania on N, Malawi, Zambia, Zimbabwe on W, South Africa, Swaziland on S. **Topography:** Coastal lowlands comprise nearly half the country with plateaus rising in steps to the mountains along the western border. **Capital:** Maputo. **Cities** (1986 est.): Maputo 882,000.

Government: Type: Socialist one-party state. **Head of state:** Pres. Joaquim Chissano; b. Oct. 22, 1939; in office: Oct. 19,

1986. **Head of Goverment:** Mario de Graca Machungo; in office: July 17, 1986. **Local divisions:** 10 provinces. **Defense:** 38% of govt. budget (1986).

Economy: Industries: Cement, alcohol, textiles. **Chief crops:** Cashews, cotton, sugar, copra, tea. **Minerals:** Coal, bauxite. **Arable land:** 4%. **Livestock** (1985): cattle: 1.3 mln. **Fish catch** (1985): 37,000 metric tons. **Electricity prod.** (1986): 1.6 bln. kwh. **Labor force:** 85% agric., 9% ind. & comm., 2% services.

Finance: Currency: Metical (Jan. 1988: 403 = $1 US). **Gross national product** (1986): $1.3 bln. **Per capita income** (1983): $220. **Imports** (1986): $525 mln.; partners: So. Afr. 11%, U.S. 13%, USSR 12%. **Exports** (1986): $90 mln.; partners: U.S. 27%, Sp. 21%, Jap. 21%. **National budget** (1983): $640 mln.

Transport: Railway traffic (1986): 263 mln. passenger-km; 303 mln. net ton-km. **Motor vehicles:** in use (1981): 49,000 passenger cars, 24,700 comm. vehicles. **Chief ports:** Maputo, Beira, Nacala, Quelimane.

Communications: Television sets: 20,000 in use (1986). **Radios:** 500,000 licensed (1986). **Telephones in use** (1986): 61,000. **Daily newspaper circ.** (1986): 5 per 1,000 pop.

Health: Life expectancy at birth (1985): 47 years. **Births** (per 1,000 pop. 1985): 44.6. **Deaths** (per 1,000 pop. 1985): 17.2. **Natural increase** (1985): 2.7%. **Hospital beds** (1986): 12,270. **Physicians** (1986): 279. **Infant mortality** (per 1,000 live births 1985): 158.

Education (1985): **Literacy:** 14%.

Major International Organization: UN (IMF, World Bank), OAU.

The first Portuguese post on the Mozambique coast was established in 1505, on the trade route to the East. Mozambique became independent June 25, 1975, after a ten-year war against Portuguese colonial domination. The 1974 revolution in Portugal paved the way for the orderly transfer of power to Frelimo (Front for the Liberation of Mozambique). Frelimo took over local administration Sept. 20, 1974, over the opposition, in part violent, of some blacks and whites. The new government, led by Maoist Pres. Samora Machel, promised a gradual transition to a communist system. Private schools were closed, rural collective farms organized, and private homes nationalized. Economic problems included the emigration of most of the country's 160,000 whites, a politically untenable economic dependence on white-ruled South Africa, and a large external debt.

In the 1980s, severe drought and civil war caused famine and heavy loss of life.

Myanmar

People: Population (1989 est.): 39,893,000. **Age distrib.** (%): 0–14: 41.2; 15–59: 52.8; 60+: 6.0. **Pop. density:** 152 per sq. mi. **Urban** (1986): 24%. **Ethnic groups:** Burmans (related to Tibetans) 68%; Karen 4%, Shan 7%, Rakhine 3%. **Languages:** Burmese (official). **Religions:** Buddhist 85%; animist, Christian.

Geography: Area: 261,789 sq. mi., nearly as large as Texas. **Location:** Between S. and S.E. Asia, on Bay of Bengal. **Neighbors:** Bangladesh, India on W, China, Laos, Thailand on E. **Topography:** Mountains surround Myanmar on W, N, and E, and dense forests cover much of the nation. N-S rivers provide habitable valleys and communications, especially the Irrawaddy, navigable for 900 miles. The country has a tropical monsoon climate. **Capital:** Yangon. **Cities** (1983 est.): Yangon 2,458,712; Mandalay 458,000; Karbe ('73 cen.): 253,600; Moulmein 188,000.

Government: Type: Military. **Head of state and head of government:** Gen. Saw Maung; in office: Sept. 21, 1988. **Local divisions:** 7 states and 7 divisions. **Defense:** 3.0% of GNP (1985).

Economy: Chief crops: Rice, sugarcane, peanuts, beans. **Minerals:** Oil, lead, silver, tin, tungsten, precious stones. **Crude oil reserves** (1985): 733 mln. bbls. **Other resources:** Rubber, teakwood. **Arable land:** 15%. **Livestock.** (1988): cattle: 9.9 mln.; pigs: 3.1 mln. **Fish catch** (1987): 643,000 metric tons. **Electricity prod.** (1986): 1.7 bln. kwh. **Labor force:** 66% agric; 12% ind.

Finance: Currency: Kyat (Mar. 1989: 6.64 = $1 US). **Gross national product** (1985): $6.5 bln. **Per capita income** (1989): $210. **Imports** (1988): $244 mln.; partners: Jap. 50%, EEC 20%. **Exports** (1988): $138 mln.; partners: SE Asian countries 30%; EEC 12%. **Tourism** (1986): $14 mln. receipts. **National budget** (1986): $4.3 bln. **International reserves less gold** (Mar. 1989): $79.5 mln. **Gold:** 251,000 oz t. **Consumer prices** (change in 1988): 19%.

Transport: Railway traffic (1987): 3.1 bln. passenger-km; 552 mln. net ton-km. **Motor vehicles:** in use (1980): 43,000 passenger cars, 44,000 comm. vehicles. **Civil aviation** (1988): 214 mln. passenger-km.; 2.1 mln. net ton-km. **Chief ports:** Yangon, Sittwe, Bassein, Moulmein, Tavoy.

Communications: Television sets: 67,000 (1987), **Radios:** 800,000 in use (1986). **Telephones in use** (1987): 66,000. **Daily newspaper circ.** (1987): 14 per 1,000 pop.

Health: Life expectancy at birth (1987): 51.9 male; 55.0 female. **Births** (per 1,000 pop. 1987): 32.6. **Deaths** (per 1,000 pop. 1987): 13.2. **Natural increase** (1987): 1.9%. **Hospital beds** (1987): 26,839. **Physicians** (1987): 10,579. **Infant mortality** (per 1,000 live births 1986): 96.

Education (1989): **Literacy:** 66%. **Years compulsory:** 4; **Attendance:** 84%.

Major International Organizations: UN (World Bank, IMF, GATT).

Embassy: 2300 S St. NW 20008; 332-9044.

The Burmese arrived from Tibet before the 9th century, displacing earlier cultures, and a Buddhist monarchy was established by the 11th. Burma was conquered by the Mongol dynasty of China in 1272, then ruled by Shans as a Chinese tributary, until the 16th century.

Britain subjugated Burma in 3 wars, 1824-84, and ruled the country as part of India until 1937, when it became self-governing. Independence outside the Commonwealth was achieved Jan. 4, 1948.

Gen. Ne Win dominated politics from 1962 to 1988, when he abdicated power, following waves of anti-government demonstrations. He led a Revolutionary Council set up in 1962, which drove Indians from the civil service and Chinese from commerce. Socialization of the economy was advanced, isolation from foreign countries enforced.

In 1987 Burma, once the richest nation in SE Asia, was granted least developed country status by the UN. Following Ne Win's resignation, Sein Lwin and later Maung Maung, a civilian, took power but rioting and street violence continued. In Sept., Gen. Saw Maung, a close associate of Ne Win, seized power.

In 1989 the country's name was changed to Myanmar.

Nauru

Republic of Nauru

Naoero

People: Population (1989): 8,100. **Pop density:** 987 per sq. mi. **Ethnic groups:** Nauruans 57%, Pacific Islanders 26%, Chinese 8%, European 8%. **Languages:** Nauruan (official), English. **Religions:** Predominately Christian.

Geography: Area: 8 sq. mi. **Location:** In Western Pacific O. just S of Equator. **Neighbors:** Nearest are Solomon Is. **Topography:** Mostly a plateau bearing high grade phosphate deposits, surrounded by a coral cliff and a sandy shore in concentric rings. **Capital:** Yaren.

Government: Type: Republic. **Head of state:** Pres. Hammer DeRoburt, b. Sept. 25, 1922; in office: May 11, 1978. **Local divisions:** 14 districts.

Economy: Phosphate mining. **Electricity prod.** (1986): 48 mln. kwh.

Finance: Currency: Australian dollar. **Gross national product** (1984): $160 mln. **Per capita income** (1981): $21,400. **Imports** (1984): $14 mln. **Exports** (1984): $93 mln.

Communications: Radios: 4,000 in use (1985). **Telephones in use** (1980): 1,500.

Health: Births (per 1,000 pop. 1985): 21. **Deaths** (per 1,000 pop. 1985): 5. **Natural increase** (1985): 1.6%. **Infant mortality** (per 1,000 live births 1985): 26.

Education (1988): Literacy 99%; compulsory ages 6-16.

The island was discovered in 1798 by the British but was formally annexed to the German Empire in 1886. After World War I, Nauru became a League of Nations mandate administered by Australia. During World War II the Japanese occupied the island and shipped 1,200 Nauruans to the fortress island of Truk as slave laborers.

In 1947 Nauru was made a UN trust territory, administered by Australia. Nauru became an independent republic Jan. 31, 1968.

Phosphate exports provide one of the world's highest per capita revenues for the Nauru people. The deposits are expected to be nearly exhausted by 1990.

Nepal
Kingdom of Nepal
Sri Nepala Sarkar

People: Population (1989 est.): **18,760,000. Age distrib.** (%): 0–14: 42.2; 15–59: 52.9; 60+: 4.9. **Pop. density:** 334 per sq. mi. **Urban** (1985): 8%. **Ethnic groups:** The many tribes are descendants of Indian, Tibetan, and Central Asian migrants. **Languages:** Nepali (official) (an Indic language), 12 others. **Religions:** Hindu (official) 90%, Buddhist 7%.

Geography: Area: 56,136 sq. mi., the size of North Carolina. **Location:** Astride the Himalaya Mts. **Neighbors:** China on N, India on S. **Topography:** The Himalayas stretch across the N, the hill country with its fertile valleys extends across the center, while the southern border region is part of the flat, subtropical Ganges Plain. **Capital:** Kathmandu. **Cities** (1987 est.): Kathmandu 422,000, Pokhara, Biratnagar, Birganj.

Government: Type: Constitutional monarchy. **Head of state:** King Birendra Bir Bikram Shah Dev; b. Dec. 28, 1945; in office: Jan. 31, 1972. **Head of government:** Prime Min. Marich Man Singh Shrestha; in office: July 15, 1986. **Local divisions:** 14 zones; 75 districts. **Defense:** 1.2% of GNP (1985).

Economy: Industries: Sugar, jute mills, tourism. **Chief crops:** Jute, rice, grain. **Minerals:** Quartz. **Other resources:** Forests. **Arable land:** 17%. **Livestock** (1986): cattle: 7 mln. **Electricity prod.** (1986): 395 mln. kwh. **Labor force:** 91% agric.

Finance: Currency: Rupee (Mar. 1989: 26.20 = $1 US). **Gross national product** (1986): $2.4 bln. **Per capita income** (1986): $160. **Imports** (1987): $570 mln.; partners: India 47%, Jap. 25%. **Exports** (1987): $151 mln.; partners: India 68%. **Tourists** (1987): receipts: $55 mln. **National budget** (1987): $618 mln. **International reserves less gold** (Mar. 1989): $244 mln. **Gold:** 152,000 oz t. **Consumer prices** (change in 1987): 10.0%.

Transport: Civil aviation (1986): 300 mln. passenger-km. **Communications: Radios:** 2 mln. in use (1986). **Telephones in use** (1987): 25,000. **Daily newspaper circ.** (1985): 5 per 1,000 pop.

Health: Life expectancy at birth (1987): 53.9 male; 51.1 female. **Births** (per 1,000 pop. 1987): 40.4. **Deaths** (per 1,000 pop. 1987): 14.4. **Natural increase** (1987): 2.6%. **Hospital beds** (1987): 3,842. **Physicians** (1987): 863. **Infant mortality** (per 1,000 live births 1987): 106.

Education (1987): Literacy: 29%. **Years compulsory:** 3; Attendance: 79% primary, 22% secondary.
Major International Organizations: UN (IMF).
Embassy: 2131 Leroy Pl. NW 20008; 667-4550.

Nepal was originally a group of petty principalities, the inhabitants of one of which, the Gurkhas, became dominant about 1769. In 1951 King Tribhubana Bir Bikram, member of the Shah family, ended the system of rule by hereditary premiers of the Ranas family, who had kept the kings virtual prisoners, and established a cabinet system of government.

Virtually closed to the outside world for centuries, Nepal is now linked to India and Pakistan by roads and air service and to Tibet by road. Polygamy, child marriage, and the caste system were officially abolished in 1963.

Netherlands
Kingdom of the Netherlands
Konindrijk der Nederlanden

People: Population (1989 est.) 14,689,000. **Age distrib.** (%): 0–14: 18.8; 15–60: 64.2; 60+: 17.0. **Pop. density:** 931 per sq. mi. **Urban** (1987): 88.3%. **Ethnic groups:** Dutch 97%. **Languages:** Dutch. **Religions:** Roman Catholic 36%, Dutch Reformed 19.3%.

Geography: Area: 15,770 sq. mi., the size of Mass., Conn., and R.I. combined. **Location:** In NW Europe on North Sea. **To-**pography: The land is flat, an average alt. of 37 ft. above sea level, with much land below sea level reclaimed and protected by 1,500 miles of dikes. Since 1927 the government has been draining the IJsselmeer, formerly the Zuider Zee. By 1972, 410,000 of a planned 550,000 acres had been drained and reclaimed. **Capital:** Amsterdam. **Cities** (1987): Amsterdam 682,000; Rotterdam 572,100; Hague 443,500.

Government: Type: Parliamentary democracy under a constitutional monarch. **Head of state:** Queen Beatrix; b. Jan. 31, 1938; in office: Apr. 30, 1980. **Head of government:** Prime Min. Ruud Lubbers; in office: Nov. 4, 1982. **Seat of govt.:** The Hague. **Local divisions:** 12 provinces. **Defense:** 3.2% of GNP (1987).

Economy: Industries: Metals, machinery, chemicals, oil refinery, diamond cutting, electronics, tourism. **Chief crops:** Grains, potatoes, sugar beets, vegetables, fruits, flowers. **Minerals:** Natural gas, oil. **Crude oil reserves** (1987): 195 mln. bbls. **Arable land:** 26%. **Livestock** (1986): cattle: 5 mln.; pigs: 13.4 mln. **Fish catch** (1985): 480,000 metric tons. **Electricity prod.** (1986): 63.0 bln. kwh. **Crude steel prod.** (1987): 5.0 mln. metric tons. **Labor force:** 1% agric.; 47% ind. and commerce, 44% services, 15% govt.

Finance: Currency: Guilder (June 1989: 2.26 = $1 US). **Gross national product** (1987): $189.8 bln. **Per capita income** (1987): $13,065. **Imports** (1988): $99.4 bln.; partners: W. Ger. 22%, Belg. 11%, U.S. 9%, U.K. 9%. **Exports** (1988): $103.1 bln.; partners: W. Ger. 30%, Belg. 14%, Fr. 10%, UK 9%. **Tourists** (1986): receipts: $2.2 bln. **National budget** (1985): $49 bln. expenditures. **International reserves less gold** (Mar. 1989): $15.8 bln. **Gold:** 43.94 mln. oz t. **Consumer prices** (change in 1988): 0.8%.

Transport: Railway traffic (1986): 8.9 bln. passenger-km; 3.0 bln. net ton-km. **Motor vehicles:** in use (1986): 4.9 mln. passenger cars, 401,000 comm. vehicles. **Civil aviation** (1987): 27.7 bln. passenger-km; 5.0 bln. freight ton-km. **Chief ports:** Rotterdam, Amsterdam, IJmuiden.

Communications: Television sets: 4.6 mln. licensed (1987). **Radios:** 4.8 mln. licensed (1986). **Telephones in use** (1987): 6 mln. **Daily newspaper circ.** (1984): 312 per 1,000 pop.

Health: Life expectancy at birth (1986): 73 male; 79 female. **Births** (per 1,000 pop. 1986): 12.7 **Deaths** (per 1,000 pop. 1987): 8.6 **Natural increase** (1987): .4%. **Hospital beds** (1987): 67,545. **Physicians** (1987): 33,330. **Infant mortality** (per 1,000 live births 1986): 6.4

Education (1985): Literacy: 99%. **Years compulsory:** 10; attendance: 100%.
Major International Organizations: UN and all of its specialized agencies, NATO, EC, OECD.
Embassy: 4200 Linnean Ave. NW 20008; 244-5300.

Julius Caesar conquered the region in 55 BC, when it was inhabited by Celtic and Germanic tribes.

After the empire of Charlemagne fell apart, the Netherlands (Holland, Belgium, Flanders) split among counts, dukes and bishops, passed to Burgundy and thence to Charles V of Spain. His son, Philip II, tried to check the Dutch drive toward political freedom and Protestantism (1568-1573). William the Silent, prince of Orange, led a confederation of the northern provinces, called Estates, in the Union of Utrecht, 1579. The Estates retained individual sovereignty, but were represented jointly in the States-General, a body that had control of foreign affairs and defense. In 1581 they repudiated allegiance to Spain. The rise of the Dutch republic to naval, economic, and artistic eminence came in the 17th century.

The United Dutch Republic ended 1795 when the French formed the Batavian Republic. Napoleon made his brother Louis king of Holland, 1806; Louis abdicated 1810 when Napoleon annexed Holland. In 1813 the French were expelled. In 1815 the Congress of Vienna formed a kingdom of the Netherlands, including Belgium, under William I. In 1830, the Belgians seceded and formed a separate kingdom.

The constitution, promulgated 1814, and subsequently revised, assures a hereditary constitutional monarchy.

The Netherlands maintained its neutrality in World War I, but was invaded and brutally occupied by Germany from 1940 to 1945.

In 1949, after several years of fighting, the Netherlands granted independence to Indonesia, where it had ruled since the 17th century. In 1963, West New Guinea was turned over to Indonesia, after five years of controversy and seizure of Dutch property in Indonesia.

The independence of former Dutch colonies has instigated mass emigrations to the Netherlands, adding to problems of unemployment.

Though the Netherlands has been heavily industrialized, its productive small farms export large quantities of pork and dairy foods.

The Netherlands has agreed to allow NATO to deploy cruise missles on their soil.

Rotterdam, located along the principal mouth of the Rhine, handles the most cargo of any ocean port in the world. Canals, of which there are 3,478 miles, are important in transportation.

Netherlands Antilles

The **Netherlands Antilles,** constitutionally on a level of equality with the Netherlands homeland within the kingdom, consist of 2 groups of islands in the West Indies. **Curacao, Aruba, and Bonaire** are near the South American coast; **St. Eustatius, Saba,** and the southern part of **St. Maarten** are SE of Puerto Rico. Northern two-thirds of St. Maarten belong to French Guadeloupe; the French call the island St. Martin. Total area of the 2 groups is 385 sq. mi., including: Aruba 75, Bonaire 111, Curacao 171, St. Eustatius 11, Saba 5, St. Maarten (Dutch part) 13.

Aruba was separated from The Netherlands Antilles on Jan. 1, 1986; it is an autonomous member of The Netherlands, the same status as the Netherland Antilles.

Total pop. (est. 1989) was 187,000. Willemstad, on Curacao, is the capital. Chief products are corn, pulse, salt and phosphate; principal industry is the refining of crude oil from Venezuela. Tourism is an important industry, as are electronics and shipbuilding.

New Zealand

People: Population: (1989 est.): 3,397,000. **Age distrib.** (%): 0–14: 23.7, 15–59: 61.4; 60+: 14.9 **Pop. density:** 32 per sq. mi. **Urban** (1986): 84.0%. **Ethnic groups:** European (mostly British) 87%, Polynesian (mostly Maori) 9%. **Languages:** English (official), Maori. **Religions:** Anglican 29%, Presbyterian 18%, Roman Catholic 15%, others.

Geography: Area: 103,736 sq. mi., the size of Colorado. **Location:** In SW Pacific O. **Neighbors:** Nearest are Australia on W, Fiji, Tonga on N. **Topography:** Each of the 2 main islands (North and South Is.) is mainly hilly and mountainous. The east coasts consist of fertile plains, especially the broad Canterbury Plains on South Is. A volcanic plateau is in center of North Is. South Is. has glaciers and 15 peaks over 10,000 ft. **Capital:** Wellington. **Cities** (1987 est.): Auckland 149,000; Christchurch 168,000; Wellington 137,000; Manukau 181,000.

Government: Type: Parliamentary. **Head of state:** Queen Elizabeth II, represented by Gov.-Gen. Paul Reeves. **Head of government:** Prime Min. David Lange; b. Aug. 4, 1942; elected: July 14, 1984. **Local divisions:** 90 counties, 128 boroughs, 10 towns & districts. **Defense:** 1.9% of GNP (1985).

Economy: Industries: Food processing, textiles, machinery, fish, forest prods. **Chief crops:** Grain. **Minerals:** Oil, gas, iron, coal **Crude oil reserves** (1987); 182 mln. bbls. **Other resources:** Wool, timber. **Arable land:** 2%. **Livestock** (1987): cattle: 8.2 mln.; sheep: 64 mln. **Fish catch** (1986): 339,000 metric tons. **Electricity prod.** (1986): 27.0 bln. kwh. **Labor force:** 11% agric. & mining; 21% ind. and commerce, 66% services and gov.

Finance: Currency: Dollar (May 1989: 1.68 = $1 US). **Gross national product** (1986): $23.2 bln. **Per capita income** (1986): $7,282. **Imports** (1988): $7.3 bln.; partners: Austral. 18%, U.S. 16%, Jap. 20%. **Exports** (1988): $8.8 bln.; partners: UK 9%, U.S. 15%, Jap. 15%, Austral. 16%. **Tourists** (1987): receipts $286 mln. **National budget** (1985): $7.4 bln. **International reserves less gold** (Feb. 1989): $2.8 bln. **Gold:** 22,000 oz t. **Consumer prices** (change in 1988): 6.4%.

Transport: Railway traffic (1986): 458 mln. passenger-km; 3.1 bln. net ton-km. **Motor vehicles:** in use (1987): 1.5 mln. passenger cars; 334,000 comm. vehicles. **Civil aviation:** (1987): 9.0 bln. passenger-km, 354 mln. freight ton-km. **Chief ports:** Auckland, Wellington, Lyttleton, Tauranga.

Communications: Television sets: 940,000 in use (1986). **Radios:** 2.8 mln. in use (1986). **Telephones in use** (1987): 2.2 mln. **Daily newspaper circ.** (1985): 323 per 1,000 pop.

Health: Life expectancy at birth (1987): 71.8 male; 77.8 female. **Births** (per 1,000 pop. 1987): 16.7. **Deaths** (per 1,000 pop. 1987): 8.3. **Natural increase** (1987): .8%. **Hospital beds**

(1987): 30,708. **Physicians** (1987): 8,312. **Infant mortality** (per 1,000 live births 1985): 10.

Education (1987): **Literacy:** 99%. Compulsory ages 6-15; attendance: 100%.

Major International Organizations: UN (GATT, World Bank, IMF), Commonwealth of Nations, OECD.

Embassy: 37 Observatory Cir. NW 20008; 328-4800.

The Maoris, a Polynesian group from the eastern Pacific, reached New Zealand before and during the 14th century. The first European to sight New Zealand was Dutch navigator Abel Janszoon Tasman, but Maoris refused to allow him to land. British Capt. James Cook explored the coasts, 1769-1770.

British sovereignty was proclaimed in 1840, with organized settlement beginning in the same year. Representative institutions were granted in 1853. Maori Wars ended in 1870 with British victory. The colony became a dominion in 1907, and is an independent member of the Commonwealth.

New Zealand fought on the side of the Allies in both world wars, and signed the ANZUS Treaty of Mutual Security with the U.S. and Australia in 1951. New Zealand's refusal to allow U.S. ships with nuclear weapons to use their port facilities caused an end to the alliance in 1986. New Zealand joined with Australia and Britain in a pact to defend Singapore and Malaysia.

In July 1985, the *Rainbow Warrior*, flagship of the Greenpeace organization, was bombed and sunk in Auckland harbour by French secret service agents.

A labor tradition in politics dates back to the 19th century. Private ownership is basic to the economy, but state ownership or regulation affects many industries. Transportation, broadcasting, mining, and forestry are largely state-owned.

The native Maoris number about 250,000. Four of 92 members of the House of Representatives are elected directly by the Maori people.

New Zealand comprises **North Island,** 44,035 sq. mi.; **South Island,** 58,304 sq. mi.; **Stewart Island,** 674 sq. mi.; **Chatham Islands,** 372 sq. mi.

In 1965, the **Cook Islands** (pop. 1983 est., 16,900; area 93 sq. mi.) became self-governing although New Zealand retains responsibility for defense and foreign affairs. **Niue** attained the same status in 1974; it lies 400 mi. to W (pop. 1981 est., 3,400; area 100 sq. mi.). **Tokelau Is.,** (pop. 1981 est., 1,600; area 4 sq. mi.) are 300 mi. N of Samoa.

Ross Dependency, administered by New Zealand since 1923, comprises 160,000 sq. mi. of Antarctic territory.

Nicaragua

Republic of Nicaragua

Republica de Nicaragua

People: Population: (1989 est.): 3,692,000. **Age distrib.** (%): 0–14: 46.6; 15–59: 49.3; 60+: 4.1. **Pop. density:** 73 per sq. mi. **Urban** (1986): 58%. **Ethnic groups:** Mestizo 69%, Caucasian 17%, black 9%, Indian 5%. **Languages:** Spanish, (official), English (on Caribbean coast). **Religion:** Roman Catholic 95%.

Geography: Area: 50,193 sq. mi., about the size of Iowa. **Location:** In Central America. **Neighbors:** Honduras on N, Costa Rica on S. **Topography:** Both Atlantic and Pacific coasts are over 200 mi. long. The Cordillera Mtns., with many volcanic peaks, runs NW-SE through the middle of the country. Between this and a volcanic range to the E lie Lakes Managua and Nicaragua. **Capital:** Managua. **Cities** (1986): Managua 1 mln.

Government: Type: Republic. **Head of Government:** Daniel Ortega Saavedra; in office Jan. 10, 1985. **Local divisions:** 16 departments. **Defense:** 16.8% of GNP (1985).

Economy: Industries: Oil refining, food processing, chemicals, textiles. **Chief crops:** Bananas, cotton, fruit, yucca, coffee, sugar, corn, beans, cocoa, rice, sesame, tobacco, wheat. **Minerals:** Gold, silver, copper, tungsten. **Other resources:** Forests, shrimp. **Arable land:** 10%. **Livestock** (1986): cattle: 2.1 mln.; pigs: 750,000. **Fish catch:** (1986): 2,400 metric tons. **Electricity prod.** (1986): 1.2 bln. kwh. **Labor force:** 41% agric.; 13% ind.; 46% services.

Finance: Currency: Cordoba (June 1989: 20,000 = $1 US). **Gross national product** (1986): $2.6 bln. **Per capita income** (1985): $868. **Imports** (1987): $923 mln.; partners Comecon, CACM, EC. **Exports** (1987): $300 mln.; partners EC, Japan, Comecon. **National budget** (1984): $1.4 bln. expenditures. **Consumer prices** (change in 1988): 10,205%.

Transport: Railway traffic (1986): 25.5 mln. passenger-miles; 68 mln. net ton-miles. **Motor vehicles:** in use (1986): 46,000 passenger cars, 30,000 comm. vehicles. **Chief ports:** Corinto, Puerto Somoza, San Juan del Sur.

Communications: Television sets: 175,000 in use (1987). **Radios:** 300,000 in use (1986). **Telephones in use** (1984): 51,000. **Daily newspaper circ.** (1987): 62 per 1,000 pop.

Health: Life expectancy at birth (1985): 58.7 male; 61.0 female. **Births** (per 1,000 pop. 1985): 44. **Deaths** (per 1,000 pop. 1985): 9. **Natural increase** (1985): 3.5%. **Hospital beds** (1985): 5,083. **Physicians** (1985): 2,172. **Infant mortality** (per 1,000 live births 1986): 37.0.

Education (1986): **Literacy:** 66%. **Years compulsory:** 11 years or 16 years old.

Major International Organizations: UN and all of its specialized agencies, OAS.

Embassy: 1627 New Hampshire Ave. NW 20009; 387-4371.

Nicaragua, inhabited by various Indian tribes, was conquered by Spain in 1552. After gaining independence from Spain, 1821, Nicaragua was united for a short period with Mexico, then with the United Provinces of Central America, finally becoming an independent republic, 1838.

U.S. Marines occupied the country at times in the early 20th century, the last time from 1926 to 1933.

Gen. Anastasio Somoza-Debayle was elected president 1967. He resigned 1972, but was elected president again in 1974. Martial law was imposed in Dec. 1974, after officials were kidnapped by the Marxist Sandinista guerrillas. The country's Roman Catholic bishops charged in 1977 that the government had mistreated civilians in its anti-guerrilla campaign. Violent opposition spread to nearly all classes, 1978; a nationwide strike called against the government Aug. 25 touched off a state of civil war at Matagalpa.

Months of simmering civil war erupted when Sandinist guerrillas invaded Nicaragua May 29, 1979, touching off a 7-week-offensive that culminated in the resignation and exile of Somoza, July 17.

Relations with the U.S. have been strained due to Nicaragua's military aid to leftist guerrillas in El Salvador and the U.S. backing anti-Sandinista contra guerrilla groups. Nicaragua accused the U.S. CIA of directing the mining of its ports, Apr. 6, 1984. It asked the International Court of Justice in The Hague to order the U.S. to halt the mining and cease aiding attacks on its territory. The Court ruled, May 10, that the U.S. should immediately halt any actions to blockade or mine Nicaragua's ports.

In 1983, Nicaragua accused the U.S. of aiding anti-Sandinista contras who were invading from Honduras. The charge sparked a debate in the U.S. Congress over funds for covert aid to the contras. In 1985, the U.S. House rejected Pres. Reagan's request for military aid to the contras; but in June voted to provide $27 mln. in humanitarian aid.

In June 1986, the House approved $100 mln. in aid for the contras. It was the first time that the House had granted overt military aid to the contras. The diversion of funds to the contras from the proceeds of a secret arms sale to Iran caused a major scandal in the U.S. The plan, masterminded by the administration's national security advisor and his deputy, took place at a time when military aid to the contras was forbidden by law.

Cease-fire talks between the Sandinista government and the contras were held in 1988. Elections were scheduled for Feb. 1990.

Niger
Republic of Niger
République du Niger

People: Population (1989 est.): 7,440,000. **Age distrib. (%):** 0–14: 46.7; 15–59: 48.5; 60+: 4.8. **Pop. density:** 15 per sq. mi. **Urban** (1988): 21%. **Ethnic groups:** Hausa 56%, Djerma 22%, Fulani 8%, Tuareg 8%. **Languages:** French (official), Hausa, Djerma. **Religions:** Sunni Moslem 80%.

Geography: Area: 489,189 sq. mi., almost 3 times the size of California. **Location:** In the interior of N. Africa. **Neighbors:** Libya, Algeria on N, Mali, Burkina Faso on W, Benin, Nigeria on S, Chad on E. **Topography:** Mostly arid desert and mountains. A narrow savanna in the S and the Niger R. basin in the SW contain most of the population. **Capital:** Niamey. **Cities** (1987 est.): Niamey 350,000.

Government: Type: Republic; military in power. **Head of state:** Col. Ali Seibou; in office: Nov. 10, 1987. **Head of government:** Prime Min. Mamane Oumarou; in office: July 15, 1988. **Local divisions:** 7 departments. **Defense:** 0.8% of GNP (1985).

Economy: Chief crops: Peanuts, cotton. **Minerals:** Uranium, coal, iron. **Arable land:** 3%. **Livestock** (1986): cattle: 3.5 mln.; sheep 505,000. **Electricity prod.** (1985): 51 mln. kwh. **Labor force:** 90% agric.

Finance: Currency: CFA franc (Mar. 1989: 319 = $1 US). **Gross domestic product** (1986): $1.6 bln. **Per capita income** (1984) : $200. **Imports** (1985): $354 mln.; partners: Fr. 36%, Nig. 13%. **Exports** (1985): $251 mln.; partners: Fr. 36%, Nig. 17%. **National budget** (1986): $317 mln. **International reserves less gold** (Jan. 1989): $232 mln. **Gold:** 11,000 oz t. **Consumer prices** (change in 1988): −1.4%.

Transport: Motor vehicles: in use (1984): 23,000 passenger cars, 9,500 comm. vehicles.

Communications: Television sets: 25,000 (1986). **Radios:** 300,000 in use (1986). **Telephones in use** (1985): 11,000. **Daily newspaper cir.** (1986): 1 per 1,000 pop.

Health: Life expectancy at birth (1987): 44 years. **Births** (per 1,000 pop. 1985): 51.0. **Deaths** (per 1,000 pop. 1985): 22.9. **Natural increase** (1985): 2.8%. **Health** (1982): 2 hospitals, 36 medical centers. **Infant mortality** (per 1,000 live births 1986): 145.

Education (1987): **Literacy:** 13%. **Years compulsory:** 6; attendance: 15%.

Major International Organizations: UN (GATT, IMF, WHO, FAO), OAU.

Embassy: 2204 R St. NW 20008; 483-4224.

Niger was part of ancient and medieval African empires. European explorers reached the area in the late 18th century. The French colony of Niger was established 1900-22, after the defeat of Tuareg fighters, who had invaded the area from the N a century before. The country became independent Aug. 3, 1960. The next year it signed a bilateral agreement with France retaining close economic and cultural ties, which have continued. Hamani Diori, Niger's first president, was ousted in a 1974 coup. Drought and famine struck in 1973-74, and again in 1975.

Nigeria
Federal Republic of Nigeria

People: Population (1989 est.): 115,152,000. **Pop. density:** 322 per sq. mi. **Urban** (1985): 23%. **Ethnic groups:** Hausa 21%, Yoruba 20%, Ibo 17%, Fulani 9%, others. **Languages:** English (official), Hausa, Yoruba, Ibo. **Religions:** Moslem 50% (in N), Christian 40% (in S), others.

Geography: Area: 356,667 sq. mi., more than twice the size of California. **Location:** On the S coast of W. Africa. **Neighbors:** Benin on W, Niger on N, Chad, Cameroon on E. **Topography:** 4 E-W regions divide Nigeria: a coastal mangrove swamp 10-60 mi. wide, a tropical rain forest 50-100 mi. wide, a plateau of savanna and open woodland, and semidesert in the N. **Capital:** Lagos. **Cities:** (1988): Lagos 1,243,000; Ibadan 1,172,000.

Government: Type: Military. **Head of state:** Gen. Ibrahim Babangida; b. Aug. 17, 1941; in office: Aug. 30, 1985. **Local divisions:** 21 states plus federal capital territory. **Defense:** 8.2% of govt. budget (1986).

Economy: Industries: Crude oil (95% of export), food processing, assembly of vehicles, textiles. **Chief crops:** Cocoa (main export crop), tobacco, palm products, peanuts, cotton, soybeans. **Minerals:** Oil, gas, coal, iron, limestone, columbium, tin. **Crude oil reserves** (1987): 16.8 bln. bbls. **Other resources:** Timber, rubber, hides. **Arable land:** 34%. **Livestock** (1987): cattle: 12.1 mln.; goats: 26.3 mln.; sheep: 13.1 mln. **Fish catch** (1987): 268,000 metric tons. **Electricity prod.** (1986): 10.7 bln. kwh. **Labor force:** 54% agric., 19% ind., comm. and serv.

Finance: Currency: Naira (Feb. 1989: 1.00 = $.13 US). **Gross national product** (1986): $66.2 bln. **Per capita income** (1984): $790. **Imports** (1987): $7.8 bln.; partners: U.S., EC. **Exports** (1987): $7.3 bln.; partners: U.S., EC. **Tourist receipts** (1986): $125 mln. **National budget** (1986): $15.6 bln. **International reserves less gold** (Jan. 1989): $651 mln. **Gold:** 687,000 oz t. **Consumer prices** (change in 1987): 10.2%.

Transport: Motor vehicles: in use (1981): 262,000 passenger cars, 90,000 comm. vehicles. **Civil aviation** (1986): 2.2 bln.

passenger-km; 44 mln. freight ton-km. **Chief ports:** Port Harcourt, Lagos, Warri, Calabar.

Communications: Television sets: 2 mln. (1987). **Radios:** 15 mln. (1986). **Telephones in use** (1986): 265,000. **Daily newspaper circ.** (1987): 12 per 1,000 pop.

Health: Life expectancy at birth (1983): 48.3 male; 51.7 female. **Births** (per 1,000 pop. 1985): 46. **Deaths** (per 1,000 pop. 1985): 18. **Natural increase** (1985): 2.8%. **Hospital beds** (1983): 60,840. **Physicians** (1983): 11,294. **Infant mortality** (per 1,000 live births 1985): 127.

Education (1987): **Literacy:** 42%. **Primary school attendance:** 42%.

Major International Organizations: UN (GATT, IMO, WHO), OPEC, OAU, Commonwealth of Nations.

Embassy: 2201 M St. NW 20037; 822-1500.

Early cultures in Nigeria date back to at least 700 BC. From the 12th to the 14th centuries, more advanced cultures developed in the Yoruba area, at Ife, and in the north, where Moslem influence prevailed.

Portuguese and British slavers appeared from the 15th-16th centuries. Britain seized Lagos, 1861, during an anti-slave trade campaign, and gradually extended control inland until 1900. Nigeria became independent Oct. 1, 1960, and a republic Oct. 1, 1963.

On May 30, 1967, the Eastern Region seceded, proclaiming itself the Republic of Biafra, plunging the country into civil war. Casualties in the war were est. at over 1 million, including many "Biafrans" (mostly Ibos) who died of starvation despite international efforts to provide relief. The secessionists, after steadily losing ground, capitulated Jan. 12, 1970. Within a few years, the Ibos were reintegrated into national life, but mistrust among the regions persists.

Oil revenues have made possible a massive economic development program, largely using private enterprise, but agriculture has lagged. Oil revenues continued to decline in 1987.

After 13 years of military rule, the nation experienced a peaceful return to civilian government, Oct., 1979.

Military rule returned to Nigeria, Dec. 31, 1983 as a coup ousted the democratically-elected government. The government has promised a return to democracy by 1992.

Norway
Kingdom of Norway
Kongeriket Norge

People: Population (1989 est.): 4,204,000. **Age distrib. (%):** 0–14: 19.4; 15–59: 59.3; 60+: 21.3. **Pop. density:** 33 per sq. mi. **Urban** (1985): 80%. **Ethnic groups:** Germanic (Nordic, Alpine, Baltic), minority Lapps. **Languages:** Norwegian (official), Lappish. **Religions:** Evangelical Lutheran 94%.

Geography: Area: 125,181 sq. mi., slightly larger than New Mexico. **Location:** Occupies the W part of Scandinavian peninsula in NW Europe (extends farther north than any European land). **Neighbors:** Sweden, Finland, USSR on E. **Topography:** A highly indented coast is lined with tens of thousands of islands. Mountains and plateaus cover most of the country, which is only 25% forested. **Capital:** Oslo. **Cities** (1988): Oslo 449,000; Bergen 207,000.

Government: Type: Hereditary constitutional monarchy. **Head of state:** King Olav V, b. July 2, 1903; in office: Sept. 21, 1957. **Head of government:** Prime Min. Gro Harlem Brundtland; b. April. 20, 1939; in office: May, 2, 1986. **Local divisions:** Oslo, Svalbard and 18 fylker (counties). **Defense:** 3.2% of GNP (1985).

Economy: Industries: Paper, shipbuilding, engineering, metals, chemicals, food processing oil, gas. **Chief crops:** Grains, potatoes, fruits. **Minerals:** Oil, copper, pyrites, nickel, iron, zinc, lead. **Crude oil reserves** (1987): 11.1 bln. bbls. **Other resources:** Timber. **Arable land:** 3%. **Livestock** (1986): sheep: 2.3 mln.; cattle: 967,000; pigs: 837,000. **Fish catch** (1986): 1.8 mln. metric tons. **Electricity prod.** (1986): 96.3 bln. kwh. **Crude steel prod.** (1987): 900,000 metric tons. **Labor force:** 7% agric.; 47% ind., banking, comm.; 18% services, 26% govt.

Finance: Currency: Kroner (May 1989: 7.22 = $1 US). **Gross national product** (1986): $64.4 bln. **Per capita income** (1984): $13,790. **Imports** (1988): $23.1 mln.; partners: Swed. 17%, W. Ger. 16%, UK 10%, U.S. 9%. **Exports** (1988): $22.0

bln.; partners: UK 27%, W. Ger. 17%, Swed. 9%. **Tourists** (1987): receipts: $1.2 bln. **National budget** (1986): $32.5 bln. expenditures. **International reserves less gold** (Mar. 1989): $13.7 bln. **Gold:** 1.18 mln. oz t. **Consumer prices** (change in 1988): 6.7%.

Transport: Railway traffic (1986): 2.2 bln. passenger-km; 2.9 bln. net ton-km. **Motor vehicles:** in use (1986): 1.5 mln. passenger cars, 282,000 comm. vehicles. **Civil aviation:** (1987): 8.8 bln. passenger-km; 908 mln. net ton-km. **Chief ports:** Bergen, Stavanger, Oslo, Tonsberg.

Communications: Television sets: 1.4 mln. licensed (1987). **Radios:** 1.5 mln. in use (1986) **Telephones in use** (1985): 2.5 mln. **Daily newspaper circ.** (1986): 482 per 1,000 pop.

Health: Life expectancy at birth (1986): 72.7 male; 79.5 female. **Births** (per 1,000 pop. 1987): 13.0. **Deaths** (per 1,000 pop. 1987): 10.7. **Natural increase** (1987): .2%. **Hospital beds** (1986): 24,951. **Physicians** (1986): 10,110. **Infant mortality** (per 1,000 live births 1986): 7.8.

Education (1987): **Literacy:** 100%. **Years Compulsory:** 9.

Major International Organizations: UN and all of its specialized agencies, NATO, OECD.

Embassy: 2720 34th St. NW 20008; 333-6000.

The first supreme ruler of Norway was Harald the Fairhaired who came to power in 872 AD. Between 800 and 1000, Norway's Vikings raided and occupied widely dispersed parts of Europe.

The country was united with Denmark 1381-1814, and with Sweden, 1814-1905. In 1905, the country became independent with Prince Charles of Denmark as king.

Norway remained neutral during World War I. Germany attacked Norway Apr. 9, 1940, and held it until liberation May 8, 1945. The country abandoned its neutrality after the war, and joined the NATO alliance. Norway rejected membership in the Common Market in a 1972 referendum.

Abundant hydroelectric resources provided the base for Norway's industrialization, producing one of the highest living standards in the world.

Norway's merchant marine is one of the world's largest.

Norway and the Soviet Union have disputed their territorial waters boundary in the Barents Sea, north of the 2 countries' common border.

Petroleum output from oil and mineral deposits under the continental shelf has raised state revenues.

Svalbard is a group of mountainous islands in the Arctic O., c. 23,957 sq. mi., pop. varying seasonally from 1,500 to 3,600. The largest, Spitsbergen (formerly called West Spitsbergen), 15,060 sq. mi., seat of governor, is about 370 mi. N of Norway. By a treaty signed in Paris, 1920, major European powers recognized the sovereignty of Norway, which incorporated it in 1925. Both Norway and the USSR mine rich coal deposits. Mt. Newton (Spitsbergen) is 5,633 ft. tall.

Oman
Sultanate of Oman
Saltanat 'Uman

People: Population (1989 est.): 1,389,000. **Pop. density:** 16 per sq. mi. **Urban** (1986): 9%. **Ethnic groups:** Arab 88%, Baluchi 4%, Persian 3%, Indian 2%, African 2%. **Languages:** Arabic (official), English, Urdu, others. **Religions:** Ibadhi Moslem 75%, Sunni Moslem.

Geography: Area: 82,030 sq. mi., about the size of New Mexico. **Location:** On SE coast of Arabian peninsula. **Neighbors:** United Arab Emirates, Saudi Arabia, South Yemen on W. **Topography:** Oman has a narrow coastal plain up to 10 mi. wide, a range of barren mountains reaching 9,900 ft. and a wide, stony, mostly waterless plateau, avg. alt. 1,000 ft. Also the tip of the Ruus-al-Jebal peninsula controls access to the Persian Gulf. **Capital:** Muscat. **Cities** (1982 est.): Muscat 85,000.

Government: Type: Absolute monarchy. **Head of state:** Sultan Qabus bin Said; b. Nov. 18, 1942; in office: July 23, 1970. **Local divisions:** 1 province, numerous districts. **Defense:** 24% of GNP (1985).

Economy: Chief crops: Dates, fruits vegetables, wheat, bananas. **Minerals:** Oil (95% of exports). **Crude oil reserves** (1987): 4.5 bln. bbls. **Fish catch** (1986): 96,000 metric tons. **Electricity prod.** (1986): 2.9 bln. kwh. **Labor force:** 80% agric. & fishing.

Finance: Currency: Rial Omani (Mar. 1989: .38 = $1 US). Gross national product (1986): $6.4 bln. Imports (1987): $1.8 bln.; partners: Jap. 21%, UAE 17%, UK 14%. Exports (1987): $3.4 bln.; partners: Jap. 58%, Europe 30%. National budget (1985): $4.4 bln. revenues; $5.4 bln. expenditures. International reserves less gold (Mar. 1989): $1.0 bln. Gold: 289,000 oz t.

Transport: Chief ports: Matrah, Muscat.

Communications: Television sets: 400,000 in use (1986). Radios: 500,000 in use (1986). Telephones in use (1986): 41,000.

Health: Life expectancy at birth (1986): 53.7 male; 56.0 female. Hospital beds (1986): 2,861; Physicians (1986): 581. Infant Mortality (per 1,000 live births 1986): 110.5

Education (1986): Literacy: 20%. Attendance: 60% primary, 10% secondary.

Major International Organizations: UN (World Bank, IMF), Arab League.

Embassy: 2342 Massachusetts Ave. NW 20008; 387-1980.

A long history of rule by other lands, including Portugal in the 16th century, ended with the ouster of the Persians in 1744. By the early 19th century, Muscat and Oman was one of the most important countries in the region, controlling much of the Persian and Pakistan coasts, and ruling far-away Zanzibar, which was separated in 1861 under British mediation.

British influence was confirmed in a 1951 treaty, and Britain helped suppress an uprising by traditionally rebellious interior tribes against control by Muscat in the 1950s. Enclaves on the Pakistan coast were sold to that country in 1958.

On July 23, 1970, Sultan Said bin Taimur was overthrown by his son. The new sultan changed the nation's name to Sultanate of Oman. He launched a domestic development program, and battled leftist rebels in the southern Dhofar area to their defeat, Dec. 1975.

Oil has been the major source of income. Oman has close political ties to the U.S. and established diplomatic relations with the USSR in 1985.

Pakistan
Islamic Republic of Pakistan

People: Population (1989 est.): 110,358,000. Pop. density: 335 per sq. mi. Urban (1985): 30%. Ethnic groups: Punjabi 66%, Sindhi 13%, Pushtun (Iranian) 8.5%, Urdu 7.6%, Baluchi 2.5%, others. Languages: Urdu, English are both official. Religions: Moslem 97%.

Geography: Area: 310,403 sq. mi., about the size of Texas. Location: In W part of South Asia. Neighbors: Iran on W, Afghanistan, China on N, India on E. Topography: The Indus R. rises in the Hindu Kush and Himalaya mtns. in the N (highest is K2, or Godwin Austen, 28,250 ft., 2d highest in world), then flows over 1,000 mi. through fertile valley and empties into Arabian Sea. Thar Desert, Eastern Plains flank Indus Valley. Capital: Islamabad. Cities (1981 cen.): Karachi 5.1 mln.; Lahore 2.9 mln.; Faisalabad 1 mln.; Hyderabad 795,000; Rawalpindi 928,000.

Government: Type: Parliamentary democracy in a federal setting. Head of government: Pres. Ishaq Khan; in office: Dec. 12, 1988. Head of state: Prime Min. Benazir Bhutto; in office: Dec. 2, 1988. Local divisions: Federal capital, 4 provinces, tribal areas. Defense: 6.4% of GNP (1985).

Economy: Industries: Textiles, food processing, chemicals, tobacco, Chief crops: Rice, wheat. Minerals: Natural gas, iron ore. Crude oil reserves (1987): 116 mln. bbls. Other resources: Wool. Arable land: 26%. Livestock (1986): cattle: 16.7 mln.; sheep: 26.6 mln.; goats: 31.9 mln. Fish catch (1985): 399,000 metric tons. Electricity prod. (1986): 22.5 bln. kwh. Labor force: 53% agric.; 19% ind; 28% services.

Finance: Currency: Rupee (June 1989: 20.70 = $1 US). Gross national product (1986): $32 bln. Per capita income (1984): $360. Imports (1988): $6.5 bln.; partners: Sau. Ar. 5%, Jap. 16%, U.S. 11%, Kuwait 7%. Exports (1988): $4.5 bln.; partners: Jap. 10%, U.S. 10%. Tourist (1986): $180 mln. receipts. National budget (1987): $7.2 bln. International reserves less gold (Mar. 1989): $597 mln. Gold: 1.94 mln. oz t. Consumer prices (change in 1988): 10.4%.

Transport: Railway traffic (1987): 16.9 bln. passenger-km; 7.8 bln. net ton-km. Motor vehicles: in use (1986): 500,000 passenger cars, 154,000 comm. vehicles. Civil aviation (1986): 7 bln. passenger-km; 309 mln. freight ton-km. Chief ports: Karachi.

Communications: Television sets: 1.4 mln. in use (1987). Radios: 5.2 mln. in use (1986). Telephones in use (1986): 583,000. Daily newspaper circ. (1986): 22 per 1,000 pop.

Health: Life expectancy at birth (1987): 53.7 male; 51.9 female. Births (per 1,000 pop. 1987): 41.9 Deaths (per 1,000 pop. 1987): 14.1. Natural increase 1987: 2.7%. Hospital beds (1987): 60,000. Physicians (1987): 51,000. Infant mortality (per 1,000 live births 1985): 125.

Education (1985): Literacy: 26%.

Major International Organizations: UN (GATT, ILO, IMF, WHO).

Embassy: 2315 Massachusetts Ave. NW 20008; 939-6200.

Present-day Pakistan shares the 5,000-year history of the India-Pakistan sub-continent. At present day Harappa and Mohenjo Daro, the Indus Valley Civilization, with large cities and elaborate irrigation systems, flourished c. 4,000-2,500 BC.

Aryan invaders from the NW conquered the region around 1,500 BC, forging a Hindu civilization that dominated Pakistan as well as India for 2,000 years.

Beginning with the Persians in the 6th century BC, and continuing with Alexander the Great and with the Sassanians, successive nations to the west ruled or influenced Pakistan, eventually separating the area from the Indian cultural sphere.

The first Arab invasion, 712 AD, introduced Islam. Under the Mogul empire (1526-1857), Moslems ruled most of India, yielding to British encroachment and resurgent Hindus.

After World War I the Moslems of British India began agitation for minority rights in elections. Mohammad Ali Jinnah (1876-1948) was the principal architect of Pakistan. A leader of the Moslem League from 1916, he worked for dominion status for India; from 1940 he advocated a separate Moslem state.

When the British withdrew Aug. 14, 1947, the Islamic majority areas of India acquired self-government as Pakistan, with dominion status in the Commonwealth. Pakistan was divided into 2 sections, West Pakistan and East Pakistan. The 2 areas were nearly 1,000 mi. apart on opposite sides of India.

Pakistan became a republic in 1956. Pakistan had a National Assembly (legislature) with equal membership from East and West Pakistan, and 2 Provincial Assemblies. In Oct. 1958, Gen. Mohammad Ayub Khan took power in a coup. He was elected president in 1960, reelected in 1965.

As a member of the Central Treaty Organization, Pakistan had been aligned with the West. Following clashes between India and China in 1962, Pakistan made commercial and aid agreements with China.

Ayub resigned Mar. 25, 1969, after several months of violent rioting and unrest, most of it in East Pakistan, which demanded autonomy. The government was turned over to Gen. Agha Mohammad Yahya Khan and martial law was declared.

The Awami League, which sought regional autonomy for East Pakistan, won a majority in Dec. 1970 elections to a National Assembly which was to write a new constitution. In March, 1971 Yahya postponed the Assembly. Rioting and strikes broke out in the East.

On Mar. 25, 1971, government troops launched attacks in the East. The Easterners, aided by India, proclaimed the independent nation of Bangladesh. In months of widespread fighting, countless thousands were killed. Some 10 million Easterners fled into India.

Full scale war between India and Pakistan had spread to both the East and West fronts by December 3. Pakistan troops in the East surrendered Dec. 16; Pakistan agreed to a cease-fire in the West Dec. 17. On July 3, 1972, Pakistan and India signed a pact agreeing to withdraw troops from their borders and seek peaceful solutions to all problems. Diplomatic relations were resumed in 1976.

Zulfikar Ali Bhutto, leader of the Pakistan People's Party, which had won the most West Pakistan votes in the Dec. 1970 elections, became president Dec. 20.

Bhutto was overthrown in a military coup July, 1977. Convicted of complicity in a 1974 political murder, Bhutto was executed Apr.4, 1979. Benazir Bhutto, his daughter, returned to Pakistan from exile in 1986. Her efforts to relaunch the Pakistan People's Party sparked violence and antigovernment riots.

Pres. Mohammad Zia ul-Haq was killed when his plane exploded in Aug. 1988. Following Nov. elections, Benazir Bhutto was named Prime Minister, the first woman leader of a Moslem nation.

There are several million Afghan refugees now in Pakistan.

Panama

Republic of Panama
República de Panamá

People: Population (1989 est.): 2,370,000. **Age distrib. (%):** 0–14: 37.0; 15–59: 56.3; 60+: 6.7. **Pop. density:** 81 per sq. mi. **Urban** (1985): 53%. **Ethnic groups:** Mestizo 70%, West Indian 14%, Caucasian 10%, Indian 6%. **Languages:** Spanish (official), English. **Religions:** Roman Catholic 93%, Protestant.

Geography: Area: 29,208 sq. mi., slightly larger than West Virginia. **Location:** In Central America. **Neighbors:** Costa Rica on W., Colombia on E. **Topography:** 2 mountain ranges run the length of the isthmus. Tropical rain forests cover the Caribbean coast and eastern Panama. **Capital:** Panama. **Cities** (1987 est.): Panama 439,000.

Government: Type: Constitutional democracy, centralized republic. **Head of state and head of government:** Pres. Manual Solis Palma; in office: Feb. 26, 1988. **Local divisions:** 9 provinces, 1 territory. **Defense:** 2% of GNP (1985).

Economy: Industries: Oil refining, international banking. **Chief crops:** Bananas, pineapples, cocoa, corn, coconuts, sugar. **Minerals:** Copper. **Other resources:** Forests (mahogany), shrimp. **Arable land:** 8%. **Livestock** (1986): cattle: 1.4 mln.; pigs: 215,000. **Fish catch** (1985): 245,000 metric tons. **Electricity prod.** (1986): 3.1 bln. kwh. **Labor force:** 28% agric., 29.4% ind. and commerce, 30% services.

Finance: Currency: Balboa (Apr. 1989: 1.00 = $1 US). **Gross national product** (1985): $5.1 bln. **Per capita income** (1984): $1,970. **Imports** (1988): $709 mln.; partners: U.S. 34%, Mexico 15%. **Exports** (1987): $357 mln.; partners: U.S. 66%, EC 16%. **Tourists** (1986): $205 mln. receipts. **National budget** (1985): $2.7 bln. **International reserves less gold** (Jan. 1989): $72 mln. **Consumer prices** (change in 1988): 0.3%.

Transport: Motor vehicles: in use (1984): 104,000 passenger cars, 35,000 comm. vehicles. **Civil aviation** (1985): 551 mln. passenger-km; 55 mln. net ton-km. **Chief ports:** Balboa, Cristobal.

Communications: Television sets: 476,000 in use (1987). **Radios:** 900,000 in use (1986). **Telephones in use** (1986): 231,000. **Daily newspaper circ.** (1986): 89 per 1,000 pop.

Health: Life expectancy at birth (1985): 69.2 male; 72.9 female. **Births** (per 1,000 pop. 1987): 25.7. **Deaths** (per 1,000 pop. 1987): 3.8. **Natural increase** (1987): 2.1%. **Hospital beds** (1987): 7,799. **Physicians** (1987): 2,596. **Infant mortality** (per 1,000 live births 1985): 25.

Education (1985): **Literacy:** 87%. **Primary school attendance:** almost 100%.

Major International Organizations: UN (IMF, IMO, World Bank), OAS.

Embassy: 2862 McGill Terrace NW 20008; 483-1407.

The coast of Panama was sighted by Rodrigo de Bastidas, sailing with Columbus for Spain in 1501, and was visited by Columbus in 1502. Vasco Nunez de Balboa crossed the isthmus and "discovered" the Pacific O. Sept. 13, 1513. Spanish colonies were ravaged by Francis Drake, 1572-95, and Henry Morgan, 1668-71. Morgan destroyed the old city of Panama which had been founded in 1519. Freed from Spain, Panama joined Colombia in 1821.

Panama declared its independence from Colombia Nov. 3, 1903, with U.S. recognition. U.S. naval forces deterred action by Colombia. On Nov. 18, 1903, Panama granted use, occupation and control of the Canal Zone to the U.S. by treaty, ratified Feb. 26, 1904.

New treaties were proposed in 1967 and 1974. In 1978, a new treaty provided for a gradual takeover by Panama of the canal, and withdrawal of U.S. troops, to be completed by 1999. U.S. payments were substantially increased in the interim. The permanent neutrality of the canal was also guaranteed.

Due to easy Panama ship regulations and strictures in the U.S., merchant tonnage registered in Panama since World War II ranks high in size.

President Delvalle was ousted by the National Assembly, Feb. 26, 1988, after he tried to fire the head of the Panama Defense

Forces, Gen. Manuel Antonio Noriega. Noreiga had been indicted by 2 U.S. federal grand juries on drug charges. A general strike followed. Despite U.S.-imposed economic sanctions Noriega remained in power. Voters went to the polls to elect a new president May 7, 1989. Noriega claimed victory but foreign observers said that the opposition had won overwhelmingly and that Noriega was trying to steal the election. The government voided the election May 10, charging foreign interference.

Papua New Guinea

People: Population (1989 est.): 3,613,000. **Age distrib. (%):** 0–14: 41.6; 15–59: 52.8; 60+: 5.6. **Pop. density:** 20 per sq. mi. **Urban** (1985): 14.0%. **Ethnic groups:** Papuans (in S and interior), Melanesian (N,E), pygmies, minorities of Chinese, Australians, Polynesians. **Languages:** English (official), Melanesian Pidgin, Police Motu, numerous local languages. **Religions:** Protestant 63%, Roman Catholic 31%, local religions.

Geography: Area: 176,280 sq. mi., slightly larger than California. **Location:** Occupies eastern half of island of New Guinea. **Neighbors:** Indonesia (West Irian) on W, Australia on S. **Topography:** Thickly forested mtns. cover much of the center of the country, with lowlands along the coasts. Included are some of the nearby islands of Bismarck and Solomon groups, including Admiralty Is., New Ireland, New Britain, and Bougainville. **Capital:** Port Moresby. **Cities** (1987): Port Moresby 152,000; Lae 79,000.

Government: Type: Parliamentary democracy. **Head of state:** Queen Elizabeth II, represented by Gov. Gen. Sir Kingsford Dibela; in office: Mar. 1, 1983. **Head of government:** Prime Min. Rabbie Namaliu; in office: July 4, 1988. **Local divisions:** National capital and 19 provinces with elected legislatures. **Defense:** approx. 1.5% of GDP (1985).

Economy: Chief crops: Coffee, coconuts, cocoa. **Minerals:** Gold, copper, silver, gas. **Arable land:** 1%. **Livestock** (1986): pigs: 1.4 mln. **Electricity prod.** (1986): 1.7 bln. kwh. **Labor force:** 75% agric., 8% ind. and commerce, 2% services.

Finance: Currency: Kina (Mar. 1989: 1.00 = $1.18 US). **Gross national product** (1984): $2.4 bln. **Per capita income** (1984): $760. **Imports** (1987): $1.2 bln.; partners: Austral. 34%, Jap. 14%, Sing. 12%. **Exports** (1987): $1.2 bln.; partners: Jap. 29%, W. Ger. 21%, Austral. 8%. **National budget** (1986): $976 mln. **International reserves less gold** (Mar. 1989): $425 mln. **Gold:** 63,000 oz t. **Consumer prices** (change in 1987): 3.3%.

Transport: Motor vehicles: in use (1986): 19,000 passenger cars, 30,000 comm. vehicles. **Chief ports:** Port Moresby, Lae.

Communications: Television sets (1986): 230,000. **Radios:** 225,000 in use (1986). **Telephones in use** (1986): 63,000. **Daily newspaper circ.** (1986): 8 per 1,000 pop.

Health: Life expectancy at birth (1987): 53.0 male; 54.6 female. **Births** (per 1,000 pop. 1987): 35.6. **Deaths** (per 1,000 pop. 1987): 12.9. **Natural increase** (1987): 2.2%. **Hospital beds** (1984): 14,661. **Physicians** (1984): 280. **Infant mortality** (per 1,000 live births 1987): 63.0.

Education (1986): **Literacy:** 32%. **Attendance:** 65% primary school; 13% secondary school.

Major International Organizations: UN (GATT), Commonwealth of Nations.

Embassy: 1330 Connecticut Ave., NW 20036.

Human remains have been found in the interior of New Guinea dating back at least 10,000 years and possibly much earlier. Successive waves of peoples probably entered the country from Asia through Indonesia. Europeans visited in the 15th century, but land claims did not begin until the 19th century, when the Dutch took control of the western half of the island.

The southern half of eastern New Guinea was first claimed by Britain in 1884, and transferred to Australia in 1905. The northern half was claimed by Germany in 1884, but captured in World War I by Australia, which was granted a League of Nations mandate and then a UN trusteeship over the area. The 2 territories were administered jointly after 1949, given self-government Dec. 1, 1973, and became independent Sept. 16, 1975.

The indigenous population consists of a huge number of tribes, many living in almost complete isolation with mutually unintelligible languages.

Paraguay
Republic of Paraguay
República del Paraguay

People: Population (1989 est.): 4,518,000. **Age distrib. (%):** 0–14: 41.0; 15–59: 52.0; 60+: 7.0. **Pop. density:** 28 per sq. mi. **Urban** (1985): 43%. **Ethnic groups:** Mestizo 95%, small Caucasian, Indian, black minorities. **Languages:** Spanish (official), Guarani (used by 90%). **Religions:** Roman Catholic (official) 97%.

Geography: Area: 157,047 sq. mi., the size of California. **Location:** One of the 2 landlocked countries of S. America. **Neighbors:** Bolivia on N, Argentina on S, Brazil on E. **Topography:** Paraguay R. bisects the country. To E are fertile plains, wooded slopes, grasslands. To W is the Chaco plain, with marshes and scrub trees. Extreme W is arid. **Capital:** Asunción. **Cities** (1985 cen.): Asunción 477,000.

Government: Type: Republic; under authoritarian rule. **Head of state:** Pres. Gen. Andres Rodriguez; in office: Feb. 3, 1989. **Local divisions:** 19 departments. **Defense:** 18.3% of govt. budget (1986).

Economy: Industries: Food processing, wood products, textiles, cement. **Chief crops:** Corn, cotton, beans, sugarcane. **Minerals:** Iron, manganese, limestone. **Other resources:** Forests. **Arable land:** 5%. **Livestock** (1986): cattle: 7.1 mln.; pigs: 1.4 mln. **Electricity prod.** (1986): 1.1 bln. kwh. **Labor force:** 44% agric., 34% ind. and commerce, 18% services.

Finance: Currency: Guarani (Mar. 1989 550.00 = $1 US). **Gross national product** (1986): $3.8 bln. **Per capita income** (1984): $1,260. **Imports** (1987): $324 mln.; partners: Braz. 32%, Arg. 8%, U.S. 8%. **Exports** (1987): $208 mln.; partners: Arg. 12%, Neth. 18%, Braz. 17%. **Tourists** (1986): $111 mln. receipts. **National budget** (1986): $762 mln. **International reserves less gold** (Mar. 1989): $287 mln. **Gold:** 35,000 oz t. **Consumer prices** (change in 1988): 24.5%.

Transport: Motor vehicles: in use (1985): 84,000 passenger cars, 41,000 comm. vehicles. **Civil aviation** (1982): 479 mln. passenger-km; 2.9 mln. net ton-km. **Chief ports:** Asuncion.

Communications: Television sets: 266,000 in use (1986). **Radios:** 624,000 in use (1986). **Telephones in use** (1986): 92,000. **Daily newspaper circ.** (1987): 32 per 100,000 pop.

Health: Life expectancy at birth (1984): 63 yrs. **Births** (per 1,000 pop. 1985): 36.0. **Deaths** (per 1,000 pop. 1985): 7.2. **Natural increase** (1985): 2.8%. **Hospital beds** (1982): 3,345. **Physicians** (1982): 2,201. **Infant mortality** (per 1,000 live births 1985): 52.

Education (1987): **Literacy:** 81%. **Years compulsory:** 7; **Attendance:** 83%.

Major International Organizations: UN (IMF, WHO, ILO), OAS.

Embassy: 2400 Massachusetts Ave. NW 20008; 483-6960.

The Guarani Indians were settled farmers speaking a common language before the arrival of Europeans.

Visited by Sebastian Cabot in 1527 and settled as a Spanish possession in 1535, Paraguay gained its independence from Spain in 1811. It lost much of its territory to Brazil, Uruguay, and Argentina in the War of the Triple Alliance, 1865-1870. Large areas were won from Bolivia in the Chaco War, 1932-35.

Gen. Alfredo Stroessner, who ruled since 1954, was ousted in a military coup led by Gen. Andres Rodriguez on Feb. 3, 1989. Rodriguez was elected president May 1.

Peru
Republic of Peru
República del Peru

People: Population (1989 est.): 21,792,000. **Age distrib. (%):** 0–14: 40.5; 15–59: 46.0; 60+: 5.5. **Pop. density:** 43 per sq. mi. **Urban** (1987): 70%. **Ethnic groups:** Indians 45%, Mestizos 37%, Caucasians 15%, blacks, Asians. **Languages:** Spanish, Quechua both official, Aymara; 30% speak no Spanish. **Religions:** Roman Catholic 90%.

Geography: Area: 496,222 sq. mi., 3 times larger than California. **Location:** On the Pacific coast of S. America. **Neighbors:** Ecuador, Colombia on N, Brazil, Bolivia on E, Chile on S. **Topography:** An arid coastal strip, 10 to 100 mi. wide, supports much of the population thanks to widespread irrigation. The Andes cover 27% of land area. The uplands are well-watered, as are the eastern slopes reaching the Amazon basin, which covers half the country with its forests and jungles. **Capital:** Lima. **Cities** (1987 est.): Lima 4,330,000; Arequipa 572,000; Callao 545,000.

Government: Type: Constitutional republic. **Head of state:** Pres. Alan Garcia Perez; b. May 23, 1949; in office: July 28, 1985. **Head of government:** Prime Min. Alberto Sanchez del Campo; in office: May 11, 1989. **Local divisions:** 24 departments, 1 province. **Defense:** 4.0% of GNP (1987).

Economy: Industries: Fish meal, mineral processing, light industry, textiles. **Chief crops:** Cotton, sugar, coffee, corn. **Minerals:** Copper, lead, molybdenum, silver, zinc, iron, oil. **Crude oil reserves** (1987): 535 mln. bbls. **Other resources:** Wool, sardines. **Arable land:** 3%. **Livestock** (1986): cattle: 3.8 mln.; pigs: 2.1 mln.; sheep: 13.5 mln. **Fish catch** (1985): 3.1 mln. metric tons. **Electricity prod.** (1985): 12.1 bln. kwh. **Labor force:** 38% agric.; 17% ind. and mining; 45% govt. and other services.

Finance: Currency: Inti (May 1989: 2,709 = $1 US). **Gross national product** (1986): $17.0 bln. **Per capita income** (1984): $940. **Imports** (1988): $3.0 bln.; partners: U.S. 25%, EC 19%. **Exports** (1988): $2.6 bln.; partners: U.S. 36%, EC 23%, Jap. 10%. **Tourists** (1985): $188 mln. receipts. **National budget** (1987): $3.9 bln. **International reserves less gold** (Mar. 1989): $491 mln. **Gold:** 1.7 mln. oz t. **Consumer prices** (change in 1987): 85.8%.

Transport: Railway traffic (1986): 485 mln. passenger-km; 1.0 bln. net ton-km. **Motor vehicles** in use (1986): 377,000 passenger cars, 226,000 comm. vehicles. **Civil aviation** (1986): 2.1 bln. passenger-km; 267 mln. net ton-km. **Chief ports:** Callao, Chimbate, Mollendo.

Communications: Television sets: 1.6 mln. in use (1987). **Radios:** 3.9 mln. in use (1986). **Telephones in use** (1985): 599,000. **Daily newspaper circ.** (1985): 57 per 1,000 pop.

Health: Life expectancy at birth (1988): 60.1 male; 64.0 female. **Births** (per 1,000 pop. 1988): 34.2. **Deaths** (per 1,000 pop. 1988): 9.0. **Natural increase** (1988): 2.5%. **Hospital beds** (1985): 30,443. **Physicians** (1986): 19,237. **Infant mortality** (per 1,000 live births 1985): 82.

Education (1987): **Literacy:** 79%. **Years compulsory:** 10.

Major International Organizations: UN and all of its specialized agencies, OAS.

Embassy: 1700 Massachusetts Ave. NW 20036; 833-9860.

The powerful Inca empire had its seat at Cuzco in the Andes covering most of Peru, Bolivia, and Ecuador, as well as parts of Colombia, Chile, and Argentina. Building on the achievements of 800 years of Andean civilization, the Incas had a high level of skill in architecture, engineering, textiles, and social organization.

A civil war had weakened the empire when Francisco Pizarro, Spanish conquistador, began raiding Peru for its wealth, 1532. In 1533 he had the seized ruling Inca, Atahualpa, fill a room with gold as a ransom, then executed him and enslaved the natives.

Lima was the seat of Spanish viceroys until the Argentine liberator, Jose de San Martin, captured it in 1821; Spain was defeated by Simon Bolivar and Antonio J. de Sucre; recognized Peruvian independence, 1824. Chile defeated Peru and Bolivia, 1879-84, and took Tarapaca, Tacna, and Arica; returned Tacna, 1929.

On Oct. 3, 1968, a military coup ousted Pres. Fernando Belaunde Terry. In 1968-74, the military government put through sweeping agrarian changes, and nationalized oil, mining, fishmeal, and banking industries.

Food shortages, escalating foreign debt, and strikes led to another coup, Aug. 29, 1976, and to a slowdown of socialist programs.

After 12 years of military rule, Peru returned to democratic leadership under former Pres. Fernando Belaunde Terry, July 1980.

There were strikes by police, oil workers, and other labor unions in 1987 and 1988. Terrorist activity, mostly by Maoist groups, continued; the government said that guerrilla insurgency caused nearly 13,000 deaths in the 1980s.

Philippines

Republic of the Philippines

People: Population (1989 est.): 61,971,000. **Age distrib.** (%): 0–14: 39.0; 15–59: 56.2; 60+: 4.8. **Pop. density:** 535 per sq. mi. **Urban** (1987): 41%. **Ethnic groups:** Malays the large majority, Chinese, Americans, Spanish are minorities. **Languages:** Pilipino (based on Tagalog), English both official; numerous others spoken. **Religions:** Roman Catholics 83%, Protestants 9%, Moslems 5%.

Geography: Area: 115,831 sq. mi., slightly larger than Nevada. **Location:** An archipelago off the SE coast of Asia. **Neighbors:** Nearest are Malaysia, Indonesia on S, Taiwan on N. **Topography:** The country consists of some 7,100 islands stretching 1,100 mi. N-S. About 95% of area and population are on 11 largest islands, which are mountainous, except for the heavily indented coastlines and for the central plain on Luzon. **Capital:** Quezon City (Manila is de facto capital). **Cities** (1985 est.): Manila 1.7 mln.; Quezon City 1.3 mln.; Cebu 552,000.

Government: Type: Republic. **Head of state:** Pres. Corazon C. Aquino; b. 1932; in office: Feb. 25, 1986. **Local divisions:** 12 regions, 74 provinces, 60 cities. **Defense:** 1.3% of GNP (1985).

Economy: Industries: Food processing, textiles, clothing, drugs, wood prods., appliances. **Chief crops:** Sugar, rice, corn, pineapple, coconut. **Minerals:** Cobalt, copper, gold, nickel, silver, iron, petroleum. **Crude oil reserves** (1987): 19 mln. bbls. **Other resources:** Forests (42% of area). **Arable land:** 34%. **Livestock** (1986): cattle: 1.7 mln.; pigs: 7.2 mln. **Fish catch** (1984): 1.8 mln. metric tons. **Electricity prod.** (1986): 22.0 bln. kwh. **Labor force:** 47% agric., 20% ind. and comm., 13% services.

Finance: Currency: Peso (May 1989: 21.10 = $1 US). **Gross national product** (1986): $34.5 bln. **Per capita income** (1985): $598. **Imports** (1987): $7.1 bln.; partners: U.S. 25%, Jap. 16%. **Exports** (1986): $5.6 bln.; partners: U.S. 35%, Jap. 17%. **Tourists** (1986): $647 mln. receipts. **National budget** (1986): $5.7 bln. expenditures. **International reserves less gold** (Mar. 1989): $675 mln. **Gold:** 3.0 mln. oz t. **Consumer prices** (change in 1988): 8.8%.

Transport: Railway traffic (1986): 168 mln. passenger-km; 60 mln. net ton-km. **Motor vehicles:** in use (1986): 773,000 passenger cars, 110,000 comm. vehicles. **Civil aviation** (1987): 9.2 bln. passenger-km; 246 mln. freight ton-km. **Chief ports:** Cebu, Manila, Iloilo, Davao.

Communications: Television sets: 4.1 mln. in use (1987). **Radios:** 7.5 mln. in use (1986). **Telephones in use** (1985): 820,000. **Daily newspaper circ.** (1985): 44 per 1,000 pop.

Health: Life expectancy at birth (1987): 61.9 male; 65.5 female. **Births** (per 1,000 pop. 1987): 34.6. **Deaths** (per 1,000 pop. 1987): 7.9. **Natural increase** (1987): 2.6%. **Hospital beds** (1985): 79,703. **Physicians** (1982): 46,579. **Infant mortality** (per 1,000 live births 1987): 56.0.

Education (1986): **Literacy:** 88%. **Attendance:** 95% in elementary, 57% secondary.

Major International Organizations: UN (World Bank, IMF, GATT), ASEAN.

Embassy: 1617 Massachusetts Ave. NW 20036; 483-1414

The Malay peoples of the Philippine islands, whose ancestors probably migrated from Southeast Asia when first visited by Europeans.

The archipelago was visited by Magellan, 1521. The Spanish founded Manila, 1571. The islands, named for King Philip II of Spain, were ceded by Spain to the U.S. for $20 million, 1898, following the Spanish-American War. U.S. troops suppressed a guerrilla uprising in a brutal 6-year war, 1899-1905.

Japan attacked the Philippines Dec. 8, 1941 (Far Eastern time). Japan occupied the islands during WW II.

On July 4, 1946, independence was proclaimed in accordance with an act passed by the U.S. Congress in 1934. A republic was established.

A rebellion by Communist-led Huk guerrillas was put down by 1954. But urban and rural political violence periodically reappears.

The Philippines and the U.S. have treaties for U.S. military and naval bases and a mutual defense treaty. Riots by radical youth groups and terrorism by leftist guerrillas and outlaws, increased from 1970. On Sept. 21, 1972, President Marcos declared martial law. Ruling by decree, he ordered some land reform and sta-

bilized prices. But opposition was suppressed, and a high population growth rate aggravated poverty and unemployment. Political corruption was believed to be widespread. On Jan. 17, 1973, Marcos proclaimed a new constitution with himself as president. His wife received wide powers in 1978 to supervise planning and development.

Government troops battled Moslem (Moro) secessionists, 1973-76, in southern Mindanao. Fighting resumed, 1977, after a Libyan-mediated agreement on autonomy was rejected by the region's mainly Christian voters.

Martial law was lifted Jan. 17, 1981. Marcos turned over legislative power to the National Assembly, released political prisoners, and said he would no longer rule by decree. He was reelected to a new 6-year term as president.

The assassination of prominent opposition leader Benigno S. Aquino Jr, Aug. 21, 1983, sparked demonstrations calling for the resignation of Marcos. An independent commission appointed by Marcos concluded that a military conspiracy was responsible for Aquino's death. The May 1984 elections saw Marcos retain his majority in the National Assembly although opponents made a strong showing in key areas like Manila.

A bitter presidential election campaign ended Feb. 7, 1986 as elections were held amid allegations of widespread fraud. On Feb. 16, Marcos was declared the victor over Corazon Aquino, widow of slain opposition leader Benigno Aquino. Aquino declared herself president and announced a nonviolent "active resistance" to overthrow the Marcos government; the 2 held separate inaugurals on Feb. 25.

On Feb. 22, 2 leading military allies of Marcos quit their posts to protest the rigged elections. Marcos, Feb. 24, declared a state of emergency as his military and religious support continued to erode. That same day U.S. President Ronald Reagan urged Marcos to resign. Marcos ended his 20-year tenure as president Feb. 26 as he fled the country. Aquino was recognized immediately as president by the U.S. and other nations.

In 1987, Aquino announced the start of land reforms. Candidates endorsed by Aquino won large majorities in legislative elections held in May, attesting to her popularity. She is plagued, however, by a weak economy, widespread poverty, communist insurgents, and lukewarm support from the military.

The archipelago has a coastline of 10,850 mi. Manila Bay, with an area of 770 sq. mi., and a circumference of 120 mi., is the finest harbor in the Far East.

All natural resources of the Philippines belong to the state; their exploitation is limited to citizens of the Philippines or corporations of which 60% of the capital is owned by citizens.

Poland

Polish People's Republic

Polska Rzeczpospolita Ludowa

People: Population (1989 est.): 38,389,000. **Age distrib.** (%): 0–14: 25.7; 15–59: 60.2; 60+: 14.1. **Pop. density:** 317 per sq. mi. **Urban** (1987): 60%. **Ethnic groups:** Polish 98%, Germans, Ukrainians, Byelorussians. **Language:** Polish. **Religion:** Roman Catholic 94%.

Geography: Area: 120,727 sq. mi. **Location:** On the Baltic Sea in E Central Europe. **Neighbors:** E. Germany on W, Czechoslovakia on S, USSR (Lithuania, Byelorussia, Ukraine) on E. **Topography:** Mostly lowlands forming part of the Northern European Plain. The Carpathian Mts. along the southern border rise to 8,200 ft. **Capital:** Warsaw. **Cities** (1987 est.): Warsaw 1.6 mln., Lodz 848,000, Kracow 740,000, Wroclaw 631,000, Poznan 570,000.

Government: Type: Communist. **Head of state:** Pres. Wojciech Jaruzelski; in office: Oct. 18, 1981. **Head of government: Prime Min.:** Tadeusz Mazowiecki; in office: Aug. 19, 1989. **Head of Communist Party:** Mieczyslaw Rakowski; in office: Sept. 27, 1988. **Local divisions:** 49 provinces. **Defense:** 6% of GNP (1985).

Economy: Industries: Shipbuilding, chemicals, metals, autos, food processing. **Chief crops:** Grains, potatoes, sugar beets, tobacco, flax. **Minerals:** Coal, copper, zinc, silver, zinc, sulphur, natural gas. **Arable land:** 49%. **Livestock** (1987): cattle: 10.9 mln.; pigs: 18.9 mln.; sheep: 5 mln. **Fish catch** (1985): 650,000 metric tons. **Electricity prod.** (1986): 141 bln. kwh. **Crude steel prod.** (1987): 17.1 mln. metric tons. **Labor force:** 30% agric.; 44% ind. & comm.; 11% services.

Finance: Currency: Zloty (Mar. 1989: 572 = $1 US). **Gross national product** (1986): $259 bln. **Per capita income** (1986): $2,000. **Imports** (1988): $12.6 bln.; partners: USSR 38%, E. Ger. 7% W. Ger. 10% Czech. 5%. **Exports** (1988): $10.5 bln.; partners: USSR 30%, E. Ger. 6%, Czech. 6%, W. Ger. 10%. **National budget** (1984): $23.3 bln. **Tourists** (1986): $136 mln. receipts. **International Reserves Less Gold** (Mar. 1989): $2.0 bln. **Gold:** 472,000. **Consumer prices** (change in 1988): 57.7%.

Transport: Railway traffic (1986): 48 bln. passenger-km; 120 bln. net ton-km. **Motor vehicles:** in use (1986): 3.9 mln. passenger cars, 912,000 comm. vehicles. **Civil aviation** (1986): 2.1 bln. passenger-km; 12 mln. freight ton-km. **Chief ports:** Gdansk, Gdynia, Szczecin.

Communications: Television sets: 10.0 mln. (1986). **Radios:** 9.4 mln. (1986). **Telephones in use** (1986): 4.2 mln. **Daily newspaper circ.** (1986): 217 per 1,000 pop.

Health: Life expectancy at birth (1985): 66.5 male; 74.8 female. **Births** (per 1,000 pop. 1986): 19. **Deaths** (per 1,000 pop. 1986): 10.1 **Natural increase** (1986): .6%. **Hospital beds** (1987): 247,000. **Physicians** (1987): 75,000. **Infant mortality** (per 1,000 live births 1985): 18.

Education (1987): **Literacy:** 98%. **Years compulsory:** 8; attendance 97%.

Major International Organizations: UN (GATT, WHO), Warsaw Pact.

Embassy: 2640 16th St. NW 20009; 234-3800.

Slavic tribes in the area were converted to Latin Christianity in the 10th century. Poland was a great power from the 14th to the 17th centuries. In 3 partitions (1772, 1793, 1795) it was apportioned among Prussia, Russia, and Austria. Overrun by the Austro-German armies in World War I, its independence, self-declared on Nov.11, 1918, was recognized by the Treaty of Versailles, June 28, 1919. Large territories to the east were taken in a war with Russia, 1921.

Nazi Germany and the USSR invaded Poland Sept. 1-27, 1939, and divided the country. During the war, some 6 million Polish citizens were killed by the Nazis, half of them Jews. With Germany's defeat, a Polish government-in-exile in London was recognized by the U.S., but the USSR pressed the claims of a rival group. The election of 1947 was completely dominated by the Communists.

In compensation for 69,860 sq. mi. ceded to the USSR, 1945, Poland received approx. 40,000 sq. mi. of German territory E of the Oder-Neisse line comprising Silesia, Pomerania, West Prussia, and part of East Prussia.

In 12 years of rule by Stalinists, large estates were abolished, industries nationalized, schools secularized, and Roman Catholic prelates jailed. Farm production fell off. Harsh working conditions caused a riot in Poznan June 28-29, 1956.

A new Politburo, committed to development of a more independent Polish Communism, was named Oct. 1956, with Wladyslaw Gomulka as first secretary of the Communist Party. Collectivization of farms was ended and many collectives were abolished.

In Dec. 1970 workers in port cities rioted because of price rises and new incentive wage rules. On Dec. 20 Gomulka resigned as party leader; he was succeeded by Edward Gierek; the incentive rules were dropped, price rises were revoked.

Poland was the first communist state to get most-favored-nation trade terms from the U.S.

A law promulgated Feb. 13, 1953, required government consent to high Roman Catholic church appointments. In 1956 Gomulka agreed to permit religious liberty and religious publications, provided the church kept out of politics. In 1961 religious studies in public schools were halted. Government relations with the Church improved in the 1970s. The number of priests and churches was greater in 1971 than in 1939.

After 2 months of labor turmoil had crippled the country, the Polish government, Aug. 30, 1980, met the demands of striking workers at the Lenin Shipyard, Gdansk. Among the 21 concessions granted were the right to form independent trade unions and the right to strike — unprecedented political developments in the Soviet bloc. By 1981, 9.5 mln. workers had joined the independent trade union (Solidarity). Farmers won official recognition for their independent trade union in May. Solidarity leaders proposed, Dec. 12, a nationwide referendum on establishing a non-Communist government if the government failed to agree to a series of demands which included access to the mass media and free and democratic elections to local councils in the provinces.

Spurred by the fear of Soviet intervention, the government, Dec. 13, imposed martial law. Public gatherings, demonstrations, and strikes were banned and an internal and external blackout was imposed. Solidarity leaders called for a nationwide strike, but there were only scattered work stoppages. Lech Walesa and other Solidarity leaders were arrested. The U.S. imposed economic sanctions which were lifted when martial law was suspended December 1982.

On Apr. 5, 1989, an accord was reached between the government and opposition factions on a broad range of political and economic reforms incl. free elections. In the first free elections in over 40 years, candidates endorsed by Solidarity swept the parliamentary elections, June 4. On Aug. 19, Tadeusz Mazowiecki became the first non-Communist to head an Eastern bloc nation, when he became prime minister. President Bush visited Poland in July. He praised the reforms and pledged modest U.S. economic aid. (*See Chronology*).

Portugal
Republic of Portugal
República Portuguesa

People: Population (1989 est.): 10,240,000. **Age distrib.** (%): 0–14: 22.7; 15–59: 59.9; 60+: 17.4. **Pop. density:** 281 per sq. mi. **Urban** (1983): 30%. **Ethnic groups:** Homogeneous Mediterranean stock with small African minority. **Languages:** Portuguese. **Religions:** Roman Catholics 97%.

Geography: Area: 36,390 sq. mi., incl. the Azores and Madeira Islands, slightly smaller than Indiana. **Location:** At SW extreme of Europe. **Neighbors:** Spain on N, E. **Topography:** Portugal N of Tajus R, which bisects the country NE-SW, is mountainous, cool and rainy. To the S there are drier, rolling plains, and a warm climate. **Capital:** Lisbon. **Cities** (1987 est.): Lisbon 2 mln. (met.), Oporto, 1.5 mln. (met.).

Government: Type: Parliamentary democracy. **Head of state:** Pres. Mario Soares; b. Dec. 7, 1924; in office: Mar. 9, 1986. **Head of government:** Prime Min. Anibal Cavaco Silva; in office: Nov. 6, 1985. **Local divisions:** 18 districts, 2 autonomous regions, one dependency. **Defense:** 2.9% of GNP (1987).

Economy: Industries: Textiles, footwear, cork, chemicals, fish canning, wine, paper. **Chief crops:** Grains, potatoes, rice, grapes, olives, fruits. **Minerals:** Tungsten, uranium, copper, iron. **Other resources:** Forests (world leader in cork production). **Arable land:** 39%. **Livestock** (1987): sheep: 2.4 mln.; pigs: 1.2 mln; cattle: 1 mln. **Fish catch** (1985): 254,000 metric tons. **Electricity prod.** (1986): 17.2 bln. kwh. **Crude steel prod.** (1985): 420,000 metric tons. **Labor force:** 21% agric.; 34% ind. and comm.; 44% services and govt.

Finance: Currency: Escudo (May 1989: 165.90 = $1 US). **Gross national product** (1986): $28.9 bln. **Per capita income** (1986): $2,970. **Imports** (1988): $16.1 bln.; partners: W. Ger. 12%, UK 8%, Fr. 11%. **Exports** (1988): $10.5 bln.; partners: UK 15%, W. Ger. 13%, Fr. 13%. **Tourists** (1986): $1.5 bln. receipts. **National budget** (1987): $11.3 bln. expenditures. **International reserves less gold** (Mar. 1989): $5.5 bln. **Gold:** 16.0 mln. oz t. **Consumer prices** (change in 1988): 9.6%.

Transport: Railway traffic (1986): 5.8 bln. passenger-km; 1.4 bln. net ton-km. **Motor vehicles:** in use (1986): 1.9 mln. passenger cars, 500,000 comm. vehicles. **Civil aviation** (1986): 4.4 bln. passenger-km; 133 mln. freight ton-km. **Chief ports:** Lisbon, Setubal, Leixoes.

Communications: Television sets: 1.6 mln. in use (1986). **Radios:** 2.1 mln. in use (1986). **Telephones in use** (1986): 1.9 mln. **Daily newspaper circ.** (1986): 84 per 1,000 pop.

Health: Life expectancy at birth (1985): 67.6 male; 74.1 female. **Births** (per 1,000 pop. 1986): 12.4. **Deaths** (per 1,000 pop. 1986): 9.4. **Natural increase** (1986): .3%. **Hospital beds** (1987): 43,000. **Physicians** (1987): 25,000. **Infant mortality** (per 1,000 live births 1987): 11.

Education (1985): **Literacy:** 83%, **Years compulsory:** 6; attendance 60%.

Major International Organizations: UN (GATT, IMF, WHO), NATO, EC, OECD.

Embassy: 2125 Kalorama Rd. NW 20008; 328-8610.

Portugal, an independent state since the 12th century, was a kingdom until a revolution in 1910 drove out King Manoel II and a republic was proclaimed.

From 1932 a strong, repressive government was headed by Premier Antonio de Oliveira Salazar. Illness forced his retirement in Sept. 1968; he was succeeded by Marcello Caetano.

On Apr. 25, 1974, the government was seized by a military junta led by Gen. Antonio de Spinola, who was named president.

The new government reached agreements providing independence for Guinea-Bissau, Mozambique, Cape Verde Islands, Angola, and Sao Tome and Principe. Spinola resigned Sept. 30, 1974, in face of increasing pressure from leftist officers. Despite a 64% victory for democratic parties in April 1975, the Soviet-supported Communist party increased its influence. Banks, insurance companies, and other industries were nationalized.

Parliament approved, June 1, 1989, a package of reforms that did away with the socialist economy and created a "democratic" economy and the denationalization of industries.

Azores Islands, in the Atlantic, 740 mi. W. of Portugal, have an area of 888 sq. mi. and a pop. (1987) of 252,000. A 1951 agreement gave the U.S. rights to use defense facilities in the Azores. The **Madeira Islands**, 350 mi. off the NW coast of Africa, have an area of 307 sq. mi. and a pop. (1987) of 269,000. Both groups were offered partial autonomy in 1976.

Macau, area of 6 sq. mi., is an enclave, a peninsula and 2 small islands, at the mouth of the Canton R. in China. Portugal granted broad autonomy in 1976. In 1987, Portugal and China agreed that Macau would revert to China in 1999. Macao, like Hong Kong, was guaranteed 50 years of noninterference in its way of life and capitalist system. Pop. (1986 est.): 433,000.

Qatar
State of Qatar
Dawlet al-Qatar

People: Population (1989 est.): 342,000. **Pop. density:** 80 per sq. mi. **Ethnic groups:** Arab 45%, Pakistani 15%, Indian 21%, Iranian 6%, others. **Languages:** Arabic (official), English. **Religions:** Moslem 95%.

Geography: Area: 4,247 sq. mi., smaller than Connecticut and Rhode Island combined. **Location:** Occupies peninsula on W coast of Persian Gulf. **Neighbors:** Saudi Arabia on W, United Arab Emirates on S. **Topography:** Mostly a flat desert, with some limestone ridges, vegetation of any kind is scarce. **Capital:** Doha. **Cities** (1987 est.): Doha 250,000.

Government: Type: Traditional emirate. **Head of state and head of government:** Khalifah ibn Hamad ath-Thani; b. 1932; in office: Feb. 22, 1972 (amir), 1970 (prime min.) **Defense:** 47% of GNP (1985).

Economy: Crude oil reserves (1987): 3.3 mln. bbls. **Arable land:** 2.9%. **Electricity prod.** (1986): 4.0 bln. kwh. **Labor force:** 10% agric., 70% ind., services and commerce.

Finance: Currency: Riyal (Mar. 1989: 1.00 = .27 US). **Gross national product** (1986): $4.1 bln. **Per capita income** (1985): $27,000. **Imports** (1987): $1.1 bln.; partners: Jap. 20%, UK 16%, U.S. 11%. **Exports** (1987): $2.6 bln.; partners: Jap. 52%, Fr. 10%. **National budget** (1987): $3.4 bln. expenditures.

Transport: Chief ports: Doha, Musayid.

Communications: Television sets: 160,000 (1986). **Radios:** 120,000 in use (1986). **Telephones in use** (1986): 115,000.

Health: Life expectancy at birth (1986): 65.2 male; 67.6 female. **Hospital beds** (1986): 915. **Physicians** (1986): 514. **Infant mortality** (per 1,000 live births 1986): 37.4.

Education (1987): **Literacy:** 60%. **Compulsory:** ages 6-16; attendance: 98%.

Major International Organizations: UN (FAO, GATT, IMF, World Bank), Arab League, OPEC.

Embassy: 600 New Hampshire Ave. NW 20037; 338-0111.

Qatar was under Bahrain's control until the Ottoman Turks took power, 1872 to 1915. In a treaty signed 1916, Qatar gave Great Britain responsibility for its defense and foreign relations. After Britain announced it would remove its military forces from the Persian Gulf area by the end of 1971, Qatar sought a federation with other British protected states in the area; this failed and Qatar declared itself independent, Sept. 1 1971.

Oil revenues give Qatar a per capita income among the highest in the world, but lack of skilled labor hampers development plans.

Romania
Socialist Republic of Romania
Republica Socialistă România

People: Population (1989 est.): 23,155,000. **Age distrib.** (%): 0-14: 24.7; 15-59; 60.9; 60+: 14.4. **Pop. density:** 252 per sq. mi. **Urban** (1987): 51%. **Ethnic groups:** Romanians 89%, Hungarians 7.9%, Germans 1.6%. **Languages:** Romanian (official), Hungarian, German. **Religions:** Orthodox 80%, Roman Catholic 6%.

Geography: Area: 91,699 sq. mi., slightly smaller than New York and Pennsylvania combined. **Location:** In SE Europe on the Black Sea. **Neighbors:** USSR on E (Moldavia) and N (Ukraine), Hungary, Yugoslavia on W, Bulgaria on S. **Topography:** The Carpathian Mts. encase the north-central Transylvanian plateau. There are wide plains S and E of the mountains, through which flow the lower reaches of the rivers of the Danube system. **Capital:** Bucharest. **Cities** (1986 est.): Bucharest 1,900,000, Brasov 346,000, Timisoara 319,000, Constanta 323,000.

Government: Type: Communist. **Head of state:** Pres. Nicolae Ceausescu; b. Jan. 26, 1918; in office; Dec. 9, 1967. **Head of government:** Prime Min. Constantin Dascalescu; in office; May 21, 1982. **Head of Communist Party:** Pres. Nicolae Ceausescu; in office: Mar. 23, 1965. **Local divisions:** Bucharest and 40 counties. **Defense:** 4.3% of GNP (1985).

Economy: Industries: Steel, metals, machinery, oil products, chemicals, textiles, shoes, tourism. **Chief crops:** Grains, sunflower, vegetables, potatoes. **Minerals:** Oil, gas, coal. **Other resources:** Timber. **Arable land:** 45%. **Livestock** (1988): cattle: 7.2 mln.; pigs: 14.7 mln.; sheep: 18.7 mln. **Fish catch** (1986): 293,000 metric tons. **Electricity prod.** (1988): 75.3 bln. kwh. **Crude steel prod.** (1987): 15.0 mln. metric tons. **Labor force:** 30% agric.; 38% ind. & comm.

Finance: Currency: Leu (Mar. 1989: 14.81 = $1 US). **Gross national product** (1986): $137 bln. **Per capita income** (1984): $2,020. **Imports** (1986): $10.6 bln.; partners: USSR 22%, Egypt 10%, Iran 8%. **Exports** (1986): $12.6 bln.; partners: USSR 21%, W. Ger. 7%. **Tourists** (1984): $230 mln. receipts. **National budget** (1982): $142 mln. expenditures.

Transport: Railway traffic (1987): 33 bln. passenger-km; 78.1 bln. net ton-km. **Motor vehicles:** in use (1986): 105,000 passenger cars; 100,000 comm. vehicles. **Civil aviation** (1987): 3.9 bln. passenger-km; 73 mln. freight ton-km. **Chief ports:** Constanta, Galati, Braila.

Communications: Television sets: 3.8 mln. licensed (1987). **Radios:** 2.5 mln. in use (1987). **Telephones in use** (1985): 1.9 mln. **Daily newspaper circ.** (1987): 159 per 1,000 pop.

Health: Life expectancy at birth (1984): 67.0 male; 72.6 female. **Births** (per 1,000 pop. 1985): 15. **Deaths** (per 1,000 pop. 1984): 10. **Natural increase** (1985): 0.5%. **Hospital beds** (1987): 214,000. **Physicians** (1987): 48,000. **Infant mortality** (per 1,000 live births 1986): 25.6.

Education (1988): **Literacy:** 98%. **Years compulsory:** 10; attendance 98%.

Major International Organizations: UN (World Bank, IMF, GATT), Warsaw Pact.

Embassy: 1607 23d St. NW 20008; 232-4748.

Romania's earliest known people merged with invading Proto-Thracians, preceding by centuries the Dacians. The Dacian kingdom was occupied by Rome, 106 AD-271 AD; people and language were Romanized. The principalities of Wallachia and Moldavia, dominated by Turkey, were united in 1859, became Romania in 1861. In 1877 Romania proclaimed independence from Turkey, became an independent state by the Treaty of Berlin, 1878, a kingdom, 1881, under Carol I. In 1886 Romania became a constitutional monarchy with a bicameral legislature.

Romania helped Russia in its war with Turkey, 1877-78. After World War I it acquired Bessarabia, Bukovina, Transylvania, and Banat. In 1940 it ceded Bessarabia and Northern Bukovina to the USSR, part of southern Dobrudja to Bulgaria, and Transylvania to Hungary.

In 1941, Romanian premier Marshal Ion Antonescu led his country in support of Germany against the USSR. In 1944 Antonescu was overthrown by King Michael and Romania joined the Allies.

With occupation by Soviet troops the communist-headed National Democratic Front displaced the National Peasant party. A

People's Republic was proclaimed, Dec. 30, 1947; Michael was forced to abdicate. Land owners were dispossessed; most banks, factories and transportation units were nationalized.

On Aug. 22, 1965, a new constitution proclaimed Romania a Socialist, rather than a People's Republic. Since 1959, USSR troops have not been permitted to enter Romania.

Internal policies remain oppressive. Ethnic Hungarians have protested cultural and job discrimination, which has led to strained relations with Hungary.

Romania has become industrialized, but lags in consumer goods and in personal freedoms. There is strong resistance to the reforms proposed by Soviet leader Gorbachev. All industry is state owned, and state farms and cooperatives own over 90% of arable land.

A major earthquake struck Bucharest in March, 1977, killing over 1,300 people and causing extensive damage to housing and industry.

Rwanda

Republic of Rwanda

Republika y'u Rwanda

People: Population (1989 est.): 7,276,000. **Age distrib. (%):** 0–14: 48.7; 15–59: 47.1; 60+: 4.2. **Pop. density:** 715 per sq. mi. **Urban** (1985): 5.1%. **Ethnic groups:** Hutu 85%, Tutsi 14%, Twa (pygmies) 1%. **Languages:** French, Kinyarwandu (both official), Swahili. **Religions:** Christian 74%, traditional 25%, Moslem 1%.

Geography: Area: 10,169 sq. mi., the size of Maryland. **Location:** In E central Africa. **Neighbors:** Uganda on N, Zaire on W, Burundi on S, Tanzania on E. **Topography:** Grassy uplands and hills cover most of the country, with a chain of volcanoes in the NW. The source of the Nile R. has been located in the headwaters of the Kagera (Akagera) R., SW of Kigali. **Capital:** Kigali. **Cities** (1989 est.): Kigali 300,000.

Government: Type: Republic. **Head of state:** Pres. Juvenal Habyarimana; b. Mar. 8, 1937; in office: July 5, 1973. **Local divisions:** 10 prefectures, 143 communes. **Defense:** 1.7% of GNP (1985).

Economy: Chief crops: Coffee, tea. **Minerals:** Tin, gold, wolframite. **Arable land:** 48%. **Electricity prod.** (1986): 110 mln. kwh. **Labor force:** 91% agric.

Finance: Currency: Franc (Apr. 1989: 79 = $1 US). **Gross national product** (1986): $1.7 bln. **Per capita income** (1986): $323. **Imports** (1987): $354 mln.; partners: Ken. 21%, Belg. 16%, Jap. 12%, W. Ger. 9%. **Exports** (1987): $113 mln.; partners: Belg.-Lux. 17%, Ugan. 12%. **National budget** (1987): $247 mln. revenues; $280 mln. expenditures. **International reserves less gold** (Mar. 1989): $107 mln. **Consumer prices** (change in 1988): 3.0%.

Transport: Motor vehicles: in use (1986): 7,000 passenger cars, 10,000 comm. vehicles.

Communications: Radios: 250,000 in use (1986). **Telephones in use** (1986): 9,000.

Health: Life expectancy at birth (1985): 48 years. **Births** (per 1,000 pop. 1985): 54.0. **Deaths** (per 1,000 pop. 1985): 16.0. **Natural increase** (1985): 3.8%. **Hospital beds** (1984): 9,000. **Physicians** (1984): 177. **Infant mortality** (per 1,000 live births 1988): 122.

Education (1989): **Literacy:** 50%. **Years compulsory:** 8; **attendance:** 70%.

Major International Organizations: UN (GATT, IMF, WHO), OAU.

Embassy: 1714 New Hampshire Ave. NW 20009; 232-2882.

For centuries, the Tutsi (an extremely tall people) dominated the Hutus (90% of the population). A civil war broke out in 1959 and Tutsi power was ended. A referendum in 1961 abolished the monarchic system.

Rwanda, which had been part of the Belgian UN trusteeship of Rwanda-Urundi, became independent July 1, 1962. The government was overthrown in a 1973 military coup. Rwanda is one of the most densely populated countries in Africa. All available arable land is being used, and is being subject to erosion. The government has carried out economic and social improvement programs, using foreign aid and volunteer labor on public works projects.

St. Christopher (St. Kitts) and Nevis

St. Christopher Nevis

People: Population (1989 est.): 40,000. **Ethnic groups:** black 95%. **Language:** English. **Religion:** Protestant 76%.

Geography: Area: 101 sq. mi. in the northern part of the Leeward group of the Lesser Antilles in the eastern Caribbean Sea. **Capitol:** Basseterre. (1984 est.): 18,500.

Government: Head of State: Queen Elizabeth represented by Sir Clement Arrindell. **Head of Government:** Prime Minister Kennedy A. Simmonds; b. Apr. 12, 1936; in office: Sept. 19, 1983.

Economy: Sugar is the principal industry.

Finance: Currency: E. Caribbean Dollar (Mar. 1987): 2.70 = $1 U.S. **Gross national product** (1986): $66 mln. **Tourists** (1986): $34 mln. receipts.

Communications: 7,000 telephones (1987).

Health: Infant mortality (per 1,000 live births, 1985): 39.

Education: Literacy (1987): 90%; school compulsory ages 5–14.

St. Christopher (known by the natives as Liamuiga) and Nevis were discovered and named by Columbus in 1493. They were settled by Britain in 1623, but ownership was disputed with France until 1713. They were part of the Leeward Islands Federation, 1871-1956, and the Federation of the W. Indies, 1958-62. The colony achieved self-government as an Associated State of the UK in 1967, and became fully independent Sept. 19, 1983. Nevis, the smaller of the islands, has the right of secession.

Saint Lucia

People: Population (1989 est.): 128,000. **Age distrib. (%):** 0–20: 44.5; 21–64: 47.5; 65+: 8.0. **Pop. density:** 537 per sq. mi. **Ethnic groups:** Predominantly African descent. **Languages:** English (official), French patois. **Religions:** Roman Catholic 90%.

Geography: Area: 238 sq. mi., about one-fifth the size of Rhode Island. **Location:** In Eastern Caribbean, 2d largest of the Windward Is. **Neighbors:** Martinique to N, St. Vincent to SW. **Topography:** Mountainous, volcanic in origin; Soufriere, a volcanic crater, in the S. Wooded mountains run N-S to Mt. Gimie, 3,145 ft., with streams through fertile valleys. **Capital:** Castries. **City:** Castries (1986 est.): 52,000.

Government: Type: Parliamentary democracy. **Head of state:** Queen Elizabeth II, represented by Gov.-Gen. Vincent Floissac; **Head of government:** Prime Min. John Compton; in office: May 3, 1982. **Local divisions:** 11 quarters

Economy: Industries: Agriculture, tourism, manufacturing. **Chief crops:** Bananas, coconuts, cocoa, citrus fruits. **Other resources:** Forests. **Arable land:** 28%. **Electricity prod.** (1986): 80 mln. kwh. **Labor force:** 36% agric., 20% ind. & commerce, 18% services.

Finance: Currency: East Caribbean dollar (Mar. 1989: 2.70 = $1 US). **Gross national product** (1985): $146 mln. **Per capita income** (1984): $1,120. **Imports** (1986): $155 mln.; partners: U.S. 36%, UK 12%, Trin./Tob. 11%. **Exports** (1986): $83 mln.; partners: U.S. 28%, UK 25%. **Tourists** (1986): receipts: $69 mln.

Transport: Motor vehicles: in use (1984): 7,000 passenger cars, 2,000 comm. vehicles. **Chief ports:** Castries, Vieux Fort.

Communications: Television sets: 5,000 in use (1986). **Radios:** 92,000 in use (1985). **Telephones in use** (1986): 14,500.

Health: Life expectancy at birth (1987): 70.3 male; 74.9 female. **Births** (per 1,000 pop. 1986): 28.0. **Deaths** (per 1,000 pop. 1986): 6.0. **Natural increase** (1986): 2.2%. **Hospital beds** (1986): 501. **Infant mortality** (per 1,000 live births 1986): 20.

Education: Literacy (1987) 78%; **Years compulsory:** ages 5-15; **Attendance:** 80%.

Major International Organizations: UN (IMF, ILO), CARICOM, OAS.

St. Lucia was ceded to Britain by France at the Treaty of Paris, 1814. Self government was granted with the West Indies Act, 1967. Independence was attained Feb. 22, 1979.

Saint Vincent and the Grenadines

People: Population (1986 est.): 112,000. **Pop. density:** 746 per sq. mi. **Ethnic groups:** Mainly of African descent. **Languages:** English. **Religions:** Methodists, Anglicans, Roman Catholics.

Geography: Area: 150 sq. mi., about twice the size of Washington, D.C. **Location:** In the eastern Caribbean, St. Vincent (133 sq. mi.) and the northern islets of the Grenadines form a part of the Windward chain. **Neighbors:** St. Lucia to N, Barbados to E, Grenada to S. **Topography:** St. Vincent is volcanic, with a ridge of thickly-wooded mountains running its length; Soufriere, rising in the N, erupted in Apr. 1979. **Capital:** Kingstown. **Cities** (1985 est.): Kingstown 18,378.

Government: Head of state: Queen Elizabeth II, represented by Gov.-Gen. Henry Harvey-Williams; in office: Feb. 29, 1988. **Head of government:** James Mitchell; in office: July 30, 1984.

Economy: Industries: Agriculture, tourism. **Chief crops:** Bananas (62% of exports), arrowroot, coconuts. **Arable land:** 50%. **Electricity prod.** (1986): 31 mln. kwh. **Labor force:** 30% agric.

Finance: Currency: East Caribbean dollar (Mar. 1989: 2.70 = $1 US). **Gross national product** (1987): $188 mln. **Per capita income** (1984): $920. **Tourists** (1986): $27 mln. receipts. **National budget** (1984): $34 mln. expenditures.

Transport: Motor vehicles: in use (1986): 5,000 passenger cars, 2,000 comm. vehicles. **Chief port:** Kingstown.

Communications: Telephones in use (1985): 9,000.

Health: Life expectancy at birth (1985): 67.5 male; 71.4 female. **Births** (per 1,000 pop. 1986): 24.5. **Deaths** (per 1,000 pop. 1986): 5.9. **Natural increase** (1986): 1.8%. **Infant mortality** (per 1,000 live births 1985): 40.

Education (1984): **Literacy:** 85%.

Columbus landed on St. Vincent on Jan. 22, 1498 (St. Vincent's Day). Britain and France both laid claim to the island in the 17th and 18th centuries; the Treaty of Versailles, 1783, finally ceded it to Britain. Associated State status was granted 1969; independence was attained Oct. 27, 1979.

The entire economic life of St. Vincent is dependent upon agriculture and tourism.

San Marino

Most Serene Republic of San Marino

Serenissima Republica di San Marino

People: Population (1989 est.): 23,000. **Age distrib. (%):** 0–14: 19.0; 15–59: 63.7; 60+: 17.3. **Pop. density:** 958 per sq. mi. **Urban** (1988): 90.5%. **Ethnic groups:** Sanmarinese 88%, Italian 11%. **Languages:** Italian. **Religion:** mostly Roman Catholic.

Geography: Area: 24 sq. mi. **Location:** In N central Italy near Adriatic coast. **Neighbors:** Completely surrounded by Italy. **Topography:** The country lies on the slopes of Mt. Titano. **Capital:** San Marino. **City** (1987 est.): San Marino 4,179.

Government: Type: Independent republic. **Head of state:** Two co-regents appt. every 6 months. **Local divisions:** 11 districts, 9 sectors.

Economy: Industries: Postage stamps, tourism, woolen goods, paper, cement, ceramics. **Arable land:** 17%.

Finance: Currency: Italian lira. **Gross national product** (1986): $188 mln. **Tourists** (1986): 2.7 mln; $56 mln. receipts.

Communications: Television sets: 6,000 (1986). **Radios:** 11,000 licensed (1986). **Telephones in use** (1986): 13,000. **Daily newspaper circ.** (1985): 60 per 1,000 pop.

Births (per 1,000 pop. 1985): 11. **Deaths** (per 1,000 pop. 1985): 7.2. **Natural increase** (1985): 0.4%. **Infant mortality** (per 1,000 live births 1987): 9.6.

Education (1987): **Literacy:** 97%. **Years compulsory:** 8. **Attendance:** 93%.

San Marino claims to be the oldest state in Europe and to have been founded in the 4th century. A communist-led coalition ruled 1947-57; a similar coalition ruled 1978-86. It has had a treaty of friendship with Italy since 1862.

Sao Tome and Principe

Democratic Republic of Sao Tome and Principe

República Democrática de Sao Tome e Principe

People: Population (1989 est.): 114,000. **Pop. density:** 306 per sq. mi. **Ethnic groups:** Portuguese-African mixture, African minority (Angola, Mozambique immigrants). **Languages:** Portuguese. **Religions:** Christian 80%.

Geography: Area: 372 sq. mi., slightly larger than New York City. **Location:** In the Gulf of Guinea about 125 miles off W Central Africa. **Neighbors:** Gabon, Equatorial Guinea on E. **Topography:** Sao Tome and Principe islands, part of an extinct volcano chain, are both covered by lush forests and croplands. **Capital:** Sao Tome. **Cities** (1988 est.): Sao Tome 40,000.

Government: Type: Republic. **Head of state:** Pres. Manuel Pinto da Costa; b. 1910; in office: July 12, 1975. **Head of government:** Prime Min. Celestino Rocha da Costa; in office: Jan. 8, 1988. **Local divisions:** 7 counties.

Economy: Chief crops: Cocoa (82% of exports), coconut products. **Arable land:** 38%. **Electricity prod.** (1986): 27 mln. kwh.

Finance: Currency: Dobra (Jan. 1989: 77 = $1 US). **Gross national product** (1986): $43 mln. **Per capita income** (1986): $384. **Imports** (1986): $25.6 mln.; partners: Port. 61%, Angola 13%. **Exports** (1986): $9.3 mln.; partners: Neth. 52%, Port. 33%, W. Ger. 8%.

Transport: Motor vehicles: in use (1979): 1,300 passenger cars, 1,900 comm. vehicles. **Chief ports:** Sao Tome, Santo Antonio.

Communications: Radios: 28,000 in use (1986).

Health: Births (per 1,000 pop. 1985): 28. **Deaths** (per 1,000 pop. 1985): 7. **Natural increase** (1985): 2.1%. **Hospital beds** (1978): 665. **Physicians** (1985): 53. **Infant mortality** (per 1,000 live births 1985): 65.

Education (1988): **Literacy:** 50%.

Major International Organizations: UN, OAU.

Embassy: 801 2d Ave., New York, NY 10017; 212-697-4211.

The islands were uninhabited when discovered in 1471 by the Portuguese, who brought the first settlers — convicts and exiled Jews. Sugar planting was replaced by the slave trade as the chief economic activity until coffee and cocoa were introduced in the 19th century.

Portugal agreed, 1974, to turn the colony over to the Gabon-based Movement for the Liberation of Sao Tome and Principe, which proclaimed as first president its East German-trained leader Manuel Pinto da Costa. Independence came July 12, 1975. Democratic reforms were instituted in 1987.

Agriculture and fishing are the mainstays of the economy.

Saudi Arabia

Kingdom of Saudi Arabia

al-Mamlaka al-'Arabiya as-Sa'udiya

People: Population (1989 est.): 12,678,000. **Pop. density:** 15 per sq. mi. **Urban** (1986): 73%. **Ethnic groups:** Arab tribes, immigrants from other Arab and Moslem countries. **Languages:** Arabic. **Religions:** Moslem 99%.

Geography: Area: 839,996 sq. mi., one-third the size of the U.S. **Location:** Occupies most of Arabian Peninsula in Middle East. **Neighbors:** Kuwait, Iraq, Jordan on N, Yemen, South Yemen, Oman on S, United Arab Emirates, Qatar on E. **Topography:** The highlands on W, up to 9,000 ft., slope as an arid, barren desert to the Persian Gulf. **Capital:** Riyadh. **Cities** (1986 est.): Riyadh 1,380,000; Jidda 1,210,000; Mecca 463,000.

Government: Type: Monarchy with council of ministers. **Head of state and head of government:** King Fahd; b. 1922; in office: June 13, 1982. **Local divisions:** 14 provinces. **Defense:** 24.4% of GNP (1985).

Economy: Industries: Oil products. **Chief crops:** Dates, wheat, barley, fruit. **Minerals:** Oil, gas, gold, copper, iron. **Crude oil reserves** (1987): 169 bln. bbls. **Arable land:** 2%. **Livestock** (1986): sheep: 3.8 mln.; goats: 2.3 mln. **Electricity prod.** (1986): 43 bln. kwh. **Labor force:** 14% agric.; 11% ind; 53% serv., comm., & govt.; 20% construction.

Finance: Currency: Riyal (May 1989: 3.74 = $1 US). **Gross national product** (1986): $98.1 bln. **Per capita income** (1979): $11,500. **Imports** (1987): $24.3 bln.; partners: US 18%, Jap. 18%, W. Ger. 7%. **Exports** (1987): $26.9 bln.; partners: U.S. 19%, Jap., 22%. **International reserves less gold** (Mar. 1989): $21.5 bln. **Gold:** 4.59 mln. oz t. **Consumer prices** (change in 1988): 1.1%.

Transport: Railway traffic (1987): 70 mln. passenger-km; 321 mln. net ton-km. **Motor vehicles:** in use (1987): 2.2 mln. passenger cars, 1.9 mln. comm. vehicles. **Civil aviation** (1987): 16.1 bln. passenger-km. 490 mln. net ton-km. **Chief ports:** Jidda, Ad-Dammam, Ras Tannurah.

Communications: Television sets: 3.7 mln. in use (1986). **Radios:** 3.2 mln. in use (1986). **Telephones in use** (1986): 980,000. **Daily newspaper circ.** (1986): 41 per 1,000 pop.

Health: Life expectancy at birth (1986): 60 years. **Births** (per 1,000 pop. 1986): 37.3. **Deaths** (per 1,000 pop. 1986): 12.8. **Natural increase** (1986): 2.3%. **Hospital beds** (1986): 23,862. **Physicians** (1986): 13,996. **Infant mortality** (per 1,000 live births 1986): 108.

Education (1986): **Literacy:** 50% (men).

Major International Organizations: UN (IMF, WHO, FAO), Arab League, OPEC.

Embassy: 601 New Hampshire Ave. NW 20037; 342-3800.

Arabia was united for the first time by Mohammed, in the early 7th century. His successors conquered the entire Near East and North Africa, bringing Islam and the Arabic language. But Arabia itself soon returned to its former status.

Nejd, long an independent state and center of the Wahhabi sect, fell under Turkish rule in the 18th century, but in 1913 Ibn Saud, founder of the Saudi dynasty, overthrew the Turks and captured the Turkish province of Hasa; took the Hejaz in 1925 and by 1926, most of Asir. The discovery of oil in the 1930s transformed the new country.

Crown Prince Khalid was proclaimed king on Mar. 25, 1975, after the assassination of King Faisal. Fahd became king on June 13, 1982 following Khalid's death. There is no constitution and no parliament. The king exercises authority together with a Council of Ministers. The Islamic religious code is the law of the land. Alcohol and public entertainments are restricted, and women have an inferior legal status.

Saudi units fought against Israel in the 1948 and 1973 Arab-Israeli wars. Many billions of dollars of advanced arms have been purchased from Britain, France, and the U.S., including jet fighters, missiles, and, in 1981, 5 airborne warning and control system (AWACS) aircraft from the U.S., despite strong opposition from Israel. Beginning with the 1967 Arab-Israeli war, Saudi Arabia provided large annual financial gifts to Egypt; aid was later extended to Syria, Jordan, and Palestinian guerrilla groups, as well as to other Moslem countries. The country has aided anti-radical forces in Yemen and Oman.

Faisal played a leading role in the 1973-74 Arab oil embargo against the U.S. and other nations in an attempt to force them to adopt an anti-Israel policy. Saudi Arabia joined most other Arab states, 1979, in condemning Egypt's peace treaty with Israel.

Between 1973 and 1976, Saudi Arabia acquired full ownership of Aramco (Arabian American Oil Co.). In the 1980s, Saudi Arabia's moderate position on crude oil prices has often prevailed at OPEC meetings.

The Hejaz contains the holy cities of Islam — Medina where the Mosque of the Prophet enshrines the tomb of Mohammed, who died in the city June 7, 632, and Mecca, his birthplace. More than 600,000 Moslems from 60 nations pilgrimage to Mecca annually. The regime faced its first serious opposition when Moslem fundamentalists seized the Grand Mosque in Mecca, Nov. 20, 1979.

Two Saudi oil tankers were attacked May 1984, as Iran and Iraq began air attacks against shipping in the Persian Gulf. On May 29, the U.S., citing grave concern over the growing escalation of the Iran-Iraq war in the Persian Gulf, authorized the sale of 400 Stinger antiaircraft missiles. In 1986, U.S. President Reagan vetoed a congressional resolution that would have blocked sale of advanced U.S. missiles to the Saudis.

In 1987, Iranians making a pilgrimage to Mecca clashed with anti-Iranian pilgrims and Saudi police; over 400 were killed. Saudi Arabia broke diplomatic relations with Iran in 1988.

Senegal
Republic of Senegal
République du Sénégal

People: Population (1989 est.): 7,704,000. **Age distrib.** (%): 0–14: 46.5; 15–59: 48.9; 60+: 4.6. **Pop. density:** 101 per sq. mi. **Urban** (1986): 30%. **Ethnic groups:** Wolof 36%, Serer 17%, Peulh 17%, Diola 9%, Toucouleur 9%, Mandingo 6%. **Languages:** French (official), tribal languages. **Religions:** Moslems 92%, Christians 2%.

Geography: Area: 75,750 sq. mi., the size of South Dakota. **Location:** At western extreme of Africa. **Neighbors:** Mauritania on N, Mali on E, Guinea, Guinea-Bissau on S, Gambia surrounded on three sides. **Topography:** Low rolling plains cover most of Senegal, rising somewhat in the SE. Swamp and jungles are in SW. **Capital:** Dakar. **Cities** (1986): Dakar 1.3 mln. Thies 156,000; Kaolack 132,000.

Government: Type: Republic. **Head of state:** Pres. Abdou Diouf; b. Sept. 7, 1935; in office: Jan. 1, 1981. **Local divisions:** 10 regions. **Defense:** 2.0% of GNP (1986).

Economy: Industries: Food processing, fishing. **Chief crops:** Peanuts are chief export; millet, rice. **Minerals:** Phosphates. **Arable land:** 27%. **Livestock** (1986): cattle: 2.2 mln.; sheep: 2.2 mln.; goats: 1 mln. **Fish catch** (1986): 255,000 metric tons. **Electricity prod.** (1986): 737 mln. kwh. **Labor force:** 70% agric.

Finance: Currency: CFA franc (Mar. 1989: 319 = $1 US). **Gross national product** (1986): $3.8 bln. **Per capita income** (1984): $380. **Imports** (1986): $705 mln.; partners Fr. 37%, U.S. 6%. **Exports** (1986): $483 mln.; partners Fr. 25%, UK 6%. **Tourists** (1985): $81 mln. receipts. **International reserves less gold** (Jan. 1989): $10.5 mln. **Gold:** 29,000 oz t. **Consumer prices** (change in 1988): −1.8%.

Transport: Railway traffic (1984): 133 mln. passenger-km; 309 mln. net ton-km. **Motor vehicles:** in use (1985): 76,000 passenger cars, 36,000 comm. vehicles. **Chief ports:** Dakar, Saint-Louis.

Communications: Television sets: 55,000 in use (1986). **Radios:** 450,000 in use (1986). **Telephones in use** (1985): 33,000. **Daily newspaper circ.** (1984): 4 per 1,000 pop.

Health: Life expectancy at birth (1984): 45.0 male, 48.0 female. **Births** (per 1,000 pop. 1985): 47.9. **Deaths** (per 1,000 pop. 1985): 21.1. **Natural increase** (1985): 2.6%. **Hospital beds** (1982): 6,200. **Physicians** (1982): 470. **Infant mortality** (per 1,000 live births 1988): 112.

Education (1988): **Literacy:** 10%. **Attendance:** 48% primary, 11% secondary.

Major International Organizations: UN and all of its specialized agencies, OAU.

Embassy: 2112 Wyoming Ave. NW 20008; 234-0540.

Portuguese settlers arrived in the 15th century, but French control grew from the 17th century. The last independent Moslem state was subdued in 1893. Dakar became the capital of French West Africa.

Independence as part, along with the Sudanese Rep., of the Mali Federation, came June 20, 1960. Senegal withdrew Aug. 20 that year. French political and economic influence is strong.

A long drought brought famine, 1972-73, and again in 1978. Senegal is recognized as the most democratic of the French-speaking West African nations.

Senegal, Dec. 17, 1981, signed an agreement with The Gambia for confederation of the 2 countries under the name of Senegambia. The confederation began Feb. 1, 1982. The 2 nations retained their individual sovereignty but adopted joint defense and monetary policies.

In 1989, a border incident sparked ethnic violence against Senegalese in Mauritania and, in retaliation, against Mauritanians in Senegal.

Seychelles
Republic of Seychelles

People: Population (1989 est.): 70,000. **Age distrib.** (%): 0–14: 36.3; 15–64; 57.3; 65+: 6.4. **Pop. density:** 409 per sq. mi. **Urban** (1986): 50% **Ethnic groups:** Creoles (mixture of Asians,

Africans, and French) predominate. **Languages:** English and French (both official), Creole. **Religions:** Roman Catholic 90%.

Geography: Area: 171 sq. mi. **Location:** In the Indian O. 700 miles NE of Madagascar. **Neighbors:** Nearest are Madagascar on SW, Somalia on NW. **Topography:** A group of 86 islands, about half of them composed of coral, the other half granite, the latter predominantly mountainous. **Capital:** Victoria. **Cities** (1986): Victoria 23,000.

Government: Type: Single party republic. **Head of state:** Pres. France-Albert Rene, b. Nov. 16, 1935; in office: June 5, 1977. **Defense:** 5.6% of GNP (1984).

Economy: Industries: Food processing. **Chief crops:** Coconut products, cinnamon, vanilla, patchouli. **Other resources:** Guano, shark fins, tortoise shells, fish. **Electricity prod.** (1986): 59 mln. kwh. **Labor force:** 18.5% agric.; 19.4% ind. & comm.; 13.5% serv.; 49% govt.

Finance: Currency: Rupee (Mar. 1989: 5.59 = $1 US). **Gross national product** (1986): $203 mln. **Per capita income** (1985): $2,100. **Imports** (1987): $114 mln.; partners: UK 20%, So. Afr. 13%. **Exports** (1987): $22 mln.; partners: Pak. 38%; Jap. 26%. **National Budget** (1985): $65 mln. **Tourists** (1985): $51 mln. receipts. **International reserves less gold** (Mar. 1989): $11.4 mln. **Consumer prices** (change in 1988): 2.6%.

Transport: Motor vehicles: in use (1985): 3,500 passenger cars, 1,000 comm. vehicles. **Port:** Victoria.

Communications: Radios: 19,000 in use (1986). **Telephones in use** (1985): 11,000. **Daily newspaper circ.** (1986): 48 per 1,000 pop.

Health: Life expectancy at birth (1986): 66 years. **Births** (per 1,000 pop. 1986): 26.2 **Deaths** (per 1,000 pop. 1986): 7.5 **Natural increase** (1986): 1.8%. **Hospital beds** (1987): 373. **Physicians** (1987): 37. **Infant mortality** (per 1,000 live births 1987): 18.4.

Education (1986): **Literacy:** 80%. **Years compulsory** 9; attendance 95%.

Major International Organizations: UN, OAU, Commonwealth of Nations.

The islands were occupied by France in 1768, and seized by Britain in 1794. Ruled as part of Mauritius from 1814, the Seychelles became a separate colony in 1903. The ruling party had opposed independence as impractical, but pressure from the OAU and the UN became irresistible, and independence was declared June 29, 1976. The first president was ousted in a coup a year later by a socialist leader.

A new constitution, announced Mar. 1979, turned the country into a one-party state.

Sierra Leone
Republic of Sierra Leone

People: Population (1989 est.): 4,318,000. **Age distrib.** (%): 0–14: 41.4; 15–59: 53.5; 60+: 5.1. **Pop. density:** 154 per sq. mi. **Ethnic groups:** Temne 30%, Mende 29%, others. **Languages:** English (official), tribal languages. **Religions:** animist 30%, Moslem 30%, Christian 10%.

Geography: Area: 27,925 sq. mi., slightly smaller than South Carolina. **Location:** On W coast of W. Africa. **Neighbors:** Guinea on N, E, Liberia on S. **Topography:** The heavily-indented, 210-mi. coastline has mangrove swamps. Behind are wooded hills, rising to a plateau and mountains in the E. **Capital:** Freetown. **Cities** (1985 est.): Freetown 469,000; Bo, Kenema, Makeni.

Government: Type: Republic. **Head of state and head of government:** Pres. Gen. Joseph Saidu Momoh; b. Jan. 26, 1937; in office: Nov. 28, 1985. **Local divisions:** 12 districts and one region including Freetown.

Economy: Industries: Mining, tourism. **Chief crops:** Cocoa, coffee, palm kernels, rice, ginger. **Minerals:** Diamonds, bauxite. **Arable land:** 25%. **Fish catch** (1985): 52,000 metric tons. **Electricity prod.** (1986): 85 mln. kwh. **Labor force:** 75% agric.; 15% ind. & serv.

Finance: Currency: Leone (Mar. 1989: 1.00 = $.02 US). **Gross national product** (1986): $1.1 bln. **Per capita income** (1984): $320. **Imports** (1987): $137 mln.; partners: UK 22%, Fr. 11%. **Exports** (1987): $129 mln.; partners: Neth. 31%; UK 15%, U.S. 9%. **National budget** (1986): $138 mln. expenditures. **International reserves less gold** (Mar. 1989): $6.2 mln. **Consumer prices** (change in 1987): 178%.

Transport: Motor Vehicles: in use (1985): 23,000 passenger cars, 36,000 comm. vehicles. **Chief ports:** Freetown, Bonthe.

Communications: Television sets: 25,000 in use (1986). **Radios:** 225,000 in use (1986). **Telephones in use** (1986): 15,000. **Daily newspaper circ.** (1987): 3 per 1,000 pop.

Health: Life expectancy at birth (1986): 46 yrs. **Births** (per 1,000 pop. 1985): 45.3. **Deaths** (per 1,000 pop. 1985): 17.4. **Natural increase** (1985): 2.7%. **Hospital beds** (1984): 4,754. **Physicians** (1984): 197. **Infant mortality** (per 1,000 live births 1985): 195.

Education (1986): **Literacy:** 15%.

Major International Organizations: UN (GATT, IMF, WHO), Commonwealth of Nations, OAU.

Embassy: 1701 19th St. NW 20009; 939-9261.

Freetown was founded in 1787 by the British government as a haven for freed slaves. Their descendants, known as Creoles, number more than 60,000.

Successive steps toward independence followed the 1951 constitution. Full independence arrived Apr. 27, 1961. Sierra Leone became a republic Apr. 19, 1971. A one-party state approved by referendum 1978, brought political stability, but the economy has been plagued by inflation, corruption, and dependence upon the International Monetary Fund and creditors.

Singapore
Republic of Singapore

People: Population (1989 est.): 2,668,000. **Age distrib.** (%): 0–14: 23.4; 15–59: 68.4; 60+: 8.2. **Pop. density:** 11,910 per sq. mi. **Ethnic groups:** Chinese 77%, Malays 15%, Indians 6%. **Languages:** Chinese, Malay, Tamil, English all official. **Religions:** Buddhism, Taoism, Islam, Hinduism, Christianity.

Geography: Area: 224 sq. mi., smaller than New York City. **Location:** Off tip of Malayan Peninsula in S.E. Asia. **Neighbors:** Nearest are Malaysia on N, Indonesia on S. **Topography:** Singapore is a flat, formerly swampy island. The nation includes 40 nearby islets. **Capital:** Singapore. **Cities** (1978 est.): Singapore 2,334,400.

Government: Type: Parliamentary democracy. **Head of state:** Pres. Wee Kim Wee; in office: Sept. 3, 1985. **Head of government:** Prime Min. Lee Kuan Yew; b. Sept. 16, 1923; in office: June 5, 1959. **Defense:** 6% of GNP (1985).

Economy: Industries: Shipbuilding, oil refining, electronics, banking, textiles, food, rubber, lumber processing, tourism. **Arable land:** 11%. **Livestock** (1986): pigs: 700,000. **Fish catch** (1987): 15,000 metric tons. **Electricity prod.** (1986): 10.0 bln. kwh. **Crude steel prod.** (1985): 350,000 metric tons. **Labor force:** 1% agric.; 58% ind. & comm.; 35% services.

Finance: Currency: Dollar (May 1989: 1.95 = $1 US). **Gross national product** (1986): $19.1 bln. **Per capita income** (1985): $6,200. **Imports** (1988): $43.8 bln.; partners: Jap. 18%, Malay. 13%, U.S. 13%, Sau. Ar. 9%. **Exports** (1988): $39.3 bln., partners: U.S. 20%, Malay. 16%, Jap. 11%, HK 6%. **Tourists** (1986): $1.7 bln. receipts. **National budget** (1986): $10 bln. expenditures. **Consumer prices** (change in 1988): 1.5%.

Transport: Motor vehicles: in use (1987): 236,000 passenger cars, 114,000 comm. vehicles. **Civil aviation:** (1986) 22.8 bln. passenger-km; 1.1 bln. freight ton-km.

Communications: Television sets: 516,000 (1987). **Radios:** 111,000 in use (1986). **Telephones in use** (1987): 1.1 mln. **Daily newsp per circ.** (1986): 270 per 1,000 pop.

Health: Life expectancy at birth (1987): 70.0 male; 76.3 female. **Births** (per 1,000 pop. 1987): 16.8 **Deaths** (per 1,000 pop. 1987): 5.0 **Natural increase** (1987): 1.1%. **Hospital beds** (1985): 9,866. **Physicians** (1985): 2,631. **Infant mortality** (per 1,000 live births 1987): 7.4

Education (1987): **Literacy:** 85%. **Years compulsory:** none; attendance 85%.

Major International Organizations: UN (GATT, IMF, WHO), ASEAN.

Embassy: 1824 R St. NW 20009; 667-7555.

Founded in 1819 by Sir Thomas Stamford Raffles, Singapore was a British colony until 1959 when it became autonomous within the Commonwealth. On Sept. 16, 1963, it joined with Malaya, Sarawak and Sabah to form the Federation of Malaysia.

Tensions between Malayans, dominant in the federation, and ethnic Chinese, dominant in Singapore, led to an agreement under which Singapore became a separate nation, Aug. 9, 1965.

Singapore is one of the world's largest ports. Standards in health, education, and housing are high. International banking has grown.

Solomon Islands

People: Population (1989 est.): 314,000. **Age distrib. (%):** 0–14: 49; 15–59: 45.5; 60+: 5.5. **Pop. density:** 29 per sq. mi. **Urban** (1986): 15%. **Ethnic groups:** Melanesian 93%, Polynesian 4%. **Languages:** English (official), Pidgin, local languages. **Religions:** Anglican 34%, Roman Catholic 19%, Evangelical 24%, traditional religions.
Geography: Area: 10,640 sq. mi., slightly larger than Maryland. **Location:** Melanesian archipelago in the western Pacific O. **Neighbors:** Nearest is Papua New Guinea on W. **Topography:** 10 large volcanic and rugged islands and 4 groups of smaller ones. **Capital:** Honiara. **Cities:** (1988): Honiara 30,000.
Government: Type: Parliamentary democracy within the Commonwealth of Nations. **Head of state:** Queen Elizabeth II, represented by Gov.-Gen. Baddeley Devesi; b. Oct. 16, 1941; in office: July 7, 1978. **Head of government:** Prime Min. Ezekial Alebua; in office: Dec. 1, 1986. **Local divisions:** 7 provinces and Honiara.
Economy: Industries: Fish canning. **Chief crops:** Coconuts, rice, bananas, yams. **Other resources:** Forests, marine shell. **Arable land:** 2%. **Fish catch** (1984): 35,000 metric tons. **Electricity prod.** (1986): 30.0 mln. kwh. **Labor force:** 32% agric., 32% services, 18% ind. & comm.
Finance: Currency: Dollar (Mar. 1989: 2.20 = $1 US). **Gross national product** (1986): $100 mln. **Per capita income** (1985): $628. **Imports** (1986): $58 mln.; partners: Austral. 31%, Jap. 14%, Sing. 18%. **Exports** (1986): $77 mln.; partners: Jap. 37%, UK 11%.
Communications: Radios: 40,000 in use (1986). **Telephones in use** (1987): 5,000.
Health: Life expectancy at birth: 54 years. **Births:** (per 1,000 pop. 1985): 47. **Deaths** (per 1,000 pop. 1985): 10. **Natural increase** (1985): 3.7%. **Infant mortality** (per 1,000 live births 1988): 46.
Education (1984): **Literacy:** 54%. **Primary school** 78%. **Secondary school:** 21%.
Major International Organizations: UN, Commonwealth of Nations.

The Solomon Islands were sighted in 1568 by an expedition from Peru. Britain established a protectorate in the 1890s over most of the group, inhabited by Melanesians. The islands saw major World War II battles. Self-government came Jan. 2, 1976, and independence was formally attained July 7, 1978.

Somalia
Somali Democratic Republic
Jamhuriyadda Dimugradiga Somaliya

People: Population (1989 est.): 8,552,000. **Pop. density:** 34 per sq. mi. **Ethnic groups:** mainly Hamitic, others. **Languages:** Somali, Arabic (both official). **Religions:** Sunni Moslems 99%.
Geography: Area: 246,300 sq. mi., slightly smaller than Texas. **Location:** Occupies the eastern horn of Africa. **Neighbors:** Djibouti, Ethiopia, Kenya on W. **Topography:** The coastline extends for 1,700 mi. Hills cover the N; the center and S are flat. **Capital:** Mogadishu. **Cities** (1986 est.): Mogadishu 700,000.
Government: Type: Independent republic. **Head of state:** Pres. Mohammed Siad Barrah; b. 1919; in office: Oct. 21, 1969. **Head of government:** Prime Min. Gen. Muhammad Ali Samatar; in office: Feb. 1, 1987. **Local divisions:** 15 regions. **Defense:** 6.5% of GNP (1984).
Economy: Chief crops: Incense, sugar, bananas, sorghum, corn, gum. **Minerals:** Iron, tin, gypsum, bauxite, uranium. **Arable land:** 2%. **Livestock** (1986): cattle: 4 mln.; goats: 18 mln.; sheep: 6 mln. **Fish catch** (1986): 16,000 metric tons. **Electricity prod.** (1986): 137 mln. kwh. **Labor force:** 82% agric.
Finance: Currency: Shilling (Mar. 1989: 340 = $1 US). **Gross national product** (1986): $1.5 bln. **Per capita income** (1985): $300. **Imports** (1985): $470 mln.; partners: It. 35%, UK 8%, U.S. 9%. **Exports** (1985): $110 mln.; partners: Saudi Ar. 66%, It. 12%. **International reserves less gold** (Nov. 1988):

$15.3 mln. **Gold:** 19,000 oz t. **Consumer prices** (change in 1987): 28.2%.
Transport: Motor vehicles: in use (1986): 17,000 passenger cars, 9,500 comm. vehicles. **Chief ports:** Mogadishu, Berbera.
Communications: Radios: 250,000 in use (1986).
Health: Life expectancy at birth (1985): 43.9 yrs. **Births** (per 1,000 pop. 1985): 47. **Deaths** (per 1,000 pop. 1985): 152. **Natural increase** (1985): 3.0%. **Hospital beds** (1985): 5,536. **Physicians** (1985): 321. **Infant mortality** (per 1,000 live births 1985): 163.
Education (1986): Literacy: 40%. 50% attend primary school, 7% attend secondary school.
Major International Organizations: UN, OAU, Arab League.
Embassy: 600 New Hampshire Ave. NW 20037; 342-1575.

Arab trading posts developed into sultanates. The Italian Protectorate of Somalia, acquired from 1885 to 1927, extended along the Indian O. from the Gulf of Aden to the Juba R. The UN in 1949 approved eventual creation of Somalia as a sovereign state and in 1950 Italy took over the trusteeship held by Great Britain since World War II.

British Somaliland was formed in the 19th century in the NW. Britain gave it independence June 26, 1960; on July 1 it joined with the former Italian part to create the independent Somali Republic.

On Oct. 21, 1969, a Supreme Revolutionary Council seized power in a bloodless coup, named a Council of Secretaries of State, and abolished the Assembly. In May, 1970, several foreign companies were nationalized.

A severe drought in 1975 killed tens of thousands, and spurred efforts to resettle nomads on collective farms.

Somalia has laid claim to Ogaden, the huge eastern region of Ethiopia, peopled mostly by Somalis. Ethiopia battled Somali rebels and accused Somalia of sending troops and heavy arms in 1977. Russian forces were expelled in 1977 in retaliation for Soviet support of Ethiopia. Some 11,000 Cuban troops with Soviet arms defeated Somali army troops and ethnic Somali rebels in Ethiopia, 1978. As many as 1.5 mln. refugees entered Somalia. Guerrilla fighting in Ogaden continued until 1988 when a peace agreement was reached with Ethiopia.

South Africa
Republic of South Africa
Republiek van Suid-Afrika

People: Population (1989 est.): 35,625,000. **Age distrib. (%):** 0–14: 41.0; 15–59: 52.8; 60+: 6.2. **Pop. density:** 75 per sq. mi. **Urban** (1985): 55%. **Ethnic groups:** black 68%, white 18%, coloured 10%, Asian 3%. **Religions:** Mainly Christian, Hindu, Moslem minorities. **Languages:** Afrikaans, English (both official), Bantu languages predominate.
Geography: Area: 472,359 sq. mi., about twice the size of Texas. **Location:** At the southern extreme of Africa. **Neighbors:** Namibia (SW Africa), Botswana, Zimbabwe on N, Mozambique, Swaziland on E; surrounds Lesotho. **Topography:** The large interior plateau reaches close to the country's 2,700-mi. coastline. There are few major rivers or lakes; rainfall is sparse in W, more plentiful in E. **Capitals:** Cape Town (legislative), Pretoria (administrative), and Bloemfontein (judicial). **Cities** (1985 met.): Durban 982,000; Cape Town 1,900,000; Johannesburg 1,600,000; Pretoria 822,000.
Government: Type: Tricameral parliament with one chamber each for whites, coloureds, and Asians. **Head of State:** State President F.W. De Klerk in office: Aug. 15, 1989. **Local divisions:** 4 provinces, 10 "homelands" for black Africans. **Defense:** 3.7 of GNP (1986).
Economy: Industries: Steel, tires, motors, textiles, plastics. **Chief crops:** Corn, wool, dairy products, grain, tobacco, sugar, fruit, peanuts, grapes. **Minerals:** Gold (largest producer), chromium, antimony, coal, iron, manganese, nickel, phosphates, tin, uranium, gem diamonds, platinum, copper, vanadium. **Other resources:** Wool. **Arable land:** 12%. **Livestock** (1987): cattle: 12.7 mln.; sheep: 30.3 mln. **Fish catch** (1986): 649,000 metric tons. **Electricity prod.** (1986): 148 bln. kwh. **Crude steel prod.** (1987): 8.7 mln. metric tons. **Labor force:** 30% agric.; 29% ind. and commerce; 34% serv.; 7% mining.
Finance: Currency: Rand (May 1989: 2.78 = $1 US). **Gross national product** (1986): $59.9 bln. **Per capita income** (1985): $4,000. **Imports** (1988): $18.7 bln.; partners: W. Ger. 15%, U.S.

19%, UK. 12%. **Exports** (1988): $21.5 bln.; partners: U.S. 9%, Jap. 9%. **Tourism** (1986): $388 mln. receipts. **National budget** (1984): $20.7 bln. **International reserves less gold** (Mar. 1989): $569 mln. **Gold:** 4.1 mln. oz t. **Consumer prices** (change in 1988): 12.8%.

Transport: Railway traffic (1986): 17.8 bln. passenger-km; 92.8 bln. net ton-km. **Motor vehicles:** in use (1986): 3.1 mln. passenger cars, 1.2 mln. comm. vehicles. **Civil aviation:** (1985): 8.7 bln. passenger-km: 397 mln. freight ton-km. **Chief ports:** Durban, Cape Town, East London, Port Elizabeth.

Communications: Television sets (1986): 4.0 mln.; **Radios:** 10 mln. in use (1986). **Telephones in use** (1986): 4.0 mln. **Daily newspaper circ.** (1986): 41 per 1,000 pop.

Health: Life expectancy at birth (1982): Whites: 70 years; Asians: 65 years; Africans: 59 years. **Births** (per 1,000 pop. 1985): 33. **Deaths** (per 1,000 pop. 1985): 10. **Natural increase** (1985): 2.3%. **Physicians** (1986): 22,500. **Infant mortality** (per 1,000 live births 1982): Africans 94, Asians 25.3, whites 14.9.

Education (1987): **Literacy:** 99% (whites), 69% (Asians), 62% (coloureds), 50% (Africans).

Major International Organizations: UN (GATT).

Embassy: 3051 Massachusetts Ave. NW 20008; 232-4400.

Bushmen and Hottentots were the original inhabitants. Bantus, including Zulu, Xhosa, Swazi, and Sotho, had occupied the area from Transvaal to south of Transkei before the 17th century.

The Cape of Good Hope area was settled by Dutch, beginning in the 17th century. Britain seized the Cape in 1806. Many Dutch trekked north and founded 2 republics, the Transvaal and the Orange Free State. Diamonds were discovered, 1867, and gold, 1886. The Dutch (Boers) resented encroachments by the British and others; the Anglo-Boer War followed, 1899-1902. Britain won and, effective May 31, 1910, created the Union of South Africa, incorporating the British colonies of the Cape and Natal, the Transvaal and the Orange Free State. After a referendum, the Union became the Republic of South Africa, May 31, 1961, and withdrew from the Commonwealth.

With the election victory of Daniel Malan's National party in 1948, the policy of separate development of the races, or apartheid, already existing unofficially, became official. This called for separate development, separate residential areas, and ultimate political independence for the whites, Bantus, Asians, and Coloreds. In 1959 the government passed acts providing the eventual creation of several Bantu nations or Bantustans on 13% of the country's land area, though most black leaders have opposed the plan.

Under apartheid, blacks are severely restricted to certain occupations, and are paid far lower wages than are whites for similar work. Only whites may vote or run for public office, and militant white opposition has been curbed. There is an advisory Indian Council, partially elected, partly appointed. In 1969, a Colored People's Representative Council was created. Some liberalization measures were allowed in the 1980s.

At least 600 persons, mostly Bantus, were killed in 1976 riots protesting apartheid. Black protests continued through 1985 as violence broke out in several black townships. Police reaction to the protests caused several hundred deaths. A new constitution was approved by referendum, Nov. 1983, which extended the parliamentary franchise to the Coloured and Asian minorities. Laws banning interracial sex and marriage were repealed in 1985.

In 1963, the Transkei, an area in the SE, became the first of these partially self-governing territories or "Homelands." Transkei became independent on Oct. 26, 1976, Bophuthatswana on Dec. 6, 1977, and Venda on Sept. 13, 1979; none received international recognition.

In 1981, So. Africa launched military operations in Angola and Mozambique to combat terrorists groups; So. African troops attacked the South West African People's Organization (SWAPO) guerrillas in Angola, March, 1982. South Africa and Mozambique signed a non-agression pact in 1984.

A car bomb exploded outside air force headquarters in Pretoria, May 20, 1983, killing or injuring hundreds of people. The African National Congress (ANC), a black nationalist group, claimed responsibility. In the U.S., there were numerous antiapartheid protests in the 1980's.

In 1986, Nobel Peace Prize winner Bishop Desmond Tutu called for Western nations to apply sanctions against S. Africa to force an end to apartheid. President Botha announced in Apr.

the end to the nation's system of racial pass laws and offered blacks an advisory role in government.

On May 19, S. Africa attacked 3 neighboring countries—Zimbabwe, Botswana, Zambia—to strike at guerrilla strongholds of the African National Congress.

A nationwide state of emergency was declared June 12, giving almost unlimited power to the security forces. On Apr. 22, 1987, a 6-week-old walkout by railway workers erupted into violence after the dismissal of 16,000 strikers. As confrontation between blacks and government increased, there was widespread support in Western nations for a complete trade embargo on S. Africa.

Some 2 million South African black workers staged a massive strike, June 6-8, 1988, to protest the government's new labor laws and the banning of political activity by trade unions and antiapartheid groups.

Bophuthatswana: Population (1987 est.): 2,005,000. **Area:** 15,444 sq. mi., 6 discontinuous geographic units. **Capital:** Mmabatho. **Head of state:** Pres. Kgosi Lucas Manyane Mangope, b. Dec. 27, 1923; in office: Dec. 6, 1977.

Ciskei: Population (1987 est.): 8,946,000. **Area:** 2,080 sq. mi. **Capitol:** Bisho. **Head of State:** Pres. Lennox Sebe.

Transkei: Population (1987 est.): 2,832,000. **Area:** 16,816 sq. mi., 3 discontinuous geographic units. **Capital:** Umtata. **Head of government:** Gen. Bantu Holomisa; in office: Dec. 30, 1987.

Venda: Population (1988 est.): 547,000. **Area:** 2,390 sq. mi., 2 discontinuous geographic units. **Capital:** Thohoyandou. **Head of state:** Frank Ravele; in office: Apr. 18, 1988.

Namibia (South-West Africa)

South-West Africa is a sparsely populated land twice the size of California. Made a German protectorate in 1884, it was surrendered to South Africa in 1915 and was administered by that country under a League of Nations mandate. S. Africa refused to accept UN authority under the trusteeship system.

Other African nations charged S. Africa imposed apartheid, built military bases, and exploited S-W Africa. The UN General Assembly, May 1968, created an 11-nation council to take over administration of S-W Africa and lead it to independence. The council charged that S. Africa had blocked its efforts to visit S-W Africa.

In 1968 the UN General Assembly gave the area the name Namibia. In Jan. 1970 the UN Security Council condemned S. Africa for "illegal" control of the area. In an advisory opinion, June 1971, the International Court of Justice declared S. Africa was occupying the area illegally.

In a 1977 referendum, white voters backed a plan for a multiracial interim government to lead to independence. The Marxist South-West Africa People's Organization (SWAPO) rejected the plan, and launched a guerrilla war. Both S. Africa and Namibian rebels agreed to a UN plan for independence by the end of 1978. S. Africa rejected the plan, Sept. 20, 1978, and held elections, without UN supervision, for Namibia's constituent assembly, Dec., that were ignored by the major black opposition parties.

The UN peace plan, proposed 1980, called for a cease-fire and a demilitarized zone 31 miles deep on each side of S-W Africa's borders with Angola and Zambia that would be patrolled by UN peacekeeping forces against guerrilla actions. In 1982, So. African and SWAPO agreed in principle on a cease-fire and the holding of UN-supervised elections. So. Africa, however, insisted on the withdrawal of Cuban forces from Angola as a precondition to Namibian independence. On Jan. 18, 1983, South Africa dissolved the Namibian National Assembly and resumed direct control of the territory.

In 1988, A U.S. mediated plan was agreed upon by So. Africa, Angola, and Cuba, which called for withdrawal of Cuban troops from Angola and black majority rule in Namibia.

Most of Namibia is a plateau, 3,600 ft. high, with plains in the N, Kalahari Desert to the E, Orange R. on the S, Atlantic O. on the W. Area is 320,827 sq. mi.; pop. (1988 est.) 1,228,000; capital, Windhoek.

Products include cattle, sheep, diamonds, copper, lead, zinc, fish. People include Nama (Hottentots), Ovambo (Bantus), Kavango, and others.

Walvis Bay, the only deepwater port in the country, was turned over to South African administration in 1922. S. Africa said in 1978 it would discuss sovereignty only after Namibian independence.

Spain
España

People: Population (1989 est.): 39,784,000 **Age distrib. (%):** 0–14: 24.6; 15–59: 59.5; 60+: 15.9. **Pop. density:** 204 per sq. mi. **Urban** (1987): 75%. **Ethnic groups:** Spanish (Castilian, Valencian, Andalusian, Asturian) 72.8%, Catalan 16.4%, Galician 8.2%, Basque 2.3%. **Languages:** Spanish (official), Catalan, Galician, Basque. **Religions:** Roman Catholic 90%.

Geography: Area: 194,896 sq. mi., the size of Arizona and Utah combined. **Location:** In SW Europe. **Neighbors:** Portugal on W. France on N. **Topography:** The interior is a high, arid plateau broken by mountain ranges and river valleys. The NW is heavily watered, the south has lowlands and a Mediterranean climate. **Capital:** Madrid. **Cities** (1987 est.): Madrid 3,500,000; Barcelona 2,000,000; Valencia 700,000; Seville 580,000.

Government: Type: Constitutional monarchy. **Head of state:** King Juan Carlos I de Borbon y Borbon, b. Jan. 5, 1938; in office: Nov. 22, 1975. **Head of government:** Prime Min. Felipe Gonzalez Marquez; in office: Dec. 2, 1982. **Local divisions:** 50 provinces, 2 territories, 3 islands. **Defense:** 2.2% of GNP (1985).

Economy: Industries: Machinery, steel, textiles, shoes, autos, processed foods. **Chief crops:** Grains, olives, grapes, citrus fruits, vegetables, olives. **Minerals:** Mercury, uranium, lead, iron, copper, zinc, coal. **Crude oil reserves** (1987): 34 mln. bbls. **Other resources:** Forests (cork). **Arable land:** 41%. **Livestock** (1986): cattle: 4.9 mln.; pigs: 11.9 mln.; sheep: 17.3 mln. **Fish catch** (1986): 1.3 mln. tons. **Electricity prod.** (1986): 134.3 bln. kwh. **Crude steel prod.** (1987): 11.8 mln. metric tons. **Labor force:** 16% agric.; 24% ind. and comm.; 52% serv.

Finance: Currency: Peseta (May 1989: 125.60 = $1 US). **Gross national product** (1986): $187.6 bln. **Per capita income** (1984): $4,490. **Imports** (1988): $60.5 bln.; partners: U.S. 11%, EC 33%. **Exports** (1988): $40.3 bln.; partners: EC 49%, U.S. 10%. **Tourists** (1986): $12.0 bln. receipts. **National budget** (1985): $35 bln. expenditures. **International reserves less gold** (Mar. 1989): $36.0 bln. **Gold:** 16.1 mln. oz t. **Consumer prices** (change in 1988): 4.8%.

Transport: Railway traffic (1987): 15 bln. passenger-km; 11.2 bln. net ton-km. **Motor vehicles:** in use (1987): 9.7 mln. passenger cars, 1.7 mln. comm. **Civil aviation:** (1986): 19.1 bln. passenger-km; 568 mln. freight ton-km. **Chief ports:** Barcelona, Bilbao, Valencia, Cartagena, Gijon.

Communications: Television sets: 14.8 mln. in use (1987). **Radios:** 10.8 mln. in use (1986). **Telephones** in use (1986): 14.2 mln. **Daily newspaper circ.** (1983): 89 per 1,000 pop.

Health: Life expectancy at birth (1985): 71.3 male; 77.5 female. **Births** (per 1,000 pop. 1985): 11. **Deaths** (per 1,000 pop. 1985): 8. **Natural increase** (1985): .3%. **Hospital beds** (1986): 193,000. **Physicians** (1986): 131,000. **Infant mortality** (per 1,000 live births 1985): 9.

Education (1987): Literacy: 97%. **School compulsory:** to age 14.

Major International Organizations: UN and all of its specialized agencies, NATO, OECD, EC.

Embassy: 2700 15th St. NW 20009; 265-0190.

Spain was settled by Iberians, Basques, and Celts, partly overrun by Carthaginians, conquered by Rome c.200 BC. The Visigoths, in power by the 5th century AD, adopted Christianity but by 711 AD lost to the Islamic invasion from Africa. Christian reconquest from the N led to a Spanish nationalism. In 1469 the kingdoms of Aragon and Castile were united by the marriage of Ferdinand II and Isabella I, and the last Moorish power was broken by the fall of the kingdom of Granada, 1492. Spain became a bulwark of Roman Catholicism.

Spain obtained a colonial empire with the discovery of America by Columbus, 1492, the conquest of Mexico by Cortes, and Peru by Pizarro. It also controlled the Netherlands and parts of Italy and Germany. Spain lost its American colonies in the early 19th century. It lost Cuba, the Philippines, and Puerto Rico during the Spanish-American War, 1898.

Primo de Rivera became dictator in 1923. King Alfonso XIII revoked the dictatorship, 1930, but was forced to leave the country 1931. A republic was proclaimed which disestablished the church, curtailed its privileges, and secularized education. A conservative reaction occurred 1933 but was followed by a Popular Front (1936-1939) composed of socialists, communists, republicans, and anarchists.

Army officers under Francisco Franco revolted against the government, 1936. In a destructive 3-year war, in which some one million died, Franco received massive help and troops from Italy and Germany, while the USSR, France, and Mexico supported the republic. War ended Mar. 28, 1939. Franco was named caudillo, leader of the nation. Spain was neutral in World War II but its relations with fascist countries caused its exclusion from the UN until 1955.

In July 1969, Franco and the Cortes designated Prince Juan Carlos as the future king and chief of state. After Franco's death, Nov. 20, 1975, Juan Carlos was sworn in as king. He presided over the formal dissolution of the institutions of the Franco regime. In free elections June 1977, moderates and democratic socialists emerged as the largest parties.

Catalonia and the Basque country were granted autonomy, Jan. 1980, following overwhelming approval in home-rule referendums. Basque extremists, however, have continued their campaign for independence.

The **Balearic Islands** in the western Mediterranean, 1,935 sq. mi., are a province of Spain; they include **Majorca** (Mallorca), with the capital, Palma; **Minorca, Cabrera, Ibiza** and **Formentera.** The **Canary Islands,** 2,807 sq. mi., in the Atlantic W of Morocco, form 2 provinces, including the islands of **Tenerife, Palma, Gomera, Hierro, Grand Canary, Fuerteventura,** and **Lanzarote** with Las Palmas and Santa Cruz thriving ports. **Ceuta** and **Melilla,** small enclaves on Morocco's Mediterranean coast, are part of Metropolitan Spain.

Spain has sought the return of Gibraltar, in British hands since 1704.

Sri Lanka
Democratic Socialist Republic of Sri Lanka
Sri Lanka Prajathanthrika Samajavadi Janarajaya

People: Population (1989 est.): 17,541,000. **Age distrib. (%):** 0–14: 35.3; 15–59: 58.1; 60+: 6.6. **Pop. density:** 692 per sq. mi. **Urban** (1985): 21.5%. **Ethnic groups:** Sinhalese 74%, Tamils 17%, Moors 7%. **Languages:** Sinhala (official), Tamil, English. **Religions:** Buddhist 69%, Hindu 15%, Christian 8%, Moslem 7%.

Geography: Area: 25,332 sq. mi. about the size of W. Va. **Location:** In Indian O. off SE coast of India. **Neighbors:** India on NW. **Topography:** The coastal area and the northern half are flat; the S-central area is hilly and mountainous. **Capital:** Colombo. **Cities** (1986): Colombo 664,000.

Government: Type: Republic. **Head of state:** Pres. Ranasinghe Premadasa; b. June 24, 1924; in office: Jan. 2, 1989. **Head of government:** Prime Minister Dingiri Banda Wijetunge, b. 1923, in office: Mar. 3, 1989. **Local divisions:** 9 provinces, 24 districts. **Defense:** 2.7% of GNP (1985).

Economy: Industries: Plywood, paper, milling, chemicals, textiles. **Chief crops:** Tea, coconuts, rice. **Minerals:** Graphite, limestone, gems, phosphate. **Other resources:** Forests, rubber. **Arable land:** 33%. **Livestock** (1986): cattle: 1.7 mln. **Fish catch** (1986): 183,000 metric tons. **Electricity prod.** (1986): 3.2 bln. kwh. **Labor force:** 46% agric.; 27% ind. and comm.; 26% serv.

Finance: Currency: Rupee (Mar. 1989: 33.85 = $1 US). **Gross national product** (1986): $6.4 bln. **Per capita income** (1984): $340. **Imports** (1987): $2.0 bln.; partners: Jap. 15%, Saudi Ar. 12%, UK 7%. **Exports** (1987): $1.3 bln.; partners: U.S. 22%, UK 7%. **Tourists** (1986): $75 mln. receipts. **National budget** (1984): $1.5 bln. revenues; $1.8 bln. expenditures. **International reserves less gold** (Mar. 1989): $213 mln. **Gold:** 63,000 oz t. **Consumer prices** (change in 1988): 14.0%.

Transport: Railway traffic (1986): 1.9 bln. passenger-km; 203 mln. net ton-km. **Motor vehicles:** in use (1986): 165,000 passenger cars, 137,000 comm. vehicles. **Civil aviation** (1986): 2.1 bln. passenger-km; 56 mln. freight ton-km. **Chief ports:** Colombo, Trincomalee, Galle.

Communications: Television sets: 500,000 (1987). **Radios:** 2 mln. (1986). **Telephones** (1986): 106,000.

Health: Life expectancy at birth (1987): 68.3 male; 71.5 female. **Births** (per 1,000 pop. 1987): 23.4 **Deaths** (per 1,000 pop. 1987): 6.1 **Natural increase** (1987): 1.7%. **Hospital beds** (1986): 45,000. **Physicians** (1986): 2,222. **Infant mortality** (per 1,000 live births 1987): 29.

Education (1985): **Literacy:** 87%. **Years compulsory:** To age 12; attendance 84%.

Major International Organizations: UN (World Bank, IMF), Commonwealth of Nations.

Embassy: 2148 Wyoming Ave. NW 20008; 483-4025.

The island was known to the ancient world as Taprobane (Greek for copper-colored) and later as Serendip (from Arabic). Colonists from northern India subdued the indigenous Veddahs about 543 BC; their descendants, the Buddhist Sinhalese, still form most of the population. Hindu descendants of Tamil immigrants from southern India account for one-fifth of the population. Parts were occupied by the Portuguese in 1505 and by the Dutch in 1658. The British seized the island in 1796. As Ceylon it became an independent member of the Commonwealth in 1948. On May 22, 1972, Ceylon became the Republic of Sri Lanka.

Prime Min. W. R. D. Bandaranaike was assassinated Sept. 25, 1959. In new elections, the Freedom Party was victorious under Mrs. Sirimavo Bandaranaike, widow of the former prime minister. In Apr., 1962, the government expropriated British and U.S. oil companies. In Mar. 1965 elections, the conservative United National Party won; the new government agreed to pay compensation for the seized oil companies.

After May 1970 elections, Mrs. Bandaranaike became prime minister again. In 1971 the nation suffered economic problems and terrorist activities by ultra-leftists, thousands of whom were executed. Massive land reform and nationalization of foreign-owned plantations was undertaken in the mid-1970s. Mrs. Bandaranaike was ousted in 1977 elections by the United Nationals. A presidential form of government was installed in 1978 to restore stability.

Tension between the Sinhalese and Tamil separatists has often erupted into violence. In 1987, hundreds died in an attack by Tamil rebels Apr. 17. Sri Lanka forces retaliated in June with attacks on the rebel-held Jaffna peninsula. Over 10,000 have died in the civil war since 1983.

Sudan

Republic of the Sudan

Jamhuryat as-Sudan

People: Population (1989 est.): 25,008,000. **Pop. density:** 25 per sq. mi. **Urban** (1983): 35%. **Ethnic groups:** black 52%, Arab 39%, Beja 6%. **Languages:** Arabic (official), various tribal languages. **Religions:** Sunni Moslem 70%, animist 18%, Christians 5%.

Geography: Area: 966,757 sq. mi., the largest country in Africa, over one-fourth the size of the U.S. **Location:** At the E end of Sahara desert zone. **Neighbors:** Egypt on N, Libya, Chad, Central African Republic on W, Zaire, Uganda, Kenya on S, Ethiopia on E. **Topography:** The N consists of the Libyan Desert in the W, and the mountainous Nubia desert in E, with narrow Nile valley between. The center contains large, fertile, rainy areas with fields, pasture, and forest. The S has rich soil, heavy rain. **Capital:** Khartoum. **Cities** (1983 est.): Khartoum 476,000; Omdurman 526,000; North Khartoum 341,000; Port Sudan 206,000.

Government: Type: Republic. **Head of government:** Prime Min. Sadiq al Mahdi; b. 1936; in office: May 6, 1986. **Local divisions:** 9 regions. **Defense:** 2.1% of GNP (1985).

Economy: Industries: Textiles, food processing. **Chief crops:** Gum arabic (principal world source), durra (sorghum), cotton (main export), sesame, peanuts, rice, coffee, sugar cane, wheat, dates. **Minerals:** Chrome, copper, **Other resources:** Mahogany. **Arable land:** 5%. **Livestock** (1986): cattle: 22 mln.; sheep: 12 mln.; goats: 15 mln. **Electricity prod.** (1986): 1.2 bln. kwh. **Labor force:** 78% agric.; 9% ind., comm.

Finance: Currency: Pound (Mar. 1989: 1.00 = $.22 US). **Gross national product** (1986): $7.2 bln. **Per capita income** (1982 est.): $361. **Imports** (1987): $871 mln.; partners: US. 13%, W. Ger. 8%, Saudi Ar. 11%. **Exports** (1987): $504 mln.; partners: China 6%, It. 9%, Saudi Ar. 21%. **National budget** (1986): $1.0 bln. expenditures. **International reserves less gold** (Mar. 1989): $18.2 mln.

Transport: Railway traffic (1987): 1.6 bln. net ton-km. **Motor vehicles:** in use (1985): 99,000 passenger cars, 17,000 comm. vehicles. **Civil aviation:** (1982): 657 mln. passenger-km; 6.3 mln. freight ton-km. **Chief ports:** Port Sudan.

Communications: Television sets: 250,000 in use (1987). **Radios:** 1.5 mln. (1986). **Telephones in use** (1985): 77,000. **Daily newspaper circ.** (1985): 6 per 1,000 pop.

Health: Life expectancy at birth (1985): 48.0 male; 50.0 female. **Births** (per 1,000 pop. 1985): 45.3. **Deaths** (per 1,000 pop. 1985): 16.6. **Natural increase** (1985): 2.8%. **Hospital beds** (1985): 17,328. **Physicians** (1983): 2,169. **Infant mortality** (per 1,000 live births 1985): 118.

Education (1986): **Literacy:** 20%. **Years compulsory:** 9; attendance 50%.

Major International Organizations: UN (IMF, WHO, FAO), Arab League, OAU.

Embassy: 2210 Massachusetts Ave. NW 20008; 338-8565.

Northern Sudan, ancient Nubia, was settled by Egyptians in antiquity, and was converted to Coptic Christianity in the 6th century. Arab conquests brought Islam in the 15th century.

In the 1820s Egypt took over the Sudan, defeating the last of earlier empires, including the Fung. In the 1880s a revolution was led by Mohammed Ahmed who called himself the Mahdi (leader of the faithful) and his followers, the dervishes.

In 1898 an Anglo-Egyptian force crushed the Mahdi's successors. In 1951 the Egyptian Parliament abrogated its 1899 and 1936 treaties with Great Britain, and amended its constitution, to provide for a separate Sudanese constitution.

Sudan voted for complete independence as a parliamentary government effective Jan. 1, 1956. Gen. Ibrahim Abboud took power 1958, but resigned under pressure, 1964.

In 1969, in a second military coup, a Revolutionary Council took power, but a civilian premier and cabinet were appointed; the government announced it would create a socialist state. The northern 12 provinces are predominantly Arab-Moslem and have been dominant in the central government. The 3 southern provinces are black and predominantly pagan. A 1972 peace agreement gave the South regional autonomy. The 2 halves of the nation began a civil war in 1988.

Sudan charged Libya with aiding an unsuccessful coup in Sudan in 1976. Sudan claimed that Libyan planes bombed several border towns, Sept. 1981, and the city of Omdurman, 1984.

Economic problems plagued the nation in the 1980s, aggravated by a hugh influx of refugees from neighboring countries. After 16 years in power, Pres. Nimeiry was overthrown in a bloodless military coup, Apr. 6, 1985. The Sudan held its first democratic parliamentary elections in 18 years in 1986. Some 2 million were made homeless by torrential rains, Aug. 1988.

Suriname

Republic of Suriname

People: Population (1989 est.): 400,000. **Pop. density:** 6 per sq. mi. **Ethnic groups** Hindustanis 37%, Creole 31%, Javanese 15%. **Languages:** Dutch (official), Sranan (Creole), English, others. **Religions:** Moslem 23%, Hindu 27%, Christian 25%.

Geography: Area: 63,037 sq. mi., slightly larger than Georgia. **Location:** On N shore of S. America. **Neighbors:** Guyana on W, Brazil on S, French Guiana on E. **Topography:** A flat Atlantic coast, where dikes permit agriculture. Inland is a forest belt; to the S, largely unexplored hills cover 75% of the country. **Capital:** Paramaribo. **Cities** (1984): Paramaribo 180,000.

Government: Type: Republic. **Head of State:** Pres. Ramsewak Shankar; in office: Jan. 25, 1988. **Head of government:** Prime Min. Henck Arron; in office: Jan. 29, 1988. **Local divisions:** 9 districts.

Economy: Industries: Aluminum. **Chief crops:** Rice, sugar, fruits. **Minerals:** Bauxite. **Other resources:** Forests, shrimp. **Arable land:** 1%. **Electricity prod.** (1986): 1.6 bln. kwh. **Labor force:** 29% agric.; 15% ind. and commerce; 42% govt.

Finance: Currency: Guilder (Mar. 1989: 1.78 = $1 US). **Gross national product** (1985): $1.1 bln. **Per capita income** (1985): $2,920. **Imports** (1986): $487 mln.; partners: U.S. 30%, Neth. 9%, Trin./Tob. 21%, Jap. 7%. **Exports** (1986): $482 mln.; partners: U.S. 13%, Neth. 26%. **Tourists** (1986): receipts: $6 mln. **National budget** (1985): $469 mln. expenditures. **International reserves less gold** (Mar. 1989): $11.5 mln. **Gold:** 54,000 oz t.

Transport: Motor vehicles: in use (1986): 33,000 passenger cars, 14,000 comm. vehicles. **Chief ports:** Paramaribo, Nieuw-Nickerie.

Communications: Television sets: 48,000 in use (1987). **Radios:** 246,000 in use (1986). **Telephones in use** (1986): 38,000. **Daily newspaper circ.** (1987): 80 per 1,000 pop.

Health: Life expectancy at birth (1987): 65.0 male; 70.0 female. **Births** (per 1,000 pop. 1985): 26. **Deaths** (per 1,000 pop. 1985): 8. **Natural increase** (1985): 2.1%. **Infant mortality** (per 1,000 live births 1985): 21.

Education (1984): Literacy: 65%; compulsory ages 6–12.

Major International Organizations: UN (WHO, ILO, FAO, World Bank, IMF), OAS.

Embassy: 2600 Virginia Ave. NW 20037; 338-6980.

The Netherlands acquired Suriname in 1667 from Britain, in exchange for New Netherlands (New York). The 1954 Dutch constitution raised the colony to a level of equality with the Netherlands and the Netherlands Antilles. In the 1970s the Dutch government pressured for Suriname independence, which came Nov. 25, 1975, despite objections from East Indians. Some 40% of the population (mostly East Indians) emigrated to the Netherlands in the months before independence.

The National Military Council took over control of the government, Feb. 1982. The government came under democratic leadership in 1988.

Swaziland
Kingdom of Swaziland

People: Population (1989 est.): 757,000. **Age distrib.** (%): 0–14: 47.3; 15–59: 47.4; 60+: 5.3. **Pop. density:** 112 per sq. mi. **Urban** (1985): 26%. **Ethnic groups:** Swazi 90%, Zulu 2.3%, European 2.1%, other African, non-African groups. **Languages:** siSwati, English, (both official). **Religions:** Christians 57%, indigenous beliefs 43%.

Geography: Area: 6,704 sq. mi., slightly smaller than New Jersey. **Location:** In southern Africa, near Indian O. coast. **Neighbors:** South Africa on N, W, S, Mozambique on E. **Topography:** The country descends from W-E in broad belts, becoming more arid in the lowveld region, then rising to a plateau in the E. **Capital:** Mbabane. **Cities** (1986 est.): Mbabane 52,000.

Government: Type: Monarchy. **Head of state:** King Mswati 3d; as of: Apr. 25, 1986. **Head of government:** Prime Min. Sotsha Dlamini; in office: Oct. 6, 1986. **Local divisions:** 4 districts, 2 municipalities, 40 regions.

Economy: Industries: Wood pulp. **Chief crops:** Sugar, corn, cotton, rice, pineapples, sugar, citrus fruits. **Minerals:** Asbestos, iron, coal. **Other resources:** Forests. **Arable land:** 18%. **Electricity prod.** (1986): 120 mln. kwh. **Labor force:** 53% agric.; 9% ind. and commerce; 9% serv.

Finance: Currency: Lilangeni (Mar. 1989: 1.00 = \$.39 US). **Gross national product** (1986): \$470 mln. **Per capita income** (1983 est.): \$790. **Imports** (1987): \$416 mln.; partners: So. Afr. 96%. **Exports** (1987): \$311 mln.; partners: UK 33%, So. Afr. 20%. **National budget** (1986): \$120 mln. **International reserves less gold** (Feb. 1989): \$133 mln. **Consumer prices** (change in 1987): 12.5%.

Transport: Motor vehicles: in use (1985): 18,000 passenger cars, 10,000 comm. vehicles.

Communications: Radios: 95,000 in use (1986). **Telephones in use** (1986): 12,000. **Daily newspaper circ.** (1985): 35 per 1,000 pop.

Health: Life expectancy at birth (1983): 46.8 male; 50.0 female. **Births** (per 1,000 pop. 1985): 47.5. **Deaths** (per 1,000 pop. 1986): 24. **Natural increase** (1985): 3.0%. **Hospital beds** (1984): 1,608. **Physicians** (1984): 80. **Infant mortality rate** (per 1,000 live births 1985): 156.

Education (1985): Literacy: 65%. Almost all attend primary school.

Major International Organizations: UN (IMF, WHO, FAO), OAU, Commonwealth of Nations.

Embassy: 4301 Connecticut Ave. NW 20008; 362-6683.

The royal house of Swaziland traces back 400 years, and is one of Africa's last ruling dynasties. The Swazis, a Bantu people, were driven to Swaziland from lands to the N by the Zulus in 1820. Their autonomy was later guaranteed by Britain and Transvaal, with Britain assuming control after 1903. Independence came Sept. 6, 1968. In 1973 the king repealed the constitution and assumed full powers.

Under the constitution political parties are forbidden; parliament's role in government is limited to debate and advice.

Sweden
Kingdom of Sweden
Konungariket Sverige

People: Population (1989 est.): 8,371,000. **Age distrib.** (%): 0–14: 17.9; 15–59: 59.0; 60+: 23.1. **Pop. density:** 48 per sq. mi. **Urban** (1985): 85%. **Ethnic groups:** Swedish 91%, Finnish 3%, Lapps, European immigrants. **Languages:** Swedish, Finnish. **Religions:** Lutheran (official) 95%.

Geography: Area: 173,731 sq. mi., larger than California. **Location:** On Scandinavian Peninsula in N. Europe. **Neighbors:** Norway on W, Denmark on S (across Kattegat), Finland on E. **Topography:** Mountains along NW border cover 25% of Sweden, flat or rolling terrain covers the central and southern areas, which includes several large lakes. **Capital:** Stockholm. **Cities** (1988): Stockholm 663,000; Goteborg 429,000; Malmo 230,000.

Government: Type: Constitutional monarchy. **Head of state:** King Carl XVI Gustaf; b. Apr. 30, 1946; in office: Sept. 19, 1973. **Head of government:** Prime Min. Ingvar Carlsson; b. Nov. 9, 1934; in office: Mar. 1, 1986. **Local divisions:** 24 lan (counties), 284 municipalities. **Defense:** 3.0% of GNP (1985).

Economy: Industries: Steel, machinery, instruments, autos, shipbuilding, shipping, paper. **Chief crops:** Grains, potatoes, sugar beets. **Minerals:** Zinc, iron, lead, copper, gold, silver. **Other resources:** Forests (half the country); yield one fourth exports. **Arable land:** 7%. **Livestock** (1986): cattle: 1.7 mln.; pigs: 2.4 mln. **Fish catch** (1986): 201,000 metric tons. **Electricity prod.** (1985): 136 bln. kwh. **Crude steel prod.** (1987): 4.6 mln. metric tons. **Labor force:** 5% agric.; 30% ind; 21% comm. & finance; 44% services.

Finance: Currency: Krona (May 1989: 6.74 = \$1 US). **Gross national product** (1986): \$109 bln. **Per capita income** (1985): \$11,989. **Imports** (1988): \$45.6 bln.; partners: W. Ger. 21%, UK 9%, U.S. 7%. **Exports** (1988): \$49.7 bln.; partners: UK 10%, W. Ger. 12%, Nor. 10%. **Tourists** (1986): \$1.5 bln. receipts. **National budget** (1989): \$60.5 bln. expenditures. **International reserves less gold** (Mar. 1989): \$7.5 bln. **Gold:** 6.06 mln. oz t. **Consumer prices** (change in 1988): 5.8%.

Transport: Railway traffic (1986): 6.1 bln. passenger-km; 17.7 bln. net ton-km. **Motor vehicles:** in use (1987): 3.2 mln. passenger cars, 243,000 comm. vehicles. **Civil aviation** (1986): 5.3 bln. passenger-km: 190 mln. freight ton-km. **Chief ports:** Goteborg, Stockholm, Malmo.

Communications: Television sets: 3.2 mln. licensed (1987). **Radios:** 3.3 mln. (1986). **Telephones in use** (1984): 7.4 mln. **Daily newspaper circ.** (1986): 586 per 1,000 pop.

Health: Life expectancy at birth (1984): 73.1 male; 79.1 female. **Births** (per 1,000 pop. 1987): 12.5 **Deaths** (per 1,000 pop. 1987): 11.1 **Natural increase** (1987): .1%. **Hospital beds** (1985): 115,000. **Physicians** (1984): 20,200. **Infant mortality** (per 1,000 live births 1986): 3.3.

Education (1987): Literacy: 99%. **Years compulsory:** 9; attendance 100%.

Major International Organizations: UN and all of its specialized agencies, EFTA, OECD.

Embassy: 600 New Hampshire Ave. NW 20037; 944-5600.

The Swedes have lived in present-day Sweden for at least 5,000 years, longer than nearly any other European people. Gothic tribes from Sweden played a major role in the disintegration of the Roman Empire. Other Swedes helped create the first Russian state in the 9th century.

The Swedes were Christianized from the 11th century, and a strong centralized monarchy developed. A parliament, the Riksdag, was first called in 1435, the earliest parliament on the European continent, with all classes of society represented.

Swedish independence from rule by Danish kings (dating from 1397) was secured by Gustavus I in a revolt, 1521-23; he built up the government and military and established the Lutheran Church. In the 17th century Sweden was a major European power, gaining most of the Baltic seacoast, but its international position subsequently declined.

The Napoleonic wars, in which Sweden acquired Norway (it became independent 1905), were the last in which Sweden participated. Armed neutrality was maintained in both world wars.

Over 4 decades of Social Democratic rule was ended in 1976 parliamentary elections but the party was returned to power in the 1982 elections. Although 90% of the economy is in private hands, the government holds a large interest in water power production and the railroads are operated by a public agency.

Consumer cooperatives are in extensive operation and also are important in agriculture and housing. Per capita GNP is among the highest in the world.

A labor crisis of strikes locking out more than 800,000 workers, May 1980, brought the country to an industrial standstill.

A Soviet submarine went aground inside Swedish territorial waters near the Karlskrona Naval Base, Oct. 27, 1981. Sweden claimed the submarine was armed with nuclear weapons and the incident was a "flagrant violation" of Swedish neutrality. The submarine was towed back to international waters Nov. 6.

Premier Olof Palme was shot and killed on a Stockholm street Feb. 28, 1986. An unemployed man with a history of substance abuse and psychiatric treatment was formally charged with the crime, May 29, 1989.

Switzerland
Swiss Confederation

People: Population (1989 est.): 6,485,000. **Age distrib.** (%): 0–14: 17.8; 15–59: 63.2; 60+: 19.0. **Pop. density:** 406 per sq. mi. **Urban** (1985): 60.4%. **Ethnic groups:** Mixed European stock. **Languages:** German 65%, French 18%, Italian 12%, Romansh 1%. (all official). **Religions:** Roman Catholic 49%, Protestant 48%.

Geography: Area: 15,941 sq. mi., as large as Mass., Conn., and R.I., combined. **Location:** In the Alps Mts. in Central Europe. **Neighbors:** France on W, Italy on S, Austria on E, W. Germany on N. **Topography:** The Alps cover 60% of the land area, the Jura, near France, 10%. Running between, from NE to SW, are midlands, 30%. **Capital:** Bern. **Cities** (1987): Zurich 351,000; Basel 174,200; Geneva 159,000.

Government: Type: Federal republic. **Head of government:** Pres. Otto Stich; in office: Jan. 1, 1988. **Local divisions:** 20 full cantons, 6 half cantons. **Defense:** 2.2% of GNP (1985).

Economy: Industries: Machinery, machine tools, steel, instruments, watches, textiles, foodstuffs (cheese, chocolate), chemicals, drugs, banking, tourism. **Chief crops:** Grains, potatoes, sugar beets, vegetables, tobacco. **Minerals:** Salt. **Other resources:** Hydro power potential. **Arable land:** 10%. **Livestock** (1986): cattle: 1.9 mln.; pigs: 1.9 mln. **Electricity prod.** (1986): 54.8 bln. kwh. **Crude steel prod.** (1987): 870,000 metric tons. **Labor force:** 39% ind. and commerce, 7% agric., 50% serv.

Finance: Currency: Franc (May 1989: 1.78 = $1 US). **Gross national product** (1987): $171 bln. **Per capita income** (1987): $26,309. **Imports** (1988): $56.4 bln.; partners: W. Ger. 30%, Fr. 11%, It. 10%, U.K. 5%. **Exports** (1988): $50.6 bln.; partners: W. Ger. 18%, Fr. 9%, It. 8%, U.S. 8%. **Tourists** (1986); receipts: $4.2 bln. **National budget** (1988): $17.4 bln. **International reserves less gold** (Mar. 1989): $21.9 bln. **Gold:** 83.28 mln. oz t. **Consumer prices** (change in 1988): 1.9%.

Transport: Railway traffic (1986): 9.2 bln. passenger-km; 6.9 bln. net ton-km. **Motor vehicles:** in use (1986): 2.6 mln. passenger cars, 211,000 comm. vehicles. **Civil aviation** (1986): 12.8 bln. passenger-km; 725 mln. freight ton-km.

Communications: Television sets: 2.2 mln. (1987). **Radios:** 2.5 mln. (1986). **Telephones in use** (1986): 5.6 mln. **Daily newspaper circ.** (1986): 491 per 1,000 pop.

Health: Life expectancy at birth (1988): 73.6 male; 80.8 female. **Births** (per 1,000 pop. 1986): 11.7 **Deaths** (per 1,000 pop. 1986): 9.2 **Natural increase** (1986): .2%. **Hospital beds** (1984): 66,192. **Physicians** (1985): 17,667. **Infant mortality** (per 1,000 live births 1986): 6.9.

Education (1989): **Literacy:** 99%. **Years compulsory:** 9; attendance 100%.

Major International Organizations: Many UN specialized agencies (though not a member). **Embassy:** 2900 Cathedral Ave. NW 20008; 745-7900.

Switzerland, the Roman province of Helvetia, is a federation of 23 cantons (20 full cantons and 6 half cantons), 3 of which in 1291 created a defensive league and later were joined by other districts. Voters in the French-speaking part of Canton Bern voted for self-government, 1978; Canton Jura was created Jan. 1, 1979.

In 1648 the Swiss Confederation obtained its independence from the Holy Roman Empire. The cantons were joined under a federal constitution in 1848, with large powers of local control retained by each canton.

Switzerland has maintained an armed neutrality since 1815, and has not been involved in a foreign war since 1515. Switzerland is a member of several UN agencies and of the European Free Trade Assoc. and has ties with the EC. It is also the seat of many UN and other international agencies.

Switzerland is a leading world banking center; stability of the currency brings funds from many quarters.

Syria
Syrian Arab Republic
al-jamhouriya al Arabia as-Souriya

People: Population (1989 est.): 12,210,000. **Age distrib.** (%): 0–14: 49.3; 15–59: 44.2; 60+: 6.5. **Pop. density:** 170 per sq. mi. **Urban** (1987): 49%. **Ethnic groups:** Arab 90%, Kurd, Armenian, others. **Languages:** Arabic (official), Kurdish, Armenian, French, English. **Religions:** Sunni Moslem 74%, other Moslem 16%, Christian 10%.

Geography: Area: 71,498 sq. mi., the size of North Dakota. **Location:** At eastern end of Mediterranean Sea. **Neighbors:** Lebanon, Israel on W, Jordan on S, Iraq on E, Turkey on N. **Topography:** Syria has a short Mediterranean coastline, then stretches E and S with fertile lowlands and plains, alternating with mountains and large desert areas. **Capital:** Damascus. **Cities** (1987 est.): Damascus 1,200,000; Aleppo 1,200,000; Homs 431,000.

Government: Type: Socialist. **Head of state:** Pres. Hafez al-Assad; b. Mar. 1930; in office: Feb. 22, 1971. **Head of government:** Prime Min. Mahmoud Zuabi; in office: Nov. 1, 1987. **Local divisions:** Damascus and 13 provinces. **Defense:** 22.8% of GNP (1985).

Economy: Industries: Oil products, textiles, cement, tobacco, glassware, sugar, brassware. **Chief crops:** Cotton, grain, olives, fruits, vegetables. **Minerals:** Oil, phosphate, gypsum. **Crude oil reserves** (1987): 1.4 bln. bbls. **Other resources:** Wool. **Arable land:** 31%. **Livestock** (1986): sheep: 13 mln., goats: 1 mln. **Electricity prod.** (1986): 8.0 bln. kwh. **Labor force:** 32% agric.; 29% ind. & comm.; 39% services.

Finance: Currency: Pound (Mar. 1989: 11.22 = $1 US). **Gross national product** (1986): $17.0 bln. **Imports** (1987): $7.1 bln.; partners: Iran, It., W. Ger., Fr. **Exports** (1987): $3.8 bln.; partners: It. 20%, Rom. 28%. **Tourists** (1986): receipts: $395 mln. **Consumer prices** (change in 1987): 59.5%.

Transport: Railway traffic (1987): 900 mln. passenger-km; 1.4 bln. net ton-km. **Motor vehicles:** in use (1987): 112,000 passenger cars, 127,000 comm. vehicles **Civil aviation** (1987): 847 mln. passenger-km; 89.8 mln. net ton-km. **Chief ports:** Latakia, Tartus.

Communications: Television sets: 400,000 in use (1986). **Radios:** 2.0 mln. in use (1986). **Telephones in use** (1986): 637,000. **Daily newspaper circ.** (1986): 19 per 1,000 pop.

Health: Life expectancy at birth (1986): 64.3 male; 61.9 female. **Births** (per 1,000 pop. 1986): 42.4. **Deaths** (per 1,000 1987): 7.5. **Natural increase** (1987): 3.4%. **Hospital beds** (1987): 12,606. **Physicians** (1987): 8,146. **Infant mortality** (per 1,000 live births 1986): 48.1.

Education (1986): **Literacy:** 78% males. **Years compulsory:** 6; attendance: 94%.

Major International Organizations: UN (IMF, WHO, FAO), Arab League.

Embassy: 2215 Wyoming Ave. NW 20008; 232-6313.

Syria contains some of the most ancient remains of civilization. It was the center of the Seleucid empire, but later became absorbed in the Roman and Arab empires. Ottoman rule prevailed for 4 centuries, until the end of World War I.

The state of Syria was formed from former Turkish districts, made a separate entity by the Treaty of Sevres 1920 and divided into the states of Syria and Greater Lebanon. Both were administered under a French League of Nations mandate 1920-1941.

Syria was proclaimed a republic by the occupying French Sept. 16, 1941, and exercised full independence effective Jan. 1, 1944. Syria joined in the Arab invasion of Israel in 1948.

Syria joined with Egypt in Feb. 1958 in the United Arab Republic but seceded Sept. 30, 1961. The Socialist Baath party and military leaders seized power in Mar. 1963. The Baath, a pan-Arab organization, became the only legal party. The government has been dominated by members of the minority Alawite sect.

In the Arab-Israeli war of June 1967, Israel seized and occupied the Golan Heights area inside Syria, from which Israeli settlements had for years been shelled by Syria.

Syria aided Palestinian guerrillas fighting Jordanian forces in Sept. 1970 and, after a renewal of that fighting in July 1971, broke off relations with Jordan. But by 1975 the 2 countries had entered a military coordination pact.

On Oct. 6, 1973, Syria joined Egypt in an attack on Israel. Arab oil states agreed in 1974 to give Syria $1 billion a year to aid anti-Israel moves. Military supplies used or lost in the 1973 war were replaced by the USSR in 1974. Some 30,000 Syrian troops entered Lebanon in 1976 to mediate in a civil war, and fought Palestinian guerrillas and, later, fought Christian militiamen. Syrian troops again battled Christian forces in Lebanon, Apr. 1981, ending a ceasefire that had been in place.

Following the June 6, 1982 Israeli invasion of Lebanon, Israeli planes destroyed 17 Syrian antiaircraft missile batteries in the Bekka Valley, June 9. Some 25 Syrian planes were downed during the engagement. Syrian and Israeli troops exchanged fire in central Lebanon. Israel and Syria agreed to a cease fire June 11. In 1983, Syria backed the PLO rebels who ousted Yasir Arafat's forces from Tripoli.

In Feb. 1982, an uprising by antigovernment Moslem brotherhood militants brought heavy fighting and caused some 5,000 deaths.

Syria's alleged role in promoting acts of international terrorism led to the breaking of diplomatic relations with Great Britain and the implementation of limited sanctions by the European Communities in 1986.

Taiwan
Republic of China
Chung-hua Min-kuo

People: Population (1989 est.): 20,283,000. **Age distrib. (%):** 0-14: 29.6; 15-59: 53.2; 60+: 8.1. **Pop. density:** 1,460 per sq. mi. **Urban** (1987): 72%. **Ethnic groups:** Taiwanese 85%, Chinese 14%. **Languages:** Mandarin Chinese (official), Taiwan, Hakka dialects. **Religions:** Buddhism, Taoism, Confucianism prevail.

Geography: Area: 13,885 sq. mi., about the size of Connecticut & New Hampshire combined. **Location:** Off SE coast of China, between E. and S. China Seas. **Neighbors:** Nearest is China. **Topography:** A mountain range forms the backbone of the island; the eastern half is very steep and craggy, the western slope is flat, fertile, and well-cultivated. **Capital:** Taipei. **Cities** (1987): Taipei (met.) 2,575,000; Kaohsiung 1,320,000; Taichung 695,000; Tainan 646,000.

Government: Type: One-party system. **Head of state and Nationalist Party chmn.:** Pres. Lee Teng-Hui; b. Jan. 15, 1923; in office: Jan. 13, 1988. **Head of government:** Prime Min. Lee Huan; in office: May 24, 1989. **Local divisions:** 16 counties, 5 cities, Taipei & Kao-Hsiung. **Defense:** 7% of GNP (1987).

Economy: Industries: Textiles, clothing, electronics, processed foods, chemicals, plastics. **Chief crops:** Rice, bananas, pineapples, sugarcane, sweet potatoes, peanuts. **Minerals:** Coal, limestone, marble. **Crude oil reserves** (1987): 10 mln. bbls. **Arable land:** 25%. **Livestock** (1986): pigs: 6.6 mln. **Fish catch** (1986): 1.0 mln. metric tons. **Electricity prod.** (1986): 54.0 bln. kwh. **Crude steel prod.** (1987): 5.7 mln. metric tons. **Labor force:** 17% agric.; 41% ind. & comm.; 42% services.

Finance: Currency: New Taiwan dollar (June 1989: 25.89 = $1 US). **Gross national product** (1986): $72.6 bln. **Per capita income** (1984): $3,000. **Imports** (1987): $34.8 bln.; partners: U.S. 22%, Jap. 34%. **Exports** (1987): $53.8 bln.; partners: U.S. 44%, Jap. 13%, Hong Kong 8%. **Tourists** (1985): $963 mln. receipts. **National budget** (1988): $15.6 bln. **Consumer prices** (change in 1986): 0.7%.

Transport: Motor vehicles: in use (1987): 1.2 mln. passenger cars, 472,000 commercial vehicles. **Civil Aviation** (1987): 14.4 bln. passenger-km; 2.9 mln. net ton-km. **Chief ports:** Kaohsiung, Keelung, Hualien, Taichung.

Communications: Television sets: 6 mln. in use (1987). **Radios:** 13 mln. in use (1986). **Telephones in use** (1986): 6.0 mln. **Daily newspaper circ.** (1987): 179 per 1,000 pop.

Health: Life expectancy at birth (1986): 70.0 male; 75.9 female. **Births** (per 1,000 pop. 1987): 16.0 **Deaths** (per 1,000 pop. 1987): 4.9 **Natural increase** (1987): 1.1%. **Physicians** (1987): 17,900. **Hospital beds** (1987): 81,000. **Infant mortality** (per 1,000 live births 1987): 6.3.

Education (1988): **Literacy:** 90%. Years compulsory 9; attendance 99%.

Large-scale Chinese immigration began in the 17th century. The island came under mainland control after an interval of Dutch rule, 1620-62. Taiwan (also called Formosa) was ruled by Japan 1895-1945. Two million Kuomintang supporters fled to Taiwan in 1949. Both the Taipei and Peking governments consider Taiwan an integral part of China. Taiwan has rejected Peking's efforts at reunification, but unofficial dealings with the mainland are growing more flexible.

The U.S. upon its recognition of the People's Republic of China, Dec. 15, 1978, severed diplomatic ties with Taiwan. It maintains the unofficial American Institute in Taiwan, while Taiwan has established the Coordination Council for North American Affairs in Washington, D.C.

Land reform, government planning, U.S. aid and investment, and free universal education have brought huge advances in industry, agriculture, and mass living standards. In 1987, martial law was lifted after 38 years.

The **Penghu** (Pescadores), 50 sq. mi., pop. 120,000, lie between Taiwan and the mainland. **Quemoy** and **Matsu**, pop. (1980) 61,000 lie just off the mainland.

Tanzania
United Republic of Tanzania
Jamhuri ya Mwungano wa Tanzania

People: Population (1989 est.) 24,746,000. **Pop. density:** 67 per sq. mi. **Urban** (1988): 18%. **Ethnic groups:** African. **Languages:** Swahili, English are official. **Religions:** Moslems 35%, Christians 30%, traditional beliefs 35%.

Geography: Area: 364,886 sq. mi., more than twice the size of California. **Location:** On coast of E. Africa. **Neighbors:** Kenya, Uganda on N, Rwanda, Burundi, Zaire on W, Zambia, Malawi, Mozambique on S. **Topography:** Hot, arid central plateau, surrounded by the lake region in the W, temperate highlands in N and S, the coastal plains. Mt. Kilimanjaro, 19,340 ft., is highest in Africa. **Capital:** Dar-es-Salaam. **Cities** (1986): Dar-es-Salaam 1.4 mln.

Government: Type: Republic. **Head of state:** Pres. Ali Hassan Mwinyi; b. May 8, 1925; in office: Nov. 5, 1985. **Head of government:** Prime Min. Joseph Warioba. **Local divisions:** 25 regions (20 on mainland). **Defense:** 3.4% of GNP (1985).

Economy: Industries: Food processing, clothing. **Chief crops:** Sisal, cotton, coffee, tea, tobacco. **Minerals:** Diamonds, gold, nickel. **Other resources:** Hides. **Arable land:** 6%. **Livestock** (1986): cattle: 14 mln.; goats: 6.4 mln.; sheep: 4.1 mln. **Fish catch** (1986): 309,000 metric tons. **Electricity prod.** (1986): 870 mln. kwh. **Labor force:** 85% agric., 15% ind., comm. & govt.

Finance: Currency: Shilling (Mar. 1989: 134 = $1 US). **Gross national product** (1986): $5.3 bln. **Per capita income** (1984): $200. **Imports** (1987): $923 mln.; partners: UK 14%, Jap. 12%, W. Ger. 10%. **Exports** (1987): $288 mln.; partners: W. Ger. 15%, UK 13%. **Tourists** (1986): $11 mln. receipts. **National budget** (1985): $1.0 bln. expenditures. **International reserves less gold** (Jan. 1989): $49.1 mln. **Consumer prices** (change in 1987): 29.9%.

Transport: Motor vehicles: in use (1984): 84,000 passenger and comm. vehicles. **Civil aviation** (1987): $249 mln. passenger-km. **Chief ports:** Dar-es-Salaam, Mtwara, Tanga.

Communications: Radios: 2 mln. in use (1986). **Telephones in use** (1986): 117,000. **Daily newspaper circ.** (1986): 5 per 1,000 pop.

Health: Life expectancy at birth (1986): 52 yrs. **Births** (per 1,000 pop. 1985): 49. **Deaths** (per 1,000 pop. 1985): 16.0. **Natural increase** (1985): 3.4%. **Hospital beds** (1984): 22,800. **Physicians** (1984): 1,065. **Infant mortality** (per 1,000 live births 1986): 110.

Education (1987): **Literacy:** 85%. **Attendance:** 87% attend primary school.

Major International Organizations: UN and all of its specialized agencies, OAU, Commonwealth of Nations.

Embassy: 2139 R. St. NW 20008; 939-6125.

The Republic of Tanganyika in E. Africa and the island Republic of Zanzibar, off the coast of Tanganyika, joined into a single nation, the United Republic of Tanzania, Apr. 26, 1964. Zanzibar retains internal self-government.

Tanganyika. Arab colonization and slaving began in the 8th century AD; Portuguese sailors explored the coast by about 1500. Other Europeans followed.

In 1885 Germany established German East Africa of which Tanganyika formed the bulk. It became a League of Nations mandate and, after 1946, a UN trust territory, both under Britain. It became independent Dec. 9, 1961, and a republic within the Commonwealth a year later.

In 1967 the government set on a socialist course; it nationalized all banks and many industries. The government also ordered that Swahili, not English, be used in all official business. Nine million people have been moved into cooperative villages.

Tanzanian forces drove Idi Amin from Uganda, Mar., 1979.

Zanzibar, the Isle of Cloves, lies 23 mi. off the coast of Tanganyika; its area is 640 sq. mi. The island of Pemba, 25 mi. to the NE, area 380 sq. mi., is included in the administration. The total population (1985 est.) is 571,000.

Chief industry is the production of cloves and clove oil of which Zanzibar and Pemba produce the bulk of the world's supply.

Zanzibar was for centuries the center for Arab slave-traders. Portugal ruled for 2 centuries until ousted by Arabs around 1700. Zanzibar became a British Protectorate in 1890; independence came Dec. 10, 1963. Revolutionary forces overthrew the Sultan Jan. 12, 1964. The new government ousted Western diplomats and newsmen, slaughtered thousands of Arabs, and nationalized farms. Union with Tanganyika followed, 1964. The ruling parties of Tanganyika and Zanzibar were united in 1977, as political tension eased.

Thailand
Kingdom of Thailand
Muang Thai or Prathet Thai

People: Population (1989 est.): 55,017,000. **Age distrib.** (%): 0–14: 36.2; 15–59: 58.1; 60+: 5.7. **Pop. density:** 277 per sq. mi. **Urban** (1985): 20%. **Ethnic groups:** Thais 84%, Chinese 12%, others 11%. **Languages:** Thai, regional dialects. **Religions:** Buddhist 95%, Moslem 4%.

Geography: Area: 198,456 sq. mi., about the size of Texas. **Location:** On Indochinese and Malayan Peninsulas in S.E. Asia. **Neighbors:** Burma on W. Laos on N, Cambodia on E, Malaysia on S. **Topography:** A plateau dominates the NE third of Thailand, dropping to the fertile alluvial valley of the Chao Phraya R. in the center. Forested mountains are in N, with narrow fertile valleys. The southern peninsula region is covered by rain forests. **Capital:** Bangkok. **Cities** (1980 est.): Bangkok (met.): 4.7 mln.

Government: Type: Constitutional monarchy. **Head of state:** King Bhumibol Adulyadej; b. Dec. 5, 1927; in office: June 9, 1946. **Head of government:** Prime Min. Chatichai Choonhavan; in office: Aug. 2, 1988. **Local divisions:** 73 provinces. **Defense:** 4.2% of GNP (1985).

Economy: Industries: Textiles, mining, wood products. **Chief crops:** Rice (a major export), corn tapioca, sugarcane. **Minerals:** Antimony, tin (among largest producers), tungsten, iron, gas. **Other resources:** Forests (teak is exported), rubber. **Arable land:** 38%. **Livestock** (1986): cattle: 4.8 mln.; pigs: 4.2 mln. **Fish catch** (1986): 2.1 mln. metric tons. **Electricity prod.** (1986): 24.0 bln. kwh. **Labor force:** 59% agric.; 26% ind. & comm.; 10% serv.; 8% govt.

Finance: Currency: Baht (Mar. 1989: 25.70 = $1 US). **Gross national product** (1986): $40 bln. **Per capita income** (1986): $771. **Imports** (1988): $19.7 bln.; partners: Jap. 24%, U.S. 13%. **Exports** (1988): $11.6 bln.; partners: Jap. 14%, U.S. 17%, Sing. 14%. **Tourists** (1988): $1.4 mln. receipts. **National budget** (1988): $9.4 bln. **International reserves less gold** (Mar. 1989): $7.3 bln. **Gold:** 2.47 mln. oz t. **Consumer prices** (change in 1988): 3.9%.

Transport: Railway traffic (1986): 9.2 bln. passenger-km; 2.5 bln. net ton-km. **Motor vehicles:** in use (1986): 545,000 passenger cars, 856,000 comm. vehicles. **Civil aviation** (1986): 11.2

bln. passenger-km; 485 mln. freight ton-km. **Chief ports:** Bangkok, Sattahip.

Communication: Television sets: 3 mln. in use (1985). **Radios:** 7.7 mln. in use (1985). **Telephones in use** (1986): 999,000. **Daily newspaper circ.** (1985): 50 per 1,000 pop.

Health: Life expectancy at birth (1987): 61.6 male; 67.6 female. **Births** (per 1,000 pop. 1987): 24.8 **Deaths** (per 1,000 pop. 1987): 7.3 **Natural increase** (1987): 1.7%. **Hospital beds** (1985): 81,000. **Physicians** (1985): 8,650. **Infant mortality** (per 1,000 live births 1987): 40.0.

Education (1988): **Literacy:** 89%. **Years compulsory:** 6; attendance 96%.

Major International Organizations: UN (GATT, World Bank). **Embassy:** 2300 Kalorama Rd. NW 20008; 483-7200.

Thais began migrating from southern China in the 11th century. Thailand is the only country in SE Asia never taken over by a European power, thanks to King Mongkut and his son King Chulalongkorn who ruled from 1851 to 1910, modernized the country, and signed trade treaties with both Britain and France. A bloodless revolution in 1932 limited the monarchy.

Japan occupied the country in 1941. After the war, Thailand followed a pro-West foreign policy.

The military took over the government in a bloody 1976 coup. Kriangsak Chomanan, prime minister resigned, Feb. 1980, under opposition over soaring inflation, oil price increases, labor unrest and growing crime.

Vietnamese troops have crossed the border and been repulsed by Thai forces in the 1980s.

Togo
Republic of Togo
République Togolaise

People: Population (1986 est.): 3,423,000. **Age distrib. (%):** 0–14: 49.8; 15–59: 44.6; 60+:5.6.**Pop. density:** 158 per sq. mi. **Urban** (1981): 15.2%. **Ethnic groups:** Ewe 35%, Mina 6%, Kabye 22%. **Languages:** French (official), others. **Religions:** Traditional 58%, Christian 22%, Moslem 20%.

Geography: Area: 21,622 sq. mi., slightly smaller than West Virginia. **Location:** On S coast of W. Africa. **Neighbors:** Ghana on W, Burkina Faso on N, Benin on E. **Topography:** A range of hills running SW-NE splits Togo into 2 savanna plains regions. **Capital:** Lomé. **Cities** (1985 est.): Lomé 300,000.

Government: Type: Republic; one-party presidential regime. **Head of state:** Pres. Gnassingbe Eyadema; b. Dec. 26, 1937; in office: Apr. 14, 1967. **Local divisions:** 21 prefectures.

Economy: Industries: Textiles, shoes. **Chief crops:** Coffee, cocoa, yams, manioc, millet, rice. **Minerals:** Phosphates. **Arable land:** 26%. **Electricity prod.** (1986): 203 mln. kwh. **Labor force:** 67% agric.; 15% industry.

Finance: Currency: CFA franc (Mar. 1989: 319 = $1 US). **Gross national product** (1986): $780 mln. **Per capita income** (1985): $240. **Imports** (1985): $262 mln.; partners: Fr., U.K., W. Ger. **Exports** (1985): $242 mln.; partners: Neth., Fr., W. Ger. **Tourists** (1986): $41 mln. receipts. **International reserves less gold** (Jan. 1989): $232 mln. **Gold:** 13,000 oz t. **Consumer prices** (change in 1987): .01%.

Transport: Railway traffic (1987): 105 mln. passenger-km; 16 mln. net ton-km. **Motor vehicles:** in use (1985): 2,000 passenger cars, 228,000 comm. vehicles. **Chief ports:** Lome.

Communications: Television sets: 23,000 (1987). **Radios:** 250,000 (1986). **Telephones** (1983): 11,000. **Daily newspaper circ.** (1986): 3 per 1,000 pop.

Health: Life expectancy at birth (1984): 47 yrs. **Births** (per 1,000 pop. 1985): 48. **Deaths** (per 1,000 pop. 1985): 17. **Natural increase** (1985): 3.1%. **Hospital beds** (1985): 3,655. **Physicians** (1985): 230. **Infant mortality** (per 1,000 live births 1985): 107.

Education (1985): **Literacy:** 45% (males).

Major International Organizations: UN (GATT, IMF), OAU. **Embassy:** 2208 Massachusetts Ave. NW 20008; 234-4212.

The Ewe arrived in southern Togo several centuries ago. The country later became a major source of slaves. Germany took control in 1884. France and Britain administered Togoland as UN trusteeships. The French sector became the republic of Togo Apr. 27, 1960.

The population is divided between Bantus in the S and Hamitic tribes in the N. Togo has actively promoted regional integration, as a means of stimulating the economy.

Tonga

Kingdom of Tonga

Pule 'anga Tonga

People: Population (1989 est.): 108,000. **Age distrib. (%):** 0–14: 44.4; 15–59: 50.5; 60+:5.1. **Pop. density:** 400 per sq. mi. **Ethnic groups:** Tongans 98%, other Polynesian, European. **Languages:** Tongan, English. **Religions:** Free Wesleyan 47%, Roman Catholics 14%, Free Church of Tonga 14%, Mormons 9%, Church of Tonga 9%.
Geography: Area: 270 sq. mi., smaller than New York City. **Location:** In western S. Pacific O. **Neighbors:** Nearest is Fiji, on W, New Zealand, on S. **Topography:** Tonga comprises 169 volcanic and coral islands, 45 inhabited. **Capital:** Nuku'alofa. **Cities** (1986): Nuku'alofa (met.) 29,000.
Government: Type: Constitutional monarchy. **Head of state:** King Taufa'ahau Tupou IV; b. July 4, 1918; in office: Dec. 16, 1965. **Head of government:** Prime Min. Fatafehi Tu'ipelehake; b. Jan. 7, 1922; in office: Dec. 16, 1965. **Local divisions:** 3 main island groups.
Economy: Industries: Tourism. **Chief crops:** Coconut products, bananas are exported. **Other resources:** Fish. **Arable land:** 77%. **Electricity prod.** (1986): 18 mln. kwh. **Labor force:** 45% agric, 27% services.
Finance: Currency: Pa'anga (Jan. 1988: 1.40 = $1 US). **Gross national product** (1986): $70 mln. **Imports** (1985): $41 mln.; partners: N Z 37%, Austral. 31%, Jap. 6%, Fiji 7%. **Exports** (1985): $7 mln.; partners: Aust. 36%, N Z 34%.
Transport: Motor vehicles: in use (1983): 443 passenger cars, 1,300 comm. vehicles. **Chief ports:** Nuku'alofa.
Communications: Radios: 5,000 in use (1986). **Telephones in use** (1984): 3,996.
Health: Life expectancy at birth (1988): 59 years. **Births** (per 1,000 pop. 1985): 28. **Deaths** (per 1,000 pop. 1985): 8. **Natural increase** (1985): 2.0%. **Infant mortality** (per 1,000 live births 1987): 40.
Education (1988): **Literacy:** 93%. **Years compulsory:** 8. **Attendance:** 77%.

The islands were first visited by the Dutch in the early 17th century. A series of civil wars ended in 1845 with establishment of the Tupou dynasty. In 1900 Tonga became a British protectorate. On June 4, 1970, Tonga became independent and a member of the Commonwealth.

Trinidad and Tobago

Republic of Trinidad and Tobago

People: Population (1989 est.): 1,261,000. **Age distrib. (%):** 0–14: 32.9; 15–59: 58.7; 60+: 8.4. **Pop. density:** 636 per sq. mi. **Ethnic groups:** Africans 43%, East Indians 40%, mixed 14%. **Languages:** English (official). **Religions:** Roman Catholic 32%, Protestant 29%, Hindu 25%, Moslem 6%.
Geography: Area: 1,980 sq. mi., the size of Delaware. **Location:** Off eastern coast of Venezuela. **Neighbors:** Nearest is Venezuela on SW. **Topography:** Three low mountain ranges cross Trinidad E-W, with a well-watered plain between N and Central Ranges. Parts of E and W coasts are swamps. Tobago, 116 sq. mi., lies 20 mi. NE. **Capital:** Port-of-Spain. **Cities** (1989 met. est.): Port-of-Spain 300,000; San Fernando 50,000.
Government: Type: Parliamentary democracy. **Head of state:** Pres. Noor Hassanali; in office: Mar. 19, 1987. **Head of government:** Prime Min. A.N.R. Robinson; in office: Dec. 18, 1986. **Local divisions:** 7 counties, Tobago.
Economy: Industries: Oil products, rum, cement, tourism. **Chief crops:** Sugar, cocoa, coffee, citrus fruits, bananas. **Minerals:** Asphalt, oil, **Crude oil reserves** (1987): 567 mln. bbls. **Arable land:** 30%. **Electricity prod.** (1986): 2.7 bln. kwh. **Labor force:** 18% construction-utilities, 14% manuf., mining, commerce, 47% services.
Finance: Currency: Dollar (Jan. 1989: 4.25 = $1 US). **Gross national product** (1987): $4.5 bln. **Per capita income** (1987): $3,731. **Imports** (1987): $1.1 bln.; partners: U.S. 37%, UK 11%.

Exports (1987): $1.4 bln.; partners: U.S. 62%. **Tourists** (1986): $190 mln. receipts. **National budget** (1986): $1.7 bln. expenditures. **International reserves less gold** (Mar. 1989): $242 mln. **Gold:** 54,000 oz t. **Consumer prices** (change in 1987): 10.8%.
Transport: Motor vehicles: in use (1985): 241,000 passenger cars, 82,000 comm. vehicles. **Civil aviation:** (1986): 2.1 bln. passenger-km; 12.5 mln. freight ton-km. **Chief ports:** Port-of-Spain.
Communications: Television sets: 345,000 in use (1987). **Radios:** 552,000 (1986). **Telephones in use** (1987): 196,000. **Daily newspaper circ.** (1986): 146 per 1,000 pop.
Health: Life expectancy at birth (1989): 67.8 male; 72.6 female. **Births** (per 1,000 pop. 1985): 27. **Deaths** (per 1,000 pop. 1985): 7. **Natural increase** (1985): 2.0%. **Hospital beds** (1987): 4,241. **Physicians** (1987): 1,164. **Infant mortality** (per 1,000 pop. 1985): 21.
Education (1988): **Literacy:** 97%. **Years compulsory:** 8. **Major International Organizations:** UN (GATT, IMF, WHO), Commonwealth of Nations, OAS.
Embassy: 1708 Massachusetts Ave. NW 20036; 467-6490.

Columbus sighted Trinidad in 1498. A British possession since 1802, Trinidad and Tobago won independence Aug. 31, 1962. It became a republic in 1976. The People's National Movement party has held control of the government since 1956.
The nation is one of the most prosperous in the Caribbean. Oil production has increased with offshore finds. Middle Eastern oil is refined and exported, mostly to the U.S.

Tunisia

Republic of Tunisia

al Jumhuriyah at-Tunisiyah

People: Population (1989 est.): 7,930,000. **Age distrib. (%)** 0–14: 39.0; 15–59: 54.2; 60+: 6.8. **Pop. density:** 125 per sq. mi. **Ethnic groups:** Arab 98%. **Languages:** Arabic (official), French. **Religions:** Moslem 99%.
Geography: Area: 63,170 sq. mi., about the size of Missouri. **Location:** On N coast of Africa. **Neighbors:** Algeria on W; Libya on E. **Topography:** The N is wooded and fertile. The central coastal plains are given to grazing and orchards. The S is arid, approaching Sahara Desert. **Capital:** Tunis. **Cities** (1984 est.) Tunis 1,000,000, Sfax 475,000.
Government: Type: Republic. **Head of state:** Pres. Gen. Zine al-Abidine Ben Ami; b. Sept 3, 1936; in office: Nov. 7, 1987. **Head of government:** Prime Min. Hedi Baccouche; in office: Nov. 17, 1987. **Local divisions:** 21 governorates. **Defense:** 3.6% of GNP (1985).
Economy: Type: Industries: Food processing, textiles, oil products, construction materials, tourism. **Chief crops:** Grains, dates, olives, citrus fruits, figs, vegetables, grapes. **Minerals:** Phosphates, iron, oil, lead, zinc. **Crude oil reserves** (1987): 1.7 bln. bbls. **Arable land:** 30%. **Livestock** (1986): sheep: 5.4 mln.; goats: 1 mln. **Fish catch** (1986): 93,000 metric tons. **Electricity prod.** (1986): 3.7 bln. kwh. **Crude steel prod.** (1986): 188,000 metric tons. **Labor force:** 35% agric.; 22% industry; 11% serv.
Finance: Currency: Dinar (Mar. 1989: .95 = $1 US). **Gross national product** (1986): $8.3 bln. **Per capita income** (1986) $1,163. **Imports** (1988): $3.8 bln.; partners: Fr. 26%, It. 12%. **Exports** (1988): $2.3 bln.; partners: It. 17%, Fr. 26%, W. Ger. 10%, U.S. 19%. **Tourists** (1986): $488 mln. receipts. **National budget** (1986): $3.3 bln. expenditures. **International reserves less gold** (Mar. 1989): $814 mln. **Gold:** 187,000 oz t. **Consumer prices** (change in 1988): 6.4%.
Transport: Railway traffic (1987): 792 mln. passenger-km; 1.9 bln. net ton-km. **Motor vehicles:** in use (1987): 271,000 passenger cars, 182,000 comm. vehicles. **Civil aviation:** (1987): 2.3 bln. passenger-km; 21.5 mln. freight ton-km. **Chief ports:** Tunis, Sfax, Bizerte.
Communications: Television sets: 500,000 (1987). **Radios:** 1.1 mln. (1986). **Telephones** (1986): 291,000. **Daily newspaper circ.** (1987): 30 per 1,000 pop.
Health: Life expectancy at birth (1985): 60.1 male; 61.1 female. **Births** (per 1,000 pop. 1987): 29.3 **Deaths** (per 1,000 pop. 1987): 6.3. **Natural increase** (1987): 2.3%. **Hospital beds** (1987): 15,838. **Physicians** (1987): 3,474. **Infant mortality** (per 1,000 pop. live births 1985): 53.
Education (1985): **Literacy:** 46%. **Years compulsory:** 8; attendance 85%.

Major International Organizations: UN, Arab League, OAU. **Embassy:** 1515 Massachusetts Ave. NW 20005; 862-1850.

Site of ancient Carthage, and a former Barbary state under the suzerainty of Turkey, Tunisia became a protectorate of France under a treaty signed May 12, 1881. The nation became independent Mar. 20, 1956, and ended the monarchy the following year. Habib Bourguiba has headed the country since independence.

Although Tunisia is a member of the Arab League, Bourguiba in the 1960s urged negotiations to end Arab-Israeli disputes and was denounced by other members.

Tunisia survived a Libyan-engineered raid against the southern mining center of Gafsa, Jan. 1980.

Turkey

Republic of Turkey

Turkiye Cumhuriyeti

People: Population (1989 est.): 55,377,000. **Age distrib. (%):** 0–14: 38.5; 15–59: 54.9; 60+: 6.6. **Pop. density:** 183 per sq. mi. **Urban** (1987): 55%. **Ethnic groups:** Turks 85%, Kurds 12%. **Languages:** Turkish (official), Kurdish, Arabic. **Religions:** Moslem 98%, Christian, Jewish.

Geography: Area: 301,381 sq. mi., twice the size of California. **Location:** Occupies Asia Minor, between Mediterranean and Black Seas. **Neighbors:** Bulgaria, Greece on W, USSR (Georgia, Armenia) on N, Iran on E, Iraq, Syria on S. **Topography:** Central Turkey has wide plateaus, with hot, dry summers and cold winters. High mountains ring the interior on all but W, with more than 20 peaks over 10,000 ft. Rolling plains are in W; mild, fertile coastal plains are in S, W. **Capital:** Ankara. **Cities** (1988 est.): Istanbul 5,800,000; Ankara 1,700,000; Izmir 2,300,000; Adana 1,700,000.

Government: Type: Republic. **Head of state:** Pres. Kenan Evren; b. 1918; in office: Oct. 27, 1980. **Head of government:** Prime Min. Turgut Ozal; b. 1927; in office: Dec. 13, 1983. **Local divisions:** 67 provinces, with appointed governors. **Defense:** 4.5% of GNP (1986).

Economy: Industries: Iron, steel, machinery, metal prods., cars, processed foods. **Chief crops:** Tobacco, cereals, cotton, barley, corn, fruits, potatoes, sugar beets. **Minerals:** Antimony, chromium, mercury, borate, copper, coal. **Crude oil reserves** (1987): 139 mln. bbls. **Other resources:** Wool, silk, forests. **Arable land:** 34%. **Livestock** (1986): cattle: 17.4 mln.; sheep: 40.4 mln. **Fish catch** (1986): 579,000 metric tons. **Electricity prod.** (1987): 44.3 bln. kwh. **Crude steel prod.** (1987): 7.0 mln. metric tons. **Labor force:** 58% agric.; 17% ind. and comm.; 25% serv.

Finance: Currency: Lira (Mar. 1989: 2,059 = $1 US). **Gross national product** (1986): $52 bln. **Per capita income** (1986): $1,160 **Imports** (1987): $14.1 bln.; partners: W. Ger. 16%, U.S. 10%. **Exports** (1987): $10.1 bln.; partners: W. Ger. 19%. **Tourists** (1986): 950 mln. receipts. **National budget** (1986): $10.7 bln. expenditures. **International reserves less gold** (Feb. 1989): $2.5 bln. **Gold:** 3.8 mln. oz t. **Consumer prices** (change in 1987): 38.8%.

Transport: Railway traffic (1987): 6.1 bln. passenger-km; 7.2 bln. net ton-km. **Motor vehicles** in use (1987): 1.1 mln. passenger cars, 553,000 comm. vehicles. **Civil aviation** (1986): 2.6 bln. passenger-km; 45 mln. freight ton-km. **Chief ports:** Istanbul, Izmir, Mersin, Samsun.

Communications: Television sets: 5 mln. in use (1986). **Radios:** 8.2 mln. in use (1986). **Telephones in use** (1987): 3.7 mln.

Health: Life expectancy at birth (1985): 57 years. **Births** (per 1,000 pop. 1985): 33.6. **Deaths** (per 1,000 pop. 1985): 9.3. **Natural increase** (1985): 2.4%. **Hospital beds** (1986): 106,000. **Physicians** (1986): 37,000. **Infant mortality** (per 1,000 live births 1988): 12.3

Education (1988): Literacy: 70%. **Years compulsory:** 8; attendance 95%.

Major International Organizations: UN (GATT, WHO, IMF), NATO, OECD.

Embassy: 1606 23d St. NW 20008; 387-3200.

Ancient inhabitants of Turkey were among the worlds first agriculturalists. Such civilizations as the Hittite, Phrygian, and Lydian flourished in Asiatic Turkey (Asia Minor), as did much of

Greek civilization. After the fall of Rome in the 5th century, Constantinople was the capital of the Byzantine Empire for 1,000 years. It fell in 1453 to Ottoman Turks, who ruled a vast empire for over 400 years.

Just before World War I, Turkey, or the Ottoman Empire, ruled what is now Syria, Lebanon, Iraq, Jordan, Israel, Saudi Arabia, Yemen, and islands in the Aegean Sea.

Turkey joined Germany and Austria in World War I and its defeat resulted in loss of much territory and fall of the sultanate. A republic was declared Oct. 29, 1923. The Caliphate (spiritual leadership of Islam) was renounced 1924.

Long embroiled with Greece over Cyprus, off Turkey's south coast, Turkey invaded the island July 20, 1974, after Greek officers seized the Cypriot government as a step toward unification with Greece. Turkey sought a new government for Cyprus, with Greek Cypriot and Turkish Cypriot zones. In reaction to Turkey's moves, the U.S. cut off military aid in 1975. Turkey, in turn, suspended the use of most U.S. bases. Aid was restored in 1978. There was a military takeover, Sept. 12, 1980.

Religious and ethnic tensions and active left and right extremists have caused endemic violence. Martial law, imposed in 1978, was lifted in 1984. The military formally transferred power to an elected parliament in 1983.

Tuvalu

People: Population (1989 est.): 9,000. **Pop. density:** 900 per sq. mi. **Ethnic group:** Polynesian. **Languages:** Tuvaluan, English. **Religions:** mainly Protestant.

Geography: Area: 10 sq. mi., less than one-half the size of Manhattan. **Location:** 9 islands forming a NW-SE chain 360 mi. long in the SW Pacific O. **Neighbors:** Nearest are Samoa on SE, Fiji on S. **Topography:** The islands are all low-lying atolls, nowhere rising more than 15 ft. above sea level, composed of coral reefs. **Capital:** Funafuti (pop. 1985): 2,800.

Government: Head of state: Queen Elizabeth II, represented by Gov.-Gen. Tupua Leupena; in office: Mar. 1, 1986. **Head of government:** Prime Min. Tomasi Puapua; in office: Sept. 8, 1981. **Local divisions:** 8 island councils on the permanently inhabited islands.

Economy: Industries: Copra. **Chief crops:** Coconuts. **Labor force:** Approx. 1,500 Tuvaluans work overseas in the Gilberts' phosphate industry, or as overseas seamen.

Finance: Currency: Australian dollar.

Transport: Chief port: Funafuti.

Health: (including former Gilbert Is.) Life expectancy at birth (1987): 59 male; 62 female. **Births** (per 1,000 pop. 1985): 27. **Deaths** (per 1,000 pop. 1985): 11. **Natural increase** (1985): 1.6%. **Infant mortality** (per 1,000 live births 1985) : 35.

Education (1985): Literacy: 96%.

The Ellice Islands separated from the British Gilbert and Ellice Islands colony, 1975, and became independent Tuvalu Oct. 1, 1978.

Britain and New Zealand provide extensive economic aid.

Uganda

Republic of Uganda

People: Population (1989 est.): 16,811,000. **Age distrib. (%):** 0–14: 48.5; 15–59: 47.3; 60+: 4.2. **Pop. density:** 180 per sq. mi. **Urban** (1984): 14%. **Ethnic groups:** Bantu, Nilotic, Nilo-Hamitic, Sudanic tribes. **Languages:** English (official), Luganda, Swahili. **Religions:** Christian 63%, Moslem 6%, traditional beliefs.

Geography: Area: 93,354 sq. mi., slightly smaller than Oregon. **Location:** In E. Central Africa. **Neighbors:** Sudan on N, Zaire on W, Rwanda, Tanzania on S, Kenya on E. **Topography:** Most of Uganda is a high plateau 3,000-6,000 ft. high, with high Ruwenzori range in W (Mt. Margherita 16,750 ft.), volcanoes in SW, NE is arid, W and SW rainy. Lakes Victoria, Edward, Albert form much of borders. **Capital:** Kampala. **Cities** (1988): Kampala 331,000.

Government: Type: Military. **Head of state:** Pres. Yoweri Kaguta Museveni; b. 1944; in office: Jan. 29, 1986. **Head of government:** Prime Min. Samson Kisekka; in office: Jan. 3, 1986. **Local divisions:** 10 provinces, 34 districts. **Defense:** 1% of GNP (1984).

Economy: Chief Crops: Coffee, cotton, tea, corn, bananas, sugar. **Minerals:** Copper, cobalt. **Arable land:** 32%. **Livestock** (1987): cattle: 5.2 mln.; goats: 3.3 mln.; sheep: 1.3 mln. **Fish catch** (1986): 212,000 metric tons. **Electricity prod.** (1986): 287 mln. kwh. **Labor force:** 90% agric.

Finance: Currency: Shilling (Mar. 1989: 200 = $1 US). **Gross national product** (1986): $3.2 bln. **Per capita income** (1976): $240. **Imports** (1987): $477 mln.; partners: Kenya 39%, U.K. 17%. **Exports** (1985): $352 mln.; partners: U.S. 27%, U.K. 9%. **National budget** (1981): $641 mln. revenues; $871 mln. expenditures. **International reserves less gold** (Jan. 1989): $49.3 mln. **Consumer prices** (change in 1987): 238%.

Transport: Motor vehicles: in use (1986): 32,000 passenger cars, 6,000 comm. vehicles.

Communications: Television sets: 90,000 in use (1987). **Radios:** 600,000 in use (1986). **Telephones in use** (1983): 55,000. **Daily newspaper circ.** (1984): 2 per 1,000 pop.

Health: Life expectancy at birth (1985): 49.0 male; 53.0 female. **Births** (per 1,000 pop. 1985): 48.0. **Deaths** (per 1,000 pop. 1985): 17. **Natural increase** (1985): 3.1%. **Hospital beds** (1983): 19,650. **Physicians** (1983): 655. **Infant mortality** (per 1,000 live births 1985): 113.

Education (1985): **Literacy:** 52%. About 50% attend primary school.

Major International Organizations: UN (GATT, WHO, IMF), OAU, Commonwealth of Nations.

Embassy: 5909 16th St. NW 20011; 726-7100.

Britain obtained a protectorate over Uganda in 1894. The country became independent Oct. 9, 1962, and a republic within the Commonwealth a year later. In 1967, the traditional kingdoms, including the powerful Buganda state, were abolished and the central government strengthened.

Gen. Idi Amin seized power from Prime Min. Milton Obote in 1971. As many as 300,000 of his opponents were reported killed in subsequent years. Amin was named president for life in 1976.

In 1972 Amin expelled nearly all of Uganda's 45,000 Asians. In 1973 the U.S. withdrew all diplomatic personnel.

A June 1977 Commonwealth conference condemned the Amin government for its "disregard for the sanctity of human life."

Amid worsening economic and domestic crises, Uganda's troops exchanged invasion attacks with long-standing foe Tanzania, 1978 to 1979. Tanzanian forces, coupled with Ugandan exiles and rebels, ended the dictatorial rule of Amin, Apr. 11, 1979.

The U.S. reopened its embassy, reinstated economic aid, and ended its trade embargo in 1979.

Union of Soviet Socialist Republics
Soyuz Sovetskykh Sotsialisticheskikh Respublic

People: Population (1989 est.): 287,015,000. **Age distrib.** (%): 0–19: 25.5; 20–59: 61.0; 60+: 13.5. **Pop. density:** 33 per sq. mi. **Urban** (1988): 66%. **Ethnic groups:** Russians 52% Ukrainians 16%, Uzbeks 5%, Byelorussians 4%, many others. **Languages:** Slavic (Russian, Ukrainian, Byelorussian, Polish), Altaic (Turkish, etc.), other Indo-European, Uralian, Caucasian. **Religions:** Russian Orthodox 31%, Moslem 11%, non-religious or atheist 51%.

Geography: Area: 8,649,496 sq. mi., the largest country in the world, nearly 2½ times the size of the U.S. **Location:** Stretches from E. Europe across N Asia to the Pacific O. **Neighbors:** Finland, Poland, Czechoslovakia, Hungary, Norway, Romania on W, Turkey, Iran, Afghanistan, China, Mongolia, N. Korea on S. **Topography:** Covering one-sixth of the earth's land area, the USSR contains every type of climate except the distinctly tropical, and has a varied topography.

The European portion has a low plain, grassy in S, wooded in N with Ural Mtns. on the E. Caucasus Mts. on the S. Urals stretch N-S for 2,500 mi. The Asiatic portion is also a vast plain, with mountains on the S and in the E; tundra covers extreme N, with forest belt below; plains, marshes are in W, desert in SW. **Capital:** Moscow. **Cities** (1987 est.): Moscow 8.8 mln.; Leningrad 4.9 mln.; Kiev 2.5 mln.; Tashkent 2.1 mln.; Kharkov 1.5 mln.; Baku 1.7 mln.; Gorky 1.4 mln.; Novosibirsk 1.4 mln.; Minsk 1.5 mln.; Kuibyshev 1.2 mln.; Sverdlovsk 1.3 mln.

Government: Type: Federal Union controlled by the Communist Party. **Head of state:** Pres. Mikhail S. Gorbachev; b. Mar. 2, 1931; in office: Oct. 1, 1988. **Head of government:** Premier

Nikolai I. Ryzhkov; b. 1929; in office: Sept. 27, 1985. **Head of Communist Party:** Mikhail Gorbachev; in office: Mar. 11, 1985. **Local divisions:** 15 union republics, within which are 20 autonomous republics, 6 krays (territories), 123 oblasts (regions), 8 autonomous oblasts. **Defense:** 12-19% of GNP (1988).

Economy: Industries: Steel, machinery, machine tools, vehicles, chemicals, cement, textiles, appliances, paper. **Chief crops:** Grain, cotton, sugar beets, potatoes, vegetables, sunflowers. **Minerals:** Iron, manganese, mercury, potash, antimony, bauxite, cobalt, chromium, copper, coal, gold, lead, molybdenum, nickel, phosphates, silver, tin, tungsten, zinc, oil (59%), potassium salts. **Crude oil reserves** (1987): 60 bln. bbls. **Other resources:** Forests (25% of world reserves). **Arable land:** 11%. **Livestock** (1988): cattle: 121 mln.; sheep: 140 mln.; pigs: 6.5 mln. **Fish catch** (1988): 11.2 mln. metric tons. **Electricity prod.** (1986): 1,600 bln. kwh. **Crude steel prod.** (1987): 161 mln. metric tons. **Labor force:** 19% agric.; 29% industry, 26% services.

Finance: Currency: Ruble (Jan. 1989: 1.00 = $1.61 US). **Gross national product** (1986): $2.3 trl. **Per capita income** (1987): $3,000. **Imports** (1985): $82.9 bln.; partners: E. Ger. 10%, Pol. 7%, Czech. 8%, Bulg. 8%. **Exports** (1985): $86.9 bln.; partners: E. Ger. 10%, Pol. 8%, Bulg. 8%, Czech. 8%. **National budget** (1982): $350 bln. **Tourists** (1984): 7.2 mln.

Transport: Railway traffic (1987): 402 bln. passenger-km; 3.8 bln. net ton-km. **Motor vehicles:** in use (1986): 9.2 mln. passenger cars, 7.9 mln. comm. vehicles; manuf. (1982): 1.3 mln. passenger cars; 874,000 comm. vehicles. **Civil aviation** (1987): 204 bln. passenger-km; 3.4 bln. freight ton-km. **Chief ports:** Leningrad, Odessa, Murmansk, Kaliningrad, Archangelsk, Riga, Vladivostok.

Communications: Television sets: 88 mln. in use (1987). **Radios:** 182 mln. in use (1986). **Telephones in use** (1987): 41.8 mln. **Daily newspaper circ.** (1986): 345 per 1,000 pop.

Health: Life expectancy at birth (1986): 64.0 male; 73.0 female. **Births** (per 1,000 pop. 1987): 19.8. **Deaths** (per 1,000 pop. 1987): 9.9. **Natural increase** (1987): .9%. **Hospital beds** (1986): 3.7 mln. **Physicians** (1988): 1.2 mln. **Infant mortality** (per 1,000 live births 1987): 25.2.

Education (1985): **Literacy:** 99%. Most receive 11 years of schooling.

Major International Organizations: UN (ILO, UNESCO, WHO), Warsaw Pact.

Embassy: 1125 16th St. NW 20036; 628-8548.

The USSR is nominally a federation consisting of 15 union republics, the largest being the Russian Soviet Federated Socialist Republic. Important positions in the republics are filled by centrally chosen appointees, often ethnic Russians.

Beginning in 1939 the USSR by means of military action and negotiation overran contiguous territory and independent republics, including all or part of Lithuania, Latvia, Estonia, Poland, Czechoslovakia, Romania, Germany, Finland, Tannu Tuva, and Japan. Census figures released in 1989 showed a 9.3 percent increase in the Soviet population in the past decade, with the largest increases in the central Asian republics. The figures also showed an increase in persons leaving rural areas to live in cities. The union republics are:

Republic	Area sq. mi.	Pop. (1988 est.)
Russian SFSR	6,592,800	284,496,000
Ukrainian SSR	233,100	51,377,000
Uzbek SSR	172,700	19,569,000
Kazakh SSR	1,049,200	16,470,000
Byelorussian SSR	80,200	10,141,000
Azerbaijan SSR	33,400	6,921,000
Georgian SSR	26,911	5,297,000
Tadzhik SSR	54,019	4,969,000
Moldavian SSR	13,012	4,224,000
Kirghiz SSR	76,642	4,238,000
Lithuanian SSR	26,173	3,682,000
Armenian SSR	11,306	3,459,000
Turkmen SSR	188,417	3,455,000
Latvian SSR	24,695	2,673,000
Estonian SSR	17,413	1,571,000

The **Russian Soviet Federated Socialist Republic** contains over 50% of the population of the USSR and includes 76% of its territory. It extends from the old Estonian, Latvian, and Finnish borders and the Byelorussian and Ukrainian lines on the W, to the shores of the Pacific, and from the Arctic on the N to the Black and Caspian seas and the borders of Kazakh SSR, Mongolia, and Manchuria on the S. Siberia encompasses a large part of the RSFSR area. Capital: Moscow.

Parts of eastern and western Siberia have been transformed by steel mills, huge dams, oil and gas industries, electric railroads, and highways.

Many of the republics experienced ethnic unrest in 1989; Pres. Gorbachev warned that the unrest posed an "enormous danger" to the USSR.

The **Ukraine**, the most densely populated of the republics, borders on the Black Sea, with Poland, Czechoslovakia, Hungary, and Romania on the W and SW. Capital: Kiev.

The Ukraine contains the arable black soil belt, the chief wheat-producing section of the Soviet Union. Sugar beets, potatoes, and livestock are important.

The Donets Basin has large deposits of coal, iron and other metals. There are chemical and machine industries and salt mines.

Byelorussia (White Russia). Capital: Minsk. Chief industries include machinery, tools, appliances, tractors, clocks, cameras, steel, cement, textiles, paper, leather, glass. Main crops are grain, flax, potatoes, sugar beets.

Azerbaijan boasts near Baku, the capital, important oil fields. Its natural wealth includes deposits of iron ore, cobalt, etc. A high-yield winter wheat is grown, as are fruits. It produces iron, steel, cement, fertilizers, synthetic rubber, electrical and chemical equipment. It borders on Iran and Turkey. In 1988, clashes were reported between Moslem Azerbaijanis and the minority Christian ethnic Armenians.

Georgia, in the western part of Transcaucasia, contains the largest manganese mines in the world. There are rich timber resources and coal mines. Basic industries are food, textiles, iron, steel. Grain, tea, tobacco, fruits, grapes are grown. Capital: Tbilisi (Tiflis). Despite massive party and government purges since 1972, illegal private enterprise and Georgian nationalist feelings persist; attempts to repress them have led to violence.

Armenia is mountainous, sub-tropical, extensively irrigated. Copper, zinc, aluminum, molybdenum, and marble are mined. Instrument making is important. Armenia has sought a reunification with the Nagorno-Karabakh autonomous region of neighboring Azerbaijan. On Dec. 7, 1988, an earthquake struck in the north killing over 55,000 and leaving 500,000 homeless. An international relief effort was mounted. Capital: Erevan.

Uzbekistan, most important economically of the Central Asia republics, produces 67% of USSR cotton, 50% of rice, 33% of silk, 34% of astrakhan, 85% of hemp. Industries include iron, steel, cars, tractors, TV and radio sets, textiles, food. Mineral wealth includes coal, sulphur, copper, and oil. Capital: Tashkent.

Turkmenistan in Central Asia, produces cotton, maize, carpets, chemicals. Minerals: oil, coal, sulphur, barite, lime, salt, gypsum. The Kara Kum desert occupies 80% of the area. Capital: Ashkhabad.

Tadzhikistan borders on China and Afghanistan. Over half the population are Tadzhiks, mostly Moslems, speaking an Iranian dialect. Chief occupations are farming and cattle breeding. Cotton, grain, rice, and a variety of fruits are grown. Heavy industry, based on rich mineral deposits, coal and hydroelectric power, has replaced handicrafts. Capital: Dushanbe.

Kazakhstan extends from the lower reaches of the Volga in Europe to the Altai Mtns. on the Chinese border. It has vast deposits of coal, oil, iron, tin, copper, lead, zinc, etc. Fish for its canning industry are caught in Lake Balkhash and the Caspian and Aral seas. The capital is Alma-Ata. About 50% of the population is Russian or Ukrainian, working in the virgin-grain lands opened up after 1954, and in the growing industries. Capital: Alma-Ata.

Kirghizia is the eastern part of Soviet Central Asia, on the frontier of Xinjiang, China. The people breed cattle and horses and grow tobacco, cotton, rice, sugar beets. Industries include machine and instrument making, chemicals. Capital: Frunze.

Moldavia, in the SW part of the USSR, is a fertile black earth plain bordering Romania and includes Bessarabia. It is an agricultural region that grows grains, fruits, vegetables, and tobacco. Textiles, wine, food and electrical equipment industries have been developed. Capital: Kishinev. The region was taken from Romania in 1940; the people speak Romanian.

Lithuania, on the Baltic, produces cattle, hogs, electric motors, and appliances. The capital is Vilnius (Vilna). The supreme Soviet agreed to allow Lithuania to develop a market-oriented economy beginning in 1990.

Latvia, on the Baltic, is the main producer electric railway passenger cars and long distance telephone exchanges in the

USSR. From 1917, Latvia was occupied by the Soviets, Germans, and the British. The Aug. 1939 Soviet-German agreement assigned it to the Soviet sphere of influence. It was officially accepted as part of the USSR on Aug. 5, 1940. Capital: Riga.

Estonia, also on the Baltic, has textiles, shipbuilding, timber, roadmaking and mining equipment industries and a shale oil refining industry. Capital: Tallinn. The 3 Baltic states were provinces of imperial Russia before World War I, were independent nations between World Wars I and II, but were conquered by Russia in 1940. The supreme soviety agreed to allow Estonia to develop a market—oriented economy beginning in 1990.

Economy. Almost all legal economic enterprises are state-owned. A huge illegal black market plays an important role in distribution.

The USSR is rich in natural resources; distant Siberian reserves are being exploited. Its heavy industry is 2d only to the U.S. It leads the world in oil and steel production. Consumer industries have lagged comparatively. Agricultural output has expanded, but in poor crop years the USSR has been forced to make huge grain purchases from the West. Shortages and rationing of basic food products periodically occur.

Industrial growth has dropped, due to short falls in oil, coal, and steel industries.

History. Slavic tribes began migrating into Russia from the W in the 5th century AD. The first Russian state, founded by Scandinavian chieftains, was established in the 9th century, centering in Novgorod and Kiev.

In the 13th century the Mongols overran the country. It recovered under the grand dukes and princes of Muscovy, or Moscow, and by 1480 freed itself from the Mongols. Ivan the Terrible was the first to be formally proclaimed Tsar (1547). Peter the Great (1682-1725), extended the domain and in 1721, founded the Russian Empire.

Western ideas and the beginnings of modernization spread through the huge Russian empire in the 19th and early 20th centuries. But political evolution failed to keep pace.

Military reverses in the 1905 war with Japan and in World War I led to the breakdown of the Tsarist regime. The 1917 Revolution began in March with a series of sporadic strikes for higher wages by factory workers. A provisional democratic government under Prince Georgi Lvov was established but was quickly followed in May by the second provisional government, led by Alexander Kerensky. The Kerensky government and the freely-elected Constituent Assembly were overthrown in a communist coup led by Vladimir Ilyich Lenin Nov. 7.

Lenin's death Jan. 21, 1924, resulted in an internal power struggle from which Joseph Stalin eventually emerged the absolute ruler of Russia. Stalin secured his position at first by exiling opponents, but from the 1930s to 1953, he resorted to a series of "purge" trials, mass executions, and mass exiles to work camps. These measures resulted in millions of deaths, according to most estimates.

Germany and the USSR signed a non-aggression pact Aug. 1939; Germany launched a massive invasion of the Soviet Union, June 1941. Notable heroic episode was the "900 days" siege of Leningrad, lasting to Jan. 1944, and causing a million deaths; the city was never taken. Russian winter counterthrusts, 1941 to '42 and 1942 to '43, stopped the German advance. Turning point was the failure of German troops to take and hold Stalingrad, Sept. 1942 to Feb. 1943. With British and U.S. Lend-Lease aid and sustaining great casualties, the Russians drove the German forces from eastern Europe and the Balkans in the next 2 years.

After Stalin died, Mar. 5, 1953, Nikita Khrushchev was elected first secretary of the Central Committee. In 1956 he condemned Stalin. "De-Stalinization" of the country on all levels was effected after Stalin's body was removed from the Lenin-Stalin tomb in Moscow.

Under Khrushchev the open antagonism of Poles and Hungarians toward domination by Moscow was brutally suppressed in 1956. He advocated peaceful co-existence with the capitalist countries, but continued arming the USSR with nuclear weapons. He aided the Cuban revolution under Fidel Castro but withdrew Soviet missiles from Cuba during confrontation by U.S. Pres. Kennedy, Sept.-Oct. 1962.

Khrushchev was suddenly deposed, Oct. 1964, and replaced as party first secretary by Leonid I. Brezhnev.

In Aug. 1968 Russian, Polish, East German, Hungarian, and Bulgarian military forces invaded Czechoslovakia to put a curb on liberalization policies of the Czech government.

The USSR in 1971 continued heavy arms shipments to Egypt. In July 1972 Egypt ordered most of the 20,000 Soviet military personnel in that country to leave. When Egypt and Syria attacked Israel in Oct. 1973, the USSR launched huge arms airlifts to the 2 Arab nations. In 1974, the Soviet replenished the arms used or lost by the Syrians in the 1973 war, and continued some shipments to Egypt.

Massive Soviet military aid to North Vietnam in the late 1960s and early 1970s helped assure communist victories throughout Indo-China. Soviet arms aid and advisers were sent to several African countries in the 1970s, including Algeria, Angola, Somalia, and Ethiopia.

More than 130,000 Jews and over 40,000 ethnic Germans were allowed to emigrate from the USSR in the 1970s, following pressure from the West. Many leading figures in the arts also left the country.

In 1979, Soviet forces entered Afghanistan to support that government against rebels. In 1988, the Soviets announced withdrawal of their troops, which will end a futile 8-year war.

There werer serious food shortages reported in the early 1980s and a new agricultural proofram, covering 1982-90, was announced amid Soviet fears of becoming dependent on foreign, especially U.S., grain imports.

Mikhail Gorbachev was chosen Gen. Secy. of the Communist Party, Mar. 1985. He was the youngest member of the Politburo and signaled a change in Soviet leadership from those whose attitudes were shaped by Stalinism and World War II.

He held summit meetings with U.S. Pres. Reagan in 1985, 1986 and in 1987, in Washington, at which time an INF treaty was signed. The 2 leaders met in Moscow in 1988.

In 1987, Gorbachev initiated a program of reforms, including expanded freedoms and the democratization of the political process, through openness (*glasnost*) and restructuring (*perestroika*). The reforms were opposed by some Eastern bloc countries and many old-line communists in the USSR. In June, 1988 a Soviet Communist Party Conference was held, the first since 1941, to discuss the economic, political, and social reforms initiated by Gorbachev.

Gorbachev called upon NATO to begin negotiation on the reduction of short-range nuclear missiles in 1989.

The Soviets received worldwide criticism for their secrecy regarding the Apr. 25, 1986 accident at the Chernobyl nuclear plant.

Government. The Communist Party leadership dominates all areas of national life. A Politburo of 14 full members and 8 candidate members makes all major political, economic, and foreign policy decisions.

United Arab Emirates

Ittihād al-Imarat al-Arabiyah

People: Population (1989 est.): 1,455,000. **Pop. density:** 45 per sq. mi. **Ethnic groups:** Arab, Iranian, Pakistani, Indian. **Languages:** Arabic (official), Farsi, English, Hindi, Urdu. **Religions:** Moslem 94%, Christian, Hindu.

Geography: Area: 32,000 sq. mi., the size of Maine. **Location:** On the S shore of the Persian Gulf. **Neighbors:** Qatar on N, Saudi Ar. on W, S, Oman on E. **Topography:** A barren, flat coastal plain gives way to uninhabited sand dunes on the S. Hajar Mtns. are on E. **Capital:** Abu Dhabi. **Cities** (1984 est.): Abu Dhabi 537,000; Dubai 278,000.

Government: Type: Federation of emirates. **Head of state:** Pres. Zaid ibn Sultan an-Nahayan b. 1923; in office: Dec. 2, 1971. **Head of government:** Prime Min. Rashid ibn Said al-Maktum; in office: June 25, 1979. **Local divisions:** 7 autonomous emirates: Abu Dhabi, Ajman, Dubai, Fujaira, Ras al-Khaimah, Sharjah, Umm al-Qaiwain. **Defense:** 5.7% of GNP (1985).

Economy: Chief crops: Vegetables, dates, limes. **Minerals:** Oil. **Crude oil reserves** (1987): 33 bln. bbls. **Arable land:** 1%. **Electricity prod.** (1986): 5.1 bln. kwh. **Labor force:** 5% agric.; 85% ind. and commerce; 5% serv.; 5% gvt.

Finance: Currency: Dirham (Apr. 1989: 3.67 = $1 US). **Gross national product** (1986): $24 bln. **Per capita income** (1983 est.) $23,000. **Imports** (1987): $7.2 bln.; partners: Jap. 18%, UK 11%, W. Ger. 6%. **Exports** (1987): $15.0 bln.; partners: Jap. 36%, U.S. 7%, Fr. 10%. **International reserves less gold** (Feb. 1989): $4.7 bln. **Gold:** 817,000 oz t.

Transport: Motor Vehicles (1985): 62,000 passenger cars; 17,000 commercial vehicles. **Chief ports:** Dubai, Abu Dhabi.

Communications: Television sets: 145,000 in use (1986). **Radios:** 434,000 in use (1986). **Telephones in use** (1984): 308,000.

Health: Life Expectancy at Birth (1986): 68.4 male, 71.7 female. **Hospital beds** (1984): 4,853. **Physicians** (1984): 1,840. **Infant mortality** (per 1,000 live births 1986): 39.9%.

Education (1985): **Literacy:** 56%. **Years Compulsory:** ages 6-12.

Major International Organizations: UN (World Bank, IMF, ILO), Arab League, OPEC.

Embassy: 600 New Hampshire Ave. NW 20037; 338-6500.

The 7 "Trucial Sheikdoms" gave Britain control of defense and foreign relations in the 19th century. They merged to become an independent state Dec. 2, 1971.

The Abu Dhabi Petroleum Co. was fully nationalized in 1975. Oil revenues have given the UAE one of the highest per capita GNPs in the world. International banking has grown in recent years.

United Kingdom of Great Britain and Northern Ireland

People: Population (1989 est.): 56,648,000. **Age distrib.** (%): 0–14: 18.8; 15–59: 60.4; 60+: 20.8. **Pop. density:** 601 per sq. mi. **Urban** (1985): 92.5%. **Ethnic groups:** English 81.5%, Scottish 9.6%, Irish 2.4%, Welsh 1.9%, Ulster 1.8%; West Indian, Indian, Pakistani over 2%; others. **Languages:** English, Welsh spoken in western Wales; Gaelic. **Religions:** Church of England, Roman Catholic.

Geography: Area: 94,226 sq. mi., slightly smaller than Oregon. **Location:** Off the NW coast of Europe, across English Channel, Strait of Dover, and North Sea. **Neighbors:** Ireland to W, France to SE. **Topography:** England is mostly rolling land, rising to Uplands of southern Scotland; Lowlands are in center of Scotland, granite Highlands are in N. Coast is heavily indented, especially on W. British Isles have milder climate than N Europe, due to the Gulf Stream, and ample rainfall. Severn, 220 mi., and Thames, 215 mi., are longest rivers. **Capital:** London. **Cities** (1986 est.): London 6,700,000; Birmingham 1,008,000; Glasgow 733,000; Leeds 710,000; Sheffield 542,000; Liverpool 492,000; Manchester 451,000; Edinburgh 440,000; Bradford 463,000; Bristol 394,000.

Government: Type: Constitutional monarchy. **Head of state:** Queen Elizabeth II; b. Apr. 21, 1926; in office: Feb. 6, 1952. **Head of government:** Prime Min. Margaret Thatcher; b. Oct. 13, 1925; in office: May 4, 1979. **Local divisions:** England and Wales: 47 non-metro counties, 6 metro counties, Greater London; Scotland: 9 regions, 3 island areas; N. Ireland: 26 districts. **Defense:** 5.3% of GDP (1985).

Economy: Industries: Steel, metals, vehicles, shipbuilding, shipping, banking, insurance, textiles, chemicals, electronics, aircraft, machinery, distilling. **Chief crops:** Grains, sugar beets, fruits, vegetables. **Minerals:** Coal, tin, oil, gas, limestone, iron, salt, clay, chalk, gypsum, lead, silica. **Crude oil reserves** (1987): 5.8 bln. bbls. **Arable land:** 30%. **Livestock** (1987): cattle: 12.6 mln.; pigs: 7.9 mln.; sheep: 38.7 mln. **Fish catch** (1987): 716,000 metric tons. **Electricity prod.** (1986): 312 bln. kwh. **Crude steel prod.** (1987): 17.4 mln. metric tons. **Labor force:** 1.7% agric.; 26% manuf. & eng., 64% services.

Finance: Currency: Pound (June 1989: .63 = $1 US). **Gross national product** (1986): $504 bln. **Per capita income** (1979): $7,216. **Imports** (1988): $189 bln.; partners: W. Ger. 17%, U.S. 12%, Fr. 7%, Neth. 8%. **Exports** (1988): $145 bln.; partners: U.S. 13%, W. Ger. 10%, Fr. 8%, Neth. 8%. **Tourists** (1986): receipts: $7.9 bln.; **National budget** (1986): $232 bln. expenditures. **International reserves less gold** (Mar. 1989): $41.4 bln. **Gold:** 19.0 mln. oz t. **Consumer prices** (change in 1988): 4.9%.

Transport: Railway traffic (1987): 32.1 bln. passenger-km; 14.4 bln. net ton-km. **Motor vehicles:** in use (1987): 17.4 mln. passenger cars, 2.4 mln. comm. vehicles. **Civil aviation** (1986): 51.0 bln. passenger-km: 1.8 bln. freight ton-km. **Chief ports:** London, Liverpool, Glasgow, Southampton, Cardiff, Belfast.

Communications: Television sets: 18.9 mln. licensed (1987). **Radios:** 63 mln. licensed (1986). **Telephones in use** (1984): 29 mln. **Daily newspaper circ.** (1986): 443 per 1,000 pop.

Health: Life expectancy at birth: (1983): 70.2 male; 76.2 female. **Births:** (per 1,000 pop. 1987): 13.6 **Deaths:** (per 1,000 pop. 1987): 11.2 **Natural increase:** (1987): .01%. **Hospital**

beds (1986): 410,000. **Physicians** (1986): 88,000. **Infant mortality:** (per 1,000 live births 1987): 9.1.

Education (1987): **Literacy:** 99%. **Years compulsory:** 12; attendance 99%.

Major International Organizations: UN all of and its specialized agencies, NATO, EC, OECD.

Embassy: 3100 Massachusetts Ave. NW 20008; 462-1340.

The United Kingdom of Great Britain and Northern Ireland comprises England, Wales, Scotland, and Northern Ireland.

Queen and Royal Family. The ruling sovereign is Elizabeth II of the House of Windsor, born Apr. 21, 1926, elder daughter of King George VI. She succeeded to the throne Feb. 6, 1952, and was crowned June 2, 1953. She was married Nov. 20, 1947, to Lt. Philip Mountbatten, born June 10, 1921, former Prince of Greece. He was created Duke of Edinburgh, Earl of Merioneth, and Baron Greenwich, and given the style H.R.H., Nov. 19, 1947; he was given the title Prince of the United Kingdom and Northern Ireland Feb. 22, 1957. Prince Charles Philip Arthur George, born Nov. 14, 1948, is the Prince of Wales and heir apparent. His son, William Philip Arthur Louis, born June 21, 1982, is second in line to the throne.

Parliament is the legislative governing body for the United Kingdom, with certain powers over dependent units. It consists of 2 houses: The **House of Lords** includes 763 hereditary and 314 life peers and peeresses, certain judges, 2 archbishops and 24 bishops of the Church of England. Total membership is over 1,000. The **House of Commons** has 650 members, who are elected by direct ballot and divided as follows: England 516; Wales 36; Scotland 71; Northern Ireland 12.

Resources and Industries. Great Britain's major occupations are manufacturing and trade. Metals and metal-using industries contribute more than 50% of the exports. Of about 60 million acres of land in England, Wales and Scotland, 46 million are farmed, of which 17 million are arable, the rest pastures.

Large oil and gas fields have been found in the North Sea. Commercial oil production began in 1975. There are large deposits of coal.

The railroads, nationalized since 1948, have been reduced in total length, with a basic network, Dec. 1978, of 11,123 mi. The merchant marine totaled 126,000 gross registered tons in 1982.

A year-long coal strike costing some $3 bln. ended March 1985. The issue of the closing of uneconomic mines was unresolved.

Britain imports all of its cotton, rubber, sulphur, 80% of its wool, half of its food and iron ore, also certain amounts of paper, tobacco, chemicals. Manufactured goods made from these basic materials have been exported since the industrial age began. Main exports are machinery, chemicals, woolen and synthetic textiles, clothing, autos and trucks, iron and steel, locomotives, ships, jet aircraft, farm machinery, drugs, radio, TV, radar and navigation equipment, scientific instruments, arms, whisky.

Religion and Education. The Church of England is Protestant Episcopal. The queen is its temporal head, with rights of appointments to archbishoprics, bishoprics, and other offices. There are 2 provinces, Canterbury and York, each headed by an archbishop. The most famous church is Westminster Abbey (1050-1760), site of coronations, tombs of Elizabeth I, Mary of Scots, kings, poets, and of the Unknown Warrior.

The most celebrated British universities are Oxford and Cambridge, each dating to the 13th century. There are about 40 other universities.

History. Britain was part of the continent of Europe until about 6,000 BC, but migration of peoples across the English Channel continued long afterward. Celts arrived 2,500 to 3,000 years ago. Their language survives in Welsh and Gaelic enclaves.

England was added to the Roman Empire in 43 AD. After the withdrawal of Roman legions in 410, waves of Jutes, Angles, and Saxons arrived from German lands. They contended with Danish raiders for control from the 8th through 11th centuries.

The last successful invasion was by French speaking Normans in 1066, who united the country with their dominions in France.

Opposition by nobles to royal authority forced King John to sign the Magna Carta in 1215, a guarantee of rights and the rule of law. In the ensuing decades, the foundations of the parliamentary system were laid.

English dynastic claims to large parts of France led to the Hundred Years War, 1338-1453, and the defeat of England. A long civil war, the War of the Roses, lasted 1455-85, and ended with the establishment of the powerful Tudor monarchy. A dis-

tinct English civilization flourished. The economy prospered over long periods of domestic peace unmatched in continental Europe. Religious independence was secured when the Church of England was separated from the authority of the Pope in 1534.

Under Queen Elizabeth I, England became a major naval power, leading to the founding of colonies in the new world and the expansion of trade with Europe and the Orient. Scotland was united with England when James VI of Scotland was crowned James I of England in 1603.

A struggle between Parliament and the Stuart kings led to a bloody civil war, 1642-49, and the establishment of a republic under the Puritan Oliver Cromwell. The monarchy was restored in 1660, but the "Glorious Revolution" of 1688 confirmed the sovereignty of Parliament: a Bill of Rights was granted 1689.

In the 18th century, parliamentary rule was strengthened. Technological and entrepreneurial innovations led to the Industrial Revolution. The 13 North American colonies were lost, but replaced by growing empires in Canada and India. Britain's role in the defeat of Napoleon, 1815, strengthened its position as the leading world power.

The extension of the franchise in 1832 and 1867, the formation of trade unions, and the development of universal public education were among the drastic social changes which accompanied the spread of industrialization and urbanization in the 19th century. Large parts of Africa and Asia were added to the empire during the reign of Queen Victoria, 1837-1901.

Though victorious in World War I, Britain suffered huge casualties and economic dislocation. Ireland became independent in 1921, and independence movements became active in India and other colonies.

The country suffered major bombing damage in World War II, but held out against Germany singlehandedly for a year after the fall of France in 1940.

Industrial growth continued in the postwar period, but Britain lost its leadership position to other powers. Labor governments passed socialist programs nationalizing some basic industries and expanding social security. The Thatcher government has however, tried to increase the role of private enterprise. In 1987, Margaret Thatcher became the first British leader in 160 years to be elected to a 3d consecutive term as prime minister.

Britain broke diplomatic relations with Libya, Apr. 22, 1984, 5 days after a policewoman was killed and 10 Libyan exile demonstrators wounded by machine-gun fire from within the Libyan embassy in London. The embassy occupants, including the killer, left Britain, Apr. 27.

Wales

The Principality of Wales in western Britain has an area of 8,019 sq. mi. and a population (1986 est.) of 2,821,000. Cardiff is the capital, pop. (1981 est.) 273,856.

England and Wales are administered as a unit. Less than 20% of the population of Wales speak both English and Welsh; about 32,000 speak Welsh solely. A 1979 referendum rejected, 4-1, the creation of an elected Welsh Assembly.

Early Anglo-Saxon invaders drove Celtic peoples into the mountains of Wales, terming them Waelise (Welsh, or foreign). There they developed a distinct nationality. Members of the ruling house of Gwynedd in the 13th century fought England but were crushed, 1283. Edward of Caernarvon, son of Edward I of England, was created Prince of Wales, 1301.

Scotland

Scotland, a kingdom now united with England and Wales in Great Britain, occupies the northern 37% of the main British island, and the Hebrides, Orkney, Shetland and smaller islands. Length, 275 mi., breadth approx. 150 mi., area, 30,405 sq. mi., population (1986 est.) 5,121,000.

The Lowlands, a belt of land approximately 60 mi. wide from the Firth of Clyde to the Firth of Forth, divide the farming region of the Southern Uplands from the granite Highlands of the North, contain 75% of the population and most of the industry. The Highlands, famous for hunting and fishing, have been opened to industry by many hydroelectric power stations.

Edinburgh, pop. (1986 est.) 439,000, is the capital. Glasgow, pop. (1986 est.) 733,000, is Britain's greatest industrial center. It is a shipbuilding complex on the Clyde and an ocean port. Aberdeen, pop. (1986 est.) 215,000, NE of Edinburgh, is a major port, center of granite industry, fish processing, and North Sea oil exploitation. Dundee, pop. (1986 est.) 177,000, NE of Edinburgh, is an industrial and fish processing center. About 90,000 persons speak Gaelic as well as English.

History. Scotland was called Caledonia by the Romans who battled early Celtic tribes and occupied southern areas from the 1st to the 4th centuries. Missionaries from Britain introduced Christianity in the 4th century; St. Columba, an Irish monk, converted most of Scotland in the 6th century.

The Kingdom of Scotland was founded in 1018. William Wallace and Robert Bruce both defeated English armies 1297 and 1314, respectively.

In 1603 James VI of Scotland, son of Mary, Queen of Scots, succeeded to the throne of England as James I, and effected the Union of the Crowns. In 1707 Scotland received representation in the British Parliament, resulting from the union of former separate Parliaments. Its executive in the British cabinet is the Secretary of State for Scotland. The growing Scottish National Party urges independence. A 1979 referendum on the creation of an elected Scotland Assembly was defeated.

There are 8 universities. Memorials of Robert Burns, Sir Walter Scott, John Knox, Mary, Queen of Scots draw many tourists, as do the beauties of the Trossachs, Loch Katrine, Loch Lomond and abbey ruins.

Industries. Engineering products are the most important industry, with growing emphasis on office machinery, autos, electronics and other consumer goods. Oil has been discovered offshore in the North Sea, stimulating on-shore support industries.

Scotland produces fine woolens, worsteds, tweeds, silks, fine linens and jute. It is known for its special breeds of cattle and sheep. Fisheries have large hauls of herring, cod, whiting. Whisky is the biggest export.

The Hebrides are a group of c. 500 islands, 100 inhabited, off the W coast. The Inner Hebrides include **Skye, Mull,** and **Iona,** the last famous for the arrival of St. Columba, 563 AD. The Outer Hebrides include **Lewis** and **Harris.** Industries include sheep raising and weaving. The **Orkney Islands,** c. 90, are to the NE. The capital is Kirkwall, on Pomona Is. Fish curing, sheep raising and weaving are occupations. NE of the Orkneys are the 200 **Shetland Islands,** 24 inhabited, home of Shetland pony. The Orkneys and Shetlands have become centers for the North Sea oil industry.

Northern Ireland

Six of the 9 counties of Ulster, the NE corner of Ireland, constitute Northern Ireland, with the parliamentary boroughs of Belfast and Londonderry. Area 5,463 sq. mi., 1986 est. pop. 1,568,000, capital and chief industrial center, Belfast, (1986 cen.) 322,000.

Industries. Shipbuilding, including large tankers, has long been an important industry, centered in Belfast, the largest port. Linen manufacture is also important, along with apparel, rope, and twine. Growing diversification has added engineering products, synthetic fibers, and electronics. They are large numbers of cattle, hogs, and sheep, potatoes, poultry, and dairy foods are also produced.

Government. An act of the British Parliament, 1920, divided Northern from Southern Ireland, each with a parliament and government. When Ireland became a dominion, 1921, and later a republic, Northern Ireland chose to remain a part of the United Kingdom. It elects 12 members to the British House of Commons.

During 1968-69, large demonstrations were conducted by Roman Catholics who charged they were discriminated against in voting rights, housing, and employment. The Catholics, a minority comprising about a third of the population, demanded abolition of property qualifications for voting in local elections. Violence and terrorism intensified, involving branches of the Irish Republican Army (outlawed in the Irish Republic), Protestant groups, police, and British troops.

A succession of Northern Ireland prime ministers pressed reform programs but failed to satisfy extremists on both sides. Over 2,000 were killed in over 15 years of bombings and shootings through 1988, many in England itself. Britain suspended the Northern Ireland parliament Mar. 30, 1972, and imposed direct British rule. A coalition government was formed in 1973 when moderates won election to a new one-house Assembly. But a Protestant general strike overthrew the government in 1974 and direct rule was resumed.

The turmoil and agony of Northern Ireland was dramatized in 1981 by the deaths of 10 imprisoned Irish nationalist hunger strikers in Maze Prison near Belfast. The inmates had starved themselves to death in an attempt to achieve status as political prisoners, but the British government refused to yield to their demands. In 1985, the Hillsborough agreement gave the Rep. of Ireland a voice in the governing of Northern Ireland; the accord was strongly opposed by Ulster loyalists.

Education and Religion. Northern Ireland is 2/3 Protestant, 1/3 Roman Catholic. Education is compulsory through age 15. There are 2 universities and 24 technical colleges.

Channel Islands

The Channel Islands, area 75 sq. mi., est. pop. 1986 145,000, off the NW coast of France, the only parts of the one-time Dukedom of Normandy belonging to England, are **Jersey, Guernsey** and the dependencies of Guernsey — **Alderney, Brechou, Great Sark, Little Sark, Herm, Jethou and Lihou.** Jersey and Guernsey have separate legal existences and lieutenant governors named by the Crown. The islands were the only British soil occupied by German troops in World War II.

Isle of Man

The Isle of Man, area 227 sq. mi., 1982 est. pop. 61,000, is in the Irish Sea, 20 mi. from Scotland, 30 mi. from Cumberland. It is rich in lead and iron. The island has its own laws and a lieutenant governor appointed by the Crown. The Tynwald (legislature) consists of the Legislative Council, partly elected, and House of Keys, elected. Capital: Douglas. Farming, tourism (413,000 visitors in 1982), fishing (kippers, scallops) are chief occupations. Man is famous for the Manx tailless cat.

Gibraltar

Gibraltar, a dependency on the southern coast of Spain, guards the entrance to the Mediterranean. The Rock has been in British possession since 1704. The Rock is 2.75 mi. long, 3/4 of a mi. wide and 1,396 ft. in height; a narrow isthmus connects it with the mainland. Est. pop. 1987, 29,048.

In 1966 Spain called on Britain to give "substantial sovereignty" of Gibraltar to Spain and imposed a partial blockade. In 1967, residents voted for remaining under Britain. A new constitution, May 30, 1996, gave an elected House of Assembly more control in domestic affairs. A UN General Assembly resolution requested Britain to end Gibraltar's colonial status by Oct. 1, 1996. No settlement has been reached.

British West Indies

Swinging in a vast arc from the coast of Venezuela NE, then N and NW toward Puerto Rico are the Leeward Islands, forming a coral and volcanic barrier sheltering the Caribbean from the open Atlantic. Many of the islands are self-governing British possessions. Universal suffrage was instituted 1951-54; ministerial systems were set up 1956-1960.

The **Leeward Islands,** still associated with the UK are **Montserrat** (1980 pop. 11,600, area 32 sq. mi., capital Plymouth), the small **British Virgin Islands** (pop. 1987: 12,000), and **Anguilla** (pop. 1985: 7,000), the most northerly of the Leeward Islands.

The three **Cayman Islands,** a dependency, lie S of Cuba, NW of Jamaica. Pop. 23,000 (1987), most of it on Grand Cayman. It is a free port; in the 1970s Grand Cayman became a tax-free refuge for foreign funds and branches of many Western banks were opened there. Total area 102 sq. mi., capital Georgetown.

The **Turks and Caicos Islands,** at the SE end of the Bahama Islands, are a separate possession. There are about 30 islands, only 6 inhabited, 1987 pop. est. 9,000, area 193 sq. mi., capital Grand Turk. Salt, crayfish and conch shells are the main exports.

Bermuda

Bermuda is a British dependency governed by a royal governor and an assembly, dating from 1620, the oldest legislative body among British dependencies. Capital is Hamilton.

It is a group of 360 small islands of coral formation, 20 inhabited, comprising 20.6 sq. mi. in the western Atlantic, 580 mi. E of North Carolina. Pop., 1987 est., was 57,800 (about 61% of African descent). Density is high.

The U.S. has air and naval bases under long-term lease, and a NASA tracking facility.

Bermuda boasts many resort hotels. Receipts from tourists totalled $407 mln. in 1986. The government raises most revenue from import duties. Exports: petroleum products, drugs.

South Atlantic

Falkland Islands and Dependencies, a British dependency, lies 300 mi. E of the Strait of Magellan at the southern end of South America.

The Falklands or Islas Malvinas include about 200 islands, area 4,700 sq. mi., pop. (1980 est.) 1,800. Sheep-grazing is the main industry; wool is the principal export. There are indications of large oil and gas deposits. The islands are also claimed by Argentina though 97% of inhabitants are of British origin. Argentina invaded the islands Apr. 2, 1982. The British responded by sending a task force to the area, landing their main force on the Falklands, May 21, and forcing an Argentine surrender at Port Stanley, June 14. **South Georgia**, area 1,450 sq. mi., and the uninhabited **South Sandwich Is.** are dependencies of the Falklands.

British Antarctic Territory, south of 60° S lat., was made a separate colony in 1962 and comprises mainly the **South Shetland Islands**, the **South Orkneys** and **Graham's Land**. A chain of meteorological stations is maintained.

St. Helena, an island 1,200 mi. off the W coast of Africa and 1,800 E of South America, has 47 sq. mi. and est. pop., 1981 of 5,300. Flax, lace and rope making are the chief industries. After Napoleon Bonaparte was defeated at Waterloo the Allies exiled him to St. Helena, where he lived from Oct. 16, 1815, to his death, May 5, 1821. Capital is Jamestown.

Tristan da Cunha is the principal of a group of islands of volcanic origin, total area 40 sq. mi., half way between the Cape of Good Hope and South America. A volcanic peak 6,760 ft. high erupted in 1961. The 262 inhabitants were removed to England, but most returned in 1963. The islands are dependencies of St. Helena.

Ascension is an island of volcanic origin, 34 sq. mi. in area, 700 mi. NW of St. Helena, through which it is administered. It is a communications relay center for Britain, and has a U.S. satellite tracking center. Est. pop., 1976, was 1,179, half of them communications workers. The island is noted for sea turtles.

Hong Kong

A Crown Colony at the mouth of the Canton R. in China, 90 mi. S of Canton. Its nucleus is Hong Kong Is., 35½ sq. mi., acquired from China 1841, on which is located Victoria, the capital. Opposite is Kowloon Peninsula, 3 sq. mi. and Stonecutters Is., ¼ sq. mi., added, 1860. An additional 355 sq. mi. known as the New Territories, a mainland area and islands, were leased from China, 1898, for 99 years. Britain and China, Dec. 19, 1985, signed an agreement under which Hong Kong would be allowed to keep its capitalist system for 50 years after 1997, the year that the 99-year lease will expire. Total area of the colony is 409 sq. mi., with a population, 1988 est., of 5.7 million including fewer than 20,000 British. From 1949 to 1962 Hong Kong absorbed more than a million refugees from China.

Hong Kong harbor was long an important British naval station and one of the world's great trans-shipment ports.

Principal industries are textiles and apparel; also tourism, 2.5 mln. visitors, $2.2 bln. expenditures (1986), shipbuilding, iron and steel, fishing, cement, and small manufactures.

Spinning mills, among the best in the world, and low wages compete with textiles elsewhere and have resulted in the protective measures in some countries. Hong Kong also has a booming electronics industry.

British Indian Ocean Territory

Formed Nov. 1965, embracing islands formerly dependencies of Mauritius or Seychelles: the Chagos Archipelago (including Diego Garcia), Aldabra, Farquhar and Des Roches. The latter 3 were transferred to Seychelles, which became independent in 1976. Area 22 sq mi. No civilian population remains.

Pacific Ocean

Pitcairn Island is in the Pacific, halfway between South America and Australia. The island was discovered in 1767 by Carteret but was not inhabited until 23 years later when the mutineers of the Bounty landed there. The area is 18 sq. mi. and pop. 1983, was 61. It is a British colony and is administered by a British Representative in New Zealand and a local Council. The uninhabited islands of **Henderson, Ducie** and **Oeno** are in the Pitcairn group.

United States of America

People: Population (1989 est.): 247,498,000. **Age distrib.(%):** 0–14: 21.5; 15–59: 61.8; 60+: 16.7. **Pop. density:** 68 per sq. mi. **Urban** (1980) 79.2%.

Defense: 5.7% of GNP (1988).

Economy: Minerals: Coal, copper, lead, molybdenum, phosphates, uranium, bauxite, gold, iron, mercury, nickel, potash, silver, tungsten, zinc. **Crude oil reserves** (1987): 27 bln. bbls. **Arable land:** 21%. **Livestock** (1987): cattle: 105.4 mln.; pigs: 50.9 mln.; sheep: 10.3 mln. **Fish catch** (1987): 3.1 mln. metric tons. **Electricity prod.** (1987): 2,571 bln. kwh. **Crude steel prod.** (1987): 89.1 mln. metric tons.

Finance: Gross national product (1987): 4.5 trl. **Per capita income** (1988): $16,444. **Imports** (1988): $459 bln.; partners: Can. 17%, Jap. 20%, Mex. 6%. **Exports** (1988): $321 bln.; partners: Can. 22%, Jap. 10%, Mex. 6%, UK 5%. **Tourists** (1986): receipts $12.9 bln. **International reserves less gold** (Mar. 1989): $38.7 bln. **Gold:** 261.0 mln. oz t. **Consumer prices** (change in 1988): 4.0%.

Transport: Railway traffic (1986): 19.2 bln. passenger-km; 1,266 bln. net ton-km. **Motor vehicles:** in use (1986): 135 mln. passenger cars, 40 mln. comm. vehicles. **Civil aviation** (1987): 614 bln. passenger-km; 11.9 bln. freight ton-km.

Communications: Television sets: 145 mln. in use (1985). **Radios:** 480 mln. in use (1986). **Telephones in use** (1986): 122 mln. **Daily newspaper circ.** (1987): 267 per 1,000 pop.

Health: Life expectancy at birth (1986): 71.5 male; 78.5 female. **Births** (per 1,000 pop. 1988): 15.9. **Deaths** (per 1,000 pop. 1988): 9.0. **Natural increase** (1988): .6%. **Hospital beds** (1985): 1.3 mln. **Physicians** (1986): 576,900. **Infant mortality** (per 1,000 live births 1988): 10.0.

Major International Organizations: UN (GATT, IMF, WHO, FAO), OAS, NATO, OECD.

Education (1987): **Literacy:** 99%.

Uruguay
Oriental Republic of Uruguay
República Oriental del Uruguay

People: Population (1989 est.): 2,983,000. **Age distrib. (%):** 0–14: 26.9; 15–59: 57.7; 60+: 15.4. **Pop. density:** 43 per sq. mi. **Urban** (1985): 86.0%. **Ethnic groups:** Caucasians (Iberians, Italians) 89%, mestizos 10%, mulatto and black. **Languages:** Spanish. **Religions:** 66% Roman Catholic.

Geography: Area: 68,037 sq. mi., the size of Washington State. **Location:** In southern S. America, on the Atlantic O. **Neighbors:** Argentina on W, Brazil on N. **Topography:** Uruguay is composed of rolling, grassy plains and hills, well-watered by rivers flowing W to Uruguay R. **Capital:** Montevideo. **Cities** (1986 est.): Montevideo 1,246,000.

Government: Type: Republic. **Head of state:** Pres. Julio Maria Sanguinetti Cairolo; b. Jan. 6, 1936; in office: Mar. 1, 1985. **Local divisions:** 19 departments. **Defense:** 2.7% of GNP (1985).

Economy: Industries: Meat-packing, metals, textiles, wine, cement, oil products. **Chief crops:** Corn, wheat, citrus fruits, rice, oats, linseed. **Arable land:** 8%. **Livestock** (1987): cattle: 9.9 mln.; sheep: 20.6 mln. **Fish catch** (1987): 134,000 metric tons. **Electricity prod.** (1986): 7.4 bln. kwh. **Labor force** 4% agric.; 37% ind. and commerce; 15% serv.; 21% govt.

Finance: Currency: New Peso (May 1989: 552 = $1 US). **Gross national product** (1986): $5.2 bln. **Per capita income** (1986): $1,701. **Imports** (1987): $1.4 bln.; partners: EC 23%, Braz. 24%, Arg. 14%, U.S. 8%. **Exports** (1987): $1.1 bln.; partners: Braz. 17%, U.S. 14%, Arg. 14%, EC 30%. **Tourists** (1986): $259 mln. receipts. **National budget** (1986): $901 mln. expeditures. **International reserves less gold** (Jan. 1989): $542 mln. **Gold:** 2.60 mln. oz t. **Consumer prices** (change in 1988): 62.2%.

Transport: Railway traffic (1986): 330 mln. passenger-km; 204 mln. net ton-km. **Motor vehicles:** in use (1981): 281,000 passenger cars, 43,000 comm. vehicles. **Civil aviation** (1985): 240 mln. passenger-km; 36 mln. freight ton-km. **Chief ports:** Montevideo.

Communications: Television sets: 500,000 in use (1987). **Radios:** 1.8 mln. in use (1987). **Telephones in use** (1987): 400,000. **Daily newspaper circ.** (1985): 185 per 1,000 pop.

Health: Life expectancy at birth (1986): 67.1 male; 73.7 female. **Births** (per 1,000 pop. 1986): 18.2. **Deaths** (per 1,000 pop. 1986): 9.8. **Natural increase** (1986): .8%. **Hospital beds** (1985): 23,400. **Physicians** (1986): 6,500. **Infant mortality** (per 1,000 live births 1986): 27.

Education (1984): Literacy: 96%.
Major International Organizations: UN (GATT, IMF, WHO), OAS.
Embassy: 1919 F St. NW 20006; 331-1313.

Spanish settlers did not begin replacing the indigenous Charrua Indians until 1624. Portuguese from Brazil arrived later, but Uruguay was attached to the Spanish Viceroyalty of Rio de la Plata in the 18th century. Rebels fought against Spain beginning in 1810. An independent republic was declared Aug. 25, 1825.

Liberal governments adopted socialist measures as far back as 1911. The state owns the power, telephone, railroad, cement, oil-refining and other industries. Social welfare programs are among the most advanced in the world.

Uruguay's standard of living was one of the highest in South America, and political and labor conditions among the freest. Economic stagnation, inflation, plus floods, drought in 1967 and a general strike in 1968 brought attempts by the government to strengthen the economy through a series of devaluations of the peso and wage and price controls. But inflation continued in the 1980s and the country was forced to ask international creditors to restructure $2.7 billion in debt in 1983.

Tupamaros, leftist guerrillas drawn from the upper classes, increased terrorist actions in 1970. Violence continued and in Feb. 1973 Pres. Juan Maria Bordaberry agreed to military control of his administration. In June he abolished Congress and set up a Council of State in its place. By 1974 the military had apparently defeated the Tupamaros, using severe repressive measures. Bordaberry was removed by the military in a 1976 coup. Civilian government was restored to the country in 1985.

Vanuatu
Republic of Vanuatu
Ripablik Blong Vanuatu

People: Population (1989 est.): 150,000. **Population density:** 26 per sq. mi. **Ethnic groups:** Mainly Melanesian, some European, Polynesian, Micronesian. **Languages:** Bislama (national), French and English both official. **Religions:** Presbyterian 40%, Anglican 14%, Roman Catholic 16%, animist 15%.

Geography: Area: 5,700 sq. mi. **Location:** SW Pacific, 1,200 mi NE of Brisbane, Australia. **Topography:** dense forest with narrow coastal strips of cultivated land. **Capital:** Vila. **Cities:** Vila (1987): 15,000.

Government: Type: Republic. **Head of state:** Pres. George Sokomanu; in office: July 30, 1980. **Head of gov't:** Prime Min. Rev. Walter Lini; in office: July 30, 1980.

Economy: Industries: Fish-freezing, meat canneries, tourism. **Chief crops:** Copra (38% of export), cocoa, coffee. **Other resources:** Forests, cattle. **Fish catch** (1987): 2.9 metric tons.

Finance: Currency: Australian dollar and Vanuatu franc (Mar. 1989: 110 vatu = $1 US). **Imports** (1987): $68 mln.; partners: Aus. 36%, Fr. 8%, Japan 13%. **Exports** (1987): $17 mln.; partners: Neth. 48%, Jap. 17%, Fr. 12%, Belg.-Lux. 14%.

Health: Life expectancy at birth (1986): 61.1 male, 59.3 female. **Infant mortality** (per 1,000 live births 1985): 78.

Education: Education not compulsory, but 85-90% of children of primary school age attend primary schools.

The Anglo-French condominium of the New Hebrides, administered jointly by France and Great Britain since 1906, became the independent Republic of Vanuatu on July 30, 1980.

Vatican City
The Holy See

People: Population (1989 est.): 750. **Ethnic groups:** Italians, Swiss. **Languages:** Italian, Latin.

Geography: Area: 108.7 acres. **Location:** In Rome, Italy. **Neighbors:** Completely surrounded by Italy.

Currency: Lira.

Apostolic Nunciature in U.S.: 3339 Massachusetts Ave. NW 20008; 333-7121.

The popes for many centuries, with brief interruptions, held temporal sovereignty over mid-Italy (the so-called Papal States), comprising an area of some 16,000 sq. mi., with a population in

the 19th century of more than 3 million. This territory was incorporated in the new Kingdom of Italy, the sovereignty of the pope being confined to the palaces of the Vatican and the Lateran in Rome and the villa of Castel Gandolfo, by an Italian law, May 13, 1871. This law also guaranteed to the pope and his successors a yearly indemnity of over $620,000. The allowance, however, remained unclaimed.

A Treaty of Conciliation, a concordat and a financial convention were signed Feb. 11, 1929, by Cardinal Gasparri and Premier Mussolini. The documents established the- independent state of Vatican City, and gave the Catholic religion special status in Italy. The treaty (Lateran Agreement) was made part of the Constitution of Italy (Article 7) in 1947. Italy and the Vatican reached preliminary agreement in 1976 on revisions of the concordat, that would eliminate Roman Catholicism as the state religion and end required religious education in Italian schools.

Vatican City includes St. Peter's, the Vatican Palace and Museum covering over 13 acres, the Vatican gardens, and neighboring buildings between Viale Vaticano and the Church. Thirteen buildings in Rome, outside the boundaries, enjoy extraterritorial rights; these buildings house congregations or officers necessary for the administration of the Holy See.

The legal system is based on the code of canon law, the apostolic constitutions and the laws especially promulgated for the Vatican City by the pope. The Secretariat of State represents the Holy See in its diplomatic relations. By the Treaty of Conciliation the pope is pledged to a perpetual neutrality unless his mediation is specifically requested. This, however, does not prevent the defense of the Church whenever it is persecuted.

The present sovereign of the State of Vatican City is the Supreme Pontiff John Paul II, Karol Wojtyla, born in Wadowice, Poland, May 18, 1920, elected Oct. 16, 1978 (the first non-Italian to be elected Pope in 456 years).

The U.S. restored formal relations in 1984 after the U.S. Congress repealed an 1867 ban on diplomatic relations with the Vatican.

Venezuela
Republic of Venezuela
Republica de Venezuela

People: Population (1989 est.): 19,246,000. **Age distrib.** (%): 0–14: 38.8; 15–59: 55.7; 60+: 5.5. **Pop. density:** 54 per sq. mi. **Urban** (1988): 83%. **Ethnic groups:** Mestizo 69%, white (Spanish, Portuguese, Italian) 20%, black 9%, Indian 2%. **Languages:** Spanish (official), Indian languages 2%. **Religions:** Roman Catholic 96%.

Geography: Area: 352,143 sq. mi., more than twice the size of California. **Location:** On the Caribbean coast of S. America. **Neighbors:** Colombia on W, Brazil on S, Guyana on E. **Topography:** Flat coastal plain and Orinoco Delta are bordered by Andes Mtns. and hills. Plains, called llanos, extend between mountains and Orinoco. Guyana Highlands and plains are S of Orinoco, which stretches 1,600 mi. and drains 80% of Venezuela. **Capital:** Caracas. **Cities** (1988 est.): Caracas 1,261,000; Maracaibo 1,151,000; Barquisimeto 681,000; Valencia 889,000.

Government: Type: Federal republic. **Head of state:** Pres. Carlos Andres Perez; in office: Feb. 2, 1989. **Local divisions:** 20 states, 2 federal territories, federal district, federal dependency. **Defense:** 1.4% of GNP (1985).

Economy: Industries: Steel, oil products, textiles, containers, paper, shoes. **Chief crops:** Coffee, rice, fruits, sugar. **Minerals:** Oil (5th largest producer), iron (extensive reserves and production), gold. **Crude oil reserves** (1987): 55 bln. bbls. **Arable land:** 4%. **Livestock** (1986): cattle: 12.3 mln.; pigs: 2.8 mln. **Fish catch** (1986): 303,000 metric tons. **Electricity prod.** (1986): 50.2 bln. kwh. **Crude steel prod.** (1987): 3.7 mln. metric tons. **Labor force:** 15% agric.; 28% ind.; 56% services.

Finance: Currency: Bolivar (Apr. 1989: 14.50 = $1 US). **Gross national product** (1986): $57 bln. **Per capita income** (1985): $2,629. **Imports** (1987): $8.8 bln.; partners: U.S. 48%, W. Ger. 6%, Jap. 8%. **Exports** (1987): $8.4 bln.; partners: U.S. 25%, Neth Ant. 21%, Can. 9%. **Tourists** (1986): $353 mln. receipts. **National budget** (1987): $16.6 bln. expenditures. **International reserves less gold** (Mar. 1989): $3.3 bln. **Gold:** 11.46 mln. oz t. **Consumer prices** (change in 1988): 26.1%.

Transport: Railway traffic (1986): 17 mln. passenger-km; 11 mln. net ton-km. **Motor vehicles:** in use (1986): 2.3 mln. passenger cars, 1.2 mln. mm. vehicles. **Civil aviation** (1985): 2.4 mln. passenger-km; 215 mln. freight ton-km. **Chief ports:** Maracaibo, La Guaira, Puerto Cabello.

Communications: Television sets: 2.8 mln. in use (1987). **Radios:** 6.7 mln. in use (1986). **Telephones in use** (1987): 1.5 mln. **Daily newspaper circ.** (1982): 120 per 1,000 pop.

Health: Life expectancy at birth (1985): 65 male; 70.6 female. **Births** (per 1,000 pop. 1986): 28.3. **Deaths** (per 1,000 pop. 1986): 4.4. **Natural increase** (1986): 2.3%. **Hospital beds** (1986): 47,000. **Physicians** (1986): 24,600. **Infant mortality** (per 1,000 live births 1986): 25.8

Education (1987): **Literacy:** 88%. **Years compulsory:** 8; attendance 82%.

Major International Organizations: UN (IMF, WHO, FAO), OAS, OPEC.

Embassy: 2445 Massachusetts Ave. NW 20008; 797-3800.

Columbus first set foot on the South American continent on the peninsula of Paria, Aug. 1498. Alonso de Ojeda, 1499, found Lake Maracaibo, called the land Venezuela, or Little Venice, because natives had houses on stilts. Venezuela was under Spanish domination until 1821. The republic was formed after secession from the Colombian Federation in 1830.

Military strongmen ruled Venezuela for most of the 20th century. They promoted the oil industry; some social reforms were implemented. Since 1959, the country has enjoyed progressive, democratically-elected governments.

Venezuela helped found the Organization of Petroleum Exporting States (OPEC). The government, Jan. 1, 1976, nationalized the oil industry with compensation. Development has begun of the Orinoco tar belt, believed to contain the world's largest oil reserves. Oil accounts for much of total export earnings and the economy suffered a severe cash crisis in the 1980s as the result of falling oil revenues.

Government-imposed price increases sparked riots, Feb-Mar., 1989, that caused over 300 deaths and 1,000 injuries.

Vietnam
Socialist Republic of Vietnam
Cong Hoa Xa Hoi Chu Nghia Viet Nam

People: Population (1989 est.): 66,708,000. **Age distrib.** (%): 0-14: 40.8; 15-59: 53.6; 60+: 5.6 **Pop. density:** 519 per sq. mi. **Urban** (1986): 19%. **Ethnic groups:** Vietnamese 84%, Chinese 2%, remainder Muong, Thai, Meo, Khmer, Man, Cham. **Languages:** Vietnamese (official), French, English. **Religions:** Buddhists, Confucians, and Taoists most numerous, Roman Catholics, animists, Muslims, Protestants.

Geography: Area: 128,401 sq. mi., the size of New Mexico. **Location:** On the E coast of the Indochinese Peninsula in SE Asia. **Neighbors:** China on N, Laos, Cambodia on W. **Topography:** Vietnam is long and narrow, with a 1,400-mi. coast. About 24% of country is readily arable, including the densely settled Red R. valley in the N, narrow coastal plains in center, and the wide, often marshy Mekong R. Delta in the S. The rest consists of semi-arid plateaus and barren mountains, with some stretches of tropical rain forest. **Capital:** Hanoi. **Cities** (1981): Ho Chi Minh City 3.5 mln.; Hanoi 2 mln.

Government: Type: Communist. **Head of state:** Pres. Vo Chi Cong; in office: June 18, 1987. **Head of government:** Prime Min. Do Muoi; in office: June 22, 1988. **Head of Communist Party:** Nguyen Van Linh; in office: Dec. 18, 1986. **Local divisions:** 39 provinces. **Defense:** 7.2% of GNP (1985 est.)

Economy: Type: Communist. **Industries:** Food processing, textiles, cement, chemical fertilizers, steel. **Chief crops:** Rice, rubber, fruits and vegetables, corn, manioc, sugarcane. **Minerals:** Phosphates, coal, iron, manganese, bauxite, apatite, chromate. **Other resources:** Forests. **Arable land:** 23%. **Livestock** (1986): cattle: 5 mln.; pigs: 11.7 mln.; sheep & goats: 262,000. **Fish catch** (1984): 765,000 metric tons. **Electricity prod.** (1986): 5.4 bln. kwh. **Labor force:** 70% agric.; 8% ind. and commerce.

Finance: Currency: Dong (Jan. 1989: 368 = $1 US). **Gross national product** (1986): $12.4 bln. **Per capita income** (1987): $180. **Imports** (1986): $1.0 bln.; partners: USSR 67%, Jap. 6%. **Exports** (1986): $800 mln.; partners: Hong Kong 12%; USSR 53%, Jap. 17%.

Transport: Motor vehicles: in use (1976): 100,000 passenger cars, 200,000 comm. vehicles. **Civil Aviation** (1986): 295

mln. passenger km. **Chief ports:** Ho Chi Minh City, Haiphong, Da Nang.

Communications: Television sets (1984) 2.2 mln. **Radios:** 6 mln. in use (1984). **Daily newspaper circ.** (1984): 8 per 1,000 pop.

Health: Life expectancy at birth (1987): 58.5 male; 62.9 female. **Births** (per 1,000 pop. 1987): 33.1. **Deaths** (per 1,000 pop. 1987): 10.0. **Natural increase** (1987): 2.3%. **Hospital beds** (1986): 216,000. **Physicians** (1986): 19,100. **Infant mortality** (per 1,000 live births 1987): 68.

Education (1983): **Literacy:** 94%.

Major International Organizations: UN (IMF, WHO).

Vietnam's recorded history began in Tonkin before the Christian era. Settled by Viets from central China, Vietnam was held by China, 111 BC-939 AD, and was a vassal state during subsequent periods. Vietnam defeated the armies of Kublai Khan, 1288. Conquest by France began in 1858 and ended in 1884 with the protectorates of Tonkin and Annam in the N. and the colony of Cochin-China in the S.

In 1940 Vietnam was occupied by Japan; nationalist aims gathered force. A number of groups formed the Vietminh (Independence) League, headed by Ho Chi Minh, communist guerrilla leader. In Aug. 1945 the Vietminh forced out Bao Dai, former emperor of Annam, head of a Japan-sponsored regime. France, seeking to reestablish colonial control, battled communist and nationalist forces, 1946-1954, and was finally defeated at Dienbienphu, May 8, 1954. Meanwhile, on July 1, 1949, Bao Dai had formed a State of Vietnam, with himself as chief of state, with French approval. China backed Ho Chi Minh.

A cease-fire accord signed in Geneva July 21, 1954, divided Vietnam along the Ben Hai R. It provided for a buffer zone, withdrawal of French troops from the North and elections to determine the country's future. Under the agreement the communists gained control of territory north of the 17th parallel, 22 provinces with area of 62,000 sq. mi. and 13 million pop., with its capital at Hanoi and Ho Chi Minh as president. South Vietnam came to comprise the 39 southern provinces with approx. area of 65,000 sq. mi. and pop. of 12 million. Some 900,000 North Vietnamese fled to South Vietnam. Neither South Vietnam nor the U.S. signed the agreement.

On Oct. 26, 1955, Ngo Dinh Diem, premier of the interim government of South Vietnam, proclaimed the Republic of Vietnam and became its first president.

The Democratic Republic of Vietnam, established in the North, adopted a constitution Dec. 31, 1959, based on communist principles and calling for reunification of all Vietnam. North Vietnam sought to take over South Vietnam beginning in 1954. Fighting persisted from 1956, with the communist Vietcong, aided by North Vietnam, pressing war in the South and South Vietnam receiving U.S. aid. Northern aid to Vietcong guerrillas was intensified in 1959, and large-scale troop infiltration began in 1964, with Soviet and Chinese arms assistance. Large Northern forces were stationed in border areas of Laos and Cambodia.

A serious political conflict arose in the South in 1963 when Buddhists denounced authoritarianism and brutality. This paved the way for a military coup Nov. 1-2, 1963, which overthrew Diem. Several military coups followed.

In 1964, the U.S. began air strikes against North Vietnam. Beginning in 1965, the raids were stepped up and U.S. troops became combatants. U.S. troop strength in Vietnam, which reached a high of 543,400 in Apr. 1969, was ordered reduced by President Nixon in a series of withdrawals, beginning in June 1969. U.S. bombings were resumed in 1972-73.

A ceasefire agreement was signed in Paris Jan. 27, 1973 by the U.S., North and South Vietnam, and the Vietcong. It was never implemented. U.S. aid was curbed in 1974 by the U.S. Congress. Heavy fighting continued for two years throughout Indochina.

North Vietnamese forces launched attacks against remaining government outposts in the Central Highlands in the first months of 1975. Government retreats turned into a rout, and the Saigon regime surrendered April 30. A Provisional Revolutionary Government assumed control, aided by officials and technicians from Hanoi, and first steps were taken to transform society along communist lines. All businesses and farms were collectivized.

The U.S. accepted over 165,000 Vietnamese refugees, while scores of thousands more sought refuge in other countries.

The war's toll included — Combat deaths: U.S. 47,752; South Vietnam over 200,000; other allied forces 5,225. Civilian casualties were over a million. Displaced war refugees in South Vietnam totaled over 6.5 million.

After the fighting ended, 8 Northern divisions remained stationed in the South. Over 1 million urban residents and 260,000 Montagnards were resettled in the countryside by 1978.

The first National Assembly of both parts of the country met and the country was officially reunited July 2, 1976. The Northern capital, flag, anthem, emblem, and currency were applied to the new state. Nearly all major government posts went to officials of the former Northern government.

Heavy fighting with Cambodia took place, 1977-80, amid mutual charges of aggression and atrocities against civilians. Increasing numbers of Vietnamese civilians, ethnic Chinese, escaped the country, via the sea, or the overland route across Cambodia. Vietnam launched an offensive against Cambodian refugee strongholds along the Thai-Cambodian border in 1985; they also engaged Thai troops. Vietnam has declared that it will remove its troops from Cambodia by 1990.

Relations with China soured as 140,000 ethnic Chinese left Vietnam charging discrimination; China cut off economic aid. Reacting to Vietnam's invasion of Cambodia, China attacked 4 Vietnamese border provinces, Feb., 1979, instigating heavy fighting.

Vietnam announced a package of reforms aimed at reducing central control of the economy in 1987, as many of the old revolutionary followers of Ho Chi Minh were removed from office.

Progress has been made with the U.S. over the repatriating of "Amerasians," the children fathered by U.S. servicemen.

Western Samoa
Independent State of Western Samoa
Malotuto'atasi o Samoa i Sisifo

People: Population (1989 est.): 169,000. **Age distrib.** (%): 0–14: 50.4; 15–59: 45.4; 60+: 4.3. **Pop. density:** 149 per sq. mi. **Urban** (1981): 21.2%. **Ethnic groups:** Samoan (Polynesian) 88%, Euronesian (mixed) 10%, European, other Pacific Islanders. **Languages:** Samoan, English both official. **Religions:** Protestant 70%, Roman Catholic 20%.

Geography: Area: 1,133 sq. mi., the size of Rhode Island. **Location:** In the S. Pacific O. **Neighbors:** Nearest are Fiji on W, Tonga on S. **Topography:** Main islands, Savai'i (670 sq. mi.) and Upolu (429 sq. mi.), both ruggedly mountainous, and small islands Manono and Apolima. **Capital:** Apia. **Cities** (1983 est.): Apia 35,000.

Government: Type: Parliamentary democracy. **Head of state:** King Malietoa Tanumafili II; b. Jan. 4, 1913; in office: Jan. 1, 1962. **Head of government:** Prime Min. Tofilau Eti Alesana; in office: Apr. 11, 1988. **Local divisions:** 24 districts.

Economy: Chief crops: Cocoa, copra, bananas. **Other resources:** Hardwoods, fish. **Arable land:** 43%. **Electricity prod.** (1986): 79 mln. kwh. **Labor force:** 67% agric.

Finance: Currency: Tala (Mar. 1989: 1.00 = $.44 US). **Gross national product** (1986): $110 mln. **Imports** (1988): $76 mln.; partners: NZ 28% Austral. 10%, Jap. 13%, U.S. 30%. **Exports** (1988): $15 mln.; partners: W. Ger. 31%, NZ 26%, U.S. 12%. **International reserves less gold** (Mar. 1989): $48.6 mln.

Consumer prices (change in 1988): 8.5%.

Transport: Motor vehicles: in use (1985): 1,700 passenger cars, 2,400 comm. vehicles. **Chief ports:** Apia, Asau.

Communications: Radios: 70,000 in use (1985). **Telephones in use** (1985): 6,000.

Health: Life expectancy at birth (1986): 62.6 male; 65.6 female. **Births** (per 1,000 pop. 1985): 38. **Deaths** (per 1,000 pop. 1985): 8. **Natural increase** (1985): 3.0%. **Hospital beds** (1982): 735. **Physicians** (1981): 63. **Infant mortality** (per 1,000 live births 1986): 52.

Education (1983): **Literacy:** 90%. 95% attend elementary school.

Major International Organizations: UN (IMF, World Bank), Commonwealth of Nations.

Western Samoa was a German colony, 1899 to 1914, when New Zealand landed troops and took over. It became a New Zealand mandate under the League of Nations and, in 1945, a New Zealand UN Trusteeship.

An elected local government took office in Oct. 1959 and the country became fully independent Jan. 1, 1962.

North Yemen
Yemen Arab Republic
al-Jumhuriyat al-Arabiyah al-Yamaniyah

People: Population (1989 est.): 6,937,000. **Pop. density:** 92 per sq. mi. **Ethnic groups:** Arabs, some Negroids. **Languages:** Arabic. **Religions:** Sunni Moslem 50%, Shiite Moslem 50%.

Geography: Area: 75,290 sq. mi., slightly smaller than South Dakota. **Location:** On the southern Red Sea coast of the Arabian Peninsula. **Neighbors:** Saudi Arabia on NE, South Yemen on S. **Topography:** A sandy coastal strip leads to well-watered fertile mountains in interior. **Capital:** Sanaa. **Cities** (1986 est.): Sanaa 427,000.

Government: Type: Republic; military in power. **Head of state:** Pres. Ali Abdullah Saleh, b. 1942; in office: July 17, 1978. **Head of government:** Prime Min. Abdul Aziz Abdel Ghani; in office: Nov. 13, 1983. **Local divisions:** 10 provinces. **Defense:** 10% of GNP (1985).

Economy: Industries: Food processing. **Chief crops:** Wheat, sorghum, fruits, coffee, cotton. **Minerals:** Salt. **Crude oil reserves** (1984): 600 mln. bbls. **Arable land:** 7%. **Livestock** (1986): goats: 2.2 mln.; sheep: 1.8 mln. **Fish catch** (1986): 22,000 metric tons. **Electricity prod.** (1986): 556 mln. kwh. **Labor force:** 64% agric.; 22% ind. and commerce; 14% serv.

Finance: Currency: Rial (Apr. 1989: 9.76 = $1 US). **Gross national product** (1986): $4.5 bln. **Imports** (1987): $7.1 bln.; partners: Saudi Ar. 20%, Fr. 8%, Jap. 16%. **Exports** (1987): $3.8 mln.; partners: S. Yemen 23%, Saudi Ar. 8%, Pak. 19%. **National budget** (1985): 946 mln. **International reserves less gold** (Mar. 1989): $562 mln.

Transport: Motor vehicles in use (1986): 121,000 passenger cars, 176,000 commercial vehicles. **Chief ports:** Al-Hudaydah, Al-Mukha.

Communications: Television sets: (1987): 150,000. **Radios:** 200,000 in use (1986). **Telephones in use** (1984): 63,000.

Health: Life expectancy at birth (1986): 45.6 male; 48.9 female. **Births** (per 1,000 pop. 1986): 49.1. **Deaths** (per 1,000 pop. 1986): 20.8. **Natural increase** (1986): 2.8%. **Hospital beds** (1986): 5,900. **Infant mortality** (per 1,000 live births 1986): 164.

Education (1987): **Literacy:** 20%. **Primary school attendance:** 59%.

Major International Organizations: UN (IMF, WHO), Arab League.

Embassy: 600 New Hampshire Ave. NW 20037; 965-4760.

Yemen's territory once was part of the ancient kindgom of Sheba, or Saba, a prosperous link in trade between Africa and India. A Biblical reference speaks of its gold, spices and precious stones as gifts borne by the Queen of Sheba to King Solomon.

Yemen became independent in 1918, after years of Ottoman Turkish rule, but remained politically and economically backward. Imam Ahmed ruled 1948-1962. The king was reported assassinated Sept. 26, 1962, and a revolutionary group headed by Brig. Gen. Abdullah al-Salal declared the country to be the Yemen Arab Republic.

The Imam Ahmed's heir, the Imam Mohamad al-Badr, fled to the mountains where tribesmen joined royalist forces; internal warfare between them and the republican forces continued. Egypt sent troops and Saudi Arabia military aid to the royalists. About 150,000 people died in the fighting.

There was a bloodless coup Nov. 5, 1967.

In April 1970 hostilities ended with an agreement between Yemen and Saudi Arabia and appointment of several royalists to the Yemen government. There were border skirmishes with forces of South Yemen in 1972-73.

On June 13, 1974, an army group, led by Col. Ibrahim al-Hamidi, seized the government. Hamidi pursued close Saudi and U.S. ties; he was assassinated in 1977.

The People's Democratic Republic of Yemen went to war with Yemen on Feb. 24, 1979. Swift Arab mediation led to a ceasefire and a mutual withdrawal of forces, Mar. 19. An Arab League-sponsored agreement between North and South Yemen on unification of the 2 countries was signed Mar. 29th. An agreement providing for widespread political and economic cooperation was signed in 1988.

The remittances from 400,000 Yemenis living in Arab oil countries provide most of foreign earnings.

South Yemen

People's Democratic Republic of Yemen

Jumhuriyat al-Yaman ad-Dimuqratiyah ash-Sha'biyan

People: Population (1989 est.): 2,488,000. **Age distrib. (%):** 0–14: 47.8; 15–59: 45.7; 60+: 6.5. **Pop. density:** 19 per sq. mi. **Urban** (1986): 40%. **Ethnic groups:** Arabs, 75%, Indians 11%, Somalis 8%, others. **Languages:** Arabic. **Religions:** Sunni Moslem 91%, Christian 4%, Hindu 3.5%.

Geography: Area: 128,559 sq. mi., the size of Nevada. **Location:** On the southern coast of the Arabian Peninsula. **Neighbors:** Yemen on W, Saudi Arabia on N, Oman on E. **Topography:** The entire country is very hot and very dry. A sandy coast rises to mountains which give way to desert sands. **Capital:** Aden. **Cities** (1985 est.): Aden 318,000.

Government: Type: Republic. **Head of state:** Chairman, Council of Ministers and President: Haidar Abu Bakr al-Attas; in office: Nov. 6, 1986. **Head of Government:** Prime Min. Yasin Said Numan; in office: Feb. 8, 1986. **Local divisions:** 6 governorates. **Defense:** 17.4% of GNP (1985).

Economy: Industries: Transshipment. **Chief crops:** Cotton (main export), grains. **Arable land:** 1%. **Livestock** (1986): sheep: 1 mln.; goats: 1.3 mln. **Fish catch** (1986): 91,000 metric tons. **Electricity prod.** (1986) 556 mln. kwh. **Labor force:** 43.8% agric.; 28% ind. and commerce; 28% serv.

Finance: Currency: Dinar (Mar. 1989: 1.00 = $2.89 US). **Gross national product** (1986): $1.1 bln. **Per capita income** (1977): $310. **Imports** (1985) $762 mln.; partners: USSR 14%, Aust. 9%. **Exports** (1985): $316 mln.; partners: Jap. 36%; N. Yem. 23%. **International reserves less gold** (Jan. 1989): $79.8 mln. **Gold:** 42,000 oz t.

Transport: Motor vehicles: in use (1984): 24,000 passenger cars, 27,000 comm. vehicles. **Chief ports:** Aden.

Communications: Television sets: 47,000 in use (1987). **Radios:** 300,000 in use (1986). **Daily newspaper circ.** (1986): 10 per 1,000 pop.

Health: Life expectancy at birth (1986): 47.1 male; 50.9 female. **Births** (per 1,000 pop. 1986): 49.7. **Deaths** (per 1,000 pop. 1986): 17.8. **Natural increase** (1986): 3.1%. **Hospital beds** (1986): 4,499. **Physicians** (1986): 652. **Infant mortality rate** (per 1,000 live births in 1985): 131.

Major International Organizations: UN (IMF, WHO), Arab League.

Education (1980): **Literacy:** 39%. About 90% attend primary school.

Aden, mentioned in the Bible, has been a port for trade in incense, spice and silk between the East and West for 2,000 years. British rule began in 1839. Aden provided Britain with a controlling position at the southern entrance to the Red Sea.

A war for independence began in 1963. The National Liberation Front (NLF) and the Egypt-supported Front for the Liberation of Occupied South Yemen, waged a guerrilla war against the British and local dynastic rulers. The 2 groups vied with each other for control. The NLF won out. Independence came Nov. 30, 1967. In 1969, the left wing of the NLF seized power and inaugurated a thorough nationalization of the economy and regimentation of daily life.

The new government broke off relations with the U.S. and nationalized some foreign firms.

In 1972-73 there were border skirmishes with forces of the Yemen Arab Republic. South Yemen aided leftist guerrillas in neighboring Oman. Relations with Saudi Arabia later improved. S. Yemen troops fought in Ethiopia against Eritrean rebels in 1978.

Pres. Salem Robaye Ali, who had tried to improve relations with Yemen, Saudi Arabia, Oman, and the U.S., was executed after a bloody coup June 1978. N. Yemen, Egypt, and Saudi Arabia froze ties with S. Yemen in July.

South Yemen went to war with North Yemen on Feb. 24, 1979. Swift Arab mediation led to a cease-fire and a mutual withdrawal of forces, Mar. 19th. An Arab League-sponsored agreement between North and South Yemen on unification of the 2 countries was signed Mar. 29th. An agreement providing for widespread political and economic cooperation was signed in 1988.

The government was overthrown in a bloody coup on Jan. 13, 1986, which escalated into civil war. Some 10,000 were killed and 12,000 fled the country before order was restored.

The Port of Aden is the country's most valuable resource.

Socotra, the largest island in the Arabian Sea, Kamaran, an island in the Red Sea near the coast of North Yemen, and Perim, an island in the strait between the Gulf of Aden and the Red Sea, are controlled by South Yemen.

Yugoslavia

Socialist Federal Republic of Yugoslavia

Socijalistička Federativna Republika Jugoslavija

People: Population (1989 est.): 23,753,000. **Age distrib. (%):** 0–14: 23.5; 15-59: 63.7; 60+: 12.8. **Pop. density:** 240 per sq. mi. **Urban** (1985): 46.5%. **Ethnic groups:** Serbs 36%, Croats 20%, Bosnian Moslems 9%, Slovenes 8%, Macedonians 6%, Albanians 8%. **Languages:** Serbo-Croatian, Macedonian, Slovenian (all official), Albanian. **Religions:** Eastern Orthodox 41%, Roman Catholic 12%, Moslem 3%.

Geography: Area: 98,766 sq. mi., the size of Wyoming. **Location:** On the Adriatic coast of the Balkan Peninsula in SE Europe. **Neighbors:** Italy on W, Austria, Hungary on N, Romania, Bulgaria on E, Greece, Albania on S. **Topography:** The Dinaric Alps run parallel to the Adriatic coast, which is lined by offshore islands. Plains stretch across N and E river basins. S and NW are mountainous. **Capital:** Belgrade. **Cities** (1980 est.): Belgrade 1,300,000; Zagreb 700,000; Skopje 440,000; Sarajevo 400,000; Ljubljana 300,000.

Government: Type: Communist state; Federal republic in form. **Head of state:** Pres. Janez Drnovsek; in office: May 15, 1989. **Head of government:** Prime Min. Ante Markovic; in office: Jan. 19 1989. **Head of Communist Party:** Milan Pancevski; b. May 16, 1935; in office: May 17, 1989. **Local divisions:** 6 republics, 2 autonomous provinces. **Defense:** 4.8% of GNP (1987).

Economy: Industries: Steel, wood products, cement, textiles, tourism. **Chief crops:** Corn, grains, tobacco, sugar beets. **Minerals:** Antimony, bauxite, lead, mercury, coal, iron, copper, chrome, zinc, salt. **Crude oil reserves** (1987): 263 mln. bbls. **Arable land:** 33%. **Livestock** (1986): cattle: 5 mln.; pigs: 7.8 mln.; sheep: 7.6 mln. **Fish catch:** (1986): 77,000 metric tons. **Electricity prod.** (1986): 77.3 bln. kwh. **Crude steel prod.** (1987): 4.6 mln. metric tons. **Labor force:** 30% agric.; 70% ind.

Finance: Currency: Dinar (Mar. 1989: 1,276 = $1 US). **Gross national product** (1986): $144.8 bln. **Per capita income:** $3,109. **Imports** (1987): $12.6 bln.; partners: W. Ger. 19%, USSR 15%, It. 8%, U.S. 6%. **Exports** (1987): $11.4 bln.; partners: USSR 17%, W. Ger. 12%, It. 13%. **Tourists** (1986): $1 bln. receipts. **National budget** (1987): $4.3 bln. expenditures. **International reserves less gold** (Mar. 1989): $1.8 bln. **Gold:** 1.90 mln. oz t. **Consumer prices** (change in 1987): 120.8%.

Transport: Railway traffic (1987): 12.3 bln. passenger-km; 27.5 bln. net ton-km. **Motor vehicles:** in use (1987): 2.9 mln. passenger cars, 283,000 comm. vehicles. **Civil aviation** (1986): 7.0 bln. passenger-km; 110 mln. freight ton-km. **Chief ports:** Rijeka, Split, Koper, Bar, Ploce.

Communications: Television sets: 4.0 mln. in use (1986). **Radios:** 4.7 mln. licensed (1986). **Telephones in use** (1986): 3.3 mln. **Daily newspaper circ.** (1986): 107 per 1,000 pop.

Health: Life expectancy at birth (1983): 68 male; 73 female. **Births** (per 1,000 pop. 1986): 15.4. **Deaths** (per 1,000 pop. 1986): 9.1. **Natural increase** (1986): .6%. **Hospital beds** (1986): 141,000. **Physicians** (1986): 40,000. **Infant mortality** (per 1,000 live births 1986): 27.1.

Education (1989): **Literacy:** 90%. Almost all attend primary school.

Major International Organizations: UN (IMF, World Bank, GATT).

Embassy: 2410 California St. NW 20008; 462-6566.

Serbia, which had since 1389 been a vassal principality of Turkey, was established as an independent kingdom by the Treaty of Berlin, 1878. Montenegro, independent since 1389, also obtained international recognition in 1878. After the Balkan wars Serbia's boundaries were enlarged by the annexation of Old Serbia and Macedonia, 1913.

When the Austro-Hungarian empire collapsed after World War I, the Kingdom of the Serbs, Croats, and Slovenes was formed from the former provinces of Croatia, Dalmatia, Bosnia, Herzegovina, Slovenia, Voyvodina and the independent state of Montenegro. The name was later changed to Yugoslavia.

Nazi Germany invaded in 1941. Many Yugoslav partisan troops continued to operate. Among these were the Chetniks led by Draja Mikhailovich, who fought other partisans led by Josip Broz, known as Marshal Tito. Tito, backed by the USSR and Britain from 1943, was in control by the time the Germans had been driven from Yugoslavia in 1945. Mikhailovich was executed July 17, 1946, by the Tito regime.

A constituent assembly proclaimed Yugoslavia a republic Nov. 29, 1945. It became a federated republic Jan. 31, 1946, and Marshal Tito, a communist, became head of the government.

The Stalin policy of dictating to all communist nations was rejected by Tito. He accepted economic aid and military equipment from the U.S. and received aid in foreign trade also from France and Great Britain. Tito also supported the liberal government of Czechoslovakia in 1968 before the Soviet invasion.

A separatist movement among Croatians, 2d to the Serbs in numbers, brought arrests and a change of leaders in the Croatian Republic in Jan. 1972. Violence by extreme Croatian nationalists and fears of Soviet political intervention led to restrictions on political and intellectual dissent. Serbians, Montenegrins, and Macedonians use Cyrillic, Croatians and Slovenians use Latin letters. Croatia and Slovenia have been the most prosperous republics.

Most industry is socialized and private enterprise is restricted to small-scale production. Management of industrial enterprises is handled by workers' councils. Farmland is mostly privately owned but farms are restricted to 25 acres.

Beginning in 1965, reforms designed to decentralize the administration of economic development and to force industries to produce more efficiently in competition with foreign producers were introduced. Yugoslavia has developed considerable trade with the West.

Pres. Tito died May 4, 1980; with his death, the post as head of the Collective Presidency and also that as head of the League of Communists became a rotating system of succession among the members representing each republic and autonomous province.

Zaire

Republic of Zaire

République du Zaïre

People: Population (1989 est.): 33,991,000. **Pop. density:** 37 per sq. mi. **Urban** (1988): 44.2%. **Ethnic groups:** Bantu tribes 80%, over 200 other tribes. **Languages:** French (official), Bantu dialects. **Religions:** Christian 70%, Moslem 10%.

Geography: Area: 905,563 sq. mi., one-fourth the size of the U.S. **Location:** In central Africa. **Neighbors:** Congo on W, Central African Republic, Sudan on N, Uganda, Rwanda, Burundi, Tanzania on E, Zambia, Angola on S. **Topography:** Zaire includes the bulk of the Zaire (Congo) R. Basin. The vast central region is a low-lying plateau covered by rain forest. Mountainous terraces in the W, savannas in the S and SE, grasslands toward the N, and the high Ruwenzori Mtns. on the E surround the central region. A short strip of territory borders the Atlantic O. The Zaire R. is 2,718 mi. long. **Capital:** Kinshasa. **Cities** (1985 est.): Kinshasa 3,000,000; Kananga 601,239.

Government: Type: Republic with strong presidential authority. **Head of state:** Pres. Mobutu Sese Seko; b. Oct. 14, 1930; in office: Nov. 25, 1965. **Head of Government:** Prime Min. Kengo Wa Dondo; in office: Nov. 26, 1988. **Local divisions:** 9 regions, Kinshasa. **Defense:** 1.7% of GNP (1985).

Economy: Chief crops: Coffee, rice, sugar cane, bananas, plantains, manioc, mangoes, tea, cocoa, palm oil. **Minerals:** Cobalt (60% of world reserves), copper, cadmium, gold, silver, tin, germanium, zinc, iron, manganese, uranium, radium. **Crude oil reserves** (1987): 111 mln. bbls. **Other resources:** Forests, rubber, ivory. **Arable land:** 3%. **Livestock** (1986): cattle: 1.3 mln.; goats: 2.9 mln. **Fish catch** (1986): 102,000 metric tons. **Electricity prod.** (1986): 5.2 bln. kwh. **Labor force:** 75% agric..

Finance: Currency: Zaire (Mar. 1989: 341 = $1 US). **Gross national product** (1988): $5.0 bln. **Imports** (1987): $756 mln.; partners: Chi. 38%, Belg. 16%, W. Ger. 7%, Fra. 7%. **Exports** (1986): $1.0 bln.; partners: Belg.-Lux. 36%, U.S. 19%. **Interna-**

tional reserves less gold (Mar. 1989): $137 mln. **Gold:** 277,000 oz t. **Consumer prices** (change in 1987): 90.4%.

Transport: Railway traffic (1986): 291 mln. passenger-km; 1.9 bln. net ton-km. **Motor vehicles:** in use (1985): 24,000 passenger cars, 60,000 comm. vehicles. **Civil aviation** (1987): 486 mln. passenger-km. 52.5 mln. freight ton-km. **Chief ports:** Matadi, Boma.

Communications: Television sets: 16,000 in use (1987). **Radios:** 500,000 mln. in use (1986). **Telephones in use** (1987): 38,000. **Daily newspaper circ.** (1986): 1 per 1,000 pop.

Health: Life expectancy at birth (1985): 48.3 male; 51.7 female. **Births** (per 1,000 pop. 1985): 45.2. **Deaths** (per 1,000 pop. 1985): 15.8. **Natural increase** (1985): 2.9%. **Hospital beds** (1982): 74,000. **Physicians** (1982): 2,000. **Infant mortality** (per 1,000 live births 1988): 130.

Education (1988): **Literacy:** 55%.

Major International Organizations: UN and all of its specialized agencies, OAU.

Embassy: 1800 New Hampshire Ave. NW 20008; 234-7690.

The earliest inhabitants of Zaire may have been the pygmies, followed by Bantus from the E and Nilotic tribes from the N. The large Bantu Bakongo kingdom ruled much of Zaire and Angola when Portuguese explorers visited in the 15th century.

Leopold II, king of the Belgians, formed an international group to exploit the Congo in 1876. In 1877 Henry M. Stanley explored the Congo and in 1878 the king's group sent him back to organize the region and win over the native chiefs. The Conference of Berlin, 1884-85, organized the Congo Free State with Leopold as king and chief owner. Exploitation of native laborers on the rubber plantations caused international criticism and led to granting of a colonial charter, 1908.

Belgian and Congolese leaders agreed Jan. 27, 1960, that the Congo would become independent June 30. In the first general elections, May 31, the National Congolese movement of Patrice Lumumba won 35 of 137 seats in the National Assembly. He was appointed premier June 21, and formed a coalition cabinet.

Widespread violence caused Europeans and others to flee. The UN Security Council Aug. 9, 1960, called on Belgium to withdraw its troops and sent a UN contingent. President Kasavubu removed Lumumba as premier. Lumumba fought for control backed by Ghana, Guinea and India; he was murdered in 1961.

The last UN troops left the Congo June 30, 1964, and Moïse Tshombe became president.

On Sept. 7, 1964, leftist rebels set up a "People's Republic" in Stanleyville. Tshombe hired foreign mercenaries and sought to rebuild the Congolese Army. In Nov. and Dec. 1964 rebels slew scores of white hostages and thousands of Congolese; Belgian paratroops, dropped from U.S. transport planes, rescued hundreds. By July 1965 the rebels had lost their effectiveness.

In 1965 Gen. Joseph D. Mobutu was named president. He later changed his name to Mobutu Sese Seko. The country changed its name to Republic of Zaire on Oct. 27, 1971; in 1972 Zairians with Christian names were ordered to change them to African names.

In 1969-74, political stability under Mobutu was reflected in improved economic conditions. In 1974 most foreign-owned businesses were ordered sold to Zaire citizens, but in 1977 the government asked the original owners to return.

In 1977, a force of Zairians invaded Shaba province (Katanga) from Angola. Zaire repelled the attack, with the aid of Egyptian pilots and Moroccan troops flown in by France. But many European mining experts failed to return after a 2d unsuccessful invasion from Angola in May 1978.

Serious economic difficulties, amid charges of corruption by government officials, have plagued Zaire in the 1980s.

Zambia

Republic of Zambia

People: Population (1989 est.): 7,770,000. **Age distrib. (%):** 0-14: 48.2; 15-59: 47.8; 60+: 4.0. **Pop. density:** 26 per sq. mi. **Urban** (1985): 49%. **Ethnic groups:** Mostly Bantu tribes. **Languages:** English (official), Bantu dialects. **Religions:** Predominantly animist, Roman Catholic 21%, Protestant, Hindu, Moslem minorities.

Geography: Area: 290,586 sq. mi., larger than Texas. **Location:** In southern central Africa. **Neighbors:** Zaire on N, Tanzania, Malawi, Mozambique on E, Zimbabwe, Namibia on S, Angola on W. **Topography:** Zambia is mostly high plateau country covered with thick forests, and drained by several important rivers, including the Zambezi. **Capital:** Lusaka. **Cities** (1987 est.): Lusaka 818,000; Kitwe 449,000; Ndola 418,000.

Government: Type: Republic. **Head of state:** Pres. Kenneth David Kaunda; b. Apr. 28, 1924; in office: Oct. 24, 1964. **Head of government:** Prime Min. Kebby Musokotwane; in office: Apr. 24, 1985. **Local divisions:** 9 provinces. **Defense:** 6.8% of GDP (1985).

Economy: Chief crops: Corn, tobacco, peanuts, cotton, sugar. **Minerals:** Cobalt, copper, zinc, gold, lead, vanadium, manganese, coal. **Other resources:** Rubber, ivory. **Arable land:** 7%. **Livestock** (1985): cattle: 2.6 mln. **Fish catch** (1985): 64,000 metric tons. **Electricity prod.** (1986): 11.1 bln. kwh. **Labor force:** 60% agric.; 40% ind. and commerce.

Finance: Currency: Kwacha (Mar. 1989: 1.00 = $.09 US). **Gross national product** (1986): $2.1 bln. **Per capita income** (1986): $304. **Imports** (1986): $714 mln.; partners: UK 26%, Saudi Ar. 18%, W. Ger. 18%, U.S. 9%. **Exports** (1986): $431 mln.; partners: Jap. 19%, Fr. 15%, UK 13%, U.S. 10%, W. Ger. 9%. **National budget** (1984): $733 mln. expenditures. **International reserves less gold** (Jan. 1989): $138.8 mln. **Gold:** 12,000 oz t. **Consumer prices** (change in 1987): 43.0%.

Transport: Motor vehicles: in use (1982): 105,000 passenger cars, 97,000 comm. vehicles. **Civil aviation** (1986): 630 mln. passenger-km.

Communications: Television sets: 200,000 in use (1987). **Radios:** 528,000 in use (1986). **Telephones in use** (1986): 85,000. **Daily newspaper circ.** (1987): 15 per 1,000 pop.

Health: Life expectancy at birth (1984): 47 yrs. **Births** (per 1,000 pop. 1985): 47.4. **Deaths** (per 1,000 pop. 1985): 15.4. **Natural increase** (1985): 3.2%. **Hospital beds** (1985): 21,668. **Physicians** (1985): 800. **Infant mortality** (per 1,000 live births 1988): 87.

Education (1988): **Literacy:** 54%. **Attendance:** less than 50% in grades 1–7.

Major International Organizations: UN (GATT, IMF, WHO), OAU, Commonwealth of Nations.

Embassy: 2419 Massachusetts Ave. NW 20008; 265-9717.

As Northern Rhodesia, the country was under the administration of the South Africa Company, 1889 until 1924, when the office of governor was established, and, subsequently, a legislature. The country became an independent republic within the Commonwealth Oct. 24, 1964.

After the white government of Rhodesia declared its independence from Britain Nov. 11, 1965, relations between Zambia and Rhodesia became strained and use of their jointly owned railroad was disputed.

Britain gave Zambia an extra $12 million aid in 1966 after imposing an oil embargo on Rhodesia, and Zambia set up a temporary airlift to carry copper out from its mines and gasoline in. In Aug. 1968 a 1,058-mi. pipeline was completed, bringing oil from Tanzania. In 1973 a truck road to carry copper to Tanzania's port of Dar es Salaam was completed with U.S. aid. A railroad, built with Chinese aid across Tanzania, reached the Zambian border in 1974.

As part of a program of government participation in major industries, a government corporation in 1970 took over 51% of the ownership of 2 foreign-owned copper mining companies. Privately-held land and other enterprises were nationalized in 1975, as were all newspapers. In the 1980s, decline in copper prices has hurt the economy and severe drought has caused famine.

Zimbabwe

People: Population (1989 est.): 9,987,000. **Age distrib.** (%): 0–14: 44.9; 15–59: 51.1; 60+: 4.0. **Pop. density:** 66 per sq. mi. **Urban** (1985): 25%. **Ethnic groups:** Shona 80%, Ndebele 19%. **Languages:** English (official), Shona, Sindebele. **Religions:** Predominantly traditional tribal beliefs, Christian minority.

Geography: Area: 150,803 sq. mi., slightly larger than Montana. **Location:** In southern Africa. **Neighbors:** Zambia on N, Botswana on W, S. Africa on S, Mozambique on E. **Topography:** Rhodesia is high plateau country, rising to mountains on eastern border, sloping down on the other borders. **Capital:** Harare. **Cities** (1988 est.): Harare 730,000; Bulawayo (met.) 415,000.

Government: Type: One-party socialist state. **Head of state:** Pres. Robert Mugabe; b. Apr. 14, 1928; in office: Jan. 1, 1988. **Local divisions:** 8 provinces. **Defense:** 6.2% of GNP (1985).

Economy: Industries: Clothing, chemicals, light industries. **Chief crops:** Tobacco, sugar, cotton, corn, wheat. **Minerals:** Chromium, gold, nickel, asbestos, copper, iron, coal. **Arable land:** 7%. **Livestock** (1985): cattle: 5.3 mln.; goats: 1.8 mln. **Electricity prod.** (1986): 4.5 bln. kwh. **Labor force:** 35% agric.; 30% ind. and commerce; 20% serv.; 15% gvt.

Finance: Currency: Dollar (Mar. 1989: 1.00 = $.49 US). **Gross national product** (1986): $4.7 bln. **Per capita income** (1986): $275. **Imports** (1987): $1.2 bln. partners: UK 10%, So. Afr. 27%, U.S. 7%, W. Ger. 7%. **Exports** (1987): $1.4 bln.; partners: UK 7%, So. Afr. 22%, W. Ger. 8%. **Total reserves less gold** (Mar. 1989): $128.2 mln. **Consumer prices** (change in 1987): 12.5%.

Transport: Railway traffic (1986): 13.7 bln. net ton-km. **Motor vehicles:** in use (1985): 253,000 passenger cars, 28,000 comm. vehicles. **Civil aviation** (1986): 648 mln. passenger-km.

Communications: Television sets: 112,000 in use (1986). **Radios:** 315,000 in use (1986). **Telephones in use** (1985): 245,000. **Daily newspaper circ.** (1985): 23 per 1,000 pop.

Health: Life expectancy at birth (1987): 57.9 male; 61.4 female. **Births** (per 1,000 pop. 1985): 53.0. **Deaths** (per 1,000 pop. 1985): 13. **Natural increase** (1985): 4.0%. **Physicians** (1986): 1,257. **Infant mortality** (per 1,000 live births 1985): 77.

Education (1988): **Literacy:** 50%. **Attendance:** 90% primary, 15% secondary for Africans; higher for whites, Asians.

Major International Organizations: UN (IMF, World Bank), OAU, Commonwealth of Nations.

Embassy: 2852 McGill Terrace NW 20008; 332-7100.

Britain took over the area as Southern Rhodesia in 1923 from the British South Africa Co. (which, under Cecil Rhodes, had conquered the area by 1897) and granted internal self-government. Under a 1961 constitution, voting was restricted to maintain whites in power. On Nov. 11, 1965, Prime Min. Ian D. Smith announced his country's unilateral declaration of independence. Britain termed the act illegal, and demanded Rhodesia broaden voting rights to provide for eventual rule by the majority Africans.

Urged by Britain, the UN imposed sanctions, including embargoes on oil shipments to Rhodesia. Some oil and gasoline reached Rhodesia, however, from South Africa and Mozambique, before the latter became independent in 1975. In May 1968, the UN Security Council ordered a trade embargo.

A new constitution came into effect, Mar. 2, 1970, providing for a republic with a president and prime minister. The election law effectively prevented full black representation through income tax requirements.

A proposed British-Rhodesian settlement was dropped in May 1972 when a British commission reported most Rhodesian blacks opposed it. Intermittent negotiations between the government and various black nationalist groups failed to prevent increasing skirmishes. By mid-1978, over 6,000 soldiers and civilians had been killed. Rhodesian troops battled guerrillas within Mozambique and Zambia. An "internal settlement" signed Mar. 1978 in which Smith and 3 popular black leaders share control until transfer of power to the black majority was rejected by guerrilla leaders.

In the country's first universal-franchise election, Apr. 21, 1979, Bishop Abel Muzorewa's United African National Council gained a bare majority control of the black-dominated parliament. Britain, in 1979, began efforts to normalize its relationship with Zimbabwe. A British cease-fire was accepted by all parties, Dec. 5th. Independence was finally achieved Apr. 18, 1980.

World Population and Growth, by Continent and Region: 1960 to 1990

Source: U.S. Bureau of the Census

Continent and Region	Midyear Population (millions)								Annual Rate of Growth (percent)			
	1960	1965	1970	1975	1980	1985	1988	1990	1965-1970	1970-1975	1975-1980	1980-1990
World total. . . .	3,049	3,358	3,721	4,103	4,473	4,882	5,143	5,320	2.1	2.0	1.7	1.7
More developed regions.	945	1,002	1,049	1,096	1,136	1,176	1,198	1,211	.9	.9	.7	.6
Less developed regions.	2,104	2,356	2,672	3,007	3,336	3,706	3,945	4,109	2.5	2.4	2.1	2.1
Percent of world .	69	70	72	73	75	76	77	77	(x)	(x)	(x)	(x)
Africa[1]	293	330	375	427	491	569	622	660	2.5	2.6	2.8	2.9
Asia	1,685	1,871	2,112	2,364	2,593	2,844	3,004	3,111	2.4	2.3	1.8	1.8
East Asia	796	874	992	1,104	1,182	1,255	1,304	1,334	2.5	2.2	1.4	1.2
South Asia	889	998	1,120	1,260	1,411	1,588	1,700	1,777	2.3	2.3	2.3	2.3
Latin America[1] . . .	218	250	286	324	364	409	436	455	2.7	2.5	2.3	2.2
Middle America[1] . .	51	60	70	81	93	104	112	116	3.1	3.0	2.7	2.2
Caribbean[1]	20	23	24	27	29	32	33	34	1.9	1.8	1.4	1.4
South America[1]. . .	146	168	191	216	242	272	291	304	2.6	2.4	2.3	2.3
North America[2] . . .	199	214	226	239	252	265	272	277	1.1	1.1	1.1	0.9
Europe[2]	425	44	460	474	484	492	497	499	.7	.6	.4	.3
Soviet Union[2]	214	231	243	254	266	279	286	291	1.0	.9	.9	.9
Oceania	16	17	19	21	23	24	26	26	2.1	1.9	1.3	1.5
Australia and New Zealand[2]	13	14	15	17	18	19	20	20	1.9	1.7	1.0	1.2

(x) Not applicable. (1) Less developed region. (2) More developed region.

Population Projections, by Region and for Selected Countries: 1990 to 2025

Source: Population Division of the United Nations

(in millions)

Region and Country	1990	1995	2000	2025	Region and Country	1990	1995	2000	2025
World, total	5,248.5	5,679.3	6,127.1	8,177.1	Mexico.	89.0	99.2	109.2	154.1
More developed[1]. . .	1,208.8	1,242.8	1,275.7	1,396.7	Nicaragua.	3.9	4.5	5.3	9.2
Less developed[1] . . .	4,039.7	4,436.4	4,851.5	6,780.4	Temperate South				
Africa.	645.3	753.2	877.4	1,642.9	America[2]	49.1	52.3	55.5	70.1
Eastern Africa[2] . . .	189.7	224.7	266.2	531.4	Argentina	32.9	35.1	37.2	47.4
Burundi	5.3	6.1	7.0	11.0	Chile	13.1	14.0	14.9	18.8
Ethiopia	42.7	50.1	58.4	112.0	Uruguay	3.1	3.2	3.4	3.9
Kenya	25.4	31.4	38.5	82.9	Tropical South				
Madagascar . . .	11.6	13.4	15.6	29.7	America[2]	249.8	276.9	304.1	436.3
Malawi.	8.3	9.8	11.7	23.2	Bolivia	7.3	8.4	9.7	18.3
Mozambique . . .	16.2	18.8	21.8	39.7	Brazil	150.4	165.1	179.5	245.8
Rwanda	7.3	8.8	10.6	22.2	Colombia	31.8	34.9	38.0	51.7
Somalia	5.9	6.2	7.1	13.2	Ecuador	10.9	12.7	14.6	25.7
Uganda	18.8	22.5	26.8	52.3	Paraguay	4.2	4.8	5.4	8.6
Tanzania	27.0	32.5	39.1	83.8	Peru	22.3	25.1	28.0	41.0
Zambia	7.9	9.4	11.2	23.8	Venezuela	21.3	24.2	27.2	42.8
Zimbabwe.	10.5	12.6	15.1	32.7	Northern America[2]. .	275.2	286.8	297.7	347.3
Middle Africa[2] . . .	71.9	83.0	96.1	183.5	Canada	27.1	28.3	29.4	34.4
Angola.	10.0	11.5	13.2	24.5	United States . . .	248.0	258.3	268.1	312.7
Cameroon.	11.1	12.6	14.4	25.2	East Asia[2]	1,317.2	1,390.4	1,470.0	1,696.1
Cen. African Rep.	2.9	3.3	3.7	6.7	China: Mainland. .	1,119.6	1,184.2	1,255.7	1,460.1
Chad.	5.7	6.4	7.3	13.1	Hong Kong.	6.1	6.6	6.9	7.9
Zaire	38.4	44.8	52.4	104.4	Japan.	122.7	125.1	127.7	127.6
Northern Africa[2]. . .	143.8	164.3	185.7	295.0	Korea, Dem. People's Rep. of .	22.4	24.9	27.3	37.6
Algeria.	26.0	30.5	35.2	57.3	Korea, Rep. of . . .	43.8	46.8	49.5	58.6
Egypt.	52.7	58.9	65.2	97.4	South Asia	1,740.2	1,909.4	2,073.7	2,770.6
Libya.	4.3	5.2	6.1	11.1	Eastern So. Asia[2] . .	440.4	480.8	519.7	684.7
Morocco.	27.6	31.9	36.3	59.9	Indonesia	178.4	191.9	204.5	255.3
Sudan	24.9	28.7	32.9	55.4	Kampuchea	8.4	9.2	9.9	12.5
Tunisia.	8.1	8.9	9.7	13.6	Laos	5.0	5.6	6.2	9.2
Southern Africa[2]. . .	42.3	48.1	54.5	90.7	Malaysia.	17.3	19.1	20.6	26.9
South Africa. . . .	36.8	41.6	46.9	76.3	Myanmar[5]	44.5	49.8	55.2	82.2
Western Africa[2] . . .	197.6	233.1	275.0	542.4	Philippines	61.4	68.3	74.8	102.3
Benin	4.7	5.4	6.4	12.2	Singapore	2.7	2.9	3.0	3.2
Burkina Faso[3]. . .	8.0	9.1	10.5	19.5	Thailand.	56.2	61.1	66.1	86.3
Côte d'Ivoire[4]. . .	11.5	13.4	15.6	28.1	Vietnam	65.4	71.7	78.1	105.1
Ghana	15.9	18.7	21.9	37.7	Middle So. Asia[2]. . .	1,169.9	1,279.9	1,385.7	1,815.9
Guinea	6.1	7.0	7.9	13.9	Afghanistan	19.3	21.7	24.2	35.9
Mali	9.3	10.7	12.4	21.4	Bangladesh	115.2	130.3	145.8	219.4
Niger.	7.1	8.3	9.8	18.9	India	831.9	899.1	961.5	1,188.5
Nigeria.	113.3	135.5	161.9	338.1	Iran.	51.8	58.7	65.5	96.2
Senegal	7.5	8.7	10.0	18.9	Nepal	18.5	20.7	23.0	33.9
Togo	3.4	3.9	4.6	9.0	Pakistan.	113.3	128.0	142.6	212.8
Latin America	453.2	501.3	550.0	786.6	Sri Lanka	18.0	19.5	20.8	26.2
Caribbean[2].	34.6	37.7	40.8	57.7	Western So. Asia[2]. .	129.9	148.7	168.3	270.0
Cuba.	10.5	11.2	11.7	13.6	Iraq.	18.5	21.6	24.9	42.7
Dominican Rep.. .	7.0	7.7	8.4	12.2	Israel.	4.7	5.0	5.4	7.0
Haiti	7.5	8.6	9.9	18.3	Jordan.	4.3	5.2	6.4	13.4
Middle America[2]. . .	119.7	134.4	149.6	222.6	Lebanon.	3.0	3.3	3.6	5.2
El Salvador	6.5	7.5	8.7	15.0	Saudi Arabia . . .	13.5	16.1	18.9	33.5
Guatemala	9.7	11.1	12.7	21.7					
Honduras	5.1	6.0	7.0	13.3					

(continued)

Region and Country	1990	1995	2000	2025	Region and Country	1990	1995	2000	2025
Syria	12.8	15.3	18.1	32.3	Southern Europe²	146.4	150.0	153.1	162.8
Turkey	56.0	62.4	68.5	99.3	Albania	3.4	3.8	4.1	5.8
Yemen Arab Rep.	7.5	8.6	9.9	16.5	Greece	10.2	10.5	10.7	11.8
Europe (excl. Soviet Union)	499.5	506.5	513.1	526.9	Italy	57.4	57.9	58.2	56.9
Eastern Europe	115.7	118.2	121.0	131.2	Portugal	10.4	10.7	11.0	11.9
Bulgaria	9.4	9.6	9.7	10.2	Spain	40.5	42.0	43.4	49.2
Czechoslovakia	16.0	16.3	16.8	18.8	Yugoslavia	23.9	24.6	25.2	26.6
German Dem. Rep.	16.6	16.5	16.6	16.1	Western Europe²	154.8	155.3	155.6	149.3
Hungary	10.8	10.8	10.9	10.9	Austria	7.5	7.5	7.5	7.3
Poland	39.0	40.2	41.4	45.9	Belgium	9.9	9.9	9.9	9.8
Romania	23.9	24.8	25.6	29.2	France	55.4	56.3	57.1	58.5
Northern Europe²	82.6	83.0	83.4	83.6	Germany, Fed. Rep. of	60.7	60.3	59.8	53.8
Denmark	5.2	5.1	5.1	4.8	Netherlands	14.7	14.9	15.0	14.6
Finland	4.9	5.0	5.0	4.8	Switzerland	6.2	6.0	5.9	4.9
Ireland	3.8	4.0	4.2	5.2	Soviet Union	291.3	303.1	314.8	367.1
Norway	4.2	4.2	4.2	4.3	Oceania²	26.7	28.5	30.4	39.5
Sweden	8.2	8.2	8.1	7.5	Australia	16.7	17.7	18.7	23.5
United Kingdom	55.8	56.0	56.2	56.4	New Zealand	3.4	3.6	3.7	4.2
					Papua New Guinea	4.2	4.8	5.3	8.2

(1) Regions. (2) Includes countries not shown separately. (3) Formerly Upper Volta. (4) Ivory Coast. (5) Formerly Burma.

Population of World's Largest Cities

Source: U.S. Bureau of the Census

The table below represents one attempt at comparing the world's largest cities. The cities are defined as population clusters of continuous built-up areas with a population density of a least 5,000 persons per square mile. The boundary of the city was determined by examining detailed maps of each city in conjunction with the most recent official population statistics. Exclaves of areas exceeding the minimum population density were added to the city if the intervening gap was less than one mile. To the extent practical, nonresidential areas such as parks, airports, industrial complexes and water were excluded from the area reported for each city, thus making the population density reflective of the concentrations in the residential portions of the city. By using a consistent definition for the city, it is possible to make comparisons of the cities on the basis of total population, area, and population density.

Political and administrative boundaries were disregarded in determining the population of the city. Berlin includes both East and West Berlin, as well as population from East Germany. Detroit includes Windsor, Canada.

The population of each city was projected based on the proportion each city was of its country total at the time of the last 2 censuses and projected country populations. The areal expansion of the city was not projected, hence density figures are valid only for 1985. Figures in the table below may differ from city population figures elsewhere in the World Almanac because of different methods of determining population.

City, Country	1985 (thousands)	2000 (thousands projected)	Area (sq. mi.)	Density (pop per sq. mi.)	City, Country	1985 (thousands)	2000 (thousands projected)	Area (sq. mi.)	Density (pop per sq. mi.)
Tokyo-Yokohama, Japan	25,434	29,971	1,089	23,356	Shenyang, China	4,086	4,684	39	104,769
Mexico City, Mexico	16,901	27,872	522	32,377	Philadelphia, U.S.	4,025	3,979	471	8,546
Sao Paolo, Brazil	14,911	25,354	451	33,062	Pusan, S. Korea	3,996	6,700	54	74,000
New York, U.S.	14,598	14,648	1,274	11,458	Barcelona, Spain	3,842	4,834	87	44,161
Seoul, South Korea	13,665	21,976	342	39,956	San Francisco, U.S.	3,790	4,214	428	8,855
Osaka-Kobe-Kyoto, Japan	13,562	14,333	495	27,397	Bangalore, India	3,685	6,764	50	73,700
Buenos Aires, Argentina	10,750	12,911	535	20,093	Lahore, Pakistan	3,603	5,864	57	63,211
Calcutta, India	10,462	14,088	209	50,057	Sydney, Australia	3,396	3,708	338	10,047
Bombay, India	10,137	15,357	95	106,705	Baghdad, Iraq	3,371	5,237	97	34,753
Rio de Janeiro, Brazil	10,116	14,169	260	38,907	Dhaka, Bangladesh	3,283	6,492	32	102,594
Moscow, USSR	9,873	11,121	379	26,050	Athens, Greece	3,252	3,866	116	28,034
Los Angeles, U.S.	9,638	10,714	1,110	8,682	Ho Chi Minh City, Vietnam	3,250	4,481	31	104,839
London, U.K.	9,442	8,574	874	10,803	Guangzhou, China	3,248	3,652	79	41,114
Paris, France	8,633	8,803	432	19,983	Detroit, U.S.	3,133	2,735	468	6,694
Cairo, Egypt	8,595	12,512	104	82,644	Miami, U.S.	3,123	3,894	448	6,971
Manila, Philippines	8,485	12,846	188	45,132	Belo Horizonte, Brazil	3,059	5,125	79	38,722
Jakarta, Indonesia	8,122	12,804	76	106,868	Wuhan, China	3,048	3,495	65	46,892
Essen, W. Germany	7,604	7,239	704	10,801	Ahmadabad, India	3,037	4,837	32	94,906
Teheran, Iran	7,354	14,251	112	65,660	Greater Berlin, Germany	3,033	3,006	274	11,069
Delhi, India	6,993	11,849	138	50,673	Hyderabad, India	3,022	4,765	88	34,341
Shanghai, China	6,698	7,540	78	85,871	Caracas, Venezuela	2,993	3,435	54	55,426
Chicago, U.S.	6,511	6,568	762	8,544	Toronto, Canada	2,972	3,296	154	19,299
Karachi, Pakistan	6,351	11,299	190	33,426	Surabaya, Indonesia	2,962	3,632	43	68,884
Lagos, Nigeria	6,054	12,528	56	108,107	Rome, Italy	2,944	3,129	69	42,667
Beijing, China	5,608	5,993	151	37,139	Naples, Italy	2,862	3,134	62	46,161
Taipei, Taiwan	5,550	8,516	138	40,217	Melbourne, Australia	2,852	2,968	327	8,722
Lima, Peru	5,447	9,241	120	45,392	Montreal, Canada	2,827	3,071	164	17,238
Hong Kong	5,415	5,956	20	270,750	Kinshasa, Zaire	2,794	5,646	57	49,018
Istanbul, Turkey	5,389	8,875	165	32,661	Guadalajara, Mexico	2,746	4,451	78	35,205
Bangkok, Thailand	4,998	7,587	102	49,000	Alexandria, Egypt	2,660	3,304	35	76,000
Madras, India	4,983	7,384	115	43,330	Yangon, Myanmar	2,558	3,332	47	54,426
Bogota, Colombia	4,711	7,935	79	59,633	Singapore, Singapore	2,556	2,913	78	32,769
Santiago, Chile	4,700	6,294	128	36,719	Porto Allegre, Brazil	2,536	4,109	231	10,978
Milan, Italy	4,635	4,839	344	13,474	Harbin, China	2,518	2,887	30	83,933
Tianjin, China	4,622	5,298	49	94,327	Casablanca, Morocco	2,495	3,795	35	71,286
Leningrad, USSR	4,569	4,738	139	32,871	Kiev, USSR	2,489	3,237	62	40,145
Nagoya, Japan	4,452	5,303	307	14,502	Dallas, U.S.	2,486	3,257	419	5,933
Manchester, U.K.	4,151	3,827	357	11,627	Boston, U.S.	2,470	2,485	303	8,152
Madrid, Spain	4,137	5,104	66	62,682					(continued)

City, Country	1985 (thousands)	2000 (thousands projected)	Area (sq. mi.)	Density (pop per sq. mi.)	City, Country	1985 (thousands)	2000 (thousands projected)	Area (sq. mi.)	Density (pop per sq. mi.)
Washington, U.S.	2,456	2,707	357	6,880	Chengdu, China	2,260	2,591	25	90,400
Monterrey, Mexico	2,351	3,974	77	30,532	Birmingham, U.K.	2,211	2,078	223	9,915
Ankara, Turkey	2,338	3,777	55	42,509	Houston, U.S.	2,104	2,651	310	6,787
Budapest, Hungary	2,297	2,335	138	16,645	Bucharest, Romania	2,095	2,271	52	40,288

The World's Refugees in 1988

The following information is from the *World Refugee Survey 1988*, a publication of the U.S. Committee for Refugees, a nonprofit corp. The refugees in this table include only those who are in need of protection and/or assistance, and do not include refugees who have resettled.

In some areas, the United States and Western Europe for example, there are large numbers of undocumented aliens and asylum seekers. These individuals are not included although many might be considered refugees. There is, however, no reliable way to document their number.

Country of Asylum	From	Number	Country of Asylum	From	Number
Total Africa		**4,088,260**	Thailand	Burma, Laos, Cambodia	439,860
Algeria	Mostly Western Sahara	167,000[1]	Vietnam	Cambodia	25,000
Angola	Namibia, Zaire, S. Africa	95,700			
Benin	Chad	3,000	**Total Europe**		**356,000**
Botswana	Zimbabwe, S. Africa	2,700	Austria	various	15,700
Burkina Faso	Chad	200	Greece	Asia, E. Europe	4,600
Burundi	Rwanda, Zaire	76,000[1]	Hungary	Romania	10,000
Cameroon	Chad	4,700	Italy	various	13,000
Central African Rep.	Chad	3,000	Portugal	various	900
Congo	Chad, Zaire	2,100	Spain	various	9,200
Côte d'Ivoire	Ghana, SE Asia	800	Turkey	Iran, Iraq	301,200[1]
Djibouti	Ethiopia	2,000	Yugoslavia	various	1,400
Egypt	Palestinians	5,660			
Ethiopia	Sudan, Somalia	700,500[1]	**Total Latin America/Caribbean**		**279,850**
Gabon	various	100	Argentina	Chile, SE Asia	4,900
Ghana	various	100	Belize	El Salvador, Guatemala	4,100
Kenya	Ethiopia, Rwanda, Uganda	10,660	Bolivia	Guatemala, Chile	300
Lesotho	South Africa	4,000[1]	Brazil	Europe, other	250
Liberia	various	200	Chile	Europe	450
Malawi	Mozambique	630,000	Colombia	Europe	410
Morocco	various	800	Costa Rica	El Salvador, Nicaragua	38,700
Mozambique	S. Africa	400	Cuba	Haiti	2,000
Nigeria	Chad, others	5,000	Dominican Rep.	Haiti	6,000[1]
Rwanda	Burundi	20,600[1]	Ecuador	Chile, various	700
Senegal	Guinea Bissau	5,200	El Salvador	Nicaragua	400
Sierra Leone	Namibia	100	French Guiana	Suriname	8,000
Somalia	Ethiopia	365,000[1]	Guatemala	El Salvador, Nicaragua	2,100
S. Africa	Mozambique	180,000[1]	Honduras	El Salvador, Nicaragua	38,540
Sudan	Ethiopia, Chad, Zaire	693,600[1]	Mexico	El Salvador, Guatemala	162,600[1]
Swaziland	South Africa, Mozambique	70,700[1]	Nicaragua	El Salvador, Guatemala	7,600
Tanzania	Burundi, Mozambique	266,200	Panama	El Salvador, others	1,400
Togo	Ghana	500	Peru	various	700
Tunisia	various	100	Uruguay	various	200
Uganda	Rwanda, Zaire, Sudan	125,500[1]	Venezuela	Caribbean	500
Zaire	Angola, Rwanda, Burundi	325,700			
Zambia	Angola, Mozambique, Zaire	149,000	**Total Middle East/South Asia**		**9,071,910**
Zimbabwe	Mozambique	171,500[1]	India	Bangladesh, Tibet, Sri Lanka	246,820
			Iran	Afghanistan, Iraq	2,807,000[1]
Total East Asia/Pacific		**625,780**	Iraq	Iran	75,000[1]
Hong Kong	Vietnam	25,260	Nepal	Tibet	12,000
Indonesia	Vietnam	2,310	Pakistan	Afghanistan	3,594,600
Japan	Vietnam	520	Yemen, North	S. Yemen, Ethiopia	62,000[1]
Korea	Vietnam	120	Palestinians		
Macau	Vietnam	440	Gaza Strip		459,070
Malaysia	Philippines, Vietnam	102,880	Jordan		870,490
Papua New Guinea	Indonesia	8,000	Lebanon		294,080
Philippines	Vietnam, Cambodia, Laos	20,920	Syria		265,220
Singapore	Vietnam	290	West Bank		385,630
Taiwan	Indochina	180			
			Total Refugees		**14,421,800**

(1) Significant variance among sources in number reported.

Principal Sources of Refugees

Afghanistan	5,927,180[1]	Somalia	350,000	Philippines	90,000[1]
Palestinians	2,273,090	Iran	348,800[1]	Namibia	81,400
Mozambique	1,147,000[1]	Rwanda	217,800[1]	Laos	78,890
Ethiopia	1,101,200[1]	Burundi	186,600	Vietnam	73,920
Iraq	508,200	Western Sahara	165,000	Yemen (Aden)	55,000[1]
Angola	395,700	El Salvador	152,500[1]	Nicaragua	54,760[1]
Sudan	355,000	Tibet	112,000	Zaire	53,200
Cambodia	354,190[1]	Sri Lanka	91,500		

(1) Significant variance among sources in number reported.

Major International Organizations

Association of Southeast Asian Nations (ASEAN), was formed in 1967 to promote economic, social, and cultural cooperation and development among the non-communist states of the region. Members in 1989 are Brunei Darussalam, Indonesia, Malaysia, Philippines, Singapore, Thailand. Annual ministerial meetings set policy; a central Secretariat in Jakarta and specialized intergovernmental committees work in trade, transportation, communications, agriculture, science, finance, and culture.

Caribbean Community (Caricom) was established July 4, 1973. Its function is to further co-operation in economics, health, education, culture, science and technology, and tax administration, as well as the co-ordination of foreign policy. Members in 1989 are Antigua, Bahamas, Barbados, Belize, Dominica, Grenada, Guyana, Jamaica, Montserrat, St. Kitts, St. Lucia, St. Vincent, Trinidad & Tobago. Observers are Dominican Republic, Haiti, and Suriname.

Commonwealth of Nations originally called the British Commonwealth of Nations, is an association of nations and dependencies loosely joined by a common interest based on having been parts of the old British Empire. The British monarch is the symbolic head of the Commonwealth.

There are 47 self-governing independent nations in the Commonwealth, plus various colonies and protectorates. As of May 1989, the members were the United Kingdom of Great Britain and Northern Ireland and 17 other nations recognizing the British monarch, represented by a governor-general, as their head of state: Antigua and Barbuda, Australia, Bahamas, Barbados, Belize, Canada, Grenada, Jamaica, Mauritius, New Zealand, Papua New Guinea, St. Kitts-Nevis, St. Lucia, St. Vincent and the Grenadines, Solomon Islands, and Tuvalu (a special member); and 30 countries with their own heads of state: Bangladesh, Botswana, Brunei, Cyprus, Dominica, The Gambia, Ghana, Guyana, India, Kenya, Kiribati, Lesotho, Malawi, Malaysia, The Maldives, Malta, Nauru (a special member), Nigeria, Samoa, Seychelles, Sierra Leone, Singapore, Sri Lanka, Swaziland, Tanzania, Tonga, Trinidad and Tobago, Uganda, Vanuatu, Zambia, and Zimbabwe. In addition various Caribbean dependencies take part in certain Commonwealth activities.

The Commonwealth facilitates consultation among member states through meetings of prime ministers and finance ministers, and through a permanent Secretariat. Members consult on economic, scientific, educational, financial, legal, and military matters, and try to coordinate policies.

European Communities (EC, the Common Market) is the collective designation of three organizations with common membership: the European Economic Community (Common Market), the European Coal and Steel Community, and the European Atomic Energy Community (Euratom). The 12 full members are: Belgium, Denmark, France, West Germany, Greece, Ireland, Italy, Luxembourg, Netherlands, Portugal, Spain, United Kingdom. Some 60 nations in Africa, the Caribbean, and the Pacific are affiliated under the Lomé Convention.

A merger of the 3 communities executives went into effect July 1, 1967, though the component organizations date back to 1951 and 1958. A Council of Ministers, a Commission, a European Parliament, and a Court of Justice comprise the permanent structure. The communities aim to integrate their economies, coordinate social developments, and bring about political union of the democratic states of Europe.

The members have agreed that a single European market which will remove all barriers to free trade and free movement of capital and people will take affect at the end of 1992.

European Free Trade Association (EFTA), consisting of Austria, Iceland, Norway, Portugal, Sweden, Switzerland and associated member Finland, was created Jan. 4, 1960, to gradually reduce customs duties and quantitative restrictions between members on industrial products. By Dec. 31, 1966, all tariffs and quotas had been eliminated. The association entered into free trade agreements with the EC, Jan. 1, 1973. Trade barriers were removed July 1, 1976.

League of Arab States (The Arab League) was created Mar. 22, 1945, by Egypt, Iraq, Jordan, Lebanon, Saudi Arabia, Syria, and Yemen. Joining later were Algeria, Bahrain, Djibouti, Egypt, Kuwait, Libya, Mauritania, Morocco, Oman, Qatar, The Palestine Liberation Org., Somalia, Sudan, Tunisia, United Arab Emirates. The League fosters cultural, economic, and communication ties and mediates disputes among the Arab states; it represents Arab states in certain international negotiations, and coordinates a military, economic, and diplomatic offensive against Israel. As a result of Egypt signing a peace treaty with Israel, the League, Mar. 1979, suspended Egypt's membership and transferred the League's headquarters from Cairo to Tunis. Egypt was readmitted to the organization in 1989.

North Atlantic Treaty Org. (NATO) was created by treaty (signed Apr. 4, 1949; in effect Aug. 24, 1949) among Belgium, Canada, Denmark, France, Iceland, Italy, Luxembourg, Netherlands, Norway, Portugal, United Kingdom, and the U.S. Greece, Turkey, West Germany, and Spain have joined since. The members agreed to settle disputes by peaceful means; to develop their individual and collective capacity to resist armed attack; to regard an attack on one as an attack on all, and to take necessary action to repel an attack under Article 51 of the United Nations Charter.

The NATO structure consists of a Council and a Military Committee of 3 commands (Allied Command Europe, Allied Command Atlantic, Allied Command Channel) and the Canada-U.S. Regional Planning Group.

Following announcement in 1966 of nearly total French withdrawal from the military affairs of NATO, organization hq. moved, 1967, from Paris to Brussels. In August, 1974, Greece announced a total withdrawal of armed forces from NATO, in response to Turkish intervention in Cyprus. Greece rejoined NATO's military wing, Oct. 10, 1980.

Organization of African Unity (OAU), formed May 25, 1963, by 32 African countries (50 in 1989) to coordinate cultural, political, scientific and economic policies; to end colonialism in Africa; and to promote a common defense of members' independence. It holds annual conferences of heads of state. Hq. is in Addis Ababa, Ethiopia.

Organization of American States (OAS) was formed in Bogota, Colombia, in 1948. Hq. is in Washington, D.C. It has a Permanent Council, Inter-American Economic and Social Council, and Inter-American Council for Education, Science and Culture, a Juridical Committee and a Commission on Human Rights. The Permanent Council can call meetings of foreign ministers to deal with urgent security matters. A General Assembly meets annually. A secretary general and assistant are elected for 5-year terms. There are 32 members, each with one vote in the various organizations: Antigua, Argentina, Bahamas, Barbados, Bolivia, Brazil, Chile, Colombia, Costa Rica, Cuba, Dominica, Dominican Republic, Ecuador, El Salvador, Grenada, Guatemala, Haiti, Honduras, Jamaica, Mexico, Nicaragua, Panama, Paraguay, Peru, St. Kitts-Nevis, St. Lucia, St. Vincent, Suriname, Trinidad & Tobago, U.S., Uruguay, Venezuela. In 1962, the OAS excluded Cuba from OAS activities but not from membership.

Organization for Economic Cooperation and Development (OECD) was established Sept. 30, 1961 to promote economic and social welfare in member countries, and to stimulate and harmonize efforts on behalf of developing nations. Nearly all the industrialized "free market" countries belong, with Yugoslavia as an associate member. OECD collects and disseminates economic and environmental information. Members in 1989 are: Australia, Austria, Belgium, Canada, Denmark, Finland, France, West Germany, Greece, Iceland, Ireland, Italy, Japan, Luxembourg, Netherlands, New Zealand, Norway, Portugal, Spain, Sweden, Switzerland, Turkey, United Kingdom, United States, Yugoslavia (special member). Hq. is in Paris.

Organization of Petroleum Exporting Countries (OPEC) was created Nov. 14, 1960 at Venezuelan initiative. The group attempts to set world oil prices by controlling oil production. It is also involved in advancing members' interests in trade and development dealings with industrialized oil-consuming nations. Members in 1989 are Algeria, Ecuador, Gabon, Indonesia, Iran, Iraq, Kuwait, Libya, Nigeria, Qatar, Saudi Arabia, United Arab Emirates, Venezuela.

Warsaw Pact was created May 14, 1955, as a mutual defense alliance. Members in 1989 are Bulgaria, Czechoslovakia, East Germany, Hungary, Poland, Romania, and the USSR. Hq. is in Moscow. It provides for a unified military command; if one member is attacked, the others will aid it with all necessary steps including armed force.

United Nations

The 44th regular session of the United Nations General Assembly opened in September, 1989.

UN headquarters are in New York, N.Y., between First Ave. and Roosevelt Drive and E. 42d St. and E. 48th St. The General Assembly Bldg., Secretariat, Conference and Library bldgs. are interconnected.

A European office at Geneva includes Secretariat and agency staff members. Other offices of UN bodies and related organizations with a staff of some 23,000 from some 150 countries are scattered throughout the world.

The UN has a post office originating its own stamps.

Proposals to establish an organization of nations for maintenance of world peace led to the United Nations Conference on International Organization at San Francisco, Apr. 25-June 26, 1945, where the charter of the United Nations was drawn up. It was signed June 26 by 50 nations, and by Poland, one of the original 51, on Oct. 15, 1945. The charter came into effect Oct. 24, 1945, upon ratification by the permanent members of the Security Council and a majority of other signatories.

Purposes: To maintain international peace and security; to develop friendly relations among nations; to achieve international cooperation in solving economic, social, cultural, and humanitarian problems and in promoting respect for human rights and fundamental freedoms; to be a center for harmonizing the actions of nations in attaining these common ends.

Roster of the United Nations
(As of mid-1989)

The 159 members of the United Nations, with the years in which they became members.

Member	Year	Member	Year	Member	Year	Member	Year
Afghanistan	1946	Djibouti	1977	Lesotho	1966	Samoa (Western)	1976
Albania	1955	Dominica	1978	Liberia	1945	Sao Tome e Principe	1975
Algeria	1962	Dominican Rep.	1945	Libya	1955	Saudi Arabia	1945
Angola	1976	Ecuador	1945	Luxembourg	1945	Senegal	1960
Antigua and Barbuda	1981	Egypt[2]	1945	Madagascar (Malagasy)	1960	Seychelles	1976
Argentina	1945	El Salvador	1945	Malawi	1964	Sierra Leone	1961
Australia	1945	Equatorial Guinea	1968	Malaysia[1]	1957	Singapore[1]	1965
Austria	1955	Ethiopia	1945	Maldives	1965	Solomon Islands	1978
Bahamas	1973	Fiji	1970	Mali	1960	Somalia	1960
Bahrain	1971	Finland	1955	Malta	1964	South Africa[5]	1945
Bangladesh	1974	France	1945	Mauritania	1961	Spain	1955
Barbados	1966	Gabon	1960	Mauritius	1968	Sri Lanka	1955
Belgium	1945	Gambia	1965	Mexico	1945	Sudan	1956
Belize	1981	Germany, East	1973	Mongolia	1961	Suriname	1975
Benin	1960	Germany, West	1973	Morocco	1956	Swaziland	1968
Bhutan	1971	Ghana	1957	Mozambique	1975	Sweden	1946
Bolivia	1945	Greece	1945	Myanmar (Burma)	1948	Syria[2]	1945
Botswana	1966	Grenada	1974	Nepal	1955	Tanzania[3]	1961
Brazil	1945	Guatemala	1945	Netherlands	1945	Thailand	1946
Brunei	1984	Guinea	1958	New Zealand	1945	Togo	1960
Bulgaria	1955	Guinea-Bissau	1974	Nicaragua	1945	Trinidad & Tobago	1962
Burkina Faso	1960	Guyana	1966	Niger	1960	Tunisia	1956
Burundi	1962	Haiti	1945	Nigeria	1960	Turkey	1945
Byelorussia	1945	Honduras	1945	Norway	1945	Uganda	1962
Cambodia	1955	Hungary	1955	Oman	1971	Ukraine	1945
Cameroon	1960	Iceland	1946	Pakistan	1947	USSR	1945
Canada	1945	India	1945	Panama	1945	United Arab Emirates	1971
Cape Verde	1975	Indonesia[6]	1950	Papua New Guinea	1975	United Kingdom	1945
Central Afr. Rep.	1960	Iran	1945	Paraguay	1945	United States	1945
Chad	1960	Iraq	1945	Peru	1945	Uruguay	1945
Chile	1945	Ireland	1955	Philippines	1945	Vanuatu	1981
China[4]	1945	Israel	1949	Poland	1945	Venezuela	1945
Colombia	1945	Italy	1955	Portugal	1955	Vietnam	1977
Comoros	1975	Jamaica	1962	Qatar	1971	Yemen	1947
Congo	1960	Japan	1956	Romania	1955	Yemen, South	1967
Costa Rica	1945	Jordan	1955	Rwanda	1962	Yugoslavia	1945
Côte d'Ivoire	1960	Kenya	1963	Saint Christopher & Nevis	1983	Zaire	1960
Cuba	1945	Kuwait	1963	Saint Lucia	1979	Zambia	1964
Cyprus	1960	Laos	1955	Saint Vincent and the Grenadines	1980	Zimbabwe	1980
Czechoslovakia	1945	Lebanon	1945				
Denmark	1945						

(1) Malaya joined the UN in 1957. In 1963, its name was changed to Malaysia following the accession of Singapore, Sabah, and Sarawak. Singapore became an independent UN member in 1965. (2) Egypt and Syria were original members of the UN. In 1958, the United Arab Republic was established by a union of Egypt and Syria and continued as a single member of the UN. In 1961, Syria resumed its separate membership. (3) Tanganyika was a member of the United Nations from 1961 and Zanzibar was a member from 1963. Following the ratification in 1964 of Articles of Union between Tanganyika and Zanzibar, the United Republic of Tanganyika and Zanzibar continued as a single member of the United Nations, later changing its name to United Republic of Tanzania. (4) The General Assembly voted in 1971 to expel the Chinese government on Taiwan and admit the Peking government in its place. (5) The General Assembly rejected the credentials of the South African delegates in 1974, and suspended the country from the Assembly. (6) Indonesia withdrew from the UN in 1965 and rejoined in 1966.

Organization of the United Nations

The text of the UN Charter, and further information, may be obtained from the Office of Public Information, United Nations, New York, NY 10017.

General Assembly. The General Assembly is composed of representatives of all the member nations. Each nation is entitled to one vote.

The General Assembly meets in regular annual sessions and in special session when necessary. Special sessions are convoked by the Secretary General at the request of the Security Council or of a majority of the members of the UN.

On important questions a two-thirds majority of members present and voting is required; on other questions a simple majority is sufficient.

The General Assembly must approve the budget and apportion expenses among members. A member in arrears will have no vote if the amount of arrears equals or exceeds the amount of the contributions due for the preceeding two full years.

Security Council. The Security Council consists of 15 members, 5 with permanent seats. The remaining 10 are elected for 2-year terms by the General Assembly; they are not eligible for immediate reelection.

Permanent members of the Council: China, France, USSR, United Kingdom, United States.

Non-permanent members are Algeria, Brazil, Nepal, Senegal, and Yugoslavia (until Dec. 31, 1989); Canada, Colombia, Ethiopia, Finland, and Malaysia (until Dec. 31, 1990).

The Security Council has the primary responsiblity within the UN for maintaining international peace and security. The Council may investigate any dispute that threatens international peace and security.

Any member of the UN at UN headquarters may participate in its discussions and a nation not a member of UN may appear if it is a party to a dispute.

Decisions on procedural questions are made by an affirmative vote of 9 members. On all other matters the affirmative vote of 9 members must include the concurring votes of all permanent members; it is this clause which gives rise to the so-called "veto." A party to a dispute must refrain from voting.

The Security Council directs the various truce supervisory forces deployed throughout the world.

Economic and Social Council. The Economic and Social Council consists of 54 members elected by the General Assembly for 3-year terms of office. The council is responsible under the General Assembly for carrying out the functions of the United Nations with regard to international economic, social, cultural, educational, health and related matters. The council meets usually twice a year.

Trusteeship Council. The administration of trust territories is under UN supervision. The only remaining trust territory is Palau, administered by the U.S.

Secretariat. The Secretary General is the chief administrative officer of the UN. He may bring to the attention of the Security Council any matter that threatens international peace. He reports to the General Assembly.

Budget: The General Assembly approved a total budget for 90-91 of $1.56 billion.

International Court of Justice (World Court). The International Court of Justice is the principal judicial organ of the United Nations. All members are *ipso facto* parties to the statute of the Court, as are three nonmembers — Liechtenstein, San Marino, and Switzerland. Other states may become parties to the Court's statute.

The jurisdiction of the Court comprises cases which the parties submit to it and matters especially provided for in the charter or in treaties. The Court gives advisory opinions and renders judgments. Its decisions are only binding between the parties concerned and in respect to a particular dispute. If any party to a case fails to heed a judgment, the other party may have recourse to the Security Council.

The 15 judges are elected for 9-year terms by the General Assembly and the Security Council. Retiring judges are eligible for re-election. The Court remains permanently in session, except during vacations. All questions are decided by majority. The Court sits in The Hague, Netherlands.

Judges: 9-year term of office ending 1997: Mohamed Shahabuddeen, Bahamas. Roberto Ago, Italy. Stephen Schwebel, U.S. Nikolai K. Tarasov, USSR. Mohammed Bedjaoui, Algeria. **9-year term in office ending 1994:** Ni Zhengyo, China. Jens Evensen, Norway. Manfred Lachs, Poland. Taslim Olawala Elias, Nigeria, Shigeru Oda, Japan. **9-year term in office ending 1991:** Nagendra Singh, India. Jose Maria Ruda, Argentina. Robert Y. Jennings, United Kingdom. Guy Ladreit de Lacharriere, France. Keba Mbaye, Senegal.

United Nations Secretaries General

Year	Secretary, Nation	Year	Secretary, Nation	Year	Secretary, Nation
1946	Trygve Lie, Norway	1961	U Thant, Burma	1982	Javier Perez de Cuellar, Peru
1953	Dag Hammarskjold, Sweden	1972	Kurt Waldheim, Austria		

U.S. Representatives to the United Nations

The U.S. Representative to the United Nations is the Chief of the U.S. Mission to the United Nations in New York and holds the rank and status of Ambassador Extraordinary and Plenipotentiary.

Year	Representative	Year	Representative	Year	Representative
1946	Edward R. Stettinius Jr.	1968	George W. Ball	1976	William W. Scranton
1946	Herschel V. Johnson (act.)	1968	James Russell Wiggins	1977	Andrew Young
1947	Warren R. Austin	1969	Charles W. Yost	1979	Donald McHenry
1953	Henry Cabot Lodge Jr.	1971	George Bush	1981	Jeane J. Kirkpatrick
1960	James J. Wadsworth	1973	John A. Scali	1985	Vernon A. Walters
1961	Adlai E. Stevenson	1975	Daniel P. Moynihan	1989	Thomas R. Pickering
1965	Arthur J. Goldberg				

Visitors to the United Nations

United Nations headquarters is open to the public every day of the year except Christmas and New Year's Day. The public entrance is at 46th Street and First Avenue and opens at 9 a.m.

Guided tours begin from the main lobby of the General Assembly building and are given approximately every half hour from 9:15 a.m. to 4:45 p.m. daily. The tours last about one hour. Tours in languages other than English may be arranged.

Groups of 15 or more persons should make arrangements as far in advance as possible by writing to the Group Program Unit, Visitors' Service, Room GA-56, United Nations, New York, NY 10017, or telephone (212) 963-7713. Children under 5 are not permitted on tours.

Specialized and Related Agencies

These agencies are autonomous, with their own memberships and organs which have a functional relationship or working agreement with the UN (headquarters.)

Food & Agriculture Org. (FAO) aims to increase production from farms, forests, and fisheries; improve distribution, marketing, and nutrition; better conditions for rural people. (Viale delle Terme di Caracalla, 00100 Rome, Italy.)

General Agreement on Tariffs and Trade (GATT) is the only treaty setting rules for world trade. Provides a forum for settling trade disputes and negotiating trade liberalization. (Centre William Rappard, 154 rue de Lausanne, 1211 Geneva 21, Switzerland.)

International Atomic Energy Agency (IAEA) aims to promote the safe, peaceful uses of atomic energy. (Vienna International Centre, PO Box 100, A-1400, Vienna, Austria.)

International Bank for Reconstruction and Development (IBRD) (World Bank) provides loans and technical assistance for economic development projects in developing member countries; encourages cofinancing for projects from other public and private sources. **International Development Association (IDA)**, an affiliate of the Bank, provides funds for development projects on concessionary terms to the poorer developing member countries. (both 1818 H St., NW, Washington, DC 20433.) **International Finance Corporation (IFC)** an affiliate of the Bank, promotes the growth of the private sector in developing member countries; encourages the development of local capital markets; stimulates the international flow of private capital. (1818 H St., NW, Washington, DC 20433.)

International Civil Aviation Org. (ICAO) promotes international civil aviation standards and regulations. (1000 Sherbrooke St. W., Montreal, Quebec, Canada H3A 2R2.)

International Fund for Agricultural Development (IFAD) aims to mobilize funds for agricultural and rural projects in developing countries. (107 Via del Serafico, Rome, Italy.)

International Labor Org. (ILO) aims to promote employment; improve labor conditions and living standards. (4 route de Morillons, CH-1211, Geneva 22, Switzerland.)

International Maritime Org. (IMO) aims to promote co-operation on technical matters affecting international shipping. (4 Albert Embankment, London, SE1 7SR, England.)

International Monetary Fund (IMF) aims to promote international monetary co-operation and currency stabilization; expansion of international trade. (700 19th St., NW, Washington, DC, 20431.)

International Telecommunication Union (ITU) sets up international regulations of radio, telegraph, telephone and space radio-communications. Allocates radio frequencies. (Place des Nations, 1211 Geneva 20, Switzerland.)

United Nations Educational, Scientific, & Cultural Org. (UNESCO) aims to promote collaboration among nations through education, science, and culture. The U.S. withdrew from this organization in 1985 because of UNESCO's anti-Western bias. (9 Place de Fontenoy, 75700 Paris, France.)

United Nations Children's Fund (UNICEF) provides aid and development assistance to children and mothers in developing countries. (1 UN Plaza, New York, NY 10017.)

Universal Postal Union (UPU) aims to perfect postal services and promote international collaboration. (Weltpoststrasse 4, 3000 Berne, 15 Switzerland.)

World Health Org. (WHO) aims to aid the attainment of the highest possible level of health. (1211 Geneva 27, Switzerland.)

World Intellectual Property Organization (WIPO) seeks to protect, through international cooperation, literary, industrial, scientific, and artistic works. (34, Chemin des Colom Bettes, 1211 Geneva, Switzerland.)

World Meteorological Org. (WMO) aims to co-ordinate and improve world meteorological work. (Case Postale 5, CH-1211, Geneva 20, Switzerland.)

U.S. Immigration Law

Source: Immigration and Naturalization Service, U.S. Justice Department

The Immigration and Nationality Act, as amended, provides for the numerical limitation of most immigration. Not subject to any numerical limitations are immigrants classified as immediate relatives who are spouses or children of U.S. citizens, or parents of citizens who are 21 years of age or older; returning residents; certain former U.S. citizens; ministers of religion; and certain long-term U.S. government employees.

The Refugee Act of 1980 (P.L. 96-212) became effective on April 1, 1980. Congress stated that the objectives of the Refugee Act are to provide a permanent and systematic procedure for the admission of refugees who are of special humanitarian concern to the U.S. and to provide uniform provisions for the effective settlement and absorption of those refugees. The number of refugees who may be admitted is determined by the President, after consultation with the Committees on the Judiciary of the Senate and of the House of Representatives.

Numerical Limitation of Immigrants

Immigration to the U.S. is numerically limited to 270,000 per year. Within this quota there is an annual limitation of 20,000 for each country. The colonies and dependencies of foreign states are limited to 600 (5,000 in 1988) per year, chargeable to the country limitation of the mother country.

Visa Categories

Of those immigrants subject to numerical limitations, applicants for immigration are classified as either preference or nonpreference. The preference visa categories are based on certain relationships to persons in the U.S., i.e., unmarried sons and daughters over 21 of U.S. citizens, spouses and unmarried sons and daughters of resident aliens, married sons and daughters of U.S. citizens, brothers and sisters of U.S. citizens 21 or over (first, 2d, 4th, and 5th preference, respectively); members of the professions or persons of exceptional ability in the sciences and arts whose services are sought by U.S. employers (3d preference); and skilled and unskilled workers in short supply (6th preference). Spouses and children of preference applicants are entitled to the same preference if accompanying or following to join such persons.

Preference status is based upon approved petitions, filed with the Immigration and Naturalization Service, by the appropriate relative or employer (or in the 3d preference by the alien himself).

Other immigrants not within one of the above-mentioned preference groups may qualify as nonpreference applicants and receive only those visa numbers not needed by preference applicants. The nonpreference category has not been available since 1978 due to 6 preferences using the allocation.

Labor Certification

The Act of October 3, 1965, established controls to protect the U.S. labor market from an influx of skilled and unskilled foreign labor. Prior to the issuance of a visa, the potential 3d, 6th, and nonpreference immigrant must obtain the Secretary of Labor's certification, establishing that there are not sufficient workers in the U.S. at the alien's destination who are able, willing, and qualified to perform the job; and that the employment of the alien will not adversely affect the wages and working conditions of workers in the U.S. similarly employed; or that there is satisfactory evidence that the provisions of that section do not apply to the alien's case.

The Immigration Reform and Control Act of 1986

The Immigration Reform and Control Act, PL 99-603, was signed into law on November 6, 1986. The legislation contains 3 major segments—legalization, employer sanctions, and temporary agricultural worker provisions. The

(continued)

legalization segment of the law provides a method for legalizing the status of many of the aliens who have been in the U.S. unlawfully since before January 1, 1982. Legalization is a 2-tiered program which provides for temporary resident status for qualified applicants. After 18 months residence in the U.S., temporary residents are eligible to apply to adjust to permanent resident status. Aliens who were employed in seasonal agricultural work for a minimum of 90 days between May 1985 and May 1986 are also eligible to apply for temporary residence. The agricultural workers will adjust to permanent resident status beginning in December, 1989.

The employer sanctions section of the legislation, for the first time, imposes civil and criminal penalties on employers who knowingly hire, recruit, or refer aliens who are not authorized to work in the U.S. The civil fines range from $250 to $10,000 per alien. Criminal penalties are possible for habitual violators. Employer sanction provisions were to begin in May 1987 but were delayed by Congress until Sept. 1 when a 12-month education period will begin.

The temporary agricultural worker provisions of the act expand the existing temporary worker (H2) program. The law divides H2 workers into two categories: temporary workers for agricultural labor or services, and all other temporary H2 workers. The changes made by the law affect only the agricultural area and are effective as of June 1, 1987. A grower wishing to hire H2 workers must file a petition with the Department of Labor. The Department will grant the petition provided there are insufficient workers who are able, willing, qualified, and available where and when needed to perform the labor, and there will be no adverse effect on the wages and working conditions of workers similarly employed in the U.S.

In addition to these major provisions, there are many other provisions of the act, including anti-discrimination provisions as well as increasing the numerical limitation for colonies of foreign states from 600 to 5,000 immigrant visas a year. Qualified aliens who are in the category Cuban/Haitian Entrant (Status Pending) are eligible to adjust to permanent resident status. The act also provides an additional 5,000 nonpreference visa numbers to be made available in fiscal years 1987 and 1988 to natives of countries which were adversely effected by the changes in the preference system created by the 1965 Immigration and Nationality Act amendments. Section 2 of the Immigration Amendments of 1988, extended this category through fiscal years 1989 and 1990, with 15,000 visa numbers provided for each of those years.

As of May 12, 1989, about 1,768,100 aliens have sought legal status under the pre-1982 provisions of the new immigration law and 1,301,800 have applied for legal status under the agricultural worker provision.

Naturalization: How to Become an American Citizen

Source: The Federal Statutes

A person who desires to be naturalized as a citizen of the United States may obtain the necessary application form as well as detailed information from the nearest office of the Immigration and Naturalization Service or from the clerk of a court handling naturalization cases.

An applicant must be at least 18 years old. He must have been a lawful resident of the United States continuously for 5 years. For husbands and wives of U.S. citizens the period is 3 years in most instances. Special provisions apply to certain veterans of the Armed Forces.

An applicant must have been physically present in this country for at least half of the required 5 years' residence.

Every applicant for naturalization must:

(1) demonstrate an understanding of the English language, including an ability to read, write, and speak words in ordinary usage in the English language (persons physically unable to do so, and persons who, on the date of their examinations, are over 50 years of age and have been lawful permanent residents of the United States for 20 years or more are exempt).

(2) have been a person of good moral character, attached to the principles of the Constitution, and well disposed to the good order and happiness of the United States for five years just before filing the petition or for whatever other period of residence is required in his case and continue to be such a person until admitted to citizenship; and

(3) demonstrate a knowledge and understanding of the fundamentals of the history, and the principles and form of government, of the U.S.

When the applicant files his petition he pays the court clerk $50. At the preliminary hearing he may be represented by a lawyer or social service agency. There is a 30-day wait. If action is favorable, there is a final hearing before a judge, who administers the following oath of allegiance:

I hereby declare, on oath, that I absolutely and entirely renounce and abjure all allegiance and fidelity to any foreign prince, potentate, state or sovereignty, to whom or which I have heretofore been a subject or citizen; that I will support and defend the Constitution and laws of the United States of America against all enemies, foreign and domestic; that I will bear true faith and allegiance to the same; that I will bear arms on behalf of the United States when required by the law; that I will perform noncombatant service in the armed forces of the United States when required by the law; that I will perform work of national importance under civilian direction when required by the law; and that I take this obligation freely without any mental reservation or purpose of evasion; so help me God.

Customs Exemptions and Advice to Travelers

Source: U.S. Customs Service

U.S. residents returning after a stay abroad of at least 48 hours are usually granted customs exemptions of $400 each. The duty-free articles must accompany the traveler at the time of his return, be for personal or household use, have been acquired as an incident of his trip, and be properly declared to Customs. Not more than one liter of alcoholic beverages may be included in the $400 exemption.

If a U.S. resident arrives directly or indirectly from American Samoa, Guam, or the U.S. Virgin Islands, the purchase may be valued up to $800 fair retail value, but not more than $400 of the exemption may be applied to the value of articles acquired elsewhere than in such insular possessions, and 5 liters of alcoholic beverages may be included in the exemption, but not more than 1 liter of such beverages may have been acquired elsewhere than in the designated islands.

The exemption for alcoholic beverages is accorded only when the returning resident has attained 21 years of age at the time of his arrival. One hundred cigars and 200 cigarettes may be included in either exemption. Cuban cigars may be included if obtained in Cuba and all articles acquired there do not exceed $100 in retail value.

The $400 or $800 exemption may be granted only if the exemption, or any part of it, has not been used within the preceding 30-day period and the stay abroad was for at least 48 hours. The 48-hour absence requirement does not apply if you return from Mexico or the U.S. Virgin Islands.

Gifts costing no more than $50 fair retail value or $100 from American Samoa, Guam, or the Virgin Islands, may be mailed duty-free.

Most items—including alcoholic beverages, cigars, cigarettes and perfume—made in designated Caribbean and Central American countries may enter the U.S. duty-free under the Caribbean Basin Economic Recovery Act. Countries currently designated for such duty-free treatment are: Aruba, Antigua and Barbuda, Bahamas, Barbados, Belize, British Virgin Islands, Costa Rica, Dominica, Dominican Republic, El Salvador, Grenada, Guatemala, Haiti, Honduras, Jamaica, Montserrat, Netherlands Antilles, Panama, Saint Christopher-Nevis, Saint Lucia, Saint Vincent and the Grenadines, and Trinidad and Tobago. Exceptions are: most textiles (incl. clothing), footwear, handbags, luggage, flat goods, work gloves and leather wearing apparel, and certain watches and watch parts. Alcoholic beverages and perfumes, remain subject to IRS tax.

U.S. Aid to Foreign Nations

Source: Bureau of Economic Analysis, U.S. Commerce Department

Figures are in millions of dollars. (*Less than $500,000.) Data include military supplies and services furnished under the Foreign Assistance Act and direct Defense Department appropriations, and include credits extended to private entities.

Net grants and credits take into account all known returns to the U.S., including reverse grants, returns of grants, and payments of principal. A minus sign (−) indicates that the total of these returns is greater than the total of grants or credits. Nations with net grant or credit under $2 mln. not incl.

Other assistance represents the transfer of U.S. farm products in exchange for foreign currencies, less the government's disbursements of the currencies as grants, credits, or for purchases.

Amounts do not include investments in the following: Asian Development Bank, $111 mln.; Inter-American Development Bank, $124 mln.; International Development Assn., $826 mln.; International Bank for Reconstruction and Development, $95 mln.; African Development Bank, $9 mln.; African Development Fund, $40 mln; International Finance Corp., $25 mln.; Special Facility for Sub-Saharan Africa, $48 mln; Inter American Investment Corp., $13 mln; Multilateral Investment Guaranty Agency, $22 mln.

Calendar Year 1988	Total	Net grants	Net credits	Net other		Total	Net grants	Net credits	Net other
Total	6,735	10,805	−4,046	−23	Cameroon	20	24	−4	—
					Cape Verde	3	3	—	—
Western Europe	92	440	−348	(*)	Cen. African Rep.	4	4	—	—
Austria	−9	(*)	−9	—	Chad	36	36	—	—
Belgium	−9	—	−9	—	Cote D'Ivoire	28	3	25	(*)
Denmark	−6	—	−6	—	Djibouti	5	5	—	—
Finland	6	(*)	6	(*)	Ethiopia	49	56	−7	(*)
France	−14	(*)	−14	—	Gabon	14	2	13	—
Iceland	−4	(*)	−4	—	Gambia	10	10	—	—
Ireland	−6	—	−6	—	Ghana	8	11	−1	(*)
Italy	−28	(*)	−29	—	Guinea	15	17	−2	(*)
Portugal	66	92	−26	—	Guinea-Bissau	3	3	—	—
Spain	−113	5	−117	(*)	Kenya	42	47	−4	−2
Sweden	−3	—	−3	—	Lesotho	20	20	—	—
United Kingdom	−103	3	−107	—	Liberia	19	25	−6	—
Yugoslavia	−29	(*)	−29	(*)	Madagascar	11	11	(*)	(*)
Fund for Ireland	35	35	—	—	Malawi	31	32	−1	—
Other & unspecified	303	303	(*)	—	Mali	42	42	(*)	(*)
Eastern Europe	−125	8	−107	−25	Mauritania	9	10	(*)	—
Poland	−57	8	−40	−25	Mauritius	6	1	5	—
Romania	−1	—	−1	—	Morocco	172	60	111	(*)
USSR	−66	—	−66	—	Mozambique	39	39	—	—
Near East & South Asia	1,934	5,486	−3,530	−22	Niger	21	21	(*)	—
Afghanistan	29	32	−3	(*)	Nigeria	169	2	167	—
Bangladesh	129	129	(*)	(*)	Rwanda	13	13	(*)	(*)
Cyprus	14	15	−1	(*)	Senegal	37	34	4	(*)
Egypt	3,480	1,503	1,976	1	Sierra Leone	8	4	4	—
Greece	488	5	482	1	Somalia	55	32	23	(*)
India	61	122	−55	−6	South Africa	9	9	—	—
Iran	−19	—	−19	—	Sudan	94	65	29	(*)
Iraq	29	—	29	—	Swaziland	10	10	(*)	—
Israel	1,831	2,869	−4,700	—	Tanzania	12	12	(*)	—
Jordan	−232	93	−325	(*)	Togo	7	8	−1	—
Lebanon	−12	20	−32	—	Tunisia	−176	43	−221	1
Nepal	16	16	(*)	—	Uganda	20	16	4	—
Oman	9	7	1	—	Zaire	138	32	106	1
Pakistan	346	265	99	−17	Zambia	17	5	12	(*)
Sri Lanka	39	12	27	(*)	Zimbabwe	5	10	−5	—
Turkey	−720	299	−1,019	(*)	Other & unspecified	58	58	(*)	—
Yemen, North	29	19	10	—	**Western Hemisphere**	1,299	1,266	7	26
Other & unspecified	80	80	—	—	Antigua & Barbuda	3	(*)	2	—
East Asia & Pacific	277	532	−255	1	Argentina	16	1	16	—
Australia	−26	—	−26	—	Belize	11	11	(*)	—
Burma	8	10	−1	—	Bolivia	59	62	−3	—
Cambodia	4	4	(*)	—	Brazil	−20	8	−27	—
China	48	(*)	48	—	Canada	−50	—	−50	—
Hong Kong	−8	(*)	−8	—	Chile	9	3	7	—
Indonesia	−17	45	−62	(*)	Colombia	−21	10	−31	—
Japan	−4	—	−4	—	Costa Rica	106	99	9	2
Korea, South	−383	1	−384	—	Dominican Republic	41	30	−8	19
Malaysia	−9	1	−10	—	Ecuador	43	32	11	—
New Zealand	−4	—	−4	—	El Salvador	394	362	32	—
Philippines	403	228	175	(*)	Guatemala	136	118	15	3
Taiwan	−8	(*)	−8	1	Guyana	5	(*)	5	—
Thailand	68	38	31	—	Haiti	34	43	−10	(*)
Trust Terr. Pacific	9	9	—	—	Honduras	188	167	21	(*)
Fed. States of Micronesia	98	98	—	—	Jamaica	98	28	60	5
Marshall Islands	40	40	—	—	Mexico	38	46	−8	—
Other & unspecified	59	59	(*)	(*)	Panama	10	10	—	—
Africa	1,068	882	188	−2	Peru	59	44	15	—
Algeria	−58	(*)	−58	—	St. Kitts-Nevis	4	1	3	—
Angola	1	5	−4	—	St. Vincent & Grenadines	2	(*)	2	—
Benin	4	4	(*)	—	Trinidad-Tobago	−13	(*)	−13	—
Botswana	18	20	−3	—	Uruguay	9	12	−3	—
Burkina Faso	13	13	—	(*)	Venezuela	−28	1	−29	—
Burundi	4	4	—	(*)	Other & unspecified	171	177	−6	(*)
					Intl. orgs. & unspecified	2,190	2,190	−1	—

Ambassadors and Envoys

As of mid-1989

The address of U.S. embassies abroad is the appropriate foreign capital. The U.S. does not have diplomatic relations with the following countries: Albania,[1] Angola,[2] Cambodia,[3] Taiwan,[4] Cuba,[5] Iran,[6] Libya,[6] Vietnam.[3] S. Yemen.[3] N. Korea, Mongolia. There are informal relations with Bhutan and Vanuatu.

Countries	Envoys from United States	Envoys to United States
Afghanistan	Jon Glassman, Chargé	Alishah Masood, Chargé
Algeria	Christopher W.S. Ross, Amb.	Rabah Kerouaz, Chargé
Antigua & Barbuda	John Clark, Chargé	Edmund H. Lake, Amb.
Argentina	Theodore E. Gildred, Amb.	Enrique J.A. Candioti, Amb.
Australia	Melvin F. Sembler, Amb.	F. Rawdon Dalrymple, Amb.
Austria	Henry A. Grunwald, Amb.	Friedrich Hoess, Amb.
Bahamas	Carol Boyd Hallett, Amb.	Margaret E. McDonald, Amb.
Bahrain	Sam H. Zakhem, Amb.	Ghazi M. Algosaibi, Amb.
Bangladesh	Willard De Pree, Amb.	A.H.S. Ataul Karim, Amb.
Barbados	John Clark, Chargé	William Douglas, Amb.
Belgium	Maynard W. Glitman, Amb.	Herman Dehennin, Amb.
Belize	Robert G. Rich, Jr., Amb.	Edward A. Laing, Amb.
Benin	Walter E. Stadtler, Amb.	Theophile Nata, Amb.
Bolivia	Robert S. Gelbard, Amb.	Carlos Delius, Amb.
Botswana	John F. Kordek, Amb.	Cecil Manyeula, Chargé
Brazil	Harry Shlaudeman, Amb.	Marcilio M. Moreira, Amb.
Brunei	Thomas C. Ferguson, Amb.	D.P.H. Mohammad Suni, Amb.
Bulgaria	Sol Polansky, Amb.	Velichko F. Velichkov Amb.
Burkina Faso	David H. Shinn, Amb.	Paul-Désiré Kabore, Amb.
Burma	Burton Levin, Amb.	U. Myo Aung, Amb.
Burundi	James Daniel Phillips, Amb.	Edouard Kadigiri, Amb.
Cameroon	Mark L. Edelman, Amb.	Paul Pondi, Amb.
Canada	Thomas M. T. Niles, Amb.	Derek H. Burney, Amb.
Cape Verde	Vernon D. Penner Jr., Amb.	Jose Luis Fernandes Lopes, Amb.
Central African Rep.	David C. Fields, Amb.	Christian Lingama-Toleque, Amb.
Chad	Robert L. Pugh, Amb.	Mahamat Ali Adoum, Amb.
Chile	Charles A. Gillespie Jr., Amb.	Patricio Maturana, Amb.
China	Winston Lord, Amb.	Han Xu, Amb.
Colombia	Thomas E. McNamara, Amb.	Victor Mosquera, Amb.
Comoros	Patricia G. Lynch, Amb.	Amini Ali Moumin, Amb.
Congo	Leonard G. Shurtleff, Amb.	Benjamin Bounkoulou, Amb.
Costa Rica	Deane R. Hinton, Amb.	Danilo Jimenez, Amb.
Côte d'Ivoire	Dennis Kux, Amb.	Charles Gomis, Amb.
Cyprus	Bill K. Perrin, Amb.	Andrew J. Jacovides, Amb.
Czechoslovakia	Shirley Temple Black, Amb.	Mirolsav Houstecky, Amb.
Denmark	Keith L. Brown, Amb.	Eigil Jorgensen, Amb.
Djibouti	Robert S. Barrett, Amb.	Roble Olhale, Amb.
Dominica	John Clark, Chargé	McDonald P. Benjamin, Amb.
Dominican Republic	Lowell C. Kilday, Amb.	Eduardo Leon, Amb.
Ecuador	Richard N. Holwill, Amb.	Jaime Moncayo, Amb.
Egypt	Frank G. Wisner, Amb.	El Sayed A. R. El Reedy, Amb.
El Salvador	William G. Walker, Amb.	Ernesto Rivas-Gallont, Amb.
Equatorial Guinea	Chester E. Norris Jr., Amb.	Damaso Obiang Ndong, Amb.
Estonia[7]		Ernst Jaakson, Consul General
Ethiopia	Robert G. Houdek, Chargé	Girma Amare, Chargé
Fiji	Leonard Rochwarger, Amb.	Abdul H. Yusuf, Chargé
Finland	Rockwell A. Schnabel, Amb.	Jukka Valtasaari, Amb.
France	Walter J.P. Curley Jr., Amb.	Emmanuel de Margerie, Amb.
Gabon	Warren Clark Jr., Amb.	Jean Robert Odzaga, Amb.
Gambia, The	Herbert E. Horowitz, Amb.	Ousman A. Sallah
Germany, East	Francis J. Meehan, Amb.	Gerhard Herder, Amb.
Germany, West	Vernon A. Walters, Amb.	Juergen Ruhfus, Amb.
Ghana	Stephen R. Lyne, Amb.	Eric K. Otoo, Amb.
Greece	Robert V. Keeley, Amb.	George D. Papaulias, Amb.
Grenada	James F. Cooper, Chargé	Albert O. Xavier, Amb.
Guatemala	James H. Michel, Amb.	Rodolfo Rohrmoser, Amb.
Guinea	Samuel E. Lupo, Amb.	Kekoura Camara, Amb.
Guinea-Bissau	John D. Blacken, Amb.	Alfredo Lopes Cabral, Amb.
Guyana	Theresa A. Tull, Amb.	Cedric H. Grant, Amb.
Haiti	Brunson McKinley, Amb.	Francois Benoit, Amb.
Honduras	Everett E. Briggs, Amb.	Jorge Hernandez-Alcerro, Amb.
Hungary	Mark H. Palmer, Amb.	Vencel Hazi, Amb.
Iceland	L. Nicholas Ruwe, Amb.	Ingvi S. Ingvarsson, Amb.
India	R. Grant Smith, Amb.	P. K. Kaul, Amb.
Indonesia	Paul Wolfowitz, Amb.	Abdul Rachman Ramly, Amb.
Iraq	April C. Glaspie, Amb.	Abdul-Amir Ali Al-Anbari, Amb.
Ireland	Margaret M. Heckler, Amb.	Padraic N. McKernan, Amb.
Israel	Vacancy	Moshe Arad, Amb.
Italy	Peter Secchia, Amb.	Rinaldo Petrignani, Amb.
Jamaica	Michael G. Sotirhos, Amb.	Keith Johnson, Amb.
Japan	Michael H. Armacost, Amb.	Nobuo Matsunaga, Amb.
Jordan	Roscoe S. Suddarth, Amb.	Hussein A. Hammami, Amb.
Kenya	Elinor G. Constable, Amb.	Dennis D. Afande, Amb.
Kiribati	Leonard Rochwarger, Amb.	Vacancy
Korea, South	Donald P. Gregg, Amb.	Tong-Jin Park, Amb.
Kuwait	W. Nathaniel Howell, Amb.	Shaikh S. N. Al-Sabah, Amb.
Laos	Harriet Isom, Amb.	Done Somvorachit, Chargé
Latvia[7]		Anatol Dinbergs, Chargé
Lebanon	John T. McCarthy, Amb.	Adballah Bouhabib, Amb.
Lesotho	Robert M. Smalley, Amb.	W. T. van Tonder, Amb.
Liberia	James K. Bishop, Amb.	Eugenia A. Wordsworth-Stevenson, Amb.

Countries	Envoys from United States	Envoys to United States
Lithuania[7]		Stasys Lozoraitis Jr., Chargé
Luxembourg	Vacancy	Andre Philippe, Amb.
Madagascar	Patricia G. Lynch, Amb.	Leon M. Rajaobelina, Amb.
Malawi	George A. Trail 3d, Amb.	Robert Mbaya, Amb.
Malaysia	John C. Monjo, Amb.	Albert S. Talalla, Amb.
Mali	Robert M. Pringle, Amb.	Nouhoum Samassekou, Amb.
Malta	Peter R. Sommer, Amb.	Salv Stellini, Amb.
Mauritania	William H. Twaddell, Amb.	Abdellah Ould Daddah, Amb.
Mauritius	Robert D. Palmer, Amb.	Chitmansing Jesseramsing, Amb.
Mexico	John Negroponte, Amb.	Gustavo Petricioli Iturbide, Amb.
Morocco	John Hawes, Chargé.	Ali Bengelloun, Amb.
Mozambique	Melissa F. Wells, Amb.	Valeriano Ferrao, Amb.
Nauru	Melvin F. Sembler, Amb.	T.W. Star, Amb.
Nepal	Milton Frank, Amb.	Mohan Man Sainju, Amb.
Netherlands	John S. Shad, Amb.	Richard H. Fein, Amb.
New Zealand	Paul M. Cleveland, Amb.	Harold H. Francis, Amb.
Nicaragua	John P. Leonard, Chargé	Leonor de Huper, Chargé
Niger	Carl C. Cundiff, Amb.	Moumouni A. Djermakoye, Amb.
Nigeria	Princeton N. Lyman, Amb.	Hamzat Ahmadu, Amb.
Norway	Robert D. Stuart, Amb.	Kjeld Vibe, Amb.
Oman	C. Cranwell Montgomery, Amb.	Awadh Bader Al-Shanfari, Amb.
Pakistan	Robert B. Oakley, Amb.	Jamsheed K. A. Marker, Amb.
Panama	Arthur H. Davis Amb.	Juan B. Sosa, Amb.
Papua New Guinea	Everett E. Bierman, Amb.	Renagi Lohia, Amb.
Paraguay	Timothy L. Towell, Amb.	Marcos Martinez Mendieta, Amb.
Peru	Alexander F. Watson, Amb.	Cesar G. Atala, Amb.
Philippines	Nicholas Platt, Amb.	Emmanuel Pelaez, Amb.
Poland	John R. Davis Jr., Chargé	Jan Kinast, Amb.
Portugal	Edward M. Rowell, Amb.	Joao Eduardo M. Periera Bastos, Amb.
Qatar	Joseph Ghougassian, Amb.	Ahmed A.Z. Al-Mahmoud, Amb.
Romania	Roger Kirk, Amb.	Ion Stoichici, Amb.
Rwanda	Leonard H.O. Spearman Sr., Amb.	Aloys Uwimana, Amb.
St. Christopher & Nevis	John Clark, Chargé	Erstein Edwards, Chargé
St. Lucia	John Clark, Chargé	Joseph E. Edmunds, Amb.
St. Vincent and The Grenadines	John Clark, Chargé	Vacancy
Samoa, Western	Paul Cleveland, Amb.	Maiava I. Toma, Amb.
Sao Tome and Principe	Warren Clark Jr., Amb.	Joaquim R. Branco, Amb.
Saudi Arabia	Walter L. Cutler, Amb.	Bandar Bin Sultan, Amb.
Senegal	George E. Moose, Amb.	Ibra Deguene Ka, Amb.
Seychelles	James Moran, Amb.	Marc Marengo, Chargé
Sierra Leone	Cynthia S. Perry, Amb.	George Carew, Amb.
Singapore	Daryl Arnold, Amb.	Tommy T. B. Koh, Amb.
Solomon Islands	Everett Bierman, Amb.	Francis Saemala, Amb.
Somalia	T. Frank Crigler, Amb.	Abdullahi Ahmed Addou, Amb.
South Africa	William L. Swing, Amb.	Piet G.J. Koornhof, Amb.
Spain	Joseph Zappala, Amb.	Julian Santamaria, Amb.
Sri Lanka	James Spain, Amb.	W. Susanta de Alwis, Amb.
Sudan	G. Norman Anderson, Amb.	Hassan Elamin El-Bashir, Amb.
Suriname	Richard Howland, Amb.	Arnolt T. Halfhide, Amb.
Swaziland	Mary A. Ryan, Amb.	Absalom V. Mamba, Amb.
Sweden	Gregory J. Newell, Amb.	Wilhelm Wachtmeister, Amb.
Switzerland	Philip D. Winn, Amb.	Edouard Brunner, Amb.
Syria	Edward P. Djerejian, Amb.	Bushra Kanafani, Amb.
Tanzania	Donald K. Petterson, Amb.	Asterius M. Hyera, Amb.
Thailand	Daniel A. O' Donohue, Amb.	Vitthya Vejjajiva, Amb.
Togo	Rush W. Taylor Jr., Amb.	Ellom-Kodjo Schuppius, Amb.
Tonga	Leonard Rochwarger, Amb.	Siaosi Taimani Aho, Amb.
Trinidad and Tobago	Charles A. Gargano, Amb.	Angus A. Khan, Amb.
Tunisia	Robert H. Pelletreau, Jr., Amb.	Abdelaziz Hamzaoui, Amb.
Turkey	Robert Strausz-Hupe, Amb.	Sukru Elekdag, Amb.
Tuvalu	Leonard Rochwarger, Amb.	Vacancy
Uganda	John A. Burroughs Jr., Amb.	Stephen K. Katenta-Apuli, Amb.
USSR	John F. Matlock, Jr., Amb.	Yuri Dubinin, Amb.
United Arab Emirates	David L. Mack, Amb.	A.S. Al-Mokarrab, Amb.
United Kingdom	Henry E. Catto, Amb.	Antony Acland, Amb.
Uruguay	Malcolm R. Wilkey, Amb.	Hector Luisi, Amb.
Vatican	Frank Shakespeare, Amb.	Pio Laghi, Pro-Nuncio
Venezuela	Otto J. Reich, Amb.	Valentin Hernandez, Amb.
Yemen Arab Rep.	Charles F. Dunbar, Amb.	Mohsin A. Alaini, Amb.
Yugoslavia	John D. Scanlon, Amb.	Zivorad Kovacevic, Amb.
Zaire	William C. Harrop, Amb.	Mushobekwa Kalimba wa Katana, Amb.
Zambia	Jeffrey Davidow, Amb.	Lazarous Kapambwe, Chargé
Zimbabwe	James W. Rawlings, Amb.	Jonathan Wutawunashe, Chargé

Ambassadors at Large: Richard T. Kennedy, Jewell S. Lafontant.

Special Missions

U.S. Mission to North Atlantic Treaty Organization, Brussels—Alton G. Keel
U.S. Mission to the European Communities, Brussels—Alfred H. Kingon, Amb.
U.S. Mission to the United Nations, New York—Thomas P. Pickering, Amb.
U.S. Mission to the European Office of the UN, Geneva—Joseph C. Petrone
U.S. Mission to the Organization for Economic Cooperation and Development, Paris—Dennis Lamb, Amb.
U.S. Mission to the Organization of American States, Washington—Richard T. McCormick, Amb.
U.S. Mission to International Civic Aviation Organization, Montreal—Edmond P. Stohr

(1) Relations severed in 1939. (2) Post closed in 1975. (3) U.S. embassy closed in 1975. (4) U.S. severed relations in 1978; unofficial relations are maintained. (5) Relations severed in 1961; limited ties restored in 1977. (6) U.S. severed relations on Apr. 7, 1980. (7) U.S. does not officially recognize 1940 annexation by USSR. (8) Embassy closed, May 2, 1980. U.S. closed the Libyan mission, May 6, 1981.

NATIONAL DEFENSE

Data as of July, 1989

Chairman, Joint Chiefs of Staff
Gen. Colin L. Powell

The Joint Chiefs of Staff consists of the Chairman and Vice Chairman of the Joint Chiefs of Staff; the Chief of Staff, U.S. Army; the Chief of Naval Operations; the Chief of Staff, U.S. Air Force; and the Commandant of the Marine Corps.

Army

Chief of Staff—Carl E. Vuono
Generals

	Date of Rank
Galvin, John R.	Feb. 25, 1985
Lindsay, James J.	Oct. 10, 1986
Menetrey, Louis C.	June 24, 1987
Powell, Colin L.	Jan. 17, 1989
RisCassi, Robert W.	Apr. 4, 1989
Saint, Crosbie E.	June 24, 1988
Thurman, Maxwell R.	June 23, 1983
Vuono, Carl E.	July 1, 1986
Wagner, Louis C.	Apr. 13, 1987

Air Force

Chief of Staff—Larry D. Welch
Generals

	Date of Rank
Cassidy, Duane H.	Nov. 8, 1985
Chain, John T., Jr.	July 1, 1985
Dugan, Michael J.	—
Hansen, Alfred G.	Aug. 1, 1987
Hatch, Monroe W. Jr.	Jan. 29, 1987
Herres, Robert T.	Aug. 1, 1984
McPeak, Merrill, A.	—
Piotrowski, John L.	Aug. 1, 1985
Randolph, Bernard P.	Aug. 1, 1987
Richards, Thomas C.	Dec. 1, 1986
Russ, Robert D.	May 22, 1985
Shaud, John A.	June 6, 1988
Welch, Larry D.	Aug. 1, 1984

Navy

Chief of Naval Operations
Admiral Carlisle A.H. Trost (submariner)
Admirals

	Date of Rank
Busey, James B. (aviator)	Oct. 17, 1985
Carter, Powell F., Jr. (submariner)	Oct. 1, 1987
DeMars, Bruce (submariner)	Nov. 1, 1988
Edney, Leon A. (aviator)	Oct. 1, 1988
Hardisty, Huntington (aviator)	Mar. 11, 1987
Hogg, James R. (surface warfare)	Dec. 1, 1988
Jeremiah, David E. (surface warfare)	Oct. 1, 1987
Kelso, Frank B., II (submariner)	June 30, 1986
Trost, Carlisle A.H. (submariner)	Oct. 4, 1985

Marine Corps

Corps Commandant, with rank of General
Alfred M. Gray .... July 1, 1987

Chief of Staff, with rank of Lt. Gen.
Joseph J. Went .... July 1, 1988

Coast Guard

Commandant, with rank of Admiral
P. A. Yost, Jr. .... May 30, 1986

Vice Commandant, with rank of Vice Admiral
Clyde T. Lusk .... June 22, 1988

Unified Defense Commands Commanders-in-Chief

U.S. European Command, Brussels — Gen. John R. Galvin (USA) (concurrently NATO Supreme Allied Commander).

U.S. Southern Command, Quarry Heights, Panama Canal Zone — Gen. Maxwell R. Thurman (USA).

U.S. Atlantic Command, Norfolk, Virginia — Adm. Lee Baggett, Jr., (USN) (concurrently NATO Supreme Allied Commander, Atlantic).

U.S. Pacific Command, Hawaii — Admiral Ronald J. Hays (USN)

U.S. Space Command, Gen. John L. Piotrowski (USAF)

*Strategic Air Command, Omaha — General John T. Chain (USAF)

*US Forces Command — vacant

*U.S. Transportation Command, General Duane H. Cassidy (USAF)

U.S. Special Operations Command, MacDill AFB, Fla. — General James J. Lindsay (USA)

U.S. Central Command, Gen. George B. Crist (USMC)

*A Specified Command.

North Atlantic Treaty Organization International Commands

Supreme Allied Commander, Europe (SACEUR) — Gen. John R. Galvin (USA)

Deputy Supreme Allied Commander Europe (DSACEUR) — Gen. Sir John Akehurst (UKA)

Deputy Supreme Allied Commander Europe (DSACEUR) — Gen. Eberhard Eimler (GEAF)

Commander-in-Chief Allied Forces Northern Europe — Gen. Sir Geoffrey Howlett, KBE, MC (UKA)

Commander-in-Chief Allied Forces Central Europe — Gen. Hans-Henning von Sandrart (GEA)

Commander-in-Chief Allied Forces Southern Europe — Adm. James Buchanan Busey (USN)

Commander-in-Chief United Kingdom Air Forces — Air Chief Marshal Sir Patrick Hine (UKAF)

Chairman, NATO Military Committee — Gen. Wolfgang Altenburg (GEA)

Principal U.S. Military Training Centers
Army

Name, P.O. address	Zip	Nearest city	Name, P.O. address	Zip	Nearest city
Aberdeen Proving Ground, MD	21005	Aberdeen	Fort Knox, KY	40121	Louisville
Carlisle Barracks, PA	17013	Carlisle	Fort Leavenworth, KS	66027	Leavenworth
Fort Belvoir, VA	22060	Alexandria	Fort Lee, VA	23801	Petersburg
Fort Benning, GA	31905	Columbus	Fort McClellan, AL	36205	Anniston
Fort Bliss, TX	79916	El Paso	Fort Monmouth, NJ	07703	Red Bank
Fort Bragg, NC	28307	Fayetteville	Fort Rucker, AL	36362	Dothan
Fort Devens, MA	01433	Ayer	Fort Sill, OK	73503	Lawton
Fort Dix, NJ	08640	Trenton	Fort Leonard Wood, MO	65473	Rolla
Fort Eustis, VA	23604	Newport News	Joint Readiness, Ft. Chaffee, AR	72905	Fort Smith
Fort Gordon, GA	30905	Augusta	National Training Center	92311	Barstow, CA
Fort Benjamin Harrison, IN	46216	Indianapolis	Redstone Arsenal, AL	35809	Huntsville
Fort Sam Houston, TX	78234	San Antonio	The Judge Advocate		Charlottes-
Fort Huachuca, AZ	85613	Sierra Vista	General School, VA	22901	ville
Fort Jackson, SC	29207	Columbia	U.S. Military Acad., NY	10996	Wet Point

Navy Recruit Training Centers

	Zip			Zip	
Great Lakes, IL	60088	North Chicago	Orlando, FL	32813	Orlando
San Diego, CA	92133	San Diego			

Major Marine Corps Facilities

Name, P.O. address	Zip	Nearest city	Name, P.O. address	Zip	Nearest city
MCB Camp Lejeune, NC	28542	Jacksonville	MCAS Iwakuni, Japan.	FPO Seattle	Iwakuni
MCB Camp Pendleton, CA	92055	Oceanside		98764	
MCB Camp Butler, Okinawa	FPO Seattle	Futenma,	MCAS Kaneohe Bay,		
	98773	Okinawa	Oahu, HI.	San Francisco	Kailua
MCAGCC Twentynine Palms, CA	92278	Palm Springs		96863	
MCCDC Quantico, VA.	22134	Quantico	MCAS Futenma,		
MCRD Parris Island, SC.	29905	Beaufort	Okinawa FPO Seattle.	98772	Futenma
MCRD San Diego, CA.	92140	San Diego	MCAS Beaufort, SC	29904	Beaufort
MCAS Cherry Point, NC.	28533	Havelock	MCAS Yuma, AZ.	85369	Yuma
MCAS El Toro (Santa Ana), CA .	92709	Santa Ana	MCMWTC Bridgeport, CA. . . .	93517	Bridgeport
MCAS Tustin, CA.	92780	Santa Ana	MCLB Albany, GA	31704	Albany
MCAS New River, NC.	28545	Jacksonville	MCLB Barstow, CA.	92311	Barstow

MCB = Marine Corps Base. MCCDC = Marine Corps Combat Development Command. MCAS = Marine Corps Air Station. Helo = Helicopter. MCAGCC = Marine Corps Air-Ground Combat Center. MCMWTC = Marine Corps Mountain Warfare Training Center. MCLB = Marine Corps Logistics Base.

Air Force*

Chanute AFB, IL	61868	Rantoul	Mather AFB, CA	95655	Sacramento
Columbus AFB, MS	39701	Columbus	Maxwell AFB, AL**.	36112	Montgomery
Goodfellow AFB, TX	76903	San Angelo	Randolph AFB, TX	78150	San Antonio
Gunter AFS, AL**	36114	Montgomery	Reese AFB, TX	79489	Lubbock
Keesler AFB, MS	39534	Biloxi	Sheppard AFB, TX	76311	Wichita Falls
Lackland AFB, TX	78236	San Antonio	Vance AFB, OK.	73702	Enid
Laughlin AFB, TX.	78843	Del Rio	Williams AFB, AZ.	85224	Phoenix
Lowry AFB, CO.	80230	Denver	Wright Patterson AFB, OH	45433	Dayton

*Air Training Command Bases. **Air University Bases.

Personal Salutes and Honors

The United States national salute, 21 guns, is also the salute to a national flag. The independence of the United States is commemorated by the salute to the union — one gun for each state — fired at noon on July 4 at all military posts provided with suitable artillery.

A 21-gun salute on arrival and departure, with 4 ruffles and flourishes, is rendered to the President of the United States, to an ex-President and to a President-elect. The national anthem or *Hail to the Chief*, as appropriate, is played for the President, and the national anthem for the others. A 21-gun salute on arrival and departure with 4 ruffles and flourishes, also is rendered to the sovereign or chief of state of a foreign country or a member of a reigning royal family; the national anthem of his or her country is played. The music is considered an inseparable part of the salute and will immediately follow the ruffles and flourishes without pause.

Rank	Salute—guns Arrive—Leave		Ruffles, flour- ishes	Music
Vice President of United States.	19		4	Hail Columbia
Speaker of the House	19		4	March
American or foreign ambassador.	19		4	Nat. anthem of official
Premier or prime minister	19		4	Nat. anthem of official
Secretary of Defense, Army, Navy or Air Force	19	19	4	Honors March
Other Cabinet members, Senate President pro tempore, Governor, or Chief Justice of U.S.	19		4	Honors March
Chairman, Joint Chiefs of Staff.	19	19	4	
Army Chief of Staff, Chief of Naval Operations, Air Force Chief of Staff, Marine Commandant	19	19	4	General's or Admiral's March
General of the Army, General of the Air Force, Fleet Admiral. . . .	19	19	4	
Generals, Admirals	17	17	4	
Assistant Secretaries of Defense, Army, Navy or Air Force	17	17	4	Honors March
Chairman of a Committee of Congress	17		4	Honors March

Other salutes (on arrival only) include 15 guns for American envoys or ministers and foreign envoys or ministers accredited to the United States; 15 guns for a lieutenant general or vice admiral; 13 guns for a major general or rear admiral (upper half); 13 guns for American ministers resident and ministers resident accredited to the U.S.; 11 guns for a brigadier general or rear admiral (lower half); 11 guns for American charges d'affaires and like officials accredited to U.S.; and 11 guns for consuls general accredited to U.S.

Military Units, U.S. Army and Air Force

Army units. Squad. In infantry usually ten men under a staff sergeant. **Platoon.** In infantry 4 squads under a lieutenant. **Company.** Headquarters section and 4 platoons under a captain. (Company in the artillery is a battery; in the cavalry, a troop.) **Battalion.** Hdqts. and 4 or more companies under a lieutenant colonel. (Battalion size unit in the cavalry is a squadron.) **Brigade.** Hdqts. and 3 or more battalions under a colonel. **Division.** Hdqts. and 3 brigades with artillery, combat support, and combat service support units under a major general. **Army Corps.** Two or more divisions with corps troops under a lieutenant general. **Field Army.** Hdqts. and two or more corps with field Army troops under a general.

Air Force Units. Flight. Numerically designated flights are the lowest level unit in the Air Force. They are used primarily where there is a need for small mission elements to be incorporated into an organized unit. **Squadron.** A squadron is the basic unit in the Air Force. It is used to designate the mission units in operational commands. **Group.** The group is a flexible unit composed of two or more squadrons whose functions may be either tactical, support or administrative in nature. **Wing.** An operational wing normally has two or more assigned mission squadrons in an area such as combat, flying training or airlift. **Air Division.** The organization of the air division may be similar to that of the numbered air force, though on a much smaller scale. Functions are usually limited to operations and logistics. **Numbered Air Forces.** Normally an operationally oriented agency, the numbered air force is designed for the control of two or more air divisions or units of comparable strength. It is a flexible organization and may be of any size. Its wings may be assigned to air divisions or directly under the numbered air force. **Major Command.** A major subdivision of the Air Force that is assigned a major segment of the USAF mission.

U.S. Army Insignia and Chevrons

Source: Department of the Army

Grade	Insignia

General of the Armies

General John J. Pershing, the only person to have held this rank, was authorized to prescribe his own insignia, but never wore in excess of four stars. The rank originally was established by Congress for George Washington in 1799, and he was promoted to the rank by joint resolution of Congress, approved by Pres. Ford Oct. 19, 1976.

General of Army... Five silver stars fastened together in a circle and the coat of arms of the United States in gold color metal with shield and crest enameled.

General . . . . Four silver stars
Lieutenant General . . . . Three silver stars
Major General . . . . Two silver stars
Brigadier General . . . . . One silver star
Colonel . . . . Silver eagle
Lieutenant Colonel . . . . Silver oak leaf
Major . . . . Gold oak leaf
Captain . . . . Two silver bars
First Lieutenant . . . . . . One silver bar
Second Lieutenant . . . . . One gold bar

Warrant officers

Grade Four—Silver bar with 4 enamel black squares.
Grade Three—Silver bar with 3 enamel black squares.

Grade Two—Silver bar with 2 enamel black squares.
Grade One—Silver bar with 1 enamel black square.

Non-commissioned Officers

Sergeant Major of the Army (E-9). Same as Command Sergeant Major (below) but with 2 stars. Also wears distinctive red and white shield on lapel.

Command Sergeant Major (E-9). Three chevrons above three arcs with a 5-pointed star with a wreath around the star between the chevrons and arcs.

Sergeant Major (E-9). Three chevrons above three arcs with a five-pointed star between the chevrons and arcs.

First Sergeant (E-8). Three chevrons above three arcs with a lozenge between the chevrons and arcs.

Master Sergeant (E-8). Three chevrons above three arcs.

Platoon Sergeant or Sergeant First Class (E-7). Three chevrons above two arcs.

Staff Sergeant (E-6). Three chevrons above one arc.

Sergeant (E-5). Three chevrons.

Corporal (E-4). Two chevrons.

Specialists

Specialist (E-4). Eagle device only.

Other enlisted

Private First Class (E-3). One chevron above one arc.

Private (E-2). One chevron.

Private (E-1). None.

U.S. Army

Source: Department of the Army

Army Military Personnel on Active Duty[1]

June 30[2]	Total strength	Commissioned officers			Warrant officers		Enlisted personnel		
		Total	Male	Female[3]	Male[4]	Female	Total	Male	Female
1940	267,767	17,563	16,624	939	763	——	249,441	249,441	——
1942	3,074,184	203,137	190,662	12,475	3,285	——	2,867,762	2,867,762	——
1943	6,993,102	557,657	521,435	36,222	21,919	0	6,413,526	6,358,200	55,325
1944	7,992,868	740,077	692,351	47,726	36,893	10	7,215,888	7,144,601	71,287
1945	8,266,373	835,403	772,511	62,892	56,216	44	7,374,710	7,283,930	90,780
1946	1,889,690	257,300	240,643	16,657	9,826	18	1,622,546	1,605,847	16,699
1950	591,487	67,784	63,375	4,409	4,760	22	518,921	512,370	6,551
1955	1,107,606	111,347	106,173	5,174	10,552	48	985,659	977,943	7,716
1960	871,348	91,056	86,832	4,224	10,141	39	770,112	761,833	8,279
1965	967,049	101,812	98,029	3,783	10,285	23	854,929	846,409	8,520
1969	1,509,637	148,836	143,699	5,137	23,734	20	1,327,047	1,316,326	10,721
1970	1,319,735	143,704	138,469	5,235	23,005	13	1,153,013	1,141,537	11,476
1975	781,316	89,756	85,184	4,572	13,214	22	678,324	640,621	37,703
1980 (Sept 30) . . .	772,661	85,339	77,843	7,496	13,265	113	673,944	612,593	61,351
1984 (Sept. 30) . . .	775,594	92,484	82,497	9,987	15,156	243	667,711	601,695	66,616
1985 (Sept. 30) . . .	776,244	94,103	83,563	10,540	15,296	288	666,557	598,639	67,918
1987 (Mar. 30) . . .	770,075	93,973	82,886	11,087	14,923	332	660,847	589,789	71,058
1988 (Mar. 30) . . .	764,247	93,173	81,904	11,269	14,664	363	656,047	584,305	71,742
1989 (Mar. 30) . . .	760,237	91,550	80,113	11,437	14,517	417	653,753	581,106	72,647

(1) Represents strength of the active Army, including Philippine Scouts, retired Regular Army personnel on extended active duty, and National Guard and Reserve personnel on extended active duty; excludes U.S. Military Academy cadets, contract surgeons, and National Guard and Reserve personnel not on extended active duty.
(2) Data for 1940 to 1947 include personnel in the Army Air Forces and its predecessors (Air Service and Air Corps).
(3) Includes: women doctors, dentists, and Medical Service Corps officers for 1946 and subsequent years, women in the Army Nurse Corps for all years, and the Women's Army Corps and Women's Medical Specialists Corps (dieticians, physical therapists, and occupational specialists) for 1943 and subsequent years.
(4) Act of Congress approved April 27, 1926, directed the appointment as warrant officers of field clerks still in active service. Includes flight officers as follows: 1943, 5,700; 1944, 13,615; 1945, 31,117; 1946, 2,580.

The Federal Service Academies

U.S. Military Academy, West Point, N.Y. Founded 1802. Awards B.S. degree and Army commission for a 5-year service obligation. For admissions information, write Admissions Office, USMA, West Point, NY 10996.

U.S. Naval Academy, Annapolis, Md. Founded 1845. Awards B.S. degree and Navy or Marine Corps commission for a 5-year service obligation. For admissions information, write Dean of Admissions, Naval Academy, Annapolis, MD 21402.

U.S. Air Force Academy, Colorado Springs, Colo. Founded 1954. Awards B.S. degree and Air Force commission for a 5-year service obligation. For admissions information, write Registrar, U.S. Air Force Academy, CO 80840.

U.S. Coast Guard Academy, New London, Conn. Founded 1876. Awards B.S. degree and Coast Guard commission for a 5-year service obligation. For admissions information, write Director of Admissions, Coast Guard Academy, New London, CT 06320.

U.S. Merchant Marine Academy, Kings Point, N.Y. Founded 1943. Awards B.S. degree, a license as a deck, engineer, or dual officer, and a U.S. Naval Reserve commission. Service obligations vary according to options taken by the graduate. For admissions information, write Admission Office, U.S. Merchant Marine Academy, Kings Point, NY 11024.

U.S. Navy Insignia

Source: Department of the Navy

Navy

Stripes and corps device are of gold embroidery.

	Stripes
Fleet Admiral	1 two inch with 4 one-half inch.
Admiral	1 two inch with 3 one-half inch.
Vice Admiral.	1 two inch with 2 one-half inch.
Rear Admiral (upper half)	1 two inch with 1 one-half inch.
Rear Admiral (lower half)	1 two inch.
Captain.	4 one-half inch.
Commander	3 one-half inch.
Lieut. Commander . .	2 one-half inch, with 1 one-quarter inch between.
Lieutenant	2 one-half inch.
Lieutenant (j.g.)	1 one-half inch with one-quarter inch above.
Ensign	1 one-half inch.

Warrant Officers—One 1/2" broken with 1/2" intervals of blue as follows:

Warrant Officer W-4—1 break

Warrant Officer W-3—2 breaks, 2" apart
Warrant Officer W-2—3 breaks, 2" apart
The breaks are symmetrically centered on outer face of the sleeve.
Enlisted personnel (non-Commissioned petty officers). . .A rating badge worn on the upper left arm, consisting of a spread eagle, appropriate number of chevrons, and centered specialty mark.

Marine Corps

Marine Corps and Army officer insignia are similar. Marine Corps and Army enlisted insignia, although basically similar, differ in color, design, and fewer Marine Corps subdivisions. The Marine Corps' distinctive cap and collar ornament is a combination of the American eagle, globe, and anchor.

Coast Guard

Coast Guard insignia follow Navy custom, with certain minor changes such as the officer cap insignia. The Coast Guard shield is worn on both sleeves of officers and on the right sleeve of all enlisted personnel.

U.S. Navy Personnel on Active Duty

June 30	Officers	Nurses	Enlisted	Off. Cand.	Total
1940.	13,162	442	144,824	2,569	160,997
1945.	320,293	11,086	2,988,207	61,231	3,380,817
1950.	42,687	1,964	331,860	5,037	381,538
1960.	67,456	2,103	544,040	4,385	617,984
1970.	78,488	2,273	605,899	6,000	692,660
1980.	63,100[1]	—	464,100[2]	—	527,200
1985 (Jan.).	70,291[1]	—	500,810[2]	—	571,101
1988 (Jan.).	72,038[1]	—	510,208[2]	—	582,246
1989 (Jan.).	73,943	—	524,570	—	598,513

(1) Nurses are included. (2) Officer candidates are included.

Marine Corps Personnel On Active Duty

Yr.	Officers	Enl.	Total	Yr.	Officers	Enl.	Total	Yr.	Officers	Enl.	Total
1955 . .	18,417	186,753	205,170	1970 . .	24,941	234,796	259,737	1986 . .	21,099	178,615	199,714
1960 . .	16,203	154,418	170,621	1980 . .	18,198	170,271	188,469	1987 . .	20,047	179,478	199,525
1965 . .	17,258	172,955	190,213	1985 . .	20,175	177,850	198,025	1988 . .	20,142	175,997	196,139

Veteran Population

Source: Dept. of Veterans Affairs

	March 1989
Veterans in civil life, end of month — Total[a,b]	27,227,000
War Veterans — Total	21,137,000
Vietnam Era — Total	8,293,000
And service in Korean Conflict.	604,000
No service in Korean Conflict.	7,690,000
Korean Conflict — Total	4,933,000
And service in WW II.	908,000
No service in WW II	4,025,000
World War II	9,312,000
World War I	111,000
Prior periods of war	(c)
Peacetime Veterans — Total	6,090,000
Post-Vietnam Era	2,784,000
Peacetime service between Korean Conflict and Vietnam Era only	2,963,000
Peacetime Service — other	342,000

NOTE: Detail may not add to total shown due to rounding. (a) The category "War veterans" equals the sum of Vietnam era (no service in Korean conflict), Korean conflict (no service in World War II), World War II and World War I. The data refer only to veterans living in the U.S. and Puerto Rico since data on veterans living elsewhere are not available. (b) The March 1989 figures reflect updated estimates of mortality for the 1980–89 period. These new estimates of mortality are used to improve the accuracy of the veteran population data. As a result, the March 1989 figures are not totally comparable with data from earlier years. (c) The number of living Spanish-American War veterans in March 1989 was 1. The number of Mexican Border period veterans reported on the compensation and pension rolls for March 1989 was 59.

Compensation and Pension Case Payments

Fiscal year	Living veteran cases No.	Deceased veteran cases No.	Total cases No.	Total disbursement Dollars	Fiscal year	Living veteran cases No.	Deceased veteran cases No.	Total cases No.	Total disbursement Dollars
1900. . .	752,510	241,019	993,529	138,462,130	1950. . .	2,368,238	658,123	3,026,361	2,009,462,298
1910. . .	602,622	318,461	921,083	159,974,056	1960. . .	3,008,935	950,802	3,959,737	3,314,761,383
1920. . .	419,627	349,916	769,543	316,418,029	1970. . .	3,127,338	1,487,176	4,614,514	5,113,649,490
1930. . .	542,610	298,223	840,833	418,432,808	1980. . .	3,195,395	1,450,785	4,646,180	11,045,412,000
1940. . .	610,122	239,176	849,298	429,138,465	1988 . . .	2,804,426	920,613	3,725,039	14,711,284,897

USAF and Air Reserve Forces Personnel by Categories

Category	FY '85[2]	FY '86[2]	FY '87[2]	FY '88[2]	FY '89	FY '90
Air Force Military						
Officers	108,400	109,400	109,400	105,538	105,538	102,300
Airmen	488,600	494,700	493,000	465,648	465,645	464,400
Cadets	4,500	4,500	4,400	4,400	4,400	4,400
Total, Air Force Military	601,500	608,200	606,800	575,603	575,600	571,000
Career Reenlistments	36,000	38,900	43,000	40,400	37,100	39,000
Rate	89%	88%	88%	89%	89%	89%
First-Term Reenlistments	25,700	23,500	22,100	23,000	25,300	22,500
Rate	54%	58%	58%	65%	65%	60%
Civilian Personnel						
Direct Hire (including Technicians)	250,400	249,604	250,266	252,188	250,416	249,044
Indirect Hire—Foreign Nationals	13,468	13,644	13,496	13,237	13,340	13,399
Total, Civilian Personnel	263,868	263,248	263,762	265,425	263,756	262,443
Total, Military and Civilian[1]	865,368	871,448	870,562	841,028	839,356	833,543
Technicians (included above as Direct Hire Civilians)						
AFRES Technicians	8,064	8,866	9,178	9,994	10,004	10,124
ANG Technicians	22,671	22,497	23,221	23,530	23,613	23,948
Air Reserve Forces						
Air National Guard, Selected Reserve	109,398	112,592	113,767	115,900	115,200	116,300
Air Force Reserve, Paid	75,214	78,519	79,562	82,400	83,600	84,800
Air Force Reserve, Nonpaid	42,371	47,153	49,941	49,920	31,225	43,900
Total, Ready Reserve	226,983	238,264	243,270	248,220	230,055	245,000
Standby	28,321	25,823	28,325	26,200	26,200	26,200
Total, Air Reserve Forces[3]	255,304	264,087	271,595	274,420	256,255	271,200

Note: Totals may not add due to rounding. (1) President's budget request. (2) FY '84-87 are actual figures; FY '88-89 are estimates; excludes nonchargeable personnel. (3) Excludes Retired Air Force Reserve.

U.S. Air Force Personnel Strength: 1907-1990

Year[2]	Strength	Year	Strength	Year	Strength	Year	Strength
1907	3	1941	152,125	1950	411,277	1987	606,900
1918	195,023	1942	764,415	1960	814,213	1988	575,603
1920	9,050	1943	2,197,114	1970	791,078	1989	570,965
1930	13,531	1944	2,372,292	1980	557,969	1990	571,100[1]
1940	51,165	1945	2,282,259	1986	608,200		

(1) Programmed. (2) Prior to 1947, data are for U.S. Army Air Corps and Air Service of the Signal Corps.

Coast Guard Personnel on Active Duty: 1970-1987

Source: U.S. Dept. of Transportation. *Annual Report of the Secretary of Transportation.*

Year	Total	Officers	Cadets	Enlisted	Year	Total	Officers	Cadets	Enlisted
1970	37,689	5,512	653	31,524	1982	38,248	6,431	902	30,915
1975	36,788	5,630	1,177	29,981	1983	39,708	6,535	811	32,362
1979	38,559	6,340	806	31,413	1984	38,705	6,790	759	31,156
1980	39,381	6,463	877	32,041	1985	38,595	6,775	733	31,087
1981	39,760	6,519	981	32,260	1986	37,284	6,577	754	29,953
					1987	38,576	6,644	859	31,073

Women in the Armed Forces

Women in the Army, Navy, Air Force, Marines, and Coast Guard are all fully integrated with male personnel. Expansion of military women's programs began in the Department of Defense in fiscal year 1973.

Although women are prohibited by law and directives based on law from serving in combat positions, policy changes in the Department of Defense have made possible the assignment of women to almost all other career fields. Career progression for women is now comparable to that for male personnel. Women are routinely assigned to overseas locations formerly closed to female personnel. Women are in command of activities and units that have missions other than administration of women.

Admission of women to the service academies began in the fall of 1976. The academies provide single-track education, allowing only for minor variations in the cadet program based on physiological differences between men and women.

Army — Information: Chief, Office of Public Affairs, Dept. of Army, Wash., DC 20310; (as of Mar. 1989): 84,501 women, 72,647 enlisted women, 11,437 women commissioned officers, 417 women warrant officers.

Army Nurse Corps — Brig. Gen. Clara Adams-Ender,

Chief Army Nurse Corps, Office of the Surgeon General, Dept. of Army, 5111 Leesburg Pike, Falls Church, VA 22041.

Navy — Information: Chief of Information, Dept. of Navy, Wash., DC 20350-1200; 7,335 women officers; 71,516 enlisted women; 433 cadets and midshipwomen, as of 9/30/88.

Navy Nurse Corps — Rear Adm. Mary F. Hall, Dir., Navy Nurse Corps, Dept. of Navy, Wash., DC 20372-2000; 2,205 women officers; 779 men. (As of 3/31/89).

Air Force — Information: Office of Public Affairs, Dept. of the Air Force, Wash., DC 20330; 12,899 women officers; 60,981 enlisted women.

Air Force Nurse Corps — Brig. Gen. Barbara A. Goodwin, Chief, Air Force Nurse Corps, Office of the Surgeon Gen., USAF, Bolling AFB, Wash., DC 20332.

Marine Corps — Information: Commandant of the Marine Corps (Code PA), Headquarters, Marine Corps, Wash., DC 20380-0001; 665 women officers; 8,976 enlisted women.

Coast Guard — Information: Commandant (G-CP), U.S. Coast Guard, 2100 Second St., SW, Wash., DC 20593-0001; 219 women commissioned officers; 8 woman warrant officer; 1,337 enlisted women.

U.S. Military Personnel Strengths—Worldwide

(As of September 30, 1988)

Source: U.S. Department of Defense

U.S. Territories & Special Locations						
Continental U.S.	1,304,547	Netherlands	2,872	**Africa, Near East & South Asia**	
Alaska	22,634	Norway	1,674	Bahrain	153
Hawaii	45,843	Portugal	1,664	British Indian Ocean Terr.	1,001
Guam	8,519	Spain	8,724	Egypt	1,468
Johnston Atoll	136	Turkey	5,034	Saudi Arabia	421
Puerto Rico	3,361	United Kingdom	28,497	Afloat	14,512
Transients	46,890	Afloat	33,199	**Total¹**	**18,373**
Afloat	165,568	**Total¹**	**356,251**	**Other Western Hemisphere**	
Total¹	**1,597,625**	**European Nato**	**322,905**	Bermuda	1,844
Western & Southern Europe		**East Asia & Pacific**		Canada	533
		Australia	753	Cuba (Guantanamo)	2,337
Belgium	3,317	Japan	49,680	Honduras	1,573
W. Germany	249,411	Philippines	16,655	Panama	11,100
Greece	3,284	Rep. of Korea	45,501	Afloat	6,375
Greenland	202	Thailand	110	**Total¹**	**24,496**
Iceland	3,234	Afloat	28,056	**Total Worldwide**	**2,138,213**
Italy	14,829	**Total¹**	**140,967**	Ashore	1,890,503
				Afloat	247,710

(1) Area totals include countries with less than 100 assigned U.S. military members.

Major U.S. Military Forces: 1980-1988

Source: The Congress of the United States, Congressional Budget Office. *An Analysis of the President's Budgetary Proposals for Fiscal Year 1989.* Data from Dept. of Defense.

	1980	1981	1982	1983	1984	1985	1986	1987	1988
Strategic forces:									
Land-based ICBMs	1,054	1,053	1,053	1,042	1,037	1,028	1,013	1,005	1,000
Sea-launched BMs	576	600	592	568	640	648	640	640	674
Strategic bombers	413	410	410	356	328	328	347	389	423
Strategic interceptors	292	279	261	261	266	264	264	252	252
General purpose forces (active):									
Army Divisions	16	16	16	16	16	17	18	18	18
Marine Corps Divisions	3	3	3	3	3	3	3	3	3
Air Force Tactical Aircraft	3,813	3,991	4,133	4,303	4,352	4,406	4,461	4,396	4,470
Navy/Marine Corps Tactical Aircraft	2,013	2,029	1,968	1,929	1,905	1,970	1,974	1,982	1,962
Naval forces:									
Aircraft carriers	13	12	13	13	13	13	13	14	14
Battleships	-	-	-	1	2	2	3	3	3
Nuclear attack submarines	74	82	91	93	94	96	97	98	96
Other warships	180	188	197	191	197	204	204	206	195
Amphibious assaults¹	63	59	59	61	59	60	60	61	62
Airlift and sealift forces:									
C-5 aircraft (PAA)	70	70	70	70	70	70	75	84	102
Other Air Force aircraft (PAA)	820	808	795	782	769	787	789	789	781
Navy and Marine Corps Tactical Support Aircraft (PAA)	88	88	88	88	88	88	88	87	87
Ships (NDRF)	164	173	183	192	202	214	220	221	209

(-) Represents zero.   (1) Excludes reserve forces' amphibious ships.

The Medal of Honor

The Medal of Honor is the highest military award for bravery that can be given to any individual in the United States. The first Army Medals were awarded on March 25, 1863, and the first Navy Medals went to sailors and Marines on April 3, 1863.

The Medal of Honor, established by Joint Resolution of Congress, 12 July 1862 (amended by Act of 9 July 1918 and Act of 25 July 1963) is awarded in the name of Congress to a person who, while a member of the Armed Forces, distinguishes himself conspicuously by gallantry and intrepidity at the risk of his life above and beyond the call of duty while engaged in an action against any enemy of the United States; while engaged in military operations involving conflict with an opposing foreign force; or while serving with friendly foreign forces engaged in an armed conflict against an opposing armed force in which the United States is not a belligerent party. The deed performed must have been one of personal bravery or self-sacrifice so conspicuous as to clearly distinguish the individual above his comrades and must have involved risk of life. Incontestable proof of the performance of service is exacted and each recommendation for award of this decoration is considered on the standard of extraordinary merit.

Prior to World War I, the 2,625 Army Medal of Honor awards up to that time were reviewed to determine which past awards met new stringent criteria. The Army removed 911 names from the list, most of them former members of a volunteer infantry group during the Civil War who had been induced to extend their enlistments when they were promised the Medal.

Since that review Medals of Honor have been awarded in the following numbers:

World War I	123	Korean War	131
World War II	433	Vietnam (to date)	239

Armed Services Senior Enlisted Adviser

The U.S. Army, Navy and Air Force in 1966-67 each created a new position of senior enlisted adviser whose primary job is to represent the point of view of his services' enlisted men and women on matters of welfare, morale, and any problems concerning enlisted personnel. The senior adviser will have direct access to the military chief of his branch of service and policy-making bodies.

The senior enlisted adviser for each Dept. is:

Army—Sgt. Major of the Army Julius W. Gates.

Navy—Master Chief Petty Officer of the Navy Duane R. Bushey.

Air Force—Chief Master Sgt. of the AF James C. Binnicker.

Marines—Sgt. Major of the Marine Corps David W. Sommers.

Estimated U.S. Strategic Nuclear Forces: 1987

Source: The Congress of the U.S., Congressional Budget Office. *Modernizing U.S. Strategic Offensive Forces: The Administration's Program and Alternatives,* May 1983; *Trident II Missiles: Capability, Costs, and Alternatives,* July 1986; and unpublished data.

Represents weapons with intercontinental range. U.S. strategic nuclear forces consist of three parts: Land-based intercontinental ballistic missiles (ICBMs), long-range bombers, and submarine-launched ballistic missiles (SLBMs). Together these three parts are known as the TRIAD.

Launcher	Number	Total warheads	Yield in megatons[1]	Total megatons	Equivalent megatons[2]	Circular error probable[3] (feet)
Total	2,023	11,861	X	3,114	3,447	X
ICBMs, total	1,000	2,289	X	1,046	1,277	X
Minuteman II	450	450	1.2	540	508	2,100
Minuteman III	523	1,569	.17/.335	415	639	600
Peacekeeper	27	270	.335	91	130	300
SLBMs, total	640	5,632	X	410	961	X
Trident (C–4)	192	1,536	0.1	154	331	900
Poseidon (C–3)	256	2,560	.04	102	299	1,500
Poseidon (C–4)	192	1,536	0.1	154	331	900
Bombers, total	383	3,940	X	1,658	1,209	X
B–52 G/H	116	928	NA	557	259	NA
B–52 G/H (cruise missile)	147	1,754	0.2	353	603	300
FB–111[4]	56	224	NA	134	62	NA
B–1B	64	1,024	NA	614	285	NA

Estimated Soviet Union Strategic Nuclear Forces: 1987

Launcher	Number	Total warheads	Yield in megatons[1]	Total megatons	Equivalent megatons[2]	Circular error probable[3] (feet)
Total	2,671	10,388	X	5,844	6,920	X
ICBMs total	1,418	6,440	X	3,687	4,420	X
SS–11	440	440	.95	418	425	3,600
SS–13	60	60	.60	36	43	6,100
SS–17	150	600	.75	450	495	1,200
SS–18	308	3,080	.50	1,540	1,940	700
SS–19	360	2,160	.55	1,188	1,450	1,300
SS–25	100	100	.55	55	67	600
SLBMs, total	928	2,448	X	957	1,242	X
SS–N–6	272	272	.75	204	225	4,200
SS–N–8	292	292	.75	219	241	4,900
SS–N–17	12	12	.5	6	8	4,600
SS–N–18	224	672	.5	336	423	3,000
SS–N–20	80	720	.1	72	155	1,800
SS–N–23	48	480	.25	120	190	2,000
Bombers, total	325	1,500	X	1,200	1,259	X
Bear	100	400	1.0	400	400	NA
Bear–H (cruise missile)	50	400	.25	100	159	NA
Bison	15	60	1.0	60	60	NA
Backfire	160	640	1.0	640	640	NA

X = Not applicable. NA = Not available. (1) A megaton is the yield of a nuclear weapon equivalent to 1 million tons of TNT. (2) A commonly used measure of the urban area destructive power of a nuclear weapon. (3) A measure of the delivery accuracy of a weapon system. It is the radius of a circle around the target at which a missile is aimed within which the warhead has a .5 probability of falling. (4) Medium bombers.

Nuclear Weapon Tests

Source: Natural Resources Defense Council

(Known nuclear tests, 1945-1988)

	United States	Soviet Union	Britain	France	China		United States	Soviet Union	Britain	France	China
1945-49	8	1	0	0	0	1970-79[3]	190	196	5	59	15
1950-59[1]	188	71	21	0	0	1980-88	141	179	11	80	7
1960-69[2]	383	170	4	31	10	Total	910	617	41	170	32

(1) Stockholm International Peace Research Institute and the Swedish National Defense Research Institute report 18 additional Soviet tests conducted between 1949 and 1958. (2) Since 1962, British underground nuclear tests have been conducted jointly with the United States in Nevada. (3) French Ministry of Defense reports 16 additional Soviet tests conducted between 1963 and 1977. India reported one test in 1974.

General and Commander in Chief

	Date of Rank
George Washington	15 June 1775

General of the Armies

John J. Pershing	3 Sept. 1919

General of the Army

	Date of Rank
George C. Marshall	16 Dec. 1944
Douglas MacArthur	18 Dec. 1944
Dwight D. Eisenhower	20 Dec. 1944
Henry H. Arnold	21 Dec. 1944
Omar N. Bradley	20 Sept. 1950

Fleet Admiral

	Date of Rank
Ernest J. King	17 Dec. 1944
Chester W. Nimitz	19 Dec. 1944
William D. Leahy	15 Dec. 1944
William F. Halsey	11 Dec. 1945

Nuclear Arms Treaties and Negotiations: An Historical Overview

Aug. 4, 1963—Nuclear Test Ban Treaty, signed in Moscow by the U.S., USSR, and Great Britain, prohibited testing of nuclear weapons in space, above ground, and under water.

Jan. 1967—Outer Space Treaty banned the introduction of nuclear weapons into space.

1968—Non-proliferation of Nuclear Weapons Treaty, with U.S., USSR, and Great Britain as major signers, limited the spread of military nuclear technology by agreement not to assist nonnuclear nations in getting or making nuclear weapons.

May 26, 1972—SALT I (Strategic Arms Limitations Talks) agreement, in negotiation since Nov. 17, 1969, signed in Moscow by U.S. and USSR. In the area of defensive nuclear weapons, the treaty limited antiballistic missiles to 2 sites of 100 antiballistic missile launchers in each country (amended in 1974 to one site in each country). The treaty also imposed a 5-year freeze on testing and deployment of intercontinental ballistic missiles and submarine-launched ballistic missiles. An interim short-term agreement putting a ceiling on numbers of offensive nuclear weapons was also signed. SALT I was in effect until Oct. 3, 1977.

July 3, 1974—Protocol on antiballistic missile systems and a treaty and protocol on limiting underground testing of nuclear weapons was signed by U.S. and USSR in Moscow.

Nov. 24, 1974—Vladivostok Agreement announced establishing the framework for a more comprehensive agreement on offensive nuclear arms, setting the guidelines of a second SALT treaty.

Sept. 1977—U.S. and USSR agreed to continue to abide by SALT I, despite its expiration date.

June 18, 1979—SALT II, signed in Vienna by the U.S. and USSR, constrained offensive nuclear weapons, limiting each side to 2,400 missile launchers and heavy bombers with

that ceiling to apply until Jan. 1, 1985. The treaty also set a combined total of 1,320 ICBMs and SLBMs with multiple warheads on each side. Although approved by the U.S. Senate Foreign Relations Committee, the treaty never reached the Senate floor because Pres. Jimmy Carter withdrew his support for the treaty following the December 1979 invasion of Afghanistan by Soviet troops.

Nov. 18, 1981—U.S. Pres. Ronald Reagan proposed his controversial "zero option" to cancel deployment of new U.S. intermediate-range missiles in Western Europe in return for Soviet dismantling of comparable forces (600 SS-20, SS-4, and SS-5 missiles already stationed in the European part of its territory).

Nov. 30, 1981—Geneva talks on limiting intermediate nuclear forces based in and around Europe began.

May 9, 1982—U.S. Pres. Ronald Reagan proposed 2-step plan for strategic arms reductions and announced that he had proposed to the USSR that START (Strategic Arms Reduction Talks) begin in June.

May 18, 1982—Soviet Pres. Leonid Brezhnev rejected Reagan's plan as one-sided, but responded positively to the call for arms reduction talks.

June 29, 1982—START (Strategic Arms Reduction Talks) began in Geneva.

1985-1987—Disarmament talks between the U.S. and the USSR began in Geneva, Switzerland on March 12, 1985.

Dec. 8, 1987—I.N.F. (Intermediate-Range Nuclear Forces) Treaty signed in Washington, D.C. by USSR leader Mikhail Gorbachev and U.S. Pres. Ronald Reagan eliminating all medium- and shorter-range nuclear missiles; ratified with conditions by U.S Senate on May 27, 1988.

(For details see Index and Chronology.)

Estimates of Total Dollar Costs of American Wars

(In millions of dollars, except percent)

Source: *The Military Budget and National Economic Priorities,* revised and updated by James L. Clayton, Univ. of Utah.

Item	World War II	Vietnam Conflict	Korean Conflict	World War I	Civil War: Union	Civil War: Confederacy	Spanish American War	American Revolution	War of 1812	Mexican War
Original increment, direct costs:[1]										
Current dollars	360,000	140,600	50,000	32,700	2,300	1,000	270	100-140	89	82
Constant (1967) dollars	816,300	148,800	69,300	100,000	8,500	3,700	1,100	400-680	170	300
Percent 1 year's GNP	188	14	15	43	74	123	2	104	14	4
Service-connected veterans' benefits[2]	87,629	26,175	17,024	19,273	3,290	—	2,111	28	20	26
Interest, pmts. on war loans[3]	[5]	[5]	[5]	11,000	1,200	[5]	60	20	14	10
Current cost to 1986[4]	447,629	166,775	67,024	62,973	6,790	[5]	2,441	170	120	120

(1) Figures are rounded and taken from Claudia D. Goldin, *Encyclopedia of American Economic History.* (2) Total cost to Oct. 1, 1986. For World War I and later wars, benefits are actual service-connected figures from 1986 *Annual Report* of Veterans Administration. For earlier wars, service-connected veterans' benefits are estimated at 40 percent of total, the approximate ratio of service-connected to total benefits since World War I. (3) Total cost to 1986. Interest payments are a very rough approximation based on the percentage of the original costs of each war financed by money creation and debt, the difference between the level of public debt at the beginning of the war and at its end, and the approximate time required to pay off the war debts. (4) Figures are rounded estimates. (5) Unknown.

Armed Forces Personnel—Number and Rate, 1986

Source: U.S. Arms Control and Disarmament Agency, *World Military Expenditures and Arms Transfers 1986*

(Number (1,000), Rate per 1,000 population)

Armed forces refer to active-duty military personnel, including paramilitary forces where those forces resemble regular units in their organization, equipment, training or mission. Reserve forces are not included.

	Number	Rate		Number	Rate		Number	Rate
United States	2,279	9.3	Greece	203	20.3	Nigeria	138	1.3
Argentina	118	3.8	India	1,502	1.9	Pakistan	573	5.5
Brazil	541	3.7	Indonesia	281	1.6	Poland	441	11.7
Bulgaria	191	21.3	Iran	350	7.0	Romania	248	10.8
Chile	127	10.2	Iraq	900	53.0	Soviet Union	4,400	15.5
China	3,530	3.3	Israel	180	42.6	Sudan	59	2.5
Cuba	297	28.9	Italy	531	9.3	Syria	400	35.9
Czechoslovakia	215	13.8	Japan	244	2.0	Taiwan	365	18.5
Egypt	450	8.7	Korea, Dem. People's Rep. of			Thailand	275	5.1
El Salvador	49	9.3		838	39.1	Turkey	879	16.6
France	559	10.1	Korea, Rep. of	604	14.3	United Kingdom	328	5.8
German Dem. Rep.	241	14.5	Nicaragua	80	24.1	Vietnam	1,300	20.4
Germany, Fed. Rep.	495	8.1						

Casualties in Principal Wars of the U.S.

Data on Revolutionary War casualties is from **The Toll of Independence**, Howard H. Peckham, ed., U. of Chicago Press, 1974. Data prior to World War I are based on incomplete records in many cases. Casualty data are confined to dead and wounded personnel and therefore exclude personnel captured or missing in action who were subsequently returned to military control. Dash (—) indicates information is not available.

Wars	Branch of service	Number serving	Casualties — Battle deaths	Other deaths	Wounds not mortal[a]	Total
Revolutionary War	Total	—	6,824	18,500	8,445	33,769
1775-1783	Army	184,000	5,992	—	7,988	13,980
	Navy &	to	—	—	—	—
	Marines	250,000	832	—	457	1,289
War of 1812	Total	³286,730	2,260	—	4,505	6,765
1812-1815	Army	—	1,950	—	4,000	5,950
	Navy	—	265	—	439	704
	Marines	—	45	—	66	111
Mexican War	Total	³78,718	1,733	11,550	4,152	17,435
1846-1848	Army	—	1,721	11,500	4,102	17,373
	Navy	—	1	—	3	4
	Marines	—	11	—	47	58
Civil War	Total	³2,213,363	140,414	224,097	281,881	646,392
(Union forces only)	Army	2,128,948	138,154	221,374	280,040	639,568
1861-1865	Navy	—	2,112	2,411	1,710	6,233
	Marines	84,415	148	312	131	591
Confederate forces	Total	—	74,524	59,297	—	133,821
(estimate)[1]	Army	600,000	—	—	—	—
1863-1866	Navy	to	—	—	—	—
	Marines	1,500,000	—	—	—	—
Spanish-American	Total	306,760	385	2,061	1,662	4,108
War	Army[4]	280,564	369	2,061	1,594	4,024
1898	Navy	22,875	10	0	47	57
	Marines	3,321	6	0	21	27
World War I	Total	4,743,826	53,513	63,195	204,002	320,710
April 6, 1917-	Army[5]	4,057,101	50,510	55,868	193,663	300,041
Nov. 11, 1918	Navy	599,051	431	6,856	819	8,106
	Marines	78,839	2,461	390	9,520	12,371
	Coast Gd.	8,835	111	81	—	192
World War II	Total	16,353,659	292,131	115,185	670,846	1,078,162
Dec. 7, 1941-	Army[6]	11,260,000	234,874	83,400	565,861	884,135
Dec. 31, 1946[2]	Navy[7]	4,183,466	36,950	25,664	37,778	100,392
	Marines	669,100	19,733	4,778	67,207	91,718
	Coast Gd.	241,093	574	1,343	—	1,917
Korean War	Total	5,764,143	33,629	20,617	103,284	157,530
June 25, 1950-	Army	2,834,000	27,704	9,429	77,596	114,729
July 27, 1953[3]	Navy	1,177,000	458	4,043	1,576	6,077
	Marines	424,000	4,267	1,261	23,744	29,272
	Air Force	1,285,000	1,200	5,884	368	7,452
	Coast Gd.	44,143	—	—	—	—
Vietnam (preliminary)[10]	Total	8,744,000	47,356	10,795	153,303	211,324
Aug. 4, 1964-	Army	4,368,000	30,904	7,274	96,802	134,972
Jan. 27, 1973	Navy	1,842,000	1,626	923	4,178	6,697
	Marines	794,000	13,082	1,754	51,392	66,213
	Air Force	1,740,000	1,739	842	931	3,435
	Coast Gd.	—	5	2	—	7

(1) Authoritative statistics for the Confederate Forces are not available. An estimated 26,000-31,000 Confederate personnel died in Union prisons.

(2) Data are for the period Dec. 1, 1941 through Dec. 31, 1946 when hostilities were officially terminated by Presidential Proclamation, but few battle deaths or wounds not mortal were incurred after the Japanese acceptance of Allied peace terms on Aug. 14, 1945. Numbers serving from Dec. 1, 1941-Aug. 31, 1945 were: Total—14,903,213; Army—10,420,000; Navy—3,883,520; and Marine Corps—599,693.

(3) Tentative final data based upon information available as of Sept. 30, 1954, at which time 24 persons were still carried as missing in action.

(4) Number serving covers the period April 21-Aug. 13, 1898, while dead and wounded data are for the period May 1-Aug. 31, 1898. Active hostilities ceased on Aug. 13, 1898, but ratifications of the treaty of peace were not exchanged between the United States and Spain until April 11, 1899.

(5) Includes Air Service Battle deaths and wounds not mortal include casualties suffered by American forces in Northern Russia to Aug. 25, 1919 and in Siberia to April 1, 1920. Other deaths covered the period April 1, 1917-Dec. 31, 1918.

(6) Includes Army Air Forces.

(7) Battle deaths and wounds not mortal include casualties incurred in Oct. 1941 due to hostile action.

(8) Marine Corps data for World War II, the Spanish-American War and prior wars represent the number of individuals wounded, whereas all other data in this column represent the total number (incidence) of wounds.

(9) As reported by the Commissioner of Pensions in his Annual Report for Fiscal Year 1903.

(10) Number serving covers the period Aug. 4 1964-Jan. 27, 1973 (date of ceasefire). Number of casualties incurred in connection with the conflict in Vietnam from Jan. 1, 1961-Sept. 30, 1977. Includes casualties incurred in Mayaguez Incident. Wounds not exclude 150,375 persons not requiring hospital care.

POSTAL INFORMATION

U.S. Postal Service

The Postal Reorganization Act, creating a government-owned postal service under the executive branch and replacing the old Post Office Department, was signed into law by President Nixon on Aug. 12, 1970. The service officially came into being on July 1, 1971.

The new U.S. Postal Service is governed by an 11-person Board of Governors. Nine members are appointed to 9-year terms by the president with Senate approval. These 9, in turn, choose a postmaster general, who is no longer a member of the president's cabinet. The board and the new postmaster general choose the 11th member, who serves as deputy postmaster general. An independent Postal Rate Commission of 5 members, appointed by the president, recommends postal rates to the governors for their approval.

As of July 28, 1989, there were 29,083 post offices throughout the U.S. and possessions.

U.S. Domestic Rates

In effect from April 3, 1988.

Domestic includes the U.S., territories and possessions, APO and FPO.

First Class

Letters written, and matter sealed against inspection, 25¢ for 1st oz. or fraction, 20¢ for each additional oz. or fraction. U.S. Postal cards; single 15¢; double 30¢; private postcards, same.

First class includes written matter, namely letters, postal cards, postcards (private mailing cards) and all other matter wholly or partly in writing, whether sealed or unsealed, except manuscripts for books, periodical articles and music, manuscript copy accompanying proofsheets or corrected proofsheets of the same and the writing authorized by law on matter of other classes. Also matter sealed or closed against inspection, bills and statements of accounts.

Express Mail

Express Mail Service is available for any mailable article up to 70 pounds, and guarantees delivery between major U.S. cities or your money back. Articles received by the acceptance time authorized by the postmaster at a postal facility offering Express Mail will be delivered by 3 p.m. the next day to some locations or will be delivered by noon the next day to other destinations. Or, if you prefer, your shipment can be picked up as early as 10 a.m. the next business day. Second day service is available to locations not on the Next Day Delivery Network. Rates include insurance, Shipment Receipt, and Record of Delivery at the destination post office.

Consult Postmaster for other Express Mail Services and rates. (The Postal Service will refund, upon application to originating office, the postage for any Express Mail shipment not meeting the service standard except for those delayed by strike or work stoppage, delay or cancellation of flights, or governmental action beyond the control of the Postal Service.)

Third Class

Third class (limit up to but not including 16 ounces): Mailable matter not in 1st and 2d classes.

Single mailing: Publications, small parcels, printed matter, booklets and catalogs, 25¢ the first ounce, 45¢ for over 1 to 2 ozs., 65¢ for over 2 to 3 ozs., 85¢ for over 3 to 4 ozs., $1.00 for over 4 to 6 ozs., $1.10 for over 6 to 8 ozs., $1.20 for over 8 to 10 ozs., $1.30 for over 10 to 12 ozs., $1.40 for over 12 to 14 ozs., $1.50 for over 14 but less than 16 ozs.

Bulk mailing: At least 200 pieces or 50 pounds of such items as solicitations, newsletters, advertising materials, books and cassettes, each item of which individually weighs less than one pound. Minimum rate per piece: Basic presort, $0.167; Basic presort ZIP+4, $0.162; 5-Digit presort, $0.132; 5-Digit presort ZIP+4, $0.127; ZIP+4 Barcoded, $0.122; Carrier route presort, $0.101. For pieces weighing more than 3.3667 ounces, the following rates apply: Basic presort, 48¢ per pound + 6.6¢ per piece; 5-Digit presort, 48¢ per pound + 3.1¢ per piece; Carrier route presort, 48¢ per pound.

Separate rates for some nonprofit organizations. Bulk mailing fee, $60 per calendar year. Apply to postmaster for permit. One-time fee for permit imprint, $60.

Parcel Post—Fourth Class

Fourth class or parcel post (16 ounces and over): merchandise, printed matter, etc., may be sealed, subject to inspection.

Priority Mail

First class mail of more than 11 ounces can be sent "Priority Mail" service. The most expeditious handling and transportation available will be used for fastest delivery.

On parcels weighing less than 15 lbs. and measuring more than 84 inches, but not more than 108 inches in length and girth combined, the minimum postal charge shall be the zone charge applicable to a 15-pound parcel.

Forwarding Addresses

The mailer, in order to obtain a forwarding address, must endorse the envelope or cover "Address Correction Requested." The destination post office then will determine whether a forwarding address has been left on file and provide it for a fee of 30¢.

Priority Mail

Packages weighing up to 70 pounds and not exceeding 108 inches in length and girth combined, including written and other material of the first class, whether sealed or unsealed, fractions of a pound being charged as a full pound.

Rates according to zone apply between the U.S. and Puerto Rico and Virgin Islands.

Parcels weighing less than 15 pounds, measuring over 84 inches but not exceeding 108 inches in length and girth combined are chargeable with a minimum rate equal to that for a 15 pound parcel for the zone to which addressed.

Zones	To 2	3	4	5	Zones	To 2	3	4	5
1, 2, 3, ...	$2.40	$2.74	$3.18	$3.61	6	$2.40	$3.74	$4.53	$5.27
4	2.40	3.16	3.75	4.32	7	2.40	3.96	4.92	5.81
5	2.40	3.45	4.13	4.86	8	2.40	4.32	5.33	6.37

*Consult postmaster for parcels over 5 lbs.

Special Handling

Third and fourth class parcels will be handled and delivered as expeditiously as practicable (but not special delivery) upon payment, in addition to the regular postage: up to 10 lbs., $1.55; over 10 lbs., $2.25. Such parcels must be endorsed, Special Handling.

Special Delivery

First class mail up to 2 lbs. $5.35, over 2 lbs. and up to 10 lbs., $5.75; over 10 lbs. $7.25. All other classes up to 2 lbs. $5.65, over 2 and up to 10 lbs., $6.50, over 10 lbs. $8.10.

Bound Printed Matter Rates
(Single Piece Zone Rate)

Weight				Zones				
lbs.	Local	1&2	3	4	5	6	7	8
1.5	$0.67	$0.92	$0.96	$1.04	$1.16	$1.28	$1.43	$1.56
2	0.69	0.96	1.02	1.12	1.28	1.44	1.64	1.81
2.5	0.71	0.99	1.07	1.20	1.39	1.60	1.85	2.06
3	0.73	1.03	1.12	1.27	1.51	1.76	2.06	2.31
3.5	0.75	1.07	1.17	1.35	1.63	1.91	2.26	2.56
4	0.77	1.10	1.22	1.43	1.74	2.07	2.47	2.81
4.5	0.79	1.14	1.27	1.50	1.86	2.23	2.68	3.06
5	0.81	1.18	1.33	1.58	1.98	2.39	2.89	3.31
6	0.85	1.25	1.43	1.73	2.21	2.70	3.30	3.80
7	0.89	1.32	1.53	1.89	2.44	3.02	3.72	4.30
8	0.93	1.39	1.63	2.04	2.67	3.33	4.13	4.80
9	0.97	1.47	1.74	2.20	2.91	3.65	4.55	5.30
10	1.01	1.54	1.84	2.35	3.14	3.96	4.96	5.80

(Bound printed matter must weigh at least 1 pound and not more than 10 pounds. Bound printed matter includes catalogs, directories and books not eligible for special fourth-class rates.)

Domestic Mail Special Services

Registry — Only matter prepaid with postage at First-class postage rates may be registered. Stamps or meter stamps must be attached. The face of the article must be at least 5″ long, 3½″ high. The mailer is required to declare the value of mail presented for registration.

Registered Mail

	Insured	Uninsured
$0.00 to $100	$4.50	$4.40
$100.01 to $500 . . .	4.85	4.70
$500.01 to $1,000 . . .	5.25	5.05
$1,000.01 to $2,000 . .	5.65	5.35
$2,000.01 to $3,000 . .	6.05	5.70
$3,000.01 to $4,000 . .	6.45	6.00
$4,000.01 to $5,000 . .	6.85	6.35
$5,000.01 to $6,000 . .	7.25	6.65
$6,000.01 to $7,000 . .	7.65	7.00
$7,000.01 to $8,000 . .	8.10	7.30
$8,000.01 to $9,000 . .	8.55	7.65
$9,000.01 to $10,000 . .	9.00	7.95

Consult postmaster for registry rates above $10,000.

C.O.D.: Unregistered — is applicable to first-, third-, fourth-class, and express mail matter. Such mail must be based on bona fide orders or be in conformity with agreements between senders and addressees. **Registered** — for details consult postmaster.

Insurance — is applicable to third and fourth class matter. Matter for sale addressed to prospective purchasers who have not ordered it or authorized its sending will not be insured.

Insured Mail

$0.01 to $50	$0.70
50.01 to 100	1.50
100.01 to 150	1.90
150.01 to 200	2.20
200.01 to 300	3.15
300.01 to 400	4.30
400.01 to 500	5.00

Liability for insured mail is limited to $500.

Certified mail — service is available for any matter having no intrinsic value on which 1st class or air mail postage is paid. Receipt is furnished at time of mailing and evidence of delivery obtained. The fee is 85¢ in addition to postage. Return receipt, restricted delivery, and special delivery are available upon payment of additional fees. No indemnity.

Special Fourth Class Rate
(limit 70 lbs.)

First pound or fraction, 90¢ (65¢ if 500 pieces or more of special rate matter are presorted to 5 digit ZIP code or 83¢ if 500 pieces or more are presorted to Bulk Mail Cntrs.); each additional pound or fraction through 7 pounds, 35¢; each additional pound, 20¢. Only the following specific articles: Books of at least 8 printed pages consisting wholly of reading matter or scholarly bibliography, or reading matter with incidental blank spaces for notations and containing no advertising matter other than incidental announcements of books; 16-millimeter or narrower width films in final form and catalogs of such films of 24 pages or more (at least 22 of which are printed) except films and film catalogs sent to or from commercial theaters; printed music in bound or sheet form; printed objective test materials; sound recordings, playscripts and manuscripts for books, periodicals, and music; printed educational reference charts; loose-leaf pages and binders thereof consisting of medical information for distribution to doctors, hospitals, medical schools, and medical students; computer-readable media containing prerecorded information and guides for use with such media. Package must be marked "Special 4th Class Rate" stating item contained.

Library Rate (limit 70 lbs.)

First pound 64¢, each additional pound through 7

Parcel Post Rate Schedule
(Inter BMC/ASF Zip Codes Only, Machinable Parcels, No Discount, No Surcharge)

Weight up to but not exceeding—(pounds)	Zones						
	1 and 2	3	4	5	6	7	8
2.	$1.69	$1.81	$1.97	$2.24	$2.35	$2.35	$2.35
3.	1.78	1.95	2.20	2.59	2.98	3.42	4.25
4.	1.86	2.10	2.42	2.94	3.46	4.05	5.25
5.	1.95	2.24	2.65	3.29	3.94	4.67	6.25
6.	2.04	2.39	2.87	3.64	4.43	5.30	7.34
7.	2.12	2.53	3.10	4.00	4.91	5.92	8.30
8.	2.21	2.68	3.32	4.35	5.39	6.55	9.26
9.	2.30	2.82	3.55	4.70	5.87	7.17	10.22
10.	2.38	2.97	3.78	5.05	6.35	7.79	11.18
11.	2.47	3.11	4.00	5.40	6.83	8.42	12.14
12.	2.56	3.25	4.22	5.75	7.30	9.03	13.09
13.	2.64	3.40	4.44	6.10	7.78	9.65	14.03
14.	2.69	3.48	4.56	6.27	8.02	9.96	14.50
15.	2.75	3.55	4.67	6.44	8.24	10.24	14.94
16.	2.79	3.63	4.78	6.60	8.45	10.52	15.35
17.	2.84	3.70	4.88	6.75	8.66	10.77	15.74
18.	2.89	3.76	4.98	6.90	8.85	11.02	16.11
19.	2.93	3.83	5.07	7.03	9.03	11.25	16.45
20.	2.98	3.89	5.16	7.16	9.20	11.47	16.79
21.	3.02	3.95	5.25	7.29	9.37	11.68	17.10
22.	3.06	4.01	5.33	7.41	9.53	11.88	17.41
23.	3.10	4.07	5.41	7.53	9.68	12.08	17.70
24.	3.14	4.12	5.49	7.64	9.83	12.26	17.97
25.	3.18	4.18	5.56	7.75	9.97	12.44	18.24

pounds, 23¢; each additional pound, 12¢. Books when loaned or exchanged between and sent to or from schools, colleges, public libraries, and certain non-profit organizations; books, printed music, bound academic theses, periodicals, sound recordings, other library materials, museum materials (specimens, collections), scientific or mathematical kits, instruments or other devices; also catalogs, guides or scripts for some of these materials. Must be marked "Library Rate".

Also qualifying for library rate are: Books mailed from publishers or distributors to schools, libraries, colleges or universities or to bookstores owned, operated and controlled by schools, colleges or universities.

Postal Union Mail Special Services

Registration — available to practically all countries. Fee $4.40. The maximum indemnity payable — generally only in case of complete loss (of both contents and wrapper) — is $24.60. To Canada only the fee is $4.50 providing indemnity for loss up to $100, $4.85 for loss up to $500, and $5.25 for loss up to $1,000.

Return receipt — showing to whom and date deliv'd, 90¢.

Special delivery — Available to most countries. Consult post office. Fees for International Special Delivery same for air or surface: for letters, letter packages and post cards not over 2 pounds, $5.35. If over 2 pounds, $5.75, for printed matter, matter for the blind, or small packets, $5.65 if not over 2 pounds; if over 2 pounds, $6.50.

Marking — an article intended for special delivery service must have affixed to the cover near the name of the country of destination "EXPRES" (special delivery) label, obtainable at the post office, or it may be marked on the cover boldly in red "EXPRES" (special delivery).

Special handling — entitles AO surface packages to priority handling between mailing point and U.S. point of dispatch. Fees: $1.55 for packages to 10 pounds, and $2.25 for packages over 10 pounds.

Airmail — there is daily air service to practically all countries.

Prepayment of replies from other countries — a mailer who wishes to prepay a reply by letter from another country may do so by sending his correspondent one or more international reply coupons, which may be purchased at United States post offices. One coupon should be accepted in any country in exchange for stamps to prepay a surface letter of the first unit of weight to the U.S.

Additional international special services: Insurance: Available to many countries for loss of or damage to items paid at parcel post rate. Consult postmaster for indemnity limits for individual countries.

Limit of Indemnity		Fees
Not Over	Canada	All other Countries
$50	$0.70	$1.50
100	1.50	1.90
150	1.90	3.15
200	2.20	3.15
300	3.15	4.30
400	4.30	5.00
500	5.00	5.70

Restricted Delivery: Available to many countries for registered mail, limits who may receive an item. Fee: $2.00.

Post Office-Authorized 2-Letter State Abbreviations

The abbreviations below are approved by the U.S. Postal Service for use in addresses only. They do not replace the traditional abbreviations in other contexts. The official list follows, including the District of Columbia, Guam, Puerto Rico, the Canal Zone, and the Virgin Islands (all capital letters are used):

Alabama	AL	Idaho	ID	Nebraska	NE	South Carolina	SC
Alaska	AK	Illinois	IL	Nevada	NV	South Dakota	SD
American Samoa	AS	Indiana	IN	New Hampshire	NH	Tennessee	TN
Arizona	AZ	Iowa	IA	New Jersey	NJ	Texas	TX
Arkansas	AR	Kansas	KS	New Mexico	NM	Trust Territories	TT
California	CA	Kentucky	KY	New York	NY	Utah	UT
Canal Zone	CZ	Louisiana	LA	North Carolina	NC	Vermont	VT
Colorado	CO	Maine	ME	North Dakota	ND	Virginia	VA
Connecticut	CT	Maryland	MD	Northern Mariana Is.	CM	Virgin Islands	VI
Delaware	DE	Massachusetts	MA	Ohio	OH	Washington	WA
Dist. of Col.	DC	Michigan	MI	Oklahoma	OK	West Virginia	WV
Florida	FL	Minnesota	MN	Oregon	OR	Wisconsin	WI
Georgia	GA	Missouri	MO	Pennsylvania	PA	Wyoming	WY
Guam	GU	Mississippi	MS	Puerto Rico	PR		
Hawaii	HI	Montana	MT	Rhode Island	RI		

Also approved for use in addressing mail are the following abbreviations:

Alley	Aly	Court	Ct	Grove	Grv	Rural	R
Arcade	Arc	Courts	Cts	Heights	Hts	Square	Sq
Avenue	Ave	Crescent	Cres	Highway	Hwy	Street	St
Boulevard	Blvd	Drive	Dr	Lane	Ln	Terrace	Ter
Branch	Br	Expressway	Expy	Manor	Mnr	Trail	Trl
Bypass	Byp	Extended	Ext	Place	Pl	Turnpike	Tpke
Causeway	Cswy	Extension	Ext	Plaza	Plz	Viaduct	Via
Center	Ctr	Freeway	Fwy	Point	Pt	Vista	Vis
Circle	Cir	Gardens	Gdns	Road	Rd		

Size Standards for Domestic Mail

Minimum Size

Pieces which do not meet the following requirements are prohibited from the mails:

    a. All pieces must be at least .007 of an inch thick, and

    b. All pieces (except keys and identification devices) **which are ¼ inch or less thick** must be:
        (1) Rectangular in shape,
        (2) At least 3½ inches high, and
        (3) At least 5 inches long.

Note: Pieces greater than ¼ inch thick can be mailed even if they measure less than 3½ by 5 inches.

Nonstandard Mail

All First-Class Mail, except presort and carrier route First-Class mail, weighing one ounce or less and all single-piece rate Third-Class mail weighing one ounce or less is nonstandard (and subject to a 10¢ surcharge in addition to the applicable postage and fees) if:

    1. Any of the following dimensions are exceeded:
        Length—11½ inches,
        Height—6⅛ inches,
        Thickness—¼ inch, or

    2. The length divided by the height is not between 1.3 and 2.5, inclusive. The nonstandard surcharge for presort and carrier route First-Class mail is 5¢.

Air Mail, Parcel Post International Rates

Aerogrammes — 39¢ each to all countries.
Air mail postcards (single) - 36¢ to all countries except Canada (21¢) and Mexico (15¢)

Country	First pound	Air parcel post rates — Each add'l pound or fraction up to first 5 lbs.	Each add'l pound or fraction
Afghanistan	$10.30	$5.80	$5.00
Albania	8.70	4.80	4.00
Algeria	10.30	5.80	5.00
Andorra	7.15	4.00	6.00
Angola	11.95	6.80	6.00
Anguilla	5.50	2.80	2.00
Antigua & Barbados	5.50	2.80	2.00
Argentina	10.30	5.80	5.00
Aruba	5.50	2.80	2.00
Ascension	No Air Service		
Australia	10.30	5.80	5.00
Austria	7.15	4.00	3.00
Azores	8.70	4.80	4.00
Bahamas	5.50	2.80	2.00
Bahrain	10.30	5.80	5.00
Bangladesh	11.95	6.80	3.00
Barbados	7.15	4.00	3.00
Belgium	10.30	5.80	5.00
Belize	5.50	2.80	2.00
Benin	8.70	4.80	4.00
Bermuda	5.50	2.80	2.00
Bhutan	11.95	6.80	6.00
Bolivia	7.15	4.00	3.00
Botswana	11.95	6.80	6.00
Brazil	11.95	6.80	6.00
British Virgin Islands	5.50	2.80	2.00
Brunei	10.30	5.80	5.00
Bulgaria	10.30	5.80	5.00
Burkina Faso	10.30	5.80	5.00
Burma	10.30	5.80	5.00
Burundi	11.95	6.80	6.00
Cameroon	10.30	5.80	5.00
Canada¹	Separate rate schedule		
Cape Verde	10.30	5.80	5.00
Cayman Islands	5.50	2.80	2.00
Central African Rep.	11.95	6.80	6.00
Chad	10.30	5.80	5.00
Chile	10.30	5.80	5.00
China (People's Republic of)	10.30	5.80	5.00
Colombia	7.15	4.00	3.00
Comoros	11.95	6.80	6.00
Congo	10.30	5.80	5.00
Corsica	11.95	6.80	6.00
Costa Rica	5.50	2.80	2.00
Cuba	No Parcel Post Service		
Cyprus	8.70	4.80	4.00
Czechoslovakia	8.70	4.80	4.00
Denmark	8.70	4.80	4.00
Djibouti	10.30	5.80	5.00
Dominica	5.50	2.80	2.00
Dominican Republic	5.50	2.80	2.00
East Timor	No Parcel Post Service		
Ecuador	8.70	4.80	4.00
Egypt	10.30	5.80	5.00
El Salvador	7.15	4.00	3.00
Equatorial Guinea	10.30	5.80	5.00
Estonia	11.95	6.80	6.00
Ethiopia	10.30	5.80	5.00
Faeroe Islands	8.70	4.80	4.00
Falkland Islands	10.30	5.80	5.00
Fiji	7.15	4.00	3.00
Finland	10.30	5.80	
France (Including Monaco)	11.95	6.80	6.00
French Guiana	8.70	4.80	4.00
French Polynesia	10.30	5.80	5.00
Gabon	10.30	5.80	5.00
Gambia	7.15	4.00	3.00
German Democratic Republic (East Germany)	8.70	4.80	4.00
Germany, Federal Rep. of (West Germany)	8.70	4.80	4.00
Ghana	10.30	5.80	5.00
Gibraltar	8.70	4.80	4.00
Great Britain	8.70	4.80	4.00
Greece	8.70	4.80	4.00
Greenland	10.30	5.80	5.00
Grenada	$5.50	$2.80	$2.00
Guadeloupe	5.50	2.80	2.00
Guatemala	5.50	2.80	2.00
Guinea	7.15	4.00	3.00
Guinea-Bissau	7.15	4.00	3.00
Guyana	7.15	4.00	3.00
Haiti	5.50	2.80	2.00
Honduras	7.15	4.00	3.00
Hong Kong	8.70	4.80	4.00
Hungary	8.70	4.80	4.00
Iceland	8.70	4.80	4.00
India	10.30	5.80	5.00
Indonesia	11.95	6.80	6.00
Iran	10.30	5.80	5.00
Iraq	10.30	5.80	5.00
Ireland (Eire)	8.70	4.80	4.00
Israel	8.70	4.80	4.00
Italy	8.70	4.80	4.00
Ivory Coast	10.30	5.80	5.00
Jamaica	5.50	2.80	2.00
Japan	11.95	6.80	6.00
Jordan	8.70	4.80	4.00
Kampuchea	No Parcel Post Service		
Kenya	10.30	5.80	5.00
Kiribati	7.15	4.00	3.00
Korea, Democratic People's Rep. (North)	No Parcel Post Service		
Korea, Rep. of (South)	8.70	4.80	4.00
Kuwait	8.70	4.80	4.00
Lao	11.95	6.80	6.00
Latvia	11.95	6.80	6.00
Lebanon	8.70	4.80	4.00
Leeward Islands	5.50	2.80	2.00
Lesotho	11.95	6.80	6.00
Liberia	8.70	4.80	4.00
Libya	10.30	5.80	5.00
Liechtenstein	7.15	4.00	3.00
Lithuania	11.95	6.80	6.00
Luxembourg	7.15	4.00	3.00
Macao	8.70	4.80	4.00
Madagascar	11.95	6.80	3.00
Madeira Islands	7.15	4.00	3.00
Malawi	10.30	5.80	5.00
Malaysia	10.30	5.80	5.00
Maldives	10.30	5.80	5.00
Mali	8.70	4.80	4.00
Malta	8.70	4.80	4.00
Martinique	5.50	2.80	2.00
Mauritania	10.30	5.80	5.00
Mauritius	11.95	6.80	6.00
Mexico	5.50	2.80	2.00
Mongolia	No Parcel Post Service		
Morocco	8.70	4.80	4.00
Mozambique	11.95	6.80	6.00
Nauru	8.70	4.80	4.00
Nepal	10.30	5.80	5.00
Netherlands	8.70	4.80	4.00
Netherlands Antilles	5.50	2.80	2.00
New Caledonia	10.30	5.80	5.00
New Zealand	10.30	5.80	5.00
Nicaragua	7.15	4.00	3.00
Niger	10.30	5.80	5.00
Nigeria	8.70	4.80	4.00
Norway	10.30	5.80	5.00
Oman	10.30	5.80	5.00
Pakistan	10.30	5.80	5.00
Panama	5.50	2.80	2.00
Papua New Guinea	10.30	5.80	5.00
Paraguay	10.30	5.80	5.00
Peru	7.15	4.00	3.00
Philippines	10.30	5.80	5.00
Pitcairn Islands	7.15	4.00	3.00
Poland	7.15	4.00	3.00
Portugal	8.70	4.80	4.00
Qatar	8.70	4.80	4.00
Reunion	11.95	6.80	6.00
Romania	8.70	4.80	4.00
Rwanda	10.30	5.80	5.00

Country	First pound	Air parcel post rates—Each add'l. pound or fraction up to first 5 lbs.	Each add'l pound or fraction	Country	First pound	Air parcel post rates—Each add'l. pound or fraction up to first 5 lbs.	Each add'l pound or fraction
St. Helena	$8.70	$4.80	$4.00	Thailand	$10.30	$5.80	$5.00
St. Lucia	5.50	2.80	2.00	Togo	10.30	5.80	5.00
St. Pierre & Miquelon	5.50	2.80	2.00	Tonga	7.15	4.00	3.00
St. Thomas & Principe	10.30	5.80	5.00	Trinidad & Tobago	7.15	4.00	3.00
St. Vincent & The Grenadines	5.50	2.80	2.00	Tristan da Cunha	11.95	6.80	6.00
San Marino	8.70	4.80	4.00	Tunisia	8.70	4.80	4.00
Santa Cruz Islands	8.70	4.80	4.00	Turkey	8.70	4.80	4.00
Saudi Arabia	10.30	4.80	5.00	Turks & Caicos Islands	5.50	2.80	2.00
Senegal	10.30	5.80	5.00	Tuvalu (Ellice Islands)	7.15	4.00	3.00
Seychelles	10.30	5.80	5.00	Uganda	10.30	5.80	5.00
Sierra Leone	10.30	5.80	5.00	USSR[2]	11.95	6.80	6.00
Singapore	10.30	5.80	5.00	United Arab Emirates	10.30	5.80	5.00
Solomon Islands	8.70	4.80	4.00	Uruguay	7.15	4.00	3.00
Somalia	10.30	5.80	5.00	Vanuatu	7.15	4.00	3.00
South Africa	10.30	5.80	5.00	Vatican City State	8.70	4.80	4.00
Spain	8.70	4.80	4.00	Venezuela	7.15	4.00	3.00
Sri Lanka	10.30	5.80	5.00	Vietnam[1]	No Parcel Post Service		
Sudan	10.30	5.80	5.00	Wallis & Futura Islands	10.30	5.80	5.00
Suriname	7.15	4.00	3.00	Western Samoa	7.15	4.00	3.00
Swaziland	10.30	5.80	5.00	Yemen Arab Republic	10.30	5.80	5.00
Sweden	10.30	5.80	5.00	Yemen, Peoples Democratic Republic of	11.95	6.80	6.00
Switzerland	7.15	4.00	3.00	Yugoslavia	8.70	4.80	4.00
Syria	8.70	4.80	4.00	Zaire	11.95	6.80	6.00
Taiwan	8.70	4.80	4.00	Zambia	11.95	6.80	6.00
Tanzania	11.95	6.80	6.00	Zimbabwe	11.95	6.80	6.00

Weight limits: minimum 1 lb., maximum 66 lbs.; up to 2 lbs., $4.32; each add'l pound or fraction, $1.24.

(1) Restrictions apply; consult post office. (2) To facilitate distribution and delivery, include "Union of Soviet Socialist Republics" or "USSR" as part of the address.

Miscellaneous International Rates

Letters and Letter Pkgs (Surface)

Weight steps Over Lbs.	Ozs.	Through Lbs.	Ozs.	Canada	Mexico	All other countries
0	0	0	1	$.30	$.25	$.40
0	1	0	2	.52	.45	.63
0	2	0	3	.74	.65	.86
0	3	0	4	.96	.85	1.09
0	4	0	5	1.18	1.05	1.32
0	5	0	6	1.40	1.25	1.55
0	6	0	7	1.62	1.45	1.78
0	7	0	8	1.84	1.65	2.01
0	8	0	9	2.06	1.85	3.80
0	9	0	10	2.28	2.05	3.80
0	10	0	11	2.50	2.25	3.80
0	11	0	12	2.72	2.45	3.80
0	12	1	0	3.08	3.25	3.80
1	0	1	8	3.70	4.05	5.20
1	8	2	0	4.32	4.85	6.60
2	0	2	8	4.94	5.65	7.60
2	8	3	0	5.56	6.45	8.60
3	0	3	8	6.18	7.25	9.60
3	8	4	0	6.80	8.05	10.60

Maximum limit: 66 pounds to Canada, 4 pounds to Mexico and all other countries.

Letters and Letter Pkgs (Air)

Canada and Mexico: Refer to rates listed under Letter and Letter Pkgs. (Surface). Mail paid at this rate receives First-Class service in the United States and air service in Canada and Mexico.

All Other Countries: 45 cents per half ounce up to and including 2 ounces; 42 cents each additional half ounce up to and including 32 ounces; 42 cents per additional ounce over 32 ounces.

Parcel Post (Surface)

Canada: $3.95 for over 1 lb. and up to 2 lbs.; $1.20 each add'l lb.

Mexico, Central America, The Caribbean Islands, Bahamas, Bermuda, St. Pierre and Miquelon: $4.40 for the first 2 pounds and $1.40 each additional pound or fraction.

All Other Countries: $4.60 for the first 2 pounds and $1.50 for each additional pound or fraction.

For Parcel Post air rates, see tables, pages 796-797.

Postcards

Surface rates to Canada, 21¢, and Mexico, 15¢; to all other countries, 28¢. By air, Canada, 21¢, and Mexico, 15¢; to all other countries, 36¢. Maximum size permitted, 6 x 4¼ in.; minimum, 5½ x 3½.

Gross Postal Revenues at Large Cities

Fiscal year	Boston	Chicago	L.A.	New York	Phila.	St. Louis	Wash., D.C.
1975	$136,453,079	$365,378,795	$193,229,077	$453,905,277	$134,571,376	$85,591,774	$115,489,343
1980	224,428,760	528,233,991	271,136,828	666,377,778	221,161,624	127,427,555	187,334,312
1981	256,524,082	551,988,015	301,159,594	741,286,845	235,116,018	142,548,957	201,191,995
1982	292,971,572	597,246,568	338,798,409	848,507,590	265,242,959	160,596,946	215,772,861
1983	294,932,399	589,476,264	330,734,928	856,569,717	273,210,529	165,000,437	212,117,368
1984	314,230,399	598,141,605	338,760,060	907,426,500	295,917,848	177,041,331	225,378,646
1985	339,550,469	563,693,370	358,859,412	938,829,064	300,811,081	194,786,119	236,131,464
1986	378,861,842	579,432,633	381,254,469	960,987,314	330,671,509	211,134,497	253,607,563
1987	405,124,317	612,014,066	389,819,485	962,000,684	367,123,549	221,972,462	290,840,099
1988	428,049,178	618,237,375	415,847,750	999,747,864	384,189,378	245,040,401	341,131,117

Other cities for fiscal year 1988: Dallas, $442,248,303; Atlanta, $395,280,927; Houston, $330,335,486; Minneapolis, $272,742,154; San Francisco, $259,704,306; Baltimore, $241,938,631; Hartford, CT, $229,668,252; Columbus, OH, $237,024,215.

SOCIAL SECURITY

Social Security Programs

Source: Social Security Administration, U.S. Department of Health and Human Services

Old-Age, Survivors, and Disability Insurance; Medicare; Supplemental Security Income

Social Security Benefits

Social Security benefits are based on a worker's primary insurance amount (PIA), which is related by law to the average indexed monthly earnings (AIME) on which social security contributions have been paid. The full PIA is payable to a retired worker who becomes entitled to benefits at age 65 and to an entitled disabled worker at any age. Spouses and children of retired or disabled workers and survivors of deceased workers receive set proportions of the PIA subject to a family maximum amount. The PIA is calculated by applying varying percentages to succeeding parts of the AIME. The formula is adjusted annually to reflect changes in average annual wages in the economy in employment covered by Social Security.

Automatic increases in Social Security benefits are initiated whenever the Consumer Price Index (CPI) of the Bureau of Labor Statistics for the third calendar quarter of a year increases relative to the CPI for the base quarter, which is either the third calendar quarter of the preceding year or the quarter in which an increase legislated by Congress becomes effective. The size of the benefit increase is determined by the actual percentage rise of the CPI between the quarters measured. However, if the balance in the combined OASDI trust funds falls below a specified level, the automatic benefit increase will be based on the lesser of the increase in the CPI or the increase in average wages. If one or more benefit increases are based on the increase in average wages, a "catch up" benefit increase will be made in a subsequent year when the combined trust fund balance reaches a higher specified level.

Average monthly benefits payable to all retired workers was $536.00 in December 1988. The average amount for disabled workers in that month was $530.00.

Minimum and maximum monthly retired-worker benefits payable to individuals who retired at age 65[1]

Year of attainment of age 65[2]	Minimum benefit Payable at the time of retirement	Minimum benefit Payable effective December 1988	Maximum benefit Payable at the time of retirement Men[3]	Maximum benefit Payable at the time of retirement Women	Maximum benefit Payable effective December 1988 Men[3]	Maximum benefit Payable effective December 1988 Women
1965 . . .	$44.00	$221.50	$131.70	$135.90	$592.10	$611.00
1970 . . .	64.00	221.50	189.80	196.40	656.20	679.40
1980 . . .	133.90	221.50	572.00	. . .	946.50	. . .
1985 . . .	(4)	(4)	717.20	. . .	811.60	. . .
1986 . . .	(4)	(4)	838.60	. . .	872.10	. . .

(1) Assumes retirement at beginning of year. (2) The final benefit amount payable after SMI premium or any other deductions is rounded to next lower $1 (if not already a multiple of $1). (3) Benefit for both men and women are shown in men's columns except where women's benefit appears separately. (4) Minimum eliminated for workers who reach age 62 after 1981.

Amount of Work Required

To qualify for benefits, the worker must have worked in covered employment long enough to become insured. Just how long depends on when the worker reaches age 62 or, if earlier, when he or she dies or becomes disabled.

A person is fully insured if he or she has one quarter of coverage for every year after 1950 (or year age 21 is reached, if later) up to but not including the year in which the worker reaches age 62, dies, or becomes disabled. In 1989, a person earns one quarter of coverage for each $500 of annual earnings in covered employment, up to a maximum of 4 quarters per year.

The law permits special monthly payments under the Social Security program to certain very old persons who are not eligible for regular social security benefits since they had little or no opportunity to earn social security work credits during their working lifetime.

To get disability benefits, in addition to being fully insured, the worker must also have credit for 20 quarters of coverage out of the 40 calendar quarters before he or she becomes disabled. A disabled blind worker need meet only the fully insured requirement. Persons disabled before age 31 can qualify with a briefer period of coverage. Certain survivor benefits are payable if the deceased worker had 6 quarters of coverage in the 13 quarters preceding death.

Work credit for fully insured status for benefits
Born after 1929; die, become disabled, or reach age 62 in

	Years needed
1981	7½
1982	7¾
1983	8
1984	8¼
1985	8½
1986	8¾
1987	9
1988	9¼
1989	9½

Contribution and benefit base

Calendar year	Base
1979	$22,900
1980	25,900
1981	29,700
1982	32,400
1983	35,700
1984	37,800
1985	39,600
1986	42,000
1987	43,800
1988	45,000
1989	48,000

Tax-rate schedule
[Percent of covered earnings]

Year	Total Employees and employers, each	OASDI	HI
1979-80	6.13	5.08	1.05
1981	6.65	5.35	1.30
1982-83	6.70	5.40	1.30
1984	7.00	5.70	1.30
1985	7.05	5.70	1.35
1986-87	7.15	5.70	1.45
1988-89	7.51	6.06	1.45
1990 and after	7.65	6.20	1.45
Self-employed			
1979-80	8.10	7.05	1.05
1981	9.30	8.00	1.30
1982-83	9.35	8.05	1.30
1984	14.00	11.40	2.60
1985	14.10	11.40	2.70
1986-87	14.30	11.40	2.90
1988-89	15.02	12.12	2.90
1990 and after	15.30	12.40	2.90

What Aged Workers Get

When a person has enough work in covered employment and reaches retirement age (currently 65 for full benefit, 62 for reduced benefit), he or she may retire and get monthly old-age benefits. The age at which unreduced benefits are payable will be increased gradually from 65 to 67 over a 21-year period beginning with workers age 62 in the year 2000; (reduced benefits will still be available as early as age 62 but with a larger reduction at age 62.) If a person aged 65 or older continues to work and has earnings of more than $8,800 in 1989, $1 in benefits will be withheld for every $2 above $8,800. The annual exempt amount for people under age 65 is $6,480 in 1989. The annual exempt amount is raised automatically as the general earnings level rises. The eligible worker who is 70 receives the full benefit regardless of earnings. Beginning in 1990, benefits for persons who reach the normal retirement age will be reduced $1 for each $3 of excess earnings.

For workers who reach age 65 after 1981, the worker's benefit will be raised by 3% for each year for which the worker between 65 and 70 (72 before 1984) did not receive benefits because of earnings from work or because the worker had not applied for benefits. The delayed retirement credit is 1 percent a year for workers reaching age 65 before 1982. The delayed retirement credit will gradually rise from the current 3% per year to 8% per year from 1990 through 2008.

Effective December 1988, the special benefit for persons aged 72 or over who do not meet the regular coverage requirements is $151.90 a month. Like the monthly benefits, these payments are subject to cost-of-living increases. The special payment is not made to persons on the public assistance or supplemental security income rolls.

Workers retiring before age 65 have their benefits permanently reduced by 5/9 of 1% for each month they receive benefits before age 65. Thus, workers entitled to benefits in the month they reach age 62 receive 80% of the PIA, while a worker retiring at age 65 receives a benefit equal to 100% of the PIA. The nearer to age 65 the worker is when he or she begins collecting a benefit, the larger the benefit will be.

Benefits for Worker's Spouse

The spouse of a worker who is getting Social Security retirement or disability payments may become entitled to a spouse's insurance benefit when he or she reaches 65 or one-half of the worker's PIA. Reduced spouse's benefits are available at age 62 (25/36 of 1% reduction for each month of entitlement before age 65). Benefits are also payable to the aged-divorced spouse of an insured worker if he or she was married to the worker for at least 10 years.

Benefits for Children of
Retired or Disabled Workers

If a retired or disabled worker has a child under 18 the child will get a benefit that is half of the worker's unreduced benefit, and so will the worker's spouse, even if he or she is under 62 if he or she is caring for an entitled child of the worker who is under 16 or who became disabled before age 22. Total benefits paid on a worker's earnings record are subject to a maximum and if the total that would be part of a family exceeds that maximum, the individual dependents' benefits are adjusted downward. (Total benefits paid to the family of a worker who retired in January 1988 at age 65 and who always had the maximum amount of earnings creditable under Social Security can be no higher than $1,575.60.)

When entitled children reach 18, their benefits will generally stop, except that a child disabled before 22 may get a benefit as long as his or her disability meets the definition in the law. Additionally, benefits will be paid to a child until age 19 if the child is in full-time attendance at an elementary or secondary school.

Benefits may also be paid to a grandchild or step-grandchild of a worker or of his or her spouse, in special circumstances.

OASDI	May 1989	May 1988	May 1987
Monthly beneficiaries, total (in thousands)	38.835	38,419	37,942
Aged 65 and over, total	28,393	27,875	27,386
Retired workers	21,455	21,009	20,591
Survivors and dependents . . .	6,926	6,849	6,744
Special age-72 beneficiaries. .	12	16	22
Under age 65, total	10,442	10,544	10,556
Retired workers	2,560	2,575	2,555
Disabled workers	2,850	2,804	2,749
Survivors and dependents . . .	5,032 .	5,165	5,252
Total monthly benefits (in millions)	$18,870	$17,787	$16,706

What Disabled Workers Get

If a worker becomes so severely disabled that he or she is unable to work, he or she may be eligible to receive a monthly disability benefit. Benefits continue until it is determined that the individual is no longer disabled. Each beneficiary's eligibility is reviewed periodically. When a disabled worker beneficiary reaches 65, the disability benefit becomes a retired-worker benefit.

Benefits generally like those provided for dependents of retired-worker beneficiaries may be paid to dependents of disabled beneficiaries. However, the maximum family benefit in disability cases is generally lower than in retirement cases.

Survivor Benefits

If an insured worker should die, one or more types of benefits may be payable to survivors, again subject to a maximum family benefit as described above.

1. If claiming benefits at 65, the surviving spouse will receive a benefit that is 100% of the deceased worker's PIA. The surviving spouse may choose to get the benefit as early as age 60, but the benefit is then reduced by 19/40 of 1% for each month it is paid before age 65. However, for those aged 62 and over whose spouses claimed their benefits before 65, the benefit is the reduced amount the worker would be getting if alive but not less than 82 1/2% of the worker's PIA.

Disabled widows and widowers may under certain circumstances qualify for benefits after attaining age 50 at the rate of 71.5% of the deceased worker's PIA. The widow or widower must have become totally disabled before or within 7 years after the spouse's death, the last month in which he or she received mother's or father's insurance benefits, or the last month he or she previously received surviving spouse's benefits.

2. A benefit for each child until the child reaches 18. The monthly benefit of each child of a worker who has died is three-quarters of the amount the worker would have received if he or she had lived and drawn full retirement benefits. A child with a disability that began before age 22 may receive benefits. Also, a child may receive benefits until age 19 if he or she is in full-time attendance at an elementary or secondary school.

3. A mother's or father's benefit for the widow(er), if children of the worker under 16 are in his or her care. The benefit is 75% of the PIA and he or she draws it until the youngest child reaches 16, at which time payments stop even if the child's benefit continues. They may start again when he or she is 60 (50 if disabled) unless he or she is married. If he or she marries and the marriage is ended, he or she regains benefit rights (A marriage after age 60, 50 if disabled, is deemed not to have occurred for benefit purposes.). If he or she has a disabled child beneficiary aged 16 or over in care, benefits also continue. This benefit may also be paid to the divorced spouse, if the marriage lasted for at least 10 years.

4. Dependent parents may be eligible for benefits, if they have been receiving at least half their support from the worker before his or her death, have reached age 62, and (except in certain circumstances) have not remarried since the worker's death. Each parent gets 75% of the worker's PIA; if only one parent survives the benefit is 82 1/2%.

5. A lump sum cash payment of $255. Payment is made only when there is a spouse who was living with the worker or a spouse or child eligible for immediate monthly survivor benefits.

Self-Employed

A self-employed person who has net earnings of $400 or more in a year must report such earnings for social security tax and credit purposes. The person reports net returns from the business. Income from real estate, savings, dividends, loans, pensions or insurance policies may not be included unless they are part of the business.

A self-employed person gets a quarter of coverage for each $500 (for 1989), up to a maximum of 4 quarters of coverage.

The nonfarm self-employed have the option of reporting their earnings as 2/3 of their gross income from self-employment but not more than $1,600 a year and not less than their actual net earnings. This option can be used only if actual net earnings from self-employment income is less than

$1,600 and may be used only 5 times. Also, the self-employed person must have actual net earnings of $400 or more in 2 of the 3 taxable years immediately preceding the year in which he or she uses the option.

When a person has both taxable wages and earnings from self-employment, the wages are credited for Social Security purposes first; only as much of the self-employment income as will bring total earnings up to the current taxable maximum is subject to the self-employment tax.

Farm Owners and Workers

Self-employed farmers whose gross annual earnings from farming are $2,400 or less may report ²/₃ of their gross earnings instead of net earnings for social security purposes. Farmers whose gross income is over $2,400 and whose net earnings are less than $1,600 can report $1,600. Cash or crop shares received from a tenant or share farmer count if the owner participated materially in production or management. The self-employed farmer pays contributions at the same rate as other self-employed persons.

Agricultural employees. A worker's earnings from farm work count toward benefits (1) if the employer pays him $150 or more in cash during the year; or (2) if the employer spends $2,500 or more in the year for agricultural labor. Under these rules a person gets credit for one calendar quarter for each $500 in cash pay in 1989 up to four quarters.

Foreign farm workers admitted to the United States on a temporary basis are not covered.

Household Workers

Anyone working as maid, cook, laundress, nursemaid, baby-sitter, chauffeur, gardener and at other household tasks in the house of another is covered by Social Security if he or she is paid $50 or more in cash in a calendar quarter by any one employer. Room and board do not count, but carfare counts if paid in cash. The job does not have to be regular or fulltime. The employee should get a Social Security card at the social security office and show it to the employer.

The employer deducts the amount of the employee's social security tax from the worker's pay, adds an identical amount as the employer's social security tax and sends the total amount to the federal government, with the employee's social security number.

Medicare

Under Medicare, protection against the costs of hospital care is provided for Social Security and Railroad Retirement beneficiaries aged 65 and over and, for persons entitled for 24 months to receive a social security disability benefit, certain persons (and their dependents) with end-stage renal disease, and, on a voluntary basis with payment of a special premium, persons aged 65 and over not otherwise eligible for hospital benefits; all those eligible for hospital benefits may enroll for medical benefits and pay a monthly premium and so may persons aged 65 and over who are not eligible for hospital benefits.

Persons eligible for both hospital and medical insurance may choose to have their covered services provided through a Health Maintenance Organization.

Medicare benefits were significantly enlarged by the Catastrophic Coverage Act of 1988. The expansion of Hospital insurance benefits begins on Jan. 1, 1989; the expansion of medical insurance benefits begins on Jan. 1, 1990; and new prescription drug benefits become effective on Jan. 1, 1991.

Hospital insurance.—In 1988, nearly $52.7 billion was withdrawn from the hospital insurance trust fund for hospital and related benefits.

The hospital insurance program pays the cost of covered services for hospital and posthospital care as follows:

- Medicare will cover all *medically necessary* inpatient hospital care 365 days a year. The Medicare hospital patient must pay a deductible sum each year (about $560 in 1987).
- Up to 150 days' care in a skilled-nursing facility (skilled-nursing home) in each year. Hospital insurance pays for all covered services except for coinsurance for the first 8 days of SNF care each year (about $20.50 per day in 1989).

- Visits by nurses or other health workers (not doctors) from a home health agency.
- Hospice care for terminally ill individuals.

Medical insurance. Aged persons can receive benefits under this supplementary program only if they sign up for them and agree to a monthly premium ($24.80 in 1988). The Federal Government pays the rest of the cost.

In 1988, about $35 billion was paid out for medical insurance benefits. As of September 1987, about 33 million persons were enrolled — 3 million of them disabled persons under age 65.

The medical insurance program pays 80% of the reasonable charges (after the first $75 in each calendar year) for the following services:

- Physicians' and surgeons' services, whether in the doctor's office, a clinic, or hospital or at home (but physician's charges for X-ray or clinical laboratory services for hospital bed-patients are paid in full and without meeting the deductible).
- Other medical and health services, such as diagnostic tests, surgical dressings and splints, and rental or purchase of medical equipment. Services of a physical therapist in independent practice, furnished in his office or the patient's home. A hospital or extended-care facility may provide covered outpatient physical therapy services under the medical insurance program to its patients who have exhausted their hospital insurance coverage.
- Physical therapy services furnished under the supervision of a practicing hospital, clinic, skilled nursing facility, or agency.
- Certain services by podiatrists.
- All outpatient services of a participating hospital (including diagnostic tests).
- Outpatient speech pathology services, under the same requirements as physical therapy.
- Services of licensed chiropractors who meet uniform standards, but only for treatment by means of manual manipulation of the spine and treatment of subluxation of the spine demonstrated by X-ray.
- Supplies related to colostomies are considered prosthetic devices and payable under the program.
- Home health services even without a hospital stay are paid up to 100% *when medically necessary.*

To get medical insurance protection, persons approaching age 65 may enroll in the 7-month period that includes 3 months before the 65th birthday, the month of the birthday, and 3 months after the birthday, but if they wish coverage to begin in the month they reach 65 they must enroll in the 3 months before their birthday. Persons not enrolling within their first enrollment period may enroll later, during the first 3 months of each year but their premium is 10% higher for each 12-month period elapsed since they first could have enrolled.

The monthly premium is deducted from the cash benefit for persons receiving Social Security, Railroad Retirement, or Civil Service retirement benefits. Income from the medical premiums and the federal matching payments are put in a Supplementary Medical Insurance Trust Fund, from which benefits and administrative expenses are paid.

Medicare card. Persons qualifying for hospital insurance under Social Security receive a health insurance card similar to cards now used by Blue Cross and other health agencies. The card indicates whether the individual has taken out medical insurance protection. It is to be shown to the hospital, skilled-nursing facility, home health agency, doctor, or whoever provides the covered services.

Payments are made only in the 50 states, Puerto Rico, the Virgin Islands, Guam, and American Samoa, except that hospital services may be provided in border areas immediately outside the U.S. if comparable services are not accessible in the U.S. for a beneficiary who becomes ill or is injured in the U.S.

Social Security Financing

Social Security is paid for by a tax on earnings (for 1989, up to $48,000; the taxable earnings base is now subject to automatic adjustment to reflect increases in average wages).

The employed worker and his or her employer share the tax equally.

Employers remit amounts withheld from employee wages for Social Security and income taxes to the Internal Revenue Service; employer Social Security taxes are also payable at the same time. (Self-employed workers pay their Social Security taxes along with their regular income tax forms). The Social Security taxes (along with revenues arising from partial taxation of the Social Security benefits of certain high-income people) are transferred to the Social Security Trust Funds (Federal Old-Age and Survivors Insurance Trust Fund, the Federal Disability Insurance Trust Fund, and the Federal Hospital Insurance Trust Fund); they can be used only to pay benefits, the cost of rehabilitation services, and administrative expenses. Money not immediately needed for these purposes is by law invested in obligations of the Federal Government, which must pay interest on the money borrowed and must repay the principal when the obligations are redeemed or mature.

Supplemental Security Income

On Jan. 1, 1974, the Supplemental Security Income (SSI)

program established by the 1972 Social Security Act amendments replaced the former federal grants to states for aid to the needy aged, blind, and disabled in the 50 states and the District of Columbia. The program provides both for federal payments based on uniform national standards and eligibility requirements and for state supplementary payments varying from state to state. The Social Security Administration administers the federal payments financed from general funds of the Treasury—and the state supplements as well, if the state elects to have its supplementary program federally administered. The states may supplement the federal payment for all recipients and must supplement it for persons otherwise adversely affected by the transition from the former public assistance programs. In May 1989, the number of persons receiving federal payments and federally administered state payments was 4,516,351 and the amount of these payments was $1.23 billion.

The maximum monthly federal SSI payment for an individual with no other countable income, living in his own household, was $368.00 in 1989. For a couple it was $553.00.

Examples of monthly cash benefit awards for selected beneficiary families with first entitlement in 1989, effective January 1989

| Beneficiary Family | Career Earnings Level | | |
	Low Earnings ($6,968 in 1989)	Average Earnings ($18,611 in 1989)[1]	Maximum Earnings ($45,000 in 1989)
Primary Insurance amount (worker retiring at 65)	$439.50	$668.50	$899.60
Maximum family benefit (worker retiring at 65)	687.80	1,217.90	1,575.60
Disability maximum family benefit (worker disabled at 55)	683.20	1,033.00	1,403.00
Disabled worker: (worker disabled at 55)			
Worker alone	455.00	688.00	935.00
Worker, spouse, and 1 child	683.00	1,033.00	1,403.00
Retired worker claiming benefits at age 62:			
Worker alone[2]	362.00	550.00	734.00
Worker with spouse claiming benefits at—			
Age 65 or over	589.00	894.00	1,192.00
Age 62[2]	532.00	808.00	1,078.00
Widow or widower claiming benefits at—			
Age 65 or over[3]	439.00	668.00	899.00
Age 60	314.00	477.00	643.00
Disabled widow or widower claiming benefits at age 50-59[4]	314.00	477.00	643.00
1 surviving child	329.00	501.00	674.00
Widow or widower age 65 or over and 1 child[5]	687.00	1,169.00	1,573.00
Widowed mother or father and 1 child[5]	659.00	1,002.00	1,349.00
Widowed mother or father and 2 children[5]	687.00	1,217.00	1,575.00

(1) Estimate. (2) Assumes maximum reduction. (3) A widow(er)'s benefit amount is limited to the amount the spouse would have been receiving if still living but not less than 82.5 percent of the PIA. (4) Effective January 1984, disabled widow(er)s claiming benefit at ages 50-59 will receive benefit equal to 71.5 percent of the PIA (based on 1983 Social Security Amendment provision). (5) Based on worker dying at age 65.

Social Security Trust Funds

Old-Age and Survivors Insurance Trust Fund, 1940-1988

[in millions]

| Fiscal year[1] | Income | | | | | | Disbursements | | | | Net increase in fund | Fund at end of period |
	Total	Net contributions[2]	Income from taxation of benefits	Payments from the general fund of the Treasury[2]	Net interest[4]	Total	Benefit payments[5]	Administrative expenses	Transfers to Railroad Retirement program	Interfund borrowing transfers[6]		
1940	$592	$550	—	—	$42	$28	$16	$12	—	—	$564	$1,745
1950	2,367	2,106	—	$4	257	784	727	57	—	—	1,583	12,893
1960	10,360	9,843	—	—	517	11,073	10,270	202	$600	—	−713	20,829
1970	31,746	29,955	—	442	1,350	27,321	26,268	474	579	—	4,425	32,616
1980	100,051	97,608	$3,151	557	1,886	103,228	100,626	1,160	1,442	—	−3,177	24,566
1985	179,881	175,305	3,151	1,321	169,210	165,310	1,589	2,310	$−4,364	6,308	33,877
1986	195,331	187,007	3,329	2,293	2,701	178,534	174,340	1,609	2,585	−13,155	3,642	37,519
1987	206,846	199,554	3,323	69	3,900	186,101	182,003	1,541	2,557	—	20,745	58,265
1988	235,720	226,409	3,335	55	5,922	197,021	192,502	1,729	2,790	—	38,700	96,964

(1) Under the Congressional Budget Act of 1974 (Public Law 93-344), fiscal years 1977 and later consist of the 12 months ending on September 30 of each year. The act further provides that the calendar quarter July-September 1976 is a period of transition from fiscal year 1976, which ended on June 30, 1976, to fiscal year 1977, which began on October 1, 1976.

(2) Beginning in 1983, includes government contributions on deemed wage credits for military service in 1957 and later. The amount shown for 1983 includes, in addition to the annual contributions on 1983 wage credits, a net amount of $5,388 million representing (1) retroactive contributions on deemed wage credits for military service in 1957-82, less (2) all reimbursements received prior to 1983 for the costs of such credits. An adjustment to these amounts totaling $466 million was transferred to the trust fund from the general fund of the Treasury in 1984.

(continued)

(3) Includes payments (1) in 1947-52 and in 1967 and later, for costs of noncontributory wage credits for military service performed before 1957; (2) in 1972-83, for costs of deemed wage credits for military service performed after 1956; and (3) in 1969 and later, for costs of benefits to certain uninsured persons who attained age 72 before 1968.

(4) Net interest includes net profits or losses on marketable investments. Beginning in 1967, administrative expenses are charged currently to the trust fund on an estimated basis, with a final adjustment, including interest, made in the following fiscal year. The amounts of these interest adjustments are included in net interest. For years prior to 1967, a description of the method of accounting for administative expenses is contained in the 1970 Annual Report. Beginning in 1983, these figures reflect payments from a borrowing trust fund to a lending trust fund for interest on amounts owed under the interfund borrowing provisions. Also, beginning in 1983, interest paid from the trust fund to the general fund on advance tax transfers is reflected. The amount shown for 1983 includes $6,677 million in interest on (1) retroactive government contributions on deemed wage credits for military service in 1957-82, and (2) unnegotiated benefit checks issued before 1983. The amount shown for 1984 includes an interest adjustment of $1,732 million on government contributions on deemed wage credits for military service in 1957-83. The amounts shown for 1985 and 1986 include interest adjustments of $76.5 million and $11.5 million, respectively, on unnegotiated checks issued before April 1985.

(5) Beginning in 1967, includes payments for vocational rehabilitation services furnished to disabled persons receiving benefits because of their disabilities. Beginning in 1983, amounts are reduced by amount of reimbursement for unnegotiated benefit checks. The amount shown for 1983 is reduced by $288 million for all unnegotiated checks issued before 1983; reductions in subsequent years are relatively small.

(6) Positive figure represents amounts lent to the OASI Trust Fund from the DI and HI Trust Funds. Negative figures represent amounts repaid from the OASI Trust Fund to the DI and HI Trust Funds.

Disability Insurance Trust Fund, 1960-1988

[in millions]

Fiscal year[1]	Income					Disbursements					Net increase in fund	Fund at end of period
	Total	Net contributions[2]	Income from taxation of benefits	Payments from the general fund of the Treasury[2]	Net interest[4]	Total	Benefit payments[5]	Administrative expenses	Transfers to Railroad Retirement program	Interfund borrowing transfers[6]		
1960	$1,034	$987	—	—	$47	$533	$528	$32	−$27	—	$501	$2,167
1970	4,380	4,141	—	$16	223	2,954	2,795	149	10	—	1,426	5,104
1980	17,376	16,805	—	118	453	15,320	14,998	334	−12	—	2,056	7,680
1985	17,984	16,876	$217	—	891	19,294	18,648	603	43	$2,540	1,230	5,873
1987	20,047	19,324	−16[7]	—	738	21,222	20,427	738	57	—	−1,175	7,173
1988	22,369	21,736	56	—	577	22,269	21,405	803	61	—	100	7,273

(1) Under the Congressional Budget Act of 1974 (Public Law 93-344), fiscal years 1977 and later consist of the 12 months ending on September 30 of each year. The act further provides that the calendar quarter July-September 1976 is a period of transition from fiscal year 1976, which ended on June 30, 1976, to fiscal year 1977, which began on October 1, 1976.

(2) Beginning in 1983, includes government contributions on deemed wage credits for military service in 1957 and later. The amount shown for 1983 includes, in addition to the annual contributions on 1983 wage credits, a net amount of $402 million representing (1) retroactive contributions on deemed wage credits for military service in 1957-82, less (2) all reimbursements received prior to 1983 for the costs of such credits. An adjustment to these amounts totaling $62 million was transferred to the trust fund from the general fund of the Treasury in 1984.

(3) Includes payments (1) in 1967 and later, for costs of noncontributory wage credits for military service performed before 1957; and (2) in 1972-83, for costs of deemed wage credits for military service performed after 1956.

(4) Net interest includes net profits or losses on marketable investments. Beginning in 1967, administrative expenses are charged currently to the trust fund on an estimated basis, with a final adjustment, including interest, made in the following fiscal year. The amounts of these interest adjustments are included in net interest. For years prior to 1967, a description of the method of accounting for administrative expenses is contained in the 1970 Annual Report. Beginning in 1983, these figures reflect payments from a borrowing trust fund to a lending trust fund for interest on amounts owed under the interfund borrowing provisions. Also, beginning in 1983, interest paid from the trust fund to the general fund on advance tax transfers is reflected. The amount shown for 1983 includes $660 million in interest on (1) retroactive government contributions on deemed wage credits for military service in 1957-82, and (2) unnegotiated benefit checks issued before 1983. The amount shown for 1984 includes an interest adjustment of $169 million on government contributions on deemed wage credits for military service in 1957-83. The amount shown for 1985 includes an interest adjustment of $14.8 million on unnegotiated benefit checks issued before April 1985.

(5) Beginning in 1967, includes payments for vocational rehabilitation services furnished to disabled persons receiving benefits because of their disabilities. Beginning in 1983, amounts are reduced by amount of reimbursement for unnegotiated benefit checks. The amount shown for 1983 is reduced by $48 million for all unnegotiated checks issued before 1983; reductions in subsequent years are relatively small.

(6) Negative figure represents amounts lent by the DI Trust Fund to the OASI Trust Fund. Positive figures represent repayment of these amounts.

(7) Reflects $195 million in transfers from the DI Trust Fund to the general fund of the Treasury to correct estimated amounts transferred for calendar years 1984 and 1985.

Supplementary Medical Insurance Trust Fund, 1970-1988

[In millions]

Fiscal year[1]	Income				Disbursements			Balance in fund at end of year[4]
	Premium from participants	Government contributions[2]	Interest and other income[3]	Total income	Benefit payments	Administrative expenses	Total disbursements	
1970	$ 936	$ 928	$ 12	$1,876	$ 1,979	$ 217	$ 2,196	$ 57
1975	1,887	2,330	105	4,322	3,765	405	4,170	1,424
1980	2,928	6,932	415	10,275	10,144	593	10,737	4,532
1985	5,524	17,898	1,155	24,577	21,808	922	22,730	10,646
1987	6,480	20,299	1,018	27,797	29,937	900	30,837	6,392
1988	8,756	25,418	828	35,002	33,682	1,265	34,947	6,447

(1) For 1967 through 1976, fiscal years cover the interval from July 1 through June 30; fiscal year 1977-86 cover the interval from October 1 through September 30. (2) The payments shown as being from the general fund of the Treasury include certain interest-adjustment items. (3) Other income includes recoveries of amounts reimbursed from the trust fund which are not obligations of the trust fund and other miscellaneous income. (4) The financial status of the program depends on both the total net assets and the liabilities of the program.

LANGUAGE

Sources for this section: *The World Almanac Guide to Good Word Usage; The Columbia Encyclopedia; Webster's Third New International Dictionary; The Oxford English Dictionary, 2nd ed.; The Associated Press Stylebook and Libel Manual; The Encyclopedia Americana.*

Neologisms

("New" words; from the Second Edition of the *Oxford English Dictionary*, Oxford Univ. Press, 1989.)

antiquark: the antiparticle of a quark.

arcade game: a (mechanical or electronic) game of a type orig. popularized in amusement arcades.

assertiveness training: a technique by which diffident persons are trained to behave (more) assuredly.

astroturfed: carpeted with astroturf.

birth parent: a natural (as opposed to an adoptive) parent.

build-down: a systematic reduction of nuclear armaments, by destroying two or more for each new one deployed.

bulimarexic: suffering from or characteristic of bulimia nervosa; one who suffers from bulimia nervosa.

camp-on: a facility of some telephone systems by which the caller of an engaged number can arrange for the system to ring it automatically as soon as it becomes free (in some cases ringing the caller also if he has replaced his receiver).

car-phone: a radio-telephone designed for use in a motor vehicle.

designer drug: a drug synthesized to mimic a legally restricted or prohibited drug without itself being subject to restriction.

fast tracker: a high-flyer; an ambitious or thrusting person.

foodie: also foody. One who is particular about food, a gourmet.

gender gap: the difference in (esp. political) attitudes between men and women.

hate mail: letters (often anonymous) in which the senders express their hostility towards the recipient.

Jazzercise: a proprietary name for a program of physical exercises arranged to be carried out in a class to the accompaniment of jazz music; also, exercise of this kind.

microwavable: of food and food containers: suitable for cooking or heating in a microwave oven.

NIMBY, nimby: "not in my backyard," a slogan expressing objection to the siting of something considered unpleasant, such as nuclear waste, in one's own locality.

passive smoking: the inhalation of smoke involuntarily from the tobacco being smoked by others, considered as a health risk.

rainbow coalition: a political grouping of minority peoples and other disadvantaged elements, esp. for the purpose of electing a candidate.

right to die: the alleged right of a brain-damaged or otherwise incurably ill person to the termination of life-sustaining treatment.

skanking: a style of West Indian dancing to reggae music, in which the body bends forward at the waist, and the knees are raised and the hands claw the air in time to the beat; dancing in this style.

street credibility: popularity with, or accessibility to, ordinary people, esp. those involved in urban street culture; the appearance or fact of being "street-wise"; hence (apparent) familiarity with contemporary trends, fashions, social issues.

yuppiedom: the condition or fact of being a yuppie; the domain of yuppies; yuppies as a class.

Eponyms (words named for people)

Bloody Mary—a vodka and tomato juice drink; after the nickname of Mary I, Queen of England, 1553-58, notorious for her persecution of Protestants.

Bloomers—full, loose trousers gathered at the knee; after Mrs. Amelia Bloomer, an American social reformer who advocated such clothing, 1851.

Bobbies—in Great Britain, police officers; after Sir Robert Peel, the statesman who organized the London police force, 1850.

Bowdlerize—to delete written matter considered indelicate; after Thomas Bowdler, British editor of an expurgated Shakespeare, 1825.

Boycott—to combine against in a policy of nonintercourse for economic or political reasons; after Charles C. Boycott, an English land agent in County Mayo, Ireland, ostracized in 1880 for refusing to reduce rents.

Braille—a system of writing for the blind; after Louis Braille, the French teacher of the blind who invented it, 1852.

Caesarean section—surgical removal of a child from the uterus through an abdominal incision; after Julius Caesar, born c. 102 B.C., in this manner, according to legend.

Casanova—a man who is a promiscuous and unscrupulous lover; after Giovanni Casanova, an Italian adventurer, 1725-98.

Chauvinist—excessively patriotic; after Nicolas Chauvin, a legendary French soldier devoted to Napoleon.

Derby—a stiff felt hat with a dome-shaped crown and rather narrow rolled brim; after Edward Stanley, 12th Earl of Derby, who in 1780 founded the Derby horse race at Epsom Downs, England, to which these hats are worn.

Gerrymander—to divide an election district in an unnatural way, to favor one political party; after Elbridge Gerry, and the salamander, for the salamander-like shape of a Mass. election district created, 1912, during Gerry's governorship.

Guillotine—a machine for beheading; after Joseph Guillotine, a French physician who proposed its use in 1789 as more humane than hanging.

Leotard—a close-fitting garment for the torso, worn by dancers, acrobats, and the like; after Julius Leotard, a 19th-century French aerial gymnast.

Silhouette—an outline image; from Etienne de Silhouette, the French finance minister, 1757, who advocated economies that included buying such paper portraits instead of painted miniatures.

Foreign Words and Phrases

(L = Latin; F = French; Y = Yiddish; R = Russian; G = Greek; I = Italian; S = Spanish)

ad hoc (L; ad HOK): for the particular end or purpose at hand

ad infinitum (L; ad in-FI-NITE-UM): endless

ad nauseum (L; ad NAWZ-ee-um): to a sickening degree

apropos (L; ap-ruh-POH): to the point; appropriate

bête noir (F; BET NWAHR): a thing or person viewed with particular dislike.

bon appetit (F; BOH nap-uh-teet): good appetite

bona fide (L; BOH nuh-feyed): genuine

carte blanche (F; kahrt BLANNSH): full discretionary power

cause celebre (F; kawz suh-LEB-ruh): a notorious incident

C'est la vie (F; se lah VEE): That's life

chutzpah (Y; KHOOT-spuh): amazing nerve bordering on arrogance

coup de grace (F; kooh duh GRAHS): the final blow

coup d'etat (F; kooh duh tah): forceful overthrow of a government

creme de la creme (F; KREM duh luh KREM): the best of the best

cum laude/magna cum laude/summa cum laude (L; KUHM loud-ay; MAHN-ya . . .; SOO-ma . . .): with praise or honor; with great praise or honor; with the highest praise or honor

de facto (L; di FAK-toh): in fact; generally agreed to without a formal decision

deja vu (F; DAY-zhah VOOH): the sensation that something happening has happened before

de jure (L; dee JOOR-ee, day YOOR-ay): determined by law, as opposed to de facto

de rigueur (F; duh ree-GUR): necessary according to convention

detente (F; day-TAHNT): an easing or relaxation of strained relations

éminence grise (F; ay-meh-NAHNN-suh GREEZ): one who wields power behind the scenes

enfant terrible (F; ahnn-FAHNN te-REE-bluh): one whose unconventional behavior causes embarrassment

en masse (F; ahn MAHS): in a large body

ergo (L; ER-goh): therefore

esprit de corps (F; es-PREE duh KAWR): group spirit; feeling of camaraderie

Eureka (G; YOOR-EE-kuh): I have found it

ex post facto (L; eks pohst FAK-toh): an explanation or regulation concocted after the event

fait accompli (F; fayt uh-kom-PLEE): an accomplished fact

faux pas (F; fowe PAH): a social blunder

glasnost (R; glahs-nust): openness, candor

hoi polloi (G; hoy puh-LOY): the masses

in loco parentis (L; in LO H-Koh puh-REN-tis): in place of a parent

in memoriam (L; in muh-MAWR-ee-uhm): in memory of

in situ (L; in SEYE-tyooh): in the original arrangement

in toto (L; in TOH-toh): totally

je ne sais quoi (F; zhuh nuh say KWAH): I don't know what; the little something that eludes description

joi de vivre (F; zhwah duh VEEV-ruh): joy of living, love of life

mea culpa (L; MAY-uh CUL-puh): my fault

meshugga (Y; meh-SHOOG-uh): crazy

modus operandi (L; MOH-duhs op-uh-RAN-dee): method of operation

noblesse oblige (F; noh-BLES uh-BLEEZH); the obligation of nobility to help the less fortunate

non compos mentis (L; non KOM-puhs MEN-tis): out of control of the mind; insane

nouveau riche (L; nooh-voh REESH); pejorative for recent rich who spend money conspicuously

perestroika (R; PAIR-es TROY-kuh): restructuring

persona non grata (L; per-SOH-nah non GRAH-tah): unacceptable person

post-mortem (L; pohst-MORE-tuhm): after death; autopsy; analysis after event

prima donna (I; pree-muh DAH-nuh): temperamental person

pro tempore (L; proh TEM-puh-ree): for the time being

que sera sera (S; keh sair-ah sair-AH): what will be, will be

quid pro quo (L; kwid proh KWOH): something given or received for something else

raison d'etre (F; RAY-zohnn DET-ruh): reason for being

shlemiel (Y; shleh-MEEL): an unlucky bungling person

savoir-faire (F; sav-wahr-FAIR): dexterity in social and practical affairs

semper fidelis (L; SEM-puhr fee-DAY-lis): always faithful

status quo (L; STAY-tus QWOH): existing order of things

tour de force (L; TOOR duh FAWRS): feat accomplished through great skill

terra firma (L; TER-uh FUR-muh): solid ground

verbatim (L; ver-BAY-tuhm): word for word

vis-a-vis (F; vee-ZUH-VEE): compared with

Esperanto

In 1887, Dr. L. L. Zamenhof, a linguist and physician, published a slim textbook on his "Internacia Lingvo" (International Language) under the pseudonym "Doktoro Esperanto." The term "Esperanto" became attached to the language itself as it gained adherents rapidly until the outbreak of World War I. Hardly recovered from the effects of the war, Esperanto was savaged by Nazism, Stalinism, Fascism, the Japanese militarists of the 1930's, and chauvinistic groups in many other countries. Not until the late 1950's did the number of speakers begin to show the steady increase which continues as Esperanto begins its second century.

Controlled experiments show that because of its logical structure, phonemic spelling, and regular grammar Esperanto can be learned to a given criterion of performance in from one-twentieth to one-fifth the time needed for the learning of a typical national language.

Inteligenta persono lernas la lingvon Esperanto rapide kaj facile. Esperanto estas la moderna, kultura lingvo por la tuta mondo.

Commonly Confused English Words

adverse: unfavorable
averse: opposed

affect: to influence
effect: to cause

aggravate: to make worse
annoy: to irritate

allusion: an indirect reference
illusion: an unreal impression

anxious: apprehensive
eager: avid

censor: to subject to examination by an official empowered to demand alteration or withdrawal
censure: a judgment involving condemnation

complement: to make complete; something that completes
compliment: to praise; praise

capital: the seat of government
capitol: the building in which a legislative body meets

emigrate: to leave for another place of residence

immigrate: to come to another place of residence

elicit: to draw or bring out
illicit: illegal

denote: to mean
connote: to suggest beyond the explicit meaning

farther: more distant in space
further: an extension of time or degree

historic: an important occurrence
historical: any occurrence in the past

imply: to relay information but not explicitly
infer: to understand information that is not relayed explicitly

imminent: ready to take place
eminent: standing out

incredible: unbelievable
incredulous: skeptical

include: used when the items following are part of a whole

comprise: used when the items following are all of a whole

ingenious: clever
ingenuous: innocent

insidious: intended to trick
invidious: detrimental to reputation

literally: actually
figuratively: metaphorically

oral: spoken, as opposed to written
verbal: referring to skill with language, as opposed to other skills

prevaricate: to lie
procrastinate: to put off

pestilence: a contagious or infectious epidemic disease
petulance: rudeness

prostate: stretched out flat, face down
prostrate: of or relating to the prostate gland

qualitative: relating to quality
quantitative: relating to number

National Spelling Bee Champions

The Scripps Howard National Spelling Bee, conducted by Scripps Howard Newspapers and other leading newspapers since 1939, was instituted by the Louisville (Ky.) Courier-Journal in 1925. Children under 16 years of age and not beyond the eighth grade are eligible to compete for cash prizes at the finals, which are held annually in Washington, D.C. The 1989 winners are: first prize, **Scott Isaacs**, Englewood, Colo. (*Rocky Mountain News,* Denver); second prize, **Ojas Tejani**, Hixon, Tenn. (*Chattanooga Times*); third prize, **Arthur Hodge**, Pottsville, Pa. (*Pottsville Republican*); fourth prize, **Samantha Cassell**, Johnson City, Tenn. (*Knoxville News-Sentinel*).

Winning Words

These were the last words given in each of the years 1965-1989 at the Scripps Howard National Spelling Bee. They were all correctly spelled, thereby determining the national champion.

1965 — eczema	1972 — macerate	1978 — deification	1984 — luge
1966 — ratoon	1973 — vouchsafe	1979 — maculature	1985 — milieu
1967 — chihuahua	1974 — hydrophyte	1980 — elucubrate	1986 — odontalgia
1968 — abalone	1975 — incisor	1981 — sarcophagus	1987 — staphylococci
1969 — interlocutory	1976 — narcolepsy	1982 — psoriasis	1988 — elegiacal
1970 — croissant	1977 — cambist	1983 — purim	1989 — spoliator
1971 — shalloon			

Commonly Misspelled English Words

accidentally	convenience	government	miniature
accommodate	deceive	grammar	mysterious
acquainted	describe	humorous	necessary
all right	description	hurrying	opportunity
already	desirable	incidentally	optimistic
amateur	despair	independent	performance
appearance	desperate	inoculate	permanent
appropriate	eliminate	irresistible	rhythm
bureau	embarrass	laboratory	ridiculous
character	fascinating	lightning	similar
commitment	finally	maintenance	sincerely
conscious	foreign	marriage	transferred
conscientious	forty		

A Collection of Animal Collectives

The English language boasts an abundance of names to describe groups of things, particularly pairs or aggregations of animals. Some of these words have fallen into comparative disuse, but many of them are still in service, helping to enrich the vocabularies of those who like their language to be precise, who tire of hearing a group referred to as "a bunch of," or who enjoy the sound of words that aren't overworked.

band of gorillas
bed of clams, oysters
bevy of quail, swans
brace of ducks
brood of chicks
cast of hawks
cete of badgers
charm of goldfinches
chattering of choughs
cloud of gnats
clowder of cats
clutch of chicks
clutter of cats
colony of ants
congregation of plovers
covey of quail, partridge

crash of rhinoceri
cry of hounds
down of hares
drift of swine
drove of cattle, sheep
exaltation of larks
flight of birds
flock of sheep, geese
gaggle of geese
gam of whales
gang of elks
grist of bees
herd of elephants
horde of gnats
husk of hares
kindle or **kendle** of kittens

knot of toads
leap of leopards
leash of greyhounds, foxes
litter of pigs
mob of kangaroos
murder of crows
muster of peacocks
mute of hounds
nest of vipers
nest, nide of pheasants
pack of hounds, wolves
pair of horses
pod of whales, seals
pride of lions
school of fish
sedge or **siege** of cranes

shoal of fish, pilchards
skein of geese
skulk of foxes
sleuth of bears
sounder of boars, swine
span of mules
spring of teals
swarm of bees
team of ducks, horses
tribe or **trip** of goats
troop of kangaroos, monkeys
volery of birds
watch of nightingales
wing of plovers
yoke of oxen

Young of Animals Have Special Names

The young of many animals, birds and fish have come to be called by special names. A young eel, for example, is an elver. Many young animals, of course, are often referred to simply as infants, babies, younglets, or younglings.

bunny: rabbit.
calf: cattle, elephant, antelope, rhino, hippo, whale, etc.
cheeper: grouse, partridge, quail.
chick, chicken: fowl.
cockerel: rooster.
codling, sprag: codfish.
colt: horse (male).
cub: lion, bear, shark, fox, etc.
cygnet: swan.
duckling: duck.
eaglet: eagle.
elver: eel.
eyas: hawk, others.
fawn: deer.

filly: horse (female).
fingerling: fish generally.
flapper: wild fowl.
fledgling: birds generally.
foal: horse, zebra, others.
fry: fish generally.
gosling: goose.
heifer: cow.
joey: kangaroo, others.
kid: goat.
kit: fox, beaver, rabbit, cat.
kitten, kitty, catling: cats, other fur-bearers.
lamb, lambkin, cosset, hog: sheep.
leveret: hare.

nestling: birds generally.
owlet: owl.
parr, smolt, grilse: salmon.
piglet, shoat, farrow, suckling: pig.
polliwog, tadpole: frog.
poult: turkey.
pullet: hen.
pup: dog, seal, sea lion, fox.
puss, pussy: cat.
spike, blinker, tinker: mackerel.
squab: pigeon.
squeaker: pigeon, others.
whelp: dog, tiger, beasts of prey.
yearling: cattle, sheep, horse, etc.

The Principal Languages of the World

Source: Sidney S. Culbert, Guthrie Hall NI-25 — University of Washington, Seattle, Wash. 98195

Total number of speakers (native plus non-native) of languages spoken by at least one million persons (midyear 1989)

Language	Millions	Language	Millions	Language	Millions
Achinese (N Sumatra, Indonesia)	3	Cantonese (or Yue) (China; Hong-kong)	62	Fon (SC Benin; S Togo)	1
Afrikaans (So. Africa)	10			French	119
Akan (or Twi-Fante) Ghana	7	Catalan (NE Spain; S France; Andorra)	9	Fula (or Peulh) (Cameroon; Nigeria)	12
Albanian (Albania; Yugoslavia)	5	Cebuano (Bohol Sea area, Philippines)	12	Fulakunda (Senegambia; Guinea Bissau)	1
Amharic (Ethiopia)	16	Chagga (Kilimanjaro area, Tanzania)	1	Futa Jalon (NW Guinea; Sierra Leone)	2
Arabic	192	Chiga (Ankole, Uganda)	1		
Armenian (USSR)	5	Chinese[5]		Galician (Galicia, NW Spain)	3
Assamese[1] (Assam, India; Bangladesh)	21	Chuvash (Chuvash ASSR, USSR)	2	Galla (see Oromo)	
Aymara (Bolivia; Peru)	2	Czech (Czechoslovakia)	12	Ganda (or Luganda) (S Uganda)	3
Azerbaijani (Iran; Azer. SSR, USSR)	14	Danish (Denmark)	5	Georgian (Georgian SSR, USSR)	4
Balinese (Indonesia)	3	Dimli (EC Turkey)	1	German	118
Baluchi (Baluchistan, Pakistan)	4	Dogri (Jammu-Kashmir, C and E India)	1	Gilaki (Gilan, NW Iran)	2
Bashkir (Bashkir ASSR, USSR)	1			Gogo (Riff Valley; Tanzania)	1
Batak Toda (including Anakola) Indonesia (see also Karo-Dairi)	4	Dong (Guizhou, Hunan, Guangxi, China)	2	Gondi (Central India)	2
Baule (Côte d' Ivoire)	2	Dutch-Flemish (Netherlands; Belgium)	21	Greek (Greece)	12
Beja (Kassala, Sudan; Ethiopia)	1			Guarani (Paraguay)	4
Bemba (Zambia)	2	Dyerma (SW Niger)	2	Gujarati[1] (W and C India; S Pakistan)	38
Bengali[1]	181	Edo (Bendel, S Nigeria)	1	Gusii (Kisii District, Nyanza, Kenya)	2
Berber[2]		Efik (incl. Ibibio) (SE Nigeria; W. Cam.)	6	Hadiyya (Arusi, Ethiopia)	2
Beti (Cameroon; Gabon; Eq. Guinea)	2			Hakka (or Kejia) (SE China)	31
Bhili (India)	3	English	437	Hani (S China)	1
Bikol (SE Luzon, Philippines)	3	Esperanto	2	Hausa (N Nigeria; Niger; Cameroon)	33
Brahui (Pakistan; Afghan.; Iran)	1	Estonian (Estonian SSR, USSR)	1	Haya (Kagera, NW Tanzania)	1
Bugis (Indonesia, Malaysia)	3	Ewe (SE Ghana; S Togo)	3	Hebrew (Israel)	4
Bulgarian (Bulgaria)	9	Fang-Bulu (Dialects of Beti, q. v.)		Hindi[1,4]	338
Burmese (Burma)	29	Farsi (Iranian form of Persian, q. v.)		Ho (Bihar and Orissa States, India)	1
Buyi (S Guizhou, S China)	2	Finnish (Finland; Sweden)	6	Hungarian (or Magyar) (Hungary)	14
Byelorussian (Byelorussian SSR, USSR)	10	Flemish (see Dutch-Flemish)		Iban (Kalimantan, Indonesia; Malaysia)	1
				Ibibio (see Efik)	

Language	Millions	Language	Millions	Language	Millions
Igbo (or Ibo) (lower Niger R., Nigeria)	15	Meithei (NE India; Bangladesh)	1	Sinhalese (Sri Lanka)	12
Ijaw (Niger River delta, Nigeria)	2	Mende (Central, S and E Sierra Leone)	2	Slovak (Czechoslovakia)	5
Ilocano (NW Luzon, Philippines)	7	Meru (Eastern Province, C Tanzania)	1	Slovene (Slovenia, NW Yugoslavia)	2
Indonesian (see Malay-Indonesian)		Miao (or Hmong) (S China; SE Asia)	5	Soga (Busoga, Uganda)	1
Italian (Italy)	63	Mien (China; Viet.; Laos; Thailand)	2	Somali (Somalia; Eth.; Ken.; Djibouti)	7
Japanese	124	Min (SE China; Taiwan; Malaysia)	46	Songye (Kasai Or., NW Shala, Zaire)	1
Javanese (Java, Indonesia)	57	Minangkabau (W Sumatra, Indonesia)	6	Soninke (Mali; countries to W S E)	1
Kabyle (W Kabylia, N Algeria)	2	Moldavian (included with Romanian)		Sotho, Northern (So. Africa)	3
Kamba (E Kenya)	3	Mongolian (Mongolia, NE China)	5	Sotho, Southern (So. Africa; Lesotho)	4
Kannada[1] (S India)	40	Mordvin (in and near Mord. SSR, USSR)	1	Spanish	331
Kanuri (Nigeria; Niger; Chad; Cam.)	4	Moré (central part of Burkina Faso)	4	Sundanese (Sunda Strait, Indonesia)	23
Karen (see Pho and Sgaw)		Nepali (Nepal; NE India; Bhutan)	13	Swahili (Kenya; Tanz.; Zaire; Uganda)	42
Karo-Dairi (N Sumatra, Indonesia)	2	Ngulu (Zambezia, Mozambique; Malawi)	2	Swati (Swaziland; So. Africa)	1
Kashmiri[1] (N India; NE Pakistan)	4	Nkole (Western Prov., Uganda)	1	Swedish (Sweden; Finland)	9
Kazakh (Kazakh SSR, USSR)	8	Norwegian (Norway)	5	Sylhetti (Bangladesh)	5
Kenuzi-Dongola (S Egypt; Sudan)	1	Nung (NE of Hanoi, Vietnam; China)	1	Tagalog (Philippines)	34
Khalka (see Mongolian)		Nupe (Kwara, Niger States, Nigeria)	1	Tajiki (Tajik Uzbek Kirghiz SSRs, USSR)	4
Khmer (Kampuchea; Vietnam; Thailand)	7	Nyamwezi-Sukuma (NW Tanzania)	4	Tamazight (N Morocco; W Algeria)	3
Khmer, Northern (Thailand)	1	Nyanja (Malawi; Zambia; N Zimbabwe)	4	Tamil[1] (Tamil Nadu, India; Sri Lanka)	64
Kikuyu (or Gekoyo) (W and C Kenya)	5	Oriya[1] (Central and E India)	30	Tatar (Tatar SSR, USSR)	7
Kirghiz (Kirghiz SSR, USSR)	2	Oromo (W Ethiopia; N Kenya)	10	Tausug (Philippines; Malaysia)	1
Kituba (Bas-Zaire, Bandundu, Zaire)	4	Pampangan (NW of Manila, Philippines)	2	Telugu[1] (Andhra Pradesh, SE India)	67
Kongo (W Zaire; S Congo; NW Angola)	3	Panay-Hiligaynon (Philippines)	6	Temne (central Sierra Leone)	1
Konkani (Maharashtra and SW India)	4	Pangasinan (Lingayen G., Philippines)	2	Thai[5] (Thailand)	47
Korean (So., No. Korea; China; Japan)	69	Pashtu (Pakistan; Afghanistan; Iran)	21	Tho (N Vietnam; S China)	1
Kurdish (south-west of Caspian Sea)	9	Pedi (see Sotho, Northern)		Thonga (Mozambique; So. Africa)	3
Kurukh (or Oraon) (C and E India)	2	Persian (Iran; Afghanistan)	32	Tibetan (SW China; N India; Nepal)	5
Lao[5] (Laos)	4	Polish (Poland)	42	Tigrinya (S Eritrea, Tigre, Ethiopia)	4
Lampung (Sumatra, Indonesia)	1	Portuguese	171	Tiv (SE Nigeria; Cameroon)	2
Latvian (Latvian SSR, USSR)	2	Provençal (S France)	4	Tong (see Dong)	
Lingala (including Bangala) (Zaire)	6	Punjabi[1] (Punjab, Pakistan; NW India)	81	Tonga (SW Zambia; NW Zimbabwe)	1
Lithuanian (Lithuanian SSR, USSR)	3	Pushto (see Pashtu) (many spellings)		Tswana (Botswana; So. Africa)	3
Luba-Lulua (or Chiluba) (Kasai, Zaire)	6	Quechua (Peru; Bol. Ec.; Arg.)	8	Tudza (N Vietnam; S China)	1
Luba-Shaba (Shaba, Zaire)	1	Rejang (SW Sumatra, Indonesia)	1	Tulu (S India)	2
Lubu (E Sumatra, Indonesia)	1	Riff (N Morocco; Algerian coast)	1	Tumbuka (N Malawi; NE Zambia)	2
Luhya (W Kenya)	3	Romanian (Romania; Moldavia, USSR)	25	Turkish (Turkey)	54
Luo (Kenya; Nyanza, Tanzania)	3	Romany (Vlach only) (Europe; Amer.)	1	Turkmen (S USSR; NE Iran; Afghanistan)	2
Luri (SW Iran; Iraq)	3	Ruanda (Rwanda; S Uganda; E Zaire)	8	Twi-Fante (see Akan)	
Lwena (E Angola; W Zambia)	1	Rundi (Burundi)	5	Uighur (Xinjiang, NW China; SC USSR)	7
Macedonian (Macedonia, Yugoslavia)	2	Russian	291	Ukrainian (Ukraine, USSR; Poland)	45
Madurese (Madura, Indonesia)	9	Samar-Leyte (Central E Philippines)	3	Urdu[1,4] (Pakistan; India)	90
Magindanaon (Moro Gulf, S Philippines)	1	Sango (Central African Republic)	3	Uzbek (Uzbek SSR, USSR)	13
Makassar (S Sulawesi, Indonesia)	2	Santali (E India; Nepal)	5	Vietnamese (Vietnam)	55
Makua (S Tanzania; N Mozambique)	3	Sasak (Lombok, Alas Strait, Indonesia)	1	Wolaytta (SW Ethiopia)	2
Malagasy (Madagascar)	11	Serbo-Croation (Yugoslavia)	20	Wolof (Senegal)	6
Malay-Indonesian	138	Sgaw (SW W N of Rangoon, SW Burma)	1	Wu (Shanghai and nearby prov., China)	61
Malay, Pattani (SE pennisular Thailand)	1	Shan (Shan, E Burma)	3	Xhosa (SW Cape Province, So. Africa)	7
Malayalam[1] (Kerala, India)	33	Shilha (W Algeria; S Morocco)	3	Yao (Malawi; Tanzania; Mozambique) (see Mien)	
Malinke-Bambara-Dyula (W Africa)	8	Shona (Zimbabwe)	7	Yi (S and SW China)	6
Mandarin	844	Sidamo (Sidamo, S Ethiopia)	1	Yiddish[6]	
Marathi[1] (Maharashtra, India)	63	Sindhi[1] (SE Pakistan; W India)	16	Yoruba (SW Nigeria; Zou, Benin)	17
Mazandarani (S Mazandaran, N Iran)	3			Zande (NE Zaire; SW Sudan)	1
Mbundu (or Umbundu) (Benguela, Angola)	3			Zhuang (S China)	14
Mbundu (or Kimbundu) (Luanda, Angola)	3			Zulu (N Natal, So. Africa; Lesotho)	7

(1) One of the fifteen languages of the Constitution of India. (2) See Kabyle, Riff, Shilha, and Tamazight. (3) See Mandarin, Cantonese, Wu, Min, and Hakka. The "common speech" (Putonghua) or the "national language" (Guoyu) is a standardized form of Mandarin as spoken in the area of Beijing. (4) Hindi and Urdu are essentially the same language, Hindustani. As the official language of Pakistan it is written in a modified Arabic script and called Urdu. As the official language of India it is written in the Devanagari script and called Hindi. (5) The distinctions between some Thai dialects and Lao is political rather than linguistic. (6) Yiddish is usually considered a variant of German, though it has its own standard grammar, dictionaries, a highly developed literature, and is written in Hebrew characters.

Computer Language

Source: The Computer Glossary, Computer Language Co., 1989

Access: the ability to get information or use a computer or program.

Acoustic coupler: a device that allows other electronic devices to communicate by making, and also listening to sounds made over an ordinary telephone. See Modem.

Address: designates the location of an item of information stored in the computer's memory.

Artificial intelligence: a broad range of computer applications that resemble human intelligence and behavior. Machines or robots with sensory capabilities.

ASCII: acronym for American Standard Code for Information Interchange. A 7-bit code used to represent alphanumeric characters.

Assembly language: a machine oriented language using mnemonics to represent each machine-language instruction. Each CPU has its own assembly language.

Authorization code: an identification number or password used to gain access to a computer system.

Backup file: a copy of a current file used if the current file is destroyed.

(continued)

BASIC: Beginner's All-purpose Symbolic Instruction Code; a computer language used by many small and personal computer systems.

Baud rate: serial-data transmission speed. Originally a telegraph term, expressed as the number of events that take place in one second. One baud equals one bit per second.

Binary: refers to the base-2 number system in which the only allowable digits are 0 and 1.

Bit: short for binary digit, the smallest unit of information stored in a computer. It always has the binary value of "O" or "1."

Bubble memory: a relatively new type of computer memory, it uses tiny magnetic "bubbles" to store data.

Buffer: a place to put information before further processing.

Bug: a mistake that occurs in a program within a computer or in the unit's electrical system. When a mistake is found and corrected, it's called debugging.

Byte: an 8-bit sequence of binary digits. Each byte corresponds to 1 character of data, representing a single letter, number, or symbol. Bytes are the most common unit for measuring computer and disk storage capacity.

CAD/CAM: abbreviation for computer-aided design/computer-aided manufacturing.

Cathode Ray Tube Terminal: a device used as a computer terminal which contains a television-like screen for displaying data. Most CRT terminals also have a typewriter-like keyboard.

CD-ROM Drive: Information is retrieved by a laser beam that scans tracks of microscopic holes in a rotating compact disk. They can store 550 million characters, but cannot store new information.

COBOL: Common Business Oriented Language; one of the most widely used business programming languages.

Command: an action statement or order to the computer.

Compiler: a program that translates a high-level language, such as BASIC, into machine language.

Connect time: the time a user at a terminal (a work station away from the main computer) is logged-on to a computer system.

CPU: the Central Processing Unit within the computer that executes the instructions the user gives the system.

Chip: a term for the integrated circuit and its package which contains coded signals.

Cursor: the symbol on the computer monitor that marks the place where the operator is working.

Database: a large amount of data stored in a well organized format. A database management system is a program that allows access to the information.

Dedicated: designed for a single use.

Density: the amount of data that can be stored on one sector of one track of a disk.

Desktop publishing: using a personal computer to produce high-quality printed output camera ready for the printer.

Diagnostics: software programs that test the operational capability of hardware components.

Directory: an index to the location of files on a disk.

Disk: a revolving plate on which information and programs are stored. See also **Floppy disk.**

Disk Drive: a peripheral machine that stores information on disks.

Documentation: user or operator instructions that come with some hardware and software that tells how to use the material.

DOS: Disk Operating System, a collection of programs designed to facilitate the use of a disk drive and floppy disk.

Download: to transmit data from a central to a remote computer or from a file server to a personal computer.

Dump: a printout of the contents of any file.

Error Message: a statement by the computer indicating that the user has done something incorrectly.

Fax: facsimile, the communication of a printed page between remote locations.

Field: the physical unit of data in a record.

File: a logical group of pieces of information labelled by a specific name; considered a single unit by the computer; used commonly on microcomputers and word processors.

Floppy disk: a small inexpensive disk used to record and store information. It must be used in conjunction with a disk drive.

Font: a set of characters of a particular design and size.

Foreground/Background: an operating system prioritizing method in multitasking computer systems. Programs running in the foreground have highest priority.

Format: the arrangement by which information is stored.

Function: in programming, a routine, or set of instructions, that performs a particular task.

Hacker: a very technical person in the computer field; the term is used in a derogatory manner to refer to people who use their technical knowledge to gain unauthorized access into computer systems and data banks.

Hardware: the physical apparatus that makes up a computer, silicon chips, transformers, boards and wires. Also used to describe various pieces of equipment including the CPU, printer, modem, CRT (cathode ray tube).

Hexadecimal: refers to the base-16 number system. Machine language programs are often written in hexadecimal notation.

Intelligent terminal: a terminal with built-in processing capability. It has memory, but no disk or tape storage.

Interface: the hardware or software necessary to connect one device or system to another.

K: abbreviation for Kilo-byte used to denote 1,024 units of stored matter.

Language: any set of compiled, unified, or related commands or instructions that are acceptable to a computer.

Laptop computer: a portable computer that usually weighs less than 12 pounds and has a self-contained power supply.

Light pen: an input device that uses a light-sensitive stylus connected by a wire to a video terminal.

Load: the actual operation of putting information and data into the computer or memory.

Loop: in programming, the repetition of some function within the program.

Machine readable: any paper form or storage medium that can be automatically read by the computer.

Master file: a collection of records pertaining to one of the main subjects of an information system.

Memory: the internal storage of information.

Menu: programs, functions or other choices displayed on the monitor for user selection.

Microcomputer: a small, complete computer system. Most personal computers now in use are microcomputers.

Minicomputer: an intermediate computer system sized between the very small microcomputer and the large computer.

Modem: Modulating-demodulating; an acoustic or non-acoustic coupler, used with a telephone or on a direct-line, for transmitting information from one computer to another.

Mouse: a puck-like object that is used as a pointing and drawing device.

Network: in communications, the path between terminals and computers. In database management, a database design.

Noise: random disturbances that degrade or disrupt data communications.

Operating system: a master control program that runs the computer and acts as a scheduler and traffic cop.

Password: a word or code used to identify an authorized user.

Peripheral: any hardware device connected to a computer, such as printers or joy sticks.

Pixel: picture element, the smallest display element on a video display screen.

Program: coded instructions telling a computer how to perform a specific function.

RAM: Random-access-memory; a type of microchip, its patterns can be changed by the user and the information it generates stored on tape, disk, or in printed form.

Random access: the ability to retrieve records in a file without reading any previous records.

Record: a group of related fields that are used to store data about a subject. A collection of records is a *file*, and a collection of files is a *database*.

ROM: abbreviation for read-only-memory. A type of microchip that is different from RAM in that it cannot be altered by the user.

Semiconductor: a solid state substance that can be electrically altered, such as a transistor.

Software: the programs, or sets of instructions, procedural

(continued)

rules, and, in some cases, documentation that make the computer function.

Spreadsheet: a software program that simulates a paper spreadsheet, or worksheet, in which columns of numbers are totaled.

Superconductor: a material that has almost no resistance to the flow of electricity.

Telecommuting: working at home and communicating via computer with the office.

User friendly: hardware or software designed to help people become familiar with their computer. Usually includes simple and easy to follow instructions.

Virus: a "rogue" program designed to reproduce and infiltrate itself through links between computers.

Voice recognition: the understanding of spoken words by a machine.

Window: portion of a video display screen devoted to displaying specific categories of information.

Word Processor: a text-editing program or system that allows electronic writing and correcting of articles, etc.

Economic and Financial Glossary

Acquisition: The purchase of one company by another.

Balanced Budget: The federal government budget is balanced when receipts are equal to current expenditure.

Balance of payments: The difference between all payments made to and from foreign countries over a set period of time. A *favorable* balance exists when more payments are coming in than going out; an *unfavorable* balance, when the reverse is true. Payments include gold, the cost of merchandise and services, interest and dividend payments, money spent by travelers, and repayment of principal on loans.

Balance of trade (trade gap): The difference between exports and imports, both in actual funds and credit. A nation's balance of trade is *favorable* when exports exceed imports and *unfavorable* when the reverse is true.

Bear Market: A market in which prices are falling.

Bearer Bond: A bond issued in bearer form rather than being registered in the owner's name. Ownership is determined by possession.

Bond: A written promise or IOU by the issuer to repay a fixed amount of borrowed money on a specified date and to pay a set annual rate of interest in the meantime, usually at semi-annual intervals. Bonds are generally considered safe because the borrower (whether a company or the government) usually must make interest payments before the money is spent on anything else.

Bull Market: A market in which prices are on the rise.

Commercial Paper: An extremely short-term corporate IOU, generally due in 270 days or less. Available in face amounts of $100,000, $250,000, $500,000, $1,000,000 and combinations thereof.

Convertible Bond: A corporate bond (see below) which may be converted into a stated number of shares of common stock. Its price tends to fluctuate along with fluctuations in the price of the stock and with changes in interest rates.

Corporate Bond: Evidence of debt by a corporation. The bond normally has a stated life and pays a fixed rate of interest. Considered safer than the common or preferred stock of the same company.

Cost of living: The cost of maintaining a standard of living measured in terms of purchased goods and services. A rise in the cost of living mirrors the rate of inflation.

Cost-of-living benefits: Benefits that go to those persons whose money receipts increase automatically as prices rise.

Credit crunch (liquidity crisis): The period when cash for lending to business and consumers is in short supply.

Debenture: An unsecured long-term debt obligation backed only by the general credit of the issuing corporation.

Deficit spending: The practice whereby a government goes into debt to finance some of its expenditures.

Depression: A long period of economic decline when prices are low, unemployment is high, and there are many business failures.

Devaluation: The official lowering of a nation's currency, decreasing its value in relation to foreign currencies.

Discount Rate: The rate of interest set by the Federal Reserve that member banks are charged when borrowing money through the Federal Reserve System.

Disposable income: Income after taxes which is available to persons for spending and saving.

Dividend: Payment by a corporation to its shareholders, usually in the form of cash, stock shares, or other property.

Dow-Jones Industrial Average: A measure of stock market prices, based on 30 leading companies on the New York Stock Exchange.

Economic Growth: The steady process of increasing productive capacity of the economy, and hence of increasing national income.

Federal Deposit Insurance Corporation (FDIC): A government-sponsored corporation that insures accounts in national banks and other qualified institutions.

Federal Reserve System: The entire banking system of the U.S., incorporating 12 Federal Reserve banks (one in each of 12 Federal Reserve districts), and 24 Federal Reserve branch banks, all national banks and state-chartered commercial banks and trust companies that have been admitted to its membership. The system greatly influences the nation's monetary and credit policies.

Federal Savings and Loan Insurance Corporation (FSLIC): Agency that operates under the Federal Home Loan Bank Board. It insures the accounts in U.S. savings and loan associations.

Full employment: The economy is said to be at full employment when only fractional unemployment exists. That is, everyone who wishes to work at the going wage-rate for his type of labor is employed. Since it takes time to switch from one job to another, there will be at any given time a small amount of unemployment.

Golden Parachute: Provisions in the employment contracts of executives guaranteeing substantial severance benefits if they lose their position in a corporate takeover.

Government Bond: An IOU of the U.S. Treasury, considered the safest security in the investment world. They are divided into two categories, those that are not marketable and those that are. *Savings Bonds* cannot be bought and sold once the original purchase is made. These include the familiar Series EE bonds. You buy them at 50 percent of their face value and when they mature, 5 years later, they will pay you back 100 percent of face value if you cash them in. Another type, Series H, are not discounted, but issued in amounts of $500, $1,000, $5,000, and $10,000 and pay their interest in semiannual checks. Marketable bonds fall into 3 categories. *Treasury Bills* are short-term U.S. obligations, maturing in 3, 6, or 12 months. They are sold at a discount of the face value, and the minimum denomination is $10,000. *Treasury Notes* mature in up to 10 years. Denominations range from $500, $1,000 to $5,000, $10,000 and up. *Treasury Bonds* mature in 10 to 30 years. The minimum investment is $1,000.

Greenmail: A company buys back its own shares from a suitor for more than the going market price to avoid a hostile takeover.

Gross National Product (GNP): The market value of all goods and services that have been bought for final use during a year. The GNP is generally considered to be the most comprehensive measure of a nation's economic activity. The *Real* GNP is the GNP adjusted for inflation.

Individual Retirement Account (IRA): A self-funded retirement plan that allows employed individuals to contribute a maximum yearly sum toward their retirement. Interest earned in the account is tax deferred.

(continued)

Inflation: An increase in the average level of prices; double-digit inflation occurs when the percent increase rises above 9.9.

Insider Information: Important facts about the condition or plans of a corporation that have not been released to the general public.

Junk Bonds: Debt securities that sell at relatively low prices, because of the low credit rating of their issuers. They pay significantly higher yields than top-grade bonds to reflect their added risk. In the 1980s, they have been used to finance hostile takeovers.

Key leading indicators: A series of a dozen indicators from different segments of the economy used by the Commerce Department to foretell what will happen in the economy in the near future.

Leveraged Buy-Out: An acquisition of a public company by a small group, often including the company's management, which takes the company private. Much of the purchase price is borrowed with the debt repaid from company profits or by selling company assets.

Liquid Assets: Assets that include cash or those items that are easily converted into cash.

Margin Account: A brokerage account that allows a person to trade securities on credit.

Money supply: The currency held by the public plus checking accounts in commercial banks and savings institutions.

Mortgage-Backed Securities: Created when a bank, builder or government agency gathers together a group of mortgages and then sells bonds to other institutions and the public. The investors receive their proportionate share of the interest payments on the loans as well as the principal payments. Usually, these mortgages are guaranteed by the government, making them a fairly safe investment despite the fact that their market value does fluctuate.

Municipal Bond: Issued by governmental units such as states, cities, local taxing authorities and other agencies. Interest is exempt from U.S. — and sometimes state and local — income tax. *Municipal Bond Unit Investment Trusts* allow you to invest with as little as $1,000 in a portfolio of many different municipal bonds chosen by professionals. The income is exempt from federal income taxes.

Mutual Fund: A portfolio, or selection, of professionally bought and managed stocks in which you pool your money along with thousands of other people. A share price is based on net asset value, or the value of all the investments owned by the funds, less any debt, and divided by the total number of shares. The major advantage is less risk — it is spread out over many stocks and, if one or two do badly, the remainder may shield you from the losses. *Bond Funds* are mutual funds that deal in the bond market exclusively. *Money Market Mutual Funds* buy in the so-called "Money Market" — institutions that need to borrow large sums of money for short terms. Usually the individual investor cannot afford the denominations required in the "Money Market" (i.e. treasury bills, commercial paper, certificates of deposit), but through a money market mutual fund he can take advantage of these instruments when interest rates are high. These funds offer special checking account advantages. The minimum investment is generally $1,000.

National debt: The debt of the national government as distinguished from the debts of the political subdivisions of the nation and private business and individuals.

National debt ceiling: Limit set by Congress beyond which the national debt cannot rise. This limit is periodically raised by congressional vote.

Option: A contractual agreement between a buyer and a seller to buy or sell shares of a security. A *Call* option contract gives the right to purchase shares of a specific stock at a stated price within a given period of time. A *Put* option contract gives the buyer the right to sell shares of a specific stock at a stated price within a given period of time.

Per capita income: The nation's total income divided by the number of people in the nation.

Prime interest rate: The rate charged by banks on short-term loans to large commercial customers with the highest credit rating.

Producer price index: A statistical measure of the change in the price of wholesale goods. It is reported for 3 different stages of the production chain: crude, intermediate, and finished goods.

Program Trading: A term used for trading techniques involving large numbers and large blocks of stocks, usually used in conjunction with computer programs. Techniques include *Index Arbitrage* in which traders profit from price differences between stocks and futures contracts on stock indexes, and *Portfolio Insurance* which is the use of stock-index futures to protect stock investors from large losses when the market drops.

Public debt: The total of the nation's debts owed by state, local, and national government. This is considered a good measure of how much of the nation's spending is financed by borrowing rather than taxation.

Recession: A mild decrease in economic activity marked by a decline in real GNP, employment, and trade, usually lasting 6 months to a year, and marked by widespread decline in many sectors of the economy.

Seasonal adjustment: Statistical changes made to compensate for regular fluctuations in data that are so great they tend to distort the statistics and make comparisons meaningless. For instance, seasonal adjustments are made in midwinter for a slowdown in housing construction and for the rise in farm income in the fall after the summer crops are harvested.

Stagnation: A period of economic slowdown in which there is little growth in GNP, capital investment, and real income.

Stock: *Common Stocks* are shares of ownership in a corporation; they are the most direct way to participate in the fortunes of a company. There can be wide swings in the prices of this kind of stock. *Preferred Stock* is a type of stock on which a fixed dividend must be paid before holders of common stock are issued their share of the issuing corporation's earnings. Prices are higher and yields lower than comparable bonds. However, they are attractive to corporate investors because 85 percent of preferred dividends are tax exempt to corporations. *Convertible Preferred Stock* can be converted into the common stock of the company that issued the preferred. This stock has the advantage of producing a higher yield than common stock and it also has appreciation potential. *Over-the-Counter Stock* is not traded on the major or regional exchanges, but rather through dealers from whom you buy directly. These stocks tend to belong to smaller companies. Prices of OTC stocks are based on the dealer's supply and demand. *Blue Chip* stocks are so called because they have been leading stocks for a long time. *Growth* stocks are stocks whose earnings have grown over several years.

Stock-index Futures: A futures contract is an agreement to buy or sell a specific amount of a commodity or financial instrument at a particular price at a set date. Futures on a stock index (such as the Standard & Poor's 500) are bets on the future price of that group of stocks.

Supply-side economics: The school of economic thinking which stresses the importance of the costs of production as a means of revitalizing the economy. Advocates policies that raise capital and labor output by increasing the incentives to produce.

Takeover: The passing of control of one company by another company or group by sale or merger. A friendly takeover occurs when the acquired company's management is agreeable to the merger; when management is opposed to the merger it is an unfriendly takeover. Takeover *arbitrage* is the purchase and/or selling of the securities of companies involved in takeover situations in order to realize a profit.

Tender Offer: A public offer to buy a company's stock; usually priced at a premium above the market.

Unit Investment Trust: A portfolio of many different corporate bonds, preferred stocks, government-backed securities or utility common stocks in which you can invest with as little as $1,000. Professional managers choose the securities, arrange for safe-keeping and collect the income. You receive your pro rata share of income every month.

Zero Coupon Bond: A corporate or government bond that is issued at a deep discount from the maturity value and pays no interest during the life of the bond. It is redeemable at face value.

CONSUMER INFORMATION

Consumer Information Catalog

Source: Consumer Information Center, U.S. General Services Administration

The *Consumer Information Catalog* is a free listing of about 200 of the best federal consumer publications. They range from booklets on financial planning to planning a diet, from learning about federal benefits to getting an education, from fixing a car to dealing effectively with consumer problems. It also lists many resources that will help you get a passport or a birth certificate, find government documents or national parks, learn your rights and stand up for them. Many of these booklets are free.

The *Consumer Information Catalog* is published quarterly by the Consumer Information Center of the U.S. General Services Administration, so you will be able to send for the most current booklets. For your free copy of the *Consumer Information Catalog*, send your name and address to: Consumer Information Catalog, Pueblo, CO 81002. Educators, libraries, and other non-profit groups who are able to distribute 25 or more copies of the *Consumer Information Catalog* on a quarterly basis should write to the same address for an application to be placed on the mailing list. Costs prevent the Consumer Information Center from maintaining a mailing list for individuals.

The booklets listed below are available *free* from the *Consumer Information Catalog* as of Fall, 1989. Quantities of some may be limited. There is a $1 fee for handling. To order, please send your name and address, the item numbers of the booklets you want, and the $1 fee to: S. James, Consumer Information Center-M, P.O. Box 100, Pueblo, CO 81002.

Free Publications

Children

Handbook on Child Support Enforcement. The basic steps to follow if you need child support enforcement services; tips on solving enforcement problems. 40 pp. (1985) **505V.**

Kidsummit Against Drugs. Detailed instructions, forms, and resources to help you organize students in 4th grade and up to stop drug abuse. 20 pp. (1988) **589V.**

Plain Talk about Raising Children. Suggestions and advice from experienced parents. 4 pp. (1985) **599V.**

Education

Schools Without Drugs. Guide for parents, schools, students, and communities on how to fight drug use by children. Describes extent of the problem, effects of various drugs, and signs of use. Includes legal considerations and an extensive list of resources. 78 pp. (1989) **510V.**

Schools That Work: What Works in Educating Disadvantaged Children. Strategies to improve the achievement of disadvantaged students; describes successful schools in poor communities; for parents, teachers, administrators, & community leaders. 80 pp. (1987) **509V.**

AIDS and the Education of Our Children. Facts about AIDS, its transmission, and how teens are at risk. Methods of protection, guidelines for selecting educational materials, and sources for more information. 28 pp. (1988) **507V.**

Choosing a School for Your Child. How to find the right public or private school. Includes a checklist to help you evaluate schools and suggestions on how to transfer from one public school district to another. 30 pp. (1989) **597V.**

Federal Benefits

Social Security ... How It Works for You. Answers questions on how the system pays retirement, disability, and survivors' benefits. 20 pp. (1988) **515V.**

Guide to Health Insurance for People with Medicare. What Medicare pays for and what to look for in private insurance. 34 pp. (1989) **512V.**

Hospice Benefits Under Medicare. Describes the scope of medical and support services available to Medicare beneficiaries with a terminal illness. 5 pp. (1989) **600V.**

Catastrophic Protection and Other New Medicare Benefits. The Medicare Catastrophic Coverage Act limits your out-of-pocket expenses for hospital care, physician services, medical supplies, outpatient care, and drugs; and increases coverage for home-health care, hospice care and skilled nursing facility care. 12 pp. (1988) **582V.**

The Student Guide to Financial Aid from the U.S. Dept. of Education. Describes federal grants, loans, and work-study programs for college, vocational and technical school students after high school. 81 pp. (1989) **516V.**

Nutrition

Consumer's Guide to Food Labels. Explains dating, symbols, grades, and nutrition information on food labels. 4 pp. (1985) **517V.**

A Word About Low Sodium Diets. Tips on how to reduce your sodium intake. Gives recipes for salt substitutes. 5 pp. (1986) **524V.**

Diet, Nutrition, and Cancer Prevention: The Good News. An estimated one-third of all cancer deaths may be related to what we eat. This booklet will help you select, prepare and serve healthier food. Includes lists of high-fiber and low-fat foods. 11 pp. (1986) **518V.**

Planning a Diet for a Healthy Heart. How dietary fat and cholesterol increase the risk of heart disease; what to eat to reduce that risk. Includes a chart of fat and cholesterol levels in many common foods. 6 pp. (1987) **521V.**

Some Facts and Myths about Vitamins. What vitamins are and are not, and which foods are the best sources. 4 pp. (1987) **522V.**

Purchase, Preparation & Food Storage

Talking about Turkey. A complete guide with recipes and charts on thawing, cooking, and stuffing. 20 pp. (1984) **527V.**

The Safe Food Book: Your Kitchen Guide. Common causes and symptoms of food poisoning; what you can do to reduce the risks with specific instructions for handling meat and poultry, home canning, what to do when the freezer fails, and more. 32 pp. (1985) **526V.**

Health

Quakery. How to protect yourself from health fraud. Discusses how bogus remedies for cancer, arthritis, and the "battle of the bulge" can hurt you much more than help. 4 pp. (1985) **528V.**

(continued)

Who Donates Better Blood for You Than You? Discusses the advantages for donating blood to yourself before undergoing planned surgery. 3 pp. (1988) **530V.**

Comparing Contraceptives. Discusses effectiveness and possible side effects of 9 types of birth control with a comparison chart and statistics on use. 8 pp. (1985) **534V.**

A Doctor's Advice on Self-Care. There are more over-the-counter drugs available now than ever before which can cure, prevent, and diagnose illnesses. The U.S. Commissioner of Food and Drugs tells how to use them safely and effectively. 7 pp. (1989) **588V.**

Breast Exams: What You Should Know. Eighty percent of breast lumps are not cancer: how to check for lumps, how doctors examine them, what types of treatment are available. 17 pp. (1986) **544V.**

Clearing the Air: A Guide to Quitting Smoking. No-nonsense tips on kicking the habit. 32 pp. (1985) **547V.**

Facing Surgery: Why Not Get a Second Opinion? Answers this and other questions of the prospective patient. Includes toll-free number for locating specialists. 5 pp. (1979) **551V.**

Mental Health

Plain Talk about Stress. What stress is and how to deal with it. 2 pp. (1985) **561V.**

Plain Talk About Wife Abuse. The causes, emotional and physical consequences, and where an abused wife can get help. 3 pp. (1983) **562V.**

Schizophrenia: Questions and Answers. Describes this chronic, debilitating illness affecting millions of Americans: its nature, causes, treatments, how others can help, and the outlook for recovery. 25 pp. (1986) **563V.**

Money Management

Investment Swindles: How They Work and How to Avoid Them. How to spot investment fraud and protect yourself. Includes examples of common schemes used to entice investors. 20 pp. (1987) **568V.**

Investors' Bill of Rights. Tips to help you make an informed decision on investment risks and costs. 6 pp. (1987) **569V.**

How to Get the Most for Your Money

Source: *Consumer's Resource Handbook.*

Before Making a Purchase:

(1) Analyze what you need and what features are important to you.

(2) Compare brands. Use word-of-mouth recommendations and formal product comparison reports. Check with your local library for magazines and other publicatons containing consumer information.

(3) Compare stores. Look for a store with a good reputation and take advantage of sales.

(4) Check for any additional charges, such as delivery and service costs.

(5) Compare warranties.

(6) Read terms of contracts carefully.

(7) Check the return or exchange policy.

After Your Purchase:

(1) Follow proper use and care instructions for products.

(2) Read and understand the warranty provisions. Keep in mind that you may have additional warranty rights in your state. Check with your state or local consumer office to find out.

(3) If trouble develops, report the problem as soon as possible. Do not try to fix the product yourself as this may void the warranty.

(4) Keep a record of efforts to have your problem remedied. This record should include names of people you speak to, times, dates, and other relevant information.

(5) Send for the *Consumer's Resource Handbook* (see Source, above) to find out where and how to get your problem resolved.

(6) Clearly state your problem and the solution you want.

(7) Include all relevant details, along with copies of documents (proof of purchase).

(8) Briefly describe what you have done to resolve the problem.

(9) Allow each person you contact a reasonable period of time to resolve your problem before contacting another source for assistance.

Handling Your Own Complaint:

(1) Identify your problem and what you believe would be a fair settlement. Do you want your money back? Would you like the product repaired? Will an exchange do?

(2) Gather documentation regarding your complaint. Sales receipts, repair orders, warranties, cancelled checks, or contracts will back up your complaint and help the company solve your problem.

(3) Go back to where you made the purchase. Contact the person who sold you the item or performed the service. Calmly and accurately explain the problem and what action you would like taken. If that person is not helpful, ask for the supervisor or manager and repeat your complaint. A large percentage of consumer problems are resolved at this level. Chances are yours will be too.

(4) Don't give up if you are not satisfied with the response. If the company operates nationally or the product is a national brand, write a letter to the person responsible for consumer complaints at the company's headquarters. A listing of many of these companies can be found in the World Almanac's Business Directory on pages 781–787. If the company doesn't have a consumer office, direct your letter to the president of the company.

How to Write a Complaint Letter:

(1) If you have already contacted the person who sold you the product or service or the company is out of town, you will need to write a letter to pursue your complaint.

(2) If you need the president's name and the address of the company, first check in your phone directory to see if the company has a local office. If it does, call and ask for the name and address of the company's president. If there is no local listing, check *Standard & Poor's Register of Corporations, Directors and Executives.* It lists over 37,000 American business firms and can be found in most libraries.

(3) If you don't have the name of the manufacturer of the product, check your local library for the *Thomas Register.* It lists the manufacturers of thousands of products.

Basic Tips on Letter Writing:

(1) Include your name, address, and home and work phone numbers.

(2) Type your letter if possible. If it is handwritten, make sure it is neat and easy to read.

(3) Make your letter brief and to the point. Include all important facts about your purchase, including the date and place where you made the purchase, and any information you can give about the product or service such as serial or model numbers or specific type of service.

(4) State exactly what you want done about the problem and how long you are willing to wait to get it resolved. Be reasonable.

(5) Include all documents regarding your problems. Be sure to send COPIES, not originals.

(6) Avoid writing an angry, sarcastic, or threatening letter. The person reading your letter probably was not responsible for your problem, but may be very helpful in resolving it.

(7) Keep a copy of the letter for your records.

Who Owns What: Familiar Consumer Products

The following is a list of familiar consumer products and their parent companies. The address of the parent company can be found on pages 814-820.

Admiral appliances: Maytag
Ajax cleanser: Colgate-Palmolive
Allstate Insurance Co.: Sears, Roebuck
Almond Joy candy: Hershey
Anacin: American Home Products
Arrid anti-perspirant: Carter-Wallace

Ban anti-perspirant: Bristol-Myers
Beech Aircraft: Raytheon
Benson & Hedges cigarettes; Philip Morris
Betty Crocker products: General Mills
Big Boy restaurants: Marriott
Budweiser beer: Anheuser-Busch
Bufferin: Bristol-Myers
Business Week magazine: McGraw-Hill
Buster Brown shoes: Brown Group

Cap'n Crunch cereal: Quaker Oats
Carrier air conditioners: United Technologies
Celeste Pizza: Quaker Oats
Chap Stick: A.H. Robins
Charmin toilet tissues: Procter & Gamble
Chef Boy-ar-dee products: American Home Products
Cheer detergent: Procter & Gamble
Cheerios cereal: General Mills
Chicken of the Sea tuna: Ralston Purina
Clairol hair products: Bristol-Myers
Clorets mints: Warner-Lambert
Columbia Pictures: Coca Cola
Continental Airlines: Texas Air.
Copenhagen snuff: UST
Cover Girl cosmetics: Noxell
Cracker Jack: Borden
Crest toothpaste: Procter & Gamble
Crisco shortening: Procter & Gamble

Dean Witter financial services: Sears, Roebuck
Doritos chips: PepsiCo
Drano: Bristol-Meyers
Dristan: American Home Products
Duncan Hines cookies: Procter & Gamble
Easy-Off oven cleaner: American Home Products
Efferdent dental cleanser: Warner-Lambert
ESPN: Capital Cities/ABC
Eveready batteries: Ralston Purina
Excedrin: Bristol-Myers

Fab detergent: Colgate-Palmolive
Family Circle magazine: New York Times
Fisher Price toys: Quaker Oats
Flagg Bros. shoe stores: Genesco
Foamy shaving cream: Gillette
Folger coffee: Procter & Gamble
Formula 409 spray cleaner: Clorox
Franco-American foods: Campbell Soup
Frito-Lay snacks: PepsiCo
Fuller Brush prods.: Sara Lee
Gatorade: Quaker Oats
Gleem toothpaste: Procter & Gamble
Handy Wipes: Colgate-Palmolive
Hanes hosiery: Sara Lee
Head and Shoulders shampoo: Procter & Gamble
Hellman's mayonnaise: CPC International
Hi-C fruit drinks: Coca Cola
Hillshire Farm meats: Sara Lee
Home Box Office: Time
Hostess baked goods: Ralston Purina
Hush Puppies shoes: Wolverine World Wide
Ivory soap products: Procter & Gamble
Jack Daniel bourbon: Brown-Forman
Jell-o: Philip Morris
Jim Beam whiskey: American Brands
Ken-L-Ration pet foods: Quaker Oats
Kent cigarettes: Loews
Kinney shoe stores: Woolworth
Knorr soups: CPC International
Kool Aid: Philip Morris
La Menu frozen dinners: Campbell Soup
Ladies Home Journal magazine: Meredith
Lee jeans: VF Corp.
Lenox china: Brown-Forman
Lerner stores: The Limited
Lestoil: Noxell
Lipton tea: Unilever

Listerine mouth wash: Warner-Lambert
Log Cabin syrup: Philip Morris
Lord & Taylor dept. stores: May Dept. Stores
Lucite paints: Clorox

Maalox: Rorer Group
Marlboro cigarettes: Philip Morris
Mazola oil: CPC International
Maxwell House coffee: Philip Morris
Michelob beer: Anheuser-Busch
Midas automotive centers: Whitman
Miller beer: Philip Morris
Minute Rice: Philip Morris
Milton Bradley games: Hasbro
Minute Rice: Philip Morris
Mrs. Paul's frozen fish: Campbell Soup
Mueller's pasta prods.: CPC International
NBC Broadcasting: General Electric
Newsweek magazine: Washington Post
9-Lives cat food: H.J. Heinz
North American Van Lines: Norfolk Southern
Noxzema skin products: Noxell

Ore-Ida frozen foods: H.J. Heinz
Oscar Mayer meats: Philip Morris
Pampers: Procter & Gamble
Paper Mate pens: Gillette
People magazine: Time
Pepto-Bismol: Procter & Gamble
Pepperidge Farm products: Campbell Soup
Pizza Hut restaurants: PepsiCo
Plax oral rinse: Pfizer
Playskool toys: Hasbro
Prego spaghetti sauce: Campbell Soup
Prell shampoo: Procter & Gamble
Purex detergent: Greyhound
Q-Tips: Unilever

Radio Shack retail outlets: Tandy
Ramblin root beer: Coca Cola
Red Lobster Inns: General Mills
Reese's peanut butter cups: Hershey
Right Guard deodorant: Gillette
Rise shave lathers: Carter-Wallace
Robitussin cough syrup: A. H. Robins
Rolaids antacid: Warner-Lambert
Ronzoni pasta: Philip Morris
Roy Rogers restaurants: Marriott
Ruffles chips: PepsiCo

Sealy bedding: Ohio Mattress
San Giorgio pasta: Hershey
Sergeant's pet care products: A.H. Robins
Skippy peanut butter: CPC International
Simon & Schuster publishing: Paramount
Southern Comfort liquor: Brown-Forman
Sports Illustrated magazine: Time
Sprite soda: Coca-Cola
Sugartwin: Alberto Culver
Sunkist soft drink: General Cinema
Taco Bell restaurants: PepsiCo
Tagamet: Smithkline Beckman
Thom McAn shoe stores: Melville
Thomas English muffins: CPC International
Tide detergent: Procter & Gamble
Tiparillo's: Culbro
Trojan condoms: Carter-Wallace
Tupperware: Premark
Tylenol: Johnson & Johnson
Ultra Brite toothpaste: Colgate-Palmolive
V-8 vegetable juice: Campbell Soup
Vanity Fair apparel: VF Corp.
Velveeta cheese prods.: Philip Morris
Vicks cough medicines: Procter & Gamble
Virginia Slims cigarettes: Philip Morris
Walden Book stores: K mart
Wall Street Journal: Dow Jones
Weight Watchers: H.J. Heinz
West Bend appliances: Premark
Wheaties cereal: General Mills
White Owl cigars: Culbro
White Rain shampoo: Gillette
Wizard air freshener: American Home Products
Wyler's drink mixes: Borden

Business Directory

Listed below are major U.S. corporations, and major foreign corporations, **whose operations—products and services—directly concern the American consumer.** At the end of each listing is a **representative sample** of some of the company's products.

Company...Address...Phone Number...Chief executive officer...Business.

AMR Corp....PO Box 619616, Dallas/Ft. Worth Airport, TX 75261...(817) 355-1234...R.L. Crandell...Air transportation (American Airlines).

Abbott Laboratories... Abbott Park, No. Chicago, IL 60664...(312) 937-6100...R.A. Schoellhorn...health care prods.

Aetna Life & Casualty Co....151 Farmington Ave., Hartford, CT 06156...(203) 273-0123...James T. Lynn...insurance, financial services.

H.F. Ahmanson & Co....660 S. Figueroa St., Los Angeles, CA 90017...(213) 955-4200...R.H. Deihi...operates largest S&L assn. in U.S. (Home Savings of America).

Alberto-Culver Co....2525 Armitage Ave., Melrose Park, IL 60160...(312) 450-3000...Leonard H. Lavin...hair care preparations, feminine hygiene products, household and grocery items.

Albertson's Inc....250 Partcenter Blvd., Boise, ID 83726...(208) 385-6200...W.E. McCain...supermarkets

Alcan Aluminium Ltd....1188 Sherbrooke St. W., Montreal, Que., Canada H3C 3G2...(514) 848-8050...D.M. Culver...aluminum producer.

Alexander & Alexander Services...1211 Ave. of the Amer., New York, NY 10036...(212) 840-8500...T.H. Irvin...insurance & financial services.

Allied-Signal Inc.... Box 2245R, Morristown, NJ 07960 (201) 455-2000...Edward L. Hennessy Jr....aerospace, engineered materials, automotive prods.

Alltel Corp....100 Executive Pkwy., Hudson, OH 44236...(216) 650-7000...J.T. Ford...telephone service in Midwest, South, and Eastern U.S.

Aluminum Co. of America...1501 Alcoa Bldg., Pittsburgh, PA 15219...(412) 553-4545...P.H. O'Neill...mining, refining, & processing of aluminum.

Amerada Hess Corp....1185 Ave. of the Americas, N.Y., NY 10036...(212) 997-8500...L. Hess...integrated petroleum co.

American Brands, Inc....1700 E. Putnam Ave., Old Greenwich, CT 06870 (203) 698-5000...W.J. Alley...tobacco (Pall Mall, Carlton, Benson & Hedges cigarettes, Half and Half, Paleden pipe tobacco), whiskey (Jim Beam), snack foods, life insurance, office prods., food, financial services, toiletries.

American Cyanamid Co.... One Cyanamid Plaza, Wayne, NJ 07470...(201) 831-2000...G.J. Sella Jr....medical, agricultural, chemical, and consumer prods.

American Express Co.... American Express Tower, N.Y., NY 10285 (212) 640-2000...J.D. Robinson 3d...travelers checks, credit card services, insurance, investment services (Shearson Lehman Bros.).

American Greetings Corp....10500 American Rd., Cleveland, OH 44144...(216) 252-7300...M. Weiss...greeting cards, stationery, gift items.

American Home Products Corp....685 3d Ave., N.Y., NY 10017...(212) 986-1000...J.R. Stafford...prescription drugs, household prods. (Woolite, Easy-Off oven cleaner; Black Flag, Wizard air fresheners), food (Chef Boy-ar-dee), drugs (Anacin, Advil, Dristan).

American Medical International Inc....414 N. Camden Dr., Beverly Hills, CA 90210...(213) 278-6200...R.A. Gilleland...hospital management.

American Stores Co....19100 Von Karman Ave., Irvine, CA 92715 (714) 476-4400...J.L. Scott...retail food markets, dept. & drug stores.

American Telephone & Telegraph Co....550 Madison Ave. N.Y., NY 10022...(212) 605-5500...R.E. Allen...communications.

Ames Department Stores, Inc....2418 Main St., Rocky Hill, CT 06067...(203) 563-8234...P.B. Hollis...self-service discount stores.

Amoco Corp....200 E. Randolph Dr., Chicago, IL 60601...(312) 856-6111...R.M. Morrow...oil and gas exploration, production, and marketing.

Anheuser-Busch, Inc.... One Busch Place, St. Louis, MO 63118...(314) 577-2000...A.A. Busch 3d...brewing (Budweiser, Michelob, Bud Light, Natural Light, King Cobra, Busch).

Armstrong World Industries...W. Liberty St., Lancaster, PA 17604...(717) 397-0611...W.W. Adams...interior furnishings.

Arvin Industries, Inc....1531 13th St., Columbus, IN 47201...(812) 379-3000...J.K. Baker...auto exhaust systems, electric heaters, stereos.

Ashland Oil, Inc....1000 Ashland Dr., Russell, KY 41169...(606) 329-3333...J.R. Hall...petroleum refiner, chemicals.

Atlantic Richfield Co....515 S. Flower St., Los Angeles, CA 90071...(213) 486-3511...L.M. Cook...petroleum, chemicals, other natural resources.

Avery International Corp....150 N. Orange Grove Blvd., Pasadena, CA 91103...(818) 304-2000...Charles D. Miller...self-adhesive labels.

Avon Products, Inc....9 West 57th St., N.Y., NY 10019...(212) 546-6015...J. E. Preston...cosmetics, fragrances, toiletries, health care.

Bally Manufacturing Corp....8700 W. Bryn Mawr Ave., Chicago, IL 60631...(312) 399-1300...R.E. Mullane...lottery and gaming equip., hotel-casino operator, health & fitness centers.

Bausch & Lomb... One Lincoln First Square, Rochester, NY 14601...(716) 338-6000...D.E. Gill...manuf. of vision care products, accessories.

Baxter Travenol Labs Inc.... One Baxter Pky., Deerfield, IL 60015...(312) 948-2000...Vernon R. Loucks Jr....medical care prods & services.

Bell Atlantic Corp....1600 Market St., Philadelphia, PA 19103...(215) 963-6000...R.W. Smith...telephone service in mid-Atlantic region.

BellSouth Corp....675 W. Peachtree NE, Atlanta, GA 30367...(404) 249-2000...J.L. Clendenin...telephone service in the South.

Bethlehem Steel Corp....8th & Eaton Ave., Bethlehem, PA 18016...(215) 694-2424...W.F. Williams...steel & steel prods.

Bic Corporation... Wiley Street, Milford, CT 06401...(203) 783-2000...Bruno Bich...writing instruments, disposable lighters, and shavers.

Black & Decker Mfg. Co....701 E. Joppa Rd., Towson, MD 21204...(301) 583-3900...N.D. Archibald...manuf. power tools, household prods., small appliances.

H & R Block, Inc....4410 Main St., Kansas City, MO 64111...(816) 753-6900...Henry W. Bloch...tax preparation.

Boeing Company...7755 E. Marginal Way So., Seattle, WA 98108...(206) 655-6123...F.A. Shrontz...aircraft manuf.

Boise Cascade Corp.... One Jefferson Square, Boise, ID 83728...(208) 384-6161...J.B. Fery...timber, paper, wood prod.

Borden, Inc....277 Park Ave., N.Y., NY 10172...(212) 573-4000...R.J. Ventres...food, cheese and cheese products, snacks (Cracker Jack), beverages.

Bristol-Myers Co....345 Park Ave., N.Y., NY 10154...(212) 546-4000...Richard L. Gelb...toiletries (Ban anti-perspirant), hair items (Clairol), drugs (Bufferin, Comtrex, Excedrin), household prods.(Drano), infant formula (Enfamil). (Announced merger with Squibb in 1989).

Brown-Forman Corp....850 Dixie Hwy., Louisville, KY 40210...(502) 585-1100...W.L.L. Brown Jr....distilled spirits (Jack Daniel, Early Times), wines (Bolla, Cella), champagne (Korbel), liquor (Southern Comfort), Lenox china and crystal.

Brown Group, Inc....8400 Maryland Ave., St. Louis, MO 63166...(314) 854-4000...B.A. Brightwater Jr...manuf. and wholesaler of women's and children's shoes (Buster Brown, Regal Shoes); specialty retailing.

Brunswick Corp.... One Brunswick Plaza, Skokie, IL 60077...(312) 470-4700...J.F. Reichert...marine, recreation prods, bowling centers & equip., fishing equip.

Burlington Coat Factory Warehouse Corp.... Route 130 North, Burlington, NJ 08016...(609) 387-7800...M.G. Milstein...discount apparel stores.

Burlington Northern Inc....999 3d Ave., Seattle, WA 98104...(206) 467-3838...R.M. Bressler...rail transportation.

CBS Inc....51 W. 52d St., N.Y., NY 10019...(212) 975-4321...L.A. Tisch...broadcasting, video cassettes, recorded music, leisure prods.

CPC International, Inc....International Plaza, Englewood Cliffs, NJ 07632...(201) 894-4000...J.R. Eiszner...branded food items (Hellman's, Best Foods, Mazola oil, Skippy peanut butter, Knorr Soups, Mueller's pasta prods., Thomas English muffins), corn wet milling prods.

Caesar's World, Inc....1801 Century Park East, Los Angeles, CA 90067...(213) 552-2711...H. Gluck...hotels & casinos.

Campbell Soup Co....Campbell Pl., Camden, NJ 08103...(609) 342-4800...R. G. McGovern...canned soups, spaghetti (Franco-American), vegetable juice (V-8), pork and beans, pet foods, restaurants, confections, Le Menu frozen dinners, Prego spaghetti sauce, Mrs. Paul's frozen fish, Pepperidge Farm breads.

Capital Cities/ABC Inc....77 W. 66th Street, New York, NY 10023...(212) 456-7777...T.S. Murphy...operates television and radio stations, newspapers, cable TV (ESPN).

Carter Hawley Hale Stores, Inc....550 S. Flower St., Los Angeles, CA 90071...(213) 620-0150...P.M. Hawley...dept. stores, specialty stores.

Carter-Wallace, Inc....767 5th Ave., New York, NY 10153...(212) 758-4500...H.H. Hoyt Jr....personal care items, anti-perspirant (Arrid), shave lathers (Rise), condoms (Trojan), laxative (Carter's Pills), pet products.

Castle & Cooke, Inc....10900 Wilshire Blvd., Los Angeles, CA 90024...(213) 842-1500...D.H. Murdock... food processing, Dole.

Caterpillar Inc....100 N.E. Adams St., Peoria, IL 61629...(309) 675-1000...G.A. Schaefer...heavy duty earth-moving equip.

Champion International Corp....1 Champion Plaza, Stamford, CT 06921...(203) 358-7000...A.C. Sigler...forest prods.

Chase Manhattan Corp....1 Chase Manhattan Plaza, New York, NY 10081...(212) 552-2222...W.C. Butcher...Bank holding co.

Chevron Corp....225 Bush St., San Francisco, CA 94104...(415) 894-7700...K.T. Derr...integrated oil co.

Chrysler Corp....12000 Chrysler Dr., Detroit, MI 48288...(313) 956-5252...Lee Iacocca...cars, trucks.

Circle K Corp....1601 N 7th St., Phoenix, AZ 85006...(602) 253-9600...R.M. Reade...convenience store chain.

Circuit City Stores, Inc....2040 Thalbro St., Richmond, VA 23230...(804) 257-4292...R.L. Sharp...retailer of electronic equip., consumer appliances.

Circus Circus Enterprises, Inc....2880 Las Vegas Blvd., S. Las Vegas, NV 89109...(702) 734-0410...W.G. Bennett...casino operator.

Citicorp...399 Park Ave., N.Y., NY 10043...(212) 559-1000...J.S. Reed...largest U.S. commercial bank.

Clayton Homes...P.O. Box 15169, Knoxville, TN 37901...(615) 970-7200...J.L. Clayton...produces & sells manufactured homes.

Clorox Co....1221 Broadway, Oakland, CA 94612...(415) 271-7000...C.R. Weaver...retail consumer prods (Formula 409, Twice As Fresh, Lucite paints, Kingsford charcoal briquets, Hidden Valley Ranch salad dressing).

Coachman Industries Inc....601 E. Beardsley Ave., Elkhart, IN 46515...(219) 262-0123...T.H. Corson...manuf. recreational vehicles.

Coca-Cola Co....One Coca-Cola Plaza, Atlanta, GA 30313...(404) 676-2121...R.C. Goizueta...soft drink (Coca Cola, Sprite, Ramblin root beer), syrups, citrus and fruit juices (Minute Maid, Hi-C), films (Columbia Pictures).

Colgate-Palmolive Co....300 Park Ave., N.Y., NY 10022...(212) 310-2000...R. Mark...soaps (Palmolive, Irish Spring), detergents (Fab, Ajax, Fresh Start), tooth paste (Colgate, Ultra Brite), household prods. (Handy Wipes, Curad bandages).

Commodore International Ltd....P.O. Box N-10256, Nassau, Bahamas...(215) 431-9100...I. Gould...microcomputer systems, semiconductors component, consumer electronics, office equipment.

Compaq Computer Corp....20555 FM 149, Houston, TX 77070...(713) 370-0670...J.R. Canion...portable, desktop computers.

Control Data Corp....8100 34th Ave. South, Minneapolis, MN 55420...(612) 853-8100...R.M. Price...computer systems & services.

Adolph Coors Co....East of Town, Golden, CO 80401...(303) 279-6565...W. K. Coors...brewery.

Corning Glass Works...Houghton Park, Corning, NY 14831...(607) 974-9000...J.R. Houghton...glass mfg.

Crane Co....737 3d Ave., N.Y., NY 10017...(212) 415-7300...R.S. Evans...fluid & pollution controls, aircraft and aerospace, building prods.

A.T. Cross Co....One Albion Rd., Lincoln, RI 02865...(401) 333-1200...B.R. Boss...writing instruments.

Crystal Brands, Inc....Crystal Brands Rd., Southport, CT 06490...(203) 254-6200...R.F. Kral...apparel, accessories.

Culbro Corp....387 Park Avenue South, New York, NY 10016...(212) 561-8700...E. M. Cullman...cigars (Corina, Robert Burns, White Owl, Tiparillo's), snack foods.

Dana Corp....4500 Dorr St., Toledo, OH 43697...(419) 535-4500...Gerald B. Mitchell...truck and auto parts supplies.

Data General Corp....4400 Computer Dr., Westboro, MA 01580...(508) 366-8911...E. D. deCastro...computer & communications sytems manuf.

Dayton-Hudson Corp....777 Nicollet Mall, Minneapolis, MN 55402...(612) 370-6948...K.A. Macke...department, specialty, stores, Mervyn's, Target.

Deere & Company...John Deere Rd., Moline, IL 61265...(309) 765-8000...Robert A. Hanson...farm, industrial, and outdoor power equip.

Delta Air Lines, Inc....Hartsfield Atlanta Intl. Airport, Atlanta, GA 30320...(404) 765-2600...R.W. Allen...air transportation.

Diebold, Inc....P.O. Box 8230, Canton, OH 44711...(216) 489-4000...R. Mahoney...equip. for financial insts.

Digital Equipment Corp....146 Main St., Maynard, MA 01754...(508) 493-5111...Kenneth H. Olsen...computer manuf.

Walt Disney Co....500 S. Buena Vista St., Burbank, CA 91521...(818) 560-1000...M.D. Eisner...motion pictures, CATV, amusement parks, Disneyland, Walt Disney World, Epcot Center.

Donnelly & Sons Co....2223 Martin Luther King Drive, Chicago, IL 60616...(312) 326-8000...J.R. Walter...largest commercial printer.

Dow Chemical Co....2030 Dow Center, Midland, MI 48674...(517) 636-1000...F.P. Popoff...chemicals, plastics, metals, consumer prods.

Dow Jones & Co....World Financial Center, New York, NY 10281...(212) 416-2000...W. H. Phillips...financial news service, publishing (Wall Street Journal, Barron's, Ottaway Newspapers).

Dresser Industries, Inc....1600 Pacific Ave., Dallas, TX 75201...(214) 740-6000...J.J. Murphy...supplier of technology and services to energy related industries.

Dun & Bradstreet Corp....299 Park Ave., New York, NY 10171...(212) 593-6800...C.W. Moritz...business information and computer services, publishing, broadcasting.

E.I. du Pont de Nemours & Co....1007 Market St., Wilmington, DE 19898...(302) 774-1000...E.S. Woolard Jr....chemicals, petroleum, consumer prods., coal.

Eastman Kodak Co....343 State St., Rochester, NY 14650...(716) 724-4000...C.H. Chandler...photographic prods, chemicals, health care (Sterling Drug).

Eaton Corp....Eaton Center, Cleveland, OH 44114...(216) 523-5000...J.R. Stover...manuf. of electronic, electrical prods., vehicle components.

Emerson Electric Co....8000 W. Florissant Ave., St. Louis, MO 63136...(314) 553-2000...C.F. Knight...electrical/electronics products & systems

Ethyl Corp....330 S. 4th St., Richmond, VA 23217...(804) 788-5000...Floyd D. Gottwald Jr....petroleum and industrial chemicals.

Exxon Corp....1251 Ave. of the Americas, N.Y., NY 10020...(212) 333-6900...L.G. Rawl...world's largest oil co.

Family Dollars Stores, Inc....10401 Old Monroe Rd., Charlotte, NC 28212...(704)847-6961...L.E. Levine...discount variety stores.

Federal Express Corp....2990 Corporate Ave., Memphis, TN 38132...(901) 369-3600...F.W. Smith...small package delivery service.

Fieldcrest Cannon, Inc....326 East Stadium Dr., Eden, NC 27288...(919) 627-3000...J.B. Ely...household textile prods., rugs (Karastan, Laurelcrest).

Fleetwood Enterprises, Inc....3125 Myers St., Riverside, CA 92523...(714) 351-3500...John C. Crean...manufactured homes, recreational vehicles.

Fluor Corp....3333 Michelson Dr., Irvine, CA 92730...(714) 975-2000...D.S. Tappan Jr....engineering and construction, natural resources.

Ford Motor Co....The American Rd., Dearborn, MI 48121...(313) 845-8540...D.E. Peterson...motor vehicles, Ford Tractor, Lincoln-Mercury.

GTE Corp....One Stamford Forum, Stamford, CT 06904...(203) 965-2000...J.L. Johnson...communications prods. (U.S. Sprint), electronics.

Gannett Co., Inc....P.O. Box 7858, Washington, DC 20044...(703) 284-6000...J.J. Curley...newspaper publishing (USA Today), TV stations, outdoor advertising.

The GAP, Inc...900 Cherry Ave., San Bruno, CA 94066...(415) 952-4400...D.G. Fisher...casual and activewear retailer.

Gencorp...175 Ghent Rd., Fairlawn, OH 44313...(216) 869-4200...A.W. Reynolds...aerospace, auto prods., polymer prods.

Genentech, Inc....460 Point San Bruno Blvd., S. San Francisco, CA 94080...(415) 266-1000...R.A. Swanson...world's largest biotechnology corp.

General Cinema Corp....27 Boylston St., Chestnut Hill, MA 02167...(617) 232-8200...R. A. Smith...movie exhibitor, soft drinks (Sunkist), speciality retailing.

General Dynamics Corp....Pierre Laclede Ctr., St. Louis, MO 63105...(314) 889-8200...S.C. Pace...military and commercial aircraft, tactical missiles.

General Electric Co....3135 Easton Ave., Fairfield, CT 06431...(203) 373-2211...J. F. Welch Jr....electrical, electronic equip, finance (Kidder, Peabody & Co.), radio, television (NBC), polymer plastic prods.

General Instrument Corp....767 5th Ave., New York, NY 10153...(212) 207-6230...F. G. Hickey...race track betting systems, CATV, semiconductors, electronic equip.

General Mills, Inc....9200 Wayzata Blvd., Minneapolis, MN 55440...(612) 540-2311...H.B. Atwater Jr....foods, toys, restaurants, fashion and specialty retailing, Total, Bisquick, Wheaties, Cheerios, Hamburger Helper, Betty Crocker, Red Lobster Inns).

General Motors Corp....Gen. Motors Bldg., Detroit, MI 48202...(313) 556-5000...R. B. Smith...world's largest auto manuf.

Genesco Inc....Genesco Park, Nashville, TN 37202...(615) 367-7000...W.S. Wire 2d...footwear and men's clothing, Hardy, Laredo, Jarman, Flagg Bros., Johnston & Murphy.

Genuine Parts Co....2999 Circle 75 Pkwy, Atlanta, GA 30339...(404) 953-1700...W. Looney...distributes auto replacement parts (NAPA).

Georgia-Pacific Corp....133 Peachtree St., NE, Atlanta, GA 30303...(404) 521-4720...T.M. Hahn Jr....building prods., pulp, paper, chemicals.

Gerber Products Co....445 State St., Fremont, MI 49412...(616) 928-2000...D.W. Johnson...baby foods, clothing, nursery accessories.

Giant Food Inc....P.O. Box 1804, Washington, DC 20013...(301) 341-4100...I. Cohen...supermarkets.

Gillette Co....Prudential Tower Bldg., Boston, MA 02199...(617) 421-7000...Colman M. Mockler Jr....razors, pens (Paper Mate; Flair), toiletries (Right Guard deodorants, Foamy shaving cream, Earth Born shampoo), hair products (Toni, Adorn, White Rain).

Golden Nugget, Inc....129 Freemont St., Las Vegas, NV 89101...(702) 385-7111...Steve Wynn...operates casino-hotels.

B.F. Goodrich Company...3925 Embassy Pkwy, Akron, OH 44313...(216) 374-3985...John D. Ong...chemical, aerospace prods.

Goodyear Tire & Rubber Co....1144 E. Market St., Akron, OH 44316...(216) 796-2121...T.H. Barrett...tires, rubber prods.

Gordon Jewelry Corp....820 Fannin St., Houston TX 77002...(713) 222-8080...D.P. Gordon...largest jewelry retailer.

W.R. Grace & Co....Grace Plaza, 1114 Ave. of the Americas, N.Y., NY 10036...(212) 819-5500...J. Peter Grace...-

chemicals, natural resources, consumer prods. and services, restaurants, Channel Home Centers.

Great Atlantic & Pacific Tea Co....2 Paragon Dr., Montvale, NJ 07645...(201) 573-9700...James Wood...supermarket chain.

Greyhound Corp....Greyhound Tower, Phoenix, AZ 85077...(602) 248-4000...John W. Teets...bus manuf., household prods. (Dial soap, Purex, Armour Star), financial services, food services.

Grumman Corp....1111 Stewart, Bethpage, NY 11714...(516) 575-0574...J. O'Brien...aerospace, truck bodies, electronics.

Hannaford Bros. Co....145 Pleasant Hill Rd., Scarborough, ME 04074...(207) 883-2911...J.L. Moody Jr....operates supermarkets, drug stores.

Harcourt Brace Jovanovich, Inc....Orlando, FL 32887...(305) 345-2000...R.O. Caulo...textbook publisher, amusement parks, insurance.

Harley-Davidson, Inc....3700 W. Junear Ave., Milwaukee, WI 53208...(414) 342-4680...R.F. Terrlink...manuf. of motorcycles, parts & accessories.

Hartmarx...101 N. Wacker Dr., Chicago, IL 60606...(312) 372-6300...H.A. Weinberg...apparel manufacturer and retailer (Hickey-Freeman).

Hasbro Inc....1027 Newport Ave., P.O. Box 1059, Pawtucket, R.I. 02862...(401) 727-5000...S.D. Hassenfeld...toy manuf. & marketer (Milton Bradley, Playskool, G.I. Joe).

H.J. Heinz Co....P.O. Box 57, Pittsburgh, PA 15230...(412) 456-5700...Anthony J.F. O'Reilly...foods (Star-Kist, Ore-Ida, '57 Varieties), 9-Lives cat food, Weight Watchers.

Helene Curtis Industries, Inc....325 N. Wells St., Chicago, IL 60610...(312) 292-2224...R.J. Gidwitz...hair care prods. (Finesse, Sauve, Salon Selectives).

Hershey Foods Corp....100 Mansion Rd., Hershey, PA 17033...(717) 534-4000...R.A. Zimmerman...chocolate & confectionery prods., (Reese's peanut butter cups, Kit Kat, Peter Paul Mounds, Almond Joy), pasta (San Giorgio).

Hewlett-Packard Co....3000 Hanover Street, Palo Alto, CA 94304...(415) 857-1501...John A. Young...electronic instruments.

Hillenbrand Industries, Inc....Highway 46, Batesville, IN 47006...(812) 934-7000...D.A. Hillenbrand...manuf. burial caskets, electronically operated hospital beds.

Holiday Corp....1023 Cherry Rd., Memphis, TN 38117...(901) 762-8600...M.D. Rose...hotels, (Holiday Inn, Hampton Inn Hotels, Embassy Suite Hotels), motels, casinos (Harrah's).

Holly Farms Corp....P.O. Box 17236, Memphis, TN 38119...(901) 761-3610...R.L. Taylor 2d...poultry, other food prods.

Home Depot, Inc....2727 Paces Ferry Rd., Atlanta, GA 30339...(404) 433-8211...Bernard Marcus...retailer of building materials & home improvement prods.

Honda Motor Co., LTD...1270 Ave. of the Americas, N.Y., NY 10020...(212) 765-3804...Tadashi Kume...manuf. autos, motorcycles.

Honeywell, Inc....Honeywell Plaza, Minneapolis, MN 55408...(612) 870-5200...J.J. Renier...industrial systems & controls, aerospace guidance systems, information systems.

Geo. A. Hormel & Co....501 16th Ave. N.E., Austin, MN 55912...(507) 437-5611...R.L. Knowlton...meat packaging, pork and beef prods (Spam, Light & Lean, Dinty Moore, Mary Kitchen).

Houghton-Mifflin Co....One Beacon St., Boston, MA 02108...(617) 725-5000...H.T. Miller...book publishing.

Household International Inc....2700 Sanders Rd., Prospect Heights, IL 60070...(312) 564-3663...D.C. Clark...financial and insurance services.

Huffy Corp....7701 Byers Rd., Miamisburg, OH 45342...(513) 866-6251...H.A. Shaw 3d...bicycle manuf.

Humana, Inc....500 W. Main St., Louisville, KY 40201...(502) 580-1000...D. A. Jones...operates hospitals, provides health care plans.

ITT Corp....320 Park Ave., N.Y., NY 10022...(212) 752-6000...R.V. Araskog...manuf., installs communication and electronic equip., auto equip., insurance, financial services, hotels, educational services.

Imperial Oil Ltd....111 St. Clair Ave. W., Toronto, Ont., Canada M5W 113...(416) 968-5076...A.R. Haynes...Canada's largest oil co.

Interco Inc....101 S. Hanley Rd., St. Louis, MO 63105...(314) 863-1100...H. Saligman...apparel, footwear mfg., specialty apparel shops.

International Business Machines Corp....Old Orchard Rd., Armonk, NY 10504...(914) 765-1900...J.F. Akers...information-handling systems, equip., and services.

International Paper Co....2 Manhattanville Rd., Purchase, NY 10577...(901) 763-6000...J.A. Georges...paper, wood prods.

Johnson & Johnson...One Johnson & Johnson Plaza, Brunswick, NJ 08933...(201) 524-0400...R.S. Larsen...surgical dressings, pharmaceuticals (Tylenol, Medipren), health and baby prods.

Jostens, Inc....5501 Norman Center Dr., Minneapolis, MN 55437...(612) 830-3287...H. W. Lurton...school rings, yearbooks.

K mart Corp....3300 W. Big Beaver Rd., Troy, MI 48084...(313) 643-1000...J. E. Antonini...largest U.S. chain of discount stores, book stores (Walden Book), cafeterias, drug stores (Pay Less Drug Stores), home improvement retail stores.

Kellogg Co....One Kellogg Sq., Battle Creek, MI 49016...(616) 961-2000...William E. LaMothe...ready to eat cereals & other food prods., Mrs. Smith's Pie Co., Salada Foods, Eggo.

Kimberly-Clark Corp....P.O. Box 619100, Dallas, TX 75261...(214) 830-1200...Darwin E. Smith...paper and lumber prods., consumer prods. (Kleenex, Huggies).

King World Productions, Inc....830 Morris Turnpike, Short Hills, NJ 07078...(201) 376-1313...M. King...syndicator of first-run TV programs.

Knight-Ridder, Inc....One Herold Plaza, Miami, FL 33132...(305) 376-3800...J.K. Batten...newspaper publishing, TV broadcasting, book publishing, information services.

Kroger Co....1014 Vine St., Cincinnati, OH 45201...(513) 762-4000...Lyle Everingham...grocery chain, drugstores (SupeRx).

L.A. Gear, Inc....4221 Redwood Ave., Los Angeles, CA 91204...(213) 822-1995...R.Y. Greenberg...athletic & leisure footwear, casual apparel.

La-Z-Boy Chair Co....1284 N. Telegraph Rd., Monroe, MI 48161...(313) 242-1444...C. T. Knabusch...reclining chair mfg.

Land's End, Inc....One Land's End Lane, Dodgeville, WI 53595...(608) 935-9341...R.C. Anderson...direct-mail catalog co.

Eli Lilly & Company...Lilly Corp. Center, Indianapolis, IN 46285...(317) 276-6070...Richard D. Wood...mfg. human health and agricultural products.

The Limited, Inc....Two Limited Pkwy., Columbus, OH 43216...(614) 479-7000...L.H. Wexner...women's apparel stores (Lane Bryant, Lerner, Victoria's Secret), Abercrombie & Fitch.

Litton Industries, Inc....360 N. Crescent Dr., Beverly Hills, CA 90210...(213) 859-5000...O.L. Hoch...industrial systems & services, advanced electronic systems, electronic & electrical prods., marine engineering.

Lockheed Corp....4500 Park Granada Blvd., Calabasas, CA 91399...(818) 712-2380...D.M. Tellup...commercial and military aircraft, missiles.

Loews Corp....667 Madison Ave., N.Y., NY 10021...(212) 545-2000...Laurence A. Tisch...tobacco prods. (Kent, Newport, True), watches, hotels, real estate, insurance.

Long's Drug Stores Corp....141 North Civic Dr., Walnut Creek, CA 94596...(415) 937-1170...R.M. Long...drug store chain.

Lowe's Cos., Inc....Hway 268 East, N. Wilkesboro, NC 28659...(919) 651-4000...L.G. Herring...retailer of building materials & related prods.

Luby's Cafeterias, Inc....211 Northeast Loop 410, San Antonio, TX 78265...(512) 654-9000...J.B. Lahourcade...operates cafeterias in SW U.S.

MCA Inc....100 Universal City Plaza, Universal City, CA 91608...(818) 777-1000...Lew R. Wasserman...motion pictures, television, music publishing, mail order, novelty, and gift merchandise.

Manor Care, Inc....10750 Columbia Pike, Silver Spring, MD 20901...(301) 681-9400...S. Bainum...operates nursing centers.

Marriott Corp....Marriott Dr., Wash., DC 20058...(301) 380-9000...J. Willard Marriott Jr....restaurants (Roy Rogers, Big Boy), hotels, food services.

Martin Marietta Corp....6801 Rockledge Dr., Bethesda, MD 20817...(301) 897-6000...N.R. Augustine...electronics, aerospace.

Mattel, Inc....5150 Rosecrans Ave., Hawthorne, CA 90250...(213) 978-5150...J.W. Amerman...toy & hobby prods (Barbie doll, Masters of the Universe, Hot Wheels).

May Department Stores Co....611 Olive Street, St. Louis, MO 63101...(314) 342-6300...D.C. Farrell...department stores (Hecht's, Famous Barr, G. Fox, Lord & Taylor, Foley's, Filene's), discount chain (Caldor).

Maytag Corp....403 W. 4th St. North, Newton, IA 50208...(515) 792-7000...Daniel J. Krumm...manuf. home laundry equip, appliances (Magic Chef prods).

McCormick & Co., Inc....11350 McCormick Rd., Hunt Valley, MD 21031...(301) 771-7301...C.P. McCormick...world's leading manuf. of seasoning & flavoring prods.

McDonald's Corp....McDonald's Plaza, Oak Brook, IL 60521...(312) 575-3000...M.R. Quinlan...fast service restaurants.

McDonnell Douglas Corp....P.O. Box 516, St. Louis, MO 63166...(314) 232-0232...J. F. McDonnell...commercial & military aircraft, space systems & missiles.

McGraw-Hill, Inc....1221 Ave. of the Americas, New York, NY 10020...(212) 512-2000...J.L. Dionne...book, magazine publishing (Business Week), information & financial services (Standard and Poor's), TV stations.

Mead Corporation...Courthouse Plaza Northeast, Dayton, OH 45463...(513) 222-6323...B.R. Roberts...printing and writing paper, paperboard, packaging, shipping containers, pulp and lumber.

Media General, Inc....333 E. Grace St., Richmond, VA 23219...(804) 649-6000...J.S. Evans...broadcasting, newspaper publishing.

Medtronic, Inc....7000 Central Ave., Minneapolis, MN 55432...(612) 574-4000...W.R. Wallin...manuf. prosthetic and theraputic devices.

Melville Corp....3000 Westchester Ave., Harrison, NY 10528...(914) 253-8000...S.P. Goldstein...shoe stores (Thom McAn), apparel (Marshalls, Chess King), drug stores.

Merck & Co., Inc....P.O. Box 2000, Rahway, NJ 07065...(201) 594-4000...P. Roy Vagelos...human & animal health care prods.

Meredith Corp....1716 Locust St., Des Moines, IA 50336...(515) 284-3000...J.O. Rehm...magazine publishing (Better Homes and Gardens, Ladies Home Journal), book publishing, broadcasting, commercial printing.

Merrill Lynch & Co., Inc....World Financial Center, N.Y., NY 10281...(212) 449-1000...W.A Schreyer...securities broker, financial services, real estate.

Minnesota Mining & Manuf. Co....3M Center, St. Paul, MN 55144...(612) 733-1100...A.F. Jacobson...abrasives, adhesives, building services & chemicals, electrical, health care, photographic, printing, recording materials.

Mobil Corp....150 E. 42d St., N.Y., NY 10017...(212) 883-4242...A.E. Murray...international oil co., chemicals.

Monsanto Company...800 N. Lindbergh Blvd., St. Louis, MO 63167...(314) 694-1000...R. J. Mahoney...chemicals, electronics, agricultural prods., pharmaceuticals, consumer prods. (NutraSweet).

Motorola, Inc....1303 E. Algonquin Rd., Schaumburg, IL 60196...(312) 397-5000...G.M.C. Fisher...electronic equipment and components.

NCR Corp....1700 S. Patterson Blvd., Dayton, OH 45479...(513) 445-5000...Charles E. Exley Jr....business information processing systems.

National Medical Enterprises, Inc....11620 Wilshire Blvd, Los Angeles, CA 90025...(213) 479-5526...R.K. Eamer...operates hospitals.

National Semiconductor Corp....2900 Semiconductor Dr., Santa Clara, CA 95051...(408) 721-5000...Charles E. Sporck...manuf. of semiconductors.

Navistar Intl. Corp....401 N. Michigan Ave, Chicago, IL 60611...(312) 836-2000...J.C. Cotting...manuf. heavy duty trucks, parts.

New York Times Co....229 W. 43rd St., N.Y., NY 10036...(212) 556-1234...A. O. Sulzberger...newspapers, radio, CATV stations, magazines (Family Circle, Golf Digest).

Norfolk Southern Corp....One Commercial Place, Norfolk, VA 23510...(804) 629-2680...A.B. McKinnon...operates

Norfolk & Southern railways, freight carrier (North American Van Lines).

Northrop Corp....1840 Century Park E., Los Angeles, CA 90067...(213) 553-6262...Thomas V. Jones...aircraft, electronics, communications.

Noxell Corp....11050 York Rd., Hunt Valley, MD 21030...(301) 785-7300...G. L. Bunting Jr....toiletry, household, consumer prods. (Noxzema, Lestoil, Clarion, Cover Girl).

Nynex Corp....335 Madison Ave., N.Y., NY 10017...(212) 370-7400...D.C. Staley...telephone co. in northeast U.S.

Occidental Petroleum Corp....10889 Wilshire Blvd., Los Angeles, CA 90024...(213) 879-1700...Dr. Armand Hammer...oil, gas, chemicals, coal, agriculture.

Ogden Corp....2 Pennsylvania Plaza, New York NY 10121...(212) 868-6100...R. E. Ablon...transportation, foods, metals, financial services.

Ohio Mattress Co....1501 Bond Court Bldg., Cleveland OH 44114...(216) 522-1310...E.M. Wuliger...bedding manuf. (Sealy, Sterns & Foster).

Olin Corp....120 Long Ridge Rd., Stamford, CT 06904...(203) 356-2000...J.W. Johnstone Jr....chemicals, water treatment prods., aerospace.

Olsten Corp....One Merrick Ave., Westbury, NY 11590...(516) 832-8200...W. Olsten...provides temporary workers.

Outboard Marine Corp....100 Sea Horse Dr., Waukegan, IL 60085...(312) 689-6200...C.D. Strang...outboard motors (Evinrude, Johnson), boats (Four Winns, Stratos, Hydra-Sports), mowers (Lawn Boy).

Owens-Corning Fiberglas Corp....Fiberglas Tower, Toledo, OH 43659...(419) 248-8000...W.W. Boeschenstein...glass fiber and related prods.

Oxford Industries, Inc....222 Piedmont Ave., N.E., Atlanta, GA 30308...(404) 659-2424...J.H. Lanier...men's and women's apparel products.

Pacific Telesis Group...130 Kearny St., San Francisco, CA 94108...(415) 882-8000...S. L. Ginn...telephone service.

Pan Am Corp....Pan Am Bldg., 200 Park Ave. N.Y., NY 10166...(212) 880-1234...T. G. Plaskett...air transportation.

Paramount Communications Inc.,...15 Columbus Circle, N.Y., NY 10023...(212) 373-8000...M.S. Davis...financial services, consumer and food products, home furnishings, entertainment (Paramount Pictures, Madison Square Garden), publishing (Simon & Schuster).

J.C. Penney Co....14841 N. Dallas Pkwy., Dallas, TX 75240...(214) 591-2010...W. R. Howell, chmn....dept. stores, catalog sales, drug stores, insurance.

Pennzoil Co....P.O. Box 2967, Houston, TX 77252...(713) 546-4000...J.H. Liedtke...integrated oil and gas co.

Pep Boys—Manny, Moe & Jack...3111 W. Allegheny Ave., Philadelphia, Pa. 19132...(215) 229-9000...B. Strauss...automotive parts and accessories, retail stores, household items, hardware, bicycles.

PepsiCo, Inc....Anderson Hill Rd., Purchase, NY 10577...(914) 253-2000...D.W. Calloway...soft drinks, (Pepsi-Cola, Slice), snack foods (Ruffles, Lays, Doritos) restaurants (Pizza Hut, Kentucky Fried Chicken, Taco Bell).

Perry Drug Stores, Inc....5400 Perry Dr., Pontiac, MI 48056...(313) 334-1300...J.A. Robinson...drug stores, health care.

Petrie Stores Corp....70 Enterprise Ave., Seacaucus, NJ 07094...(201) 866-3600...M.J. Petrie...operates chain of women's specialty stores.

Pfizer Inc....235 E. 42d St., N.Y., NY 10017...(212) 573-2323...E.T. Pratt Jr....pharmaceutical, hospital, agricultural, chemical prods., consumer prods. (Plax oral rinse).

Philip Morris Cos., Inc....120 Park Ave., N.Y., NY 10017...(212) 880-5000...H. Maxwell...cigarettes (Marlboro, Benson & Hedges, Virginia Slims), beer (Miller High Life, Lite, Lowenbrau brands), packaged foods (Jell-o, Oscar Meyer meats, Ronzoni pasta, Entenmann baked goods, Maxwell House coffee, Kool Aid, Tang, Cheez Whiz & Velveeta cheese prods.).

Phillips-Van Heusen Corp....1290 Ave. of the Americas, New York, NY 10104...(212) 541-5200...L. S. Phillips...manuf. apparel for men & women; operates retail stores.

Pitney Bowes, Inc.,...Stamford, CT 06926...(203) 356-5000...G. B. Harvey...postage meters, mail handling equip., office equipment.

Playboy Enterprises, inc....919 N. Michigan Ave., Chicago, IL 60611...(312) 751-8000...C. Hefner...magazine publishing, CATV, merchandising.

Polaroid Corp....549 Technology Sq., Cambridge, MA 02139...(617) 577-2000...I.M. Booth...photographic equip., supplies and optical goods.

Premark Intl., Inc....1717 Deerfield Rd. Deerfield, IL 60015...(312) 405-6000...W.L. Batts...consumer prods. (Tupperware, Hobart, West Bend).

Primerica, Corp....American Lane, Greenwich, CT 06836...(203) 552-2000...G. Tsai...financial services (Smith Barney), retailing (Fingerhut, Musicland, Durham's).

Procter & Gamble Co....One Procter & Gamble Plaza, Cincinnati, OH 45202...(513) 983-1100...J. G. Smale...soap & detergent (Ivory, Cheer, Tide, Spic and Span), shortenings (Crisco), toiletries (Crest toothpaste, Prell, and Head and Shoulders shampoos), pharmaceuticals (Pepto-Bismol), Pampers disposable diapers, Folgers coffee, Charmin toilet tissues, Bounty towels, Vicks cough medicines.

Quaker Oats Co....321 N. Clark St., Chicago, IL 60610...(312) 222-7111...William D. Sithburg...foods, cereal (Quaker Oat Bran, Life, Cap'n Crunch, Puffed Wheat, Puffed Rice), foods (Aunt Jemima, Celeste pizza, Van Camp's pork and beans, Gatorade), pet foods (Ken-L-Ration, Gaines, Puss 'Boots), Fisher Price toys, Magic Pan restaurants.

Quaker State Corp....255 Elm St., Oil City, PA 16301...(814) 676-7676...J.W. Corn refining, marketing petroleum prods., filters, mining & marketing coal.

Ralston Purina Co....Checkerboard Sq., St. Louis, MO 63164...(314) 982-1000...W. R. Stritz...pet and livestock food, consumer prods. (Chex cereal, Chicken of the Sea tuna, Wonder bread, Hostess baked goods, Eveready batteries.)

Ramada Inc....2390 E. Cammelback Rd., Phoenix, AZ 85072...(602) 273-4000...Richard Snell...casino/hotels operator.

Raytheon Company...141 Spring St., Lexington, MA 02173...(617) 862-6600...Thomas L. Phillips...electronics, aviation, appliances...Amana Refrigeration, Beech Aircraft.

Reebok Intl. Ltd....150 Royall St., Canton, MA 02021...(617) 821-2800...P.B. Fireman...athletic & casual footwear, sportswear.

Reynolds Metals Co....6601 W. Broad St., Richmond, VA 23261...(804) 281-2000...W.O. Bourke...aluminum prods.

Rite Aid Corp....Shiremanstown, PA 17011...(717) 761-2633...A. Grass...discount drug stores, beauty aid stores, auto parts stores.

A.H. Robins Co., Inc....1407 Cummings Dr., Richmond, VA 23261...(804) 257-2000...E.C. Robins Jr....health care, consumer prods. (Chap Stick, Quencher, Robitussin cough syrups).

Rockwell Intl. Corp....2230 E. Imperial Hwy., El Segundo, CA...(213) 647-5000...D. R. Beall...aerospace, electronic, automotive prods.

Rorer Group Inc....500 Virginia Dr., Ft. Washington, PA 19034...(215) 628-6000...R.E. Cawthorn...pharmaceuticals (Maalox, Ascriptin).

Rubbermaid Inc....1147 Akron Rd., Wooster, OH 44691...(216) 264-6464...S. C. Gault...rubber and plastic consumer prods.

Russell Corp....P.O. Box 272, Alexander City, AL 35010...(205) 329-4000...D.L. Carlisle Jr....leisure apparel, athletic uniforms.

Ryder System, Inc....3600 NW 82d Ave., Miami, FL 33166...(305) 593-3726...M. A. Burns...truck leasing service.

Santa Fe Pacific Corp.,...224 S. Michigan Ave., Chicago, IL 60604...(312) 786-6422...Robert Krebs...railroad, real estate, construction, natural resources.

Sara Lee Corp....3 First National Plaza, Chicago, IL 60602...(312) 726-2600...J.H. Bryan Jr....baked goods, fresh and processed meats, fresh and frozen fruits and vegetables and other packaged foods, beverages, tobacco products, hosiery, intimate apparel and knitwear, Electrolux, Fuller Brush, Hanes, Gant, Kiwi, Shasta, Hillshire Farm, L' eggs, isotoner.

Schering-Plough Corp....One Giralda Farms, Madison, NJ 07940...(201) 822-7000...R. P. Luciano...pharmaceuticals, consumer prods, radio stations.

Schlumberger Ltd....277 Park Ave., New York, NY 10172...(212) 350-9400...E. Baird...oilfield services, electronics, measurement and control devices.

Scott Paper Co....Scott Plaza, Phila., PA 19113...(215) 522-5000...P. E. Lippincott...sanitary paper prods.

Seagram Co. Ltd....1430 Peel St., Montreal, Que., Canada H3A 1S9...(514) 849-5271...E.M. Bronfman...distilled spirits & wine (Crown Royal, Chivas Regal, Calvert, Wolfschmidt Vodka, Paul Masson, Christian Brothers, Martell, Myer's Jamaica Rum).

Sears, Roebuck & Co....Sears Tower, Chicago, IL 60684...(312) 875-2500...E.A. Brennan...merchandising, insurance (Allstate), financial services (Dean Witter).

Service Merchandise, Inc....P.O. Box 24600, Nashville, TN 37202...(615) 251-6666...R. Zimmerman...operates catalog showrooms.

Shaw Industries, Inc....616 E. Walnut Ave., Dalton, GA 30722...(404) 278-3812...R.E. Shaw...manuf. tufted carpeting (Magee, Philadelphia).

Sherwin-Williams Co....101 Prospect Ave. N.W., Cleveland, OH 44115...(216) 566-2000...John G. Breen...world's largest paint producer (Dutch Boy, Kem-Tone).

Skyline Corp....2520 By-Pass Rd., Elkhart, IN 46515...(219) 294-6521...Arthur J. Decio...mfg. housing and recreational vehicles.

Smithkline Beckman Corp....One Franklin Plaza, Phila., PA 19101...(215) 751-4000...K. N. Kermes...pharmaceuticals (Tagamet, Dyazide), animal health prods., diagnostic instruments.

Smucker (J.M.) Co....Strawberry Lane, Orville, OH 44667...(216) 682-0015...P. H. Smucker...preserves, jams, jellies, toppings.

Snap-on Tools Corp....2801 80th St., Kenosha, WI 53141...(414) 656-5200...M. F. Gregory...manuf. mechanic's tools, equip.

Sony Corp....9 W. 57th St., New York, NY 10019...(212) 418-9470...A. Morita...manuf. televisions, radios, tape recorders, audio equip., video tape recorders.

Southwest Airlines Co....P.O. Box 37611, Love Field, Dallas, TX 75235...(214) 902-1100...H.D. Kelleher...air transportation.

Southwestern Bell Corp....One Bell Center, St. Louis, MO 63101...(314) 235-9800...Z.E. Barnes...telephone communications.

Squibb Corp....P.O. Box 4000, Princeton, NJ 08540...(609) 921-4000...Richard M. Furlaud...drugs (Capoten, Capozide), confectionery, household prods, Charles of the Ritz. (Announced merger with Bristol-Myers in 1989.).

Standard Brands Paint Co....4300 W 190th St., Torrance, CA 90509...(213) 214-2411...S.D. Buchalter...retailer of home decorating prods.

Stanley Works...1000 Stanley Drive, P.O. Box 7000, New Britain CT 06050...(203) 225-5111...R.H. Ayers...hand tools, hardware, door opening equipment.

Stride Rite Corp....5 Cambridge Center, Cambridge, MA 02142...(617) 491-8800...A. Hiatt...manuf. & retailer children's footwear.

Sun Company, Inc....100 Matsonford Rd., Radnor, PA 19087...(215) 293-6000...R. McClements Jr....energy resources co.

Syms Corp....Syms Way, Secaucus, NJ 07094...(201) 902-9600...S. Syms...operates off-price apparel stores.

Talley Industries, Inc....2800 N. 44th St., Phoenix, AZ 85008...(602) 957-7711...W.H. Mallender...clocks (West Clox, Seth Thomas), technical prods.

Tambrands Inc....One Marcus Ave., Lake Success, NY 11042...(516) 358-8300...M.F. Emmett...menstrual tampons (Tampax, Maxithins).

Tandem Computers...19333 Vallco Pkwy., Cupertino, CA 95014...(408) 725-6000...T.G. Treybig...supplier of computer systems and networks.

Tandy Corp....1800 One Tandy Center, Fort Worth, TX 76102...(817) 390-3700...J.V. Roach...consumer electronics retailing & mfg, Radio Shack.

Teledyne, Inc....1901 Ave. of the Stars, Los Angeles, CA 90067...(213) 277-3311...G. A. Roberts...electronics, aerospace prods., industrial prods., insurance, finance.

Tenneco, Inc....P.O. Box 2511, Houston, TX 77252...(713) 757-2131...J. L. Ketelsen...oil, natural gas pipelines, manuf.

Texaco Inc....2000 Westchester Ave., White Plains, NY 10650...(914) 253-4000...J.W. Kinnear...petroleum and petroleum prods.

Texas Air Corp....333 Clay St., Houston, TX 77002...(713) 658-9588...F.A. Lorenzo...air transportation (Continental, Eastern airlines).

Texas Instruments Inc....P.O. Box 655774, Dallas, TX 75265...(214) 995-2011...J.R. Junkins...electrical & electronics prods.

Textron Inc....40 Westminster St., Providence, RI 02903...(401) 421-2800...B.F. Dolan...aerospace, consumer, industrial, metal prods, consumer finance, insurance, management services.

Tidewater Inc....1440 Canal St., New Orleans, LA 70112...(504) 568-1010...J.P. Laborde...marine equip. and services for oil industry.

Time Inc....Time & Life Bldg., New York, NY 10020...(212) 522-1212...J.R. Munro...magazine publisher (Time, Sports Illustrated, Fortune, Money, People), CATV (HBO, Cinemax), publishing (Little, Brown and Co.). (Merged with Warner Communications in 1989).

Tonka Corp....6000 Clearwater Dr., Minnetonka, MN 55343...(612) 936-3300...S.G. Shank...toy manuf. (Monopoly, Play-Doh, Pound Puppies, Trivial Pursuit, Risk, Clue).

Tootsie Roll Industries, Inc.,...7401 S. Cicero Ave., Chicago, IL 60629...(312) 838-3400...M.J. Gordon...candy (Tootsie Roll, Mason Dots, Mason Crows, Bonomo Turkish Taffy, Charms).

The Toro Company...8111 Lyndale Ave. South, Bloomington, MN 55420...(612) 887-8526...K. B. Melrose...lawn and turf maintenance, snow removal equipment.

Toys "R" Us...461 From Rd., Paramus, NJ 07652...(201) 262-7800...Charles Lazarus...toy retailer, clothing stores (Kids "R" Us).

Transamerica Corp....600 Montgomery St., San Francisco, CA 94111...(415) 983-4000...J.R. Harvey...insurance, financial, business services (Occidental Life Ins.).

Travelers Corp....One Tower Sq., Hartford, CT 06183...(203) 277-0111...E. H. Budd...insurance.

Tribune Co....435 N. Michigan Ave., Chicago, IL 60611...(312) 222-9100...S.R. Cook...newpaper publishing, broadcasting, entertainment (Chicago Cubs baseball team).

Trinity Industries, Inc....2525 Stemmons Freeway, P.O. Box 10587, Dallas, TX 75207...(214) 631-4420...W.R. Wallace...manufactures variety of metal products.

TRW Inc....1900 Richmond Rd., Cleveland, OH 44124...(216) 291-7000...J.T. Gorman...car and truck operations, electronics, and space systems.

TW Services, Inc....Mark Center IV, Paramus, NJ 07652...(201) 712-0500...F. L. Salizzoni...food service, restaurants (Denny's), nursing homes.

USAIR Group, Inc....1911 Jefferson Hwy., Arlington, VA 22002...(703) 892-7000...E.I. Colodny...air carrier of passengers, property, and mail (Piedmont).

UST Inc....100 W. Putnam Ave., Greenwich, CT 06830...(203) 661-1100...L.F. Bantle...smokeless tobacco (Copenhagen, Skoal, Happy Days), pipes, pipe tobacco.

USX Corp....600 Grant St., Pittsburgh, PA 15230...C.A. Corry...steel manuf., oil & gas.

Unilever, N.V....Burgemeester's Jacobplein 1, Rotterdam, The Netherlands...F. A. Maljers, Chmn....soap, detergent, margarine, frozen food, toothpaste, tea, dried soups, ice cream (Lever Brothers, Lipton, Pond's Vaseline Intensive Care, Q-Tips, Cutex).

Union Carbide Corp....39 Old Ridgebury Rd., Danbury, CT 06817...(203) 794-2000...R.D. Kennedy...chemicals, industrial gases.

Union Pacific Corp....Martin Tower, Bethlehem, PA 18018...(215) 861-3200...D. Lewis...railroad, natural resources.

Unisys Corp....P.O. Box 500, Blue Bell, PA...(215) 542-6050...W. Michael Blumenthal...business equip., data processing prods.

United Brands Co....250 E. 5th St., Cincinnati, OH 45202...(513) 784-8011...C. H. Lindner...food prods. (Chiquita, John Morrell).

U.S. Home Corp....1800 W. Loop South, Houston, TX 77252...(713) 877-2311...R. J. Strudler...leading single-family homebuilder in U.S.

United States Shoe Corp....One Eastwood Dr., Cincinnati, OH 45227...(513) 527-7000...P. G. Barach...apparel, retailer (Casual Corner), shoes (Red Cross, Joyce).

United Technologies Corp....United Technologies Bldg., Hartford, CT 06101...(203) 728-7000...R.F. Daniell...aerospace, industrial prods. & services, Carrier Corp., Otis Elevator; Pratt & Whitney, Sikorsky Aircraft.

Univar, Corp....1600 Norton Building, Seattle, WA 98104...(206) 447-5911...J.W. Bernard...industrial and agricultural chemicals, laboratory and graphic arts products distributor, home furnishing supplies and fabrics distributors.

Universal Foods Corp....433 East Michigan St., Milwaukee, WI 53202...(414) 271-6755...G.A. Osborn...yeast products, cheese products, dehydrated seasonings, food colors and flavors, imported gourmet foods.

Upjohn Co....7000 Portage Rd., Kalamazoo, MI 49001...(616) 323-4000...T. Cooper...pharmaceuticals (Motrin, Nuprin, Xanax, Halcion, Cleocin), chemicals, agricultural and health care prods.

VF Corp....1047 No. Park Rd., Wyomissing, PA 19610...(215) 378-1151...L.R. Pugh...apparel, Vanity Fair, Lee jeans, Bassett-Walker, Jantzen.

Vulcan Materials Co....One Metroplex Dr., Birmingham, AL 35209...(205) 877-3000...H.A. Sklenar...construction materials, chemicals, metals.

Wal-Mart Stores Inc....702 W. 8th St., Bentonville, AR 72716...(501) 273-4000...D.D. Glass...discount dept. stores.

Walgreen Co....200 Wilmot Rd., Deerfield, IL 60015...(312) 940-2500...Charles R. Walgreen 3d...retail drug chain, restaurants.

Wang Laboratories, Inc....One Industrial Ave., Lowell, MA 01851...(617) 459-5000...R. Miller...word processors.

Warner Communications Inc....75 Rockefeller Plaza, N.Y., NY 10019...(212) 484-8000...Steven J. Ross...filmed entertainment, records & music publishing (Atlantic Records), book publishing, CATV system, consumer prods. (Merged with Time Inc. in 1989).

Warner-Lambert Co....201 Tabor Rd., Morris Plains, NJ 07950...(201) 540-2000...J.D. Williams...health care prods. (Benadryl), consumer prods. (Efferdent dental cleanser, Hall cough tablets, Schick razors, Clorets breath mints, Rolaids antacid, Listerine mouth wash).

Washington Post Co....1150 15th St., N.W., Washington, DC 20071...(202) 334-6000...Katharine Graham...newspapers, magazines (Newsweek), TV stations.

Weis Markets, Inc....1000 South Second Street, Sunbury, PA 17801...(717) 286-4571...S. Weis...operates supermarkets, distributes frozen foods and grocery items.

Wells Fargo & Co....420 Montgomery St., San Francisco, CA 94163...(415) 396-0123...C.E. Reichardt...banking.

Wendy's Intl., Inc....4288 W. Dublin-Granville, Dublin, OH 43017...(614) 764-3100...R. L. Barney...quick service restaurants.

Westinghouse Electric Corp....Westinghouse Bldg., Gateway Center, Pittsburgh, PA 15222...(412) 244-2000...J. C. Marous...manuf. electrical, mechanical equip., radio and television stations.

Westvaco Corp....299 Park Avenue, New York, NY 10171...(212) 688-5000...J.A. Lake...manufactures paper for graphic reproduction, communications, and packaging (largest producer of envelopes in the world).

Weyerhaeuser Co....Tacoma, WA 98477...(206) 924-2345...George H. Weyerhaeuser...manuf., distribution of forest prods.

Whirlpool Corp....Administrative Center, Benton Harbor, MI 49022...(616) 926-5000...D.R. Whitwam...major home appliances.

Whitman Corp. ...One Illinois Ctr., 111 E. Wacker Dr., Chicago, IL 60601...(312) 565-3000...K.D. Bays...diversified prods. and services, consumer products, food, auto prods (Midas).

Willamette Industries, Inc....3800 1st Interstate Tower, Portland, OR 97201...(503) 227-5581...William Swindells Jr....building materials and paper prods.

Winn-Dixie Stores, Inc....5050 Edgewood Ct., Jacksonville, FL 32205...(904) 783-5000...A.D. Davis, chmn....retail grocery chain.

Winnebago Industries, Inc....P.O. Box 152, Forest City, IA 50436...(515) 582-3535...J.K. Hanson, chmn....manuf. of motor homes, recreation vehicles.

Wolverine World Wide, Inc....9341 Courtland Dr., Rockford, MI 49351...(616) 866-5500...T.D. Gleason...manuf. footwear (Hush Puppies).

F.W. Woolworth Co....233 Broadway, N.Y., NY 10279...(212) 553-2000...H.E. Seils...variety stores, shoe stores (Kinney), men's clothing (Richman Brothers), children's apparel (Little Folk shop), athletic footwear (Foot Locker).

Wm. Wrigley Jr. Co....410 N. Michigan Ave., Chicago, IL 60611...(312) 644-2121...William Wrigley...chewing gum.

Xerox Corp....P.O. Box 1600, Stamford, CT 06904...(203) 968-3000...D. T. Kearns...equip. for reproduction, reduction, and transmission of printed information.

Zenith Electronics Corp....1000 Milwaukee Ave., Glenview, IL 60025...(312) 391-7000...Jerry K. Pearlman...consumer electronic prods.

Complaints Against Airlines Decrease

Complaints against U.S. airlines decreased to 13,122 for the period January through June, 1988 compared with 14,042 complaints during the same period in 1987, according to the Dept. of Transportation. During all of 1986, 10,802 complaints were made; during all of 1987, 40,885 complaints were made. The most frequent complaints during all three years—1986, 1987, and 1988—were about flight cancellations and delays; problems with baggage were second in frequency during all three years.

Shopping for Credit: Ask the Right Questions

Source: New York State Banking Department

Under federal law, all institutions that extend or arrange for the extension of consumer credit must give the borrower meaningful information about the cost of each loan. The cost must be expressed as the dollar amount of the interest or finance charge, and as the annual percentage rate computed on the amount financed.

To be sure the loan or credit agreement you are considering suits both your budget and your individual needs, shop around. Ask questions to compare and evaluate a lender's rate and services. For instance:

1. What is the annual percentage rate?
2. What is the total cost of the loan in dollars?
3. How long do you have to pay off the loan?
4. What are the number, amounts, and due dates of payments?
5. What is the cost of deferring or extending the time period of the loan?
6. What is the cost of late charges for overdue payments?
7. If you pay the loan off early, are there any prepayment penalties?
8. Does the loan have to be secured? If so, what collateral is required?
9. What is the cost of credit life or other insurance that is being offered or may be required?
10. Are there any other charges you may have to pay?

Bank Credit Cards in 1988

Bank credit-card users had average monthly balances of about $1,200 last year, according to a report by the American Bankers Assn. About 35 percent of credit-card users paid off those balances in full each month, down from 40 percent in 1987.

The national survey of 453 commercial banks found that more than 25 percent of the 201-million Visa and Master-Card accounts didn't use the cards at all in 1988. The survey also noted that the average sale on a bank card was $63, up from $60 in 1987; 2.19 percent of bank card accounts were 30 or more days overdue at year end compared with 2.33 percent at the end of 1987; and losses from bad debts reached $3.3 billion in 1988 compared with $3 billion in 1987.

How to Check Your Credit File

Any individual can investigate the contents of his or her credit file by directly contacting one or more of the approximately 2,000 credit bureaus, or consumer credit clearinghouses, in the United States. The nearest ones can be found by calling a local Better Business Bureau or by looking in the telephone Yellow Pages under "Credit Rating or Reporting Agencies."

Although the Fair Credit Reporting Act requires that a bureau give a person no more than an oral or written credit history review, many bureaus will go beyond the technical requirements of the law and furnish the same computer-generated compilation of facts that they give the banks, retailers and other companies that subscribe to their service. An individual who has been denied credit on the basis of negative information from a credit bureau can obtain this review without charge within 30 days of the denial. Otherwise, the fee typically ranges from $8 to $12 for such a credit check.

After inspecting this record of past credit behavior, a consumer can question any item believed to be inaccurate, misleading or vague. The credit bureau must then investigate and remove any item that cannot be substantiated.

When a bureau affirms, rather than removes, a questionable item, an individual can present a 100-word explanation that must be placed in his or her file. And whenever an adverse item is deleted from the file or an explantory statement is added to one, a consumer may request that the credit bureau inform every credit grantor who received a report within the last six months.

Credit Card Rates

(As of Aug. 1, 1989)
(Prepared by Christian T. Jones, San Diego, CA)

Nearly all states have special laws dealing with rates charged for credit cards issued by state banks and other financial institutions. Although some state laws apply only to banks, under Federal parity law, the same charges can be made by other financial institutions. A national bank can charge the highest rates allowed for revolving credit extended by any other creditor in the state where the bank is located for similar types of credit, and such rates may also be charged to residents of any other state. Rates are yearly.

Ala.	No limit.	La.	18%; 4% cash advance and $12 annual fees.	Oh.	25% to 1/1/92.
Alas.	17% plus fee.			Okla.	30-21-15% @ $750, $2,400; or
Ariz.	No limit.	Me.	18%; $12 annual fee.		21%.
Ark.	5% over FRB discount rate (max. 17%).	Md.	24%; 2% fee.	Ore.	No limit.
		Mass.	23% to $6,000; no limit over $6,000; $20 annual fee.	Pa.	12% loans; 15% purchases; $15 annual fee.
Cal.	No limit.	Mich.	18%; no limit on annual fee.	P.R.	17% loans; 26% purchases.
Colo.	21%.	Minn.	18%; $50 annual fee.	R.I.	18%.
Conn.	15%; $10 annual fee.	Miss.	21%; or 18% plus $12 annual fee.	S.C.	No limit.
D.C.	24%.			S.D.	No limit.
Del.	No limit.	Mo.	22-10% @ $1,000.	Tenn.	24%.
Fla.	18%.	Mont.	No limit.	Tex.	18%.
Ga.	No limit on rate or fee.	Neb.	18% plus fees.	Utah	No limit.
Ha.	24%.	Nev.	No limit.	Vt.	18%; no limit on annual fee.
Ida.	No limit.	N.H.	No limit.	Va.	No limit.
Ill.	No limit; plus fees.	N.J.	30%; $15 annual fee or $50 over $5,000.	Wash.	12% or 4% over U.S. T-bill rate.
Ind.	36-21-15%, @ $810, $2,700; or 21%.			W.Va.	18%.
		N.M.	No limit.	Wis.	No limit to 11/1/90; thereafter
Ia.	No limit.	N.Y.	25% plus annual fee to 6/30/93.		18%.
Kan.	18-14.45% @ $1,000.	N.C.	18%; $20 annual fee.	Wyo.	36-21% @ $1,000; no limit over
Ky.	21%; $20 annual fee.	N.D.	No limit.		$25,000.

Fair Credit: What You Should Know

Source: Federal Trade Commission

Federal legislation has made it easier for you to be treated fairly in credit-related areas:

Billing. The Fair Credit Billing Act permits you to dispute the accuracy of charges listed on your credit card statement and provides other important rights (such as limits on liability for unauthorized charges). To file a notice of a "billing error," send a letter to the card issuer at the address specified for "billing inquiries" within 60 days of the date that the card issuer mailed the first statement that shows the alleged error. Be sure to include your name, address, account number, the amount of the charge you dispute, and why you think an error was made. Do not send the letter in the same envelope as your payment. Keep a copy to prove you sent the letter.

Equal Credit. The Equal Credit Opportunity Act (ECOA) prohibits discrimination on the grounds of sex, marital status, age (provided the applicant has the capacity under state law to enter a contract), race, color, religion, or national origin. The ECOA also protects applicants whose income derives in whole or in part from any public assistance program, or those who have in good faith exercised any right under the Federal Consumer Credit Protection Act, which includes the FCBA and ECOA, among other provisions.

The creditor may inquire about your marital status, for example, if it needs to do so to determine its rights and not to discriminate in a determination of creditworthiness. Another example involves considering the age of the applicant if the inquiry is for the purpose of determining the amount and probable continuation of income levels or other elements of creditworthiness. However, a creditor may not consider race, national origin, or religion in deciding whether to extend credit.

The ECOA also requires the creditor to respond to applications within 30 days of receiving a completed application and to provide rejected applicants with a statement of specific reasons why credit was denied or a notice disclosing the consumer's rights to have the reasons if he or she requests them in writing.

Mail-Order Merchandise. By law, you have the right to have merchandise ordered through the mail shipped within 30 days, unless another shipping date has been specified in the advertisement for the merchandise. Promises such as "one week" or "4 to 6 weeks" must be met. However, if the seller is unable to ship your order when promised (or within the 30-day limit), the seller must provide you with a notice informing you that you have the right to cancel your order and get a prompt refund. If you experience a problem with late or non-delivery of merchandise ordered through the mail, contact the Federal Trade Commission. This will help the Commission to identify problem companies.

Interest Laws and Consumer Finance Loan Rates

Source: Revised by Christian T. Jones, Editor, Consumer Finance Law Bulletin, San Diego, Ca.

All states have laws regulating interest rates. These laws fix a legal or conventional rate which applies when there is no contract for interest. They also fix a general maximum contract rate, but there are so many exceptions that the general contract maximum actually applies only to exceptional cases. Also, federal law has preempted state limits on first home mortgages, subject to each state's right to reinstate its own law, and given depository institutions parity with other state lenders.

Legal rate of interest. The legal or conventional rate of interest applies to money obligations when no interest rate is contracted for and also to judgments. The rate is usually somewhat below the general interest rate.

General maximum contract rates. General interest laws in most states set the maximum rate between 8% and 16% per year. The general maximum is fixed by the state constitution at 5% over the Federal Reserve Discount rate in Arkansas. Loans to corporations are frequently exempted or subject to a higher maximum. In recent years, it has also been common to provide special rates for home mortgage loans and variable usury rates that are indexed to market rates.

Specific enabling acts. In many states special statutes permit industrial loan companies, second mortgage lenders, and banks to charge 1.5% a month or more. Laws regulating revolving loans, charge accounts and credit cards generally limit charges between 1.5% and 2% per month plus annual fees for credit cards. Rates for installment sales contracts in most states are somewhat higher. Credit unions may generally charge 1% to 1.5% a month. Pawnbrokers' rates vary widely. Savings and loan associations, and loans insured by federal agencies, are also specially regulated. A number of states allow regulated lenders to charge any rate agreed to with the customer either for all credit or over a certain dollar amount.

Consumer finance loan statutes. Most consumer finance loan statutes are based on early models drafted by the Russell Sage Foundation (1916-42) to provide small loans to wage earners under license and other protective regulations. Since 1969 the model has frequently been the Uniform Consumer Credit Code which applies to credit sales and loans for consumer purposes. In general, licensed lenders may charge 3% a month and reduced rates for additional amounts. An add-on of 17% ($17 per $100) per year yields about 2.5% per month if paid in equal monthly installments. Discount rates produce higher yields than add-on rates of the same amount. In the table below, unless otherwise stated, monthly and annual rates are based on reducing principal balances, annual add-on rates are based on the original principal for the full term, and two or more rates apply to different portions of balance or original principal.

States with consumer finance loan laws and the rates of charge as of August 1, 1989
Maximum monthly rates computed on unpaid balances, unless otherwise stated.

Ala.. . . Annual add-on: 15% to $750, 10% to $2,000 (min. 1.5% on unpaid balances). Higher rates for loans up to $749. Over $2,000, any agreed rate. Fee: 2% (max. $20); 5% real estate.

Alas. . . 3% to $850, 2% to $10,000. Over $10,000, any agreed rate.

Ariz. . . To $1,000: 3%. Over $1,000: 3% to $500, 2% to $10,000. Over $10,000, any agreed rate.

Cal. . . 2.5% to $225, 2% to $900, 1.5% to $1,650, 1% to $2,500 (1.6% min.). Over $2,500, any agreed rate. 5% fee (max. $50) to $2,500

Colo. . . 36% per year to $630, 21% to $2,100, 15% to $25,000 (21% min.).

Conn. . Annual Add-on: 17% to $600, 11% to $5,000; 11% over $1,800 to $5,000 for certain secured loans. Any agreed rate for second mortgages.

Del.. . . Any agreed rate.

D.C. . . 24% per year.

Fla.. . . 30% per year to $500, 24% to $1,000, 18% to $5,000; 18% per year on entire amount over $5,000.

Ga.. . . 10% per year discount to 18 months, add-on to 36½ months; 8% fee to $600, 4% on excess plus $2 per month. Over $3,000, any agreed rate.

Ha.. . . 3.5% to $100, 2.5% to $300; 2% on entire balance over $300 or discount rates.

Ida.. . . Any agreed rate.

Ill.. . . Any agreed rate.

Ind.. . . 36% per year to $810, 21% to $2,700, 15% to $25,000 (21% min.).

Ia. . . . 3% to $1,000, 2% to $2,800, 1.5% to $25,000; or equivalent flat rate. Over $25,000: 21% per year.

Kan. . . 36% per year to $630, 21% to $2,100, 14.45% to $25,000 (18% min.). Fee: 2% (max. $100); 3% real estate.

Ky. . . . 3% to $1,000, 2% to $3,000. Over $3,000, 2%.

La. . . . 36% per year to $1,400, 27% to $4,000, 24% to $7,000, 21% over $7,000, plus $25 fee.

Me.. . . 30% per year to $700, 21% to $2,000, 15% to $25,000 (18% min.).

Md.. . . 2.75% to $1,000, 2% to $2,000. Over $2,000, 2%.

Mass. . 23% per year plus $20 fee to $6,000; any agreed rate over $6,000.

Mich.. . 31% per year to $500, 13% to $3,000 (18% min.); 18% for second mortgages, plus 2% fee (max. $200).

Minn.. . 33% per year to $455, 19% over $455 (21.75% min.).

Miss.. . 36% per year to $1,000, 33% to $1,800, 24% to $5,000, 14% over $5,000. Over $25,000, 18%. 2% fee (max. $50).

Mo.. . . 2.218% to $1,200, 1.67% over $1,200, plus 5% fee (max. $15); 1.67% plus 2% for second mortgages.

Mont.. . Any agreed rate.

Neb. . . 24% per year to $1,000. 21% over, plus fee of 7% to $2,000 and 5% over (max. $500).

Nev.. . Any agreed rate.

N.H. . . 2% to $600, 1.5% to $1,500; Any agreed rate over $1,500 or for real estate mortgages.

N.J.. . . 30% per year to $5,000 or for second mortgages.

N.M.. . Any agreed rate.

N.Y. . . 25% per year to 6/30/93.

N.C. . . 3% to $1,000, 1.5% to $7,500; 1.5% on entire amount to $10,000. 1.5% or variable plus 2% fee for second mortgages.

N.D. . . 2.5% to $250, 2% to $500, 1.75% to $750, 1.5% to $1,000; any agreed rate over $1,000.

Ohio . . 28% per year to $1,000, 22% to $5,000; 25% on entire amount over $5,000; plus fee.

Okla.. . 30% per annum to $750, 21% to $2,500, 15% to $45,000. (21% min.). Special rates to $500.

Ore. . . Any agreed rate.

Pa. . . . 9.5% per year discount to 48 months, 6% for remaining time plus 2% fee (max. $100); or 2% on unpaid balances; 1.85% for second mortgages over $5,000, plus 2% fee.

P.R. . . 24% per year.

R.I.. . . 3% to $300, 2.5% for loans between $300 and $800; 2% for larger loans to $5,000. 1.75% over $5,000.

S.C. . . Any agreed and posted rate.

S.D. . . Any agreed rate.

Tenn. . Over $100, 24% per year or discount rates plus fees.

Texas . Annual add-on: 18% to $1,020, 8% to $8,500 or formula rate (18% to 24% per year on unpaid balances.)

Utah . . Any agreed rate.

Vt. . . . 2% to $1,000, 1% to $3,000 (min. 1.5%); 1.5% for second mortgages.

Va.. . . 2¼% to $600, 2% to $1,800, 1.5% to $2,800; or annual add-on of 19% to $600, 15% to $1,800, 12% to $2,800; 2% fee. Any agreed rate over $2,800 for second mortgages, plus 2% fee.

Wash. . 2.5% to $500, 1.5% to $1,000, 1% to $2,500. Over $2,500, 25% per year or discount rates.

W.Va. . 36% per year to $500, 24% to $1,500, 18% to $2,000. Over $2,000, 27% per year to $2,000, 25% to $10,000, 18% on remainder, 2% fee.

Wis. . . Any agreed rate, to 11/1/90 thereafter 23% per year to $5,000, any agreed rate over $5,000.

Wyo.. . 36% per year to $1,000, 21% to $25,000. No limit over $25,000.

U.S. Passport, Visa, and Health Requirements

Source: Passport Services, U.S. State Department as of June, 1989

Passports are issued by the U.S. Department of State to citizens and nationals of the United States for the purpose of documenting them for foreign travel and identifying them as Americans.

How to Obtain a Passport

Applicants who have never been issued a passport in their own name must execute an application in person before (1) a passport agent; (2) a clerk of any federal court or state court of record or a judge or clerk of any probate court accepting applications; (3) a postal employee designated by the postmaster at a post office which has been selected to accept passport applications; or (4) a U.S. diplomatic or consular officer abroad. A DSP-11 is the correct form to use for applicants who must apply in person. All persons are required to obtain individual passports in their own name. An applicant who is 13 years of age or older is required to appear in person before the clerk or agent executing the application. A parent or legal guardian may execute the application for children under 13.

A passport previously issued to the applicant, or one in which he was included, will be accepted as proof of U.S. citizenship. If the applicant has no prior passport and was born in the U.S. a certified copy of their birth certificate shall be presented to the agent accepting the passport application. To be acceptable, the certificate must show the given name and surname, the date and place of birth, and that the birth record was filed shortly after birth. A delayed birth certificate (a record filed more than one year after the date of birth) is acceptable provided that it shows acceptable secondary evidence was used for creating this record.

If such primary evidence is not obtainable, a notice from state registrar shall be submitted stating that no birth record exists. The notice shall be accompanied by the best obtainable secondary evidence such as a baptismal certificate, or a hospital birth record.

A naturalized citizen with no previous passport should present a Certificate of Naturalization. A person born abroad claiming U.S. citizenship through either a native-born or naturalized citizen parent must submit a certificate of citizenship issued by the Immigration and Naturalization Service; or a Consular Report of Birth or Certification of Birth issued by the Dept. of State. If one of the above documents has not been obtained, evidence of citizenship of the parent(s) through whom citizenship is claimed and evidence which would establish the parent/child relationship must be submitted. Additionally, if citizenship is derived through birth to citizen parent(s), the following documents will be required: parents' marriage certificate plus an affidavit from parent(s) showing periods and places of residence or physical presence in the U.S. and abroad, specifying periods spent abroad in the employment of the U.S. government, including the armed forces, or with certain international organizations. If citizenship is derived through naturalization of parents, evidence of admission to the U.S. for permanent residence also will be required.

Persons who possess a passport in their own name issued within the last 12 years and after their 16th birthday may be eligible to apply for a new passport by mail. A form DSP-82, Application for Passport by Mail must be filled out and mailed to the nearest passport agency, together with their previous passport, 2 recent identical photographs and $35.00.

Contract Employees — Persons traveling because of a contract with the U.S. Government must submit with their application: letters from their employer stating position, destination and purpose of travel, armed forces contract number, and expiration date of contract when pertinent.

Photographs, Fees and Identity

Photographs — Submit 2 identical photographs which are sufficiently recent (normally not more than 6 months old) to be a good likeness of and satisfactorily identify the applicant. Photographs should be 2×2 inches in size. The image size measured from the bottom of the chin to the top of the head (including hair) should be not less than one inch nor more than 1 3/8 inches. Photographs should be portrait-type prints. They must be clear, front view, full face, with a plain, white or off-white background. Photographs which depict the applicant as relaxed and smiling are encouraged.

Fees — The passport fee is $20.00 for passports issued to persons under 18 years of age. These passports are valid for 5 years from the date of issue. The passport fee is $35.00 for passports issued to persons 18 and older. These passports are valid for 10 years from the date of issuance. An additional fee of $7.00 is charged for the execution of the application. There is no acceptance fee when using DSP-82, "Application For Passport By Mail." Applicants eligible to use this form pay only the $35.00 passport fee.

Identity—Applicants must also establish their identity to the satisfaction of the person accepting the application. To establish identity, applicants may use a previous U.S. passport, a Certificate of Naturalization, a valid driver's license, or a government identification card. Applicants may not use a Social Security card, learner's or temporary driver's license, credit card, or expired identity card. Applicants unable to establish their identity must take the identification cards they have in their own name (i.e. Social Security card) and in addition, they must be accompanied by a person who has known them for at least 2 years and who is a U.S. citizen or legal U.S. permanent resident alien. That person must sign an affidavit before the individual who executes the passport application. The witness will be required to establish his or her own identity.

The loss or theft of a valid passport is a serious matter and should be reported immediately to Passport Services, 1425 K Street, N.W., Dept. of State, Wash., D.C. 20524, tel: (202) 647-0518 or to the nearest passport agency if you are in the U.S. or the nearest U.S. embassy or consulate when abroad.

Foreign Regulations

A visa, usually rubber stamped in a passport by a representative of the country to be visited, indicates that the bearer of the passport is permitted to enter that country for a certain purpose and length of time. In most instances, you must obtain necessary visas before you leave the U.S. Apply directly to the embassy or nearest consulate of each country you plan to visit, or consult a travel agent.

The State Dept. publication, "Foreign Visa Requirements," contains entry requirements and application instructions for most foreign countries and is available for 50¢ from the Consumer Information Center, Dept. 438T, Pueblo, CO 81009.

The process may take several weeks, so it is important to apply well in advance and verify requirements with the embassy or nearest consulate of each country before applying.

Aliens — An alien leaving the U.S. must request a passport from the embassy of the country of their nationality, must have a permit from his local Collector of Internal Revenue, and if they wish to return, should request a re-entry permit from the Immigration and Naturalization Service if it is required.

How to Obtain Birth, Marriage, Death Records

The United States government has published a series of inexpensive booklets entitled: Where to Write for Birth & Death Records; Where to Write for Marriage Records; Where to Write for Divorce Records; Where to Write for Birth and Death Records of U. S. Citizens Who were Born or Died Outside of the U. S.; Birth Certifications for Alien Children Adopted by U. S. Citizens; You May Save Time Proving Your Age and Other Birth Facts. They tell where to write to get a certified copy of an original vital record. Supt. of Documents, Government Printing Office, Washington, DC 20402.

Marriage Laws

Source: Gary N. Skoloff, Skoloff & Wolfe, Livingston, N.J.; as of June 1, 1989.

State	Age with parental consent Male	Female	Age without consent Male	Female	Physical exam & blood test for male and female Maximum period between exam and license	Scope of medical exam	Waiting period Before license	After license
Alabama*	14a	14a	18	18	—	b	—	s
Alaska	16z	16z	18	18	—	b	3 da., w	—
Arizona	16z	16z	18	18	—	—	—	—
Arkansas	17c	16c	18	18	—	—	v	—
California	aa	aa	18	18	30 da., w	bb	—	h
Colorado*	16z	16z	18	18	—	b	—	s
Connecticut	16z	16z	18	18	w	bb	4 da., w	ttt
Delaware	18c	16c	18	18	—	—	—	e, s
Florida	16a, c	16a, c	18	18	60 da.	b	3 da.	s
Georgia*	aa	aa	16	16	—	b	3 da., g	s*
Hawaii	16d	16d	18	18	—	b	—	—
Idaho*	16z	16z	18	18	—	bb	—	—
Illinois	16	16	18	18	30 da.	b, n	—	ee
Indiana	17c	17c	18	18	—	bb	72 hrs.	t
Iowa*	18z	18z	18	18	—	—	3 da., v	tt
Kansas*y	18z	18z	18	18	—	—	3 da., w	—
Kentucky	18c, z	18c, z	18	18	—	none	—	—
Louisiana	18z	18z	18	18	10 da.	b	—	72 hrs., w
Maine	16z	16z	18	18	—	—	3 da., v, w	t
Maryland	16c, f	16c, f	18	18	—	—	48 hrs., w	ff
Massachusetts	18d	18d	18	18	33-90 da.	bb	3 da., v	—
Michigan	16c, d	16c	18	18	30 da.	b	3 da., w	—
Minnesota	16z	16z	18	18	—	—	5 da., w	—
Mississippi	17	15	21	21	30 da.	b	3 da., w	—
Missouri	15d, 18z	15d, 18z	18	18	—	—	—	—
Montana*w	16	16	18	18	6 mos.	b	—	ff
Nebraskaw	17	17	18	18	—	bb	—	—
Nevada	16z	16z	18	18	—	—	—	—
New Hampshire	14j	13j	18	18	30 da.	b, l	3 da., v	h
New Jersey	16z, c	16z, c	18	18	30 da.	b	72 hrs., w	s
New Mexicoy	16d	16d	18	18	30 da.	b	—	—
New York	14j	14j	18	18	—	nn	—	24 hrs., w, t
North Carolina	16c, g	16c, g	18	18	—	m	v	—
North Dakota	16	16	18	18	—	b	—	—
Ohio*	18c, z	16c, z	18	18	30 da.	b	5 da.	t, w
Oklahoma*	16c	16c	18	18	30 da., w	b	—	—
Oregon	17	17	18	18	—	b	3 da., w	t
Pennsylvania*	16d	16d	18	18	30 da.	b	3 da., w	t
Puerto Ricoy	18c, d, z	16c, d, z	21	21	—	b	—	—
Rhode Island*	18d	16d	18	18	—	bb	—	—
South Carolina*	16c	14c	18	18	—	—	1 da.	—
South Dakota	16c	16c	18	18	—	—	—	tt
Tennessee	16d	16d	18	18	—	—	3 da., cc	s
Texas*y	14j, k	14j, k	18	18	—	—	—	s
Utah	14	14	18x	18x	30 da.	b	—	s
Vermont	16z	16z	18	18	30 da.	b	—	3 da., w
Virginia	16a, c	16a, c	18	18	—	b	—	t
Washington	17d	17d	18	18	—	b	3 da.	t
West Virginia	18c	18c	18	18	—	b	3 da., w	—
Wisconsin	16	16	18	18	—	b	5 da., w	s
Wyoming	16d	16d	18	18	—	bb	—	—
Dist. of Columbia*	16a	16a	18	18	30 da., w	b	3 da., w	—

*Indicates 1987 common-law marriage recognized; in many states, such marriages are only recognized if entered into many years before. (a) Parental consent not required if minor was previously married. (aa) No age limits. (b) Veneral diseases. (bb) Veneral diseases and Rubella (for female). In Colorado, Rubella for female under 45 and Rh type. (c) Younger parties may obtain license in case of pregnancy or birth of child. (cc) Unless parties are over 18 years of age. (d) Younger parties may obtain license in special circumstances. (e) Residents before expiration of 24-hour waiting period; non-residents formerly residents, before expiration of 96-hour waiting period; others 96 hours. (ee) License effective 1 day after issuance, unless court orders otherwise, valid for 60 days only. (f) If parties are under 16 years of age, proof of age and the consent of parents in person is required. If a parent is ill, an affidavit by the incapacitated parent and a physician's affidavit to that effect required. (ff) License valid for 180 days only. (g) Unless parties are 18 years of age or more, or female is pregnant, or applicants are the parents of a living child born out of wedlock. (h) License valid for 90 days only. (j) Parental consent and/or permission of judge required. (k) Below age of consent parties need parental consent and permission of judge. (l) With each certificate issued to couples, a list of family planning agencies and services available to them is provided. (m) Mental incompetence, infectious tuberculosis, venereal diseases and Rubella (certain counties only). (n) Venereal diseases; test for sickle cell anemia given at request of examining physician. (nn) Tests for sickle cell anemia may be required for certain applicants. Marriage prohibited unless it is established that procreation is not possible. (p) If one or both parties are below the age for marriage without parental consent (3 day waiting period). (s) License valid for 30 days only. (t) License valid for 60 days only. (tt) License valid for 20 days only. (ttt) License valid for 65 days. (v) Parties must file notice of intention to marry with local clerk. (w) Waiting period may be avoided. (x) Authorizes counties to provide for premarital counseling as a requisite to issuance of license to persons under 19 and persons previously divorced. (y) Marriages by proxy are valid. (yy) Proxy marriages are valid under certain conditions. (z) Younger parties may marry with parental consent and/or permission of judge. In Connecticut, judicial approval. (zz) With consent of court.

Divorce Laws

Adapted from a revision by Gary N. Skoloff of the N.J. Bar, as of June 1, 1989. Important: almost all states also have other laws, as well as qualifications of the laws shown below and proposed divorce-reform laws pending. It would be wise to consult a lawyer in conjunction with the use of this chart.

Some grounds for absolute divorce

	Residence	Adultery	Cruelty	Desertion	Alcoholism	Impotency	Non-support	Insanity	Pregnancy at marriage	Bigamy	Separation	Felony conviction or imprisonment	Drug addiction	Fraud force, duress
PR	1 yr.	Yes	Yes	1 yr.	Yes	Yes	No	Yes	No	A	2 yrs.	Yes*	Yes	No
AL	6 mos.*	Yes	Phys. only	1 yr.	Yes	Yes*	2 yrs.	5 yrs.	Yes	A	2 yrs.*	*	Yes	A
AK	*	Yes	Yes	1 yr.	1 yr.	Yes	No	18 mos.	No	A	No	Yes	Yes	A
AZ	90 da.	No	No	No	No	No	No	No	No	A	No	No	No	No
AR	60 da.	Yes	Yes	1 yr.	1 yr.	Yes	Yes	3 yrs.	No	No	3 yrs.	Yes	No	A
CA	6 mos.	No	No	No	No	A	No	Yes, A	No	A	No	No	No	A
CO	90 da.	No	No	No	No	No	No	No	No	A	No	No	No	A
CT	1 yr.*	Yes	Yes	1 yr.	Yes	A	No	5 yrs.	Yes*	A	18 mos.*	life*	No	Yes
DE	6 mos.	Yes	Yes	Yes	Yes	Yes, A	No	A	No	Yes	6 mos.	Yes	Yes, A	No
FL	6 mos.	No	No	No	No	No	No	3 yrs.	No	No	No	No	No	No
GA	6 mos.	Yes	Yes	1 yr.	Yes	Yes	No	2 yrs.	Yes	A	No	Yes*	Yes	Yes
HI	6 mos.*	No	No	No	No	No	No	A	No	A	2 yrs.*	No	No	A
ID	6 wks.	Yes	Yes	Yes	Yes	A	1 yr.	3 yrs.	Yes	A	5 yrs.	Yes	No	A
IL	90 da.	Yes	Yes	1 yr.	2 yrs.	Yes	No	No	No	Yes	2 yrs.*	Yes	2 yrs.	No
IN	6 mos.*	No	No	No	No	Yes	No	2 yrs.	Yes	A	No	Yes	No	A
IA	1 yr.	No	No	No	No	A	No	A	No	A	No	No	No	No
KS	60 da.	No	No	No	No	No	Yes	2 yrs.	A	A	No	No	No	A
KY	180 da.	No	No	No	No	A	No	No	No	No	No	No	No	A
LA	1 yr.*	Yes	Yes	Yes	Yes	No	Yes	No	No	A	6 mos.	Yes*	No	A
ME	6 mos.*	Yes	Yes	3 yrs.	Yes	Yes	Yes	No	No	No	No	No	Yes	No
MD	1 yr.	Yes	Yes	1 yr.*	No	No	No	3 yrs.	No	A	1 yr.*	1 yr.*	No	A
MA	1 yr.*	Yes	Yes	1 yr.	Yes	Yes	Yes	No	No	A	No	5 yrs.	Yes	No
MI	1 yr.*	No	No	No	No	No	No	No	No	A	No	No	No	A
MN	180 da.	No	No	No	No	No	No	No	No	No	180 da.	No	No	A
MS	6 mos.	Yes	Yes	1 yr.	Yes	Yes	No	3 yrs.	Yes	Yes	No	Yes*	Yes	A
MO	90 da.	No	No	No	No	No	No	No	No	No	No	No	No	A
MT	90 da.	No	No	No	No	A	No	No	No	No	180 da.*	No	No	A
NE	1 yr.*	No	No	No	No	No	No	No	No	A	No	No	No	A
NV	6 wks.	No	No	No	No	No	No	2 yrs.	No	A	1 yr.	No	No	A
NH	1 yr.*	Yes	Yes	2 yrs.	2 yrs.	Yes	2 yrs.	No	No	No	No	*	No	No
NJ	1 yr.*	Yes	Yes	1 yr.	1 yr.	A	No	2 yrs.	No	A	18 mos.	18 mos.	1 yr.	A
NM	6 mos.	Yes	Yes	Yes*	No	No	No	No	No	No	No	No	No	No
NY	1 yr.*	Yes	Yes	1 yr.	No	No	No	No	No	A	1 yr.	3 yrs.	No	No
NC	6 mos.	No	No	No	No	A	No	3 yrs.	No	A	1 yr.	No	No	No
ND	6 mos.	Yes	Yes	1 yr.	1 yr.	A	1 yr.	5 yrs.*	No	A	No	Yes	1 yr.	A
OH	6 mos.	Yes	Yes	1 yr.	Yes	Yes	Yes	No	No	Yes, A	1 yr.	Yes	No	Yes
OK	6 mos.	Yes	Yes	1 yr.	Yes	Yes	Yes	5 yrs.	Yes	Yes	No	Yes	Yes	Yes
OR	6 mos.*	No	No	No	No	No	No	No	No	No	No	No	No	No
PA	6 mos.	Yes	Yes	1 yr.	No	No	No	18 mos.*	No	Yes	2 yrs.*	Yes	No	No
RI	1yr.	Yes	Yes	5 yrs.*	Yes	Yes	1 yr.	No	Yes	Yes	3 yrs.	No	Yes	No
SC	1 yr.*	Yes	Phys. only	1 yr.	Yes	No	No	No	No	No	1 yr.	Yes	Yes	No
SD	none*	Yes	Yes	1 yr.	1 yr.	A	1 yr.	5 yrs.	No	A	No	Yes	No	A*
TN	6 mos.	Yes	Yes	1 yr.	Yes	Yes	Yes	No	Yes	Yes	3 yrs.	Yes	Yes	A
TX	6 mos.*	Yes	Yes	1 yr.	*	A	No	3 yrs.	No	A	3 yrs.	1 yr.	No	No
UT	3 mos.	Yes	Yes	1 yr.	Yes	Yes	Yes	Yes	No	A	3 yrs.*	Yes	No	A
VT	6 mos.*	Yes	Yes	7 yrs.*	No	No	Yes	5 yrs.	No	No	6 mos.	3 yrs.	No	A
VA	6 mos.*	Yes	Phys.* only	1 yr.	No	A	No	No	A	A	1 yr.*	1 yr.*	No	A
WA	bona fide res.	No	No	No	No	No	No	No	No	No	No	No	No	No
WV	1 yr.	Yes	Yes	6 mos.	Yes	A	A	3 yrs.	A	A	1 yr.	Yes	Yes	No
WI	6 mos.	No	No	No	No	A	No	No	No	A	No	No	No	A
WY	2 mos.*	No	No	No	No	No	No	2 yrs.	No	A	No	No	No	No
DC	6 mos.	No	No	No	No	No	No	A*	No	A	6 mos.-1 yr.	No	No	A

(*) indicates qualification-check local statutes; (A) indicates grounds for annulment.

Wedding Anniversaries

The traditional names for wedding anniversaries go back many years in social usage. As such names as wooden, crystal, silver, and golden were applied it was considered proper to present the married pair with gifts made of these products or of something related. The list of traditional gifts, with a few allowable revisions in parentheses, is presented below, followed by modern gifts in **bold** face.

1st-Paper, **clocks**
2d-Cotton, **china**
3d-Leather, **crystal & glass**
4th-Linen (silk), **electrical appliances**
5th-Wood, **silverware**
6th-Iron, **wood**
7th-Wool (copper), **desk sets**
8th-Bronze, **linens & lace**
9th-Pottery (china), **leather**

10th-Tin (aluminum), **diamond jewelry**
11th-Steel, **fashion jewelry, accessories**
12th-Silk, **pearls or colored gems**
13th-Lace, **textiles & furs**
14th-Ivory, **gold jewelry**
15th-Crystal, **watches**
20th-China, **platinum**

25th-Silver, **sterling silver jubliee**
30th-Pearl, **diamond**
35th-Coral (jade), **jade**
40th-Ruby, **ruby**
45th-Sapphire, **sapphire**
50th-Gold, **gold**
55th-Emerald, **emerald**
60th-Diamond, **diamond**

Copyright Law of The United States

Source: Copyright Office, Library of Congress

What Copyright Is

Copyright is a form of protection provided by the laws of the United States (title 17, U.S. Code) to the authors of "original works of authorship" including literary, dramatic, musical, artistic, and certain other intellectual works. This protection is available to both published and unpublished works. Section 106 of the Copyright Act generally gives the owner of copyright the exclusive right to do and to authorize others to do the following:

• To *reproduce* the copyrighted work in copies or phonorecords;

• To prepare *derivative works* based upon the copyrighted work;

• To *distribute copies or phonorecords* of the copyrighted work to the public by sale or other transfer of ownership, or by rental, lease, or lending;

• To *perform the copyrighted work publicly*, in case of literary, musical, dramatic, and choreographic works, pantomimes, and motion pictures and other audiovisual works; and

• To *display the copyrighted work publicly*, in the case of literary, musical, dramatic, and choreographic works, pantomimes, and pictorial, graphic, or sculptural works, including the individual images of a motion picture or other audiovisual work.

It is illegal for anyone to violate any of the rights provided by the Act to the owner of copyright. These rights, however, are not unlimited in scope. Sections 107 through 118 of the Copyright Act establish limitations on these rights. In some cases, these limitations are specified exemptions from copyright liability. One major limitation is the doctrine of "fair use," which is given a statutory basis by section 107 of the Act. In other instances, the limitation takes the form of a "compulsory license" under which certain limited uses of copyrighted works are permitted upon payment of specified royalties and compliance with statutory conditions.

Copyright protection subsists from the time the work is created in fixed form; that is, it is an incident of the process of authorship. The copyright in the work of authorship *immediately* becomes the property of the author who created it. Only the author or those deriving their rights through the author can rightfully claim copyright.

In the case of works made for hire, the employer and not the employee is presumptively considered the author. Section 101 of the copyright statute defines a "work made for hire" as:

(1) a work prepared by an employee within the scope of his or her employment; or

(2) a work specially ordered or commissioned for use as a contribution to a collective work, as a part of a motion picture or other audio visual work, as a translation, as a supplementary work, as a compilation, as an instructional text, as a test, as answer material for a test, or as an atlas, if the parties expressly agree in a written instrument signed by them that the work shall be considered a work made for hire . . . .

The authors of a joint work are co-owners of the copyright in the work, unless there is an agreement to the contrary.

Copyright in each separate contribution to a periodical or other collective work is distinct from copyright in the collective work as a whole and vests initially with the author of the contribution.

Works published on or after January 1, 1978, are subject to protection under the copyright statute if, on the date of first publication, one or more of the authors is a national or domiciliary of the U.S., or is a national, domiciliary, or soverign authority of a foreign nation that is a party to a copyright treaty to which the U.S. is also a party, or is a stateless person, regardless of domicile, or if the work is first published either in the U.S. or in a foreign nation that on the date of first publication is a party to the Universal Copyright Convention or the Berne Union.

What Works Are Protected

Copyright protects "original works of authorship" that are fixed in a tangible form of expression. The fixation need not be directly perceptible, so long as it may be communicated with the aid of a machine or device. Copyrightable works include the following categories:

(1) literary works;

(2) musical works, including any accompanying words;

(3) dramatic works, including any accompanying music;

(4) pantomimes and choreographic works;

(5) pictorial, graphic, and sculptural works;

(6) motion pictures and other audiovisual works; and

(7) sound recordings.

These categories should be viewed quite broadly: for example, computer programs and most "compilations" are registrable as "literary works"; maps and architectural plans are registrable as "pictorial, graphic, and sculptural works."

What Is Not Protected By Copyright

Several categories of material are generally not eligible for statutory copyright protection. These include among others:

• Works that have *not* been fixed in a tangible form of expression. For example: choreographic works that have not been notated or recorded, or improvisational speeches or performances that have not been written or recorded.

• Titles, names, short phrases, and slogans; familiar symbols or designs; mere variations of typographic ornamentation, lettering, or coloring; mere listings of ingredients or contents.

• Ideas, procedures, methods, systems, processes, concepts, principles, discoveries, or devices, as distinguished from a description, explanation, or illustration.

• Works consisting *entirely* of information that is common property and containing no original authorship. For example: standard calendars, height and weight charts, tape measures and rulers, and lists or tables taken from public documents or other common sources.

Notice of Copyright

For works first published on and after March 1, 1989, use of the copyright notice is optional, though highly recommended. Before March 1, 1989, the use of the notice was mandatory on all published works, and any work first published before that date *must* bear a notice or risk loss of copyright protection.

Use of the notice is recommended because it informs the public that the work is protected by copyright, identifies the copyright owner, and shows the year of

(continued)

first publication. Furthermore, in the event that a work is infringed, if the work carries a proper notice, the court will not allow a defendant to claim "innocent infringement"—that is, that he or she did not realize that the work is protected. (A successful innocent infringement claim may result in a reduction in damages that the copyright owner would otherwise receive.)

The use of the copyright notice is the responsibility of the copyright owner and does not require advance permission from, or registration with, the Copyright Office.

For visually perceptible copies, the form of the notice consists of the following: © (the letter C in a circle), the word "Copyright," or "Copr.," and the year of first publication, and the name of the owner of copyright in the work. Example: © 1989 Judy Smith. The notice must be affixed in such manner and location as to give reasonable notice of the claim of copyright.

The notice of copyright prescribed for all published phonorecords of sound recordings consists of the symbol ℗ (the letter P in a circle), the year of first publication of the sound recording, and the name of the owner of copyright in the sound recording. Example ℗ XYZ Records, Inc. The notice on phonorecords may appear on the surface of the phonorecord or on the phonorecord label or container, provided the manner of placement and location give reasonable notice of the claim.

How Long Copyright Protection Endures

Works Originally Copyrighted on or After January 1, 1978

A work that is created (fixed in tangible form for the first time) on or after January 1, 1978, is automatically protected from the moment of its creation, and is ordinarily given a term enduring for the author's life, plus an additional 50 years after the author's death. In the case of "a joint work prepared by two or more authors who did not work for hire," the term lasts for 50 years after the last surviving author's death. For works made for hire, and for anonymous and pseudonymous works (unless the author's identity is revealed in Copyright Office records), the duration of copyright will be 75 years from publication or 100 years from creation, whichever is shorter.

Works that were created but not published or registered for copyright before January 1, 1978, have been automatically brought under the statute and are now given Federal copyright protection. The duration of copyright in these works will generally be computed in the same way as for works created on or after January 1, 1978: the life-plus-50 or 75/100-year terms will apply to them as well. The law provides that in no case will the term of copyright for works in this category expire before December 31, 2002, and for works published on or before December 31, 2002, the term of copyright will not expire before December 31, 2027.

Works Copyrighted Before January 1, 1978

Under the law in effect before 1978, copyright was secured either on the date a work was published or on the date of registration if the work was registered in unpublished form. In either case, the copyright endured for a first term of 28 years from the date it was secured. During the last (28th) year of the first term, the copyright was eligible for renewal. The current copyright law has extended the renewal term from 28 to 47 years for copyrights that were subsisting on January 1, 1978, making these works eligible for a total term of protection of 75 years. However, the copyright *must* be renewed to receive the 47-year period of added protection. This is accomplished by filing a properly completed Form RE accompanied by a $6 filing fee in the Copyright Office before the end of the 28th calendar year of the original term.

International Copyright Protection

There is no such thing as an "international copyright" that will automatically protect an author's writings throughout the entire world. Protection against unauthorized use in a particular country depends, basically, on the national laws of that country. However, most countries do offer protection to foreign works under certain conditions, and these conditions have been greatly simplified by international copyright treaties and conventions. The U.S. belongs to both global, multilateral copyright treaties—the Universal Copyright Convention (UCC) and the Berne Convention for the Protection of Literary and Artistic Works.

A U.S. author may obtain copyright protection in all countries that are members of the Berne Union and the International Copyright Convention. A work first published in the U.S. or another Berne Union country (or first published in a non-Berne Union country, followed by publication within 30 days in a Berne Union country) is eligible for protection in all Berne member countries. There are no special requirements. In member countries of the UCC, where no formalities are required, the works of U.S. authors are also automatically protected. Member countries whose laws impose formalities protect U.S. works if all published copies bear a convention notice, which consists of the symbol ©, together with the name of the copyright owner and the year of publication. Example: © JOHN DOE 1990.

For a list of countries that maintain copyright relations with the U.S., write or call the Copyright Office and ask for Circular 38a.

Copyright Registration

Copyright registration is a legal formality intended to make a public record of the basic facts of a particular copyright and is not a condition of copyright protection. Even though registration is not generally a requirement for protection, the copyright law provides several inducements or advantages to encourage copyright owners to register. Among these advantages are the following:

• Registration establishes a public record of the copyright claim;

• Before an infringement suit may be filed in court, registration is necessary for works of U.S. origin and for foreign works not originating in a Berne Union country. (For more information on when a work is of U.S. origin, contact the Copyright Office);

• If made before or within 5 years of publication, registration will establish prima facie evidence in court of the validity of the copyright and of the facts stated in the certificate; and

• If registration is made within 3 months after publication of the work or prior to an infringement of the work, statutory damages and attorney's fees will be available to the copyright owner in court actions. Otherwise, only an award of actual damages and profits is available to the copyright owner.

Registration may be made at any time within the life of the copyright. When a work has been registered in unpublished form, it is not necessary to make another registration when the work becomes published (although the copyright owner may register the published edition, if desired).

The process of registration is quite simple. An appropriate form is requested from the Copyright Office

(continued)

and completed. It is returned to the Copyright Office along with a $10 nonrefundable filing fee and the appropriate deposit(s) of the work for which registration is sought. In a common example—a published book—the deposit is two copies of the best edition of the book. A certificate of registration is sent once the paperwork is completed, a process that usually takes several months due to the large volume of registrations the Office must handle.

Although a copyright registration is not required, the Copyright Act establishes a mandatory deposit requirement for works published in the U.S. In general, the owner of copyright, or the owner of the exclusive right of publication in the work, has a legal obligation to deposit in the Copyright Office, within three months of publication in the U.S., two copies (or, in the case of

sound recordings, two phonorecords) for the use of the Library of Congress. Failure to make the deposit can result in fines and other penalties, but does not affect copyright protection. Certain categories of works are *exempt entirely* from the mandatory deposit requirements, and the obligation is reduced for certain other categories.

Information on registration and application forms may be obtained free of charge by writing the Copyright Office, Information Section, LM-455, Library of Congress, Washington, DC 20559. Registration application forms and circulars may be ordered on a 24-hour basis by calling (202) 707-9100. Request Circular 1 for additional general information on copyright, including a list of which application forms to use when registering specific types of works.

Birthstones

Source: Jewelry Industry Council

Month	Ancient	Modern
January	Garnet	Garnet
February	Amethyst	Amethyst
March	Jasper	Bloodstone or Aquamarine
April	Sapphire	Diamond
May	Agate	Emerald
June	Emerald	Pearl, Moonstone, or Alexandrite

Month	Ancient	Modern
July	Onyx	Ruby
August	Carnelian	Sardonyx or Peridot
September	Chrysolite	Sapphire
October	Aquamarine	Opal or Tourmaline
November	Topaz	Topaz
December	Ruby	Turquoise or Zircon

Home Buyer's Glossary

Amortization: The gradual repayment of a mortgage over time, usually according to a predetermined schedule.

Appraisal: An opinion or estimate of the value of property, usually made by lenders before they will determine how much of a mortgage they will extend.

Assumable mortgage: The purchaser takes ownership of real estate encumbered by an existing mortgage and assumes responsibility as the guarantor for the unpaid balance of the mortgage.

Balloon payment: The final payment on a loan, usually substantially larger than previous payments, which repays the loan in full.

Binder: A preliminary and temporary agreement between the seller and the buyer, generally agreeing to the price of a house before a formal contract.

Broker: Usually, a licensed agent of, and paid by, the seller to serve as an intermediary in real estate transactions.

Closing: The day of judgment, when after writing numerous checks to cover various fees, the title passes to the buyer.

Commission: The fee paid by a seller to a broker for the sale of the house. Fee is negotiable.

Condominium: A form of ownership, not a kind of development, in which the owner gets title to a housing unit and an interest in the common areas.

Cooperative: A type of ownership in which buyers get shares in the cooperative corporation that owns the building. Those shares give the buyer a proprietary lease on an apartment in that building.

Deed: A written document that conveys title to the property.

Equity: The value of property minus the mortgage and other liens against it.

Escrow: Money paid monthly to the lender, along with the mortgage payment, for use in paying taxes and sometimes insurance. The lender keeps the funds separately and pays bills when due.

Foreclosure: Forced sale of property to meet debt obligations; usually to a lending or taxing institution.

Freddie Mac: The Federal Home Loan Mortgage Corp., a major secondary mortgage market agency that buys mortgages from lenders, allowing them to make new loans with the proceeds.

FHA: The Federal Housing Administration, a division of the Department of Housing and Urban Development that insures, but does not make, mortgages.

Fannie Mae: Federal National Mortgage Association, the largest secondary mortgage agency.

Ginnie Mae: Government National Mortgage Association, a government-owned secondary market agency that buys FHA-insured loans from lenders.

Indexing: Adjusting the interest rate on a loan in accordance with the movements of an index or economic indicator, i.e., the U.S. Treasury bill rate or the consumer price index.

Interest: Money paid for the use of money. There are two kinds of interest. Simple interest is interest that is earned and paid. Compound interest is the accumulated interest that is added to the principal amount.

Lien: A right to property obtained as collateral to a loan or debt. A mortgage is a lien.

Mortgage: A written pledge of property as collateral for a loan.

The most common type of mortgage is the *fixed rate mortgage*, in which the monthly payments remain the same over the life of the loan; and the *adjustable rate mortgage* (ARM) where the interest rate is tied to a financial index (the one-year Treasury bill rate and the savings and loan cost-of-funds index are most common). With an ARM, the monthly payments usually vary over the life of the loan. In some cases, the total number of monthly payments can be increased or decreased with the amount remaining the same. In 1989, nearly half of new mortgages were ARMs.

Another type of mortgage is the *graduated payment mortgage*, which has a fixed interest rate but lower initial payments, usually for the first 5 years of the loan. This type of mortgage is advantageous to the first-time homeowner. There is also the *shared-appreciation mortgage*, in which a borrower agrees to share the appreciation of the property with the lender in return for a lower interest rate. *Reverse mortgages* allow elderly homeowners to convert some of their accumulated housing equity into cash.

Origination Fee: A fee paid by a borrower for the cost of evaluating and documenting a loan.

Points: Additional payments made by a borrower to a lender; a point equals 1 percent of the loan.

Prepayment penalty: An extra fee charged for paying off a mortgage before it is due.

Principal: The total amount of a mortgage debt. The amount upon which the interest is computed.

Title: Evidence of a person's ownership of a piece of property.

Median Price of Existing Single-Family Homes

Source: National Association of Realtors

The median sale price for existing single-family homes rose 3.4 percent in the first quarter of 1989 from the same period in 1988.

City[1]	Median price first quarter 1988	1989	Pct. chng.	City[1]	Median price First quarter 1988	1989	Pct. chng.
Akron, Oh.	$57,100	$56,000	−1.9	Los Angeles, Cal.	$159,100	$201,000	+26.3
Albuquerque, N.M.	79,700	82,000	+2.9	Louisville, Ky.	52,200	56,700	+8.6
Anaheim/Santa Ana, Cal.	182,700	237,900	+30.2	Madison, Wis.	67,700	74,700	+10.3
Atlanta, Ga.	NA	80,300	NA	Memphis, Tenn.	77,500	77,000	−0.6
Baltimore, Md.	83,600	92,200	+10.3	Miami/Hialeah, Fla.	78,000	82,600	+5.9
Baton Rouge, La.	65,700	61,100	−7.0	Milwaukee, Wis.	72,600	74,500	+2.6
Birmingham, Ala.	73,100	77,300	+5.7	Minneapolis/St. Paul, Minn.	84,400	85,900	+1.8
Boston, Mass.	176,900	178,500	+0.9	Mobile, Ala.	50,600	50,900	+0.6
Buffalo, N.Y.	64,100	68,700	+7.2	Nashville/Davidson, Tenn.	77,600	79,600	+2.6
Charleston, S.C.	72,600	72,400	−0.3	New Haven, Conn.	168,900	166,700	−1.3
Charlotte, N.C.	NA	85,200	NA	New Orleans, La.	73,000	71,200	−2.5
Chattanooga, Tenn.	61,200	65,600	+7.2	New York, N.Y.	187,000	181,700	−2.8
Chicago, Ill.	92,800	99,300	+7.0	Oklahoma City, Okla.	56,500	52,300	−7.4
Cincinnati, Oh.	66,700	73,200	+9.7	Omaha, Neb.	58,300	60,900	+4.5
Cleveland, Oh.	66,500	69,400	+4.4	Orlando, Fla.	78,700	79,100	+0.5
Columbia, S.C.	68,300	71,900	+5.3	Philadelphia, Pa.	97,700	100,400	+2.8
Columbus, Oh.	66,200	73,900	+11.6	Phoenix, Ariz.	79,000	78,500	−0.6
Corpus Christi, Tex.	63,200	63,200	unch.	Pittsburgh, Pa.	60,900	62,400	+2.5
Dallas, Tex.	86,100	88,400	+2.7	Portland, Ore.	62,900	67,100	+6.7
Daytona Beach, Fla.	59,300	59,500	+0.3	Providence, R.I.	123,300	128,800	+4.5
Denver, Col.	83,700	80,800	−3.5	Raleigh/Durham, N.C.	87,700	102,000	+16.3
Des Moines, Ia.	54,500	57,300	+5.1	Sacramento, Cal.	88,200	100,300	+13.7
Detroit, Mich.	71,500	71,900	+0.6	St. Louis, Mo.	74,100	81,400	+9.9
El Paso, Tex.	57,800	57,200	−1.0	San Antonio, Tex.	63,400	60,800	−4.1
Grand Rapids, Mich.	55,400	59,600	+7.6	San Diego, Cal.	134,400	163,900	+21.9
Hartford, Conn.	166,400	165,500	−0.5	San Francisco, Cal.	185,100	243,900	+31.8
Honolulu, Hi.	198,400	236,000	+19.0	Seattle, Wash.	88,200	99,700	+13.0
Houston, Tex.	60,200	62,900	+4.5	Spokane, Wash.	49,900	50,200	+0.6
Indianapolis, Ind.	61,800	68,000	+10.0	Syracuse, N.Y.	68,100	76,900	+12.9
Jacksonville, Fla.	68,900	65,900	−4.4	Tampa, Fla.	60,200	71,700	+19.1
Kansas City, Mo.	70,900	73,800	+4.1	Toledo, Oh.	56,500	57,700	+2.1
Knoxville, Tenn.	66,300	69,800	+5.3	Tulsa, Okla.	63,500	60,500	−4.7
Las Vegas, Nev.	75,700	80,500	+6.3	Washington, D.C.	132,400	143,700	+8.5
Little Rock, Ark.	63,000	63,400	+0.6	U.S. average	$88,600	$91,600	+3.4

(1) All areas are metropolitan statistical areas as defined by the U.S. Office of Management and Budget. They include the named central city and surrounding suburban areas.

Housing Affordability

Source: National Assn. of Realtors

	Median-priced existing home	Average mortgage rate	Monthly principal and interest payment	Payment as percentage of median income		Median-priced existing home	Average mortgage rate	Monthly principal and interest payment	Payment as percentage of median income
1980	$62,200	12.95%	$549	31.3%	1985	$75,500	11.74%	$609	26.2%
1981	66,400	15.12	677	36.3	1986	80,300	10.25	563	23.0
1982	67,800	15.38	702	35.9	1987	85,600	9.28	565	21.8
1983	70,300	12.85	616	30.1	1988	90,600	9.31	599	22.5
1984	72,400	12.49	618	28.2	1989	93,200	10.59	687	25.2

Note: The average mortgage rate is based on the effective rate of loans closed on existing homes monitored by the Federal Home Loan Bank Board.
The 1988 and 1989 numbers are for June.

Income Needed to Get a Mortgage

Source: National Association of Realtors

The following shows the minimum annual gross income needed for various size home loans at different rates. The figures are based on a 30-year loan and assume that the borrower's monthly payments can't exceed 28% of gross income, the ceiling most lenders use. The figures do not include property taxes and insurance as part of the monthly payment.

Interest rate (Percent)	$50,000	$75,000	Loan amount $100,000 income needed	$150,000	$200,000
8	$15,724	$23,586	$31,447	$47,171	$62,895
8½	16,477	24,715	32,954	49,430	65,907
9	17,242	25,863	34,484	51,726	68,968
9½	18,018	27,028	36,037	54,055	72,074
10	18,085	28,208	37,611	56,415	75,221
10½	19,602	29,403	39,203	58,805	78,406
11	20,407	30,611	40,814	61,221	81,628
11½	21,221	31,831	42,441	63,662	84,883
12	22,042	33,063	44,084	66,125	88,167
12½	22,870	34,305	45,740	68,610	91,479
13	23,704	35,556	47,409	71,113	94,817

Mortgage Payment Tables

Source: *The Mortgage Money Guide*, Federal Trade Commission

8% Annual Percent Rate

Monthly Payments (Principal and Interest)*

Amount Financed	10 Years	15 Years	20 Years	25 Years	30 Years
$ 25,000	303.32	238.91	209.11	192.95	183.44
30,000	363.98	286.70	250.93	231.54	220.13
35,000	424.65	334.48	292.75	270.14	256.82
40,000	485.31	382.26	334.58	308.73	293.51
45,000	545.97	430.04	376.40	347.32	330.19
50,000	606.64	477.83	418.22	385.91	366.88
60,000	727.97	573.39	501.86	463.09	440.26
70,000	849.29	668.96	585.51	540.27	513.64
80,000	970.62	764.52	669.15	617.45	587.01
90,000	1091.95	860.09	752.80	694.63	660.39
100,000	1213.28	955.65	836.44	771.82	733.76
120,000	1455.94	1146.78	1003.72	926.18	880.52
140,000	1698.58	1337.92	1171.02	1080.54	1027.28
160,000	1941.24	1529.04	1338.30	1234.90	1174.02
180,000	2183.90	1720.18	1505.60	1389.26	1320.78
200,000	2426.56	1911.30	1672.88	1543.64	1467.52

9% Annual Percent Rate

Monthly Payments (Principal and interest)*

Amount Financed	10 Years	15 Years	20 Years	25 Years	30 Years
$ 25,000	316.69	253.57	224.93	209.80	201.16
30,000	380.03	304.28	269.92	251.76	241.39
35,000	443.36	354.99	314.90	293.72	281.62
40,000	506.70	405.71	359.89	335.68	321.85
45,000	570.04	456.42	404.88	377.64	362.08
50,000	633.38	507.13	449.86	419.60	402.31
60,000	760.05	608.56	539.84	503.52	482.77
70,000	886.73	709.99	629.81	587.44	563.24
80,000	1013.41	811.41	719.78	671.36	643.70
90,000	1140.08	912.84	809.75	755.28	724.16
100,000	1266.76	1014.27	899.73	839.20	804.62
120,000	1520.10	1217.12	1079.68	1007.04	965.54
140,000	1773.46	1419.98	1259.62	1174.88	1126.48
160,000	2026.82	1622.82	1439.56	1342.72	1287.40
180,000	2280.16	1825.68	1619.50	1510.56	1448.32
200,000	2533.52	2028.54	1799.46	1678.40	1609.24

10% Annual Percentage Rate

Monthly Payments (Principal and interest)*

Amount Financed	10 Years	15 Years	20 Years	25 Years	30 Years
$ 25,000	330.38	268.65	241.26	227.18	219.39
30,000	396.45	322.38	289.51	272.61	263.27
35,000	462.53	376.11	337.76	318.05	307.15
40,000	528.60	429.84	386.01	363.48	351.03
45,000	594.68	483.57	434.26	408.92	394.91
50,000	660.75	537.30	482.51	454.35	438.79
60,000	792.90	644.76	579.01	545.22	526.54
70,000	925.06	752.22	675.52	636.09	614.30
80,000	1057.20	859.68	772.02	726.96	702.06
90,000	1189.36	967.14	868.52	817.83	789.81
100,000	1321.51	1074.61	965.02	908.70	877.57
120,000	1585.80	1289.52	1158.02	1090.44	1053.08
140,000	1850.12	1504.44	1351.04	1272.18	1228.60
160,000	2114.40	1719.36	1544.04	1453.92	1404.12
180,000	2378.72	1934.28	1737.04	1635.66	1579.62
200,000	2643.02	2149.22	1930.04	1817.40	1755.14

11% Annual Percentage Rate

Monthly Payments (Principal and interest)*

Amount Financed	10 Years	15 Years	20 Years	25 Years	30 Years
$ 25,000	344.38	284.15	258.05	245.03	238.08
30,000	413.25	340.98	309.66	294.03	285.70
35,000	482.13	397.81	361.27	343.04	333.31
40,000	551.00	454.64	412.88	392.05	380.93
45,000	619.88	511.47	464.48	441.05	428.55
50,000	688.75	568.30	516.09	490.06	476.16

	60,000	826.50	681.96	619.31	588.07	571.39
	70,000	964.25	795.62	722.53	686.08	666.63
	80,000	1102.00	909.28	825.75	784.09	761.86
	90,000	1239.75	1022.94	928.97	882.10	857.09
	100,000	1377.50	1136.60	1032.19	980.11	952.32
	120,000	1653.00	1363.92	1238.62	1176.14	1142.78
	140,000	1928.50	1591.24	1445.06	1372.16	1333.26
	160,000	2204.00	1818.56	1651.50	1568.18	1523.72
	180,000	2479.50	2045.88	1857.94	1764.20	1714.18
	200,000	2755.00	2273.20	2064.38	1960.22	1904.64

12% Annual Percentage Rate

Monthly Payments (Principal and interest)*

Amount Financed	10 Years	15 Years	20 Years	25 Years	30 Years
$ 25,000	358.68	300.05	275.28	263.31	257.16
30,000	430.42	360.06	330.33	315.97	308.59
35,000	502.15	420.06	385.39	368.63	360.02
40,000	573.89	480.07	440.44	421.29	411.45
45,000	645.62	540.08	495.49	473.96	462.88
50,000	717.36	600.09	550.55	526.62	514.31
60,000	860.83	720.11	660.66	631.93	617.17
70,000	1004.30	840.12	770.77	737.26	720.03
80,000	1147.77	960.14	880.87	842.58	822.90
90,000	1291.24	1080.15	990.98	947.90	925.75
100,000	1434.71	1200.17	1101.09	1053.23	1028.62
120,000	1721.66	1440.22	1321.32	1263.86	1234.34
140,000	2008.60	1680.24	1541.54	1474.52	1440.06
160,000	2295.54	1920.28	1761.74	1685.16	1645.80
180,000	2582.48	2160.30	1981.96	1895.80	1851.50
200,000	2869.42	2400.34	2202.18	2106.46	2057.24

13% Annual Percentage Rate

Monthly Payments (Principal and interest)*

Amount Financed	10 Years	15 Years	20 Years	25 Years	30 Years
$ 25,000	373.28	316.32	292.90	281.96	276.55
30,000	447.94	379.58	351.48	338.36	331.86
35,000	522.59	442.84	410.06	394.75	387.17
40,000	597.25	506.10	468.64	451.14	442.48
45,000	671.90	569.36	527.21	507.53	497.79
50,000	746.56	632.63	585.79	563.92	553.10
60,000	895.87	759.15	702.95	676.71	663.72
70,000	1045.18	885.67	820.11	789.49	774.34
80,000	1194.49	1012.20	937.27	902.27	884.96
90,000	1343.80	1138.72	1054.42	1015.05	995.58
100,000	1493.11	1265.25	1171.58	1127.84	1106.20
120,000	1791.74	1518.30	1405.90	1353.42	1327.44
140,000	2090.36	1771.34	1640.22	1578.98	1548.68
160,000	2388.98	2024.40	1874.54	1804.54	1769.92
180,000	2687.60	2277.44	2108.84	2030.10	1991.16
200,000	2986.22	2530.50	2343.16	2255.68	2212.40

14% Annual Percentage Rate

Monthly Payments (Principal and interest)*

Amount Financed	10 Years	15 Years	20 Years	25 Years	30 Years
$ 25,000	388.17	332.94	310.89	300.95	296.22
30,000	465.80	399.53	373.06	361.13	355.47
35,000	543.44	466.11	435.24	421.32	414.71
40,000	621.07	532.70	497.41	481.51	473.95
45,000	698.70	599.29	559.59	541.70	533.20
50,000	776.34	665.88	621.77	601.89	592.44
60,000	931.60	799.05	746.12	722.26	710.93
70,000	1086.87	932.22	870.47	842.64	829.42
80,000	1242.14	1065.40	994.82	963.01	947.90
90,000	1397.40	1198.57	1119.17	1083.38	1066.38
100,000	1552.67	1331.75	1243.53	1203.77	1184.88
120,000	1863.20	1598.10	1492.24	1444.52	1421.86
140,000	2173.74	1864.44	1740.94	1685.28	1658.84
160,000	2484.28	2130.80	1989.64	1926.02	1895.80
180,000	2794.80	2397.14	2238.34	2166.76	2132.76
200,000	3105.34	2663.50	2487.06	2407.54	2369.76

(continued)

15% Annual Percentage Rate

Monthly Payments (Principal and Interest)*

Amount Financed	10 Years	15 Years	20 Years	25 Years	30 Years	Amount Financed	10 Years	15 Years	20 Years	25 Years	30 Years
$ 25,000	403.34	349.90	329.90	320.21	316.12	$80,000	1290.68	1119.67	1053.44	1024.67	1011.56
30,000	484.01	419.88	395.04	384.25	379.34	90,000	1452.63	1259.63	1185.11	1152.75	1138.00
35,000	564.68	489.86	460.88	448.30	442.56	100,000	1613.35	1399.59	1316.79	1280.84	1264.45
40,000	645.34	559.84	526.72	512.34	505.78	120,000	1936.02	1679.52	1580.16	1537.00	1517.34
45,000	726.11	629.82	592.56	576.38	569.00	140,000	2258.70	1959.44	1843.52	1793.18	1770.24
50,000	806.68	699.80	658.40	640.42	632.23	160,000	2581.36	2239.34	2106.88	2049.34	2023.12
60,000	968.01	839.76	790.08	768.50	758.67	180,000	2904.02	2519.26	2370.22	2305.50	2276.00
70,000	1129.35	979.72	921.76	896.59	885.12	200,000	3226.70	2799.18	2633.58	2561.68	2528.90

*For loans that fully pay off the debt over the loan term.

Tips on Cutting Energy Costs in Your Home

Source: Con Edison Conservation Services, New York City

Heating

In many homes, in areas where temperatures drop during the winter, more energy is used for heating than anything else. Installing the right amount of insulation, storm windows and doors, caulking and weatherstripping pays off. Also consider the following advice:

- Make sure the thermostat and heating system are in good working order. An annual checkup is recommended.
- If your heating system has air filters, make sure they are clean.
- Set the thermostat no higher than 68 degrees. When no one is home, or when everyone is sleeping, the setting should be turned down to 60 degrees or lower. An automatic setback thermostat can raise and lower your home's temperature at times you specify.
- Close off and do not heat unused areas.
- Cover all air conditioner units.
- If you do not have conventional storm windows or doors, use kits to make plastic storm windows.
- Special glass fireplace doors help keep a room's heat from being drawn up the chimney when the fire is burning low. Close the damper when a fireplace is not in use.
- Use the sun's heat by opening blinds and draperies on sunny days.
- Keep radiators and warm air outlets clean. Do not block them with furniture or draperies.

Water Heater

In many homes, the water heater ranks second only to the heating system in total energy consumption.

- Put an insulation blanket on your water heater; when you go on vacation turn it to a minimum setting.
- If you have a dishwasher, set the water heater thermostat no higher than 140 degrees. If not, or if you have a separate water heater for baths, a setting as low as 110 degrees may be sufficient.
- Run the dishwasher and clothes washer only when you have a full load. Use warm or cold water cycles for laundry when you can.
- Take showers instead of tub baths. About half as much hot water is used for a shower.
- Install a water-saver shower head.
- Install aerators or restrictors on all your sink faucets.
- Do not leave the hot water running when rinsing dishes or shaving. Plug and partially fill the basin, or fill a pan with water.
- Use the right size water heater for your needs. An oversized unit wastes energy heating unneeded water. An undersized unit will not deliver all the hot water you want when you need it.
- When shopping for a water heater, look for the yellow-and-black federal EnergyGuide label to learn the estimated yearly energy cost of a unit.

Air Conditioning

- Clean or replace the filter in an air conditioner at the beginning of the cooling season. Then check it once a month and clean or change the filter if necessary. A dirty filter blocks the flow of air.
- Adjust the temperature control setting to provide a room temperature no lower than 78 degrees. Use a good wall thermometer to tell which setting will provide the desired temperature.
- Close windows and doors when the air conditioner is running.
- When the outside temperature is 78 degrees or cooler, turn off the air conditioner and open windows to cool your home.
- Always keep your air conditioner turned off when you are away from home or not using the areas that it cools. An air conditioner timer can be set to turn on just before family members arrive home.
- Close draperies and shades to block out the sun's heat.
- When shopping for a new room air conditioner, look for the yellow-and-black federal EnergyGuide label to learn the Energy Efficiency Rating (EER) and the estimated yearly operating cost. The higher the EER, the less electricity will be used for a cooling job.
- Read the manufacturer's instructions; follow closely.
- If you have a central air conditioning system, run your hands along the ducts while it is operating to check for air leaks. Repair leaks with duct tape. Make sure the duct system is properly insulated.
- On many days, a window fan can cool an apartment as effectively as an air conditioner, and it is less costly.

Refrigerators and Freezers

The refrigerator operates 24 hours a day, every day, so it is one of the biggest users of energy in the home all year.

- Keep the condenser coils clean. The coils are on the back or at the bottom of the refrigerator. Carefully wipe, vacuum or brush the coils to remove dust and dirt at least once a year.
- Examine door gaskets and hinges regularly for air leaks. The doors should fit tightly. To check, place a piece of paper between the door and the cabinet. Close the door

(continued)

with normal force, then try to pull the paper straight out. There should be a slight resistance. Test all around the door, including the hinge side. If there are any places where the paper slides out easily, you need to adjust the hinges or replace the gasket, or both.

- Pause before opening your refrigerator door. Think of everything you will need before you open the door so you do not have to go back several times. When you open the door, close it quickly to keep the cool air in.

- Adjust the temperature-setting dial of the refrigerator as the manufacturer recommends. Use a thermometer to check the temperature (38 to 40 degrees is usually recommended for the refrigerator; zero degrees for the freezer). Settings that are too cold waste electricity.

- If you have a manual-defrost refrigerator, do not allow the ice to build up more than 1/4 inch thick.

- Keep your refrigerator well-stocked but allow room for air to circulate around the food.

- The freezer, on the other hand, should be packed full. If necessary, fill empty spaces with bags of ice cubes or fill milk cartons with water and freeze.

- When you are going to be away from home for a week or more, turn off and unplug the refrigerator, empty and clean it, and prop the door open.

- If you are buying a new refrigerator, look for one with a humid-dry ("power-saver") switch. This switch is used to turn off "anti-sweat" heaters in the doors to save electricity when the heaters are not needed.

- When shopping for a new refrigerator or freezer, eliminate those too large for your needs; look for the federal EnergyGuide label to help you select an efficient unit.

Cooking

- Cook as many dishes in the oven at one time as you can instead of cooking each separately. If recipes call for slightly different temperatures, say 325, 350, and 375 degrees, pick the middle temperature of 350 to cook all 3 dishes and remove each dish as it's done.

- Don't preheat the oven unnecessarily. Usually, any food that takes more than an hour of cooking can be started in a cold oven.

- Turn off your oven or range just before the cooking is done. The heat that is left will usually finish the cooking.

- Whenever you peek into an oven by opening a door, the temperature drops about 25 degrees. So open the oven door as little as possible.

- Use tight-fitting covers on pots and pans to retain heat and cook foods more quickly.

- Use the lowest possible heat setting to cook foods on top of the range.

- Match the pot to the size of the surface unit. Putting a small pot on a large surface unit wastes energy without cooking the food any faster.

- Adjust the flame on a gas burner so that it does not extend beyond the base of the pot. Using too high a flame wastes energy, and can be dangerous.

- On gas ranges, the flame should burn in a firm, blue cone. If not, get a service representative to check it.

Lighting

- Get all family members in the habit of turning off lights when they leave a room, even if they will be gone only for a short time.

- During the day, try to get along with as few lights as possible. Let the daylight do the work. White or light-colored walls make a room seem brighter.

- Use bulbs of lower wattage.

- When possible, use one large bulb rather than several smaller ones. One 100-watt incandescent bulb, for example, produces more light than three 40-watt. However, never use bulbs of a higher wattage than a fixture is designed to take.

- Use three-way bulbs wherever possible.

- Buy energy-saving incandescent bulbs to replace standard bulbs with slightly higher wattage. There's a ten percent energy cost saving.

- Modern solid-state dimmer controls let you save energy by reducing your lighting level and wattage. Many are easy to install.

- Use plug-in timers to turn lights on and off automatically.

- Consider changing to fluorescent lighting, especially in kitchens, bathrooms, and work areas. Fluorescent tubes give more light at lower energy cost than incandescent bulbs with the same wattage.

- For outdoor lighting, replace standard incandescent floodlights with the new energy-saving halogen type.

Measuring Energy

Source: Energy Information Administration, U.S. Energy Dept.

The following tables of equivalents contain those figures commonly used to compare different types of energy sources and their various measurements.

Btu — a British thermal unit — the amount of heat required to raise one pound of water one degree Fahrenheit. Equivalent to 1,055 joules or about 252 gram calories. A therm is usually 100,000 Btu but is sometimes used to refer to other units.

Calorie — The amount of heat required to raise one gram of water one degree Centigrade; abbreviated cal.; equivalent to about .003968 Btu. More common is the kilogram calorie, also called a kilocalorie and abbreviated Cal. or Kcal; equivalent to about 3.97 Btu. (One Kcal is equivalent to one food calorie.)

Btu Values of Energy Sources
(These are conventional or average values, not precise equivalents.)

Coal (per 2,000 lb. ton of U.S. production):
Anthracite = 22.9×10^6 Btu
Bituminous coal and lignite = 22.6×10^6
Average heating value of coal used to generate electricity in 1979 was 21.4×10^6 Btu per metric ton.
Natural Gas:
Dry (per cubic foot) = 1,028 Btu
Liquefied Natural Gas (Methane) (per barrel) = 3.0×10^6
Electricity — 1 kwh = 3,412 Btu
Petroleum (per barrel):
Crude oil = 5.80×10^6 Btu
Residual fuel oil = 6.29×10^6
Distillate fuel oil = 5.83×10^6
Gasoline (including aviation gas) = 5.25×10^6

Jet fuel (kerosene)	=	5.67×10^6
Jet fuel (naphtha)	=	5.36×10^6
Kerosene	=	5.67×10^6

Nuclear — (per
kilowatt hour) = 10,769
The Btu and calorie, being small amounts of energy, are usually expressed as follows when large numbers are involved.

1×10^3 Btu	=	1,000
1×10^6	=	1,000,000
1×10^9	=	1,000,000,000
1×10^{12}	=	1 trillion
1×10^{15}	=	1 quadrillion
1×10^{18}	=	1 quintillion or 1 Q unit
One Q unit	=	44.3 billion short tons of coal
	=	172.4 billion tons of oil
	=	980 trillion cubic feet of natural gas

Other Conversion Factors

Electricity — 1 kwh	=	0.3 pounds of coal
	=	0.025 gallon of crude oil
	=	3.3 cubic feet of natural gas
Natural gas — 1 tcf		
(trillion cubic feet)	=	45×10^6 short tons of bituminous and lignite coal produced
	=	176×10^6 barrels of crude oil

Coal — 1 mstce
(million short tons of
coal equivalent)

=	3.9×10^6 barrels of crude oil
=	1.7×10^6 short tons of crude oil
=	22.1×10^9 cubic feet of natural gas

Oil — 1 million short tons
(6.65×10^6 barrels)

=	4×10^9 kwh of electricity (when used to generate power)
=	12×10^9 kwh unconverted
=	1.7×10^6 short tons of coal
=	37×10^9 cubic feet of natural gas

Approximate Conversion Factors for Oils

To convert	Barrels to metric tons	Metric tons to barrels	Barrels/ day to tons/ year	Tons/year to barrels/ day
		Multiply by:		
Crude oil[1] . .	.136	7.33	49.8	.0201
Gasoline . .	.118	8.45	43.2	.0232
Kerosene . .	.128	7.80	46.8	.0214
Diesel fuel .	.133	7.50	48.7	.0205
Fuel oil . . .	.149	6.70	54.5	.0184

(1) Based on world average gravity (excluding natural gas liquids).

Fuel Economy in 1990 Cars: Comparative Miles per Gallon

Source: U.S. Environmental Protection Agency

Highest and Lowest in Each Size

Size Class	Highest Model	City	Hwy.	Avg. Annual Fuel Cost	Lowest Model	City	Hwy.	Avg. Annual Fuel Cost
2-seater	Honda Civic CRX	32	35	$477	Ferrari Testarossa.	10	15	$1,432
Minicompact. .	Honda Civic CRX HF	49	52	315	Lamborghini Countach	6	10	2,250
Subcompact. .	Geo Metro XFI	53	58	287	Rolls-Royce Bentley Continental . . .	10	13	1,636
					Rolls-Royce Corniche II.	10	13	1,636
Compact. . . .	Volkswagen Jetta	37	43	338	BMW 535I	15	23	876
Mid Size	Chevrolet Corsica	24	34	562	BMW 750IL	12	18	1,125
Large.	Volkswagen Passat	21	30	657	Rolls-Royce Silver Spirit II/Silver S . .	10	13	1,636
Small Wagon .	Honda Civic Wagon	31	34	477	Mitsubishi Town Car	17	24	788
Mid-Size W. . .	Plymouth Colt Wagon	28	34	524	Audi 200 Quattro Wagon.	17	24	788
Large Wagon .	Volvo 740 Wagon	21	28	657	Buick LeSabre/Electra Wagon	17	24	788
					Chevrolet Caprice Wagon	17	24	788
					Ford LTD Crown Victoria Wagon . . .	17	24	788
					Lincoln-Mercury Grand Marquis Wag.	17	24	788
					Oldsmobile Custom Cruiser	17	24	788

Selected Cars

Size Class	Model	City	Hwy.	Avg. Annual Fuel Cost		Model	City	Hwy.	Avg. Annual Fuel Cost
2-Seater	Alfa Romeo Spider	23	30	$693		Oldsmobile Cutlass Ciera	20	29	685
	Cadillac Allante	15	22	1,001	Large	Buick LeSabre	18	27	717
	Chevrolet Corvette	16	24	947		Chevrolet Caprice	16	25	788
	Nissan 300ZX	18	24	900		Chrysler New Yorker			
Minicompact	Lotus Espirit Turbo	17	27	857		5th Ave.	18	25	788
	Maserati 222E	15	18	1,125		Ford LTD Crown			
	Mazda RX-7	17	23	828		Victoria	13	19	1,051
	Volkswagen Cabriolet	23	28	630	Small Wagon	Dodge Colt Vista	22	23	717
Subcompact	Acura Integra	23	27	657		Mitsubishi Mirage			
	BMW 325I Convertible	18	23	788		Wagon	27	29	562
	Ford Festiva	31	33	491		Nissan Sentra Wagon	26	30	562
	Izusu Impulse	24	32	583		Pontiac Bonneville	18	27	750
Compact	Buick Skylark	23	31	606	Mid-Size W.	Buick Century Wagon	21	27	685
	Chevrolet Tercel	29	32	524		Oldsmobile Cutlass			
	Dodge Shadow	23	28	630		Cruiser	21	27	685
	Eagle Summit	27	29	562		Peugeot 405 Wagon	20	24	717
	Lincoln-Mercury Topaz	19	23	750		Volkswagen Fox			
	Nissan Stanza	21	27	685		Wagon	25	30	583
	Saab 900	19	23	750	Large Wagon	Pontiac 6000 Wagon	21	27	685
	Subaru Lebacy	21	28	657		Volkswagen Passat			
Mid-Size	Audi 100	18	22	788		Wagon	20	29	685
	Cadillac Eldorado	16	25	947		Volvo 240 Wagon	21	28	657
	Hyundai Sonata	21	26	685					

Note: Many car models come in 2 or more versions, differing by such factors as engine and transmission type. Estimated miles per gallon differ from version to version.

VITAL STATISTICS
Source: National Center for Health Statistics, U.S. Department of Health and Human Services

Births
According to provisional statistics for the first quarter of 1989, there were 932,000 live births, less than 1 percent more than the estimated number reported for the same 3-month period in 1988 (926,000). The birth rate (15.3) was the same for both periods.

During the 12 months ending with March 1989, there were an estimated 3,917,000 live births, 2 percent more than the number reported for the comparable period ending a year earlier (3,835,000). The birth rate was 15.9, 1 percent above the rate for the 12 months ending with March 1988 (15.7).

Natural Increase
The rate of natural increase for the first quarter of 1989 was 6.3 persons per 1,000 population, 11 percent above the rate for the first 3 months of 1988 (5.7). The increase was due to both the rise in the birth rate and the decline in the death rate.

Marriages
The total number of marriages for the first quarter of 1989 was 409,000. The marriage rate was 6.7 per 1,000 population, 1 percent below the rate for the first quarter of 1988 (6.8). Marriage rates for the first quarter of the year typically are lower than rates for the rest of the year.

During the 12 months ending with March 1989, an estimated 2,382,000 couples married, less than 1 percent below the number who married during the previous 12-month period. The marriage rate for the 12 months ending with March 1989 was 9.7 per 1,000 population, 1 percent below the rate for the previous 12-month period (9.8).

Divorces
A total of 279,000 couples divorced during the first quarter of 1989. The divorce rate was 4.6 per 1,000 population, 2 percent above the rate for the first quarter of 1988 (4.5).

During the 12 months ending with March 1989, an estimated 1,186,000 couples divorced. The divorce rate was 4.8 per 1,000 population, 2 percent above the figure for the comparable period a year earlier.

Deaths
According to provisional statistics, there were 573,000 deaths during the first quarter of 1989, 3 percent less than estimated for the first quarter of 1988 (592,000). The death rate was 9.4 per 1,000 population, 3 percent lower than the Jan.-March 1988 rate. Among the 573,000 deaths for the first quarter of 1989, were 9,900 deaths at ages under 1 year, yielding an infant mortality rate of 10.3 per 1,000 live births, 4 percent lower than the rate of 10.7 for the 12-month period ending with March 1988.

The death rate for the 12 months ending with March 1988 (8.9 deaths per 1,000 population) was 3 percent higher than the rate of 8.6 for the comparable 12-month period a year earlier. The infant mortality rate for this 12-month-period was 10.0 per 1,000 live births, 3 percent lower than the rate of 10.3 for the 12 months ending with March 1987.

Provisional Statistics
12 months ending with March

	Number		Rate*	
	1989	1988	1989	1988
Live births	3,917,000	3,835,000	15.9	15.7
Deaths	2,152,000	2,166,000	8.7	8.9
Natural increase.	1,765,000	1,669,000	7.2	6.8
Marriages	2,382,000	2,398,000	9.7	9.8
Divorces	1,186,000	1,159,000	4.8	4.8
Infant deaths. . .	38,400	38,500	9.8	10.1
Population base (in millions)			246.3	243.9

*Per 1,000 population
Note: Rates are based on the 1980 Census of Population.

Annual Report for the Year 1988 (Provisional Statistics)

Highlights
The provisional number of live births in 1988 was higher than the number reported in 1987, and was the largest number reported since 1964. The birth rate and the fertility rate also increased in 1988 and were the highest since 1982.

In 1988 the provisional number of marriages fell by 1 percent from 1987. The marriage rate decreased 2 percent to the lowest level since 1967. The number of divorces increased 2 percent between 1987 and 1988, and the divorce rate remained the same.

The number of deaths increased in 1988 to the highest number ever recorded. The infant mortality rate declined to the lowest recorded level for the U.S.

Births
During 1988 an estimated 3,913,000 babies were born in the United States, 2 percent more than in 1987 (3,829,000). This was the largest number reported since 1964. The birth rate was 15.9 per 1,000 total population, 1 percent above the rate for 1987. The fertility rate was 67.3 live births per 1,000 women aged 15-44 years, 2 percent higher than 1987 rate.

The birth and fertility rates, which increased dramatically in the 1940's and 1950's, followed by rapid declines in the 1960's and early 1970's, have been fairly steady since 1975. The current birth and fertility rates are the highest since 1982. The 2-percent increase in the general fertility rate between 1987 and 1988 indicates that there were increases in at least some of the age-specific birth rates. These increases, coupled with a less than 1-percent increase in the number of women in the childbearing years, resulted in the 2-percent rise in the number of births.

Deaths
The provisional count of deaths in the United States during 1988 totaled 2,171,000, the greatest number ever recorded. The provisional death rate of 883.0 deaths per 100,000 population was slightly higher than the provisional rate for 1987 (874.0). The record 1988 number is consistent with a general increase in the size of the population, especially for ages 65 and over, and the occurence in the first few months of 1988 of an influenza outbreak.

The infant mortality rate for 1988 was 9.9 per 1,000 live births, compared with the rate of 10.0 for 1987. It was the lowest rate ever recorded in the U.S.

Marriages and Divorces
The number of marriages in 1988 was 2,389,000, 1 percent fewer than in 1987 (2,421,000). The national marriage rate fell by 2 percent, from 9.9 per 1,000 population in 1987 to 9.7 in 1988. This was the lowest marriage rate since 1967, and the fourth consecutive drop after a period of fairly steady rates from 1980-84.

According to provisional data, 1,183,000 couples were divorced during 1988, 2 percent more than in 1987. The divorce rate for 1988, 4.8 per 1,000 population, was the same as the rate for 1987. This rate was the lowest since 1975.

Births and Deaths in the U.S.
Refers only to events occurring within the U.S., including Alaska and Hawaii beginning in 1960. Excludes fetal deaths. Rates per 1,000 population enumerated as of April 1 for 1960, and 1970; estimated as of July 1 for all other years. (p) provisional. (NA) not available. Beginning 1970 excludes births and deaths occurring to nonresidents of the U.S.

	Births		Deaths	
Year	Total number	Rate	Total number	Rate
1955.	4,097,000	25.0	1,528,717	9.3
1960.	4,257,850	23.7	1,711,982	9.5
1965.	3,760,358	19.4	1,828,136	9.4
1970.	3,731,386	18.4	1,921,031	9.5
1975.	3,144,198	14.6	1,892,879	8.8
1980.	3,612,258	15.9	1,986,000	8.7
1985.	3,749,000	15.7	2,084,000	8.7
1988.	3,913,000	15.9	2,171,000	8.8

Births and Deaths by States and Regions

Source: National Center for Health Statistics, U.S. Department of Health and Human Services

	Births 1988 Number	Births 1988 Rate	Births 1987 Number	Births 1987 Rate	Deaths 1988 Number	Deaths 1988 Rate	Deaths 1987 Number	Deaths 1987 Rate
New England	195,022	15.0	187,816	14.6	121,658	9.4	118,594	9.2
Maine	15,961	13.2	16,155	13.6	11,331	9.4	11,434	9.6
New Hampshire	17,186	15.8	16,435	15.5	8,658	8.0	8,226	7.8
Vermont	8,538	15.3	7,226	13.2	5,267	9.5	4,518	8.2
Massachusetts	91,988	15.6	86,934	14.8	57,715	9.8	56,273	9.6
Rhode Island	14,481	14.6	14,519	14.7	9,930	10.0	9,886	10.0
Connecticut	46,868	14.5	46,547	14.5	28,757	8.9	28,257	8.8
Middle Atlantic	558,553	14.8	548,021	14.6	373,228	9.9	367,861	9.8
New York	277,291	15.5	270,390	15.2	174,299	9.7	172,380	9.7
New Jersey	114,118	14.8	111,344	14.5	71,773	9.3	69,712	9.1
Pennsylvania	167,144	13.9	166,287	13.9	127,156	10.6	125,769	10.5
East North Central	637,327	15.1	618,999	14.8	374,467	8.9	366,920	8.8
Ohio	165,258	15.2	156,900	14.5	100,625	9.3	97,774	9.1
Indiana	81,421	14.7	77,694	14.0	50,396	9.1	48,925	8.8
Illinois	180,526	15.5	177,564	15.3	101,165	8.7	99,002	8.5
Michigan	140,229	15.2	136,374	14.8	78,882	8.5	78,871	8.6
Wisconsin	69,893	14.4	70,467	14.7	43,399	8.9	42,348	8.8
West North Central	265,917	15.0	262,637	14.9	167,896	9.5	165,615	9.4
Minnesota	66,579	15.5	64,068	15.1	35,246	8.2	34,644	8.2
Iowa	38,506	13.6	38,736	13.7	27,753	9.8	26,958	9.5
Missouri	75,844	14.8	75,950	14.9	54,495	10.6	54,574	10.7
North Dakota	11,433	17.1	11,545	17.2	6,055	9.1	5,827	8.7
South Dakota	11,297	15.8	11,514	16.2	6,564	9.2	6,683	9.4
Nebraska	24,363	15.2	23,657	14.8	15,123	9.4	15,207	9.5
Kansas	37,895	15.2	37,167	15.0	22,660	9.1	21,695	8.8
South Atlantic	655,130	15.4	629,371	15.1	390,957	9.2	378,595	9.1
Delaware	10,915	16.5	10,032	15.6	5,866	8.9	5,675	8.8
Maryland	68,412	14.8	64,692	14.3	37,789	8.2	37,233	8.2
District of Columbia	19,290	31.3	20,406	32.8	8,972	14.5	8,602	13.8
Virginia	90,498	15.0	87,002	14.7	46,984	7.8	46,015	7.8
West Virginia	22,585	12.0	23,572	12.4	19,649	10.5	19,978	10.5
North Carolina	98,183	15.1	93,405	14.6	58,164	9.0	55,396	8.6
South Carolina	53,285	15.4	50,693	14.8	28,348	8.2	27,705	8.1
Georgia	107,108	16.9	104,881	16.9	52,815	8.3	49,872	8.0
Florida	184,854	15.0	174,688	14.5	132,370	10.7	128,119	10.7
East South Central	230,975	15.1	222,131	14.5	149,298	9.7	143,384	9.4
Kentucky	51,109	13.7	51,075	13.7	35,557	9.5	33,959	9.1
Tennessee	79,140	16.2	71,343	14.7	50,720	10.4	48,370	10.0
Alabama	59,611	14.5	59,207	14.5	39,016	9.5	37,188	9.1
Mississippi	41,115	15.7	40,506	15.4	24,005	9.2	23,867	9.1
West South Central	463,380	17.2	462,452	17.2	217,606	8.1	209,856	7.8
Arkansas	34,554	14.4	33,375	14.0	25,278	10.6	23,464	9.8
Louisiana	75,170	17.1	75,313	16.9	38,640	8.8	36,516	8.2
Oklahoma	46,874	14.5	45,535	13.9	29,174	9.0	27,972	8.5
Texas	306,782	18.2	308,229	18.4	124,514	7.4	121,904	7.3
Mountain	235,526	17.7	235,177	17.9	96,664	7.3	93,736	7.1
Montana	11,356	14.1	11,976	14.8	6,736	8.4	6,524	8.1
Idaho	15,564	15.5	15,956	16.0	7,391	7.4	6,992	7.0
Wyoming	6,697	14.0	7,107	14.5	3,042	6.4	2,878	5.9
Colorado	53,014	16.1	54,314	16.5	21,712	6.6	21,487	6.5
New Mexico	27,438	18.2	30,169	20.1	10,476	7.0	10,437	7.0
Arizona	65,608	18.8	63,449	18.7	28,446	8.2	27,552	8.1
Utah	37,260	22.0	35,927	21.4	9,695	5.7	9,339	5.6
Nevada	18,589	17.6	16,279	16.2	9,166	8.7	8,557	8.5
Pacific	653,886	17.5	637,640	17.5	227,784	7.4	282,066	7.7
Washington	68,242	14.7	73,836	16.3	36,372	7.8	34,992	7.7
Oregon	41,305	14.9	39,708	14.6	24,868	9.0	24,130	8.9
California	514,247	18.2	494,053	17.9	208,161	7.4	214,486	7.8
Alaska	11,037	21.1	11,441	21.8	2,059	3.9	2,075	4.0
Hawaii	19,055	17.4	18,602	17.2	6,324	5.8	6,383	5.9

Infant Mortality Rates by Race and Sex

Source: National Center for Health Statistics

	All races Both sexes	All races Male	All races Female	White Both sexes	White Male	White Female	Black Both sexes	Black Male	Black Female
1986	10.4	11.5	9.1	8.9	10.0	7.8	18.0	20.0	16.0
1985	10.6	11.9	9.3	9.3	10.6	8.0	18.2	19.9	16.5
1984	10.8	11.9	9.6	9.4	10.5	8.3	18.4	19.8	16.9
1983	11.2	12.3	10.0	9.7	10.8	8.6	19.2	21.1	17.2
1982	11.5	12.8	10.2	10.1	11.2	8.9	19.6	21.5	17.7
1981	11.9	13.1	10.7	10.5	11.7	9.2	20.0	21.7	18.3
1980	12.6	13.9	11.2	11.0	12.3	9.6	21.4	23.3	19.4
1970	20.0	22.4	17.5	17.8	20.0	15.4	32.6	36.2	29.0
1960	26.0	29.3	22.6	22.9	26.0	19.6	44.3	49.1	39.4

Estimated Death Rates for Selected Causes, 1987-88

Source: Natl. Center for Health Statistics, U.S. Depart. of Health and Human Services

Cause of death (est.)	Rate* 1987	Rate*p 1988	Cause of death (est.)	Rate* 1986	Rate* 1987
All causes	874.0	883.0	Influenza and pneumonia.	28.8	31.5
Viral hepatitis	0.6	0.5	Influenza	0.3	0.8
Tuberculosis, all forms	0.7	0.8	Pneumonia	28.6	30.7
Septicemia.	8.1	8.5	Chronic obstructive pulmonary diseases	32.2	33.3
Syphilis	0.0	0.0	Chronic and unspecified bronchitis .	1.4	1.4
All other infectious and parasitic dis-			Emphysema	6.0	6.4
eases.	7.9	9.2	Asthma	1.7	1.9
Malignant neoplasms, including			Ulcer of stomach and duodenum	2.4	2.6
neoplasms of lymphatic and			Hernia and intestinal obstruction	2.3	2.1
hematopoietic tissues	196.1	198.6	Cirrhosis and chronic liver disease . . .	10.7	10.6
Diabetes mellitus	15.6	16.1	Cholelithiasis, cholecystitis, and cholan-		
Meningitis	0.5	0.5	gitis	1.3	1.3
Major cardiovascular diseases	397.0	395.5	Nephritis, nephrosis and nephrotic syn..	9.5	8.9
Diseases of heart	313.4	312.2	Infections of kidney	0.8	0.6
Rheumatic fever and			Hyperplasia of prostate.	0.2	0.2
rheumatic heart disease	2.5	2.7	Congenital anomalies.	5.0	5.2
Hypertensive heart disease . . .	8.3	8.3	Certain causes of mortality in early in-		
Ischemic heart disease	211.0	207.9	fancy	7.6	7.5
Acute myocardial infarction. . . .	104.0	101.7	Symptoms, signs, ill-defined conditions.	12.9	12.9
All other forms of heart disease .	85.8	87.8	All other diseases.	66.4	68.1
Hypertension.	3.3	3.3	Accidents	39.0	39.7
Cerebrovascular diseases	61.3	61.1	Motor vehicle accidents.	20.1	20.4
Artherosclerosis	9.5	9.6	Suicide	12.7	12.3
Other diseases of arteries,			Homicide.	8.5	9.0
arterioles, and capillaries	9.5	9.2	All other external causes.	1.2	1.2
Acute bronchitis and bronchiolitis	0.2	0.3			

*Per 100,000 population; based on a 10-percent sample of deaths. p = provisional.

Principal Types of Accidental Deaths

Source: National Safety Council

Year	Motor vehicle	Falls	Drowning	Fires, Burns	Injestion of Food, Object	Firearms	Poison (solid, liquid)	Poison by Gas
1970 . .	54,633	16,926	7,860	6,718	2,753	2,406	3,679	1,620
1975 . .	45,853	14,896	8,000	6,071	3,106	2,380	4,694	1,577
1980 . .	53,172	13,294	7,257	5,822	3,249	1,955	3,089	1,242
1981 . .	51,385	12,628	6,277	5,697	3,331	1,871	3,243	1,280
1982 . .	45,779	12,077	6,351	5,210	3,254	1,756	3,474	1,259
1983 . .	44,452	12,024	6,353	5,028	3,387	1,695	3,382	1,251
1985 . .	45,901	12,001	5,316	4,938	3,551	1,649	4,091	1,079
1986 . .	48,300	11,200	5,600	4,600	3,500	1,600	4,400	1,000
1987 . .	48,700	11,300	5,300	4,800	3,200	1,400	4,400	1,000
1988 . .	49,000	12,000	5,000	5,000	3,600	1,400	5,300	1,000
Death rates per 100,000 population								
1970 . .	26.8	8.3	3.9	3.3	1.4	1.2	1.8	0.8
1975 . .	21.3	6.9	3.7	2.8	1.4	1.1	2.2	0.7
1980 . .	23.4	5.9	3.2	2.6	1.4	0.9	1.4	0.5
1981 . .	22.4	5.5	2.7	2.5	1.5	0.8	1.4	0.6
1982 . .	19.7	5.2	2.7	2.2	1.4	0.8	1.4	0.5
1983 . .	19.0	5.1	2.7	2.1	1.4	0.7	1.4	0.5
1985 . .	19.2	5.0	2.2	2.1	1.5	0.7	1.7	0.5
1986 . .	20.0	4.6	2.3	1.9	1.5	0.7	1.8	0.4
1987 . .	20.0	4.6	2.2	2.0	1.3	0.6	1.8	0.4
1988 . .	19.9	4.9	2.0	1.5	1.5	0.6	2.2	0.4

U.S. Civil Aviation Accidents

Source: National Safety Council

1988	Accidents Total	Accidents Fatal	Deaths[1]	Per 100,000 Aircraft-Hours Total	Per 100,000 Aircraft-Hours Fatal	Per million Aircraft-Miles Total	Per million Aircraft-Miles Fatal
Large airlines	29	3	285	0.275	0.020	0.007	0.007
Commuter airlines. . .	20	2	21	0.99	0.10	0.06	0.01
On-demand air taxis . .	97	28	57	3.36	0.97	—	—
General aviation	2,332	438	782	7.95	1.49	—	—

(1) Includes passengers, crew members and others.

Transportation Accident Passenger Death Rates, 1987

Source: National Safety Council

Kind of transportation	Passenger miles (billions)	Passenger deaths	Rate per 100 mln. pass. miles	1985-1987 aver. death rate
Passenger automobiles and taxis[1]	2,578.7	24,909	0.97	0.97
Buses	116.5	34	0.03	0.03
Intercity buses	22.8	10	0.04	0.04
Railroad passenger trains	12.1	16	0.13	0.07
Scheduled airlines	329.1	253	0.07	0.05

(1) Drivers of passenger automobiles are considered passengers.

Motor Vehicle Traffic Deaths by State
Source: National Safety Council

Place of accidents	Number 1988	Number 1987	Mileage Rate[2] 1988	Mileage Rate[2] 1987	Place of accidents	Number 1988	Number 1987	Mileage Rate[2] 1988	Mileage Rate[2] 1987
Total U.S.[1]	49,000	48,400	2.5	2.5					
Alabama	1,023	1,116	2.7	3.0	Montana	198	234	2.4	2.9
Alaska	97	76	2.3	1.9	Nebraska	291	297	1.9	2.3
Arizona	944	939	3.0	3.0	Nevada	286	262	3.2	3.1
Arkansas	610	639	3.2	3.5	New Hampshire	163	179	1.7	2.0
California	5,381	5,500	2.3	2.4	New Jersey	1,052	1,023	1.8	1.8
Colorado	496	591	1.8	2.2	New Mexico	487	568	3.1	3.8
Connecticut	486	451	1.7	1.7	New York	2,237	2,327	2.3	2.4
Delaware	164	147	2.6	2.4	North Carolina	1,587	1,601	2.7	2.9
Dist. of Col.	63	56	1.9	1.7	North Dakota	104	101	1.7	1.8
Florida	3,092	2,891	3.1	3.1	Ohio	1,748	1,692	2.2	2.1
Georgia	1,633	1,604	2.5	2.7	Oklahoma	642	611	2.1	1.9
Hawaii	149	138	2.0	1.9	Oregon	677	618	3.0	2.6
Idaho	257	260	3.0	3.2	Pennsylvania	1,932	2,006	2.4	2.6
Illinois	1,862	1,685	2.4	2.2	Rhode Island	125	100	2.1	1.7
Indiana	1,104	1,056	2.5	2.4	South Carolina	1,034	1,087	3.1	3.6
Iowa	556	491	2.6	2.4	South Dakota	147	134	2.3	2.2
Kansas	483	491	2.2	2.4	Tennessee	1,266	1,247	3.0	3.0
Kentucky	840	849	2.6	2.8	Texas	3,395	3,261	2.2	2.2
Louisiana	923	827	3.1	2.7	Utah	297	297	2.3	2.3
Maine	246	228	2.1	2.1	Vermont	128	120	2.4	2.4
Maryland	793	830	2.0	2.3	Virginia	1,069	1,022	1.9	1.9
Massachusetts	731	690	1.7	1.6	Washington	785	790	2.0	2.1
Michigan	1,699	1,632	2.2	2.2	West Virginia	460	471	3.2	3.4
Minnesota	615	530	1.6	1.5	Wisconsin	813	813	1.9	2.0
Mississippi	722	756	3.4	3.7	Wyoming	155	129	2.7	2.4
Missouri	1,104	1,058	2.5	2.4					

(1) Includes both traffic and nontraffic motor-vehicle deaths. (2) The mileage death rate is deaths per 100,000,000 vehicle miles. 1987 mileage death rates are National Safety Council estimates.

Accidental Deaths and Injuries by Severity of Injury
Source: National Safety Council

In 1988 accidental deaths were estimated to number 96,000, an increase of 1,500 or 2 percent from the 1987 total. This was the seventh consecutive year that accidental deaths were estimated at less than 100,000. The death rate per 100,000 population was 39.1, up 1 percent from 1987.

1988 Severity of injury	Total*	Motor vehicle	Work	Home	Public
Deaths*	96,000	49,000	10,600	22,500	18,000
Disabling injuries*	9,100,000	1,800,000	1,800,000	3,400,000	2,300,000
Permanent impairments	340,000	150,000	60,000	90,000	50,000
Temporary total disabilities	8,700,000	1,700,000	1,700,000	3,300,000	2,200,000
Certain Costs of Accidental Deaths or Injuries, 1988 ($ billions)					
Total*	$143.4	$70.2	$47.1	$17.4	$10.9
Wage loss	37.1	20.3	7.9	5.8	4.7
Medical expense	23.6	5.0	8.1	6.7	4.4
Insurance administration	28.7	21.3	6.0	0.8	0.6

*Duplication between motor vehicle, work, and home are eliminated in the total column.

Home Accident Deaths
Source: National Safety Council

Year	Total home	Falls	Fires, burns[2]	Suffo., ingesting object	Suffo., mech- anical	Poison (solid, liquid)	Poison by gas	Fire- arms	Other
1950	29,000	14,800	5,000	(1)	1,600	1,300	1,250	950	4,100
1955	28,500	14,100	5,400	(1)	1,250	1,150	900	1,100	4,600
1960	28,000	12,300	6,350	1,850	1,500	1,350	900	1,200	2,550
1965	28,500	11,700	6,100	1,300*	1,200	1,700	1,100	1,300	4,100
1970	27,000	9,700	5,600	1,800	1,100	3,000	1,100	1,400	3,300
1975	25,000	8,000	5,000	1,800	800	3,700	1,000	1,300	3,400
1980	22,800	7,100	4,800	2,000	500	2,500	700	1,100	4,100[3]
1985	21,600	6,500	4,000	2,400	600	3,200	700	900	3,300
1987	20,500	6,200	3,900	2,000	600	3,500	600	700	3,000
1988	22,500	6,500	4,100	2,400	500	4,300	600	800	3,300

*Data for this year and subsequent years not comparable with previous years due to classification changes. (1) Included in Other. (2) Includes deaths resulting from conflagration, regardless of nature of injury. (3) Includes about 1,000 excessive deaths due to summer heat wave.

Pedalcycle Accidents
Source: National Safety Council

Year	Pedalcycles (millions)	Deaths	Death Rate[a]	Percent of Deaths by Age 0-14	15-24	25 & over
1940	7.8	750	9.59	48	39	13
1950	13.8	440	3.18	82	9	9
1960	28.2	460	1.63	78	9	13
1970	56.5	780	1.38	66	15	19
1980	100.0	1,200	1.20	35	36	29
1985	108.0	1,100	1.02	49	24	27
1987	111.0	1,400	1.26	31	32	37
1988	111.0	1,100	0.99	36	26	38

(a) Deaths per 100,000 pedalcycles.

Accidental Deaths by Month and Type, 1985 and 1988

Source: National Safety Council
1986 Details by Type

Month	1988 totals	1985 totals	Motor vehicle	Falls	Drown- ing†	Fires, burns*	Ingest. of food, object	Fire- arms	Poison (solid, liquid)	Poison by gas
All months	96,000	93,457	47,865	11,444	5,700	4,835	3,692	1,452	4,731	1,009
January	8,000	7,510	3,274	1,026	180	702	337	130	395	142
February	6,700	6,509	2,814	900	230	512	324	115	397	99
March	7,450	7,192	3,559	1,042	340	521	327	117	408	101
April	7,250	7,281	3,607	863	400	379	325	104	410	64
May	8,000	7,906	4,331	957	620	374	286	120	470	40
June	8,550	8,562	4,460	937	960	241	274	100	456	52
July	9,100	8,757	4,704	979	1,130	264	267	114	434	47
August	8,900	8,707	4,895	950	770	250	306	122	393	43
September	7,850	7,748	4,197	941	400	252	273	110	308	56
October	8,300	7,823	4,244	997	260	339	309	103	354	86
November	7,800	7,596	3,920	893	230	421	328	178	339	126
December	8,100	7,866	3,860	959	180	580	336	139	367	153
Average	8,000	7,788	3,989	954	475	403	308	121	394	84

†Partly estimated; includes drowning in water transport accidents. *Includes deaths resulting from conflagration regardless of nature of injury.

Accidental Deaths by Age, Sex, and Type, 1986

Age and Sex	1986 totals	Motor- vehicle	Falls	Drown- ing	Fires,* burns	Ingest. of food, object	Fire- arms	Poison (solid, liquid)	Poison by gas	% Male all types
All ages . .	95,277	47,865	11,444	5,700	4,835	3,692	1,452	47,311	1,009	69
Under 5	3,843	1,188	117	754	768	280	34	59	34	60
5 to 14	4,226	2,350	55	649	434	49	200	26	28	69
15 to 24	19,975	15,227	399	1,341	395	74	443	473	200	77
25 to 44	27,201	15,844	1,035	1,665	1,003	320	471	2,885	343	79
45 to 64	14,733	6,799	1,519	716	841	600	196	716	207	72
65 to 74	8,499	3,096	1,554	270	562	643	61	243	92	60
75 & over . . .	16,800	3,361	6,765	305	832	1,726	47	329	105	47
Male	65,570	34,088	6,043	4,704	2,984	2,003	1,254	3,341	764	
Female	29,707	13,777	5,401	996	1,851	1,689	198	1,390	245	
Percent male.	69	71	53	83	62	54	86	71	76	

†Partly estimated; includes drowning in water transport accidents. *Includes deaths resulting from conflagration regardless of nature of injury.

Ownership of Life Insurance in the U.S. and Assets of U.S. Life Insurance Companies

Source: American Council of Life Insurance

Legal Reserve Life Insurance Companies (millions of dollars)

Year	Purchases of life insurance				Insurance in force					Assets
	Ordi- nary	Group	Indus- trial	Total	Ordi- nary	Group	Indus- trial	Credit	Total	
1940	6,689	691	3,350	10,730	79,346	14,938	20,866	380	115,530	30,802
1950	17,326	6,068	5,402	28,796	149,116	47,793	33,415	3,844	234,168	64,020
1960	52,883	14,645	6,880	74,408	341,881	175,903	39,563	29,101	586,448	119,576
1965	83,485	51,385*	7,296	142,166*	499,638	308,078	39,818	53,020	900,554	158,884
1970	122,820	63,690*	6,612	193,122*	734,730	551,357	38,644	77,392	1,402,123	207,254
1975	188,000	95,190*	6,729	289,922*	1,083,421	904,695	39,423	112,032	2,139,571	289,304
1980	385,575	183,418	3,609	572,602	1,760,474	1,579,355	35,994	165,215	3,541,038	479,210
1981	481,895	346,702*	2,517	831,114*	1,978,080	1,888,612	34,547	162,356	4,063,595	525,803
1982	585,444	250,532	1,898	837,874	2,216,388	2,066,361	32,766	161,144	4,476,659	588,163
1983	753,444	271,609	1,388	1,026,441	2,544,275	2,219,573	31,354	170,659	4,965,861	654,948
1984	820,315	293,521	943	1,114,779	2,887,574	2,392,558	30,104	189,951	5,499,987	722,979
1985	910,944	319,503	722	1,231,169	3,247,289	2,561,595	28,250	215,973	6,053,107	825,901
1986	933,592	374,741*	418	1,308,751*	3,658,203	2,801,049	27,168	233,859	6,720,279	937,551
1987	986,660	365,529	324	1,352,513	4,139,071	3,043,782	26,668	242,977	7,452,498	1,044,459
1988	995,686	410,848	320	1,406,854	4,511,608	3,232,080	25,446	251,015	8,020,159	1,166,870

*Includes Servicemen's Group Life Insurance $27.8 billion in 1965, $17.1 billion in 1970, $1.7 billion in 1975, $45.6 billion in 1981, and $51.0 in 1986, as well as $84.4 billion of Federal Employees' Group Life Insurance in 1981 and $10.8 billion in 1986.

Births to Unmarried Women, 1987-1988

Source: National Center for Health Statistics

(Data for women who had a child between June, 1987 and June, 1988. The number of out-of-wedlock births is under-represented, since it excludes single women under 18, who comprised about 15%—133,000—of the births to unmarried women in 1986).

Race, age	Women who gave birth			Race, age	Women who gave birth		
		Unmarried women[1]				Unmarried women[1]	
	All women	Number	%		All women	Number	%
All Races				**Black**			
Total, 18 to 44 years .	3,667	803	21.9	Total, 18 to 44 years .	595	335	56.3
18-24 years	1,146	465	40.6	18-24 years	290	214	73.8
25-29 years	1,238	177	14.3	25-29 years	152	66	43.4
30-44 years	1,283	163	12.7	30-44 years	153	56	36.6
White				**Hispanic origin[2]**			
Total, 18 to 44 years .	2,894	440	15.2	Total, 18 to 44 years .	406	104	25.6
18-24 years	824	237	28.8	18-24 years	144	42	29.2
25-29 years	1,035	102	9.9	25-29 years	125	32	25.6
30-44 years	1,035	101	9.8	30-44 years	138	31	22.5

(1) Women either widowed, divorced or single at the survey date. (2) Persons of Hispanic origin may be of any race.

Marriages and Divorces by States and Regions

Source: National Center for Health Statistics, U.S. Department of Health and Human Services

	Marriages[1]				Divorces			
	1988		1987		1988		1987	
	Number	Rate	Number	Rate	Number	Rate	Number	Rate
New England	116,059	9.0	119,193	9.3	44,558	3.4	43,960	3.4
Maine	12,487	10.4	11,879	10.0	5,763	4.8	5,811	4.9
New Hampshire	11,270	10.4	10,506	9.9	4,755	4.4	4,844	4.6
Vermont	6,486	11.6	5,668	10.3	2,748	4.9	2,201	4.0
Massachusetts	49,981	8.5	55,925	9.6	17,244	2.9	17,755	3.0
Rhode Island	8,379	8.4	8,026	8.1	3,785	3.8	3,681	3.7
Connecticut	27,456	8.5	27,189	8.5	10,263	3.2	9,668	3.0
Middle Atlantic	314,638	8.4	317,164	8.5	130,828	3.5	134,678	3.6
New York	165,421	9.2	169,184	9.5	64,571	3.6	68,965	3.9
New Jersey	61,052	7.9	60,129	7.8	26,897	3.5	27,222	3.5
Pennsylvania	88,165	7.3	87,851	7.4	39,360	3.3	38,491	3.2
East North Central[2]	343,963	8.2	352,585	8.4	153,086	4.2	152,356	4.2
Ohio	97,334	9.0	95,647	8.9	49,778	4.6	48,162	4.5
Indiana	51,874	9.3	48,451	8.8	—	—	—	—
Illinois	79,100	6.8	95,598	8.3	46,433	4.0	46,681	4.0
Michigan	74,150	8.0	75,159	8.2	39,887	4.3	40,493	4.4
Wisconsin	41,505	8.5	37,730	7.8	16,978	3.5	17,020	3.5
West North Central	155,858	8.8	149,838	8.5	77,487	4.4	72,063	4.1
Minnesota.	33,481	7.8	32,765	7.7	14,945	3.5	14,865	3.5
Iowa	25,006	8.8	23,100	8.2	10,761	3.8	10,791	3.8
Missouri	49,867	9.7	48,167	9.4	24,864	4.8	24,289	4.8
North Dakota	4,923	7.4	5,025	7.5	2,371	3.6	2,249	3.3
South Dakota.	7,262	10.2	6,983	9.8	2,657	3.7	2,692	3.8
Nebraska	12,349	7.7	11,749	7.4	6,379	4.0	6,317	4.0
Kansas	22,970	9.2	22,049	8.9	15,510	6.2	10,860	4.4
South Atlantic	454,498	10.7	443,768	10.6	218,983	5.2	215,454	5.2
Delaware	5,616	8.5	5,209	8.1	2,972	4.5	2,910	4.5
Maryland	44,064	9.5	45,436	10.0	16,439	3.6	15,932	3.5
District of Columbia . . .	4,947	8.0	5,146	8.3	3,610	5.9	4,150	6.7
Virginia	69,022	11.5	67,073	11.4	26,065	4.3	25,568	4.3
West Virginia	14,400	7.7	13,451	7.1	9,149	4.9	9,071	4.8
North Carolina	51,664	8.0	50,506	7.9	32,367	5.0	31,630	4.9
South Carolina	54,339	15.7	53,489	15.6	14,637	4.2	13,961	4.1
Georgia	73,330	11.6	65,284	10.5	35,709	5.6	33,546	5.4
Florida.	137,116	11.1	138,174	11.5	78,035	6.3	79,686	6.6
East South Central	188,658	12.3	173,024	11.3	88,086	5.7	87,975	5.8
Kentucky	49,910	13.4	47,583	12.8	20,456	5.5	19,933	5.3
Tennessee	69,354	14.2	57,530	11.8	31,990	6.5	31,012	6.4
Alabama	44,546	10.9	44,045	10.8	23,411	5.7	24,658	6.0
Mississippi	24,848	9.5	23,866	9.1	12,229	4.7	12,372	4.7
West South Central[3] . . .	276,138	10.3	289,459	10.8	134,464	6.0	133,432	5.9
Arkansas	34,820	14.5	32,198	13.5	16,675	7.0	16,197	6.8
Louisiana	33,870	7.7	36,764	8.2	—	—	—	—
Oklahoma.	32,923	10.2	31,823	9.7	23,048	7.1	23,919	7.3
Texas	174,525	10.4	188,674	11.2	94,741	5.6	93,316	5.6
Mountain	240,308	18.0	242,467	18.6	87,751	6.6	86,912	6.6
Montana.	6,765	8.4	6,518	8.1	4,074	5.1	4,135	5.1
Idaho	11,213	11.2	13,080	13.1	6,058	6.0	5,873	5.9
Wyoming	4,696	9.8	4,600	9.4	3,307	6.9	3,209	6.5
Colorado	31,536	9.6	31,388	9.5	18,792	5.7	18,558	5.6
New Mexico	13,025	8.6	13,518	9.0	7,943	5.3	8,608	5.7
Arizona	35,737	10.2	39,415	12.4	24,940	7.1	23,808	7.0
Utah	16,611	9.8	16,294	9.7	7,824	4.6	8,879	5.3
Nevada	120,725	114.5	117,654	116.8	14,813	14.1	13,842	13.7
Pacific.	319,810	8.6	333,182	9.1	186,112	5.0	173,830	4.8
Washington.	44,042	9.5	43,460	9.6	26,436	5.7	26,045	5.7
Oregon	22,581	8.2	23,325	8.6	14,891	5.4	15,694	5.8
California	229,983	8.1	244,440	8.8	136,076	4.8	124,090	4.5
Alaska.	5,803	11.1	5,509	10.5	3,633	6.9	3,530	6.7
Hawaii	17,401	15.8	16,448	15.2	5,076	4.6	4,471	4.1

p = provisional; (1) Data are either marriages reported or marriage licenses issued; (2) Divorce data exclude figures for Indiana; (3) Divorce data exclude figures for Louisiana. NA = not available.

Marriages, Divorces, and Rates in the U.S.

Source: National Center for Health Statistics; U.S. Department of Health and Human Services

Data refer only to events occurring within the United States, including Alaska and Hawaii beginning with 1960. Rates per 1,000 population.

Year	Marriages[1] No.	Rate	Divorces[2] No.	Rate	Year	Marriages[1] No.	Rate	Divorces[2] No.	Rate
1895	620,000	8.9	40,387	0.6	1945	1,612,992	12.2	485,000	[3]3.5
1900	709,000	9.3	55,751	0.7	1950	1,667,231	11.1	385,144	2.6
1905	842,000	10.0	67,976	0.8	1955	1,531,000	9.3	377,000	2.3
1910	948,166	10.3	83,045	0.9	1960	1,523,000	8.5	393,000	2.2
1915	1,007,595	10.0	104,298	1.0	1965	1,800,000	9.3	479,000	2.5
1920	1,274,476	12.0	170,505	1.6	1970	2,158,802	10.6	708,000	3.5
1925	1,188,334	10.3	175,449	1.5	1975	2,152,662	10.0	1,036,000	4.8
1930	1,126,856	9.2	195,961	1.6	1980	2,413,000	10.6	1,182,000	5.2
1935	1,327,000	10.4	218,000	1.7	1985	2,425,000	10.2	1,187,000	5.0
1940	1,595,879	12.1	264,000	2.0	1988	2,389,000	9.7	1,183,000	4.8

(1) Includes estimates and marriage licenses for some states for all years. (2) Includes reported annulments. (3) Divorce rates for 1945 based on population including armed forces overseas.

Median Age at First Marriage, 1890-1988

Source: U.S. Bureau of the Census

Year	Men	Women	Year	Men	Women
1988	25.9	23.6	1950	22.8	20.3
1985	25.5	23.3	1940	24.3	21.5
1980	24.7	22.0	1930	24.3	21.3
1975	23.5	21.1	1920	24.6	21.2
1970	23.2	20.8	1910	25.1	21.6
1965	22.8	20.6	1900	25.9	21.9
1960	22.8	20.3	1890	26.1	22.0
1955	22.6	20.2			

Percent of Population Never Married

Source: U.S. Bureau of the Census

	Women				Men			
	1988	1980	1970*	1960	1988	1980	1970*	1960
Total, 15 years and over...	22.9	22.5	22.1	17.3	29.9	29.6	28.1	23.2
Under 40 years	40.4	38.8	38.5	28.1	51.1	48.8	47.7	39.6
40 years and over	5.1	5.1	6.2	7.5	5.5	5.7	7.4	7.6
15-17 years	97.7	97.0	97.3	93.2	99.3	99.4	99.4	98.8
18 years	92.4	88.0	82.0	75.6	98.0	97.4	95.1	94.6
19 years	86.0	77.6	68.8	59.7	95.1	90.9	89.9	87.1
20-24 years	61.1	50.2	35.8	28.4	77.7	68.8	54.7	53.1
20 years	78.7	66.5	56.9	46.0	88.5	86.0	78.3	75.8
21 years	71.6	59.7	43.9	34.6	88.7	77.2	66.2	63.4
22 years	58.9	48.3	33.5	25.6	80.4	69.9	52.3	51.6
23 years	56.0	41.7	22.4	19.4	72.7	59.1	42.1	40.5
24 years	43.7	33.5	17.9	15.7	61.2	50.0	33.2	33.4
25-29 years	29.5	20.9	10.5	10.5	43.3	33.1	19.1	20.8
25 years	39.0	28.6	14.0	13.1	56.6	44.3	26.6	27.9
26 years	32.6	22.7	12.2	11.4	49.5	36.5	20.9	23.5
27 years	27.4	22.2	9.1	10.2	44.5	31.5	16.5	19.8
28 years	26.3	16.0	8.9	9.2	33.2	26.8	17.0	17.5
29 years	22.2	14.6	8.0	8.7	31.9	24.0	13.8	16.0
30-34 years	16.1	9.5	6.2	6.9	25.0	15.9	9.4	11.9
35-39 years	9.0	6.2	5.4	6.1	14.0	7.8	7.2	8.8
40-44 years	6.2	4.8	4.9	6.1	7.5	7.1	6.3	7.3
45-54 years	5.1	4.7	4.9	7.0	5.6	6.1	7.5	7.4
55-64 years	4.0	4.5	6.8	8.0	4.9	5.3	7.8	8.0
65 years and over	5.3	5.9	7.7	8.5	4.6	4.9	7.5	7.7

*Figures for 1970 include persons 14 years of age.

Divorced Persons Per 1,000 Married Persons With Spouse Present, 1960-1988

Source: U.S. Bureau of the Census

		Race					Race		
	Total	White	Black	Hispanic[1]		Total	White	Black	Hispanic[1]
Both sexes:					1970	35	32	62	40
1988	133	124	263	137	1960	28	27	45	(NA)
1980	100	92	203	98	Female:				
1970	47	44	83	61	1988	156	146	311	167
1960	35	33	62	(NA)	1980	120	110	258	132
Male:					1970	60	56	104	81
1988	110	102	216	106	1960	42	38	78	(NA)
1980	79	74	149	64					

NA-Not available. (1) Persons of Hispanic origin may be of any race.

Children Involved in Divorces, 1950-1986

Year	Esti-mated # of children Involved	Avg. # of children per decree	Rate per 1,000 children under 18 yrs.	Year	Esti-mated # of children Involved	Avg. # of children per decree	Rate per 1,000 children under 18 yrs.	Year	Esti-mated # of children Involved	Avg. # of children per decree	Rate per 1,000 children under 18 yrs.
1986	1,064,000	0.90	16.8	1973	1,079,000	1.17	15.7	1961	516,000	1.25	7.8
1985	1,091,000	0.92	17.3	1972	1,021,000	1.20	14.7	1960	463,000	1.18	7.2
1984	1,081,000	0.92	17.2	1971	946,000	1.22	13.6	1959	468,000	1.18	7.5
1983	1,091,000	0.94	17.4	1970	870,000	1.22	12.5	1958	398,000	1.08	6.5
1982	1,108,000	0.94	17.6	1969	840,000	1.31	11.9	1957	379,000	0.99	6.4
1981	1,180,000	0.97	18.7	1968	784,000	1.34	11.1	1956	361,000	0.95	6.3
1980	1,174,000	0.98	17.3	1967	701,000	1.34	9.9	1955	347,000	0.92	6.3
1979	1,181,000	1.00	18.4	1966	669,000	1.34	9.5	1954	341,000	0.90	6.4
1978	1,147,000	1.01	17.7	1965	630,000	1.32	8.9	1953	330,000	0.85	6.4
1977	1,095,000	1.00	16.7	1964	613,000	1.36	8.7	1952	318,000	0.81	6.2
1976	1,117,000	1.03	16.9	1963	562,000	1.31	8.2	1951	304,000	0.80	6.1
1975	1,123,000	1.08	16.7	1962	532,000	1.29	7.9	1950	299,000	0.78	6.3
1974	1,099,000	1.12	16.2								

Note: Data refer to divorces and annulments in the U.S., involving children under 18 years at age. Beginning in 1960, estimates are made from frequencies based on sample data; for 1950-59, estimates are made from total counts.

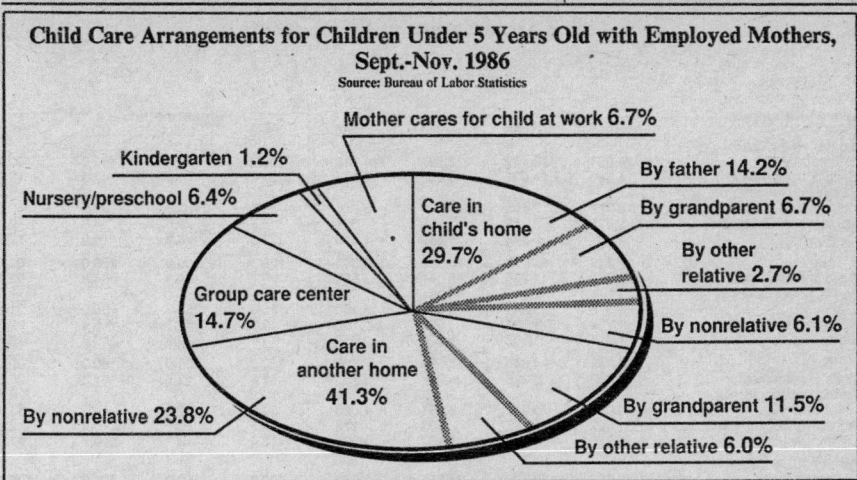

Child Care Arrangements for Children Under 5 Years Old with Employed Mothers, Sept.-Nov. 1986

Source: Bureau of Labor Statistics

- Mother cares for child at work 6.7%
- Kindergarten 1.2%
- Nursery/preschool 6.4%
- Care in child's home 29.7%
  - By father 14.2%
  - By grandparent 6.7%
  - By other relative 2.7%
  - By nonrelative 6.1%
- Group care center 14.7%
- Care in another home 41.3%
  - By grandparent 11.5%
  - By other relative 6.0%
- By nonrelative 23.8%

Living Arrangements of Children

Source: Bureau of the Census; March, 1988

(numbers in thousands)

	Both parents	Total	Mother only — Marital status of mother — Divorced	Married, spouse absent	Widowed	Never married	Father only — Marital status of father — Divorced	Married, spouse absent	Widowed	Never married
All Races										
Children under 18 years......	45,942	13,521	5,010	3,371	838	4,302	861	443	132	371
# of siblings in house hold:										
None..........	9,759	3,880	1,566	679	272	1,362	384	159	49	168
One	18,894	4,835	2,020	1,125	317	1,373	340	176	66	115
Two	10,837	2,872	931	926	181	834	77	104	15	30
Three.........	4,108	1,159	336	418	43	363	42	3	–	23
Four	1,286	441	94	129	7	212	18	–	–	16
Five or more......	1,057	334	63	94	19	158	–	–	2	19
Age of parent:										
15-19..........	72	473	29	32	5	407	–	–	–	49
20-24..........	1,349	1,640	199	319	16	1,107	19	28	–	95
25-29..........	6,100	2,769	729	749	47	1,245	76	68	9	84
30-34..........	10,444	3,396	1,400	886	127	984	183	92	13	85
35-39..........	11,714	2,696	1,427	729	174	367	246	100	29	43
40-44..........	8,935	1,586	838	425	176	147	162	73	17	9
45-49..........	4,261	608	276	151	152	29	122	49	28	6
50-54..........	1,834	202	64	56	73	10	24	18	13	1
55-59..........	737	88	23	22	36	6	17	4	16	1
Education of parent:										
Elementary: 0-8 years	3,471	1,490	275	489	149	577	33	49	22	49
High school: 1-3 years	4,317	3,018	721	776	159	1,363	100	67	11	137
4 years	17,256	5,881	2,262	1,393	369	1,857	408	193	42	120
College 1-3 years...	8,898	2,138	1,170	472	76	420	165	74	38	44
4 years	6,209	589	349	133	49	58	78	20	14	14
5 or more years ..	5,791	404	234	109	35	26	77	40	6	6
Percent high school graduates.....	83.0	66.7	80.1	62.5	63.2	54.9	84.5	73.9	75.6	49.8
Employment status of parent:										
In the labor force ...	42,146	8,157	3,848	1,891	457	1,962	781	406	104	267
Employed.....	40,386	7,075	3,575	1,655	384	1,461	729	358	91	203
Both parents employed ..	24,366	(X)	(X)	(X)	(X)	(X)	(X)	(X)	(X)	(X)
Full time	38,454	5,737	3,039	1,325	260	1,113	649	351	87	176
Part time	1,932	1,337	536	329	124	348	80	7	4	27
Unemployed	1,760	1,083	273	236	73	501	52	47	13	64
Not in the labor force .	3,796	5,364	1,162	1,481	381	2,340	80	37	28	104
Presence of adults other than parent:										
Other relatives present only	6,669	3,504	942	871	259	1,432	158	94	43	86
Nonrelatives present only	244	1,402	686	207	71	439	176	82	11	176
Other relatives and nonrelatives present	125	196	67	41	10	78	36	18	–	37

Living Arrangements of Young Adults

Source: U.S. Bureau of the Census
(numbers in thousands)

Living arrangement	1988	1980	1970	1960	Percent distribution 1988	1980	1970	1960
Adults 18-24 Years								
Total	26,061	29,122	22,357	14,718	100.0	100.0	100.0	100.0
Child of householder	14,190	14,091	10,582	6,333	54.4	48.4	47.3	43.0
Family householder or spouse.	6,009	8,408	8,740	6,186	23.1	28.9	37.9	42.0
Nonfamily householder. . .	2,275	2,776	1,066	354	8.7	9.5	4.8	2.4
Other.	3,587	3,848	2,239	1,845	13.8	13.2	10.0	12.5
Male.	12,835	14,278	10,398	6,842	100.0	100.0	100.0	100.0
Child of householder	7,792	7,755	5,641	3,583	60.7	54.3	54.3	52.4
Family householder or spouse.	1,976	3,041	3,119	2,160	15.4	21.3	30.0	31.6
Nonfamily householder. . .	1,253	1,581	563	182	9.8	11.1	5.4	2.7
Other.	1,814	1,902	1,075	917	14.1	13.3	10.3	13.4
Female.	13,226	14,844	11,959	7,876	100.0	100.0	100.0	100.0
Child of householder	6,398	6,336	4,941	2,750	48.4	42.7	41.3	34.9
Family householder or spouse.	4,033	5,367	5,351	4,026	30.5	36.2	44.7	51.1
Nonfamily householder. . .	1,022	1,195	503	172	7.7	8.1	4.2	2.2
Other.	1,773	1,946	1,164	928	13.4	13.1	9.7	11.8
Adults 25-34 Years								
Total	42,636	36,796	24,556	22,483	100.0	100.0	100.0	100.0
Child of householder	4,726	3,194	1,958	2,038	11.1	8.7	8.0	9.1
Family householder or spouse.	28,392	26,615	20,332	18,538	66.6	72.3	82.8	82.5
Nonfamily householder. . .	5,391	4,411	1,215	642	12.6	12.0	4.9	2.9
Other.	4,127	2,577	1,061	1,265	9.7	7.0	4.3	5.6
Male.	21,320	18,107	11,929	10,896	100.0	100.0	100.0	100.0
Child of householder	3,207	1,894	1,129	1,185	15.0	10.5	9.5	10.9
Family householder or spouse.	12,184	12,024	9,455	8,557	57.1	66.4	79.3	78.5
Nonfamily householder. . .	3,410	2,765	775	398	16.0	15.3	6.5	3.7
Other.	2,519	1,424	570	756	11.8	7.9	4.8	6.9
Female.	21,649	18,689	12,637	11,587	100.0	100.0	100.0	100.0
Child of householder	1,791	1,300	829	853	8.3	7.0	6.6	7.4
Family householder or spouse.	15,977	14,591	10,877	9,981	73.8	78.1	86.1	86.1
Nonfamily householder. . .	2,166	1,646	440	244	10.0	8.8	3.5	2.1
Other.	1,715	1,153	491	509	7.9	6.2	3.9	4.4

Note: Child of householder includes unmarried college students living in dormitories.

Families with Employed Mothers: Weekly Child Care Expenditures, Sept.-Nov., 1986

Source: Bureau of the Census
(in thousands)

	No. of women	No. of payments made	Weekly child care expenses Mean	Percent of income spent on child care per month		No. of women	No. of payments made	Weekly child care expenses Mean	Percent of income spent on child care per month
Total Race:	18,244	12,413	$45.2	6.4	1 child	9,255	6,607	40.7	5.9
White	14,864	9,991	45.6	6.4	2 or more children	8,989	5,806	48.9	6.8
Black	2,769	2,070	36.8	7.1	Number of children less than 5 years old:				
Hispanic:					1 child	6,030	2,520	45.9	6.6
Hispanic	1,659	936	43.9	7.8	2 or more children	1,496	577	63.0	8.0
Not Hispanic	16,585	11,477	45.3	6.3	**Employment status:**				
Marital status:					Part time	6,123	4,705	40.9	5.4
Married, spouse present	13,800	9,275	46.9	5.9	Full time	12,121	7,709	46.5	6.8
All other marital status	4,444	3,139	39.1	10.2	**Monthly family income:**				
Age of youngest child:					Less than $1,250	3,142	2,281	35.2	17.8
Less than 1 year	1,473	667	52.7	6.4	$1,250 to $2,499	5,930	4,119	38.3	8.7
1 and 2 years	3,451	1,337	52.1	7.4	$2,500 to $3,749	4,901	3,263	46.5	6.6
3 and 4 years	2,602	1,093	44.0	6.6	$3,750 or more	4,271	2,750	57.6	4.4
5 years old and over	10,718	9,316	31.6	4.7	**Poverty level:**				
Number of children:					Below poverty level	1,675	1,322	32.0	21.7
					Above poverty level	16,569	11,091	46.0	6.2

Average Family Size, 1940-1988

Source: U.S. Bureau of the Census

1940 . . . . 3.76	1965 . . . . 3.70	1985 . . . . 3.23
1950 . . . . 3.54	1970 . . . . 3.58	1986 . . . . 3.21
1955 . . . . 3.59	1975 . . . . 3.54	1987 . . . . 3.19
1960 . . . . 3.67	1980 . . . . 3.29	1988 . . . . 3.17

Children Awaiting Adoption

Source: Child Welfare League; Nov. 1988 survey of 151 U.S. adoption agencies.

State	Children to adopt	Percent minority	Percent with special needs	Parents waiting	State	Children to adopt	Percent minority	Percent with special needs	Parents waiting
Ala.	259	51	87	263	Mont.	80	10	100	0
Alaska	n/a	n/a	n/a	n/a	Neb.	82	13	100	0
Ariz.	125	43	95	0	Nev.	67	47	100	1,200
Ark.	279	30	80	60	N.H.	29	7	100	20
Calif.	9,547	52	86	3,695	N.J.	1,850	85	100	n/a
Colo.	40	25	100	80	N.M.	504	60	85	250
Conn.	203	58	65	3,000	N.Y.	2,727	71	n/a	1,000
Del.	14	57	100	0	N.C.	395	48	72	n/a
D.C.	53	100	100	24	N.D.	7	0	100	433
Fla.	1,200	35	100	200	Ohio	1,500	60	90	n/a
Ga.	443	60	92	2,000	Okla.	338	30	86	900
Hawaii	206	n/a	90	28	Ore.	250	10	90	150
Idaho	18	2	70	39	Pa.	1,663	n/a	n/a	n/a
Ill.	2,600	48	70	1,183	R.I.	75	32	99	90
Ind.	426	33	90	152	S.C.	636	65	72	1,535
Iowa	90	1	95	160	S.D.	34	70	100	60
Kan.	243	17	90	138	Tenn.	605	33	82	612
Ky.	n/a	n/a	n/a	n/a	Texas	768	40	70	200
La.	670	54	25	n/a	Utah	n/a	n/a	n/a	n/a
Maine	50	0	100	135	Vt.	9	10	100	49
Md.	n/a	n/a	n/a	n/a	Va.	368	56	74	310
Mass.	1,757	33	70	n/a	Wash.	559	10	n/a	200
Mich.	1,388	49	90	0	W.Va.	n/a	n/a	n/a	148
Minn.	667	12	75	0	Wis.	257	32	100	135
Miss.	125	70	90	1,000	Wyo.	3	0	100	0
Mo.	419	41	91	1,049					

NA = Not available

Women, Age 18-44, Who Gave Birth from June 1987 to June 1988

Source: U.S. Bureau of the Census (numbers in thousands)

	Number of women	% Childless	Women who had a child June 87-June 88		
			Number	Total births per 1,000 women	First births per 1,000 women
Age					
Total	52,586	38.0	3,667	69.7	24.4
18-29 years old	24,006	59.8	2,384	99.3	42.0
18-24 years old	13,167	74.2	1,146	87.1	47.7
25-29 years old	10,839	42.2	1,238	114.2	35.2
30-44 years old	28,580	19.7	1,283	44.9	9.6
30-34 years old	10,838	25.1	884	81.6	20.3
35-39 years old	9,586	17.7	324	33.8	5.1
40-44 years old	8,155	14.7	75	9.2	.5
Race of Origin					
White	43,870	39.2	2,894	66.0	23.4
Black	6,835	30.3	595	87.0	28.4
Hispanic	4,326	33.6	406	94.0	32.9
Marital Status					
Currently married	31,489	19.3	2,864	90.9	29.9
Married, husband present	29,275	19.8	2,700	92.2	30.7
Married, husband absent[1]	2,214	13.1	164	73.9	19.5
Widowed or divorced	5,357	21.1	197	36.8	5.1
Single	15,739	81.0	606	38.5	19.9
Educational Attainment					
Not a high school graduate	7,552	27.1	656	86.9	24.2
High school, 4 years	21,977	32.0	1,583	72.0	25.0
College: 1 or more years	23,057	47.3	1,428	61.9	23.8
1 to 3 years	12,798	46.5	778	60.8	22.9
4 or more years	10,259	48.3	649	63.3	25.0
4 years	6,781	49.4	435	64.1	25.3
5 or more years	3,478	46.1	215	61.7	24.5
Labor Force Status					
In labor force	38,537	43.9	1,866	48.4	19.2
Employed	36,143	44.0	1,661	46.0	17.9
Unemployed	2,394	42.4	204	85.3	38.9
Not in labor force	14,049	21.8	1,802	128.2	38.6

(1) Includes separated women.

Hospitals, 1960-1986

Source: American Hospital Association, *Hospital Statistics*, 1987 © 1986

	1960	1970	1975	1980	1982	1984	1986
Number							
All hospitals	6,876	7,123	7,156	6,965	6,915	6,872	6,841
With 100 beds or more	2,903	3,488	3,691	3,755	3,807	3,808	3,765
Non-Federal	6,441	6,715	6,774	6,606	6,569	6,531	6,499
Short-term general and special	5,407	5,859	5,979	5,904	5,863	5,814	5,728
Nongovernmental nonprofit	3,291	3,386	3,364	3,339	3,354	3,366	3,338
For profit	856	769	775	730	748	786	834
State and local government	1,260	1,704	1,840	1,835	1,761	1,662	1,556
Long-term general and special	308	236	215	157	138	131	133
Psychiatric	488	519	544	534	558	579	634
Tuberculosis	238	101	36	11	10	7	4
Federal	435	408	382	359	346	341	342
Beds (1,000)							
All hospitals	1,658	1,616	1,466	1,365	1,360	1,339	1,283
Rate per 1,000 population[1]	9.3	7.9	6.8	6.0	5.9	5.7	5.4
Beds per hospital	241	227	205	196	197	195	188
Non-Federal	1,481	1,455	1,334	1,248	1,246	1,226	1,172
Short-term general and special	639	848	947	992	1,015	1,020	997
Rate per 1,000 population[1]	3.6	4.2	4.4	4.4	4.4	4.3	4.1
Nongovernmental nonprofit	446	592	659	693	712	717	686
For profit	37	53	73	87	91	100	106
State and local government	156	204	215	212	212	203	184
Long-term general and special	67	60	51	39	34	30	30
Psychiatric	722	527	330	215	195	175	165
Tuberculosis	52	20	6	2	1	1	(z)
Federal	177	161	132	117	114	112	111
Occupancy rate[2]							
All hospitals	84.6	80.3	76.7	77.7	77.4	72.5	68.8
Non-Federal	(NA)	(NA)	76.3	77.4	77.2	71.9	68.3
Short-term general and special	74.7	78.0	74.8	75.4	75.2	68.9	64.6
Nongovernmental nonprofit	76.6	80.1	77.4	78.2	77.8	71.4	67.1
For profit	65.4	72.2	65.9	65.2	65.5	57.0	50.9
State and local government	71.6	73.2	69.7	70.7	70.7	65.9	62.8
Long-term general and special	86.9	82.0	82.1	85.9	87.9	88.7	86.1
Psychiatric	93.1	84.8	80.3	85.2	86.1	86.3	86.8
Tuberculosis	75.4	61.8	57.7	67.0	62.3	63.4	59.0
Federal	87.2	79.6	80.7	80.1	79.4	79.0	74.2
Personnel per 100 patients[3]							
All hospitals	114	196	269	329	376	374	413
Non-Federal	113	198	272	333	380	379	419
Short-term general and special	226	292	339	385	434	430	481
Nongovernmental nonprofit	232	292	336	385	438	434	487
For profit	196	256	288	334	374	375	423
State and local government	215	298	365	401	443	438	483
Long-term general and special	95	140	162	170	200	203	212
Psychiatric	35	68	110	150	167	172	183
Tuberculosis	99	146	216	290	334	342	365
Federal	120	169	240	297	335	327	360

(NA) Not available. (Z) Less than 500 beds. (1) Based on Bureau of the Census estimated resident population as of July 1; (2) Ratio of average daily census to every 100 beds; (3) Includes full-time equivalents of part-time personnel. Note: short-term hospitals have an average patient stay of less than 30 days; special hospitals include eye, ear, nose, and throat; obstetrics & gynecology; orthopedic; rehabilitation; and chronic.

U.S. Health Expenditures

Source: Health Care Financing Administration, U.S. Department of Health and Human Services

Type of expenditure	1965	1970	1980	1985	1986	1987
Total	$41.9	$75.0	$248.1	$419.0	$455.7	$500.3
Health services and supplies	38.4	69.6	236.2	403.4	439.3	483.2
Personal health care	35.9	65.4	219.7	368.3	401.6	442.6
Hospital care	14.0	28.0	101.6	166.7	178.4	194.7
Physician services	8.5	14.3	46.8	81.4	91.6	102.7
Dentist services	2.8	4.7	15.4	27.1	29.6	32.8
Other professional services	1.0	1.6	5.7	12.4	14.1	16.2
Drugs and medical sundries	5.2	8.0	18.8	28.5	31.3	34.0
Eyeglasses and appliances	1.2	1.9	5.1	7.8	8.7	9.5
Nursing home care	2.1	4.7	20.4	34.7	37.4	40.6
Other personal health care	1.1	2.1	5.9	9.8	10.7	12.0
Program administration and net cost of private health insurance	1.7	2.8	9.2	22.6	23.9	25.9
Government public health activities	0.8	1.4	7.3	12.5	13.8	14.7
Research and construction of medical facilities	3.5	5.4	11.9	15.6	16.4	17.1
Noncommercial research[1]	1.5	2.0	5.4	7.5	8.3	8.8
Construction	2.0	3.4	6.5	8.1	8.0	8.3

(1) Research and development expenditures of drug companies and other manufacturers and providers of medical equipment and supplies are excluded from "research expenditures," but included in the expenditure class in which the product falls.

Physicians by Age, Sex, and State

Source: American Medical Association, Jan. 1, 1988

	Total Physicians*		Under 35 yrs.		35–44 yrs.		45–54 yrs.		55–64 yrs.	
	Male	Female	Male	Female	Male	Female	Male	Female	Male	Female
Total Physicians	492,879	92,718	103,735	37,188	139,522	30,397	95,482	12,158	75,098	6,457
Alabama	6,065	788	1,472	367	1,745	271	1,120	75	892	42
Alaska	748	139	114	31	305	71	187	20	102	10
Arizona	6,961	1,040	1,228	435	1,905	347	1,333	117	1,083	69
Arkansas	3,501	412	731	180	1,031	138	695	42	505	28
California	64,777	11,861	10,861	4,180	18,835	4,178	13,047	1,570	10,666	891
Colorado	6,559	1,145	1,250	492	2,079	416	1,347	111	957	62
Connecticut	8,633	1,697	1,896	718	2,369	550	1,635	193	1,349	112
Delaware	1,149	246	207	85	280	73	257	43	219	30
Dist. of Col.	3,313	991	708	405	850	297	743	141	523	83
Florida	26,729	3,337	4,160	1,070	7,037	1,048	5,161	511	3,967	310
Georgia	10,207	1,544	2,290	660	3,006	538	2,177	173	1,488	92
Hawaii	2,482	455	463	158	786	146	457	57	370	47
Idaho	1,318	99	152	31	420	42	292	11	202	1
Illinois	21,414	5,147	5,132	2,024	5,929	1,730	4,191	755	2,937	325
Indiana	7,969	1,181	1,606	517	2,218	358	1,480	141	1,336	79
Iowa	4,062	528	924	277	1,156	139	702	54	627	24
Kansas	4,129	655	919	269	1,105	231	768	74	639	39
Kentucky	5,648	926	1,234	396	1,670	306	1,100	122	843	64
Louisiana	7,629	1,218	1,856	540	2,232	394	1,459	137	1,108	87
Maine	2,125	317	270	114	642	105	405	37	344	22
Maryland	13,888	3,386	3,327	1,391	4,222	1,173	2,775	459	1,836	206
Massachusetts	16,593	4,090	3,972	1,833	4,836	1,407	3,113	417	2,051	205
Michigan	15,201	3,015	3,602	1,199	4,083	1,030	2,960	444	2,482	200
Minnesota	8,493	1,559	2,089	778	2,500	495	1,492	143	1,260	71
Mississippi	3,341	438	720	195	938	127	654	57	539	29
Missouri	8,923	1,655	2,253	830	2,464	465	1,698	202	1,329	89
Montana	1,299	110	128	35	403	46	303	14	234	6
Nebraska	2,633	312	582	162	774	98	477	33	412	9
Nevada	1,648	154	229	44	535	65	370	21	272	16
New Hampshire	2,026	293	326	99	652	96	374	40	286	21
New Jersey	15,887	3,830	3,055	1,128	4,492	1,425	3,219	750	2,593	293
New Mexico	2,526	517	422	183	829	217	504	52	349	25
New York	47,712	12,142	11,404	4,615	12,186	3,626	8,728	1,898	7,364	1,011
North Carolina	11,120	1,732	2,669	861	3,190	520	2,021	137	1,620	99
North Dakota	1,148	102	232	47	377	32	236	12	180	9
Ohio	19,072	3,639	4,497	1,533	4,925	1,119	3,508	524	3,115	244
Oklahoma	4,601	685	963	298	1,315	225	937	75	696	44
Oregon	5,379	839	677	319	1,695	312	1,213	96	820	45
Pennsylvania	24,710	5,134	5,970	2,203	6,684	1,593	4,374	615	3,661	366
Rhode Island	2,204	474	478	231	554	123	425	59	362	32
South Carolina	5,408	656	1,233	322	1,572	203	982	60	782	39
South Dakota	1,036	102	185	51	339	30	186	10	158	4
Tennessee	8,741	1,197	2,074	576	2,600	369	1,603	114	1,274	79
Texas	27,383	4,576	6,077	2,081	8,126	1,511	5,371	474	4,210	259
Utah	2,974	346	566	177	1,012	101	555	34	418	15
Vermont	1,311	242	248	90	402	86	236	26	162	15
Virginia	11,528	2,151	2,619	924	3,272	683	2,232	278	1,793	132
Washington	9,502	1,553	1,493	594	3,111	618	1,923	129	1,375	114
West Virginia	3,027	467	562	155	904	183	675	73	419	27
Wisconsin	8,398	1,290	1,775	588	2,436	416	1,646	124	1,358	91
Wyoming	700	64	120	25	222	26	143	6	105	7

*Includes those 65 years and over, those living in U.S. possessions, APO's and FPO's, and those with addresses unknown.

Physicians by Age, Sex, and Selected Specialties

Source: American Medical Association, Jan. 1, 1988

	Total Physicians*		Under 35 yrs.		35–44 yrs.		45–54 yrs.		55–64 yrs.	
	Male	Female	Male	Female	Male	Female	Male	Female	Male	Female
Total Physicians	482,490	86,670	103,735	37,188	139,522	30,397	95,482	12,158	75,098	6,457
Anesthesiology	20,069	4,189	5,654	1,327	6,121	1,454	3,980	877	3,183	377
Cardiovascular Disease	14,361	771	2,876	291	5,513	313	3,221	107	1,773	44
Dermatology	5,705	1,336	830	589	1,995	490	1,466	168	819	58
Diagnostic Radiology	12,382	2,146	3,921	1,121	4,768	772	2,483	180	897	60
Emergency Medicine	11,180	1,745	2,986	765	5,424	722	1,508	177	895	69
Family Practice	37,882	7,062	11,615	3,861	12,947	2,240	5,001	580	5,527	253
Gastroenterology	6,510	358	1,376	154	2,919	160	1,423	32	543	8
General Practice	22,014	2,381	771	261	2,491	698	3,982	571	6,835	467
General Surgery	35,642	2,150	9,707	1,400	8,516	570	7378	105	6,180	47
Internal Medicine	77,634	17,040	24,216	9,017	25,230	5,560	12,868	1,537	9,450	647
Neurology	7,359	1,304	1,688	502	2,914	529	1,696	183	787	69
Obstetrics/Gynecology	25,644	6,634	4,487	3,345	7,641	2,056	6,290	759	4,808	299
Ophthalmology	14,205	1,376	2,793	643	4,122	479	3,758	142	2,090	72
Orthopedic Surgery	17,886	348	4,373	196	5,408	116	4,509	15	2,477	14
Otolaryngology	7,451	361	1,519	184	2,152	136	2,137	20	964	14
Pathology-Anat./Clin.	12,685	3,527	2,199	1,132	3,594	1,304	3,257	673	2,657	310
Pediatrics	24,199	14,032	6,160	6,149	7,953	4,868	4,847	1,867	3,503	784
Plastic surgery	4,085	271	546	91	1,569	117	1,225	39	520	17
Psychiatry	26,304	7,375	3,812	2,198	7,179	2,424	6,628	1,391	5,587	865
Pulmonary Diseases	5,324	452	1,117	170	2,544	176	1,010	56	405	31
Radiology	7,665	710	362	133	1,388	277	2,773	184	2,184	90
Urological Surgery	9,037	118	1,586	72	2,622	34	2,608	9	1,478	2
Other	5,565	817	381	123	1,135	230	1,267	182	1,473	177
Unspecified	4,282	1,190	2,265	775	708	219	432	106	410	53

*Includes those 65 years and over, those living in U.S. possessions, APO's and FPO's, and those with addresses unknown.

Mental Health Facilities

Source: Department of Health and Human Services; Alcohol, Drug Abuse and Mental Health Administration, Jan. 1986.

	Number of Organizations	Inpatient Care	Residential Treatment	Residential Supportive Care	Outpatient Care	Partial Care
Total	5,022	2,188	958	1,049	2,967	1,955
Total (Excl. Territories)	4,990	2,179	954	1,047	2,946	1,943
State & County Mental Hospitals	288	288	5	27	83	57
Traditional	208	208	5	23	55	37
Children's	31	31	-	2	11	14
Forensic	19	19	—	1	4	—
Wisconsin and New Jersey	21	21	—	1	7	3
Teaching Hospitals	9	9	—	—	6	3
Private Psychiatric Hospitals	315	315	27	31	114	102
For Profit	230	230	15	4	52	54
Not-for-Profit	85	85	12	27	62	48
VA Psychiatric Organizations	140	125	7	17	138	63
Psychiatric Outpatient Clinics	9	—	—	—	9	—
VA Multiserve	131	125	7	17	129	63
RTC'S FOR EDC'S	437	—	437	81	99	123
Psychiatric Outpatient Clinics	780	—	—	—	780	—
State and Local Governments	233	—	—	—	233	—
For Profit	45	—	—	—	45	—
Not-for-Profit	502	—	—	—	502	—
Psychiatric Day/Night Orgs.	97	—	—	—	—	97
Multiservice MHO's NEC	1,363	171	424	703	1,254	1,232
State and Local Governments	385	69	113	174	379	357
For Profit	16	7	4	6	12	10
Not-for-Profit	962	95	307	523	863	865
Other Residential Organizations	248	—	58	190	—	—
State and Local Governments	23	—	10	13	—	—
For Profit	66	—	23	43	—	—
Not-for-Profit	159	—	25	134	—	—
General Hospitals	1,354	1,289	—	—	499	281
State and Local Governments	220	211	—	—	97	45
For Profit	110	108	—	—	22	12
Not-for-Profit	1,024	970	—	—	380	224

Note: All data are preliminary.

Characteristics of Women Obtaining Legal Abortions, 1972-1985

Source: U.S. Dept. of Health and Human Services, Centers for Disease Control

	1972	1976	1980	1981	1982	1983	1984	1985
Reported no. of legal abortions	586,760	988,267	1,297,606	1,300,70	1,303,980	1,268,987	1,333,521	1,328,570
Ratio[1]	180.1	312.0	359.2	358.4	354.3	348.7	364.1	353.8
Rate[2]	13	21	25	24	24	23	24	24
			Pecentage distribution[3]					
Age (yrs)								
19 and under	32.6	32.1	29.2	28.0	27.1	27.1	26.2	26.3
20-24	32.5	33.3	35.5	35.3	35.1	34.7	35.3	34.7
25 and over	34.9	34.6	35.3	36.7	37.8	38.2	38.5	39.0
Race								
White	77.0	66.6	69.6	69.9	68.5	67.6	67.4	66.6
Black and other	23.0	33.4	30.1	30.1	31.5	32.4	32.6	33.4
Marital status								
Married	29.7	24.6	23.1	22.1	22.0	21.4	20.8	19.3
Unmarried	70.3	75.4	76.9	77.9	78.0	78.6	79.2	80.7
No. live births[4]								
0	49.4	47.7	58.4	58.3	57.8	57.1	56.9	56.6
1	18.2	20.7	19.5	19.7	20.3	20.7	20.9	21.3
2	13.3	15.4	13.7	13.7	13.9	14.2	14.4	14.5
3	8.7	8.3	5.3	5.3	5.1	5.2	5.1	5.1
4 and over	10.4	7.9	3.2	3.0	2.9	2.8	2.7	2.5
Type procedure								
Curettage	88.6	92.8	95.5	96.1	96.4	96.8	96.6	97.8
Suction	65.2	82.6	89.8	90.4	90.6	91.1	92.8	92.9
Sharp	23.4	10.2	5.7	5.7	5.8	5.7	3.8	5.0
Intrauterine installation	10.4	6.0	3.1	2.8	2.5	2.1	2.0	1.5
Hysterotomy/hysterectomy	0.6	0.2	0.1	0.1	0.0[5]	0.0[5]	0.0[5]	0.0[5]
Other	0.5	0.9	1.3	1.0	1.0	1.1	1.4	0.7
Weeks gestation								
8 and under	34.0	47.0	51.7	51.2	50.6	49.7	49.7	50.8
9-10	30.7	28.0	26.2	26.8	26.7	26.8	26.8	26.2
11-12	17.5	14.4	12.2	12.1	12.4	12.8	12.9	12.3
13-15	8.4	4.5	5.2	5.2	5.3	5.8	5.9	5.9
16-20	8.2	5.1	3.9	3.7	3.9	3.9	3.9	3.9
21 and over	1.3	0.9	0.9	1.0	1.1	1.0	0.8	0.8

(1) Abortions per 1000 live births; (2) Abortions per 1000 women 15-44 years of age; (3) Excludes unknowns. Because the number of states reporting each characteristic varies from year to year, temporal comparisons should be made with caution; (4) For 1972 and 1976, data indicate number of living children; (5) 0.05% or less.

The 15 Leading Causes of Death, 1988

Source: Natl. Center for Health Statistics

Rank		Number	Death rate	Percent of total deaths
	All causes.	2,171,000	883.0	100.0
1	Diseases of heart. . . .	767,400	312.2	35.3
2	Malignant neoplasms, including neoplasms of lymphatic and hematopoietic tissues .	488,240	198.6	22.5
3	Cerebrovascular diseases.	150,300	61.1	6.9
4	Accidents and adverse effects	97,500	39.7	4.5
	Motor vehicle accidents	50,060	20.4	2.3
	All other accidents and adverse effects	47,440	19.3	2.2
5	Chronic obstructive pulmonary diseases and allied conditions	81,960	33.3	3.8
6	Pneumonia and influ-			

Rank		Number	Death rate	Percent of total deaths
	enza	77,330	31.5	3.6
7	Diabetes mellitus	39,610	16.1	1.8
8	Suicide.	30,260	12.3	1.4
9	Chronic liver disease and cirrhosis.	26,080	10.6	1.2
10	Atherosclerosis	23,700	9.6	1.1
11	Homicide and legal intervention	22,190	9.0	1.0
12	Nephritis, nephrotic syndrome, and nephrosis .	21,890	8.9	1.0
13	Septicemia.	20,850	8.5	1.0
14	Certain conditions originating in the perinatal period	18,510	7.5	0.9
15	Human immunodeficiency virus infection . .	16,210	6.6	0.7
...	All other causes.	288,970	117.6	13.3

Note: Data are provisional, estimated from a 10-percent sample of deaths. Rates per 100,000 population.

Inpatient Surgeries, 1983 and 1987

Source: National Center for Health Statistics

(Data are for non-federal short-stay hospitals and exlude newborn infants)

	Number in thousands 1983	1987	Rate per 10,000 population 1983	1987
All surgical procedures.	26,220	26,655	1,128.8	1,061.6
Operations on the nervous system	648	563	27.9	23.3
Operations on the endocrine system	105	109	4.5	4.5
Operations on the eye . .	1,558	497	67.1	20.5
Operations on the ear. . .	372	176	16.0	7.3
Operations on the nose, mouth, and pharynx . . .	1,496	930	64.4	38.5
Operations on the respiratory system	624	745	26.9	30.8
Operations on the cardiovascular system.	1,836	2,978	79.0	123.2
Operations on the hemic				

	Number in thousands 1983	1987	Rate per 10,000 population 1983	1987
and lymphatic system. . .	365	398	15.7	16.5
Operations on the digestive system	4,202	4,288	180.9	177.4
Operations on the urinary system	1,073	1,083	46.2	44.8
Operations on male genital organs	845	747	36.4	30.9
Operations on female genital organs	3,849	2,870	165.7	118.8
Obstetrical procedures . .	3,914	5,358	168.5	221.7
Operations on the musculoskeletal system	3,502	3,313	150.8	137.1
Operations on the integumentary system	1,830	1,600	78.8	66.2

Persons with Selected Chronic Conditions, 1986

Source: National Center for Health Statistics

Chronic Condition	Number of conditions (1,000)	Rate per 1,000 persons Total	Under 18 yrs	18-44 yrs.	45-64 yrs.	65-74 yrs.	75 yrs. and over	Male	Female
Heart conditions	18,458	78.1	21.7	39.3	123.2	250.0	319.4	74.3	81.7
High blood pressure (Hypertension)	28,969	122.6	1.9[1]	67.2	250.6	385.2	409.2	109.4	134.9
Varicose veins of lower extremities	6,856	29.0	(¹)	22.6	56.3	76.2	71.9	9.1	47.7
Hemorrhoids	9,909	41.9	.9[1]	46.7	73.2	70.2	64.1	40.0	43.8
Chronic bronchitis . . .	11,379	48.1	63.2	36.5	45.8	62.9	55.4	41.2	54.7
Asthma	9,690	41.0	51.1	36.4	36.3	46.4	36.3	40.8	41.1
Chronic sinusitis	34,386	145.5	65.8	170.4	187.0	168.6	170.7	128.0	161.9
Hay fever, allergic rhinitus without asthma . .	21,702	91.8	64.3	113.1	95.8	72.4	67.2	88.7	94.8
Dermatitis, including eczema	9,547	40.4	42.0	44.3	35.4	33.6	25.2	33.7	46.7
Arthritis	30,911	130.8	2.0[1]	47.9	284.6	443.3	540.1	94.0	165.2
Diabetes.	6,585	27.9	2.4[1]	8.7	63.7	91.9	108.5	25.8	29.8
Migraine	8,516	36.0	14.6	49.4	45.5	21.3	20.1[1]	18.1	52.8
Diseases of urinary system	7,736	32.7	6.8	32.8	45.4	58.3	92.3	15.9	48.5
Visual impairments. . .	8,352	35.3	12.2	28.7	46.3	69.3	136.3	43.7	27.5
Cataracts	5,031	21.3	.6[1]	1.5	21.1	84.3	233.2	13.4	28.7
Hearing impairments. .	20,732	87.7	20.1	51.8	136.2	244.2	378.4	102.6	73.8
Tinnitus	6,315	26.7	3.6[1]	15.3	49.2	83.2	88.3	29.6	24.0
Deformities or orthopedic impairments	27,381	115.9	32.5	132.1	161.6	158.4	195.7	113.6	118.0
Frequent indigestion . .	5,315	22.5	3.9[1]	25.4	31.3	43.3	35.6	21.9	23.0
Frequent constipation . .	4,539	19.2	5.6	14.3	22.1	51.2	83.9	8.8	29.0

NA = Not available. (1) Figure does not meet standards of reliability or precision.

U.S. Crime Rate Up 2.1% in 1988

Source: 1988 Uniform Crime Reports, FBI

The crime rate rose 2.1 percent in 1988, according to the FBI's Uniform Crime Reports. From 1987 to 1988, overall violent crime increased by 4.5 percent, and property crime increased by 1.8 percent.

Overall, the number of crimes committed nationwide rose to 13.9 million in 1988.

The rate of murders was up 1.2 percent; rape, up 0.5 percent; robbery, 3.9 percent; aggravated assault 5.4 percent; burglary, down 1.5 percent; larceny, up 1.7 percent; and auto theft, up 10.1 percent.

The FBI urged caution in interpreting the figures.

Crime Rates by Region, Geographic Division, and State

Source: 1988 Uniform Crime Reports, FBI

(Per 100,000)

Area	Total	Violent Crime[1]	Property crime[2]	Murder	Rape	Robbery	Aggravated Assault	Burglary	Larceny-theft	Motor vehicle theft
United States Total . .	5,664.2	637.2	5,027.1	8.4	37.6	220.9	370.2	1,309.2	3,134.9	582.9
Northeast	5,005.6	680.3	4,325.3	7.5	29.1	298.7	345.0	1,018.2	2,594.1	713.0
New England	4,730.1	458.1	4,272.1	3.8	28.2	140.4	285.6	1,062.6	2,541.6	667.9
Connecticut	5,097.6	455.4	4,642.2	5.4	26.2	187.6	236.2	1,218.0	2,810.2	614.0
Maine	3,577.7	157.4	3,420.3	3.1	18.6	25.8	110.0	816.9	2,398.7	204.7
Massachusetts	4,990.9	619.6	4,371.3	3.5	32.0	176.3	407.8	1,061.3	2,417.5	892.5
New Hampshire. . . .	3,333.9	147.9	3,186.1	2.3	25.2	21.1	99.4	682.7	2,275.7	227.7
Rhode Island	5,204.4	396.7	4,807.7	4.1	30.5	115.2	246.9	1,261.3	2,718.5	827.9
Vermont	4,240.5	142.3	4,098.2	2.0	23.0	16.0	101.3	1,096.8	2,804.1	197.3
Middle Atlantic	5,100.4	756.9	4,343.6	8.8	29.4	353.2	365.4	1,002.9	2,612.1	728.6
New Jersey	5,295.3	582.8	4,712.5	5.3	33.7	245.2	298.6	980.2	2,837.9	894.4
New York	6,309.8	1,097.3	5,212.0	12.5	30.6	544.4	509.8	1,218.3	3,133.8	859.9
Pennsylvania	3,176.4	362.0	2,814.4	5.5	24.9	138.1	193.5	696.7	1,690.9	426.8
Midwest	4,872.9	511.1	4,361.8	6.4	38.3	169.2	297.2	1,039.2	2,876.8	445.8
East North Central . .	5,086.9	577.2	4,509.7	7.3	43.3	200.0	326.6	1,072.9	2,926.7	510.1
Illinois	5,620.9	810.4	4,810.4	8.6	38.5	312.7	450.6	1,128.7	3,076.5	605.3
Indiana	4,150.0	380.0	3,770.0	6.4	31.0	89.0	253.5	935.2	2,481.3	353.5
Michigan	6,084.4	741.7	5,342.7	10.8	69.5	241.1	420.3	1,314.6	3,287.0	741.1
Ohio	4,645.3	452.0	4,193.2	5.4	42.6	161.4	242.7	1,031.4	2,762.6	399.2
Wisconsin	3,972.0	214.4	3,757.6	3.0	19.9	67.1	124.5	729.2	2,759.3	269.2
West North Central . .	4,364.5	354.0	4,010.5	4.3	26.6	95.9	227.2	958.9	2,758.2	293.3
Iowa	4,076.7	256.8	3,819.8	1.7	15.7	39.9	199.5	854.3	2,803.4	162.2
Kansas.	4,879.9	365.2	4,514.7	3.4	31.3	85.9	244.6	1,179.0	3,093.2	242.5
Minnesota	4,314.7	290.1	4,024.7	2.9	31.0	94.7	161.4	909.6	2,775.8	339.3
Missouri	4,844.7	552.5	4,292.2	8.0	29.3	168.1	347.1	1,140.4	2,717.4	434.4
Nebraska	4,140.0	273.2	3,866.8	3.6	24.0	56.1	189.4	765.2	2,912.8	188.8
North Dakota	2,728.1	59.1	2,668.9	1.8	11.2	8.1	38.0	437.7	2,112.7	118.6
South Dakota	2,581.0	113.7	2,467.3	3.1	26.9	12.2	71.6	517.9	1,853.8	95.5
South.	6,093.4	645.7	5,447.7	10.3	39.9	208.5	387.0	1,583.3	3,338.1	526.2
South Atlantic	6,263.3	733.2	5,530.1	10.4	39.4	246.0	437.4	1,553.5	3,459.8	516.8
Delaware	4,799.1	451.7	4,347.4	5.2	74.4	118.8	253.3	1,040.6	3,003.6	303.2
District of Columbia .	9,914.7	1,921.6	7,993.1	59.5	26.6	917.7	917.7	1,983.9	4,616.8	1,392.4
Florida	8,937.6	1,117.7	7,819.9	11.4	49.7	403.3	653.3	2,294.3	4,760.6	765.1
Georgia	6,326.6	665.3	5,661.2	11.7	46.4	243.6	363.7	1,610.8	3,495.8	554.6
Maryland	5,704.6	806.8	4,897.9	9.7	37.1	301.3	458.7	1,178.6	3,047.1	672.1
North Carolina	4,862.2	501.9	4,360.4	7.8	28.1	108.6	357.4	1,391.2	2,718.8	250.4
South Carolina	5,412.3	741.2	4,671.2	9.3	42.7	124.7	564.4	1,416.2	2,950.3	304.7
Virginia	4,176.7	299.2	3,877.5	7.8	27.1	112.5	151.8	818.4	2,757.6	301.6
West Virginia	2,238.8	131.4	2,107.4	4.9	18.7	34.2	73.6	610.9	1,334.8	161.7
East South Central . .	4,022.2	455.3	3,566.9	8.6	33.9	118.2	294.7	1,144.8	2,104.0	318.2
Alabama	4,561.7	558.6	4,003.1	9.9	29.8	117.8	401.2	1,233.8	2,502.6	266.7
Kentucky.	3,134.8	330.1	2,804.7	6.2	22.4	74.3	227.3	826.3	1,792.8	185.5
Mississippi	3,592.8	325.2	3,267.6	8.6	36.2	77.2	203.3	1,281.0	1,820.3	166.4
Tennessee.	4,469.4	532.7	3,936.7	9.4	44.7	173.6	305.1	1,237.9	2,156.0	542.8
West South Central . .	7,010.0	616.1	6,393.9	11.1	44.0	200.9	360.1	1,881.7	3,852.0	660.2
Arkansas	4,219.6	422.7	3,796.9	8.7	32.2	84.1	297.6	1,091.8	2,492.3	212.9
Louisiana	5,760.7	717.4	5,043.3	11.6	38.5	209.0	458.3	1,444.4	3,148.0	450.9
Oklahoma	5,589.1	434.5	5,154.6	7.4	37.7	105.1	284.4	1,643.4	2,954.9	556.3
Texas	8,017.7	652.6	7,365.1	12.1	48.4	234.2	357.9	2,157.2	4,407.9	800.1
West	6,543.0	729.3	5,813.7	8.5	41.6	225.0	454.2	1,460.6	3,642.4	710.7
Mountain	6,150.9	480.3	5,670.6	6.6	36.1	105.5	332.1	1,330.0	3,965.4	375.2
Arizona.	7,471.3	610.1	6,861.2	8.5	38.8	137.0	425.8	1,580.3	4,821.7	459.1
Colorado.	6,178.3	472.6	5,705.7	5.7	38.6	98.8	329.5	1,383.1	3,900.6	422.0
Idaho	3,973.0	234.7	3,738.2	3.6	17.9	20.2	193.0	870.0	2,692.0	176.3
Montana	4,267.0	123.0	4,144.0	2.6	16.8	22.6	81.0	703.6	3,224.0	216.4
Nevada	6,453.1	780.7	5,672.5	10.5	73.8	291.2	405.2	1,544.9	3,528.4	599.2
New Mexico.	6,606.3	658.1	5,948.1	11.5	38.4	103.1	505.2	1,836.9	3,721.3	389.9
Utah	5,578.5	243.1	5,335.5	2.8	23.6	54.1	162.6	881.0	4,238.7	215.7
Wyoming.	3,967.1	314.0	3,653.1	2.5	24.0	15.1	272.4	658.8	2,851.8	142.5
Pacific	6,683.3	818.4	5,864.9	9.2	43.5	267.8	497.9	1,507.3	3,526.8	830.8
Alaska	4,921.6	522.8	4,398.8	5.7	57.7	72.9	386.5	842.3	3,101.6	455.0
California	6,635.5	929.8	5,705.7	10.4	41.8	305.8	571.8	1,447.1	3,314.5	944.0
Hawaii	5,989.0	257.1	5,731.9	4.0	32.5	84.1	136.5	1,255.8	4,112.2	364.0
Oregon.	7,058.7	545.7	6,513.0	5.1	40.5	193.0	307.2	1,764.1	4,154.4	594.4
Washington	7,113.0	466.4	6,646.6	5.7	56.5	145.9	258.3	1,855.6	4,358.1	432.9
Puerto Rico	3,327.1	666.9	2,660.2	17.8	12.8	382.3	254.0	1,079.8	1,030.4	550.0

(1) Violent crimes are murder, rape, robbery and aggravated assault; (2) Property crimes are burglary, larceny-theft, and motor vehicle theft.

Crime in the U.S., 1981-1988

Source: Uniform Crime Reports, FBI

Population[1]	Crime Index total[2]	Violent crime[3]	Property crime[4]	Murder and non-negligent man-slaughter	Forcible rape	Robbery	Burglary	Larceny theft
Number of offenses:								
1981-229,146,000...	13,423,800	1,361,820	12,061,900	22,520	82,500	592,910	3,779,700	7,194,400
1982-231,534,000...	12,974,400	1,322,390	11,652,000	21,010	78,770	553,130	3,447,100	7,142,500
1983-233,981,000...	12,108,600	1,258,090	10,850,500	19,310	78,920	506,570	3,129,900	6,712,800
1984-236,158,000...	11,881,800	1,273,280	10,608,500	18,690	84,230	485,010	2,984,400	6,591,900
1985-238,740,000...	12,431,400	1,328,870	11,102,600	18,980	87,670	497,870	3,073,300	6,926,400
1986-241,077,000...	13,211,900	1,489,170	11,722,700	20,610	91,460	542,780	3,241,400	7,257,200
1987-243,400,000...	13,508,700	1,484,000	12,024,700	20,100	91,110	517,700	3,236,200	7,499,900
1988-245,807,000...	13,923,100	1,566,220	12,356,900	20,680	92,490	542,970	3,218,100	7,705,900
Percent change; number of offenses:								
1988/1987......	+3.1	+5.5	+2.8	+2.9	+1.5	+4.9	−0.6	+2.7
1988/1984......	+17.2	+23.0	+16.5	+10.6	+9.8	+12.0	+7.8	+16.9
1988/1979......	+13.7	+29.7	+11.9	−3.6	+21.1	+13.0	−3.3	+16.7
Rate per 100,000 inhabitants:								
1981	5,858.2	594.3	5,263.9	9.8	36.0	258.7	1,649.5	3,139.7
1982	5,603.6	571.1	5,032.5	9.1	34.0	238.9	1,488.8	3,084.8
1983	5,175.0	537.7	4,637.4	8.3	33.7	216.5	1,337.7	2,868.9
1984	5,031.3	539.2	4,492.1	7.9	35.7	205.4	1,263.7	2,791.3
1985	5,207.1	556.6	4,650.5	7.9	37.1	208.5	1,287.3	2,901.2
1986	5,480.4	617.3	4,862.6	8.6	37.9	225.1	1,344.6	3,010.3
1987	5,550.0	609.7	4,904.3	8.3	37.4	212.7	1,329.6	3,081.3
1988	5,664.2	637.2	5,027.1	8.4	37.6	220.9	1,309.2	3,134.9
Percent change; rate per 100,000 inhabitants:								
1988/1987......	+2.1	+4.5	+1.8	+1.2	+0.5	+3.9	−1.5	+1.7
1988/1984......	+12.6	+18.2	+11.9	+6.3	+5.3	+7.5	+3.6	+12.3
1988/1979......	+1.8	+16.1	+0.2	−13.4	+8.4	+1.1	−13.4	+4.5

(1) Populations are Bureau of the Census provisional estimates as of July 1, except April 1, 1980, preliminary census counts, and are subject to change. (2) Because of rounding, the offenses may not add to totals. (3) Violent crimes are offenses of murder, forcible rape, robbery, and aggravated assault. Property crimes are offenses of burglary, larceny-theft, and motor vehicle theft. Data are not included for the property crime of arson. (4) All rates were calculated on the offenses before rounding.

Law Enforcement Officers

Source: 1988 Uniform Crime Reports, FBI

The Nation's law enforcement community employed an average of 2.1 full-time officers for every 1,000 inhabitants as of October 31, 1988. Considering full-time civilians, the overall law enforcement employee rate was 2.8 per 1,000 inhabitants according to 12,269 city, county, and state police agencies reporting in 1988. These agencies collectively offered law enforcement service to a population of nearly 231 million, employing 485,566 officers and 166,877 civilians.

The law enforcement employee average for all cities nationwide in 1988 was 2.7 per 1,000 inhabitants. City law enforcement employee averages ranged from 2.1 per 1,000 inhabitants in those with populations from 10,000 to 49,999 to 3.4 for those with populations of 250,000 or more. Rural and suburban counties averaged full-time law enforcement employee rates of 3.4 and 3.0 per 1,000 population, respectively.

Regionally, the highest law enforcement employee rate was in the Northeast with 2.9. Following were the South with 2.8, and both the Midwest, and West with 2.4.

Nationally, males comprised 92 percent of all sworn employees. Ninety-four percent of the officers in rural counties and 93 percent of those in cities were males, while in suburban counties they accounted for 89 percent.

Civilians made up 26 percent of the total U.S. law enforcement employee force for 1988. They represented 21 percent of the police employees in cities, 32 percent of those in rural counties, and 34 percent of the suburban law enforcement strength.

Seventy-eight law enforcement officers were feloniously slain in the line of duty during 1988, 3 more lives lost than in 1987. Another 77 officers were killed due to accidents occurring while performing their official duties in 1988.

Murder Weapons, 1983-1988

Source: 1988 Uniform Crime Reports, FBI

Weapon	1984	1985	1986	1987	1988
Total	17,260	17,545	19,257	17,859	18,269
Total Firearms.............	10,175	10,296	11,381	10,556	11,084
Handguns................	7,557	7,548	8,460	7,807	8,278
Rifles.................	785	810	788	772	764
Shotguns................	1,194	1,188	1,296	1,095	1,117
Other guns	19	24	22	16	15
Firearms-not stated.......	620	726	815	866	910
Cutting or stabbing instruments	3,653	3,694	3,957	3,619	3,496
Blunt objects (clubs, hammers, etc.)	1,007	972	1,099	1,039	1,143
Personal weapons (hands, fists, feet, etc.)[1]	1,134	1,180	1,310	1,162	1,139
Poison	6	7	14	34	15
Explosives	8	11	16	12	35
Fire	196	243	230	199	258
Narcotics....................	20	31	23	24	36
Drowning....................	47	43	49	51	38
Strangulation.................	322	311	341	357	335
Asphyxiation.................	113	115	160	115	72
Other weapons or weapons not stated	579	642	677	691	618

(1) Pushing is included in personal weapons.

State and Federal Prison Population; Death Penalty

Source: Prison population: Bureau of Justice Statistics, U.S. Dept. of Justice, Dec. 31, 1988; death penalty: NAACP Legal Defense and Educational Fund; "Executions" and "Death penalty" as of Dec. 31, 1988; "Under sentence of death" as of July, 1989.

The number of prisoners under jurisdiction of Federal or State correction authorities at year end 1988 reached a record 627,402. From 1980 through 1988 there was an increase of about 90% in the prison population. The 1988 growth rate (7.4%) was greater than the percentage increase recorded during 1987 (7.2%), and the number of new prisoners added during 1988 was about 3,500 higher than the number added during 1987. The 1988 increase meant a nationwide need for more than 800 new prison bedspaces per week. Total prison population rose most rapidly during 1988 in Rhode Island (33.5%), Colorado (24.7%), New Hampshire (17.5%), Michigan (16.1%), and California (13.7%).

	Sentenced to more than 1 yr.		Incarcer- ation rate 1988[a]	Death penalty		
	1988[p]	% change 1987-88		Under sentence of death	Executions	Death penalty
Total	603,928	7.8%	244	2,210	11	—
Federal institutions	42,738	8.1	17	5	0	Yes
State institutions	561,190	7.7	227	2,205	11	36
Northeast	94,770	8.7%	187	141	0	—
Connecticut	4,723	1.9	146	1	0	Yes
Maine	1,214	-4.2	100	0	0	No
Massachusetts	6,733	7.5	114	0	0	No
New Hampshire	1,019	17.5	93	0	0	Yes
New Jersey[b]	16,936	8.9	219	25	0	Yes
New York	44,560	9.1	248	0	0	No
Pennsylvania	17,862	9.9	148	115	0	Yes
Rhode Island	1,179	19.0	118	0	0	No
Vermont	544	7.7	97	0	0	No
Midwest	120,008	8.6%	200	348	0	—
Illinois	21,081	6.2	181	120	0	Yes
Indiana	11,271	6.0	202	50	0	Yes
Iowa	3,034	6.4	107	0	0	No
Kansas	5,936	2.7	237	0	0	No
Michigan	27,714	16.1	299	0	0	No
Minnesota	2,799	9.9	64	0	0	No
Missouri	12,354	10.8	239	73	0	Yes
Nebraska	2,111	7.5	131	13	0	Yes
North Dakota	414	8.9	62	0	0	No
Ohio	26,113	7.8	240	92	0	Yes
South Dakota	1,020	-10.0	143	0	0	Yes
Wisconsin	6,161	1.3	126	0	0	No
South	226,444	5.0%	266	1,285	10	—
Alabama	12,357	-1.9	300	93	1	Yes
Arkansas	5,519	1.4	230	31	0	Yes
Delaware	2,359	11.5	354	7	0	Yes
District of Columbia[b]	6,340	12.9	1,031	0	0	No
Florida	34,681	7.2	278	294	2	Yes
Georgia	18,018	1.7	281	102	1	Yes
Kentucky[b]	7,119	10.6	191	28	0	Yes
Louisiana	16,149	5.0	368	39	3	Yes
Maryland	13,572	5.1	291	19	0	Yes
Mississippi	7,304	8.7	279	45	0	Yes
North Carolina	16,326	1.3	250	81	1	Yes
Oklahoma	10,448	8.4	323	98	0	Yes
South Carolina	12,938	9.1	370	46	1	Yes
Tennessee	7,491	-1.7	152	69	0	Yes
Texas	40,437	4.2	240	283	3	Yes
Virginia	13,928	7.7	230	40	1	Yes
West Virginia	1,458	-0.2	78	0	0	No
West	119,968	11.5%	234	441	1	—
Alaska	1,862	5.4	355	0	0	No
Arizona	11,639	10.2	329	86	0	Yes
California	73,780	13.8	257	247	0	Yes
Colorado	5,997	24.7	181	3	0	Yes
Hawaii	1,510	-1.7	136	0	0	No
Idaho	1,548	7.9	154	16	0	Yes
Montana	1,272	7.2	158	10	0	Yes
Nevada	4,881	10.1	452	45	0	Yes
New Mexico	2,723	3.7	180	2	0	Yes
Oregon	5,991	9.3	215	15	0	Yes
Utah	1,987	6.9	117	8	1	Yes
Washington	5,816	-5.1	124	7	0	Yes
Wyoming	962	5.0	203	2	0	Yes

P = preliminary. (a) The number of prisoners sentenced to more than 1 year per 100,000 resident population on Dec. 31, 1988 (b) Figures for 1987 and 1988 are not comparable to those for previous years because of the inclusion of additional jail inmates.

Juvenile Arrests, 1988

Source: 1988 Uniform Crime Reports, FBI

	Total all ages	Number of persons arrested				Percent of total all ages		
		Under 15	Under 18	Under 21	Under 25	Under 15	Under 18	Under 21
Total	7,938,517	456,722	1,381,909	2,512,306	3,825,324	5.8	17.4	31.6
Murder and nonnegligent man-slaughter	12,575	172	1,514	3,714	6,069	1.4	12.0	29.5
Forcible rape.	21,941	1,123	3,372	6,059	9,710	5.1	15.4	27.6
Robbery	99,438	6,066	22,535	39,886	58,892	6.1	22.7	40.1
Aggravated assault	240,212	9,719	32,769	60,584	100,274	4.0	13.6	25.2
Burglary	251,502	33,842	85,869	128,939	166,283	13.5	34.1	51.3
Larceny-theft	999,521	137,986	309,869	446,012	572,726	13.8	31.0	44.6
Motor vehicle theft	124,962	13,566	51,838	74,470	91,690	10.9	41.5	59.6

Change in the State and Federal Prison Populations, 1980-1987

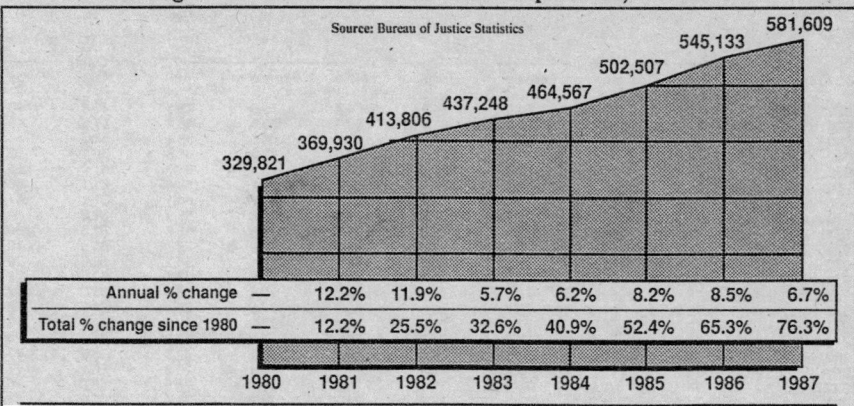

Source: Bureau of Justice Statistics

	1980	1981	1982	1983	1984	1985	1986	1987
	329,821	369,930	413,806	437,248	464,567	502,507	545,133	581,609
Annual % change —		12.2%	11.9%	5.7%	6.2%	8.2%	8.5%	6.7%
Total % change since 1980 —		12.2%	25.5%	32.6%	40.9%	52.4%	65.3%	76.3%

Note: All counts are for December 31 of each year and may differ from previously reported numbers because of revision.

U.S. Fires, 1987

Source: National Fire Protection Association, Quincy, Mass.

Fires
- Fires attended by public fire departments increased by 2.6 percent to 2,330,000.
- Fires in outside properties increased by 8.5 percent to 1,101,000.
- Residential properties accounted for 73 percent, or 551,500, of all structure fires.
- Fires in structures decreased by 5.3 percent to 758,000.
- The South's fire incident rate was highest, at 11.3 percent per thousand population.

Fire Deaths
- Civilian fire deaths decreased by 0.7 percent to 5,810.
- 127 firefighters died in fires, 11 more than in 1986, and 102,600 firefighters were injured, compared with 96,450 in 1986.
- Residential fire deaths, which accounted for 80.2 percent of all fire fatalities, decreased by 2.3 percent to 4,660.
- The South had the highest rate of civilian fire deaths, at 29 per million population, 21 percent higher than the national average.

Fire Injuries
- Civilian injuries increased 5.2 percent to 28,215.
- Residential properties were the site of 72.5 percent, or 20,440, of civilian injuries, while nonresidental structures saw 12 percent, or 3,375.

- The Northeast had the highest civilian injury rate, with 126.4 per million population.

Property Damage
- Property losses increased by 6.7 percent to $7.159 billion.
- Structure fires caused $6.226 billion, or 87 percent, of all property damage, with an average loss per structure fire of $8,212, up 12.6 percent.
- Residential properties incurred $3.699 billion, or 61 percent, of all structure property loss.
- The South's property loss rate was 28 percent higher than the national average, at $37.5 per person.

Incendiary and Suspicious Fires
- The number of structure fires that were deliberately set, or are suspected of having been set, was down 5.4 percent to 105,000.
- Incendiary and suspicious fires accounted for 13.8 percent of all structure fires and 25.5 percent of all structure property loss.
- Incendiary and suspicious structure fires resulted in 730 civilian deaths, an increase of 3.6 percent, and $1.590 billion in property damage, a decrease of 5.2 percent.
- Incendiary and suspicious vehicle fires decreased 10.5 percent to 51,000 and resulted in $135 million in property damage, down 10.6 percent.

Civilian Fire Deaths and Injuries

Source: National Fire Protection Association, Quincy, Mass.

	Deaths	%	Injuries	%
Residential (total)	4,660	80.2	20,440	72.5
One-and Two-Family Dwellings[1]	3,780	65.0	15,200	53.9
Apartments	790	13.6	4,765	16.9
Hotels and Motels	50	0.9	300	1.1
Other Residential	40	0.7	175	0.6
Non Residential Structures[2]	220	3.8	3,375	12.0
Highway Vehicles	775	13.0	2,900	10.2
Other Vehicles[3]	50	0.9	250	0.9
All Other[4]	125	2.1	1,250	4.4
Total	**5,810**		**28,215**	

Structure Fires by Property Use

	No. of fires	Property loss (thousands)
Public assembly	21,000	$300,000
Educational	11,000	96,000
Institutional	19,000	141,000
Residential	551,500	3,699,000
One-/2-family dwellings[1]	433,000	3,078,000
Apartments	103,500	521,000
Hotels, motels	8,000	60,000
Other residential	7,000	20,000
Stores and offices	45,000	632,000
Industry, utility, defense[5]	28,000	596,000
Storage in structures[5]	48,500	633,000
Special structures	34,000	129,000
Total	**758,000**	**$6,226,000**

(1) Includes mobile homes. (2) Includes public assembly, educational, institutional, stores and offices, industry, utility, storage, and special structure properties. (3) Includes trains, boats, ships, aircraft, farm vehicles and construction vehicles. (4) Includes properties outside with value, brush, rubbish, and other. (5) Excludes incidence handled only by private fire brigades or fixed suppression systems.

Years of Life Expected at Birth

Source: National Center for Health Statistics

Year	Total	Total Male	Total Female	White Total	White Male	White Female	Black and Other Total	Black and Other Male	Black and Other Female
1920*	54.1	53.6	54.6	54.9	54.4	55.6	45.3	45.5	45.2
1930	59.7	58.1	61.6	61.4	59.7	63.5	48.1	47.3	49.2
1940	62.9	60.8	65.2	64.2	62.1	66.6	53.1	51.5	54.9
1950	68.2	65.6	71.1	69.1	66.5	72.2	60.8	59.1	62.9
1955	69.6	66.7	72.8	70.5	67.4	73.7	63.7	61.4	66.1
1960	69.7	66.6	73.1	70.6	67.4	74.1	63.6	61.1	66.3
1965	70.2	66.8	73.7	71.0	67.6	74.7	64.1	61.1	67.4
1970	70.8	67.1	74.7	71.7	68.0	75.6	65.3	61.3	69.4
1971	71.1	67.4	75.0	72.0	68.3	75.8	65.6	61.6	69.8
1972	71.2	67.4	75.1	72.0	68.3	75.9	65.7	61.5	70.1
1973	71.4	67.6	75.3	72.2	68.5	76.1	66.1	62.0	70.3
1974	72.0	68.2	75.9	72.8	69.0	76.7	67.1	62.9	71.3
1975	72.6	68.8	76.6	73.4	69.5	77.3	68.0	63.7	72.4
1976	72.9	69.1	76.8	73.6	69.9	77.5	68.4	64.2	72.7
1977	73.3	69.5	77.2	74.0	70.2	77.9	68.9	64.7	73.2
1979	73.9	70.0	77.8	74.6	70.8	78.4	69.8	65.4	74.1
1980	73.7	70.0	77.5	74.4	70.7	78.1	69.5	65.3	73.6
1981	74.2	70.4	77.8	74.8	71.1	78.4	70.3	66.1	74.4
1982	74.5	70.9	78.1	75.1	71.5	78.7	71.0	66.8	75.0
1983	74.6	71.0	78.1	75.2	71.7	78.7	71.1	67.2	74.3
1984	74.7	71.2	78.2	75.3	71.8	78.7	71.3	67.4	75.0
1985	74.7	71.2	78.2	75.3	71.9	78.7	71.2	67.2	75.0
1986	74.8	71.3	78.3	75.4	72.0	78.9	71.2	67.2	75.1
1987p	74.9	71.4	78.3	75.5	72.1	78.8	71.6	67.6	75.4
1988p	74.9	71.5	78.3	75.5	72.1	78.9	71.5	67.4	75.5

p = preliminary * Data prior to 1940 for death-registration states only.

Average Height and Weight for Children

Source: *Physicians Handbook*, 1983

Age Years (Boys)	ft (Boys Height)	in (Boys Height)	cm (Boys Height)	lb (Boys Weight)	kg (Boys Weight)	Age Years (Girls)	ft (Girls Height)	in (Girls Height)	cm (Girls Height)	lb (Girls Weight)	kg (Girls Weight)
(Birth)	1	8	50.8	7½	3.4	(Birth)	1	8	50.8	7½	3.4
½	2	2	66.0	17	7.7	½	2	2	66.0	16	7.2
1	2	5	73.6	21	9.5	1	2	5	73.6	20	9.1
2	2	9	83.8	26	11.8	2	2	9	83.8	25	11.3
3	3	0	91.4	31	14.0	3	3	0	91.4	30	13.6
4	3	3	99.0	34	15.4	4	3	3	99.0	33	15.0
5	3	6	106.6	39	17.7	5	3	5	104.1	38	17.2
6	3	9	114.2	46	20.9	6	3	8	111.7	45	20.4
7	3	11	119.3	51	23.1	7	3	11	119.3	49	22.2
8	4	2	127.0	57	25.9	8	4	2	127.0	56	25.4
9	4	4	132.0	63	28.6	9	4	4	132.0	62	28.1
10	4	6	137.1	69	31.3	10	4	6	137.1	69	31.3
11	4	8	142.2	77	34.9	11	4	8	142.2	77	34.9
12	4	10	147.3	83	37.7	12	4	10	147.3	86	39.0
13	5	0	152.4	92	41.7	13	5	0	152.4	98	45.5
14	5	2	157.5	107	48.5	14	5	2	157.5	107	48.5

This table gives a general picture of American children at specific ages. When used as a standard, the individual variation in children's growth should not be overlooked. In most cases the height-weight relationship is probably a more valid index of weight status than a weight-for-age assessment.

Average Weight of Americans by Height and Age

Source: Society of Actuaries; from the *1979 Build and Blood Pressure Study*
The figures represent weights in ordinary indoor clothing and shoes, and heights with shoes.

Height (Men)	20-24	25-29	30-39	40-49	50-59	60-69	Height (Women)	20-24	25-29	30-39	40-49	50-59	60-69
5'2"	130	134	138	140	141	140	4'10"	105	110	113	118	121	123
5'3"	136	140	143	144	145	144	4'11"	110	112	115	121	125	127
5'4"	139	143	147	149	150	149	5'0"	112	114	118	123	127	130
5'5"	143	147	151	154	155	153	5'1"	116	119	121	127	131	133
5'6"	148	152	156	158	159	158	5'2"	120	121	124	129	133	136
5'7"	153	156	160	163	164	163	5'3"	124	125	128	133	137	140
5'8"	157	161	165	167	168	167	5'4"	127	128	131	136	141	143
5'9"	163	166	170	172	173	172	5'5"	130	132	134	139	144	147
5'10"	167	171	174	176	177	176	5'6"	133	134	137	143	147	150
5'11"	171	175	179	181	182	181	5'7"	137	138	141	147	152	155
6'0"	176	181	184	186	187	186	5'8"	141	142	145	150	156	158
6'1"	182	186	190	192	193	191	5'9"	146	148	150	155	159	161
6'2"	187	191	195	197	198	196	5'10"	149	150	153	158	162	163
6'3"	193	197	201	203	204	200	5'11"	155	156	159	162	166	167
6'4"	198	202	206	208	209	207	6'0"	157	159	164	168	171	172

SPORTS IN 1989

Olympic Games Records

The modern Olympic Games, first held in Athens, Greece in 1896, were the result of efforts by Baron Pierre de Coubertin, a French educator, to promote interest in education and culture, also to foster better international understanding through the universal medium of youth's love of athletics.

His source of inspiration for the Olympic Games was the ancient Greek Olympic Games, most notable of the four Panhellenic celebrations. The games were combined patriotic, religious, and athletic festivals held every four years. The first such recorded festival was held in 776 B.C., the date from which the Greeks began to keep their calendar by "Olympiads," or four-year spans between the games.

The first Olympiad is said to have consisted merely of a 200-yard foot race near the small city of Olympia, but the games gained in scope and became demonstrations of national pride. Only Greek citizens — amateurs — were permitted to participate. Winners received laurel, wild olive, and palm wreaths and were accorded many special privileges. Under the Roman emperors, the games deteriorated into professional carnivals and circuses. Emperor Theodosius banned them in 394 A.D.

Baron de Coubertin enlisted 9 nations to send athletes to the first modern Olympics in 1896; now more than 100 nations compete. Winter Olympic Games were started in 1924.

Sites of Olympic Games

1896 Athens	1920 Antwerp	1952 Helsinki	1976 Montreal
1900 Paris	1924 Paris	1956 Melbourne	1980 Moscow
1904 St. Louis	1928 Amsterdam	1960 Rome	1984 Los Angeles
1906 Athens	1932 Los Angeles	1964 Tokyo	1988 Seoul
1908 London	1936 Berlin	1968 Mexico City	1992 Barcelona
1912 Stockholm	1948 London	1972 Munich	

Games not recognized by International Olympic Committee. Games 6 (1916), 12 (1940), and 13 (1944) were not celebrated. The 1980 games were boycotted by 62 nations, including the U.S. The 1984 games were boycotted by the USSR and most eastern bloc nations. East and West Germany began competing separately in 1968.

Olympic Games Champions, 1896—1988

(*Indicates Gold Medal-Winning Record)

Track and Field — Men

100-Meter Run

1896	Thomas Burke, United States	12s
1900	Francis W. Jarvis, United States	11.0s
1904	Archie Hahn, United States	11s
1908	Reginald Walker, South Africa	10.8s
1912	Ralph Craig, United States	10.8s
1920	Charles Paddock, United States	10.8s
1924	Harold Abrahams, Great Britain	10.6s
1928	Percy Williams, Canada	10.8s
1932	Eddie Tolan, United States	10.3s
1936	Jesse Owens, United States	10.3s
1948	Harrison Dillard, United States	10.3s
1952	Lindy Remigino, United States	10.4s
1956	Bobby Morrow, United States	10.5s
1960	Armin Hary, Germany	10.2s
1964	Bob Hayes, United States	10.0s
1968	Jim Hines, United States	9.95s
1972	Valery Borzov, USSR	10.14s
1976	Hasely Crawford, Trinidad	10.06s
1980	Allan Wells, Great Britain	10.25s
1984	Carl Lewis, United States	9.99s
1988	Carl Lewis, United States	9.92s*

200-Meter Run

1900	Walter Tewksbury, United States	22.2s
1904	Archie Hahn, United States	21.6s
1908	Robert Kerr, Canada	22.6s
1912	Ralph Craig, United States	21.7s
1920	Allan Woodring, United States	22s
1924	Jackson Scholz, United States	21.6s
1928	Percy Williams, Canada	21.8s
1932	Eddie Tolan, United States	21.2s
1936	Jesse Owens, United States	20.7s
1948	Mel Patton, United States	21.1s
1952	Andrew Stanfield, United States	20.7s
1956	Bobby Morrow, United States	20.6s
1960	Livio Berruti, Italy	20.5s
1964	Henry Carr, United States	20.3s
1968	Tommie Smith, United States	19.83s
1972	Valeri Borzov, USSR	20.00s
1976	Donald Quarrie, Jamaica	20.23s
1980	Pietro Mennea, Italy	20.19s
1984	Carl Lewis, United States	19.80s
1988	Joe DeLoach, United States	19.75s*

400-Meter Run

1896	Thomas Burke, United States	54.2s
1900	Maxey Long, United States	49.4s
1904	Harry Hillman, United States	49.2s
1908	Wyndham Halsweile, Great Britain, walkover	50s
1912	Charles Reidpath, United States	48.2s
1920	Bevil Rudd, South Africa	49.6s
1924	Eric Liddell, Great Britain	47.6s
1928	Ray Barbuti, United States	47.8s
1932	William Carr, United States	46.2s
1936	Archie Williams, United States	46.5s
1948	Arthur Wint, Jamaica, B W I	46.2s
1952	George Rhoden, Jamaica, B W I	45.9s
1956	Charles Jenkins, United States	46.7s
1960	Otis Davis, United States	44.9s
1964	Michael Larrabee, United States	45.1s
1968	Lee Evans, United States	43.8s*
1972	Vincent Matthews, United States	44.66s
1976	Alberto Juantorena, Cuba	44.26s
1980	Viktor Markin, USSR	44.60s
1984	Alonzo Babers, United States	44.27s
1988	Steven Lewis, United States	43.87s

800-Meter Run

1896	Edwin Flack, Australia	2m. 11s
1900	Alfred Tysoe, Great Britain	2m. 1.2s
1904	James Lightbody, United States	1m. 56s
1908	Mel Sheppard, United States	1m. 52.8s
1912	James Meredith, United States	1m. 51.9s
1920	Albert Hill, Great Britain	1m. 53.4s
1924	Douglas Lowe, Great Britain	1m. 52.4s
1928	Douglas Lowe, Great Britain	1m. 51.8s
1932	Thomas Hampson, Great Britain	1m. 49.8s
1936	John Woodruff, United States	1m. 52.9s
1948	Mal Whitfield, United States	1m. 49.2s
1952	Mal Whitfield, United States	1m. 49.2s
1956	Thomas Courtney, United States	1m. 47.7s
1960	Peter Snell, New Zealand	1m. 46.3s
1964	Peter Snell, New Zealand	1m. 45.1s
1968	Ralph Doubell, Australia	1m. 44.3s
1972	Dave Wottle, United States	1m. 45.9s
1976	Alberto Juantorena, Cuba	1m. 43.50s
1980	Steve Ovett, Great Britain	1m. 45.40s
1984	Joaquim Cruz, Brazil	1m. 43.00s*
1988	Paul Ereng, Kenya	1m. 43.45s

1,500-Meter Run

1896	Edwin Flack, Australia	4m. 33.2s
1900	Charles Bennett, Great Britain	4m. 6.2s
1904	James Lightbody, United States	4m. 5.4s
1908	Mel Sheppard, United States	4m. 3.4s
1912	Arnold Jackson, Great Britain	3m. 56.8s
1920	Albert Hill, Great Britain	4m. 1.8s
1924	Paavo Nurmi, Finland	3m. 53.6s
1928	Harry Larva, Finland	3m. 53.2s
1932	Luigi Beccali, Italy	3m. 51.2s
1936	Jack Lovelock, New Zealand	3m. 47.8s
1948	Henri Eriksson, Sweden	3m. 49.8s
1952	Joseph Barthel, Luxemburg	3m. 45.2s
1956	Ron Delany, Ireland	3m. 41.2s
1960	Herb Elliott, Australia	3m. 35.6s
1964	Peter Snell, New Zealand	3m. 38.1s
1968	Kipchoge Keino, Kenya	3m. 34.9s
1972	Pekka Vasala, Finland	3m. 36.3s
1976	John Walker, New Zealand	3m. 39.17s
1980	Sebastian Coe, Great Britain	3m. 38.4s
1984	Sebastian Coe, Great Britain	3m. 32.53s*
1988	Peter Rono, Kenya	3m. 35.96s

3,000-Meter Steeplechase

1920	Percy Hodge, Great Britain	10m. 0.4s
1924	Willie Ritola, Finland	9m. 33.6s
1928	Toivo Loukola, Finland	9m. 21.8s
1932	Volmari Iso-Hollo, Finland	10m. 33.4s
	(About 3,450 mtrs. extra lap by error)	
1936	Volmari Iso-Hollo, Finland	9m. 3.8s
1948	Thore Sjoestrand, Sweden	9m. 4.6s
1952	Horace Ashenfelter, United States	8m. 45.4s
1956	Chris Brasher, Great Britain	8m. 41.2s
1960	Zdzislaw Krzyszkowiak, Poland	8m. 34.2s
1964	Gaston Roelants, Belgium	8m. 30.8s
1968	Amos Biwott, Kenya	8m. 51s
1972	Kipchoge Keino, Kenya	8m. 23.6s
1976	Anders Garderud, Sweden	8m. 08.2s
1980	Bronislaw Malinowski, Poland	8m. 09.7s
1984	Julius Korir, Kenya	8m. 11.8s
1988	Julius Kariuki, Kenya	8m. 05.51s*

5,000-Meter Run

1912	Hannes Kolehmainen, Finland	14m. 36.6s
1920	Joseph Guillemot, France	14m. 55.6s
1924	Paavo Nurmi, Finland	14m. 31.2s
1928	Willie Ritola, Finland	14m. 38s
1932	Lauri Lehtinen, Finland	14m. 30s
1936	Gunnar Hockert, Finland	14m. 22.2s
1948	Gaston Reiff, Belgium	14m. 17.6s
1952	Emil Zatopek, Czechoslovakia	14m. 6.6s
1956	Vladimir Kuts, USSR	13m. 39.6s
1960	Murray Halberg, New Zealand	13m. 43.4s
1964	Bob Schul, United States	13m. 48.8s
1968	Mohamed Gammoudi, Tunisia	14m. 05.0s
1972	Lasse Viren, Finland	13m. 26.4s
1976	Lasse Viren, Finland	13m. 24.76s
1980	Miruts Yifter, Ethiopia	13m. 21.0s
1984	Said Aouita, Morocco	13m. 05.59s*
1988	John Ngugi, Kenya	13m. 11.70s

10,000-Meter Run

1912	Hannes Kolehmainen, Finland	31m. 20.8s
1920	Paavo Nurmi, Finland	31m. 45.8s
1924	Willie Ritola, Finland	30m. 23.2s
1928	Paavo Nurmi, Finland	30m. 18.8s
1932	Janusz Kusocinski, Poland	30m. 11.4s
1936	Ilmari Salminen, Finland	30m. 15.4s
1948	Emil Zatopek, Czechoslovakia	29m. 59.6s
1952	Emil Zatopek, Czechoslovakia	29m. 17.0s
1956	Vladimir Kuts, USSR	28m. 45.6s
1960	Pyotr Bolotnikov, USSR	28m. 32.2s
1964	Billy Mills, United States	28m. 24.4s
1968	Naftali Temu, Kenya	29m. 27.4s
1972	Lasse Viren, Finland	27m. 38.4s
1976	Lasse Viren, Finland	27m. 40.38s
1980	Miruts Yifter, Ethiopia	27m. 42.7s
1984	Alberto Cova, Italy	27m. 47.54
1988	Brahim Boutaib, Morocco	27m. 21.46s*

Marathon

1896	Spiridon Loues, Greece	2h. 58m. 50s
1900	Michel Theato, France	2h. 59m. 45s
1904	Thomas Hicks, United States	3h. 28m. 63s
1908	John J. Hayes, United States	2h. 55m. 18.4s
1912	Kenneth McArthur, South Africa	2h. 36m. 54.8s
1920	Hannes Kolehmainen, Finland	2h. 32m. 35.8s

1924	Albin Stenroos, Finland	2h. 41m. 22.6s
1928	A.B. El Ouafi, France	2h. 32m. 57s
1932	Juan Zabala, Argentina	2h. 31m. 36s
1936	Kijung Son, Japan (Korean)	2h. 29m. 19.2s
1948	Delfo Cabrera, Argentina	2h. 34m. 51.6s
1952	Emil Zatopek, Czechoslovakia	2h. 23m. 03.2s
1956	Alain Mimoun, France	2h. 25m.
1960	Abebe Bikila, Ethiopia	2h. 15m. 16.2s
1964	Abebe Bikila, Ethiopia	2h. 12m. 11.2s
1968	Mamo Wolde, Ethiopia	2h. 20m. 26.4s
1972	Frank Shorter, United States	2h. 12m. 19.8s
1976	Waldemar Cierpinski, E. Germany	2h. 09m. 55s
1980	Waldemar Cierpinski, E. Germany	2h. 11m. 03s
1984	Carlos Lopes, Portugal	2h. 09m. 21 s*
1988	Gelindo Bordin, Italy	2h. 10m. 32s

20-Kilometer Walk

1956	Leonid Spirin, USSR	1h. 31m. 27.4s
1960	Vladimir Golubnichy, USSR	1h. 33m. 7.2s
1964	Kenneth Mathews, Great Britain	1h. 29m. 34.0s
1968	Vladimir Golubnichy, USSR	1h. 33m. 58.4s
1972	Peter Frenkel, E. Germany	1h. 26m. 42.4s
1976	Daniel Bautista, Mexico	1h. 24m. 40.6s
1980	Maurizio Damilano, Italy	1h. 23m. 35.5s
1984	Ernesto Canto, Mexico	1h. 23m. 13.0s
1988	Josef Pribilinec, Czech.	1h. 19m. 57.0s*

50-Kilometer Walk

1932	Thomas W. Green, Great Britain	4h. 50m. 10s
1936	Harold Whitlock, Great Britain	4h. 30m. 41.4s
1948	John Ljunggren, Sweden	4h. 41m. 52s
1952	Giuseppe Dordoni, Italy	4h. 28m. 07.8s
1956	Norman Read, New Zealand	4h. 30m. 42.8s
1960	Donald Thompson, Great Britain	4h. 25m. 30s
1964	Abdon Pamich, Italy	4h. 11m. 12.4s
1968	Christoph Hohne, E. Germany	4h. 20m. 13.6s
1972	Bern Kannenberg, W. Germany	3h. 56m. 11.6s
1980	Hartwig Gauter, E. Germany	3h. 49m. 24.0s
1984	Raul Gonzalez, Mexico	3h. 47m. 26.0
1988	Vayachslav Ivanenko, USSR	3h. 38m. 29.0s*

110-Meter Hurdles

1896	Thomas Curtis, United States	17.6s
1900	Alvin Kraenzlein, United States	15.4s
1904	Frederick Schule, United States	16s
1908	Forrest Smithson, United States	15s
1912	Frederick Kelly, United States	15.1s
1920	Earl Thomson, Canada	14.8s
1924	Daniel Kinsey, United States	15s
1928	Sydney Atkinson, South Africa	14.8s
1932	George Saling, United States	14.6s
1936	Forrest Towns, United States	14.2s
1948	William Porter, United States	13.9s
1952	Harrison Dillard, United States	13.7s
1956	Lee Calhoun, United States	13.5s
1960	Lee Calhoun, United States	13.8s
1964	Hayes Jones, United States	13.6s
1968	Willie Davenport, United States	13.3s
1972	Rod Milburn, United States	13.24s
1976	Guy Drut, France	13.30s
1980	Thomas Munkelt, E. Germany	13. 39s
1984	Roger Kingdom, United States	13.20s
1988	Roger Kingdom, United States	12.98*

400-Meter Hurdles

1900	J.W.B. Tewksbury, United States	57.6s
1904	Harry Hillman, United States	53s
1908	Charles Bacon, United States	55s
1920	Frank Loomis, United States	54s
1924	F. Morgan Taylor, United States	52.6s
1928	Lord Burghley, Great Britain	53.4s
1932	Robert Tisdall, Ireland	51.7s
1936	Glenn Hardin, United States	52.4s
1948	Roy Cochran, United States	51.1s
1952	Charles Moore, United States	50.8s
1956	Glenn Davis, United States	50.1s
1960	Glenn Davis, United States	49.3s
1964	Rex Cawley, United States	49.6s
1968	Dave Hemery, Great Britain	48.12s
1972	John Akii-Bua, Uganda	47.82s
1976	Edwin Moses, United States	47.64s
1980	Volker Beck, E. Germany	48.70s
1984	Edwin Moses, United States	47.75s
1988	Andre Phillips, United States	47.19s*

High Jump

1896	Ellery Clark, United States	5ft. 11 1-4 in.
1900	Irving Baxter, United States	6ft. 2 4-5 in.
1904	Samuel Jones, United States	5ft. 11 in.
1908	Harry Porter, United States	6ft. 3 in.
1912	Alma Richards, United States	6ft. 4 in.
1920	Richmond Landon, United States	6ft. 4 in.
1924	Harold Osborn, United States	6ft. 6 in.
1928	Robert W. King, United States	6ft. 4 1-2 in.
1932	Duncan McNaughton, Canada	6ft. 5 5-8 in.
1936	Cornelius Johnson, United States	6ft. 8 in.
1948	John L. Winter, Australia	6ft. 6 in.
1952	Walter Davis, United States	6ft. 8.32 in.
1956	Charles Dumas, United States	6ft. 11 1-2 in.
1960	Robert Shavlakadze, USSR	7ft. 1 in.
1964	Valery Brumel, USSR	7ft. 1 3-4 in.
1968	Dick Fosbury, United States	7ft. 4 1-4 in.
1972	Yuri Tarmak, USSR	7ft. 3 3-4 in.
1976	Jacek Wszola, Poland	7ft. 4 1-2 in.
1980	Gerd Wessig, E. Germany	7ft. 8 3-4 in.
1984	Dietmar Mogenburg, W. Germany	7ft. 8 1-2 in.
1988	Guennadi Avdeenko, USSR	7ft 9 1-2 in.*

Long Jump

1896	Ellery Clark, United States	20ft. 10 in.
1900	Alvin Kraenzlein, United States	23ft. 6 3-4 in.
1904	Myer Prinstein, United States	24ft. 1 in.
1908	Frank Irons, United States	24ft. 6 1-2 in.
1912	Albert Gutterson, United States	24ft. 11 1-4 in.
1920	William Pettersson, Sweden	23ft. 5 1-2 in.
1924	DeHart Hubbard, United States	24ft. 5 in.
1928	Edward B. Hamm, United States	25ft. 4 1-2 in.
1932	Edward Gordon, United States	25ft. 3-4 in.
1936	Jesse Owens, United States	26ft. 5 1-2 in.
1948	William Steele, United States	25ft. 8 in.
1952	Jerome Biffle, United States	24ft. 10 in.
1956	Gregory Bell, United States	25ft. 8 1-4 in.
1960	Ralph Boston, United States	26ft. 7 3-4 in.
1964	Lynn Davies, Great Britain	26ft. 5 3-4 in.
1968	Bob Beamon, United States	29ft. 2 1-2 in.*
1972	Randy Williams, United States	27ft. 1-2 in.
1976	Arnie Robinson, United States	27ft. 4 1-2 in.
1980	Lutz Dombrowski, E. Germany	28ft. 1-4 in.
1984	Carl Lewis, United States	28ft. 1-4 in.
1988	Carl Lewis, United States	28ft. 7 1-4 in.

400-Meter Relay

1912	Great Britain	42.4s
1920	United States	42.2s
1924	United States	41s
1928	United States	41s
1932	United States	40s
1936	United States	39.8s
1948	United States	40.6s
1952	United States	40.1s
1956	United States	39.5s
1960	Germany (U.S. disqualified)	39.5s
1964	United States	39.0s
1968	United States	38.2s
1972	United States	38.19s
1976	United States	38.33s
1980	USSR	38.26s
1984	United States	37.83s*
1988	USSR	38.19s

1,600-Meter Relay

1908	United States	3m. 29.4s
1912	United States	3m. 16.6s
1920	Great Britain	3m. 22.2s
1924	United States	3m. 16s
1928	United States	3m. 14.2s
1932	United States	3m. 8.2s
1936	Great Britain	3m. 9s
1948	United States	3m. 10.4s
1952	Jamaica, B.W.I.	3m. 03.9s
1956	United States	3m. 04.8s
1960	United States	3m. 02.2s
1964	United States	3m. 00.7s
1968	United States	2m. 56.16s
1972	Kenya	2m. 59.8s
1976	United States	2m. 58.65s
1980	USSR	3m. 01.1s
1984	United States	2m. 57.91 s
1988	United States	2m. 56.16s*

Pole Vault

1896	William Hoyt, United States	10ft. 10 in.
1900	Irving Baxter, United States	10ft. 10 in.
1904	Charles Dvorak, United States	11ft. 5 3-4 in.
1908	A. C. Gilbert, United States	
	Edward Cook Jr., United States	12ft. 2 in.
1912	Harry Babcock, United States	12ft. 11 1-2 in.
1920	Frank Foss, United States	13ft. 5 in.
1924	Lee Barnes, United States	12ft. 11 1-2 in.
1928	Sabin W. Carr, United States	13ft. 9 1-4 in.
1932	William Miller, United States	14ft. 1 3-4 in.
1936	Earle Meadows, United States	14ft. 3 1-4 in.
1948	Guinn Smith, United States	14ft. 1 1-4 in.
1952	Robert Richards, United States	14ft. 11 in.
1956	Robert Richards, United States	14ft. 11 1-2 in.
1960	Don Bragg, United States	15ft. 5 in.
1964	Fred Hansen, United States	16ft. 8 3-4 in.
1968	Bob Seagren, United States	17ft. 8 1-2 in.
1972	Wolfgang Nordwig, E. Germany	18ft. 1-2 in.
1976	Tadeusz Slusarski, Poland	18ft. 1-2 in.
1980	Wladyslaw Kozakiewicz, Poland	18ft. 11 1-2 in.
1984	Pierre Quinon, France	18ft. 10 1-4 in.
1988	Sergei Bubka, USSR	19ft. 9 1-4 in.*

Hammer Throw

1900	John Flanagan, United States	163ft. 1 in.
1904	John Flanagan, United States	168ft. 1 in.
1908	John Flanagan, United States	170ft. 4 1-4 in.
1912	Matt McGrath, United States	179ft. 7 1-8 in.
1920	Pat Ryan, United States	173ft. 5 5-8 in.
1924	Fred Tootell, United States	174ft. 10 1-8 in.
1928	Patrick O'Callaghan, Ireland	168ft. 7 1-2 in.
1932	Patrick O'Callaghan, Ireland	176ft. 11 1-8 in.
1936	Karl Hein, Germany	185ft. 4 in.
1948	Imre Nemeth, Hungary	183ft. 11 1-2 in.
1952	Jozsef Csermak, Hungary	197ft. 11 9-16 in.
1956	Harold Connolly, United States	207ft. 3 1-2 in.
1960	Vasily Rudenkov, USSR	220ft. 1 5-8 in.
1964	Romuald Klim, USSR	228ft. 9 1-2 in.
1968	Gyula Zsivotsky, Hungary	240ft. 8 in.
1972	Anatoli Bondarchuk, USSR	247ft. 8 in.
1976	Yuri Syedykh, USSR	254ft. 4 in.
1980	Yuri Syedykh, USSR	268ft. 4 1-2 in.
1984	Juha Tiainen, Finland	256ft. 2 in.
1988	Sergei Litinov, USSR	278ft. 2 1-2 in.*

Discus Throw

1896	Robert Garrett, United States	95ft. 7 1-2 in.
1900	Rudolf Bauer, Hungary	118ft. 3 in.
1904	Martin Sheridan, United States	128ft. 10 1-2 in.
1908	Martin Sheridan, United States	134ft. 2 in.
1912	Armas Taipale, Finland	148ft. 3 in.
	Both hands—Armas Taipale, Finland	271ft. 10 1-4 in.
1920	Elmer Niklander, Finland	146ft. 7 in.
1924	Clarence Houser, United States	151ft. 4 in.
1928	Clarence Houser, United States	155ft. 3 in.
1932	John Anderson, United States	162ft. 4 in.
1936	Ken Carpenter, United States	165ft. 7 in.
1948	Adolfo Consolini, Italy	173ft. 2 in.
1952	Sim Iness, United States	180ft. 6.85 in.
1956	Al Oerter, United States	184ft. 10 1-2 in.
1960	Al Oerter, United States	194ft. 2 in.
1964	Al Oerter, United States	200ft. 1 1-2 in.
1968	Al Oerter, United States	212ft. 6 1-2 in.
1972	Ludvik Danek, Czechoslovakia	211ft. 3 in.
1976	Mac Wilkins, United States	221ft. 5.4 in.
1980	Viktor Rashchupkin, USSR	218ft. 8 in.
1984	Rolf Dannenberg, W. Germany	218ft. 6 in.
1988	Jurgen Schult, E. Germany	225ft. 9 1-4 in.*

Triple Jump

1896	James Connolly, United States	44ft. 11 3-4 in.
1900	Myer Prinstein, United States	47ft. 5 3-4 in.
1904	Myer Prinstein, United States	47 ft.
1908	Timothy Ahearne, Great Britain, Ireland	48ft. 11 1-4 in.
1912	Gustaf Lindblom, Sweden	48ft. 5 1-4 in.
1920	Vilho Tuulos, Finland	47ft. 7 in.
1924	Anthony Winter, Australia	50ft. 11 1-4 in.
1928	Mikio Oda, Japan	49ft. 11 in.
1932	Chuhei Nambu, Japan	51ft. 7 in.
1936	Naoto Tajima, Japan	52ft. 6 in.
1948	Arne Ahman, Sweden	50ft. 6 1-4 in.
1952	Adhemar da Silva, Brazil	53ft. 2 3-4 in.
1956	Adhemar da Silva, Brazil	53ft. 7 3-4 in.
1960	Jozef Schmidt, Poland	55ft. 2 in.
1964	Jozef Schmidt, Poland	55ft. 3 1-2 in.

(continued)

1968	Viktor Saneev, USSR	57ft. 3-4 in.
1972	Viktor Saneev, USSR	56ft. 11 in.
1976	Viktor Saneev, USSR	56ft. 8 3-4 in.
1980	Jaak Uudmae, USSR	56ft. 11 1-4 in.
1984	Al Joyner, United States	56ft. 7 1-2 in.
1988	Hristo Markov, Bulgaria	57ft. 9 1-4 in.*

16-lb. Shot Put

1896	Robert Garrett, United States	36ft. 9 3-4 in.
1900	Richard Sheldon, United States	46ft. 3 1-4 in.
1904	Ralph Rose, United States	48ft. 7 in.
1908	Ralph Rose, United States	46ft. 7 1-2 in.
1912	Pat McDonald, United States	50ft. 4 in.
	Both hands—Ralph Rose,	
	United States	90ft. 5 1-2 in.
1920	Ville Porhola, Finland	48ft. 7 1-4 in.
1924	Clarence Houser, United States	49ft. 2 1-4 in.
1928	John Kuck, United States	52ft. 3-4 in.
1932	Leo Sexton, United States	52ft. 6 in.
1936	Hans Woellke, Germany	53ft. 1 3-4 in.
1948	Wilbur Thompson, United States	56ft. 2 in.
1952	Parry O'Brien, United States	57ft. 1-2 in.
1956	Parry O'Brien, United States	60ft. 11 1-4 in.
1960	William Nieder, United States	64ft. 6 3-4 in.
1964	Dallas Long, United States	66ft. 8 1-2 in.
1968	Randy Matson, United States	67ft. 4 3-4 in.
1972	Wladyslaw Komar, Poland	69ft. 6 in.
1976	Udo Beyer, E. Germany	69ft. 3-4 in.
1980	Vladimir Kiselyov, USSR	70ft. 1-2 in.
1984	Alessandro Andrei, Italy	69ft. 9 in.
1988	Ulf Timmermann, E. Germany	73ft. 8 3-4 in.*

Javelin

1908	Erik Lemming, Sweden	178ft. 7 1-2 in.
	Held in middle—Erik Lemming,	
	Sweden	179ft. 10 1-2 in.
1912	Erik Lemming, Sweden	198ft. 11 1-4 in.
	Both hands, Julius Saaristo, Finland	358ft. 11 7-8 in.
1920	Jonni Myrra, Finland	215ft. 9 3-4 in.
1924	Jonni Myrra, Finland	206ft. 6 3-4 in.
1928	Eric Lundkvist, Sweden	218ft. 6 1-8 in.

1932	Matti Jarvinen, Finland	238ft. 6 in.
1936	Gerhard Stoeck, Germany	235ft. 8 5-16 in.
1948	Kaj Rautavaara, Finland	228ft. 10 1-2 in.
1952	Cy Young, United States	242ft. 0.79 in.
1956	Egil Danielson, Norway	281ft. 2 1-4 in.
1960	Viktor Tsibulenko, USSR	277ft. 8 3-8 in.
1964	Pauli Nevala, Finland	271ft. 2 1-2 in.
1968	Janis Lusis, USSR	295ft. 7 1-4 in.
1972	Klaus Wolfermann, W. Germany	296ft. 10 in.
1976	Miklos Nemeth, Hungary	310ft. 4 in.*
1980	Dainis Kula, USSR	299ft. 2 3-8 in.
1984	Arto Haerkoenen, Finland	284ft. 8 in.
1988	Tapio Korjus, Finland	276ft. 6 in.

Decathlon

1912	Hugo Wieslander, Sweden	7,724.49 pts.(a)
1920	Helge Lovland, Norway	6,804.35 pts.
1924	Harold Osborn, United States	7,710.77 pts.
1928	Paavo Yrjola, Finland	8,053.29 pts.
1932	James Bausch, United States	8,462.23 pts.
1936	Glenn Morris, United States	7,900 pts.
1948	Robert Mathias, United States	7,139 pts.
1952	Robert Mathias, United States	7,887 pts.
1956	Milton Campbell, United States	7,937 pts.
1960	Rafer Johnson, United States	8,392 pts.
1964	Willi Holdorf, Germany	7,887 pts.
1968	Bill Toomey, United States	8,193 pts.
1972	Nikolai Avilov, USSR	8,454 pts.
1976	Bruce Jenner, United States	8,617 pts.
1980	Daley Thompson, Great Britain	8,495 pts.
1984	Daley Thompson, Great Britain	8,798 pts.*(b)
1988	Christian Schenk, E. Germany	8,488 pts.

Former point systems used prior to 1964.

(a) Jim Thorpe of the U.S. won the 1912 Decathlon with 8,413 pts. but was disqualified and had to return his medals because he had played professional baseball prior to the Olympic games. The medals were restored posthumously in 1982. (b) Scoring change effective Apr., 1985.

Track and Field—Women

100-Meter Run

1928	Elizabeth Robinson, United States	12.2s
1932	Stella Walsh, Poland	11.9s
1936	Helen Stephens, United States	11.5s
1948	Francina Blankers-Koen, Netherlands	11.9s
1952	Marjorie Jackson, Australia	11.5s
1956	Betty Cuthbert, Australia	11.5s
1960	Wilma Rudolph, United States	11.0s
1964	Wyomia Tyus, United States	11.4s
1968	Wyomia Tyus, United States	11.0s
1972	Renate Stecher, E. Germany	11.07s
1976	Annegret Richter, W. Germany	11.08s
1980	Lyudmila Kondratyeva, USSR	11.6s
1984	Evelyn Ashford, United States	10.97s
1988	Florence Griffith-Joyner, United States	10.54s*

200-Meter Run

1948	Francina Blankers-Koen, Netherlands	24.4s
1952	Marjorie Jackson, Australia	23.7s
1956	Betty Cuthbert, Australia	23.4s
1960	Wilma Rudolph, United States	24.0s
1964	Edith McGuire, United States	23.0s
1968	Irena Szewinska, Poland	22.5s
1972	Renate Stecher, E. Germany	22.40s
1976	Barbel Eckert, E. Germany	22.37s
1980	Barbel Wockel, E. Germany	22.03
1984	Valerie Brisco-Hooks, United States	21.81s
1988	Florence Griffith-Joyner, United States	21.34s*

400-Meter Run

1964	Betty Cuthbert, Australia	52s
1968	Colette Besson, France	52s
1972	Monika Zehrt, E. Germany	51.08s
1976	Irena Szewinska, Poland	49.29s
1980	Marita Koch, E. Germany	48.88s
1984	Valerie Brisco-Hooks, United States	48.83s
1988	Olga Bryzgina, USSR	48.65s*

800-Meter Run

1928	Lina Radke, Germany	2m. 16.8s
1960	Ludmila Shevtsova, USSR	2m. 4.3s
1964	Ann Packer, Great Britain	2m. 1.1s

1968	Madeline Manning, United States	2m. 0.9s
1972	Hildegard Falck, W. Germany	1m. 58.6s
1976	Tatyana Kazankina, USSR	1m. 54.94s
1980	Nadezhda Olizarenko, USSR	1m. 53.5s*
1984	Doina Melinte, Romania	1m. 57.6s
1988	Sigrun Wodars, E. Germany	1m. 56.10s

1,500-Meter Run

1972	Lyudmila Bragina, USSR	4m. 01.4s
1976	Tatyana Kazankina, USSR	4m. 05.48s
1980	Tatyana Kazankina, USSR	3m. 56.6s
1984	Gabriella Dorio, Italy	4m. 03.25s
1988	Paula Ivan, Romania	3m. 53.96s*

3,000-Meter Run

1984	Maricica Puica, Romania	8:35.96s
1988	Tatyana Samolenko, USSR	8:26.53s*

10,000-Meter Run

1988	Olga Boldarenko, USSR	31m. 44.69s*

400-Meter Relay

1928	Canada	48.4s
1932	United States	46.9s
1936	United States	46.9s
1948	Netherlands	47.5s
1952	United States	45.9s
1956	Australia	44.5s
1960	United States	44.5s
1964	Poland	43.6s
1968	United States	42.8s
1972	West Germany	42.81s
1976	East Germany	42.55s
1980	East Germany	41.60s*
1984	United States	41.65s
1988	United States	41.98s

1,600-Meter Relay

1972	East Germany	3m. 23s
1976	East Germany	3m. 19.23s

1980	USSR.	3m. 20.02s
1984	United States	3m. 18.29s
1988	USSR.	3 m. 15.18s*

80-Meter Hurdles

1932	"Babe" Didrikson, United States.	11.7s
1936	Trebisonda Valla, Italy.	11.7s
1948	Francina Blankers-Koen, Netherlands.	11.2s
1952	Shirley Strickland de la Hunty, Australia	10.9s
1956	Shirley Strickland de la Hunty, Australia	10.7s
1960	Irina Press, USSR.	10.8s
1964	Karin Balzer, Germany	10.5s
1968	Maureen Caird, Australia	10.3s*

100-Meter Hurdles

1972	Annelie Ehrhardt, E. Germany	12.59s
1976	Johanna Schaller, E. Germany.	12.77s
1980	Vera Komisova, USSR.	12.56s
1984	Benita Brown-Fitzgerald, United States	12.84s
1988	Jordanka Donkova, Bulgaria.	12.38s*

400-Meter Hurdles

| 1984 | Nawal el Moutawakii, Morocco . . . . | 54.61s |
| 1988 | Debra Flintoff-King, Australia . . . . | 53.17s* |

10,000-Meter Run

| 1988 | Olga Boldarenko, USSR. . . . . | 31m. 44.69s* |

Heptathlon

| 1984 | Glynis Nunn, Australia . . . . | 6,390 pts. |
| 1988 | Jackie Joyner-Kersee, United States . . . . . | 7,215 pts.* |

High Jump

1928	Ethel Catherwood, Canada	5ft. 2 1-2 in.
1932	Jean Shiley, United States.	5ft. 5 1-4 in.
1936	Ibolya Csak, Hungary.	5ft. 3 in.
1948	Alice Coachman, United States.	5ft. 6 1-8 in.
1952	Esther Brand, South Africa	5ft. 5 3-4 in.
1956	Mildred L. McDaniel, United States.	5ft. 9 1-4 in.
1960	Iolanda Balas, Romania	6ft. 3-4 in.
1964	Iolanda Balas, Romania	6ft. 2 3-4 in.
1968	Miloslava Reskova, Czechoslovakia	5ft. 11 1-2 in.
1972	Ulrike Meyfarth, W. Germany	6ft. 4 in.
1976	Rosemarie Ackermann, E. Germany	6ft. 3 3-4 in.
1980	Sara Simeoni, Italy.	6ft. 5 1-2 in.
1984	Ulrike Meyfarth, W. Germany	6ft. 7 1-2 in.
1988	Louise Ritter, United States.	6ft. 8 in.*

Discus Throw

1928	Helena Konopacka, Poland.	129ft. 11 3-4 in.
1932	Lillian Copeland, United States.	133ft. 2 in.
1936	Gisela Mauermayer, Germany	156ft. 3 in.
1948	Micheline Ostermeyer, France.	137ft. 6 1-2 in.
1952	Nina Romaschkova, USSR.	168ft. 8 in.

1956	Olga Fikotova, Czechoslovakia.	176ft. 1 in.
1960	Nina Ponomareva, USSR.	180ft. 8 1-4 in.
1964	Tamara Press, USSR	187ft. 10 in.
1968	Lia Manoliu, Romania	191ft. 2 in.
1972	Faina Melnik, USSR.	218ft. 7 in.
1976	Evelin Schlaak, E. Germany	226ft. 4 in.
1980	Evelin Jahl, E. Germany.	229ft. 6 in.
1984	Ria Stalman, Netherlands.	214ft. 5 in.
1988	Martina Hellmann, E. Germany.	237ft. 2 1-4 in.*

Javelin Throw

1932	"Babe" Didrikson, United States.	143ft. 4 in.
1936	Tilly Fleischer, Germany	148ft. 2 3-4 in.
1948	Herma Bauma, Austria	149ft. 6 in.
1952	Dana Zatopkova, Czechoslovakia	165ft. 7 in.
1956	Inese Jaunzeme, USSR.	176ft. 8 in.
1960	Elvira Ozolina, USSR	183ft. 8 in.
1964	Mihaela Penes, Romania	198ft. 7 1-2 in.
1968	Angela Nemeth, Hungary	198ft. 1-2 in.
1972	Ruth Fuchs, E. Germany	209ft. 7 in.
1976	Ruth Fuchs, E. Germany	216ft. 4 in.
1980	Maria Colon, Cuba.	224ft. 5 in.
1984	Tessa Sanderson, Great Britain	228ft. 2 in.
1988	Petra Felke, E. Germany	245ft.*

Shot Put (8lb., 13oz.)

1948	Micheline Ostermeyer, France.	45ft. 1 1-2 in.
1952	Galina Zybina, USSR	50ft. 1 3-4 in.
1956	Tamara Tishkyevich, USSR	54ft. 5 in.
1960	Tamara Press, USSR.	56ft. 10 in.
1964	Tamara Press, USSR.	59ft. 6 1-4 in.
1968	Margitta Gummel, E. Germany.	64ft. 4 in.
1972	Nadezhda Chizova, USSR.	69ft.
1976	Ivanka Hristova, Bulgaria.	69ft. 5 1-4 in.
1980	Ilona Slupianek, E. Germany	73ft. 6 1-4 in.*
1984	Claudia Losch, W. Germany	67ft. 2 1-4 in.
1988	Natalya Lisovskaya, USSR.	72ft. 11 1-2 in.

Long Jump

1948	Olga Gyarmati, Hungary.	18ft. 8 1-4 in.
1952	Yvette Williams, New Zealand.	20ft. 5 3-4 in.
1956	Elzbieta Krzeskinska, Poland	20ft. 9 3-4 in.
1960	Vyera Krepkina, USSR.	20ft. 10 3-4 in.
1964	Mary Rand, Great Britain.	22ft. 2 1-4 in.
1968	Viorica Viscopoleanu, Romania	22ft. 4 1-2 in.
1972	Heidemarie Rosendahl, W. Germany . . .	22ft. 3 in.
1976	Angela Voigt, E. Germany.	22ft. 3-4 in.
1980	Tatyana Kolpakova, USSR.	23ft. 2 in.
1984	Anisoara Stanciu, Romania.	22ft. 10 in.
1988	Jackie Joyner-Kersee, United States. . . .	24ft 3 1-2 in.*

Marathon

| 1984 | Joan Benoit, United States . . . . | 2h. 24m. 52s* |
| 1988 | Rosa Mota, Portugal . . . . | 2h. 25m. 40s |

Swimming—Men

50-Meter Freestyle

| 1988 | Matt Biondi, U.S. . . . . | 22.14* |

100-Meter Freestyle

1896	Alfred Hajos, Hungary	1:22.2
1904	Zoltan de Halmay, Hungary (100 yards)	1:02.8
1908	Charles Daniels, U.S..	1:05.6
1912	Duke P. Kahanamoku, U.S..	1:03.4
1920	Duke P. Kahanamoku, U.S..	1:01.4
1924	John Weissmuller, U.S..	59.0
1928	John Weissmuller, U.S..	58.6
1932	Yasuji Miyazaki, Japan.	58.2
1936	Ferenc Csik, Hungary.	57.6
1948	Wally Ris, U.S..	57.3
1952	Clark Scholes, U.S..	57.4
1956	Jon Henricks, Australia.	55.4
1960	John Devitt, Australia.	55.2
1964	Don Schollander, U.S..	53.4
1968	Mike Wenden, Australia	52.2
1972	Mark Spitz, U.S..	51.22
1976	Jim Montgomery, U.S..	49.99
1980	Jorg Woithe, E. Germany	50.40
1984	Rowdy Gaines, U.S..	49.80
1988	Matt Biondi, United States	48.63*
1968	Mike Wenden, Australia	1:55.2

200-Meter Freestyle

1972	Mark Spitz, U.S.	1:52.78
1976	Bruce Furniss, U.S.	1:50.29
1980	Sergei Kopliakov, USSR	1:49.81
1984	Michael Gross, W. Germany	1:47.44
1988	Duncan Armstrong, Australia	1:47.25*

400-Meter Freestyle

1904	C. M. Daniels, U.S. (440 yards)	6:16.2
1908	Henry Taylor, Great Britain.	5:36.8
1912	George Hodgson, Canada.	5:24.4
1920	Norman Ross, U.S..	5:26.8
1924	John Weissmuller, U.S..	5:04.2
1928	Albert Zorilla, Argentina	5:01.6
1932	Clarence Crabbe, U.S..	4:48.4
1936	Jack Medica, U.S..	4:44.5
1948	William Smith, U.S..	4:41.0
1952	Jean Boiteux, France	4:30.7
1956	Murray Rose, Australia.	4:27.3
1960	Murray Rose, Australia.	4:18.3
1964	Don Schollander, U.S..	4:12.2
1968	Mike Burton, U.S..	4:09.0
1972	Brad Cooper, Australia	4:00.27
1976	Brian Goodell, U.S..	3:51.93

(continued)

1980	Vladimir Salnikov, USSR	3:51.31
1984	George DiCarlo, U.S.	3:51.23
1988	Ewe Dassler, E. Germany	3:46.95*

1,500-Meter Freestyle

1908	Henry Taylor, Great Britain	22:48.4
1912	George Hodgson, Canada	22:00.0
1920	Norman Ross, U.S.	22:23.2
1924	Andrew Charlton, Australia	20:06.6
1928	Arne Borg, Sweden	19:51.8
1932	Kusuo Kitamura, Japan	19:12.4
1936	Noboru Terada, Japan	19:13.7
1948	James McLane, U.S.	19:18.5
1952	Ford Konno, U.S.	18:30.3
1956	Murray Rose, Australia	17:58.9
1960	Jon Konrads, Australia	17:19.6
1964	Robert Windle, Australia	17:01.7
1968	Mike Burton, U.S.	16:38.9
1972	Mike Burton, U.S.	15:52.58
1976	Brian Goodell, U.S.	15:02.40
1980	Vladimir Salnikov, USSR	14:58.27*
1984	Michael O'Brien, U.S.	15:05.20
1988	Vladimir Salnikov, USSR	15:00.40

400-Meter Medley Relay

1960	United States	4:05.4
1964	United States	3:58.4
1968	United States	3:54.9
1972	United States	3:48.16
1976	United States	3:42.22
1980	Australia	3:45.70
1984	United States	3:39.30
1988	United States	3:36.93*

400-Meter Freestyle Relay

1964	United States	3:31.2
1968	United States	3:31.7
1972	United States	3:26.42
1984	United States	3:19.03
1988	United States	3:16.53*

800-Meter Freestyle Relay

1908	Great Britain	10:55.6
1912	Australia	10:11.6
1920	United States	10:04.4
1924	United States	9:53.4
1928	United States	9:36.2
1932	Japan	8:58.4
1936	Japan	8:51.5
1948	United States	8:46.0
1952	United States	8:31.1
1956	Australia	8:23.6
1960	United States	8:10.2
1964	United States	7:52.1
1968	United States	7:52.33
1972	United States	7:35.78
1976	United States	7:23.22
1980	USSR	7:23.50
1984	United States	7:15.69
1988	United States	7:12.51*

100-Meter Backstroke

1904	Walter Brack, Germany (100 yds.)	1:16.8
1908	Arno Bieberstein, Germany	1:24.6
1912	Harry Hebner, U.S.	1:21.2
1920	Warren Kealoha, U.S.	1:15.2
1924	Warren Kealoha, U.S.	1:13.2
1928	George Kojac, U.S.	1:08.2
1932	Masaji Kiyokawa, Japan	1:08.6
1936	Adolph Kiefer, U.S.	1:05.9
1948	Allen Stack, U.S.	1:06.4
1952	Yoshi Oyakawa, U.S.	1:05.4
1956	David Thiele, Australia	1:02.2
1960	David Thiele, Australia	1:01.9
1968	Roland Matthes, E. Germany	58.7
1972	Roland Matthes, E. Germany	56.58
1976	John Naber, U.S.	55.49
1980	Bengt Baron, Sweden	56.33
1984	Rick Carey, U.S.	55.79
1988	Daichi Suzuki, Japan	55.05*

200-Meter Backstroke

1964	Jed Graef, U.S.	2:10.3
1968	Roland Matthes, E. Germany	2:09.6
1972	Roland Matthes, E. Germany	2:02.82
1976	John Naber, U.S.	1:59.19*

1980	Sandor Wladar, Hungary	2:01.93
1984	Rick Carey, U.S.	2:00.23
1988	Igor Polianski, USSR	1:59.37

100-Meter Breaststroke

1968	Don McKenzie, U.S.	1:07.7
1972	Nobutaka Taguchi, Japan	1:04.94
1976	John Hencken, U.S.	1:03.11
1980	Duncan Goodhew, Great Britain	1:03.44
1984	Steve Lundquist, U.S.	1:01.65*
1988	Adrian Moorhouse, Great Britain	1:02.04

200-Meter Breaststroke

1908	Frederick Holman, Great Britain	3:09.2
1912	Walter Bathe, Germany	3:01.8
1920	Haken Malmroth, Sweden	3:04.4
1924	Robert Skelton, U.S.	2:56.6
1928	Yoshiyuki Tsuruta, Japan	2:48.8
1932	Yoshiyuki Tsuruta, Japan	2:45.4
1936	Tetsuo Hamuro, Japan	2:41.5
1948	Joseph Verdeur, U.S.	2:39.3
1952	John Davies, Australia	2:34.4
1956	Masura Furukawa, Japan	2:34.7
1960	William Mulliken, U.S.	2:37.4
1964	Ian O'Brien, Australia	2:27.8
1968	Felipe Munoz, Mexico	2:28.7
1972	John Hencken, U.S.	2:21.55
1976	David Wilkie, Great Britain	2:15.11
1980	Robertas Zhulpa, USSR	2:15.85
1984	Victor Davis, Canada	2:13.34*
1988	Jozsef Szabo, Hungary	2:13.52

100-Meter Butterfly

1968	Doug Russell, U.S.	55.9
1972	Mark Spitz, U.S.	54.27
1976	Matt Vogel, U.S.	54.35
1980	Par Arvidsson, Sweden	54.92
1984	Michael Gross, W. Germany	53.08
1988	Anthony Nesty, Suriname	53.00*

200-Meter Butterfly

1956	William Yorzyk, U.S.	2:19.3
1960	Michael Troy, U.S.	2:12.8
1964	Kevin J. Berry, Australia	2:06.6
1968	Carl Robie, U.S.	2:08.7
1972	Mark Spitz, U.S.	2:00.70
1976	Mike Bruner, U.S.	1:59.23
1980	Sergei Fesenko, USSR	1:59.76
1984	Jon Sieben, Australia	1:57.04
1988	Michael Gross, W. Germany	1:56.94*

200-Meter Individual Medley

1968	Charles Hickcox, U.S.	2:12.0
1972	Gunnar Larsson, Sweden	2:07.17
1984	Alex Baumann, Canada	2:01.42
1988	Tamas Darnyi, Hungary	2:00.17*

400-Meter Individual Medley

1964	Dick Roth, U.S.	4:45.4
1968	Charles Hickcox, U.S.	4:48.4
1972	Gunnar Larsson, Sweden	4:31.98
1976	Rod Strachan, U.S.	4:23.68
1980	Aleksandr Sidorenko, USSR	4:22.89
1984	Alex Baumann, Canada	4:17.41
1988	Tamas Darnyi, Hungary	4:14.75*

Springboard Diving

		Points
1908	Albert Zurner, Germany	85.5
1912	Paul Guenther, Germany	79.23
1920	Louis Kuehn, U.S.	675.40
1924	Albert White, U.S.	97.46
1928	Pete Desjardins, U.S.	185.04
1932	Michael Galitzen, U.S.	161.38
1936	Richard Degener, U.S.	163.57
1948	Bruce Harlan, U.S.	163.64
1952	David Browning, U.S.	205.29
1956	Robert Clotworthy, U.S.	159.56
1960	Gary Tobian, U.S.	170.00
1964	Kenneth Sitzberger, U.S.	159.90
1968	Bernie Wrightson, U.S.	170.15
1972	Vladimir Vasin, USSR	594.09
1976	Phil Boggs, U.S.	619.52
1980	Aleksandr Portnov, USSR	905.02
1984	Greg Louganis, U.S.	754.41
1988	Greg Louganis, U.S.	730.80

Platform Diving

		Points
1904	Dr. G.E. Sheldon, U.S................	12.75
1908	Hjalmar Johansson, Sweden...........	83.75
1912	Erik Adlerz, Sweden................	73.94
1920	Clarence Pinkston, U.S..............	100.67
1924	Albert White, U.S..................	97.46
1928	Pete Desjardins, U.S...............	98.74
1932	Harold Smith, U.S..................	124.80
1936	Marshall Wayne, U.S................	113.58
1948	Sammy Lee, U.S...................	130.05
1952	Sammy Lee, U.S...................	156.28
1956	Joaquin Capilla, Mexico.............	152.44
1960	Robert Webster, U.S................	165.56
1964	Robert Webster, U.S................	148.58
1968	Klaus Dibiasi, Italy................	164.18
1972	Klaus Dibiasi, Italy................	504.12
1976	Klaus Dibiasi, Italy................	600.51
1980	Falk Hoffmann, E. Germany..........	835.65
1984	Greg Louganis, U.S................	710.91
1988	Greg Louganis, U.S................	638.61

Swimming—Women

50-Meter Freestyle

1988	Kristin Otto, E. Germany.............	25.49*

100-Meter Freestyle

1912	Fanny Durack, Australia.............	1:22.2
1920	Ethelda Bleibtrey, U.S..............	1:13.6
1924	Ethel Lackie, U.S.................	1:12.4
1928	Albina Osipowich, U.S..............	1:11.0
1932	Helene Madison, U.S...............	1:06.8
1936	Hendrika Mastenbroek, Holland.......	1:05.9
1948	Greta Andersen, Denmark...........	1:06.3
1952	Katalin Szoke, Hungary.............	1:06.8
1956	Dawn Fraser, Australia.............	1:02.0
1960	Dawn Fraser, Australia.............	1:01.2
1964	Dawn Fraser, Australia.............	59.5
1968	Jan Henne, U.S...................	1:00.0
1972	Sandra Neilson, U.S................	58.59
1976	Kornelia Ender, E. Germany.........	55.65
1980	Barbara Krause, E. Germany.........	54.79*
1984	(tie) Carrie Steinseifer, U.S..........	55.92
	Nancy Hogshead, U.S..............	55.92
1988	Kristin Otto, E. Germany.............	54.93

200-Meter Freestyle

1968	Debbie Meyer, U.S................	2:10.5
1972	Shane Gould, Australia.............	2:03.56
1976	Kornelia Ender, E. Germany.........	1:59.26
1980	Barbara Krause, E. Germany.........	1:58.33
1984	Mary Wayte, U.S..................	1:59.23
1988	Heike Friedrich, E. Germany.........	1:57.65*

400-Meter Freestyle

1924	Martha Norelius, U.S...............	6:02.2
1928	Martha Norelius, U.S...............	5:42.8
1932	Helene Madison, U.S...............	5:28.5
1936	Hendrika Mastenbroek, Netherlands....	5:26.4
1948	Ann Curtis, U.S...................	5:17.8
1952	Valerie Gyenge, Hungary............	5:12.1
1956	Lorraine Crapp, Australia............	4:54.6
1960	Susan Chris von Saltza, U.S.........	4:50.6
1964	Virginia Duenkel, U.S..............	4:43.3
1968	Debbie Meyer, U.S................	4:31.8
1972	Shane Gould, Australia.............	4:19.44
1976	Petra Thuemer E. Germany..........	4:09.89
1980	Ines Diers, E. Germany.............	4:08.76
1984	Tiffany Cohen, U.S................	4:07.10
1988	Janet Evans, U.S.................	4:03.85*

800-Meter Freestyle

1968	Debbie Meyer, U.S................	9:24.0
1972	Keena Rothhammer, U.S............	8:53.68
1976	Petra Thuemer, E. Germany.........	8:37.14
1980	Michelle Ford, Australia.............	8:28.90
1984	Tiffany Cohen, U.S................	8:24.95
1988	Janet Evans, U.S.................	8:20.20*

100-Meter Backstroke

1924	Sybil Bauer, U.S..................	1:23.2
1928	Marie Braun, Netherlands...........	1:22.0
1932	Eleanor Holm, U.S................	1:19.4
1936	Dina Senff, Netherlands............	1:18.9
1948	Karen Harup, Denmark.............	1:14.4
1952	Joan Harrison, South Africa.........	1:14.3
1956	Judy Grinham, Great Britain.........	1:12.9
1960	Lynn Burke, U.S..................	1:09.3
1964	Cathy Ferguson, U.S...............	1:07.7
1968	Kaye Hall, U.S...................	1:06.2
1972	Melissa Belote, U.S...............	1:05.78
1976	Ulrike Richter, E. Germany..........	1:01.83
1980	Rica Reinisch, E. Germany..........	1:00.86*
1984	Theresa Andrews, U.S..............	1:02.55
1988	Kristin Otto, E. Germany.............	1:00.89

200-Meter Backstroke

1968	Pokey Watson, U.S................	2:24.8
1972	Melissa Belote, U.S...............	2:19.19
1976	Ulrike Richter, E. Germany..........	2:13.43
1980	Rica Reinisch, E. Germany..........	2:11.77
1984	Jolanda De Rover, Netherlands.......	2:12.38
1988	Krisztina Egerszegi, Hungary........	2:09.29*

100-Meter Breaststroke

1968	Djurdjica Bjedov, Yugoslavia........	1:15.8
1972	Cathy Carr, U.S..................	1:13.58
1976	Hannelore Anke, E. Germany........	1:11.16
1980	Ute Geweniger, E. Germany.........	1:10.22
1984	Petra Van Staveren, Netherlands.....	1:09.88
1988	Tania Dangalakova, Bulgaria.........	1:07.95*

200-Meter Breaststroke

1924	Lucy Morton, Great Britain..........	3:33.2
1928	Hilde Schrader, Germany...........	3:12.6
1932	Clare Dennis, Australia.............	3:06.3
1936	Hideko Maehata, Japan............	3:03.6
1948	Nelly Van Vliet, Netherlands.........	2:57.2
1952	Eva Szekely, Hungary..............	2:51.7
1956	Ursula Happe, Germany............	2:53.1
1960	Anita Lonsbrough, Great Britain......	2:49.5
1964	Galina Prozumenschikova, USSR......	2:46.4
1968	Sharon Wichman, U.S..............	2:44.4
1972	Beverly Whitfield, Australia..........	2:41.71
1976	Marina Koshevaia, USSR...........	2:33.35
1980	Lina Kachushite, USSR.............	2:29.54
1984	Anne Ottenbrite, Canada...........	2:30.38
1988	Silke Hoerner, E. Germany..........	2:26.71*

200-Meter Individual Medley

1968	Claudia Kolb, U.S.................	2:24.7
1972	Shane Gould, Australia.............	2:23.07
1984	Tracy Caulkins, U.S...............	2:12.64
1988	Daniela Hunger, E. Germany.........	2:12.59*

400-Meter Individual Medley

1964	Donna de Varona, U.S.............	5:18.7
1968	Claudia Kolb, U.S.................	5:08.5
1972	Gail Neall, Australia...............	5:02.97
1976	Ulrike Tauber, E. Germany..........	4:42.77
1980	Petra Schneider, E. Germany........	4:36.29*
1984	Tracy Caulkins, U.S...............	4:39.24
1988	Janet Evans, U.S.................	4:37.76

100-Meter Butterfly

1956	Shelley Mann, U.S................	1:11.0
1960	Carolyn Schuler, U.S..............	1:09.5
1964	Sharon Stouder, U.S...............	1:04.7
1968	Lynn McClements, Australia.........	1:05.5
1972	Mayumi Aoki, Japan...............	1:03.34
1976	Kornelia Ender, E. Germany.........	1:00.13
1980	Caren Metschuck, E. Germany.......	1:00.42
1984	Mary T. Meagher, U.S..............	59.26
1988	Kristin Otto, E. Germany.............	59.00*

200-Meter Butterfly

1968	Ada Kok, Netherlands..............	2:24.7
1972	Karen Moe, U.S..................	2:15.57
1976	Andrea Pollack, E. Germany.........	2:11.41
1980	Ines Geissler, E. Germany..........	2:10.44
1984	Mary T. Meagher, U.S..............	2:06.90*
1988	Kathleen Nord, E. Germany.........	2:09.51

400-Meter Medley Relay

1960	United States...................	4:41.1
1960	United States...................	4:33.9
1968	United States...................	4:28.3

(continued)

1972	United States	4:20.75
1976	East Germany	4:07.95
1980	East Germany	4:06.67
1984	United States	4:08.34
1988	E. Germany	4:03.74*

400-Meter Freestyle Relay

1912	Great Britain	5:52.8
1920	United States	5:11.6
1924	United States	4:58.8
1928	United States	4:47.6
1932	United States	4:38.0
1936	Netherlands	4:36.0
1948	United States	4:29.2
1952	Hungary	4:24.4
1956	Australia	4:17.1
1960	United States	4:08.9
1964	United States	4:03.8
1968	United States	4:02.5
1972	United States	3:55.19
1976	United States	3:44.82
1980	East Germany	3:42.71
1984	United States	3:43.43
1988	E. Germany	3:40.63*

Springboard Diving — Points

1920	Aileen Riggin, U.S.	539.90
1924	Elizabeth Becker, U.S.	474.50
1928	Helen Meany, U.S.	78.62
1932	Georgia Coleman U.S.	87.52

1936	Marjorie Gestring, U.S.	89.27
1948	Victoria M. Draves, U.S.	108.74
1952	Patricia McCormick, U.S.	147.30
1956	Patricia McCormick, U.S.	142.36
1960	Ingrid Kramer, Germany	155.81
1964	Ingrid Engel-Kramer, Germany	145.00
1968	Sue Gossick, U.S.	150.77
1972	Micki King, U.S.	450.03
1976	Jenni Chandler, U.S.	506.19
1980	Irina Kalinina, USSR	725.91
1984	Sylvie Bernier, Canada	530.70
1988	Gao Min, China	580.23

Platform Diving — Points

1912	Greta Johansson, Sweden	39.90
1920	Stefani Fryland-Clausen, Denmark	34.60
1924	Caroline Smith, U.S.	33.20
1928	Elizabeth B. Pinkston, U.S.	31.60
1932	Dorothy Poynton, U.S.	40.26
1936	Dorothy Poynton Hill, U.S.	33.93
1948	Victoria M. Draves, U.S.	68.87
1952	Patricia McCormick, U.S.	79.37
1956	Patricia McCormick, U.S.	84.85
1960	Ingrid Kramer, Germany	91.28
1964	Lesley Bush, U.S.	99.80
1968	Milena Duchkova, Czech	109.59
1972	Ulrika Knape, Sweden	390.00
1976	Elena Vaytsekhouskaya, USSR	406.59
1980	Martina Jaschke, E. Germany	596.25
1984	Zhou Jihong, China	435.51
1988	Xu Yanmei, China	445.20

Boxing

Light Flyweight (106 lbs)
1968 Francisco Rodriguez, Venezuela
1972 Gyorgy Gedo, Hungary
1976 Jorge Hernandez, Cuba
1980 Shamil Sabyrov, USSR
1984 Paul Gonzalez, U.S.
1988 Ivailo Hristov, Bulgaria

Flyweight (112½ lbs)
1904 George Finnegan, U.S.
1920 William Di Gennara, U.S.
1924 Fidel LaBarba, U.S.
1928 Antal Kocsis, Hungary
1932 Istvan Enekes, Hungary
1936 Willi Kaiser, Germany
1948 Pascual Perez, Argentina
1952 Nathan Brooks, U.S.
1956 Terence Spinks, Great Britain
1960 Gyula Torok, Hungary
1964 Fernando Atzori, Italy
1968 Ricardo Delgado, Mexico
1972 Georgi Kostadinov, Bulgaria
1976 Leo Randolph, U.S.
1980 Peter Lessov, Bulgaria
1984 Steve McCrory, U.S.
1988 Kim Kwang Sun, S. Korea

Bantamweight (119½ lbs)
1904 Oliver Kirk, U.S.
1908 A Henry Thomas, Great Britain
1920 Clarence Walker, South Africa
1924 William Smith, South Africa
1928 Vittorio Tamagnini, Italy
1932 Horace Gwynne, Canada
1936 Ulderico Sergo, Italy
1948 Tibor Csik, Hungary
1952 Pentti Hamalainen, Finland
1956 Wolfgang Behrendt, E. Germany
1960 Oleg Grigoryev, USSR
1964 Takao Sakurai, Japan
1968 Valery Sokolov, USSR
1972 Orlando Martinez, Cuba
1976 Yong-Jo Gu, N. Korea
1980 Juan Hernandez, Cuba
1984 Maurizio Stecca, Italy
1988 Kennedy McKinney, U.S.

Featherweight (126 lbs)
1904 Oliver Kirk, U.S.
1908 Richard Gunn, Great Britain
1920 Paul Fritsch, France
1924 John Fields, U.S.
1928 Lambertus van Klaveren, Netherlands
1932 Carmelo Robledo, Argentina
1936 Oscar Casanovas, Argentina
1948 Ernesto Formenti, Italy
1952 Jan Zachara, Czech.
1956 Vladimir Safronov, USSR
1960 Francesco Musso, Italy
1964 Stanislav Stephashkin, USSR
1968 Antonin Roldan, Mexico
1972 Boris Kousnetsov, USSR
1976 Angel Herrera, Cuba
1980 Rudi Fink, E. Germany
1984 Meldrick Taylor, U.S.
1988 Giovanni Parisi, Italy

Lightweight (132 lbs)
1904 Harry Spanger, U.S.
1908 Frederick Grace, Great Britain
1920 Samuel Mosberg, U.S.
1924 Hans Nielsen, Denmark
1928 Carlo Orlandi, Italy
1932 Lawrence Stevens, South Africa
1936 Imre Harangi, Hungary
1948 Gerald Dreyer, South Africa
1952 Aureliano Bolognesi, Italy
1956 Richard McTaggart, Great Britain
1960 Kazimierz Pazdzior, Poland
1964 Jozef Grudzien, Poland
1968 Ronald Harris, U.S.
1972 Jan Szczepanski, Poland
1976 Howard Davis, U.S.
1980 Angel Herrera, Cuba
1984 Pernell Whitaker, U.S.
1988 Andreas Zuelow, E. Germany

Light Welterweight (140 lbs)
1952 Charles Adkins, U.S.
1956 Vladimir Yengibaryan, USSR
1960 Bohumil Nemecek, Czech.
1964 Jerzy Kulej, Poland
1968 Jerzy Kulej, Poland
1972 Ray Seales, U.S.
1976 Ray Leonard, U.S.
1980 Patrizio Oliva, Italy
1984 Jerry Page, U.S.
1988 Viatcheslav Janovski, USSR

Welterweight (148 lbs)
1904 Albert Young, U.S.
1920 Albert Schneider, Canada
1924 Jean Delarge, Belgium
1928 Edward Morgan, New Zealand
1932 Edward Flynn, U.S.
1936 Sten Suvio, Finland
1948 Julius Torma, Czech.
1952 Zygmunt Chychla, Poland
1956 Nicolae Linca, Romania
1960 Giovanni Benvenuti, Italy
1964 Marian Kasprzyk, Poland

Welterweight (continued)
1968 Manfred Wolke, E. Germany
1972 Emilio Correa, Cuba
1976 Jochen Bachfeld, E. Germany
1980 Andres Aldama, Cuba
1984 Mark Breland, U.S.
1988 Robert Wangila, Kenya

Light Middleweight (156 lbs)
1952 Laszlo Papp, Hungary
1956 Laszlo Papp, Hungary
1960 Wilbert McClure, U.S.
1964 Boris Lagutin, USSR
1968 Boris Lagutin, USSR
1972 Dieter Kottysch, W. Germany
1976 Jerzy Rybicki, Poland
1980 Armando Martinez, Cuba
1984 Frank Tate, U.S.
1988 Park Si Hun, S. Korea

Middleweight (165½ lbs)
1904 Charles Mayer, U.S.
1908 John Douglas, Great Britain
1920 Harry Mallin, Great Britain
1924 Harry Mallin, Great Britain
1928 Piero Toscani, Italy
1932 Carmen Barth, U.S.
1936 Jean Despeaux, France
1948 Laszlo Papp, Hungary
1952 Floyd Patterson, U.S.
1956 Gennady Schatkov, USSR
1960 Edward Crook, U.S.
1964 Valery Popenchenko, USSR
1968 Christopher Finnegan, Great Britain
1972 Vyacheslav Lemechev, USSR
1976 Michael Spinks, U.S.
1980 Jose Gomez, Cuba
1984 Joon-Sup Shin, S. Korea
1988 Henry Maske, E. Germany

Light Heavyweight (179 lbs)
1920 Edward Eagan, U.S.
1924 Harry Mitchell, Great Britain
1928 Victor Avendano, Argentina
1932 David Carstens, South Africa
1936 Roger Michelot, France
1948 George Hunter, South Africa
1952 Norvel Lee, U.S.
1956 James Boyd, U.S.
1960 Cassius Clay, U.S.
1964 Cosimo Pinto, Italy
1968 Dan Poznyak, USSR
1972 Mate Parlov, Yugoslavia
1976 Leon Spinks, U.S.
1980 Slobodan Kacar, Yugoslavia
1984 Anton Josipovic, Yugoslavia

1988	Andrew Maynard, U.S.	1920	Ronald Rawson, Great Britain	1960	Franco De Piccoli, Italy
	Heavyweight (200½ lbs)	1924	Otto von Porat, Norway	1964	Joe Frazier, U.S.
1984	Henry Tillman, U.S.	1928	Arturo Rodriguez Jurado,	1968	George Foreman, U.S.
1988	Ray Mercer, U.S.		Argentina	1972	Teofilo Stevenson, Cuba
	Super Heavyweight (Unlimited)	1932	Santiago Lovell, Argentina	1976	Teofilo Stevenson, Cuba
	(known as heavyweight from 1904-1980)	1936	Herbert Runge, Germany	1980	Teofilo Stevenson, Cuba
1904	Samuel Berger, U.S.	1948	Rafael Inglesias, Argentina	1984	Tyrell Biggs, U.S.
1908	Albert Oldham, Great Britain	1952	H. Edward Sanders, U.S.	1988	Lennox Lewis, Canada
		1956	T. Peter Rademacher, U.S.		

24th Summer Olympics

Seoul, S. Korea, Sept. 17-24, 1988

A record 13,674 athletes gathered in Seoul, South Korea in September for 16 days to compete in the Games of the XXIV Olympiad. The athletes represented 161 nations, 21 more than had participated in any previous Olympics, and competed for 237 gold medals in 26 sports at a cost of $3.1 billion to the South Korean government. The Soviet Union won the most medals, East Germany finished second, and the United States third.

The 1988 games will be remembered mostly for the long-awaited showdown in the 100-meter race between Ben Johnson, the Canadian sprinter and world record holder, and his archrival, Carl Lewis of the United States. Johnson won the race in world record time. Three days later, Johnson was stripped of his gold medal and world record because he had tested positive for the anabolic steroid stanozolol. Two weightlifters from Bulgaria were also stripped of their gold medals for taking drugs. In all, 10 of the athletes tested were disqualified by the International Olympic Committee for using banned substances.

Sports fans in the United States had much to cheer about. Swimmers Matt Biondi won 5 gold medals and Janet Evans won gold in three events. Greg Louganis repeated his 1984 performance by winning the springboard and platform diving events. Florence Griffith-Joyner won the 100 and 200-meter races while her sister-in-law, Jackie Joyner-Kersee was the Heptathlon and long jump champion. The U.S. men won the volleyball gold medal. The biggest disappointment was the defeat of the men's basketball team by the Soviet Union, only the second loss in history for a U.S. Olympic basketball team.

Final Medal Standings

	Gold	Silver	Bronze	Total		Gold	Silver	Bronze	Total
					Spain	1	1	2	4
USSR	55	31	46	132	Switzerland	0	2	2	4
East Germany	37	35	30	102	Morocco	1	0	2	3
United States	36	31	27	94	Turkey	1	1	0	2
West Germany	11	14	15	40	Jamaica	0	2	0	2
Bulgaria	10	12	13	35	Argentina	0	1	1	2
South Korea	12	10	11	33	Belgium	0	0	2	2
China	5	11	12	28	Mexico	0	0	2	2
Romania.	7	11	6	24	Austria.	1	0	0	1
Great Britain	5	10	9	24	Portugal	1	0	0	1
Hungary	11	6	6	23	Suriname	1	0	0	1
France	6	4	6	16	Chile	0	1	0	1
Poland	2	5	9	16	Costa Rica	0	1	0	1
Italy	6	4	4	14	Indonesia	0	1	0	1
Japan	4	3	7	14	Iran.	0	1	0	1
Australia.	3	6	5	14	Netherlands Antilles . . .	0	1	0	1
New Zealand	3	2	8	13	Peru	0	1	0	1
Yugoslavia	3	4	5	12	Senegal	0	1	0	1
Sweden	0	4	7	11	Virgin Islands	0	1	0	1
Canada	3	2	5	10	Columbia	0	0	1	1
Kenya	5	2	2	9	Djibouti	0	0	1	1
Netherlands.	2	2	5	9	Greece	0	0	1	1
Czechoslovakia	3	3	2	8	Mongolia	0	0	1	1
Brazil	1	2	3	6	Pakistan	0	0	1	1
Norway	2	3	0	5	Philippines.	0	0	1	1
Denmark	2	1	1	4	Thailand	0	0	1	1
Finland.	1	1	2	4					

Olympic Information

Symbol: Five rings or circles, linked together to represent the sporting friendship of all peoples. The rings also symbolize the 5 continents—Europe, Asia, Africa, Australia, and America. Each ring is a different color—blue, yellow, black, green, and red.

Flag: The symbol of the 5 rings on a plain white background.

Motto: "Citius, Altius, Fortius." Latin meaning "faster, higher, braver," or the modern interpretation "swifter, higher, stronger". The motto was coined by Father Didon, a French educator, in 1895.

Creed: "The most important thing in the Olympic Games is not to win but to take part, just as the most important thing in life is not the triumph but the struggle. The essential thing is not to have conquered but to have fought well."

Oath: An athlete of the host country recites the following at the opening ceremony. "In the name of all competitors I promise that we will take part in these Olympic Games, respecting and abiding by the rules which govern them, in the true spirit of sportsmanship for the glory of sport and the honor of our teams." Both the oath and the creed were composed by Pierre de Coubertin, the founder of the modern Games.

Flame: Symbolizes the continuity between the ancient and modern Games. The modern version of the flame was adopted in 1936. The torch used to kindle the flame is first lit by the sun's rays at Olympia, Greece, and then carried to the site of the Games by relays of runners. Ships and planes are used when necessary.

Other Summer Olympics Gold Medalists in 1988

Archery

Men—Jay Barrs, U.S.
Men's Team—S. Korea.
Women—Kim Soo-Nyung, S. Korea.
Women's Team—S. Korea.

Basketball

Men—1. USSR; 2. Yugoslavia; 3. U.S.
Women—1. U.S.; 2. Yugoslavia; 3. USSR.

Canoeing—Men

K1-500M—Zsolt Gyulay, Hungary.
K2-500M—Ian Ferguson, Paul MacDonald, New Zealand.
K1-1,000M—Greg Barton, U.S.
K2-1,000M—Greg Barton, N. Bellingham, U.S.
K4-1,000m—Hungary.
C1-500M—Olaf Heukrodt, E. Germany.
C2-500M—Victor Reneiski, Nikolai Jouravski, USSR.
C1-1,000M—Ivan Klementiev, USSR.
C2-1,000M—Victor Reneiski, Nikolai Jouravski, USSR.

Canoeing—Women

K1-500M—Vania Guecheva, Bulgaria.
K2-500M—Birgit Schmidt, Anke Nothnagel, E. Germany.
K4-500M—E. Germany.

Cycling

4,000 Individual Pursuit—Gintaoutas Umaras, USSR.
Sprint—Lutz Hesslich, E. Germany.
4,000 Team Pursuit—USSR.
50 Km Points Race—Dan Forst, Denmark.
1K Time Trial—Alexandr Kiritchenko, USSR.
100K Team Time Trial—E. Germany.
Road Race—Olaf Ludwig, E. Germany.
Women's Sprint—Erika Saloumiae, USSR.
Women's Road Race—Monique Knol, Netherlands.

Diving

Women's Platform—Xu Yanmei, China.
Women's Springboard—Gao Min, China.
Men's Springboard—Greg Louganis, U.S.
Men's Platform—Greg Louganis, U.S.

Equestrian

Individual 3-Day Event—Mark Todd, New Zealand.
Team 3-Day Event—W. Germany.
Individual Dressage—Nicole Uphoff, W. Germany.
Team Dressage—W. Germany.
Individual Jumping—Pierre Durand, France.
Team Jumping—W. Germany.

Fencing—Men

Foil Individual—Stefano Cerioni, Italy.
Team Foil—USSR.
Sabre Individual—Jean-Francois Lamour, France.
Team Sabre—Hungary.
Epée Individual—Arnd Schmitt, W. Germany.
Epée Team—France.

Fencing—Women

Foil Individual—Anja Fichtel, W. Germany.
Team Foil—W. Germany.

Field Hockey

Men—1. Great Britain; 2. W. Germany; 3. Netherlands.
Women—1. Australia; 2. S. Korea; 3. Netherlands.

Gymnastics—Men

Team—USSR.
All Around—Vladimir Artemov, USSR.
Floor Exercise—Sergei Kharikov, USSR.
Pommel Horse—Dimitri Bilozerchev, USSR.
Rings—Dimitri Bilozerchev, USSR.
Vault—Lou Yun, China.

Parallel Bars—Vladimir Artemov, USSR.
Horizontal Bar—Vladimir Artemov, USSR.

Gymnastics—Women

Team—USSR.
All-Around—Yelena Shoushunova, USSR.
Vault—Svetlana Boguinskaya, USSR.
Uneven Parallel Bars—Daniela Silivas, Romania.
Balance Beam—Daniela Silivas, Romania.
Floor Exercise—Daniela Silivas, Romania.

Rhythmic Gymnastics

Marina Lobatch, USSR.

Judo

133 Pounds—Kim Jae Yup, S. Korea.
143 Pounds—Lee Kyung-Keun, S. Korea.
156 Pounds—Marc Alexandre, France.
172 Pounds—Waldemar Legien, Poland.
189 Pounds—Peter Seisenbacher, Austria.
209 Pounds—Aurelio Miguel, Brazil.
Over 209 Pounds—Hitoshi Saito, Japan.

Modern Pentathlon

Individual—Janos Martinek, Hungary.
Team—Hungary.

Rowing—Men

Single Sculls—Tomas Lange, E. Germany.
Double Sculls—Netherlands.
Coxless Pairs—Great Britain.
Coxed Pairs—Italy.
Coxed Fours—E. Germany.
Coxless Fours—E. Germany.
Quadruple Sculls—Italy.
Eights—W. Germany.

Rowing—Women

Single Sculls—Jutta Behrendt, E. Germany.
Double Sculls—E. Germany.
Coxless Pairs—Romania.
Coxless Fours—E. Germany.
Quadruple Sculls—E. Germany.
Eights—E. Germany.

Shooting—Men

Smallbore Standard Rifle—Miroslav Varga, Czechoslovakia.
Smallbore Free Rifle—Malcolm Cooper, Great Britain.
Free Pistol—Sorin Babii, Romania.
Air Rifle—Goran Maksimovic, Yugoslavia.
Rapid-Fire Pistol—Afanasi Kouzmine, USSR.
Running Target—Tor Heiestad, Norway.
Air Pistol—Taniou Kiruakov, Bulgaria.

Shooting—Women

Air Rifle—Irina Cilova, USSR.
Sport Pistol—Nino Saloukvadze, USSR.
Air Pistol—Jasna Sekaric, Yugoslavia.
Smallbore Standard Rifle—Silvia Sperber, W. Germany.

Shooting—Mixed

Skeet—Axel Wegner, E. Germany.
Trap—Dmitri Monakov, USSR.

Soccer

Championship—1. USSR; 2. Brazil; 3. W. Germany.

Synchronized Swimming

Solo—Carolyn Waldo, Canada.
Duet—Michelle Cameron, Carolyn Waldo, Canada.

Table Tennis—Men

Singles—Yoo Nam Kyu, S. Korea.

Doubles—Chen Longcan, Wei Qingquang, China.

Table Tennis—Women

Singles—Chen Jing, China.
Doubles—Hyun Jung Hwa, Yang Young Ja, S. Korea.

Team Handball

Men—1. USSR. S. Korea; 3. Yugoslavia.
Women—1. S. Korea. Norway; 3. USSR.

Tennis—Men

Singles—Miloslav Mecir, Czech.
Doubles—Ken Flach, Robert Seguso, U.S.

Tennis—Women

Singles—Steffi Graf, W. Germany.
Doubles—Pam Shriver, Zina Garrison, U.S.

Volleyball

Men—1. U.S.; 2. USSR; 3. Argentina.
Women—1. USSR; 2. Peru; 3. China.

Water Polo

Championship—1. Yugoslavia; 2. U.S.; 3. USSR.

Weight Lifting

115 Pounds—Sevdalin Marinov, Bulgaria.
123 Pounds—Oxen Mirzoian, USSR.
132 Pounds—Naim Suleymanoglu, Turkey.
149 Pounds—Joachim Kunz, E. Germany.
165 Pounds—Borislav Guidikov, Bulgaria.
182 Pounds—Israil Arsamakov, USSR.
198 Pounds—Anatoli Khrapatyi, USSR.

220 Pounds—Pavel Kouzntsov, USSR.
242 Pounds—Yuri Zakharevitch, USSR.
Over 242 Pounds—Aleksandr Kourlovich, USSR.

Wrestling—Greco-Roman

106 Pounds—Vicenzo Maenza, Italy.
115 Pounds—Jon Ronningen, Norway.
126 Pounds—Andras Sike, Hungary.
137 Pounds—Kamandar Madjidov, USSR.
150 Pounds—Levon Djoulfalakian, USSR.
163 Pounds—Kim Young Nam, S. Korea.
181 Pounds—Mikhail Mamiachvili, USSR.
198 Pounds—Atanas Komchev, Bulgaria.
220 Pounds—Andrzej Wronski, Poland.
286 Pounds—Alexander Kareline, USSR.

Wrestling—Freestyle

106 Pounds—Takashi Kobayashi, Japan.
115 Pounds—Mitsuru Sato, Japan.
126 Pounds—Serguei Beloglazov, USSR.
137 Pounds—John Smith, U.S.
150 Pounds—Arsen Fadzaev, USSR.
163 Pounds—Ken Monday, U.S.
181 Pounds—Han Myang-Woo, S. Korea.
198 Pounds—Makharbek Khadartsev, USSR.
220 Pounds—Vasile Puscasu, Romania.
286 Pounds—David Gobedjichvili, USSR.

Yachting

Board Sailing—Bruce Kendall, New Zealand.
Finn—José Luis Doreste, Spain.
Flying Dutchman—Denmark.
Soling—E. Germany.
Star—Great Britain.
Tornado—France.
Men's 470—France.
Women's 470—U.S.

Winter Olympic Games Champions, 1924-1988

Sites of Games

1924 Chamonix, France
1928 St. Moritz, Switzerland
1932 Lake Placid, N.Y.
1936 Garmisch-Partenkirchen, Germany
1948 St. Moritz, Switzerland
1952 Oslo, Norway

1956 Cortina d'Ampezzo, Italy
1960 Squaw Valley, Cal.
1964 Innsbruck, Austria
1968 Grenoble, France
1972 Sapporo, Japan

1976 Innsbruck, Austria
1980 Lake Placid, N.Y.
1984 Sarajevo, Yugoslavia
1988 Calgary, Alberta
1992 Albertville, France (scheduled)

Bobsledding
4-Man Bob

	(Driver in parentheses)	Time
1924	Switzerland (Eduard Scherrer)	5:45.54
1928	United States (William Fiske) (5-man)	3:20.50
1932	United States (William Fiske)	7:53.68
1936	Switzerland (Pierre Musy)	5:19.85
1948	United States (Francis Tyler)	5:20.10
1952	Germany (Andreas Ostler)	5:07.84
1956	Switzerland (Franz Kapus)	5:10.44
1964	Canada (Victor Emery)	4:14.46
1968	Italy (Eugenio Monti) (2 races)	2:17.39
1972	Switzerland (Jean Wicki)	4:43.07
1976	E. Germany (Meinhard Nehmer)	3:40.43
1980	E. Germany (Meinhard Nehmer)	3:59.92
1984	E. Germany (Wolfgang Hoppe)	3:20.22
1988	Switzerland (Ekkehard Fasser)	3:47.51

2-Man Bob

		Time
1932	United States (Hubert Stevens)	8:14.74
1936	United States (Ivan Brown)	5:29.29
1948	Switzerland (F. Endrich)	5:29.20
1952	Germany (Andreas Ostler)	5:24.54
1956	Italy (Dalla Costa)	5:30.14
1964	Great Britain (Anthony Nash)	4:21.90
1968	Italy (Eugenio Monti)	4:41.54
1972	W. Germany (Wolfgang Zimmerer)	4:57.07
1976	E. Germany (Meinhard Nehmer)	3:44.42
1980	Switzerland (Erich Schaerer)	4:09.36
1984	E.Germany (Wolfgang Hoppe)	3:25.56
1988	USSR (Janis Kipours)	3:54.19

Luge
Men's Singles

		Time
1964	Thomas Keohler, Germany	3:26.77
1968	Manfred Schmid, Austria	2:52.48
1972	Wolfgang Scheidel, E. Germany	3:27.58
1976	Detlef Guenther, E. Germany	3:27.688
1980	Bernhard Glass, E. Germany	2:54.796
1984	Paul Hildgartner, Italy	3:04.258
1988	Jens Mueller, E. Germany	3:05.548

Men's Pairs

		Time
1964	Austria	1:41.62
1968	E. Germany	1:35.85
1972	Italy, E. Germany (tie)	1:28.35
1976	E. Germany	1:25.604
1980	E. Germany	1:19.331
1984	W. Germany	1:23.620
1988	E. Germany	1:31.940

Women's Singles

		Time
1964	Ortun Enderlein, Germany	3:24.67
1968	Erica Lechner, Italy	2:28.66
1972	Anna M. Muller, E. Germany	2:59.18
1976	Margit Schumann, E. Germany	2:50.621
1980	Vera Zozulya, USSR	2:36.537
1984	Steffi Martin, E. Germany	2:46.570
1988	Steffi Walter, E. Germany	3:03.973

Biathlon

10 Kilometers

		Time
1980	Frank Ullrich, E. Germany	32:10.69
1984	Eirik Kvalfoss, Norway	30:53.80
1988	Frank-Peter Roetsch, E. Germany	25:08.10

20 Kilometers

		Time
1960	Klas Lestander, Sweden	1:33:21.6
1964	Vladimir Melanin, USSR	1:20:26.8
1968	Magnar Solberg, Norway	1:13:45.9
1972	Magnar Solberg, Norway	1:15:55.50
1976	Nikolai Kruglov, USSR	1:14:12.26
1980	Anatoly Aljabiev, USSR	1:08:16.31
1984	Peter Angerer, W. Germany	1:11:52.7
1988	Frank-Peter Roetsch, E. Germany	0:56:33.33

30-Kilometer Relay

		Time
1968	USSR, Norway, Sweden	2:13:02.4
1972	USSR, Finland, E. Germany	1:51:44.92
1976	USSR, Finland, E. Germany	1:57:55.64
1980	USSR, E. Germany, W. Germany (30 km.)	1:34:03.27
1984	USSR, Norway, W. Germany	1:38:51.70
1988	USSR, W. Germany, Italy	1:22:30.00

Figure Skating

Men's Singles

1908	Ulrich Salchow, Sweden
1920	Gillis Grafstrom, Sweden
1924	Gillis Grafstrom, Sweden
1928	Gillis Grafstrom, Sweden
1932	Karl Schaefer, Austria
1936	Karl Schaefer, Austria
1948	Richard Button, U.S.
1952	Richard Button, U.S.
1956	Hayes Alan Jenkins, U.S.
1960	David W. Jenkins, U.S.
1964	Manfred Schnelldorfer, Germany
1968	Wolfgang Schwartz, Austria
1972	Ondrej Nepela, Czechoslovakia
1976	John Curry, Great Britain
1980	Robin Cousins, Great Britain
1984	Scott Hamilton, U.S.
1988	Brian Boitano, U.S.

Women's Singles

1908	Madge Syers, Great Britain
1920	Magda Julin-Mauroy, Sweden
1924	Herma von Szabo-Planck, Austria
1928	Sonja Henie, Norway
1932	Sonja Henie, Norway
1936	Sonja Henie, Norway
1948	Barbara Ann Scott, Canada
1952	Jeanette Altwegg, Great Britain
1956	Tenley Albright, U.S.
1960	Carol Heiss, U.S.
1964	Sjoukje Dijkstra, Netherlands
1968	Peggy Fleming, U.S.
1972	Beatrix Schuba, Austria
1976	Dorothy Hamill, U.S.
1980	Anett Poetzsch, E. Germany
1984	Katarina Witt, E. Germany
1988	Katarina Witt, E. Germany

Pairs

1908	Anna Hubler & Heinrich Burger, Germany
1920	Ludovika & Walter Jakobsson, Finland
1924	Helene Engelman & Alfred Berger, Austria
1928	Andree Joly & Pierre Brunet, France
1932	Andree Joly & Pierre Brunet, France
1936	Maxi Herber & Ernst Baier, Germany
1948	Micheline Lannoy & Pierre Baugniet, Belgium
1952	Ria and Paul Falk, Germany
1956	Elisabeth Schwartz & Kurt Oppelt, Austria
1960	Barbara Wagner & Robert Paul, Canada
1964	Ludmila Beloussova & Oleg Protopopov, USSR
1968	Ludmila Beloussova & Oleg Protopopov, USSR
1972	Irina Rodnina & Alexei Ulanov, USSR
1976	Irina Rodnina & Aleksandr Zaitzev, USSR
1980	Irina Rodnina & Aleksandr Zaitzev, USSR
1984	Elena Valova & Oleg Vassiliev, USSR
1988	Ekaterina Gordeeva & Sergei Grinkov, USSR

Ice Dancing

1976	Ludmila Pakhomova & Aleksandr Gorschkov, USSR
1980	Natalya Linichuk & Gennadi Karponosov, USSR
1984	Jayne Torvill & Christopher Dean, Great Britain
1988	Natalia Bestemianova & Andrei Bukin, USSR

Ice Hockey

1920	Canada, U.S., Czechoslovakia
1924	Canada, U.S., Great Britain
1928	Canada, Sweden, Switzerland
1932	Canada, U.S., Germany
1936	Great Britain, Canada, U.S.
1948	Canada, Czechoslovakia, Switzerland
1952	Canada, U.S., Sweden
1956	USSR, U.S., Canada
1960	U.S., Canada, USSR
1964	USSR, Sweden, Czechoslovakia
1968	USSR, Czechoslovakia, Canada
1972	USSR, U.S., Czechoslovakia
1976	USSR, Czechoslovakia, W. Germany
1980	U.S., USSR, Sweden
1984	USSR, Czechoslovakia, Sweden
1988	USSR, Finland, Sweden

Alpine Skiing

Men's Downhill

		Time
1948	Henri Oreiller, France	2:55.0
1952	Zeno Colo, Italy	2:30.8
1956	Anton Sailer, Austria	2:52.2
1960	Jean Vuarnet, France	2:06.0
1964	Egon Zimmermann, Austria	2:18.16
1968	Jean-Claude Killy, France	1:59.85
1972	Bernhard Russi, Switzerland	1:51.43
1976	Franz Klammer, Austria	1:45.73
1980	Leonhard Stock, Austria	1:45.50
1984	Bill Johnson, U.S.	1:45:59
1988	Pirmin Zurbriggen, Switzerland	1:59.63

Men's Super Giant Slalom

		Time
1988	Franck Piccard, France	1:39.66

Men's Giant Slalom

		Time
1952	Stein Eriksen, Norway	2:25.0
1956	Anton Sailer, Austria	3:00.1
1960	Roger Staub, Switzerland	1:48.3
1964	Francois Bonlieu, France	1:46.71
1968	Jean-Claude Killy, France	3:29.28
1972	Gustavo Thoeni, Italy	3:09.62
1976	Heini Hemmi, Switzerland	3:26.97
1980	Ingemar Stenmark, Sweden	2:40.74
1984	Max Julen, Switzerland	2:41.18
1988	Alberto Tomba, Italy	2:06:37

Men's Slalom

		Time
1948	Edi Reinalter, Switzerland	2:10.3
1952	Othmar Schneider, Austria	2:00.0
1956	Anton Sailer, Austria	194.7 pts.
1960	Ernst Hinterseer, Austria	2:08.9
1964	Josef Stiegler, Austria	2:11.13
1968	Jean-Claude Killy, France	1:39.73
1972	Francisco Fernandez Ochoa, Spain	1:49.27
1976	Piero Gros, Italy	2:03.29
1980	Ingemar Stenmark, Sweden	1:44.26
1984	Phil Mahre, U.S.	1:39.41
1988	Alberto Tomba	1:39.47

Men's Combined

		Points
1988	Hubert Strolz, Austria	36.55

Women's Downhill

		Time
1948	Hedi Schlunegger, Switzerland	2:28.3
1952	Trude Jochum-Beiser, Austria	1:47.1
1956	Madeleine Berthod, Switzerland	1:40.7
1960	Heidi Biebl, Germany	1:37.6
1964	Christl Haas, Austria	1:55.39
1968	Olga Pall, Austria	1:40.87
1972	Marie Therese Nadig, Switzerland	1:36.68
1976	Rosi Mittermaier, W. Germany	1:46.16
1980	Annemarie Proell Moser, Austria	1:37.52
1984	Michela Figini, Switzerland	1:13.36
1988	Marina Kiehl, W. Germany	1:25.86

Women's Super Giant Slalom

	Time
1988 Sigrid Wolf, Austria	1:19.03

Women's Giant Slalom

	Time
1952 Andrea Mead Lawrence, U.S.	2:06.8
1956 Ossi Reichert, Germany	1:56.5
1960 Yvonne Ruegg, Switzerland	1:39.9
1964 Marielle Goitschel, France	1:52.24
1968 Nancy Greene, Canada	1:51.97
1972 Marie Therese Nadig, Switzerland	1:29.90
1976 Kathy Kreiner, Canada	1:29.13
1980 Hanni Wenzel, Liechtenstein (2 runs)	2:41.66
1984 Debbie Armstrong, U.S.	2:20.98
1988 Vreni Schneider, Switzerland	2:06.49

Women's Slalom

	Time
1948 Gretchen Fraser, U.S.	1:57.2
1952 Andrea Mead Lawrence, U.S.	2:10.6
1956 Renee Colliard, Switzerland	112.3 pts.
1960 Anne Heggtveigt, Canada	1:49.6
1964 Christine Goitschel, France	1:29.86
1968 Marielle Goitschel, France	1:25.86
1972 Barbara Cochran, U.S.	1:31.24
1976 Rosi Mittermaier, W. Germany	1:30.54
1980 Hanni Wenzel, Liechtenstein	1:25.09
1984 Paoletta Magoni, Italy	1:36.47
1988 Vreni Schneider, Switzerland	1:36.69

Women's Combined

	Points
1988 Anita Wachter, Austria	29.25

Nordic Skiing

Men's Cross-Country Events

15 kilometers (9.3 miles)

	Time
1924 Thorleif Haug, Norway	1:14:31
1928 Johan Grottumsbraaten, Norway	1:37:01
1932 Sven Utterstrom, Sweden	1:23:07
1936 Erik-August Larsson, Sweden	1:14:38
1948 Martin Lundstrom, Sweden	1:13:50
1952 Hallgeir Brenden, Norway	1:01:34
1956 Hallgeir Brenden, Norway	49:39.0
1960 Haakon Brusveen, Norway	51:55.5
1964 Eero Maentyranta, Finland	50:54.1
1968 Harald Groenningen, Norway	47:54.2
1972 Sven-Ake Lundback, Sweden	45:28.24
1976 Nikolai Balukov, USSR	43:58.47
1980 Thomas Wassberg, Sweden	41:57.63
1984 Gunde Svan, Sweden	41:25.6
1988 Mikhail Deviatiarov, USSR	41:18.9

(Note: approx. 18-km. course 1924-1952)

30 kilometers (18.6 miles)

	Time
1956 Veikko Hakulinen, Finland	1:44:06.0
1960 Sixten Jernberg, Sweden	1:51:03.9
1964 Eero Maentyranta, Finland	1:30:50.7
1968 Franco Nones, Italy	1:35:39.2
1972 Vyacheslav Vedenine, USSR	1:36:31.15
1976 Sergei Saveliev, USSR	1:30:29.38
1980 Nikolai Zimyatov, USSR	1:27:02.80
1984 Nikolai Zimyatov, USSR	1:28:56.3
1988 Aleksei Prokourorov, USSR	1:24:26.3

50 kilometers (31.2 miles)

	Time
1924 Thorleif Haug, Norway	3:44:32.0
1928 Per Erik Hedlund, Sweden	4:52:03.0
1932 Veli Saarinen, Finland	4:28:00.0
1936 Elis Wiklund, Sweden	3:30:11.0
1948 Nils Karlsson, Sweden	3:47:48.0
1952 Veikko Hakulinen, Finland	3:33:33.0
1956 Sixten Jernberg, Sweden	2:50:27.0
1960 Kalevi Hamalainen, Finland	2:59:06.3
1964 Sixten Jernberg, Sweden	2:43:52.6
1968 Ole Ellefsaeter, Norway	2:28:45.8
1972 Paal Tyldum, Norway	2:43:14.75
1976 Ivar Formo, Norway	2:37:30.05
1980 Nikolai Zimyatov, USSR	2:27:24.60
1984 Thomas Wassberg, Sweden	2:15:55.8
1988 Gunde Svan, Sweden	2:04:30.9

40-km. Relay

	Time
1936 Finland, Norway, Sweden	2:41:33.0
1948 Sweden, Finland, Norway	2:32:08.0
1952 Finland, Norway, Sweden	2:20:16.0
1956 USSR, Finland, Sweden	2:15:30.0
1960 Finland, Norway, USSR	2:18:45.6
1964 Sweden, Finland, USSR	2:18:34.6

Combined Cross-Country & Jumping

	Points
1924 Thorleif Haug, Norway	453.800
1928 Johan Grottumsbraaten, Norway	427.800
1932 Johan Grottumsbraaten, Norway	446.000
1936 Oddbjorn Hagen, Norway	430.300
1948 Heikki Hasu, Finland	448.800
1952 Simon Slattvik, Norway	451.621
1956 Sverre Stenersen, Norway	455.000
1960 Georg Thoma, Germany	457.952
1964 Tormod Knutsen, Norway	469.280
1968 Franz Keller, W. Germany	449.040
1972 Ulrich Wehling, E. Germany	413.340
1976 Ulrich Wehling, E. Germany	423.390
1980 Ulrich Wehling, E. Germany	432.200
1984 Tom Sandberg, Norway	422.595
1988 Hippolyt Kempf, Switzerland	235.8

Men's Team Ski Jumping (90 meters)

	Points
1988 Finland, Yugoslavia, Norway	634.400

Ski Jumping (90 meters)

	Points
1924 Jacob Thams, Norway	227.5
1928 Alfred Andersen, Norway	230.5
1932 Birger Ruud, Norway	228.1
1936 Birger Ruud, Norway	232.0
1948 Petter Hugsted, Norway	228.1
1952 Arnfinn Bergmann, Norway	226.0
1956 Antti Hyvarinen, Finland	227.0
1960 Helmut Recknagel, Germany	227.2
1964 Toralf Engan, Norway	230.7
1968 Vladimir Beloussov, USSR	231.3
1972 Wojiech Fortuna, Poland	219.9
1976 Karl Schnabl, Austria	234.8
1980 Jouko Tormanen, Finland	271.0
1984 Matti Nykaenen, Finland	231.2
1988 Matti Nykaenen, Finland	224.0

Men's Team Combined

	Time
1988 W. Germany, Switzerland, Austria	1:20:46.0

Ski Jumping (70 meters)

	Points
1964 Veikko Kankkonen, Finland	229.9
1968 Jiri Raska, Czechoslovakia	216.5
1972 Yukio Kasaya, Japan	244.2
1976 Hans Aschenbach, E. Germany	252.0
1980 Anton Innauer, Austria	266.3
1984 Jens Weissflog, E. Germany	215.2
1988 Matti Nykaenen, Finland	229.1

Women's Events

5 kilometers (approx. 3.1 miles)

	Time
1964 Claudia Boyarskikh, USSR	17:50.5
1968 Toini Gustafsson, Sweden	16:45.2
1972 Galina Koulacova, USSR	17:00.50
1976 Helena Takalo, Finland	15:48.69
1980 Raisa Smetanina, USSR	15:06.92
1984 Marja-Liisa Haemaelainen, Finland	17:04.0
1988 Marjo Matikainen, Finland	15:04.0

10 kilometers

	Time
1952 Lydia Wideman, Finland	41:40.0
1956 Lyubov Kosyreva, USSR	38:11.0
1960 Maria Gusakova, USSR	39:46.6
1964 Claudia Boyarskikh, USSR	40:24.3
1968 Toini Gustafsson, Sweden	36:46.5
1972 Galina Koulacova, USSR	34:17.82
1976 Raisa Smetanina, USSR	30:13.41
1980 Barbara Petzold, E. Germany	30:31.54
1984 Marja-Liisa Haemaelainen, Finland	31:44.2
1988 Vida Ventsene, USSR	30:08.3

20 kilometers

	Time
1984 Marja-Liisa Haemaelainen, Finland	1:01:45.0
1988 Tamara Tikhonova, USSR	55:53.6

20-km. Relay

	Time
1956 Finland, USSR, Sweden (15 km.)	1:09:01.0
1960 Sweden, USSR, Finland (15 km.)	1:04:21.4
1964 USSR, Sweden, Finland (15 km.)	59:20.2
1968 Norway, Sweden, USSR (15 km.)	57:30.0

(continued)

1972 USSR, Finland, Norway (15 km.) 48:46.15
1976 USSR, Finland, E. Germany . . . . . ? . . 1:07:49.75
1980 E. Germany, USSR, Norway 1:02:11.10
1984 Norway, Czechoslovakia, Finland 1:06:49.70
1988 USSR, Norway, Finland 59:51.1

Speed Skating

Men's 500 meters	Time
1924 Charles Jewtraw, U.S.	0:44.0
1928 Thunberg, Finland & Evensen, Norway (tie)	0:43.4
1932 John A. Shea, U.S.	0:43.4
1936 Ivar Ballangrud, Norway	0:43.4
1948 Finn Helgesen, Norway	0:43.1
1952 Kenneth Henry, U.S.	0:43.2
1956 Evgeniy Grishin, USSR	0:40.2
1960 Evgeniy Grishin, USSR	0:40.2
1964 Terry McDermott, U.S.	0:40.1
1968 Erhard Keller, W. Germany	0:40.3
1972 Erhard Keller, W. Germany	0:39.44
1976 Evgeny Kulikov, USSR	0:39.17
1980 Eric Heiden, U.S.	0:38.03
1984 Sergei Fokichev, USSR	0:38.19
1988 Jens-Uwe Mey, E. Germany	0:36.45

Men's 1,000 meters	Time
1976 Peter Mueller, U.S.	1:19.32
1980 Eric Heiden, U.S.	1:15.18
1984 Gaetan Boucher, Canada	1:15.80
1988 Nikolai Guiliaev, USSR	1:13.03

Men's 1,500 meters	Time
1924 Clas Thunberg, Finland	2:20.8
1928 Clas Thunberg, Finland	2:21.1
1932 John A. Shea, U.S.	2:57.5
1936 Charles Mathiesen, Norway	2:19.2
1948 Sverre Farstad, Norway	2:17.6
1952 Hjalmar Andersen, Norway	2:20.4
1956 Grishin, & Mikhailov, both USSR (tie) . . .	2:08.6
1960 Aas, Norway & Grishin, USSR (tie)	2:10.4
1964 Ants Antson, USSR	2:10.3
1968 Cornelis Verkerk, Netherlands	2:03.4
1972 Ard Schenk, Netherlands	2:02.96
1976 Jan Egil Storholt, Norway	1:59.38
1980 Eric Heiden, U.S.	1:55.44
1984 Gaetan Boucher, Canada	1:58.36
1988 Andre Hoffmann, E. Germany	1:52.06

Men's 5,000 meters	Time
1924 Clas Thunberg, Finland	8:39.0
1928 Ivar Ballangrud, Norway	8:50.5
1932 Irving Jaffee, U.S.	9:40.8
1936 Ivar Ballangrud, Norway	8:19.6
1948 Reidar Liaklev, Norway	8:29.4
1952 Hjalmar Andersen, Norway	8:10.6
1956 Boris Shilkov, USSR	7:48.7
1960 Viktor Kosichkin, USSR	7:51.3
1964 Knut Johannesen, Norway	7:38.4
1968 F. Anton Maier, Norway	7:22.4
1972 Ard Schenk, Netherlands	7:23.61
1976 Sten Stensen, Norway	7:24.48
1980 Eric Heiden, U.S.	7:02.29
1984 Sven Tomas Gustafson, Sweden	7:12:28
1988 Tomas Gustafson, Sweden	6:44:63

Men's 10,000 meters	Time
1924 Julius Skutnabb, Finland.	18:04.8
1928 Event not held, thawing of ice	
1932 Irving Jaffee, U.S.	19:13.6
1936 Ivar Ballangrud, Norway	17:24.3
1948 Ake Seyffarth, Sweden	17:26.3
1952 Hjalmar Andersen, Norway	16:45.8
1956 Sigvard Ericsson, Sweden	16:35.9
1960 Knut Johannesen, Norway	15:46.6
1964 Jonny Nilsson, Sweden	15:50.1
1968 Jonny Hoeglin, Sweden	15:23.6
1972 Ard Schenk, Netherlands	15:01.35
1976 Piet Kleine, Netherlands	14:50.59
1980 Eric Heiden, U.S.	14:28.13
1984 Igor Malkov, USSR	14:39.90
1988 Tomas Gustafson, Sweden	13:48.20

Women's 500 meters	Time
1960 Helga Haase, Germany	0:45.9
1964 Lydia Skoblikova, USSR	0:45.0
1968 Ludmila Titova, USSR	0:46.1
1972 Anne Henning, U.S.	0:43.33
1976 Sheila Young, U.S.	0:42.76
1980 Karin Enke, E. Germany	0:41.78
1984 Christa Rothenburger, E. Germany	0:41.02
1988 Bonnie Blair, U.S.	0:39.10

Women's 1,000 meters	Time
1960 Klara Guseva, USSR	1:34.1
1964 Lydia Skoblikova, USSR	1:33.2
1968 Carolina Geijssen, Netherlands	1:32.6
1972 Monika Pflug, W. Germany	1:31.40
1976 Tatiana Averina, USSR	1:28.43
1980 Natalya Petruseva, USSR	1:24.10
1984 Karin Enke, E. Germany	1:21.61
1988 Christa Rothenburger, E. Germany	1:17.65

Women's 1,500 meters	Time
1960 Lydia Skoblikova, USSR	2:52.2
1964 Lydia Skoblikova, USSR	2:22.6
1968 Kaija Mustonen, Finland	2:22.4
1972 Dianne Holum, U.S.	2:20.85
1976 Galina Stepanskaya, USSR	2:16.58
1980 Anne Borckink, Netherlands	2:10.95
1984 Karin Enke, E. Germany	2:03.42
1988 Yvonne van Gennip, Netherlands	2:00.68

Women's 3,000 meters	Time
1960 Lydia Skoblikova, USSR	5:14.3
1964 Lydia Skoblikova, USSR	5:14.9
1968 Johanna Schut, Netherlands	4:56.2
1972 Christina Baas-Kaiser, Netherlands	4:52.14
1976 Tatiana Averina, USSR	4:45.19
1980 Bjoerg Eva Jensen, Norway	4:32.13
1984 Andrea Schoene, E. Germany	4:24.79
1988 Yvonne van Gennip, Netherlands	4:11.94

Women's 5,000 meters	Time
1988 Yvonne van Gennip, Netherlands	7:14:13

Winter Olympic Medal Winners in 1988

Calgary, Alberta, Canada, Feb. 13-28, 1988

	Gold	Silver	Bronze	Total		Gold	Silver	Bronze	Total
Soviet Union	11	9	9	29	United States	2	1	3	6
East Germany	9	10	6	25	Italy	2	1	2	5
Switzerland	5	5	5	15	Norway	0	3	2	5
Austria	3	5	2	10	Canada	0	2	3	5
West Germany	2	4	2	8	Yugoslavia	0	2	1	3
Finland	4	0	3	7	Czechoslovakia	0	1	2	3
The Netherlands	3	2	2	7	France	1	0	1	2
Sweden	4	0	2	6	Japan	0	0	1	1
					Liechtenstein	0	0	1	1

National Hockey League, 1988-89

Final Standings

Wales Conference

Adams Division

	W	L	T	Pts	GF	GA
Montreal	53	18	9	115	315	218
Boston	37	29	14	88	289	256
Buffalo	38	35	7	83	291	299
Hartford	37	38	5	79	299	290
Quebec	27	46	7	61	269	342

Patrick Division

	W	L	T	Pts	GF	GA
Washington	41	29	10	92	305	259
Pittsburgh	40	33	7	87	347	349
N.Y. Rangers	37	35	8	82	310	307
Philadelphia	36	36	8	80	307	285
New Jersey	27	41	12	66	281	325
N.Y. Islanders	28	47	5	61	265	325

Campbell Conference

Norris Division

	W	L	T	Pts	GF	GA
Detroit	34	34	12	80	313	316
St. Louis	33	35	12	78	275	285
Minnesota	27	37	16	70	258	278
Chicago	27	41	12	66	297	335
Toronto	28	46	6	62	259	342

Smythe Division

	W	L	T	Pts	GF	GA
Calgary	54	17	9	117	354	226
Los Angeles	42	31	7	91	376	335
Edmonton	38	34	8	84	325	306
Vancouver	33	39	8	74	251	253
Winnipeg	26	42	12	64	300	355

Stanley Cup Playoff Results

Wales Conference

Pittsburgh defeated N.Y. Rangers 4-0.
Montreal defeated Hartford 4-0.
Boston defeated Buffalo 4-1.
Philadelphia defeated Washington 4-2.
Montreal defeated Boston 4-1.
Philadelphia defeated Pittsburgh 4-2.
Montreal defeated Philadelphia 4-2.

Campbell Conference

St. Louis defeated Minnesota 4-1.
Chicago defeated Detroit 4-2.
Calgary defeated Vancouver 4-3.
Los Angeles defeated Edmonton 4-3.
Calgary defeated Los Angeles 4-0.
Chicago defeated St. Louis 4-1.
Calgary defeated Chicago 4-1.

Finals

Calgary defeated Montreal 4-2.

Stanley Cup Champions Since 1927

Year	Champion	Coach	Final opponent	Year	Champion	Coach	Final opponent
1927	Ottawa	Dave Gill	Boston	1959	Montreal	Toe Blake	Toronto
1928	N.Y. Rangers	Lester Patrick	Montreal	1960	Montreal	Toe Blake	Toronto
1929	Boston	Cy Denneny	N.Y. Rangers	1961	Chicago	Rudy Pilous	Detroit
1930	Montreal	Cecil Hart	Boston	1962	Toronto	Punch Imlach	Chicago
1931	Montreal	Cecil Hart	Chicago	1963	Toronto	Punch Imlach	Detroit
1932	Toronto	Dick Irvin	N.Y. Rangers	1964	Toronto	Punch Imlach	Detroit
1933	New York	Lester Patrick	Toronto	1965	Montreal	Toe Blake	Chicago
1934	Chicago	Tommy Gorman	Detroit	1966	Montreal	Toe Blake	Detroit
1935	Montreal Maroons	Tommy Gorman	Toronto	1967	Toronto	Punch Imlach	Montreal
1936	Detroit	Jack Adams	Toronto	1968	Montreal	Toe Blake	St. Louis
1937	Detroit	Jack Adams	N.Y. Rangers	1969	Montreal	Claude Ruel	St. Louis
1938	Chicago	Bill Stewart	Toronto	1970	Boston	Harry Sinden	St. Louis
1939	Boston	Art Ross	Toronto	1971	Montreal	Al MacNeil	Chicago
1940	N.Y. Rangers	Frank Boucher	Toronto	1972	Boston	Tom Johnson	N.Y. Rangers
1941	Boston	Cooney Weiland	Detroit	1973	Montreal	Scotty Bowman	Chicago
1942	Toronto	Hap Day	Detroit	1974	Philadelphia	Fred Shero	Boston
1943	Detroit	Jack Adams	Boston	1975	Philadelphia	Fred Shero	Buffalo
1944	Montreal	Dick Irvin	Chicago	1976	Montreal	Scotty Bowman	Philadelphia
1945	Toronto	Hap Day	Detroit	1977	Montreal	Scotty Bowman	Boston
1946	Montreal	Dick Irvin	Boston	1978	Montreal	Scotty Bowman	Boston
1947	Toronto	Hap Day	Montreal	1979	Montreal	Scotty Bowman	N.Y. Rangers
1948	Toronto	Hap Day	Detroit	1980	N.Y. Islanders	Al Arbour	Philadelphia
1949	Toronto	Hap Day	Detroit	1981	N.Y. Islanders	Al Arbour	Minnesota
1950	Detroit	Tommy Ivan	N.Y. Rangers	1982	N.Y. Islanders	Al Arbour	Vancouver
1951	Toronto	Joe Primeau	Montreal	1983	N.Y. Islanders	Al Arbour	Edmonton
1952	Detroit	Tommy Ivan	Montreal	1984	Edmonton	Glen Sather	N.Y. Islanders
1953	Montreal	Dick Irvin	Boston	1985	Edmonton	Glen Sather	Philadelphia
1954	Detroit	Tommy Ivan	Montreal	1986	Montreal	Jean Perron	Calgary
1955	Detroit	Jimmy Skinner	Montreal	1987	Edmonton	Glen Sather	Philadelphia
1956	Montreal	Toe Blake	Detroit	1988	Edmonton	Glen Sather	Boston
1957	Montreal	Toe Blake	Boston	1989	Calgary	Terry Crisp	Montreal
1958	Montreal	Toe Blake	Boston				

Conn Smythe Trophy (MVP in Playoffs)

1965	Jean Beliveau, Montreal	1974	Bernie Parent, Philadelphia	1982	Mike Bossy, N.Y. Islanders
1966	Roger Crozier, Detroit	1975	Bernie Parent, Philadelphia	1983	Billy Smith, N.Y. Islanders
1967	Dave Keon, Toronto	1976	Reg Leach, Philadelphia	1984	Mark Messier, Edmonton
1968	Glenn Hall, St. Louis	1977	Guy Lafleur, Montreal	1985	Wayne Gretzky, Edmonton
1969	Serge Savard, Montreal	1978	Larry Robinson, Montreal	1986	Patrick Roy, Montreal
1970	Bobby Orr, Boston	1979	Bob Gainey, Montreal	1987	Ron Hextall, Philadelphia
1971	Ken Dryden, Montreal	1980	Bryan Trottier, N.Y. Islanders	1988	Wayne Gretzky, Edmonton
1972	Bobby Orr, Boston	1981	Butch Goring, N.Y. Islanders	1989	Al MacInnis, Calgary
1973	Yvan Cournoyer, Montreal				

Individual Leaders

Points

Mario Lemieux, Pittsburgh, 199; Wayne Gretzky, Los Angeles, 168; Steve Yzerman, Detroit, 155; Bernie Nicholls, Los Angeles, 150; Rob Brown, Pittsburgh, 115.

Goal Scoring

Mario Lemieux, Pittsburgh, 85; Bernie Nicholls, Los Angeles, 70; Steve Yzerman, Detroit, 65; Wayne Gretzky, Los Angeles, 54; Joe Nieuwendyk, Calgary, 51; Joe Mullen, Calgary, 51.

Assists

Mario Lemieux, Pittsburgh, 114; Wayne Gretzky, Los Angeles, 114; Steve Yzerman, Detroit, 90; Paul Coffey, Pittsburgh, 83; Bernie Nicholls, Los Angeles, 80.

Power-play goals

Mario Lemieux, Pittsburgh, 31; Tim Kerr, Philadelphia, 25; Rob Brown, Pittsburgh, 24; Bernie Nicholls, Los Angeles, 21; Kevin Dineen, Hartford, 20; Andrew McBain, Winnipeg, 20.

Short hand goals

Mario Lemieux, Pittsburgh, 13; Dirk Graham, Chicago, 10; Esa Tikkanen, Edmonton, 8; Bernie Nicholls, Los Angeles, 8; Mark Messier, Edmonton, 6.

Shooting percentage

(minimum 80 shots)

Rob Brown, Pittsburgh, 29.0; Craig Simpson, Edmonton, 28.9; Mario Lemieux, Pittsburgh, 27.2; Pat Elynuik, Winnipeg, 26.0; Ron Sutter, Philadelphia, 24.5.

Game-winning goals

Joe Nieuwendyk, Calgary, 11; Guy Carbonneau, Montreal, 10; Mike Ridley, Washington, 9.

Plus/Minus

Joe Mullen, Calgary, 51; Doug Gilmour, Calgary, 45; Colin Patterson, Calgary, 44; Craig Muni, Edmonton, 43; Brad McCrimmon, Calgary, 43.

Goaltending Leaders

(minimum 25 games)

Goals against average

Patrick Roy, Montreal, 2.47; Mike Vernon, Calgary, 2.65; Pete Peeters, Washington, 2.85; Brian Hayward, Montreal, 2.90; Rick Wamsley, Calgary, 2.96.

Wins

Mike Vernon, Calgary, 37; Patrick Roy, Montreal, 33; Ron Hextall, Philadelphia, 30; John Vanbiesbrouck, N.Y. Rangers, 28; Kelly Hrudey, N.Y. Islanders-L.A., 28.

Save percentage

Patrick Roy, Montreal, .908; Jon Casey, Minnesota, .900; Kari Takko, Minnesota, .899; Mike Vernon, Calgary, .897; Steve Weeks, Vancouver, .892.

Shutouts

Greg Millen, St. Louis, 6; Pete Peeters, Washington, 4; Kirk McLean, Vancouver, 4; Peter Sidorkiewicz, Hartford, 4; Patrick Roy, Montreal, 4.

Individual Scoring

(40 or more games played)

Boston Bruins

	GP	G	A	Pts	+/−	PIM
Cam Neely	74	37	38	75	14	190
Ken Linseman	78	27	45	72	15	164
Craig Janney	62	16	46	62	20	12
Randy Burridge	80	31	30	61	19	39
Ray Bourque	60	18	43	61	20	52
Glen Wesley	77	19	35	54	23	61
Bob Joyce	77	18	31	49	8	46
Greg Hawgood	56	16	24	40	4	84
Bob Carpenter	57	16	24	40	7	26
Andy Brickley	71	13	22	35	4	20
Keith Crowder	69	15	18	33	6	147
Garry Galley	78	8	21	29	7−	80
Bob Sweeney	75	14	14	28	19−	99
John Carter	44	12	10	22	1−	24
Greg Johnston	57	11	10	21	7	32
Michael Thelven	40	3	18	21	10	71
Ray Neufeld	45	6	5	11	11	80
Allen Pedersen	51	0	6	6	3−	69
Lyndon Byers	49	0	4	4	8−	218
Rejean Lemelin	40	0	1	1	0	6
Andy Moog	41	0	1	1	0	6

Buffalo Sabres

	GP	G	A	Pts	+/−	PIM
Pierre Turgeon	80	34	54	88	3−	26
Phil Housley	72	26	44	70	6	47
Christian Ruuttu	67	14	46	60	13	98
Rick Vaive	58	31	26	57	2	124
Dave Andreychuk	56	28	24	52	1	40
Doug Bodger	71	8	44	52	15	59
Mike Foligno	75	27	22	49	7−	156
Benoit Hogue	69	14	30	44	4−	120
John Tucker	60	13	31	44	4	31
Ray Sheppard	67	22	21	43	7−	15
Scott Arniel	80	18	23	41	10	46
Mark Napier	66	11	17	28	4−	33
Grant Ledyard	74	4	16	20	2	51
Jeff Parker	57	9	9	18	3	82
Kevin Maguire	70	8	10	18	9	241
Uwe Krupp	70	5	13	18	0	55
Mike Hartman	70	8	9	17	8	316
Mike Ramsey	56	2	14	16	5	84
Larry Playfair	48	0	6	6	7−	110
Clint Malarchuk	49	0	1	1	0	18

Calgary Flames

	GP	G	A	Pts	+/−	PIM
Joe Mullen	79	51	59	110	51	16
Hakan Loob	79	27	58	85	28	44
Doug Gilmour	72	26	59	85	45	44
Joe Nieuwendyk	77	51	31	82	26	40
Al MacInnis	79	16	58	74	38	126
Gary Suter	63	13	49	62	26	78
Jiri Hrdina	70	22	32	54	19	26
Joel Otto	72	23	30	53	12	213
Brian Maclellan	72	18	26	44	3	118
Gary Roberts	71	22	16	38	32	250
Colin Patterson	74	14	24	38	44	56
Jim Peplinski	79	13	25	38	6	241
Mark Hunter	66	22	8	30	4	194
Jamie Macoun	72	8	19	27	40	76
Brad McCrimmon	72	5	17	22	43	96
Dana Murzyn	63	3	19	22	26	142
Lanny McDonald	51	11	7	18	1−	26
Rob Ramage	68	3	13	16	26	156
Tim Hunter	75	3	9	12	22	375
Mike Vernon	52	0	4	4	0	18

Chicago Black Hawks

	GP	G	A	Pts	+/−	PIM
Steve Larmer	80	43	44	87	2	54
Denis Savard	58	23	59	82	5−	110
Dirk Graham	80	33	45	78	8	89
Doug Wilson	66	15	47	62	8	69
Dave Manson	79	18	36	54	5	352
Troy Murray	79	21	30	51	0	113
Adam Creighton	67	22	24	46	9−	136
Steve Thomas	45	21	19	40	2−	69
Wayne Presley	72	21	19	40	3−	100
Trent Yawney	69	5	19	24	5−	116
Mike Hudson	41	7	16	23	12−	20
Greg Gilbert	59	8	13	21	2	45
Bob Bassen	68	5	16	21	5−	83
Steve Konroyd	78	6	12	18	16−	42
Keith Brown	74	2	16	18	5−	84
Duane Sutter	75	7	9	16	11−	214
Mike Eagles	47	5	11	16	8−	44
Brian Noonan	45	4	12	16	2−	28
Dan Vincelette	66	11	4	15	5−	119
Everett Sanipass	50	6	9	15	7−	164
Alain Chevrier	49	0	4	4	0	2
Bob McGill	68	0	4	4	9	155

Detroit Red Wings

	GP	G	A	Pts	+/−	PIM
Steve Yzerman	80	65	90	155	17	61
Gerard Gallant	76	39	54	93	7	230
Adam Oates	69	16	62	78	1−	14
Paul MacLean	76	36	35	71	7	118
Dave Barr	73	27	32	59	12	69
Steve Chiasson	65	12	35	47	6−	149
Shawn Burr	79	19	27	46	5	78
Lee Norwood	66	10	32	42	6	100
Petr Klima	51	25	16	41	5	44
Rick Zombo	75	1	20	21	23	106
Joey Kocur	60	9	9	18	4−	213
Mike O'Connell	66	1	15	16	8−	41
Jim Nill	71	8	7	15	1−	83
Tim Higgins	42	5	9	14	0	62
Jeff Sharples	46	4	9	13	5	26
Doug Houda	57	2	11	13	17	67
Adam Graves	56	7	5	12	5−	60
John Chabot	52	2	10	12	18−	6
Kris King	55	2	3	5	7−	168
Gilbert Delorme	42	1	3	4	11−	51
Greg Stefan	46	0	2	2	0	41

Edmonton Oilers

	GP	G	A	Pts	+/−	PIM
Jari Kurri	76	44	58	102	19	69
Jimmy Carson	80	49	51	100	3	36
Mark Messier	72	33	61	94	5−	130
Esa Tikkanen	67	31	47	78	10	92
Craig Simpson	66	35	41	76	3−	80
Glenn Anderson	79	16	48	64	16−	93
Craig MacTavish	80	21	31	52	10	55
Charlie Huddy	76	11	33	44	0	52
Tomas Jonsson	73	10	33	43	25−	56
Normand Lacombe	64	17	11	28	2	57
Kevin Lowe	76	7	18	25	26	98
Kevin McClelland	79	6	14	20	10−	161
Craig Muni	69	5	13	18	43	71
Randy Gregg	57	3	15	18	9−	28
Kelly Buchberger	66	5	9	14	14−	234
Dave Hunter	66	6	6	12	8−	83
Chris Joseph	44	4	5	9	9−	54
Doug Halward	42	0	8	8	14−	61
Dave Brown	72	0	5	5	12−	156
Grant Fuhr	59	0	1	1	0	6

Hartford Whalers

	GP	G	A	Pts	+/−	PIM
Kevin Dineen	79	45	44	89	6−	167
Ron Francis	69	29	48	77	4	36
Ray Ferraro	80	41	35	76	1	86
Scott Young	76	19	40	59	21−	27
Dave Babych	70	6	41	47	5−	54
Paul MacDermid	74	17	27	44	1	141
Brian Lawton	65	17	26	43	11−	67
Dave Tippett	80	17	24	41	6−	45
John Anderson	62	16	24	40	15	28
Ulf Samuelsson	71	9	26	35	23	181
Jody Hull	60	16	18	34	6	10
Norm Maciver	63	1	32	33	3−	38
Sylvain Turgeon	42	16	14	30	11−	40
Dean Evason	67	11	17	28	9−	60
Don Maloney	52	7	20	27	3	39
Sylvain Cote	78	8	9	17	7−	49
Brent Peterson	66	4	13	17	2	61
Tom Martin	42	8	7	15	9	117
Grant Jennings	55	3	10	13	17	159
Joel Quenneville	69	4	7	11	3	32
Jim Pavese	44	3	6	9	2−	135
Randy Ladouceur	75	2	5	7	23−	95
Peter Sidorkiewicz	44	0	3	3	0	0

Los Angeles Kings

	GP	G	A	Pts	+/−	PIM
Wayne Gretzky	78	54	114	168	15	26
Bernie Nicholls	79	70	80	150	30	96
Luc Robitaille	78	46	52	98	5	65
Steve Duchesne	79	25	50	75	31	92
John Tonelli	77	31	33	64	9	110
Dave Taylor	70	26	37	63	10	80
Mike Krushelnyski	78	26	36	62	9	110
Steve Kasper	78	19	31	50	2−	63
Mike Allison	55	14	22	36	7	122
Dale Degray	63	6	22	28	3	97
Marty McSorley	66	10	17	27	3	350

	GP	G	A	Pts	+/−	PIM
Doug Crossman	74	10	15	25	11−	53
Ron Duguay	70	7	17	24	23	48
Tim Watters	76	3	18	21	17	168
Tom Laidlaw	70	3	17	20	30	63
Jay Miller	66	7	7	14	9−	301
Dean Kennedy	67	3	11	14	17	103
Ken Baumgartner	49	1	3	4	9−	286
Kelly Hrudey	66	0	3	3	0	19
Glenn Healy	48	0	1	1	0	28

Minnesota North Stars

	GP	G	A	Pts	+/−	PIM
Dave Gagner	75	35	43	78	13	104
Mike Gartner	69	33	36	69	11	73
Neal Broten	68	18	38	56	1	57
Marc Habscheid	76	23	31	54	2	40
Brian Bellows	60	23	27	50	14−	55
Larry Murphy	78	11	35	46	0	82
Reed Larson	54	9	29	38	10−	68
David Archibald	72	14	19	33	11−	14
Basil McRae	78	12	19	31	8−	365
Stewart Gavin	73	8	18	26	3	34
Shawn Chambers	72	5	19	24	4−	80
Frantisek Musil	55	1	19	20	4	54
Bob Brooke	57	7	9	16	12−	57
Curt Giles	76	5	10	15	2	77
Dusan Pasek	48	4	10	14	8−	30
Perry Berezan	51	5	8	13	6	25
Ville Siren	50	3	10	13	0	72
Larry DePalma	43	5	7	12	14−	102
Mark Tinordi	47	2	3	5	9−	107
Jon Casey	55	0	1	1	0	10

Montreal Canadiens

	GP	G	A	Pts	+/−	PIM
Mats Naslund	77	33	51	84	34	14
Bobby Smith	80	32	51	83	25	69
Chris Chelios	80	15	58	73	35	185
Stephane Richer	68	25	35	60	4	61
Guy Carbonneau	79	26	30	56	37	44
Claude Lemieux	69	29	22	51	14	136
Shayne Corson	80	26	24	50	1−	193
Petr Svoboda	71	8	37	45	28	147
Russ Courtnall	73	23	18	41	9	19
Mike McPhee	73	19	22	41	14	74
Brian Skrudland	71	12	29	41	22	84
Mike Keane	69	16	19	35	9	69
Ryan Walter	78	14	17	31	23	48
Larry Robinson	74	4	26	30	23	22
Brent Gilchrist	49	8	16	24	9	16
Bob Gainey	49	10	7	17	13	34
Craig Ludwig	74	3	13	16	33	73
Rick Green	72	1	14	15	19	25
Patrick Roy	48	0	6	6	0	2

New Jersey Devils

	GP	G	A	Pts	+/−	PIM
John MacLean	74	42	45	87	26	127
Kirk Muller	80	31	43	74	23−	119
Patrik Sundstrom	65	28	41	69	22	36
Tom Kurvers	74	16	50	66	11	38
Aaron Broten	80	16	43	59	7−	81
Brendan Shanahan	68	22	28	50	2	115
Pat Verbeek	77	26	21	47	18−	189
Mark Johnson	40	13	25	38	1−	24
Tommy Albelin	60	9	28	37	12	67
Jim Korn	65	15	16	31	3−	212
Doug Brown	63	15	10	25	7−	15
Joe Cirella	80	3	19	22	14−	155
Claude Loiselle	74	7	14	21	10−	209
Randy Velischek	80	4	14	18	2−	70
Pat Conacher	55	7	5	12	7	14
Anders Carlsson	47	4	8	12	3	20
David Maley	68	5	6	11	27−	249
Craig Wolanin	56	3	8	11	9−	69
Ken Daneyko	80	5	5	10	22−	283
Sean Burke	62	0	3	3	0	54

New York Islanders

	GP	G	A	Pts	+/−	PIM
Pat LaFontaine	79	45	43	88	6−	26
Brent Sutter	77	29	34	63	12−	77
Dave Volek	77	25	34	59	11−	24

(continued)

	GP	G	A	Pts	+/-	PIM
Bryan Trottier	73	17	28	45	7—	44
Mikko Makela	76	17	28	45	16—	22
Derek King	60	14	29	43	10	14
Alan Kerr	71	20	18	38	5—	144
Gerald Diduck	65	11	21	32	9	155
Jeff Norton	69	1	30	31	24—	74
Randy Wood	77	15	13	28	18—	44
Patrick Flatley	41	10	15	25	5—	31
Brad Dalgarno	55	11	10	21	8—	86
Gary Nylund	69	7	10	17	19—	137
Marc Bergevin	69	2	13	15	1—	80
Richard Pilon	62	0	14	14	9—	242
Wayne McBean	52	0	6	6	13—	35
Mick Vukota	48	2	2	4	17—	237

New York Rangers

	GP	G	A	Pts	+/-	PIM
Tomas Sandstrom	79	32	56	88	5	148
Carey Wilson	75	32	45	77	11—	59
Brian Leetch	68	23	48	71	8	50
Brian Mullen	78	29	35	64	7	60
Tony Granato	78	36	27	63	17	140
Kelly Kisio	70	26	36	62	14	91
James Patrick	68	11	36	47	3	41
Guy Lafleur	67	18	27	45	1	12
Ulf Dahlen	56	24	19	43	6—	50
John Ogrodnick	60	13	29	42	0	14
Lucien Deblois	73	9	24	33	6—	107
Michel Petit	69	8	25	33	15—	154
Lindy Ruff	76	6	16	22	23—	117
Mark Hardy	60	4	16	20	9—	71
David Shaw	63	6	11	17	14	88
Jan Erixon	44	4	11	15	3—	27
Ron Greschner	58	1	10	11	9	94
Rudy Poeschek	52	0	2	2	8—	199
John Vanbiesbrouck	56	0	2	2	0	30

Philadelphia Flyers

	GP	G	A	Pts	+/-	PIM
Tim Kerr	69	48	40	88	4—	73
Rick Tocchet	66	45	36	81	1—	183
Brian Propp	77	32	46	78	16	37
Pelle Eklund	79	18	51	69	5	23
Mike Bullard	74	27	38	65	2	106
Scott Mellanby	76	21	29	50	13—	183
Ron Sutter	55	26	22	48	25	80
Terry Carkner	78	11	32	43	6—	149
Keith Acton	71	14	25	39	10	111
Mark Howe	52	9	29	38	7	45
Murray Craven	51	9	28	37	4	52
Dave Poulin	69	18	17	35	4	49
Gordon Murphy	75	4	31	35	3—	68
Derrick Smith	74	16	14	30	4—	43
Jay Wells	67	2	19	21	3—	184
Moe Mantha	46	4	14	18	4—	43
Kjell Samuelsson	69	3	14	17	13	140
Al Secord	60	6	10	16	20—	109
Doug Sulliman	52	6	6	12	8—	8
Ron Hextall	64	0	8	8	0	113
Jeff Chychrun	80	1	4	5	11	245
Craig Berube	53	1	1	2	15—	199

Pittsburgh Penguins

	GP	G	A	Pts	+/-	PIM
Mario Lemieux	76	85	114	199	41	100
Rob Brown	68	49	66	115	27	118
Paul Coffey	75	30	83	113	10—	193
Dan Quinn	79	34	60	94	37—	102
Bob Errey	76	26	32	58	40	124
John Cullen	79	12	37	49	25—	112
Zarley Zalapski	58	12	33	45	9	57
Randy Cunneyworth	70	25	19	44	22—	156
Phil Bourque	80	17	26	43	22—	97
Dave Hannan	72	10	20	30	12—	157
Randy Hillier	68	1	23	24	4—	141
Troy Loney	69	10	6	16	5—	165
Jim Johnson	76	2	14	16	7	163
Tom Barrasso	54	0	8	8	0	70
Dan Frawley	46	3	4	7	1—	66
Steve Dykstra	65	1	6	7	12—	126
Chris Dahlquist	43	1	5	6	8—	42
Rod Buskas	52	1	5	6	2—	105
Jay Caufield	58	1	4	5	4—	285
Gord Dineen	40	1	3	4	9—	44

Quebec Nordiques

	GP	G	A	Pts	+/-	PIM
Peter Stastny	72	35	50	85	23—	117
Walt Poddubny	72	38	37	75	18—	107
Jeff Brown	78	21	47	68	22—	62
Michel Goulet	69	26	38	64	20—	67
Joe Sakic	70	23	39	62	36—	24
Iiro Jarvi	75	11	30	41	13—	40
Paul Gillis	79	15	25	40	14—	163
Marc Fortier	57	20	19	39	18—	45
Anton Stastny	55	7	30	37	19—	12
Gaetan Duchesne	70	8	21	29	0	56
Randy Moller	74	7	22	29	2	136
Robert Picard	74	7	14	21	28—	61
Mike Hough	46	9	10	19	7—	39
Mario Marois	49	3	12	15	21—	118
Curtis Leschyshyn	71	4	9	13	32—	71
Alain Cote	55	2	8	10	1—	14
Trevor Stienberg	55	6	3	9	17—	125
Steven Finn	77	2	6	8	21—	235

St. Louis Blues

	GP	G	A	Pts	+/-	PIM
Brett Hull	78	41	43	84	17—	33
Peter Zezel	78	21	49	70	14—	42
Bernie Federko	66	22	45	67	20—	54
Cliff Ronning	64	24	31	55	3	18
Greg Paslawski	75	26	26	52	8	18
Tony Hrkac	70	17	28	45	10—	8
Gino Cavallini	74	20	23	43	2	79
Tony McKegney	71	25	17	42	1—	58
Brian Benning	66	8	26	34	23—	102
Rick Meagher	78	15	14	29	9	53
Sergio Momesso	53	9	17	26	1—	139
Gordie Roberts	77	2	24	26	7	90
Steve Tuttle	53	13	12	25	3	6
Paul Cavallini	65	4	20	24	25	128
Tom Tilley	70	1	22	23	1	47
Mike Lalor	48	2	18	20	14	69
Doug Evans	53	7	12	19	3	81
Herb Raglan	50	7	10	17	8—	144
Gaston Gingras	52	3	10	13	1	6
Craig Coxe	41	0	7	7	3	127
Dave Richter	66	1	5	6	21—	99
Greg Millen	52	0	0	0	0	4

Toronto Maple Leafs

	GP	G	A	Pts	+/-	PIM
Ed Olczyk	80	38	52	90	0	75
Gary Leeman	61	32	43	75	0	66
Vincent Damphousse	80	26	42	68	8—	75
Tom Fergus	80	22	45	67	38—	48
Dan Marois	76	31	23	54	4—	76
Mark Osborne	75	16	30	46	5—	112
Al Iafrate	65	13	20	33	3	72
Dave Reid	77	9	21	30	12	22
Todd Gill	59	11	14	25	3—	72
Craig Laughlin	63	10	13	23	22—	41
Borje Salming	63	3	17	20	7	86
Brad Marsh	80	1	15	16	16—	79
Derek Laxdal	41	9	6	15	11—	65
Chris Kotsopoulos	57	1	14	15	4—	44
Dan Daoust	68	7	5	12	20—	54
Luke Richardson	55	2	7	9	15—	106
Brian Curran	47	1	4	5	0	185
John Kordic	52	1	2	3	14—	198
Allan Bester	43	0	2		0	2

Vancouver Canucks

	GP	G	A	Pts	+/-	PIM
Petri Skriko	74	30	36	66	3—	57
Trevor Linden	80	30	29	59	10—	41
Paul Reinhart	64	7	50	57	4—	44
Tony Tanti	77	24	25	49	10—	69
Brian Bradley	71	18	27	45	5—	42
Barry Pederson	62	15	26	41	5	22
Robert Nordmark	80	6	35	41	4—	97
Jim Sandlak	72	20	20	40	8	99
Steve Bozek	71	17	18	35	1	64
Greg Adams	61	19	14	33	21—	24
Rich Sutter	75	17	15	32	3	122
Stan Smyl	75	7	18	25	0	102
Doug Lidster	63	5	17	22	4—	78
Garth Butcher	78	0	20	20	4	227
Greg C. Adams	61	8	7	15	3	117

	GP	G	A	Pts	+/-	PIM
David Bruce	53	7	7	14	16-	65
Larry Melnyk	74	3	11	14	3-	82
Jim Benning	65	3	9	12	4-	48
Harold Snepsts	59	0	8	8	3-	69
Kevan Guy	45	2	2	4	14-	34
Kirk McLean	42	0	1	1	0	6

	GP	G	A	Pts	+/-	PIM
Lou Franceschetti	63	7	10	17	4-	123
John Druce	48	8	7	15	7-	62
Neil Sheehy	72	3	4	7	1-	179

Winnipeg Jets

	GP	G	A	Pts	+/-	PIM
Dale Hawerchuk	75	41	55	96	30-	28
Thomas Steen	80	27	61	88	14-	80
Andrew McBain	80	37	40	77	35-	71
Brent Ashton	75	31	37	68	5-	36
Fredrik Olausson	75	15	47	62	6	32
Dave Ellett	75	22	34	56	18-	62
Pat Elynuik	56	26	25	51	5	29
Iain Duncan	57	14	30	44	17-	74
Randy Carlyle	78	6	38	44	19-	78
Laurie Boschman	70	10	26	36	17-	163
Doug Smail	47	14	15	29	12	52
Paul Fenton	80	16	12	28	16-	39
Gord Donnelly	73	10	10	20	20-	274
Peter Taglianetti	66	1	14	15	23-	226
Teppo Numminen	69	1	14	15	11-	36
Jim Kyte	74	3	9	12	25-	190
Hannu Jarvenpaa	53	4	7	11	14-	41
Randy Gilhen	64	5	3	8	24-	38
Eldon Reddick	41	0	1	1	0	6

Washington Capitals

	GP	G	A	Pts	+/-	PIM
Mike Ridley	80	41	48	89	17	49
Geoff Courtnall	79	42	38	80	11	112
Dino Ciccarelli	76	44	30	74	6-	76
Bengt Gustafsson	72	18	51	69	13	18
Scott Stevens	80	7	61	68	1	225
Dave Christian	80	34	31	65	2	12
Dale Hunter	80	20	37	57	3-	219
Kelly Miller	78	19	21	40	13	45
Kevin Hatcher	62	13	27	40	19	101
Stephen Leach	74	11	19	30	4	94
Michal Pivonka	52	8	19	27	9	30
Calle Johansson	59	3	18	21	6-	37
Rod Langway	76	2	19	21	12	65
Bob Rouse	79	4	15	19	3-	160
Bob Gould	75	5	13	18	2-	65

NHL All Star Team, 1989

First team	Position	Second team
Patrick Roy, Montreal	Goalie	Mike Vernon, Calgary
Chris Chelios, Montreal	Defense	Al Macinnis, Calgary
Paul Coffey, Pittsburgh	Defense	Ray Bourquè, Boston
Mario Lemieux, Pittsburgh	Center	Wayne Gretzky, Los Angeles
Joe Mullen, Calgary	Right Wing	Jari Kurri, Edmonton
Luc Robitaille, Los Angeles	Left Wing	Gerald Gallant, Detroit

Ross Trophy (Leading Scorer)

Year	Winner	Year	Winner	Year	Winner
1927	Bill Cook, N.Y. Rangers	1948	Elmer Lach, Montreal	1969	Phil Esposito, Boston
1928	Howie Morenz, Montreal	1949	Roy Conacher, Chicago	1970	Bobby Orr, Boston
1929	Ace Bailey, Toronto	1950	Ted Lindsay, Detroit	1971	Phil Esposito, Boston
1930	Cooney Weiland, Boston	1951	Gordie Howe, Detroit	1972	Phil Esposito, Boston
1931	Howie Morenz, Montreal	1952	Gordie Howe, Detroit	1973	Phil Esposito, Boston
1932	Harvey Jackson, Toronto	1953	Gordie Howe, Detroit	1974	Phil Esposito, Boston
1933	Bill Cook, N.Y. Rangers	1954	Gordie Howe, Detroit	1975	Bobby Orr, Boston
1934	Charlie Conacher, Toronto	1955	Bernie Geoffrion, Montreal	1976	Guy Lafleur, Montreal
1935	Charlie Conacher, Toronto	1956	Jean Beliveau, Montreal	1977	Guy Lafleur, Montreal
1936	Dave Schriner, N.Y. Americans	1957	Gordie Howe, Detroit	1978	Guy Lafleur, Montreal
1937	Dave Schriner, N.Y. Americans	1958	Dickie Moore, Montreal	1979	Bryan Trottier, N.Y. Islanders
1938	Gordie Drillon, Toronto	1959	Dickie Moore, Montreal	1980	Marcel Dionne, Los Angeles
1939	Toe Blake, Montreal	1960	Bobby Hull, Chicago	1981	Wayne Gretzky, Edmonton
1940	Milt Schmidt, Boston	1961	Bernie Geoffrion, Montreal	1982	Wayne Gretzky, Edmonton
1941	Bill Cowley, Boston	1962	Bobby Hull, Chicago	1983	Wayne Gretzky, Edmonton
1942	Bryan Hextall, N.Y. Rangers	1963	Gordie Howe, Detroit	1984	Wayne Gretzky, Edmonton
1943	Doug Bentley, Chicago	1964	Stan Mikita, Chicago	1985	Wayne Gretzky, Edmonton
1944	Herbie Cain, Boston	1965	Stan Mikita, Chicago	1986	Wayne Gretzky, Edmonton
1945	Elmer Lach, Montreal	1966	Bobby Hull, Chicago	1987	Wayne Gretzky, Edmonton
1946	Max Bentley, Chicago	1967	Stan Mikita, Chicago	1988	Mario Lemieux, Pittsburgh
1947	Max Bentley, Chicago	1968	Stan Mikita, Chicago	1989	Mario Lemieux, Pittsburgh

Hart Memorial Trophy (MVP)

Year	Winner	Year	Winner	Year	Winner
1927	Herb Gardiner, Montreal	1948	Buddy O'Connor, N.Y. Rangers	1969	Phil Esposito, Boston
1928	Howie Morenz, Montreal	1949	Sid Abel, Detroit	1970	Bobby Orr, Boston
1929	Roy Worters, N.Y. Americans	1950	Chuck Rayner, N.Y. Rangers	1971	Bobby Orr, Boston
1930	Nels Stewart, Montreal Maroons	1951	Milt Schmidt, Boston	1972	Bobby Orr, Boston
1931	Howie Morenz, Montreal	1952	Gordie Howe, Detroit	1973	Bobby Clarke, Philadelphia
1932	Howie Morenz, Montreal	1953	Gordie Howe, Detroit	1974	Phil Esposito, Boston
1933	Eddie Shore, Boston	1954	Al Rollins, Chicago	1975	Bobby Clarke, Philadelphia
1934	Aurel Joliat, Montreal	1955	Ted Kennedy, Toronto	1976	Bobby Clarke, Philadelphia
1935	Eddie Shore, Boston	1956	Jean Beliveau, Montreal	1977	Guy Lafleur, Montreal
1936	Eddie Shore, Boston	1957	Gordie Howe, Detroit	1978	Guy Lafleur, Montreal
1937	Babe Siebert, Montreal	1958	Gordie Howe, Detroit	1979	Bryan Trottier, N.Y. Islanders
1938	Eddie Shore, Boston	1959	Andy Bathgate, N.Y. Rangers	1980	Wayne Gretzky, Edmonton
1939	Toe Blake, Montreal	1960	Gordie Howe, Detroit	1981	Wayne Gretzky, Edmonton
1940	Ebbie Goodfellow, Detroit	1961	Bernie Geoffrion, Montreal	1982	Wayne Gretzky, Edmonton
1941	Bill Cowley, Boston	1962	Jacques Plante, Montreal	1983	Wayne Gretzky, Edmonton
1942	Tom Anderson, N.Y. Americans	1963	Gordie Howe, Detroit	1984	Wayne Gretzky, Edmonton
1943	Bill Cowley, Boston	1964	Jean Beliveau, Montreal	1985	Wayne Gretzky, Edmonton
1944	Babe Pratt, Toronto	1965	Bobby Hull, Chicago	1986	Wayne Gretzky, Edmonton
1945	Elmer Lach, Montreal	1966	Bobby Hull, Chicago	1987	Wayne Gretzky, Edmonton
1946	Max Bentley, Chicago	1967	Stan Mikita, Chicago	1988	Mario Lemieux, Pittsburgh
1947	Maurice Richard, Montreal	1968	Stan Mikita, Chicago	1989	Wayne Gretzky, Los Angeles

*Vezina Trophy (Leading Goalie)

		1949	Bill Durnan, Montreal		Rangers
		1950	Bill Durnan, Montreal	1972	Esposito, Smith, Chicago
1927	George Hainsworth, Montreal	1951	Al Rollins, Toronto	1973	Ken Dryden, Montreal
1928	George Hainsworth, Montreal	1952	Terry Sawchuk, Detroit	1974	Bernie Parent, Philadelphia;
1929	George Hainsworth, Montreal	1953	Terry Sawchuk, Detroit		Tony Esposito, Chicago
1930	Tiny Thompson, Boston	1954	Harry Lumley, Toronto	1975	Bernie Parent, Philadelphia
1931	Roy Worters, N.Y. Americans	1955	Terry Sawchuk, Detroit	1976	Ken Dryden, Montreal
1932	Charlie Gardiner, Chicago	1956	Jacques Plante, Montreal	1977	Dryden, Larocque, Montreal
1933	Tiny Thompson, Boston	1957	Jacques Plante, Montreal	1978	Dryden, Larocque, Montreal
1934	Charlie Gardiner, Chicago	1958	Jacques Plante, Montreal	1979	Dryden, Larocque, Montreal
1935	Lorne Chabot, Chicago	1959	Jacques Plante, Montreal	1980	Sauve, Edwards, Buffalo
1936	Tiny Thompson, Boston	1960	Jacques Plante, Montreal	1981	Sevigny, Larocque, Herron,
1937	Normie Smith, Detroit	1961	John Bower, Toronto		Montreal
1938	Tiny Thompson, Boston	1962	Jacques Plante, Montreal	1982	Bill Smith, N.Y. Islanders
1939	Frank Brimsek, Boston	1963	Glenn Hall, Chicago	1983	Pete Peeters, Boston
1940	Dave Kerr, N.Y. Rangers	1964	Charlie Hodge, Montreal	1984	Tom Barrasso, Buffalo
1941	Turk Broda, Toronto	1965	Sawchuk, Bower, Toronto	1985	Pelle Lindbergh, Philadelphia
1942	Frank Brimsek, Boston	1966	Worsley, Hodge, Montreal	1986	John Vanbiesbrouck, N.Y.
1943	Johnny Mowers, Detroit	1967	Hall, DeJordy, Chicago		Rangers
1944	Bill Durnan, Montreal	1968	Worsley, Vachon, Montreal	1987	Ron Hextall, Philadelphia
1945	Bill Durnan, Montreal	1969	Hall, Plante, St. Louis	1988	Grant Fuhr, Edmonton
1946	Bill Durnan, Montreal	1970	Tony Esposito, Chicago	1989	Patrick Roy, Montreal
1947	Bill Durnan, Montreal	1971	Giacomin, Villemure, N.Y.		
1948	Turk Broda, Toronto				

* Awarded to goalie who played a minimum 25 games for the team which allowed the fewest goals; since 1982, awarded to outstanding goalie.

Calder Memorial Trophy (Rookie of the Year)

1933	Carl Voss, Detroit	1952	Bernie Geoffrion, Montreal	1971	Gilbert Perreault, Buffalo
1934	Russ Blinco, Montreal Maroons	1953	Gump Worsley, N.Y. Rangers	1972	Ken Dryden; Montreal
1935	Dave Schriner, N.Y. Americans	1954	Camille Henry, N.Y. Rangers	1973	Steve Vickers, N.Y. Rangers
1936	Mike Karakas, Chicago	1955	Ed Litzenberger, Chicago	1974	Denis Potvin, N.Y. Islanders
1937	Syl Apps, Toronto	1956	Glenn Hall, Detroit	1975	Eric Vail, Atlanta
1938	Cully Dahlstrom, Chicago	1957	Larry Regan, Boston	1976	Bryan Trottier, N.Y. Islanders
1939	Frank Brimsek, Boston	1958	Frank Mahovlich, Toronto	1977	Willi Plett, Atlanta
1940	Kilby Macdonald, N.Y. Rangers	1959	Ralph Backstrom, Montreal	1978	Mike Bossy, N.Y. Islanders
1941	John Quilty, Montreal	1960	Bill Hay, Chicago	1979	Bobby Smith, Minnesota
1942	Grant Warwick, N.Y. Rangers	1961	Dave Keon, Toronto	1980	Ray Bourque, Boston
1943	Gaye Stewart, Toronto	1962	Bobby Rousseau, Montreal	1981	Peter Stastny, Quebec
1944	Gus Bodnar, Toronto	1963	Kent Douglas, Toronto	1982	Dale Hawerchuk, Winnipeg
1945	Frank McCool, Toronto	1964	Jacques Laperriere, Montreal	1983	Steve Larmer, Chicago
1946	Edgar Laprade, N.Y. Rangers	1965	Roger Crozier, Detroit	1984	Tom Barrasso, Buffalo
1947	Howie Meeker, Toronto	1966	Brit Selby, Toronto	1985	Mario Lemieux, Pittsburgh
1948	Jim McFadden, Detroit	1967	Bobby Orr, Boston	1986	Gary Suter, Calgary
1949	Pentti Lund, N.Y. Rangers	1968	Derek Sanderson, Boston	1987	Luc Robitaille, Los Angeles
1950	Jack Gelineau, Boston	1969	Danny Grant, Minnesota	1988	Joe Nieuwendyk, Calgary
1951	Terry Sawchuk, Detroit	1970	Tony Esposito, Chicago	1989	Brian Leetch, N.Y. Rangers

Lady Byng Memorial Trophy (Most Gentlemanly Player)

1925	Frank Nighbor, Ottawa	1947	Bobby Bauer, Boston	1969	Alex Delvecchio, Detroit
1926	Frank Nighbor, Ottawa	1948	Buddy O'Connor, N.Y. Rangers	1970	Phil Goyette, St. Louis
1927	Billy Burch, N.Y. Americans	1949	Bill Quackenbush, Detroit	1971	John Bucyk, Boston
1928	Frank Boucher, N.Y. Rangers	1950	Edgar Laprade, N.Y. Rangers	1972	Jean Ratelle, N.Y. Rangers
1929	Frank Boucher, N.Y. Rangers	1951	Red Kelly, Detroit	1973	Gil Perreault, Buffalo
1930	Frank Boucher, N.Y. Rangers	1952	Sid Smith, Toronto	1974	John Bucyk, Boston
1931	Frank Boucher, N.Y. Rangers	1953	Red Kelly, Detroit	1975	Marcel Dionne, Detroit
1932	Joe Primeau, Toronto	1954	Red Kelly, Detroit	1976	Jean Ratelle, N.Y. R.-Boston
1933	Frank Boucher, N.Y. Rangers	1955	Sid Smith, Toronto	1977	Marcel Dionne, Los Angeles
1934	Frank Boucher, N.Y. Rangers	1956	Earl Reibel, Detroit	1978	Butch Goring, Los Angeles
1935	Frank Boucher, N.Y. Rangers	1957	Andy Hebenton, N.Y. Rangers	1979	Bob MacMillan, Atlanta
1936	Doc Romnes, Chicago	1958	Camille Henry, N.Y. Rangers	1980	Wayne Gretzky, Edmonton
1937	Marty Barry, Detroit	1959	Alex Delvecchio, Detroit	1981	Butch Goring, N.Y. Islanders
1938	Gordie Drillon, Toronto	1960	Don McKenney, Boston	1982	Rick Middleton, Boston
1939	Clint Smith, N.Y. Rangers	1961	Red Kelly, Toronto	1983	Mike Bossy, N.Y. Islanders
1940	Bobby Bauer, Boston	1962	Dave Keon, Toronto	1984	Mike Bossy, N.Y. Islanders
1941	Bobby Bauer, Boston	1963	Dave Keon, Toronto	1985	Jari Kurri, Edmonton
1942	Syl Apps, Toronto	1964	Ken Wharram, Chicago	1986	Mike Bossy, N.Y. Islanders
1943	Max Bentley, Chicago	1965	Bobby Hull, Chicago	1987	Joe Mullen, Calgary
1944	Clint Smith, Chicago	1966	Alex Delvecchio, Detroit	1988	Mats Naslund, Montreal
1945	Bill Mosienko, Chicago	1967	Stan Mikita, Chicago	1989	Joe Mullen, Calgary
1946	Toe Blake, Montreal	1968	Stan Mikita, Chicago		

Frank J. Selke Trophy (Best Defensive Forward)

1978	Bob Gainey, Montreal	1982	Steve Kasper, Boston	1986	Troy Murray, Chicago
1979	Bob Gainey, Montreal	1983	Bobby Clarke, Philadelphia	1987	Dave Poulin, Philadelphia
1980	Bob Gainey, Montreal	1984	Doug Jarvis, Washington	1988	Guy Carbonneau, Montreal
1981	Bob Gainey, Montreal	1985	Craig Ramsay, Buffalo	1989	Guy Carbonneau, Montreal

James Norris Memorial Trophy (Outstanding Defenseman)

1954	Red Kelly, Detroit	1966	Jacques Laperriere, Montreal	1978	Denis Potvin, N.Y. Islanders
1955	Doug Harvey, Montreal	1967	Harry Howell, N.Y. Rangers	1979	Denis Potvin, N.Y. Islanders
1956	Doug Harvey, Montreal	1968	Bobby Orr, Boston	1980	Larry Robinson, Montreal
1957	Doug Harvey, Montreal	1969	Bobby Orr, Boston	1981	Randy Carlyle, Pittsburgh
1958	Doug Harvey, Montreal	1970	Bobby Orr, Boston	1982	Doug Wilson, Chicago
1959	Tom Johnson, Montreal	1971	Bobby Orr, Boston	1983	Rod Langway, Washington
1960	Doug Harvey, Montreal	1972	Bobby Orr, Boston	1984	Rod Langway, Washington
1961	Doug Harvey, Montreal	1973	Bobby Orr, Boston	1985	Paul Coffey, Edmonton
1962	Doug Harvey, N.Y. Rangers	1974	Bobby Orr, Boston	1986	Paul Coffey, Edmonton
1963	Pierre Pilote, Chicago	1975	Bobby Orr, Boston	1987	Ray Bourque, Boston
1964	Pierre Pilote, Chicago	1976	Denis Potvin, N.Y. Islanders	1988	Ray Bourque, Boston
1965	Pierre Pilote, Chicago	1977	Larry Robinson, Montreal	1989	Chris Chelios, Montreal

All-Time NHL Scoring Leaders

At end of 1988-89 season. *Active player.

	Games	G	A	Pts		Games	G	A	Pts
					Gil Perreault	1,191	512	814	1,326
Gordie Howe	1,767	801	1,049	1,850	Guy Lafleur*	1,028	536	755	1,291
Wayne Gretzky*	774	637	1,200	1,837	Alex Delvecchio	1,549	456	825	1,281
Marcel Dionne*	1,348	731	1,040	1,771	Jean Ratelle	1,281	491	776	1,267
Phil Esposito	1,282	717	873	1,590	Norm Ullman	1,410	490	739	1,229
Stan Mikita	1,394	541	926	1,467	Jean Beliveau	1,215	507	712	1,219
John Bucyk	1,540	556	813	1,369	Bobby Clarke	1,144	358	852	1,210
Bryan Trottier*	1,064	487	842	1,329	Bobby Hull	1,063	610	560	1,170

NCAA Hockey Champions

1948	Michigan	1959	North Dakota	1970	Cornell	1981	Wisconsin
1949	Boston College	1960	Denver	1971	Boston Univ.	1982	North Dakota
1950	Colorado College	1961	Denver	1972	Boston Univ	1983	Wisconsin
1951	Michigan	1962	Michigan Tech	1973	Wisconsin	1984	Bowling Green
1952	Michigan	1963	North Dakota	1974	Minnesota	1985	RPI
1953	Michigan	1964	Michigan	1975	Michigan Tech	1986	Michigan State
1954	RPI	1965	Michigan Tech	1976	Minnesota	1987	North Dakota
1955	Michigan	1966	Michigan State	1977	Wisconsin	1988	Lake Superior St.
1956	Michigan	1967	Cornell	1978	Boston Univ.	1989	Harvard
1957	Colorado College	1968	Denver	1979	Minnesota		
1958	Denver	1969	Denver	1980	North Dakota		

Curling Champions

Source: North American Curling News

World Champions

Year	Country, skip	Year	Country, skip	Year	Country, skip
1972	Canada, Crest Melesnuk	1978	United States, Bob Nichols	1984	Norway, Eigil Ramsfjell
1973	Sweden, Kjell Oscarius	1979	Norway, Kristian Soerum	1985	Canada, Al Hackner
1974	United States, Bud Somerville	1980	Canada, Rich Folk	1986	Canada, Ed Luckowich
1975	Switzerland, Otto Danieli	1981	Switzerland, Jurg Tanner	1987	Canada, Russ Howard
1976	United States, Bruce Roberts	1982	Canada, Al Hackner	1988	Norway, Eigil Ramsfjell
1977	Sweden, Ragnar Kamp	1983	Canada, Ed Werenich	1989	Canada, Pat Ryan

U.S. Men's Champions

Year	State, skip	Year	State, skip	Year	State, skip
1972	North Dakota, Bob LaBonte	1978	Wisconsin, Bob Nichols	1984	Minnesota, Bruce Roberts
1973	Massachusetts, Barry Blanchard	1979	Minnesota, Scotty Baird	1985	Illinois, Tim Wright
1974	Wisconsin, Bud Somerville	1980	Minnesota, Paul Pustover	1986	Wisconsin, Steve Brown
1975	Washington, Ed Risling	1981	Wisconsin, Somerville-Nichols	1987	Washington, Jim Vukich
1976	Minnesota, Bruce Roberts	1982	Wisconsin, Steve Brown	1988	Washington, Doug Jones
1977	Minnesota, Bruce Roberts	1983	Colorado, Don Cooper	1989	Washington, Jim Vukich

U.S. Ladies Champions

Year	State, skip	Year	State, skip	Year	State, skip
1978	Wisconsin, Sandy Robarge	1982	Illinois, Ruth Schwenker	1986	Minnesota, Gerri Tilden
1979	Washington, Nancy Langley	1983	Washington, Nancy Langley	1987	Washington, Sharon Good
1980	Washington, Sharon Kozai	1984	Minnesota, Amy Hatten	1988	Washington, Nancy Langey
1981	Washington, Nancy Langley	1985	Alaska, Bev Birklid	1989	North Dakota, Jan Lagasse

Major Indoor Soccer League in 1989

The San Diego Sockers defeated the Baltimore Blast 6-5 in the seventh and deciding game to win the Major Indoor Soccer League championship series. It was the 5th title in seven years for the San Diego team.

IGFA Freshwater & Saltwater All-Tackle World Records

Source: International Game Fish Association. Records confirmed to June, 1989

Saltwater Fish

Species	Weight	Where caught	Date	Angler
Albacore	88 lbs. 2 oz.	Pt. Mogan, Canary Islands	Nov. 19, 1977	Siegfried Dickemann
Amberjack, greater	155 lbs. 10 oz.	Bermuda	June 24, 1981	Joseph Dawson
Amberjack, Pacific	104 lbs.	Baja, Mexico	July 4, 1984	Richard Cresswell
Barracuda, great	83 lbs.	Lagos, Nigeria	Jan. 13, 1952	K.J.W. Hackett
Barracuda, Mexican	21 lbs.	Costa Rica	Mar. 27, 1987	E. Greg Kent
Barracuda, slender	17 lbs. 4 oz.	Sitra Channel, Bahrain	Nov. 21, 1985	Roger Cranswick
Bass, barred sand	11 lbs. 4 oz.	Imperial Beach, Cal.	Aug. 16, 1986	Dale Barrington
Bass, black sea	9 lbs. 8 oz.	Virginia Beach, Va.	Jan. 9, 1987	Joe Mizelle Jr.
Bass, European	20 lbs. 11 oz.	Stes Maries de la Mer, France	May 6, 1986	Jean Baptiste Bayle
Bass, giant sea	563 lbs. 8 oz.	Anacaba Island, Cal.	Aug. 20, 1968	James D. McAdam Jr.
Bass, striped	78 lbs. 8 oz.	Atlantic City, N.J.	Sept. 21, 1982	Albert McReynolds
Bluefish	31 lbs. 12 oz.	Hatteras Inlet, N.C.	Jan. 30, 1972	James M. Hussey
Bonefish	19 lbs.	Zululand, S. Africa	May 26, 1962	Brian W. Batchelor
Bonito, Atlantic	18 lbs. 14 oz.	Fayal I., Azores	July 8, 1953	D. G. Higgs
Bonito, Pacific	23 lbs. 8 oz.	Victoria, Mahe Seychelles	Feb. 19, 1975	Anne Cochain
Cabezon	18 lbs.	Pt. Townsend, Wash.	Apr. 28, 1988	Mark Mokodean
Cobia	135 lbs. 9 oz.	Shark Bay, Australia	July 9, 1985	Peter W. Goulding
Cod, Atlantic	98 lbs. 12 oz.	Isle of Shoals, N.H.	June 8, 1969	Alphonse Bielevich
Cod, Pacific	30 lbs.	Andrew Bay, Alaska	June 7, 1984	Donald Vaughn
Conger	102 lbs. 8 oz.	Devon, England	July 18, 1983	Raymond E. Street
Dolphin	87 lbs.	Papagallo Gulf, Costa Rica	Sept. 25, 1976	Manual Salazar
Drum, black	113 lbs. 1 oz.	Lewes, Del.	Sept. 15, 1975	Gerald Townsend
Drum, red	94 lbs. 2 oz.	Avon, N.C.	Nov. 7, 1984	David Deuel
Eel, African mottled	36 lbs. 1 oz.	Durban, So. Africa	June 10, 1984	Ferdie van Nooten
Eel, American	4 lb. 7 oz.	Lake Ronkonkoma, N.Y.	Nov. 15, 1986	William C. Cummings
Flounder, southern	20 lbs. 9 oz.	Nassau Sound, Fla.	Dec. 23, 1983	Larenza Mungin
Flounder, summer	22 lbs. 7 oz.	Montauk, N.Y.	Sept. 15, 1975	Charles Nappi
Grouper, Warsaw	436 lbs. 12 oz.	Gulf of Mexico, Destin, Fla.	Dec. 22, 1985	Steve Haeusler
Halibut, Atlantic	250 lbs.	Gloucester, Mass.	July 3, 1981	Louis Sirard
Halibut, California	53 lbs. 4 oz.	Santa Rosa Is., Cal.	July 7, 1988	Russell Harmon
Halibut, Pacific	350 lbs.	Homer, Alaska	June 30, 1982	Vern S. Foster
Jack, crevalle	54 lbs. 7oz.	Pt. Michel, Gabon	Jan. 15, 1982	Thomas Gibson Jr.
Jack, horse-eye	24 lbs. 8 oz.	Miami, Fla.	Dec. 20, 1982	Tito Schnau
Jack, Pacific crevalle	24 lbs.	Baja, Cal., Mex.	Apr. 30, 1987	Sharon Swanson
Jewfish	680 lbs.	Fernandina Beach, Fla.	May 20, 1961	Lynn Joyner
Kawakawa	29 lbs.	New South Wales, Australia	Dec. 17, 1986	Ronald Nakamura
Lingcod	64 lbs.	Elfin Cove, Alaska	Aug. 2, 1988	David Bauer
Mackerel, cero	17 lbs. 2 oz.	Islamorada, Fla.	Apr. 5, 1986	G. Michael Mills
Mackerel, king	90 lbs.	Key West, Fla.	Feb. 16, 1976	Norton Thomton
Mackeral, Spanish	13 lbs.	Ocracoke Inlet, N.C.	Nov. 4, 1987	Robert Cranton
Marlin, Atlantic blue	1,282 lbs.	St. Thomas, Virgin Islands	Aug. 6, 1977	Larry Martin
Marlin, black	1,560 lbs.	Cabo Blanco, Peru	Aug. 4, 1953	A. C. Glassell Jr.
Marlin, Pacific blue	1,376 lbs.	Kaaiwa Pt., Hawaii	May. 31, 1982	J.W. deBeaubien
Marlin, striped	494 lbs.	Tutukaka, New Zealand	Jan. 16, 1986	Bill Boniface
Marlin, white	181 lbs. 14 oz.	Vitoria, Brazil	Dec. 8, 1979	Evandro Luiz Caser
Permit	51 lbs. 8 oz.	Lake Worth, Fla.	Apr. 28, 1978	William M. Kenney
Pollack	26 lbs. 7 oz.	Devon, England	Dec. 30, 1984	Robert Perry
Pollock	46 lbs. 7 oz.	Brielle, N.J.	May 26, 1975	John Tomes Holton
Pompano, African	49 lbs.	Stuart, Fla.	Feb. 4, 1977	Lawrence Hofman
Roosterfish	114 lbs.	La Paz, Mexico	June 1, 1960	Abe Sackheim
Runner, blue	6 lbs. 8 oz.	Barnegat Light, N.J.	Aug. 24, 1987	Sandra B. Good
Runner, rainbow	33 lbs. 10 oz.	Clarion Is., Mexico	Mar. 14, 1976	Ralph A. Mikkelsen
Sailfish, Atlantic	128 lbs. 1 oz.	Luanda, Angola	Mar. 27, 1974	Harm Steyn
Sailfish, Pacific	221 lbs.	Santa Cruz Is., Ecuador	Feb. 12, 1947	C. W. Stewart
Seabass, white	83 lbs. 12 oz.	San Felipe, Mexico	Mar. 31, 1953	L.C. Baumgardner
Seatrout, spotted	16 lbs.	Mason's Beach, Va.	May 28, 1977	William Katko
Shark, blue	437 lbs.	Catherine Bay, N.S.W. Australia	Oct. 2, 1976	Peter Hyde
Shark, Greenland	1,708 lbs. 9 oz.	Trondheim, Norway	Oct. 18, 1987	Terje Nordtvedt
Shark, hammerhead	991 lbs.	Sarasota, Fla.	May 30, 1982	Allen Ogle
Shark, man-eater or white	2,664 lbs.	Ceduna, Australia	Apr. 21, 1959	Alfred Dean
Shark, mako	1,115 lbs.	Black R., Mauritius	Nov. 16, 1988	Patrick Guillanton
Shark, porbeagle	465 lbs.	Cornwall, England	July 23, 1976	Jorge Potier
Shark, thresher	802 lbs.	Tutukaka, New Zealand	Feb. 8, 1981	Dianne North
Shark, tiger	1,780 lbs.	Cherry Grove, S.C.	June 14, 1964	Walter Maxwell
Skipjack, black	20 lbs. 5 oz.	Baja, Mexico	Oct. 14, 1983	Roger Torriero
Snapper, cubera	121 lbs. 8 oz.	Cameron, La.	July 5, 1982	Mike Hebert
Snook	53 lbs. 10 oz.	Costa Rica	Oct. 18, 1978	Gilbert Ponzi
Spearfish	90 lbs. 13 oz.	Madeira Island, Portugal	June 2, 1980	Joseph Larkin
Swordfish	1,182 lbs.	Iquique, Chile	May 7, 1953	L. Marron
Tanguigue	99 lbs.	Natal, So. Africa	Mar. 14, 1982	Michael J. Wilkinson
Tarpon	283 lbs.	Lake Maracaibo, Venezuela	Mar. 19, 1956	M. Salazar
Tautog	24 lbs.	Wachapreagee, Va.	Aug. 25, 1987	Gregory Bell
Tope	72 lbs. 12 oz.	Parengarenga Harbor, New Zealand	Dec. 19, 1986	Melanie Feldman
Trevally, bigeye	15 lbs.	Isla Coiba, Panama	Jan. 18, 1984	Sally Timms
Trevally, giant	137 lbs. 9 oz.	McKenzie St. Park, Hawaii	July 13, 1983	Roy Gushiken
Tuna, Atlantic bigeye	375 lbs. 8 oz.	Ocean City, Md.	Aug. 26, 1977	Cecil Browne
Tuna, blackfin	42 lbs.	Bermuda	June 2, 1978	Alan J. Card
Tuna, bluefin	1,496 lbs.	Aulds Cove, Nova Scotia	Oct. 26, 1979	Ken Fraser

Species	Weight	Where caught	Date	Angler
Tuna, longtail	79 lbs. 2 oz.	Montague Is., N.S.W., Australia	Apr. 12, 1982	Tim Simpson
Tuna, Pacific bigeye	435 lbs.	Cabo Blanco, Peru	Apr. 17, 1957	Dr. Russel Lee
Tuna, skipjack	41 lbs. 14 oz.	Mauritius	Nov. 12, 1985	Edmund Heinzen
Tuna, southern bluefin	348 lbs. 5 oz.	Whakatane, New Zealand	Jan. 16, 1981	Rex Wood
Tuna, yellowfin	388 lbs. 12 oz.	San Benedicto Island, Mexico	Apr. 1, 1977	Curt Wiesenhutter
Tunny, little	35 lbs. 2 oz.	Cape de Garde, Algeria	Dec. 14, 1988	Jean Yves Chatard
Wahoo	149 lbs.	Cay Cay, Bahamas	June 15, 1962	John Pirovano
Weakfish	19 lbs. 2 oz.	Jones Beach Inlet, N.Y.	Oct. 11, 1984	Dennis Rooney
Yellowtail, California	78 lbs.	Alijos Rocks, Mexico	June 27, 1987	Richard Cresswell
Yellowtail, southern	114 lbs. 10 oz.	Tauranga, New Zealand	Feb. 5, 1984	Mike Godfrey

Freshwater Fish

Species	Weight	Where caught	Date	Angler
Barramundi	59 lbs. 12 oz.	Pt. Stuart, Australia	Apr. 7, 1983	Andrew Davern
Bass, largemouth	22 lbs. 4 oz.	Montgomery Lake, Ga.	June 2, 1932	George W. Perry
Bass, peacock	26 lbs. 8 oz.	Matevini R., Colombia	Jan. 26, 1982	Rod Neubert
Bass, redeye	8 lbs. 3 oz.	Flint River, Ga.	Oct. 23, 1977	David A. Hubbard
Bass rock	3 lbs.	York River, Ont.	Aug. 1, 1974	Peter Gulgin
Bass, smallmouth	11 lbs. 15 oz.	Dale Hollow Lake, Ky.	July 9, 1955	David L. Hayes
Bass, Suwannee	3 lbs. 14 oz.	Suwannee River, Fla.	Mar. 2, 1985	Ronnie Everett
Bass, white	5 lbs. 14 oz.	Kerr Lake, N.C.	Mar. 15, 1986	Jim King
Bass, whiterock	22 lbs. 6 oz.	New Savannah Dam, Ga.	July 20, 1986	Jerry L. Adams
Bass, yellow	2 lbs. 4 oz.	Lake Monroe, Ind.	Mar. 27, 1977	Donald L. Stalker
Bluegill	4 lbs. 12 oz.	Ketona Lake, Ala.	Apr. 9, 1950	T.S. Hudson
Bowfin	21 lbs. 8 oz.	Florence, S.C.	Jan. 29, 1980	Robert Harmon
Buffalo, bigmouth	70 lbs. 5 oz.	Bastrop, La.	Apr. 21, 1980	Delbert Sisk
Buffalo, black	55 lbs. 8 oz.	Cherokee L., Tenn.	May 3, 1984	Edward McLain
Buffalo, smallmouth	68 lbs. 8 oz.	L. Hamilton, Ark.	May 16, 1984	Jerry Dolezal
Bullhead, brown	5 lbs. 8 oz.	Veal Pond, Ga.	May 22, 1975	Jimmy Andrews
Bullhead, yellow	4 lbs. 4 oz.	Mormon Lake, Ariz.	May 11, 1984	Emily Williams
Burbot	18 lbs. 4 oz.	Pickford, Mich.	Jan. 31, 1980	Thomas Courtemanche
Carp	75 lbs. 11 oz.	Lac de St. Cassien, France	May 21, 1987	Leo van der Gugten
Catfish, blue	97 lbs.	Missouri River, S.D.	Sept. 16, 1959	E.B. Elliott
Catfish, channel	58 lbs.	Santee-Cooper Res., S.C.	July 7, 1964	W.B. Whaley
Catfish, flathead	98 lbs.	Lewisville, Tex.	June 2, 1986	William Stephens
Catfish, white	17 lbs. 7 oz.	Success L., Tulare, Cal.	Nov. 15, 1981	Chuck Idell
Char, Arctic	32 lbs. 9 oz.	Tree River, Canada	July 30, 1981	Jeffrey Ward
Crappie, white	5 lbs. 3 oz.	Enid Dam, Miss.	July 31, 1957	Fred L. Bright
Dolly Varden	12 lbs.	Noatak R., Alaska	July 10, 1987	Kenneth Alt
Dorado	51 lbs. 5 oz.	Corrientes, Argentina	Sept. 27, 1984	Armando Giudice
Drum, freshwater	54 lbs. 8 oz.	Nickajack Lake, Tenn.	Apr. 20, 1972	Benny E. Hull
Gar, alligator	279 lbs.	Rio Grande River, Tex.	Dec. 2, 1951	Bill Valverde
Gar, Florida	21 lbs. 3 oz.	Boca Raton, Fla.	June 3, 1981	Jeff Sabol
Gar, longnose	50 lbs. 5 oz.	Trinity River, Tex.	July 30, 1954	Townsend Miller
Gar, shortnose	5 lbs.	Sally Jones L., Oklahoma	Apr. 26, 1985	Buddy Croslin
Gar, spotted	8 lbs. 12 oz.	Tennessee R., Ala.	Aug. 26, 1987	Winston Baker
Grayling, Arctic	5 lbs. 15 oz.	Katseyedie River, N.W.T.	Aug. 16, 1967	Jeanne P. Branson
Inconnu	53 lbs.	Pah R., Alaska	Aug. 20, 1986	Lawrence Hudnall
Kokanee	9 lbs. 6 oz.	Okanagan Lake, Vernon, B.C.	June 18, 1988	Norm Kuhn
Muskellunge	69 lbs. 15 oz.	St. Lawrence River, N.Y.	Sept. 22, 1957	Arthur Lawton
Muskellunge, tiger	51 lbs. 3 oz.	Lac Vieux-Desert, Wis., Mich.	July 16, 1919	John Knobla
Perch, Nile	132 lbs. 4 oz.	L. Turkana, Kenya	Jan. 28, 1988	Jerry Tricomi
Perch, white	4 lbs. 12 oz.	Messalonskee Lake, Me.	June 4, 1949	Mrs. Earl Small
Perch, yellow	4 lbs. 3 oz.	Bordentown, N.J.	May, 1865	Dr. C.C. Abbot
Pickerel, chain	9 lbs. 6 oz.	Homerville, Ga.	Feb. 17, 1961	Baxley McQuaig Jr.
Pike, northern	55 lbs. 1 oz.	Lake of Grefeern, W., Germany	Oct. 16, 1986	Lothar Louis
Redhorse, shorthead	9 lbs. 3 oz.	Salmon R., Pulaski, N.Y.	May 11, 1985	Jason Wilson
Redhorse, silver	11 lbs. 7 oz.	Plum Creek, Wis.	May 29, 1985	Neal Long
Salmon, Atlantic	79 lbs. 2 oz.	Tana River, Norway	1928	Henrik Henriksen
Salmon, chinook	97 lbs. 4 oz.	Kenai R., Alas.	May 17, 1985	Les Anderson
Salmon, chum	32 lbs.	Behm Canal, Alas.	June 7, 1985	Fredrick Thynes
Salmon, coho	31 lbs.	Cowichan Bay, B.C.	Oct. 11, 1947	Mrs. Lee Hallberg
Salmon, pink	12 lbs. 9 oz.	Morse, Kenai rivers, Alas.	Aug. 17, 1974	Steven A. Lee
Salmon, sockeye	15 lbs. 3 oz.	Kenai R., Alaska	Aug. 9, 1987	Stan Roach
Sauger	8 lbs. 12 oz.	Lake Sakakawea, N.D.	Oct. 6, 1971	Mike Fischer
Shad, American	11 lbs. 4 oz.	Connecticut R., Mass.	May 19, 1986	Bob Thibodo
Sturgeon, white	468 lbs.	Benicia, Cal.	July 9, 1983	Joey Pallotta 3d
Sunfish, green	2 lbs. 2 oz.	Stockton Lake, Mo.	June 18, 1971	Paul M. Dilley
Sunfish, redbreast	1 lb. 12 oz.	Suwannee R., Fla.	May 29, 1984	Alvin Buchanan
Sunfish, redear	4 lbs. 13 oz.	Marianna, Fla.	Mar. 13, 1986	Joey Floyd
Tigerfish	97 lbs.	Zaire R., Kinshasa, Zaire	July 9, 1988	Raymond Houtmans
Tilapia	4 lbs. 5 oz.	Mittry L., Ariz.	Sept. 17, 1984	John B. Adkins
Trout, Apache	1 lb. 8 oz.	Apache Res., Ariz.	Oct. 19, 1984	Burton Leed
Trout, brook	14 lbs. 8 oz.	Nipigon River, Ont.	July 1916	Dr. W.J. Cook
Trout, brown	35 lbs. 15 oz.	Nahuel Huapi, Argentina	Dec. 16, 1952	Eugenio Cavaglia
Trout, bull	32 lbs.	L. Pend Oreille, Ida.	Oct. 27, 1949	N.L. Higgins
Trout, cutthroat	41 lbs.	Pyramid Lake, Nev.	Dec. 1925	J. Skimmerhorn
Trout, golden	11 lbs.	Cook's Lake, Wyo.	Aug. 5, 1948	Charles S. Reed
Trout, lake	65 lbs.	Great Bear Lake, N.W.T.	Aug. 8, 1970	Larry Daunis
Trout, rainbow	42 lbs. 2 oz.	Bell Island, Alas.	June 22, 1970	David Robert White
Trout, tiger	20 lbs. 13 oz.	Lake Michigan, Wis.	Aug. 12, 1978	Pete Friedland
Walleye	25 lbs.	Old Hickory Lake, Tenn.	Aug. 1, 1960	Mabry Harper
Warmouth	2 lbs. 7 oz.	Yellow R., Holt, Fla.	Oct. 19, 1985	Tony D. Dempsey
Whitefish, lake	14 lbs. 6 oz.	Meaford, Ont.	May 21, 1984	Dennis Laycock
Whitefish, mountain	5 lbs. 2 oz.	Columbia R., Wash.	Nov. 30, 1983	Steven Becken
Whitefish, river	11 lbs. 2 oz.	Nymoua, Sweden	Dec. 9, 1984	Jorgen Larsson
Whitefish, round	6 lbs.	Putahow R., Manitoba	June 14, 1984	Allen Ristori
Zander	22 lbs. 2 oz.	Trosa, Sweden	June 12, 1986	Harry Lee Tennison

COLLEGE BASKETBALL
Final Regular Season Conference Standings, 1988–89

Atlantic Coast

Team	Conf W	Conf L	Non-Conf W	Non-Conf L
N.C. State	10	4	20	7
Duke	9	5	22	6
North Carolina	9	5	24	7
Virginia	9	5	18	9
Georgia Tech	8	6	20	10
Clemson	7	7	18	9
Wake Forest	3	11	13	14
Maryland	1	13	8	19

Tournament Champion—N. Carolina.

Atlantic 10

Team	Conf W	Conf L	Non-Conf W	Non-Conf L
West Virginia	17	1	25	4
Temple	15	3	18	11
Rutgers	13	5	17	12
Penn St.	12	6	19	10
Rhode Island	9	9	13	15
St. Bonaventure	7	11	13	15
Duquesne	7	11	13	16
Massachusetts	5	13	10	18
St. Joseph's	4	14	8	21
George Washington	1	17	1	27

Tournament Champion—Rutgers.

Big East

Team	Conf W	Conf L	Non-Conf W	Non-Conf L
Georgetown	13	3	23	4
Seton Hall	11	5	25	5
Syracuse	10	6	25	6
Pittsburgh	9	7	16	11
Providence	7	9	18	9
Villanova	7	9	16	14
Connecticut	6	10	16	11
St. John's	6	10	15	12
Boston College	3	13	11	16

Tournament Champion—Georgetown.

Big Eight

Team	Conf W	Conf L	Non-Conf W	Non-Conf L
Oklahoma	12	2	26	4
Missouri	10	4	24	7
Kansas St.	8	6	18	9
Iowa St.	7	7	16	10
Oklahoma St.	7	7	16	11
Kansas	6	8	19	11
Nebraska	4	10	16	14
Colorado	2	12	7	20

Tournament Champion—Missouri.

Big Sky

Team	Conf W	Conf L	Non-Conf W	Non-Conf L
Idaho	13	3	23	5
Boise St.	13	3	22	5
Montana	11	5	19	10
Nevada-Reno	10	6	16	11
Weber St.	9	7	16	10
Montana St.	6	10	14	14
E. Washington	5	11	8	22
Idaho St.	4	12	9	18
N. Arizona	1	15	2	25

Tournament Champion—Idaho.

Big Ten

Team	Conf W	Conf L	Non-Conf W	Non-Conf L
Indiana	15	3	25	7
Illinois	14	4	27	4
Michigan	12	6	24	7
Iowa	10	8	22	9
Minnesota	9	9	17	11
Wisconsin	8	10	17	11
Purdue	8	10	15	16
Ohio St.	6	12	17	14
Michigan St.	6	12	15	13
Northwestern	2	16	9	19

East Coast

Team	Conf W	Conf L	Non-Conf W	Non-Conf L
Bucknell	11	3	22	7
Towson St.	10	4	19	10
Lafayette	8	6	20	9
Hofstra	7	7	14	15
Drexel	7	7	12	16
Delaware	6	8	14	14
Lehigh	3	9	10	18
Rider	2	12	5	23

Tournament Champion—Bucknell.

Big West

Team	Conf W	Conf L	Non-Conf W	Non-Conf L
UNLV	16	2	23	7
New Mexico St.	12	6	19	9
UC-Santa Barbara	11	7	20	7
CS-Fullerton	10	8	15	12
Long Beach St.	10	8	13	14
Utah St.	10	8	12	15
Fresno St.	9	9	14	13
UC-Irvine	8	10	11	16
Pacific Univ.	3	15	7	20
San Jose St.	1	17	5	22

Tournament Champion—UNLV.

Colonial

Team	Conf W	Conf L	Non-Conf W	Non-Conf L
Richmond	13	1	20	9
George Mason	10	4	20	10
American Univ.	9	5	17	11
N.C.-Wilmington	9	5	16	14
James Madison	6	8	16	14
East Carolina	6	8	15	14
William & Mary	2	12	5	23
Navy	1	13	6	22

Tournament Champion—George Mason.

ECAC North Atlantic

Team	Conf W	Conf L	Non-Conf W	Non-Conf L
Siena	16	1	21	4
Boston Univ.	14	4	19	8
Northeastern	12	5	16	10
Canisius	11	7	13	14
Hartford	10	7	14	12
Maine	7	11	9	18
Niagara	6	12	9	18
Colgate	5	13	6	21
Vermont	4	14	6	21
New Hampshire	3	14	4	22

Tournament Champion—Siena.

Ivy League

Team	Conf W	Conf L	Non-Conf W	Non-Conf L
Princeton	11	3	19	7
Dartmouth	10	4	17	9
Penn	9	5	13	13
Harvard	7	7	11	15
Cornell	7	7	10	16
Yale	6	8	11	17
Columbia	4	10	8	18
Brown	2	12	7	19

Metro

Team	Conf W	Conf L	Non-Conf W	Non-Conf L
Florida St.	9	3	21	6
Louisville	8	4	20	8
Memphis St.	8	4	21	9
South Carolina	8	4	18	9
Cincinnati	5	7	15	12
Virginia Tech	2	10	11	17
Southern Miss	2	10	10	16

Tournament Champion—Louisville.

Metro Atlantic

Team	Conf W	Conf L	Non-Conf W	Non-Conf L
La Salle	13	1	26	5
St. Peter's	11	3	22	8
Iona	8	6	15	15
Fordham	8	6	14	15
Army	6	8	12	16
Holy Cross	5	9	13	15
Manhattan	3	11	7	21
Fairfield	2	12	7	21

Tournament Champion—La Salle.

Mid-American

Team	Conf W	Conf L	Non-Conf W	Non-Conf L
Ball St.	14	2	25	2
Kent St.	11	5	18	9
Toledo	9	7	15	14
Miami (Ohio)	8	8	13	14
E. Michigan	7	9	15	12
Bowling Green	6	10	12	15
Cent. Michigan	6	10	12	15
W. Michigan	6	10	12	15
Ohio Univ.	5	11	11	16

Tournament Champion—Ball St.

Mid-Continent

Team	Conf W	Conf L	Non-Conf W	Non-Conf L
SW Missouri St.	10	2	19	9
N. Iowa	8	4	19	9
E. Illinois	7	5	16	15
Wisconsin-Green Bay	6	6	14	14
Valparaiso	4	8	10	18
W. Illinois	4	8	9	19
Ill.-Chicago	3	9	12	16
Cleveland St.	0	12	16	12

Tournament Champion—SW Missouri St.

Mid-Eastern

Team	Conf W	Conf L	Non-Conf W	Non-Conf L
S. Carolina St.	14	2	25	7
Florida A&M	12	4	20	10
Coppin St.	11	5	18	11
Morgan St.	9	7	15	14
Bethune-Cookman	8	8	12	16
Delaware St.	6	10	11	17
N. Carolina A&T	6	10	9	18
Howard Univ.	1	9	1	19
Maryland-E. Shore	1	15	1	26

Tournament Champion—South Carolina St.

Midwestern

Team	Conf W	Conf L	Non-Conf W	Non-Conf L
Evansville	10	2	23	4
St. Louis	8	4	22	8
Xavier (Ohio)	7	5	18	11
Dayton	6	6	11	16
Loyola (Ill.)	4	8	11	16
Detroit	4	8	7	20
Butler	3	9	11	16

Tournament Champion—Xavier.

Missouri Valley

Team	Conf W	Conf L	Non-Conf W	Non-Conf L
Creighton	11	3	19	10
Wichita St.	10	4	18	10
Tulsa	10	4	18	13
Bradley	7	7	13	14
S. Illinois	6	8	20	12
Illinois St.	6	8	13	17
Drake	6	8	12	17
Indiana St.	0	14	4	24

Tournament Champion—Creighton.

Ohio Valley

Team	Conf W	Conf L	Non-Conf W	Non-Conf L
Middle Tennessee	10	2	20	7
Murray St.	10	2	19	9
Austin Peay	8	4	17	11
Morehead St.	5	7	15	16
E. Kentucky	4	8	7	21
Tennessee Tech	3	9	10	20
Tennessee St.	2	10	4	24

Tournament Champion—Middle Tenn.

Pacific-10

Team	Conf W	Conf L	Non-Conf W	Non-Conf L
Arizona	17	1	24	3
Stanford	15	3	24	5
Oregon St.	13	5	21	6
UCLA	13	5	19	8
California	10	8	19	11
Washington	8	10	12	15
Arizona St.	5	13	12	15
Washington St.	4	14	9	18
Oregon	3	15	8	20
USC	2	16	9	21

Tournament Champion—Arizona.

Southern

Team	Conf W	Conf L	Non-Conf W	Non-Conf L
Tenn.-Chattanooga	10	4	18	12
Furman	9	5	17	12
Appalachian St.	8	6	20	8
E. Tennessee St.	7	7	20	10
Citadel	7	7	16	12
Marshall	6	8	15	15
VMI	5	9	11	17
W. Carolina	4	10	12	16

Tournament Champion—E. Tenn. St.

Southeastern

	Conference W	L	Non-Conference W	L
Florida	13	5	19	11
Alabama	12	6	20	7
Vanderbilt	12	6	18	12
LSU	11	7	20	10
Tennessee	11	7	18	9
Mississippi	8	10	14	13
Kentucky	8	10	13	18
Mississippi St.	7	11	13	14
Georgia	6	12	14	15
Auburn	2	16	9	18

Tournament Champion—Alabama.

Southland

	Conference W	L	Non-Conference W	L
North Texas	10	4	13	14
NE Louisiana	9	5	16	11
McNeese St.	9	5	14	13
Sam Houston St.	8	6	12	16
NW Louisiana	7	7	12	15
SW Texas St.	6	8	13	16
Texas-Arlington	4	10	7	20
S.F. Austin	3	11	10	18

Tournament Champion—McNeese St.

Southwest

	Conference W	L	Non-Conference W	L
Arkansas	13	3	21	6
Texas	12	4	22	7
Texas Christian	9	7	16	12
Houston	9	8	18	13
Texas A&M	8	8	15	13
Texas Tech	8	8	13	14
SMU	7	9	13	15
Rice	6	10	12	15
Baylor	1	15	5	22

Tournament Champion—Arkansas.

Southwestern

	Conference W	L	Non-Conference W	L
Southern Univ.	10	4	17	10
Texas So.	10	4	15	12
Grambling St.	10	4	14	13
Jackson St.	7	7	15	12
Alabama St.	7	7	12	15
Prairie View	5	9	11	15
Alcorn St.	4	10	5	22
Mississippi Valley	3	11	8	19

Tournament Champion—Southern Univ.

Sun Belt

	Conference W	L	Non-Conference W	L
South Alabama	11	3	22	8
N.C.-Charlotte	10	4	17	11
Va. Commonwealth	9	5	13	15
Alabama-Birmingham	8	6	18	11
Old Dominion	7	7	15	13
Jacksonville	5	9	14	16
W. Kentucky	4	10	14	15
South Florida	2	12	7	21

Tournament Champion—South Alabama.

Trans America

	Conference W	L	Non-Conference W	L
Georgia Southern	16	2	23	4
Arkansas-Little Rock	14	4	20	7
Stetson	10	8	16	11
Centenary	9	9	14	13
Georgia St.	9	9	14	13
Mercer	9	9	14	13
Texas-San Antonio	8	10	15	12
Houston Baptist	6	12	8	19
Samford	5	13	8	19
Hardin Simmons	4	14	8	19

Tournament Champion—Arkansas-Little Rock.

West Coast

	Conference W	L	Non-Conference W	L
St. Mary's	12	2	25	4
Loyola, Marymount	10	4	20	10
Pepperdine	10	4	19	12
San Francisco	8	6	16	12
Santa Clara	7	7	20	10
Gonzaga	5	9	14	14
San Diego	2	12	8	20
Portland	2	12	2	26

Tournament Champion—Loyola, Marymount.

Western Athletic

	Conference W	L	Non-Conference W	L
Colorado St.	12	4	20	8
Texas-El Paso	11	5	22	6
New Mexico	11	5	19	9
Hawaii	9	7	16	11
Brigham Young	7	9	14	14
Air Force	6	10	14	13
Utah	6	10	15	16
Wyoming	6	10	14	16
San Diego St.	4	12	12	16

Tournament Champion—Texas-El Paso.

Independents

	W	L
Akron	21	7
Notre Dame	20	8
De Paul	20	11
Miami, Fla.	19	12
Md. Baltimore Co.	17	11
Wright St.	17	11
Marquette	13	15
Chicago St.	12	16
Mt. St. Mary's, Md.	12	15
Nicholls St.	12	16
N. Illinois	11	17
U.S. International	11	17
Liberty	10	17
Central Connecticut	10	18
Florida International	10	18
S. Utah	10	18
Oral Roberts	8	20
Central Florida	7	20
Davidson	7	24
Youngstown St.	5	23
Brooklyn	4	23
SE Louisiana	4	23

Division I College Basketball Leaders in 1988-1989 Season

(regular season)

Scoring

	G	Pts	Avg
Gathers, Loyola-Marymount	30	987	32.9
Jackson, LSU	31	932	30.1
Simmons, LaSalle	31	882	28.5
Glass, Mississippi	29	812	28.0
Edwards, E. Carolina	29	773	26.7
Dudley, Air Force	28	746	26.6
Coles, Va. Tech	27	717	26.6
Smith, BYU	29	765	26.4
King, Oklahoma	30	788	26.3

Assists

	G	No.	Avg
Williams, Holy Cross	28	278	9.9
Douglas, Syracuse	34	294	8.6
Corchaini, N. Carolina St.	28	241	8.6
Payton, Oregon St.	29	234	8.1
Manuel, Bradley	27	216	8.0
Timberlake, Boston U.	30	238	7.9

Rebounds

	G	No.	Avg
Gathers, Loyola-Marymount	30	409	13.6
Hill, Xavier	32	397	12.4
Draper, American	28	336	12.0
Coleman, Syracuse	34	393	11.6
Battles, Southern	30	345	11.5
Mack, S. Carolina St.	32	361	11.3
Simmons, LaSalle	31	349	11.3
Burton, Long Island	28	309	11.0
Washington, Weber	28	303	10.8

Field-Goal Percentage

	FG	FGA	Pct
Davis, Florida	175	243	72.0
Vaught, Michigan	184	265	69.4
Burns, Mississippi St.	167	249	67.1
Mack, S. Carolina St.	200	299	66.9
Davis, Clemson	138	207	66.7

Blocked Shots Per Game

	G	NO	AVG
Mourning, Georgetown	30	150	5.0
Causwell, Temple	29	123	4.2
Ogg, Ala.-Birmingham	29	113	3.9
Coleman, Syracuse	34	122	3.6
Butts, Bucknell	30	100	3.3

3-Pt. FG Percentage

	FG	FGA	Pct
Calloway, Monmouth	48	82	58.5
Tribelhorn, Colo. St.	70	125	56.0
Joseph, Bucknell	60	108	55.6
Bays, Towson	71	131	54.2
Anglavar, Marquette	53	99	53.5

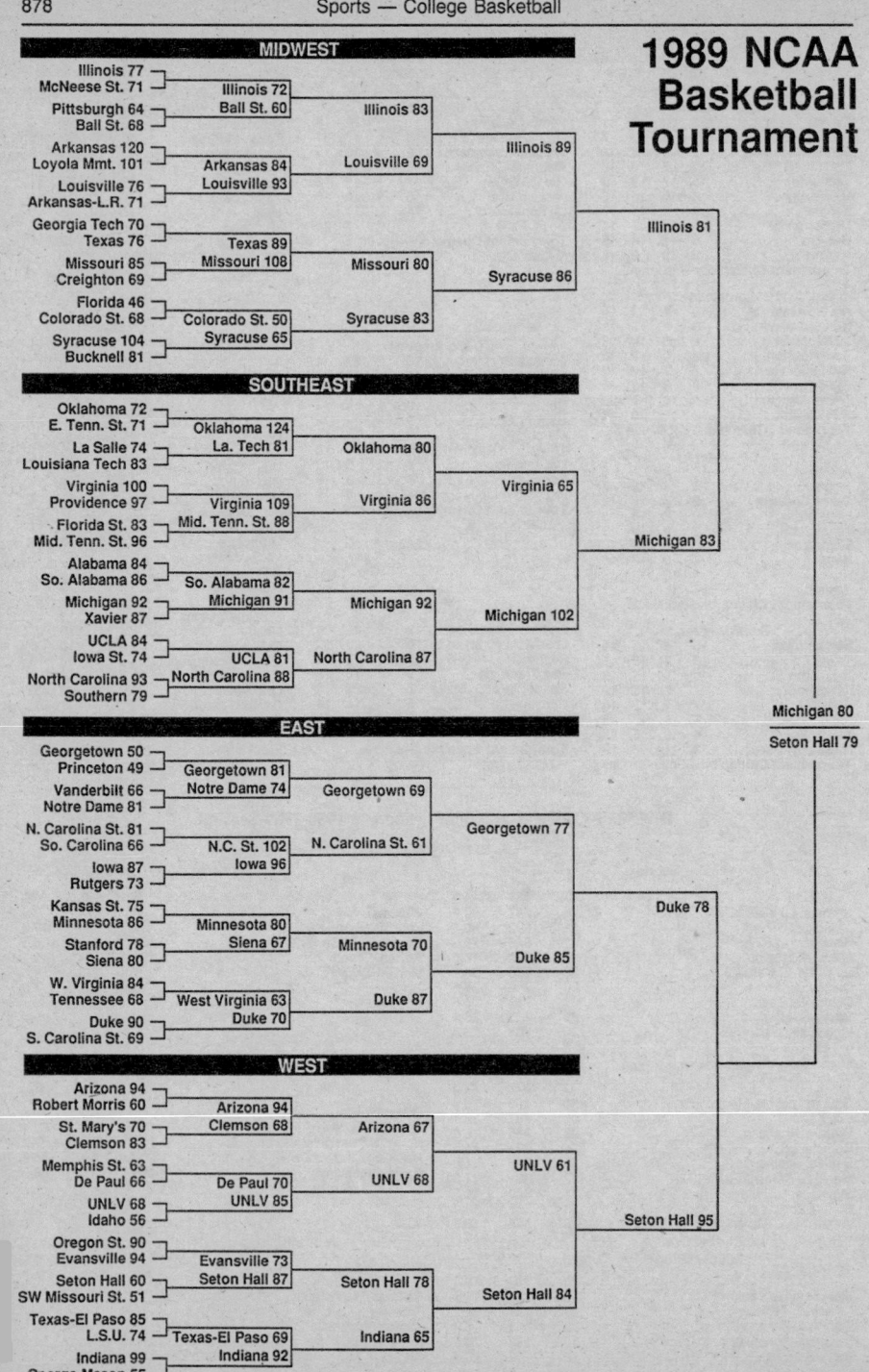

NCAA Division I Champions

Year	Champion	Coach	Final opponent	Score	Outstanding player	Site
1939	Oregon	Howard Hobson	Ohio St.	46-33	None	Evanston, Ill.
1940	Indiana	Branch McCracken	Kansas	60-42	Marvin Huffman, Indiana	Kansas City, Mo.
1941	Wisconsin	Harold Foster	Washington St.	39-34	John Kotz, Wisconsin	Kansas City, Mo.
1942	Stanford	Everett Dean	Dartmouth	53-38	Howard Dallmar, Stanford	Kansas City, Mo.
1943	Wyoming	Everett Shelton	Georgetown	46-34	Ken Sailors, Wyoming	New York, N.Y.
1944	Utah	Vadal Peterson	Dartmouth	42-40(1)	Arnold Ferrin, Utah	New York, N.Y.
1945	Oklahoma St.(2)	Henry Iba	NYU	49-45	Bob Kurland, Oklahoma St.	New York, N.Y.
1946	Oklahoma St.(2)	Henry Iba	North Carolina	43-40	Bob Kurland, Oklahoma St.	New York, N.Y.
1947	Holy Cross	Alvin Julian	Oklahoma	58-47	George Kaftan, Holy Cross	New York, N.Y.
1948	Kentucky	Adolph Rupp	Baylor	58-42	Alex Groza, Kentucky	New York, N.Y.
1949	Kentucky	Adolph Rupp	Oklahoma St.	46-36	Alex Groza, Kentucky	Seattle, Wash.
1950	CCNY	Nat Holman	Bradley	71-68	Irwin Dambrot, CCNY	New York, N.Y.
1951	Kentucky	Adolph Rupp	Kansas St.	68-58	None	Minneapolis, Minn.
1952	Kansas	Forrest Allen	St. John's	80-63	Clyde Lovellette, Kansas	Seattle, Wash.
1953	Indiana	Branch McCracken	Kansas	69-68	B.H. Born, Kansas	Kansas City, Mo.
1954	La Salle	Kenneth Loeffler	Bradley	92-76	Tom Gola, La Salle	Kansas City, Mo.
1955	San Francisco	Phil Woolpert	LaSalle	77-63	Bill Russell, San Francisco	Kansas City, Mo.
1956	San Francisco	Phil Woolpert	Iowa	83-71	Hal Lear, Temple	Evanston, Ill.
1957	N. Carolina	Frank McGuire	Kansas	54-53(1)	Wilt Chamberlain, Kansas	Kansas City, Mo.
1958	Kentucky	Adolph Rupp	Seattle	84-72	Elgin Baylor, Seattle	Louisville, Ky.
1959	California	Pete Newell	W. Virginia	71-70	Jerry West, W. Virginia	Louisville, Ky.
1960	Ohio St.	Fred Taylor	California	75-55	Jerry Lucas, Ohio St.	San Francisco, Cal.
1961	Cincinnati	Edwin Jucker	Ohio St.	70-65(1)	Jerry Lucas, Ohio St.	Kansas City, Mo.
1962	Cincinnati	Edwin Jucker	Ohio St.	71-59	Paul Hogue, Cincinnati	Louisville, Ky.
1963	Loyola (Ill.)	George Ireland	Cincinnati	60-58(1)	Art Heyman, Duke	Louisville, Ky.
1964	UCLA	John Wooden	Duke	98-83	Walt Hazzard, UCLA	Kansas City, Mo.
1965	UCLA	John Wooden	Michigan	91-80	Bill Bradley, Princeton	Portland, Ore.
1966	Texas-El Paso(3)	Don Haskins	Kentucky	72-65	Jerry Chambers, Utah	College Park, Md.
1967	UCLA	John Wooden	Dayton	79-64	Lew Alcindor, UCLA	Louisville, Ky.
1968	UCLA	John Wooden	N. Carolina	78-55	Lew Alcindor, UCLA	Los Angeles, Cal.
1969	UCLA	John Wooden	Purdue	92-72	Lew Alcindor, UCLA	Louisville, Ky.
1970	UCLA	John Wooden	Jacksonville	80-69	Sidney Wicks, UCLA	College Park, Md.
1971	UCLA	John Wooden	Villanova*	68-62	Howard Porter, Villanova*	Houston, Tex.
1972	UCLA	John Wooden	Florida St.	81-76	Bill Walton, UCLA	Los Angeles, Cal.
1973	UCLA	John Wooden	Memphis St.	87-66	Bill Walton, UCLA	St. Louis, Mo.
1974	N. Carolina St.	Norm Sloan	Marquette	76-64	David Thompson, N.C. St.	Greensboro, N.C.
1975	UCLA	John Wooden	Kentucky	92-85	Richard Washington, UCLA	San Diego, Cal.
1976	Indiana	Bob Knight	Michigan	86-68	Kent Benson, Indiana	Philadelphia, Pa.
1977	Marquette	Al McGuire	N. Carolina	67-59	Butch Lee, Marquette	Atlanta, Ga.
1978	Kentucky	Joe Hall	Duke	94-88	Jack Givens, Kentucky	St. Louis, Mo.
1979	Michigan St.	Jud Heathcote	Indiana St.	75-64	Magic Johnson, Michigan St.	Salt Lake City, Ut.
1980	Louisville	Denny Crum	UCLA*	59-54	Darrell Griffith, Louisville	Indianapolis, Ind.
1981	Indiana	Bob Knight	N. Carolina	63-50	Isiah Thomas, Indiana	Philadelphia, Pa.
1982	N. Carolina	Dean Smith	Georgetown	63-62	James Worthy, No. Carolina	New Orleans, La.
1983	N. Carolina St.	Jim Valvano	Houston	54-52	Akeem Olajuwon, Houston	Albuquerque, N.M.
1984	Georgetown	John Thompson	Houston	84-75	Patrick Ewing, Georgetown	Seattle, Wash.
1985	Villanova	Rollie Massimino	Georgetown	66-64	Ed Pinckney, Villanova	Lexington, Ky.
1986	Louisville	Denny Crum	Duke	72-69	Pervis Ellison, Louisville	Dallas, Tex.
1987	Indiana	Bob Knight	Syracuse	74-73	Keith Smart, Indiana	New Orleans, La.
1988	Kansas	Larry Brown	Oklahoma	83-79	Danny Manning, Kansas	Kansas City, Mo.
1989	Michigan	Steve Fisher	Seton Hall	80-79(1)	Glen Rice, Michigan	Seattle, Wash.

*Declared ineligible subsequent to the tournament. (1) Overtime. (2) Known as Oklahoma A&M at that time. (3) Known as Texas Western at that time.

NCAA Division I Career Scoring Leaders

Player, team	Seasons	G	FG	FT	Pts.	Avg.
Pete Maravich, Louisiana State	1968-70	83	1387	893	3667	44.2
Austin Carr, Notre Dame	1969-71	74	1017	526	2560	34.6
Oscar Robertson, Cincinnati	1958-60	88	1052	869	2973	33.8
Calvin Murphy, Niagara	1968-70	77	947	654	2548	33.1
Dwight Lamar, SW Louisiana	1972-73	57	768	326	1862	32.7
Frank Selvy, Furman	1952-54	78	922	694	2538	32.5
Rick Mount, Purdue	1968-70	72	910	503	2323	32.3
Darrell Floyd, Furman	1954-56	71	868	545	2281	32.1
Nick Werkman, Seton Hall	1962-64	71	812	649	2273	32.0
Willie Humes, Idaho State	1970-71	48	565	380	1510	31.5
William Averitt, Pepperdine	1972-73	49	615	311	1541	31.4
Elgin Baylor, Col. Idaho, Seattle	55, 57-58	80	956	588	2500	31.3
Elvin Hayes, Houston	1966-68	93	1215	454	2884	31.0
Freeman Williams, Portland State	1975-1978	106	1369	511	3249	30.7
Larry Bird, Indiana State	1977-79	94	1154	542	2850	30.3

John R. Wooden Award

Awarded annually to the nation's outstanding college basketball playing student-athlete by a poll of sports writers and broadcasters.

1977 Marques Johnson, UCLA	1982 Ralph Sampson, Virginia	1986 Walter Berry, St. John's
1978 Phil Ford, North Carolina	1983 Ralph Sampson, Virginia	1987 David Robinson, Navy
1979 Larry Bird, Indiana State	1984 Michael Jordan, North Carolina	1988 Danny Manning, Kansas
1980 Darrell Griffith, Louisville	1985 Chris Mullin, St. John's	1989 Sean Elliott, Arizona
1981 Danny Ainge, Brigham Young		

National Invitation Tournament Champions

Year	Champion	Year	Champion	Year	Champion	Year	Champion
1938	Temple	1951	Brigham Young	1964	Bradley	1977	St. Bonaventure
1939	Long Island Univ.	1952	LaSalle	1965	St. John's	1978	Texas
1940	Colorado	1953	Seton Hall	1966	Brigham Young	1979	Indiana
1941	Long Island Univ.	1954	Holy Cross	1967	Southern Illinois	1980	Virginia
1942	West Virginia	1955	Duquesne	1968	Dayton	1981	Tulsa
1943	St. John's	1956	Louisville	1969	Temple	1982	Bradley
1944	St. John's	1957	Bradley	1970	Marquette	1983	Fresno State
1945	De Paul	1958	Xavier (Ohio)	1971	North Carolina	1984	Michigan
1946	Kentucky	1959	St. John's	1972	Maryland	1985	UCLA
1947	Utah	1960	Bradley	1973	Virginia Tech	1986	Ohio State
1948	St. Louis	1961	Providence	1974	Purdue	1987	Southern Mississippi
1949	San Francisco	1962	Dayton	1975	Princeton	1988	Connecticut
1950	CCNY	1963	Providence	1976	Kentucky	1989	St. John's

NCAA Division I Women's Champions

Year	Champion	Coach	Final opponent	Year	Champion	Coach	Final opponent
1982	Louisiana Tech	Sonja Hogg	Cheyney	1986	Texas	Jody Conradt	USC
1983	USC	Linda Sharp	Louisiana Tech	1987	Tennessee	Pat Head Summitt	Louisiana Tech
1984	USC	Linda Sharp	Tennessee	1988	Louisiana Tech	Leon Barmore	Auburn
1985	Old Dominion	Marianne Stanley	Georgia	1989	Tennessee	Pat Head Summitt	Auburn

NCAA Division I Basketball Statistical Trends

Averages and percentages are for both teams, per game.

Year	Games	FG Made	FG Att.	Pct.	FT Made	FT Att.	Pct.	PF	Pts.
1948	3945	40.6	138.7	29.3	25.3	42.2	59.8	36.9	106.5
1950	3659	43.2	136.8	31.6	28.7	46.5	61.8	39.0	115.1
1952	4009	47.5	140.6*	33.7	31.6	50.5	62.6	44.9*	126.6
1953	3754	48.0	138.1	34.7	42.1	65.8*	64.0	42.5	138.1
1955	3829	51.1	138.6	36.9	43.1*	64.7	66.5	37.9	145.3
1958	4153	51.6	134.2	38.4	33.6	50.5	66.4	36.4	136.8
1960	4295	52.6	132.3	39.8	34.7	51.5	67.4	36.7	139.9
1961	4238	53.3	131.1	40.7	34.7	50.9	68.2	36.4	141.3
1963	4180	53.2	127.6	41.7	32.6	47.8	68.2	36.4	139.0
1965	4520	58.3	135.4	43.1	34.7	50.3	69.0	38.5	151.4
1967	4602	57.7	131.9	43.8	34.4	49.8	69.0	38.3	149.8
1969	4883	58.2	132.8	43.8	34.8	50.8	68.4	37.9	151.2
1971	5232	60.2	135.6	44.4	35.0	51.3	68.1	38.5	155.4*
1973	5582	62.3*	139.2	44.8	26.2	38.3	68.4	38.4	150.9
1975	6147	62.9	136.7	46.0	27.4	39.7	69.0	40.3	153.1
1977	6676	60.7	129.8	46.7	28.4	41.0	69.4	40.2	149.7
1979	7131	59.2	124.1	47.7	29.5	42.2	69.7*	41.1	147.9
1981	7407	55.6	115.9	48.0	29.0	42.0	68.9	40.2	140.2
1983	7957	54.3	114.0	47.7	29.0	42.3	68.5	39.7	138.7
1985	8269	54.5	113.9	47.9	29.3	42.5	68.9	39.3	138.3
1986	8360	54.7	114.6	47.7	29.4	42.5	69.1	39.1	138.7
1987	8580	54.4	117.3	46.6	29.7	43.0	69.1	39.3	145.5
1988	8587*	54.8	116.6	47.0	30.2	43.8	68.9	39.4	147.8

*All-time high.

World Almanac All-America Team in 1989

First team	Position	Second team
Stacey King, Oklahoma	Center	Derrick Coleman, Syracuse
Danny Ferry, Duke	Forward	Hank Gathers, Loyola, Marymount
Sean Elliott, Arizona	Forward	Glen Rice, Michigan
Sherman Douglas, Syracuse	Guard	Jay Edwards, Indiana
Chris Jackson, LSU	Guard	Mookie Blaylock, Oklahoma

Coach of the Year — Bob Knight, Indiana   **Player of the Year — Stacey King**

World Almanac All-America Women's Team in 1989

First team	Position	Second team
Clarissa Davis, Texas	Center	Shanda Berry, Iowa
Bridgette Gordon, Tennessee	Forward	Vickie Orr, Auburn
Vicky Bullett, Maryland	Forward	Venus Lacy, Louisiana Tech
Penny Toler, Long Beach St.	Guard	Tracy Waits, Long Beach St.
Andrea Stinson, North Carolina St.	Guard	Lisa Cline, Ohio St.

Coach of the Year — Joe Ciampi, Auburn   **Player of the Year — Clarissa Davis**

NATIONAL BASKETBALL ASSOCIATION, 1988-89

Final Standings

Eastern Conference

Atlantic Division

Club	W	L	Pct	GB
New York	52	30	.634	...
Philadelphia	46	36	.561	6
Boston	42	40	.512	10
Washington	40	42	.488	12
New Jersey	26	56	.317	26
Charlotte	20	62	.244	32

Central Division

Club	W	L	Pct	GB
Detroit	63	19	.768	...
Cleveland	57	25	.695	6
Atlanta	52	30	.634	11
Milwaukee	49	33	.598	14
Chicago	47	35	.573	16
Indiana	28	54	.341	35

Western Conference

Midwest Division

Club	W	L	Pct	GB
Utah	51	31	.622	...
Houston	45	37	.549	6
Denver	44	38	.537	7
Dallas	38	44	.463	13
San Antonio	21	61	.256	30
Miami	15	67	.183	36

Pacific Division

Club	W	L	Pct	GB
L.A. Lakers	57	25	.695	...
Phoenix	55	27	.671	2
Seattle	47	35	.573	10
Golden State	43	39	.524	14
Portland	39	43	.476	18
Sacramento	27	55	.329	30
L.A. Clippers	21	61	.256	36

Pistons Win Title by Sweeping Lakers

The Detroit Pistons won their first NBA championship by defeating the defending-champion Los Angeles Lakers in 4 straight games. It was the 5th sweep in the history of the league's championship series. Joe Dumars of the Pistons was chosen the most valuable player in the series. The Lakers' Magic Johnson, the regular season MVP, was injured in the second game and did not play (other than 4 minutes of game 3) the rest of the series.

L.A. Lakers

	FG M-A	FT M-A	Reb	PF	Avg Pts
Worthy	39-81	23-31	17	14	25.5
Abdul-Jabbar	20-46	10-12	20	7	12.5
Cooper	17-45	5-6	6	27	12.0
E. Johnson	12-26	10-11	11	24	11.7
Campbell	15-24	13-17	10	4	11.0
Thompson	13-30	14-22	19	3	10.0
Woolridge	11-18	16-19	21	6	9.5
Green	11-25	13-19	37	2	8.8
Rivers	4-12	4-5	3	5	4.0
Lamp	2-3	1-2	1	0	1.3
McNamara	0-0	0-0	0	0	0.0
Totals	144-310	108-144	189	92	102.3

Detroit Pistons

	FG M-A	FT M-A	Reb	PF	Avg Pts
Dumars	38-66	33-38	7	24	27.3
Thomas	32-66	19-25	10	29	21.3
V. Johnson	30-50	7-11	13	11	17.3
Edwards	12-27	12-16	14	1	9.0
Laimbeer	12-22	6-7	21	9	8.0
Salley	13-19	4-7	10	5	7.5
Aguirre	12-33	6-8	24	6	7.5
Mahorn	10-18	4-6	21	6	6.0
Rodman	7-15	6-7	40	5	5.0
Long	1-1	0-0	0	0	2.0
Dembo	0-0	0-0	0	0	0.0
Williams	0-0	0-0	0	1	0.0
Totals	167-317	97-125	191	97	109.0

NBA Playoff Results

Eastern Division

New York defeated Philadelphia 3 games to 0.
Detroit defeated Boston 3 games to 0.
Milwaukee defeated Atlanta 3 games to 2.
Chicago defeated Cleveland 3 games to 2.
Detroit defeated Milwaukee 4 games to 0.
Chicago defeated New York 4 games to 2.
Detroit defeated Chicago 4 games to 2.

Western Division

L.A. Lakers defeated Portland 3 games to 0.
Golden State defeated Utah 3 games to 0.
Phoenix defeated Denver 3 games to 0.
Seattle defeated Houston 3 games to 1.
L.A. Lakers defeated Seattle 4 games to 0.
Phoenix defeated Golden State 4 games to 1.
L.A. Lakers defeated Phoenix 4 games to 0.

Championship

Detroit defeated L.A. Lakers 4 games to 0.

1988-1989 NBA Individual Highs

Minutes played, season — 3255, Jordan, Chicago.
Points, game — 53, Jordan, Chicago vs. Phoenix, 1/21.
Field goals made, game — 24, Jordan, Chicago at Philadelphia, 11/16; English, Denver at Miami, 3/10 (2 OT).
Field goal attempts, game — 35, English, Denver at Miami, 3/10 (2 OT).
3-pt. field goals made, game — 8, Adams, Denver vs. Milwaukee, 1/21.
3-pt. field goal attempts, game — 14, Berry, Sacramento vs. Golden State, 2/9.
Free throws made, game — 19, Malone, Utah vs. Milwaukee, 1/20; K. Johnson, Phoenix at New York, 3/7.
Free throw attempts, game — 22, Jordan, Chicago vs. L.A. Lakers, 12/20; Malone, Utah vs. Milwaukee, 1/20; Malone, Atlanta at Chicago, 4/10.

Rebounds, game — 29, Williams, Indiana vs. Denver, 1/23.
Offensive rebounds, game — 14, Oakley, New York vs. Boston, 1/3 (OT).
Defensive rebounds, game — 25, Williams, Indiana vs. Denver, 1/23.
Offensive rebounds, season — 403, Barkley, Philadelphia.
Defensive rebounds, season — 767, Olajuwon, Houston.
Assists, game — 24, Stockton, Utah at Houston, 1/3.
Blocked shots, game — 14, Eaton, Utah vs. San Antonio, 2/18.
Steals, game — 10, Robertson, San Antonio vs. Houston, 1/11 (OT).
Personal fouls, season — 337, Long, Miami.
Games disqualified, season — 14, Smits, Indiana.

NBA Champions 1947-1989

Year	Regular season Eastern Conference	Western Conference	Playoffs Winner	Coach	Runner-up
1947	Washington	Chicago	Philadelphia	Ed Gottlieb	Chicago
1948	Philadelphia	St. Louis	Baltimore	Buddy Jeannette	Philadelphia
1949	Washington	Rochester	Minneapolis	John Kundla	Washington
1950	Syracuse	Minneapolis	Minneapolis	John Kundla	Syracuse
1951	Philadelphia	Minneapolis	Rochester	Lester Harrison	New York
1952	Syracuse	Rochester	Minneapolis	John Kundla	New York
1953	New York	Minneapolis	Minneapolis	John Kundla	New York
1954	New York	Minneapolis	Minneapolis	John Kundla	Syracuse
1955	Syracuse	Ft. Wayne	Syracuse	Al Cervi	Ft. Wayne
1956	Philadelphia	Ft. Wayne	Philadelphia	George Senesky	Ft. Wayne
1957	Boston	St. Louis	Boston	Red Auerbach	St. Louis
1958	Boston	St. Louis	St. Louis	Alex Hannum	Boston
1959	Boston	St. Louis	Boston	Red Auerbach	Minneapolis
1960	Boston	St. Louis	Boston	Red Auerbach	St. Louis
1961	Boston	St. Louis	Boston	Red Auerbach	St. Louis
1962	Boston	Los Angeles	Boston	Red Auerbach	Los Angeles
1963	Boston	Los Angeles	Boston	Red Auerbach	Los Angeles
1964	Boston	San Francisco	Boston	Red Auerbach	San Francisco
1965	Boston	Los Angeles	Boston	Red Auerbach	Los Angeles
1966	Philadelphia	Los Angeles	Boston	Red Auerbach	Los Angeles
1967	Philadelphia	San Francisco	Philadelphia	Alex Hannum	San Francisco
1968	Philadelphia	St. Louis	Boston	Bill Russell	Los Angeles
1969	Baltimore	Los Angeles	Boston	Bill Russell	Los Angeles
1970	New York	Atlanta	New York	Red Holzman	Los Angeles

Year	Atlantic	Central	Midwest	Pacific	Winner	Coach	Runner-up
1971	New York	Baltimore	Milwaukee	Los Angeles	Milwaukee	Larry Costello	Baltimore
1972	Boston	Baltimore	Milwaukee	Los Angeles	Los Angeles	Bill Sharman	New York
1973	Boston	Baltimore	Milwaukee	Los Angeles	New York	Red Holzman	Los Angeles
1974	Boston	Capital	Milwaukee	Los Angeles	Boston	Tom Heinsohn	Milwaukee
1975	Boston	Washington	Chicago	Golden State	Golden State	Al Attles	Washington
1976	Boston	Cleveland	Milwaukee	Golden State	Boston	Tom Heinsohn	Phoenix
1977	Philadelphia	Houston	Denver	Los Angeles	Portland	Jack Ramsay	Philadelphia
1978	Philadelphia	San Antonio	Denver	Portland	Washington	Dick Motta	Seattle
1979	Washington	San Antonio	Kansas City	Seattle	Seattle	Len Wilkens	Washington
1980	Boston	Atlanta	Milwaukee	Los Angeles	Los Angeles	Paul Westhead	Philadelphia
1981	Boston	Milwaukee	San Antonio	Phoenix	Boston	Bill Fitch	Houston
1982	Boston	Milwaukee	San Antonio	Los Angeles	Los Angeles	Pat Riley	Philadelphia
1983	Philadelphia	Milwaukee	San Antonio	Los Angeles	Philadelphia	Billy Cunningham	Los Angeles
1984	Boston	Milwaukee	Utah	Los Angeles	Boston	K.C. Jones	Los Angeles
1985	Boston	Milwaukee	Denver	L.A. Lakers	L.A. Lakers	Pat Riley	Boston
1986	Boston	Milwaukee	Houston	L.A. Lakers	Boston	K.C. Jones	Houston
1987	Boston	Atlanta	Dallas	L.A. Lakers	L.A. Lakers	Pat Riley	Boston
1988	Boston	Detroit	Denver	L.A. Lakers	L.A. Lakers	Pat Riley	Detroit
1989	New York	Detroit	Utah	L.A. Lakers	Detroit	Chuck Daly	L.A. Lakers

NBA Most Valuable Player

1956	Bob Pettit, St. Louis	1973	Dave Cowens, Boston
1957	Bob Cousy, Boston	1974	Kareem Abdul-Jabbar, Milwaukee
1958	Bill Russell, Boston	1975	Bob McAdoo, Buffalo
1959	Bob Pettit, St. Louis	1976	Kareem Abdul-Jabbar, Los Angeles
1960	Wilt Chamberlain, Philadelphia	1977	Kareem Abdul-Jabbar, Los Angeles
1961	Bill Russell, Boston	1978	Bill Walton, Portland
1962	Bill Russell, Boston	1979	Moses Malone, Houston
1963	Bill Russell, Boston	1980	Kareem Abdul-Jabbar, Los Angeles
1964	Oscar Robertson, Cincinnati	1981	Julius Erving, Philadelphia
1965	Bill Russell, Boston	1982	Moses Malone, Houston
1966	Wilt Chamberlain, Philadelphia	1983	Moses Malone, Philadelphia
1967	Wilt Chamberlain, Philadelphia	1984	Larry Bird, Boston
1968	Wilt Chamberlain, Philadelphia	1985	Larry Bird, Boston
1969	Wes Unseld, Baltimore	1986	Larry Bird, Boston
1970	Willis Reed, New York	1987	Magic Johnson, L.A. Lakers
1971	Lew Alcindor, Milwaukee	1988	Michael Jordan, Chicago
1972	Kareem Abdul-Jabbar (Alcindor), Milwaukee	1989	Magic Johnson, L.A. Lakers

MVP in Playoffs

1969	Jerry West, Los Angeles	1977	Bill Walton, Portland	1984	Larry Bird, Boston
1970	Willis Reed, New York	1978	Wes Unseld, Washington	1985	Kareem Abdul-Jabbar, L.A. Lakers
1971	Lew Alcindor, Milwaukee	1979	Dennis Johnson, Seattle		
1972	Wilt Chamberlain, Los Angeles	1980	Magic Johnson, Los Angeles	1986	Larry Bird, Boston
1973	Willis Reed, New York	1981	Cedric Maxwell, Boston	1987	Magic Johnson, L.A. Lakers
1974	John Havlicek, Boston	1982	Magic Johnson, Los Angeles	1988	James Worthy, L.A. Lakers
1975	Rick Barry, Golden State	1983	Moses Malone, Philadelphia	1989	Joe Dumars, Detroit
1976	Jo Jo White, Boston				

Kareem Abdul-Jabbar Retires

The final game of the National Basketball Association championship series was the last NBA game for Kareem Abdul-Jabbar after 20 NBA seasons. Jabbar was a member of 6 NBA championship teams after leading UCLA to 3 consecutive NCAA titles. He was the only player to be chosen the league's most valuable player six times. He retired with over 23 NBA records including most points (38,387), minutes (57,446), field goals (15,832), and blocked shots (3,189).

Statistical Leaders, 1988-1989

Scoring

	G	Pts	Avg
Jordan, Chicago	81	2633	32.5
Malone, Utah	80	2326	29.1
Ellis, Seattle	82	2253	27.5
Drexler, Portland	78	2123	27.2
Mullin, Golden State	82	2176	26.5
English, Denver	82	2175	26.5
Wilkins, Atlanta	80	2099	26.2
Barkley, Philadelphia	79	2037	25.8
Chambers, Phoenix	81	2085	25.7
Olajuwon, Houston	82	2034	24.8
Cummings, Milwaukee	80	1829	22.9
Ewing, New York	80	1815	22.7
Tripucka, Charlotte	71	1606	22.6
McHale, Boston	78	1758	22.5
Johnson, L.A. Lakers	77	1730	22.5
Richmond, Golden State	79	1741	22.0
Malone, Washington	76	1651	21.7
Person, Indiana	80	1728	21.6
E. Johnson, Phoenix	70	1504	21.5
King, Washington	81	1674	20.7

Rebounds

	G	Tot	Avg
Olajuwon, Houston	82	1105	13.5
Barkley, Philadelphia	79	986	12.5
Parish, Boston	80	996	12.5
Malone, Atlanta	81	956	11.8
Malone, Utah	80	853	10.7
Oakley, New York	82	861	10.5
Eaton, Utah	82	843	10.3
Thorpe, Houston	82	787	9.6
Laimbeer, Detroit	81	776	9.6
Cage, Seattle	80	765	9.6

Field Goal Percentage

	FG	FGA	Pct
Rodman, Detroit	316	531	.595
Barkley, Philadelphia	700	1208	.579
Parish, Boston	596	1045	.570
Ewing, New York	727	1282	.567
Worthy, L.A. Lakers	702	1282	.548
McHale, Boston	661	1211	.546
Thorpe, Houston	521	961	.542
Benjamin, L.A. Clippers	491	907	.541
Nance, Cleveland	496	920	.539

Free Throw Percentage

	FT	FTA	Pct
Johnson, L.A. Lakers	513	563	.911
Sikma, Milwaukee	266	294	.905
Skiles, Indiana	130	144	.903
Price, Cleveland	263	292	.901
Mullin, Golden State	493	553	.892
K. Johnson, Phoenix	508	576	.882
Kleine, Boston	134	152	.882
Davis, Denver	175	199	.879
Gminski, Philadelphia	297	341	.871
Malone, Washington	296	340	.871

Assists Per Game

	G	Ast	Avg
Stockton, Utah	82	1118	13.6
Johnson, L.A. Lakers	77	988	12.8
K. Johnson, Phoenix	81	991	12.2
Porter, Portland	81	770	9.5
McMillan, Seattle	75	696	9.3
Floyd, Houston	82	709	8.6
Jackson, New York	72	619	8.6
Price, Cleveland	75	631	8.4
Thomas, Detroit	80	663	8.3
Jordan, Chicago	81	650	8.0

3-Point Field Goal Percentage

	FG	FGA	Pct
Sundvold, Miami	48	92	.522
Ellis, Seattle	162	339	.478
Price, Cleveland	93	211	.441
Hawkins, Philadelphia	71	166	.428
Hodges, Chicago	75	180	.417
E. Johnson, Phoenix	71	172	.413
Berry, Sacramento	65	160	.406
Pressley, Sacramento	119	295	.403
Miller, Indiana	98	244	.402
Scott, L.A. Lakers	77	193	.399
Tucker, New York	118	296	.399

Steals Per Game

	G	Stl	Avg
Stockton, Utah	82	263	3.21
Robertson, San Antonio	65	197	3.03
Jordan, Chicago	81	234	2.89
Lever, Denver	71	195	2.75
Drexler, Portland	78	213	2.73
Olajuwon, Houston	82	213	2.60
Rivers, Atlanta	76	181	2.38
Harper, Cleveland	82	185	2.26
Garland, Golden State	79	175	2.22
Conner, New Jersey	82	181	2.21

Blocked Shots Per Game

	G	Blk	Avg
Bol, Golden State	80	345	4.31
Eaton, Utah	82	315	3.84
Ewing, New York	80	281	3.51
Olajuwon, Houston	82	282	3.44
Nance, Cleveland	73	206	2.82
Benjamin, L.A. Clippers	79	221	2.80
Cooper, Denver	79	211	2.67
West, Phoenix	82	187	2.28
Lister, Seattle	82	180	2.20
Smits, Indiana	82	151	1.84

NBA All League Team in 1989

First team	Position	Second team
Karl Malone, Utah	Forward	Tom Chambers, Phoenix
Charles Barkley, Philadelphia	Forward	Chris Mullen, Golden State
Akeem Olajuwon, Houston	Center	Patrick Ewing, New York
Magic Johnson, L.A. Lakers	Guard	John Stockton, Utah
Michael Jordan, Chicago	Guard	Kevin Johnson, Phoenix

NBA All-Defensive Team in 1989

First team	Position	Second team
Dennis Rodman, Detroit	Forward	Kevin McHale, Boston
Larry Nance, Cleveland	Forward	A.C. Green, L.A. Lakers
Mark Eaton, Utah	Center	Patrick Ewing, New York
Michael Jordan, Chicago	Guard	Alvin Robertson, San Antonio
Joe Dumars, Detroit	Guard	John Stockton, Utah

Individual Statistics, 1988-1989
(Over 500 Minutes Played)

Atlanta Hawks

	Min	FG%	FT%	RBs	Ast	Pts	Avg
Wilkins	2997	.464	.844	553	211	2099	26.2
Malone	2878	.491	.789	956	112	1637	20.2
Theus	2517	.466	.851	242	387	1296	15.8
Rivers	2462	.455	.861	286	525	1032	13.6
Battle	1672	.457	.815	140	197	779	9.5
Levingston	2184	.528	.696	498	75	734	9.2
Carr	1488	.480	.855	274	91	582	7.5
Koncak	1531	.524	.553	453	56	345	4.7
Webb	1219	.459	.867	123	284	319	3.9

Boston Celtics

	Min	FG%	FT%	RBs	Ast	Pts	Avg
McHale	2876	.546	.818	637	172	1758	22.5
Parish	2840	.570	.719	996	175	1486	18.6
Lewis	2657	.486	.787	377	218	1495	18.5
Pinckney	2012	.513	.800	449	118	918	11.5
Johnson	2309	.434	.821	190	472	721	10.0
Paxson	1138	.454	.816	74	107	492	8.6
Shaw	2301	.433	.826	376	472	703	8.6
Upshaw	617	.467	.692	49	117	219	6.8
Kleine	1411	.405	.882	378	67	484	6.5
Grandison	528	.415	.738	92	42	177	2.5
Acres	632	.482	.542	146	19	137	2.2

Charlotte Hornets

	Min	FG%	FT%	RBs	Ast	Pts	Avg
Tripucka	2302	.467	.866	267	224	1606	22.6
Chapman	2219	.414	.795	187	176	1267	16.9
Reid	2152	.428	.776	302	153	1207	14.7
Curry	813	.491	.870	104	50	571	11.9
Rambis	2233	.518	.734	703	159	832	11.1
Holton	1696	.427	.839	105	424	553	8.3
Rowsom	517	.494	.802	137	24	226	6.6
Hoppen	1419	.564	.727	384	57	500	6.5
Cureton	2047	.501	.537	488	130	532	6.5
Kempton	1341	.510	.686	304	102	484	6.1
Bogues	1755	.426	.750	165	620	423	5.4
Kite	942	.430	.488	243	36	150	2.1

Chicago Bulls

	Min	FG%	FT%	RBs	Ast	Pts	Avg
Jordan	3255	.538	.850	652	650	2633	32.5
Pippen	2413	.476	.668	445	256	1048	14.4
Cartwright	2333	.475	.766	521	90	966	12.4
Grant	2809	.519	.704	681	168	950	12.0
Vincent	1703	.484	.822	190	335	656	9.4
Hodges	1204	.472	.842	89	146	529	9.0
Paxson	1738	.480	.861	94	308	567	7.3
Sellers	1732	.485	.851	227	99	551	6.9
Corzine	1483	.461	.740	315	103	479	5.9
Davis	545	.426	.731	114	31	185	3.8

Cleveland Cavaliers

	Min	FG%	FT%	RBs	Ast	Pts	Avg
Daugherty	2821	.538	.737	718	285	1475	18.9
Price	2728	.526	.901	226	631	1414	18.9
Harper	2851	.511	.751	409	434	1526	18.6
Nance	2526	.539	.799	581	159	1259	17.2
Williams	2125	.509	.748	477	108	948	11.6
Sanders	2102	.453	.719	307	133	764	9.3
Ehlo	1867	.475	.607	295	266	608	7.4
Valentine	1086	.426	.813	103	174	366	4.8
Dudley	544	.435	.364	157	21	185	3.0
Rollins	583	.449	.632	139	19	136	2.3

Dallas Mavericks

	Min	FG%	FT%	RBs	Ast	Pts	Avg
Blackman	2946	.476	.854	273	288	1534	19.7
Dantley	2422	.493	.810	317	171	1400	19.2
Harper	2968	.477	.806	228	570	1404	17.3
Tarpley	591	.541	.688	218	17	328	17.3
Perkins	2860	.464	.833	688	127	1171	15.0
Williams	2470	.436	.686	593	124	777	10.2
Donaldson	1746	.573	.766	570	38	481	9.1
Davis	1395	.483	.805	108	242	497	6.4
Tyler	1057	.469	.758	209	40	386	5.5
Wennington	1074	.433	.744	286	46	300	4.6

Denver Nuggets

	Min	FG%	FT%	RBs	Ast	Pts	Avg
English	2990	.491	.858	326	383	2175	26.5
Lever	2745	.457	.785	662	559	1409	19.8
Adams	2787	.433	.819	283	490	1424	18.5
Davis	1857	.498	.879	151	190	1267	15.6
Schayes	1918	.522	.826	500	105	969	12.8
Cook	1143	.456	.808	107	127	507	7.7
Rasmussen	1308	.445	.852	287	49	583	7.6
Greenwood	1403	.423	.750	402	96	466	7.0
Cooper	1864	.495	.745	619	78	520	6.6
Hanzlik	701	.437	.782	93	86	201	4.9
Lane	550	.426	.384	200	60	261	4.8
Turner	1746	.428	.589	287	144	337	4.3

Detroit Pistons

	Min	FG%	FT%	RBs	Ast	Pts	Avg
Aguirre	2597	.461	.733	386	278	1511	18.9
Thomas	2924	.464	.818	273	663	1458	18.2
Dumars	2408	.505	.850	172	390	1186	17.2
Johnson	2073	.464	.734	255	242	1130	13.8
Laimbeer	2640	.499	.840	776	177	1106	13.7
Rodman	2208	.595	.626	772	99	735	9.0
Edwards	1254	.500	.686	231	49	555	7.3
Mahorn	1795	.517	.748	496	59	522	7.3
Salley	1458	.498	.692	335	75	467	7.0
Long	919	.409	.921	77	80	372	5.5

Golden State Warriors

	Min	FG%	FT%	RBs	Ast	Pts	Avg
Mullin	3093	.509	.892	483	415	2176	26.5
Richmond	2717	.468	.810	468	334	1741	22.0
Teagle	1569	.476	.809	263	96	1002	15.2
Garland	2661	.434	.809	328	505	1145	14.5
Higgins	1887	.476	.821	376	160	856	10.6
O. Smith	1597	.435	.798	330	140	803	10.0
Sampson	1086	.449	.653	307	77	393	6.4
L. Smith	1897	.552	.310	652	118	456	5.7
Alford	906	.457	.820	72	92	366	5.5
Bol	1769	.369	.606	462	27	314	3.9

Houston Rockets

	Min	FG%	FT%	RBs	Ast	Pts	Avg
Olajuwon	3024	.508	.696	1105	149	2034	24.8
Thorpe	3135	.542	.729	787	202	1370	16.7
Floyd	2788	.443	.845	306	709	1162	14.2
Woodson	2259	.438	.823	194	206	1046	12.9
B. Johnson	1850	.524	.754	286	126	642	9.6
Chievous	1539	.437	.783	256	77	750	9.3
Berry	1355	.507	.699	267	77	609	8.8
Short	1157	.413	.865	179	107	482	7.4
McCormick	1257	.481	.674	261	54	425	5.2
F. Johnson	879	.443	.806	79	181	294	4.4
Leavell	627	.346	.733	53	127	179	3.3

Indiana Pacers

	Min	FG%	FT%	RBs	Ast	Pts	Avg
Person	3012	.489	.792	516	289	1728	21.6
Miller	2536	.479	.844	292	227	1181	16.0
Fleming	2552	.515	.799	310	494	1084	14.3
Thompson	2329	.489	.808	718	81	1059	13.9
Schrempf	1850	.474	.780	395	179	828	12.0
Smits	2041	.517	.722	500	70	956	11.7
Skiles	1571	.448	.903	149	390	546	6.8
Wittman	1120	.455	.683	80	111	291	4.5
Gray	783	.471	.688	245	29	188	2.6

Los Angeles Clippers

	Min	FG%	FT%	RBs	Ast	Pts	Avg
Norman	3020	.502	.630	667	277	1450	18.1
Manning	950	.494	.767	171	81	434	16.7
Benjamin	2585	.541	.744	696	157	1299	16.4
Smith	2161	.495	.725	465	103	1155	16.3
Dailey	1722	.465	.759	204	154	1114	16.1
Grant	1924	.435	.735	238	506	846	11.9
R. Williams	1303	.438	.754	179	103	642	10.2
Nixon	1318	.414	.738	78	339	362	6.8
Garrick	1499	.490	.803	156	243	454	6.4
Wolf	1450	.423	.688	271	113	386	5.8
K. Williams	547	.405	.780	70	53	209	4.2

Los Angeles Lakers

	Min	FG%	FT%	RBs	Ast	Pts	Avg
Johnson	2886	.509	.911	607	988	1730	22.5
Worthy	2960	.548	.782	489	288	1657	20.5
Scott	2605	.491	.863	302	231	1448	19.6
Green	2510	.529	.786	739	103	1088	13.3
Abdul-Jabbar	1695	.475	.739	334	74	748	10.1
Woolridge	1491	.464	.738	270	58	715	9.7
Thompson	1994	.559	.678	467	48	738	9.2
Cooper	1943	.431	.871	191	314	587	7.3
Campbell	787	.458	.843	130	47	388	6.2

Miami Heat

	Min	FG%	FT%	RBs	Ast	Pts	Avg
Edwards	2349	.425	.746	262	349	1094	13.8
Sparrow	2613	.452	.879	216	429	1000	12.5
Long	2435	.486	.749	546	149	976	11.9
Seikaly	1962	.448	.511	549	55	848	10.9
Thompson	2273	.487	.696	572	176	854	10.8
Sundvold	1338	.455	.825	87	137	709	10.4
Cummings	1096	.500	.742	281	47	466	8.8
Gray	1220	.420	.673	286	117	440	8.0
Washington	1065	.424	.788	123	226	411	7.6
Shasky	944	.488	.689	232	22	357	5.5
Hastings	1206	.436	.850	231	59	386	5.1
Neal	500	.366	.609	29	118	114	2.2

Milwaukee Bucks

	Min	FG%	FT%	RBs	Ast	Pts	Avg
Cummings	2824	.467	.787	650	198	1829	22.9
Pierce	2078	.518	.859	197	156	1317	17.6
Sikma	2587	.431	.905	623	289	1068	13.4
Krystkowiak	2472	.473	.823	610	107	1017	12.7
Pressey	2170	.474	.776	262	439	813	12.1
Moncrief	1594	.491	.865	172	188	752	12.1
Humphries	2220	.483	.816	189	405	844	11.6
Roberts	1251	.486	.806	209	66	417	5.9
Green	871	.489	.909	69	187	291	4.6
Breuer	513	.480	.549	135	22	200	4.2
Mokeski	690	.360	.784	187	36	165	2.2

New Jersey Nets

	Min	FG%	FT%	RBs	Ast	Pts	Avg
Hinson	2542	.482	.757	522	71	1308	16.0
Morris	2096	.457	.717	397	119	1074	14.1
Carroll	1996	.448	.800	473	105	902	14.1
McGee	2027	.473	.535	189	116	1038	13.0
B. Williams	2446	.531	.666	696	78	959	13.0
Hopson	1551	.419	.849	202	103	788	12.7
Conner	2532	.457	.788	355	604	843	10.3
Bagley	1642	.416	.724	144	391	500	7.4
Lee	840	.422	.746	259	42	271	4.8

New York Knickerbockers

	Min	FG%	FT%	RBs	Ast	Pts	Avg
Ewing	2896	.567	.746	740	188	1815	22.7
Jackson	2477	.467	.698	341	619	1219	16.9
Newman	2336	.475	.815	206	162	1293	16.0
G. Wilkins	2414	.451	.756	244	274	1161	14.3
Oakley	2604	.510	.773	861	187	1061	12.9
Vandeweghe	934	.469	.899	71	69	499	11.1
Strickland	1358	.467	.745	160	319	721	8.9
Tucker	1824	.454	.782	176	132	687	8.5
Green	1277	.460	.759	394	76	517	6.3
Walker	1163	.489	.776	230	36	419	5.3
E. Wilkins	584	.465	.550	148	7	289	4.1

Philadelphia 76ers

	Min	FG%	FT%	RBs	Ast	Pts	Avg
Barkley	3088	.579	.753	986	325	2037	25.8
Gminski	2739	.477	.871	769	138	1409	17.2
Anderson	2618	.491	.856	406	139	1330	16.2
Hawkins	2577	.455	.831	225	239	1196	15.1
Cheeks	2298	.483	.774	183	554	824	11.6
Smith	1295	.435	.686	167	128	568	8.7
Henderson	986	.414	.819	68	140	425	6.5
Brooks	1372	.420	.884	94	306	428	5.2
Coleman	703	.485	.792	177	17	295	5.1
Jones	669	.441	.725	111	40	238	4.9
Welp	843	.446	.658	193	29	246	3.4

Phoenix Suns

	Min	FG%	FT%	RBs	Ast	Pts	Avg
Chambers	3002	.471	.851	684	231	2085	25.7
E. Johnson	2043	.497	.868	306	162	1504	21.5
K. Johnson	3179	.505	.882	340	991	1650	20.4
Gilliam	2120	.503	.743	541	52	1176	15.9
Hornacek	2487	.495	.826	266	465	1054	13.5
Majerle	1354	.419	.614	209	130	467	8.6
Corbin	1655	.540	.788	398	118	631	8.2
West	2019	.653	.535	551	39	594	7.2
Perry	614	.537	.615	132	18	257	4.1
Lang	526	.513	.650	147	9	159	2.6

Portland Trail Blazers

	Min	FG%	FT%	RBs	Ast	Pts	Avg
Drexler	3064	.496	.799	615	450	2123	27.2
Duckworth	2662	.477	.757	635	60	1432	18.1
Porter	3102	.471	.840	367	770	1431	17.7
Kersey	2716	.469	.694	629	243	1330	17.5
Johnson	1477	.524	.527	358	105	721	10.0
Branch	811	.463	.725	132	60	498	7.4
Young	952	.460	.781	74	123	297	6.2
Anderson	1082	.417	.484	231	98	371	5.2
Bryant	803	.486	.580	179	33	280	5.0
Jones	1279	.421	.787	300	59	202	2.8

Sacramento Kings

	Min	FG%	FT%	RBs	Ast	Pts	Avg
Ainge	2377	.457	.854	255	402	1281	17.5
Tisdale	2434	.514	.773	609	128	1381	17.5
K. Smith	3145	.462	.737	226	621	1403	17.3
Thompson	1276	.461	.809	392	44	646	15.0
McCray	2435	.466	.722	514	293	854	12.6
Pressley	2257	.439	.780	485	174	981	12.3
Berry	1406	.450	.789	197	80	706	11.0
Petersen	1633	.459	.747	413	81	671	10.2
D. Smith	600	.402	.674	81	60	289	10.0
Del Negro	1556	.475	.850	171	206	569	7.1
Lohaus	1214	.432	.786	256	66	502	6.5

San Antonio Spurs

	Min	FG%	FT%	RBs	Ast	Pts	Avg
W. Anderson	2738	.498	.775	417	372	1508	18.6
Robertson	2287	.483	.723	384	393	1122	17.3
Dawkins	1083	.443	.893	101	224	454	14.2
G. Anderson	2401	.503	.514	676	61	1127	13.7
Brickowski	1822	.515	.715	406	131	875	13.7
Maxwell	2065	.432	.745	202	301	927	11.7
Cook	757	.467	.821	59	84	346	9.6
Vincent	646	.405	.667	110	27	249	8.6
Greenwood	912	.425	.800	238	55	294	7.7
King	791	.431	.771	140	79	327	7.1
Comegys	1119	.487	.658	234	30	438	6.5
M. Anderson	730	.417	.695	89	153	204	5.7
Smrek	623	.471	.645	129	12	193	4.5
Whitehead	622	.396	.660	134	19	175	3.1
Roth	536	.353	.690	64	55	181	2.9

Seattle SuperSonics

	Min	FG%	FT%	RBs	Ast	Pts	Avg
Ellis	3190	.501	.816	342	164	2253	27.5
McDaniel	2385	.489	.732	433	134	1677	20.5
McKey	2804	.502	.803	464	219	1305	15.9
Cage	2536	.498	.743	765	126	825	10.3
Threatt	1220	.494	.818	117	238	544	8.6
Lister	1806	.499	.646	545	54	657	8.0
Reynolds	737	.417	.760	100	62	428	7.6
McMillan	2341	.410	.630	388	696	532	7.1
Schoene	774	.387	.807	165	36	358	5.2
Lucas	842	.398	.701	79	260	310	4.2
Polynice	835	.506	.593	206	21	233	2.9

Utah Jazz

	Min	FG%	FT%	RBs	Ast	Pts	Avg
Malone	3126	.519	.766	853	219	2326	29.1
Bailey	2777	.483	.825	447	138	1595	19.5
Stockton	3171	.538	.863	248	1118	1400	17.1
Griffith	2382	.446	.780	330	130	1135	13.8
Hansen	964	.467	.560	128	50	341	7.4
Eaton	2914	.462	.660	843	83	508	6.2
Brown	1051	.419	.708	258	41	300	4.5
Leckner	779	.545	.699	199	16	319	4.3
Iavaroni	796	.442	.818	132	32	180	2.3
Les	781	.301	.781	87	215	138	1.7

Washington Bullets

	Min	FG%	FT%	RBs	Ast	Pts	Avg		Min	FG%	FT%	RBs	Ast	Pts	Avg
Malone	2418	.480	.871	179	219	1651	21.7	Alarie	1141	.478	.839	255	63	498	6.7
King	2559	.477	.819	384	294	1674	20.7	Colter	1425	.444	.749	182	225	534	6.7
Williams	2413	.466	.776	573	356	1120	13.7	Grant	1193	.464	.596	163	79	396	5.6
Eackles	1459	.434	.786	180	123	917	11.5	Feitl	828	.436	.831	202	36	286	5.0
Catledge	2077	.490	.602	572	75	822	10.4	C. Jones	1154	.480	.640	257	42	136	2.6
Walker	2565	.420	.772	507	496	714	9.0	C.A. Jones	516	.463	.623	140	18	110	2.6

All-Time NBA Statistical Leaders

(at the start of the 1988-89 season unless otherwise noted)

Scoring Average
(400 games or 10,000 Points Minimum)

	G	Pts.	Avg
Wilt Chamberlain	1,045	31,419	30.1
Elgin Baylor	846	23,149	27.4
Jerry West	932	25,192	27.0
Bob Pettit	792	20,880	26.4
George Gervin	791	20,708	26.2
*Dominique Wilkins	559	14,557	26.0
Oscar Robertson	1,040	26,710	25.7
*Adrian Dantley	900	22,458	24.9
*Larry Bird	717	17,899	24.9
*Kareem Abdul-Jabbar	1,560	38,387	24.6

Field Goal Percentage
(2,000 FGM Minimum)

	FGA	FGM	Pct.
Artis Gillmore	9,570	5,732	.599
James Donaldson	3,678	2,163	.588
Steve Johnson	4,245	2,463	.580
Charles Barkley	4,044	2,332	.577
Darryl Dawkins	6,060	3,468	.572
Kevin McHale	7,747	4,396	.567
Jeff Ruland	3,685	2,080	.564
Kareem Abdul-Jabbar	27,648	15,524	.561
Larry Nance	6,409	3,585	.559
James Worthy	6,182	3,449	.558

Free Throw Percentage
(1,200 FTM Minimum)

	FTA	FTM	Pct.
Rick Barry	4,243	3,818	.900
*Larry Bird	3,745	3,356	.896
Calvin Murphy	3,864	3,445	.892
Bill Sharman	3,357	3,143	.884
Mike Newlin	3,456	3,005	.870
*Kiki Vandeweghe	2,912	2,535	.870
*Jeff Malone	1,938	1,682	.867
*John Long	1,996	1,719	.861
Fred Brown	1,945	1,662	.854
Larry Siegfried	1,945	1,662	.854

Points

	Pts.
*Kareem Abdul-Jabbar	38,387
Wilt Chamberlain	31,419
Elvin Hayes	27,313
Oscar Robertson	26,710
John Havlicek	26,395
Jerry West	25,192
*Alex English	23,417
*Moses Malone	23,340
Elgin Baylor	23,149
*Adrian Dantley	22,458

Games Played

*Kareem Abdul-Jabbar	1,560
Elvin Hayes	1,303
John Havlicek	1,270
Paul Silas	1,254
Hal Greer	1,122
Len Wilkens	1,077
Dolph Schayes	1,059
Johnny Green	1,057
Don Nelson	1,053
Leroy Ellis	1,048

Assists

Oscar Robertson	9,887
*Magic Johnson	8,025
Len Wilkens	7,211
Bob Cousy	6,955
Guy Rodgers	6,917
Nate Archibald	6,476
Jerry West	6,238
*John Lucas	6,216
John Havlicek	6,114
Norm Nixon	6,047

Field Goals Made

*Kareem Abdul-Jabbar	15,837
Wilt Chamberlain	12,681
Elvin Hayes	10,976
John Havlicek	10,513
*Alex English	9,702
Oscar Robertson	9,508
Jerry West	9,016
Elgin Baylor	8,693
Hal Greer	8,504
George Gervin	8,045

Rebounds

Wilt Chamberlain	23,924
Bill Russell	21,620
*Kareem Abdul-Jabbar	17,440
Elvin Hayes	16,279
Nate Thurmond	14,464
Walt Bellamy	14,241
Wes Unseld	13,769
*Moses Malone	13,671
Jerry Lucas	12,942
Bob Pettit	12,849

*Includes 1988-89 season.

NBA Scoring Leaders

Year	Scoring champion	Pts	Avg	Year	Scoring champion	Pts	Avg
1947	Joe Fulks, Philadelphia	1,389	23.2	1969	Elvin Hayes, San Diego	2,327	28.4
1948	Max Zaslofsky, Chicago	1,007	21.0	1970	Jerry West, Los Angeles	2,309	31.2
1949	George Mikan, Minneapolis	1,698	28.3	1971	Lew Alcindor, Milwaukee	2,596	31.7
1950	George Mikan, Minneapolis	1,865	27.4	1972	Kareem Abdul-Jabbar (Alcindor), Milwau-		
1951	George Mikan, Minneapolis	1,932	28.4		kee	2,822	34.8
1952	Paul Arizin, Philadelphia	1,674	25.4	1973	Nate Archibald, Kansas City-Omaha	2,719	34.0
1953	Neil Johnston, Philadelphia	1,564	22.3	1974	Bob McAdoo, Buffalo	2,261	30.6
1954	Neil Johnston, Philadelphia	1,759	24.4	1975	Bob McAdoo, Buffalo	2,831	34.5
1955	Neil Johnston, Philadelphia	1,631	22.7	1976	Bob McAdoo, Buffalo	2,427	31.1
1956	Bob Pettit, St. Louis	1,849	25.7	1977	Pete Maravich, New Orleans	2,273	31.1
1957	Paul Arizin, Philadelphia	1,817	25.6	1978	George Gervin, San Antonio	2,232	27.2
1958	George Yardley, Detroit	2,001	27.8	1979	George Gervin, San Antonio	2,365	29.6
1959	Bob Pettit, St. Louis	2,105	29.2	1980	George Gervin, San Antonio	2,585	33.1
1960	Wilt Chamberlain, Philadelphia	2,707	37.9	1981	Adrian Dantley, Utah	2,452	30.7
1961	Wilt Chamberlain, Philadelphia	3,033	38.4	1982	George Gervin, San Antonio	2,551	32.3
1962	Wilt Chamberlain, Philadelphia	4,029	50.4	1983	Alex English, Denver	2,326	28.4
1963	Wilt Chamberlain, San Francisco	3,586	44.8	1984	Adrian Dantley, Utah	2,418	30.6
1964	Wilt Chamberlain, San Francisco	2,948	36.5	1985	Bernard King, New York	1,809	32.9
1965	Wilt Chamberlain, San Fran., Phila.	2,534	34.7	1986	Dominique Wilkins, Atlanta	2,366	30.3
1966	Wilt Chamberlain, Philadelphia	2,649	33.5	1987	Michael Jordan, Chicago	3,041	37.1
1967	Rick Barry, San Francisco	2,775	35.6	1988	Michael Jordan, Chicago	2,868	35.0
1968	Dave Bing, Detroit	2,142	27.1	1989	Michael Jordan, Chicago	2,633	32.5

NBA Rookie of the Year

Year	Player	Year	Player	Year	Player
1953	Don Meineke, Ft. Wayne	1966	Rick Barry, San Francisco	1978	Walter Davis, Phoenix
1954	Ray Felix, Baltimore	1967	Dave Bing, Detroit	1979	Phil Ford, Kansas City
1955	Bob Pettit, Milwaukee	1968	Earl Monroe, Baltimore	1980	Larry Bird, Boston
1956	Maurice Stokes, Rochester	1969	Wes Unseld, Baltimore	1981	Darrell Griffith, Utah
1957	Tom Heinsohn, Boston	1970	Lew Alcindor, Milwaukee	1982	Buck Williams, New Jersey
1958	Woody Sauldsberry, Philadelphia	1971	Dave Cowens, Boston;	1983	Terry Cummings, San Diego
1959	Elgin Baylor, Minneapolis		Geoff Petrie, Portland (tie)	1984	Ralph Sampson, Houston
1960	Wilt Chamberlain, Philadelphia	1972	Sidney Wicks, Portland	1985	Michael Jordan, Chicago
1961	Oscar Robertson, Cincinnati	1973	Bob McAdoo, Buffalo	1986	Patrick Ewing, New York
1962	Walt Bellamy, Chicago	1974	Ernie DiGregorio, Buffalo	1987	Chuck Person, Indiana
1963	Terry Dischinger, Chicago	1975	Keith Wilkes, Golden State	1988	Mark Jackson, New York
1964	Jerry Lucas, Cincinnati	1976	Alvan Adams, Phoenix	1989	Mitch Richmond, Golden State
1965	Willis Reed, New York	1977	Adrian Dantley, Buffalo		

1989 NBA Player Draft

The following are the first round picks of the National Basketball Assn.

Sacramento—Pervis Ellison, Louisville
L.A. Clippers—Danny Ferry, Duke
San Antonio—Sean Elliott, Arizona
Miami—Glen Rice, Michigan
Charlotte—J.R. Reid, North Carolina
Chicago—Stacey King, Oklahoma
Indiana—George McCloud, Florida St.
Dallas—Randy White, Louisiana Tech
Washington—Tom Hammonds, Georgia Tech
Minnesota—Pooh Richardson, UCLA
Orlando—Nick Anderson, Illinois
New Jersey—Mookie Blaylock, Oklahoma
Boston—Michael Smith, BYU
Golden State—Tim Hardaway, Texas-El Paso

Denver—Todd Lichti, Stanford
Seattle—Dana Barros, Boston College
Seattle—Shawn Kemp, Trinity C.C.
Chicago—B.J. Armstrong, Iowa
Philadelphia—Kenny Payne, Louisville
Chicago—Jeff Sanders, Georgia Southern
Utah—Blue Edwards, East Carolina
Portland—Byron Irvin, Missouri
Atlanta—Roy Marble, Iowa
Phoenix—Anthony Cook, Arizona
Cleveland—John Morton, Seton Hall
L.A. Lakers—Vlade Divac, Yugoslavia
Detroit—Kenny Battle, Illinois

Individuals in The Basketball Hall of Fame

Springfield, Mass.

Players
Arizin, Paul
Barry, Rick
Baylor, Elgin
Beckman, John
Borgmann, Bennie
Bradley, Bill
Brennan, Joseph
Barlow, Thomas
Cervi, Al
Chamberlain, Wilt
Cooper, Charles
Cousy, Bob
Cunningham, Billy
Davies, Bob
DeBernardi, Forrest
DeBusschere, Dave
Dehnert, Dutch
Endacott, Paul
Foster, Bud
Frazier, Walt
Friedman, Max
Fulks, Joe
Gale, Lauren
Gates, Pop
Gola, Tom
Greer, Hal
Gruenig, Ace
Hagan, Cliff
Hanson, Victor
Havlicek, John
Heinsohn, Tom
Holman, Nat
Houbregs, Bob
Hyatt, Chuck
Johnson, William
Jones, K.C.
Jones, Sam
Krause, Moose
Kurland, Bob
Lapchick, Joe
Lovellette, Clyde
Lucas, Jerry

Luisetti, Hank
Macauley, Ed
Maravich, Pete
Martin, Slater
McCracken, Branch
McCracken, Jack
McDermott, Bobby
Mikan, George
Murphy, Stretch
Page, Pat
Pettit, Bob
Phillip, Andy
Pollard, Jim
Ramsey, Frank
Reed, Willis
Robertson, Oscar
Roosma, John S.
Russell, Honey
Russell, Bill
Schayes, Adolph
Schmidt, Ernest
Schommer, John
Sedran, Barney
Sharman, Bill
Steinmetz, Christian
Thompson, Cat
Thurmond, Nate
Twyman, Jack
Unseld, Wes
Vandivier, Fuzzy
Wachter, Edward
Wanzer, Bobby
West, Jerry
Wilkins, Lenny
Wooden, John

Coaches
Auerbach, Red
Barry, Sam
Blood, Ernest
Cann, Howard
Carlson, Dr. H. C.
Carnevale, Ben
Case, Everett

Dean, Everett
Diddle, Edgar
Drake, Bruce
Gaines, Clarence
Gardner, Jack
Gill, Slats
Hickey, Edgar
Hobson, Howard
Holzman, Red
Iba, Hank
Julian, Alvin
Keaney, Frank
Keogan, George
Lambert, Ward
Litwack, Harry
Loeffler, Kenneth
Lonborg, Dutch
McCutchan, Arad
McGuire, Frank
McLendon, John
Meyer, Ray
Meanwell, Dr. W.E.
Miller, Ralph
Newell, Pete
Rupp, Adolph
Sachs, Leonard
Shelton, Everett
Smith, Dean
Taylor, Fred
Teague, Bertha
Wade, Margaret
Watts, Stan
Wooden, John

Referees
Enright, James
Hepbron, George
Hoyt, George
Kennedy, Matthew
Leith, Lloyd
Mihalik, Red
Nucatola, John
Quigley, Ernest

Shirley, J. Dallas
Tobey, David
Walsh, David

Contributors
Abbott, Senda B.
Allen, Phog
Bee, Clair
Brown, Walter
Bunn, John
Douglas, Bob
Duer, Al O.
Fagan, Cliff
Fisher, Harry
Gottlieb, Edward
Gulick, Dr. L. H.
Harrison, Lester
Hepp, Dr. Ferenc
Hickox, Edward
Hinkle, Tony
Irish, Ned
Jones, R. W.
Kennedy, Walter
Liston, Emil
Mokray, Bill
Morgan, Ralph
Morgenweck, Frank
Naismith, Dr. James
O'Brien, John
Olsen, Harold
Podoloff, Maurice
Porter, H. V.
Reis, William
Ripley, Elmer
St. John, Lynn
Saperstein, Abe
Schabinger, Arthur
Stagg, Amos Alonzo
Steitz, Edward
Taylor, Chuck
Tower, Oswald
Trester, Arthur
Wells, Clifford
Wilke, Lou

THOROUGHBRED RACING

Triple Crown Winners

Since 1920, colts have carried 126 lbs. in triple crown events; fillies 121 lbs.

(Kentucky Derby, Preakness, and Belmont Stakes)

Year	Horse	Jockey	Trainer	Year	Horse	Jockey	Trainer
1919	Sir Barton	J. Loftus	H. G. Bedwell	1946	Assault	Mehrtens	M. Hirsch
1930	Gallant Fox	E. Sande	J. Fitzsimmons	1948	Citation	E. Arcaro	H.A. Jones
1935	Omaha	W. Sanders	J. Fitzsimmons	1973	Secretariat	R. Turcotte	L. Laurin
1937	War Admiral	C. Kurtsinger	G. Conway	1977	Seattle Slew	J. Cruguet	W.H. Turner Jr.
1941	Whirlaway	E. Arcaro	B.A. Jones	1978	Affirmed	S. Cauthen	L.S. Barrera
1943	Count Fleet	J. Longden	G.D. Cameron				

Kentucky Derby

Churchill Downs, Louisville, Ky.; inaugurated 1875; distance 1-1/4 miles; 1-1/2 miles until 1896. 3-year olds.
Best time: 1:59.2, Secretariat, 1973

Year	Winner	Jockey	Year	Winner	Jockey	Year	Winner	Jockey
1875	Aristides	O. Lewis	1914	Old Rosebud	J. McCabe	1952	Hill Gail	E. Arcaro
1876	Vagrant	R. Swim	1915	Regret*	J. Notter	1953	Dark Star	H. Moreno
1877	Baden Baden	W. Walker	1916	George Smith	J. Loftus	1954	Determine	R. York
1878	Day Star	J. Carter	1917	Omar Khayyam	C. Borel	1955	Swaps	W. Shoemaker
1879	Lord Murphy	C. Schauer	1918	Exterminator	W. Knapp	1956	Needles	D. Erb
1880	Fonso	G. Lewis	1919	Sir Barton	J. Loftus	1957	Iron Liege	W. Hartack
1881	Hindoo	J. McLaughlin	1920	Paul Jones	T. Rice	1958	Tim Tam	I. Valenzuela
1882	Apollo	B. Hurd	1921	Behave Yourself	C. Thompson	1959	Tomy Lee	W. Shoemaker
1883	Leonatus	W. Donohue	1922	Morvich	A. Johnson	1960	Venetian Way	W. Hartack
1884	Buchanan	I. Murphy	1923	Zev	E. Sande	1961	Carry Back	J. Sellers
1885	Joe Cotton	E. Henderson	1924	Black Gold	J. D. Mooney	1962	Decidedly	W. Hartack
1886	Ben Ali	P. Duffy	1925	Flying Ebony	E. Sande	1963	Chateaugay	B. Baeza
1887	Montrose	I. Lewis	1926	Bubbling Over	A. Johnson	1964	Northern Dancer	W. Hartack
1888	Macbeth II.	G. Covington	1927	Whiskery	L. McAtee	1965	Lucky Debonair	W. Shoemaker
1889	Spokane	T. Kiley	1928	Reigh Count	C. Lang	1966	Kauai King	D. Brumfield
1890	Riley	I. Murphy	1929	Clyde Van Dusen	L. McAtee	1967	Proud Clarion	R. Ussery
1891	Kingman	I. Murphy	1930	Gallant Fox	E. Sande	1968	Dancer's Image (a)	R. Ussery
1892	Azra	A. Clayton	1931	Twenty Grand	C. Kurtsinger	1969	Majestic Prince	W. Hartack
1893	Lookout	E. Kunze	1932	Burgoo King	E. James	1970	Dust Commander	M. Manganello
1894	Chant	F. Goodale	1933	Brokers Tip	D. Meade	1971	Canonero II.	G. Avila
1895	Halma	J. Perkins	1934	Cavalcade	M. Garner	1972	Riva Ridge	R. Turcotte
1896	Ben Brush	W. Simms	1935	Omaha	W. Saunders	1973	Secretariat	R. Turcotte
1897	Typhoon II.	F. Garner	1936	Bold Venture	I. Hanford	1974	Cannonade	A. Cordero
1898	Plaudit	W. Simms	1937	War Admiral	C. Kurtsinger	1975	Foolish Pleasure	J. Vasquez
1899	Manuel	F. Taral	1938	Lawrin	E. Arcaro	1976	Bold Forbes	A. Cordero
1900	Lieut. Gibson	J. Boland	1939	Johnstown	J. Stout	1977	Seattle Slew	J. Cruguet
1901	His Eminence	J. Winkfield	1940	Galiahadion	C. Bierman	1978	Affirmed	S. Cauthen
1902	Alan-a-Dale	J. Winkfield	1941	Whirlaway	E. Arcaro	1979	Spectacular Bid	R. Franklin
1903	Judge Himes	H. Booker	1942	Shut Out	W. D. Wright	1980	Genuine Risk*	J. Vasquez
1904	Elwood	F. Prior	1943	Count Fleet	J. Longden	1981	Pleasant Colony	J. Velasquez
1905	Agile	J. Martin	1944	Pensive	C. McCreary	1982	Gato del Sol	E. Delahoussaye
1906	Sir Huon	R. Troxler	1945	Hoop, Jr.	E. Arcaro	1983	Sunny's Halo	E. Delahoussaye
1907	Pink Star	A. Minder	1946	Assault	W. Mehrtens	1984	Swale	L. Pincay
1908	Stone Street	A. Pickens	1947	Jet Pilot	E. Guerin	1985	Spend a Buck	A. Cordero
1909	Wintergreen	V. Powers	1948	Citation	E. Arcaro	1986	Ferdinand	W. Shoemaker
1910	Donau	F. Herbert	1949	Ponder	S. Brooks	1987	Alysheba	C. McCarron
1911	Meridian	G. Archibald	1950	Middleground	W. Boland	1988	Winning Colors*	G. Stevens
1912	Worth	C.H. Shilling	1951	Count Turf	C. McCreary	1989	Sunday Silence	P. Valenzuela
1913	Donerail	R. Goose						

(a) Dancer's Image was disqualified from purse money after tests disclosed that he had run with a pain-killing drug, phenylbutazone, in his system. All wagers were paid on Dancer's Image. Forward Pass was awarded first place money.

The Kentucky Derby has been won five times by two jockeys, Eddie Arcaro, 1938, 1941, 1945, 1948 and 1952; and Bill Hartack, 1957, 1960, 1962, 1964 and 1969; four times by Willie Shoemaker, 1955, 1959, 1965, and 1986; and three times by each of three jockeys, Isaac Murphy, 1884, 1890, and 1891; Earle Sande, 1923, 1925 and 1930, and Angel Cordero in 1974, 1976 and 1985. *Regret, Genuine Risk and Winning Colors are the only fillies to win the Derby.

Preakness

Pimlico, Baltimore, Md.; inaugurated 1873; 1 3-16 miles, 3 yr. olds. Best time: 1:53.2, Tank's Prospect, 1985

Year	Winner	Jockey	Year	Winner	Jockey	Year	Winner	Jockey
1873	Survivor	G. Barbee	1885	Tecumseh	J. McLaughlin	1900	Hindus	H. Spencer
1874	Culpeper	M. Donohue	1886	The Bard	S. H. Fisher	1901	The Parader	F. Landry
1875	Tom Ochiltree	L. Hughes	1887	Dunboyne	W. Donohue	1902	Old England	L. Jackson
1876	Shirley	G. Barbee	1888	Refund	F. Littlefield	1903	Flocarline	W. Gannon
1877	Cloverbrook	C. Holloway	1889	Buddhist	G. Anderson	1904	Bryn Mawr	E. Hildebrand
1878	Duke of Magenta	C. Holloway	1890	Montague	W. Martin	1905	Cairngorm	W. Davis
1879	Harold	L. Hughes	1894	Assignee	F. Taral	1906	Whimsical	W. Miller
1880	Grenada	L. Hughes	1895	Belmar	F. Taral	1907	Don Enrique	G. Mountain
1881	Saunterer	W. Costello	1896	Margrave	H. Griffin	1908	Royal Tourist	E. Dugan
1882	Vanguard	W. Costello	1897	Paul Kauvar	C. Thorpe	1909	Effendi	W. Doyle
1883	Jacobus	G. Barbee	1898	Sly Fox	W. Simms	1910	Layminster	R. Estep
1884	Knight of Ellerslie	S. H. Fisher	1899	Half Time	R. Clawson	1911	Watervale	E. Dugan

Year	Winner	Jockey	Year	Winner	Jockey	Year	Winner	Jockey
1912	Colonel Holloway	C. Turner	1938	Dauber	M. Peters	1964	Northern Dancer	W. Hartack
1913	Buskin	J. Butwell	1939	Challedon	G. Seabo	1965	Tom Rolfe	R. Turcotte
1914	Holiday	A. Schuttinger	1940	Bimelech	F.A. Smith	1966	Kauai King	D. Brumfield
1915	Rhine Maiden	D. Hoffman	1941	Whirlaway	E. Arcaro	1967	Damascus	W. Shoemaker
1916	Damrosch	L. McAtee	1942	Alsab	B. James	1968	Forward Pass	I. Valenzuela
1917	Kalitan	E. Haynes	1943	Count Fleet	J. Longden	1969	Majestic Prince	W. Hartack
1918	War Cloud	J. Loftus	1944	Pensive	C. McCreary	1970	Personality	E. Belmonte
	Jack Hare Jr.	C. Peak	1945	Polynesian	W.D. Wright	1971	Canonero II	G. Avila
1919	Sir Barton	J. Loftus	1946	Assault	W. Mehrtens	1972	Bee Bee Bee	E. Nelson
1920	Man o' War	C. Kummer	1947	Faultless	D. Dodson	1973	Secretariat	R. Turcotte
1921	Broomspun	F. Coltiletti	1948	Citation	E. Arcaro	1974	Little Current	M. Rivera
1922	Pillory	L. Morris	1949	Capot	T. Atkinson	1975	Master Derby	D. McHargue
1923	Vigil	B. Marinelli	1950	Hill Prince	E. Arcaro	1976	Elocutionist	J. Lively
1924	Nellie Morse	J. Merimee	1951	Bold	E. Arcaro	1977	Seattle Slew	J. Cruguet
1925	Coventry	C. Kummer	1952	Blue Man	C. McCreary	1978	Affirmed	S. Cauthen
1926	Display	J. Malben	1953	Native Dancer	E. Guerin	1979	Spectacular Bid	R. Franklin
1927	Bostonian	A. Abel	1954	Hasty Road	J. Adams	1980	Codex	A. Cordero
1928	Victorian	R. Workman	1955	Nashua	E. Arcaro	1981	Pleasant Colony	J. Velasquez
1929	Dr. Freeland	L. Schaefer	1956	Fabius	W. Hartack	1982	Aloma's Ruler	J. Kaenel
1930	Gallant Fox	E. Sande	1957	Bold Ruler	E. Arcaro	1983	Deputed Testamony	D. Miller
1931	Mate	G. Ellis	1958	Tim Tam	I. Valenzuela	1984	Gate Dancer	A. Cordero
1932	Burgoo King	E. James	1959	Royal Orbit	W. Harmatz	1985	Tank's Prospect	P. Day
1933	Head Play	C. Kurtsinger	1960	Bally Ache	R. Ussery	1986	Snow Chief	A. Solis
1934	High Quest	R. Jones	1961	Carry Back	J. Sellers	1987	Alysheba	C. McCarron
1935	Omaha	W. Saunders	1962	Greek Money	J.L. Rotz	1988	Risen Star	E. Delahoussaye
1936	Bold Venture	G. Woolf	1963	Candy Spots	W. Shoemaker	1989	Sunday Silence	P. Valenzuela
1937	War Admiral	C. Kurtsinger						

Belmont Stakes

Elmont, N.Y.; inaugurated 1867; 1 ½ miles, 3 year olds. Fastest time: 2:24, Secretariat

Year	Winner	Jockey	Year	Winner	Jockey	Year	Winner	Jockey
1867	Ruthless	J. Gilpatrick	1908	Colin	J. Notter	1950	Middleground	W. Boland
1868	General Duke	R. Swim	1909	Joe Madden	E. Dugan	1951	Counterpoint	D. Gorman
1869	Fenian	C. Miller	1910	Sweep	J. Butwell	1952	One Count	E. Arcaro
1870	Kingfisher	W. Dick	1913	Prince Eugene	R. Troxler	1953	Native Dancer	E. Guerin
1871	Harry Bassett	W. Miller	1914	Luke McLuke	M. Buxton	1954	High Gun	E. Arcaro
1872	Joe Daniels	J. Rowe	1915	The Finn	G. Byrne	1955	Nashua	E. Arcaro
1873	Springbok	J. Rowe	1916	Friar Rock	E. Haynes	1956	Needles	D. Erb
1874	Saxon	G. Barbee	1917	Hourless	J. Butwell	1957	Gallant Man	W. Shoemaker
1875	Calvin	R. Swim	1918	Johren	F. Robinson	1958	Cavan	P. Anderson
1876	Algerine	W. Donohue	1919	Sir Barton	J. Loftus	1959	Sword Dancer	W. Shoemaker
1877	Cloverbrook	C. Holloway	1920	Man o' War	C. Kummer	1960	Celtic Ash	W. Hartack
1878	Duke of Magenta	L. Hughes	1921	Grey Lag	E. Sande	1961	Sherluck	B. Baeza
1879	Spendthrift	S. Evans	1922	Pillory	C.H. Miller	1962	Jaipur	W. Shoemaker
1880	Grenada	L. Hughes	1923	Zev	E. Sande	1963	Chateaugay	B. Baeza
1881	Saunterer	T. Costello	1924	Mad Play	E. Sande	1964	Quadrangle	M. Ycaza
1882	Forester	J. McLaughlin	1925	American Flag	A. Johnson	1965	Hail to All	J. Sellers
1883	George Kinney	J. McLaughlin	1926	Crusader	A. Johnson	1966	Amberoid	W. Boland
1884	Panique	J. McLaughlin	1927	Chance Shot	E. Sande	1967	Damascus	W. Shoemaker
1885	Tyrant	P. Duffy	1928	Vito	C. Kummer	1968	Stage Door Johnny	H. Gustines
1886	Inspector B.	J. McLaughlin	1929	Blue Larkspur	M. Garner	1969	Arts and Letters	B. Baeza
1887	Hanover	J. McLaughlin	1930	Gallant Fox	E. Sande	1970	High Echelon	J.L. Rotz
1888	Sir Dixon	J. McLaughlin	1931	Twenty Grand	C. Kurtsinger	1971	Pass Catcher	W. Blum
1889	Eric	W. Hayward	1932	Faireno	T. Malley	1972	Riva Ridge	R. Turcotte
1890	Burlington	S. Barnes	1933	Hurryoff	M. Garner	1973	Secretariat	R. Turcotte
1891	Foxford	E. Garrison	1934	Peace Chance	W.D. Wright	1974	Little Current	M. Rivera
1892	Patron	W. Hayward	1935	Omaha	W. Saunders	1975	Avatar	W. Shoemaker
1893	Comanche	W. Simms	1936	Granville	J. Stout	1976	Bold Forbes	A. Cordero
1894	Henry of Navarre	W. Simms	1937	War Admiral	C. Kurtsinger	1977	Seattle Slew	J. Cruguet
1895	Belmar	F. Taral	1938	Pasteurized	J. Stout	1978	Affirmed	S. Cauthen
1896	Hastings	H. Griffin	1939	Johnstown	J. Stout	1979	Coastal	R. Hernandez
1897	Scottish Chieftain	J. Scherrer	1940	Bimelech	F.A. Smith	1980	Temperence Hill	E. Maple
1898	Bowling Brook	F. Littlefield	1941	Whirlaway	E. Arcaro	1981	Summing	G. Martens
1899	Jean Bereaud	R.R. Clawson	1942	Shut Out	E. Arcaro	1982	Conquistador Cielo	L. Pincay
1900	Ildrim	N. Turner	1943	Count Fleet	J. Longden	1983	Caveat	L. Pincay
1901	Commando	H. Spencer	1944	Bounding Home	G.L. Smith	1984	Swale	L. Pincay
1902	Masterman	J. Bullman	1945	Pavot	E. Arcaro	1985	Creme Fraiche	E. Maple
1903	Africander	J. Bullman	1946	Assault	W. Mehrtens	1986	Danzig Connection	C. McCarron
1904	Delhi	G. Odom	1947	Phalanx	R. Donoso	1987	Bet Twice	C. Perret
1905	Tanya	E. Hildebrand	1948	Citation	E. Arcaro	1988	Risen Star	E. Delahoussaye
1906	Burgomaster	L. Lyne	1949	Capot	T. Atkinson	1989	Easy Goer	P. Day
1907	Peter Pan	G. Mountain						

Eclipse Awards in 1988

Sponsored by the Thoroughbred Racing Assn., Daily Racing Form, and the National Turf Writers Assn.

Horse of the Year—Alysheba
Best 2-year-old colt—Easy Goer
Best 2-year-old filly—Open Mind
Best 3-year-old colt—Risen Star
Best 3-year-old filly—Winning Colors
Best colt, horse, or gelding (4-year-olds & up)—Alysheba
Best filly or mare (4-year-olds & up)—Personal Ensign
Best male turf horse—Sunshine Forever

Best turf filly or mare—Miesque
Best sprinter—Gulch
Best steeplechase horse—Jimmy Lorenzo
Best trainer—Shug McGaughey
Best jockey—Jose Santos
Best apprentice jockey—Steve Capanas
Best owner—Ogden Phipps Stable
Best breeder—Ogdon Phipps Stable

Annual Leading Money-Winning Horses

Year	Horse	Dollars	Year	Horse	Dollars	Year	Horse	Dollars
1948	Citation	709,470	1962	Never Bend	402,969	1976	Forego	491,701
1949	Ponder	321,825	1963	Candy Spots	604,481	1977	Seattle Slew	641,370
1950	Noor	346,940	1964	Gun Bow	580,100	1978	Affirmed	901,541
1951	Counterpoint	250,525	1965	Buckpasser	568,096	1979	Spectacular Bid	1,279,334
1952	Crafty Admiral	277,255	1966	Buckpasser	669,078	1980	Temperence Hill	1,130,452
1953	Native Dancer	513,425	1967	Damascus	817,941	1981	John Henry	1,148,800
1954	Determine	328,700	1968	Forward Pass	546,674	1982	Perrault	1,197,400
1955	Nashua	752,550	1969	Arts and Letters	555,604	1983	All Along	2,138,963
1956	Needles	440,850	1970	Personality	444,049	1984	Slew O'Gold	2,627,944
1957	Round Table	600,383	1971	Riva Ridge	503,263	1985	Spend a Buck	3,552,704
1958	Round Table	662,780	1972	Droll Roll	471,633	1986	Snow Chief	1,875,200
1959	Sword Dancer	537,004	1973	Secretariat	860,404	1987	Alysheba	2,511,156
1960	Bally Ache	455,045	1974	Chris Evert	551,063	1988	Alysheba	3,808,600
1961	Carry Back	565,349	1975	Foolish Pleasure	716,278			

Annual Leading Jockey—Money Won

Year	Jockey	Dollars	Year	Jockey	Dollars	Year	Jockey	Dollars
1957	Bill Hartack	3,060,501	1968	Braulio Baeza	2,835,108	1979	Laffit Pincay Jr.	8,193,535
1958	Willie Shoemaker	2,961,693	1969	Jorge Velasquez	2,542,315	1980	Chris McCarron	7,663,300
1959	Willie Shoemaker	2,843,133	1970	Laffit Pincay Jr.	2,626,526	1981	Chris McCarron	8,397,604
1960	Willie Shoemaker	2,123,961	1971	Laffit Pincay Jr.	3,784,377	1982	Angel Cordero Jr.	9,483,590
1961	Willie Shoemaker	2,690,819	1972	Laffit Pincay Jr.	3,225,827	1983	Angel Cordero Jr.	10,116,697
1962	Willie Shoemaker	2,916,844	1973	Laffit Pincay Jr.	4,093,492	1984	Chris McCarron	12,045,813
1963	Willie Shoemaker	2,526,925	1974	Laffit Pincay Jr.	4,251,060	1985	Laffit Pincay Jr.	13,353,299
1964	Willie Shoemaker	2,649,553	1975	Braulio Baeza	3,695,198	1986	Jose Santos	11,329,297
1965	Braulio Baeza	2,582,702	1976	Angel Cordero Jr.	4,709,500	1987	Jose Santos	12,375,433
1966	Braulio Baeza	2,951,022	1977	Steve Cauthen	6,151,750	1988	Jose Santos	14,877,298
1967	Braulio Baeza	3,088,888	1978	Darrel McHargue	6,029,885			

Westminster Kennel Club

Year	Best-in-show	Breed	Owner
1977	Ch. Dersade Bobby's Girl	Sealyham	Dorothy Wymer
1978	Ch. Cede Higgens	Yorkshire terrier	Barbara & Charles Switzer
1979	Ch. Oak Tree's Irishtocrat	Irish water spaniel	Anne E. Snelling
1980	Ch. Sierra Cinnar	Siberian husky	Kathleen Kanzler
1981	Ch. Dhandy Favorite Woodchuck	Pug	Robert Houslohner
1982	Ch. St. Aubrey Dragonora of Elsdon	Pekingese	Anne Snelling
1983	Ch. Kabik's The Challenger	Afghan	Chris & Marguerite Terrell
1984	Ch. Seaward's Blackbeard	Newfoundland	Elinor Ayers
1985	Ch. Braeburn's Close Encounter	Scottish terrier	Sonnie Novick
1986	Ch. Marjetta National Acclaim	Pointer	Mrs. Alan Robson & Michael Zollo
1987	Ch. Covy Tucker Hill's Manhattan	German shepherd	Shirley Braunstein & Jane Firestone
1988	Ch. Great Elms Prince Charming II	Pomeranian	Skip Piazza & Olga Baker
1989	Ch. Royal Tudor's Wild As The Wind	Doberman	Sue & Art Kemp, Richard & Carolyn Vida, Beth Wilhite

Professional Sports Directory

Baseball

Commissioner's Office
350 Park Ave.
New York, NY 10022

National League

National League Office
350 Park Ave.
New York, NY 10022

Atlanta Braves
PO Box 4064
Atlanta, GA 30302

Chicago Cubs
Wrigley Field
Chicago, IL 60613

Cincinnati Reds
100 Riverfront Stadium
Cincinnati, OH 45202

Houston Astros
Astrodome
Houston, TX 77001

Los Angeles Dodgers
Dodger Stadium
Los Angeles, CA 90012

Montreal Expos
PO Box 500, Station M
Montreal, Que. H1V 3P2

New York Mets
Shea Stadium
Flushing, NY 11368

Philadelphia Phillies
PO Box 7575
Philadelphia, PA 19101

Pittsburgh Pirates
Three Rivers Stadium
Pittsburgh, PA 15212

St. Louis Cardinals
Busch Stadium
St. Louis, MO 63102

San Diego Padres
PO Box 2000
San Diego, CA 92120

San Francisco Giants
Candlestick Park
San Francisco, CA 94124

American League

American League Office
350 Park Ave.
New York, NY 10022

Baltimore Orioles
Memorial Stadium
Baltimore, MD 21218

Boston Red Sox
4 Yawkey Way
Boston, MA 02215

California Angels
Anaheim Stadium
Anaheim, CA 92806

Chicago White Sox
324 W. 35th St.
Chicago, IL 60616

Cleveland Indians
Cleveland Stadium
Cleveland, OH 44114

Detroit Tigers
Tiger Stadium
Detroit, MI 48216

Kansas City Royals
P.O. Box 419969
Kansas City, MO 64141

Milwaukee Brewers
Milwaukee County Stadium
Milwaukee, WI 53214

Minnesota Twins
501 Chicago Ave. South
Minneapolis, MN 55415

New York Yankees
Yankee Stadium
Bronx, NY 10451

Oakland A's
Oakland Coliseum
Oakland, CA 94621

Seattle Mariners
P.O. Box 4100
Seattle, WA 98104

Texas Rangers
1250 Copeland Rd.
Arlington, TX 76010

Toronto Blue Jays
300 The Esplanade West
Toronto, Ont. M5V 3B3

National Football League

League Office
350 Park Avenue
New York, NY 10022

Atlanta Falcons
Suwanee Road
Suwanee, GA 30174

Buffalo Bills
1 Bills Drive
Orchard Park, NY 14127

Chicago Bears
250 N. Washington
Lake Forest, IL 60045

Cincinnati Bengals
200 Riverfront Stadium
Cincinnati, OH 45202

Cleveland Browns
Cleveland Stadium
Cleveland, OH 44114

Dallas Cowboys
One Cowboys Pkwy.
Irving, TX 75063

Denver Broncos
5700 Logan St.
Denver, CO 80216

Detroit Lions
1200 Featherstone Rd.
Pontiac, MI 48057

Green Bay Packers
1265 Lombardi Ave.
Green Bay, WI 54303

Houston Oilers
P.O. Box 1516
Houston, TX 77251

Indianapolis Colts
P.O. Box 53500
Indianapolis, IN 46253

Kansas City Chiefs
1 Arrowhead Drive
Kansas City, MO 64129

Los Angeles Raiders
332 Center St.
El Segundo, CA 90245

Los Angeles Rams
2327 W. Lincoln Ave.
Anaheim, CA 92801

Miami Dolphins
4770 Biscayne Blvd.
Miami, FL 33137

Minnesota Vikings
9520 Viking Dr.
Eden Prairie, MN 55344

New England Patriots
Sullivan Stadium
Foxboro, MA 02035

New Orleans Saints
6928 Saints Dr.
Metairie, LA 70003

New York Giants
Giants Stadium
E. Rutherford, NJ 07073

New York Jets
598 Madison Ave.
New York, NY 10022

Philadelphia Eagles
Veterans Stadium
Philadelphia, PA 19148

Phoenix Cardinals
51 W 3d
Tempe, AZ 85281

Pittsburgh Steelers
Three Rivers Stadium
Pittsburgh, PA 15212

San Diego Chargers
P.O. Box 20666
San Diego, CA 92120

San Francisco 49ers
4949 Centennial Blvd.
Santa Clara, CA 95054

Seattle Seahawks
11220 NE 53d St.
Kirkland, WA 98033

Tampa Bay Buccaneers
1 Buccaneer Place
Tampa, FL 33607

Washington Redskins
PO Box 17247
Dulles Intl. Airport
Washington, DC 20041

National Basketball Association

League Office
645 5th Ave.
New York, NY 10022

Atlanta Hawks
100 Techwood Drive NW
Atlanta, GA 30303

Boston Celtics
Boston Garden
Boston, MA 02114

Charlotte Hornets
2 First Union Center
Charlotte, NC 28282

Chicago Bulls
980 North Michigan Ave.
Chicago, IL 60611

Cleveland Cavaliers
2923 Statesboro Rd.
Richfield, OH 44286

Dallas Mavericks
777 Sports St.
Dallas, TX 75207

Denver Nuggets
1635 Clay St.
Denver, CO 80204

Detroit Pistons
3777 Lapeer Rd.
Auburn Hills, MI 48057

Golden State Warriors
Oakland Coliseum
Oakland, CA 94621

Houston Rockets
The Summit
Houston, TX 77046

Indiana Pacers
2 W. Washington St.
Indianapolis, IN 46204

Los Angeles Clippers
3939 S. Figueroa
Los Angeles, CA 90037

Los Angeles Lakers
PO Box 10
Inglewood, CA 90306

Miami Heat
Miami Arena
Miami, FL 33136

Milwaukee Bucks
1001 N. 4th St.
Milwaukee, WI 53203

Minnesota Timberwolves
730 Hennepin Ave.
Minneapolis, MN 55403

New Jersey Nets
Meadowlands Arena
E. Rutherford, NJ 07073

New York Knickerbockers
4 Pennsylvania Plaza
New York, NY 10001

Orlando Magic
1 Magic Place
Orlando, FL 32801

Philadelphia 76ers
PO Box 25040
Philadelphia, PA 19147

Phoenix Suns
2910 N. Central
Phoenix, AZ 85012

Portland Trail Blazers
700 NE Multnomah St.
Portland, OR 97232

Sacramento Kings
One Sports Pkwy.
Sacramento, CA 95834

San Antonio Spurs
600 E. Market St.
San Antonio, TX 78205

Seattle SuperSonics
190 Queen Ann Ave. N.
Seattle, WA 98109

Utah Jazz
5 Triad Center
Salt Lake City, UT 84180

Washington Bullets
Capital Centre
Landover, MD 20785

National Hockey League

League Headquarters
Sun Life Bldg.
Montreal, Quebec H3B 2W2

Boston Bruins
150 Causeway St.
Boston, MA 02114

Buffalo Sabres
Memorial Auditorium
Buffalo, NY 14202

Calgary Flames
P.O. Box 1540
Calgary, Alta. T2P 3B9

Chicago Black Hawks
1800 W. Madison St.
Chicago, IL 60612

Detroit Red Wings
600 Civic Center Drive
Detroit, MI 48226

Edmonton Oilers
Northlands Coliseum
Edmonton, Alta. T5B 4M9

Hartford Whalers
One Civic Center Plaza
Hartford, CT 06103

Los Angeles Kings
39 W. Manchester Blvd.
Inglewood, CA 90306

Minnesota North Stars
7901 Cedar Ave. S.
Bloomington, MN 55420

Montreal Canadiens
2313 St. Catherine St., West
Montreal, Quebec H3H 1N2

New Jersey Devils
Meadowlands Arena
E. Rutherford, NJ 07073

New York Islanders
Nassau Coliseum
Uniondale, NY 11553

New York Rangers
4 Pennsylvania Plaza
New York, NY 10001

Philadelphia Flyers
Pattison Place
Philadelphia, PA 19148

Pittsburgh Penguins
Civic Arena
Pittsburgh, PA 15219

Quebec Nordiques
2205 Ave. du Colisee
Quebec, Que. G1L 4W7

St. Louis Blues
5700 Oakland Ave.
St. Louis, MO 63110

Toronto Maple Leafs
60 Carlton St.
Toronto, Ont. M5B 1L1

Vancouver Canucks
100 North Renfrew St.
Vancouver, B.C. V5K 3N7

Washington Capitals
Capital Centre
Landover, MD 20785

Winnipeg Jets
15-1430 Maroons Road
Winnipeg, Man. R3G 0L5

COLLEGE FOOTBALL

Annual Results of Major Bowl Games

(Note: Dates indicate the year that the game was played.)

Rose Bowl, Pasadena

1902 Michigan 49, Stanford 0	1941 Stanford 21, Nebraska 13	1965 Michigan 34, Oregon St. 7
1916 Wash. State 14, Brown 0	1942 Oregon St. 20, Duke 16	1966 UCLA 14, Mich. State 12
1917 Oregon 14, Pennsylvania 0	(at Durham)	1967 Purdue 14, So. California 13
1918-19 Service teams	1943 Georgia 9, UCLA 0	1968 Southern Cal. 14, Indiana 3
1920 Harvard 7, Oregon 6	1944 So. California 29, Washington 0	1969 Ohio State 27, Southern Cal 16
1921 California 28, Ohio State 0	1945 So. California 25, Tennessee 0	1970 Southern Cal 10, Michigan 3
1922 Wash. & Jeff. 0, California 0	1946 Alabama 34, So. California 14	1971 Stanford 27, Ohio State 17
1923 So. California 14, Penn State 3	1947 Illinois 45, UCLA 14	1972 Stanford 13, Michigan 12
1924 Navy 14, Washington 14	1948 Michigan 49, So. California 0	1973 So. California 42, Ohio State 17
1925 Notre Dame 27, Stanford 10	1949 Northwestern 20, California 14	1974 Ohio State 42, So. California 21
1926 Alabama 20, Washington 19	1950 Ohio State 17, California 14	1975 So. California 18, Ohio State 17
1927 Alabama 7, Stanford 7	1951 Michigan 14, California 6	1976 UCLA 23, Ohio State 10
1928 Stanford 7, Pittsburgh 6	1952 Illinois 40, Stanford 7	1977 So. California 14, Michigan 6
1929 Georgia Tech 8, California 7	1953 So. California 7, Wisconsin 0	1978 Washington 27, Michigan 20
1930 So. California 47, Pittsburgh 14	1954 Mich. State 28, UCLA 20	1979 So. California 17, Michigan 10
1931 Alabama 24, Wash. State 0	1955 Ohio State 20, So. California 7	1980 So. California 17, Ohio State 16
1932 So. California 21, Tulane 12	1956 Mich. State 17, UCLA 14	1981 Michigan 23, Washington 6
1933 So. California 35, Pittsburgh 0	1957 Iowa 35, Oregon St. 19	1982 Washington 28, Iowa 0
1934 Columbia 7, Stanford 0	1958 Ohio State 10, Oregon 7	1983 UCLA 24, Michigan 14
1935 Alabama 29, Stanford 13	1959 Iowa 38, California 12	1984 UCLA 45, Illinois 9
1936 Stanford 7, So. Methodist 0	1960 Washington 44, Wisconsin 8	1985 So. California 20, Ohio State 17
1937 Pittsburgh 21, Washington 0	1961 Washington 17, Minnesota 7	1986 UCLA 45, Iowa 28
1938 California 13, Alabama 0	1962 Minnesota 21, UCLA 3	1987 Arizona St. 22, Michigan 15
1939 So. California 7, Duke 3	1963 So. California 42, Wisconsin 37	1988 Michigan St. 20, USC 17
1940 So. California 14, Tennessee 0	1964 Illinois 17, Washington 7	1989 Michigan 22, USC 14

Orange Bowl, Miami

1935 Bucknell 26, Miami (Fla.) 0	1954 Oklahoma 7, Maryland 0	1972 Nebraska 38, Alabama 6
1936 Catholic U. 20, Mississippi 19	1955 Duke 34, Nebraska 7	1973 Nebraska 40, Notre Dame 6
1937 Duquesne 13, Miss. State 12	1956 Oklahoma 20, Maryland 6	1974 Penn State 16, Louisiana St. 9
1938 Auburn 6, Mich. State 0	1957 Colorado 27, Clemson 21	1975 Notre Dame 13, Alabama 11
1939 Tennessee 17, Oklahoma 0	1958 Oklahoma 48, Duke 21	1976 Oklahoma 14, Michigan 6
1940 Georgia Tech 21, Missouri 7	1959 Oklahoma 21, Syracuse 6	1977 Ohio State 27, Colorado 10
1941 Miss. State 14, Georgetown 7	1960 Georgia 14, Missouri 0	1978 Arkansas 31, Oklahoma 6
1942 Georgia 40, TCU 26	1961 Missouri 21, Navy 14	1979 Oklahoma 31, Nebraska 24
1943 Alabama 37, Boston Col. 21	1962 LSU 25, Colorado 7	1980 Oklahoma 24, Florida St. 7
1944 LSU 19, Texas A&M 14	1963 Alabama 17, Oklahoma 0	1981 Oklahoma 18, Florida St. 17
1945 Tulsa 26, Georgia Tech 12	1964 Nebraska 13, Auburn 7	1982 Clemson 22, Nebraska 15
1946 Miami (Fla.) 13, Holy Cross 6	1965 Texas 21, Alabama 17	1983 Nebraska 21, Louisiana St. 20
1947 Rice 8, Tennessee 0	1966 Alabama 39, Nebraska 28	1984 Miami (Fla.) 31, Nebraska 30
1948 Georgia Tech 20, Kansas 14	1967 Florida 27, Georgia Tech 12	1985 Washington 28, Oklahoma 17
1949 Texas 41, Georgia 28	1968 Oklahoma 26, Tennessee 24	1986 Oklahoma 25, Penn State 10
1950 Santa Clara 21, Kentucky 13	1969 Penn State 15, Kansas 14	1987 Oklahoma 42, Arkansas 8
1951 Clemson 15, Miami (Fla.) 14	1970 Penn State 10, Missouri 3	1988 Miami (Fla.) 20, Oklahoma 14
1952 Georgia Tech 17, Baylor 14	1971 Nebraska 17, Louisiana St. 12	1989 Miami (Fla.) 23, Nebraska 3
1953 Alabama 61, Syracuse 6		

Sugar Bowl, New Orleans

1935 Tulane 20, Temple 14	1954 Georgia Tech 42, West Virginia 19	*1972 (Dec.) Oklahoma 14, Penn State
1936 TCU 3, LSU 2	1955 Navy 21, Mississippi 0	1973 Notre Dame 24, Alabama 23
1937 Santa Clara 21, LSU 14	1956 Georgia Tech 7, Pittsburgh 0	1974 Nebraska 13, Florida 10
1938 Santa Clara 6, LSU 0	1957 Baylor 13, Tennessee 7	1975 Alabama 13, Penn State 6
1939 TCU 15, Carnegie Tech 7	1958 Mississippi 39, Texas 7	1977 (Jan.) Pittsburgh 27, Georgia 3
1940 Texas A&M 14, Tulane 13	1959 LSU 7, Clemson 0	1978 Alabama 35, Ohio State 6
1941 Boston Col. 19, Tennessee 13	1960 Mississippi 21, LSU 0	1979 Alabama 14, Penn State 7
1942 Fordham 2, Missouri 0	1961 Mississippi 14, Rice 6	1980 Alabama 24, Arkansas 9
1943 Tennessee 14, Tulsa 7	1962 Alabama 10, Arkansas 3	1981 Georgia 17, Notre Dame 10
1944 Georgia Tech 20, Tulsa 18	1963 Mississippi 17, Arkansas 13	1982 Pittsburgh 24, Georgia 20
1945 Duke 29, Alabama 26	1964 Alabama 12, Mississippi 7	1983 Penn State 27, Georgia 23
1946 Oklahoma A&M 33, St. Mary's 13	1965 LSU 13, Syracuse 10	1984 Auburn 9, Michigan 7
1947 Georgia 20, No. Carolina 10	1966 Missouri 20, Florida 18	1985 Nebraska 28, Louisiana St. 10
1948 Texas 27, Alabama 7	1967 Alabama 34, Nebraska 7	1986 Tennessee 35, Miami (Fla.) 7
1949 Oklahoma 14, No. Carolina 6	1968 LSU 20, Wyoming 13	1987 Nebraska 30, Louisiana St. 15
1950 Oklahoma 35, LSU 0	1969 Arkansas 16, Georgia 2	1988 Syracuse 16, Auburn 16
1951 Kentucky 13, Oklahoma 7	1970 Mississippi 27, Arkansas 22	1989 Florida St. 13, Auburn 7
1952 Maryland 28, Tennessee 13	1971 Tennessee 34, Air Force 13	*Penn St. awarded game by forfeit
1953 Georgia Tech. 24, Mississippi 7	1972 Oklahoma 40, Auburn 22	

Fiesta Bowl, Tempe

1971 Arizona St. 45, Florida St. 38	1977 Penn St. 42, Arizona St. 30	1984 Ohio State 28, Pittsburgh 23
1972 Arizona St. 49, Missouri 35	1978 UCLA 10, Arkansas 10	1985 UCLA 39, Miami 37
1973 Arizona St. 28, Pittsburgh 7	1979 Pittsburgh 16, Arizona 10	1986 Michigan 27, Nebraska 23
1974 Okla. St. 16, Brigham Young 6	1980 Penn St. 31, Ohio St. 19	1987 Penn St. 14, Miami (Fla.) 10
1975 Arizona St. 17, Nebraska 14	1981 Penn St. 26, USC 10	1988 Florida St. 31, Nebraska 28
1976 Oklahoma 41, Wyoming 7	1983 (Jan.) Arizona St. 32, Oklahoma 21	1989 Notre Dame 34, W. Virginia 21

Cotton Bowl, Dallas

1937 TCU 16, Marquette 6	1939 St. Mary's 20, Texas Tech 13	1941 Texas A&M 13, Fordham 12
1938 Rice 28, Colorado 14	1940 Clemson 6, Boston Col. 3	1942 Alabama 29, Texas A&M 21

1943 Texas 14, Georgia Tech 7
1944 Randolph Field 7, Texas 7
1945 Oklahoma A&M 34, TCU 0
1946 Texas 40, Missouri 27
1947 Arkansas 0, LSU 0
1948 So. Methodist 13, Penn State 13
1949 So. Methodist 21, Oregon 13
1950 Rice 27, No. Carolina 13
1951 Tennessee 20, Texas 14
1952 Kentucky 20, TCU 7
1953 Texas 16, Tennessee 0
1954 Rice 28, Alabama 6
1955 Georgia Tech 14, Arkansas 6
1956 Mississippi 14, TCU 13
1957 TCU 28, Syracuse 27
1958 Navy 20, Rice 7

1959 TCU 0, Air Force 0
1960 Syracuse 23, Texas 14
1961 Duke 7, Arkansas 6
1962 Texas 12, Mississippi 7
1963 LSU 13, Texas 0
1964 Texas 28, Navy 6
1965 Arkansas 10, Nebraska 7
1966 LSU 14, Arkansas 7
1967 Georgia 24, So. Methodist 9
1968 Texas A&M 20, Alabama 16
1969 Texas 36, Tennessee 13
1970 Texas 21, Notre Dame 17
1971 Notre Dame 24, Texas 11
1972 Penn State 30, Texas 6
1973 Texas 17, Alabama 13
1974 Nebraska 19, Texas 3

1975 Penn State 41, Baylor 20
1976 Arkansas 31, Georgia 10
1977 Houston 30, Maryland 21
1978 Notre Dame 38, Texas 10
1979 Notre Dame 35, Houston 34
1980 Houston 17, Nebraska 14
1981 Alabama 30, Baylor 2
1982 Texas 14, Alabama 12
1983 SMU 7, Pittsburgh 3
1984 Georgia 10, Texas 9
1985 Boston Coll. 45, Houston 28
1986 Texas A&M 36, Auburn 16
1987 Ohio St. 28, Texas A&M 12
1988 Texas A&M 35, Notre Dame 10
1989 UCLA 17, Arkansas 3

Sun Bowl, El Paso

1936 Hardin Simmons 14, New Mex. St. 14
1937 Hardin-Simmons 34, Texas Mines 6
1938 West Virginia 7, Texas Tech 6
1939 Utah 26, New Mexico 0
1940 Catholic U. 0, Arizona St. 0
1941 Western Reserve 26, Arizona St. 13
1942 Tulsa 6, Texas Tech 0
1943 2d Air Force 13, Hardin-Simmons 7
1944 Southwestern (Tex.) 7, New Mexico 0
1945 Southwestern (Tex.) 35, U. of Mex. 0
1946 New Mexico 34, Denver 24
1947 Cincinnati 18, Virginia Tech 6
1948 Miami (O.) 13, Texas Tech 12
1949 West Virginia 21, Texas Mines 12
1950 Texas Western 33, Georgetown 20
1951 West Texas St. 14, Cincinnati 13
1952 Texas Tech 25, Col. Pacific 14

1953 Col. Pacific 26, Miss. Southern 7
1954 Texas Western 37, Miss. Southern 14
1955 Texas Western 47, Florida St. 20
1956 Wyoming 21, Texas Tech 14
1957 Geo. Washington 13, Tex. Western 0
1958 Louisville 34, Drake 20
1959 Wyoming 14, Hardin-Simmons 6
1960 New Mexico St. 28, No. Texas St. 8
1961 New Mexico St. 20, Utah State 13
1962 Villanova 17, Wichita 9
1963 West Texas St. 15, Ohio U. 14
1964 Oregon 21, So. Methodist 14
1965 Georgia 7, Texas Tech 0
1966 Texas Western 13, TCU 12
1967 Wyoming 28, Florida St. 20
1968 UTex El Paso 14, Mississippi 7
1969 Auburn 34, Arizona 10
1969 (Dec.) Nebraska 45, Georgia 6

1970 Georgia Tech. 17, Texas Tech. 9
1971 LSU 33, Iowa State 15
1972 North Carolina 32, Texas Tech 28
1973 Missouri 34, Auburn 17
1974 Mississippi St. 26, No. Carolina 24
1975 Pittsburgh 33, Kansas 19
1977 (Jan.) Texas A&M 37, Florida 14
1977 (Dec.) Stanford 24, Louisiana St. 14
1978 Texas 42, Maryland 0
1979 Washington 14, Texas 7
1980 Nebraska 31, Mississippi St. 17
1981 Oklahoma 40, Houston 14
1982 North Carolina 26, Texas 10
1983 Alabama 28, SMU 7
1984 Maryland 28, Tennessee 27
1985 Georgia 13, Arizona 13
1986 Alabama 28, Washington 6
1987 Oklahoma St. 35, West Virginia 33
1988 Alabama 29, Army 28

Gator Bowl, Jacksonville

1946 Wake Forest 26, So. Carolina 14
1947 Oklahoma 34, N.C. State 13
1948 Maryland 20, Georgia 20
1949 Clemson 24, Missouri 23
1950 Maryland 20, Missouri 7
1951 Wyoming 20, Wash. & Lee 7
1952 Miami (Fla.) 14, Clemson 0
1953 Florida 14, Tulsa 13
1954 Texas Tech 35, Auburn 13
1955 Auburn 33, Baylor 13
1956 Vanderbilt 25, Auburn 13
1957 Georgia Tech 21, Pittsburgh 14
1958 Tennessee 3, Texas A&M 0
1959 Mississippi 7, Florida 3
1960 Arkansas 14, Georgia Tech 7

1961 Florida 13, Baylor 12
1962 Penn State 30, Georgia Tech 15
1963 Florida 17, Penn State 7
1964 No. Carolina 35, Air Force 0
1965 Florida St. 36, Oklahoma 19
1966 Georgia Tech 31, Texas Tech 21
1967 Tennessee 18, Syracuse 12
1968 Penn State 17, Florida St. 17
1969 Missouri 35, Alabama 10
1969 (Dec.) Florida 14, Tenn. 13
1971 (Jan.) Auburn 35, Mississippi 28
1972 Georgia 7, N. Carolina 3
1973 Auburn 24, Colorado 3
1973 (Dec.) Tex. Tech. 28, Tenn. 19
1974 Auburn 27, Texas 3

1975 Maryland 13, Florida 0
1976 Notre Dame 20, Penn State 9
1977 Pittsburgh 34, Clemson 3
1978 Clemson 17, Ohio State 15
1979 No. Carolina 17, Michigan 15
1980 Pittsburgh 37, So. Carolina 9
1981 No. Carolina 31, Arkansas 27
1982 Florida St. 31, West Va. 12
1983 Florida 14, Iowa 6
1984 Oklahoma St. 21, So. Carolina 14
1985 Florida St. 34, Oklahoma St. 23
1986 Clemson 27, Stanford 21
1987 LSU 30, So. Carolina 13
1989 (Jan.) Georgia 34, Michigan St. 27

Bluebonnet Bowl, Houston

1959 Clemson 23, TCU 7
1960 Texas 3, Alabama 3
1961 Kansas 33, Rice 7
1962 Missouri 14, Georgia Tech 10
1963 Baylor 14, LSU 7
1964 Tulsa 14, Mississippi 7
1965 Tennessee 27, Tulsa 6
1966 Texas 19, Mississippi 0
1967 Colorado 31, Miami (Fla.) 21
1968 SMU 28, Oklahoma 27

1969 Houston 36, Auburn 7
1970 Oklahoma 24, Alabama 24
1971 Colorado 29, Houston 17
1972 Tennessee 24, Louisiana St. 17
1973 Houston 47, Tulane 7
1974 N. Carolina St. 31, Houston 31
1975 Texas 38, Colorado 21
1976 Nebraska 27, Texas Tech 24
1977 USC 47, Texas A&M 28
1978 Stanford 25, Georgia 22

1979 Purdue 27, Tennessee 22
1980 No. Carolina 16, Texas 7
1981 Michigan 33, UCLA 14
1982 Arkansas 28, Florida 24
1983 Oklahoma St. 24, Baylor 14
1984 W. Virginia 31, Tex. Christian 14
1985 Air Force 21, Texas 16
1986 Baylor 21, Colorado 9
1987 Texas 32, Pittsburgh 27
1988 Not played

Liberty Bowl, Memphis

1959 Penn State 7, Alabama 0
1960 Penn State 41, Oregon 12
1961 Syracuse 15, Miami 14
1962 Oregon State 6, Villanova 0
1963 Miss. State 16, N.C. State 12
1964 Utah 32, West Virginia 6
1965 Mississippi 13, Auburn 7
1966 Miami (Fla.) 14, Va. Tech 7
1967 N.C. State 14, Georgia 7
1968 Mississippi 34, Va. Tech 17

1969 Colorado 47, Alabama 33
1970 Tulane 17, Colorado 3
1971 Tennessee 14, Arkansas 13
1972 Georgia Tech 31, Iowa State 30
1973 No. Carolina St. 31, Kansas 18
1974 Tennessee 7, Maryland 3
1975 USC 20, Texas A&M 0
1976 Alabama 36, UCLA 6
1977 Nebraska 21, N. Carolina 17
1978 Missouri 20, Louisiana St. 15

1979 Penn St. 9, Tulane 6
1980 Purdue 28, Missouri 25
1981 Ohio State 31, Navy 28
1982 Alabama 21, Illinois 15
1983 Notre Dame 19, Boston Coll. 18
1984 Auburn 21, Arkansas 15
1985 Baylor 21, Louisiana St. 7
1986 Tennessee 21, Minnesota 14
1987 Georgia 20, Arkansas 17
1988 Indiana 34, S. Carolina 10

Freedom Bowl, Anaheim

1984 Iowa 55, Texas 17
1985 Washington 20, Colorado 17

1986 UCLA 31, Brigham Young 10
1987 Arizona St. 33, Air Force 28

1988 Brigham Young 20, Colorado 17

Citrus Bowl, Orlando

1947 Catawba 31, Maryville 6
1948 Catawba 7, Marshall 0

1949 Murray State 21, Sul Ross St. 21
1950 St. Vincent 7, Emory & Henry 6

1951 Morris Harvey 35, Emory & Henry 14

(continued)

1952 Stetson 35, Arkansas St. 20
1953 East Texas St. 33, Tenn. Tech 0
1954 East Texas St. 7, Arkansas St. 7
1955 Neb.-Omaha 7, Eastern Kentucky 6
1956 Juniata 6, Missouri Valley 6
1957 West Texas St. 20, So. Miss. 13
1958 East Texas St. 10, So. Miss. 9
1958 (Dec.) East Texas St. 26, Missouri Valley 7
1960 (Jan.) Middle Tenn. 21, Presbyterian 12
1960 (Dec.) Citadel 27, Tenn. Tech 0
1961 Lamar 21, Middle Tennessee 14
1962 Houston 49, Miami (O.) 21

1963 Western Ky. 27, Coast Guard 0
1964 E. Carolina 14, Massachusetts 13
1965 East Carolina 31, Maine 0
1966 Morgan State 14, West Chester 6
1967 Tenn.-Martin 25, West Chester 8
1968 Richmond 49, Ohio U. 42
1969 Toledo 56, Davidson 33
1970 Toledo 40, William & Mary 12
1971 Toledo 28, Richmond 3
1972 Tampa 21, Kent State 18
1973 Miami (O.) 16, Florida 7
1974 Miami (O.) 21, Georgia 10
1975 Miami (O.) 20, South Carolina 7

1976 Okla. St. 49, Brigham Young 21
1977 Florida St. 40, Texas Tech 17
1978 N.C. State 30, Pittsburgh 17
1979 LSU 34, Wake Forest 10
1980 Florida 35, Maryland 20
1981 Missouri 19, Southern Miss. 17
1982 Auburn 33, Boston College 26
1983 Tennessee 30, Maryland 23
1984 Georgia 17, Florida St. 17
1985 Ohio St. 10, Brigham Young 7
1986 Auburn 16, USC 7
1987 (Jan.) Clemson 35, Penn St. 10
1989 Clemson 13, Oklahoma 6

Peach Bowl, Atlanta

1968 LSU 31, Florida St. 27
1969 West Virginia 14, S. Carolina 3
1970 Arizona St. 48, N. Carolina 26
1971 Mississippi 41, Georgia Tech. 18
1972 N. Carolina 32, W. Va. 13
1973 Georgia 17, Maryland 16
1974 Vanderbilt 6, Texas Tech. 6

1975 W. Virginia 13, No. Carolina St. 10
1976 Kentucky 21, North Carolina 0
1977 N. Carolina St. 24, Iowa St. 14
1978 Purdue 41, Georgia Tech. 21
1979 Baylor 24, Clemson 18
1981 (Jan.) Miami 20, Virginia Tech. 10
1981 (Dec.) West Virginia 26, Florida 6

1982 Iowa 28, Tennessee 22
1983 Florida St. 28, North Carolina 3
1984 Virginia 27, Purdue 22
1985 Army 31, Illinois 29
1986 Va. Tech 25, N.C. State 24
1988 (Jan.) Tennessee 28, Indiana 22
1988 (Dec.) N.C. State 28, Iowa 23

Independence Bowl, Shreveport

1976 McNeese St. 20, Tulsa 16
1977 Louisiana Tech 24, Louisville 14
1978 E. Carolina 35, La. Tech 13
1979 Syracuse 31, McNeese St. 7
1980 So. Miss. 16, McNeese St. 14

1981 Texas A&M 33, Oklahoma St. 16
1982 Wisconsin 14, Kansas St. 3
1983 Air Force 9, Mississippi 3
1984 Air Force 23, Virginia Tech 7

1985 Minnesota 20, Clemson 13
1986 Mississippi 20, Texas Tech 17
1987 Washington 24, Tulane 12
1988 S. Mississippi 38, UTEP 18

All-American Bowl, Birmingham

1977 Maryland 17, Minnesota 7
1978 Texas A&M 28, Iowa St. 12
1979 Missouri 24, So. Carolina 14
1980 Arkansas 34, Tulane 15

1981 Mississippi St. 10, Kansas 0
1982 Air Force 36, Vanderbilt 28
1983 W. Virginia 20, Kentucky 16
1984 Kentucky 20, Wisconsin 19

1985 Georgia Tech 17, Michigan St. 14
1986 Florida St. 27, Indiana 13
1987 Virginia 22, Brigham Young 16
1988 Florida 14, Illinois 10

Holiday Bowl, San Diego

1978 Navy 23, Brigham Young 16
1979 Indiana 38, Brigham Young 37
1980 Brigham Young 46, SMU 45
1981 Brigham Young 38, Wash. St. 36

1982 Ohio State 47, Brigham Young 17
1983 Brigham Young 21, Missouri 17
1984 Brigham Young 24, Michigan 17
1985 Arkansas 18, Arizona St. 17

1986 Iowa 39, San Diego St. 38
1987 Iowa 20, Wyoming 19
1988 Oklahoma St. 62, Wyoming 14

Aloha Bowl, Honolulu

1982 Washington 21, Maryland 20
1983 Penn State 13, Washington 10
1984 SMU 27, Notre Dame 20

1985 Alabama 24, USC 3
1986 Arizona 30, North Carolina 21

1987 UCLA 20, Florida 16
1988 Washington St. 24, Houston 22

California Bowl, Fresno

1981 Toledo 27, San Jose St. 25
1982 Fresno St. 29, Bowling Green 28
1983 N. Illinois 20, Cal. State Fullerton 13

1984 Nevada-Las Vegas 30, Toledo 13
1985 Fresno St. 51, Bowling Green 7
1986 San Jose St. 37, Miami (Oh.) 7

1987 E. Michigan 30, San Jose St. 27
1988 Fresno St. 35, W. Michigan 30

Hall of Fame Bowl, Tampa

1986 (Dec.) Boston Coll. 27, Georgia 24

1988 (Jan.) Michigan 28, Alabama 24

1989 Syracuse 23, LSU 10

College Division I Football Teams

Team	Nickname	Team colors	Conference	Coach	1988 record (W-L-T)
Air Force	Falcons	Blue & silver	Western Athletic	Fisher De Berry	5-7-0
Akron	Zips	Blue & Gold	Independent	Gerry Faust	5-6-0
Alabama	Crimson Tide	Crimson & white	Southeastern	Bill Curry	9-3-0
Alabama State	Hornets	Black & gold	Southwestern	Houston Markham	7-3-0
Alcorn State	Braves	Purple & gold	Southwestern	Theo Danzy	6-4-0
Appalachian State	Mountaineers	Black & gold	Southern	Jerry Moore	6-4-1
Arizona	Wildcats	Red & blue	Pacific Ten	Dick Tomey	7-4-0
Arizona State	Sun Devils	Maroon & gold	Pacific Ten	Larry Marmie	6-5-0
Arkansas	Razorbacks	Cardinal & white	Southwest	Ken Hatfield	10-2-0
Arkansas State	Indians	Scarlet & black	Independent	Lawrence Lacewell	5-6-0
Army	Cadets	Black, gold, gray	Independent	Jim Young	9-3-0
Auburn	Tigers	Orange & blue	Southeastern	Pat Dye	10-2-0
Austin Peay State	Governors	Red & white	Ohio Valley	Paul Brewster	3-8-0
Ball State	Cardinals	Cardinal & white	Mid-American	Paul Schudel	8-3-0
Baylor	Bears	Green & gold	Southwest	Grant Teaff	6-5-0
Bethune-Cookman	Wildcats	Maroon & gold	Mid-Eastern	Larry Little	5-6-0
Boise State	Broncos	Orange & Blue	Big Sky	Skip Hall	8-4-0
Boston College	Eagles	Maroon & gold	Independent	Jack Bicknell	3-8-0
Boston Univ.	Terriers	Scarlet & white	Yankee	Chris Palmer	4-7-0
Bowling Green	Falcons	Orange & brown	Mid-American	Moe Ankney	2-8-1
Brigham Young	Cougars	Royal blue & white	Western Athletic	LaVell Edwards	9-4-0
Brown	Bears	Brown, cardinal, white	Ivy	John Rosenberg	0-9-1
Bucknell	Bisons	Orange & blue	Colonial	Lou Maranzana	3-7-0
California	Golden Bears	Blue & gold	Pacific Ten	Bruce Snyder	5-5-1

Team	Nickname	Team colors	Conference	Coach	1988 record (W-L-T)
Central Michigan	Chippewas	Maroon & gold	Mid-American	Herb Deromedi	7-4-0
Cincinnati	Bearcats	Red & black	Independent	Tim Murphy	3-8-0
Citadel	Bulldogs	Blue & white	Southern	Charles Taafe	8-4-0
Clemson	Tigers	Purple & orange	Atlantic Coast	Danny Ford	10-2-0
Colgate	Red Raiders	Maroon	Colonial	Mike Foley	2-9-0
Colorado State	Rams	Green & gold	Western Athletic	Earle Bruce	1-10-0
Colorado	Buffaloes	Silver, gold & blue	Big Eight	Bill McCartney	8-4-0
Columbia	Lions	Blue & white	Ivy	Ray Tellier	2-8-0
Connecticut	Huskies	Blue & white	Yankee	Tom Jackson	7-4-0
Cornell	Big Red	Carnelian & white	Ivy	Jack Fouts	7-2-1
Dartmouth	Big Green	Dartmouth green & white	Ivy	Buddy Teevens	5-5-0
Davidson	Wildcats	Red & black	Colonial	Vic Gatto	0-10-0
Delaware	Fightin' Blue Hens	Blue & gold	Yankee	Harold Raymond	7-5-0
Delaware State	Hornets	Red & blue	Mid-Eastern	William Collick	5-5-0
Duke	Blue Devils	Royal blue & white	Atlantic Coast	Steve Spurrier	7-3-1
East Carolina	Pirates	Purple & gold	Independent	Bill Lewis	3-8-0
East Tennessee St.	Buccaneers	Blue & gold	Southern	Don Riley	3-8-0
Eastern Illinois	Panthers	Blue & Gray	Gateway	Bob Spoo	5-6-0
Eastern Kentucky	Colonels	Maroon & white	Ohio Valley	Roy Kidd	11-3-0
Eastern Michigan	Hurons	Green & white	Mid-American	Jim Harkema	6-3-1
Eastern Washington	Eagles	Red & white	Big Sky	Dick Zornes	2-8-1
Florida	Gators	Orange & blue	Southeastern	Galen Hall	7-5-0
Florida A&M	Rattlers	Orange & green	Mid-Eastern	Ken Riley	7-3-1
Florida State	Seminoles	Garnet & gold	Independent	Pobby Bowden	11-1-0
Fresno State	Bulldogs	Cardinal & blue	Big West	Jim Sweeney	10-2-0
Fullerton, Cal State	Titans	Blue, orange, white	Big West	Gene Murphy	5-6-0
Furman	Paladans	Purple & white	Southern	Jimmy Satterfield	13-2-0
Georgia	Bulldogs	Red & black	Southeastern	Ray Goff	9-3-0
Georgia Southern	Eagles	Blue & white	Independent	Erskine Russell	12-3-0
Georgia Tech	Yellow Jackets	Old gold & white	Atlantic Coast	Bobby Ross	3-8-0
Grambling	Tigers	Black & gold	Southwestern	Eddie Robinson	8-3-0
Harvard	Crimson	Crimson	Ivy	Joe Restic	2-8-0
Hawaii	Rainbow Warriors	Green & white	Western Athletic	Bob Wagner	9-3-0
Holy Cross	Crusaders	Royal purple	Colonial	Mike Duffner	9-2-0
Houston	Cougars	Scarlet & white	Southwest	Jack Pardee	9-3-0
Howard	Bison	Blue & white	Mid-Eastern	Steve Wilson	7-4-0
Idaho	Vandals	Silver & gold	Big Sky	John L. Smith	11-2-0
Idaho State	Bengals	Orange & black	Big Sky	Garth Hall	0-11-0
Illinois	Fighting Illini	Orange & blue	Big Ten	John Mackovic	6-5-1
Illinois State	Redbirds	Red & white	Gateway	Jim Heacock	1-10-0
Indiana	Fightin' Hoosiers	Cream & crimson	Big Ten	Bill Mallory	8-3-1
Indiana State	Sycamores	Blue & white	Gateway	Dennis Raetz	5-6-0
Iowa	Hawkeyes	Old gold & black	Big Ten	Hayden Fry	6-4-3
Iowa State	Cyclones	Cardinal & gold	Big Eight	Jim Walden	5-6-0
Jackson State	Tigers	Blue & white	Southwestern	W.C. Gorden	8-1-2
James Madison	Dukes	Purple & gold	Independent	Joe Purzycki	5-6-0
Kansas	Jayhawks	Crimson & blue	Big Eight	Glen Mason	1-10-0
Kansas State	Wildcats	Purple & white	Big Eight	Bill Snyder	0-11-0
Kent State	Golden Flashes	Blue & gold	Mid-American	Dick Crum	5-6-0
Kentucky	Wildcats	Blue & white	Southeastern	Jerry Clairborne	5-6-0
Lafayette	Leopards	Maroon & white	Colonial	Bill Russo	8-2-1
Lamar	Cardinals	Red & white	Independent	Ray Alborn	3-8-0
Lehigh	Engineers	Brown & white	Colonial	Hank Small	6-5-0
Liberty	Flames	Red, White, Blue	Independent	Sam Rutigliano	8-3-0
Long Beach State	Forty-Niners	Brown & gold	Big West	Larry Reisbig	3-9-0
Louisiana State	Fighting Tigers	Purple & gold	Southeastern	Mike Archer	8-4-0
Louisiana Tech	Bulldogs	Red & blue	Independent	Joe Raymond Peace	4-7-0
Louisville	Cardinals	Red, black, white	Independent	Howard Schnellenberger	8-3-0
Maine	Black Bears	Blue & white	Yankee	Tom Lichtenberg	7-4-0
Marshall	Thundering Herd	Green & white	Southern	George Chaump	11-2-0
Maryland	Terps	Red, white, black & gold	Atlantic Coast	Joe Krivak	5-6-0
Massachusetts	Minutemen	Maroon & white	Yankee	Jim Reid	8-4-0
McNeese State	Cowboys	Blue & gold	Southland	Sonny Jackson	6-5-0
Memphis State	Tigers	Blue & gray	Independent	Chuck Stobart	6-5-0
Miami (Fla.)	Hurricanes	Orange, green, white	Independent	Dennis Erickson	11-1-0
Miami (Ohio)	Redskins	Red & white	Mid-American	Tim Rose	0-10-1
Michigan	Wolverines	Maize & blue	Big Ten	Bo Schembechler	9-2-1
Michigan State	Spartans	Green & white	Big Ten	George Perles	6-5-1
Middle Tennessee St.	Blue Raiders	Blue & white	Ohio Valley	Boots Donnelly	7-4-0
Minnesota	Golden Gophers	Maroon & gold	Big Ten	John Gutekunst	2-7-2
Mississippi	Rebels	Red & blue	Southeastern	Billy Brewer	5-6-0
Mississippi State	Bulldogs	Maroon & white	Southeastern	Rocky Felker	1-10-0
Miss. Valley	Delta Devils	Green & white	Southwestern	Ken Pettiford	3-8-0
Missouri	Tigers	Old gold & black	Big Eight	Bob Stull	3-7-1
Montana	Grizzlies	Copper, silver, gold	Big Sky	Don Read	8-4-0
Montana State	Bobcats	Blue & gold	Big Sky	Earle Solomonson	4-7-0
Morehead State	Eagles	Blue & gold	Ohio Valley	Bill Baldridge	3-8-0
Morgan State	Bears	Blue & orange	Mid-Eastern	Ed Wynch	1-10-0
Murray State	Racers	Blue & gold	Ohio Valley	Mike Mahoney	4-6-0
Navy	Midshipmen	Navy blue & gold	Independent	Elliot Uzelac	3-8-0
Nebraska	Cornhuskers	Scarlet & cream	Big Eight	Tom Osborne	11-2-0
Nevada-Las Vegas	Rebels	Scarlet & gray	Big West	Wayne Nunnely	4-7-0
Nevada-Reno	Wolf Pack	Silver & blue	Big Sky	Chris Ault	7-4-0

Team	Nickname	Team colors	Conference	Coach	1988 record (W-L-T)
New Hampshire	Wildcats	Blue & white	Yankee	Bill Bowes	6-5-0
New Mexico	Lobos	Cherry & silver	Western Athletic	Mike Sheppard	2-10-0
New Mexico State	Aggies	Crimson & white	Big West	Mike Knoll	1-10-0
Nicholls St.	Colonels	Red & grey	Independent	Phil Greco	7-4-0
North Carolina	Tar Heels	Blue & white	Atlantic Coast	Mack Brown	1-10-0
North Carolina A & T.	Aggies	Blue & gold	Mid-Eastern	Bill Hayes	2-9-0
North Carolina State	Wolfpack	Red & white	Atlantic Coast	Dick Sheridan	8-3-1
North Texas	Mean Green, Eagles	Green & white	Southland	Corky Nelson	8-4-0
Northeast Louisiana	Indians	Maroon & gold	Southland	Dave Roberts	5-6-0
Northeastern	Huskies	Red & black	Independent	Paul Pawlak	4-7-0
Northern Arizona	Lumberjacks	Blue & gold	Big Sky	Larry Kentera	6-5-0
Northern Illinois	Huskies	Cardinal & black	Independent	Jerry Pettibone	7-4-0
Northern Iowa	Panthers	Purple & Old Gold	Gateway	Terry Allen	5-6-0
Northwestern	Wildcats	Purple & white	Big Ten	Francis Peay	2-8-1
Northwestern State	Demons	Purple & White	Southland	Sam Goodwin	10-3-0
Notre Dame	Fighting Irish	Gold & blue	Independent	Lou Holtz	12-0-0
Ohio State	Buckeyes	Scarlet & gray	Big Ten	John Cooper	4-6-1
Ohio Univ	Bobcats	Green & white	Mid-American	Cleve Bryant	4-6-1
Oklahoma	Sooners	Crimsom & cream	Big Eight	Gary Gibbs	9-3-0
Oklahoma State	Cowboys	Orange & black	Big Eight	Pat Jones	10-2-0
Oregon	Ducks	Green & Yellow	Pacific Ten	Rich Brooks	6-6-0
Oregon State	Beavers	Orange & black	Pacific Ten	Dave Kragthrope	4-6-1
Pacific	Tigers	Orange & black	Big West	Walt Harris	2-9-0
Penn State	Nittany Lions	Blue & white	Independent	Joe Paterno	5-6-0
Pennsylvania	Red & Blue, Quakers	Red & blue	Ivy	Gary Steele	9-1-0
Pittsburgh	Panthers	Gold & blue	Independent	Mike Gottfried	6-5-0
Prairie View A & M.	Panthers	Purple & gold	Southwestern	Haney Catchings	5-5-0
Princeton	Tigers	Orange & black	Ivy	Steve Tosches	6-4-0
Purdue	Boilermakers	Old gold & black	Big Ten	Fred Akers	4-7-0
Rhode Island	Rams	Blue & white	Yankee	Bob Griffin	4-7-0
Rice	Owls	Blue & gray	Southwest	Fred Goldsmith	0-11-0
Richmond	Spiders	Red & blue	Yankee	Jim Marshall	4-7-0
Rutgers	Scarlet Knights	Scarlet	Independent	Dick Anderson	5-6-0
Sam Houston State	Bear Kats	Orange & white	Southland	Ron Randleman	3-8-0
Samford	Bulldogs	Crimson & Blue	Independent	Terry Bowden	5-6-0
San Diego State	Aztecs	Scarlet & black	Western Athletic	Al Luginbill	3-8-0
San Jose State	Spartans	Gold & white	Big West	Claude Gilbert	4-8-0
South Carolina	Fighting Gamecocks	Garnet & black	Independent	Sparky Woods	8-4-0
South Carolina State	Bulldogs	Garnet & blue	Mid-Eastern	Willie Jeffries	4-7-0
Southern-Baton Rouge	Jaguars	Blue & gold	Southwestern	Gerald Kimble	6-5-0
Southern California	Trojans	Cardinal & gold	Pacific Ten	Larry Smith	10-2-0
Southern Illinois	Salukis	Maroon & white	Gateway	Bob Smith	4-7-0
Southern Mississippi	Golden Eagles	Black & gold	Independent	Curley Hallman	10-2-0
SW Missouri St.	Bears	Maroon & white	Gateway	Jesse Branch	5-5-0
SW Texas St.	Bobcats	Maroon & gold	Southland	John O'Hara	4-7-0
Southwestern La.	Ragin' Cajuns	Vermillion & white	Independent	Nelson Stokley	6-5-0
Stanford	Cardinal	Cardinal & white	Pacific Ten	Dennis Green	3-6-2
Stephen F. Austin St.	Lumberjacks	Purple & white	Southland	Lynn Graves	10-3-0
Syracuse	Orangemen	Orange	Independent	Dick MacPherson	10-2-0
Temple	Owls	Cherry & white	Independent	Jerry Berndt	4-7-0
Tennessee	Volunteers	Orange & white	Southeastern	John Majors	5-6-0
Tenn.-Chattanooga	Moccasins	Navy blue & gold	Southern	Buddy Nix	4-7-0
Tennessee State	Tigers	Blue & white	Ohio Valley	Joe Gilliam Sr.	3-7-1
Tennessee Tech	Golden Eagles	Purple & gold	Ohio Valley	Jim Ragland	1-10-0
Texas	Longhorns	Orange & white	Southwest	David McWilliams	4-7-0
Texas-El Paso	Miners	Orange, white, blue	Western Athletic	David Lee	10-3-0
Texas A & M	Aggies	Maroon & white	Southwest	R.C. Slocum	7-5-0
Texas Christian	Horned Frogs	Purple & white	Southwest	Jim Wacker	4-7-0
Texas Southern	Tigers	Maroon & gray	Southwestern	Walter Highsmith	0-11-0
Texas Tech	Red Raiders	Scarlet & black	Southwest	Spike Dykes	5-6-0
Toledo	Rockets	Blue & gold	Mid-American	Dan Simrell	6-5-0
Towson St.	Tigers	Gold & white	Independent	Phil Albert	5-5-0
Tulane	Green Wave	Olive green & sky blue	Independent	Greg Davis	5-6-0
Tulsa	Golden Hurricane	Blue & gold	Independent	Dave Rader	4-7-0
UCLA	Bruins	Navy blue & gold	Pacific Ten	Terry Donahue	10-2-0
Utah State	Aggies	Navy blue & white	Big West	Chuck Shelton	4-7-0
Utah	Utes	Crimson & white	Western Athletic	Jim Fassel	6-5-0
Vanderbilt	Commodores	Black & gold	Southeastern	Watson Brown	3-8-0
Villanova	Wildcats	Blue & white	Yankee	Andy Talley	5-5-1
Virginia	Cavaliers	Orange & blue	Atlantic Coast	George Welsh	7-4-0
VMI	Keydets	Red, white & yellow	Southern	Jim Shuck	2-9-0
Virginia Tech	Gobblers, Hokies	Orange & maroon	Independent	Frank Beamer	3-8-0
Wake Forest	Demon Deacons	Old gold & black	Atlantic Coast	Bill Dooley	6-4-1
Washington	Huskies	Purple & gold	Pacific Ten	Don James	6-5-0
Washington State	Cougars	Crimson & gray	Pacific Ten	Mike Price	9-3-0
Weber State	Wildcats	Purple & white	Big Sky	Dave Arsianian	5-6-0
West Virginia	Mountaineers	Old gold & blue	Independent	Don Nehlen	11-1-0
Western Carolina	Catamounts	Purple & gold	Southern	Dave Strahm	2-9-0
Western Illinois	Leathernecks	Purple & Gold	Gateway	Bruce Craddock	10-2-0
Western Kentucky	Hilltoppers	Red & white	Independent	Jack Harbaugh	9-4-0
Western Michigan	Broncos	Brown & gold	Mid-American	Al Molde	9-3-0
William & Mary	Tribe	Green & gold	Independent	Jimmye Laycock	6-4-1
Wisconsin	Badgers	Cardinal & white	Big Ten	Don Morton	1-10-0
Wyoming	Cowboys	Brown & yellow	Western Athletic	Paul Roach	11-2-0
Yale	Bulldogs, Elis	Yale blue & white	Ivy	Carmen Cozza	3-6-1
Youngstown St.	Penguins	Scarlet & white	Independent	Jim Tressel	4-7-0

College Football Conference Champions

Atlantic Coast		Ivy League		Big Eight		Big Ten	
1973	No. Carolina St.	1973	Dartmouth	1973	Oklahoma	1973	Ohio State, Michigan
1974	Maryland	1974	Yale, Harvard	1974	Oklahoma	1974	Ohio State, Michigan
1975	Maryland	1975	Harvard	1975	Oklahoma, Nebraska	1975	Ohio State
1976	Maryland	1976	Yale, Brown	1976	Oklahoma, Colorado,	1976	Michigan, Ohio State
1977	North Carolina	1977	Yale		Oklahoma State	1977	Michigan, Ohio State
1978	Clemson	1978	Dartmouth	1977	Oklahoma	1978	Michigan St., Michigan
1979	No. Carolina St.	1979	Yale	1978	Nebraska, Oklahoma	1979	Ohio State
1980	North Carolina	1980	Yale	1979	Oklahoma	1980	Michigan
1981	Clemson	1981	Yale, Dartmouth	1980	Oklahoma	1981	Iowa, Ohio State
1982	Clemson	1982	Harvard, Dartmouth, Penn	1981	Nebraska	1982	Michigan
1983	Maryland	1983	Harvard, Penn	1982	Nebraska	1983	Illinois
1984	Maryland	1984	Penn	1983	Nebraska	1984	Ohio State
1985	Maryland	1985	Penn	1984	Nebraska, Oklahoma	1985	Iowa
1986	Clemson	1986	Penn	1985	Oklahoma	1986	Michigan, Ohio State
1987	Clemson	1987	Harvard	1986	Oklahoma	1987	Michigan St.
1988	Clemson	1988	Penn, Cornell	1987	Oklahoma	1988	Michigan
				1988	Nebraska		

Mid-America		Southern		Southeastern		Southwest	
1973	Miami	1973	East Carolina	1973	Alabama	1973	Texas
1974	Miami	1974	VMI	1974	Alabama	1974	Baylor
1975	Miami	1975	Richmond	1975	Alabama	1975	Texas A&M, Texas, Arkansas
1976	Ball State	1976	East Carolina	1976	Georgia	1976	Houston
1977	Miami	1977	Tenn.-Chattanooga	1977	Alabama	1977	Texas
1978	Ball State	1978	Tenn.-Chattanooga, Furman	1978	Alabama	1978	Houston
1979	Central Michigan	1979	Tenn.-Chattanooga	1979	Alabama	1979	Houston, Arkansas
1980	Central Michigan	1980	Furman	1980	Georgia	1980	Baylor
1981	Toledo	1981	Furman	1981	Georgia, Alabama	1981	SMU
1982	Bowling Green	1982	Furman	1982	Georgia	1982	SMU
1983	Northern Illinois	1983	Furman	1983	Auburn	1983	Texas
1984	Toledo	1984	Tenn.-Chattanooga	1984	Florida (title vacated)	1984	SMU, Texas
1985	Bowling Green	1985	Furman	1985	Tennessee	1985	Texas A&M
1986	Miami	1986	Appalachian St.	1986	LSU	1986	Texas A&M
1987	E. Michigan	1987	Appalachian St.	1987	Auburn	1987	Texas A&M
1988	W. Michigan	1988	Marshall, Furman	1988	Auburn, LSU	1988	Arkansas

Pacific Ten		Western Athletic		Big West	
1973	USC	1973	Arizona State, Arizona	1973	San Diego State
1974	USC	1974	Brigham Young	1974	San Diego State
1975	UCLA, Cal.	1975	Arizona State	1975	San Jose St.
1976	USC	1976	Wyoming, Brigham Young	1976	San Diego State
1977	Washington	1977	Brigham Young, Arizona St.	1977	Fresno State
1978	USC	1978	Brigham Young	1978	Utah St., San Jose St.
1979	USC	1979	Brigham Young	1979	San Jose St.
1980	Washington	1980	Brigham Young	1980	Long Beach State
1981	Washington	1981	Brigham Young	1981	San Jose State
1982	UCLA	1982	Brigham Young	1982	Fresno State
1983	UCLA	1983	Brigham Young	1983	Cal State-Fullerton
1984	USC	1984	Brigham Young	1984	Nevada-Las Vegas
1985	UCLA	1985	Brigham Young, Air Force	1985	Fresno State
1986	Arizona State	1986	San Diego State	1986	San Jose State
1987	UCLA, USC	1987	Wyoming	1987	San Jose State
1988	USC	1988	Wyoming	1988	Fresno State

Longest Division I-A Winning Streaks

Wins	Team	Years	Ended by	Score
47	Oklahoma	1953-57	Notre Dame	7-0
39	Washington	1908-14	Oregon State	0-0
37	Yale	1890-93	Princeton	6-0
37	Yale	1887-89	Princeton	10-0
35	Toledo	1969-71	Tampa	21-0
34	Pennsylvania	1894-96	Lafayette	6-4
31	Oklahoma	1948-50	Kentucky	13-7
31	Pittsburgh	1914-18	Cleveland Naval Reserve	10-9
31	Pennsylvania	1896-98	Harvard	10-0
30	Texas	1968-70	Notre Dame	24-11
29	Michigan	1901-03	Minnesota	6-6
28	Alabama	1978-80	Mississippi State	6-3
28	Oklahoma	1973-75	Kansas	23-3
28	Michigan State	1950-53	Purdue	6-0
27	Nebraska	1901-04	Colorado	6-0
26	Cornell	1921-24	Williams	14-7
26	Michigan	1903-05	Chicago	2-0
25	Michigan	1946-49	Army	21-7
25	Army	1944-46	Notre Dame	0-0
25	Southern Cal	1931-33	Oregon State	0-0
25	Brigham Young	1983-85	UCLA	27-24

National College Football Champions

The NCAA recognizes as unofficial national champion the team selected each year by the AP (poll of writers) and the UPI (poll of coaches). When the polls disagree both teams are listed. The AP poll originated in 1936 and the UPI poll in 1950.

1936	Minnesota	1950	Oklahoma	1964	Alabama
1937	Pittsburgh	1951	Tennessee	1965	Alabama, Mich. State
1938	Texas Christian	1952	Michigan State	1966	Notre Dame
1939	Texas A&M	1953	Maryland	1967	Southern Cal.
1940	Minnesota	1954	Ohio State, UCLA	1968	Ohio State
1941	Minnesota	1955	Oklahoma	1969	Texas
1942	Ohio State	1956	Oklahoma	1970	Nebraska, Texas
1943	Notre Dame	1957	Auburn, Ohio State	1971	Nebraska,
1944	Army	1958	Louisiana State	1972	Southern Cal.
1945	Army	1959	Syracuse	1973	Notre Dame, Alabama
1946	Notre Dame	1960	Minnesota	1974	Oklahoma, So. Cal.
1947	Notre Dame	1961	Alabama	1975	Oklahoma
1948	Michigan	1962	Southern Cal.	1976	Pittsburgh
1949	Notre Dame	1963	Texas	1977	Notre Dame

1978	Alabama, So. Cal.
1979	Alabama
1980	Georgia
1981	Clemson
1982	Penn State
1983	Miami (Fla.)
1984	Brigham Young
1985	Oklahoma
1986	Penn State
1987	Miami (Fla.)
1988	Notre Dame

College Football Coach of the Year

(Selected by the American Football Coaches Assn. & the Football Writers Assn. of America)

	AFCA		FWAA		AFCA
1935	Lynn Waldorf, Northwestern	1957	Woody Hayes, Ohio St.		Woody Hayes, Ohio St.
1936	Dick Harlow, Harvard	1958	Paul Dietzel, LSU		Paul Dietzel, LSU
1937	Edward Mylin, Lafayette	1959	Ben Schwartzwalder, Syracuse		Ben Schwartzwalder, Syracuse
1938	Bill Kern, Carnegie Tech	1960	Murray Warmath, Minnesota		Murray Warmath, Minnesota
1939	Eddie Anderson, Iowa	1961	Darrell Royal, Texas		Paul "Bear" Bryant, Alabama
1940	Clark Shaughnessy, Stanford	1962	John McKay, USC		John McKay, USC
1941	Frank Leahy, Notre Dame	1963	Darrell Royal, Texas		Darrell Royal, Texas
1942	Bill Alexander, Georgia Tech	1964	Ara Parseghian, Notre Dame		Frank Broyles, Arkansas; Ara Parseghian, Notre Dame
1943	Amos Alonzo Stagg, Pacific	1965	Duffy Daugherty, Michigan St.		Tommy Prothro, UCLA
1944	Carroll Widdoes, Ohio St.	1966	Tom Cahill, Army		Tom Cahill, Army
1945	Bo McMillin, Indiana	1967	John Pont, Indiana		John Pont, Indiana
1946	Earl "Red" Blaik, Army	1968	Woody Hayes, Ohio St.		Joe Paterno, Penn St.
1947	Fritz Crisler, Michigan	1969	Bo Schembechler, Michigan		Bo Schembechler, Michigan
1948	Bennie Oosterbaan, Michigan	1970	Alex Agase, Northwestern		Charles McClendon, LSU; Darrell Royal, Texas
1949	Bud Wilkinson, Oklahoma	1971	Bob Devaney, Nebraska		Paul "Bear" Bryant, Alabama
1950	Charlie Caldwell, Princeton	1972	John McKay, USC		John McKay, USC
1951	Chuck Taylor, Stanford	1973	Johnny Majors, Pittsburgh		Paul "Bear" Bryant, Alabama
1952	Biggie Munn, Michigan St.	1974	Grant Teaff, Baylor		Grant Teaff, Baylor
1953	Jim Tatum, Maryland	1975	Woody Hayes, Ohio St.		Frank Kush, Arizona St.
1954	Henry "Red" Sanders, UCLA	1976	Johnny Majors, Pittsburgh		Johnny Majors, Pittsburgh
1955	Duffy Daugherty, Michigan St.	1977	Lou Holtz, Arkansas		Don James, Washington
1956	Bowden Wyatt, Tennessee	1978	Joe Paterno, Penn St.		Joe Paterno, Penn St.
		1979	Earle Bruce, Ohio St.		Earle Bruce, Ohio St.
		1980	Vince Dooley, Georgia		Vince Dooley, Georgia
		1981	Danny Ford, Clemson		Danny Ford, Clemson
		1982	Joe Paterno, Penn St.		Joe Paterno, Penn St.
		1983	Howard Schnellenberger, Miami (Fla.)		Ken Hatfield, Air Force
		1984	LaVell Edwards, Brigham Young		LaVell Edwards, Brigham Young
		1985	Fisher De Berry, Air Force		Fisher De Berry, Air Force
		1986	Joe Paterno, Penn St.		Joe Paterno, Penn St.
		1987	Dick MacPherson, Syracuse		Dick MacPherson, Syracuse
		1988	Lou Holtz, Notre Dame		Don Nehlen, W. Virginia

All-Time Division I-A Coaching Victories

Paul "Bear" Bryant	323	Vince Dooley	201	Carl Snavely	180
Amos Alonzo Stagg	314	Dana Bible	198	Gil Dobie	180
Glenn "Pop" Warner	313	Dan McGugin	197	Ben Schwartzwalder	178
Woody Hayes	238	Fielding Yost	196	Ralph Jordan	176
Bo Schembechler	224	Howard Jones	194	Frank Kush	176
Joe Paterno	212	John Vaught	190	Lynn "Pappy" Waldorf	174
Jess Neely	207	John Heisman	185	Bob Neyland	173
Warren Woodson	203	Bobby Bowden	185	Jerry Claiborne	173
Eddie Anderson	201	Darrell Royal	184		

Eddie Robinson of Grambling State Univ. holds the record for most college football victories with 349 at the start of the 1989 season.

Outland Award

Honoring the outstanding interior lineman selected by the Football Writers' Association of America.

1946	George Connor, Notre Dame, T	1961	Merlin Olsen, Utah State, T	1975	Lee Roy Selmon, Oklahoma, DT
1947	Joe Steffy, Army, G	1962	Bobby Bell, Minnesota, T	1976	Ross Browner, Notre Dame, DE
1948	Bill Fischer, Notre Dame, G	1963	Scott Appleton, Texas, T	1977	Brad Shearer, Texas, DT
1949	Ed Bagdon, Michigan St., G	1964	Steve Delong, Tennessee, T	1978	Greg Roberts, Oklahoma, G
1950	Bob Gain, Kentucky, T	1965	Tommy Nobis, Texas, G	1979	Jim Ritcher, No. Carolina St., C
1951	Jim Weatherall, Oklahoma, T	1966	Loyd Phillips, Arkansas, T	1980	Mark May, Pittsburgh, OT
1952	Dick Modzelewski, Maryland, T	1967	Ron Yary, Southern Cal, T	1981	Dave Rimington, Nebraska, C
1953	J. D. Roberts, Oklahoma, G	1968	Bill Stanfill, Georgia, T	1982	Dave Rimington, Nebraska, C
1954	Bill Brooks, Arkansas, G	1969	Mike Reid, Penn State, DT	1983	Dean Steinkuhler, Nebraska, G
1955	Calvin Jones, Iowa, G	1970	Jim Stillwagon, Ohio State, LB	1984	Bruce Smith, Virginia Tech, DT
1956	Jim Parker, Ohio State, G	1971	Larry Jacobson, Nebraska, DT	1985	Mike Ruth, Boston College, DT
1957	Alex Karras, Iowa, T	1972	Rich Glover, Nebraska, MG	1986	Jason Buck, Brigham Young, DT
1958	Zeke Smith, Auburn, G	1973	John Hicks, Ohio State, G	1987	Chad Hennings, Air Force, DT
1959	Mike McGee, Duke, T	1974	Randy White, Maryland, DE	1988	Tracy Rocker, Auburn, DT
1960	Tom Brown, Minnesota, G				

Heisman Trophy Winners

Awarded annually to the nation's outstanding college football player.

1935	Jay Berwanger, Chicago, HB	1953	John Lattner, Notre Dame, HB
1936	Larry Kelley, Yale, E	1954	Alan Ameche, Wisconsin, FB
1937	Clinton Frank, Yale, HB	1955	Howard Cassady, Ohio St., HB
1938	David O'Brien, Tex. Christian, QB	1956	Paul Hornung, Notre Dame, QB
1939	Nile Kinnick, Iowa, HB	1957	John Crow, Texas A & M, HB
1940	Tom Harmon, Michigan, HB	1958	Pete Dawkins, Army, HB
1941	Bruce Smith, Minnesota, HB	1959	Billy Cannon, La. State, HB
1942	Frank Sinkwich, Georgia, HB	1960	Joe Bellino, Navy, HB
1943	Angelo Bertelli, Notre Dame, QB	1961	Ernest Davis, Syracuse, HB
1944	Leslie Horvath, Ohio State, QB	1962	Terry Baker, Oregon State, QB
1945	Felix Blanchard, Army, FB	1963	Roger Staubach, Navy, QB
1946	Glenn Davis, Army, HB	1964	John Huarte, Notre Dame, QB
1947	John Lujack, Notre Dame, QB	1965	Mike Garrett, USC, HB
1948	Doak Walker, SMU, HB	1966	Steve Spurrier, Florida, QB
1949	Leon Hart, Notre Dame, E	1967	Gary Beban, UCLA, QB
1950	Vic Janowicz, Ohio State, HB	1968	O. J. Simpson, USC, RB
1951	Richard Kazmaier, Princeton, HB	1969	Steve Owens, Oklahoma, RB
1952	Billy Vessels, Oklahoma, HB	1970	Jim Plunkett, Stanford, QB

1971	Pat Sullivan, Auburn, QB
1972	Johnny Rodgers, Nebraska, RB-R
1973	John Cappelletti, Penn State, RB
1974	Archie Griffin, Ohio State, RB
1975	Archie Griffin, Ohio State, RB
1976	Tony Dorsett, Pittsburgh, RB
1977	Earl Campbell, Texas, RB
1978	Billy Sims, Oklahoma, RB
1979	Charles White, USC, RB
1980	George Rogers, So. Carolina, RB
1981	Marcus Allen, USC, RB
1982	Herschel Walker, Georgia, RB
1983	Mike Rozier, Nebraska, RB
1984	Doug Flutie, Boston College, QB
1985	Bo Jackson, Auburn, RB
1986	Vinny Testaverde, Miami, QB
1987	Tim Brown, Notre Dame, WR
1988	Barry Sanders, Oklahoma St., RB

Vince Lombardi Award

Honoring the outstanding lineman, sponsored by the Rotary Club of Houston

1970	Jim Stillwagon, Ohio State, MG	1977	Ross Browner, Notre Dame, DE
1971	Walt Patulski, Notre Dame, DE	1978	Bruce Clark, Penn State, DT
1972	Rich Glover, Nebraska, MG	1979	Brad Budde, USC, G
1973	John Hicks, Ohio State, OT	1980	Hugh Green, Pittsburgh, DE
1974	Randy White, Maryland, DT	1981	Kenneth Sims, Texas, DT
1975	Lee Roy Selmon, Oklahoma, DT	1982	Dave Rimington, Nebraska, C
1976	Wilson Whitley, Houston, DT		

1983	Dean Steinkuhler, Nebraska, G
1984	Tony Degrate, Texas, DT
1985	Tony Casillas, Oklahoma, NG
1986	Cornelius Bennett, Alabama, DE
1987	Chris Spielman, Ohio State, LB
1988	Tracy Rocker, Auburn, DT

All-Time Division I-A Percentage Leaders

(Classified as Division I-A for the last 10 years; record includes bowl games; ties computed as half won and half lost)

	Years	Won	Lost	Tied	Pct.	Bowl Games W	L	T
Notre Dame	100	671	202	40	.757	9	5	0
Michigan	109	693	231	33	.741	9	11	0
Alabama	94	641	226	43	.728	23	15	3
Oklahoma	94	621	223	50	.723	18	10	1
Texas	96	656	249	31	.717	16	15	2
USC	96	596	230	49	.709	21	11	0
Ohio State	99	618	249	50	.701	11	10	0
Penn State	102	629	276	40	.687	15	8	2
Nebraska	99	625	279	39	.684	14	13	0
Tennessee	92	589	265	50	.679	15	14	0
Central Michigan	88	451	234	30	.652	3	0	0
Louisiana State	95	553	291	46	.647	11	16	1
Miami (Ohio)	100	523	280	38	.645	5	2	0
Army	99	561	299	50	.644	2	1	0
Arizona State	76	416	229	23	.640	9	5	1
Georgia	95	555	309	53	.634	13	12	3
Washington	99	516	297	49	.627	9	7	1
Minnesota	105	535	324	43	.617	2	3	0
Michigan State	92	491	301	42	.614	3	5	0
Nevada-Las Vegas	21	141	88	4	.614	1	0	0
Auburn	96	519	319	44	.613	10	9	2
UCLA	70	406	255	36	.608	9	7	1
Arkansas	95	523	333	38	.606	9	13	3
Florida State	42	262	168	16	.605	9	7	2

Canadian Football League Championships

Winners of Eastern and Western divisions meet in championship game for Grey Cup (donated by Governor-General Earl Grey in 1909). Canadian football features 3 downs, 110-yard field, and each team can have 12 players on field at one time.

1956	Edmonton Eskimos 50, Montreal Alouettes 27	1973	Ottawa Rough Riders 22, Edmonton Eskimos 18
1957	Hamilton Tiger-Cats 32, Winnipeg Blue Bombers 7	1974	Montreal Alouettes 20, Edmonton Eskimos 7
1958	Winnipeg Blue Bombers 35, Hamilton Tiger-Cats 28	1975	Edmonton Eskimos 9, Montreal Alouettes 8
1959	Winnipeg Blue Bombers 21, Hamilton Tiger-Cats 7	1976	Ottawa Rough Riders 23, Saskatchewan Roughriders 20
1960	Ottawa Rough Riders 16, Edmonton Eskimos 6	1977	Montreal Alouettes 41, Edmonton Eskimos 6
1961	Winnipeg Blue Bombers 21, Hamilton Tiger-Cats 14	1978	Edmonton Eskimos 20, Montreal Alouettes 13
1962	Winnipeg Blue Bombers 28, Hamilton Tiger-Cats 27	1979	Edmonton Eskimos 17, Montreal Alouettes 9
1963	Hamilton Tiger-Cats 21, British Columbia Lions 10	1980	Edmonton Eskimos 48, Hamilton Tiger-Cats 10
1964	British Columbia Lions 34, Hamilton Tiger-Cats 24	1981	Edmonton Eskimos 26, Ottawa Rough Riders 23
1965	Hamilton Tiger-Cats 22, Winnipeg Blue Bombers 16	1982	Edmonton Eskimos 32, Toronto Argonauts 16
1966	Saskatchewan Roughriders 29, Ottawa Rough Riders 14	1983	Toronto Argonauts 18, B.C. Lions 17
1967	Hamilton Tiger-Cats 24, Saskatchewan Roughriders 1	1984	Winnipeg Blue Bombers 47, Hamilton Tiger-Cats 17
1968	Ottawa Rough Riders 24, Calgary Stampeders 21	1985	B.C. Lions 37, Hamilton Tiger-Cats 24
1969	Ottawa Rough Riders 29, Saskatchewan Roughriders 11	1986	Hamilton Tiger-Cats 39, Edmonton Eskimos 15
1970	Montreal Alouettes 23, Calgary Stampeders 10	1987	Edmonton Eskimos 38, Toronto Argonauts 36
1971	Calgary Stampeders 14, Toronto Argonauts 11	1988	Winnipeg Blue Bombers 22, B.C. Lions 21
1972	Hamilton Tiger-Cats 13, Saskatchewan Roughriders 10		

NATIONAL FOOTBALL LEAGUE

Final 1988 Standings

National Conference

Eastern Division

	W	L	T	Pct	Pts	Opp
Philadelphia	10	6	0	.625	379	319
New York Giants	10	6	0	.625	359	304
Washington	7	9	0	.438	345	387
Phoenix	7	9	0	.438	344	398
Dallas	3	13	0	.188	265	381

Central Division

	W	L	T	Pct	Pts	Opp
Chicago	12	4	0	.750	312	215
Minnesota	11	5	0	.688	406	233
Tampa Bay	5	11	0	.313	261	350
Detroit	4	12	0	.250	220	313
Green Bay	4	12	0	.250	240	315

Western Division

	W	L	T	Pct	Pts	Opp
San Francisco	10	6	0	.625	369	294
Los Angeles Rams	10	6	0	.625	407	293
New Orleans	10	6	0	.625	312	283
Atlanta	5	11	0	.313	244	315

American Conference

Eastern Division

	W	L	T	Pct	Pts	Opp
Buffalo	12	4	0	.750	329	237
Indianapolis	9	7	0	.563	354	.315
New England	9	7	0	.563	250	284
New York Jets	8	7	1	.531	372	354
Miami	6	10	0	.375	319	380

Central Division

	W	L	T	Pct	Pts	Opp
Cincinnati	12	4	0	.750	448	329
Cleveland	10	6	0	.625	304	288
Houston	10	6	0	.625	424	365
Pittsburgh	5	11	0	.313	336	421

Western Division

	W	L	T	Pct	Pts	Opp
Seattle	9	7	0	.563	339	329
Denver	8	8	0	.500	327	352
Los Angeles Raiders	7	9	0	.438	325	369
San Diego	6	10	0	.375	231	332
Kansas City	4	11	1	.281	254	320

49ers Defeat Bengals in Super Bowl

The San Francisco 49ers drove 92 yards in the final minutes and scored a touchdown with 34 seconds left, to defeat the Cincinnati Bengals, 20-16, and win Super Bowl XXIII. The winning score came on Joe Montana's 10-yard pass to John Taylor. It was the third Super Bowl championship for San Francisco, which also won in 1982 and 1985. Wide receiver Jerry Rice of the Niners was chosen the game's most valuable player. His 11 pass receptions resulted in a Super Bowl record 215 yards gained.

Score by Quarters

Cincinnati	0	3	10	3—16
San Francisco	3	0	3	14—20

Scoring

San Francisco—Cofer 41 yd. field goal
Cincinnati—Breech 34 yd. field goal
Cincinnati—Breech 43 yd. field goal
San Francisco—Cofer 32 yd. field goal
Cincinnati—Jennings 93 yd. kickoff return (Breech kick)
San Francisco—Rice 14 yd. pass from Montana (Cofer kick)
Cincinnati—Breech 40 yd. field goal
San Francisco—Taylor 10 yd. pass from Montana (Cofer kick)

Individual Statistics

Rushing — Cincinnati, Woods 20-79, Brooks 6-24, Jennings 1-3, Esiason 1-0. San Francisco, Craig 17-74, Rathman 5-23, Montana 5-9, Rice 1-5.

Passing — Cincinnati, Esiason 11-25-1-144. San Francisco, Montana 23-36-0-357.

Receiving — Cincinnati, Brown 4-44, Collinsworth 3-40, Mc-Gee 2-23, Brooks 1-20, Hillary 1-17. San Francisco, Rice 11-215, Craig 8-101, Frank 2-15, Rathman 1-16, Taylor 1-10.

Team Statistics

	Cincinnati	San Francisco
First downs	13	23
Total net yards	229	454
Total Plays	64	67
Avg gain	3.6	6.8
Rushing yards	106	111
Passing yards	123	343
Yards per pass play	3.4	8.8
Punts-average	5-44	4-37
Penalties-yards	7-65	4-32
Fumbles-lost	1-0	4-1
Time of possession	32:43	27:17

Super Bowl

Year	Winner	Loser	Winning coach	Site
1967	Green Bay Packers, 35	Kansas City Chiefs, 10	Vince Lombardi	Los Angeles Coliseum
1968	Green Bay Packers, 33	Oakland Raiders, 14	Vince Lombardi	Orange Bowl, Miami
1969	New York Jets, 16	Baltimore Colts, 7	Weeb Ewbank	Orange Bowl, Miami
1970	Kansas City Chiefs, 23	Minnesota Vikings, 7	Hank Stram	Tulane Stadium, New Orleans
1971	Baltimore Colts, 16	Dallas Cowboys, 13	Don McCafferty	Orange Bowl, Miami
1972	Dallas Cowboys, 24	Miami Dolphins, 3	Tom Landry	Tulane Stadium, New Orleans
1973	Miami Dolphins, 14	Washington Redskins, 7	Don Shula	Los Angeles Coliseum
1974	Miami Dolphins, 24	Minnesota Vikings, 7	Don Shula	Rice Stadium, Houston
1975	Pittsburgh Steelers, 16	Minnesota Vikings, 6	Chuck Noll	Tulane Stadium, New Orleans
1976	Pittsburgh Steelers, 21	Dallas Cowboys, 17	Chuck Noll	Orange Bowl, Miami
1977	Oakland Raiders, 32	Minnesota Vikings, 14	John Madden	Rose Bowl, Pasadena
1978	Dallas Cowboys, 27	Denver Broncos, 10	Tom Landry	Superdome, New Orleans
1979	Pittsburgh Steelers, 35	Dallas Cowboys, 31	Chuck Noll	Orange Bowl, Miami
1980	Pittsburgh Steelers, 31	Los Angeles Rams, 19	Chuck Noll	Rose Bowl, Pasadena
1981	Oakland Raiders, 27	Philadelphia Eagles, 10	Tom Flores	Superdome, New Orleans
1982	San Francisco 49ers, 26	Cincinnati Bengals, 21	Bill Walsh	Silverdome, Pontiac, Mich.
1983	Washington Redskins, 27	Miami Dolphins, 17	Joe Gibbs	Rose Bowl, Pasadena
1984	Los Angeles Raiders, 38	Washington Redskins, 9	Tom Flores	Tampa Stadium
1985	San Francisco 49ers, 38	Miami Dolphins, 16	Bill Walsh	Stanford Stadium, Palo Alto, Cal.
1986	Chicago Bears, 46	New England Patriots, 10	Mike Ditka	Superdome, New Orleans
1987	New York Giants, 39	Denver Broncos, 20	Bill Parcells	Rose Bowl, Pasadena
1988	Washington Redskins, 42	Denver Broncos, 10	Joe Gibbs	San Diego Stadium
1989	San Francisco 49ers, 20	Cincinnati Bengals, 16	Bill Walsh	Joe Robbie Stadium, Miami

National Football League Champions

Year	East Winner (W-L-T)	West Winner (W-L-T)	Playoff
1933	New York Giants (11-3-0)	Chicago Bears (10-2-1)	Chicago Bears 23, New York 21
1934	New York Giants (8-5-0)	Chicago Bears (13-0-0)	New York 30, Chicago Bears 13
1935	New York Giants (9-3-0)	Detroit Lions (7-3-2)	Detroit 26, New York 7
1936	Boston Redskins (7-5-0)	Green Bay Packers (10-1-1)	Green Bay 21, Boston 6
1937	Washington Redskins (8-3-0)	Chicago Bears (9-1-1)	Washington 28, Chicago Bears 21
1938	New York Giants (8-2-1)	Green Bay Packers (8-3-0)	New York 23, Green Bay 17
1939	New York Giants (9-1-1)	Green Bay Packers (9-2-0)	Green Bay 27, New York 0
1940	Washington Redskins (9-2-0)	Chicago Bears (8-3-0)	Chicago Bears 73, Washington 0
1941	New York Giants (8-3-0)	Chicago Bears (10-1-1)(a)	Chicago Bears 37, New York 9
1942	Wash. Redskins (10-1-1)	Chicago Bears (11-0-0)	Washington 14, Chicago Bears 6
1943	Wash. Redskins (6-3-1)(a)	Chicago Bears (8-1-1)	Chicago Bears, 41, Washington 21
1944	New York Giants (8-1-1)	Green Bay Packers (8-2-0)	Green Bay 14, New York 7
1945	Wash. Redskins (8-2-0)	Cleveland Rams (9-1-0)	Cleveland 15, Washington 14
1946	New York Giants (7-3-1)	Chicago Bears (8-2-1)	Chicago Bears 24, New York 14
1947	Philadelphia Eagles (8-4-0)(a)	Chicago Cardinals (9-3-0)	Chicago Cardinals 28, Philadelphia 21
1948	Philadelphia Eagles (9-2-1)	Chicago Cardinals (11-1-0)	Philadelphia 7, Chicago Cardinals 0
1949	Philadelphia Eagles (11-1-0)	Los Angeles Rams (8-2-2)	Philadelphia 14, Los Angeles 0
1950	Cleveland Browns (10-2-0)(a)	Los Angeles Rams (9-3-0)(a)	Cleveland 30, Los Angeles 28
1951	Cleveland Browns (11-1-0)	Los Angeles Rams (8-4-0)	Los Angeles 24, Cleveland 17
1952	Cleveland Browns (8-4-0)	Detroit Lions (9-3-0)(a)	Detroit 17, Cleveland 7
1953	Cleveland Browns (11-1-0)	Detroit Lions (10-2-0)	Detroit 17, Cleveland 16
1954	Cleveland Browns (9-3-0)	Detroit Lions (9-2-1)	Cleveland 56, Detroit 10
1955	Cleveland Browns (9-2-1)	Los Angeles Rams (8-3-1)	Cleveland 38, Los Angeles 14
1956	New York Giants (8-3-1)	Chicago Bears (9-2-1)	New York 47, Chicago Bears 7
1957	Cleveland Browns (9-2-1)	Detroit Lions (8-4-0)(a)	Detroit 59, Cleveland 14
1958	New York Giants (9-3-0)(a)	Baltimore Colts (9-3-0)	Baltimore 23, New York (b)
1959	New York Giants (10-2-0)	Baltimore Colts (9-3-0)	Baltimore 31, New York 16
1960	Philadelphia Eagles (10-2-0)	Green Bay Packers (8-4-0)	Philadelphia 17, Green Bay 13
1961	New York Giants (10-3-1)	Green Bay Packers (11-3-0)	Green Bay 37, New York 0
1962	New York Giants (12-2-0)	Green Bay Packers (13-1-0)	Green Bay 16, New York 7
1963	New York Giants (11-3-0)	Chicago Bears (11-1-2)	Chicago 14, New York 10
1964	Cleveland Browns (10-3-1)	Baltimore Colts (12-2-0)	Cleveland 27, Baltimore 0
1965	Cleveland Browns (11-3-0)	Green Bay Packers (10-3-1)(a)	Green Bay 23, Cleveland 12
1966	Dallas Cowboys (10-3-1)	Green Bay Packers (12-2-0)	Green Bay 34, Dallas 27

(a) Won divisional playoff. (b) Won at 8:15 sudden death overtime period.

Year	Conference	Division	Winner (W-L-T)	Playoff
1967	East	Century	Cleveland (9-5-0)	Dallas 52, Cleveland 14
		Capitol	Dallas (9-5-0)	
	West	Central	Green Bay (9-4-1)	Green Bay 28, Los Angeles 7
		Coastal	Los Angeles (11-1-2)(a)	Green Bay 21, Dallas 17
1968	East	Century	Cleveland (10-4-0)	Cleveland 31, Dallas 20
		Capitol	Dallas (12-2-0)	
	West	Central	Minnesota (8-6-0)	Baltimore 24, Minnesota 14
		Coastal	Baltimore (13-1-0)	Baltimore 34, Cleveland 0
1969	East	Century	Cleveland (10-3-1)	Cleveland 38, Dallas 14
		Capitol	Dallas (11-2-1)	
	West	Central	Minnesota (12-2-0)	Minnesota 23, Los Angeles 20
		Coastal	Los Angeles (11-3-0)	Minnesota 27, Cleveland 7
1970	American	Eastern	Baltimore (11-2-1)	Baltimore 17, Cincinnati 0
		Central	Cincinnati (8-6-0)	Oakland 21, Miami 14
		Western	Oakland (8-4-2)	Baltimore 27, Oakland 17
	National	Eastern	Dallas (10-4-0)	Dallas 5, Detroit 0
		Central	Minnesota (12-2-0)	San Francisco 17, Minnesota 14
		Western	San Francisco (10-3-1)	Dallas 17, San Francisco 10
1971	American	Eastern	Miami (10-3-1)	Miami 27, Kansas City 24
		Central	Cleveland (9-5-0)	Baltimore 20, Cleveland 3
		Western	Kansas City (10-3-1)	Miami 21, Baltimore 0
	National	Eastern	Dallas (11-3-0)	Dallas 20, Minnesota 12
		Central	Minnesota (11-3-0)	San Francisco 24, Washington 20
		Western	San Francisco (9-5-0)	Dallas 14, San Francisco 3
1972	American	Eastern	Miami (14-0-0)	Miami 20, Cleveland 14
		Central	Pittsburgh (11-3-0)	Pittsburgh 13, Oakland 7
		Western	Oakland (10-3-1)	Miami 21, Pittsburgh 17
	National	Eastern	Washington (11-3-0)	Washington 16, Green Bay 3
		Central	Green Bay (10-4-0)	Dallas 30, San Francisco 28
		Western	San Francisco (8-5-1)	Washington 26, Dallas 3
1973	American	Eastern	Miami (12-2-0)	Miami 34, Cincinnati 16
		Central	Cincinnati (10-4-0)	Oakland 33, Pittsburgh 14
		Western	Oakland (9-4-1)	Miami 27, Oakland 10
	National	Eastern	Dallas (10-4-0)	Dallas 27, Los Angeles 16
		Central	Minnesota (12-2-0)	Minnesota 27, Washington 20
		Western	Los Angeles (12-2-0)	Minnesota 27, Dallas 10
1974	American	Eastern	Miami (11-3-0)	Oakland 28, Miami 26
		Central	Pittsburgh (10-3-1)	Pittsburgh 32, Buffalo 14
		Western	Oakland (12-2-0)	Pittsburgh 24, Oakland 13
	National	Eastern	St. Louis (10-4-0)	Minnesota 30, St. Louis 14
		Central	Minnesota (10-4-0)	Los Angeles 19, Washington 10
		Western	Los Angeles (10-4-0)	Minnesota 14, Los Angeles 10
1975	American	Eastern	Baltimore (10-4-0)	Pittsburgh 28, Baltimore 10
		Central	Pittsburgh (12-2-0)	Oakland 31, Cincinnati 28
		Western	Oakland (11-3-0)	Pittsburgh 16, Oakland 10

(continued)

Year	Conference	Division	Winner (W-L-T)	Playoff
	National	Eastern	St. Louis (11-3-0)	Dallas 17, Minnesota 14
		Central	Minnesota (12-2-0)	Los Angeles 35, St. Louis 23
		Western	Los Angeles (12-2-0)	Dallas 37, Los Angeles 7
1976	American	Eastern	Baltimore (11-3-0)	Pittsburgh 40, Baltimore 14
		Central	Pittsburgh (10-4-0)	Oakland 24, New England 21
		Western	Oakland (13-1-0)	Oakland 24, Pittsburgh 7
	National	Eastern	Dallas (11-3-0)	Minnesota 35, Washington 20
		Central	Minnesota (11-2-1)	Los Angeles 14, Dallas 12
		Western	Los Angeles (10-3-1)	Minnesota 24, Los Angeles 13
1977	American	Eastern	Baltimore (10-4-0)	Oakland 37, Baltimore 31
		Central	Pittsburgh (9-5-0)	Denver 34, Pittsburgh 21
		Western	Denver (12-2-0)	Dallas 37, Chicago 7
	National	Eastern	Dallas (12-2-0)	Minnesota 14, Los Angeles 7
		Central	Minnesota (9-5-0)	Denver 20, Oakland 17
		Western	Los Angeles (10-4-0)	Dallas 23, Minnesota 6
1978	American	Eastern	New England (11-5-0)	Pittsburgh 33, Denver 10
		Central	Pittsburgh (14-2-0)	Houston 31, New England 14
		Western	Denver (10-6-0)	Pittsburgh 34, Houston 5
	National	Eastern	Dallas (12-4-0)	Dallas 27, Atlanta 20
		Central	Minnesota (8-7-1)	Los Angeles 34, Minnesota 10
		Western	Los Angeles (12-4-0)	Dallas 28, Los Angeles 0
1979	American	Eastern	Miami (10-6-0)	Houston 17, San Diego 14
		Central	Pittsburgh (12-4-0)	Pittsburgh 34, Miami 14
		Western	San Diego (12-4-0)	Pittsburgh 27, Houston 13
	National	Eastern	Dallas (11-5-0)	Tampa Bay 24, Philadelphia 17
		Central	Tampa Bay (10-6-0)	Los Angeles 21, Dallas 19
		Western	Los Angeles (9-7-0)	Los Angeles 9, Tampa Bay 0
1980	American	Eastern	Buffalo (11-5-0)	San Diego 20, Buffalo 14
		Central	Cleveland (11-5-0)	Oakland 14, Cleveland 12
		Western	San Diego (11-5-0)	Oakland 34, San Diego 27
	National	Eastern	Philadelphia (12-4-0)	Philadelphia 31, Minnesota 16
		Central	Minnesota (9-7-0)	Dallas 30, Atlanta 27
		Western	Atlanta (12-4-0)	Philadelphia 20, Dallas 7
1981	American	Eastern	Miami (11-4-1)	San Diego 41, Miami 38
		Central	Cincinnati (12-4-0)	Cincinnati 28, Buffalo 21
		Western	San Diego (10-6-0)	Cincinnati 27, San Diego 7
	National	Eastern	Dallas (12-4-0)	Dallas 38, Tampa Bay 0
		Central	Tampa Bay (9-7-0)	San Francisco 38, N.Y. Giants 24
		Western	San Francisco (13-3-0)	San Francisco 28, Dallas 27
1982(1)	American		L.A. Raiders (8-1-0)	
	National		Washington (8-1-0)	

AFC playoffs—Miami 28, New England 13; L.A. Raiders 27, Cleveland 10; N.Y. Jets 44, Cincinnati 17; San Diego 31, Pittsburgh 28; N.Y. Jets 17, L.A. Raiders 14; Miami 34, San Diego 13; Miami 14, N.Y. Jets 0. **NFC playoffs**—Washington 31, Detroit 7; Green Bay 41, St. Louis 16; Dallas 30, Tampa Bay 17; Minnesota 30, Atlanta 24; Washington 21, Minnesota 7; Dallas 37, Green Bay 26; Washington 31, Dallas 17.

Year	Conference	Division	Winner (W-L-T)	Playoff
1983	American	Eastern	Miami (12-4-0)	Seattle 27, Miami 20
		Central	Pittsburgh (10-6-0)	L.A. Raiders 38, Pittsburgh 10
		Western	L.A. Raiders (12-4-0)	L.A. Raiders 30, Seattle 14
	National	Eastern	Washington (14-2-0)	Washington 51, L.A. Rams 7
		Central	Detroit (9-7-0)	San Francisco 24, Detroit 23
		Western	San Francisco (10-6-0)	Washington 24, San Francisco 21
1984	American	Eastern	Miami (14-2-0)	Miami 31, Seattle 10
		Central	Pittsburgh (9-7-0)	Pittsburgh 24, Denver 17
		Western	Denver (13-3-0)	Miami 45, Pittsburgh 28
	National	Eastern	Washington (11-5-0)	Chicago 23, Washington 19
		Central	Chicago (10-6-0)	San Francisco 21, N.Y. Giants 10
		Western	San Francisco (15-1-0)	San Francisco 23, Chicago 0
1985	American	Eastern	Miami (12-4-0)	New England 27, L.A. Raiders 20
		Central	Cleveland (8-8-0)	Miami 24, Cleveland 21
		Western	L.A. Raiders (12-4-0)	New England 31, Miami 14
	National	Eastern	Dallas (10-6-0)	Chicago 21, N.Y. Giants 0
		Central	Chicago (15-1-0)	L.A. Rams 20, Dallas 0
		Western	L.A. Rams (11-5-0)	Chicago 24, L.A. Rams 0
1986	American	Eastern	New England (11-5-0)	Denver 22, New England 17
		Central	Cleveland (12-4-0)	Cleveland 23, N.Y. Jets 20
		Western	Denver (11-5-0)	Denver 23, Cleveland 20
	National	Eastern	N.Y. Giants (14-2-0)	N.Y. Giants 49, San Francisco 3
		Central	Chicago (14-2-0)	Washington 27, Chicago 13
		Western	San Francisco (10-5-1)	N.Y. Giants 17, Washington 0
1987	American	Eastern	Indianapolis (9-6-0)	Cleveland 38, Indianapolis 21
		Central	Cleveland (10-5-0)	Denver 34, Houston 10
		Western	Denver (10-4-1)	Denver 38, Cleveland 33
	National	Eastern	Washington (11-4-0)	Washington 21, Chicago 7
		Central	Chicago (11-4-0)	Minnesota 36, San Francisco 24
		Western	San Francisco (13-2-0)	Washington 17, Minnesota 10
1988	American	Eastern	Buffalo (12-4-0)	Buffalo 17, Houston 10
		Central	Cincinnati (12-4-0)	Cincinnati 21, Seattle 13
		Western	Seattle (9-7-0)	Cincinnati 21, Buffalo 10
	National	Eastern	Philadelphia (10-6-0)	Chicago 20, Philadelphia 12
		Central	Chicago (12-4-0)	San Francisco 34, Minnesota 9
		Western	San Francisco (10-6-0)	San Francisco 28, Chicago 3

(1) Strike-shortened season

World Almanac/NEA Bert Bell Memorial Trophy Winners

The World Almanac/NEA Bert Bell Memorial Trophy, named after the former NFL commissioner, is awarded annually to the outstanding NFL rookie as chosen by a panel of sports experts.

1964	Charlie Taylor, Washington, WR		NFC: Steve Bartkowski, Atlanta, QB
1965	Gale Sayers, Chicago, RB	1976	AFC: Mike Haynes, New England, CB
1966	Tommy Nobis, Atlanta, LB		NFC: Sammy White, Minnesota, WR
1967	Mel Farr, Detroit, RB	1977	Tony Dorsett, Dallas, RB
1968	Earl McCullouch, Detroit, WR	1978	Earl Campbell, Houston, RB
1969	Calvin Hill, Dallas, RB	1979	Ottis Anderson, St. Louis, RB
1970	Raymond Chester, Oakland, TE	1980	Billy Sims, Detroit, RB
1971	AFC: Jim Plunkett, New England, QB	1981	Lawrence Taylor, N.Y. Giants, LB
	NFC: John Brockington, Green Bay, RB	1982	Marcus Allen, L.A. Raiders, RB
1972	AFC: Franco Harris, Pittsburgh, RB	1983	Eric Dickerson, L.A. Rams, RB
	NFC: Willie Buchanon, Green Bay, DB	1984	Louis Lipps, Pittsburgh, WR
1973	AFC: Boobie Clark, Cincinnati, RB	1985	Eddie Brown, Cincinnati, WR
	NFC: Chuck Foreman, Minnesota, RB	1986	Rueben Mayes, New Orleans, RB
1974	Don Woods, San Diego, RB	1987	Bo Jackson, L.A. Raiders, RB
1975	AFC: Robert Brazile, Houston, LB	1988	John Stephens, New England, RB

World Almanac/NEA George Halas Trophy Winners

The World Almanac/NEA Halas Trophy, named after football coach George Halas, is awarded annually to the outstanding defensive player in the NFL as chosen by a panel of sports experts.

1966	Larry Wilson, St. Louis	1974	Joe Greene, Pittsburgh	1982	Mark Gastineau, N.Y. Jets
1967	Deacon Jones, Los Angeles	1975	Curley Culp, Houston	1983	Jack Lambert, Pittsburgh
1968	Deacon Jones, Los Angeles	1976	Jerry Sherk, Cleveland	1984	Mike Haynes, L.A. Raiders
1969	Dick Butkus, Chicago	1977	Harvey Martin, Dallas	1985	Howie Long, L.A. Raiders
1970	Dick Butkus, Chicago	1978	Randy Gradishar, Denver		Andre Tippett, New England
1971	Carl Eller, Minnesota	1979	Lee Roy Selmon, Tampa Bay	1986	Lawrence Taylor, N.Y. Giants
1972	Joe Greene, Pittsburgh	1980	Lester Hayes, Oakland	1987	Reggie White, Philadelphia
1973	Alan Page, Minnesota	1981	Joe Klecko, N.Y. Jets	1988	Mike Singletary, Chicago

World Almanac/NEA All-Pro Team in 1988

Chosen by a panel of sports experts representing the World Almanac and its co-sponsoring newspapers, and its publisher, Newspaper Enterprise Assn.

First team	Offense	Second team
Henry Ellard, L.A. Rams	Wide receiver	Al Toon, N.Y. Jets
Eddie Brown, Cincinnati	Wide receiver	Jerry Rice, San Francisco
Mickey Shuler, N.Y. Jets	Tight end	Keith Jackson, Philadelphia
Anthony Munoz, Cincinnati	Tackle	Gary Zimmerman, Minnesota
Irv Pankey, L.A. Rams	Tackle	Chris Hinton, Indianapolis
Bill Fralic, Atlanta	Guard	Bruce Matthews Houston
Mike Munchak, Houston	Guard	Max Montoya, Cincinnati
Jay Hilgenberg, Chicago	Center	Ray Donaldson, Indianapolis
Boomer Esiason, Cincinnati	Quarterback	Dan Marino, Miami
Roger Craig, San Francisco	Running back	Herschel Walker, Dallas
Eric Dickerson, Indianapolis	Running back	Ickey Woods, Cincinnati
Nick Lowery, Kansas City	Placekicker	Morton Anderson, New Orleans

First team	Defense	Second team
Reggie White, Philadelphia	End	Ray Childress, Houston
Bruce Smith, Buffalo	End	Richard Dent, Chicago
Michael Carter, San Francisco	Nose tackle	Steve McMichael, Chicago
Dan Hampton, Chicago	Tackle	Keith Millard, Minnesota
Vaughan Johnson, New Orleans	Inside linebacker	John Offerdahl, Miami
Mike Singletary, Chicago	Middle linebacker	Scott Studwell, Minnestoa
Tim Harris, Green Bay	Outside Linebacker	Andre Tippett, New England
Cornelius Bennett, Buffalo	Outside linebacker	Lawrence Taylor, N.Y. Giants
Frank Minnifield, Cleveland	Cornerback	Carl Lee, Minnesota
Ronnie Lippett, New England	Cornerback	Jerry Gray, L.A. Rams
Joey Browner, Minnesota	Strong safety	Bennie Blades, Detroit
Ronnie Lott, San Francisco	Free safety	Deron Cherry, Kansas City
Jim Arnold, Detroit	Punter	Mike Horan, Denver

NFL Team Rankings in 1988

	Offense			Defense				Offense			Defense		
	Total	Rush	Pass	Total	Rush	Pass		Total	Rush	Pass	Total	Rush	Pass
Atlanta	25	14	25	25	25	21	Miami	5	28	1	26	26	14
Buffalo	12	7	15	4	12	4	Minnesota	7	20	4	1	5	2
Chicago	11	3	20	2	1	9	New England	27	9	27	5	19	3
Cincinnati	1	1	11	15	18	10	New Orleans	16	11	18	12	11	18
Cleveland	18	24	9	6	15	6	N.Y. Giants	20	23	14	11	10	18
Dallas	9	16	7	20	13	24	N.Y. Jets	13	8	19	23	21	23
Denver	8	19	6	22	27	7	Philadelphia	10	17	8	27	6	28
Detroit	28	27	28	18	17	15	Phoenix	4	13	5	14	16	12
Green Bay	24	26	13	7	20	5	Pittsburgh	15	6	21	28	14	27
Houston	14	4	22	8	4	13	San Diego	26	12	26	21	22	16
Indianapolis	21	4	24	17	8	25	San Francisco	2	2	10	3	3	8
Kansas City	22	22	16	10	28	1	Seattle	23	10	23	24	24	20
L.A. Raiders	19	18	17	19	23	11	Tampa Bay	17	21	12	13	2	26
L.A. Rams	3	15	3	9	7	17	Washington	6	25	2	16	9	22

1988 NFL Individual Leaders

National Football Conference

Passing

	Att	Comp	Pct comp	Yards	Avg gain	TD	Pct TD	Int	Rating points
Wilson, Wade, Minnesota	332	204	61.4	2746	8.27	15	4.5	9	91.5
Everett, Jim, L.A. Rams	517	308	59.6	3964	7.67	31	6.0	18	89.2
Montana, Joe, San Francisco	397	238	59.9	2981	7.51	18	4.5	10	87.9
Lomax, Neil, Phoenix	443	255	57.6	3395	7.66	20	4.5	11	86.7
Simms, Phil, N.Y. Giants	479	263	54.9	3359	7.01	21	4.4	11	82.1
Hebert, Bobby, New Orleans	478	280	58.6	3156	6.60	20	4.2	15	79.3
Cunningham, Randall, Philadelphia	560	301	53.8	3808	6.80	24	4.3	16	77.6
Williams, Doug, Washington	380	213	56.1	2609	6.87	15	3.9	12	77.4
Pelluer, Steve, Dallas	435	245	56.3	3139	7.22	17	3.9	19	73.9
Majkowski, Don, Green Bay	336	178	53.0	2119	6.31	9	2.7	11	67.8
Miller, Chris, Atlanta	351	184	52.4	2133	6.08	11	3.1	12	67.3
Wright, Randy, Green Bay	244	141	57.8	1490	6.11	4	1.6	13	58.9
Hilger, Rusty, Detroit	306	126	41.2	1558	5.09	7	2.3	12	48.9
Testaverde, Vinny, Tampa Bay	466	222	47.6	3240	6.95	13	2.8	35	48.8

Rushing

	Att	Yds	Avg	TD
Walker, Herschel, Dallas	361	1514	4.2	5
Craig, Roger, San Francisco	310	1502	4.8	9
Bell, Greg, L.A. Rams	288	1212	4.2	16
Anderson, Neal, Chicago	249	1106	4.4	12
Morris, Joe, N.Y. Giants	307	1083	3.5	5
Settle, John, Atlanta	232	1024	4.4	7
Ferrell, Earl, Phoenix	202	924	4.6	7
Hilliard, Dalton, New Orleans	204	823	4.0	5
Mitchell, Stump, Phoenix	164	726	4.4	4
Mays, Rueben, New Orleans	170	628	3.7	3

Interceptions

	No	Yds	TD
Case, Scott, Atlanta	10	47	0
Lee, Carl, Minnesota	8	118	2
Hoage, Terry, Philadelphia	8	116	0
Jackson, Vestee, Chicago	8	94	0
McKyer, Tim, San Francisco	7	11	0
Hamilton, Harry, Tampa Bay	6	123	0

Pass Receiving

	No	Yds	Avg	TD
Ellard, Henry, L.A. Rams	86	1414	16.4	10
Martin, Eric, New Orleans	85	1083	12.7	7
Smith, J.T., Phoenix	83	986	11.9	5
Jackson, Keith, Philadelphia	81	869	10.7	6
Craig, Roger, San Francisco	76	534	7.0	1
Sanders, Ricky, Washington	73	1148	15.7	12
Carter, Anthony, Minnesota	72	1225	17.0	6
Monk, Art, Washington	72	946	13.1	5
Byars, Keith, Philadelphia	72	705	9.8	4
Green, Roy, Phoenix	68	1097	16.1	7
Settle, John, Atlanta	68	570	8.4	1

Kickoff Returns

	No	Yds	Avg	TD
Elder, Donnie, Tampa Bay	34	772	22.7	0
Burbage, Cornell, Dallas	20	448	22.4	0
Clack, Darryl, Dallas	32	690	21.6	0
Gentry, Dennis, Chicago	27	578	21.4	0
Harris, Darryl, Minnesota	39	833	21.4	0
Atkins, Gene, New Orleans	20	424	21.2	0
Gray, Mel, New Orleans	32	670	20.9	0
Sikahema, Vai, Phoenix	23	475	20.7	0
Fullwood, Brent, Green Bay	21	421	20.0	0
Morris, Jamie, Washington	21	413	19.7	0

Scoring-Touchdowns

	TD	Rush	Pass	Pts
Bell, Greg, L.A. Rams	18	16	2	108
Anderson, Neal, Chicago	12	12	0	72
Sanders, Ricky, Washington	12	0	12	72
Byars, Keith, Philadelphia	10	6	4	60
Craig, Roger, San Francisco	10	9	1	60
Ellard, Henry, L.A. Rams	10	0	10	60
Rice, Jerry, San Francisco	10	1	9	60
Ferrell, Earl, Phoenix	9	7	2	54
Hill, Bruce, Tampa Bay	9	0	9	54

Punt Returns

	No	Yds	Avg	TD
Taylor, John, San Francisco	44	556	12.6	2
Gray, Mel, New Orleans	25	305	12.2	1
Futrell, Bobby, Tampa Bay	27	283	10.5	0
Sikahema, Vai, Phoenix	33	341	10.3	0
Lewis, Leo, Minnesota	58	550	9.5	0
Barnes, Lew, Atlanta	34	307	9.0	0
Martin, Kelvin, Dallas	44	360	8.2	0
McKinnon, Dennis, Chicago	34	277	8.1	0
McConkey, Phil, N.Y. Giants	40	313	7.8	0
Mandley, Pete, Detroit	37	287	7.8	0

Scoring-Kicking

	XP	XPA	FG	FGA	Pts
Cofer, Mike, San Francisco	40	41	27	38	121
Lansford, Mike, L.A. Rams	45	48	24	32	117
Andersen, Morten, N.O.	32	33	26	36	110
Nelson, Chuck, Minnesota	48	49	20	25	108
Lohmiller, Chip, Washington	40	41	19	26	97
Zendejas, Luis, Dall.-Phil.	35	36	20	27	95
Butler, Kevin, Chicago	37	38	15	19	82
Davis, Greg, Atlanta	25	27	19	30	82
Murray, Ed, Detroit	22	23	20	21	82
Del Greco, Al, Phoenix	42	44	12	21	78

Punters

	No	Yds	Avg
Arnold, Jim, Detroit	97	4110	42.4
Wagner, Bryan, Chicago	79	3282	41.5
Buford, Maury, N.Y. Giants	73	3012	41.3
Saxon, Mike, Dallas	80	3271	40.9
Horne, Greg, Phoenix	79	3228	40.9
Hansen, Brian, New Orleans	72	2913	40.5
Teltschik, John, Philadelphia	98	3958	40.4
Scribner, Bucky, Minnesota	84	3387	40.3
Donnelly, Rick, Atlanta	98	3920	40.0

Sacks

	No		No		No
White, Reggie, Philadelphia	18.0	Harris, Timothy, Green Bay	13.5	Jeter, Gary, L.A. Rams	11.5
Greene, Kevin, L.A. Rams	16.5	Cofer, Mike, Detroit	12.0	McMichael, Steve, Chicago	11.5
Taylor, Lawrence, N.Y. Giants	15.5	Haley, Charles, San Francisco	11.5	Dent, Richard, Chicago	10.5
Nunn, Freddie Joe, Phoenix	14.0				

American Football Conference

Passing

	Att	Comp	Pct comp	Yards	Avg gain	TD	Pct TD	Int	Rating points
Esiason, Boomer, Cincinnati	388	223	57.5	3572	9.21	28	7.2	14	97.4
Krieg, Dave, Seattle	228	134	58.8	1741	7.64	18	7.9	8	94.6
Moon, Warren, Houston	294	160	54.4	2327	7.91	17	5.8	8	88.4
Kosar, Bernie, Cleveland	259	156	60.2	1890	7.30	10	3.9	7	84.3
Marino, Dan, Miami	606	354	58.4	4434	7.32	28	4.6	23	80.8
O'Brien, Ken, N.Y. Jets	424	236	55.7	2567	6.05	15	3.5	7	78.6
Kelly, Jim, Buffalo	452	269	59.5	3380	7.48	15	3.3	17	78.2
DeBerg, Steve, Kansas City	414	224	54.1	2935	7.09	16	3.9	16	73.5
Elway, John, Denver	496	274	55.2	3309	6.67	17	3.4	19	71.4
Chandler, Chris, Indianapolis	233	129	55.4	1619	6.95	8	3.4	12	67.2
Beuerlein, Steve, L.A. Raiders	238	105	44.1	1643	6.90	8	3.4	7	66.6
Brister, Bubby, Pittsburgh	370	175	47.3	2634	7.12	11	3.0	14	65.3
Schroeder, Jay, L.A. Raiders	256	113	44.1	1839	7.18	13	5.1	13	64.6
Malone, Mark, San Diego	272	147	54.0	1580	5.81	6	2.2	13	58.8

Rushing

	Att	Yds	Avg	TD
Dickerson, Eric, Indianapolis	388	1659	4.3	14
Stephens, John, New England	297	1168	3.9	4
Anderson, Gary, San Diego	225	1119	5.0	3
Woods, Ickey, Cincinnati	203	1066	5.3	15
Warner, Curt, Seattle	266	1025	3.9	10
Rozier, Mike, Houston	251	1002	4.0	10
McNeil, Freeman, N.Y. Jets	219	944	4.3	6
Brooks, James, Cincinnati	182	931	5.1	8
Thomas, Thurman, Buffalo	207	881	4.3	2
Williams, John L., Seattle	189	877	4.6	4

Pass Receiving

	No	Yds	Avg	TD
Toon, Al, N.Y. Jets	93	1067	11.5	5
Clayton, Mark, Miami	86	1129	13.1	14
Hill, Drew, Houston	72	1141	15.8	10
Reed, Andre, Buffalo	71	968	13.6	6
Shuler, Mickey, N.Y. Jets	70	805	11.5	5
Johnson, Vance, Denver	68	896	13.2	5
Paige, Stephone, Kansas City	61	902	14.8	7
Givins, Ernest, Houston	60	976	16.3	5
Byner, Earnest, Cleveland	59	576	9.8	2
Jensen, Jim, Miami	58	652	11.2	5
Williams, John L., Seattle	58	651	11.2	3

Scoring-Touchdowns

	TD	Rush	Pass	Pts
Dickerson, Eric, Indianapolis	15	14	1	90
Woods, Ickey, Cincinnati	15	15	0	90
Brooks, James, Cincinnati	14	8	6	84
Clayton, Mark, Miami	14	0	14	84
Riddick, Robb, Buffalo	14	12	1	84
Hampton, Lorenzo, Miami	12	9	3	72
Warner, Curt, Seattle	12	10	2	72
Rozier, Mike, Houston	11	10	1	66
Hector, Johnny, N.Y. Jets	10	10	0	60
Hill, Drew, Houston	10	0	10	60

Scoring-Kicking

	XP	XPA	FG	FGA	Pts
Norwood, Scott, Buffalo	33	33	32	37	129
Anderson, Gary, Pittsburgh	34	35	28	36	118
Biasucci, Dean, Indianapolis	39	40	25	32	114
Zendejas, Tony, Houston	48	50	22	34	114
Leahy, Pat, N.Y. Jets	43	43	23	28	112
Johnson, Norm, Seattle	39	39	22	28	105
Karlis, Rich, Denver	36	37	23	36	105
Bahr, Matt, Cleveland	32	33	24	29	104
Lowery, Nick, Kansas City	23	23	27	32	104
Bahr, Chris, L.A. Raiders	37	39	18	29	91

Interceptions

	No	Yds	TD
McMillan, Erik, N.Y. Jets	8	168	2
Kelso, Mark, Buffalo	7	180	1
Byrd, Gill, San Diego	7	82	0
Thomas, Eric, Cincinnati	7	61	0
Cherry, Deron, Kansas City	7	51	0
Moyer, Paul, Seattle	6	79	0

Kickoff Returns

	No	Yds	Avg	TD
Brown, Tim, L.A. Raiders	41	1098	26.8	1
Holland, Jamie, San Diego	31	810	26.1	1
Miller, Anthony, San Diego	25	648	25.9	1
Humphrey, Bobby, N.Y. Jets	21	510	24.3	0
Martin, Sammy, New England	31	735	23.7	1
Woodson, Rod, Pittsburgh	37	850	23.0	1
Edmonds, Bobby Joe, Seattle	40	900	22.5	0
Young, Glen, Cleveland	29	635	21.9	0
Jennings, Stanford, Cincinnati	32	684	21.4	1
Bell, Ken, Denver	36	762	21.2	0

Punt Returns

	No	Yds	Avg	TD
Townsell, JoJo, N.Y. Jets	35	409	11.7	1
Verdin, Clarence, Indianapolis	22	239	10.9	1
Fryar, Irving, New England	38	398	10.5	0
James, Lionel, San Diego	28	278	9.9	0
Edmonds, Bobby Joe, Seattle	35	340	9.7	0
Nattiel, Ricky, Denver	23	223	9.7	0
Schwedes, Scott, Miami	24	230	9.6	0
Brown, Tim, L.A. Raiders	49	444	9.1	0
Woodson, Rod, Pittsburgh	33	281	8.5	0
McNeil, Gerald, Cleveland	38	315	8.3	0

Punters

	No	Yds	Avg
Newsome, Harry, Pittsburgh	65	2950	45.4
Mojsiejenko, Ralf, San Diego	85	3745	44.1
Horan, Mike, Denver	65	2861	44.0
Stark, Rohn, Indianapolis	64	2784	43.5
Roby, Reggie, Miami	64	2754	43.0
Gossett, Jeff, L.A. Raiders	91	3804	41.8
Rodriguez, Ruben, Seattle	70	2858	40.8
Goodburn, Kelly, Kansas City	76	3059	40.3
Runager, Max, S.F.-Cleveland	49	1959	40.0
Kidd, John, Buffalo	62	2451	39.5

Sacks

	No		No		No
Townsend, Greg, L.A. Raiders	11.5	Skow, Jim, Cincinnati	9.5	Fuller, William, Houston	8.5
Smith, Bruce, Buffalo	11.0	Fletcher, Simon, Denver	9.0	Meads, Johnny, Houston	8.0
Williams, Lee, San Diego	11.0	Green, Jacob, Seattle	9.0	Williams, Brent, New England	8.0
Bennett, Cornelius, Buffalo	9.5	Childress, Ray, Houston	8.5		

National Football Conference Leaders

(National Football League, 1960-69)

Passing / Pass-Receiving

Player, team	Atts	Com	YG	TD	Year	Player, team	Ct	YG	TD
Milt Plum, Cleveland	250	151	2,297	21	1960	Raymond Berry, Baltimore	74	1,298	10
Milt Plum, Cleveland	302	177	2,416	18	1961	Jim Phillips, L.A. Rams	78	1,092	5
Bart Starr, Green Bay	285	178	2,438	12	1962	Bobby Mitchell, Washington	72	1,384	11
Y.A. Tittle, N.Y. Giants	367	221	3,145	36	1963	Bobby Joe Conrad, St. Louis	73	967	10
Bart Starr, Green Bay	272	163	2,144	15	1964	Johnny Morris, Chicago	93	1,200	10
Rudy Bukich, Chicago	312	176	2,641	20	1965	Dave Parks, San Francisco	80	1,344	12
Bart Starr, Green Bay	251	156	2,257	14	1966	Charley Taylor, Washington	72	1,119	12
Sonny Jurgensen, Washington	508	288	3,747	31	1967	Charley Taylor, Washington	70	990	9
Earl Morrall, Baltimore	317	182	2,909	26	1968	Clifton McNeil, San Francisco	71	994	7
Sonny Jurgensen, Washington	442	274	3,102	22	1969	Dan Abramowicz, New Orleans	73	1,015	7
John Brodie, San Francisco	378	223	2,941	24	1970	Dick Gordon, Chicago	71	1,026	13
Roger Staubach, Dallas	211	126	1,882	15	1971	Bob Tucker, Giants	59	791	4
Norm Snead, N.Y. Giants	325	196	2,307	17	1972	Harold Jackson, Philadelphia	62	1,048	4
Roger Staubach, Dallas	286	179	2,428	23	1973	Harold Carmichael, Philadelphia	67	1,116	9
Sonny Jurgensen, Washington	167	107	1,185	11	1974	Charles Young, Philadelphia	63	696	3
Fran Tarkenton, Minnesota	425	273	2,294	25	1975	Chuck Foreman, Minnesota	73	691	9
James Harris, Los Angeles	158	91	1,460	8	1976	Drew Pearson, Dallas	58	806	6
Roger Staubach, Dallas	361	210	2,620	18	1977	Ahmad Rashad, Minnesota	51	681	2
Roger Staubach, Dallas	413	231	3,190	25	1978	Rickey Young, Minnesota	88	704	5
Roger Staubach, Dallas	461	267	3,586	27	1979	Ahmad Rashad, Minnesota	80	1,156	9
Ron Jaworski, Philadelphia	451	257	3,529	27	1980	Earl Cooper, San Francisco	83	567	4
Joe Montana, San Francisco	488	311	3,565	19	1981	Dwight Clark, San Francisco	85	1,105	4
Joe Thiesmann, Washington	252	161	2,033	13	1982	Dwight Clark, San Francisco	60	913	5
Steve Bartkowski, Atlanta	423	274	3,167	22	1983	Roy Green, St. Louis	78	1,227	14
						Charlie Brown, Washington	78	1,225	8
						Earnest Gray, N.Y. Giants	78	1,139	5
Joe Montana, San Francisco	432	279	3,630	28	1984	Art Monk, Washington	106	1,372	7
Joe Montana, San Francisco	494	303	3,653	27	1985	Roger Craig, San Francisco	92	1,016	6
Tommy Kramer, Minnesota	372	208	3,000	24	1986	Jerry Rice, San Francisco	86	1,570	15
Joe Montana, San Francisco	398	266	3,054	31	1987	J.T. Smith, St. Louis	91	1,117	8
Wade Wilson, Minnesota	332	204	2,746	15	1988	Henry Ellard, L.A. Rams	86	1,414	10

Scoring / Rushing

Player, team	TD	PAT	FG	Pts	Year	Player, team	Yds	Atts	TD
Paul Hornung, Green Bay	15	41	15	176	1960	Jim Brown, Cleveland	1,257	215	9
Paul Hornung, Green Bay	10	41	15	146	1961	Jim Brown, Cleveland	1,408	305	8
Jim Taylor, Green Bay	19	0	0	114	1962	Jim Taylor, Green Bay	1,474	272	19
Don Chandler, N.Y. Giants	0	52	18	106	1963	Jim Brown, Cleveland	1,863	291	12
Lenny Moore, Baltimore	20	0	0	120	1964	Jim Brown, Cleveland	1,446	280	7
Gale Sayers, Chicago	22	0	0	132	1965	Jim Brown, Cleveland	1,544	289	17
Bruce Gossett, L.A. Rams	0	29	28	113	1966	Gale Sayers, Chicago	1,231	229	8
Jim Bakken, St. Louis	0	36	27	117	1967	Leroy Kelly, Cleveland	1,205	235	11
Leroy Kelly, Cleveland	20	0	0	120	1968	Leroy Kelly, Cleveland	1,239	248	16
Fred Cox, Minnesota	0	43	26	121	1969	Gale Sayers, Chicago	1,032	236	8
Fred Cox, Minnesota	0	35	30	125	1970	Larry Brown, Washington	1,125	237	5
Curt Knight, Washington	0	27	29	114	1971	John Brockington, Green Bay	1,105	216	4
Chester Marcol, Green Bay	0	29	33	128	1972	Larry Brown, Washington	1,216	285	8
David Ray, Los Angeles	0	40	30	130	1973	John Brockington, Green Bay	1,144	265	3
Chester Marcol, Green Bay	0	19	25	94	1974	Lawrence McCutcheon, Los Angeles	1,109	236	3
Chuck Foreman, Minnesota	22	0	0	132	1975	Jim Otis, St. Louis	1,076	269	5
Mark Moseley, Washington	0	31	22	97	1976	Walter Payton, Chicago	1,390	311	13
Walter Payton, Chicago	16	0	0	96	1977	Walter Payton, Chicago	1,852	339	14
Frank Corrall, Los Angeles	0	31	29	118	1978	Walter Payton, Chicago	1,395	333	11
Mark Moseley, Washington	0	39	25	114	1979	Walter Payton, Chicago	1,610	369	14
Ed Murray, Detroit	0	35	27	116	1980	Walter Payton, Chicago	1,460	317	15
Ed Murray, Detroit	0	46	25	121	1981	George Rogers, New Orleans	1,674	378	13
Wendell Tyler, L.A. Rams	13	0	0	78	1982	Tony Dorsett, Dallas	745	177	5
Mark Moseley, Washington	0	62	33	161	1983	Eric Dickerson, L.A. Rams	1,808	390	18
Ray Werschieg, San Francisco	0	56	25	131	1984	Eric Dickerson, L.A. Rams	2,105	379	14
Kevin Butler, Chicago	0	51	31	144	1985	Gerald Riggs, Atlanta	1,719	397	10
Kevin Butler, Chicago	0	36	28	120	1986	Eric Dickerson, L.A. Rams	1,821	404	11
Jerry Rice, San Francisco	23	0	0	138	1987	Charles White, L.A. Rams	1,374	324	11
Mike Cofer, San Francisco	0	40	27	121	1988	Herschel Walker, Dallas	1,514	361	5

American Football Conference Leaders

(American Football League, 1960-1969)

Passing / Pass-Receiving

Player, team	Atts	Com	YG	TD	Year	Player, team	Ct	YG	TD
Jack Kemp, Los Angeles	406	211	3,018	20	1960	Lionel Taylor, Denver	92	1,235	12
George Blanda, Houston	362	187	3,330	36	1961	Lionel Taylor, Denver	100	1,176	4
Len Dawson, Dallas	310	189	2,759	29	1962	Lionel Taylor, Denver	77	908	4
Tobin Rote, Kansas City	286	170	2,510	20	1963	Lionel Taylor, Denver	78	1,101	10
Len Dawson, Kansas City	354	199	2,879	30	1964	Charley Hennigan, Houston	101	1,546	8
John Hadl, San Diego	348	174	2,798	20	1965	Lionel Taylor, Denver	85	1,131	6
Len Dawson, Kansas City	284	159	2,527	26	1966	Lance Alworth, San Diego	73	1,383	13
Daryle Lamonica, Oakland	425	220	3,228	30	1967	George Sauer, N.Y. Jets	75	1,189	6
Len Dawson, Kansas City	224	131	2,109	17	1968	Lance Alworth, San Diego	68	1,312	10
Greg Cook, Cincinnati	197	106	1,854	15	1969	Lance Alworth, San Diego	64	1,003	4
Daryle Lamonica, Oakland	356	179	2,516	22	1970	Marlin Briscoe, Buffalo	57	1,036	8
Bob Griese, Miami	263	145	2,089	19	1971	Fred Biletnikoff, Oakland	61	929	9

Passing

Player, team	Atts	Com	YG	TD	Year
Earl Morrall, Miami.........	150	83	1,360	11	1972
Ken Stabler, Oakland......	260	163	1,997	14	1973
Ken Anderson, Cincinnati....	328	213	2,667	18	1974
Ken Anderson, Cincinnati....	377	228	3,169	21	1975
Ken Stabler, Oakland......	291	194	2,737	27	1976
Bob Griese, Miami.......	307	180	2,252	22	1977
Terry Bradshaw, Pittsburgh....	368	207	2,915	28	1978
Dan Fouts, San Diego........	530	332	4,082	24	1979
Brian Sipe, Cleveland.......	554	337	4,132	30	1980
Ken Anderson, Cincinnati......	479	300	3,754	29	1981
Ken Anderson, Cincinnati......	309	218	2,495	12	1982
Dan Marino, Miami.......	296	173	2,210	20	1983
Dan Marino, Miami.......	564	362	5,084	48	1984
Ken O'Brien, N.Y. Jets......	488	297	3,888	25	1985
Dan Marino, Miami.......	623	378	4,746	44	1986
Bernie Kosar, Cleveland.....	389	241	3,033	22	1987
Boomer Esiason, Cincinnati....	388	223	3,572	28	1988

Pass-Receiving

Player, team	Ct	YG	TD	Year
Fred Biletnikoff, Oakland.........	58	802	7	1972
Fred Willis, Houston...........	57	371	1	1973
Lydell Mitchell, Baltimore......	72	544	2	1974
Reggie Rucker, Cleveland........	60	770	3	1975
Lydell Mitchell, Baltimore.......	60	554	4	
MacArthur Lane, Kansas City	66	686	1	1976
Lydell Mitchell, Baltimore.......	71	620	4	1977
Steve Largent, Seattle.........	71	1,168	8	1978
Joe Washington, Baltimore......	82	750	3	1979
Kellen Winslow, San Diego......	89	1,290	9	1980
Kellen Winslow, San Diego......	88	1,075	10	1981
Kellen Winslow, San Diego......	54	721	6	1982
Todd Christensen, L.A. Raiders.....	92	1,247	12	1983
Ozzie Newsome, Cleveland......	89	1,001	5	1984
Lionel James, San Diego.........	86	1,027	6	1985
Todd Christensen, L.A. Raiders.....	95	1,153	8	1986
Al Toon, N.Y. Jets........	68	976	5	1987
Al Toon, N.Y. Jets........	93	1,067	5	1988

Scoring

Player, team	TD	PAT	FG	Pts	Year
Gene Mingo, Denver........	6	33	18	123	1960
Gino Cappelletti, Boston......	8	48	17	147	1961
Gene Mingo, Denver......	4	32	27	137	1962
Gino Cappelletti, Boston......	2	35	22	113	1963
Gino Cappelletti, Boston......	7	36	25	155	1964
Gino Cappelletti, Boston......	9	27	17	132	1965
Gino Cappelletti, Boston......	6	35	16	119	1966
George Blanda, Oakland......	0	56	20	116	1967
Jim Turner, N.Y. Jets......	0	43	34	145	1968
Jim Turner, N.Y. Jets......	0	33	32	129	1969
Jan Stenerud, Kansas City....	0	26	30	116	1970
Garo Yepremian, Miami....	0	33	28	117	1971
Bobby Howfield, N.Y. Jets....	0	40	27	121	1972
Roy Gerela, Pittsburgh....	0	36	29	123	1973
Roy Gerela, Pittsburgh....	0	33	20	93	1974
O.J. Simpson, Buffalo......	23	0	0	138	1975
Toni Linhart, Baltimore....	0	49	20	109	1976
Errol Mann, Oakland.....	0	39	20	99	1977
Pat Leahy, N.Y. Jets......	0	41	22	107	1978
John Smith, New England....	0	46	23	115	1979
John Smith, New England....	0	51	26	129	1980
Jim Breech, Cincinnati....	0	49	22	115	1981
Marcus Allen, L.A. Raiders....	14	0	0	84	1982
Gary Anderson, Pittsburgh....	0	38	21	119	1983
Gary Anderson, Pittsburgh....	0	45	24	117	1984
Gary Anderson, Pittsburgh....	0	40	33	139	1985
Tony Franklin, New England....	0	44	32	140	1986
Jim Breech, Cincinnati....	0	25	24	97	1987
Scott Norwood, Buffalo......	0	33	32	129	1988

Rushing

Player, team	Yds	Atts	TD	Year
Abner Haynes, Dallas......	875	156	9	1960
Billy Cannon, Houston.......	948	200	6	1961
Cookie Gilchrest, Buffalo......	1,096	214	13	1962
Clem Daniels, Oakland.......	1,099	215	3	1963
Cookie Gilchrest, Buffalo......	981	230	6	1964
Paul Lowe, San Diego........	1,121	222	7	1965
Jim Nance, Boston.......	1,458	299	11	1966
Jim Nance, Boston.......	1,216	269	7	1967
Paul Robinson, Cincinnati.......	1,023	238	8	1968
Dick Post, San Diego........	873	182	6	1969
Floyd Little, Denver.......	901	209	3	1970
Floyd Little, Denver.......	1,133	284	6	1971
O.J. Simpson, Buffalo.......	1,251	292	6	1972
O.J. Simpson, Buffalo.......	2,003	332	12	1973
Otis Armstrong, Denver.......	1,407	263	9	1974
O.J. Simpson, Buffalo.......	1,817	329	16	1975
O.J. Simpson, Buffalo.......	1,503	290	8	1976
Mark van Eeghen, Oakland.......	1,273	324	7	1977
Earl Campbell, Houston.......	1,450	302	13	1978
Earl Campbell, Houston.......	1,697	368	19	1979
Earl Campbell, Houston.......	1,934	373	13	1980
Earl Campbell, Houston.......	1,376	361	10	1981
Freeman McNeil, N.Y. Jets.......	786	151	6	1982
Curt Warner, Seattle.......	1,446	335	13	1983
Earnest Jackson, San Diego.......	1,179	296	8	1984
Marcus Allen, L.A. Raiders.......	1,759	380	11	1985
Curt Warner, Seattle.......	1,481	319	13	1986
Eric Dickerson, L.A. Rams, Indianapolis.	1,288*	283	6	1987
Eric Dickerson, Indianapolis.........	1,659	388	14	1988

*1,011 AFC yards led conference.

World Almanac/NEA Jim Thorpe Trophy Winners

The World Almanac/NEA Jim Thorpe Trophy goes to the most valuable player as chosen by the NFL Players Association in 1987.

1955	Harlon Hill, Chicago Bears	1972	Larry Brown, Washington Redskins
1956	Frank Gifford, N.Y. Giants	1973	O.J. Simpson, Buffalo Bills
1957	John Unitas, Baltimore Colts	1974	Ken Stabler, Oakland Raiders
1958	Jim Brown, Cleveland Browns	1975	Fran Tarkenton, Minnesota Vikings
1959	Charley Conerly, N.Y. Giants	1976	Bert Jones, Baltimore Colts
1960	Norm Van Brocklin, Philadelphia Eagles	1977	Walter Payton, Chicago Bears
1961	Y.A. Tittle, N.Y. Giants	1978	Earl Campbell, Houston Oilers
1962	Jim Taylor, Green Bay Packers	1979	Earl Campbell, Houston Oilers
1963	Jim Brown, Cleveland Browns; Y.A. Tittle, N.Y. Giants	1980	Earl Campbell, Houston Oilers
1964	Lenny Moore, Baltimore Colts	1981	Ken Anderson, Cincinnati Bengals
1965	Jim Brown, Cleveland Browns	1982	Dan Fouts, San Diego Chargers
1966	Bart Starr, Green Bay Packers	1983	Joe Theismann, Washington Redskins
1967	John Unitas, Baltimore Colts	1984	Dan Marino, Miami Dolphins
1968	Earl Morrall, Baltimore Colts	1985	Walter Payton, Chicago Bears
1969	Roman Gabriel, Los Angeles Rams	1986	Phil Simms, N.Y. Giants
1970	John Brodie, San Francisco 49ers	1987	Jerry Rice, San Francisco
1971	Bob Griese, Miami Dolphins	1988	Roger Craig, San Francisco

Super Bowl MVPs

1967	Bart Starr, Green Bay	1975	Franco Harris, Pittsburgh	1983	John Riggins, Washington
1968	Bart Starr, Green Bay	1976	Lynn Swann, Pittsburgh	1984	Marcus Allen, L.A. Raiders
1969	Joe Namath, N.Y. Jets	1977	Fred Biletnikoff, Oakland	1985	Joe Montana, San Francisco
1970	Len Dawson, Kansas City	1978	Randy White, Harvey Martin, Dallas	1986	Richard Dent, Chicago
1971	Chuck Howley, Dallas	1979	Terry Bradshaw, Pittsburgh	1987	Phil Simms, N.Y. Giants
1972	Roger Staubach, Dallas	1980	Terry Bradshaw, Pittsburgh	1988	Doug Williams, Washington
1973	Jake Scott, Miami	1981	Jim Plunkett, Oakland	1989	Jerry Rice, San Francisco
1974	Larry Csonka, Miami	1982	Joe Montana, San Francisco		

All-Time Professional Football Records

NFL, AFL, and All-American Football Conference

(at start of 1989 season)

Leading Lifetime Rushers

Player	League	Yrs	Att	Yards	Avg	Player	League	Yrs	Att	Yards	Avg
Walter Payton	NFL	13	3,838	16,726	4.4	O.J. Anderson	NFL	10	1,949	8,294	4.3
Jim Brown	NFL	9	2,359	12,312	5.2	Larry Csonka	AFL-NFL	11	1,891	8,081	4.3
Tony Dorsett	NFL	12	2,936	12,739	4.3	Mike Pruitt	NFL	11	1,844	7,378	4.0
Franco Harris	NFL	13	2,949	12,120	4.1	Leroy Kelly	NFL	10	1,727	7,274	4.2
John Riggins	NFL	14	2,916	11,352	3.9	George Rogers	NFL	7	1,692	7,176	4.2
O.J. Simpson	AFL-NFL	11	2,404	11,236	4.7	Marcus Allen	NFL	7	1,712	6,982	4.1
Eric Dickerson	NFL	6	2,136	9,915	4.6	John Henry Johnson	NFL-AFL	13	1,571	6,803	4.3
Joe Perry	AAFC-NFL	16	1,929	9,723	5.0	Freeman McNeil	NFL	8	1,525	6,794	4.5
Earl Campbell	NFL	8	2,187	9,407	4.3	Wilbert Montgomery	NFL	9	1,540	6,789	4.4
Jim Taylor	NFL	10	1,941	8,597	4.4	Chuck Muncie	NFL	9	1,561	6,702	4.3

Most Yards Gained, Season — 2,105, Eric Dickerson, Los Angeles Rams, 1984.
Most Yards Gained, Game — 275, Walter Payton, Chicago Bears vs. Minnesota Vikings, Nov. 20, 1977.
Most Games, 100 Yards or more, Season — 12, Eric Dickerson, Los Angeles Rams, 1984.
Most Games, 100 Yards or more, Career — 77, Walter Payton, Chicago Bears, 1975-87.
Most Touchdowns Rushing, Career — 110, Walter Payton, Chicago Bears, 1975-1987.
Most Touchdowns Rushing, Season — 24, John Riggins, Washington Redskins, 1983.
Most Touchdowns Rushing, Game — 6, Ernie Nevers, Chicago Cardinals vs. Chicago Bears, Nov. 8, 1929.
Most Rushing Attempts, Season — 407, James Wilder, Tampa Bay Buccaneers, 1984.
Most Rushing Attempts, Game — 45, Jamie Morris, Washington Redskins vs. Cincinnati Bengals, Dec. 17, 1988.
Longest run from Scrimmage — 99 yds., Tony Dorsett, Dallas vs. Minnesota, Jan. 3, 1983 (scored touchdown).

Leading Lifetime Passers
(Minimum 1,500 attempts)

Player	League	Yrs	Att	Comp	Yds	Pts*	Player	League	Yrs	Att	Comp	Yds	Pts*
Joe Montana	NFL	10	3,673	2,322	27,533	92.0	Ken Anderson	NFL	16	4,475	2,654	32,838	81.9
Dan Marino	NFL	6	3,100	1,866	23,856	91.5	Danny White	NFL	13	2,950	1,761	21,959	81.7
Otto Graham	AAFC-NFL	10	2,626	1,464	23,584	86.6	Bart Starr	NFL	16	3,149	1,808	24,718	80.5
Boomer Esiason	NFL	5	1,830	1,038	14,825	86.2	Jim McMahon	NFL	7	1,513	874	11,203	80.4
Dave Krieg	NFL	9	2,344	1,358	17,549	85.5	Fran Tarkenton	NFL	18	6,467	3,686	47,003	80.4
Ken O'Brien	NFL	5	1,990	1,183	14,423	85.0	Dan Fouts	NFL	15	5,604	3,294	43,040	80.2
Roger Staubach	NFL	11	2,958	1,685	22,700	83.4	Johnny Unitas	NFL	18	5,186	2,830	40,239	78.2
Neil Lomax	NFL	8	3,153	1,817	22,771	82.7	Bert Jones	NFL	10	2,551	1,430	18,190	78.2
Sonny Jurgensen	NFL	18	4,262	2,433	32,224	82.6	Frank Ryan	NFL	13	2,133	1,090	16,042	77.6
Len Dawson	NFL-AFL	19	3,741	2,136	28,711	82.6	Joe Theismann	NFL	12	3,602	2,044	25,206	77.4

*Rating points based on performances in the following categories: Percentage of completions, percentage of touchdown passes, percentage of interceptions, and average gain per pass attempt.

Most Yards Gained, Season — 5,084, Dan Marino, Miami Dolphins, 1984.
Most Yards Gained, Game — 554, Norm Van Brocklin, Los Angeles Rams vs. New York Yankees, Sept. 18, 1951 (27 completions in 41 attempts).
Most Touchdowns Passing, Career — 342, Fran Tarkenton, Minnesota Vikings, 1961-66; N.Y. Giants, 1967-71; Vikings, 1972-78.
Most Touchdown Passing, Season — 48, Dan Marino, Miami Dolphins, 1984.
Most Touchdown Passing, Game — 7, Sid Luckman, Chicago Bears vs. New York Giants, Nov. 14, 1943; Adrian Burk, Philadelphia Eagles vs. Washington Redskins, Oct. 17, 1954; George Blanda, Houston Oilers vs. New York Titans, Nov. 19, 1961; Y.A. Tittle, New York Giants vs. Washington Redskins, Oct. 28, 1962; Joe Kapp, Minnesota Vikings vs. Baltimore Colts, Sept. 28, 1969.
Most Passing Attempts, Season — 623, Dan Marino, Miami Dolphins, 1986.
Most Passing Attempts, Game — 68, George Blanda, Houston Oilers vs. Buffalo Bills, Nov. 1, 1964 (37 completions).
Most Passes Completed, Season — 378, Dan Marino, Miami Dolphins, 1986.
Most Passes Completed, Game — 42, Richard Todd, N.Y. Jets vs. San Francisco 49ers, Sept. 21, 1980.
Most Consecutive Passes Completed — 22, Joe Montana, S. F. vs. Cleveland, (5), Nov. 29, & Green Bay (17), Dec. 6, 1987.
Most Consecutive Games, Touchdown Passes — 47, John Unitas, Baltimore Colts, 1956-1960.

Leading Lifetime Receivers

Player	League	Yrs	No	Yds	Avg	Player	League	Yrs	No	Yds	Avg
Steve Largent	NFL	13	791	12,686	16.0	Art Monk	NFL	9	576	7,979	13.9
Charlie Joiner	NFL	18	750	12,146	16.2	Lionel Taylor	AFL	10	567	7,195	12.7
Charley Taylor	NFL	13	649	9,110	14.0	Wes Chandler	NFL	11	559	8,966	16.0
Don Maynard	AFL-NFL	15	633	11,834	18.7	Lance Alworth	AFL-NFL	11	542	10,266	18.9
Raymond Berry	NFL	13	631	9,275	14.7	Kellen Winslow	NFL	9	541	6,741	12.5
Ozzie Newsome	NFL	11	610	7,416	12.2	John Stallworth	NFL	14	537	8,723	16.2
James Lofton	NFL	11	599	11,085	18.5	Bobby Mitchell	NFL	11	521	7,954	15.3
Harold Carmichael	NFL	14	590	8,985	15.2	Nat Moore	NFL	13	510	7,546	14.8
Fred Biletnikoff	AFL-NFL	14	589	8,974	15.2	Stanley Morgan	NFL	12	506	9,866	19.5
Harold Jackson	NFL	16	579	10,372	17.9	Dwight Clark	NFL	9	506	6,750	13.3

Most Yards Gained, Season — 1,746, Charley Hennigan, Houston Oilers, 1961.
Most Yards Gained, Game — 309, Stephone Paige, Kansas City Chiefs vs. San Diego Chargers, Dec. 22, 1985.
Most Pass Receptions, Season — 106, Art Monk, Washington Redskins, 1984.
Most Pass Receptions, Game — 18, Tom Fears, Los Angeles Rams vs. Green Bay Packers, Dec. 3, 1950 (189 yards).
Most Consecutive Games, Pass Receptions — 152, Steve Largent, Seattle Seahawks, 1976-1987.
Most Touchdown Passes, Career — 99, Don Hutson, Green Bay Packers, 1935-1945.
Most Touchdown Passes, Season — 22, Jerry Rice, San Francisco 49ers, 1987.
Most Touchdown Passes, Game — 5, Bob Shaw, Chicago Cardinals vs. Baltimore Colts, Oct. 2, 1950; Kellen Winslow, San Diego vs. Oakland, Nov. 22, 1981.

Leading Lifetime Scorers

Player	League	Yrs	TD	PAT	FG	Total	Player	League	Yrs	TD	PAT	FG	Total
George Blanda	NFL-AFL	26	9	943	335	2,002	Don Cockroft	NFL	13	0	432	216	1,080
Jan Stenerud	AFL-NFL	19	0	580	373	1,699	Garo Yepremian	AFL-NFL	14	0	444	210	1,074
Lou Groza	AAFC-NFL	21	1	810	264	1,608	Bruce Gossett	NFL	11	0	374	219	1,031
Jim Turner	AFL-NFL	16	1	521	304	1,439	Sam Baker	NFL	15	2	428	179	977
Mark Moseley	NFL	16	0	482	300	1,382	Rafael Septien	NFL	10	0	420	180	960
Jim Bakken	NFL	17	0	534	282	1,380	Lou Michaels	NFL	13	1	386	187	955*
Fred Cox	NFL	15	0	519	282	1,365	Nick Lowery	NFL	10	0	304	201	907
Pat Leahy	NFL	15	0	467	241	1,190	Roy Gerela	AFL-NFL	11	0	351	184	903
Chris Bahr	NFL	13	0	461	224	1,133	Jim Breech	NFL	10	0	381	172	897
Gino Cappelletti	AFL	11	42	350	176	1,130	*Includes safety.						
Ray Wersching	NFL	15	0	456	222	1,122							

Most Points, Season — 176, Paul Hornung, Green Bay Packers, 1960 (15 TD's, 41 PAT's, 15 FG's).
Most Points, Game — 40, Ernie Nevers, Chicago Cardinals vs. Chicago Bears, Nov. 28, 1929 (6 TD's, 4 PAT's).
Most Touchdowns, Season — 24, John Riggins, Washington Redskins, 1984 (24 rushing).
Most Touchdowns, Game — 6, Ernie Nevers, Chicago Cardinals vs. Chicago Bears, Nov. 28, 1929 (6 rushing); Dub Jones, Cleveland Browns vs. Chicago Bears, Nov. 25, 1951 (4 rushing, 2 pass receptions); Gale Sayers, Chicago Bears vs. San Francisco 49ers, Dec. 12, 1965 (4 rushing, 1 pass reception, 1 punt return).
Most Points After Touchdown, Season — 66, Uwe von Schamann, Miami Dolphins, 1984.
Most Consecutive Points After Touchdown — 234, Tommy Davis, San Francisco 49ers, 1959-1969.
Most Field Goals, Game — 7, Jim Bakken, St. Louis Cardinals vs. Pittsburgh Steelers, Sept. 24, 1967.
Most Field Goals, Season — 35, Ali Haji-Sheikh, N.Y. Giants, 1983.
Most Field Goals Attempted, Season — 49, Bruce Gossett, Los Angeles Rams, 1966; Curt Knight, Washington Redskins, 1971.
Most Field Goals Attempted, Game — 9, Jim Bakken, St. Louis Cardinals vs. Pittsburgh Steelers, Sept. 24, 1967 (7 successful).
Most Consecutive Field Goals — 23, Mark Moseley, Washington Redskins, 1981-1982.
Most Consecutive Games, Field Goal — 31, Fred Cox, Minnesota Vikings, 1968-1970.
Longest Field Goal — 63 yds., Tom Dempsey, New Orleans Saints vs. Detroit Lions, Nov. 8, 1970.
Highest Field Goal Completion Percentage, Season (20 attempts) — 95.24 Mark Moseley, Washington Redskins, 1982 (20 FG's in 21 attempts).

Pass Interceptions

Most Passes Had Intercepted, Game — 8, Jim Hardy, Chicago Cardinals vs. Philadelphia Eagles, Sept. 24, 1950 (39 attempts)
Most Passes Had Intercepted, Season — 42, George Blanda, Houston Oilers, 1962 (418 attempts).
Most Passes Had Intercepted, Career — 277, George Blanda, Chicago Bears, 1949-1958; Houston Oilers, 1960-1966; Oakland Raiders, 1967-1975 (4,000 attempts).
Most Consecutive Passes Attempted Without Interception — 294, Bart Starr, Green Bay Packers, 1964-1965.
Most Interceptions By, Season — 14, Dick Lane, Los Angeles Rams, 1952.
Most Interceptions By, Career — 81, Paul Krause, Washington Redskins, 1964-67; Minnesota Vikings, 1968-79.
Most Consecutive Games, Passes Intercepted By — 8, Tom Morrow, Oakland Raiders, 1962 (4), 1963 (4).

Punting

Most Punts, Game — 15, John Teltschick, Philadelphia Eagles vs. N.Y. Giants, Dec. 6, 1987.
Most Punts, Career — 1,154, Dave Jennings, N.Y. Giants, 1974-1984; N.Y. Jets, 1985-1987.
Most Punts, Season — 114, Bob Parsons, Chicago Bears, 1981.
Highest Punting Average, Season (20 punts) — 51.40, Sam Baugh, Washington Redskins, 1940 (35 punts).
Longest Punt — 98 yds., Steve O'Neal, New York Jets vs. Denver Broncos, Sept. 21, 1969.

Kickoff Returns

Most Yardage Returning Kickoffs, Career — 6,922, Ron Smith, Chicago Bears, 1965; Atlanta Falcons, 1966-67; Los Angeles Rams, 1968-69; Chicago Bears, 1970-72; San Diego Chargers, 1973; Oakland Raiders, 1974.
Most Yardage Returning Kickoffs, Season — 1,345, Buster Rhymes, Minnesota Vikings, 1985.
Most Yardage Returning Kickoffs, Game — 294, Wally Triplett, Detroit Lions vs. Los Angeles Rams, Oct. 29, 1950 (4 returns).
Most Touchdowns Scored via Kickoff Returns, Career — 6, Ollie Matson, Chicago Cardinals, 1952 (2), 1954, 1956, 1958 (2); Gale Sayers, Chicago Bears, 1965, 1966 (2), 1967 (3); Travis Williams, Green Bay Packers, 1967 (4), 1969; Los Angeles Rams, 1971.
Most Touchdowns Scored via Kickoff Returns, Season — 4, Travis Williams, Green Bay Packers, 1967; Cecil Turner, Chicago Bears, 1970.
Most Touchdowns Scored via Kickoff Returns, Game — 2, Tim Brown, Philadelphia Eagles vs. Dallas Cowboys, Nov. 6, 1966; Travis Williams, Green Bay Packers vs. Cleveland Browns, Nov. 12, 1967; Ron Brown, Los Angeles Rams vs. Green Bay Packers, Nov. 24, 1985.
Most Kickoff Returns, Career — 275, Ron Smith, Chicago Bears, 1965; Atlanta Falcons, 1966-67; Los Angeles Rams, 1968-69; Chicago Bears, 1970-72; San Diego Chargers, 1973; Oakland Raiders, 1974.
Most Kickoff Returns, Season — 60, Drew Hill, Los Angeles Rams, 1981.
Longest Kickoff Return — 106 yds., Al Carmichael, Green Bay Packers vs. Chicago Bears, October 7, 1956; Noland Smith, Kansas City vs. Denver, Dec. 17, 1967; Roy Green, St. Louis Cardinals vs. Dallas Cowboys, Oct. 21, 1979 (all scored TD).

Punt Returns

Most Yardage Returning Punts, Career — 3,317, Billy Johnson, Houston, 1974-80, Atlanta, 1982-87, Washington, 1988.
Most Yardage Returning Punts, Season — 692, Fulton Walker, Miami-L.A. Raiders, 1985.
Most Yardage Returning Punts, Game — 207, Leroy Irvin, Los Angeles Rams vs. Atlanta Falcons, Oct. 11. 1981.
Most Touchdowns Scored via Punt Returns, Career — 8, Jack Christiansen, Detroit Lions, 1951-1958; Rick Upchurch, Denver Broncos, 1975-83.
Most Punt Returns, Career — 282, Billy Johnson, Houston Oilers, 1974-1980; Atlanta Falcons, 1982-1987, Washington, 1988.
Most Punt Returns, Season — 70, Danny Reece, Tampa Bay Buccaneers, 1979.

Miscellaneous Records

Most Fumbles, Season — 17, Dan Pastorini, Houston Oilers, 1973; Warren Moon, Houston Oilers, 1984.
Most Fumbles, Game — 7, Len Dawson, Kansas City Chiefs vs. San Diego Chargers, Nov. 15, 1964.
Winning Streak (Regular Season) — 17 games, Chicago Bears, 1933-34.
Most Seasons, Active Player — 26, George Blanda, Chicago Bears, 1949-1958; Houston Oilers, 1960-1966 and Oakland, 67-75.
Most Consecutive Games Played, Career — 282, Jim Marshall, Cleveland Browns, 1960; Minnesota Vikings, 1961-1979.

First-Round Selections in the 1989 NFL Draft

Team	Player	Pos.	College	Team	Player	Pos.	College
1—Dallas	Troy Aikman	QB	UCLA	15—Seattle	Andy Heck	OT	Notre Dame
2—Green Bay	Tony Mandarich	OT	Michigan State	16—New England	Hart L. Dykes	WR	Oklahoma State
3—Detroit	Barry Sanders	RB	Oklahoma State	17—Phoenix	Joe Wolf	OG	Boston College
4—Kansas City	Derrick Thomas	LB	Alabama	18—N.Y. Giants	Brian Williams	OG	Minnesota
5—Atlanta	Deion Sanders	DB	Florida State	19—New Orleans	Wayne Martin	DE	Arkansas
6—Tampa Bay	Broderick Thomas	LB	Nebraska	20—Denver	Steve Atwater	DB	Arkansas
7—Pittsburgh	Tim Worley	RB	Georgia	21—L.A. Rams	Bill Hawkins	DE	Miami, Fla.
8—San Diego	Burt Grossman	DE	Pittsburgh	22—Indianapolis	Andre Rison	WR	Michigan State
9—Miami	Sammie Smith	RB	Florida State	23—Houston	David Williams	OT	Florida
10—Phoenix	Eric Hall	LB	LSU	24—Pittsburgh	Tom Ricketts	OT	Pittsburgh
11—Chicago	Donnell Woolford	DB	Clemson	25—Miami	Louis Oliver	DB	Florida
12—Chicago	Trace Armstrong	DE	Florida	26—L.A. Rams	Cleveland Gary	RB	Miami
13—Cleveland	Eric Metcalf	RB	Texas	27—Atlanta	Shawn Collins	WR	N. Arizona
14—N.Y. Jets	Jeff Lageman	LB	Virginia	28—San Francisco	Keith DeLong	LB	Tennessee

American Football League

Year	Eastern Division	Western Division	Playoff
1960	Houston Oilers (10-4-0)	L. A. Chargers (10-4-0)	Houston 24, Los Angeles 16
1961	Houston Oilers (10-3-1)	San Diego Chargers (12-2-0)	Houston 10, San Diego 3
1962	Houston Oilers (11-3-0)	Dallas Texans (11-3-0)	Dallas 20, Houston 17(b)
1963	Boston Patriots (8-6-1)(a)	San Diego Chargers (11-3-0)	San Diego 51, Boston 10
1964	Buffalo Bills (12-2-0)	San Diego Chargers (8-5-1)	Buffalo 20, San Diego 7
1965	Buffalo Bills (10-3-1)	San Diego Chargers (9-2-3)	Buffalo 23, San Diego 0
1966	Buffalo Bills (9-4-1)	Kansas City Chiefs (11-2-1)	Kansas City 31, Buffalo 7
1967	Houston Oilers (9-4-1)	Oakland Raiders (13-1-0)	Oakland 40, Houston 7
1968	New York Jets (11-3-0)	Oakland Raiders (12-2-0)(a)	New York 27, Oakland 23
1969	New York Jets (10-4-0)	Oakland Raiders (12-1-1)	Kansas City 17, Oakland 7(c)

(a) won divisional playoff (b) won at 2:45 of second overtime. (c) Kansas City defeated Jets to make playoffs.

Pro Football Hall of Fame, Canton, Ohio

Herb Adderley	Mike Ditka	Ken Houston	John (Blood) McNally	Art Shell
Lance Alworth	Art Donovan	Cal Hubbard	Mike Michalske	O.J. Simpson
Doug Atkins	Paddy Driscoll	Sam Huff	Wayne Millner	Bart Starr
Morris (Red) Badgro	Bill Dudley	Lamar Hunt	Bobby Mitchell	Roger Staubach
Cliff Battles	Turk Edwards	Don Hutson	Ron Mix	Ernie Stautner
Sammy Baugh	Weeb Ewbank	John Henry Johnson	Lenny Moore	Ken Strong
Chuck Bednarik	Tom Fears	Deacon Jones	Marion Motley	Joe Stydahar
Bert Bell	Ray Flaherty	Sonny Jurgensen	George Musso	Fran Tarkenton
Bobby Bell	Len Ford	Walt Kiesling	Bronko Nagurski	Charlie Taylor
Raymond Berry	Dr. Daniel Fortmann	Frank (Bruiser) Kinard	Joe Namath	Jim Taylor
Charles Bidwell	Frank Gatski	Curly Lambeau	Greasy Neale	Jim Thorpe
Fred Biletnikoff	Bill George	Dick (Night Train) Lane	Ernie Nevers	Y.A. Tittle
George Blanda	Frank Gifford	Jim Langer	Ray Nitschke	George Trafton
Mel Blount	Sid Gillman	Willie Lanier	Leo Nomellini	Charlie Trippi
Terry Bradshaw	Otto Graham	Yale Lary	Merlin Olsen	Emlen Tunnell
Jim Brown	Red Grange	Dante Lavelli	Jim Otto	Clyde (Bulldog) Turner
Paul Brown	Joe Greene	Bobby Layne	Steve Owen	Johnny Unitas
Roosevelt Brown	Forrest Gregg	Tuffy Leemans	Alan Page	Gene Upshaw
Willie Brown	Lou Groza	Bob Lilly	Clarence (Ace) Parker	Norm Van Brocklin
Dick Butkus	Joe Guyon	Vince Lombardi	Jim Parker	Steve Van Buren
Tony Canadeo	George Halas	Sid Luckman	Joe Perry	Doak Walker
Joe Carr	Jack Ham	Link Lyman	Pete Pihos	Paul Warfield
Guy Chamberlin	Ed Healey	Tim Mara	Hugh (Shorty) Ray	Bob Waterfield
Jack Christiansen	Mel Hein	Gino Marchetti	Dan Reeves	Arnie Weinmeister
Dutch Clark	Pete Henry	George Marshall	Jim Ringo	Bill Willis
George Connor	Arnold Herber	Ollie Matson	Andy Robustelli	Larry Wilson
Jim Conzelman	Bill Hewitt	Don Maynard	Art Rooney	Alex Wojciechowicz
Larry Csonka	Clarke Hinkle	George McAfee	Pete Rozelle	Willie Wood
Willie Davis	Elroy (Crazy Legs) Hirsch	Mike McCormack	Gale Sayers	
Len Dawson	Paul Hornung	Hugh McElhenny	Joe Schmidt	

NFL Stadiums

Name, location	Capacity	Name, location	Capacity
Anaheim Stadium, Anaheim, Cal.	69,007	Mile High Stadium, Denver, Col.	76,273
Arrowhead Stadium, Kansas City, Mo.	78,067	Milwaukee County Stadium.	56,051
Astrodome, Houston, Tex.	50,599	Pontiac Silverdome, Mich.	80,638
Atlanta-Fulton County Stadium.	59,673	Rich Stadium, Buffalo, N.Y.	80,290
Candlestick Park, San Francisco, Cal.	64,252	Riverfront Stadium, Cincinnati, Oh.	59,754
Cleveland Stadium.	80,098	Joe Robbie Stadium, Miami, Fla.	75,000
Giants Stadium, E. Rutherford, N.J.	76,891	San Diego Jack Murphy Stadium, San Diego.	60,750
Hoosier Dome, Indianapolis, Ind.	60,127	Soldier Field, Chicago, Ill.	65,793
Hubert H. Humphrey Metrodome, Minneapolis	63,000	Sullivan Stadium, Foxboro, Mass.	60,794
Robert F. Kennedy Stadium, Wash., D.C.	55,642	Sun Devil Stadium, Tempe, Ariz.	72,000
Kingdome, Seattle, Wash.	64,984	Tampa Stadium, Tampa, Fla.	74,317
Lambeau Field, Green Bay, Wis.	57,063	Texas Stadium, Irving, Tex.	63,855
Los Angeles Memorial Coliseum	92,488	Three Rivers Stadium, Pittsburgh, Pa.	59,000
Louisiana Superdome, New Orleans.	69,551	Veterans Stadium, Philadelphia, Pa.	66,356

BOWLING

PBA Leading Money Winners

Total winnings are from PBA, ABC Masters, and BPAA All-Star tournaments only, and do not include numerous other tournaments or earnings from special television shows and matches.

Year	Bowler	Dollars	Year	Bowler	Dollars	Year	Bowler	Dollars
1962	Don Carter	49,972	1971	Johnny Petraglia	85,065	1980	Wayne Webb	116,700
1963	Dick Weber	46,333	1972	Don Johnson	56,648	1981	Earl Anthony	164,735
1964	Bob Strampe	33,592	1973	Don McCune	69,000	1982	Earl Anthony	134,760
1965	Dick Weber	47,674	1974	Earl Anthony	99,585	1983	Earl Anthony	135,605
1966	Wayne Zahn	54,720	1975	Earl Anthony	107,585	1984	Mark Roth	158,712
1967	Dave Davis	54,165	1976	Earl Anthony	110,833	1985	Mike Aulby	201,200
1968	Jim Stefanich	67,377	1977	Mark Roth	105,583	1986	Walter Ray Williams Jr.	145,550
1969	Billy Hardwick	64,160	1978	Mark Roth	134,500	1987	Pete Weber	175,491
1970	Mike McGrath	52,049	1979	Mark Roth	124,517	1988	Brian Voss	225,485

Leading PBA Averages by Year

Year	Bowler	Average	Year	Bowler	Average	Year	Bowler	Average
1962	Don Carter	212.844	1971	Don Johnson	213.977	1980	Earl Anthony	218.535
1963	Billy Hardwick	210.346	1972	Don Johnson	215.290	1981	Mark Roth	216.699
1964	Ray Bluth	210.512	1973	Earl Anthony	215.799	1982	Marshall Holman	212.844
1965	Dick Weber	211.895	1974	Earl Anthony	219.394	1983	Earl Anthony	216.645
1966	Wayne Zahn	208.663	1975	Earl Anthony	219.060	1984	Marshall Holman	213.911
1967	Wayne Zahn	212.342	1976	Mark Roth	215.970	1985	Mark Baker	213.718
1968	Jim Stefanich	211.895	1977	Mark Roth	218.174	1986	John Gant	214.378
1969	Bill Hardwick	212.957	1978	Mark Roth	219.834	1987	Marshall Holman	216.801
1970	Nelson Burton Jr.	214.908	1979	Mark Roth	221.662	1988	Mark Roth	218.036

Firestone Tournament of Champions

Year	Winner	Year	Winner	Year	Winner	Year	Winner
1965	Billy Hardwick	1972	Mike Durbin	1978	Earl Anthony	1984	Mike Durbin
1966	Wayne Zahn	1973	Jim Godman	1979	George Pappas	1985	Mark Williams
1967	Jim Stefanich	1974	Earl Anthony	1980	Wayne Webb	1986	Marshall Holman
1968	Dave Davis	1975	Dave Davis	1981	Steve Cook	1987	Pete Weber
1969	Jim Godman	1976	Marshall Holman	1982	Mike Durbin	1988	Mark Williams
1970	Don Johnson	1977	Mike Berlin	1983	Joe Berardi	1989	Del Ballard Jr.
1971	Johnny Petraglia						

PBA Hall of Fame

Performance

Bill Allen
Glenn Allison
Earl Anthony
Barry Asher
Ray Bluth
Nelson Burton Jr.
Don Carter
Dave Davis
Gary Dickinson
Mike Durbin

Buzz Fazio
Jim Godman
Johnny Guenther
Billy Hardwick
Don Johnson
Larry Laub
Mike McGrath
George Pappas
Johnny Petraglia
Dick Ritger

Mark Roth
Jim St. John
Carmen Salvino
Bob Strampe
Harry Smith
Dave Soutar
Jim Stefanich
Dick Weber
Billy Welu
Wayne Zahn

Meritorious service

John Archibald
Eddie Elias
Frank Esposito
Dick Evans
Raymond Firestone
E. A. "Bud" Fisher
Lou Frantz
Harry Golden
Ted Hoffman Jr.

Joe Joseph
John Jowdy
Joseph Kelley
Steve Nagy
Chuck Pezzano
Joe Richards
Chris Schenkel
Lorraine Stilzlein

American Bowling Congress Championships in 1989

Regular Division

Individual—Pete Tetreqult, Lebanon, N.H., 813.
All Events—George Hall, Mundelein, Ill., 2,227.
Doubles—Gus Yannoras & Gary Dardzsewski, Milwaukee, Wis., 1,499.

Team—Chilton Vending, Wichita, Kan, 3,481.

Booster Division

Team—National By-Products, Wichita, Kan., 2,813.

All-Time Records for League and Tournament Play

Type of record	Holder of record	Year	Score	Competition
High team total	Budweiser Beer, St. Louis	1958	3,858	League
High team game	Sunset Bowl, Kansas City, Kan.	1987	1,382	League
High doubles total	Thomas Jordan & Ken Yonker Jr, Paterson, N.J.	1989	1,655	League
High doubles game	John Cotta and Steve Larson, Manteca, Cal.	1981	600	Tournament
High individual total	Thomas Jordan, Paterson, N.J.	1989	899	League
High all events score	Paul Andrews, East Moline, Ill.	1981	2,415	Tournament

Masters Bowling Tournament Champions

Year	Winner	Year	Winner	Year	Winner
1979	Doug Myers, El Toro, Cal.	1983	Mike Lastowski, Havre de Grace, Md.	1986	Mark Fahy, Chicago, Ill.
1980	Neil Burton, St. Louis, Mo.	1984	Earl Anthony, Dublin, Cal.	1987	Rick Steelsmith, Wichita, Kan.
1981	Randy Lightfoot, St. Charles, Mo.	1985	Steve Wunderlich, St. Louis, Mo.	1988	Del Ballard Jr., Richardson, Tex.
1982	Joe Berardi, Brooklyn, N.Y.			1989	Mike Aubly, Indianapolis, Ind.

Bowlers with 15 or More Sanctioned 300 Games

John Wilcox Jr., Shavertown, Pa.	32	Dave Heller, Highland Falls, N.Y.	21	Dave Williams, Sebastopal, Cal.	17
Jim Johnson Jr., Wilmington, Del.	31	Mark Stibora, Cleveland, Oh.	20	Don Johnson, Las Vegas, Nev.	16
Bob Learn Jr, Erie, Pa.	30	Mitch Jabczenski, Detroit, Mich.	20	Dave Davis, Tinton Falls, N.J.	15
Ron Woolet, Louisville, Ky.	29	Dave Soutar, Kansas City, Mo.	19	Ronnie Graham, Louisville, Ky.	15
Elvin Mesger, Sullivan, Mo.	27	Steve Carson, Oklahoma City, Okla	19	Byron Russell, Tulsa, Okla.	15
Tony Torrice, Wolcott, Conn.	23	Dick Weber, St. Louis, Mo.	18	Don McCune, Munster, Ind.	15
Teata Semiz, Fairfield, N.J.	22	George Billick, Old Forge, Pa.	17	Bob Hart, Columbus, Oh.	15

Women's International Bowling Congress Champions in 1989

All Events—Nancy Fehr, Cincinnati, Oh.
Singles—Lorraine Anderson, Northville, Mich.
Doubles—Diana Goodman-Rene Felming, Chino Hill Cal./

Oklahoma City, Okla.
Team—Robby's, Glendale, Cal.

Most Santioned 300 Games

Jeanne Maiden, Solon, Oh. 15	Aleta Sill, Dearborn, Mich. 7	Pam Buckner, Reno, Nev. 5
Betty Morris, Stockton, Cal. 9	Toni Gillard, Beverly, Oh. 6	Regi Jonak, St. Peters, Mo. 5
Vicki Fischel, Westminster, Cal. 9	Ann Marie Pike, Cypress, Cal. 6	Carol Norman, Ardmore, Okla. 5
Cindy Coburn, Buffalo, N.Y. 9	Linda Kelly, Union, Oh. 6	Robin Romeo, Van Nuys, Cal. 5
Donna Adamek, Victorville, Cal. 8	Alayne Blomenberg, Cranston, R.I. 5	Cheryl Daniels, Detroit, Mich. 5
Tish Johnson, Panorama City, Cal. 8		

James E. Sullivan Memorial Trophy Winners

The James E. Sullivan Memorial Trophy, named after the former president of the AAU and inaugurated in 1930, is awarded annually by the AAU to the athlete who "by his or her performance, example and influence as an amateur, has done the most during the year to advance the cause of sportmanship."

Year	Winner	Sport	Year	Winner	Sport	Year	Winner	Sport
1930	Bobby Jones	Golf	1950	Fred Wilt	Track	1970	John Kinsella	Swimming
1931	Barney Berlinger	Track	1951	Rev. Robert Richards	Track	1971	Mark Spitz	Swimming
1932	Jim Bausch	Track	1952	Horace Ashenfelter	Track	1972	Frank Shorter	Track
1933	Glenn Cunningham	Track	1953	Dr. Sammy Lee	Diving	1973	Bill Walton	Basketball
1934	Bill Bonthron	Track	1954	Mal Whitfield	Track	1974	Rick Wohlhuter	Track
1935	Lawson Little	Golf	1955	Harrison Dillard	Track	1975	Tim Shaw	Swimming
1936	Glenn Morris	Track	1956	Patricia McCormick	Diving	1976	Bruce Jenner	Track
1937	Don Budge	Tennis	1957	Bobby Joe Morrow	Track	1977	John Naber	Swimming
1938	Don Lash	Track	1958	Glenn Davis	Track	1978	Tracy Caulkins	Swimming
1939	Joe Burk	Rowing	1959	Parry O'Brien	Track	1979	Kurt Thomas	Gymnastics
1940	Greg Rice	Track	1960	Rafer Johnson	Track	1980	Eric Heiden	Speed Skating
1941	Leslie MacMitchell	Track	1961	Wilma Rudolph Ward	Track	1981	Carl Lewis	Track
1942	Cornelius Warmerdam	Track	1962	James Beatty	Track	1982	Mary Decker	Track
1943	Gilbert Dodds	Track	1963	John Pennel	Track	1983	Edwin Moses	Track
1944	Ann Curtis	Swimming	1964	Don Schollander	Swimming	1984	Greg Louganis	Diving
1945	Doc Blanchard	Football	1965	Bill Bradley	Basketball	1985	Joan Benoit Samuelson	Marathon
1946	Arnold Tucker	Football	1966	Jim Ryun	Track	1986	Jackie Joyner-Kersee	Track
1947	John Kelly Jr.	Rowing	1967	Randy Matson	Track	1987	Jim Abbott	Baseball
1948	Robert Mathias	Track	1968	Debbie Meyer	Swimming	1988	Florence Griffith Joyner	Track
1949	Dick Button	Skating	1969	Bill Toomey	Track			

Pro Rodeo Championship Standings in 1988

Event	Winner	Money won	Event	Winner	Money won
All Around	Dave Appleton, Arlington, Tex.	$121,546	Steer Roping	Shaun Burchett, Pryor, Okla.	$33,197
Saddle Bronc	Clint Johnson, Spearfish, S.D.	82,660	Team Roping	Jake Barnes, Bloomfield, N.M. &	
Bareback	Marvin Garrett, Gillette, Wyo.	100,803		Clay O'Brien Cooper, Gilbert, Ariz.	84,578
Bull Riding	Jim Sharp, Kermit, Tex.	102,588	Women's Barrel	Charmayne James Rodman, Galt,	
Calf Roping	Joe Beaver, Victoria, Tex.	91,213	Racing	Cal.	130,540
Steer Wrestling	John W. Jones Jr., Morro Bay, Cal.	82,815			

Pro Rodeo Cowboy All Around Champions

Year	Winner	Money won	Year	Winner	Money won
1968	Larry Mahan, Salem, Ore.	$49,129	1978	Tom Ferguson, Miami, Okla.	$103,734
1969	Larry Mahan, Brooks, Ore.	57,726	1979	Tom Ferguson, Miami, Okla.	96,272
1970	Larry Mahan, Brooks, Ore.	41,493	1980	Paul Tierney, Rapid City, S.D.	105,568
1971	Phil Lyne, George West, Tex.	49,245	1981	Jimmie Cooper, Monument, N.M.	105,862
1972	Phil Lyne, George West, Tex.	60,852	1982	Chris Lybert, Coyote, Cal.	123,709
1973	Larry Mahan, Dallas, Tex.	64,447	1983	Roy Cooper, Durant, Okla.	153,391
1974	Tom Ferguson, Miami, Okla.	66,929	1984	Dee Pickett, Caldwell, Ida.	122,618
1975	Leo Camarillo, Oakdale, Cal.	50,300	1985	Lewis Feild, Elk Ridge, Ut.	130,347
	Tom Ferguson, Miami, Okla.	50,300	1986	Lewis Feild, Elk Ridge, Ut.	166,042
1976	Tom Ferguson, Miami, Okla.	87,908	1988	Lewis Feild, Elk Ridge, Ut.	144,335
1977	Tom Ferguson, Miami, Okla.	76,730	1988	Dave Appleton, Arlington, Tex.	121,546

Figure Skating Champions

U.S. Champions

World Champions

Men	Women	Year	Men	Women
Dick Button	Tenley Albright	1952	Dick Button, U.S.	Jacqueline du Bief, France
Hayes Jenkins	Tenley Albright	1953	Hayes Jenkins, U.S.	Tenley Albright, U.S.
Hayes Jenkins	Tenley Albright	1954	Hayes Jenkins, U.S.	Gundi Busch, W. Germany
Hayes Jenkins	Tenley Albright	1955	Hayes Jenkins, U.S.	Tenley Albright, U.S.
Hayes Jenkins	Tenley Albright	1956	Hayes Jenkins, U.S.	Carol Heiss, U.S.
Dave Jenkins	Carol Heiss	1957	Dave Jenkins, U.S.	Carol Heiss, U.S.
Dave Jenkins	Carol Heiss	1958	Dave Jenkins, U.S.	Carol Heiss, U.S.
Dave Jenkins	Carol Heiss	1959	Dave Jenkins, U.S.	Carol Heiss, U.S.
Dave Jenkins	Carol Heiss	1960	Alain Giletti, France	Carol Heiss, U.S.
Bradley Lord	Laurence Owen	1961	none	none
Monty Hoyt	Barbara Roles Pursley	1962	Don Jackson, Canada	Sjoukje Dijkstra, Neth.
Tommy Litz	Lorraine Hanlon	1963	Don McPherson, Canada	Sjoukje Dijkstra, Neth.
Scott Allen	Peggy Fleming	1964	Manfred Schnelldorfer, W. Germany	Sjoukje Dijkstra, Neth.
Gary Visconti	Peggy Fleming	1965	Alain Calmat, France	Petra Burka, Canada
Scott Allen	Peggy Fleming	1966	Emmerich Danzer, Austria	Peggy Fleming, U.S.
Gary Visconti	Peggy Fleming	1967	Emmerich Danzer, Austria	Peggy Fleming, U.S.
Tim Wood	Peggy Fleming	1968	Emmerich Danzer, Austria	Peggy Fleming, U.S.
Tim Wood	Janet Lynn	1969	Tim Wood, U.S.	Gabriele Seyfert, E. Germany
Tim Wood	Janet Lynn	1970	Tim Wood, U.S.	Gabriele Seyfert, E. Germany
John Misha Petkevich	Janet Lynn	1971	Ondrej Nepela, Czech.	Beatrix Schuba, Austria
Ken Shelley	Janet Lynn	1972	Ondrej Nepela, Czech.	Beatrix Schuba, Austria
Gordon McKellen Jr.	Janet Lynn	1973	Ondrej Nepela, Czech.	Karen Magnussen, Canada
Gordon McKellen Jr.	Dorothy Hamill	1974	Jan Hoffmann, E. Germany	Christine Errath, E. Germany
Gordon McKellen Jr.	Dorothy Hamill	1975	Sergei Volkov, USSR	Dianne de Leeuw, Neth.-U.S.
Terry Kubicka	Dorothy Hamill	1976	John Curry, Gt. Britain	Dorothy Hamill, U.S.
Charles Tickner	Linda Fratianne	1977	Vladimir Kovalev, USSR	Linda Fratianne, U.S.
Charles Tickner	Linda Fratianne	1978	Charles Tickner, U.S.	Anett Potzsch, E. Germany
Charles Tickner	Linda Fratianne	1979	Vladimir Kovalev, USSR	Linda Fratianne, U.S.
Charles Tickner	Linda Fratianne	1980	Jan Hoffmann, E. Germany	Anett Potzsch, E. Germany
Scott Hamilton	Elaine Zayak	1981	Scott Hamilton, U.S.	Denise Biellmann, Switzerland
Scott Hamilton	Rosalynn Sumners	1982	Scott Hamilton, U.S.	Elaine Zayak, U.S.
Scott Hamilton	Rosalynn Sumners	1983	Scott Hamilton, U.S.	Rosalynn Sumners, U.S.
Scott Hamilton	Rosalynn Sumners	1984	Scott Hamilton, U.S.	Katarina Witt, E. Germany
Brian Boitano	Tiffany Chin	1985	Aleksandr Fadeev, USSR	Katarina Witt, E. Germany
Brian Boitano	Debi Thomas	1986	Brian Boitano, U.S.	Debi Thomas, U.S.
Brian Boitano	Jill Trenary	1987	Brian Orser, Canada	Katarina Witt, E. Germany
Brian Boitano	Debi Thomas	1988	Brian Boitano, U.S.	Katarina Witt, E. Germany
Christopher Bowman	Jill Trenary	1989	Kurt Browning, Canada	Midori Ito, Japan

U.S. Pairs and Dancing Champions in 1989

Kristi Yamaguchi and Rudi Galindo won the 1989 U.S. pairs figure skating championship in Baltimore, Md. Susan Wynne and Joseph Druar triumphed in ice dancing.

American Power Boat Assn. Gold Cup Champions

Year	Boat	Driver	Year	Boat	Driver
1973	Miss Budweiser	Dean Chenoweth	1982	Atlas Van Lines	Chip Hanauer
1974	Pay'N Pak	George Henley	1983	Atlas Van Lines	Chip Hanauer
1975	Pay 'N Pak	George Henley	1984	Atlas Van Lines	Chip Hanauer
1976	Miss U.S.	Tom D'Eath	1985	Miller American	Chip Hanauer
1977	Atlas Van Lines	Bill Muncey	1986	Miller American	Chip Hanauer
1978	Atlas Van Lines	Bill Muncey	1987	Miller American	Chip Hanauer
1979	Atlas Van Lines	Bill Muncey	1988	Miller American	Chip Hanauer
1980	Miss Budweiser	Dean Chenoweth	1989	Miss Budweiser	Tom D'eath
1981	Miss Budweiser	Dean Chenoweth			

NCAA Wrestling Champions

Year	Champion	Year	Champion	Year	Champion	Year	Champion	Year	Champion
1964	Oklahoma State	1970	Iowa State	1975	Iowa	1980	Iowa	1985	Iowa
1965	Iowa State	1971	Oklahoma State	1976	Iowa	1981	Iowa	1986	Iowa
1966	Oklahoma State	1972	Iowa State	1977	Iowa State	1982	Iowa	1987	Iowa State
1967	Michigan State	1973	Iowa State	1978	Iowa	1983	Iowa	1988	Arizona State
1968	Oklahoma State	1974	Oklahoma	1979	Iowa	1984	Iowa	1989	Oklahoma State
1969	Iowa State								

Iditarod Trail Sled Dog Race in 1989

Joe Runyan won the 1989 Iditarod Trail Sled Dog Race by completing the 1,168-mile racce from Anchorage to Nome, Alaska in slightly more than 11 days. Susan Butcher, who had won the race the past 3 years, finished second. Runyon's victory was worth $50,000.

Tennis

U.S. Open Champions

Men's Singles

Year	Champion	Final opponent	Year	Champion	Final opponent
1910	William Larned	T. C. Bundy	1950	Arthur Larsen	Herbert Flam
1911	William Larned	Maurice McLoughlin	1951	Frank Sedgman	E. Victor Seixas Jr.
1912	Maurice McLoughlin	Wallace Johnson	1952	Frank Sedgman	Gardnar Mulloy
1913	Maurice McLoughlin	Richard Williams	1953	Tony Trabert	E. Victor Seixas Jr.
1914	Richard Williams	Maurice McLoughlin	1954	E. Victor Seixas Jr.	Rex Hartwig
1915	William Johnston	Maurice McLoughlin	1955	Tony Trabert	Ken Rosewall
1916	Richard Williams	William Johnston	1956	Ken Rosewall	Lewis Hoad
1917	Richard Murray	N. W. Niles	1957	Malcolm Anderson	Ashley Cooper
1918	Richard Murray	Bill Tilden	1958	Ashley Cooper	Malcolm Anderson
1919	William Johnston	Bill Tilden	1959	Neale A. Fraser	Alejandro Olmedo
1920	Bill Tilden	William Johnston	1960	Neale A. Fraser	Rod Laver
1921	Bill Tilden	Wallace Johnson	1961	Roy Emerson	Rod Laver
1922	Bill Tilden	William Johnston	1962	Rod Laver	Roy Emerson
1923	Bill Tilden	William Johnston	1963	Rafael Osuna	F. A. Froehling 3d
1924	Bill Tilden	William Johnston	1964	Roy Emerson	Fred Stolle
1925	Bill Tilden	William Johnston	1965	Manuel Santana	Cliff Drysdale
1926	Rene Lacoste	Jean Borotra	1966	Fred Stolle	John Newcombe
1927	Rene Lacoste	Bill Tilden	1967	John Newcombe	Clark Graebner
1928	Henri Cochet	Francis Hunter	1968	Arthur Ashe	Tom Okker
1929	Bill Tilden	Francis Hunter	1969	Rod Laver	Tony Roche
1930	John Doeg	Francis Shields	1970	Ken Rosewall	Tony Roche
1931	H. Ellsworth Vines	George Lott	1971	Stan Smith	Jan Kodes
1932	H. Ellsworth Vines	Henri Cochet	1972	Ilie Nastase	Arthur Ashe
1933	Fred Perry	John Crawford	1973	John Newcombe	Jan Kodes
1934	Fred Perry	Wilmer Allison	1974	Jimmy Connors	Ken Rosewall
1935	Wilmer Allison	Sidney Wood	1975	Manuel Orantes	Jimmy Connors
1936	Fred Perry	Don Budge	1976	Jimmy Connors	Bjorn Borg
1937	Don Budge	Baron G. von Cramm	1977	Guillermo Vilas	Jimmy Connors
1938	Don Budge	C. Gene Mako	1978	Jimmy Connors	Bjorn Borg
1939	Robert Riggs	S. Welby Van Horn	1979	John McEnroe	Vitas Gerulaitis
1940	Don McNeill	Robert Riggs	1980	John McEnroe	Bjorn Borg
1941	Robert Riggs	F. L. Kovacs	1981	John McEnroe	Bjorn Borg
1942	F. R. Schroeder Jr.	Frank Parker	1982	Jimmy Connors	Ivan Lendl
1943	Joseph Hunt	Jack Kramer	1983	Jimmy Connors	Ivan Lendl
1944	Frank Parker	William Talbert	1984	John McEnroe	Ivan Lendl
1945	Frank Parker	William Talbert	1985	Ivan Lendl	John McEnroe
1946	Jack Kramer	Thomas Brown Jr.	1986	Ivan Lendl	Miloslav Mecir
1947	Jack Kramer	Frank Parker	1987	Ivan Lendl	Mats Wilander
1948	Pancho Gonzales	Eric Sturgess	1988	Mats Wilander	Ivan Lendl
1949	Pancho Gonzales	F. R. Schroeder Jr.	1989	Boris Becker	Ivan Lendl

Women's Singles

Year	Champion	Final opponent	Year	Champion	Final opponent
1926	Molla B. Mallory	Elizabeth Ryan	1958	Althea Gibson	Darlene Hard
1927	Helen Wills	Betty Nuthall	1959	Maria Bueno	Christine Truman
1928	Helen Wills	Helen Jacobs	1960	Darlene Hard	Maria Bueno
1929	Helen Wills	M. Watson	1961	Darlene Hard	Ann Haydon
1930	Betty Nuthall	L. A. Harper	1962	Margaret Smith	Darlene Hard
1931	Helen Wills Moody	E. B. Whittingstall	1963	Maria Bueno	Margaret Smith
1932	Helen Jacobs	Carolin A. Babcock	1964	Maria Bueno	Carole Graebner
1933	Helen Jacobs	Helen Wills Moody	1965	Margaret Smith	Billie Jean Moffitt
1934	Helen Jacobs	Sarah H. Palfrey	1966	Maria Bueno	Nancy Richey
1935	Helen Jacobs	Sarah P. Fabyan	1967	Billie Jean King	Ann Haydon Jones
1936	Alice Marble	Helen Jacobs	1968	Virginia Wade	Billie Jean King
1937	Anita Lizana	Jadwiga Jedrzejowska	1969	Margaret Court	Nancy Richey
1938	Alice Marble	Nancye Wynne	1970	Margaret Court	Rosemary Casals
1939	Alice Marble	Helen Jacobs	1971	Billie Jean King	Rosemary Casals
1940	Alice Marble	Helen Jacobs	1972	Billie Jean King	Kerry Melville
1941	Sarah Palfrey Cooke	Pauline Betz	1973	Margaret Court	Evonne Goolagong
1942	Pauline Betz	Louise Brough	1974	Billie Jean King	Evonne Goolagong
1943	Pauline Betz	Louise Brough	1975	Chris Evert	Evonne Goolagong
1944	Pauline Betz	Margaret Osborne	1976	Chris Evert	Evonne Goolagong
1945	Sarah P. Cooke	Pauline Betz	1977	Chris Evert	Wendy Turnbull
1946	Pauline Betz	Doris Hart	1978	Chris Evert	Pam Shriver
1947	Louise Brough	Margaret Osborne	1979	Tracy Austin	Chris Evert Lloyd
1948	Margaret Osborne duPont	Louise Brough	1980	Chris Evert Lloyd	Hana Mandlikova
1949	Margaret Osborne duPont	Doris Hart	1981	Tracy Austin	Martina Navratilova
1950	Margaret Osborne duPont	Doris Hart	1982	Chris Evert Lloyd	Hana Mandlikova
1951	Maureen Connolly	Shirley Fry	1983	Martina Navratilova	Chris Evert Lloyd
1952	Maureen Connolly	Doris Hart	1984	Martina Navratilova	Chris Evert Lloyd
1953	Maureen Connolly	Doris Hart	1985	Hana Mandlikova	Martina Navratilova
1954	Doris Hart	Louise Brough	1986	Martina Navratilova	Helena Sukova
1955	Doris Hart	Patricia Ward	1987	Martina Navratilova	Steffi Graf
1956	Shirley Fry	Althea Gibson	1988	Steffi Graf	Gabriela Sabatini
1957	Althea Gibson	Louise Brough	1989	Steffi Graf	Martina Navratilova

Men's Doubles

Year	Champions	Year	Champions
1944	Don McNeill—Robert Falkenburg	1967	John Newcombe—Tony Roche
1945	Gardnar Mulloy—William Talbert	1968	Robert Lutz—Stan Smith
1946	Gardnar Mulloy—William Talbert	1969	Fred Stolle—Ken Rosewall
1947	Jack Kramer—Frederick Schroeder Jr.	1970	Pierre Barthes—Nicki Pilic
1948	Gardnar Mulloy—William Talbert	1971	John Newcombe—Roger Taylor
1949	John Bromwich—William Sidwell	1972	Cliff Drysdale—Roger Taylor
1950	John Bromwich—Frank Sedgman	1973	John Newcombe—Owen Davidson
1951	Frank Sedgman—Kenneth McGregor	1974	Bob Lutz—Stan Smith
1952	Mervyn Rose—E. Victor Seixas Jr.	1975	Jimmy Connors—Ilie Nastase
1953	Rex Hartwig—Mervyn Rose	1976	Marty Riessen—Tom Okker
1954	E. Victor Seixas Jr.—Tony Trabert	1977	Bob Hewitt—Frew McMillan
1955	Kosei Kamo—Atsushi Miyagi	1978	Stan Smith—Bob Lutz
1956	Lewis Hoad—Ken Rosewall	1979	John McEnroe—Peter Fleming
1957	Ashley Cooper—Neale Fraser	1980	Bob Lutz—Stan Smith
1958	Hamilton Richardson—Alejandro Olmedo	1981	John McEnroe—Peter Fleming
1959	Neale A. Fraser—Roy Emerson	1982	Kevin Curren—Steve Denton
1960	Neale A. Fraser—Roy Emerson	1983	John McEnroe—Peter Fleming
1961	Dennis Ralston—Chuck McKinley	1984	Tomas Smid—John Fitzgerald
1962	Rafael Osuna—Antonio Palafox	1985	Ken Flach—Robert Seguso
1963	Dennis Ralston—Chuck McKinley	1986	Andres Gomez—Slobodan Zivojinovic
1964	Dennis Ralston—Chuck McKinley	1987	Stefan Edberg—Anders Jarryd
1965	Roy Emerson—Fred Stolle	1988	Sergio Casal—Emilio Sanchez
1966	Roy Emerson—Fred Stolle	1989	John McEnroe—Mark Woodforde

Women's Doubles

Year	Champions	Year	Champions
1944	A. Louise Brough—Margaret Osborne	1967	Rosemary Casals—Billie Jean King
1945	A. Louise Brough—Margaret Osborne	1968	Maria Bueno—Margaret S. Court
1946	A. Louise Brough—Margaret Osborne	1969	Francoise Durr—Darlene Hard
1947	A. Louise Brough—Margaret Osborne	1970	M. S. Court—Judy Tegart Dalton
1948	A. Louise Brough—Mrs. M. O. du Pont	1971	Rosemary Casals—Judy Tegart Dalton
1949	A. Louise Brough—Mrs. M. O. du Pont	1972	Francoise Durr—Betty Stove
1950	A. Louise Brough—Mrs. M. O. du Pont	1973	Margaret S. Court—Virginia Wade
1951	Doris Hart—Shirley Fry	1974	Billie Jean King—Rosemary Casals
1952	Doris Hart—Shirley Fry	1975	Margaret Court—Virginia Wade
1953	Doris Hart—Shirley Fry	1976	Linky Boshoff—Ilana Kloss
1954	Doris Hart—Shirley Fry	1977	Betty Stove—Martina Navratilova
1955	A. Louise Brough—Mrs. M. O. du Pont	1978	Martina Navratilova—Billie Jean King
1956	A. Louise Brough—Mrs. M. O. du Pont	1979	Betty Stove—Wendy Turnbull
1957	A. Louise Brough—Mrs. M. O. du Pont	1980	Billie Jean King—Martina Navratilova
1958	Darlene Hard—Jeanne Arth	1981	Anne Smith—Kathy Jordan
1959	Darlene Hard—Jeanne Arth	1982	Rosemary Casals—Wendy Turnbull
1960	Darlene Hard—Maria Bueno	1983	Martina Navratilova—Pam Shriver
1961	Darlene Hard—Lesley Turner	1984	Martina Navratilova—Pam Shriver
1962	Maria Bueno—Darlene Hard	1985	Claudia Kohde-Kilsch—Helena Sukova
1963	Margaret Smith—Robyn Ebbern	1986	Martina Navratilova—Pam Shriver
1964	Billie Jean Moffitt—Karen Susman	1987	Martina Navratilova—Pam Shriver
1965	Carole C. Graebner—Nancy Richey	1988	Gigi Fernandez—Robin White
1966	Maria Bueno—Nancy Richey	1989	Martina Navratilova—Hana Mandlikova

Davis Cup Challenge Round

Year	Result	Year	Result	Year	Result
1900	United States 5, British Isles 0	1930	France 4, United States 1	1962	Australia 5, Mexico 0
1901	(not played)	1931	France 3, Great Britain 2	1963	United States 3, Australia 2
1902	United States 3, British Isles 2	1932	France 3, United States 2	1964	Australia 3, United States 2
1903	British Isles 4, United States 1	1933	Great Britain 3, France 2	1965	Australia 4, Spain 1
1904	British Isles 5, Belgium 0	1934	Great Britain 4, United States 1	1966	Australia 4, India 1
1905	British Isles 5, United States 0	1935	Great Britain 5, United States 0	1967	Australia 4, Spain 1
1906	British Isles 5, United States 0	1936	Great Britain 3, Australia 2	1968	United States 4, Australia 1
1907	Australia 3, British Isles 2	1937	United States 4, Great Britain 1	1969	United States 5, Romania 0
1908	Australasia 3, United States 2	1938	United States 3, Australia 2	1970	United States 5, W. Germany 0
1909	Australasia 5, United States 0	1939	Australia 3, United States 2	1971	United States 3, Romania 2
1910	(not played)	1940-45	(not played)	1972	United States 3, Romania 2
1911	Australasia 5, United States 0	1946	United States 5, Australia 0	1973	Australia 5, United States 0
1912	British Isles 3, Australasia 2	1947	United States 4, Australia 1	1974	South Africa (default by India)
1913	United States 3, British Isles 2	1948	United States 5, Australia 0	1975	Sweden 3, Czech. 2
1914	Australasia 3, United States 2	1949	United States 4, Australia 1	1976	Italy 4, Chile 1
1915-18	(not played)	1950	Australia 4, United States 1	1977	Australia 3, Italy 1
1919	Australasia 4, British Isles 1	1951	Australia 3, United States 2	1978	United States 4, Great Britain 1
1920	United States 5, Australasia 0	1952	Australia 4, United States 1	1979	United States 5, Italy 0
1921	United States 5, Japan 0	1953	Australia 3, United States 2	1980	Czechoslovakia 4, Italy 1
1922	United States 4, Australasia 1	1954	United States 3, Australia 2	1981	United States 3, Argentina 1
1923	United States 4, Australasia 1	1955	Australia 5, United States 0	1982	United States 3, France, 0
1924	United States 5, Australasia 0	1956	Australia 5, United States 0	1983	Australia 3, Sweden 1
1925	United States 5, France 0	1957	Australia 3, United States 2	1984	Sweden 3, United States 0
1926	United States 4, France 1	1958	United States 3, Australia 2	1985	Sweden 3, W. Germany 2
1927	France 3, United States 2	1959	Australia 3, United States 2	1986	Australia 3, Sweden 2
1928	France 4, United States 1	1960	Australia 4, Italy 1	1987	Sweden 5, India 0
1929	France 3, United States 2	1961	Australia 5, Italy 0	1988	W. Germany 4, Sweden 1

All-England Champions, Wimbledon
Men's Singles

Year	Champion	Final opponent	Year	Champion	Final opponent
1933	Jack Crawford	Ellsworth Vines	1964	Roy Emerson	Fred Stolle
1934	Fred Perry	Jack Crawford	1965	Roy Emerson	Fred Stolle
1935	Fred Perry	Gottfried von Cramm	1966	Manuel Santana	Dennis Ralston
1936	Fred Perry	Gottfried von Cramm	1967	John Newcombe	Wilhelm Bungert
1937	Donald Budge	Gottfried von Cramm	1968	Rod Laver	Tony Roche
1938	Donald Budge	Wilfred Austin	1969	Rod Laver	John Newcombe
1939	Bobby Riggs	Elwood Cooke	1970	John Newcombe	Ken Rosewall
1940-45	not held		1971	John Newcombe	Stan Smith
1946	Yvon Petra	Geoff E. Brown	1972	Stan Smith	Ilie Nastase
1947	Jack Kramer	Tom P. Brown	1973	Jan Kodes	Alex Metreveli
1948	Bob Falkenburg	John Bromwich	1974	Jimmy Connors	Ken Rosewall
1949	Ted Schroeder	Jaroslav Drobny	1975	Arthur Ashe	Jimmy Connors
1950	Budge Patty	Frank Sedgman	1976	Bjorn Borg	Ilie Nastase
1951	Dick Savitt	Ken McGregor	1977	Bjorn Borg	Jimmy Connors
1952	Frank Sedgman	Jaroslav Drobny	1978	Bjorn Borg	Jimmy Connors
1953	Vic Seixas	Kurt Nielsen	1979	Bjorn Borg	Roscoe Tanner
1954	Jaroslav Drobny	Ken Rosewall	1980	Bjorn Borg	John McEnroe
1955	Tony Trabert	Kurt Nielsen	1981	John McEnroe	Bjorn Borg
1956	Lew Hoad	Ken Rosewall	1982	Jimmy Connors	John McEnroe
1957	Lew Hoad	Ashley Cooper	1983	John McEnroe	Chris Lewis
1958	Ashley Cooper	Neale Fraser	1984	John McEnroe	Jimmy Connors
1959	Alex Olmedo	Rod Laver	1985	Boris Becker	Kevin Curren
1960	Neale Fraser	Rod Laver	1986	Boris Becker	Ivan Lendl
1961	Rod Laver	Chuck McKinley	1987	Pat Cash	Ivan Lendl
1962	Rod Laver	Martin Mulligan	1988	Stefan Edberg	Boris Becker
1963	Chuck McKinley	Fred Stolle	1989	Boris Becker	Stefan Edberg

Women's Singles

Year	Champion	Year	Champion	Year	Champion	Year	Champion
1946	Pauline Betz	1957	Althea Gibson	1968	Billie Jean King	1979	Martina Navratilova
1947	Margaret Osborne	1958	Althea Gibson	1969	Ann Haydon-Jones	1980	Evonne Goolagong
1948	Louise Brough	1959	Maria Bueno	1970	Margaret Court	1981	Chris Evert Lloyd
1949	Louise Brough	1960	Maria Bueno	1971	Evonne Goolagong	1982	Martina Navratilova
1950	Louise Brough	1961	Angela Mortimer	1972	Billie Jean King	1983	Martina Navratilova
1951	Doris Hart	1962	Karen Hantze-Susman	1973	Billie Jean King	1984	Martina Navratilova
1952	Maureen Connolly	1963	Margaret Smith	1974	Chris Evert	1985	Martina Navratilova
1953	Maureen Connolly	1964	Maria Bueno	1975	Billie Jean King	1986	Martina Navratilova
1954	Maureen Connolly	1965	Margaret Smith	1976	Chris Evert	1987	Martina Navratilova
1955	Louise Brough	1966	Billie Jean King	1977	Virginia Wade	1988	Steffi Graf
1956	Shirley Fry	1967	Billie Jean King	1978	Martina Navratilova	1989	Steffi Graf

French Open Champions

Year	Men	Women	Year	Men	Women
1969	Rod Laver	Margaret Smith Court	1980	Bjorn Borg	Chris Evert Lloyd
1970	Jan Kodes	Margaret Smith Court	1981	Bjorn Borg	Hana Mandlikova
1971	Jan Kodes	Evonne Goolagong	1982	Mats Wilander	Martina Navratilova
1972	Andres Gimeno	Billie Jean King	1983	Yannick Noah	Chris Evert Lloyd
1973	Ilie Nastase	Margaret Court	1984	Ivan Lendl	Martina Navratilova
1974	Bjorn Borg	Chris Evert	1985	Mats Wilander	Chris Evert Lloyd
1975	Bjorn Borg	Chris Evert	1986	Ivan Lendl	Chris Evert Lloyd
1976	Adriano Panatta	Sue Barker	1987	Ivan Lendl	Steffi Graf
1977	Guillermo Vilas	Mima Jausovec	1988	Mats Wilander	Steffi Graf
1978	Bjorn Borg	Virginia Ruzici	1989	Michael Chang	Arantxa Sanchez
1979	Bjorn Borg	Chris Evert Lloyd			

Table Tennis in 1989
World Championships

Dortmund, W. Germany, Mar. 29—Apr. 9, 1989

Men's Singles — Jan-Ove Waldner, Sweden.
Women's Singles — Qiao Hong, China.
Men's Doubles — Steffen Fetzner & Jorg Rosskopf, W. Germany.

Women's Doubles — Deng Yaping & Qiao Hong, China.
Mixed Doubles — Yoo Nam Kyu & Hyun Jung Hwa, S. Korea.
Men's Team — Sweden.
Women's Team — China.

U.S. National Open

Miami Beach, Fla., June 7—11, 1989

Men's Singles — Jean-Michel Saive, Belgium.
Women's Singles — Xu Jin, China.
Men's Doubles — Chen Longcan & Wei Qingguang, China.
Women's Doubles — Hong Cha Ok & Lee Tae Joo, S. Korea.

Mixed Doubles — Chen Longcan & Chen Jing, China.
Men's Team — China.
Women's Team — China.

TRACK AND FIELD

World Track and Field Records
As of Sept. 1989

*Indicates pending record; some new records await confirmation. The International Amateur Athletic Federation, the world body of track and field, recognizes only records in metric distances except for the mile.

Men's Records
Running

Event	Record	Holder	Country	Date	Where made
100 meters	9.92 s.	Carl Lewis	U.S.	Sept. 24, 1987	Seoul
200 meters	19.72 s.	Pietro Mennea	Italy	Sept. 17, 1979	Mexico City
400 meters	43.29 s.	Butch Reynolds	U.S.	Aug. 17, 1988	Zurich
800 meters	1 m., 41.73 s.	Sebastian Coe	Gr. Britain	June 10, 1981	Florence, Italy
1,000 meters	2 m., 12.18 s.	Sebastian Coe	Gr. Britain	July 11, 1981	Oslo
1,500 meters	3 m., 29.46 s.	Said Aouita	Morocco	Aug. 23, 1985	W. Berlin
1 mile	3 m., 46.32 s.	Steve Cram	Gr. Britain	July 27, 1985	Oslo
2,000 meters	4 m., 50.81 s.	Said Aouita	Morocco	July 16, 1987	Paris
3,000 meters	*7 m., 29.45 s.	Said Aouita	Morocco	Aug. 20, 1989	Cologne
5,000 meters	12 m., 58.39 s.	Said Aouita	Morocco	July 22, 1987	Rome
10,000 meters	*27 m., 08.23 s.	Arturo Barrios	Mexico	Aug., 1989	W. Berlin
20,000 meters	57 m., 24.2 s.	Jos Hermens	Netherlands	May 1, 1976	Netherlands
25,000 meters	1 hr., 13 m., 55.8 s.	Toshihiko Seko	Japan	Mar. 22, 1981	New Zealand
30,000 meters	1 hr., 29 m., 18.8 s.	Toshihiko Seko	Japan	Mar. 22, 1981	New Zealand
3,000 meter stpl	*8 m., 05.35 s.	Peter Koech	Kenya	July 3, 1989	Stockholm
Marathon	2 hr., 6 m., 50 s.	Belayneh Densimo	Ethiopia	Apr. 17, 1988	Rotterdam

Hurdles

110 meters	*12.92 s.	Roger Kingdom	U.S.	Aug. 16, 1989	Zurich
400 meters	47.02 s.	Edwin Moses	U.S.	Aug. 31, 1983	Koblenz, W. Ger.

Relay Races

400 mtrs.	37.83 s.	(Graddy, Brown, Smith, Lewis)	U.S.	Aug. 11, 1984	Los Angeles
800 mtrs. (4×200)	*1 m., 19.38 s.	(Lewis, Everett, Burrell, Heard)	U.S.	Aug. 23, 1989	W. Germany
1,600 mtrs. (4×400)	2 m., 56.16 s.	(Matthews, Freeman, James, Evans)	U.S.	Oct. 20, 1968	Mexico City
		(Everett, Lewis, Robinzine, Reynolds)	U.S.	Oct 1, 1988	Seoul
3,200 mtrs. (4×800)	7 m., 03.89 s.	National team	Gr. Britain	Aug. 30, 1982	London

Field Events

High jump	*8 ft.	Javier Sotomayer	Cuba	July 29, 1989	Puerto Rico
Long jump	29 ft., 2½ in.	Bob Beamon	U.S.	Oct. 18, 1968	Mexico City
Triple jump	58 ft., 11½ in.	Willie Banks	U.S.	June 16, 1985	Indianapolis
Pole vault	*19 ft., 10½ in.	Sergei Bubka	USSR	July, 1988	Nice, France
16 lb. shot put	75 ft., 8 in.	Ulf Timmermann	E. Germany	May 22, 1988	Crete
Discus throw	243 ft.	Juergen Schult	E. Germany	June 6, 1986	E. Germany
Javelin throw(a)	287 ft., 7 in.	Jan Zelezny	Czech.	May 31, 1987	Nitra
16 lb. hammer throw	284 ft., 7 in.	Yuri Sedykh	USSR	Aug. 30, 1986	Stuttgart
Decathlon	8,647 pts.	Daley Thompson	Gr. Britain	Aug. 8-9, 1984	Los Angeles

(a) New implement.

Walking

30 km.	2 h., 7 min., 59.8 s.	Jose Martin	Spain	Aug. 4, 1979	Barcelona
50 km.	3 hr., 41 m., 38.4 s.	Raul Gonzales	Mexico	May 25, 1979	Norway

Women's Records
Running

100 meters	10.49 s.	Florence Griffith Joyner	U.S.	July 16, 1988	Indianapolis
200 meters	21.34 s.	Florence Griffith Joyner	U.S.	Sept. 29, 1988	Seoul
400 meters	47.60 s.	Marita Koch	E. Germany	Oct. 6, 1985	Canberra
800 meters	1 m., 53.28 s.	Jarmila Kratochvilova	Czech.	July 26, 1983	Munich
1,500 meters	3 m., 52.47 s.	Tatyana Kazankina	USSR	Aug. 13, 1980	Zurich
1 mile	*4 m., 15.71 s.	Paula Ivan	Romania	July 10, 1989	Nice
2,000 meters	5 m., 28.69 s.	Maricica Puica	Romania	July 11, 1986	London
3,000 meters	8 m., 22.62 s.	Tatyana Kazankina	USSR	Aug. 26, 1984	Leningrad
5,000 meters	14 m., 37.33 s.	Ingrid Kristiansen	Norway	Aug. 5, 1986	Stockholm
10,000 meters	30 m., 13.74 s.	Ingrid Kristiansen	Norway	July 5, 1986	Oslo
Marathon	2 h., 21 m., 06 s.	Ingrid Kristiansen	Norway	Apr. 21, 1985	London

Hurdles

100 meters	*12.21 s.	Yordanka Donkova	Bulgaria	Aug. 20, 1988	Bulgaria
400 meters	52.94 s.	Marina Stepanova	USSR	Sept. 17, 1986	USSR

Field Events

High jump	6 ft., 10¼ in.	Stefka Kostadinova	Bulgaria	Aug. 30, 1987	Rome
Shot put	74 ft., 3 in.	Natalya Lisouskaya	USSR	June 7, 1987	Moscow
Long jump	24 ft., 8¼ in.	Galina Chistyakova	USSR	June 11, 1988	Leningrad

(continued)

Event	Record	Holder	Country	Date	Where made
Discus throw	252 ft.	Gabriele Reinsch	E. Germany	July 9, 1988	E. Germany
Javelin	262 ft., 5 in.	Petra Felke	E. Germany	Sept. 9, 1988	Potsdam
Heptathlon	7,291 pts.	Jackie Joyner-Kersee	U.S.	Sept. 23-24, 1988	Seoul

Relay Races

400 mtrs. (4×100)	41.37 s.	National team	E. Germany	Oct. 6, 1985	Canberra
800 mtrs. (4×200)	1 m., 28.15 s.	National team	E. Germany	Aug. 9, 1980	E. Germany
1,600 mtrs. (4×400)	3 m., 15.18 s.	National team	USSR	Oct. 1, 1988	Seoul
3,200 mtrs. (4×800)	7 m., 50.17 s.	National team	USSR	Aug. 5, 1984	Moscow

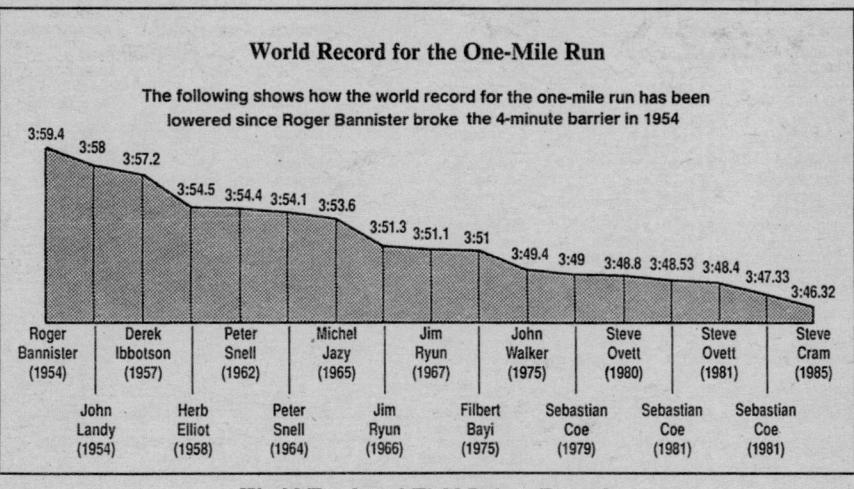

World Record for the One-Mile Run

The following shows how the world record for the one-mile run has been lowered since Roger Bannister broke the 4-minute barrier in 1954

Roger Bannister (1954) 3:59.4
John Landy (1954)
Derek Ibbotson (1957) 3:58, 3:57.2
Herb Elliot (1958)
Peter Snell (1962) 3:54.5, 3:54.4
Peter Snell (1964) 3:54.1
Michel Jazy (1965) 3:53.6
Jim Ryun (1966) 3:51.3
Jim Ryun (1967) 3:51.1
Filbert Bayi (1975) 3:51
John Walker (1975) 3:49.4
Sebastian Coe (1979) 3:49
Steve Ovett (1980) 3:48.8
Sebastian Coe (1981) 3:48.53
Steve Ovett (1981) 3:48.4
Sebastian Coe (1981) 3:47.33
Steve Cram (1985) 3:46.32

World Track and Field Indoor Records

As of Sept., 1989

The International Amateur Athletic Federation began recognizing world indoor track & field records as official on January 1, 1987. Prior to that, there were only unofficial world indoor bests. World indoor bests set prior to January 1, 1987 are subject to approval as world records providing they meet the prescribed IAAF world records criteria, including drug testing. To be accepted as a world indoor record, a performance must meet the same criteria as a world record outdoors except that a track performance can't be set on an indoor track larger than 200 meters. *record pending.

Men

Event	Record	Holder	Country	Date	Where made
60 meters	6.50	Lee McRae	U.S.	Mar. 7, 1987	Indianapolis
200 meters	20.36	Bruno Marie-Rose	France	Feb. 22, 1987	Lievin
400 meters	45.05	Thomas Schoenbe	E. Germany	Feb. 5, 1988	W. Germany
800 meters	*1:44.84	Paul Ereng	Kenya	Mar., 1989	Budapest
1,000 meters	2:16.62	Rob Druppers	Netherlands	Feb. 20, 1988	The Hague
1,500 meters	3:35.6	Eamonn Coghlan	Ireland	Feb. 20, 1981	San Diego
1 Mile	3:49.78	Eamonn Coghlan	Ireland	Feb. 27, 1983	E. Rutherford
3,000 meters	7:39.2	Emiel Puttemans	Belgium	Feb. 18, 1973	New York
5,000 meters	13:20.4	Suleiman Nyambui	Tanzania	Feb. 6, 1981	New York
50-meter hurdles	6.25	Mark McKoy	Canada	Mar. 5, 1986	Kobe
60-meter hurdles	*7.36	Roger Kingdom	U.S.	Mar. 9, 1989	Athens
High Jump	*8 ft.	Javier Sotomayor	Cuba	July 29, 1989	San Juan
Pole Vault	*19 ft. 9¼ in.	Sergey Bubka	USSR	Mar., 1989	Osaka
Long Jump	28 ft. 10¼ in.	Carl Lewis	U.S.	Feb. 27, 1984	New York
Triple Jump	58 ft. 3¼ in.	Mike Conley	U.S.	Feb. 27, 1987	New York
Shot Put	*74 ft. 4¼ in.	Randy Barnes	U.S.	Jan., 1989	Los Angeles

Women

Event	Record	Holder	Country	Date	Where made
60 meters	7.00	Nellie Cooman-Fiere	Holland	Feb. 23, 1986	Madrid
200 meters	22.27	Heike Drechsler	E. Germany	Mar. 7, 1987	Indianapolis
400 meters	49.59	Jarmila Kratochvilova	Czechoslovakia	Mar. 7, 1982	Milan
500 meters	1:07.67	Olga Nazarova	USSR	Jan. 10, 1988	Moscow
800 meters	1:56.40	Christine Wachtel	E. Germany	Feb. 13, 1988	Vienna
1,000 meters	2:34.8	Brigitte Kraus	W. Germany	Feb. 19, 1978	Dortmund
1,500 meters	4:00.8	Mary Decker-Slaney	U.S.	Feb. 8, 1980	New York
1 Mile	4:18.86	Doina Melinte	Romania	Feb. 13, 1988	E. Rutherford
3,000 meters	*8:33.82	Elly Van Hulst	Netherlands	Mar., 1989	Budapest
5,000 meters	15:25.02	Brenda Webb	U.S.	Jan. 30, 1988	Gainesville
55-meter hurdles	7:37	Cornelia Oschkenat	E. Germany	Feb., 1987	New York
		Jackie Joyner-Kersee	U.S.	Feb., 1989	New York
60-meter hurdles	7.74	Yordanka Dankova	Bulgaria	Feb. 15, 1987	Sofia
High Jump	6 ft. 9 in.	Stefka Kostadinova	Bulgaria	Feb. 20, 1988	Piraeus, Greece
Long Jump	24 ft. 2¼ in.	Heike Drechsler	E. Germany	Feb. 13, 1988	Vienna
Shot Put	73 ft. 10 in.	Helena Fibingerova	Czechoslovakia	Feb. 19, 1977	Jablonec

National Track & Field Hall of Fame

Indianapolis, Ind.

Jesse Abramson
Dave Albritton
Horace Ashenfelter
Andy Bakjian
Weems Baskin
James Bausch
Bob Beamon
Percy Beard
Greg Bell
Dee Boeckman
Tom Botts
Ralph Boston
Bill Bowerman
Avery Brundage
Jim Bush
Lee Calhoun
Milt Campbell
Alice Coachman (Davis)
Harold Connolly
Tom Courtney
Dean Cromwell
Glenn Cunningham
William Curtis
Willie Davenport
Glenn Davis
Harold Davis
Mildred (Babe) Didrikson
Harrison Dillard
Ken Doherty
Bill Easton
James (Jumbo) Elliott
Lee Evans
Barney Ewell
Ray Ewry

Mae Faggs (Starr)
Barbara Ferrell
Dan Ferris
John Flanagan
Dick Fosbury
Bob Giegengack
Fortune Gordien
John Griffith
Archie Hahn
Evelyne Hall
Brutus Hamilton
Glenn Hardin
Ted Haydon
Billy Hayes
Bob Hayes
Ward Haylett
Bud Held
Ralph Higgins
Harry Hillman
Jim Hines
Bud Houser
DeHart Hubbard
Edward Hurt
Wilbur Hutsell
Nell Jackson
Bruce Jenner
Rafer Johnson
Hayes Jones
Thomas Jones
Payton Jordan
John Kelley
Abel Kiviat
Alvin Kraenzlein
Ron Laird

Clyde Littlefield
Bob Mathias
Randy Matson
Mildred McDaniel
Edith McGuire (DuVall)
Ted Meredith
Ralph Metcalfe
Billy Mills
Madeline Manning-Mims
Jack Moakley
Tom Moore
Bobby Morrow
Michael Murphy
Lon Myers
Cordner Nelson
Parry O'Brien
Al Oerter
Harold Osborn
Jesse Owens
Charlie Paddock
Mel Patton
Eulace Peacock
Steve Prefontaine
Joie Ray
Greg Rice
Bob Richards
Betty Robinson (Schwartz)
Ralph Rose
Wilma Rudolph
Jim Ryun
Jackson Scholz
Bob Seagren
Mel Sheppard
Martin Sheridan

Frank Shorter
Dave Sime
Robert Simpson
Tommie Smith
Larry Snyder
Andy Stanfield
Les Steers
Helen Stephens
James Sullivan
Ed Temple
Dink Templeton
John Thomas
Earl Thomson
Jim Thorpe
Eddie Tolan
Bill Toomey
Forrest Towns
Wyomia Tyus
LeRoy Walker
Stella Walsh
Cornelius Warmerdam
Martha Watson
Willye White
Mal Whitfield
Fred Wilt
Lloyd "Bud" Winter
John Woodruff
Dave Wottle
Frank Wykoff
Joe Yancey
George Young

Track and Field Events in 1989

82d Annual Millrose Games

New York, N.Y., Feb. 3, 1989

Men

55 Meters—Lee McRae, Univ. of Pittsburgh. **Time—0:06.14.**
55-Meter High Hurdles—Jack Pierce, unattached. **Time—0:07.07.**
400 Meters—Antonio McKay, N.Y. AC. **Time—0:47.28.**
500 Meters—Mark Everett, Univ. of Florida. **Time—1:02.00.**
600 Meters—Ian Morris, Abilene Christian Univ. **Time—1:08.42.**
800 Meters—George Kersh, Taft Coll. **Time—1:48.32.**
1,000 Meters—Simon Hoogewerf, Canada. **Time—2:19.92.**
One Mile—Marcus O'Sullivan, Ireland. **Time—3:54.27.**
Masters Mile—Ron Bell, Great Britain. **Time—4:17.88.**
3,000 Meters—Said Aouita, Morocco. **Time—7:47.07.**

High Jump—Jake Jacoby, Reebok RC. 7 ft. 7 in.
Pole Vault—Grigoriv Yegorov, USSR. 18 ft. 8¼ in.

Women

55 meters—Gwen Torrence, Athletics West. **Time—0:06.68.**
55-Meter Hurdles—Jackie Joyner-Kersee, World Class Athletics. **Time—0:07.37.**
400 Meters—Diane Dixon, unattached. **Time—0:53.44.**
800 Meters—Joetta Clark, Athletics West. **Time—2:03.00.**
One Mile—Paula Ivan, Romania. **Time—4:23.72.**
High Jump—Louise Ritter, Mazda TC. 6ft. 5½ in.

NCAA Outdoor Championships

Provo, Ut., June 1-4, 1989

Men

100 Meters—Raymond Stewart, TCU. **Time—0:09.97.**
200 Meters—Dennis Mitchell, Florida. **Time—0:20.09.**
400 Meters—Raymond Pierre, Baylor. **Time—0:44.59.**
800 Meters—Paul Ereng, Virginia. **Time—1:47.50.**
1,500 Meters—Kip Cheruiyot, St. Mary's-Md. **Time—3:42.06.**
5,000 Meters—Marc Davis, Arizona. **Time—14:07.88.**
110-Meter Hurdles—Robert Reading, USC. **Time—0:13.19.**
400-Meter Hurdles—Winthrop Graham, Texas. **Time—0:48.55.**
High Jump—Hollis Conway, SW Louisiana. 7 ft. 9¾ in.
Long Jump—Joe Greene, Ohio St. 27 ft. 7½ in.
Triple Jump—Edrick Floreal, Arkansas. 56 ft. 8¾ in.
Shot Put—Mike Stuice, Texas A&M. 68 ft. 11¾ in.
Hammer Throw—Christoph Koch, NE Louisiana. 233 ft. 2 in.
Pole Vault—Tim McMichael, Oklahoma. 18 ft. 6½ in.
Decathlon—Derek Huff, Arizona. 8,020 pts.
Team champion—LSU.

Women

100 Meters—Dawn Sowell, LSU. **Time—0:10.78.**
200 Meters—Dawn Sowell. **Time—0:22.04.**
400 Meters—Pauline Davis, Alabama. **Time—0:50.18.**
800 Meters—Meridith Rainey, Harvard. **Time—2:03.90.**
1,500 Meters—Suzanne Favor, Wisconsin. **Time—4:15.83.**
3,000 Meters—Vicki Huber, Villanova. **Time—9:06.96.**
5,000 Meters—Valeria McGovern, Kentucky. **Time—16:17.20.**
100-Meter Hurdles—Tananjalyn Stanley, LSU. **Time—0:12.70.**
400-Meter Hurdles—Janeene Vickers, UCLA. **Time—0:55.27.**
High Jump—Melinda Clark, Texas A&M. 6 ft. ¾ in.
Long Jump—Christy Opara, Brigham Young. 21 ft. 2½ in.
Triple Jump—Renita Robinson, Nebraska. 44 ft. 7½ in.
Shot Put—Carla Garrett, Arizona. 54 ft. 8 in.
Discus—Carla Garrett. 190 ft. 4 in.
Javelin—Kim Engel, Georgia. 196 ft. 8 in.
Team champion—LSU.

USA/Mobil Outdoor Championships

Houston, Tex., June 15-17, 1989

Men

100 Meters—Leroy Burrell. Time—0:09.94.
200 Meters—Floyd Heard. Time—0:20.09.
400 Meters—Antonio Pettigrew. Time—0:44.27.
800 Meters—Johnny Gray. Time—1:46.77.
1,500 Meters—Terrance Herrington. Time—3:46.83.
5,000 Meters—Tim Hacker. Time—13:39.72.
10,000 Meters—Pat Porter. Time—28:45.78.
110-Meter Hurdles—Roger Kingdom. Time—0:13.22.
400-Meter Hurdles—David Patrick. Time—0:48.83.
High Jump—Brian Brown. 7 ft. 7¼ in.
Pole Vault—Kory Tarpenning. 19 ft.
Long Jump—Larry Myricks. 28 ft. 6½ in.
Triple Jump—Mike Conley. 57 ft. 5 in.
Discus—Kami Keshmiri. 218 ft. 2 in.
Hammer—Lance Deal. 252 ft. 5 in.
Javelin—Mike Barnett. 256 ft. 9 in.
Shot Put—Randy Barnes. 70 ft. 9 in.

Women

100 Meters—Dawn Sowell. Time—0:10.91.
200 Meters—Danette Young. Time—0:22.29.
400 Meters—Rochelle Stephens. Time—0:50.75.
800 Meters—Joetta Clark. Time—2:01.42.
1,500 Meters—Regina Jacobs. Time—4:11.80.
3,000 Meters—Patti Sue Plumber. Time—9:00.05.
5,000-Meters—Mindy Rowland. Time—16:12.36.
100-Meter Hurdles—Lynda Tolbert. Time—0:12.75.
400-Meter Hurdles—Sandra Farmer-Patrick. Time—0:53.75.
Long Jump—Claire Connor. 21 ft. 6 in.
Shot Put—Romona Pagel. 62 ft. ½ in.
Javelin—Laverne Eve. 212 ft. 6 in.
Discus—Connie Price. 201 ft. 11 in.
High Jump—Jan Wohlschlag. 6 ft. 4 in.
Triple Jump—Sheila Hudson. 45 ft. 6½ in.

Sports on Television

Source: "Sports 1988-89," Nielsen Media Research

	Household rating %	% Viewing Audience			
		Men	Women	Teens	Children
Football					
NFL Super Bowl	43.5	47	36	7	10
ABC-NFL (Monday eves.)	16.9	57	33	5	5
CBS-NFL	15.1	57	32	5	6
NBC-NFL	12.8	57	31	6	6
College bowl games	9.2	52	35	5	8
College football reg. season	6.9	56	32	5	7
Baseball					
World Series	23.9	51	39	4	6
All-star game	20.4	51	34	5	10
Regular season	6.2	53	34	5	8
Horse racing					
Breeders Cup	4.0	40	43	5	12
Basketball					
NBA average	8.1	54	31	7	8
NCAA average	5.3	54	31	7	8
Bowling					
Pro tour	4.4	44	43	4	9
Golf					
Average all	3.4	53	39	3	5
Tennis					
Wimbledon	3.6	43	42	8	7
Tournament average	3.1	44	42	7	7
Multi-sports					
ABC Wide World of Sports	5.0	45	40	6	9
CBS Sports Saturday	3.4	47	35	7	11
CBS Sports Sunday	4.8	50	34	7	9
Sportsworld-Saturday	3.2	48	39	4	9
Sportsworld-Sunday	3.5	47	35	8	10

U.S. Gymnastics Championships in 1989

Houston, Tex., July 6-9, 1989

Senior Men

Floor exercise—Mike Racnelli.
Pommel horse—Kevin Davis.
Still rings—Scott Keswick.
Vault—William Roth.
Parallel bars—Conrad Voor Sanger.
High bars—Tim Ryan.
All Around—Tim Ryan.

Senior Women

Vault—Brandy Johnson.
Uneven bars—Chelle Stack.
Balance beam—Brandy Johnson.
Floor exercise—Brandy Johnson.
All Around—Brandy Johnson.

Tour de France in 1989

Greg LeMond of the United States won the 76th Tour de France, the world's most prestigious bicycle race. His margin of victory over Laurent Fignon, the second place finisher, was 8 seconds, the smallest margin in the history of the race. LeMond rode a record 27 minutes 57 seconds in the final stage of the race, a 15-mile time trial. It was the second Tour de France victory for LeMond who completed the 21-day, about 2,000-mile race in a total time of 87 hours 36 minutes 35 seconds.

Jeannie Longo of France won the women's Tour de France, which was run in 11 stages over 482 miles.

Notable Sports Personalities

Henry Aaron, b. 1934: Milwaukee-Atlanta outfielder hit record 755 home runs; led NL 4 times.

Kareem Abdul-Jabbar, b. 1947: Milwaukee, L.A. Lakers center; MVP 6 times; leading scorer twice; playoff MVP, 1971, 1985; all-time leading NBA scorer.

Grover Cleveland Alexander, (1887-1950): pitcher won 374 NL games; pitched 16 shutouts, 1916.

Muhammad Ali, b. 1942: 3-time heavyweight champion.

Ken Anderson, b. 1949: Cinn. Bengals quarterback led AFC in passing 4 times.

Mario Andretti, b. 1940; won Indy 500, 1969; Grand Prix champ, 1978.

Eddie Arcaro, b. 1916: jockey rode 4,779 winners including the Kentucky Derby 5 times; the Preakness and Belmont Stakes 6 times each.

Henry Armstrong, b. 1912: boxer held feather-, welter-, lightweight titles simultaneously, 1937-38.

Arthur Ashe, b. 1943: U.S. singles champ, 1968, Wimbledon champ, 1975.

Red Auerbach, b. 1917: coached Boston Celtics to 9 NBA championships.

Ernie Banks, b. 1931: Chicago Cubs slugger hit 512 NL homers; twice MVP.

Roger Bannister, b. 1929: Briton ran first sub 4-minute mile, May 6, 1954.

Rick Barry, b. 1944: NBA scoring leader, 1967; ABA, 1969.

Sammy Baugh, b. 1914: Washington Redskins quarterback held numerous records upon retirement after 16 pro seasons.

Elgin Baylor, b. 1934: L.A. Lakers forward; 1st team all-star 10 times.

Bob Beamon, b. 1946: long jumper won 1968 Olympic gold medal with record 29 ft. 2½ in.

Jean Beliveau, b. 1931: Montreal Canadiens center scored 507 goals; twice MVP.

Johnny Bench, b. 1947: Cincinnati Reds catcher; MVP twice; led league in home runs twice, RBIs 3 times.

Patty Berg, b. 1918: won over 80 golf tournaments; AP Woman Athlete-of-the-Year 3 times.

Yogi Berra, b. 1925: N.Y. Yankees catcher; MVP 3 times; played in 14 World Series.

Raymond Berry, b. 1933: Baltimore Colts receiver caught 631 passes.

Matt Biondi, b. 1965: swimmer won 5 gold medals at 1988 Olympics.

Larry Bird, b. 1956: Boston Celtics forward; chosen MVP 1984-86, playoff MVP, 1984, 1986.

George Blanda, b. 1927: quarterback, kicker; 26 years as active player, scoring record 2,002 points.

Wade Boggs, b. 1958: AL Batting champ, 1983, 1985-88.

Bjorn Borg, b. 1956: led Sweden to first Davis Cup, 1975; Wimbledon champion, 5 times.

Mike Bossy, b.1957: N.Y. Islanders right wing scored over 50 goals 8 times.

Terry Bradshaw, b. 1948: Pittsburgh Steelers quarterback led team to 4 Super Bowl titles.

George Brett, b. 1953: Kansas City Royals 3d baseman led AL in batting, 1976, 1980; MVP, 1980.

Lou Brock, b. 1939: St. Louis Cardinals outfielder stole record 118 bases, 1974; record 938 career; led NL 8 times.

Jimmy Brown, b. 1936: Cleveland Browns fullback ran for 12,312 career yards; MVP 3 times.

Paul "Bear" Bryant, (1913-1983), college football coach with 323 victories.

Maria Bueno, b. 1939: U.S. singles champ 4 times; Wimbledon champ 3 times.

Dick Butkus, b. 1942: Chicago Bears linebacker twice chosen best NFL defensive player.

Dick Button, b. 1929: figure skater won 1948, 1952 Olympic gold medals; world titlist, 1948-52.

Walter Camp, (1859-1925): Yale football player, coach, athletic director; established many rules; promoted All-America designations.

Roy Campanella, b. 1921: Brooklyn Dodgers catcher; MVP 3 times.

Earl Campbell, b. 1955: NFL running back; NFL MVP 1978-1980.

Jose Canseco, b. 1964: Oakland A's outfielder; AL MVP 1988.

Rod Carew, b. 1945: AL infielder won 7 batting titles; MVP, 1977.

Steve Carlton, b. 1944: NL pitcher won 20 games 5 times, Cy Young award 4 times.

Billy Casper, b. 1931: PGA Player-of-the-Year 3 times; U.S. Open champ twice.

Wilt Chamberlain, b. 1936: center was NBA leading scorer 7 times; MVP 4 times.

Bobby Clarke, b. 1949: Philadelphia Flyers center led team to 2 Stanley Cup championships; MVP 3 times.

Roberto Clemente, (1934-1972): Pittsburgh Pirates outfielder won 4 batting titles; MVP, 1966.

Ty Cobb, (1886-1961): Detroit Tigers outfielder had record .367 lifetime batting average, 12 batting titles.

Sebastian Coe, b. 1956: Briton won Olympic 1,500-meter run, 1980, 1984.

Nadia Comaneci, b. 1961: Romanian gymnast won 3 gold medals, achieved 7 perfect scores, 1976 Olympics.

Maureen Connolly, (1934-1969): won tennis "grand slam," 1953; AP Woman-Athlete-of-the-Year 3 times.

Jimmy Connors, b. 1952: U.S. singles champ 5 times; Wimbledon champ twice.

James J. Corbett, (1866-1933): heavyweight champion, 1892-97; credited with being the first "scientific" boxer.

Angel Cordero, b. 1942: jockey won over 6,000 races; leading money winner, 1976, 1982-83.

Margaret Smith Court, b. 1942: Australian won U.S. singles championship 5 times; Wimbledon champ 3 times.

Bob Cousy, b. 1928: Boston Celtics guard led team to 6 NBA championships; MVP, 1957.

Andre Dawson, b. 1954: slugger led NL in home runs, MVP, 1987.

Dizzy Dean, (1911-1974): colorful pitcher for St. Louis Cardinals "Gashouse Gang" in the 30s; MVP, 1934.

Jack Dempsey, (1895-1983); heavyweight champion, 1919-26.

Eric Dickerson, b. 1960: running back ran for NFL record 2,105 yds., 1984; led NFC 3 times, AFC twice.

Joe DiMaggio, b. 1914: N.Y. Yankees outfielder hit safely in record 56 consecutive games, 1941; MVP 3 times.

Leo Durocher, b. 1906: manager won 3 NL pennants.

Gertrude Ederle, b. 1906: first woman to swim English Channel, broke existing men's record, 1926.

Julius Erving, b. 1950: MVP and leading scorer in ABA 3 times; NBA MVP, 1981.

Phil Esposito, b. 1942: NHL scoring leader 5 times.

Chris Evert, b. 1954: U.S. singles champ 6 times, Wimbledon champ 3 times.

Patrick Ewing, b. 1962: center led Georgetown Univ. to 1984 NCAA championship.

Ray Ewry, (1873-1937): track and field star won 8 gold medals, 1900, 1904, and 1908 Olympics.

Juan Fangio, b. 1911: World Grand Prix champion 5 times.

Bob Feller, b. 1918: Cleveland Indians pitcher won 266 games; pitched 3 no-hitters, 12 one-hitters.

Peggy Fleming, b. 1948: world figure skating champion, 1966-68; gold medalist 1968 Olympics.

Whitey Ford, b. 1928: N.Y. Yankees pitcher won record 10 World Series games.

Dick Fosbury, b. 1947: high jumper won 1968 Olympic gold medal; developed the "Fosbury Flop."

Jimmie Foxx, (1907-1967): Red Sox, Athletics slugger; MVP 3 times; triple crown, 1933.

A.J. Foyt, b. 1935: won Indy 500 4 times; U.S. Auto Club champ 7 times.

Joe Frazier, b. 1944: heavyweight champion, 1970-73.

Lou Gehrig, (1903-1941): N.Y. Yankees 1st baseman played record 2,130 consecutive games; MVP, 1936.

George Gervin, b. 1952: leading NBA scorer, 1978-80, 1982.

Althea Gibson, b. 1927: twice U.S. and Wimbledon singles champ.

Bob Gibson, b. 1935: St. Louis Cardinals pitcher won Cy Young award twice; struck out 3,117 batters.

Frank Gifford, b. 1930: N.Y. Giants back; MVP, 1956.

Dwight Gooden, b. 1964: N.Y. Mets pitcher was NL Rookie of Year, 1984; Cy Young award, 1985.

Steffi Graf, b. 1969: W. German won tennis "grand slam," 1988; U.S. champ 1988, 1989.

Otto Graham, b. 1921: Cleveland Browns quarterback; all-pro 4 times.

Red Grange, b 1903: All-America at Univ. of Illinois; played for Chicago Bears, 1925-35.

Joe Greene, b. 1946: Pittsburgh Steelers lineman; twice NFL outstanding defensive player.

Wayne Gretzky, b. 1961: Edmonton Oilers center scored record 92 goals, 212 pts., 1982; MVP, 1980-87, 1989.

Florence Griffith Joyner, b. 1959: sprinter won 3 gold medals at 1988 Olympics.

Lefty Grove, (1900-1975): pitcher won 300 AL games; 20-game winner 8 times.

Tony Gwynn, b. 1960: NL batting champ, 1984, 1987-1989.

Walter Hagen, (1892-1969): won PGA championship 5 times. British Open 4 times.

George Halas, (1895-1983): founder-coach of Chicago Bears; won 5 NFL championships.

Bill Hartack, b. 1932: jockey rode 5 Kentucky Derby winners.

John Havlicek, b. 1940: Boston Celtics forward scored over 26,000 NBA points.

Eric Heiden, b. 1958: speed skater won 5 1980 Olympic gold medals.

Rickey Henderson, b. 1958; AL outfielder stole record 130 bases, 1982.

Sonja Henie, (1912-1969): world champion figure skater, 1927-36; Olympic gold medalist, 1928, 1932, 1936.

Ben Hogan, b. 1912: won 4 U.S. Open championships, 2 PGA, 2 Masters.

Rogers Hornsby, (1896-1963): NL 2d baseman batted record .424 in 1924; twice won triple crown; batting leader, 1920-25.

Paul Hornung, b. 1935: Green Bay Packers runner-placekicker scored record 176 points, 1960.

Gordie Howe, b. 1928: hockey forward holds NHL career records in goals, assists, and points; NHL MVP 6 times.

Carl Hubbell, (1903-1988): N.Y. Giants pitcher; 20-game winner 5 consecutive years, 1933-37.

Bobby Hull, b. 1939: NHL all-star 10 times.

Catfish Hunter, b. 1946: pitched perfect game, 1968; 20-game winner 5 times.

Don Hutson, b. 1913: Green Bay Packers receiver caught NFL record 99 touchdown passes.

Reggie Jackson, b. 1946: slugged led AL in home runs 4 times; MVP, 1973; hit 5 World Series home runs, 1977.

Bruce Jenner, b. 1949: decathlon gold medalist, 1976.

Jack Johnson, (1878-1946): heavyweight champion, 1910-15.

Magic Johnson, b. 1959: NBA MVP 1987, 1989; playoff MVP 1980, 1982, 1987.

Rafer Johnson, b. 1935: decathlon gold medalist, 1960.

Walter Johnson, (1887-1946): Washington Senators pitcher won 413 games.

Bobby Jones, (1902-1971): won "grand slam of golf" 1930; U.S. Amateur champ 5 times, U.S. Open champ 4 times.

Deacon Jones, b. 1938: L.A. Rams lineman; twice NFL outstanding defensive player.

Michael Jordan, b. 1963: NBA leading scorer, 1987-89; MVP, 1988.

Sonny Jurgensen, b. 1934: quarterback named all-pro 5 times.

Duke Kahanamoku, (1890-1968): swimmer won 1912, 1920 Olympic gold medals in 100-meter freestyle.

Harmon Killebrew, b. 1936: Minnesota Twins slugger led AL in home runs 6 times.

Jean Claude Killy, b. 1943: French skier won 3 1968 Olympic gold medals.

Ralph Kiner, b. 1922: Pittsburgh Pirates slugger led NL in home runs 7 consecutive years, 1946-52.

Billie Jean King, b. 1943: U.S. singles champ 4 times; Wimbledon champ 6 times.

Bob Knight, b. 1940: Indiana U. basketball coach lead team to NCAA championships, 1976, 1981, 1987.

Olga Korbut, b. 1955: Soviet gymnast won 3 1972 Olympic gold medals.

Sandy Koufax, b. 1935: Dodgers pitcher won Cy Young award 3 times; lowest ERA in NL, 1962-66; pitched 4 no-hitters, one a perfect game.

Guy Lafleur, b. 1951: Montreal Canadiens forward led NHL in scoring 3 times; MVP, 1977, 1978.

Tom Landry, b. 1924: Dallas Cowboys head coach 1960-88.

Rod Laver, b. 1938: Australian won tennis "grand slam," 1962, 1969; Wimbledon champ 4 times.

Mario Lemieux, b. 1965: NHL leading scorer, 1988-1989; MVP, 1988.

Ivan Lendl, b. 1960: U.S. singles champ, 1985-87.

Sugar Ray Leonard, b. 1956: former world welterweight champ.

Carl Lewis, b. 1961: track and field star won 4 1984 Olympic gold medals.

Vince Lombardi, (1913-1970): Green Bay Packers coach led team to 5 NFL championships and 2 Super Bowl victories.

Joe Louis, (1914-1981): 1914: heavyweight champion, 1937-49.

Sid Luckman, b. 1916: Chicago Bears quarterback led team to 4 NFL championships; MVP, 1943.

Connie Mack, (1862-1956): Philadelphia Athletics manager, 1901-50; won 9 pennants, 5 championships.

Bill Madlock, b. 1951: NL batting leader 4 times.

Moses Malone, b. 1955: NBA center was MVP 1979, 1982, 1983.

Mickey Mantle, b. 1931: N.Y. Yankees outfielder; triple crown, 1956; 18 World Series home runs.

Pete Maravich (1948-1988): guard scored NCAA record 44.2 ppg during collegiate career; led NBA in scoring, 1977.

Rocky Marciano, (1923-1969): heavyweight champion, 1952-56; retired undefeated.

Dan Marino, b. 1961: Miami Dolphins quarterback passed for NFL record 5,084 yds, 1984.

Roger Maris, (1934-1985): N.Y. Yankees outfielder hit record 61 home runs, 1961; MVP, 1960 and 1961.

Eddie Mathews, b. 1931: Milwaukee-Atlanta 3d baseman hit 512 career home runs.

Christy Mathewson, (1880-1925): N.Y. Giants pitcher won 373 games.

Bob Mathias, b. 1930: decathlon gold medalist, 1948, 1952.

Don Mattingly, b. 1961: N.Y. Yankees 1st baseman won 1984 AL batting title; MVP, 1985.

Willie Mays, b. 1931: N.Y.-S.F. Giants center fielder hit 660 home runs; twice MVP.

Willie McCovey, b. 1938: S.F. Giants slugger hit 521 home runs; led NL 3 times.

John McEnroe, b. 1959: U.S. singles champ, 1979-81, 1984; Wimbledon champ, 1981, 1983-84.

John McGraw, (1873-1934): N.Y. Giants manager led team to 10 pennants, 3 championships.

Debbie Meyer, b. 1952: swimmer won 200-, 400-, and 800- meter freestyle events, 1968 Olympics.

George Mikan, b. 1924: Minneapolis Lakers center selected in a 1950 AP poll as the greatest basketball player of the first half of the 20th century.

Stan Mikita, b. 1940: Chicago Black Hawks center led NHL in scoring 4 times; MVP twice.

Joe Montana, b. 1956: QB led 49ers to Super Bowl championships, 1982, 1985.

Archie Moore, b. 1913: world light-heavyweight champion, 1952-62.

Howie Morenz, (1902-1937): Montreal Canadiens forward chosen in a 1950 Canadian press poll as the outstanding hockey player of the first half of the 20th century.

Joe Morgan, b. 1943: National League MVP, 1975, 1976.

Thurman Munson, (1947-1979): N.Y. Yankees catcher; MVP, 1976.

Dale Murphy, b. 1956: Atlanta Braves outfielder chosen NL MVP 1982, 1983.

Stan Musial, b. 1920: St. Louis Cardinals star won 7 NL batting titles; MVP 3 times.

Bronko Nagurski, b. 1908: Chicago Bears fullback and tackle; gained over 4,000 yds. rushing.

Joe Namath, b. 1943: quarterback led N.Y. Jets to 1969 Super Bowl title.

Martina Navratilova, b. 1956: Wimbledon champ 8 times, U.S. champ 1983-1984; 1986-87.

Byron Nelson, b. 1912: won 11 consecutive golf tournaments in 1945; twice Masters and PGA titlist.

Ernie Nevers, (1903-1976): Stanford star selected the best college fullback to play between 1919-1969.

John Newcombe, b. 1943: Australian twice U.S. singles champ; Wimbledon titlist 3 times.

Jack Nicklaus, b. 1940: PGA Player-of-the-Year, 1967, 1972; leading money winner 8 times; won Masters 6 times.

Chuck Noll, b. 1931: Pittsburgh Steelers coach led team to 4 Super Bowl titles.

Paavo Nurmi, (1897-1973): Finnish distance runner won 6 Olympic gold medals, 1920, 1924, 1928.

Al Oerter, b. 1936: discus thrower won gold medal at 4 consecutive Olympics, 1956-68.

Bobby Orr, b. 1948: Boston Bruins defenseman; Norris Trophy 8 times; led NHL in scoring twice, assists 5 times.

Mel Ott, (1909-1958): N.Y. Giants outfielder hit 511 home runs; led NL 6 times.

Jesse Owens, (1913-1980): track and field star won 4 1936 Olympic gold medals.

Satchel Paige, (1906-1982): pitcher starred in Negro leagues, 1924-48; entered major leagues at age 42.

Arnold Palmer, b. 1929: golf's first $1 million winner; won 4 Masters, 2 British Opens.

Jim Palmer, b. 1945: Baltimore Orioles pitcher; Cy Young award 3 times; 20-game winner 7 times.

Floyd Patterson, b. 1935: twice heavyweight champion.

Walter Payton, b. 1954: Chicago Bears running back has most rushing yards in NFL history; leading NFC rusher, 1976-80.

Pele, b. 1940: Brazilian soccer star scored 1,281 goals during 22-year career.

Bob Pettit, b. 1932: first NBA player to score 20,000 points; twice NBA scoring leader.

Richard Petty, b. 1937: NASCAR national champ 7 times; 7-times Daytona 500 winner.

Laffit Pincay Jr., b. 1946: leading money-winning jockey, 1970-74, 1979.

Jacques Plante, (1929-1986): goalie, 7 Vezina trophies; first goalie to wear a mask in a game.

Willis Reed, b. 1942: N.Y. Knicks center; MVP, 1970; playoff MVP, 1970, 1973.

Jerry Rice, b. 1962: S.F. 49ers receiver chosen 1989 Super Bowl MVP.

Jim Rice, b. 1953: Boston Red Sox outfielder led AL in home runs, 1977-78, 1983; MVP 1978.

Maurice Richard, b. 1921: Montreal Canadiens forward scored 544 regular season goals, 82 playoff goals.

Branch Rickey, (1881-1965): executive instrumental in breaking baseball's color barrier, 1947; initiated farm system, 1919.

Oscar Robertson, b. 1938: guard averaged career 25.7 points per game; record 9,887 career assists; MVP, 1964.

Brooks Robinson, b. 1937: Baltimore Orioles 3d baseman played in 4 World Series; MVP, 1964.

Frank Robinson, b. 1935: slugger MVP in both NL and AL; triple crown winner, 1966; first black manager in majors.

Jackie Robinson, (1919-1972): broke baseball's color barrier with Brooklyn Dodgers, 1947; MVP, 1949.

Larry Robinson, b. 1951: NHL defenseman won Norris trophy, 1977, 1980.

Sugar Ray Robinson, b. 1920: middleweight champion 5 times, welterweight champion.

Knute Rockne, (1888-1931): Notre Dame football coach, 1918-31; revolutionized game by stressing forward pass.

Pete Rose, b. 1941: won 3 NL batting titles; hit safely in 44 consecutive games, 1978; has most major league hits.

Wilma Rudolph, b. 1940: sprinter won 3 1960 Olympic gold medals.

Bill Russell, b. 1934: Boston Celtics center led team to 11 NBA titles; MVP 5 times; first black coach of major pro sports team.

Babe Ruth, (1895-1948): N.Y. Yankees outfielder hit 60 home runs, 1927; 714 lifetime; led AL 11 times.

Johnny Rutherford, b. 1938: auto racer won Indy 500 3 times.

Nolan Ryan, b. 1947: pitcher struck out record 383 batters, 1973; first to strike out 5,000 batters; pitched record 5 no-hitters.

Gene Sarazen, b. 1902: won PGA championship 3 times, U.S. Open twice; developer of sand wedge.

Gale Sayers, b. 1943: Chicago Bears back twice led NFC in rushing.

Mike Schmidt, b. 1949: Phillies 3d baseman led NL in home runs, 1974-76, 1980-81, 1983-84, 1986; NL MVP, 1980, 1981, 1986.

Tom Seaver, b. 1944: pitcher won NL Cy Young award 3 times, won 311 major league games.

Bill Shoemaker, b. 1931: jockey rode 3 Kentucky Derby and 5 Belmont Stakes winners; leading career money winner.

Eddie Shore, (1902-1985): Boston Bruins defenseman; MVP 4 times, first-team all-star 7 times.

Al Simmons, (1902-1956): AL outfielder had lifetime .334 batting average.

O.J. Simpson, b. 1947: running back rushed for 2,003 yds., 1973; AFC leading rusher 4 times.

George Sisler, (1893-1973): St. Louis Browns 1st baseman had record 257 hits, 1920; batted .340 lifetime.

Billy Smith, b. 1950: N.Y. Islanders goalie led team to 4 Stanley Cup championships.

Sam Snead, b. 1912: PGA and Masters champ 3 times each.

Warren Spahn, b. 1921: pitcher won 363 NL games; 20-game winner 13 times; Cy Young award, 1957.

Tris Speaker, (1885-1958): AL outfielder batted .344 over 22 seasons; hit record 793 career doubles.

Mark Spitz, b. 1950: swimmer won 7 1972 Olympic gold medals.

Amos Alonzo Stagg, (1862-1965): coached Univ. of Chicago football team for 41 years, including 5 undefeated seasons; introduced huddle, man-in-motion, and end-around play.

Willie Stargell, b. 1941: Pittsburgh Pirate slugger chosen NL, World Series MVP, 1979.

Bart Starr, b. 1934: Green Bay Packers quarterback led team to 5 NFL titles and 2 Super Bowl victories.

Roger Staubach, b. 1942: Dallas Cowboys quarterback; leading NFC passer 5 times.

Casey Stengel, (1890-1975): managed Yankees to 10 pennants, 7 championships, 1949-60.

Jackie Stewart, b. 1939: Scot auto racer retired with 27 Grand Prix victories.

John L. Sullivan, (1858-1918): last bareknuckle heavyweight champion, 1882-1892.

Fran Tarkenton, b. 1940: quarterback holds career passing records for touchdowns, completions, yardage.

Gustave Thoeni, b. 1951: Italian 4-time world alpine ski champ.

Jim Thorpe, (1888-1953): football All-America, 1911, 1912; won pentathlon and decathlon, 1912 Olympics.

Bill Tilden, (1893-1953): U.S. singles champ 7 times; played on 11 Davis Cup teams.

Y.A. Tittle, b. 1926: N.Y. Giants quarterback; MVP, 1961, 1963.

Lee Trevino, b. 1939: won the U.S. and British Open championships twice.

Bryan Trottier, b. 1956: N.Y. Islanders center led team to 4 consecutive Stanley Cup championships, 1980-83.

Mike Tyson, b. 1966: world heavyweight champion.

Wyomia Tyus, b. 1945: sprinter won 1964, 1968 Olympic 100-meter dash.

Johnny Unitas, b. 1933: Baltimore Colts quarterback passed for over 40,000 yds.; MVP, 1957, 1967.

Al Unser, b. 1939: Indy 500 winner 4 times.

Bobby Unser, b. 1934: Indy 500 winner 3 times.

Fernando Valenzuela, b. 1960: L.A. Dodgers pitcher won Cy Young award, 1981.

Norm Van Brocklin, (1926-1983): quarterback passed for game record 554 yds., 1951; MVP, 1960.

Honus Wagner, (1874-1955): Pittsburgh Pirates shortstop won 8 NL batting titles.

Tom Watson, b. 1949: golfer won British Open 5 times.

Johnny Weissmuller, (1903-1984): swimmer won 52 national championships, 5 Olympic gold medals; set 67 world records.

Jerry West, b. 1938: L.A. Lakers guard had career average 27 points per game; first team all-star 10 times.

Kathy Whitworth, b. 1939: women's golf leading money winner 8 times: first woman to earn over $300,000.

Ted Williams, b. 1918: Boston Red Sox outfielder won 6 batting titles; last major leaguer to hit over .400: .406 in 1941: .344 lifetime batting average.

Helen Wills, b. 1906: winner of 7 U.S., 8 British, 4 French women's singles titles.

John Wooden, b. 1910: coached UCLA basketball team to 10 national championships.

Mickey Wright, b. 1935: won LPGA championship 4 times, Vare Trophy 5 times; twice AP Woman-Athlete-of-the-Year.

Carl Yastrzemski, b. 1939: Boston Red Sox slugger won 3 batting titles, triple crown, 1967.

Cy Young, (1867-1955): pitcher won record 511 major league games.

Babe Didrikson Zaharias, (1914-1956): track star won 2 1932 Olympic gold medals; won numerous golf tournaments.

Professional Sports Arenas

The seating capacity of sports arenas can vary depending on the event being presented. The figures below are the normal seating capacity for basketball. (*) indicates hockey seating capacity. Domed stadiums can dramatically increase seating capacity for special occasions.

Name, location	Capacity
ARCO Arena, Sacramento	16,400
Arizona Veteran's Memorial Coliseum, Phoenix	14,471
Boston Garden	14,890-*14,451
Bradley Center, Milwaukee	18,400
Buffalo Memorial Auditorium	17,900-*16,433(a)
Capital Centre, Landover, Md.	19,411-*18,130
Charlotte Coliseum	23,500
Chicago Stadium	17,458-*17,317
The Coliseum, Richfield Township, Oh.	20,900
Great Western Forum	17,505-*16,005
Hartford Civic Center	*15,200
HemisFair Arena, San Antonio	15,800
Joe Louis Sports Arena, Detroit	*19,275
Kingdome, Seattle	40,192
Los Angeles Memorial Sports Arena	15,167
Madison Square Garden, New York	19,591-*17,500
Maple Leaf Gardens, Toronto	*16,382(a)
Market Square Arena, Indianapolis	16,912-*15,822
McNichols Sports Arena, Denver	17,022-*16,399
Meadowlands Arena, E. Rutherford, N.J.	20,149-*19,040
Met. Sports Center, Bloomington, Minn.	*15,449

Name, location	Capacity
Miami Arena	15,361
Montreal Forum	*16,074
Nassau Veterans Memorial Coliseum, Uniondale, N.Y.	*16,267
Northlands Coliseum, Edmonton	*17,502(a)
Oakland Coliseum Arena	15,011
Olympic Saddledome, Calgary, Alta.	*16,798
The Omni, Atlanta	16,522
Orlando Arena, Orlando, Fla.	15,500
Pacific Coliseum, Vancouver, B.C.	*16,553
Palace, Auburn Hills, Mich.	21,000
Pittsburgh Civic Arena	*16,033
Portland Memorial Coliseum	12,666
Quebec Coliseum	*15,434
Reunion Arena, Dallas	17,007
St. Louis Arena	*17,666
Salt Palace, Salt Lake City	12,212-*10,594
Seattle Center Coliseum	14,200
Spectrum, Philadelphia	17,967-*17,211
The Summit, Houston	16,279
Winnipeg Arena	*15,401
(a) includes standees	

Boxing Champions by Classes

As of Sept. 15, 1989 the only generally accepted title holder was in the heavyweight division. There are numerous governing bodies in boxing including the World Boxing Council, the World Boxing Assn., the International Boxing Federation, the United States Boxing Assn., the North American Boxing Federation, and the European Boxing Union. Other organizations are recognized by TV networks and the print media. All the governing bodies have their own champions and assorted boxing divisions. The following are the recognized champions in the principal divisions of the World Boxing Association, the World Boxing Council, and the International Boxing Federation.

Class, Weight Limit	WBA	WBC	IBF
Heavyweight	Mike Tyson, U.S.	Mike Tyson, U.S.	Mike Tyson, U.S.
Cruiserweight (195 lbs.) . . .	Evander Holyfield, U.S.	Carlos DeLeon, Puerto Rico	Glenn McCrory, England
Light Heavyweight (175 lbs.) . . .	Virgil Hill, U.S.	Jeff Harding, Australia,	Charles Williams, U.S.
Middleweight (160 lbs.)	Mike McCallum, U.S.	Roberto Duran, Panama	Michael Nunn, U.S.
Jr. Middleweight (154 lbs.) . . .	Julian Jackson, Virgin Islands	John Mugabi, U.S.	Gianfranco Rosi, Italy
Welterweight (147 lbs.)	Mark Breland, U.S.	Marlon Starling, U.S.	Simon Brown, U.S.
Jr. Welterweight (140 lbs.) . . .	Juan Coggi, Argentina	Julio Cesar Chavez, Mexico	Meldrick Taylor, U.S.
Lightweight (135 lbs.)	Edwin Rosario, Puerto Rico	Mauricio Aceves, Mexico	Pernell Whitaker, U.S.
Jr. Lightweight (130 lbs.)	Brian Mitchell, So. Africa	Pernell Whitaker, U.S.	Tony Lo Pez, U.S.
Featherweight (126 lbs.)	Antonio Esparragoza, Venezuela	Jeff Fenech, Australia	Jorge Paez, Mexico
Jr. Featherweight (122 lbs.) . . .	Juan Jose Estrada, Mexico	Daniel Zaragoza, Mexico	Fabrice Benichou, France
Bantamweight (118 lbs.)	Khaokor Galaxy, Thailand	Raul Perez, Mexico	Orlando Canizales, U.S.
Flyweight (112 lbs.)	Fidel Bassa, Colombia	Sot Chitalada, Thailand	Dave McAuley, Ireland

Ring Champions by Years

*Abandoned title

Heavyweights

1882-1892	John L. Sullivan (a)
1892-1897	James J. Corbett (b)
1897-1899	Robert Fitzsimmons
1899-1905	James J. Jeffries (c)
1905-1906	Marvin Hart
1906-1908	Tommy Burns
1908-1915	Jack Johnson
1915-1919	Jess Willard
1919-1926	Jack Dempsey
1926-1928	Gene Tunney*
1928-1930	vacant
1930-1932	Max Schmeling
1932-1933	Jack Sharkey
1933-1934	Primo Carnera
1934-1935	Max Baer
1935-1937	James J. Braddock
1937-1949	Joe Louis*
1949-1951	Ezzard Charles
1951-1952	Joe Walcott
1952-1956	Rocky Marciano*
1956-1959	Floyd Patterson
1959-1960	Ingemar Johansson
1960-1962	Floyd Patterson
1962-1964	Sonny Liston
1964-1967	Cassius Clay* (Muhammad Ali) (d)
1970-1973	Joe Frazier
1973-1974	George Foreman
1974-1978	Muhammad Ali
1978-1979	Leon Spinks (e), Muhammad Ali*
1978	Ken Norton (WBC), Larry Holmes (WBC) (f)
1979	John Tate (WBA)
1980	Mike Weaver (WBA)
1982	Michael Dokes (WBA)
1983	Gerrie Coetzee (WBA)
1984	Tim Witherspoon (WBC); Pinklon Thomas (WBC); Greg Page (WBA)
1985	Tony Tubbs (WBA); Michael Spinks (IBF)
1986	Tim Witherspoon (WBC); Trevor Berbick (WBC); Mike Tyson (WBC); James (Bonecrusher) Smith (WBA).
1987	Mike Tyson (WBA).

(a) London Prize Ring (bare knuckle champion).
(b) First Marquis of Queensberry champion.
(c) Jeffries abandoned the title (1905) and designated Marvin Hart and Jack Root as logical contenders and agreed to referee a fight between them, the winner to be declared champion. Hart defeated Root in 12 rounds (1905) and in turn was defeated by Tommy Burns (1906) who immediately laid claim to the title. Jack Johnson defeated Burns (1908) and was recognized as champion. He clinched the title by defeating Jeffries in an attempted comeback (1910).
(d) Title declared vacant by the WBA and other groups in 1967 after Clay's refusal to fulfill his military obligation. Joe Frazier was recognized as champion by 6 states, Mexico, and So. America. Jimmy Ellis was declared champion by the WBA. Frazier KOd Ellis, Feb. 16, 1970.

(e) After Spinks defeated Ali, the WBC recognized Ken Norton as champion. Norton subsequently lost his title to Larry Holmes.
(f) Holmes was stripped of his WBC title in 1984. He was the IBF champion when he lost to Michael Spinks.

Light Heavyweights

1903	Jack Root, George Gardner
1903-1905	Bob Fitzsimmons
1905-1912	Philadelphia Jack O'Brien*
1912-1916	Jack Dillon
1916-1920	Battling Levinsky
1920-1922	George Carpentier
1922-1923	Battling Siki
1923-1925	Mike McTigue
1925-1926	Paul Berlenbach
1926-1927	Jack Delaney*
1927-1929	Tommy Loughran*
1930-1934	Maxey Rosenbloom
1934-1935	Bob Olin
1935-1939	John Henry Lewis*
1939	Melio Bettina
1939-1941	Billy Conn*
1941	Anton Christoforidis (won NBA title)
1941-1948	Gus Lesnevich, Freddie Mills
1948-1950	Freddie Mills
1950-1952	Joey Maxim
1952-1960	Archie Moore
1961-1962	vacant
1962-1963	Harold Johnson
1963-1965	Willie Pastrano
1965-1966	Jose Torres
1966-1968	Dick Tiger
1968-1974	Bob Foster*, John Conteh (WBA)
1975-1977	John Conteh (WBC), Miguel Cuello (WBC), Victor Galindez (WBA)
1978	Mike Rossman (WBA), Mate Parlov (WBC), Marvin Johnson (WBC)
1979	Victor Galindez (WBA), Matthew Saad Muhammad (WBC)
1980	Eddie Mustava Muhammad (WBA)
1981	Michael Spinks (WBA), Dwight Braxton (WBC)
1983	Michael Spinks
1986	Marvin Johnson (WBA); Dennis Andries (WBC)
1987	Thomas Hearns (WBC); Leslie Stewart (WBA); Virgil Hill (WBA); Don Lalonde (WBC)
1988	Ray Leonard* (WBC)
1989	Jeff Harding (WBC)

Middleweights

1884-1891	Jack "Nonpareil" Dempsey
1891-1897	Bob Fitzsimmons*
1897-1907	Tommy Ryan*
1907-1908	Stanley Ketchel, Billy Papke
1908-1910	Stanley Ketchel
1911-1913	vacant
1913	Frank Klaus, George Chip
1914-1917	Al McCoy
1917-1920	Mike O'Dowd

1920-1923	Johnny Wilson
1923-1926	Harry Greb
1926-1931	Tiger Flowers, Mickey Walker
1931-1932	Gorilla Jones (NBA)
1932-1937	Marcel Thil
1938	Al Hostak (NBA), Solly Krieger (NBA)
1939-1940	Al Hostak (NBA)
1941-1947	Tony Zale
1947-1948	Rocky Graziano
1948	Tony Zale, Marcel Cerdan
1949-1951	Jake LaMotta
1951	Ray Robinson, Randy Turpin, Ray Robinson*
1953-1955	Carl (Bobo) Olson
1955-1957	Ray Robinson
1957	Gene Fullmer, Ray Robinson, Carmen Basilio
1958	Ray Robinson
1959	Gene Fullmer (NBA); Ray Robinson (N.Y.)
1960	Gene Fullmer (NBA); Paul Pender (New York and Mass.)
1961	Gene Fullmer (NBA); Terry Downes (New York, Mass., Europe)
1962	Gene Fullmer, Dick Tiger (NBA), Paul Pender (New York and Mass.)*
1963	Dick Tiger (universal).
1963-1965	Joey Giardello
1965-1966	Dick Tiger
1966-1967	Emile Griffith
1967	Nino Benvenuti
1967-1968	Emile Griffith
1968-1970	Nino Benvenuti
1970-1977	Carlos Monzon*
1977-1978	Rodrigo Valdez
1978-1979	Hugo Corro
1979-1980	Vito Antuofermo
1980	Alan Minter, Marvin Hagler
1987	Ray Leonard* (WBC); Thomas Hearns (WBC); Sumbu Kalambay (WBA).
1988	Iran Barkley (WBC)
1989	Mike McCallum (WBA); Roberto Duran (WBC)

Welterweights

1892-1894	Mysterious Billy Smith
1894-1896	Tommy Ryan
1896	Kid McCoy*
1900	Rube Ferns, Matty Matthews
1901	Rube Ferns
1901-1904	Joe Walcott
1904-1906	Dixie Kid, Joe Walcott, Honey Mellody
1907-1911	Mike Sullivan
1911-1915	vacant
1915-1919	Ted Lewis
1919-1922	Jack Britton
1922-1926	Mickey Walker
1926	Pete Latzo
1927-1929	Joe Dundee
1929	Jackie Fields
1930	Jack Thompson, Tommy Freeman
1931	Freeman, Thompson, Lou Brouillard
1932	Jackie Fields
1933	Young Corbett, Jimmy McLarnin
1934	Barney Ross, Jimmy McLarnin
1935-1938	Barney Ross
1938-1940	Henry Armstrong
1940-1941	Fritzie Zivic
1941-1946	Fred Cochrane
1946-1946	Marty Servo*; Ray Robinson (a)
1946-1950	Ray Robinson*
1951	Johnny Bratton (NBA)
1951-1954	Kid Gavilan
1954-1955	Johnny Saxton
1955	Tony De Marco, Carmen Basilio
1956	Carmen Basilio, Johnny Saxton, Basilio
1957	Carmen Basilio*
1958-1960	Virgil Akins, Don Jordan
1960	Benny Paret
1961	Emile Griffith, Benny Paret
1962	Emile Griffith
1963	Luis Rodriguez, Emile Griffith
1964-1966	Emile Griffith*
1966-1969	Curtis Cokes
1969-1970	Jose Napoles, Billy Backus
1971-1975	Jose Napoles
1975-1976	John Stracey (WBC), Angel Espada (WBA)
1976-1979	Carlos Palomino (WBC), Jose Cuevas (WBA)
1979	Wilfredo Benitez (WBC), Sugar Ray Leonard (WBC)
1980	Roberto Duran (WBC), Thomas Hearns (WBA), Sugar Ray Leonard (WBC)
1981-1982	Sugar Ray Leonard*

1983	Donald Curry (WBA); Milton McCrory (WBC)
1985	Donald Curry
1986	Lloyd Honeyghan (WBC)
1987	Mark Breland (WBA); Marlon Starling (WBA); Jorge Vaca (WBC).
1988	Tomas Molinares (WBA); Lloyd Honeyghan (WBC).
1989	Marlon Starling (WBC); Mark Breland (WBA)

(a) Robinson gained the title by defeating Tommy Bell in an elimination agreed to by the NY Commission and the NBA. Both claimed Robinson waived his title when he won the middleweight crown from LaMotta in 1951.

Lightweights

1896-1899	Kid Lavigne
1899-1902	Frank Erne
1902-1908	Joe Gans
1908-1910	Battling Nelson
1910-1912	Ad Wolgast
1912-1914	Willie Ritchie
1914-1917	Freddie Welsh
1917-1925	Benny Leonard*
1925	Jimmy Goodrich, Rocky Kansas
1926-1930	Sammy Mandell
1930	Al Singer, Tony Canzoneri
1930-1933	Tony Canzoneri
1933-1935	Barney Ross*
1935-1936	Tony Canzoneri
1936-1938	Lou Ambers
1938	Henry Armstrong
1939	Lou Ambers
1940	Lew Jenkins
1941-1943	Sammy Angott
1944	S. Angott (NBA), J. Zurita (NBA)
1945-1951	Ike Williams (NBA: later universal)
1951-1952	James Carter
1952	Lauro Salas, James Carter
1953-1954	James Carter
1954	Paddy De Marco; James Carter
1955	James Carter; Bud Smith
1956	Bud Smith, Joe Brown
1956-1962	Joe Brown
1962-1965	Carlos Ortiz
1965	Ismael Laguna
1965-1968	Carlos Ortiz
1968-1969	Teo Cruz
1969-1970	Mando Ramos
1970	Ismael Laguna, Ken Buchanan (WBA)
1971	Mando Ramos (WBC), Pedro Carrasco (WBC)
1972-1979	Roberto Duran* (WBA)
1972	Pedro Carrasco, Mando Ramos, Chango Carmona, Rodolfo Gonzalez (all WBC)
1974-1976	Guts Ishimatsu (WBC)
1976-1977	Esteban De Jesus (WBC)
1979	Jim Watt (WBC), Ernesto Espana (WBA)
1980	Hilmer Kenty (WBA)
1981	Alexis Arguello (WBC), Sean O'Grady (WBA), Arturo Frias (WBA)
1982-1984	Ray Mancini (WBA)
1983	Edwin Rosario (WBC)
1984	Livingstone Bramble (WBA); Jose Luis Ramirez (WBC)
1985	Hector (Macho) Camacho (WBC)
1986	Edwin Rosario (WBA); Jose Luis Ramirez (WBC).
1987	Julio Cesar Chavez (WBA).
1989	Edwin Rosario (WBA); Pernell Whitaker (WBC).

Featherweights

1892-1900	George Dixon (disputed)
1900-1901	Terry McGovern, Young Corbett*
1901-1912	Abe Attell
1912-1923	Johnny Kilbane
1923	Eugene Criqui, Johnny Dundee
1923-1925	Johnny Dundee*
1925-1927	Kid Kaplan*
1927-1928	Benny Bass, Tony Canzoneri
1928-1929	Andre Routis
1929-1932	Battling Battalino*
1932-1934	Tommy Paul (NBA)
1933-1936	Freddie Miller
1936-1937	Petey Sarron
1937-1938	Henry Armstrong*
1938-1940	Joey Archibald (b)
1940-41	Harry Jeffra
1942-1948	Willie Pep
1948-1949	Sandy Saddler (continued)

1949-1950	Willie Pep
1950-1957	Sandy Saddler*
1957-1959	Hogan (Kid) Bassey
1959-1963	Davey Moore
1963-1964	Sugar Ramos
1964-1967	Vicente Saldivar*
1968-1971	Paul Rojas (WBA), Sho Saijo (WBA)
1971	Antonio Gomez (WBA), Kuniaki Shibada (WBC)
1972	Ernesto Marcel* (WBA), Clemente Sanchez* (WBC), Jose Legra (WBC)
1973	Eder Jofre (WBC)
1974	Ruben Olivares (WBA), Alexis Arguello (WBA), Bobby Chacon (WBC)
1975	Ruben Olivares (WBC), David Kotey (WBC)
1976	Danny Lopez (WBC)
1977	Rafael Ortega (WBA)

1978	Cecilio Lastra (WBA), Eusebio Pedrosa (WBA)
1980	Salvador Sanchez (WBC)
1982	Juan LaPorte (WBC)
1984	Wilfredo Gomez (WBC); Azumah Nelson (WBC)
1985	Barry McGuigan (WBA)
1986	Steve Cruz (WBA)
1987	Antonio Esparragoza (WBA)
1988	Jeff Fenech (WBC)

(b) After Petey Scalzo knocked out Archibald in an overweight match and was refused a title bout, the NBA named Scalzo champion. The NBA title succession: Scalzo, 1938-1941; Richard Lemos, 1941; Jackie Wilson, 1941-1943; Jackie Callura, 1943; Phil Terranova, 1943-1944; Sal Bartolo, 1944-1946.

History of Heavyweight Championship Bouts

*Title Changed Hands

1889—July 8—John L. Sullivan def. Jake Kilrain, 75, Richburg, Miss. Last championship bare knuckles bout.

***1892**—Sept. 7—James J. Corbett def. John L. Sullivan, 21, New Orleans. Big gloves used for first time.

1894—Jan. 25—James J. Corbett KOd Charley Mitchell, 3, Jacksonville, Fla.

***1897**—Bob Fitzsimmons def. James J. Corbett, 14, Carson City, Nev.

***1899**—June 9—James J. Jeffries def. Bob Fitzsimmons, 11, Coney Island, N.Y.

1899—Nov. 3—James J. Jeffries def. Tom Sharkey, 25, Coney Island, N.Y.

1900—May 11—James J. Jeffries KOd James J. Corbett, 23, Coney Island, N.Y.

1901—Nov. 15—James J. Jeffries KOd Gus Ruhlin, 5, San Francisco.

1902—July 25—James J. Jeffries KOd Bob Fitzsimmons, 8, San Francisco.

1903—Aug. 14—James J. Jeffries KOd James J. Corbett, 10, San Francisco.

1904—Aug. 26—James J. Jeffries KOd Jack Monroe, 2, San Francisco.

***1905**—James J. Jeffries retired, July 3—Marvin Hart KOd Jack Root, 12, Reno. Jeffries refereed and presented the title to the victor. Jack O'Brien also claimed the title.

***1906**—Feb. 23—Tommy Burns def. Marvin Hart, 20, Los Angeles.

1906—Nov. 28—Philadelphia Jack O'Brien and Tommy Burns, 20, draw, Los Angeles.

1907—May 8—Tommy Burns def. Jack O'Brien, 20, Los Angeles.

1907—July 4—Tommy Burns KOd Bill Squires, 1, Colma, Cal.

1907—Dec. 2—Tommy Burns KOd Gunner Moir, 10, London.

1908—Feb. 10—Tommy Burns KOd Jack Palmer, 4, London.

1908—March 17—Tommy Burns KOd Jem Roche, 1, Dublin.

1908—April 18—Tommy Burns KOd Jewey Smith, 5, Paris.

1908—June 13—Tommy Burns KOd Bill Squires, 8, Paris.

1908—Aug. 24—Tommy Burns KOd Bill Squires, 13, Sydney, New South Wales.

1908—Sept. 2—Tommy Burns KOd Bill Lang, 2, Melbourne, Australia.

***1908**—Dec. 26—Jack Johnson KOd Tommy Burns, 14, Sydney, Australia. Police halted contest.

1909—May 19—Jack Johnson and Jack O'Brien, 6, draw, Philadelphia.

1909—June 30—Jack Johnson and Tony Ross, 6, draw, Pittsburgh.

1909—Sept. 9—Jack Johnson and Al Kaufman, 10, draw, San Francisco.

1909—Oct. 16—Jack Johnson KOd Stanley Ketchel, 12, Colma, Cal.

1910—July 4—Jack Johnson KOd Jim Jeffries, 15, Reno, Nev. Jeffries came back from retirement.

1912—July 4—Jack Johnson def. Jim Flynn, 9, Las Vegas, N.M. Contest stopped by police.

1913—Nov. 28—Jack Johnson KOd Andre Spaul, 2, Paris.

1913—Dec. 9—Jack Johnson and Jim Johnson, 10, draw, Paris. Bout called a draw when Jack Johnson declared he had broken his arm.

1914—June 27—Jack Johnson def. Frank Moran, 20, Paris.

***1915**—April 5—Jess Willard KOd Jack Johnson, 26, Havana, Cuba.

1916—March 25—Jess Willard and Frank Moran, 10, draw, New York.

***1919**—July 4—Jack Dempsey KOd Jess Willard, Toledo, Oh. Willard failed to answer bell for 4th round.

1920—Sept. 6—Jack Dempsey KOd Billy Miske, 3, Benton Harbor, Mich.

1920—Dec. 14—Jack Dempsey KOd Bill Brennan, 12, New York.

1921—July 2—Jack Dempsey KOd George Carpentier, 4, Boyle's Thirty Acres, Jersey City, N.J. Carpentier had held the so-called white heavyweight title since July 16, 1914, in a series established in 1913, after Jack Johnson's exile in Europe late in 1912.

1923—July 4—Jack Dempsey def. Tom Gibbons, 15, Shelby, Mont.

1923—Sept. 14—Jack Dempsey KOd Luis Firpo, 2, New York.

***1926**—Sept. 23—Gene Tunney def. Jack Dempsey, 10, Philadelphia.

1927—Sept. 22—Gene Tunney def. Jack Dempsey, 10, Chicago.

1928—July 26—Gene Tunney KOd Tom Heeney, 11, New York; soon afterward he announced his retirement.

***1930**—June 12—Max Schmeling def. Jack Sharkey, 4, New York. Sharkey fouled Schmeling in a bout which was generally considered to have resulted in the election of a successor to Gene Tunney, New York.

1931—July 3—Max Schmeling KOd Young Stribling, 15, Cleveland.

***1932**—June 21—Jack Sharkey def. Max Schmeling, 15, New York.

***1933**—June 29—Primo Carnera KOd Jack Sharkey, 6, New York.

1933—Oct. 22—Primo Carnera def. Paulino Uzcudun, 15, Rome.

1934—March 1—Primo Carnera def. Tommy Loughran, 15, Miami.

***1934**—June 14—Max Baer KOd Primo Carnera, 11, New York.

***1935**—June 13—James J. Braddock def. Max Baer, 15, New York.

***1937**—June 22—Joe Louis KOd James J. Braddock, 8, Chicago.

1937—Aug. 30—Joe Louis def. Tommy Farr, 15, New York.

1938—Feb. 23—Joe Louis KOd Nathan Mann, 3, New York.

1938—April 1—Joe Louis KOd Harry Thomas, 5, New York.

1938—June 22—Joe Louis KOd Max Schmeling, 1, New York.

1939—Jan. 25—Joe Louis KOd John H. Lewis, 1, New York.

1939—April 17—Joe Louis KOd Jack Roper, 1, Los Angeles.

1939—June 28—Joe Louis KOd Tony Galento, 4, New York.

1939—Sept. 20—Joe Louis KOd Bob Pastor, 11, Detroit.

1940—February 9—Joe Louis def. Arturo Godoy, 15, New York.

1940—March 29—Joe Louis KOd Johnny Paycheck, 2, New York.

1940—June 20—Joe Louis KOd Arturo Godoy, 8, New York.

1940—Dec. 16—Joe Louis KOd Al McCoy, 6, Boston.

1941—Jan. 31—Joe Louis KOd Red Burman, 5, New York.

1941—Feb. 17—Joe Louis KOd Gus Dorazio, 2, Philadelphia.

1941—March 21—Joe Louis KOd Abe Simon, 13, Detroit.

1941—April 8—Joe Louis KOd Tony Musto, 9, St. Louis.

1941—May 23—Joe Louis def. Buddy Baer, 7, Washington, D.C., on a disqualification.

1941—June 18—Joe Louis KOd Billy Conn, 13, New York.

1941—Sept. 29—Joe Louis KOd Lou Nova, 6, New York.

1942—Jan. 9—Joe Louis KOd Buddy Baer, 1, New York.

1942—March 27—Joe Louis KOd Abe Simon, 6, New York.

1946—June 19—Joe Louis KOd Billy Conn, 8, New York.

1946—Sept. 18—Joe Louis KOd Tami Mauriello, 1, New York.

1947—Dec. 5—Joe Louis def. Joe Walcott, 15, New York.
1948—June 25—Joe Louis KOd Joe Walcott, 11, New York.
*1949—June 22—Following Joe Louis' retirement Ezzard Charles def. Joe Walcott, 15, Chicago, NBA recognition only.
1949—Aug. 10—Ezzard Charles KOd Gus Lesnevich, 7, New York.
1949—Oct. 14—Ezzard Charles KOd Pat Valentino, 8, San Francisco; clinched American title.
1950—Aug. 15—Ezzard Charles KOd Freddy Beshore, 14, Buffalo.
1950—Sept. 27—Ezzard Charles def. Joe Louis in latter's attempted comeback, 15, New York; universal recognition.
1950—Dec. 5—Ezzard Charles KOd Nick Barone, 11, Cincinnati.
1951—Jan. 12—Ezzard Charles KOd Lee Oma, 10, New York.
1951—March 7—Ezzard Charles def. Joe Walcott, 15, Detroit.
1951—May 30—Ezzard Charles def. Joey Maxim, light heavyweight champion, 15, Chicago.
*1951—July 18—Joe Walcott KOd Ezzard Charles, 7, Pittsburgh.
1952—June 5—Joe Walcott def. Ezzard Charles, 15, Philadelphia.
*1952—Sept. 23—Rocky Marciano KOd Joe Walcott, 13, Philadelphia.
1953—May 15—Rocky Marciano KOd Joe Walcott, 1, Chicago.
1953—Sept. 24—Rocky Marciano KOd Roland LaStarza, 11, New York.
1954—June 17—Rocky Marciano def. Ezzard Charles, 15, New York.
1954—Sept. 17—Rocky Marciano KOd Ezzard Charles, 8, New York.
1955—May 16—Rocky Marciano KOd Don Cockell, 9, San Francisco.
1955—Sept. 21—Rocky Marciano KOd Archie Moore, 9, New York. Marciano retired undefeated, Apr. 27, 1956.
*1956—Nov. 30—Floyd Patterson KOd Archie Moore, 5, Chicago.
1957—July 29—Floyd Patterson KOd Hurricane Jackson, 10, New York.
1957—Aug. 22—Floyd Patterson KOd Pete Rademacher, 6, Seattle.
1958—Aug. 18—Floyd Patterson KOd Roy Harris, 12, Los Angeles.
1959—May 1—Floyd Patterson KOd Brian London, 11, Indianapolis.
*1959—June 26—Ingemar Johansson KOd Floyd Patterson, 3, New York.
*1960—June 20—Floyd Patterson KOd Ingemar Johansson, 5, New York. First heavyweight in boxing history to regain title.
1961—Mar. 13—Floyd Patterson KOd Ingemar Johansson, 6, Miami Beach.
1961—Dec. 4—Floyd Patterson KOd Tom McNeeley, 4, Toronto.
*1962—Sept. 25—Sonny Liston KOd Floyd Patterson, 1, Chicago.
1963—July 22—Sonny Liston KOd Floyd Patterson, 1, Las Vegas.
*1964—Feb. 25—Cassius Clay KOd Sonny Liston, 7, Miami Beach.
1965—May 25—Cassius Clay KOd Sonny Liston, 1, Lewiston, Maine.
1965—Nov. 11—Cassius Clay KOd Floyd Patterson, 12, Las Vegas.
1966—Mar. 29—Cassius Clay def. George Chuvalo, 15, Toronto.
1966—May 21—Cassius Clay KOd Henry Cooper, 6, London.
1966—Aug. 6—Cassius Clay KOd Brian London, 3, London.
1966—Sept. 10—Cassius Clay KOd Karl Mildenberger, 12, Frankfurt, Germany.

1966—Nov. 14—Cassius Clay KOd Cleveland Williams, 3, Houston.
1967—Feb. 6—Cassius Clay def. Ernie Terrell, 15, Houston.
1967—Mar. 22—Cassius Clay KOd Zora Folley, 7, New York. Clay was stripped of his title by the WBA and others for refusing military service.
*1970—Feb. 16—Joe Frazier KOd Jimmy Ellis, 5, New York.
1970—Nov. 18—Joe Frazier KOd Bob Foster, 2, Detroit.
1971—Mar. 8—Joe Frazier def. Cassius Clay (Muhammad Ali), 15, New York.
1972—Jan. 15—Joe Frazier KOd Terry Daniels, 4, New Orleans.
1972—May 25—Joe Frazier KOd Ron Stander, 5, Omaha.
*1973—Jan. 22—George Foreman KOd Joe Frazier, 2, Kingston, Jamaica.
1973—Sept. 1—George Foreman KOd Joe Roman, 1, Tokyo.
1974—Mar. 3—George Foreman KOd Ken Norton, 2, Caracas.
*1974—Oct. 30—Muhammad Ali KOd George Foreman, 8, Zaire.
1975—Mar. 24—Muhammad Ali KOd Chuck Wepner, 15, Cleveland.
1975—May 16—Muhammad Ali KOd Ron Lyle, 11, Las Vegas.
1975—June 30—Muhammad Ali def. Joe Bugner, 15, Malaysia.
1975—Oct. 1—Muhammad Ali KOd Joe Frazier, 14, Manila.
1976—Feb. 20—Muhammad Ali KOd Jean-Pierre Coopman, 5, San Juan.
1976—Apr. 30—Muhammad Ali def. Jimmy Young, 15, Landover, Md.
1976—May 25—Muhammad Ali KOd Richard Dunn, 5, Munich.
1976—Sept. 28—Muhammad Ali def. Ken Norton, 15, New York.
1977—May 16—Muhammad Ali def. Alfredo Evangelista, 15, Landover, Md.
1977—Sept. 29—Muhammad Ali def. Earnie Shavers, 15, New York.
*1978—Feb. 15—Leon Spinks def. Muhammad Ali, 15, Las Vegas.
*1978—Sept. 15—Muhammad Ali def. Leon Spinks, 15, New Orleans. Ali retired in 1979.

(Bouts when title changed hands only)

*1978—June 9—(WBC) Larry Holmes def. Ken Norton, 15, Las Vegas.
*1980—Mar. 31—(WBA) Mike Weaver KOd John Tate, 15, Knoxville.
*1982—Dec. 10—(WBA) Michael Dokes KOd Mike Weaver, 1, Las Vegas.
*1983—Sept. 23—(WBA) Gerrie Coetzee KOd Michael Dokes, 10, Richfield, Oh.
*1984—Mar. 10—(WBC) Tim Witherspoon def. Greg Page, 12, Las Vegas, Nev.
*1984—Aug. 31—(WBC) Pinklon Thomas def. Tim Witherspoon, 12, Las Vegas, Nev.
*1984—Dec. 2—(WBA) Greg Page KOd Gerrie Coetzee, 8, Sun City, Bophuthatswana
*1985—Apr. 29—(WBA) Tony Tubbs def. Greg Page, 15, Buffalo, N.Y.
*1985—Sept. 21—(IBF) Michael Spinks def. Larry Holmes, 15, Las Vegas, Nev.
*1986—Jan. 17—(WBA) Tim Witherspoon def. Tony Tubbs, 15, Atlanta, Ga.
*1986—Mar. 23—(WBC) Trevor Berbick def. Pinklon Thomas, 12, Miami, Fla.
*1986—Nov. 22—(WBC) Mike Tyson KOd Trevor Berbick, 2, Las Vegas.
*1986—Dec. 12—(WBA) James (Bonecrusher) Smith KOd Tim Witherspoon, 1, New York.
*(1987—Mar. 7—(WBA) Mike Tyson def. James (Bonecrusher) Smith, 12, Las Vegas.

Sports Halls of Fame

Source: Assn. of Sports Museums & Halls of Fame

Sport, location	1988 visitors
Baseball, Cooperstown, N.Y.	309,000
Pro Football, Canton, Oh.	212,541
Hockey, Toronto, Ont.	160,000
Basketball, Springfield, Mass.	130,000
Tennis, Newport, R.I.	100,000
Thoroughbred Racing, Saratoga Springs, N.Y.	55,000

Sport, location	1988 visitors
Softball, Oklahoma City, Okla.	50,000
Golf, Pinehurst, N.C.	40,000
Greyhound Racing, Abilene, Kan.	40,000
Bowling, St. Louis, Mo.	34,000
Swimming, Ft. Lauderdale, Fla.	22,000
Harness Racing, Goshen, N.Y.	20,000

World Swimming Records

As of Sept., 1989

Men's Records

Freestyle

Distance	Time	Holder	Country	Where made	Date
50 Meters	0:22.12	Tom Jager	U.S.	Tokyo	Aug. 20, 1989
100 Meters	0:48.42	Matt Biondi	U.S.	Austin, Tex.	Aug. 11, 1988
200 Meters	1:46.69	Giorgio Lamberti	Italy	Bonn	Aug. 15, 1989
400 Meters	3:46.95	Ewe Dassler	E. Germany	Seoul	Sept., 1988
800 Meters	7:50.64	Vladimir Salnikov	USSR	Moscow	July 4, 1986
1,500 Meters	14:54.76	Vladimir Salnikov	USSR	Moscow	Feb. 22, 1983

Breaststroke

100 Meters	1:01.49	Adrian Moorhouse	Gt. Britain	Bonn	Aug. 15, 1989
200 Meters	2:12.89	Mike Barrowman	Canada	Tokyo	Aug. 20, 1989

Butterfly

100 Meters	0:52.84	Pablo Morales	U.S.	Orlando, Fla.	June 23, 1986
200 Meters	1:56.24	Michael Gross	W. Germany	Bonn, W. Germany	June 24, 1986

Backstroke

100 Meters	0:54.91	David Berkoff	U.S.	Austin, Tex.	Aug. 1988
200 Meters	1:58.14	Igor Polianskiy	USSR	Erfurt, E. Germany	Mar. 3, 1985

Individual Medley

200 Meters	2:00.11	Dave Wharton	U.S.	Tokyo	Aug. 20, 1989
400 Meters	4:14.75	Tamas Darnyi	Hungary	Seoul	Sept., 1988

Freestyle Relays

400 M. (4×100)	3:16.53	Jacobs, Dalbey, Jager, Biondi	U.S.	Seoul	Sept. 23, 1988
800 M. (4×200)	7:12.51	Dalbey, Cetlinsky, Gjertsen, Biondi	U.S.	Seoul	Sept., 1988

Medley Relays

400 M. (4×100)	3:36.93	Berkoff, Schroeder, Jacobs, Biondi	U.S.	Seoul	Sept. 25, 1988

Women's Records

Freestyle

Distance	Time	Holder	Country	Where made	Date
50 Meters	0:24.98	Yang Wenyi	China	China	Apr. 11, 1988
100 Meters	0:54.73	Kristin Otto	E. Germany	Madrid	Aug. 19, 1986
200 Meters	1:57.65	Kristin Otto	E. Germany	Seoul	Sept., 1988
400 Meters	4:03.85	Janet Evans	U.S.	Seoul	Sept. 22, 1988
800 Meters	8:16.22	Janet Evans	U.S.	Tokyo	Aug. 20, 1989
1,500 Meters	15:52.10	Janet Evans	U.S.	Orlando, Fla.	Mar. 22, 1988

Breaststroke

100 Meters	1:07.91	Silke Hoerner	E. Germany	Strasbourg, France	Aug. 21, 1987
200 Meters	2:26.71	Silke Hoerner	E. Germany	Seoul	Sept., 1988

Butterfly

100 Meters	0:57.93	Mary T. Meagher	U.S.	Brown Deer, Wis.	Aug. 16, 1981
200 Meters	2:05.96	Mary T. Meagher	U.S.	Brown Deer, Wis.	Aug. 13, 1981

Backstroke

100 Meters	1:00.59	Ina Kleber	E. Germany	Moscow	Aug. 24, 1984
200 Meters	2:08.60	Betsy Mitchell	U.S.	Orlando, Fla.	June 27, 1986

Individual Medley

200 Meters	2:10.60	Petra Schneider	E. Germany	Gainesville, Fla.	Aug. 1, 1982
400 Meters	4:36.10	Petra Schneider	E. Germany	Ecuador	Aug. 1, 1982

Freestyle Relays

400 M. (4×100)	3:40.57	(Otto, Stellmach, Friedrich, Schulze)	E. Germany	Madrid	Aug. 19, 1986
800 M. (4×200)	7:55:47	Stellmach, Strauss, Mohring, Friedrich)	E. Germany	Strasbourg, France	Aug. 18, 1987

Medley Relays

400 M. (4×100)	4:03.69	National Team (Kleber, Gerasch, Geissler, Meineke)	E. Germany	Moscow	Aug. 24, 1984

U.S. Long Course Swimming Championships in 1989

Los Angeles, Cal., July 31-Aug. 4, 1989

Men

50M Freestyle—Matt Biondi. Time—0:22.36.
100M Freestyle—Lang Brent. Time—0:50.17
200M Freestyle—Doug Gjertsen. Time—1:48.70
400M Freestyle—Dan Jorgensen. Time—3:50.88
800M Freestyle—Dan Jorgensen. Time—7:56.61.
1,500M Freestyle—Lars Jorgensen. Time—15:17.33.
100M Breaststroke—Rich Schroeder. Time—1:02.46.
200M Breaststroke—Mike Barrowman. Time—2:14.74.
100M Butterfly—Wade King. Time—0:53.72.
200M Butterfly—Melvin Stewart. Time—1:57.94.
100M Backstroke—Geoff Cronin. Time—0:56.14.
200M Backstroke—Dan Veatch. Time—2:02.09.
200M Individual Medley—Dave Wharton. Time—2:01.48
400M Individual Medley—Dave Wharton. Time—4:15.93.
400M Freestyle Relay—Longhorn "A". Time—3:22.00.
800M Freestyle Relay—Longhorn "A". Time—7:22.78.
400M Medley Relay—Ft. Lauderdale. Time—3:45.26.

Women

50M Freestyle—Leigh Ann Fetter. Time—0:25.55.
100M Freestyle—Nicole Haislett. Time—0:56.15.
200M Freestyle—Julie Kole. Time—2:00.95.
400M Freestyle—Janet Evans. Time—4:06.73.
800M Freestyle—Janet Evans. Time—8:22.11
1,500M Freestyle—Julie Kole. Time—16:14.12.
100M Breaststroke—Tracy McFarlane. Time—1:09.88.
200M Breaststroke—Mary Blanchard. Time—2:31.59.
100M Backstroke—Betsy Mitchell. Time—1:02.37.
200M Backstroke—Kristen Linehan. Time—2:14.01.
100M Butterfly—Pamela Minthorn. Time—1:01.12.
200M Butterfly—Pamela Minthorn. Time—2:11.88.
200M Individual Medley—Janet Evans. Time—2:15.15.
400M Individual Medley—Janet Evans. Time—4:39.36.
400M Freestyle Relay—Longhorn "A". Time—3:45.92.
800M Freestyle Relay—Longhorn "A". Time—8:11.54

U.S. Outdoor Diving Championships in 1989

Men

One Meter—Kent Ferguson.
Three Meter—Kent Ferguson.
Platform—Matt Scoggin.

Women

One Meter—Wendy Lucero.
Three Meter—Wendy Lucero.
Platform—Wendy Wyland.

1989 Rifle and Pistol Individual Championships

Source: National Rifle Association of America

National Outdoor Rifle and Pistol Championships

Pistol — Dr. Darius Young, Alberta, Canada, 2651-137X.
Civilian Pistol — Allen Fulford, Vienna, Ga. 2639-126X.
Woman Pistol — Roxane Conrad, Quantico, Va., 2594-101X.
Collegiate Pistol — Keith Hanzel, Falls Church, Va., 2533-78X.
Smallbore Rifle Prone — David Weaver, Oil City, Pa., 6395-530X.
Civilian Smallbore Rifle Prone — David Weaver, 6395-530X.
Woman Smallbore Rifle Prone — Carolyn Millard-Sparks, Atlanta, Ga., 6391-509X.
Collegiate Smallbore Rifle Prone — William H. Dodd, Queenstown, Md., 6381-499X.
Smallbore Rifle 3-Position — Thomas Tamas, Columbus, Ga., 2271-82.

Civilian Smallbore Rifle 3-Position — Lones Wigger Jr., Colorado Springs, Co., 2255-73.
Woman Smallbore Rifle 3-Position — Kirsten Pasch, Hibbing, Minn., 2240-67.
Collegiate Smallbore Rifle 3-Position — Erin Gestl, Bethlehem, Pa., 2190-59.
Highpower Rifle — Patrick McCann, Staunton, Ill. 2371-106X.
Woman Highpower Rifle — Nancy Gallagher, Phoenix, Ariz., 2331-82X.
Civilian Highpower Rifle — Patrick McCann, 2371-106X.
Collegiate Highpower Rifle — Lowell Johnson, State College, Pa.,2335-66X.

U. S. NRA International Shooting Championships

Smallbore Free Rifle Prone — Ernest Vande Zande, Vancouver, Wash., 1187.3.
Smallbore Free Rifle Position — Glenn Dubis, Ft. Benning, Ga., 3599.6.
Men's Air Rifle — William Dodd, Queenstown, Md., 1855.2.
Women's Air Rifle — Deena Wigger, Colorado Springs, Co., 1673.5.
Women's Standard Rifle Prone — Deena Wigger, Colorado Springs, Co., 1768.
Women's Standard Rifle 3-Position — Launi Meili, Cheney, Wash., 1836.9.
Free Pistol — Eric Buljung, Ft. Benning, Ga., 1218.
Rapid Fire Pistol — John McNally, Columbus, Ga., 1458.

Center Fire Pistol — Eric Buljung, 1178.
Standard Pistol — Jerry Wilder, Plymouth, Ind., 1141.
Men's Air Pistol — Erich Buljung, 1271.4.
Women's Air Pistol — Carol Baker, Brea, Cal., 849.7
Women's Sport Pistol — Constance Petracek, Nashville, Tenn., 1242.
International Trap — Bret Erickson, Columbus, Ga., 415.
Women's International Trap — Carol Gephart, Dumfries, Va., 286.
International Skeet — Michael Schmidt, Jr. St. Paul, Minn., 417.
Women's International Skeet —Cindy Raahuage, Columbus, Ga., 305.

National Indoor Rifle and Pistol Championships

Smallbore Rifle 4-Position — James Meredith, Columbus, Ga., 800.
Smallbore Rifle NRA 3-Position — Karen Monez, Colorado Springs, Co., 1187.
Smallbore Rifle International — Robert Foth, Colorado Springs, Co., 1183.
Woman Smallbore Rifle 4-Position — Karen Monez, 799.
Woman Smallbore Rifle NRA 3-Position — Karen Monez, 1187.
Woman International Smallbore Rifle — Elizabeth Bourland, Wichita Falls, Tex., 1173.
Air Rifle — Debra Sinclair, Tigard, Ore., 592.

Woman Air Rifle — Debra Sinclair, 592.
Conventional Pistol — Charles Baxter, Argyle, Tex., 886.
Woman Conventional Pistol — Kristin Watson, Shelton, Conn., 839.
International Free Pistol — Eric Buljung, Ft. Benning, Ga., 557.
Woman International Free Pistol — Carol Baker, Brea, Cal., 513.
International Standard Pistol — Erich Buljung, 575.
Woman International Standard Pistol — Shelly Blatny, Lincoln, Neb., 544.
Air Pistol — Ronald Daniels, Peekskill, N.Y., 573.
Woman Air Pistol — Sharlein Rose, Roxbury, N.Y., 499.

Auto Racing

Indianapolis 500 Winners

Year	Winner, Car	MPH	Year	Winner, Car	MPH
1911	Ray Harroun, Marmon Wasp	74.59	1953	Bill Vukovich, Fuel Injection	128.740
1912	Joe Dawson, National	78.72	1954	Bill Vukovich, Fuel Injection	130.840
1913	Jules Goux, Peugeot	75.933	1955	Bob Sweikert, John Zink Special	128.209
1914	Rene Thomas, Delage	82.47	1956	Pat Flaherty, John Zink Special	128.490
1915	Ralph DePalma, Mercedes	89.84	1957	Sam Hanks, Belond Exhaust	135.601
1916	Dario Resta, Peugeot	84.00	1958	Jimmy Bryan, Belond A.P.	133.791
1917-18	race not held		1959	Rodger Ward, Leader Card Special	135.857
1919	Howdy Wilcox, Peugeot	88.05	1960	Jim Rathmann, Ken Paul Special	138.767
1920	Gaston Chevrolet, Monroe	88.16	1961	A.J. Foyt, Bowes Seal Fast	139.130
1921	Tommy Milton, Frontenac	89.62	1962	Rodger Ward, Leader Card Special	140.293
1922	Jimmy Murphy, Murphy Special	94.48	1963	Parnelli Jones, Agajanian Special	143.137
1923	Tommy Milton, H.C.S.	90.95	1964	A.J. Foyt, Sheraton-Thompson Special	147.350
1924	L.L. Corum-Joe Boyer, Duesenberg	98.23	1965	Jim Clark, Lotus-Ford	150.686
1925	Pete DePaolo, Duesenberg	101.13	1966	Graham Hill, American Red Ball	144.317
1926	Frank Lockhart, Miller	95.904	1967	A.J. Foyt, Sheraton-Thompson Special	151.207
1927	George Souders, Duesenberg	97.545	1968	Bobby Unser, Rislone Special	152.882
1928	Louis Meyer, Miller	99.482	1969	Mario Andretti, STP Oil Treatment Special	156.867
1929	Ray Keech, Simplex	97.585	1970	Al Unser, Johnny Lightning Special	155.749
1930	Billy Arnold, Miller-Hartz	100.448	1971	Al Unser, Johnny Lightning Special	157.735
1931	Louis Schneider, Bowes Seal Fast	96.629	1972	Mark Donohue, Sunoco McLaren	162.962
1932	Fred Frame, Miller-Hartz	104.144	1973	Gordon Johncock, STP Double Oil Filter	159.036
1933	Louis Meyer, Tydol	104.162	1974	Johnny Rutherford, McLaren	158.589
1934	Bill Cummings, Boyle Products	104.863	1975	Bobby Unser, Jorgenson Eagle	149.213
1935	Kelly Petillo, Gilmore Speedway	106.240	1976	Johnny Rutherford, Hygain McLaren	148.725
1936	Louis Meyer, Ring Free	109.069	1977	A.J. Foyt, Gilmore Coyote-Ford	161.331
1937	Wilbur Shaw, Shaw-Gilmore	113.580	1978	Al Unser, Lola Cosworth	161.363
1938	Floyd Roberts, Burd Piston Ring	117.200	1979	Rick Mears, Penske-Cosworth	158.899
1939	Wilbur Shaw, Boyle	115.035	1980	Johnny Rutherford, Chaparral-Cosworth	142.862
1940	Wilbur Shaw, Boyle	114.277	1981	Bobby Unser, Eagle-Offenhauser	139.085
1941	Floyd Davis-Mauri Rose, Knock-Out-Hose Clip	115.117	1982	Gordon Johncock, Wildcat-Cosworth	162.026
1942-45	race not held		1983	Tom Sneva, March-Cosworth	162.117
1946	George Robson, Thorne Engineering	114.820	1984	Rick Mears, March-Cosworth	163.621
1947	Mauri Rose, Blue Crown Special	116.338	1985	Danny Sullivan, March-Cosworth	152.982
1948	Mauri Rose, Blue Crown Special	119.814	1986	Bobby Rahal, March-Cosworth	170.722
1949	Bill Holland, Blue Crown Special	121.327	1987	Al Unser, March-Cosworth	162.175
1950	Johnny Parsons, Wynn Kurtis Kraft	124.002	1988	Rick Mears, Penske-Chevy V8	144.809
1951	Lee Wallard, Belanger	126.224	1989	Emerson Fittipaldi, Penske PC 18-Chevrolet	167.581
1952	Troy Ruttman, Agajanian	128.922			

The race was less than 500 miles in the following years: 1916 (300 mi.), 1926 (400 mi.), 1950 (345 mi.), 1973 (332.5 mi.), 1975 (435 mi.), 1976 (255 mi.). Race record—170.722 MPH, Bobby Rahal, 1986.

Notable One-Mile Speed Records

Date	Driver	Car	MPH	Date	Driver	Car	MPH
1/26/06	Marriott.	Stanley (Steam)	127.659	9/ 3/35	Campbell.	Bluebird Special	301.13
3/16/10	Oldfield.	Benz	131.724	11/19/37	Eyston	Thunderbolt 1	311.42
4/23/11	Burman.	Benz	141.732	9/16/38	Eyston	Thunderbolt 1	357.5
2/12/19	DePalma	Packard	149.875	8/23/39	Cobb	Railton	368.9
4/27/20	Milton.	Dusenberg	155.046	9/16/47	Cobb	Railton-Mobil	394.2
4/28/26	Parry-Thomas . .	Thomas Spl.	170.624	8/ 5/63	Breedlove	Spirit of America	407.45
3/29/27	Seagrave	Sunbeam	203.790	10/27/64	Arfons	Green Monster	536.71
4/22/28	Keech	White Triplex	207.552	11/15/65	Breedlove	Spirit of America	600.601
3/11/29	Seagrave	Irving-Napier	231.446	10/23/70	Gabelich	Blue Flame	622.407
2/ 5/31	Campbell.	Napier-Campbell	246.086	10/9/79	Barrett	Budweiser Rocket	638.637*
2/24/32	Campbell.	Napier-Campbell	253.96	10/4/83	Noble.	Thrust 2	633.6
2/22/33	Campbell.	Napier-Campbell	272.109			*not recognized as official by sanctioning bodies.	

CART Champions

(U.S. Auto Club Champions prior to 1979)

Year	Driver	Year	Driver	Year	Driver	Year	Driver
1960	A. J. Foyt	1969	Mario Andretti	1976	Gordon Johncock	1983	Al Unser
1961	A. J. Foyt	1970	Al Unser	1977	Tom Sneva	1984	Mario Andretti
1962	Rodger Ward	1971	Joe Leonard	1978	Tom Sneva	1985	Al Unser
1963	A. J. Foyt	1972	Joe Leonard	1979	Rick Mears	1986	Bobby Rahal
1964	A. J. Foyt	1973	Roger McCluskey	1980	Johnny Rutherford	1987	Bobby Rahal
1965	Mario Andretti	1974	Bobby Unser	1981	Rick Mears	1988	Danny Sullivan
1966	Mario Andretti	1975	A. J. Foyt	1982	Rick Mears	1989	Emerson Fittipaldi
1967	A. J. Foyt						
1968	Bobby Unser						

Le Mans 24-Hour Race in 1989

Joachen Mass, Manuel Reuter, and Stanley Dickens drove their Mercedes to victory in the 1989 Le Mans 24-hour race. They covered 3,271 miles at an average speed of 137.5 miles per hour.

NASCAR Racing in 1989

Winston Cup Races

Date	Race, site	Winner	Car	Average MPH
Feb. 19	Daytona 500, Daytona Beach, Fla.	Darrell Waltrip	Chevrolet	148.466
Mar. 5	Goodwrench 500, Rockingham, N.C.	Rusty Wallace	Pontiac	115.122
Mar. 19	Motorcraft 500, Atlanta, Ga.	Darrell Waltrip	Chevrolet	139.684
Mar. 26	Pontiac Excitment 400, Richmond, Va.	Rusty Wallace	Pontiac	89.619
Apr. 2	Transouth 500, Darlington, S.C.	Harry Gant	Oldsmobile	115.475
Apr. 9	Valleydale Meats 500, Bristol, Tenn.	Rusty Wallace	Pontiac	76.034
Apr. 16	First Union 400, N. Wilkesboro, N.C.	Dale Earnhardt	Chevrolet	89.937
Apr. 23	Pannill Sweatshirts 500, Martinsville, Va.	Darrell Waltrip	Chevrolet	79.025
May 7	Winston 500, Talladega, Ala.	Davey Allison	Ford	155.869
May 28	Coca Cola 600, Charlotte, N.C.	Darrell Waltrip	Chevrolet	144.077
June 11	Banquet Frozen Foods 300, Sonoma, Cal.	Ricky Rudd	Buick	76.088
June 18	Miller High Life 500, Pocono, Pa.	Terry Labonte	Ford	131.320
June 25	Miller High Life 400, Brooklyn, Mich.	Bill Elliott	Ford	139.023
July 1	Pepsi 400, Daytona Beach, Fla.	Davey Allison	Ford	132.207
July 23	AC Spark Plug 500, Pocono, Pa.	Bill Elliott	Ford	117.847
July 30	Talladega 500, Talladega, Ala.	Terry Labonte	Ford	157.354
Aug. 13	Watkins Glen International, N.Y.	Rusty Wallace	Pontiac	87.242
Aug. 26	Busch 500, Bristol, Tenn.	Darrell Waltrip	Chevrolet	85.554
Sept. 3	Southern 500, Darlington, S.C.	Dale Earnhardt	Chevrolet	135.462
Sept. 10	Miller High Life 400, Richmond, Va.	Rusty Wallace	Pontiac	88.380
Sept. 17	Delaware 500, Dover, Del.	Dale Earnhardt	Chevrolet	122.972
Sept. 24	Goody's 500, Martinsville, Va.	Darrell Waltrip	Chevrolet	76,571

Winston Cup Champions (NASCAR)

Year	Driver	Year	Driver	Year	Driver	Year	Driver
1949	Red Byron	1959	Lee Petty	1969	David Pearson	1979	Richard Petty
1950	Bill Rexford	1960	Rex White	1970	Bobby Isaac	1980	Dale Earnhardt
1951	Herb Thomas	1961	Ned Jarrett	1971	Richard Petty	1981	Darrell Waltrip
1952	Tim Flock	1962	Joe Weatherly	1972	Richard Petty	1982	Darrell Waltrip
1953	Herb Thomas	1963	Joe Weatherly	1973	Benny Parson	1983	Bobby Allison
1954	Lee Petty	1964	Richard Petty	1974	Richard Petty	1984	Terry Labonte
1955	Tim Flock	1965	Ned Jarrett	1975	Richard Petty	1985	Darrell Waltrip
1956	Buck Baker	1966	David Pearson	1976	Cale Yarborough	1986	Dale Earnhardt
1957	Buck Baker	1967	Richard Petty	1977	Cale Yarborough	1987	Dale Earnhardt
1958	Lee Petty	1968	David Pearson	1978	Cale Yarborough	1988	Bill Elliott

Daytona 500 Winners

Year	Driver, car	Avg. MPH	Year	Driver, car	Avg. MPH
1959	Lee Petty, Oldsmobile	135.521	1975	Benny Parsons, Chevrolet	153.649
1960	Junior Johnson, Chevrolet	124.740	1976	David Pearson, Mercury	152.181
1961	Marvin Panch, Pontiac	149.601	1977	Cale Yarborough, Chevrolet	153.218
1962	Fireball Roberts, Pontiac	152.529	1978	Bobby Allison, Ford	159.730
1963	Tiny Lund, Ford	151.566	1979	Richard Petty, Oldsmobile	143.977
1964	Richard Petty, Plymouth	154.334	1980	Buddy Baker, Oldsmobile	177.602
1965	Fred Lorenzen, Ford (a)	141.539	1981	Richard Petty, Buick	169.651
1966	Richard Petty, Plymouth (b)	160.627	1982	Bobby Allison, Buick	153.991
1967	Mario Andretti, Ford	146.926	1983	Cale Yarborough, Pontiac	155.979
1968	Cale Yarborough, Mercury	143.251	1984	Cale Yarborough, Chevrolet	150.994
1969	Lee Roy Yarborough, Ford	160.875	1985	Bill Elliott, Ford	172.265
1970	Pete Hamilton, Plymouth	149.601	1986	Geoff Bodine, Chevrolet	148.124
1971	Richard Petty, Plymouth	144.456	1987	Bill Elliott, Ford	176.263
1972	A. J. Foyt, Mercury	161.550	1988	Bobby Allison, Buick	137.531
1973	Richard Petty, Dodge	157.205	1989	Darrell Waltrip, Chevrolet	148.466
1974	Richard Petty, Dodge (c)	140.894			

(a) 322.5 miles. (b) 495 miles. (c) 450 miles.

World Grand Prix Champions

Year	Driver	Year	Driver	Year	Driver
1951	Jan Fangio, Argentina	1964	John Surtees, England	1977	Niki Lauda, Austria
1952	Alberto Ascari, Italy	1965	Jim Clark, Scotland	1978	Mario Andretti, U.S.
1953	Alberto Ascari, Italy	1966	Jack Brabham, Australia	1979	Jody Scheckter, So. Africa
1954	Juan Fangio, Argentina	1967	Denis Hulme, New Zealand	1980	Alan Jones, Australia
1955	Juan Fangio, Argentina	1968	Graham Hill, England	1981	Nelson Piquet, Brazil
1956	Juan Fangio, Argentina	1969	Jackie Stewart, Scotland	1982	Keke Rosberg, Finland
1957	Juan Fangio, Argentina	1970	Jochen Rindt, Austria	1983	Nelson Piquet, Brazil
1958	Mike Hawthorne, England	1971	Jackie Stewart, Scotland	1984	Niki Lauda, Austria
1959	Jack Brabham, Australia	1972	Emerson Fittipaldi, Brazil	1985	Alain Prost, France
1960	Jack Brabham, Australia	1973	Jackie Stewart, Scotland	1986	Alain Prost, France
1961	Phil Hill, United States	1974	Emerson Fittipaldi, Brazil	1987	Nelson Piquet, Brazil
1962	Graham Hill, England	1975	Nicki Lauda, Austria	1988	Ayrton Senna, Brazil
1963	Jim Clark, Scotland	1976	James Hunt, England		

Grand Prix for Formula 1 Cars in 1989

Grand Prix	Winner, car	Grand Prix	Winner, car
Belgian	Ayrton Senna, McLaren-Honda	Italian	Alain Prost, McLaren-Honda
Brazilian	Nigel Mansell, Ferrari	Mexico	Ayrton Senna, McLaren-Honda
British	Alain Prost, McLaren-Honda	Monaco	Ayrton Senna, McLaren-Honda
Canadian	Thierey Boutsen, Williams-Renault	Portuguese	Gerhard Berger, Ferrari
French	Alain Prost, McLaren-Honda	San Marino	Ayrton Senna, McLaren-Honda
German	Ayrton Senna, McLaren-Honda	Spanish	Ayrton Senna, McLaren-Honda
Hungarian	Nigel Mansell, Ferrari	United States	Alain Prost, McLaren-Honda

Lacrosse Champions in 1989

U.S. Club Lacrosse Association Championship—Baltimore, Md., June 10: Long Island Hofstra L.C. 13, Mt. Washington 8.

NCAA Division I Championship—College Park, Md., May 29: Syracuse Univ. 13, Johns Hopkins 12.

NCAA Division III Championship—Geneva, N.Y., May 20: Hobart 11, Ohio Wesleyan 8.

USILA All Star Game—Baltimore, Md., June 9: North 13, South 9.

National Junior College Championship—Garden City, N.Y., May 13: Herkimer C.C. 15, Nassau C.C. 14.

NCAA Women's Lacrosse Championship, Division I—Westchester, Pa., May 21: Penn State 7, Harvard 6.

USILA Division I All America Team

Attack: Matt Panetta, Johns Hopkins; John Zulberti, Syracuse; Mike Ruland, Loyola.

Midfield: Pait Gait, Syracuse; Gary Gait, Syracuse; Phil Willard, Maryland; Brian Keith, Navy.
Defense: Pat McCabe, Syracuse; Dave Pietramala, Johns Hopkins; Bill Ralph, Maryland.
Goal: Quint Kessenich, Johns Hopkins.
Coach of the Year: Dick Garber, Massachusetts.
Note: 4 midfielders selected for the 3 midfield positions.

NCAA Division III All America Team

Attack: William Miller, Hobart; Tim Hormes, Washington; Bill Coons, Nazareth.
Midfield: Bob Martino, Washington; Eric Stein, Hobart; Kevin Finneran, Ohio Wesleyan; Michael DeMaris, Hobart.
Defense: Matt Wilson, Washington; David Walter, Cortland; Jim Dempsey, Ohio Wesleyan.
Goal: Shawn Trell, Hobart.
Coach of the Year: Ray Rostan, Hampden-Sydney.
Note: 4 midfielders selected for the 3 midfield positions.

NCAA Divisions I Champions

Year	Champion	Year	Champion	Year	Champion	Year	Champion
1971	Cornell			1981	North Carolina		
1972	Virginia			1982	North Carolina		
1973	Maryland			1983	Syracuse		
1974	Johns Hopkins			1984	Johns Hopkins		
1975	Maryland			1985	Johns Hopkins		
1976	Cornell			1986	North Carolina		
1977	Cornell			1987	Johns Hopkins		
1978	Johns Hopkins			1988	Syracuse		
1979	Johns Hopkins			1989	Syracuse		
1980	Johns Hopkins						

Skiing in 1989

World Cup Alpine Champions

Men

1967	Jean Claude Killy, France	1975	Gustavo Thoeni, Italy	1983	Phil Mahre, U.S.
1968	Jean Claude Killy, France	1976	Ingemar Stenmark, Sweden	1984	Pirmin Zurbriggen, Switzerland
1969	Karl Schranz, Austria	1977	Ingemar Stenmark, Sweden	1985	Marc Girardelli, Luxembourg
1970	Karl Schranz, Austria	1978	Ingemar Stenmark, Sweden	1986	Marc Girardelli, Luxembourg
1971	Gustavo Thoeni, Italy	1979	Peter Luescher, Switzerland	1987	Pirmin Zurbriggen, Switzerland
1972	Gustavo Thoeni, Italy	1980	Andreas Wenzel, Liechtenstein	1988	Pirmin Zurbriggen, Switzerland
1973	Gustavo Thoeni, Italy	1981	Phil Mahre, U.S.	1989	Marc Girardelli, Luxembourg
1974	Piero Gros, Italy	1982	Phil Mahre, U.S.		

Women

1967	Nancy Greene, Canada	1975	Annemarie Proell, Austria	1983	Tamara McKinney, U.S.
1968	Nancy Greene, Canada	1976	Rose Mittermaier, W. Germany	1984	Erika Hess, Switzerland
1969	Gertrud Gabl, Austria	1977	Lise-Marie Morerod, Switzerland	1985	Michela Figini, Switzerland
1970	Michele Jacot, France	1978	Hanni Wenzel, Liechtenstein	1986	Maria Walliser, Switzerland
1971	Annemarie Proell, Austria	1979	Annemarie Proell Moser, Austria	1987	Maria Walliser, Switzerland
1972	Annemarie Proell, Austria	1980	Hanni Wenzel, Liechtenstein	1988	Michela Figini, Switzerland
1973	Annemarie Proell, Austria	1981	Marie-Theres Nadig, Switzerland	1989	Vreni Schneider, Switzerland
1974	Annemarie Proell, Austria	1982	Erika Hess, Switzerland		

World Alpine Championships

Vail, Colorado

Men	Women
Downhill—Hansjorg Tauscher, W. Germany	**Downhill**—Maria Walliser, Switzerland
Slalom—Rudolf Nierlich, Austria	**Slalom**—Mateja Svet, Yugoslavia
Giant Slalom—Rudolf Nierlich	**Giant Slalom**—Vreni Schneider, Switzerland
Super Giant Slalom—Martin Hangl, Switzerland	**Super Giant Slalom**—Ulrike Maier, Austria
Combined—Marc Girardelli, Luxembourg	**Combined**—Tamara McKinney, U.S.

The America's Cup

The United States yacht *Stars & Stripes* defeated the New Zealand yacht *New Zealand* in 2 consecutive races to win the best-of-three series in the waters off San Diego, Cal. *Stars & Stripes* was skippered by Dennis Connor, as it had been when the Cup was recaptured from Australia in 1987.

The New Zealand syndicate, however, went to court to have the result of the races invalidated, claiming that the Americans did not live up to the America's Cup Deed of Gift which, they claim, says that the competing boats must be similar. The Americans used a catamaran, the New Zealanders a monohulled ship. On Mar. 28, 1989, a New York State Supreme Court justice ruled that the San Diego Yacht Club had beaten its challenger unfairly and must forfeit the America's Cup to New Zealand. On Sept. 19, a New York appeals court overturned the ruling.

Competition for the America's Cup grew out of the first contest to establish a world yachting championship, one of the carnival features of the London Exposition of 1851. The race, open to all classes of yachts from all over the world, covered a 60-mile course around the Isle of Wight; the prize was a cup worth about $500, donated by the Royal Yacht Squadron of England, known as the "America's Cup" because it was first won by the United States yacht *America*. Successive efforts of British and Australian yachtsmen had failed to win the famous trophy until 1983 when the Australian yacht *Australia II* defeated the U.S. entry *Liberty*.

Winners of the America's Cup

1851	America	1930	Enterprise defeated Shamrock V, England, (4-0)
1870	Magic defeated Cambria, England, (1-0)	1934	Rainbow defeated Endeavour, England, (4-2)
1871	Columbia (first three races) and Sappho (last two races) defeated Livonia, England, (4-1)	1937	Ranger defeated Endeavour II, England, (4-0)
		1958	Columbia defeated Sceptre, England, (4-0)
1876	Madeline defeated Countess of Dufferin, Canada, (2-0)	1962	Weatherly defeated Gretel, Australia, (4-1)
1881	Mischief defeated Atalanta, Canada, (2-0)	1964	Constellation defeated Sovereign, England, (4-0)
1885	Puritan defeated Genesta, England, (2-0)	1967	Intrepid defeated Dame Pattie, Australia, (4-0)
1886	Mayflower defeated Galatea, England, (2-0)	1970	Intrepid defeated Gretel II, Australia, (4-1)
1887	Volunteer defeated Thistle, Scotland, (2-0)	1974	Courageous defeated Southern Cross, Australia, (4-0)
1893	Vigilant defeated Valkyrie II, England, (3-0)	1977	Courageous defeated Australia, Australia, (4-0)
1895	Defender defeated Valkyrie III, England, (3-0)	1980	Freedom defeated Australia, Australia, (4-1)
1899	Columbia defeated Shamrock, England, (3-0)	1983	Australia II, Australia defeated Liberty, (4-3)
1901	Columbia defeated Shamrock II, England, (3-0)	1987	Stars & Stripes defeated Kookaburra III, Australia, (4-0)
1903	Reliance defeated Shamrock III, England, (3-0)	1988	Stars & Stripes defeated New Zealand, New Zealand, (2-0)
1920	Resolute defeated Shamrock IV, England, (3-2)		

Chess

Chess dates back to antiquity. Its exact origin is unknown. The strongest players of their time, and therefore regarded by later generations as world champions, were Francois Philidor, France; Alexandre Deschappelles, France; Louis de la Bourdonnais, France; Howard Staunton, England; Adolph Anderssen, Germany and Paul Morphy, United States. In 1866 Wilhelm Steinitz of Austria defeated Adolph Anderssen and claimed the title of world champion. The official world champions since the title was first used follow:

1866-1894 Wilhelm Steinitz, Austria	France	1963-1969 Tigran Petrosian, USSR
1894-1921 Dr. Emanuel Lasker, Germany	1948-1957 Mikhail Botvinnik, USSR	1969-1972 Boris Spassky, USSR
1921-1927 Jose R. Capablanca, Cuba	1957-1958 Vassily Smyslov, USSR	1972-1975 Bobby Fischer, U.S. (a)
1927-1935 Dr. Alexander A. Alekhine,	1958-1959 Mikhail Botvinnik, USSR	1975-1985 Anatoly Karpov, USSR
France	1960-1961 Mikhail Tal, USSR	1985 Gary Kasparov, USSR
1935-1937 Dr. Max Euwe, Netherlands	1961-1963 Mikhail Botvinnik, USSR	
1937-1946 Dr. Alexander A. Alekhine,		

(a) Defaulted championship after refusal to accept International Chess Federation rules for a championship match, April 1975.

United States Champions

Unofficial champions	1894-1895 Albert Hodges	1961-1962 Larry Evans	1981-1983 (tie) Walter Browne,
1857-1871 Paul Morphy	1895-1897 Jackson Showalter	1962-1968 Bobby Fischer	Yasser Seirawan
1871-1876 George Mackenzie	1897-1906 Harry Pillsbury	1968-1969 Larry Evans	1983 (tie) Walter Browne
1876-1880 James Mason	1906-1909 vacant	1969-1972 Samuel Reshevsky	Larry Christiansen
1880-1889 George Mackenzie	1909-1936 Frank Marshall	1972-1973 Robert Byrne	Roman
1889-1890 S. Lipschutz	1936-1944 Samuel Reshevsky	1973-1974 Lubomir Kavalek,	Dzindzichashvili
1890 Jackson Showalter	1944-1946 Arnold Denker	John Grefe	1984-1985 Lev Alburt
1890-1891 Max Judd	1946-1948 Samuel Reshevsky	1974-1977 Walter Browne	1986 Yasser Seirawan
Official champions	1948-1951 Herman Steiner	1978-1980 Lubomir Kavalek	1987 (tie) Joel Benjamin
1891-1892 Jackson Showalter	1951-1954 Larry Evans	1980-1981 (tie) Larry Evans,	Nick DeFirmian
1892-1894 S. Lipschutz	1954-1957 Arthur Bisguier	Larry Christiansen,	1988 Michael Wilder
1894 Jackson Showalter	1957-1961 Bobby Fischer	Walter Browne	

The World Cup

The World Cup, emblematic of International soccer supremacy, was won by Argentina on June 29, 1986, with a 3-2 victory over W. Germany. It was the 2d time Argentina has won the event. Winners and sites of previous World Cup play follow:

Year	Winner	Final opponent	Site	Year	Winner	Final opponent	Site
1930	Uruguay	Argentina	Uruguay	1966	England	W. Germany	England
1934	Italy	Czechoslovakia	Italy	1970	Brazil	Italy	Mexico City
1938	Italy	Hungary	France	1974	W. Germany	Netherlands	W. Germany
1950	Uruguay	Brazil	Brazil	1978	Argentina	Netherlands	Argentina
1954	W. Germany	Hungary	Switzerland	1982	Italy	W. Germany	Spain
1958	Brazil	Sweden	Sweden	1986	Argentina	W. Germany	Mexico City
1962	Brazil	Czechoslovakia	Chile				

GOLF

United States Open

Year	Winner	Year	Winner	Year	Winner	Year	Winner
1901	Willie Anderson	1923	Bobby Jones*	1947	L. Worsham	1968	Lee Trevino
1902	L. Auchterlonie	1924	Cyril Walker	1948	Ben Hogan	1969	Orville Moody
1903	Willie Anderson	1925	Willie MacFarlane	1949	Cary Middlecoff	1970	Tony Jacklin
1904	Willie Anderson	1926	Bobby Jones*	1950	Ben Hogan	1971	Lee Trevino
1905	Willie Anderson	1927	Tommy Armour	1951	Ben Hogan	1972	Jack Nicklaus
1906	Alex Smith	1928	John Farrell	1952	Julius Boros	1973	Johnny Miller
1907	Alex Ross	1929	Bobby Jones*	1953	Ben Hogan	1974	Hale Irwin
1908	Fred McLeod	1930	Bobby Jones*	1954	Ed Furgol	1975	Lou Graham
1909	George Sargent	1931	Wm. Burke	1955	Jack Fleck	1976	Jerry Pate
1910	Alex Smith	1932	Gene Sarazen	1956	Cary Middlecoff	1977	Hubert Green
1911	John McDermott	1933	John Goodman*	1957	Dick Mayer	1978	Andy North
1912	John McDermott	1934	Olin Dutra	1958	Tommy Bolt	1979	Hale Irwin
1913	Francis Ouimet*	1935	Sam Parks Jr.	1959	Billy Casper	1980	Jack Nicklaus
1914	Walter Hagen	1936	Tony Manero	1960	Arnold Palmer	1981	David Graham
1915	Jerome Travers*	1937	Ralph Guldahl	1961	Gene Littler	1982	Tom Watson
1916	Chick Evans*	1938	Ralph Guldahl	1962	Jack Nicklaus	1983	Larry Nelson
1917-18	(Not played)	1939	Byron Nelson	1963	Julius Boros	1984	Fuzzy Zoeller
1919	Walter Hagen	1940	Lawson Little	1964	Ken Venturi	1985	Andy North
1920	Edward Ray	1941	Craig Wood	1965	Gary Player	1986	Ray Floyd
1921	Jim Barnes	1942-45	(Not played)	1966	Billy Casper	1987	Scott Simpson
1922	Gene Sarazen	1946	Lloyd Mangrum	1967	Jack Nicklaus	1988	Curtis Strange
*Amateur						1989	Curtis Strange

Professional Golfer's Association Championships

Year	Winner	Year	Winner	Year	Winner	Year	Winner
1921	Walter Hagan	1938	Paul Runyan	1956	Jack Burke	1973	Jack Nicklaus
1922	Gene Sarazen	1939	Henry Picard	1957	Lionel Hebert	1974	Lee Trevino
1923	Gene Sarazen	1940	Byron Nelson	1958	Dow Finsterwald	1975	Jack Nicklaus
1924	Walter Hagen	1941	Victor Ghezzi	1959	Bob Rosburg	1976	Dave Stockton
1925	Walter Hagen	1942	Sam Snead	1960	Jay Hebert	1977	Lanny Wadkins
1926	Walter Hagen	1944	Bob Hamilton	1961	Jerry Barber	1978	John Mahaffey
1927	Walter Hagen	1945	Byron Nelson	1962	Gary Player	1979	David Graham
1928	Leo Diegel	1946	Ben Hogan	1963	Jack Nicklaus	1980	Jack Nicklaus
1929	Leo Diegel	1947	Jim Ferrier	1964	Bob Nichols	1981	Larry Nelson
1930	Tommy Armour	1948	Ben Hogan	1965	Dave Marr	1982	Ray Floyd
1931	Tom Creavy	1949	Sam Snead	1966	Al Geiberger	1983	Hal Sutton
1932	Olin Dutra	1950	Chandler Harper	1967	Don January	1984	Lee Trevino
1933	Gene Sarazen	1951	Sam Snead	1968	Julius Boros	1985	Hubert Green
1934	Paul Runyan	1952	James Turnesa	1969	Ray Floyd	1986	Bob Tway
1935	Johnny Revolta	1953	Walter Burkemo	1970	Dave Stockton	1987	Larry Nelson
1936	Denny Shute	1954	Melvin Harbert	1971	Jack Nicklaus	1988	Jeff Sluman
1937	Denny Shute	1955	Doug Ford	1972	Gary Player	1989	Payne Stewart

Masters Golf Tournament Champions

Year	Winner	Year	Winner	Year	Winner	Year	Winner
1934	Horton Smith	1963	Jack Nicklaus	1964	Arnold Palmer	1977	Tom Watson
1935	Gene Sarazen	1950	Jimmy Demaret	1965	Jack Nicklaus	1978	Gary Player
1936	Horton Smith	1951	Ben Hogan	1966	Jack Nicklaus	1979	Fuzzy Zoeller
1937	Byron Nelson	1952	Sam Snead	1967	Gay Brewer Jr.	1980	Severiano Ballesteros
1938	Henry Picard	1953	Ben Hogan	1968	Bob Goalby	1981	Tom Watson
1939	Ralph Guldahl	1954	Sam Snead	1969	George Archer	1982	Craig Stadler
1940	Jimmy Demaret	1955	Cary Middlecoff	1970	Billy Casper	1983	Severiano Ballesteros
1941	Craig Wood	1956	Jack Burke	1971	Charles Coody	1984	Ben Crenshaw
1942	Byron Nelson	1957	Doug Ford	1972	Jack Nicklaus	1985	Bernhard Langer
1943-1945	(Not played)	1958	Arnold Palmer	1973	Tommy Aaron	1986	Jack Nicklaus
1946	Herman Keiser	1959	Art Wall Jr.	1974	Gary Player	1987	Larry Mize
1947	Jimmy Demaret	1960	Arnold Palmer	1975	Jack Nicklaus	1988	Sandy Lyle
1948	Claude Harmon	1961	Gary Player	1976	Ray Floyd	1989	Nick Faldo
1949	Sam Snead	1962	Arnold Palmer				

British Open Golf Champions

Year	Winner	Year	Winner	Year	Winner	Year	Winner
1930	Bobby Jones	1949	Bobby Locke	1963	Bob Charles	1977	Tom Watson
1931	Tommy Armour	1950	Bobby Locke	1964	Tony Lema	1978	Jack Nicklaus
1932	Gene Sarazen	1951	Max Faulkner	1965	Peter Thomson	1979	Seve Ballesteros
1933	Denny Shute	1952	Bobby Locke	1966	Jack Nicklaus	1980	Tom Watson
1934	Henry Cotton	1953	Ben Hogan	1967	Roberto de Vicenzo	1981	Bill Rogers
1935	Alf Perry	1954	Peter Thomson	1968	Gary Player	1982	Tom Watson
1936	Alf Padgham	1955	Peter Thomson	1969	Tony Jacklin	1983	Tom Watson
1937	T.H. Cotton	1956	Peter Thomson	1970	Jack Nicklaus	1984	Seve Ballesteros
1938	R.A. Whitcombe	1957	Bobby Locke	1971	Lee Trevino	1985	Sandy Lyle
1939	Richard Burton	1958	Peter Thomson	1972	Lee Trevino	1986	Greg Norman
1940-45	(Not played)	1959	Gary Player	1973	Tom Weiskopf	1987	Nick Faldo
1946	Sam Snead	1960	Kel Nagle	1974	Gary Player	1988	Seve Ballesteros
1947	Fred Daly	1961	Arnold Palmer	1975	Tom Watson	1989	Mark Calcavecchia
1948	Henry Cotton	1962	Arnold Palmer	1976	Johnny Miller		

Professional Golf Tournaments in 1989

Date	Event	Winner	Score	Prize
Jan. 8	MONY Tournament of Champions, Carlsbad, Cal.	Steve Jones	279	$135,000
Jan. 15	Bob Hope Chrysler Classic, Indian Wells, Cal.	Steve Jones	*343	180,000
Jan. 22	Phoenix Open, Ariz.	Mark Calcavecchia	263	126,000
Jan. 29	A.T.&T. National Pro-Am, Pebble Beach, Cal.	Mark O'Meara	277	180,000
Feb. 5	Los Angeles Open	Mark Calcavecchia	272	180,000
Feb. 12	Hawaiian Open, Honolulu	Gene Sauers	197	135,000
Feb. 19	San Diego Open, La Jolla, Cal.	Greg Twiggs	271	126,000
Feb. 26	Doral Ryder Open, Miami, Fla.	Bill Glasson	275	234,000
Mar. 5	Honda Classic, Coral Springs, Fla.	Blaine McCallister	266	144,000
Mar. 12	Bay Hill Classic, Orlando, Fla.	Tom Kite	*278	144,000
Mar. 19	Tournament Players Championship, Ponte Vedra, Fla.	Tom Kite	279	243,000
Mar. 26	U.S.F.&G. Classic, New Orleans, La.	Tim Simpson	274	135,000
Apr. 9	Masters Tournament, Augusta, Ga.	Nick Faldo	*283	200,000
Apr. 16	Heritage Classic, Hilton Head, S.C.	Payne Stewart	268	144,000
Apr. 23	Greater Greensboro Open, N.C.	Ken Green	277	180,000
Apr. 30	Las Vegas Invitational	Scott Hoch	*336	225,000
May 7	Byron Nelson Classic, Irving, Tex.	Jodie Mudd	265	180,000
May 14	Memorial Tournament, Dublin, Oh.	Bob Tway	277	160,000
May 21	Colonial National Tournament, Ft. Worth, Tex.	Ira Baker-Finch	270	180,000
June 4	Kemper Open, Potomac, Md.	Tom Byrum	268	162,000
June 12	Westchester Classic, Harrison, N.Y.	Wayne Grady	*277	180,000
June 18	U.S. Open, Pittsfield, N.Y.	Curtis Strange	278	200,000
June 25	Canadian Open, Oakville, Ont.	Steve Jones	271	162,000
July 9	Greater Hartford Open, Conn.	Paul Azinger	267	180,000
July 16	Anheuser-Busch Classic, Williamsburg, Va.	Mike Donald	*268	153,000
July 30	Buick Open, Grand Blanc, Mich.	Leonard Thompson	273	180,000
Aug. 6	St. Jude Classic, Memphis, Tenn.	John Mahaffey	272	180,000
Aug. 13	PGA Championship, Hawthorn Woods, Ill.	Payne Stewart	276	200,000
Aug. 20	The International, Castle Rock, Col.	Greg Norman	+2 pts.	180,000
Aug. 27	World Series of Golf, Akron, Oh.	David Frost	*276	180,000
Sept. 3	Greater Milwaukee Open	Greg Norman	269	144,000
Sept. 10	B.C. Open, Endicott, N.Y.	Mike Hulbert	*268	90,000
Sept. 17	Bank of Boston Classic, Sutton, Mass.	Blaine McCallister	271	126,000
Sept. 24	Southern Open, Columbus, Ga.	Ted Schulz	266	72,000
Oct. 1	Centel Classic, Tallahassee, Fla.	Bill Britton	200	135,000

Women

Date	Event	Winner	Score	Prize
Jan. 15	Jamaica Classic, Sandy Bay, Jamaica	Betsy King	202	$75,000
Jan. 29	Mazda Classic, Boca Raton, Fla.	Dottie Mochrie	*279	45,000
Feb. 19	Hawaiian Open, Kahuku	Sherri Turner	205	45,000
Feb. 26	Kemper Open, Princeville, Ha.	Betsy King	202	60,000
Mar. 19	Tucson Open, Tucson, Ariz.	Lori Garbacz	274	45,000
Mar. 26	Turquoise Classic, Phoenix, Ariz.	Allison Finley	282	60,000
Apr. 2	Dinah Shore Invitational, Rancho Mirage, Cal.	Juli Inkster	279	80,000
Apr. 16	All Star-Centinela Open, Los Angeles	Pat Bradley	208	67,000
Apr. 23	USX Classic, Gulfport, Fla.	Betsy King	*275	37,500
May 7	Crestar Classic, Chesapeake, Va.	Juli Inkster	210	45,000
May 14	Chrysler-Plymouth Classic, Lincroft, N.J.	Cindy Rarick	214	41,000
May 21	LPGA Championship, Kings Island, Oh.	Nancy Lopez	274	75,000
May 28	Corning Classic, Corning, N.Y.	Ayako Okamoto	272	48,000
June 4	Rochester International, N.Y.	Patty Sheehan	*278	45,000
June 18	Lady Keystone Open, Hershey, Pa.	Laura Davies	207	45,000
July 2	Du Maurier Classic, Montreal	Tammie Green	279	90,000
July 9	Jamie Farr Toledo Classic, Oh.	Penny Hammel	206	41,000
July 16	U.S. Women's Open, Lake Orion, Mich.	Betsy King	278	80,000
July 23	Boston Five Classic, Danvers, Mass.	Amy Alcott	272	52,000
Aug. 6	Greater Washington Open, Bethesda, Md.	Beth Daniel	205	45,000
Aug. 27	World Championship of Women's Golf, Buford, Ga.	Betsy King	275	85,000
Sept. 4	Rail Charity Classic, Springfield, Ill.	Beth Daniel	208	41,000
Sept. 10	Cellular One-Ping Championship, Portland, Ore.	Muffin Spencer-Devlin	214	45,000
Sept. 17	Safeco Classic, Kent, Wash.	Beth Daniel	273	45,000
Sept. 24	MBS Classic, Buena Park, Cal.	Nancy Lopez	271	45,000
Oct. 1	San Jose Classic, San Jose, Cal.	Beth Daniel	205	48,000

*Won playoff.

U.S. Women's Open Golf Champions

Year	Winner	Year	Winner	Year	Winner	Year	Winner
1948	"Babe" Zaharias	1959	Mickey Wright	1970	Donna Caponi	1980	Amy Alcott
1949	Louise Suggs	1960	Betsy Rawls	1971	JoAnne Carner	1981	Pat Bradley
1950	"Babe" Zaharias	1961	Mickey Wright	1972	Susie Maxwell Berning	1982	Janet Alex
1951	Betsy Rawls	1962	Murle Lindstrom	1973	Susie Maxwell Berning	1983	Jan Stephenson
1952	Louise Suggs	1963	Mary Mills	1974	Sandra Haynie	1984	Hollis Stacy
1953	Betsy Rawls	1964	Mickey Wright	1975	Sandra Palmer	1985	Kathy Baker
1954	"Babe" Zaharias	1965	Carol Mann	1976	JoAnne Carner	1986	Jane Geddes
1955	Fay Crocker	1966	Sandra Spuzich	1977	Hollis Stacy	· 1987	Laura Davies
1956	Mrs. K. Cornelius	1967	Catherine Lacoste*	1978	Hollis Stacy	1988	Liselotte Neumann
1957	Betsy Rawls	1968	Susie Maxwell Berning	1979	Jerilyn Britz	1989	Betsy King
1958	Mickey Wright	1969	Donna Caponi				

*Amateur

PGA Leading Money Winners

Year	Player	Dollars	Year	Player	Dollars	Year	Player	Dollars
1946	Ben Hogan	42,556	1961	Gary Player	64,540	1975	Jack Nicklaus	323,149
1947	Jimmy Demaret	27,936	1962	Arnold Palmer	81,448	1976	Jack Nicklaus	266,438
1948	Ben Hogan	36,812	1963	Arnold Palmer	128,230	1977	Tom Watson	310,653
1949	Sam Snead	31,593	1964	Jack Nicklaus	113,284	1978	Tom Watson	362,429
1950	Sam Snead	35,758	1965	Jack Nicklaus	140,752	1979	Tom Watson	462,636
1951	Lloyd Mangrum	26,088	1966	Billy Casper	121,944	1980	Tom Watson	530,808
1952	Julius Boros	37,032	1967	Jack Nicklaus	188,988	1981	Tom Kite	375,699
1953	Lew Worsham	34,002	1968	Billy Casper	205,168	1982	Craig Stadler	446,462
1954	Bob Toski	65,819	1969	Frank Beard	175,223	1983	Hal Sutton	426,668
1955	Julius Boros	65,121	1970	Lee Trevino	157,037	1984	Tom Watson	476,260
1956	Ted Kroll	72,835	1971	Jack Nicklaus	244,490	1985	Curtis Strange	542,321
1957	Dick Mayer	65,835	1972	Jack Nicklaus	320,542	1986	Greg Norman	653,296
1958	Arnold Palmer	42,407	1973	Jack Nicklaus	308,362	1987	Curtis Strange	925,941
1959	Art Wall Jr.	53,167	1974	Johnny Miller	353,201	1988	Curtis Strange	1,147,644
1960	Arnold Palmer	75,262						

LPGA Leading Money Winners

Year	Winner	Dollars	Year	Winner	Dollars	Year	Winner	Dollars
1954	Patty Berg	16,011	1966	Kathy Whitworth	33,517	1978	Nancy Lopez	189,813
1955	Patty Berg	16,492	1967	Kathy Whitworth	32,937	1979	Nancy Lopez	215,987
1956	Marlene Hagge	20,235	1968	Kathy Whitworth	48,379	1980	Beth Daniel	231,000
1957	Patty Berg	16,272	1969	Carol Mann	49,152	1981	Beth Daniel	206,977
1958	Beverly Hanson	12,629	1970	Kathy Whitworth	30,235	1982	JoAnne Carner	310,399
1959	Betsy Rawls	26,774	1971	Kathy Whitworth	41,181	1983	JoAnne Carner	291,404
1960	Louise Suggs	16,892	1972	Kathy Whitworth	65,063	1984	Betsy King	266,771
1961	Mickey Wright	22,236	1973	Kathy Whitworth	82,854	1985	Nancy Lopez	416,472
1962	Mickey Wright	21,641	1974	JoAnne Carner	87,094	1986	Pat Bradley	492,021
1963	Mickey Wright	31,269	1975	Sandra Palmer	94,805	1987	Ayako Okamoto	466,034
1964	Mickey Wright	29,800	1976	Judy Rankin	150,734	1988	Sherri Turner	347,255
1965	Kathy Whitworth	28,658	1977	Judy Rankin	122,890			

Harness Racing

Source: U.S. Trotting Assn.

The Hambletonian (3-year-old trotters)

Year	Winner	Driver	Purse	Year	Winner	Driver	Purse
1949	Miss Tilly	Fred Egan	$69,791	1970	Timothy T	John Simpson Sr.	$143,630
1950	Lusty Song	Del Miller	75,209	1971	Speedy Crown	Howard Beissinger	128,770
1951	Mainliner	Guy Crippen	95,263	1972	Super Bowl	Stanley Dancer	119,090
1952	Sharp Note	Bion Shively	87,637	1973	Flirth	Ralph Baldwin	144,710
1953	Helicopter	Harry Harvey	117,118	1974	Christopher T	Bill Haughton	160,150
1954	Newport Dream	Del Cameron	106,830	1975	Bonefish	Stanley Dancer	232,192
1955	Scott Frost	Joe O'Brien	86,863	1976	Steve Lobell	Bill Haughton	263,524
1956	The Intruder	Ned Bower	98,591	1977	Green Speed	Bill Haughton	284,131
1957	Hickory Smoke	John Simpson Sr.	111,126	1978	Speedy Somolli	Howard Beissinger	241,280
1958	Emily's Pride	Flave Nipe	106,719	1979	Legend Hanover	George Sholty	300,000
1959	Diller Hanover	Frank Ervin	125,284	1980	Burgomeister	Bill Haughton	293,570
1960	Blaze Hanover	Joe O'Brien	144,590	1981	Shiaway St. Pat.	Ray Remmen	838,000
1961	Harlan Dean	James Arthur	131,573	1982	Speed Bowl	Tommy Haughton	875,750
1962	A.C. Os Viking	Sanders Russell	116,312	1983	Duenna	Stanley Dancer	1,080,000
1963	Speedy Scot	Ralph Baldwin	115,549	1984	Historic Freight	Ben Webster	1,219,000
1964	Ayres	John Simpson Sr.	115,281	1985	Prakas	Bill O'Donnell	1,272,000
1965	Egyptian Candor	Del Cameron	122,245	1986	Nuclear Kosmos	Ulf Thoresen	1,172,082
1966	Kerry Way	Frank Ervin	122,540	1987	Mack Lobell	John Campbell	1,046,300
1967	Speedy Streak	Del Cameron	122,650	1988	Armbro Goal	John Campbell	1,156,800
1968	Nevele Pride	Stanley Dancer	116,190	1989	Park Avenue Joe	Ron Waples	1,131,000
1969	Lindy's Pride	Howard Beissinger	124,910				

Little Brown Jug (3-year-old pacers)

Year	Winner	Driver	Purse	Year	Winner	Driver	Purse
1963	Overtrick	John Patterson Sr.	$68,294	1976	Keystone Ore	Stanley Dancer	$153,799
1964	Vicar Hanover	Billy Haughton	66,590	1977	Gov. Skipper	John Chapman	150,000
1965	Bret Hanover	Frank Ervin	71,447	1978	Happy Escort	Bill Popfinger	186,760
1966	Romeo Hanover	George Sholty	74,616	1979	Hot Hitter	Herve Filion	226,455
1967	Best of All	James Hackett	84,778	1980	Niatross	Clint Galbraith	207,000
1968	Rum Customer	Billy Haughton	104,226	1981	Fan Hanover(A)	Glen Garnsey	243,779
1969	Laverne Hanover	Billy Haughton	109,731	1982	Merger	John Campbell	328,900
1970	Most Happy Fella	Stanley Dancer	100,110	1983	Ralph Hanover	Ron Waples	358,800
1971	Nansemond	Herve Filion	102,944	1984	Colt Forty Six	Chris Boring	366,717
1972	Strike Out	Keith Waples	104,916	1985	Nihilator	Bill O'Donnell	350,730
1973	Melvin's Woe	Joe O'Brien	120,000	1986	Barberry Spur	Bill O'Donnell	407,680
1974	Ambro Omaha	Billy Haughton	132,630	1987	Jaguar Spur	Dick Stillings	412,330
1975	Seatrain	Ben Webster	147,813	1988	B.J. Scott	Michel Lachance	486,050
(A) First filly to win the Little Brown Jug.				1988	Goalie Jeff	Michel Lachance	500,200

Harness Horse of the Year

(Chosen by the U.S. Trotting Assn. and the U.S. Harness Writers Assn.)

1949	Good Time	1959	Bye Bye Byrd	1969	Nevele Pride	1979	Niatross
1950	Proximity	1960	Adios Butler	1970	Fresh Yankee	1980	Niatross
1951	Pronto Don	1961	Adios Butler	1971	Albatross	1981	Fan Hanover
1952	Good Time	1962	Su Mac Lad	1972	Albatross	1982	Cam Fella
1953	Hi Lo's Forbes	1963	Speedy Scot	1973	Sir Dalrae	1983	Cam Fella
1954	Stenographer	1964	Bret Hanover	1974	Delmonica Hanover	1984	Fancy Crown
1955	Scott Frost	1965	Bret Hanover	1975	Savior	1985	Nihilator
1956	Scott Frost	1966	Bret Hanover	1976	Keystone Ore	1986	Forrest Skipper
1957	Torpid	1967	Nevele Pride	1977	Green Speed	1987	Mack Lobell
1958	Emily's Pride	1968	Nevele Pride	1978	Abercrombie	1988	Mack Lobell

Annual Leading Money-Winning Horses

Trotters

Year	Horse	Dollars	Year	Horse	Dollars	Year	Horse	Dollars
1962	Duke Rodney	206,113	1971	Fresh Yankee	293,960	1980	Classical Way	350,410
1963	Speedy Scot	144,403	1972	Super Bowl	437,108	1981	Shiaway St. Pat	480,095
1964	Speedy Scot	235,710	1973	Spartan Hanover	262,023	1982	Speed Bowl	672,084
1965	Dartmouth	252,348	1974	Delmonica Hanover	252,165	1983	Joie De Vie	1,007,705
1966	Noble Victory	210,696	1975	Savoir	351,385	1984	Baltic Speed	1,062,611
1967	Carlisle	231,243	1976	Steve Lobell	338,770	1985	Prakis	1,610,608
1968	Nevele Pride	427,440	1977	Green Speed	584,405	1986	Royal Prestige	1,052,114
1969	Lindy's Pride	323,997	1978	Speedy Somolli	362,404	1987	Mack Lobell	1,878,798
1970	Fresh Yankee	359,002	1979	Chiola Hanover	553,058	1988	Ambro Goal	1,311,234

Pacers

Year	Horse	Dollars	Year	Horse	Dollars	Year	Horse	Dollars
1962	Henry T. Adios	220,302	1971	Albatross	558,009	1980	Niatross	1,414,313
1963	Overtrick	208,833	1972	Albatross	459,921	1981	McKinzie Almahurst	936,418
1964	Race Time	199,292	1973	Sir Dalrae	307,354	1982	Fortune Teller	1,313,175
1965	Bret Hanover	341,784	1974	Armbro Omaha	345,146	1983	Ralph Hanover	1,711,990
1966	Bret Hanover	407,534	1975	Silk Stockings	336,312	1984	On The Road Again	1,751,695
1967	Romulus Hanover	277,626	1976	Keystone Ore	539,762	1985	Nihilator	1,864,286
1968	Rum Customer	355,618	1977	Governor Skipper	522,148	1986	Redskin	1,407,263
1969	Overcall	373,150	1978	Abercrombie	703,260	1987	Jate Lobell	1,645,598
1970	Most Happy Fella	387,239	1979	Hot Hitter	826,542	1988	Matt's Scooter	1,783,558

Leading Drivers

Races Won

Year	Driver		Year	Driver		Year	Driver		Year	Driver	
1963	Donald Busse	201	1970	Herve Filion	486	1977	Herve Filion	441	1983	Eddie Davis	470
1964	Bob Farrington	312	1971	Herve Filion	543	1978	Herve Filion	423	1984	Michel Lachance	466
1965	Bob Farrington	310	1972	Herve Filion	605	1979	Ron Waples	443	1985	Michel Lachance	592
1966	Bob Farrington	283	1973	Herve Filion	445	1980	Herve Filion	474	1986	Michel Lachance	770
1967	Bob Farrington	277	1974	Herve Filion	637	1981	Eddie Davis	404	1987	Michel Lachance	715
1968	Herve Filion	407	1975	Daryl Buse	360		Herve Filion	404	1988	Herve Filion	798
1969	Herve Filion	394	1976	Herve Filion	445	1982	Herve Filion	495			

Money Won

Year	Driver	Dollars	Year	Driver	Dollars	Year	Driver	Dollars
1962	Stanley Dancer	760,343	1971	Herve Filion	1,915,945	1980	John Campbell	3,732,306
1963	Bill Haughton	790,086	1972	Herve Filion	2,473,265	1981	Bill O'Donnell	4,065,608
1964	Stanley Dancer	1,051,538	1973	Herve Filion	2,233,302	1982	Bill O'Donnell	5,755,067
1965	Bill Haughton	889,943	1974	Herve Filion	3,474,315	1983	John Campbell	6,104,082
1966	Stanley Dancer	1,218,403	1975	Carmine Abbatiello	2,275,093	1984	Bill O'Donnell	9,059,184
1967	Bill Haughton	1,305,773	1976	Herve Filion	2,241,045	1985	Bill O'Donnell	10,207,372
1968	Bill Haughton	1,654,172	1977	Herve Filion	2,551,058	1986	John Campbell	9,515,055
1969	Del Insko	1,635,463	1978	Carmine Abbatiello	3,344,457	1987	John Campbell	10,186,495
1970	Herve Filion	1,647,837	1979	John Campbell	3,308,984	1988	John Campbell	11,148,565

Water Ski Champions in 1989

30th Annual Masters Tournament

Men's Overall—Carl Roberge.
Men's Slalom—Mike Kjellander.
Men's Tricks—Patrice Martin.
Men's Jump—Sammy Duvall.

Women's Overall—Karen Neville.
Women's Slalom—Helena Kjellander.
Women's Tricks—Tawn Larsen.
Women's Jump—Deena Mapple.

U.S. Open

Men's Overall—Kreg Llewellyn.
Men's Slalom—Andy Mapple.
Men's Tricks—Kreg Llewellyn.
Men's Jump—Mike Kjellander.

Women's Overall—Deena Mapple.
Women's Slalom—Deena Mapple.
Women's Tricks—Tawn Larsen.
Women's Jump—Deena Mapple.

BASEBALL
Major League Pennant Winners, 1901–1989

	National League					American League			
Year	Winner	Won	Lost	Pct	Manager	Year	Winner	Won	Lost	Pct	Manager
---	---	---	---	---	---	---	---	---	---	---	---
1901	Pittsburgh	90	49	.647	Clarke	1901	Chicago	83	53	.610	Griffith
1902	Pittsburgh	103	36	.741	Clarke	1902	Philadelphia	83	53	.610	Mack
1903	Pittsburgh	91	49	.650	Clarke	1903	Boston	91	47	.659	Collins
1904	New York	106	47	.693	McGraw	1904	Boston	95	59	.617	Collins
1905	New York	105	48	.686	McGraw	1905	Philadelphia	92	56	.622	Mack
1906	Chicago	116	36	.763	Chance	1906	Chicago	93	58	.616	Jones
1907	Chicago	107	45	.704	Chance	1907	Detroit	92	58	.613	Jennings
1908	Chicago	99	55	.643	Chance	1908	Detroit	90	63	.588	Jennings
1909	Pittsburgh	110	42	.724	Clarke	1909	Detroit	98	54	.645	Jennings
1910	Chicago	104	50	.675	Chance	1910	Philadelphia	102	48	.680	Mack
1911	New York	99	54	.647	McGraw	1911	Philadelphia	101	50	.669	Mack
1912	New York	103	48	.682	McGraw	1912	Boston	105	47	.691	Stahl
1913	New York	101	51	.664	McGraw	1913	Philadelphia	96	57	.627	Mack
1914	Boston	94	59	.614	Stallings	1914	Philadelphia	99	53	.651	Mack
1915	Philadelphia	90	62	.592	Moran	1915	Boston	101	50	.669	Carrigan
1916	Brooklyn	94	60	.610	Robinson	1916	Boston	91	63	.591	Carrigan
1917	New York	98	56	.636	McGraw	1917	Chicago	100	54	.649	Rowland
1918	Chicago	84	45	.651	Mitchell	1918	Boston	75	51	.595	Barrow
1919	Cincinnati	96	44	.686	Moran	1919	Chicago	88	52	.629	Gleason
1920	Brooklyn	93	60	.604	Robinson	1920	Cleveland	98	56	.636	Speaker
1921	New York	94	56	.614	McGraw	1921	New York	98	55	.641	Huggins
1922	New York	93	61	.604	McGraw	1922	New York	94	60	.610	Huggins
1923	New York	95	58	.621	McGraw	1923	New York	98	54	.645	Huggins
1924	New York	93	60	.608	McGraw	1924	Washington	92	62	.597	Harris
1925	Pittsburgh	95	58	.621	McKechnie	1925	Washington	96	55	.636	Harris
1926	St. Louis	89	65	.578	Hornsby	1926	New York	91	63	.591	Huggins
1927	Pittsburgh	94	60	.610	Bush	1927	New York	110	44	.714	Huggins
1928	St. Louis	95	59	.617	McKechnie	1928	New York	101	53	.656	Huggins
1929	Chicago	98	54	.645	McCarthy	1929	Philadelphia	104	46	.693	Mack
1930	St. Louis	92	62	.597	Street	1930	Philadelphia	102	52	.662	Mack
1931	St. Louis	101	53	.656	Street	1931	Philadelphia	107	45	.704	Mack
1932	Chicago	90	64	.584	Grimm	1932	New York	107	47	.695	McCarthy
1933	New York	91	61	.599	Terry	1933	Washington	99	53	.651	Cronin
1934	St. Louis	95	58	.621	Frisch	1934	Detroit	101	53	.656	Cochrane
1935	Chicago	100	54	.649	Grimm	1935	Detroit	93	58	.616	Cochrane
1936	New York	91	62	.597	Terry	1936	New York	102	51	.667	McCarthy
1937	New York	95	57	.625	Terry	1937	New York	102	52	.662	McCarthy
1938	Chicago	89	63	.586	Hartnett	1938	New York	99	53	.651	McCarthy
1939	Cincinnati	97	57	.630	McKechnie	1939	New York	106	45	.702	McCarthy
1940	Cincinnati	100	53	.654	McKechnie	1940	Detroit	90	64	.584	Baker
1941	Brooklyn	100	54	.649	Durocher	1941	New York	101	53	.656	McCarthy
1942	St. Louis	106	48	.688	Southworth	1942	New York	103	51	.669	McCarthy
1943	St. Louis	105	49	.682	Southworth	1943	New York	98	56	.636	McCarthy
1944	St. Louis	105	49	.682	Southworth	1944	St. Louis	89	65	.578	Sewell
1945	Chicago	98	56	.636	Grimm	1945	Detroit	88	65	.575	O'Neill
1946	St. Louis	98	58	.628	Dyer	1946	Boston	104	50	.675	Cronin
1947	Brooklyn	94	60	.610	Shotton	1947	New York	97	57	.630	Harris
1948	Boston	91	62	.595	Southworth	1948	Cleveland	97	58	.626	Boudreau
1949	Brooklyn	97	57	.630	Shotton	1949	New York	97	57	.630	Stengel
1950	Philadelphia	91	63	.591	Sawyer	1950	New York	98	56	.636	Stengel
1951	New York	98	59	.624	Durocher	1951	New York	98	56	.636	Stengel
1952	Brooklyn	96	57	.627	Dressen	1952	New York	95	59	.617	Stengel
1953	Brooklyn	105	49	.682	Dressen	1953	New York	99	52	.656	Stengel
1954	New York	97	57	.630	Durocher	1954	Cleveland	111	43	.721	Lopez
1955	Brooklyn	98	55	.641	Alston	1955	New York	96	58	.623	Stengel
1956	Brooklyn	93	61	.604	Alston	1956	New York	97	57	.630	Stengel
1957	Milwaukee	95	59	.617	Haney	1957	New York	98	56	.636	Stengel
1958	Milwaukee	92	62	.597	Haney	1958	New York	92	62	.597	Stengel
1959	Los Angeles	88	68	.564	Alston	1959	Chicago	94	60	.610	Lopez
1960	Pittsburgh	95	59	.617	Murtaugh	1960	New York	97	57	.630	Stengel
1961	Cincinnati	93	61	.604	Hutchinson	1961	New York	109	53	.673	Houk
1962	San Francisco	103	62	.624	Dark	1962	New York	96	66	.593	Houk
1963	Los Angeles	99	63	.611	Alston	1963	New York	104	57	.646	Houk
1964	St. Louis	93	69	.574	Keane	1964	New York	99	63	.611	Berra
1965	Los Angeles	97	65	.599	Alston	1965	Minnesota	102	60	.630	Mele
1966	Los Angeles	95	67	.586	Alston	1966	Baltimore	97	63	.606	Bauer
1967	St. Louis	101	60	.627	Schoendienst	1967	Boston	92	70	.568	Williams
1968	St. Louis	97	65	.599	Schoendienst	1968	Detroit	103	59	.636	Smith

National League

	East					West				Playoff
Year	Winner	W	L	Pct	Manager	Winner	W	L	Pct	Manager	winner
---	---	---	---	---	---	---	---	---	---	---	---
1969	N.Y. Mets	100	62	.617	Hodges	Atlanta	93	69	.574	Harris	New York
1970	Pittsburgh	89	73	.549	Murtaugh	Cincinnati	102	60	.630	Anderson	Cincinnati
1971	Pittsburgh	97	65	.599	Murtaugh	San Francisco	90	72	.556	Fox	Pittsburgh
1972	Pittsburgh	96	59	.619	Virdon	Cincinnati	95	59	.617	Anderson	Cincinnati
1973	N.Y. Mets	82	79	.509	Berra	Cincinnati	99	63	.611	Anderson	New York
1974	Pittsburgh	88	74	.543	Murtaugh	Los Angeles	102	60	.630	Alston	Los Angeles
1975	Pittsburgh	92	69	.571	Murtaugh	Cincinnati	108	54	.667	Anderson	Cincinnati
1976	Philadelphia	101	61	.623	Ozark	Cincinnati	102	60	.630	Anderson	Cincinnati

Year	Winner (East)	W	L	Pct	Manager	Winner (West)	W	L	Pct	Manager	Playoff winner
1977	Philadelphia	101	61	.623	Ozark	Los Angeles . . .	98	64	.605	Lasorda	Los Angeles
1978	Philadelphia .	90	72	.556	Ozark	Los Angeles . . .	95	67	.586	Lasorda	Los Angeles
1979	Pittsburgh. . .	98	64	.605	Tanner	Cincinnati.	90	71	.559	McNamara	Pittsburgh
1980	Philadelphia .	91	71	.562	Green	Houston	93	70	.571	Virdon	Philadelphia
1981(a)	Philadelphia .	34	21	.618	Green	Los Angeles . . .	36	21	.632	Lasorda	(c)
1981(b)	Montreal . . .	30	23	.566	Williams, Fanning	Houston	33	20	.623	Virdon	Los Angeles
1982	St. Louis . . .	92	70	.568	Herzog	Atlanta	89	73	.549	Torre	St. Louis
1983	Philadelphia .	90	72	.556	Corrales, Owens	Los Angeles . . .	91	71	.562	Lasorda	Philadelphia
1984	Chicago. . . .	96	65	.596	Frey	San Diego	92	70	.568	Williams	San Diego
1985	St. Louis . . .	101	61	.623	Herzog	Los Angeles . . .	95	67	.586	Lasorda	St. Louis
1986	N.Y. Mets. . .	108	54	.667	Johnson	Houston	96	66	.593	Lanier	New York
1987	St. Louis . . .	95	67	.586	Herzog	San Francisco . .	90	72	.556	Craig	St. Louis
1988	N.Y. Mets. . .	100	60	.625	Johnson	Los Angeles . . .	94	67	.584	Lasorda	Los Angeles
1989	Chicago. . . .	93	69	.571	Zimmer	San Francisco . .	92	70	.568	Craig	San Francisco

American League

Year	Winner (East)	W	L	Pct	Manager	Winner (West)	W	L	Pct	Manager	Playoff winner
1969	Baltimore . . .	109	53	.673	Weaver	Minnesota	97	65	.599	Martin	Baltimore
1970	Baltimore . . .	108	54	.667	Weaver	Minnesota	98	64	.605	Rigney	Baltimore
1971	Baltimore . . .	101	57	.639	Weaver	Oakland	101	60	.627	Williams	Baltimore
1972	Detroit	86	70	.551	Martin	Oakland	93	62	.600	Williams	Oakland
1973	Baltimore . . .	97	65	.599	Weaver	Oakland	94	68	.580	Williams	Oakland
1974	Baltimore . . .	91	71	.562	Weaver	Oakland	90	72	.556	Dark	Oakland
1975	Boston	95	65	.594	Johnson	Oakland	98	64	.605	Dark	Boston
1976	New York . . .	97	62	.610	Martin	Kansas City . . .	90	72	.556	Herzog	New York
1977	New York . . .	100	62	.617	Martin	Kansas City . . .	102	60	.630	Herzog	New York
1978	New York . . .	100	63	.613	Martin, Lemon	Kansas City . . .	92	70	.568	Herzog	New York
1979	Baltimore . . .	102	57	.642	Weaver	California.	88	74	.543	Fregosi	Kansas City
1980	New York . . .	103	59	.636	Howser	Kansas City . . .	97	65	.599	Frey	Kansas City
1981(a)	New York . . .	34	22	.607	Michael	Oakland	37	23	.617	Martin	(d)
1981(b)	Milwaukee . .	31	22	.585	Rodgers	Oakland	30	23	.566	Frey, Howser	New York
1982	Milwaukee . .	95	67	.586	Rodgers, Kuenn	California.	93	69	.574	Mauch	Milwaukee
1983	Baltimore . . .	98	64	.605	Altobelli	Chicago	99	63	.611	LaRussa	Baltimore
1984	Detroit	104	58	.642	Anderson	Kansas City . . .	84	78	.519	Howser	Detroit
1985	Toronto	99	62	.615	Cox	Kansas City . . .	91	71	.562	Howser	Kansas City
1986	Boston.	95	66	.590	McNamara	California.	92	70	.568	Mauch	Boston
1988	Boston.	89	73	.549	McNamara, Morgan	Oakland	104	58	.642	LaRussa	Oakland
1989	Toronto	89	73	.549	Williams, Gaston	Oakland	99	63	.611	LaRussa	Oakland

(a) First half; (b) Second half; (c) Montreal and L.A. won the divisional playoffs; (d) N.Y. and Oakland won the divisional playoffs.

Baseball Stadiums
National League

Team	Stadium	Surface	Home run distances (ft.) LF	Center	RF	Seating capacity
Atlanta Braves.	Atlanta-Fulton County Stadium	Natural grass	330	402	330	52,003
Chicago Cubs	Wrigley Field.	Natural grass	355	400	353	39,600
Cincinnati Reds	Riverfront Stadium	Artificial	330	404	330	52,392
Houston Astros	Astrodome	Artificial	330	400	330	45,000
Los Angeles Dodgers. . . .	Dodger Stadium.	Natural grass	330	395	330	56,000
Montreal Expos	Olympic Stadium	Artificial	325	404	325	59,149
New York Mets	Shea Stadium	Natural grass	338	410	338	55,300
Philadelphia Phillies	Veterans Stadium	Artificial	330	408	330	64,538
Pittsburgh Pirates	Three Rivers Stadium.	Artificial	335	400	335	58,727
St. Louis Cardinals	Busch Stadium	Artificial	330	414	330	54,224
San Diego Padres	Jack Murphy Stadium	Natural grass	327	405	327	58,433
San Francisco Giants	Candlestick Park	Natural grass	335	400	330	58,000

American League

Team	Stadium	Surface	LF	Center	RF	Seating capacity
Baltimore Orioles	Memorial Stadium.	Natural grass	309	405	309	54,017
Boston Red Sox	Fenway Park	Natural grass	315	420	302	34,182
California Angels	Anaheim Stadium	Natural grass	333	404	333	64,593
Chicago White Sox	Comiskey Park	Natural grass	347	409	347	44,087
Cleveland Indians	Cleveland Stadium	Natural grass	320	400	320	74,483
Detroit Tigers	Tiger Stadium	Natural grass	340	440	325	52,416
Kansas City Royals	Royals Stadium.	Artificial	330	410	330	40,625
Milwaukee Brewers	Milwaukee County Stadium	Natural grass	315	402	315	53,192
Minnesota Twins	Hubert H. Humphrey Metrodome	Artificial	343	408	327	55,883
New York Yankees	Yankee Stadium	Natural grass	318	408	314	57,545
Oakland A's	Oakland Coliseum	Natural grass	330	400	330	49,219
Seattle Mariners	Kingdome	Artificial	316	410	316	58,150
Texas Rangers	Arlington Stadium.	Natural grass	330	400	330	43,508
Toronto Blue Jays	Skydome.	Artificial	330	400	330	53,000

Home Run Leaders

National League		American League	
Year Player, Club	HR	Year Player, Club	HR
1901 Sam Crawford, Cincinnati	16	1901 Napoleon Lajoie, Philadelphia	14
1902 Thomas Leach, Pittsburgh	6	1902 Socks Seybold, Philadelphia	16
1903 James Sheckard, Brooklyn	9	1903 Buck Freeman, Boston	13
1904 Harry Lumley, Brooklyn	9	1904 Harry Davis, Philadelphia	10
1905 Fred Odwell, Cincinnati	9	1905 Harry Davis, Philadelphia	8
1906 Timothy Jordan, Brooklyn	12	1906 Harry Davis, Philadelphia	12
1907 David Brain, Boston	10	1907 Harry Davis, Philadelphia	8
1908 Timothy Jordan, Brooklyn	12	1908 Sam Crawford, Detroit	7
1909 Red Murray, New York	7	1909 Ty Cobb, Detroit	9
1910 Fred Beck, Bos., Frank Schulte, Chi.	10	1910 Jake Stahl, Boston	10
1911 Frank Schulte, Chicago	21	1911 J. Franklin Baker, Philadelphia	11
1912 Henry Zimmerman, Chicago	14	1912 J. Franklin Baker, Philadelphia, Tris Speaker, Boston	10
1913 Gavvy Cravath, Philadelphia	19	1913 J. Franklin, Baker, Philadelphia	12
1914 Gavvy Cravath, Philadelphia	19	1914 J. Franklin, Baker, Philadelphia	9
1915 Gavvy Cravath, Philadelphia	24	1915 Robert Roth, Chicago-Cleveland	7
1916 Dave Robertson, N.Y., Fred (Cy) Williams, Chi.	12	1916 Wally Pipp, New York	12
1917 Dave Robertson, N.Y., Gavvy Cravath, Phil.	12	1917 Wally Pipp, New York	9
1918 Gavvy Cravath, Philadelphia	8	1918 Babe Ruth, Bos., Tilly Walker, Phil.	11
1919 Gavvy Cravath, Philadelphia	12	1919 Babe Ruth, Boston	29
1920 Cy Williams, Philadelphia	15	1920 Babe Ruth, New York	54
1921 George Kelly, New York	23	1921 Babe Ruth, New York	59
1922 Rogers Hornsby, St. Louis	42	1922 Ken Williams, St. Louis	39
1923 Cy Williams, Philadelphia	41	1923 Babe Ruth, New York	41
1924 Jacques Fournier, Brooklyn	27	1924 Babe Ruth, New York	46
1925 Rogers Hornsby, St. Louis	39	1925 Bob Meusel, New York	33
1926 Hack Wilson, Chicago	21	1926 Babe Ruth, New York	47
1927 Hack Wilson, Chicago; Cy Williams, Philadelphia	30	1927 Babe Ruth, New York	60
1928 Hack Wilson, Chicago; Jim Bottomley, St. Louis	31	1928 Babe Ruth, New York	54
1929 Chuck Klein, Philadelphia	43	1929 Babe Ruth, New York	46
1930 Hack Wilson, Chicago	56	1930 Babe Ruth, New York	49
1931 Chuck Klein, Philadelphia	31	1931 Babe Ruth, Lou Gehrig, New York	46
1932 Chuck Klein, Philadelphia, Mel Ott, New York	38	1932 Jimmie Foxx, Philadelphia	58
1933 Chuck Klein, Philadelphia	28	1933 Jimmie Foxx, Philadelphia	48
1934 Rip Collins, St. Louis; Mel Ott, New York	35	1934 Lou Gehrig, New York	49
1935 Walter Berger, Boston	34	1935 Jimmie Foxx, Philadelphia, Hank Greenberg, Detroit	36
1936 Mel Ott, New York	33	1936 Lou Gehrig, New York	49
1937 Mel Ott, New York; Joe Medwick, St. Louis	31	1937 Joe DiMaggio, New York	46
1938 Mel Ott, New York	36	1938 Hank Greenberg, Detroit	58
1939 John Mize, St. Louis	28	1939 Jimmie Foxx, Boston	35
1940 John Mize, St. Louis	43	1940 Hank Greenberg, Detroit	41
1941 Dolph Camilli, Brooklyn	34	1941 Ted Williams, Boston	37
1942 Mel Ott, New York	30	1942 Ted Williams, Boston	36
1943 Bill Nicholson, Chicago	29	1943 Rudy York, Detroit	34
1944 Bill Nicholson, Chicago	33	1944 Nick Etten, New York	22
1945 Tommy Holmes, Boston	28	1945 Vern Stephens, St. Louis	24
1946 Ralph Kiner, Pittsburgh	23	1946 Hank Greenberg, Detroit	44
1947 Ralph Kiner, Pittsburgh; John Mize, New York	51	1947 Ted Williams, Boston	32
1948 Ralph Kiner, Pittsburgh; John Mize, New York	40	1948 Joe DiMaggio, New York	39
1949 Ralph Kiner, Pittsburgh	54	1949 Ted Williams, Boston	43
1950 Ralph Kiner, Pittsburgh	47	1950 Al Rosen, Cleveland	37
1951 Ralph Kiner, Pittsburgh	42	1951 Gus Zernial, Chicago-Philadelphia	33
1952 Ralph Kiner, Pittsburgh; Hank Sauer, Chicago	37	1952 Larry Doby, Cleveland	32
1953 Ed Mathews, Milwaukee	47	1953 Al Rosen, Cleveland	43
1954 Ted Kluszewski, Cincinnati	49	1954 Larry Doby, Cleveland	32
1955 Willie Mays, New York	51	1955 Mickey Mantle, New York	37
1956 Duke Snider, Brooklyn	43	1956 Mickey Mantle, New York	52
1957 Hank Aaron, Milwaukee	44	1957 Roy Sievers, Washington	42
1958 Ernie Banks, Chicago	47	1958 Mickey Mantle, New York	42
1959 Ed Mathews, Milwaukee	46	1959 Rocky Colavito, Cleve., Harmon Killebrew, Wash.	42
1960 Ernie Banks, Chicago	41	1960 Mickey Mantle, New York	40
1961 Orlando Cepeda, San Francisco	46	1961 Roger Maris, New York	61
1962 Willie Mays, San Francisco	49	1962 Harmon Killebrew, Minnesota	48
1963 Hank Aaron, Milwaukee, Willie McCovey, S.F.	44	1963 Harmon Killebrew, Minnesota	45
1964 Willie Mays, San Francisco	47	1964 Harmon Killebrew, Minnesota	49
1965 Willie Mays, San Francisco	52	1965 Tony Conigliaro, Boston	32
1966 Hank Aaron, Atlanta	44	1966 Frank Robinson, Baltimore	49
1967 Hank Aaron, Atlanta	39	1967 Carl Yastrzemski, Boston, Harmon Killebrew, Minn.	44
1968 Willie McCovey, San Francisco	36	1968 Frank Howard, Washington	44
1969 Willie McCovey, San Francisco	45	1969 Harmon Killebrew, Minnesota	49
1970 Johnny Bench, Cincinnati	45	1970 Frank Howard, Washington	44
1971 Willie Stargell, Pittsburgh	48	1971 Bill Melton, Chicago	33
1972 Johnny Bench, Cincinnati	40	1972 Dick Allen, Chicago	37
1973 Willie Stargell, Pittsburgh	44	1973 Reggie Jackson, Oakland	32
1974 Mike Schmidt, Philadelphia	36	1974 Dick Allen, Chicago	32
1975 Mike Schmidt, Philadelphia	38	1975 George Scott, Milwaukee; Reggie Jackson, Oakland	36
1976 Mike Schmidt, Philadelphia	38	1976 Graig Nettles, New York	32
1977 George Foster, Cincinnati	52	1977 Jim Rice, Boston	39
1978 George Foster, Cincinnati	40	1978 Jim Rice, Boston	46
1979 Dave Kingman, Chicago	48	1979 Gorman Thomas, Milwaukee	45
1980 Mike Schmidt, Philadelphia	48	1980 Reggie Jackson, New York; Ben Oglivie, Milwaukee	41
1981 Mike Schmidt, Philadelphia	31	1981 Bobby Grich, California; Tony Armas, Oakland; Dwight Evans, Boston; Eddie Murray, Baltimore	22
1982 Dave Kingman, New York	37	1982 Gorman Thomas, Milwaukee; Reggie Jackson, Cal.	39
1983 Mike Schmidt, Philadelphia	40	1983 Jim Rice, Boston	39

Year	Player, Club	HR	Year	Player, Club	HR
1984	Mike Schmidt, Phil.; Dale Murphy, Atlanta	36	1984	Tony Armas, Boston	43
1985	Dale Murphy, Atlanta	37	1985	Darrell Evans, Detroit	40
1986	Mike Schmidt, Philadelphia	37	1986	Jesse Barfield, Toronto	40
1987	Andre Dawson, Chicago	49	1987	Mark McGwire, Oakland	49
1988	Darryl Strawberry, New York	39	1988	Jose Canseco, Oakland	42
1989	Kevin Mitchell, San Francisco	47	1989	Fred McGriff, Toronto	36

Runs Batted In Leaders

National League

American League

Year	Player, Club	RBI	Year	Player, Club	RBI
1907	Honus Wagner, Pittsburgh	91	1907	Ty Cobb, Detroit	116
1908	Honus Wager, Pittsburgh	106	1908	Ty Cobb, Detroit	101
1909	Honus Wager, Pittsburgh	102	1909	Ty Cobb, Detroit	115
1910	Sherwood Magee, Philadelphia	116	1910	Sam Crawford, Detroit	115
1911	Frank Schulte, Chicago	121	1911	Ty Cobb, Detroit	144
1912	Henry Zimmerman, Chicago	98	1912	J. Franklin Baker, Philadelphia	133
1913	Gavvy Cravath, Philadelphia	118	1913	J. Franklin Baker, Philadelphia	126
1914	Sherwood Magee, Philadelphia	101	1914	Sam Crawford, Detroit	112
1915	Gavvy Cravath, Philadelphia	118	1915	Sam Crawford, Detroit	116
1916	Hal Chase, Cincinnati	94	1916	Wally Pipp, New York	99
1917	Henry Zimmerman, New York	100	1917	Robert Veach, Detroit	115
1918	Frederick Merkle, Chicago	71	1918	George Burns, Phila., Robert Veach, Detroit	74
1919	Hi Myers, Boston	72	1919	Babe Ruth, Boston	112
1920	George Kelly, N.Y., Rogers Hornsby, St. Louis	94	1920	Babe Ruth, New York	137
1921	Rogers Hornsby, St. Louis	126	1921	Babe Ruth, New York	171
1922	Rogers Hornsby, St. Louis	152	1922	Ken Williams, St. Louis	155
1923	Emil Meusel, New York	125	1923	Babe Ruth, New York	131
1924	George Kelly, New York	136	1924	Goose Goslin, Washington	129
1925	Rogers Hornsby, St. Louis	143	1925	Bob Meusel, New York	138
1926	Jim Bottomley, St. Louis	120	1926	Babe Ruth, New York	145
1927	Paul Waner, Pittsburgh	131	1927	Lou Gehrig, New York	175
1928	Jim Bottomley, St. Louis	136	1928	Babe Ruth, N.Y., Lou Gehrig, N.Y.	142
1929	Hack Wilson, Chicago	159	1929	Al Simmons, Philadelphia	157
1930	Hack Wilson, Chicago	190	1930	Lou Gehrig, New York	174
1931	Chuck Klein, Philadelphia	121	1931	Lou Gehrig, New York	184
1932	Don Hurst, Philadelphia	143	1932	Jimmie Foxx, Philadelphia	169
1933	Chuck Klein, Philadelphia	120	1933	Jimmie Foxx, Philadelphia	163
1934	Mel Ott, New York	135	1934	Lou Gehrig, New York	165
1935	Walter Berger, Boston	130	1935	Hank Greenberg, Detroit	170
1936	Joe Medwick, St. Louis	138	1936	Hal Trosky, Cleveland	162
1937	Joe Medwick, St. Louis	154	1937	Hank Greenburg, Detroit	183
1938	Joe Medwick, St. Louis	122	1938	Jimmie Foxx, Boston	175
1939	Frank McCormick, Cincinnati	128	1939	Ted Williams, Boston	145
1940	John Mize, St. Louis	137	1940	Hank Greenberg, Detroit	150
1941	Adolph Camilli, Brooklyn	120	1941	Joe DiMaggio, New York	125
1942	John Mize, New York	110	1942	Ted Williams, Boston	137
1943	Bill Nicholson, Chicago	128	1943	Rudy York, Detroit	118
1944	Bill Nicholson, Chicago	122	1944	Vern Stephens, St. Louis	109
1945	Dixie Walker, Brooklyn	124	1945	Nick Etten, New York	111
1946	Enos Slaughter, St. Louis	130	1946	Hank Greenberg, Detroit	127
1947	John Mize, New York	138	1947	Ted Williams, Boston	114
1948	Stan Musial, St. Louis	131	1948	Joe DiMaggio, New York	155
1949	Ralph Kiner, Pittsburgh	127	1949	Ted Williams, Bos., Vern Stephens, Bos.	159
1950	Del Ennis, Philadelphia	126	1950	Walt Dropo, Bos., Vern Stephens, Bos.	144
1951	Monte Irvin, New York	121	1951	Gus Zernial, Chicago-Philadelphia	129
1952	Hank Sauer, Chicago	121	1952	Al Rosen, Cleveland	105
1953	Roy Campanella, Brooklyn	142	1953	Al Rosen, Cleveland	145
1954	Ted Kluszewski, Cincinnati	141	1954	Larry Doby, Cleveland	126
1955	Duke Snider, Brooklyn	136	1955	Ray Boone, Detroit, Jackie Jensen, Boston	116
1956	Stan Musial, St. Louis	109	1956	Mickey Mantle, New York	130
1957	Hank Aaron, Milwaukee	132	1957	Roy Sievers, Washington	114
1958	Ernie Banks, Chicago	129	1958	Jackie Jensen, Boston	122
1959	Ernie Banks, Chicago	143	1959	Jackie Jensen, Boston	112
1960	Hank Aaron, Milwaukee	126	1960	Roger Maris, New York	112
1961	Orlando Cepeda, San Francisco	142	1961	Roger Maris, New York	142
1962	Tommy Davis, Los Angeles	153	1962	Harmon Killebrew, Minnesota	126
1963	Hank Aaron, Milwaukee	130	1963	Dick Stuart, Boston	118
1964	Ken Boyer, St. Louis	119	1964	Brooks Robinson, Baltimore	118
1965	Deron Johnson, Cincinnati	130	1965	Rocky Colavito, Cleveland	108
1966	Hank Aaron, Atlanta	127	1966	Frank Robinson, Baltimore	122
1967	Orlando Cepeda, St. Louis	111	1967	Carl Yastrzemski, Boston	121
1968	Willie McCovey, San Francisco	105	1968	Ken Harrelson, Boston	109
1969	Willie McCovey, San Francisco	126	1969	Harmon Killebrew, Minnesota	140
1970	Johnny Bench, Cincinnati	148	1970	Frank Howard, Washington	126
1971	Joe Torre, St. Louis	137	1971	Harmon Killebrew, Minnesota	119
1972	Johnny Bench, Cincinnati	125	1972	Dick Allen, Chicago	113
1973	Willie Stargell, Pittsburgh	119	1973	Reggie Jackson, Oakland	117
1974	Johnny Bench, Cincinnati	129	1974	Jeff Burroughs, Texas	118
1975	Greg Luzinski, Philadelphia	120	1975	George Scott, Milwaukee	109
1976	George Foster, Cincinnati	121	1976	Lee May, Baltimore	109
1977	George Foster, Cincinnati	149	1977	Larry Hisle, Minnesota	119
1978	George Foster, Cincinnati	120	1978	Jim Rice, Boston	139
1979	Dave Winfield, San Diego	118	1979	Don Baylor, California	139
1980	Mike Schmidt, Philadelphia	121	1980	Cecil Cooper, Milwaukee	122
1981	Mike Schmidt, Philadelphia	91	1981	Eddie Murray, Baltimore	78
1982	Dale Murphy, Atlanta; Al Oliver, Montreal	109	1982	Hal McRae, Kansas City	133

Year	Player, Club	RBI	Year	Player, Club	RBI
1983	Dale Murphy, Atlanta	121	1983	Cecil Cooper, Milwaukee; Jim Rice, Boston	126
1984	Mike Schmidt, Phil.; Gary Carter, Montreal	106	1984	Tony Armas, Boston	123
1985	Dave Parker, Cincinnati	125	1985	Don Mattingly, New York	145
1986	Mike Schmidt, Philadelphia	119	1986	Joe Carter, Cleveland	121
1987	Andre Dawson, Chicago	137	1987	George Bell, Toronto	134
1988	Will Clark, San Francisco	109	1988	Jose Canseco, Oakland	124
1989	Kevin Mitchell, San Francisco	125	1989	Ruben Sierra, Texas	119

Batting Champions

	National League				American League		
Year	Player	Club	Pct.	Year	Player	Club	Pct.
1901	Jesse C. Burkett	St. Louis	.382	1901	Napoleon Lajoie	Philadelphia	.422
1902	Clarence Beaumont	Pittsburgh	.357	1902	Ed Delahanty	Washington	.376
1903	Honus Wagner	Pittsburgh	.355	1902	Napoleon Lajoie	Cleveland	.355
1904	Honus Wagner	Pittsburgh	.349	1904	Napoleon Lajoie	Cleveland	.381
1905	James Seymour	Cincinnati	.377	1905	Elmer Flick	Cleveland	.308
1906	Honus Wagner	Pittsburgh	.339	1906	George Stone	St. Louis	.358
1907	Honus Wagner	Pittsburgh	.350	1907	Ty Cobb	Detroit	.350
1908	Honus Wagner	Pittsburgh	.354	1908	Ty Cobb	Detroit	.324
1909	Honus Wagner	Pittsburgh	.339	1909	Ty Cobb	Detroit	.377
1910	Sherwood Magee	Philadelphia	.331	1910	Ty Cobb	Detroit	.385
1911	Honus Wagner	Pittsburgh	.334	1911	Ty Cobb	Detroit	.420
1912	Henry Zimmerman	Chicago	.372	1912	Ty Cobb	Detroit	.410
1913	Jacob Daubert	Brooklyn	.350	1913	Ty Cobb	Detroit	.390
1914	Jacob Daubert	Brooklyn	.329	1914	Ty Cobb	Detroit	.368
1915	Larry Doyle	New York	.320	1915	Ty Cobb	Detroit	.369
1916	Hal Chase	Cincinnati	.339	1916	Tris Speaker	Cleveland	.386
1917	Edd Roush	Cincinnati	.341	1917	Ty Cobb	Detroit	.383
1918	Zach Wheat	Brooklyn	.335	1918	Ty Cobb	Detroit	.382
1919	Edd Roush	Cincinnati	.321	1919	Ty Cobb	Detroit	.384
1920	Rogers Hornsby	St. Louis	.370	1920	George Sisler	St. Louis	.407
1921	Rogers Hornsby	St. Louis	.397	1921	Harry Heilmann	Detroit	.394
1922	Rogers Hornsby	St. Louis	.401	1922	George Sisler	St. Louis	.420
1923	Rogers Hornsby	St. Louis	.384	1923	Harry Heilmann	Detroit	.403
1924	Rogers Hornsby	St. Louis	.424	1924	Babe Ruth	New York	.378
1925	Rogers Hornsby	St. Louis	.403	1925	Harry Heilmann	Detroit	.393
1926	Eugene Hargrave	Cincinnati	.353	1926	Henry Manush	Detroit	.378
1927	Paul Waner	Pittsburgh	.380	1927	Harry Heilmann	Detroit	.398
1928	Rogers Hornsby	Boston	.387	1928	Goose Goslin	Washington	.379
1929	Lefty O'Doul	Philadelphia	.398	1929	Lew Fonseca	Cleveland	.369
1930	Bill Terry	New York	.401	1930	Al Simmons	Philadelphia	.381
1931	Chick Hafey	St. Louis	.349	1931	Al Simmons	Philadelphia	.390
1932	Lefty O'Doul	Brooklyn	.368	1932	Dale Alexander	Detroit-Boston	.367
1933	Chuck Klein	Philadelphia	.368	1933	Jimmie Foxx	Philadelphia	.356
1934	Paul Waner	Pittsburgh	.362	1934	Lou Gehrig	New York	.363
1935	Arky Vaughan	Pittsburgh	.385	1935	Buddy Myer	Washington	.349
1936	Paul Waner	Pittsburgh	.373	1936	Luke Appling	Chicago	.388
1937	Joe Medwick	St. Louis	.374	1937	Charlie Gehringer	Detroit	.371
1938	Ernie Lombardi	Cincinnati	.342	1938	Jimmie Foxx	Boston	.349
1939	John Mize	St. Louis	.349	1939	Joe DiMaggio	New York	.381
1940	Debs Garms	Pittsburgh	.355	1940	Joe DiMaggio	New York	.352
1941	Pete Reiser	Brooklyn	.343	1941	Ted Williams	Boston	.406
1942	Ernie Lombardi	Boston	.330	1942	Ted Williams	Boston	.356
1943	Stan Musial	St. Louis	.357	1943	Luke Appling	Chicago	.328
1944	Dixie Walker	Brooklyn	.357	1944	Lou Boudreau	Cleveland	.327
1945	Phil Cavarretta	Chicago	.355	1945	George Stirnweiss	New York	.309
1946	Stan Musial	St. Louis	.365	1946	Mickey Vernon	Washington	.353
1947	Harry Walker	Philadelphia	.363	1947	Ted Williams	Boston	.343
1948	Stan Musial	St. Louis	.376	1948	Ted Williams	Boston	.369
1949	Jackie Robinson	Brooklyn	.342	1949	George Kell	Detroit	.343
1950	Stan Musial	St. Louis	.346	1950	Billy Goodman	Boston	.354
1951	Stan Musial	St. Louis	.355	1951	Ferris Fain	Philadelphia	.344
1952	Stan Musial	St. Louis	.336	1952	Ferris Fain	Philadelphia	.327
1953	Carl Furillo	Brooklyn	.344	1953	Mickey Vernon	Washington	.337
1954	Willie Mays	New York	.345	1954	Roberto Avila	Cleveland	.341
1955	Richie Ashburn	Philadelphia	.338	1955	Al Kaline	Detroit	.340
1956	Hank Aaron	Milwaukee	.328	1956	Mickey Mantle	New York	.353
1957	Stan Musial	St. Louis	.351	1957	Ted Williams	Boston	.388
1958	Richie Ashburn	Philadelphia	.350	1958	Ted Williams	Boston	.328
1959	Hank Aaron	Milwaukee	.355	1959	Harvey Kuenn	Detroit	.353
1960	Dick Groat	Pittsburgh	.325	1960	Pete Runnels	Boston	.320
1961	Roberto Clemente	Pittsburgh	.351	1961	Norm Cash	Detroit	.361
1962	Tommy Davis	Los Angeles	.346	1962	Pete Runnels	Boston	.326
1963	Tommy Davis	Los Angeles	.326	1963	Carl Yastrzemski	Boston	.321
1964	Roberto Clemente	Pittsburgh	.339	1964	Tony Oliva	Minnesota	.323
1965	Roberto Clemente	Pittsburgh	.329	1965	Tony Oliva	Minnesota	.321
1966	Matty Alou	Pittsburgh	.342	1966	Frank Robinson	Baltimore	.316
1967	Roberto Clemente	Pittsburgh	.357	1967	Carl Yastrzemski	Boston	.326
1968	Pete Rose	Cincinnati	.335	1968	Carl Yastrzemski	Boston	.301
1969	Pete Rose	Cincinnati	.348	1969	Rod Carew	Minnesota	.332
1970	Rico Carty	Atlanta	.366	1970	Alex Johnson	California	.328
1971	Joe Torre	St. Louis	.363	1971	Tony Oliva	Minnesota	.337
1972	Billy Williams	Chicago	.333	1972	Rod Carew	Minnesota	.318
1973	Pete Rose	Cincinnati	.338	1973	Rod Carew	Minnesota	.350
1974	Ralph Garr	Atlanta	.353	1974	Rod Carew	Minnesota	.364
1975	Bill Madlock	Chicago	.354	1975	Rod Carew	Minnesota	.359
1976	Bill Madlock	Chicago	.339	1976	George Brett	Kansas City	.333

Year	Player	Club	Pct.	Year	Player	Club	Pct.
1977	Dave Parker	Pittsburgh	.338	1977	Rod Carew	Minnesota	.388
1978	Dave Parker	Pittsburgh	.334	1978	Rod Carew	Minnesota	.333
1979	Keith Hernandez	St. Louis	.344	1979	Fred Lynn	Boston	.333
1980	Bill Buckner	Chicago	.324	1980	George Brett	Kansas City	.390
1981	Bill Madlock	Pittsburgh	.341	1981	Carney Lansford	Boston	.336
1982	Al Oliver	Montreal	.331	1982	Willie Wilson	Kansas City	.332
1983	Bill Madlock	Pittsburgh	.323	1983	Wade Boggs	Boston	.361
1984	Tony Gwynn	San Diego	.351	1984	Don Mattingly	New York	.343
1985	Willie McGee	St. Louis	.353	1985	Wade Boggs	Boston	.368
1986	Tim Raines	Montreal	.334	1986	Wade Boggs	Boston	.357
1987	Tony Gwynn	San Diego	.369	1987	Wade Boggs	Boston	.363
1988	Tony Gwynn	San Diego	.313	1988	Wade Boggs	Boston	.366
1989	Tony Gwynn	San Diego	.336	1989	Kirby Puckett	Minnesota	.339

Cy Young Award Winners

Year	Player, club	Year	Player, club	Year	Player, club
1956	Don Newcombe, Dodgers	1971	(NL) Ferguson Jenkins, Cubs	1980	(NL) Steve Carlton, Phillies
1957	Warren Spahn, Braves		(AL) Vida Blue, A's		(AL) Steve Stone, Orioles
1958	Bob Turley, Yankees	1972	(NL) Steve Carlton, Phillies	1981	(NL) Fernando Valenzuela, Dodgers
1959	Early Wynn, White Sox		(AL) Gaylord Perry, Indians		(AL) Rollie Fingers, Brewers
1960	Vernon Law, Pirates	1973	(NL) Tom Seaver, Mets	1982	(NL) Steve Carlton, Phillies
1961	Whitey Ford, Yankees		(AL) Jim Palmer, Orioles		(AL) Pete Vuckovich, Brewers
1962	Don Drysdale, Dodgers	1974	(NL) Mike Marshall, Dodgers	1983	(NL) John Denny, Phillies
1963	Sandy Koufax, Dodgers		(AL) Jim (Catfish) Hunter, A's		(AL) LaMarr Hoyt, White Sox
1964	Dean Chance, Angels	1975	(NL) Tom Seaver, Mets	1984	(NL) Rick Sutcliffe, Cubs
1965	Sandy Koufax, Dodgers		(AL) Jim Palmer, Orioles		(AL) Willie Hernandez, Tigers
1966	Sandy Koufax, Dodgers	1976	(NL) Randy Jones, Padres	1985	(NL) Dwight Gooden, Mets
1967	(NL) Mike McCormick, Giants		(AL) Jim Palmer, Orioles		(AL) Bret Saberhagen, Royals
	(AL) Jim Lonborg, Red Sox	1977	(NL) Steve Carlton, Phillies	1986	(NL) Mike Scott, Astros
1968	(NL) Bob Gibson, Cardinals		(AL) Sparky Lyle, Yankees		(AL) Roger Clemens, Red Sox
	(AL) Dennis McLain, Tigers	1978	(NL) Gaylord Perry, Padres	1987	(NL) Steve Bedrosian, Phillies
1969	(NL) Tom Seaver, Mets		(AL) Ron Guidry, Yankees		(AL) Roger Clemens, Red Sox
	(AL) (tie) Dennis McLain, Tigers	1979	(NL) Bruce Sutter, Cubs	1988	(NL) Orel Hershiser, Dodgers
	Mike Cuellar, Orioles		(AL) Mike Flanagan, Orioles		(AL) Frank Viola, Twins
1970	(NL) Bob Gibson, Cardinals				
	(AL) Jim Perry, Twins				

Major League Leaders in 1989

National League

Batting

Gwynn, San Diego, .336; Clark, San Francisco, .333; L. Smith, Atlanta, .315; Grace, Chicago, .314; Guerrero, St. Louis, .311.

Home Runs

Mitchell, San Francisco, 47; Johnson, New York, 36; Davis, Cincinnati, 34; Davis, Houston, 34; Sandberg, Chicago, 30.

Runs Batted In

Mitchell, San Francisco, 125; Guerrero, St. Louis, 117; Clark, San Francisco, 111; Davis, Cincinnati, 101; Johnson, New York, 101.

Hits

Gwynn, San Diego, 203; Clark, San Francisco, 196; Alomar, San Diego, 184; Guerrero, St. Louis, 177; Sandberg, Chicago, 176.

Stolen Bases

Coleman, St. Louis, 65; Alomar, San Diego, 42; Samuel, New York, 42; Johnson, New York, 41; Raines, Montreal, 41.

On-Base Pct.

L. Smith, Atlanta, .415; Clark, San Diego, .410; Clark, San Francisco, .407; Grace, Chicago, .405; Raines, Montreal, .395.

Doubles

Guerrero, St. Louis, 42; Wallach, Montreal, 42; Johnson, New York, 41; Clark, San Francisco, 38; Bonilla, Pittsburgh, 37.

Triples

Thompson, San Francisco, 11; Bonilla, Pittsburgh, 10.

Earned-Run Average

Garrelts, San Francisco, 2.28; Hershiser, Los Angeles, 2.31; Langston, Montreal, 2.39; Whitson, San Diego, 2.66; Hurst, San Diego, 2.69.

Saves

Davis, San Diego, 44; Williams, Chicago, 36; Franco, Cincinnati, 32; Burke, Montreal, 28; Howell, Los Angeles, 28.

Strikeouts

DeLeon, St. Louis, 201; Belcher, Los Angeles, 200; Fernandez, New York, 198; Cone, New York, 190.

American League

Batting

Puckett, Minnesota, .339; Lansford, Oakland, .336; Boggs, Boston, .330; Yount, Milwaukee, .318; Franco, Texas, .316; Sax, New York, 316.

Home Runs

McGriff, Toronto, 36; Carter, Cleveland, 35; McGwire, Oakland, 33; Jackson, Kansas City, 32; Esasky, Boston, 30.

Runs Batted In

Sierra, Texas, 119; Mattingly, New York, 113; Esasky, Boston, 108; Carter, Cleveland, 105; Jackson, Kansas City, 105.

Hits

Puckett, Minnesota, 215; Boggs, Boston, 205; Sax, New York, 205; Yount, Milwaukee, 195; Molitor, Milwaukee, 194.

Stolen Bases

Henderson, Oakland, 77; Espy, Texas, 45; White, California, 44; Pettis, Detroit, 43; Sax, New York, 43.

On-Base Pct.

Boggs, Boston, .430; Davis, Seattle, .424; R. Henderson, Oakland, .411; McGriff, Toronto, .399; Lansford, Oakland, .398.

Doubles

Boggs, Boston, 51; Puckett, Minnesota, 45; Reed, Boston, 42; Bell, Toronto, 41; Yount, Milwaukee, 38.

Triples

Sierra, Texas, 14; White, California, 13.

Earned Run Average

Saberhagen, Kansas City, 2.16; Finley, California, 2.57; Moore, Oakland, 2.61; Blyleven, California, 2.73; McCaskill, California, 2.93.

Saves

Russell, Texas, 38; Thigpen, Chicago, 34; Eckersley, Oakland, 33; Plesac, Milwaukee, 33; Schooler, Seattle, 33.

Strikeouts

Ryan, Texas, 301; Clemens, Boston, 230; Saberhagen, Kansas City, 193; Bosio, Milwaukee, 173.

National League Records in 1989
Final standings
Eastern Division

Club	W	L	Pct	GB	Home	Road	vs. RHP	LHP	Grass	Artif	Night	Day	1-Run Games
Chicago....	93	69	.571	—	48-33	45-36	62-52	31-17	63-51	30-18	44-31	49-38	28-23
New York...	87	75	.537	6	51-30	36-45	54-48	33-27	63-51	24-24	63-43	24-32	22-30
St. Louis .	86	76	.531	7	46-35	40-41	61-43	25-33	20-22	66-54	59-49	27-27	29-21
Montreal ...	81	81	.500	12	44-37	37-44	54-63	27-18	17-25	64-56	54-61	27-20	26-29
Pittsburgh...	74	88	.457	19	39-42	35-46	53-58	21-30	18-24	56-64	49-59	25-29	19-32
Philadelphia .	67	95	.414	26	38-42	29-53	44-58	23-37	14-28	53-67	53-67	14-28	20-23

Western Division

Club	W	L	Pct	GB	Home	Road	vs. RHP	LHP	Grass	Artif	Night	Day	1-Run Games
San Francisco	92	70	.568	—	53-28	39-42	56-50	36-20	73-47	19-23	53-44	39-26	30-25
San Diego ..	89	73	.549	3	46-35	43-38	62-54	27-19	66-54	23-19	67-48	22-25	30-18
Houston ...	86	76	.531	6	47-35	39-41	59-55	27-21	21-27	65-49	58-54	28-22	35-24
Los Angeles .	77	83	.481	14	44-37	33-46	46-53	30-30	61-57	16-26	47-64	30-19	27-31
Cincinnati...	75	87	.463	17	38-43	37-44	55-61	20-26	22-26	53-61	53-54	22-33	21-24
Atlanta	63	97	.394	28	33-46	30-51	40-59	23-38	46-71	17-25	48-74	15-23	24-31

National League Championship Series

San Francisco 11, Chicago 3　　San Francisco 5, Chicago 4　　San Francisco 3, Chicago 2
Chicago 9, San Francisco 5　　San Francisco 6, Chicago 4

Team Batting

Team	Pct	AB	R	H	HR	SB
Chicago...........	.261	5513	702	1438	124	136
St. Louis	.258	5492	632	1418	73	155
San Diego	.251	5422	642	1360	120	136
San Francisco	.250	5469	699	1365	141	87
Montreal	.247	5482	632	1353	100	160
Cincinnati........	.247	5520	632	1362	128	128
New York.........	.246	5489	683	1351	147	158
Philadelphia	.243	5447	629	1324	123	106
Pittsburgh	.241	5539	637	1334	95	155
Los Angeles	.240	5465	554	1313	89	81
Houston	.239	5516	647	1316	97	144
Atlanta	.234	5463	584	1281	128	83

Team Pitching

Team	ERA	CG	IP	H	R	BB	SO
Los Angeles	2.95	25	1463	1278	536	504	1052
New York	3.29	24	1454	1260	595	532	1108
San Francisco	3.30	12	1457	1320	600	471	802
St. Louis	3.36	18	1461	1330	608	482	844
San Diego	3.38	21	1457	1359	626	481	933
Chicago	3.43	18	1460	1369	623	532	918
Montreal	3.48	20	1468	1344	630	519	1059
Pittsburgh	3.64	20	1487	1394	680	539	827
Houston	3.64	19	1479	1379	669	551	965
Atlanta	3.70	15	1447	1370	680	468	966
Cincinnati	3.73	16	1464	1404	691	559	981
Philadelphia	4.04	10	1433	1408	735	613	899

Individual Batting (at least 135 at-bats); Individual Pitching (at least 50 innings)

Atlanta Braves

Batting	BA	AB	R	H	HR	RBI
L. Smith.........	.315	482	89	152	21	79
McDowell........	.304	280	56	85	7	24
Treadway........	.277	473	58	131	8	40
Blauser.........	.270	456	63	123	12	46
Berroa..........	.265	136	7	36	2	9
James	.259	170	15	44	1	11
Perry	.252	266	24	67	4	21
Gregg	.243	276	24	67	6	23
Murphy	.228	574	60	131	20	84
Thomas.........	.213	554	41	118	13	57
Evans	.207	276	31	57	11	39
Benedict........	.194	160	12	31	1	6
Russell.........	.182	159	14	29	2	9
Gant...........	.177	260	26	46	9	25
Davis	.169	231	12	39	4	19

Pitching	W	L	ERA	IP	BB	SO	Sv
Acker		6	2.67	97	20	68	2
Alvarez	3	3	2.86	50	24	45	2
Smoltz.........	12	11	2.94	208	72	168	
Clary	4	3	3.15	108	31	30	
Galvine	14	8	3.68	186	40	90	
Boever	4	11	3.94	82	34	68	21
Lilliquist	8	10	3.97	165	34	79	
Eichhorn........	5	5	4.35	68	19	49	
P. Smith........	5	14	4.75	142	57	115	

Chicago Cubs

Batting	Avg	AB	R	H	HR	RBI
D. Smith.........	.324	343	52	111	9	52
Grace	.314	510	74	160	13	79
Walton	.293	475	64	139	5	46
Sandberg	.290	606	104	176	30	76
McClendon	.286	259	47	74	12	40
Salazar	.282	326	34	92	9	34
Dunston	.278	471	52	131	9	60
Ramos	.263	179	18	47	1	19
Berryhill	.257	334	37	86	5	41
Webster	.257	272	40	70	3	19
Dawson	.252	416	62	105	21	77
Girardi	.248	157	15	39	1	14
Wilkerson	.244	160	18	39	1	10
Wynne	.243	342	27	83	7	39
Law	.235	408	38	96	7	42
Dascenzo.......	.165	139	20	23	1	12

Pitching	W	L	ERA	IP	BB	SO	Sv
Lancaster	4	2	1.36	72	15	56	8
Williams	4	4	2.76	81	52	67	36
Maddux	19	12	2.95	238	82	135	
Bielecki	18	7	3.14	212	81	147	
Sutcliffe	16	11	3.66	229	69	153	
Pico	3	1	3.77	90	31	38	2
Sanderson	11	9	3.94	146	31	86	
Assenmacher....	3	4	3.99	76	28	79	
Wilson	6	4	4.20	85	31	65	2
Kilgus	6	10	4.39	145	49	61	2

Cincinnati Reds

Batting	Avg	AB	R	H	HR	RBI
Larkin	.342	325	47	111	4	36
Davis	.281	462	74	130	34	101
O'Neill	.276	428	49	118	15	74
Oliver	.272	151	13	41	3	23
Roomes	.263	315	36	83	7	34
Griffey	.263	236	26	62	8	30
Sabo	.260	304	40	79	6	29
Winningham	.251	251	40	63	3	13
Duncan	.248	258	32	64	3	21
Oester	.246	305	23	75	1	14
Benzinger	.245	628	79	154	17	76
Quinones	.244	340	43	83	12	34
Reed	.223	287	16	64	3	23
Diaz	.205	132	6	27	1	8

Pitching	W	L	ERA	IP	BB	SO	Sv
Dibble	10	5	2.09	99	39	141	2
Rijo	7	6	2.84	111	48	86	
Charlton	8	3	2.93	95	40	98	
Franco	4	8	3.12	80	36	60	32
Robinson	5	3	3.35	83	28	36	
Browning	15	12	3.39	249	64	118	
Leary	8	14	3.52	207	68	123	
Birtsas	2	2	3.75	69	27	57	1
Mahler	9	13	3.83	220	51	102	
Scudder	4	9	4.49	100	61	66	
Tekulve	0	3	5.02	52	23	31	1
Sebra	2	3	5.20	55	28	35	1
Jackson	6	11	5.60	115	57	70	

Houston Astros

Batting	Avg	AB	R	H	HR	RBI
Bass	.300	313	42	94	5	44
Puhl	.271	354	41	96	0	27
Davis	.269	581	87	156	34	89
Wilson	.266	432	50	115	11	64
Biggio	.257	443	64	114	13	60
Caminiti	.255	585	71	149	10	72
Ramirez	.246	537	46	132	6	54
Young	.233	533	71	124	0	38
Doran	.219	507	65	111	8	58
Reynolds	.201	189	16	38	2	14

Pitching	W	L	ERA	IP	BB	SO	Sv
Anderson	4	4	1.54	87	24	85	3
Darwin	11	4	2.36	122	33	104	7
Smith	3	4	2.64	58	19	31	25
Portugal	7	1	2.75	108	37	86	
Deshaies	15	10	2.91	225	79	153	
Agosto	4	5	2.93	83	32	46	1
Scott	20	10	3.10	229	62	172	
Rhoden	2	6	4.28	96	41	41	
Schatzeder	4	1	4.45	56	28	46	1
Clancy	7	14	5.08	147	66	91	
Forsch	4	5	5.32	108	46	40	

Los Angeles Dodgers

Batting	Avg	AB	R	H	HR	RBI
Hatcher	.295	224	18	66	2	25
Randolph	.282	549	62	155	2	36
Gonzalez	.268	261	31	70	3	18
Marshall	.260	377	41	98	11	42
Scioscia	.250	408	40	102	10	44
Davis	.249	173	21	43	5	19
Murray	.247	594	66	147	20	88
Griffin	.247	506	49	125	0	29
Daniels	.246	171	33	42	4	17
Hamilton	.245	548	45	134	12	56
Harris	.236	335	36	79	3	26
Anderson	.229	140	15	32	1	14
Gibson	.213	253	35	54	9	28
Shelby	.183	345	28	63	1	12
Dempsey	.179	151	16	27	4	16

Pitching	W	L	ERA	IP	BB	SO	Sv
Howell	5	3	1.58	79	22	55	28
Pena	4	3	2.13	76	18	75	5
Hershiser	15	15	2.31	76	18	75	
Morgan	8	11	2.53	152	33	72	
Belcher	15	12	2.82	230	80	200	1
Martinez	6	4	3.19	98	41	89	
Crews	0	1	3.21	61	23	56	1
Valenzuela	10	13	3.43	196	98	116	
Wetteland	5	8	3.77	102	34	96	1

Montreal Expos

Batting	Avg	AB	R	H	HR	RBI
Raines	.286	517	76	148	9	60
Wallach	.277	573	76	159	13	77
Da. Martinez	.274	361	41	99	3	27
Garcia	.271	203	26	55	3	18
Brooks	.268	542	56	145	14	70
Galarraga	.257	572	76	147	23	85
Santovenia	.250	304	30	76	5	31
Hudler	.245	155	21	38	6	13
Fitzgerald	.238	290	33	69	7	42
Owen	.233	437	52	102	6	41
Foley	.229	375	34	86	7	39
Aldrete	.221	136	12	30	1	12
Nixon	.217	258	41	56	0	21

Pitching	W	L	ERA	IP	BB	SO	Sv
Langston	12	9	2.39	176	93	175	
Burke	9	3	2.55	84	22	54	28
B. Smith	10	11	2.84	215	54	129	
De. Martinez	16	7	3.18	232	49	142	
Perez	9	13	3.31	198	45	152	
Z. Smith	1	13	3.49	147	52	93	2
Gross	11	12	4.38	201	88	158	
McGaffigan	3	5	4.68	75	30	40	2

New York Mets

Batting	Avg	AB	R	H	HR	RBI
Sasser	.291	182	17	53	1	22
Johnson	.287	571	104	164	36	101
Magadan	.286	374	47	107	4	41
McReynolds	.272	545	74	148	22	85
Jefferies	.258	508	72	131	12	56
Teufel	.256	219	27	56	2	15
Lyons	.247	235	15	58	3	27
Samuel	.235	532	69	125	11	48
Hernandez	.233	215	18	50	4	19
Elster	.231	458	52	106	10	55
Miller	.231	143	15	33	1	7
Strawberry	.225	476	69	107	29	77
Wilson	.205	249	22	51	3	18
Carter	.183	153	14	28	2	15

Pitching	W	L	ERA	IP	BB	SO	Sv
Aguilera	6	6	2.34	69	21	80	7
Myers	7	4	2.35	84	40	88	24
Fernandez	14	5	2.83	219	75	198	
Gooden	9	4	2.89	108	47	101	1
Viola	5	5	3.38	85	27	73	
Ojeda	13	11	3.47	192	78	95	
Darling	14	14	3.52	217	70	153	
Cone	14	8	3.52	219	74	190	
Aase	1	5	3.94	59	26	34	2

Philadelphia Phillies

Batting	Avg	AB	R	H	HR	RBI
Kruk	.300	357	53	107	8	44
Herr	.287	561	65	161	2	37
Jordan	.285	523	63	149	12	75
Thon	.271	435	45	118	15	60
Ready	.264	254	37	67	8	26
V. Hayes	.259	540	93	140	26	78
C. Hayes	.257	304	26	78	8	43
Lake	.252	155	9	39	2	14
Jeltz	.243	263	28	64	4	25
Dykstra	.237	511	66	121	7	32
Ford	.218	142	13	31	1	13
Murphy	.218	156	20	34	9	27
Schmidt	.203	148	19	30	6	28
Daulton	.201	368	29	74	8	44
Dernier	.171	187	26	32	1	13

Pitching	W	L	ERA	IP	BB	SO	Sv
McDowell	4	8	1.96	92	38	47	23
Parrett	12	6	2.98	105	44	98	6
Howell	12	12	3.44	204	86	164	
Harris	2	2	3.58	75	43	51	1
Frohwirth	1	0	3.59	62	18	39	
Cook	7	8	3.72	121	38	67	
McWilliams	2	11	4.10	120	49	54	
Ruffin	6	10	4.44	125	62	70	
Mulholland	4	7	4.92	115	36	66	
Carman	5	15	5.24	149	86	81	

Pittsburgh Pirates

Batting	Avg	AB	R	H	HR	RBI
LaValliere	.316	190	15	60	2	23
Redus	.283	279	42	79	6	33
Bonilla	.281	616	96	173	24	86
Reynolds	.270	363	45	98	6	48
Bell	.258	271	33	70	2	27
Bonds	.248	580	96	144	19	58
Distefano	.247	154	12	38	2	15
Van Slyke	.237	476	64	113	9	53
Lind	.232	578	52	134	2	48
Hatcher	.231	481	59	111	4	51
Cangelosi	.219	160	18	35	0	9
Ortiz	.217	230	16	50	1	22
Belliard	.214	154	10	33	0	8
Quinones	.209	225	21	47	3	29
King	.195	215	31	42	5	19

Pitching	W	L	ERA	IP	BB	SO	Sv
Landrum	2	3	1.67	81	28	51	26
Bair	2	3	2.27	67	28	56	1
Drabek	14	12	2.80	244	69	123	
Smiley	12	8	2.81	205	49	123	
Kipper	3	4	2.93	83	33	58	4
Heaton	6	7	3.05	147	55	67	
Kramer	5	9	3.96	111	61	52	2
Walk	13	10	4.41	196	65	83	
Robinson	7	13	4.58	141	59	95	4
Reed	1	4	5.60	54	11	34	

St. Louis Cardinals

Batting	Avg	AB	R	H	HR	RBI
Guerrero	.311	570	60	177	17	117
Oquendo	.291	556	59	162	1	48
Thompson	.290	545	60	158	4	68
Smith	.273	593	82	162	2	50
Pendleton	.264	613	83	162	13	74
Pena	.259	424	36	110	4	37
Coleman	.254	563	94	143	2	28
Brunansky	.239	556	67	133	20	85
McGee	.236	199	23	47	3	17

Pitching	W	L	ERA	IP	BB	SO	Sv
Dipino	9	0	2.45	88	20	44	
Quisenberry	3	1	2.64	78	14	37	6
Dayley	4	3	2.87	75	30	40	12
Magrane	18	9	2.91	234	72	127	
Worrell	3	5	2.96	51	26	41	20
DeLeon	16	12	3.05	244	80	201	
Carpenter	4	4	3.18	68	26	35	
Costello	5	4	3.32	62	20	40	3
Terry	8	10	3.57	148	43	69	2
Power	7	7	3.71	97	21	43	
Hill	7	15	3.80	196	99	112	
Horton	0	3	4.85	72	21	26	

San Diego Padres

Batting	Avg	AB	R	H	HR	RBI
Gwynn	.336	604	82	203	4	62
Roberts	.301	329	81	99	3	25
R. Alomar	.295	623	82	184	7	56
Templeton	.255	506	43	129	6	40
James	.243	482	55	117	13	65
Ja. Clark	.242	455	76	110	26	94
Santiago	.236	462	50	109	16	62
Martinez	.221	267	23	59	6	39
Jackson	.218	170	17	37	4	20
Pagliarulo	.196	148	12	29	3	14
Parent	.191	141	12	27	7	21

Pitching	W	L	ERA	IP	BB	SO	Sv
Davis	4	3	1.85	92	31	92	44
Harris	8	9	2.60	135	52	106	6
Whitson	16	11	2.66	227	48	117	
Hurst	15	11	2.69	244	66	179	
Grant	8	2	3.33	116	32	69	2
Schiraldi	6	7	3.51	100	63	71	4
Benes	6	3	3.51	66	31	66	
Terrell	5	13	4.01	123	26	63	
Show	8	6	4.23	106	39	66	
Rasmussen	10	10	4.26	183	72	87	

San Francisco Giants

Batting	Avg	AB	R	H	HR	RBI
Clark	.333	588	104	196	23	11
Mitchell	.291	543	100	158	47	125
Butler	.283	594	100	168	4	36
Riles	.278	302	43	84	7	40
Oberkfell	.269	156	19	42	2	17
Nixon	.265	166	23	44	1	15
Litton	.252	143	12	36	4	17
Thompson	.241	547	91	132	13	50
Kennedy	.239	355	19	85	5	34
Uribe	.221	453	34	100	1	30
Maldonado	.217	345	39	75	9	41
Manwaring	.210	200	14	42	0	18
Sheridan	.205	161	20	33	3	14
Williams	.202	292	31	59	18	50

Pitching	W	L	ERA	IP	BB	SO	Sv
Garrelts	14	5	2.28	193	46	119	
Lefferts	2	4	2.69	107	22	71	20
Bedrosian	3	7	2.87	84	39	58	23
Reuschel	17	8	2.94	208	54	111	
Lacoss	10	10	3.17	150	65	78	6
Robinson	12	11	3.43	197	37	96	
Hammaker	6	6	3.76	76	23	30	
Brantley	7	1	4.07	97	37	69	
Downs	4	8	4.79	82	26	49	
Knepper	7	12	5.13	165	75	64	

Earned-Run Average Leaders

	National League					American League			
Year	Player, club	G	IP	ERA	Year	Player, club	G	IP	ERA
1970	Tom Seaver, New York	37	291	2.81	1970	Diego Segui, Oakland	47	162	2.56
1971	Tom Seaver, New York	36	286	1.76	1971	Vida Blue, Oakland	39	312	1.82
1972	Steve Carlton, Philadelphia	41	348	1.98	1972	Luis Tiant, Boston	43	179	1.91
1973	Tom Seaver, New York	36	290	2.07	1973	Jim Palmer, Baltimore	38	296	2.40
1974	Buzz Capra, Atlanta	39	217	2.28	1974	Catfish Hunter, Oakland	41	318	2.49
1975	Randy Jones, San Diego	37	285	2.24	1975	Jim Palmer, Baltimore	39	323	2.09
1976	John Denny, St. Louis	30	207	2.52	1976	Mark Fidrych, Detroit	31	250	2.34
1977	John Candelaria, Pittsburgh	33	231	2.34	1977	Frank Tanana, California	31	241	2.54
1978	Craig Swan, New York	29	207	2.43	1978	Ron Guidry, New York	35	274	1.74
1979	J. R. Richard, Houston	38	292	2.71	1979	Ron Guidry, New York	33	236	2.78
1980	Don Sutton, Los Angeles	32	212	2.21	1980	Rudy May, New York	41	175	2.47
1981	Nolan Ryan, Houston	21	149	1.69	1981	Steve McCatty, Oakland	22	186	2.32
1982	Steve Rogers, Montreal	35	277	2.40	1982	Rick Sutcliffe, Cleveland	34	216	2.96
1983	Atlee Hammaker, San Fran.	23	172	2.25	1983	Rick Honeycutt, Texas	25	174	2.42
1984	Alejandro Pena, Los Angeles	28	199	2.48	1984	Mike Boddicker, Baltimore	34	261	2.79
1985	Dwight Gooden, New York	35	276	1.53	1986	Dave Stieb, Toronto	36	265	2.48
1986	Mike Scott, Houston	37	275	2.22	1986	Roger Clemens, Boston	33	254	2.48
1987	Nolan Ryan, Houston	34	211	2.76	1987	Jimmy Key, Toronto	36	261	2.76
1988	Joe Magrane, St. Louis	24	165	2.18	1988	Allan Anderson, Minnesota	30	202	2.45
						Teodoro Higuera, Milwaukee	31	227	2.45
1989	Scott Garrelts, San Francisco	30	193	2.28	1989	Bret Saberhagen, Kansas City	36	262	2.16

ERA is computed by multiplying earned runs allowed by 9, then dividing by innings pitched.

National Baseball Hall of Fame and Museum
Cooperstown, N.Y.

Aaron, Hank	Comiskey, Charles A.	Grove, Lefty	Lombardi, Ernie	Ruth, Babe
Alexander, Grover Cleveland	Conlan, Jocko	Hafey, Chick	Lopez, Al	Schalk, Ray
Alston, Walt	Connolly, Thomas H.	Haines, Jesee	Lyons, Ted	Schoendienst, Red
Anson, Cap	Connor, Roger	Hamilton, Bill	Mack, Connie	Sewell, Joe
Aparicio, Luis	Coveleski, Stan	Harridge, Will	MacPhail, Larry	Simmons, Al
Appling, Luke	Crawford, Sam	Harris, Bucky	Mantle, Mickey	Sisler, George
Averill, Earl	Cronin, Joe	Hartnett, Gabby	Manush, Henry	Slaughter, Enos
Baker, Home Run	Cummings, Candy	Heilmann, Harry	Maranville, Rabbit	Snider, Duke
Bancroft, Dave	Cuyler, Kiki	Herman, Billy	Marichal, Juan	Spahn, Warren
Banks, Ernie	Dandridge, Ray	Hooper, Harry	Marquard, Rube	Spalding, Albert
Barlick, Al	Dean, Dizzy	Hornsby, Rogers	Mathews, Eddie	Speaker, Tris
Barrow, Edward G.	Delahanty, Ed	Hoyt, Waite	Mathewson, Christy	Stargell, Willie
Beckley, Jake	Dickey, Bill	Hubbard, Cal	Mays, Willie	Stengel, Casey
Bell, Cool Papa	DiHigo, Martin	Hubbell, Carl	McCarthy, Joe	Terry, Bill
Bench, Johnny	DiMaggio, Joe	Huggins, Miller	McCarthy, Thomas	Thompson, Sam
Bender, Chief	Doerr, Bobby	Hunter, Catfish	McCovey, Willie	Tinker, Joe
Berra, Yogi	Drysdale, Don	Irvin, Monte	McGinnity, Joe	Traynor, Pie
Bottomley, Jim	Duffy, Hugh	Jackson, Travis	McGraw, John	Vance, Dazzy
Boudreau, Lou	Evans, Billy	Jennings, Hugh	McKechnie, Bill	Vaughan, Arky
Bresnahan, Roger	Evers, John	Johnson, Byron	Medwick, Joe	Waddell, Rube
Brock, Lou	Ewing, Buck	Johnson, William (Judy)	Mize, Johnny	Wagner, Honus
Brouthers, Dan	Faber, Urban	Johnson, Walter	Musial, Stan	Wallace, Roderick
Brown (Three Finger), Mordecai	Feller, Bob	Joss, Addie	Nichols, Kid	Walsh, Ed.
Bulkeley, Morgan C.	Ferrell, Rick	Kaline, Al	O'Rourke, James	Waner, Lloyd
Burkett, Jesse C.	Flick, Elmer H.	Keefe, Timothy	Ott, Mel	Waner, Paul
Campanella, Roy	Ford, Whitey	Keeler, William	Paige, Satchel	Ward, John
Carey, Max	Foster, Andrew	Kell, George	Pennock, Herb	Weiss, George
Cartwright, Alexander	Foxx, Jimmie	Kelley, Joe	Plank, Ed	Welch, Mickey
Chadwick, Henry	Frick, Ford	Kelly, George	Radbourn, Charlie	Wheat, Zach
Chance, Frank	Frisch, Frank	Kelly, King	Reese, Pee Wee	Wilhelm, Hoyt
Chandler, Happy	Galvin, Pud	Killebrew, Harmon	Rice, Sam	Williams, Billy
Charleston, Oscar	Gehrig, Lou	Kiner, Ralph	Rickey, Branch	Williams, Ted
Chesbro, John	Gehringer, Charles	Klein, Chuck	Rixey, Eppa	Wilson, Hack
Clarke, Fred	Gibson, Bob	Klem, Bill	Roberts, Robin	Wright, George
Clarkson, John	Gibson, Josh	Koufax, Sandy	Robinson, Brooks	Wright, Harry
Clemente, Roberto	Giles, Warren	Lajoie, Napoleon	Robinson, Frank	Wynn, Early
Cobb, Ty	Gomez, Lefty	Landis, Kenesaw M.	Robinson, Jackie	Yastrzemski, Carl
Cochrane, Mickey	Goslin, Goose	Lemon, Bob	Robinson, Wilbert	Yawkey, Tom
Collins, Eddie	Greenberg, Hank	Leonard, Buck	Roush, Edd	Young, Cy
Collins, James	Griffith, Clark	Lindstrom, Fred	Ruffing, Red	Youngs, Ross
Combs, Earle	Grimes, Burleigh	Lloyd, Pop	Rusie, Amos	

All-Star Baseball Games, 1933-1989

Year	Winner	Score	Location	Year	Winner	Score	Location
1933	American	4-2	Chicago	1961	Called-rain	1-1	Boston
1934	American	9-7	New York	1962	National (3)	3-1	Washington
1935	American	4-1	Cleveland	1962	American	9-4	Chicago
1936	National	4-3	Boston	1963	National	5-3	Cleveland
1937	American	8-3	Washington	1964	National	7-4	New York
1938	National	4-1	Cincinnati	1965	National	6-5	Minnesota
1939	American	3-1	New York	1966	National (3)	2-1	St. Louis
1940	National	4-0	St. Louis	1967	National (4)	2-1	Anaheim
1941	American	7-5	Detroit	1968*	National	1-0	Houston
1942	American	3-1	New York	1969	National	9-3	Washington
1943*	American	5-3	Philadelphia	1970*	National (2)	5-4	Cincinnati
1944*	National	7-1	Pittsburgh	1971*	American	6-4	Detroit
1945	(not played)			1972*	National	4-3	Atlanta
1946	American	12-0	Boston	1973*	National	7-1	Kansas City
1947	American	2-1	Chicago	1974*	National	7-2	Pittsburgh
1948	American	5-2	St. Louis	1975*	National	6-3	Milwaukee
1949	American	11-7	New York	1976*	National	7-1	Philadelphia
1950	National (1)	4-3	Chicago	1977*	National	7-5	New York
1951	National	8-3	Detroit	1978*	National	7-3	San Diego
1952	National	3-2	Philadelphia	1979*	National	7-6	Seattle
1953	National	5-1	Cincinnati	1980*	National	4-2	Los Angeles
1954	American	11-9	Cleveland	1981*	National	5-4	Cleveland
1955	National (2)	6-5	Milwaukee	1982*	National	4-1	Montreal
1956	National	7-3	Washington	1983*	American	13-3	Chicago
1957	American	6-5	St. Louis	1984*	National	3-1	San Francisco
1958	American	4-3	Baltimore	1985*	National	6-1	Minneapolis
1959	National	5-4	Pittsburgh	1986*	American	3-2	Houston
1959	American	5-3	Los Angeles	1987*	National (5)	2-0	Oakland
1960	National	5-3	Kansas City	1988*	American	2-1	Cincinnati
1960	National	6-0	New York	1989*	American	5-3	Anaheim
1961	National (3)	5-4	San Francisco				

(1) 14 innings, (2) 12 innings, (3) 10 innings, (4) 15 innings (5) 13 innings. *Night game.

American League Records in 1989
Final Standings
Eastern Division

Club	W	L	Pct	GB	Home	Road	vs. RHP	LHP	Grass	Artif	Night	Day	1-Run Games
Toronto....	89	73	.549	—	46-35	43-38	62-48	27-25	38-25	51-48	67-44	22-29	25-22
Baltimore..	87	75	.537	2	47-34	40-41	60-55	27-20	77-61	10-14	71-55	16-20	18-16
Boston....	83	79	.512	6	46-35	37-44	62-58	21-21	71-66	12-13	54-52	29-27	13-25
Milwaukee..	81	81	.500	8	45-36	36-45	48-65	33-16	69-68	12-13	53-57	28-24	17-20
New York..	74	87	.460	14½	41-40	33-47	44-59	30-28	59-78	15-9	54-59	20-28	19-22
Cleveland.	73	89	.451	16	41-40	32-49	51-62	22-27	64-74	9-15	50-61	23-28	25-28
Detroit....	59	103	.364	30	38-43	21-60	36-76	24-27	55-82	4-21	38-72	21-31	19-26

Western Division

Club	W	L	Pct	GB	Home	Road	vs. RHP	LHP	Grass	Artif	Night	Day	1-Run Games
Oakland...	99	63	.611	—	54-27	45-36	67-49	32-14	87-49	12-14	52-46	47-17	29-18
Kansas City	92	70	.568	7	55-26	37-44	63-50	29-20	25-37	67-33	72-50	20-20	24-19
California	91	71	.562	8	52-29	39-42	66-46	25-25	76-59	15-12	68-55	23-16	33-21
Texas....	83	79	.512	16	45-36	38-43	57-60	26-19	72-65	11-14	67-66	16-13	20-18
Minnesota	80	82	.494	19	45-36	35-46	57-59	23-23	28-34	52-48	55-58	25-24	25-20
Seattle...	73	89	.451	26	40-41	33-48	53-72	20-17	27-35	46-54	56-64	17-25	23-28
Chicago...	69	92	.429	29½	35-45	34-47	46-56	23-36	61-76	8-16	50-68	19-24	19-26

American League Championship Series

Oakland 7, Toronto 3
Oakland 6, Toronto 3

Toronto 7, Oakland 3
Toronto 6, Oakland 5

Oakland 4, Toronto 3

Team Batting

Team	Pct	AB	R	H	HR	SB
Boston.........	.277	5666	774	1571	108	56
Minnesota......	.276	5581	740	1542	117	111
Chicago........	.271	5504	693	1493	94	97
New York......	.269	5458	698	1470	130	137
Texas.........	.263	5458	695	1433	122	101
Oakland.......	.261	5416	712	1414	127	157
Kansas City....	.261	5475	690	1428	101	154
Toronto.......	.260	5581	731	1449	142	144
Milwaukee.....	.259	5473	707	1415	126	165
Seattle........	.257	5512	694	1417	134	81
California.....	.256	5545	669	1422	145	89
Baltimore......	.252	5440	708	1369	129	118
Cleveland.....	.245	5463	604	1340	127	74
Detroit........	.242	5432	617	1315	116	103

Team Pitching

Team	ERA	CG	IP	H	R	BB	SO
Oakland.....	3.09	17	1448	1287	576	510	930
California...	3.28	32	1454	1384	578	465	897
Kansas City..	3.55	27	1451	1415	635	455	978
Toronto.....	3.58	12	1467	1408	651	478	849
Cleveland...	3.65	23	1453	1423	654	452	844
Milwaukee...	3.80	16	1432	1463	679	457	812
Texas......	3.91	26	1434	1279	714	654	1112
Seattle.....	4.00	15	1438	1422	728	560	897
Baltimore...	4.00	16	1448	1518	686	486	676
Boston.....	4.01	14	1460	1448	735	548	1054
Chicago....	4.23	9	1422	1472	750	539	778
Minnesota...	4.28	19	1429	1495	738	500	851
New York...	4.50	15	1414	1550	792	521	787
Detroit.....	4.53	24	1427	1514	816	652	831

Individual Batting (at least 115 at-bats); Individual Pitching (at least 50 innings)

Baltimore Orioles

Batting

Batting	Avg	AB	R	H	HR	RBI
Orsulak.........	.285	390	59	111	7	55
Moreland......	.278	425	45	118	6	45
Bradley........	.277	545	83	151	11	55
Milligan.......	.268	365	56	98	12	45
Devereaux.....	.266	391	55	104	8	46
Tettleton......	.258	411	72	106	26	65
C. Ripken......	.257	646	80	166	21	93
Finley.........	.249	217	35	54	2	25
Worthington...	.247	497	57	123	15	70
Jefferson......	.245	139	20	34	4	21
Sheets........	.243	304	33	74	7	33
Melvin........	.241	278	22	67	1	32
B. Ripken.....	.239	318	31	76	2	26
Gonzales......	.217	166	16	36	1	11
Traber........	.209	234	14	49	4	26
Anderson.....	.207	266	44	55	4	16

Pitching

Pitching	W	L	ERA	IP	BB	SO	Sv
Olson........	5	2	1.69	85	46	90	27
Tibbs........	5	0	2.82	54	20	30	
Williamson....	10	5	2.93	107	30	55	9
Ballard.......	18	8	3.43	215	57	62	
Milacki.......	14	12	3.74	243	88	113	
Thurmond.....	2	4	3.90	90	17	34	4
Holton.......	5	7	4.02	116	39	51	
Johnson......	4	7	4.23	89	28	26	
Harnisch.....	5	9	4.62	103	64	70	
Bautista.....	3	4	5.31	78	15	30	
Schmidt......	10	13	5.69	156	36	46	

Boston Red Sox

Batting

Batting	Avg	AB	R	H	HR	RBI
Boggs.........	.330	621	113	205	3	54
Greenwell......	.308	578	87	178	14	95
Burks.........	.303	399	73	121	12	61
Heep.........	.300	320	36	96	5	49
Reed.........	.288	524	76	151	3	40
Evans.........	.285	520	82	148	20	100
Esasky........	.277	564	79	156	30	108
Romine.......	.274	274	30	75	1	23
Rivera........	.257	323	35	83	5	29
Barrett.......	.256	336	31	86	1	27
Cerone.......	.243	296	28	72	4	48
Rice.........	.234	209	22	49	3	28
Kutcher......	.225	160	28	36	2	16
Gedman.......	.212	260	24	55	4	16

Pitching

Pitching	W	L	ERA	IP	BB	SO	Sv
Lamp.........	4	2	2.32	112	27	61	2
Murphy.......	5	7	2.74	105	41	107	9
Clemens......	17	11	3.13	253	93	230	
Smith........	6	1	3.57	70	33	96	25
Dopson.......	12	8	3.99	169	69	95	
Boddicker....	15	11	4.00	211	71	145	
Price........	2	5	4.35	70	30	52	
Boyd.........	3	2	4.42	59	19	26	
Stanley......	5	2	4.88	79	26	32	4
Smithson.....	7	14	4.95	143	35	61	2
Gardner......	3	7	5.97	86	47	81	
Hetzel.......	2	3	6.26	50	28	33	

California Angels

Batting	Avg	AB	R	H	HR	RBI
Ray	.289	530	52	153	5	62
Downing	.283	544	59	154	14	59
Joyner	.282	593	78	167	16	79
Washington	.273	418	53	114	13	42
Davis	.271	560	81	152	22	90
Armas	.257	202	22	52	11	30
White	.245	636	86	156	12	56
Parrish	.238	433	48	103	17	50
Anderson	.229	223	27	51	0	17
Schofield	.228	302	42	69	4	26
Howell	.228	474	56	108	20	52
Bichette	.210	138	13	29	3	15
Schroeder	.203	138	16	28	6	15

Pitching	W	L	ERA	IP	BB	SO	Sv
McClure	6	1	1.55	52	15	36	3
Minton	4	3	2.20	90	37	42	8
Finley	16	9	2.57	199	82	156	
Blyleven	17	5	2.73	241	44	131	
McCaskill	15	10	2.93	212	59	107	
Fraser	4	7	3.24	91	23	46	2
Harvey	3	3	3.44	55	41	78	25
Abbott	12	12	3.92	181	74	115	
Witt	9	15	4.54	220	48	123	

Chicago White Sox

Batting	Avg	AB	R	H	HR	RBI
Kittle	.302	169	26	51	11	37
Johnson	.300	180	28	54	0	16
Martinez	.300	350	44	105	5	32
Fisk	.293	375	47	110	13	68
Calderon	.286	622	83	178	14	87
Williams	.274	201	25	55	3	10
Gallagher	.266	601	74	160	1	46
Lyons	.264	443	51	117	2	50
Karkovice	.264	182	21	48	3	24
Sosa	.257	183	27	47	4	13
Guillen	.253	597	63	151	1	54
Fletcher	.253	546	77	138	1	43
Boston	.252	218	34	55	5	23
Pasqua	.248	246	26	61	11	47
Walker	.210	233	25	49	5	26

Pitching	W	L	ERA	IP	BB	SO	Sv
Hibbard	6	7	3.21	137	41	55	
Pall	4	5	3.31	87	19	58	6
King	9	10	3.39	159	64	72	
McCarthy	1	2	3.51	66	20	27	
Thigpen	2	6	3.76	79	40	47	34
Long	5	5	3.92	98	37	51	1
Dotson	5	12	4.46	151	58	69	
Patterson	6	1	4.52	65	28	43	
Hillegas	7	11	4.74	119	51	76	3
Rosenberg	4	13	4.94	142	58	77	
Perez	11	14	5.01	183	90	141	

Cleveland Indians

Batting	Avg	AB	R	H	HR	RBI
James	.306	245	26	75	4	29
Browne	.299	598	83	179	5	45
Jacoby	.272	519	49	141	13	64
O'Brien	.259	555	75	144	12	55
Carter	.243	651	84	158	35	105
Fermin	.238	484	50	115	0	21
Komminsk	.237	198	27	47	8	33
Clark	.237	253	21	60	8	29
Allanson	.232	323	30	75	3	17
Skinner	.230	178	10	41	1	13
Belle	.225	218	22	49	7	37
McDowell	.222	239	33	53	3	22
Snyder	.215	489	49	105	18	59

Pitching	W	L	ERA	IP	BB	SO	Sv
Orosco	3	4	2.08	78	26	79	3
Jones	7	10	2.34	80	13	65	32
Candiotti	13	10	3.10	206	55	124	
Black	12	11	3.36	222	52	88	
Swindell	13	6	3.37	184	51	129	
Farrell	9	14	3.63	208	71	132	
Bailes	5	9	4.28	113	29	47	
Nichols	4	6	4.40	71	24	42	
Yett	5	6	5.00	99	47	47	

Detroit Tigers

Batting	Avg	AB	R	H	HR	RBI
Bergman	.268	385	38	103	7	37
Heath	.263	396	38	104	10	43
Jones	.259	158	17	41	3	26
Pettis	.257	444	77	114	1	18
Ward	.253	292	27	74	9	30
Whitaker	.251	509	77	128	28	85
Nokes	.250	268	15	67	9	39
Trammell	.243	449	54	109	5	43
Sheridan	.242	120	16	29	3	15
Lynn	.241	353	44	85	11	46
Lemon	.237	414	45	98	7	47
Schu	.214	266	25	57	7	21
Strange	.214	196	16	42	1	14
K. Williams	.205	258	29	53	6	23
Brumley	.198	212	33	42	1	11

Pitching	W	L	ERA	IP	BB	SO	Sv
Tanana	10	14	3.58	223	74	147	
F. Williams	3	3	3.64	71	46	33	1
Henneman	11	4	3.70	90	51	69	8
Nunez	3	4	4.17	54	36	41	1
Ritz	4	6	4.38	74	44	56	
Alexander	6	18	4.44	223	76	95	
Gibson	4	8	4.64	132	57	77	
Morris	6	14	4.86	170	59	115	
Hudson	4	5	6.35	66	31	23	

Kansas City Royals

Batting	Avg	AB	R	H	HR	RBI
Eisenreich	.293	475	64	139	9	59
Brett	.282	457	67	129	12	80
Seitzer	.281	597	78	168	4	48
Boone	.274	405	33	111	1	43
Tartabull	.268	441	54	118	18	62
Stillwell	.261	463	52	121	7	54
Tabler	.259	390	36	101	2	42
Jackson	.256	515	86	132	32	105
White	.256	418	34	107	2	36
Wilson	.253	383	58	97	3	43
Wellman	.230	178	30	41	2	12
Macfarlane	.223	157	13	35	2	19
Buckner	.216	176	7	38	1	16

Pitching	W	L	ERA	IP	BB	SO	Sv
Montgomery	7	3	1.37	92	25	94	18
Saberhagen	23	6	2.16	262	43	193	
Crawford	3	1	2.83	54	19	33	
Gubicza	15	11	3.04	255	63	173	
Aquino	6	8	3.50	141	35	68	
Gordon	17	9	3.64	163	86	153	1
Farr	2	5	4.12	63	22	56	18
Leach	5	6	4.15	73	36	34	
Bannister	4	1	4.66	75	18	35	
Leibrandt	5	11	5.14	161	54	73	

Milwaukee Brewers

Batting	Avg	AB	R	H	HR	RBI
Yount	.318	614	101	195	21	103
Molitor	.315	615	84	194	11	56
Gantner	.274	409	51	112	0	34
Brock	.265	373	40	99	12	52
Spiers	.255	345	44	88	4	33
Surhoff	.248	436	42	108	5	55
Sheffield	.247	368	34	91	5	32
Braggs	.247	514	77	127	15	66
Felder	.241	315	50	76	3	23
O'Brien	.234	188	22	44	6	35
Francona	.232	233	26	54	3	23
Meyer	.224	147	13	33	7	29
Deer	.210	466	72	98	26	65
Romero	.209	163	17	34	0	9
Polidor	.194	175	15	34	0	14

Pitching	W	L	ERA	IP	BB	SO	Sv
Plesac	3	4	2.35	61	17	52	33
Crim	9	7	2.83	117	36	59	7
Bosio	15	10	2.95	234	48	173	
Navarro	7	8	3.12	109	32	56	
Knudson	8	5	3.35	123	29	47	
Higuera	9	6	3.46	135	48	91	
Fossas	2	2	3.54	61	22	42	1
Filer	7	3	3.61	72	23	20	
Krueger	3	2	3.84	93	33	72	3
Clutterbuck	2	5	4.14	67	16	29	
Reuss	9	9	5.13	140	34	40	
August	12	12	5.31	142	58	51	

Minnesota Twins

Batting	Avg	AB	R	H	HR	RBI
Puckett	.339	635	75	215	9	85
Harper	.325	385	43	125	8	57
Gladden	.295	461	69	136	8	46
Moses	.281	242	33	68	1	31
Hrbek	.272	375	59	102	25	84
Gagne	.272	460	69	125	9	48
Larkin	.267	446	61	119	6	46
Bush	.263	391	60	103	14	54
Castillo	.257	218	23	56	8	33
Newman	.253	446	62	113	0	38
Gaetti	.251	498	63	125	19	75
Backman	.231	299	33	69	1	26
Laudner	.222	239	24	53	6	27

Pitching	W	L	ERA	IP	BB	SO	Sv
Aguilera	3	5	3.21	75	17	57	
Wayne	3	4	3.30	71	36	41	1
Berenguer	9	3	3.48	106	47	93	3
Viola	8	12	3.79	175	47	138	
Anderson	17	10	3.80	196	53	69	
Smith	10	6	3.92	172	51	92	1
Reardon	5	4	4.07	73	12	46	31
Oliveras	3	4	4.53	55	15	24	
Guthrie	2	4	4.55	57	21	38	
Dyer	4	7	4.82	71	37	37	
Rawley	5	12	5.21	145	60	68	

New York Yankees

Batting	Avg	AB	R	H	HR	RBI
Sax	.315	651	88	205	5	63
Mattingly	.303	631	79	191	23	113
Kelly	.302	441	65	133	9	48
Polonia	.300	433	70	130	3	46
Geren	.288	205	26	59	9	27
Espinoza	.282	503	51	142	0	41
Hall	.260	361	54	94	17	58
Slaught	.251	350	34	88	5	38
Balboni	.237	300	33	71	17	59
Barfield	.234	521	79	122	23	67
Brookins	.226	168	14	38	4	14
Pagliarulo	.197	223	19	44	4	16
Tolleson	.164	140	16	23	1	9

Pitching	W	L	ERA	IP	BB	SO	Sv
Guetterman	5	5	2.45	103	26	51	13
Righetti	2	6	3.00	69	26	51	25
Cary	4	4	3.26	99	29	79	
Plunk	8	6	3.28	104	64	85	1
Parker	4	5	3.68	120	31	53	
Cadaret	5	5	4.05	120	57	80	
McCullers	4	3	4.57	84	37	82	3
Hawkins	15	15	4.80	208	76	98	
Mohorcic	2	1	4.99	57	18	24	2
Terrell	6	5	5.20	83	24	30	
Lapointe	6	9	5.62	113	45	51	
John	2	7	5.80	63	22	18	

Oakland Athletics

Batting	Avg	AB	R	H	HR	RBI
Lansford	.336	551	81	185	2	52
R. Henderson	.274	541	113	148	12	57
Steinbach	.273	454	37	124	7	42
Canseco	.269	227	40	61	17	57
Parker	.264	553	56	146	22	97
Phillips	.262	451	48	118	4	47
Gallego	.252	357	45	90	3	30
D. Henderson	.250	579	77	145	15	80
Javier	.248	310	42	77	1	28
Phelps	.242	194	26	47	7	29
Weiss	.233	236	30	55	3	21
Blankenship	.232	125	22	29	1	4
McGwire	.231	490	74	113	33	95
Hassey	.228	268	29	61	5	23
Hubbard	.198	131	12	26	3	12

Pitching	W	L	ERA	IP	BB	SO	Sv
Eckersley	4	0	1.56	57	3	55	33
Burns	6	5	2.24	96	28	49	8
Honeycutt	2	2	2.35	76	26	52	12
Moore	19	11	2.61	241	63	172	
Welch	17	8	3.00	209	78	137	
Nelson	3	5	3.26	80	30	70	3
Stewart	21	9	3.32	257	69	155	
C. Young	5	9	3.73	111	47	55	
Davis	19	7	4.36	169	68	91	

Seattle Mariners

Batting	Avg	AB	R	H	HR	RBI
Davis	.305	498	84	152	21	95
Reynolds	.300	613	87	184	0	43
Buhner	.275	204	27	56	9	33
Bradley	.274	270	21	74	3	37
Briley	.266	394	52	105	13	52
Cotto	.264	295	44	78	9	33
Griffey	.264	455	61	120	16	61
Leonard	.254	566	69	144	24	93
Coles	.252	535	54	135	10	59
Martinez	.240	171	20	41	2	20
Valle	.237	316	32	75	7	34
Presely	.236	390	42	92	12	41
Vizquel	.220	387	45	85	1	20

Pitching	W	L	ERA	IP	BB	SO	Sv
Schooler	1	7	2.81	77	19	69	33
Jackson	4	6	3.17	99	54	94	7
Hanson	9	5	3.18	113	32	75	
Reed	7	7	3.19	101	43	50	
Bankhead	14	6	3.34	210	63	140	
Holman	8	10	3.44	159	62	82	
Langston	4	5	3.56	73	19	60	
Johnson	7	9	4.40	131	70	104	
Swift	7	3	4.43	130	38	45	1
Zavaras	1	6	5.19	52	30	31	
Dunne	2	9	5.27	85	37	38	

Texas Rangers

Batting	Avg	AB	R	H	HR	RBI
Franco	.316	548	80	173	13	92
Baines	.309	505	73	156	16	72
Sierra	.306	634	101	194	29	119
Petralli	.304	184	18	56	4	23
Manrique	.294	378	46	111	4	52
Palmeiro	.275	559	76	154	8	64
Leach	.272	239	32	65	1	23
Kunkel	.270	293	39	79	8	29
Espy	.257	475	65	122	3	31
Stanley	.246	122	9	30	1	11
Incaviglia	.236	453	48	107	21	81
Buechele	.235	486	60	114	16	59
Sundberg	.197	147	13	29	2	8
Kreuter	.152	158	16	24	5	9

Pitching	W	L	ERA	IP	BB	SO	Sv
Russell	6	4	1.98	72	24	77	38
Rogers	3	4	2.93	73	42	63	2
Ryan	16	10	3.20	239	98	301	
Brown	12	9	3.35	191	70	104	
Jeffcoat	9	6	3.58	130	33	64	
Hall	2	1	3.70	58	33	45	
Guante	6	6	3.91	69	36	69	2
Hough	10	13	4.35	182	95	94	
Moyer	4	9	4.86	76	33	44	
Witt	12	13	5.14	194	114	166	

Toronto Blue Jays

Batting	Avg	AB	R	H	HR	RBI
Wilson	.298	238	32	71	2	17
Bell	.297	613	88	182	18	104
Gruber	.290	545	83	158	18	73
McGriff	.269	551	98	148	36	92
Liriano	.263	418	51	110	5	53
Whitt	.262	385	42	101	11	53
Lee	.260	300	27	78	3	34
Felix	.258	415	62	107	9	46
Borders	.257	241	22	62	3	29
Fernandez	.257	573	64	147	11	64
Mulliniks	.238	273	25	65	3	29
Moseby	.221	502	72	111	11	43

Pitching	W	L	ERA	IP	BB	SO	Sv
Henke	8	3	1.92	89	25	116	20
Wells	7	4	2.40	86	28	78	2
Cerutti	11	11	3.07	205	53	69	
Stieb	17	8	3.35	206	76	101	
Wills	3	1	3.66	71	30	41	
Ward	4	10	3.77	114	58	122	15
Key	13	14	3.88	216	27	118	
Stottlemyre	7	7	3.88	127	44	63	
Flanagan	8	10	3.93	171	47	47	

Most Valuable Player
Baseball Writers' Association
National League

Year	Player, team	Year	Player, team	Year	Player, team
1931	Frank Frisch, St. Louis	1951	Roy Campanella, Brooklyn	1971	Joe Torre, St. Louis
1932	Charles Klein, Philadelpha	1952	Hank Sauer, Chicago	1972	Johnny Bench, Cincinnati
1933	Carl Hubbell, New York	1953	Roy Campanella, Brooklyn	1973	Pete Rose, Cincinnati
1934	Dizzy Dean, St. Louis	1954	Willie Mays, New York	1974	Steve Garvey, Los Angeles
1935	Gabby Hartnett, Chicago	1955	Roy Campanella, Brooklyn	1975	Joe Morgan, Cincinnati
1936	Carl Hubbell, New York	1956	Don Newcombe, Brooklyn	1976	Joe Morgan, Cincinnati
1937	Joe Medwick, St. Louis	1957	Henry Aaron, Milwaukee	1977	George Foster, Cincinnati
1938	Ernie Lombardi, Cincinnati	1958	Ernie Banks, Chicago	1978	Dave Parker, Pittsburgh
1939	Bucky Walters, Cincinnati	1959	Ernie Banks, Chicago	1979	(tie) Willie Stargell, Pittsburgh
1940	Frank McCormick, Cincinnati	1960	Dick Groat, Pittsburgh		Keith Hernandez, St. Louis
1941	Dolph Camilli, Brooklyn	1961	Frank Robinson, Cincinnati	1980	Mike Schmidt, Philadelphia
1942	Mort Cooper, St. Louis	1962	Maury Wills, Los Angeles	1981	Mike Schmidt, Philadelphia
1943	Stan Musial, St. Louis	1963	Sandy Koufax, Los Angeles	1982	Dale Murphy, Atlanta
1944	Martin Marion, St. Louis	1964	Ken Boyer, St. Louis	1983	Dale Murphy, Atlanta
1945	Phil Cavarretta, Chicago	1965	Willie Mays, San Francisco	1984	Ryne Sandberg, Chicago
1946	Stan Musial, St. Louis	1966	Roberto Clemente, Pittsburgh	1985	Willie McGee, St. Louis
1947	Bob Elliott, Boston	1967	Orlando Cepeda, St. Louis	1986	Mike Schmidt, Philadelphia
1948	Stan Musial, St. Louis	1968	Bob Gibson, St. Louis	1987	Andre Dawson, Chicago
1949	Jackie Robinson, Brooklyn	1969	Willie McCovey, San Francisco	1988	Kirk Gibson, Los Angeles
1950	Jim Konstanty, Philadelphia	1970	Johnny Bench, Cincinnati		

American League

Year	Player, team	Year	Player, team	Year	Player, team
1931	Lefty Grove, Philadelphia	1951	Yogi Berra, New York	1970	John (Boog) Powell, Baltimore
1932	Jimmy Foxx, Philadelphia	1952	Bobby Shantz, Philadelphia	1971	Vida Blue, Oakland
1933	Jimmy Foxx, Philadelphia	1953	Al Rosen, Cleveland	1972	Dick Allen, Chicago
1934	Mickey Cochrane, Detroit	1954	Yogi Berra, New York	1973	Reggie Jackson, Oakland
1935	Henry Greenberg, Detroit	1955	Yogi Berra, New York	1974	Jeff Burroughs, Texas
1936	Lou Gehrig, New York	1956	Mickey Mantle, New York	1975	Fred Lynn, Boston
1937	Charley Gehringer, Detroit	1957	Mickey Mantle, New York	1976	Thurman Munson, New York
1938	Jimmy Foxx, Boston	1958	Jackie Jensen, Boston	1977	Rod Carew, Minnesota
1939	Joe DiMaggio, New York	1959	Nellie Fox, Chicago	1978	Jim Rice, Boston
1940	Hank Greenberg, Detroit	1960	Roger Maris, New York	1979	Don Baylor, California
1941	Joe DiMaggio, New York	1961	Roger Maris, New York	1980	George Brett, Kansas City
1942	Joe Gordon, New York	1962	Mickey Mantle, New York	1981	Rollie Fingers, Milwaukee
1943	Spurgeon Chandler, New York	1963	Elston Howard, New York	1982	Robin Yount, Milwaukee
1944	Hal Newhouser, Detroit	1964	Brooks Robinson, Baltimore	1983	Cal Ripken Jr., Baltimore
1945	Hal Newhouser, Detroit	1965	Zoilo Versalles, Minnesota	1984	Willie Hernandez, Detroit
1946	Ted Williams, Boston	1966	Frank Robinson, Baltimore	1985	Don Mattingly, New York
1947	Joe DiMaggio, New York	1967	Carl Yastrzemski, Boston	1986	Roger Clemens, Boston
1948	Lou Boudreau, Cleveland	1968	Denny McLain, Detroit	1987	George Bell, Toronto
1949	Ted Williams, Boston	1969	Harmon Killebrew, Minnesota	1988	Jose Canseco, Oakland
1950	Phil Rizzuto, New York				

Rookie of the Year
Baseball Writers' Association

1947—Combined selection—Jackie Robinson, Brooklyn, 1b
1948—Combined selection—Alvin Dark, Boston, N.L. ss

National League

Year	Player, team	Year	Player, team	Year	Player, team
1949	Don Newcombe, Brooklyn, p	1963	Pete Rose, Cincinnati, 2b		Pat Zachry, Cincinnati, p
1950	Sam Jethroe, Boston, of	1964	Richie Allen, Philadelphia, 3b	1977	Andre Dawson, Montreal, of
1951	Willie Mays, New York, of	1965	Jim Lefebvre, Los Angeles, 2b	1978	Bob Horner, Atlanta, 3b
1952	Joe Black, Brooklyn, p	1966	Tommy Helms, Cincinnati, 2b	1979	Rick Sutcliffe, Los Angeles, p
1953	Jim Gilliam, Brooklyn, 2b	1967	Tom Seaver, New York, p	1980	Steve Howe, Los Angeles, p
1954	Wally Moon, St. Louis, of	1968	Johnny Bench, Cincinnati c	1981	Fernando Valenzuela, Los
1955	Bill Virdon, St. Louis, of	1969	Ted Sizemore, Los Angeles, 2b		Angeles, p
1956	Frank Robinson, Cincinnati, of	1970	Carl Morton, Montreal, p	1982	Steve Sax, Los Angeles, 2b
1957	Jack Sanford, Philadelphia, p	1971	Earl Williams, Atlanta, c	1983	Darryl Strawberry, New York, of
1958	Orlando Cepeda, S.F., 1b	1972	Jon Matlack, New York, p	1984	Dwight Gooden, New York, p
1959	Willie McCovey, S.F., 1b	1973	Gary Matthews, S.F., of	1985	Vince Coleman, St. Louis, of
1960	Frank Howard, Los Angeles, of	1974	Bake McBride, St. Louis, of	1986	Todd Worrell, St. Louis, p
1961	Billy Williams, Chicago, of	1975	John Montefusco, S.F., p	1987	Benito Santiago, San Diego, c
1962	Ken Hubbs, Chicago, 2b	1976	(tie) Butch Metzger, San Diego, p	1988	Chris Sabo, Cincinnati, 3b

American League

Year	Player, team	Year	Player, team	Year	Player, team
1949	Roy Sievers, St. Louis, of	1963	Gary Peters, Chicago, p	1977	Eddie Murray, Baltimore, dh
1950	Walt Dropo, Boston, 1b	1964	Tony Oliva, Minnesota, of	1978	Lou Whitaker, Detroit, 2b
1951	Gil McDougald, New York, 3b	1965	Curt Blefary, Baltimore, of	1979	(tie) John Castino, Minnesota, 3b
1952	Harry Byrd, Philadelphia, p	1966	Tommie Agee, Chicago, of		Alfredo Griffin, Toronto, ss
1953	Harvey Kuenn, Detroit, ss	1967	Rod Carew, Minnesota, 2b	1980	Joe Charboneau, Cleveland, of
1954	Bob Grim, New York, p	1968	Stan Bahnsen, New York, p	1981	Dave Righetti, New York, p
1955	Herb Score, Cleveland, p	1969	Lou Piniella, Kansas City, of	1982	Cal Ripken Jr., Baltimore, ss, 3b
1956	Luis Aparicio, Chicago, ss	1970	Thurman Munson, New York, c	1983	Ron Kittle, Chicago, of
1957	Tony Kubek, New York, if-of	1971	Chris Chambliss, Cleveland, 1b	1984	Alvin Davis, Seattle, 1B
1958	Albie Pearson, Washington, of	1972	Carlton Fisk, Boston, c	1985	Ozzie Guillen, Chicago, ss
1959	Bob Allison, Washington, of	1973	Al Bumbry, Baltimore, of	1986	Jose Canseco, Oakland, of
1960	Ron Hansen, Baltimore, ss	1974	Mike Hargrove, Texas, 1b	1987	Mark McGwire, Oakland, 1b
1961	Don Schwall, Boston, p	1975	Fred Lynn, Boston, of	1988	Walt Weiss, Oakland, ss
1962	Tom Tresh, New York, if-of	1976	Mark Fidrych, Detroit, p		

Earthquake Causes Postponement of World Series

The third game of the 1989 World Series between the San Francisco Giants and the Oakland Athletics, scheduled for Tuesday evening, October 17, was cancelled as a result of the major earthquake, which struck the San Francisco/Oakland area just minutes before the start of the game. A capacity crowd at Candlestick Park was evacuated, as Commissioner Fay Vincent called off the game.

In the aftermath of the destructive earthquake, it was decided to play game three in Candlestick Park no sooner than October 27. Vincent said, "I don't think cancellation of the World Series is appropriate or necessary right now. I think we will play at Candlestick Park at some point." No major structural damage was found in the Giants' home field, although minor repairs and cleanup were needed. The Commissioner acknowledged that the World Series issue "is a minor one, compared to the conditions" in the Bay area after the earthquake. *See page 959 for complete coverage of the earthquake.*

Editor's Note

Due to the postponement of the World Series, *The World Almanac*, which normally waits for the series to be completed before going to press, was unable to include coverage of the conclusion because of long-standing printing and distribution schedules. We regret this inconvenience to our readers, but are confident that they will understand the unusual circumstances.

1989 World Series

First Game

San Francisco	ab	r	h	bi	Oakland	ab	r	h	bi
Butler cf	4	0	0	0	R. Henderson lf	5	0	2	1
Thompson 2b	4	0	0	0	Lansford 3b	5	0	1	0
Clark 1b	4	0	2	0	Gallego 2b	0	0	0	0
Mitchell lf	4	0	2	0	Canseco rf	3	0	0	0
Williams 3b	4	0	0	0	Parker dh	4	1	1	1
Riles dh	4	0	0	0	D. Henderson cf	3	1	0	0
Maldonado rf	4	0	0	0	McGwire 1b	4	0	3	0
Kennedy c	3	0	0	0	Steinbach c	4	1	1	0
Uribe ss	2	0	1	0	Phillips 2b	4	1	2	1
Oberkfell 3b	0	0	0	0	Weiss ss	4	1	1	1
Garretls p	0	0	0	0	Stewart p	0	0	0	0
Hammaker p	0	0	0	0					
Brantley p	0	0	0	0					
LaCoss p	0	0	0	0					
Totals	33	0	5	0	Totals	36	5	11	4

```
San Francisco . . . . . . .   0 0 0 0 0 0 0 0 0—0
Oakland . . . . . . . . . .   0 3 1 1 0 0 0 x—5
```

San Francisco	ip	h	r	er	bb	so
Garretls, L, 0-1	4	7	5	4	1	5
Hammaker	1⅔	3	0	0	0	2
Brantley	1⅓	1	0	0	1	0
LaCoss	1	0	0	0	0	1
Oakland						
Stewart, W, 1-0	9	5	0	0	1	6

LOB - San Francisco 7, Oakland 9. 2B - Clark. HR - Parker (1), Weiss (1).

How runs were scored—Three in Athletics second: D. Henderson walked. Steinbach singled. Phillips singled scoring D. Henderson. Steinbach scored on an error. R. Henderson singled scoring Phillips.

One in Athletics third: Parker hit a home run.

One in Athletics fourth: Weiss hit a home run.

Second Game

San Francisco	ab	r	h	bi	Oakland	ab	r	h	bi
Butler cf	2	0	1	0	R. Henderson lf	3	1	3	0
Thompson 2b	3	0	0	1	Lansford 3b	3	0	1	1
Clark 1b	4	0	0	0	Canseco rf	2	1	0	0
Mitchell lf	4	0	1	0	Parker dh	4	1	1	1
Williams 3b	4	0	0	0	D. Henderson cf	3	1	0	0
Riles dh	3	0	0	0	McGwire 1b	4	0	1	0
Maldonado rf	3	0	0	0	Steinbach c	4	1	1	3
Kennedy c	3	0	1	0	Phillips 2b	3	0	0	0
Uribe ss	2	1	0	0	Weiss ss	3	0	0	0
Oberkfell 3b	1	0	1	0	Moore p	0	0	0	0
Reuschel p	0	0	0	0	Honeycutt p	0	0	0	0
Downs p	0	0	0	0	Eckersly p	0	0	0	0
Lefferts p	0	0	0	0					
Bedrosian p	0	0	0	0					
Totals	29	1	4	1	Totals	29	5	7	5

```
San Francisco . . . . . . .   0 0 1 0 0 0 0 0 0—1
Oakland . . . . . . . . . . :  1 0 0 4 0 0 0 0 x—5
```

San Francisco	ip	h	r	er	bb	so
Reuschel, L, 0-1	4	5	5	5	4	2
Downs	2	1	0	0	0	2
Lefferts	1	1	0	0	1	1
Bedrosian	1	0	0	0	0	2
Oakland						
Moore, W, 1-0	7	4	1	1	2	7
Honeycutt	1⅓	0	0	0	0	1
Eckersley	⅔	0	0	0	0	0

DP - San Francisco 2, Oakland 1. LOB - San Francisco 4, Oakland 5. 2B - Lansford, Parker, McGwire. 3B - R. Henderson. HR - Steinbach (1). SB - R. Henderson (1), Butler 2 (2). Caught stealing - R. Henderson. SF - Thompson.

How runs were scored—One in Athletics first: R. Henderson walked. Lansford doubled scoring R. Henderson.

One in Giants third: Uribe reached first on a fielders choice. Butler singled. Thompson hit a sacrifice fly scoring Uribe.

Four in Athletics fourth: Canseco walked. Parker doubled scoring Canseco. D. Henderson walked. Steinbach hit a home run scoring Parker and D. Henderson.

World Series MVPs

1955 Johnny Podres, Brooklyn (NL)	1967 Bob Gibson, St. Louis (NL)	1979 Willie Stargell, Pittsburgh (NL)
1956 Don Larsen, New York (AL)	1968 Mickey Lolich, Detroit (AL)	1980 Mike Schmidt, Philadelphia (NL)
1957 Lew Burdette, Milwaukee (NL)	1969 Donn Clendenon, New York (NL)	1981 Ron Cey, Pedro Guerrero, Steve Yeager, Los Angeles (NL)
1958 Bob Turley, New York (AL)	1970 Brooks Robinson, Baltimore (AL)	
1959 Larry Sherry, Los Angeles (NL)	1971 Roberto Clemente, Pittsburgh (NL)	1982 Darrell Porter, St. Louis (NL)
1960 Bobby Richardson, New York (AL)	1972 Gene Tenace, Oakland (AL)	1983 Rick Dempsey, Baltimore (AL)
1961 Whitey Ford, New York (AL)	1973 Reggie Jackson, Oakland (AL)	1984 Alan Trammell, Detroit (AL)
1962 Ralph Terry, New York (AL)	1974 Rollie Fingers, Oakland (AL)	1985 Bret Saberhagen, Kansas City (AL)
1963 Sandy Koufax, Los Angeles (NL)	1975 Pete Rose, Cincinnati (NL)	1986 Ray Knight, New York (NL)
1964 Bob Gibson, St. Louis (NL)	1976 Johnny Bench, Cincinnati (NL)	1987 Frank Viola, Minnesota (AL)
1965 Sandy Koufax, Los Angeles (NL)	1977 Reggie Jackson, New York (AL)	1988 Orel Hershiser, Los Angeles (NL)
1966 Frank Robinson, Baltimore (AL)	1978 Bucky Dent, New York (AL)	

World Series Results, 1903-1989

1903 Boston AL 5, Pittsburgh NL 3	1932 New York AL 4, Chicago NL 0	1962 New York AL 4, San Francisco NL 3
1904 No series	1933 New York NL 4, Washington AL 1	
1905 New York NL 4, Philadelphia AL 1	1934 St. Louis NL 4, Detroit AL 3	1963 Los Angeles NL 4, New York AL 0
1906 Chicago AL 4, Chicago NL 2	1935 Detroit AL 4, Chicago NL 2	1964 St. Louis NL 4, New York AL 3
1907 Chicago AL 4, Detroit AL 0, 1 tie	1936 New York AL 4, New York NL 2	1965 Los Angeles NL 4, Minnesota AL 3
1908 Chicago NL 4, Detroit AL 1	1937 New York AL 4, New York NL 1	1966 Baltimore AL 4, Los Angeles NL 0
1909 Pittsburgh NL 4, Detroit AL 3	1938 New York AL 4, Chicago NL 0	1967 St. Louis NL 4, Boston AL 3
1910 Philadelphia AL 4, Chicago NL 1	1939 New York AL 4, Cincinnati NL 0	1968 Detroit AL 4, St. Louis NL 3
1911 Philadelphia AL 4, New York NL 2	1940 Cincinnati NL 4, Detroit AL 3	1969 New York NL 4, Baltimore AL 1
1912 Boston AL 4, New York NL 3, 1 tie	1941 New York AL 4, Brooklyn NL 1	1970 Baltimore AL 4, Cincinnati NL 1
1913 Philadelphia AL 4, New York NL 1	1942 St. Louis NL 4, New York AL 1	1971 Pittsburgh NL 4, Baltimore AL 3
1914 Boston NL 4, Philadelphia AL 0	1943 New York AL 4, St. Louis NL 1	1972 Oakland AL 4, Cincinnati NL 3
1915 Boston AL 4, Philadelphia NL 1	1944 St. Louis NL 4, St. Louis AL 2	1973 Oakland AL 4, New York NL 3
1916 Boston AL 4, Brooklyn NL 1	1945 Detroit AL 4, Chicago NL 3	1974 Oakland AL 4, Los Angeles NL 1
1917 Chicago AL 4, New York NL 2	1946 St. Louis NL 4, Boston AL 3	1975 Cincinnati NL 4, Boston AL 3
1918 Boston AL 4, Chicago NL 2	1947 New York AL 4, Brooklyn NL 3	1976 Cincinnati NL 4, New York AL 0
1919 Cincinnati NL 5, Chicago AL 3	1948 Cleveland AL 4, Boston NL 2	1977 New York AL 4, Los Angeles NL 2
1920 Cleveland AL 5, Brooklyn NL 2	1949 New York AL 4, Brooklyn NL 1	1978 New York AL 4, Los Angeles NL 2
1921 New York NL 5, New York AL 3	1950 New York AL 4, Philadelphia NL 0	1979 Pittsburgh NL 4, Baltimore AL 3
1922 New York NL 4, New York AL 0, 1 tie	1951 New York AL 4, New York NL 2	1980 Philadelphia NL 4, Kansas City AL 2
1923 New York AL 4, New York NL 2	1952 New York AL 4, Brooklyn NL 3	
1924 Washington AL 4, New York NL 3	1953 New York AL 4, Brooklyn NL 2	1981 Los Angeles NL 4, New York AL 2
1925 Pittsburgh NL 4, Washington AL 3	1954 New York NL 4, Cleveland AL 0	1982 St. Louis NL 4, Milwaukee AL 3
1926 St. Louis NL 4, New York AL 3	1955 Brooklyn NL 4, New York AL 3	1983 Baltimore AL 4, Philadelphia NL 1
1927 New York AL 4, Pittsburgh NL 0	1956 New York AL 4, Brooklyn NL 3	1984 Detroit AL 4, San Diego NL 1
1928 New York AL 4, St. Louis NL 0	1957 Milwaukee NL 4, New York AL 3	1985 Kansas City AL 4, St. Louis NL 3
1929 Philadelphia AL 4, Chicago NL 1	1958 New York AL 4, Milwaukee NL 3	1986 New York NL 4, Boston AL 3
1930 Philadelphia AL 4, St. Louis NL 2	1959 Los Angeles NL 4, Chicago AL 2	1987 Minnesota AL 4, St. Louis NL 3
1931 St. Louis NL 4, Philadelphia AL 3	1960 Pittsburgh NL 4, New York AL 3	1988 Los Angeles NL 4, Oakland AL 1
	1961 New York AL 4, Cincinnati NL 1	

All-Time Major League Leaders

(Includes 1989 season)

Games		Runs		Runs Batted In		Strikeouts	
Pete Rose	3562	Ty Cobb	2245	Hank Aaron	2297	Nolan Ryan	5076
Carl Yastrzemski	3308	Hank Aaron	2174	Babe Ruth	2204	Steve Carlton	4136
Hank Aaron	3298	Babe Ruth	2174	Lou Gehrig	1990	Tom Seaver	3640
Ty Cobb	3033	Pete Rose	2165	Ty Cobb	1961	Don Sutton	3574
Stan Musial	3026	Willie Mays	2062	Stan Musial	1951	Bert Blyleven	3562
Willie Mays	2992	Stan Musial	1949	Jimmie Foxx	1922	Gaylord Perry	3534
Rusty Staub	2951	Lou Gehrig	1888	Willie Mays	1903	Walter Johnson	3508
Brooks Robinson	2896	Tris Speaker	1881	Mel Ott	1860	Phil Niekro	3340
Al Kaline	2834	Mel Ott	1859	Carl Yastrzemski	1844	Ferguson Jenkins	3192
Eddie Collins	2826	Frank Robinson	1829	Ted Williams	1839	Bob Gibson	3117

At Bats		Hits		Stolen Bases Since 1898		Shutouts	
Pete Rose	14,043	Pete Rose	4256	Lou Brock	938	Walter Johnson	110
Hank Aaron	12,364	Ty Cobb	4191	Ty Cobb	892	Grover C. Alexander	90
Carl Yastrzemski	11,988	Hank Aaron	3771	Rickey Henderson	871	Christy Mathewson	83
Ty Cobb	11,429	Stan Musial	3630	Eddie Collins	742	Cy Young	77
Stan Musial	10,972	Tris Speaker	3515	Max Carey	738	Eddie Plank	69
Willie Mays	10,881	Honus Wagner	3430	Honus Wagner	703	Warren Spahn	63
Brooks Robinson	10,654	Carl Yastrzemski	3419	Joe Morgan	689	Mordecai Brown	63
Honus Wagner	10,427	Eddie Collins	3309	Bert Campaneris	649	Tom Seaver	61
Lou Brock	10,332	Willie Mays	3283	Maury Wills	586	Ed Walsh	58
Luis Aparicio	10,230	Nap Lajoie	3252	Tim Raines	585	Don Sutton	58

All-Time Home Run Leaders

Player	HR	Player	HR	Player	HR	Player	HR
Hank Aaron	755	Mel Ott	511	Orlando Cepeda	379	Dale Murphy	354
Babe Ruth	714	Lou Gehrig	493	Tony Perez	379	Eddie Murray	353
Willie Mays	660	Stan Musial	475	Jim Rice	379	Dick Allen	351
Frank Robinson	586	Willie Stargell	475	Norm Cash	377	George Foster	348
Harmon Killebrew	573	Carl Yastrzemski	452	Rocky Colavito	374	Ron Santo	342
Reggie Jackson	563	Dave Kingman	442	Gil Hodges	370	John (Boog) Powell	339
Mike Schmidt	548	Billy Williams	426	Ralph Kiner	369	Don Baylor	338
Mickey Mantle	536	Darrell Evans	414	Dwight Evans	366	Carlton Fisk	336
Jimmy Foxx	534	Duke Snider	407	Joe DiMaggio	361	Joe Adcock	336
Ted Williams	521	Al Kaline	399	John Mize	359	Bobby Bonds	332
Willie McCovey	521	Graig Nettles	390	Yogi Berra	358	Hank Greenberg	331
Ed Mathews	512	Johnny Bench	389	Dave Winfield	357	Willie Horton	325
Ernie Banks	512	Frank Howard	382	Lee May	354		

The Sporting News Gold Glove Awards in 1988

National League

Keith Hernandez, New York, first base.
Ryne Sandberg, Chicago, second base.
Tim Wallach, Montreal, third base.
Ozzie Smith, St. Louis, shortstop.
Andre Dawson, Chicago, outfield.
Andy Van Slyke, Pittsburgh, outfield.
Eric Davis, Cincinnati, outfield.
Benito Santaigo, San Diego, catcher.
Orel Hershiser, Los Angeles, pitcher.

American League

Don Mattingly, New York, first base.
Harold Reynolds, Seattle, second base.
Gary Gaetti, Minnesota, third base.
Tony Fernandez, Toronto, shortstop.
Gary Pettis, Detroit, outfield.
Kirby Puckett, Minnesota, outfield.
Devon White, California, outfield.
Bob Boone, California, catcher.
Mark Langston, Seattle, pitcher.

The following are the players at each position who have won the most Gold Gloves since the award was instituted in 1957.

First base:	Keith Hernandez	11	Shortstop:	Luis Aparicio	9		Dwight Evans	8
	George Scott	8		Ozzie Smith	9		Garry Maddox	8
Second base:	Bill Mazeroski	8	Outfield:	Roberto Clemente	12	Catcher:	Johnny Bench	10
	Frank White	8		Willie Mays	12		Jim Sundberg	6
Third base:	Brooks Robinson	16		Al Kaline	10		Bob Boone	6
	Mike Schmidt	10		Paul Blair	8	Pitcher:	Jim Kaat	16
							Bob Gibson	9

World Almanac All-Major League Baseball Team in 1989

The team was chosen by a panel of sports experts on behalf of the World Almanac.

Position	Player, team	Position	Player, team
First base	Will Clark, San Francisco Giants	Catcher	Mickey Tettleton, Baltimore Orioles
Second base	Ryne Sandberg, Chicago Cubs	Right-hand pitcher	Bret Saberhagen, Kansas City Royals
Third base	Howard Johnson, N.Y. Mets	Left-hand pitcher	Joe Magrane, St. Louis Cardinals
Shortstop	Cal Ripkin Jr., Baltimore Orioles	Relief pitcher	Mark Davis, San Diego Padres
Left field	Kevin Mitchell, San Francisco Giants	Rookie of the Year	Jerome Walton, Chicago Cubs
Center field	Kirby Puckett, Minnesota Twins	Player of the Year	Kevin Mitchell, San Francisco Giants
Right field	Ruben Sierra, Texas Rangers	Manager of the Year	Frank Robinson, Baltimore Orioles

Major League Perfect Games Since 1900

Year	Player	Clubs	Score	Year	Player	Clubs	Score
1904	Cy Young	Boston vs. Phil. (AL)	3-0	1964	Jim Bunning	Phil. vs. N.Y. Mets (NL)	6-0
1908	Addie Joss	Cleveland vs. Chicago (AL)	1-0	1965	Sandy Koufax	Los Angeles vs. Chic. (NL)	1-0
1917	Ernie Shore (a)	Boston vs. Wash. (AL)	4-0	1968	Jim Hunter	Oakland vs. Minn. (AL)	4-0
1922	Charles Robertson	Chicago vs. Detroit (AL)	2-0	1981	Len Barker	Cleveland vs. Toronto (AL)	3-0
1956	Don Larsen (b)	N.Y. Yankees vs. Brooklyn	2-0	1984	Mike Witt	California vs. Texas (AL)	1-0
1959	Harvey Haddix (c)	Pitts. vs. Milwaukee (NL)	0-1	1988	Tom Browning	Cincinnati vs. L.A. (NL)	1-0

(a) Babe Ruth, the starting pitcher, was ejected from the game after walking the first batter. Shore replaced him and the base-runner was out stealing. Shore retired the next 26 batters. (b) World Series. (c) Pitched 12 perfect innings, lost in 13th on an error, sacrifice bunt, walk, and double.

Hall of Famers Chosen in First Year of Eligibility

1962	Jackie Robinson,	1973	Warren Spahn	1981	Bob Gibson	1986	Willie McCovey
	Bob Feller	1974	Mickey Mantle	1982	Hank Aaron	1988	Willie Stargell
1966	Ted Williams	1977	Ernie Banks		Frank Robinson	1989	Johnny Bench,
1969	Stan Musial	1979	Willie Mays	1983	Brooks Robinson		Carl Yastrzemski
1972	Sandy Koufax	1980	Al Kaline	1985	Lou Brock		

NCAA Baseball Champions

1947	California	1958	USC	1969	Arizona St.	1980	Arizona
1948	USC	1959	Oklahoma St.	1970	USC	1981	Arizona St.
1949	Texas	1960	Minnesota	1971	USC	1982	Miami, Fla.
1950	Texas	1961	USC	1972	USC	1983	Texas
1951	Oklahoma	1962	Michigan	1973	USC	1984	Cal. St.-Fullerton
1952	Holy Cross	1963	USC	1974	USC	1985	Miami, Fla.
1953	Michigan	1964	Minnesota	1975	Texas	1986	Arizona
1954	Missouri	1965	Arizona St.	1976	Arizona	1987	Standord
1955	Wake Forest	1966	Ohio St.	1977	Arizona St.	1988	Stanford
1956	Minnesota	1967	Arizona St.	1978	USC	1989	Wichita St.
1957	California	1968	USC	1979	Cal. St.-Fullerton		

Little League World Series in 1989

The team from Trumbull, Conn. won the 1989 Little League World Series by defeating Kaohsiung, Taiwan 5-2 at Williamsport, Pa. Trumbull became the first U.S. team to win the Little League World Series since Marietta, Ga. in 1983. Little Leaguers from Taiwan had won the championship for three consecutive years, 1986-88.

Softball Champions in 1989

Source: Amateur Softball Associations of America

Men's Major Fast Pitch — Penn Corp., Sioux City, Ia.
Women's Major Fast Pitch — Southern California Raiders, Whittier, Cal.
Men's Class A Fast Pitch — Texas Flyers, Houston, Tex.
Women's Class A Fast Pitch — John DeWyse & Sons, Essexville, Mich.
Men's Class A Industrial Pitch — All-Star Chevrolet, Wilmington, Del.
Men's Major Slow Pitch — Ritch's Salvage, Harrisburg, N.C.

Women's Major Slow Pitch — Canaan's Illusions, Houston, Tex.
Men's Major Industrial Slow Pitch — Delta Allstars, Atlanta, Ga.
Women's Major Industrial Slow Pitch — Provident Vets, Chattanooga, Tenn.
Men's Major Church Slow Pitch — Choto, Knoxville, Tenn.
Women's Major Church Slow Pitch — First Baptist of Houston, Tex.
Men's Major 16-Inch Slow Pitch — Whips, Chicago, Ill.

Notable Sports Records

(Dec. 1988-Oct. 1989)

Baseball

—Nolan Ryan became the first pitcher to strike out 5,000 major league batters.
—Ryne Sandberg had a major league record 90 consecutive errorless games at second base at the end of the season.
—Kent Tekulve retired with a major league record 1,050 relief appearances.
—Ken Griffey Sr. and Ken Griffey Jr. became the first father and son to play in the major leagues at the same time.
—Kevin Elster set a NL record by going 88 consecutive games at shortstop without an error.
—Vince Coleman stole a major league record 50 consecutive bases.
—The Cincinnati Reds collected 16 hits in the first inning against the L.A. Dodgers to set a major league record.
—Wade Boggs became the first major leaguer to have 4 consecutive 200-hit, 100-walk seasons.
—Jose Canseco received the largest raise in baseball history when he agreed to a 1-year contract for $1.6 million. The raise was $1.2 million, or 351 percent, over the previous season.
—Rickey Henderson stole 4 bases in a game, and 8 in the ALCS to set records for post-season games.

Football

—Barry Sanders scored 39 TDs, 10 more than the previous Div. I record. He also set single-season records in rushing yards

(2,638), and averaged 295.5 all-purpose yards per game, breaking the record set by now Supreme Court justice Byron White in 1937.
—Tim Brown set a NFL rookie mark for all-purpose yardage with 2, 316 yards.
—Vinny Testaverde threw a NFL record 35 interceptions.
—Jerry Rice tied a Super Bowl record with 11 receptions, and set the record for receiving yardage with 215.
—Joe Montana set a Super Bowl record by passing for 357 yards.
—Houston became the first team in major-college history to gain 1,000 yards total offense as they beat SMU 95-21.

Others

—Loyola Marymount and U.S. International set a NCAA-record for most points scored in a basketball game when Loyola beat USI 181-150.
—Michael Chang, 17, became the youngest man to win a tennis grand slam event when he won the singles' title at the French Open.
—Javier Sotomayor became the first person to high jump 8 feet.
—Roger Kingdom set a world record when he ran the 110-meter hurdles in 12.92 seconds.
—Deion Sanders became the first to hit a major league home run and score a NFL touchdown in the same week.
—Wayne Gretzky scored his 1,851st point to become the leading scorer in NHL History.

Ten Most Dramatic Sports Events, Nov. 1988—Oct. 1989

Selected by The World Almanac Sports Staff

—Joe Montana threw a touchdown pass to John Taylor with 34 seconds remaining in the game to give the San Francisco 49ers a 20-16 victory over the Cincinnati Bengals in the Super Bowl. The scoring pass capped a 92-yard drive.
—Rumeal Robinson hit 2 foul shots with 3 seconds left in the game to give Michigan a 80-79 victory over Seton Hall in the NCAA championship game. It was the first NCAA basketball championship for the Wolverines.
—Nolan Ryan of the Texas Rangers struck out Rickey Henderson of the Oakland A's to become the first pitcher to strike out 5,000 major league batters.
—Notre Dame defeated previously undefeated West Virginia 34-21 in the Fiesta Bowl. The Fighting Irish finished the season 12-0, and won their eighth national football championship.
—Javier Sotomayor of Cuba became the first to break the 8-foot barrier in the high jump.

—The Detroit Pistons defeated the defending champion Los Angeles Lakers in 4 games to win their first National Basketball Association championship.
—Michael Chang of the U.S. and Arantxa Sanchez of Spain, a pair of 17-year-olds, won the singles' titles at the French Open. Chang became the youngest man to win a tennis grand slam event.
—The Calgary Flames defeated the Montreal Canadiens in 6 games to win the Stanley Cup. It was the first Stanley Cup championship for the Flames.
—Curtis Strange won the U.S. Open for the second consecutive year. He became the first golfer to win the U.S. Open in 2 consecutive years since Ben Hogan did it in 1951.
—Greg LeMond of the U.S. came from 50 seconds behind to win the Tour de France bicycle race. It was the second time that LeMond had won the event; he became the first American to win the race in 1986.

Deaths, Nov. 1, 1988—Oct. 16, 1989

A

Adamson, George, 83; environmentalist who was featured in the book and movie *Born Free;* Kenya, Aug. 20.

Allison, Fran, 81; star of the "Kukla, Fran, and Ollie" TV show of the 1940s and 1950s; Sherman Oaks, Cal., June 13.

Allott, Gordon, 82; U.S. senator from Colorado, 1955-73; Englewood, Col., Jan. 17.

Alsop, Joseph, 78; syndicated political columnist; Washington, D.C., Aug. 28.

Andrews, Harry, 77; British film, stage, and TV actor whose career spanned 56 years; Salehurst, England, Mar. 6.

Armour, Richard Willard, 82; poet and satirist; Claremont, Cal., Feb. 28.

Ashby, Hal, 59; film director, *Shampoo, Coming Home;* Malibu, Cal., Dec. 27.

B

Backus, Jim, 76; actor in the "Gilligan's Island" TV sitcom; voice of cartoon character "Mr. Magoo"; Santa Monica, Cal., July 3.

Ball, Lucille, 77; actress who starred in "I Love Lucy", one of the most popular series in TV history; Los Angeles, Apr. 26.

Barthelme, Donald, 58; short-story writer and novelist; Houston, July 23.

Berlin, Irving, 101; songwriter who wrote over 1,500 songs, many of them classics; "White Christmas", "God Bless America"; New York, Sept. 22.

Berry, Ricky, 24; basketball player for the NBA Sacramento Kings; Fair Oaks, Cal., Aug. 14.

Blaik, Earl "Red", 92; football coach at the U.S. Military Academy, 1941-58; Colorado Springs, Col., May 6.

Blake, Amanda, 60; actress who played Miss Kitty on the "Gunsmoke" TV series; Los Angeles, Aug. 16.

Blanc, Mel, 81; actor who provided the voices for numerous cartoon characters including Bugs Bunny, Woody Woodpecker, Porky Pig; Los Angeles, July 10.

Bleyer, Archie, 79; musical director and arranger long associated with Arthur Godfrey; Sheboygan, Wis., Mar. 20.

Bremigan, Nick, 43; American League umpire since 1974; Garland, Tex., Mar. 28.

Brewster Jr., Kingman, 69; president of Yale Univ., 1963-77; U.S. ambassador to Britain, 1977-81; Oxford, England, Nov. 8.

Browne, Dik, 71; cartoonist who created the "Hagar the Horrible" strip; Sarasota, Fla., June 4.

Burns, Jethro, 69; mandolin-playing partner of the "Homer and Jethro" country music team; Evanston, Ill., Feb. 4.

Busch Jr., August, 90; beer co. exec.; owner St. Louis Cardinals baseball team; St. Louis Co., Mo., Sept. 29.

C

Calhoun, Lee, 56; hurdler who won 2 Olympic gold medals; Erie, Pa., June 21.

Carradine, John, 82; character actor who appeared in over 200 films; Milan, Italy, Nov. 27.

Case, George, 73; baseball player who led the AL in stolen bases 6 times; Morrisville, Pa., Jan. 23.

Cassavetes, John, 59; actor, film writer, and director, *Woman Under the Influence, Faces;* Los Angeles, Feb. 3.

Castellano, Richard, 55; actor noted for his portrayals of Italian-Americans; North Bergen, N.J., Dec. 10.

Chapman, Graham, 48; member of the "Monte Python" comedy group; England, Oct. 4.

Chappell Jr., Bill, 67; U.S. representative from Florida, 1969-89; Bethesda, Md., Mar. 30.

Clubb, O. Edmund, 88; U.S. foreign service officer who was a "China hand" and McCarthy target in the 1950s; New York, May 9.

Conlan, Jocko, 89; hall of fame umpire who was in National League for 24 years; Scottsdale, Ariz., Apr. 16.

Coulouris, George, 85; actor who appeared in over 40 major films, usually as a villain; London, Apr. 25.

Cotton, Norris, 88; U.S. senator from New Hampshire, 1954-75; Lebanon, N.H., Feb. 24.

Cowley, Malcolm, 90; literary critic, editor, poet, and essayist; New Milford, Conn., Mar. 27.

D

Dali, Salvador, 84; Spanish painter who pioneered European Surrealism; Figueras, Spain, Jan. 23.

Davis, Bette, 81; a major film star for 50 years; won 2 best actress Oscars; Neuilly-Sur-Seine, France, Oct. 6.

Dorati, Antal, 82; Hungarian-born conductor who led the National Symphony in Washington in the 1970s; Bern, Switzerland, Nov. 13.

Douglas, Jack, 80; comedy writer who was a frequent guest on the Jack Paar TV show in the 1950s; Los Angeles, Jan. 31.

E

Eldridge, Roy, 78; jazz trumpeter; Valley Stream, N.Y., Feb. 26.

Evans, Maurice, 87; British actor noted for his Shakespearean roles; Brighton, England, Mar. 12.

F

Fitzgerald, Pegeen, 78; radio host who with husband, Ed, conducted a radio talk show for 42 years and pioneered the at-home radio format; New York, Jan. 30.

Fleisher, Larry, 58; organizer and former head of the National Basketball Players Association; New York, May 4.

French, Victor, 54; actor who starred in the "Highway to Heaven" TV series; Los Angeles, June 15.

Furillo, Carl, 66; outfielder for the Brooklyn Dodgers who led the NL in batting in 1953; Stony Creek Mills, Pa., Jan 21.

G

Gardner, Hy, 80; Broadway gossip columnist in the 1950s and 1960s; Miami, June 16.

Giamatti, A. Bartlett, 51; Major League Baseball commissioner; Martha's Vineyard, Mass., Sept. 1.

Gomez, Vernon "Lefty", 80; baseball hall of fame pitcher who won 189 games for the N.Y. Yankees; Larkspur, Cal., Feb. 17.

Graham, Sheilah, 84; Hollywood gossip columnist whose book, *Beloved Infidel,* told of her affair with F. Scott Fitzgerald; Palm Beach, Fla., Nov. 17.

Green, John, 80; film composer and arranger; songwriter, "Body and Soul"; Beverly Hills, Cal., May 15.

Gromyko, Andrei, 79; Soviet foreign minister for most of the post World War II era; USSR, July 2.

H

Halliwell, Leslie, 59; author of several encyclopedic guides to film; Surrey, England, Jan. 21.

Harrington, Michael, 61; socialist and author; Larchmont, N.Y., July 31.

Hays, Wayne L., 77; U.S. representative from Ohio, 1949-77; Wheeling, W. Va., Feb. 10.

Hicks, John Richard, 85; economist who won the 1972 Nobel Prize for Economics; Blockley, England, May 20.

Heywood, Eddie, 73; jazz pianist, arranger, and composer, "Canadian Sunset"; N. Miami, Fla., Jan. 2.

Hinkle, Clarke, 79; pro football hall of famer who led the Green Bay Packers to NFL championships in 1936 and 1939; Toronto, Oh., Nov. 9.

Hirohito, 87; emperor of Japan since 1926; Tokyo, Jan. 7.

Hoffman, Abbie, 52; political activist who founded the Yippie movement of the 1960s; New Hope, Pa., Apr. 12.

Hook Sidney, 86; political philosopher and author; Stanford, Conn., July 12.

Hu Yaobang, 73; Chinese political leader who led his country away from orthodox Marxism; China, Apr. 15.

Hubbell, Carl, 85; baseball hall of famer who won 253 games for the N.Y. Giants; Scottsdale, Ariz., Nov. 21.

J

Johnson, Judy, 89; baseball hall of famer who starred in the Negro leagues; Wilmington, Del., June 14.

Jorgensen, Christine, 62; man who in 1952 underwent the first sex change operation to be transformed into a woman; San Clemente, Cal., May 3.

K

Kadar, Janos, 77; Hungarian leader who came to power as the Soviet Army crushed the 1956 uprising; ruled for 32 years; Budapest, Hungary, July 6.

von Karajan, Herbert, 81; conductor who was one of the century's most powerful figures in classical music; Anif, Austria, July 16.

Kelly, Dan, 52; hockey play-by-play announcer; St. Louis, Feb. 10.

Khomeini, Ayatollah Ruhollah, 89; political and spiritual leader of Iran since 1979; Teheran, June 4.

Kirkwood, James, 64; actor, novelist, and playwright; co-authored the book for *A Chorus Line;* New York, Apr. 21.

Kirst, Hans Helmut, 74; German novelist, *The Night of the Generals;* Bremen, W. Germany, Feb. 23.

Klein, Norma, 50; author of young-adult novels; New York, Apr. 25.

de Kooning, Elaine, 68; painter, writer, and teacher of art; Southampton, N.Y., Feb. 1.

L

Leland, Mickey, 44; U.S. representative from Texas; Ethiopia, Aug.

Lemnitzer, Gen. Lyman, 89; World War II hero who later served as chairman of the Joint Chiefs of Staff; Washington, D.C., Nov. 12.

Leone, Sergio, 67; Italian film director famed for "spaghetti" westerns; Rome, Apr. 30.

Lillie, Beatrice, 94; comedienne and actress whose career spanned 50 years; Henley-on-Thames, England; Jan. 20.

M

Magnuson, Warren G., 84; U.S. senator from Washington, 1945-81; Seattle, May 20.

Marcos, Ferdinand, 72; leader of the Philippines for 20 years until his ouster in 1986; Honolulu, Sept. 28.

Matsushita, Konosuke, 94; Japanese industrialist; Osaka, Japan, Apr. 27.

Matuszak, John, 38; football lineman who played on 2 Oakland Raiders

Super Bowl teams; Los Angeles, June 17.

du Maurier, Daphne, 81; author of several gothic romances, *Rebecca;* Cornwall, England, Apr. 19.

McCloy, John J., 93; lawyer and diplomat who was an advisor to presidents from FDR to Reagan; Stamford, Conn., Mar. 11.

McMahon, Jack, 60; NBA player, coach, and administrator; Chicago, June 11.

McMillan, Kenneth, 56; character actor in films and the theater; Santa Monica, Cal., Jan. 8.

Milanov, Zinka, 83; leading dramatic soprano at the Metropolitan Opera for nearly 30 years; New York, May 30.

Mills, Herbert, 77; member of the Mills Brothers singing group; Las Vegas, Apr. 12.

Mitchell, John, 75; former U.S. attorney general who was a major figure in the Watergate scandal; Washington, D.C., Nov. 9.

Moore, Donnie, 35; former pitcher for the California Angels baseball team; Anaheim, Cal., July 18.

Morrison, Joe, 51; Univ. of S. Carolina football coach; played 14 seasons with N.Y. Giants; Columbia, S.C., Feb. 5

N

Newborn Jr., Phineas, 57; jazz pianist; Memphis, May 26.

Newton, Huey, 47; co-founder of the Black Panther Party of the 1960s; Oakland, Cal., Aug. 22.

Nichols, William, 70; U.S. representative from Alabama since 1967; Washington, D.C., Dec. 13.

Noguchi, Isamu, 84; Japanese sculptor; New York, Dec. 30.

O

Olivier, Laurence, 82; actor who was considered the greatest classical stage actor of his time; Steyning, England, July 11.

Onassis, Christina, 37; head of family business empire; Argentina, Nov. 19.

O'Rourke, Frank, 72; author of some 60 western and mystery novels; Tucson, Apr. 27.

Orbison, Roy, 52; singer and songwriter who was popular in the 1960s, "Oh Pretty Woman;" Hendersonville, Tenn., Dec. 6.

P

Parish, Peggy, 61; children's author who wrote 11 Amelia Bedelia novels; Manning, S.C., Nov. 19.

Patane, Giuseppe, 57; conductor who specialized in Italian opera; Munich, May 30.

Pepper, Claude, 88; U.S. representative from Florida who was famed as a champion of the elderly; Washington, D.C., May 30.

Pratt, Walter "Babe", 72; hockey hall of famer who was the NHL most valuable player in 1944; Vancouver, B.C., Dec. 16.

R

Radner, Gilda, 42; comedian who

appeared on the "Saturday Night Live" TV show in the 1970s; Los Angeles, May 20.

Raposo, Joseph G., 51; producer and composer who helped create the "Sesame Street" TV program; Bronxville, N.Y. Feb. 5.

Richmond, Tim, 34; auto racer who led the NASCAR circuit in victories in 1986; Miami, Aug. 13.

Richter, Curt, 94; psychobiologist who pioneered the study of biorhythms; Baltimore, Dec. 21.

Robinson, Max, 49; TV journalist who was the first black to anchor network news; Washington, D.C., Dec. 20.

Robinson, Sugar Ray, 67; boxer who was a 5-time world middleweight champion; Culver City, Cal., Apr. 12.

Rouse, Charlie, 64; jazz saxophonist; Seattle, Nov. 30.

Rukeyser, Merryle S., 91; financial columnist and editor; White Plains, N.Y., Dec. 21.

S

Saxon, Charles, 68; cartoonist who did 92 covers for *The New Yorker* magazine; Stamford, Conn., Dec. 6.

Schaeffer, Rebecca, 21; actress who starred in the "My Sister Sam" TV sitcom; Los Angeles, July 18.

Schaffner, Franklin, 69; film director who received 28 Oscar nominations; Santa Monica, Cal., July 2.

Secretariat, 19; thoroughbred who won racing's triple crown in 1973; Paris, Ky., Oct. 4.

Segre, Dr. Emilio G., 84; nuclear scientist who shared the 1959 Nobel Prize in physics; Lafayette, Cal., Apr. 22.

Sewell, Truett "Ripp," 82; pitcher who won 143 major league games; famed for "eephus" pitch; Plant City, Fla., Sept. 3.

Seymour, Anne, 79; actress who performed in over 5,000 radio dramas; Los Angeles, Dec. 8.

Shockley, William B., 79; scientist who shared the 1947 Nobel Prize in physics; famed for controversial views on genetic differences between the races; Stanford, Cal., Aug. 12.

Silver, Joe, 66; actor who appeared on Broadway, films, and TV during a 45-year career; New York, Feb. 27.

Simenon, Georges, 86; French author of some 200 novels including 84 Inspector Maigret mysteries; Lausanne, Switzerland, Sept. 4.

Smith, Larkin, 45; U.S. representative from Mississippi; Mississippi, Aug. 13.

Sopwith, Sir Thomas, 101; British aircraft pioneer and aviator who shot down Germany's famed Red Baron, 1917; Winchester, England, Jan. 27.

Stephenson, Sir William, 93; British spy known as "Intrepid"; Bermuda, Feb. 3.

Stone, I.F., 81; journalist who was famed for his muckraking newsletter; Boston, June 18.

Stone, Irving, 86; author of biographical novels, *Lust for Life;* Los Angeles, Aug. 26.

Stone, M.H., 85; mathematician known for synthesizing diverse areas of abstract mathematics; Madras, India, Jan. 9.

Symington, Stuart, 87; U.S. senator from Missouri, 1953-76; first secretary of the Air Force, 1947; New Canaan, Conn. Dec. 14.

T

Talvela, Martti, 54; bass who performed regularly at the Metropolitan Opera in New York; Juva, Finland, July 22.

Terry, Bill, 90; baseball hall of famer; the last player to bat .400 in the National League, 1930; Jacksonville, Fla., Jan. 9.

Thomson, Virgil, 92; composer and critic; won 1948 Pulitzer Prize for music; New York, Sept. 30.

Tinbergen, Nikolaas, 81; Dutch-born zoologist who shared the 1973 Nobel Prize for Physiology or Medicine; Oxford, England, Dec. 21.

Toran, Stacey, 27; defensive back for the L.A. Raiders football team; Marina del Rey, Cal., Aug. 5.

Tuchman, Barbara, 77; author-historian who won 2 Pulitzer Prizes, *The Guns of August,* and *Stilwell and the American Experience in China, 1911-45;* Greenwich, Conn., Feb. 6.

Tucker, Tommy, 86; big-band leader of the 1940s; Sarasota, Fla., July 11.

V

Vare, Glenna Collett, 85; pioneer golfer who won the U.S. women's national title 6 times between 1922 and 1935; Gulfstream, Fla., Feb. 3.

Voorhees, Donald, 85; conductor and musical director of the "Bell Telephone Hour" on radio and TV for 28 years; Cape May, N.J., Jan. 10.

Vreeland Diana, 80s; fashion editor who was associated with *Harper's Bazaar* and *Vogue;* New York, Aug. 22.

W

Walt, Gen. Lewis W., 76; U.S. Marine Corps general who won combat decorations in 3 wars; Gulfport, Miss., Mar. 26.

Ward, Jay, 69; cartoonist who created Bullwinkle and other TV cartoon characters; Los Angeles, Oct. 12.

Warren, Robert Penn, 84; 1st U.S. poet laureate, 1986; poet and novelist who won 3 Pulitzer Prizes, *All the King's Men;* Stratton, Vt., Sept. 15.

Webber, Robert, 64; character actor who appeared in numerous film and TV roles; Malibu, Cal., May 19.

Wilde, Cornell, 74; actor who was a leading man in some 50 films; Los Angeles, Oct. 16.

Z

Zita, 96; last empress of Austria-Hungary; Zizers, Switzerland, Mar. 14.

Off-Beat News Stories of 1989

What did you expect? — Anarchists from around the world held a convention in San Francisco to discuss history, debate philosophy, and share their visions of a stateless society. They concluded their activities with a 2-hour riot. Police said that 300 people from the annual convention threw stones and bottles, broke store windows, set trash fires, and commandeered a Coca-Cola delivery truck. There were 30 arrests. The disturbance disappointed conference organizers, who had sought to improve the public image of the anarchists. "People think we're mad bombers in pointy

hats with beards," said Joey Cain, who helped organize the conference. "We have to counteract that by showing that anarchists are responsible people." While those at the convention disagreed about what anarchism is, they did agree that they shared a distaste for the state and a belief in direct action.

Head of the Class — Kevin McQuain, a Syracuse Univ. art student, was arrested and accused of taking a skull from a mausoleum and boiling it in his dormitory to prepare it for a sculpting class. The police were notified after McQuain's roommate smelled a foul odor and found the skull. McQuain explained that he took the skull from the mausoleum to use as a model for an art class. The skull was believed to be that of John J. Crouse, who served as mayor of Syracuse from 1876 to 1880.

And let's call the cow "Edsel" — A poll conducted by the *Des Moines Register* reported that 11 percent of the people in Iowa name their cars. The most popular names were Betsy, Betty, and Bessie. Others included Lemon, Clunker, and Junker. The poll showed that younger people were most likely to name their cars, with 19 percent of the 18-24-year-olds doing so.

A repeat offender — The New Hampshire State Supreme Court was asked to decide when a belch is intentional and willful. When James Jordan was suspected of being drunk and brought to the police station for a blood-alcohol test, he belched. The result of a breath test is skewed by belching, which contaminates the mouth with alcohol from the stomach. The police told him to wait 20 minutes before belching again and warned that any further belching would be considered a test refusal and result in suspension of his license. He belched again and lost his license. Jordan maintained that he did not mean to belch and even tried to hold back. Assistant Attorney General Stephen Judge agreed that no criteria exists to determine whether belching is willful, but said that the evidence in this case supported the police.

Always leave a light on — Town officials in Blackfoot, Idaho seeking to enforce a town cleanup ordinance, broke into the home of Leo Wynn and his wife while they were out of town and threw out or gave away their belongings. The officials thought the house had been vacated because the lawn had not been mowed and inoperable vehicles were stored on the property.

What would Mr. Potato-head say? —All 3 television networks broadcast a public service announcement by the American Pediatric Academy saying that children who watch too much television could become "couch potatoes"—obese, boring, and dense. The state of Maine, where the potato is the largest cash crop, objected to the term "couch potato" and sent a lighthearted "a peel" to the academy asking for an end to the broadcasts. The Couch Potatoes, a California-based organization dedicated to television watching, also objected to the message.

Telephonathon — Ethel Scull was fined $1,000 after pleading guilty to aggravated harassment for phoning her stockbroker 1,208 times in 8 days. She made the calls—485 in one day—in January 1988 to complain that she lost money in the market due to her broker's bad advice. In reality, she had made $300,000.

Hoo sez wee kan't spel? — Americans are the worst spellers in the English-speaking world, according to a Gallup spelling quiz. The best spellers are in Australia, followed by Canada, the United Kingdom, and then the United States. The words on the quiz were: magazine, sandwich, kerosene, calamity, penitentiary, picnicking, deceive, accelerator, cauliflower, and parallel. Of the 10 test words, Americans misspelled, on average, more than 6 of them. Only one in 20 adults in all 4 countries could spell all 10 words correctly. The test also revealed that women were better spellers than men except in the United Kingdom where the sexes had equal ability. In the U.S., the best spellers were those aged 35 to 44.

But can he shoot? — A man walked into the locker room of the Charlotte Hornets basketball team and tried to put on guard Rickey Green's uniform. Security officers and police arrested Edward Paula for trespassing. As he was being led away he told the Cleveland Cavaliers Mark Price, "I'm going to shut you down." Charlotte's Kelly Tripuka said: "The sad thing is we probably could have used him."

Is this what they mean by "altered?" — The owner of the steer that was chosen grand champion at the Ohio State Fair agreed to relinquish the blue ribbon and the $28,000 earned when the steer was sold at auction. The owner had broken a rule by dying the hairs on the steer. The agreement did not reconcile, however, whether the steer, Hank, had been entered in an Illinois county fair under the name of Carl. The allegations arose because of similarities in photographs of Hank and Carl. The one difference was a shock of white navel hair on Carl that did not appear on Hank. Hank was impounded while investigators waited for the hair to grow out. Hank's hair proved to be white. The owner admitted dyeing the hair but denied that Hank and Carl were the same steer. The owner of Carl also denied the allegation, but added that since the Illinois contest, Carl had been sold to a meat packer.

Capitol loss — Former Vice President Spiro T. Agnew sought to claim a tax deduction on $142,500 that he paid Maryland in restitution for bribes he was accused of collecting while serving as governor of that state. He was appealing a 1986 decision by the California Franchise Tax Board to deny his request for a refund of $24,197. Agnew, who pleaded no contest to corruption charges and resigned as Vice President in 1973, had been accused of accepting bribes from road engineering contractors while he was governor of Maryland from 1967 to 1969. He viewed the court-ordered restitution as an expenditure and wanted to recover a percentage of it.

Numeracy — On June 7, 1989, the clock and the calendar combined to form a "date-straight" that would have made a 9-card stud player gasp. At 23 minutes and 45 seconds after one o'clock on that date, the moment could accurately be rendered as 1:23:45/6/7/89. Though the event went unnoticed by most people, there were those who could not pass up a chance to cash in on a hunch. In the New York Lottery, so many people bet on 6789 in the daily Win 4 game that the number was cut off at 8 A.M. The number didn't win but hunch players shouldn't lose heart. Next year for one second, the figures will read 12:34:56 7/8/90.

Courting — A 15-year-old sued the boy who was to take her to the high school prom, contending that he owes her about $50 for the shoes, flowers, and hairdo she never got to show off. Her date explained: "She didn't believe me when I told her I fractured my ankle." He also said that he had to go out of town that night.

"Buy Me Some Peanuts and Yakitori ..." — While they will undoubtedly continue to offer peanuts and popcorn, the San Diego Padres and the San Francisco Giants are staying current with their fan's dining habits. The Padres offered sushi at their concession stands this season, while the Giants offered yogurt, salads, and tofu hot dogs.

Donkey business — Brigitte Bardot, the French movie star, was looking after a neighbor's donkey, Charly, while the owner was away. When Charly became amorous with Bardot's donkey, a mare, Bardot called a veterinarian and had Charly castrated. The neighbor threatened to go to court and claimed, "Things will never be the same for Charly."

Volunteers needed to serve eviction papers — Sonny, an 11-year-old African elephant with a habit of breaking his cages and wearing out his welcome in a series of zoos, was moved into a home for the unwanted. His new $300,000-home is a stall in Popcorn, N.J. which contains a 160-foot-square paddock with a pool.

Powerful Earthquake Strikes Northern California

An earthquake that registered 6.9 on the Richter scale hit the San Francisco Bay area for 15 seconds at 5:04 P.M. Pacific Time, Tuesday, Oct. 17, 1989. The quake killed at least 59 people and injured at least 3,000, making it the second-worst in American history, after the 1906 San Francisco quake, which killed from 800 to 1,000 people. Physical damage was estimated at well over $1 billion. Seven counties in Northern California were declared disaster areas.

The worst damage came when a more than mile-long section of the upper level of the two-tier Nimitz Freeway, part of Interstate Highway 880, collapsed onto the lower level. This killed at least 38 people, according to official body counts as of Oct. 22. Doctors, nurses, and emergency teams were hindered in rescuing victims trapped in vehicles, because of the narrow space between the two levels of the roadway.

In addition, much of downtown Santa Cruz was leveled and 4 people were killed; a 30-foot section of the upper deck of the San Francisco-Oakland Bay Bridge collapsed, killing 1 person; a building in San Francisco collapsed, killing several people. The quake set fires in San Francisco, Oakland, and Berkeley. Hundreds of aftershocks were recorded the next day, including one that measured 4.5 on the Richter scale. Water, electricity, communication and transportation were disrupted, with 5 freeways and San Francisco Airport closed.

Some 50 million Americans whose televisions were tuned in to the warmup before the third game of the World Series between the Oakland Athletics and the San Francisco Giants at Candlestick Park could see the image on their TV screens shake as the quake oc-

curred, 16 minutes before the scheduled game time. The game was cancelled, and 58,000 people were evacuated; the stadium did not suffer major structural damage.

The earthquake occurred on a section of the San Andreas fault that geologists had established as most likely to rupture in the near future. This segment had never ruptured in recorded history, while segments to the north and south had broken in recent years, which meant that the area generating the fault had accumulated considerable strain. Some scientists maintained that the quake was an extremely delayed after-effect of the Great Earthquake of 1906, which most scientists placed at 8.3 on the Richter scale, and others at 7.9. On the Richter scale, every increase of one number signifies a tenfold increase in magnitude, so a reading of 7.9 would reflect an earthquake 10 times stronger than one of 6.9. The 1906 quake took place on April 18 at 5:12 A.M., with most San Franciscans asleep. Most of the damage was caused by fires, after broken water mains brought a drop in water pressure that impeded firefighting. If the 1989 earthquake had been as intense as the 1906 quake, 11,000 would have been killed, 12,000 would have been seriously injured, and physical damage would have totalled $25 billion, according to the Federal Emergency Management Agency.

A.T.&.T. officials estimated that 20 million attempted telephone calls were made on Tuesday from those concerned about friends and family in Northern California. Some 140 million long-distance calls were placed Wednesday, the highest number for a single day in history.

Major California Earthquakes Since 1900

Source: Associated Press

1906	San Francisco	8.3*	1980	Eureka	7.0		Mountains	6.4
1952	Tehachapi-		1940	Imperial Valley	6.7	1971	San Fernando	6.4
	Bakersfield	7.8	1911	Coyote	6.6	1933	Long Beach	6.3
1927	Offshore San Luis		1980	Mammoth Lakes (4)	6.0-6.6	1925	Santa Barbara	6.3
	Obispo	7.7	1983	Coalinga	6.5	1984	Morgan Hill	6.2
1923	North Coast	7.2	1979	Imperial Valley	6.4	1987	Los Angeles	6.1
1989	San Francisco	7.0	1968	Anza-Borrego		1986	Palm Springs	6.0

*This figure is an estimate, since the quake took place before the Richter Scale was developed.

East Germany's Leader Ousted

The East German Communist Party removed Erich Honecker, its head for 18 years, on Oct. 18, in yet another dramatic development in that nation. Honecker's protégé, Egon Krenz, age 52, was named successor. The youngest member of the Politburo, Krenz had been head of security and youth affairs. He was named to all 3 of Honecker's positions—party chief, head of state, and chairman of the Defense Council. The 77-year-old Honecker officially resigned because serious illness and surgery "no longer allow me to devote the power and energy demanded today." He proposed that the "able and decisive" Krenz succeed him.

In a nationally televised address delivered the evening of his appointment, Krenz said, "It is clear that we have not realistically appraised the social developments in our country in recent months, and have not drawn the right conclusions quickly enough. We see the seriousness of the situation." He added: "But we

also sense and recognize the major opportunity we have opened for ourselves to define the policies in dialogue with our citizens, policies that will bring us to the verge of the next century." Without directly criticizing his predecessor, Krenz used the same words Mikhail Gorbachev had used 2 weeks earlier during the Soviet leader's visit to East Berlin: "We have to see and react to the times, otherwise life will punish us."

Krenz was born on March 19, 1937 in Kolberg, Pomerania, now part of E. Germany. He worked in the Free German Youth in Bergen and Rostock, 1959-1961, and was secretary of the Free German Youth in the Central Committee, 1961-1964. Elected to the Central Committee of the Communist Party in 1973, he became the committee's secretary in 1983, and also a full Politburo member. He was named deputy chairman to Honecker in 1984.

QUICK REFERENCE INDEX

Quality printing and binding by
Arcata Graphics/Buffalo
T.C. Industrial Park
Depew, New York 14043
U.S.A.